Time-Saver Standards for Interior Design and Space Planning

TIME-SAVER STANDARDS FOR INTERIOR DESIGN AND SPACE PLANNING

Joseph De Chiara
Julius Panero
Martin Zelnik

Second Edition

McGRAW-HILL
New York Chicago San Francisco
Lisbon London Madrid Mexico City
Milan New Delhi San Juan Seoul
Singapore Sydney Toronto

Library of Congress Cataloging-in-Publication Data

Time-saver standards for interior design and space planning / [edited by]
Joseph De Chiara, Julius Panero, Martin Zelnik—2nd ed.
p. cm.
Includes index.
ISBN 0-07-134616-3 (alk. paper)
1. Interior decoration—Standards—Handbooks, manuals, etc.
2. Interior architecture—Standards—Handbooks, manuals, etc.
I. De Chiara, Joseph, date. II. Panero, Julius. III. Zelnik, Martin, date.

NK2110.T48 2001
729—dc21 2001030504

McGraw-Hill

A Division of The ***McGraw-Hill*** *Companies*

8 9 0 QPD/QPD 0 7 6 5

ISBN 0-07-134616-3

The sponsoring editor for this book was Wendy Lochner, the editing supervisor was Virginia Carroll, and the production supervisor was Sherri Souffrance. It was set in Times by North Market Street Graphics.

Printed and bound by Quebecor/Versailles.

Contents

Contributors

Marvin Affrime
Andrew Alpern, AIA *Architect*
Amon & Graecen *Architects*
David Appel, DLF, IALD
Charles Baron
Bertram L. Bassuk *Architect*
Anthony Beaumont *Architect*
David Bilger
Brian Black
Jeannie Bochette *Steelcase*
Louis Bowman *Architect*
Brennan Beer Gorman Monk/Interiors
Scott Bromley *Architect*
Bromley Caldari Architects, PC
Bromley Jacobsen *Architecture and Design*
Jerry Caldari *Architect*
Rick Carter, AIA *Architect*
Centerbrook, Architects & Planners, LLC
Tony Chi/Albert Chen Associates
Tony Chi & Associates
Will Ching *Planning and Design*
Tammy Chou
Barbara Cianci, IALD
Cameron Clark *Architect*
Davis, Brody & Wisniewski *Architects*
Di Leonardo International, Inc.
Joseph De Chiara, RA *Architect*
Henry Dreyfuss Associates
Marjorie Earthlife
Brad Elias, ASID
David Engel *Landscape Architect*
Engel/GGP *Landscape Architects*
Paul Eshelman, IDEC
Evans, Moore, Peterson & Woodbridge *Architects*
Charles D. Flayhan Associates, Inc.
Frank J. Forster *Architect*
Ulrich Franzen *Architect*
Gensler Associates
Judy Girod
Franklin H. Gottschall
Adrienne Grad
Julius Gregory *Architect*
William H. Grover, FAIA
Albert Halse
HKS Inc.
Hochheiser Elias Design Group, Inc.
Linda Holtschue
Caleb Hornbolstel *Architect*
Lees Horton
James Huang
ISD Incorporated
Lawrence Israel, AIA, FISP *Architect*
Roy Jacuzzi
Francis Joannes *Architect*
Ely Jacques Kahn *Architect*
Mary Jean Kamin, ASID
William H. Kapple, AIA
Joseph Kleiman
Dorothy Lee
Sammy Lee *Architect*
Naomi Leff
Naomi Leff & Associates
Lori Lennon, ASID
Howard Litton, ASID
Donald Long
Steve Louie
Ronald Lubman *Architect*
Harry Lunstead Design, Inc.
Michael Lynn *Architect*
Michael Lynn & Associates
Nathan Jerry Maltz, AIA *Architect*
William M. Manley, FASID
James R. Martin, AIA
Mays, Simpson & Hunsicker *Architects*
Merrill, Humble, and Taylor *Architects*
Doug Mockett
Julia Monk
Montgomery Winecoff & Associates, Inc.
William Morgan, FAIA
Marcel Morin
Bernhardt E. Muller *Architect*
Richard J. Neutra *Architect*
Julius Panero, RA *Architect*
Panero Zelnik Associates
Parish Hadley Associates, Inc.
Sal Passalacqua
Passalacqua & Toto Associates
Richard H. Penner
Perkins & Will *Architects*
Dennis Piermont, ASLA *Landscape Architect*
Nicholas Politis *Professor, Fashion Institute of Technology, Architect*
John Russel Pope *Architect*
William Pulgram *Architect*
Ramey, Himes & Buchner *Architects*
Antonin Raymond *Architect*
Jefferson B. Riley, FAIA
Frank Rispoli
Rosenblum Architects
Norman Rosenfeld, FAIA, FACHA
Norman Rosenfeld Architects, LLC
James Ryan
Saarinen, Swanson & Saarinen *Architects*
Andrew Seifer and Associates
Patricia C. Shanahan
Jacqueline Siles
Mark Simon, FAIA

Contributors

The Space Design Group
Richard Stonis
Gustin Tan
William Tarr
Andrew J. Thomas *Architect*
Thompson, Robinson,Toraby, Inc.
Darius Toraby Architects, PC
Michael Trencher *Professor, Pratt Institute*
Verna, Cook, Salomosky *Architects*
Walker & Gillette *Architects*
Walker Group/CNI
Leroy P. Ward *Architect*
Amiel Weisblum
Edgar I. Williams *Architect*
Charlie Wing
Bryan Ethan Zelnik
Martin Zelnik, RA/AIA/ASID *Architect*
Simon B. Zelnik, FAIA *Architect*

Organizations

A & J Washroom Accessories
ADL Associates
Access America
Alvarado Manufacturing Co., Inc.
American Olean Tile Company
American Parquet Association
American Sanitary Partition Corporation
American Specialties, Inc.
American Standard, Inc.
Architectural Paneling, Inc.
Architectural Woodwork Institute
Armor Elevator Company
Ascente
Audio Unlimited of East Meadow, L.I.
B & B Rare Woods
Bauman
Bobrick Washroom Equipment, Inc.
Bretford Mfg., Inc.
Brown Manufacturing Co.
Buckingham-Virginia Slate Co.
Camden Window and Millwork
Celotex Corporation
Clairson International
Closet Maid Systems
Concord Elevator Company
Conde Nast Publications, Inc.
Culter Manufacturing Corp.
Curvoflite Stairs and Millwork, Inc.
Dancker, Sellew, & Douglas
Derksen (USA), Inc.
Designers Sign Company
Doug Mockett & Company
Dover Elevator Systems
Eastern Paralyzed Veterans Association
Eggers Industries
Electric Time Company, Inc.
Eljer Plumbingware Division of Wallace-Murray Corporation
Ellens's Bracket, Inc.
Euroflair
Focal Point, Inc.
Formica Corporation
Franciscan Tile Company
Garaventa (Canada) Ltd.
General Electric Lighting/North America
General Services Administration
Glencoe Publishing Co.
Goodheart-Willcox Co., Inc.
Habitat
Hafele
Hartco Flooring/Tibbals Flooring Co.
Haws Corporation
Herman Miller, Inc.
Hollow Metal Manufacturers Association
Horton Lees Lighting Designs, Inc.
Howe Furniture Company
Hussey Seating Company
Illinois Agricultural Experiment Station
Ilttala, Inc.
Indiana Limestone Institute of America
Innerface Sign Systems, Inc.
Insulated Steel Door Systems Institute
Intergraph Corporation
Interkal, Inc.
International Steel Revolving Door Company
Jacuzzi Inc.
JG Furniture Systems, Inc.
Just Bulbs Ltd.
Kinney Shoe Corporation
Kirsch Division of Cooper Industries, Inc.
Kohler Co.
Lapeyre Stair Co.
Lehigh Furniture Corporation
Library Bureau, Inc.
Lightolier Inc.
MacIevy Health and Fitness Products
Majestic Fireplaces
Manville
Maple Flooring Manufacturers Association
Marble from Greece
Marble Institute of America, Inc.
Marvin Windows
McGraw-Hill, Inc.
McKinney/Parker
Merillat
Midwest Plan Service
Modernfold, Inc.
Montgomery KONE, Inc.
National Association of Architectural Metal Manufacturers
National Association of Ornamental Metal Manufacturers
National Cathode Corp.
National Retail Merchants Association
National Terrazzo and Mosaic Association
Nesson Lamps, Inc.
New York City Housing Authority
Nichols Publishing
Niland Company
Osram Sylvania, Inc.
PAM International
Parker/Nutone
Philips Lighting Co.
Phillips & Brooks, Inc.
Pittcon Softforms
Pittsburg Corning Corporation
Putnam Rolling Ladder Co., Inc.
Railex Corporation
Random House, Inc.

Reeve Store Equipment Co.
Roberts Step-Life Systems
Roppe Rubber Corporation
St. Charles Kitchens
Schlage Lock Company
Schulte
Selby Furniture Hardware Co., Inc.
Simon & Schuster
Sister Kenny Institute
Stairways, Inc.
StairWorld, Inc.
Stanley Hardware
Steelcase Inc.
Steel Door Institute
Sweet's Division of McGraw-Hill, Inc.
Tarkett
Tile Council of America, Inc.
Triangle Pacific Corp.
U.S. Department of Agriculture
U.S. Department of Commerce
U.S. Department of Housing and Urban Development
U.S. Department of the Interior
U.S. Department of Transportation
U.S. Gypsum Corporation
Vermont Castings
Watson Guptil
Western Wood Products Association
Whirlpool Corporation
White Consolidated Industries, Inc.
Whitney Library of Design
Winebarger Church Furniture
W. M. Shanahan Inc.
Woodwork Institute of California

Foreword to the Second Edition

I am honored and delighted that the three coauthors, who collectively have over 100 years of experience in interior design education and practice, have asked me to write a foreword to the second edition of this great resource.

Over the years, I have come to realize that the best interiors are the end result of a creative process that, at some point, must involve the collection and integration of a tremendous amount of practical information and technical data.

When the first edition of *Time Saver Standards for Interior Design and Space Planning* was published a decade ago, it immediately served as a comprehensive and well-organized resource for such information and data and soon became the must-have reference for designers of the interior environment.

This second edition is even more comprehensive than the first, with over 500 more pages. It contains sharper graphics, CADD-generated details, color representations of wood and marble finishes, as well as new and expanded sections including retail design, hospitality design, health care facilities, and conference centers. The section dealing with office spaces now includes additional information and planning data for the design of videoconferencing facilities. In addition, an entirely new section on the ADA has also been added that provides an analysis of the various federal legislation that impacts accessibility. Also included are related detailed design guidelines.

This very successful new edition reflects the increasing professionalism of the interior design field and the ever growing acknowledgment that interior design is a serious subject affecting the health, safety, and welfare of the public. There is no doubt that interior designers, architects, facility managers, design educators, and design students will find the new *Time Saver Standards for Interior Design and Space Planning* indispensable.

Scott M. Ageloff, IDEC, ASID, AIA
Dean, New York School of Design

Foreword to the First Edition

A resource of incredible range and detail, this volume was compiled by three remarkably inspired designers and educators. Because of their great knowledge of interior design and their sensitivity to the subject matter, they have created the most comprehensive sourcebook for the field ever.

The editors spent three years bringing this volume to fruition, culling the best project drawings by outstanding designers to illustrate much of the subject matter and tapping their own anthropometric expertise to address space planning and special function areas. They also address the importance of historic influence on present-day design with an impressive review of period furniture and interior details. All of these things have produced a reference work of such scope and inclusiveness that the reader will be relieved of many hours in the pursuit of details and information, time saved that can be used for more innovation and creativity in developing solutions for client needs.

The authority and abundance of this book are a testimony to the maturation of this profession of ours and to the editors' appreciation and understanding of its importance.

Jack Lowery, FASID, IDEC

My pleasure in being invited to write part of the Foreword swiftly changed to respect and, in turn, awe at the scope and depth of this book.

To say that it is an encyclopedic compilation and mass of information is obvious. But it is especially and uniquely user-friendly. It presents the written and illustrative data without a trace of pedantry; it meets a real need in our interior designer professional resources. The editors' effort, dedication, and patience, sustained during a period of over three years, are truly heroic. An astonishing number of hours of input have produced a reference of incalculable value.

I offer the same cautionary advice mentioned in the Preface: If the book is a wonderfully comprehensive reference and support for interior design standards, historical material, suggested plan and design criteria, and regulatory limitations, it is not—it will never be—a substitute for the inspired, creative design act, for imaginative solutions are always driven by new cultural conditions, programs, and functional requirements.

So to all you designers: Continue to spin your dreams, but do not stray far from this great resource.

Lawrence J. Israel, AIA, FISP

Preface to the Second Edition

Several significant changes have been incorporated into this second edition. Section 1 has been expanded to include two entirely new subsections entitled "Banking Spaces" and "Health Care Spaces." The existing subsection entitled "Hospitality Spaces" has been almost doubled in size and expanded to include planning data and layouts relative to hotels and conference centers. The subsection entitled "Retail Spaces" has also been more than doubled in size. The subsection entitled "Office Spaces" has been expanded to include additional workstation configurations and planning criteria for videoconferencing facilities. For the first time in a professional handbook of this type, color has been introduced in the form of color plates of wood veneers and marble finishes. The entire book has also been expanded by more than 500 pages.

Perhaps the most significant change, however, is the addition of a major section dealing with accessible design, including the Americans with Disabilities Act (ADA) requirements and related illustrated accessibility guidelines and legislation. It should be noted that many of the drawings throughout this book may not, in fact, conform to the requirements of the ADA for a number of reasons, as follows:

- The ADA requirements apply mostly to public accommodations, while many of the details in the various sections of this book may be used in other types of spaces.
- In certain situations, such as minor alterations to existing spaces and/or when conformance is simply not feasible, nonconforming details may be used.
- Projects located in foreign countries do not require conformance to the ADA.

Accordingly, the reader is advised that, in such cases where conformance to the ADA is required, Section 5 of this book be consulted in order to ensure conformance. The reader is also cautioned that the ADA is to some extent a work in progress and always subject to interpretation, challenges, and changes. Moreover, conditions impacting negatively on accessibility continue to be brought to the attention of the U.S. Architectural and Transportation Barriers Compliance Board and new design guidelines developed and added. It is essential, therefore, that the designer keep abreast of these ongoing changes to the law.

Joseph De Chiara
Julius Panero
Martin Zelnik

Preface to the First Edition

Time-Saver Standards for Interior Design and Space Planning is a professional handbook dealing with the planning, design, and detailing of interior spaces. Its primary goal is to provide, within a single reference, information that typically is found dispersed throughout a multitude of sources, including manufacturers' catalogs, technical literature, books dealing with historic styles, and documents and drawings from various projects.

This handbook can be used by the small and medium-size interior design or architectural firm to establish an instant reference library of design data and details by providing a broad selection of detail types and techniques. In addition, the large firm will be able to substantially augment and modify an existing library of details.

Perhaps the most unique feature of this handbook is the vast array of construction and woodwork details reproduced directly from actual working drawings contributed by some of the nation's leading interior design and architectural firms. It is this that makes the handbook particularly useful to the interior designer, architect, and student alike.

This book consists of five sections. The first, entitled "Planning and Design of Interior Spaces," deals with residential, office, hospitality, and retail spaces in terms of the relevant planning, design, and detailing data specifically associated with each. The second section, entitled "Construction Details and Finishes," deals with various basic interior construction components associated with most interior spaces. These components include partitions, wall openings, wall finishes, floors and floor finishes, doors, ceilings, stairs, fireplaces, and lighting. Details relevant to each component have been contributed by practicing interior designers and architects as well as manufacturers.

The third section, entitled "Architectural Woodwork," deals with standard joinery and casework details, customized woodwork details, cornices and moldings, and furniture hardware. The fourth section, entitled "Specialties," deals with various specialized areas of equipment, systems, furnishings, and decoration, including signage and graphics, audiovisual systems, window treatments, and accessories. Information for these subject areas is drawn from manufacturers, suppliers, and designers.

The sixth section, entitled "General Reference Data," provides the most comprehensive set of time-saving reference materials found in handbooks of this type, including tables, charts, formulas, and planning guidelines. Of particular interest to the architect, interior designer, and facility manager are tables that can be easily used to determine carpet and wall covering yardage. Charts and drawings relative to human factors and planning standards are also provided.

It should be noted that since the details and other information presented in this book have been compiled from so many different sources, it is difficult to ensure that all the data are entirely accurate or appropriate; for example, in some instances planning guidelines may reflect minimum acceptable standards and not necessarily ideal or preferred standards. In other instances the details indicated may have been perfectly adequate in the context of the total building design of which they were a part, but they may well require modification to reflect design conditions and the reader's intended use. It should also be noted that building codes, fire safety regulations, barrier-free standards, and many other laws governing the design and construction of buildings vary from state to state. Accordingly, the reader should consult all applicable local, state, and federal codes for conformance prior to applying any of the information contained in this book. Moreover, the reader is cautioned that the dimensional information provided in connection with furniture, equipment, appliances, accessories, and so on, has been obtained from manufacturers and technical literature and thus varies from supplier to supplier and from source to source. Certain items may have been discontinued, others modified, and still others replaced. Although every effort has been made to ensure the reasonableness of the information, the reader is cautioned to consult the manufacturer of the item specified for current dimensional data.

The reader is also advised that most drawings and other illustrative material have been enlarged or reduced for reasons of page layout and page size. The reader is cautioned, therefore, to disregard any scale designations and not to scale the drawings in order to determine any additional dimensional information.

Finally, as mentioned before, the plans and details contained in this book were extracted from complete sets of actual working drawings prepared by many different contributors. They were selected both because they were representative of typical situations faced by the designer of interior spaces and because they were particularly informative. The authors would like to underscore the fact that these plans and details, as well as all the other material presented in this book, are intended to serve only as a helpful point of departure in connection with the design process, and not as a substitute for original thinking and creativity.

Although every effort has been made to present reasonably accurate information, the editors and publisher assume no liability or responsibility for damage to persons or property alleged to have occurred as a direct or indirect consequence of the use and application of any of the contents of this book. The reader is advised to view the subject matter primarily as guidelines for preliminary planning and detailing, and to properly review, modify, and process it to ensure conformance with local codes and practices and appropriateness of applicability.

Joseph De Chiara
Julius Panero
Martin Zelnik

1
PLANNING AND DESIGN OF INTERIOR SPACES

RESIDENTIAL SPACES

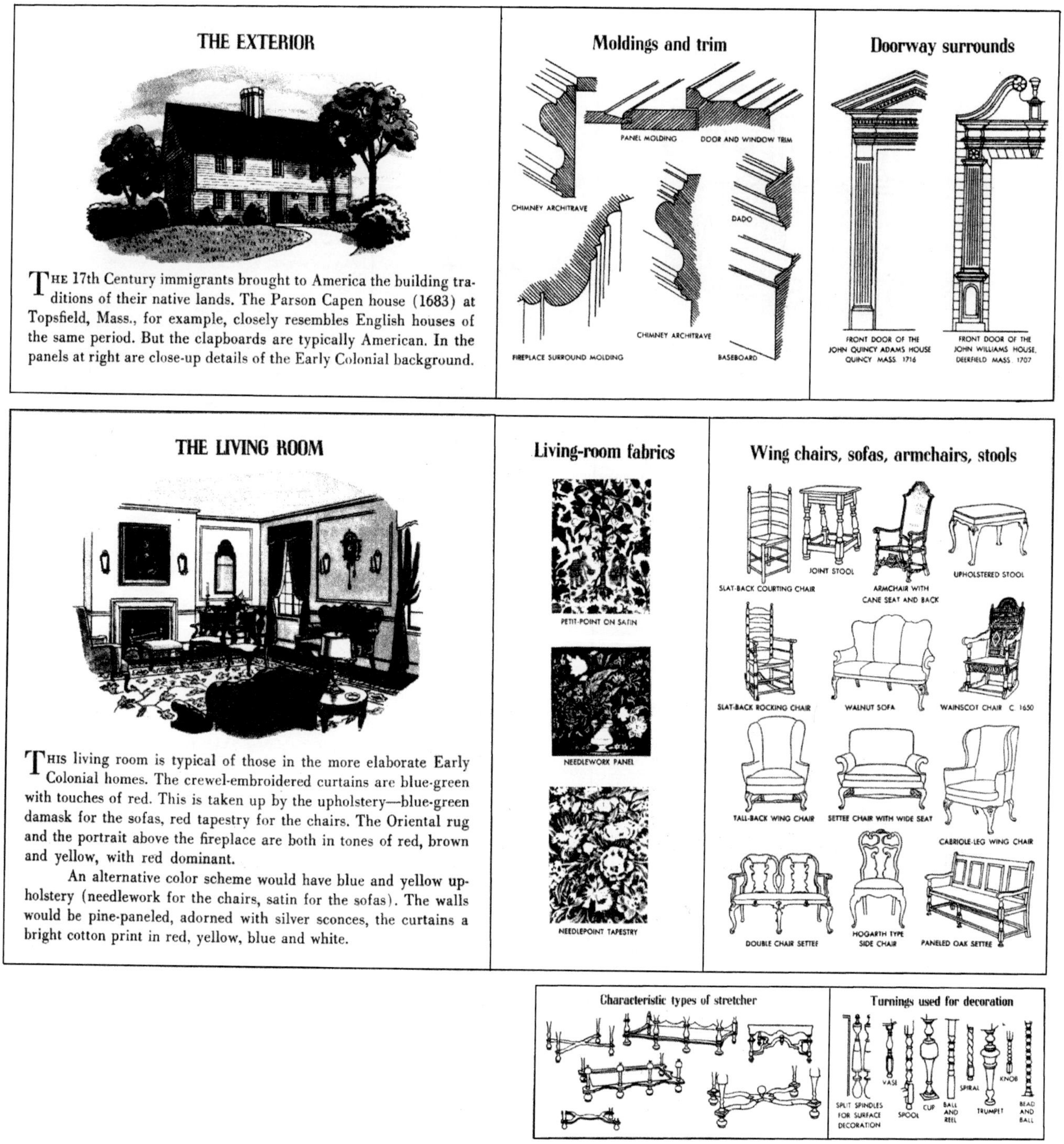
THE EXTERIOR
THE 17th Century immigrants brought to America the building traditions of their native lands. The Parson Capen house (1683) at Topsfield, Mass., for example, closely resembles English houses of the same period. But the clapboards are typically American. In the panels at right are close-up details of the Early Colonial background.
Moldings and trim
PANEL MOLDING
DOOR AND WINDOW TRIM
CHIMNEY ARCHITRAVE
DADO
CHIMNEY ARCHITRAVE
FIREPLACE SURROUND MOLDING
BASEBOARD
Doorway surrounds
FRONT DOOR OF THE JOHN QUINCY ADAMS HOUSE QUINCY MASS. 1716
FRONT DOOR OF THE JOHN WILLIAMS HOUSE, DEERFIELD MASS. 1707
THE LIVING ROOM
THIS living room is typical of those in the more elaborate Early Colonial homes. The crewel-embroidered curtains are blue-green with touches of red. This is taken up by the upholstery—blue-green damask for the sofas, red tapestry for the chairs. The Oriental rug and the portrait above the fireplace are both in tones of red, brown and yellow, with red dominant.
An alternative color scheme would have blue and yellow upholstery (needlework for the chairs, satin for the sofas). The walls would be pine-paneled, adorned with silver sconces, the curtains a bright cotton print in red, yellow, blue and white.
Living-room fabrics
PETIT-POINT ON SATIN
NEEDLEWORK PANEL
NEEDLEPOINT TAPESTRY
Wing chairs, sofas, armchairs, stools
SLAT-BACK COURTING CHAIR
JOINT STOOL
ARMCHAIR WITH CANE SEAT AND BACK
UPHOLSTERED STOOL
SLAT-BACK ROCKING CHAIR
WALNUT SOFA
WAINSCOT CHAIR C. 1650
TALL-BACK WING CHAIR
SETTEE CHAIR WITH WIDE SEAT
CABRIOLE-LEG WING CHAIR
DOUBLE CHAIR SETTEE
HOGARTH TYPE SIDE CHAIR
PANELED OAK SETTEE
Characteristic types of stretcher
Turnings used for decoration
SPLIT SPINDLES FOR SURFACE DECORATION
VASE
SPOOL
CUP
BALL AND REEL
SPIRAL
TRUMPET
KNOB
BEAD AND BALL

Fig. 1 Motifs characteristic of Early Colonial furniture

PERIOD FURNITURE

SEVENTEENTH-CENTURY AMERICAN: COLONIAL

Furniture made in America during the Early Colonial period (the seventeenth century and the first quarter of the eighteenth century) was necessarily, and possibly also by choice, of the simplest type. The early colonists, particularly those in New England, had not time or equipment to spare for any but the essentials of life.

Turning on the lathe was the simplest to achieve and thus the most common form of furniture decoration. It was also a process capable of infinite variations of design (some are shown in Fig. 1).

PERIOD FURNITURE
17th Century American: Colonial

THE DINING ROOM

THE color scheme in this dining room is keyed to the low tones of the pine paneling and walnut furniture, the soft gleam of the smooth polished brass chandelier. The bannister back chairs have rush-bottom seats. Brilliant red and white printed cotton is used for the curtains. The hooked rug is in reds and greens.

Alternatively the curtains might be of red and yellow crewel embroidery, the upholstery of red brocade. In the panels at right are furniture and fabrics suited to an Early Colonial dining room.

Dining-room fabrics

Dining tables, table chairs

THE BEDROOM

THIS little bedroom with its pine paneling and low ceiling is typical of the Early Colonial period. The bed, decorated with hangings of crewel work in an Oriental design. is the most important feature of the room. The chairs are upholstered in yellow damask. The green printed cotton used for the little draped window curtains is echoed by the greens in the hooked rug on the floor.

Alternatively the walls might be painted a dark gray-blue, the curtain material being a red printed cotton on a gray ground. The furniture is of walnut and oak.

Bedroom fabrics

Beds, daybed, cradle

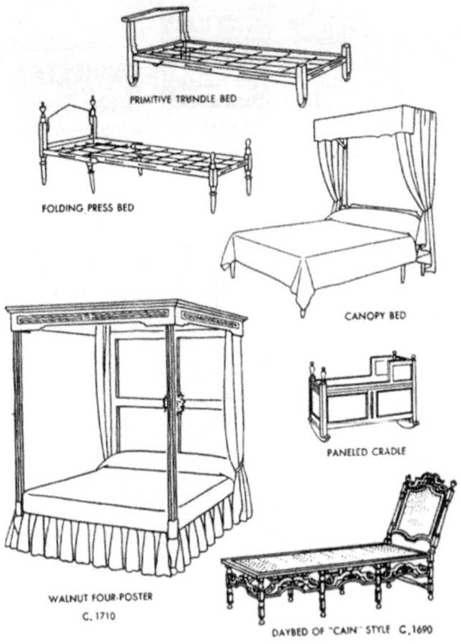

Fig. 1 *(Continued)*

Even the most costly furniture in this Early Colonial period was usually of solid wood, unfinished except for stain or waxing. Veneering and shellacking, to gain carefully patterned graining and high finish, were still unexploited. The pine paneling on the walls might be left unfinished, waxed, or painted. Other woods near at hand in the forests and so commonly used were oak, birch, maple, and walnut. Generally, American work is patterned upon English work of 10 or 20 years earlier. In Pennsylvania and Delaware, which were settled by colonists of Swedish and German descent (in addition to the English), much of the simple furniture was painted, with its motifs transferred from European peasant art.

In the later years of the Early Colonial period, when New Englanders were already beginning to trade with the Orient, much Chinese porcelain was imported. The oriental influence was strong in textiles; the Tree of Life pattern was very popular at this period. Native textiles copied the patterns and colors of India, Persia, and China. The originals, or good copies of them, were usually imported from England.

Armchair, side chairs

"CAIN" CHAIRS, FLEMISH SCROLLS AND FEET. CANE BACKS AND SEATS

BANNISTER BACK, SIMPLE TURNED LEGS

EARLY TYPE CABRIOLE LEGS

CANE SEAT, PLAIN SPLAT

LATE QUEEN ANNE TYPE, FLATTENED BALL AND CLAW FEET

BANNISTER BACK, SPANISH FEET

EARLY QUEEN ANNE TYPE WITH DUTCH SPLAT BACK

UPHOLSTERED CHAIR, WITH DUTCH FEET

SHELL CRESTING, SHALLOW SEAT

PIERCED BACK, BALL-AND-CLAW FEET

Sideboards, dressers, chests

OAK SIDEBOARD CABRIOLE LEGS C 1650

LOW CHEST WITH DRAWERS

NEW ENGLAND OAK PRESS CUPBOARD

HEAVY OAK CHEST OF DRAWERS WITH APPLIED MOLDINGS

OAK SIDEBOARD, TWISTED LEGS

WILLIAM AND MARY TYPE GLASS-FRONTED CABINET

PENNSYLVANIA SPICE CUPBOARD C. 1700

WALNUT DRESSER, PANELED DOORS

Dining-room accessories

WROUGHT-IRON ANDIRON

BRASS ANDIRON

SPICE BOX

PAINTED BELLOWS

SPOON RACK

CANDLESTICKS

17th CENTURY DUTCH WALL CLOCK

BRASS CANDELABRA

SILVER CANDLESTAND

SILVER SCONCE WITH RAISED EMBOSSED EDGE

WALNUT-FRAMED MIRRORS AMERICAN QUEEN ANNE STYLE, C. 1710

ETCHED MIRROR SCONCE, GLASS DRIP DISHES

Chests, kas, highboy, chests of drawers

MAPLE CHEST OF DRAWERS

BOX TABLE OF OAK AND MAPLE C 1670

INLAID CHEST OF DRAWERS WITH DROP HANDLES

CHEST ON FRAME, DECORATED WITH SCRATCH CARVING

HIGHBOY WITH TRUMPET-TURNED LEGS

CONNECTICUT PAINTED CHEST

DUTCH KAS WITH BALL FEET

DUTCH KAS FROM NEW YORK PAINTED IN GRAY AND WHITE

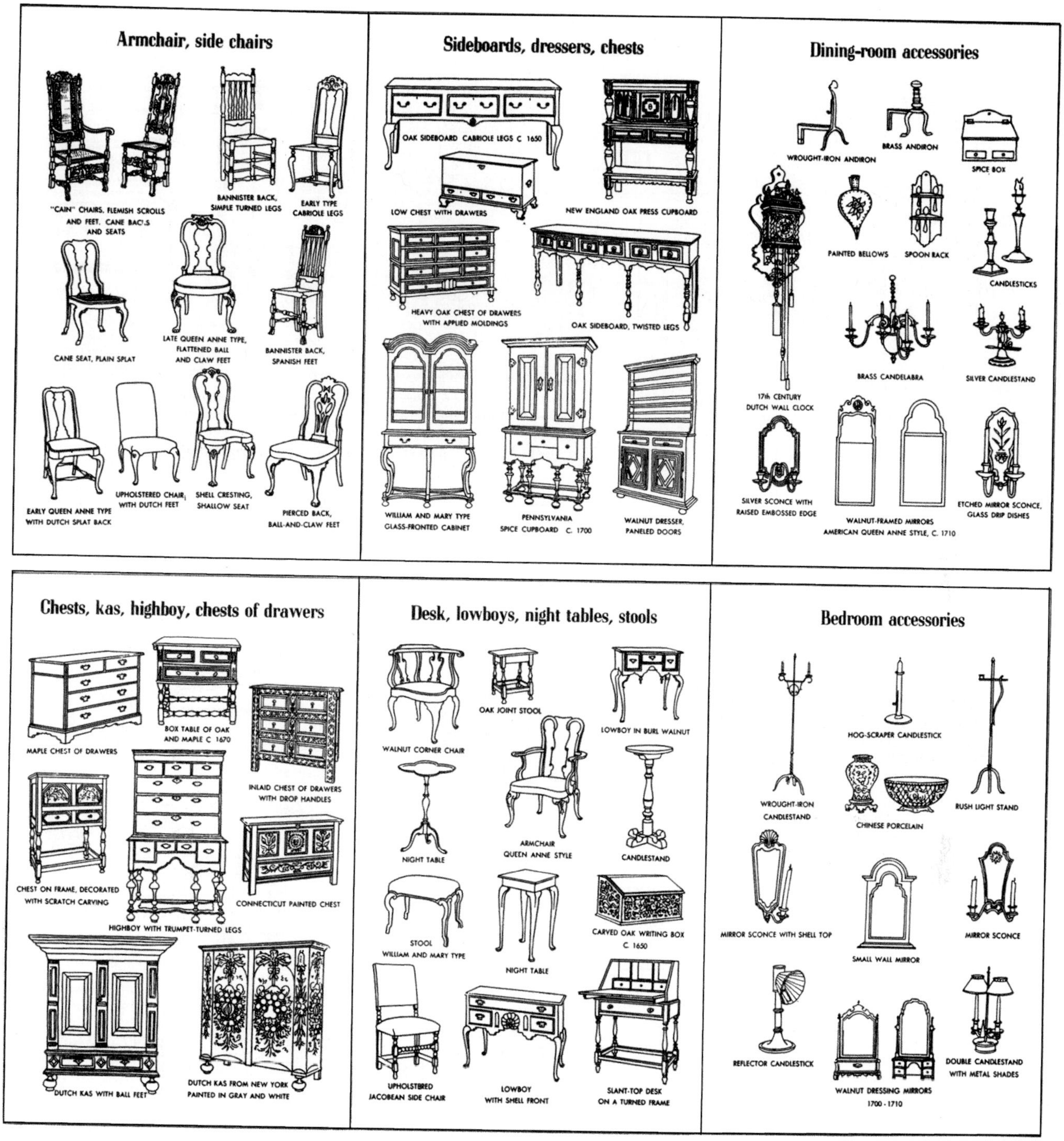

Fig. 1 ***(Continued)***

The colors in common use were of a piece with the solid, sturdy furniture. They seldom escaped from the conventional round of blue, red, gold, and natural gray. The only exceptions were imported fabrics and the occasional hard brilliance of the Chinese porcelain found in the great houses of the day. Whatever luxury there was at this time expressed itself in textiles and silver rather than in furniture. Settlers in the South, many of them English aristocrats, maintained a higher standard of comfort than those in the North; they imported most of their furniture and fabrics from England and continued to do so for a long time.

Early Colonial furniture taken as a whole is sturdy, but not subtle. Furniture patterns in this country changed slowly. Paneling relieved the larger flat areas such as cupboard doors and drawer fronts. The latter were further decorated by quite elaborate fretted brass and wrought-iron hardware (see Fig. 1).

More carefully embellished than the earliest American furniture were the pieces imported by the colonists from their various homelands. These pieces, and the memories of others left behind, later served as models for American craftsmen. The dominant influence

PERIOD FURNITURE
17th Century American: Colonial

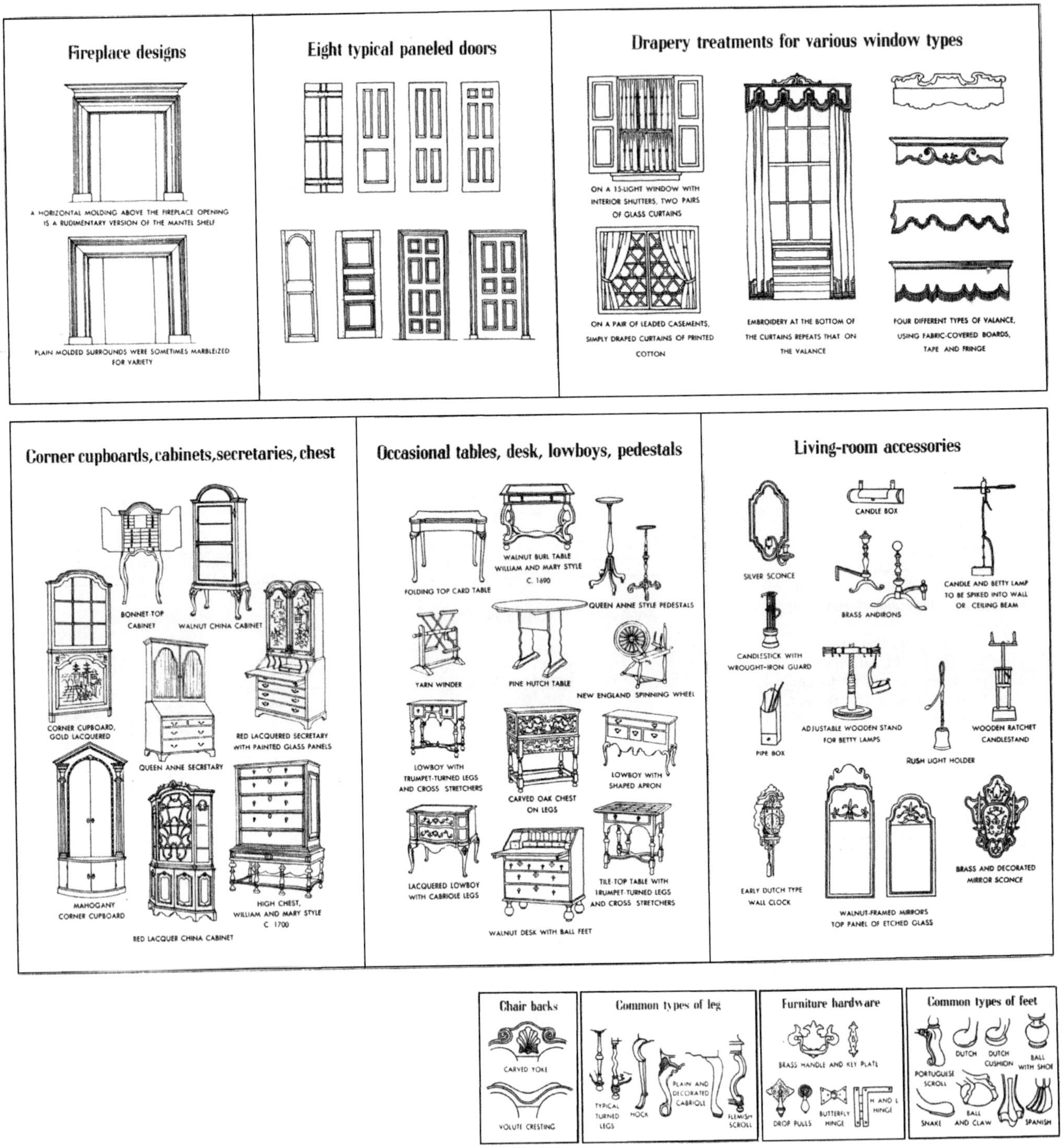

Fig. 1 *(Continued)*

was Dutch, for the English had a Hollander, William of Orange, as king. He and his queen, Mary, gave their names to a style of which elaborate stretchers (particularly on highboys, lowboys, and occasional tables) and scrolled legs are among the most obvious characteristics.

Also from Dutch, Spanish, and Portuguese sources are derived most of the carved feet which distinguish this Early Colonial furniture and often give clues to its date and place of origin.

EIGHTEENTH-CENTURY AMERICAN: COLONIAL

Whereas furniture of the Early Colonial period was often so primitive as to be referred to as "kitchen Colonial," in this succeeding era dignity and luxury prevail in the centers of taste. The furnishings reflect the fashionable contemporary styles of England and stately country homes, whether on New England farms or Virginia and Carolina plantations, followed these styles. This gave rise to a number of notable architects, craftsmen, and workers in metal and wood.

THE EXTERIOR

The architectural details shown in the five panels at right are characteristic of the background for 18th Century Colonial decoration. As one of the finest houses of the period we have pictured (at right) "Westover" the great mansion erected by William Byrd in Charles City Co., Virginia. Typical of this period are the brick walls and chimneys, the stone or white painted brick trim. In the North wood was in more common use than brick for the exterior, and the interior wooden trim was finely detailed.

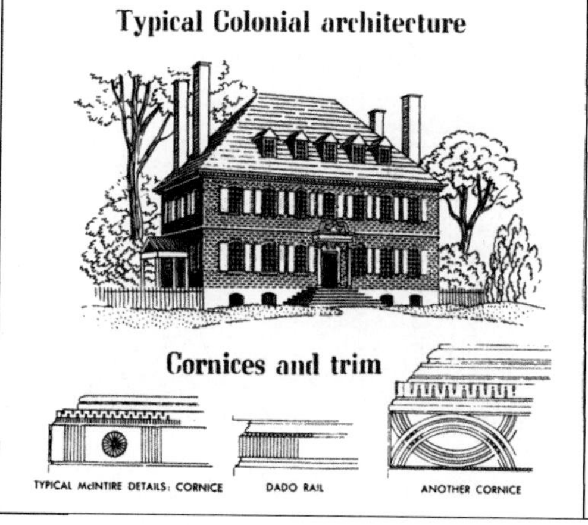
Typical Colonial architecture
Cornices and trim
TYPICAL McINTIRE DETAILS: CORNICE
DADO RAIL
ANOTHER CORNICE

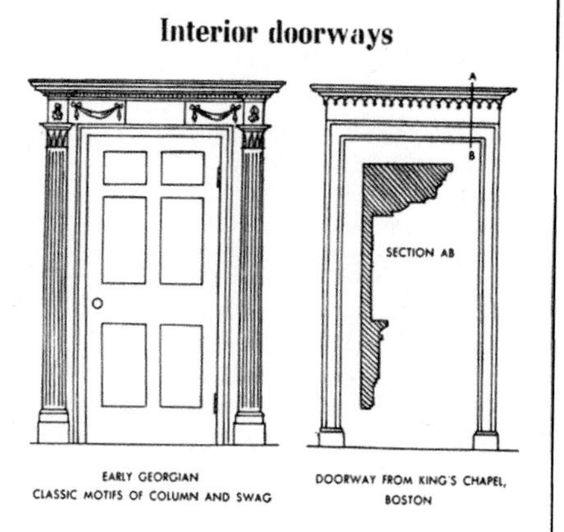
Interior doorways
SECTION AB
EARLY GEORGIAN
CLASSIC MOTIFS OF COLUMN AND SWAG
DOORWAY FROM KING'S CHAPEL, BOSTON

THE LIVING ROOM

The furniture, fabrics and accessories shown in these panels are all suitable to the living room, and they are all typical of the 18th Century Colonial style.

The interior pictured at right is a fine Colonial living room carefully restored to its 18th Century state. The walls are Naples yellow, the columns and fireplace white. Red and green are dominant in the Oriental rug, dark greens and browns in the portrait above the fireplace. So the sofa is upholstered in striped satin, the armchair in yellow Venetian brocade, the wing chair in a printed linen. The urns are of Chinese porcelain.

Another color scheme might be: pearly gray walls, oyster white columns and fireplace. Red would be dominant in the Oriental carpet, dark greens and red in the portrait. There would be red damask on the sofa, green rep on the wing chair, and gold damask for the armchair.

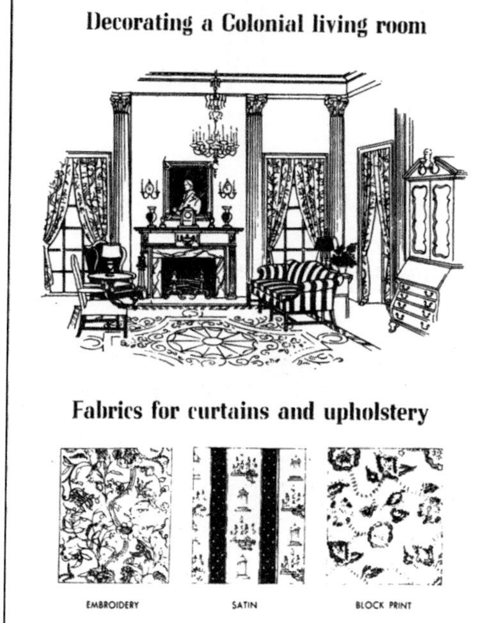
Decorating a Colonial living room
Fabrics for curtains and upholstery
EMBROIDERY
SATIN
BLOCK PRINT

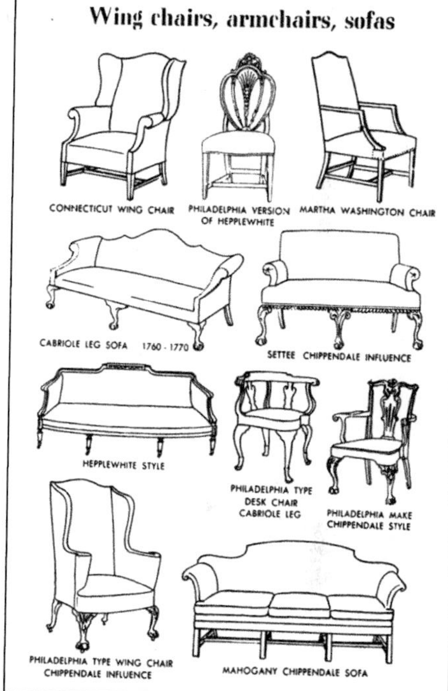
Wing chairs, armchairs, sofas
CONNECTICUT WING CHAIR
PHILADELPHIA VERSION OF HEPPLEWHITE
MARTHA WASHINGTON CHAIR
CABRIOLE LEG SOFA 1760 - 1770
SETTEE CHIPPENDALE INFLUENCE
HEPPLEWHITE STYLE
PHILADELPHIA TYPE DESK CHAIR CABRIOLE LEG
PHILADELPHIA MAKE CHIPPENDALE STYLE
PHILADELPHIA TYPE WING CHAIR CHIPPENDALE INFLUENCE
MAHOGANY CHIPPENDALE SOFA

Fig. 1 ***(Continued)***

The eighteenth-century Colonial period was the first of the really great eras in American cabinetmaking.

The manufacture of wallpaper in this country was begun by 1763. Before this it was from Europe. The "Pennsylvania fireplace" or "Franklin stove" was invented by Benjamin Franklin in 1742 and immediately became popular up and down the Atlantic seaboard. Philadelphia was a furniture style center—in fact, the most active in the creation of taste—with Boston and Charleston following.

A number of artists and craftsmen of this period bear mentioning. Among the architects were Samuel McIntire, Charles Bulfinch, John James, Richard Mundy, Peter Harrison, John Kirk, and Isaac Royall. These men were greatly influenced by the English architects Isaac Ware, James Gibbs, Robert Morris, Abraham Swan, William Halfpenny, Batty Langley, and William Pain, who in turn were in debt to the Italian masters Palladio and Giacomo Leoni. Among the cabinetmakers were Moses Dodge, Stephen Dwight, Henry Hardcastle, Gilbert Ash, Robert Wallace, Charles Shipman, John Brinner, John Tremain, Charles Warham, John Brown, Bemsley Wells, Thomas and Benjamin Laskey, Jonathan Goodhue, and Job Trask. Among the upholsterers were Stephen Callow, Richard Wenman, Joseph Cox, and John Taylor; among the metalworkers were William Coffin, Wilkins, Joseph Liddell, William Bradford, John Bassett, and Peter Harby; and among the painters were John Singleton Copley, Joseph Blackburn, John Ramage, James Peale, and Charles Wilson Peale. Important manufacturers were, of wallpaper, Jackson of Battersea (England) and, of window and bottle glass, Baron Stiegel and Caspar Wistar.

Fabrics most commonly used during the Colonial period were damask, camblet, Indian gimp and binding, moreen (woolen drapery cloth), harrateen cloth, block-printed cotton and linen, cashmere, calico, dimity, durance, stout worsted cloth, turkey work (tufted "pilelike"), padu-

PERIOD FURNITURE
18th Century American: Colonial

DINING ROOM

The furniture and fabrics shown in the five panels at right would look well in any dining room; but for your guidance in the selection of materials and colors we illustrate at right a fine Colonial dining room as it might have appeared in the 18th Century.

The pine-panelled walls are colored a light ocher, the niches Chinese red. Curtains are French blue. Blue, rust and beige predominate in the Oriental rug, dark green, blue and black in the portrait over the fireplace. Table and chairs are of walnut, the sideboard of mahogany.

An alternative color scheme would be light blue-gray walls with cream niches. Curtains would be oyster white silk, the Oriental rug having a greenish tan background.

Decorating a Colonial dining room

Fabric for curtains and upholstery

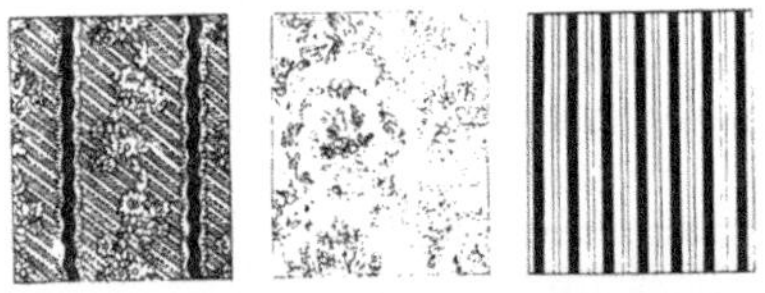

Dining tables, consoles

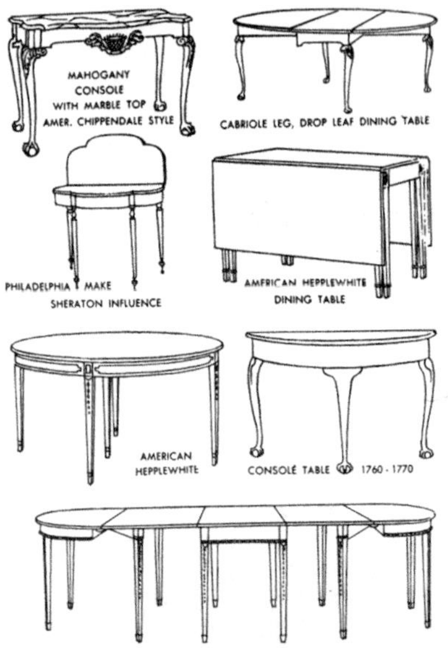

BEDROOM

In the bedroom at right, choice of color and textures was designed to achieve an impression of warmth and intimacy. The paneled walls are in two tones of gray-green, the ceiling ocher. Curtains are antique gray-green satin.

Furniture is walnut, except for the mahogany bed, which has a yellow taffeta spread. Fireside chairs are covered in crimson damask side chairs in turkey work.

An alternative color scheme would be: warm gray walls with oyster white moldings. The ceiling would be cream, the carpet solid taupe, and the curtains of blue damask. The bed would have a white moire spread and blue valance. The side chairs would be upholstered in yellow damask, the wing chair in turkey work.

Decorating a Colonial bedroom

Fabrics for curtains, upholstery, canopy

Four-poster beds

Fig. 1 *(Continued)*

asoy (strong silk), soy, shalloon, watchet, linsey-woolsey, fustian, silk muslin, chintz, Indian calico, tabby, sarcanet, taffeta, horsehair, camak, bancours, and brocade.

Woods most commonly used were oak, ash, elm, red cedar, mahogany, walnut, maple, pine, and cherry.

The Chippendale style merges at one end with Queen Anne, at the other with Hepplewhite, Sheraton, and Duncan Phyfe. The Rococo mounts to its zenith and starts to decline within these years. Walnut has a new rival in mahogany. And American craftsmen produced pieces of a quality which compares favorably with English work.

Marble was imported until after the Revolution, when domestic marbles began to be used. Marble chimney pieces, window sash, lead roofing, and hardware were all imported from London. The size of glass window panes gradually increased as the century progressed.

An order of small pilasters or columns supporting the mantel in a chimney piece was found only in imported work prior to the

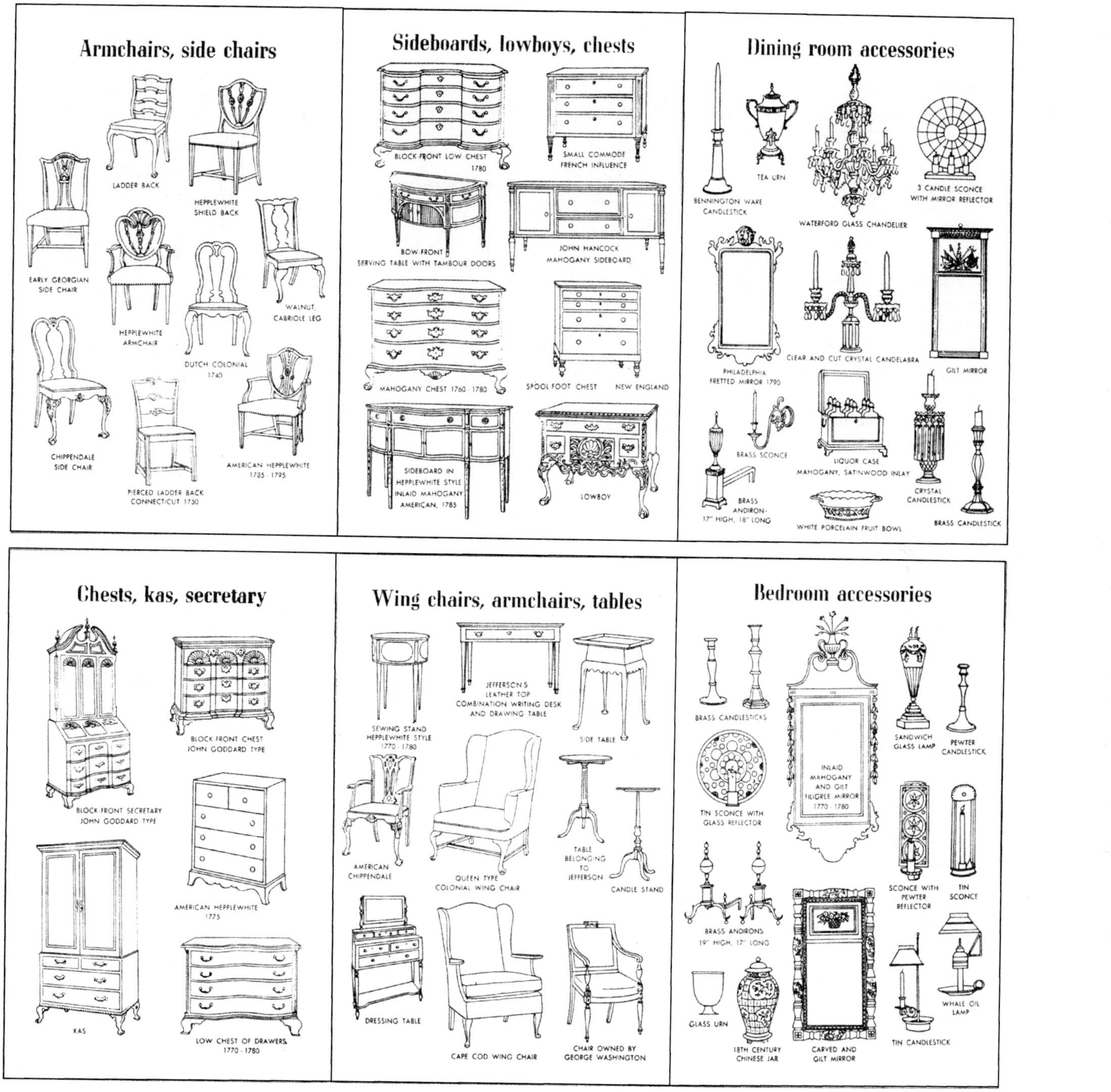

Fig. 1 ***(Continued)***

Revolution. Fireplace openings with neither cornice nor mantel shelf were long common. Ears on the architraves were almost universal, and a pediment (always broken) was very common. After 1760 the scroll pediment, or a similar treatment of the architrave, occurs.

EIGHTEENTH-CENTURY AMERICAN: FEDERAL

The Federal style is at its most suave and elegant in the furniture of Duncan Phyfe, a Scottish cabinetmaker who arrived in New York about 1795. He did not originate a style; he translated prevailing fashions into fine craftsmanship. Thomas Sheraton, then the current English favorite, and the French Directoire cabinetmakers set the style. All these designers were profoundly influenced by a rediscovery of the classic splendors of Greece and Italy.

Reeding of table, chair, and sofa legs and other framing members gives elegance to Federal furniture. Contrasting color veneer is used to outline the edges of tables and desks and to lend interest to large,

PERIOD FURNITURE
18th Century American: Federal

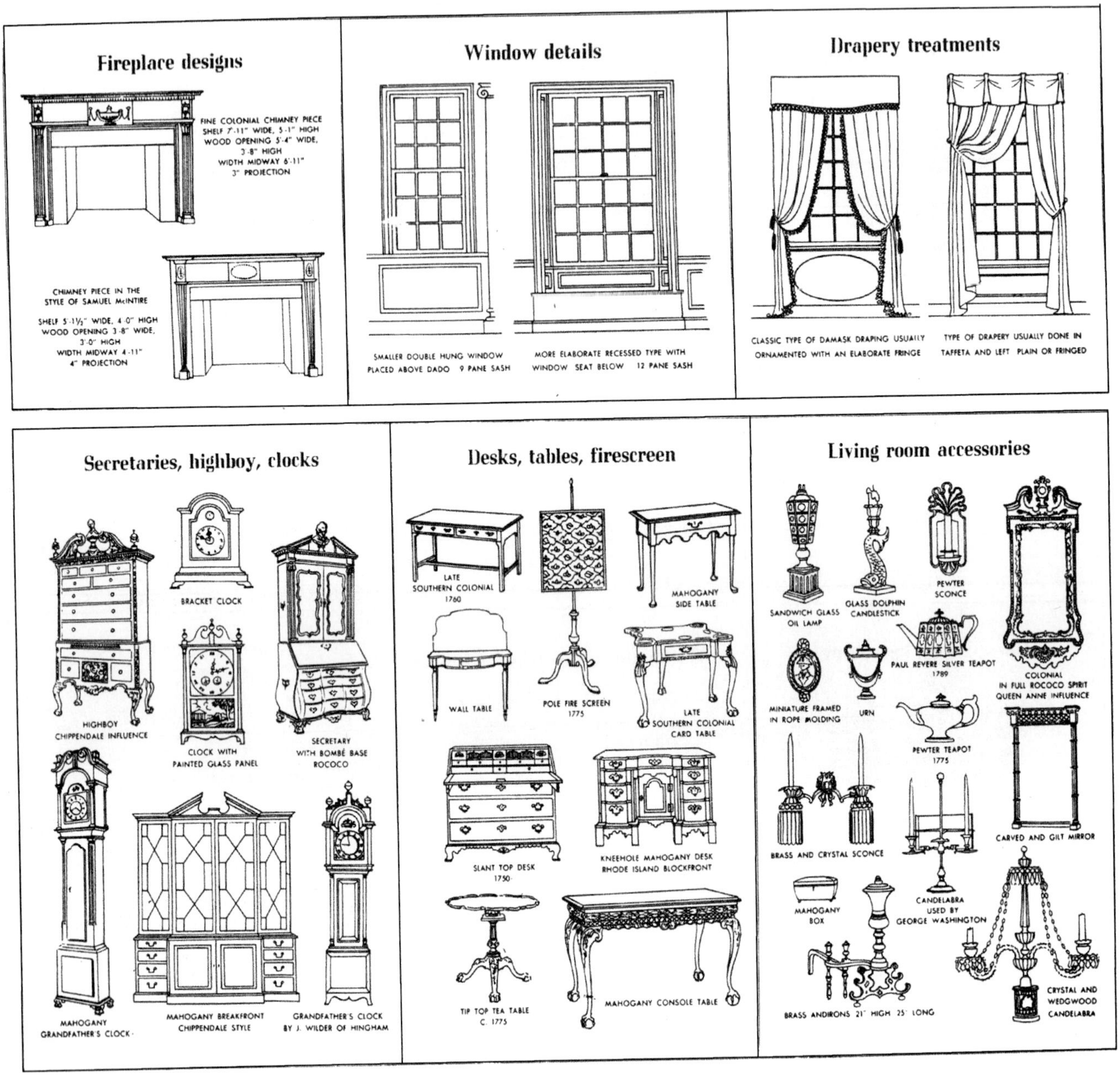

Fig. 1 ***(Continued)***

plain surfaces. Another characteristic subtlety is the raised hairline of wood, known as a cock beading, which is used to finish off the edges of drawers. Phyfe used white wood linings for the drawers in his furniture, instead of the pine linings universally employed by other American cabinetmakers of this period.

Brass ornaments (probably for the most part imported) are used extensively on Federal pieces. They have brass feet and casters, ring handles, and other types of applied ornament. Toward the end of the period, about 1825, china and glass knobs began to supplant brass rings as drawer pulls.

The new United States was in its first throes of nationalism; consequently, its emblem, the eagle, appears everywhere—on transparencies in windows, painted on fans, and inlaid in mirrors, desks, knife boxes, and brass work. The "spread eagle" became a favorite tavern sign. All kinds of historic scenes and patriotic emblems appear as decoration on clocks.

And yet, the Classic influence was even stronger than the patriotic. Earthenware and porcelain such as Crown-Derby, Worcester, and Wedgwood were molded in Classic forms and painted with delicate sepia figures in Classic robes. Silver and Sheffield plate (the latter replacing pewter) also followed Classic forms. Ireland sent Waterford glass.

Fabrics most used were damask, brocade, satin, taffeta, haircloth, toile de Jouy, printed cotton, and silk.

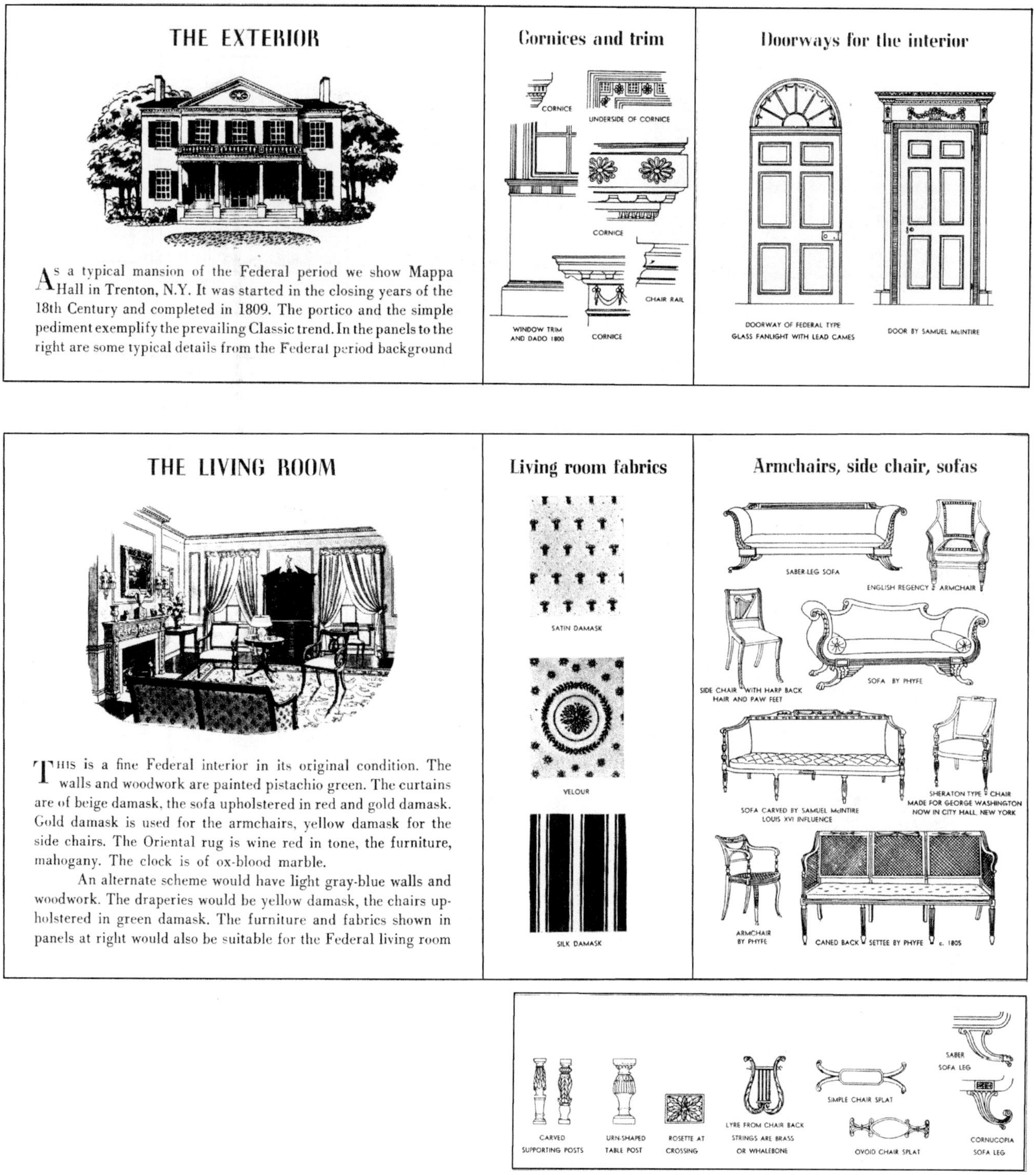
THE EXTERIOR
As a typical mansion of the Federal period we show Mappa Hall in Trenton, N.Y. It was started in the closing years of the 18th Century and completed in 1809. The portico and the simple pediment exemplify the prevailing Classic trend. In the panels to the right are some typical details from the Federal period background
Cornices and trim
CORNICE
UNDERSIDE OF CORNICE
CORNICE
CHAIR RAIL
WINDOW TRIM AND DADO 1800
CORNICE
Doorways for the interior
DOORWAY OF FEDERAL TYPE GLASS FANLIGHT WITH LEAD CAMES
DOOR BY SAMUEL McINTIRE
THE LIVING ROOM
This is a fine Federal interior in its original condition. The walls and woodwork are painted pistachio green. The curtains are of beige damask, the sofa upholstered in red and gold damask. Gold damask is used for the armchairs, yellow damask for the side chairs. The Oriental rug is wine red in tone, the furniture, mahogany. The clock is of ox-blood marble.
An alternate scheme would have light gray-blue walls and woodwork. The draperies would be yellow damask, the chairs upholstered in green damask. The furniture and fabrics shown in panels at right would also be suitable for the Federal living room
Living room fabrics
SATIN DAMASK
VELOUR
SILK DAMASK
Armchairs, side chair, sofas
SABER-LEG SOFA
ENGLISH REGENCY ARMCHAIR
SIDE CHAIR WITH HARP BACK HAIR AND PAW FEET
SOFA BY PHYFE
SOFA CARVED BY SAMUEL McINTIRE LOUIS XVI INFLUENCE
SHERATON TYPE CHAIR MADE FOR GEORGE WASHINGTON NOW IN CITY HALL, NEW YORK
ARMCHAIR BY PHYFE
CANED BACK SETTEE BY PHYFE c. 1805
CARVED SUPPORTING POSTS
URN-SHAPED TABLE POST
ROSETTE AT CROSSING
LYRE FROM CHAIR BACK STRINGS ARE BRASS OR WHALEBONE
SIMPLE CHAIR SPLAT
OVOID CHAIR SPLAT
SABER SOFA LEG
CORNUCOPIA SOFA LEG

Fig. 2 Motifs characteristic of Federal furniture

Woods most used were mahogany, cherry, and maple, and fruit woods in less splendid furniture. Curly maple often replaced the satinwood used in European models. After 1800, rosewood was used for the more costly furniture.

The Federal motifs derive almost exclusively from classical sources. The acanthus leaf, the lyre, the saber leg, the lion's mask and paw, the bowknot, rosettes, thunderbolts, trumpets, and drapery swags are all to be found on the list of standard Federal furniture motifs.

After the War of 1812, when the Federal era rose to its zenith of popularity, the laurel, cornucopia, and eagle motifs became especially popular. (See Fig. 2.)

PERIOD FURNITURE
18th Century American: Federal

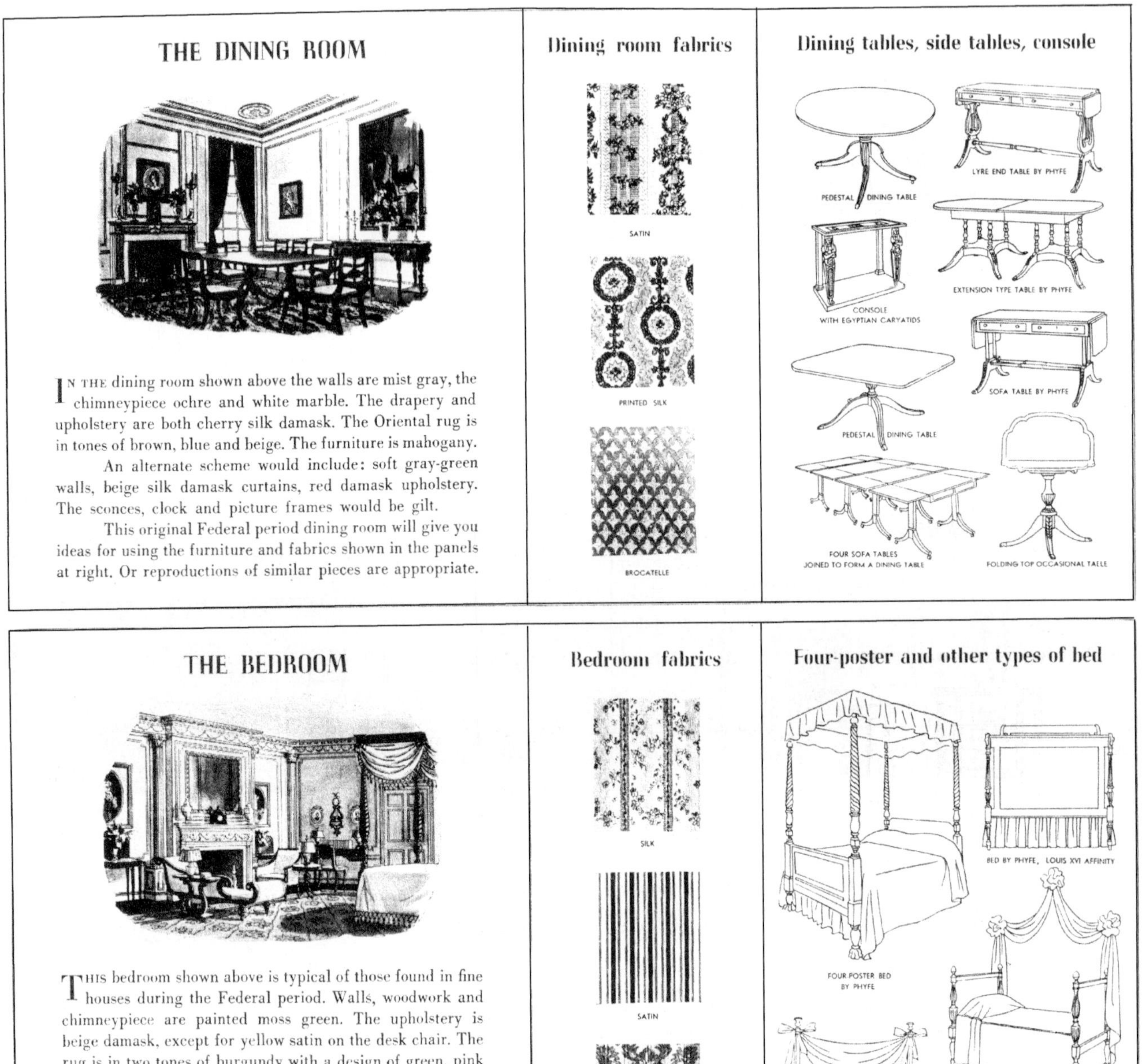

THE DINING ROOM

IN THE dining room shown above the walls are mist gray, the chimneypiece ochre and white marble. The drapery and upholstery are both cherry silk damask. The Oriental rug is in tones of brown, blue and beige. The furniture is mahogany.

An alternate scheme would include: soft gray-green walls, beige silk damask curtains, red damask upholstery. The sconces, clock and picture frames would be gilt.

This original Federal period dining room will give you ideas for using the furniture and fabrics shown in the panels at right. Or reproductions of similar pieces are appropriate.

Dining room fabrics

SATIN

PRINTED SILK

BROCATELLE

Dining tables, side tables, console

PEDESTAL DINING TABLE

LYRE END TABLE BY PHYFE

CONSOLE WITH EGYPTIAN CARYATIDS

EXTENSION TYPE TABLE BY PHYFE

PEDESTAL DINING TABLE

SOFA TABLE BY PHYFE

FOUR SOFA TABLES JOINED TO FORM A DINING TABLE

FOLDING TOP OCCASIONAL TAELE

THE BEDROOM

THIS bedroom shown above is typical of those found in fine houses during the Federal period. Walls, woodwork and chimneypiece are painted moss green. The upholstery is beige damask, except for yellow satin on the desk chair. The rug is in two tones of burgundy with a design of green, pink and white. On the walls are engravings in gilt frames.

An alternate color scheme would have walls and woodwork painted peach color. The rug would then be olive green with a design in yellow and pink. The upholstery would be blue, except for red satin on the seat of the desk chair. Other furniture and fabrics suitable for this room are shown at right

Bedroom fabrics

SILK

SATIN

DAMASK

Four-poster and other types of bed

BED BY PHYFE, LOUIS XVI AFFINITY

FOUR POSTER BED BY PHYFE

MAHOGANY BED ONE OF A PAIR BY PHYFE

BED BY PHYFE FRENCH INFLUENCE

Fig. 2 *(Continued)*

Phyfe's treatment of the acanthus leaf is so typical that many of his pieces depend upon this for their identification. It is simplified into a series of rounded grooves and ridges, with a raised tapering ridge up the center.

The lyre was used to fill in the backs of chairs, to decorate the arms of sofas, and (split apart) to support mirrors on dressing tables. Two crossed lyres are used as support for a pedestal table.

EIGHTEENTH-CENTURY ENGLISH: GEORGIAN

Thomas Chippendale was a dominating factor in the history of Georgian furniture design and his name serves as a convenient tag for the period centering in the reign of the second of the three Georges who provide the period title. Yet this English cabinetmaker achieved eminence not so much by his own work as by that of his copyists.

PERIOD FURNITURE

18th Century English: Georgian

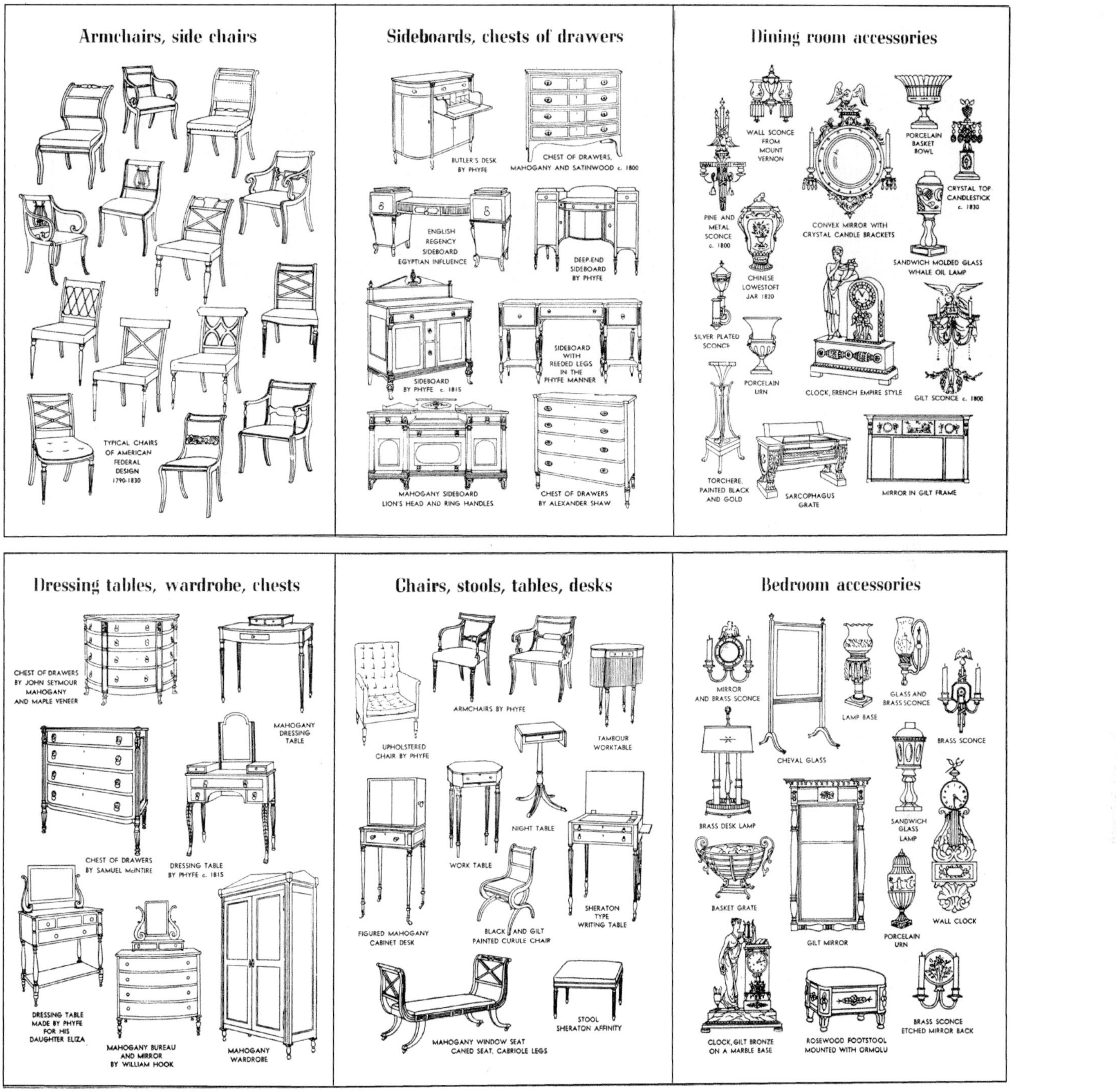

Fig. 2 ***(Continued)***

They all used the designs in *The Gentleman and Cabinet-Makers' Director,* published by Chippendale in 1754. To fill this book, Chippendale commandeered all the ideas he could lay his hands on and then embroidered them with his own fancy, adapted them to his own forms. He plundered the design manuals of China and the French Rococo, of the ancient Gothic masters, and of his immediate predecessors in the English furniture trade.

From the craftsmen of the early eighteenth century Chippendale borrowed such tested forms as the cabriole leg, the claw-and-ball foot, and the typical acanthus leaf ornament. But to each of them he added a grace and charm of which the earlier furniture makers had never been capable.

Chippendale was a typical product of that brilliant English society which flourished during the mid–eighteenth century. He was a contemporary of Josiah Wedgwood, the potter, and of Edmund Burke, the orator. Boswell and Johnson, Benjamin Franklin, Garrick, Gibbon, and Goldsmith, all added their wit and intelligence to the creation of a sturdy culture.

PERIOD FURNITURE

18th Century English: Georgian

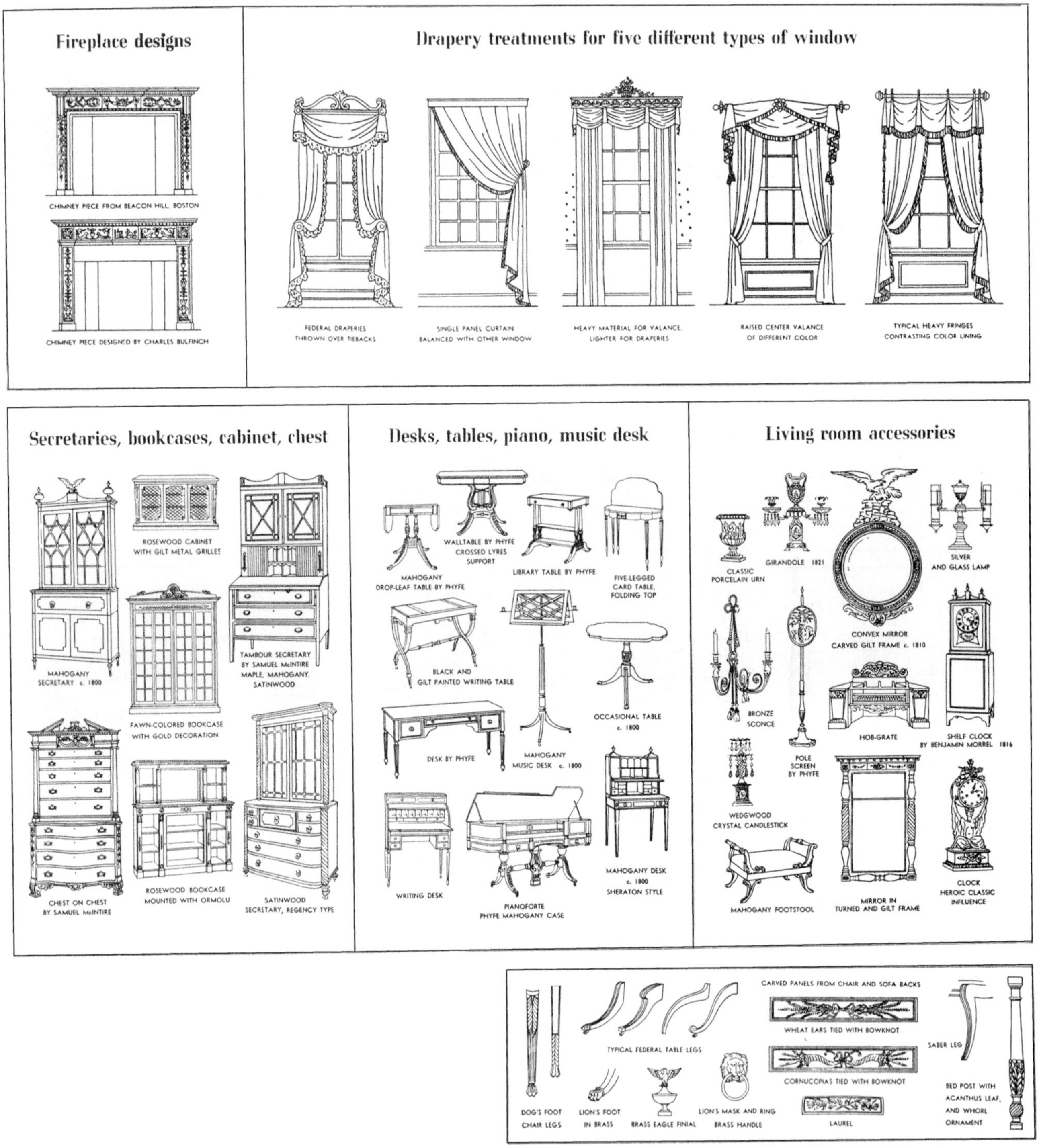

Fig. 2 ***(Continued)***

Thomas Chippendale served their changing taste and their fashionable whims. In his later years he was engaged in making furniture of classic, elegant simplicity for the brothers Adam. His earlier work to his own designs, his love of gilt and gaudy color, his fascination with the exotic—all typical of the age in which he lived—suggest that he might have made a brilliant stage designer.

Chippendale is the first personality in the history of furniture style. This was due less to his fine craftsmanship than to his ability as a publicist. He was the first cabinetmaker to publish a book of furniture designs. The influence of his *Director* was particularly strong in Philadelphia, but the American cabinetmakers usually simplified his exuberant ornament to suit their clients' taste and their workers' skill

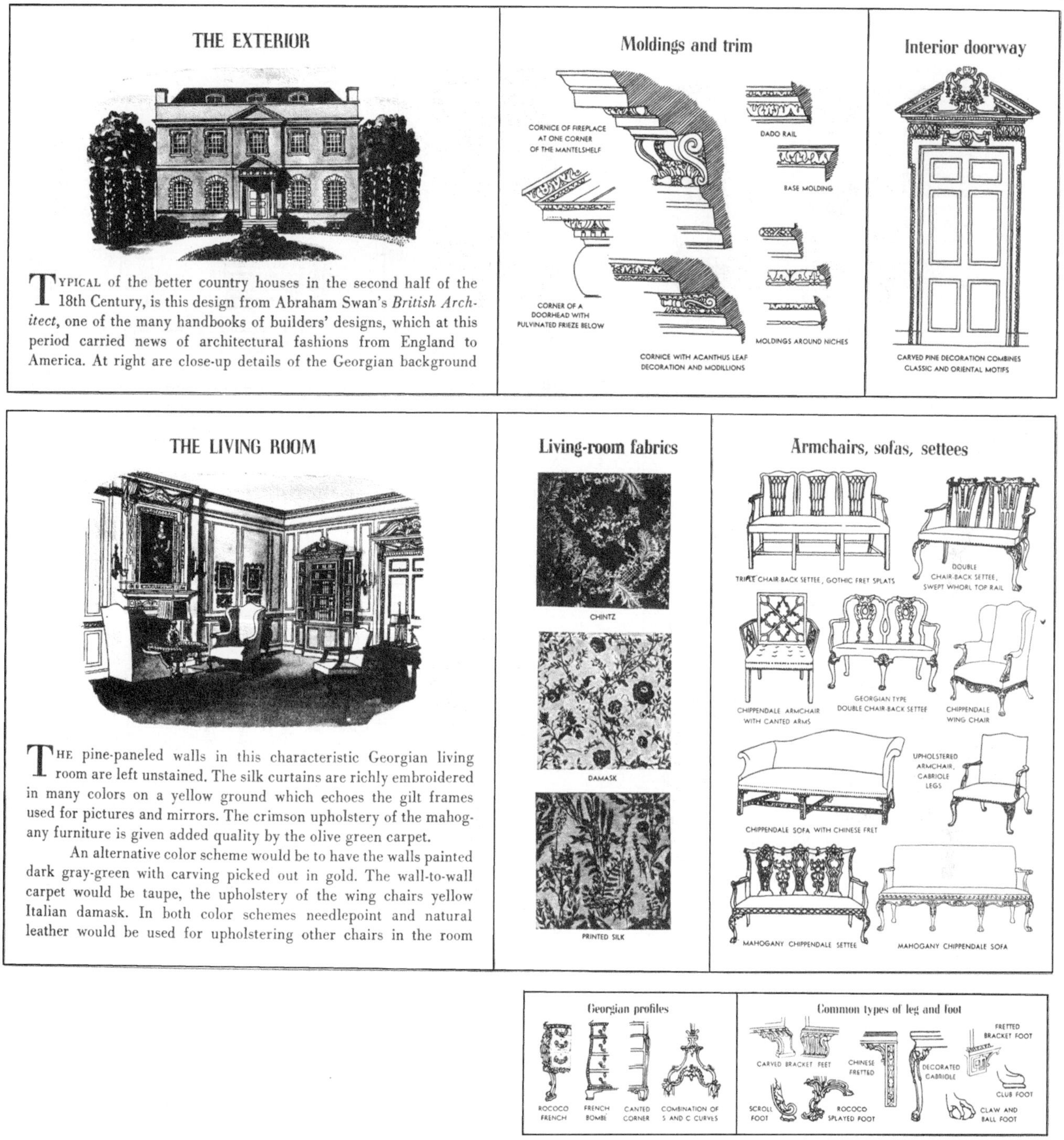
THE EXTERIOR
TYPICAL of the better country houses in the second half of the 18th Century, is this design from Abraham Swan's British Architect, one of the many handbooks of builders' designs, which at this period carried news of architectural fashions from England to America. At right are close-up details of the Georgian background
Moldings and trim
CORNICE OF FIREPLACE AT ONE CORNER OF THE MANTELSHELF
DADO RAIL
BASE MOLDING
CORNER OF A DOORHEAD WITH PULVINATED FRIEZE BELOW
MOLDINGS AROUND NICHES
CORNICE WITH ACANTHUS LEAF DECORATION AND MODILLIONS
Interior doorway
CARVED PINE DECORATION COMBINES CLASSIC AND ORIENTAL MOTIFS
THE LIVING ROOM
THE pine-paneled walls in this characteristic Georgian living room are left unstained. The silk curtains are richly embroidered in many colors on a yellow ground which echoes the gilt frames used for pictures and mirrors. The crimson upholstery of the mahogany furniture is given added quality by the olive green carpet.
An alternative color scheme would be to have the walls painted dark gray-green with carving picked out in gold. The wall-to-wall carpet would be taupe, the upholstery of the wing chairs yellow Italian damask. In both color schemes needlepoint and natural leather would be used for upholstering other chairs in the room
Living-room fabrics
CHINTZ
DAMASK
PRINTED SILK
Armchairs, sofas, settees
TRIPLE CHAIR-BACK SETTEE, GOTHIC FRET SPLATS
DOUBLE CHAIR-BACK SETTEE, SWEPT WHORL TOP RAIL
CHIPPENDALE ARMCHAIR WITH CANTED ARMS
GEORGIAN TYPE DOUBLE CHAIR-BACK SETTEE
CHIPPENDALE WING CHAIR
UPHOLSTERED ARMCHAIR, CABRIOLE LEGS
CHIPPENDALE SOFA WITH CHINESE FRET
MAHOGANY CHIPPENDALE SETTEE
MAHOGANY CHIPPENDALE SOFA
Georgian profiles
ROCOCO FRENCH
FRENCH BOMBÉ
CANTED CORNER
COMBINATION OF S AND C CURVES
Common types of leg and foot
CARVED BRACKET FEET
CHINESE FRETTED
DECORATED CABRIOLE
FRETTED BRACKET FOOT
CLUB FOOT
SCROLL FOOT
ROCOCO SPLAYED FOOT
CLAW AND BALL FOOT

Fig. 3 Motifs characteristic of Georgian furniture

in carving. For it must be remembered that many of the published designs were too complex for reproduction in the solid, even by the most highly skilled English carvers. Such designs were intended for inspiration only.

The introduction of mahogany about 1725 was a fundamental influence on furniture design. Rosewood was another material in favor. Pine was used for paneling and also for intricate carving as, for example, on mirror frames. In the latter case it was usually gilt. Amboyna was occasionally used, mostly for inlays. But the considerable use of inlay is not found until the late Georgian period.

From China come the rectangular leg and an infinite variety of fretted ornament, as well as the more obviously oriental pagoda forms. From the France of Louis XV come the elaborate combinations of foliated C and S scrolls so typical of the Rococo style of ornament. These came to a lush flowering in furniture hardware and gilt mirror frames. Serpentine fronts and sides broke down even the solid rectangular

PERIOD FURNITURE
18th Century English: Georgian

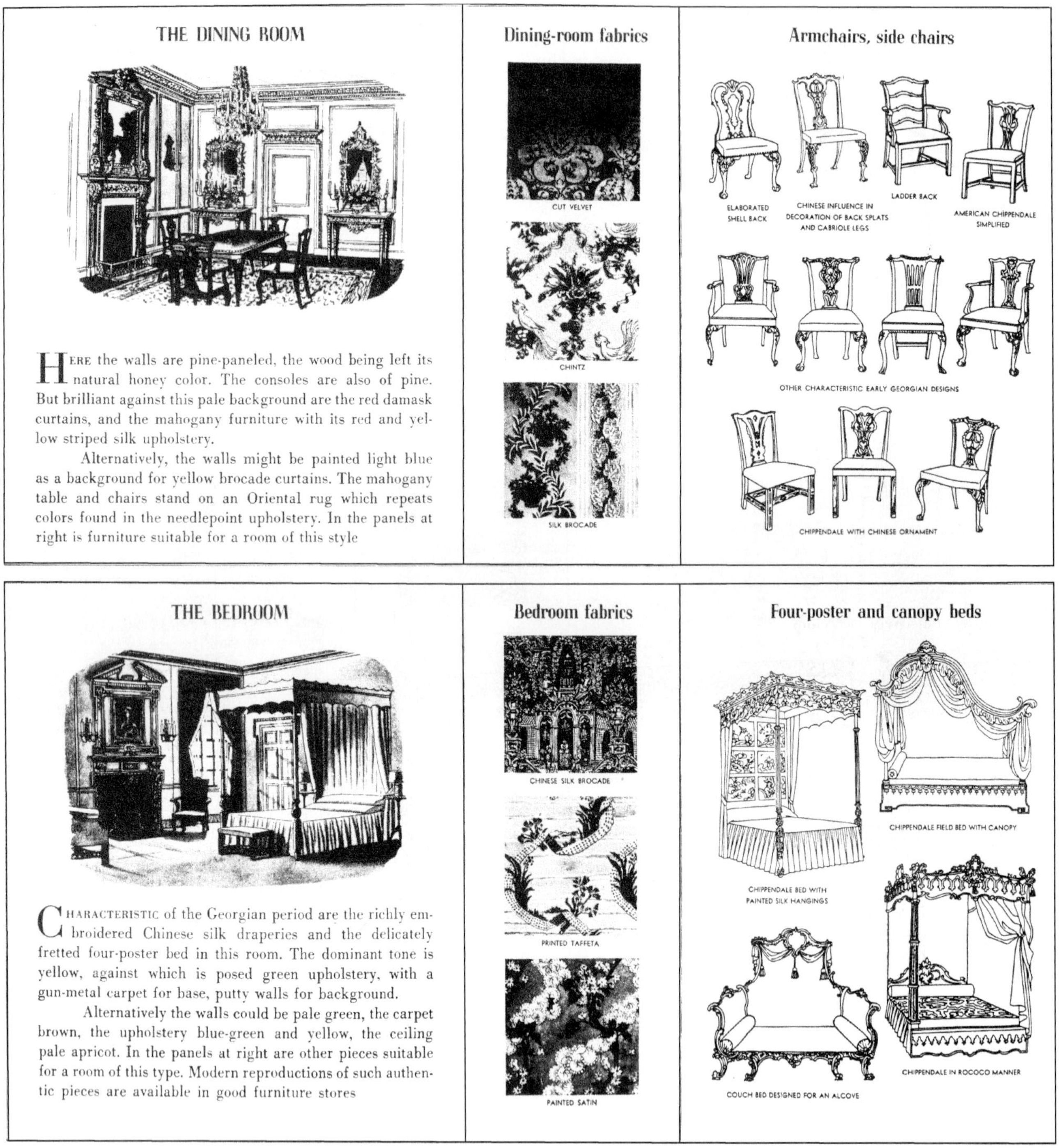
THE DINING ROOM
HERE the walls are pine-paneled, the wood being left its natural honey color. The consoles are also of pine. But brilliant against this pale background are the red damask curtains, and the mahogany furniture with its red and yellow striped silk upholstery.
Alternatively, the walls might be painted light blue as a background for yellow brocade curtains. The mahogany table and chairs stand on an Oriental rug which repeats colors found in the needlepoint upholstery. In the panels at right is furniture suitable for a room of this style
Dining-room fabrics
CUT VELVET
CHINTZ
SILK BROCADE
Armchairs, side chairs
ELABORATED SHELL BACK
CHINESE INFLUENCE IN DECORATION OF BACK SPLATS AND CABRIOLE LEGS
LADDER BACK
AMERICAN CHIPPENDALE SIMPLIFIED
OTHER CHARACTERISTIC EARLY GEORGIAN DESIGNS
CHIPPENDALE WITH CHINESE ORNAMENT
THE BEDROOM
CHARACTERISTIC of the Georgian period are the richly embroidered Chinese silk draperies and the delicately fretted four-poster bed in this room. The dominant tone is yellow, against which is posed green upholstery, with a gun-metal carpet for base, putty walls for background.
Alternatively the walls could be pale green, the carpet brown, the upholstery blue-green and yellow, the ceiling pale apricot. In the panels at right are other pieces suitable for a room of this type. Modern reproductions of such authentic pieces are available in good furniture stores
Bedroom fabrics
CHINESE SILK BROCADE
PRINTED TAFFETA
PAINTED SATIN
Four-poster and canopy beds
CHIPPENDALE FIELD BED WITH CANOPY
CHIPPENDALE BED WITH PAINTED SILK HANGINGS
COUCH BED DESIGNED FOR AN ALCOVE
CHIPPENDALE IN ROCOCO MANNER

Fig. 3 ***(Continued)***

forms of such traditionally four-square pieces as chests of drawers and tables. (For typical profiles and decorative motifs see Fig. 3.)

Romance was sought in the past as well as the East; the pointed Gothic arch and burgeoning crockets turn up in all kinds of furniture and decoration.

EIGHTEENTH-CENTURY ENGLISH: LATE GEORGIAN

Chippendale went for inspiration to Chinese and Gothic decoration. The great designers of the later Georgian period—the brothers Adam, George Hepplewhite, and Thomas Sheraton—were entranced by the recently discovered Classic glories of Pompeii and Herculaneum, and by the slim prettiness in vogue at the French court.

The motifs most characteristic of the later Georgian period (see Fig. 4) are all of Classic origin: acanthus leaf and honeysuckle, ram's head, winged griffin and lion, laurel, and garland.

Characteristic of this period is the perfect coordination between architects, painters, and furniture designers. The four Adam brothers—John, Robert, James, and William, who trademarked themselves the Adelphi

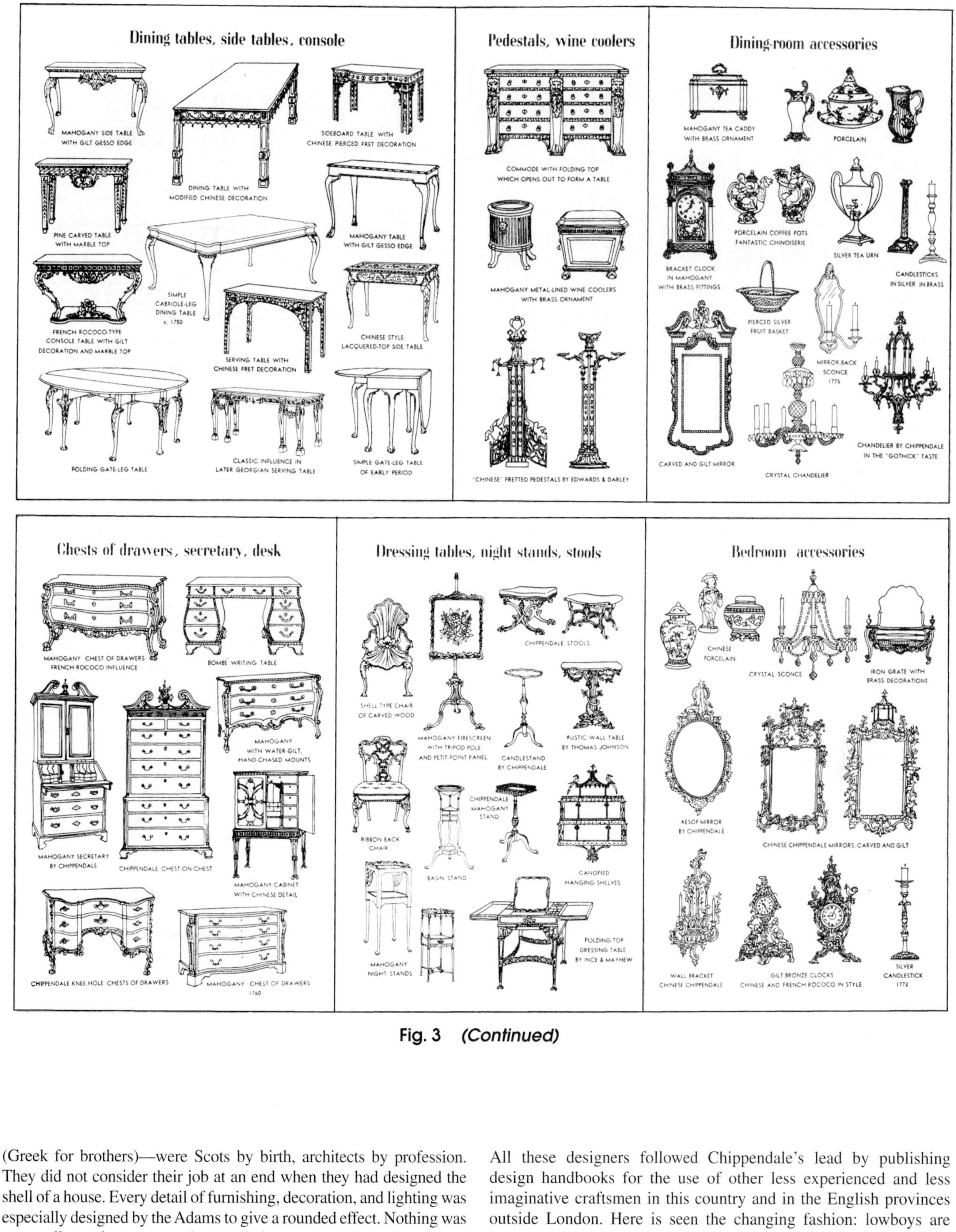

Fig. 3 ***(Continued)***

(Greek for brothers)—were Scots by birth, architects by profession. They did not consider their job at an end when they had designed the shell of a house. Every detail of furnishing, decoration, and lighting was especially designed by the Adams to give a rounded effect. Nothing was too small or unimportant to deserve their attention. The best craftsmen would then be employed to carry out their designs. Chippendale and Hepplewhite, perhaps Sheraton also, made furniture for the Adams.

All these designers followed Chippendale's lead by publishing design handbooks for the use of other less experienced and less imaginative craftsmen in this country and in the English provinces outside London. Here is seen the changing fashion: lowboys are being supplanted by dressing tables, highboys by wardrobes. Color and inlay become more popular than carving, with Sheraton as the champion of inlay against painting.

PERIOD FURNITURE
18th Century English: Late Georgian

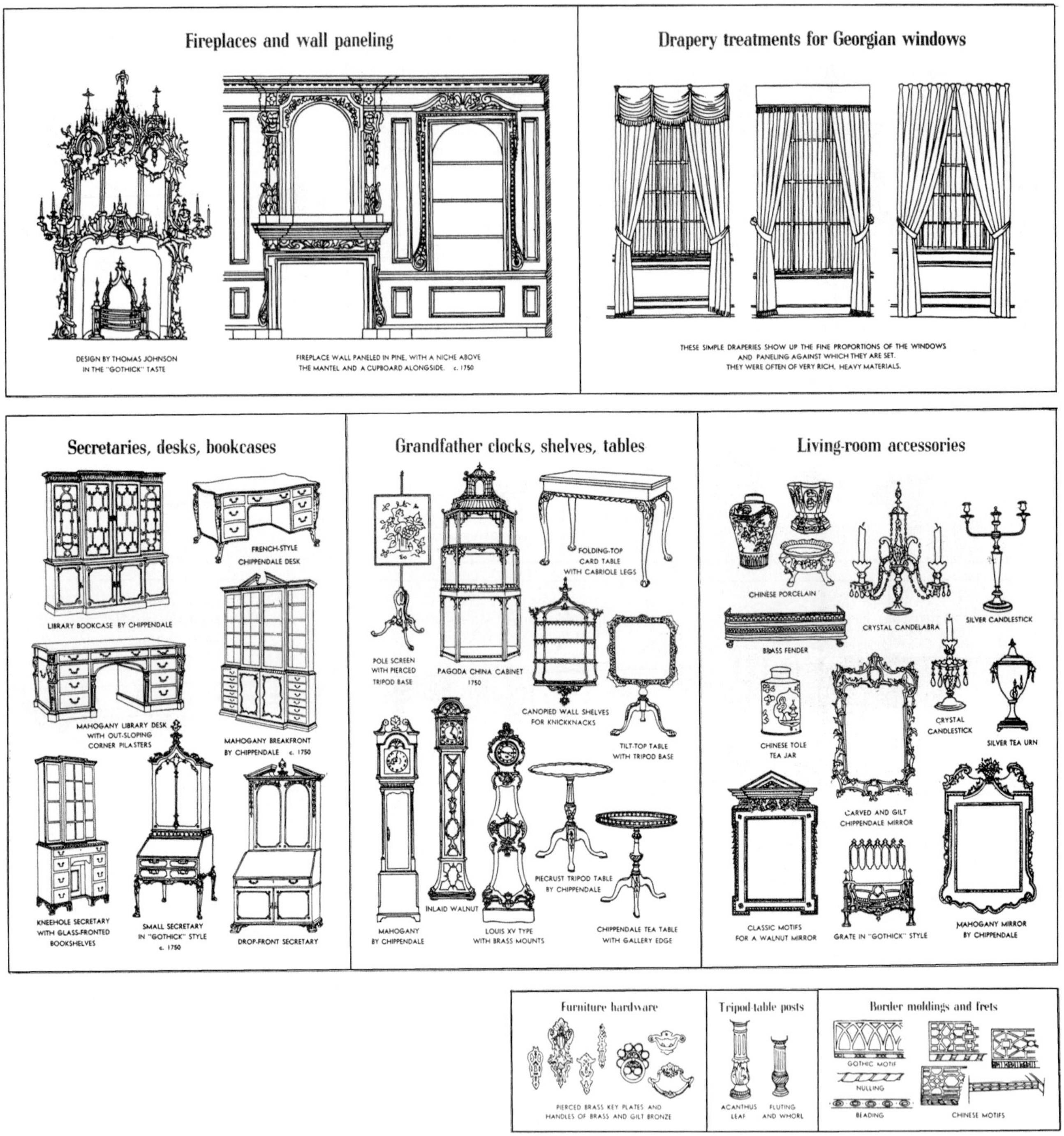

Fig. 3 ***(Continued)***

Hepplewhite's work is usually characterized by his affection for curves, Sheraton's by a preference for straight lines. This was probably because Hepplewhite was more strongly influenced than Sheraton by contemporary French work, which was enlivened by a profusion of delicate curves. Of particular interest in Sheraton's work are his designs for ingenious folding and multipurpose furniture such as folding beds, combined bookcases and washstand, and couches that folded up to become tables. These were designed for use in those bedrooms which were now doubling as parlors during the day.

This later Georgian period has often been labeled the Age of Satinwood. All the designers eagerly exploited the possibilities of veneering and inlay with woods such as satinwood and amboyna, ebony, sycamore, holly, kingwood, and lime. Ivory and brass inlay were often used to mark key plates.

Some of these motifs (the acanthus leaf, for example) had been in use by English designers for more than half a century. But now, reintroduced from Italy by means of measured drawings, they take on a

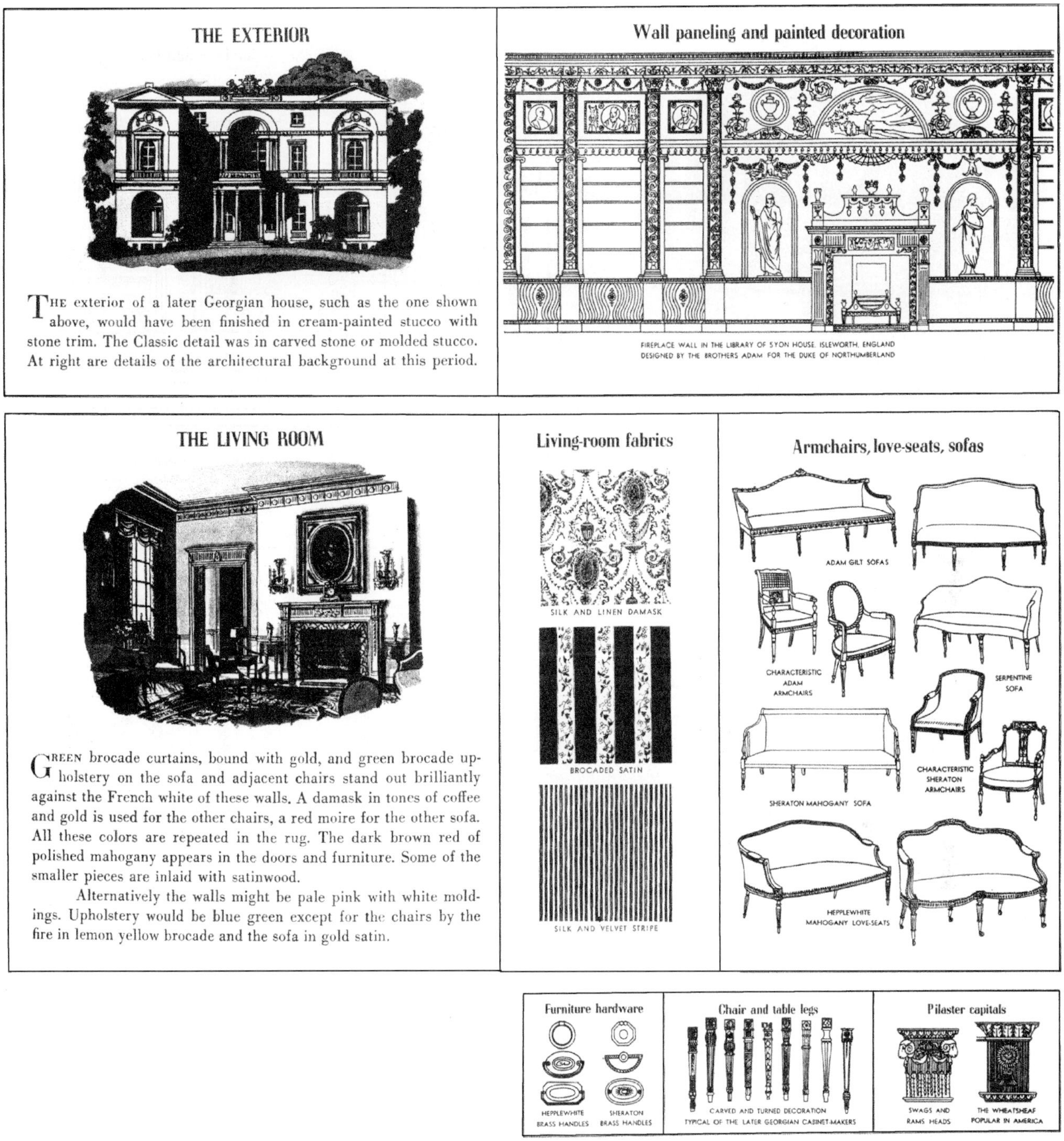
THE EXTERIOR
THE exterior of a later Georgian house, such as the one shown above, would have been finished in cream-painted stucco with stone trim. The Classic detail was in carved stone or molded stucco. At right are details of the architectural background at this period.
Wall paneling and painted decoration
FIREPLACE WALL IN THE LIBRARY OF SYON HOUSE, ISLEWORTH, ENGLAND
DESIGNED BY THE BROTHERS ADAM FOR THE DUKE OF NORTHUMBERLAND
THE LIVING ROOM
GREEN brocade curtains, bound with gold, and green brocade upholstery on the sofa and adjacent chairs stand out brilliantly against the French white of these walls. A damask in tones of coffee and gold is used for the other chairs, a red moire for the other sofa. All these colors are repeated in the rug. The dark brown red of polished mahogany appears in the doors and furniture. Some of the smaller pieces are inlaid with satinwood.
Alternatively the walls might be pale pink with white moldings. Upholstery would be blue green except for the chairs by the fire in lemon yellow brocade and the sofa in gold satin.
Living-room fabrics
SILK AND LINEN DAMASK
BROCADED SATIN
SILK AND VELVET STRIPE
Armchairs, love-seats, sofas
ADAM GILT SOFAS
CHARACTERISTIC ADAM ARMCHAIRS
SERPENTINE SOFA
SHERATON MAHOGANY SOFA
CHARACTERISTIC SHERATON ARMCHAIRS
HEPPLEWHITE MAHOGANY LOVE-SEATS
Furniture hardware
HEPPLEWHITE BRASS HANDLES
SHERATON BRASS HANDLES
Chair and table legs
CARVED AND TURNED DECORATION TYPICAL OF THE LATER GEORGIAN CABINET-MAKERS
Pilaster capitals
SWAGS AND RAMS HEADS
THE WHEATSHEAF POPULAR IN AMERICA

Fig. 4 Motifs characteristic of the later Georgian period

fresh elegance. Italian painters were brought in—Pergolesi, Zucchi, and Cipriani—to provide the background of decoration. Angelica Kaufmann, a Swiss, filled their wreathed panels with neo-Classic figures.

Yet the solid tradition of English craftsmanship remained intact beneath all these changing fashions. The basic proportions remain almost inviolate. Hepplewhite attempted (in his own words) "to unite elegance with utility, and to blend the useful with the agreeable."

LATE EIGHTEENTH- TO EARLY NINETEENTH-CENTURY FRENCH: DIRECTOIRE AND EMPIRE

The Directoire was France's recovery period after the shock of a six-year revolution. The Directoire, established in 1795, lasted only a brief four years, but this was long enough for the designers to sketch in the outlines of a new style. Those outlines were to be filled in later as Directoire merged into Empire; these are but two stages in a single style.

PERIOD FURNITURE

Late 18th–Early 19th Century French: Directoire and Empire

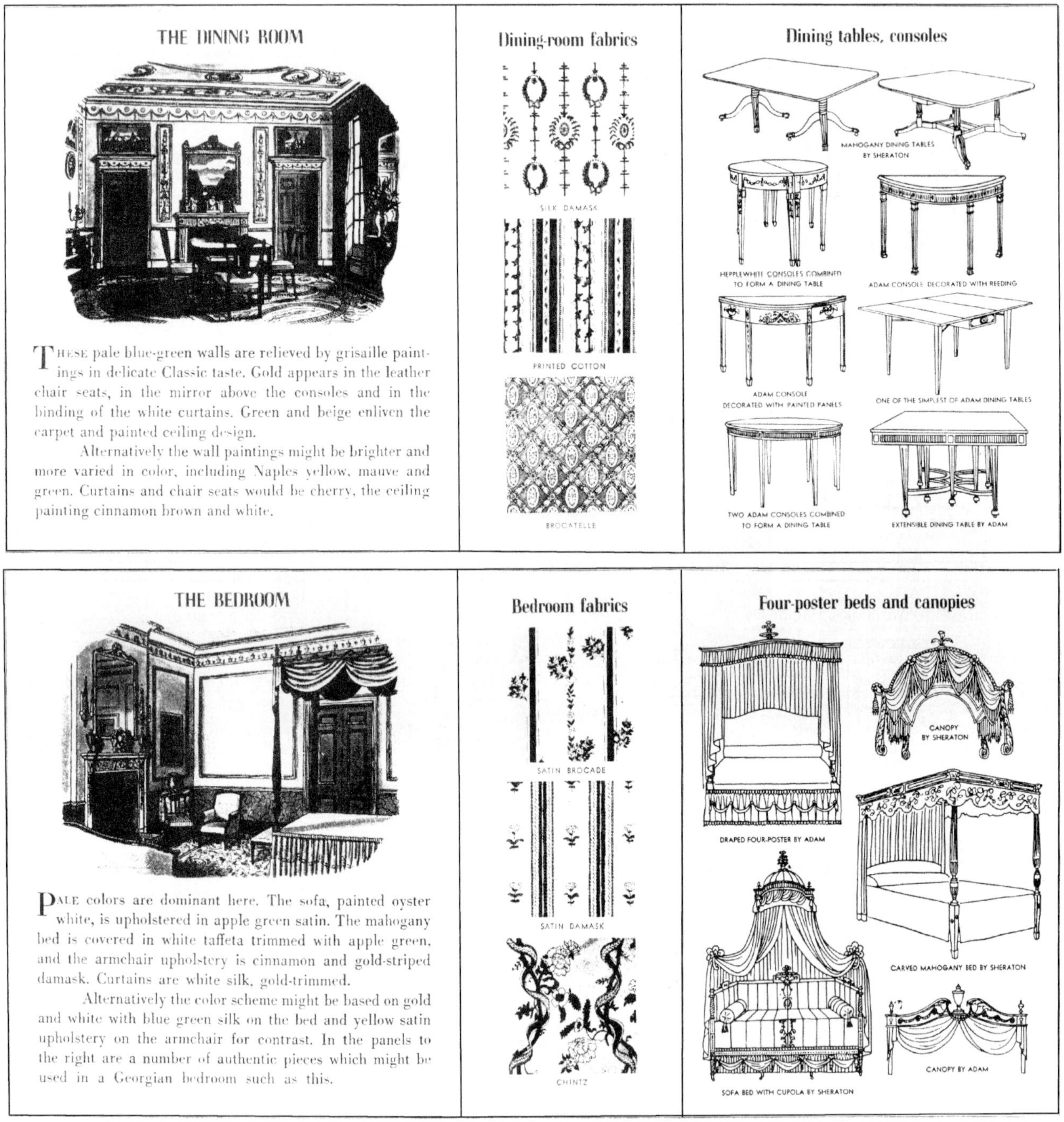
THE DINING ROOM
THESE pale blue-green walls are relieved by grisaille paintings in delicate Classic taste. Gold appears in the leather chair seats, in the mirror above the consoles and in the binding of the white curtains. Green and beige enliven the carpet and painted ceiling design.
Alternatively the wall paintings might be brighter and more varied in color, including Naples yellow, mauve and green. Curtains and chair seats would be cherry, the ceiling painting cinnamon brown and white.
Dining-room fabrics
SILK DAMASK
PRINTED COTTON
BROCATELLE
Dining tables, consoles
MAHOGANY DINING TABLES BY SHERATON
HEPPLEWHITE CONSOLES COMBINED TO FORM A DINING TABLE
ADAM CONSOLE DECORATED WITH REEDING
ADAM CONSOLE DECORATED WITH PAINTED PANELS
ONE OF THE SIMPLEST OF ADAM DINING TABLES
TWO ADAM CONSOLES COMBINED TO FORM A DINING TABLE
EXTENSIBLE DINING TABLE BY ADAM
THE BEDROOM
PALE colors are dominant here. The sofa, painted oyster white, is upholstered in apple green satin. The mahogany bed is covered in white taffeta trimmed with apple green, and the armchair upholstery is cinnamon and gold-striped damask. Curtains are white silk, gold-trimmed.
Alternatively the color scheme might be based on gold and white with blue green silk on the bed and yellow satin upholstery on the armchair for contrast. In the panels to the right are a number of authentic pieces which might be used in a Georgian bedroom such as this.
Bedroom fabrics
SATIN BROCADE
SATIN DAMASK
CHINTZ
Four-poster beds and canopies
CANOPY BY SHERATON
DRAPED FOUR-POSTER BY ADAM
CARVED MAHOGANY BED BY SHERATON
CANOPY BY ADAM
SOFA BED WITH CUPOLA BY SHERATON

Fig. 4 ***(Continued)***

With the rise of Napoleon to absolute power, the delicate style of the Directoire was taken over and developed "for the good of the State." It was to be made into a French national style thoroughly imbued with the political principles which were to guide the new state.

Imperial Rome was found to provide the dignity and impressiveness required in the prototype, so all the imperial symbols were converted to use. The symmetrical shapes of heavy proportion were taken over unchanged, copied in wood instead of being reproduced in stone or bronze.

Most pieces displayed large surfaces of highly polished wood, usually mahogany. They were not, as a rule, decorated by molding or paneling, or even by carving. Ornamentation was almost always applied or inlaid. Most typically it took the form of gilded bas reliefs tacked to the smooth wood surfaces. Painted decoration was more commonly used on walls and ceilings than for furniture.

The general color scheme is rich, dark, and somewhat heavy. Rich, deep mahogany, French polished and often stained red, was the favorite material. Rosewood and ebony were also in favor. Where

PERIOD FURNITURE

Late 18th–Early 19th Century French: Directoire and Empire

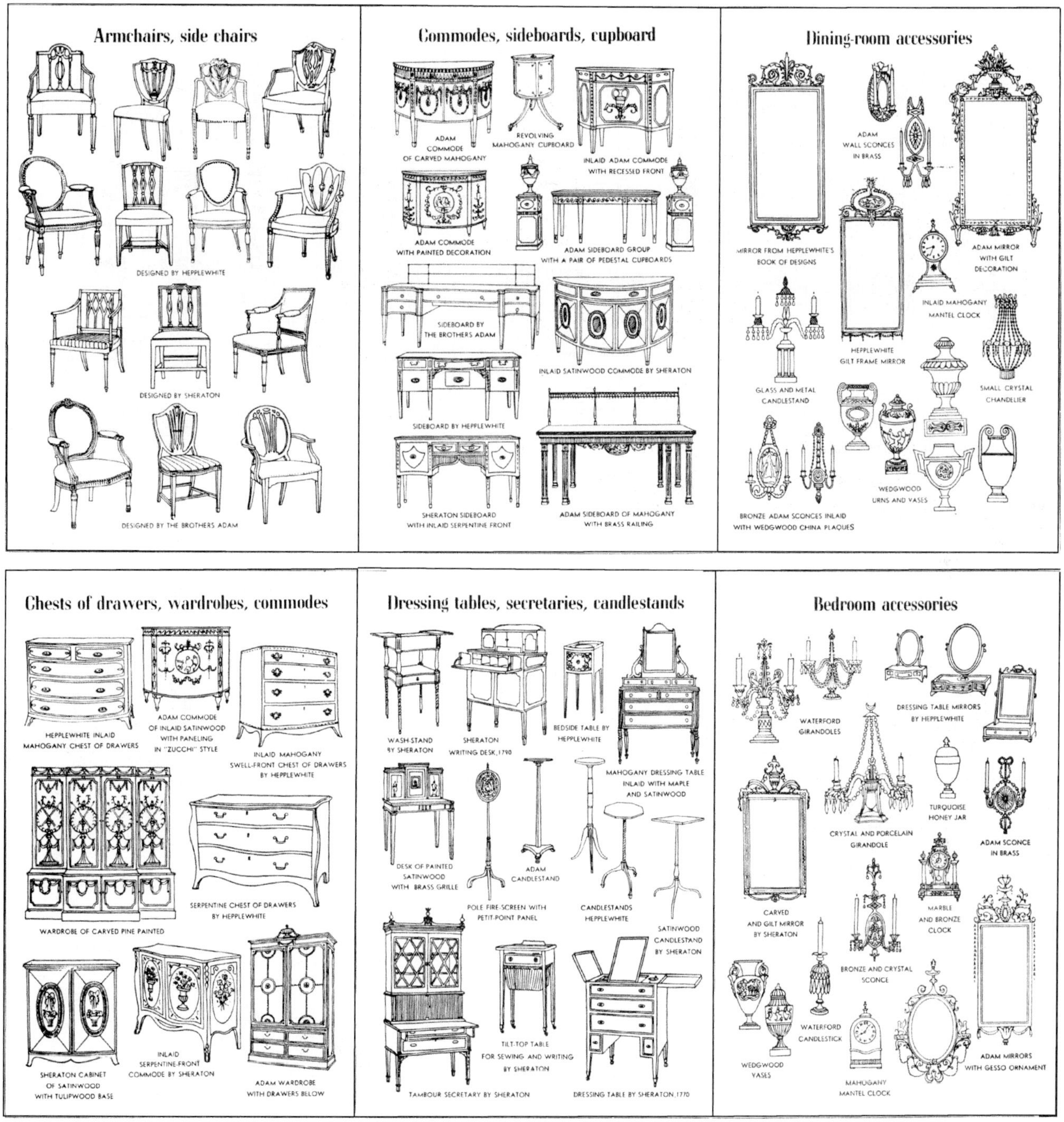

Fig. 4 ***(Continued)***

other woods were used, their nature was concealed by staining to imitate the more popular species.

Round tables were popular. They usually stood on a pedestal or tripod vase. The top was commonly of porphyry or marble. Beds developed into Classic ceremonial couches with scrolled ends. The popular craze for all things Roman extended to include women's dresses and Lucullan banquets.

In the early (Directoire) part of the period, fabrics were quite delicately colored, the decorative motifs still possessed some Grecian delicacy of form, and much of the furniture was painted and gilt. Later, under Napoleon's fist, fabrics were usually in deep primary colors, the motifs of Imperial Roman heaviness, the furniture of dark red polished mahogany.

From each of his campaigns he brought home some new decorative motif, which he would turn over to his craftsmen for use in the next batch of furniture made to his order.

The Egyptian campaign yielded an impressive collection of sphinxes, pyramids, obelisks, and lotus leaf capitals. From Italy came all the

PERIOD FURNITURE

Late 18th–Early 19th Century French: Directoire and Empire

Fig. 4 ***(Continued)***

paraphernalia of Imperial Roman decoration—acanthus leaves, laurel wreaths, torches, winged victories, cornucopias, and the rest, including the famous wreath of bees Napoleon is usually accused of having appropriated from the arms of an old Italian family, the Barberini.

The early Empire pieces (Directoire) are simplified versions of the styles current under Louis XVI. These pieces have grace, simplicity, and charm. The hampering restrictions on foreign trade led to the use of native fruitwoods instead of mahogany.

THE EXTERIOR

THE typical Directoire château shows French Renaissance tradition crossed with the newer Classic vogue. The center panel of this façade is of stone, the remainder in two shades of painted stucco, perhaps in such gay colors as salmon, tan and blue.

Typical Directoire wall treatments

THE LIVING ROOM

A CHARACTERISTICALLY pale range of colors keeps this room in period. The walls are a pinkish gray, the doors gray and gold. The curtains are oyster white bound in gray and the rug predominantly white except for green and gold in the center. Green recurs in the upholstery of the armchair, side chairs and sofa, and gold (satin) in the sofa and méridienne by the fireplace.

For added color the fireside pieces might be upholstered in red satin, the other furniture in gold and blue striped satin. In panels at right are other pieces suitable for such a room.

Living-room fabrics

Settees, méridienne, sofas

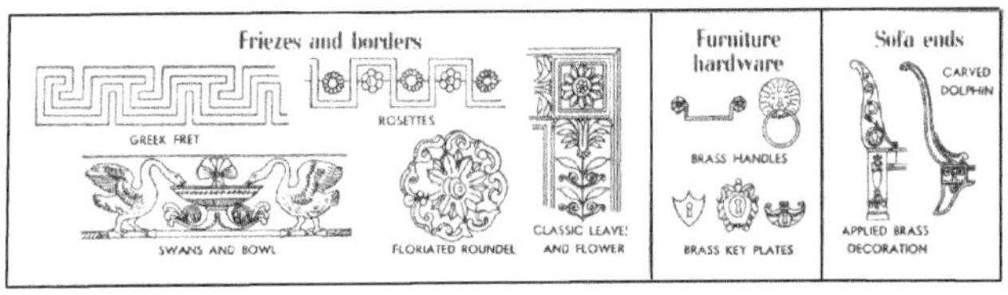

Fig. 5 Motifs characteristic of Directoire and Empire

PERIOD FURNITURE

Late 18th–Early 19th Century French: Directoire and Empire

THE DINING ROOM

THE rich brown of polished mahogany in this table is surrounded by chairs painted gold and white, upholstered in blue satin. The walls are painted oyster white picked out with yellow moldings. Above the doors are white Classic figure paintings with a blue background which is echoed in the blue taffeta curtains.

Alternatively the walls might be painted green with the cornice picked out in white and gold. The chairs would then be upholstered in red. Other pieces suitable for a room of this type are shown in the panels at right.

Dining-room fabrics

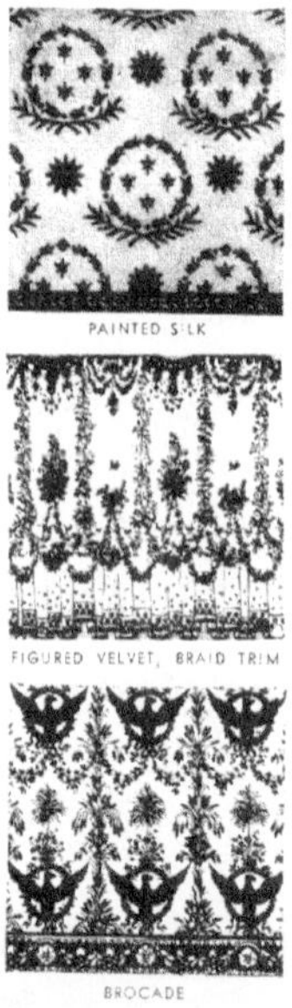

Side chairs, armchair

THE BEDROOM

PINK WALLS decorated in white and gold provide a good background for this mahogany and rosewood furniture relieved with brass mounts. Fabrics are gayly colored here: blue taffeta for curtains and bed canopy, striped yellow and red satin for the chairs, and yellow satin for the two stools (which have white-painted frames).

An alternative color scheme would have dark beige walls, green taffeta for the curtains and bed canopy. Most of the furniture would be painted white and gold. At right are other pieces and fabrics suitable for this type of room.

Bedroom fabrics

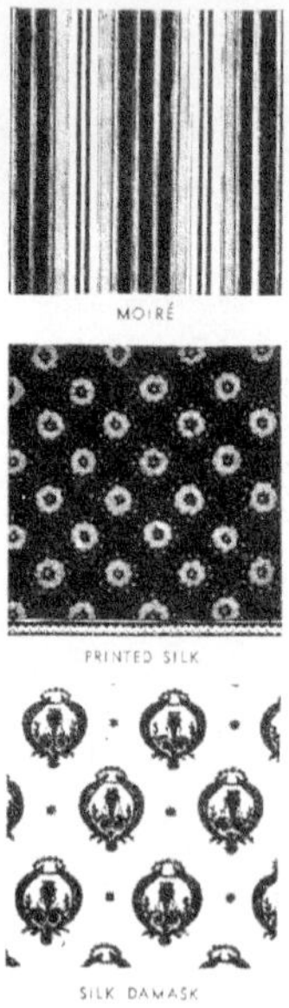

Beds, chaises longues, méridiennes

Fig. 5 ***(Continued)***

PERIOD FURNITURE

Late 18th–Early 19th Century French: Directoire and Empire

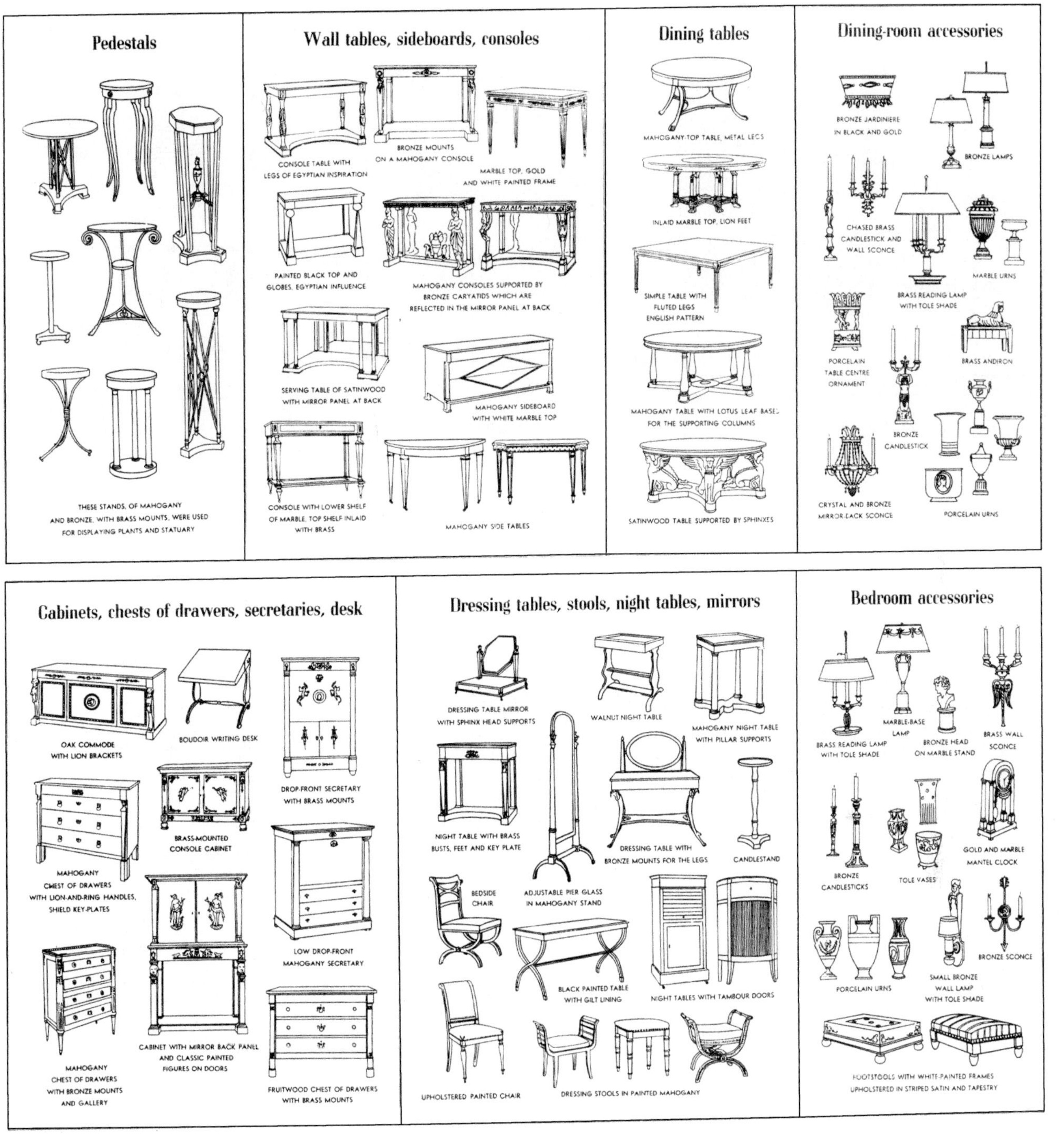
Pedestals
THESE STANDS, OF MAHOGANY AND BRONZE, WITH BRASS MOUNTS, WERE USED FOR DISPLAYING PLANTS AND STATUARY
Wall tables, sideboards, consoles
CONSOLE TABLE WITH LEGS OF EGYPTIAN INSPIRATION
BRONZE MOUNTS ON A MAHOGANY CONSOLE
MARBLE TOP, GOLD AND WHITE PAINTED FRAME
PAINTED BLACK TOP AND GLOBES, EGYPTIAN INFLUENCE
MAHOGANY CONSOLES SUPPORTED BY BRONZE CARYATIDS WHICH ARE REFLECTED IN THE MIRROR PANEL AT BACK
SERVING TABLE OF SATINWOOD WITH MIRROR PANEL AT BACK
MAHOGANY SIDEBOARD WITH WHITE MARBLE TOP
CONSOLE WITH LOWER SHELF OF MARBLE, TOP SHELF INLAID WITH BRASS
MAHOGANY SIDE TABLES
Dining tables
MAHOGANY-TOP TABLE, METAL LEGS
INLAID MARBLE TOP, LION FEET
SIMPLE TABLE WITH FLUTED LEGS ENGLISH PATTERN
MAHOGANY TABLE WITH LOTUS LEAF BASE; FOR THE SUPPORTING COLUMNS
SATINWOOD TABLE SUPPORTED BY SPHINXES
Dining-room accessories
BRONZE JARDINIERE IN BLACK AND GOLD
BRONZE LAMPS
CHASED BRASS CANDLESTICK AND WALL SCONCE
MARBLE URNS
BRASS READING LAMP WITH TOLE SHADE
PORCELAIN TABLE CENTRE ORNAMENT
BRASS ANDIRON
BRONZE CANDLESTICK
CRYSTAL AND BRONZE MIRROR-BACK SCONCE
PORCELAIN URNS
Cabinets, chests of drawers, secretaries, desk
OAK COMMODE WITH LION BRACKETS
BOUDOIR WRITING DESK
DROP-FRONT SECRETARY WITH BRASS MOUNTS
BRASS-MOUNTED CONSOLE CABINET
MAHOGANY CHEST OF DRAWERS WITH LION-AND-RING HANDLES, SHIELD KEY-PLATES
LOW DROP-FRONT MAHOGANY SECRETARY
CABINET WITH MIRROR BACK PANEL AND CLASSIC PAINTED FIGURES ON DOORS
MAHOGANY CHEST OF DRAWERS WITH BRONZE MOUNTS AND GALLERY
FRUITWOOD CHEST OF DRAWERS WITH BRASS MOUNTS
Dressing tables, stools, night tables, mirrors
DRESSING TABLE MIRROR WITH SPHINX HEAD SUPPORTS
WALNUT NIGHT TABLE
MAHOGANY NIGHT TABLE WITH PILLAR SUPPORTS
NIGHT TABLE WITH BRASS BUSTS, FEET AND KEY PLATE
DRESSING TABLE WITH BRONZE MOUNTS FOR THE LEGS
CANDLESTAND
BEDSIDE CHAIR
ADJUSTABLE PIER GLASS IN MAHOGANY STAND
BLACK PAINTED TABLE WITH GILT LINING
NIGHT TABLES WITH TAMBOUR DOORS
UPHOLSTERED PAINTED CHAIR
DRESSING STOOLS IN PAINTED MAHOGANY
Bedroom accessories
BRASS READING LAMP WITH TOLE SHADE
MARBLE-BASE LAMP
BRONZE HEAD ON MARBLE STAND
BRASS WALL SCONCE
BRONZE CANDLESTICKS
TOLE VASES
GOLD AND MARBLE MANTEL CLOCK
PORCELAIN URNS
SMALL BRONZE WALL LAMP WITH TOLE SHADE
BRONZE SCONCE
FOOTSTOOLS WITH WHITE-PAINTED FRAMES UPHOLSTERED IN STRIPED SATIN AND TAPESTRY

Fig. 5 *(Continued)*

PERIOD FURNITURE
Late 18th–Early 19th Century French: Directoire and Empire

Fig. 5 ***(Continued)***

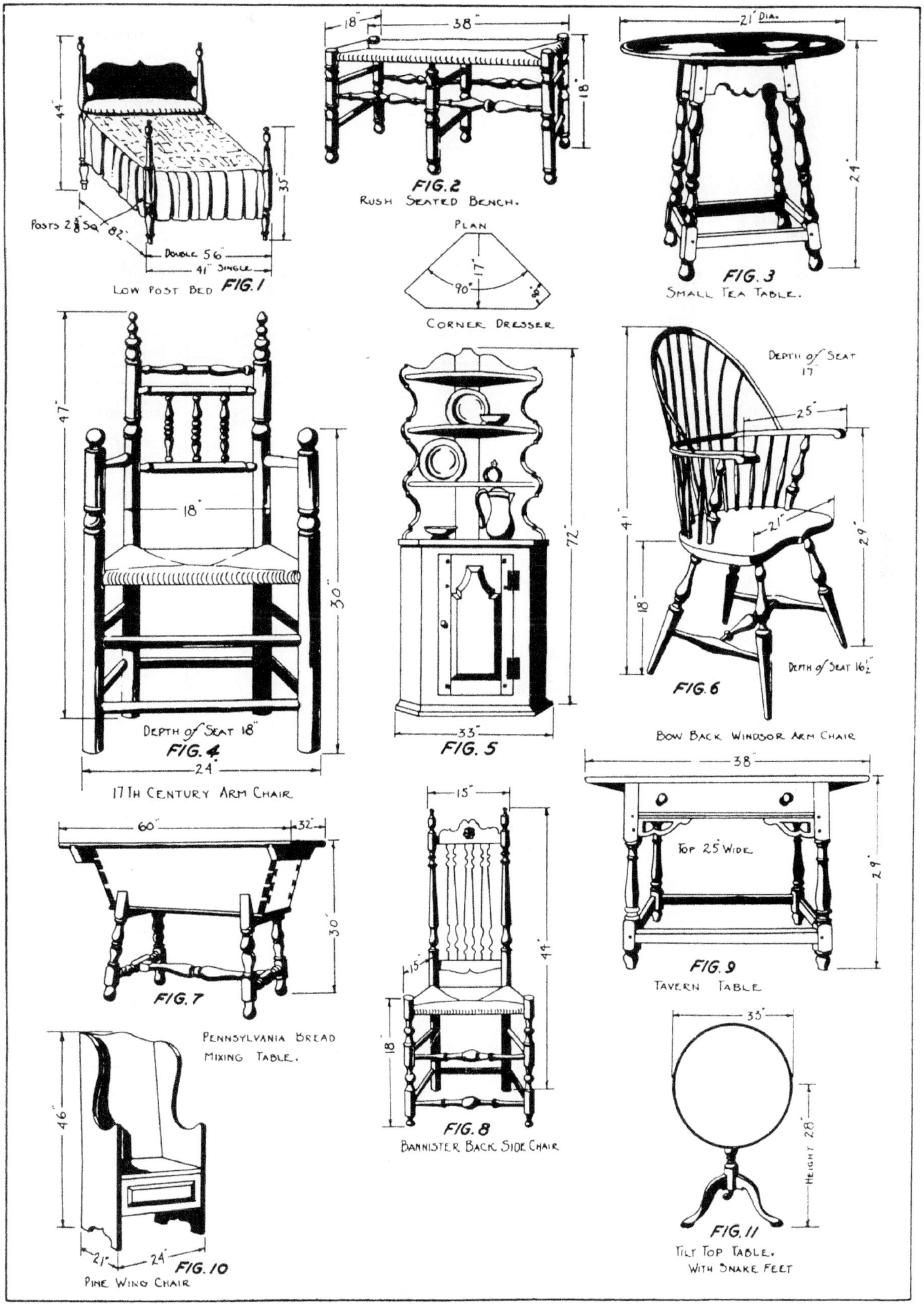
FIG. 1
LOW POST BED
POSTS 2 3/8 SQ.
82"
DOUBLE 56"
41" SINGLE
44"
35"
FIG. 2
RUSH SEATED BENCH.
18"
38"
18"
PLAN
17"
90°
90°
CORNER DRESSER
FIG. 3
SMALL TEA TABLE.
21" DIA.
24"
FIG. 4
17TH CENTURY ARM CHAIR
DEPTH of SEAT 18"
47"
18"
30"
24"
FIG. 5
72"
33"
FIG. 6
BOW BACK WINDSOR ARM CHAIR
DEPTH of SEAT 17"
25"
21"
41"
29"
18"
DEPTH of SEAT 16½"
FIG. 7
PENNSYLVANIA BREAD MIXING TABLE.
60"
32"
30"
FIG. 8
BANNISTER BACK SIDE CHAIR
15"
44"
15"
18"
FIG. 9
TAVERN TABLE
38"
TOP 25" WIDE
29"
FIG. 10
PINE WING CHAIR
46"
21"
24"
FIG. 11
TILT TOP TABLE, WITH SNAKE FEET
33"
HEIGHT 28"

Colonial style

PERIOD FURNITURE

17th and 18th Century American: Colonial

Colonial style

FIG. 1
Depth of Seat At Center Line 16"
Duncan Phyfe Side Chair Reeded Horseshoe Shaped Seat.
FIG. 2
Depth of Seat 17"
Side Chair With Lyre Back.
FIG. 3
Depth of Seat At Center Line 18"
Duncan Phyfe Arm Chair.
FIG. 4
Two Back Settee With Lyre Ends. These May Be Made With Three Backs & Are Sometimes Caned. They Sometimes Have Animal Feet.
FIG. 5
Console Table. Veneered Apron.
FIG. 6
Cock Bead
Sewing Table. The Silk Bag Is Fastened To The Lower Drawer Which Has No Bottom. The Semi-Circular Ends Are Boxes & The Lids Have Invisible Hinges.
Though Duncan Phyfe Adapted Freely From The Work of Sheraton, Hepplewhite & Others He Developed A Distinct Style.
FIG. 7
Library Table With Lyre Ends.
FIG. 8
Small Veneered Sideboard.
FIG. 9
Plinth
Lyre Base Card Table
FIG. 10
Dining Table. These May Be Made In Two, Three Or Five Sections. Wide Boards May Also Be Added Between Each Section To Lengthen The Tables.
The Principle Pieces of Furniture Made By Phyfe Were Chairs, Tables, Sofas & Settees. He Also Made Sideboards, Bedsteads, Mirrors, Washstands, Writing Desks, Etc. Some of His Favorite Motifs Were The Lyre, The Acanthus Leaf, Turned & Reeded Legs, Turned Pedestals Supported On Curved Legs, & Animal Feet of Brass. The Principal Wood Used Was Mahogany Often Veneered.

Duncan Phyfe style

PERIOD FURNITURE

16th Century English: Early Jacobean

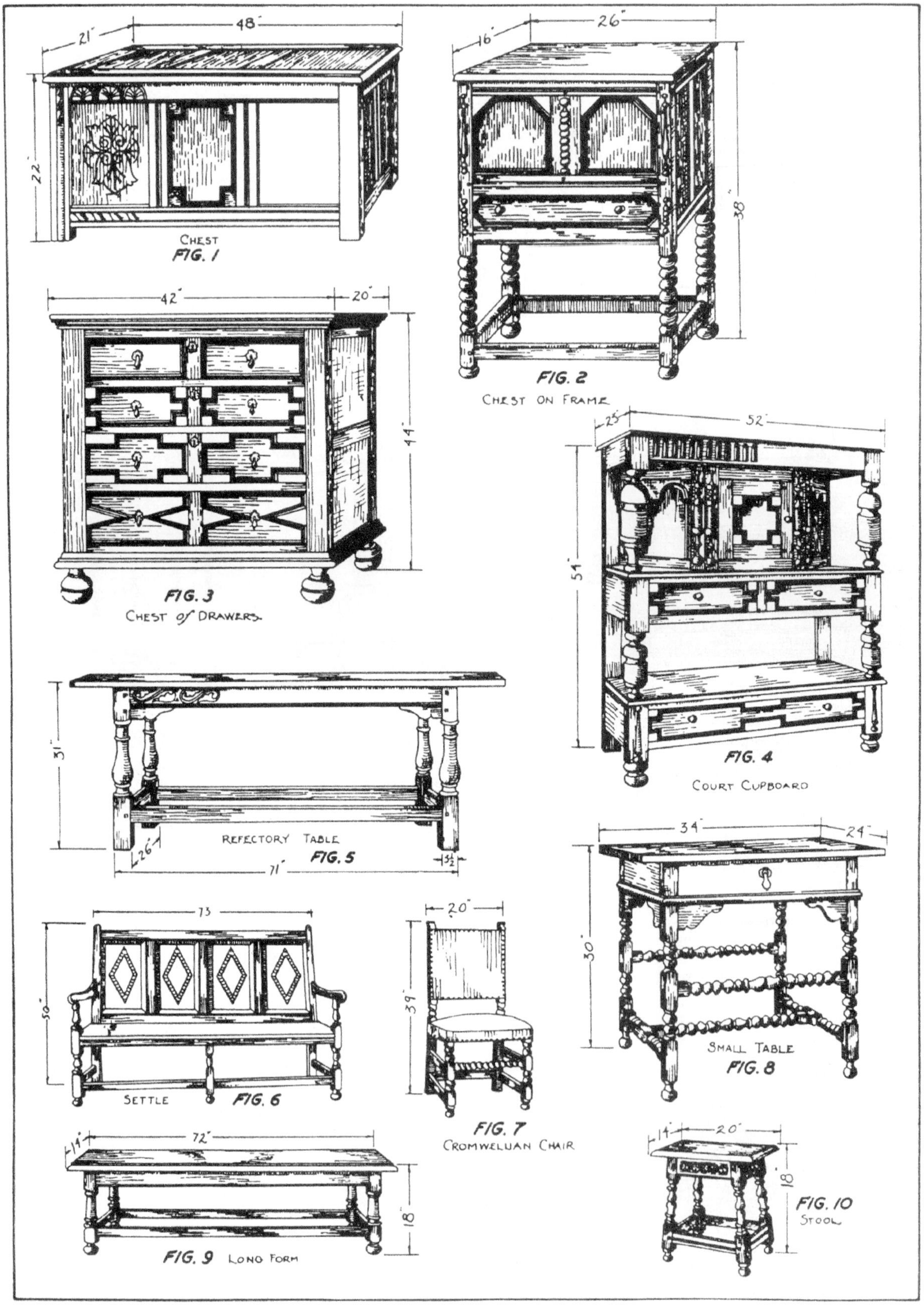

Early Jacobean period

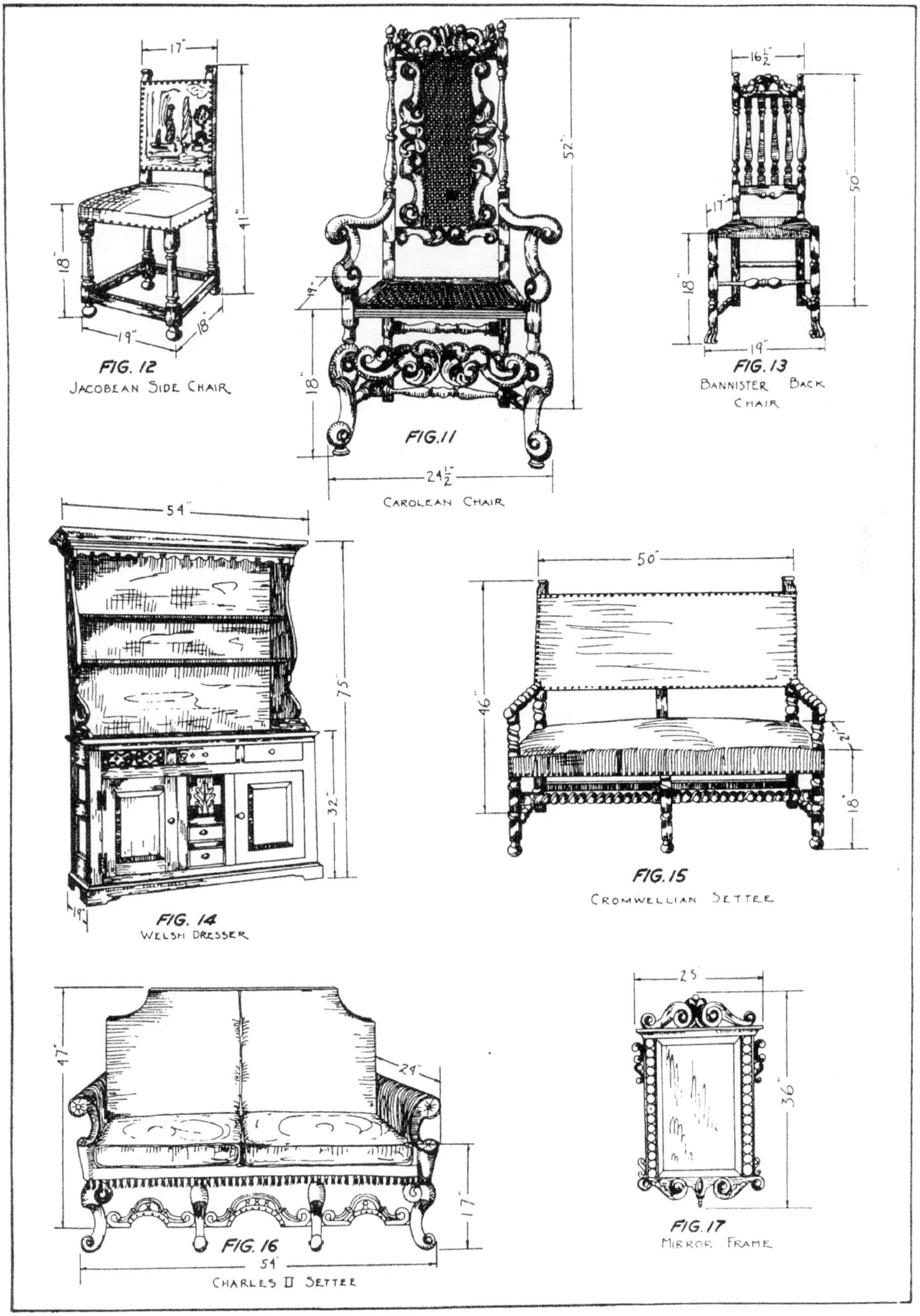

Jacobean period

FIG. 12
JACOBEAN SIDE CHAIR

FIG. 11
CAROLEAN CHAIR

FIG. 13
BANNISTER BACK CHAIR

FIG. 14
WELSH DRESSER

FIG. 15
CROMWELLIAN SETTEE

FIG. 16
CHARLES II SETTEE

FIG. 17
MIRROR FRAME

PERIOD FURNITURE

17th Century English: William & Mary

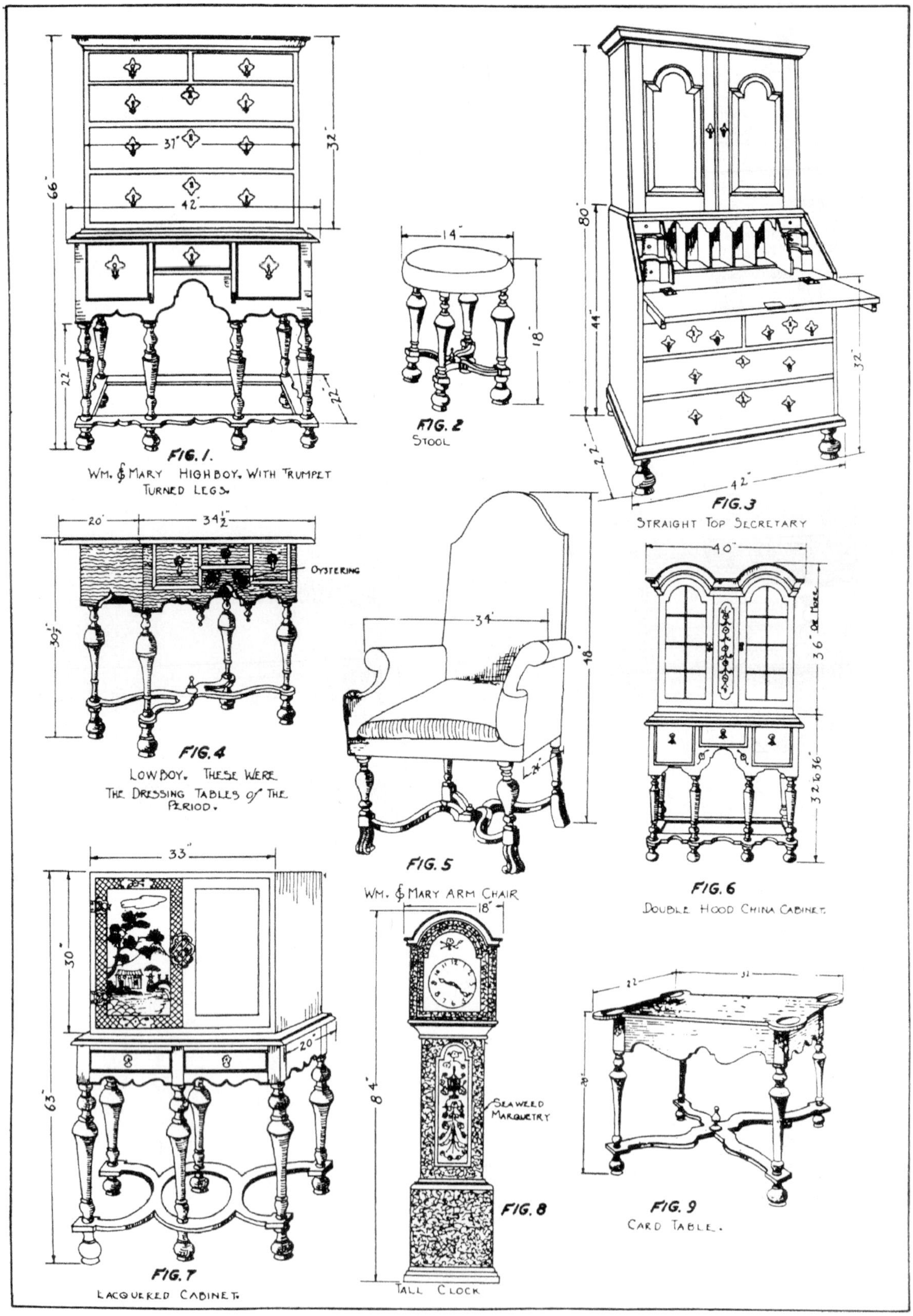

William and Mary period

FIG. 1
HIGHBOY
FIG. 2
LOWBOY
FIG. 3
SMALL TABLE
FIG 4
SOFA
FIG. 5
HALL TABLE
FIG. 6
SMALL TEA TABLE
Top 40" IN DIAMETER WHEN OPEN.
FIG. 7
LIGHT DROP-LEAF TABLE
FIG. 8
GATE LEG TABLE
FIG. 9
ARM CHAIR
SEAT 18" HIGH
SEAT 24" WIDE 18" DEEP
40 TO 46" HIGH
Top 22 By 72
FIG. 10
SIDEBOARD
FIG. 11
WRITING DESK
FIG. 12
SIDE CHAIR
WIDTH of SEAT 21" DEPTH 17"
FIG. 13
STOOL
THE PROPER WOOD FOR QUEEN ANNE FURNITURE IS WALNUT. MAHOGANY WAS SOMETIMES USED.

Queen Anne period

PERIOD FURNITURE

18th Century English: Georgian (Chippendale)

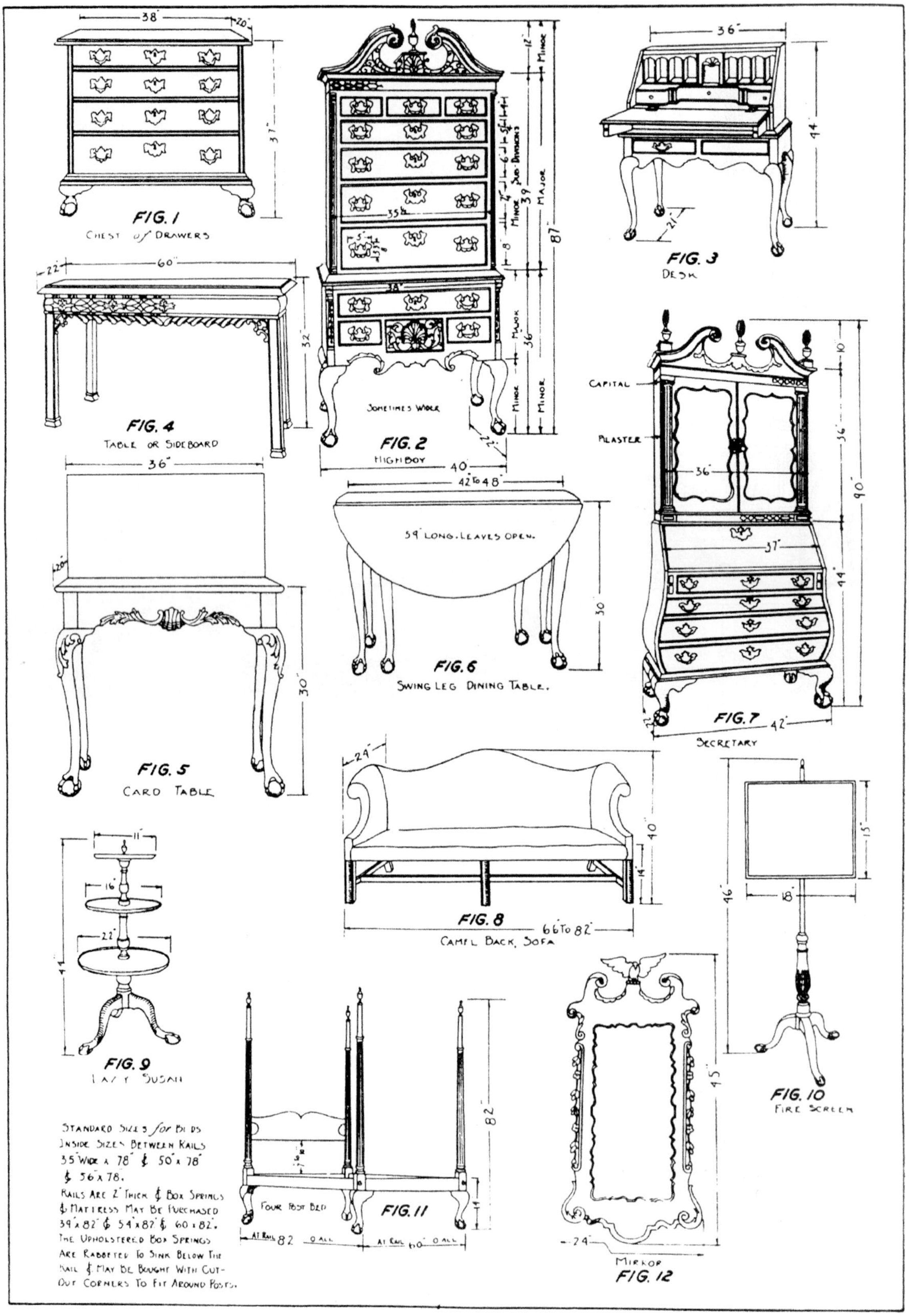

Chippendale style

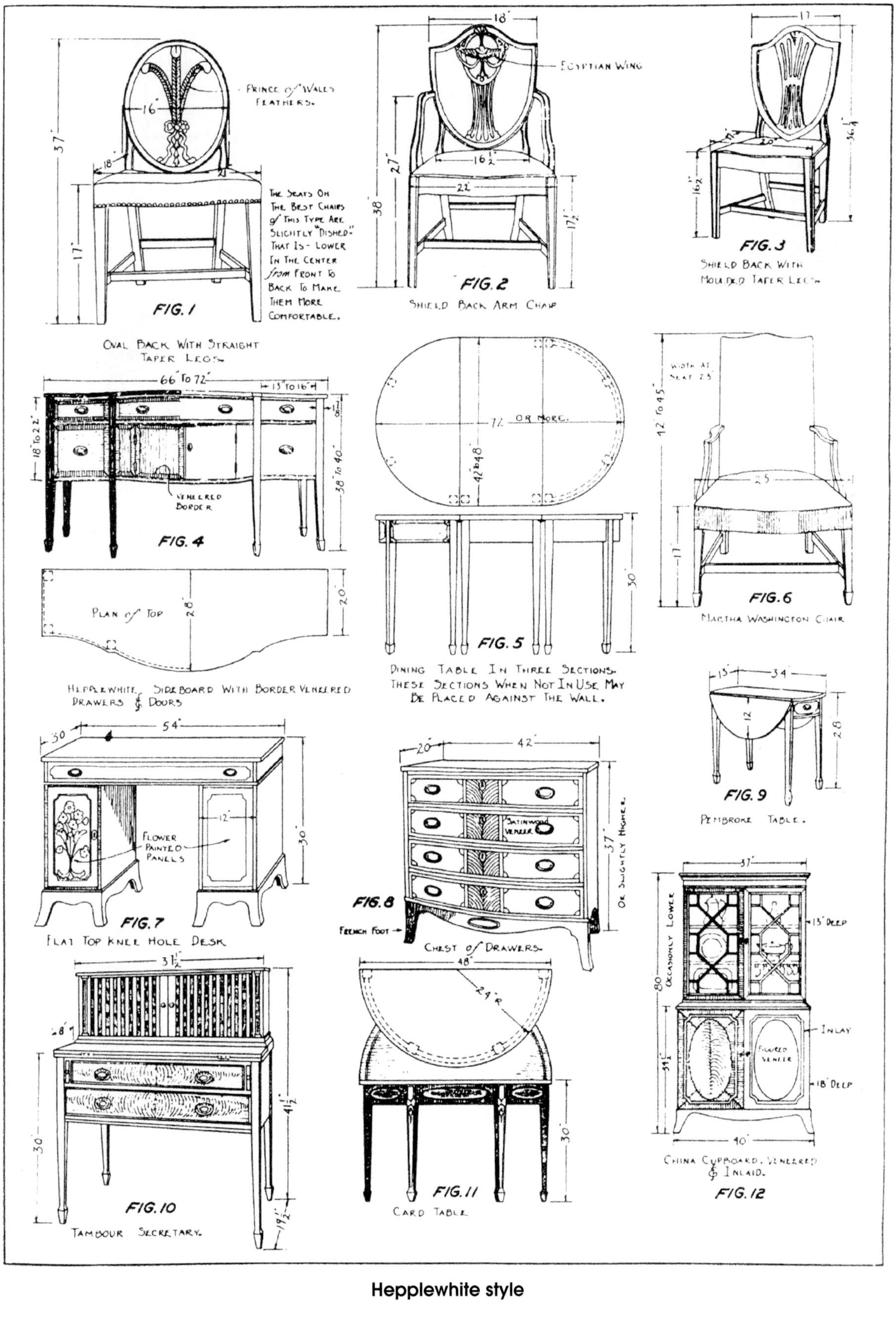

Hepplewhite style

PERIOD FURNITURE

18th Century English: Late Georgian (Sheraton)

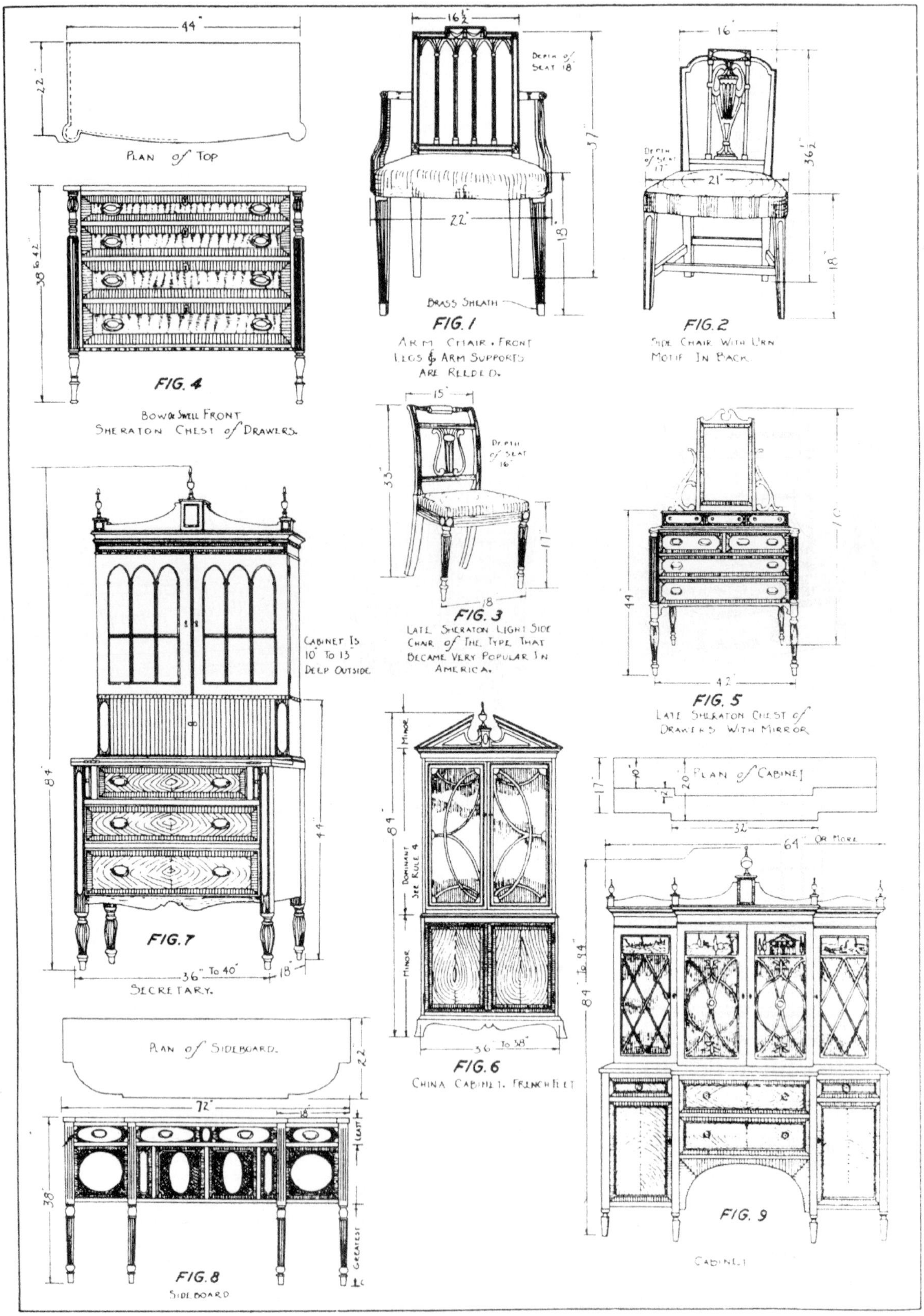

Sheraton style

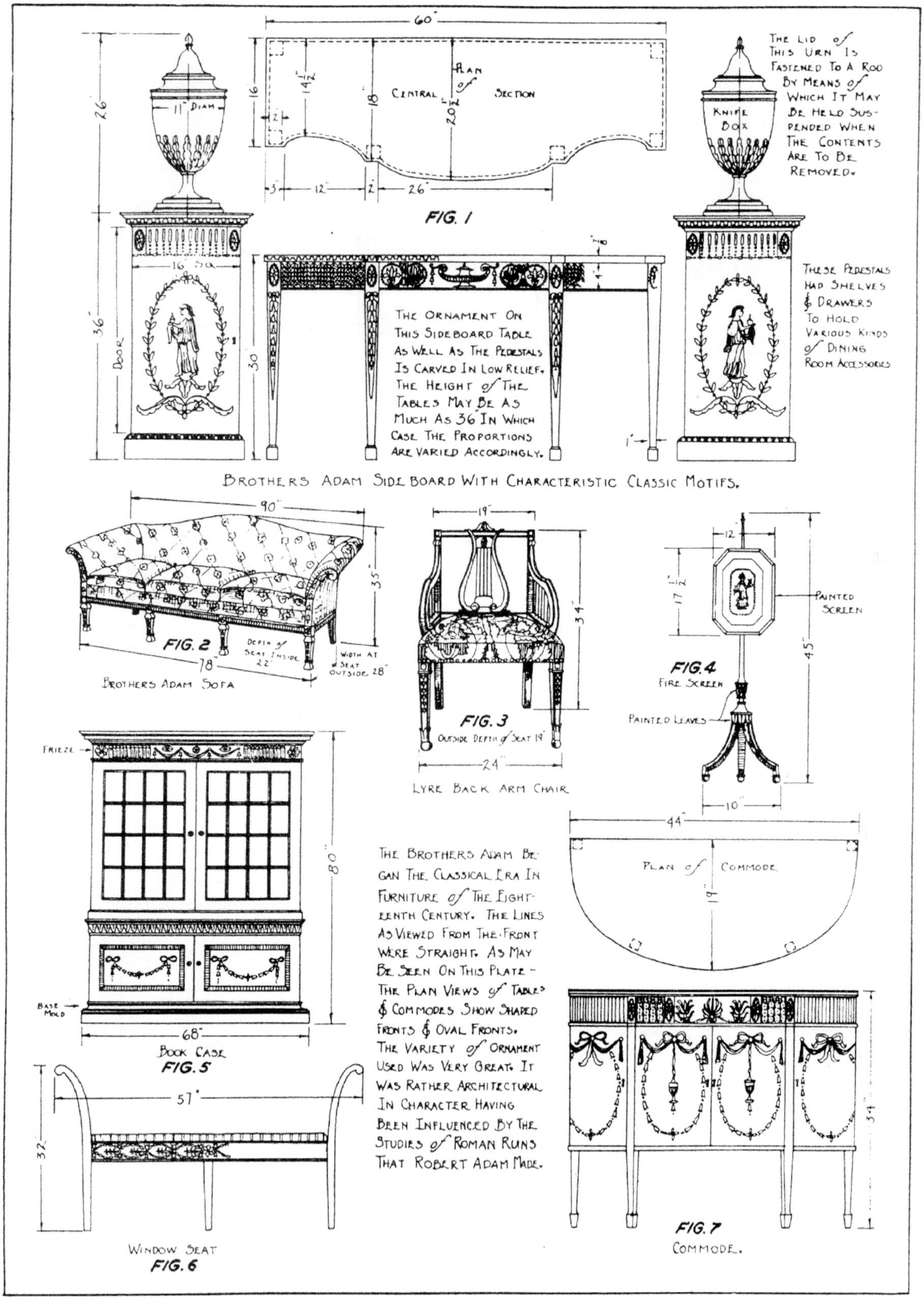
60"
Plan of Central Section
FIG. 1
The lid of this urn is fastened to a rod by means of which it may be held suspended when the contents are to be removed.
Knife Box
11" Diam
16" Sq
Door
These pedestals had shelves & drawers to hold various kinds of dining room accessories
The ornament on this sideboard table as well as the pedestals is carved in low relief. The height of the tables may be as much as 36" in which case the proportions are varied accordingly.
Brothers Adam Side Board With Characteristic Classic Motifs.
90"
35"
78"
FIG. 2
Depth of seat inside 22"
Width at seat outside 28"
Brothers Adam Sofa
19"
34"
24"
FIG. 3
Outside depth of seat 19"
Lyre Back Arm Chair
12"
17 1/2"
Painted Screen
45"
FIG. 4
Fire Screen
Painted Leaves
10"
Frieze
80"
Base Mold
68"
Book Case
FIG. 5
The Brothers Adam began the classical era in furniture of the eighteenth century. The lines as viewed from the front were straight. As may be seen on this plate - the plan views of tables & commodes show shaped fronts & oval fronts. The variety of ornament used was very great. It was rather architectural in character having been influenced by the studies of Roman ruins that Robert Adam made.
44"
Plan of Commode
19"
57"
32"
Window Seat
FIG. 6
34"
FIG. 7
Commode.

Brothers Adam

PERIOD FURNITURE

18th Century English: Late Georgian (Brothers Adam)

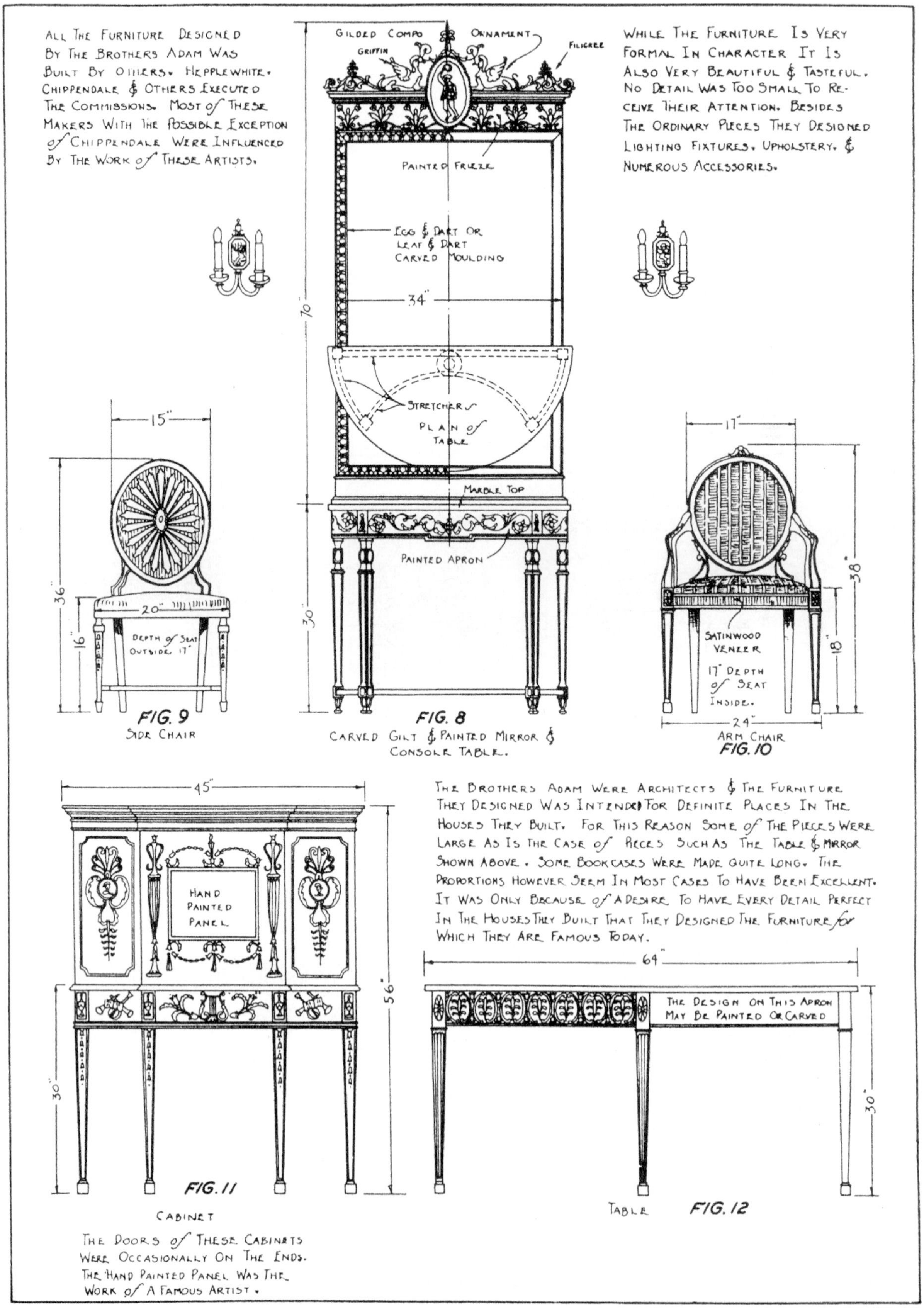
All The Furniture Designed By The Brothers Adam Was Built By Others. Hepplewhite. Chippendale & Others Executed The Commissions. Most of These Makers With The Possible Exception of Chippendale Were Influenced By The Work of These Artists.
While The Furniture Is Very Formal In Character It Is Also Very Beautiful & Tasteful. No Detail Was Too Small To Receive Their Attention. Besides The Ordinary Pieces They Designed Lighting Fixtures. Upholstery. & Numerous Accessories.
Gilded Compo
Griffin
Ornament
Filigree
Painted Frieze
Egg & Dart or Leaf & Dart Carved Moulding
34"
70"
Stretchers
Plan of Table
Marble Top
Painted Apron
30"
15"
36"
20"
16"
Depth of Seat Outside 17"
FIG. 9
Side Chair
FIG. 8
Carved Gilt & Painted Mirror & Console Table.
17"
38"
Satinwood Veneer
17" Depth of Seat Inside.
18"
24"
Arm Chair
FIG. 10
45"
Hand Painted Panel
56"
30"
FIG. 11
Cabinet
The Doors of These Cabinets Were Occasionally On The Ends. The Hand Painted Panel Was The Work of A Famous Artist.
The Brothers Adam Were Architects & The Furniture They Designed Was Intended For Definite Places In The Houses They Built. For This Reason Some of The Pieces Were Large As Is The Case of Pieces Such As The Table & Mirror Shown Above. Some Bookcases Were Made Quite Long. The Proportions However Seem In Most Cases To Have Been Excellent. It Was Only Because of A Desire To Have Every Detail Perfect In The Houses They Built That They Designed The Furniture for Which They Are Famous Today.
64"
The Design On This Apron May Be Painted Or Carved
30"
Table
FIG. 12

Brothers Adam

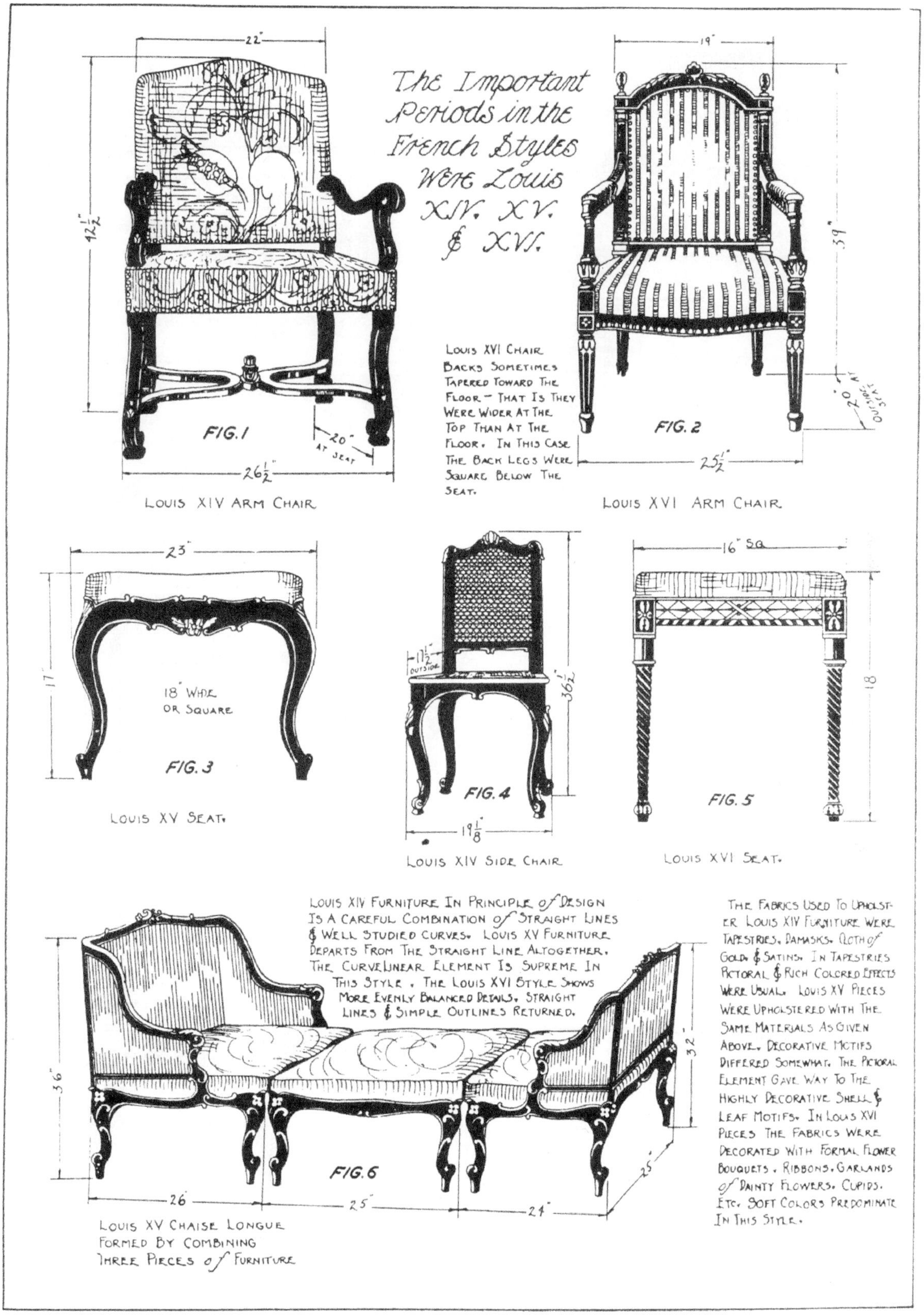
The Important Periods in the French Styles Were Louis XIV, XV. & XVI.
22"
42½"
FIG. 1
20" AT SEAT
26½"
LOUIS XIV ARM CHAIR
Louis XVI Chair Backs Sometimes Tapered Toward The Floor – That Is They Were Wider At The Top Than At The Floor. In This Case The Back Legs Were Square Below The Seat.
19"
39"
20" OUTSIDE AT SEAT
FIG. 2
25½"
LOUIS XVI ARM CHAIR
23"
17"
18" WIDE OR SQUARE
FIG. 3
LOUIS XV SEAT.
17½" OUTSIDE
36½"
FIG. 4
19⅛"
LOUIS XIV SIDE CHAIR
16" SQ.
18"
FIG. 5
LOUIS XVI SEAT.
LOUIS XIV FURNITURE IN PRINCIPLE OF DESIGN IS A CAREFUL COMBINATION OF STRAIGHT LINES & WELL STUDIED CURVES. LOUIS XV FURNITURE DEPARTS FROM THE STRAIGHT LINE ALTOGETHER. THE CURVELINEAR ELEMENT IS SUPREME IN THIS STYLE. THE LOUIS XVI STYLE SHOWS MORE EVENLY BALANCED DETAILS. STRAIGHT LINES & SIMPLE OUTLINES RETURNED.
THE FABRICS USED TO UPHOLSTER LOUIS XIV FURNITURE WERE TAPESTRIES, DAMASKS, CLOTH OF GOLD & SATINS. IN TAPESTRIES PICTORAL & RICH COLORED EFFECTS WERE USUAL. LOUIS XV PIECES WERE UPHOLSTERED WITH THE SAME MATERIALS AS GIVEN ABOVE. DECORATIVE MOTIFS DIFFERED SOMEWHAT. THE PICTORAL ELEMENT GAVE WAY TO THE HIGHLY DECORATIVE SHELL & LEAF MOTIFS. IN LOUIS XVI PIECES THE FABRICS WERE DECORATED WITH FORMAL FLOWER BOUQUETS, RIBBONS, GARLANDS OF DAINTY FLOWERS, CUPIDS, ETC. SOFT COLORS PREDOMINATE IN THIS STYLE.
36"
32"
FIG. 6
25"
26"
25"
24"
LOUIS XV CHAISE LONGUE FORMED BY COMBINING THREE PIECES OF FURNITURE

French styles

PERIOD FURNITURE
16th and 17th Century Spanish

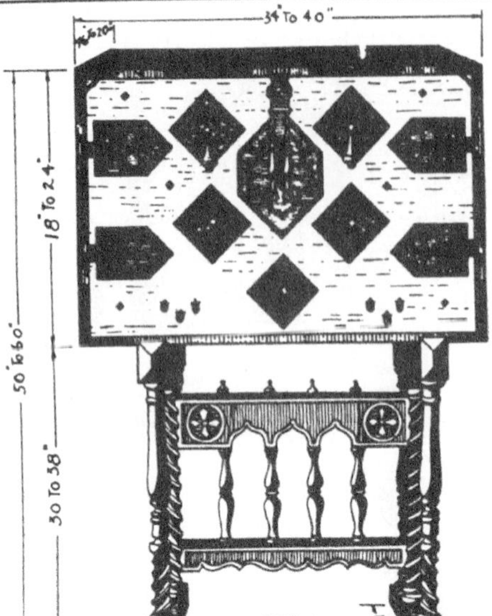

FIG. 1
VARGUENO

THESE CABINETS ORIGINATED IN SPAIN DURING THE 16 TH CENTURY. THEY WERE OFTEN USED AS A DESK & ARE EASILY THE MOST IMPORTANT CONTRIBUTION OF SPAIN TO THE FURNITURE WORLD.

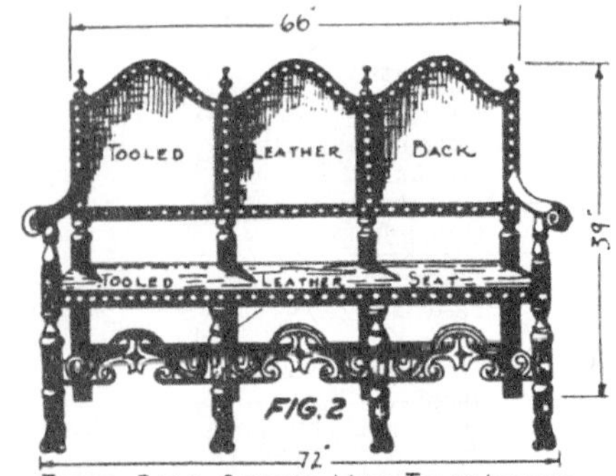

FIG. 2

THREE BACK SETTEE WITH TOOLED LEATHER BACK & SEAT FASTENED WITH LARGE HEADED BRASS NAILS CIRCA. 1700

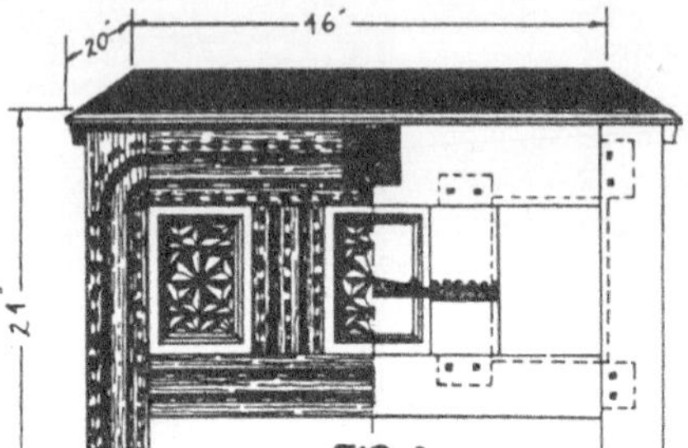

FIG. 3

17 TH CENTURY CHEST WITH CHIP CARVED PANELS LAID OUT IN GEOMETRIC DESIGNS INTERUPTED CHANNEL GROOVES ON LEGS. RAILS & STILES. SPANISH CHESTS VARY GREATLY IN CHARACTER. SOME ARE DESIGNED WITH ROUND LIDS. SOME ARE FASTENED TO TURNED LEGGED FRAMES. OTHERS ARE COVERED WITH TOOLED LEATHER OR CARVED IN GOTHIC MOTIFS. ETC.

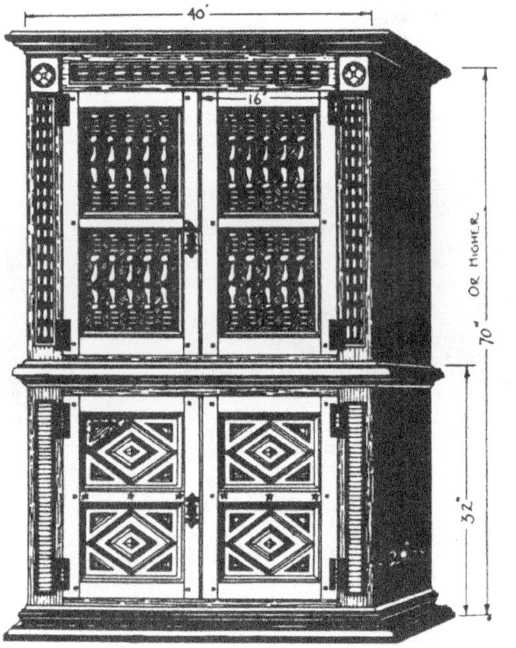

CUPBOARD OF THE 16 TH CENTURY. RENAISSANCE PERIOD. THESE CUPBOARDS WERE USED TO HOLD FOOD SUCH AS BREAD & CHEESE & WINE. FIG. 4

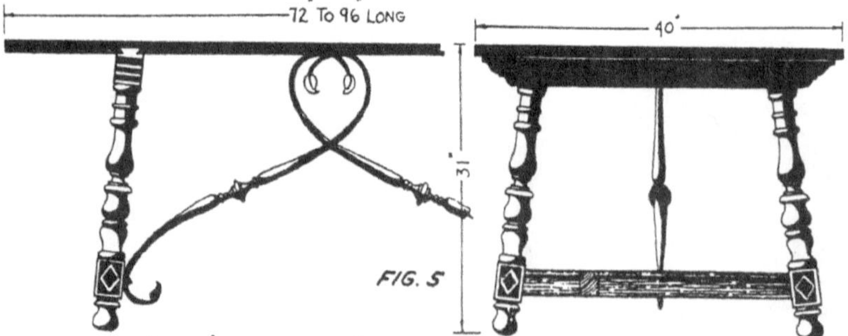

FIG. 5

FRONT & END VIEWS OF TURNED LEGGED TABLE WITH WROUGHT IRON BRACES.

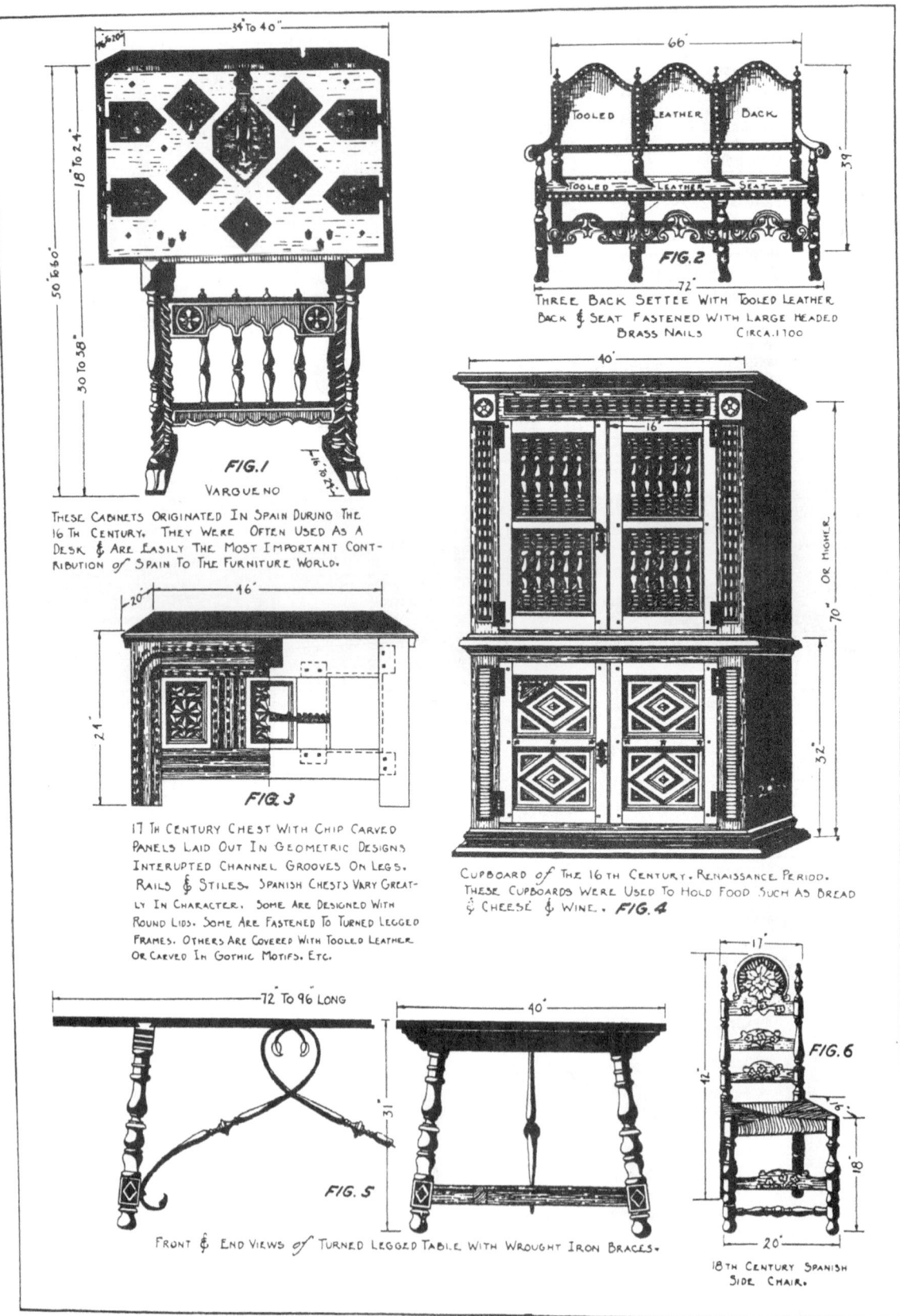

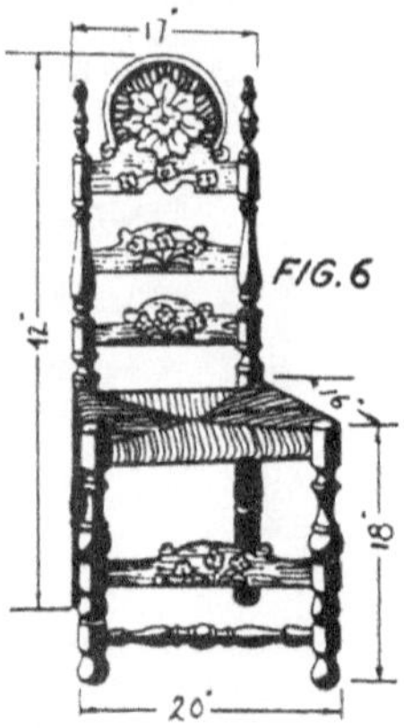

FIG. 6

18 TH CENTURY SPANISH SIDE CHAIR.

Spanish styles

TABLE 1 Period Styles and Finishes

Period style	Associated styles	Walls and ceilings	Floors	Floor coverings
Early English Tudor Jacobean Charles II	Italian Renaissance Spanish Renaissance William & Mary Larger pieces of Queen Anne	Oak panels Rough plaster with oak trim Parquetry ceilings	Hardwood stained, dark strips and planks on flooring Stone Tiles	Oriental and large-patterned domestic rugs Plain rugs
Anglo-Dutch William & Mary Queen Anne	Chippendale Early Georgian Louis XVI Smaller pieces of Jacobean, such as gate-leg table or Windsor chair	Papered Painted (in light tones) Hung with fabrics Paneled	Hardwood flooring Parquetry	Oriental and large-patterned domestic rugs Plain rugs
Early Georgian Chippendale	Chippendale Early Georgian Louis XVI Smaller pieces of Jacobean, such as gate-leg table or Windsor chair	Painted dado Painted Paneled Papered upper section	Hardwood flooring Parquetry	Plain or small-patterned rugs or carpets Oriental rugs
Late Georgian Adam Hepplewhite Sheraton Empire Federal	Chinese Chippendale Louis XVI Duncan Phyfe Directoire	Plain plaster Painted Papered Large wood panels painted Gesso ceilings	Hardwood flooring Parquetry	Plain or small-patterned rugs or carpets Oriental rugs
Louis XIV, XV, and XVI	All late Georgian styles 1 or 2 pieces of Directoire	Large wood panels painted and decorated Wallpaper in Chinese motifs	Hardwood flooring Parquetry	Plain or small-patterned rugs or carpets Oriental rugs
Spanish Renaissance	Italian Renaissance Early English Louis XIV	Rough plaster painted Ceilings same or beamed	Hardwood flooring Tiles Vinyls in tile pattern	Spanish or Oriental rugs
Early Colonial	All Early English styles William & Mary Queen Anne wing chair	Oak panels Rough plaster with oak Parquetry ceilings	Hardwood flooring or planks Vinyls in jaspe pattern	Braided or hooked rugs
Early American	Late Georgian Chippendale Queen Anne Duncan Phyfe French Provincial	Smooth plaster, light trim Wallpaper, scenic and Chinese designs Paneling Ceiling plaster	Dark hardwood flooring Vinyls in plain or jaspe patterns	Hooked, braided, Oriental, or domestic rugs Carpet, plain, two-toned patterned
Modern	Swedish Modern Chinese Chippendale	Painted solid colors, striped, figured Plain papers Combinations of above	Hardwood flooring Parquetry Vinyls in modern pattern	Carpet Rugs in solid colors, geometric patterns
French Provincial	18th-century American Colonial Federal	Smooth plaster Wallpaper in scenic or geometric designs	Hardwood flooring Parquetry	Aubussons Homespun carpet, small-patterned Oriental rugs
Victorian	Colonial William & Mary Queen Anne	Large-patterned paper	Hardwood flooring	Carpet in large patterns Oriental rugs

FURNITURE DIMENSIONS
Children's Furniture and Tables

CHILDREN'S FURNITURE

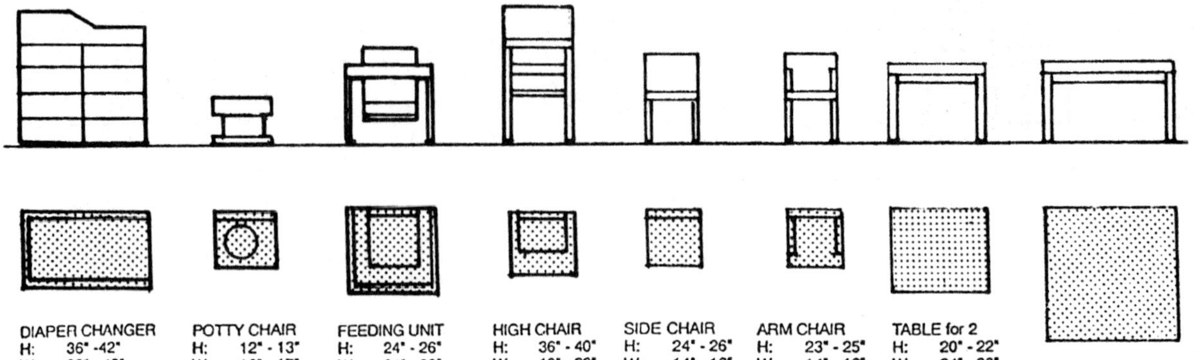

DIAPER CHANGER
H: 36" - 42"
W: 32" - 42"
D: 21" - 24"

POTTY CHAIR
H: 12" - 13"
W: 16" - 17"
D: 14" - 16"

FEEDING UNIT
H: 24" - 26"
W: 24" - 28"
D: 24" - 25"

HIGH CHAIR
H: 36" - 40"
W: 18" - 22"
D: 18" - 20"

SIDE CHAIR
H: 24" - 26"
W: 14" - 16"
D: 15" - 17"

ARM CHAIR
H: 23" - 25"
W: 14" - 16"
D: 16" - 17"

TABLE for 2
H: 20" - 22"
W: 24" - 30"
D: 24" - 25"

TABLE for 4
H: 20" - 22"
W: 36" - 42"
D: 36" - 42"

TABLES

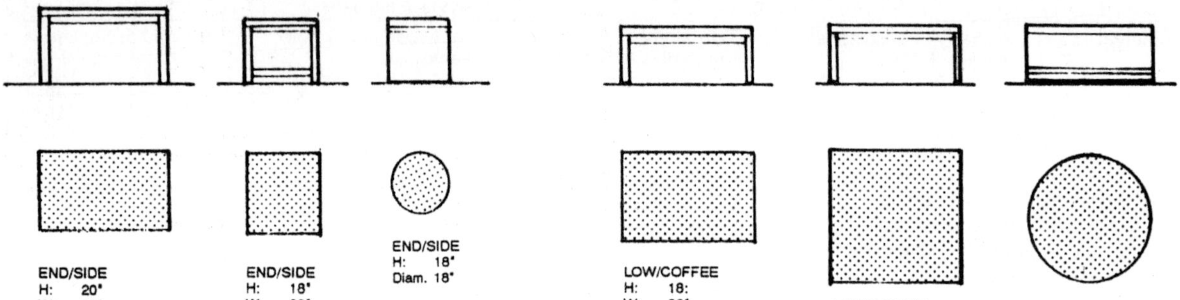

END/SIDE
H: 20"
W: 36"
D: 20"

END/SIDE
H: 18"
W: 20"
D: 20"

END/SIDE
H: 18"
Diam. 18"

LOW/COFFEE
H: 18:
W: 36"
D: 24"

LOW/COFFEE
H: 18"
W: 36"
D: 36"

LOW/COFFEE
H: 18"
Diam. 36"

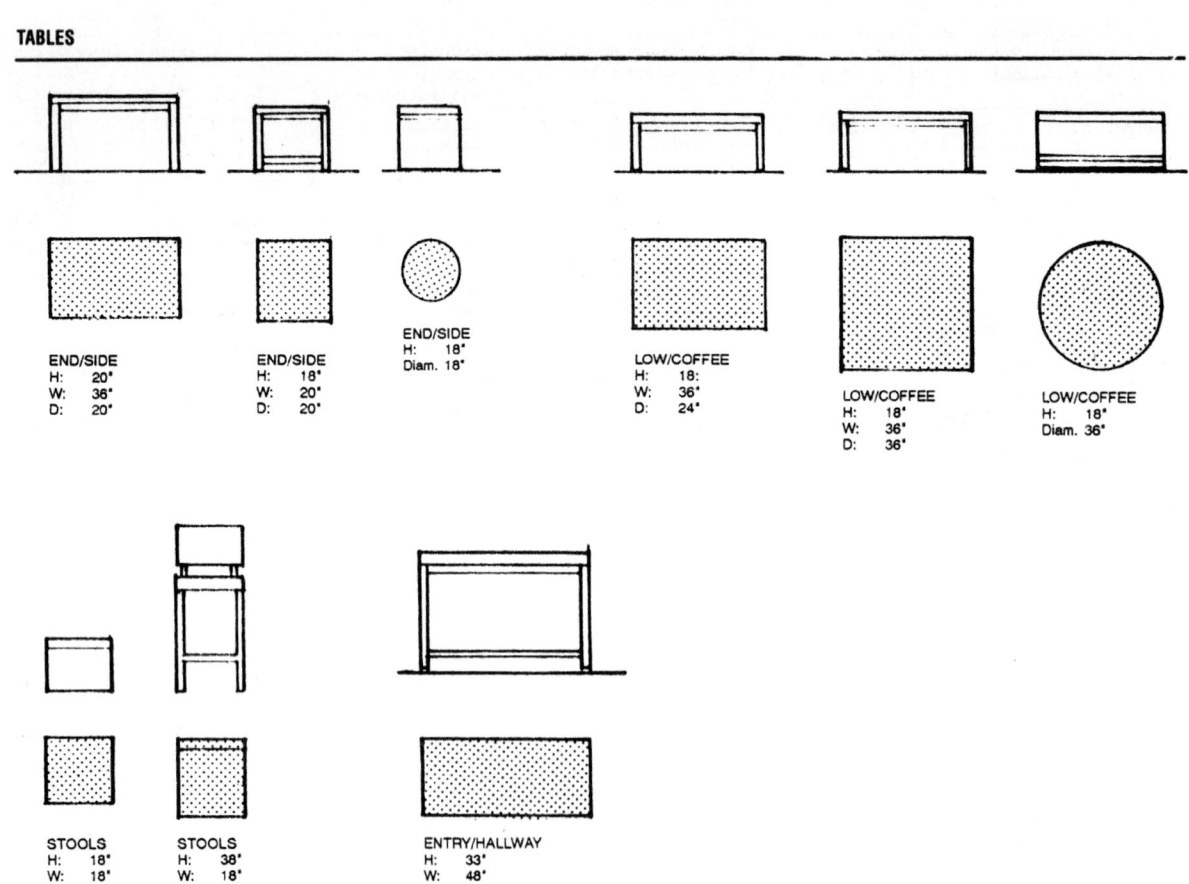

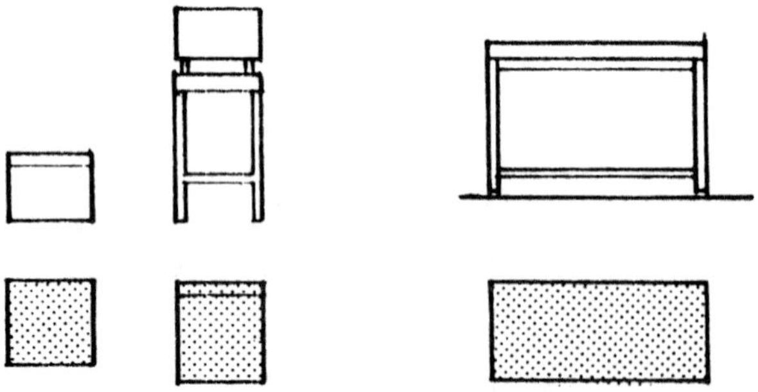

STOOLS
H: 18"
W: 18"
D: 18"

STOOLS
H: 38"
W: 18"
D: 20"

ENTRY/HALLWAY
H: 33"
W: 48"
D: 20"

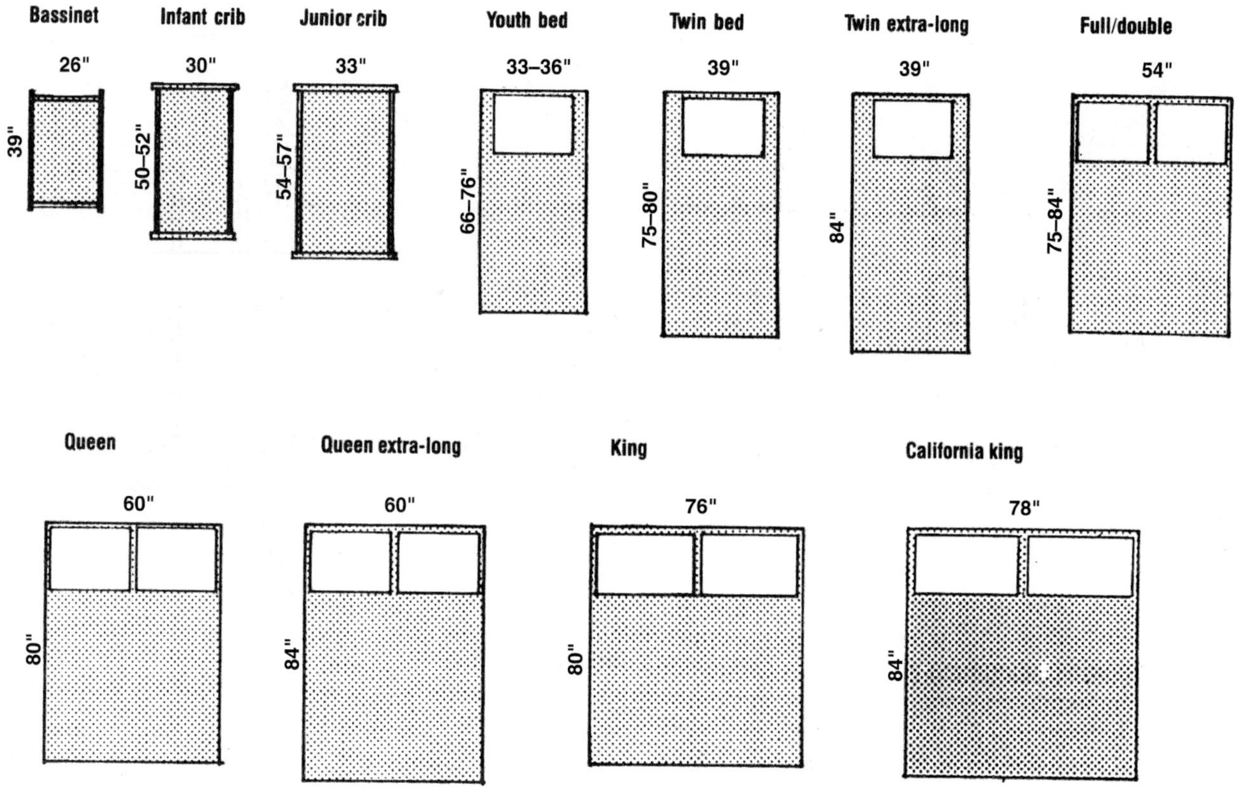

Fig. 1

BED/MATTRESS TYPES AND SIZES

Figure 1 provides the designer with an array of typical bed and mattress sizes with which rooms can be planned. Tables 1 and 2, however, suggest that within the bedding and mattress industries there exists a wide range of sizes from which to select. Many manufacturers use bed/mattress terminology that reflects different dimensional standards than those of other manufacturers. Ultimately, the designer, in consultation with the client, must verify exact measurements. Be sure to take your clients to see and test the bed or mattress selected. After all, they are the ones who will have to sleep on it.

WATERBEDS, SOFA BEDS/CONVERTIBLE SOFAS, AND WALL BEDS

TELEVISION VIEWING AREAS

The shape of the viewing area is approximately as shown in Fig. 2. Its size is always based on the size of the image to be viewed. The human eye comprehends detail only within a limited cone angle (about 2½ minutes of arc), and the length of chord subtending this arc—that is, the image of width—varies with its distance from the observer. Thus an object 20 ft away and 6 ft long appears the same as a similar object 10 ft away and 3 ft long. The size of the viewing area is determined by three dimensions:

- The minimum distance (1), which is the distance from the nearest part of the image to the eye of the closest viewer
- The maximum distance (2), which is the distance from the furthermost part of the image to the most distant viewer
- The maximum viewing angle (3), which is the angle between the projection axis and the line of sight of a person located as far from this axis as he or she can be and still see all image detail in proper brilliance

TABLE 1 Juvenile, Youth, and Adult Mattress Types and Sizes

	Width (in)		Length (in)	
Mattress type	Min	Max	Min	Max
Bassinet	17	23	36	40
Portable crib	22	26	45	52
Junior crib	24	32½	46	58
Youth bed	33	36	66	76
Bunk bed	30	33	75	76
Dorm bed	32	36	75	80
Hospital bed	36	36	75	80
Narrow twin	36	36	74	75
Twin bed	39	39	75	80, 84
Full-size or double bed	54	54	74	75
Queen-size bed	60	60	80	84
King-size bed	76	78	80	84
Extra-long double	54	54	80	80
Super twin	45	45	75	80

TABLE 2 Pillow Types and Sizes

	Width (in)		Length (in)	
Pillow type	Min	Max	Min	Max
Standard	18	20	26	27
Queen	19	21	29	30
King	20	22	35	36

Note: Many manufacturers also make and sell undersized pillows for cribs and youth beds as well as oversized pillows for the larger beds.

FURNITURE DIMENSIONS
Waterbeds, Sofa Beds/Convertible Sofas, and Wall Beds

WATERBEDS

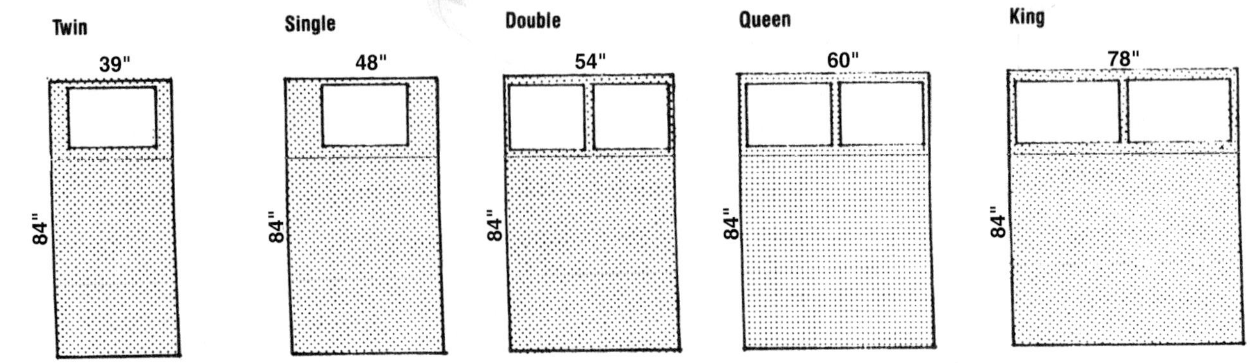

SOFA BEDS/CONVERTIBLE SOFAS

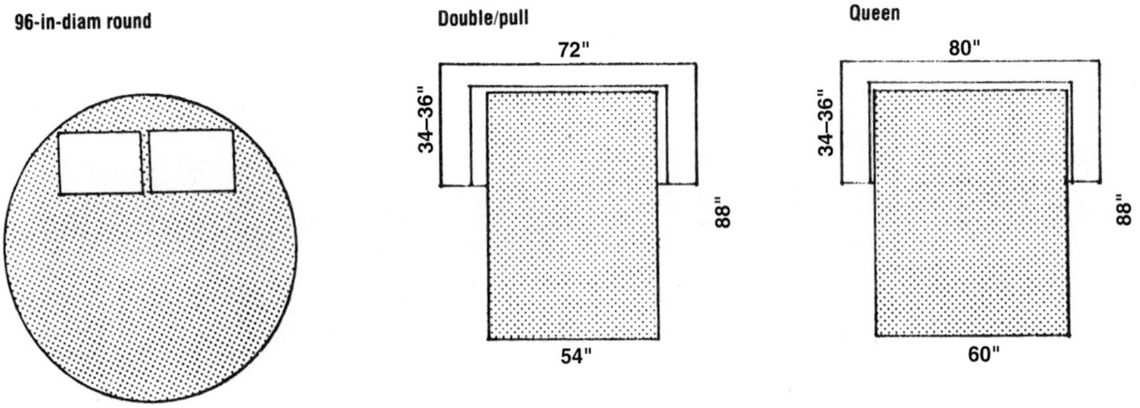

WALL AND SIDE BEDS

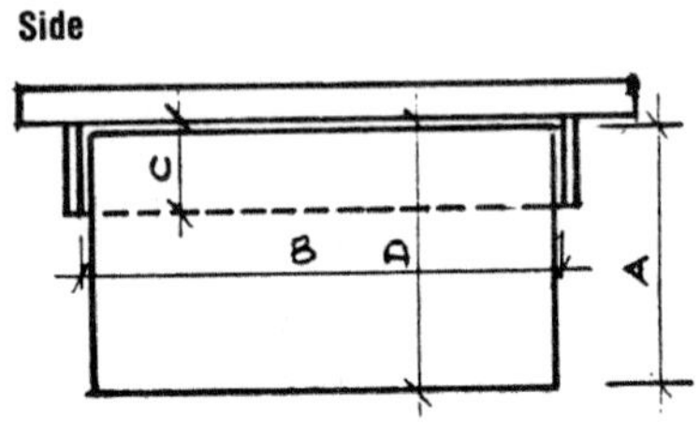

A Width of Bed	B Width of Clear Door Opening	C Depth From Back Of Closet To Back of Doors	D Projection of Bed in Use From Back of Closet
39"	79"	13"	43½"
48"	79"	13"	52½"
54"	79"	13"	57"

HEIGHT: FLOOR TO TOP OF OPENING
44½" for 39" Bed. 53½" for 48" Bed. 59" for 54" Bed.

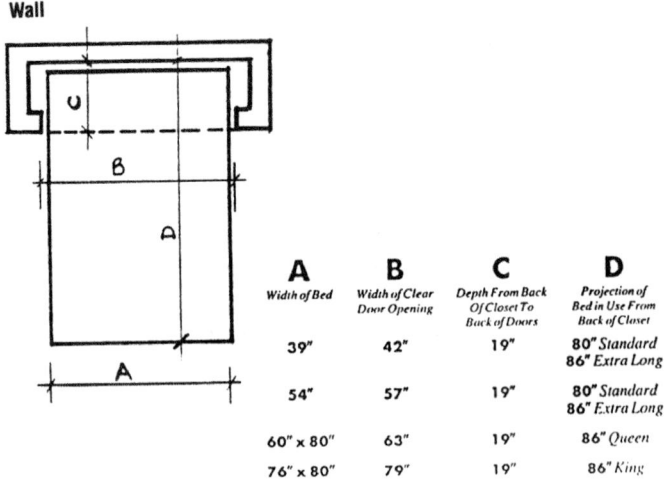

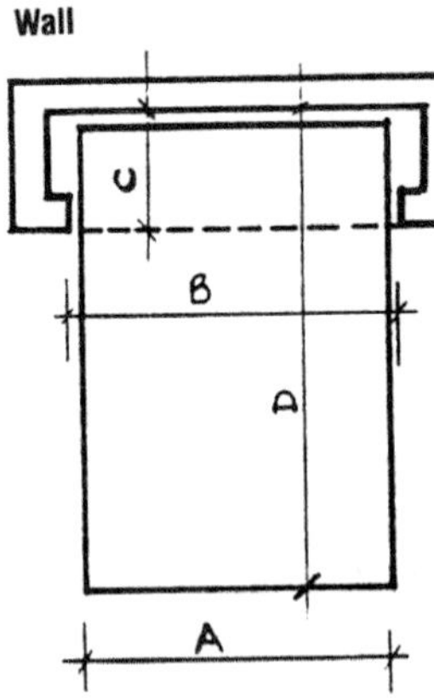

A Width of Bed	B Width of Clear Door Opening	C Depth From Back Of Closet To Back of Doors	D Projection of Bed in Use From Back of Closet
39"	42"	19"	80" Standard 86" Extra Long
54"	57"	19"	80" Standard 86" Extra Long
60" x 80"	63"	19"	86" Queen
76" x 80"	79"	19"	86" King

HEIGHT: FLOOR TO TOP OF OPENING
80" - *For 39" and 54" Beds of Standard 75" Length*
86" - *For Queen, King and Extra Long Beds 80" in Length*

Practical minimum and maximum distances are both expressed as multiples of the image width (W). They vary both with the medium being used and with the type and quality of material being projected, and may be affected also, in some degree, by personal preferences. They have not yet been precisely determined by scientific methods, and it's doubtful that such data would have much practical value anyway. The generally accepted values, resulting from numerous studies, are these:

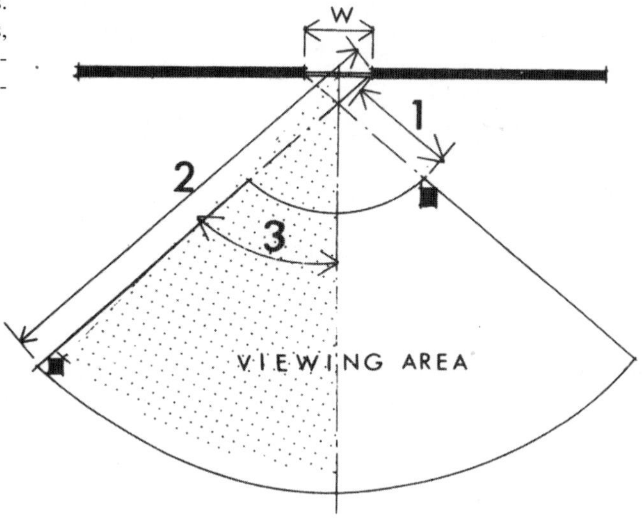

	Film, slides, and projected TV	TV receivers
Minimum distance	2W	4W
Maximum distance	6W to 10W	12W

Size of TV tube	Minimum viewing distance 4W	Maximum viewing distance 12W
17 in	4 ft 11 in	14 ft 9 in
19 in	5 ft 1 in	15 ft 2 in
21 in	6 ft 4 in	19 ft 0 in
23 in	6 ft 6 in	19 ft 4 in
24 in	7 ft 5 in	21 ft 5 in
27 in	9 ft 8 in	24 ft 5 in

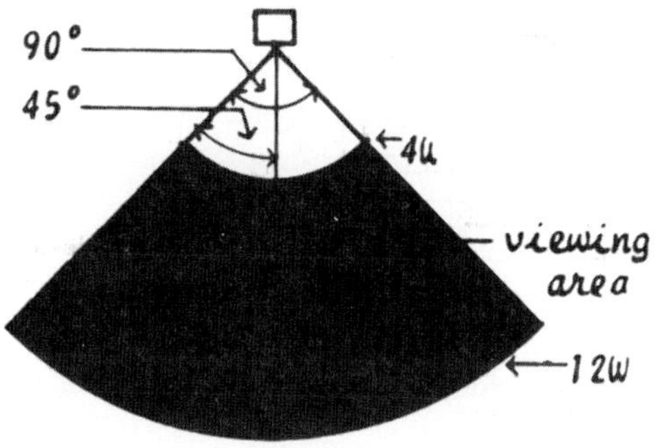

FURNITURE DIMENSIONS
Dining/Living Room

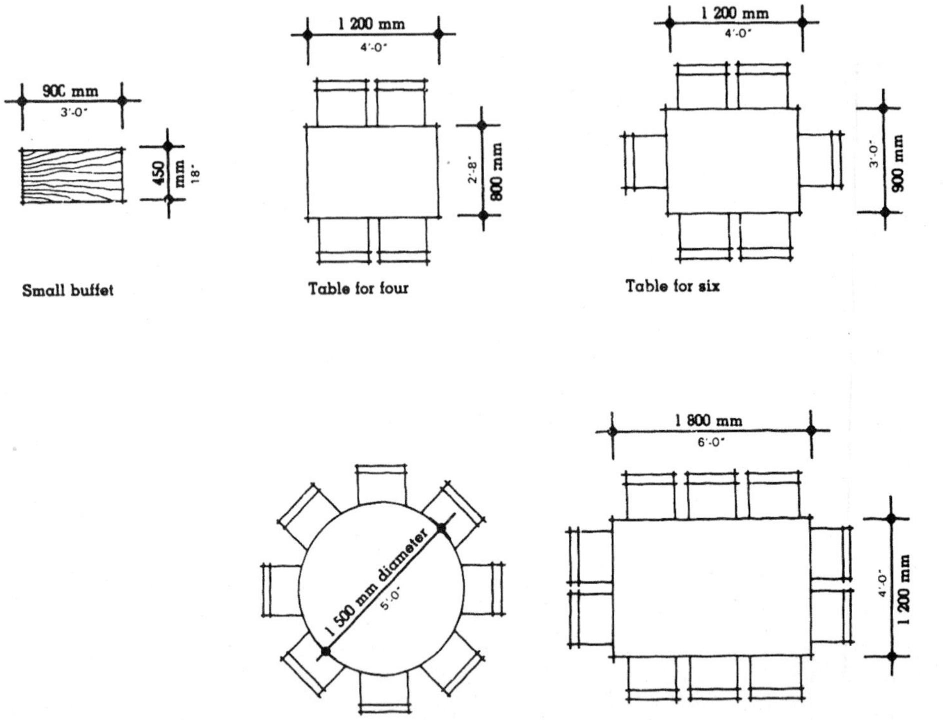

Fig. 3 Typical dining room furniture

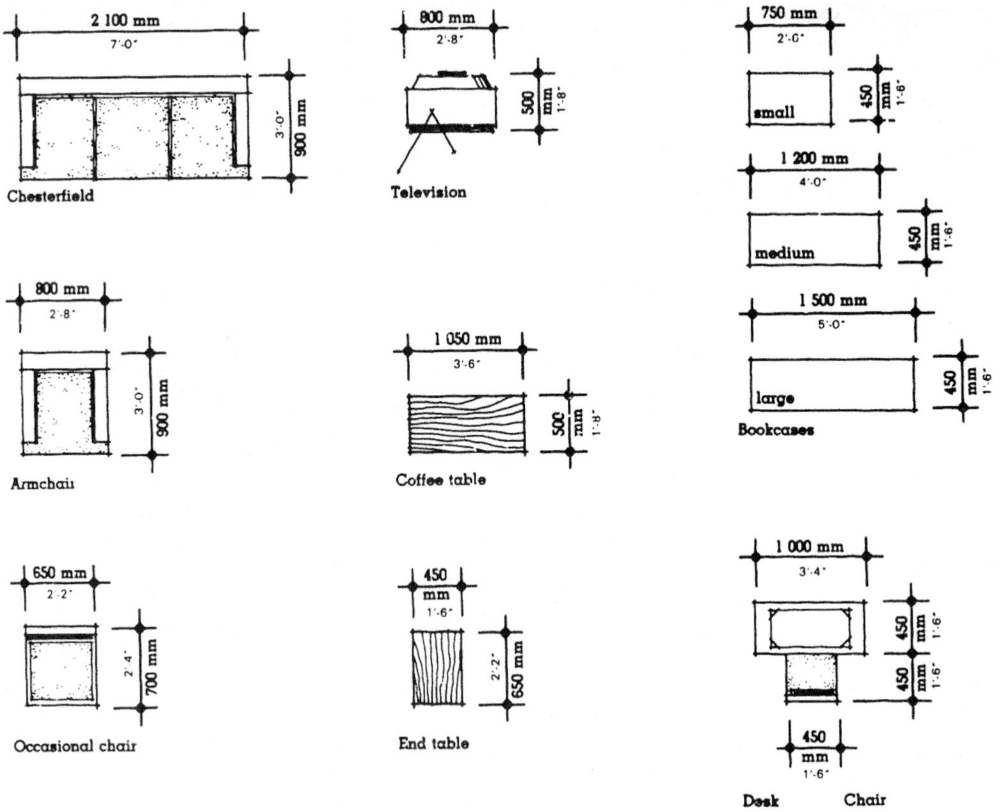

Fig. 4 Typical living room furniture

FURNITURE DIMENSIONS
20th Century Classic Chairs

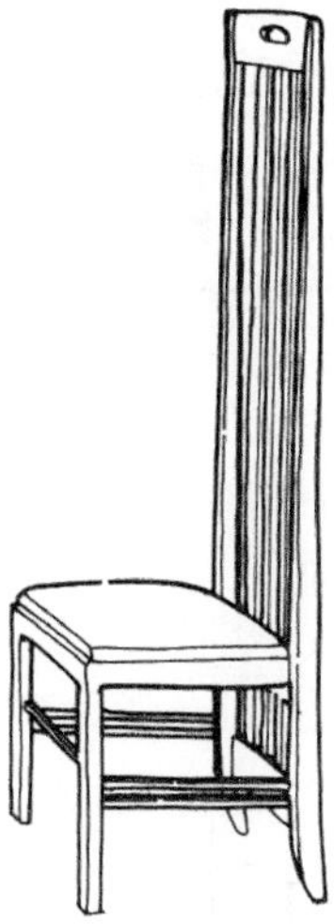

INGRAM HIGH CHAIR
DESIGNER:
Charles R. Macintosh
YEAR: 1900
MANUFACTURER:
Atelier International
DIMENSIONS:
18½"W x 17½"D x 59¼"H

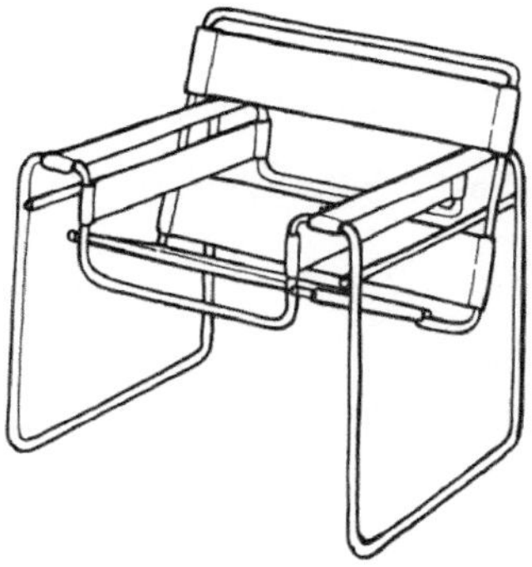

WASSILY CHAIR
DESIGNER:
Marcel Breuer
YEAR: 1925
MANUFACTURER:
Knoll International
DIMENSIONS:
30¾"W x 29"D x 28½"H

KUBUS CHAIR
DESIGNER:
Joseph Hoffman
YEAR: 1910
DIMENSIONS:
36"W x 30½"D x 28½"H

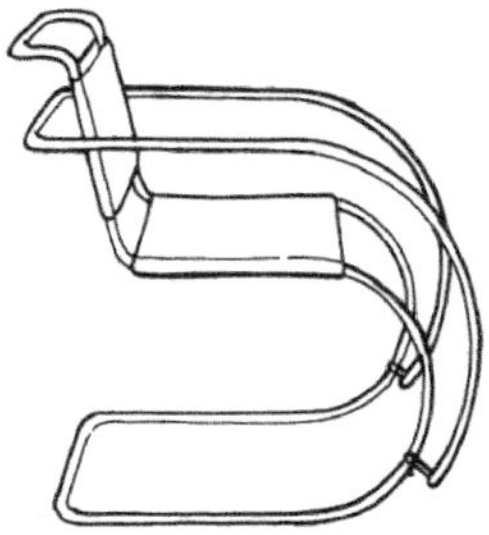

MR. CHAIR
DESIGNER:
Mies Van Der Rohe
YEAR: 1927
MANUFACTURER:
Stendig
DIMENSIONS:
21¾"W x 32¼"D x 32¼"H

HAU KOLLER CHAIR
DESIGNER:
Joseph Hoffman
YEAR: 1911
DIMENSIONS:
35½"W x 32"D x 37"H

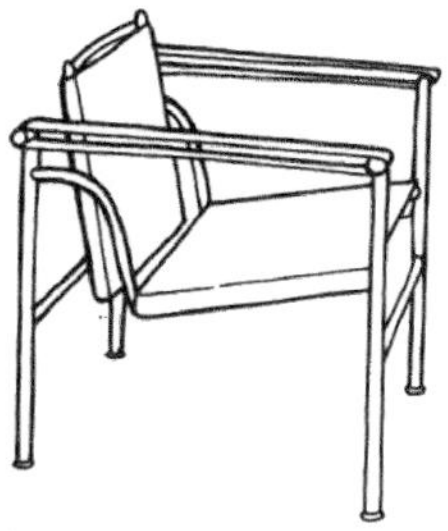

LC1 SLING CHAIR
DESIGNER:
Le Corbusier
YEAR: 1928
MANUFACTURER:
Atelier International
DIMENSIONS:
23⅝"W x 25⅝"D x 25¼"H

MIDWAY CHAIR
DESIGNER:
Frank Lloyd Wright
YEAR: 1914
MANUFACTURER:
Atelier International
DIMENSIONS:
16"W x 13"D x 35"H

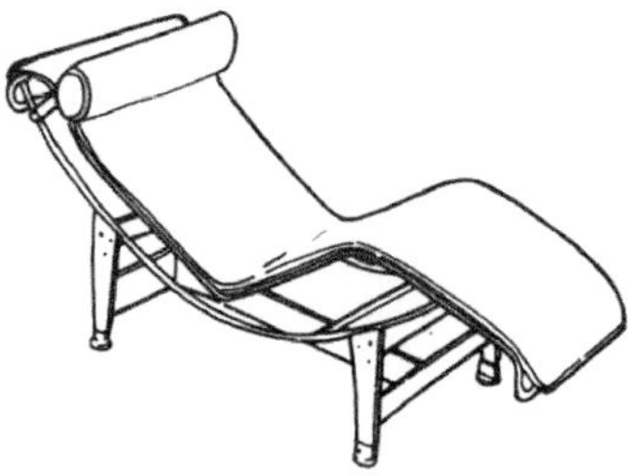

LC9 LOUNGE CHAIR
DESIGNER:
Le Corbusier
YEAR: 1928
MANUFACTURER:
Atelier International
DIMENSIONS:
22"W x 63"D

FURNITURE DIMENSIONS
20th Century Classic Chairs

CESCA ARMCHAIR
DESIGNER:
Marcel Breuer
YEAR: 1928
MANUFACTURER:
Knoll International
DIMENSIONS:
22⅝"W x 21⅝"D x 31¾"H

BARCELONA STOOL
DESIGNER:
Mies Van Der Rohe
YEAR: 1929
MANUFACTURER:
Knoll International
DIMENSIONS:
23"W x 22"D x 14½"H

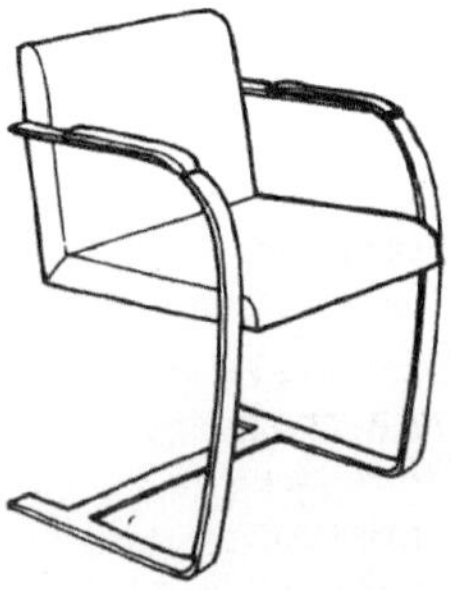

BRNO ARMCHAIR
DESIGNER:
Mies Van Der Rohe
YEAR: 1929
MANUFACTURER:
Stendig
DIMENSIONS:
18"W x 23"D x 31½"H

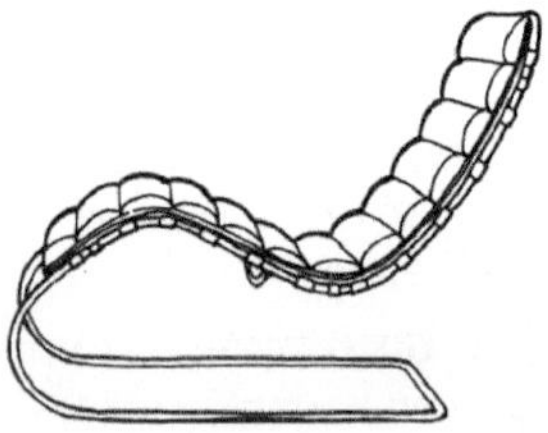

CHAISE LOUNGE
DESIGNER:
Mies Van Der Rohe
YEAR: 1931
MANUFACTURER:
Knoll International
DIMENSIONS:
23⅝"W x 47½"D x 37½"H

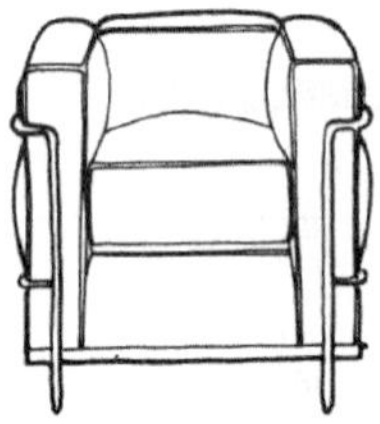

LC2 ARMCHAIR
DESIGNER:
Le Corbusier
YEAR: 1929
MANUFACTURER:
Atelier International
DIMENSIONS:
30"W x 27½"D x 26½"H

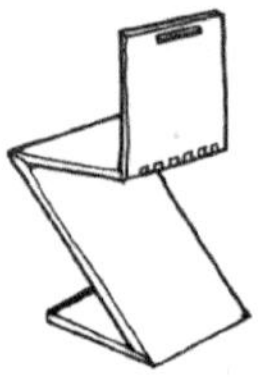

ZIG-ZAG CHAIR
DESIGNER:
Gerrit Rietveld
YEAR: 1934
MANUFACTURER:
Atelier International
DIMENSIONS:
14½"W x 17"D x 29"H

BARCELONA CHAIR
DESIGNER:
Mies Van Der Rohe
YEAR: 1929
MANUFACTURER:
Knoll International
DIMENSIONS:
30"W x 30"D x 30"H

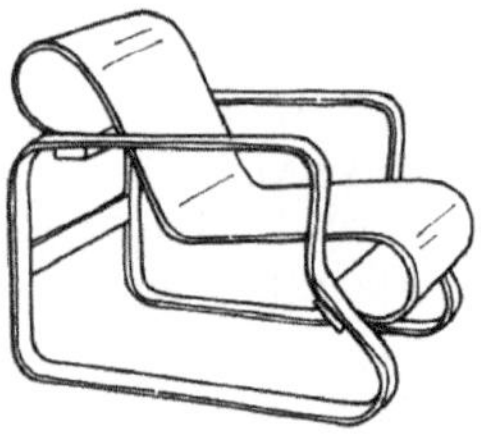

PAIMO CHAIR
DESIGNER:
Alvar Aalto
YEAR: 1935
MANUFACTURER:
Palazetti
DIMENSIONS:
23½"W x 31½"D x 25"H

FURNITURE DIMENSIONS
20th Century Classic Chairs

BARREL CHAIR
DESIGNER:
Frank Lloyd Wright
YEAR: 1937
MANUFACTURER:
Atelier International
DIMENSIONS:
21½"W x 22"D x 32"H

MOLDED FIBERGLAS CHAIR
DESIGNER:
Charles Eames
YEAR: 1949
MANUFACTURER:
Herman Miller
DIMENSIONS:
25"W x 25½"D x 31"H

BUTTERFLY CHAIR
DESIGNER:
Harday, Boner & Kurchan
YEAR: 1938
DIMENSIONS:
28"W x 27½"D x 35½"H

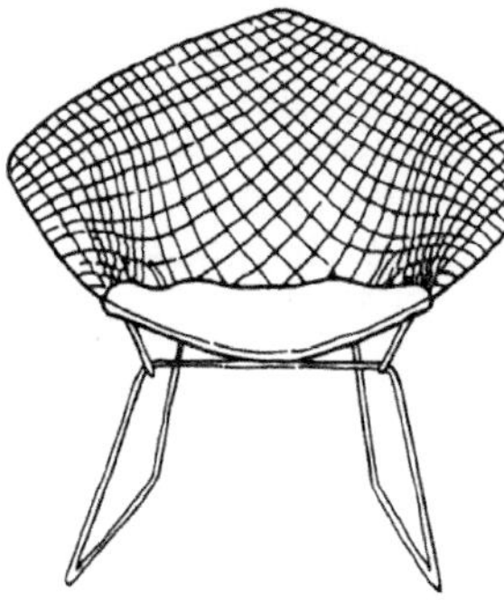

DIAMOND CHAIR
DESIGNER:
Harry Bertoia
YEAR: 1952
MANUFACTURER:
Knoll International
DIMENSIONS:
33¾"W x 28"D x 30½"H

MOLDED PLYWOOD CHAIR
DESIGNER:
Charles Eames
YEAR: 1946
MANUFACTURER:
Herman Miller
DIMENSIONS:
21½"W x 19¼"D x 29⅜"H

LOUNGE CHAIR
DESIGNER:
Charles Eames
YEAR: 1956
MANUFACTURER:
Herman Miller
DIMENSIONS:
32½"W x 32¾"D x 33½"H

WOMB CHAIR
DESIGNER:
Eero Saarinen
YEAR: 1948
MANUFACTURER:
Knoll International
DIMENSIONS:
40"W x 39"D x 35½"H

OTTOMAN
DESIGNER:
Charles Eames
YEAR: 1956
MANUFACTURER:
Herman Miller
DIMENSIONS:
26"W x 21"D x 15"H

FURNITURE DIMENSIONS
20th Century Classic Chairs

ALUMINUM GROUP CHAIR
DESIGNER:
Charles Eames
YEAR: 1958
MANUFACTURER:
Herman Miller
DIMENSIONS:
28½"W x 24¾"D x 33¾"H

LOUNGE CHAIR
DESIGNER:
Richard Schultz
YEAR: 1966
MANUFACTURER:
Knoll International
DIMENSIONS:
26"W x 28¼"D x 26½"H

SHERRIFF CHAIR
DESIGNER:
Sergio Rodriguez
YEAR: 1958
MANUFACTURER:
OCA

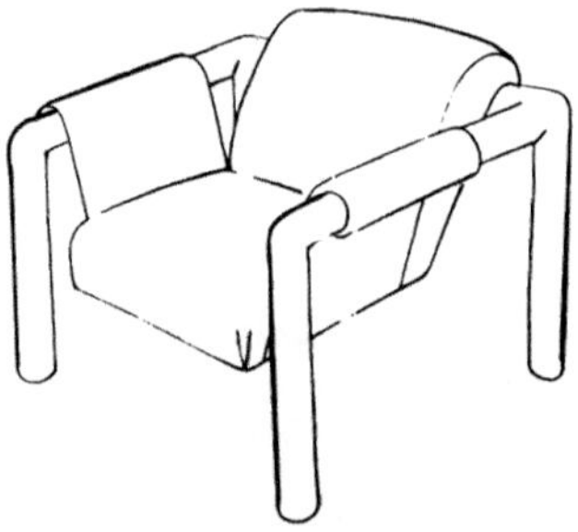

TUBO CHAIR
DESIGNER:
John Mascheroni
YEAR: 1968
MANUFACTURER:
Vecta
DIMENSIONS:
32"W x 32"D x 32"H

HAND CHAIR
DESIGNER:
Pedro Freidberg
YEAR: 1963
MANUFACTURER:
Hand Crafted

SAPPER COLLECTION
DESIGNER:
Richard Sapper
YEAR: 1977
MANUFACTURER:
Knoll International
DIMENSIONS:
28⅜"W x 27½"D x 38½-41⅜"H

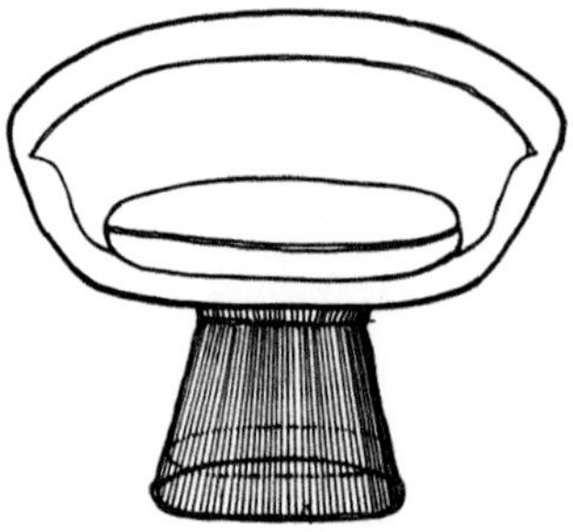

PLATNER CHAIR
DESIGNER:
Warren Platner
YEAR: 1966
MANUFACTURER:
Knoll International
DIMENSIONS:
36½"W x 25½"D x 30½"H

BASIC OPERATIONAL
DESIGNER:
Niels Diffrient
YEAR: 1979
MANUFACTURER:
Knoll International
DIMENSIONS:
25½"W x 21"D x 32½-36½"H

FURNITURE DIMENSIONS
20th Century Classic Chairs

NOTHING CONTINUES TO HAPPEN CHAIR
DESIGNER:
Horward Meisper
YEAR: 1981
MANUFACTURER:
Art et Industrie
DIMENSIONS:
17"W x 16"D x 37"H

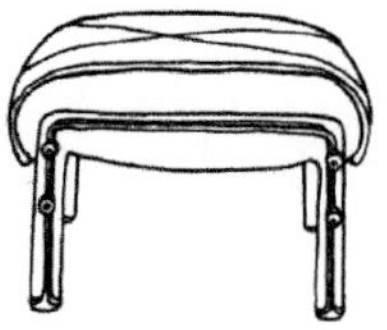

OTTOMAN
DESIGNER:
Niels Diffrient
YEAR: 1986
MANUFACTURER:
Sunar/Hauserman
DIMENSIONS:
25"W x 24"D x 17⅛"H

LOUNGE CHAIR
DESIGNER:
Michael Graves
YEAR: 1982
MANUFACTURER:
Sunar/Hauserman
DIMENSIONS:
32"W x 29"D x 29"H

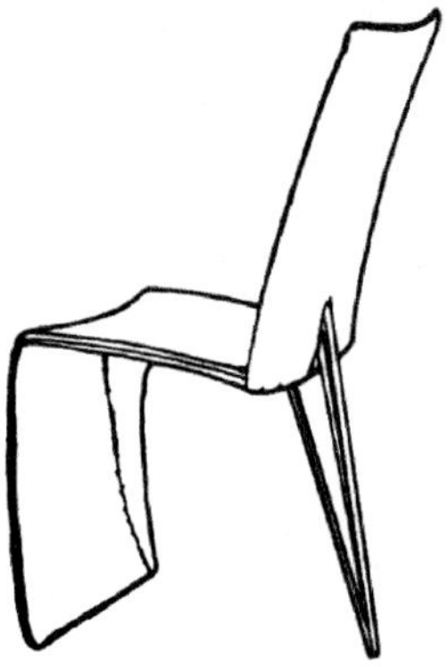

ED ARCHER CHAIR
DESIGNER:
Philippe Starck
YEAR: 1987
MANUFACTURER:
Driade Italy
DIMENSIONS:
18½"W x 21½"D x 38½"H

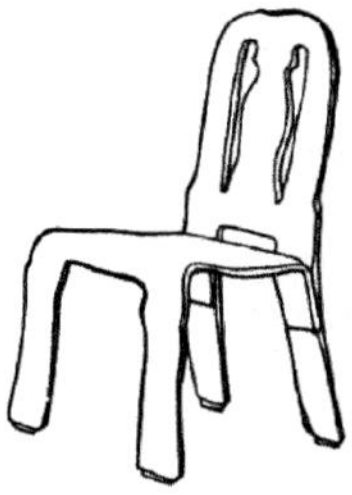

QUEENE ANNE CHAIR
DESIGNER:
Robert Venturi
YEAR: 1984
MANUFACTURER:
Knoll International
DIMENSIONS:
26½"W x 23½"D x 38½"H

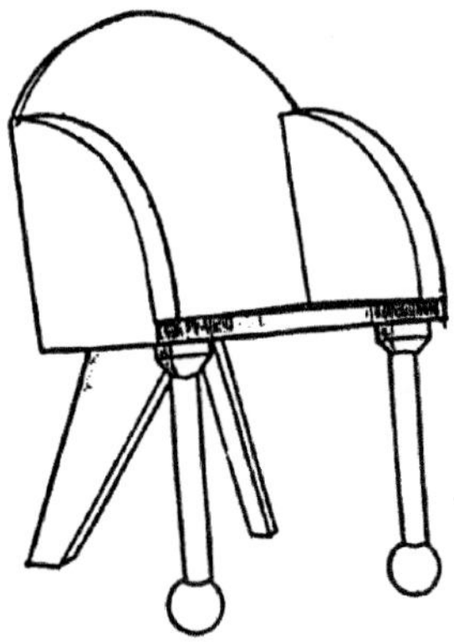

STONE CHAIR
DESIGNER:
James Kutasi
YEAR: 1988
MANUFACTURER:
James Kutasi Australia
DIMENSIONS:
19⅝"W x 19⅝"D x 35½"H

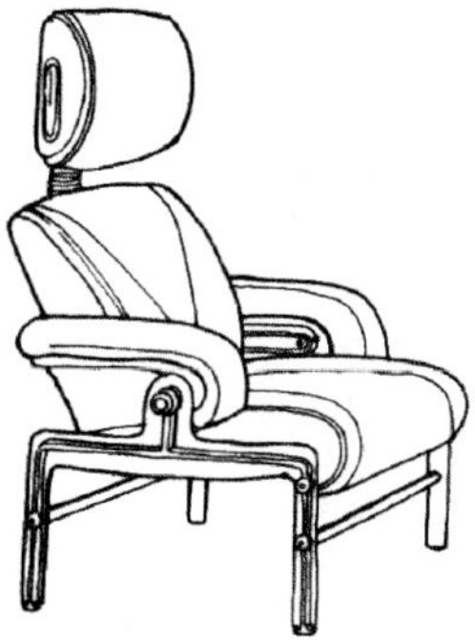

JEFFERSON CHAIR
DESIGNER:
Neils Diffrient
YEAR: 1986
MANUFACTURER:
Sunar/Hauserman
DIMENSIONS:
32⅜"W x 34"D x 43½"H

FURNITURE DIMENSIONS

Traditional Bedroom and Dining Room Furniture

BEDROOM FURNITURE

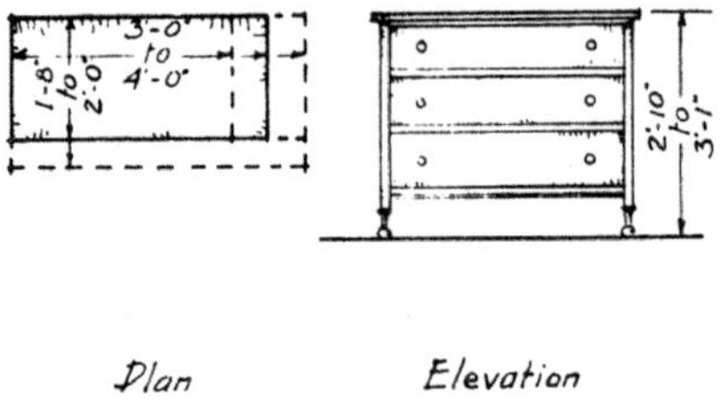

Bureau

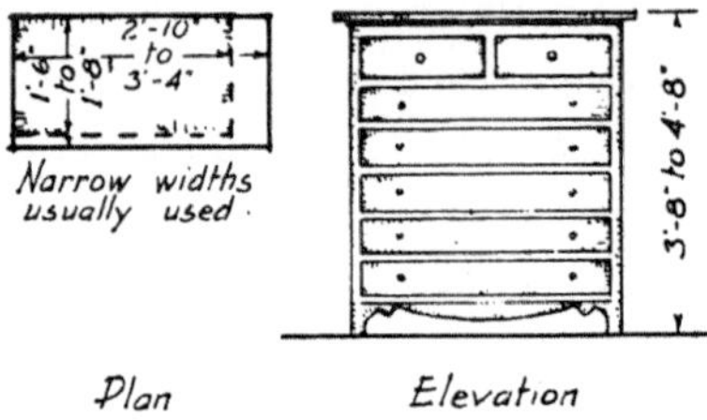

Chiffonier

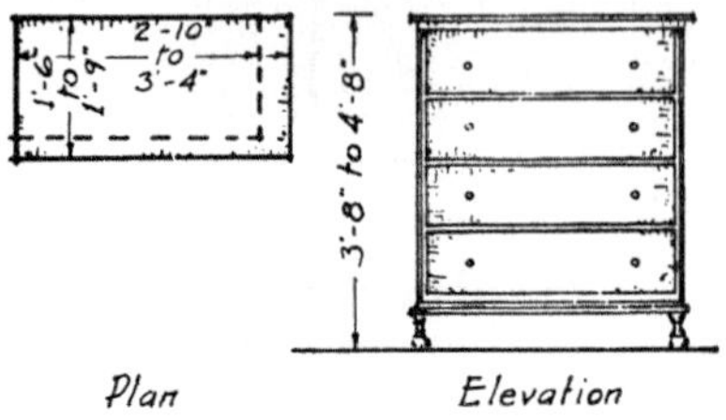

Chest of drawers

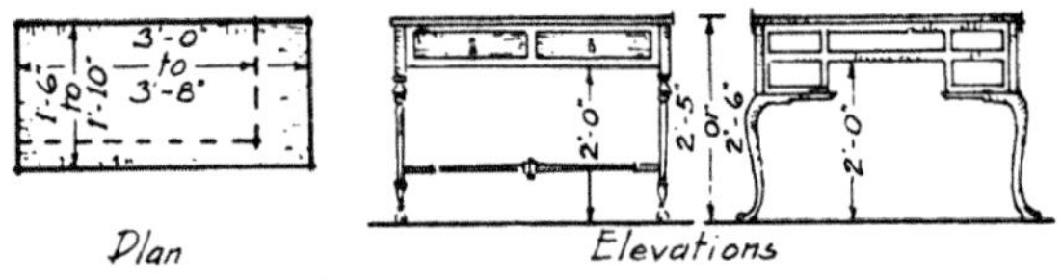

Dressing table

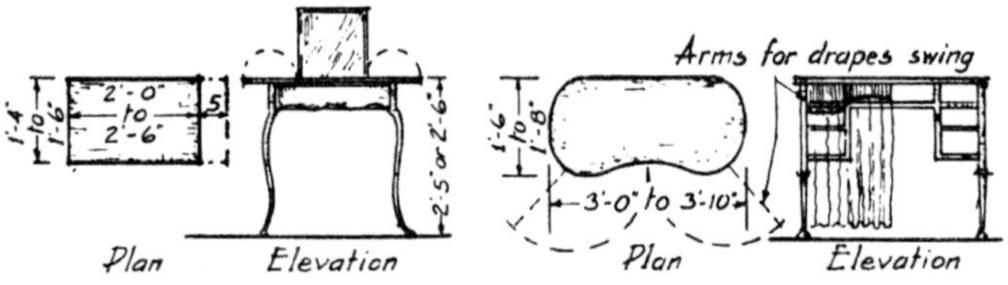

Makeup or powder table

DINING ROOM FURNITURE

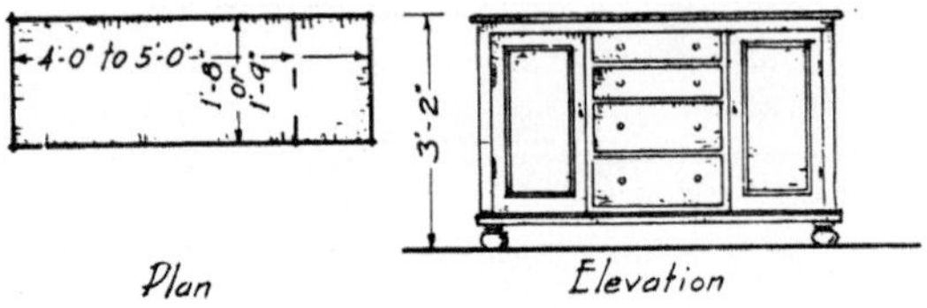

Sideboard

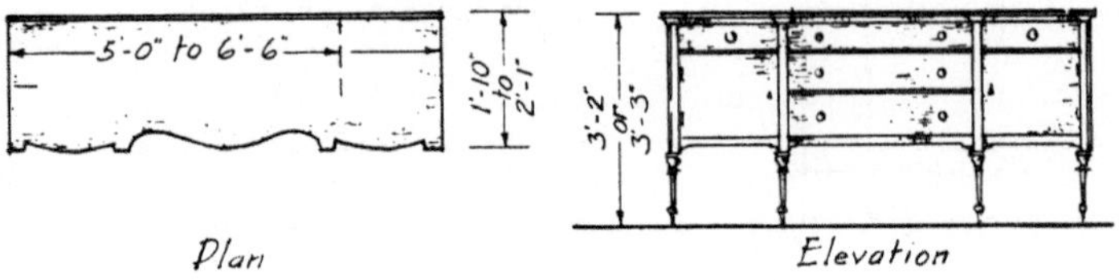

Buffet

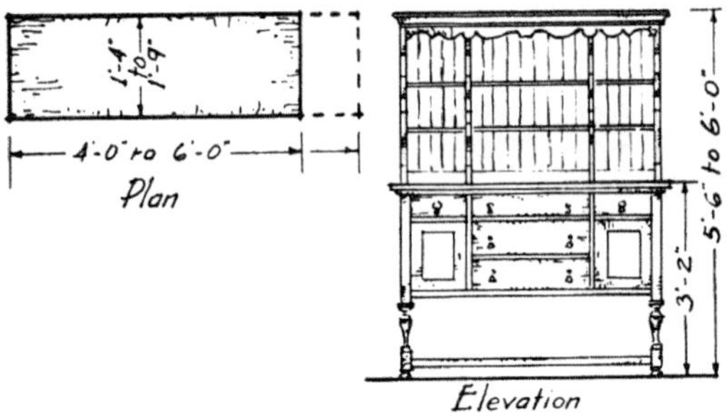

Dresser

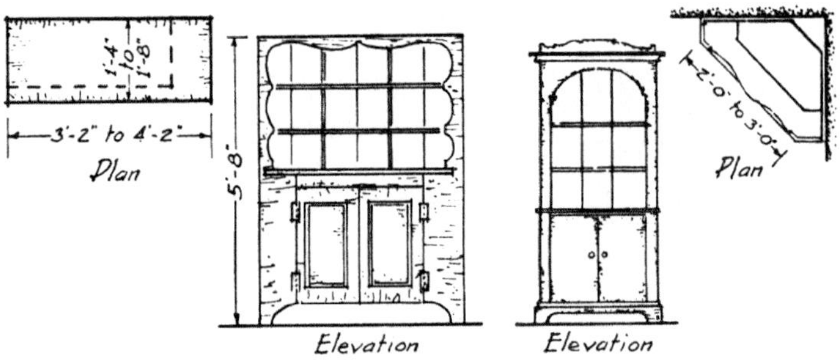

Cupboards

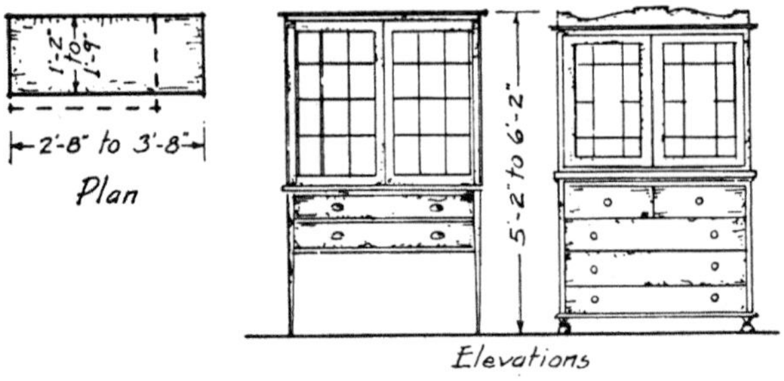

China cabinets

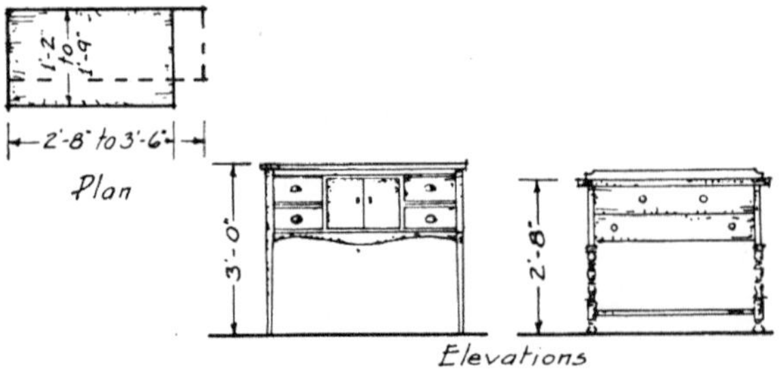

Servers

FURNITURE DIMENSIONS
Traditional Sofas, Settees, and Benches

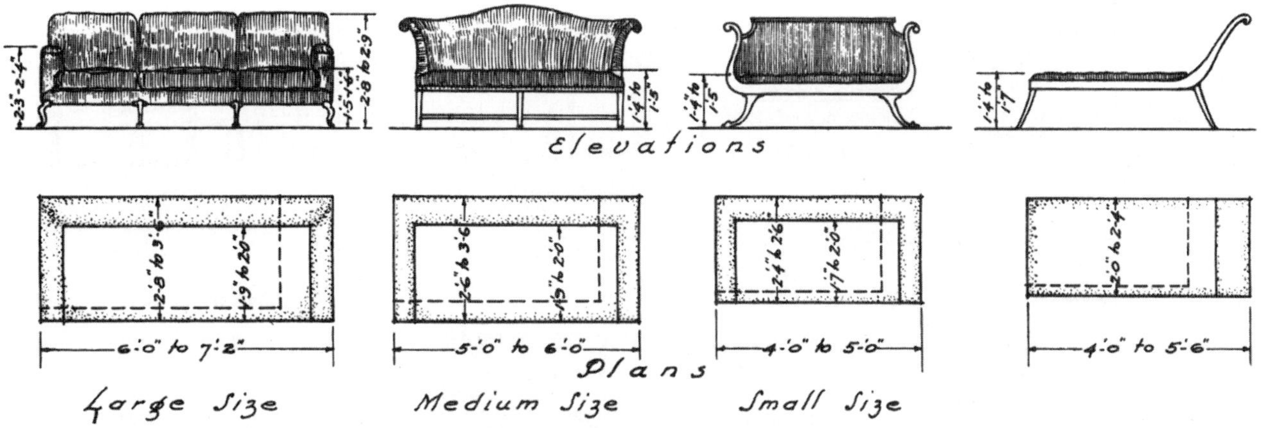

Sofas, couches, davenports, divans, lounges

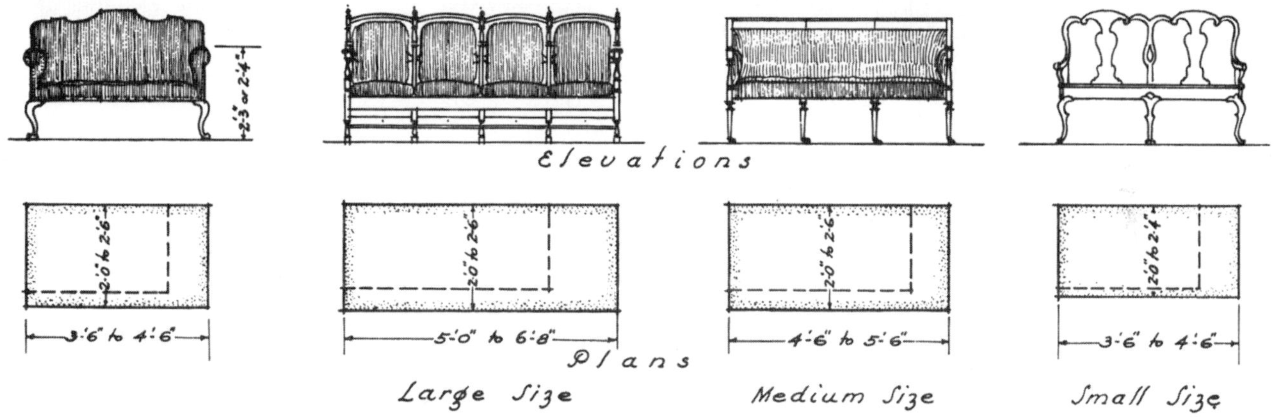

Settees

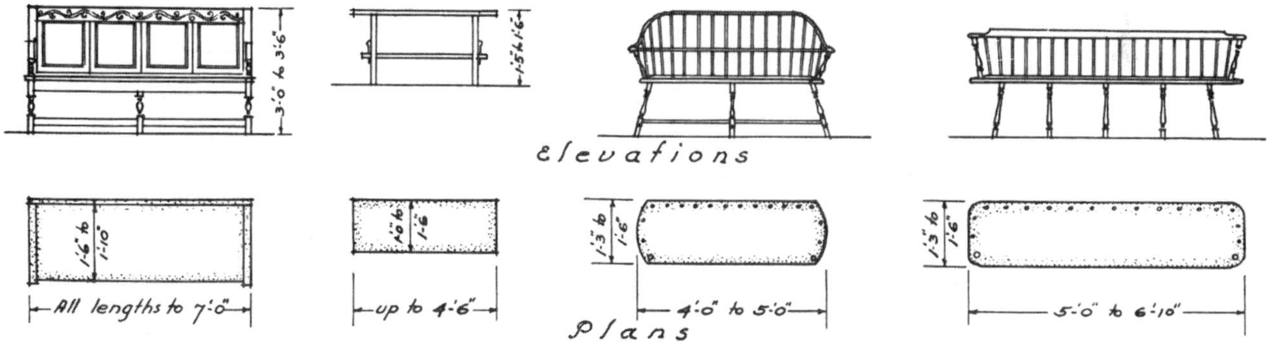

Settle **Bench** **Seats (Windsor)**

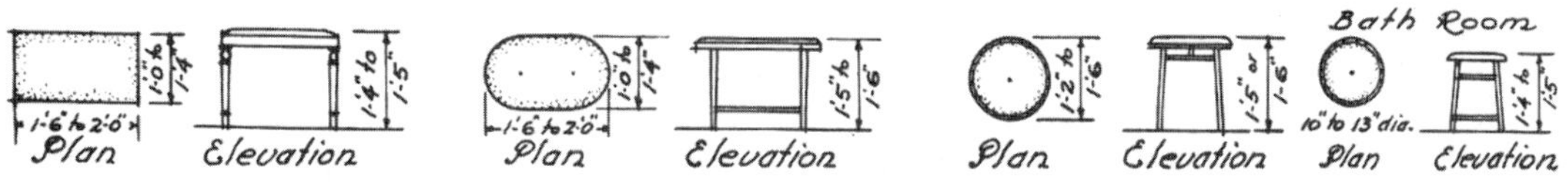

Dressing stools and benches

FURNITURE DIMENSIONS
Traditional Desks, Bookcases, and Chests

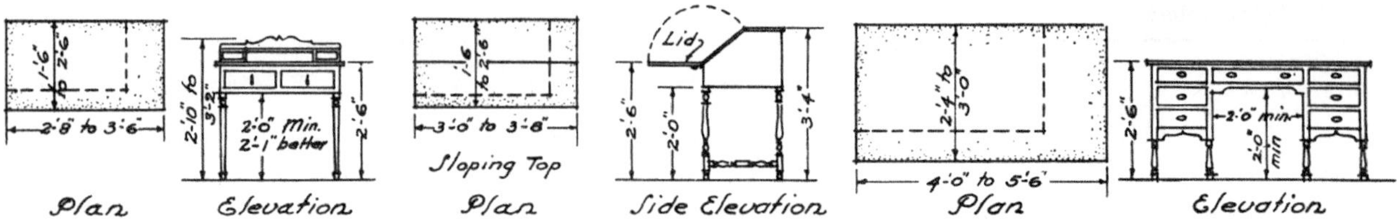

Desks

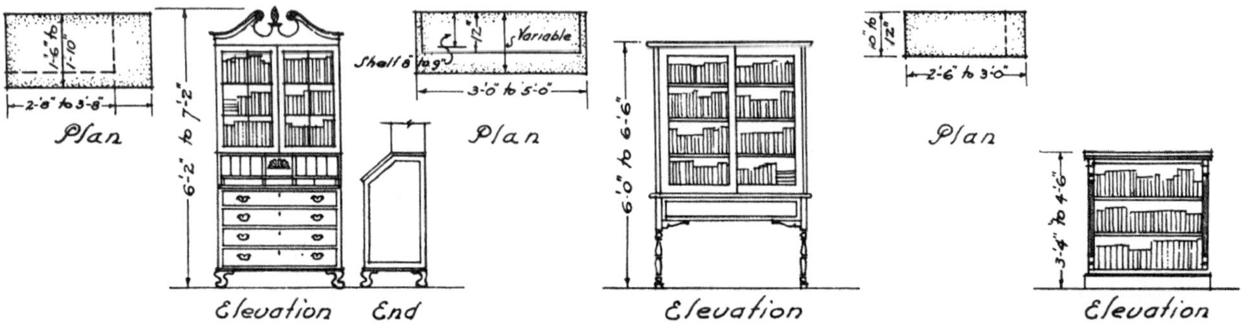

Secretary

Bookcases

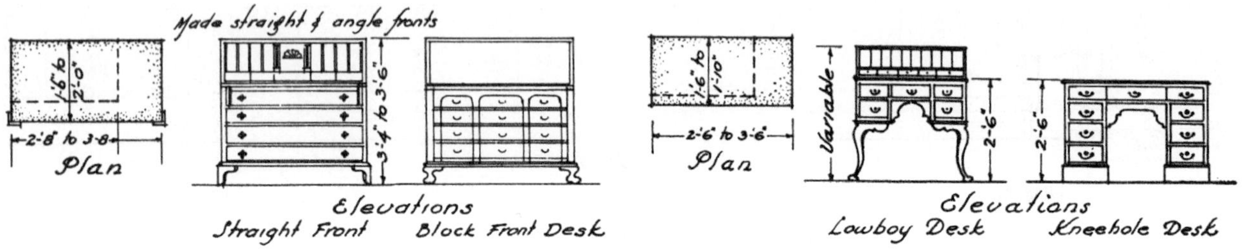

Desks

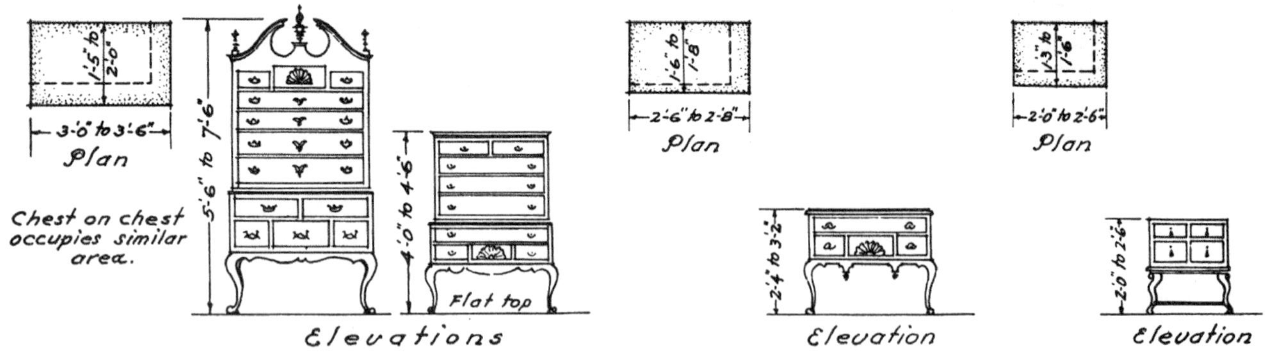

Highboys

Lowboy

Cabinet or chest

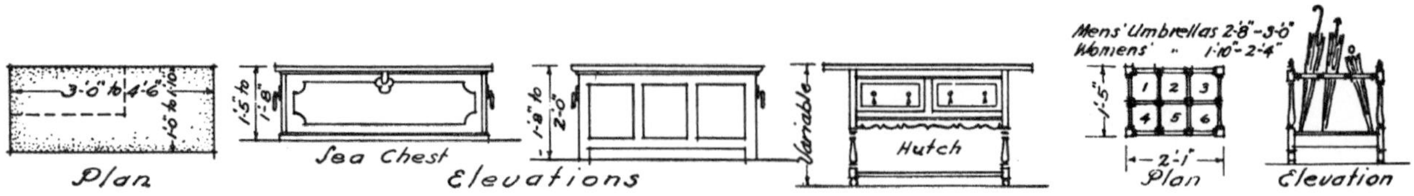

Chests

Umbrella stand

UNUPHOLSTERED CHAIRS

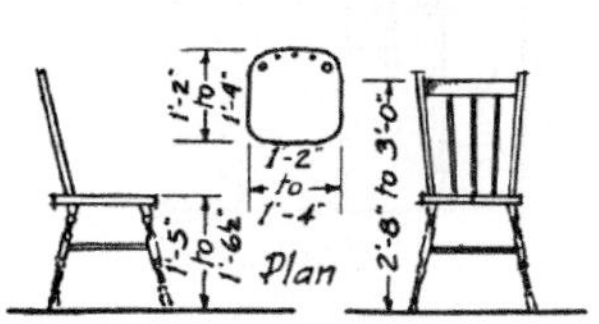

Kitchen chair

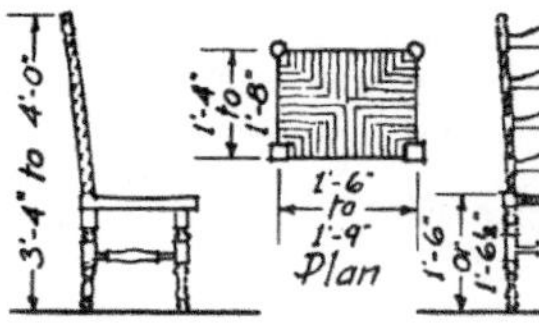

Side chair

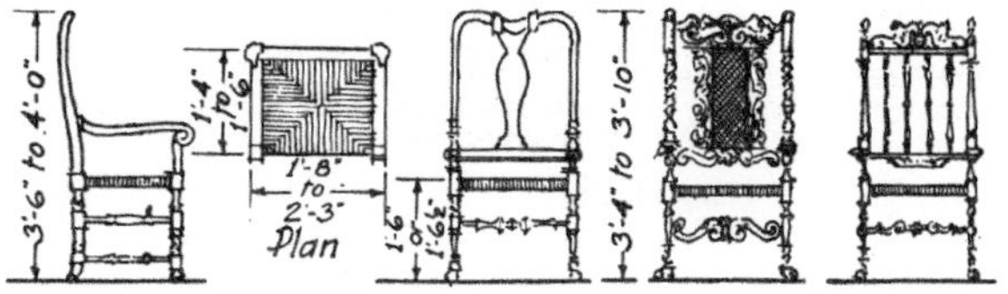

Arm chairs

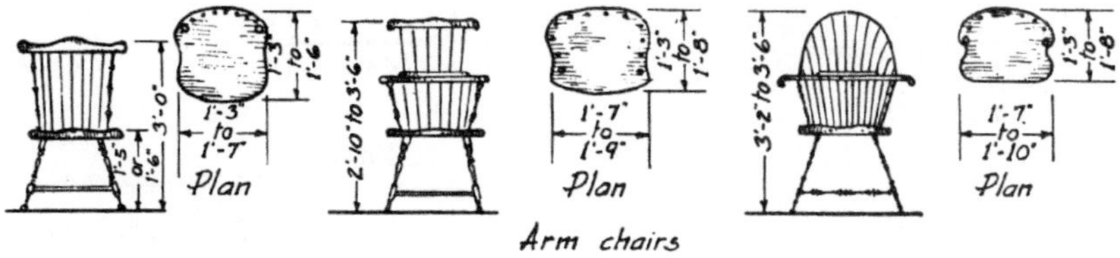

Windsor chairs

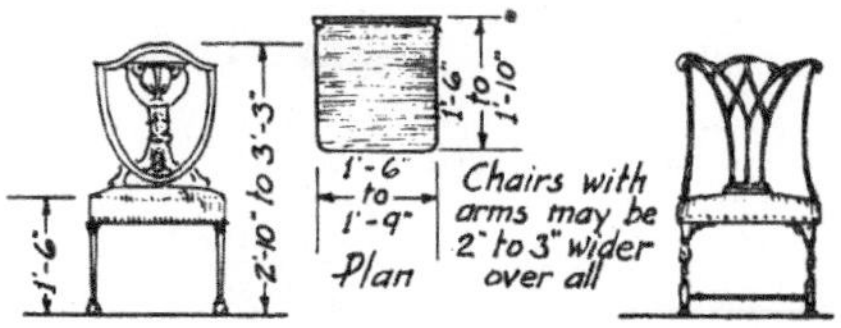

Dining room chairs

UPHOLSTERED CHAIRS

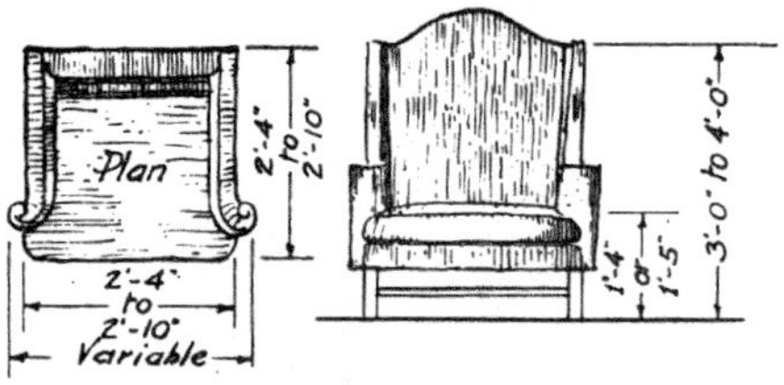

Wing chair

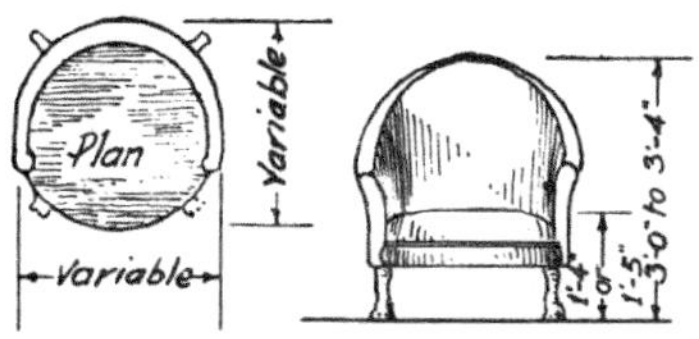

Barrel chair

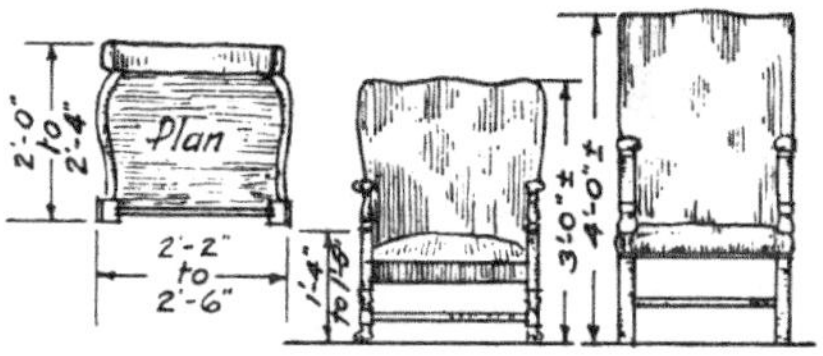

Arm chairs

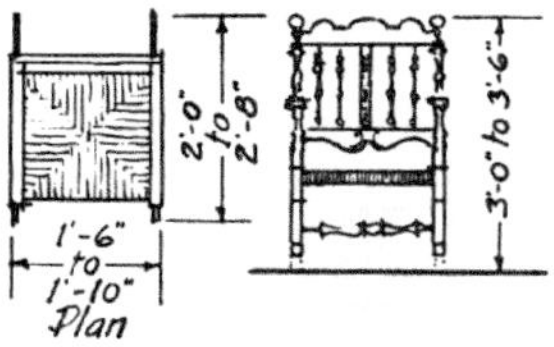

Rocking chair

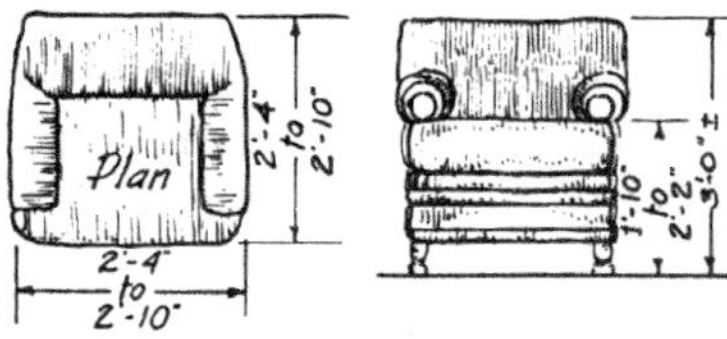

Club chair

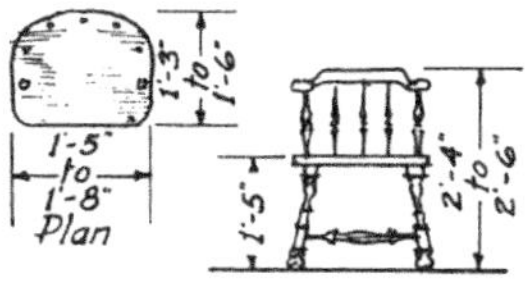

Tavern chair

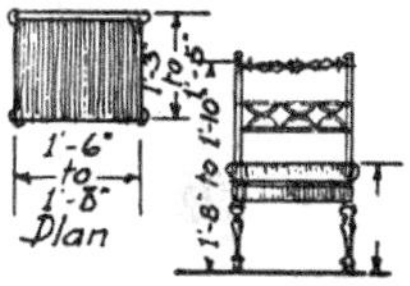

Side chair

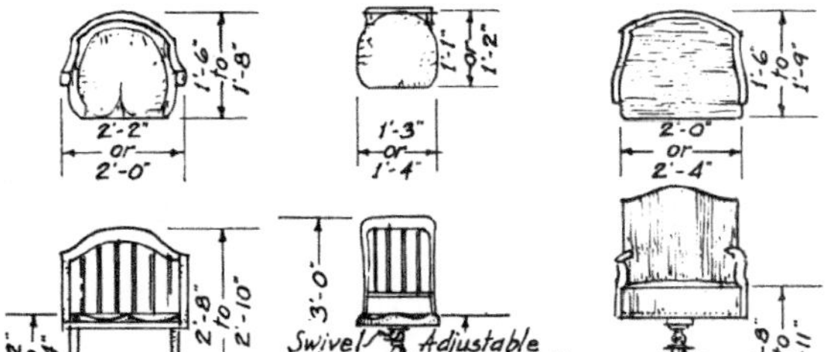

Office chairs

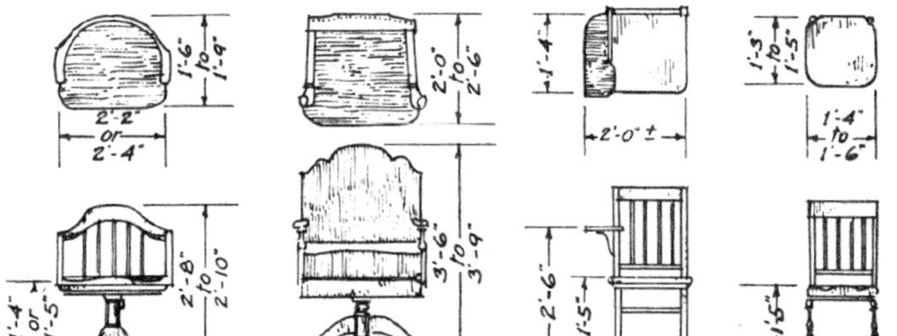

Special chairs

FURNITURE DIMENSIONS

Traditional Tables

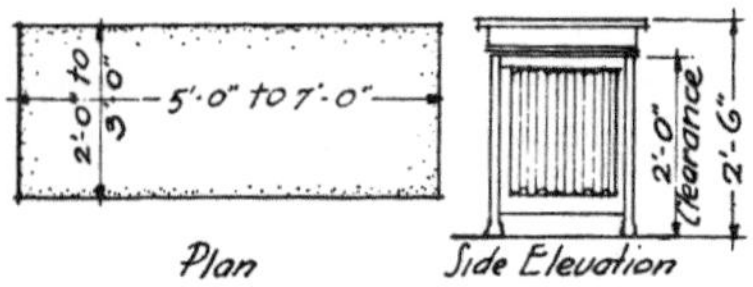

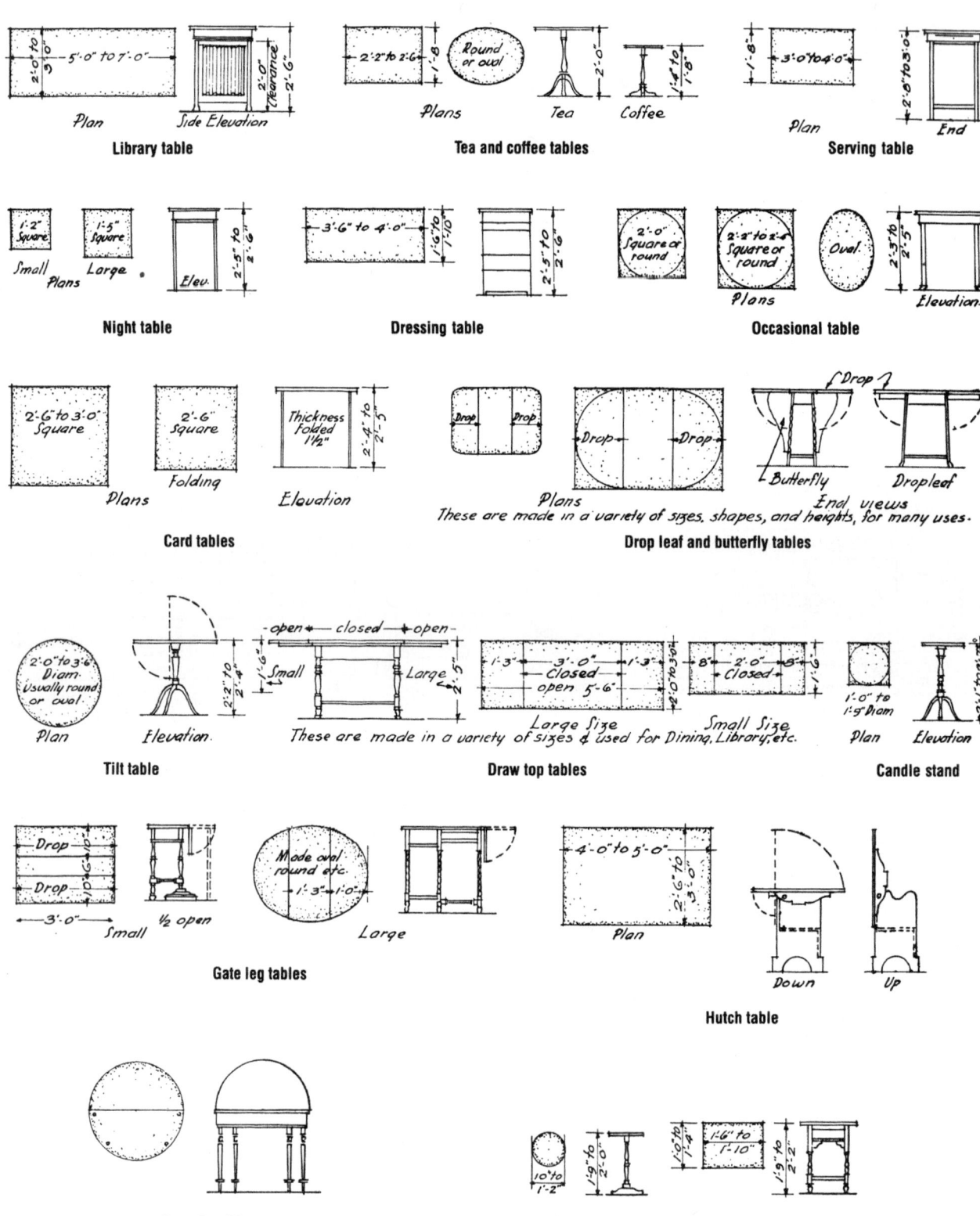

Library table

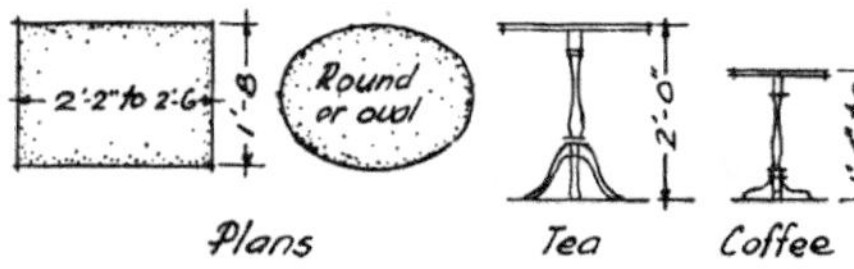

Tea and coffee tables

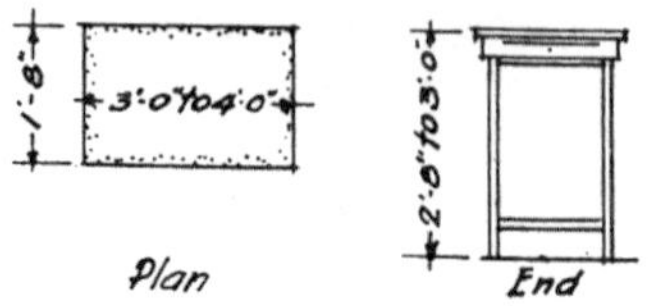

Serving table

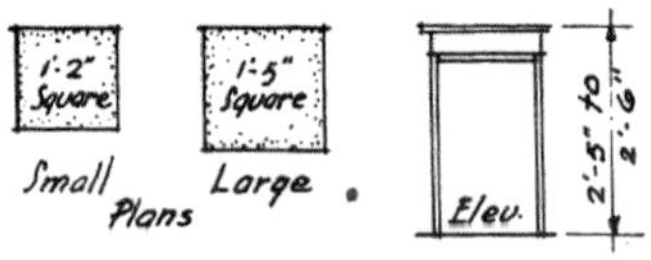

Night table

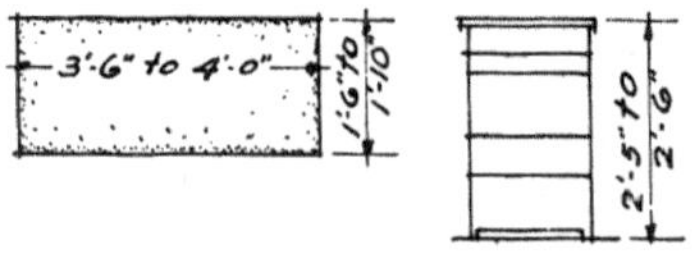

Dressing table

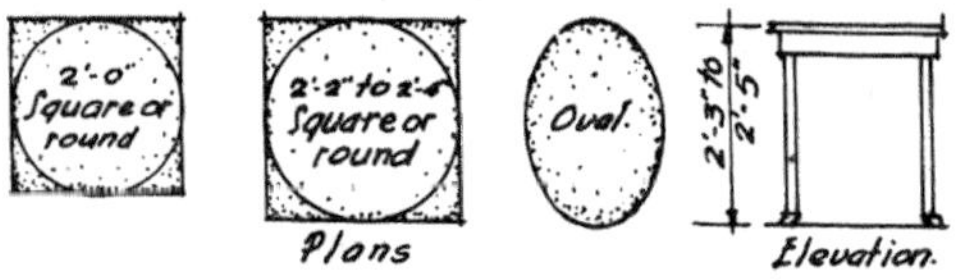

Occasional table

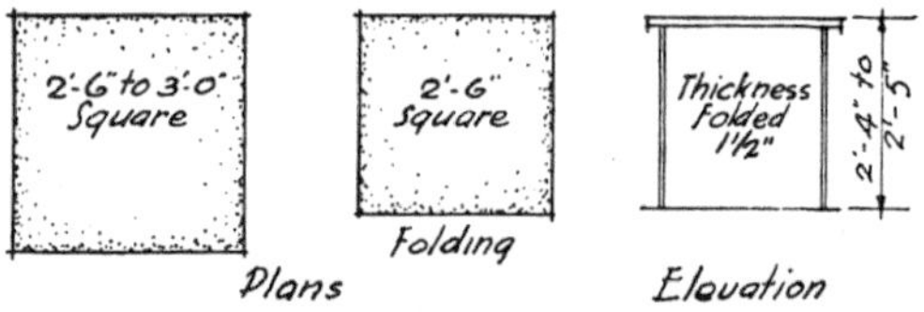

Card tables

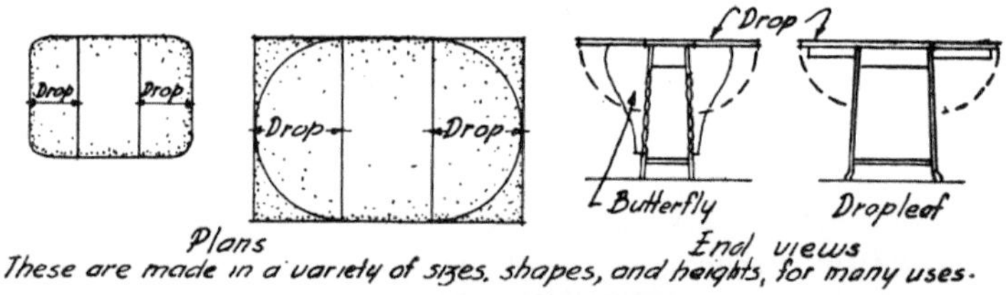

Drop leaf and butterfly tables

These are made in a variety of sizes, shapes, and heights, for many uses.

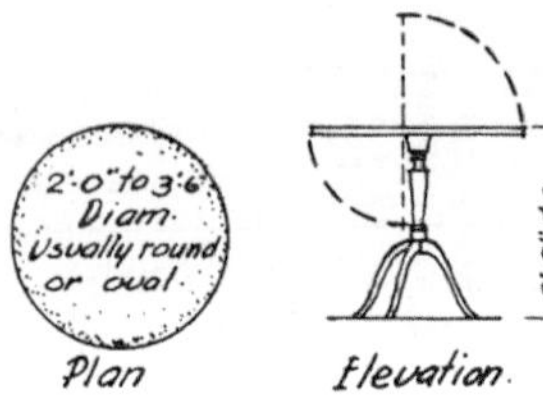

Tilt table

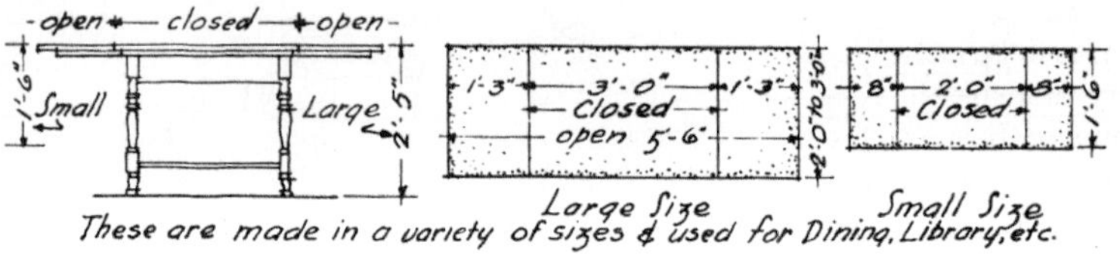

Draw top tables

These are made in a variety of sizes & used for Dining, Library, etc.

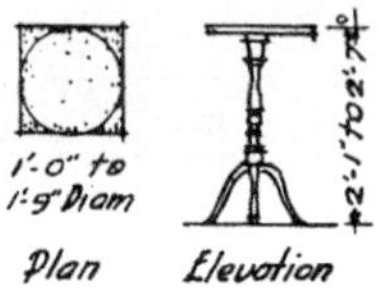

Candle stand

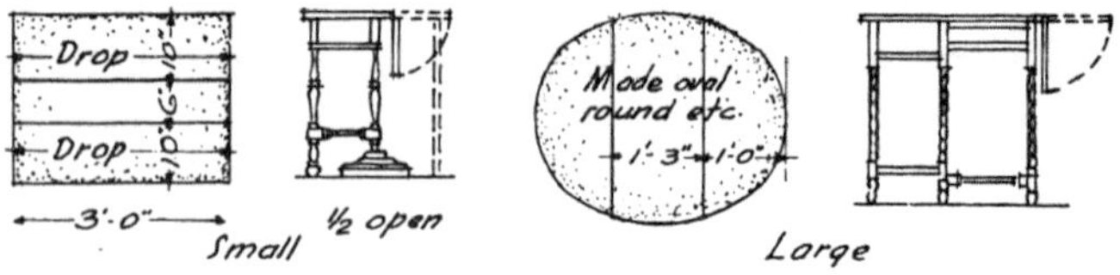

Gate leg tables

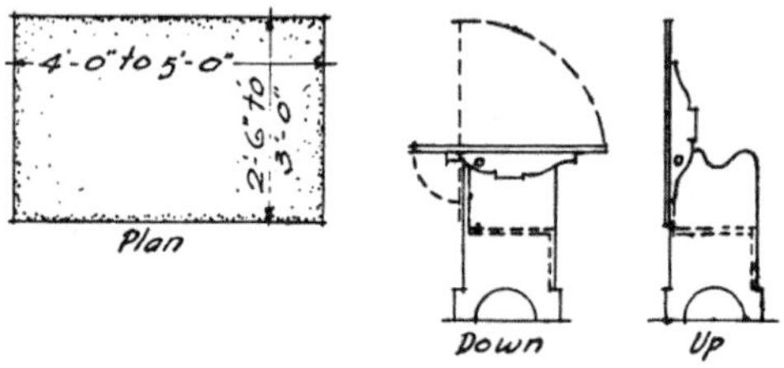

Hutch table

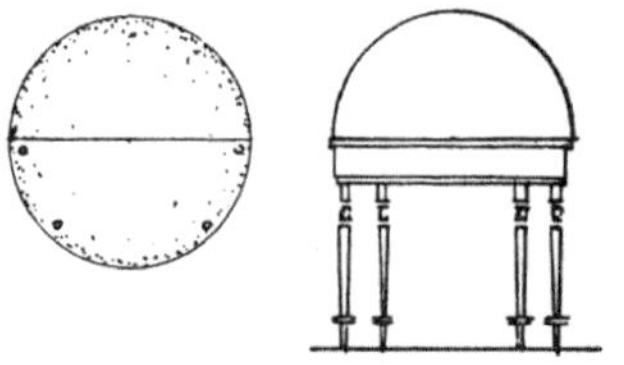

Console table

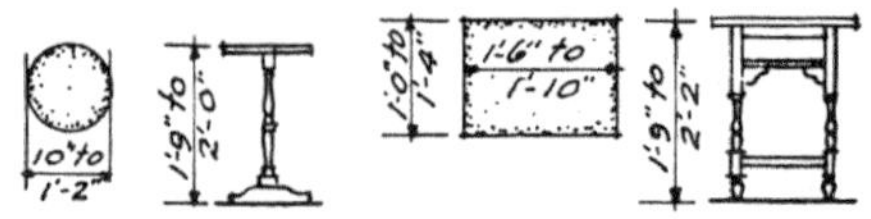

Stands

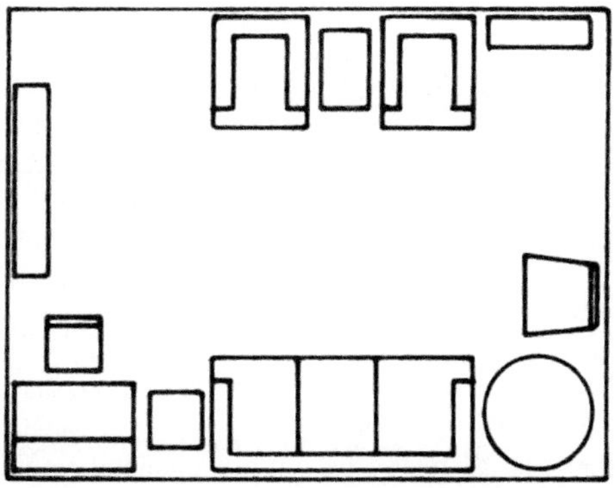

Fig. 1 Typical furniture arrangement for a one- or two-bedroom apartment (12.5 ft × 16 ft, 200 ft²)

LIVING ROOMS

FURNITURE ARRANGEMENTS

The sizes of living rooms and the furniture arrangements contained within such spaces vary dramatically, depending on the size of the dwelling, the economic status and lifestyle of the user, and the relationship of the room to other areas of the dwelling. With regard to the luxury end of the scale, there are few limitations and no attempt has been made to identify the endless planning options possible. There are, however, minimum requirements and basic planning considerations that are applicable whatever the size of the space.

Minimum Requirements

A living room for a three- or four-bedroom dwelling unit requires more space for its occupants than one for a one- or two-bedroom dwelling unit. Luxury units will necessarily need more space to accommodate more furnishings. In any case, the minimum living room with no dining facilities should be approximately 180 ft² but preferably around 200 ft². Figures 1 and 2 show two living rooms with typical furniture groupings (no dining facilities).

Figure 3 shows a living room with one end used for dining. This area often is arranged in an "L" shape to achieve greater definition or privacy from the living activities. Dwelling units with three or more bedrooms should have separate dining rooms or clearly defined dining areas.

The minimum width of a living room should be 11 to 12 ft. This is extremely tight, however, and if at all possible the width should be at least 14 ft.

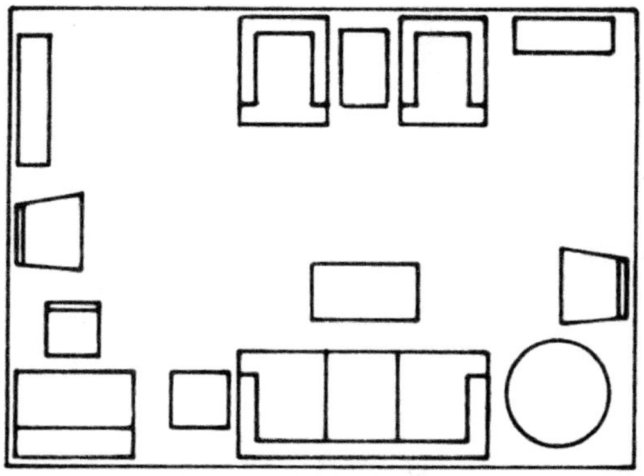

Fig. 2 Typical furniture arrangement for a three-bedroom apartment (12.5 ft × 20 ft, 250 ft²)

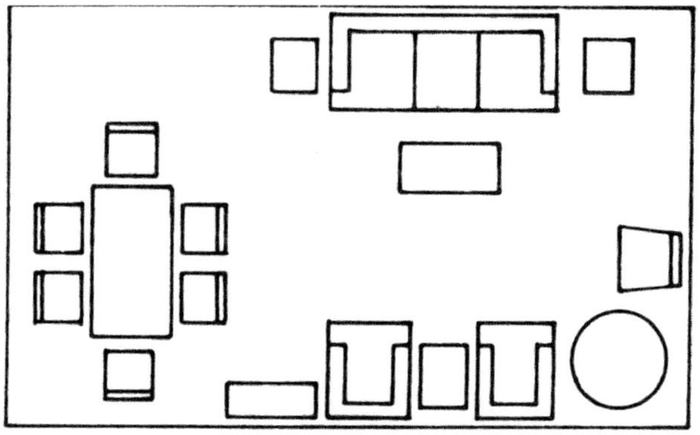

Fig. 3 Another typical furniture arrangement for a three-bedroom apartment (12.5 ft × 22 ft, 275 ft²)

LIVING ROOMS
Circulation

Planning Considerations

Planning considerations should include adequate floor and wall space for furniture groupings, separation of trafficways from centers of activity, and ease of access to furniture and windows.

Circulation within the living room should be as direct as possible and yet not interfere with furniture placement. Ideally, there should be no through traffic. If such traffic is necessary, it should be at one end, with the remaining portion of the room a dead-end space.

During social activities, people tend to gather or congregate in relatively small groups. Desirable conversation distance is also relatively small, approximately 10 ft in diameter.

When the living room is combined with the dining area, the dining area should be offset into an alcove or be clearly identified as an entity in itself.

CIRCULATION

FURNITURE CLEARANCES

Figures 5 to 10 show various groupings and related clearances. Figure 5 shows that a space 12 ft 6 in × 15 ft 6 in should be provided in order to accommodate seating for five around a 56-in-diameter cocktail table. The piano, sofa, and cocktail table arrangement shown in Fig. 6 requires a space at least 11 ft 0 in × 16 ft 0 in. Figure 7 suggests that a space at least 12 ft 9 in × 13 ft 3 in is required to accommodate a grouping to seat six or seven persons, while Fig. 8 indicates that a corner arrangement for two requires a space at least 6 ft 3 in × 6 ft 6 in.

When planning furniture arrangements, allowances for clearances should take into account the human dimension as well, as illustrated in Figs. 9 and 10.

It should be noted that these diagrams are not intended as models for complete living room layouts. They are intended only as guidelines to illustrate minimum clearances for preliminary planning purposes.

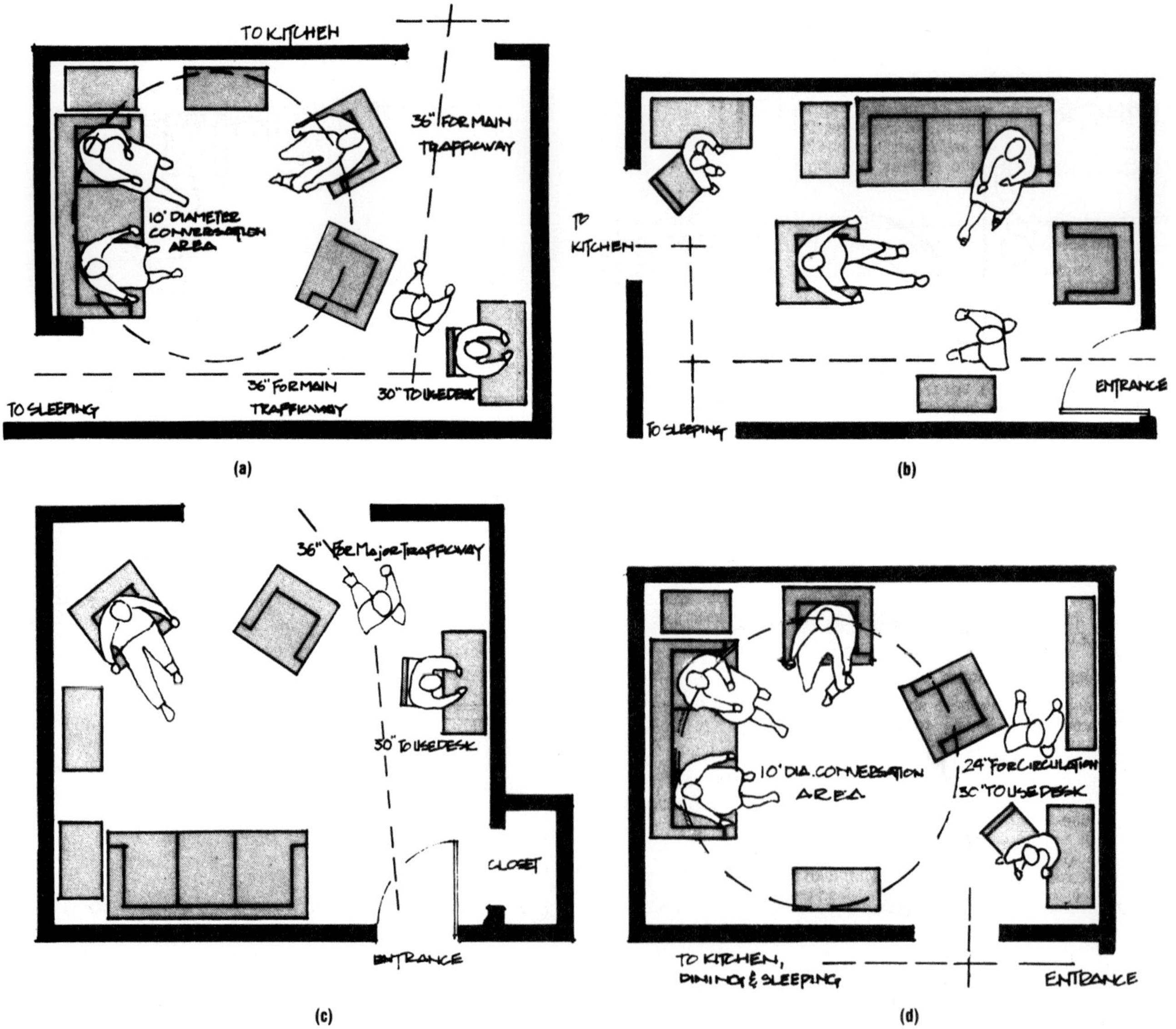

Fig. 4 When through traffic is unavoidable, pathways should skirt conversational or activity centers, as illustrated in (*a*), (*b*), and (*c*); (*d*) illustrates a more ideal layout in which the entire room is bypassed

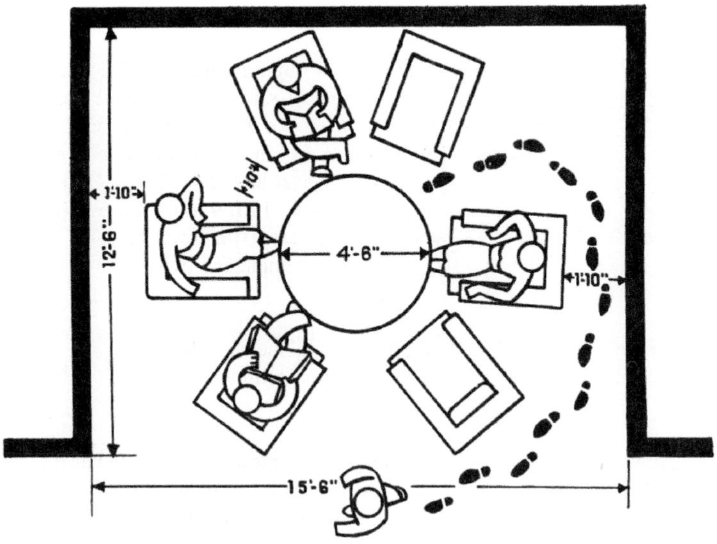

Fig. 5

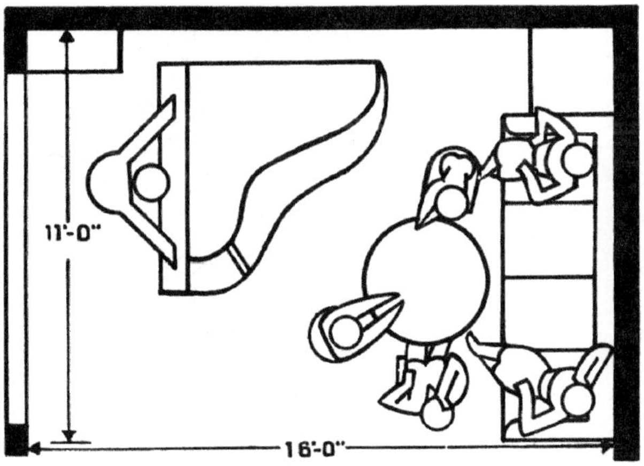

Fig. 6

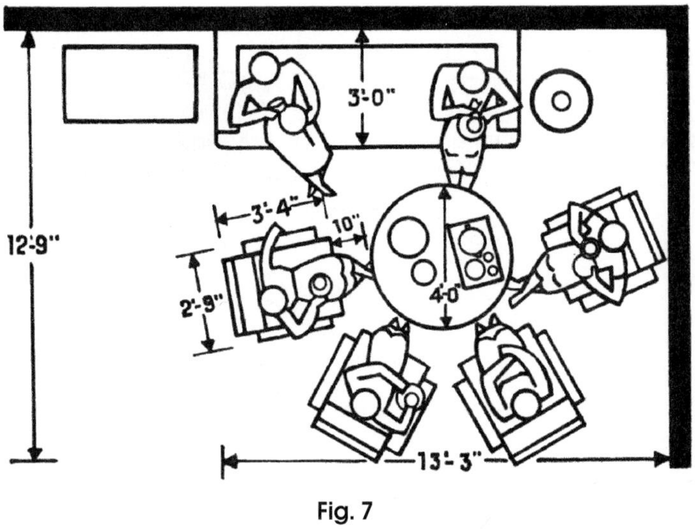

Fig. 7

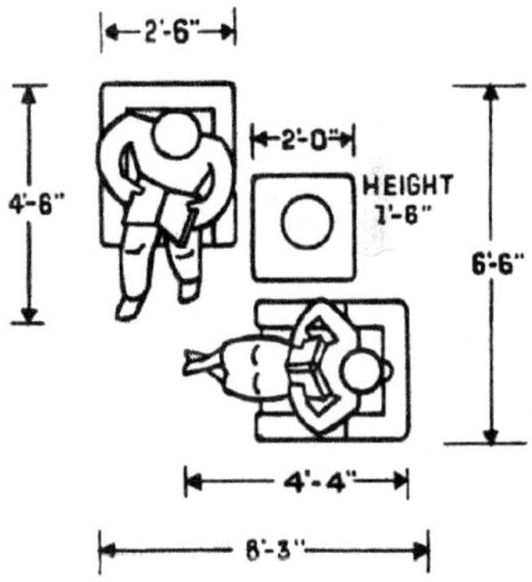

Fig. 8

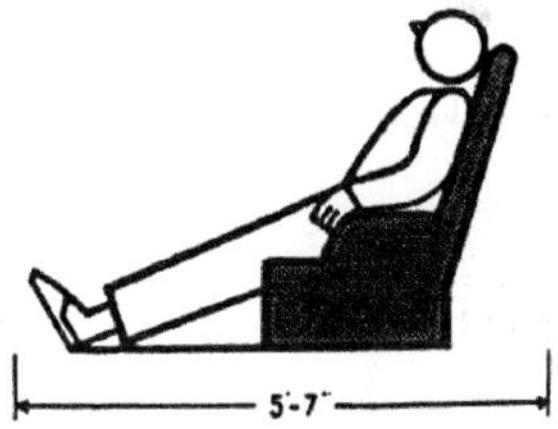

Fig. 9

Fig. 10

LIVING ROOMS

Media Cabinet Details

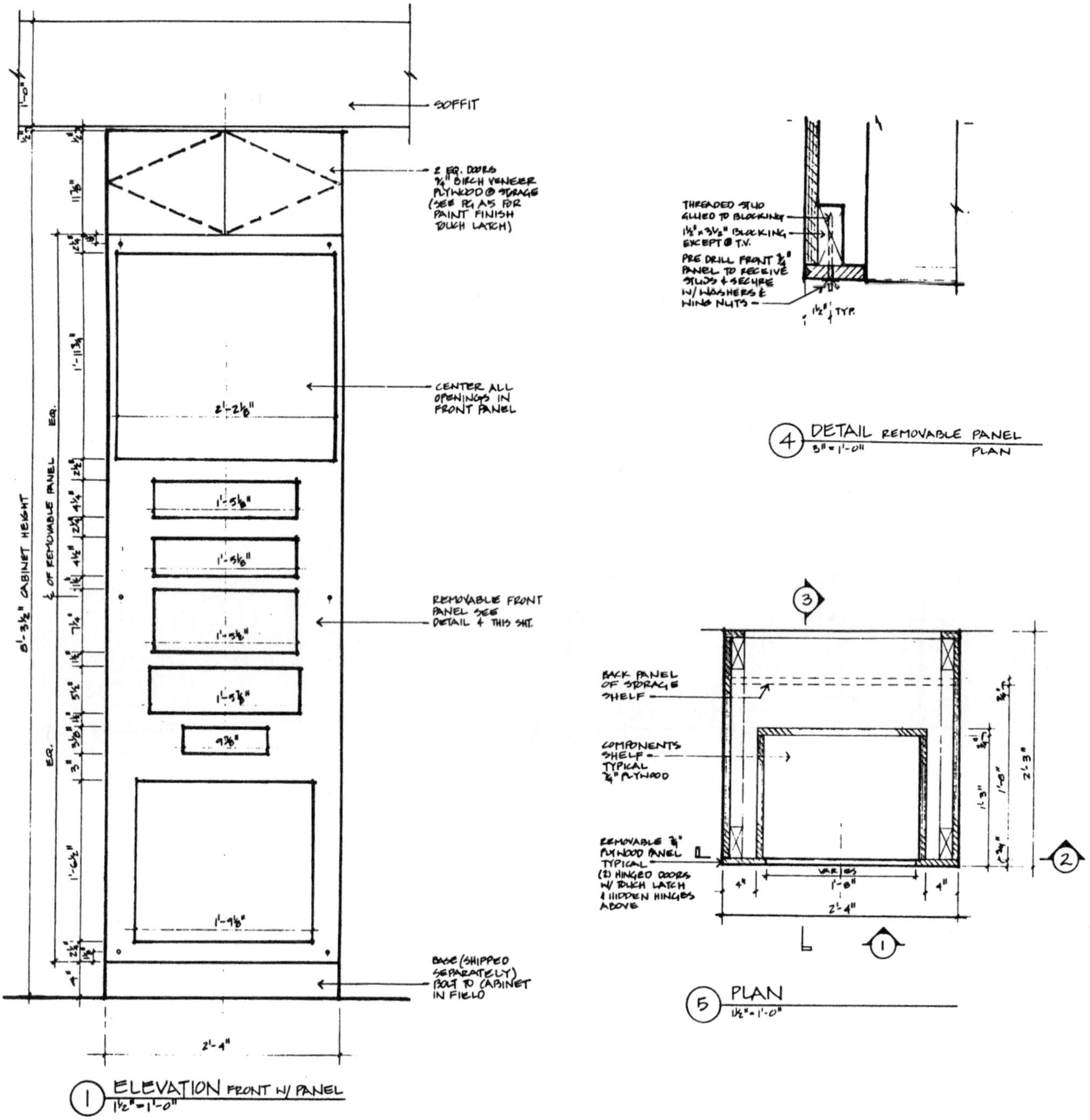

Fig. 11 Working drawings of a media cabinet, including plans, elevations, and sections of the installation. The design of the cabinet should take into account the actual electronic and other equipment to be housed and the clearances involved for operation. Power outlets should be coordinated and located so as to conceal unsightly wires and cables

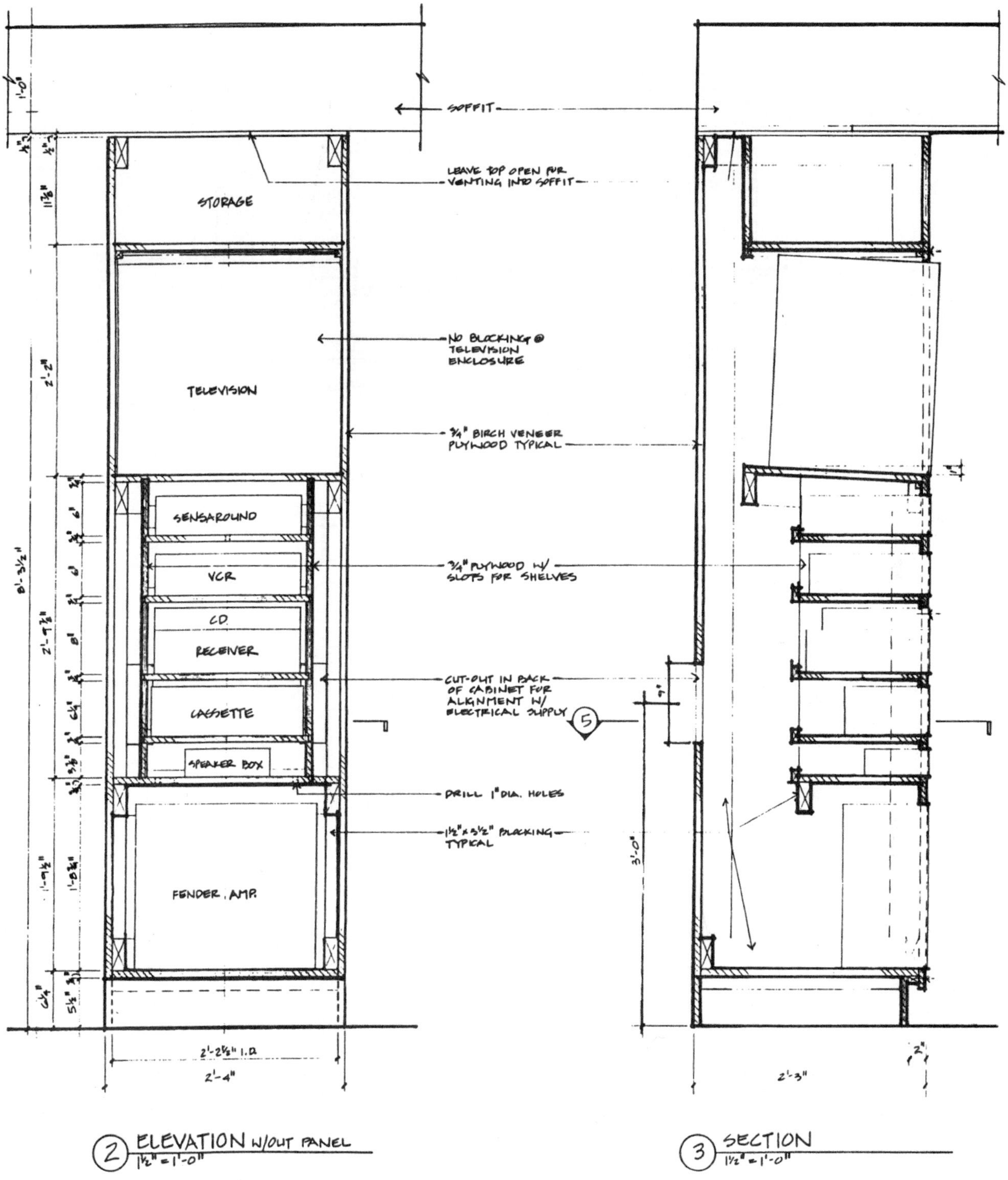
SOFFIT
LEAVE TOP OPEN FOR VENTING INTO SOFFIT
STORAGE
NO BLOCKING @ TELEVISION ENCLOSURE
TELEVISION
3/4" BIRCH VENEER PLYWOOD TYPICAL
SENSAROUND
VCR
3/4" PLYWOOD W/ SLOTS FOR SHELVES
CD
RECEIVER
CUT-OUT IN BACK OF CABINET FOR ALIGNMENT W/ ELECTRICAL SUPPLY
CASSETTE
SPEAKER BOX
DRILL 1" DIA. HOLES
1½" x 3½" BLOCKING TYPICAL
FENDER AMP.
2'-2½" I.D.
2'-4"
2'-3"
2 ELEVATION W/OUT PANEL
1½" = 1'-0"
3 SECTION
1½" = 1'-0"

Fig. 11 *(Continued)*

LIVING ROOMS
Plans, Elevations, and Details

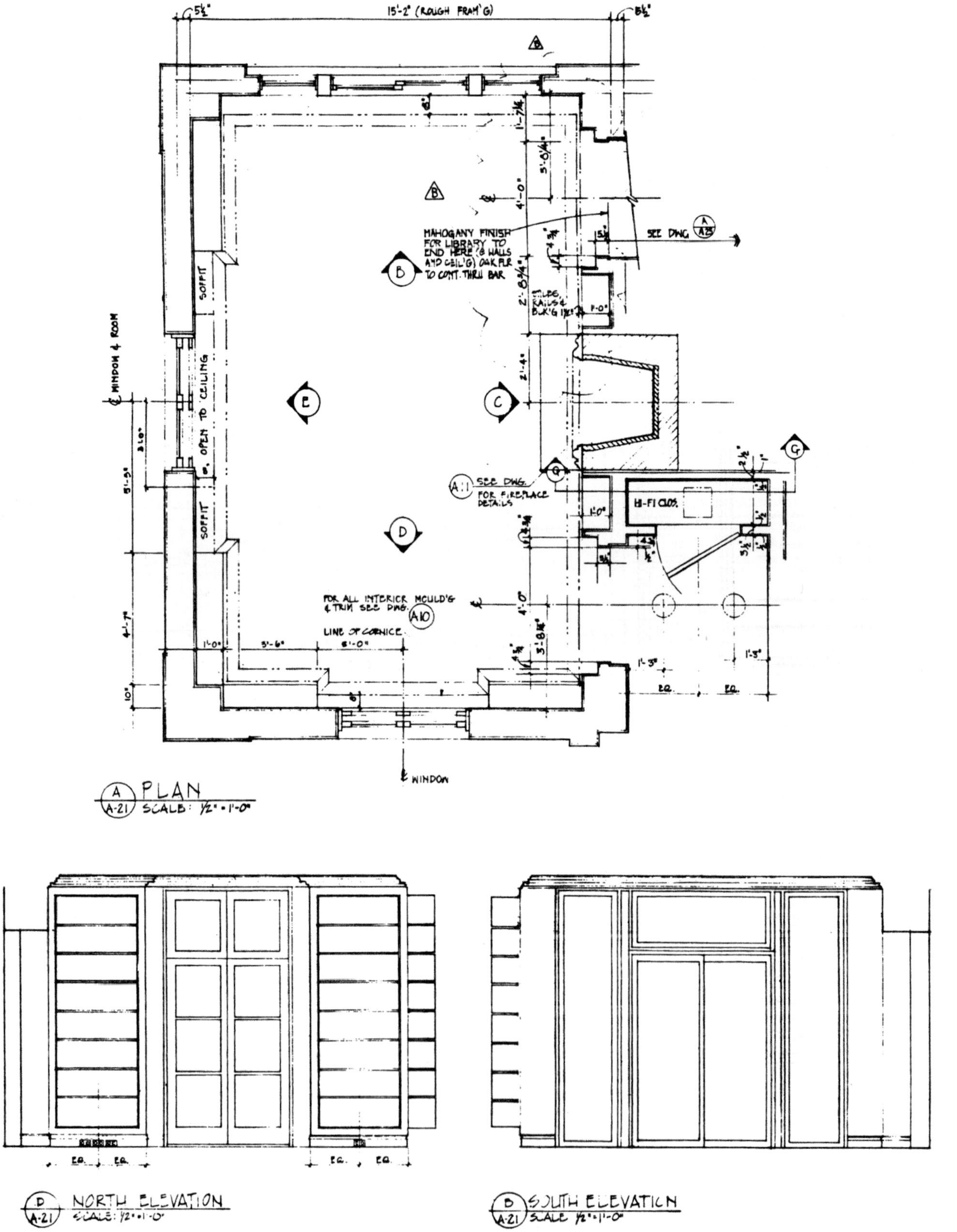

Fig. 12 Working drawings of a library/living room, including a plan of the space, wall elevations, and some of the many details involved

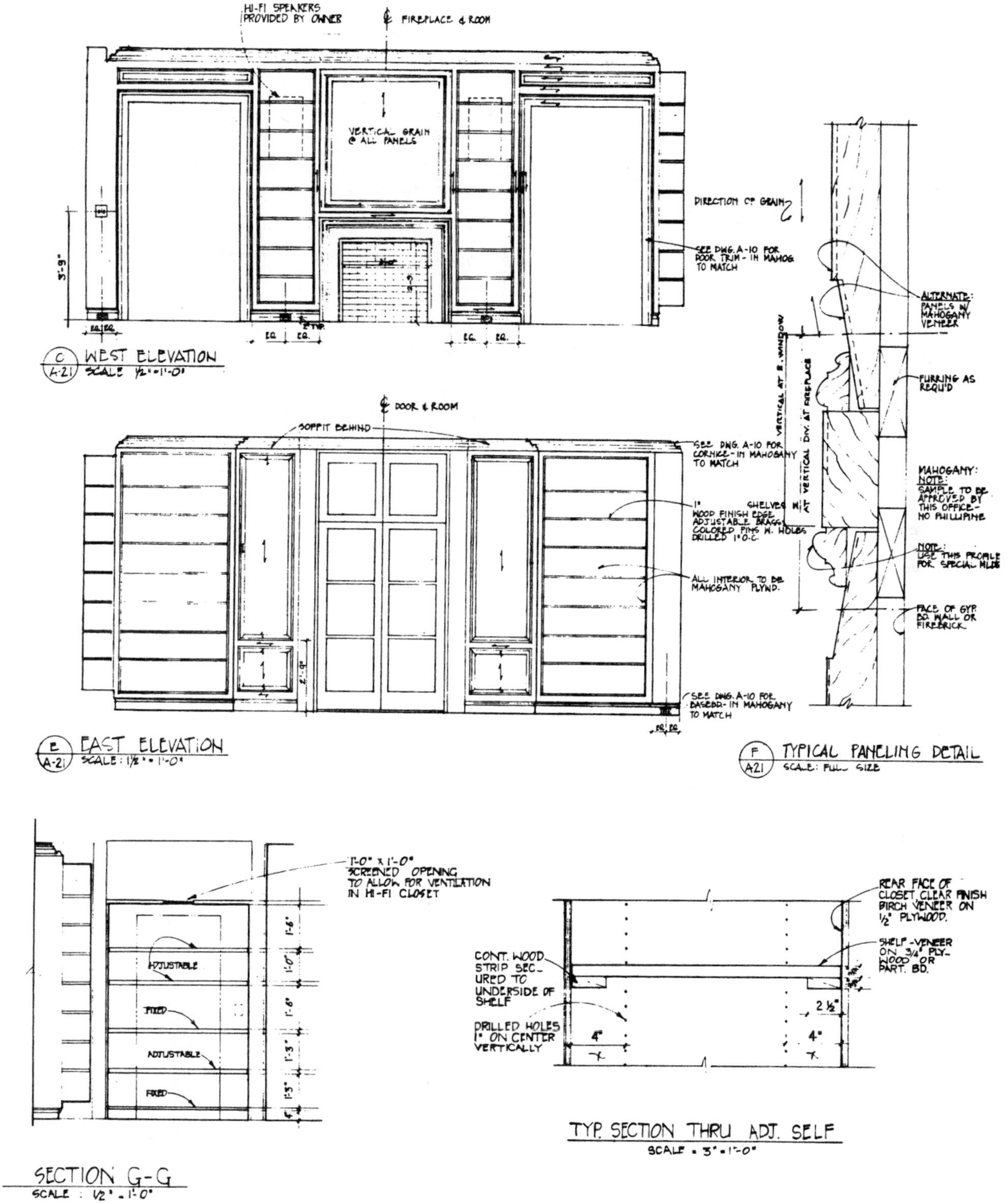

Fig. 12 *(Continued)*

LIVING ROOMS
Fireplace Wall Elevation and Details

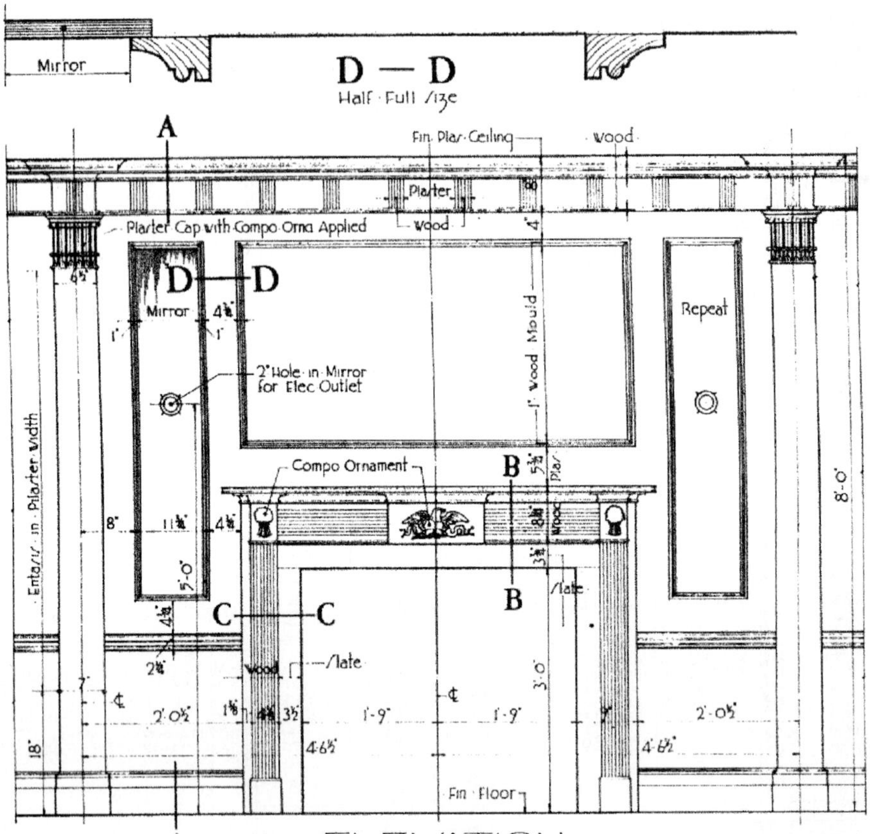

ELEVATION
Scale: ½" = 1' – 0"

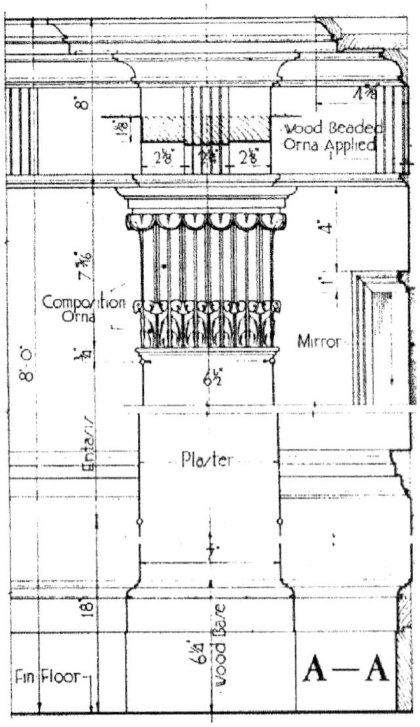

1½" Scale: DETAIL · OF · PILASTER & CORNICE

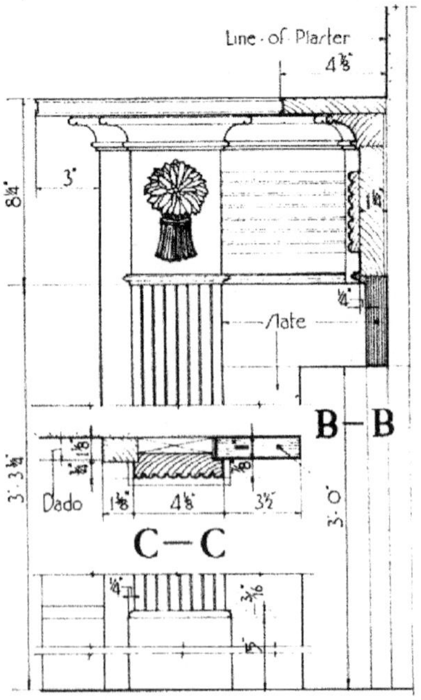

DETAIL · OF · MANTEL
Scale: 1½" = 1' - 0"

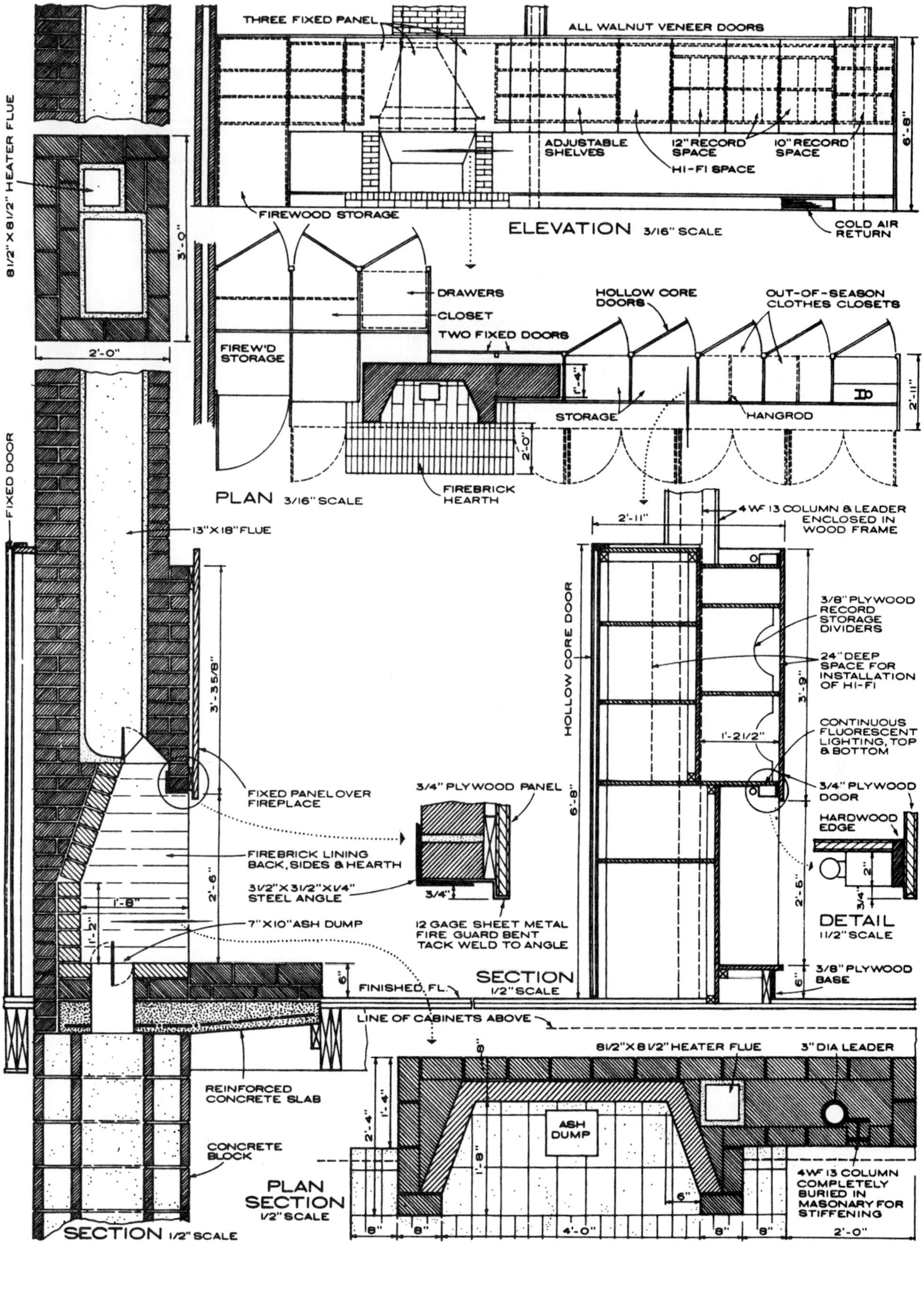
THREE FIXED PANEL
ALL WALNUT VENEER DOORS
ADJUSTABLE SHELVES
12" RECORD SPACE
10" RECORD SPACE
HI-FI SPACE
6'-8"
FIREWOOD STORAGE
ELEVATION 3/16" SCALE
COLD AIR RETURN
8 1/2" X 8 1/2" HEATER FLUE
3'-0"
2'-0"
DRAWERS
CLOSET
TWO FIXED DOORS
HOLLOW CORE DOORS
OUT-OF-SEASON CLOTHES CLOSETS
FIREW'D STORAGE
1'-4"
2'-11"
STORAGE
HANGROD
2'-0"
PLAN 3/16" SCALE
FIREBRICK HEARTH
FIXED DOOR
13" X 18" FLUE
4 WF 13 COLUMN & LEADER ENCLOSED IN WOOD FRAME
2'-11"
HOLLOW CORE DOOR
3/8" PLYWOOD RECORD STORAGE DIVIDERS
24" DEEP SPACE FOR INSTALLATION OF HI-FI
3'-9"
1'-2 1/2"
CONTINUOUS FLUORESCENT LIGHTING, TOP & BOTTOM
3/4" PLYWOOD DOOR
HARDWOOD EDGE
3'-3 5/8"
6'-8"
FIXED PANEL OVER FIREPLACE
3/4" PLYWOOD PANEL
FIREBRICK LINING BACK, SIDES & HEARTH
3 1/2" X 3 1/2" X 1/4" STEEL ANGLE
3/4"
12 GAGE SHEET METAL FIRE GUARD BENT TACK WELD TO ANGLE
2'-6"
1'-8"
1'-2"
7" X 10" ASH DUMP
2'-5"
2"
3/4
DETAIL 1 1/2" SCALE
6"
FINISHED FL.
SECTION 1/2" SCALE
3/8" PLYWOOD BASE
6"
LINE OF CABINETS ABOVE
REINFORCED CONCRETE SLAB
8 1/2" X 8 1/2" HEATER FLUE
3" DIA LEADER
2'-4"
1'-4"
ASH DUMP
1'-8"
CONCRETE BLOCK
4 WF 13 COLUMN COMPLETELY BURIED IN MASONARY FOR STIFFENING
PLAN SECTION 1/2" SCALE
6"
8"
8"
4'-0"
8"
8"
2'-0"
SECTION 1/2" SCALE

LIVING ROOMS
Fireplace Mantel Details

Figure 13 shows a plan and elevations of modifications to an existing fireplace. Based on these drawings and inspection and measurement of existing conditions, the contractor prepares and submits shop drawings for the designer's approval. Since at least two trades are involved, coordination of the trades by the contractor and a thorough review of the shop drawings by both contractor and designer are essential. It is important, also, that modifications conform with all applicable codes. The extent of hearth extension, the materials used, and the distance of combustible materials from the firebox are among the numerous items governed by codes.

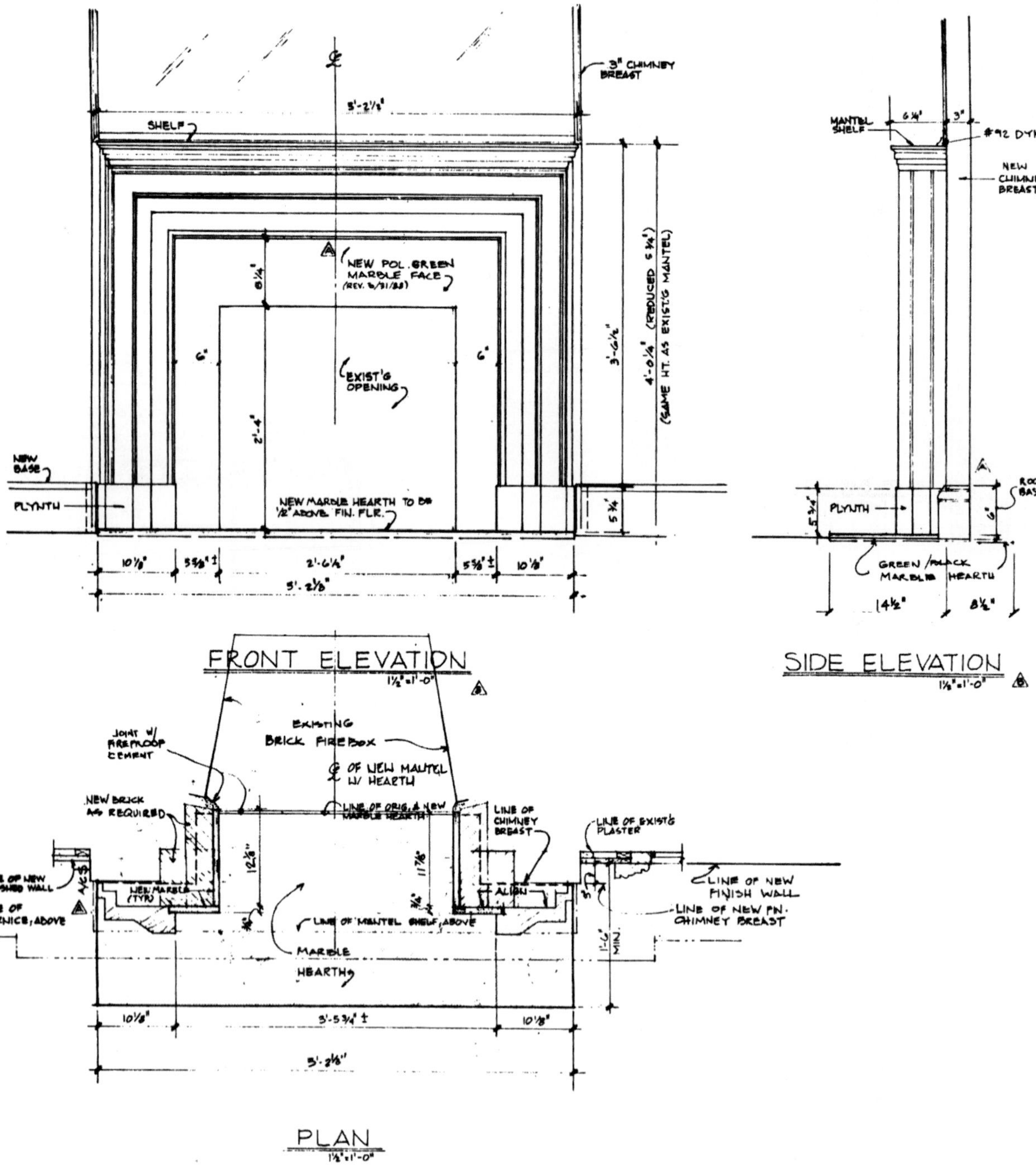

Fig. 13

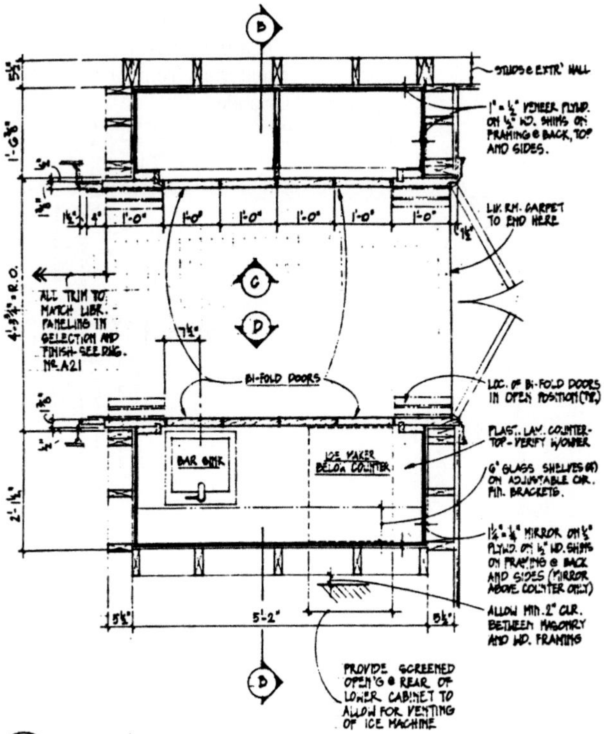

A / A-25 PLAN OF BAR VESTIBULE
SCALE: ¾" = 1'-0"

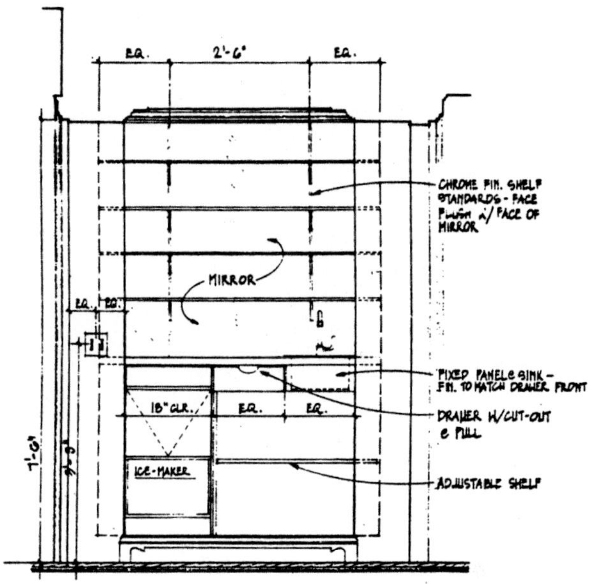

D / A-25 SECTION LKG. NORTH (SHOWN W/OUT DOORS)
¾" = 1'-0"

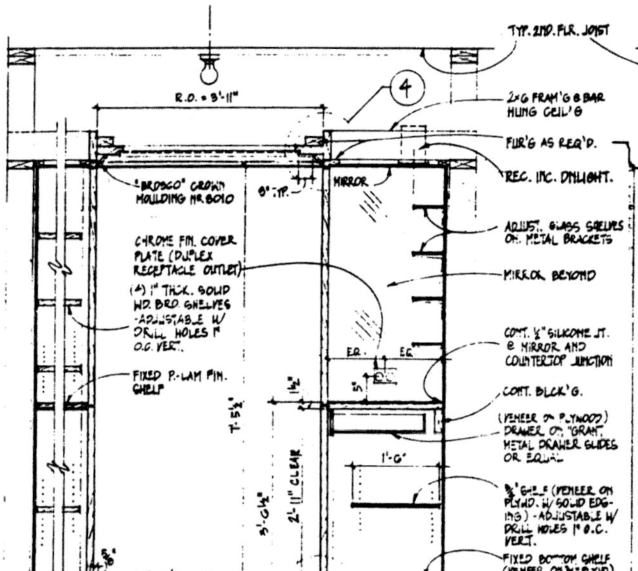

B / A-25 SECTION LOOKING TOWARDS LIV RM.
¾" = 1'-0"

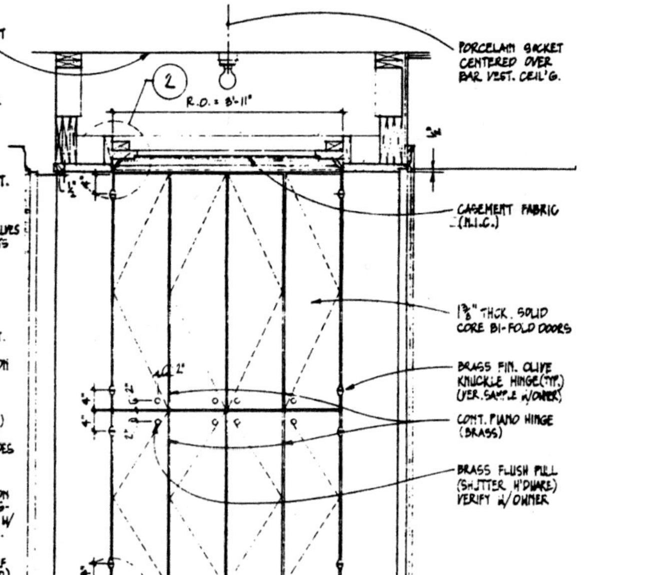

C / A-25 SECTION LOOKING SOUTH
¾" = 1'-0"

LIVING ROOMS
Electrical Plan

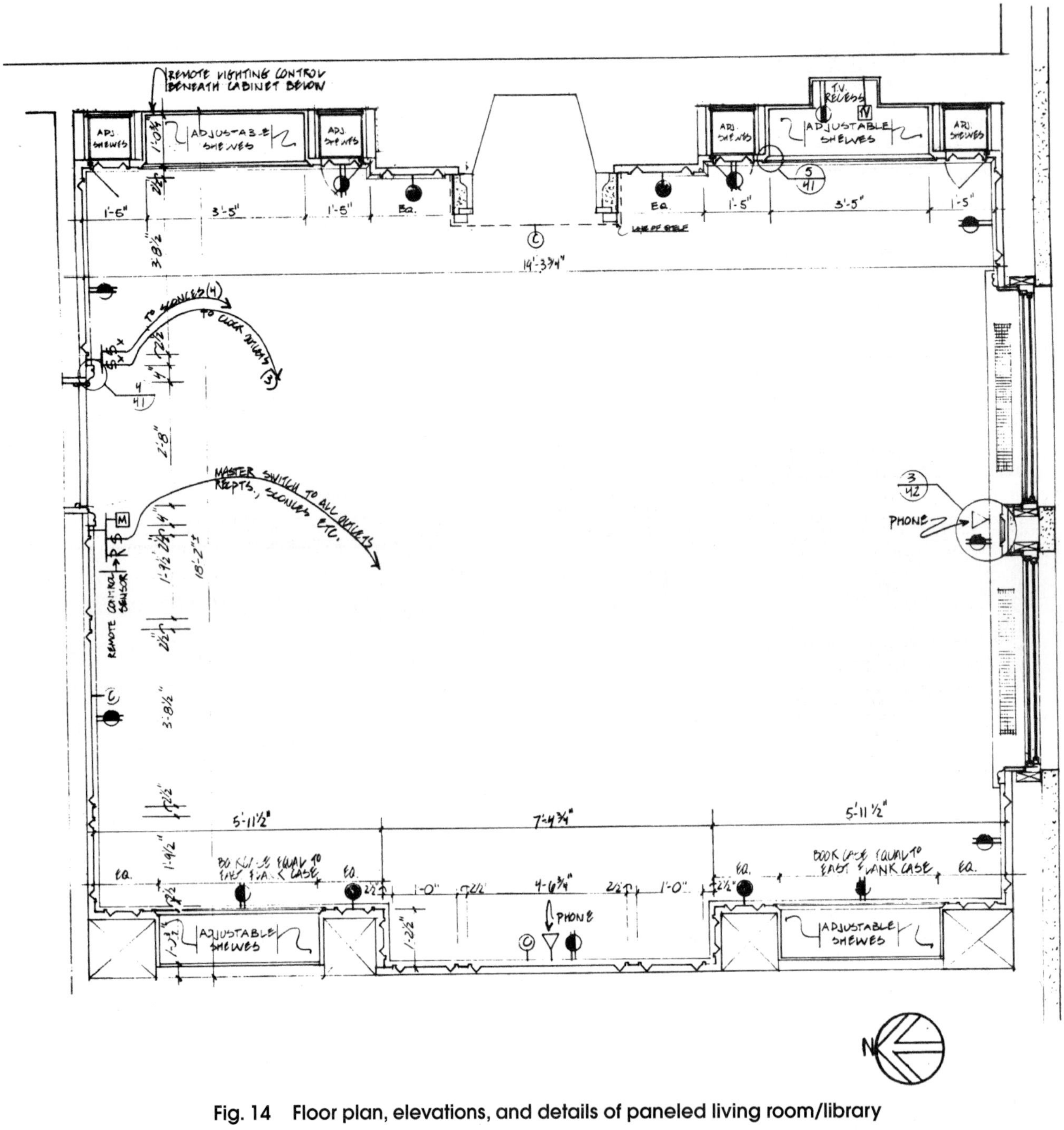

Fig. 14 Floor plan, elevations, and details of paneled living room/library

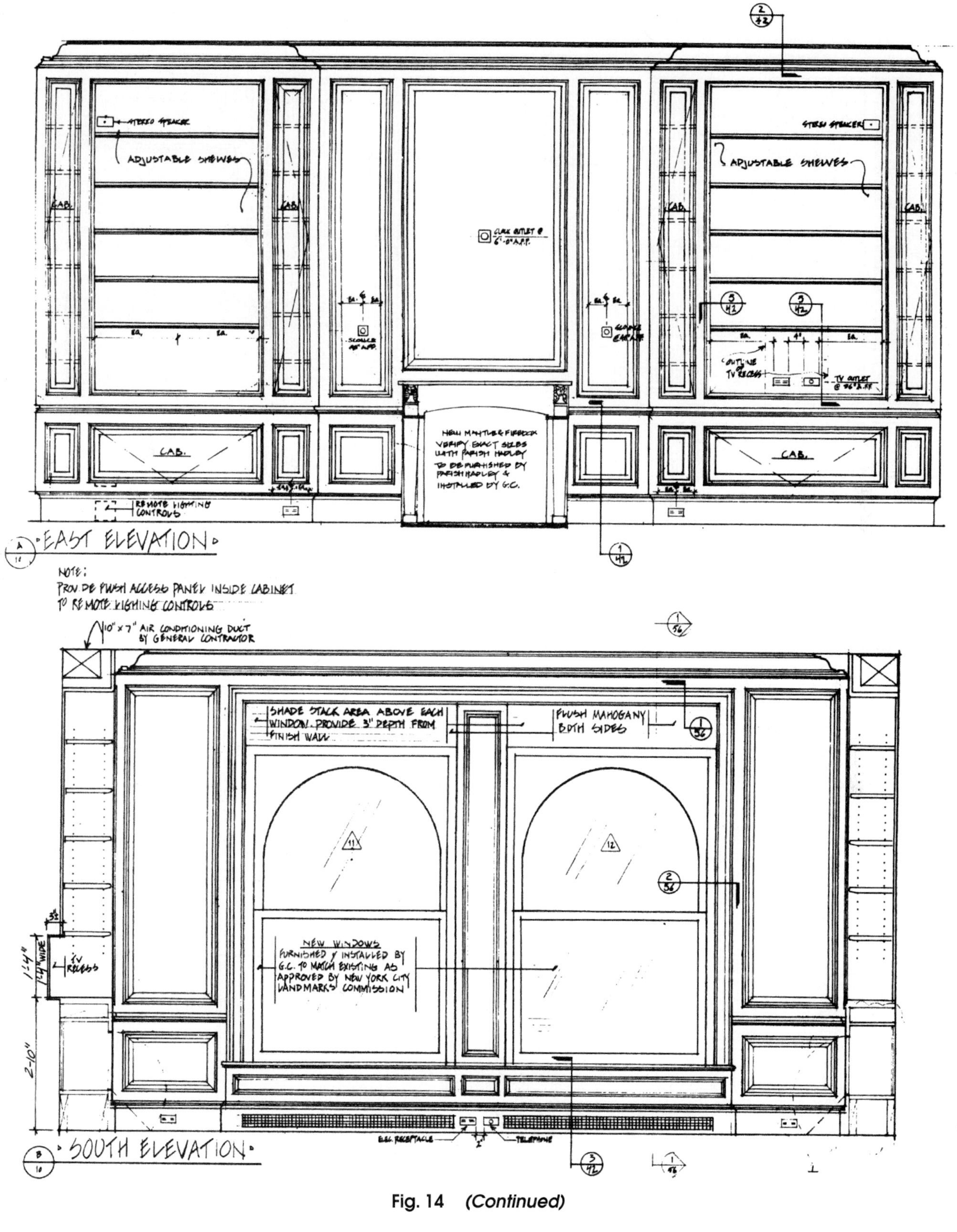

Fig. 14 *(Continued)*

LIVING ROOMS
Wall Elevations

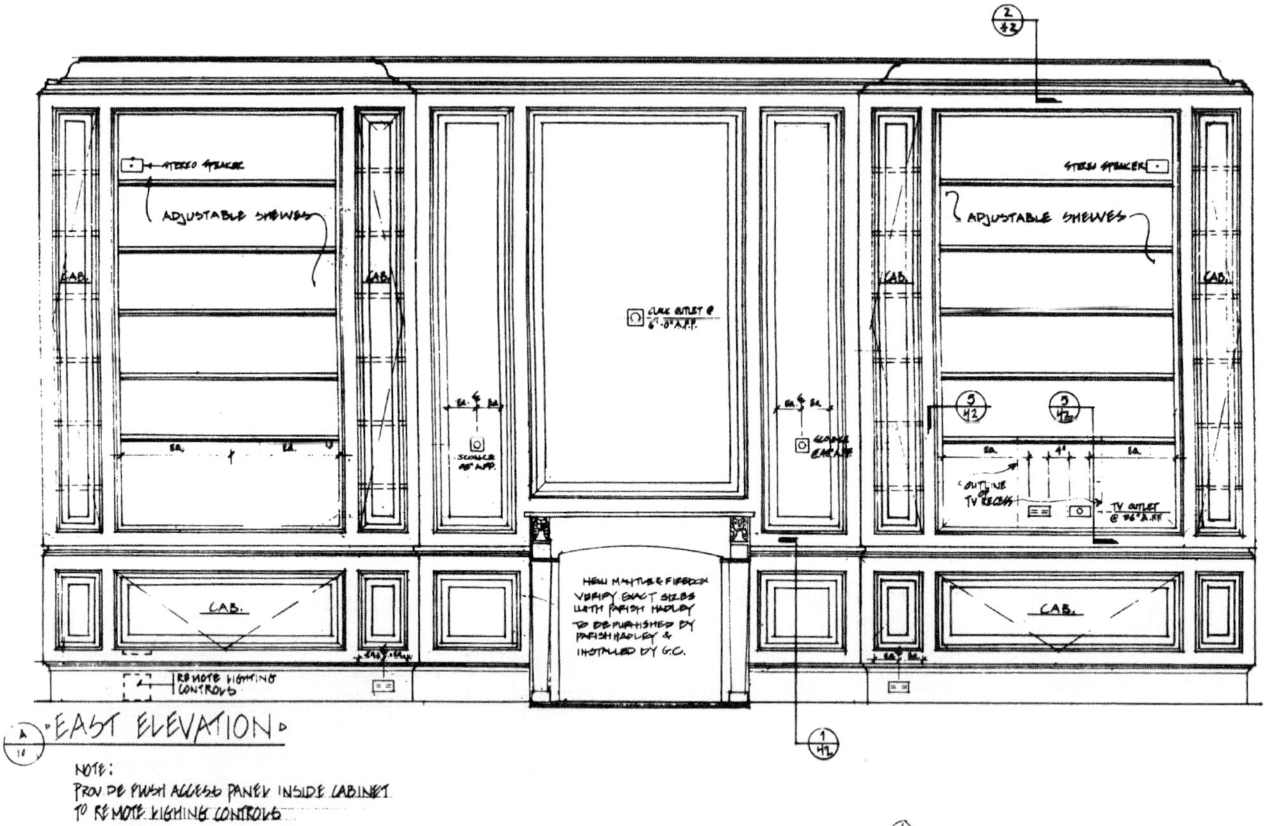

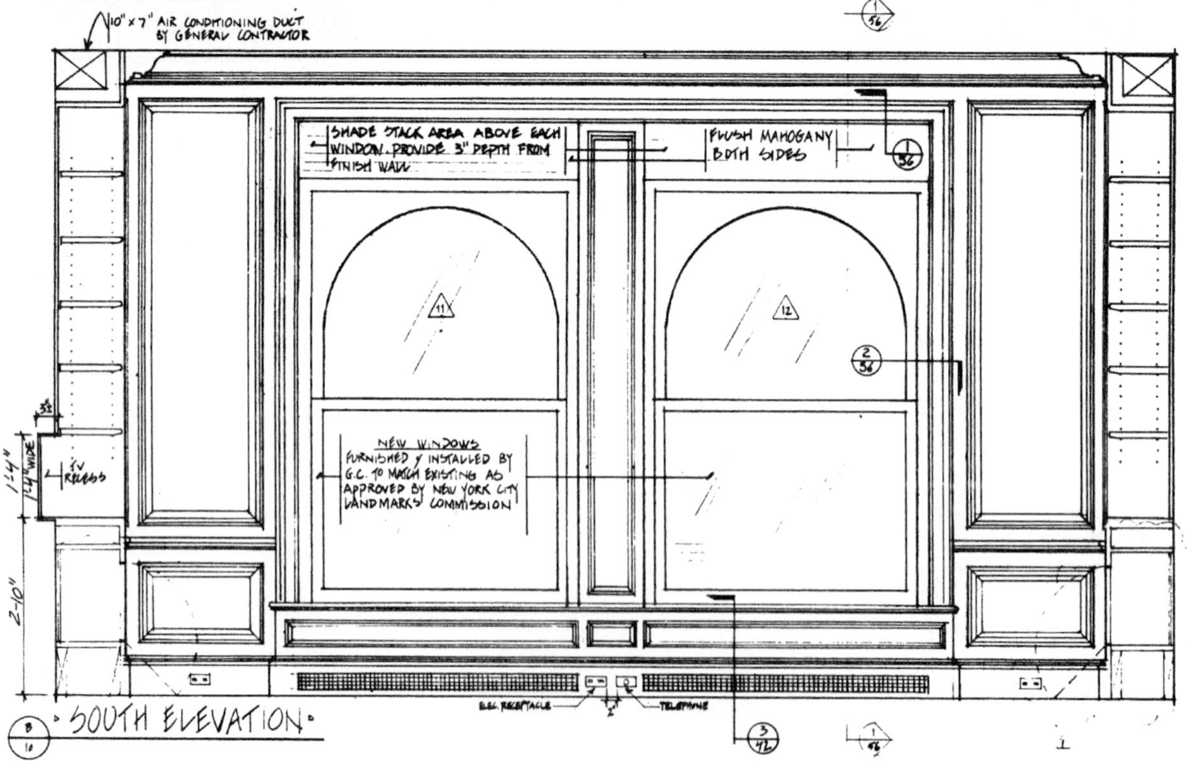

Fig. 14 *(Continued)*

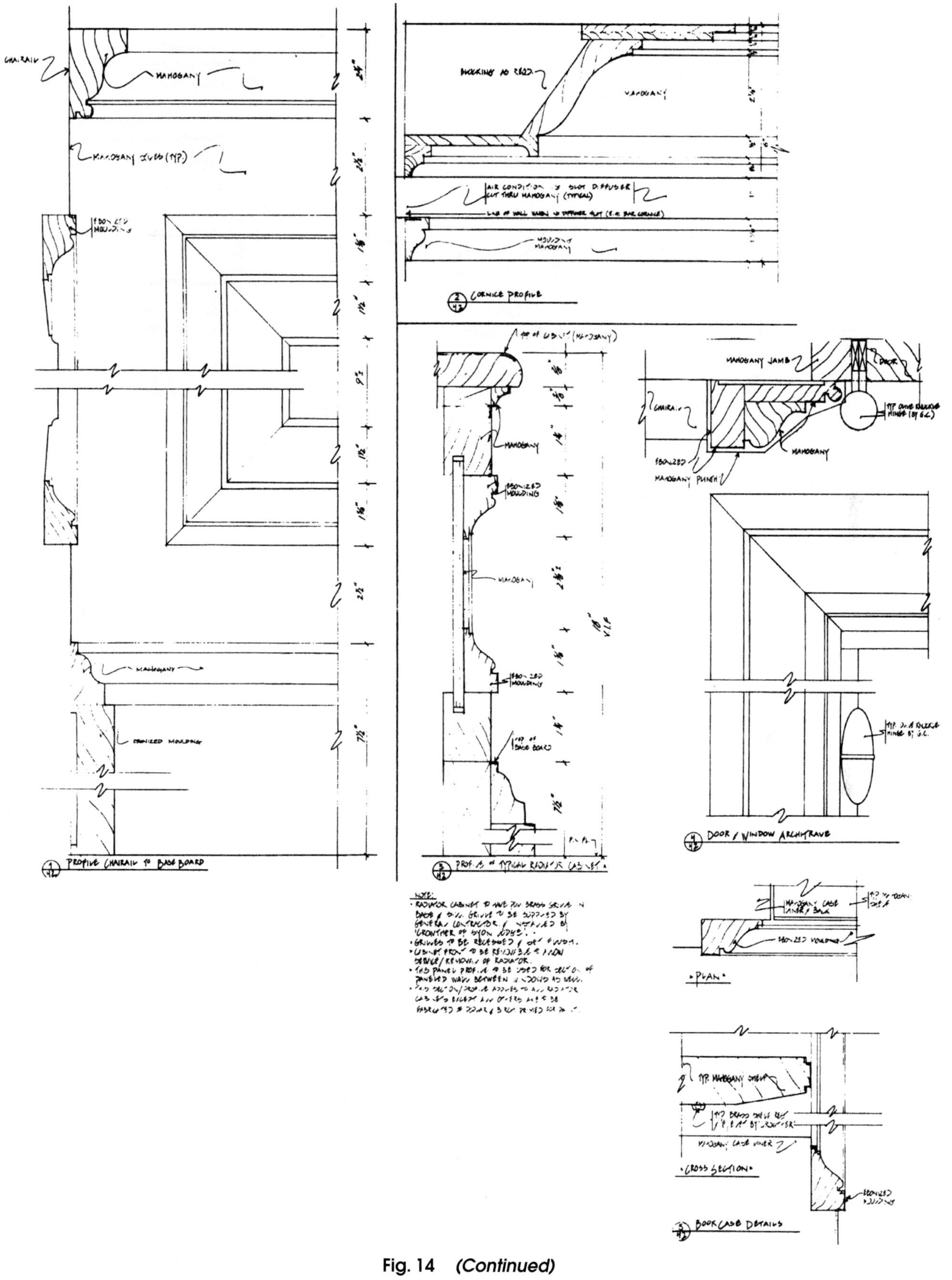

Fig. 14 *(Continued)*

LIVING ROOMS
Planning Data: Sofas

Traditional: roll arms, loose-cushion back, kidney shape, solid base

Traditional: roll arms, fixed-cushion back, tailored skirt

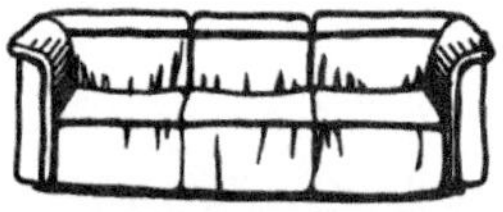
Contemporary: curved arms, fixed-cushion back, solid base

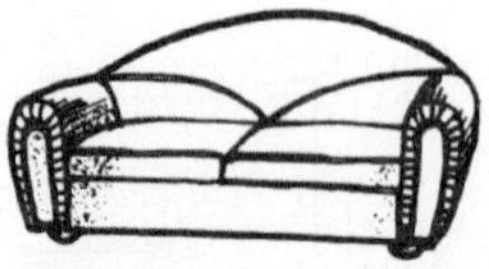
Contemporary: dome arms, solid back, solid base

Traditional: roll arms, fixed-cushion back, tailored skirt

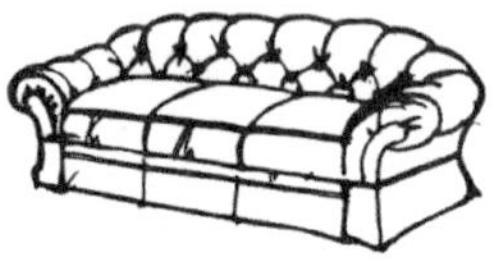
Traditional: roll arms, tufted

Traditional: roll arms, one-piece back, skirted base

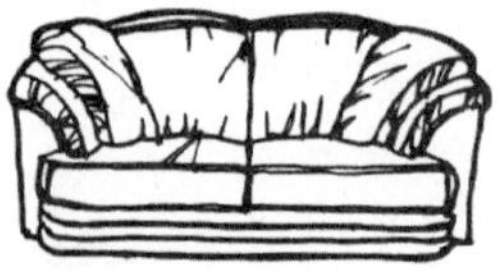
Contemporary: slanted cushion arms, fixed-cushion back, solid base

Traditional: roll arms, one-piece back, solid base

Traditional: roll arms, loose-pillow back, shirred base

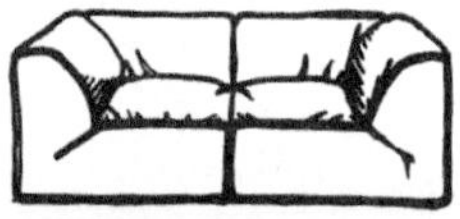
Contemporary: curved arms, fixed-cushion back, solid base

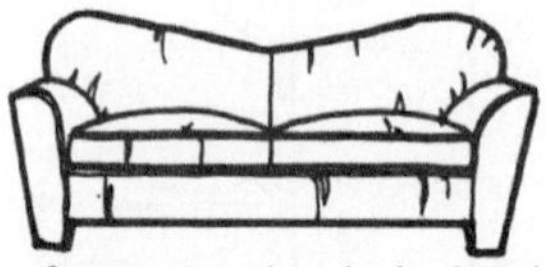
Contemporary: shaped sofa, shaped front view

Traditional: roll arms

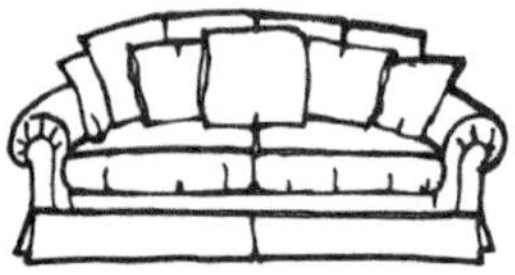
Traditional: roll arms, loose-pillow back, tailored skirt

Traditional: roll arms

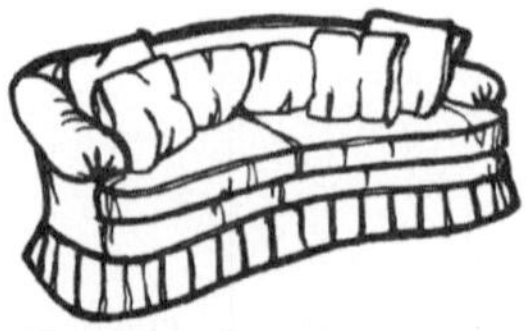
Traditional: roll arms, loose-cushion back, kidney shape, pleated skirt, solid base

Traditional: roll arms

Contemporary: shaped sofa, shaped base

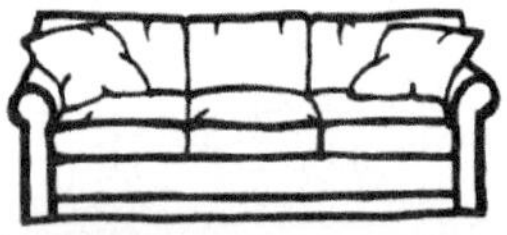
Traditional: roll arms, fixed-cushion back, solid base

Contemporary: square arms, loose-cushion back, solid base

Contemporary: miscellaneous slanted arms

Traditional: roll arms, fixed-cushion back, shirred skirt

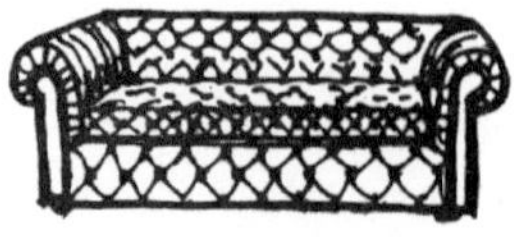
Traditional: roll arms, tufted

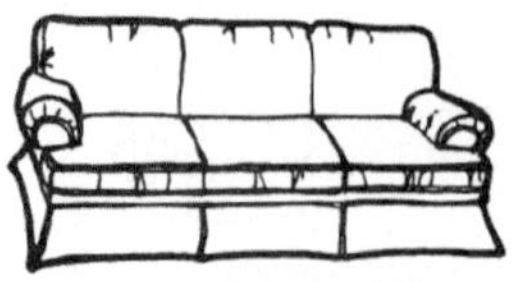
Traditional: roll arms, fixed-cushion back, tailored skirt

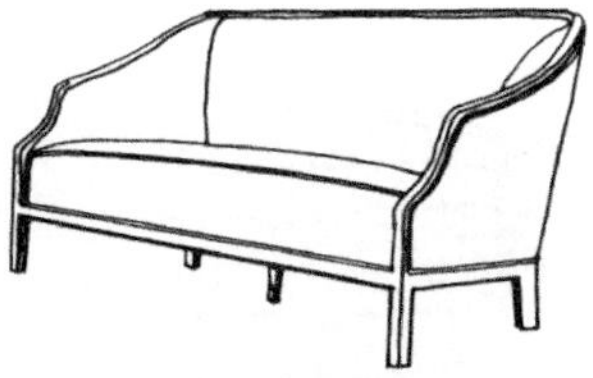

Contemporary: straight arms, one-piece back, open base

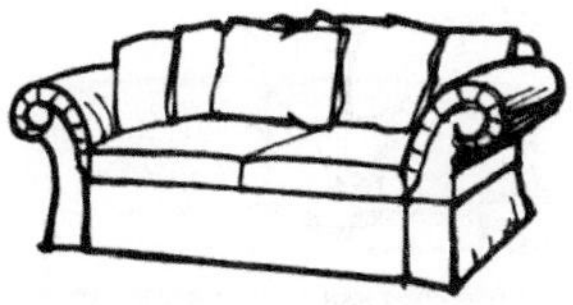

Traditional: roll arms, loose-pillow back, full skirt

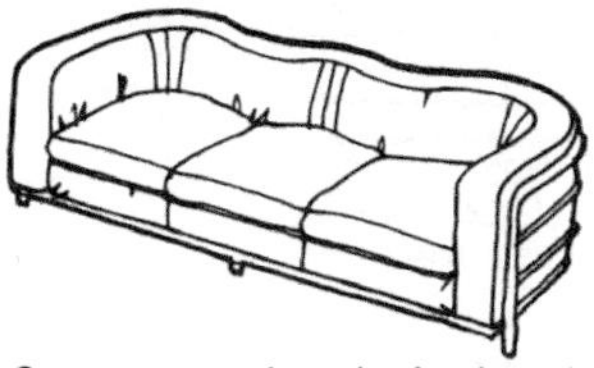

Contemporary: shaped sofa, shaped plan

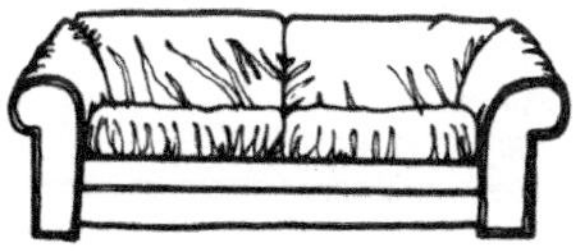

Contemporary: roll arms, fixed-cushion back, solid base

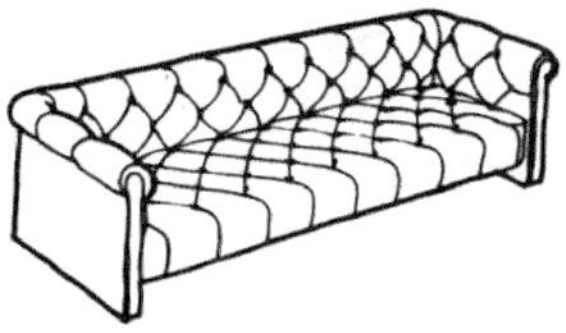

Traditional: roll arms, tufted

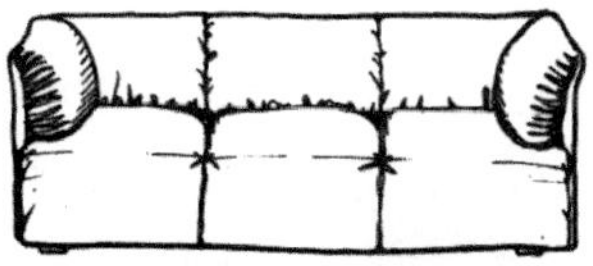

Contemporary: miscellaneous slanted arms

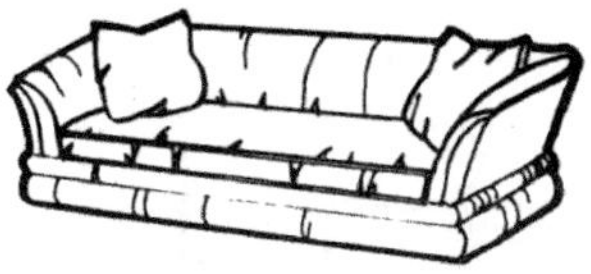

Contemporary: shaped sofa, partitioned back

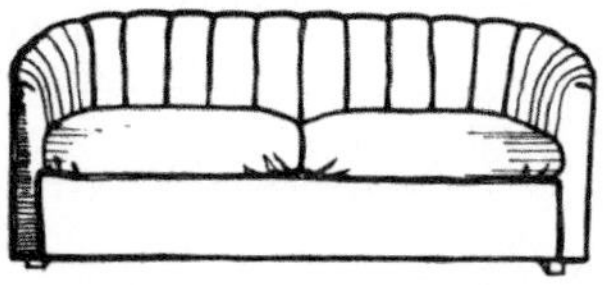

Contemporary: curved arms, fixed-cushion back, solid base

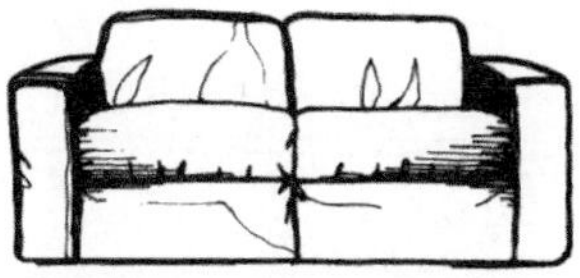

Contemporary: square arms, loose-cushion back, solid base

Contemporary: straight arms, one-piece back, open base

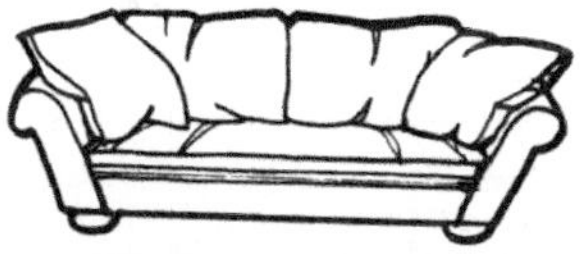

Contemporary: miscellaneous slanted arms

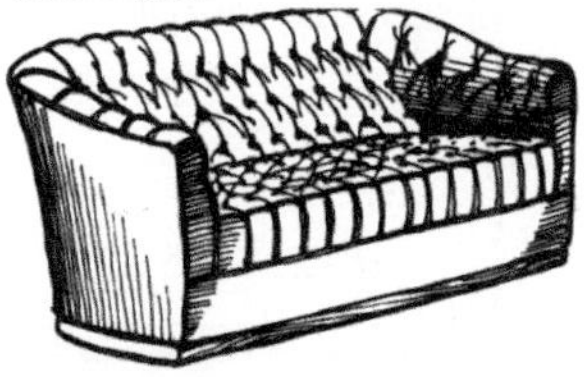

Contemporary: dome arms, one-piece tufted back, solid base

Contemporary: roll arms, loose-cushion back, solid base

Contemporary: square arms, fixed-cushion back, open base

Contemporary: dome arms, loose-cushion back, solid base

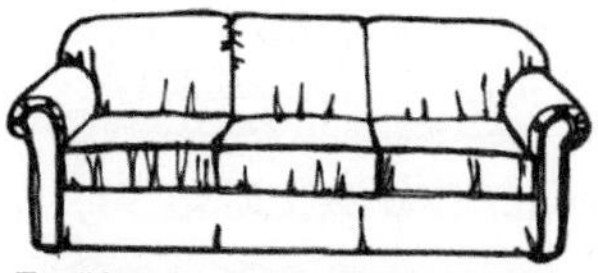

Traditional: roll arms, fixed-cushion back

Contemporary: square arms, fixed-cushion back, open base

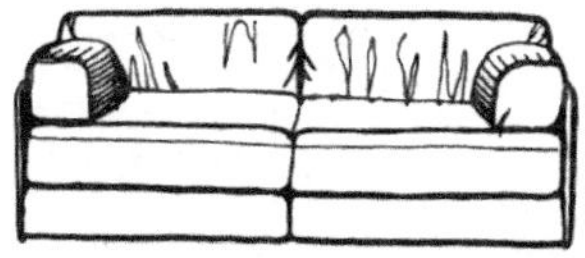

Contemporary: curved arms, fixed-cushion back, solid base

Contemporary: roll arms, fixed-cushion back, solid base

Contemporary: square arms, fixed-cushion back, open base

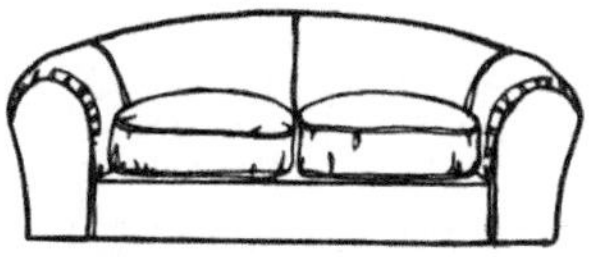

Contemporary: dome arms, solid back, solid base

LIVING ROOMS
Planning Data: Sofas

Contemporary: wood frame arms and legs, one-piece curved back, open base

Contemporary: square arms, fixed-cushion back, wood trim, open base

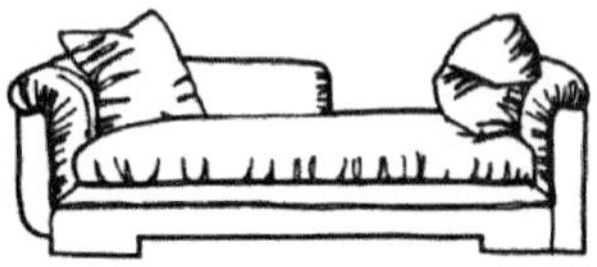

Contemporary: sofa/daybed

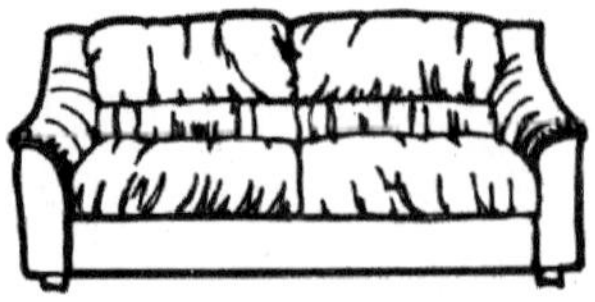

Contemporary: curved arms, fixed-cushion back, solid base

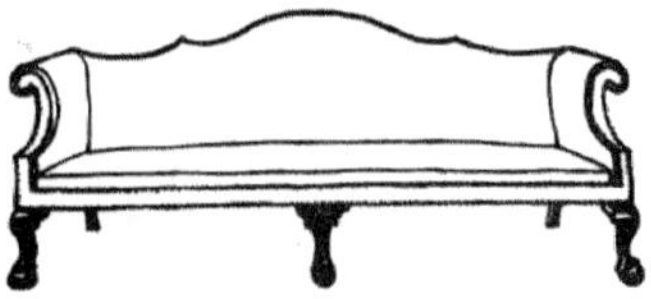

Traditional: roll arms, one-piece back, open base

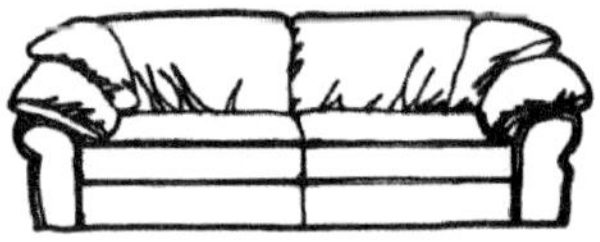

Contemporary: slanted cushion arms, fixed-cushion back, solid base

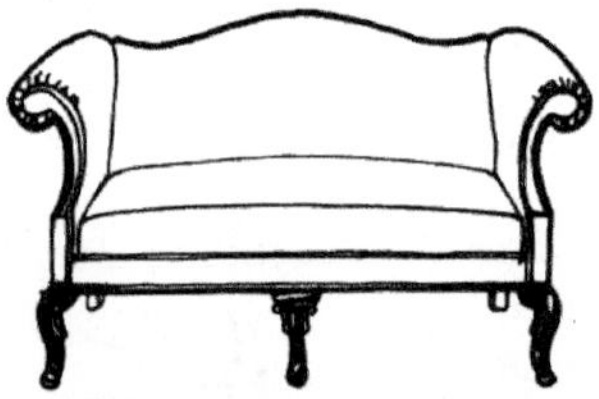

Traditional: roll arms, one-piece back, open base

Contemporary: dome arms, channel quilted back, seat, and arms, solid base

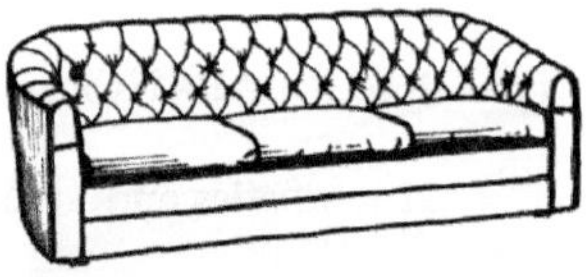

Contemporary: dome arms, one-piece tufted back and seat, solid base

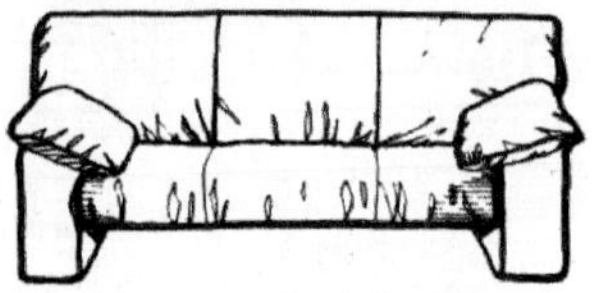

Contemporary: slanted cushion arms, fixed-cushion back, open base

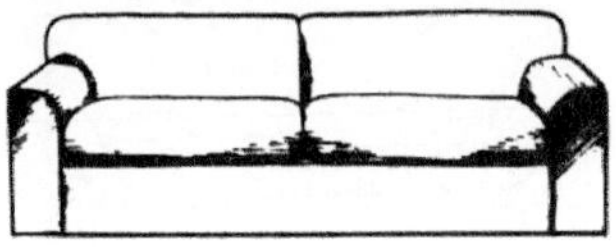

Contemporary: curved arms, fixed-cushion back, solid base

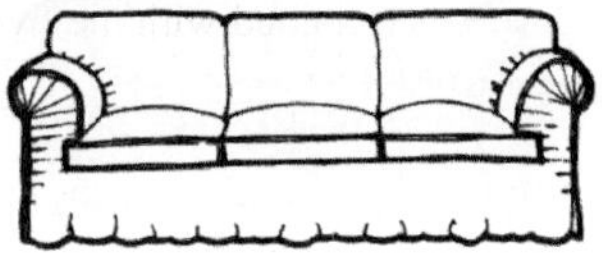

Contemporary: roll arms, fixed-cushion back, soft skirt

Contemporary: one-piece curved back and arms, wood legs, open base

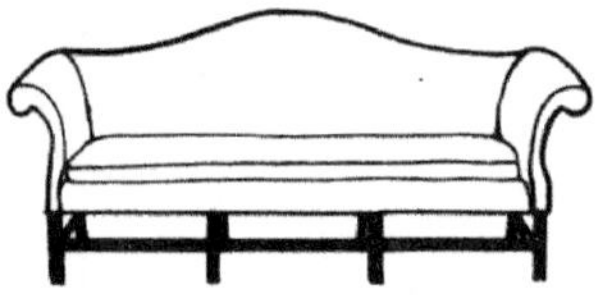

Traditional: roll arms, one-piece back, open base

Contemporary: shaped sofa, partitioned back

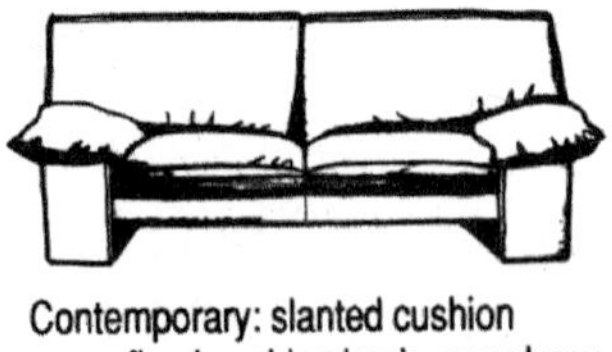

Contemporary: slanted cushion arms, fixed-cushion back, open base

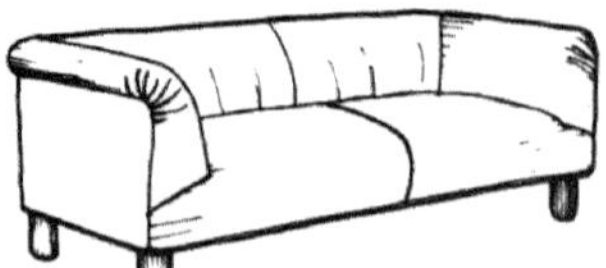

Contemporary: curved arms, fixed-cushion back, solid base

Contemporary: curved arms, fixed-cushion back, solid base

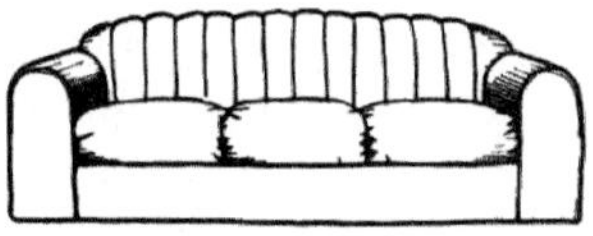

Contemporary: dome arms, solid back

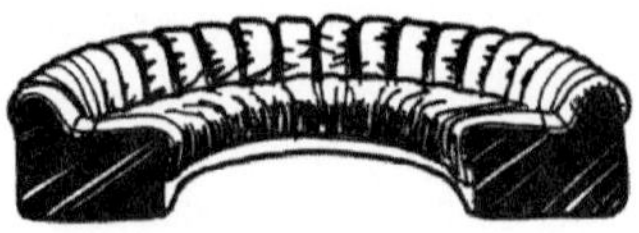

Contemporary: modular

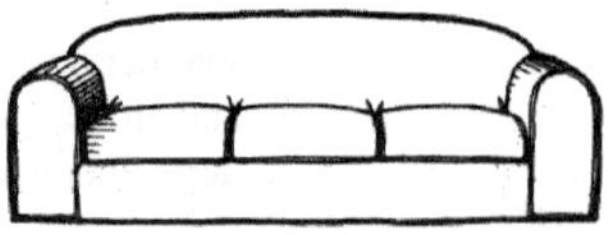

Contemporary: dome arms, solid back

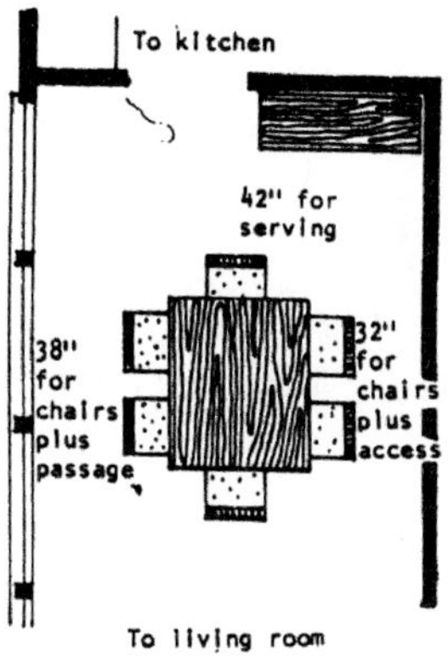

Fig. 1 Dining room for six-person, three-bedroom living unit

DINING ROOMS

FURNITURE CLEARANCES

Spatial Characteristics and Arrangement

Requirement

Each living unit should contain space for the purpose of dining. This area may be combined with the living room or kitchen, or it may be a separate room.

Criterion

The amount of space allocated to dining should be based on the number of persons to be served and the proper circulation space. Appropriate space should be provided for the storage of china and large dining articles, either in the dining area itself or in the adjacent kitchen.

Space for accommodating the following sizes of tables and chairs in the dining area should be provided, according to the intended occupancy, as shown:

1 or 2 persons: 2 ft 6 in × 2 ft 6 in
4 persons: 2 ft 6 in × 3 ft 2 in
6 persons: 3 ft 4 in × 4 ft 0 in or 4 ft 0 in round
8 persons: 3 ft 4 in × 6 ft 0 in or 4 ft 0 in × 4 ft 0 in
10 persons: 3 ft 4 in × 8 ft 0 in or 4 ft 0 in × 6 ft 0 in
12 persons: 4 ft 0 in × 8 ft 0 in
Dining chairs: 1 ft 6 in × 1 ft 6 in
Buffet or storage unit: 1 ft 6 in × 3 ft 6 in

Figures 1 to 6 show the minimum requirements of the U.S. Department of Housing and Urban Development.

Commentary

The size of the individual eating space on the table should be based on a frontage of 24 in and an area of approximately 2 ft^2. In addition, table space should be large enough to accommodate serving dishes.

Desirable room for seating is a clear 42 in all around the dining table. The following minimum clearances from the edge of the table should

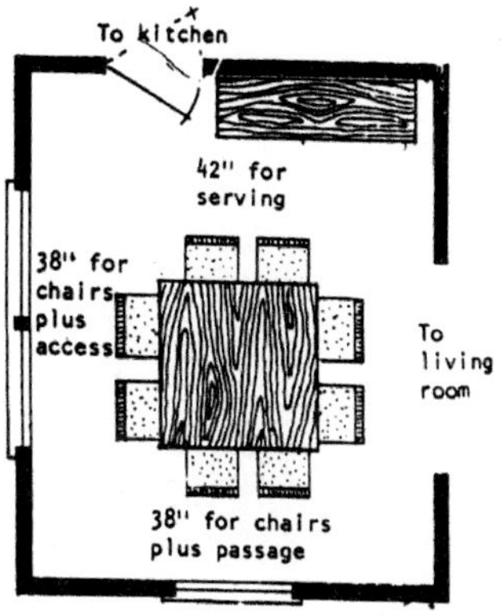

Fig. 2 Dining room for eight-person, four-bedroom living unit

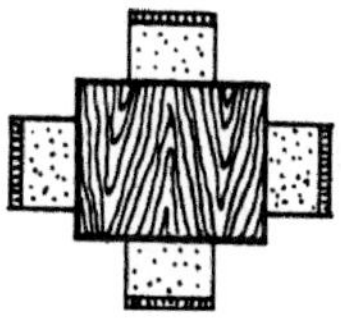

Fig. 3 Table for two, 2′6″ × 2′6″
Fig. 4 Table for four, 2′6″ × 3′2″

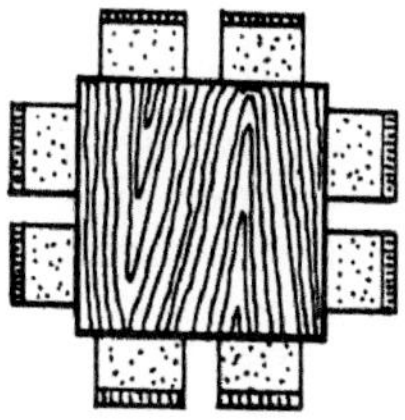

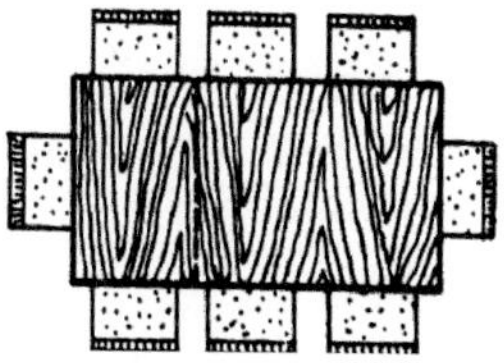

Fig. 5 Table for eight, 4′0″ × 4′0″
Fig. 6 Table for eight, 3′4″ × 6′0″

DINING ROOMS

Furniture Clearances

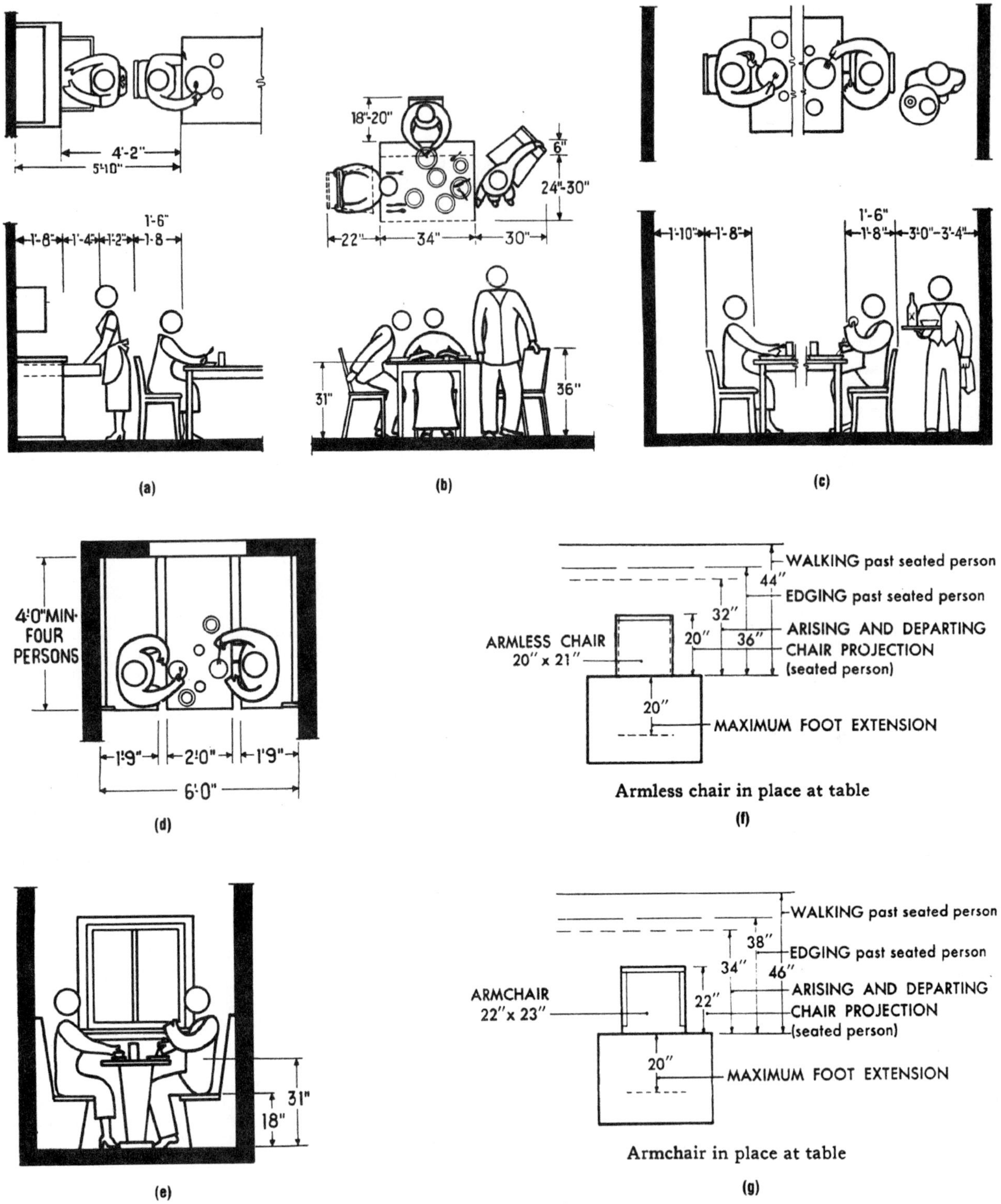

Fig. 7 *(a)* to *(e)* illustrate, in plan and elevation, seating requirements and clearances for various dining table arrangements; *(f)* and *(g)* illustrate clearance guidelines for a typical armless dining chair and a dining chair with arms, respectively. It should be noted that the clearances indicated relate to chairs with depth dimensions of 20 in and 22 in; clearances should be adjusted depending on the chair size finally selected

be provided: 32 in for chairs plus access thereto, 38 in for chairs plus access and passage, 42 in for serving from behind chair, 24 in for passage only, 48 in from table to base cabinet (in kitchen).

In sizing the separate dining room, provision should be made for circulation through the room in addition to space for dining.

The location of the dining area in the kitchen is desirable for small houses and small apartments. This preference appears to stem from two needs: (1) housekeeping advantages; (2) the dining table in the kitchen provides a meeting place for the entire family. Where only one dining location is feasible, locating the dining table in the living room is not recommended.

Figures 8 and 9 show clearances and room sizes for various dining arrangements. Since these data come from two sources, there may be slight disparities in suggested dimensions for similar conditions. Since these illustrations are intended only as guidelines for preliminary planning purposes, either set of any differing dimensions can be used.

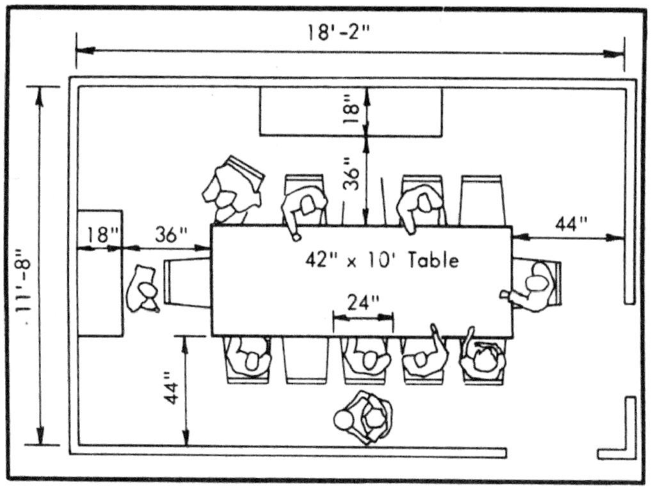

A dining room for 12.
A hutch or buffet is typically about 18" deep. A 42" wide table is common. There is space behind the chairs to edge past one side and one end, and to walk past on the other side and end. Table space is 24" per person, the minimum place setting zone. With arm chairs at the ends, allow an extra 2" for each; add 4" to the room length.

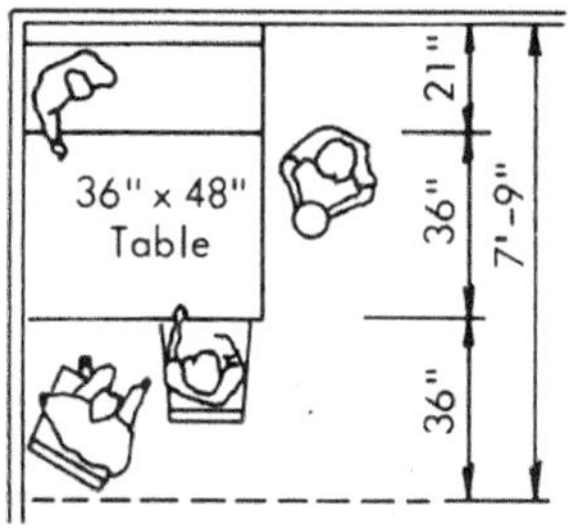

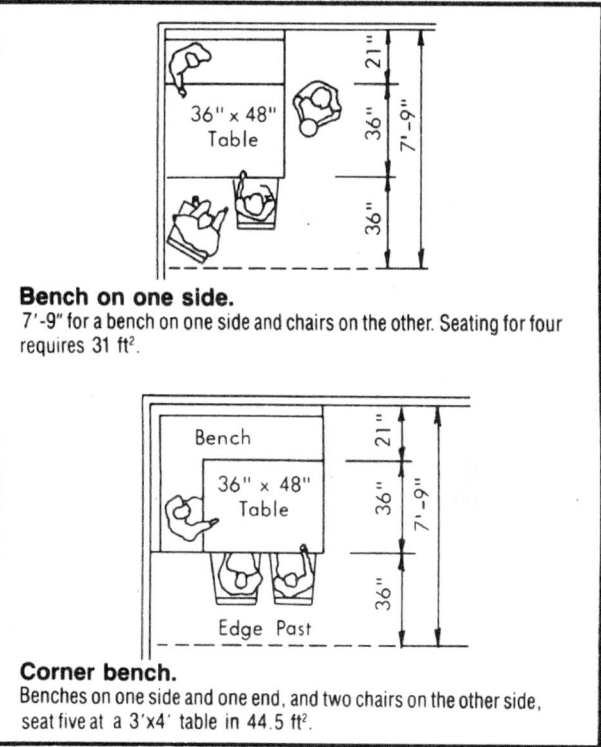

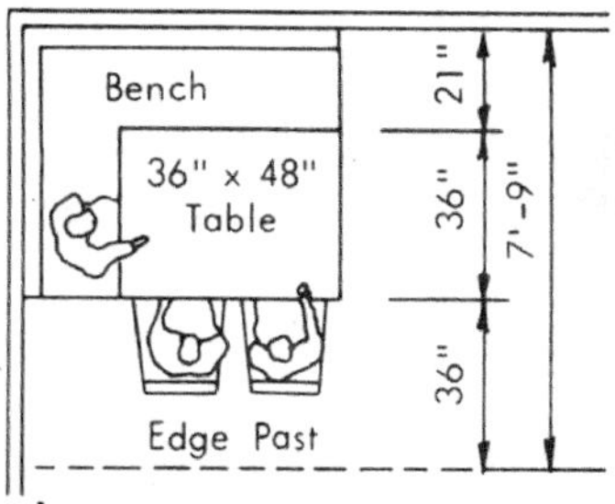

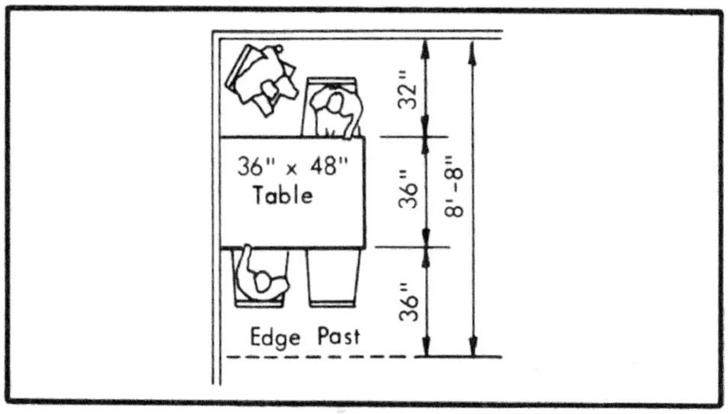

Minimum width for table and chairs.
8'-8" for 36" wide table, 32" on one side to rise from the table and 36" on the other side to edge past. A 48" long table seats 4 and requires 34.6 ft².

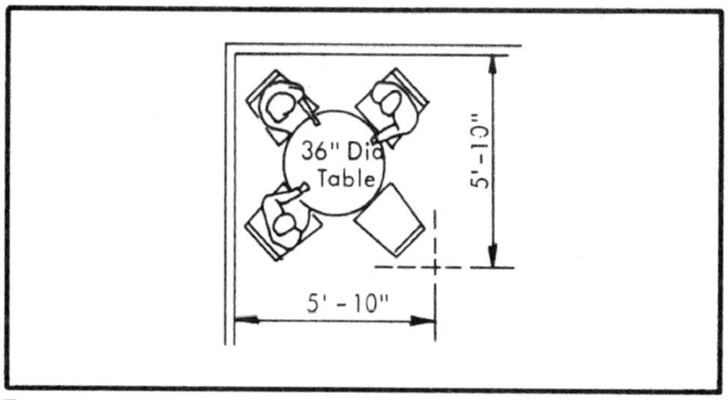

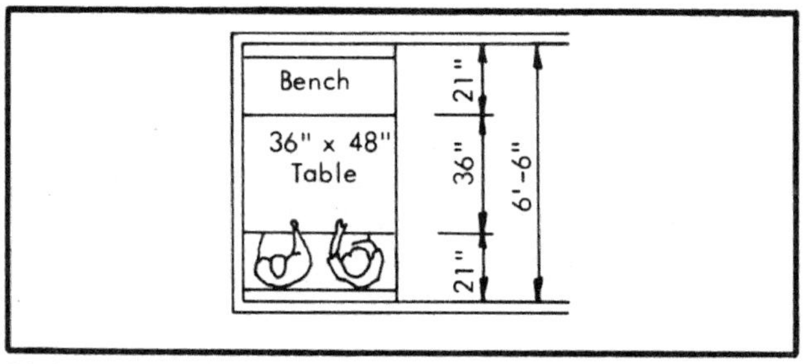

Dining space with benches.
6'-6" for benches on both sides of a 36" table. A 48" long table seats 4 and requires 26 ft².

Bench on one side.
7'-9" for a bench on one side and chairs on the other. Seating for four requires 31 ft².

Corner bench.
Benches on one side and one end, and two chairs on the other side, seat five at a 3'x4' table in 44.5 ft².

Bench and chair dining.

Round tables.
A 36" round table with four swivel chairs fit in a 5'-10"x5'-10" or 34 ft² corner space.

Fig. 8

DINING ROOMS

Furniture Clearances and Room Sizes

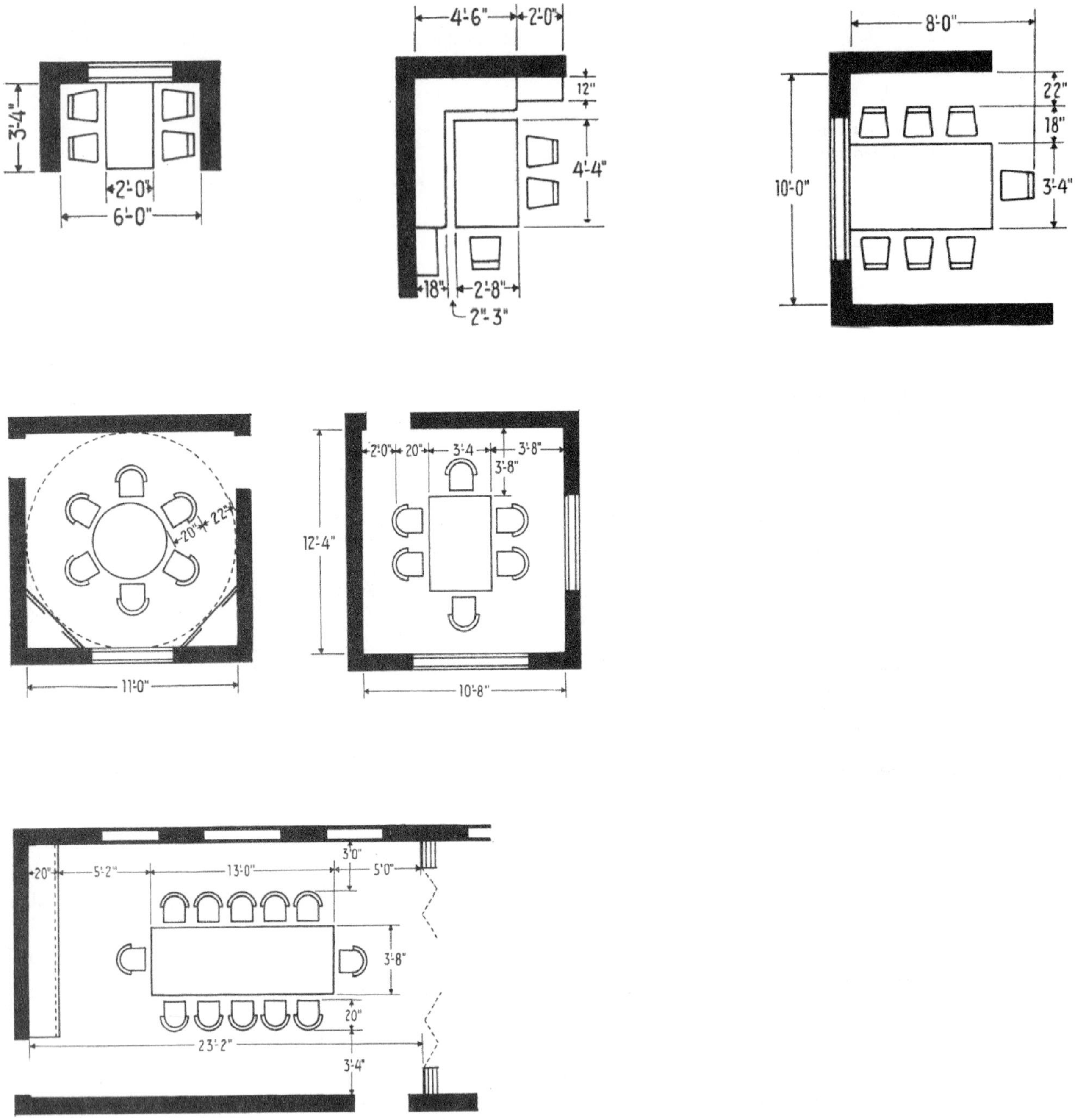

Fig. 9

To assure adequate space for convenient use of the dining area, not less than the following clearances from the edge of the dining table should be observed:

32 in for chair plus access thereto
38 in for chairs plus access and passage
42 in for serving from behind chair
24 in for passage only
48 in from table to base cabinet (in dining-kitchen)

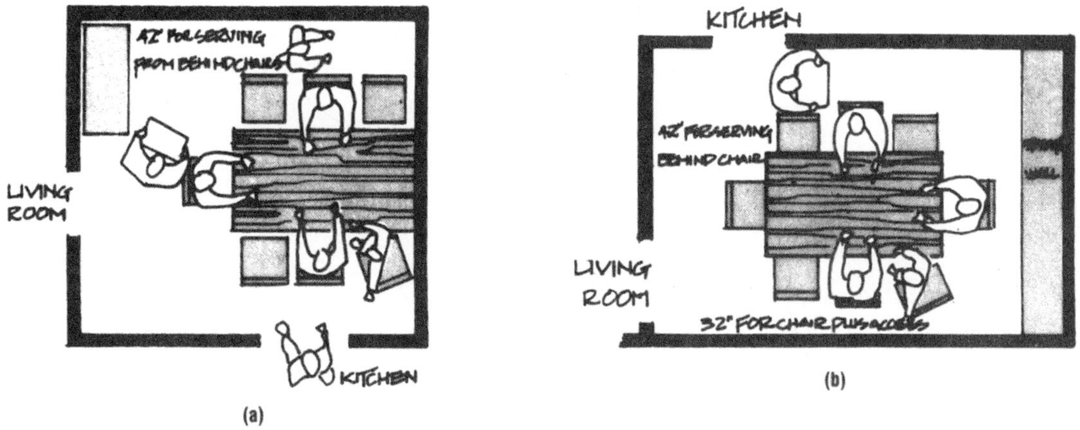

Fig. 10 Minimum clearances for dining areas: (*a*) one end of table against wall; (*b*) serving from one end and one side of table

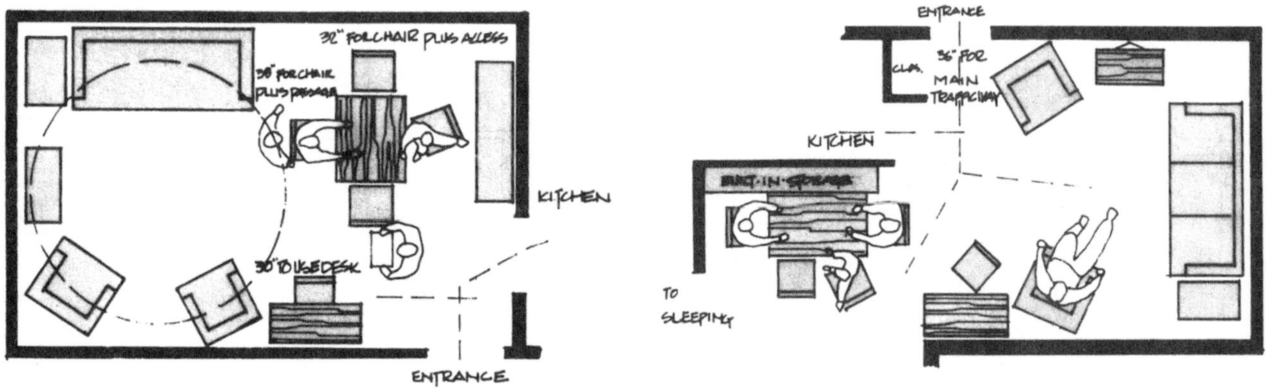

Fig. 11 Minimum clearances and circulation for combined living-dining areas

ROUND TABLES

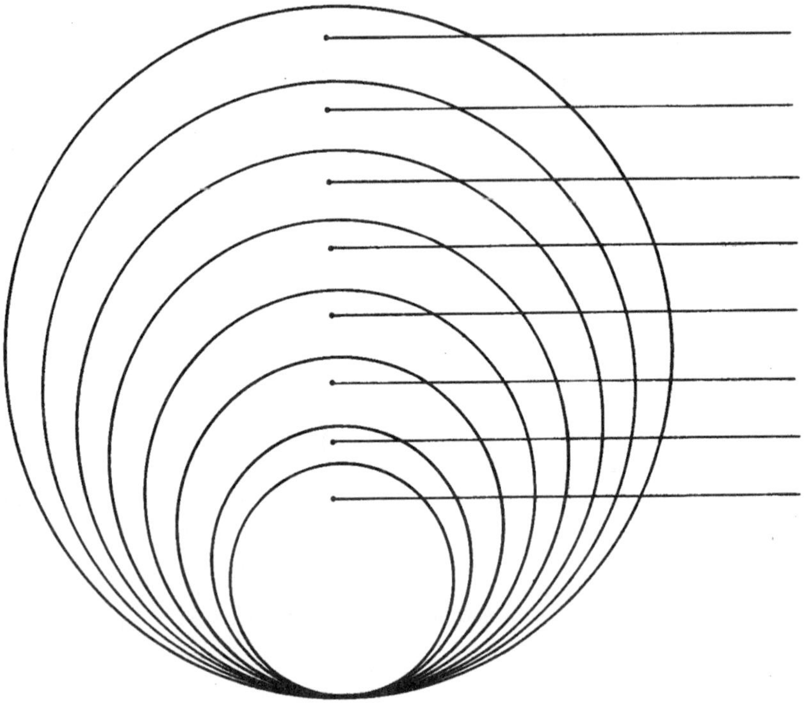

Diam.	Circum.	Approx. Seating	Recommended Minimum Room Size
10′0″	31′5″	12–15	20′0″ x 20′0″
9′0″	28′2″	11–14	19′0″ x 19′0″
8′0″	25′1″	10–12	18′3″ x 18′3″
7′0″	22′0″	9–11	16′0″ x 16′0″
6′0″	18′10″	8–9	14′6″ x 14′6″
5′0″	15′9″	7–8	13′0″ x 13′0″
4′0″	12′6″	5–6	11′6″ x 11′6″
3′6″	11′0″	4–5	10′6″ x 10′6″

SQUARE TABLES

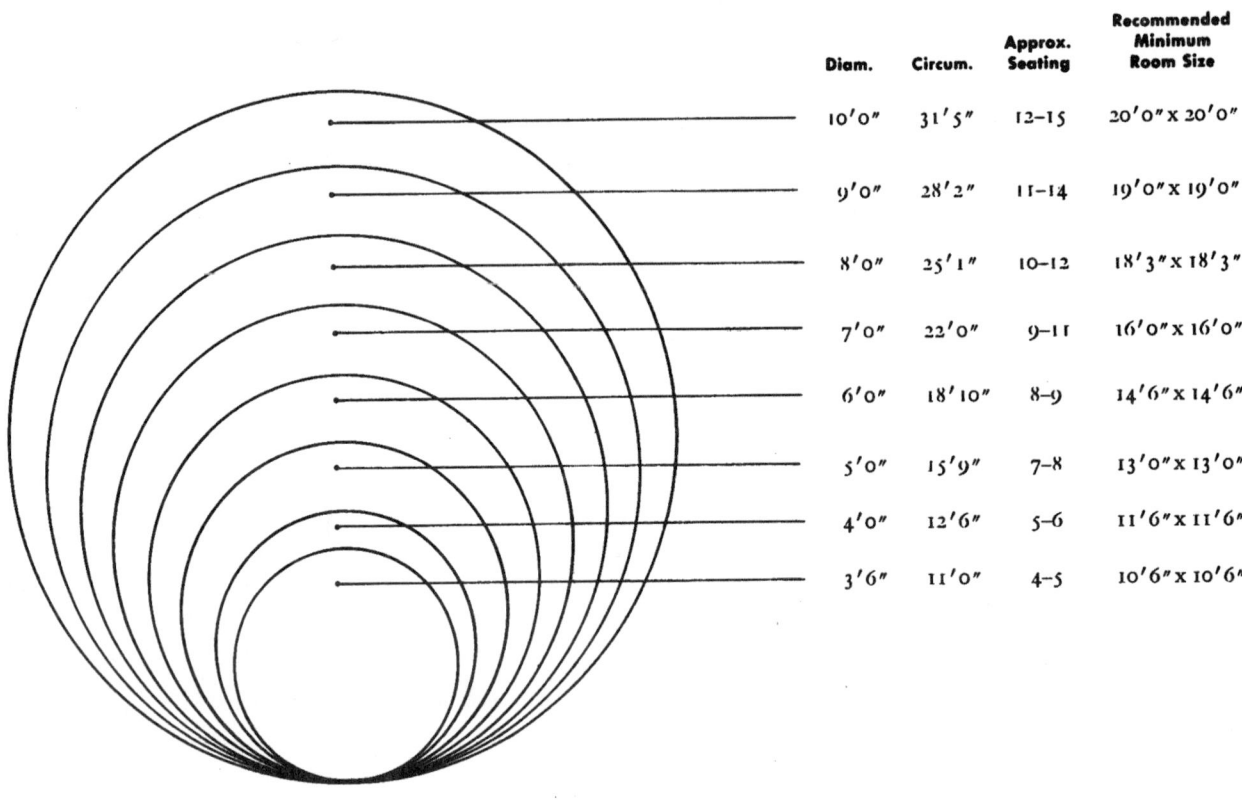

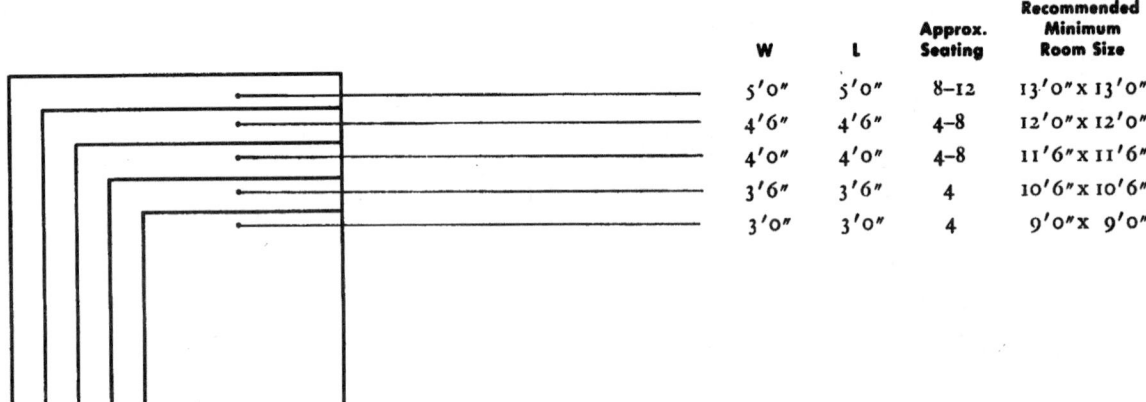

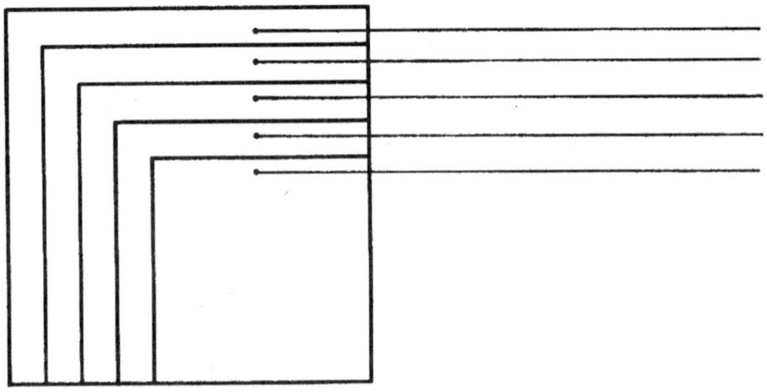

W	L	Approx. Seating	Recommended Minimum Room Size
5′0″	5′0″	8–12	13′0″ x 13′0″
4′6″	4′6″	4–8	12′0″ x 12′0″
4′0″	4′0″	4–8	11′6″ x 11′6″
3′6″	3′6″	4	10′6″ x 10′6″
3′0″	3′0″	4	9′0″ x 9′0″

Fig. 12 Seating capacities for round, square, rectangular, and boat-shaped tables of various sizes, and the recommended minimum room sizes to accommodate each

RECTANGULAR TABLES

W	L	Approx. Seating	Recommended Minimum Room Size
6'0"	28'0"	28–30	18'0"x 40'0"
6'0"	26'0"	26–28	18'0"x 38'0"
6'0"	24'0"	24–26	18'0"x 36'0"
5'0"	22'0"	22–24	15'0"x 32'0"
5'0"	20'0"	20–22	15'0"x 30'0"
4'6"	18'0"	18–20	13'6"x 27'0"
4'6"	16'0"	16–18	13'6"x 25'0"
4'6"	14'0"	14–16	13'6"x 23'0"
4'0"	13'0"	12–14	12'0"x 21'0"
4'0"	12'0"	12–14	12'0"x 20'0"
4'0"	11'0"	10–12	12'0"x 19'0"
4'0"	10'0"	10–12	12'0"x 17'0"
4'0"	9'6"	8–10	12'0"x 16'6"
3'6"	9'0"	8–10	10'6"x 16'0"
3'6"	8'6"	8–10	10'6"x 15'6"
3'6"	8'0"	8–10	10'6"x 15'0"
3'6"	7'6"	6–8	10'6"x 14'6"
3'6"	7'0"	6–8	10'6"x 14'0"
3'0"	6'6"	6–8	10'0"x 13'6"
3'0"	6'0"	6–8	10'0"x 13'0"
2'6"	5'6"	4–6	9'0"x 12'6"
2'6"	5'0"	4–6	9'0"x 12'0"

BOAT SHAPED TABLES

W	L	Approx. Seating	Recommended Minimum Room Size
3'5"	8'0"	8–10	10'0"x 15'0"
3'8"	9'0"	8–10	11'0"x 16'0"
3'11"	10'0"	10–12	12'0"x 17'0"
4'3"	11'0"	10–12	13'0"x 19'0"
4'7"	12'0"	12–14	14'0"x 21'0"
4'11"	14'0"	14–16	15'0"x 23'0"
5'3"	16'0"	16–18	16'0"x 26'0"
5'7"	18'0"	20–22	17'0"x 29'0"
6'0"	20'0"	20–24	18'0"x 32'0"

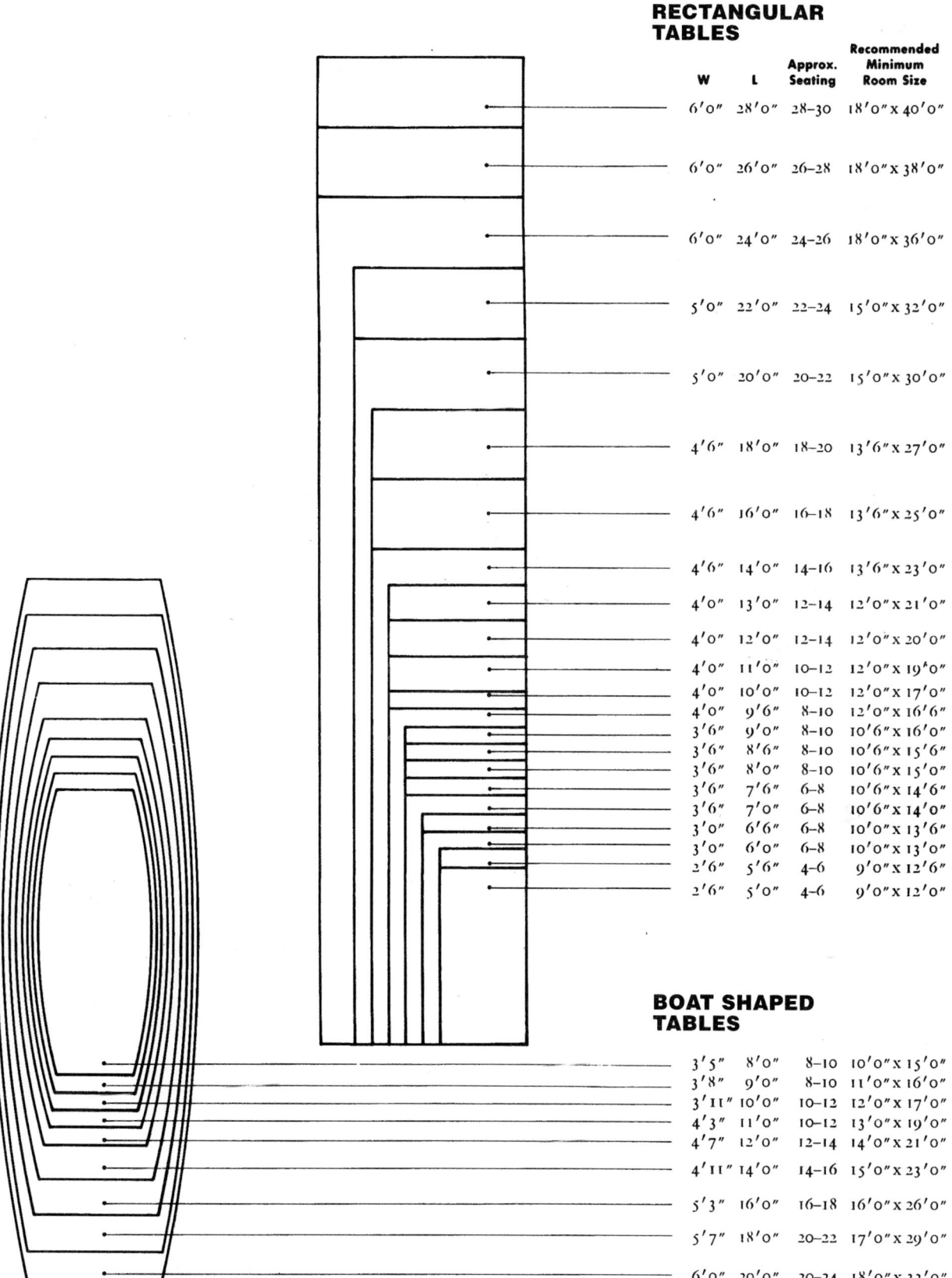

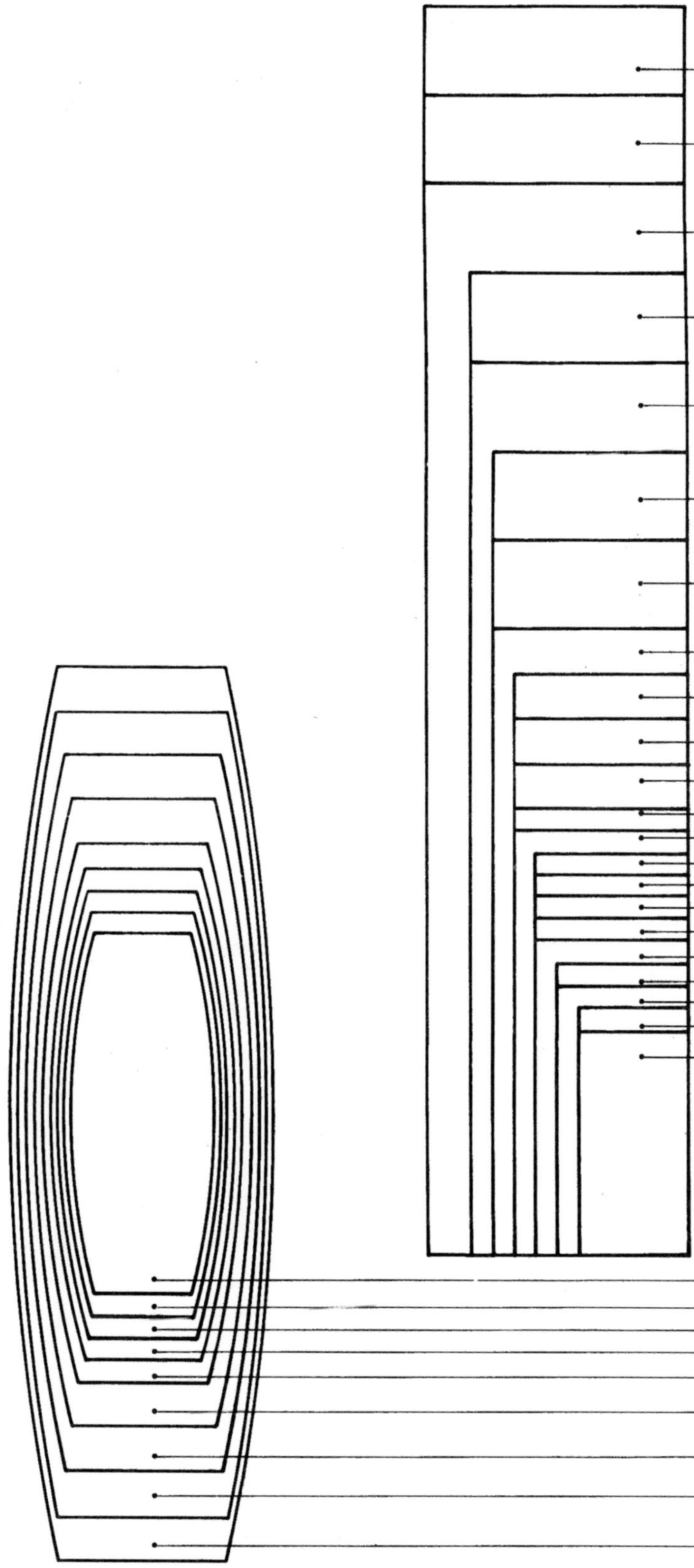

Fig. 12 *(Continued)*

DINING ROOMS

Sideboard and Wall Panel Details

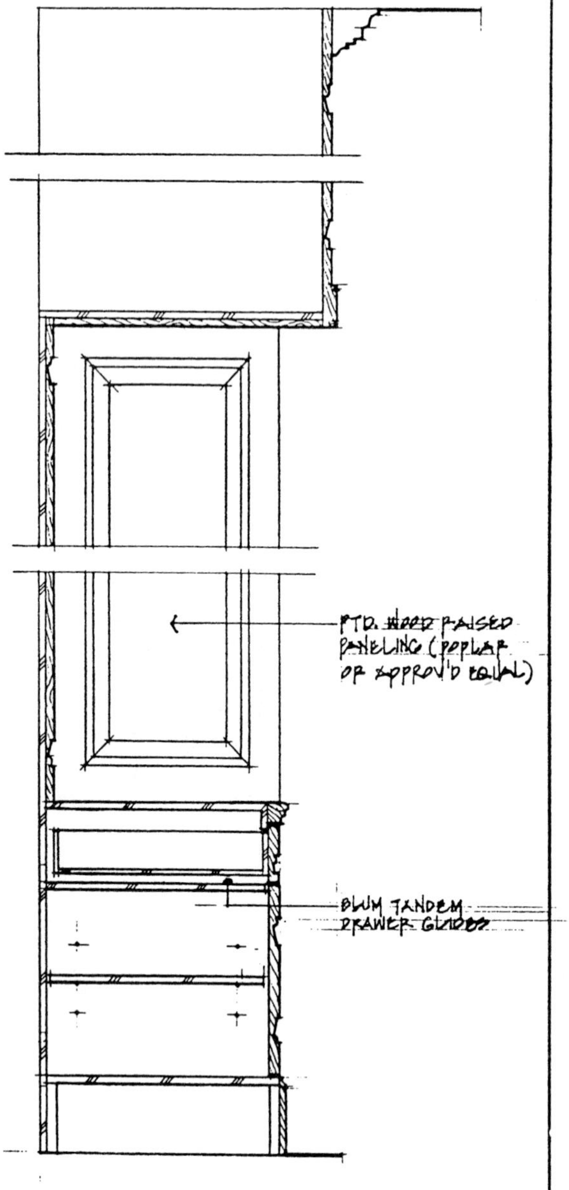

3 Sideboard - Dining Rm.

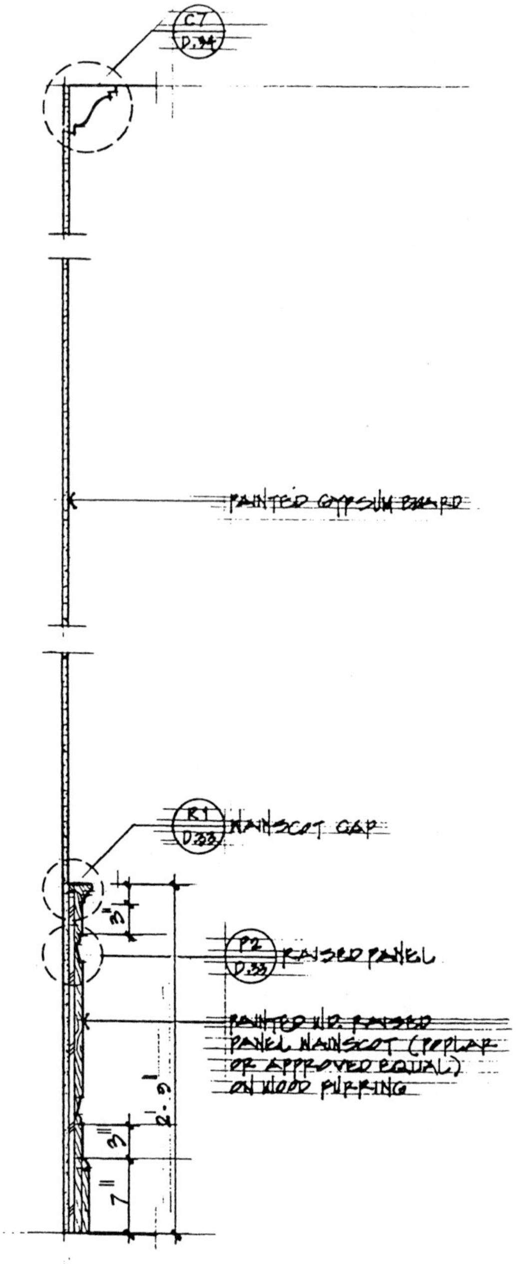

4 Typ. Wall-L.R., 1st. Fl., Halls, Foyer

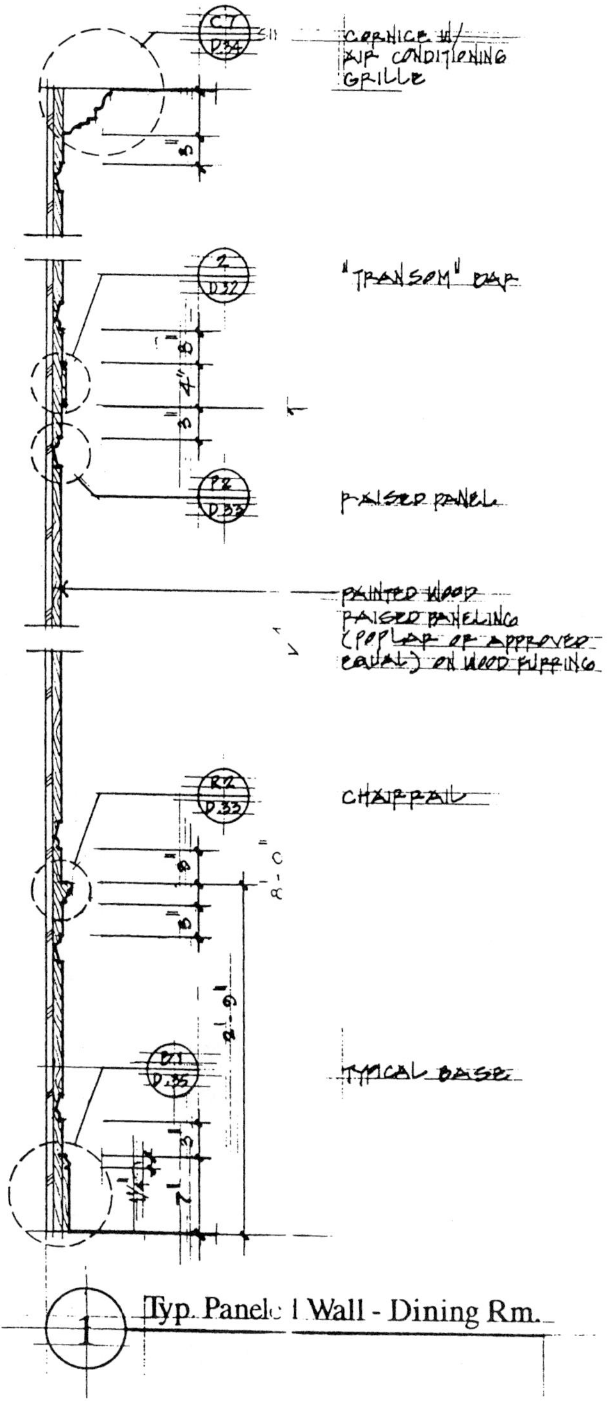

1 Typ. Paneled Wall - Dining Rm.

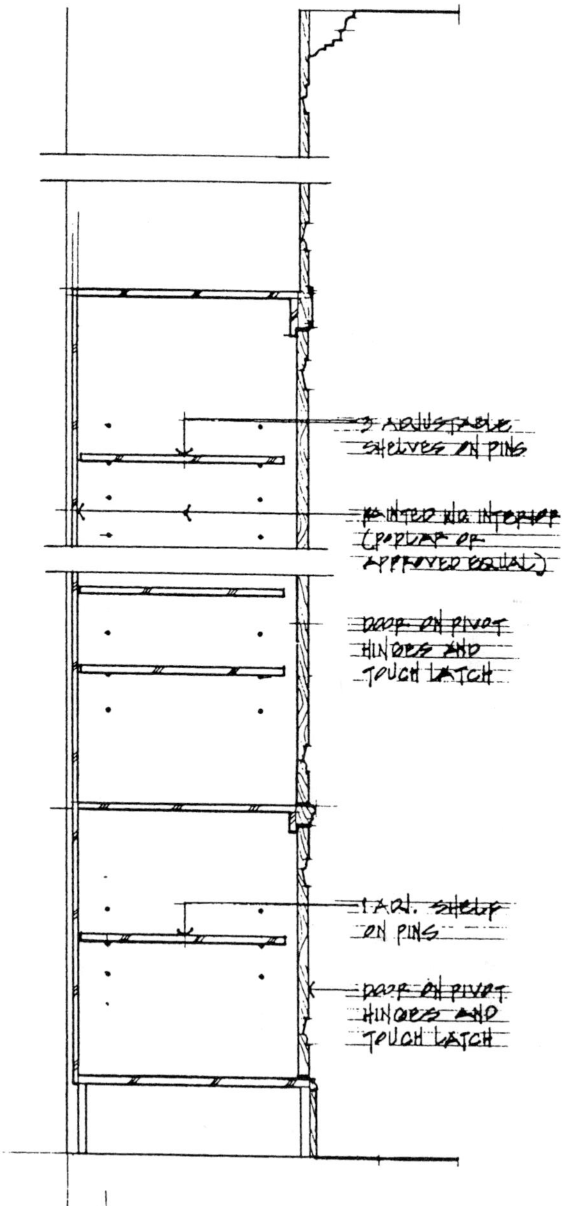

2 Cabinet - Dining Rm.

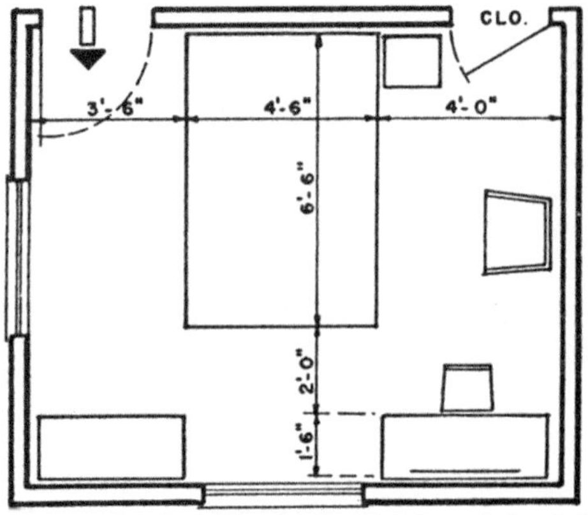

DOUBLE BED - ONE CLOS. 10'-3"x12'-0"

Fig. 1

BEDROOMS

FURNITURE CLEARANCES AND ARRANGEMENTS

Most of the clearances and bedroom sizes shown here are minimum and intended primarily for preliminary planning purposes. Some building codes permit rooms of even smaller sizes, while rooms in many private homes and luxury apartments are much larger. Moreover, in the final analysis, lifestyle, the size and scale of furniture, the activities to be accommodated, and barrier-free design are all factors that should be taken into account during the design process.

Ideally, the recommended minimum bedroom size should be 10 ft 0 in × 12 ft 0 in exclusive of closets, while the recommended minimum size for a larger bedroom or master bedroom should be 12 ft 0 in × 16 ft 0 in exclusive of closets.

A larger proportion of the bedroom floor area is occupied by furniture than is the case with any other room; windows and doors account for a large percentage of the wall and partition space. These two factors complicate the planning of bedrooms, especially when the rooms are small.

Because of the room layout, some bedrooms with smaller areas better meet the needs than larger ones. The location of doors, windows, and closets must be properly planned to allow the best placement of the bed and other furniture.

Privacy, both visual and sound, are desirable for the bedroom. Children's bedrooms should be located away from the living room, because conversation in the living room prevents the children from sleeping. Closets should be used between all bedrooms wherever possible.

Each child needs a space that is his or her own to develop a sense of responsibility and a respect for the property rights of others. The ideal plan would provide a bedroom for each child, but since this is not always possible, there should be a bed for each.

The minimum room width shall be determined by the space required for the bed, activity space, and any furniture facing the bed. Widths less than 9 ft 0 in will usually require extra area to accommodate comparable furniture.

Aside from sleeping, the bedroom is the center of dressing and undressing activities. An interrelationship exists between dressing, storage of clothes, and the bedroom.

Inevitably, in a small apartment, it is not only economical but necessary to plan the use of the bedroom for more than one activity. It is essential to incorporate in the bedroom other functions such as relaxation, work, or entertainment.

A master bedroom should accommodate at least one double bed 4 ft 6 in × 6 ft 6 in or two single beds 3 ft 3 in × 6 ft 6 in each, one crib 2 ft 4 in × 1 ft 5 in if necessary, one dresser 3 ft 6 in × 1 ft 10 in, one chest of drawers 2 ft 6 in × 1 ft 10 in, one or two chairs 1 ft 6 in × 1 ft 6 in each, two night tables, and possibly a small desk or table 1 ft 6 in × 3 ft 0 in. Figures 1 to 3 illustrate three configurations and the furniture clearances and room sizes required.

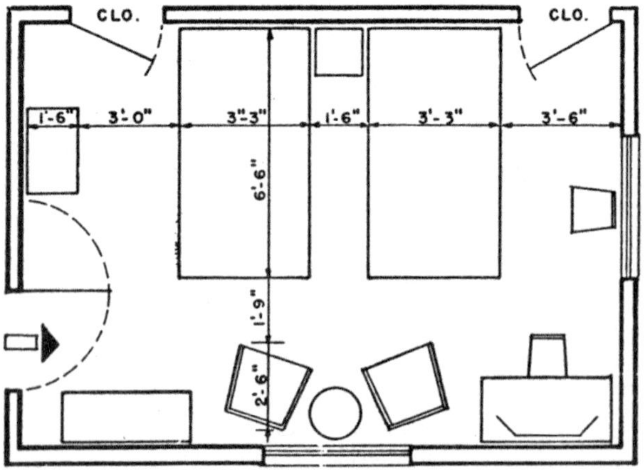

TWIN BED - SEPARATED 11'-0"x16'-0"

Fig. 2

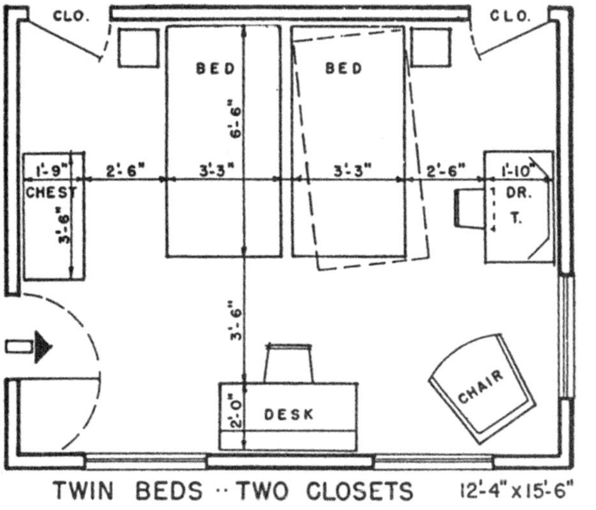

Fig. 3

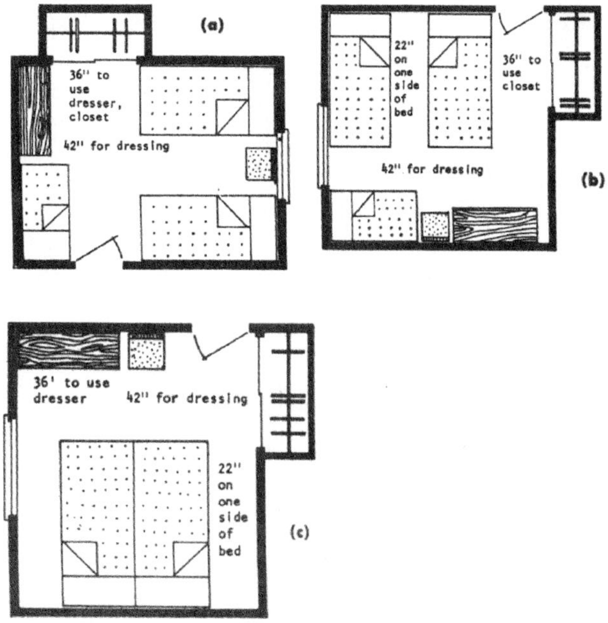

Fig. 4 (*a*), (*b*) Primary bedroom; (*c*) primary bedroom without crib

Ample storage is essential. Each bedroom requires at least one clothes closet. For master bedrooms, at least 5 linear ft of closet length is needed. For secondary bedrooms, at least 3 linear ft is needed. Clothes closets require a clear depth of 2 ft.

Each bedroom shall have at least one closet that meets or exceeds the following standards:

1. Depth: 2 ft clear
2. Length (for primary bedroom): 5 linear ft clear
3. Height:
   a. At least 5 ft 4 in clear hanging space
   b. Lowest shelf shall not be over 6 ft 2 in above the floor of room.
4. One shelf and rod with at least 12 in clear space above shelf
5. At least one-half the closet floor shall be level and not more than 12 in above floor of adjacent room.

FURNITURE CLEARANCES

To ensure adequate space for convenient use of furniture in the bedroom, not less than the following clearances should be observed (Figs. 4 and 5):

42 in at one side or foot of bed for dressing
6 in between side of bed and side of dresser or chest

FURNITURE ARRANGEMENTS

The location of doors and windows should permit alternate furniture arrangements.

36 in in front of dresser, closet, and chest of drawers
24 in for major circulation path (door to closet, etc.)
22 in on one side of bed for circulation
12 in on least used side of double bed.

The least-used side of a single or twin bed can be placed against the wall, except in bedrooms for the elderly.

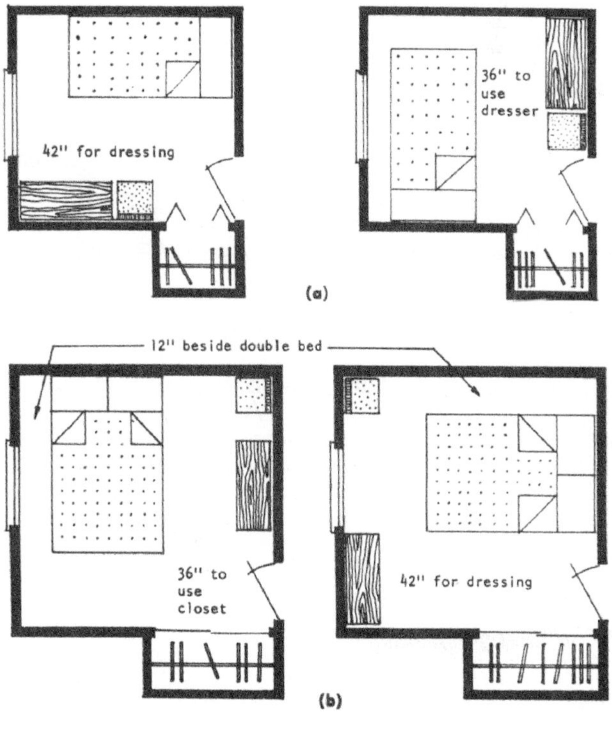

Fig. 5 (*a*) Single-occupancy bedroom; (*b*) double-occupancy bedroom

BEDROOMS
General Planning Data

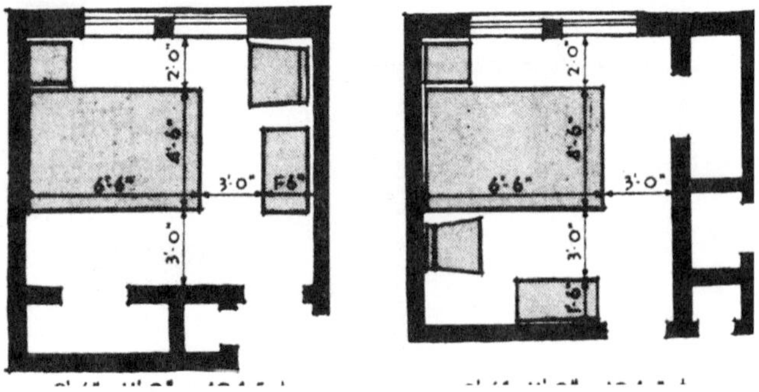

Fig. 6 Although the recommended minimum size for a secondary bedroom is 10 ft 0 in × 12 ft 0 in, these diagrams indicate how a double bed, night table, chair, and dresser can be accommodated in a room only 9 ft 6 in × 11 ft 0 in

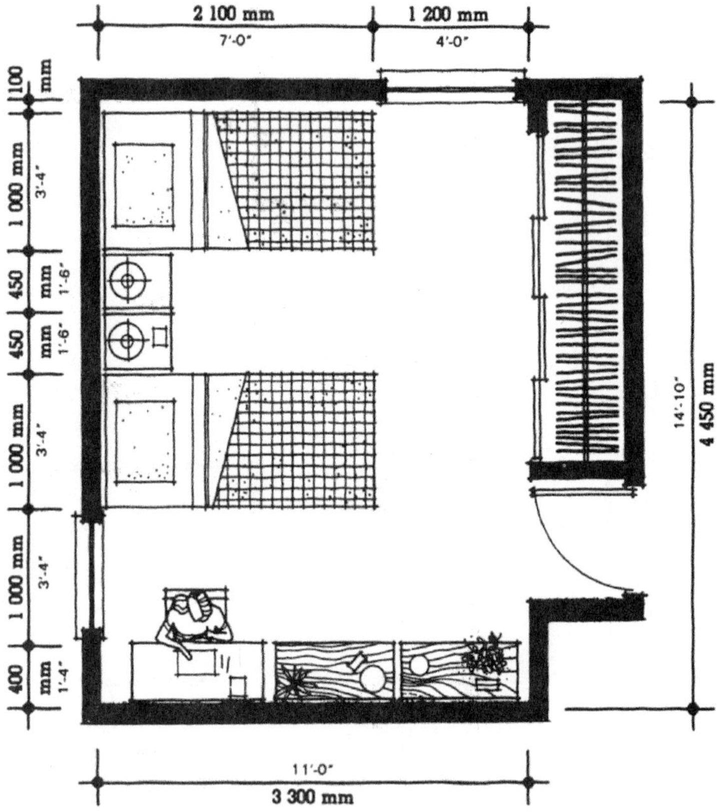

Fig. 7 Double-occupancy bedroom. Net area: 14.7 m^2 (160 ft^2). The most likely occupants of this type of bedroom are adults, school-age children of the same sex, children of different sexes who are less than 9 years old, and preschoolers

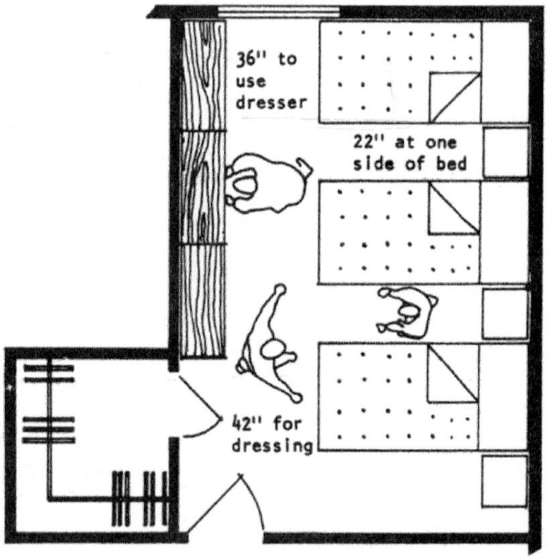

Fig. 8 Occupancy of a bedroom by more than two persons is not recommended. In cases where budgetary and/or space limitations offer no alternative, however, a dormitory arrangement may be necessary. The U.S. Department of Housing and Urban Development recommends the arrangement illustrated in this diagram

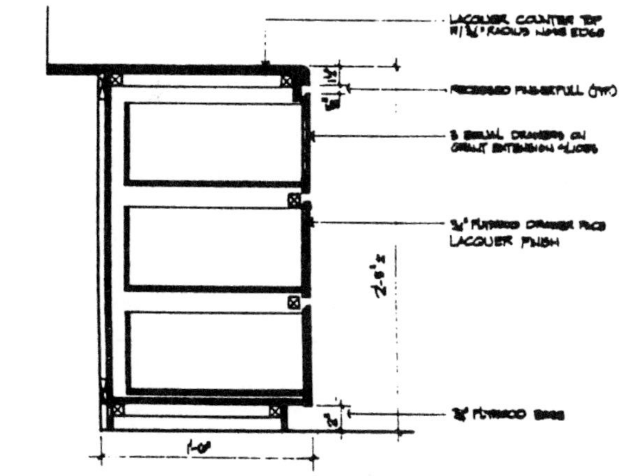

14/A12 SECTION THRU CABINET @ BEDROOM #1
1½"=1'-0"

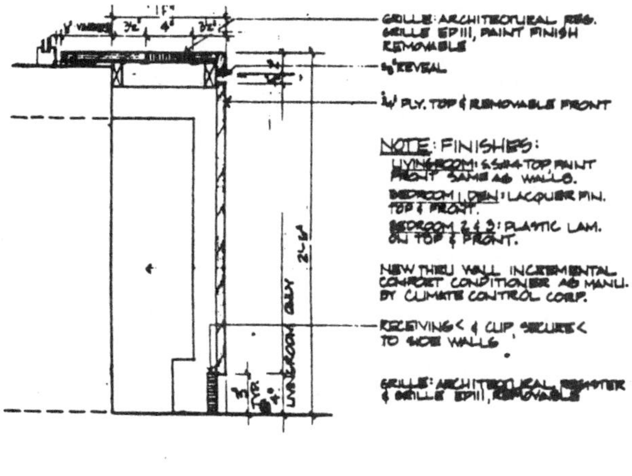

3/A7 SECTION THRU RADIATOR COVER, TYP.
1½"=1'-0"

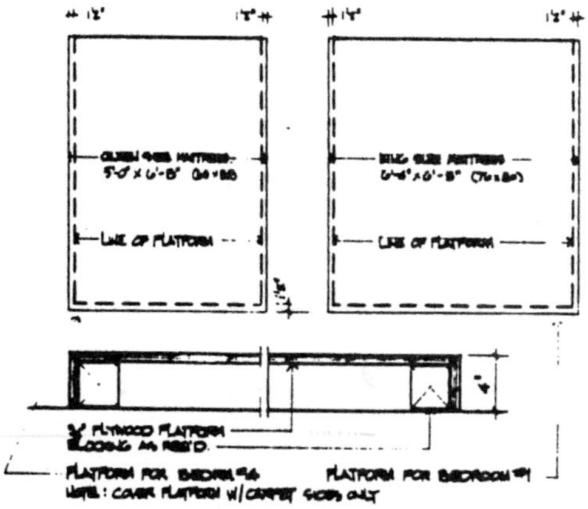

15/A12 PLAN & ELEVATION OF PLATFORMS @ BED #1 & #4
1/2"=1'-0"

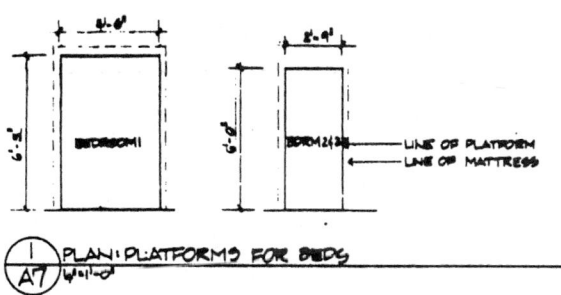

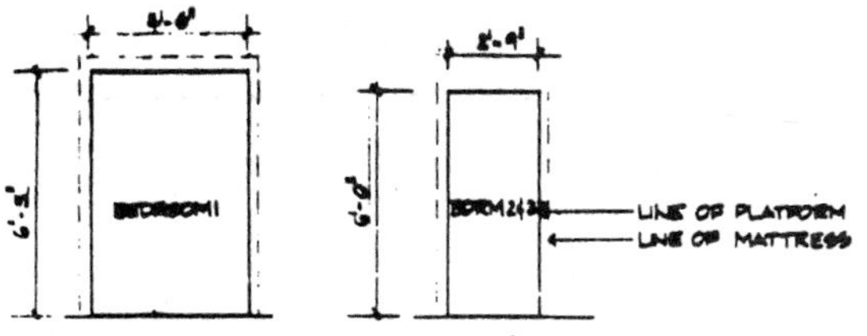

1/A7 PLAN: PLATFORMS FOR BEDS
1/4"=1'-0"

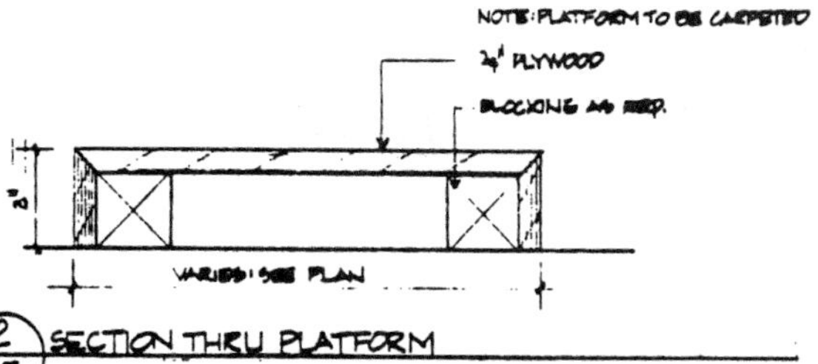

2/A7 SECTION THRU PLATFORM

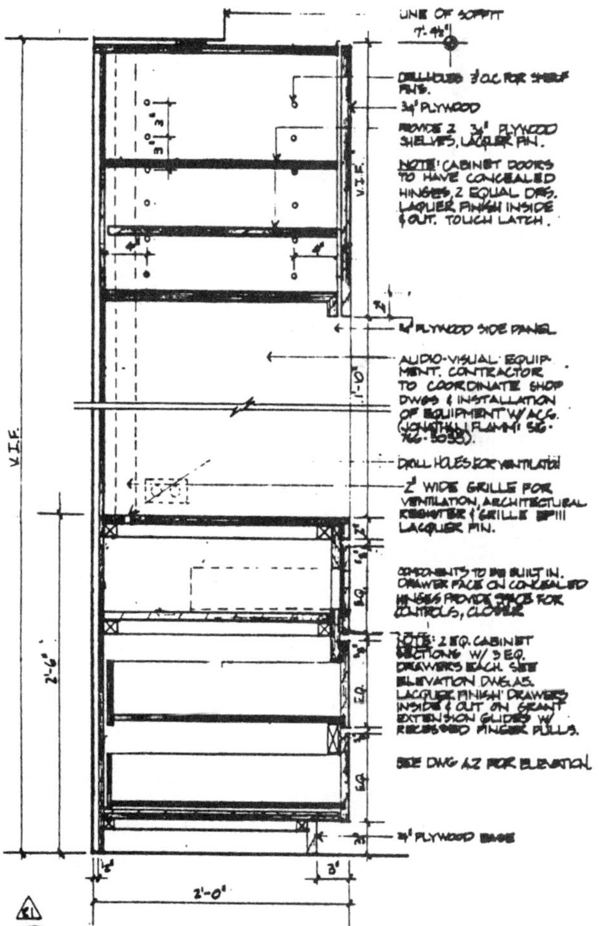

4/A7 SECTION: ARMOIRE BEDROOM 1
1½"=1'-0"

BEDROOMS

Built-in Furniture

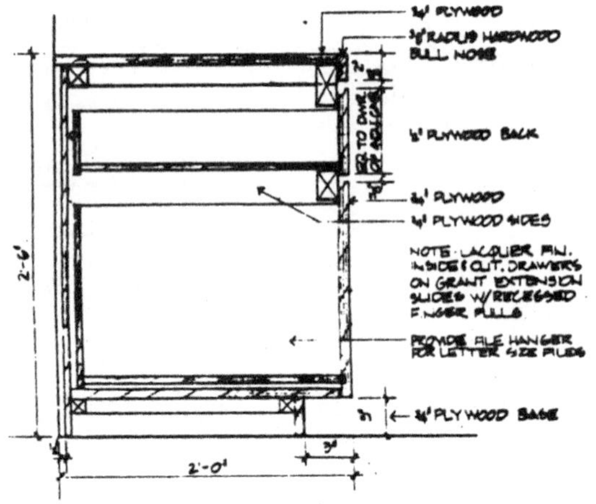

5 A6 SECTION THRU FILE CAB. @ BEDROOM 1
1½"=1'-0"

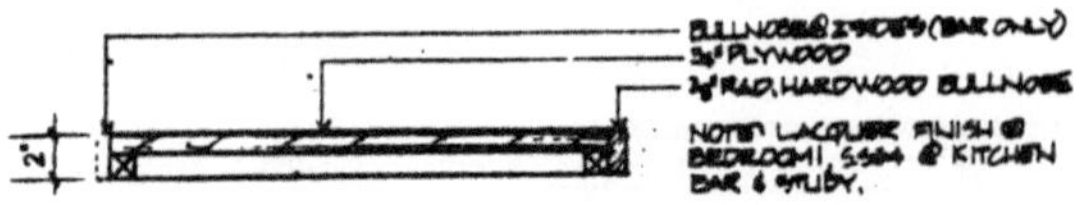

7 A7 SECTION THRU DESKTOP-BDRM 1, BAR, STUDY
1½"=1'-0"

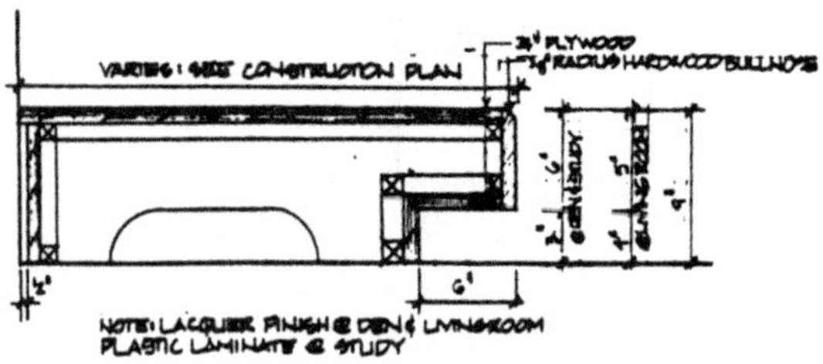

8 A7 SECTION THRU BANQUETTE - TYPICAL
1½"=1'-0"

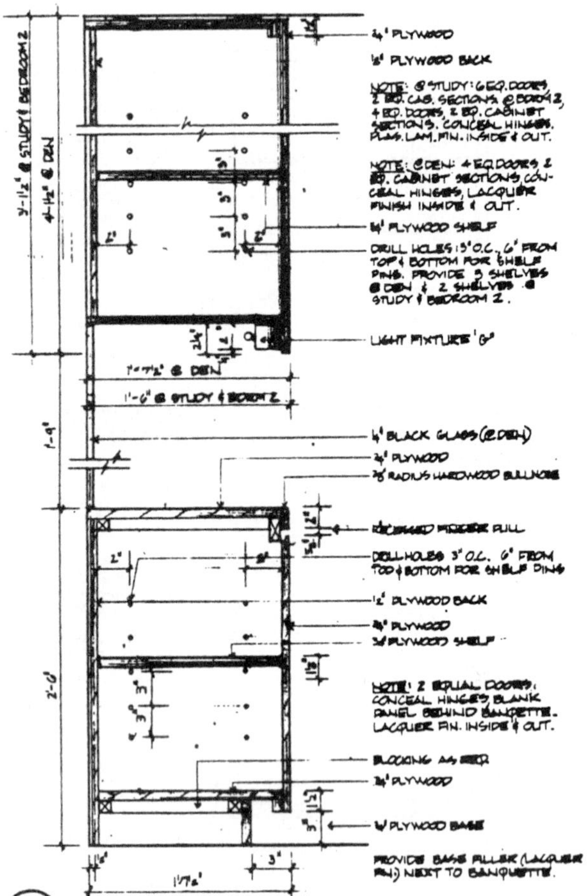

6 A7 SECTION THRU CAB @ DEN WALL @ DEN, STUDY, BDRM 2
1½"=1'-0"

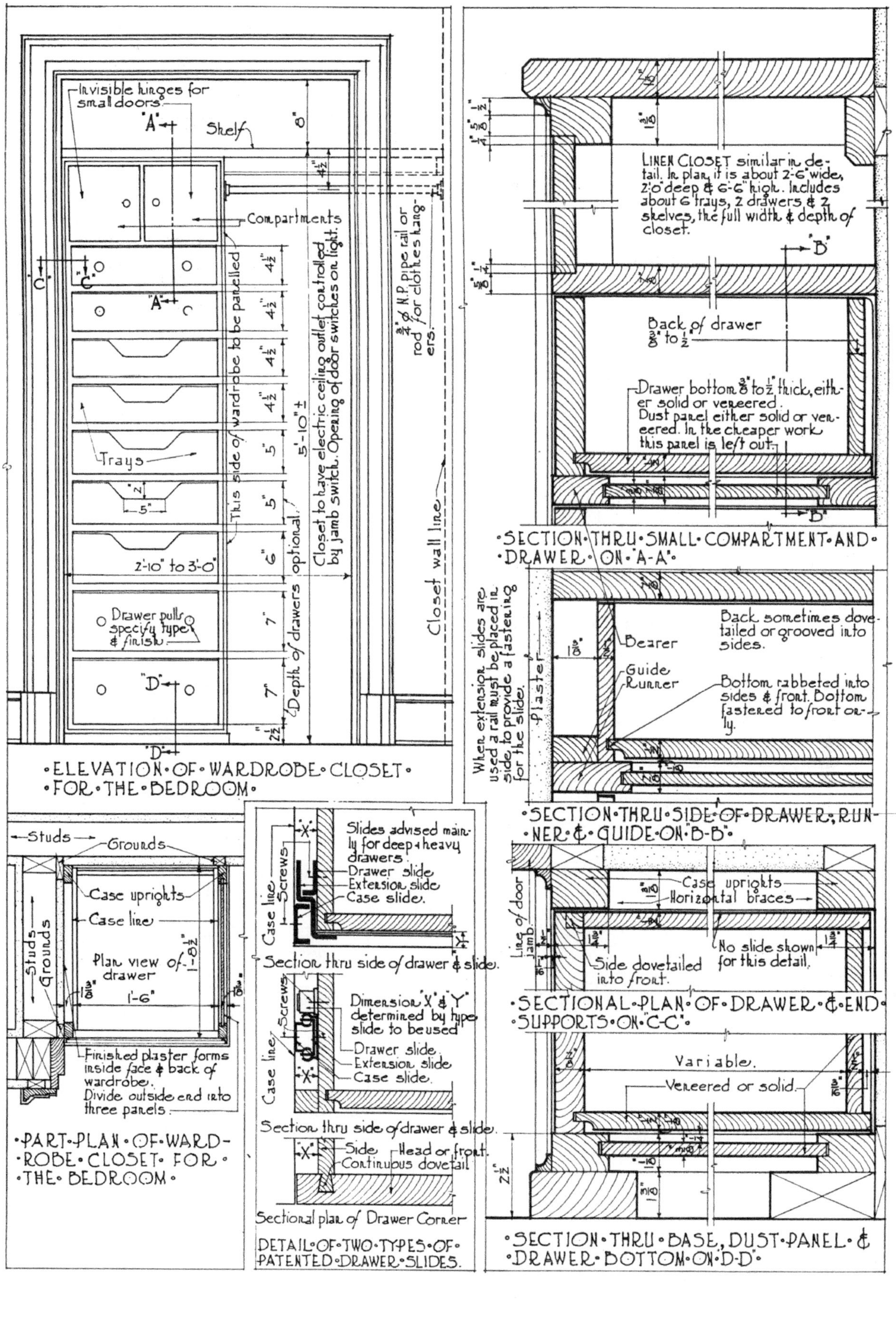
Invisible hinges for small doors
Shelf
Compartments
Trays
Drawer pulls specify type & finish
This side of wardrobe to be panelled
Closet to have electric ceiling outlet controlled by jamb switch. Opening of door switches on light.
3/4" ø N.P. pipe rail or rod for clothes hangers.
Depth of drawers optional
Closet wall line
2'-10" to 3'-0"
5'-10" ±
•ELEVATION•OF•WARDROBE•CLOSET•
•FOR•THE•BEDROOM•
LINEN CLOSET similar in detail. In plan it is about 2'-6" wide, 2'-0" deep & 6'-6" high. Includes about 6 trays, 2 drawers & 2 shelves, the full width & depth of closet.
Back of drawer 3/8" to 1/2"
Drawer bottom 3/8" to 1/2" thick, either solid or veneered. Dust panel either solid or veneered. In the cheaper work this panel is left out.
•SECTION•THRU•SMALL•COMPARTMENT•AND•
•DRAWER•ON•"A-A"•
When extension slides are used a rail must be placed in side to provide a fastening for the slide.
Plaster
Bearer
Guide
Runner
Back sometimes dovetailed or grooved into sides.
Bottom rabbeted into sides & front. Bottom fastened to front only.
•SECTION•THRU•SIDE•OF•DRAWER, RUNNER•&•GUIDE•ON•"B-B"•
Studs
Grounds
Case uprights
Case line
Plan view of drawer
1'-6"
Finished plaster forms inside face & back of wardrobe.
Divide outside end into three panels.
•PART•PLAN•OF•WARDROBE•CLOSET•FOR•THE•BEDROOM•
Slides advised mainly for deep & heavy drawers.
Drawer slide
Extension slide
Case slide
Screws
Case line
Section thru side of drawer & slide.
Dimension "X" & "Y" determined by type slide to be used
Side
Head or front.
Continuous dovetail
Sectional plan of Drawer Corner
DETAIL•OF•TWO•TYPES•OF•PATENTED•DRAWER•SLIDES.
Line of door jamb
Case uprights
Horizontal braces
No slide shown for this detail.
Side dovetailed into front.
•SECTIONAL•PLAN•OF•DRAWER•&•END•SUPPORTS•ON•"C-C"•
Variable.
Veneered or solid.
•SECTION•THRU•BASE, DUST•PANEL•&•DRAWER•BOTTOM•ON•"D-D"•

BEDROOMS
Built-in Wardrobe Details

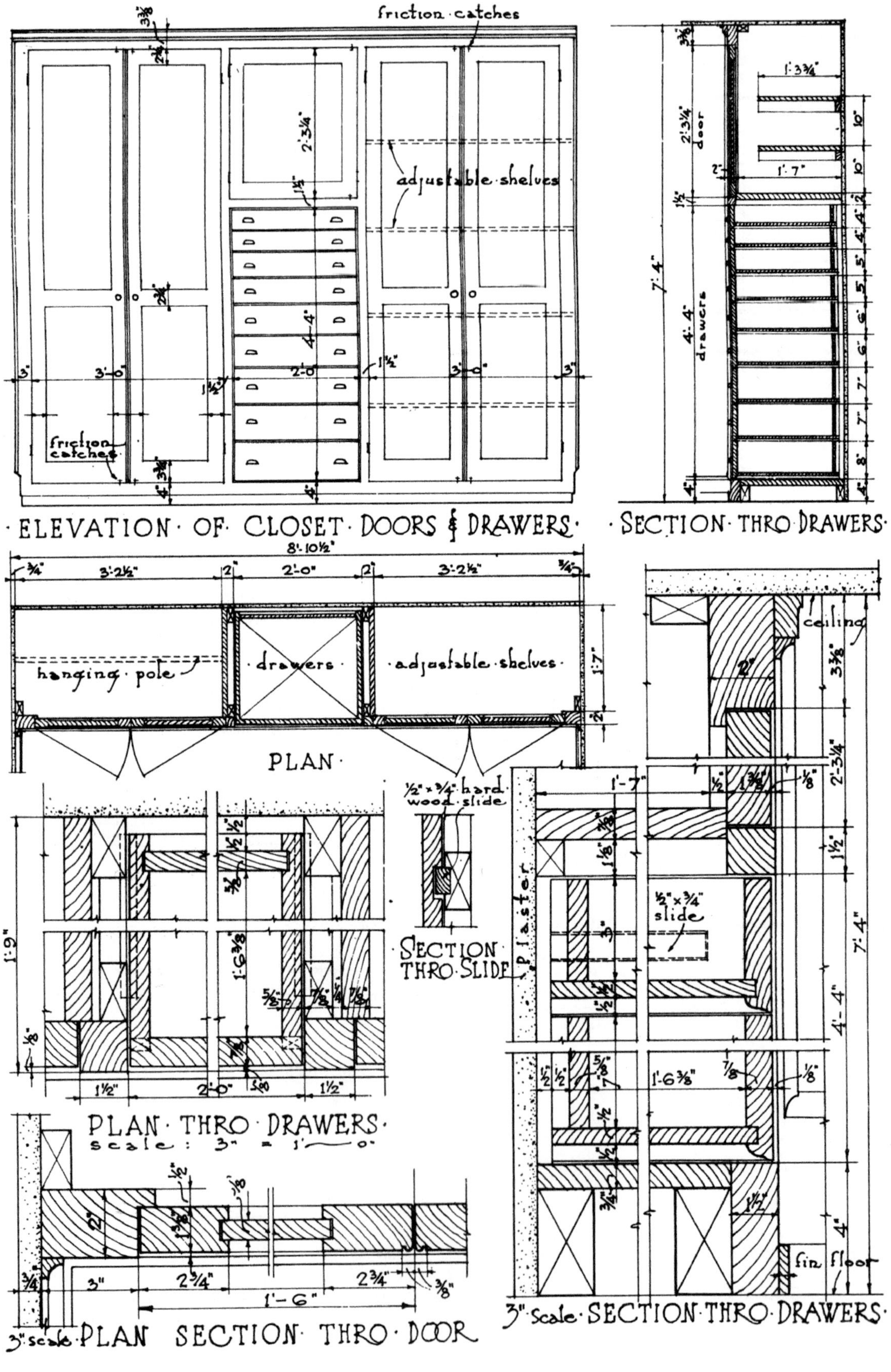
friction catches
adjustable shelves
friction catches
·ELEVATION· OF· CLOSET· DOORS & DRAWERS·
door
drawers
·SECTION· THRO DRAWERS·
8'-10½"
3'-2½"
2'-0"
3'-2½"
hanging pole
drawers
adjustable shelves
PLAN·
½" x ¾" hard wood slide
·SECTION THRO·SLIDE
PLAN· THRO· DRAWERS·
scale: 3" = 1'—0·
ceiling
plaster
½" x ¾" slide
fin floor
3" Scale· SECTION·THRO·DRAWERS·
3" scale PLAN SECTION· THRO· DOOR

BEDROOMS
Plan and Elevation of Walk-in Closet

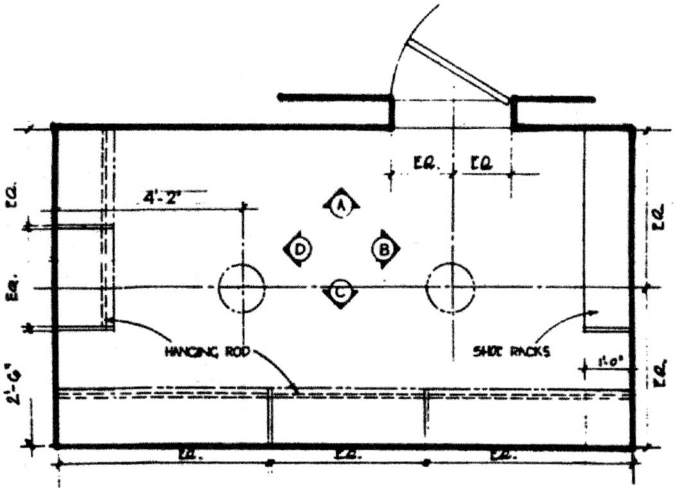

PLAN

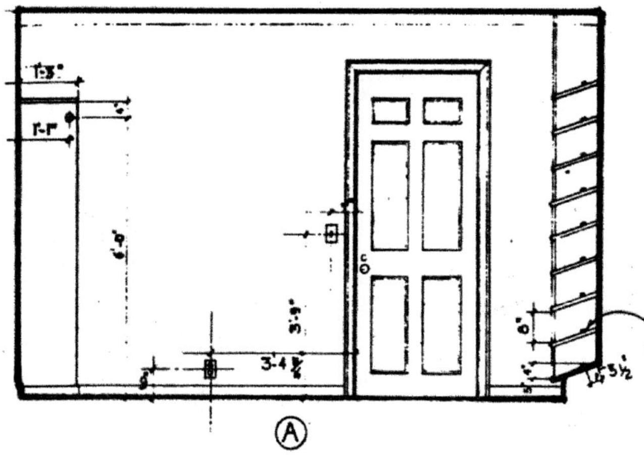

Ⓐ

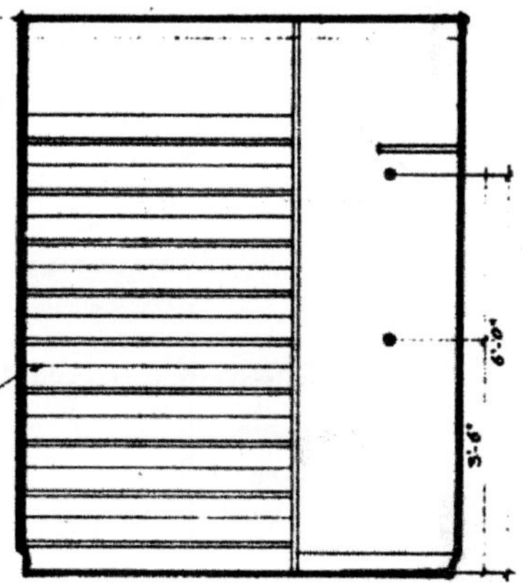

Ⓑ

NOTE: ALL HANG'G RODS TO BE METAL

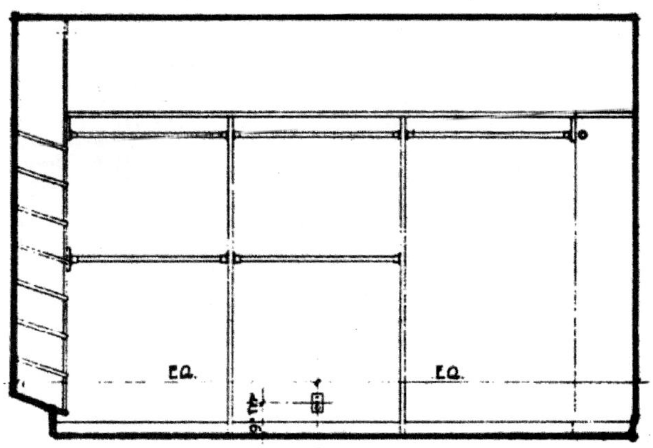

Ⓒ

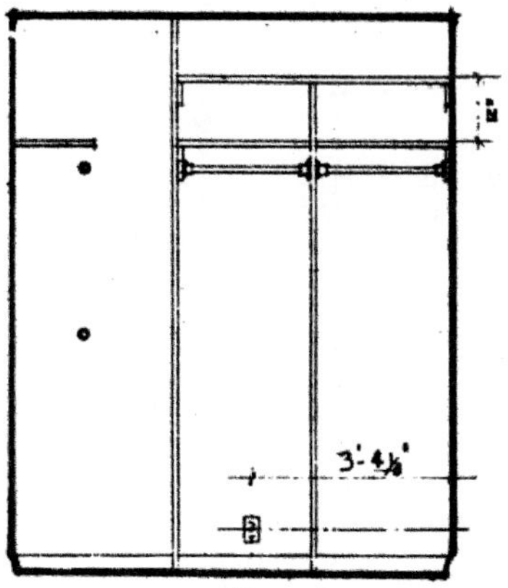

Ⓓ

BEDROOMS

Built-in Furniture and Closet Details

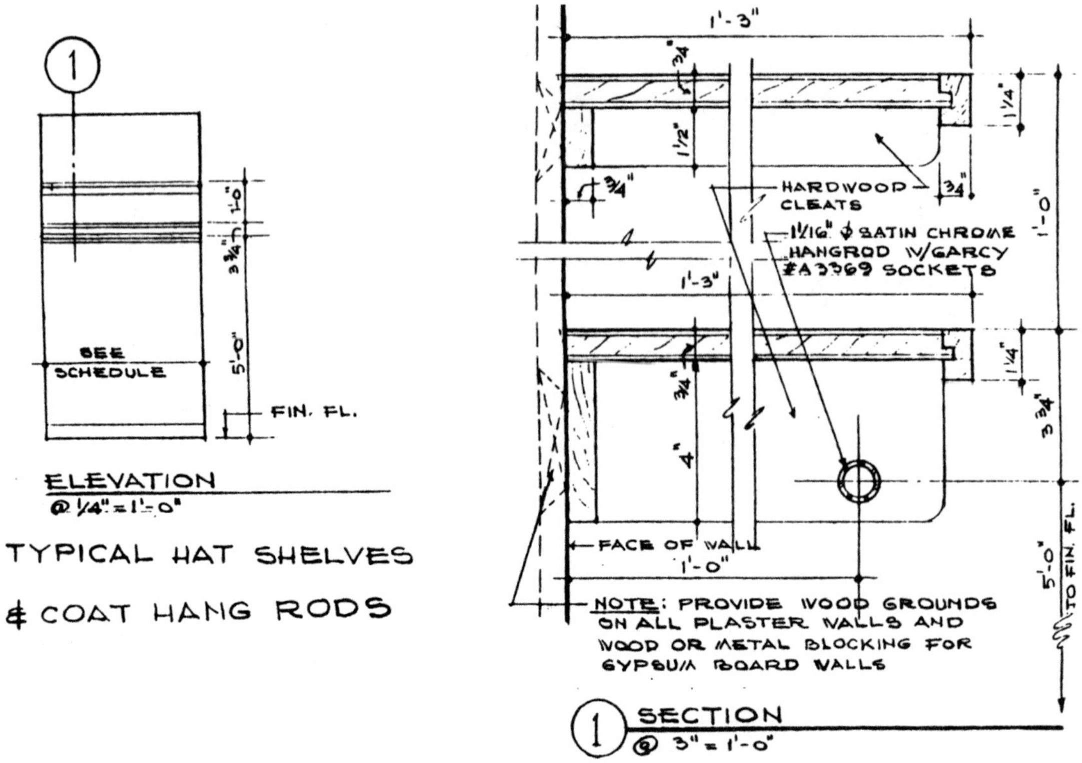

(a)

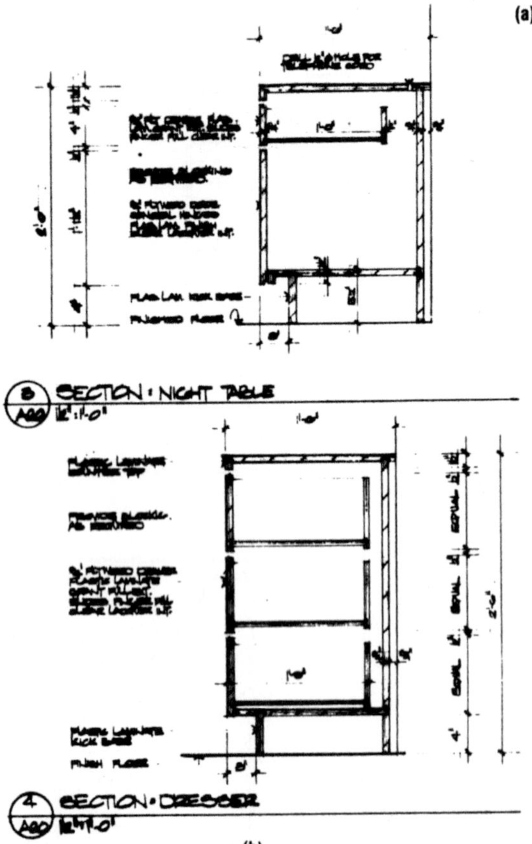

(b)

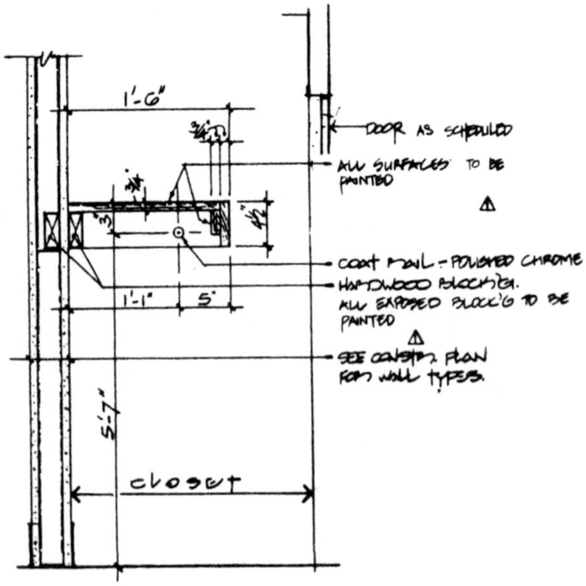

(c)

Fig. 9 (*a*) illustrates a typical hat shelf and coat rod, while (*b*) shows relatively typical sections through a night table and a dresser; (*c*) illustrates a typical closet

BATHROOMS

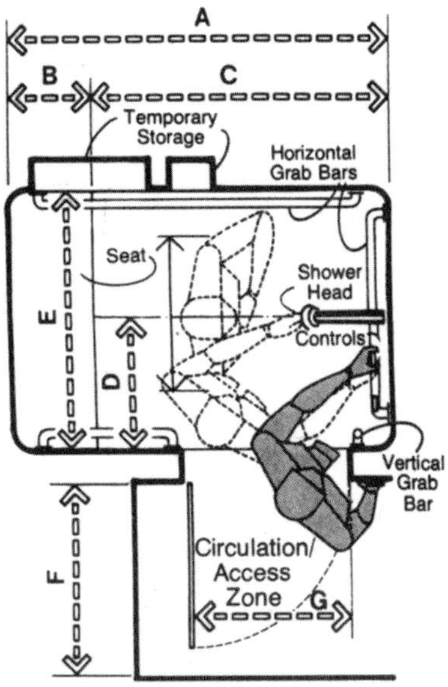

MINIMUM SHOWER CLEARANCES

	in	cm
A	54	137.2
B	12	30.5
C	42 min.	106.7 min.
D	18	45.7
E	36 min.	91.4 min.
F	30	76.2
G	24	61.0
H	12 min.	30.5 min.
I	15	38.1
J	40–48	101.6–121.9
K	40–50	101.6–127.0
L	72 min.	182.9 min.

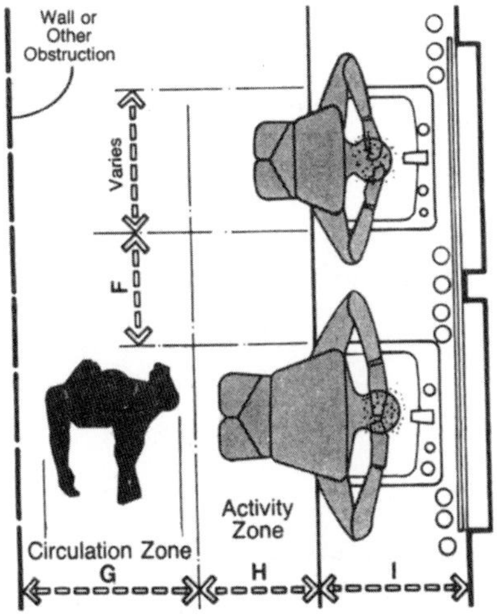

DOUBLE LAVATORY CLEARANCES

	in	cm
A	15–18	38.1–45.7
B	28–30	71.1–76.2
C	37–43	94.0–109.2
D	32–36	81.3–91.4
E	26–32	66.0–81.3
F	14–16	35.6–40.6
G	30	76.2
H	18	45.7
I	21–26	53.3–66.0

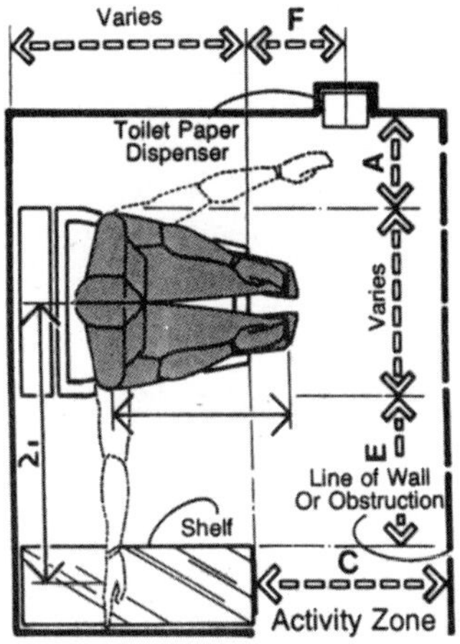

WATER CLOSET

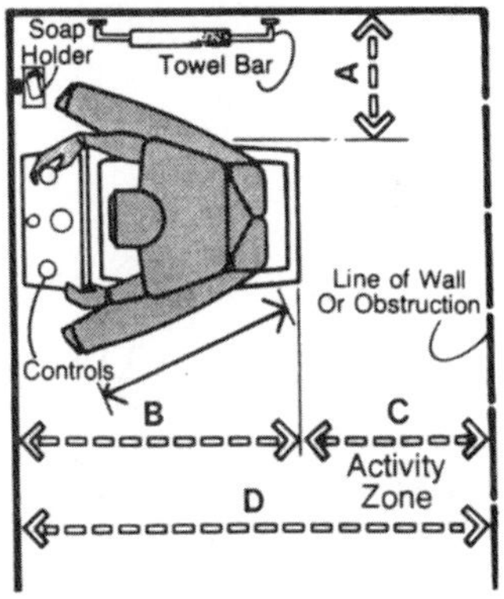

BIDET

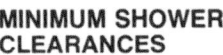

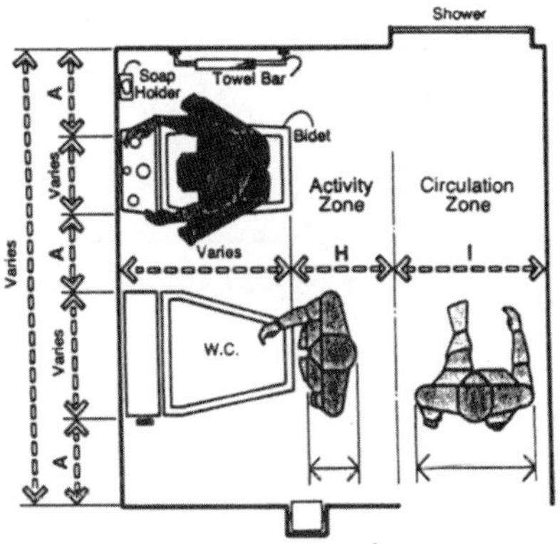

BIDET AND WATER CLOSET

	in	cm
A	12 min.	30.5 min.
B	28 min.	71.1 min.
C	24 min.	61.0 min.
D	52 min.	132.1 min.
E	12–18	30.5–45.7
F	12	30.5
G	40	101.6
H	18	45.7
I	30	76.2

BATHROOMS
Planning Data

PLANNING DATA AND FIXTURE ARRANGEMENTS

A bathroom should have enough area to accommodate a lavatory, a water closet, and a bathtub or shower. Arrangement for fixtures should provide for comfortable use of each fixture and permit at least 90° door swing unless sliding doors are used.

The bathroom should be convenient to the bedroom zone and accessible from the living and work areas. Linen storage should be accessible from the bathroom, but not necessarily located within the bathroom.

Each complete bathroom should be provided with the following:

1. Grab-bar and soap dish at bathtub
2. Toilet paper holder at water closet
3. Soap dish at lavatory (may be integral with lavatory)
4. Towel bar
5. Mirror and medicine cabinet or equivalent enclosed shelf space
6. In all cases where shower head is installed, provide a shower rod or shower door

Each half-bath should be provided with items 2 to 6 from this list.

PLANNING DATA

Figure 1 deals primarily with some of the more critical male anthropometric considerations. A lavatory height above the floor of 37 to 43 in, or 94 to 109.2 cm, is suggested to accommodate the majority of users. It should be noted, however, that common practice is to locate the lavatory in the neighborhood of 31 in above the floor. In order to establish the location of mirrors above the lavatory, eye height should be taken into consideration.

Figure 2 explores, in much the same manner, the anthropometric considerations related to women and children. Given the great variability in body sizes to be accommodated within a single family, a strong

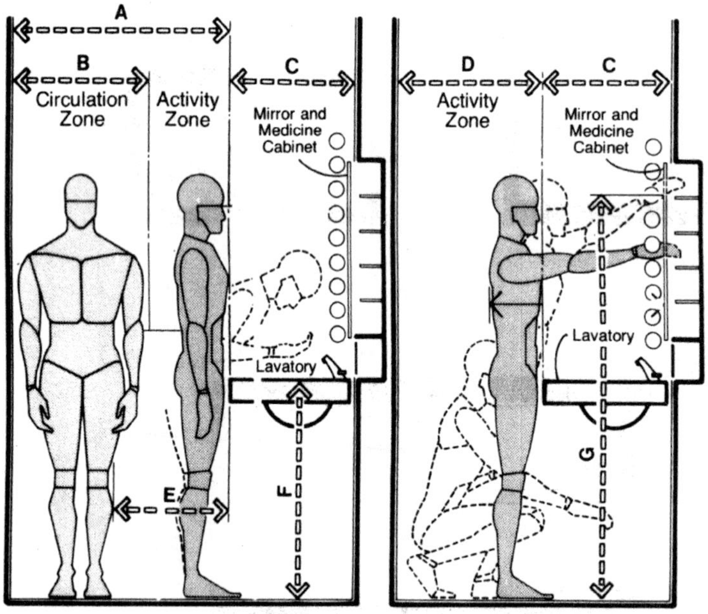

Fig. 1 Lavatory: male anthropometric considerations

	in	cm
A	48	121.9
B	30	76.2
C	19–24	48.3–61.0
D	27 min.	68.6 min.
E	18	45.7
F	37–43	94.0–109.2
G	72 max.	182.9 max.
H	32–36	81.3–91.4
I	69 max.	175.3 max.
J	16–18	40.6–45.7
K	26–32	66.0–81.3
L	32	81.3
M	20–24	50.8–61.0

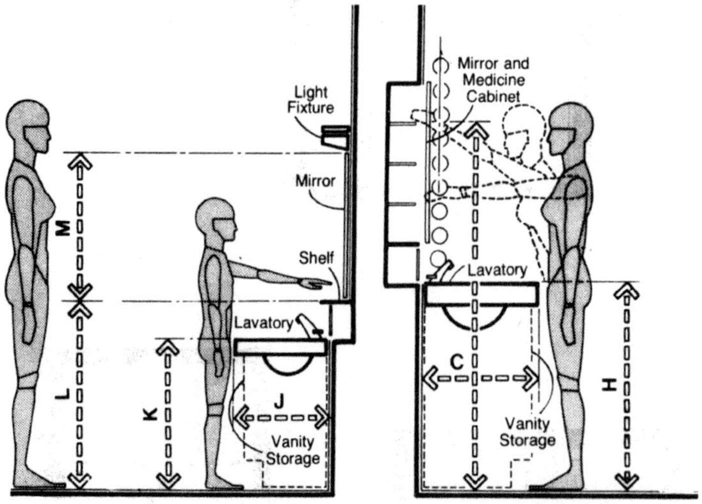

Fig. 2 Lavatory: female and child anthropometric considerations

case can be presented for the development of a height adjustment capability for the lavatory. Until that is developed, there is no reason, on custom installations, why the architect or interior designer cannot take anthropometric measurements of the client to ensure proper interface between the user and the lavatory.

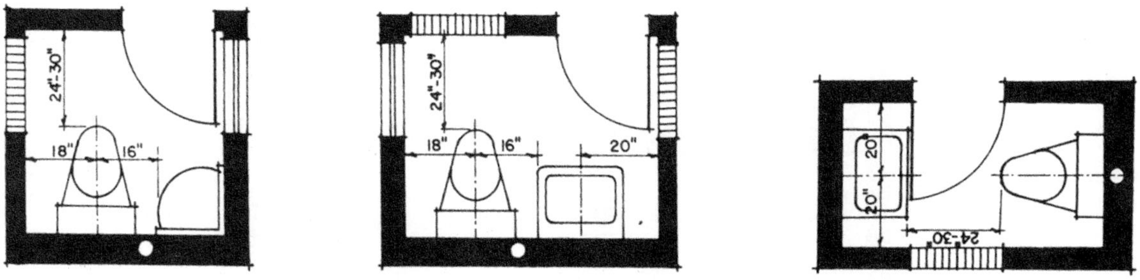

Fig. 3 Two-fixture plans: water closet and washbasin

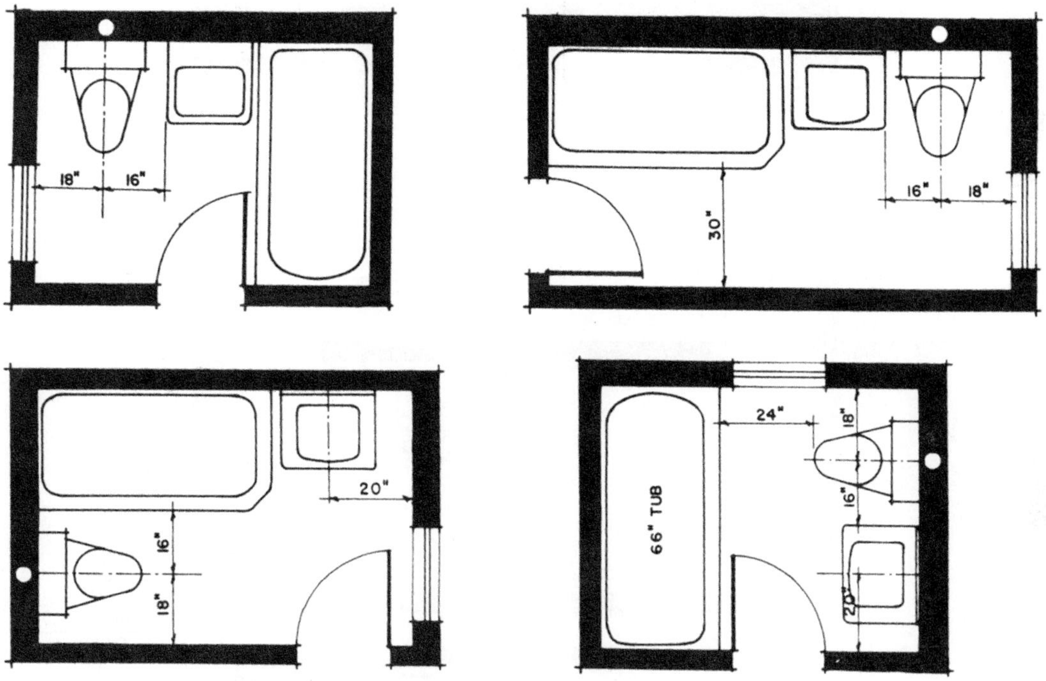

Fig. 4 Three-fixture plans: water closet, washbasin, and tub

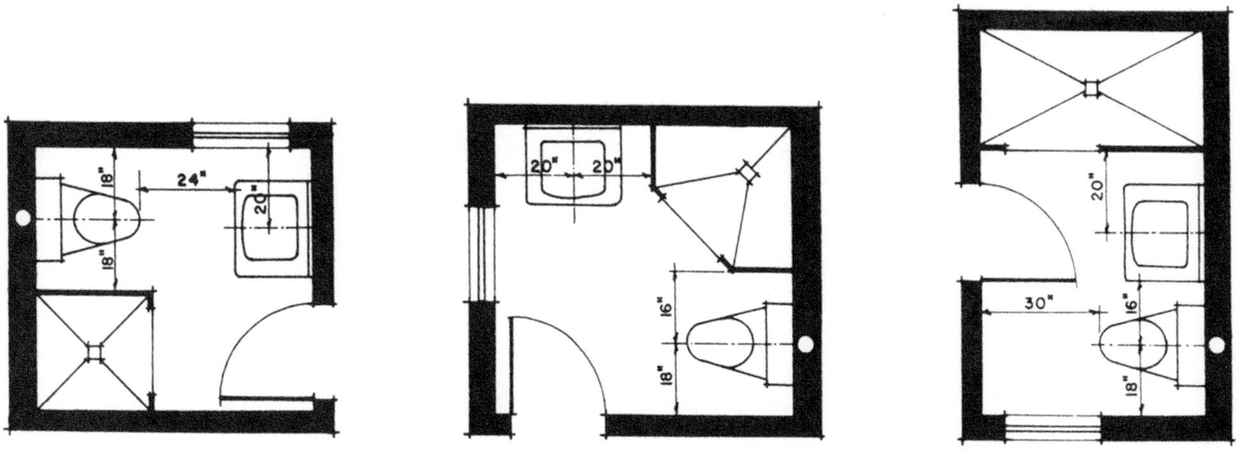

Fig. 5 Two- and three-fixture noncompartmented plans: water closet, washbasin, and shower

BATHROOMS
Typical Plans and Fixture Arrangements

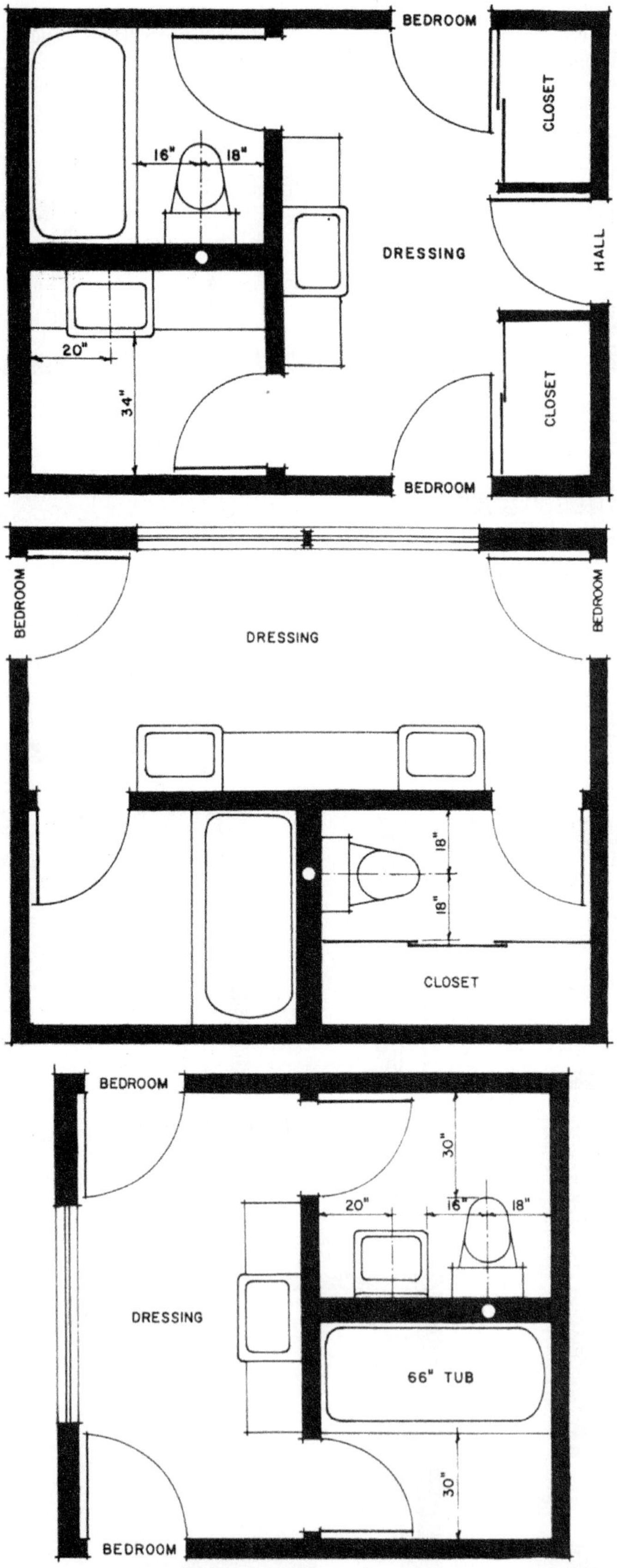

Fig. 6 Four-fixture compartmented plans: water closet, tub, and two washbasins

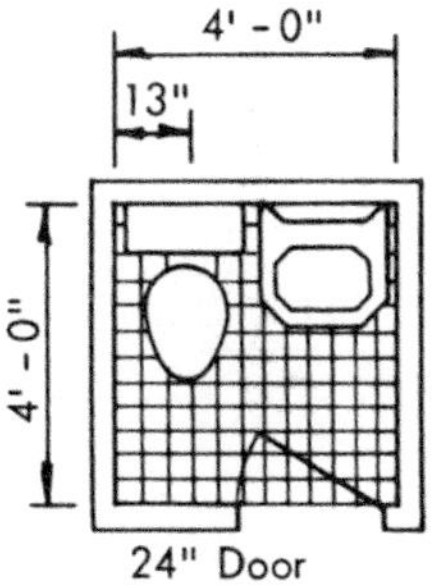

Minimum half-bath.
16 ft² is about minimum for standard fixtures; 4'-6"x4'-6" gives a more spacious feeling.

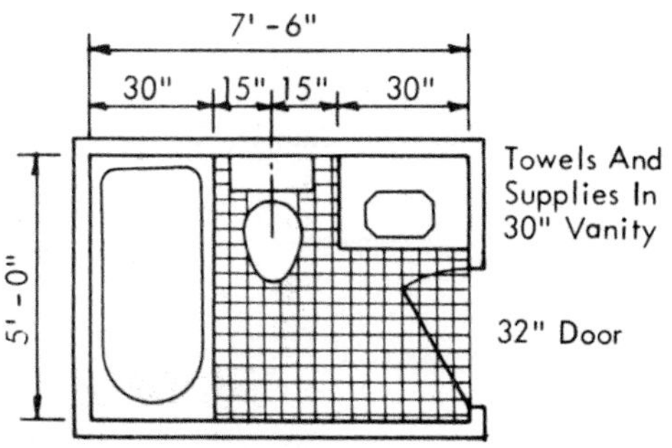

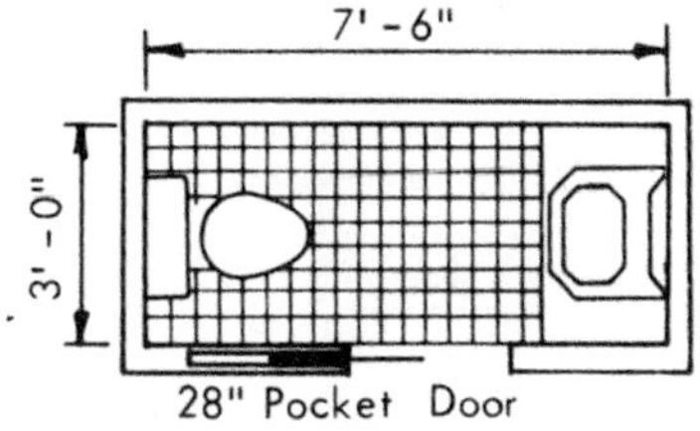

Generous half-bath.
22.5 ft² is a generous half-bath. A wall-hung lavatory instead of a vanity squeezes into 2'-6" width and 16.3 ft².

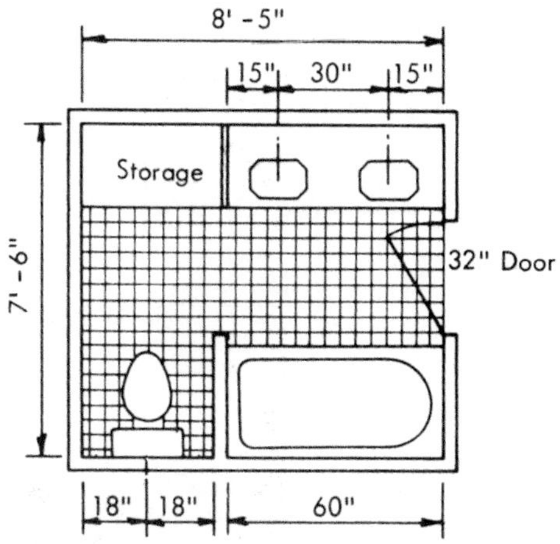

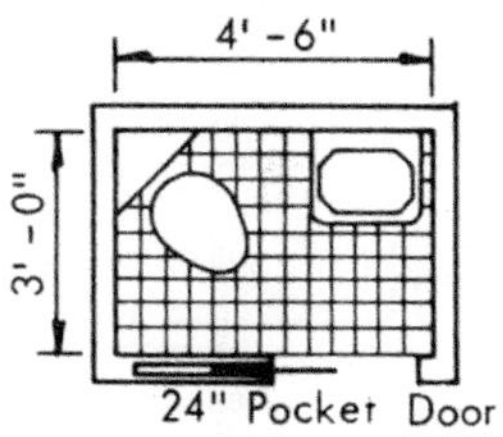

Corner toilet in a half-bath.
A corner toilet and a small lavatory fit 13.5 ft². Consider this idea for installing a half-bath in a closet or under a stairway.

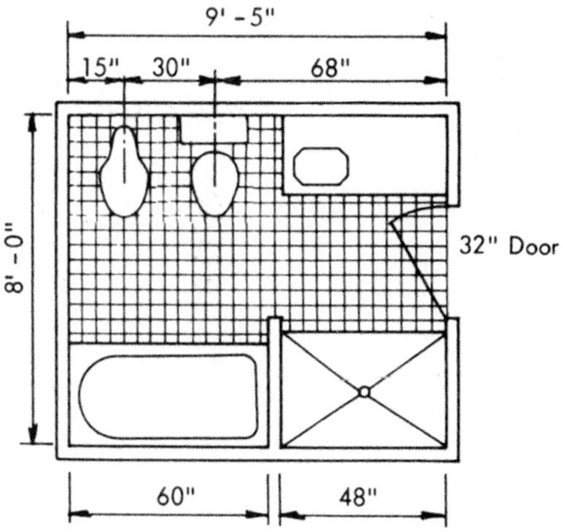

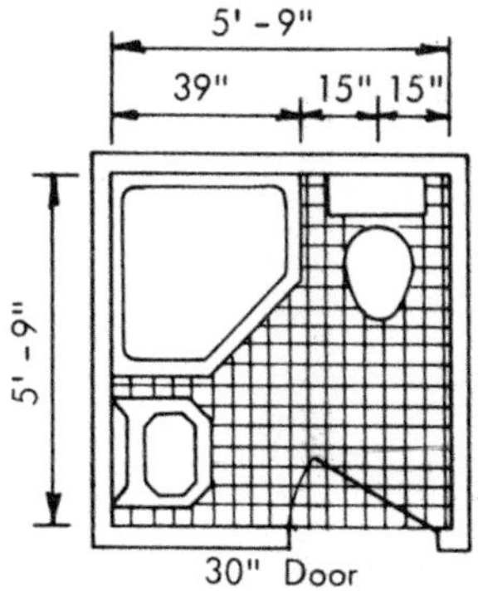

Corner shower.
A corner shower, toilet, and lavatory fit in 33 ft². Very little storage space available.

Small, 3-fixture bathroom.
A small 3-fixture bathroom with limited storage in a built-in vanity meets basic bathroom requirements in a space 37.5 ft². The door is 32" wide for a person with a cane or crutches. This bathroom is too small for a wheelchair.

Two-lavatory bathroom.
A 2-lavatory bathroom with adequate room at the toilet and each lavatory. Note storage space under the lavatories and in a floor-to-ceiling unit. Area: 63 ft².

Separate tub and shower.
This plan also includes a bidet. Storage is in the 48" long vanity. Area: 75.3 ft².

Fig. 7   A wide array of two-, three-, four-, and five-fixture toilet plans

BATHROOMS

Typical Plans and Fixture Arrangements

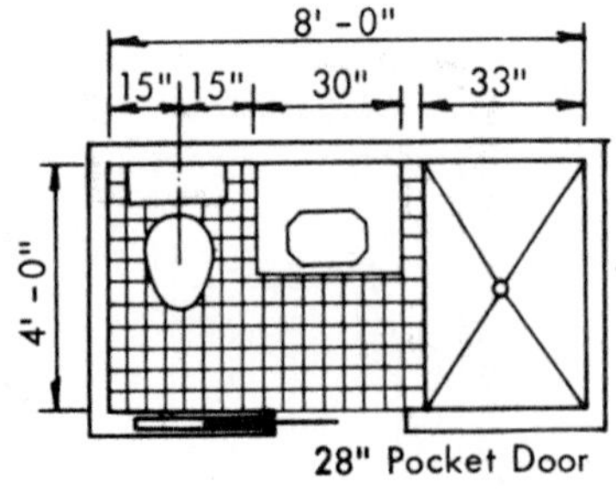

Large shower.
A generous 33"x48" shower is featured in this 32 ft² bathroom. Storage is under the 30" vanity and on shelves over the toilet.

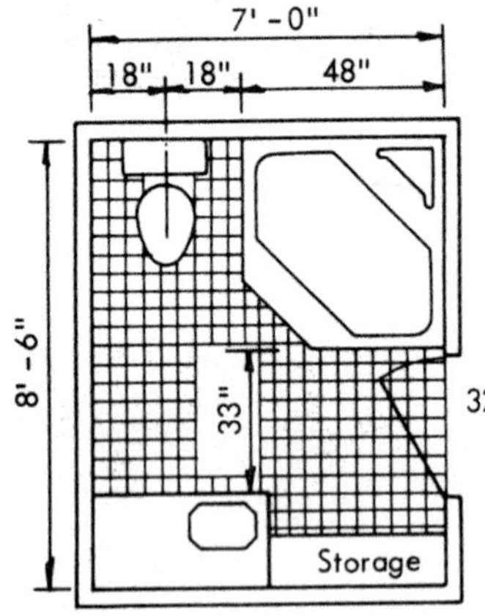

Corner square tub.
Although not usually a space saver, a square tub fits some situations better than a rectangular one. This 3-fixture bathroom has excellent storage but is only 59.5 ft².

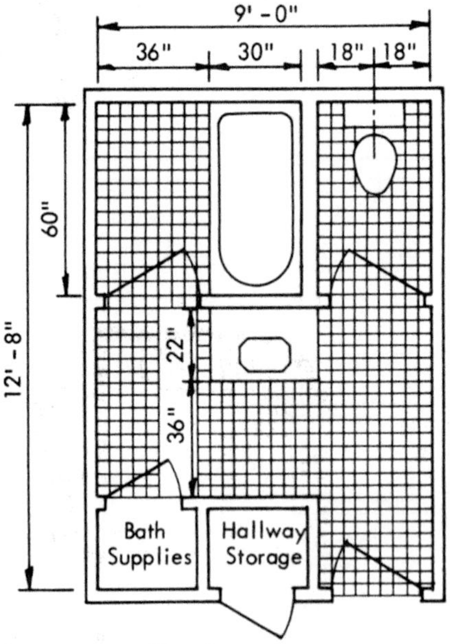

Large 3-fixture bathroom.
With fixtures in separate compartments, this layout can replace a second bath by accommodating more than one person at a time. It is as large as two bathrooms but costs less because of fewer fixtures and less plumbing. Area: 106 ft² plus hallway storage.

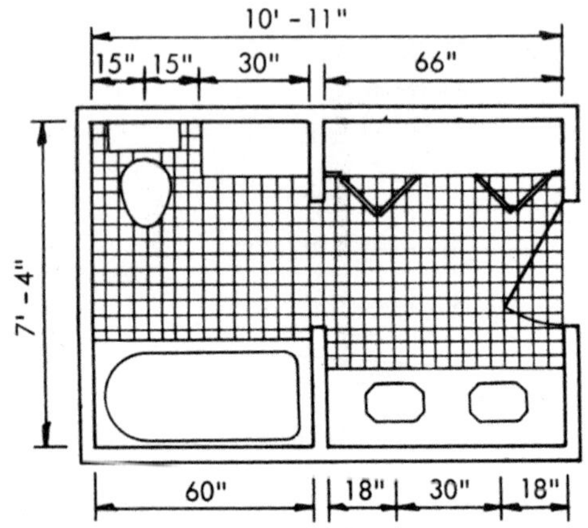

Four-fixtures, two compartments.
Three people can use this bathroom at the same time. Consider a pocket door between the compartments. Even with generous storage space it takes only the same space as many non-compartmented bathrooms, about 80.5 ft².

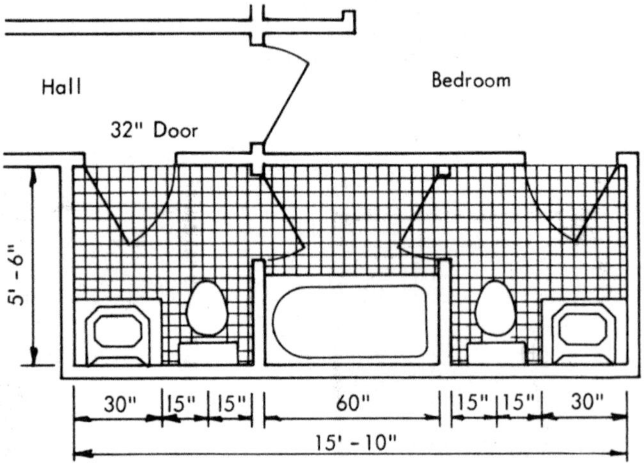

Five fixtures, three compartments.
This bathroom serves as two full bathrooms in 87 ft². Two doors to each compartment are undesirable. Limited storage space available.

Fig. 7 *(Continued)*

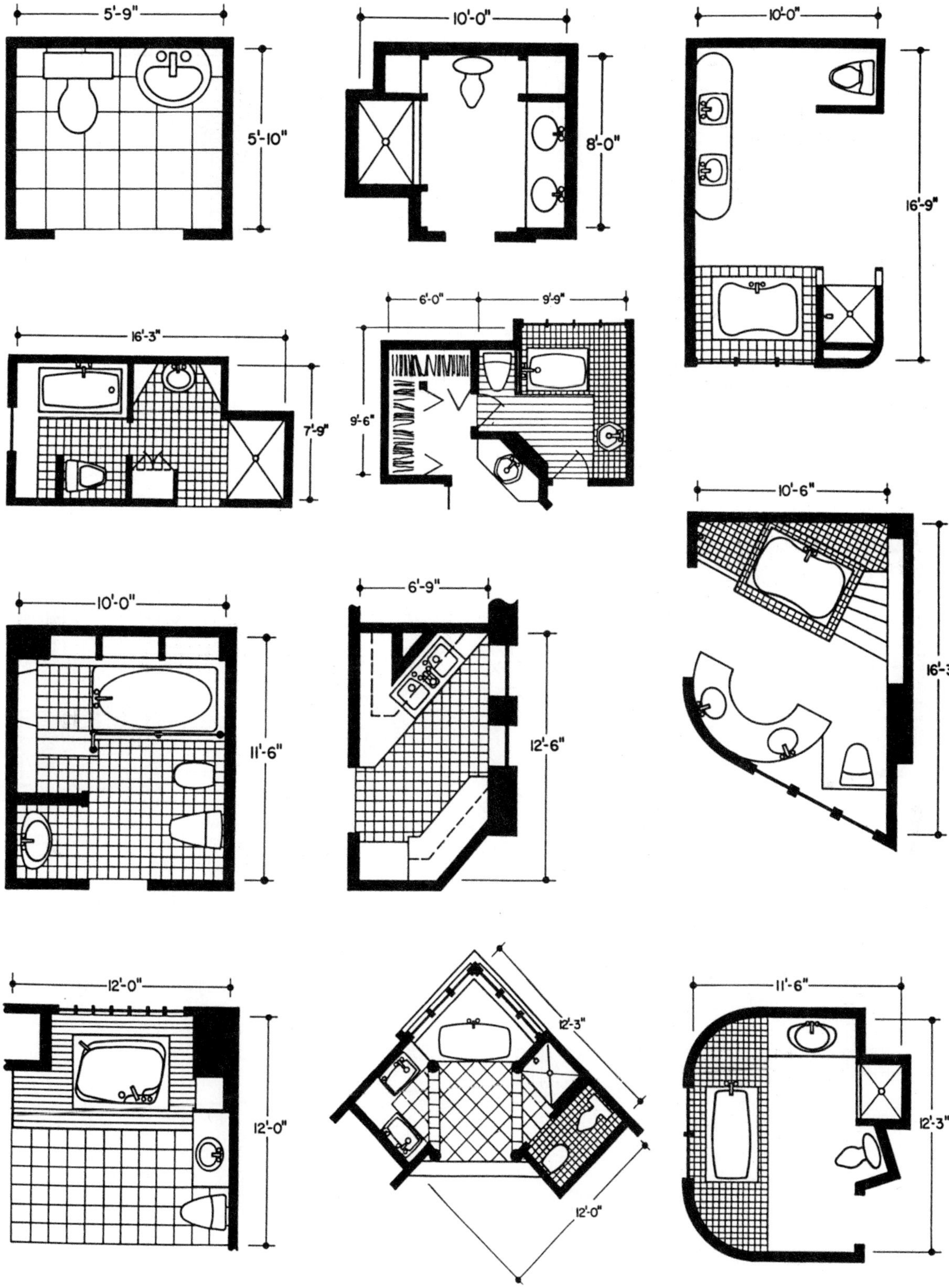

Fig. 8 A variety of design possibilities for the more customized bathroom

BATHROOMS

Custom Designs

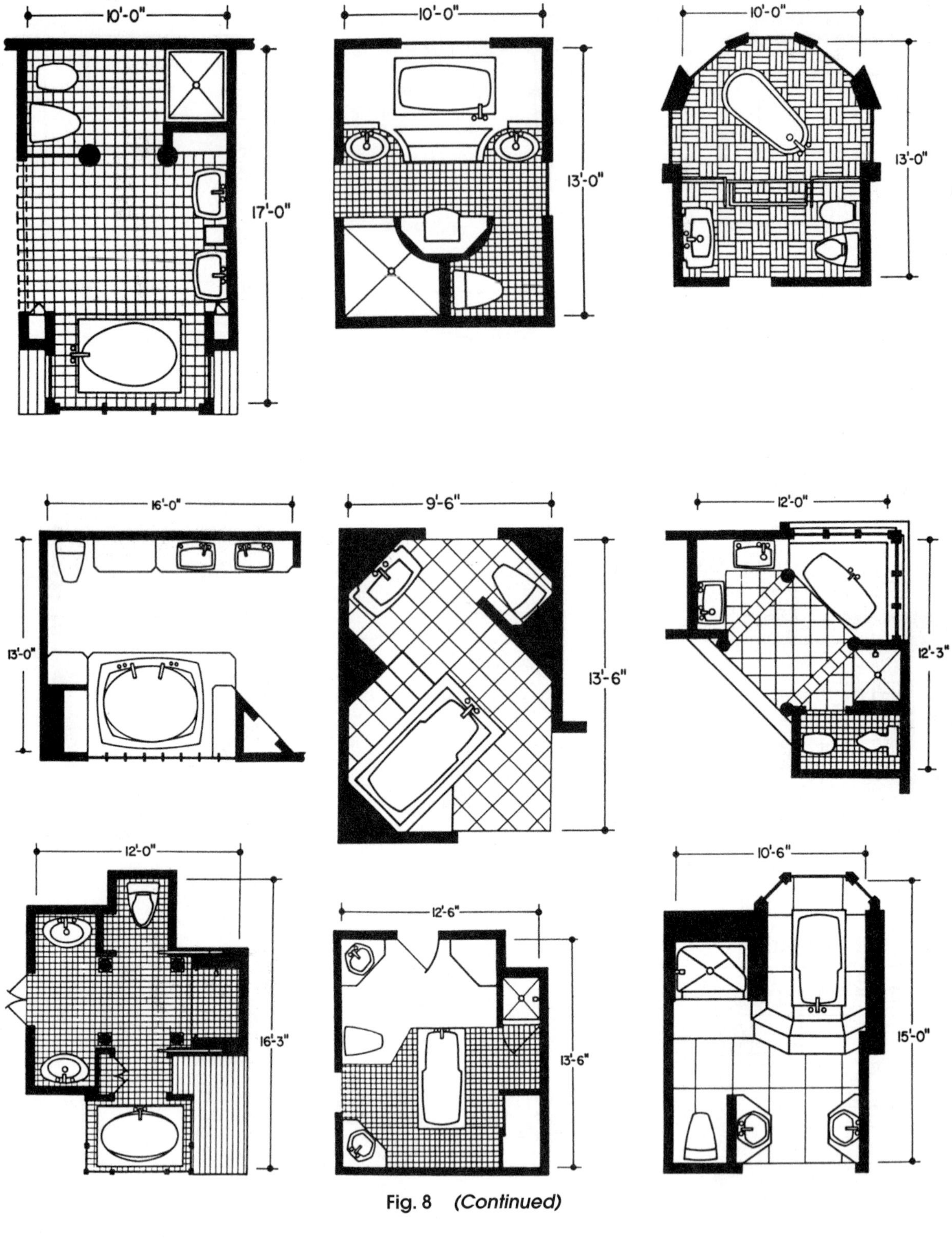

Fig. 8 ***(Continued)***

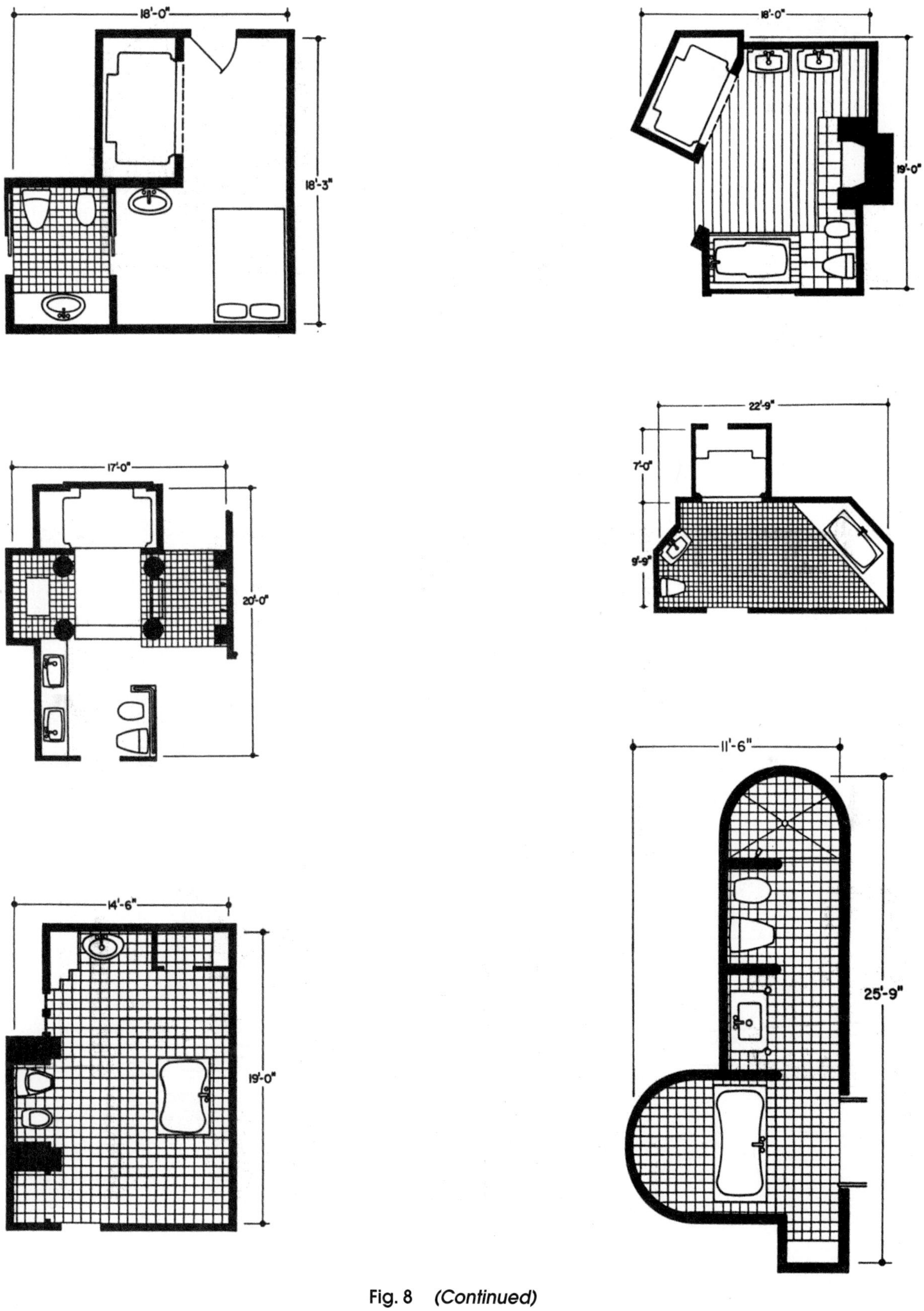

Fig. 8 *(Continued)*

BATHROOMS
Lavatory Types and Dimensions

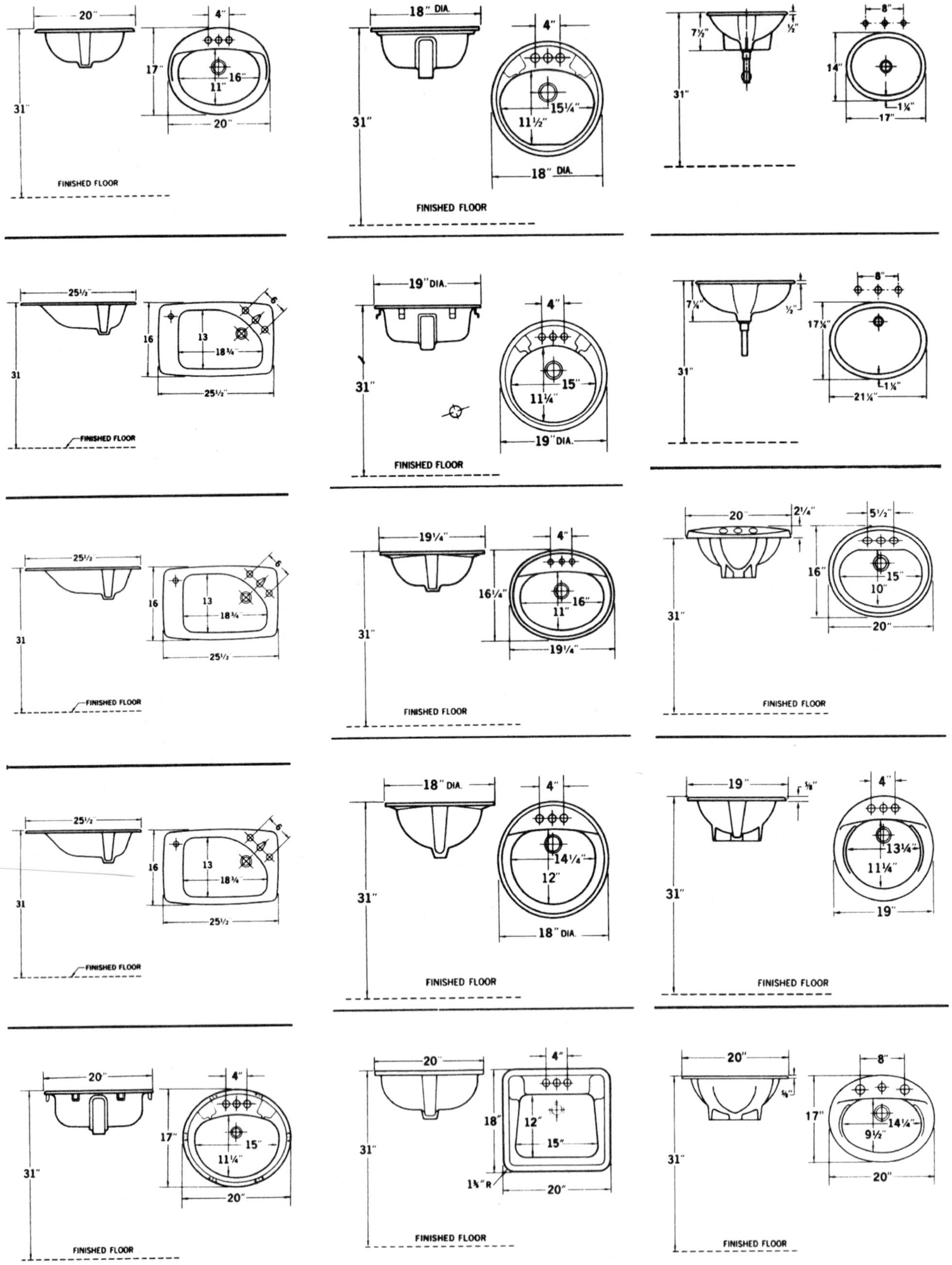

Fig. 9 A selection of countertop lavatories

BATHROOMS
Lavatory Types and Dimensions

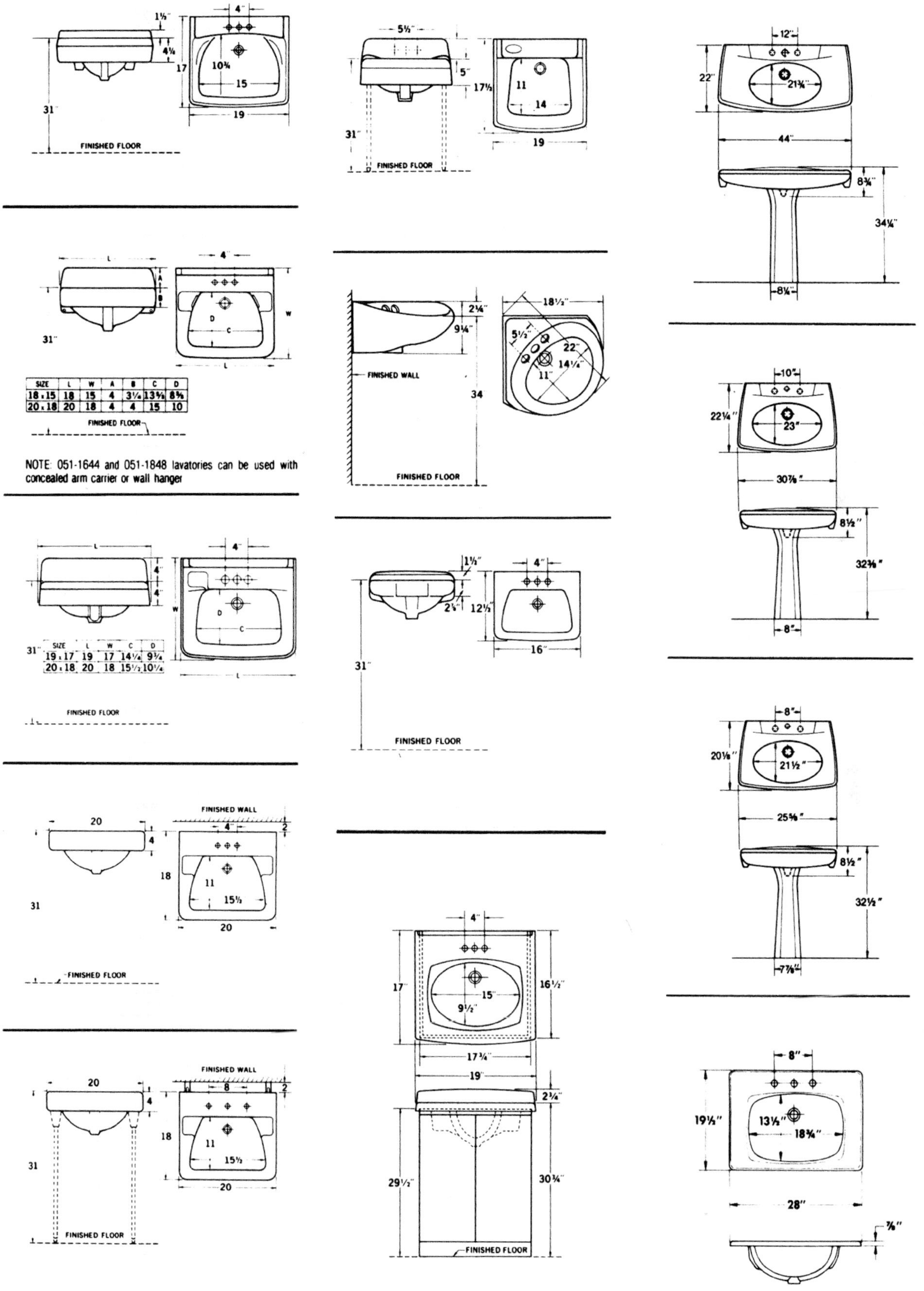

SIZE	L	W	A	B	C	D
18 x 15	18	15	4	3¼	13⅝	8⅝
20 x 18	20	18	4	4	15	10

NOTE: 051-1644 and 051-1848 lavatories can be used with concealed arm carrier or wall hanger

SIZE	L	W	C	D
19 x 17	19	17	14¼	9¾
20 x 18	20	18	15½	10¼

Fig. 10 A selection of wall-hung and pedestal-type lavatories

BATHROOMS

Lavatory Types and Dimensions

Fig. 11 Another selection of lavatories

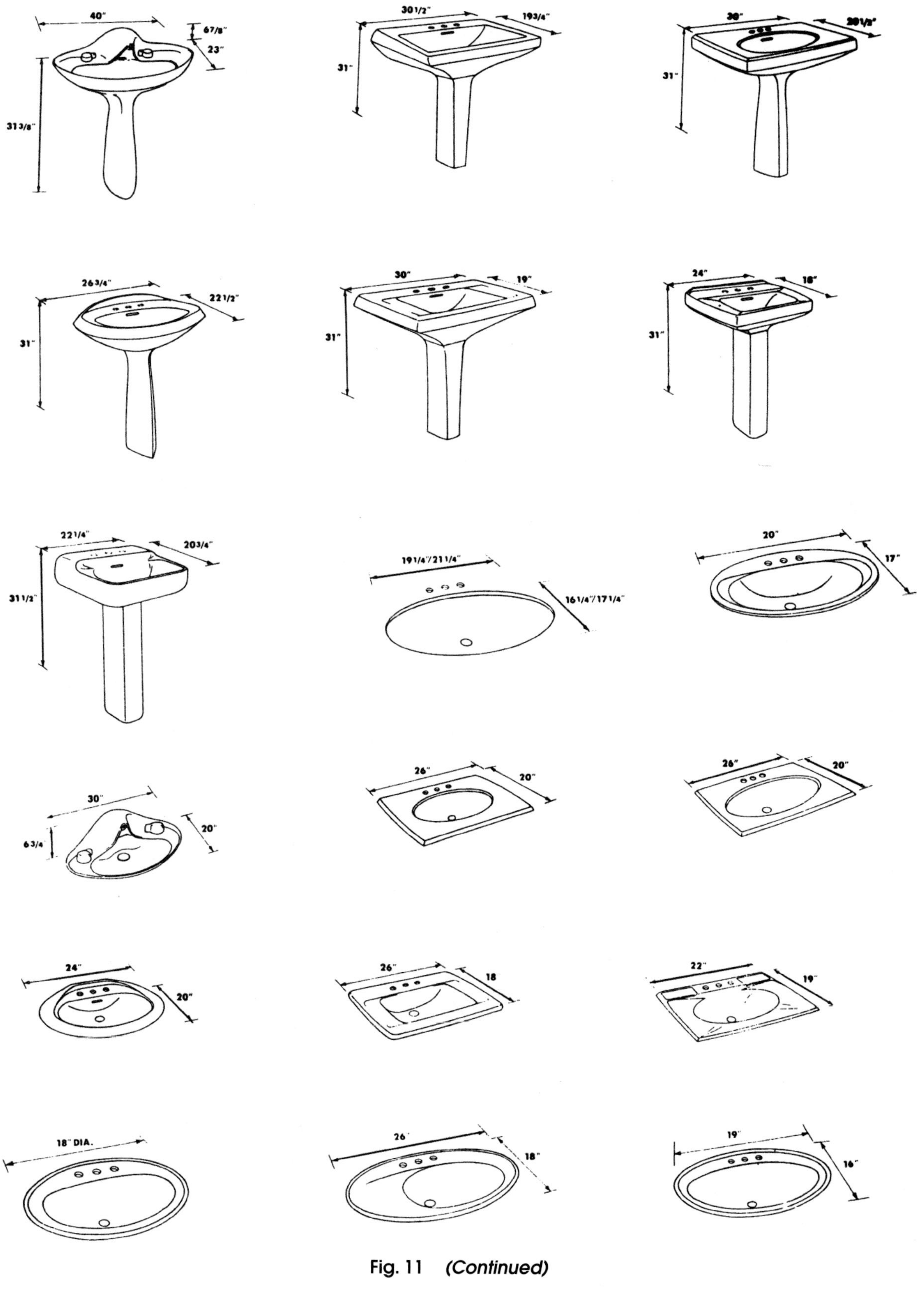

Fig. 11 *(Continued)*

BATHROOMS

Whirlpool Types and Dimensions

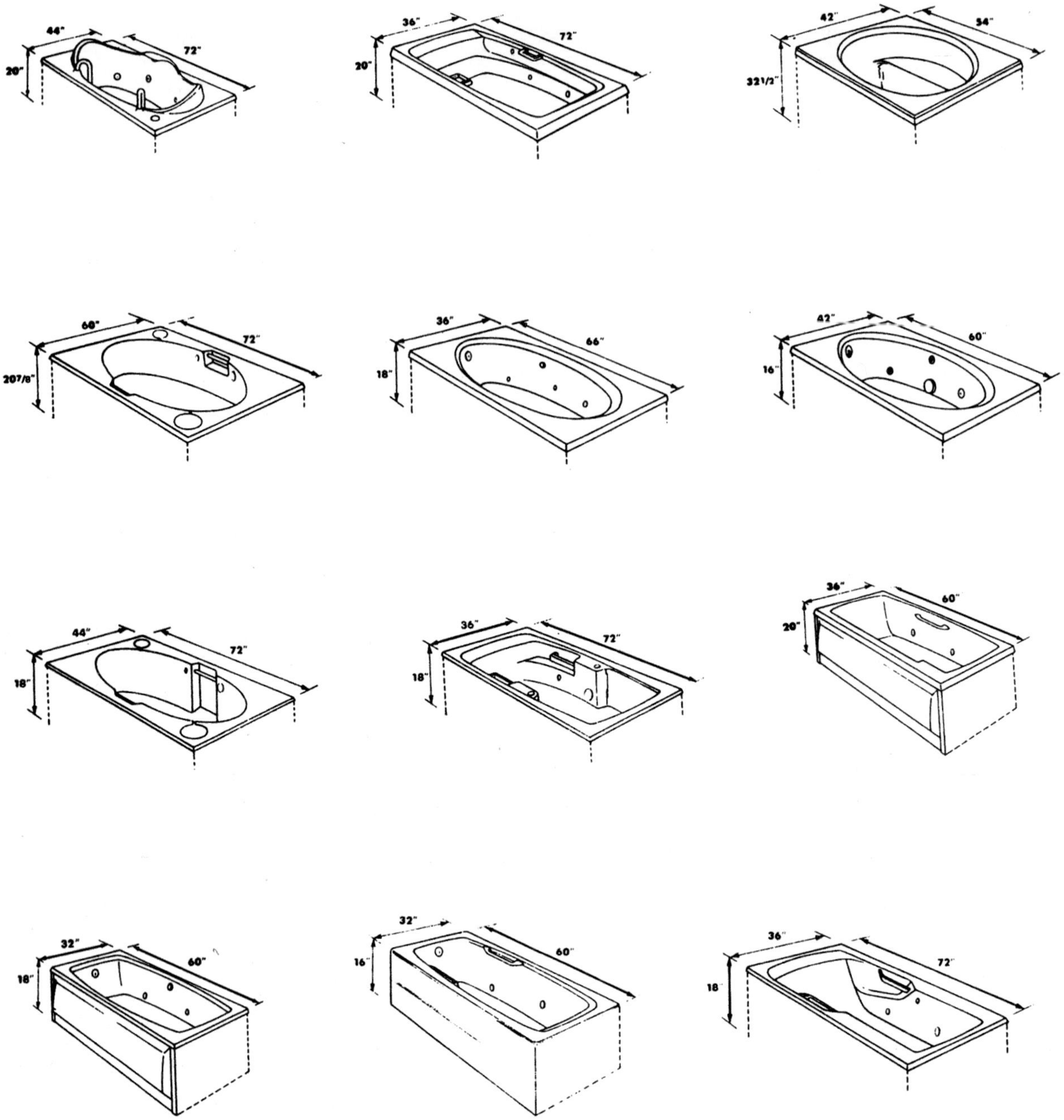

Fig. 12 A selection of whirlpool baths

BATHROOMS
Bathtub Types and Dimensions

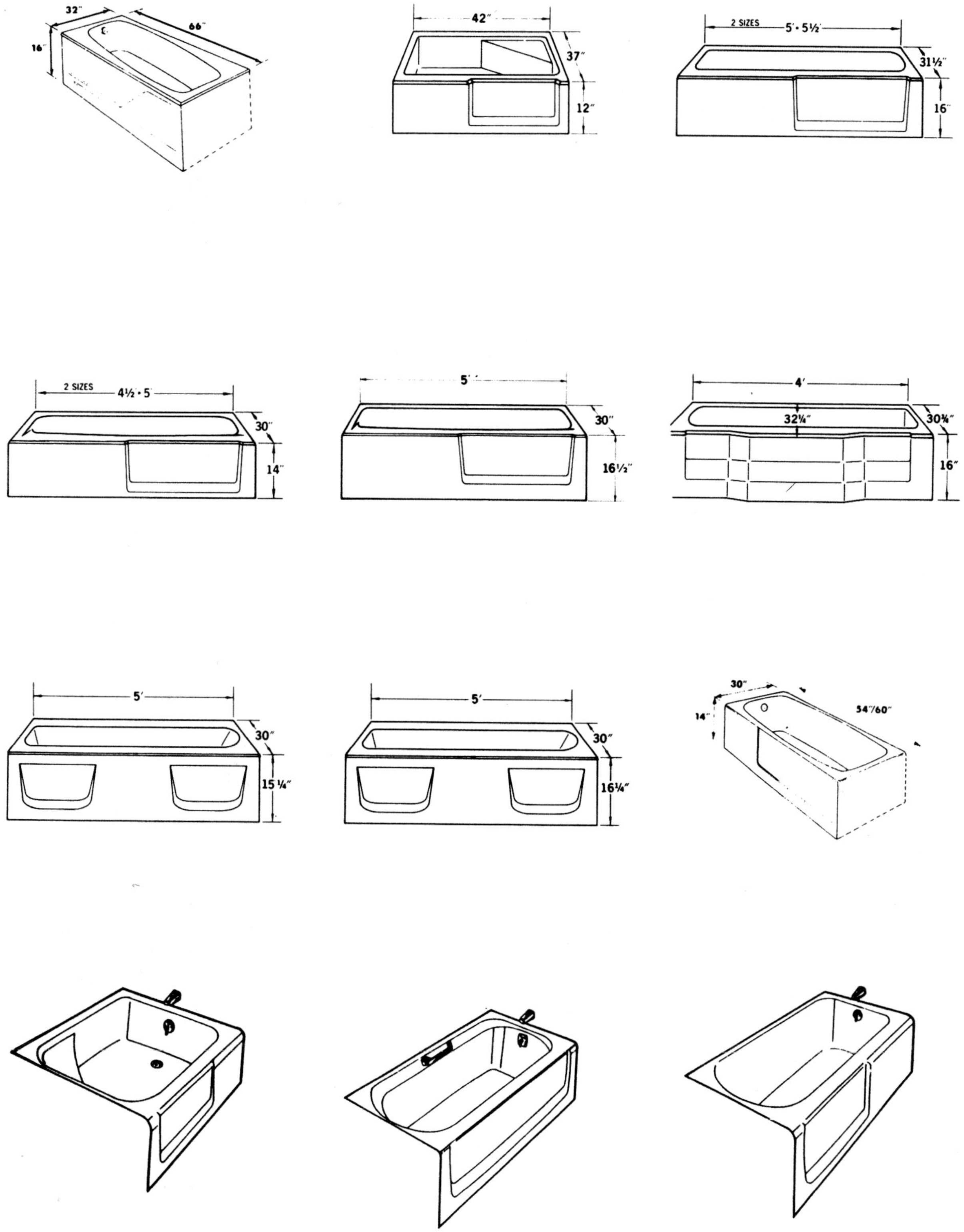

Dimensions: 42" x 37" x 12"

Dimensions: 60" x 31½" x 16"

Dimensions: 60" x 31½" x 16"

Fig. 13 A selection of standard baths

BATHROOMS

Watercloset Types and Dimensions

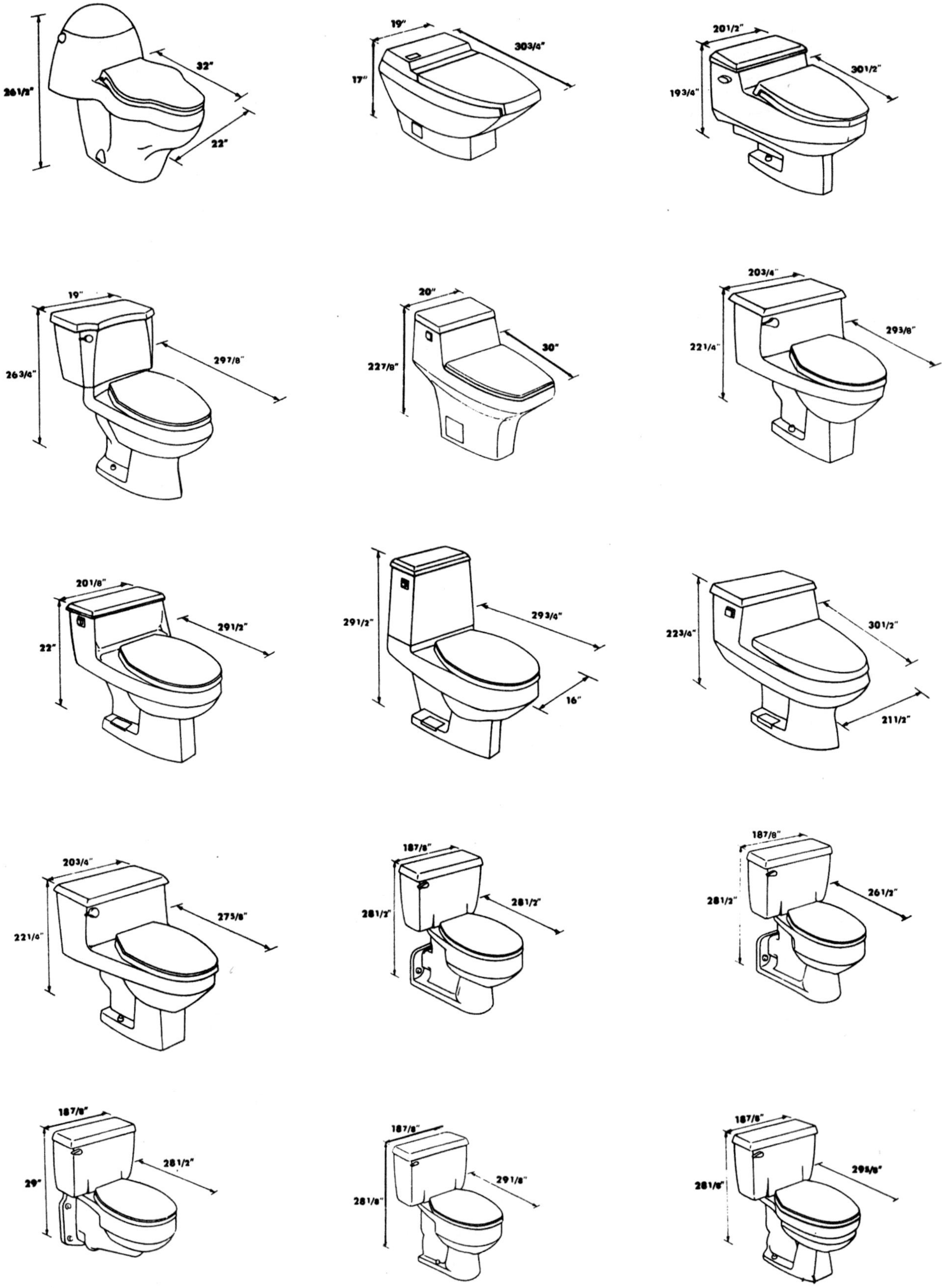

Fig. 14 A selection of water closets

BATHROOMS
Bidet Types and Dimensions

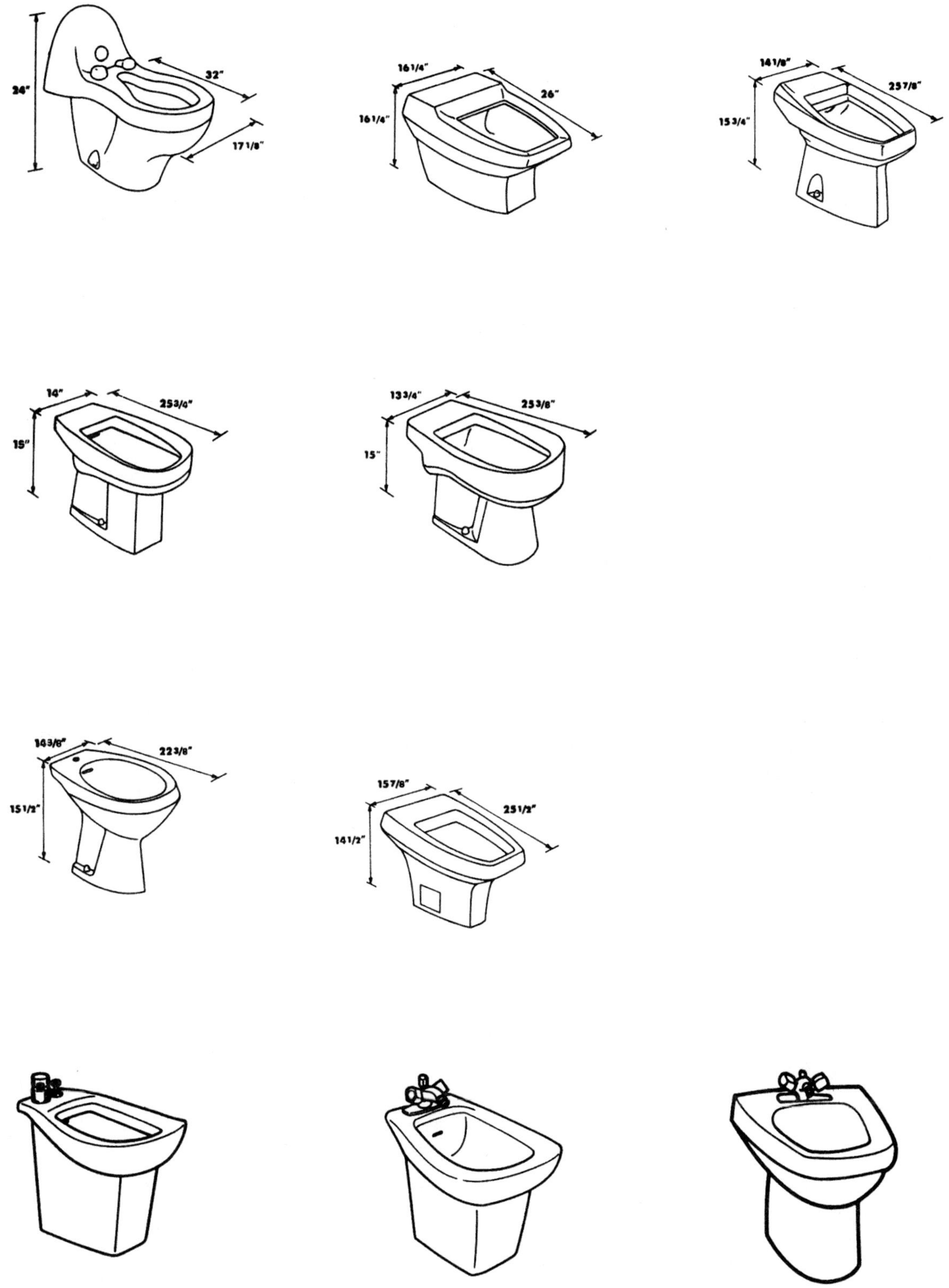

Fig. 15 A selection of bidets

BATHROOMS
Accessories

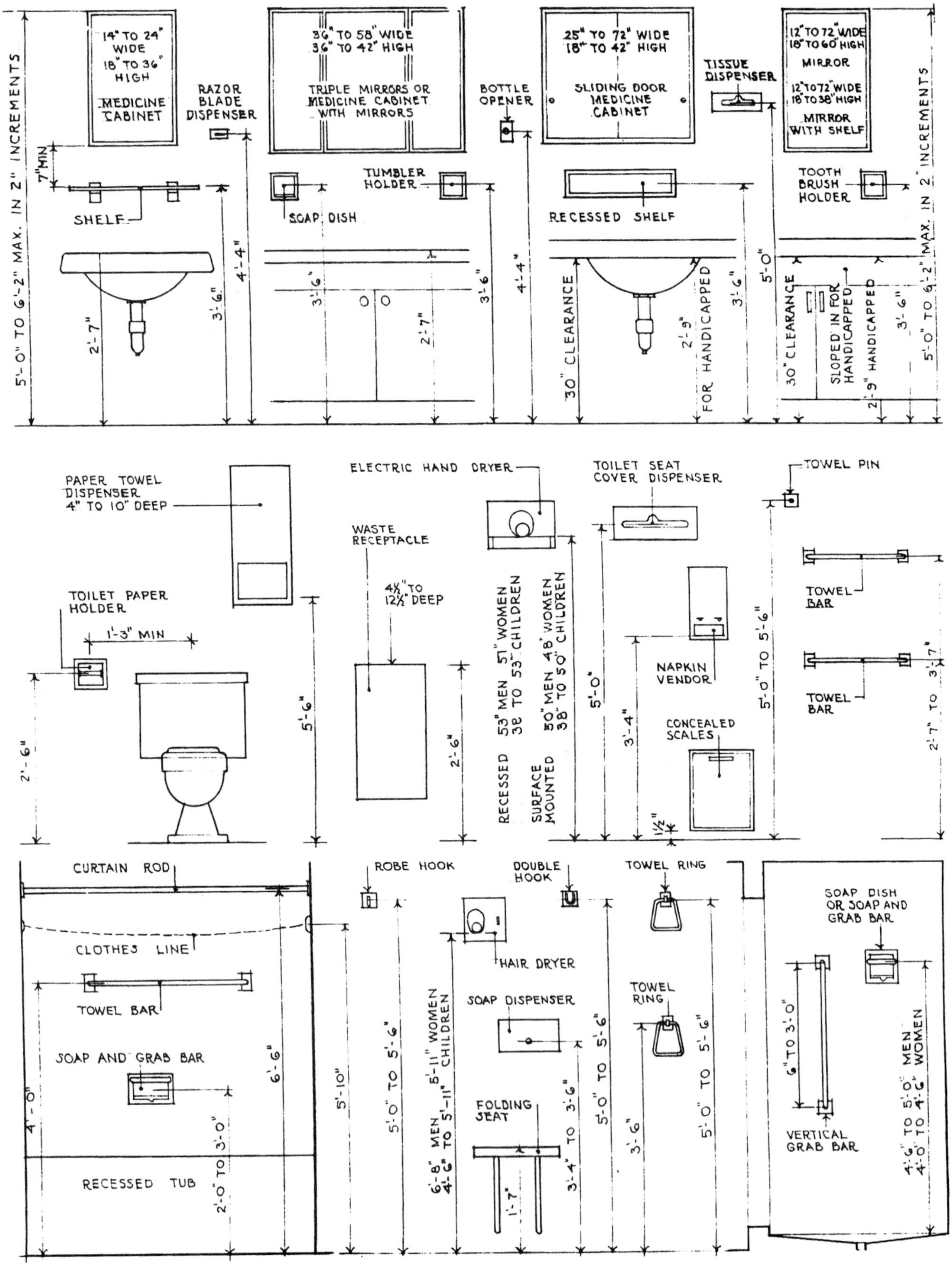

BATHROOMS
Plans, Elevations, and Details

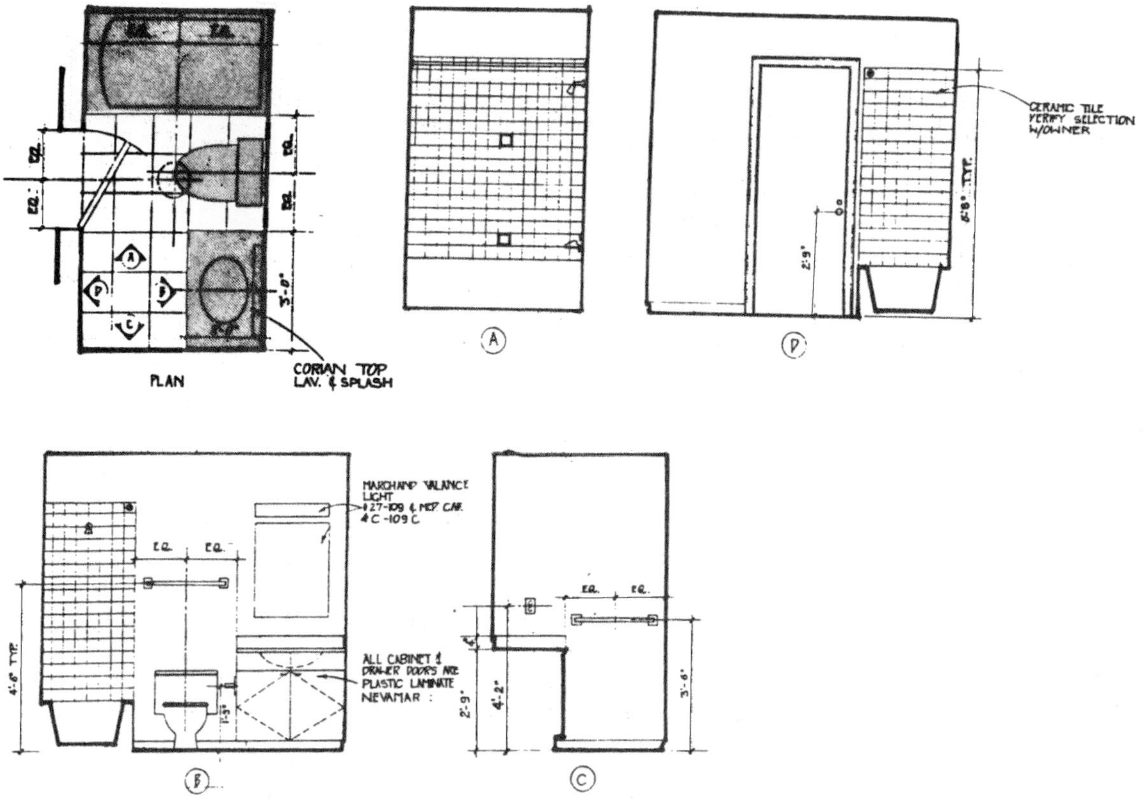

Three-fixture bathroom with tub

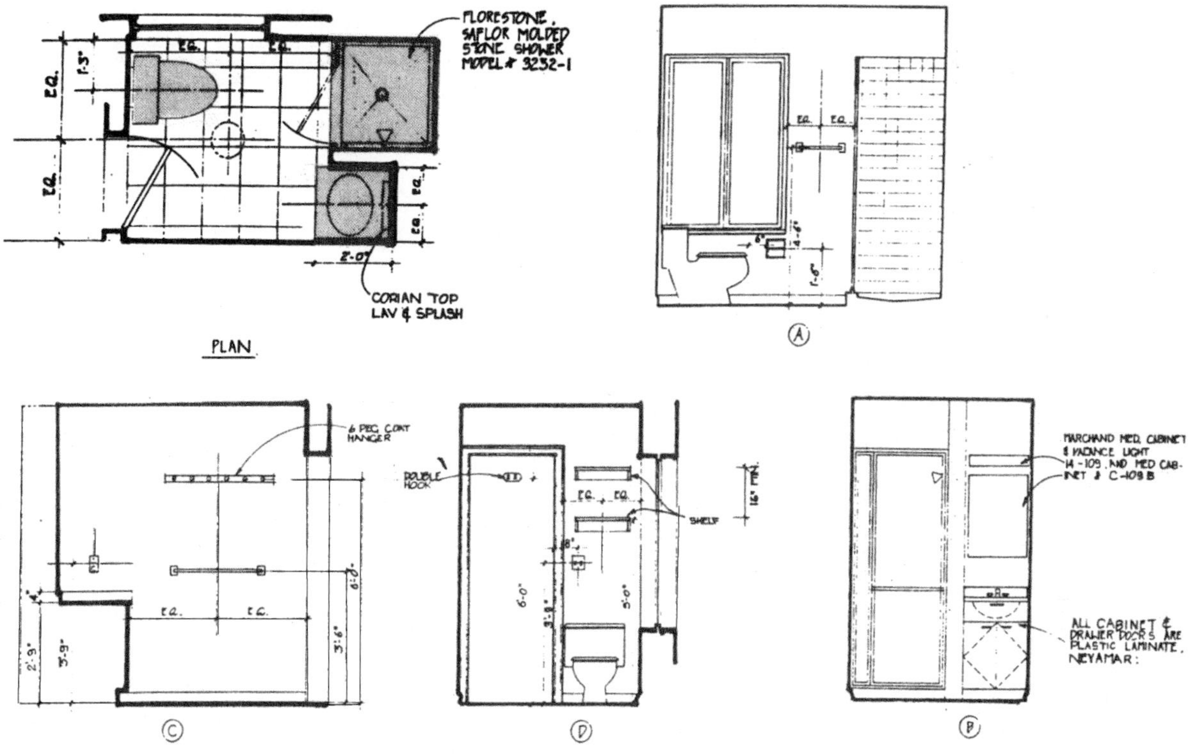

Three-fixture bathroom with shower

BATHROOMS

Plans, Elevations, and Details

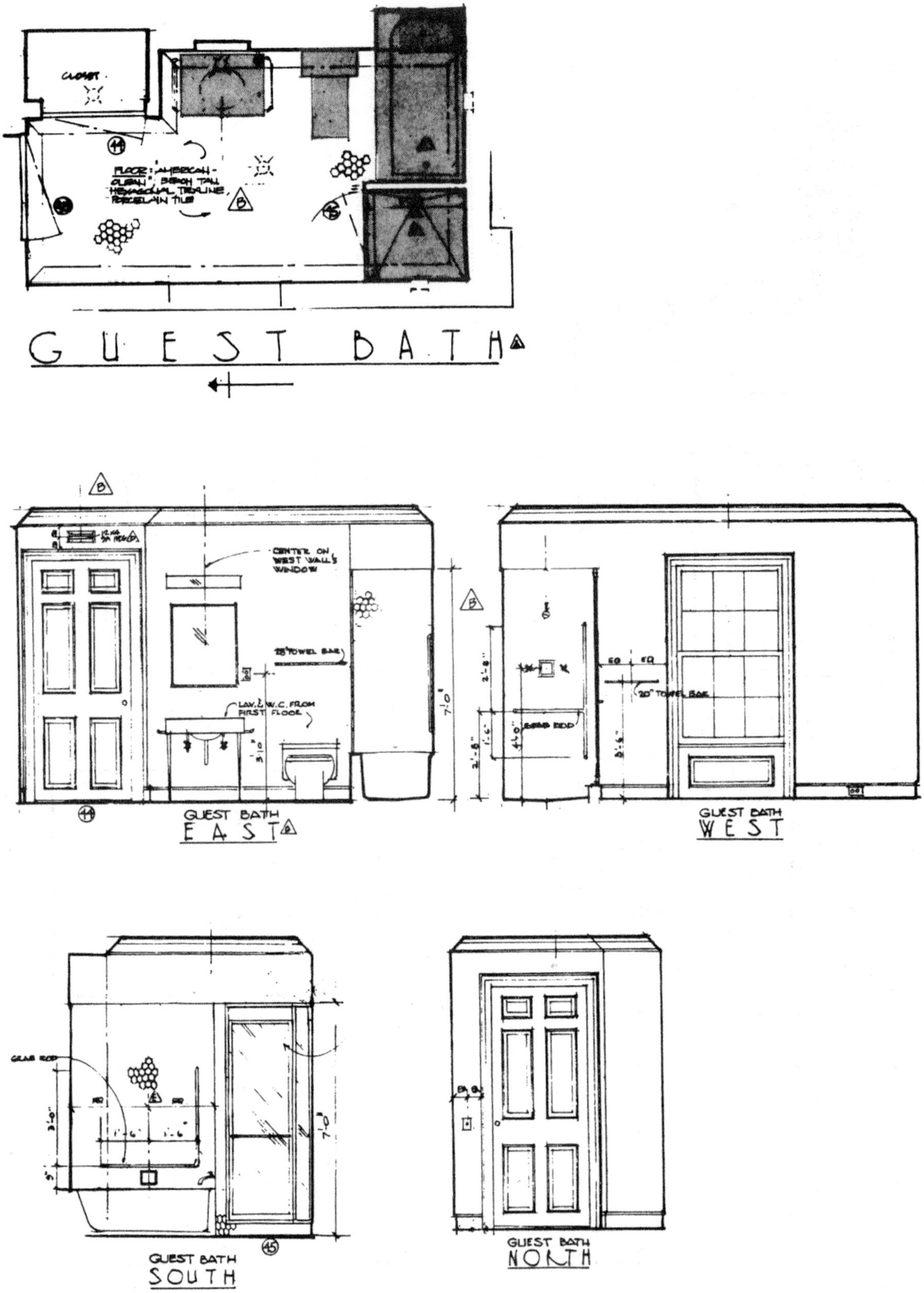

Four-fixture bathroom with tub and shower

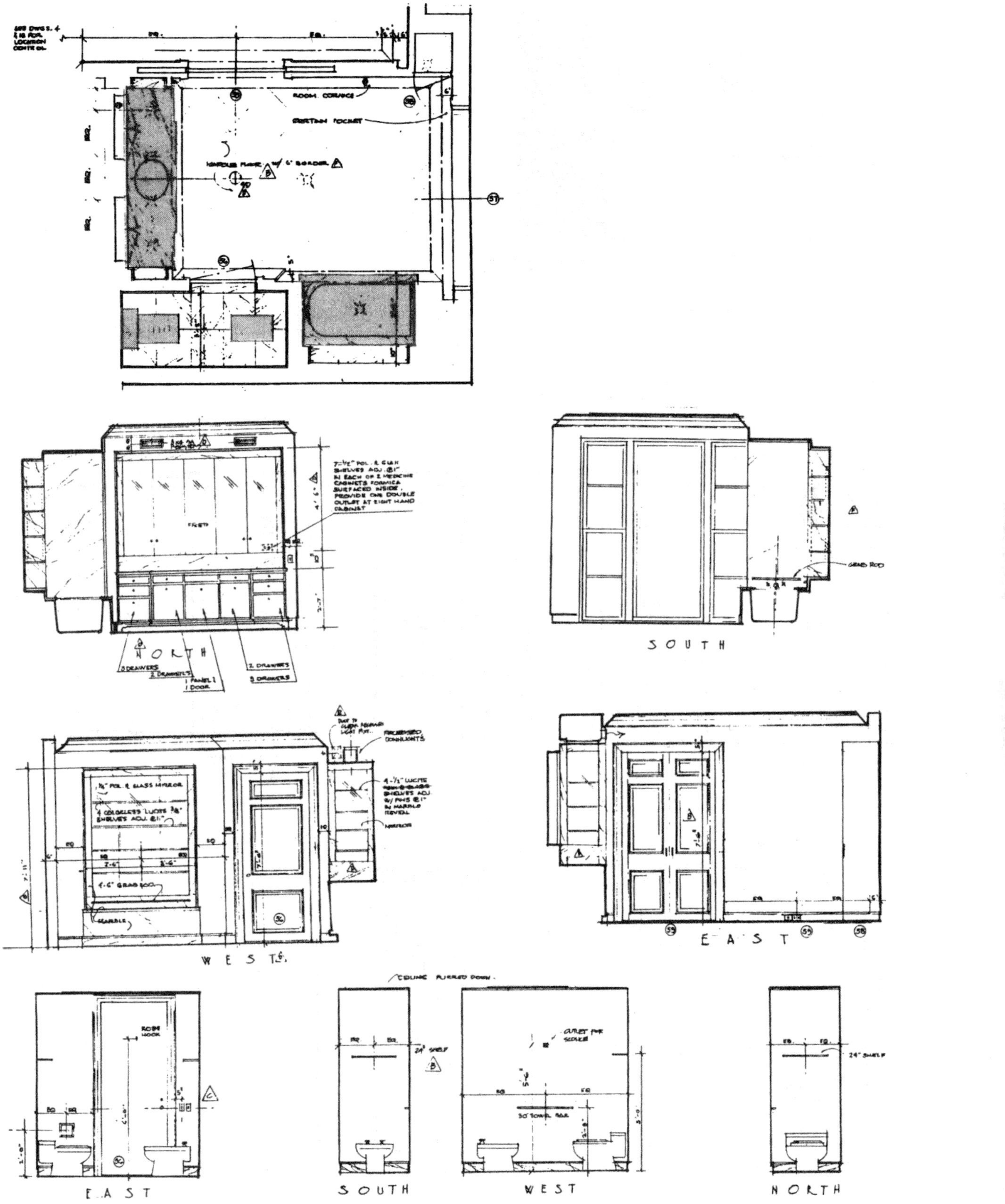

Four-fixture bathroom with bidet and tub

BATHROOMS
Plans, Elevations, and Details

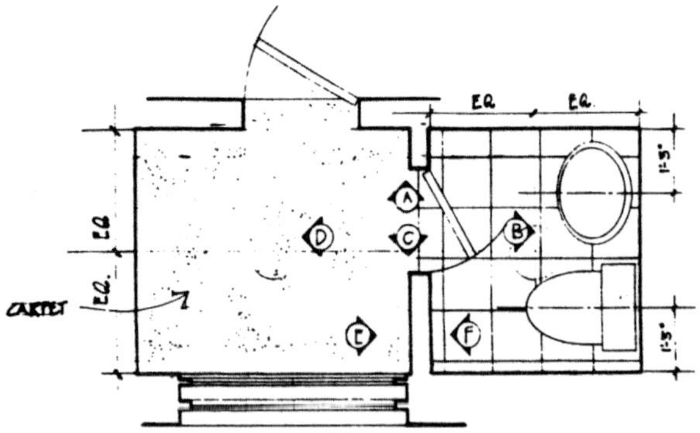

PLAN

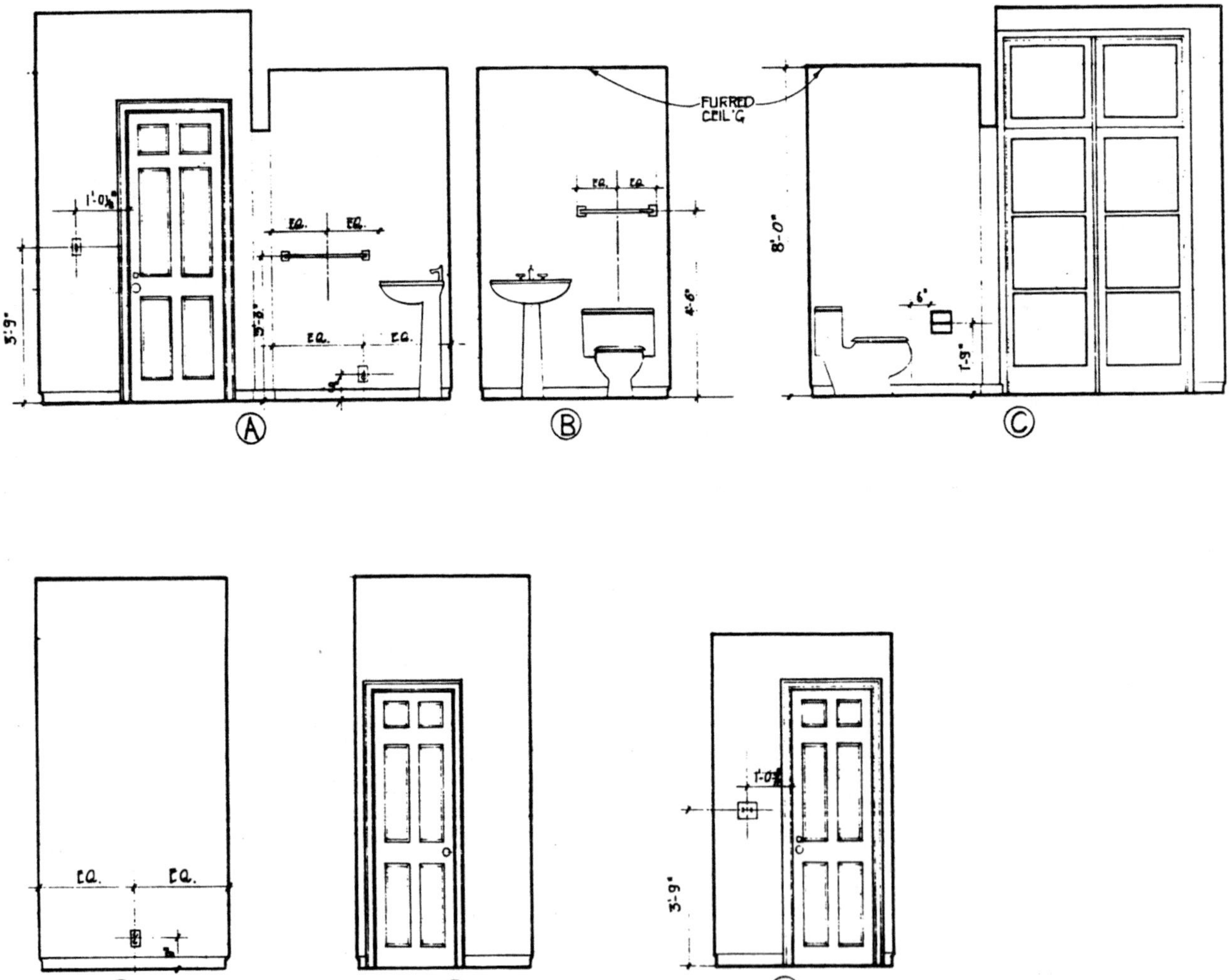

Powder room

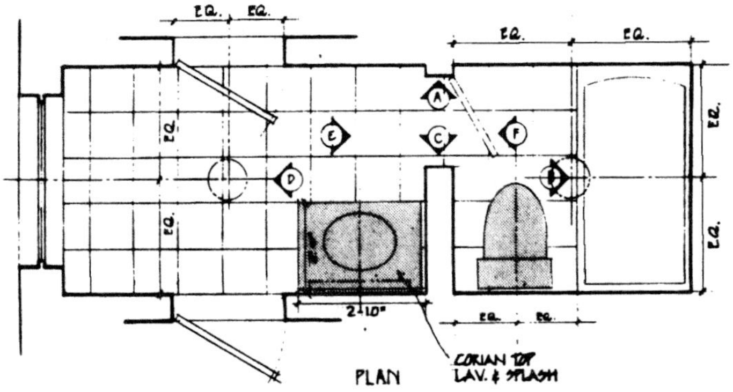
EQ.
EQ.
2'-10"
CORIAN TOP
LAV. & SPLASH
PLAN

B A T H R O O M

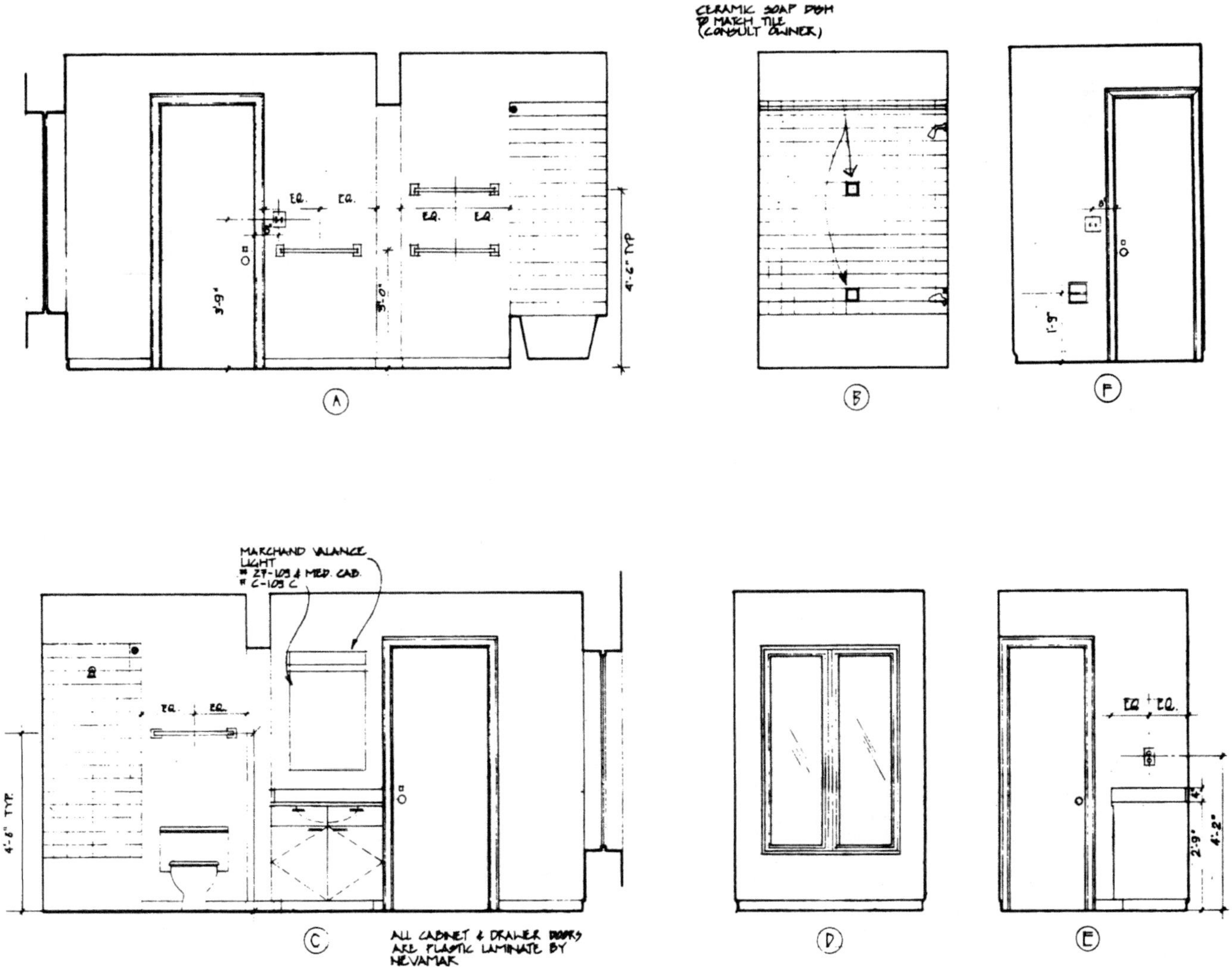
CERAMIC SOAP DISH
TO MATCH TILE
(CONSULT OWNER)
4'-6" TYP
3'-9"
3'-0"
A
B
F
MARCHAND VALANCE
LIGHT
27-103 & MED. CAB.
C-103 C
4'-6" TYP.
C
ALL CABINET & DRAWER DOORS
ARE PLASTIC LAMINATE BY
NEVAMAR
D
E
2'-9"
4'-2"

BATHROOMS
Plans, Elevations, and Details

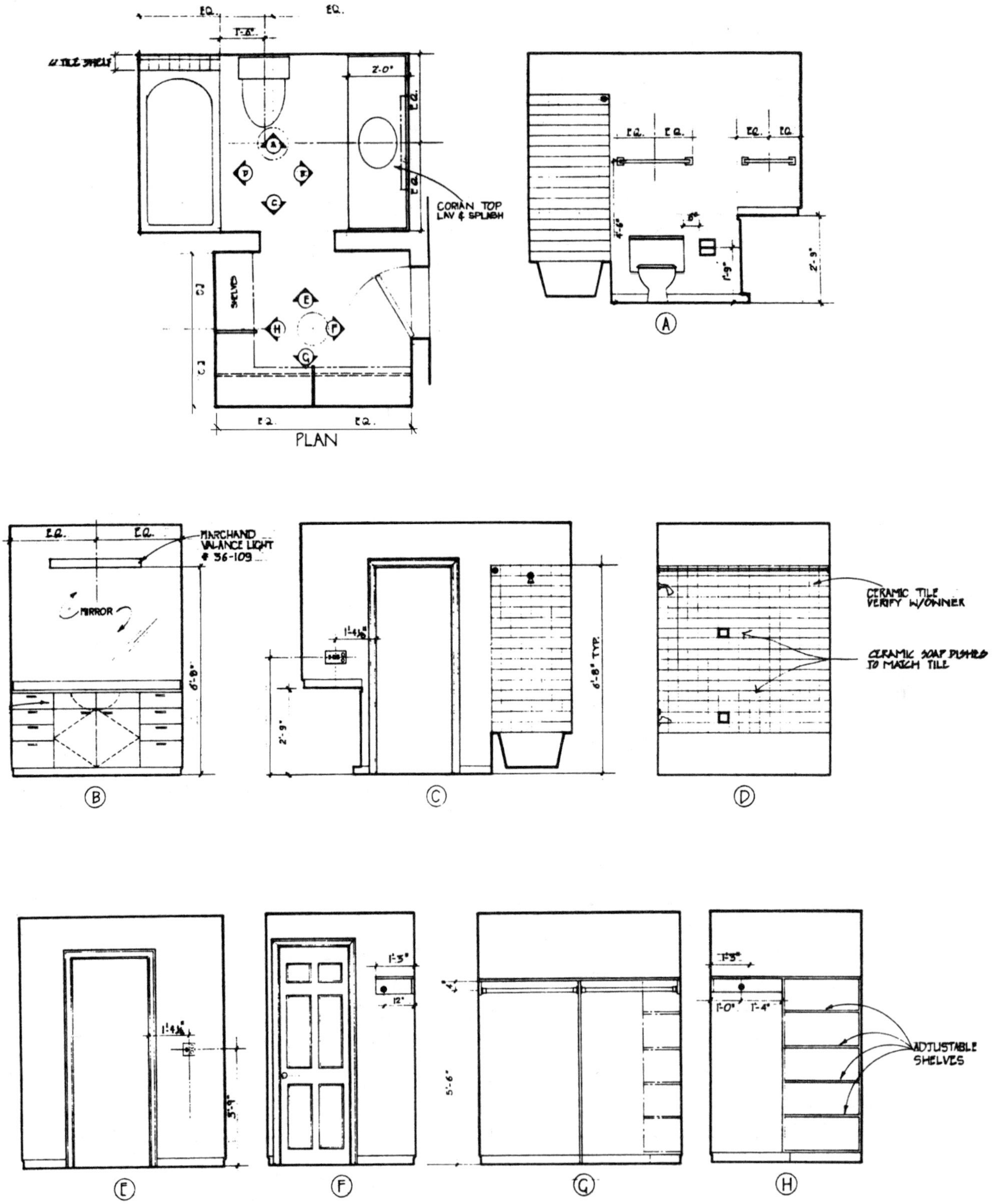

Powder room

BATHROOMS
Plans, Elevations, and Details

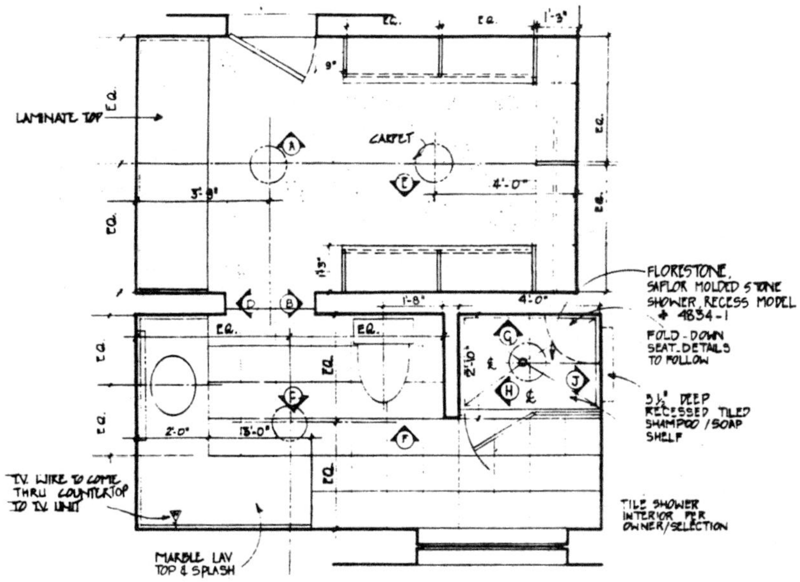

PLAN

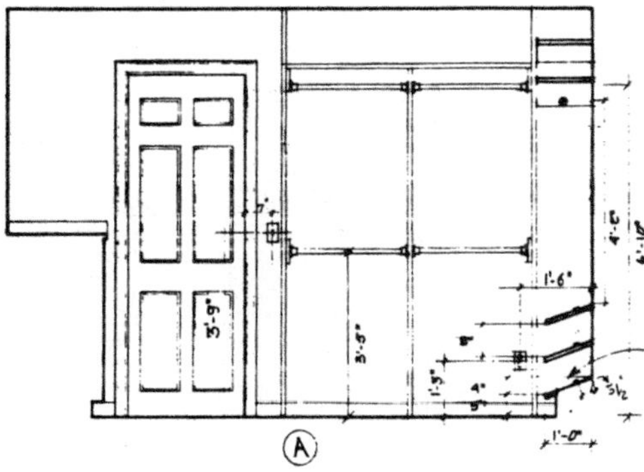

(A)

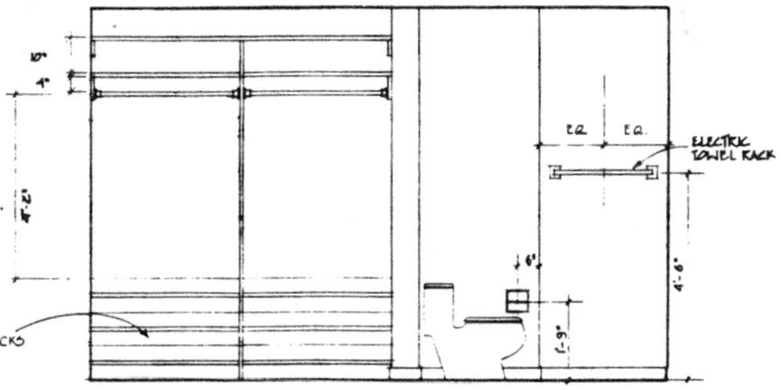

(B)

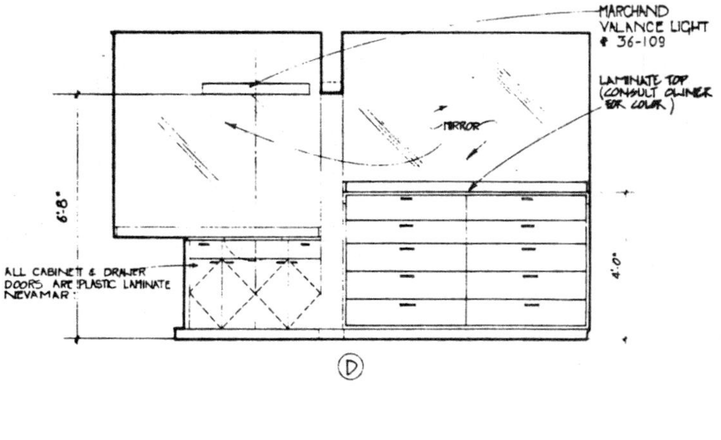

(D)

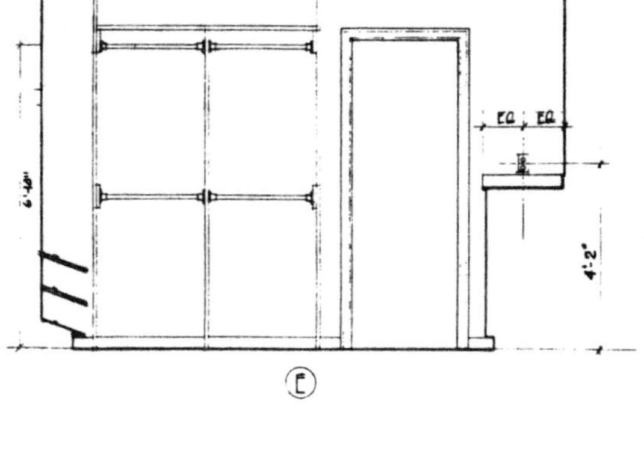

(E)

BATHROOMS

Dressing Room Elevations

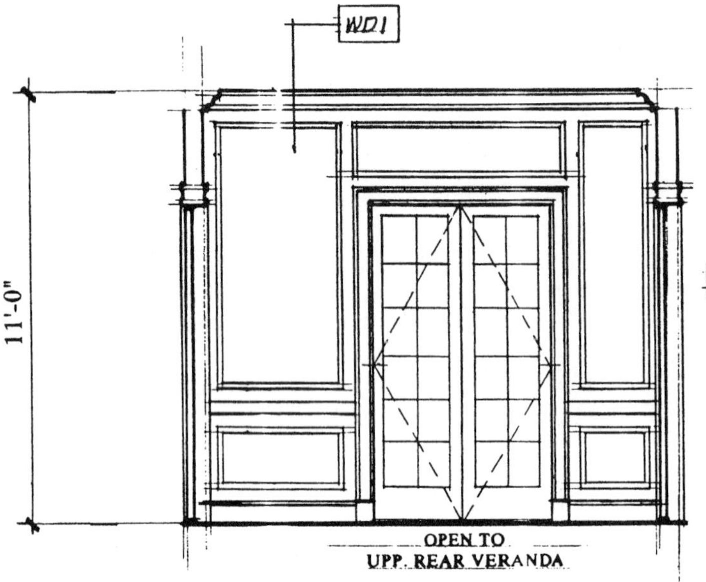

1 His Dressing Rm.-South

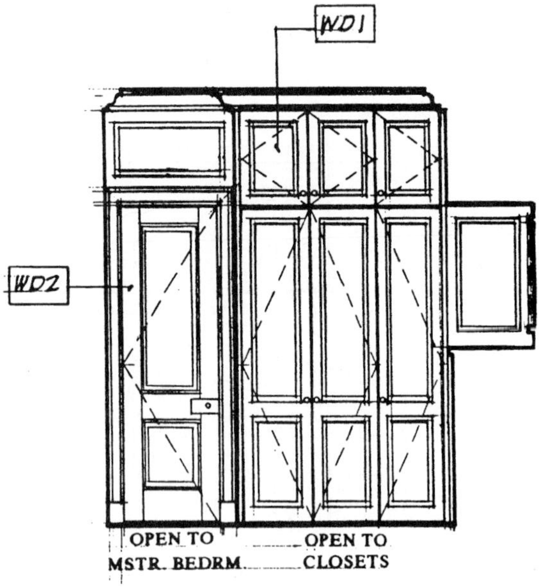

2 His Dressing Rm.-West

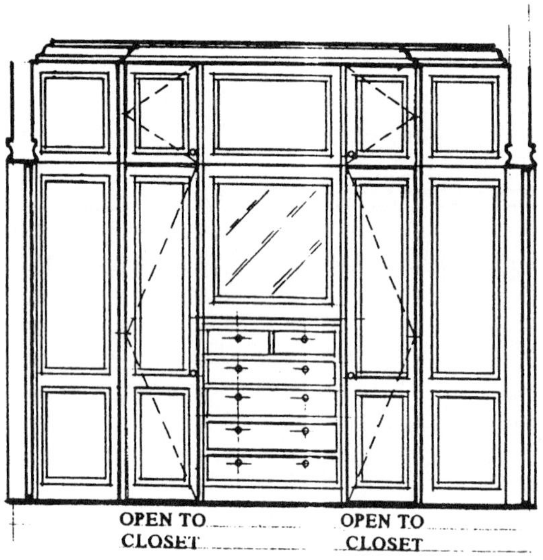

3 His Dressing Rm.-North

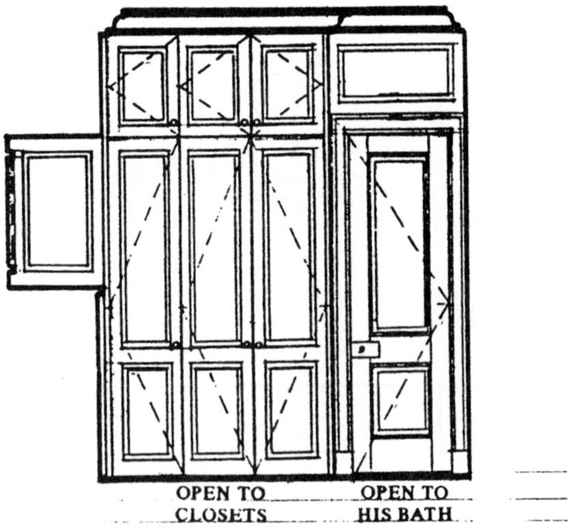

4 His Dressing Rm.-East

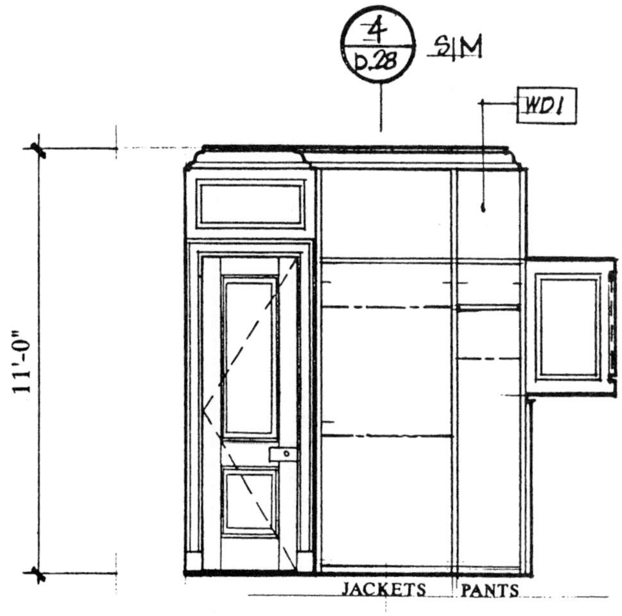

5 His Dressing Rm.-West
(Cl. Doors Open)

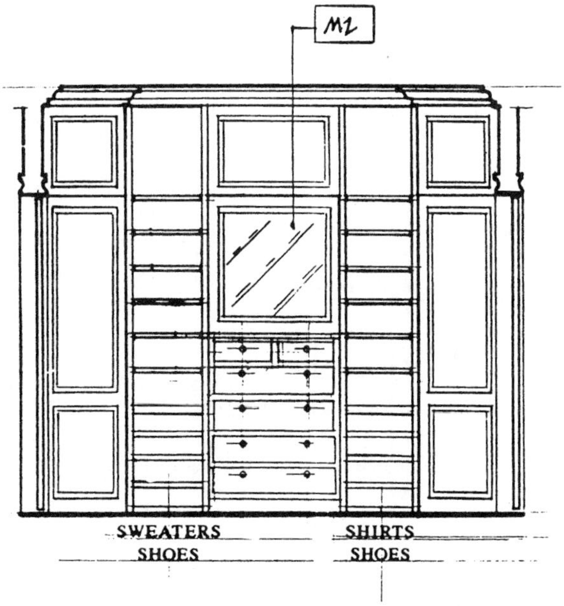

6 His Dressing Rm.-North
(Cl. Doors Open)

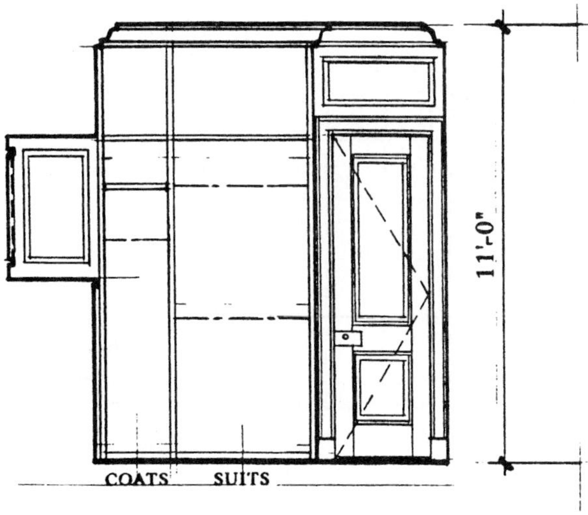

7 His Dressing Rm.-East
(Cl. Doors Open)

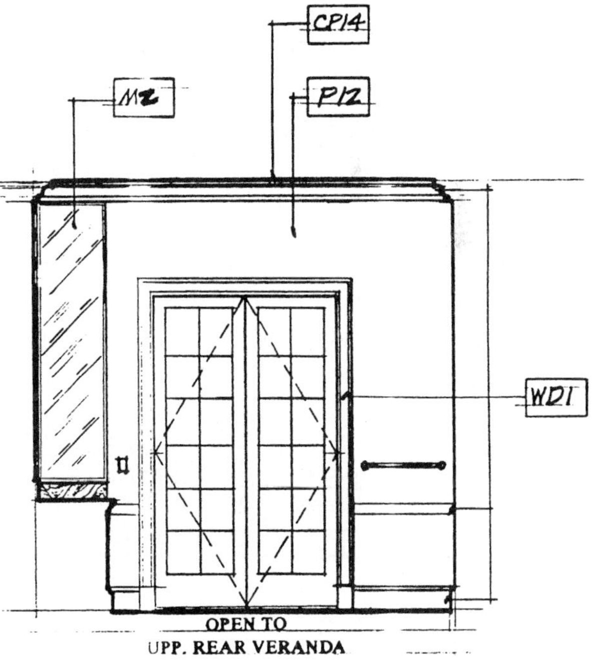

8 His Bath-South

BATHROOMS

Dressing Room/Bathroom Elevations

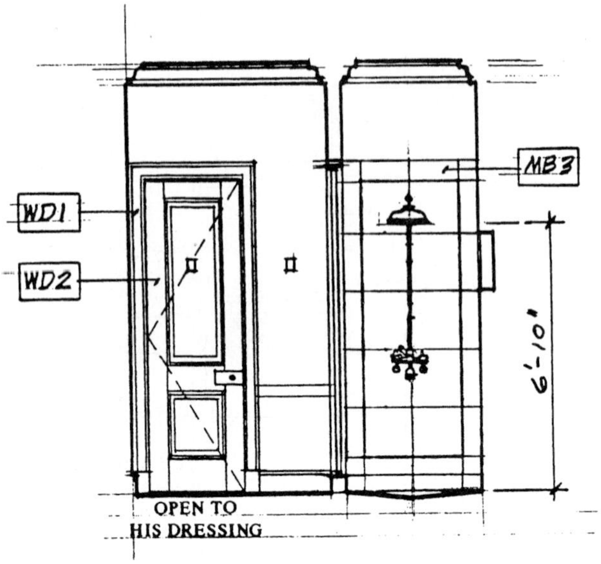

9 His Bath-West

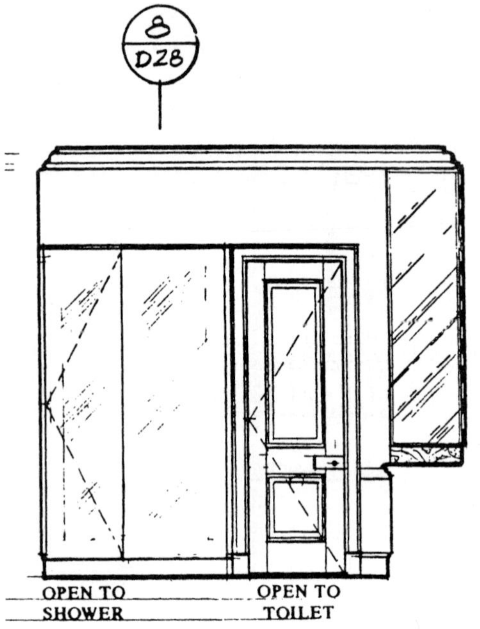

10 His Bath-North

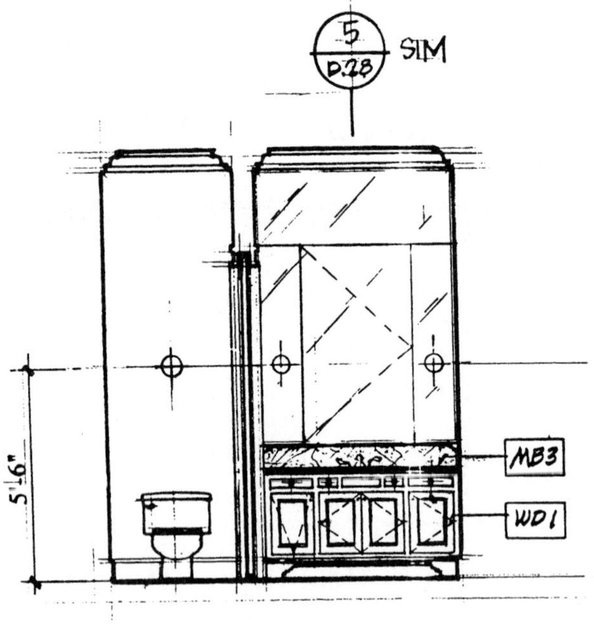

11 His Bath-East

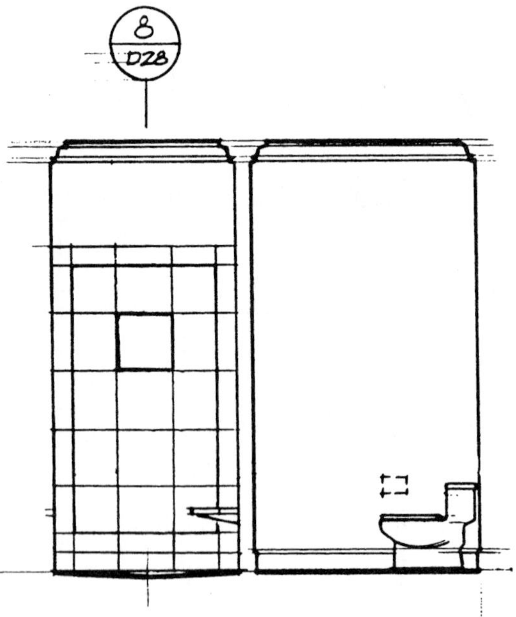

12 Shower/Toilet-North

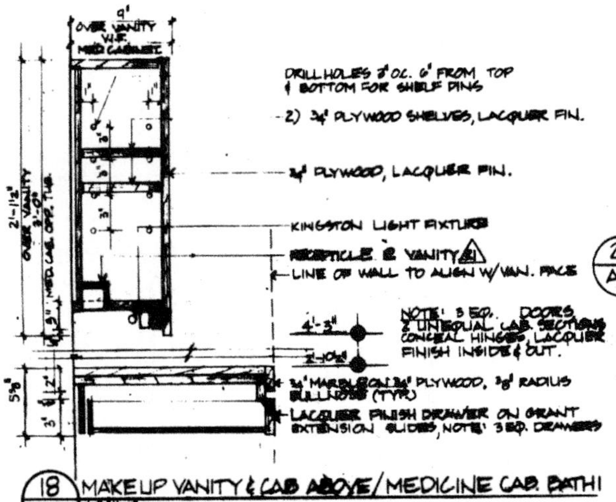

18 / A6 MAKE UP VANITY & CAB ABOVE/MEDICINE CAB. BATH 1
1½"=1'-0"

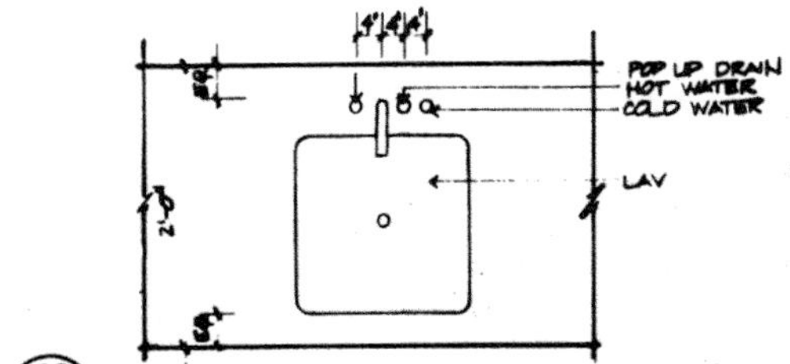

22 / A6 PLAN, FITTINGS ARRANGEMENT @ LAV. BATH 2
1"=1'-0"

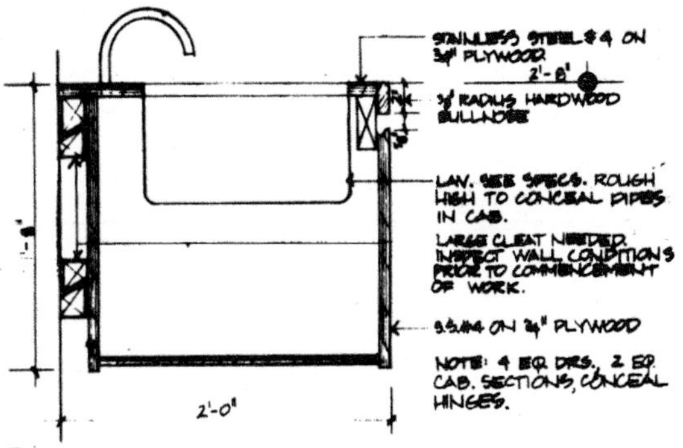

23 / A6 LAV. VANITY, BATH 2
1½"=1'-0"

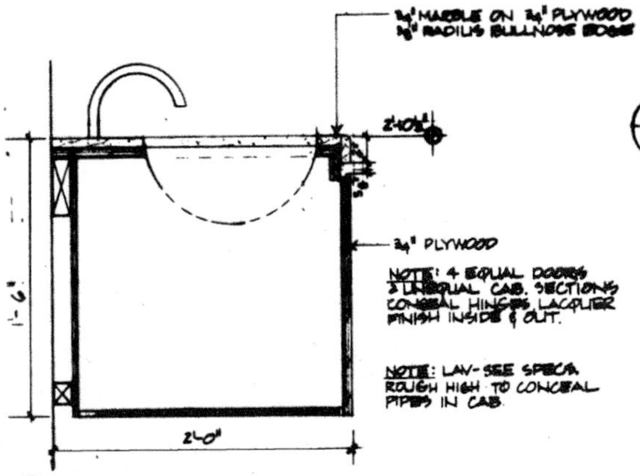

19 / A6 LAV. VANITY, BATH 1
1½"=1'-0"

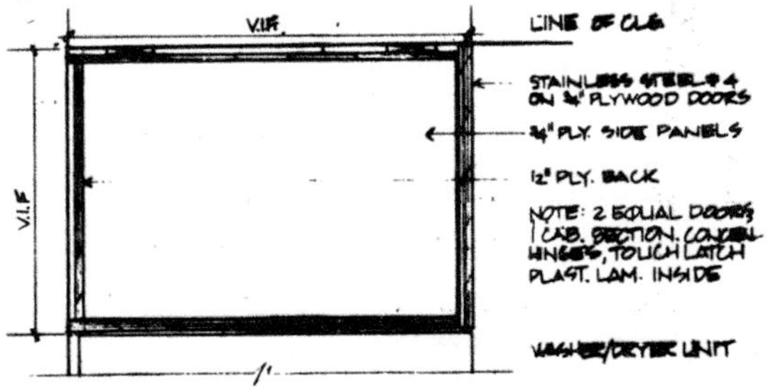

24 / A6 SECTION THRU CAB. OVER WASHER/DRYER UNIT
1½"=1'-0"

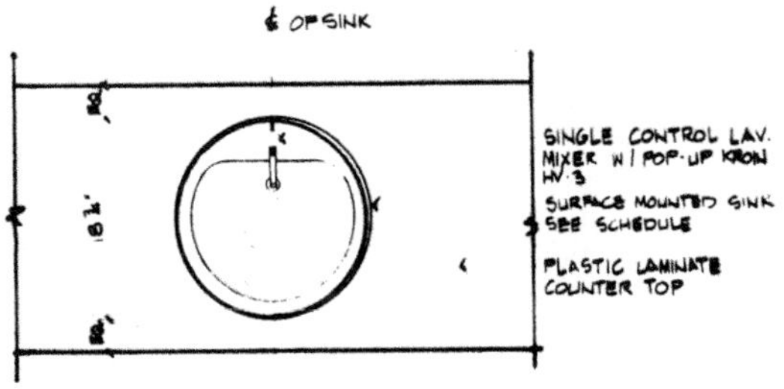

12 / A11 TYPICAL LAVATORY FITTINGS ARRANGEMENT
1"=1'-0"

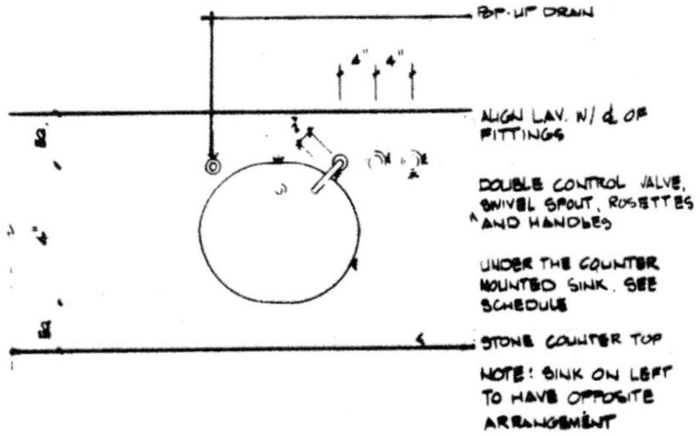

17 / A11 LAVATORY FITTING ARRANGEMENT @ BATH #1
1"=1'-0" SIMILAR BATH #5

BATHROOMS
Vanities

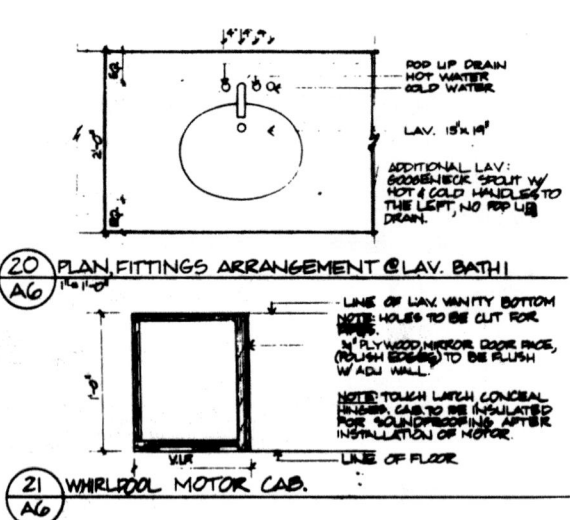

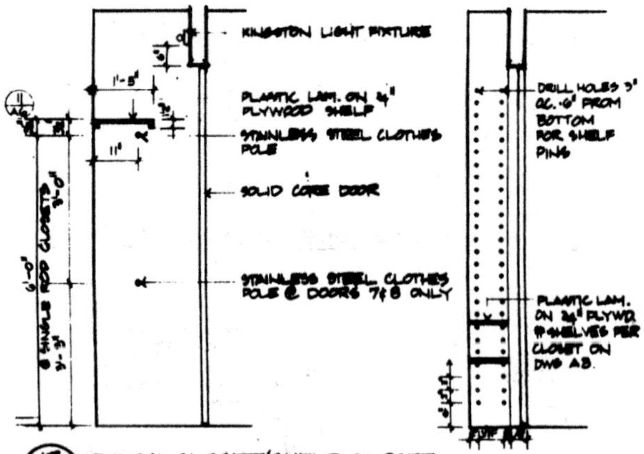

17/A6 TYPICAL CLOSET/SHELF CLOSET

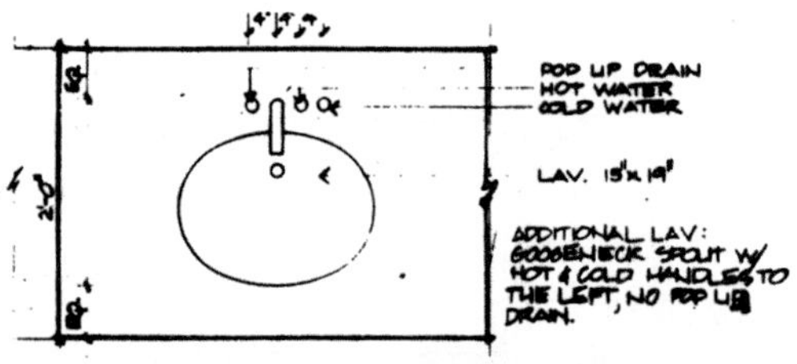

20/A6 PLAN, FITTINGS ARRANGEMENT @ LAV. BATH 1
1½"=1'-0"

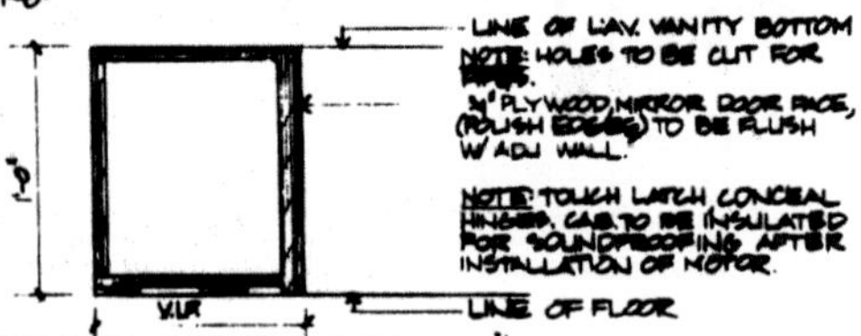

21/A6 WHIRLPOOL MOTOR CAB.

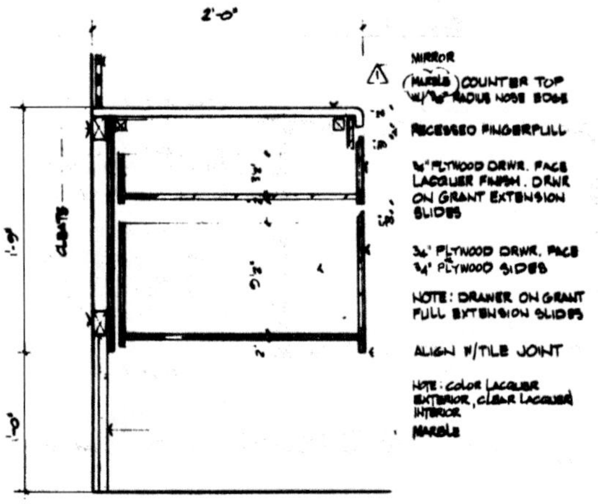

1/A11 SECTION THRU LAV. CAB. @ BATH #1
1½"=1'-0"

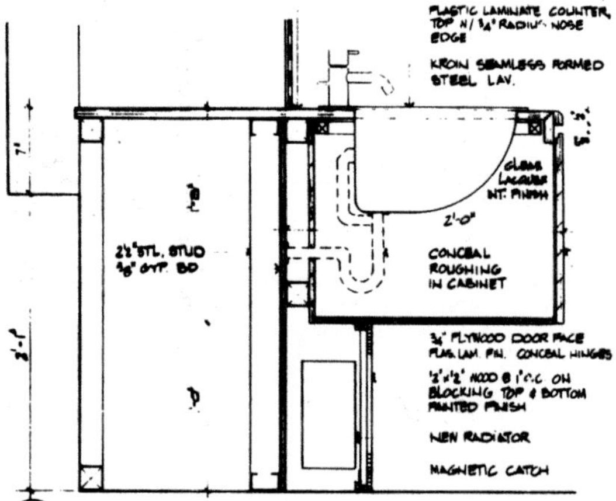

3/A11 SECTION THRU LAV. CAB. @ BATH #4
1½"=1'-0"

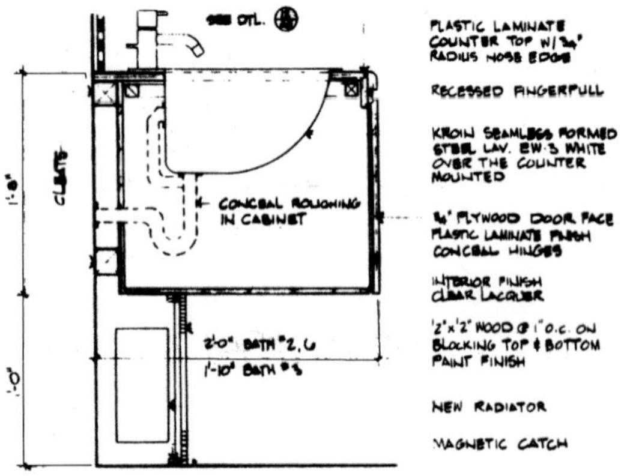

2/A11 SECTION THRU LAV. CAB. @ BATH #2 & BATH #3, #6 (SIMILAR)
1½"=1'-0"

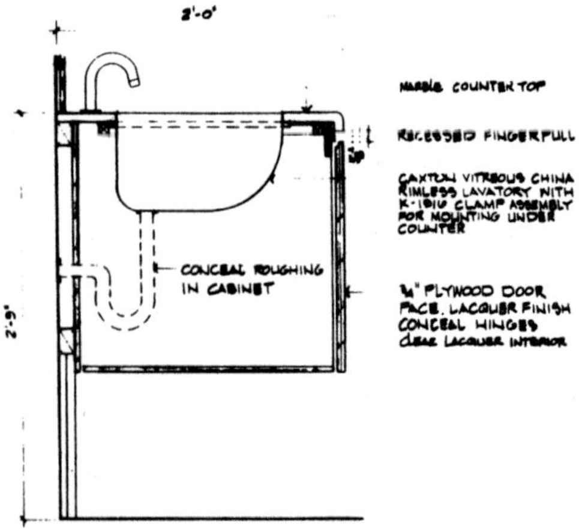

5/A11 SECTION THRU LAV. CAB. @ BATH #1
1½"=1'-0"

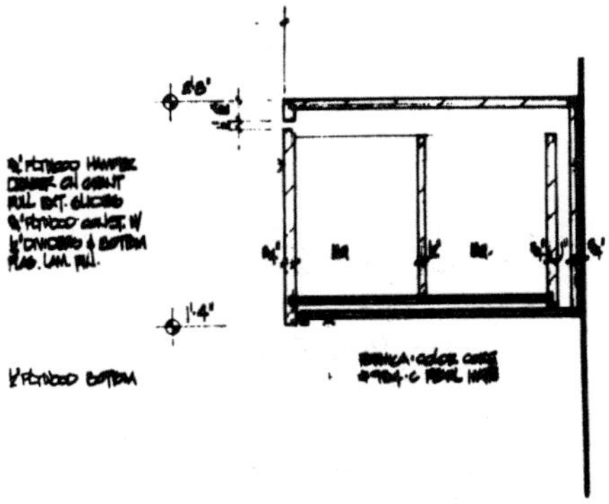

5/A17 DETAIL: VANITY HAMPER
½": 1'-0"

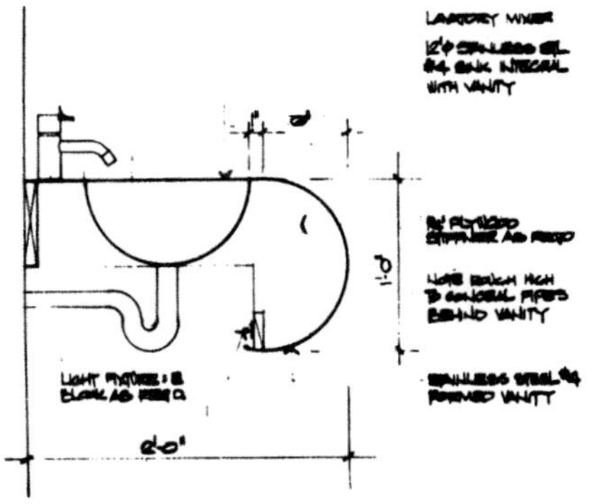

7/A17 SECTION: POWDER RM. VANITY
½": 1'-0"

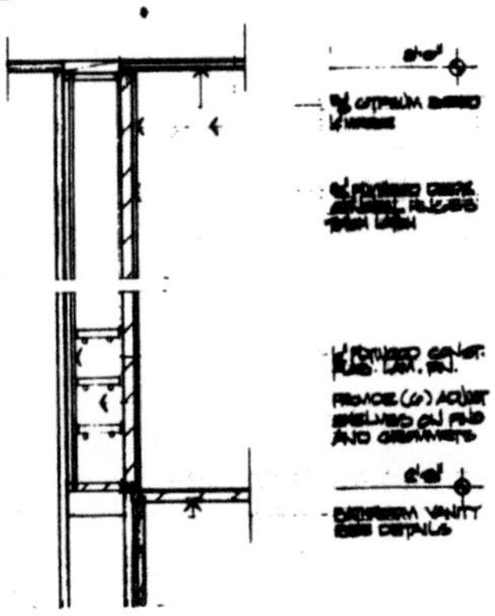

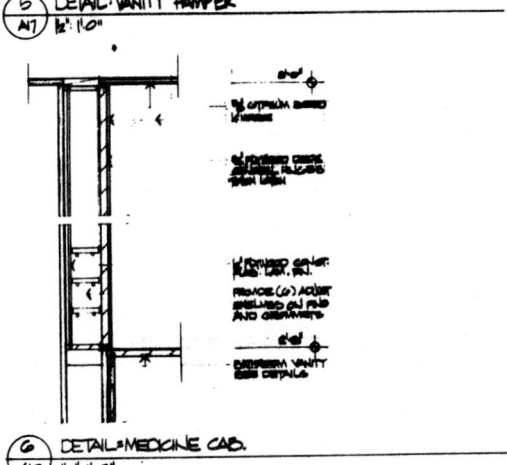

6/A17 DETAIL: MEDICINE CAB.
½": 1'-0"

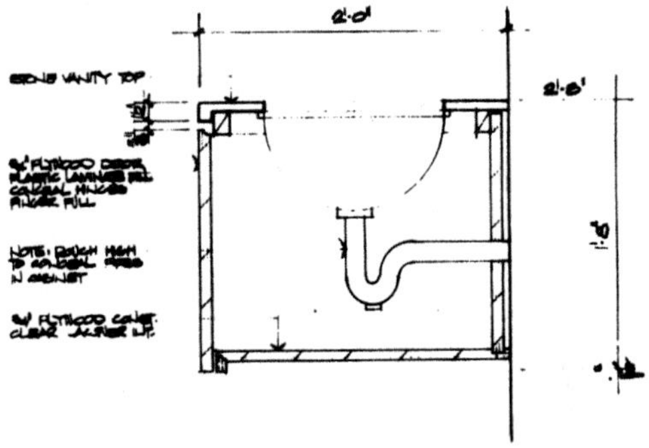

8/A17 DETAIL: VANITY MASTER BATHROOM
½": 1'-0"

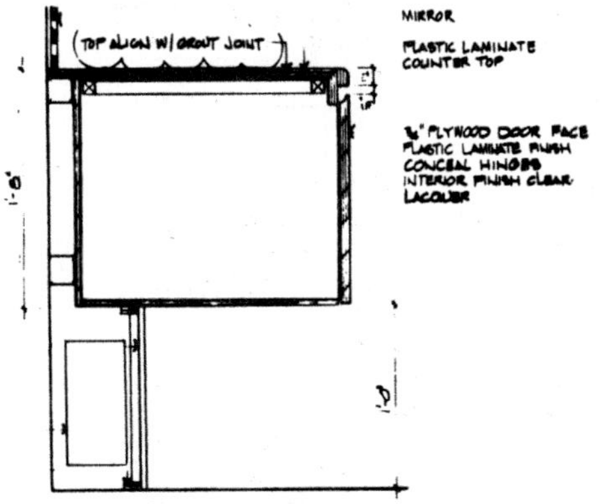

6/A11 SECTION THRU LAV. CAB. @ BATH #2 & BATH #3 (SIMILAR)

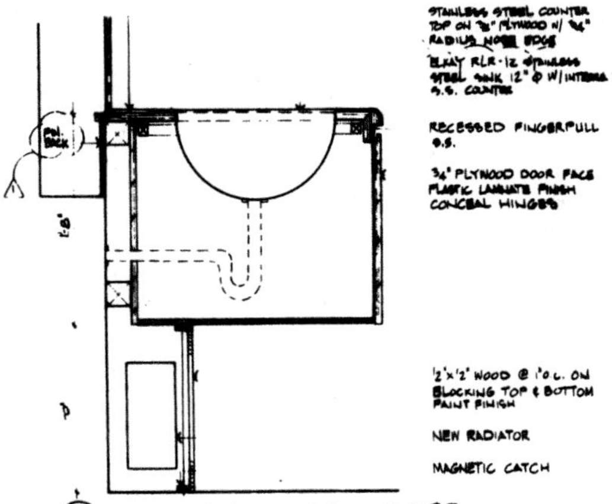

7/A11 SECTION THRU LAV. CAB. @ BATH #5
1½" = 1'-0"

BATHROOMS
Vanity Details

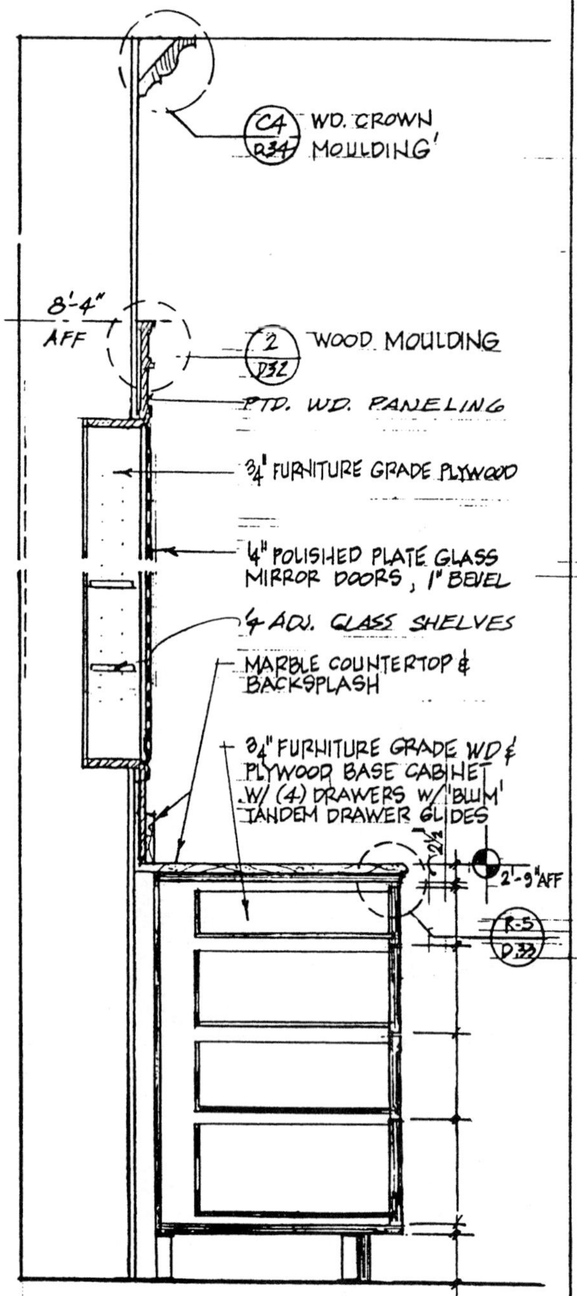

5 Vanity - Her Bath

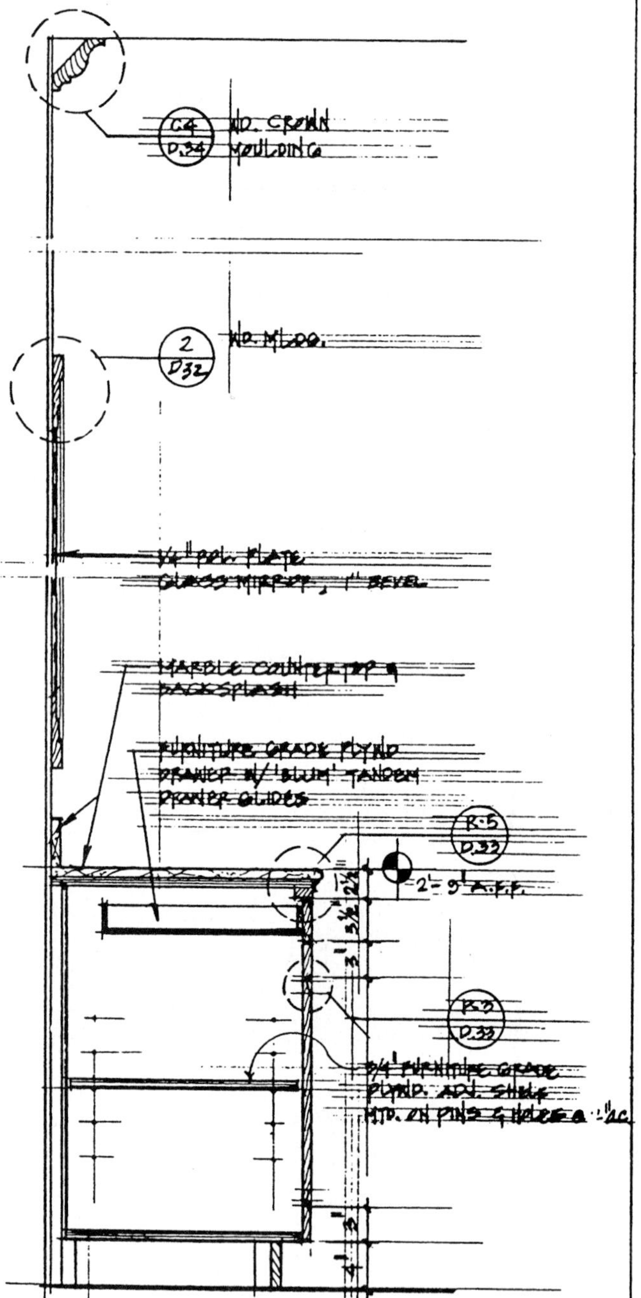

6 Vanity - Guest Baths

BATHROOMS

Accessory and Control Placement

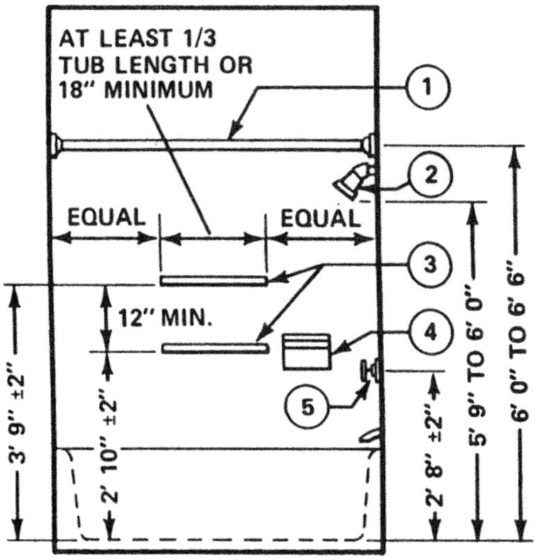

ELEVATION
OF TUB W/SHOWER

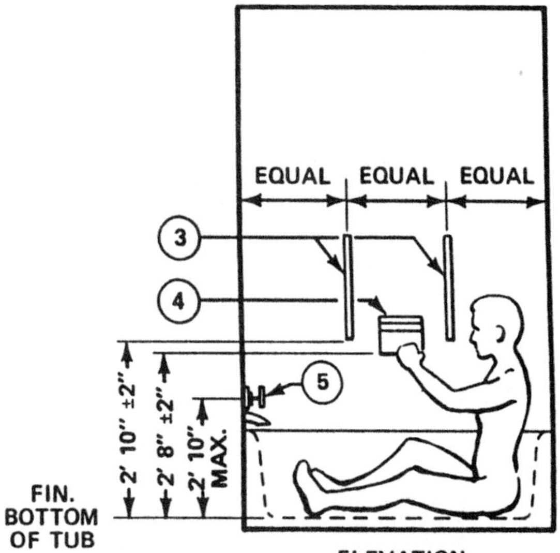

ELEVATION
OF TUB W/O SHOWER

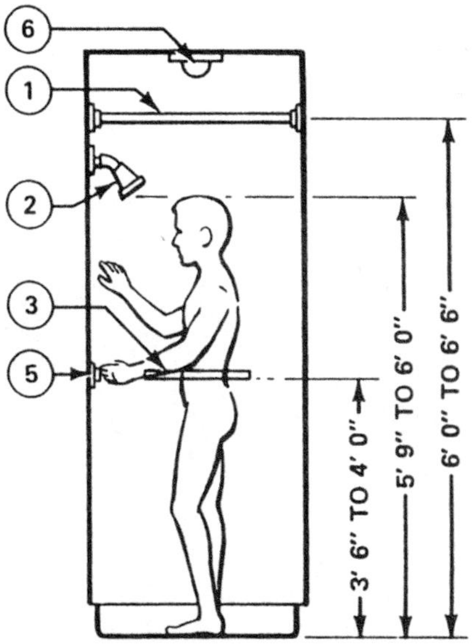

SECTION AT SHOWER

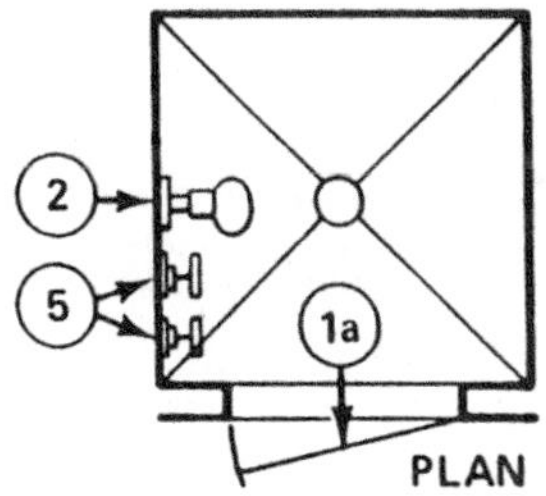

PLAN

(1.) SHOWER CURTAIN ROD: KEEP WITHIN INSIDE OF TUB OR SHOWER.

1a. ENCLOSURE DOORS: IF SWINGING DOORS ARE USED, PLACE HINGES ON THE SIDE OPPOSITE CONTROL VALVES.

(2.) SHOWER HEAD: SEE ELEVATION OF TUB AND SHOWER STALL FOR RECOMMENDED HEIGHTS.

(3.) GRAB BARS SHALL BE MANUFACTURED OF SHATTER-RESISTANT MATERIAL, FREE FROM BURRS, SHARP EDGES AND PINCH POINTS. KNURLING OR SLIP-RESISTANT SURFACE IS DESIRABLE.

(4.) RECESSED SOAP DISH SHALL BE FREE FROM BURRS AND SHARP EDGES. WHERE GRAB BAR IS AN INTEGRAL PART OF THE SOAP DISH, IT MAY HAVE A MINIMUM LENGTH OF 6 INCHES.

(5.) FAUCET SHALL BE MANUFACTURED OF SHATTER-RESISTANT MATERIAL, FREE FROM BURRS AND SHARP EDGES. ALL FAUCET SETS IN SHOWERS, TUBS AND LAVATORIES SHALL BE EQUIPPED WITH A WATER-MIXING VALVE DELIVERING A MAXIMUM WATER TEMPERATURE OF 110° ±5°F.

(6.) SHOWER STALL LIGHT: SHALL BE OF A VAPOR-PROOF FIXTURE WITH THE ELECTRICAL LIGHT SWITCH A MINIMUM OF 72 INCHES AWAY FROM SHOWER STALL.

BATHROOMS

Vanities: Lavatory Counters

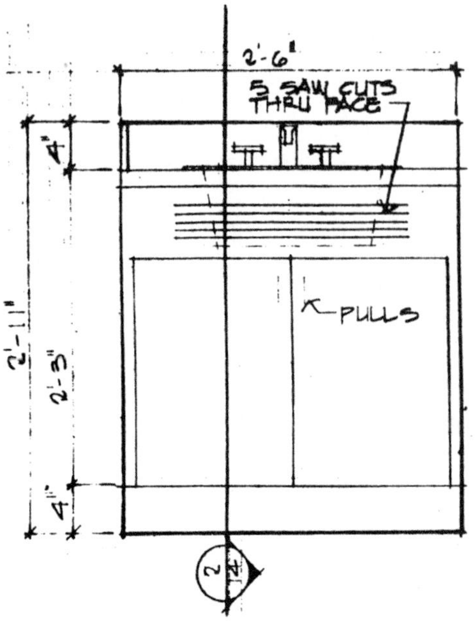

1/14 TOILET ROOM CAB. ELEV.

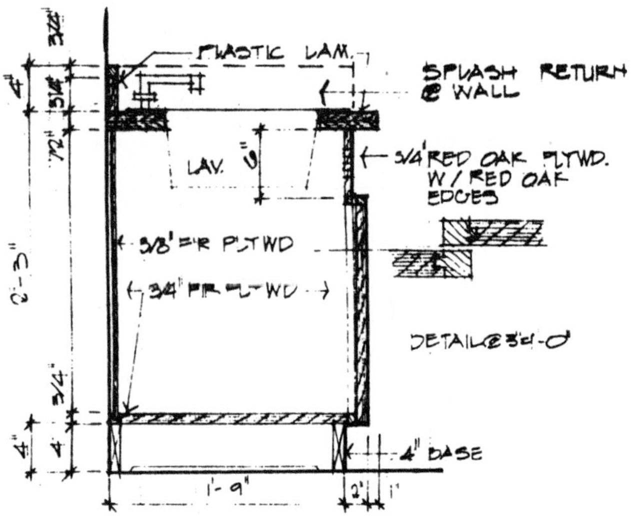

2/14 TOILET ROOM CAB. SECT.

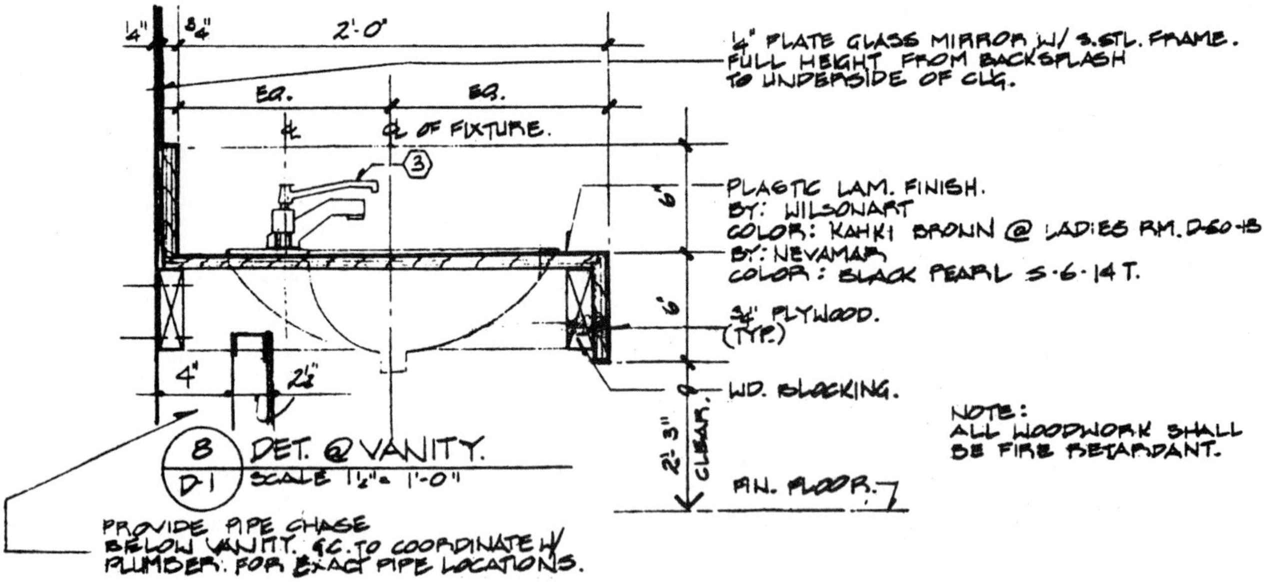

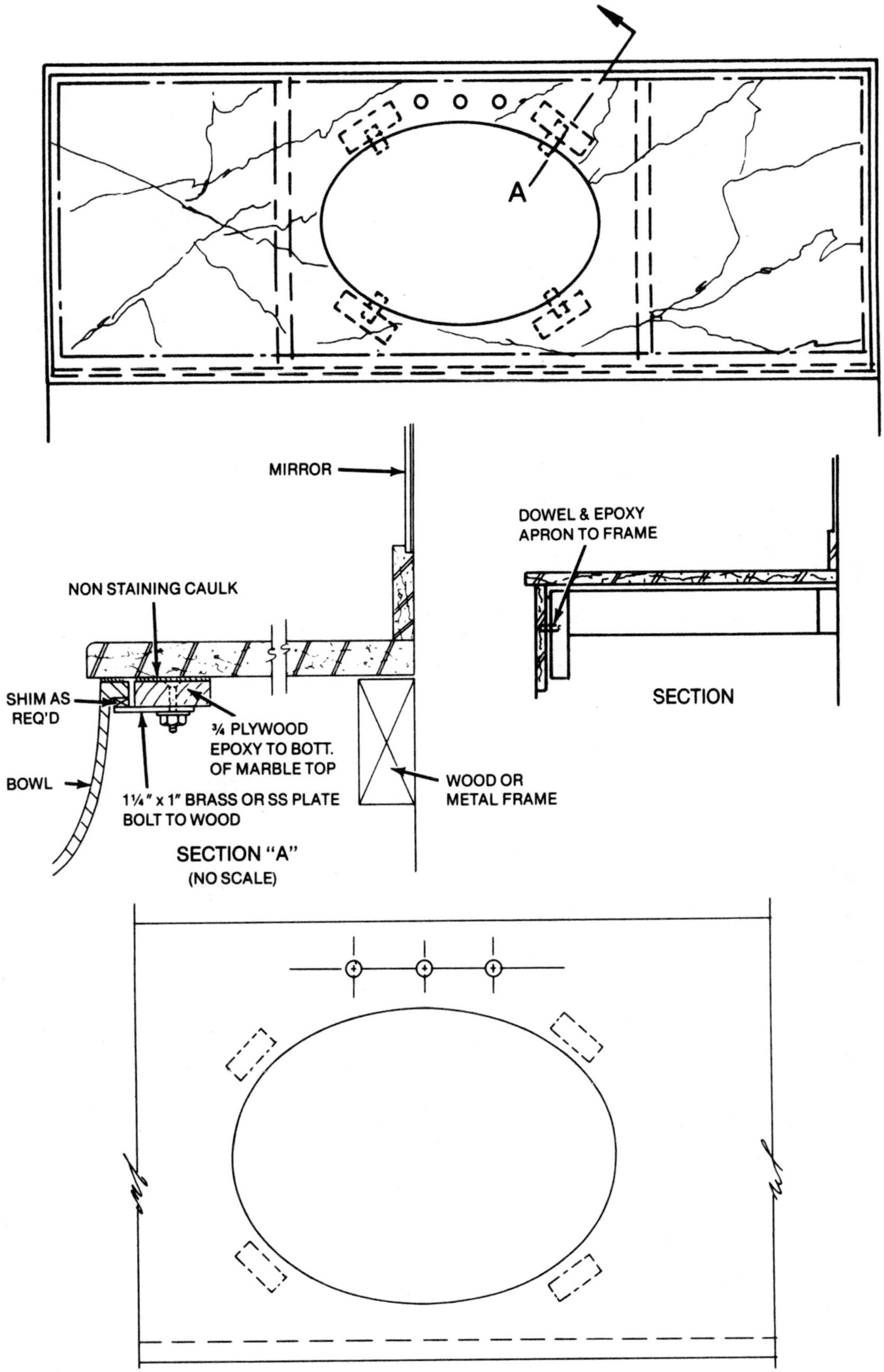

Fig. 16 Typical details of a marble vanity-top installation

BATHROOMS
Lavatory Counters

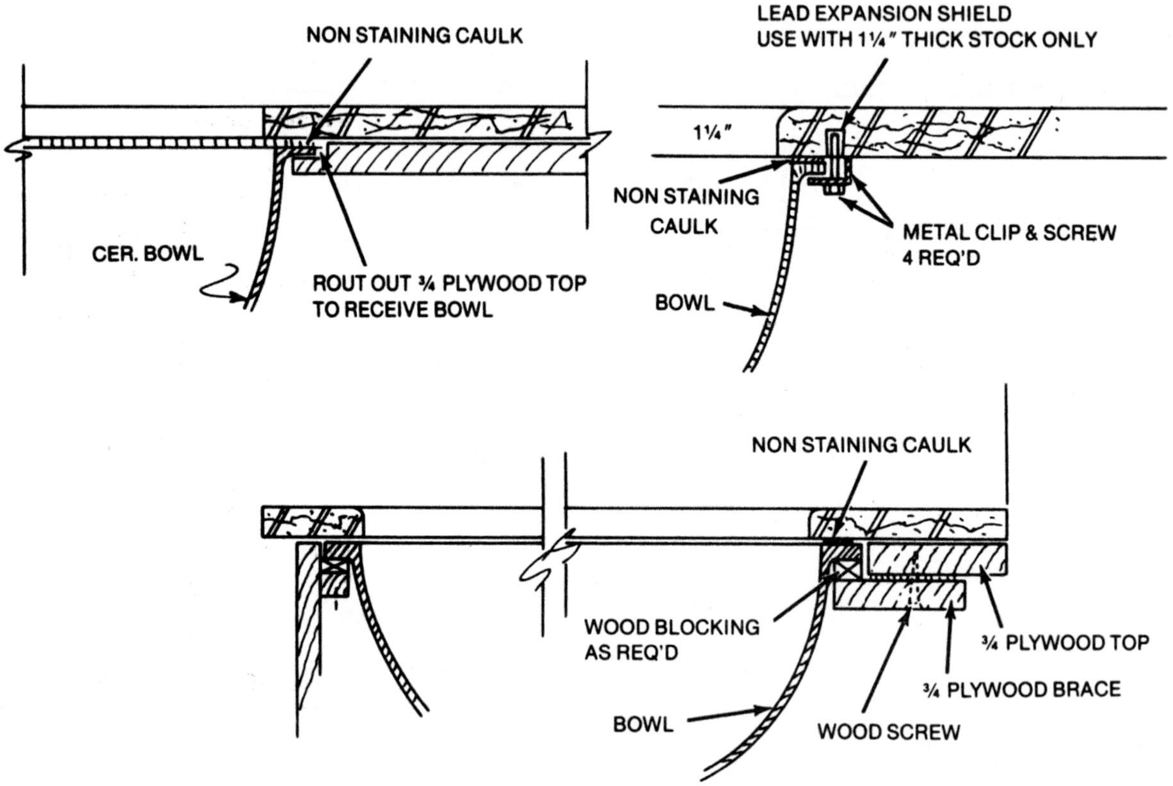

TYPICAL SECTIONS BOWL CARRIER

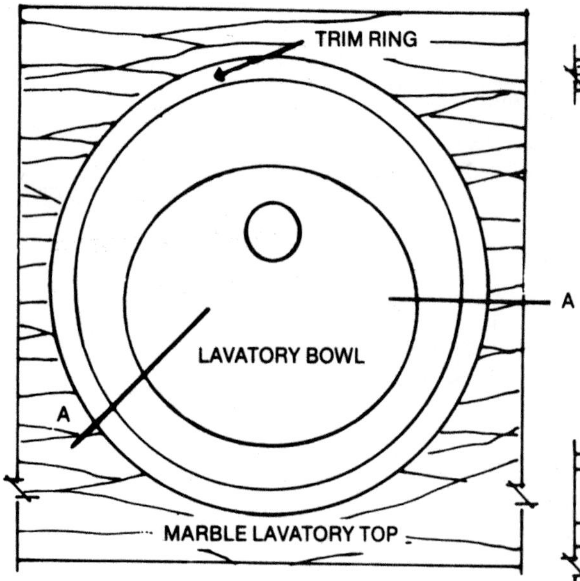

PLAN

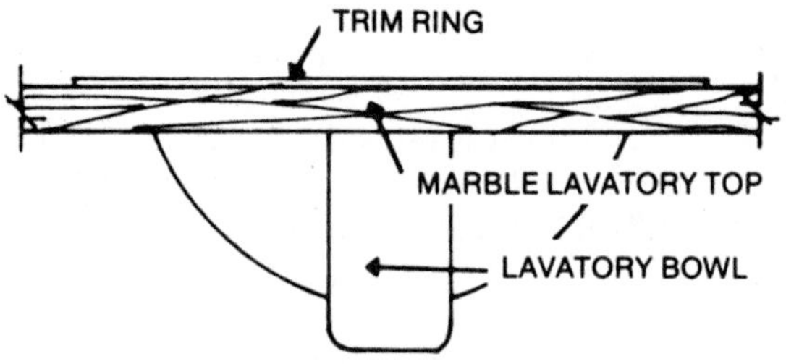

ELEVATION

SECT - "A"
NO SCALE

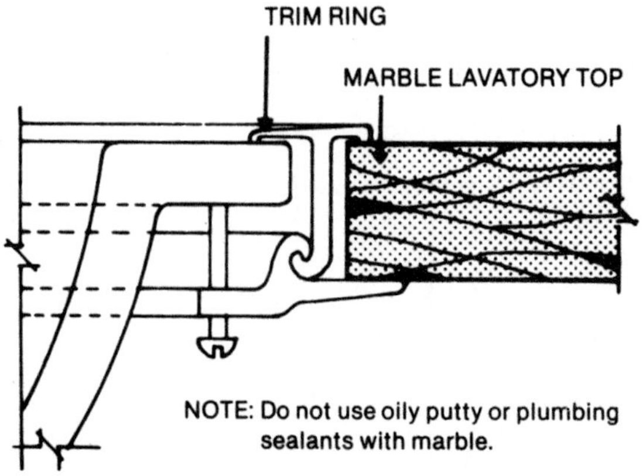

NOTE: Do not use oily putty or plumbing sealants with marble.

CONCEALED MARBLE EDGE
SECTION

Tile

When detailing a ceramic tile wall or ceiling for wet or damp locations, it is especially important to consider the performance of the entire assembly. Although ceramic tile, adhesives, and grout aren't generally harmed by water, the setting bed and/or structure may be susceptible to moisture penetration. Keeping moisture out is usually achieved by the appropriate combination of setting bed and waterproofing membrane, which is generally either a flexible sheet or a trowel-applied system.

Flexible Sheets

The three common types of flexible sheet membranes are tar-saturated felt paper (also called tar paper), 4-mil polyethylene film, and chlorinated polyethylene (CPE) waterproofing sheet. The tar paper and polyethylene are applied behind the setting bed, so the setting bed must be able to withstand exposure to moisture. They are attached with staples, either directly to the framing or to a rigid backing. They are the least expensive, but also least reliable, waterproofing membranes.

CPE is laminated to the surface of the setting bed with an appropriate setting material. CPE sheets are the most expensive waterproofing membranes, but the most effective, and may allow the use of a less expensive setting bed.

Trowel-Applied Waterproofing

Single or multicomponent trowel-applied waterproofing membranes are available. The single-component system consists of a liquid or paste that cures into a continuous membrane. It is applied to the surface of the setting bed.

The multicomponent system is a combination of liquid latex and fabric applied to the surface of the setting bed. The liquid is first spread on the setting bed and the fabric is embedded in it. A second coat of liquid is then applied over the fabric.

Trowel-applied waterproofing typically costs about the same as the CPE membrane, but is more versatile and effective in complicated installations.

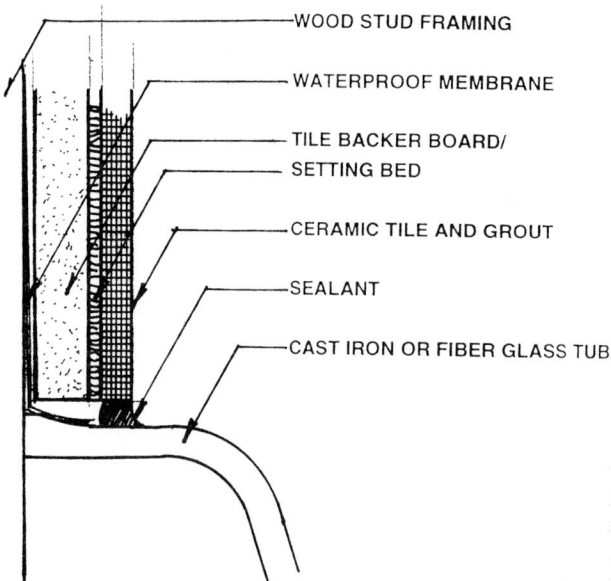

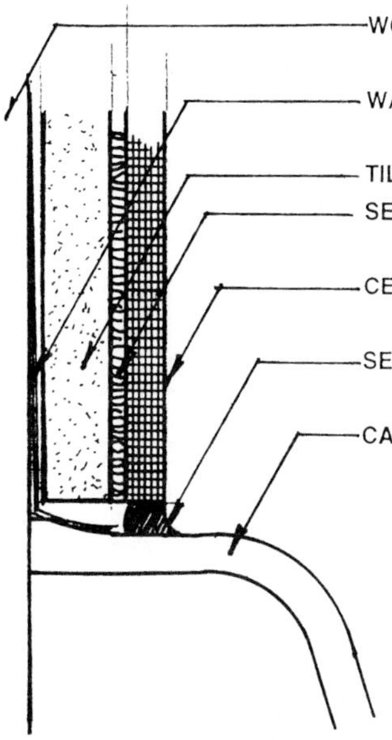

DETAIL OF TUB AT WALL

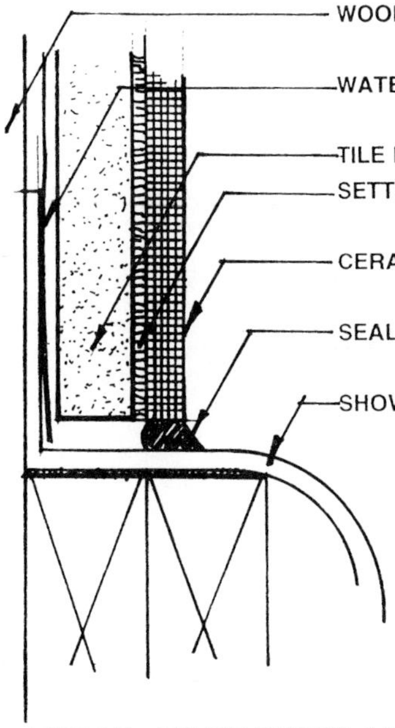

DETAIL OF SHOWER AT WALL

The designer must give careful consideration to the selection of an appropriate assembly of materials for all bathroom surfaces, especially those surfaces that will be subject to a high concentration of moisture and water. Special tile backer boards and/or flexible sheet waterproof membranes are best suited for such installations.

The most common types of flexible sheet waterproof membranes are polyethylene film and chlorinated polyethylene waterproofing sheets, although some contractors still rely on tar paper (tar saturated felt paper).The polyethylene film and tar paper are fastened to the vertical wall framing members, to which one applies either a galvanized metal lath (a more traditional method) or a tile backer board. The finished ceramic tile is then applied to the setting bed or the tile backer board using an appropriate tile setting material. (Caution: Many contractors will often substitute "green board" or a moisture resistant ("MR") gypsum board in wet and damp areas. This is not an acceptable use of that material and will eventually result in a failed assembly)

Depending upon the detail of the tub or shower, the flexible membrane should lap over the flange of the tub or the shower.

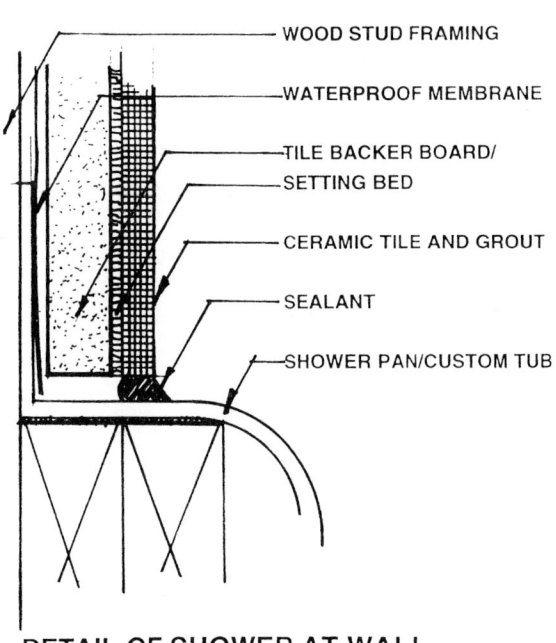

BATHROOMS

Bathtub and Shower Details

BATHTUB WALLS

Wood or Metal Studs

Cement Mortar

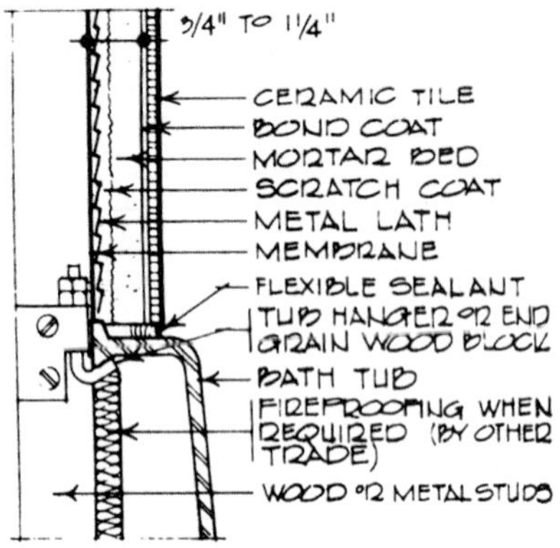

Recommended uses

- over dry, well-braced wood studs, furring, or metal studs
- preferred method of installation over wood studs for bathtubs

Glass Mesh Mortar Units

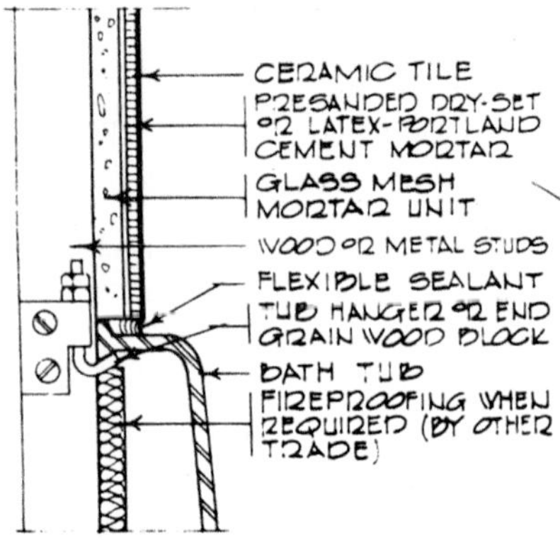

Recommended use

- in tub enclosures and tub showers over dry, well-braced wood studs, furring, or metal studs

Gypsum Board

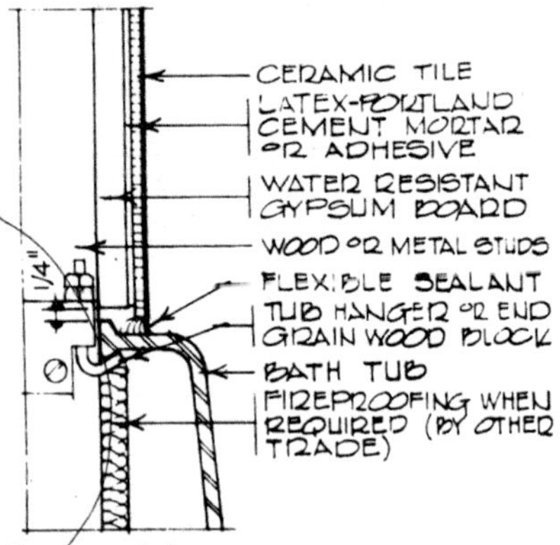

Recommended use

- in tub enclosures and tub showers over water-resistant gypsum backing board on wood or metal studs

TILE TUBS AND FOUNTAINS

Membrane

Cement Mortar

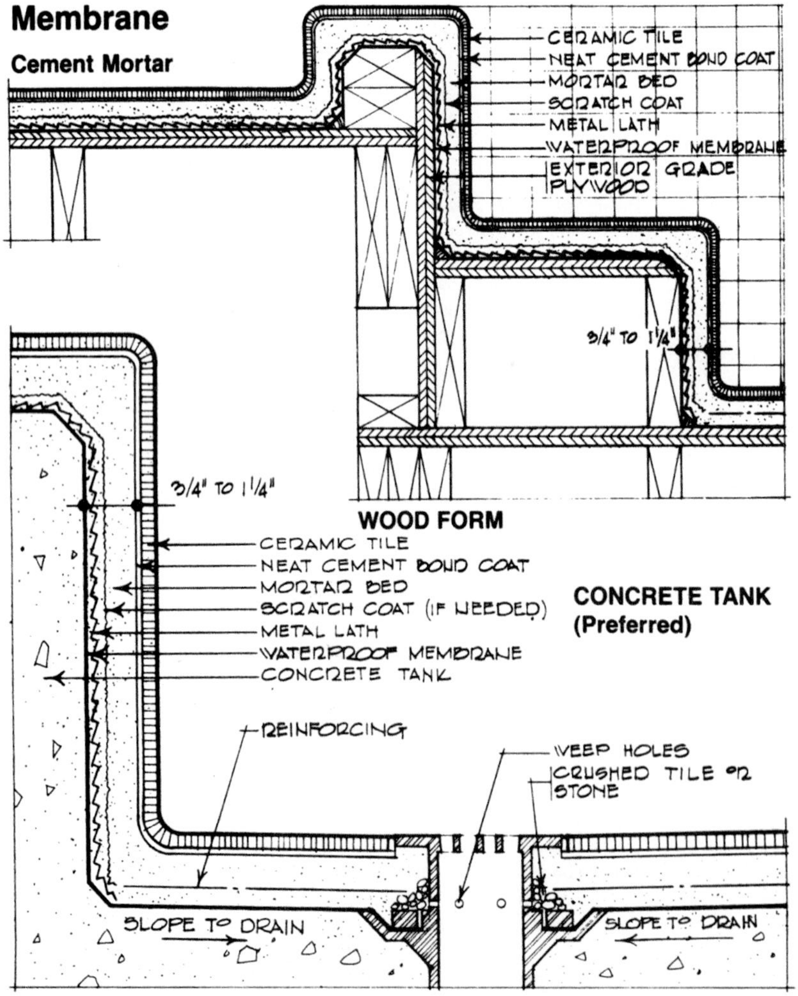

SHOWER RECEPTOR RENOVATION

Cement Mortar

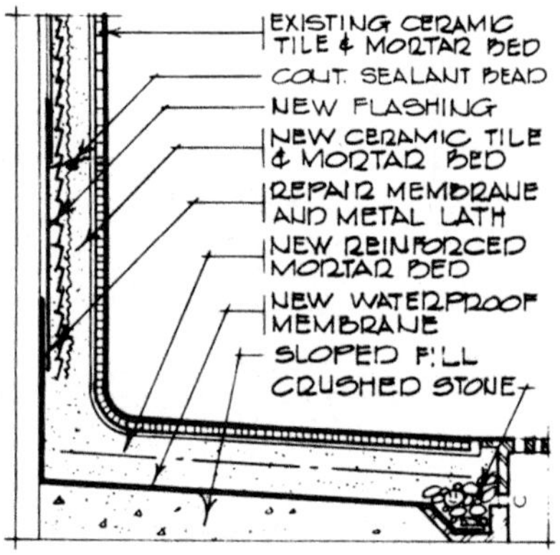

Recommended use

- over wood or concrete subfloors; where old shower pan has failed

Requirements

- waterproof membrane required except in slab-on-grade installations where membrane may be omitted
- slope tank so that membrane will slope to the drain
- flange drain with weep holes required
- wood framing, if used, should be pressure treated and designed to resist deflection and movement

Fig. 17 Typical installation details for bathtub walls, tile tubs, and shower receptors

SHOWER RECEPTORS, WALLS

Wood or Metal Studs

Cement Mortar

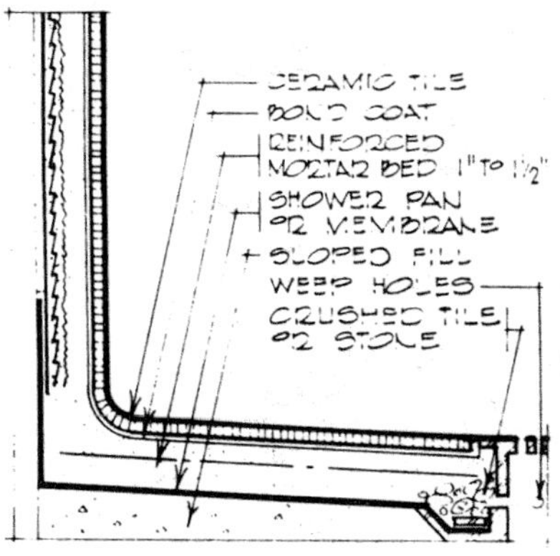

Recommended use

- over wood or concrete subfloors

Glass Mesh Mortar Units

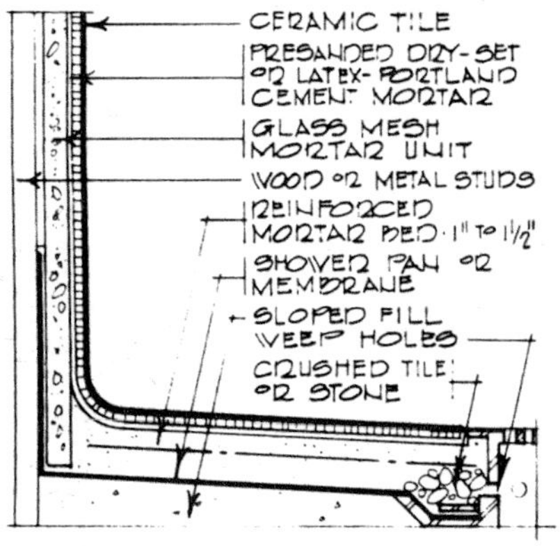

Recommended use

- in showers over dry, well-braced wood studs, furring, or metal studs

Gypsum Board Organic Adhesive

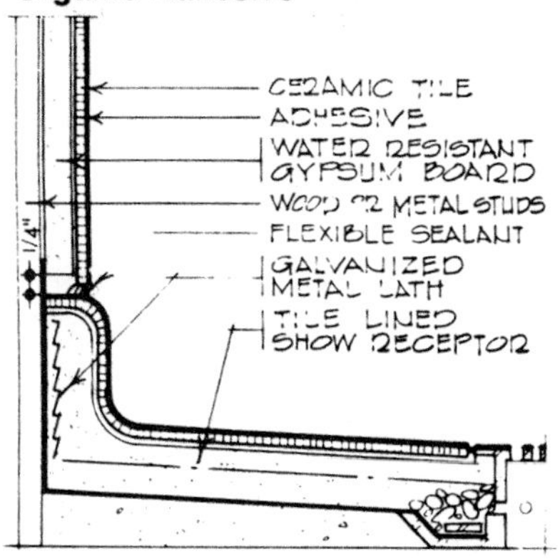

Recommended use

- in showers over water-resistant gypsum backing board on wood or metal studs

COUNTERTOPS

Wood Base

Cement Mortar

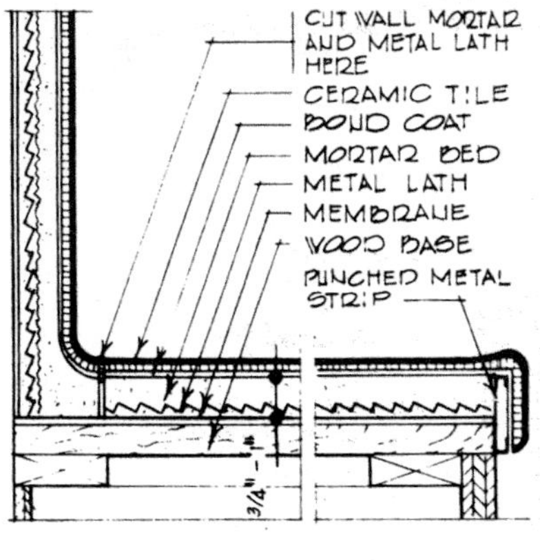

Recommended uses

- on countertops, drainboards, lavatory tops, etc.
- preferred method where sink or lavatory is to be recessed

Thin-Bed

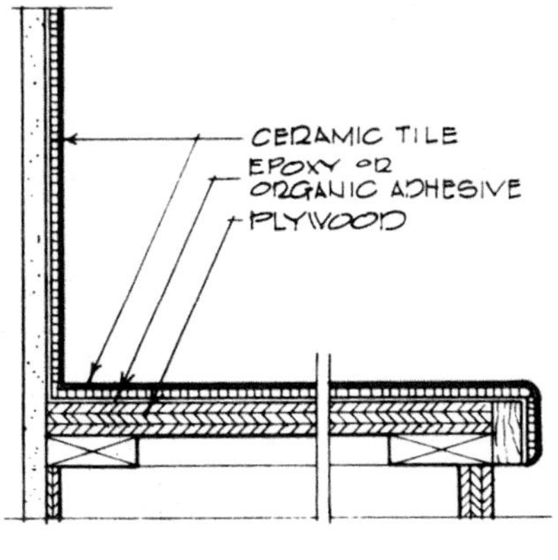

Recommended use

- on countertops where thin-set method is desired

Glass Mesh Mortar Unit

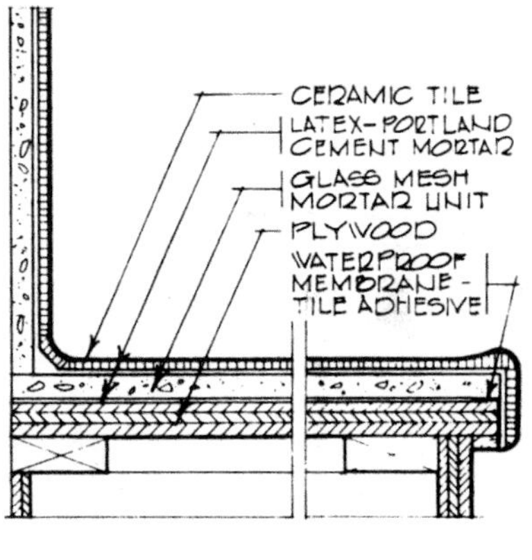

Recommended uses

- preferred thin-set mortar method on countertops, drainboards, lavatory tops, and similar uses
- preferred method where self-rimming sinks and lavatories are desired

Fig. 18 Typical installation details for shower receptors, walls, and countertops

BATHROOMS

Bathtub and Shower Details

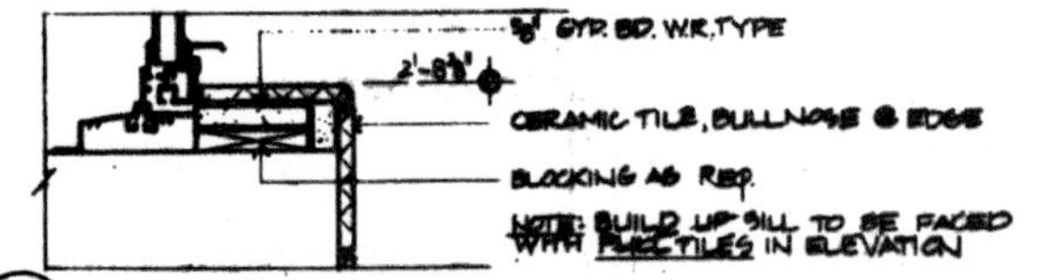

10 / A6 SILL DETAIL @ BATH 2

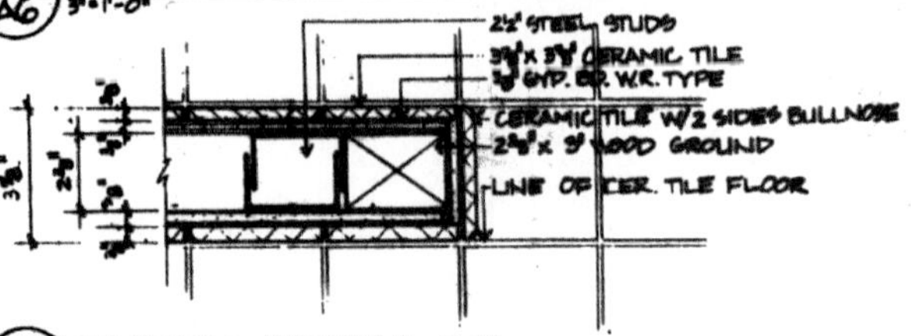

11 / A6 WING WALL @ BATH 2 : TYP.

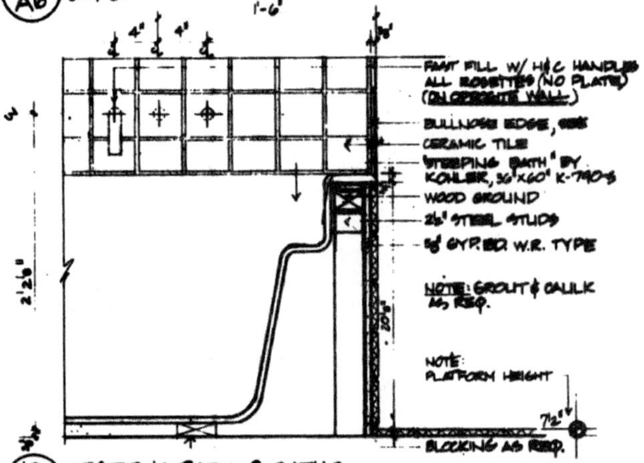

12 / A6 SECTION: BATH @ BATH 2

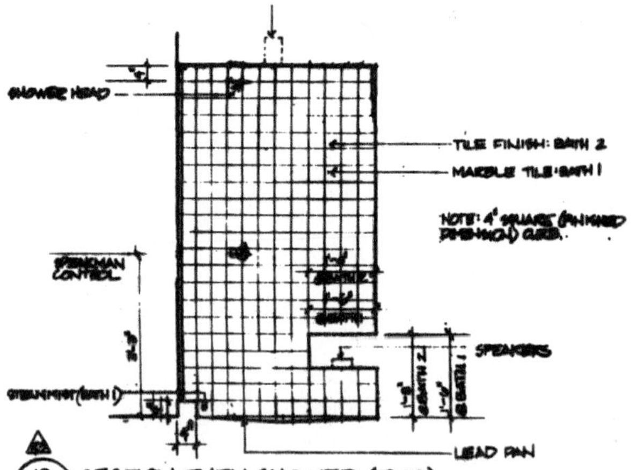

13 / A6 SECTION THRU SHOWER (TYP.)

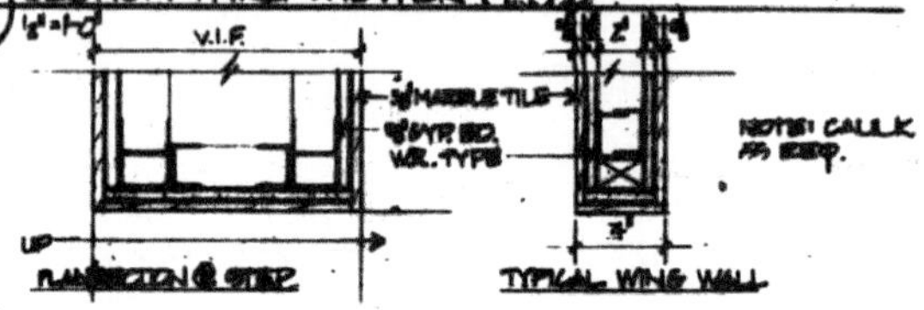

14 / A6 SECTION THRU MARLE TILE WALL @ BATH 1

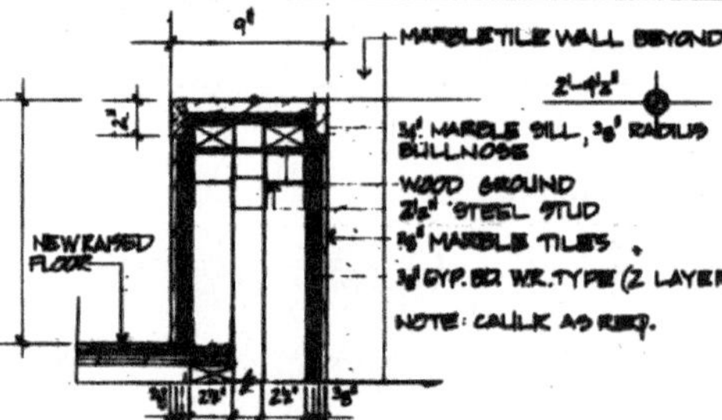

15 / A6 SECTION THRU KNEE WALL & SILL @ BATH 1

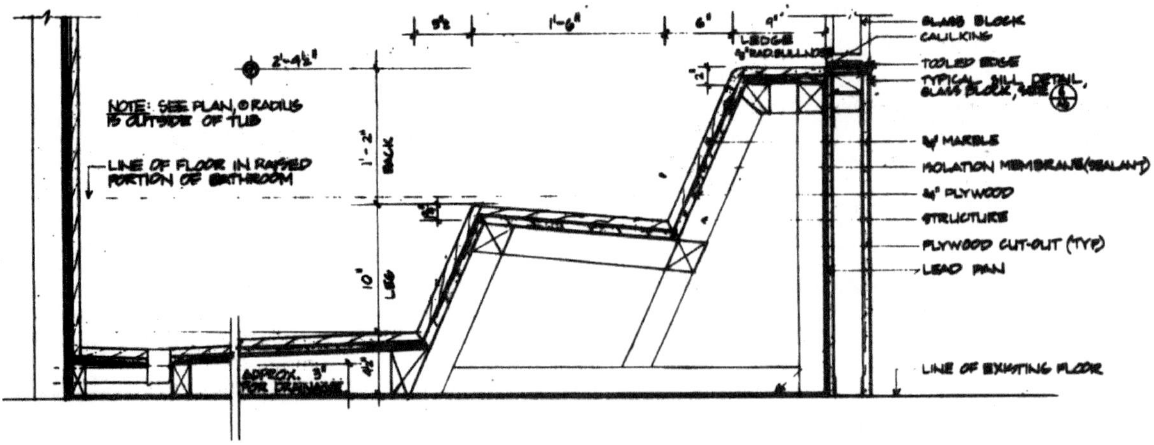

16 / A6 SECTION THRU BATHTUB @ BATH #1 (TYP.)

BATHROOMS
Whirlpool Details

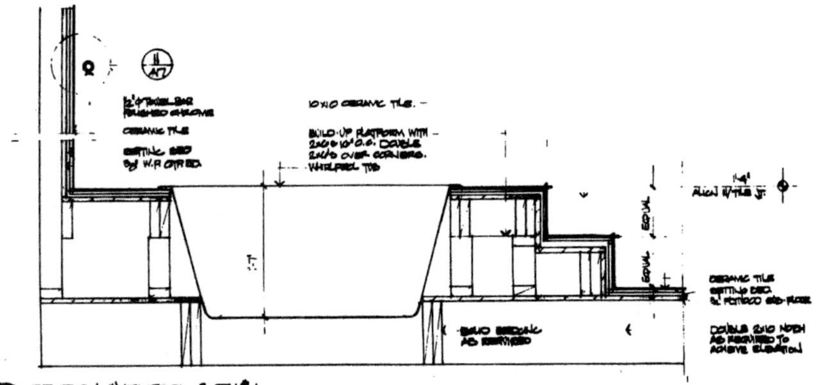

12/A17 SECTION: WHIRLPOOL BATH #1
1"=1'-0"

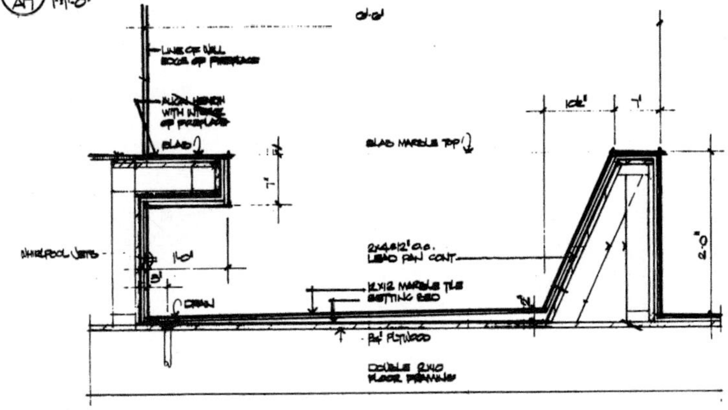

13/A17 SECTION: WHIRLPOOL TUB, MASTER BATH
1"=1'-0"

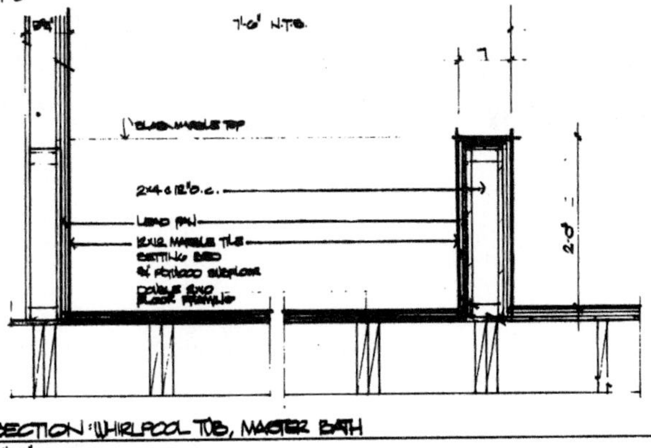

14/A17 SECTION: WHIRLPOOL TUB, MASTER BATH
1"=1'-0"

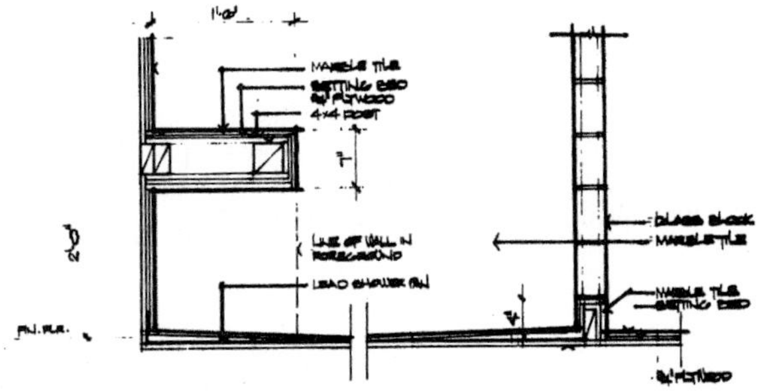

10/A17 SECTION: M. BATH SHOWER
1"=1'-0"

BATHROOMS
Ceramic Tile Details

Interior Walls

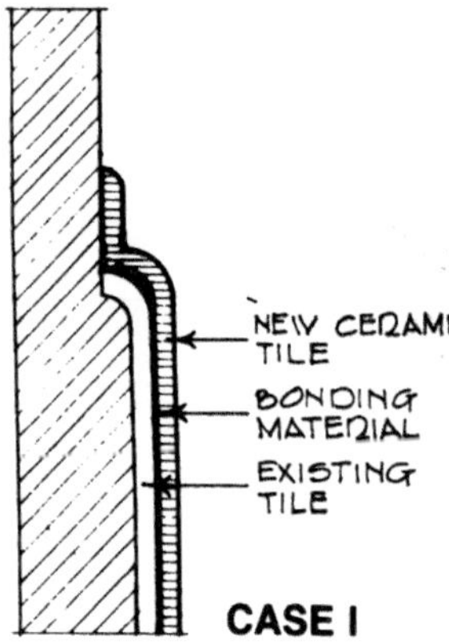

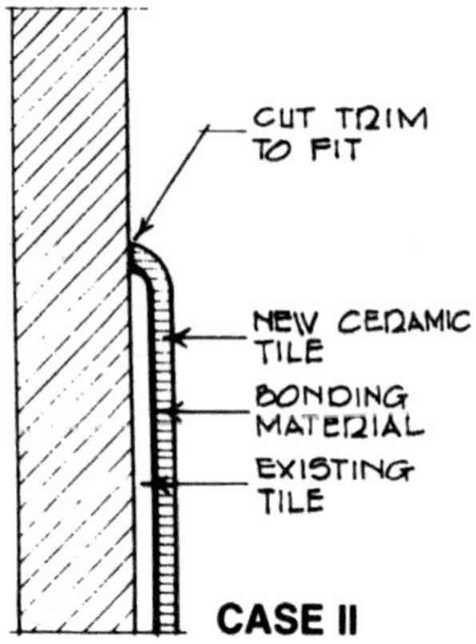

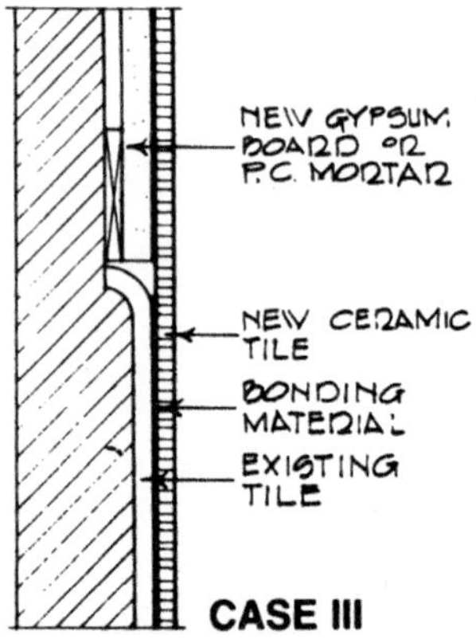

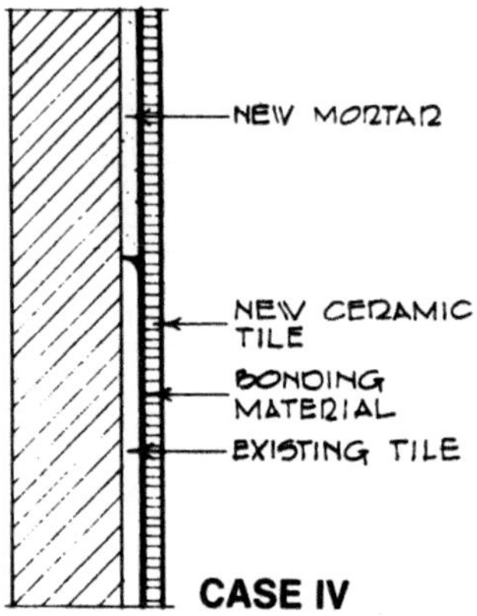

Recommended uses

■ for alteration of ceramic-tiled areas where modernization or a change of design is desired in residences, motels and hotels, restaurants, public rest rooms, etc.

■ also applicable to smooth walls of marble, stone, slate, etc.

Requirements

■ existing installation must be sound, well bonded, and without major structural cracks

Materials, grouting, expansion joints, installation specifications

■ for organic adhesive installation see Method W223

■ for Dry-Set or latex-portland cement mortar installation see Method W202

■ for epoxy adhesive installation refer to manufacturer's literature

Interior Floors

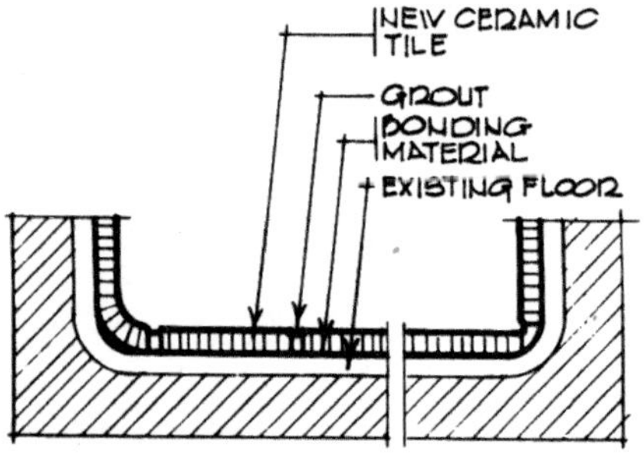

Recommended uses

■ for alteration of ceramic-tiled areas where modernization or a change of design is desired in residences, motels and hotels, restaurants, public rest rooms, etc.

■ also applicable to smooth floors of terrazzo, stone, slate, etc.

Fig. 19 Typical installation details for tile over tile

Accessibility

It is essential that the design of interior spaces, as well as exterior spaces, be responsive to the needs of those having physical disabilities. There is a proliferation of state and local legislation in this regard, and, more recently, federal legislation (Americans with Disabilities Act of 1990) that provides design guidelines and requirements. The designer should become familiar with those codes and other requirements in her or his area prior to initiation of design and, where possible, go beyond the very minimum standards.

The design of the bathroom is perhaps one of those areas where the interface between the physically disabled and the interior space is the most critical. Accordingly, this page and the following pages present design guidelines prepared by the Veterans Administration and the U.S. Department of Housing and Urban Development.

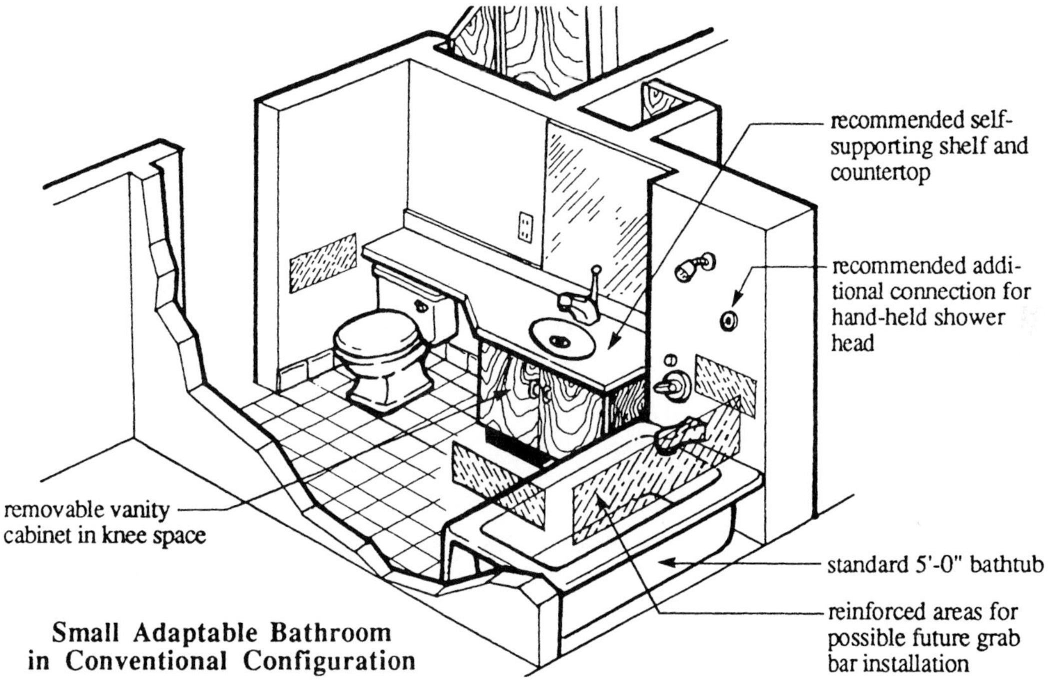

Small Adaptable Bathroom in Conventional Configuration

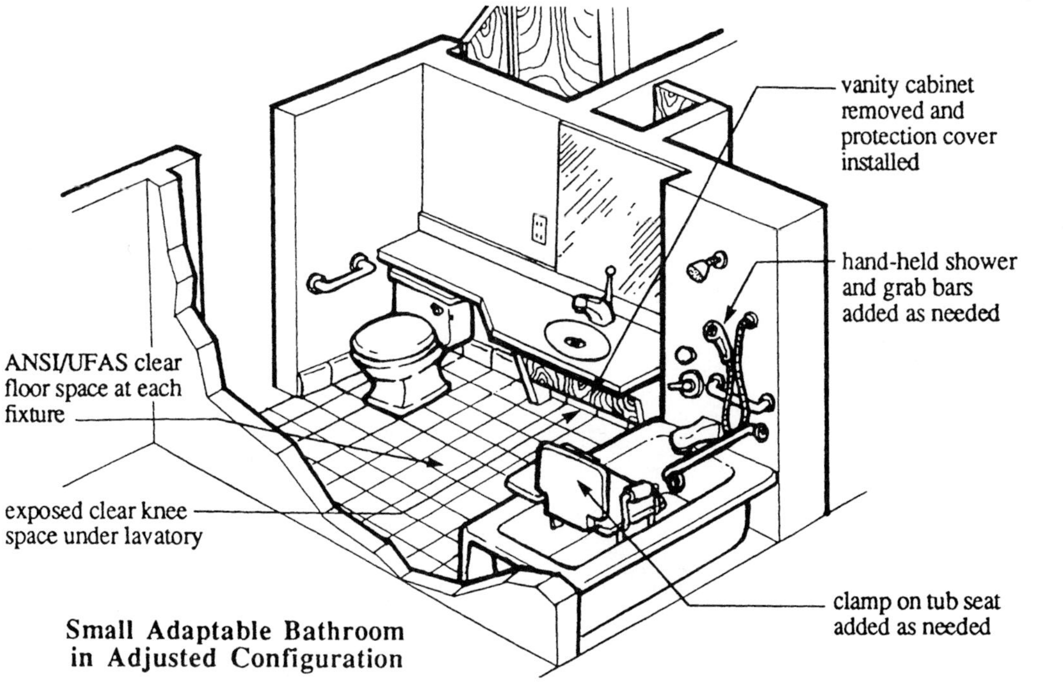

Small Adaptable Bathroom in Adjusted Configuration

BATHROOMS
Adaptable Bathrooms

This sample bathroom meets the minimum space requirements of both ANSI and UFAS; note, however, that the space is very small and many wheelchair users will have difficulty using such a bathroom. More space should be allocated when possible.

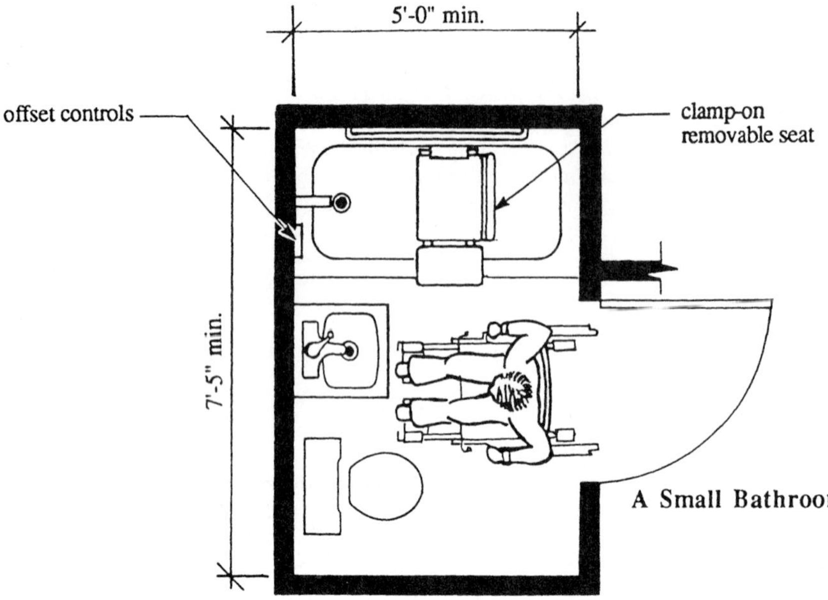

A Small Bathroom with Adaptable Features
Plan

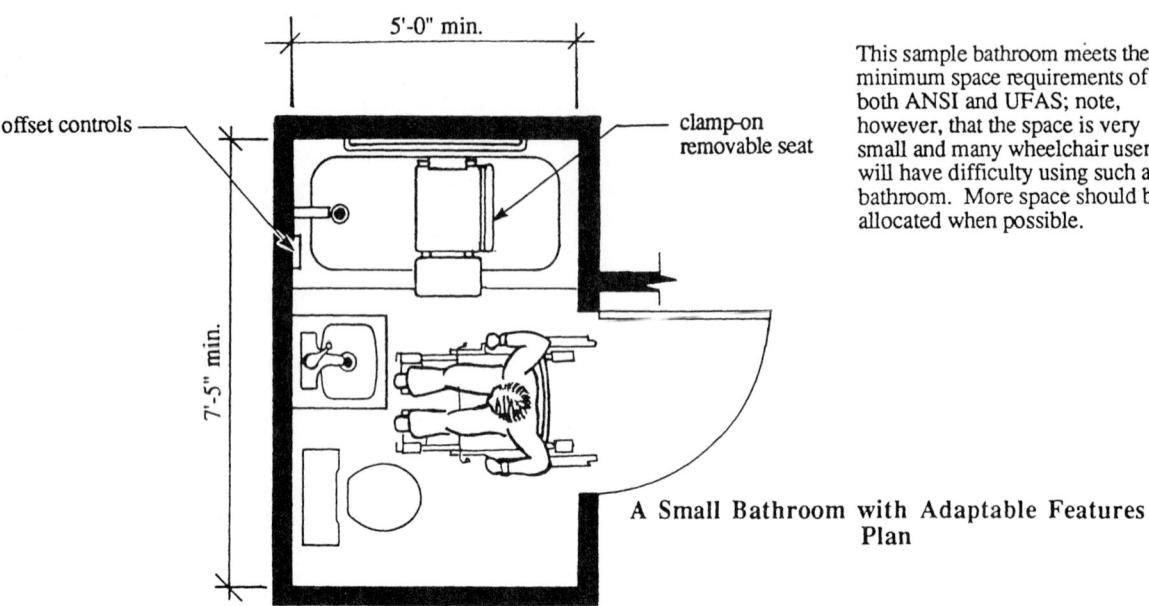

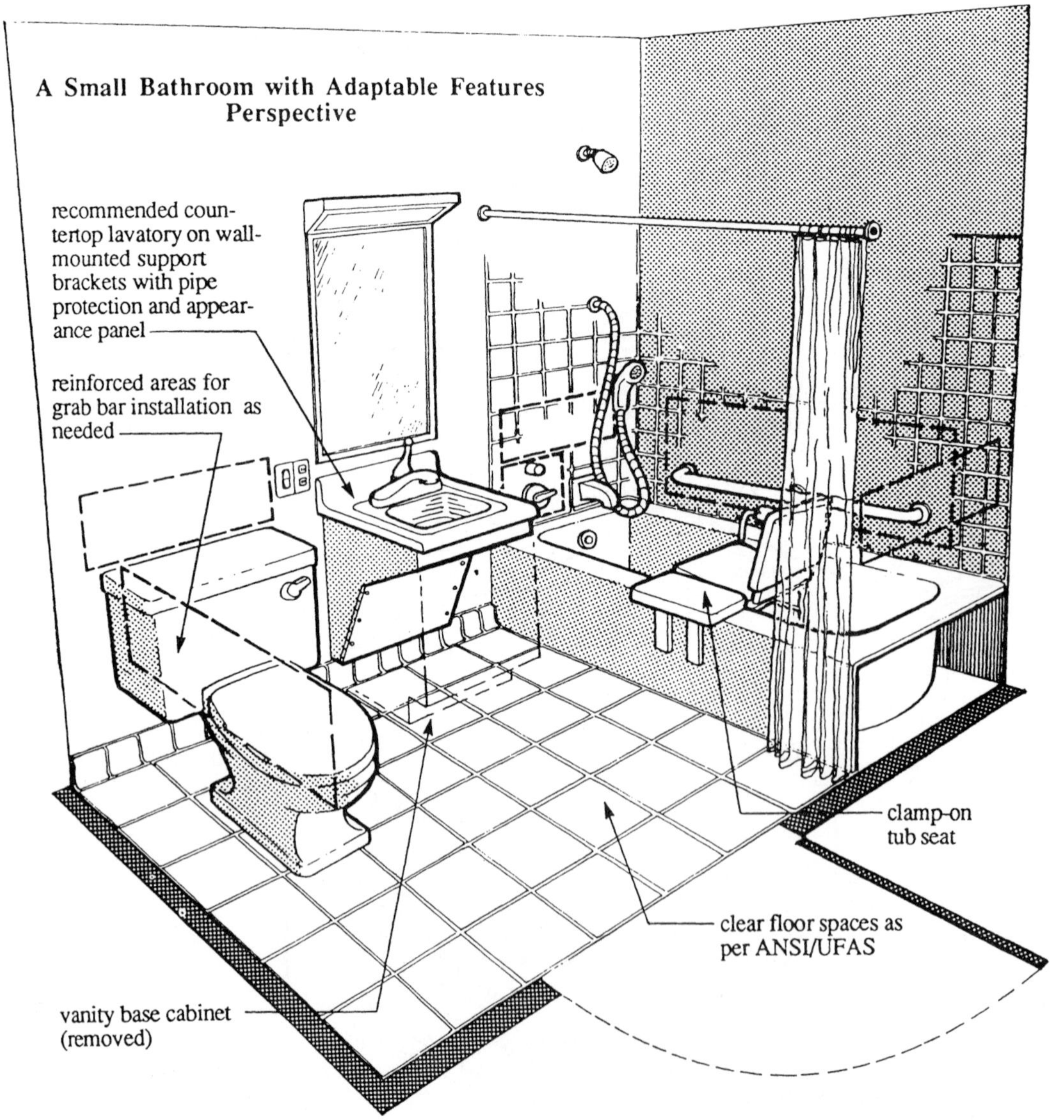

A Small Bathroom with Adaptable Features
Perspective

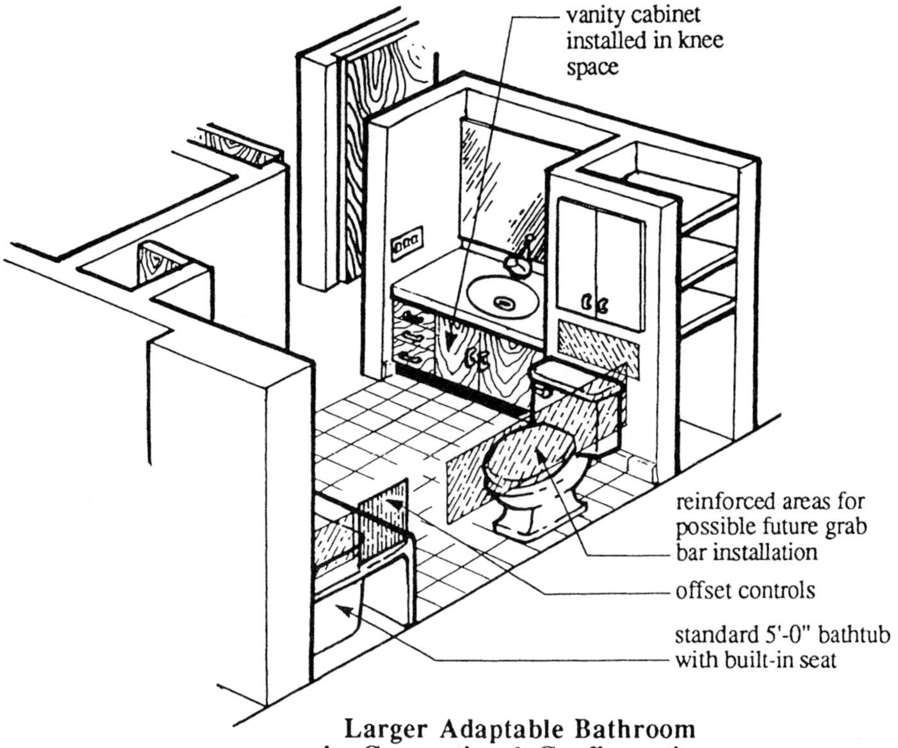

Larger Adaptable Bathroom in Conventional Configuration

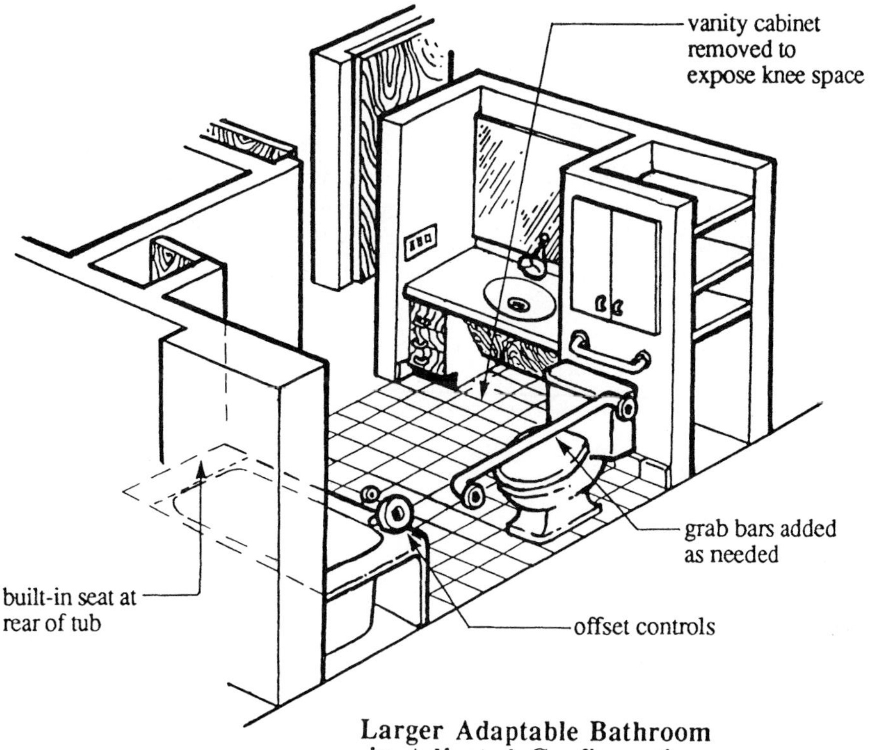

Larger Adaptable Bathroom in Adjusted Configuration

BATHROOMS
Adaptable Bathrooms

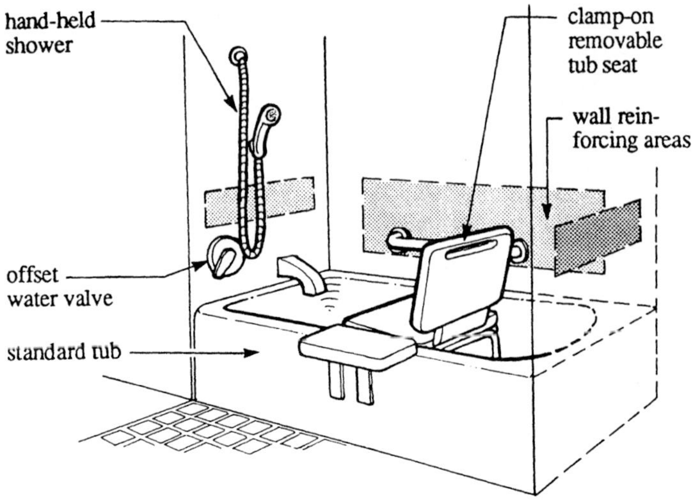

Standard Bathtub with Removable Seat

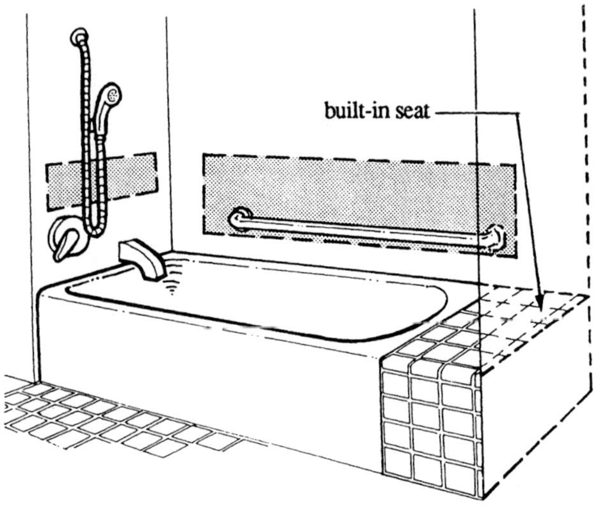

Standard Bathtub with Built-in Seat

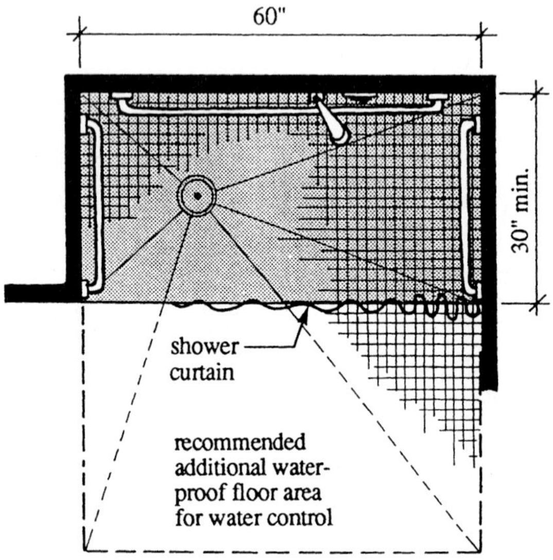

ANSI Minimum Roll-in Shower

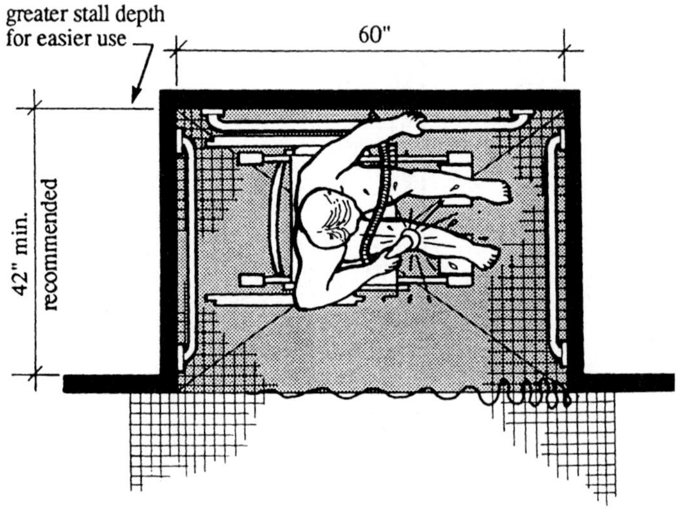

Preferred Deeper Roll-in Shower

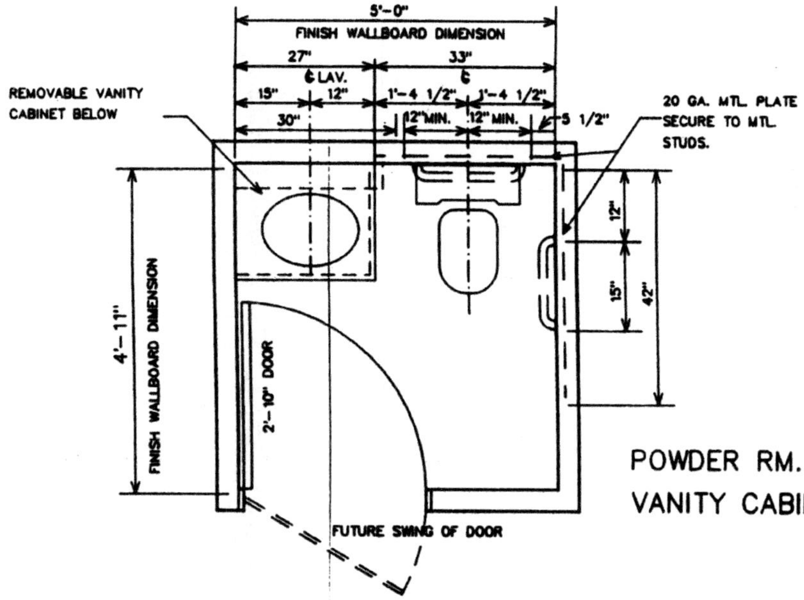

POWDER RM. PLAN WITH 27" REMOVABLE VANITY CABINET

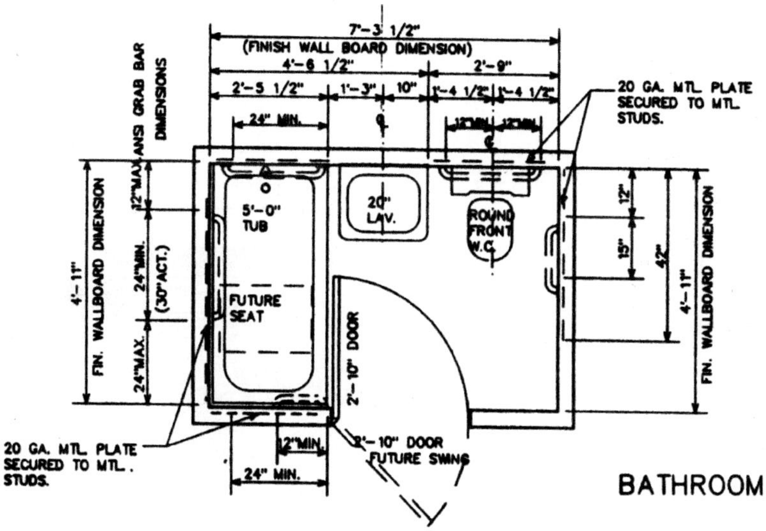

BATHROOM PLAN W/20" LAVATORY

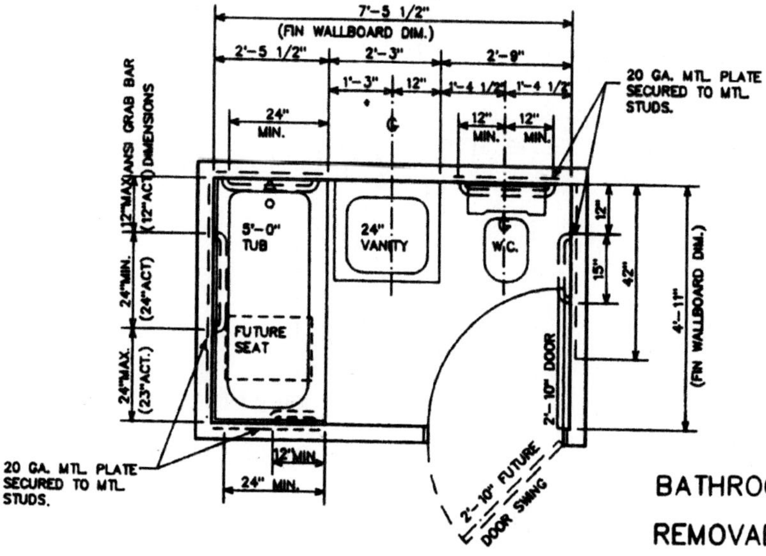

BATHROOM TYPE WITH 24" REMOVABLE VANITY CABINET

BATHROOMS
Adaptable Bathrooms

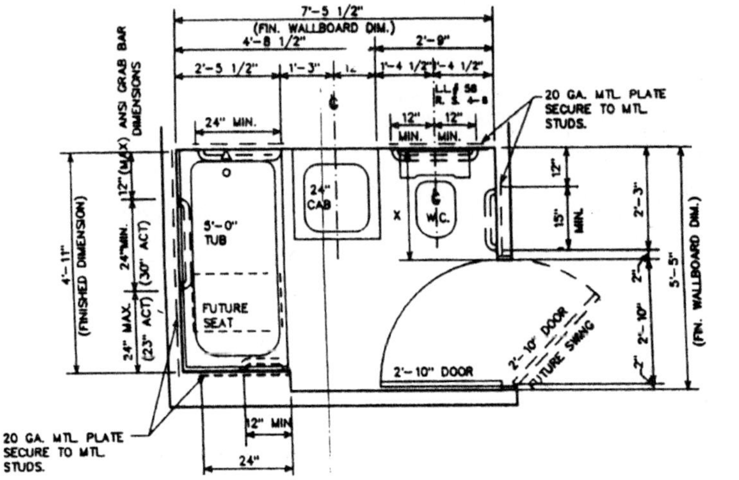

BATHROOM PLAN WITH 24" REMOVABLE VANITY CABINET

X = THE OUTER EDGE OF THE WATER CLOSET WILL NOT EXTEND INTO THE CLEAR SPACE REQUIRED FROM THE DOOR OPENING.

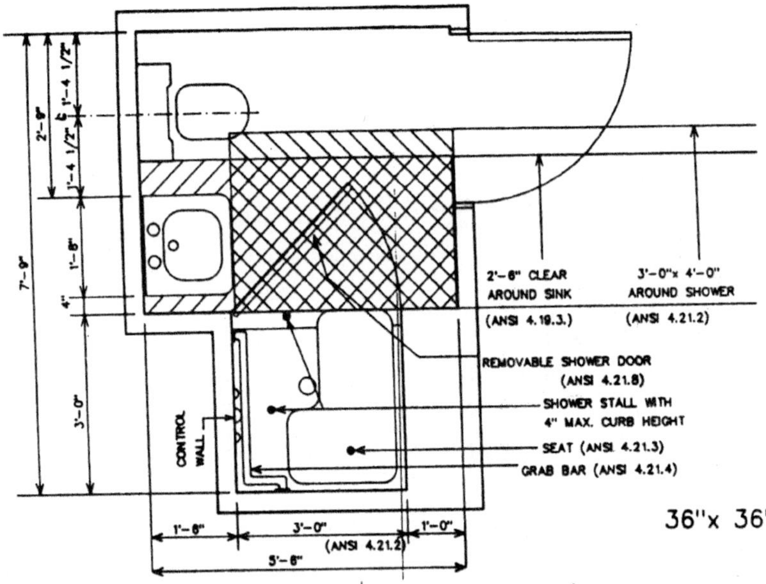

36"x 36" ADAPTABLE SHOWER STALL

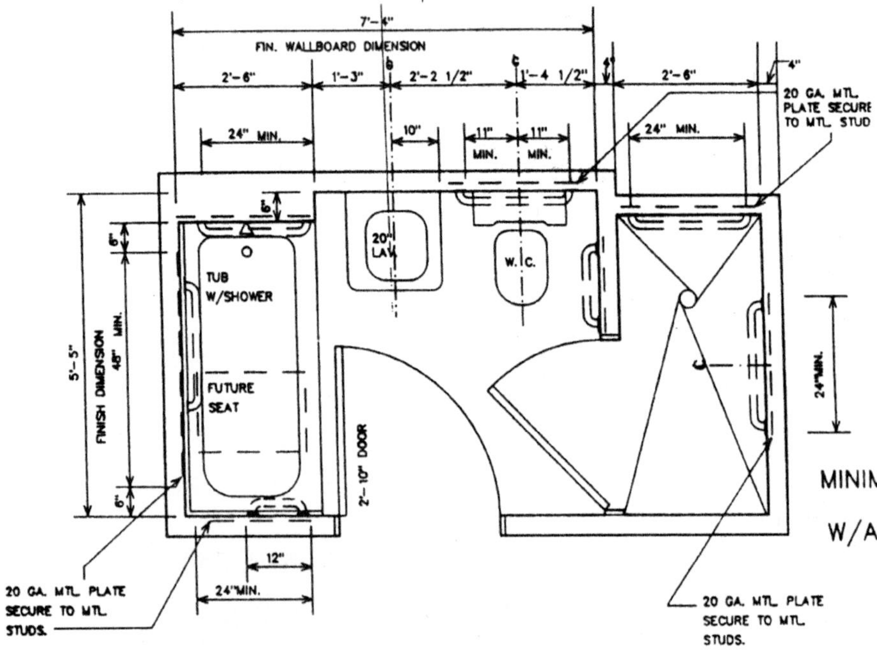

MINIMUM BATHROOM REQUIRED W/ADDITIONAL SHOWER

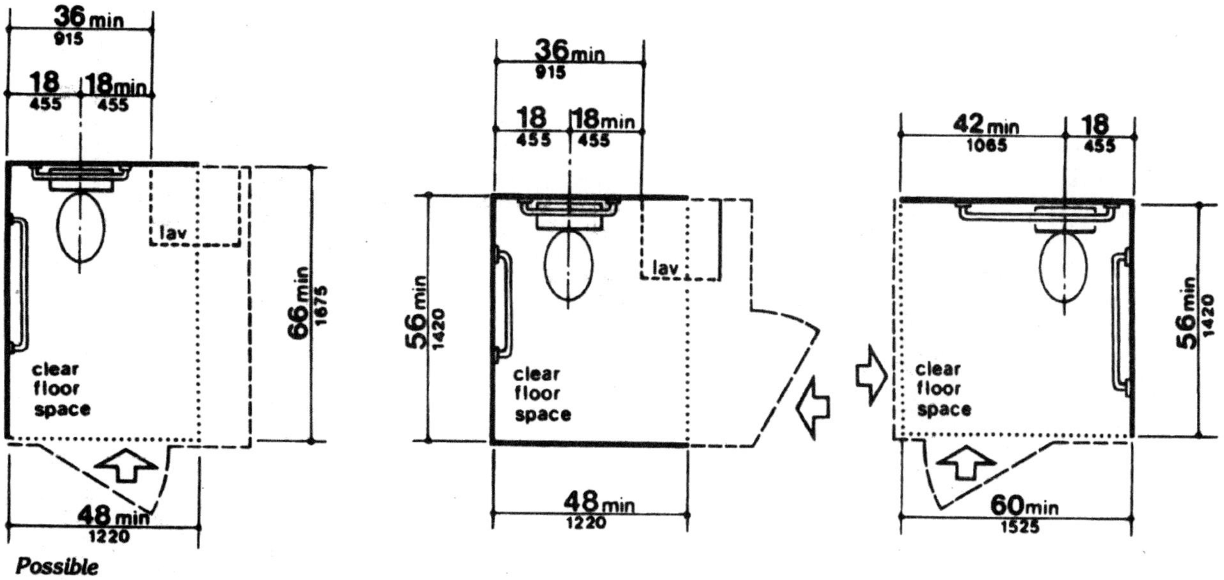

Clear Floor Space at Water Closets

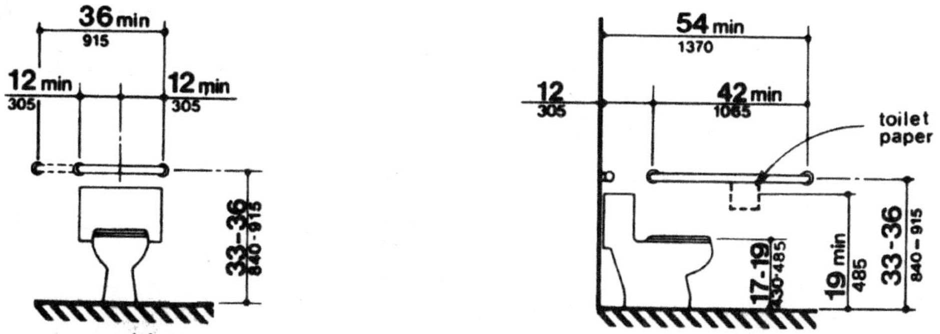

(a)
Back Wall

(b)
Side Wall

Grab Bars at Water Closets

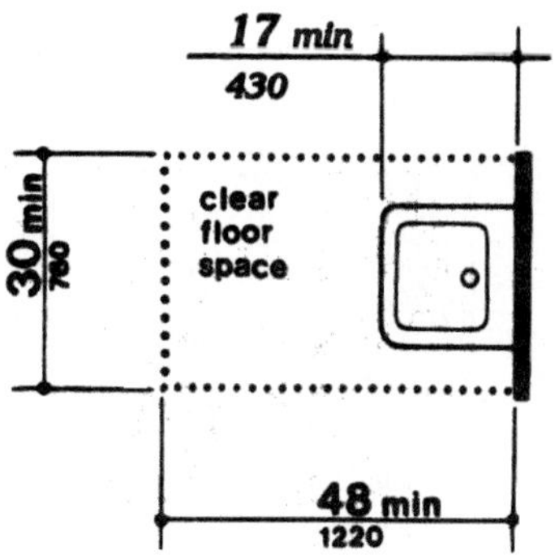

Clear Floor Space at Lavatories

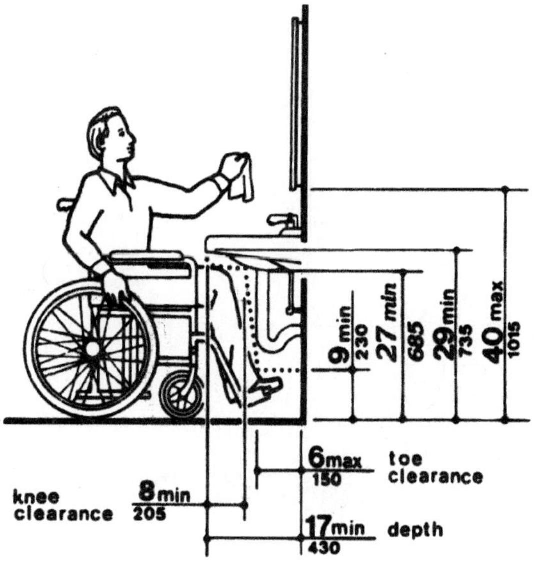

Lavatory Clearances

BATHROOMS
Wheelchair-Accessible Clearances

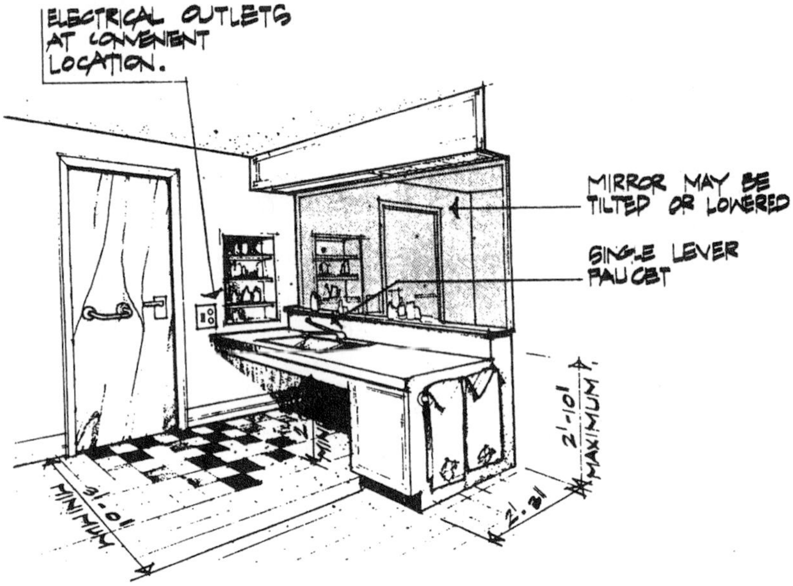

Vanity

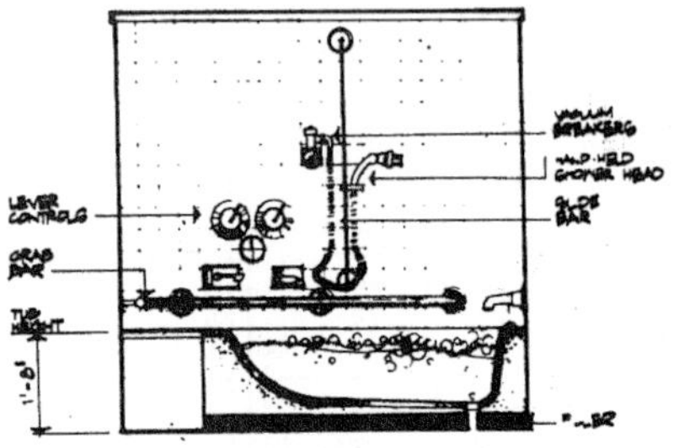

Combination bathtub/shower.

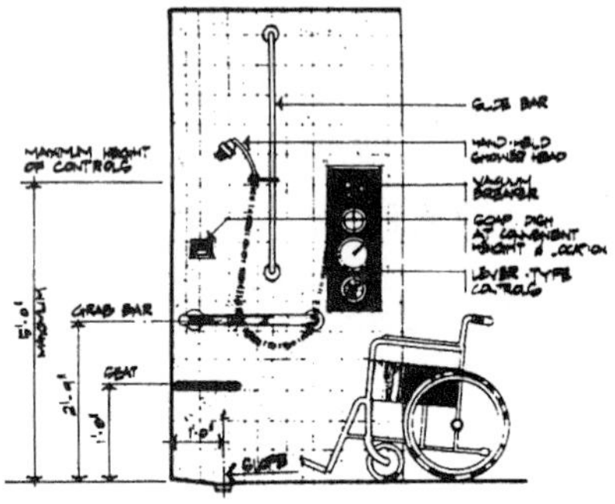

Shower

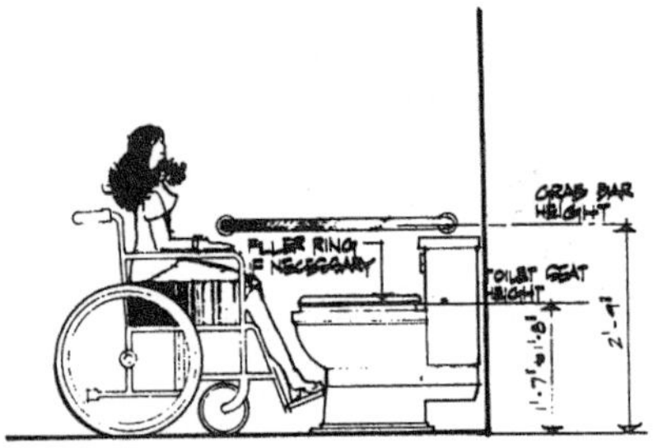

Floor-mounted water closet

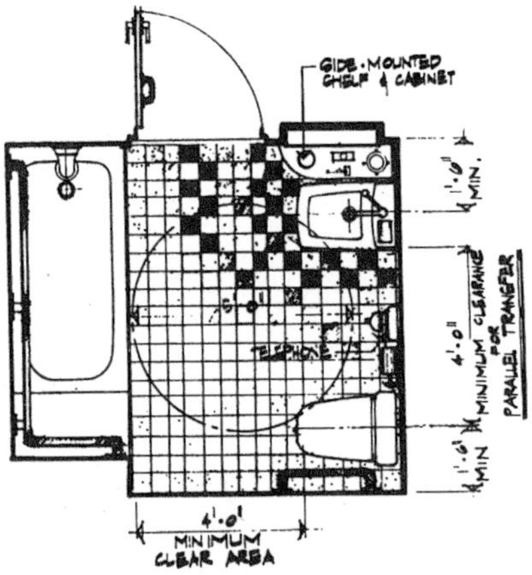

Typical bathroom arrangement

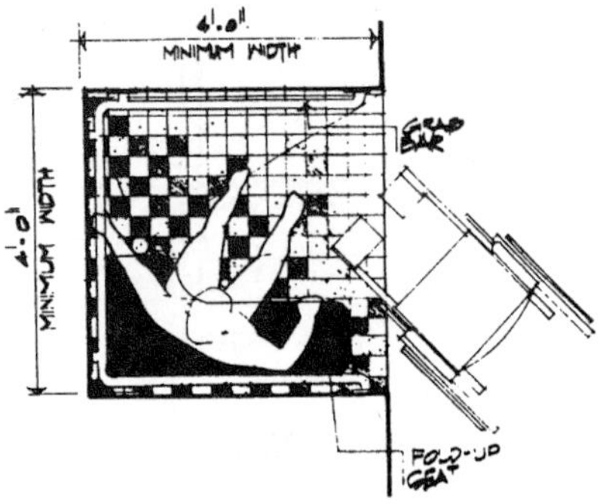

Shower seat

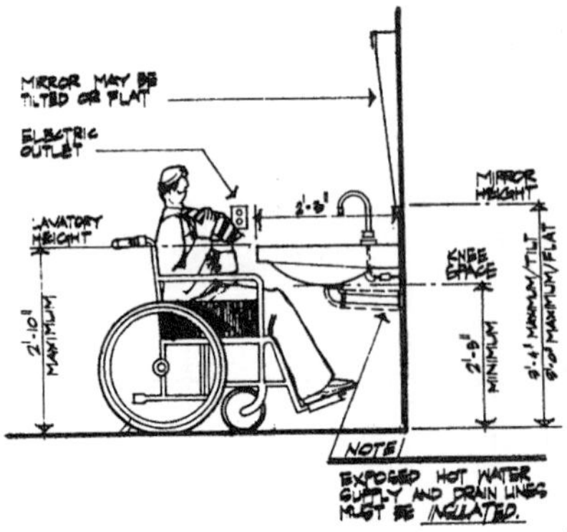

Lavatory

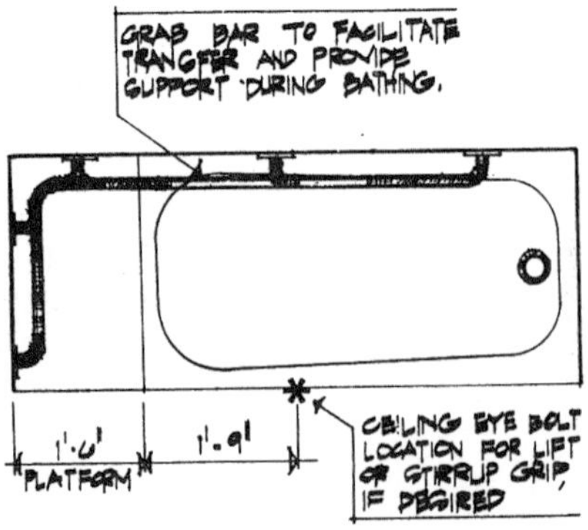

Bathtub

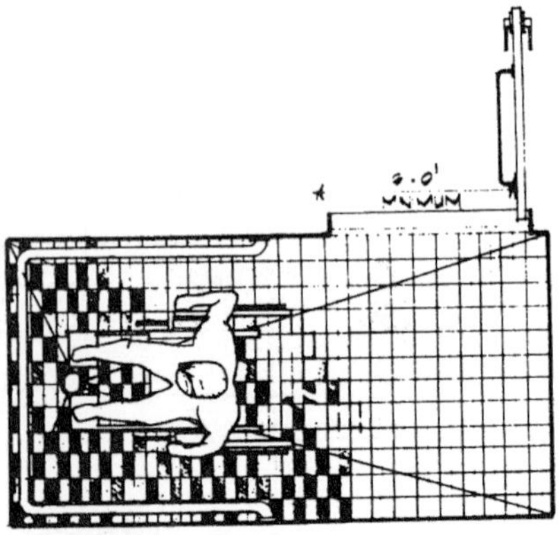

"Roll-in" shower

BATHROOMS
Wheelchair-Accessible Design

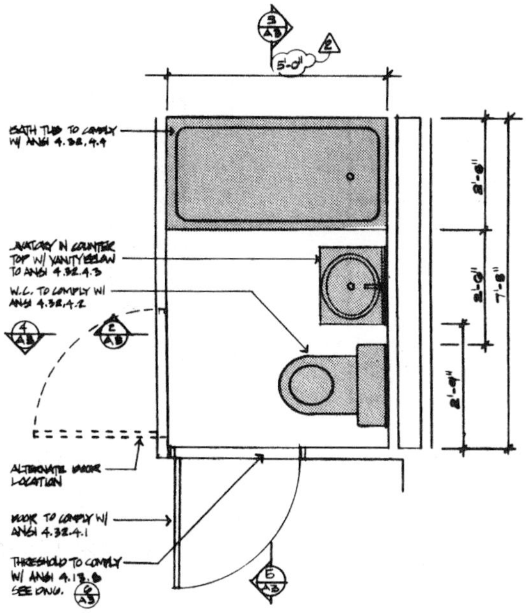

1 A3 PLAN: TYPICAL ADAPTABLE BATHROOM
1/2" = 1'-0"

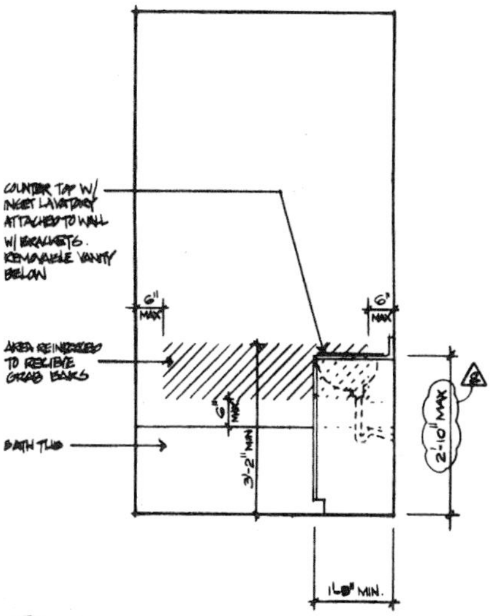

2 A3 ELEVATION: TYPICAL ADAPTABLE BATHROOM
1/2" = 1'-0"

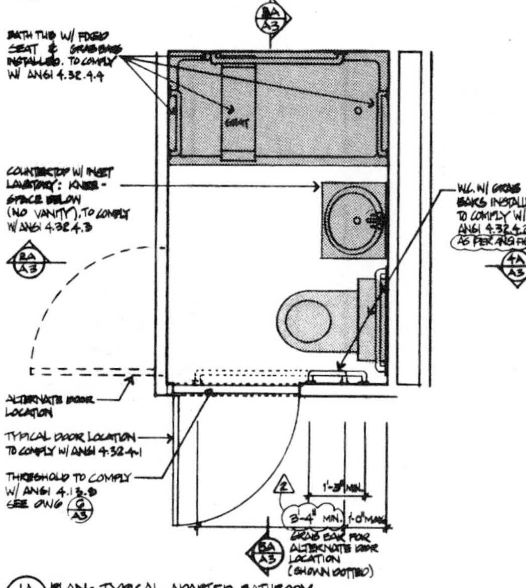

1A A3 PLAN: TYPICAL ADAPTED BATHROOM
1/2" = 1'-0"

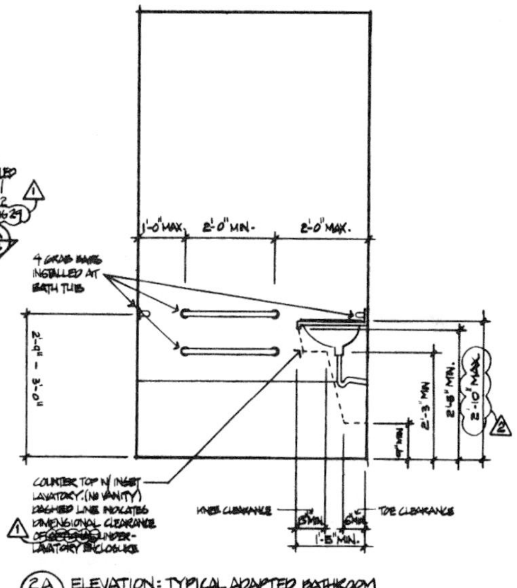

2A A3 ELEVATION: TYPICAL ADAPTED BATHROOM
1/2" = 1'-0"

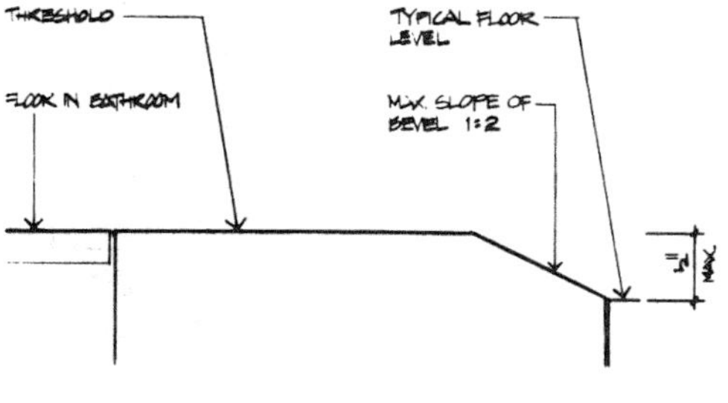

6 A3 SECTION THRU THRESHOLD: TO COMPLY W/ ANSI 4.13.8
FULL SIZE

BATHROOMS
Wheelchair-Accessible Clearance

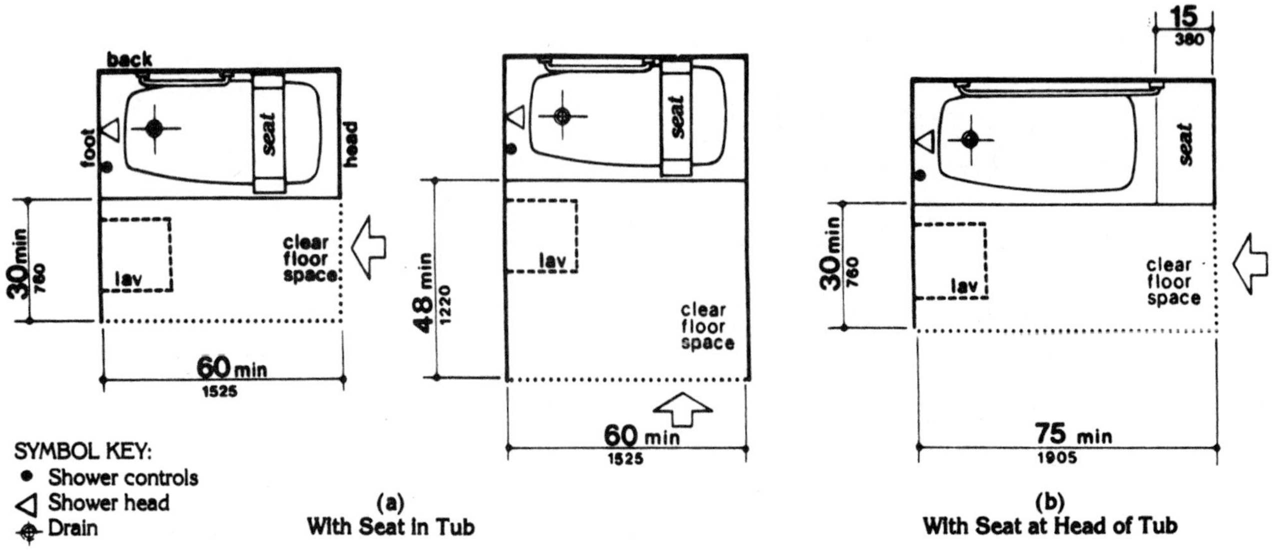

(a) With Seat in Tub

(b) With Seat at Head of Tub

Clear Floor Space at Bathtubs

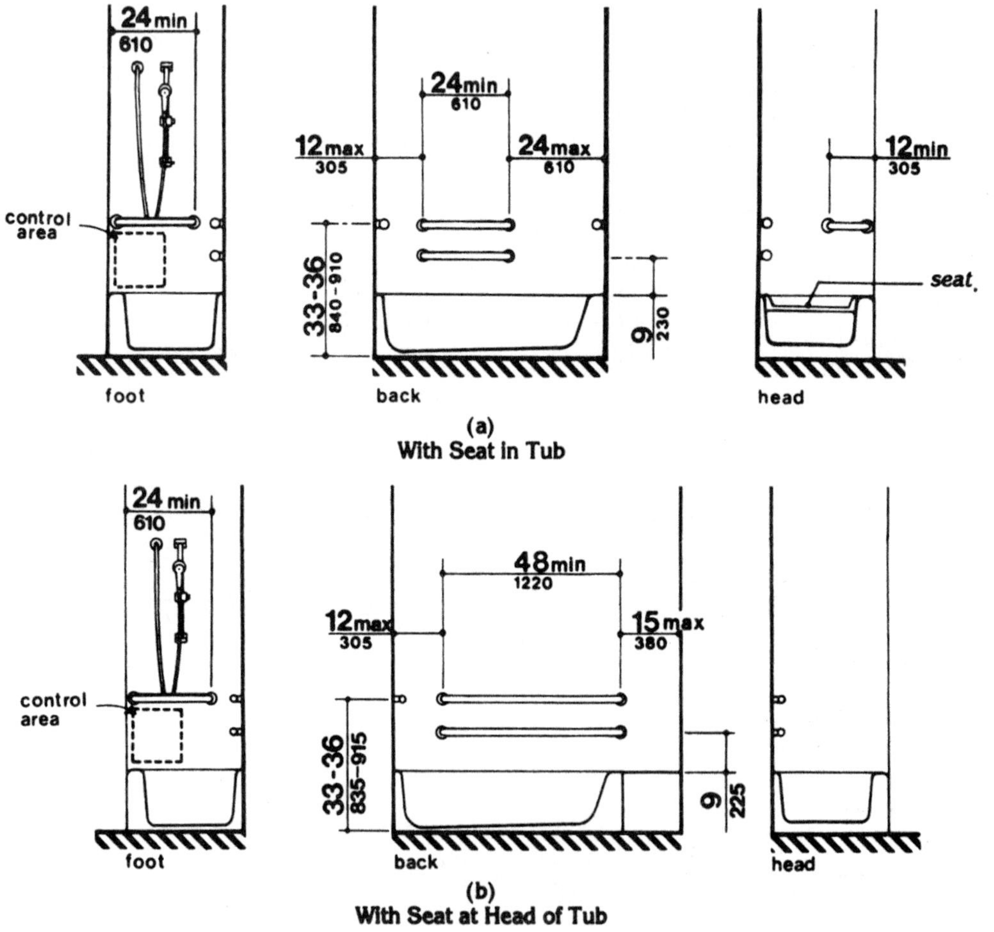

(a) With Seat in Tub

(b) With Seat at Head of Tub

Grab Bars at Bathtubs

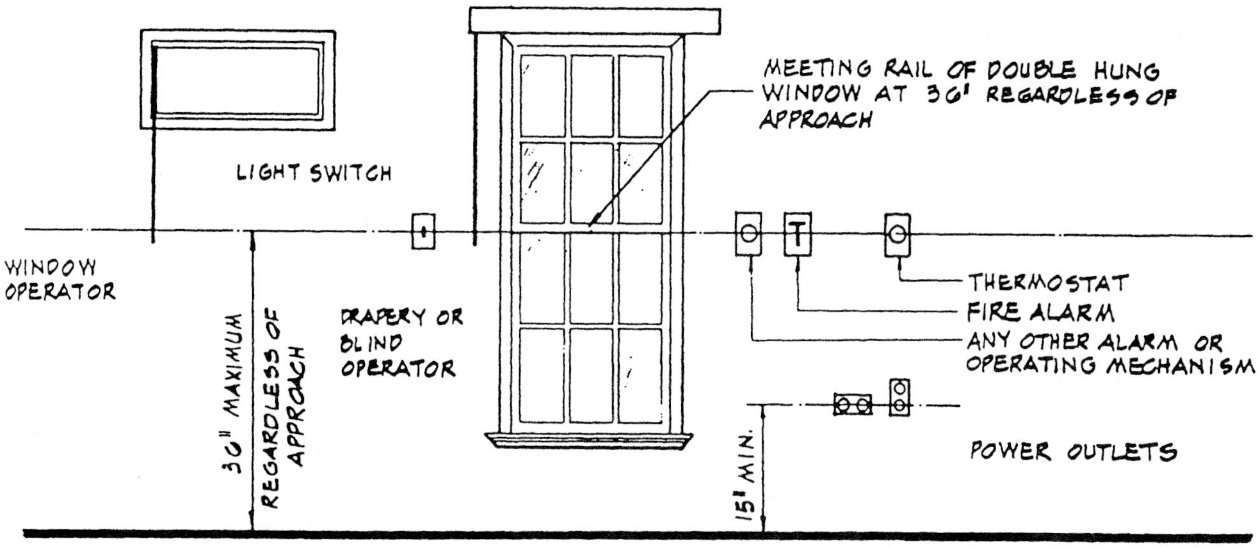

Fig. 1 Height requirements for controls and operating mechanisms

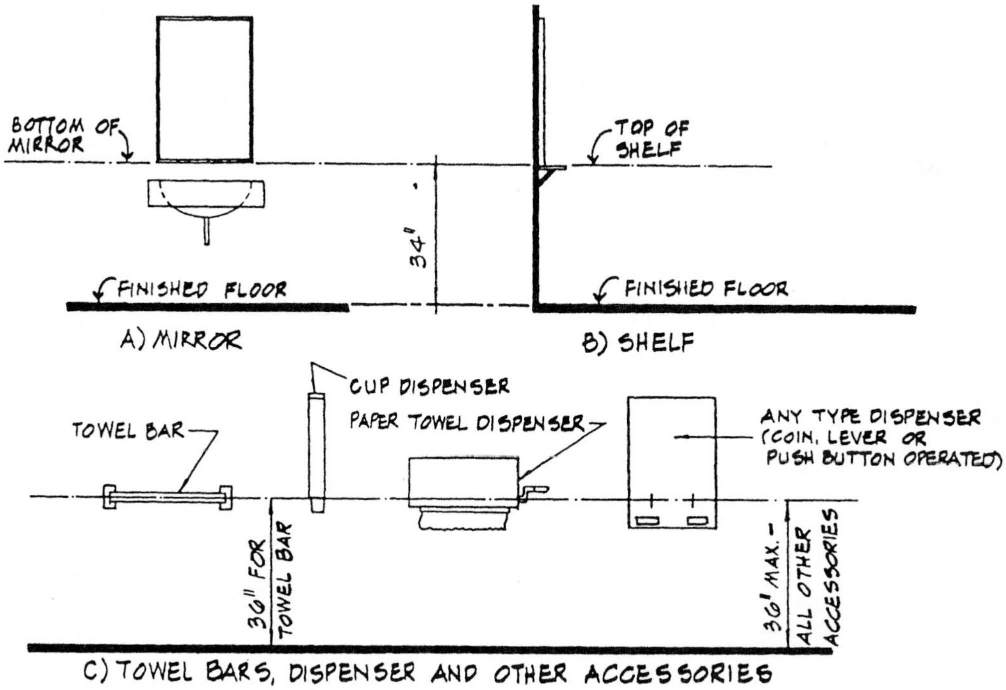

Fig. 2 Accessible toilet accessories

BATHROOMS

Accessible Bathroom Plans

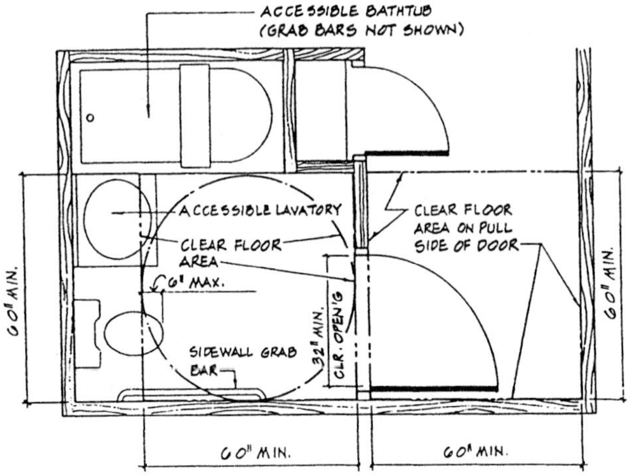

Fig. 3 Floor clearances for bathroom with outswing door

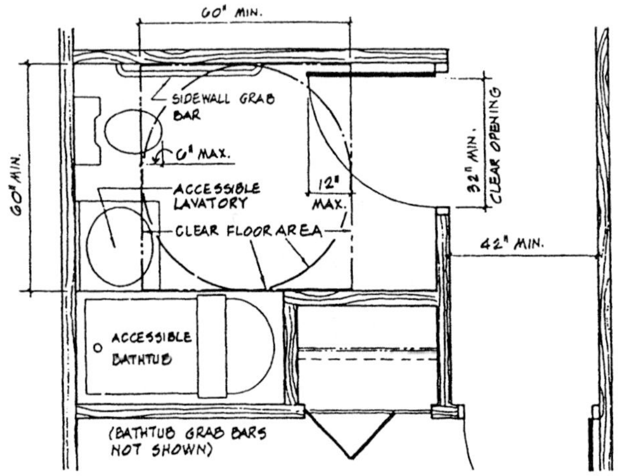

Fig. 5 Floor clearances for bathroom with inswing door

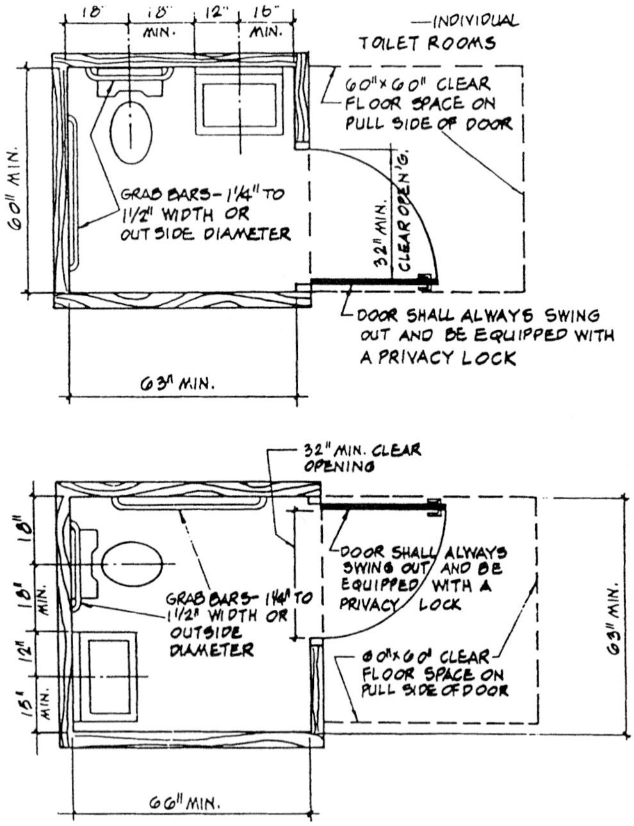

Fig. 4 Individual toilet rooms

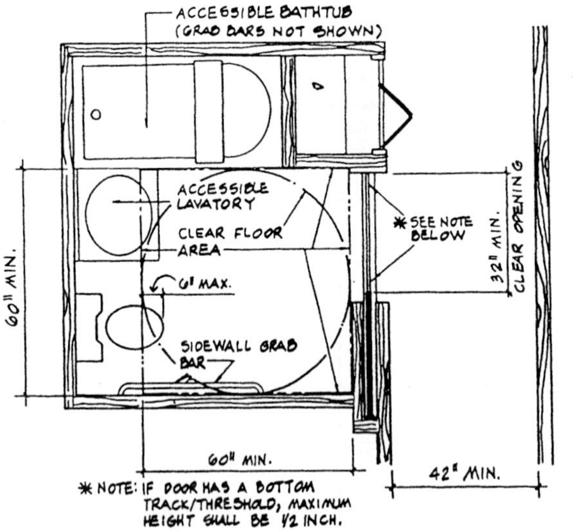

Fig. 6 Floor clearances for bathroom with sliding door

BATHROOMS

Accessible Bathroom Elevations

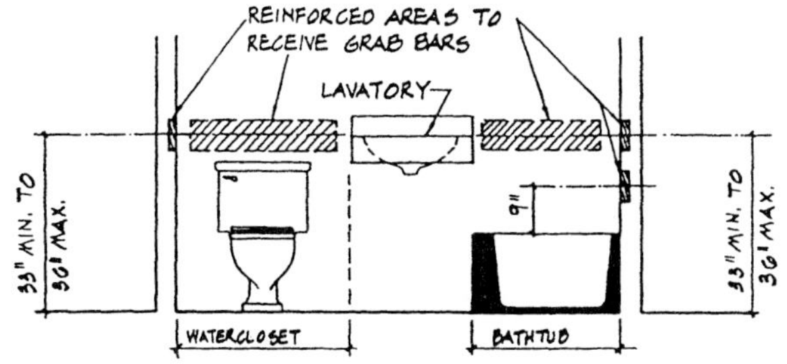

—WALLS OR PARTITIONS ADJACENT TO AND BEHIND WATERCLOSETS AND SURROUNDING BATHTUBS SHALL BE SUITABLY REINFORCED TO SUPPORT BOTH THE GRAB BAR ITSELF AND A 250 POUND LOAD.

Fig. 7 Blocking for grab bars

GRAB BARS SHALL BE 1¼" TO 1½" OUTSIDE DIAMETER WITH A 1½" HAND SPACE BETWEEN THE INNER FACE OF THE BAR AND THE FINISHED FACE OF THE WALL OR PARTITION. GRAB BARS SHALL SUPPORT A LOAD OF 250 POUNDS.

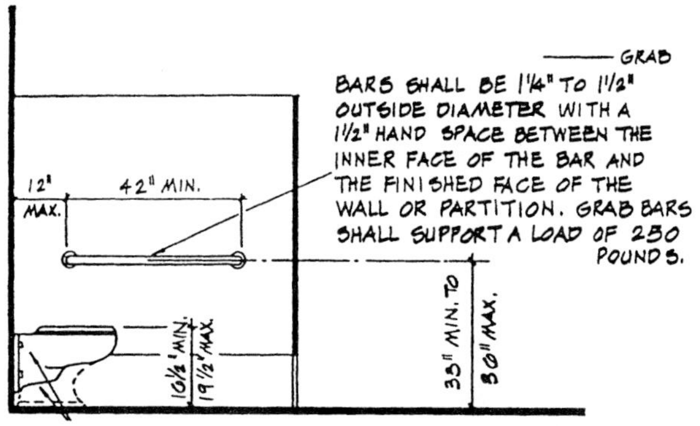

—ACCESSIBLE WATERCLOSETS, WHETHER FLOOR MOUNTED OR WALL MOUNTED, SHALL HAVE THE SEAT (NOT THE RIM) AT 16½" MINIMUM TO 19½ INCHES MAXIMUM ABOVE THE FINISHED FLOOR.

—GRAB BARS IN STANDARD SIZE TOILET STALLS SHALL HAVE ONE GRAB BAR LOCATED ON EACH SIDEWALL.

Fig. 9 Toilet stall grab bars

SIDE ELEVATION

—LARGE SIZE TOILET STALLS SHALL HAVE ONE SIDEWALL AND ONE REAR WALL MOUNTED GRAB BAR.

FRONT ELEVATION

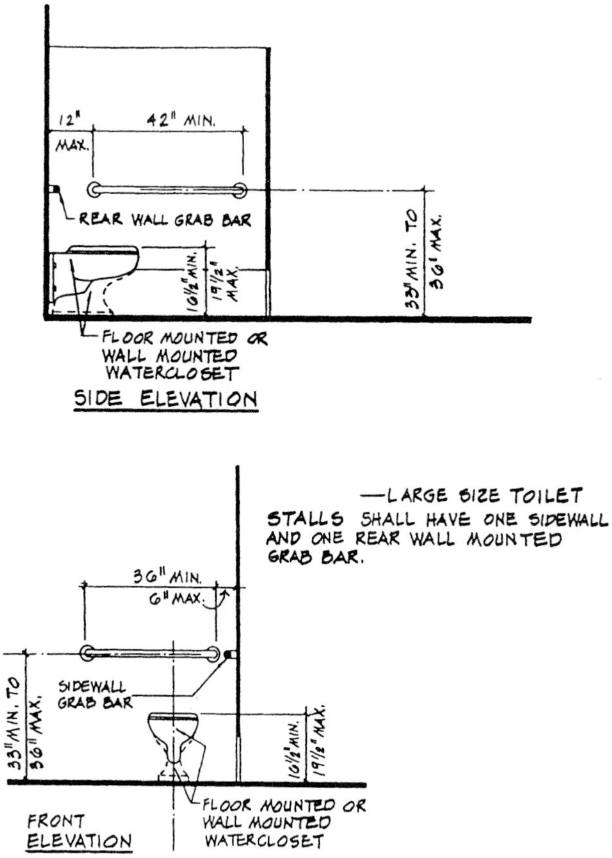

Fig. 8 Toilet stall grab bars

SIDE ELEVATION

—INDIVIDUAL TOILET ROOMS SHALL HAVE A 24" LONG REAR WALL GRAB BAR AND A 42" LONG SIDEWALL GRAB BAR.

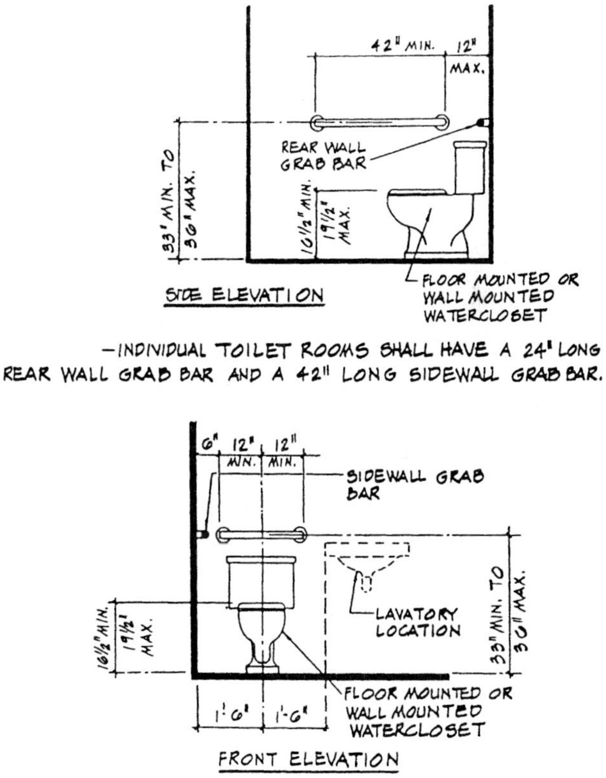

Fig. 10 Individual toilet room grab bars

BATHROOMS

Accessible Toilet and Urinal Plans and Elevations

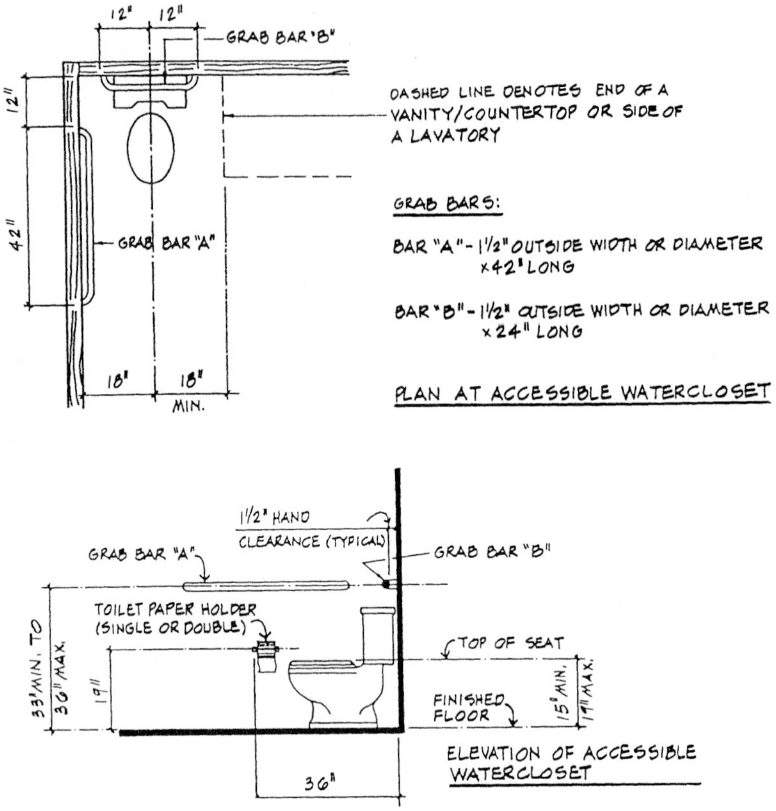

Fig. 11 Accessible water closet, showing requirements of the ANSI code

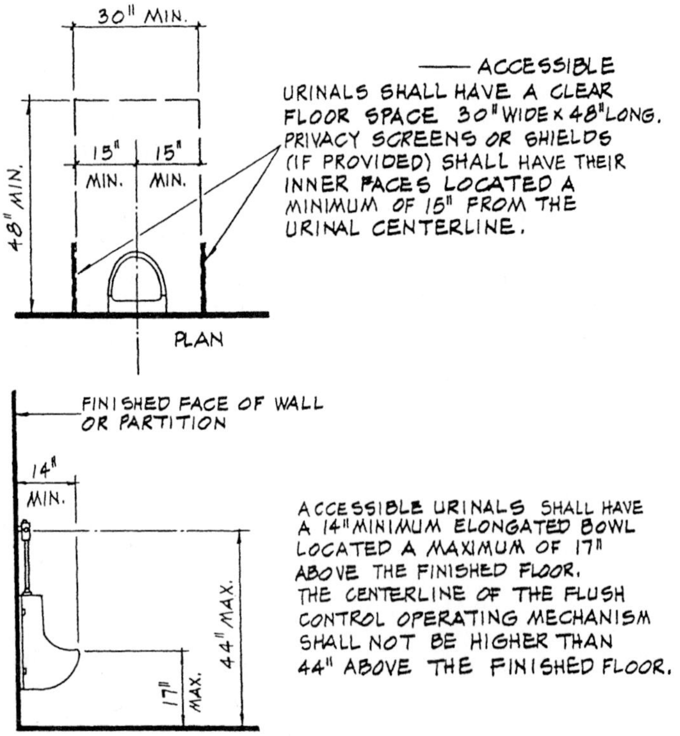

Fig. 12 Accessible urinals

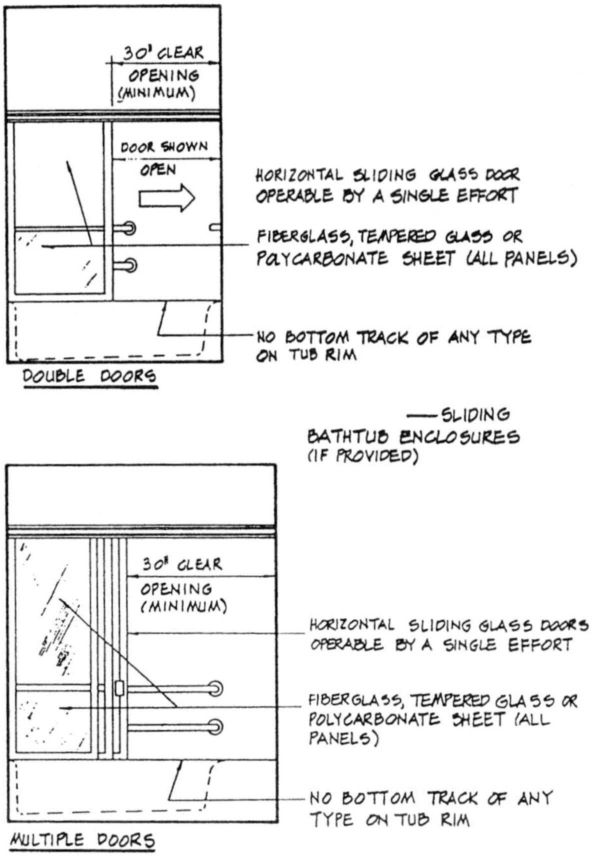

Fig. 13 Sliding door bathtub enclosures

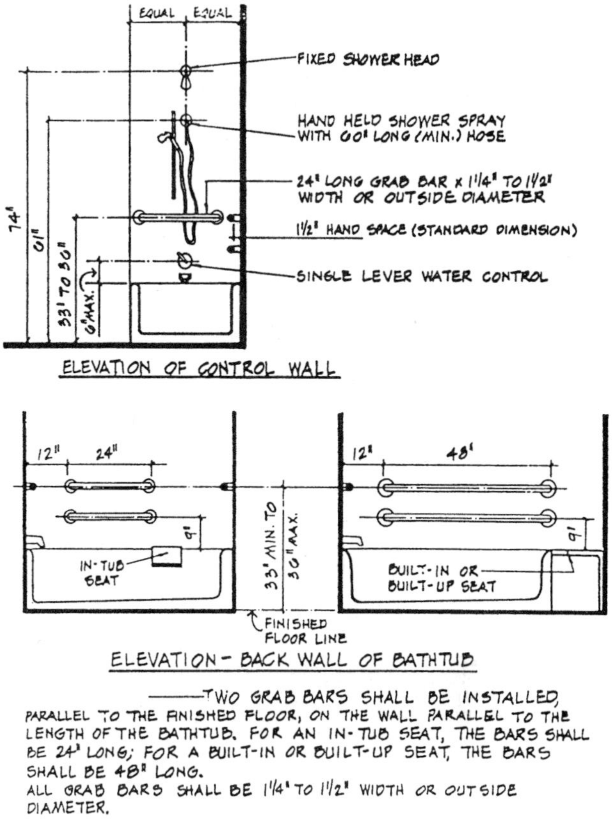

Fig. 15 Bathtub grab bar locations

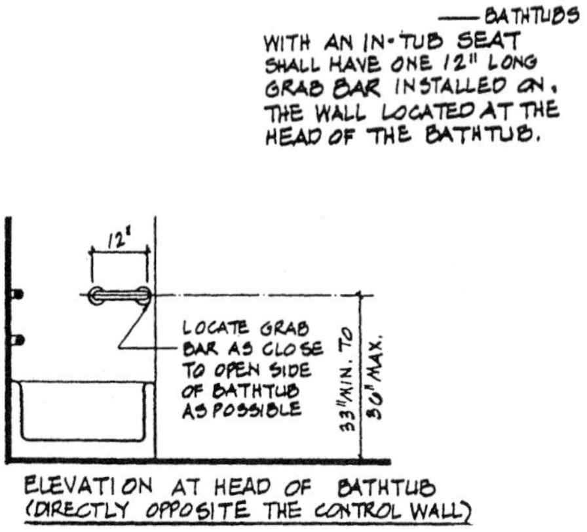

Fig. 14 Grab bar location for bathtub with built-in seat

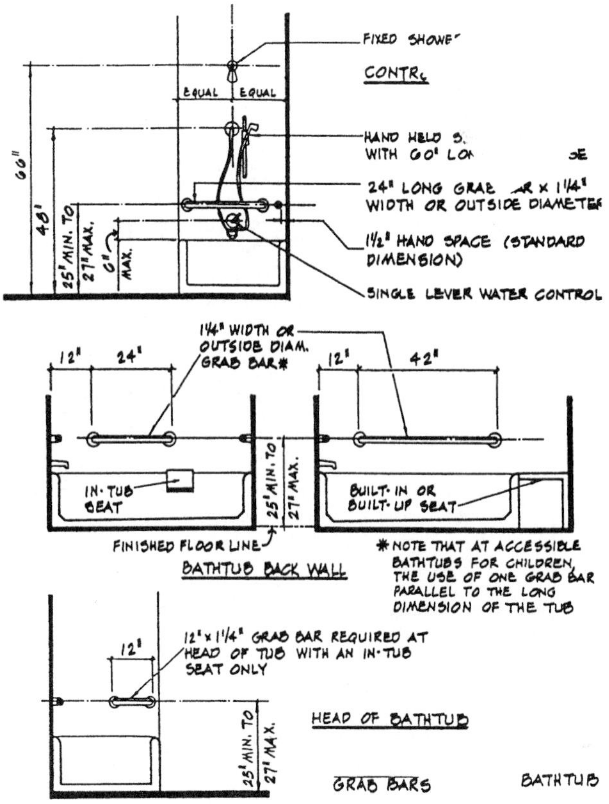

Fig. 16 Bathtub grab bar locations

BATHROOMS
Shower Elevations

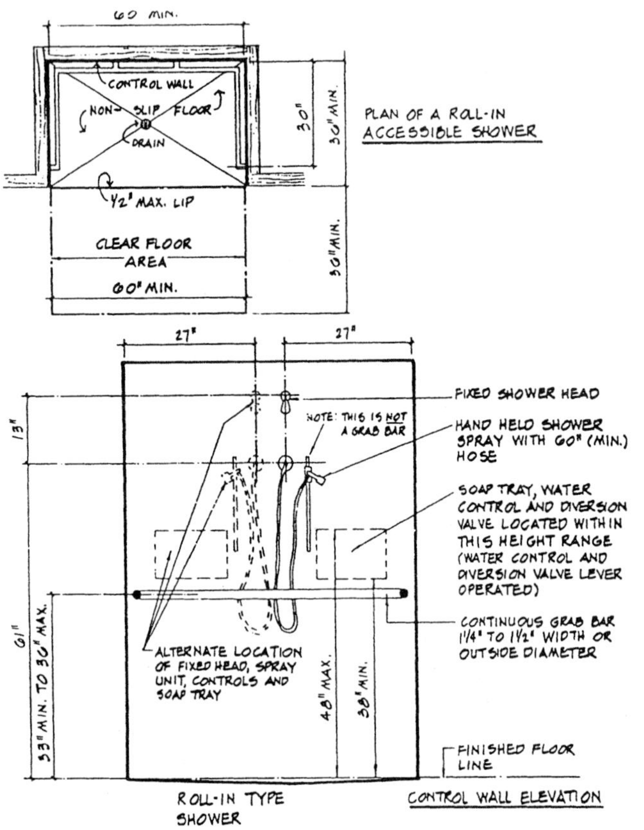

Fig. 17 Roll-in showers

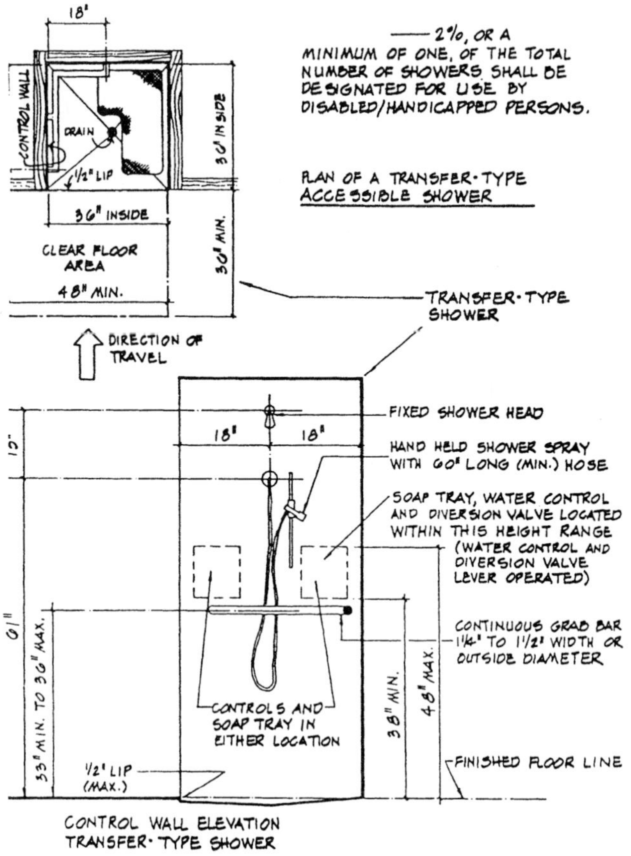

Fig. 19 Transfer-type showers

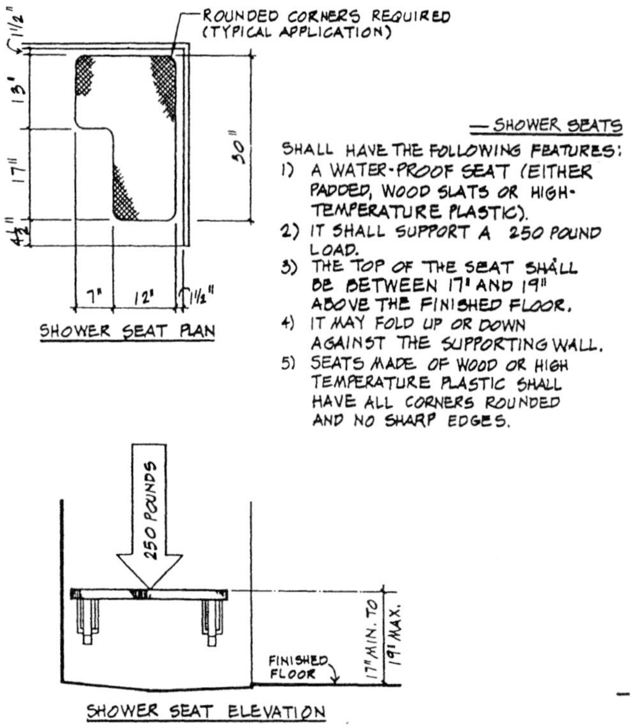

Fig. 18 Shower seats

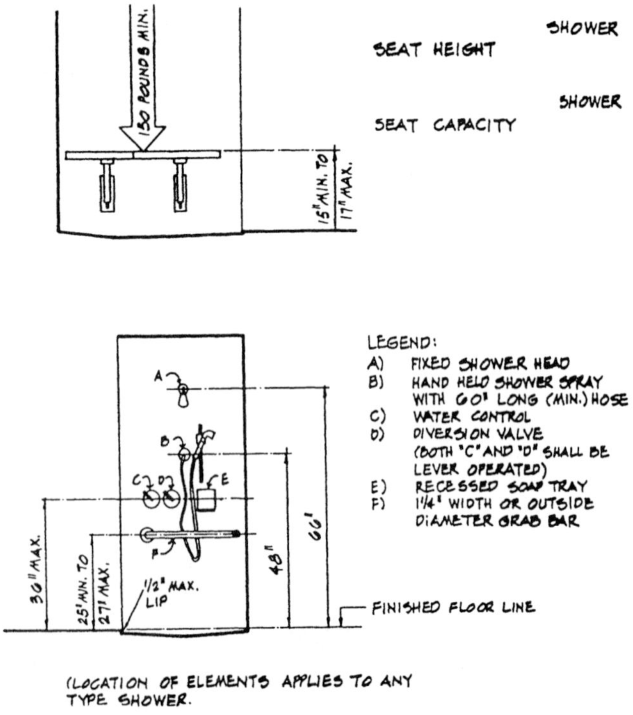

Fig. 20 Accessible showers

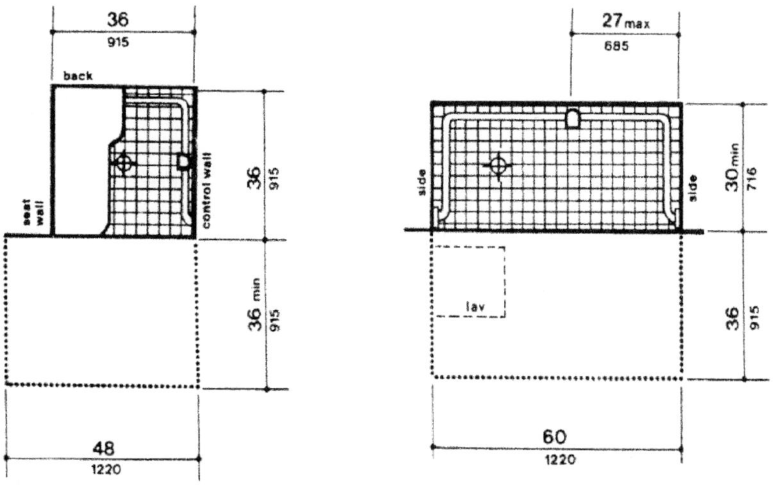

(a)
36-in by 36-in
(915-mm by 915-mm) Stall

(b)
30-in by 60-in
(760-mm by 1525-mm) Stall

Shower Size and Clearances

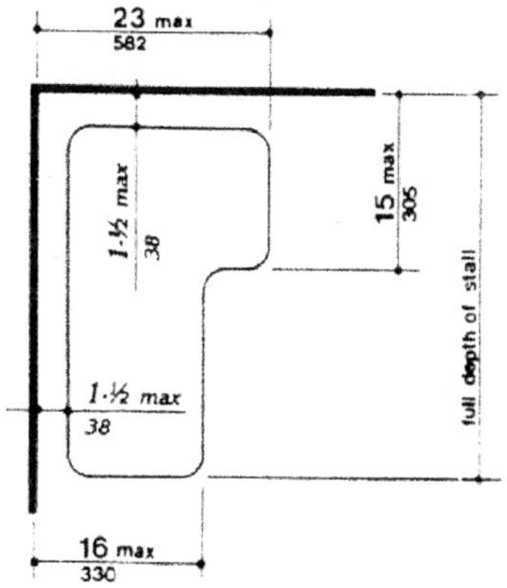

Shower Seat Design

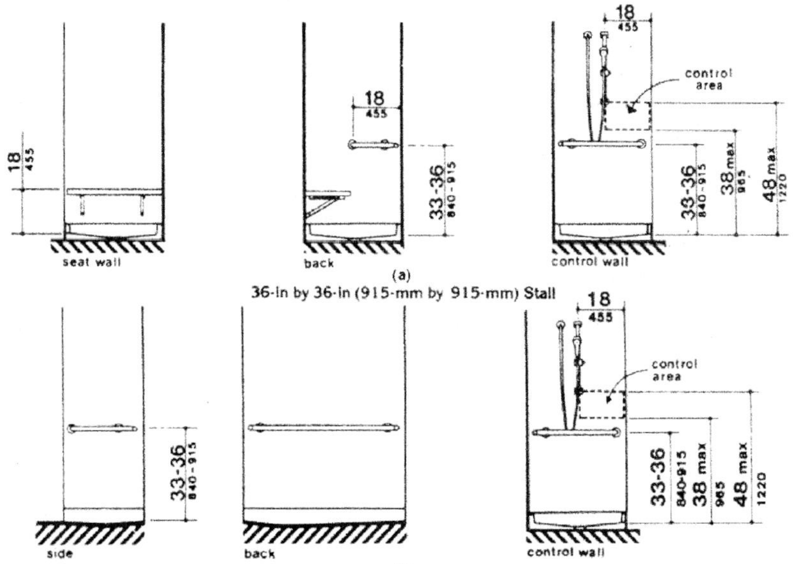

(b)
30-in by 60-in (760-mm by 1525-mm) Stall

Grab Bars at Shower Stalls

BATHROOMS

Wheelchair-Accessible Design

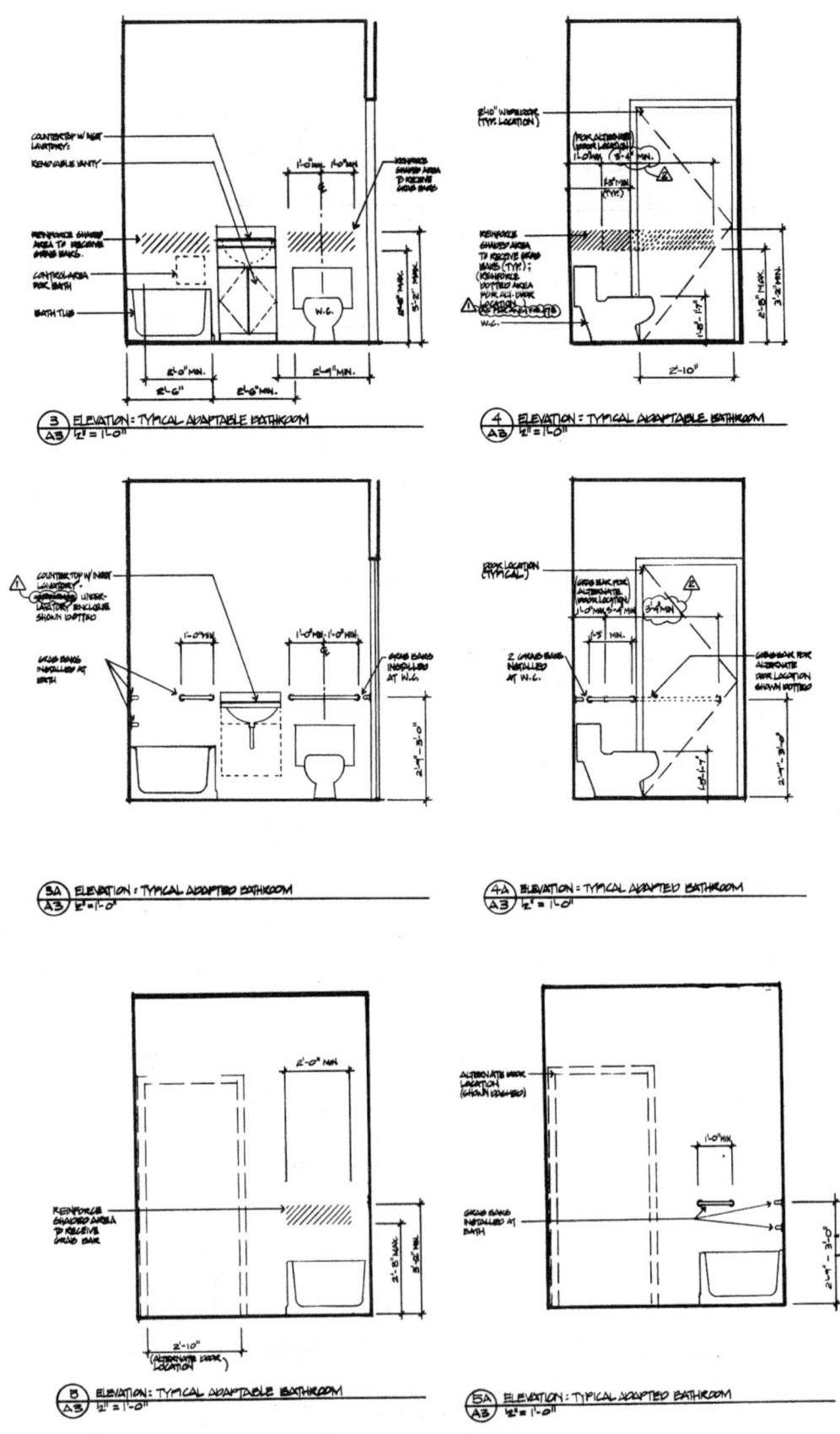

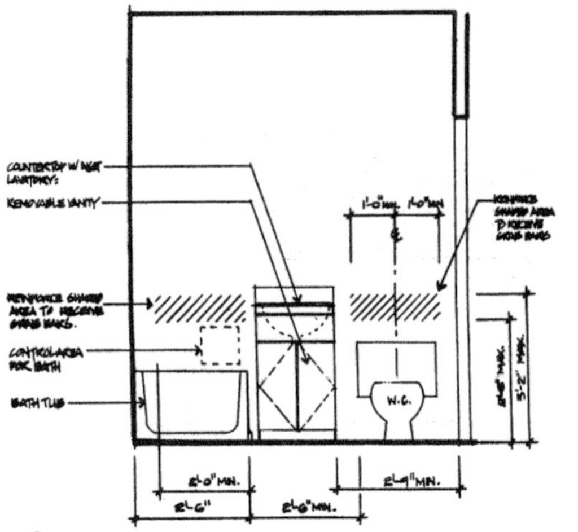

3/A3 ELEVATION: TYPICAL ADAPTABLE BATHROOM 1/2" = 1'-0"

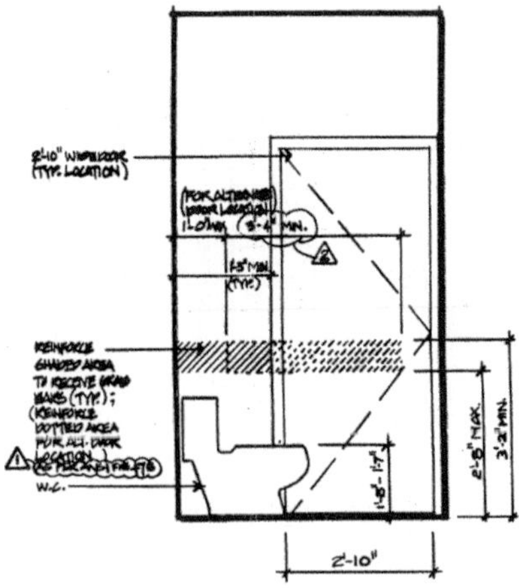

4/A3 ELEVATION: TYPICAL ADAPTABLE BATHROOM 1/2" = 1'-0"

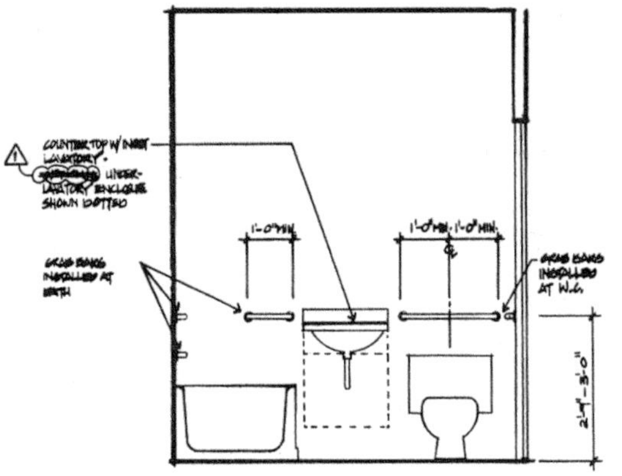

3A/A3 ELEVATION: TYPICAL ADAPTED BATHROOM 1/2" = 1'-0"

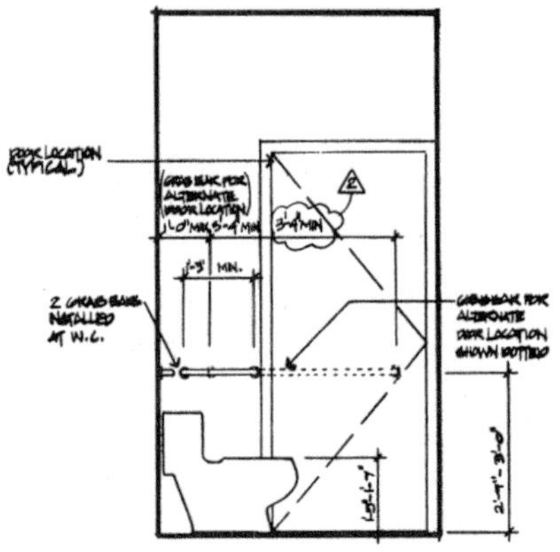

4A/A3 ELEVATION: TYPICAL ADAPTED BATHROOM 1/2" = 1'-0"

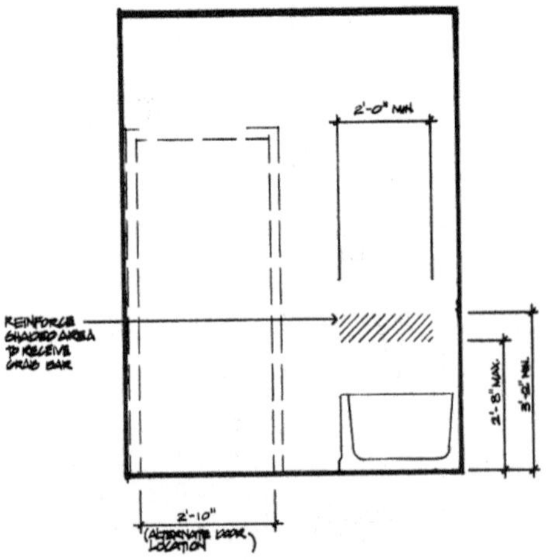

5/A3 ELEVATION: TYPICAL ADAPTABLE BATHROOM 1/2" = 1'-0"

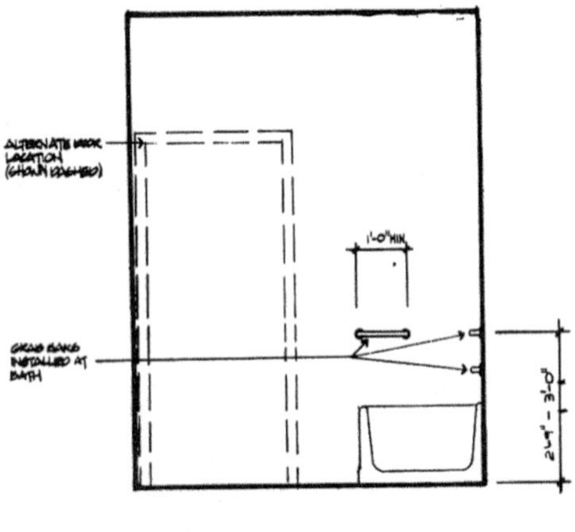

5A/A3 ELEVATION: TYPICAL ADAPTED BATHROOM 1/2" = 1'-0"

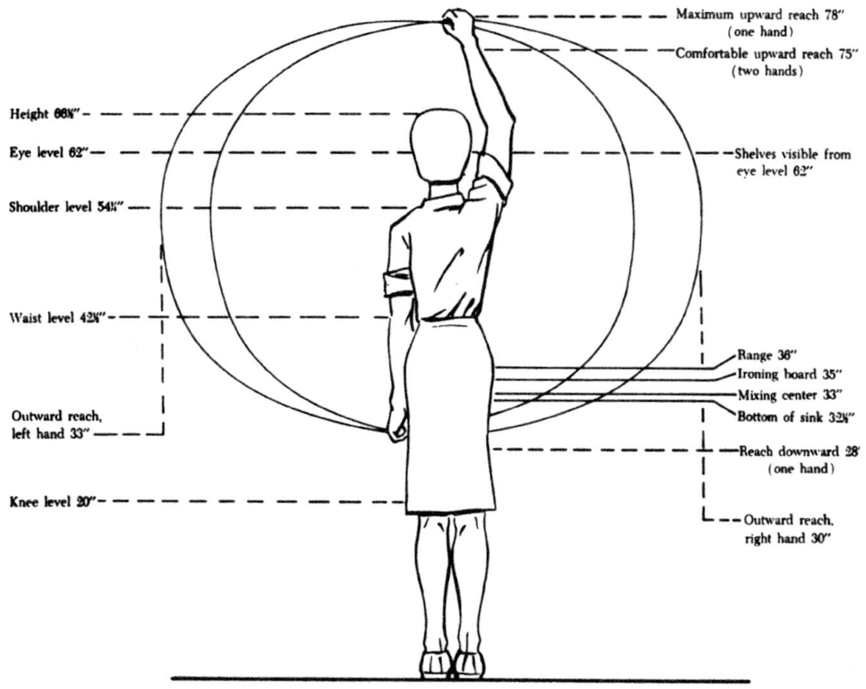

Fig. 1

KITCHENS

ANTHROPOMETRIC DATA

The height of a kitchen work counter, the proper clearance between cabinets or appliances for circulation, the accessibility to overhead or undercounter storage, and proper visibility are among the primary considerations in the design of cooking spaces. All must be responsive to human dimension and body size if the quality of interface between the user and the components of the interior space are to be adequate. In establishing clearances between counters, the maximum body breadth and depth of the user of larger body size must be taken into account as well as the projections of the appliances. Refrigerator doors, cabinet drawers, dishwashing machine doors, and cabinet doors all project to some degree in their open position into the space within which the user must circulate and must be accommodated.

Standard kitchen counter heights manufactured are all about 36 in, or 91.4 cm. But such a height does not necessarily accommodate the body dimension of all users for all tasks. Certain cooking activities, for example, may be more efficiently performed from a standing position, but with a counter height less than 36 in. In overhead cabinets the upper shelves are usually inaccessible to the smaller person, while the lower shelves are usually inaccessible to most without bending or kneeling. The logical answer is the development of kitchen cabinet systems capable of total adjustability to accommodate the human dimension of the individual user. Such a system could accommodate not only those of smaller and larger body size, but also elderly and disabled people.

Figure 1 provides some general anthropometric data for establishing basic heights of cabinetry and appliances above the floor. Figures 2 and 3 show in more detail the interface of the human body and the kitchen environment.

Figures 2 and 3 illustrate the clearances related to range centers. Figure 2 indicates a minimum clearance between appliances of 48 in, or 121.9 cm. The anthropometric basis for the clearances are amplified in Fig. 3.

The 40-in, or 101.6-cm, wall oven work zone clearance is adequate to accommodate the projected wall oven door, in addition to the maximum body depth dimension of the user. The standing figure shown in broken line, however, indicates both dimensionally and graphically that the 40-in clearance will not permit comfortable circulation when appliances on both sides are in operation at the same time. The range work zone clearance, also 40 in, is adequate to accommodate the open range door and the body size of the kneeling user.

An extremely important, but frequently overlooked, anthropometric consideration in kitchen design is eye height. In this regard, the distance from the top of the range to the underside of the hood should allow the rear burners to be visible to the user.

KITCHENS
Anthropometric Data

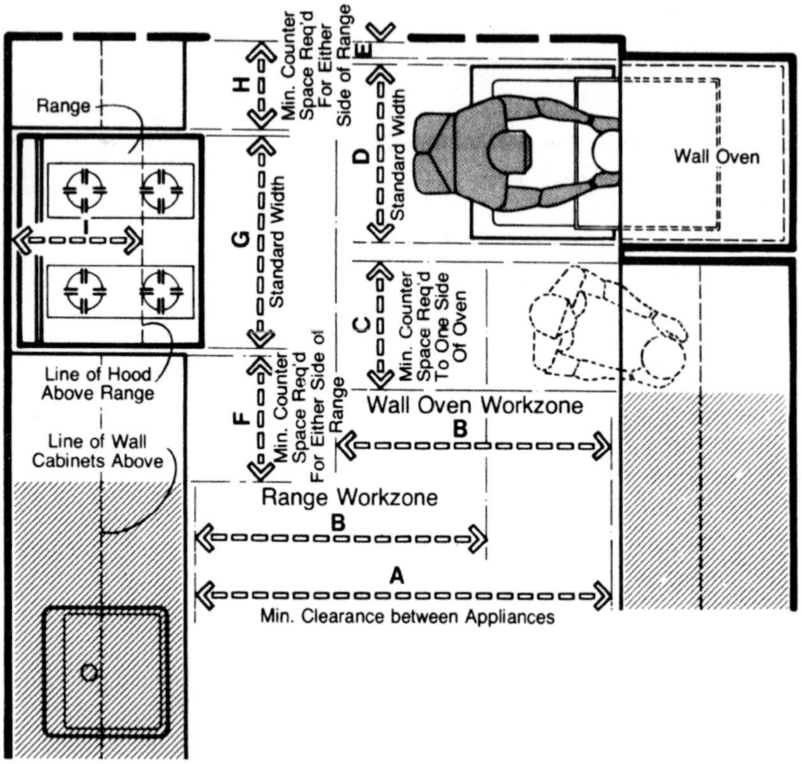

RANGE CENTER

	in	cm
A	48 min.	121.9 min.
B	40	101.6
C	15	38.1 min.
D	21–30	53.3–76.2
E	1–3	2.5–7.6
F	15 min.	38.1 min.
G	19.5–46	49.5–116.8
H	12 min.	30.5 min.
I	17.5 max.	44.5 max
J	96–101.5	243.8–257.8
K	24–27.5	61.0–69.9
L	24–26	61.0–66.0
M	30	76.2
N	60 min.	152.4 min.
O	35–36.25	88.9–92.1
P	24 min.	61.0 min.
Q	35 max.	88.9 max.

Fig. 2

TYPICAL LAYOUTS

The U-shaped plan is the most efficient. When not broken, it provides the opportunity and floor space for several simultaneous activities. The corridor or gallery kitchen is typically accessible from both ends, often converting it from a work space to a corridor. It sometimes is closed off on one end, thereby creating a variation of the U-shaped plan, which, although small, can produce a fairly comfortable kitchen.

The broken U-shaped plan often results from the necessity of locating a door along one or two of the three walls of a typical U-shaped scheme. The resulting through traffic reduces the compactness and efficiency of the plan.

The typical L-shaped kitchen allows for the location of a small breakfast area in the opposite corner.

STORAGE AND CABINETS

Kitchen Storage

Each kitchen or kitchenette should have (1) accessible storage space for food and utensils, (2) sufficient space for the average kitchen accessories, and (3) sufficient storage space for those items of household equipment normally used and for which storage is not elsewhere provided.

Clearances over Cooking Ranges

In Fig. 10, dimension A: 2 ft 6 in minimum clearance between the top of the range and the bottom of an unprotected wood or metal cabinet, or 2 ft 0 in minimum when the bottom of a wood or metal cabinet is protected.

Dimension B: 2 ft 0 in minimum when hood projection X is 18 in or more, or 1 ft 10 in min. when hood projection X is less than 18 in.

Dimension C: not less than width of range or cooking unit.

Dimension D: 10-in minimum when vertical side surface extends above countertops.

Dimension E: when range is not provided by builder, 40-in minimum.

Dimension F: Minimum clearance should be not less than 3 in.

Cabinet protection should be at least ¼-in asbestos millboard covered with not less than 28-gauge sheet metal (0.015 stainless steel, 0.024 aluminum, or 0.020 copper).

Clearance for D, E, or F should be not less than listed UL or AGA clearances.

	in	cm
A	48 min.	121.9 min.
B	40	101.6
C	15	38.1 min.
D	21–30	53.3–76.2
E	1–3	2.5–7.6
F	15 min.	38.1 min.
G	19.5–46	49.5–116.8
H	12 min.	30.5 min.
I	17.5 max.	44.5 max
J	96–101.5	243.8–257.8
K	24–27.5	61.0–69.9
L	24–26	61.0–66.0
M	30	76.2
N	60 min.	152.4 min.
O	35–36.25	88.9–92.1
P	24 min.	61.0 min.
Q	35 max.	88.9 max.

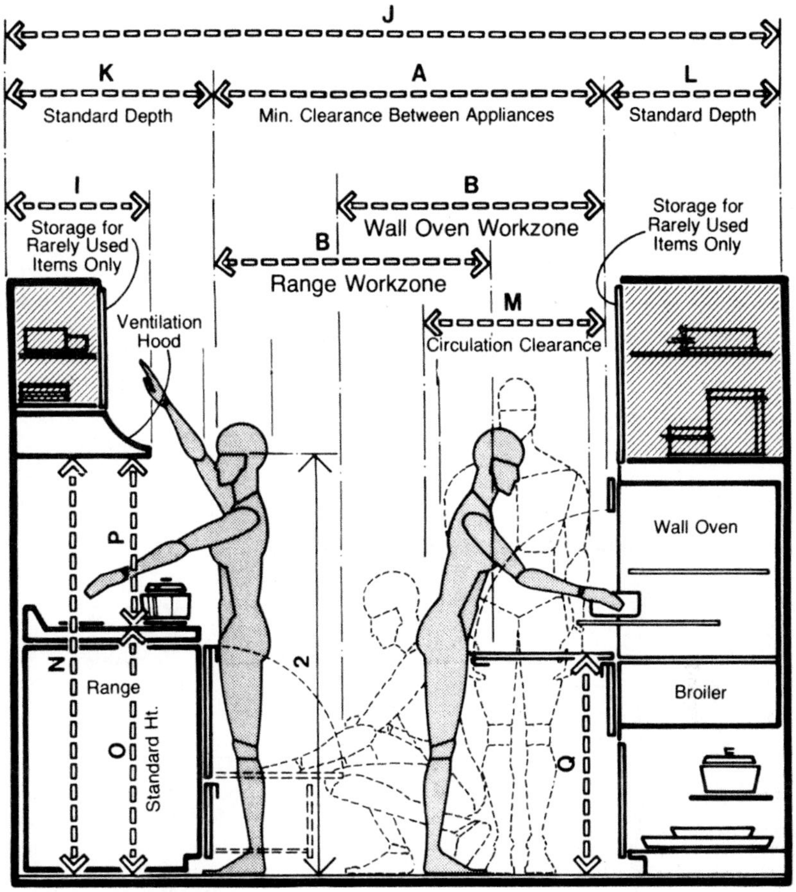

RANGE CENTER

Fig. 3

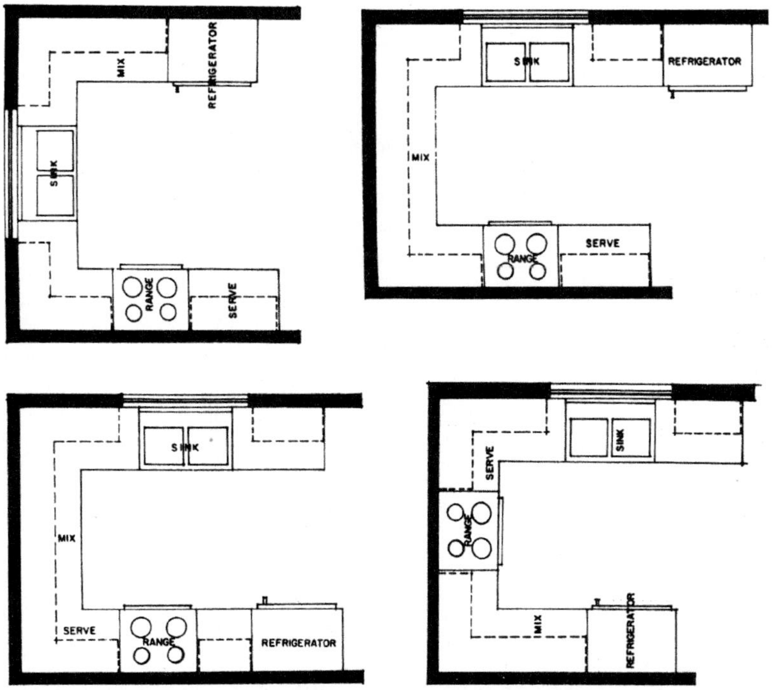

Fig. 4 U-shaped plans. If dishwasher is desired, it should be located at sink center

KITCHENS
Typical Layouts

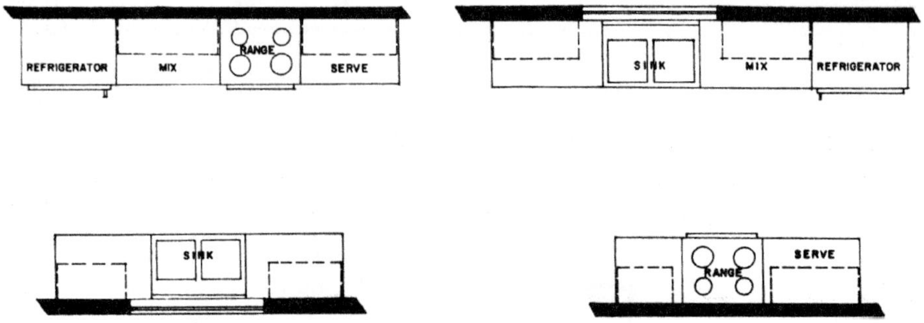

Fig. 5 Corridor plans. If dishwasher is desired, it should be located at sink center

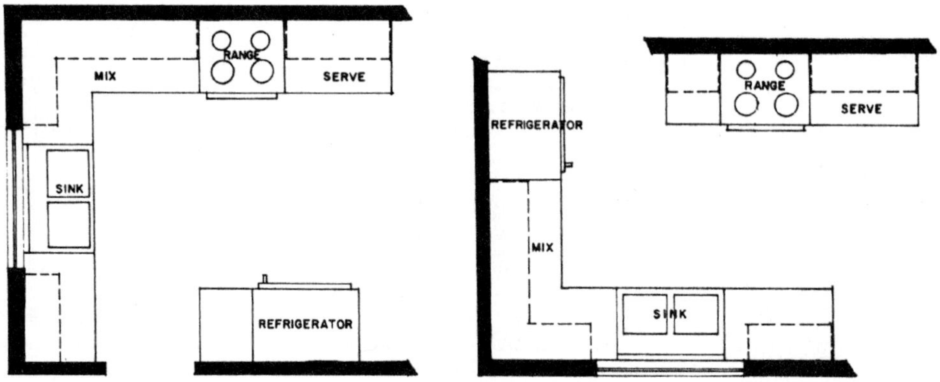

Fig. 6 Broken U-shaped plans. If dishwasher is desired, it should be located at sink center

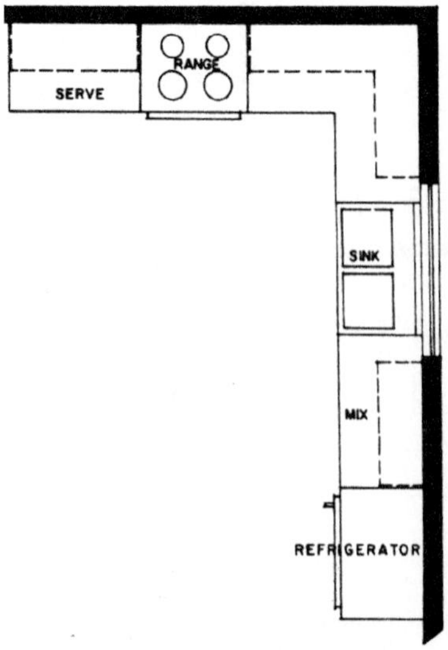

Fig. 7 L-shaped plan. If dishwasher is desired, it should be located at sink center

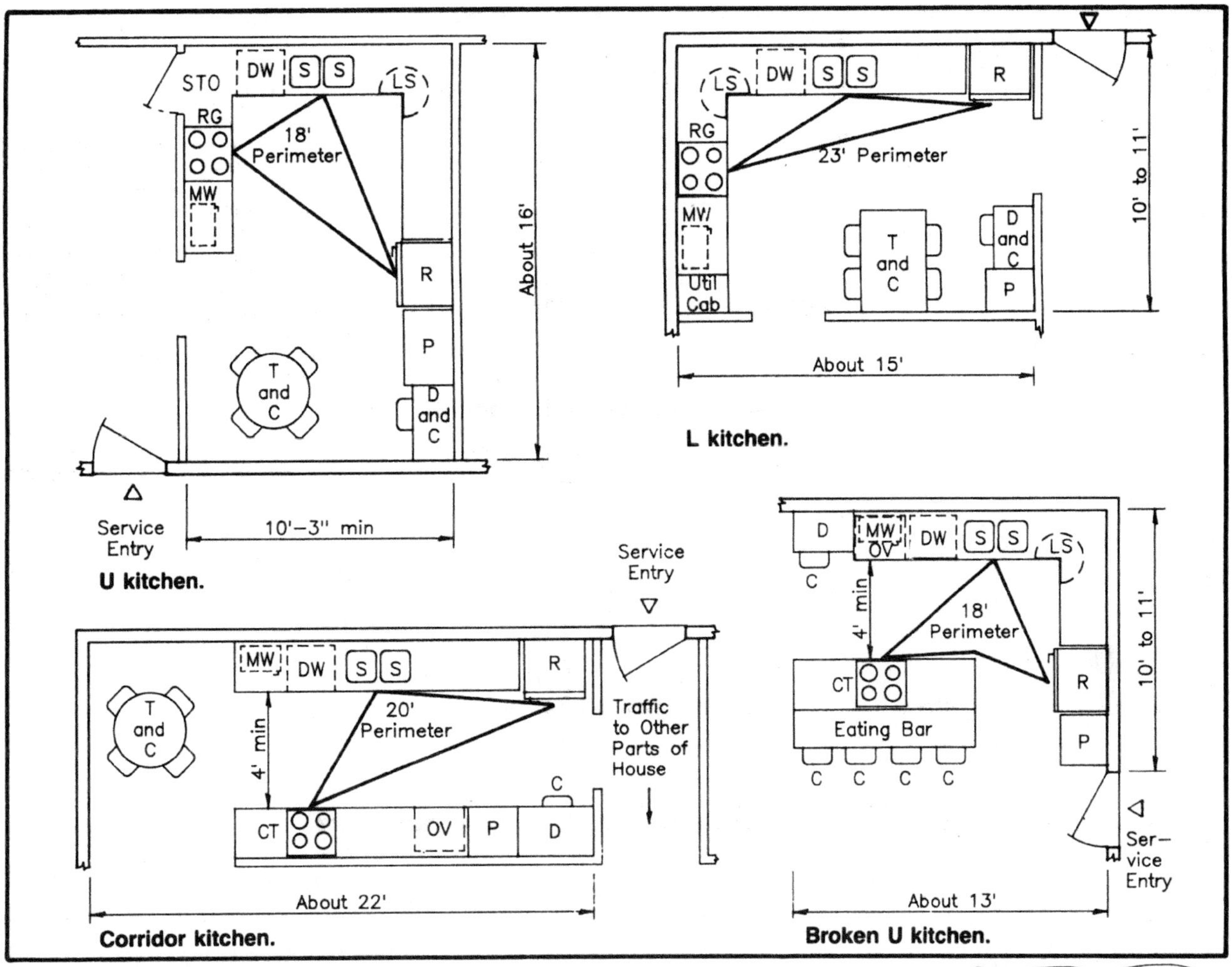

U kitchen.

L kitchen.

Corridor kitchen.

Broken U kitchen.

Fig. 8 These diagrams illustrate further variations of the typical plans shown in Figs. 4 to 7. A triangle perimeter of 23 ft 0 in or less is usually indicative of a relatively efficient kitchen layout

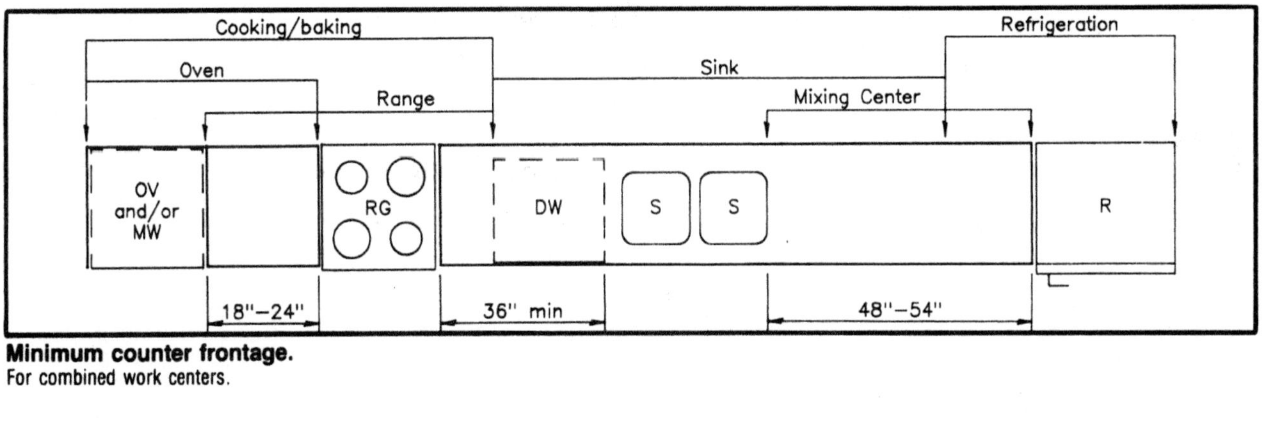

Minimum counter frontage.
For combined work centers.

KITCHENS
Storage and Cabinets

KITCHEN STORAGE

Each kitchen or kitchenette should have (1) accessible storage space for food and utensils, (2) sufficient space for the average kitchen accessories, (3) sufficient storage space for those items of household equipment normally used and for which storage is not elsewhere provided.

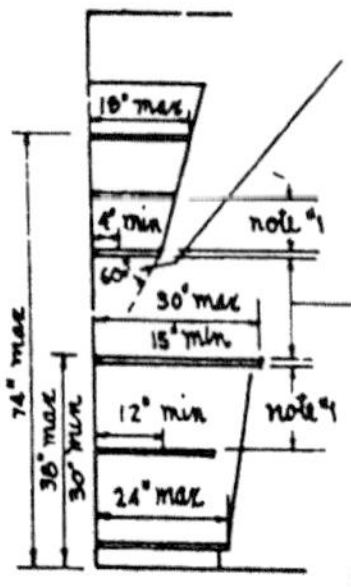

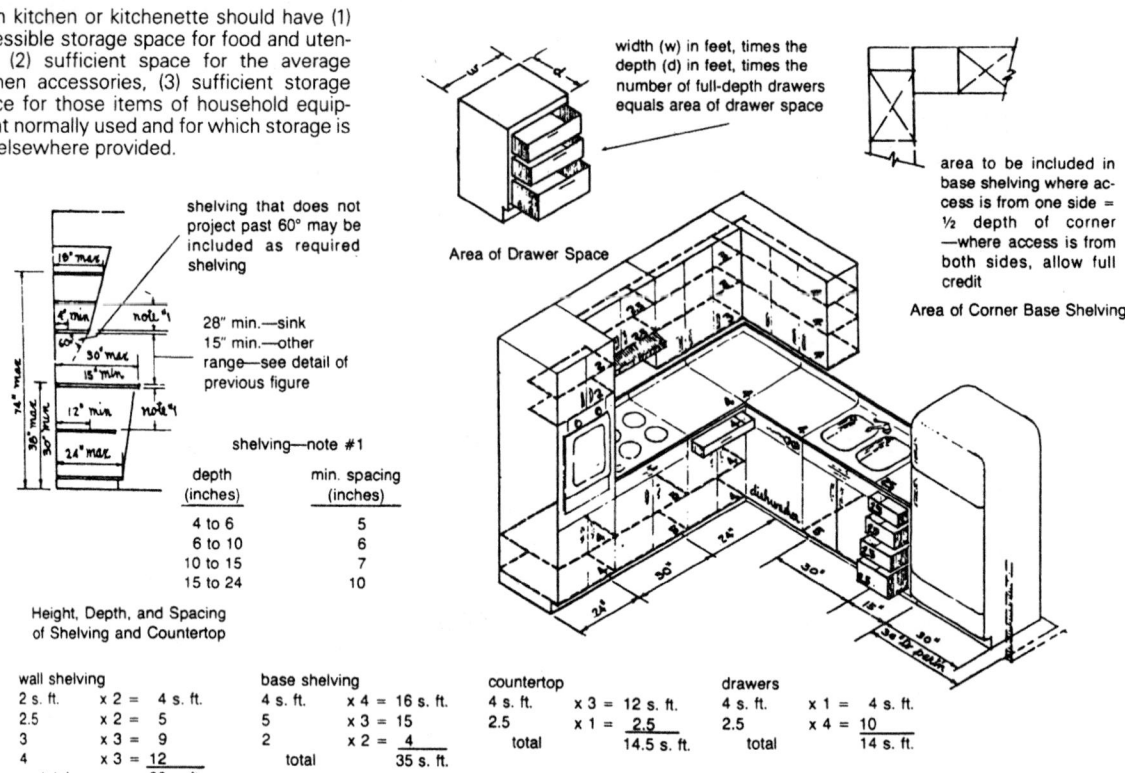

shelving that does not project past 60° may be included as required shelving

28" min.—sink
15" min.—other range—see detail of previous figure

shelving—note #1

depth (inches)	min. spacing (inches)
4 to 6	5
6 to 10	6
10 to 15	7
15 to 24	10

Height, Depth, and Spacing of Shelving and Countertop

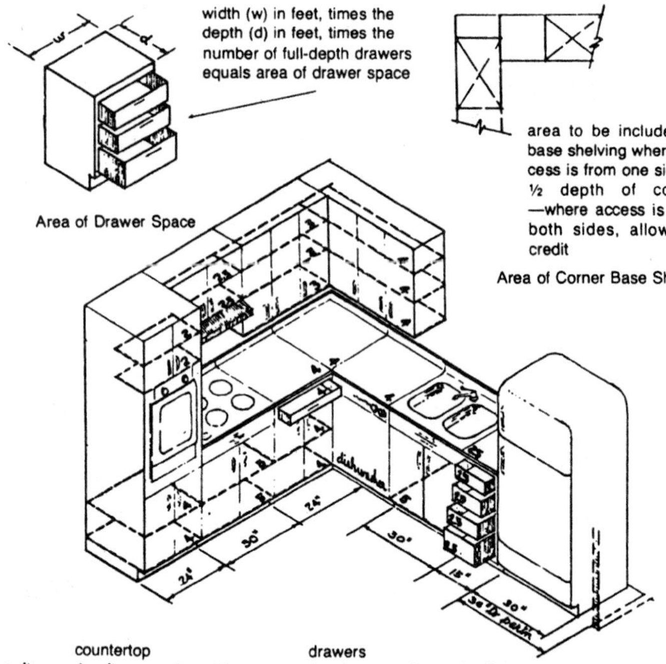

width (w) in feet, times the depth (d) in feet, times the number of full-depth drawers equals area of drawer space

Area of Drawer Space

area to be included in base shelving where access is from one side = ½ depth of corner —where access is from both sides, allow full credit

Area of Corner Base Shelving

wall shelving

2 s. ft.	x 2 =	4 s. ft.
2.5	x 2 =	5
3	x 3 =	9
4	x 3 =	12
total		30 s. ft.

base shelving

4 s. ft.	x 4 =	16 s. ft.
5	x 3 =	15
2	x 2 =	4
total		35 s. ft.

countertop

4 s. ft.	x 3 =	12 s. ft.
2.5	x 1 =	2.5
total		14.5 s. ft.

drawers

4 s. ft.	x 1 =	4 s. ft.
2.5	x 4 =	10
total		14 s. ft.

Fig. 9 Example: measurement of shelf and countertop areas

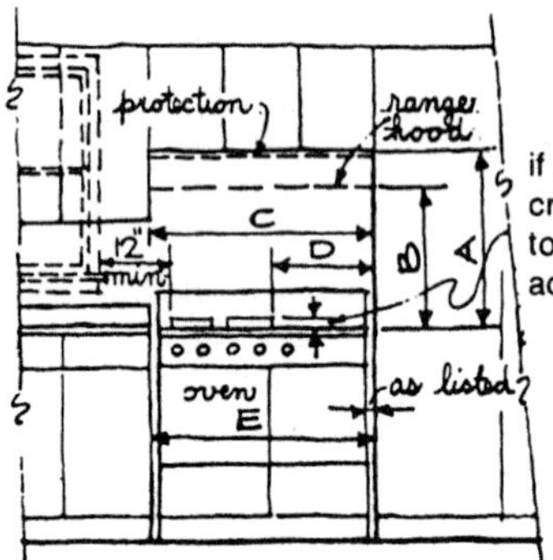

if more than ¾" increase clearance to cabinet by the additional amount

elevation
free-standing range

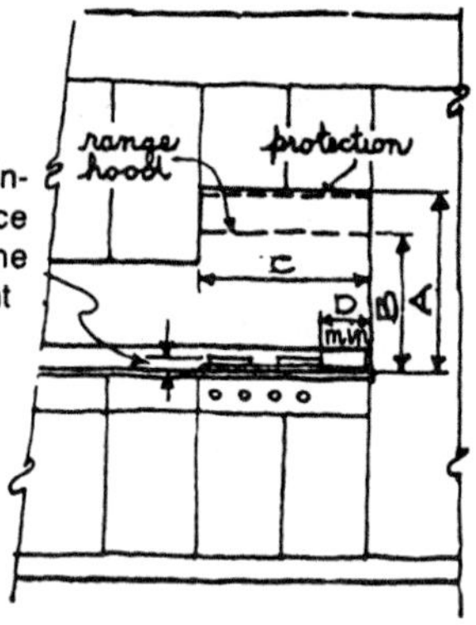

elevation

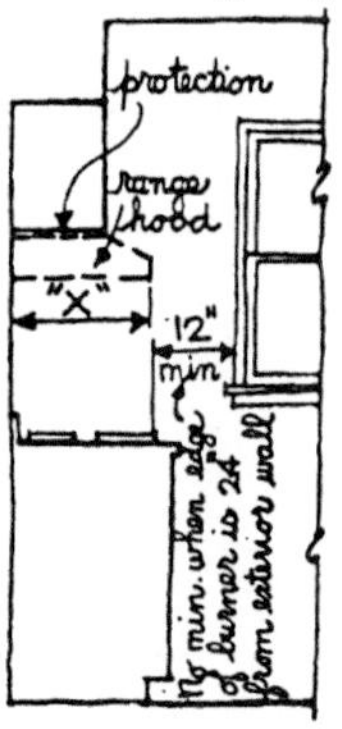

section

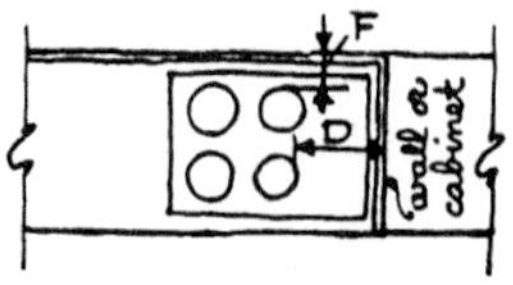

plan
built-in cooking unit

Fig. 10

CLEARANCES OVER COOKING RANGES

In Fig. 10, dimension A: 2 ft 6 in minimum clearance between the top of the range and the bottom of an unprotected wood or metal cabinet, or 2 ft 0 in minimum when the bottom of a wood or metal cabinet is protected.

Dimension B: 2 ft 0 in minimum when hood projection X is 18 in or more, or 1 ft 10 in min. when hood projection X is less than 18 in.

Dimension C: not less than width of range or cooking unit.

Dimension D: 10 in minimum when vertical side surface extends above countertops.

Dimension E: when range is not provided by builder, 40 in minimum.

Dimension F: Minimum clearance should be not less than 3 in.

Cabinet protection should be at least ¼ in asbestos millboard covered with not less than 28-gauge sheet metal (0.015 stainless steel, 0.024 aluminum, or 0.020 copper).

Clearance for D, E, or F should be not less than listed UL or AGA clearances.

KITCHENS
Storage and Cabinets

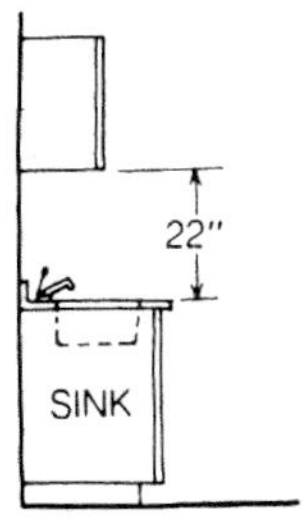

ABOVE SINK

Above a sink, plan for a minimum of 22 in to the bottom of a wall cabinet. Since the wall behind a sink often holds a window, measurement for a cabinet is academic. But if wall space is minimal, a cabinet over the sink makes good sense.

The use of large pans, pancake flips, and similar cooking maneuvers dictate a distance of 30 in between rangetop and wall cabinet bottom. A fan mounted in the wall is the means here to exhaust cooking fumes to the outside.

A range of 15 to 18 in is the proper span between standard base and wall cabinets. Opt for the 15-in distance if you are 5 ft 4 in or less; a wider span if you're taller. For the highest shelf, 6 ft from the floor is a reachable distance.

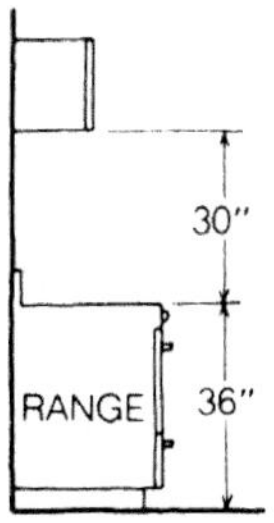

ABOVE RANGE

Kitchen activities become tiresome in poor light. A single fixture centered on the ceiling is insufficient. Your need for light is greatest over the work centers. A good light there reduces the danger of cutting yourself, eases the task of monitoring color changes during a mix, and so on. The best place to install fixtures for this purpose is beneath the wall cabinets (with a shield to prevent glare when you're seated in the kitchen). A workable alternative is found in fixtures installed in an extended soffit. Plan for light above a rangetop and over the sink as well. Choose incandescent deluxe warm white or deluxe cool white lamps for the fixtures to avoid poor color rendition.

Utensil and General Storage

Space for utensils includes storage for dishes, pots and pans, utensils, and appliances. With the increased use of such electrical appliances, their storage becomes a significant problem. General storage requires space for linens, towels, and kitchen supplies. Included in this category are brooms, mops, and other cleaning equipment and supplies.

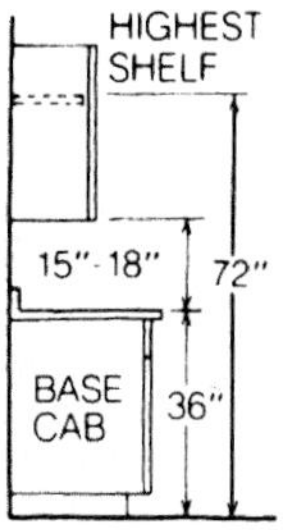

ABOVE BASE CAB

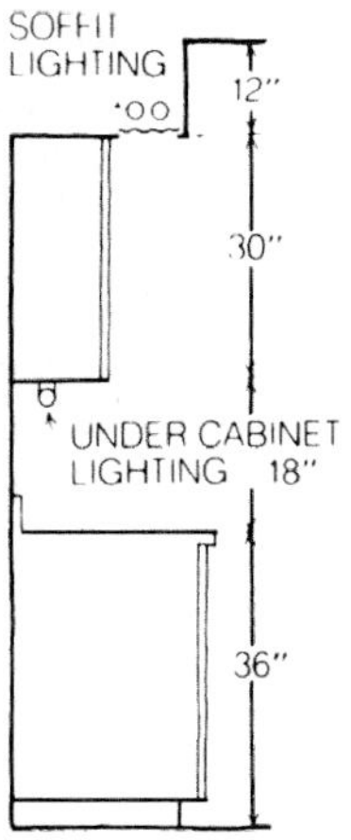

KITCHEN LIGHTING

TABLE 1 Minimum Kitchen Storage Required

Item	0-bedroom living unit,* ft²	1-bedroom living unit,* ft²
40 to 60 ft² Area – Kitchenette		
Total shelving in wall and base cabinets	24	30
Shelving in either wall or base cabinets	10	12
Drawer area	4	5
Countertop area	5	6
60 ft² Area and Over – Kitchen		
Item	1- and 2-bedroom living units, ft²	3- and 4-bedroom living units, ft²
Total shelving in wall and base cabinets	48	54
Shelving in either wall or base cabinets	18	20
Drawer area	8	10
Countertop area	10	12

*Kitchen unit assemblies serving the kitchen function and occupying less than 40 ft² area in 0-BR living units shall not be less than 5 ft in length and shall provide at least 12 ft² of total shelving in wall and base cabinets. Drawer and countertop space shall also be provided. No room count is allowable for this type facility.

KITCHENS

Cabinet Dimensions

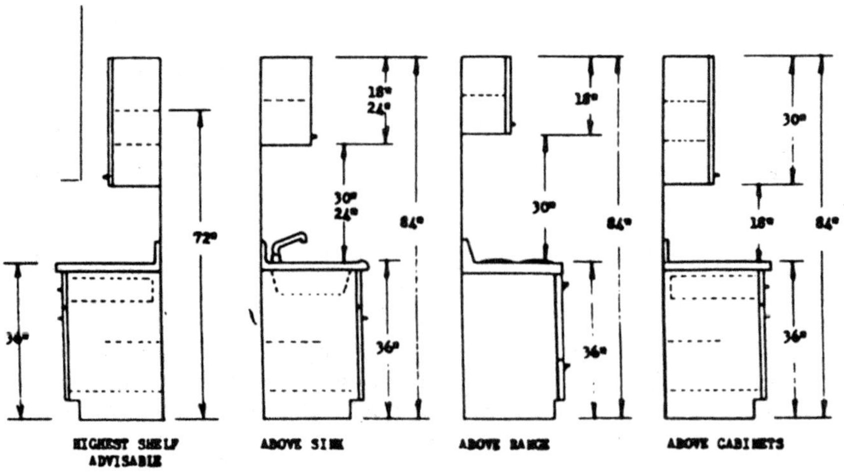

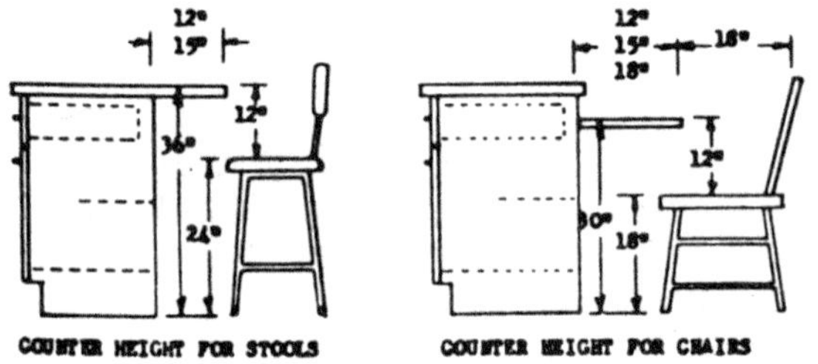

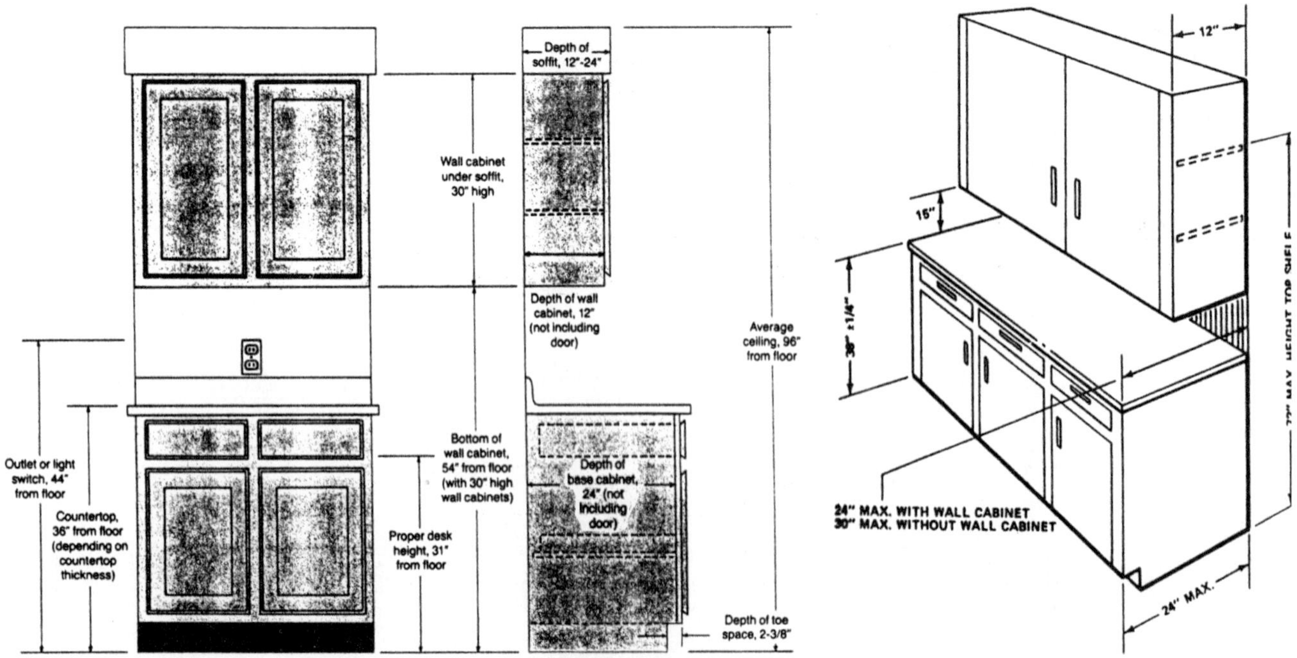

Example of the proper dimensional limits and relative placement of kitchen base cabinets and wall cabinets

FRAMED CABINETRY

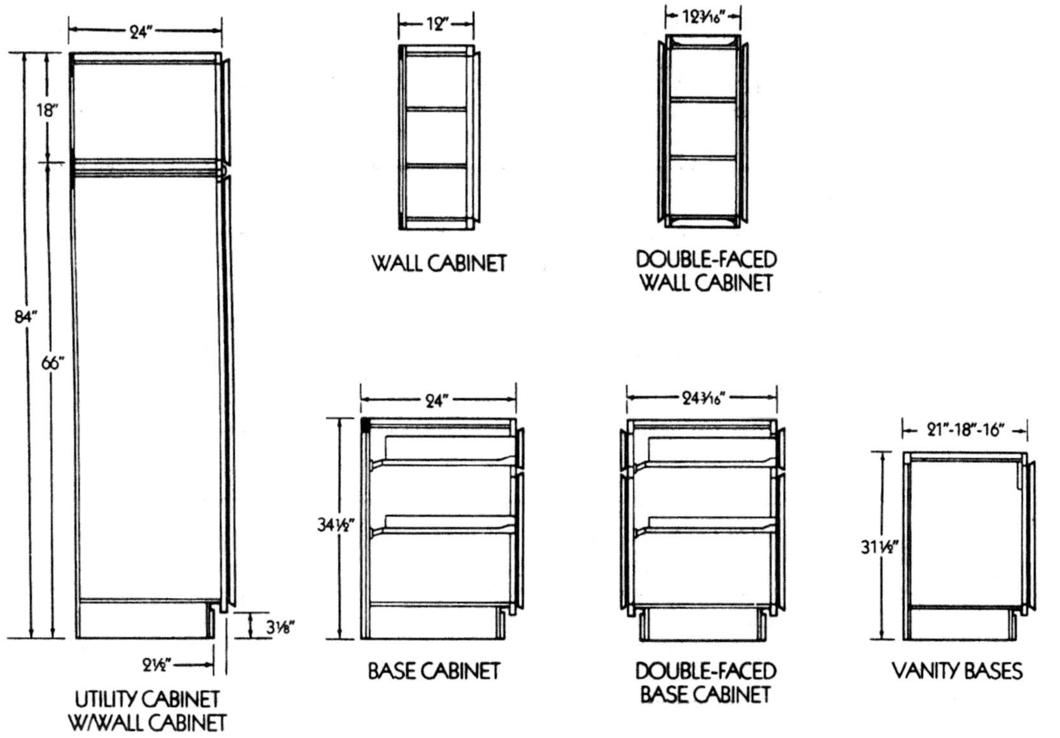

FRAMELESS CABINETRY

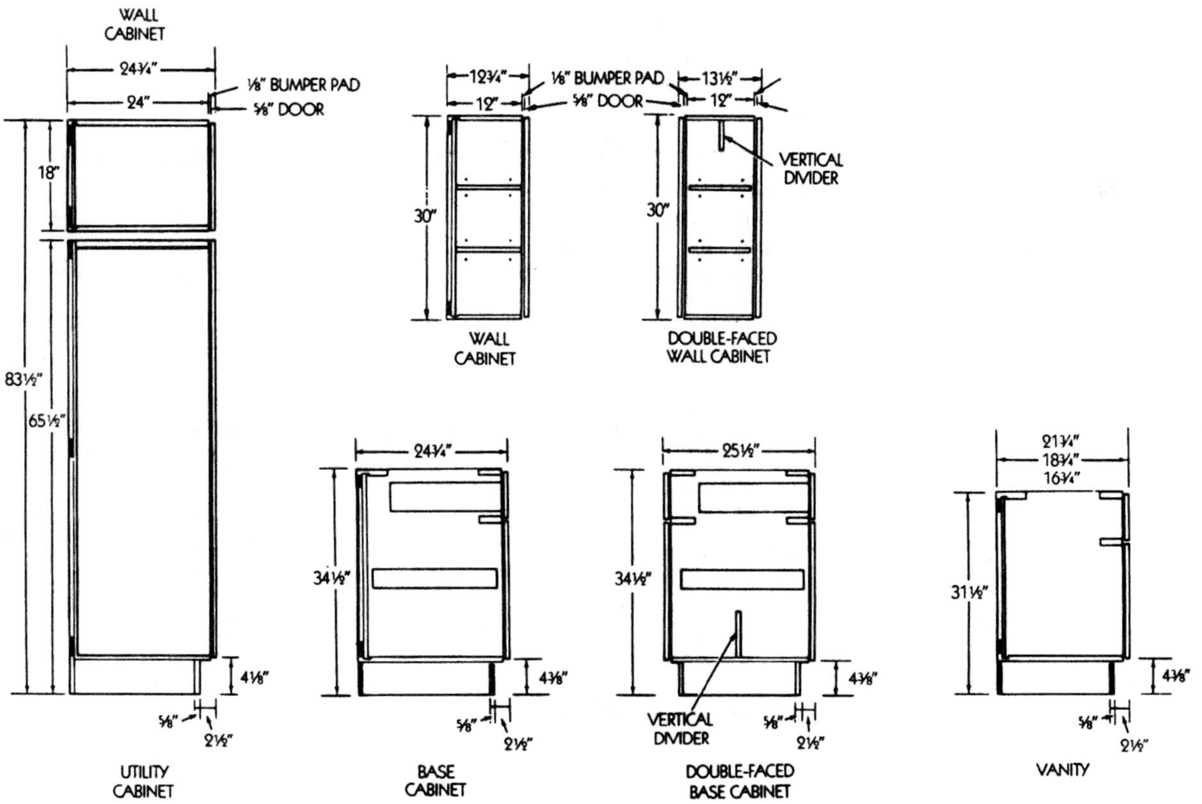

KITCHENS
Cabinet Sizes

FRAMED FRAMELESS

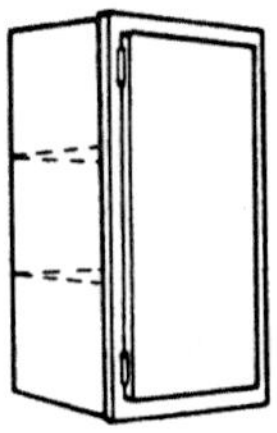
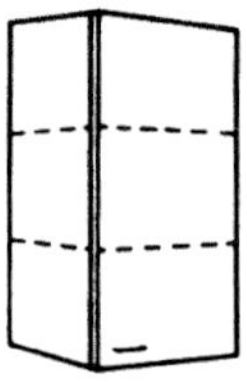

WALL CABINETS

Wall cabinets are available in heights of 42", 30", 24", 18", 15", and 12". Most cabinets are available in widths ranging from 9" to 48", in 3" increments. Framed wall cabinets are 12" deep, not including doors. Frameless wall cabinets are 12¾" deep, including doors.

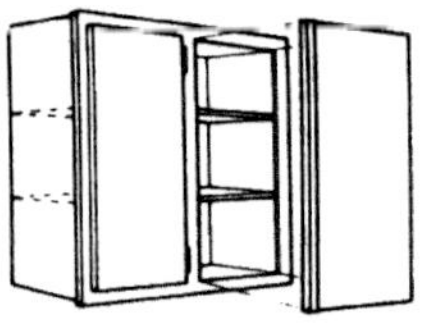
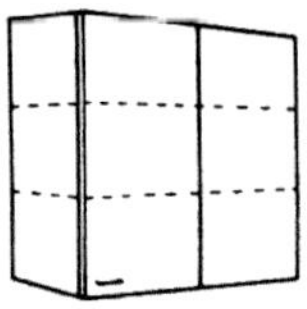

WALL BLIND CORNER CABINETS

Wall blind corner cabinets are available in heights of 42", 30" and 24". Most wall blind corner cabinets are available in widths of 24", 27", 30", 33", 36", 42", and 48".

DOUBLE-FACE WALL CABINETS

Double-face wall cabinets are available in heights of 30", 24" and 18". Most are available in widths of 18", 24", 30", 36", 42" and 48". Framed cabinets are 13$\frac{15}{16}$" deep with doors. Frameless are 13½" deep with doors.

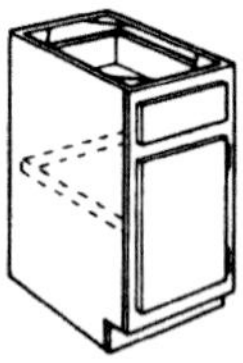
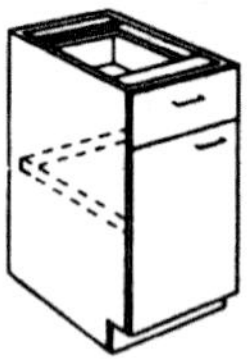

BASE CABINETS

All base cabinets are 34½" tall. Most are available in widths ranging from 9" to 48", in 3" increments. Framed base cabinets are 24" deep, not including doors. Frameless base cabinets are 24¾" deep, including doors.

Four-drawer base cabinets are available in widths ranging from 12" to 24", in 3" increments. Frameless base cabinets are also available in a three-drawer style in widths of 30" and 36".

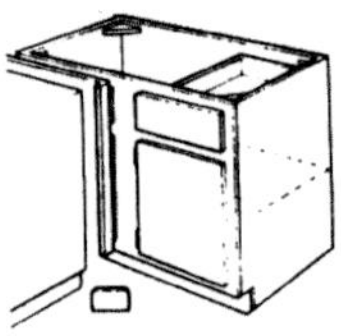
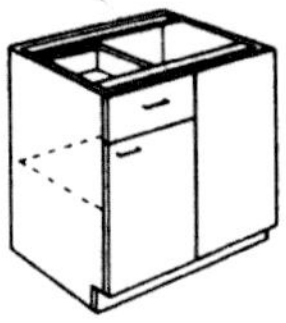

BASE BLIND CORNER CABINETS

All base blind corner cabinets are 34½" high. Most are available in widths of 24", 30", 36", 39", 42", and 48".

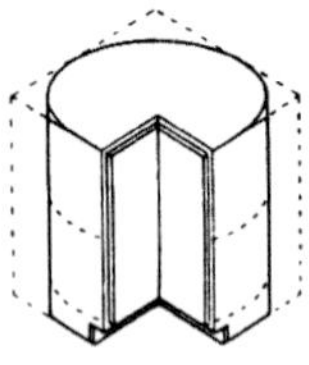
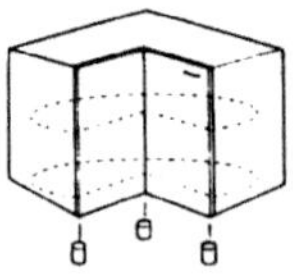

SPECIALTY CABINETS

Lazy Susans:
36"-Wide

Range Hoods: (framed only)
36" & 30"-Wide

Wall What-Not Shelves: (framed only)
30"-High

Base Open Shelves: (framed only)
34½"-High

Pantries: (framed only)
36" x 66"

Utility Cabinets: (framed)
24" x 66"
18" x 66"
In 12" and 24" Depths

Utility Cabinets: (frameless)
24" x 65½"
18" x 65½"
In 12¾" and 24¾" Depths

Tilt-Out Range Hoods: (frameless only)
30" x 24"

Glass Door Wall Cabinets: (frameless only)
30" & 36"-Wide

Microwave Cabinets: (framed only)
30" x 21"

Microwave Shelves:
30" x 22⅝" (framed)
30" x 18" (frameless)

Oven Cabinets: (framed)
27" x 66"
30" x 66"
33" x 66"

Oven Cabinets: (frameless)
27" x 65½"
30" x 65½"
33" x 65½"

Up to six 6" drawers can be added to frameless oven cabinets.

Sink Cabinets & Fronts

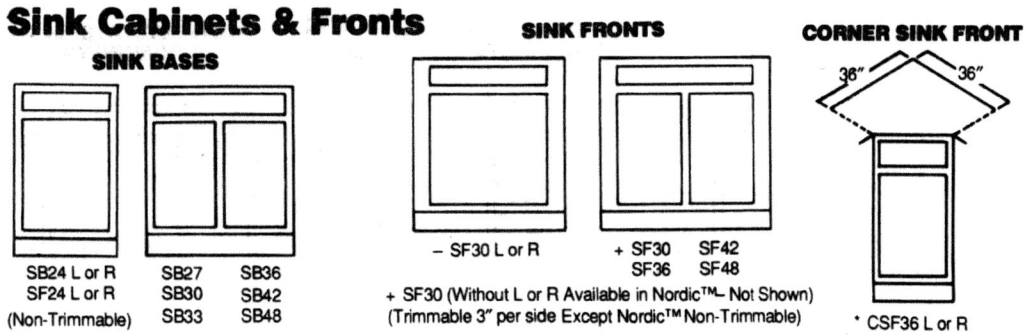

SINK BASES

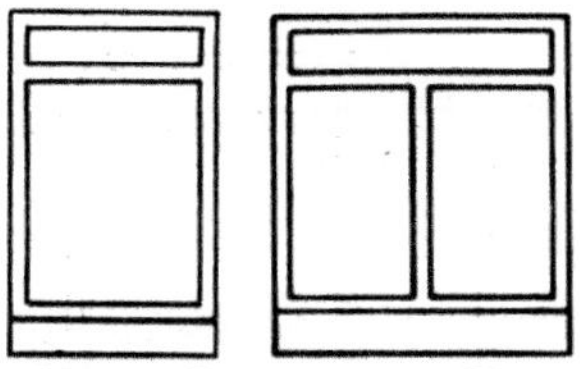

SB24 L or R
SF24 L or R
(Non-Trimmable)

SB27 SB36
SB30 SB42
SB33 SB48

SINK FRONTS

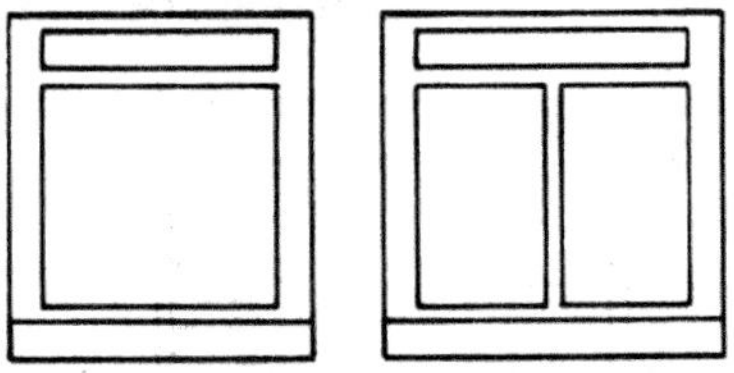

– SF30 L or R

+ SF30 SF42
SF36 SF48

+ SF30 (Without L or R Available in Nordic™– Not Shown)
(Trimmable 3″ per side Except Nordic™ Non-Trimmable)

CORNER SINK FRONT

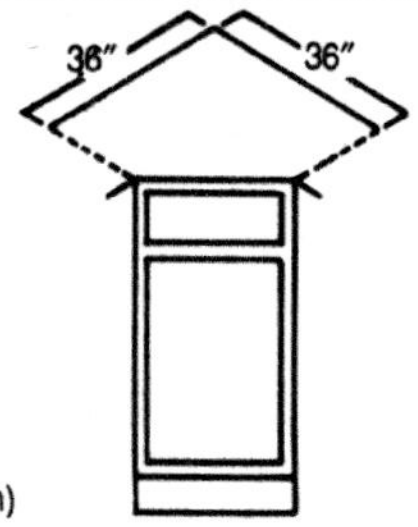

* CSF36 L or R

Oven Cabinets & Drop-In Range Fronts

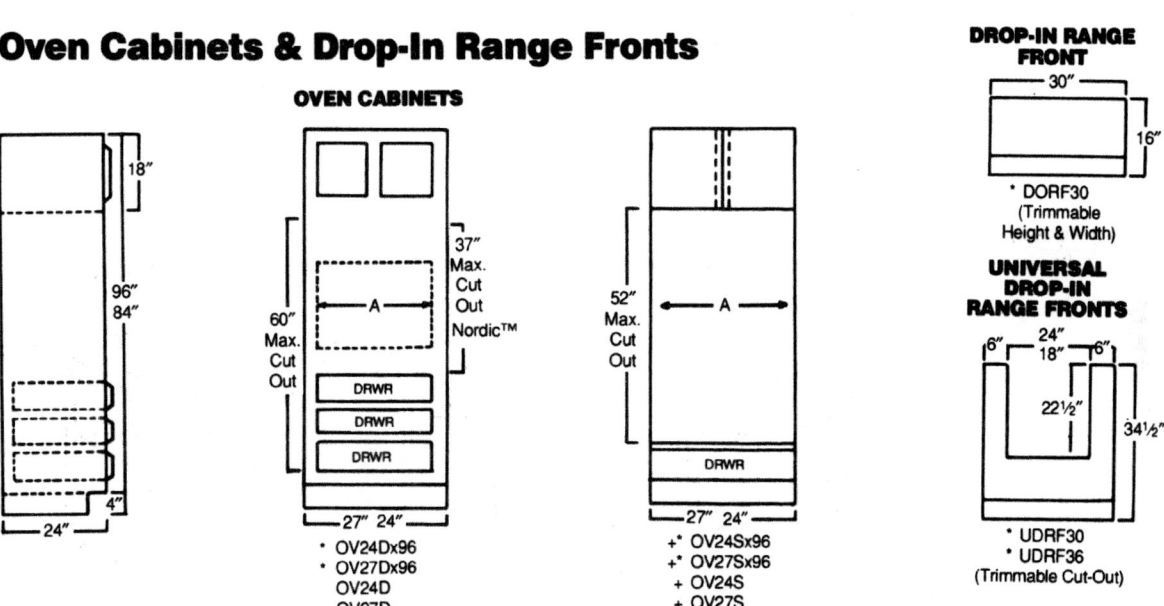

OVEN CABINETS

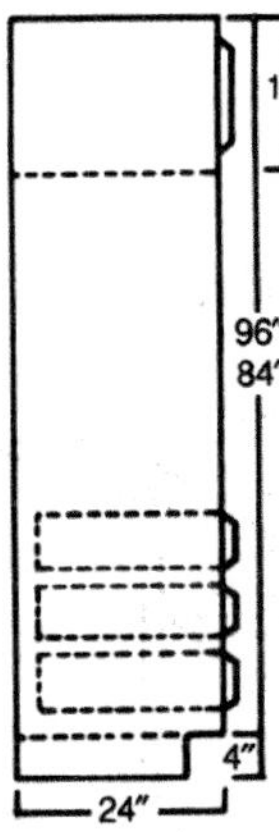

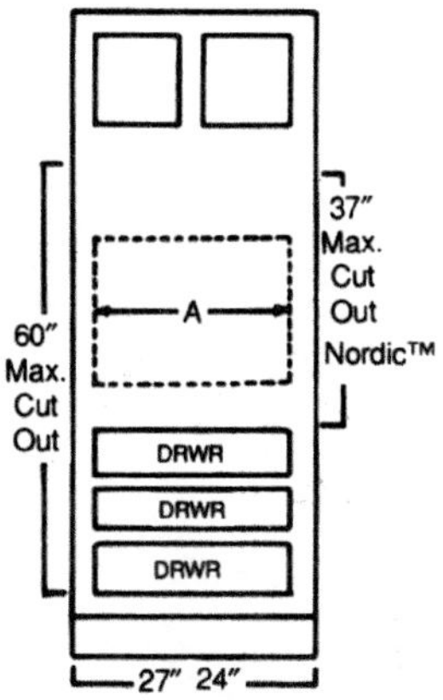

* OV24Dx96
* OV27Dx96
OV24D
OV27D

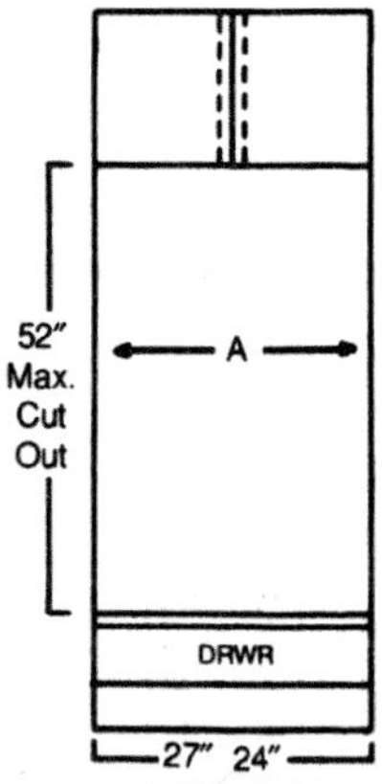

+* OV24Sx96
+* OV27Sx96
+ OV24S
+ OV27S

DROP-IN RANGE FRONT

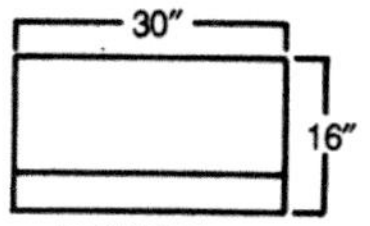

* DORF30
(Trimmable
Height & Width)

UNIVERSAL DROP-IN RANGE FRONTS

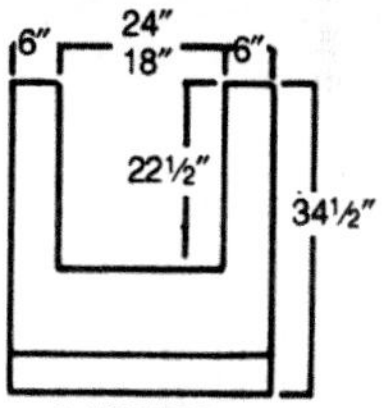

* UDRF30
* UDRF36
(Trimmable Cut-Out)

Utility Cabinets/Fronts & Pantry Cabinet

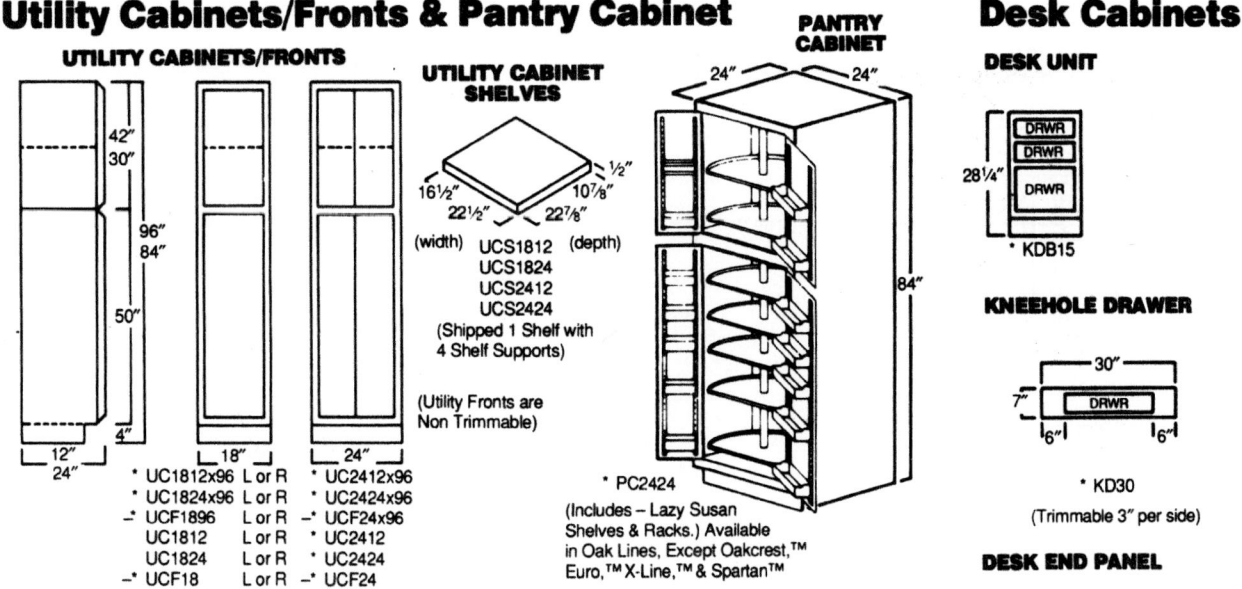

UTILITY CABINETS/FRONTS

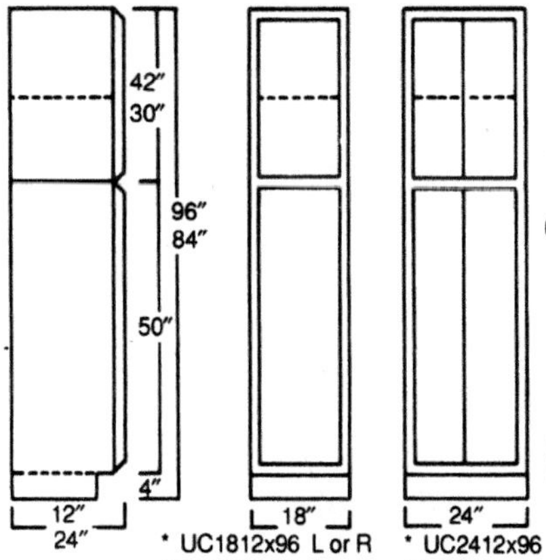

* UC1812x96	L or R	* UC2412x96
* UC1824x96	L or R	* UC2424x96
–* UCF1896	L or R	–* UCF24x96
UC1812	L or R	* UC2412
UC1824	L or R	* UC2424
–* UCF18	L or R	–* UCF24

UTILITY CABINET SHELVES

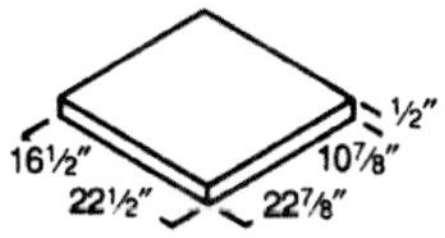

(width) UCS1812 (depth)
UCS1824
UCS2412
UCS2424
(Shipped 1 Shelf with
4 Shelf Supports)

(Utility Fronts are
Non Trimmable)

PANTRY CABINET

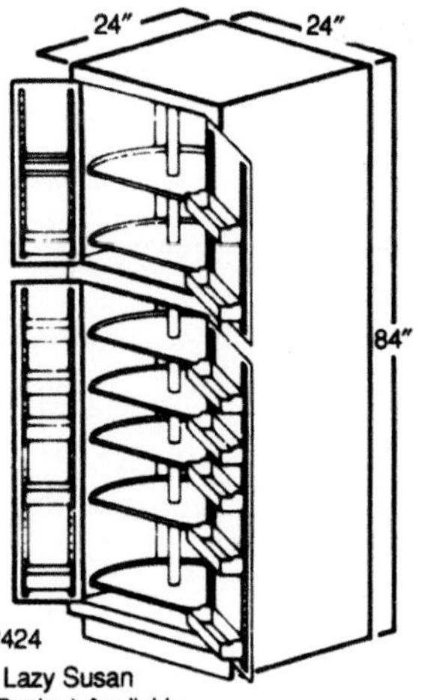

* PC2424

(Includes – Lazy Susan
Shelves & Racks.) Available
in Oak Lines, Except Oakcrest,™
Euro,™ X-Line,™ & Spartan™

Desk Cabinets

DESK UNIT

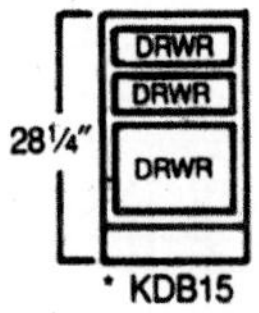

* KDB15

KNEEHOLE DRAWER

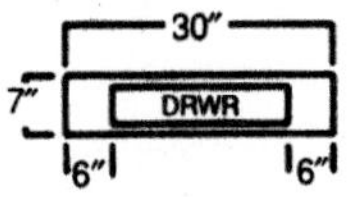

* KD30

(Trimmable 3″ per side)

DESK END PANEL

KITCHENS
Cabinet Types and Dimensions

BASE CABINETS

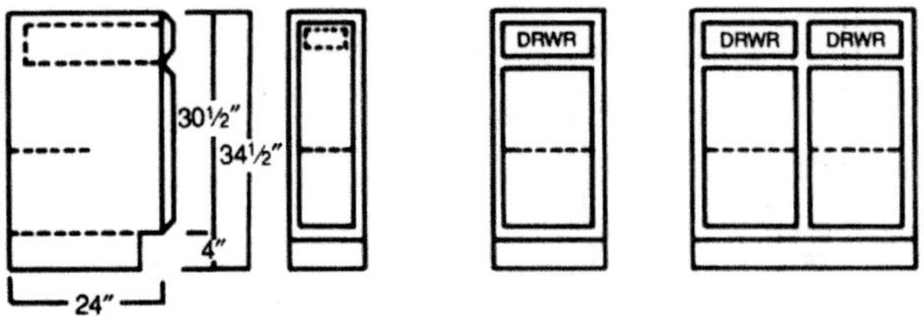

▲■ B9 L or R
(Concealed Drawer)

B12 L or R
B15 L or R
B18 L or R
B21 L or R
B24 L or R

B27 B36
B30 B42
B33 B48

DRAWER BASE CABINETS

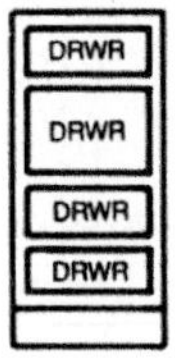

DB12
DB15
DB18
DB21
DB24

SPECIAL DRAWER BASE CABINET

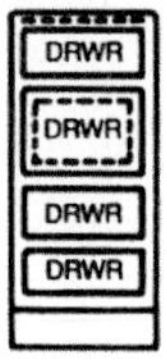

– DB18CB
(Includes — Cutting Board, Cutlery Divider & Metal Bread Box.)

COMBINATION SINK BASE CABINETS

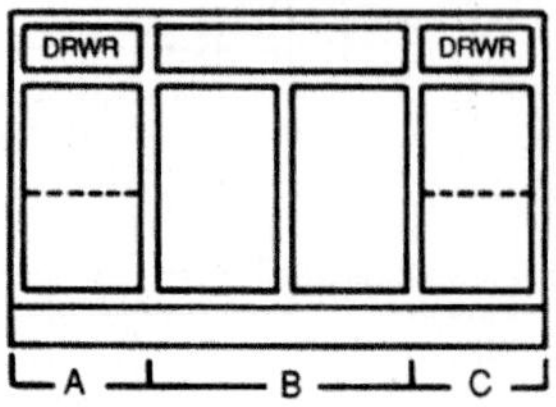

	A	B	C
–* SB60	15″	30″	15″
–* SB66	15″	36″	15″
–* SB72	18″	36″	18″

▲ No Arched Door.
■ No Center Medallion. (Saxony)

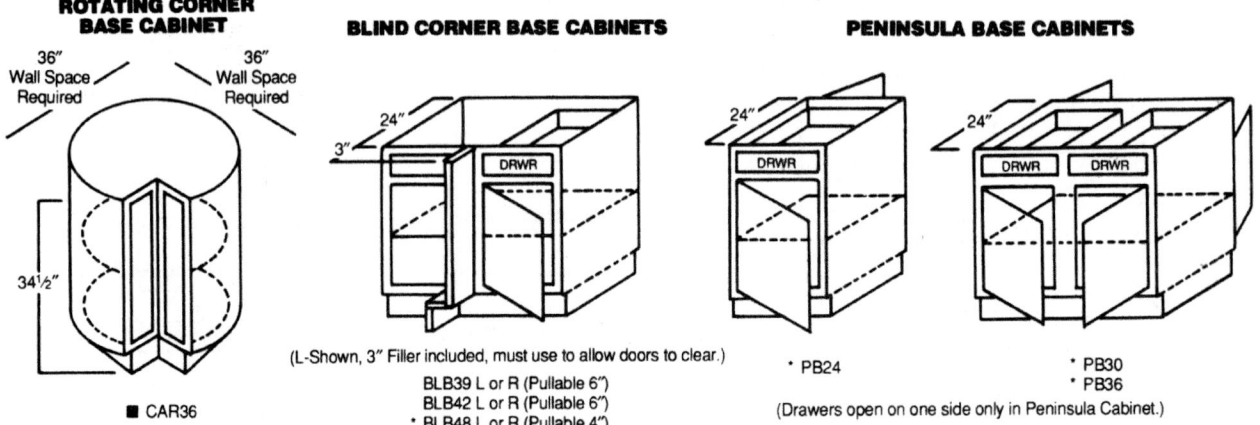

ROTATING CORNER BASE CABINET

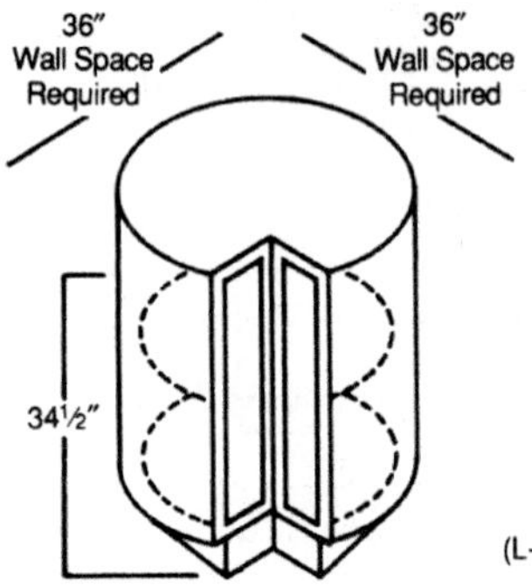

■ CAR36

BLIND CORNER BASE CABINETS

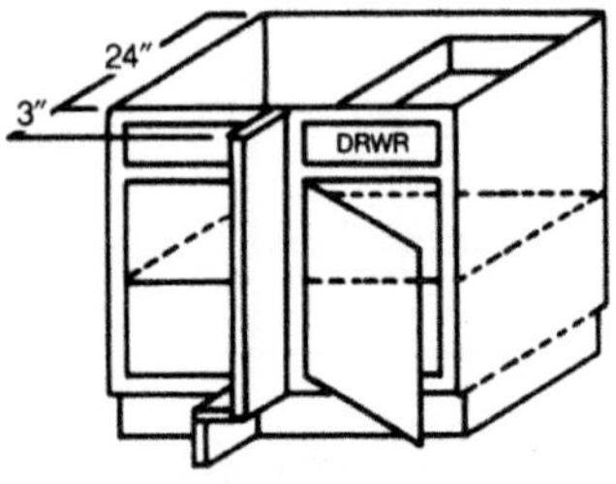

(L-Shown, 3″ Filler included, must use to allow doors to clear.)

BLB39 L or R (Pullable 6″)
BLB42 L or R (Pullable 6″)
* BLB48 L or R (Pullable 4″)

PENINSULA BASE CABINETS

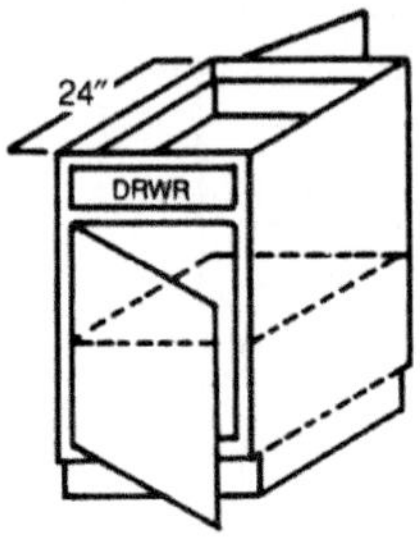

* PB24

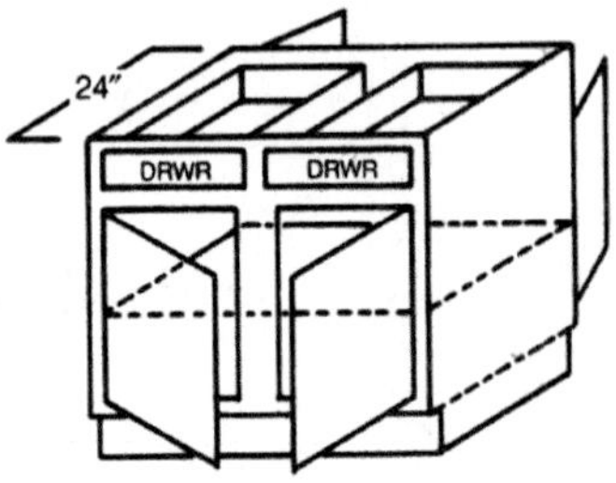

* PB30
* PB36

(Drawers open on one side only in Peninsula Cabinet.)

BLIND PENINSULA BASE CABINETS

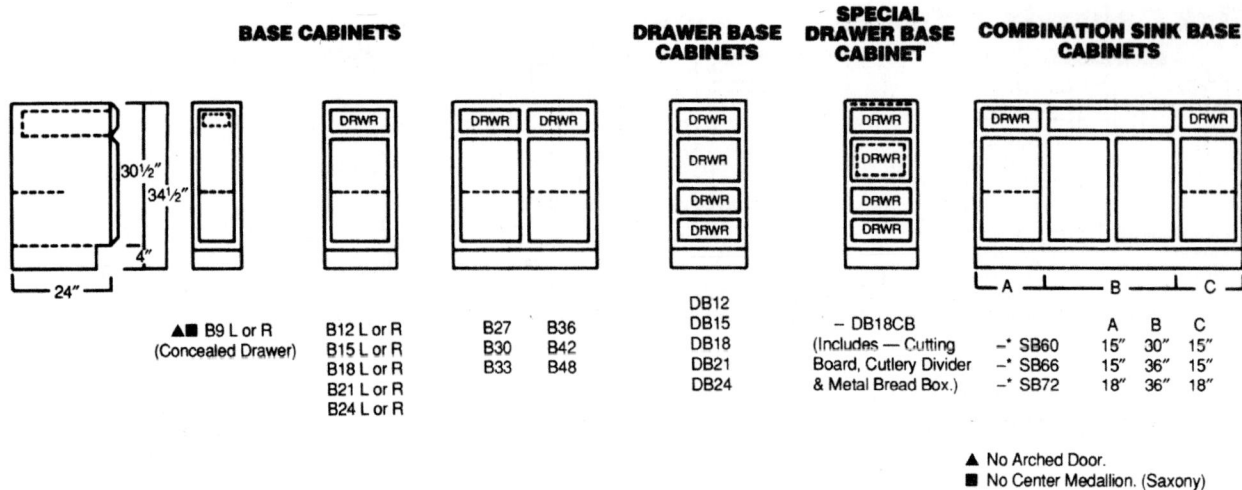

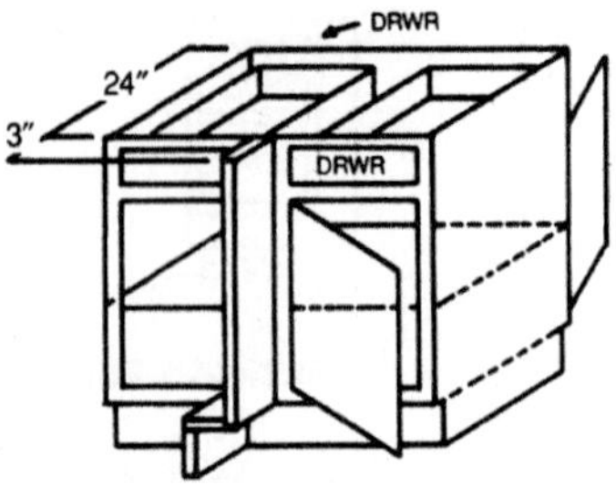

(L-Shown, 3″ Filler included, must use to allow doors to clear.)

* BLPB42 L or R (Pullable 6″)
* BLPB48 L or R (Pullable 6″)

WALL CABINETS

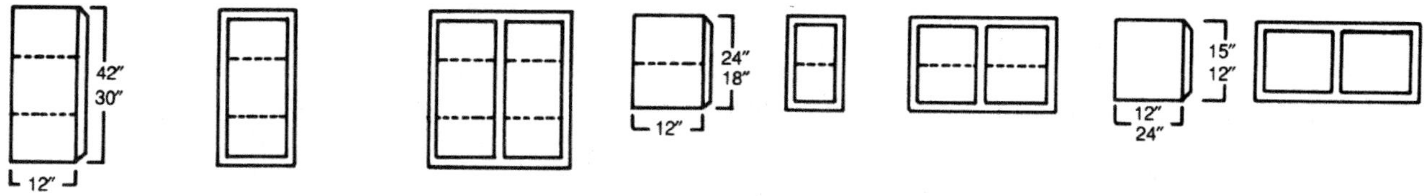

* W1242 L or R
* W1542 L or R
* W1842 L or R
* W2142 L or R
* W2442 L or R

▲■ * W930 L or R
W1230 L or R
W1530 L or R
W1830 L or R
W2130 L or R
W2430 L or R

* W2742 W2730
* W3042 W3030
* W3342 W3330
* W3642 W3630
* W4242 W4230
* W4842 W4830

* W1224 L or R
* W1524 L or R
* W1824 L or R
* W2124 L or R
* W2424 L or R

W3024
* W3624
* W4224
* W4824

W2418
W3018
W3318
W3618
W4218

W3015 * W3015x24 ■ W3012
W3315 * W3315x24 ■ W3612
W3615 * W3615x24

COMBINATION WALL CABINETS

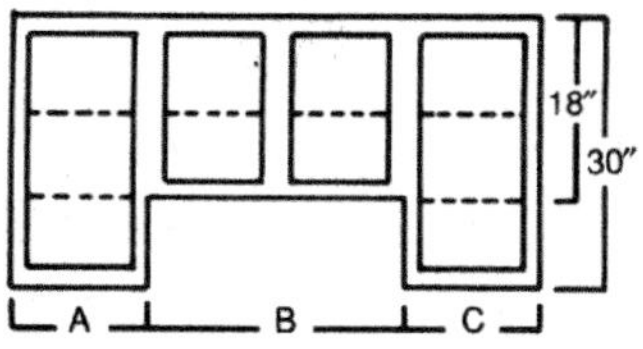

	A	B	C
–* CWC60	15"	30"	15"
–* CWC66	18"	30"	18"
–* CWC72	21"	30"	21"

(Fixed Shelves)

CORNER WALL CABINET

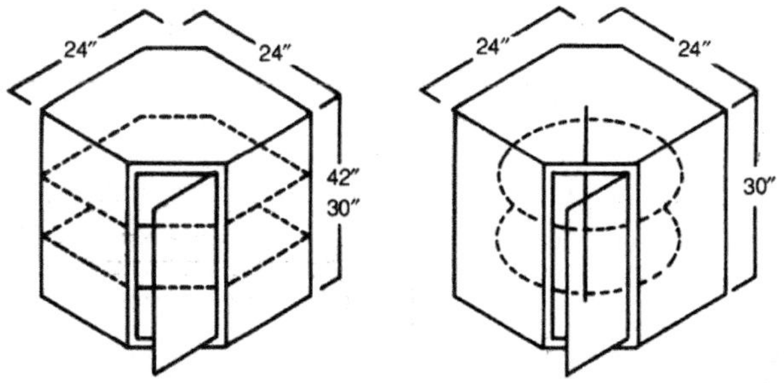

* CW2442 L or R
CW2430 L or R
(Fixed Shelves)

CWS2430 L or R
(2 Adjustable Rotary Shelves)

BLIND CORNER WALL CABINETS

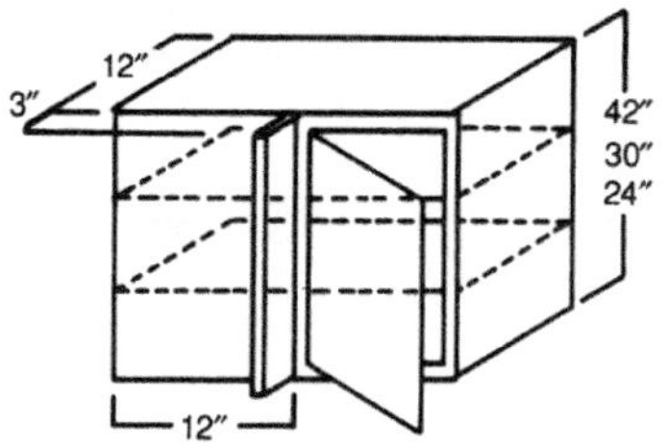

(L-Shown, 3" Filler included, must use to allow doors to clear.)

* BLW2742 L or R
* BLW3042 L or R
* BLW3642 L or R
* BLW4242 (2 Doors) L or R
* BLW4842 (2 Doors) L or R

BLW2730 L or R
BLW3030 L or R
BLW3630 L or R
BLW4230 (2 Doors) L or R
* BLW4830 (2 Doors) L or R

* BLW2724 L or R
* BLW3624 L or R

PENINSULA WALL CABINETS

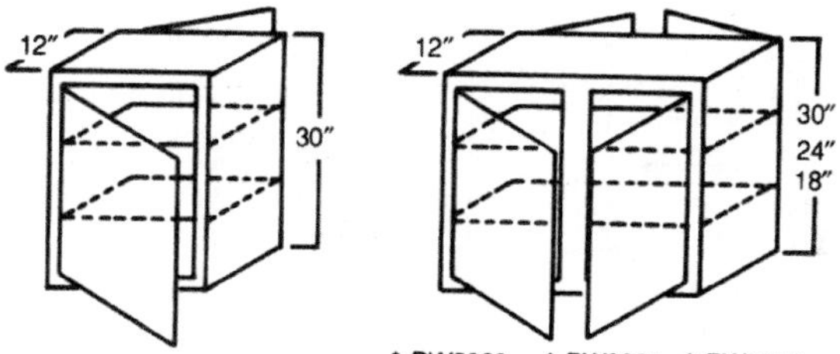

* PW2430

* PW3030 * PW3024 * PW3018
* PW3630 * PW3624 * PW3618
* PW4218

MICROWAVE CABINET

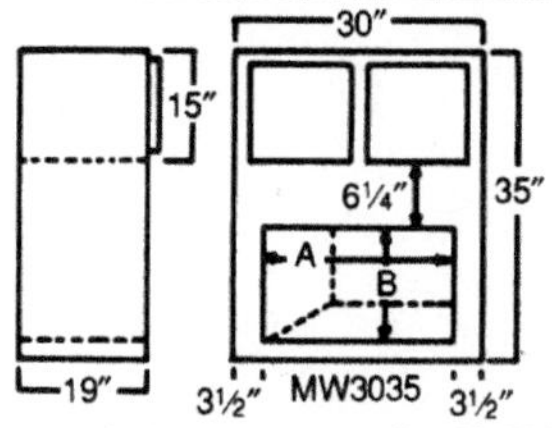

A: 22" Minimum 28" Maximum
B: 13¾" Minimum 19⅛" Maximum

MICROWAVE CABINET W/SHELF

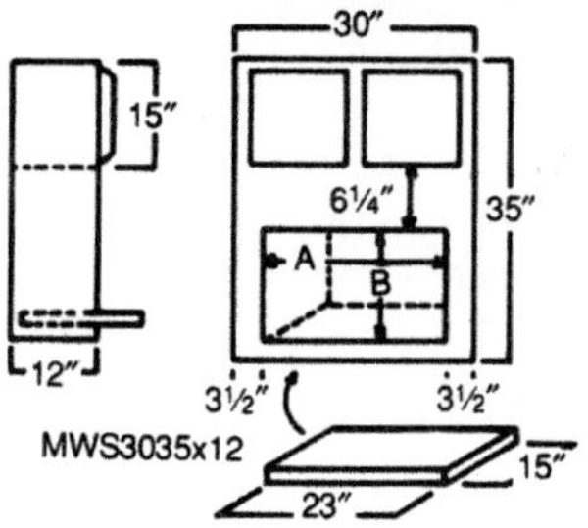

BLIND PENINSULA CORNER WALL CABINET

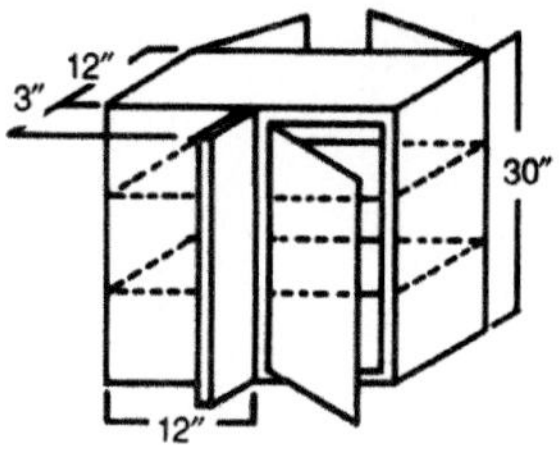

(L-Shown, 3" Filler included, must use to allow doors to clear.)

* BLPW2730 L or R

KITCHENS

Cabinet Types and Dimensions

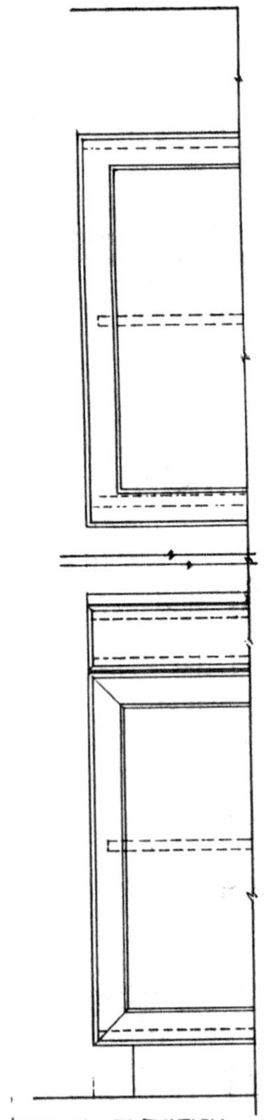

PARTIAL ELEVATION
SCALE: 3"=1'-0"

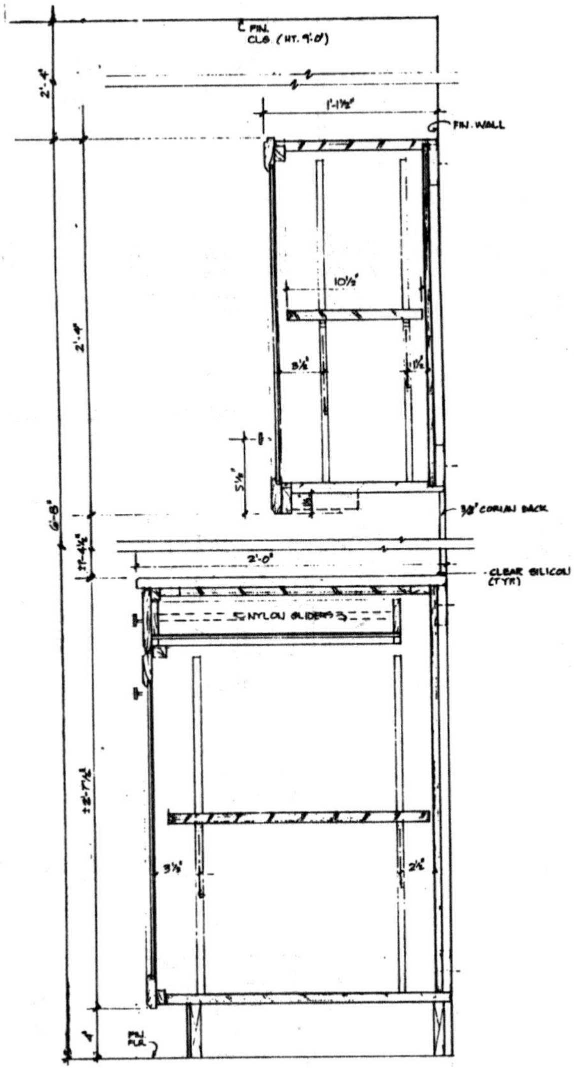

SECTION 'A'

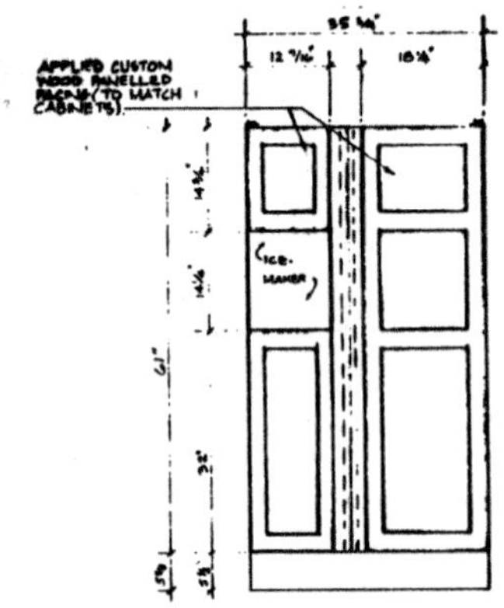

REFRIGERATOR ELEVATION
SCALE: 1"=1'-0"

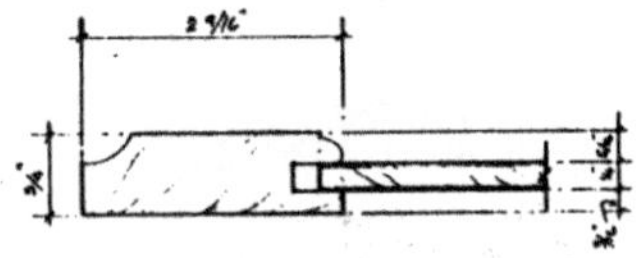

SECTION OF WOOD PANEL FACING
SCALE: FULL SIZE

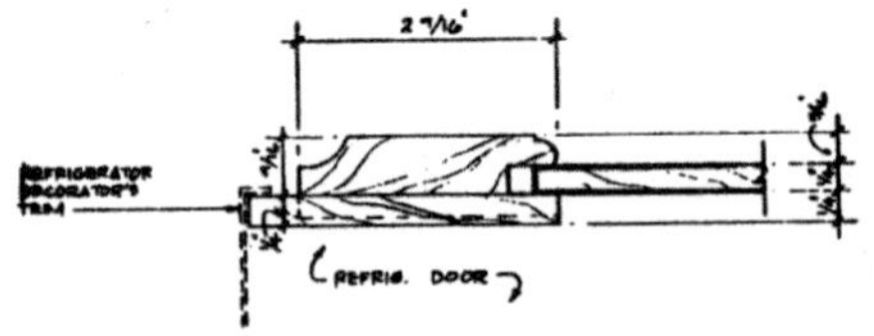

SECTION

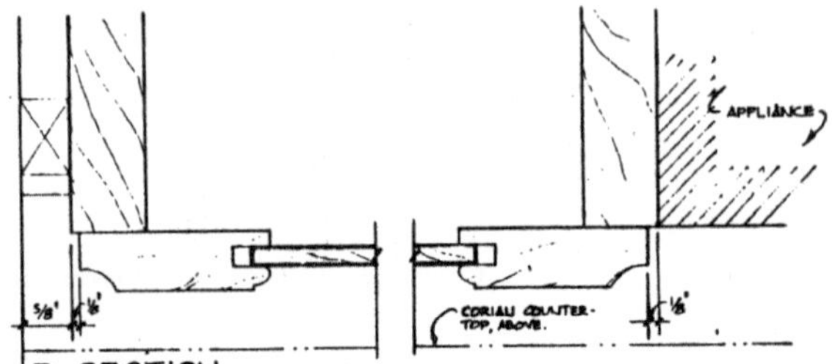

SECTION

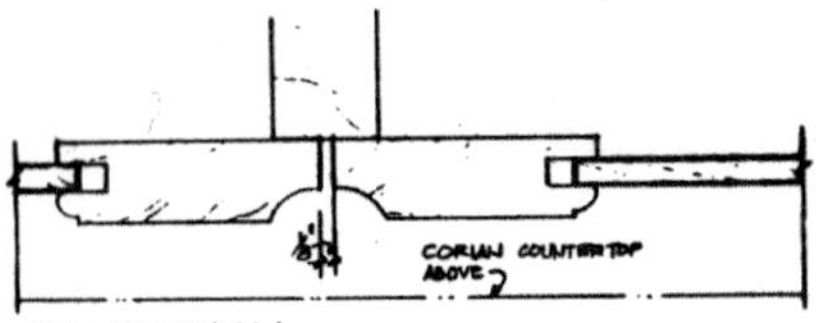

SECTION

KITCHENS
Cabinet Details

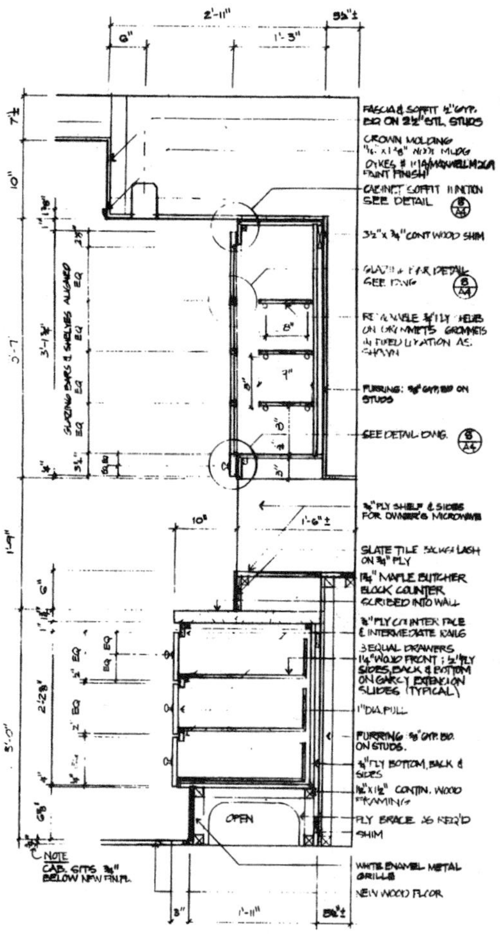

1 A4 SECTION: TYPICAL KITCHEN CABINET @ DRAWERS
1" = 1'-0"

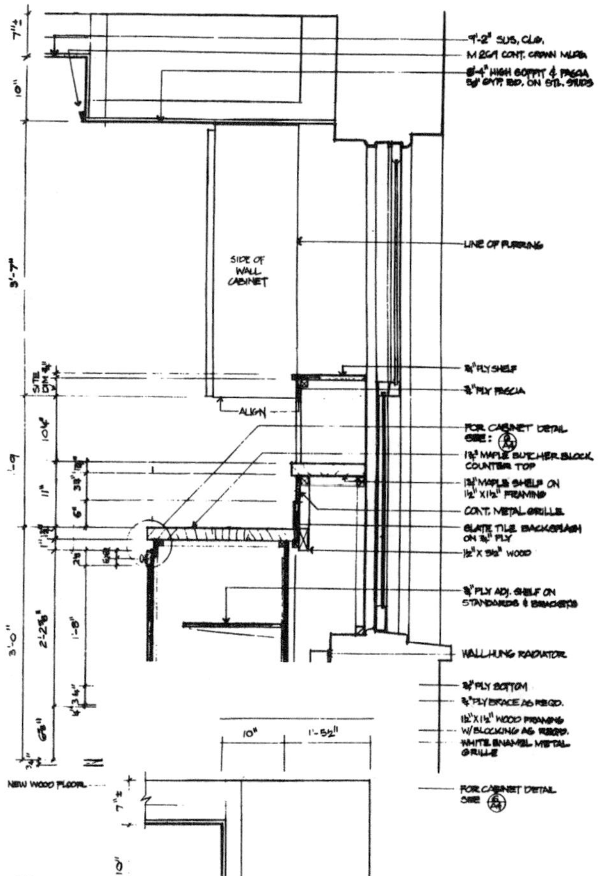

3 A4 SECTION
1" = 1'-0"

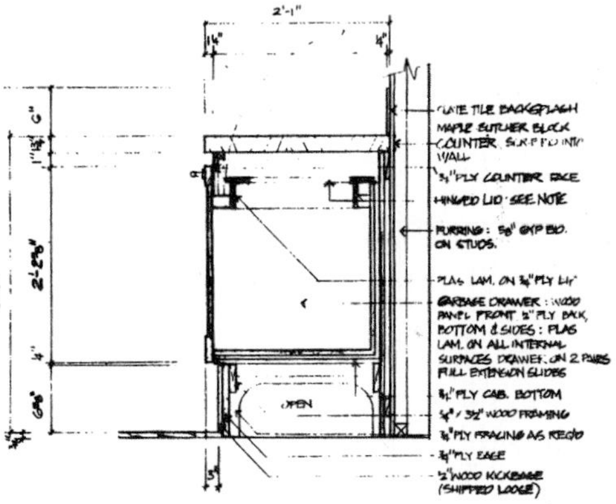

2 A4 SECTION: KITCHEN CABINET @ GARBAGE DRAWER
1" = 1'-0"

*NOTE: PLAS. LAM. ON ¾" PLY W/ CUT-OUT FOR GARBAGE BAG, ATTACH LID TO DRAWER W/ CONTIN. PIANO HINGE.

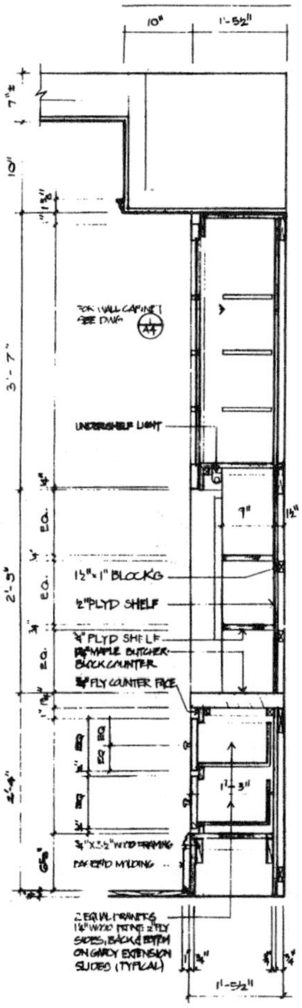

4 A4 SECTION @ NEW WOOD DESK
1" = 1'-0"

KITCHENS
Cabinet Details

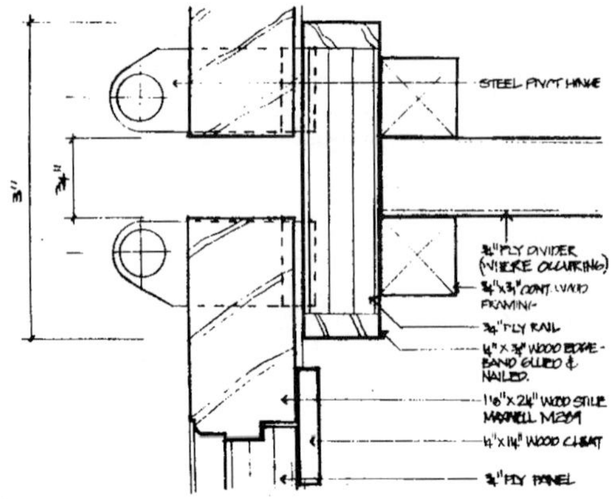

5 / A4 KITCHEN CABINET - PLAN @ JAMB (TYPICAL)
FULL SIZE

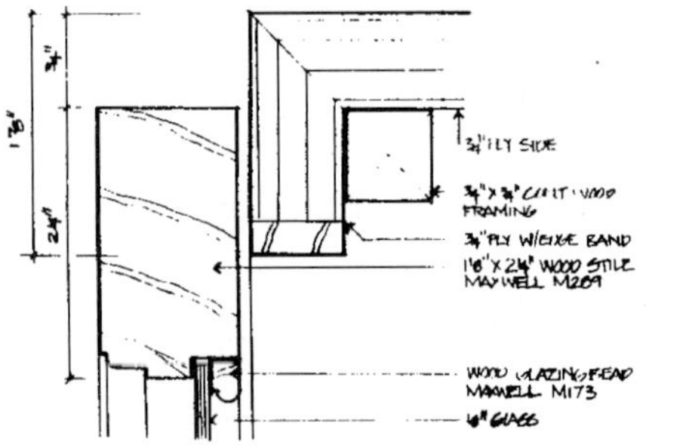

7 / A4 KITCHEN CABINET - PLAN @ CORNER JAMB (TYPICAL)
FULL SIZE

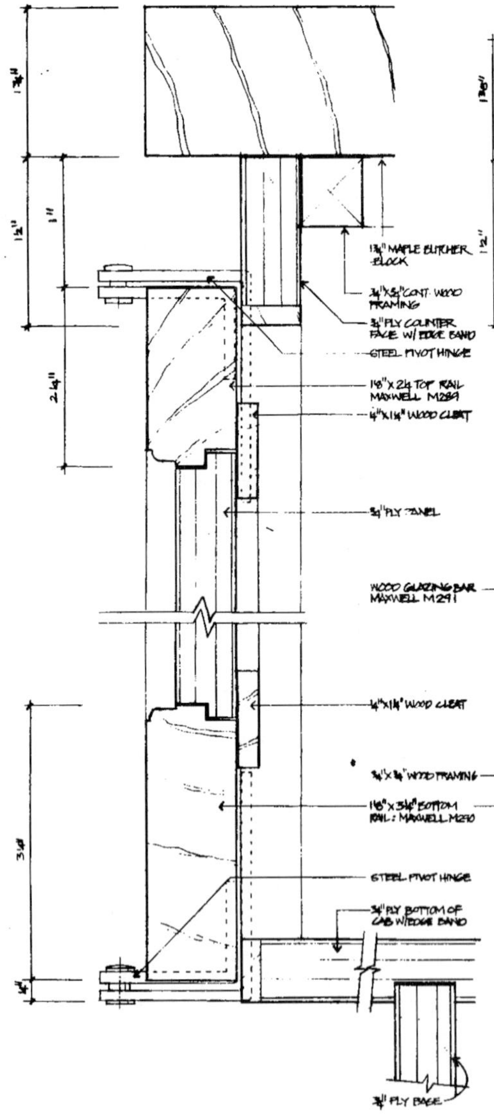

6 / A4 KITCHEN BASE CABINET @ DOOR - TYPICAL SECTION
FULL SIZE

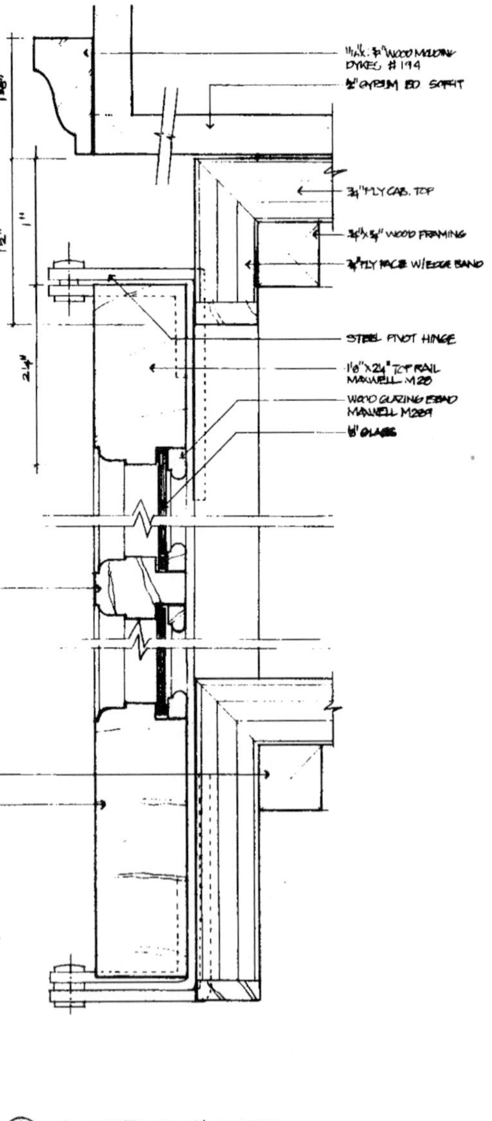

8 / A4 WALL CABINET - TYPICAL SECTION
FULL SIZE

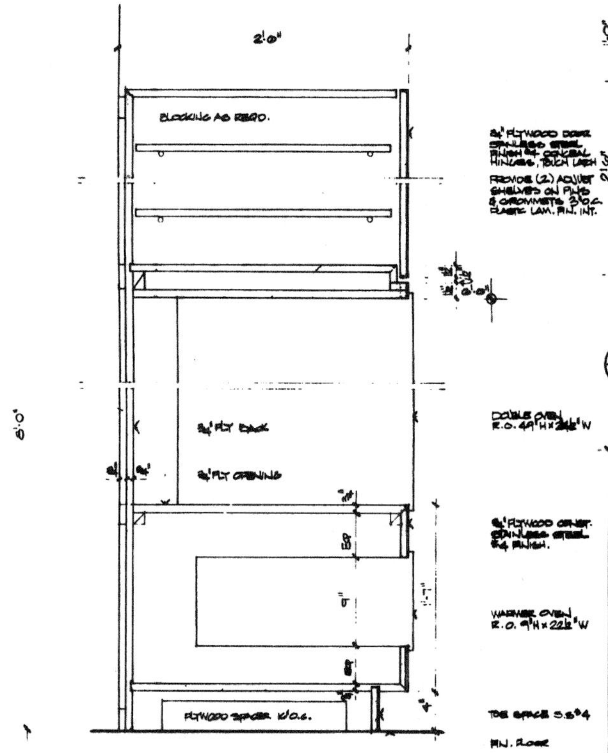

6 SECTION : DBLE OVEN
A13 1/2"=1'-0"

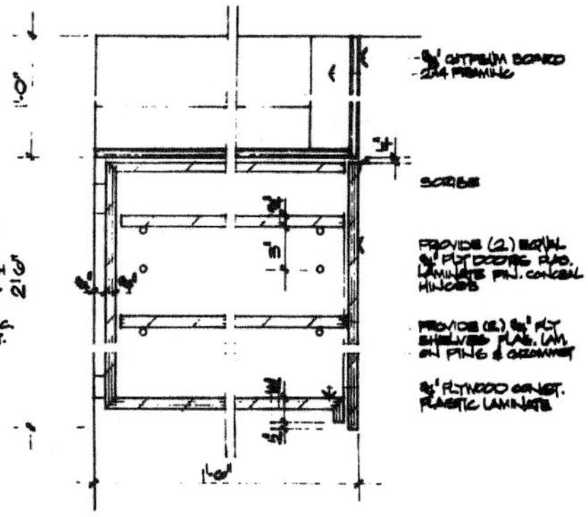

8 SECTION : PANTRY
A13 1/2"=1'-0"

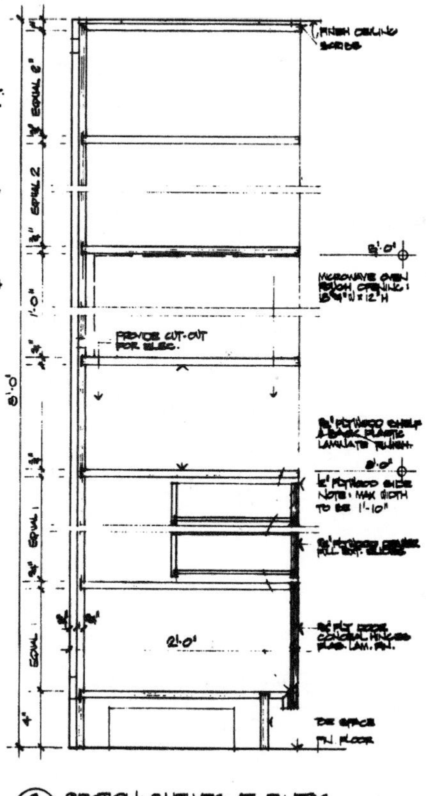

9 SECTION: SHELVES AT PANTRY
A13 1/2"=1'-0"

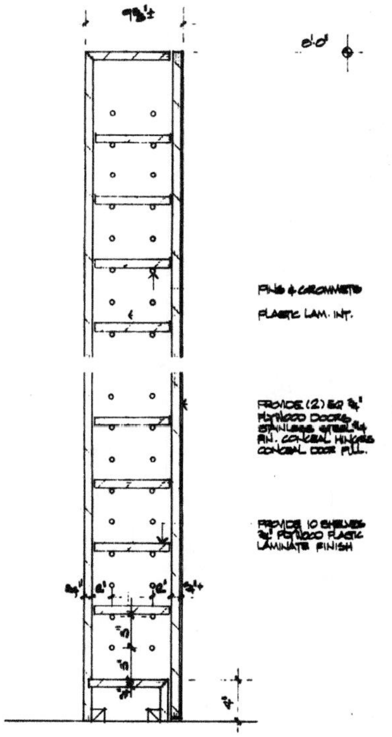

7 SECTION : PANTRY @ KITCHEN
A13 1/2"=1'-0"

KITCHENS

Cabinet Types and Dimensions

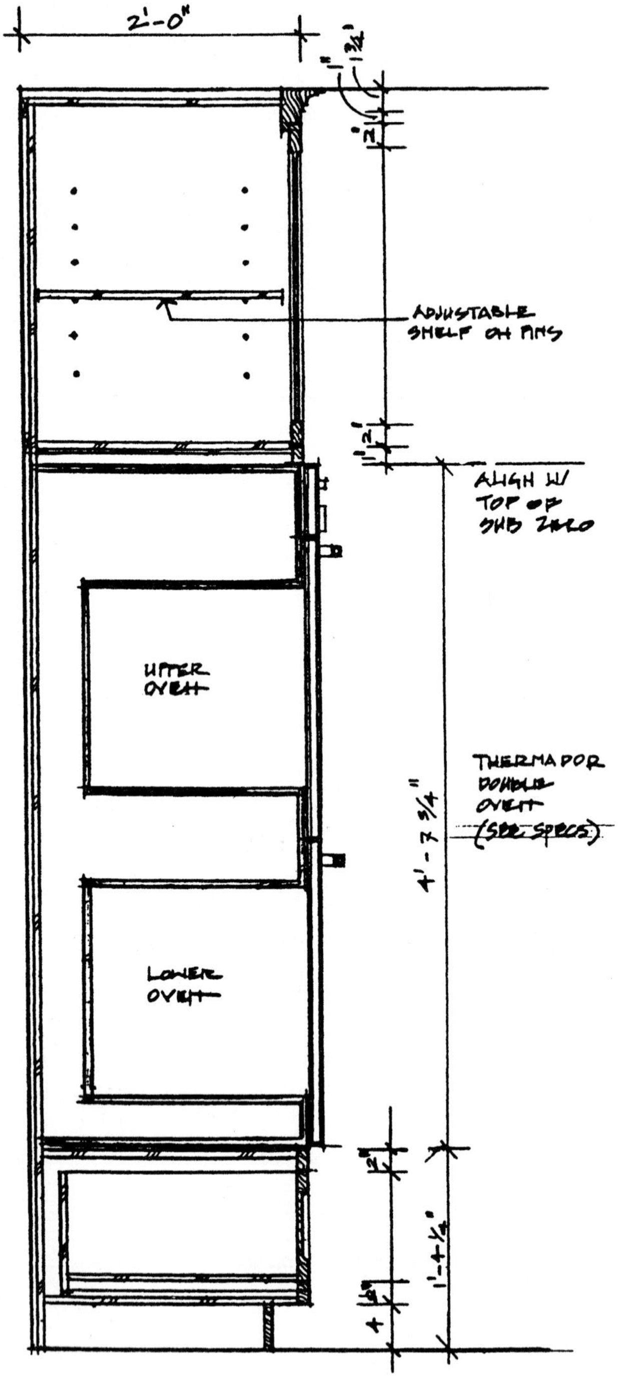

1/1 Double Oven Cabinet

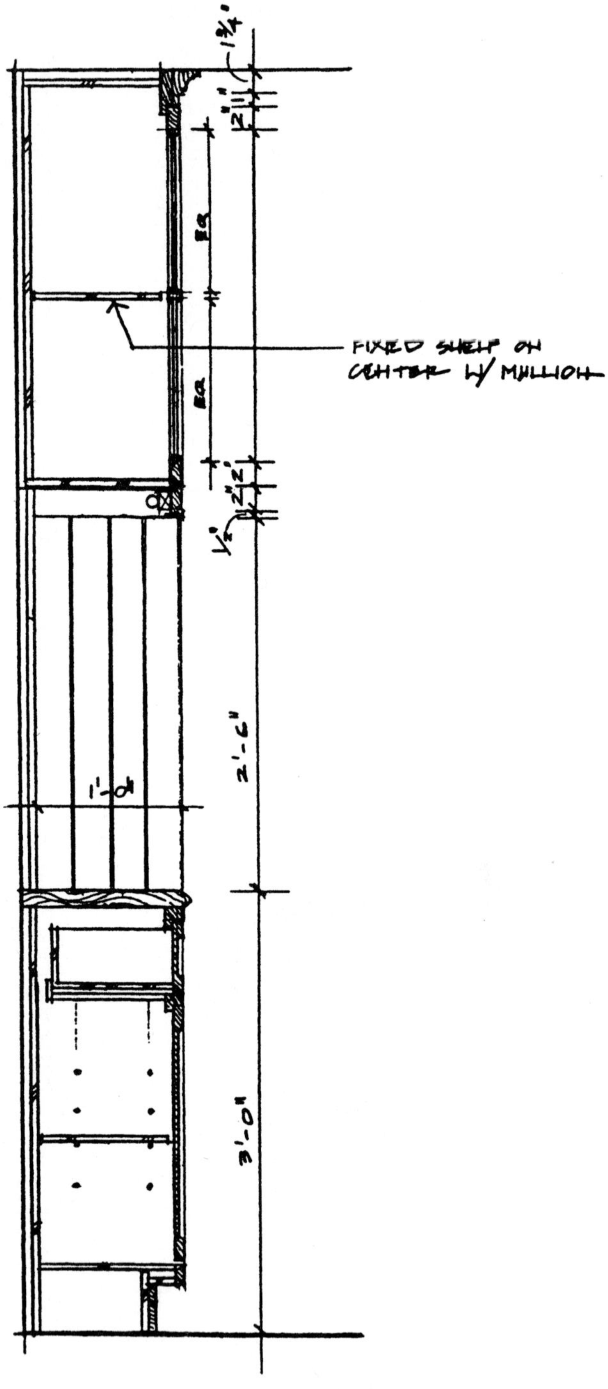

1/2 Ledge W/ Cabinet Above

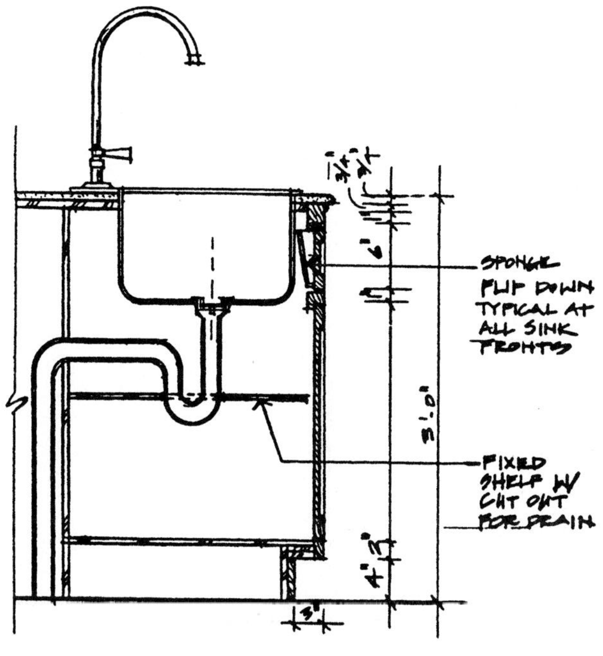

9 Island Cabinet

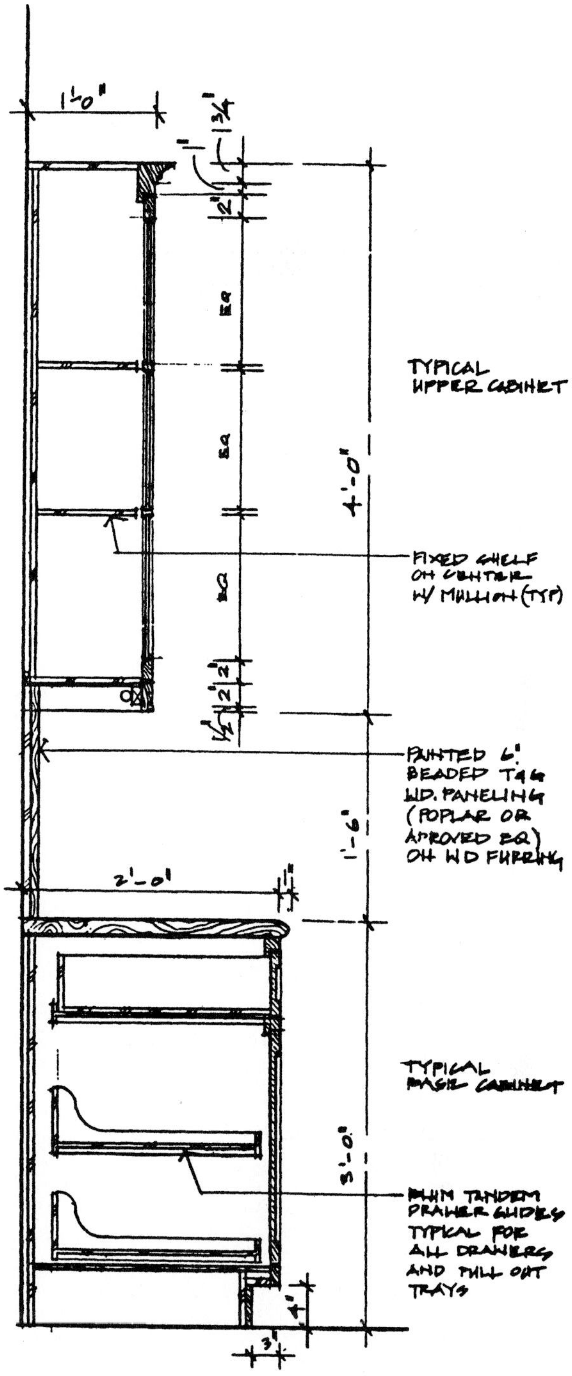

10 Typ. Base & Upper Cabinet

KITCHENS
Sink Types and Dimensions

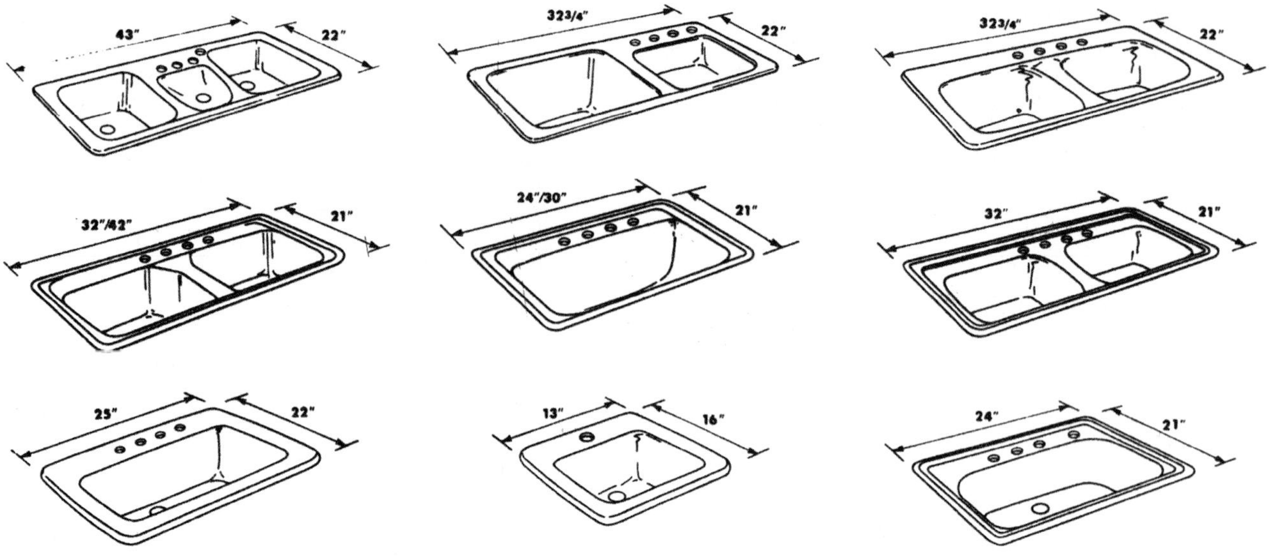

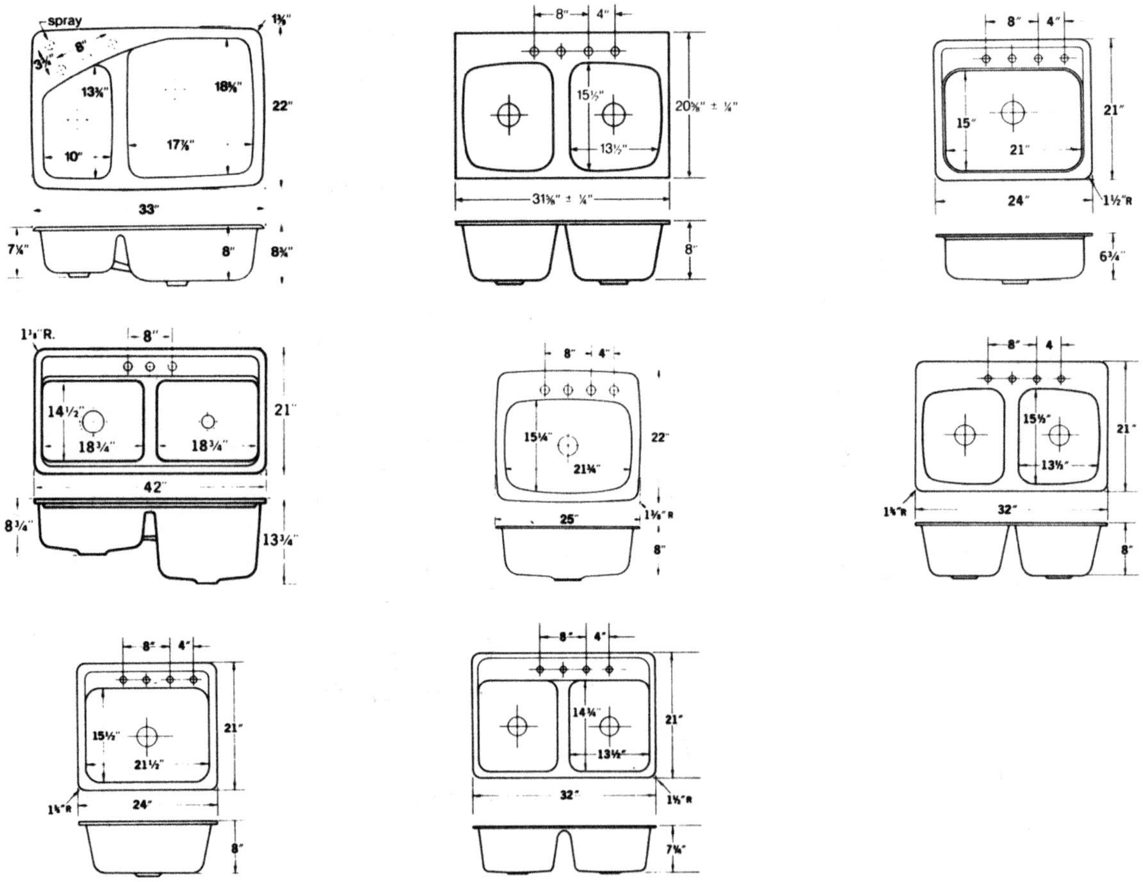

Ranges and Built-in Ovens

Freestanding ranges and built-in ovens come in a variety of sizes and configurations. Some of the larger ranges consist of modular cooktops providing anywhere from two to seven heating elements as well as modular grills, griddles, and even downdraft built-in ventilators. Normally, a minimum clearance of 30 in is required above any range or cooktop, but the designer is cautioned to carefully verify local code requirements. Manufacturers' specifications should be carefully reviewed for rough opening requirements and any venting requirements, particularly for self-cleaning ovens.

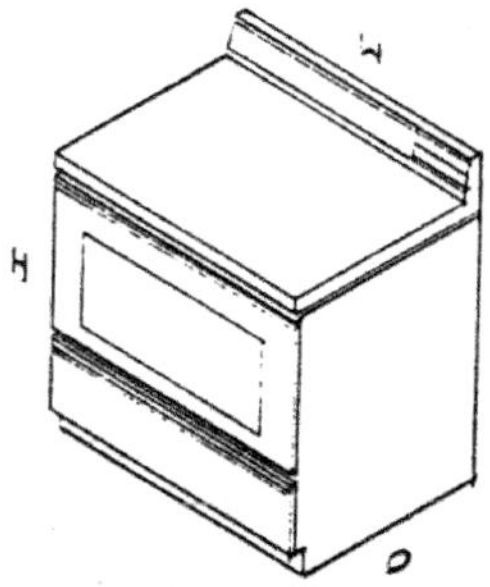

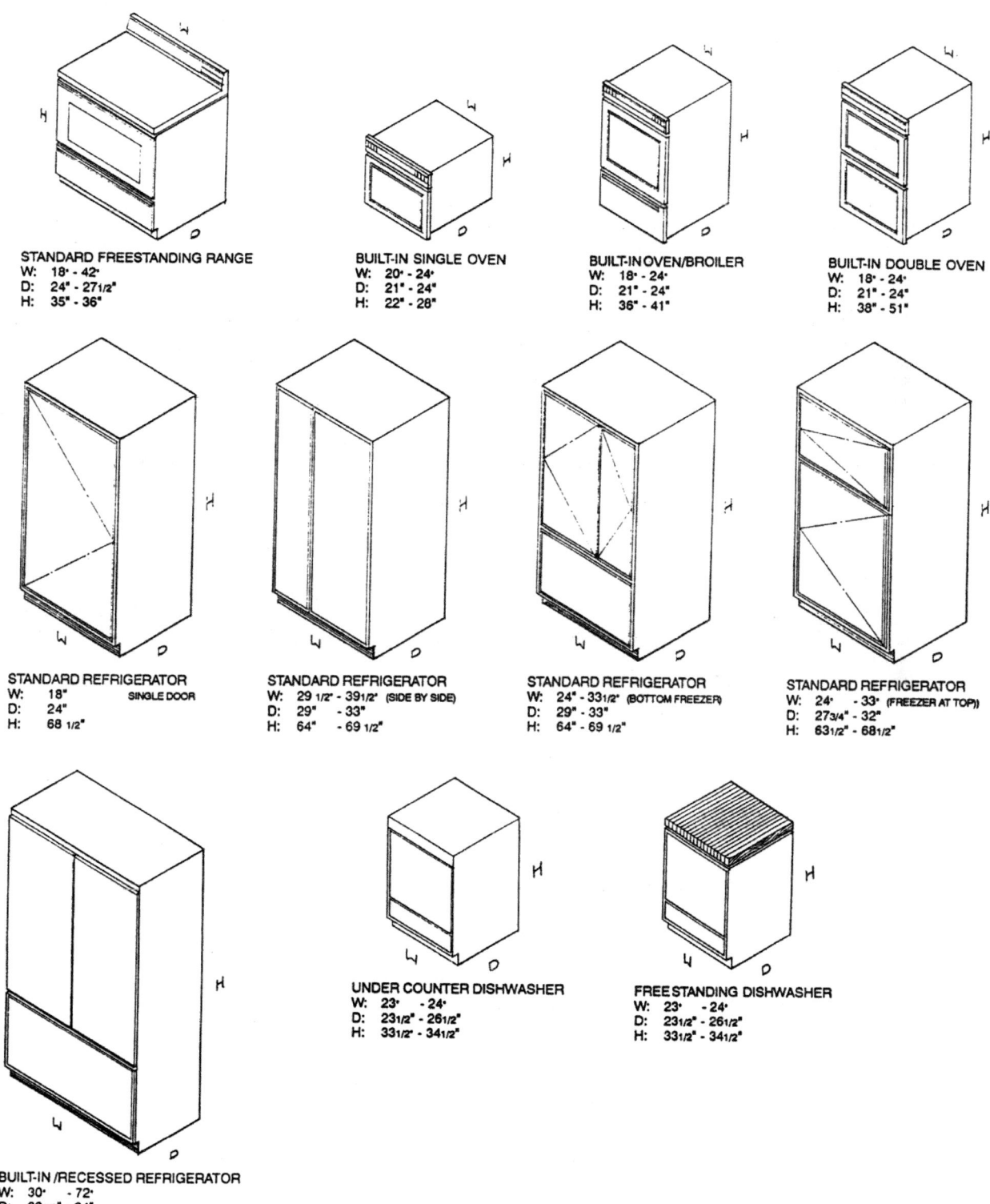

STANDARD FREESTANDING RANGE
W: 18" - 42"
D: 24" - 27 1/2"
H: 35" - 36"

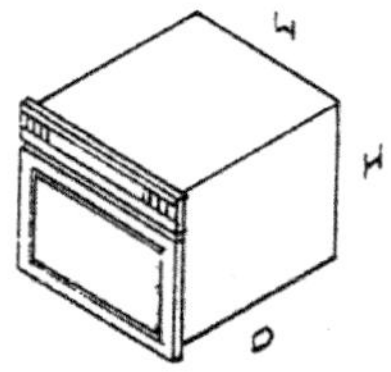

BUILT-IN SINGLE OVEN
W: 20" - 24"
D: 21" - 24"
H: 22" - 28"

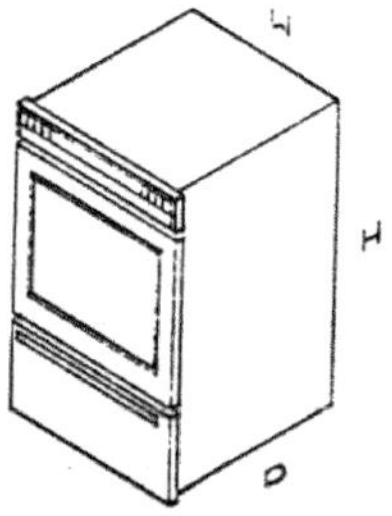

BUILT-IN OVEN/BROILER
W: 18" - 24"
D: 21" - 24"
H: 36" - 41"

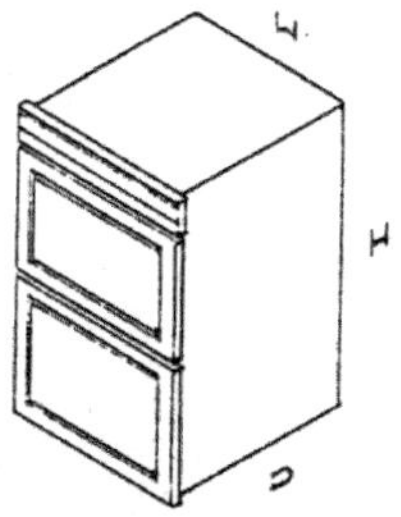

BUILT-IN DOUBLE OVEN
W: 18" - 24"
D: 21" - 24"
H: 38" - 51"

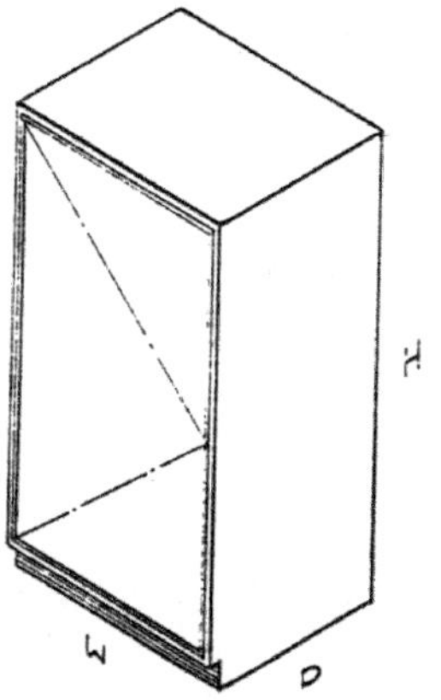

STANDARD REFRIGERATOR
W: 18" SINGLE DOOR
D: 24"
H: 68 1/2"

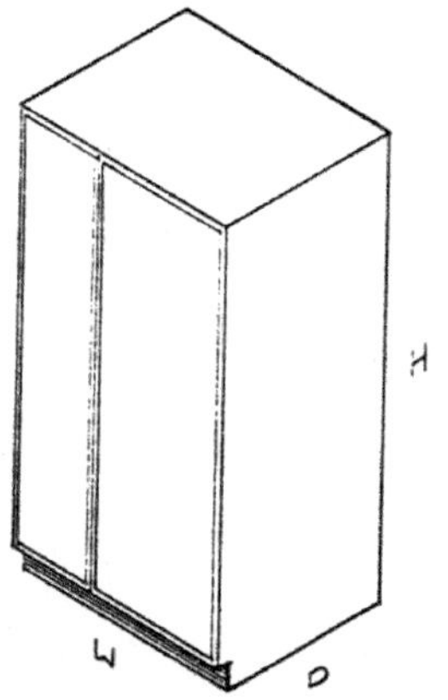

STANDARD REFRIGERATOR
W: 29 1/2" - 39 1/2" (SIDE BY SIDE)
D: 29" - 33"
H: 64" - 69 1/2"

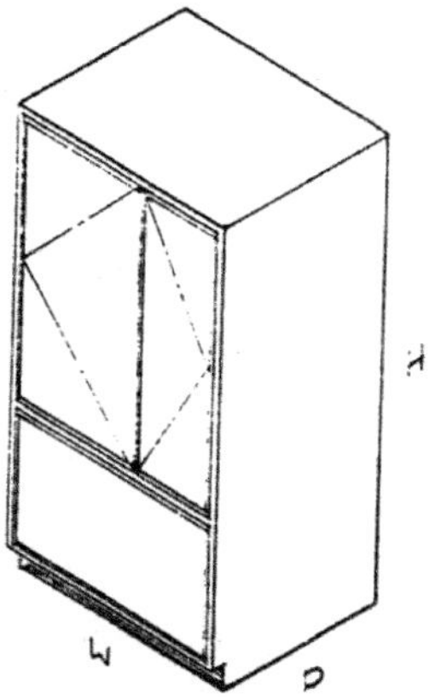

STANDARD REFRIGERATOR
W: 24" - 33 1/2" (BOTTOM FREEZER)
D: 29" - 33"
H: 64" - 69 1/2"

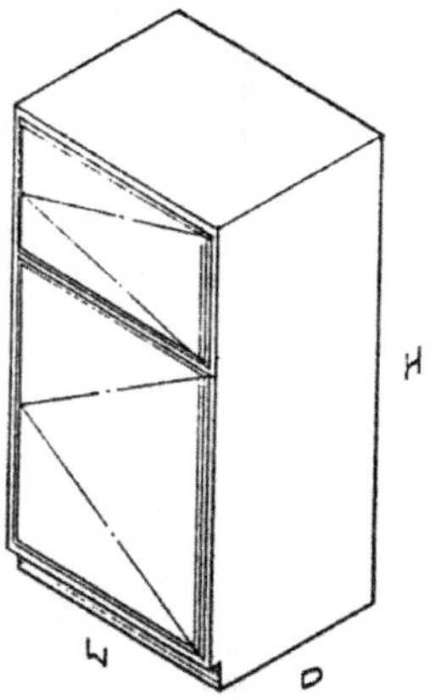

STANDARD REFRIGERATOR
W: 24" - 33" (FREEZER AT TOP)
D: 27 3/4" - 32"
H: 63 1/2" - 68 1/2"

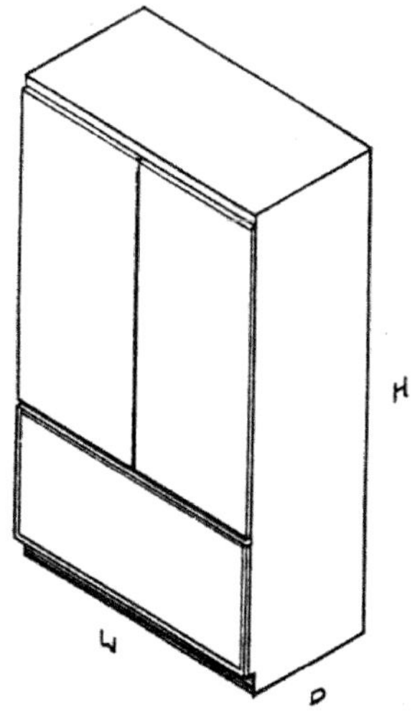

BUILT-IN /RECESSED REFRIGERATOR
W: 30" - 72"
D: 23 1/2" - 24"
H: 84"

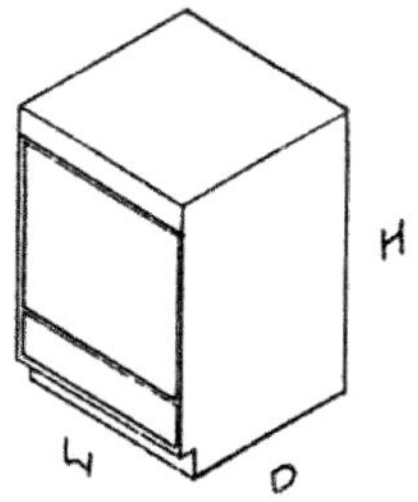

UNDER COUNTER DISHWASHER
W: 23" - 24"
D: 23 1/2" - 26 1/2"
H: 33 1/2" - 34 1/2"

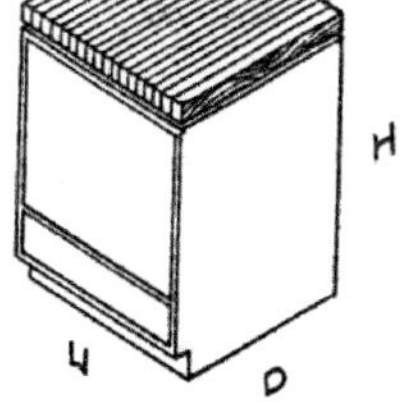

FREE STANDING DISHWASHER
W: 23" - 24"
D: 23 1/2" - 26 1/2"
H: 33 1/2" - 34 1/2"

KITCHENS
Dishwashers and Refrigerators

Dishwashers

Built-in, freestanding, and undersink dishwashers are fairly well standardized in terms of overall dimensions. Access to plumbing and waste lines is the major consideration, as is the method of securing the dishwasher in order to minimize vibration.

Refrigerators

Refrigerator door swings and clearances are of critical importance. While a 90° door swing may provide sufficient room for a person to observe storage within a refrigerator or freezer, a 180° door swing may be required to clean a refrigerator and remove storage bins. This is particularly true of the side-by-side door configuration. In addition, adequate clearance should be allowed between the sides and top of the refrigerator and any adjoining cabinet work, especially if a built-in look is desired. The designer should check requirements with the manufacturer.

While these drawings can be used for preliminary planning, final dimensions and clearance must be verified with the manufacturer. Often overlooked are clearances for refrigerator handles or pulls as well as coils mounted at the rear of the refrigerator.

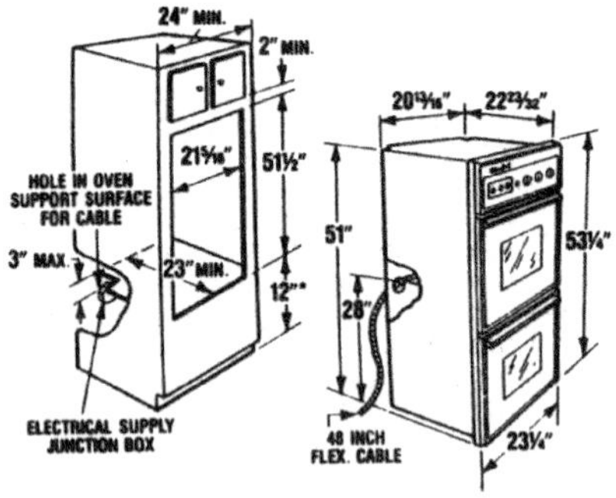

24″ electric built-in double oven

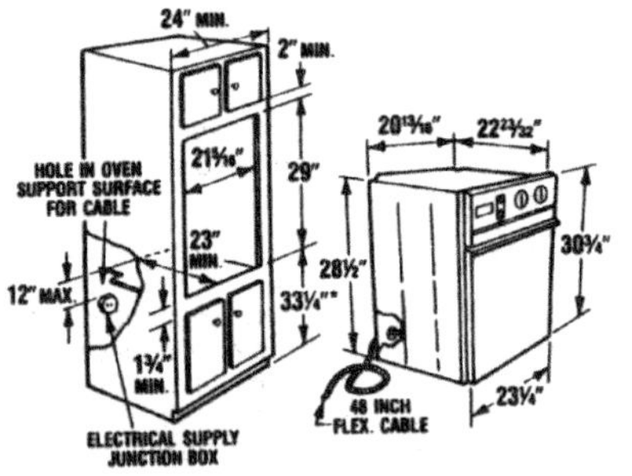

24″ electric built-in single oven

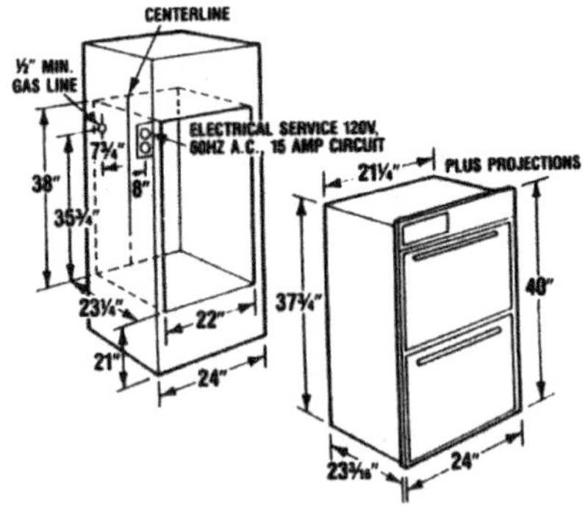

Gas built-in oven

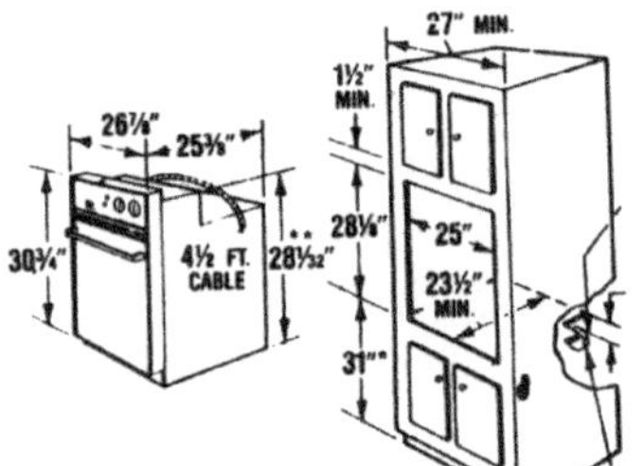

Electric built-in single oven

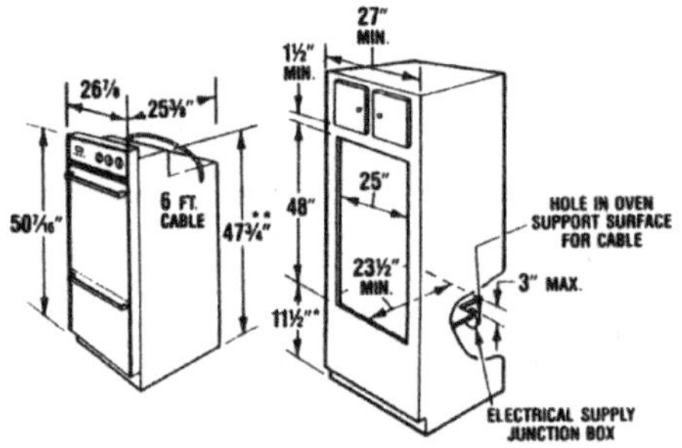

27″ electric built-in double oven

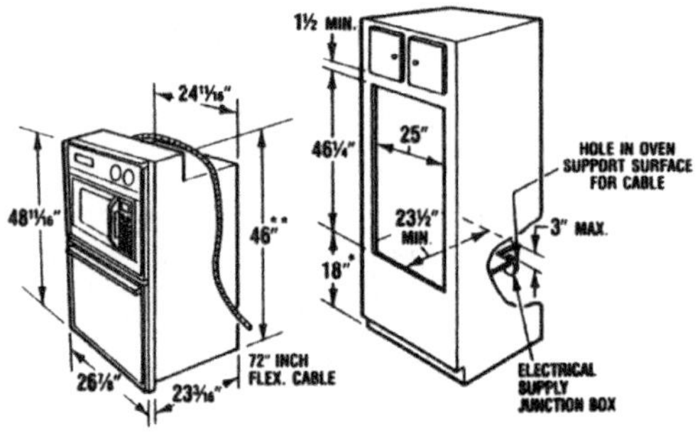

27″ built-in microwave oven

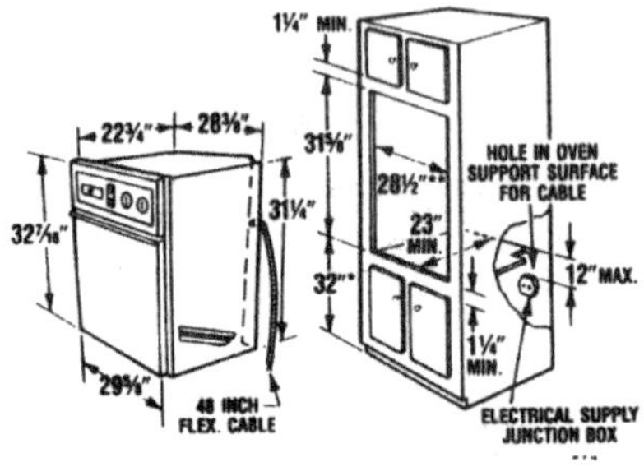

30″ electric built-in single oven

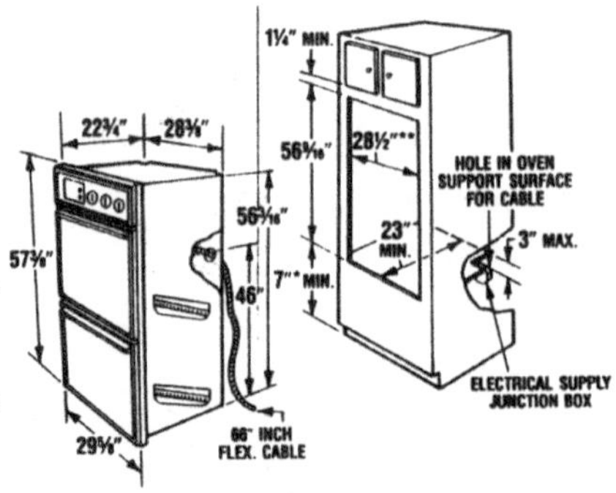

30″ electric built-in double oven

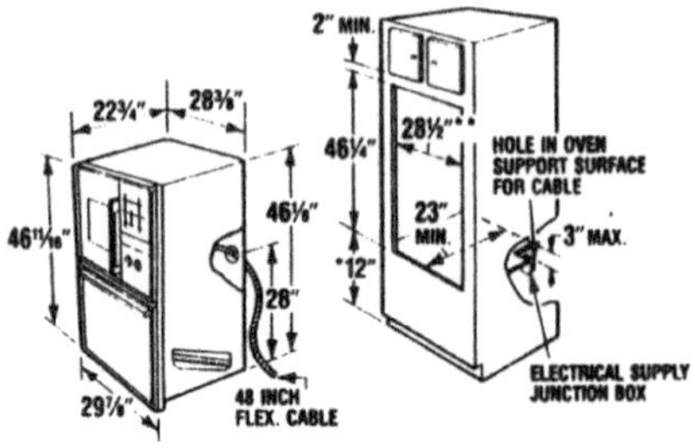

30″ built-in microwave oven

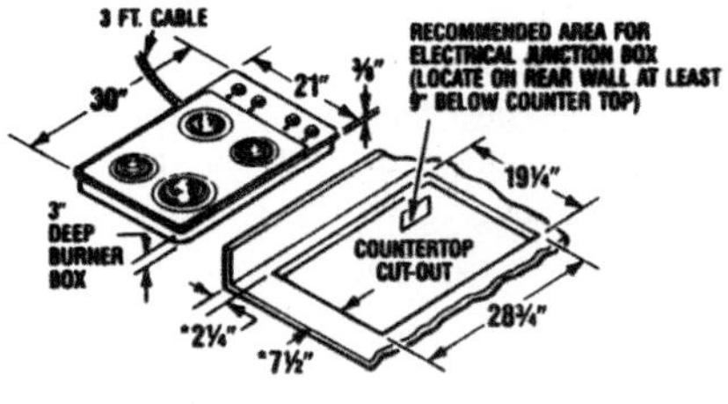

Conventional electric cooktop

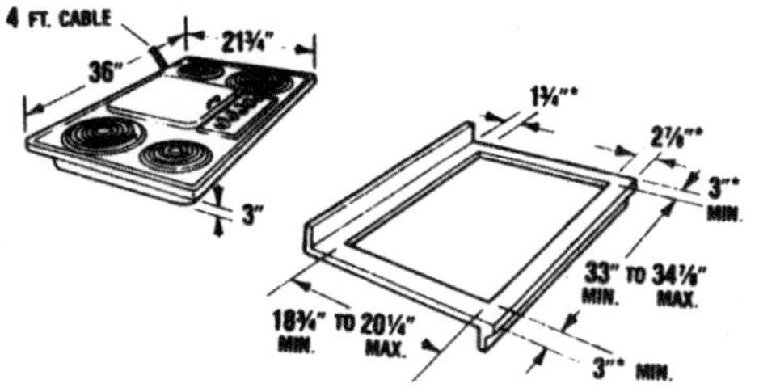

36″ electric cooktop

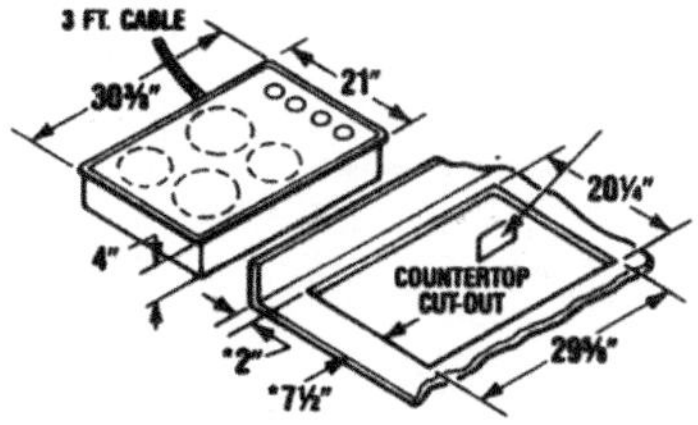

Glass cooktop

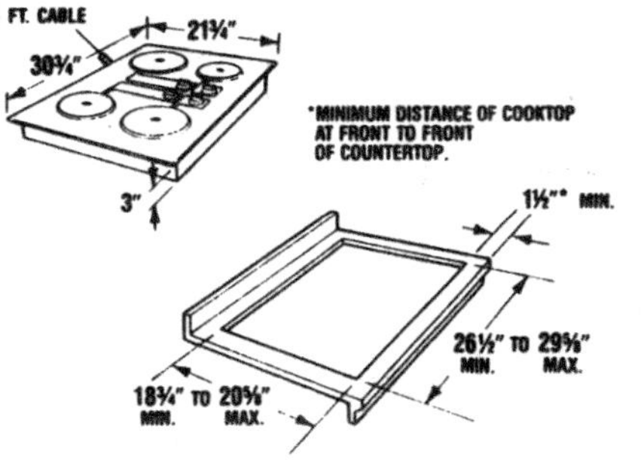

30″ solid elements/glass cooktop

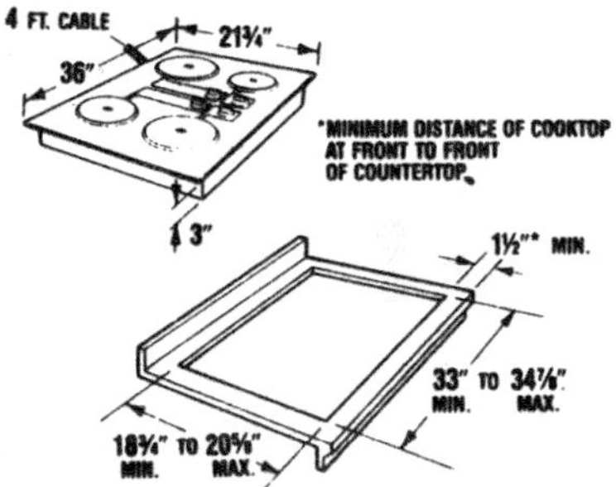

36″ solid element/glass cooktop

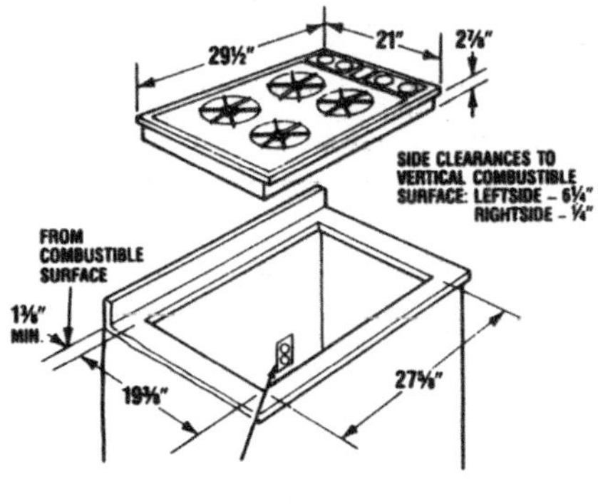

30″ gas cooktop

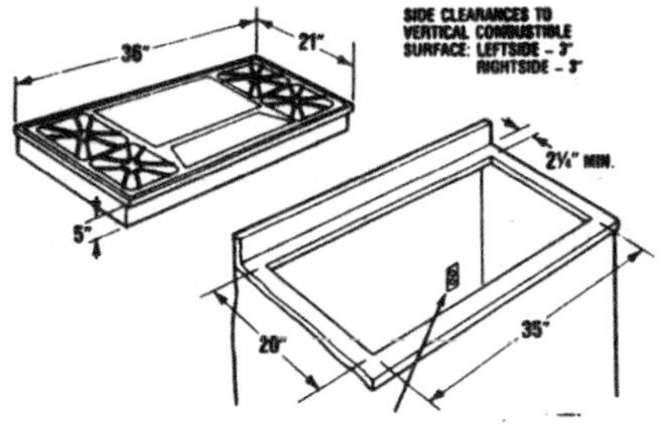

30″ gas cooktop

KITCHENS
Countertops

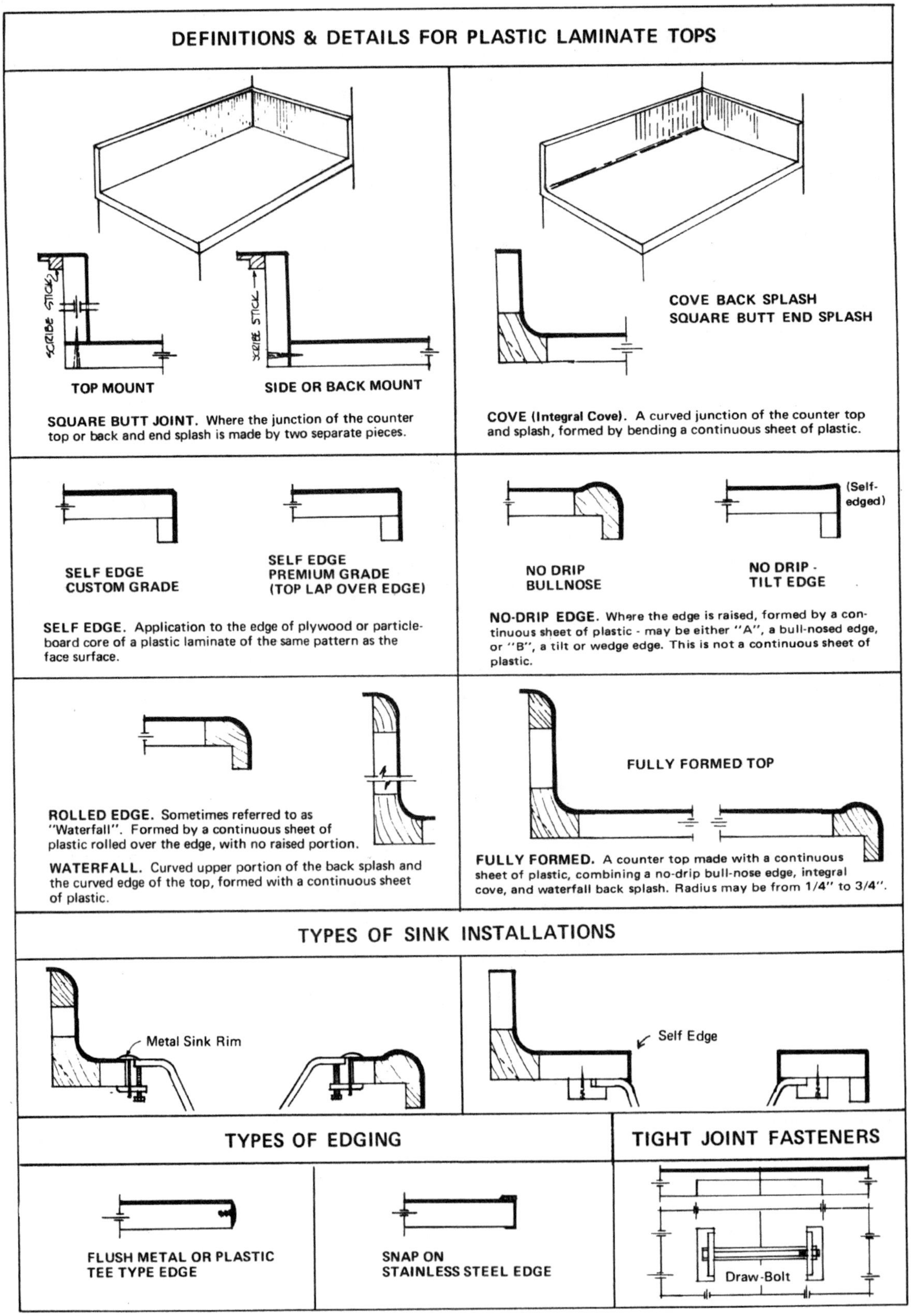
DEFINITIONS & DETAILS FOR PLASTIC LAMINATE TOPS
SCRIBE STICK
SCRIBE STICK
TOP MOUNT
SIDE OR BACK MOUNT
SQUARE BUTT JOINT. Where the junction of the counter top or back and end splash is made by two separate pieces.
COVE BACK SPLASH
SQUARE BUTT END SPLASH
COVE (Integral Cove). A curved junction of the counter top and splash, formed by bending a continuous sheet of plastic.
SELF EDGE
CUSTOM GRADE
SELF EDGE
PREMIUM GRADE
(TOP LAP OVER EDGE)
SELF EDGE. Application to the edge of plywood or particle-board core of a plastic laminate of the same pattern as the face surface.
NO DRIP
BULLNOSE
(Self-edged)
NO DRIP -
TILT EDGE
NO-DRIP EDGE. Where the edge is raised, formed by a continuous sheet of plastic - may be either "A", a bull-nosed edge, or "B", a tilt or wedge edge. This is not a continuous sheet of plastic.
ROLLED EDGE. Sometimes referred to as "Waterfall". Formed by a continuous sheet of plastic rolled over the edge, with no raised portion.
WATERFALL. Curved upper portion of the back splash and the curved edge of the top, formed with a continuous sheet of plastic.
FULLY FORMED TOP
FULLY FORMED. A counter top made with a continuous sheet of plastic, combining a no-drip bull-nose edge, integral cove, and waterfall back splash. Radius may be from 1/4" to 3/4".
TYPES OF SINK INSTALLATIONS
Metal Sink Rim
Self Edge
TYPES OF EDGING
FLUSH METAL OR PLASTIC
TEE TYPE EDGE
SNAP ON
STAINLESS STEEL EDGE
TIGHT JOINT FASTENERS
Draw-Bolt

Fig. 11 Definitions and details for plastic laminate tops

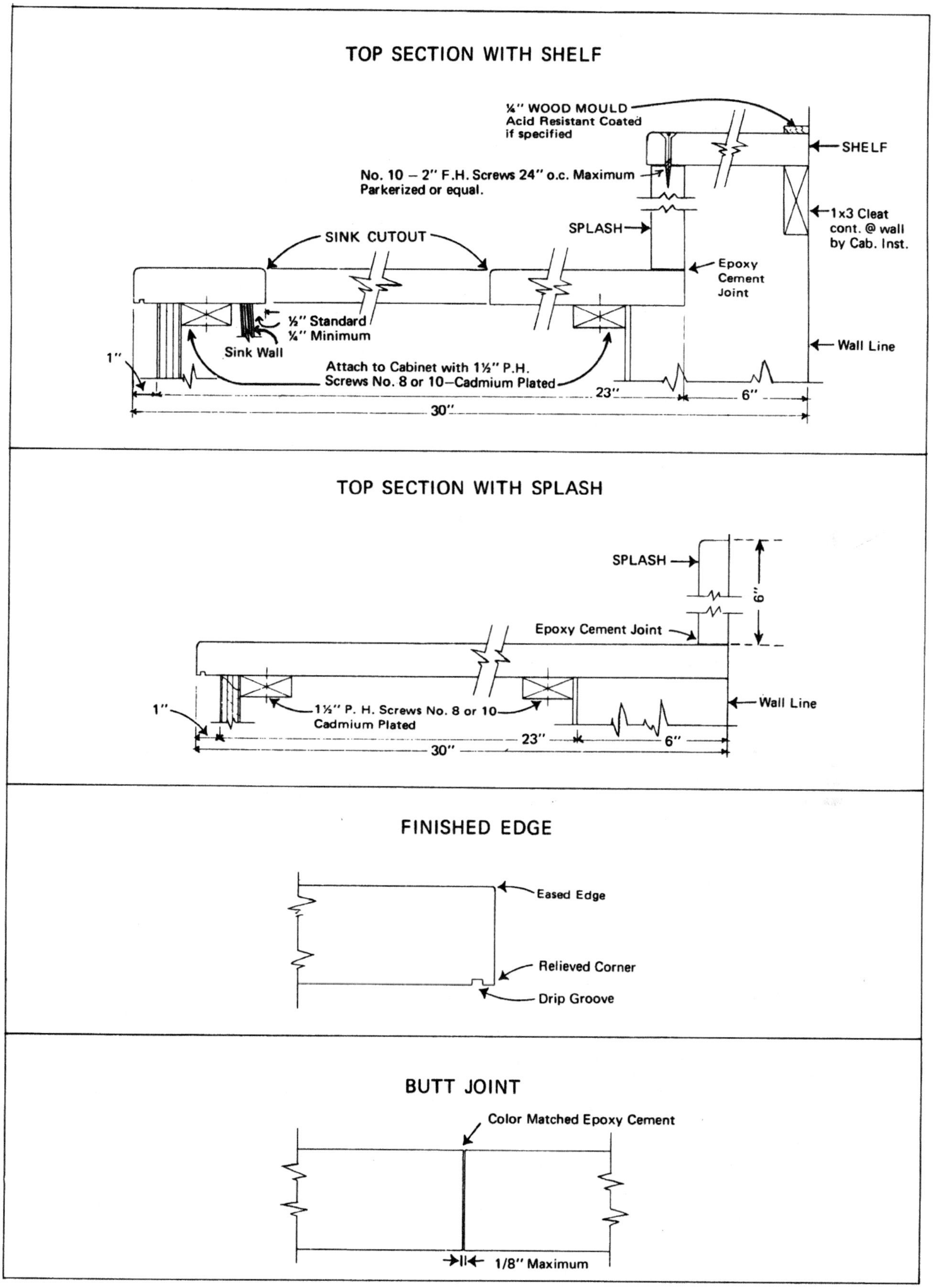

Fig. 12 Composition stone top and sink details

KITCHENS

Plans and Elevations

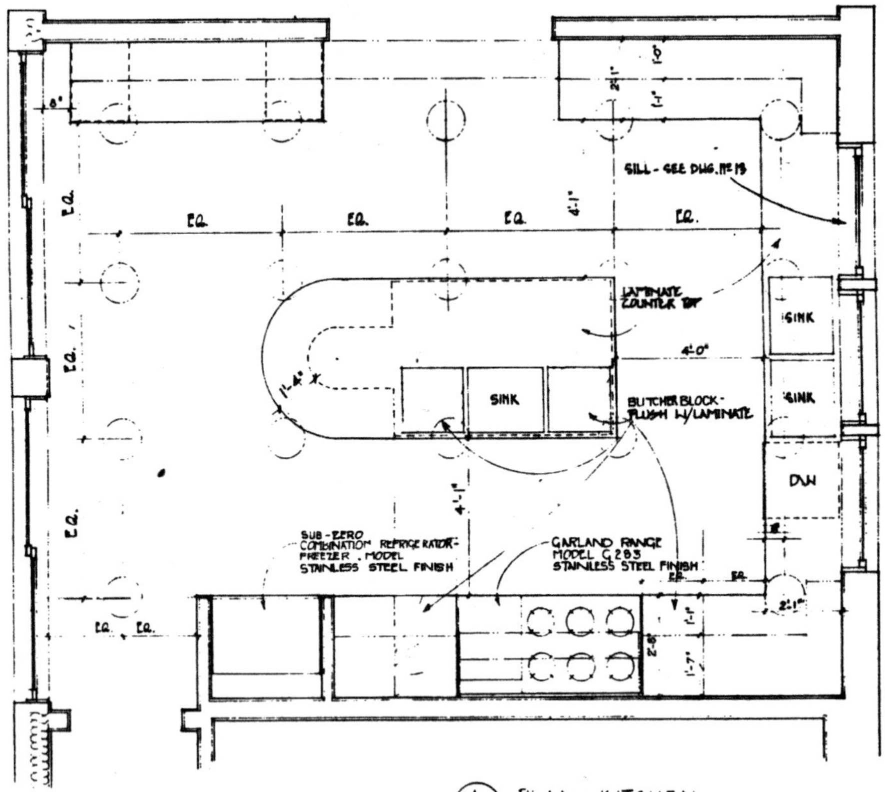

A/A20 PLAN - KITCHEN
SCALE: 1/2" = 1'-0"

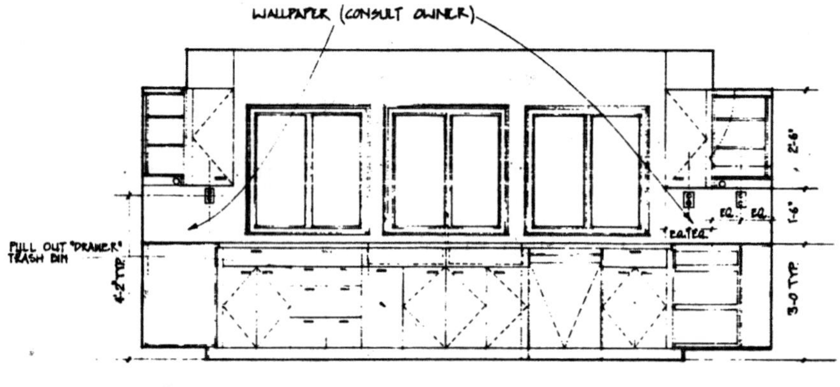

C/A20 WEST KITCHEN ELEVATION
SCALE: 1/2" = 1'-0"

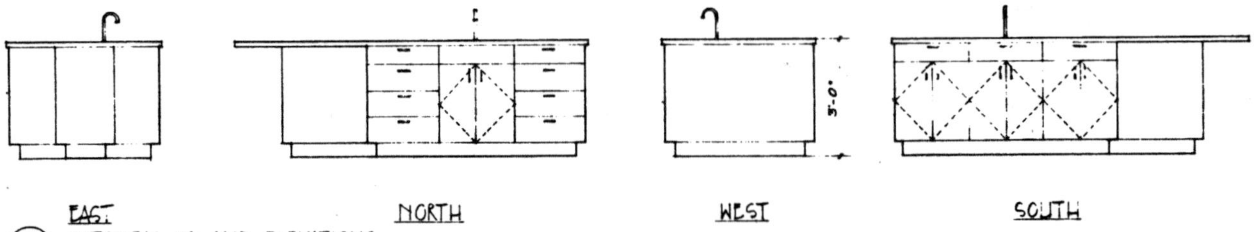

F/A-20 KITCHEN ISLAND ELEVATIONS
SCALE: 1/2" = 1'-0"

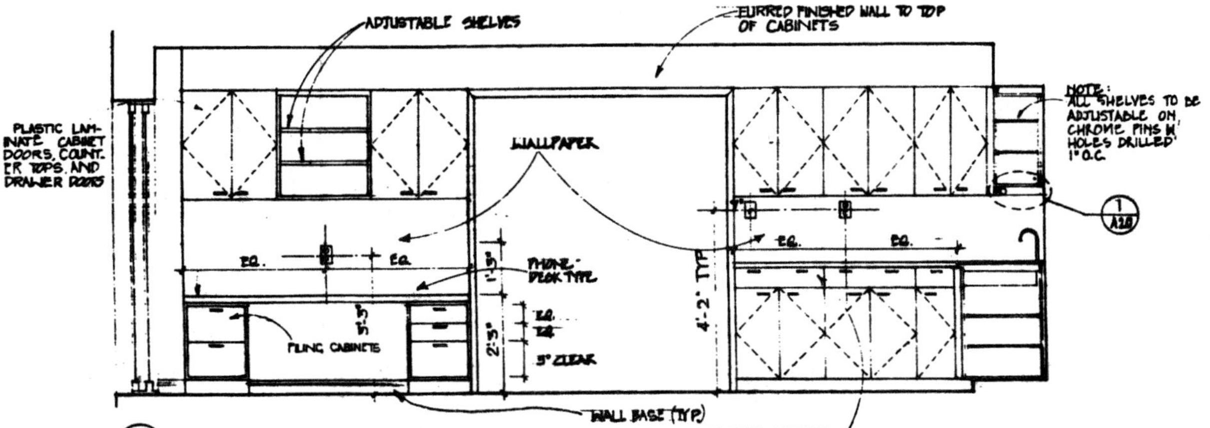

B / A20 SOUTH KITCHEN ELEVATION
SCALE: 1/2" = 1'-0"

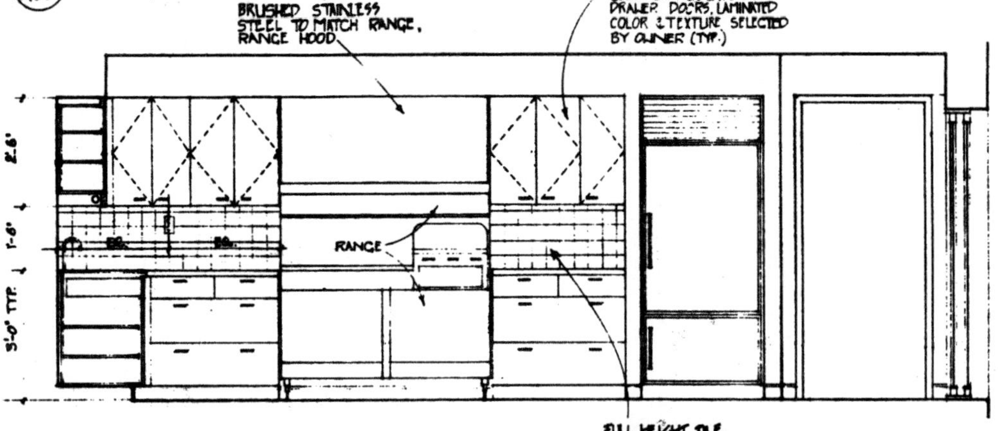

D / A20 NORTH KITCHEN ELEVATION
SCALE: 1/2" = 1'-0"

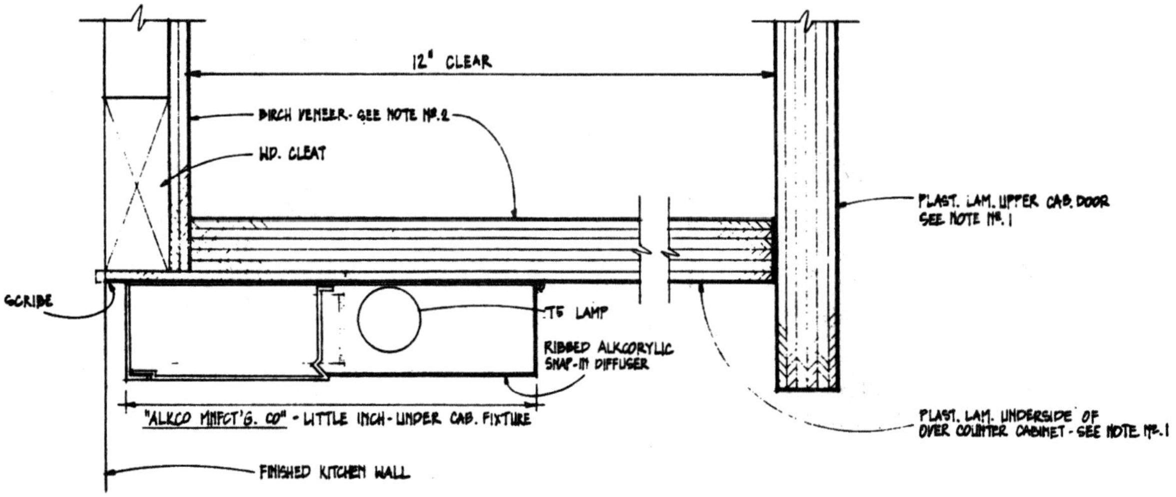

1 / A20 SECTION DETAIL @ UPPER CABINET
FULL SIZE

KITCHENS
Wheelchair-Accessible Design

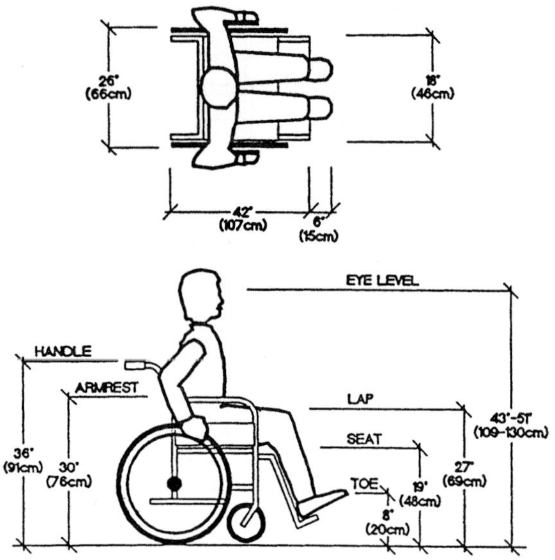

Dimensions of Adult- Sized Wheel-

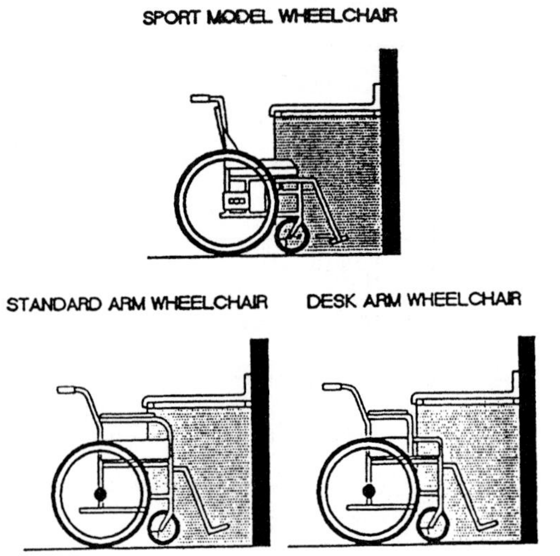

Common wheelchair styles.

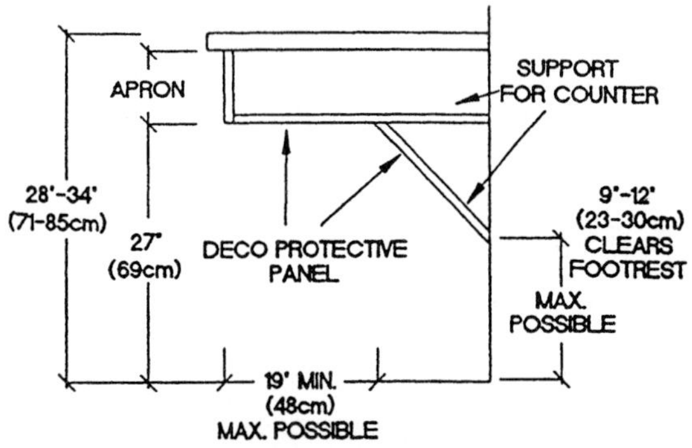

Figure 8 - Kneespace considerations.

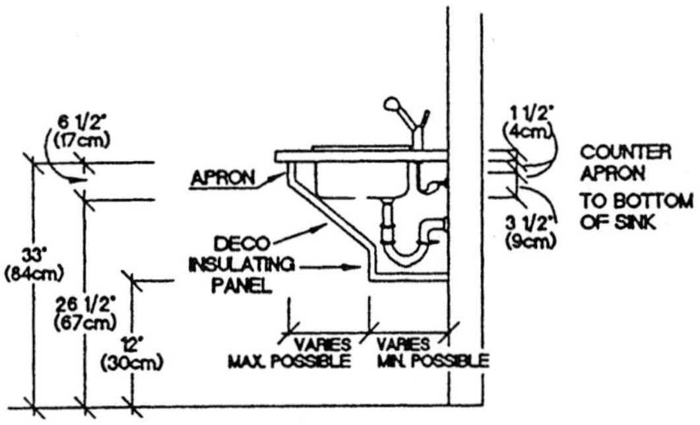

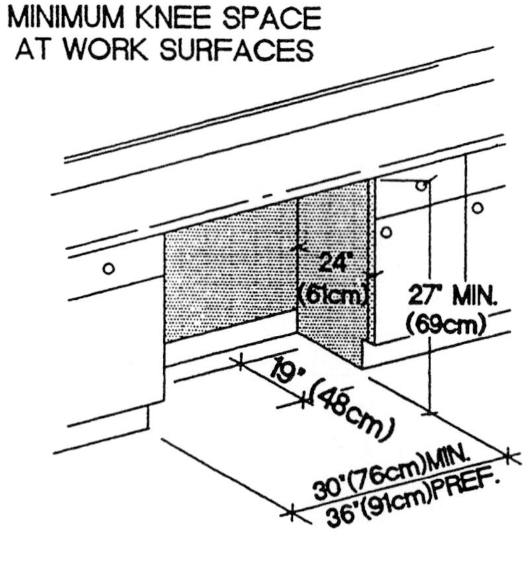

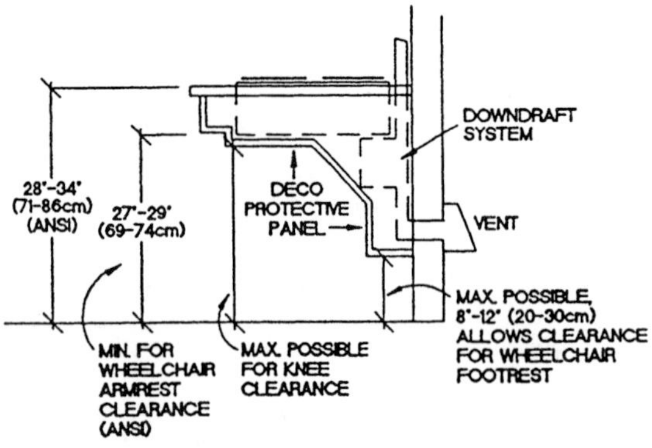

KITCHENS
Wheelchair-Accessible Design

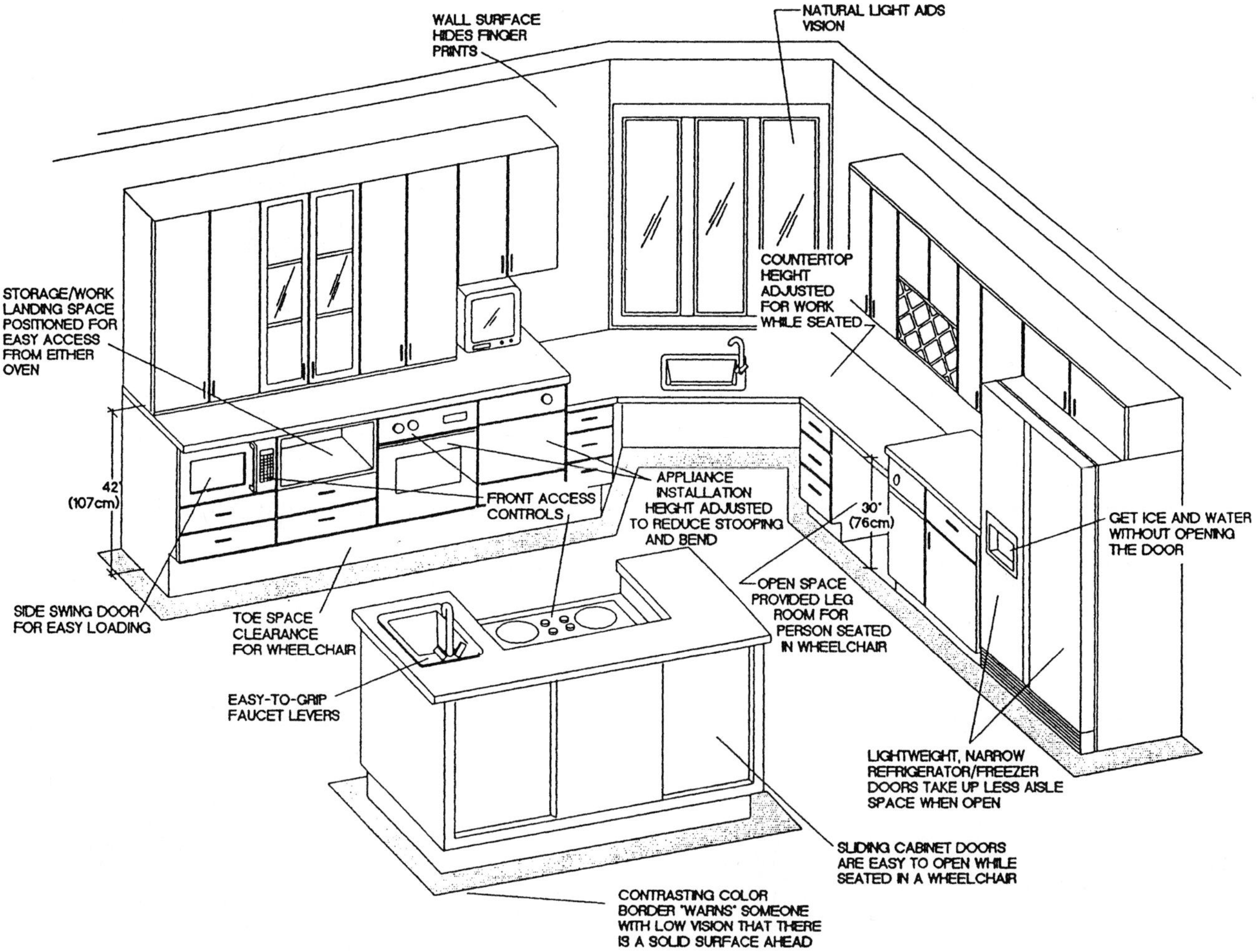
WALL SURFACE HIDES FINGER PRINTS
NATURAL LIGHT AIDS VISION
COUNTERTOP HEIGHT ADJUSTED FOR WORK WHILE SEATED
STORAGE/WORK LANDING SPACE POSITIONED FOR EASY ACCESS FROM EITHER OVEN
42" (107cm)
APPLIANCE INSTALLATION HEIGHT ADJUSTED TO REDUCE STOOPING AND BEND
FRONT ACCESS CONTROLS
30" (76cm)
GET ICE AND WATER WITHOUT OPENING THE DOOR
OPEN SPACE PROVIDED LEG ROOM FOR PERSON SEATED IN WHEELCHAIR
SIDE SWING DOOR FOR EASY LOADING
TOE SPACE CLEARANCE FOR WHEELCHAIR
EASY-TO-GRIP FAUCET LEVERS
LIGHTWEIGHT, NARROW REFRIGERATOR/FREEZER DOORS TAKE UP LESS AISLE SPACE WHEN OPEN
SLIDING CABINET DOORS ARE EASY TO OPEN WHILE SEATED IN A WHEELCHAIR
CONTRASTING COLOR BORDER "WARNS" SOMEONE WITH LOW VISION THAT THERE IS A SOLID SURFACE AHEAD

Whirlpool Corporation "The Less Challenging Home" - Modified to accommodate a person using a wheelchair, this design eliminates many of the common barriers in kitchens. Pointed out in the drawing are examples of concepts that create a more accessible space.

KITCHENS
Wheelchair-Accessible Design

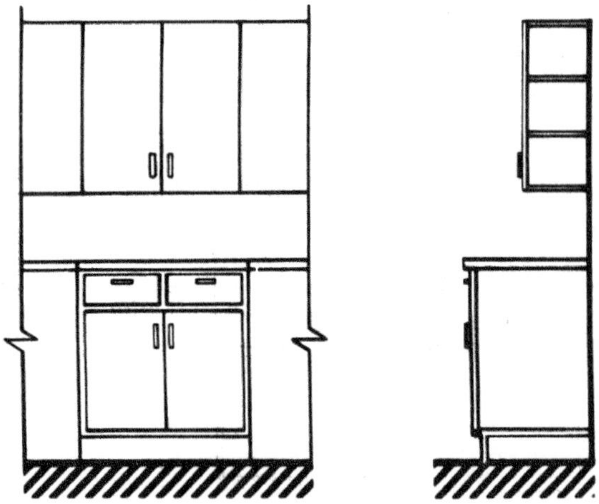

(a)
Before Removal of Cabinets and Base

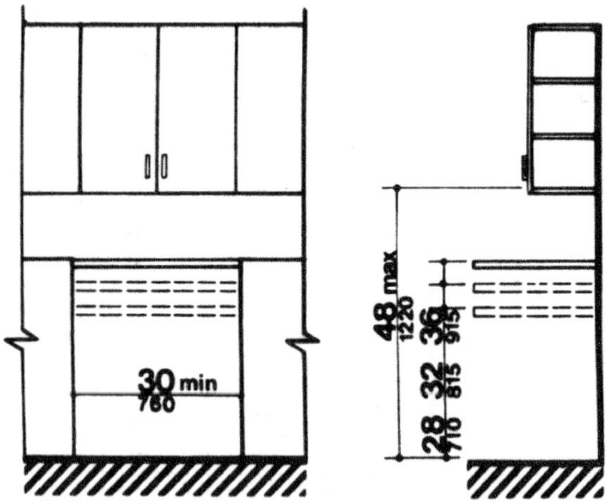

(b)
Cabinets and Base Removed and Height Alternatives

Counter Work Surface

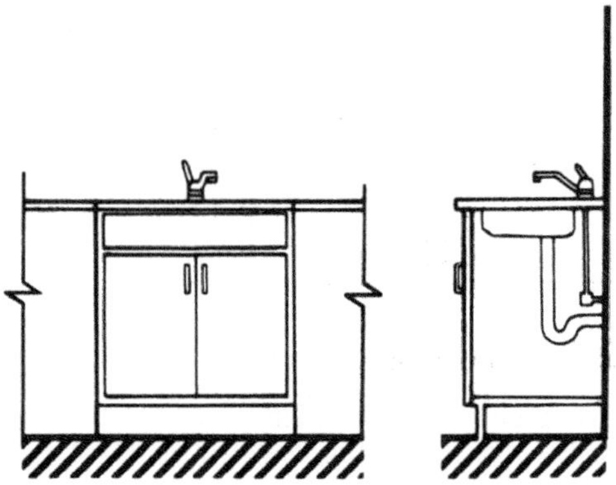

(a)
Before Removal of Cabinets and Base

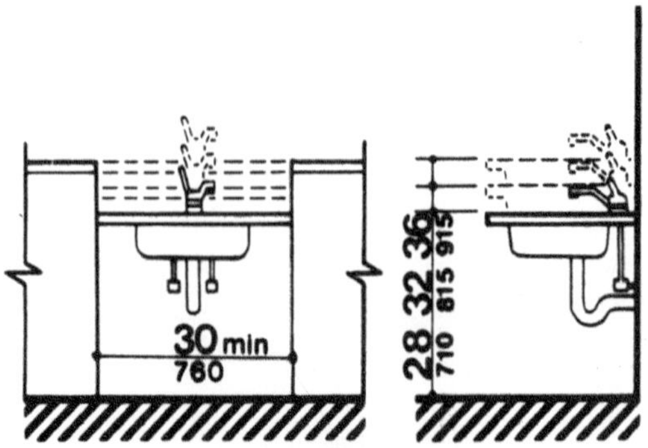

(b)
Cabinets and Base Removed and Height Alternatives

Kitchen Sink

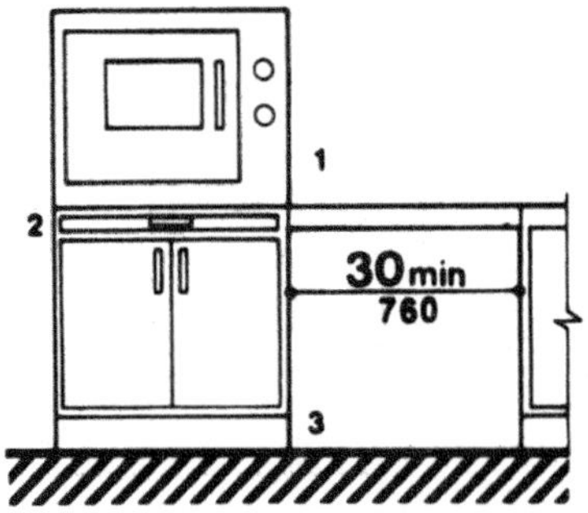

(a)
Side-Hinged Door

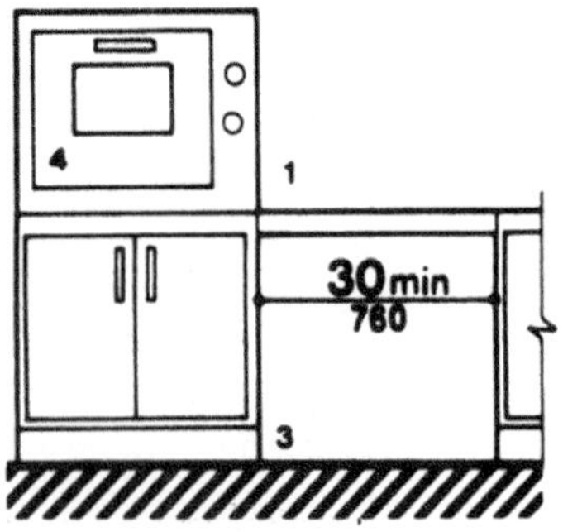

(b)
Bottom-Hinged Door

SYMBOL KEY:
1. Countertop or wall-mounted oven.
2. Pull-out board preferred with side-opening door.
3. Clear open space.
4. Bottom-hinged door.

Ovens without Self-Cleaning Feature

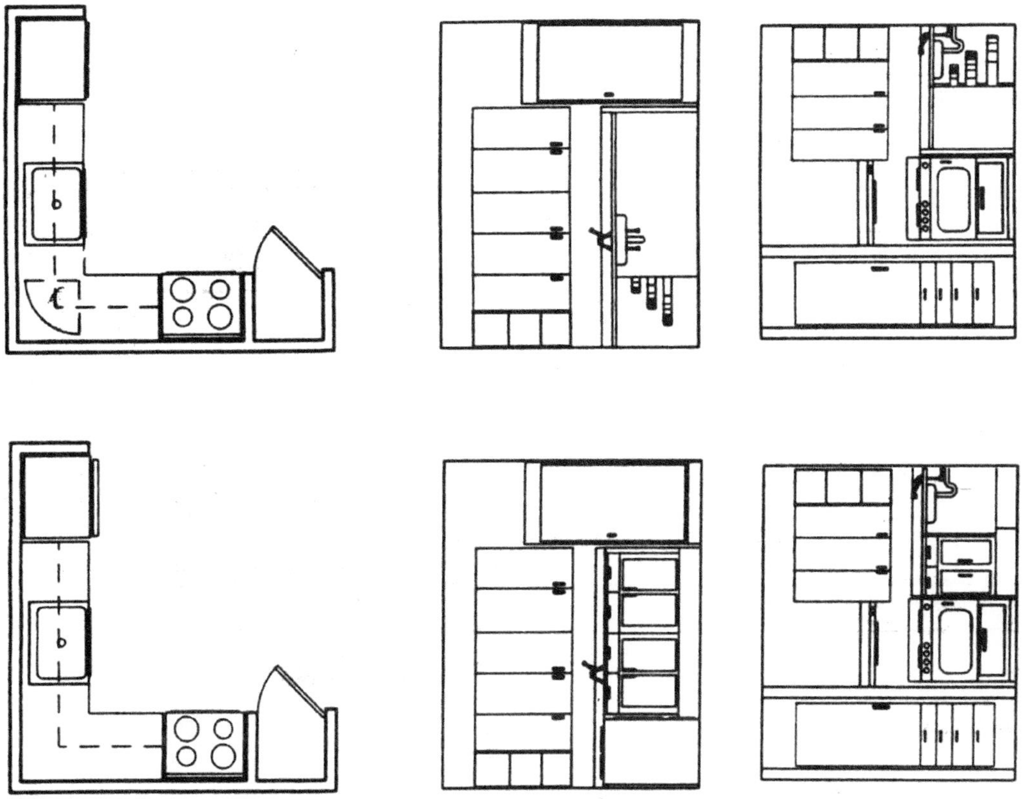

ACCESSIBLE; BEFORE REMOVAL OF CABINETS AND BASE.

CABINETS AND BASE REMOVED, COUNTER HEIGHT LOWERED.

EXAMPLE OF ADAPTABLE KITCHEN –L– SHAPED PLAN

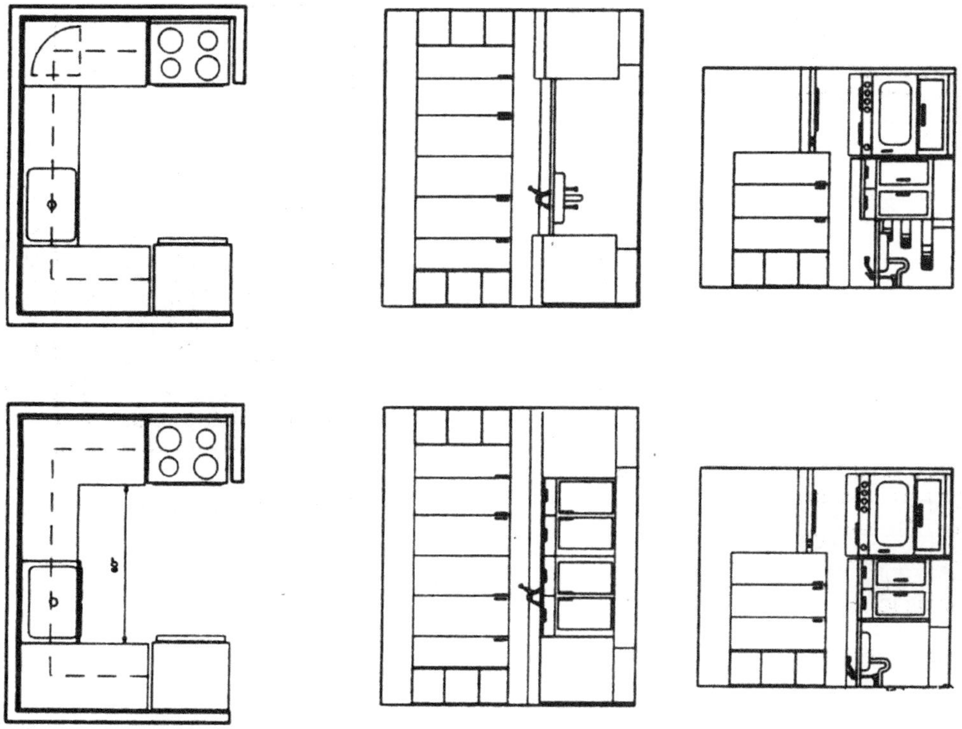

ACCESSIBLE ; BEFORE REMOVAL OF CABINETS AND BASE.

CABINETS AND BASE REMOVED, COUNTER HEIGHT LOWERED.

EXAMPLE OF ADAPTABLE KITCHEN –U– SHAPED PLAN

KITCHENS
Wheelchair-Accessible Design

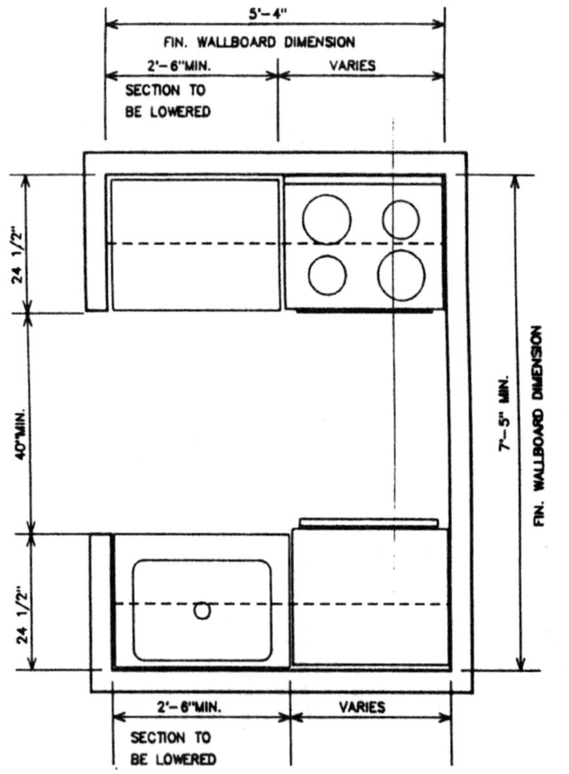

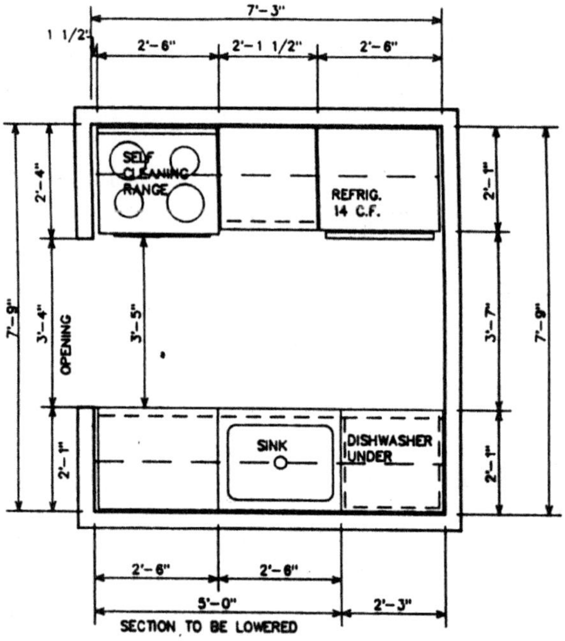

Minimum-sized adaptable kitchen or kitchenette

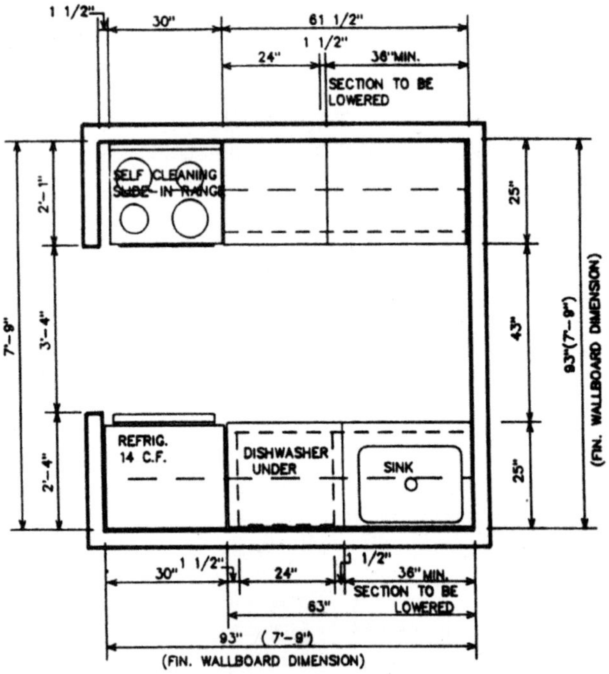

Minimum-sized adaptable kitchen (galley type)

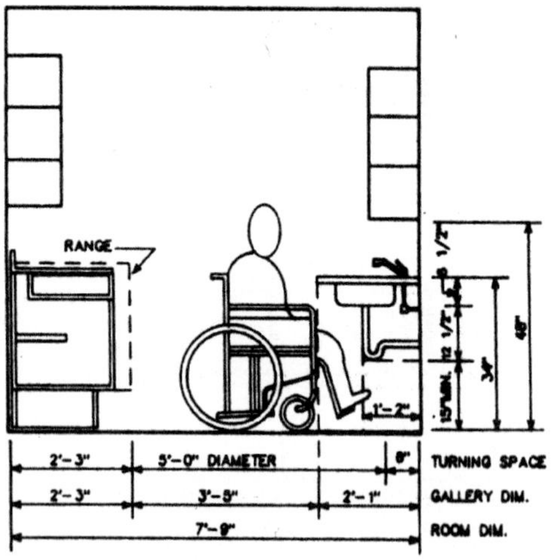

Kitchen clearance dimensions (not to scale)

Requirements

The ANSI and UFAS standards require accessible and adaptable features which make the kitchen usable by most people. The fixed accessible features specified in ANSI 4.32.5 and UFAS 4.34.6 include requirements for doors, clearances, clear floor space, appliances, storage, controls, and knee space. The adaptable features are removable base cabinets at knee spaces and counters that can be adjusted in height or fixed at a lower-than-standard height.

The adaptable features for kitchens specified in the standards are shown in Figs. 13 and 14. In Fig. 13, the kitchen is shown in a standard configuration with the counter height at 36 in and the knee spaces covered with base cabinets.

In Fig. 14, the kitchen has been adapted by exposing the knee spaces and lowering the work surface and sink counter segments. No other changes have been made to the kitchen.

Since removable base cabinets and adjustable height counters are not now products that are readily available for purchase, they are usually custom-made items.

The kitchen shown in Figs. 17 and 18 is an example of a more elaborate kitchen having ANSI/UFAS-accessible/adaptable features. This kitchen exceeds the ANSI/UFAS minimum requirements.

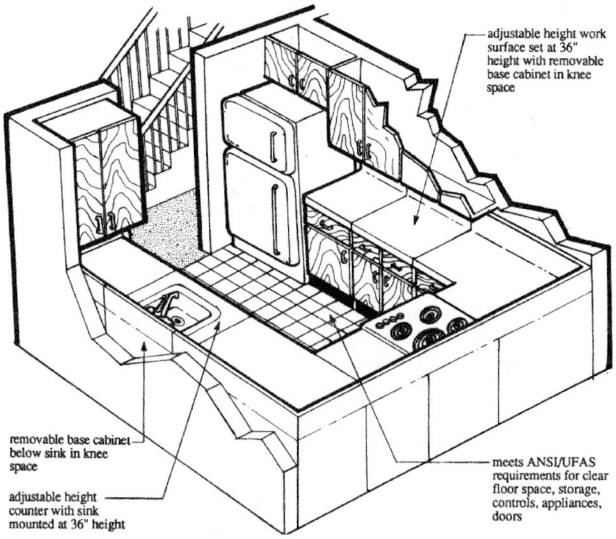

Fig. 13 An adaptable kitchen in conventional configuration

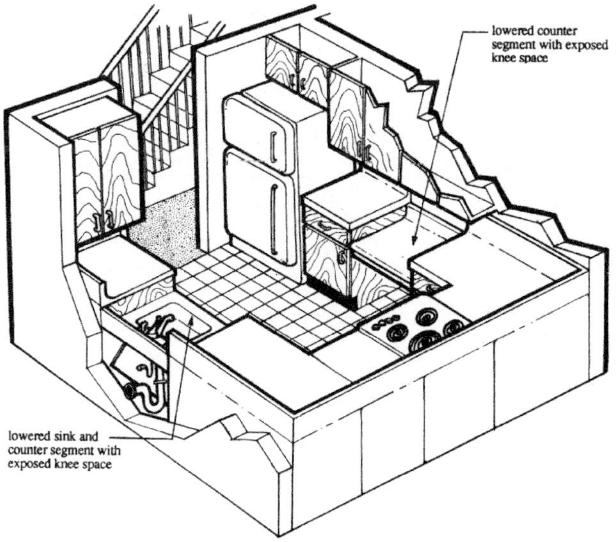

Fig. 14 An adaptable kitchen in the adjusted configuration

Work Surfaces

People who use wheelchairs and other people who must or wish to sit down while preparing food need at least one work surface lower than the usual 36-in-high counter (Fig. 19).

The standards (ANSI 4.32.5.4 and UFAS 4.34.6.4) require that at least one 30-in-wide, adjustable-height work surface be provided in an adaptable kitchen, although a wider size is preferred. The wider work surface provides space for pots, dishes, and other utensils as well as small appliances, and makes it easier to work on several things at once or to cook using many ingredients.

Work surfaces at ovens

If a wall oven is installed, a lowered work surface with knee space should be installed next to the wall oven. The standards specify that when the wall oven is not self-cleaning, a knee space must be located next to the oven to permit a disabled person in a wheelchair to pull up close enough to clean the oven.

Even if a self-cleaning oven is installed, locating the knee space next to the oven makes it easier and safer for a disabled person to remove hot items from the oven.

When an oven with a side-opening door is used, a pull-out shelf located beneath the oven must be installed. The shelf is used as a transfer surface for dishes as they are placed into or taken out of the oven. When not needed, the shelf is pushed back into the oven cabinet (Fig. 23). When an oven with a drop-front door is used (Fig. 21), the pull-out shelf is not needed because the door serves as a transfer shelf.

See ANSI 4.32.5.7 and UFAS 4.34.6.7 for dimensions and details of oven.

Cooktops in Adjustable-Height Counter Segments

ANSI 4.32.5.6 and UFAS 4.34.6.6 permit use of a standard range if the controls comply with ANSI 4.25 or UFAS 4.27. The controls must be placed along the front or the side of the range so that a seated person need not reach across a hot burner to adjust the controls (Fig. 24).

Some wheelchair users cannot use conventional ranges because the surface is too high and there is no knee space for maneuvering.

KITCHENS
Wheelchair-Accessible Design

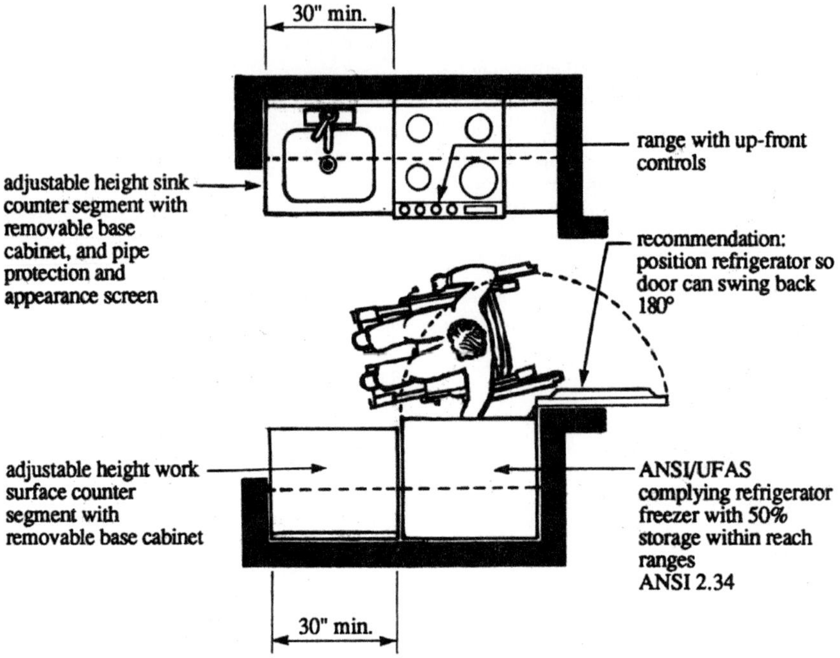

Fig. 15 A small kitchen with adaptable features: plan

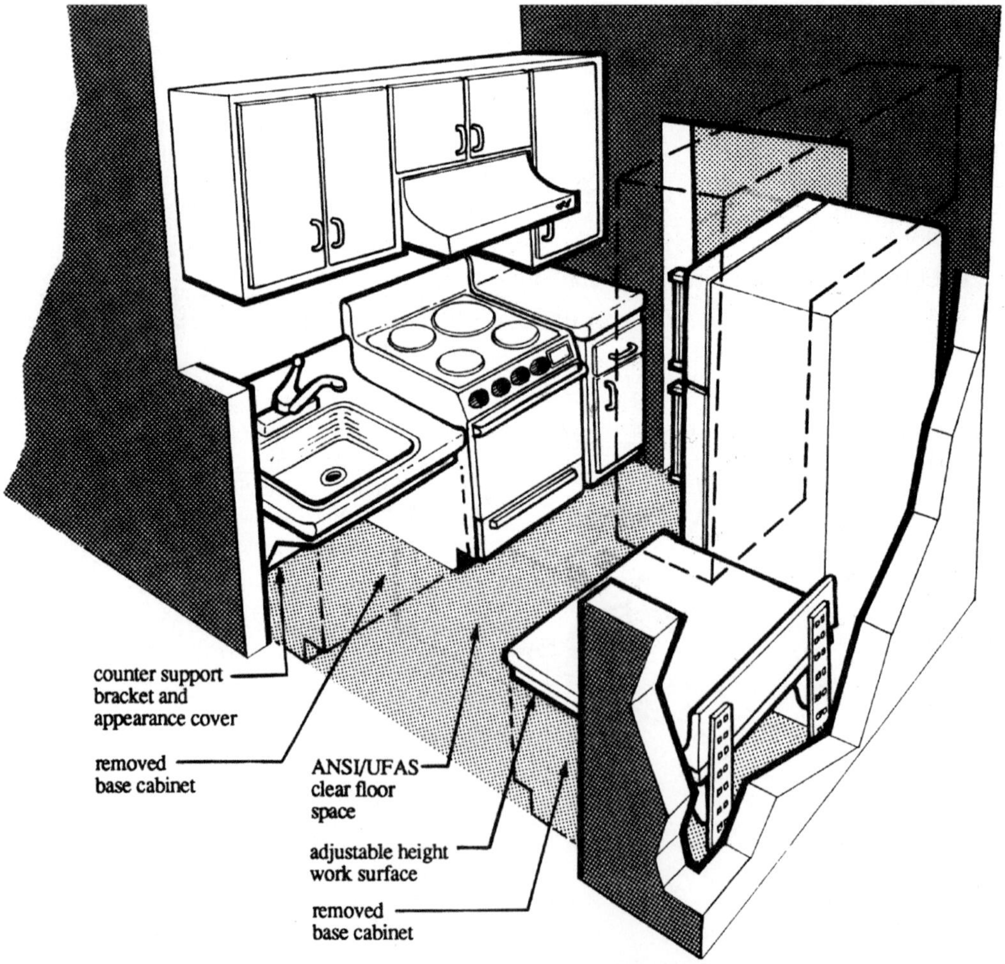

Fig. 16 A small kitchen with adaptable features: perspective

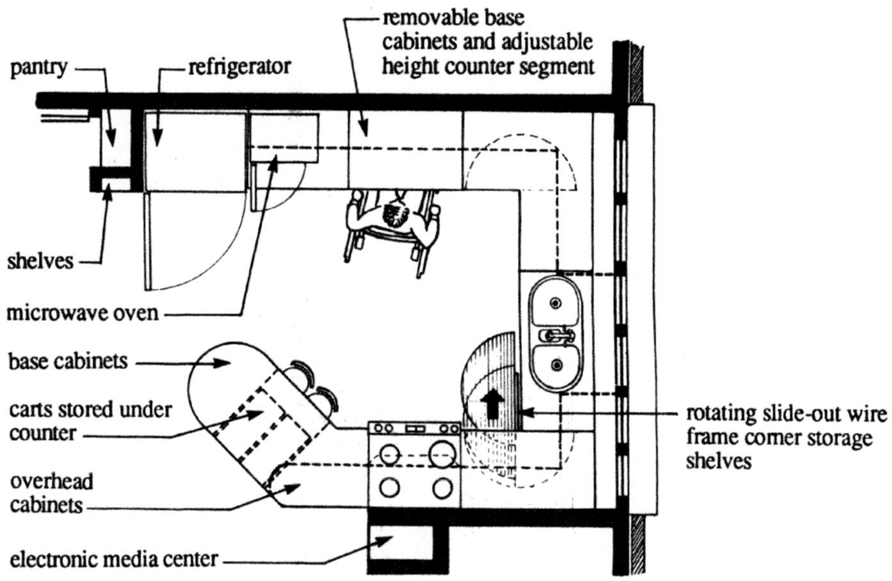

Fig. 17 An elaborate kitchen with adaptable features: plan

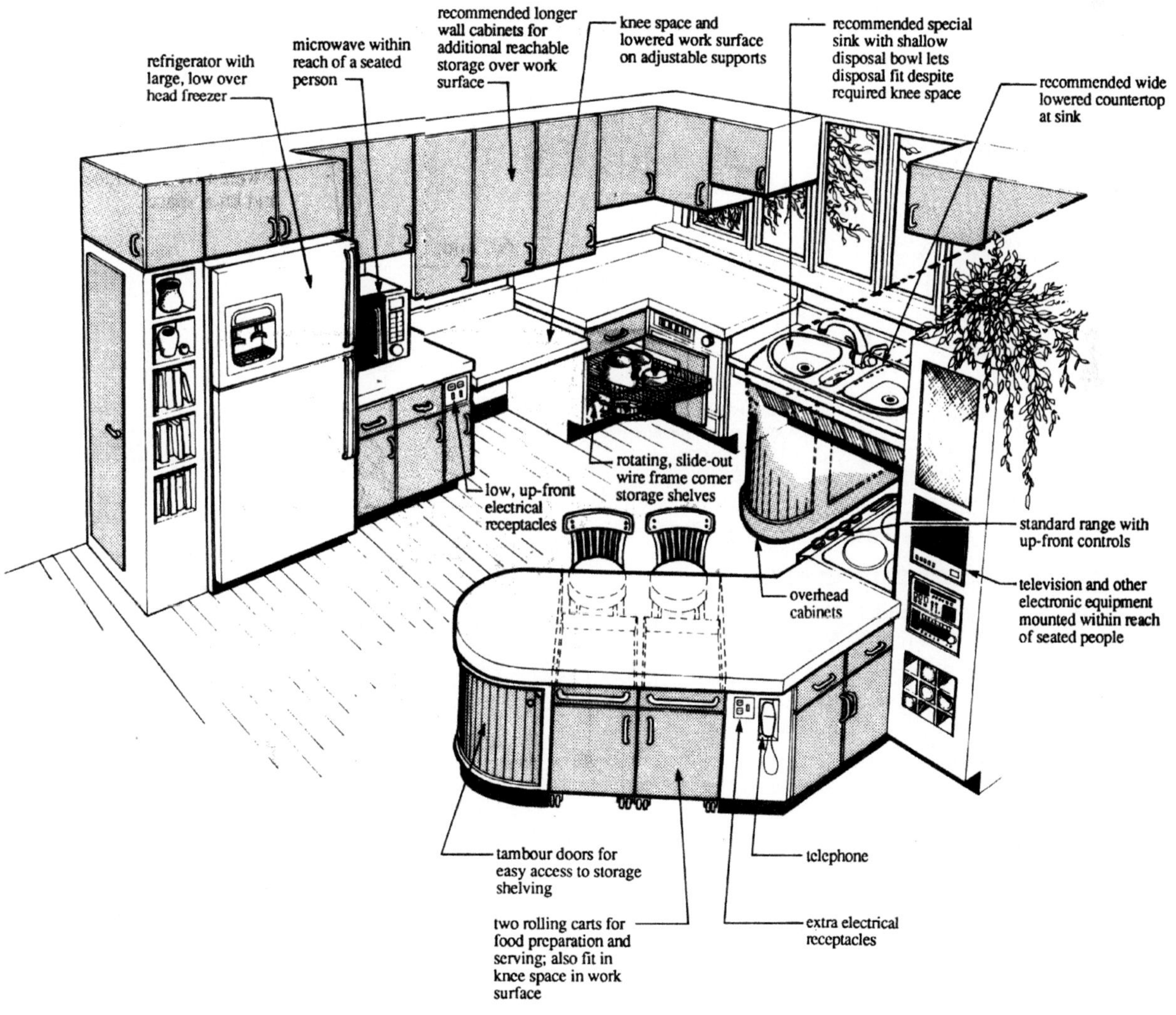

Fig. 18 An elaborate kitchen with adaptable features: perspective

KITCHENS
Wheelchair-Accessible Design

Fig. 19 Seated person at lowered work surface

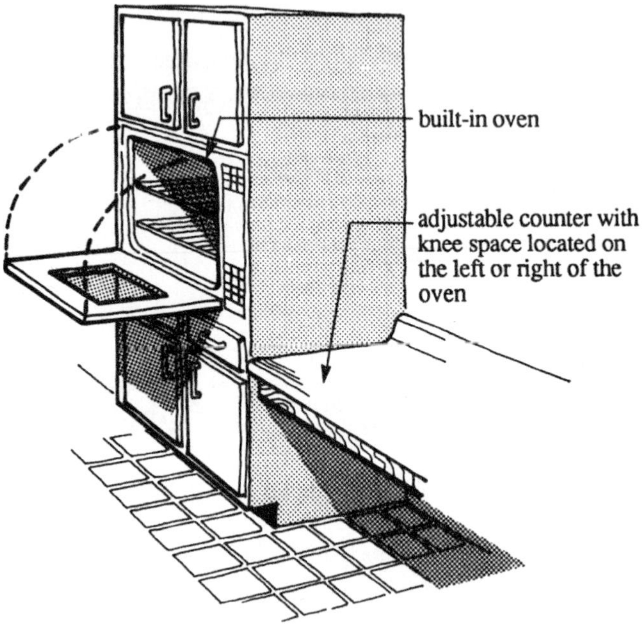

Fig. 21 Work surface at non-self-cleaning oven with drop-front door

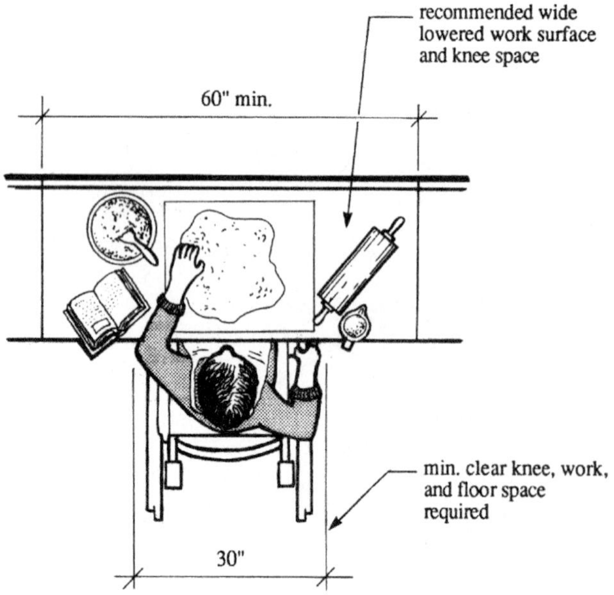

Fig. 20 Use of a wider, lowered work surface

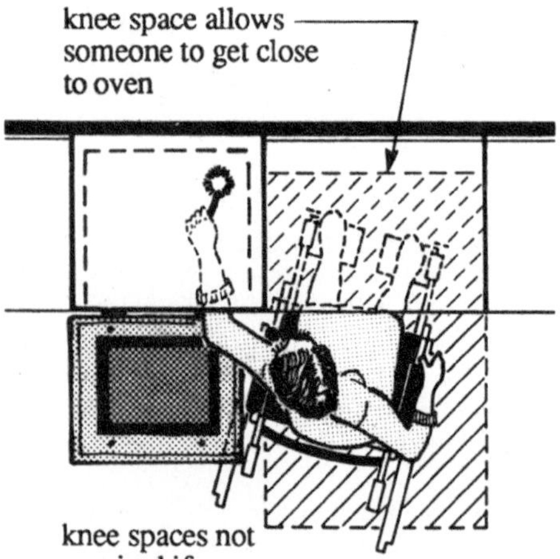

Fig. 22 Use of knee space next to oven

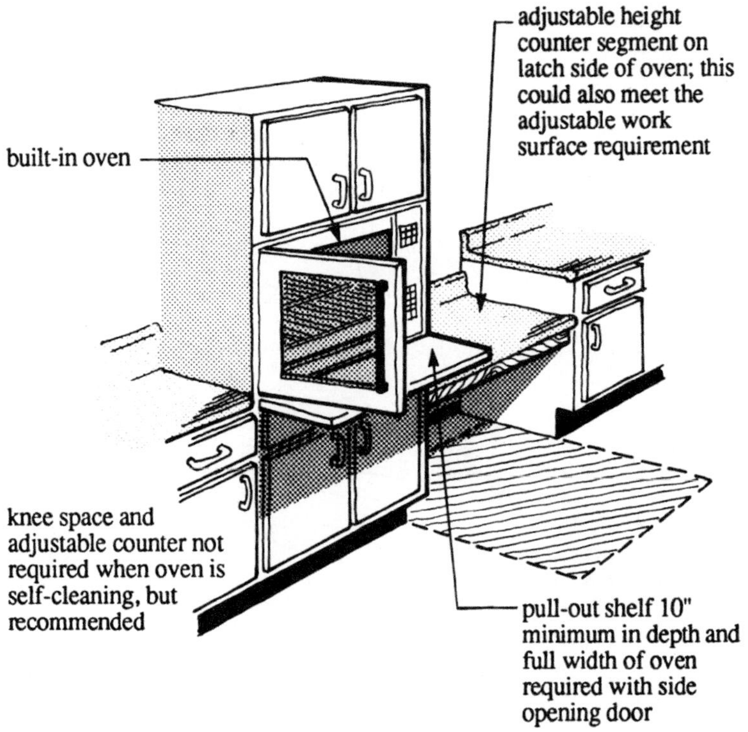

Fig. 23 Pull-out shelf at non-self-cleaning oven with side-opening door

Cooktops in lowered counter segments with knee space below allow some wheelchair users to get close enough to operate the controls and move heavy pots and pans (Fig. 25).

Cooktops with smooth surfaces are preferred by people with limited hand and arm strength because they can slide pots of hot food on and off the cooktop rather than lifting them over raised burners and knobs.

When a cooktop is installed in a lowered counter, the width of the counter segment and knee space should be at least 30 in and should provide space to the side of the cooktop for utensils and maneuvering. An additional 30 in to the side is recommended (Fig. 26).

When the knee space is under a cooktop, the standards require that the bottom of the cooktop be insulated to protect against accidental burns.

While this type of installation may be the only way that some people can cook, it does expose a person in a wheelchair to the hazard of spilling hot food in his/her lap. People who pull up beneath the cooktop must exercise extreme care and cool hot foods before moving them.

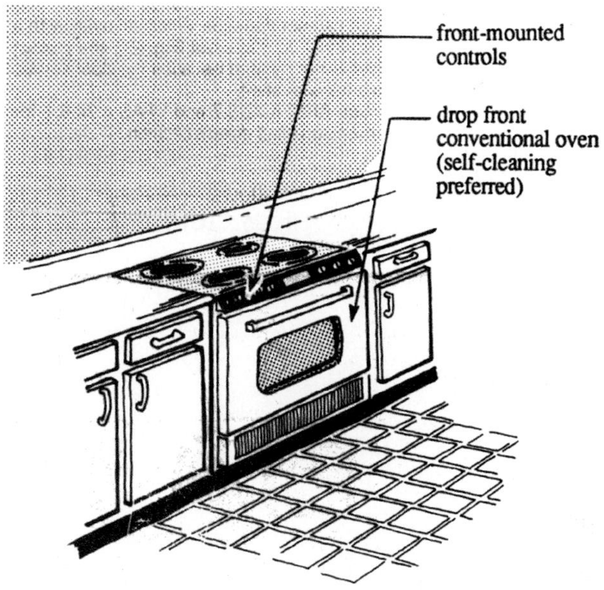

Fig. 24 Standard range

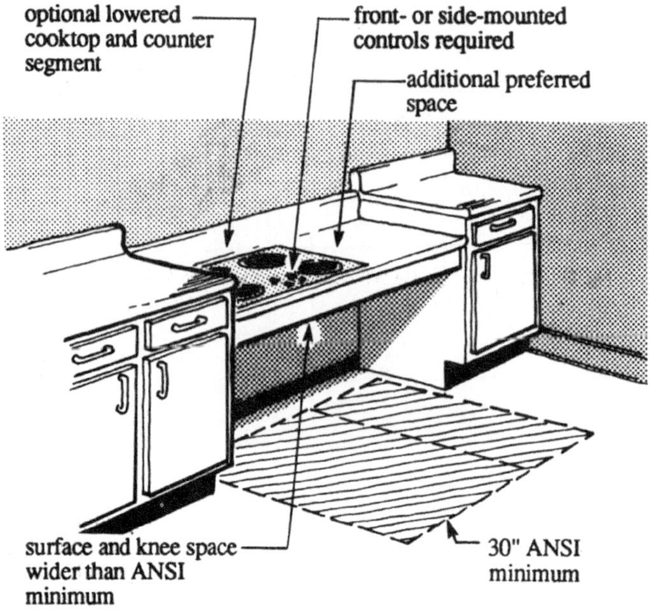
optional lowered cooktop and counter segment
front- or side-mounted controls required
additional preferred space
surface and knee space wider than ANSI minimum
30" ANSI minimum

Fig. 25 Use of cooktop with knee space

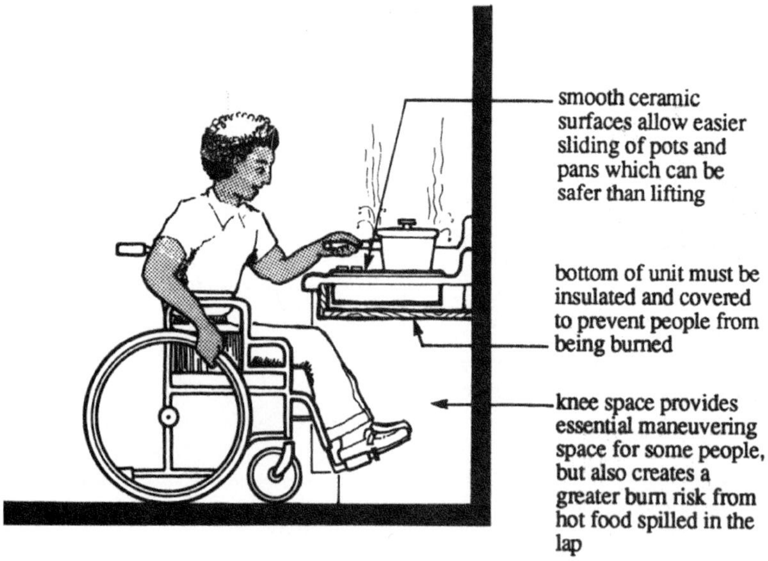
smooth ceramic surfaces allow easier sliding of pots and pans which can be safer than lifting
bottom of unit must be insulated and covered to prevent people from being burned
knee space provides essential maneuvering space for some people, but also creates a greater burn risk from hot food spilled in the lap

Fig. 26 Lowered cooktop with knee space and wide counter

KITCHENS
Wheelchair-Accessible Design

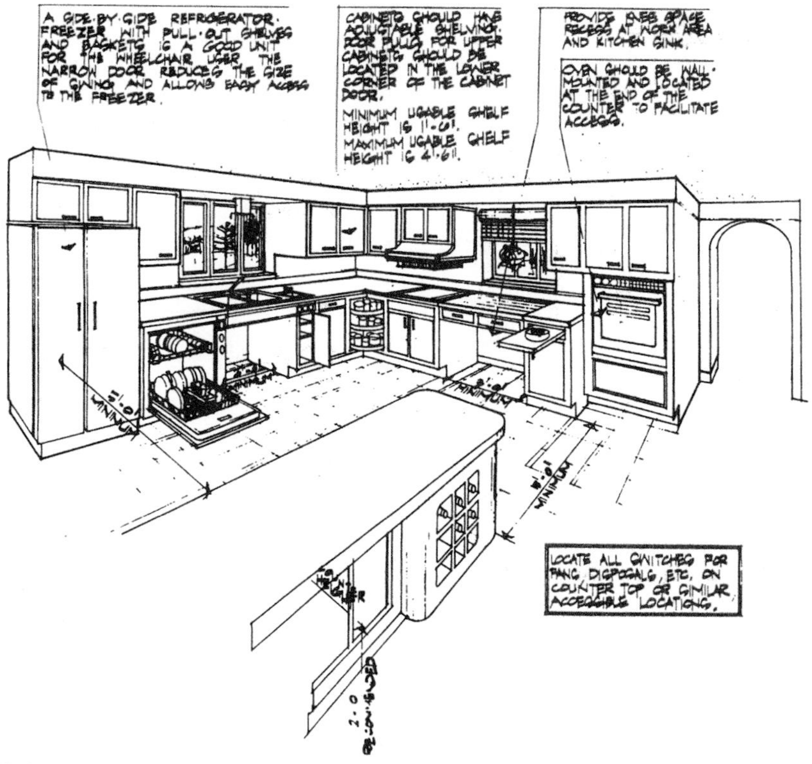
A SIDE-BY-SIDE REFRIGERATOR-FREEZER WITH PULL-OUT SHELVES AND BASKETS IS A GOOD UNIT FOR THE WHEELCHAIR USER. THE NARROW DOOR REDUCES THE SIZE OF SWING AND ALLOWS EASY ACCESS TO THE FREEZER.
CABINETS SHOULD HAVE ADJUSTABLE SHELVING. DOOR PULLS FOR UPPER CABINETS SHOULD BE LOCATED IN THE LOWER CORNER OF THE CABINET DOOR.
MINIMUM USABLE SHELF HEIGHT IS 1'-0".
MAXIMUM USABLE SHELF HEIGHT IS 4'-6".
PROVIDE KNEE SPACE RECESS AT WORK AREA AND KITCHEN SINK.
OVEN SHOULD BE WALL-MOUNTED AND LOCATED AT THE END OF THE COUNTER TO FACILITATE ACCESS.
5'-0" MINIMUM
5'-0" MINIMUM
LOCATE ALL SWITCHES FOR FANS, DISPOSALS, ETC. ON COUNTER TOP OR SIMILAR ACCESSIBLE LOCATIONS.

Kitchen arrangements

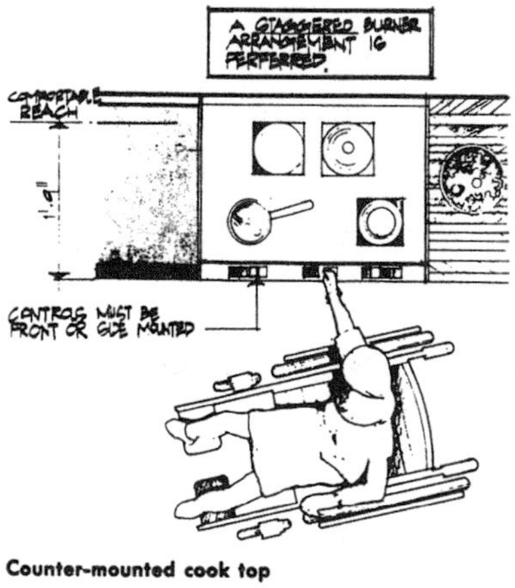
A STAGGERED BURNER ARRANGEMENT IS PREFERRED.
COMFORTABLE REACH
CONTROLS MUST BE FRONT OR SIDE MOUNTED

Counter-mounted cook top

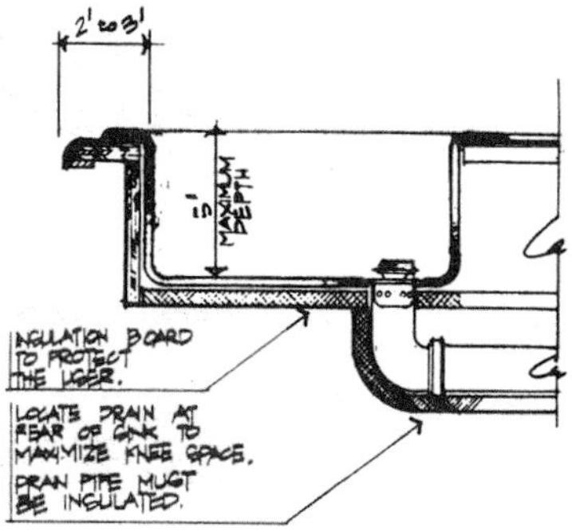
2' to 3'
MAXIMUM DEPTH
INSULATION BOARD TO PROTECT THE USER.
LOCATE DRAIN AT REAR OF SINK TO MAXIMIZE KNEE SPACE.
DRAIN PIPE MUST BE INSULATED.

Sink

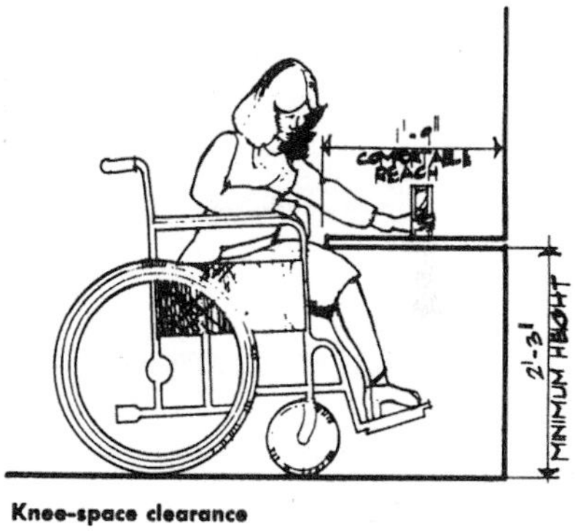
COMFORTABLE REACH
2'-3" MINIMUM HEIGHT

Knee-space clearance

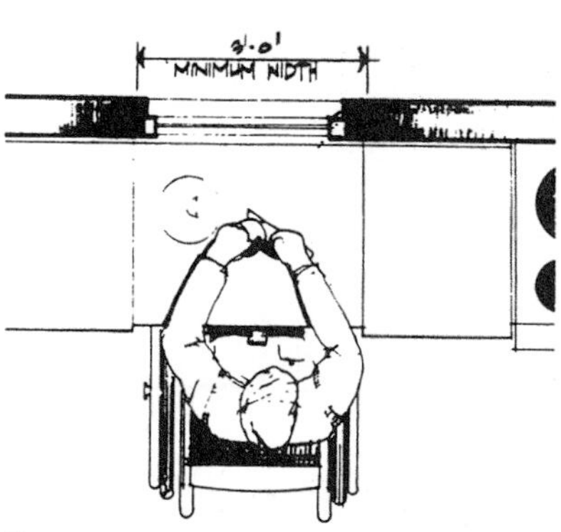
3'-0" MINIMUM WIDTH

Knee-recess work area

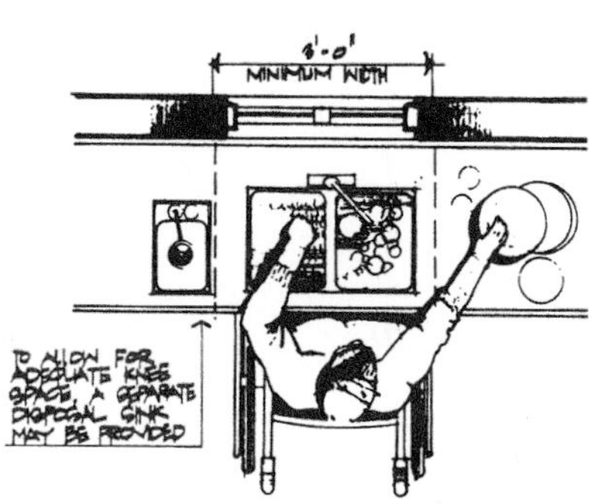
3'-0" MINIMUM WIDTH
TO ALLOW FOR ADEQUATE KNEE SPACE, A SEPARATE DISPOSAL SINK MAY BE PROVIDED

Disposal sink

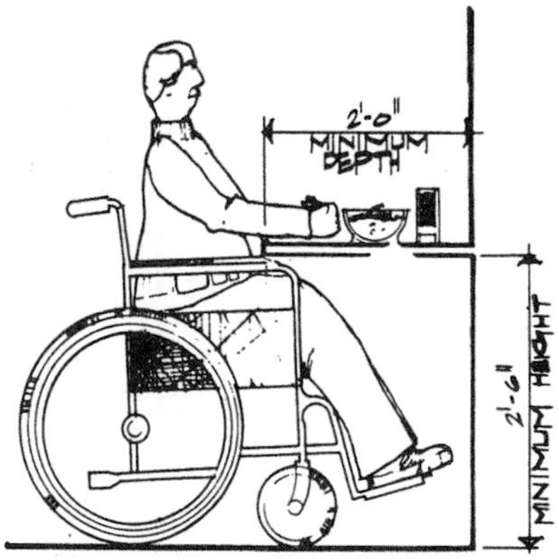
2'-0" MINIMUM DEPTH
2'-6" MINIMUM HEIGHT

Armrest clearance

KITCHENS
Wheelchair-Accessible Design

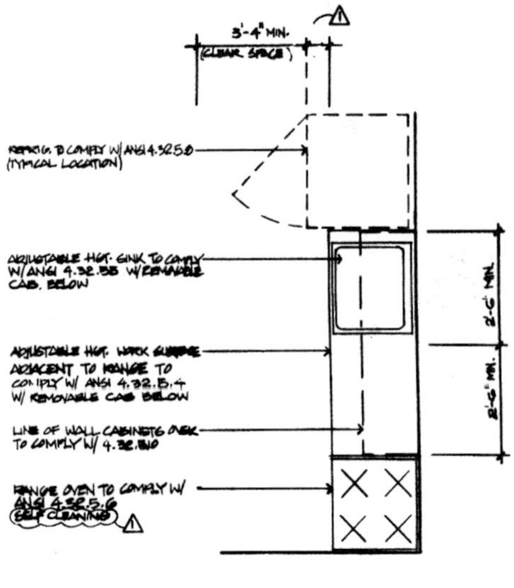

1/A4 PLAN: TYPICAL ADAPTABLE KITCHEN: LINEAR
1" = 1'-0"

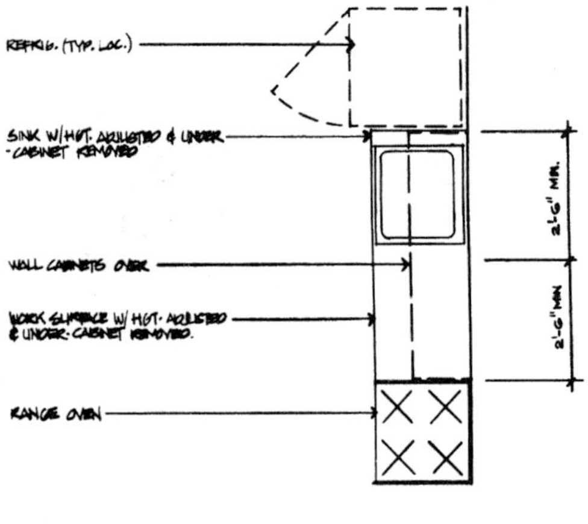

1A/A4 PLAN: TYPICAL ADAPTED KITCHEN: LINEAR
½" = 1'-0"

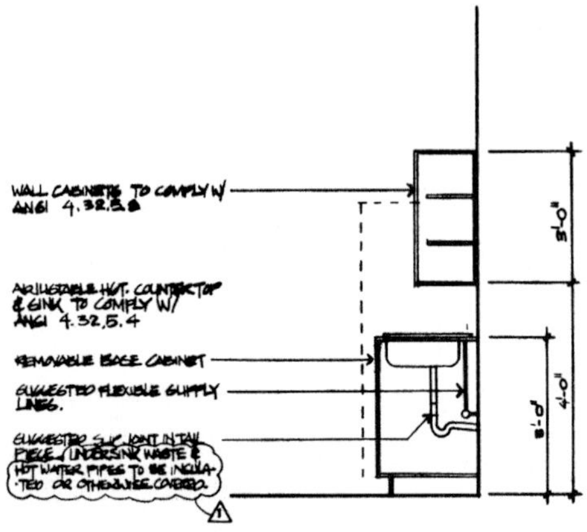

2/A4 SECTION: TYPICAL ADAPTABLE KITCHEN: LINEAR
1" = 1'-0"

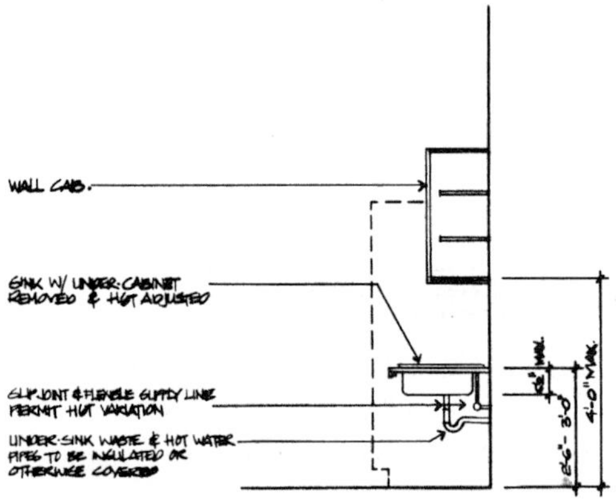

2A/A4 SECTION: TYPICAL ADAPTED KITCHEN: LINEAR
½" = 1'-0"

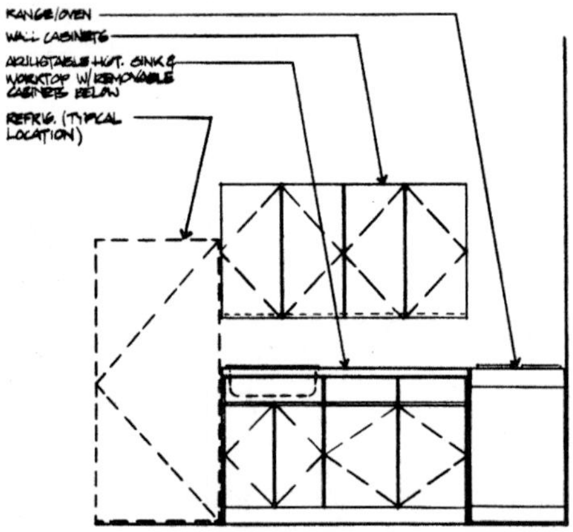

3/A4 ELEVATION: TYPICAL ADAPTABLE KITCHEN: LINEAR
1" = 1'-0"

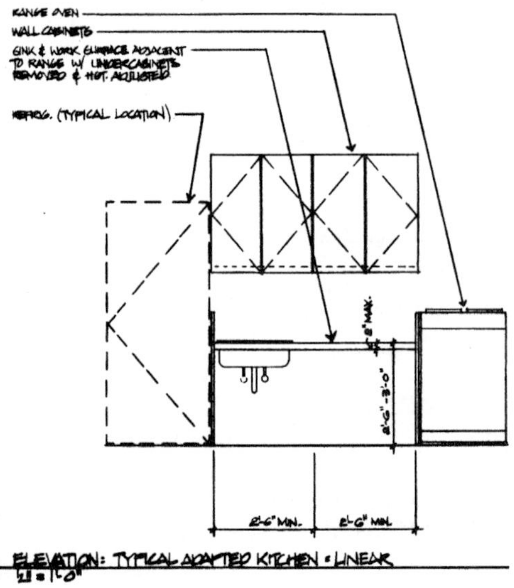

3A/A4 ELEVATION: TYPICAL ADAPTED KITCHEN: LINEAR
½" = 1'-0"

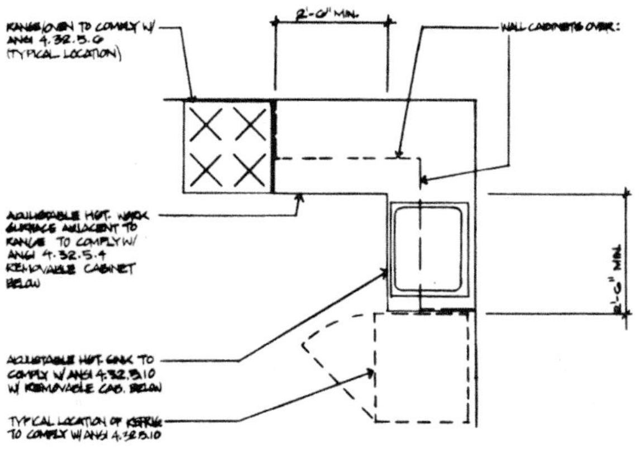

4/A4 PLAN: TYPICAL ADAPTABLE KITCHEN : L-SHAPED
½" = 1'-0"

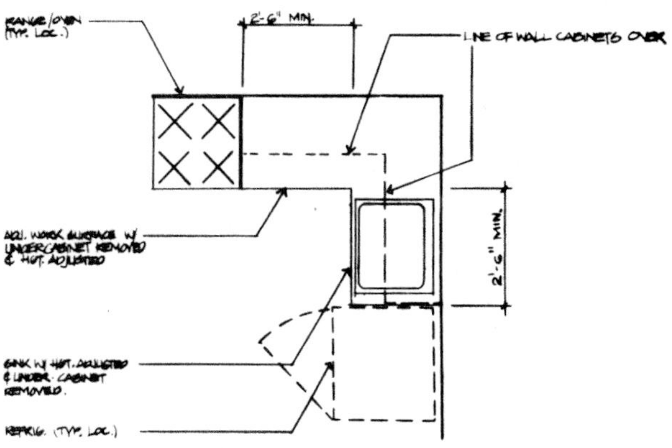

4A/A4 PLAN: TYPICAL ADAPTED KITCHEN : L-SHAPED
½" = 1'-0"

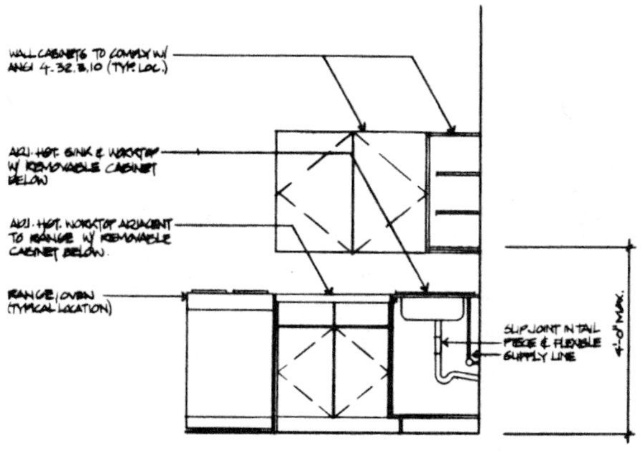

5/A4 ELEVATION: TYPICAL ADAPTABLE KITCHEN : L-SHAPED
½" = 1'-0"

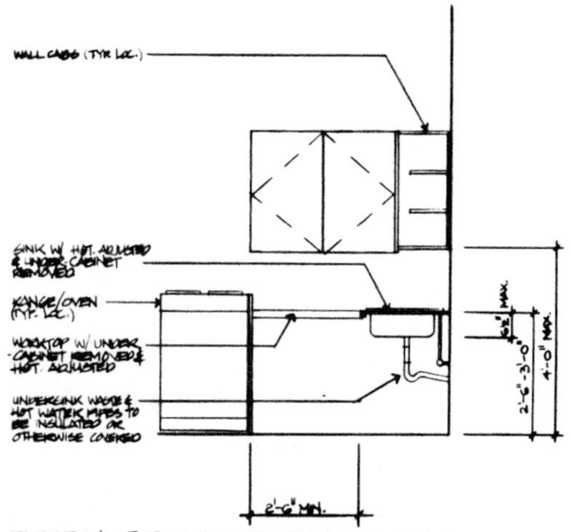

5A/A4 ELEVATION: TYPICAL ADAPTED KITCHEN: L-SHAPED
½" = 1'-0"

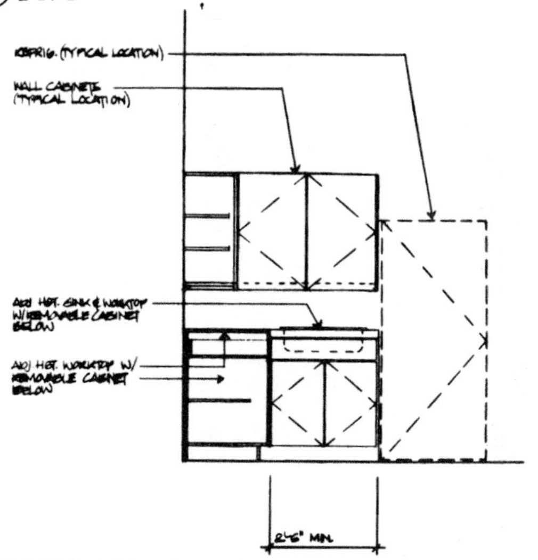

6/A4 ELEVATION: TYPICAL ADAPTABLE KITCHEN : L-SHAPED
½" = 1'-0"

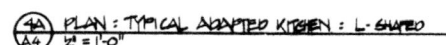

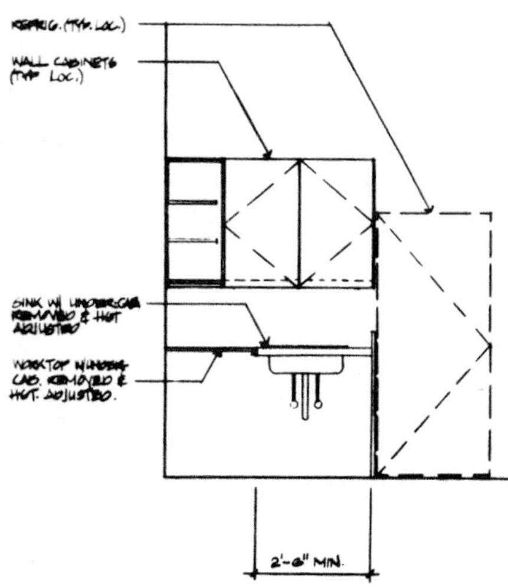

6A/A4 ELEVATION: TYPICAL ADAPTED KITCHEN : L-SHAPED
½" = 1'-0"

LIBRARY/STUDY
Anthropometric Data

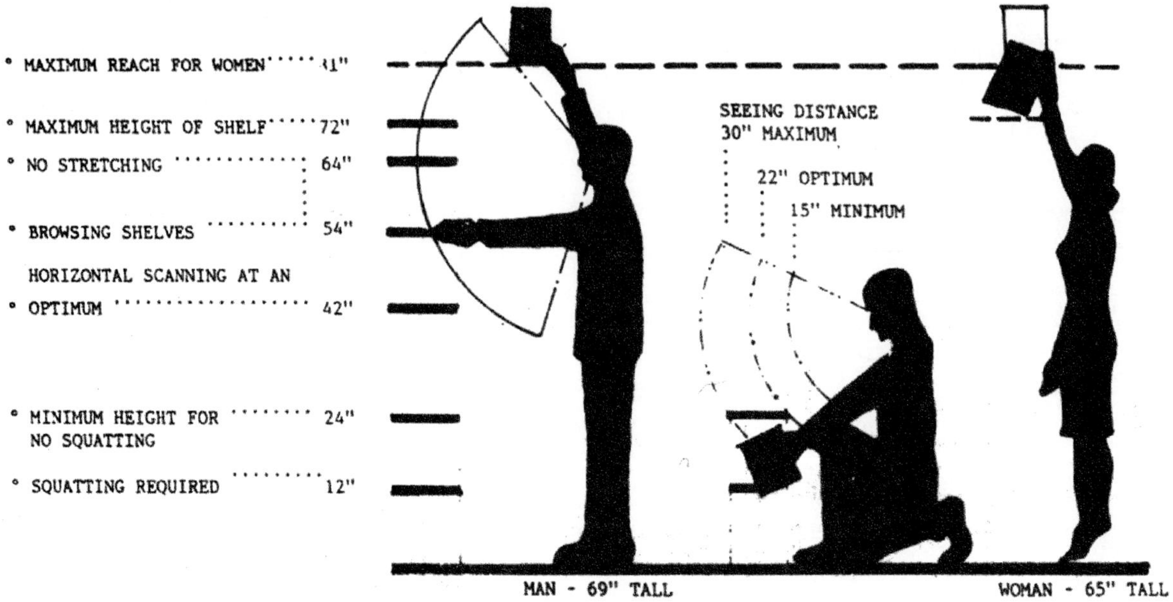

Fig. 1 Optimum shelving conditions for adults

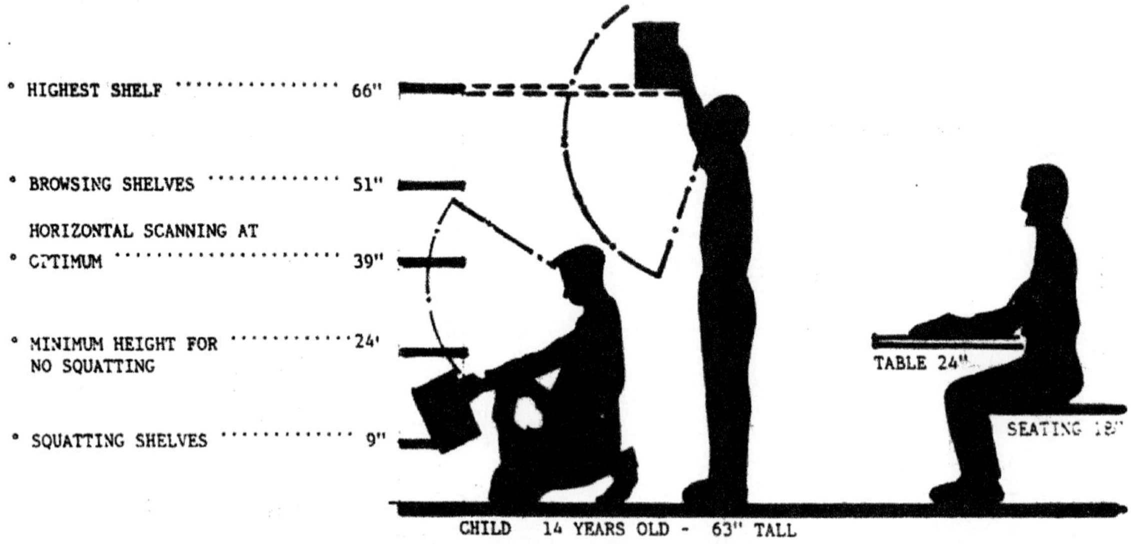

Fig. 2 Optimum shelving conditions for teenagers

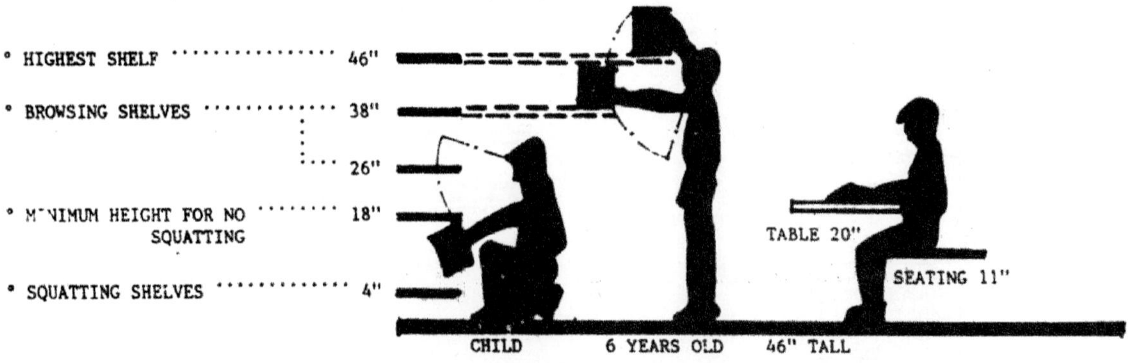

Fig. 3 Optimum shelving conditions for children

It is difficult to develop precise formulas by which to design residential library shelving or to project the number of books that can be accommodated on a unit base because of the many variables involved. The size of books, the types of books and other reading materials, the reach limitations of the user, and so on, all have an impact on the design requirements.

It is possible, however, for preliminary planning purposes, to apply the broad guidelines indicated in Figs. 1 to 3. Seven volumes per foot of shelving can be used as a rule of thumb to project capacity. The height of the highest shelf above the floor should be limited to between 78 and 81 in; 24 in is the minimum height above the floor to gain access to a shelf without squatting. Limitations for shelving to serve children will differ and are indicated in Fig. 3.

PLANS AND ELEVATIONS

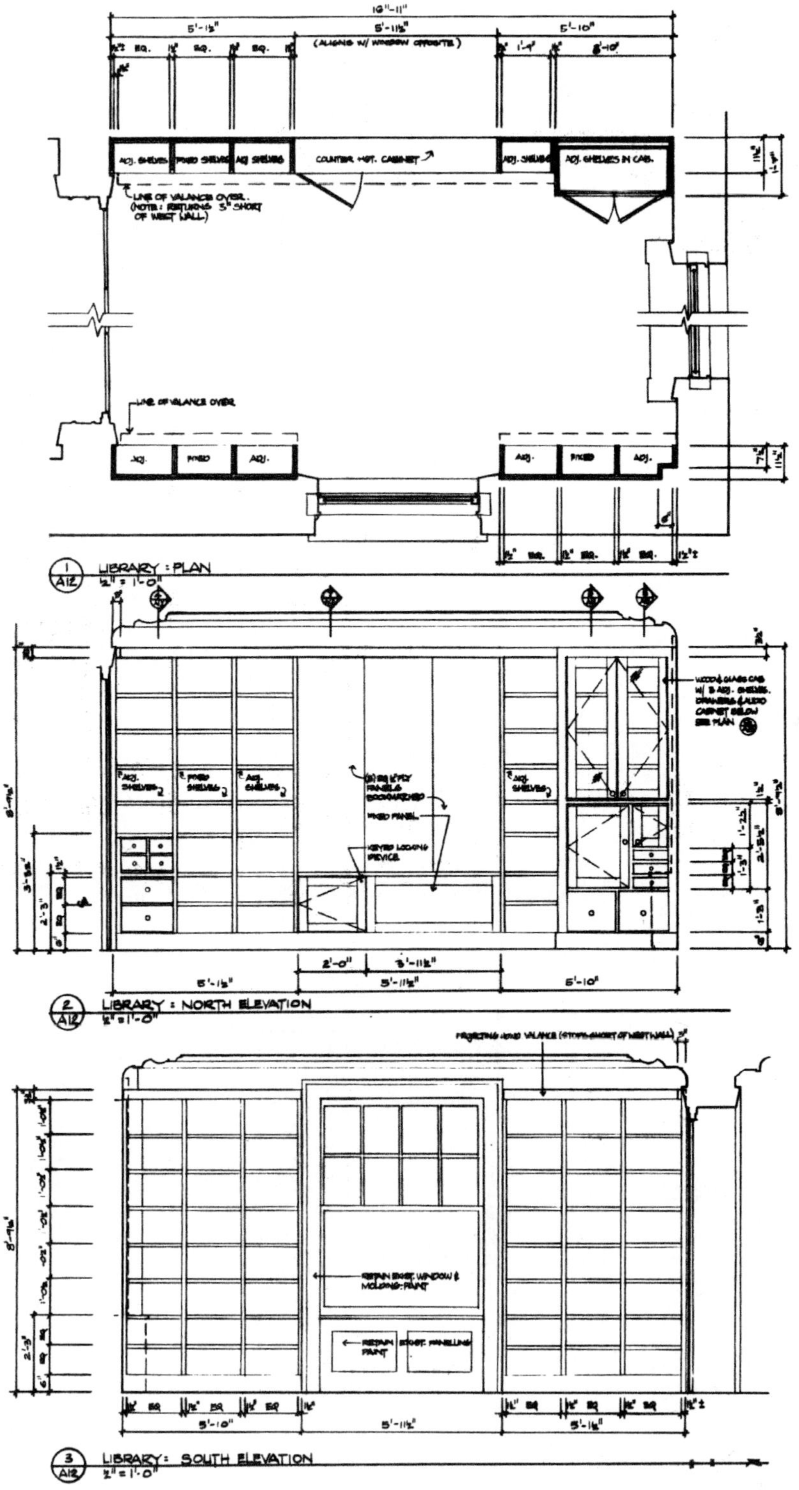

LIBRARY/STUDY
Library Shelving Details

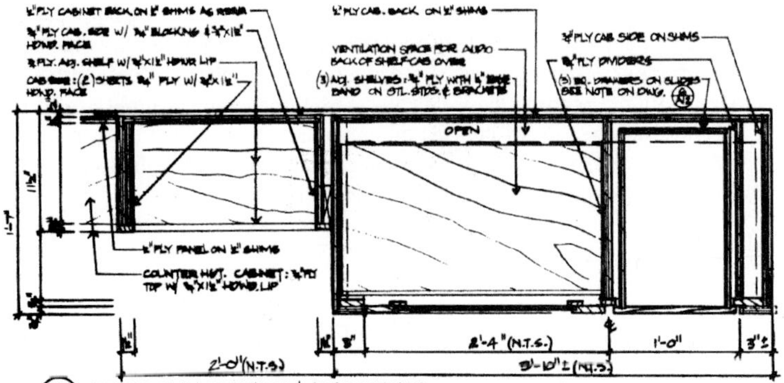

6/A12 LIBRARY: PLAN OF SHELVES & AUDIO CABINET
1½" = 1'-0"

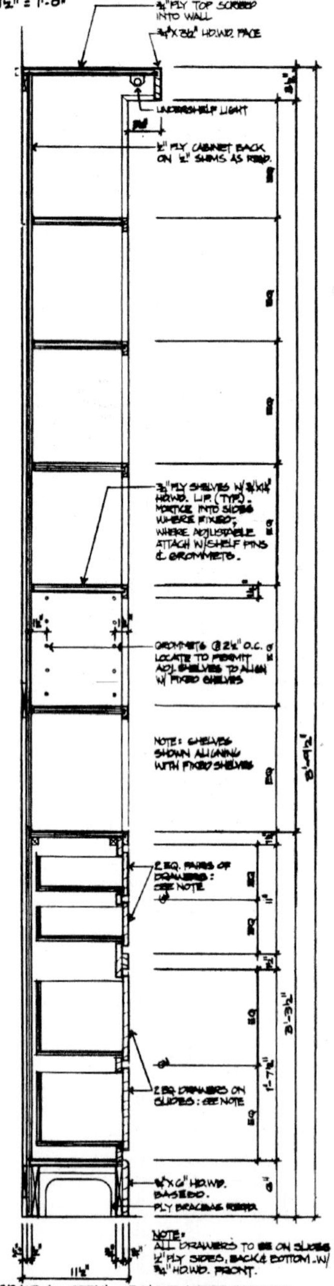

4/A12 LIBRARY: DETAIL OF NORTHWEST CABINET
1½" = 1'-0"

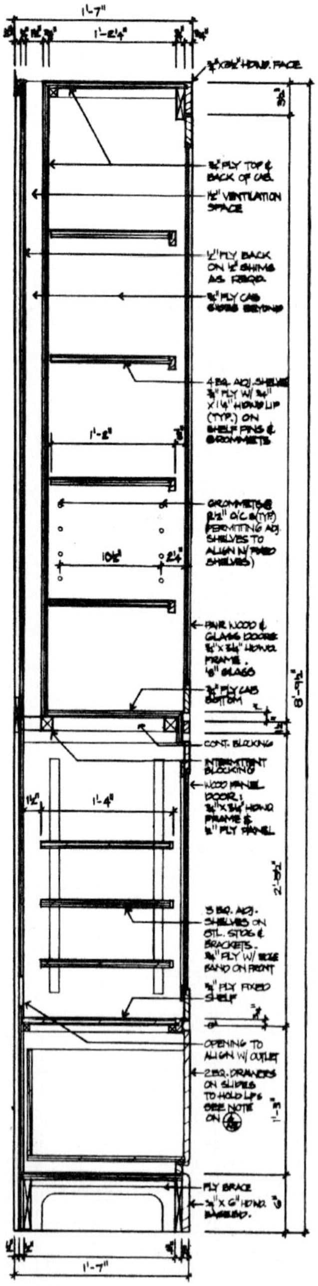

5/A12 LIBRARY: DETAIL @ AUDIO CABINET
1½" = 1'-0"

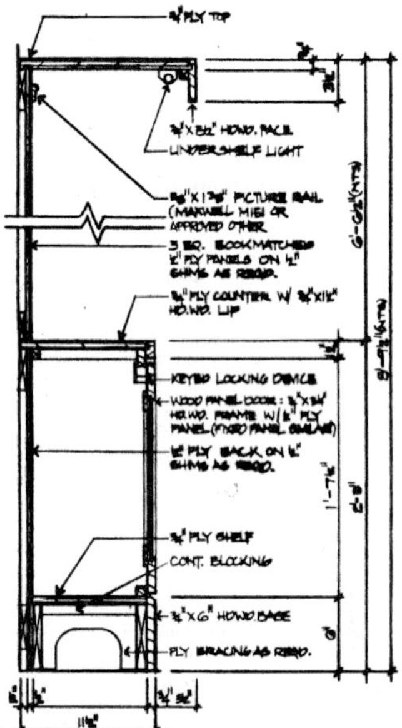

7/A12 LIBRARY: COUNTER HGT. CABINET
1½" = 1'-0"

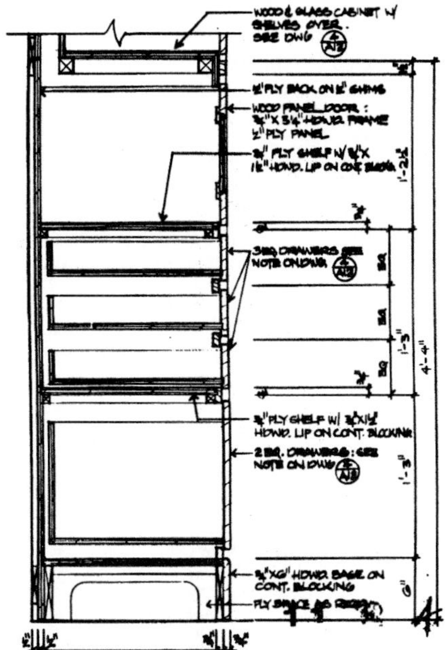

B/A12 LIBRARY: DETAIL @ NORTHEAST CABINET 1½" = 1'-0"

DETAIL·OF·SHELVING·

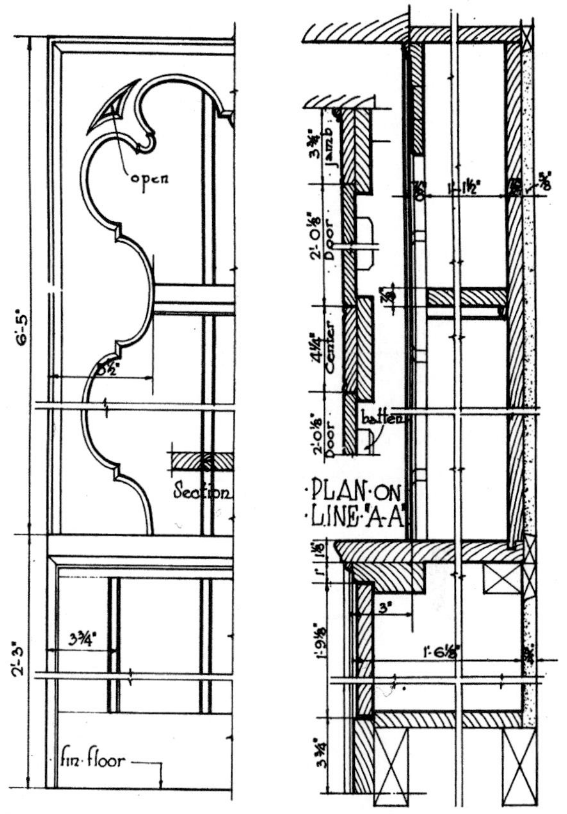

Note: All woodwork in Bookcase and Cupboards is White Oak

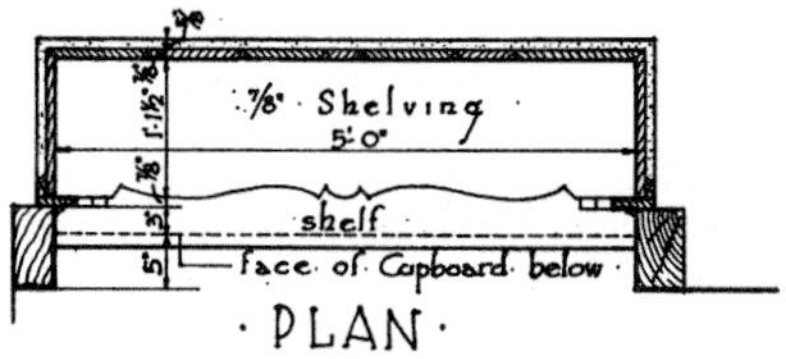

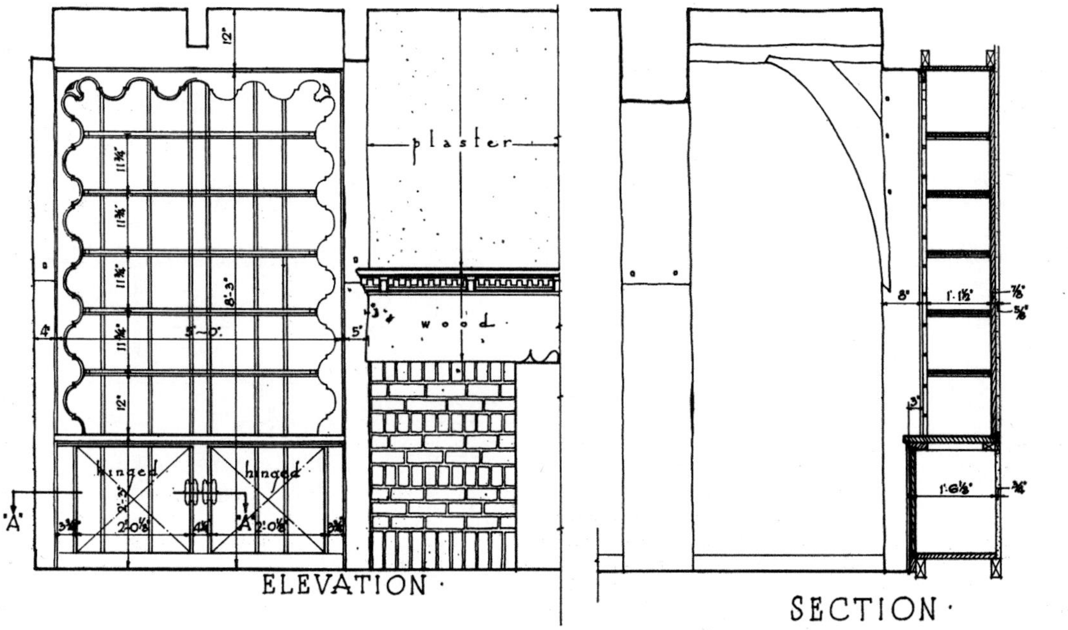

LIBRARY/STUDY
Built-in Bookshelves

TABLE 1 Library Shelving: Volumes per Linear Foot of Shelf Based on Subject
(Standard stack section 3 ft wide × 7½ ft high with 7 shelves)

Subject	Volumes per foot of shelf	Volumes per single face section
Art (excluding oversize)	7	147
Nonfiction	8	168
Economics	8	168
Fiction	8	168
General literature	7	147
History	7	147
Law	4	84
Medical	5	105
Periodicals, bound	5	105
Public documents	5	105
Technical and scientific	6	126
Average for overall estimating		125

Here is a simple method of building in bookshelves, bar units, and the like, for residences and other types of buildings by using an egg-crate system. The front of the shelf is supported by the vertical members and the back of the shelf is nailed to the plywood back. These built-in bookshelves and bar unit were developed for a residence on the Eastern Shore of Maryland. In this design Hugh Newell Jacobsen, FAIA, divided the built-in bookcases into units of three shelf widths and introduced a recessed vertical divider 3 in deep by 7½ in wide between bookcase units. The major trim piece is solid wood 1⅛ in × 1⅛ in with a ⅜ in wide by ⅜ in deep groove at the middle. This simple trim piece acts as framing for sides, top, and bottom of the bookshelves and also for the bar unit with glass shelves and mirrored back, sides, top, and bottom.

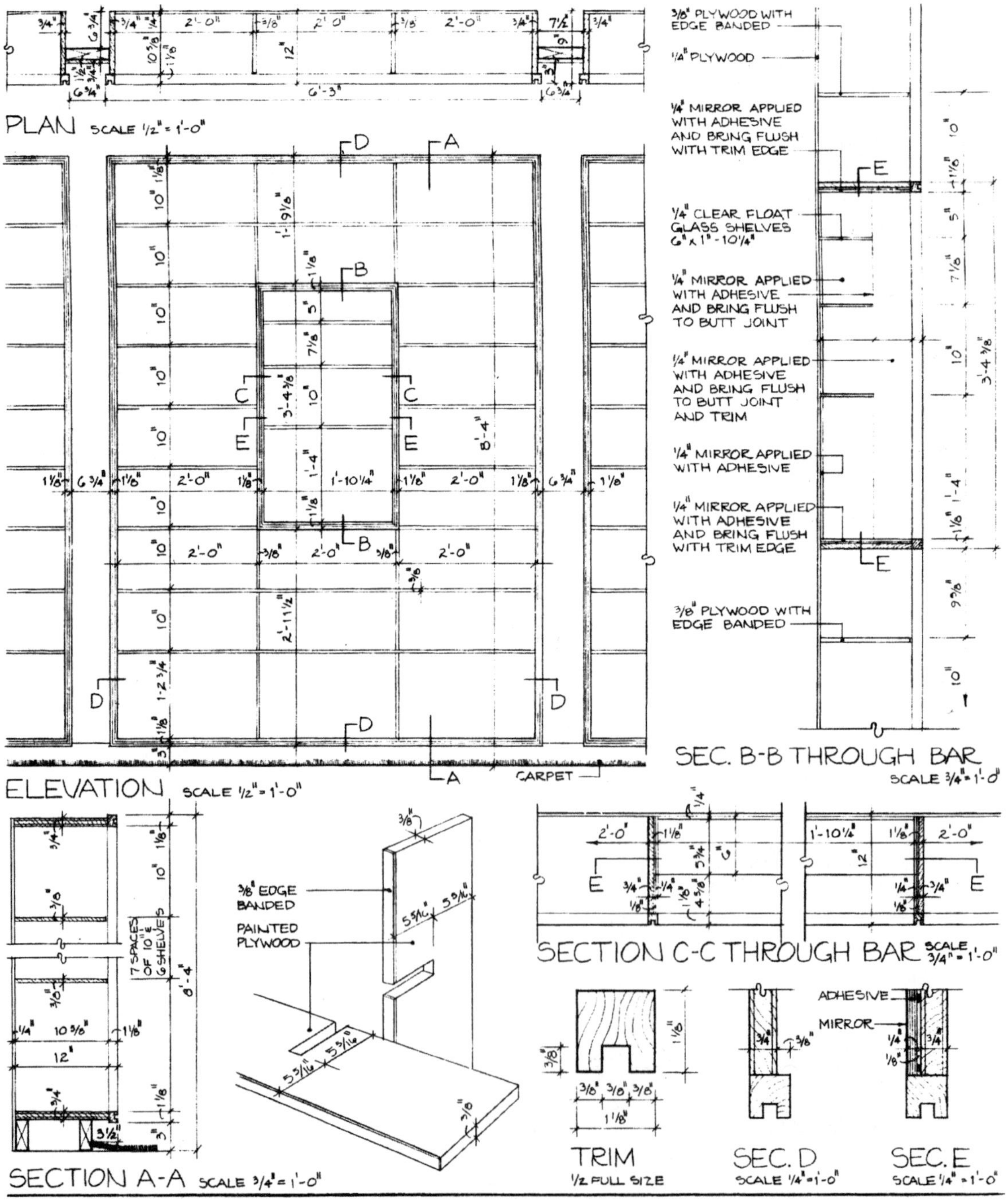

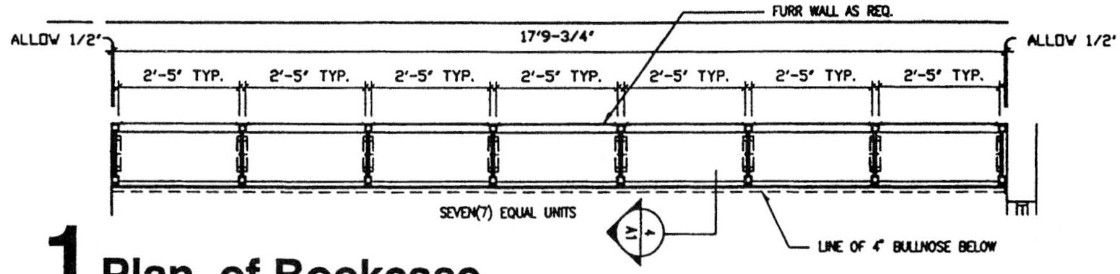

1 Plan of Bookcase

1/2" = 1' – 0"

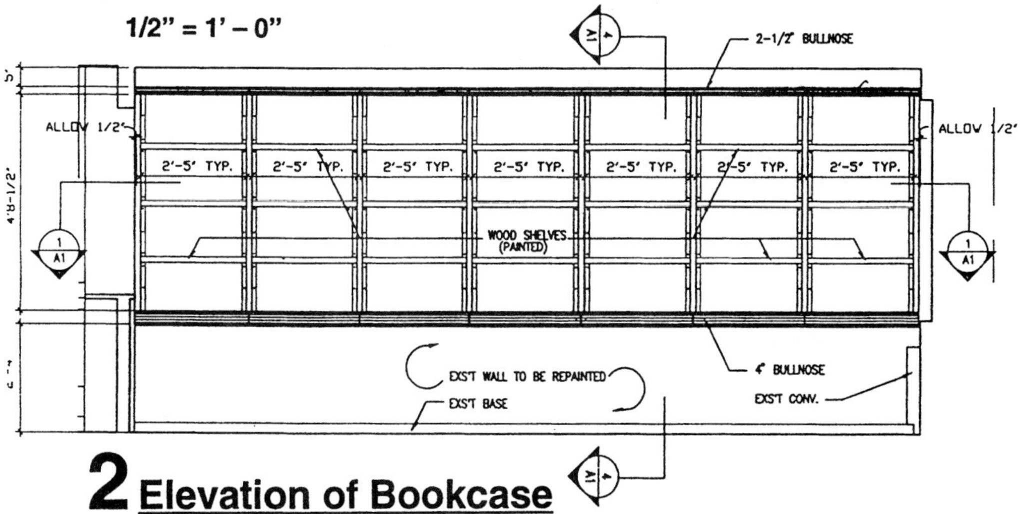

2 Elevation of Bookcase

1/2" = 1' – 0"

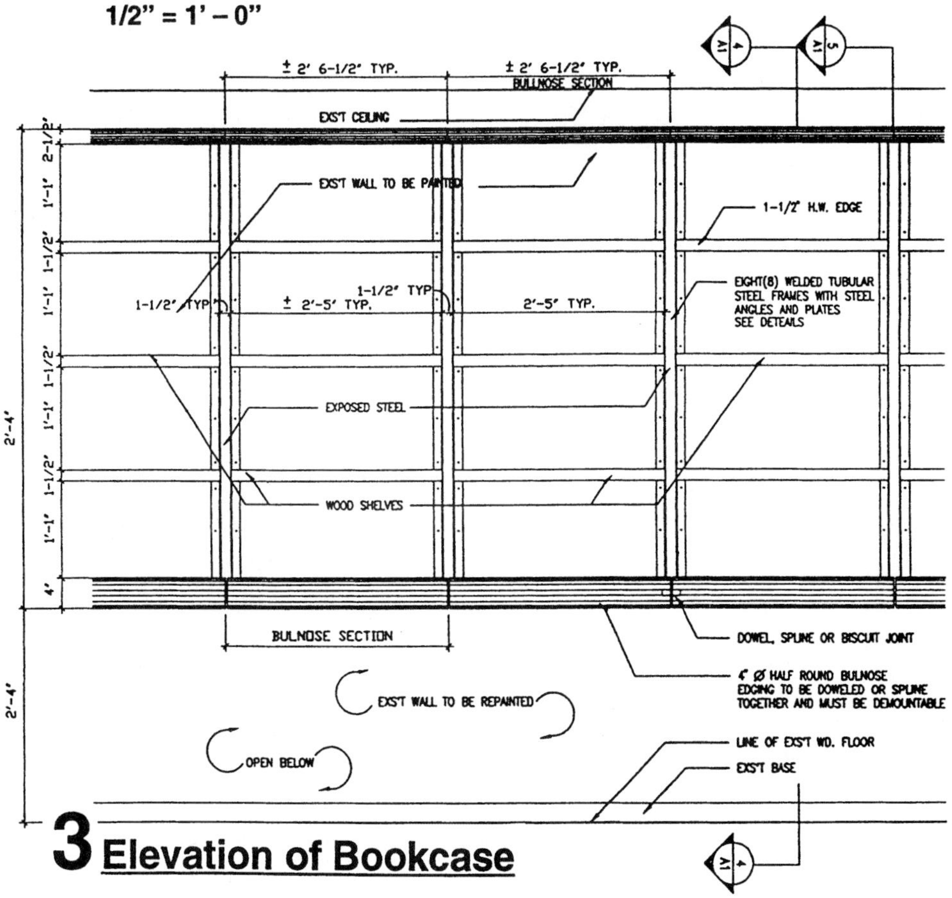

3 Elevation of Bookcase

LIBRARY/STUDY

Steel and Wood Bookcase and Storage

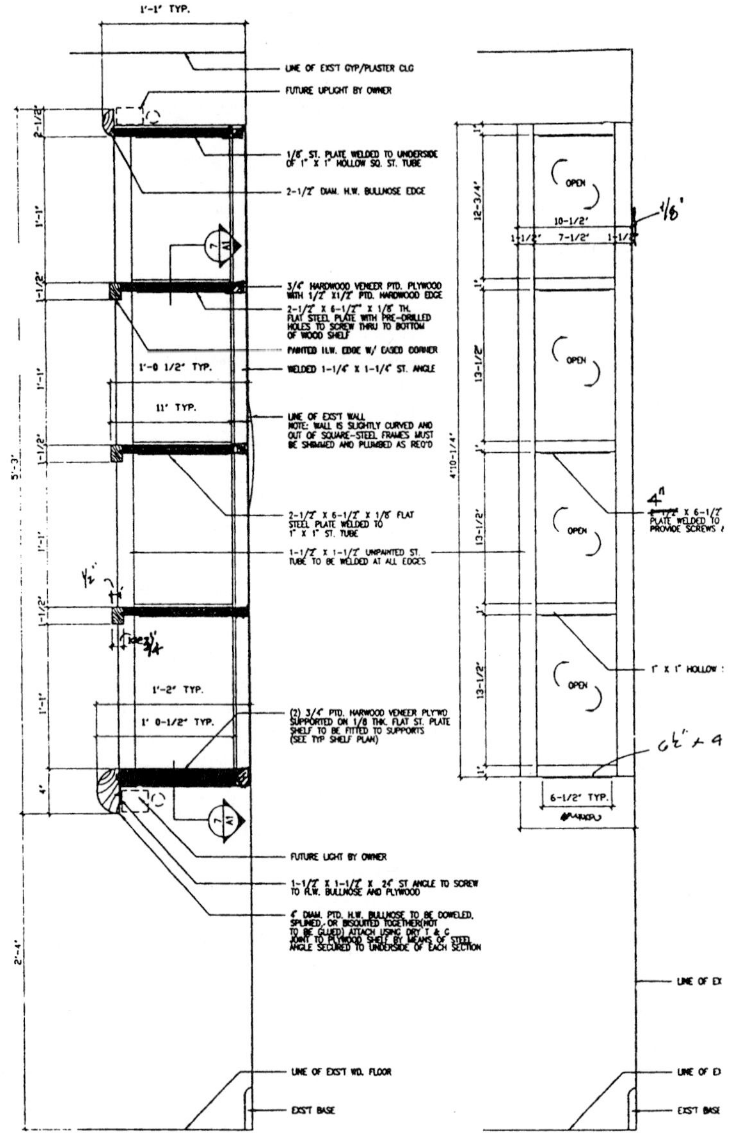

4 & 5 Sections through Bookcase

3/4" = 1'- 0"

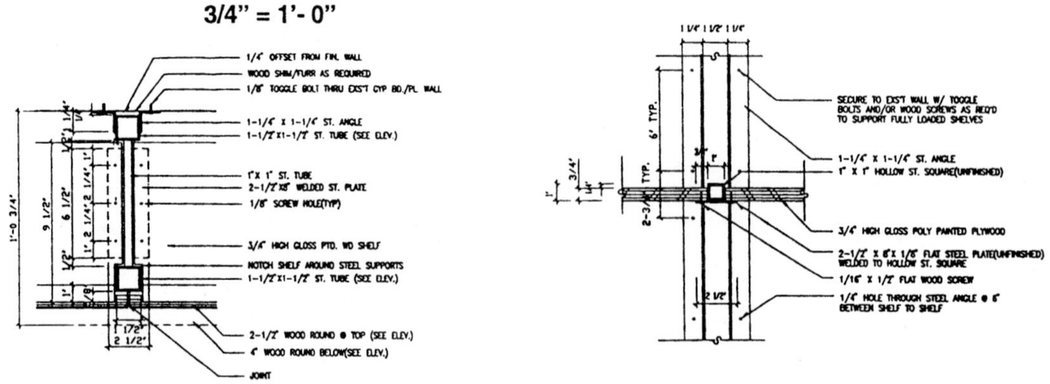

6 & 7 Sections @ Typical Steel Frame

3/4" = 1' – 0"

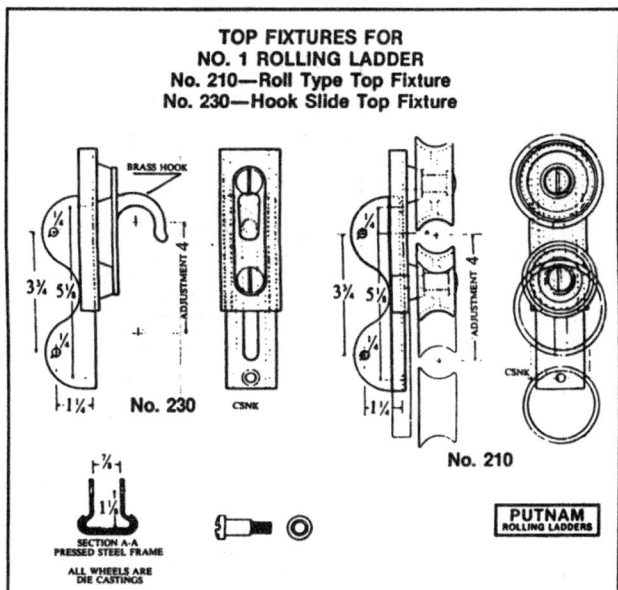

TOP FIXTURES FOR NO. 1 ROLLING LADDER
No. 210—Roll Type Top Fixture
No. 230—Hook Slide Top Fixture

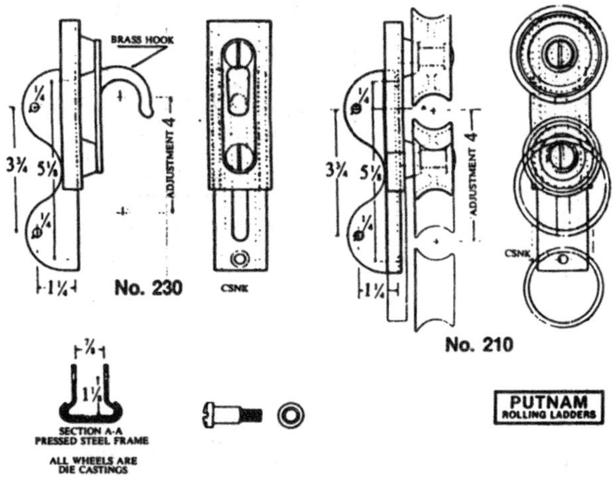

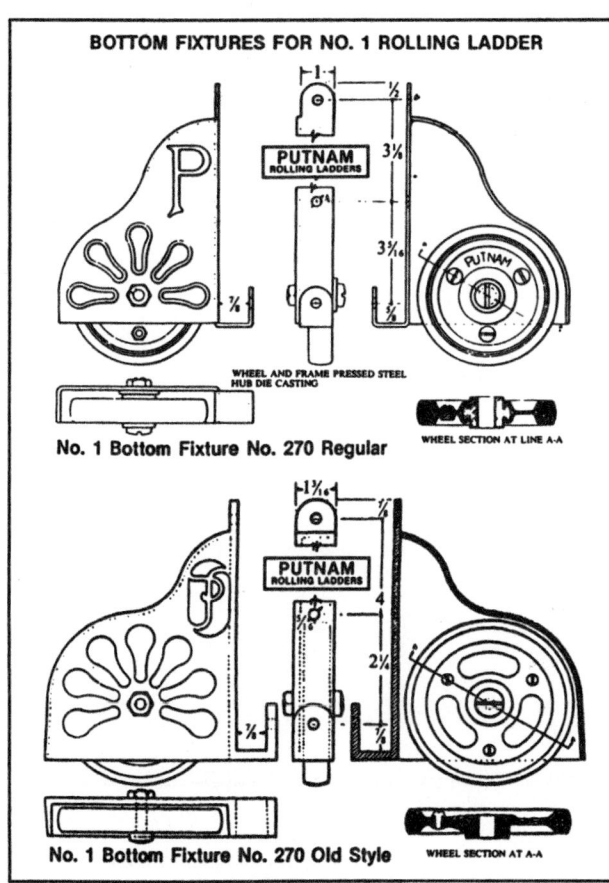

BOTTOM FIXTURES FOR NO. 1 ROLLING LADDER

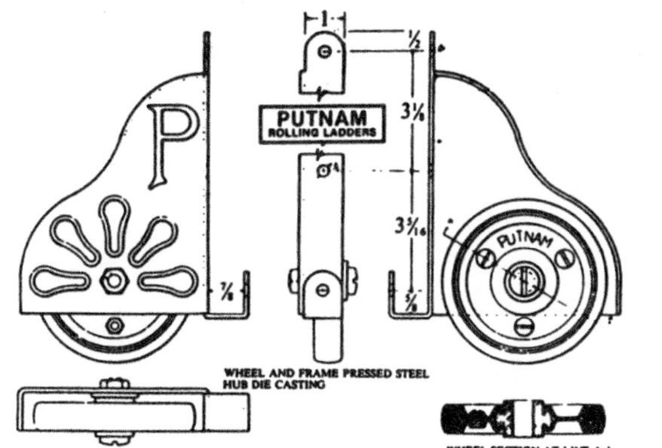

No. 1 Bottom Fixture No. 270 Regular

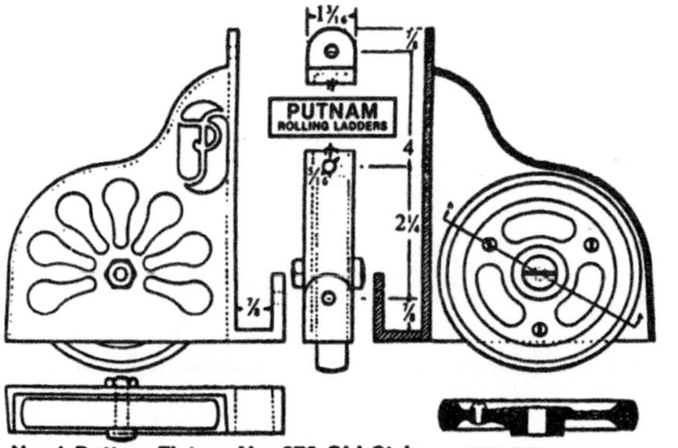

No. 1 Bottom Fixture No. 270 Old Style

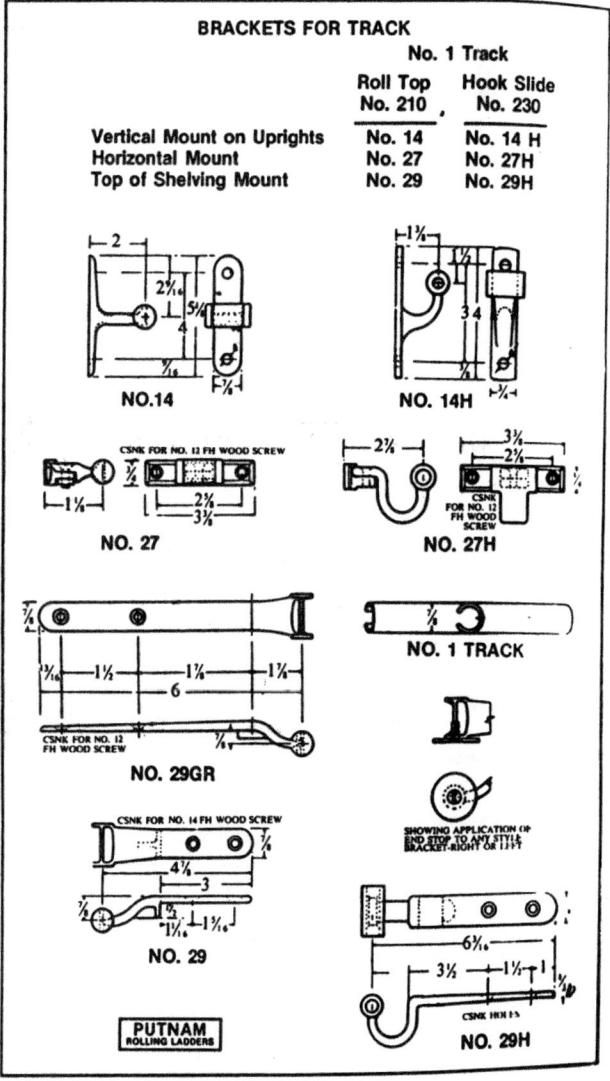

BRACKETS FOR TRACK

	No. 1 Track	
	Roll Top No. 210	Hook Slide No. 230
Vertical Mount on Uprights	No. 14	No. 14 H
Horizontal Mount	No. 27	No. 27H
Top of Shelving Mount	No. 29	No. 29H

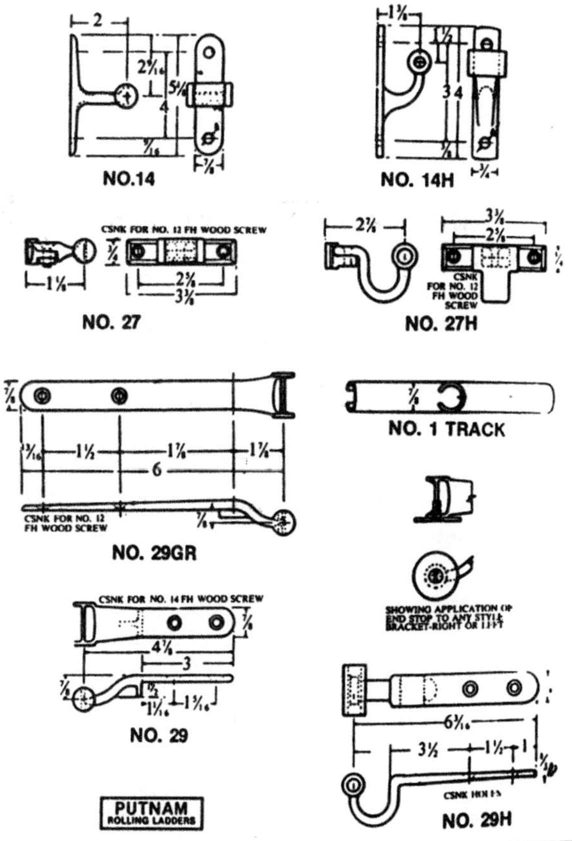

FAMILY/RECREATION ROOMS
Arrangements and Clearances

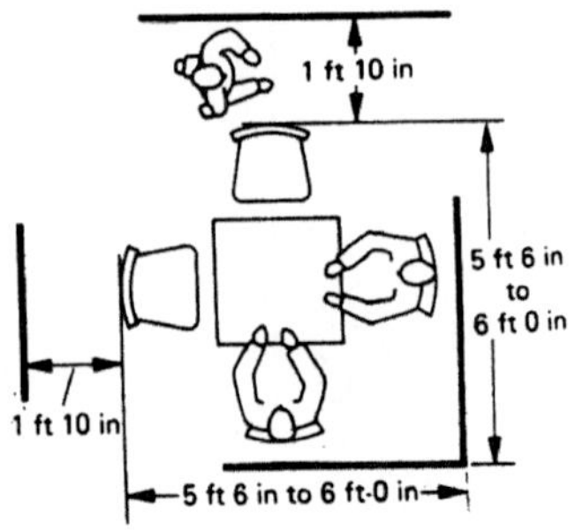

Clearances for playing bridge

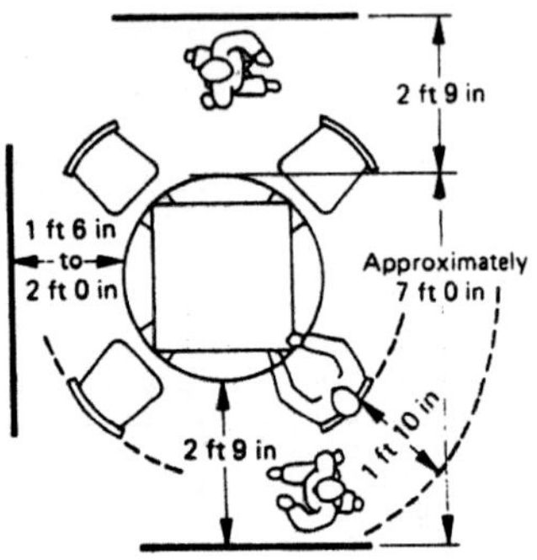

Clearances for playing poker

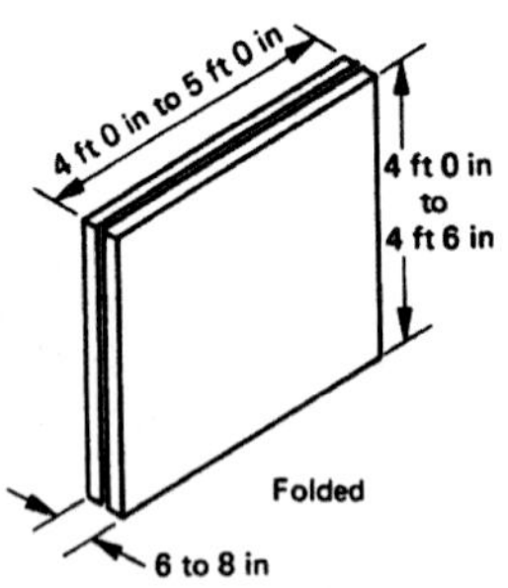

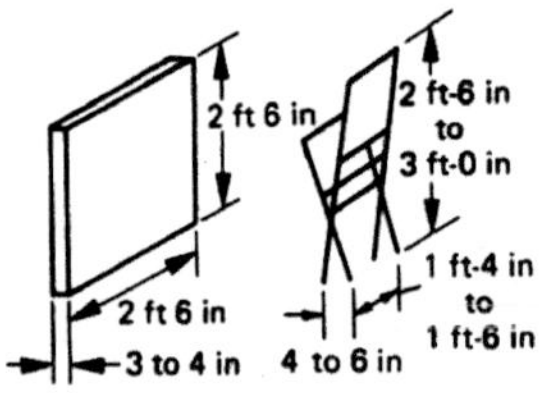

Folded bridge table

Folded chair

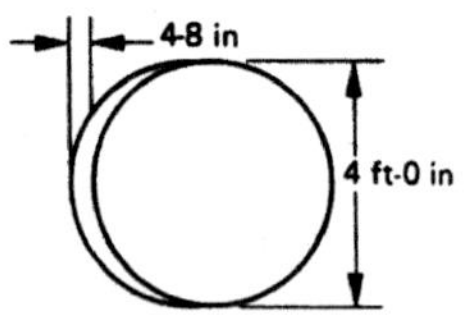

Folded poker table

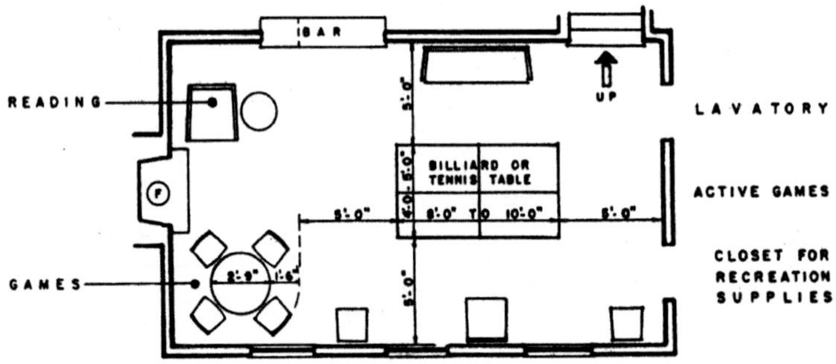

Fig. 1 Play room

FAMILY/RECREATION ROOMS

ARRANGEMENTS AND CLEARANCES

Recreational Activities

Indoor recreational activities invariably require definite spaces for equipment and clearances for using it. Not all games occupy floor areas indicated as necessary for those diagrammed on this page. But if interiors are planned to accommodate large units of equipment such as that required for table tennis and provide necessary playing clearances, spaces will be adequate for many other uses as well.

Dimensions of game equipment and floor areas required for its use are both subject to variation. Sizes noted here are comfortable averages, not absolute minima.

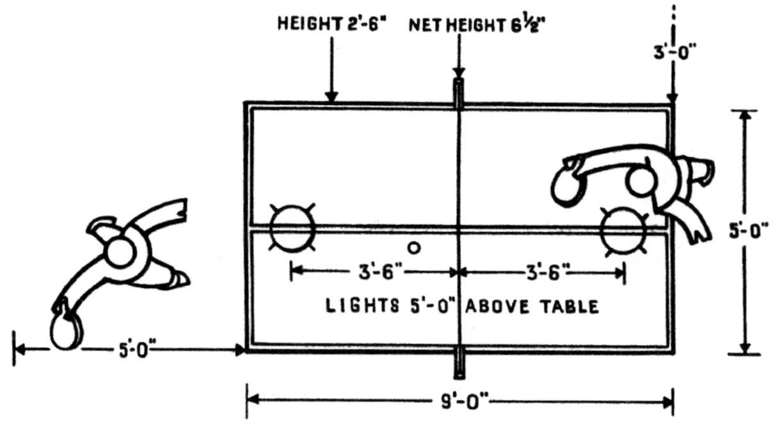

PING PONG

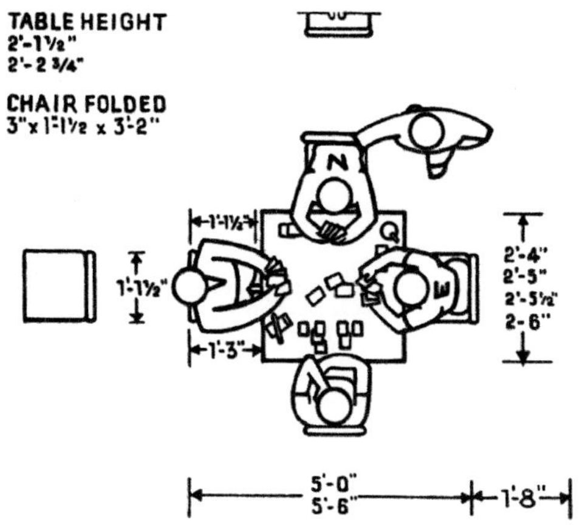

CARD PLAYING

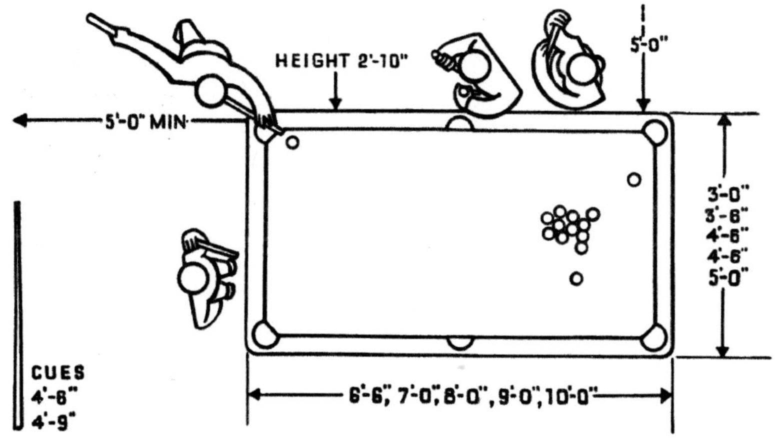

POOL AND BILLIARDS

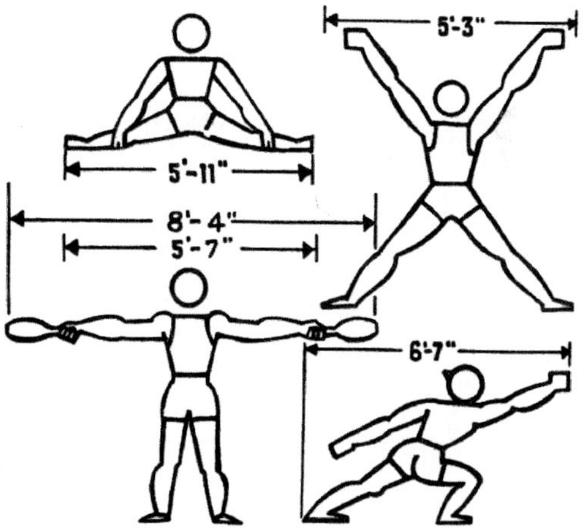

GYMNASTICS

Standard ping pong table sizes are 3 ft x 6 ft; 3 ft 6 in x 7 ft 0 in; 4 ft 0 in x 8 ft 0 in; 4 ft 8 in x 8 ft 6 in; 5 ft 0 in x 9 ft 2 in; 5 ft 6 in x 10 ft 2 in; 6 ft 8 in x 12 ft 8 in.

TABLE 1 Pool and Billiard Table Sizes (in feet)

Size	Where used
3 × 6	Home
3½ × 7	Home
4 × 8	Home Commercial standard in South America, Mexico, and Spain
4½ × 9	Popular U.S. commercial standard
5 × 10	U.S. professional standard
6 × 12	Commercial standard in Canada and England

FAMILY/RECREATION ROOMS
Entertainment Center Plan and Elevation

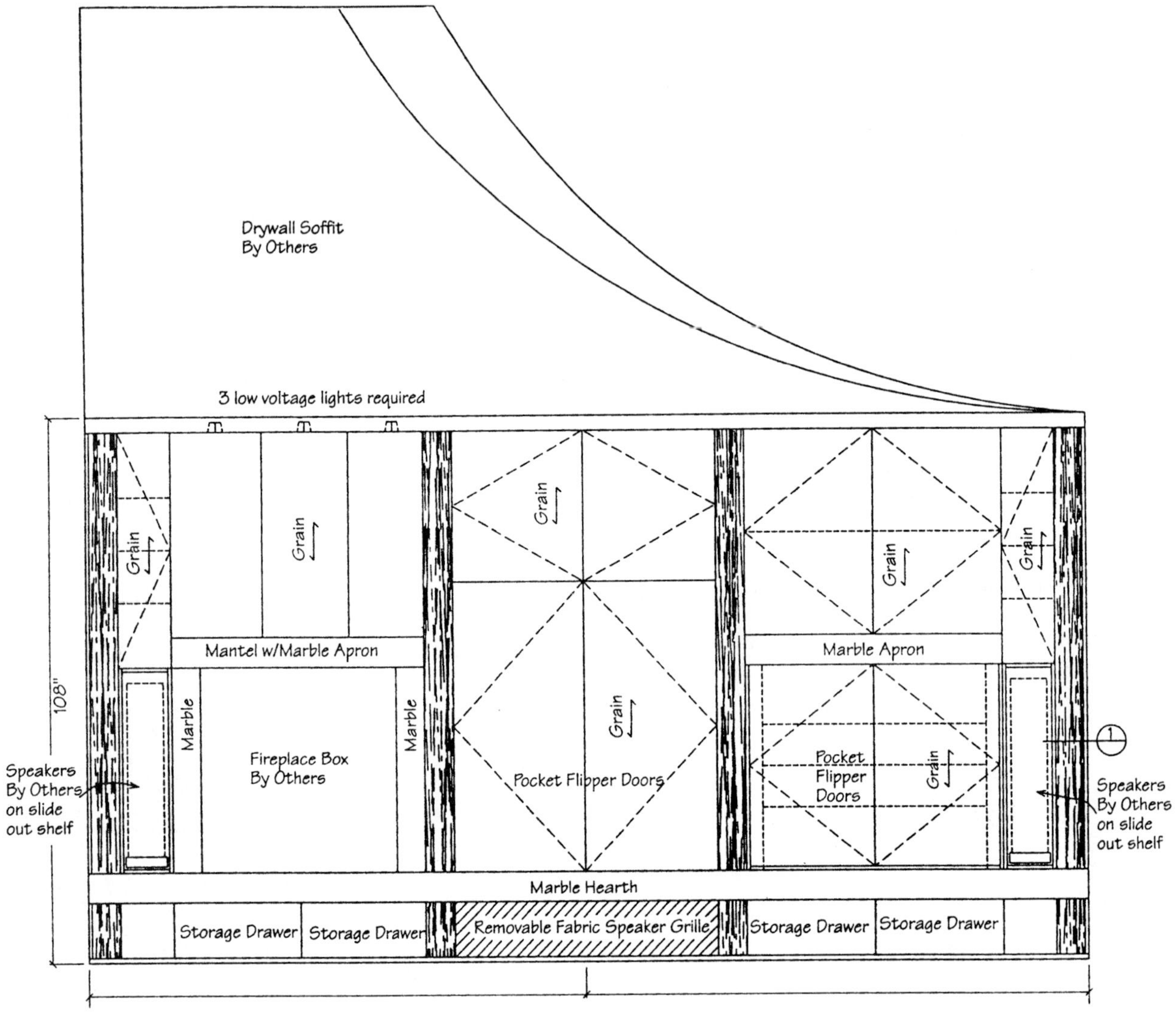

Elevation

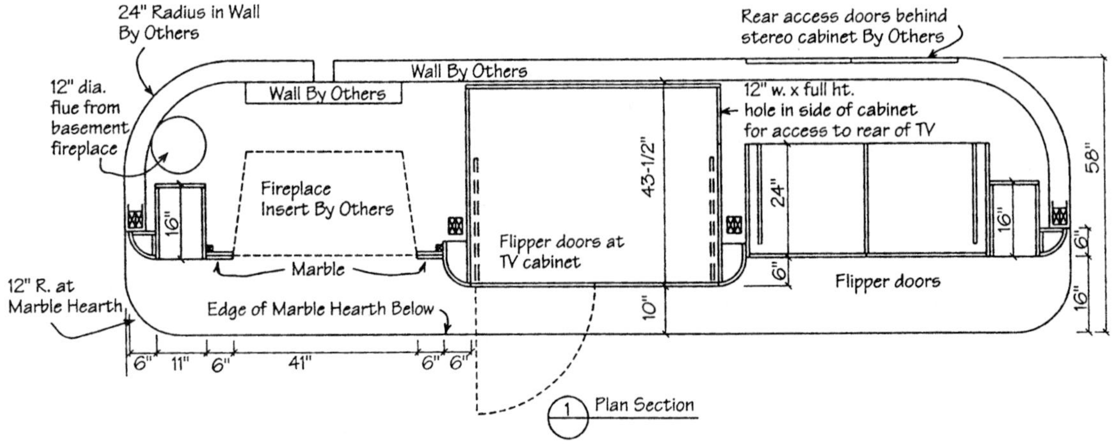

1 Plan Section

FAMILY/RECREATION ROOMS
Television Cabinet Section and Paneled Wall Section

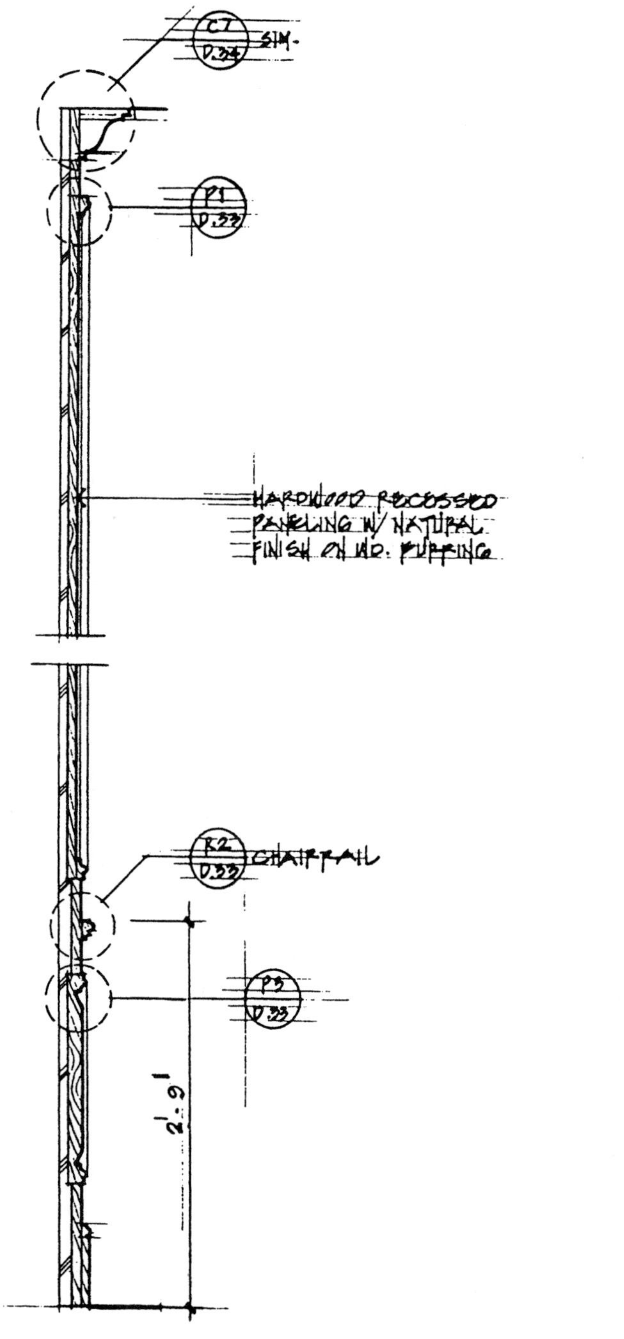

5 Typ. Paneled Wall - Family Rm.

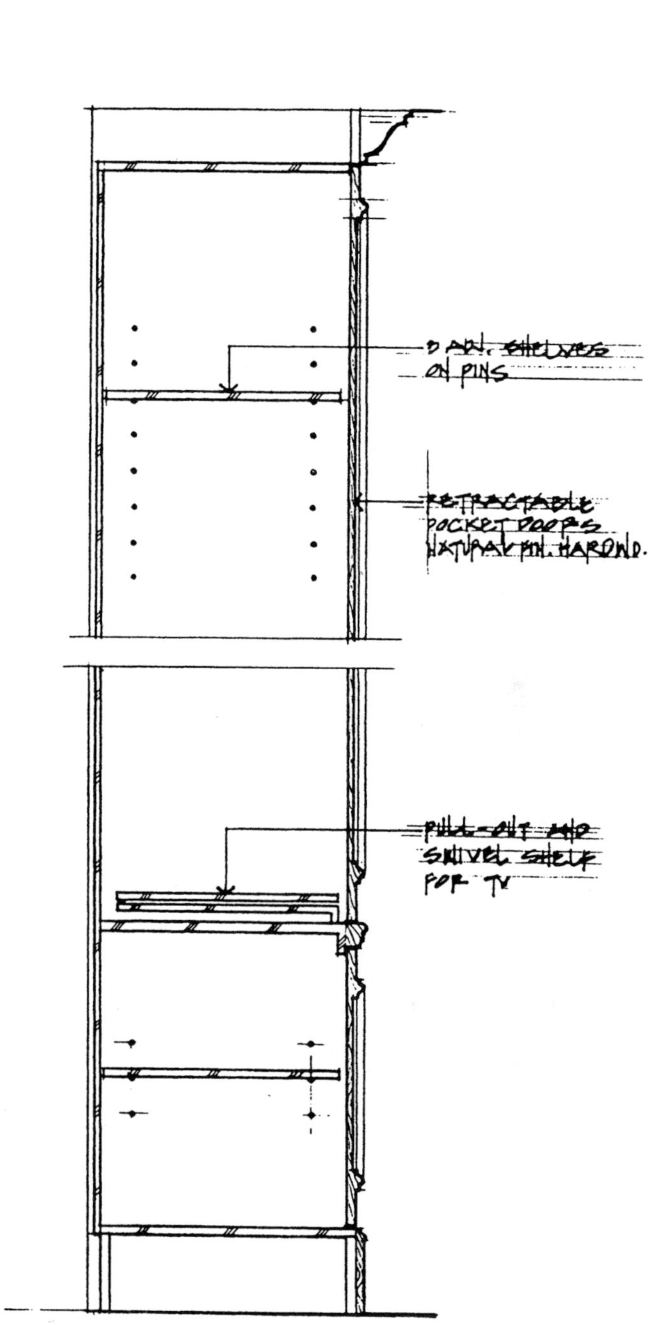

6 Tv Cabinet - Family Rm.

FAMILY/RECREATION ROOMS
Piano Sizes and Bar Details

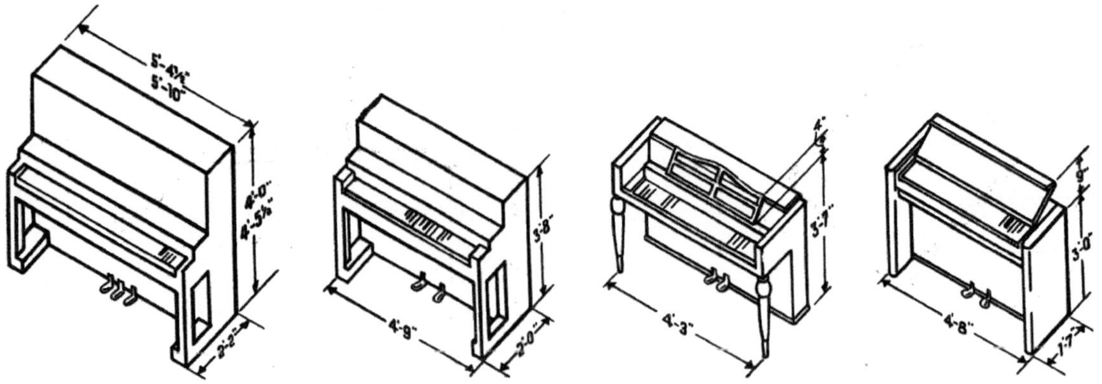

UPRIGHT PIANO SIZES

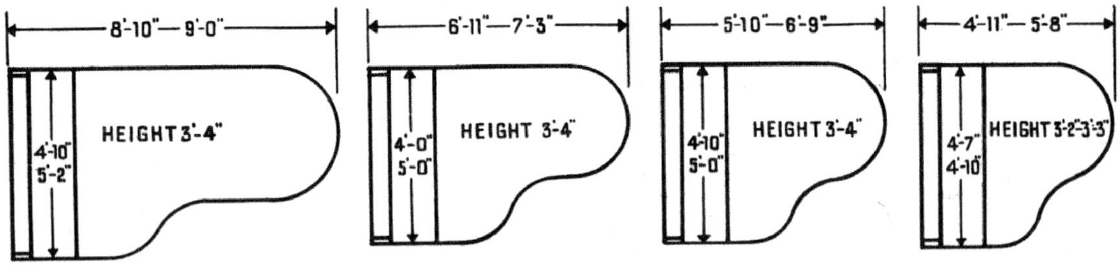

GRAND PIANO SIZES

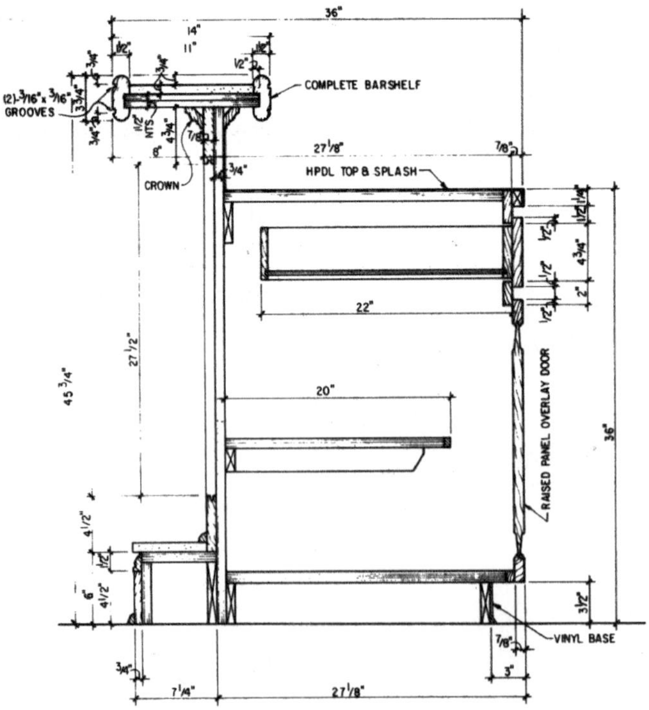

SECTION THRU BAR CABINET

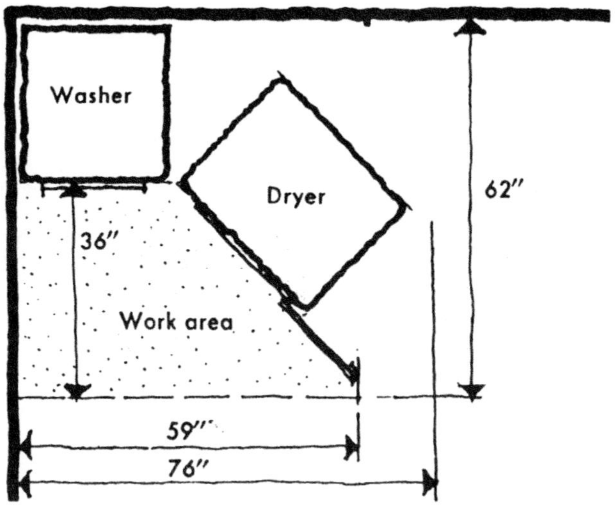

Fig. 1 Angle arrangement

LAUNDRY/SEWING ROOMS

LAUNDRY ROOM LAYOUTS

Home Laundry Activities

Home laundry encompasses the processes from sorting through ironing of clothes and household linens, including pretreating, washing, drying, and sprinkling.

General Planning Suggestions

1. It is desirable to plan space for specific laundry processes.
2. Moistureproof surfaces are needed for pretreating and sprinkling of clothes.
3. Drying areas should be accessible for use under all climatic conditions.
4. To control moisture in the room, dryers should be located to permit venting to the outside of the house.
5. Adequate storage for washing equipment and supplies should be located near the place of first use.
6. Facilities for hanging drip-dry garments after washing should be provided.
7. In locating the washing equipment, consideration should be given to convenience of interrelated household activities, distances from the source of soiled clothes, and the drying areas, and the isolation of clutter.

Figures 1 and 2 illustrate arrangements of laundry equipment. Space needed by a single worker in front of equipment or between equipment placed opposite is indicated. Overall dimensions of areas will vary with type and size of equipment selected. No allowance has been made between the back of equipment and the wall for electrical, plumbing, and dryer vent connections. The space required will depend on the type of installation used.

Counter space is provided for sorting and folding three washer loads of clothes. The space under the counters has been used for bins, one for soiled clothing and the other for dry, clean articles that require further treatment before use or storage. Additional counter space can be provided by the tops of the dryer and washer, depending on the type selected.

A tall storage cabinet for laundry supplies would complement each arrangement. In this cabinet, an ironing board, iron, mops, and buckets (needed for cleaning the laundry area) may also be stored.

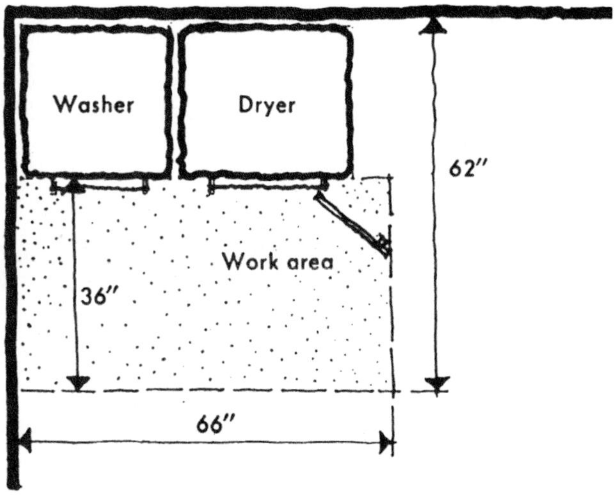

Fig. 2 Conventional arrangement

LAUNDRY/SEWING ROOMS

Laundry Room Layouts

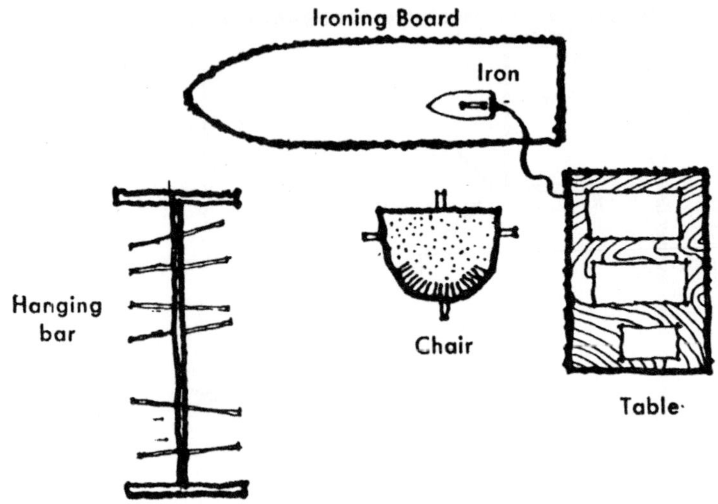

Fig. 3 Arrangement of ironing equipment based on flow of work

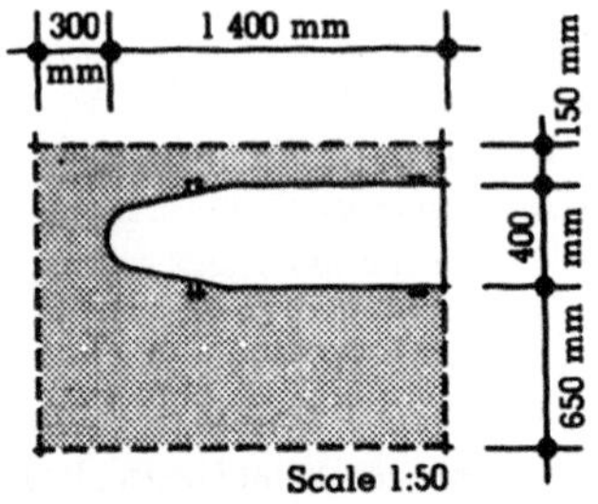

Fig. 4 Space around ironing board

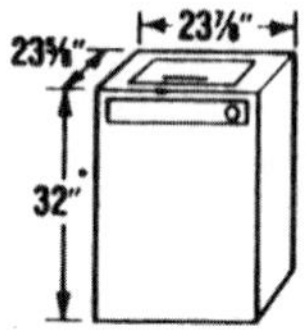

Fig. 7 Compact washer

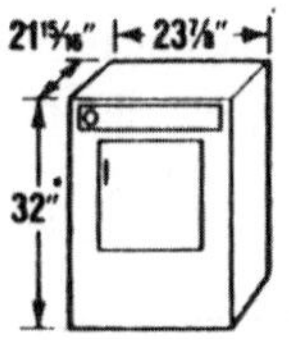

Fig. 8 Compact dryer

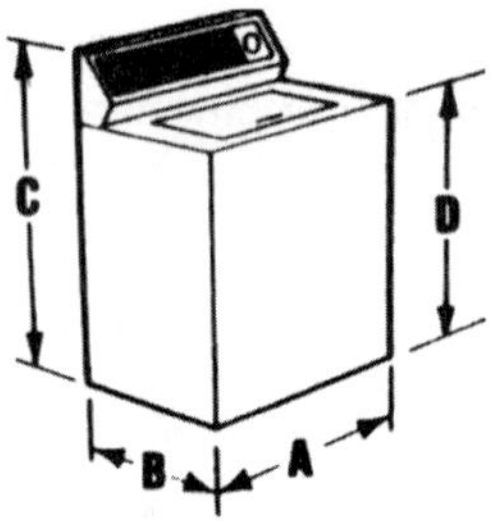

Fig. 5 Automatic washer. A = 24–30 in, B = 26–30 in, C = 42 in, D = 36 in

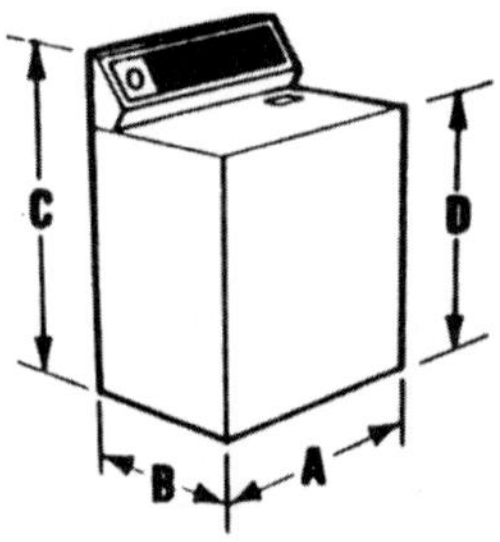

Fig. 6 Automatic dryer. A = 24–28 in, B = 24–26 in, C = 42 in, D = 36 in

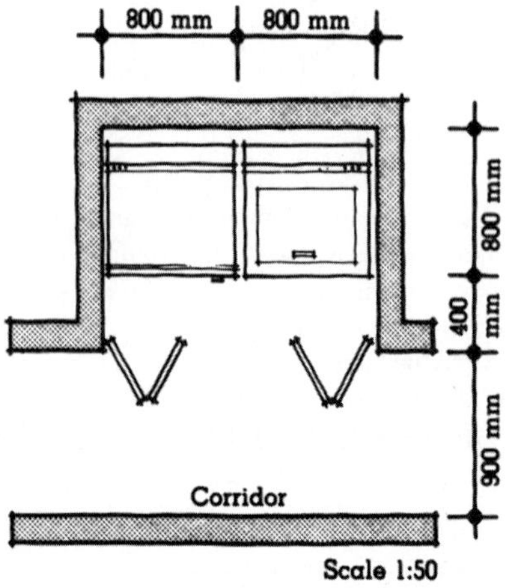

Fig. 9 When space is limited, it may be possible to locate the laundry space next to a corridor

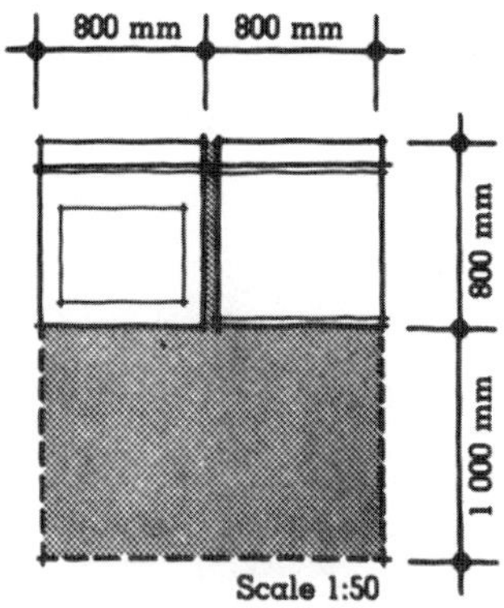

Fig. 10 Clearance in front of automatic washer and dryer. If the space in front of the automatic washer and dryer is a corridor, this dimension should be increased to at least 1200 mm (4 ft). This will permit a second person to pass through when someone is doing the laundry. If a washer and dryer are located opposite each other, this dimension should also be 1200 mm (4 ft)

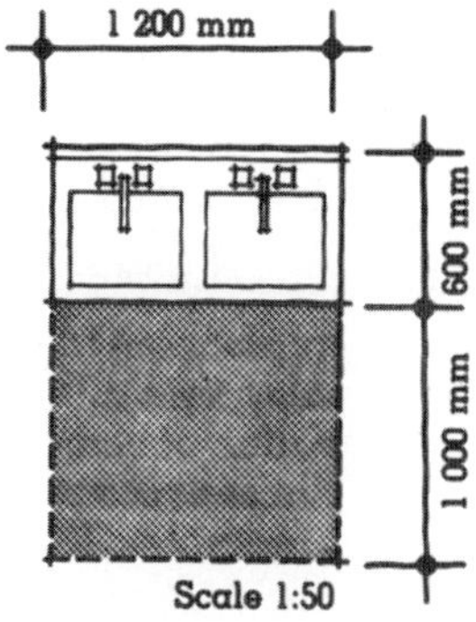

Fig. 11 Clearance in front of laundry tub

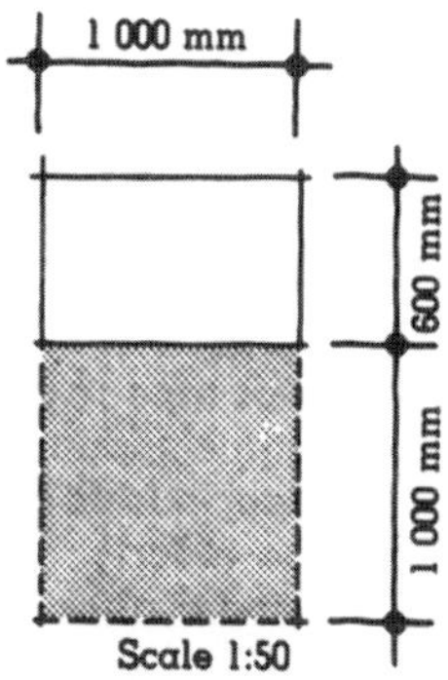

Fig. 12 Clearance in front of sorting counter or table

TABLE 1 Space Requirements for Washer-Dryer Arrangements

Type and size of equipment	Auxiliary equipment	Work area, in	Total floor area, in	
			Width	Depth
Stacked arrangement: washer, 31 × 26 in; dryer, 31 × 26 in	Basket, 19-in diameter	43 × 37	43	63
Angle arrangement: washer 26 × 26 in; dryer, 31 × 26 in	Basket, 19-in diameter	36 × 59	62	76
Straight-line arrangement: washer, 26 × 26 in; dryer, 31 × 26 in	Basket, 19-in diameter	36 × 66	62	66

Laundry Location

The ideal location of the laundry space is a matter of preference. The laundry area may be separate or combined with the bathroom, the kitchen, the utility space, or the corridor. The most frequently mentioned advantages and disadvantages of these various options are listed as follows.

Separate Laundry

Advantages

A separate space can be used for other activities such as sewing and hobbies, if it is large enough.

Clothes may be hung for air drying without interfering with other household activities.

Noise from laundry appliances can be shut off from the rest of the dwelling.

Temporary holding or storage of clothing to be washed or ironed is made easier.

Disadvantages

Providing this extra room increases the cost of the dwelling.

Laundry in Combination with Bathroom

Advantages

When the bathroom is located near the bedrooms, the washer and dryer are close to where most laundry originates. This facilitates gathering soiled articles and putting away clean linen and clothing.

Combining the laundry space with a half bathroom adjacent to the kitchen provides many of the advantages of a separate laundry room.

The tops of the laundry appliances provide useful horizontal space on which to lay clothes.

Floor and wall finishes in bathrooms are usually resistant to high humidities.

Usually, additional plumbing costs are minimal.

The bathroom sink may be used for hand washing.

Mechanical ventilation can be provided economically for both functions.

Disadvantages

A bathroom will usually accommodate only washing and drying facilities. Other laundry-related activities such as ironing, will have to be carried out elsewhere in the dwelling.

Occupants may wish to use the bathroom when laundry is being washed or dried.

Laundry in Combination with Kitchen

Advantages

Suitable in housing for young families because the person doing the laundry can keep an eye on the washing machine while doing other jobs and supervising the children.

Direct access to the outside for clothes drying is likely to be easier than from laundries located in a basement or on a second story.

LAUNDRY/SEWING ROOMS

Laundry Room Layouts

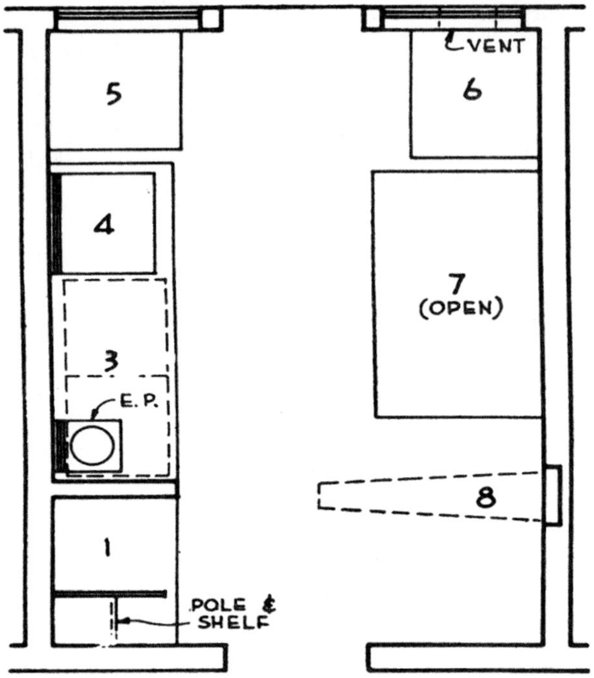

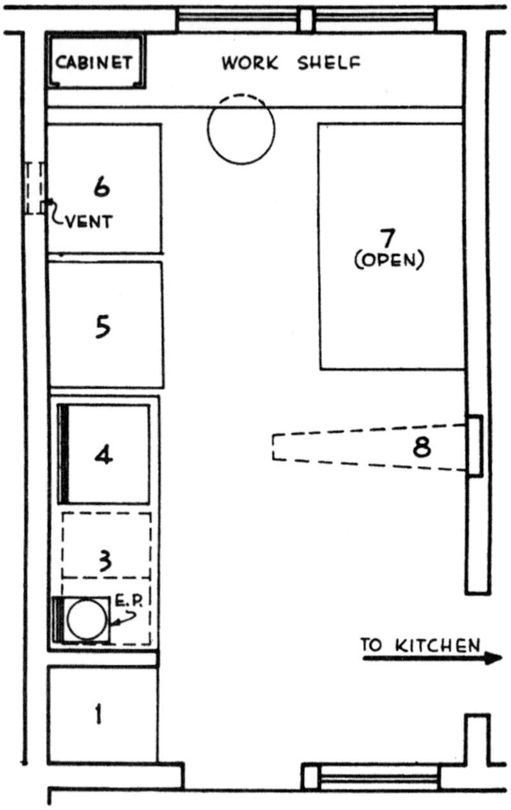

KEY

1. STORAGE CLOSET
2. CLOTHES CHUTE
3. SORTING SHELF
4. LAUNDRY TRAY
5. WASHING MACHINE
6. DRYER
7. IRONER
8. IRONING BOARD

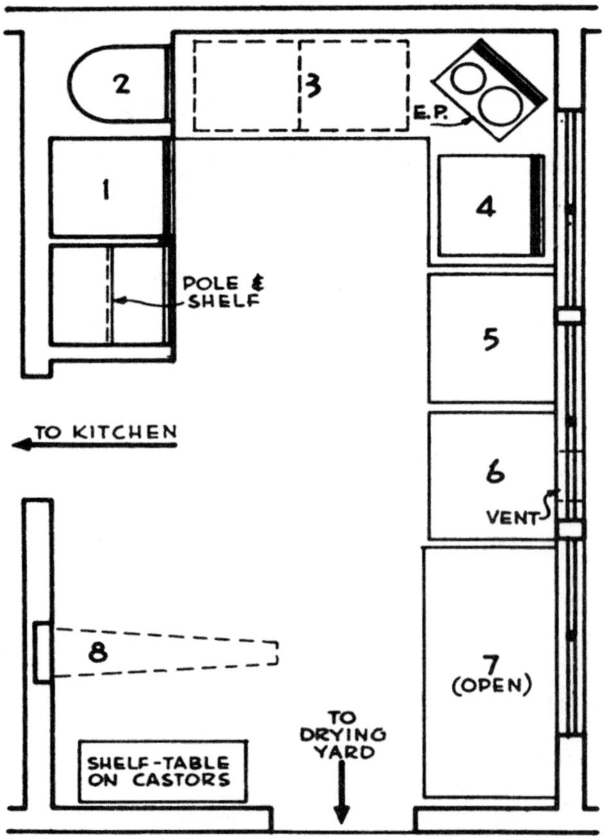

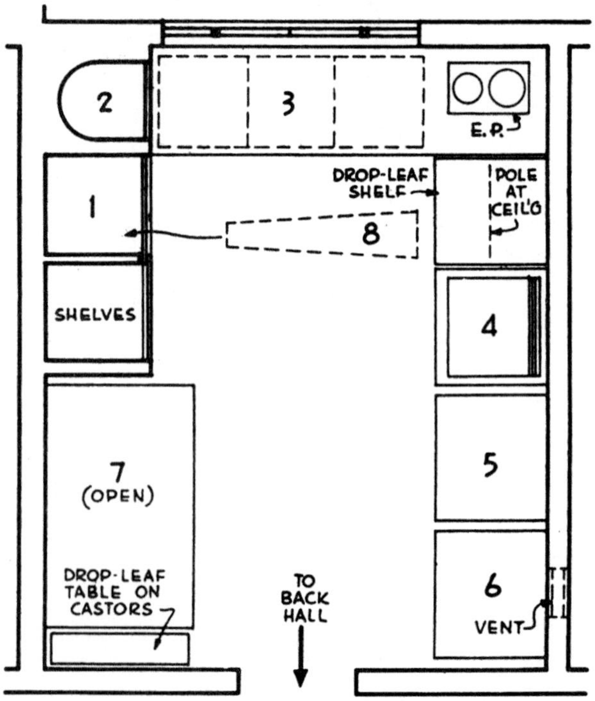

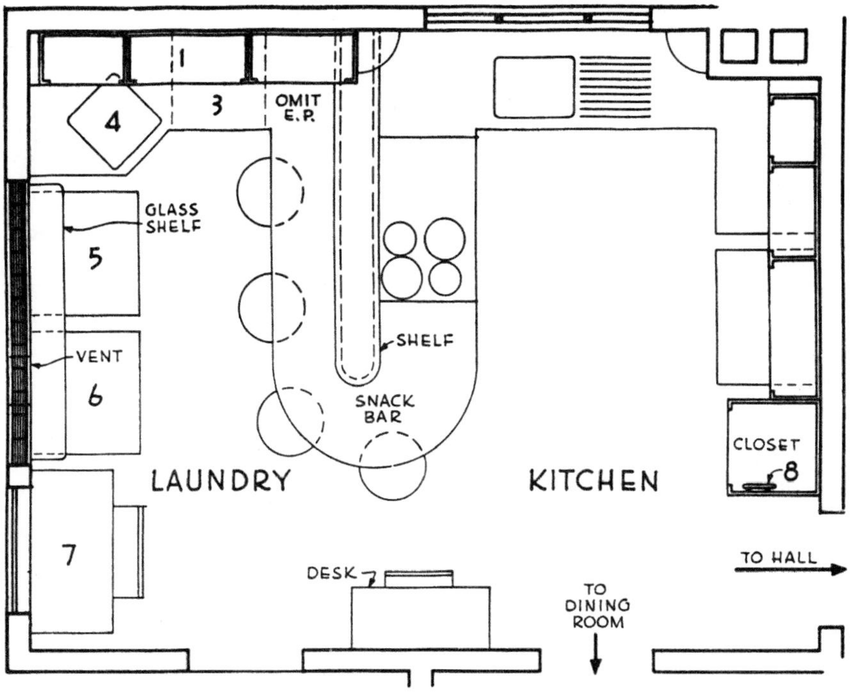

KEY

1. STORAGE CLOSET
2. CLOTHES CHUTE
3. SORTING SHELF
4. LAUNDRY TRAY
5. WASHING MACHINE
6. DRYER
7. IRONER
8. IRONING BOARD

KITCHEN AND LAUNDRY LAYOUT

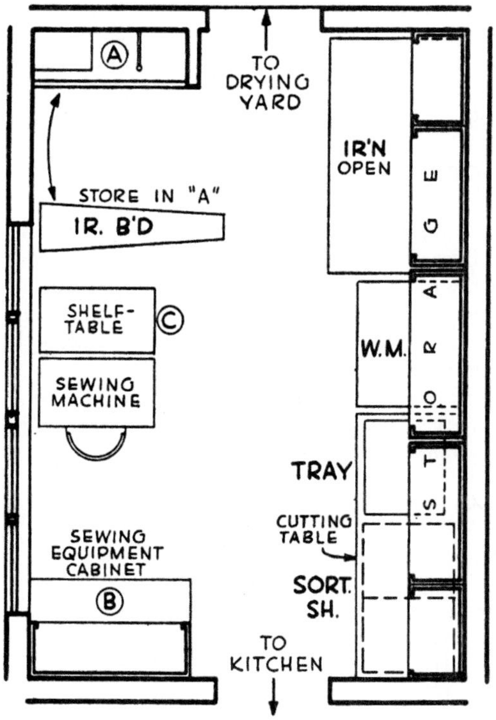

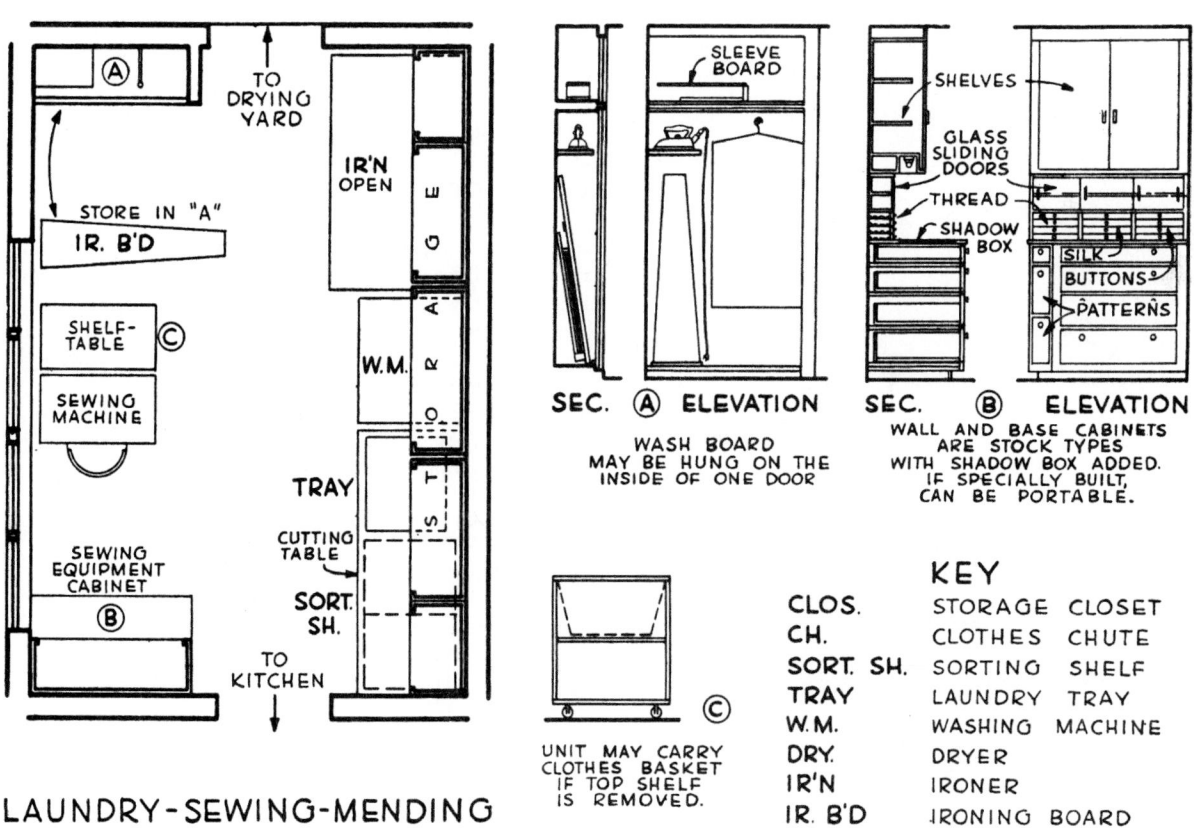

LAUNDRY-SEWING-MENDING

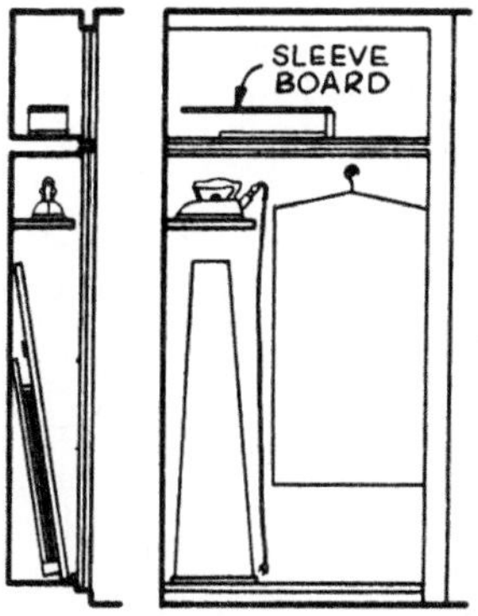

SEC. Ⓐ ELEVATION

WASH BOARD MAY BE HUNG ON THE INSIDE OF ONE DOOR

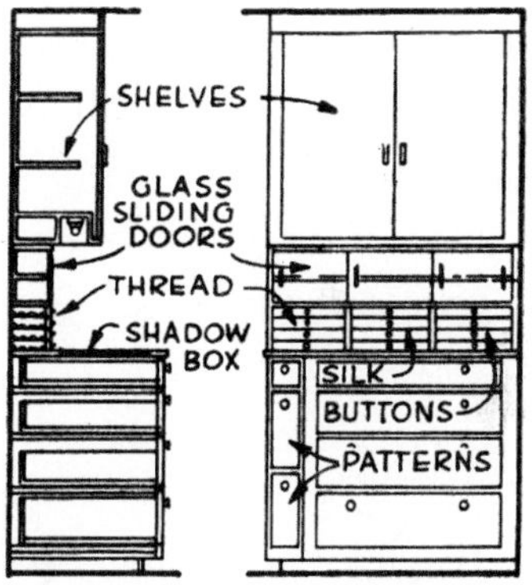

SEC. Ⓑ ELEVATION

WALL AND BASE CABINETS ARE STOCK TYPES WITH SHADOW BOX ADDED. IF SPECIALLY BUILT, CAN BE PORTABLE.

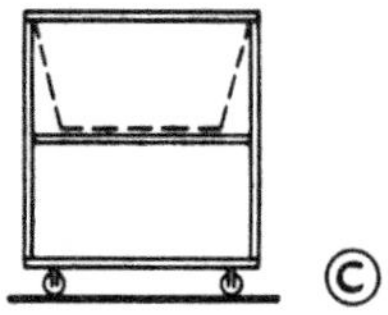

Ⓒ

UNIT MAY CARRY CLOTHES BASKET IF TOP SHELF IS REMOVED.

KEY

CLOS.	STORAGE CLOSET
CH.	CLOTHES CHUTE
SORT. SH.	SORTING SHELF
TRAY	LAUNDRY TRAY
W.M.	WASHING MACHINE
DRY.	DRYER
IR'N	IRONER
IR. B'D	IRONING BOARD

LAUNDRY/SEWING ROOMS
Sewing Center Clearances

Kitchen sinks are usually sizeable and can be used for laundering. Additional plumbing costs are usually small.

Disadvantages

Danger of cross-contamination through the handling of dirty washing during food preparation.
Grease and cooking smells can be passed on to clean clothes.
Noise generated by running appliances cannot easily be shut off from the rest of the dwelling.

Laundry in Combination with Utility Space in Basement

Advantages

Generally, as much space as needed can be provided.
Noise generated by running appliances can be easily shut off from the rest of the dwelling.

Disadvantages

Laundry must be carried up and down stairs, although automatic dryers have eased the problem of carrying heavy baskets of damp clothes to outdoor clotheslines.

Laundry in Combination with Corridor

Advantages

The space is used more economically (Fig. 9).
The space above the appliances may be used as a linen closet.
The appliances can be hidden from sight when they are not in use; they can be recessed into the wall and enclosed with doors.

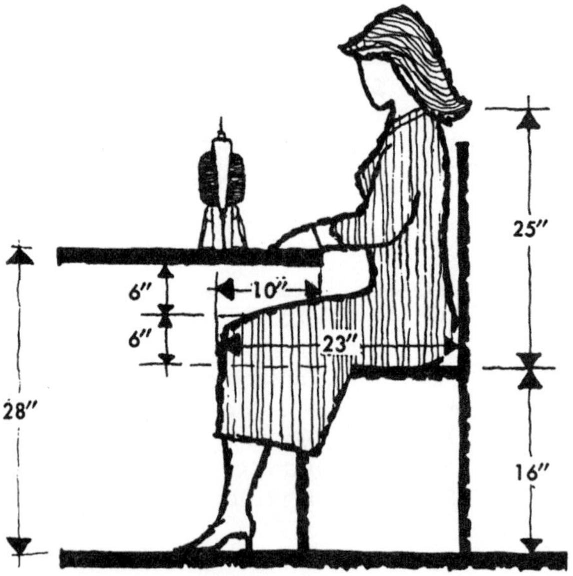

Fig. 13 Mean heights and clearances for sewing machine use

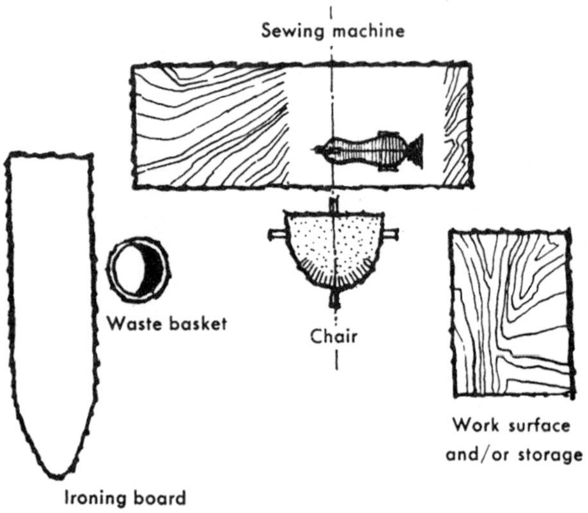

Fig. 14 Arrangement of sewing equipment based on flow of work

Disadvantages

Noise generated by running appliances cannot be easily shut off from the rest of the dwelling.
An alcove adjacent to a corridor will accommodate only a minimum-sized laundry area. Other laundry-related activities, such as ironing, will have to be carried out elsewhere in the dwelling.

Planning for Efficiency

The sequence of laundering operations determines the planning of space and facilities and the placing of equipment. Convenience and time-and-step saving are easily achieved by placing the elements in their natural order of use: (1) clothes chute (with or without bins or hampers), (2) sorting table or counter, (3) washing machine, (4) laundry trays, (5) dryer, (6) ironer or mangle, (7) ironing board, (8) rack, "horse," or table for finished laundry. In addition, storage closet or cabinets will be necessary for soaps, powders, bluing, bleaches, starch, basket, clothespins, iron, and so on.

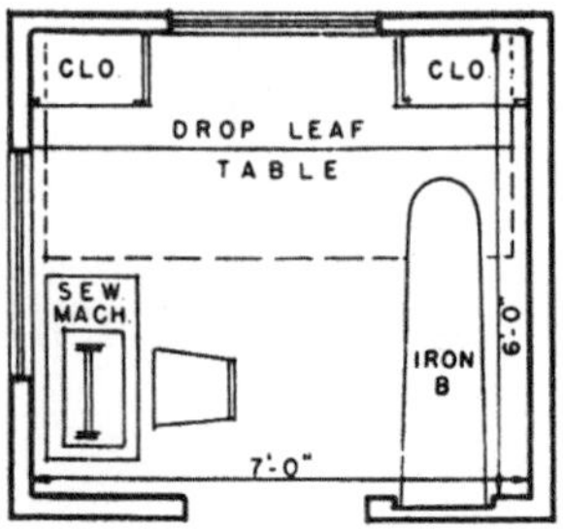

Fig. 15 Sewing room

TABLE 2 Dimensions of Area for Layout and Cutting Garments

Measurement	Dimensions, in	
	Minimum	Adequate
Working surface		
Length	56	72
Width		
Table, free-standing	28	36
Table obstructed on one side	28	32
Height	34–40 (range)	36 (median)
Clearance for worker	18	24

TABLE 3 Dimensions of Fitting Space

Use of Space	Minimum	Adequate
Viewing in mirror:		
Mirror dimensions, in		
Width	16	18
Length	42	60
Top to floor	70	72
Clearance in front of mirror, ft		
Width	3	4
Length	6–8	10
Clearance while fitting self, ft	6 × 4	
Clearance while being fitted, ft	8½ × 4	
Fitting garment on dress form, ft	5 × 4	7 × 6

SEWING CENTER CLEARANCES

General Planning Suggestions

1. An area especially planned for sewing, convenient to other activity areas, is desirable.
2. Most houses need storage space for sewing materials and equipment. The amount and kind of storage required varies according to the quality and frequency of sewing.
3. A minimum sewing area should include the machine, auxiliary work surfaces, a chair that permits freedom of motion, and storage arrangements. The work surface for layout and cutting may be outside the area for sewing machine operations and serve multiple purposes.
4. Consideration should be given to work surfaces at comfortable heights for the varying activities of sewing.
5. Light should be adequate for the activity.

CLOSETS/STORAGE AREAS
Anthropometric Data

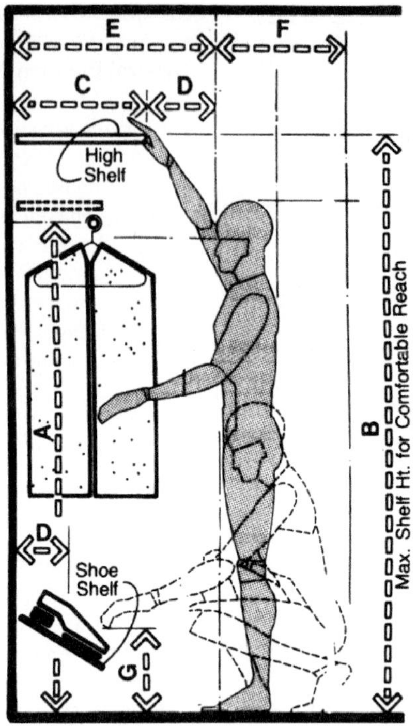

Fig. 1 Closet and storage facilities: male

CLOSETS/STORAGE AREAS

Figures 1 and 2 show the vertical clearances related to male and female closet and storage facilities. Wherever possible or practical, the closet shelf should be located within human reach. The height shown for the high shelf has been established based on fifth-percentile male and female data in order to place it within reach of individuals of smaller body size. Any shelf located at a greater distance should be used primarily for storage that requires only infrequent access. The location of the shelf just above the rod is essentially a function of rod height. The clearance between the bottom of the shelf and the top of the rod should allow for easy removal of the hanger.

Figure 3 illustrates two various types of walk-in storage facilities. Undoubtably, it can be argued that the 36-in, or 91.4-cm, clearance shown between the hanging garment and the storage shelf or between opposite garments could be reduced about 50 percent. The authors contend, however, that in order to achieve any degree of comfort in the selection and removal of the desired garment, a minimum of 36 in. shold be maintained. The degree to which this dimension can be reduced is a question of the level of comfort the user is prepared to tolerate in exchange for the floor space saved. The two drawings of the plan view of the human figure illustrate clearances required for donning a coat or putting on a pair of stockings.

Clothes Closet

The capacity of a clothes closet depends on h accessible length of rod. Three types of closets are common.

Reach-in closet The minimum front-to-back depth of space for hanging clothes is 24 in. The accessible rod length is equal to the width of the door opening plus 6 in on each side.

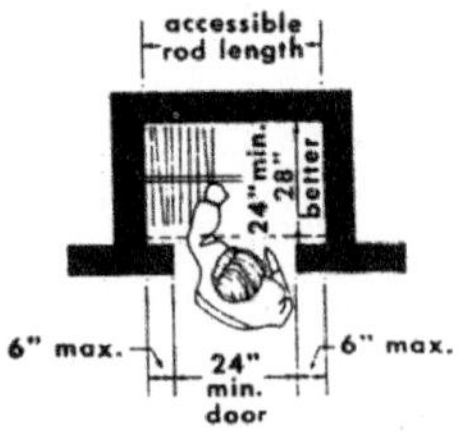

Edge-in closet By providing an edge-in space of at least 18 in the accessible rod length can be much longer than the door width. This requires less wall space than a full front opening.

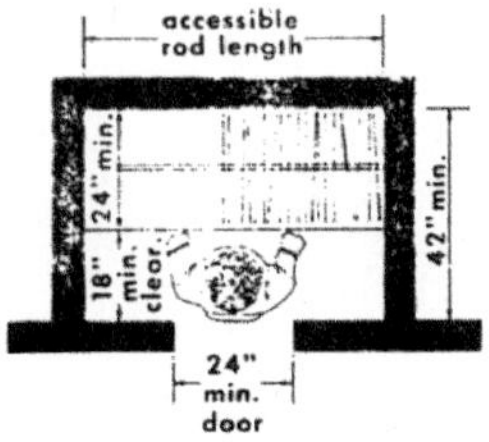

CLOSETS/STORAGE AREAS
Anthropometric Data

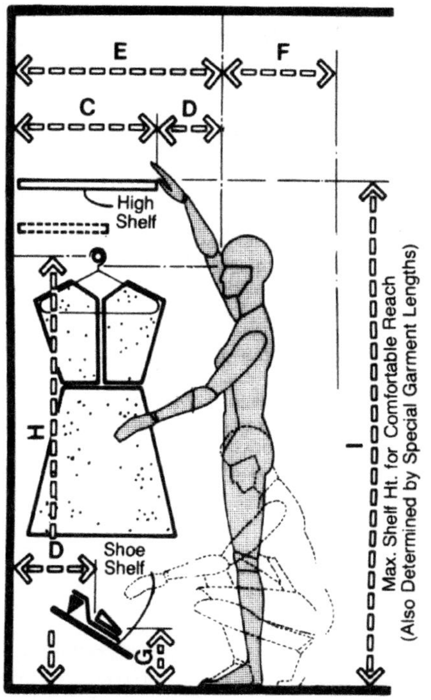

Fig. 2 Closet and storage facilities: female

Walk-in closet This type provides rods on one or borth sides of an access space within the closet may be used as a dressing area.

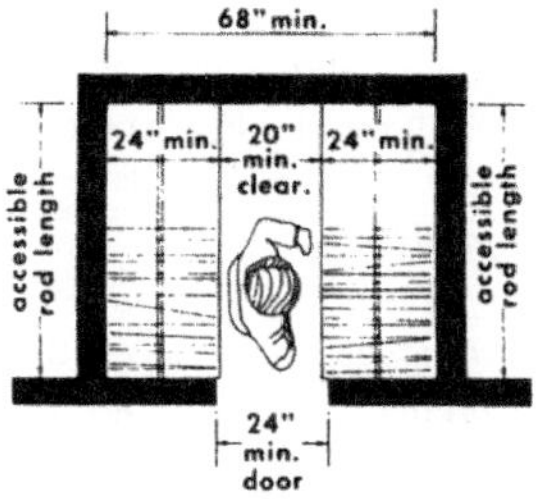

Rod Lengths and Heights

The Minimum Property Standards of HUD (1973) require that each bedroom have a closet, with rod and shelf, with minimum dimensions as follows:

Double-occupancy bedrooms: 24 in by 60 in
Single-occupancy bedrooms: 24 in by 36 in
Closet at entrance to house: 24 in by 24 in

A more desireable front-to-back depth would be 28 in for bedroom closets and 30 in for entrance closets to accommodate bulky outer garments.

	in	cm
A	64–68	162.6–172.7
B	72–76	182.9–193.0
C	12–18	30.5–45.7
D	8–10	20.3–25.4
E	20–28	50.8–71.1
F	34–36	86.4–91.4
G	10–12	25.4–30.5
H	60–70	152.4–177.8
I	69–72	175.3–182.9
J	76	193.0
K	68	172.7
L	42	106.7
M	46	116.8
N	30	76.2
O	18	45.7

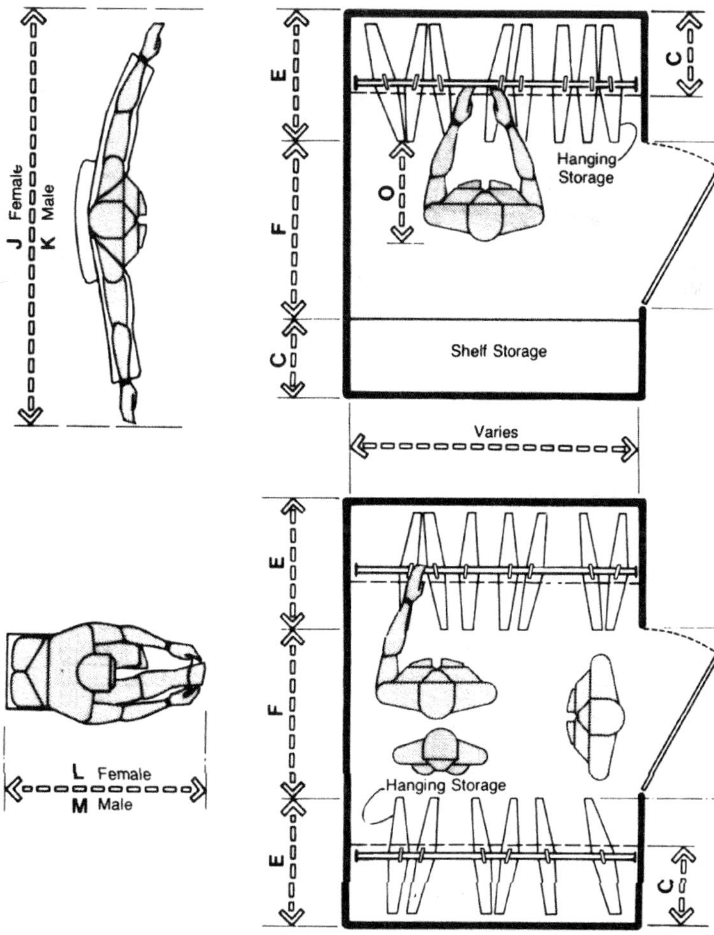

Fig. 3 Walk-in closet and storage facilities

CLOSETS/STORAGE AREAS

Types of Closets

The average rod space per garment is about 2 in for women's clothing, 2¼ in for men's clothing, and 4 in for heavy coats.

Recommended heights of rods are 68 i nfor long robes, 63 in for adult clothing, and 32 in for children's clothing.

Shelf Space and Lighting

The shelf is normally located 2 in above the rod and another shelf may be located 12 higher. Shelves higher than the rod may also be installed at the end of the closet.

A fluorescent fixture over the door is recommended for lighting a closet. Deluxe cool white tubes match daylight for selecting clothing

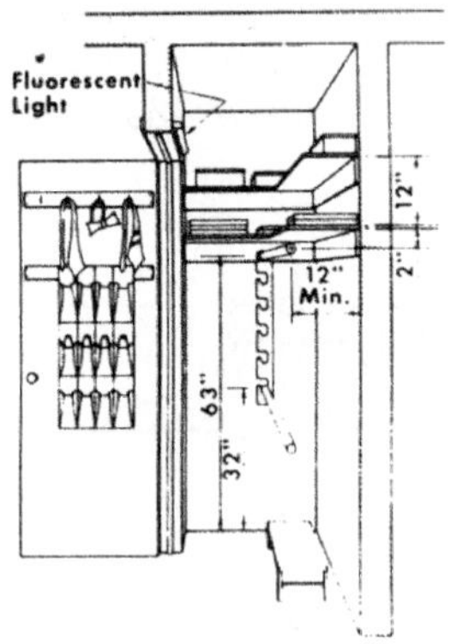

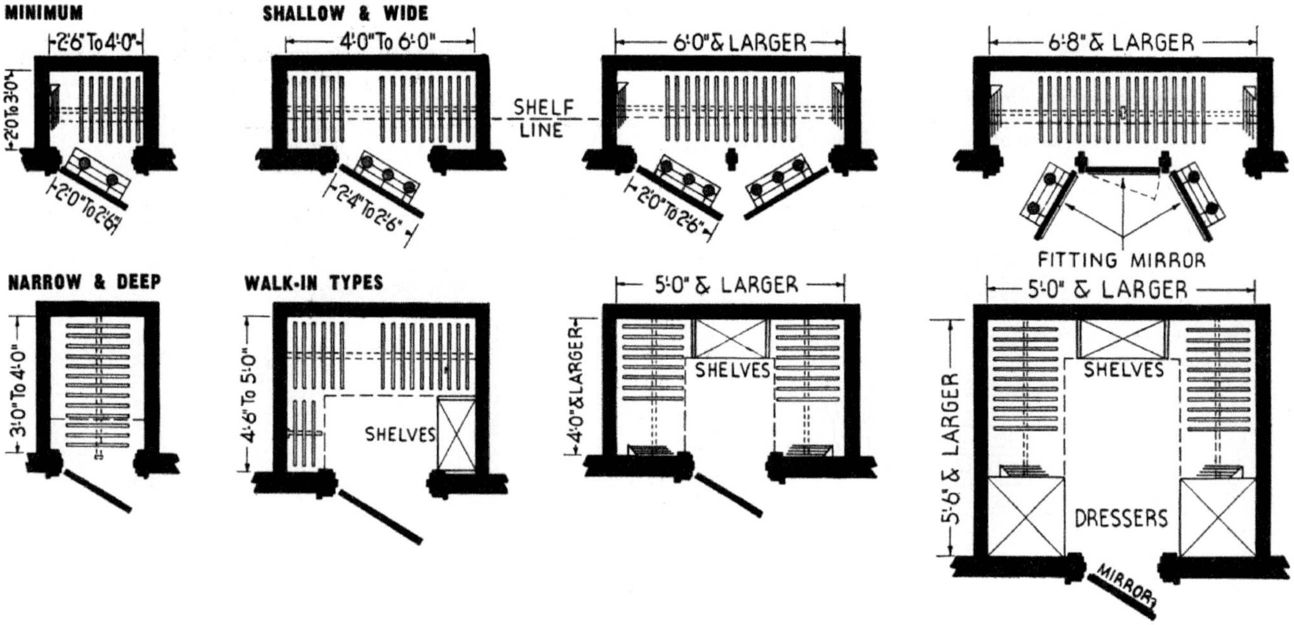

CLOSETS/STORAGE AREAS

Clothes Closet Details

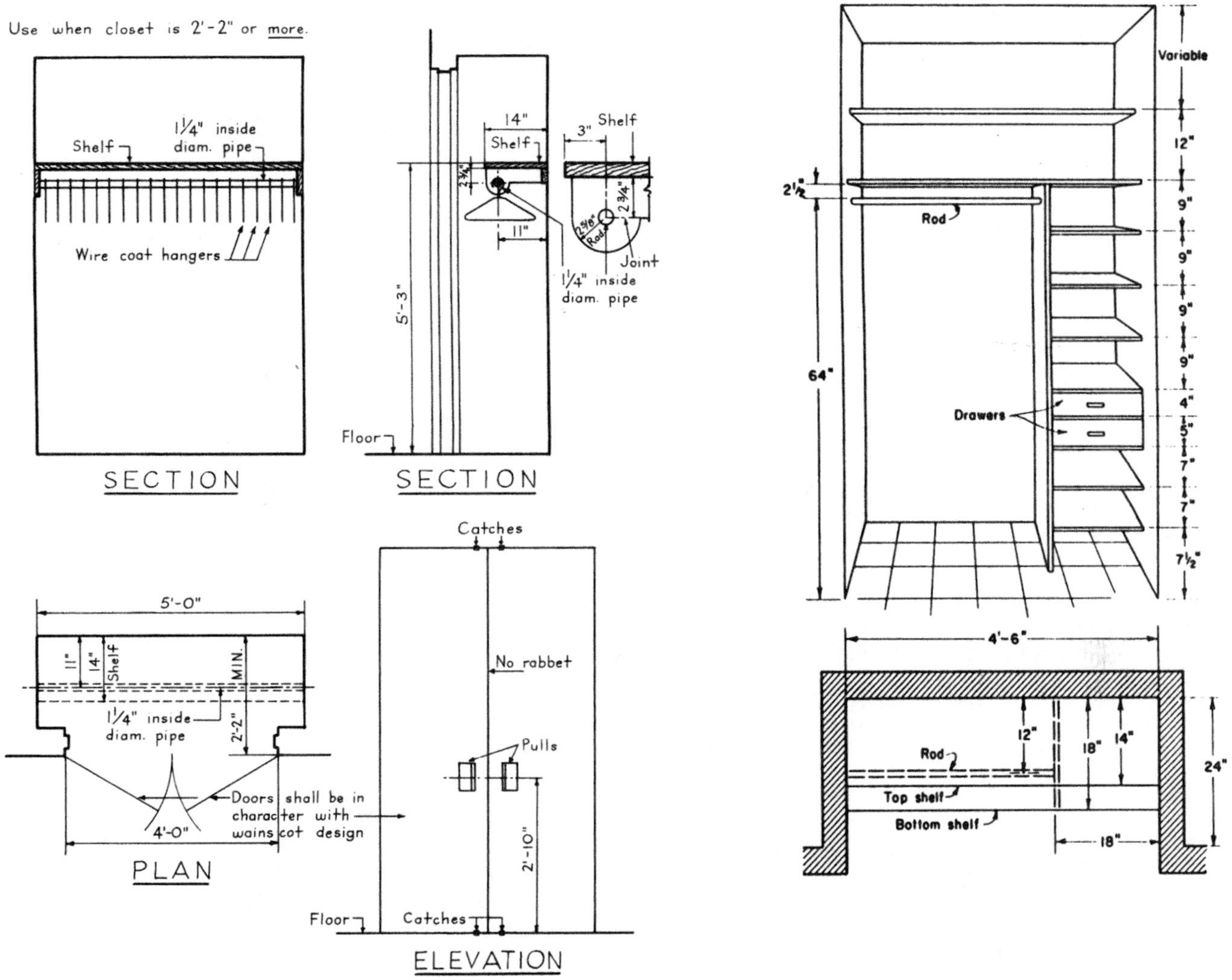

Fig. 4 Bedroom closet designed for one person. This diagram shows dimensions for rods, shelves, and drawers to hold underwear, sweaters, shoes, hats, purses, and ties. Research shows that each person needs at least 48 in of rod space for hanging clothing.

TABLE 1 Garment Dimensions

Men's garments	Allowance per garment, in	Women's garments	Allowance per garment, in
Heavy jackets and coats	3	Coats and jackets:	
Medium-weight jackets, coats, and raincoats	2	Heavy	3
Sweaters, light-weight jackets, and raincoats	1	Medium	2
Work pants:		Light	1
Folded on hanger	2¼	Sweaters	1¼
Hung full length	1¾	Other garments:	
Other garments:		Dress coats, winter	3½
Top coats	2½	Robes	2
Robes	2	Suits, wool (skirt under jacket)	2½
Suits (trousers full length under jacket)	3	Skirts	1
Trousers	1½	Jackets	2
Jackets	2	Blouses	1
Sweater jacket	1	House dresses	1¾
Shirts (all kinds)	1½	Other dresses:	
		Average	2
		Full-skirted	2½
		Straight-line	1¼

Men's garments	Range of lengths, in	Women's garments	Range of lengths, in
Suit jackets, other jackets, shirts	31–40	Blouses, jackets	25–35
Trousers:		Skirts, medium and short coats	31–43
Folded over hanger	29–37	Dresses, long coats, short robes	48–55
Full length	47–53	Long robes, long evening dresses	61–68
Overcoats, robes	48–54		

CLOSETS/STORAGE AREAS

Clothes Closet Details

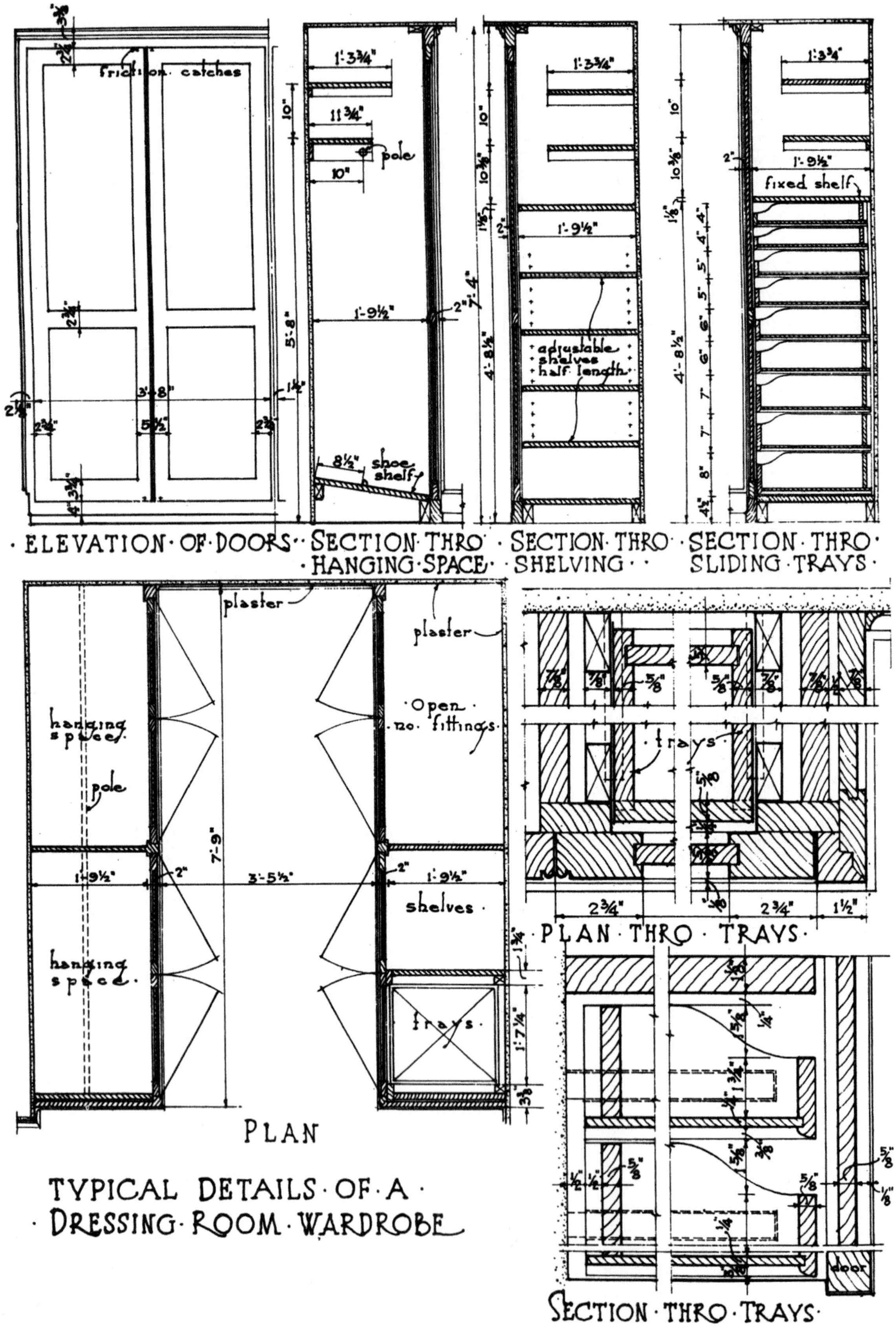

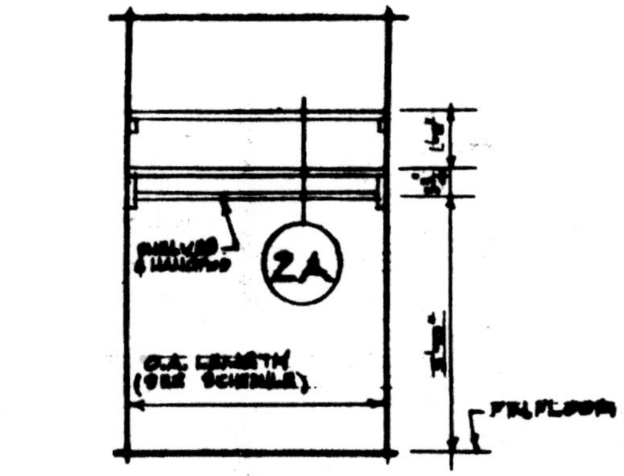

ELEVATION OF UNIT
@1/4"=1'-0"

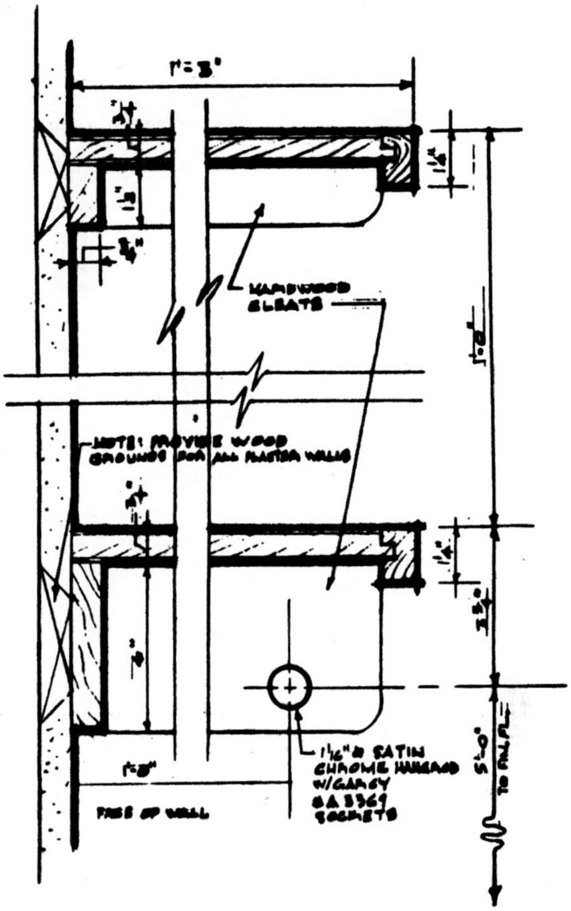

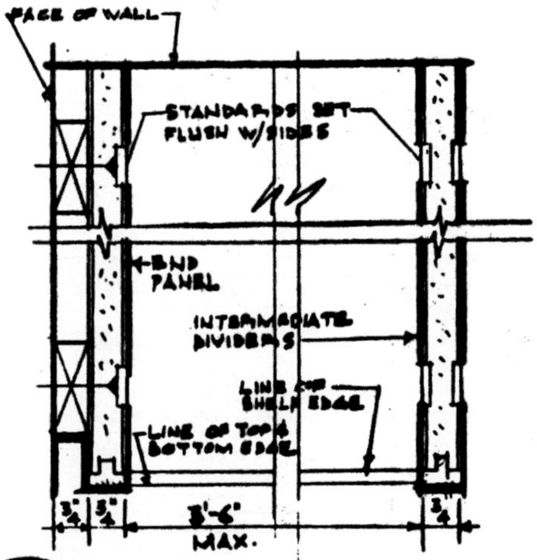

4D
@ 3"=1'-0"

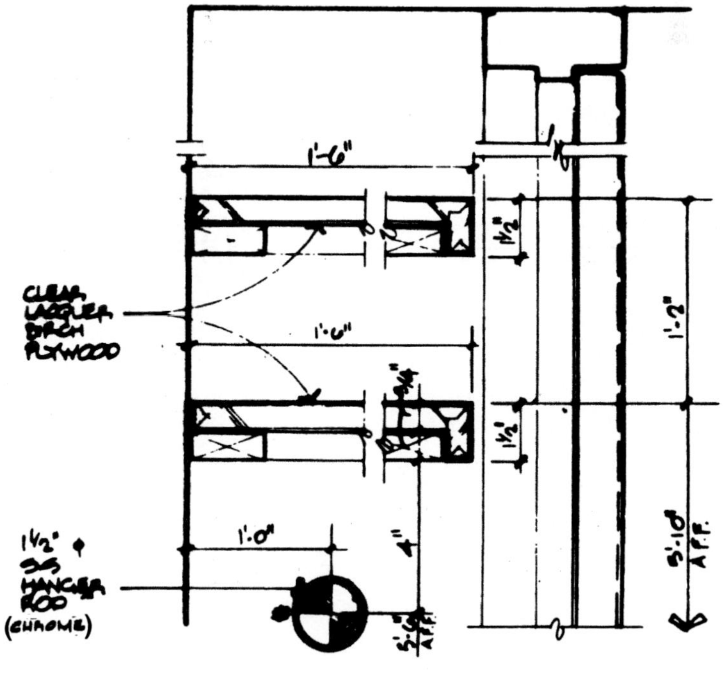

CLOSETS/STORAGE AREAS
Clothes Closet Details

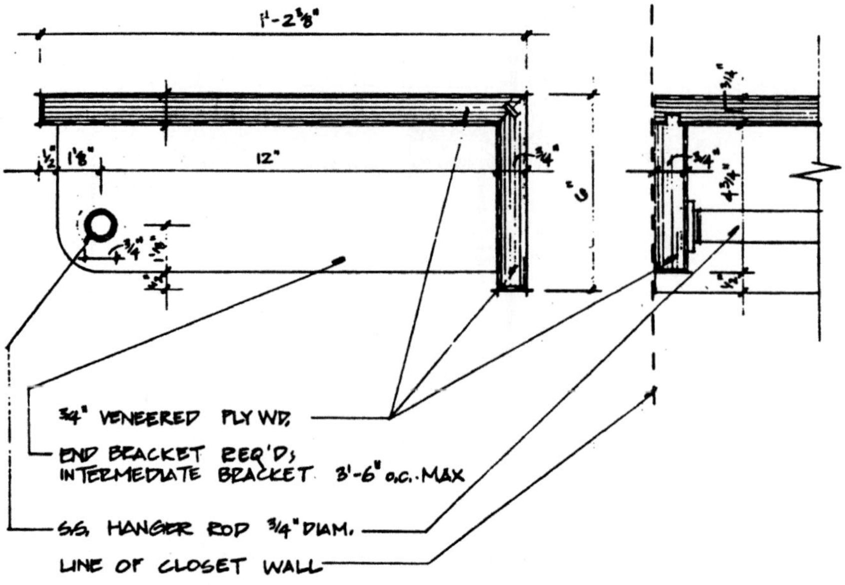

CLOSET SHELF DETAIL

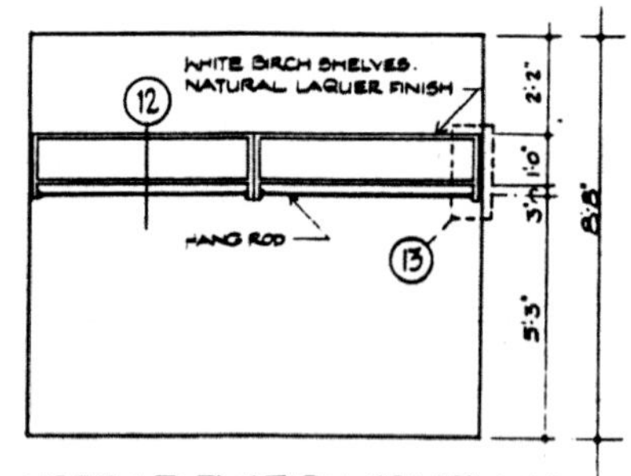

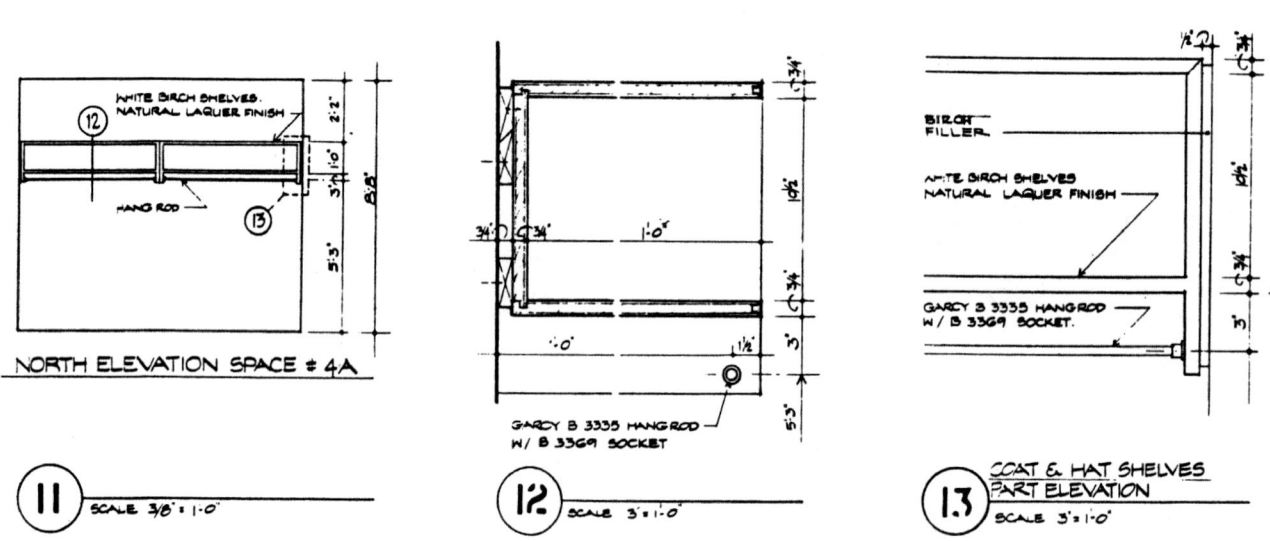

NORTH ELEVATION SPACE # 4A

11 SCALE 3/8" = 1'-0"

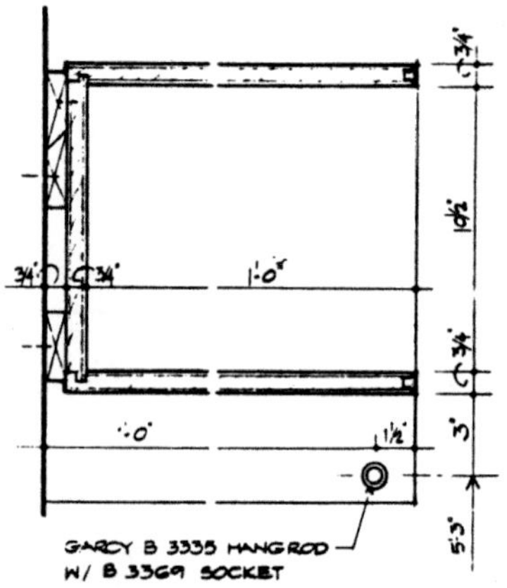

12 SCALE 3" = 1'-0"

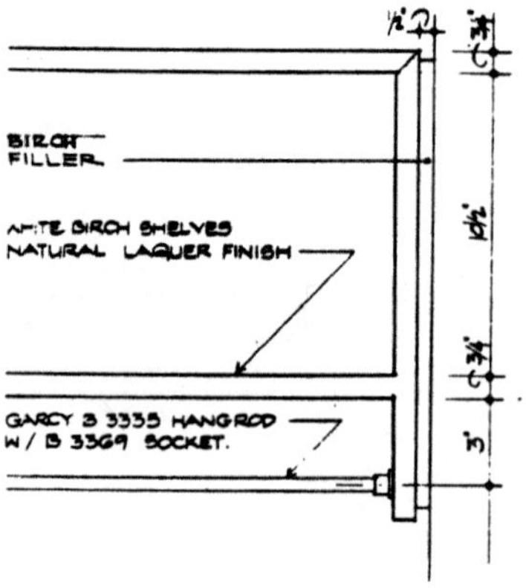

13 COAT & HAT SHELVES PART ELEVATION
SCALE 3" = 1'-0"

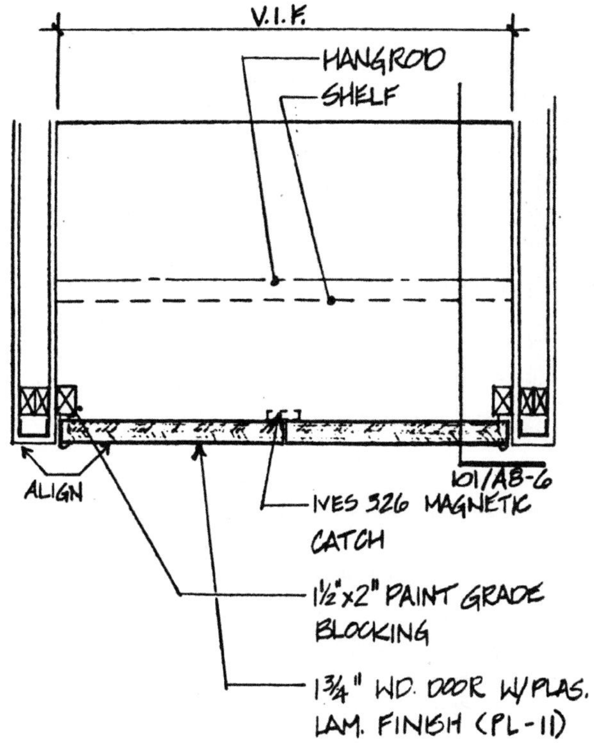

PLAN SECTION AT COAT CLOSET

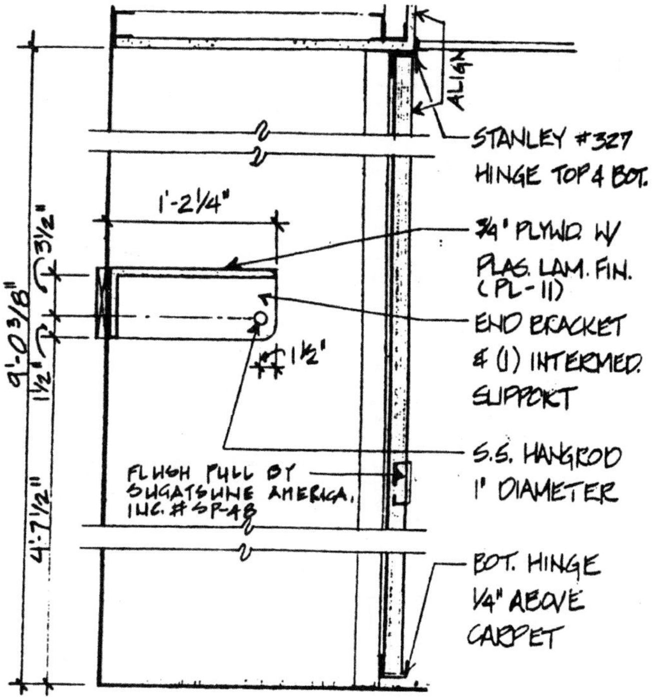

VERT. SECTION AT COAT CLOSET

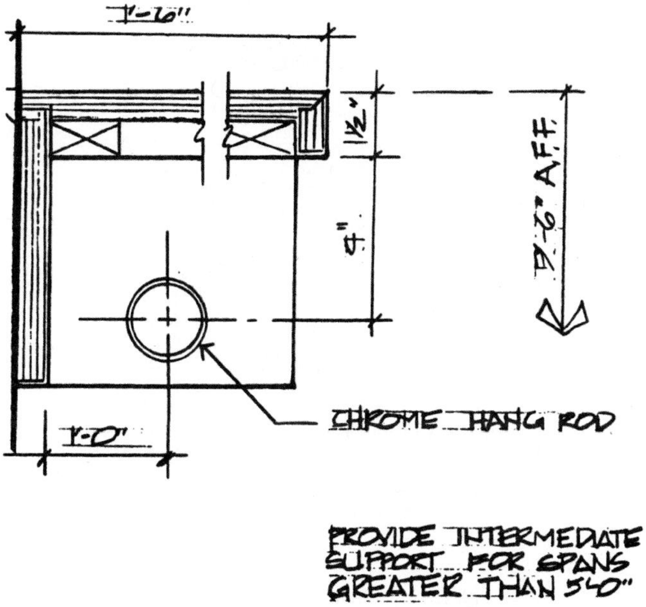

COAT CLOSET SHELF

CLOSETS/STORAGE AREAS
General Storage Shelving

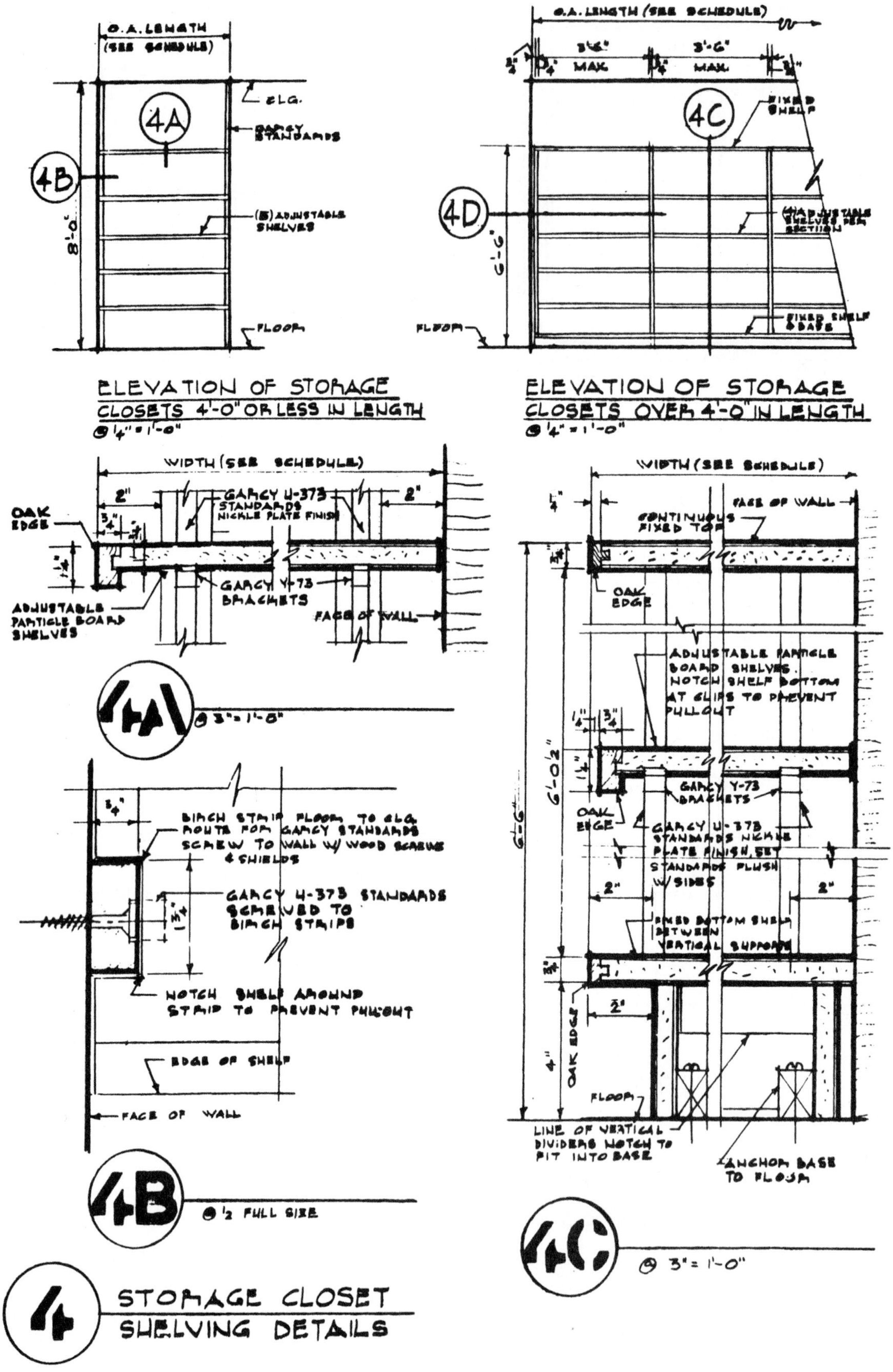

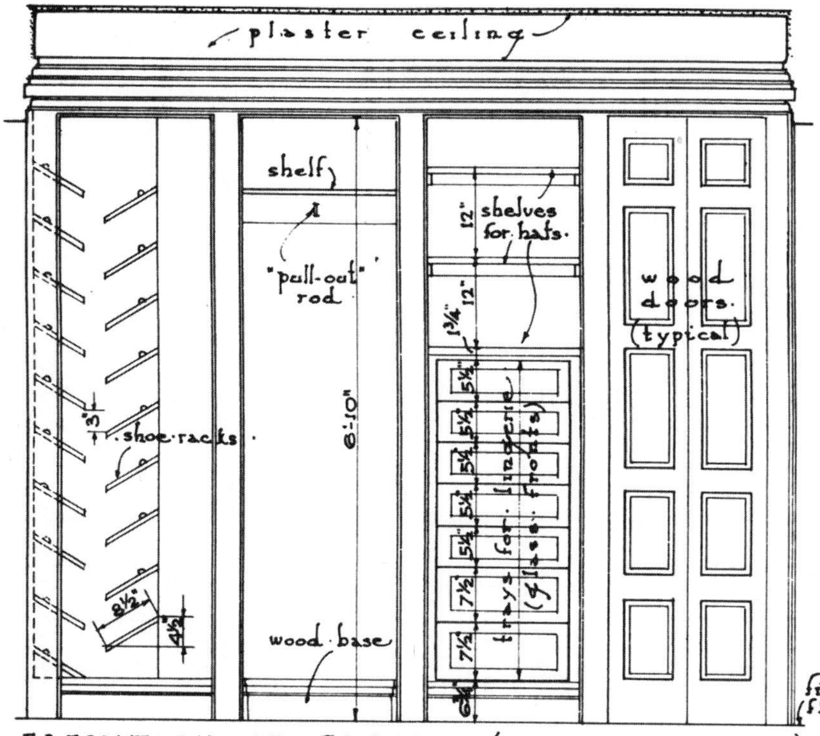

ELEVATION OF CLOSETS (DOORS REMOVED)

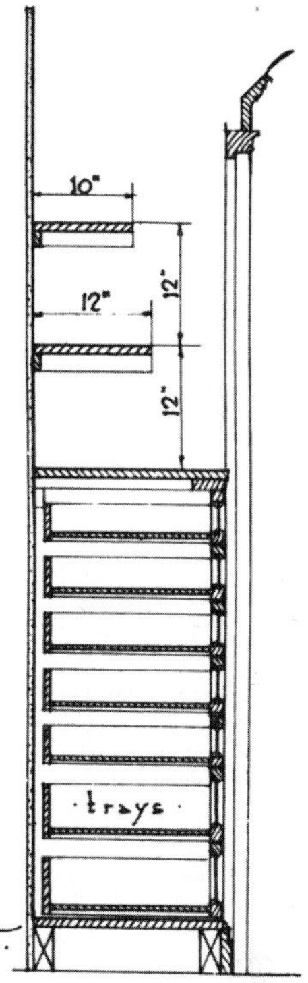

SECTION THRO TRAYS

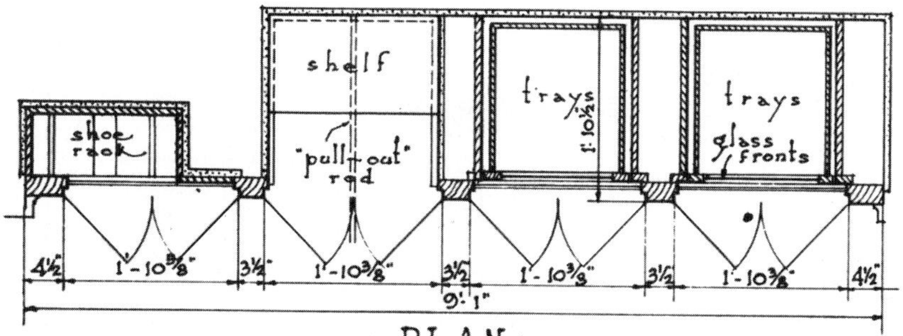

PLAN

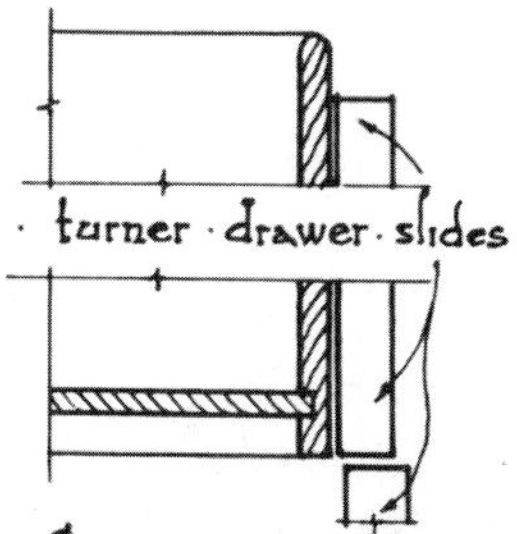

SECTION THRO SIDE OF TRAY

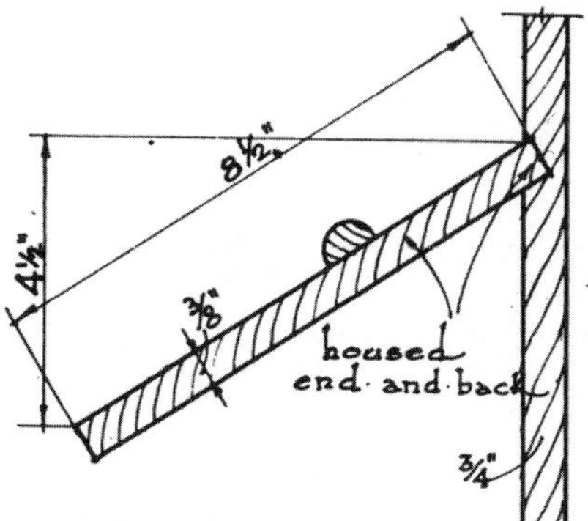

SECTION THRO SHOE SHELVING

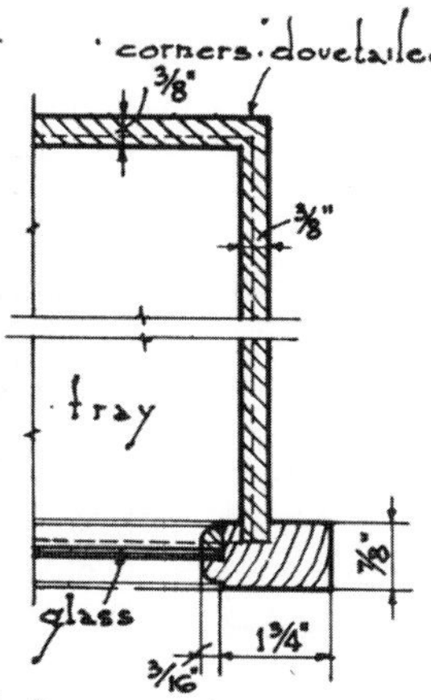

PLAN SECTION THRO TRAYS

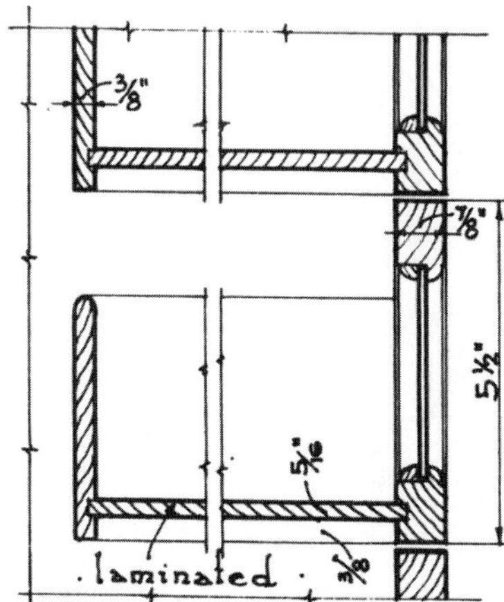

VERTICAL SECTION THRO TRAYS

CLOSETS/STORAGE AREAS

Closet Wall Details

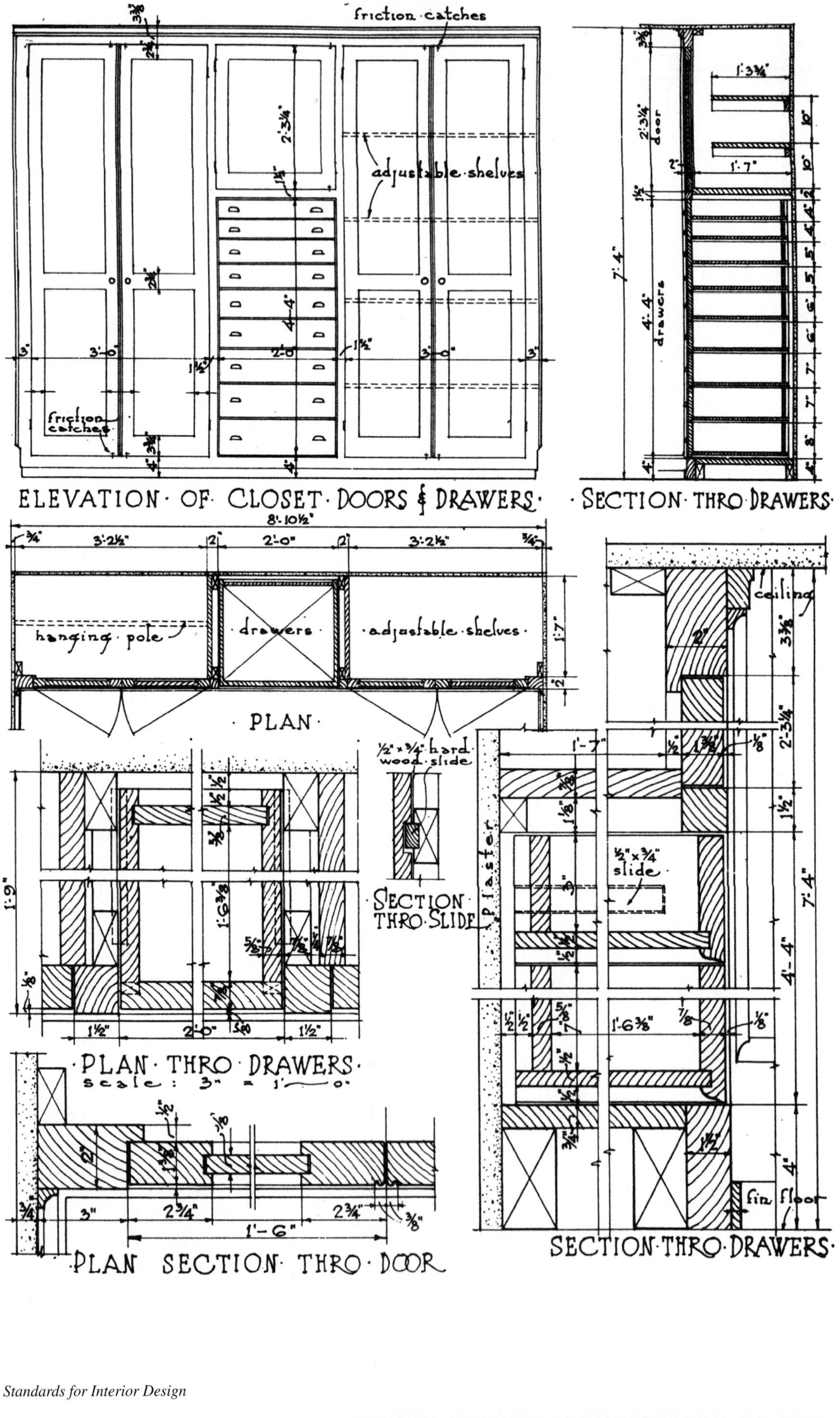

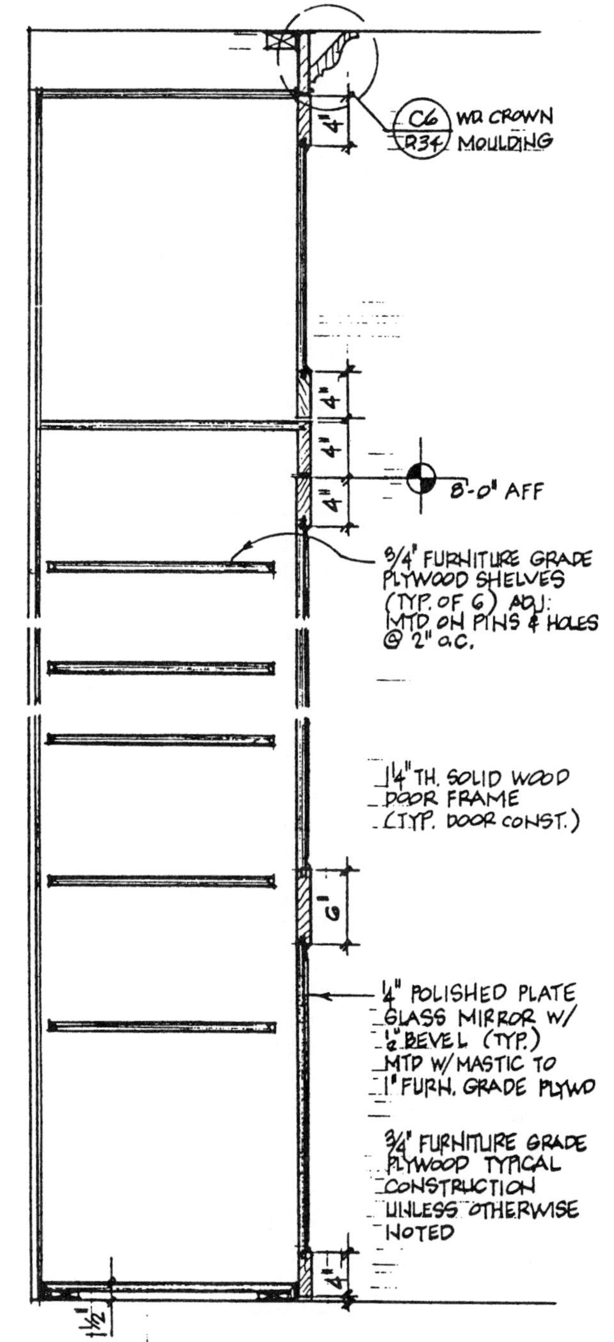
C6
R34
WD. CROWN MOULDING
4"
4"
4"
4"
8'-0" AFF
3/4" FURNITURE GRADE PLYWOOD SHELVES (TYP. OF 6) ADJ. MTD ON PINS & HOLES @ 2" O.C.
1 1/4" TH. SOLID WOOD DOOR FRAME (TYP. DOOR CONST.)
6"
1/4" POLISHED PLATE GLASS MIRROR W/ 1/2" BEVEL (TYP.) MTD W/ MASTIC TO 1" FURN. GRADE PLYWD
3/4" FURNITURE GRADE PLYWOOD TYPICAL CONSTRUCTION UNLESS OTHERWISE NOTED
4"
1 1/2"

3 Closet - Her Dressing

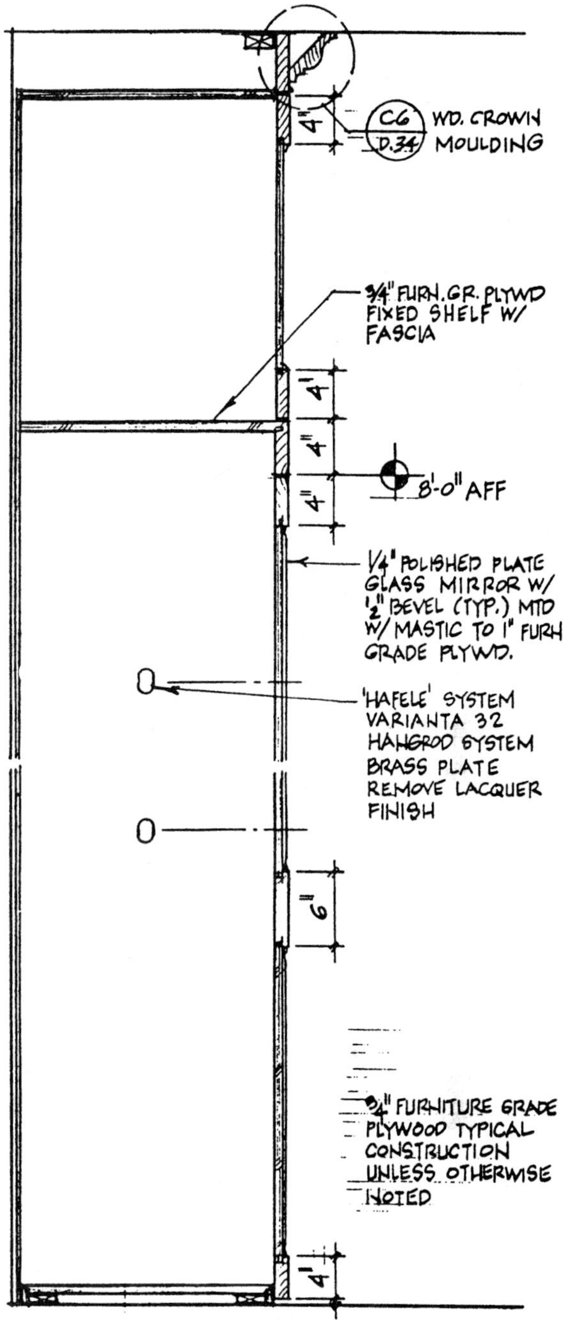
C6
D.34
WD. CROWN MOULDING
4"
3/4" FURN. GR. PLYWD FIXED SHELF W/ FASCIA
4'
4"
4"
8'-0" AFF
1/4" POLISHED PLATE GLASS MIRROR W/ 1/2" BEVEL (TYP.) MTD W/ MASTIC TO 1" FURN GRADE PLYWD.
'HAFELE' SYSTEM VARIANTA 32 HANGROD SYSTEM BRASS PLATE REMOVE LACQUER FINISH
6"
3/4" FURNITURE GRADE PLYWOOD TYPICAL CONSTRUCTION UNLESS OTHERWISE NOTED
4'

4 Closet - Her Dressing

CLOSETS/STORAGE AREAS
Clothes Closet Sections

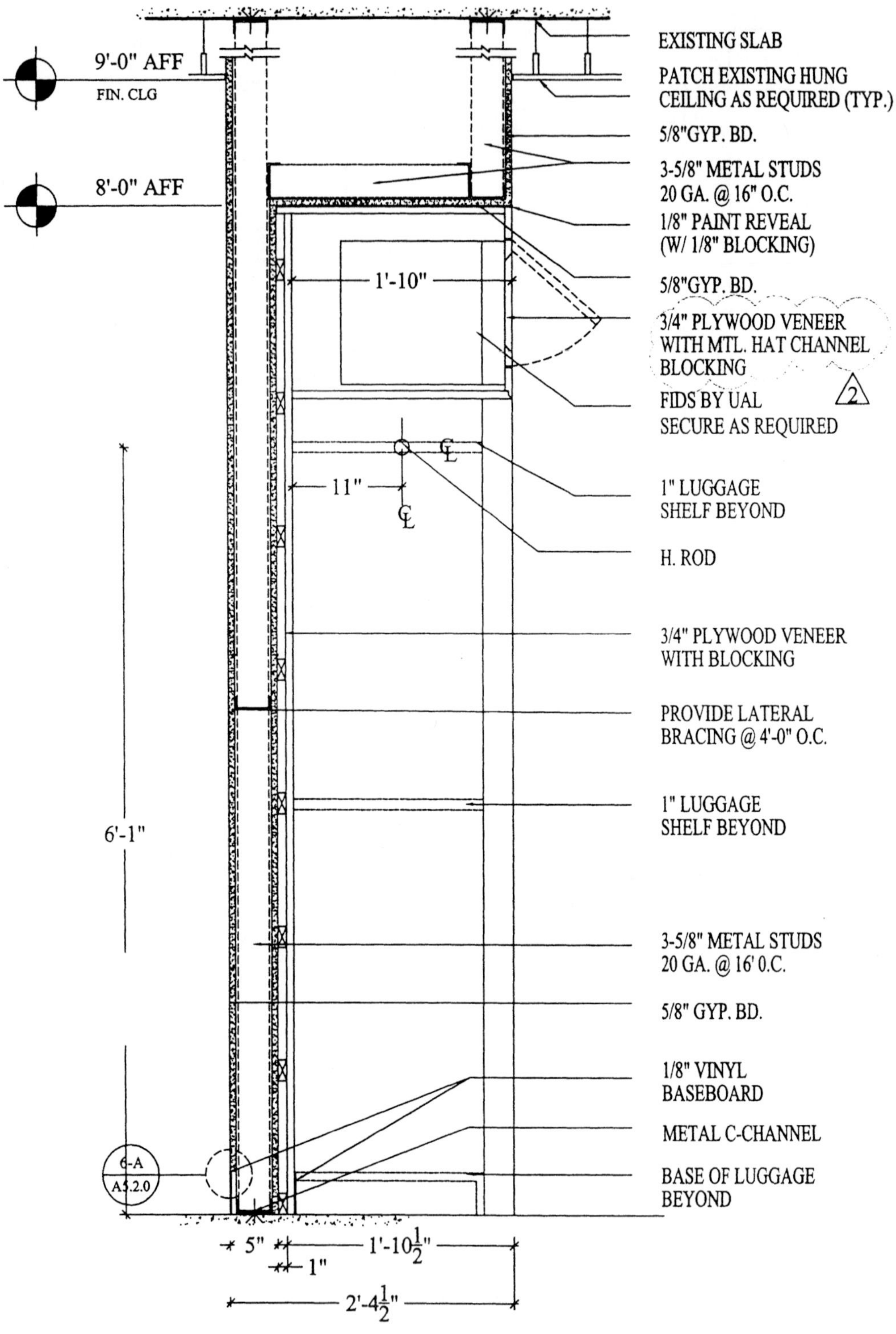

8 FIDS/ COAT CLOSET
3/4"=1'-0"

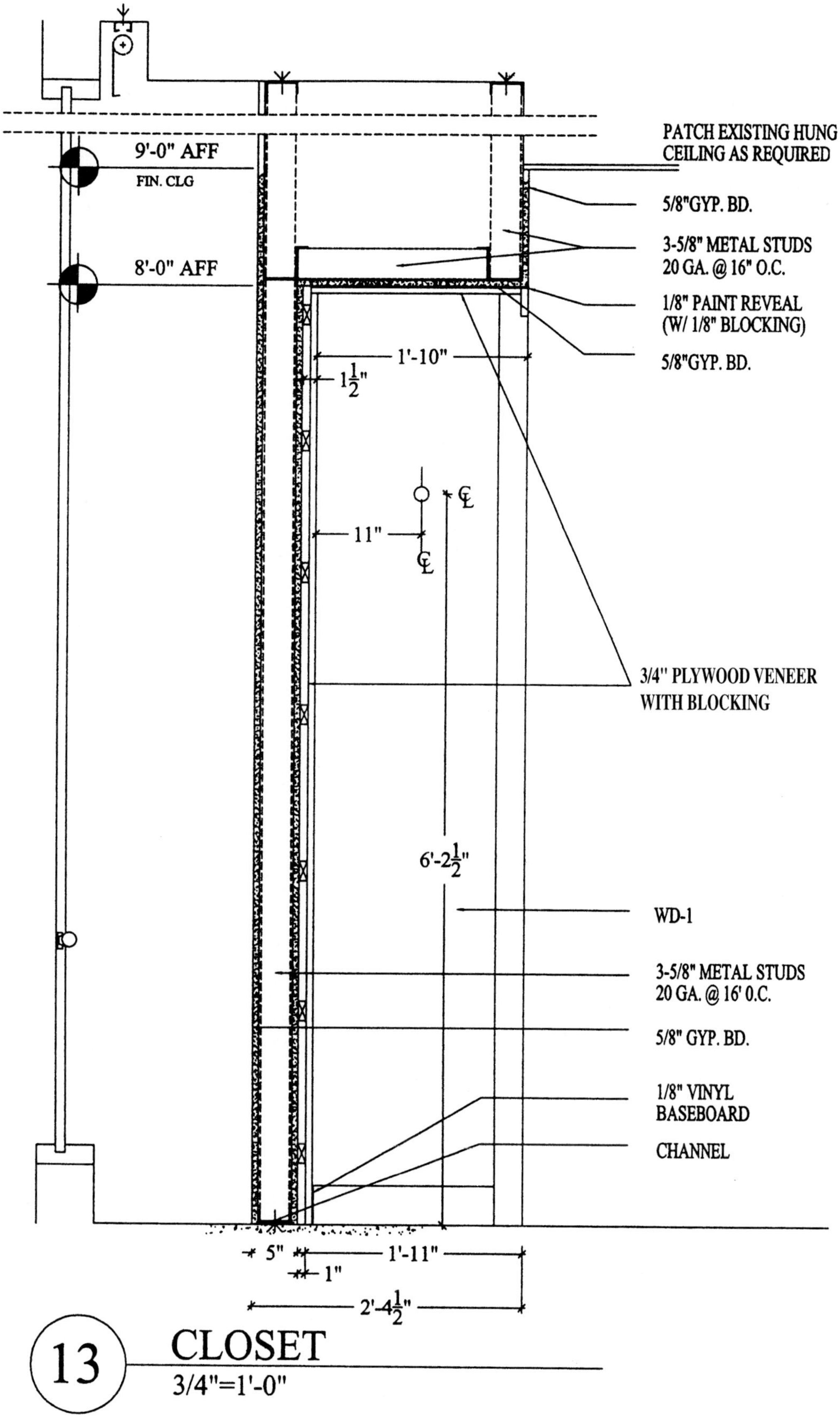
9'-0" AFF
FIN. CLG
8'-0" AFF
PATCH EXISTING HUNG CEILING AS REQUIRED
5/8"GYP. BD.
3-5/8" METAL STUDS 20 GA. @ 16" O.C.
1/8" PAINT REVEAL (W/ 1/8" BLOCKING)
5/8"GYP. BD.
1'-10"
1½"
11"
3/4" PLYWOOD VENEER WITH BLOCKING
6'-2½"
WD-1
3-5/8" METAL STUDS 20 GA. @ 16' 0.C.
5/8" GYP. BD.
1/8" VINYL BASEBOARD
CHANNEL
5"
1'-11"
1"
2'-4½"

13 CLOSET
3/4"=1'-0"

CLOSETS/STORAGE AREAS
Wire Basket and Shelving Systems

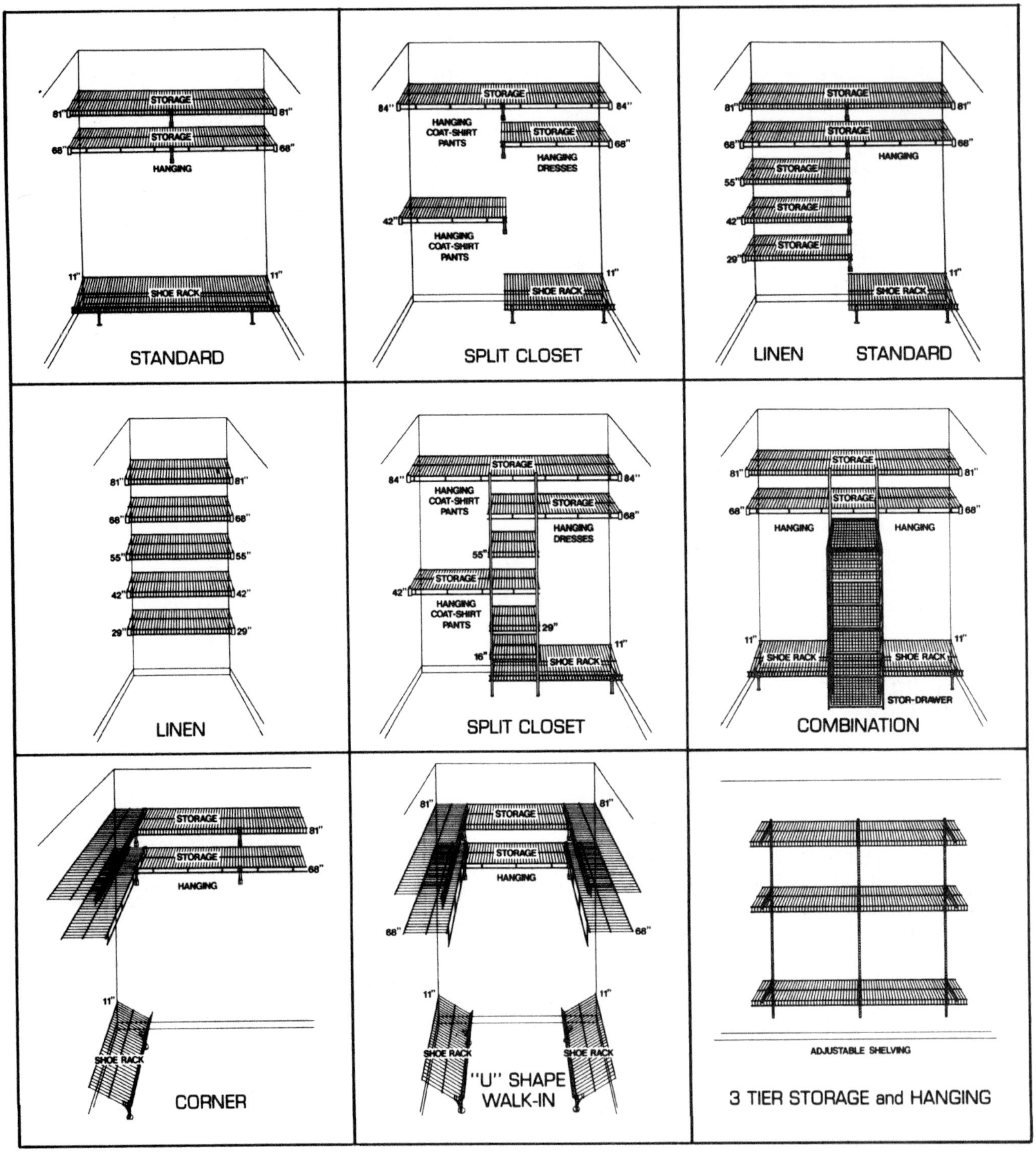

PANTRY

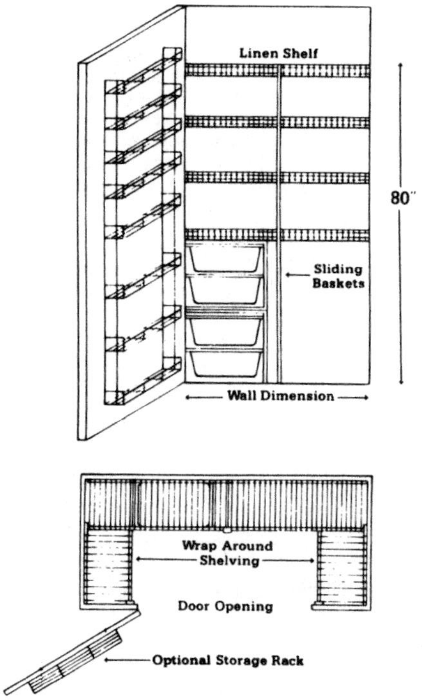

Front View
Multiple-stacked, wrap-around storage shelving. Optional baskets and door racks. (9", 12", 16" and 20" widths available)

Top View
All the shelving you'll ever need for full-size family food storage. Sliding baskets hold fruit, vegetables and other kitchen supplies. Optional door racks maximize storage area by utilizing all available space.

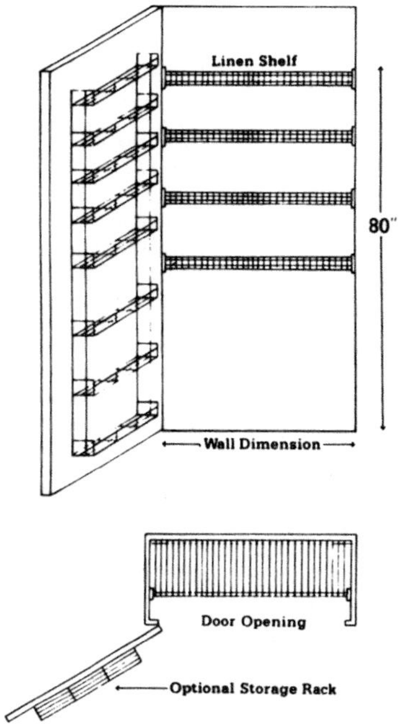

Front View
Multiple-stacked storage shelving. Optional full-height door storage rack. (9", 12", 16" and 20" widths available)

Top View
Standard pantry design provides ample shelving and storage for canned goods and other food items. Center pole gives extra support. Optional door racks provide easy access to your most needed items.

HOUSEKEEPING/UTILITY ROOM

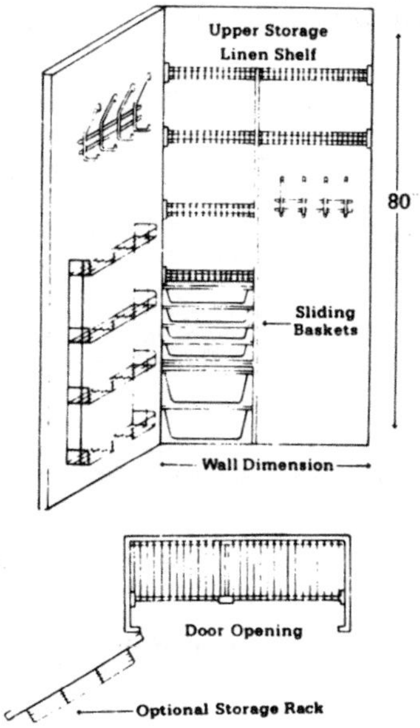

Front View
Double, full-width upper storage shelving with stacked storage shelving. (12", 16" widths available)

Top View
Makes housework easier to handle by storing household cleaning items just where you need them. Plenty of shelving space for cloths, detergents and brushes. Wide storage area holds vacuum cleaner, brooms, mops and small appliances.

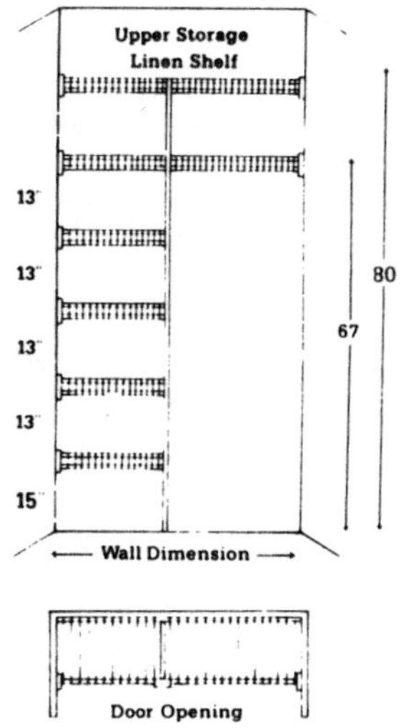

Front View
Double, full-width storage shelving with side-mounted shelving and basket unit and optional door/wall storage rack. (12", 16" widths available)

Top View
Make a clean sweep of cleaning with full-length shelves that hold a variety of utensils. Storage baskets pack brushes, cloths and sundry items. Bottled detergents and cleaning products can be stored neatly and safely in optional door racks.

CLOSETS/STORAGE AREAS
Wire Basket and Shelving Systems

BEDROOM APPLICATIONS

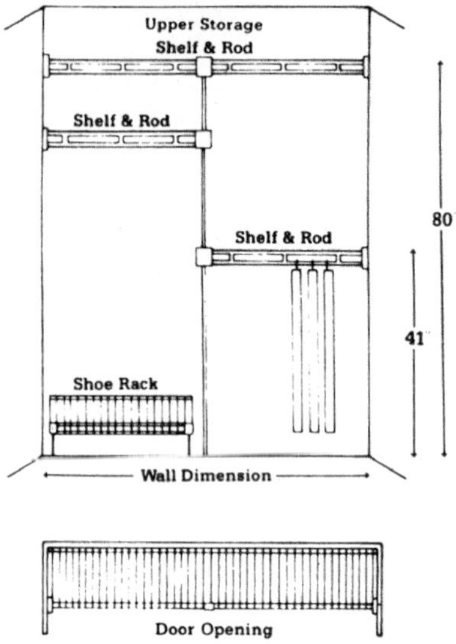

Front View
Single and double hang with upper storage, center pole support and shoe racks. (12", 16" widths available)

Top View
Combination convenience for single and double hanging clothes. The perfect his and hers closet. Extra wide shelf space for clothing, linen and blankets in your master bedroom. Plus lots of room for her long dresses and coats — his shirts, suits and slacks. Shoe racks on both sides.

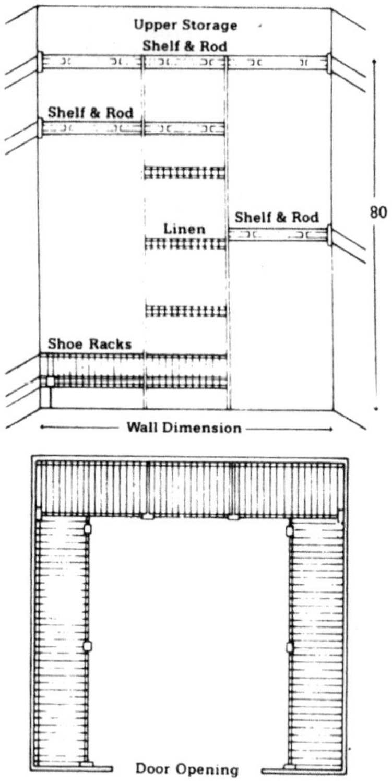

Front View
Walk-In. Single and double hang with upper storage and central shelving unit with additional clearance and shoe racks. (12", 16" widths available)

Top View
Single hanging space for coats and other long garments. Double hanging convenience for shorter garments. Full shelves with central storage unit allow easy storage of sweaters, boots, sports equipment, tall and over-sized items. Tailor-made for couples with a 2nd bedroom.

CHILDREN'S CLOSETS

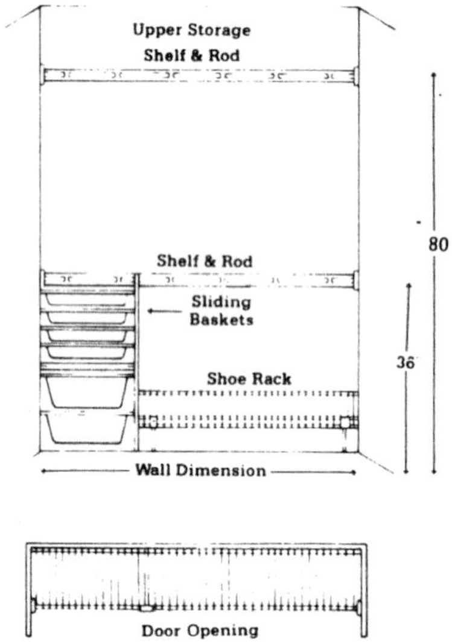

Front View
Full-width, double hanging with lower shelving height. Sliding basket system and shoe racks. (12", 16" widths available)

Top View
Specially designed for the children's room. Extra low-hanging shelf makes it easy for kids to reach. Stores toys and sports equipment in easy-access sliding baskets. Shoe rack keeps sneakers and other footwear neatly organized.

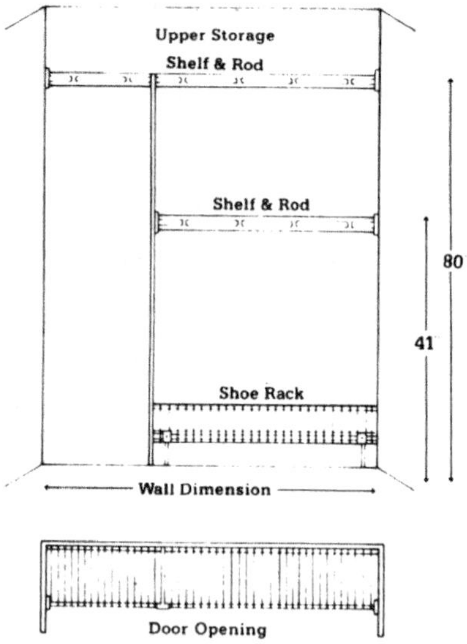

Front View
Standard. Double hang with shoe rack and off-center pole support. (12", 16" widths available)

Top View
Makes kids stuff out of chaos in any teen-ager's room. Plenty of storage space for footballs, beach equipment, basket-balls, skates and other cumbersome items. Doubles as storage area for dresses and coats. Conveniently placed hanging rod for all your teenager's clothing.

LINEN

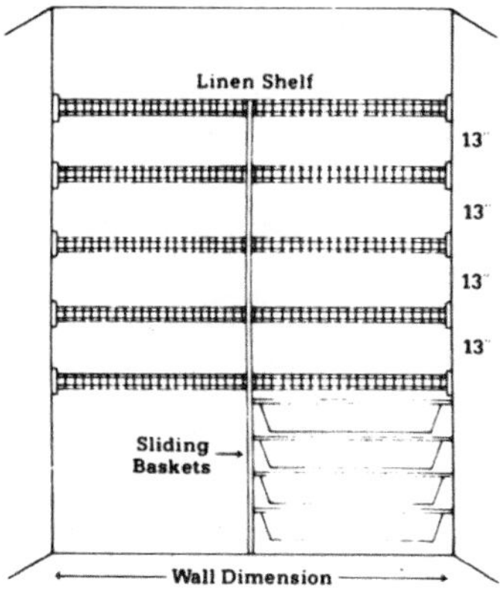

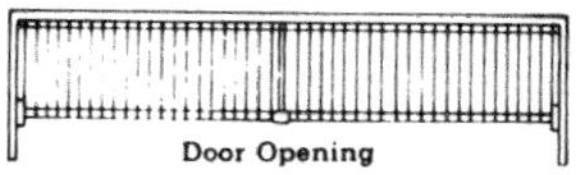

Front View
Multiple-stacked linen shelving with pole support and sliding basket system. (9", 12", 16" and 20" widths available)

Top View
Four extra-wide shelves for linen and blankets. Storage baskets slide out and hold dish cloths, pillowcases and smaller items. The perfect linen closet.

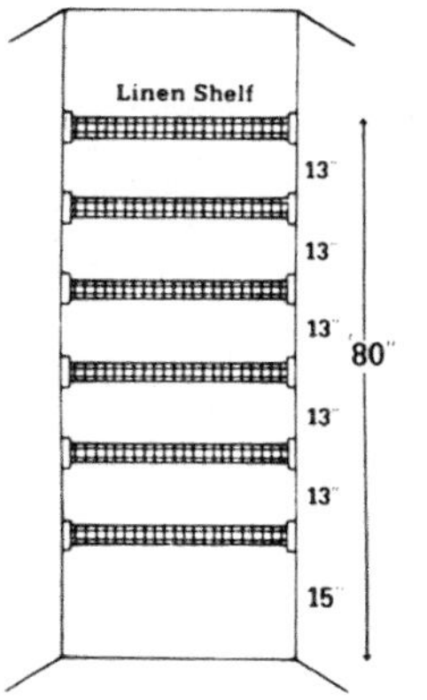

Front View
Multiple-stacked linen shelving. (9", 12", 16" and 20" widths available)

Top View
Bathroom linen closet stores towels, sheets and cleaning supplies in one easy-access area.

FOYER/FRONT ENTRY CLOSET

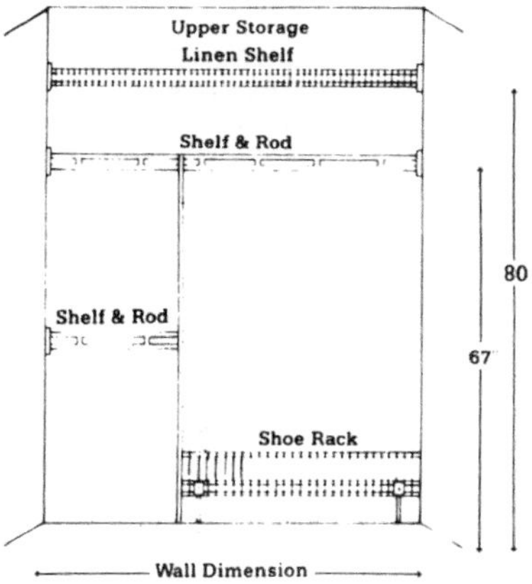

Front View
Single hang with upper storage and off-center storage unit and shoe racks. (12", 16" widths available)

Top View
A welcome addition to any home. Full-width, upper storage holds hats, gloves and sweaters. Off-center storage for umbrellas and winter items. Shelves, shoe racks and generous hanging space lets guests know they're welcome.

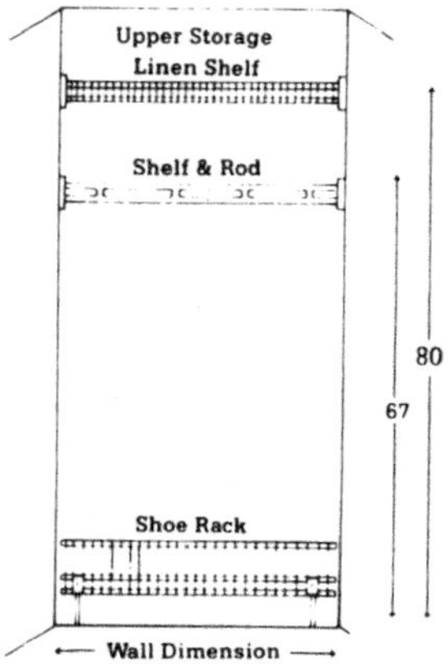

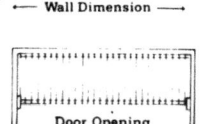

Front View
Single hang with half-length shoe racks and upper storage. (12", 16" widths available)

Top View
Holds coats, hats, shoes and guest clothing with care. Upper storage area for visitor's bags and small cases.

CLOSETS/STORAGE AREAS
Wire Basket and Shelving Systems

MASTER BEDROOMS

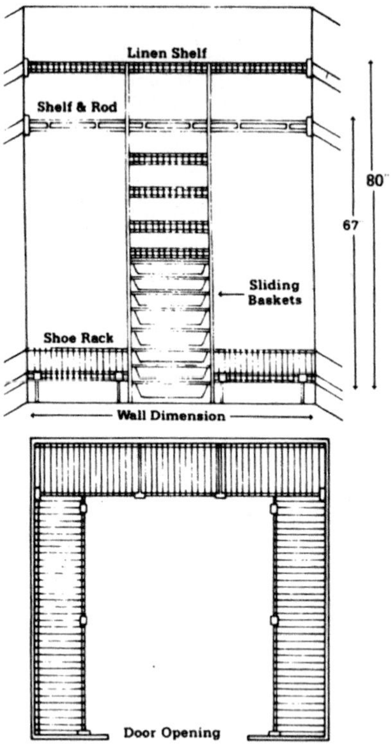

Front View
Walk-In. Single hang with upper storage and central shelving/ basket unit and shoe racks. (12," 16" widths available)

Top View
Keeps shoes, shirts and clothing neatly organized. Sliding baskets for easy access to linen, underwear, etc. Full-length clothes storage for dresses, shirts and suits. Ideal for master bedroom.

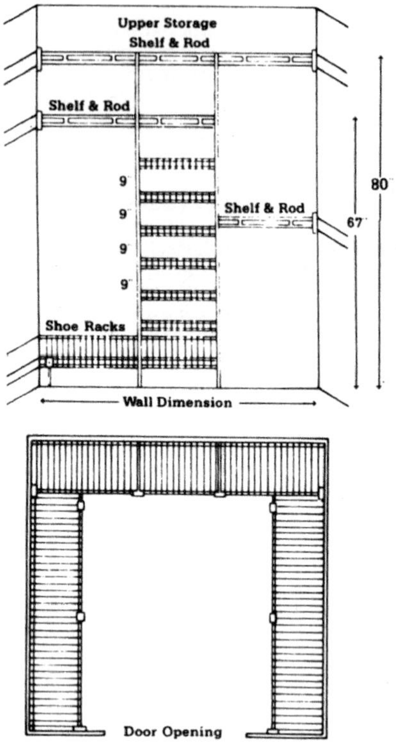

Front View
Walk-In. Single and double hang with upper storage, central shelving and shoe racks. (12," 16" widths available)

Top View
Hang dresses and coats on one side, suits and shorter garments on the other. Central shelving actually replaces a piece of furniture in the master bedroom!

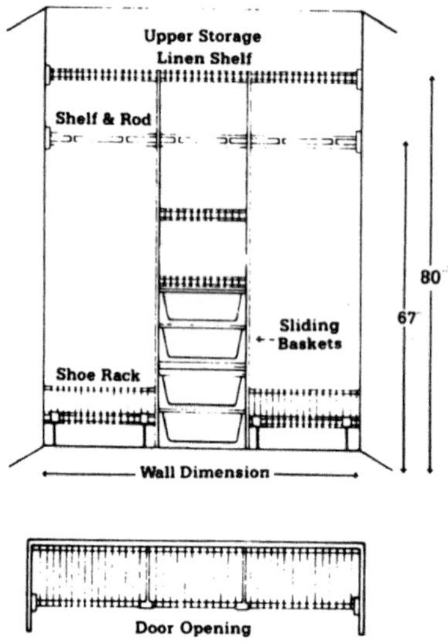

Front View
Single hang with upper storage and central shelving and basket unit, additional clearance and shoe racks. (12," 16" widths available)

Top View
So well designed it actually replaces a piece of furniture! Four sliding baskets provide multiple storage capacity for shirts, underwear, socks and sweaters. Full-length clothes hanging space, full-width shoe racks and lots of shelf space make this system a must for your 2nd bedroom.

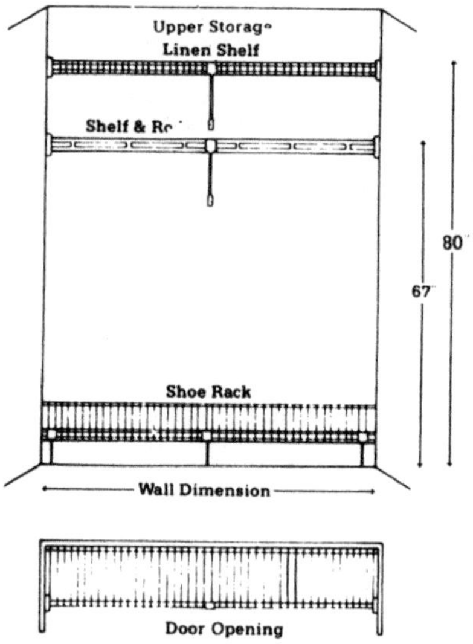

Front View
Single hang with upper storage and full-width shoe racks. (12," 16" widths available)

Top View
Doubles shelf/storage space. Single hanging for clothes, coats, shirts and jackets. Expands easily to accommodate future needs. Two full-length shoe racks.

OFFICE SPACES

INTRODUCTION

The amount of office space built during the past few decades can be measured in the hundreds of billions of square feet. Within these buildings, workers spend nearly half their waking hours and a third of their entire lives.

Over the life span of a typical office building, the same spaces may be occupied by a succession of different tenants, each with their own programmatic requirements. Consequently, interior spaces may be recycled and redesigned many times, simply to accommodate the changing needs of new corporate users. In many instances redesign may be necessitated solely by the effect of technological change on the methodology of transacting business. Moreover, the escalating costs of land acquisition and construction and the increasing scarcity of urban building sites make it essential that the redesign reflects an efficient, cost-effective utilization of space, as well as one that is responsive to the human factors involved. It is necessary, therefore, for the designer to be familiar not only with the general planning criteria associated with office design, but with the architectural detailing of some of the typical interior elements contained within these spaces.

Accordingly, this section includes general planning criteria and examples of actual working drawings of typical interior conditions, prepared by various design professionals. The details referred to include such items as trading desks, elevated computer floors, library furniture, built-in storage cabinets, work counters, wall paneling, vanities, reception desks, and conference room elements. Also included are illustrations and dimensional data pertaining to typical office furniture, equipment, and electronic media storage.

GENERAL OFFICES AND MULTIPLE WORKSTATIONS
Planning Data: Basic Workstations

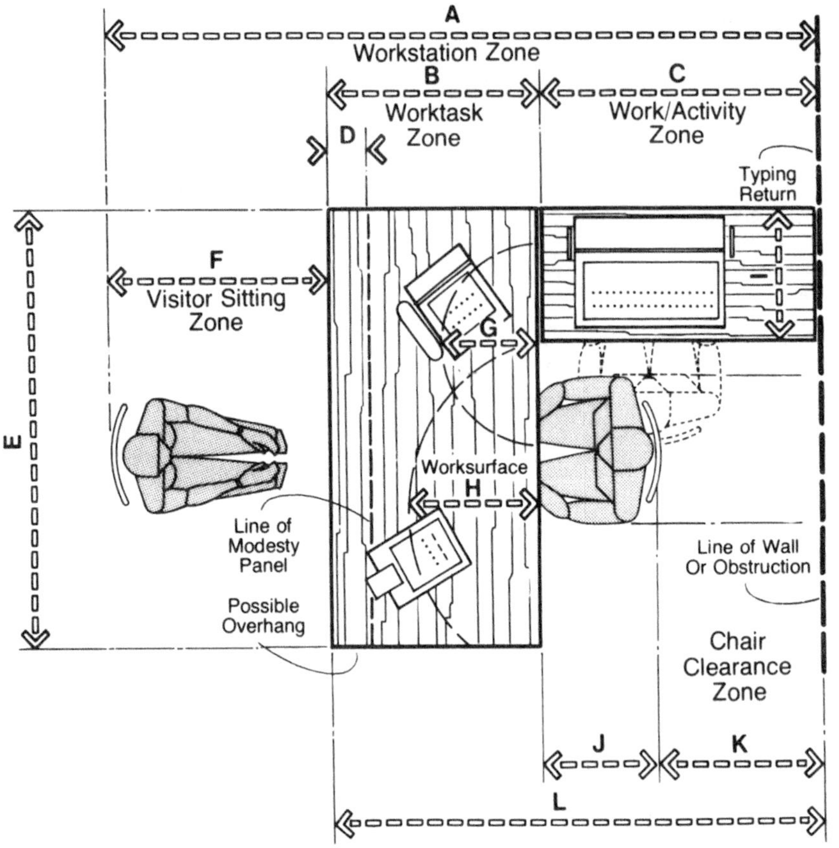

	in	cm
A	90–126	228.6–320.0
B	30–36	76.2–91.4
C	30–48	76.2–121.9
D	6–12	15.2–30.5
E	60–72	152.4–182.9
F	30–42	76.2–106.7
G	14–18	35.6–45.7
H	16–20	40.6–50.8
I	18–22	45.7–55.9
J	18–24	45.7–61.0
K	6–24	15.2–61.0
L	60–84	152.4–213.4
M	24–30	61.0–76.2
N	29–30	73.7–76.2
O	15–18	38.1–45.7

Fig. 1 Basic workstation with visitor seating

GENERAL OFFICES AND MULTIPLE WORKSTATIONS

The so-called general office takes on a variety of forms and configurations. In its simplest variation, it may be nothing more complex than several standard desks with returns located within a room or space. In its more sophisticated and ergonomically designed form, the general office may be based on an open planning or office landscaping concept, involving a system of workstations. The workstations include desk surfaces, files, acoustic partitions, and a host of other optional components to suit the nature of the particular work tasks involved. The systems are extremely flexible, allowing the workstations to be configured in a variety of shapes. Provision for power and lighting is quite common.

The design of the general office, like the design of the private office, requires a knowledge of the basic dimensional requirements and clearances of the workstation and, where applicable, of the visitor seating to be accommodated.

In certain instances, where customized and/or built-in storage elements, work counters, credenzas, and so on, are required, a knowledge of architectural woodworking, as may be related to the design of such elements, can be quite helpful.

Accordingly, this part includes basic planning criteria for general office design, in addition to examples of architectural woodwork details in connection with some of the more common customized components of general office spaces.

The basic workstation, as illustrated in plan in Fig. 1, is the fundamental building block in understanding the anthropometric considerations for the planning and design of the general office. The work-task zone must be large enough to accommodate the paperwork, equipment, and other accessories that support the user's function. The work/activity zone dimension, shown in Fig. 1, is established by the space requirements needed for use of the typical return. In no case should this distance be less than the 30 in, or 76.2 cm, needed to provide adequate space for the chair clearance zone. The visitor seating zone, ranging in depth from 30 to 42 in, or 76.2 to 106.7 cm, requires the designer to accommodate both the buttock-knee and buttock-toe length body dimensions of the larger user. If an overhang is provided or the desk's modesty panel is recessed, the visitor seating zone can be reduced due to the additional knee and toe clearances provided. The specific type and size of the seating (i.e., if it swivels or if it has casters) also influence these dimensions.

Minimum Square Footage Standards for the Open and Screened Workstation

The Nonautomated Task. *Square footage workstation standards for the nonautomated task are developed primarily according to task profile, equipment, conferencing, and privacy requirements.*

Open
No requirement of equipment or task for privacy, concentration

Screened
Privacy required for reading, working, thinking, calculating, meetings, confidential phone calls, elimination of visual and acoustical distractions

---

Task Profile: Processing paper on work surface with quick turnaround.

- Continued flow of material is processed as it arrives at the workspace and is passed on to either another function or to group storage.
- Storage for permanent files and reference materials minimal.
- Reference material accessed infrequently. Telephone tasks may require concentration.

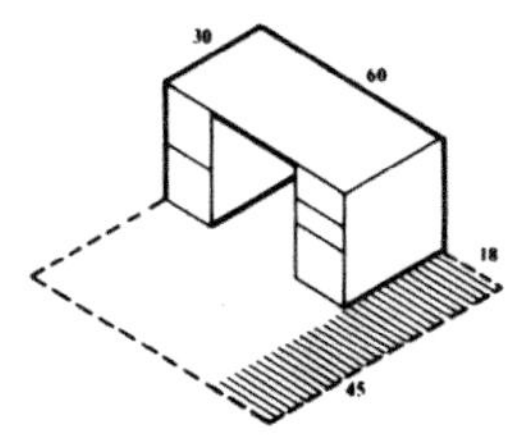

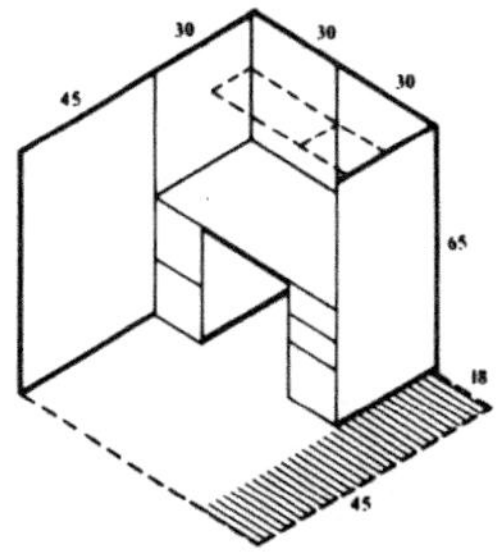

No	Guest chair
30 x 60 (76 x 152 cm)	Primary work surface
No	Secondary work surface
3–4	File drawers
0–2	Shelves

41 sq. ft.

Task Profile: Typewriter the primary tool for processing paper.

- Continued flow of material is processed as it arrives at the workspace and is passed on to either another function or to group storage.
- Storage for permanent files and reference materials minimal.
- Reference material access may be frequent. Tasks may require concentration.

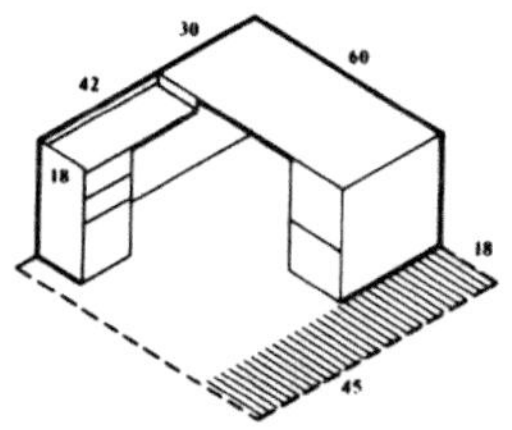

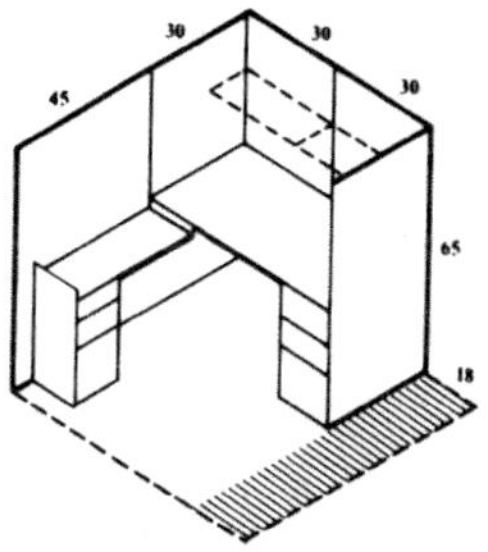

No	Guest chair
30 x 60	Primary work surface
18 x 42 (46 x 107 cm)	Secondary work surface
3–4	File drawers
0–2	Shelves

41 sq. ft.

Task Profile: Typewriter the primary tool for processing paper.

- Continued flow of material is processed as it arrives at the workspace and is passed on to either another function or to group storage.
- Storage for permanent files and reference materials minimal.
- Reference material access may be frequent. Tasks may require concentration. Limited conferencing required at the workspace.
- Need to see and hear co-workers or subordinates of secondary priority.

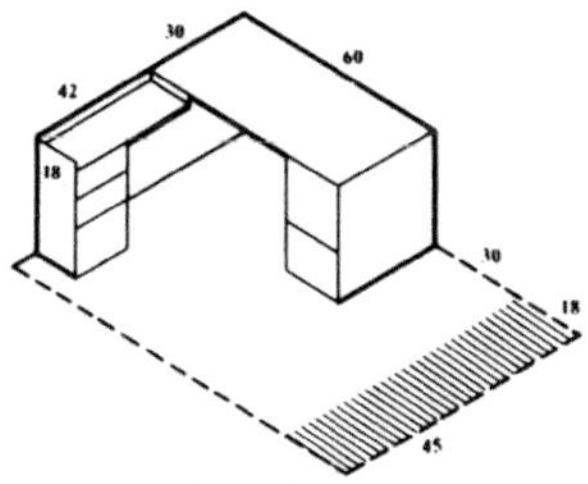

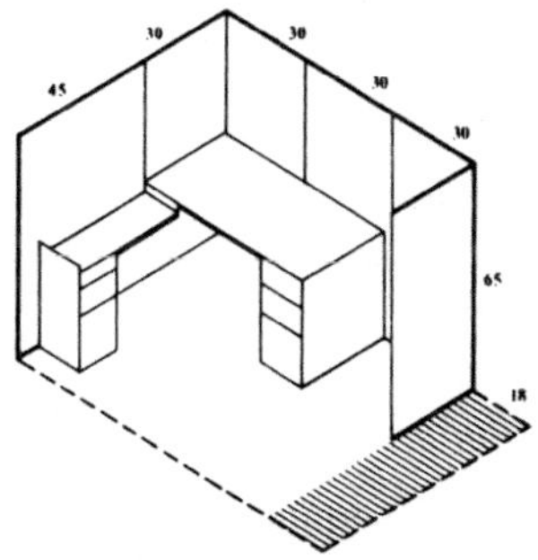

1	Guest chair
30 x 60	Primary work surface
18 x 42	Secondary work surface
3–4	File drawers
0–2	Shelves

56 sq. ft.

GENERAL OFFICES AND MULTIPLE WORKSTATIONS
Planning Data: Basic Workstations

The Nonautomated Task	Open	Screened
	No requirement of equipment or task for privacy, concentration	Privacy required for reading, working, thinking, calculating, meetings, confidential phone calls, elimination of visual and acoustical distractions

Task Profile: Same as 1 with addition of extended conferencing requirements at individual workstation.

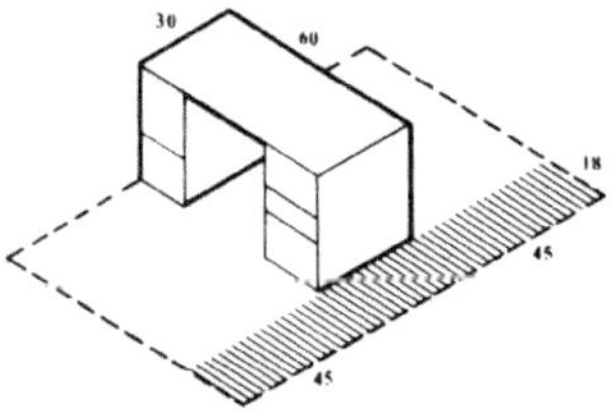

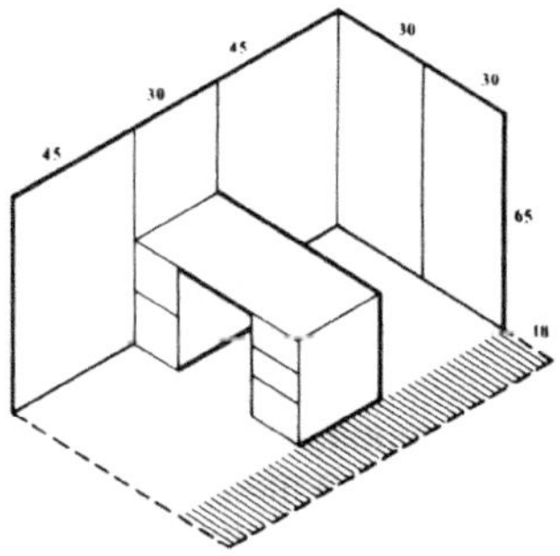

2	Guest chair
30 x 60	Primary work surface
No	Secondary work surface
3–4	File drawers
No	Shelves

65 sq. ft.

Task Profile: Same as 3 with addition of extended conferencing requirements at individual workstation.

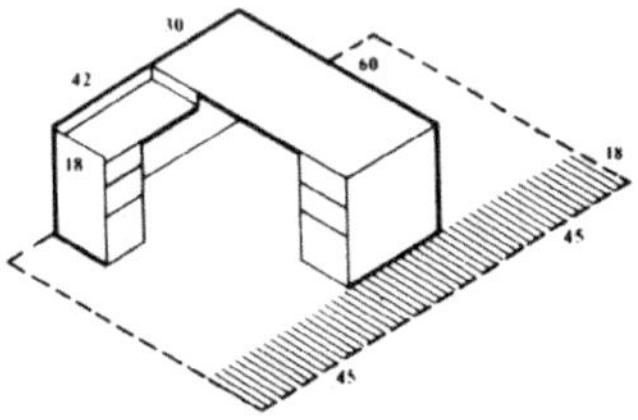

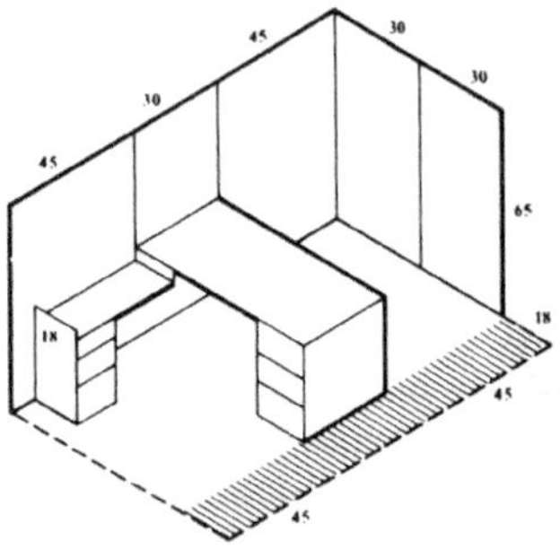

2	Guest chair
30 x 60	Primary work surface
18 x 42	Secondary work surface
3–4	File drawers
No	Shelves

65 sq. ft.

Task Profile: Data Entry.

- □ Paper, material, or information processed and/or maintained.
- □ Multiple reference sources may be used on a task.
- □ Reference materials used frequently.
- □ Limited volume of supplies and permanent records kept at the workspace.
- □ Electronic equipment used for keeping records current, information inputting, and maintaining data and records.
- □ Ability to see and hear co-workers may be desirable.
- □ Tasks may also require screening for concentration.

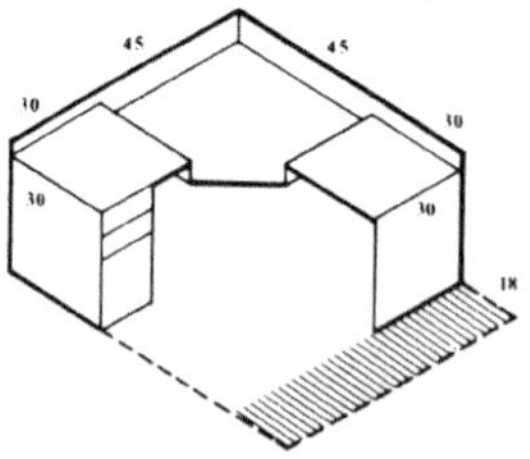

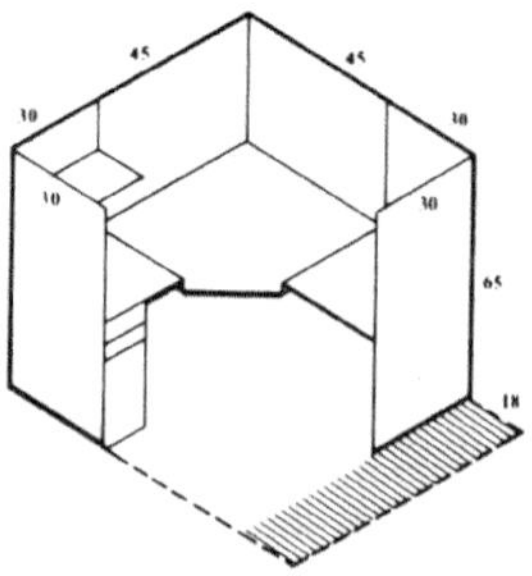

No	Guest chair
45 x 45 (114 x 114 cm)	Primary work surface
30 x 30 (76 x 76 cm)	Secondary work surface
1–2	File drawers
0–2	Shelves

48 sq. ft.

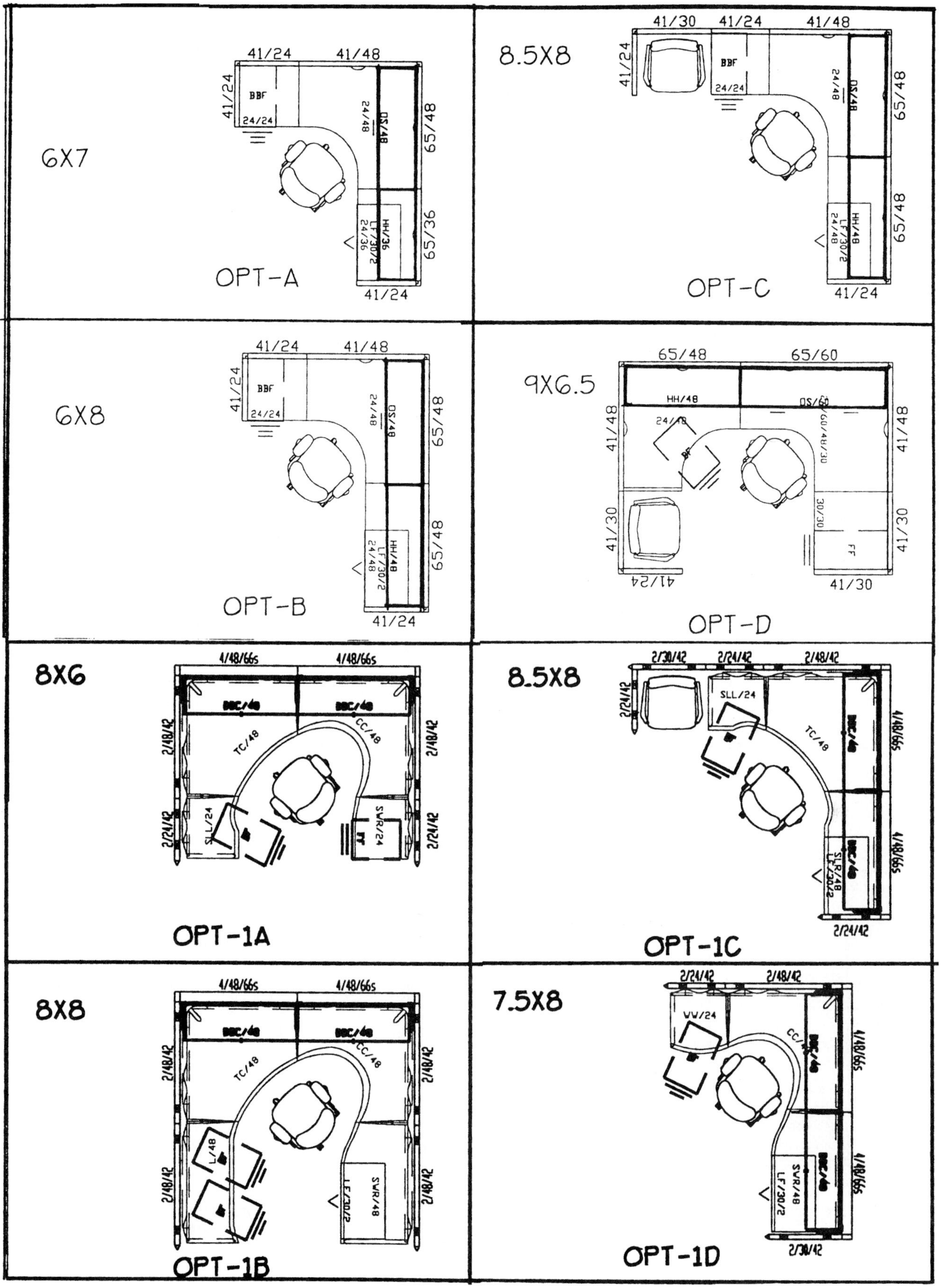
6X7
41/24
41/48
41/24
BBF
24/24
24/48
DS/48
65/48
HH/36
LF/30/2
24/36
65/36
OPT-A
41/24
8.5X8
41/30
41/24
41/48
41/24
BBF
24/24
24/48
DS/48
65/48
HH/48
LF/30/2
24/48
65/48
OPT-C
41/24
6X8
41/24
41/48
41/24
BBF
24/24
24/48
DS/48
65/48
HH/48
LF/30/2
24/48
65/48
OPT-B
41/24
9X6.5
65/48
65/60
HH/48
DS/60
41/48
41/48
41/30
30/30
41/30
FF
41/24
41/30
OPT-D
8X6
4/48/66s
4/48/66s
BBC/48
BBC/48
TC/48
CC/48
2/48/42
2/48/42
2/24/42
SLL/24
SWR/24
2/24/42
OPT-1A
8.5X8
2/30/42
2/24/42
2/48/42
2/24/42
SLL/24
TC/48
BBC/48
4/48/66S
SWR/48
LF/30/2
4/48/66S
2/24/42
OPT-1C
8X8
4/48/66s
4/48/66s
BBC/48
BBC/48
TC/48
CC/48
2/48/42
2/48/42
L/48
2/48/42
SWR/48
LF/30/2
2/48/42
OPT-1B
7.5X8
2/24/42
2/48/42
VV/24
CC/48
BBC/48
4/48/66S
SWR/48
LF/30/2
4/48/66S
2/30/42
OPT-1D

GENERAL OFFICES AND MULTIPLE WORKSTATIONS

Planning Data: Multiple Workstations

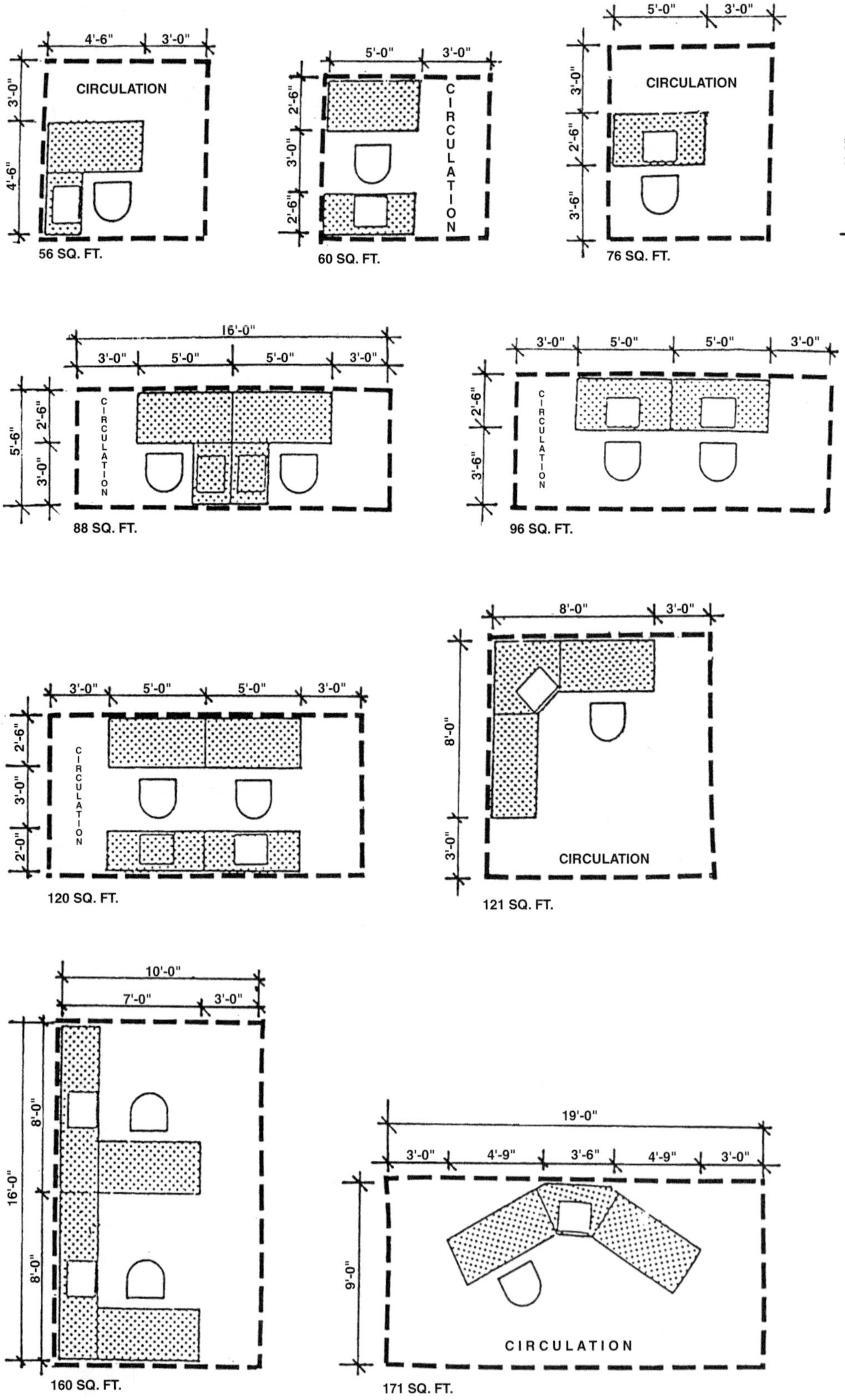

Fig. 2 Depending on function, the sizes of individual and multiple workstations vary dramatically. Size of work surface, length and depth of return, chair size, and circulation patterns all influence the gross square footage requirements

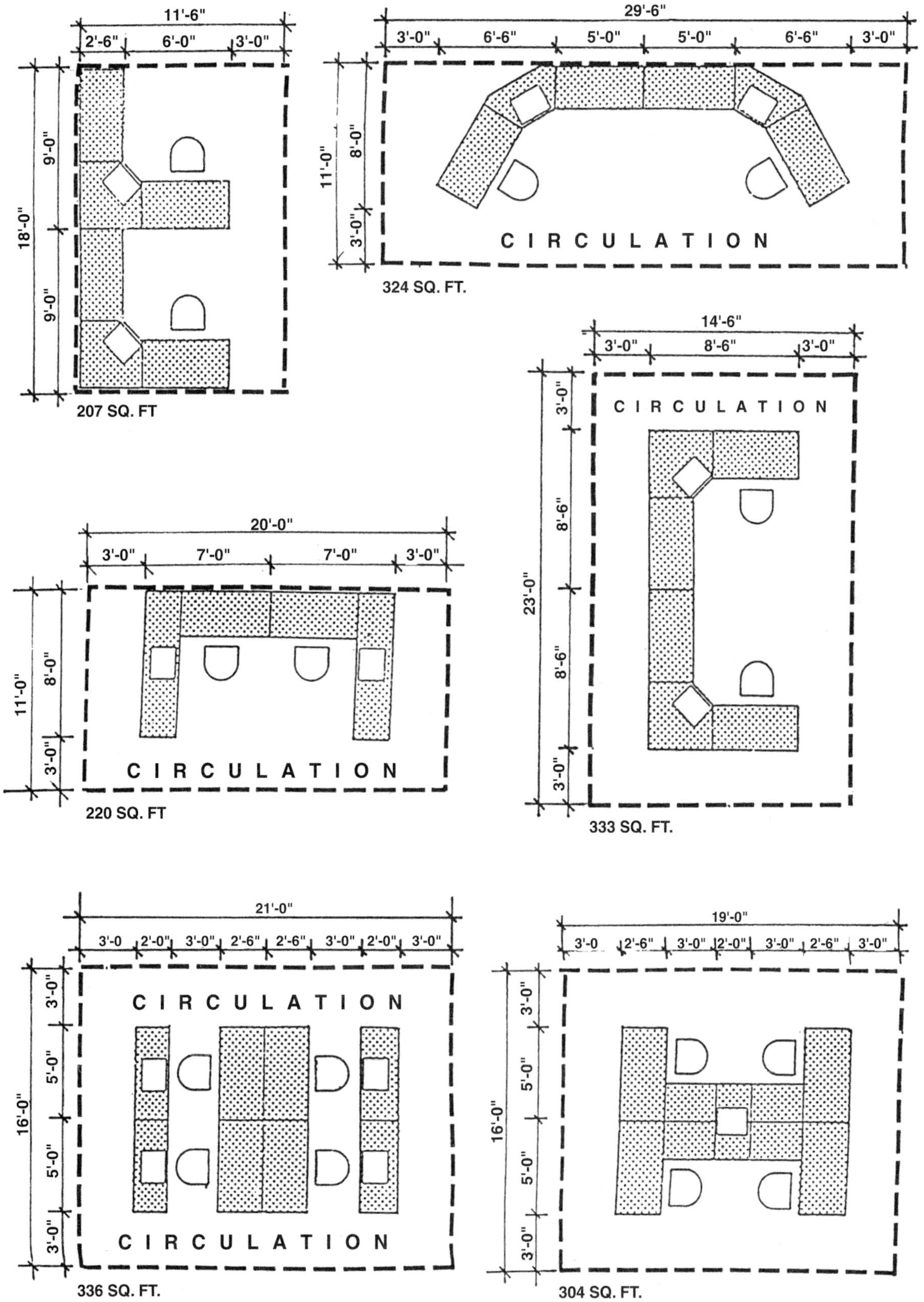

Fig. 3 Floating or free-standing workstations tend to utilize more floor area than workstations placed against a wall or sharing the same wall panel. Clustering of workstations will ultimately result in the use of less floor area, but at the expense of major ergonomic considerations. Decisions relative to both acoustical privacy and personal space are often sacrificed in the name of economy

GENERAL OFFICES AND MULTIPLE WORKSTATIONS
Planning Data: Multiple Workstations

Multiple workstations can result in efficient utilization of space and sharing of expensive computer terminals and equipment. If use of computer terminals is intensive, individual CRTs should be provided. Figures 4, 5, and 6 each show eight workstations, yet the setups range in area from 448 to 1012 ft². Furniture size, function, and ergonomic considerations all affect setup.

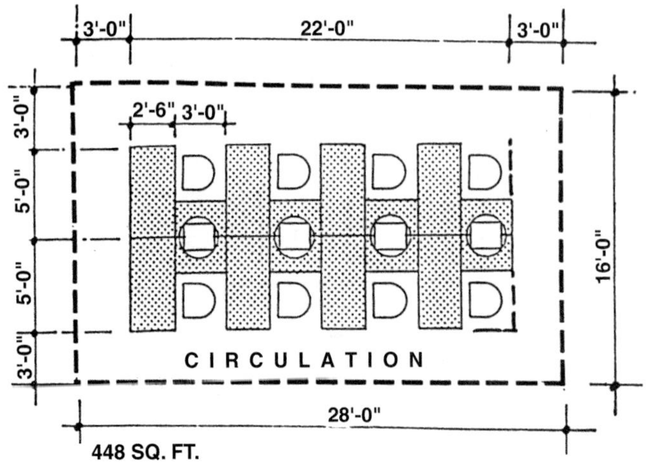

Fig. 4

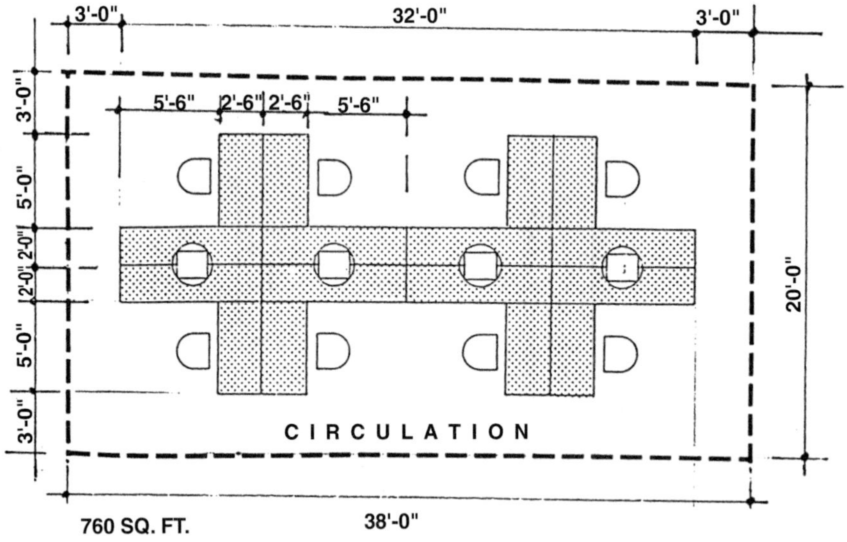

Fig. 5

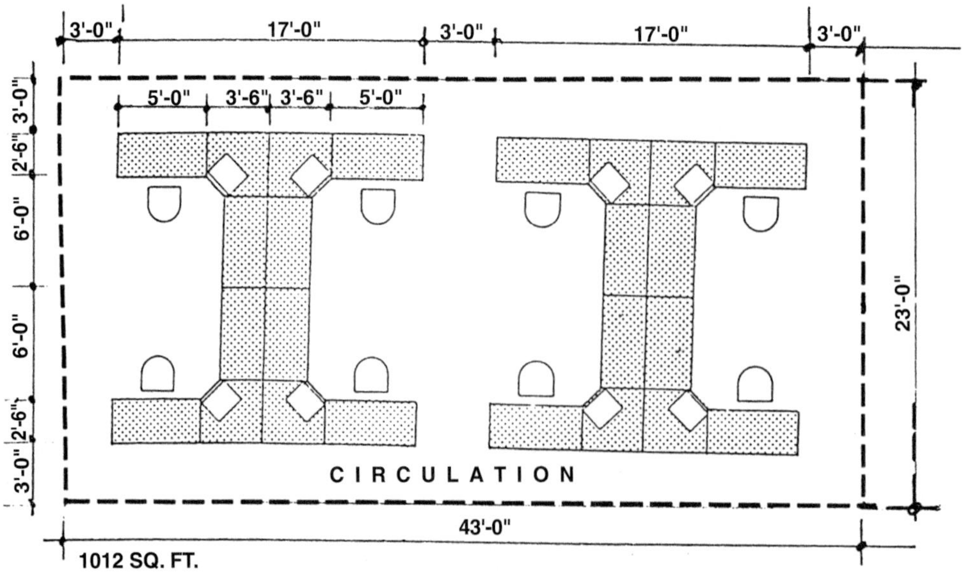

Fig. 6

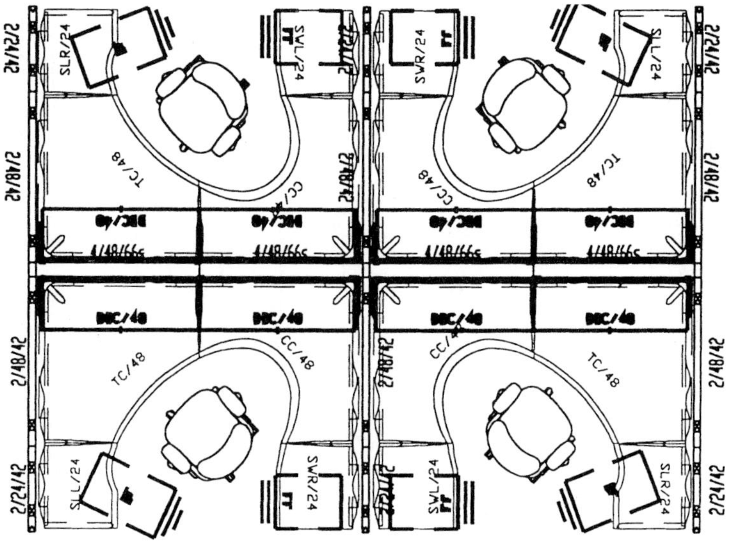

8'-0" x 6'-0" MODULES IN 4-UNIT CLUSTER

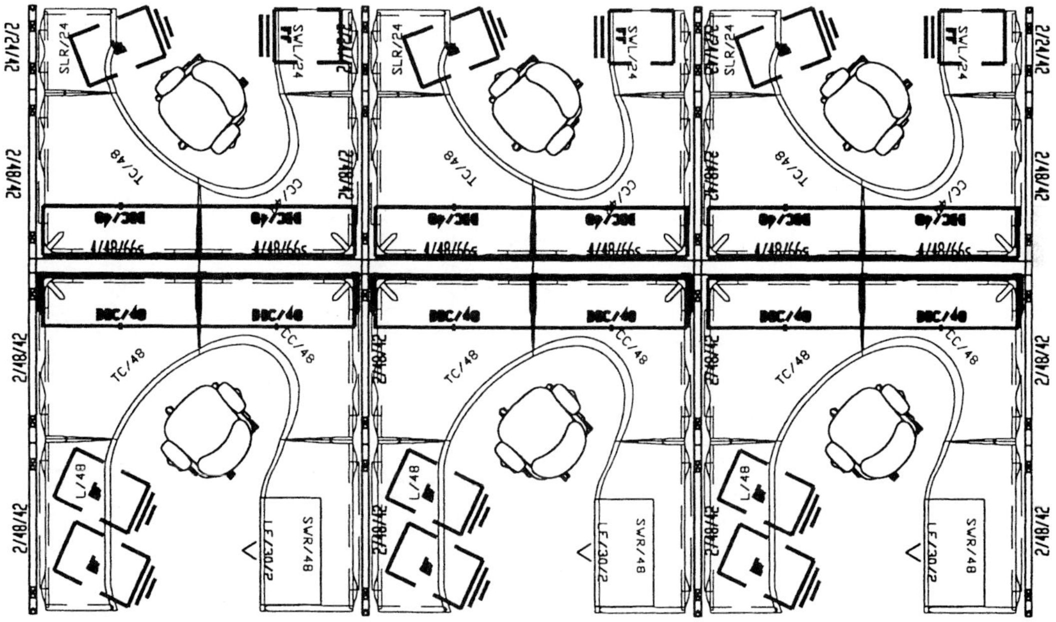

8'-0" x 8'-0" MODULES IN 6-UNIT CLUSTER

GENERAL OFFICES AND MULTIPLE WORKSTATIONS

Planning Data: Multiple Workstations

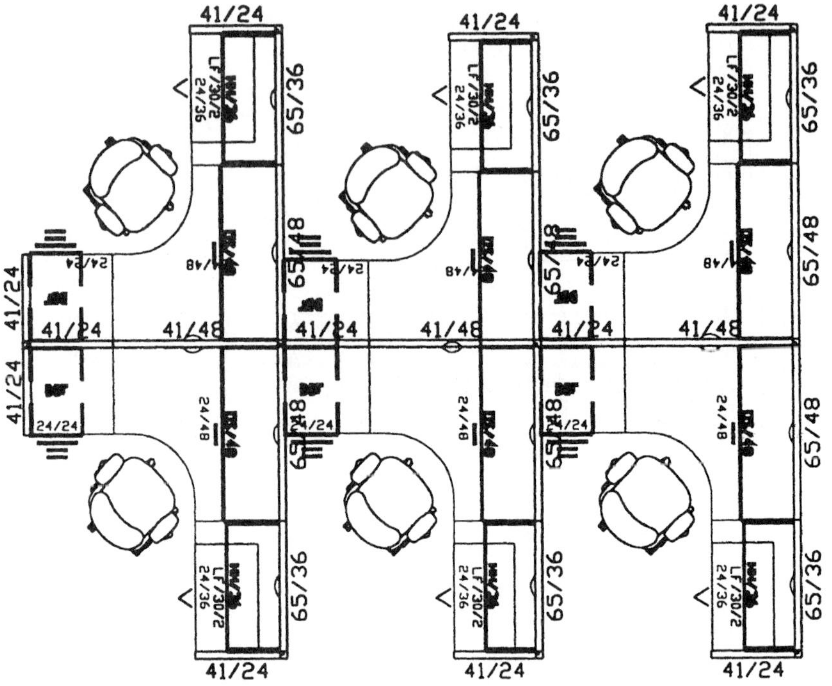

6'-0" x 7'-0" MODULES IN 6-UNIT CLUSTER

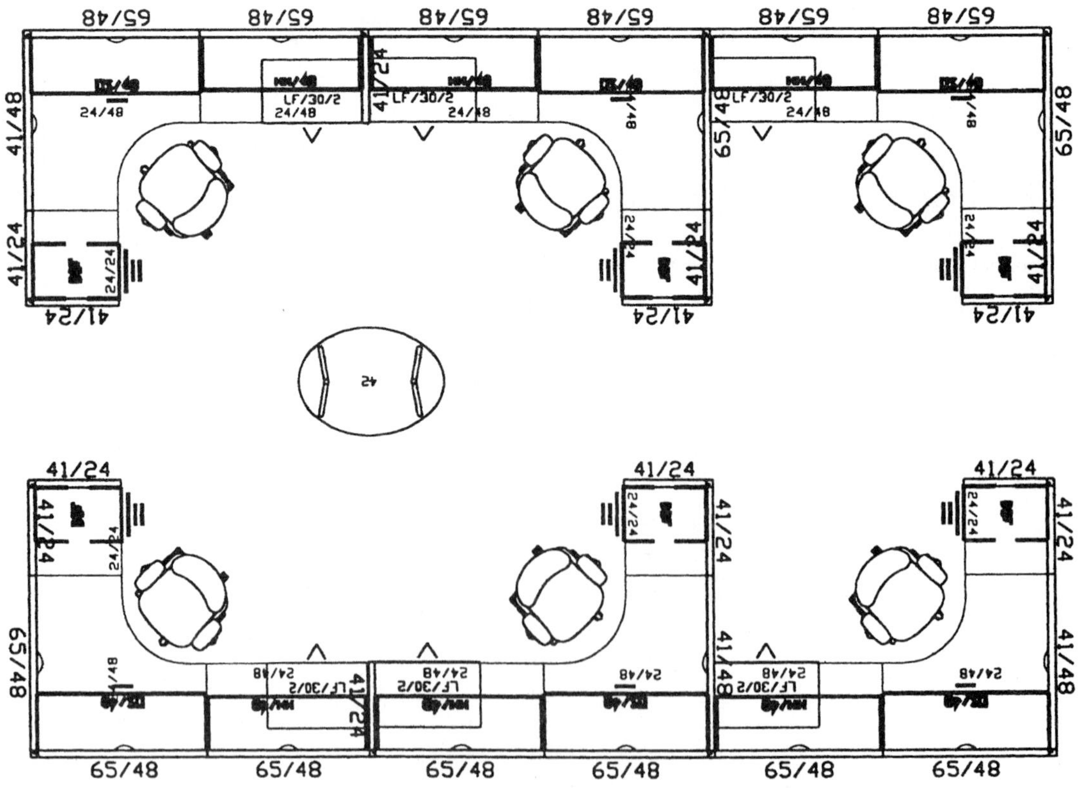

6'-0" x 8'-0" MODULES IN 6-UNIT CLUSTER

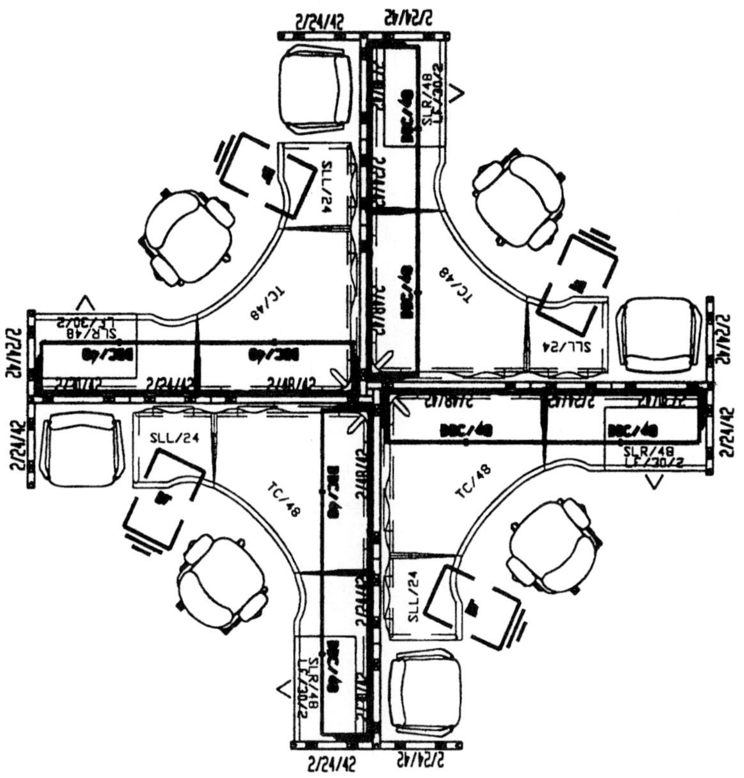

8'-6" x 8'-0" MODULES IN 4-UNIT CLUSTER

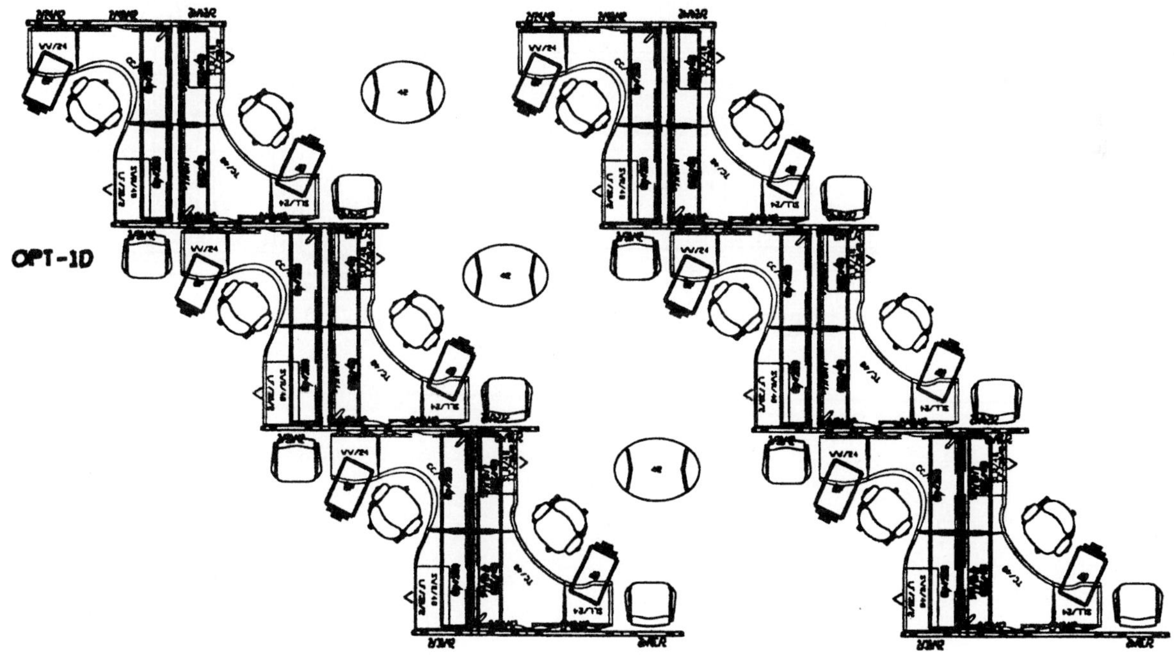

8'-6" x 8'-0" MODULES IN 6-UNIT DIAGONAL CLUSTERS

GENERAL OFFICES AND MULTIPLE WORKSTATIONS

Planning Data: Secretarial Workstations

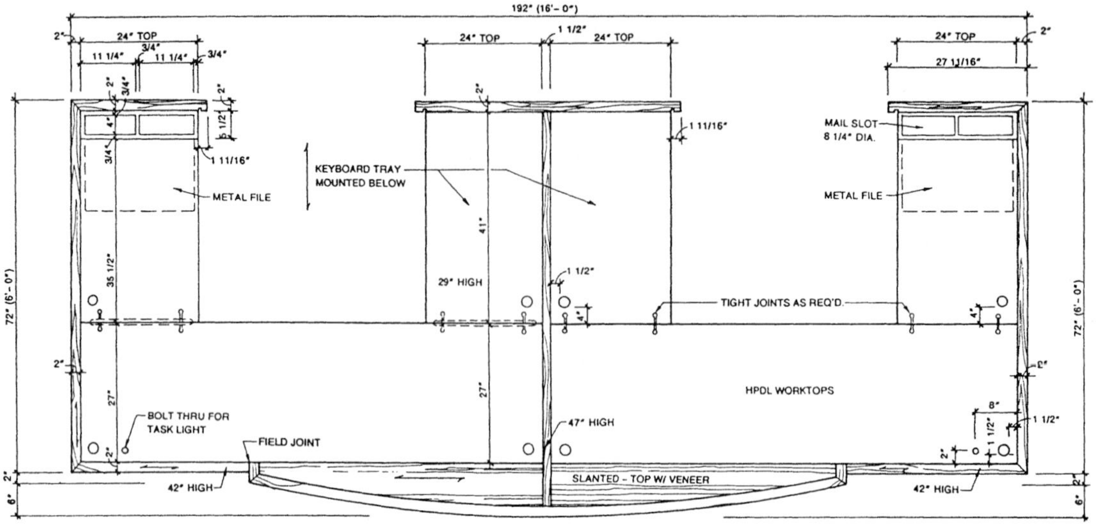

PLAN AT SECRETARIAL STATION

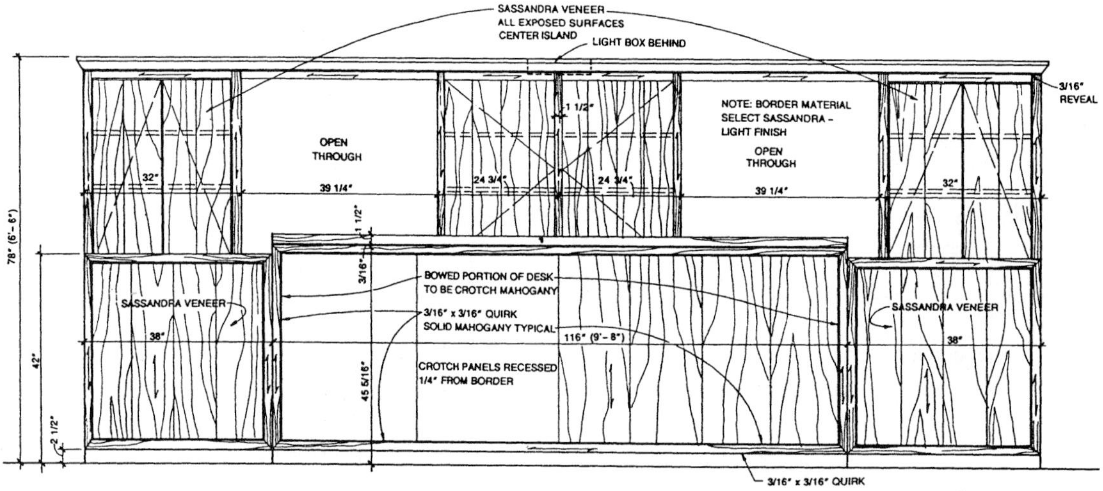

ELEVATION AT SECRETARIAL STATION

It is not unusual to have two or more persons share an enclosed office space. In planning this type of office space, both circulation and clearance become critically important. Door swings, the extension of file drawers, and points of entry must all be carefully considered.

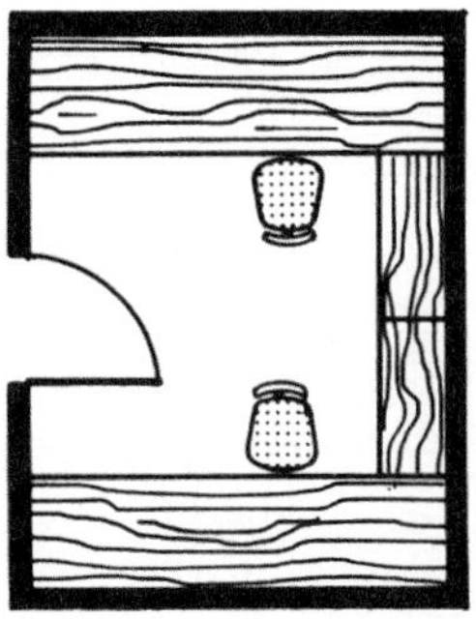

Fig. 7 9 ft × 12 ft, 108 ft²

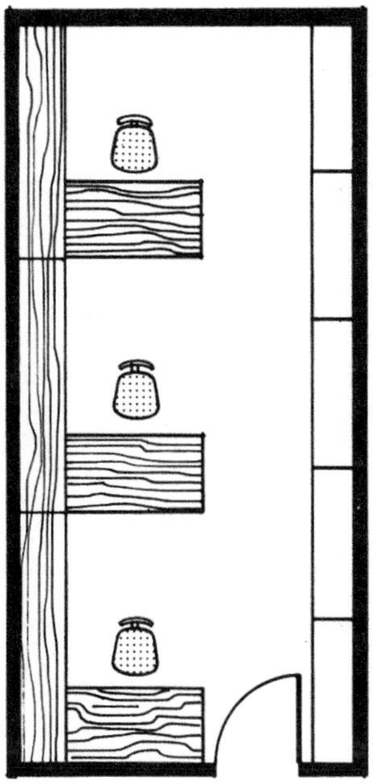

Fig. 10 12 ft × 25 ft, 300 ft²

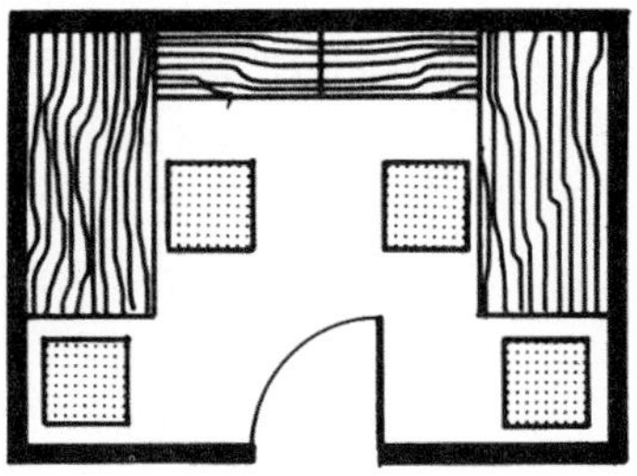

Fig. 8 9 ft × 14 ft, 126 ft²

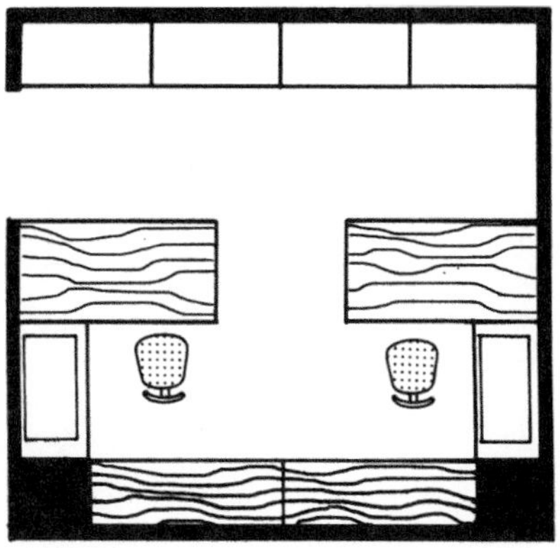

Fig. 9 15 ft × 16 ft, 240 ft²

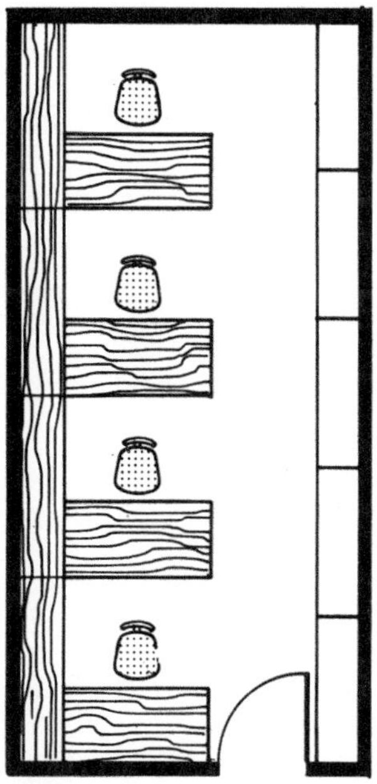

Fig. 11 12 ft × 25 ft, 300 ft²

GENERAL OFFICES AND MULTIPLE WORKSTATIONS
Planning Data: Office Layout

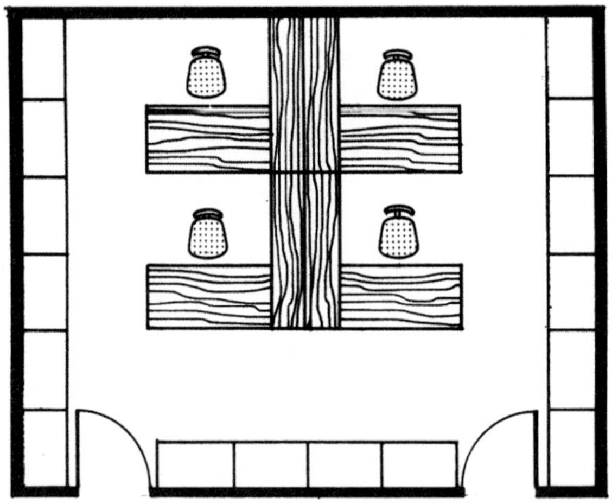

Fig. 12 18 ft × 25 ft, 414 ft²

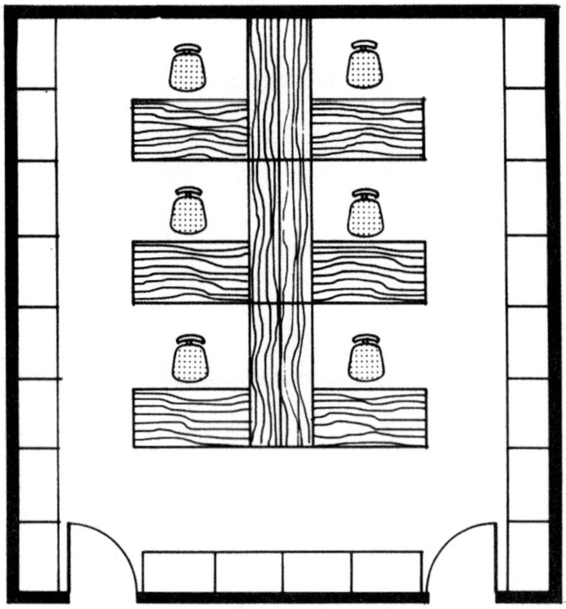

Fig. 13 24 ft × 23 ft, 552 ft²

The design of the private office requires a knowledge of the basic dimensional requirements and clearances of the executive workstation and, where applicable, of visitor seating accommodations. In certain instances where various aspects of the office interior are customized and/or built into the construction, a knowledge of architectural woodwork detailing is also desirable.

This page and the following pages include the necessary planning criteria required, as well as details of certain customized components.

Executive workstation and/or desk size and configuration can be customized, depending on desired image, scale, and ambience. Desks are also available in generally accepted standard sizes. It is these standard desks that are most used in the design of the private office. Figure 1 illustrates the range of desk dimensions, chair dimensions, and clearances involved.

Many private executive offices are being designed with desks that do not conform with the basic rectangular shape. Such a situation is illustrated in Fig. 2, which shows a circular executive desk. Such a desk is often selected if the executive in question plans to hold conferences within the office and prefers the psychology of having either visitors or employees gather around the work surface in an egalitarian fashion. While a minimum desk size of 48 in, or 121.9 cm, is shown, this dimension is also influenced by the number of side chairs to be grouped around the desk.

A circular executive desk must be supported by supplementary credenza or file storage within easy reach of the executive chair. Side arm reach relative to the work/activity zone must always be studied carefully.

Figure 3 illustrates a typical circular lounge grouping found within an executive office. Providing for the appropriate leg clearance of 12 to 18 in, or 30.5 to 45.7 cm, is also determined by the sitting zone requirements. Buttock-knee length must also be considered.

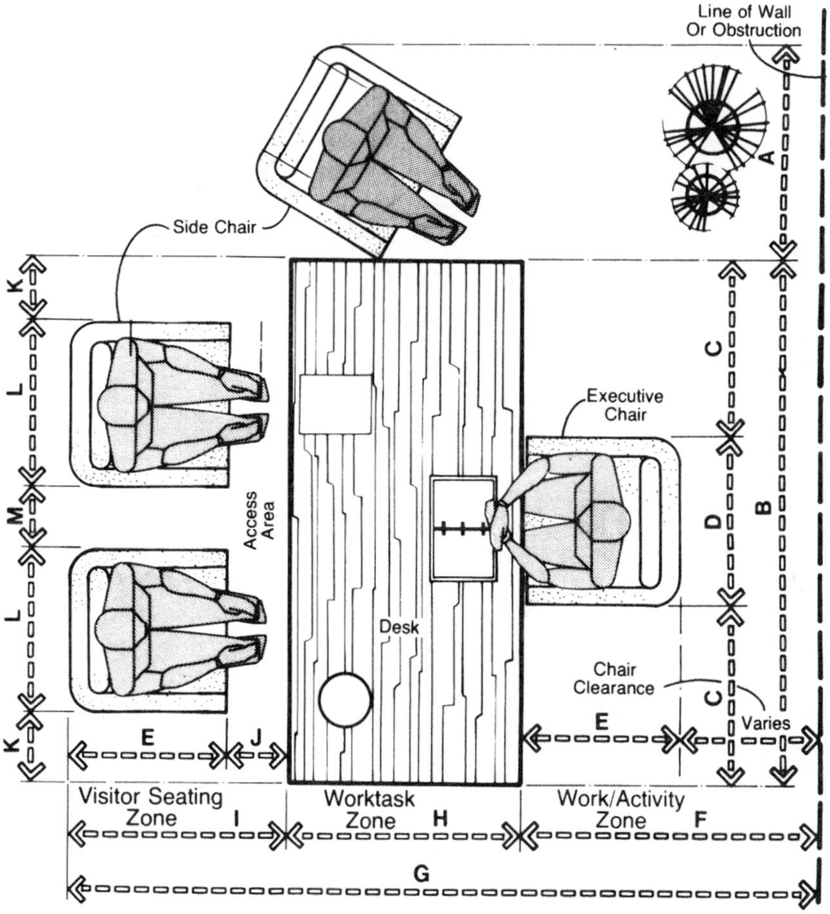

	in	cm
A	30–39	76.2–99.1
B	66–84	167.6–213.4
C	21–28	53.3–71.1
D	24–28	61.0–71.1
E	23–29	58.4–73.7
F	42 min.	106.7 min.
G	105–130	266.7–330.2
H	30–45	76.2–114.3
I	33–43	83.8–109.2
J	10–14	25.4–35.6
K	6–16	15.2–40.6
L	20–26	50.8–66.0
M	12–15	30.5–38.1
N	117--148	297.2–375.9
O	45–61	114.3–154.9
P	30–45	76.2–114.3
Q	12–18	30.5–45.7
R	29–30	73.7–76.2
S	22–32	55.9–81.3

Fig. 1 Executive desk/visitor seating

PRIVATE OFFICES

Executive Workstation

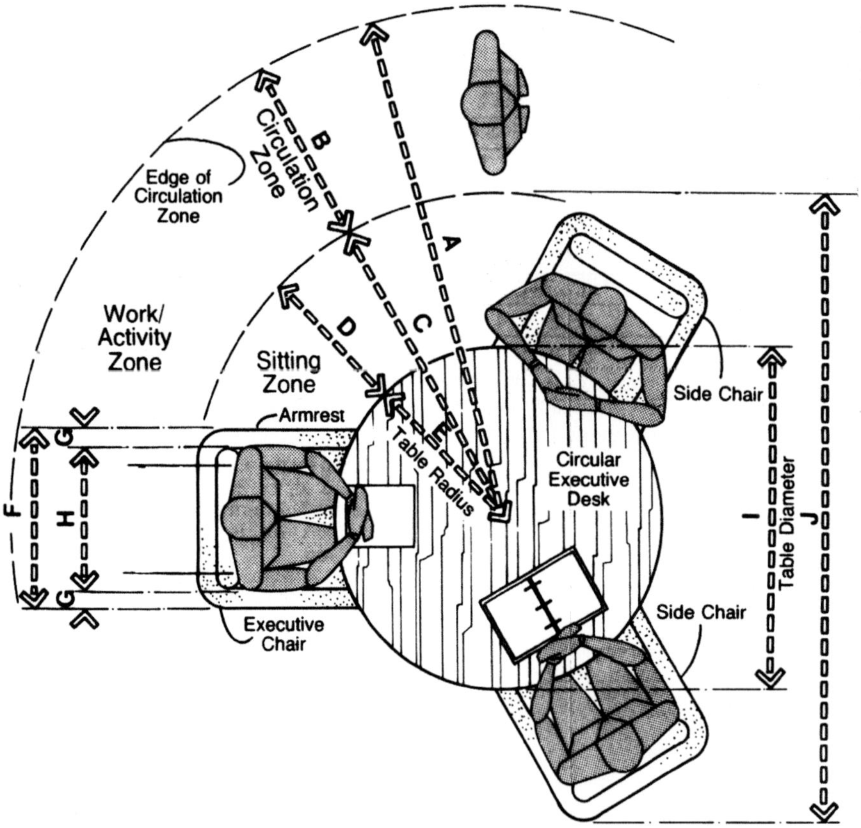

	in	cm
A	77–88	195.6–223.5
B	30	76.2
C	46–58	116.8–147.3
D	22–28	55.9–71.1
E	24–30	61.0–91.4
F	24–28	61.0–71.1
G	2–3	5.1–7.6
H	20–22	50.8–55.9
I	48–60	121.9–152.4
J	92–116	233.7–294.6
K	36–42	91.4–106.7
L	6–9	15.2–22.9
M	24	61.0
N	42–60	106.7–152.4
O	36–48	91.4–121.9
P	57–78	144.8–198.1
Q	33–48	83.8–121.9
R	12–18	30.5–45.7
S	21–30	53.3–76.2
T	24–32	61.0–81.3

Fig. 2 Circular executive desk

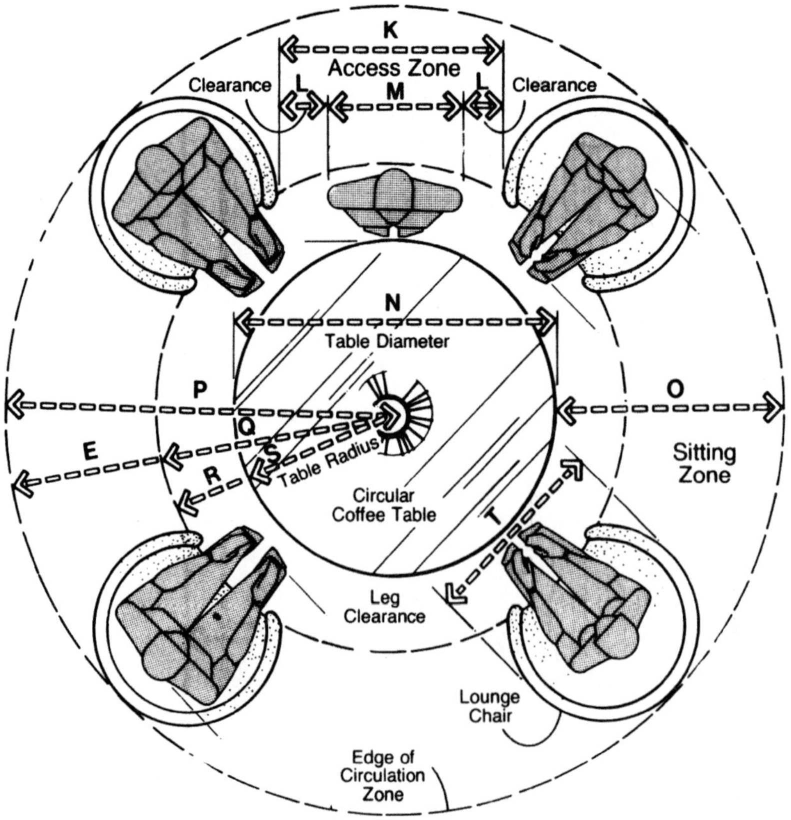

Fig. 3 Circular lounge grouping

PRIVATE OFFICES

Planning Data: Typical Room Arrangements

The private offices illustrated in Figs. 4 to 17 reflect middle to senior management functional, as well as status, requirements. Each office layout should be carefully reviewed with the client to ensure that all programmatic functions have been met. Offices of this size do not easily accommodate an independent conference function.

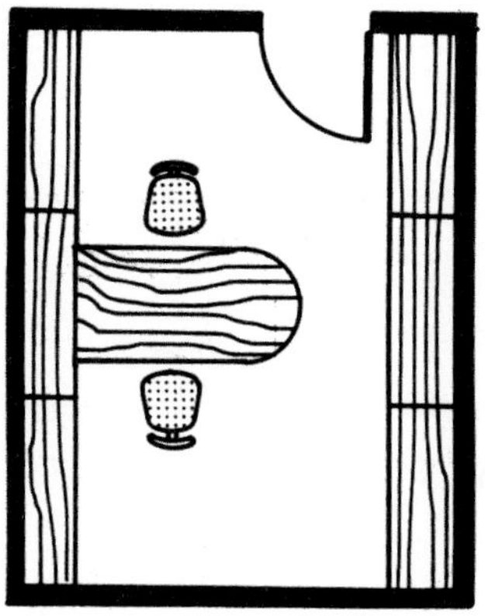

Fig. 4 12 ft × 15 ft, 180 ft²

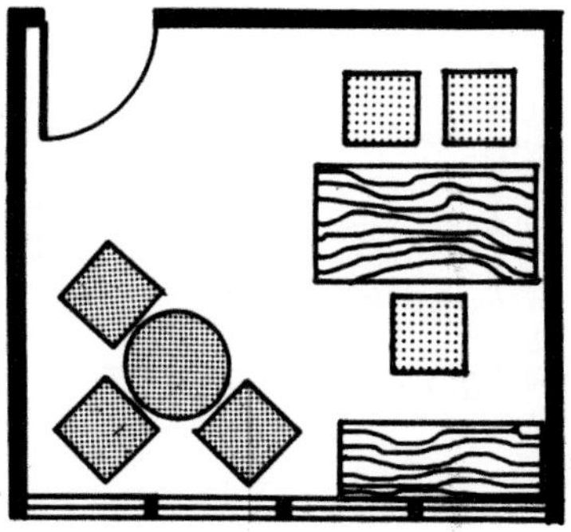

Fig. 5 14 ft × 12 ft, 168 ft²

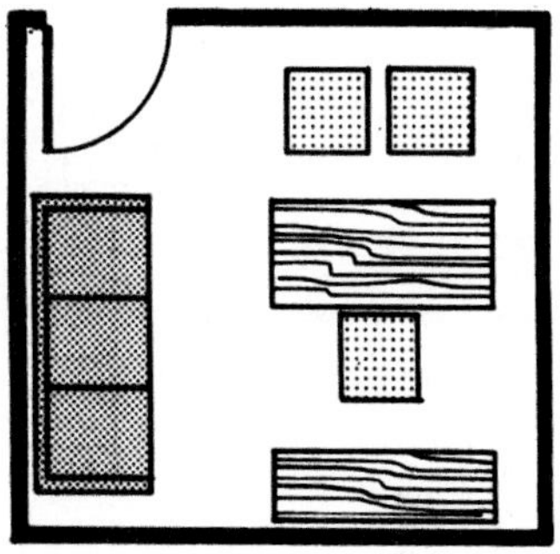

Fig. 6 13 ft × 12 ft, 156 ft²

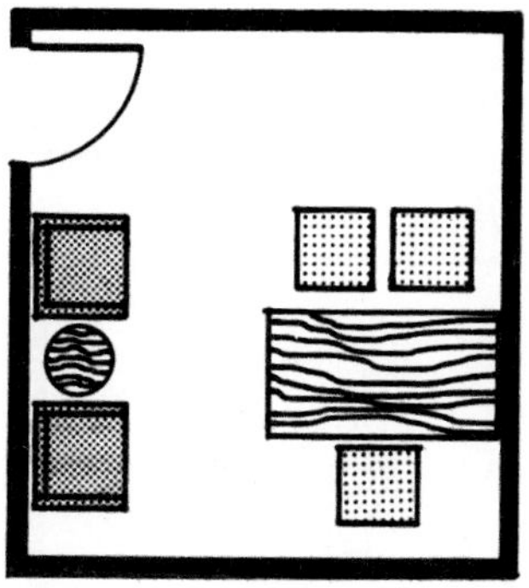

Fig. 7 12 ft × 13 ft, 156 ft²

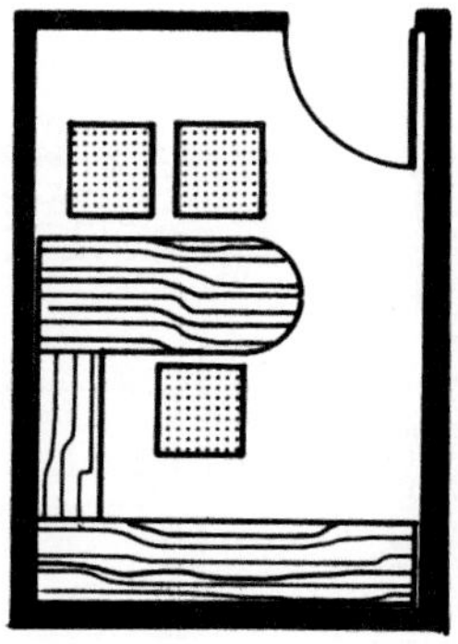

Fig. 8 9 ft × 15 ft, 135 ft²

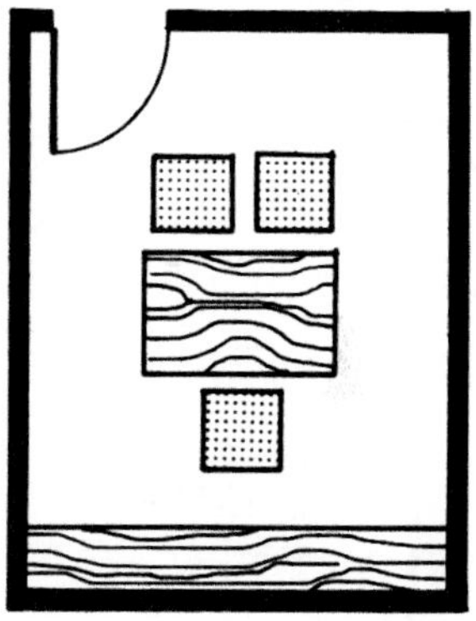

Fig. 9 11 ft × 14 ft, 154 ft²

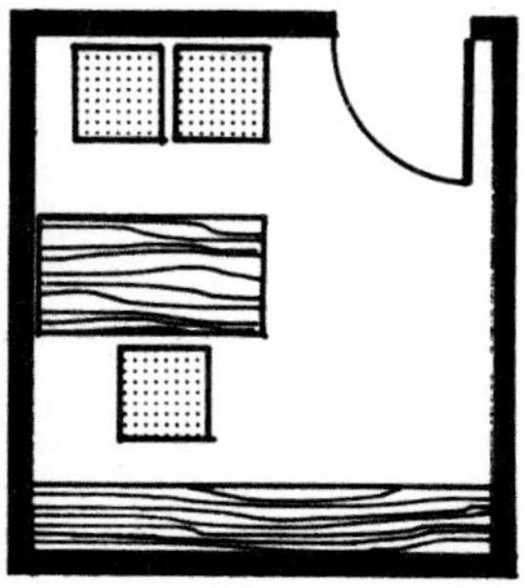

Fig. 10 10 ft × 11 ft, 110 ft²

Fig. 11 9 ft × 12 ft, 108 ft²

PRIVATE OFFICES
Planning Data: Typical Room Arrangements

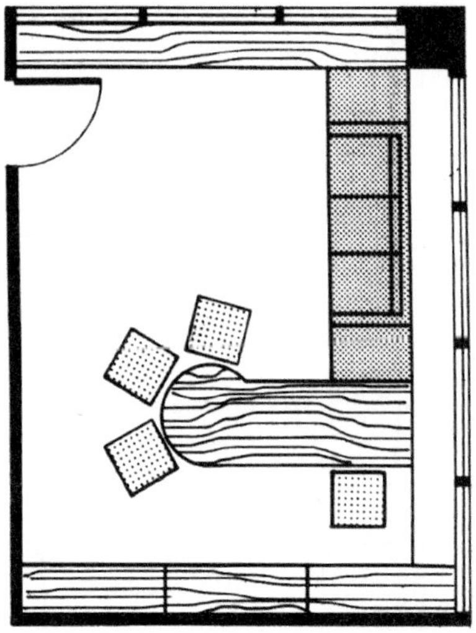
Fig. 12 16 ft × 21 ft, 336 ft²

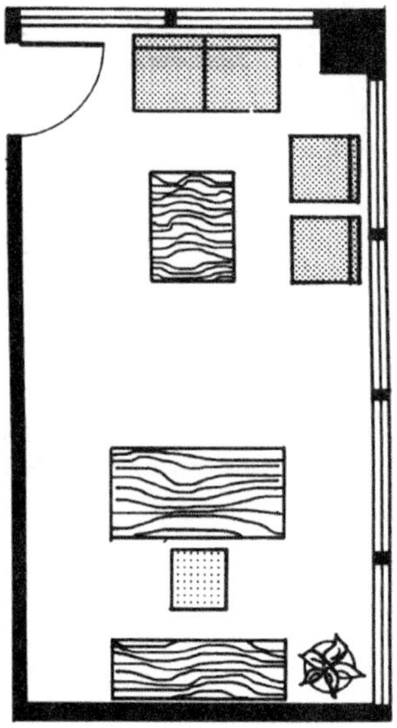
Fig. 13 12 ft × 23 ft, 276 ft²

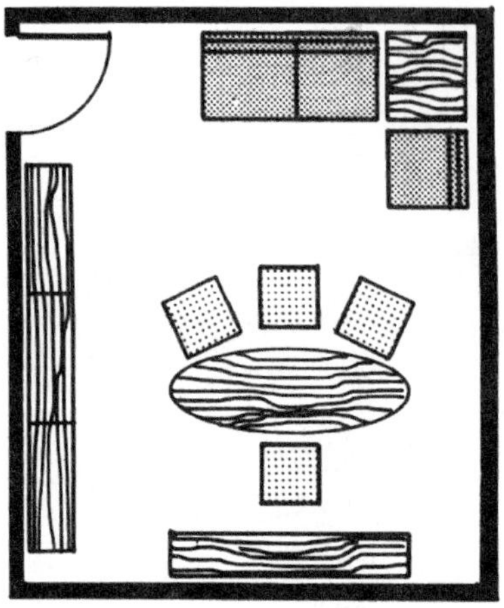
Fig. 14 15 ft × 18 ft, 270 ft²

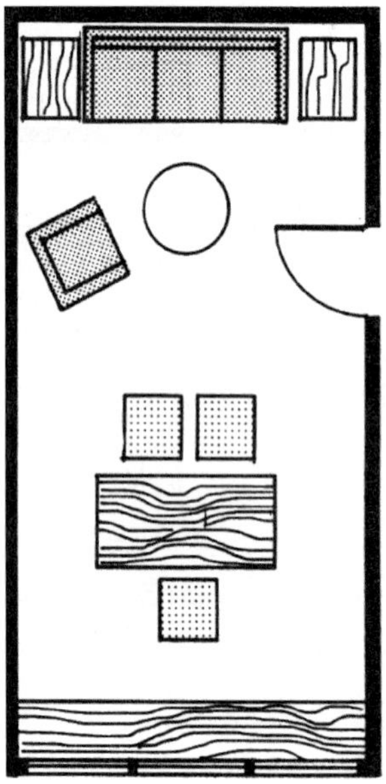
Fig. 15 12 ft × 24 ft, 288 ft²

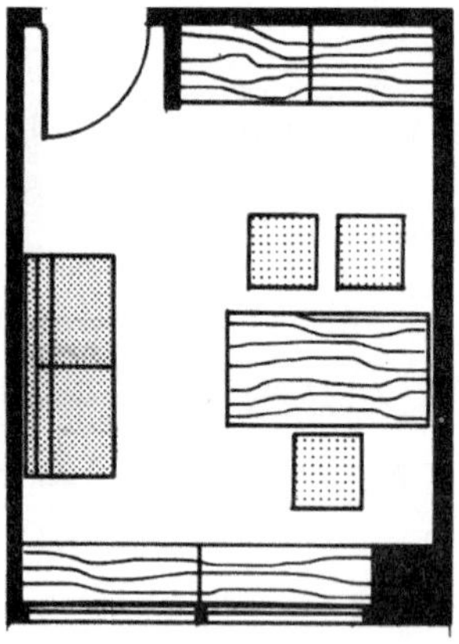
Fig. 16 12 ft × 16 ft, 192 ft²

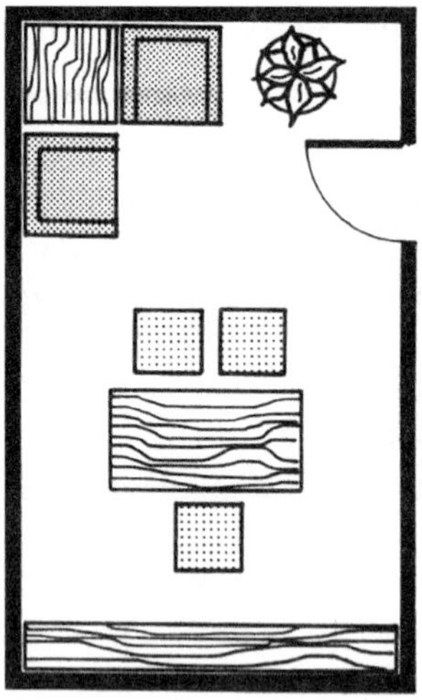
Fig. 17 12 ft × 20 ft, 240 ft²

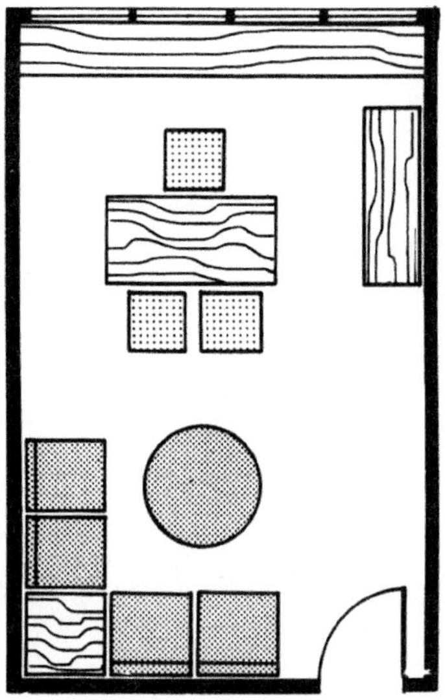

Fig. 18 14 ft × 22 ft, 308 ft²

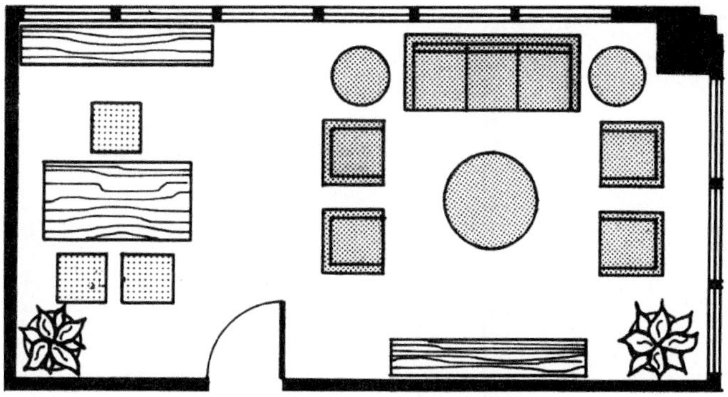

Fig. 19 14 ft × 28 ft, 392 ft²

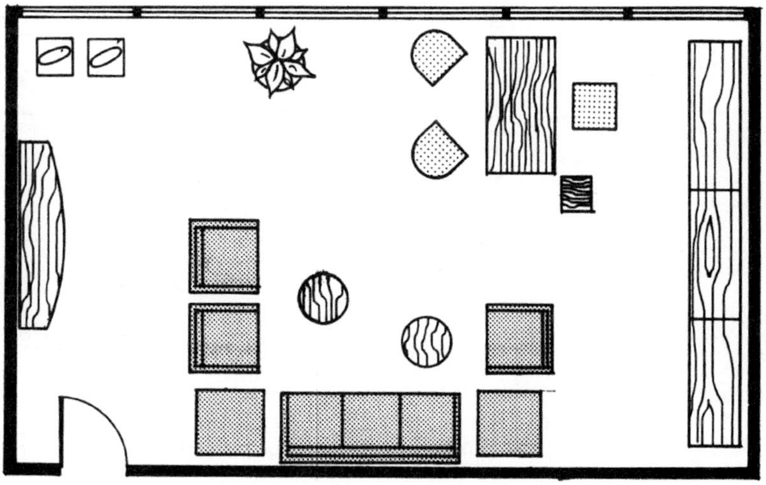

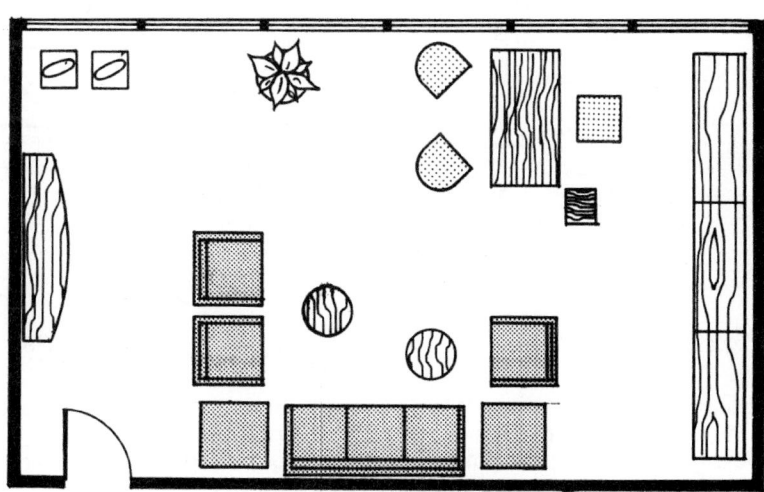

Fig. 20 19 ft × 33 ft, 627 ft²

PRIVATE OFFICES

Wall Unit Details

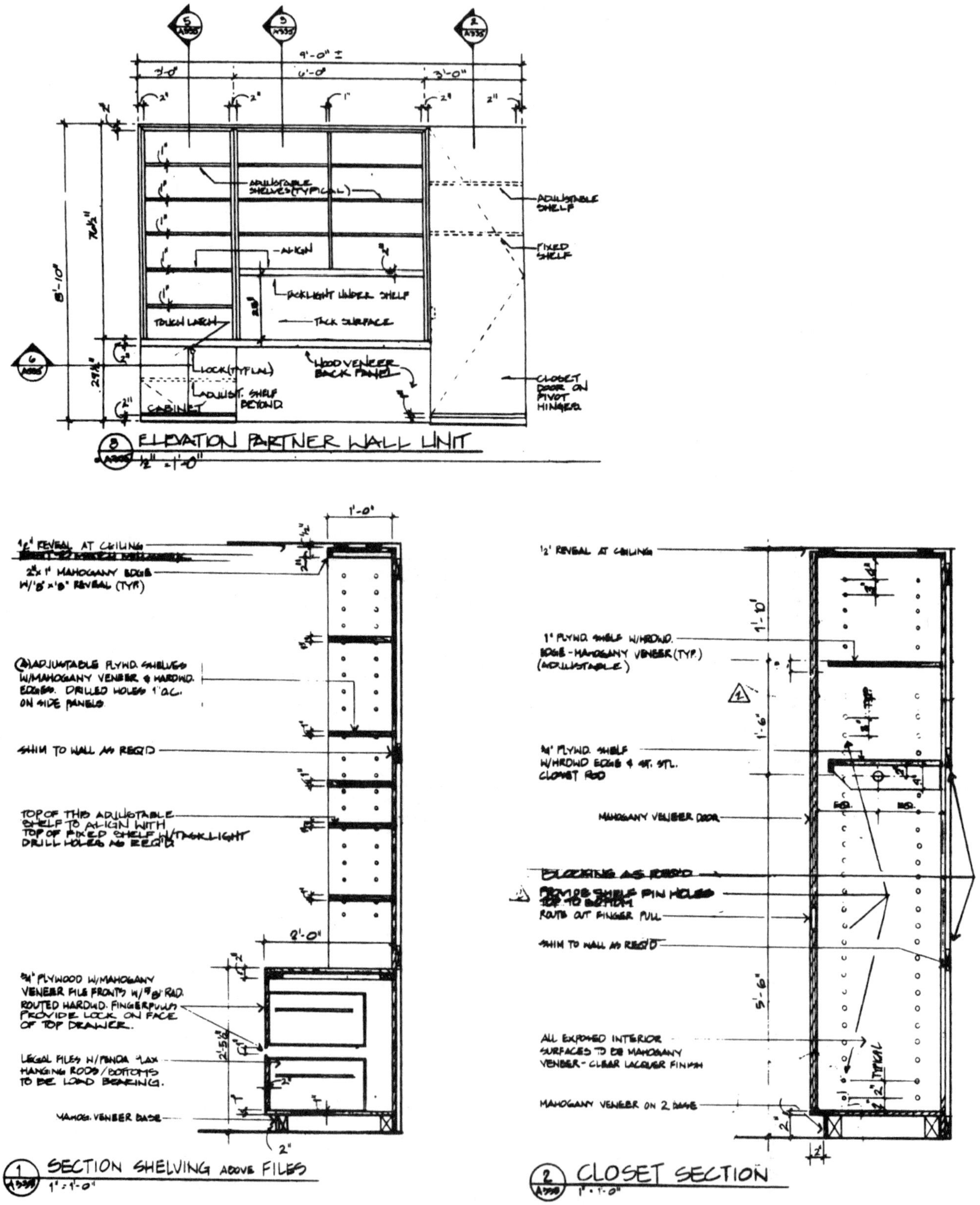

Fig. 21 Custom architectural woodwork (or "built-ins") is often required for executive offices. These architectural working drawings reflect the custom design of a storage wall for a partner in a law office. Careful analysis shows the incorporation of file, book, and coat storage within a floor-to-ceiling mahogany wood unit

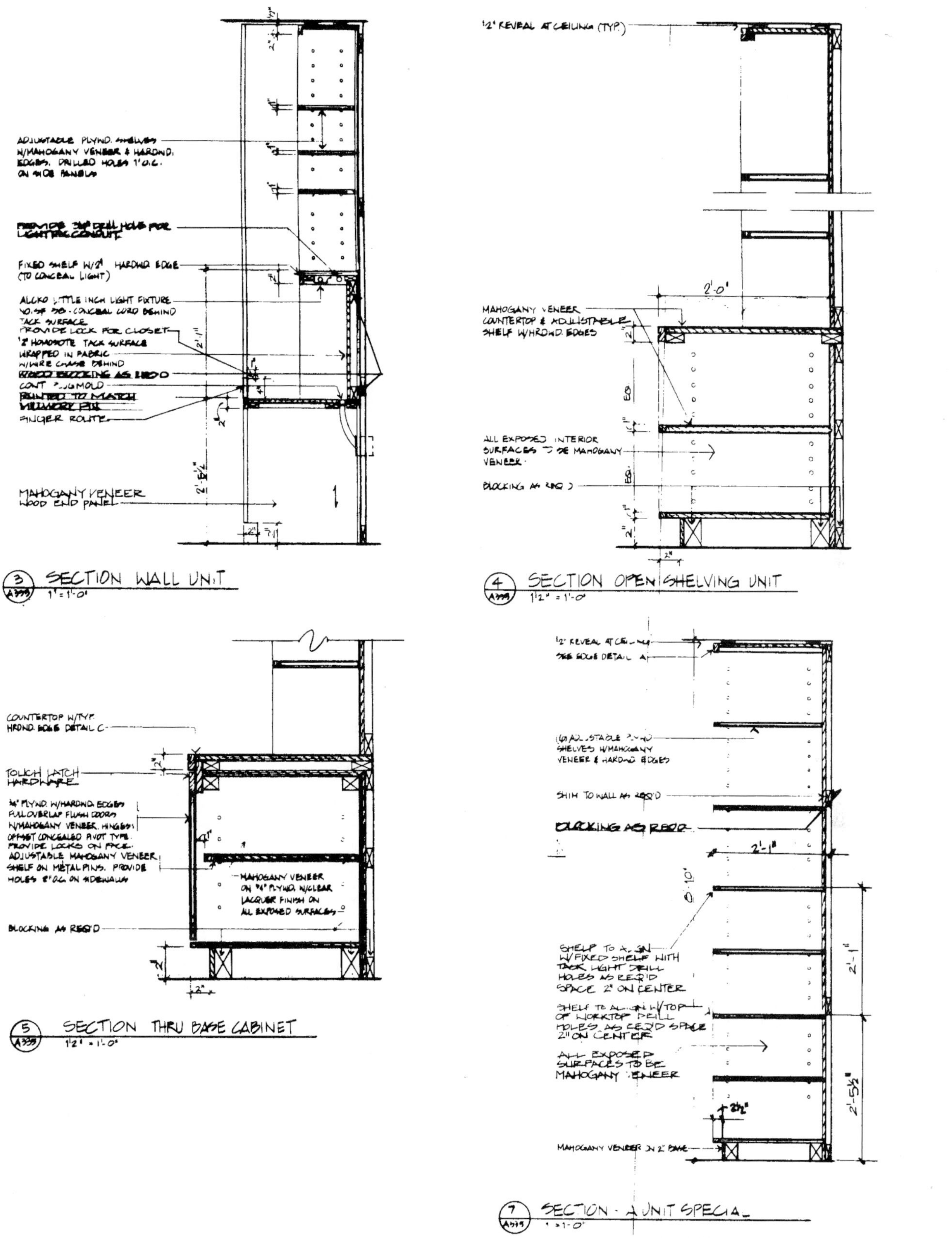

Fig. 22 These details represent typical vertical sections taken through various storage components for the partner wall unit shown in Fig. 21. Careful attention must be given to integration of electronic equipment, electrical wiring, and task lighting

PRIVATE OFFICES

Wall Unit Details

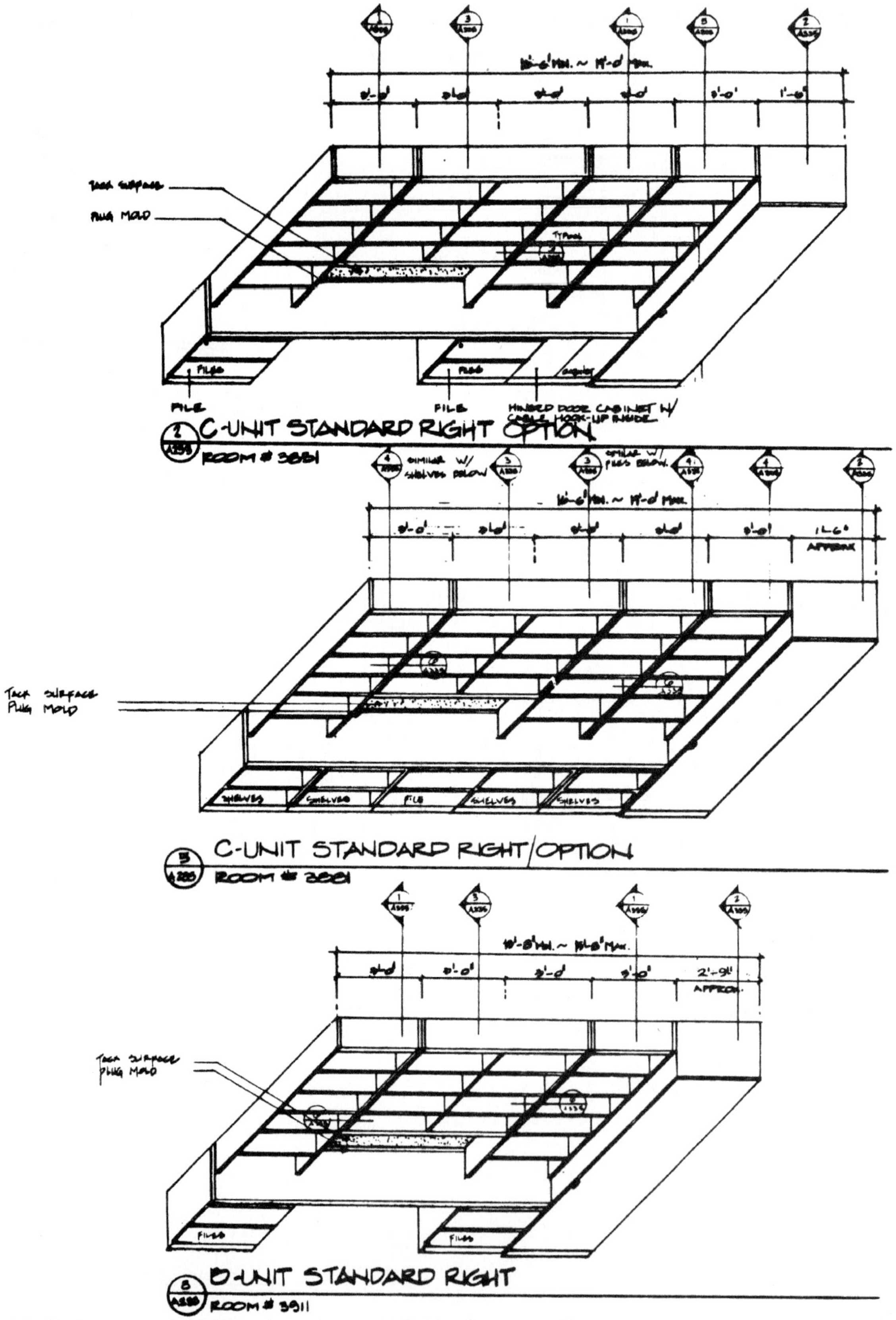

Fig. 23 These plan oblique drawings provide detailed design information to both client and architectural woodwork contractor. These drawings are particularly helpful when the office project for which these wall units are intended consists of many offices, and each office is to be customized within certain constraints

Many private offices require the detailing of custom credenzas and storage units. The sophistication and complexity of such details can significantly influence the budget for the space as well as the time of installation. Figure 24 represents a high-end approach, while Fig. 25 is more appropriate for offices with a moderate budget.

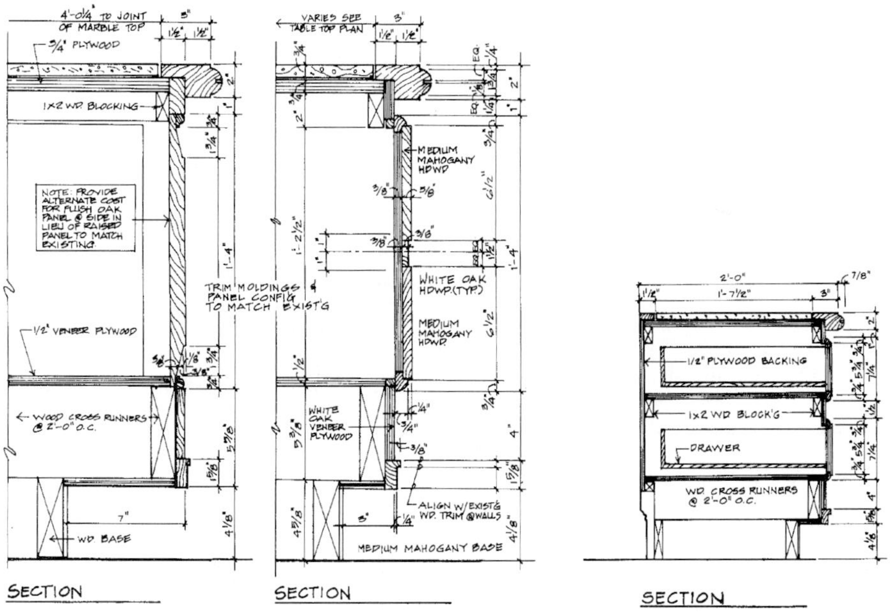

Fig. 24

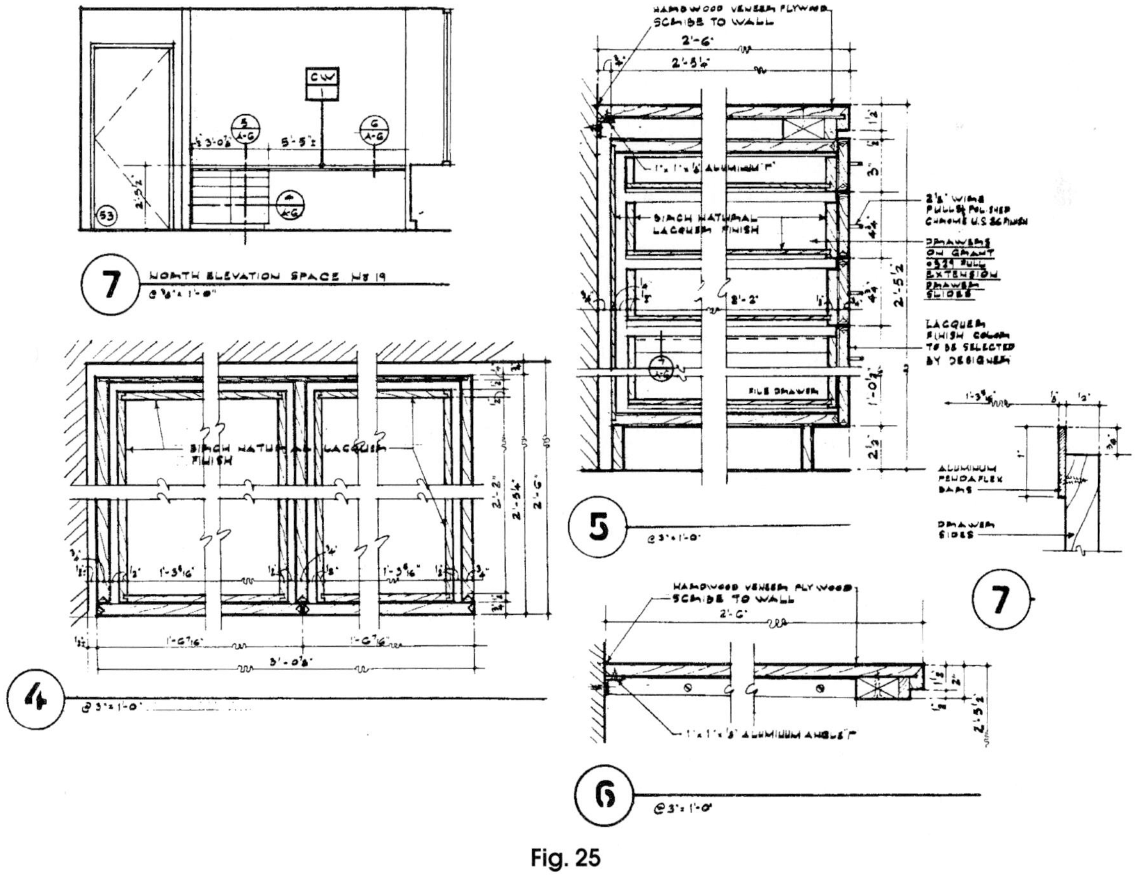

Fig. 25

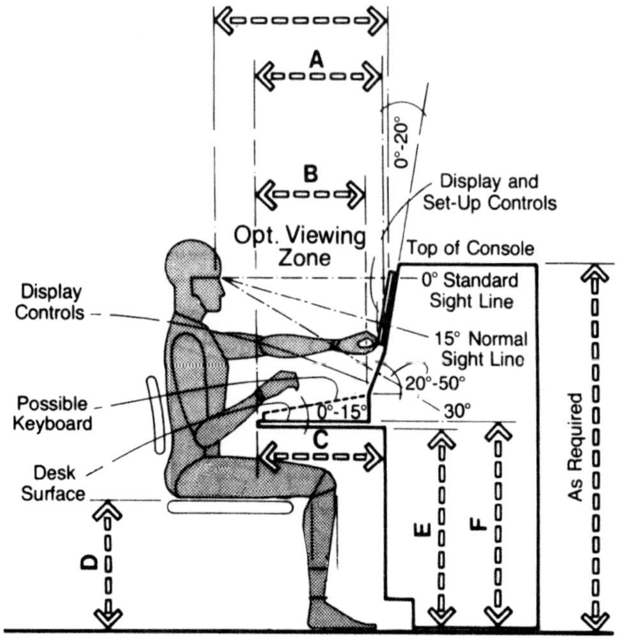

	in	cm
A	16–18	40.6–45.7
B	16 min.	40.6 min.
C	18 min.	45.7 min.
D	15–18 adjust.	38.1–45.7
E	26.5 min.	67.3 min.
F	30	76.2

Fig. 1

ELECTRONIC WORKSTATIONS

PLANNING DATA: ANTHROPOMETRICS

New electronic technologies, together with the advent and proliferation of the microcomputer and the availability of inexpensive packaged software, have changed the complexion of the office workplace. The ergonomic considerations related to this new work environment have necessitated a reevaluation of the traditional interface between the seated office worker and his or her workplace. It is essential that the design of this electronic workstation be responsive to human factors in order to avoid physical discomfort for the user. The location of the keyboard, angle of the visual display terminal, adjustability of the chair, field of vision, provisions for back support, and height of the seat above the floor are a few of the considerations in the design process.

This page and the following pages provide a variety of anthropometric and ergonomic planning data and details for use as reference in the design of the electronic workstation.

Figure 1 illustrates guidelines for use in establishing preliminary design assumptions for a workstation display console. Since the types of displays and the nature of the tasks associated with those displays can vary considerably, Fig. 1 cannot be taken too literally. The configuration shown, however, is fairly representational. Certain basic factors should be noted anthropometrically. The use of an adjustable chair will permit the eye height of the seated viewer to be raised or lowered to view the display, as may be required depending on body size. An adjustment range between 15 and 18 in, or 38.1 and 45.7 cm, should be adequate to accommodate the eye height sitting requirements of about 90 percent of all viewers. Adjustability, however, will be of little value if the vertical distance between the underside of the desk and the floor is insufficient to accommodate the knee height and thigh clearance when the seat is adjusted to the appropriate position. If such distance is not less than 26.5 in, or 67.3 cm, the majority of viewers will be accommodated.

The location of the top of the display should align with the standard sightline for optimum viewing conditions. Since the eye and the head can rotate within certain limitations and, in so doing, increase the area that can be scanned, displays can be located above the standard sightline when absolutely necessary. It should also be noted that the more perpendicular the normal sightline is to the display plane, the greater the viewing comfort. Accordingly, consideration should be given to sloping the display plane since the normal sightline is about 15° below the horizontal.

Stature is the vertical distance from the floor to the top of the head, measured while the subject stands erect, looking straight ahead.

Elbow height is the distance measured vertically from the floor to the depression formed at the elbow where the forearm meets the upper arm.

Eye height is the vertical distance from the floor to the inner corner of the eye, measured with the subject looking straight ahead and standing erect.

Sitting height erect is the vertical distance from the sitting surface to the top of the head with the subject sitting erect.

Sitting height normal is the vertical distance from the sitting surface to the top of the head, measured with the subject sitting relaxed.

Eye height is the vertical distance from the inner corner of the eye to the sitting surface.

Shoulder height is the distance taken vertically from the sitting surface to a point on the shoulder midway between the neck and acromion.

Shoulder breadth is the maximum horizontal distance across the deltoid muscles.

Elbow to elbow is the distance across the lateral surfaces of the elbows measured with elbows flexed and resting lightly against the body, with the forearms extended horizontally.

Hip breadth is the breadth of the body as measured across the widest portion of the hips. Note that a hip breadth measurement can also be taken with the subject in a standing position, in which case the definition would be the maximum breadth of the lower torso.

Elbow rest height is the height from the top of the sitting surface to the bottom of the tip of the elbow.

Thigh clearance is the distance taken vertically from a sitting surface to the top of the thigh at the point where the thigh and the abdomen intersect.

Knee height is the vertical distance from the floor to the midpoint of the kneecap.

Popliteal height is the distance, taken vertically, from the floor to the underside of the portion of the thigh, just behind the knee, while the subject is seated with body erect. The knees and ankles are usually perpendicular, with the bottom of the thigh and the back of the knees barely touching the sitting surface.

Buttock-popliteal length is the horizontal distance from the rearmost surface of the buttock to the back of the lower leg.

Buttock-knee length is the horizontal distance from the rearmost surface of the buttocks to the front of the kneecaps.

Buttock-toe length is the horizontal distance from the rearmost surface of the buttocks to the tip of the toe.

Buttock-heel length is the horizontal distance from the base of the heel to a wall against which the subject sits erect with his leg maximally extended forward along the sitting surface. This is sometimes referred to as *buttock-leg length.*

Vertical reach is the height above the sitting surface of the tip of the middle finger when the arm, hand, and fingers are extended vertically.

Vertical grip reach is usually measured from the floor to the top of a bar grasped in the right hand while the subject stands erect and the hand within which the bar is grasped is raised as high as it can be conveniently without experiencing discomfort or strain.

Side arm reach is the distance from the center line of the body to the outside surface of a bar grasped in the right hand while the subject stands erect and the arm is conveniently outstretched horizontally without experiencing discomfort or strain.

Thumb tip reach is the distance from the wall to the tip of the thumb, measured with the subject's shoulders against the wall, arm extended forward, and index finger touching the tip of the thumb.

Maximum body depth is the horizontal distance between the most anterior point on the body to the most posterior. Anterior points are usually located on the chest or abdomen while the posterior points are usually found in the buttock or shoulder region.

Maximum body breadth is the maximum distance, including arms, across the body.

- Both the work surface and the display monitors must be lowered and raised as a unit, with 31.8 cm of travel.
- The work surface must be tilted anywhere between a horizontal position to 35° below horizontal. The work surface, at its lowest setting and with a 10° tilted angle, as is common in use, must be 63.5 cm in height at its front edge.
- The work surface must raise to a horizontal height of 104 cm, accommodating a majority of people in a standing position.
- The monitor screens must be tiltable to any position between 15° forward of vertical and 15° back. This lets the user adjust the screen to avoid reflective glare, and it accommodates various working positions of different lines of sight.
- Adjustment controls designed for hand operation must be located within the operator's extended reach envelope.
- All surfaces must have matte or dull finishes. This reduces the likelihood of reflective glare.

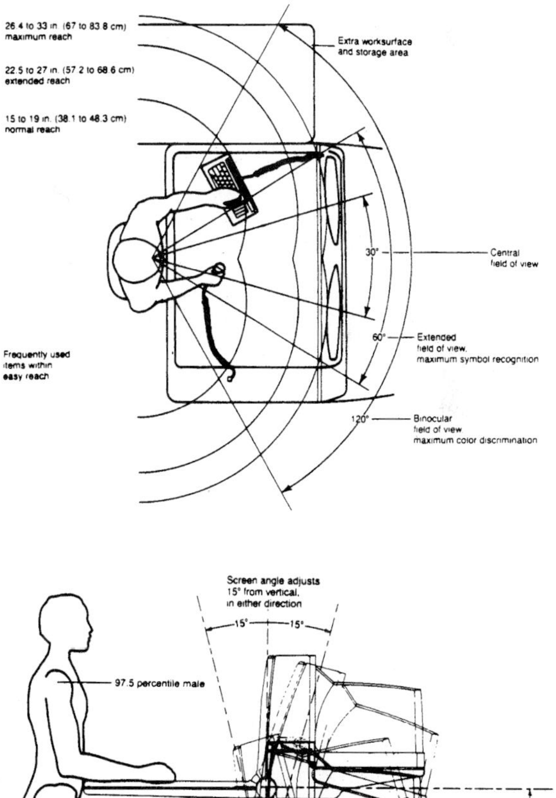

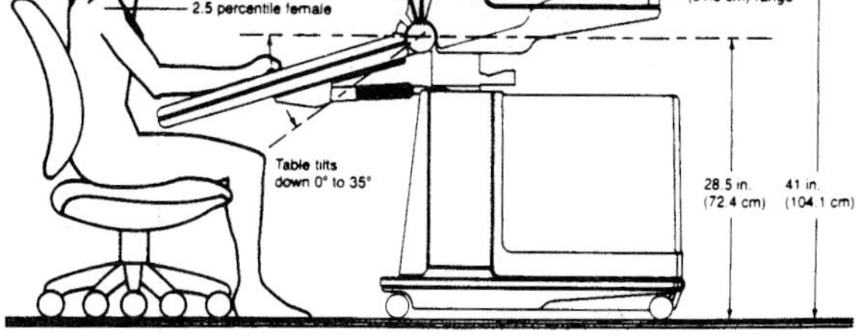

ELECTRONIC WORKSTATIONS

Planning Data: Anthropometrics

- The workstation must be compact and relatively easy to move through a standard 81-cm doorway.
- No structural components shall exist which inhibit the workstation's operation by users in wheelchairs, ensuring a barrier-free workstation.
- Service personnel must have easy access to electrical components.
- The digitizing surface must accommodate standard European and American D-size drawings.
- Screen depth of view must allow alphanumeric characters to be viewed at an angle between 20 and 28 arc minutes.

The Automated Task. *Square footage workstation standards for the automated task are also developed primarily according to task profile, equipment, conferencing, and privacy requirements.*	**Open** No requirement of equipment or task for privacy, concentration	**Screened** Privacy required for reading, working, thinking, calculating, meetings, confidential phone calls, elimination of visual and acoustical distractions

Task Profile: Data Retrieval.

- □ Paper, material, or information processed, analyzed, and/or maintained.
- □ Multiple reference sources may be used on a task.
- □ Reference materials used frequently.
- □ Limited volume of supplies and permanent records kept at the workspace.
- □ Electronic equipment may be used for easy reference, retrieval, keeping records current, and maintaining data and records.
- □ Additional equipment such as microfilm viewers may be required.
- □ Ability to see and hear co-workers may be desirable.
- □ Tasks may also require screening for concentration.

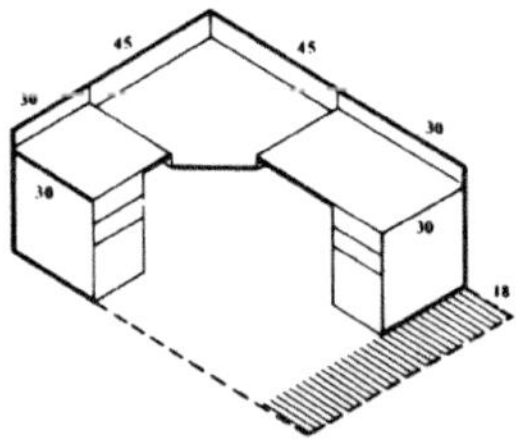

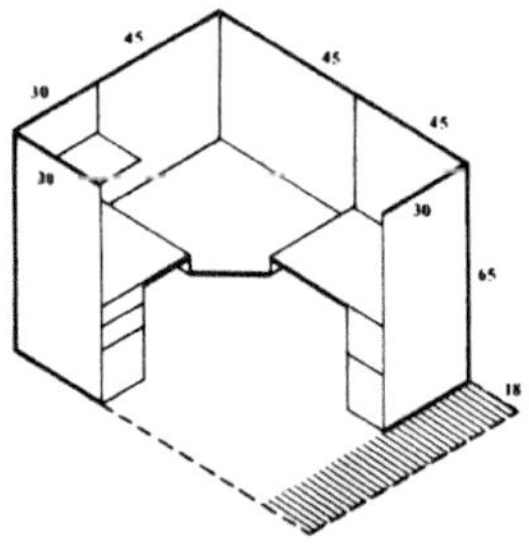

No	Guest chair
45 x 45	Primary work surface
30 x 45 (76 x 114 cm)	Secondary work surface
3–4	File drawers
0–2	Shelves

56 sq. ft.

Task Profile: Shared Tasks.

- □ Paper, material, or information processed, analyzed, and/or maintained.
- □ More than one task may be performed concurrently.
- □ More than one operator uses same equipment.
- □ Multiple reference sources may be used on a task.
- □ Reference materials used may be used frequently.
- □ Electronic equipment may be used for easy reference, inputting/maintaining data and records, retrieval, keeping records current.
- □ Storage requirements vary according to task.

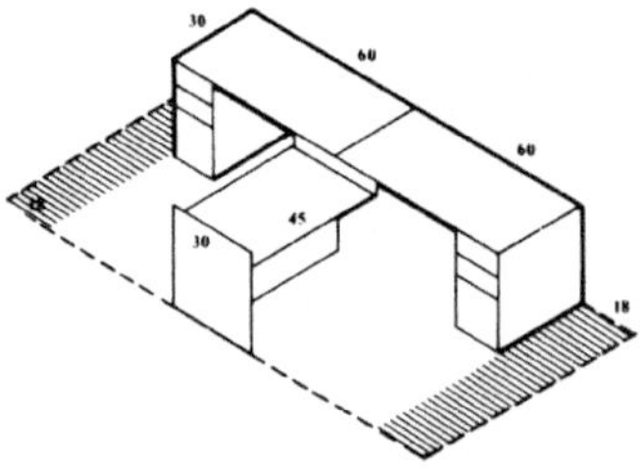

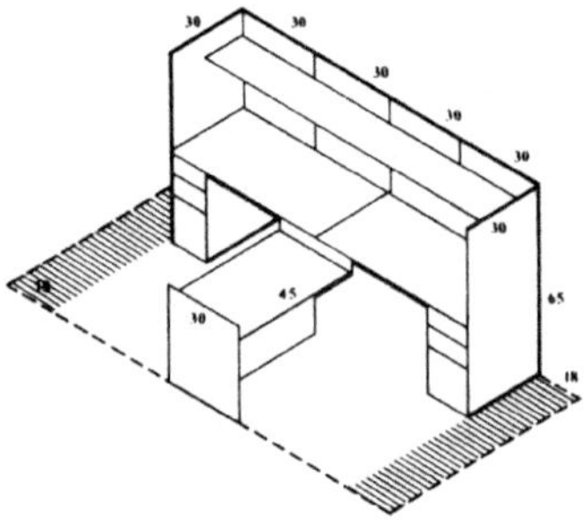

No	Guest chair
30 x 45	Primary work surface
30 x 60 (76 x 152 cm)	Secondary work surface
1–2	File drawers
0–4	Shelves

81 sq. ft.

Task Profile: Administrative Specialist/Secretarial.

- □ Paper, material, or information processed, analyzed, and/or maintained.
- □ More than one task may be performed concurrently.
- □ Multiple reference sources may be used on a task.
- □ Reference materials used frequently.
- □ Electronic equipment may be used for easy reference, retrieval, keeping records current, inputting/maintaining data and records.
- □ If supervising, ability to see subordinates may be desirable to direct activities.
- □ If monitoring, visual access may be desirable.
- □ Moderate amount of storage required at the workspace, that is, casework, client accounts, supplies.

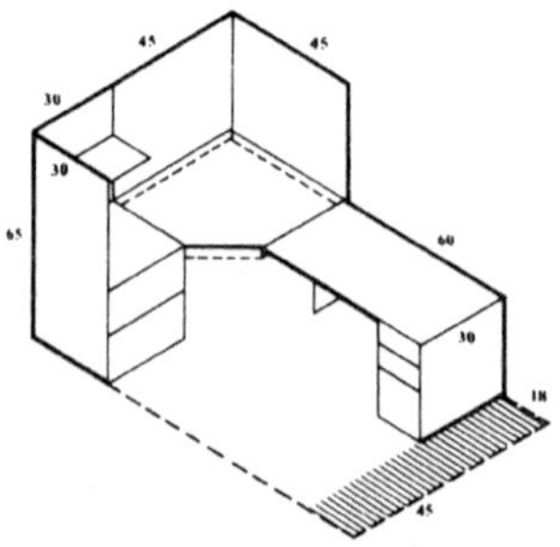

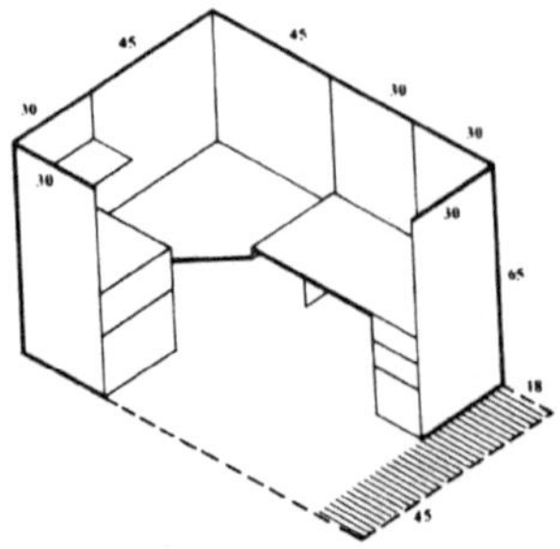

No	Guest chair
45 x 45	Primary work surface
30 x 60	Secondary work surface
3–4	File drawers
1–2	Shelves

64 sq. ft.

ELECTRONIC WORKSTATIONS
Planning Data: Square Footage

The Automated Task	Open	Screened
	No requirement of equipment or task for privacy, concentration	Privacy required for reading, working, thinking, calculating, meetings, confidential phone calls, elimination of visual and acoustical distractions

Task Profile: Administrative Specialist/Secretarial (+ Guest).

- □ Paper, material, or information processed, analyzed, and/or maintained.
- □ More than one task performed concurrently.
- □ Multiple reference sources used on a task.
- □ Reference materials used frequently.
- □ Limited volume of supplies and permanent records kept at the workspace.
- □ Electronic equipment may be used for easy reference, retrieval, keeping records current
- □ Tasks are complex enough to require concentration.
- □ Extensive use of telephone and additional equipment such as desk-top printer and microfilm viewer may be required.
- □ Need to see and hear co-workers is secondary priority.
- □ Limited conferencing required at workspace.
- □ If supervising, ability to see subordinates may be desirable to direct activities.
- □ If monitoring, visual access may be desirable.

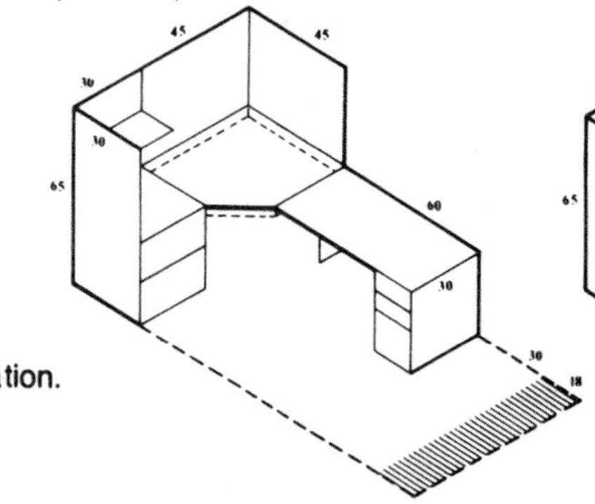

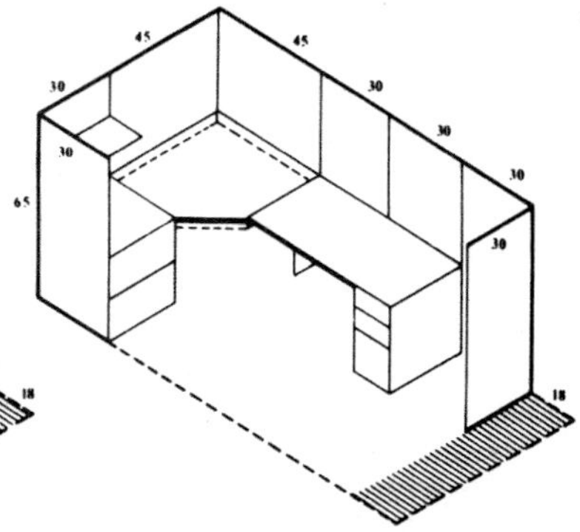

1	Guest chair
45 x 45	Primary work surface
30 x 60	Secondary work surface
3–4	File drawers
1–2	Shelves

80 sq. ft.

Task Profile: Word Processing.

- □ Time divided among administrative, processing paper, material, or information.
- □ More than one task may be performed concurrently.
- □ Multiple reference sources may be used on a task.
- □ Reference materials moderate but used frequently.
- □ Limited storage primarily for supplies.
- □ Ability to see and hear co-workers or subordinates is desirable.
- □ Typewriter and/or electronic equipment may be used to expedite processing and administrative tasks, for example, VDT, printer, transcriber, OCR, microfilm viewer, separate disk drives.

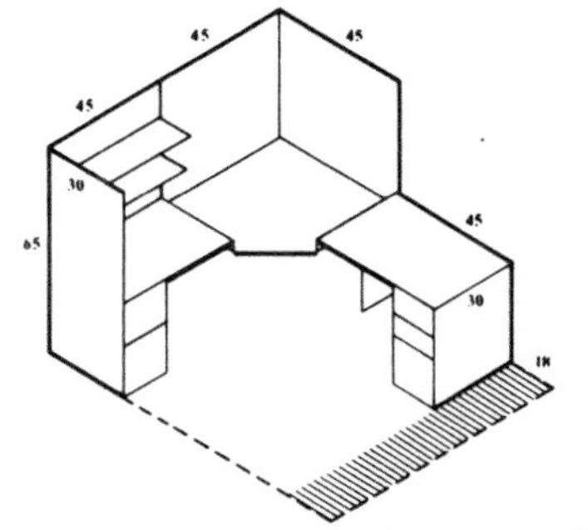

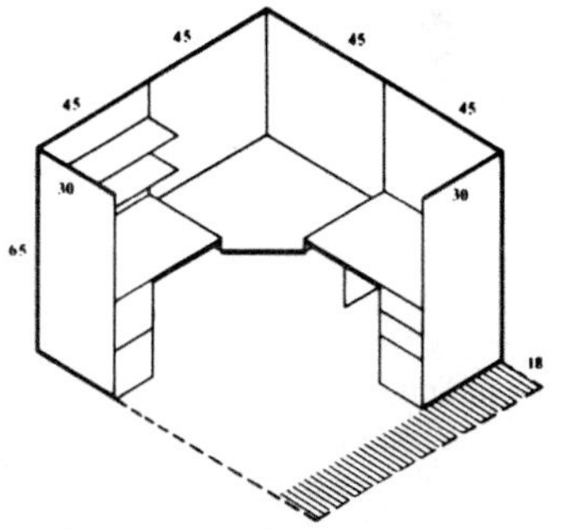

No	Guest chair
45 x 45 (114 x 114 cm)	Primary work surface
30 x 45 (76 x 114 cm)	Secondary work surface
3–4	File drawers
1–2	Shelves

67 sq. ft.

Task Profile: Word Processing (+ Guest).

- □ Time divided among administrative, processing paper, material, or information, and limited conferencing at workspace.
- □ More than one task may be performed concurrently.
- □ Multiple reference sources may be used on a task.
- □ Reference materials moderate but used frequently.
- □ Limited storage primarily for supplies.
- □ Typewriter and/or electronic equipment (VDT, printer, and so on) may be used to expedite processing and administrative tasks.
- □ Tasks are complex enough to require concentration for analysis, or heavy equipment operations require acoustical screening.
- □ Work surface needed for organization of work.

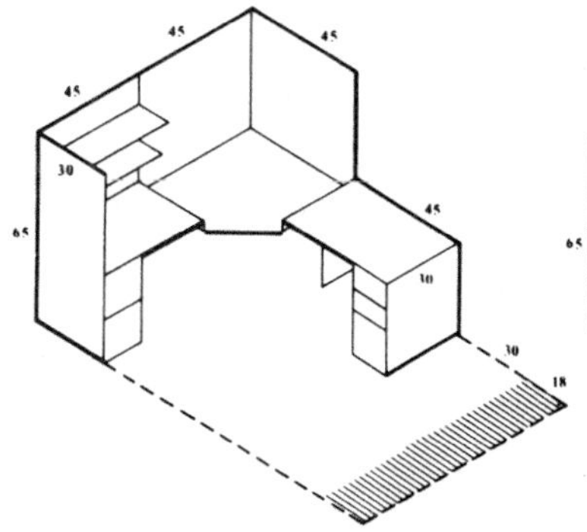

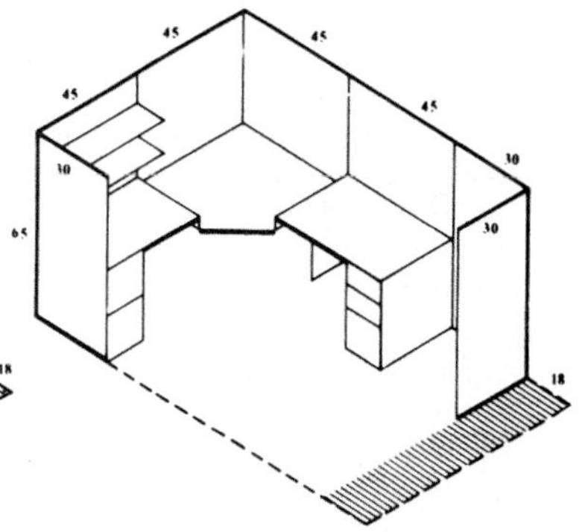

1	Guest chair
45 x 45	Primary work surface
30 x 45	Secondary work surface
3–4	File drawers
1–2	Shelves

86 sq. ft.

ELECTRONIC WORKSTATIONS
Planning Data: Square Footage

The Automated Task	Open	Screened
	No requirement of equipment or task for privacy, concentration	Privacy required for reading, working, thinking, calculating, meetings, confidential phone calls, elimination of visual and acoustical distractions

Task Profile: Technical/Systems Analyst/ Programmer.

- □ Time divided among administrative, processing paper, material, or information, and limited conferencing at workspace.
- □ More than one task may be performed concurrently.
- □ Multiple reference sources may be used on a task.
- □ Reference materials may be extensive and used frequently.
- □ Ability to see and hear co-workers or subordinates desirable.
- □ Typewriter and electronic equipment (VDT, printer, and so on) may be used to expedite processing and administrative tasks.
- □ Moderate to extensive amount of storage required at the workspace for manuals, binders, computer printouts, coding sheets, supplies, permanent files, reference materials.

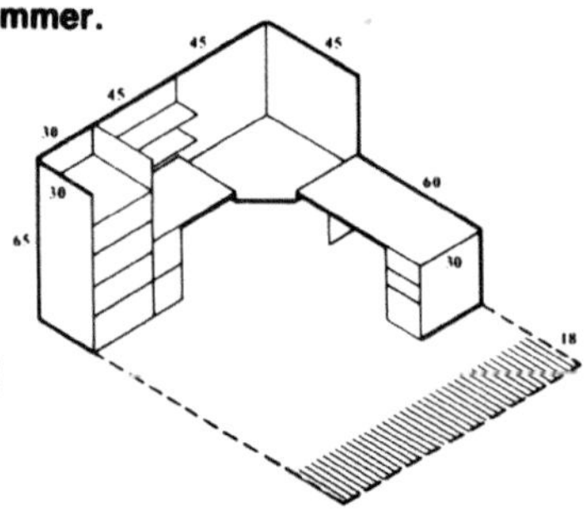

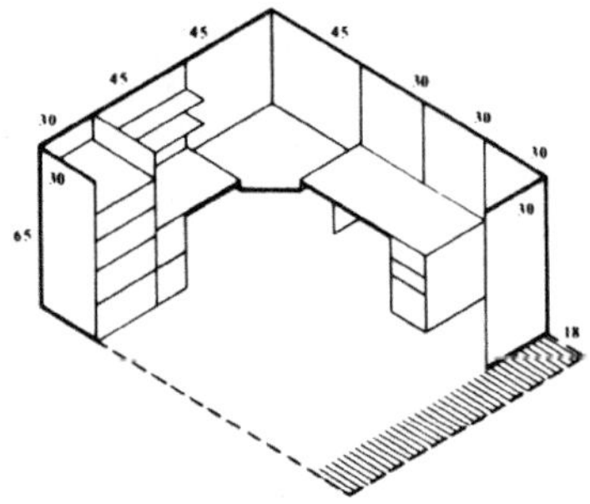

1	Guest chair
45 x 45	Primary work surface
30 x 60 (76 x 152 cm)	Secondary work surface
6–8	File drawers
3–5	Shelves

128 sq. ft.

Task Profile: Administrative/Managerial.

- □ Extensive conferencing at individual workspace.
- □ Analysis of reports, computerized materials, and so on.
- □ Varied tasks or projects performed simultaneously on an ongoing basis.
- □ Large amounts of storage extensively used.
- □ Storage for client/project files, reference manuals, documentation, correspondence.
- □ Telephone used extensively.
- □ Supervision of subordinates almost universal.
- □ Electronic equipment accommodation is secondary priority, used primarily for communication/electronic mail, scheduling.

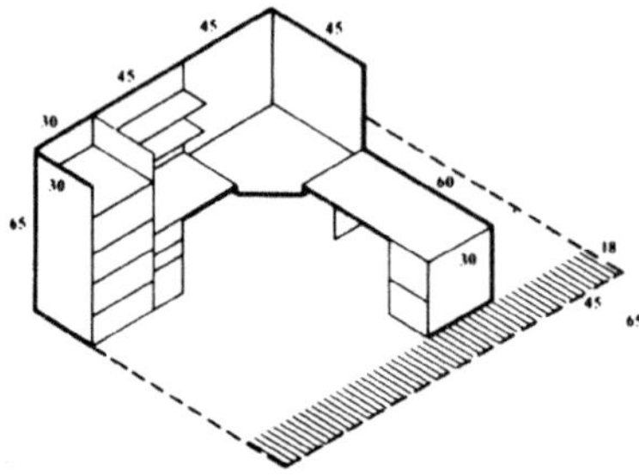

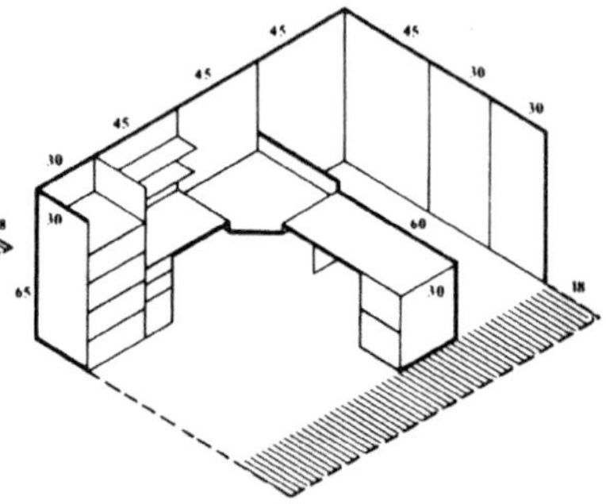

2	Guest chair
45 x 45	Primary work surface
30 x 60 (76 x 152 cm)	Secondary work surface
5–8	File drawers
3–5	Shelves

154 sq. ft.

Task Profile: Administrative/Total Enclosure.

- □ Extensive conferencing at individual workspace.
- □ Analysis of reports, computerized materials, and so on.
- □ Varied tasks on projects performed simultaneously on an ongoing basis.
- □ Large amounts of storage extensively used.
- □ Storage for client/project files, reference manuals, documentation, correspondence.
- □ Telephone used extensively.
- □ Supervision of subordinates almost universal.
- □ Electronic equipment accommodation is secondary priority, used primarily for communication/electronic mail, scheduling.
- □ Subject matter of job responsibilities requires confidentiality.

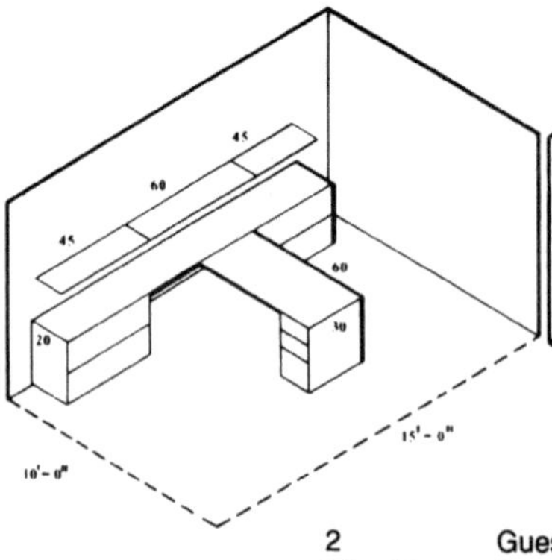

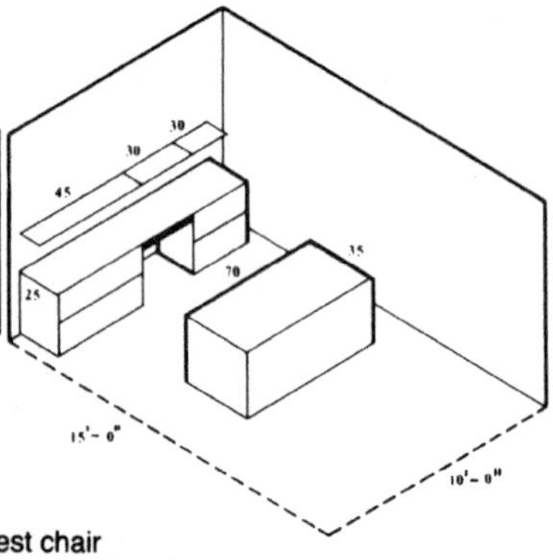

2	Guest chair
30 x 60	Primary work surface
20 sq ft (15 sq m)	Secondary work surface
5–8	File drawers
3–5	Shelves

150 sq. ft.

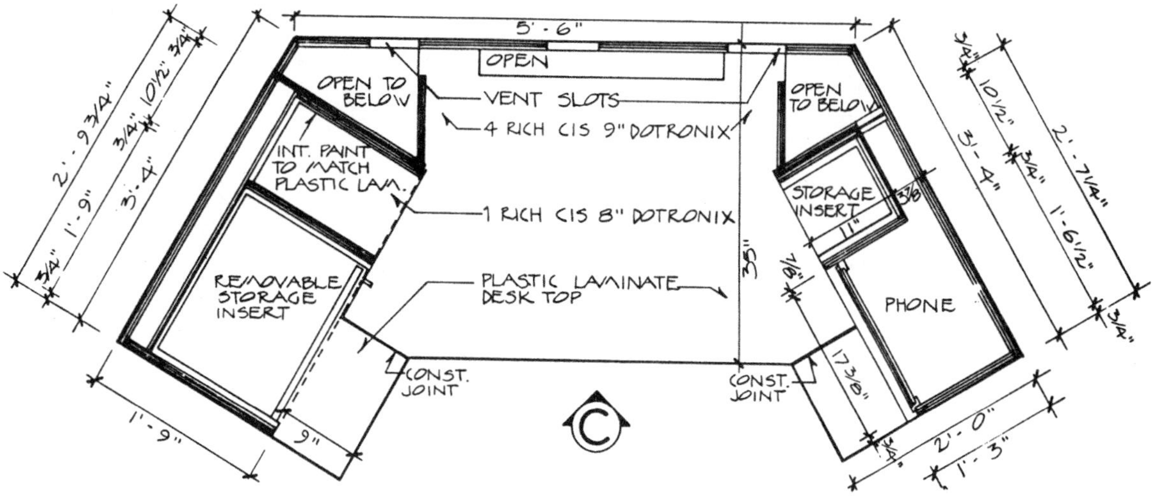

A PLAN / SECTION TRADING DESK TYPE 'A'

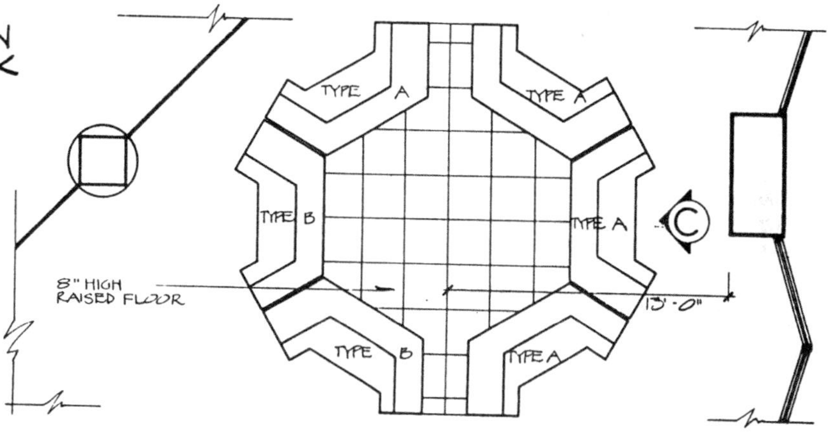

B PLAN - 20TH FLOOR TRADING ROOM

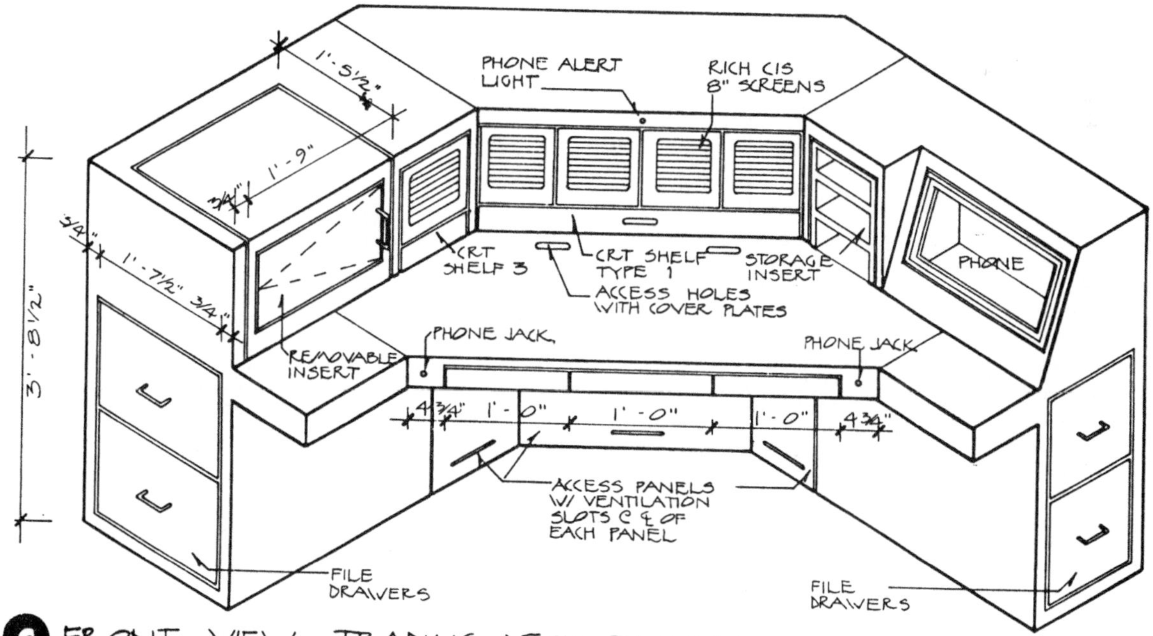

C FRONT VIEW - TRADING DESK TYPE 'A'

Fig. 2 Technologically and electronically complex trading desks must be ergonomically correct in every respect. With little, if any, margin for error when designing and detailing multiple workstations of this type, a full-size mock-up is always required

ELECTRONIC WORKSTATIONS
Trading Desk Details

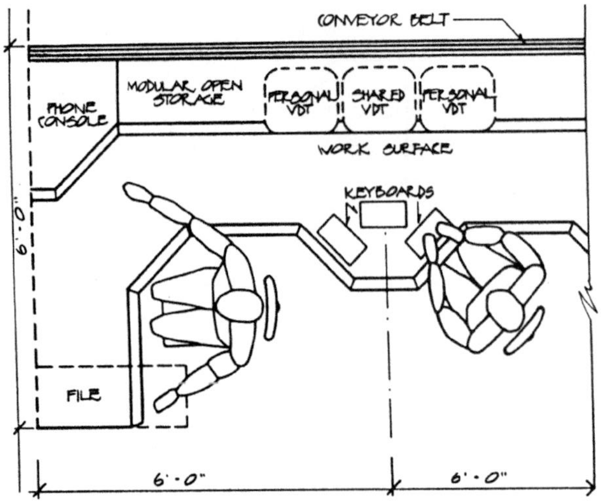

A ERGONOMIC FACTORS - PLAN

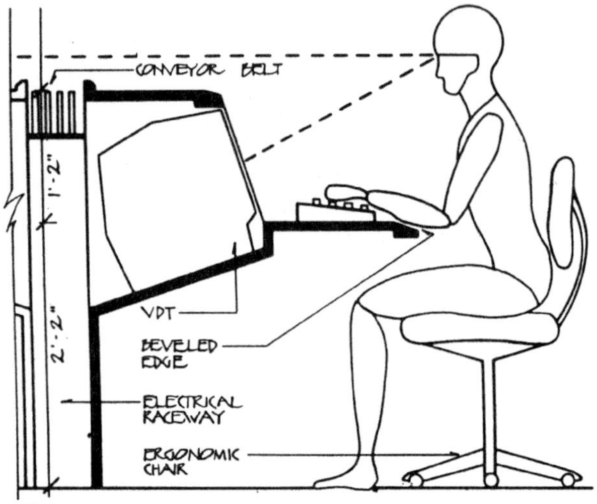

C ELEVATION/SECTION

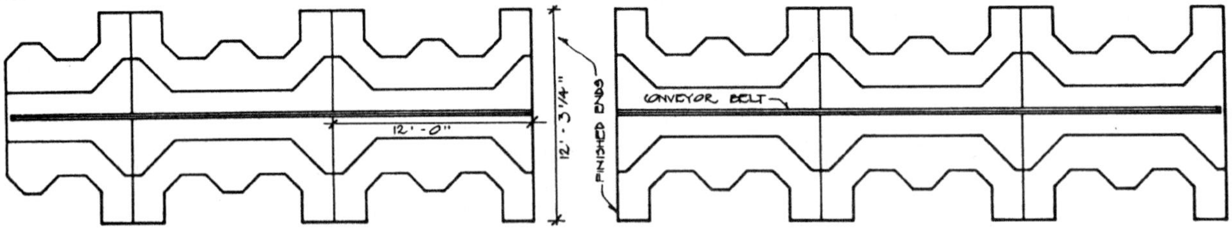

B TYPICAL PLAN LAYOUT

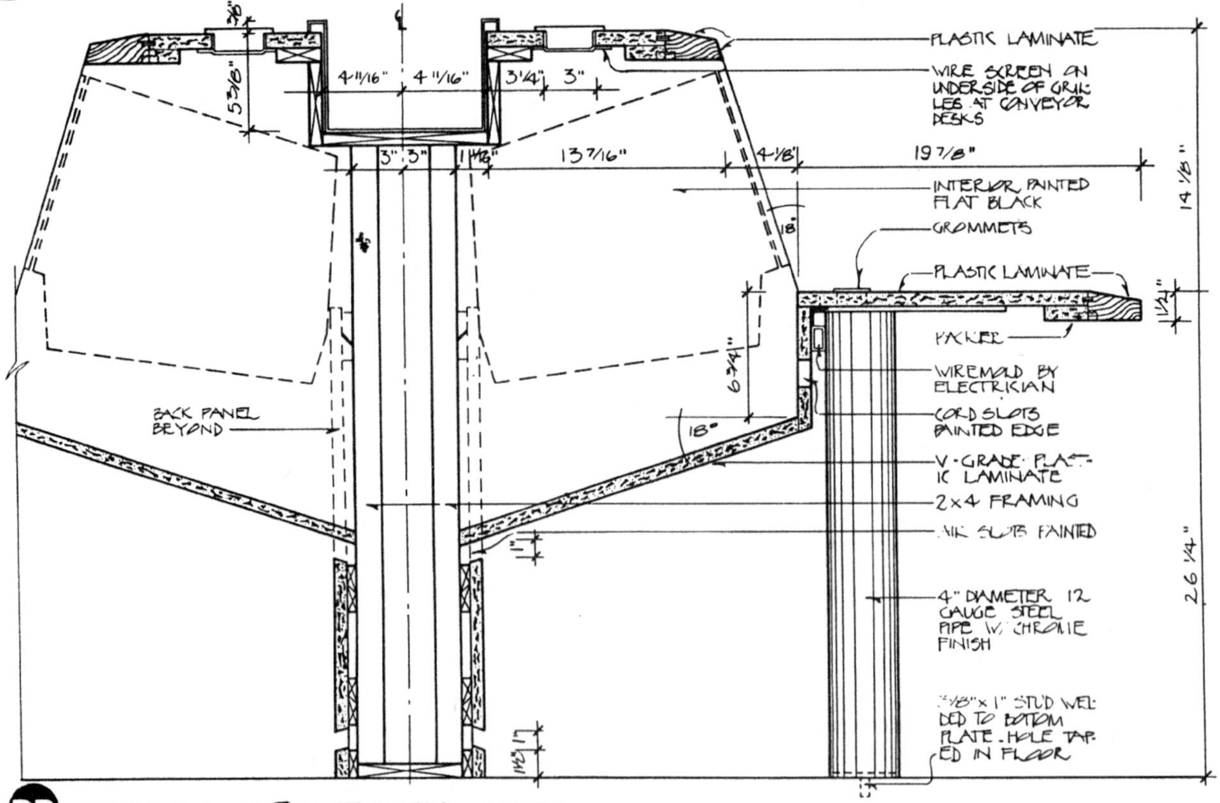

DD SECTION THRU TYPICAL DESK

ELECTRONIC WORKSTATIONS

Trading Table Details

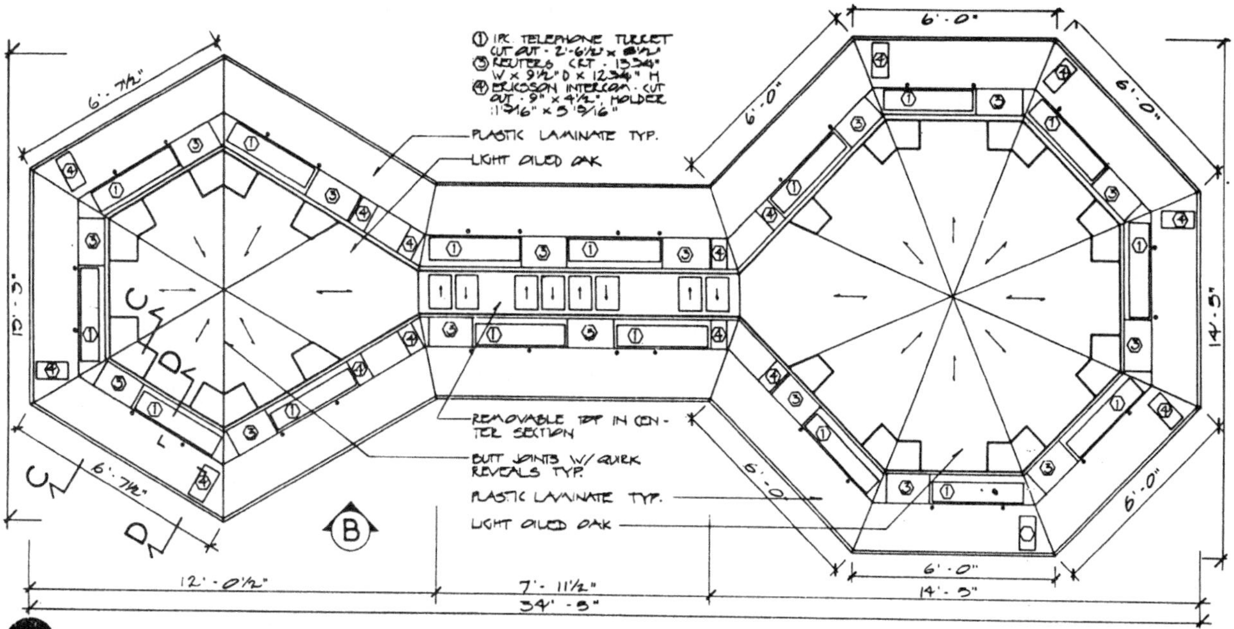

A PLAN OF TREASURY TRADING TABLE

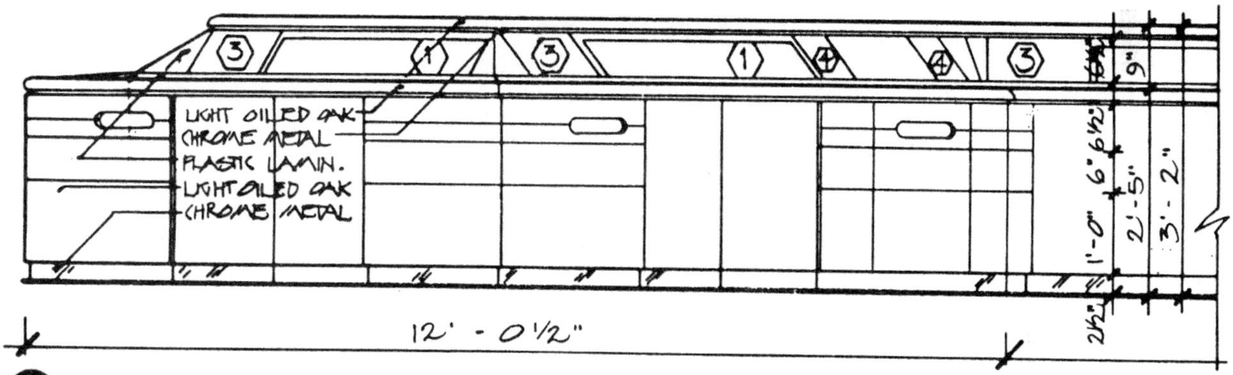

B PARTIAL ELEVATION

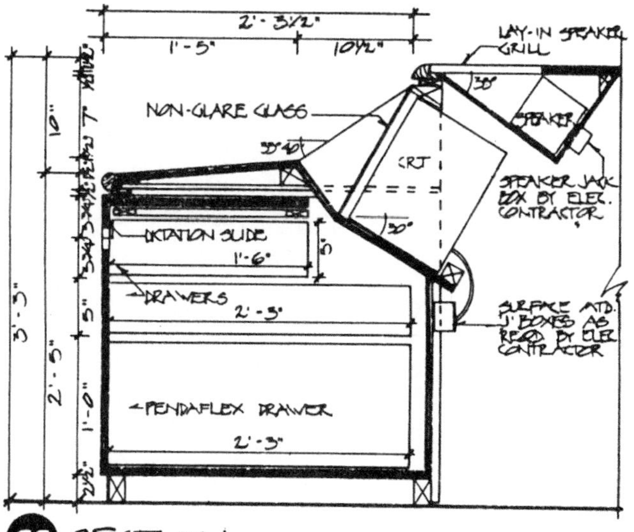

CC SECTION

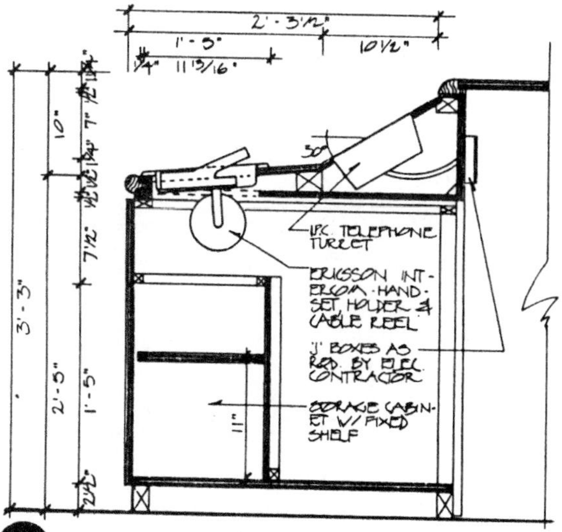

DD SECTION

CONFERENCE ROOMS
Planning Data: Table Sizes and Seating Capacities

Consideration must be given to clearances and circulation around the larger conference table, as indicated in Figs. 1 and 2. A minimum of 48 in, or 121.9 cm, is suggested from the edge of the table to the wall or nearest obstruction. This dimension under ordinary circumstance allows for a circulation zone beyond the sitting zone of 30 to 36 in, or 76.2 to 91.4 cm, based on a maximum body breadth measurement of the larger person. The greater dimension is recommended to allow for the chair in a pulled-out position.

The actual dimensions of the conference table are a function of the number of people to be seated. The square table illustrated in Fig. 1 provides for eight people, with each side ranging from 54 to 60 in, or 137.2 to 152.4 cm. The larger dimension is more appropriate to accommodate people of larger body size and to allow for a more generous work zone for each person. This translates into 30 in, or 76.2 cm, per person, which constitutes a comfortable perimeter allocation. The circular table shown in Fig. 2 comfortably accommodates five people while allowing for a 30-in, or 76.2-cm, access zone between chairs. To accommodate both sitting zone and circulation zone, a space with a radius ranging from 72 to 81 in, or 182.9 to 205.7 cm, must be provided.

Round conference tables offer the advantages of intimacy, equality, and compactness. On the other hand, if status is an issue, or if one wall within the space is an audiovisual wall, this table shape can be less than satisfactory. The same problems can arise with a square conference table. In both instances, however, the total seating around each table shape must be viewed in the context of chair size, chair spacing, and tasks to be performed at the table.

	in	cm
A	48–60	121.9–152.4
B	4–6	10.2–15.2
C	20–24	50.8–61.0
D	6–10	15.2–25.4
E	18–24	45.7–61.0
F	30–36	76.2–91.4
G	54–60	137.2–152.4
H	30	76.2
I	72–81	182.9–205.7
J	42–51	106.7–129.5
K	24–27	61.0–68.6
L	48–54	121.9–137.2

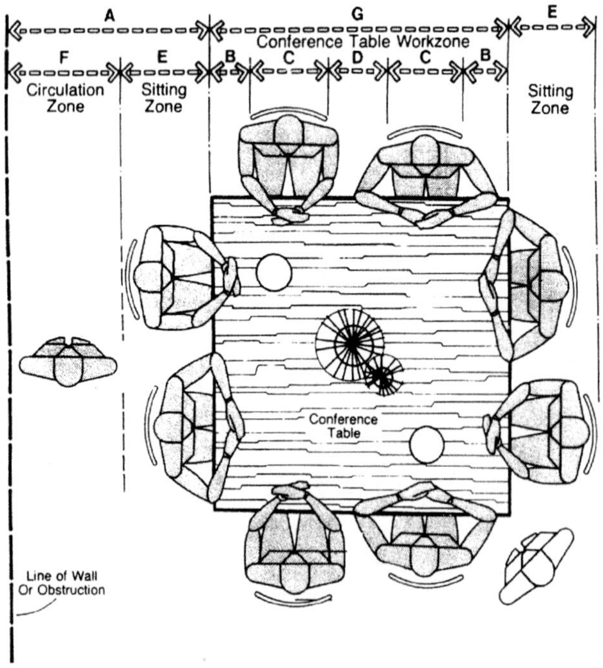

Fig. 1 Square conference table

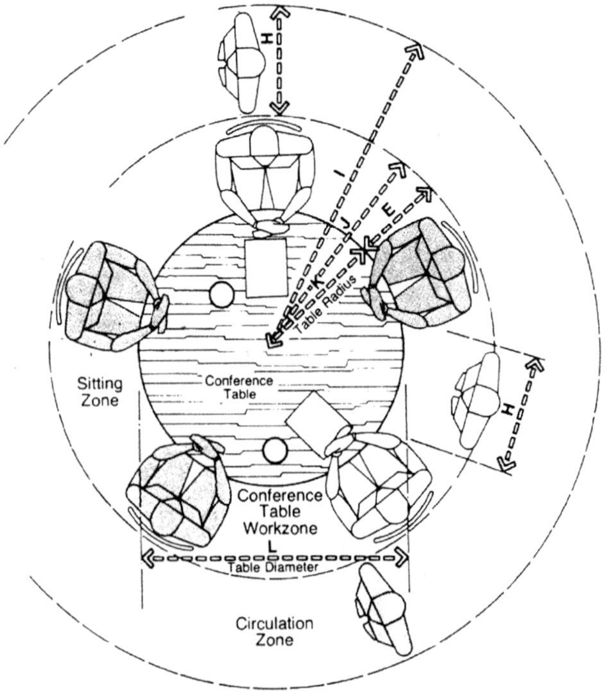

Fig. 2 Circular conference table

CONFERENCE ROOMS
Planning Data: Table Sizes and Seatig Capacities

ROUND TABLES

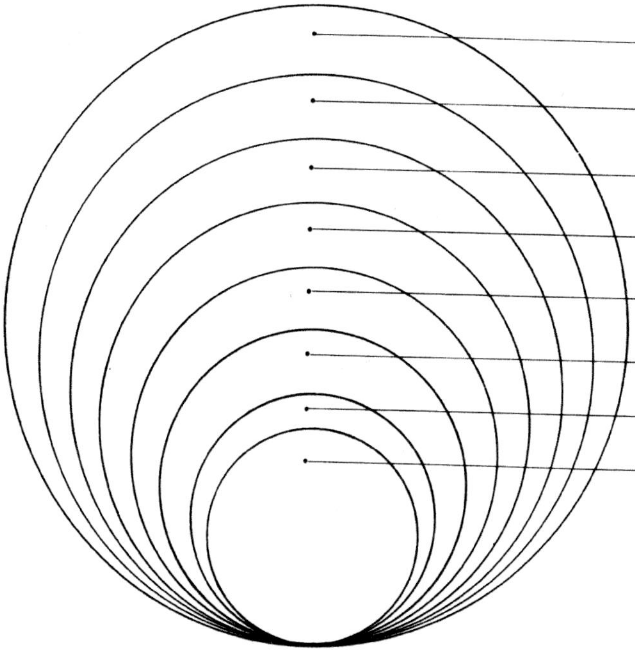

Diam.	Circum.	Approx. Seating	Recommended Minimum Room Size
10′0″	31′5″	12–15	20′0″ x 20′0″
9′0″	28′2″	11–14	19′0″ x 19′0″
8′0″	25′1″	10–12	18′3″ x 18′3″
7′0″	22′0″	9–11	16′0″ x 16′0″
6′0″	18′10″	8–9	14′6″ x 14′6″
5′0″	15′9″	7–8	13′0″ x 13′0″
4′0″	12′6″	5–6	11′6″ x 11′6″
3′6″	11′0″	4–5	10′6″ x 10′6″

SQUARE TABLES

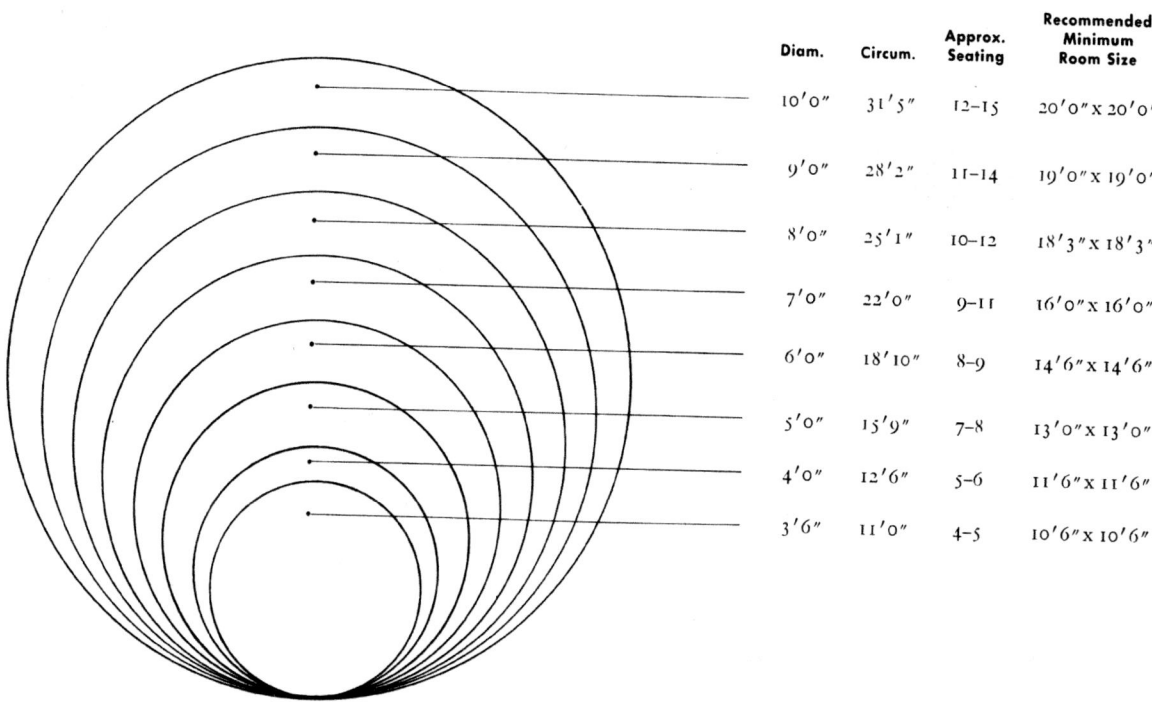

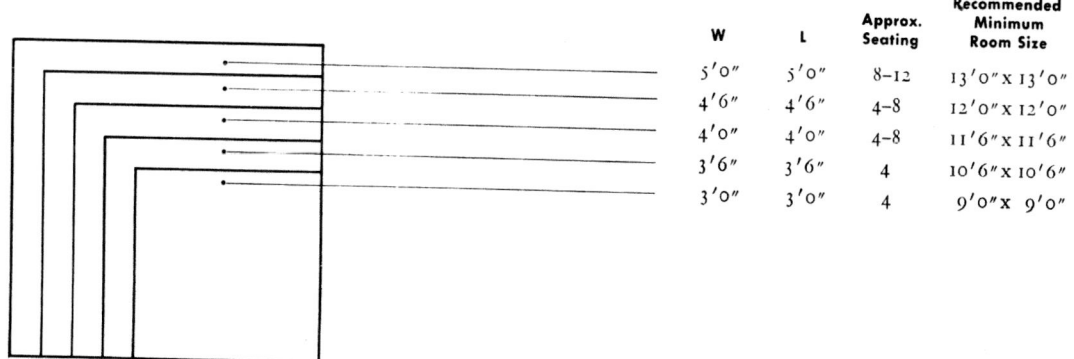

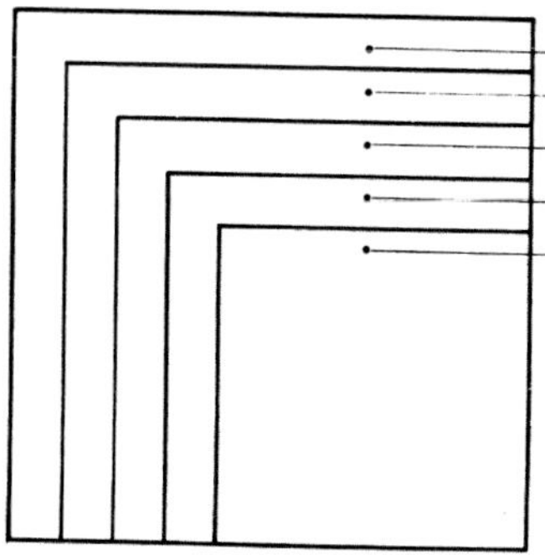

W	L	Approx. Seating	Recommended Minimum Room Size
5′0″	5′0″	8–12	13′0″ x 13′0″
4′6″	4′6″	4–8	12′0″ x 12′0″
4′0″	4′0″	4–8	11′6″ x 11′6″
3′6″	3′6″	4	10′6″ x 10′6″
3′0″	3′0″	4	9′0″ x 9′0″

CONFERENCE ROOMS

Planning Data: Table Sizes and Seating Capacities

Rectangular and boat-shaped conference tables lend themselves to formal settings where status and hierarchy are important. Both table shapes are also more suitable in a room where an audiovisual wall is placed at one end of the space, or where speakers are making presentations. The boat-shaped table also offers greater visibility of others seated at the table, as well as ease of circulation around its perimeter.

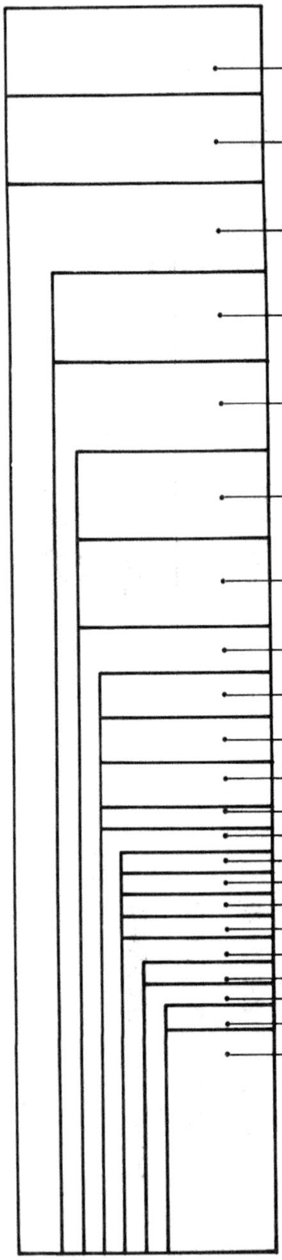

RECTANGULAR TABLES

W	L	Approx. Seating	Recommended Minimum Room Size
6′0″	28′0″	28–30	18′0″ x 40′0″
6′0″	26′0″	26–28	18′0″ x 38′0″
6′0″	24′0″	24–26	18′0″ x 36′0″
5′0″	22′0″	22–24	15′0″ x 32′0″
5′0″	20′0″	20–22	15′0″ x 30′0″
4′6″	18′0″	18–20	13′6″ x 27′0″
4′6″	16′0″	16–18	13′6″ x 25′0″
4′6″	14′0″	14–16	13′6″ x 23′0″
4′0″	13′0″	12–14	12′0″ x 21′0″
4′0″	12′0″	12–14	12′0″ x 20′0″
4′0″	11′0″	10–12	12′0″ x 19′0″
4′0″	10′0″	10–12	12′0″ x 17′0″
4′0″	9′6″	8–10	12′0″ x 16′6″
3′6″	9′0″	8–10	10′6″ x 16′0″
3′6″	8′6″	8–10	10′6″ x 15′6″
3′6″	8′0″	8–10	10′6″ x 15′0″
3′6″	7′6″	6–8	10′6″ x 14′6″
3′6″	7′0″	6–8	10′6″ x 14′0″
3′0″	6′6″	6–8	10′0″ x 13′6″
3′0″	6′0″	6–8	10′0″ x 13′0″
2′6″	5′6″	4–6	9′0″ x 12′6″
2′6″	5′0″	4–6	9′0″ x 12′0″

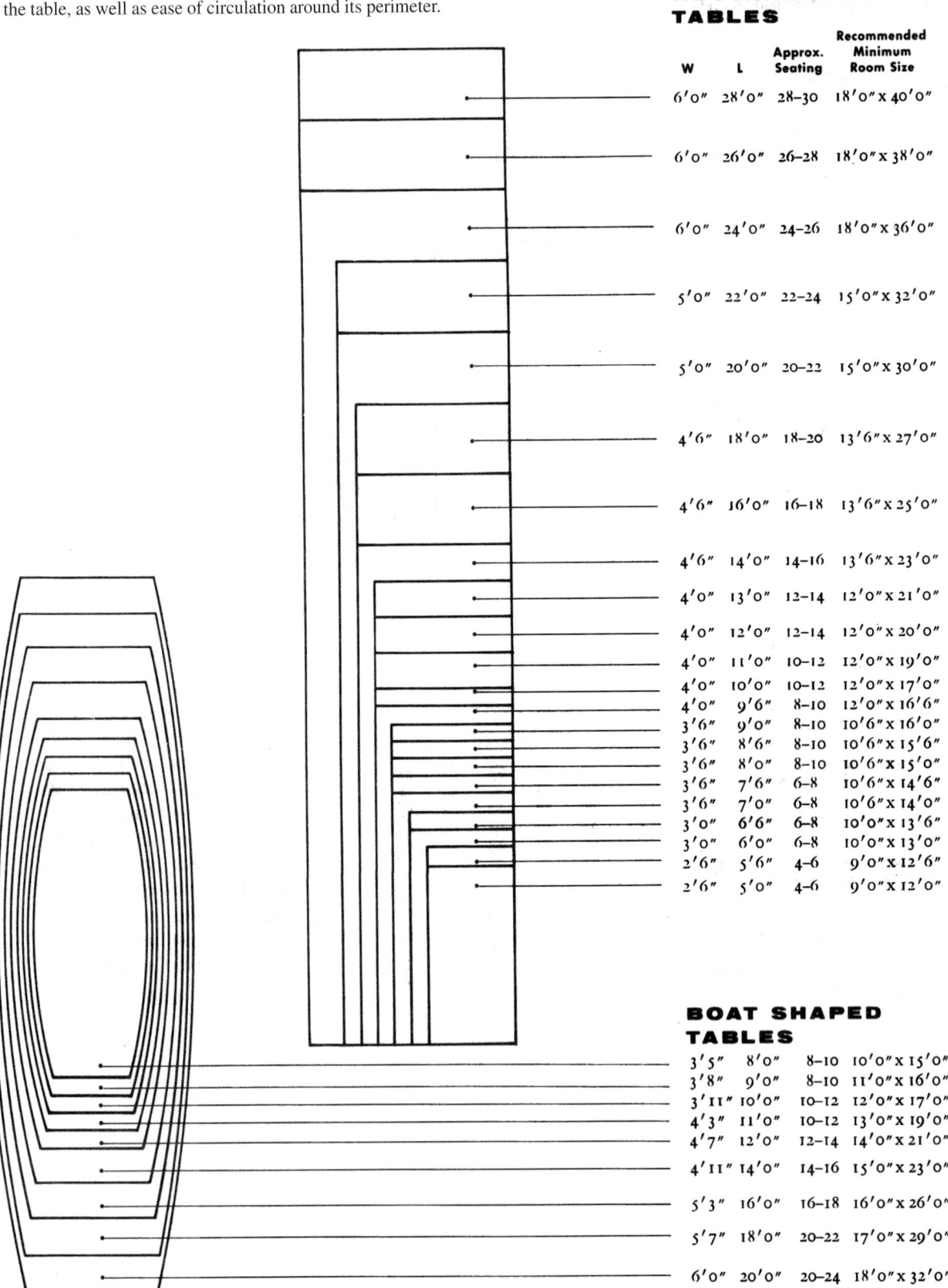

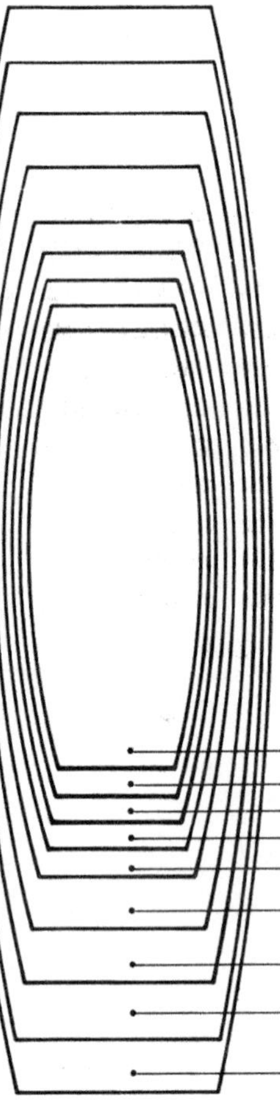

BOAT SHAPED TABLES

W	L	Approx. Seating	Recommended Minimum Room Size
3′5″	8′0″	8–10	10′0″ x 15′0″
3′8″	9′0″	8–10	11′0″ x 16′0″
3′11″	10′0″	10–12	12′0″ x 17′0″
4′3″	11′0″	10–12	13′0″ x 19′0″
4′7″	12′0″	12–14	14′0″ x 21′0″
4′11″	14′0″	14–16	15′0″ x 23′0″
5′3″	16′0″	16–18	16′0″ x 26′0″
5′7″	18′0″	20–22	17′0″ x 29′0″
6′0″	20′0″	20–24	18′0″ x 32′0″

CONFERENCE ROOMS
Planning Data: Table Sizes and Seating Capacities

Solid Conference
For 20 people

4-30"x72" tables
2-30"x 60" tables

Race Track
For 26 people

6-30"x72" tables
4-30" wide crescents

Trapezoid/Round
For 12 people

6-30"x30"x30"x 60" tables

V-Shape
For 20 people

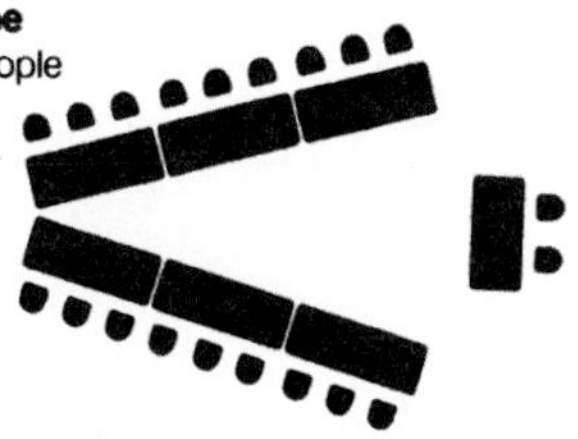

Boat Shape
For 28 people

BANQUET ROOMS

60" diameter tables
Capacity: 180 people

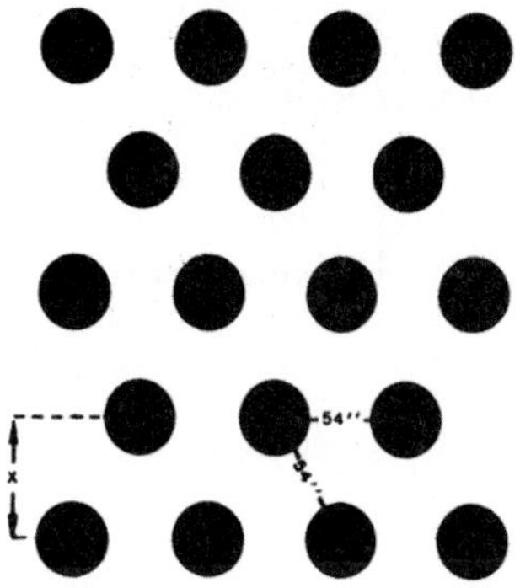

Table Size	Capacity	Centerline Spread *
48" dia.	6 persons	7'5"
54" dia.	6-8 persons	7'10"
60" dia.	8-10 persons	8'3"
66" dia.	10 persons	8'8"
72" dia.	10-12 persons	9'1"

30" x 96" tables
Capacity: 180 people

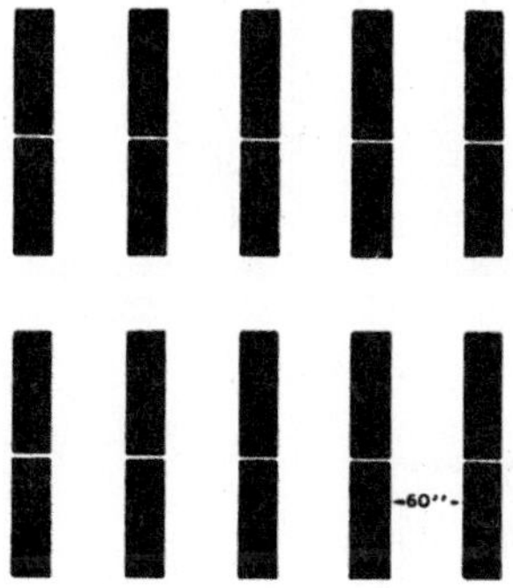

Table Size	Capacity
30"x48"	4-6 persons
30"x60"	6 persons
30"x72"	8 persons
30"x96"	10 persons

18" x 72" classroom style tables
Capacity: 162 people

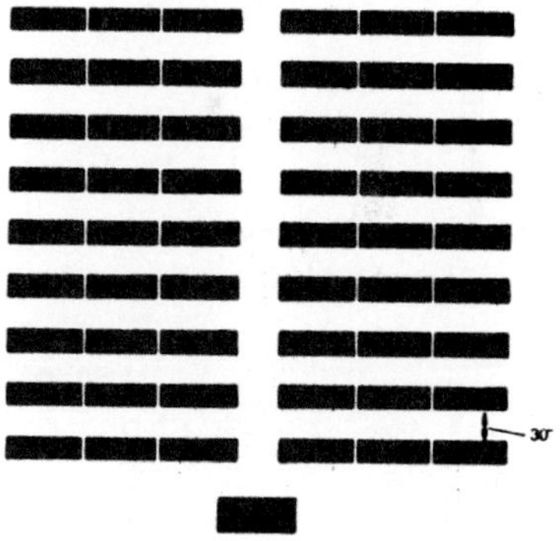

Table Size	Capacity
18"x60"	2 persons
18"x72"	3 persons
18"x96"	4 persons

CONFERENCE ROOMS

Planning Data: Table Sizes and Seating Capacities

Seats 8, 323 ft²

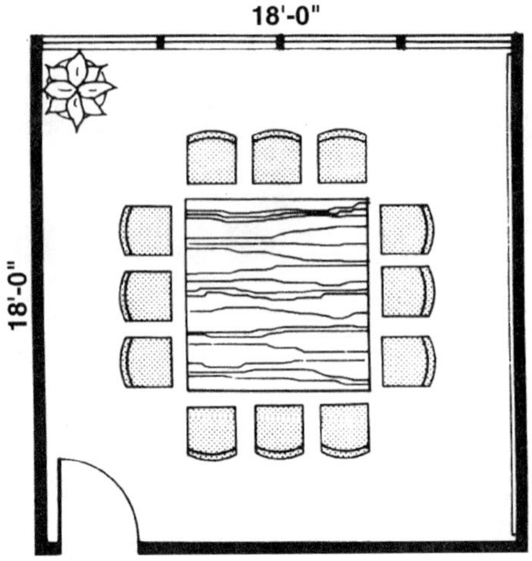

Seats 12, 324 ft²

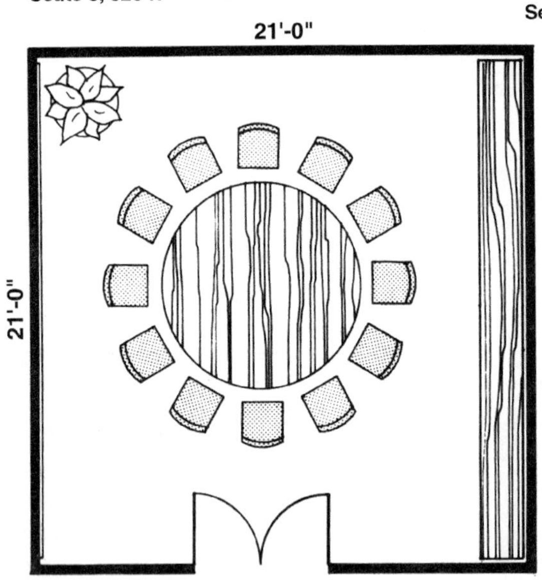

Seats 12, 441 ft²

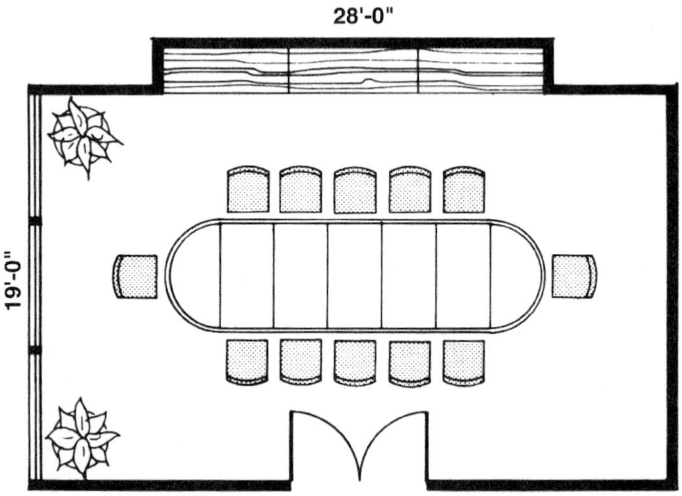

Seats 12, 532 ft²

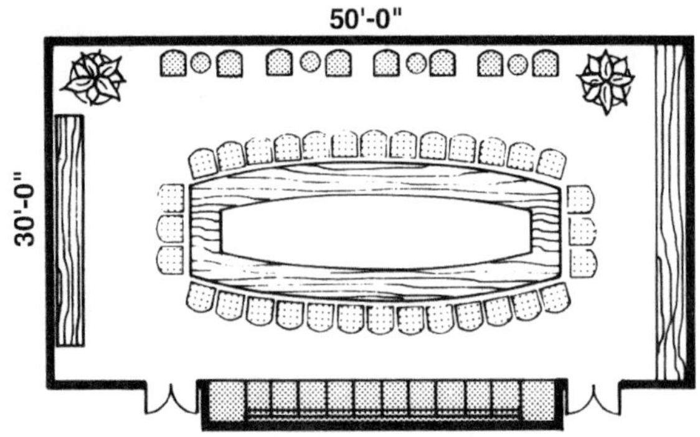

Seats 50, 1500 ft²

PLANNING DATA: ROOM LAYOUTS

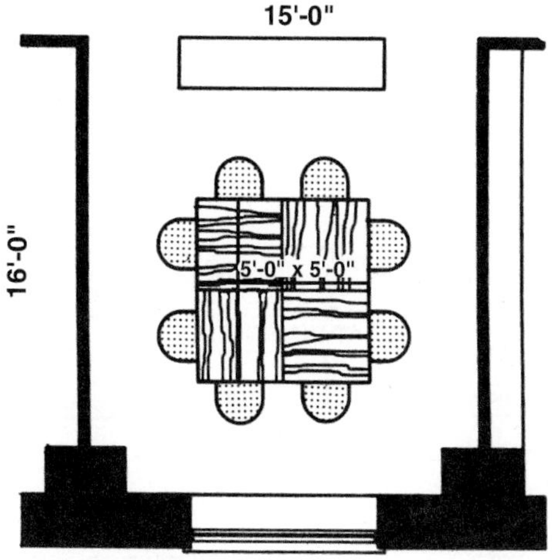

Seats 8, 240 ft^2

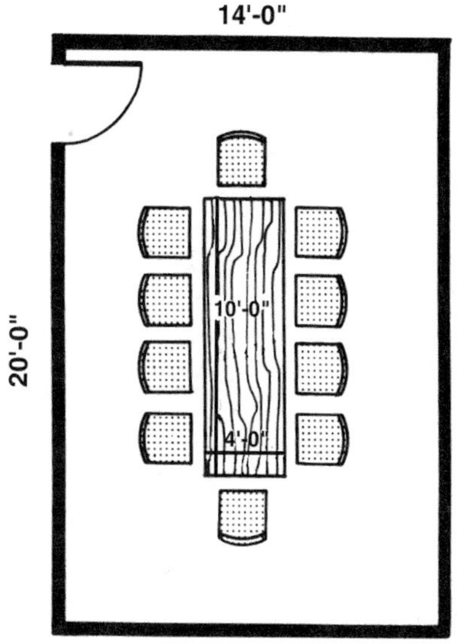

Seats 10, 280 ft^2

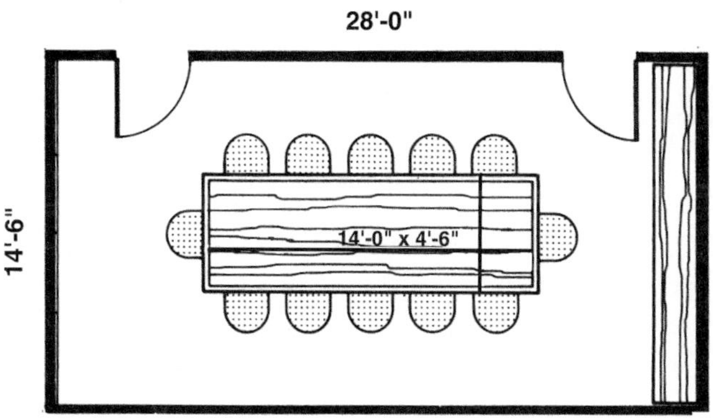

Seats 12, 406 ft^2

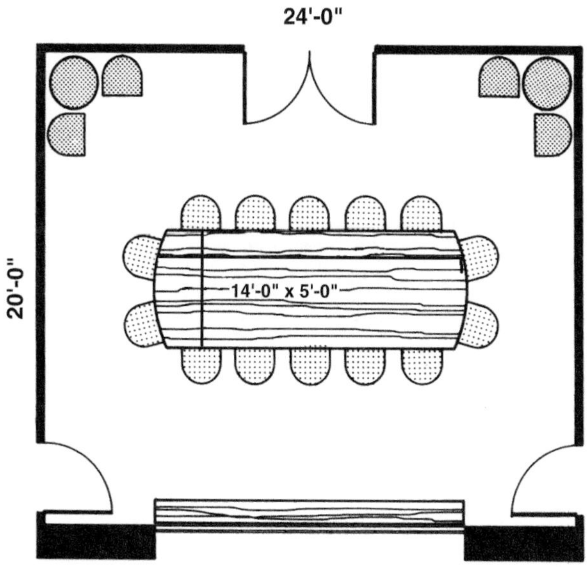

Seats 18, 480 ft^2

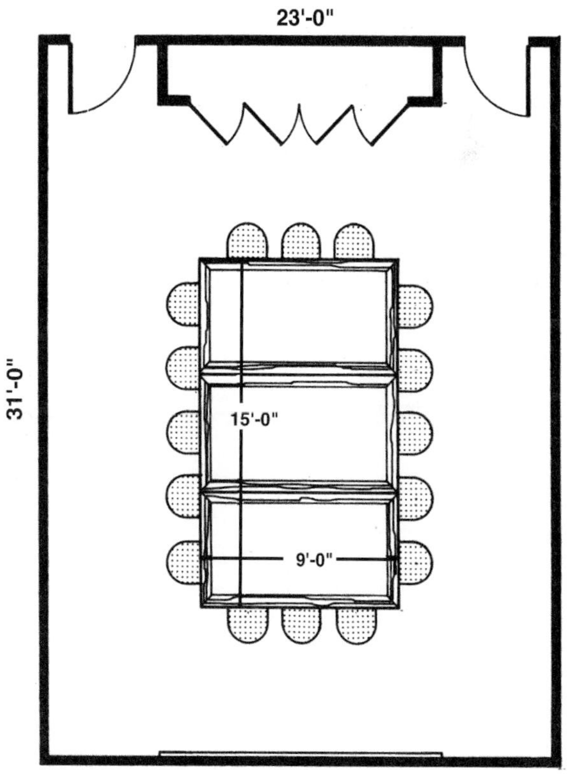

Seats 16, 713 ft^2

CONFERENCE ROOMS

Table Base and Edge Treatments

It is important for the designer to understand and appreciate some of the important details that make up a conference table. The base treatments shown in Fig. 4 are but a few of the myriad possibilities. Perhaps even more important to consider are the finished edges of glass and wood conference tables, representative details of which are shown in Figs. 5 and 6. Other edge details could be made of marble, granite, or even leather. Fingers, hands, and arms make intimate contact with these edge details something that should be carefully considered.

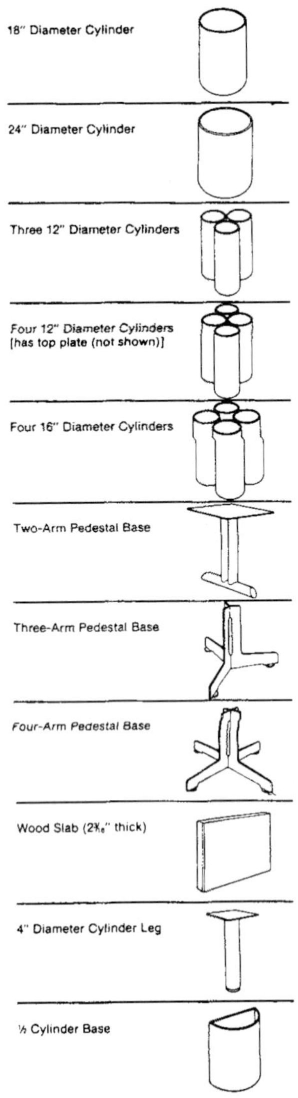

Fig. 4 Base treatment

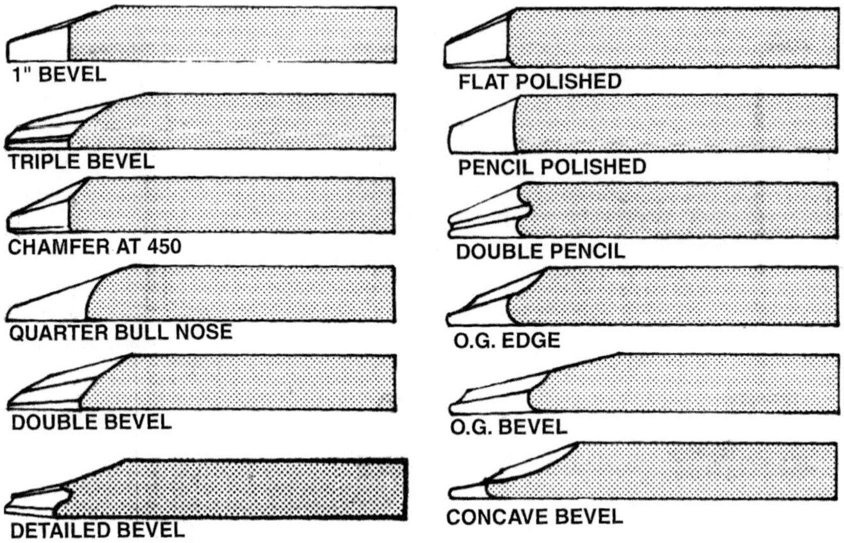

Fig. 5 Glass edge treatment

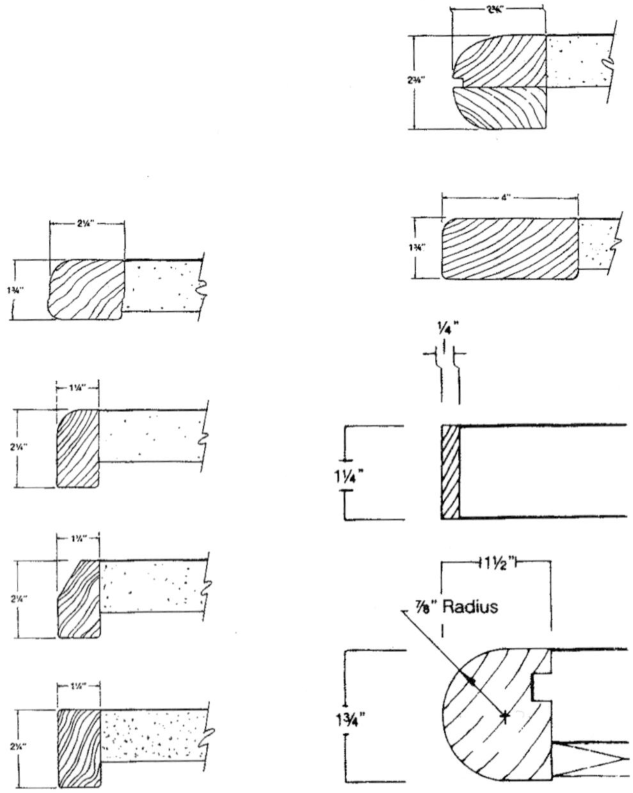

Fig. 6 Wood edge treatment

CONFERENCE ROOMS

Conference Table Details

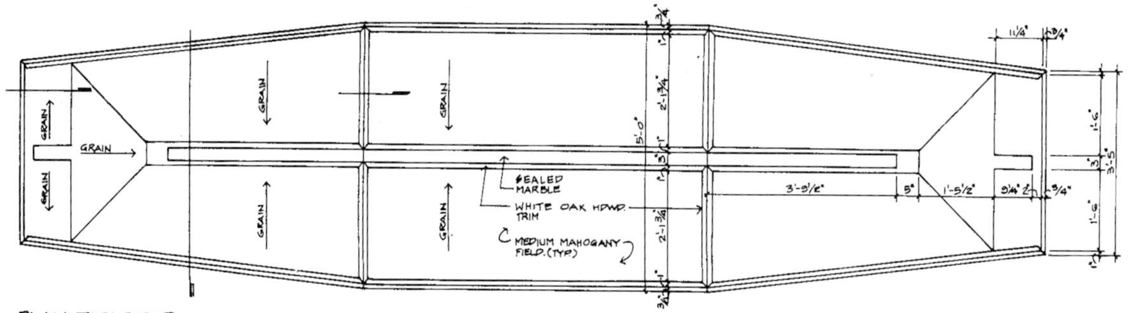

PLAN TABLE TOP

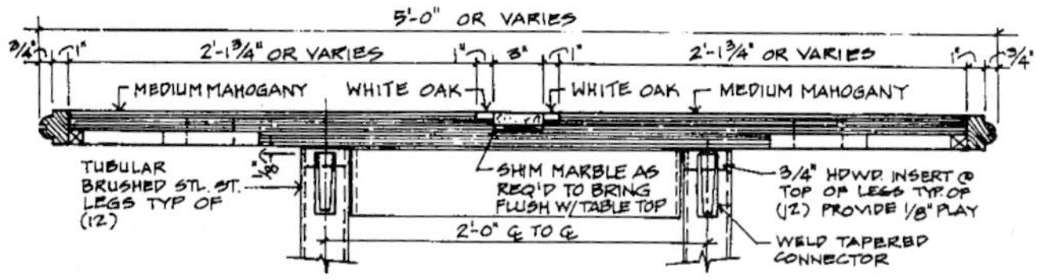

SECTION TABLE TOP

NOTE! FOR WELDED TAPERED CONN. PREPARE SUBSTRATE AS REQ'D FOR WELDING. CLEAN & DRESS WELDS AS REQ'D.

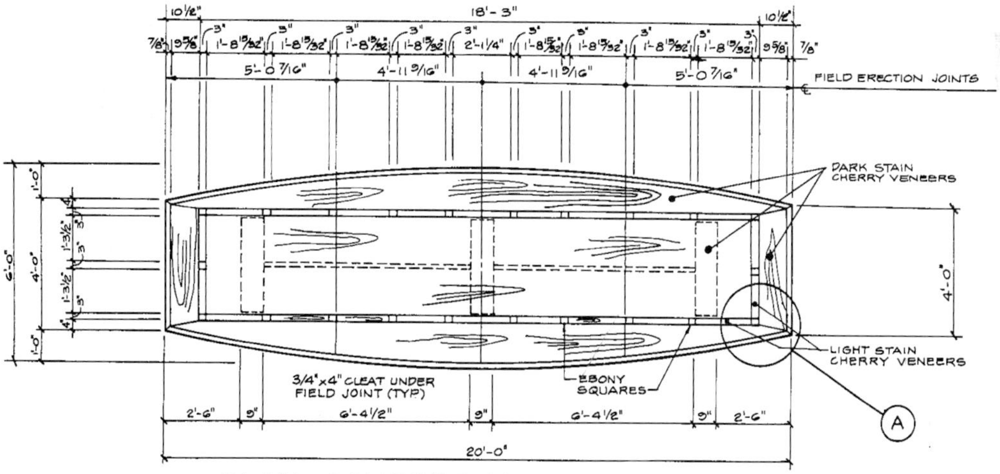

PLAN - CONFERENCE TABLE

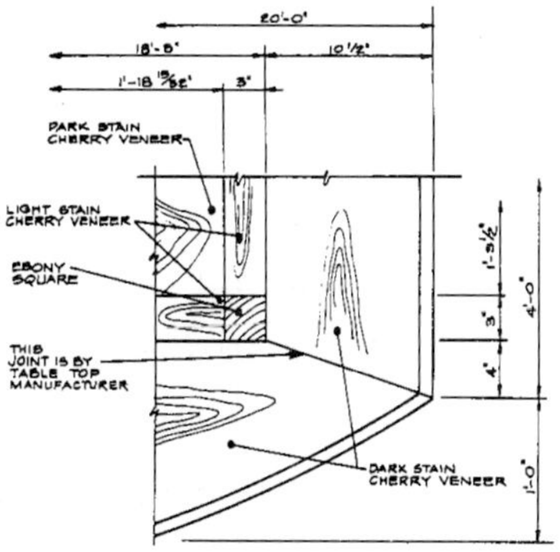

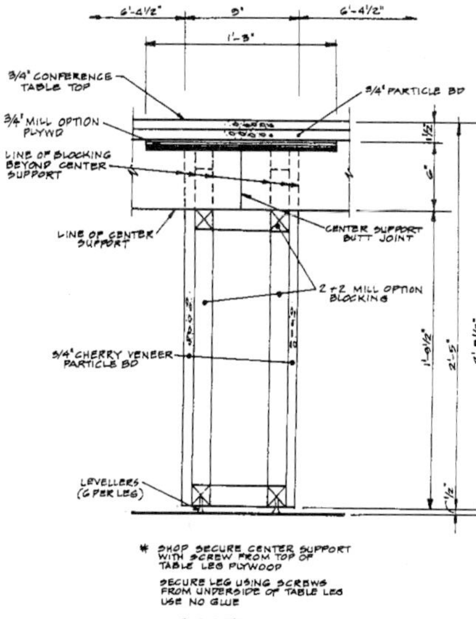

* SHOP SECURE CENTER SUPPORT WITH SCREW FROM TOP OF TABLE LEG PLYWOOD

SECURE LEG USING SCREWS FROM UNDERSIDE OF TABLE LEG USE NO GLUE

SECTION

CONFERENCE ROOMS
Conference Table Details

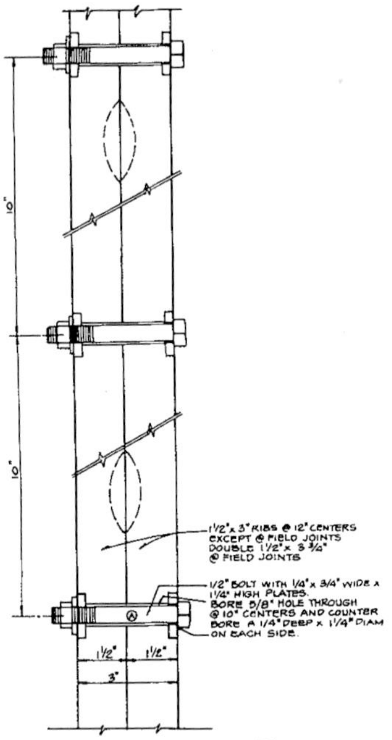

TOP SECTION @ FIELD JOINT CONFERENCE TABLE

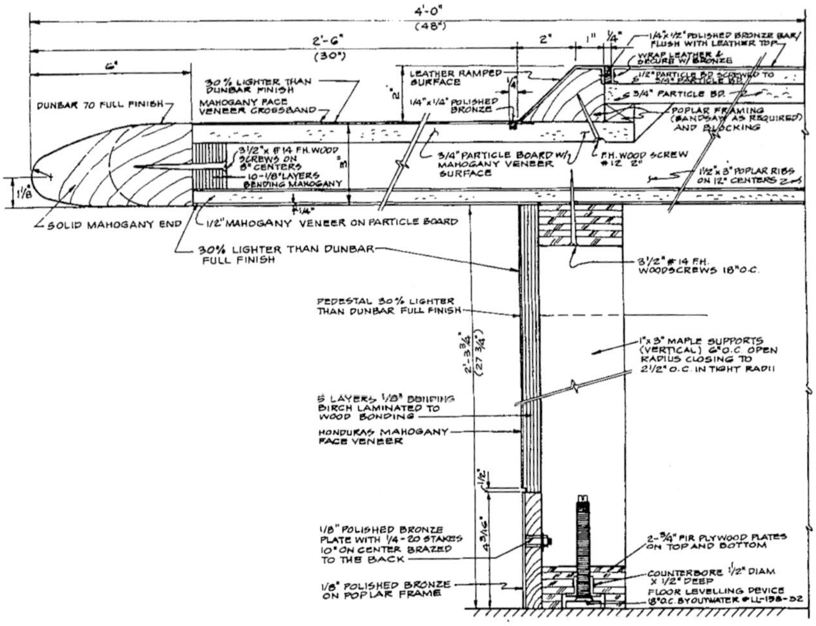

TYPICAL SECTION CONFERENCE TABLE

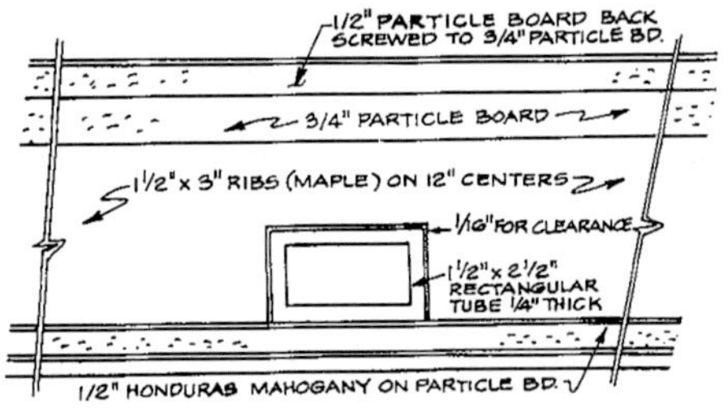

SECTION THROUGH SUPPORT FRAME

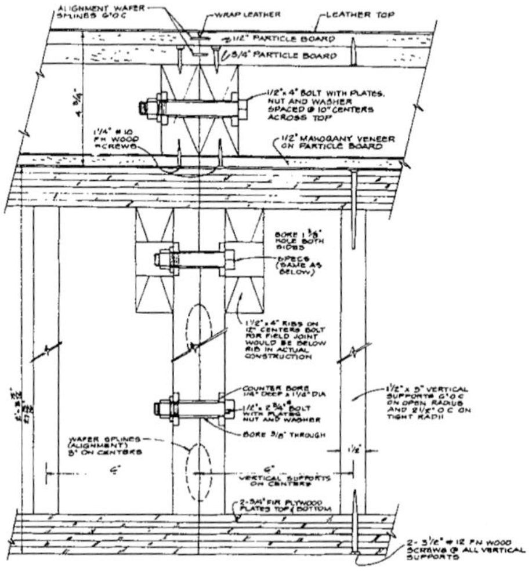

FIELD JOINT SIDE SECTION CONFERENCE TABLE

* CAN USE A THREE INCH BOLT LENGTH

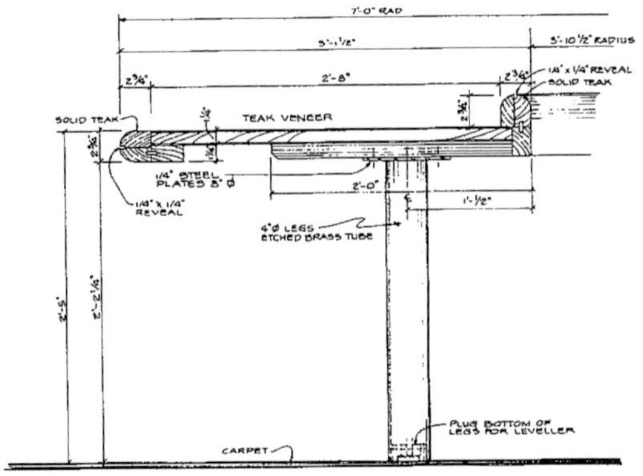

SECTION AT CONFERENCE TABLE

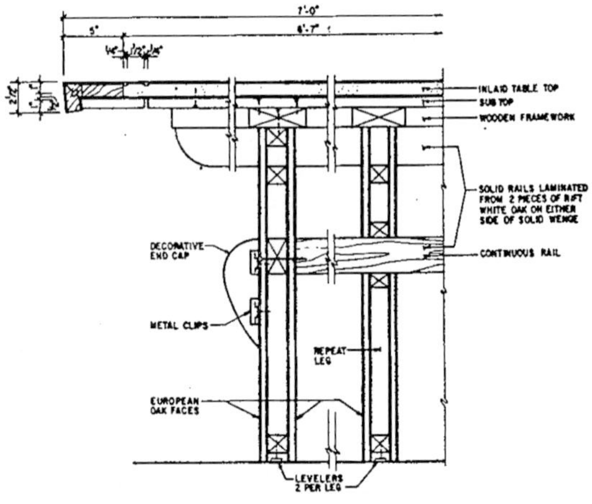

SECTION AT CONFERENCE TABLE

Custom credenza units are often designed to complement the details of a conference table. They serve multiple functions, including storage, incorporation of electronic media equipment, and display, as well as serving as a work surface. In addition, architectural woodwork is used to enclose existing convector covers and to frame window openings. It is important for the designer to consider providing ease of access to the heating and air-handling elements behind the woodwork, as well as allowing the appropriate flow of air.

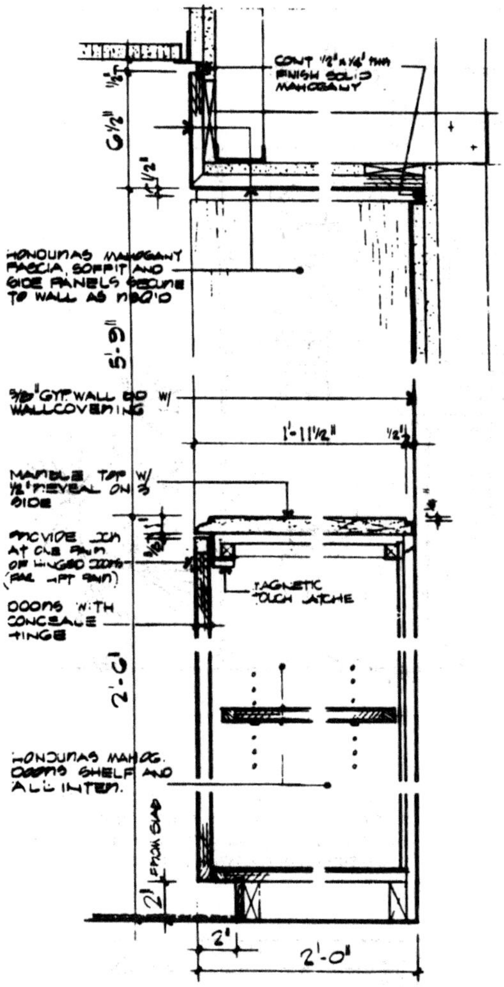

TYP. SECTION THRU CONF CENTER CREDENZA

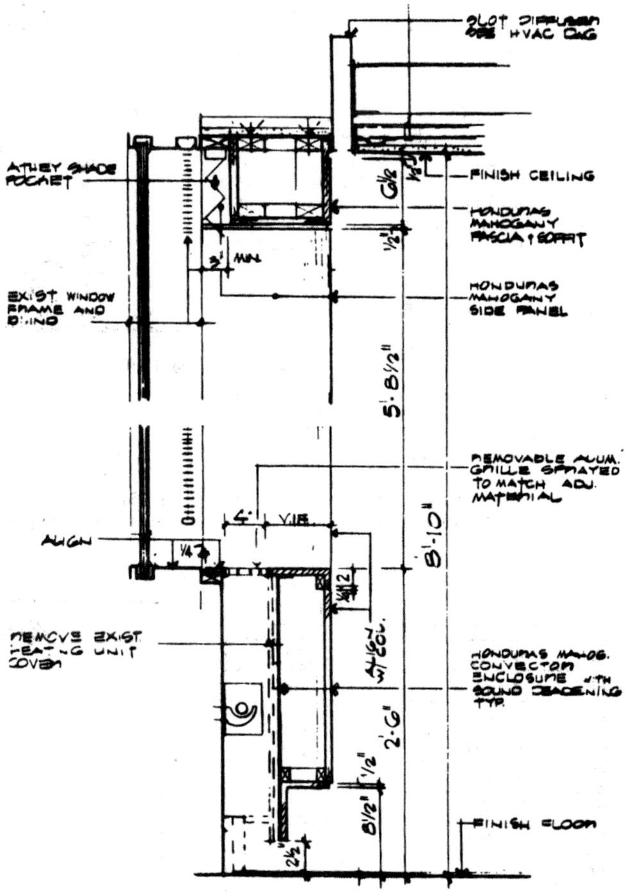

SECTION THRU MILLWORK HEATING UNIT ENCLOSURE

VIDEOCONFERENCE ROOMS
Seating Arrangement and Capacity

Small Videoconference Rooms

ROUND TABLE CONFIGURATION

- The round table is perfect for small video conferences.
- Make sure to place the camera higher to avoid broadcasting the view under the table.
- A camera with a 48° viewing angle will work well.
- The CA2642 Cart will adjust up to 42" high. The Cart will hold one small monitor, and the camera can sit on top. It also has a locking cabinet and wheels.

ROOM DIMENSIONS

- Y = 12'-0", Z = 9'-5"
- Camera distance: X = 5'-0"

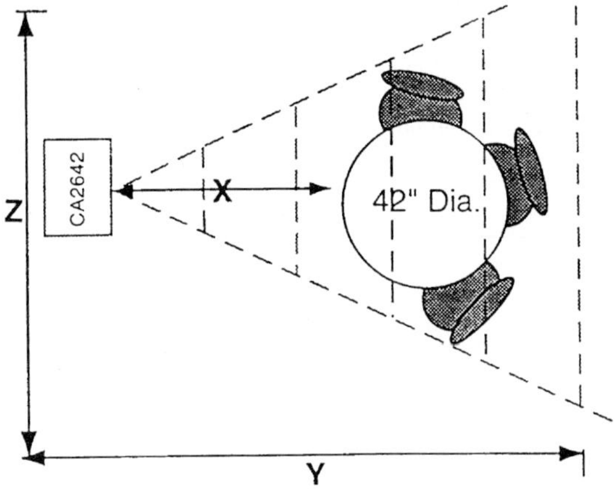

Fig. 1 Seating for three

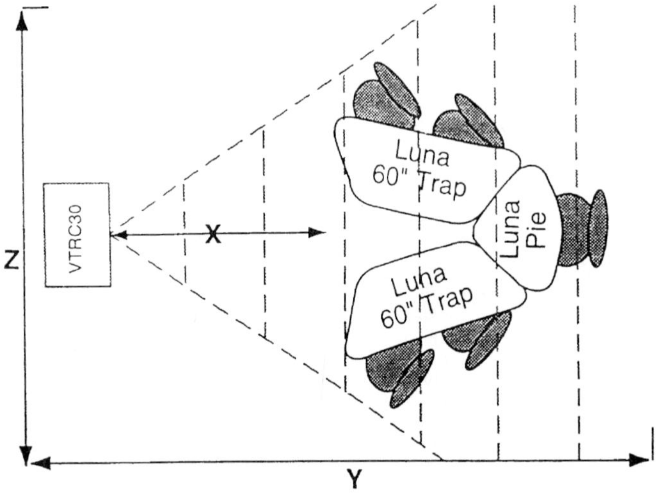

THE LUNA FOR 5 PEOPLE

- Luna Pie Scooters can join to trapezoids to make the perfect V-shape for video conferencing. Additional trapezoids cannot be added on.
- The VTRC30 can be custom finished to match your Luna™ Tables. It houses a 27" monitor and locks for security.
- We used one 66° camera video system with one monitor.

ROOM DIMENSIONS

- Y = 16'-0", Z = 11'-0"
- Camera distance: X = 5'-10"

Fig. 2 Seating for five

THE TRAPEZOID CONFIGURATION FOR 3

- With smaller trapezoids and less people, we are able to capture everyone in a 66° angle.
- With only one monitor, this group can easi ly see the party they are conferencing with. If that party would like to show them a document, they will temporarily not be able to see the participants faces while the document is being presented.

ROOM DIMENSIONS

- Y = 16'-0", Z = 12'-0"
- Camera distance: X = 6'-5"

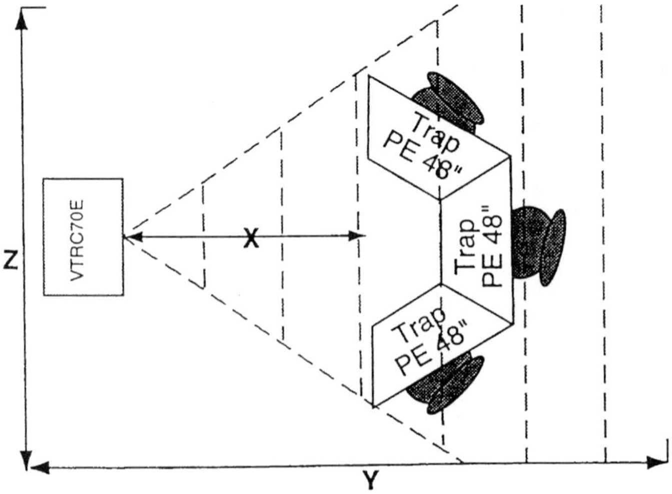

Fig. 3 Seating for three

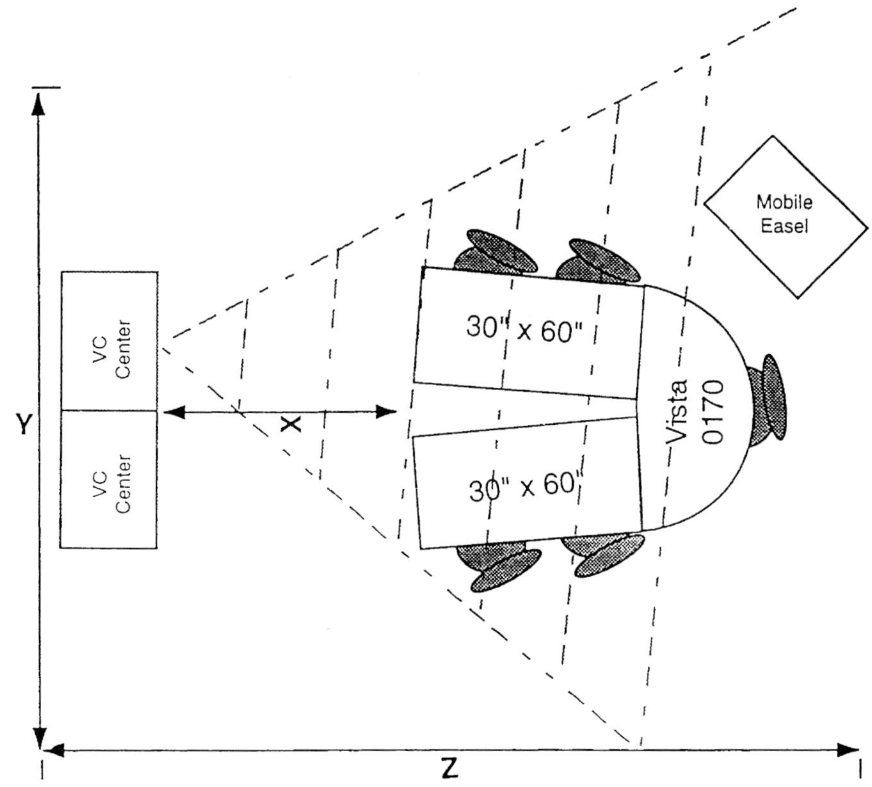

Fig. 4 Seating for five

VISTA CONFIGURATION FOR 5

- The latest table configuration for video conferencing is shaped like the letter "V" to provide excellent sight lines for all participants. The taper is more extreme and allows the room to be re-configured for other activities.
- We have used one 66° camera and two monitors.
- One monitor displays the alternate party. The other monitor can display the meeting agenda or proposal from the alternate party's document camera. The second monitor can also display what the camera sees at this location so they can view themselves while conferencing. As vain as this may seem, it is nice to know who the camera is spotlighting and what image you are projecting to the other party.
- The starter unit VC Center houses the video system. The other VC Center houses a VCR and scan converter with the additional monitor.
- Use 3 standard microphones or one PowerMic on the head table.

ROOM DIMENSIONS

- Y = 14'-9", Z = 18'-9"
- Camera distance: X = 5'=10"

TRAPEZOID CONFIGURATION FOR 6

- Ten years ago, this was the prime configuration of tables to use for video conferencing.
- We have used two 48° cameras and two monitors. One 48° camera would not fit everyone in the picture. The users can switch the camera views from input #1 to input #2 with the remote control to capture a different participant speaking.
- One monitor should display the alternate party. The second monitor should display what the camera sees at this location due to multiple camera views. It can also display documents.
- Use 3 standard or one Boundry microphone at the head table. A voice-activated camera is not recommended when using two camera views.

ROOM DIMENSIONS

- Y = 17'-0", Z = 15'-3"
- Camera distance: XA & XB = 10'-0"

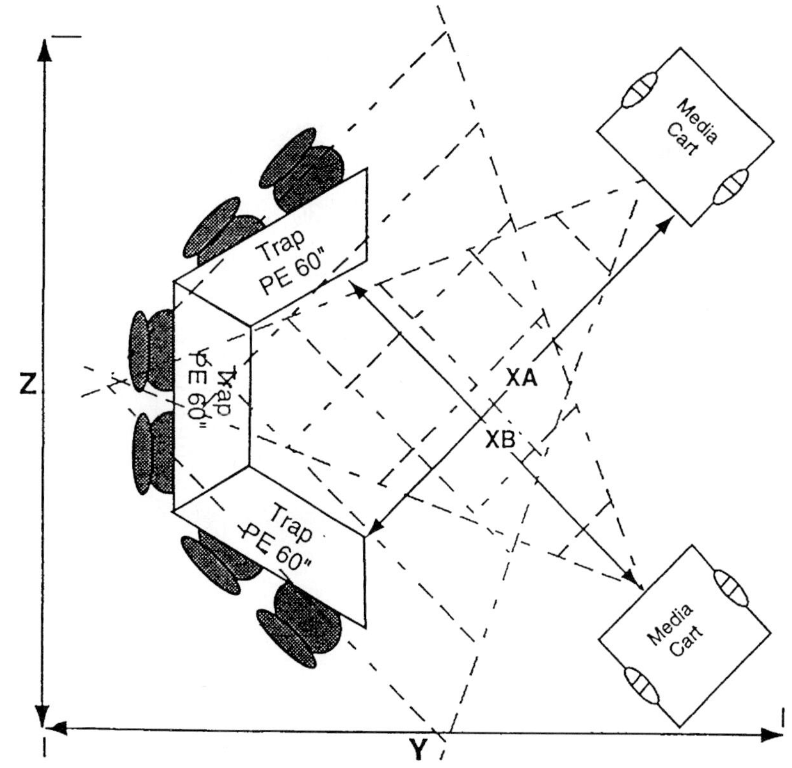

Fig. 5 Seating for six

VIDEOCONFERENCE ROOMS
Seating Arrangement and Capacity

Large Videoconference Rooms

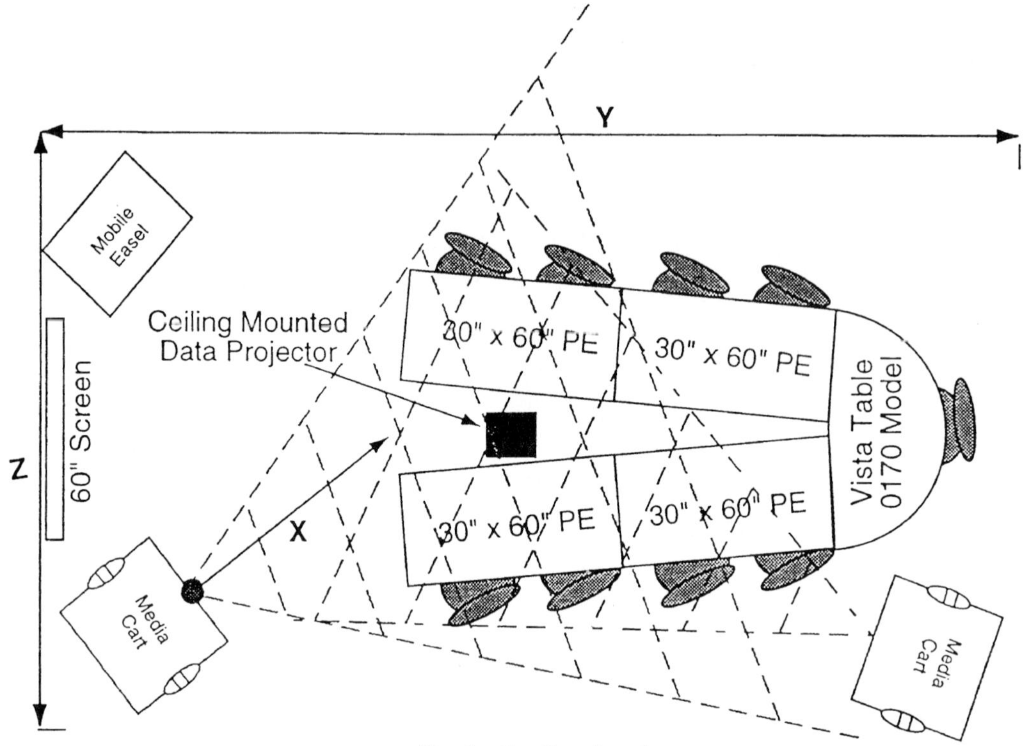

Fig. 6 Seating for nine

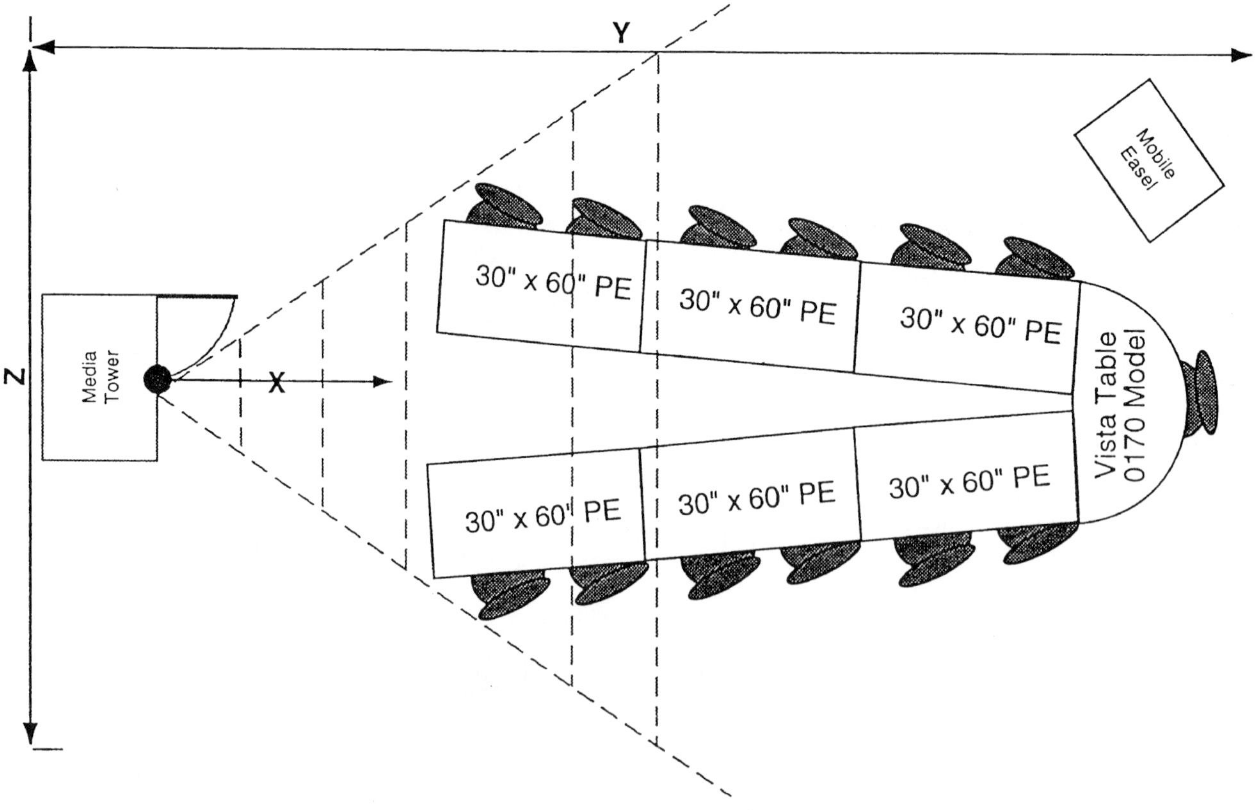

Fig. 7 Seating for thirteen

VISTA CONFIGURATION FOR 9 (See Fig. 6)

- This room was designed for corporate training or distance learning.
- The camera angle at the front of the room is 66° to capture most of the participants' faces. The camera in the back is 48.8°. It projects over the back of the participants' heads to view the instructor at the front.
- The instructor can lecture, write notes on the white board, or project a PowerPoint presentation or video onto the screen. When a student/trainee asks a question the instructor can switch cameras to spotlight the student.

ROOM DIMENSIONS

- Y = 23'-3", Z = 13'-6"
- Camera distance: 6'-0"

VISTA CONFIGURATION FOR 13 (See Fig. 7)

- Having the camera centered allows everyone to participate. In the example at the top left, the camera was off center because the participants were merely an audience.
- Most cameras will be able to zoom in to view notes on an easel/white board from this distance.
- We used a 75° angle camera. The 48.8° would not work well in this situation.

ROOM DIMENSIONS

- Y = 29'-0", Z = 16'-0"
- Camera distance: 5'-9"

VISTA CONFIGURATION FOR 17 (See Fig. 8)

- This is the best configuration available for such a large group. It provides excellent sight lines and flexibility to re-configure the room for other tasks. If you have a room that is wider on the Z axis, the larger Vista PXM 1600 can be used for even better sightlines.
- We have used three 48.8° cameras and three monitors. Your A/V Specialist should be able to splice the view from 3 cameras onto one monitor. In essence you have a wide-angle view of everyone involved without switching inputs or preset views on cameras. You may have to just zoom in and out once in a while.
- One monitor displays the alternate party. The second monitor should display what the camera sees at this location due to multiple camera views. The third monitor is able to display documents from the document camera at this location or from the alternate location.
- Additional monitors on TV mounts along the side walls may be necessary since the person at the head table is 28 feet away from the monitor.
- Use one microphone per two people. Bretford's PowerTrak™ is useful in this situation to conceal the 9 wires that typically would be trailing down the center of the tables.

ROOM DIMENSIONS

- Y = 31'-0", Z = 15'-0"
- Camera distance: X = 4'-6"

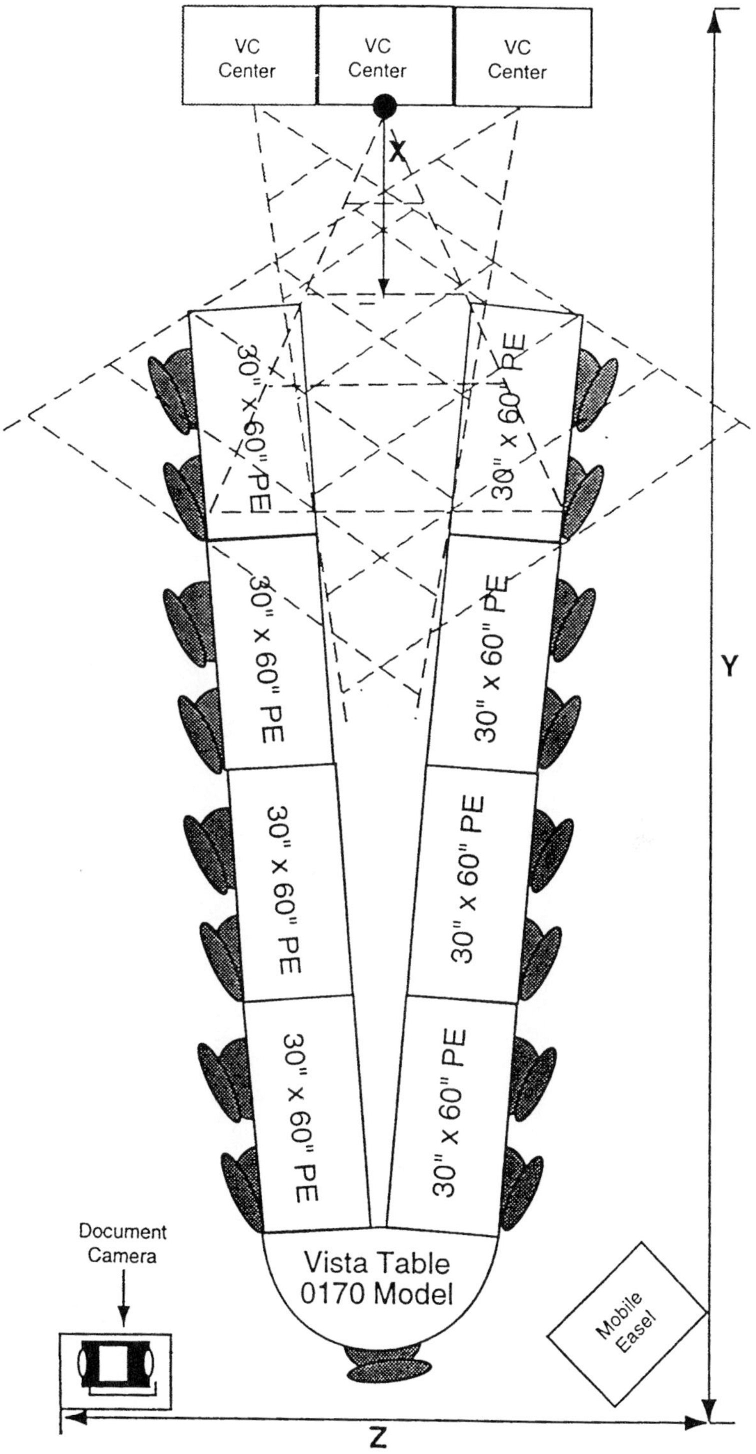

Fig. 8 Seating for seventeen

VIDEOCONFERENCE ROOMS
Seating Arrangement and Capacity

CONFERENCE TABLES 8' - 20'

- On the 8'-0" and 10'-0" conference table, we used the Bretford's 48/36" EZ View Conference table to provide a slight taper and offer clear sight lines to all participants. For table sizes 12'-0" and over, we recommend the Bretford 60"/36"Super EZ View Conference table which provides the maximum amount of taper for larger groups.
- Due to the narrow attributes of most conference tables, a camera with a 48° angle best captures this configuration.
- Use one microphone per 4 people, or one Boundry microphone for tables up to 168" long. For 192" to 240" long tables, piggyback two Boundry microphones. Bretford's powered conference tables have a trough to conceal all of these wires and route than to the floor.

ROOM DIMENSIONS

- As a minimum, the width of the room should be 13 feet. Add more space if the room requires additional equipment.

CAMERA DISTANCE

- 6'-0" will capture a 48" wide table.
- If you have a wider table, use your template to determine the distance between the camera and the table. You may also consider using a wider camera angle instead of increasing the length of the room since the person at the head of the table is already far away from viewing the monitor.

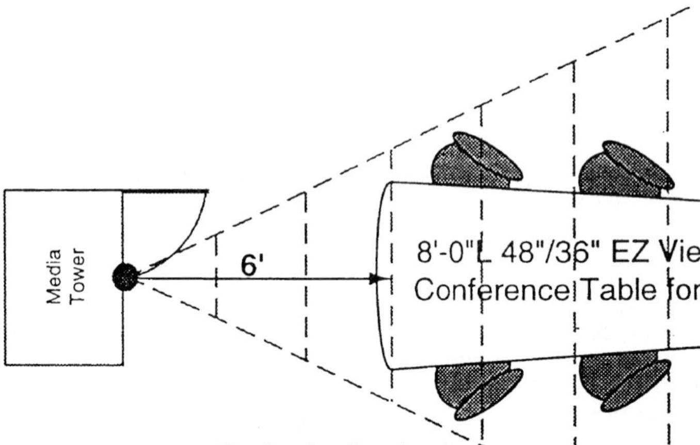

Fig. 9 Seating for six

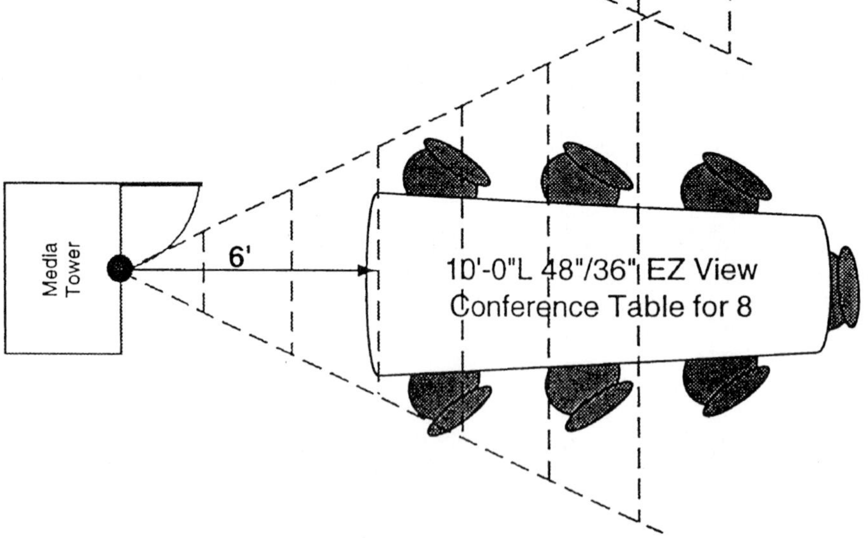

Fig. 10 Seating for eight

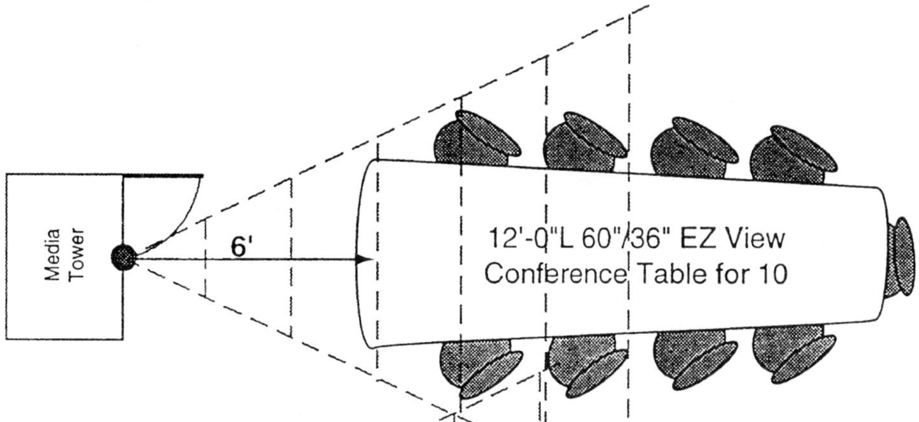

Fig. 11 Seating for 10

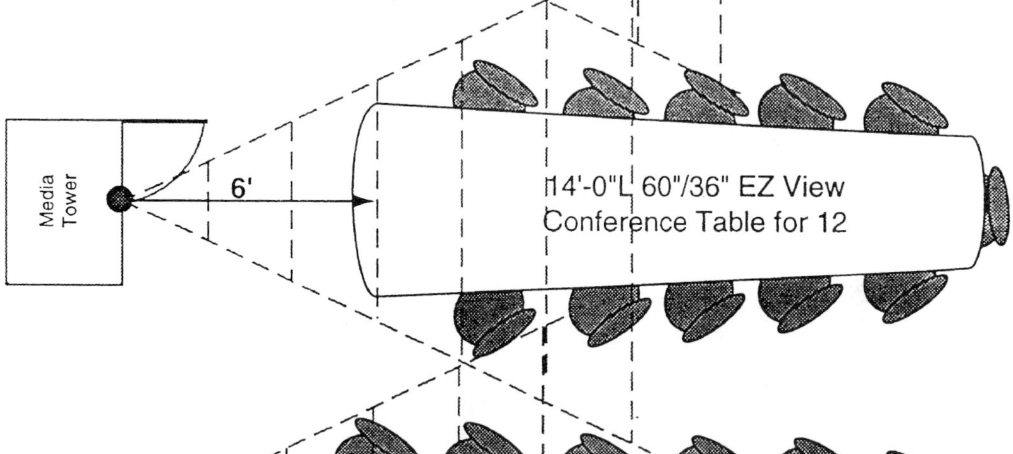

Fig. 12 Seating for 12

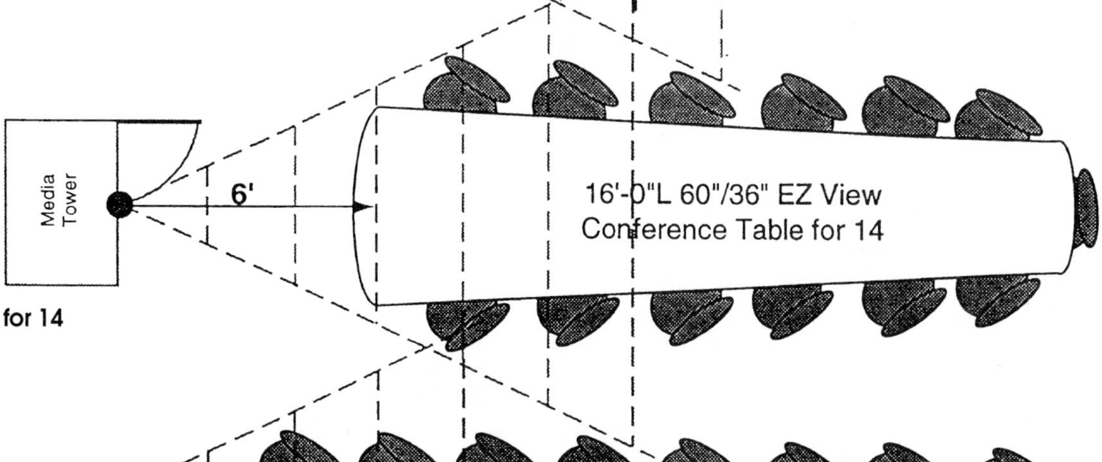

Fig. 13 Seating for 14

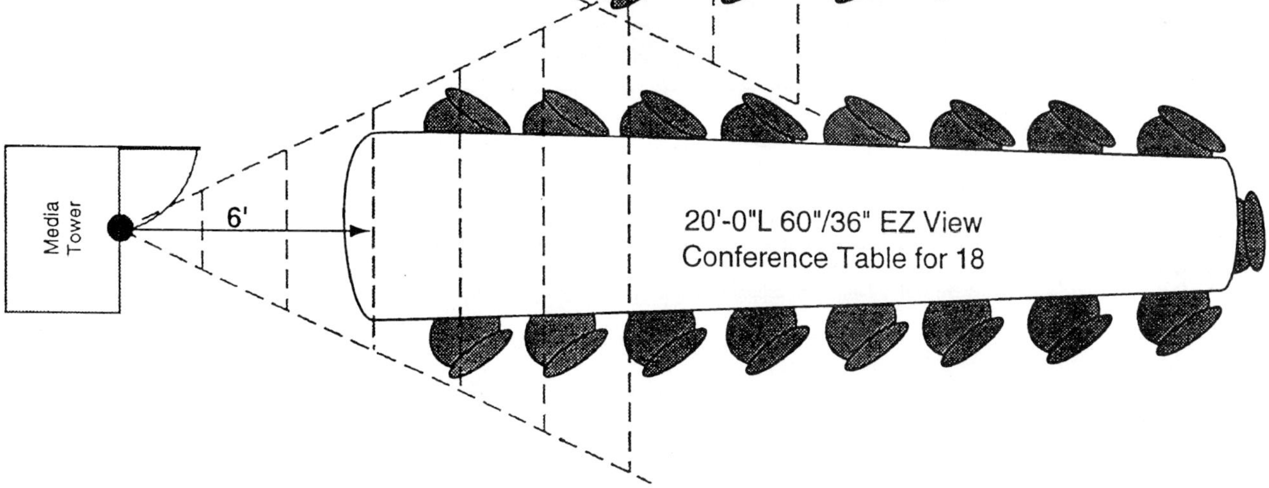

Fig. 14 Seating for 18

VIDEOCONFERENCE ROOMS
Classroom Form

Lecture Videoconference Rooms

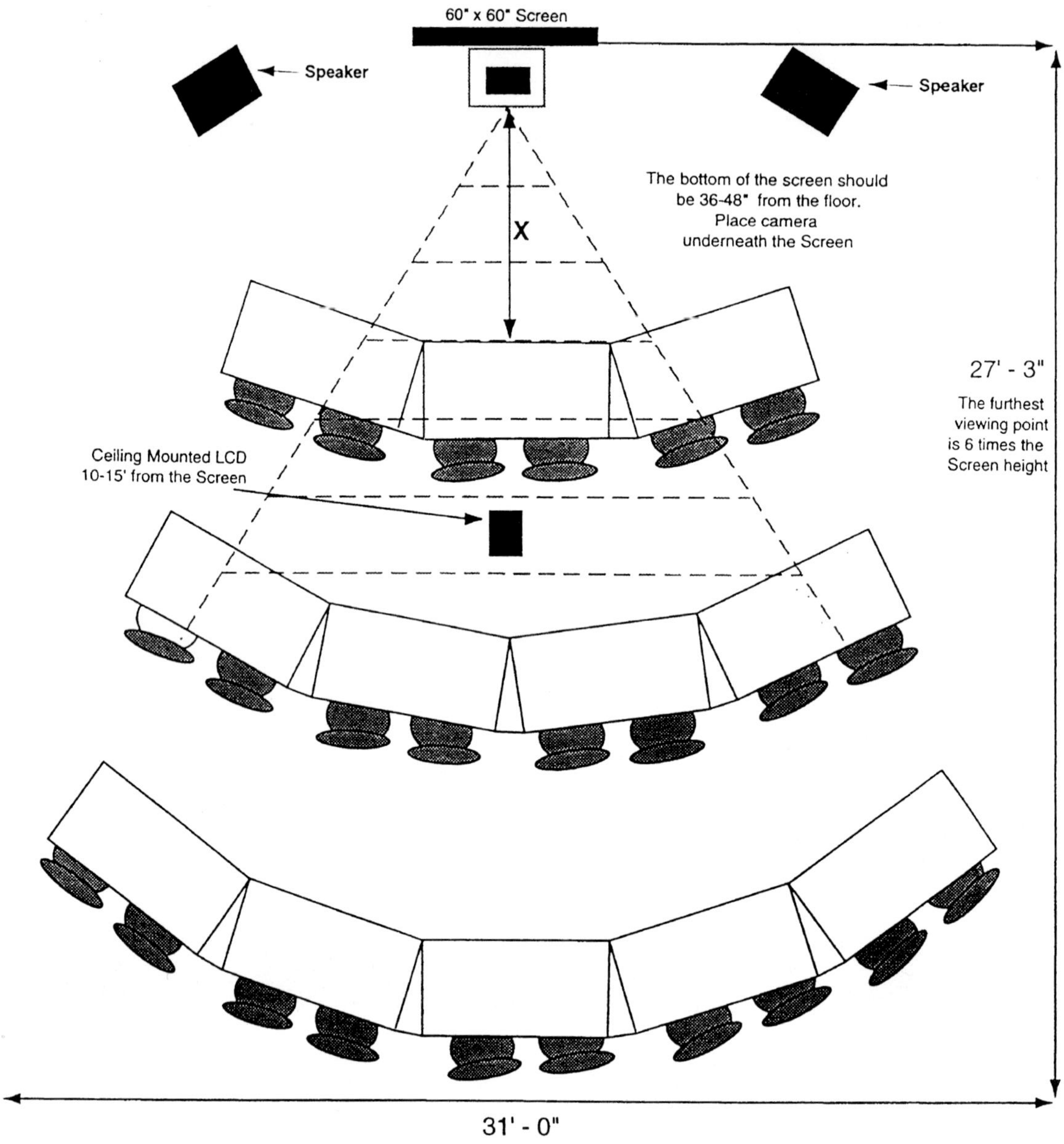

CLASSROOM FOR 24 PEOPLE

- This floor plan is perfect for corporate training, distance learning, or meetings.
- One camera is sufficient for this configuration. It does not capture everyone at once, but the camera can sweep from left to right to identify the group.
- It is best to use a video system with a built-in microphone and a voice tracking feature. You could also use five Boundry mics that are piggybacked together.
- The tables provide writing surface, modesty panels, wire mangement, and power. Bretford's PowerHouse™ can supply power and data directly to the table tops if laptops are necessary.
- We have replaced the monitors with a screen and a ceiling-mounted data projector. The group will be able to see their trainer from a remote location, and he/she will be able to see them.
- The trainer's voice will be heard through the speakers at the front of the room. If you are only using one speaker, place it directly under the camera. If you have a pair of speakers, it is okay to separate the trainers voice from their face, because it will be in stereo sound.

ROOM DIMENSIONS

- 31'-0" x 27'-11"
- Camera distance: X = 6'-0"

Fig. 15 Seating for 24

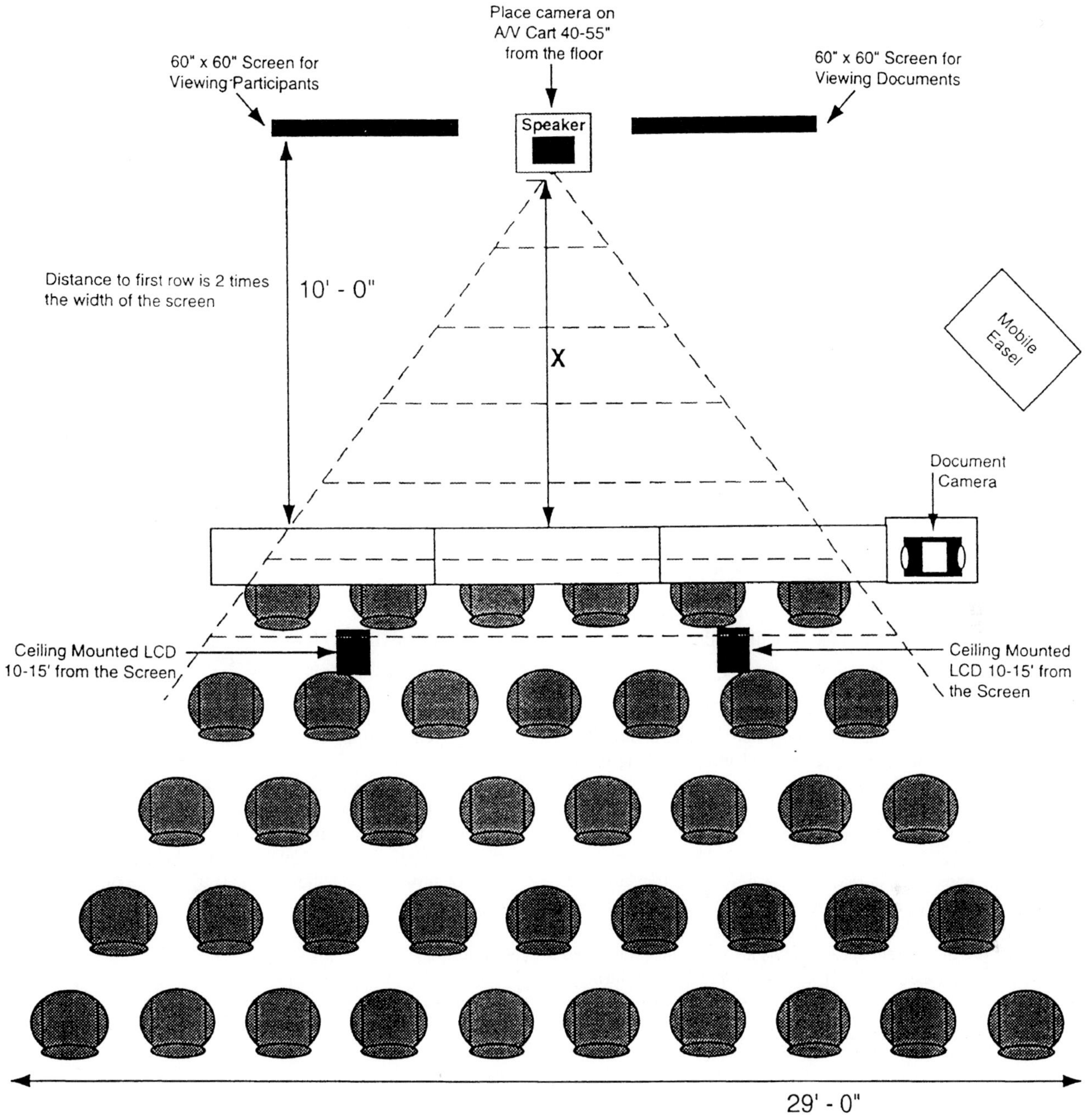

CONFERENCE FOR 40 PEOPLE

- This room can be used for corporate training, shareholder's meetings, distance learning and much more.
- We have used one 75° camera and two projection screens with ceiling-mounted LCD projectors.
- One person would act like a talkshow host and transport a wireless microphone to each participant with a question. The camera would zoom in on each participant with the use of a remove control or automatic voice tracking.
- The three tables are in front to provide modesty panels for the group.

ROOM DIMENSIONS

- 29'-0" x 26'-0"
- Camera distance: X = 9'-0"

Fig. 16 Seating for 40

VIDEOCONFERENCE ROOMS

Equipment Requirements

Cameras

You will require one to three cameras.

- The first camera is to focus on the participants' faces.
- The second camera provides an alternate view of the participants. If it is not possible to get everyone in the view of one camera, have one camera on each side of the room. A button on your remote control will alternate the views.
- A document camera is used to transfer images of documents or 3D objects that the participants want to display to the other group in their presentation.

When planning a videoconference room, the most important factor is where the camera is placed.

- At the beginning of a meeting, it is nice to see an overall view of the participants. Make sure that the camera is not too close to the table to capture everyone.
- Place the camera between 36 in and 60 in above the floor.
- At 36 in high, your participants will be seen at eye level, but their feet will also be in the picture. Make sure you choose a table with a modesty panel if you are placing the camera at this level.
- Place the camera directly on top or in front of the monitor. If the camera is too far away from the monitor the participants will seem as if they are not making eye contact with the alternate party.
- If the camera is over 60 in high, it will spotlight the follically challenged users.
- If someone is standing up to make a presentation, adjust the camera height to their height. It is also a good idea to mark the floor with tape to emphasize the boundary of the camera's view. This will prevent a mobile speaker from accidentally walking out of the picture.

Microphones

There are many choices to be made concerning sound transmission. Many video systems have built-in microphones that track where a voice is coming from within a 12- to 15-ft diameter and direct the camera to capture the current speaker. This also eliminates the need for tabletop microphones and the use of a remote control during a conference.

- The best type of microphone to purchase is a boundary microphone, which can pick up voices from 14 ft away. It can also be daisy-chained from one microphone to another. Only one or two are necessary for your entire group.
- When a participant is standing up to give a presentation, use a lapel microphone.
- Ask your videoconference dealer or sound contractor which solution is best for your facility.

Single or Dual Monitors

You will require one or two monitors. The first monitor is to display the participants you will be conferencing with or to display documents or 3D objects they want to share with you. The optional second monitor is to display your own picture. As vain as this may seem, it is very useful to show who the camera is spotlighting. Most monitors have Picture in Picture (PIP) to display both groups. Groups larger than four people will not be able to see the PIP box, so an alternate monitor is recommended.

- When a group of 2 to 5 people will be meeting, use a 27- to 32-inch monitor.
- For a group of 6 to 12 people, use a 32- to 37-inch monitor.
- When a group of 13 to 20 will be meeting, use two 37- to 45-inch monitors.
- When a group of 21 or more will be meeting, use two projection screens with data projector ceiling mounts.
- You must purchase a monitor, not a TV. Remember, monitor screens are measured diagonally on the glass portion only.
- Offer an additional monitor or screen whenever a document camera, DVD, VCR, data projector, white board, or other display equipment will be used.

ISDN Lines (Integrated Services Digital Network)

ISDN lines can be installed and maintained by the local telephone company.

- In each ISDN line there are two channels.
- Your videoconferencing system will require one to four ISDN lines. If only one line is ordered, the user's voices and movements could be choppy. If you have ever watched a kung fu movie that was translated to English, you know what one-line videoconferencing is like. With the addition of each line, the picture and transmission will become smoother.

DESIGN CONSIDERATIONS

Room Size

- A few general rules remain constant when planning any size room. There are specific color schemes, lighting, furniture, and acoustics that are standards for videoconferencing.
- When getting started, your primary focus should be the number of people that will be participating in the videoconferences. The number of people will dictate what size the room should be, what kind of furniture you should use, and the type of system that is required.

Room Shape

- For smaller meetings, a square room is acceptable.
- For meetings with four or more people, a rectangular room is best.

Entrances

- Two entrances to the room are ideal so participants are able to enter the room and sit down without walking in front of the camera.
- The entrances should be on the camera wall or the walls perpendicular to the camera. They should be as close to the camera wall as possible.
- The wall behind the participants should not have any doors or windows.

Acoustics

- Pay close attention to the ventilation system in the room. Does it create a lot of noise that could muffle the participants' voices? If the vent is directly over the microphone, the sound will amplify like a hurricane. Try placing a cover over the vent that redirects the airflow in a different direction rather than straight down.

- Does the room have a lot of exposed wood or high ceilings? Pad as much in the room as possible to prevent echoed or amplified voices in a large room. Upholstery on chairs, carpet on the floor, and ceiling tile will absorb most of the reverberations in the room.
- The videoconference room should be in a remote area that is away from the cafeteria or other gathering places in the office. It is also a good idea to place a red light or a sign outside the room to forewarn others that a conference is in progress.

Color

- The best choice for wall paint color is a light blue or light gray. Bretford recommends Benjamin Moore paint numbers 1627, 829, 996, and HC-169. The worst wall color to use is white. White creates too much of a contrast and can literally erase the faces of participants with dark skin tones from the camera's view.
- A light- to medium-colored conference table will reflect light upward and make shadows disappear from users' faces. Do not use a white or black laminate or other high-intensity colors that could reflect too much light and wash out the participants' faces. Also keep in mind that the pattern on the laminate should be camera friendly. Bretford recommends the following laminate colors by Wilson Art from Bretford's finish card: Featherstone, Pebble, Pewter, Sea Breeze, Bronze Legacy, Grey Tigris, Saffron Tigris, Fusion Maple, or Wild Cherry. If you plan to use a veneer conference table, natural cherry, medium cherry, and natural maple are excellent choices.
- Avoid patterns that are large or repeated on furniture, walls, or clothing.
- The room does not have to be monochromatic, but keep it simple.

Accessories

- Logos can be placed behind the users as long as they do not reflect or detract from the participants.
- Artwork or plants are okay as long as they are not on the table or in the camera's view.
- Additional wall clocks are an excellent idea to hang in the room to display alternate time zones.

Furniture

- Use tables that taper to allow the camera to see all of the participants' faces. Tables should also have modesty panels and provide access to power and data.
- Chairs should be padded and comfortable. They should not rock or roll. Wheels squeak when they roll, and the rocking motion provides a distracting activity for camera-shy users.
- Carts or cabinetry for the video equipment should provide power, cord management, and rear access to fix technical difficulties. A cart should also lock and have wheels to stow it in the corner when not in use.

Lighting

- The room should have indirect fluorescent lighting.
- The light should shine upward and reflect evenly off of the ceiling. Lights that shine down create shadows on the participants' faces.
- If there are windows in the room, make sure to use light-blocking shades. Hunter Douglas Light-Lines or Levelor's Mark One miniblinds are recommended because they provide the best light control. You will be amazed to compare the room with and without sunlight. If sunlight is shining directly into the camera, the participants will look like silhouettes.

RECEPTION AREAS

Planning Data: Receptionist's Workstation

Proper design of the reception area is critical in communicating an organization's desired corporate image. Reception spaces are both the first and the last areas with which the visitor interacts and, accordingly, have considerable visual impact in communicating that image.

Not only must the reception space look attractive, but it must function properly as well. The two most important planning elements in this regard are the visitor's seating area and the receptionist's workstation or desk.

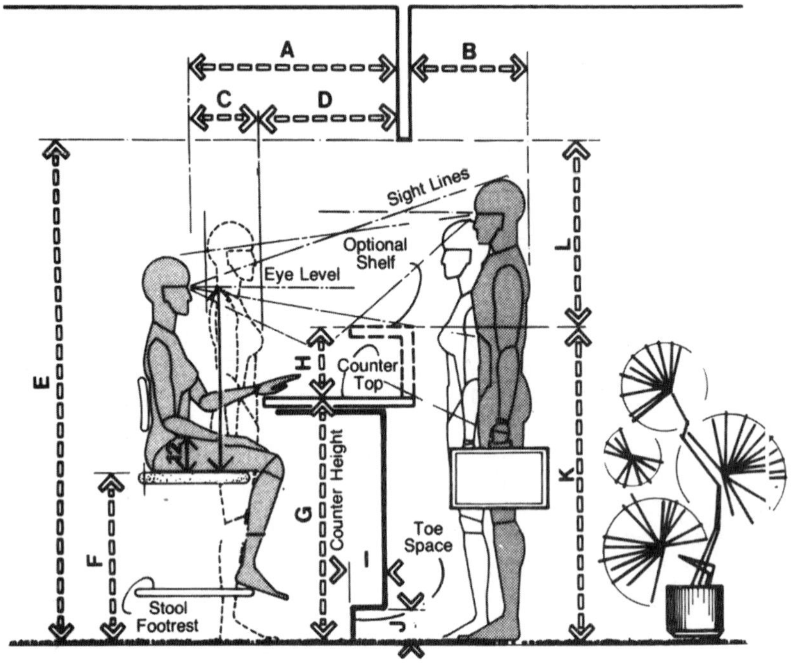

Fig. 1 Receptionist's workstation/counter height

	in	cm
A	40–48	101.6–121.9
B	24 min.	61.0 min.
C	18	45.7
D	22–30	55.9–76.2
E	78 min.	198.1 min.
F	24–27	61.0–68.6
G	36–39	91.4–99.1
H	8–9	20.3–22.9
I	2–4	5.1–10.2
J	4	10.2
K	44–48	111.8–121.9
L	34 min.	86.4 min.
M	44–48	111.8–121.9
N	54	137.2
O	26–30	66.0–76.2
P	24	61.0
Q	30	76.2
R	15–18	38.1–45.7
S	29–30	73.7–76.2
T	10–12	25.4–30.5
U	6–9	15.2–22.9
V	39–42	99.1–106.7

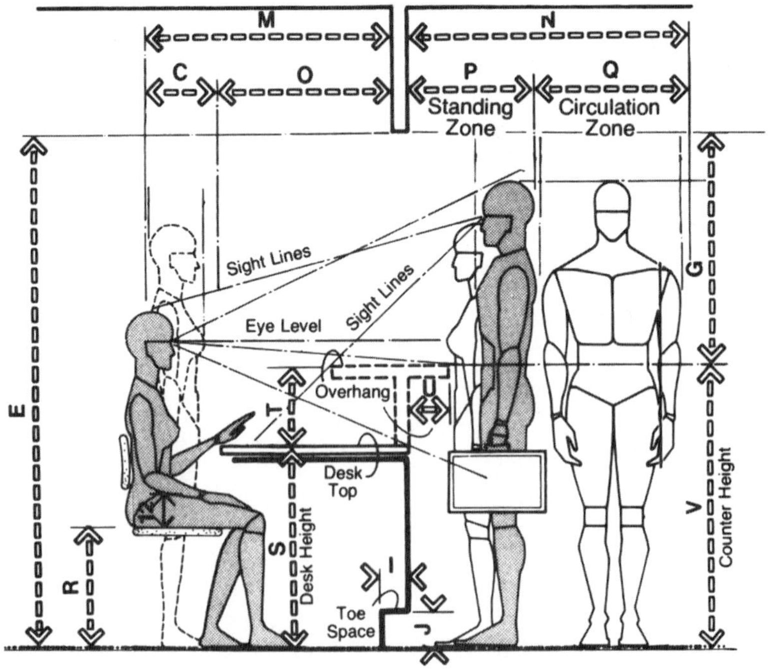

Fig. 2 Receptionist's workstation/desk height

While most of the examples in this part are drawn from corporate interiors, the designer is urged to take into consideration the needs of special user groups who must interact with a receptionist. If small children are to communicate (or see or be seen), how high is the privacy wall? If a wheelchair-bound user is to approach the reception desk, is there room for the footrests to be accommodated? The designer must consider all user populations.

This part deals primarily with basic planning data relative to the design of a receptionist's workstation and furniture arrangements of the seating areas. Also included are related details directly from the working drawings of design firms.

For the purpose of privacy or security, the receptionist's workstation is often an area physically separated by built-in furniture and/or partitions. Figure 1 shows a counter height receptionist's workstation. While the relationship of work surface to seat height is key, other anthropometric considerations are eye height and sitting height normal. The minimum height of the opening above the floor has been established at 78 in, or 198.1 cm. Sitting height and eye height are significant in providing unobstructed vision. Figure 2 depicts a desk height receptionist's workstation. The depth of the work surface ranges from 26 to 30 in, or 66 to 76.2 cm, allowing for thumb tip reach required for the exchange of papers and packages. Both Figs. 1 and 2 show in broken line an added countertop element often provided for security or as a visual screen of the work surface top.

PLANNING DATA: SEATING ARRANGEMENTS

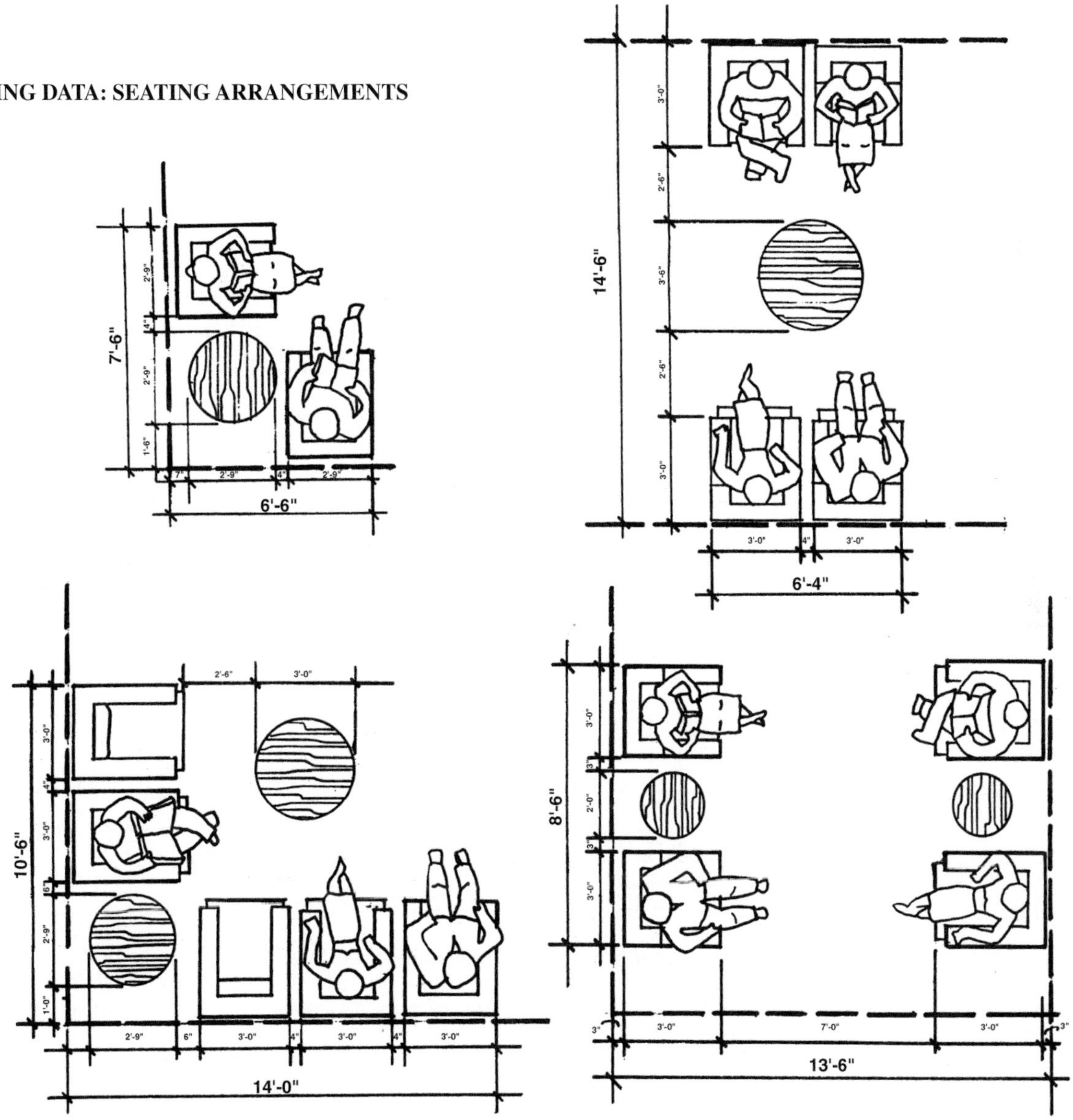

Fig. 3 The seating arrangements illustrated here provide some typical conditions that the designer must address. Individual seats are preferred over sofas. Corner seating arrangements must always consider leg clearance. Circulation between low tables and the edges of chairs must be adequate to allow for the legs of persons seated in the chairs. Convenient locations for side tables, so that magazines, ashtrays, artwork, or portable lighting can be placed on them, are important

RECEPTION AREAS

Reception Desk Details

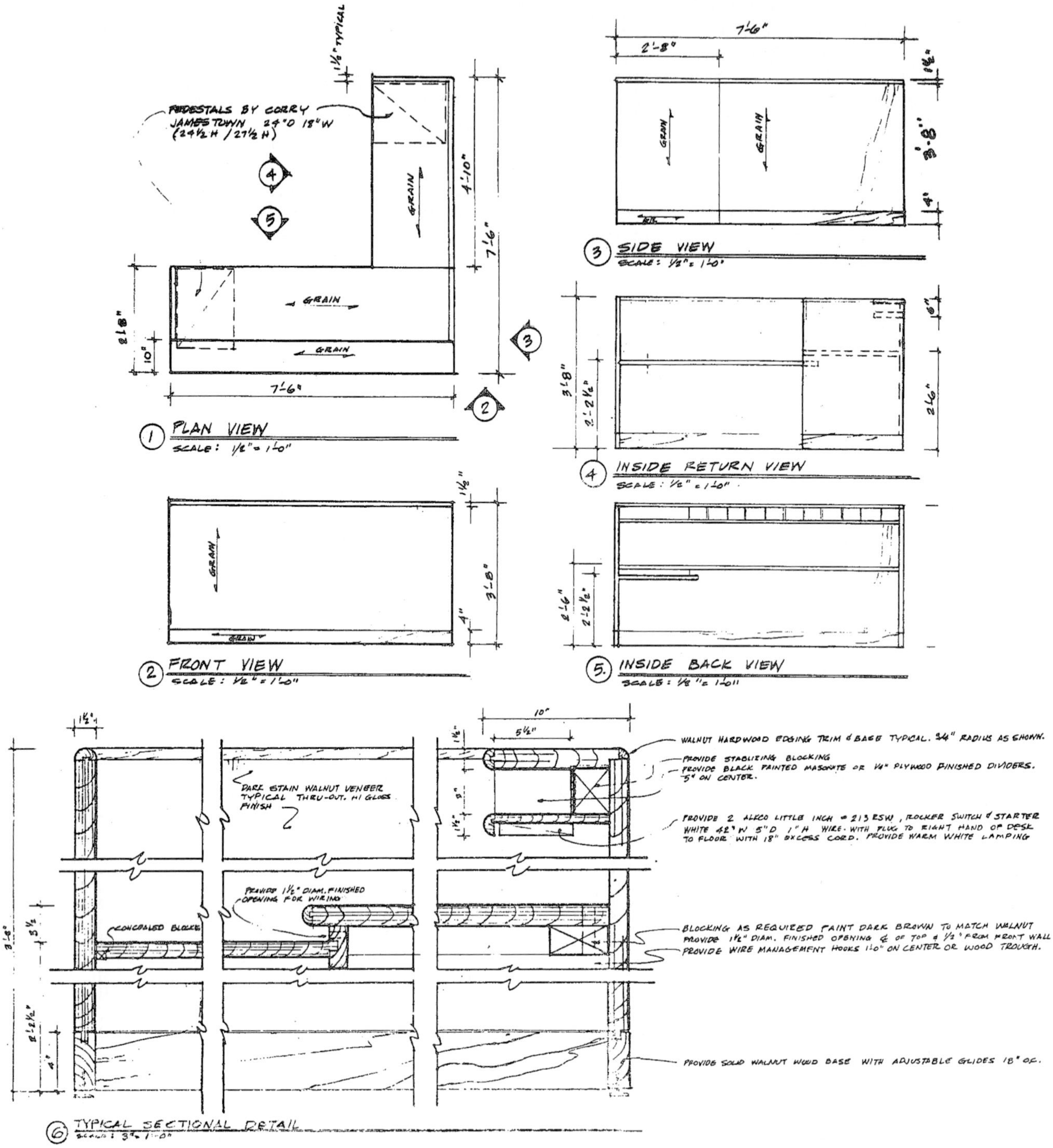

Fig. 4 Depending on the size of an office, a reception desk can be either relatively simple and small in scale or relatively complex and large in scale, sometimes staffed by two or more persons. The reception desk illustrated here shows a typical L-shaped unit with 44-in-high privacy panel. Reception desks of this type can either be custom designed or purchased from a manufacturer

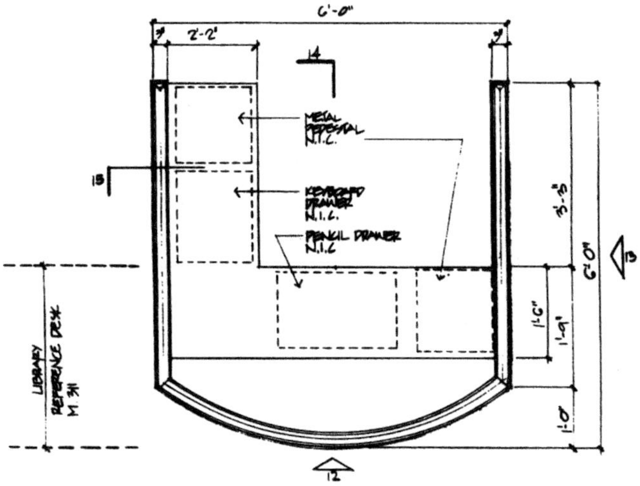

(11) PLAN - M.305

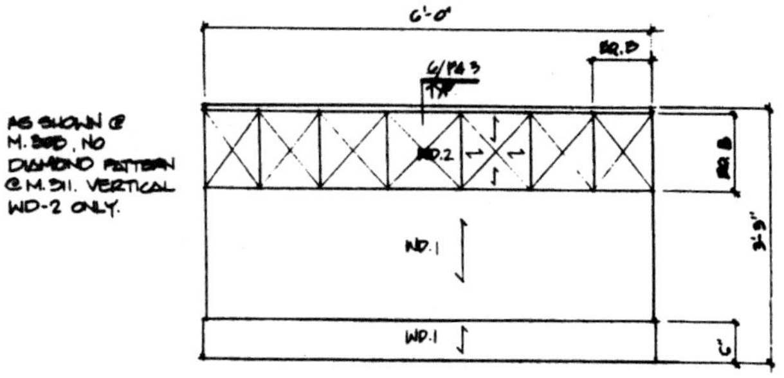

(12) ELEVATION

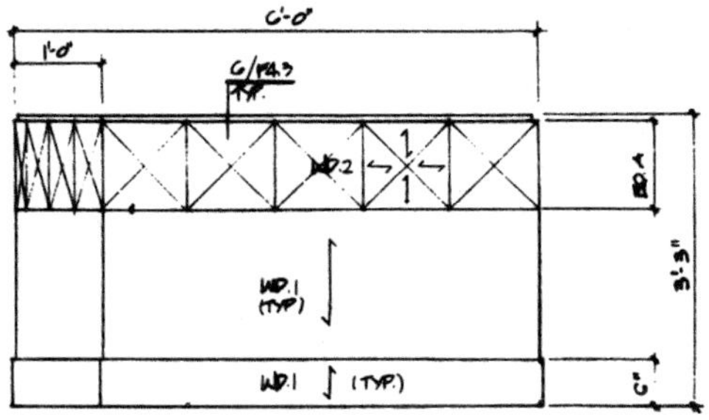

(13) ELEVATION - LEFT

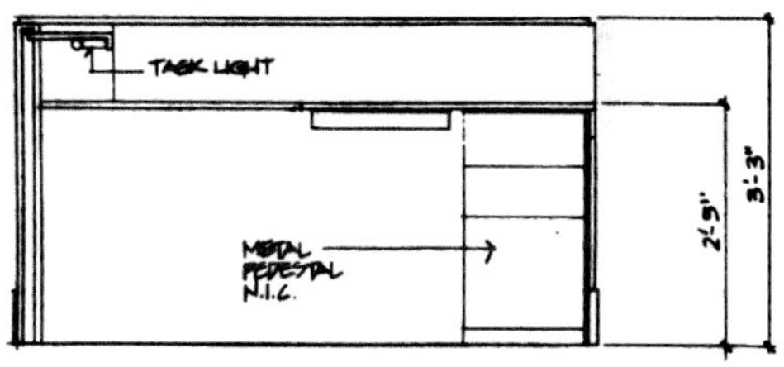

(14) SECTION-

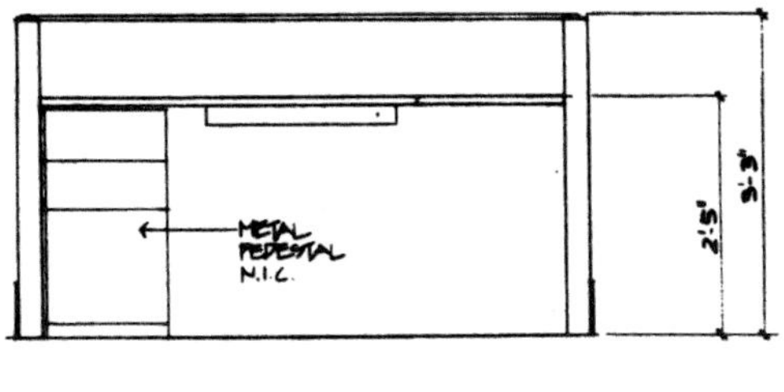

(15) SECTION-

M.311
M.305

Fig. 5 More privacy can be achieved in the design of a reception desk when there is enclosure on three sides, as is shown here. When designing custom reception desks, it is important to fully understand the tasks that the person working there will be asked to perform, in order to provide for adequate storage, work surfaces at the appropriate height, the incorporation of electronic equipment, and task lighting

RECEPTION AREAS

Reception Desk Details

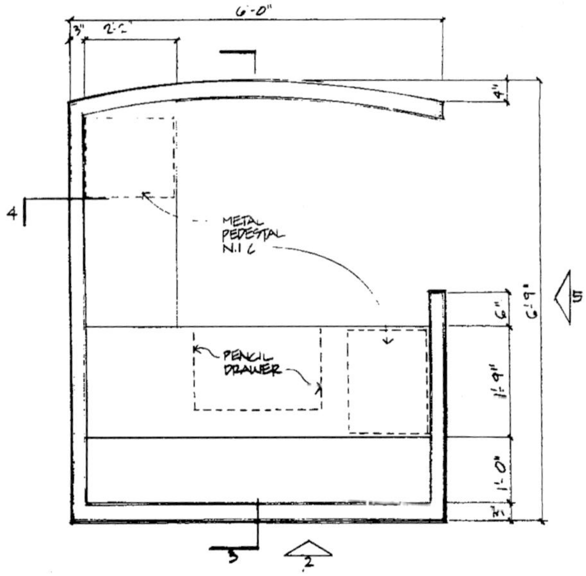

1 PLAN M.308

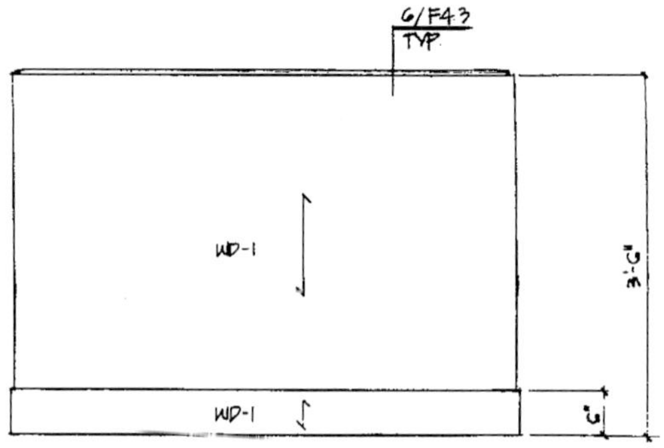

2 ELEVATION - FRONT

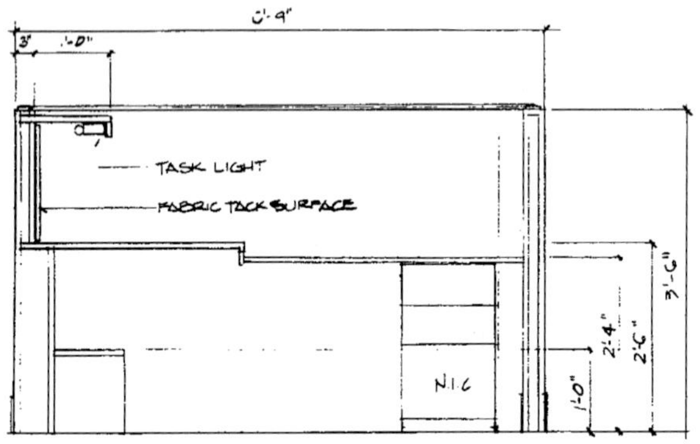

3 SECTION -

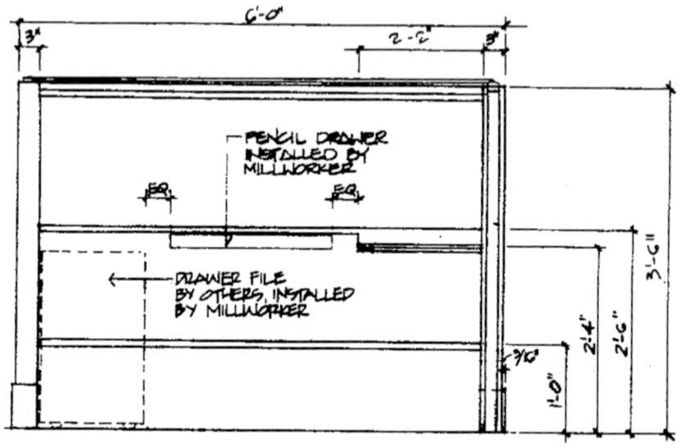

4 SECTION -

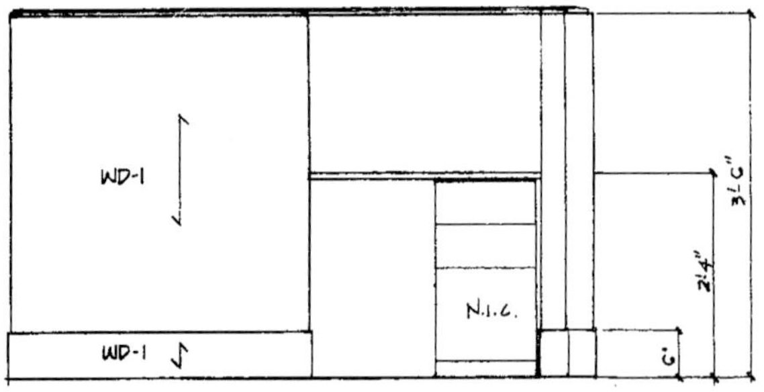

5 ELEVATION - LEFT

Fig. 6 The reception desk shown here is designed in order to provide privacy on three sides, with partial privacy on the fourth side. In this example, a right-hand typing return has been provided. Careful consideration should always be given to the height and placement of task lighting in order to ensure that the surface or task below is being lit properly. Many designers do not give this adequate thought. Overall costs of custom-designed reception desks can be reduced by integrating standard metal file components into the architectural woodwork

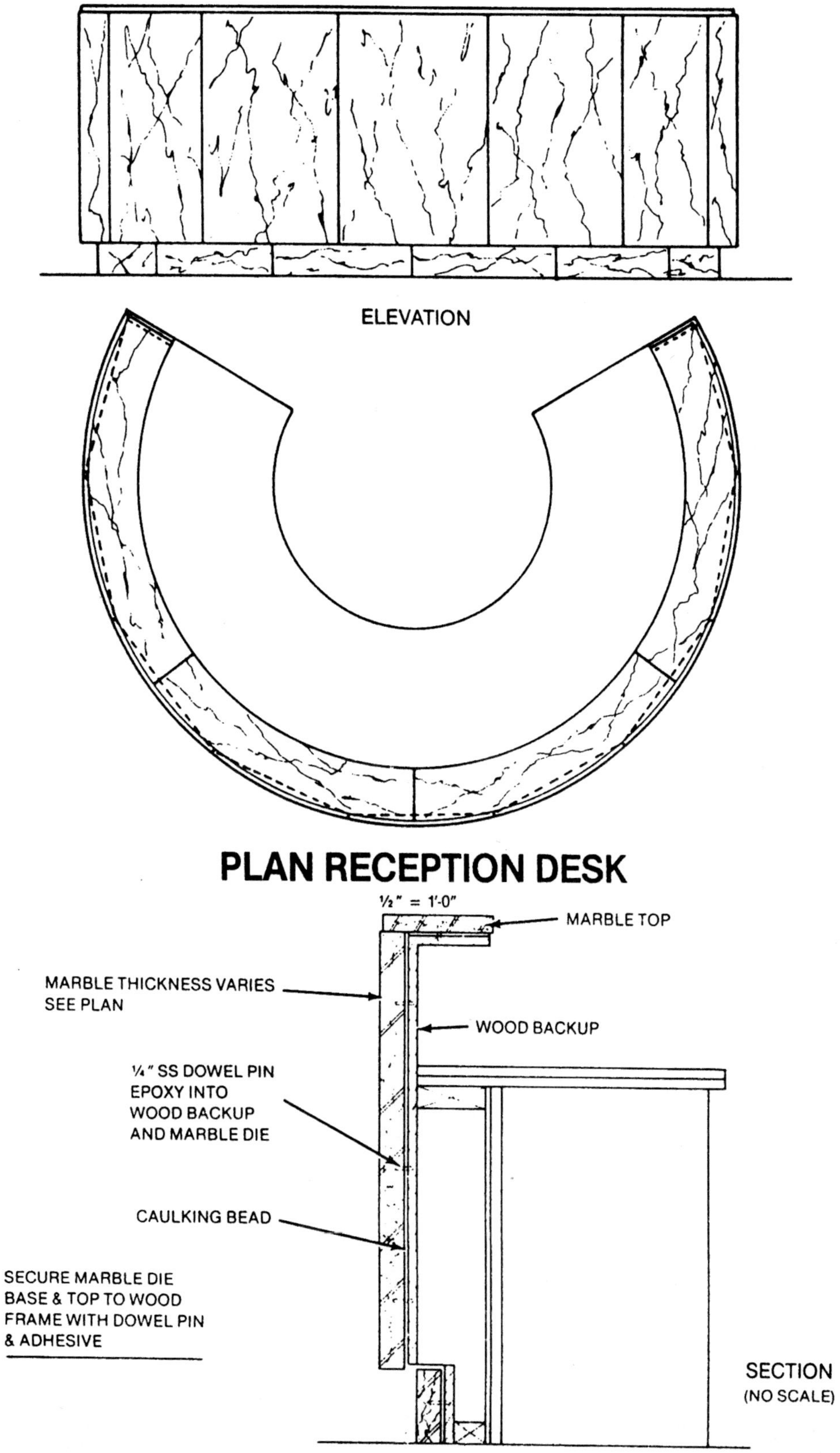

Fig. 7 A larger reception desk can accommodate work surfaces on three sides, as shown here. With this type of configuration, however, the designer must be concerned with the orientation of the open side. As with all custom reception desks, the designer must anticipate the integration of wiring and electronic equipment within the architectural woodwork

RECEPTION AREAS

Reception Desk Details

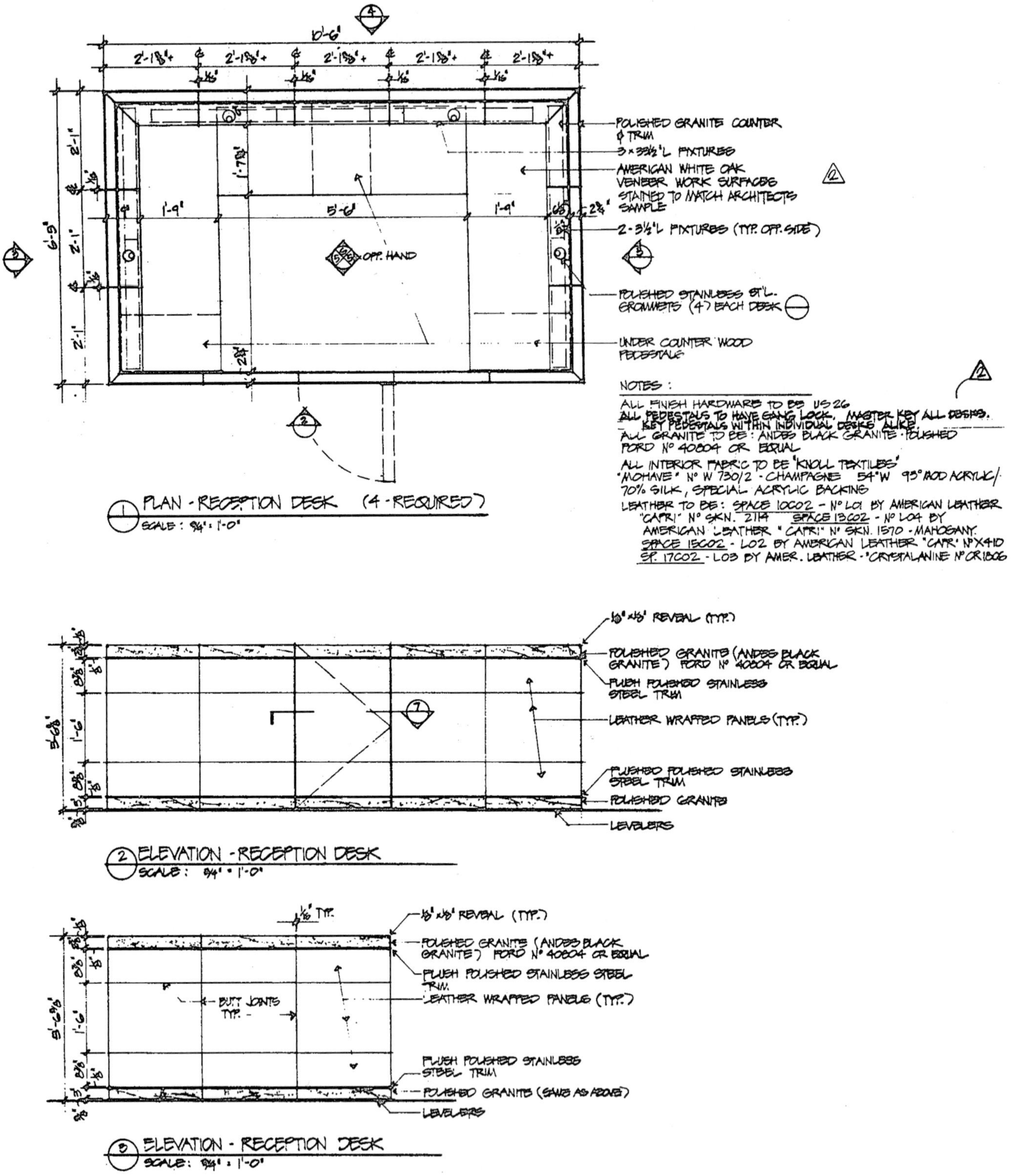

Fig. 8 Total privacy of the receptionist's workstation can be achieved through enclosure on all four sides. In addition to enhancing visual privacy, such a design can also provide added security and control by the addition of a door. Such a design might be particularly appropriate for a reception area where the designer might wish to control access by children

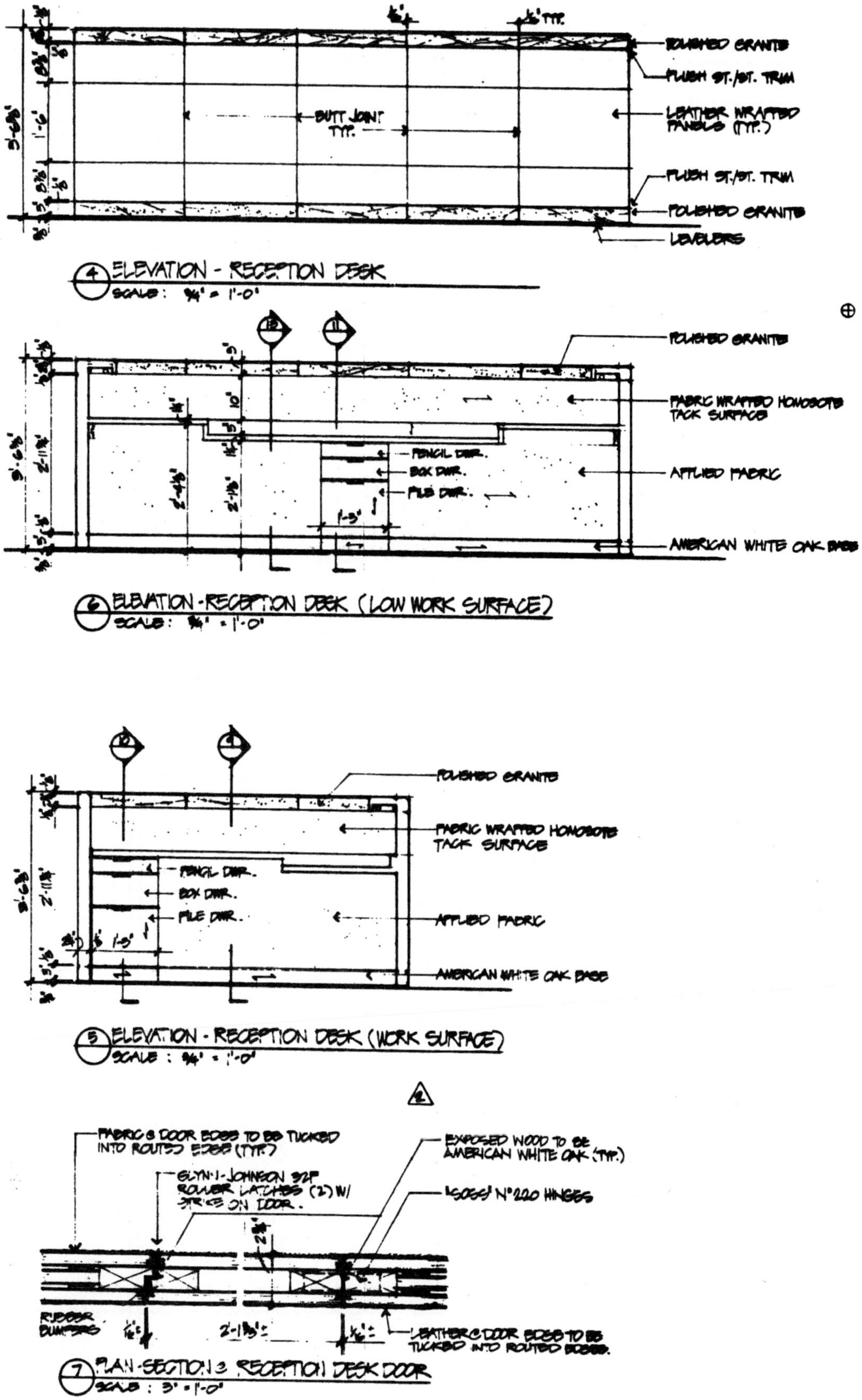

Fig. 8 *(Continued)*

④ ELEVATION - RECEPTION DESK
SCALE : ¾" = 1'-0"

⑥ ELEVATION - RECEPTION DESK (LOW WORK SURFACE)
SCALE : ¾" = 1'-0"

⑤ ELEVATION - RECEPTION DESK (WORK SURFACE)
SCALE : ¾" = 1'-0"

⑦ PLAN - SECTION RECEPTION DESK DOOR
SCALE : 3" = 1'-0"

RECEPTION AREAS

Reception Desk Details

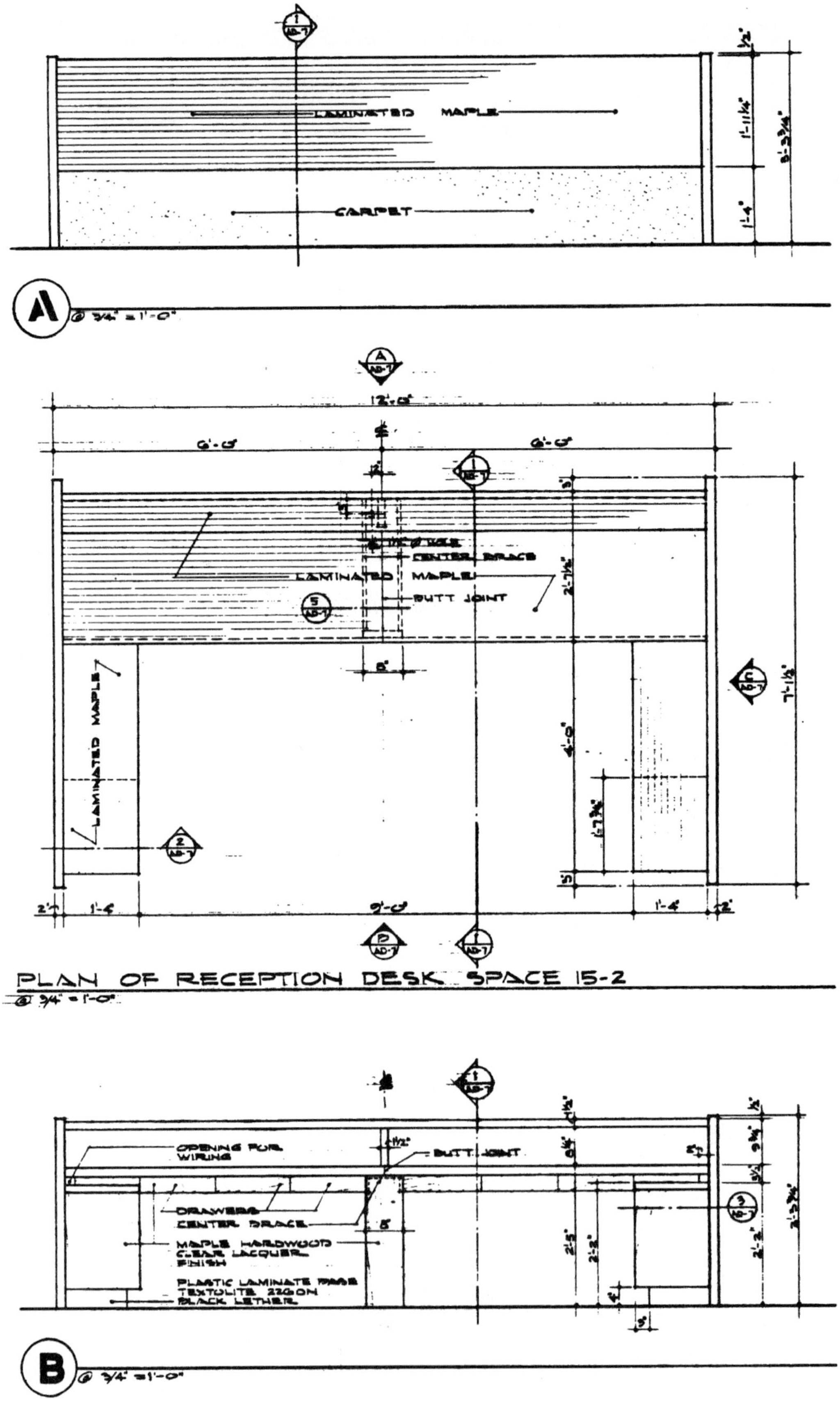

Fig. 9 A reception desk can often consist of two workstations

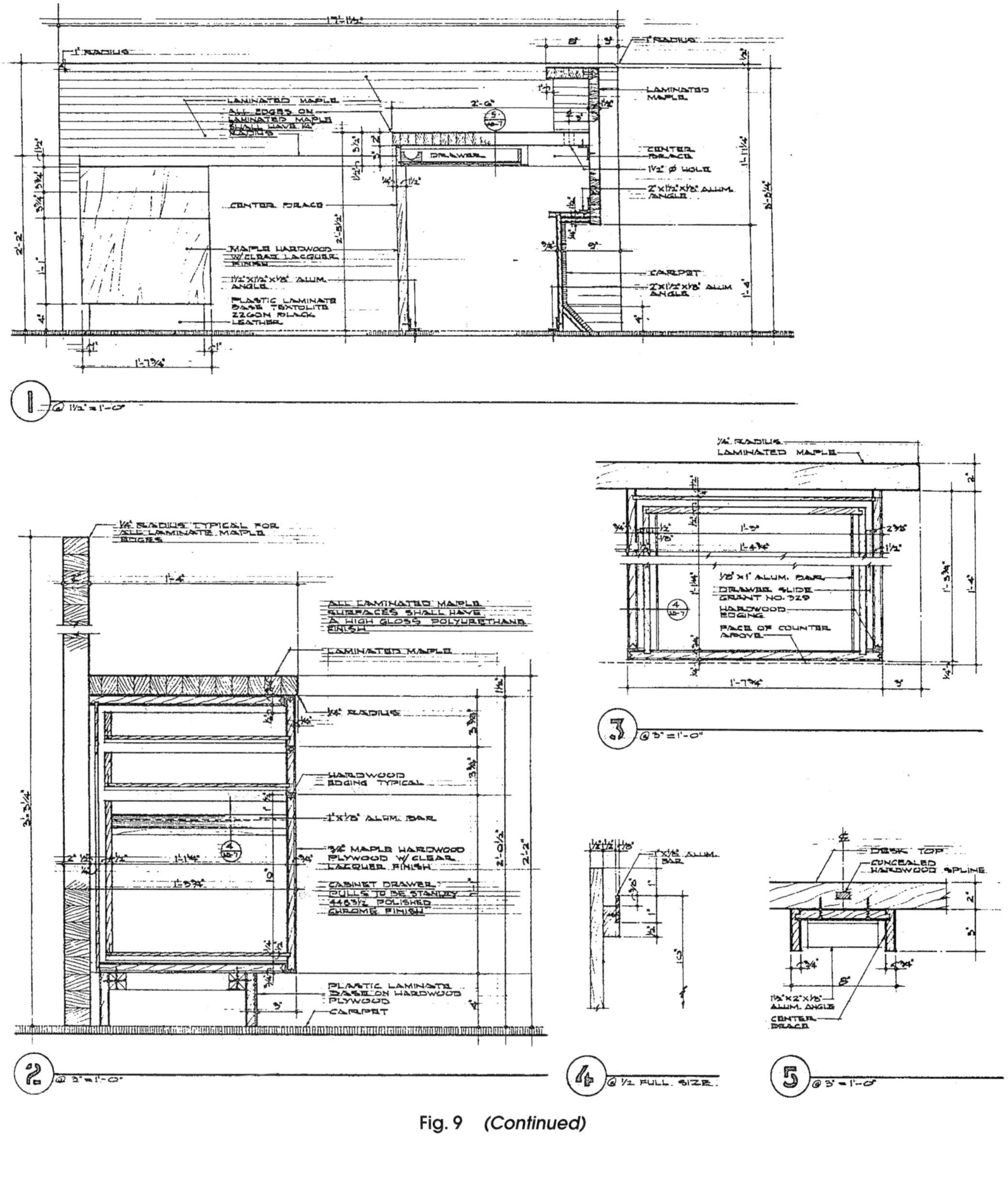

Fig. 9 *(Continued)*

RECEPTION AREAS

Reception Desk Details

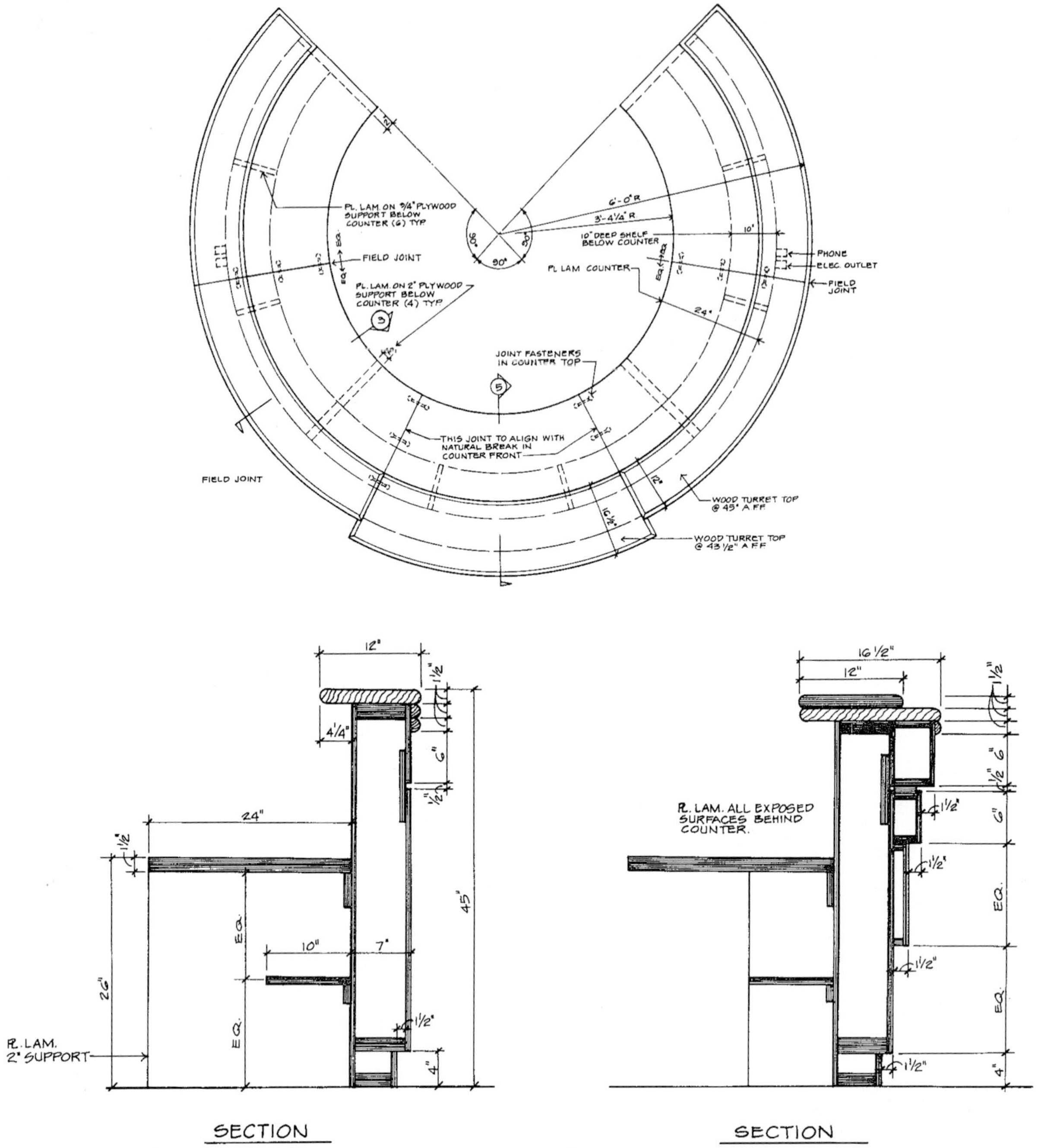

Fig. 10 A circular reception desk can make a bold and sophisticated corporate statement. The designer is cautioned, however, to carefully analyze the minimum radius required for chair movement. Custom built-in files and drawers, if also curved, can become costly and sometimes impractical

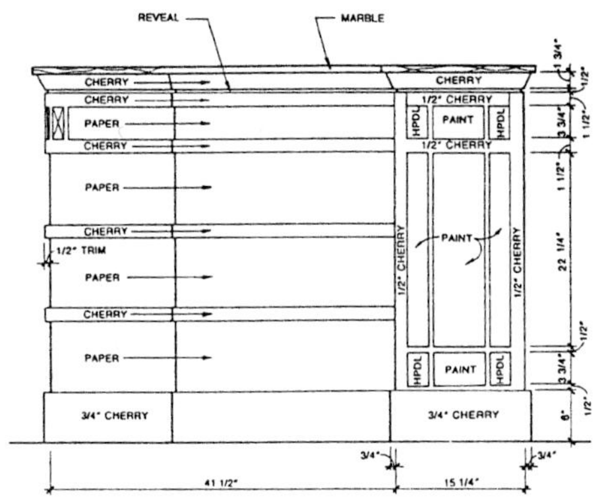

SIDE ELEVATION - RECEPTION DESK - CAMBRIDGE

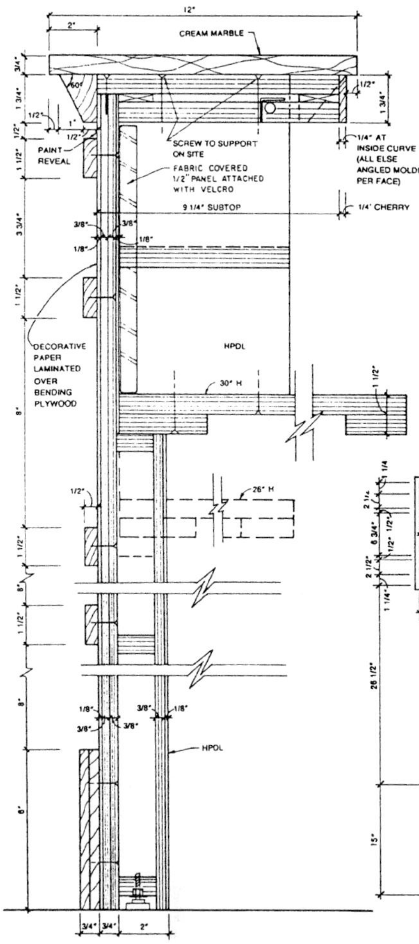

SECTION - RECEPTION DESK - CAMBRIDGE

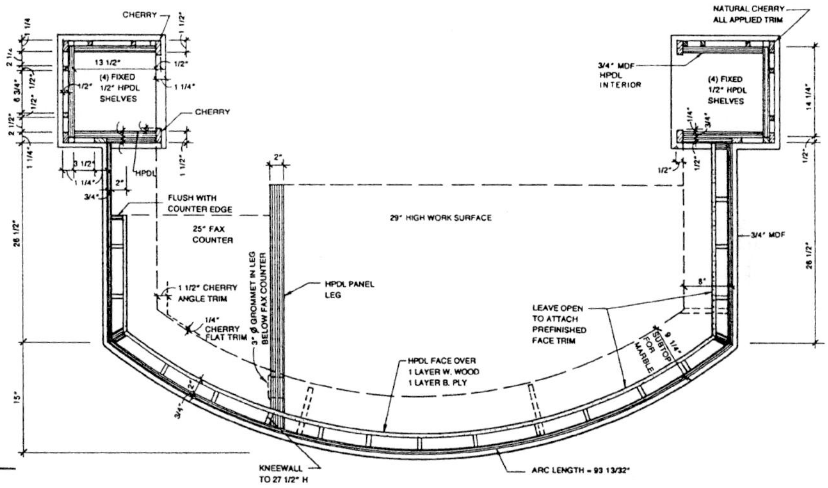

PLAN - RECEPTION DESK - CAMBRIDGE

RECEPTION AREAS

Reception Desk Details

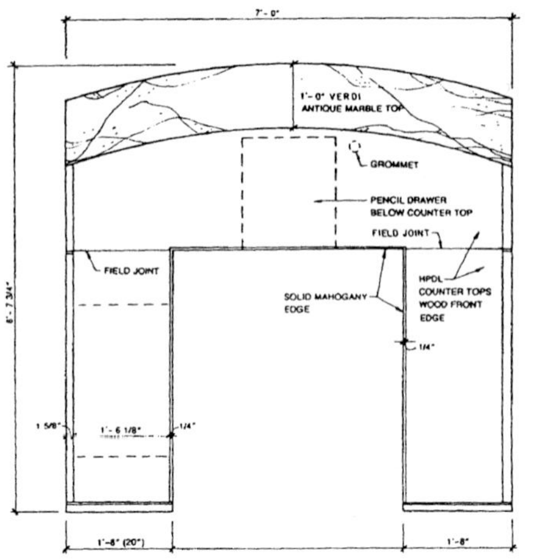

PLAN AT RECEPTION DESKS

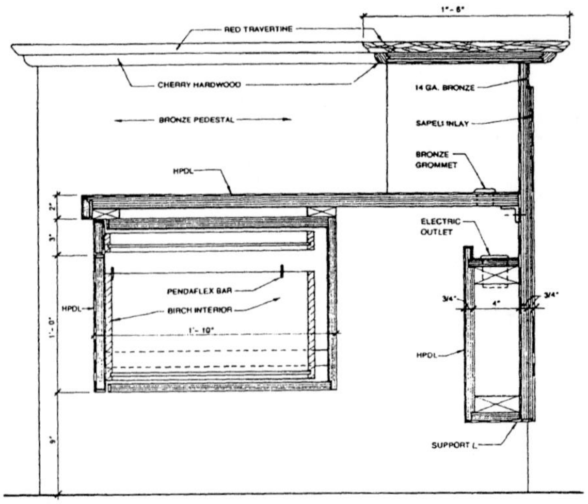

SECTION AT RECEPTION DESK

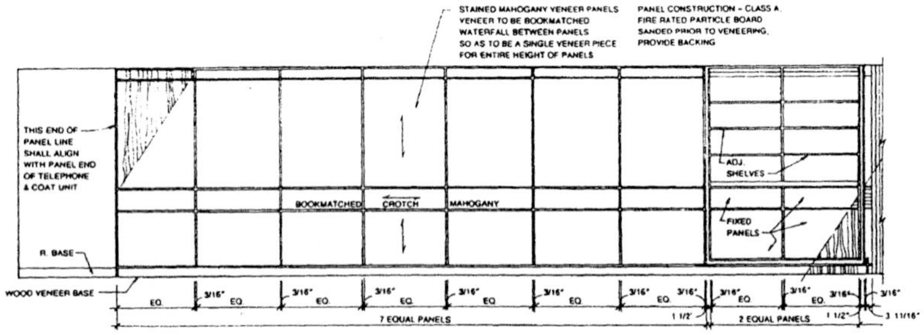

ELEVATION AT RECEPTION AREA

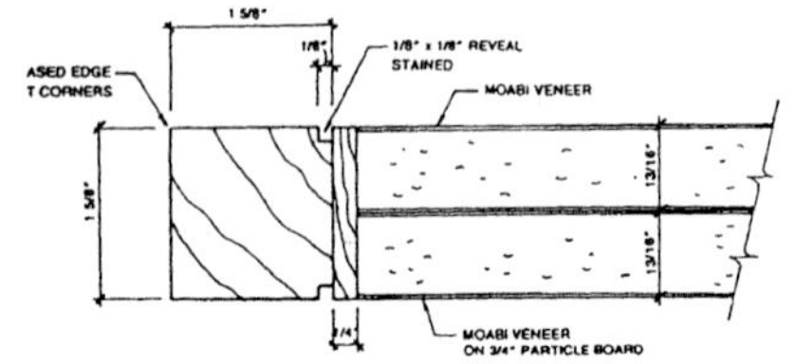

SECTION AT RAIL

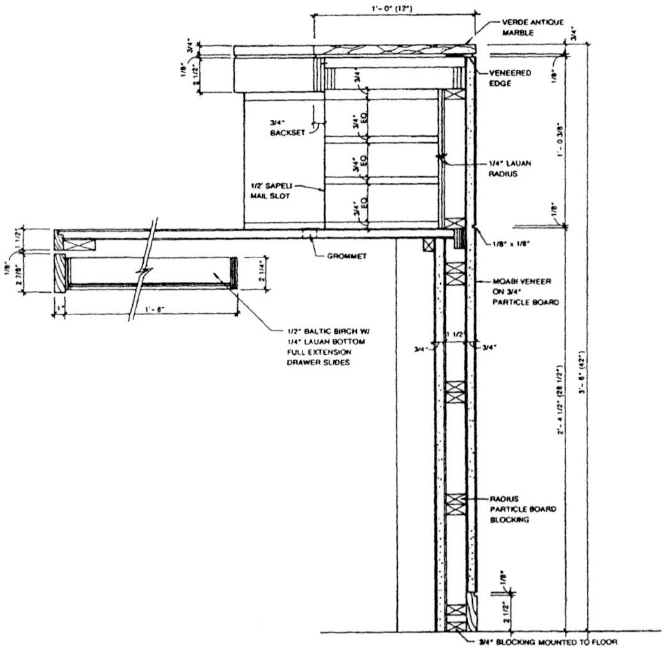

SECTION AT DESK FRONT

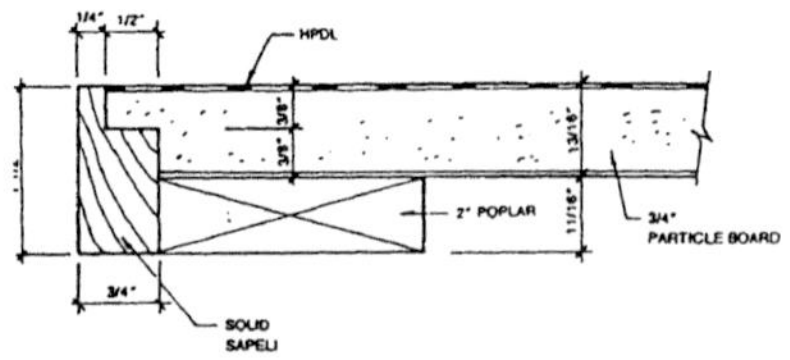

EDGE DETAIL

RECEPTION AREAS
Reception Desk Details

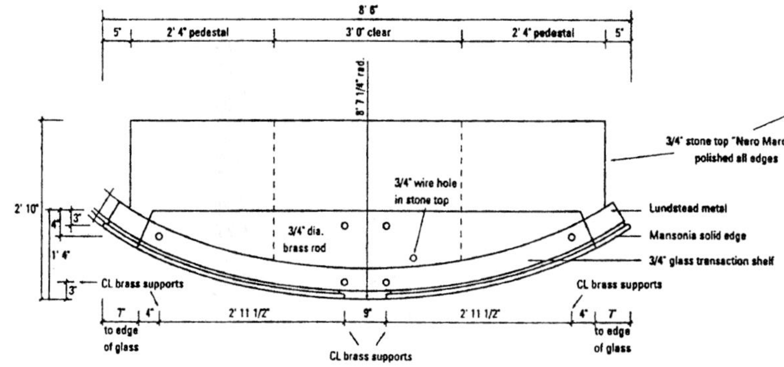

PLAN

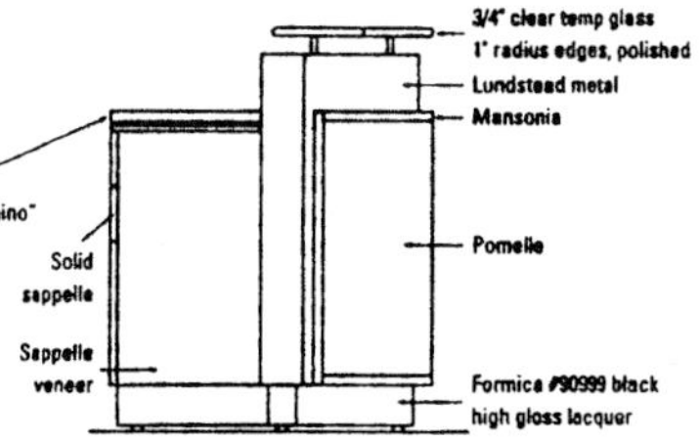

SECTION

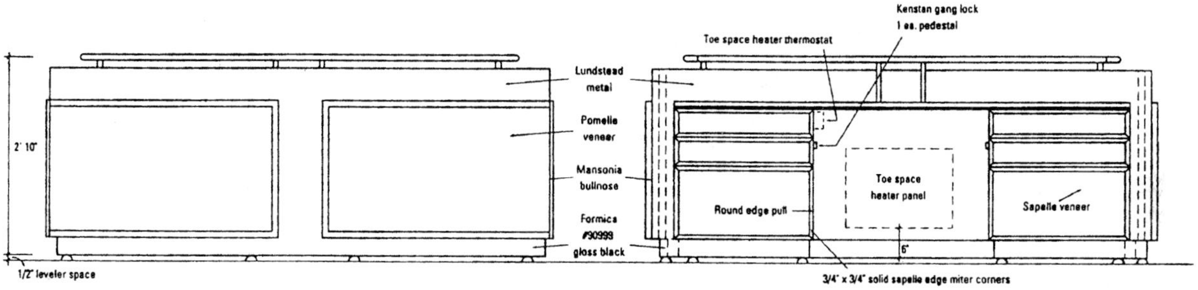

ELEVATION

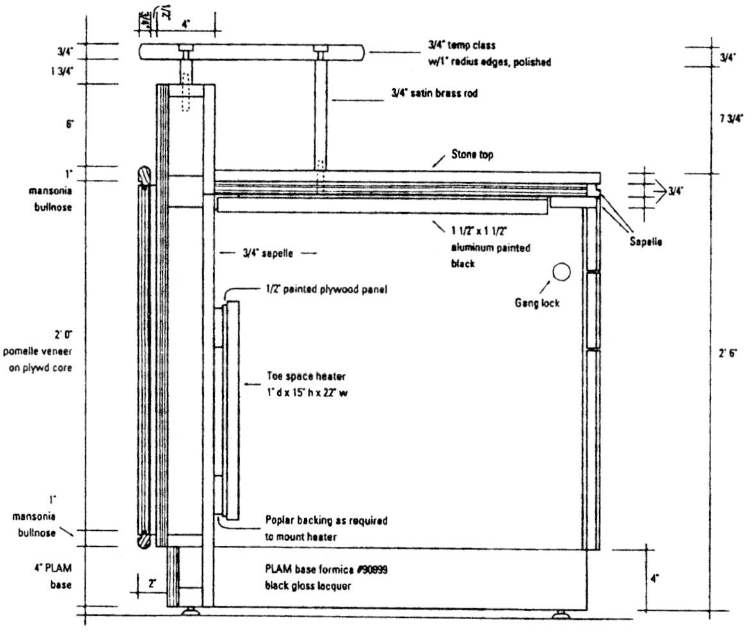

SECTION THROUGH KNEE SPACE

RECEPTION AREAS

Reception Desk Details

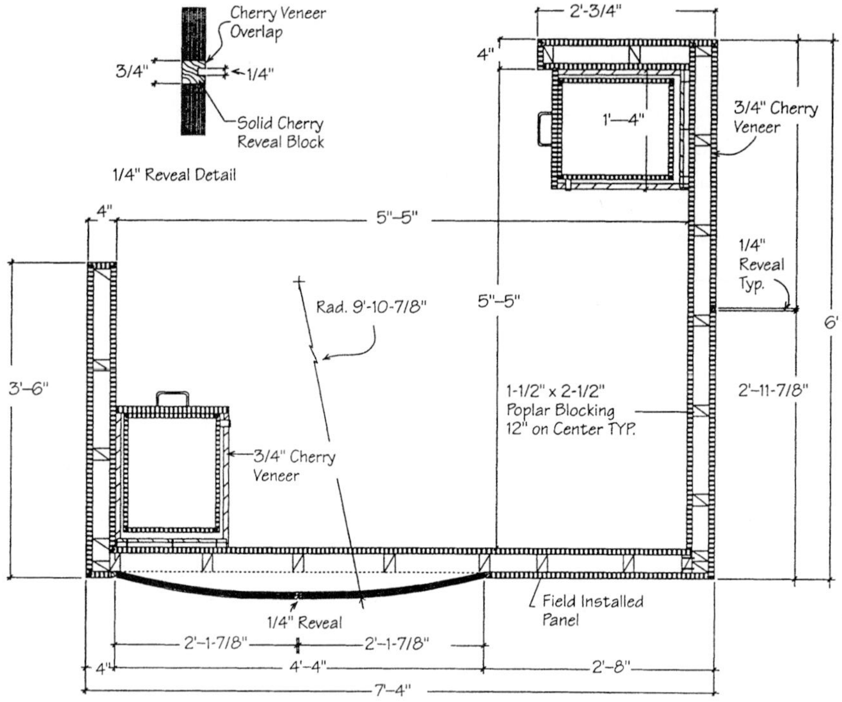

Reception Desk Details

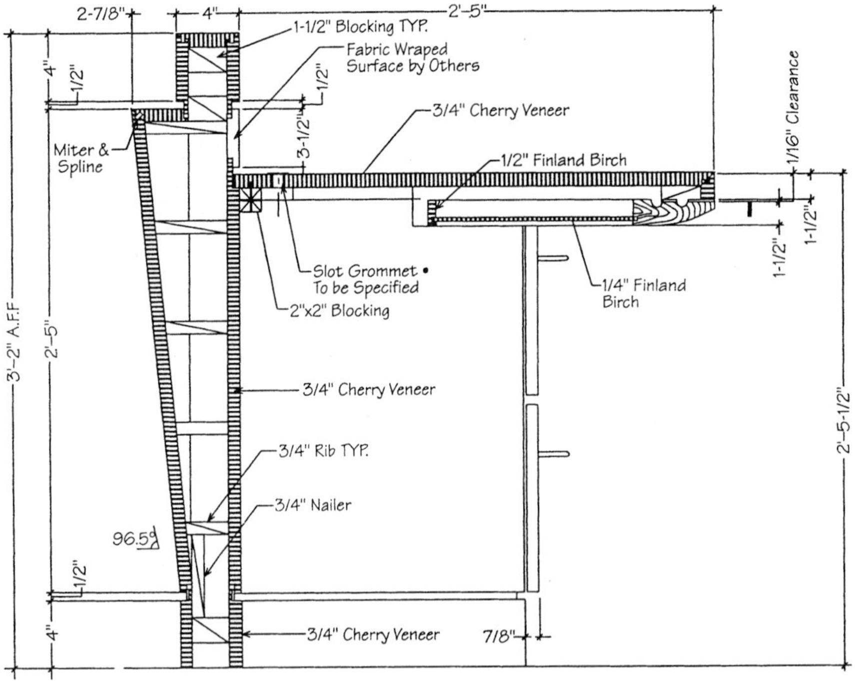

Vertical Section: Pencil Drawer

RECEPTION AREAS

Reception Desk Details

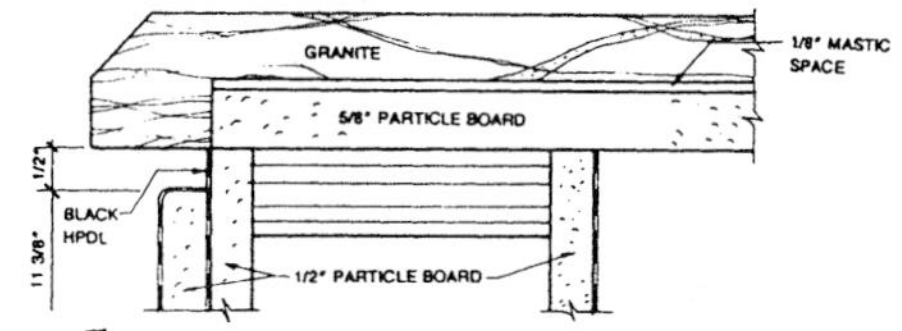

SECTION EDGE DETAIL

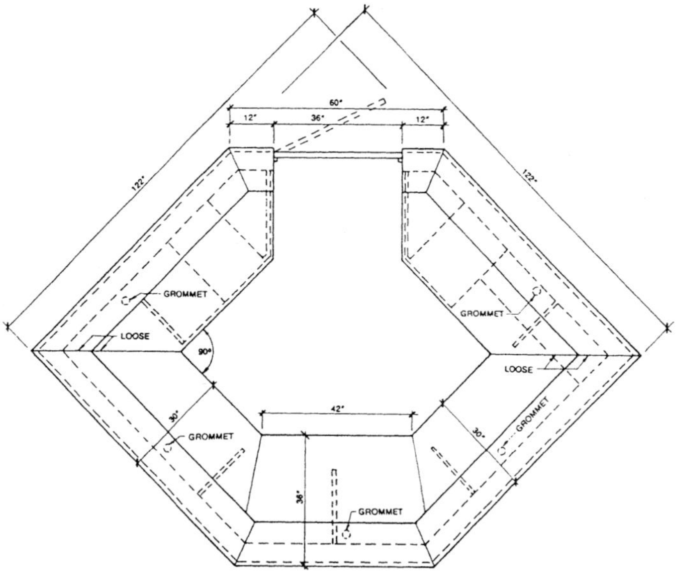

PLAN VIEW – RECEPTION DESK

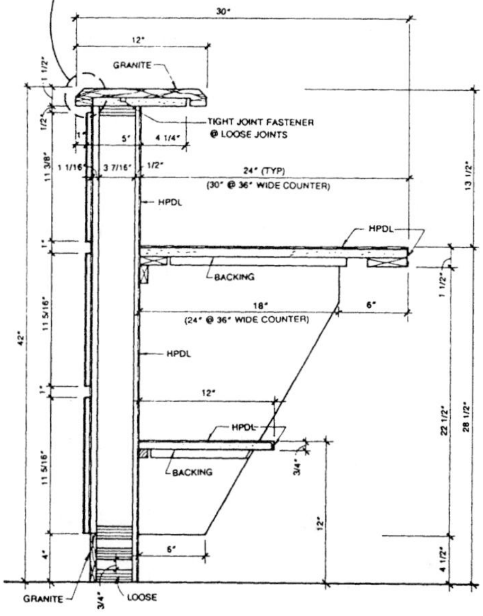

SECTION AT DESK

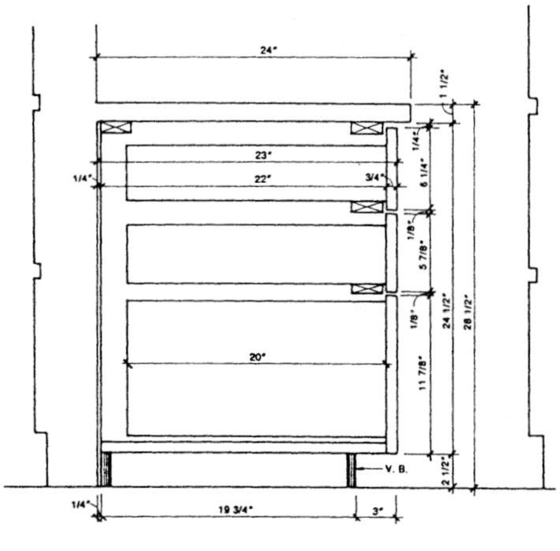

SECTION AT DESK

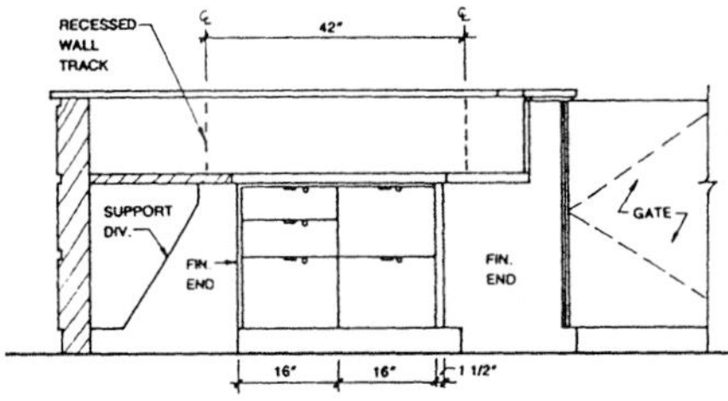

ELEVATION – INTERIOR DESK FRONT

RECEPTION AREAS
Reception Desk Details

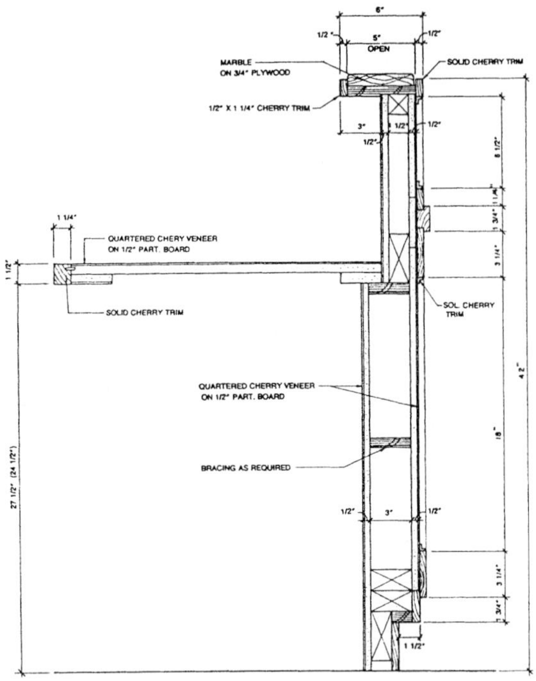

SECTION AT RECEPTION DESK

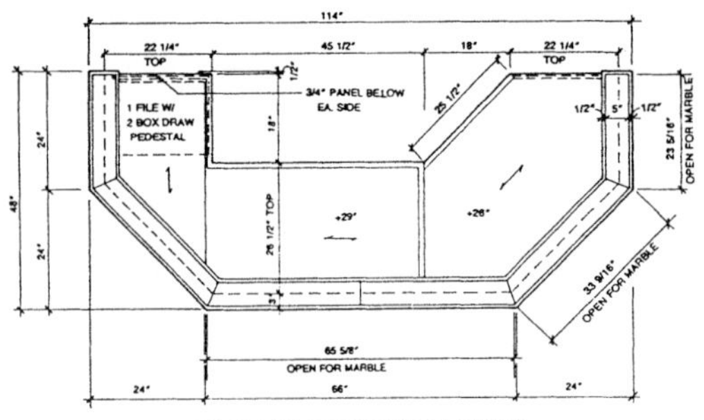

PLAN AT RECEPTION DESK

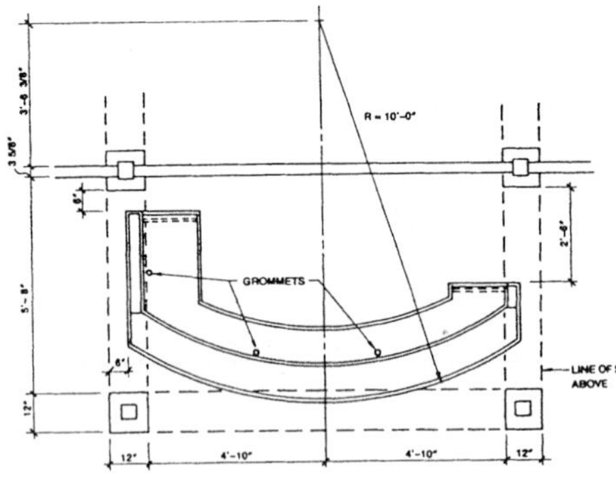

PLAN - RECEPTION DESK

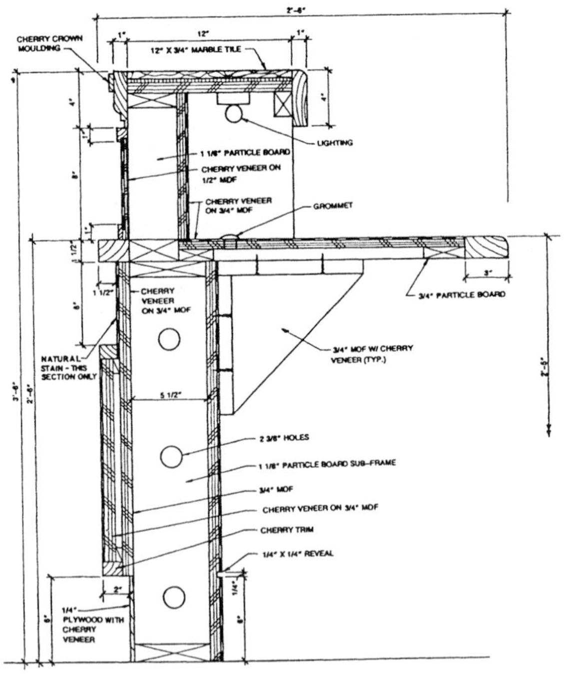

SECTION AT RECEPTION DESK

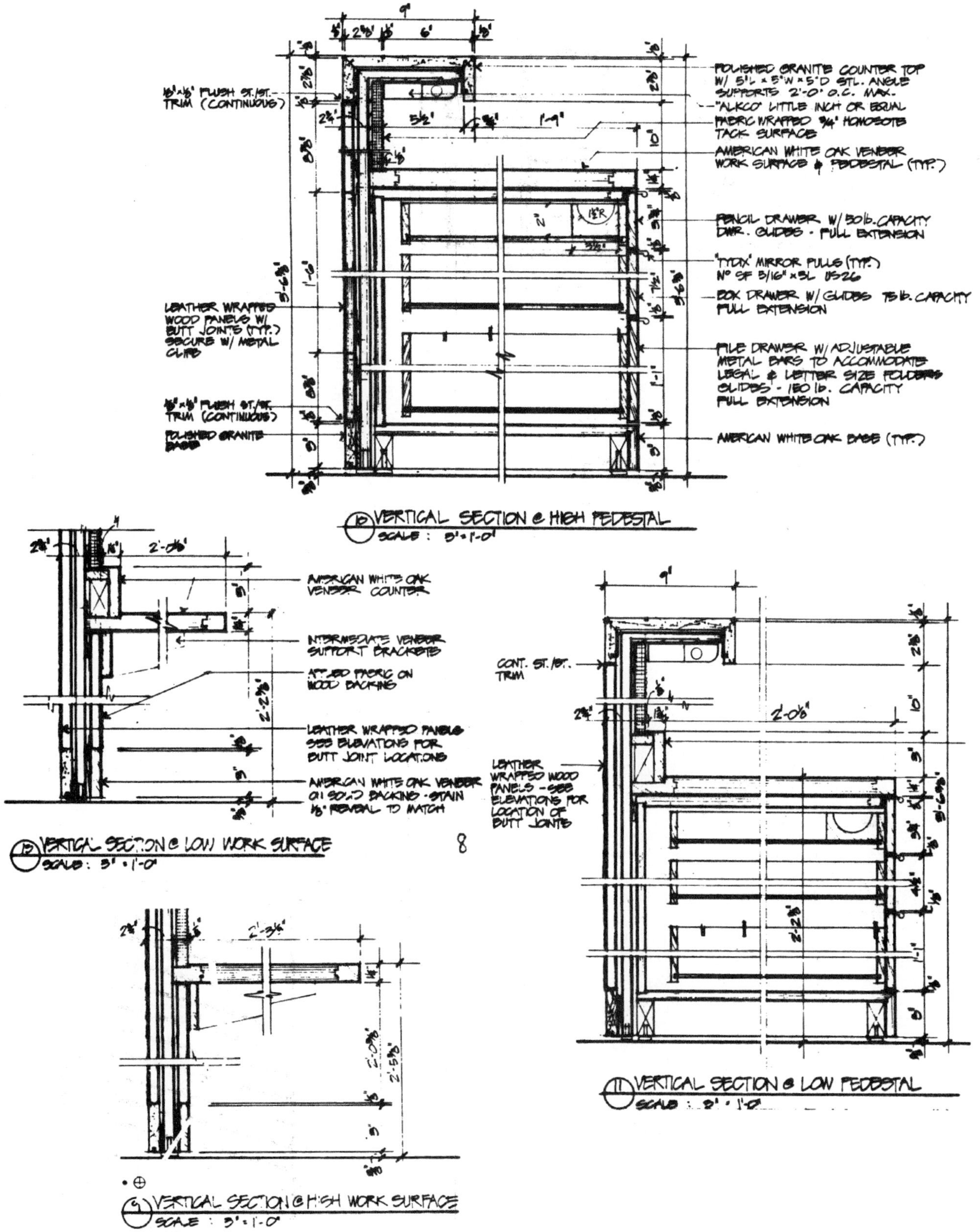

Fig. 11 A fully detailed reception desk will require many large-scale vertical sections to explain the various storage, drawer, work surface, lighting, and electrical requirements. Examples of such details are shown here

RECEPTION AREAS

Reception Desk Details

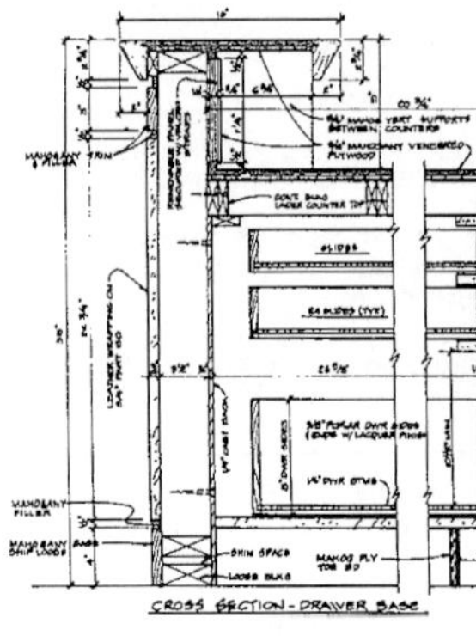

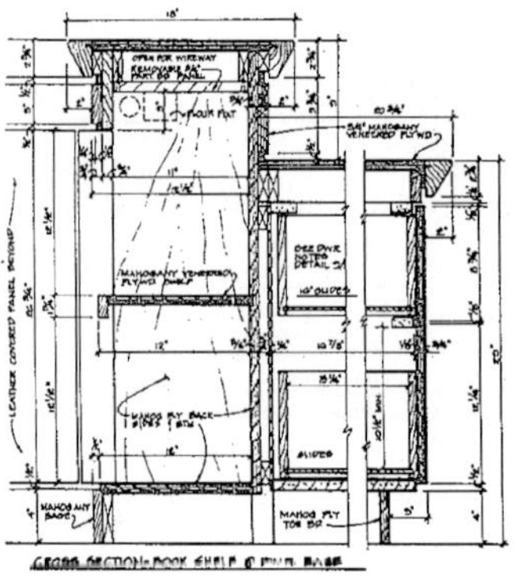

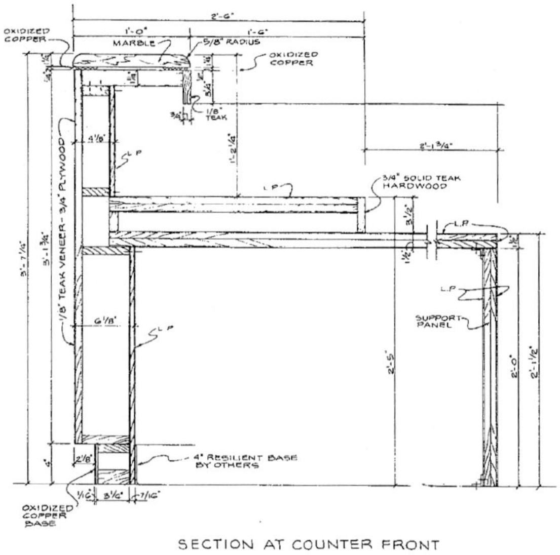

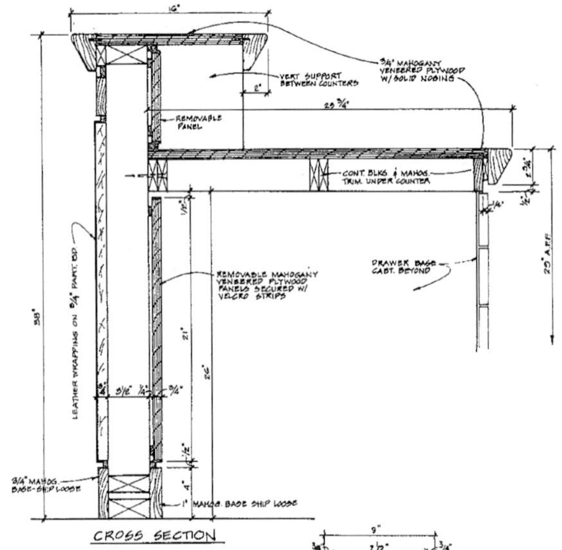

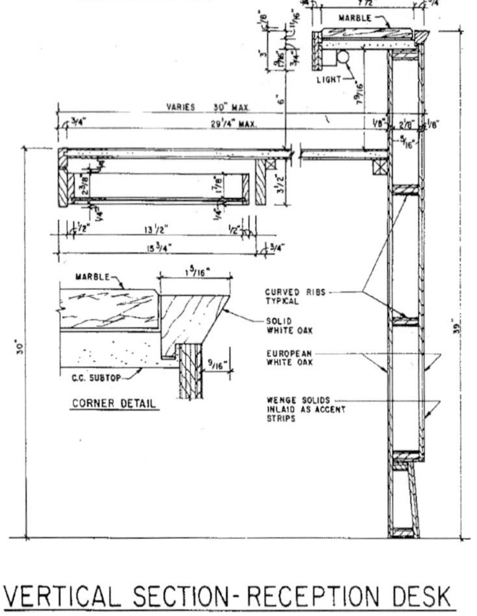

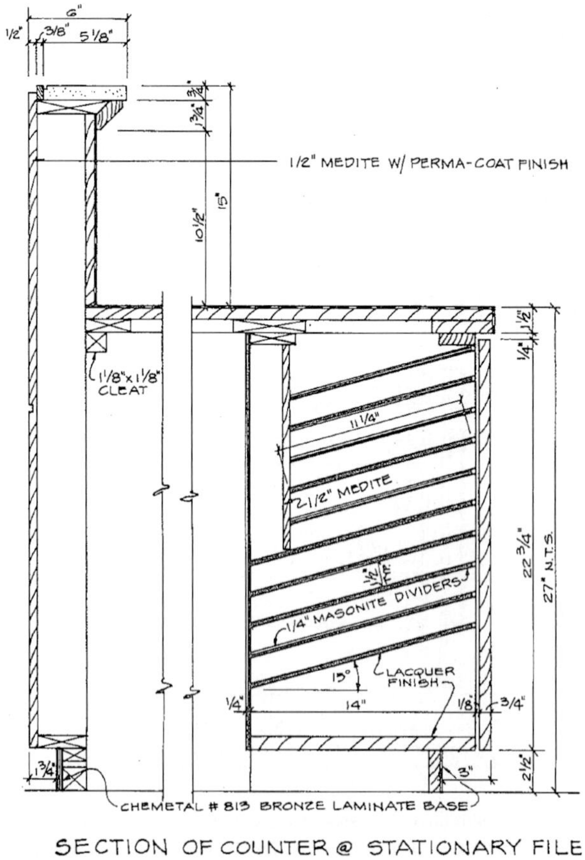

Fig. 11 ***(Continued)***

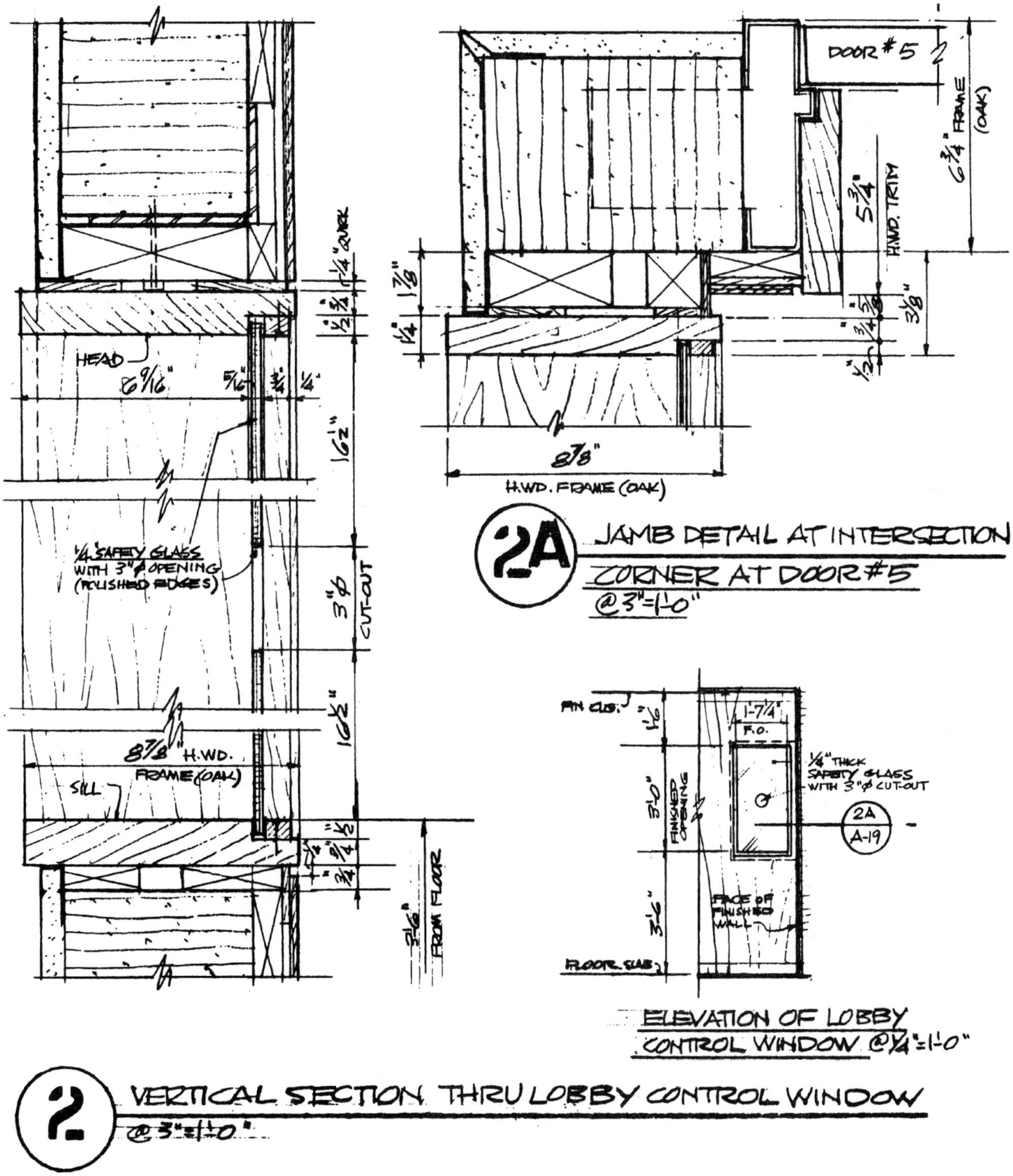

Fig. 12 A receptionist's workstation need not be freestanding within a reception area, where security and privacy are of critical importance. A receptionist may be located on the opposite side of a glass partition, as shown here. Such a solution is often suggested when the receptionist performs multiple tasks such as typing and answering phones

RECEPTION AREAS
Reception Window/Pass-Through

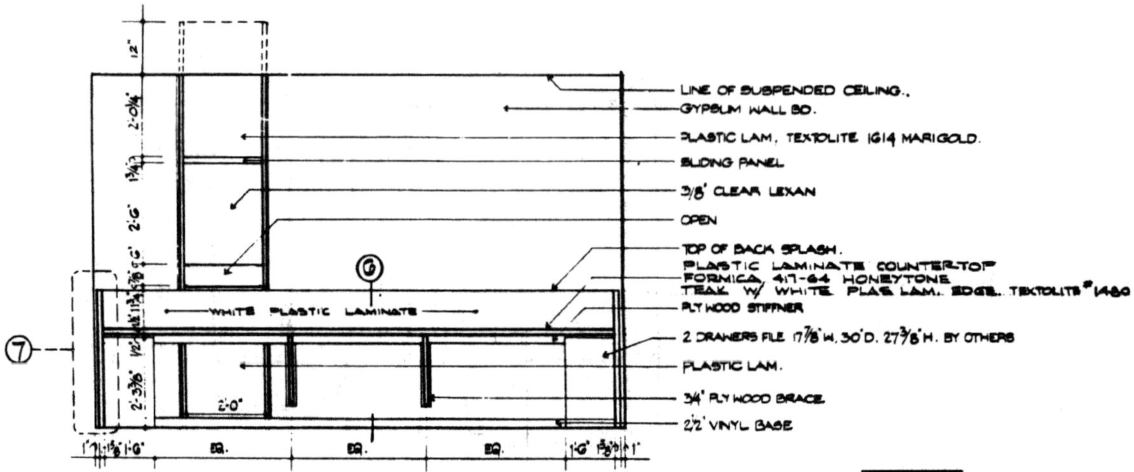

5 NORTH ELEVATION FROM SPACE NO. 13
SCALE 1/2" = 1'-0"

CW
5

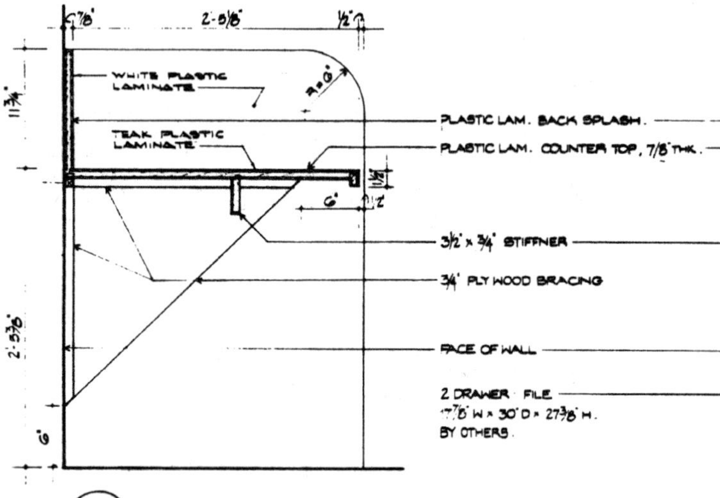

6
SCALE 1 1/2" = 1'-0"

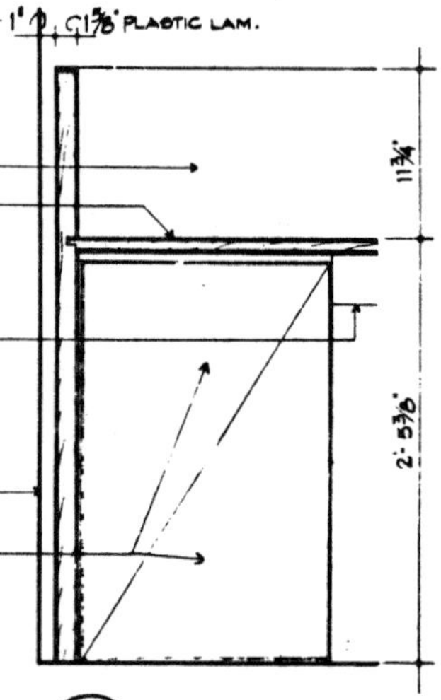

7
SCALE 1 1/2" = 1'-0"

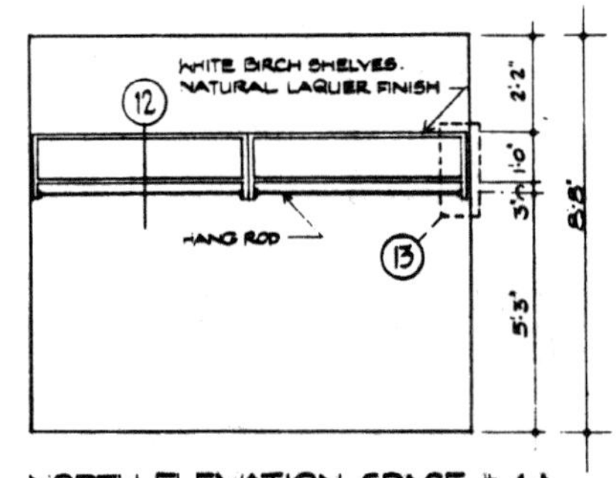

NORTH ELEVATION SPACE # 4A

11
SCALE 3/8" = 1'-0"

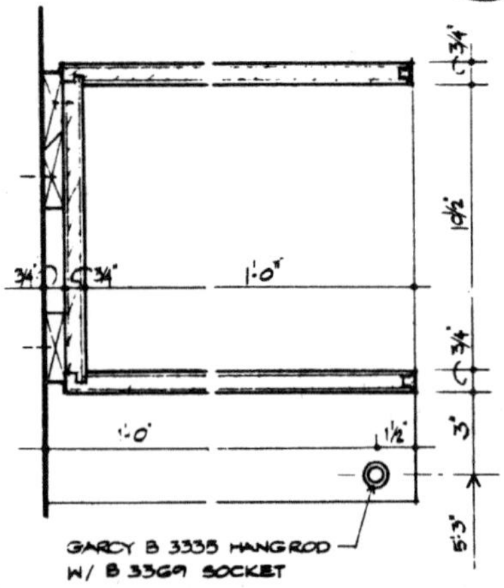

12
SCALE 3" = 1'-0"

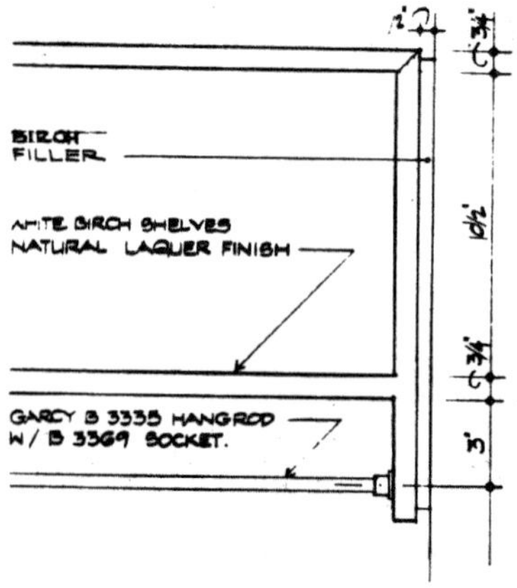

13 COAT & HAT SHELVES
PART ELEVATION
SCALE 3" = 1'-0"

Fig. 12 *(Continued)*

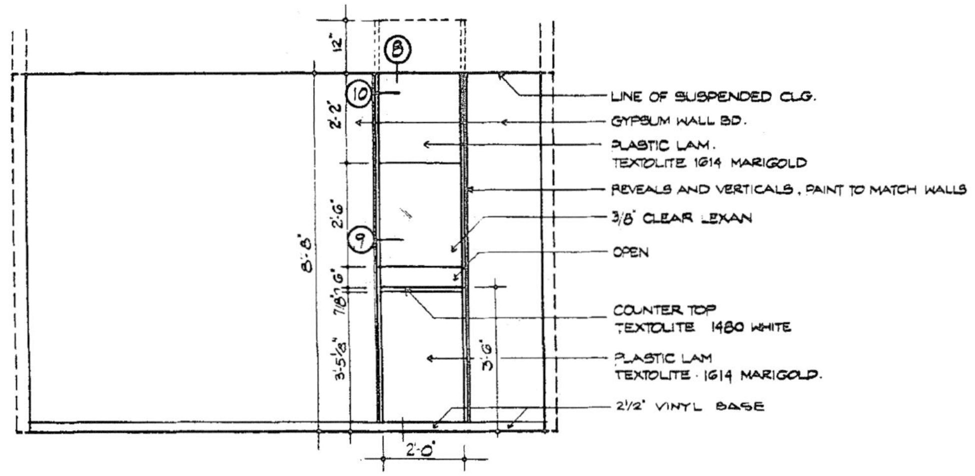

4 SOUTH ELEVATION FROM SPACE NO. 14
SCALE 1/2" = 1'-0"

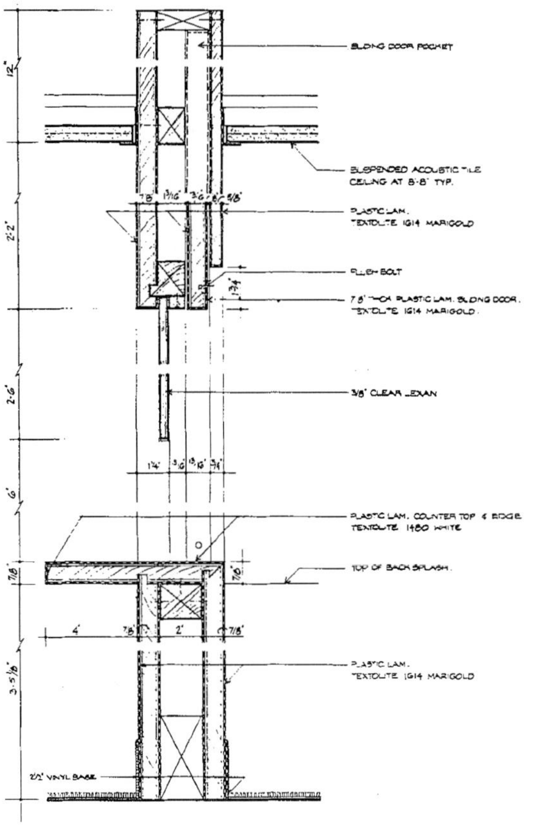

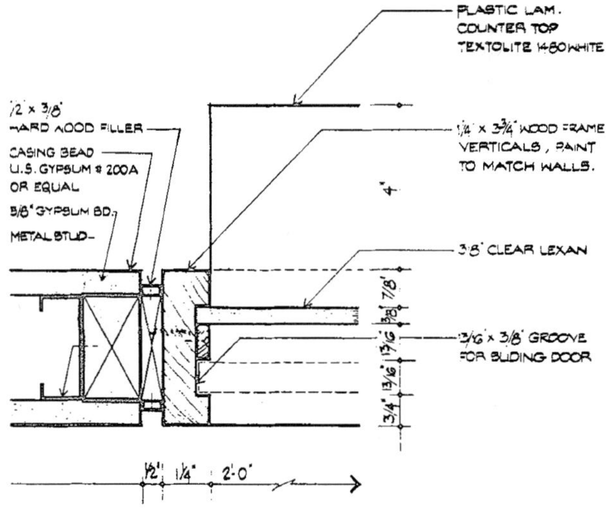

9 SCALE : HALF FULL SIZE

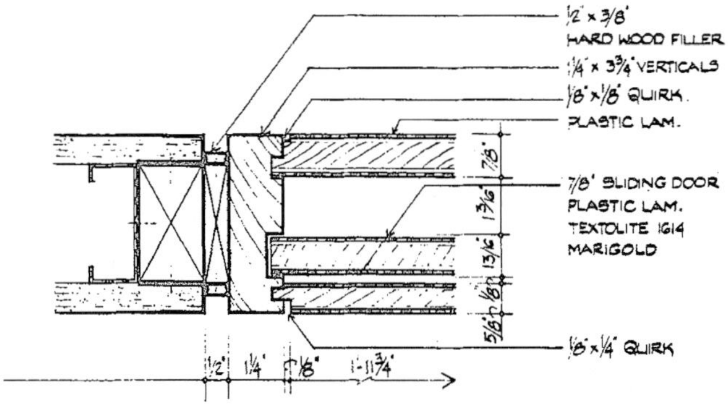

10 SCALE : HALF FULL SIZE.

Fig. 12 *(Continued)*

RECEPTION AREAS

Reception Window/Pass-Through

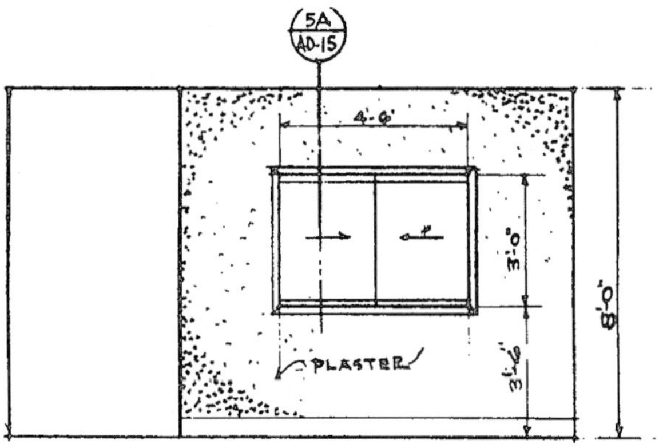

ELEVATION FROM SPACE 202
1/4" = 1'-0"

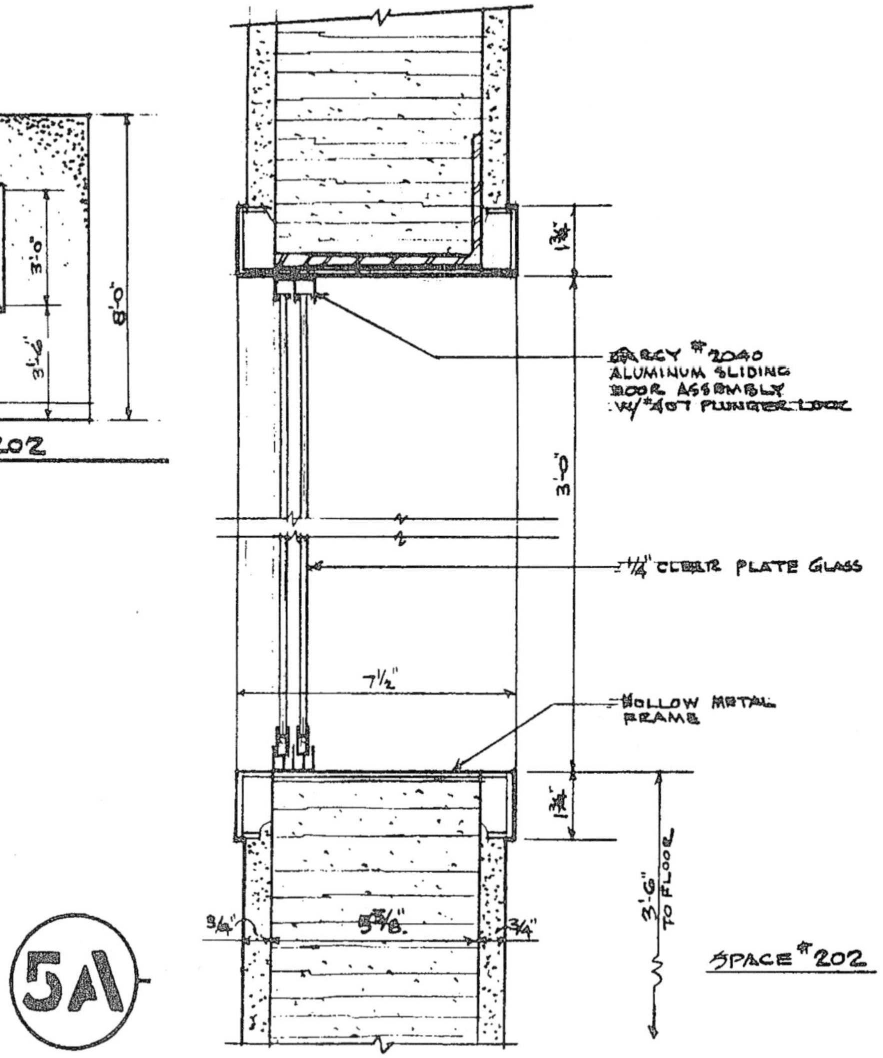

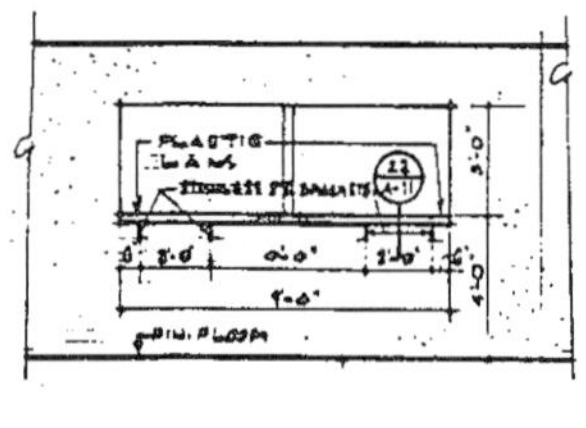

21 EAST ELEVATION
1/4" = 1'-0"

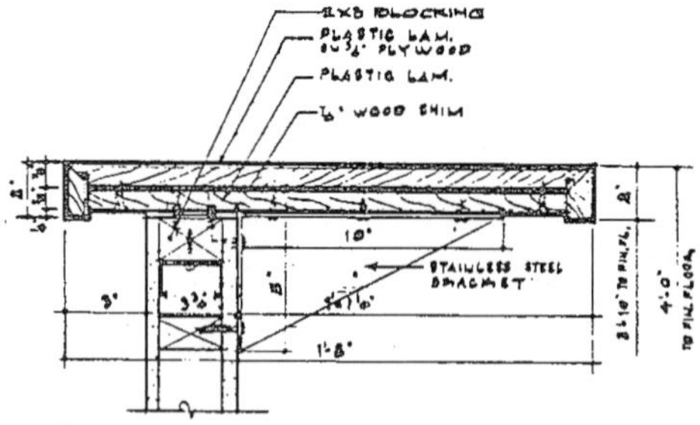

22 3" = 1'-0"

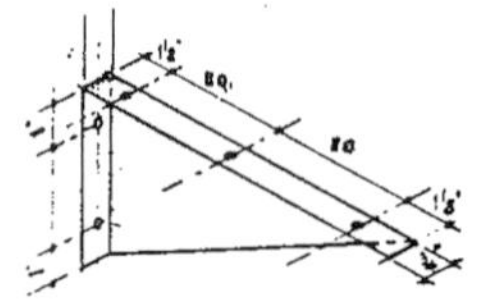

ISOMETRIC OF STAINLESS STEEL BRACKET
NOT TO SCALE

Fig. 12 ***(Continued)***

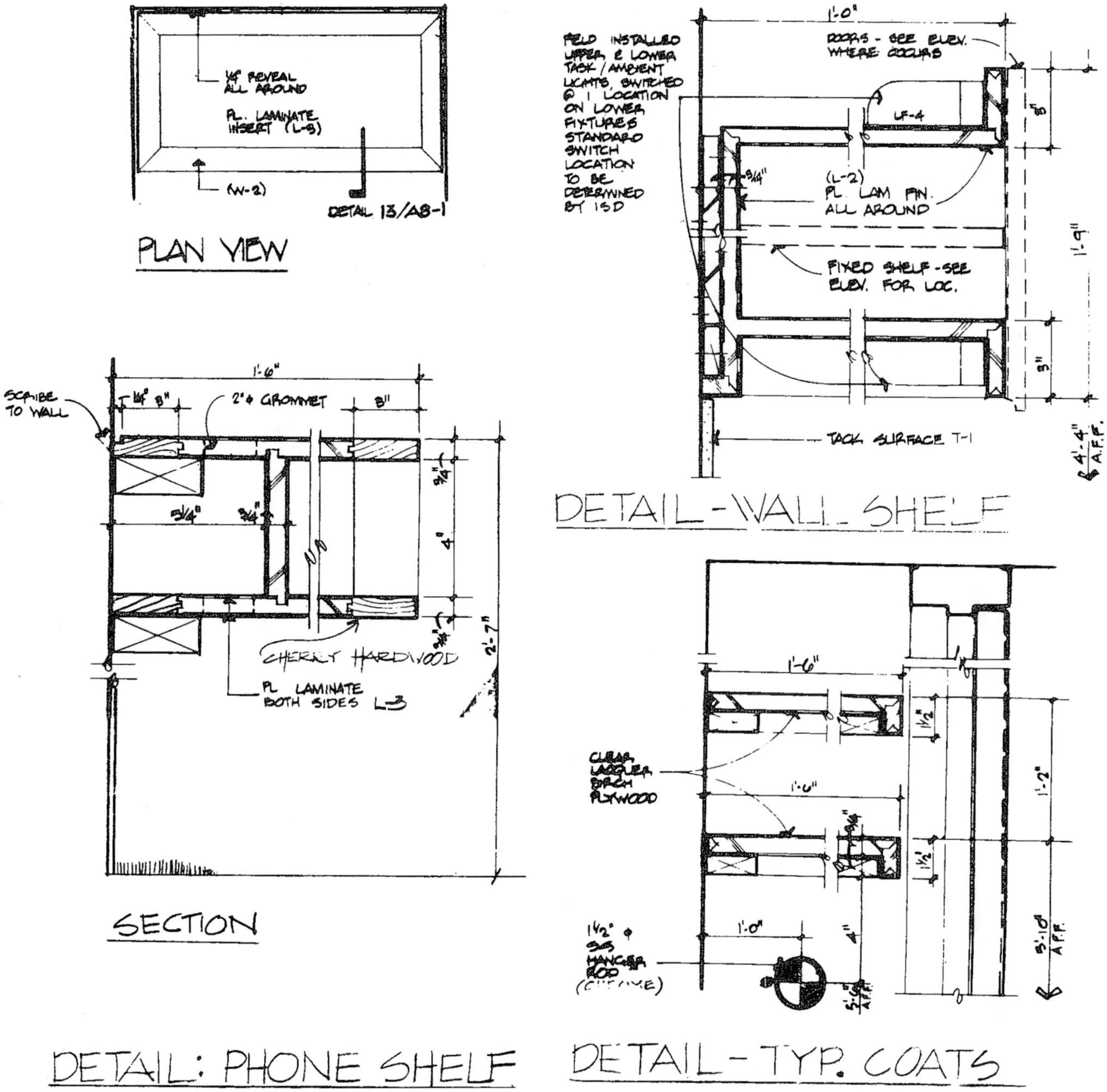

Fig. 13 While the reception desk is typically the major element to be designed and detailed for a reception area, other custom-designed components must also be carefully considered. A phone shelf, a wall shelf, a coat hanging area, and a work surface are often items that must be carefully designed and detailed

FURNITURE, FURNISHINGS, AND EQUIPMENT
Desks and Seating

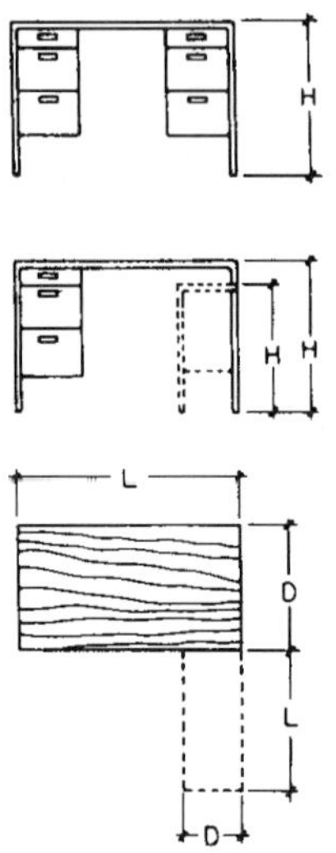

DESK DIMENSIONS

	DESKS				RETURNS	
	DOUBLE PEDESTAL		SINGLE PEDESTAL		FOR EXECUTIVE DESK RETURNS ARE AVAILABLE AT SAME HEIGHT AS DESK	
	STANDARD	RANGE	STANDARD	RANGE	STANDARD	RANGE
D	2'-6"	2'-0"-3'-3"	2'-6"	2'-0"-3'-3"	1'-6"	1'-3"-1'-8"
H	2'-5"	2'-4"-2'-6"	2'-5"	2'-4"-2'-6"	2'-2"	2'-1"-2'-3"
L	5'-0"	4'-6"-7'-0"	5'-0'	3'-9"-7'-0"	3'-0"	2'-0"-5'-0"

DESKS-SINGLE OR DOUBLE PEDESTAL

WORK TABLES ARE OF SIMILAR DIMENSIONS.

FOR EXECUTIVE DESKS WITH RETURNS, RETURNS ARE AVAILABLE AT THE SAME HEIGHT AS THE DESK SURFACE.

A MINIMUM CLEAR WIDTH OF 22" SHOULD BE PROVIDED FOR KNEE ROOM, 24" IS NORMAL.

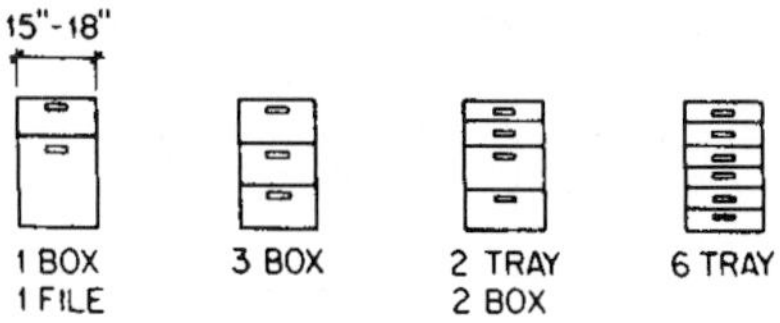

VARIOUS DRAWER ARRANGEMENTS FOR PEDESTALS

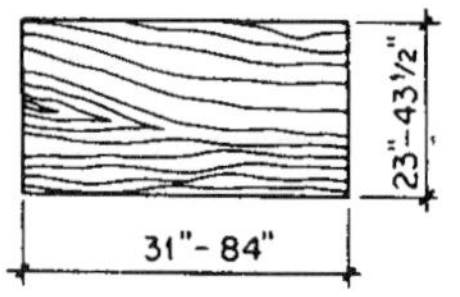

ARTIST AND DRAFTING DESKS OR TABLES

PEDESTALS FOR SECRETARIAL RETURNS WILL BE REDUCED IN HEIGHT THE EQUIVALENT OF ONE PENCIL DRAWER.

STANDARD SIZE ENGINEERING OR ARCHITECTURAL DRAFTING TABLES ARE 37½"x 43½" D x 60"-72"-84" W x 37" H.

Fig. 1 Office planning: desks—sizes

FURNITURE, FURNISHINGS, AND EQUIPMENT

DESKS AND SEATING

Furniture, furnishings, and equipment are the basic building blocks in the design of office spaces. The illustrations and dimensional data contained in this part are based on the product lines available from particular manufacturers.

Although the data, to a great extent, are fairly standard throughout the industry, there will be some variations according to manufacturer. Accordingly, although the information presented is adequate for preliminary planning purposes, the designer is cautioned to reconcile preliminary assumptions with the actual dimensional data of the manufacturer whose product is ultimately specified.

Included in the data provided in this part are examples of filing cabinets, storage cabinets, conference tables, desks, and electronic media.

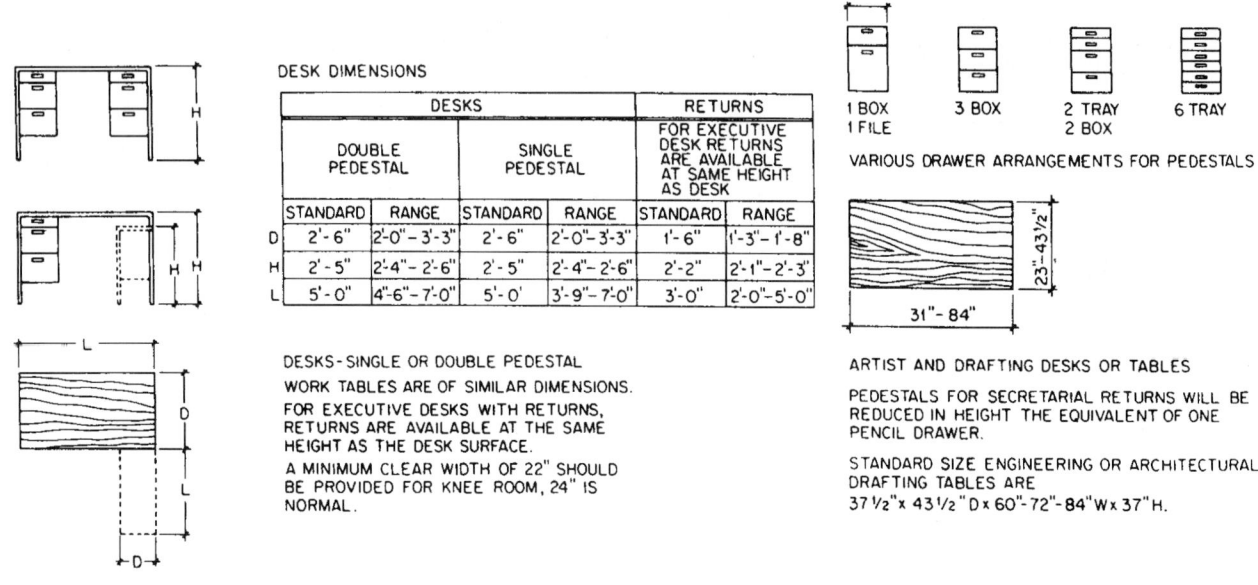

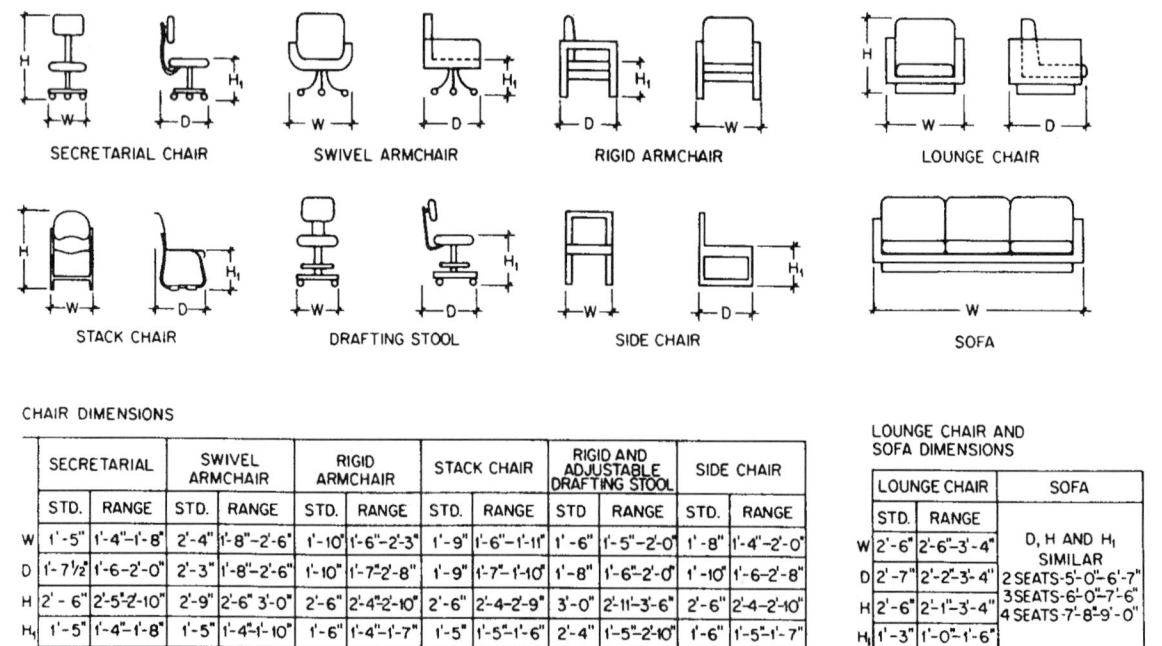

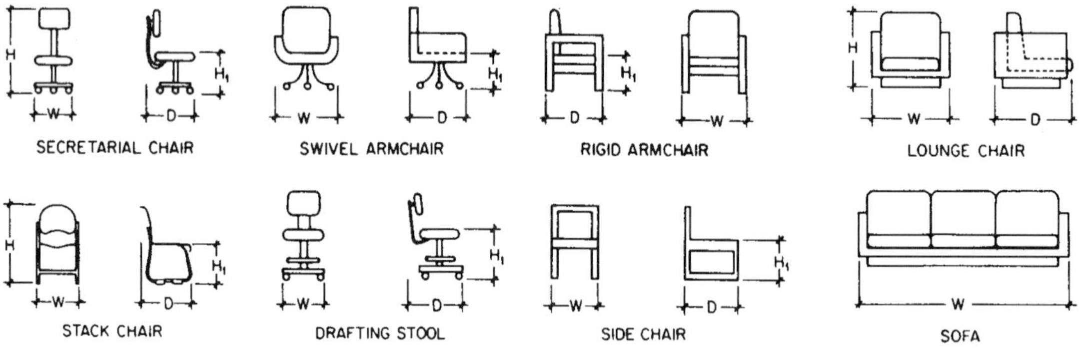

CHAIR DIMENSIONS

	SECRETARIAL		SWIVEL ARMCHAIR		RIGID ARMCHAIR		STACK CHAIR		RIGID AND ADJUSTABLE DRAFTING STOOL		SIDE CHAIR	
	STD.	RANGE	STD.	RANGE	STD.	RANGE	STD.	RANGE	STD	RANGE	STD.	RANGE
W	1'-5"	1'-4"-1'-8"	2'-4"	1'-8"-2'-6"	1'-10"	1'-6"-2'-3"	1'-9"	1'-6"-1'-11"	1'-6"	1'-5"-2'-0"	1'-8"	1'-4"-2'-0"
D	1'-7½"	1'-6-2'-0"	2'-3"	1'-8"-2'-6"	1'-10"	1'-7"-2'-8"	1'-9"	1'-7"-1'-10"	1'-8"	1'-6"-2'-0"	1'-10"	1'-6-2'-8"
H	2'-6"	2'-5"-2'-10"	2'-9"	2'-6" 3'-0"	2'-6"	2'-4"-2'-10"	2'-6"	2'-4-2'-9"	3'-0"	2'-11-3'-6"	2'-6"	2'-4-2'-10"
H_1	1'-5"	1'-4"-1'-8"	1'-5"	1'-4"-1'-10"	1'-6"	1'-4"-1'-7"	1'-5"	1'-5"-1'-6"	2'-4"	1'-5"-2'-10"	1'-6"	1'-5"-1'-7"

LOUNGE CHAIR AND SOFA DIMENSIONS

	LOUNGE CHAIR		SOFA
	STD.	RANGE	D, H AND H_1 SIMILAR 2 SEATS-5'-0"-6'-7" 3 SEATS-6'-0"-7'-6" 4 SEATS-7'-8"-9'-0"
W	2'-6"	2'-6"-3'-4"	
D	2'-7"	2'-2"-3'-4"	
H	2'-6"	2'-1"-3'-4"	
H_1	1'-3"	1'-0"-1'-6"	

Fig. 2 Office planning: seating—sizes

FURNITURE, FURNISHINGS, AND EQUIPMENT
Chairs

Chair types are often associated with certain generic job titles. The designer, however, is cautioned not to make assumptions about chair selection without a thorough understanding of the tasks the individual is to perform. Ergonomic considerations are to be carefully reviewed in order to select a chair with appropriate attributes—that is, seat height, adjustability, back and arm support, firmness, and so on. Overall chair size must be understood within the context of available clearances and workstation configuration.

operator sled base

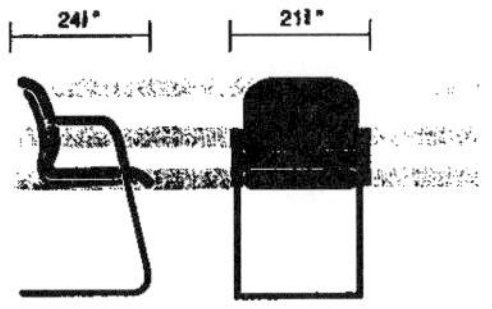

height range:
33"
arm height range:
25[illegible]"
seat height range:
18"

operator stool

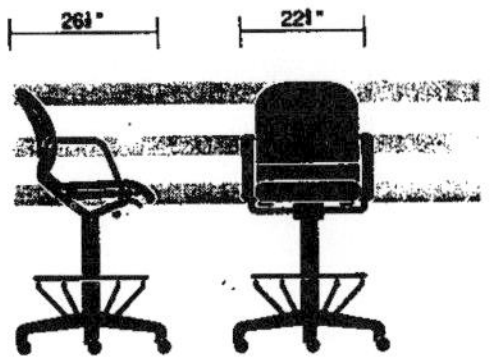

height range:
39[illegible]"-46[illegible]" pneumatic
39[illegible]"-46[illegible]" vecmatic
arm height range:
31"-38[illegible]" pneumatic
31"-38[illegible]" vecmatic
seat height range:
22[illegible]"-29[illegible]" pneumatic
22[illegible]"-29[illegible]" vecmatic

operator

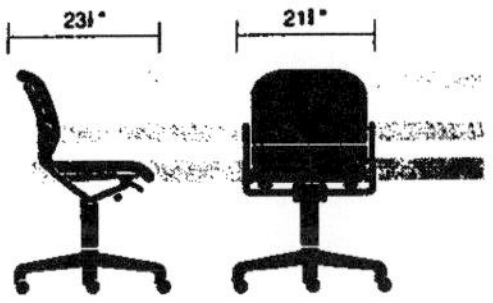

height range:
33"-37" pneumatic
33"-37" vecmatic
34" fixed
seat height range:
16[illegible]"-20[illegible]" pneumatic
16[illegible]"-20[illegible]" vecmatic
17[illegible]" fixed

operator

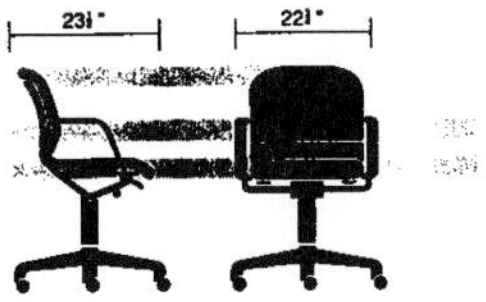

height range:
33"-37" pneumatic
33"-37" vecmatic
34" fixed
arm height range:
25[illegible]"-29[illegible]" pneumatic
25[illegible]"-29[illegible]" vecmatic
26" fixed
seat height range:
16[illegible]"-20[illegible]" pneumatic
16[illegible]"-20[illegible]" vecmatic
17[illegible]" fixed

mid-manager

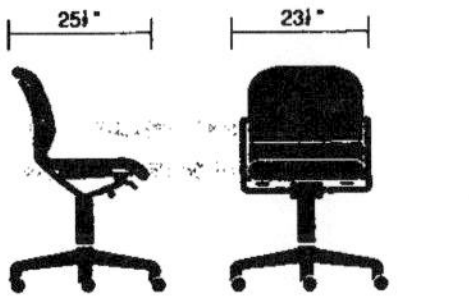

height range:
33[illegible]"-37[illegible]" pneumatic
33[illegible]"-37[illegible]" vecmatic
34[illegible]" fixed
seat height range:
17"-21" pneumatic
17"-21" vecmatic
17[illegible]" fixed

mid-manager sled base

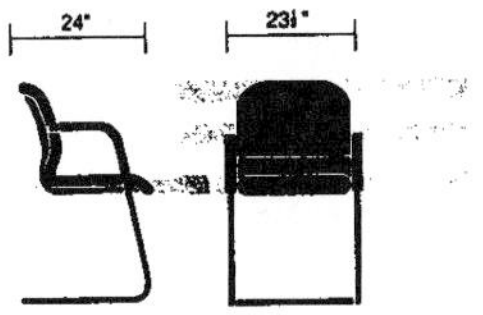

height:
33"
arm height:
25[illegible]"
seat height:
18[illegible]"

mid-manager

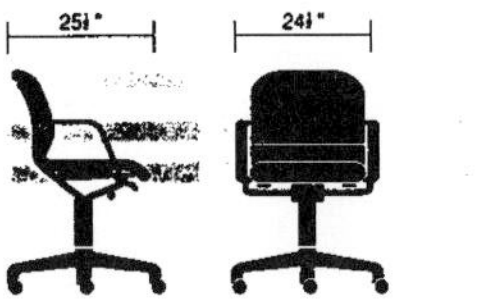

height range:
33[illegible]"-37[illegible]" pneumatic
33[illegible]"-37[illegible]" vecmatic
34[illegible]" fixed
arm height range:
25[illegible]"-29[illegible]" pneumatic
25[illegible]"-29[illegible]" vecmatic
25[illegible]" fixed
seat height range:
17"-21" pneumatic
17"-21" vecmatic
17[illegible]" fixed

high back mid-manager

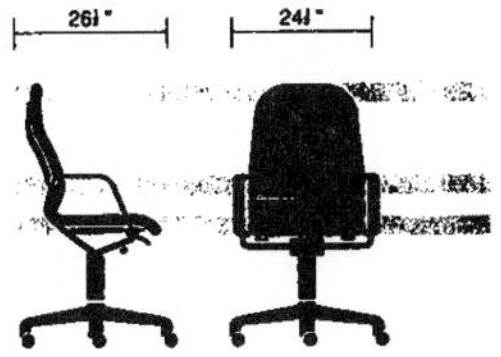

height range:
39[illegible]"-43[illegible]" pneumatic
39[illegible]"-43[illegible]" vecmatic
arm height range:
25[illegible]"-29[illegible]" pneumatic
25[illegible]"-29[illegible]" vecmatic
seat height range:
17"-21" pneumatic
17"-21" vecmatic
45 pounds
Shipped Set-Up

manager sled base

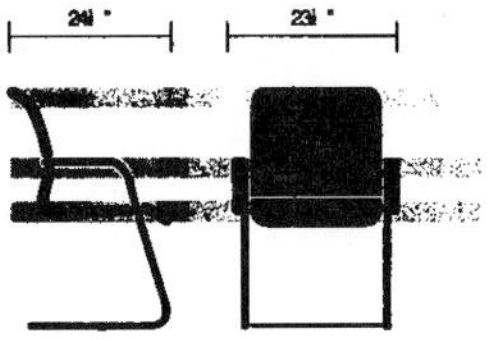

height:
35"
arm height:
25[illegible]"
seat height:
18[illegible]"

executive manager sled bases

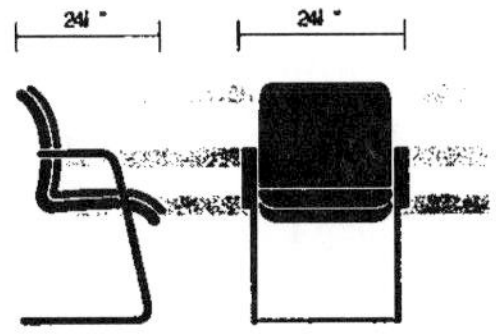

height:
35"
arm height:
25[illegible]"
seat height:
18[illegible]"

manager high back

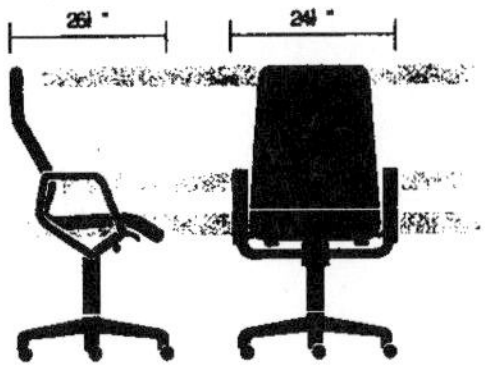

height range:
42"-46" pneumatic
42"-46" vecmatic
arm height range:
25[illegible]"-29[illegible]" pneumatic
25[illegible]"-29[illegible]" vecmatic
seat height range:
17[illegible]"-21[illegible]" pneumatic
17[illegible]"-21[illegible]" vecmatic

grand class manager sled bases

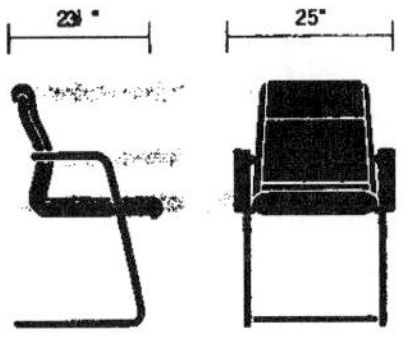

height:
33[illegible]"
arm height:
25"
seat height:
18[illegible]"

manager

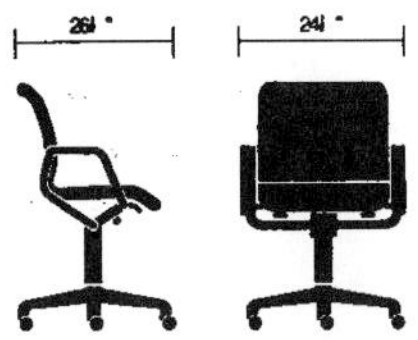

height range:
34[illegible]"-39[illegible]" pneumatic
34[illegible]"-39[illegible]" vecmatic
35" fixed
arm height range:
25[illegible]"-29[illegible]" pneumatic
25[illegible]"-29[illegible]" vecmatic
26" fixed
seat height range:
17[illegible]"-21[illegible]" pneumatic
17[illegible]"-21[illegible]" vecmatic
18" fixed

grand class manager

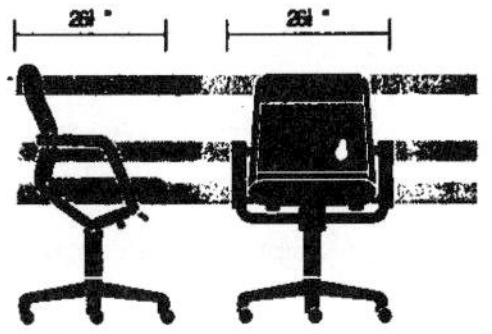

height range:
34[illegible]"-38[illegible]" pneumatic
34[illegible]" fixed
arm height range:
25[illegible]"-29[illegible]" pneumatic
25[illegible]" fixed
seat height range:
17[illegible]"-21[illegible]" pneumatic
17[illegible]" fixed

executive

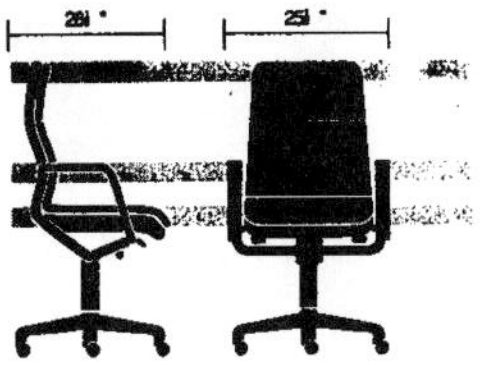

height range:
42-46" high back
34[illegible]"-39[illegible]" manager
arm height range:
25[illegible]"-29[illegible]"
seat height range:
17[illegible]"-21[illegible]"

50 pounds
Shipped Set-Up

grand class high back

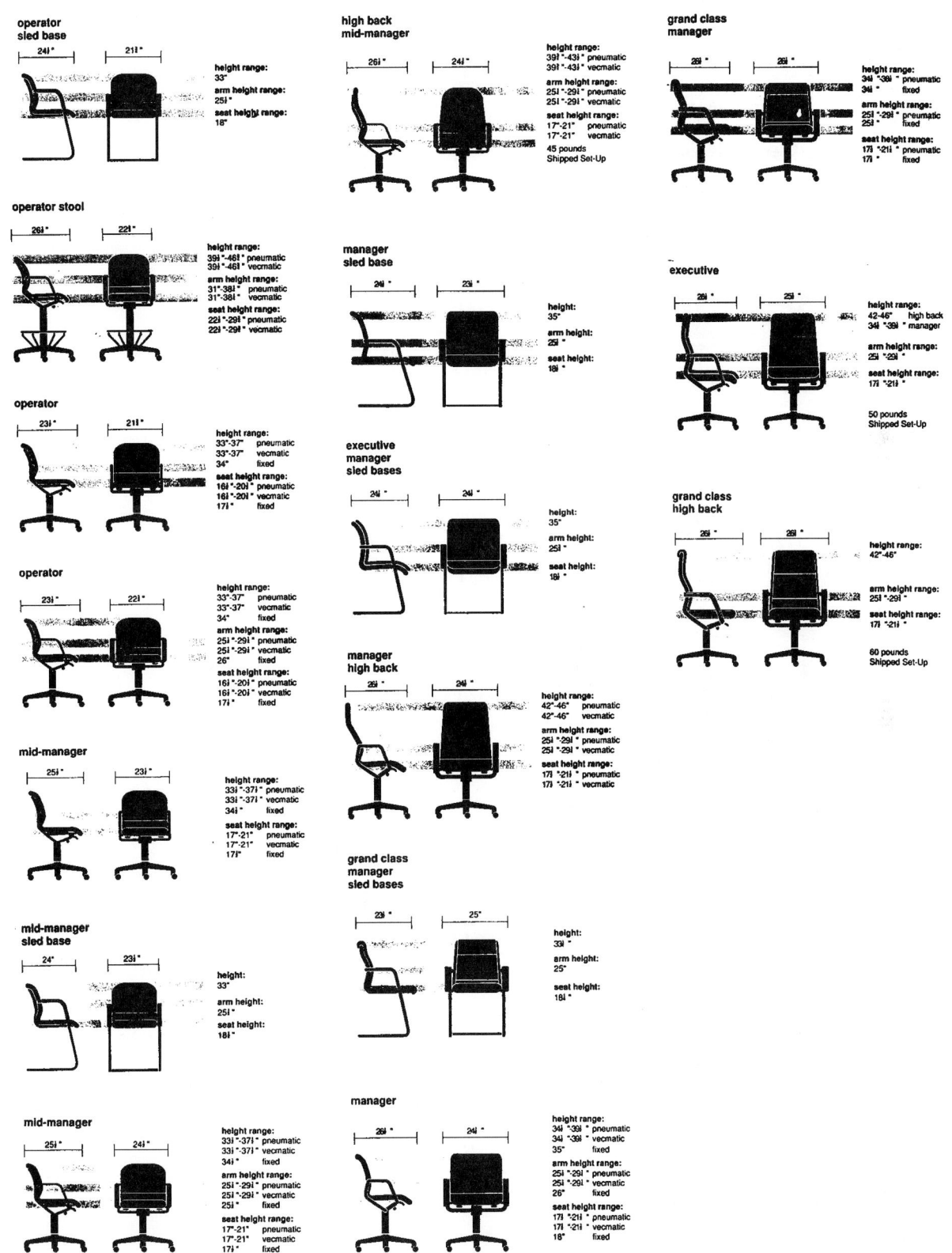

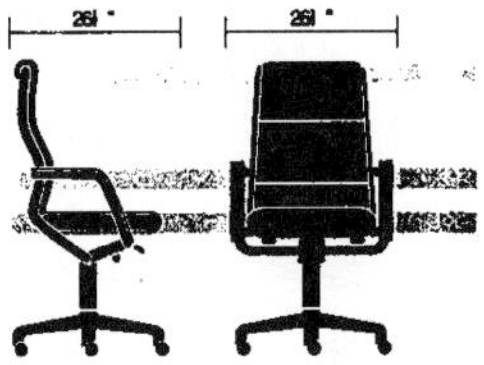

height range:
42"-46"
arm height range:
25[illegible]"-29[illegible]"
seat height range:
17[illegible]"-21[illegible]"

60 pounds
Shipped Set-Up

FURNITURE, FURNISHINGS, AND EQUIPMENT

Chairs

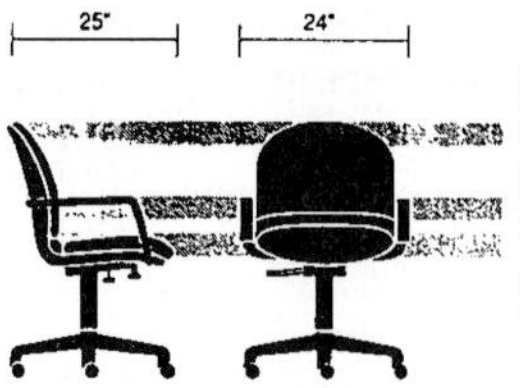

height range:
33ł"-37ł" pneumatic
31"-35" vecmatic
33" fixed
arm height range:
24ł"-28ł" pneumatic
22ł"-26ł" vecmatic
24ł" fixed
seat height range:
18"-22" pneumatic
16"-20" vecma'
18" fixed

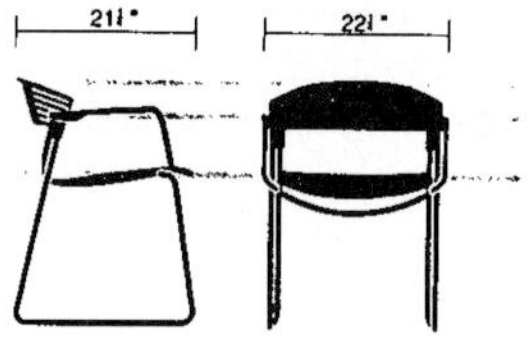

height:
29ł"
arm height:
25ł"
seat height:
17ł"

15 pounds
Shipped Set-Up

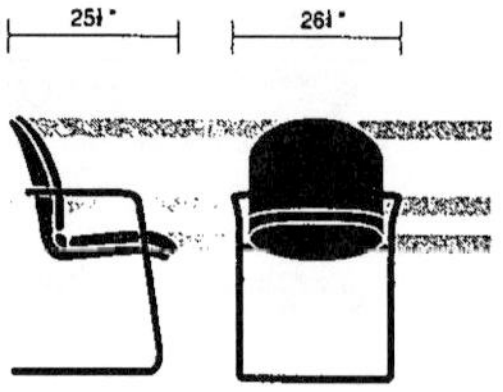

height range:
33ł"
arm height range:
25"
seat height range:
18ł"

43 pounds
Shipped Set-Up

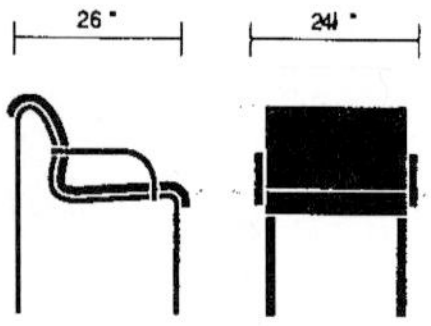

height:
31"
arm height:
25"
seat height:
19"

36 pounds
Shipped Set-Up

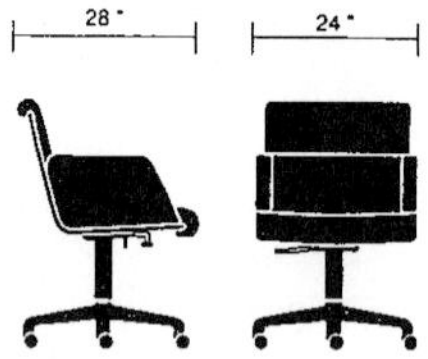

height range:
41 "-45" high back
33ł"-37" mid back
arm height range:
24ł"-28"
seat height range:
18ł"-21ł"

67 pounds
Shipped Set-Up

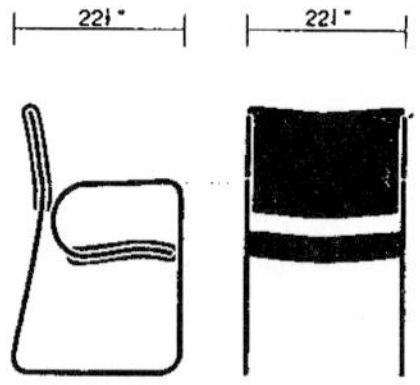

height range:
33ł"
arm height range:
25ł"
seat height range:
17ł"

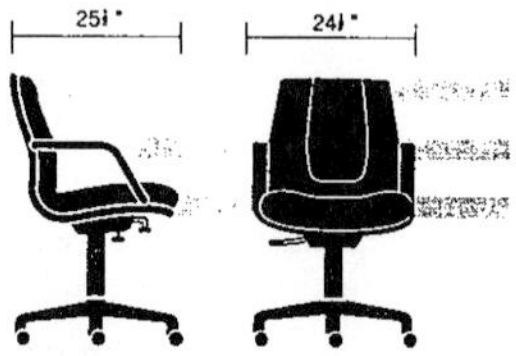

height range:
41ł"-44ł" high back
37ł"-40ł" mid back
35"-38ł" low back
arm height range:
25ł"-29"
seat height range:
17ł"-20ł"

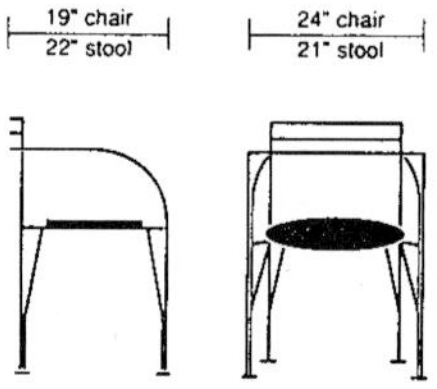

height:
30" chair
33ł" stool
arm height:
26"
seat height:
17ł" chair
30" stool

21 pounds
Shipped Set-Up

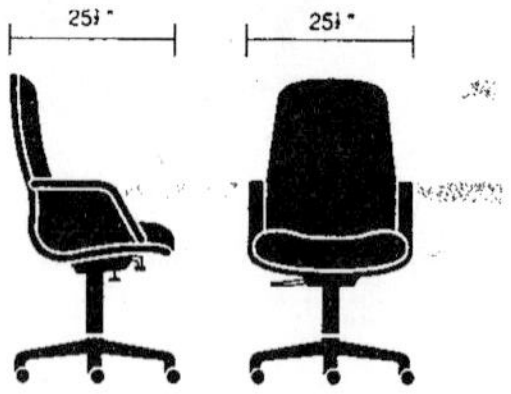

height range:
41ł"-44ł" high back
37ł"-40ł" mid back

arm height range:
26"-29ł"

seat height range:
17ł"-20ł"

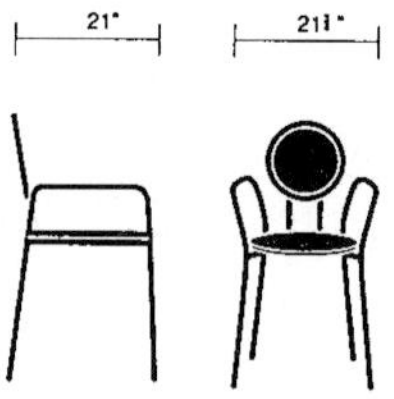

height:
33ł"
arm height:
25ł"
seat height:
17ł"

20 pounds
Shipped Set-l

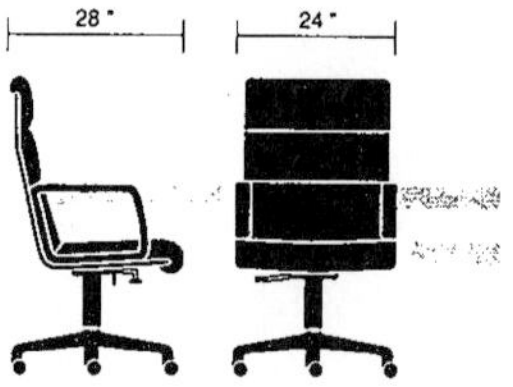

height range:
41 "-45" high back
33ł"-37" mid back

arm height range:
24ł"-28"
seat height range:
18ł"-21ł"

67 pounds
Shipped Set-Up

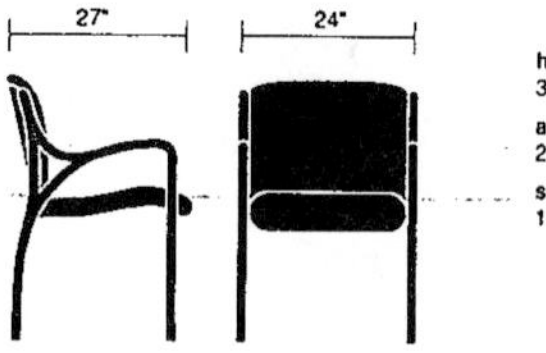

height:
32"
arm height:
25"
seat height:
17ł"

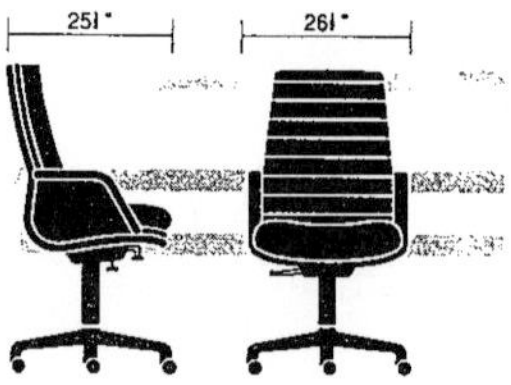

height range:
42ł"-45ł" high back
38ł"-41ł" mid back
arm height range:
24ł"-27ł"
seat height range:
18ł"-21ł"
64 pounds
Shipped Set-Up

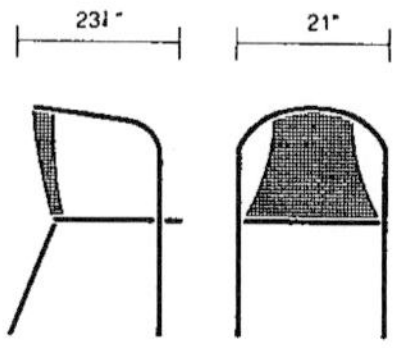

height:
28"
seat height:
16ł"

Executive Chairs

Tilt-Swivel Chair with Casters

Option: CA

Non-Swivel Lounge Chair

Swivel Lounge Chair

Non-Swivel Lounge Arm Chair

Swivel Lounge Arm Chair

Tilt-Swivel Reclining Arm Chair

Ottoman

Lounge

Non-Swivel Lounge Chair

Swivel Lounge Chair

Non-Swivel Lounge Armchair

Swivel Lounge Armchair

Tilt-Swivel Reclining Armchair

Ottoman

Straight Module

Side/Pull-up Chairs

Non-Swivel Side Chair

Swivel Side Chair

Non-Swivel Arm Chair

Swivel Arm Chair

Tilt-Swivel Arm Chair with Glides

Tilt-Swivel Arm Chair with Casters

Option: CA

Executive Chairs

Tilt-Swivel Chair with Glides

Lounge Chair

Ottoman

Lounge Chair and Ottoman

Eames™ Chaise

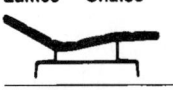

Sofa Compact

Nelson Sling Sofa

Eames Executive Lounge Chairs

Executive Swivel Lounge Chair

Adjustable Executive Tilt-Swivel Lounge Chair

Adjustable Tilt-Swivel

FURNITURE, FURNISHINGS, AND EQUIPMENT

Reception and Lounge Seating

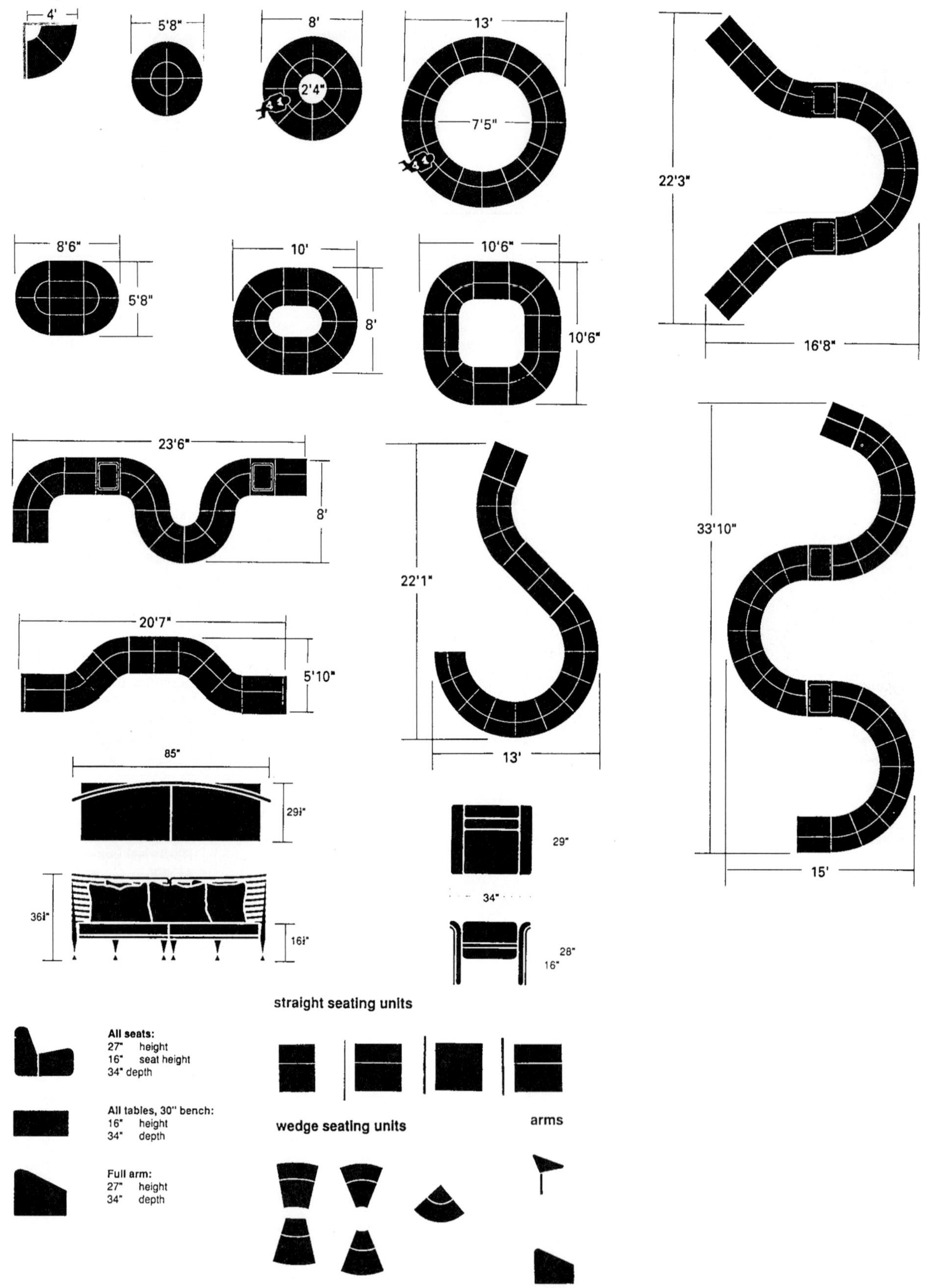

Fig. 3 Reception and lounge seating can assume various sizes, shapes, and configurations. Modular seating units can offer a custom built-in look, and can often incorporate table and storage components. Overall sizes will vary from manufacturer to manufacturer

Conference tables come in an infinite variety of shapes and sizes. Figures 4 to 6 attempt to provide a representative sampling of such tables, along with dimensional information and seating capacities. The designer is cautioned to use such information as a preliminary planning tool only, and to carefully lay out conference rooms with actual furniture pieces that have been selected. Chair width and spacing will ultimately dictate conference table seating capacity.

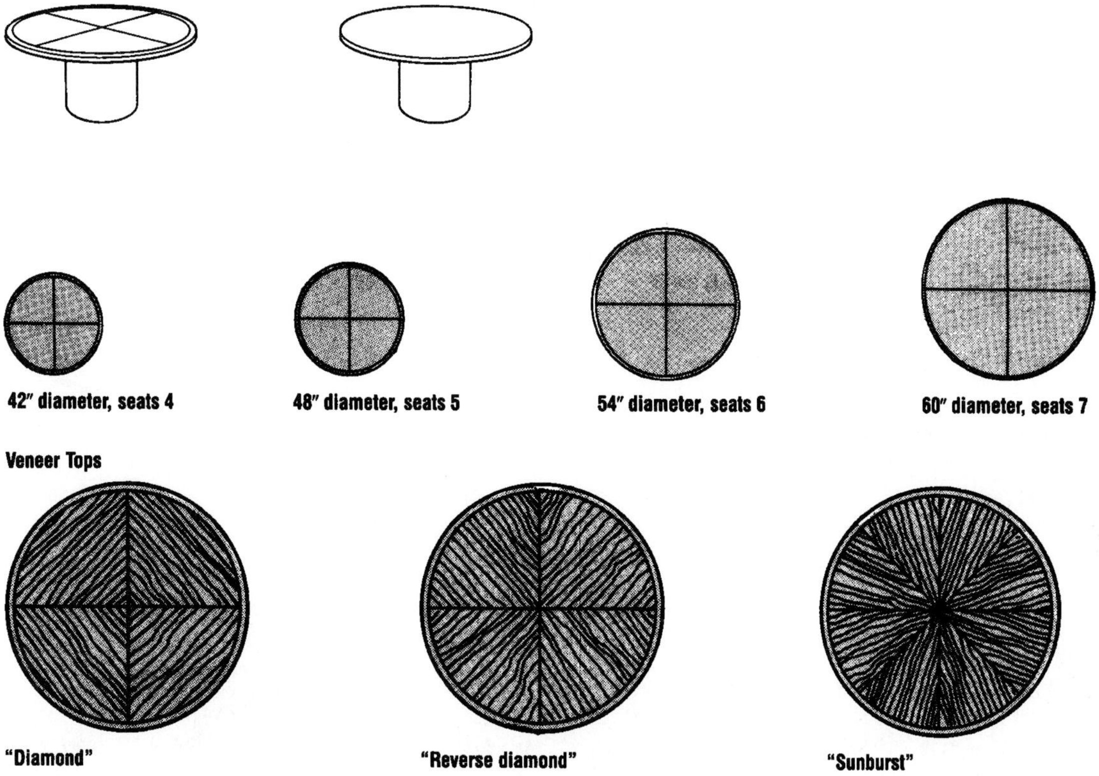

Fig. 4

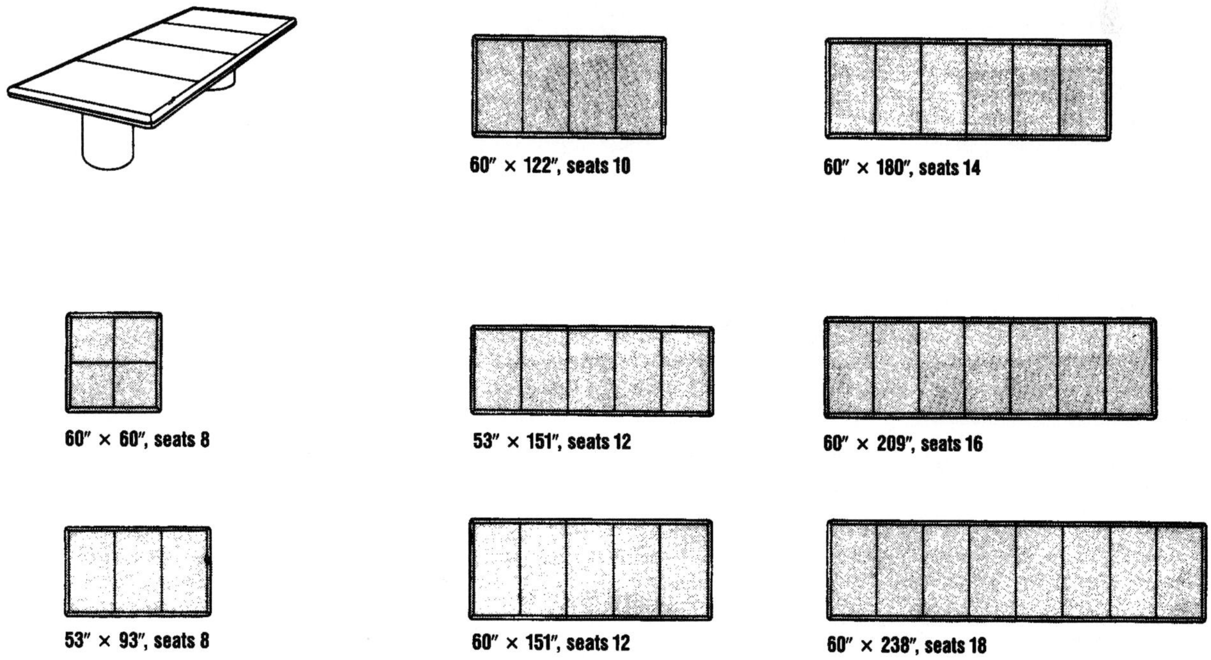

Fig. 5

FURNITURE, FURNISHINGS, AND EQUIPMENT

Conference Tables

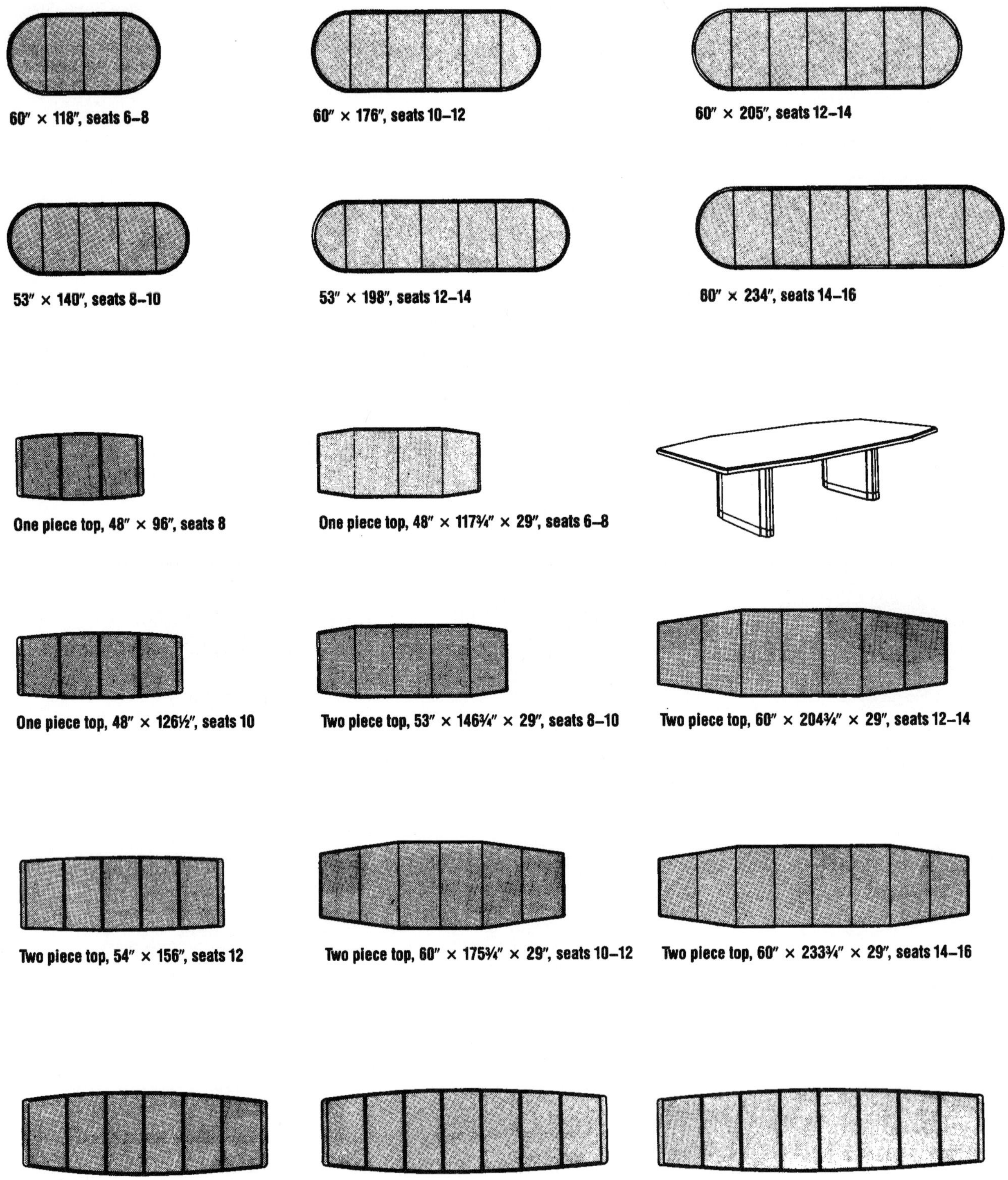
60″ × 118″, seats 6–8
60″ × 176″, seats 10–12
60″ × 205″, seats 12–14
53″ × 140″, seats 8–10
53″ × 198″, seats 12–14
60″ × 234″, seats 14–16
One piece top, 48″ × 96″, seats 8
One piece top, 48″ × 117¾″ × 29″, seats 6–8
One piece top, 48″ × 126½″, seats 10
Two piece top, 53″ × 146¾″ × 29″, seats 8–10
Two piece top, 60″ × 204¾″ × 29″, seats 12–14
Two piece top, 54″ × 156″, seats 12
Two piece top, 60″ × 175¾″ × 29″, seats 10–12
Two piece top, 60″ × 233¾″ × 29″, seats 14–16
Two piece top, 60″ × 185¾″, seats 14
Two piece top, 60″ × 216″, seats 16
Two piece top, 60″ × 245¼″, seats 18

Fig. 6

Standard vertical file cabinets are usually designed to accommodate standard-height drawers and half-height file insert drawers (optional). Cabinets are available in letter-size widths (14⅞ in) and legal-size widths (17⅞ in). Vertical file drawers are usually 12 in high and accommodate front-to-back filing.

Standard cabinets are available in four heights: five-drawer (58⅝ in), four-drawer (52⅜ in), three-drawer (41¼ in), and two-drawer (29⅜ in or 27⅜ in). The depths of the three-, four-, and five-drawer cabinets are 28 9/16 in, while the depth of the 2-drawer cabinets is 30 in. Table 1 lists these dimensional data. It should be noted that, although adequate for preliminary planning purposes, the data are based on Steelcase cabinets.

Guidelines for Customizing Vertical Files

Depending on the manufacturer, vertical file cabinets can be customized. Usually two half-height file insert drawers may be substituted for a 12-in-high drawer in any or all positions. Table 2 indicates the dimensions and linear capacities of such insert drawers, while Fig. 7 illustrates basic guidelines for customizing.

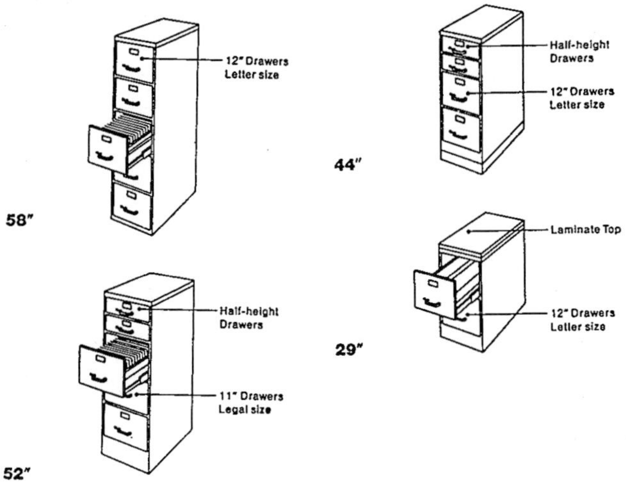

Fig. 7

Table 1 Vertical file cabinets

Description	Cabinet height		Outside dimensions: Depth	Width	Height
	58⅝"	Letter	28 9/16"	14⅞"	58⅜"
		Legal	28 9/16"	17⅞"	58⅜"
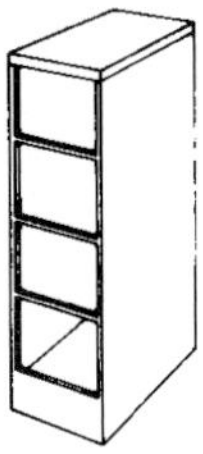	52⅜"	Letter	28 9/16"	14⅞"	52⅜"
		Legal	28 9/16"	17⅞"	52⅜"
		Card	28 9/16"	14⅞"	52⅜"
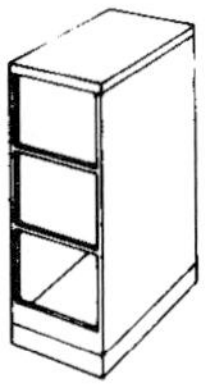	41¼"	Letter	28 9/16"	14⅞"	41¼"
		Legal	28 9/16"	17⅞"	41¼"
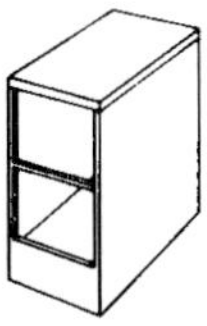	29⅜"	Letter	30"	14⅞"	29⅜"
		Legal	30"	17⅞"	29⅜"
	27⅜"	Letter	30"	14⅞"	27⅞"
		Legal	30"	17⅞"	27⅞"

FURNITURE, FURNISHINGS, AND EQUIPMENT

Vertical File Drawers; Overfile Cabinets; Roll-Away Carts

Table 2 Vertical file insert drawers

Description	Inside dimensions: Depth	Width	Height	Linear capacity
Half-height (3x5 or 4x6 cards) 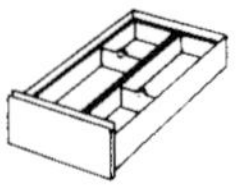	26⅞"	6"(2)	4⅜"	53⅞"* (2 rows)
Half-height (checks)	26⅞"*	10¾"	4⅜"	26⅞"
Half-height (cash)	8¼"	3¼"	1⅞"	Bills
	8½"	11½"	1⅞"	Storage
	4⅜"	2¼"	1¾"	Coin tray
Half-height (box)	26⅞"	12¼"	4¾"	26⅞" front-to-back 12¼" side-to-side
Half-height (microfilm)	26¼"*	4"(3)	4⅜"	80¾"* (3 compartments)
Full height (letter size)	26⅞"*	6"(2)	10⅛"	53⅞"* (2 compartments)
Full height (letter size)	26⅞"*	4"(3)	10⅛"	80¾"* (3 compartments)
Full height (box)	26⅞"	15¼"	4¾"	–
Full height (3x5 cards)	26⅞"*	5"(3)	4½"	80¾"* (3 compartments)
Full height (4x6 cards)	26⅞"*	6¼"(2)	4⅜"	53⅞" (2 compartments)
Full height (legal size)	26⅞"*	7½"(2)	10⅛"	See style no. C
Full height (legal size)	26⅞"*	5"(3)	10⅛"	See style no. D

*Deduct ⅝" when compressor is used.

Table 3 Drawers, overfile cabinets, and roll-away file cart

Description	Width	Inside dimensions: Depth	Width	Height	Linear capacity
12" Letter-size drawer 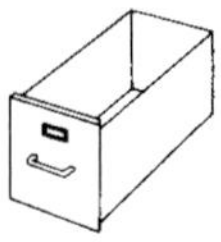	–	27⅜"	12¼"	10½"	27⅜" front-to-back*
12" Legal-size drawer 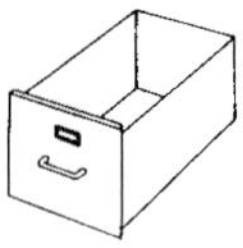	–	27⅜"	15¼"	10½"	27⅜" front-to-back
		Outside/inside dimensions			
Overfile cabinet Fits over two letter-size files 	29¾"	28⅝"/28½"†	29¾"/27⅞"	28⅛" /25⅜"	55¾" side-to-side on 2 shelves (1 adj., ¾" thick)
Overfile cabinet Fits over two legal-size files	35¾"	28⅝"/28½"†	35¾"/33⅞"	28⅛"/25⅜"	67¾" side-to-side on 2 shelves (1 adj., ¾" thick)
Overfile cabinet Fits over three letter size files	44⅝"	28⅝"/28½"†	44⅝"/42¾"	28⅛"/25⅜"	85½" side-to-side on 2 shelves (1 adj., ¾" thick)
Overfile cabinet Fits over three legal-size files	53⅝"	28⅝"/28½"†	53⅝"/51¾"	28⅛"/25⅜"	103½" side-to-side on 2 shelves (1 adj., ¾" thick)
Roll-away file cart 		30¼"/28"	15⅛"/12⅛"	22⅞"/13⅜"	25" Letter/legal

*Deduct ⅝" when compressor is used.
†Deduct 1½" when ordered with sliding doors.

Standard lateral file cabinets are usually available in three widths—30 in, 36 in, and 42 in—and with 12-in-high drawers or roll-out shelves. Some cabinets are designed on a 3-in module to accommodate 3-, 6-, 9-, 12-, and 15-in-high drawers and shelves.

Ganging hardware is usually included with each file cabinet. Cabinets should be ganged with adjacent files or bolted to the floor. Counterbalance weights should be used for single-application files.

Table 4 shows the outside and inside dimensions of four lateral file cabinets and their loaded floor weights based on 12-in-high drawers filled to capacity.

It should be noted that the dimensional data and load factors are based on Steelcase cabinets. Although these data are adequate for preliminary planning purposes, it is essential that the data of the equipment being specified be verified with its manufacturer.

Table 4 Lateral file cabinets

Description (cabinet inside height)	Cabinet width	Outside/inside dimensions		
		Depth	Width	Height
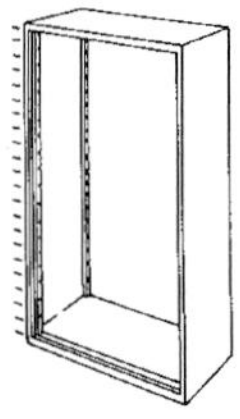 60″	30″	18″/17⅛″*	30″/28½″	64⅝″/60″
	36″	18″/17⅛″*	36″/34½″	64⅝″/60″
	42″	18″/17⅛″*	42″/40½″	64⅝″/60″
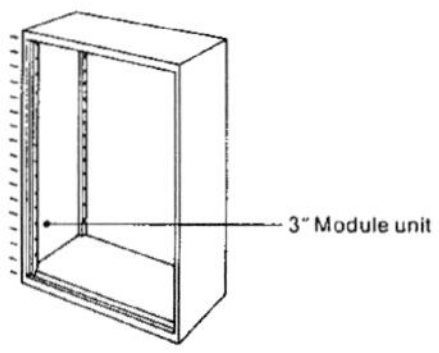 48″	30″	18″/17⅛″*	30″/28½″	52⅜″/48″
	36″	18″/17⅛″*	36″/34½″	52⅜″/48″
	42″	18″/17⅛″*	42″/40½″	52⅜″/48″
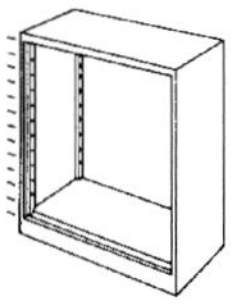 36″	30″	18″/17⅛″*	30″/28½″	41¼″/36″
	36″	18″/17⅛″*	36″/34½″	41¼″/36″
	42″	18″/17⅛″*	42″/40½″	41¼″/36″
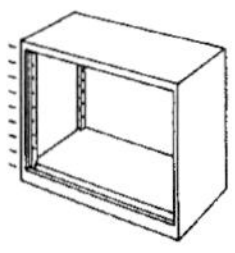 24″	30″	18″/17⅛″*	30″/28½″	28¼″/24″
	36″	18″/17⅛″*	36″/34½″	28¼″/24″
	42″	18″/17⅛″*	42″/40½″	28¼″/24″

Loaded Weights												
	Cabinet inside height											
Description	24″			36″			48″			60″		
Cabinet width	30″	36″	42″	30″	36″	42″	30″	36″	42″	30″	36″	42″
Loaded weight in pounds	285	336	391	401	475	553	524	645	720	610	725	843

*Deduct ⅝″ when compressor is used.

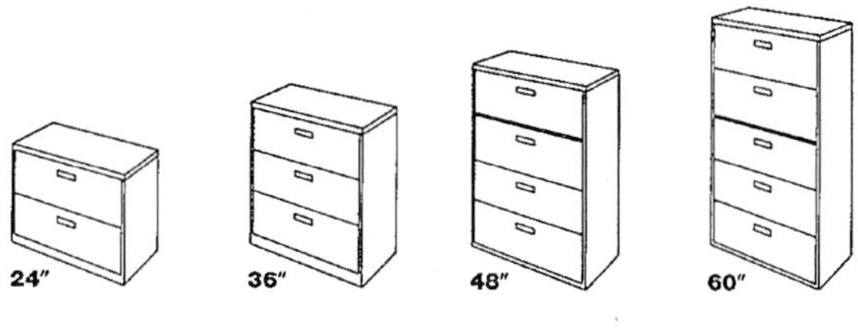

FURNITURE, FURNISHINGS, AND EQUIPMENT

Filing Arrangements

Most lateral file drawers are designed for filing both letter-size and legal-size documents, in addition to EDP printouts. Lateral file drawers can usually accommodate materials in a front-to-back (F-to-B) arrangement or in a side-to-side (S-to-S) arrangement. In some instances, a combination of the two is possible. The actual capacity in linear inches for each arrangement and for each particular drawer or shelf has been calculated and is shown in the "Linear capacity" column in Tables 2, 3, 6, 7, and 8. It should be noted that the dimensional data in Table 5 are based on Steelcase drawers.

Table 5 Filing arrangements

Description	30" width	36" width	42" width
Letter/legal, 12" drawer			
	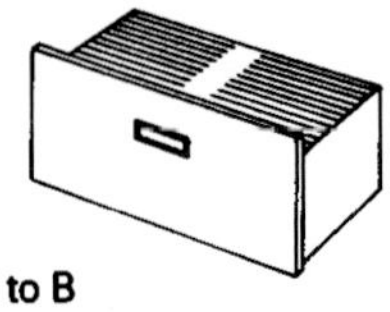 F to B	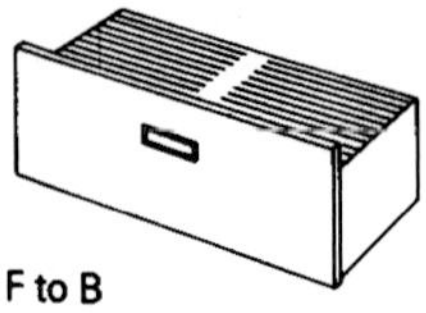 F to B	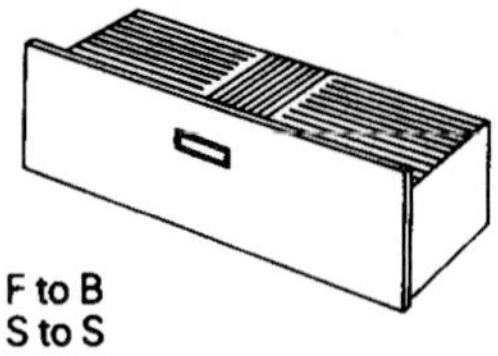 F to B S to S
	 F to B S to S	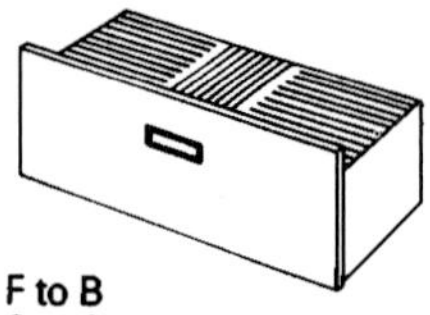 F to B S to S	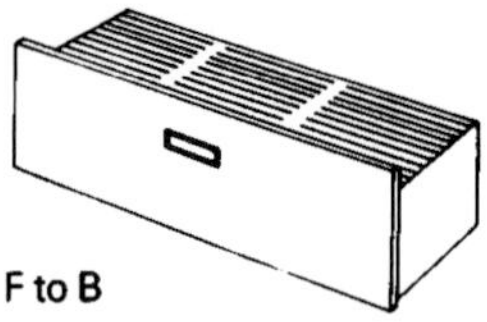 F to B
EDP binders, 15" drawer			
	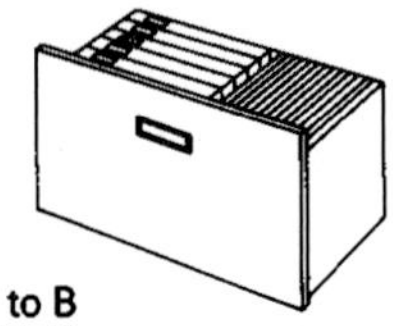 F to B S to S	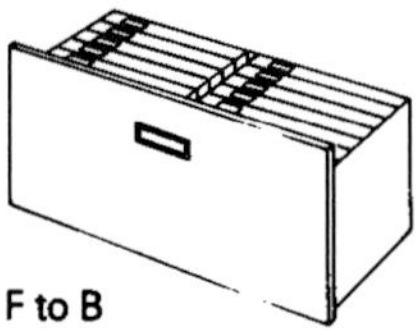 F to B	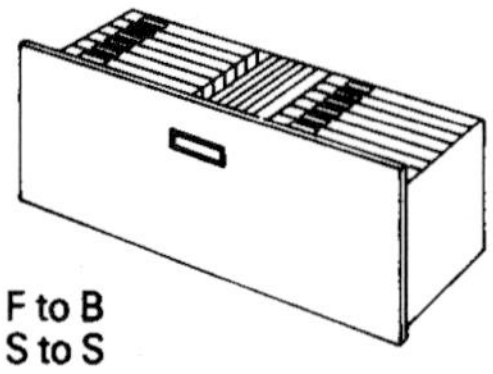 F to B S to S
EDP folders, 15" drawer			
	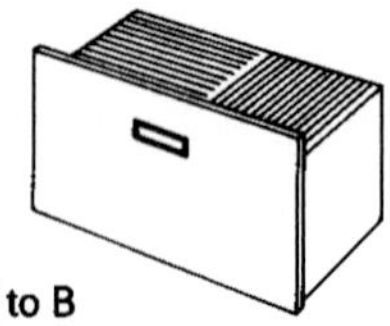 F to B S to S	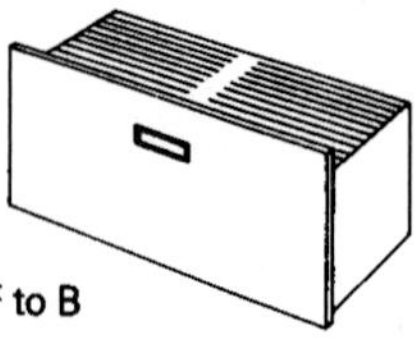 F to B	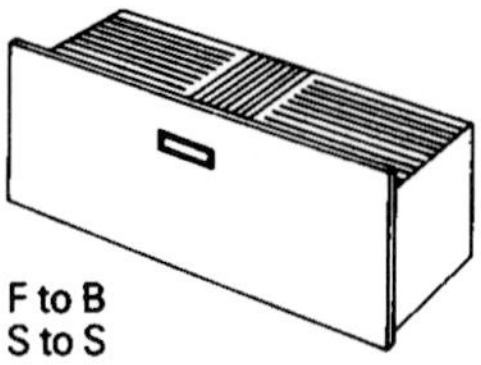 F to B S to S

Table 6 Drawers, shelves, add-on cabinets

Description	File cabinet width	Style no.	Outside/inside dimensions			Linear capacity
			Depth	Width	Height	
12" legal fixed shelf with door	30"		16½"	28½"	10½"*	28½" side-to-side
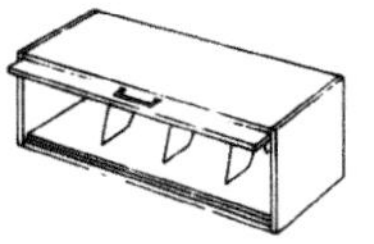	36"		16½"	34½"	10½"*	34½" S to S
	42"		16½"	40½"	10½"*	40½" S to S
15" legal fixed shelf with door	30"		16½"	28½"	13½"	28½" S to S
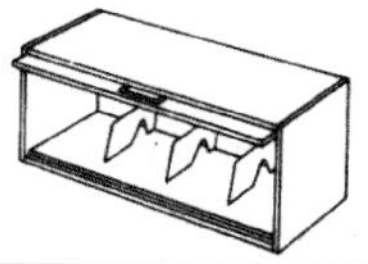	36"		16½"	34½"	13½"	34½" S to S
	42"		16½"	40½"	13½"	40½" S to S
Center hook filing hanger bar	30"		17"	28½"	10⅝" (12" high door) 12¾" (15" high door)	28½" S to S 28½" S to S
	36"		17"	34½"	10⅝" (12" high door) 12¾" (15" high door)	34½" S to S 34½" S to S
	42"		17"	40½"	10⅝" (12" high door) 12¾" (15" high door)	40½" S to S 40½" S to S
T-bar	30"		17"	28½"	10¼" (12" high door) 12⅜" (15" high door)	28½" S to S 28½" S to S
	36"		17"	34½"	10¼" (12" high door) 12¾" (15" high door)	34½" S to S 34½" S to S
	42"		17"	40½"	10¼" (12" high door) 12⅜" (15" high door)	40½" S to S 40½" S to S
Wire tape rack	30"		17"	28½"	7⅛" (9" high door) 10⅛" (12" high door) 13⅛" (15" high door)	28½" S to S 28½" S to S 28½" S to S
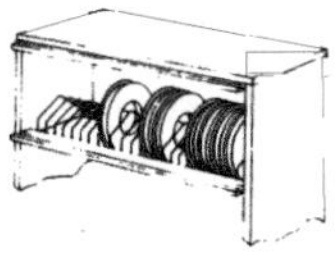	36"		17"	34½"	7⅛" (9" high door) 10⅛" (12" high door) 13⅛" (15" high door)	34½" S to S 34½" S to S 34½" S to S
	42"		17"	40½"	7⅛" (9" high door) 10⅛" (12" high door) 13⅛" (15" high door)	40½" S to S 40½" S to S 40½" S to S
Add-on cabinet	30"	830-610	18"/16⅜"*	30"/28⅛"	15¾/13⅛"	28⅛" S to S
	36"	836-610	18"/16⅜"*	36"/34⅛"	15¾"/13⅛"	34⅛" S to S
	42"	842-610	18"/16⅜"*	42"/40⅛"	15¾"/13⅛"	40⅛" S to S
	30"	830-710	18"/16⅜"*	30"/28⅛"	28⅛"/25⅛"	28⅛" S to S
	36"	836-710	18"/16⅜"*	36"/34⅛"	28⅛"/25⅛"	34⅛" S to S
	42"	842-710	18"/16⅜"*	42"/40⅛"	28⅛"/25⅛"	40⅛" S to S

*Deduct ⅝" when compressor is used.

FURNITURE, FURNISHINGS, AND EQUIPMENT
Storage Cabinets

Standard cabinets often provide a fast, flexible, and economical solution to many storage problems. Table 7 provides dimensional data and capacities for four typical cabinet types. These cabinets are manufactured by Steelcase. The dimensions of cabinets of other manufacturers will differ somewhat. The data in Table 7, however, are adequate for preliminary planning purposes.

Table 7 Storage cabinets

	Outside/inside dimensions			
Description	Depth	Width	Height	Linear capacity
Storage cabinet	18″/17″	36″/33⅛″	41¼″/35⅝″	99½″ side-to-side on 3 shelves (2 adj., 1″ thick)
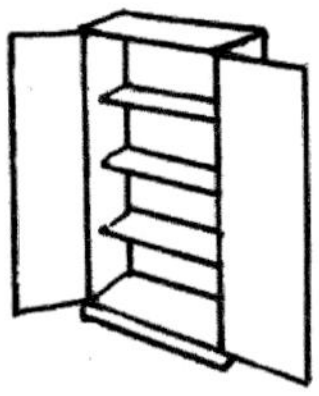	18″/17″	36″/33⅛″	52⅜″/46⅜″	99½″ S to S on 3 shelves (2 adj., 1″ thick)
	18″/17″	36″/33⅛″	64⅝″/58¾″	132¾″ S to S on 4 shelves (3 adj., 1″ thick)
	18″/17″	36″/33⅛″	80½″/74½″	165⅞″ S to S on 5 shelves (4 adj., 1″ thick)
	24″/23″	36″/33⅛″	64⅝″/58¾″	132¾″ S to S on 4 shelves (3 adj., 1″ thick)
	24″/23″	36″/33⅛″	80½″/74½″	165⅞″ S to S on 5 shelves (4 adj., 1″ thick)
Wardrobe cabinet	18″/17″	36″/33⅛″	52⅜″/46⅜″	Not for filing
	18″/17″	36″/33⅛″	64⅝″/58¾″	Not for filing
	18″/17″	36″/33⅛″	80½″/74½″	Not for filing
	24″/23″	36″/33⅛″	64⅝″/58¾″	Not for filing
	24″/23″	36″/33⅛″	80½″/74½″	Not for filing
Wardrobe/storage cabinet	18″/17″	36″/33⅛″	52⅜″/46⅜″	43¼″ S to S on 3 shelves (2 adj., 1″ thick)
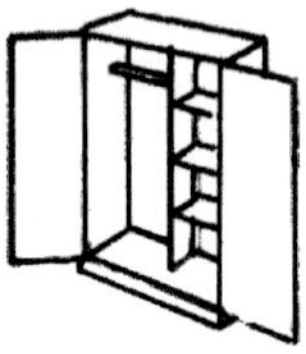	18″/17″	36″/33⅛″	64⅝″/58¾″	58″ S to S on 4 shelves (3 adj., 1″ thick)
	18″/17″	36″/33⅛″	80½″/74½″	58″ S to S on 4 shelves (3 adj., 1″ thick)
	24″/23″	36″/33⅛″	64⅝″/58¾″	58″ S to S on 4 shelves (3 adj., 1″ thick)
	24″/23″	36″/33⅛″	80½″/74½″	58″ S to S on 4 shelves (3 adj., 1″ thick)
Wardrobe	18″/16⅝″	18″/15⅛″	41⅛″/35⅞″	15⅛″ on bar
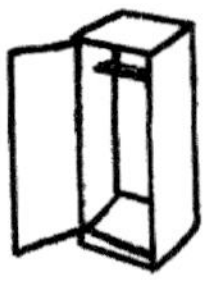	18″/16⅝″	18″/15½″	52¼″/47″	15½″ on bar
	18″/16⅝″	18″/15⅛″	64½″/59¼″	15⅛″ on bar

Table 8 Interior card trays

(For use in vertical or lateral files)

Description	Style No.	Inside dimensions: Depth	Width	Height	Linear capacity
3 x 5 card	4335	11⅞"	5"	3¼"	10¼"
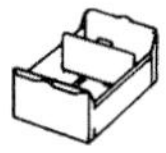					
3 x 5 card	4337M	14⅞"	5"	3¼"	13¼"
5 x 8 card	4355	11⅞"	8⅛"	4¾"	11¼"
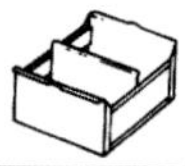					
5 x 8 card	4357	14⅞"	8⅛"	4¾"	13¼"
4 x 6 card	800-TN-46	12"	6⅛"	4⅜"	11⅜"

4 x 6 card	800-TW-46	15"	6⅛"	4⅜"	14⅜"
Tab card	7201	11⅞"	7½"	3⅝"	10⅜"
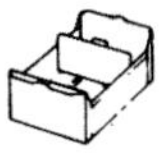					
Tab card	7204	14⅞"	7½"	3⅝"	13⅜"
Coin and bill	4388	8¼" 5⅞"	3⅛" 11 1/12"	1⅞" 1⅞"	* †

Coin and bill	4389	7⅞" 2⅜"	3¾" 2¼"	1⅞" 1¾"	* †

Description	Style No.	Number of card trays accommodated per 6"-high drawer or shelf: 4337M	800TW46‡	4357	7204M
6" high shelves/drawers	842 DWDV-6	7	5	4	5
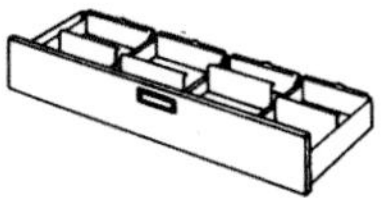	842 SWDV-6	7	5	–	5
	836 DWDV-6	6	4	3	4
	836 SWDV-6	6	4	–	4
	830 DWDV-6	5	3	3	3
	830 SWDV-6	5	3	3	3
	830 SWDV-3	5	3	–	3

*Dimensions of each of 6 bill compartments.
†Dimensions of each of 5 coin compartments.
‡Card trays cannot be installed in 6"-high shelf located directly below a door. Use 3"-high shelf and refer to guidelines.

FURNITURE, FURNISHINGS, AND EQUIPMENT

Storage Components Glossary

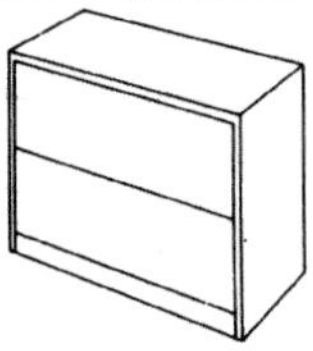

Lower storage/Lateral file
Free-standing wall- or panel-mounted files with width dimension greater than depth dimension.

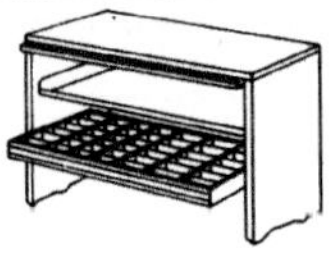

Media compartment kit
Can be retrofit or factory assembled to 800/900 Series 6" roll-out shelf. Provides dividers and partitions adjustable for storing a variety of media-cassettes, mini-cassettes, cartridges, floppy disks, and more.

Mobile pedestal
Supports drawers in several combinations and has casters for mobility.

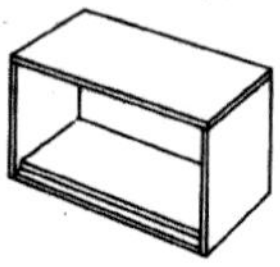

Overfile cabinet
For use above lateral or vertical files. Sliding door, lock, and shelf-modifier options.

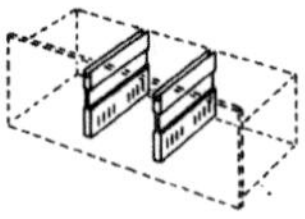

Partition
A double metal wall that mounts into a lateral file drawer to divide drawer.

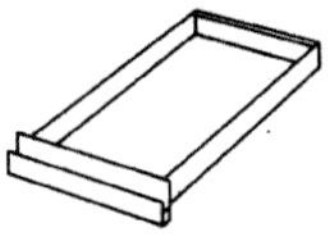

Personal drawer
For personal items. An adjustable divider is included. 3" high.

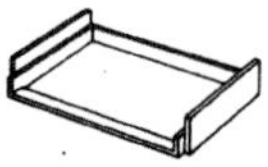

Pull-out keyboard shelf
Attaches beneath work-surface for computer keyboard support and storage.

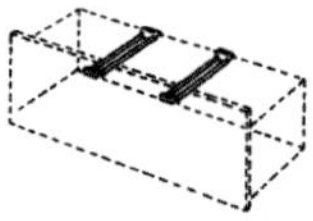

Rails
Mount in lateral file for drawer suspended filing, front-to-back or side-to-side.

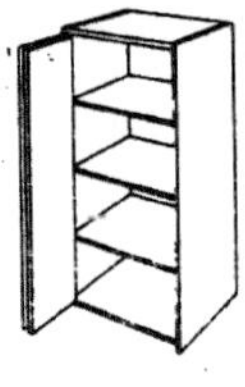

Storage cabinet
Storage for general supplies. Available in 2, 3, or 4 adjustable shelves.

T-bar filing for bound printouts
Accepts EDP printouts in T-bar type binders.

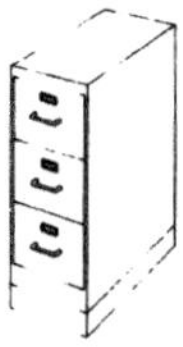

Vertical file
Letter- or legal-size filing cabinet with depth dimension greater than width dimension. For front-to-back filing only.

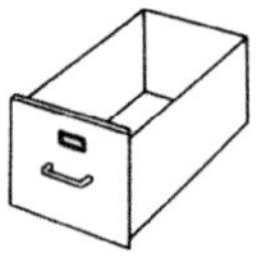

Vertical file drawer
6" high and 12" high drawers for letter or legal-size filing cabinets.

Wardrobe
Provides full-width coat rod for hanging clothes mounted beneath full-width shelf.

Wire tape racks
Racks can be freestanding or built-in to lateral files for storage of magnetic tapes and disk cartridges on edge. Dividers can be positioned to accommodate media of different thicknesses.

FURNITURE, FURNISHINGS, AND EQUIPMENT
Storage Components Glossary

Bookcase
Units have adjustable shelves which can accommodate rows of standard ring binders and other bound materials.

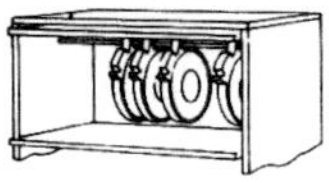

Center hook filing hanging bar
Accepts printouts and magnetic tape reels with center hooks.

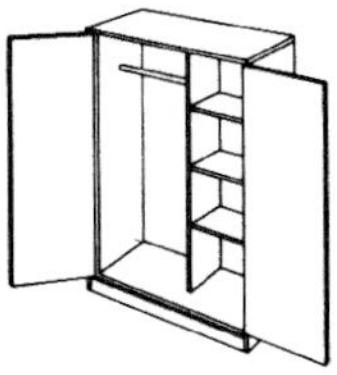

Combination wardrobe and storage cabinet
Units are divided – space for hanging clothes and two or three vertically adjustable shelves.

Compressor
A spring-loaded plate that supports file material. Can be moved and locked in position. Used in vertical and lateral file drawers, pedestal file drawers and card trays.

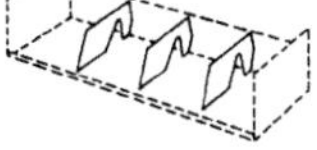

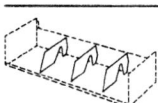

Divider
Metal plate used to separate and support file material. For lateral file and pedestal file drawers, fixed and roll-out shelves.

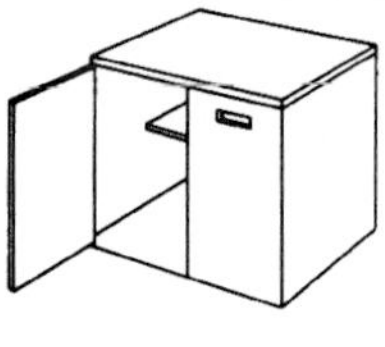

Double-door storage cabinet
For miscellaneous storage below worksurface. Includes one adjustable shelf and two swing-arm doors.

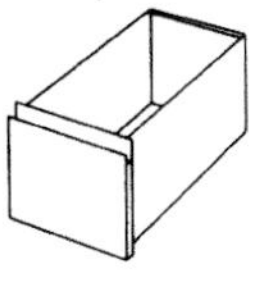

File drawer
For letter- or legal-size documents 12" and 15" high. 15" high drawers can also be used for computer printouts. For front-to-back or side-to-side or combination filing.

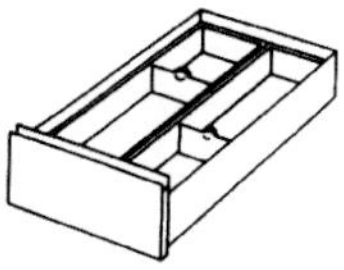

File insert drawers
For use in vertical files instead of card trays.

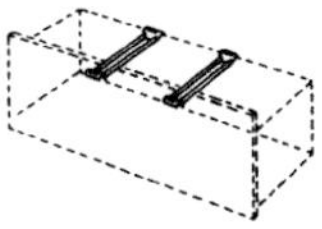

Hanging folder frame
A metal rod mounted in lateral and vertical files for suspended file material. Can be mounted on partitions for front-to-back filing.

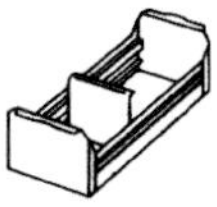

Interior card trays
Portable trays in various sizes for common card sizes: 3 x 5, 4 x 6, etc. Compressor included.

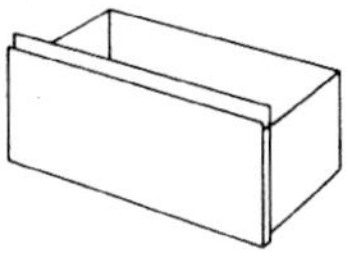

Later file drawer
3" tray drawer, 6" card drawer, and 9", 12" and 15" high file drawers. Letter or legal-size filing. Dividers, three sway blocks, compressor, hanging folder frames, rails, or partitions available.

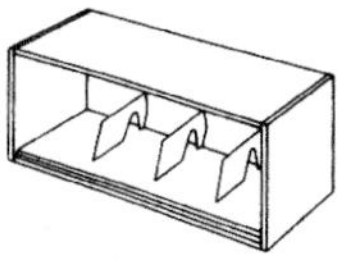

Lateral file fixed shelf
12" or 15" high shelves with or without doors and with three dividers.

Lateral file posting shelf
Metal pull-out shelf option on 48" and 60" interior height lateral files. When not specified, the space will be filled by a posting shelf filler.

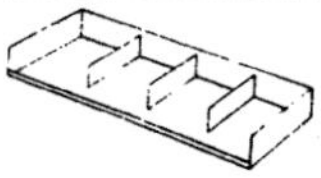

Lateral file roll-out shelf
3", 6", 12", and 15" high shelves extend for accessibility.

Lateral file workshelf
3" high roll-out worksheIf with laminate surface.

FURNITURE, FURNISHINGS, AND EQUIPMENT
Electronic Media Storage

Microfiche

Microfiche is a 4- × 6-in film transparency containing multiple rows of greatly reduced page images of any written, printed, or graphic material. Image reductions range from 13 up to several hundred times smaller than the originals. A microfiche viewer enlarges the images so that they are readable. Labeling information is written or printed on a narrow strip along the long edge at the top of the microfiche.

Microfiche may be stored in interior card trays, in lateral file 6-in-high roll-out shelves, and in a lateral file media compartment.

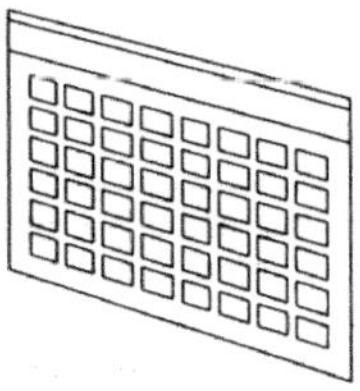

4″ x 6″

Microfilm

Microfilm is roll photographic film on a reel or in a square cartridge that contains images of pages of written, graphic, or printed material reduced hundreds of times. A microfilm viewer enlarges the images so that they are readable. Microfilm on a reel is kept in a square plastic or cardboard box for protection and ease of handling. Microfilm is most conveniently stored on edge. Labeling is placed on one of the edges of the reel or box.

Microfilm may be stored in the lateral file media compartment kit, in an interior card tray, and in lateral file 6-in-high drawers or shelves.

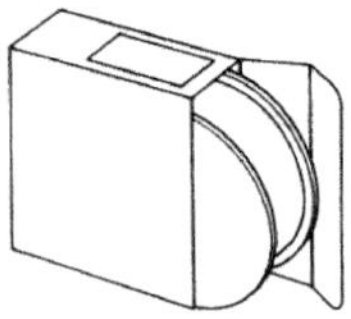

1″ x 4″ diameter reel
(1¼″ x 4¼″ x 4¼″ box)

Printout Paper

Printout paper, also known as continuous form data processing paper, is used in almost all computer printers and some word processing equipment. The most common types are recognizable by:

- Small pin-feed holes along both edges, which are used by the printer to grip and advance the paper.
- Green or gray-shaded stripes across the paper, which serve to organize the printed information.

After printing, the printout may exist in a fan-folded stack or it may be "burst," that is, separated into individual sheets along the perforations that exist at the fold lines.

If the printout consists of a significant number of sheets, it may be bound for easier handling. Fan-folded printouts *must* be bound along the top or long edge. Printouts that have been burst may be bound along either the long edge or the short edge. The binding may consist of only a narrow metal or plastic clamp or it may include a stiff plastic or fiberboard cover. Frequently the binding may include hooks at both ends so the printout may be hung from two rails like a hanging file folder. Other hooks may be used to suspend it from special bars or rails.

Identification information may be marked on one of the edges (depending on how the printout is stored) or on the front sheet of the binding cover.

Printout paper may be stored in Steelcase lateral and vertical files, depending on the paper size. Check the file which will accommodate your paper. Boxed paper can be stored in storage cabinets.

Cartridges

Cartridges have ¼-in-wide magnetic tape loaded into a reel-to-reel cartridge generally made of clear plastic with metal back plate. They look similar to an oversize recording cassette. Cartridges come in and are sometimes stored in flip-open plastic or cardboard boxes. Labels and identification information are located on the long edge or on the side along the long edge of the cartridge or the box.

Cartridges may be stored in interior card trays or in a media compartment kit in lateral file 6-in-high drawers or shelves.

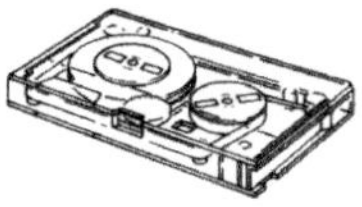

⅝″ x 4″ x 6″ (cartridge)
⅞″ x 4¼″ x 6¼″ (cartridge in case)

Cassettes

Cassettes are available in standard and mini sizes and consist of magnetic tape loaded into a reel-to-reel configuration in a plastic case. Standard cassettes for electronic equipment are identical in size and appearance to those used for home recording. Cassettes may be used in microcomputers and in word processing or dictation equipment. They come in and are frequently stored in flip-open plastic cases. Labels or identification information may be located on the long edge or side of the cassette or its case.

Cassettes may be stored in a lateral file media compartment kit.

Standard Cassette Case
1 1/16″ x 2¾″ x 4 5/16″

Mini Cassette Case
7/16″ x 1½″ x 2⅞″

Disk Cartridges

Disk cartridges are round plastic cases which contain a series of rotating platters (or disks) on which data is magnetically recorded. The number of platters in a case varies with the height of the case. In use, the entire case is inserted in a computer disk drive unit, where recording arms, which read/record information, enter the case through a slot with a spring door.

Disk cartridges are flat in appearance with an elongated Y-shaped protrusion on the top. They can be stored flat or on edge.

Labels for identification are usually located on the edge of the disk cartridge. Frequently disk cartridges have to be stored in a temperature/humidity-controlled environment.

Disk cartridges may be stored in lateral file 6-in-high roll-out shelves, storage cabinets, and bookcases.

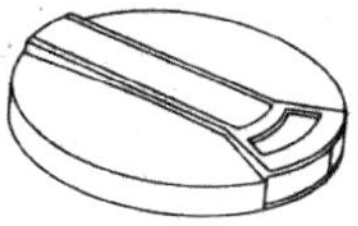

1" x 10" diameter
3" x 10" diameter
1" x 15" diameter
3" x 15" diameter

Disk Packs

Disk packs are round plastic cases which contain a series of rotating platters (or disks) on which data is magnetically recorded. The number of platters in a unit varies with the height of the plastic case. In use, the entire case is inserted in a computer disk drive unit, where recording arms, to read/record information, enter the case through a slot with a spring door. Disk packs are flat on the bottom and upright, with the handle on top. Identification is generally located on the edge of the disk pack. These units should be stored in a temperature/humidity-controlled environment. Disk packs *must not* be stored on top of one another.

Disk packs may be stored in storage cabinets, bookcases, and on 3-in- and 6-in-high lateral file shelves.

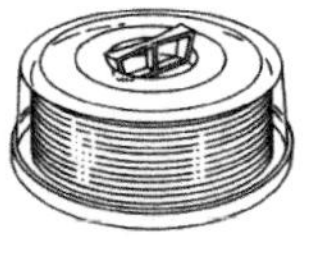

7" x 10" diameter
7" x 15" diameter

Floppy (Flexible) Disks

Floppy disks, also called diskettes or flexible disks, are small, record-like disks, each permanently enclosed in a square, stiff paper envelope. They are used to magnetically record information in all types of small computer and word processing equipment. Labels are placed on the paper envelope.

Floppy disks may be stored in 12-in-high lateral file drawers and shelves.

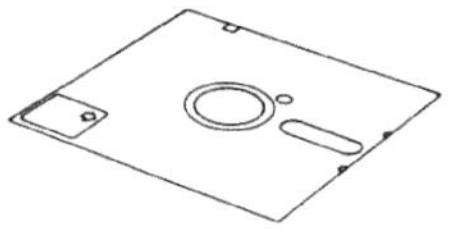

8" x 8"
5¼" x 5¼"
3½" x 3½"

Laser Disks

Laser disks look like long-play record albums, complete with a paper protective sleeve. Data are stored and retrieved by laser beam.

Laser disks may be stored in 15-in-high lateral file drawers and shelves.

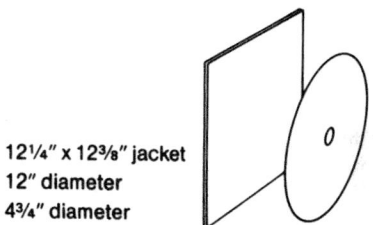

12¼" x 12⅜" jacket
12" diameter
4¾" diameter

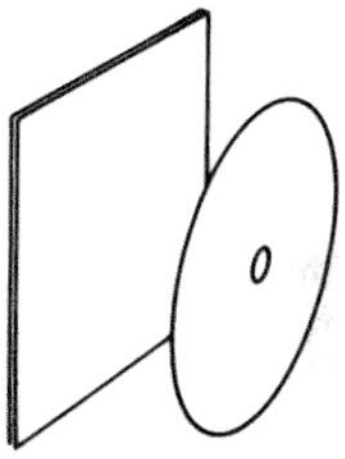

Magnetic, Tab, and Aperture Cards

Magnetic cards, also known as mag cards, are a tab-size black plastic card with magnetic material coated on one or both sides. The cards are used to record or reproduce information in word processing equipment. In some cases, one or more of the cards will be kept in a paper envelope. Identifying information will be marked on the face of the envelope.

Tab cards, also known as keypunch cards, are 80-column cards or punch cards with small holes in them to represent bits of data. Although they may be stored in a workstation or central storage area, they are usually used and produced in a mainframe computer room or keypunch department, and are stored in specially separated decks. The decks are most frequently identified by markings across the edges of the cards.

Aperture cards are tab cards with a piece of microfilm mounted over a hole in their center. They are most frequently used for microfilm images of engineering or architectural drawings. Aperture card reader/printers enlarge the image on a screen for reference and, if required, reproduce a full-size copy of the drawing. Identifying information is printed in a narrow band along the top (long edge) of the card.

These cards may be stored in interior card trays and in lateral file 6-in-high drawers and roll-out shelves.

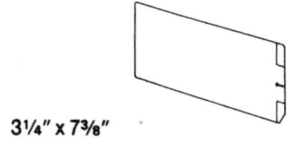

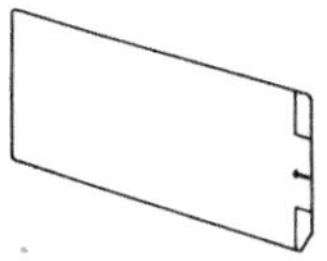

3¼" x 7⅜"

FURNITURE, FURNISHINGS, AND EQUIPMENT
Electronic Media Storage

Magnetic Tape Reels

Magnetic tape is typically ½-in wide and loaded on reels of varying diameters. A flexible plastic strip locks around the outside of the reel to protect the tape and prevent unraveling when it is not in use. This medium is used in large tape drive units that are generally found only in computer rooms. The long-term storage of magnetic tapes is subject to strict temperature and humidity requirements to prevent damage. Tapes are labeled both on the side and on the flexible strip that is placed around the edge of the reel. They can be stored flat or on edge. For flat storage, handle like disk cartridges.

Magnetic tape reels may be stored in the lateral file add-on cabinets, storage cabinets, or in freestanding wire racks on lateral file shelves.

1" x 7½" diameter
1" x 8½" diameter
1" x 10½" diameter
1" x 15" diameter

FILE COUNTERTOP

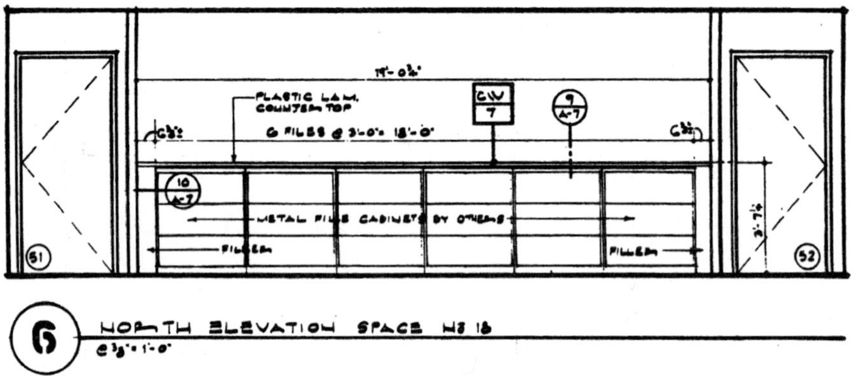

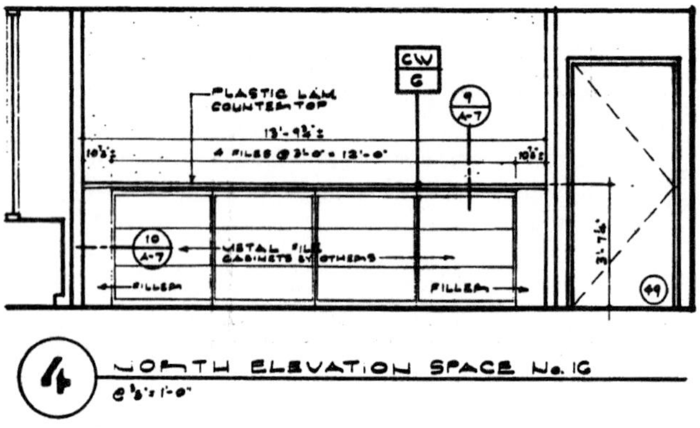

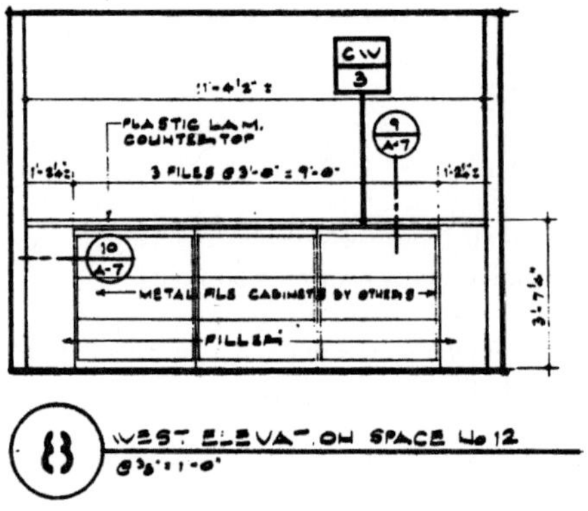

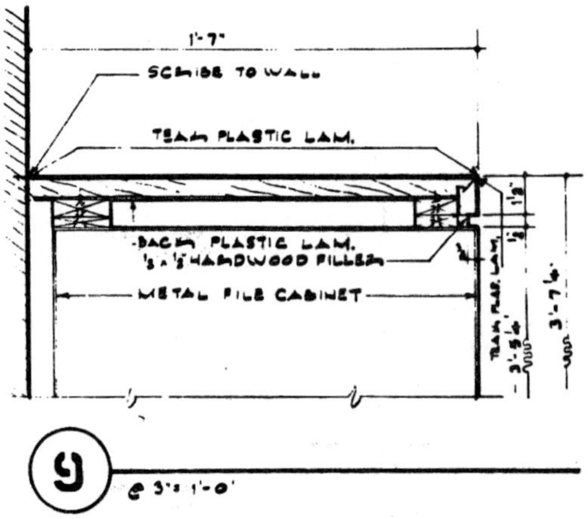

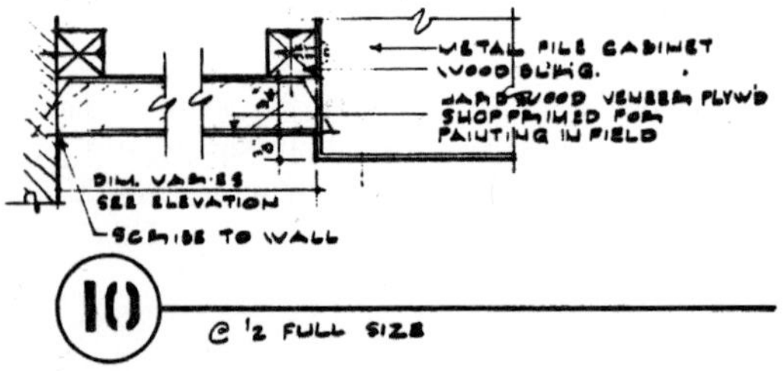

FURNITURE, FURNISHINGS, AND EQUIPMENT

File Countertop With Shelf Light

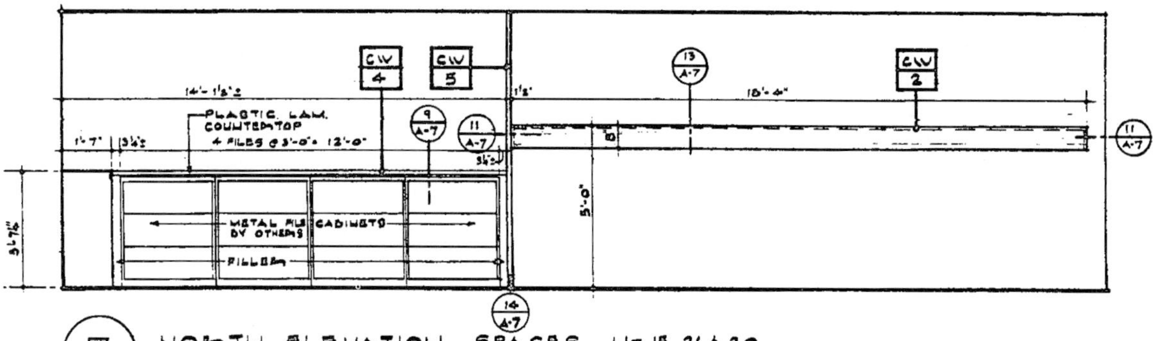

3 NORTH ELEVATION SPACES N8 15, 21 & 20

@ 3/8" = 1'-0"

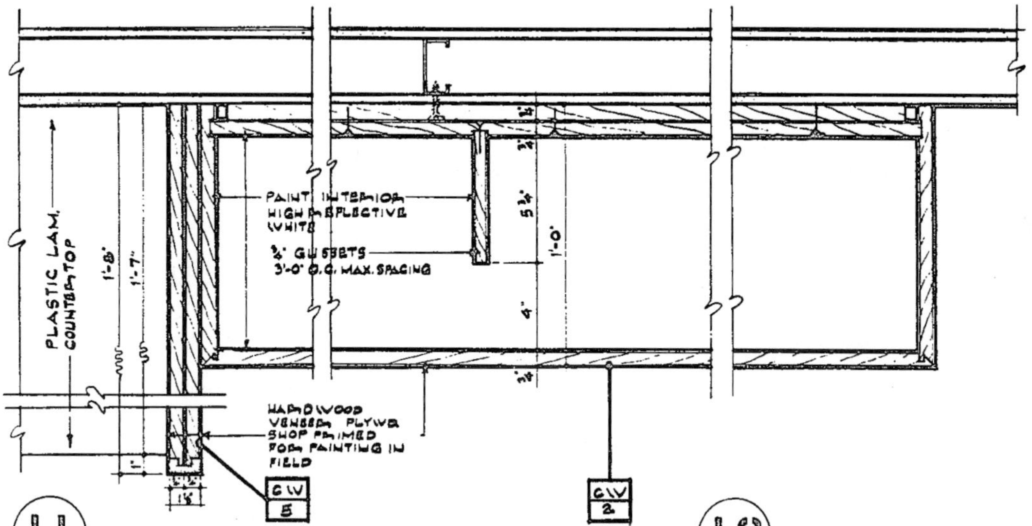

11 @ 3" = 1'-0"

12 @ 3" = 1'-0"

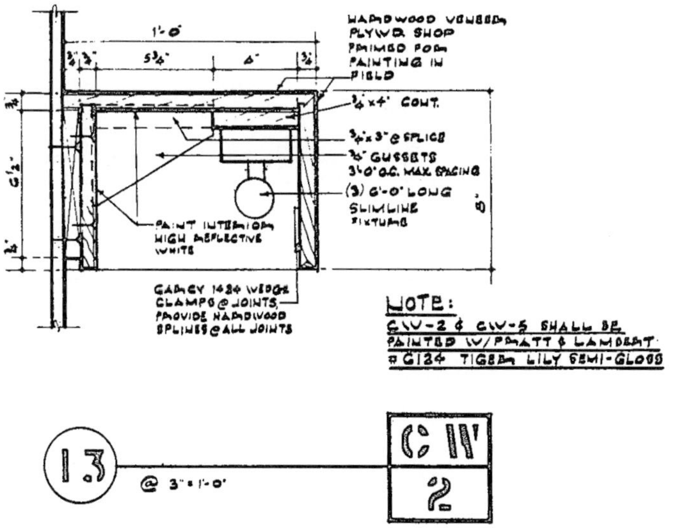

NOTE:
CW-2 & CW-5 SHALL BE PAINTED W/ PRATT & LAMBERT #G134 TIGER LILY SEMI-GLOSS

13 @ 3" = 1'-0"

CW 2

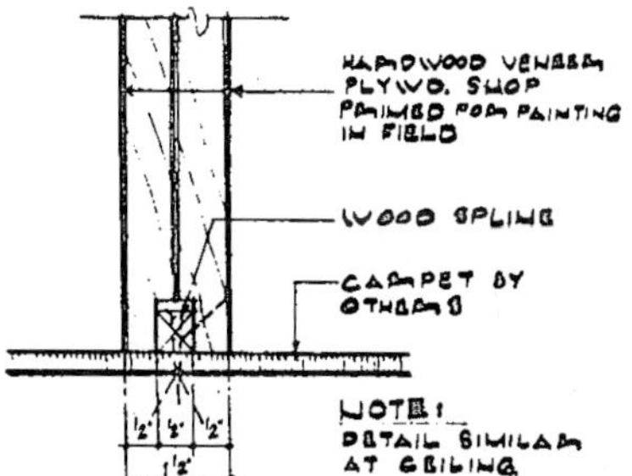

14 @ 1/2 FULL SIZE

CW 5

FURNITURE, FURNISHINGS, AND EQUIPMENT

File Storage Walls with Overhead Cabinets

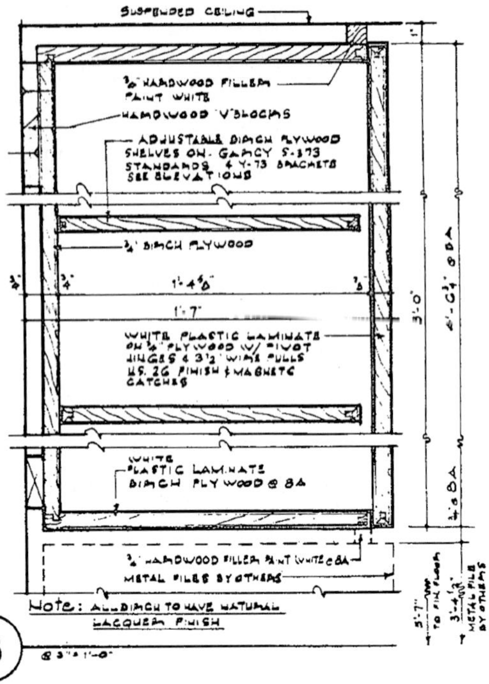

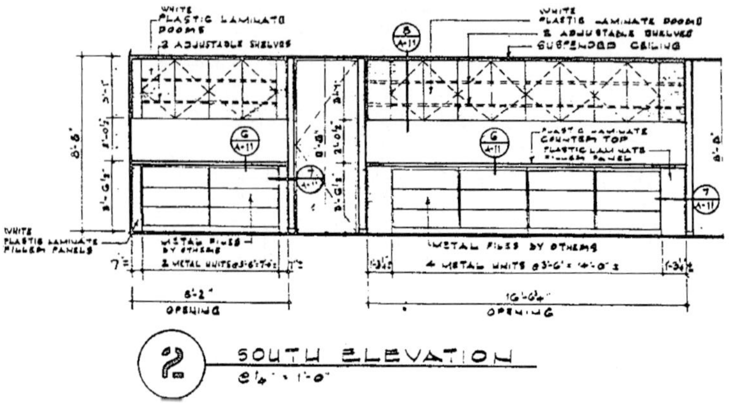

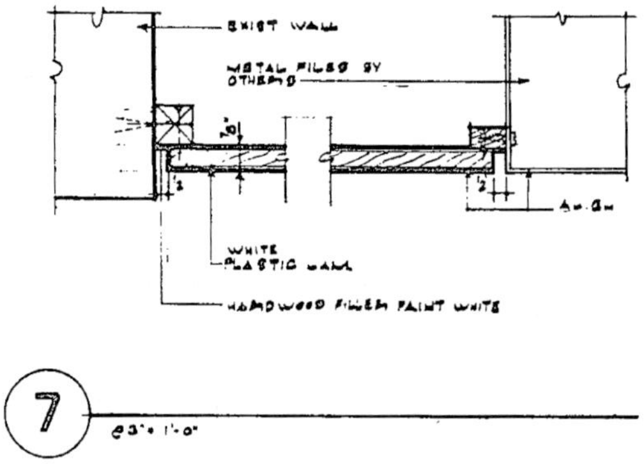

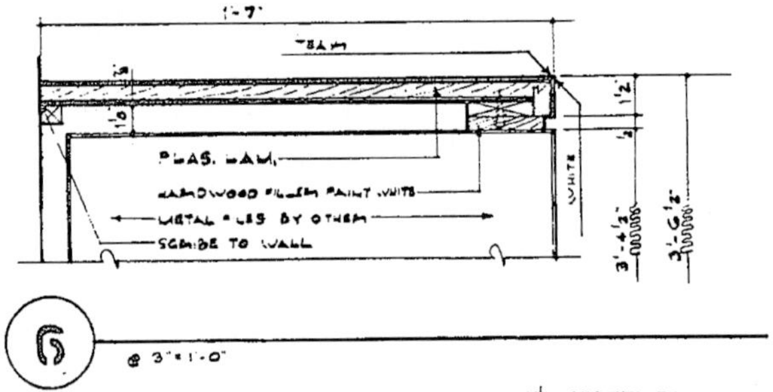

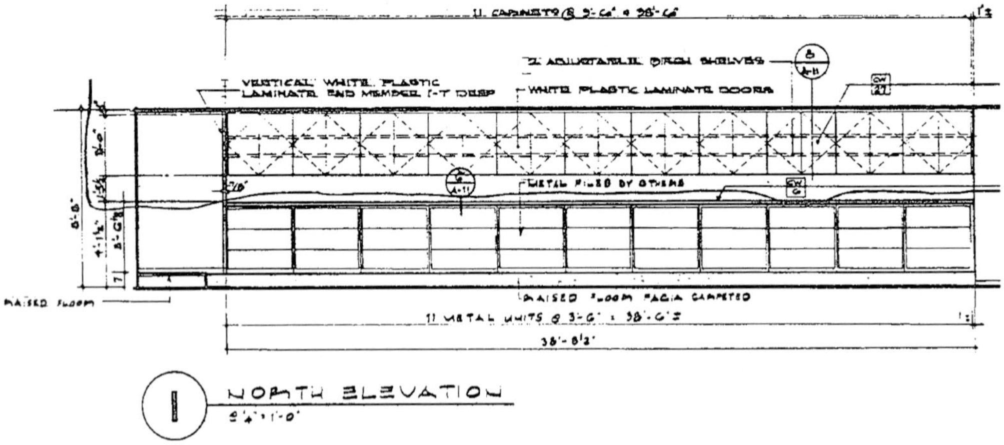

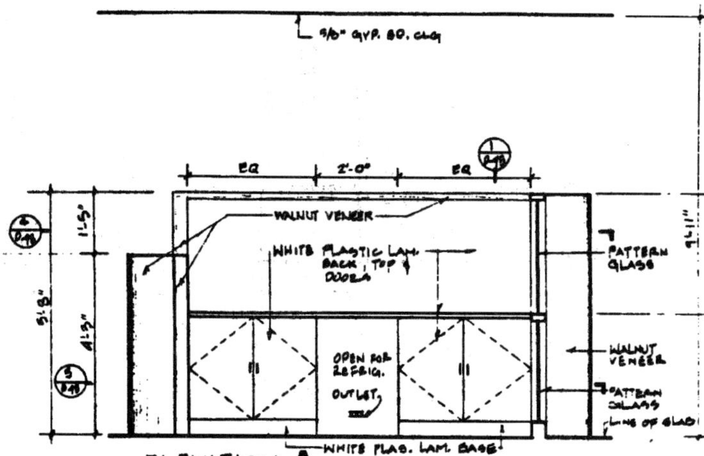

ELEVATION A
SCALE: 1/2"=1'-0"

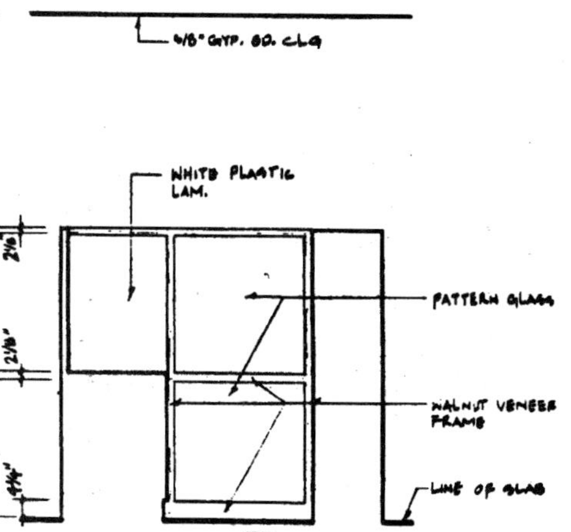

ELEVATION B
SCALE: 1/2"=1'-0"

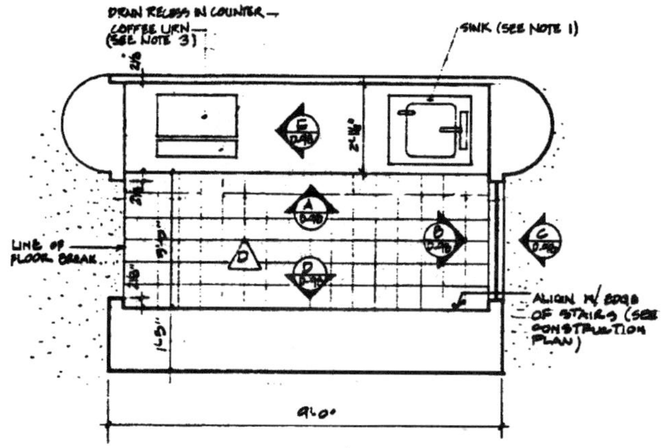

PLAN
SCALE: 1/2"=1'-0"

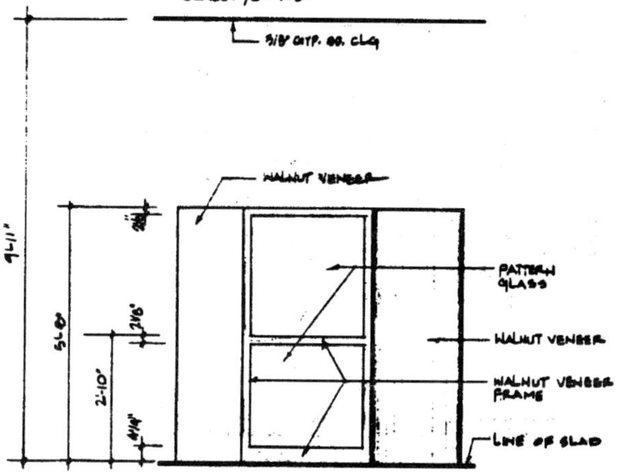

ELEVATION C
SCALE: 1/2"=1'-0"

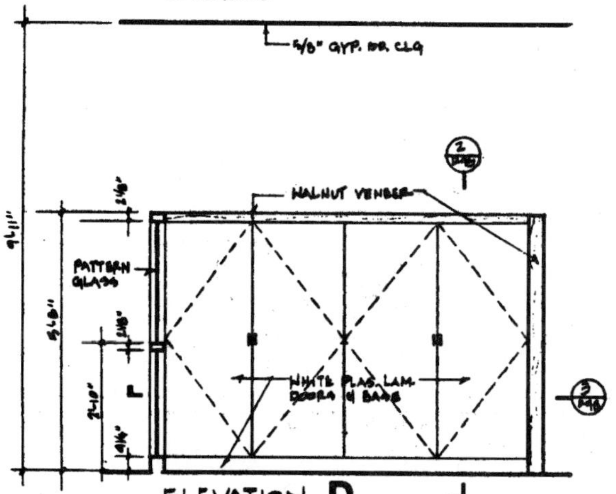

ELEVATION D
SCALE: 1/2"=1'-0"

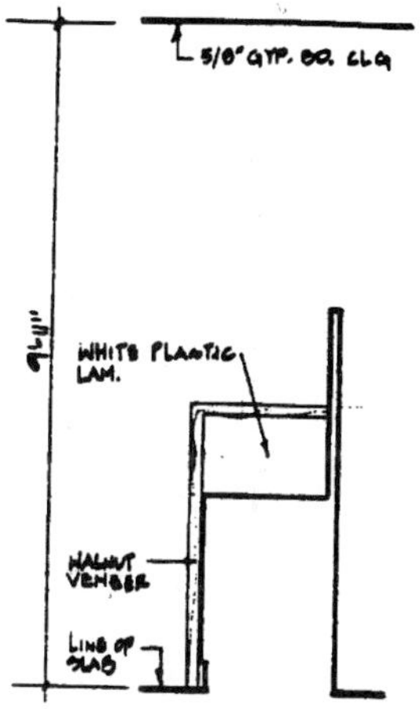

ELEVATION E
SCALE: 1/2"=1'-0"

FURNITURE, FURNISHINGS, AND EQUIPMENT

Office Pantry

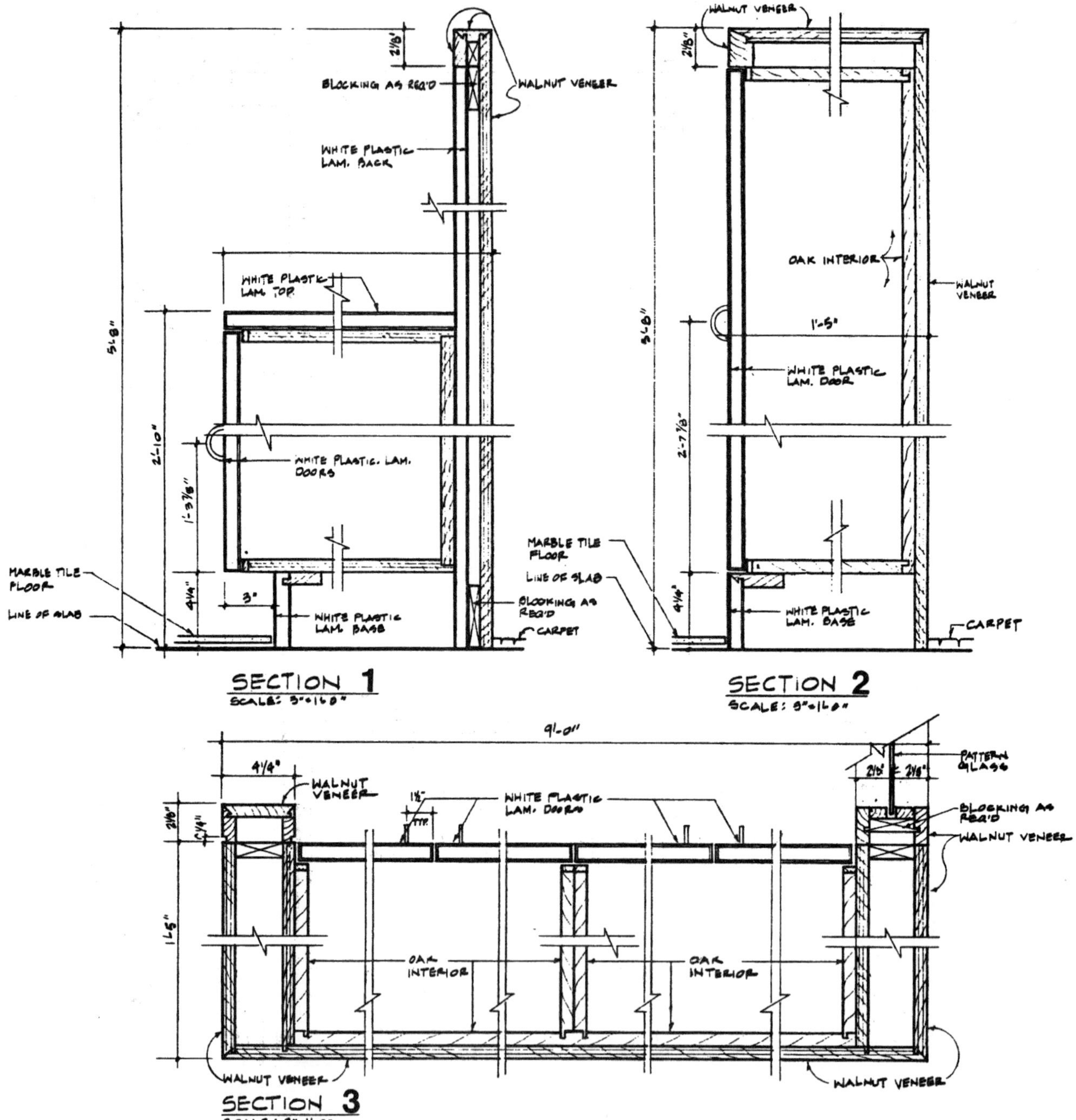

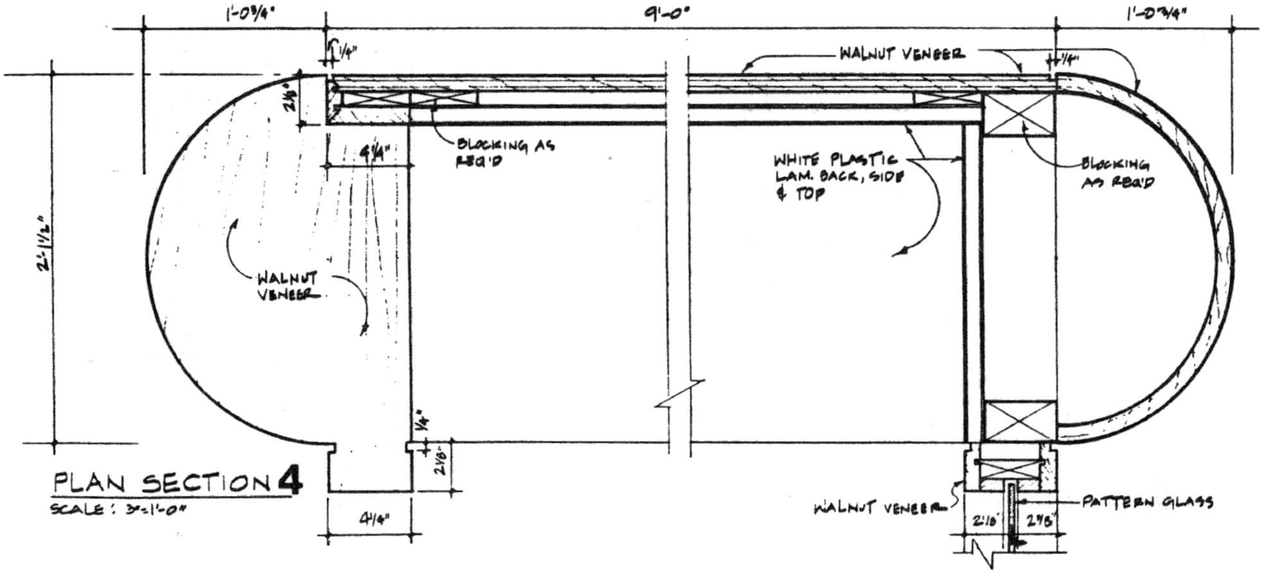
1'-0¾"
9'-0"
1'-0¾"
¼"
WALNUT VENEER
¼"
2⅛"
4¼"
BLOCKING AS REQ'D
WHITE PLASTIC LAM. BACK, SIDE & TOP
BLOCKING AS REQ'D
2'-1½"
WALNUT VENEER
¼"
2⅛"
4¼"
WALNUT VENEER
PATTERN GLASS
2⅛"
2⅛"
PLAN SECTION 4
SCALE: 3"=1'-0"

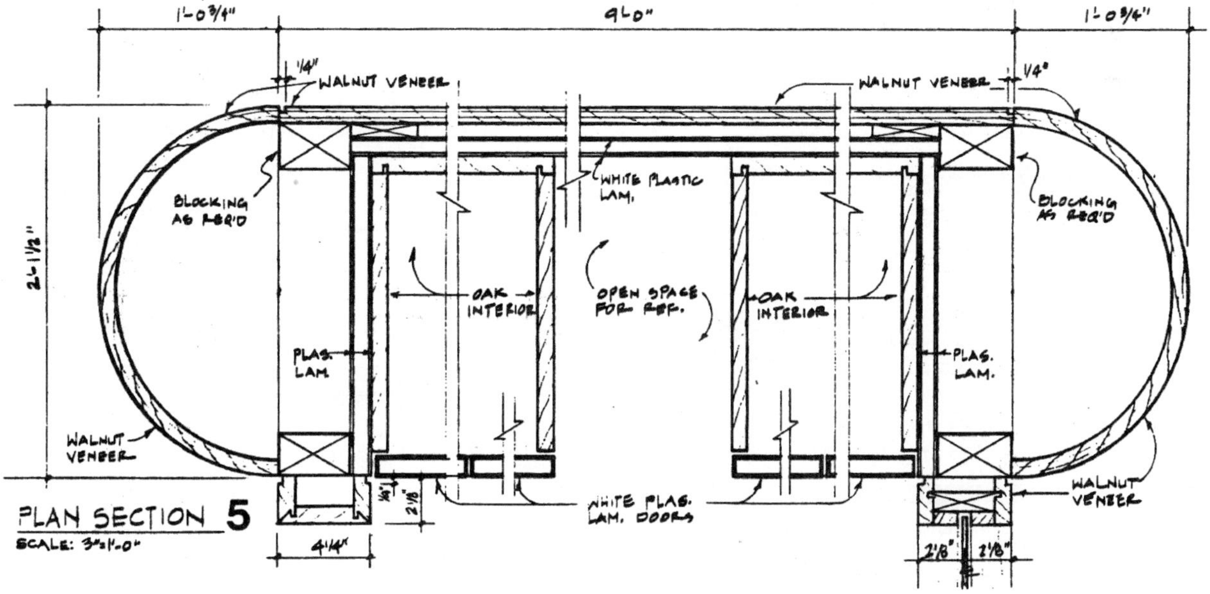
1'-0¾"
9'-0"
1'-0¾"
¼"
WALNUT VENEER
WALNUT VENEER
¼"
WHITE PLASTIC LAM.
BLOCKING AS REQ'D
BLOCKING AS REQ'D
2'-1½"
OAK INTERIOR
OPEN SPACE FOR REF.
OAK INTERIOR
PLAS. LAM.
PLAS. LAM.
WALNUT VENEER
WALNUT VENEER
¼"
2⅛"
WHITE PLAS. LAM. DOORS
PLAN SECTION 5
SCALE: 3"=1'-0"
4¼"
2⅛"
2⅛"

FURNITURE, FURNISHINGS, AND EQUIPMENT

Countertop with Base Cabinets

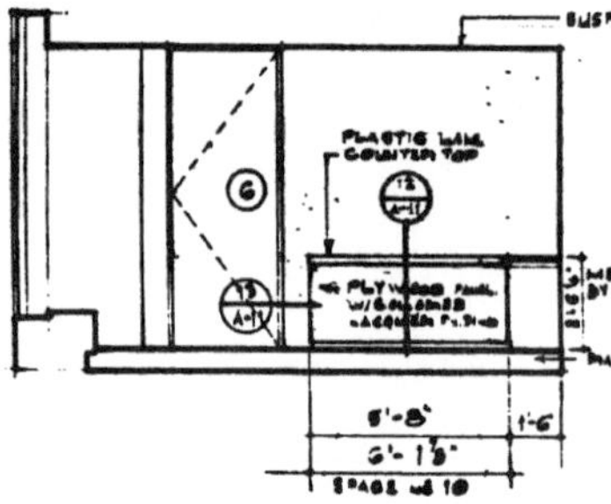

9 NORTH ELEVATION
SPACE N# 9 @ 1/4"=1'-0"

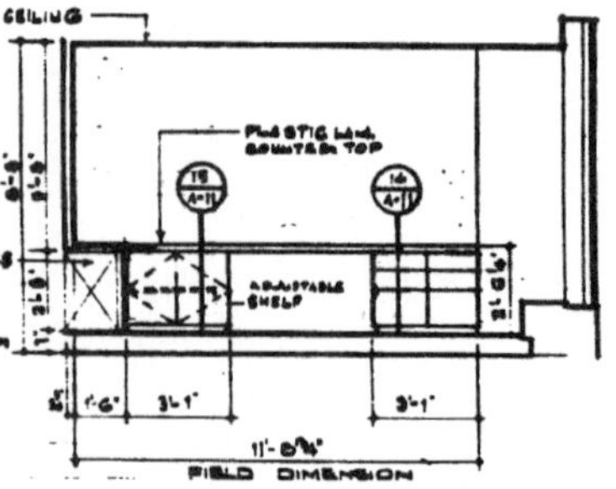

10 EAST ELEVATION
SPACE N# 9 @ 1/4"=1'-0"

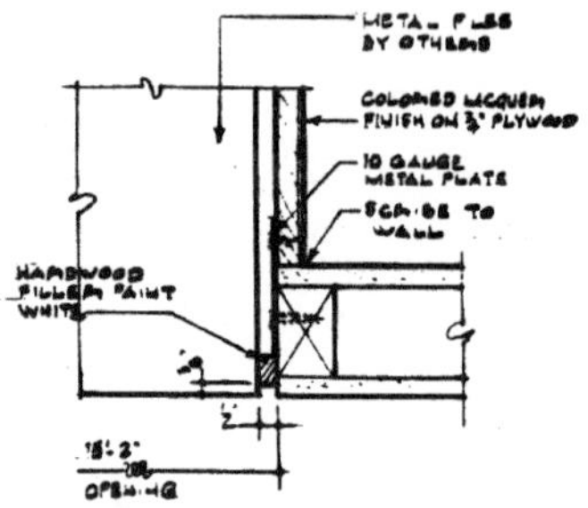

13 @ 3"=1'-0"

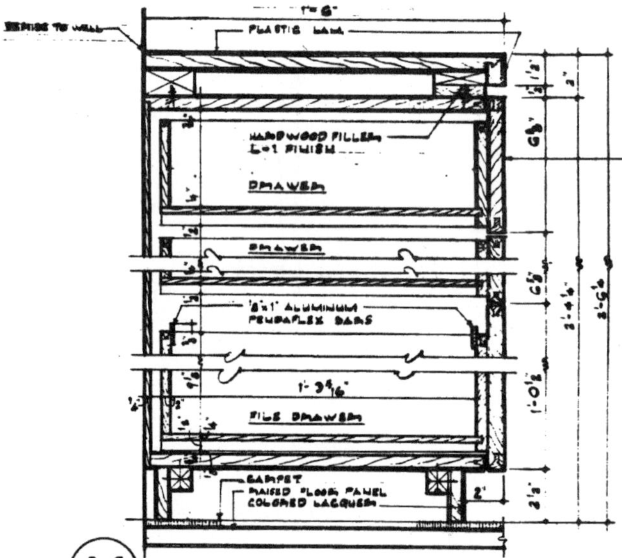

14 @ 3"= 1'-0"

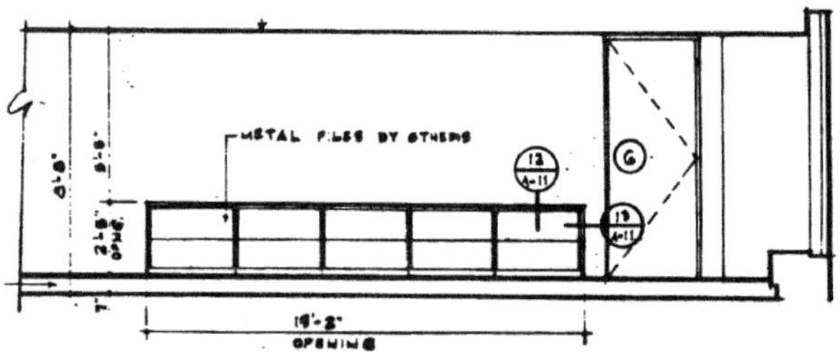

11 SOUTH ELEVATION SPACE N# 8
@ 1/4"= 1'-0"

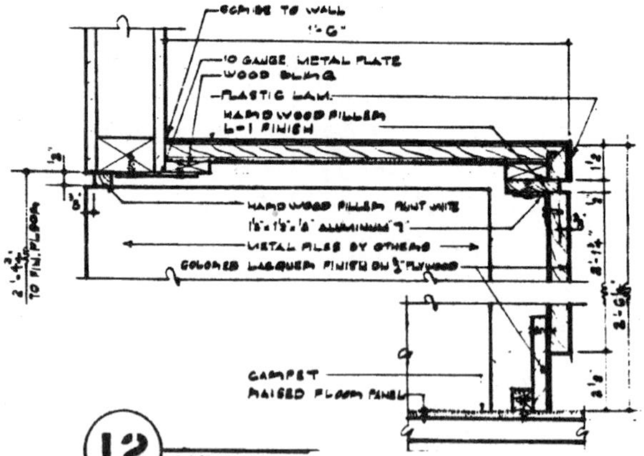

12 @ 3"= 1'-0"

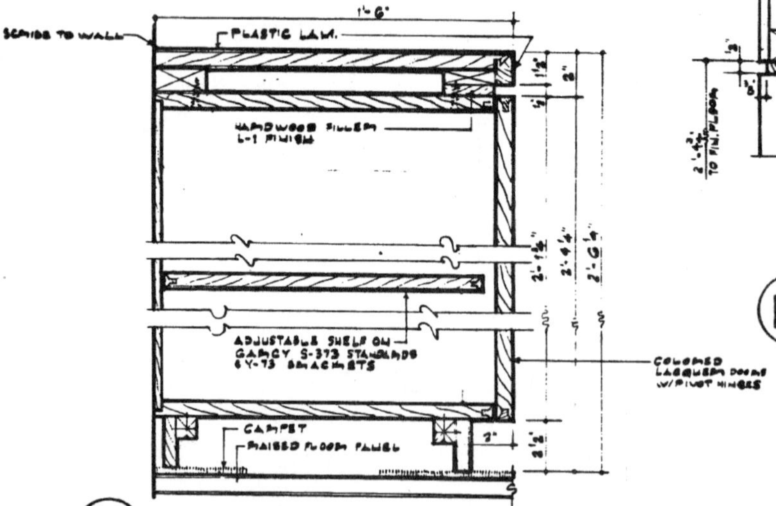

15 @ 3"= 1'-0"

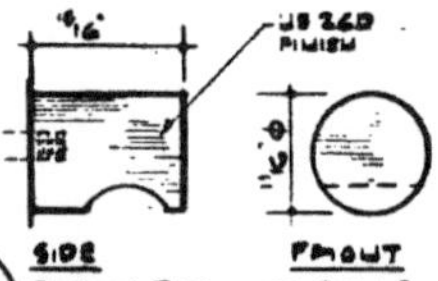

16 ELEVATION OF PULLS
@ 1/2 FULL SIZE

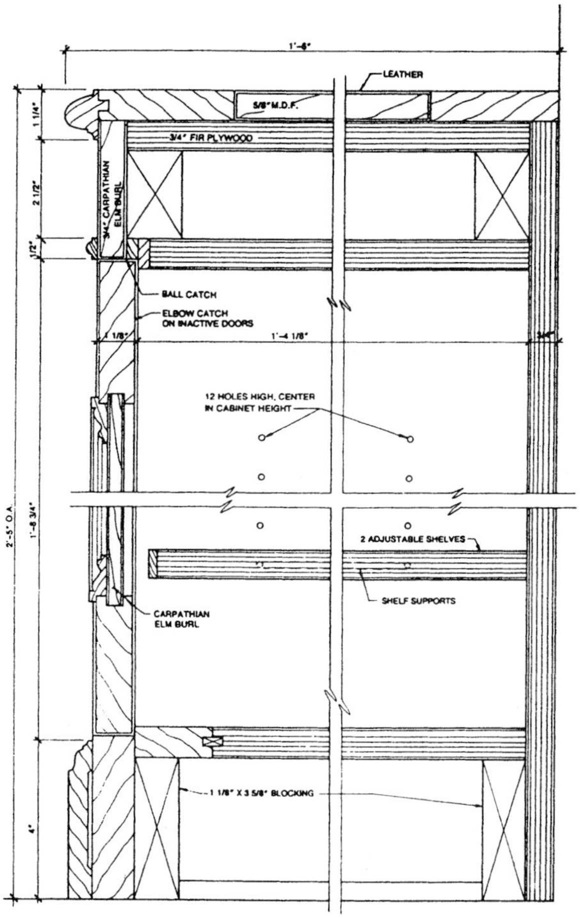

SECTION AT CREDENZA

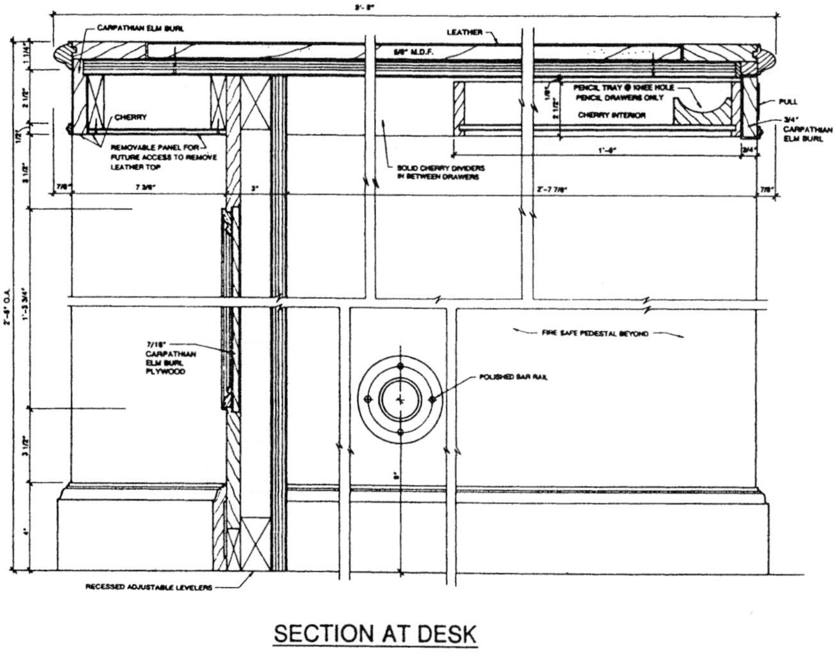

SECTION AT DESK

FURNITURE, FURNISHINGS, AND EQUIPMENT
Island File Counter; Compact Kitchen

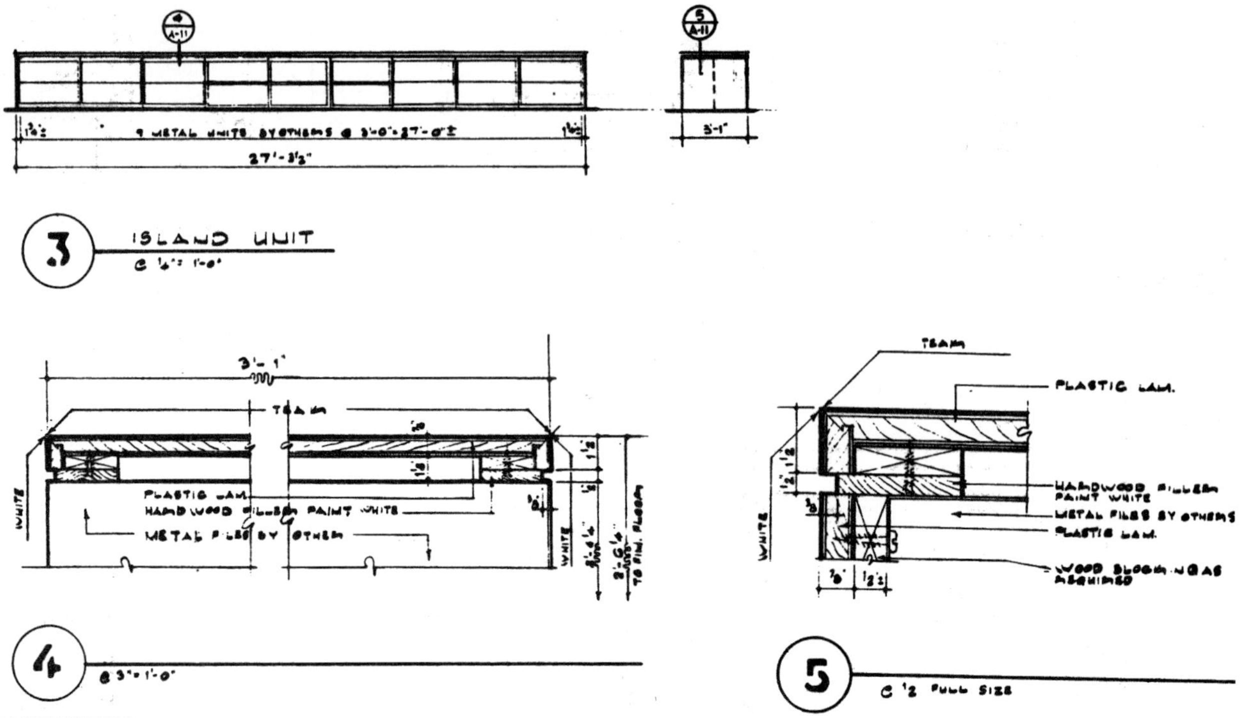

ISLAND FILE COUNTER

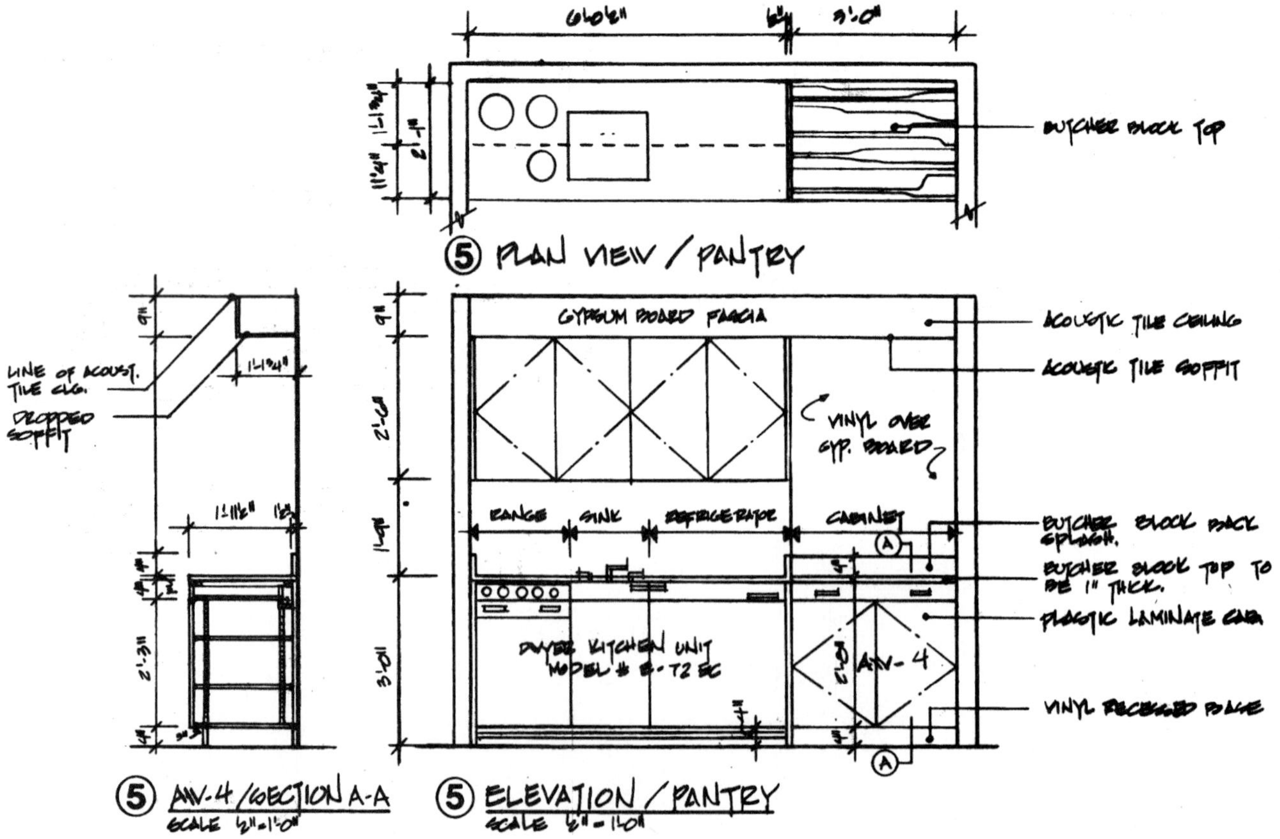

COMPACT KITCHEN

HOSPITALITY SPACES

The basic components of any restaurant interior are the chair and the table. Depending on restaurant type, menu, service, table setting, furniture selection, and degree of intimacy required, table size and overall chair space requirements can, and should, vary greatly. A restaurant that encourages rapid turnover of customers will normally provide small tabletop and chair sizes. On the other hand, those restaurants that encourage limited turnover and emphasize the wining and dining experience will typically provide larger tabletop sizes and larger, more comfortable chairs, with greater distance between table groupings.

There is no agreement among even the most experienced restaurateurs and restaurant designers as to what the optimal table and chair dimensions should be. In addition, many other design factors will influence the final decision, including circulation and egress, accessibility standards, methods of service, and the overall dimensions of any given space.

Figures 1 to 19 provide the designer with restaurant planning standards that have been developed by many experienced architects and interior designers. These drawings not only show the various individual table and chair arrangements, but provide the designer with groupings of these arrangements, as well as an indication of overall size, floor area, and number of persons accommodated. These arrangements, however, should be utilized only for preliminary planning information.

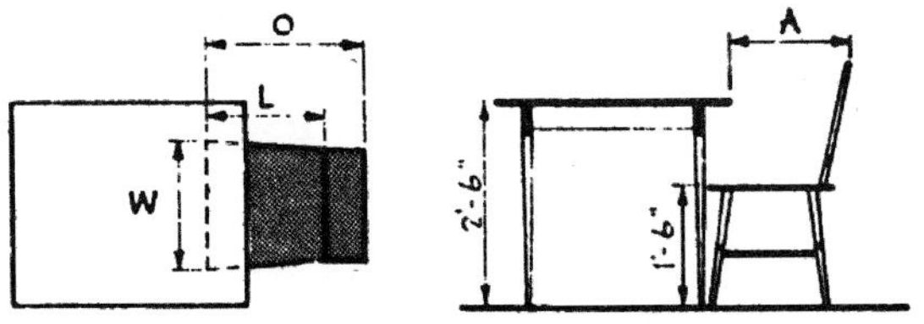

	O	L	W	A
LUXURIOUS	22"	18"	18"-20"	18"
INTERMEDIATE	19"-20"	16"	16"	18"
ECONOMICAL	17"-18"	15"	14"	18"

CHAIR DIMENSIONS

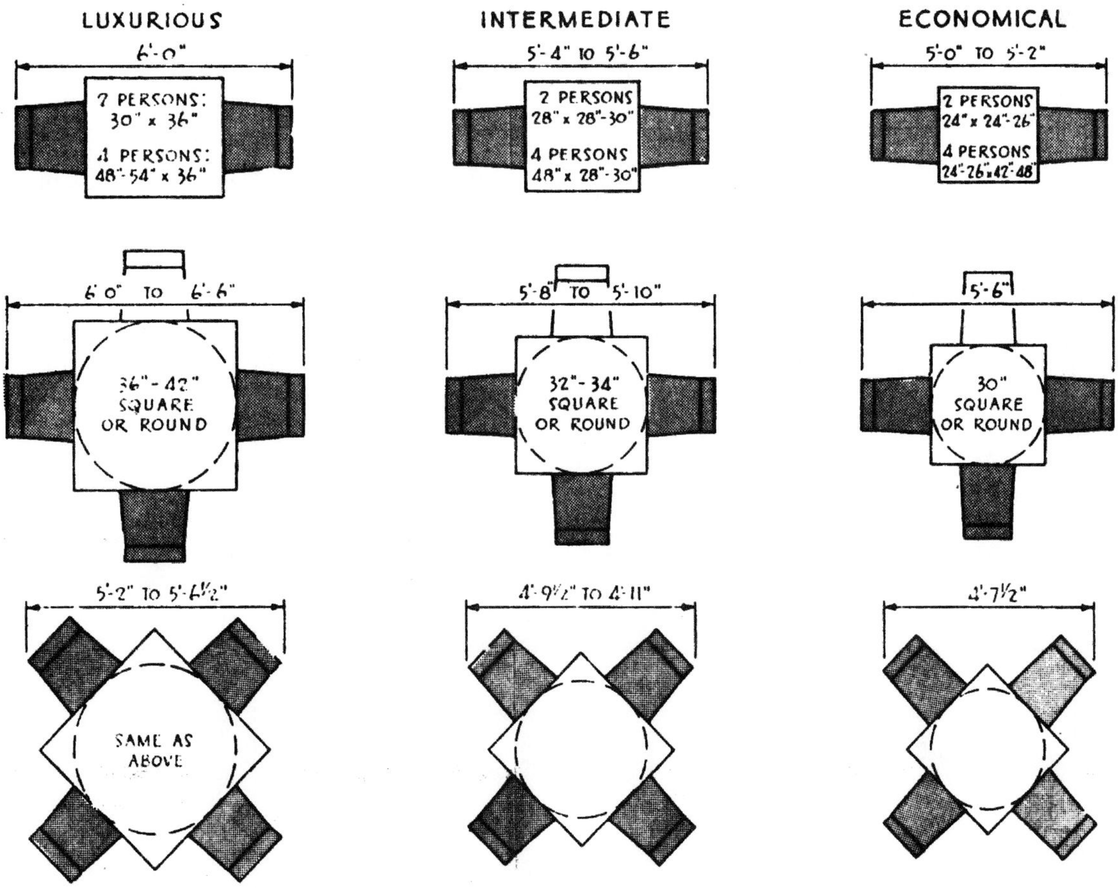

CHAIR-AND-TABLE UNITS (OCCUPIED)

AISLE WIDTHS:	FOR PUBLIC CIRCULATION: 36" MINIMUM CLEAR WIDTH	FOR SERVICE ONLY: 24" MIN. BETWEEN CHAIR BACKS	FOR MAIN ENTRANCE: LARGE AS POSSIBLE

Fig. 1

RESTAURANTS

Types and Sizes of Table Arrangements

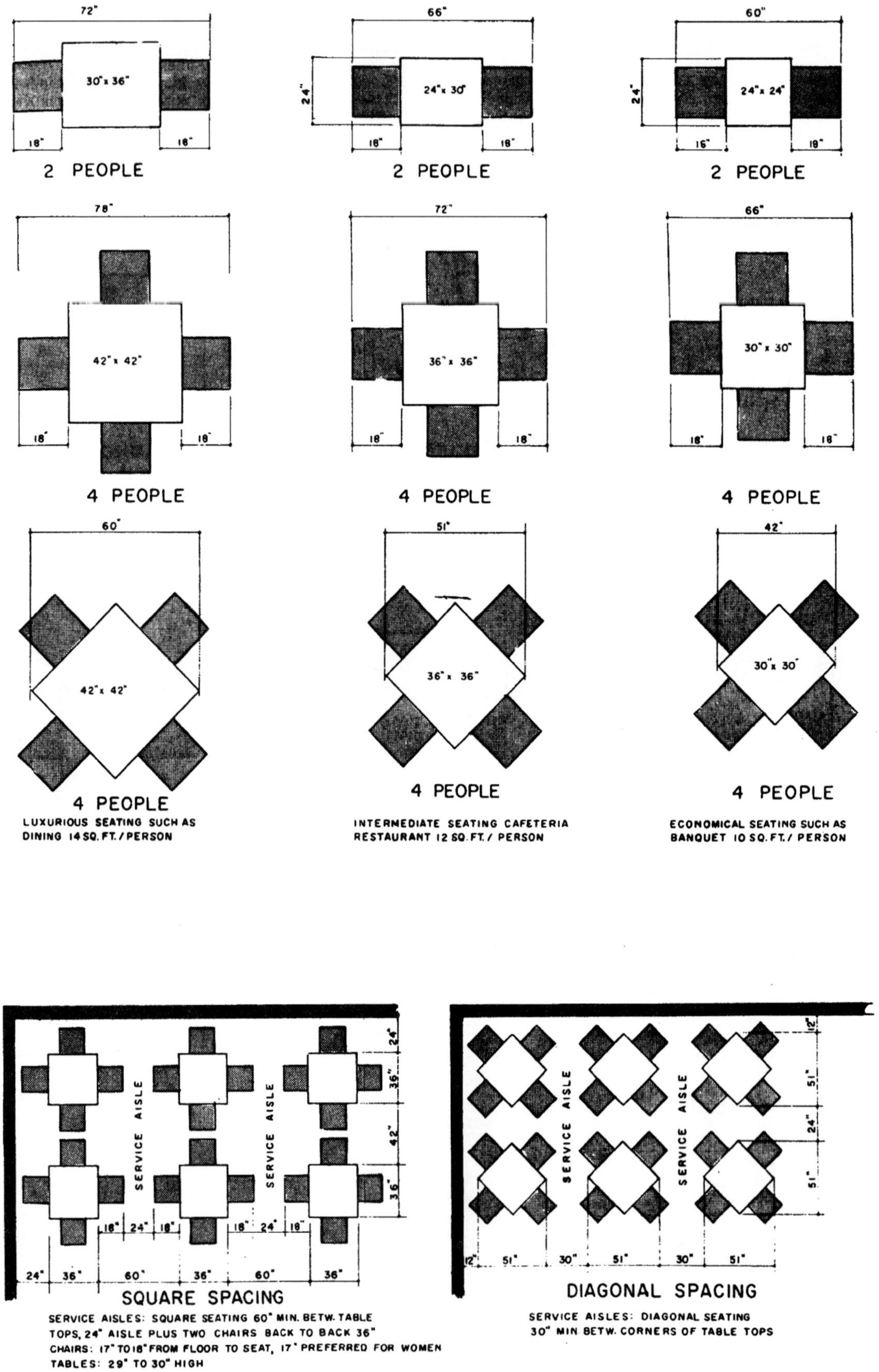

Fig. 2

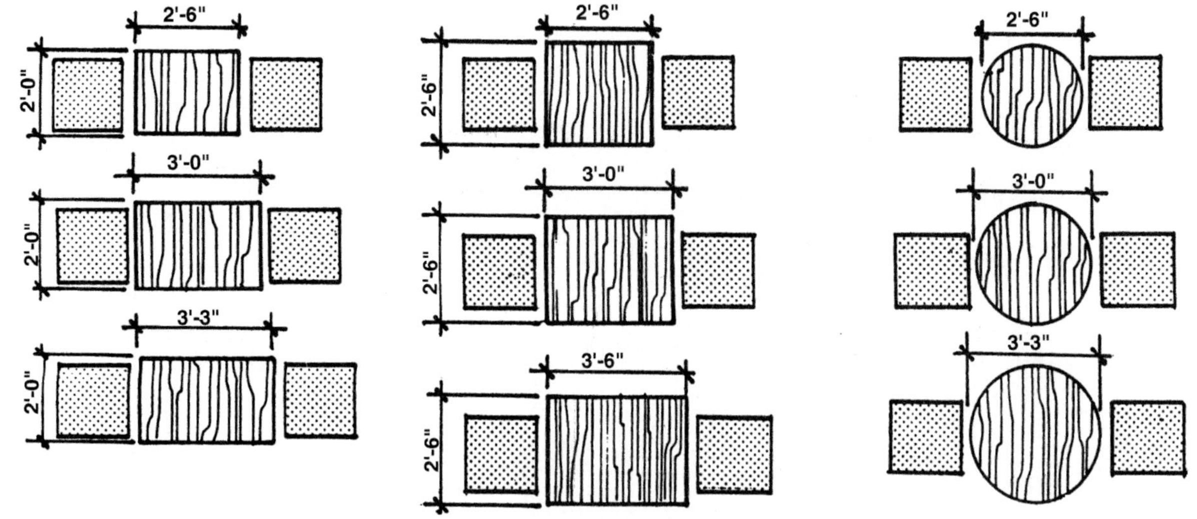

Fig. 3 Seating for two

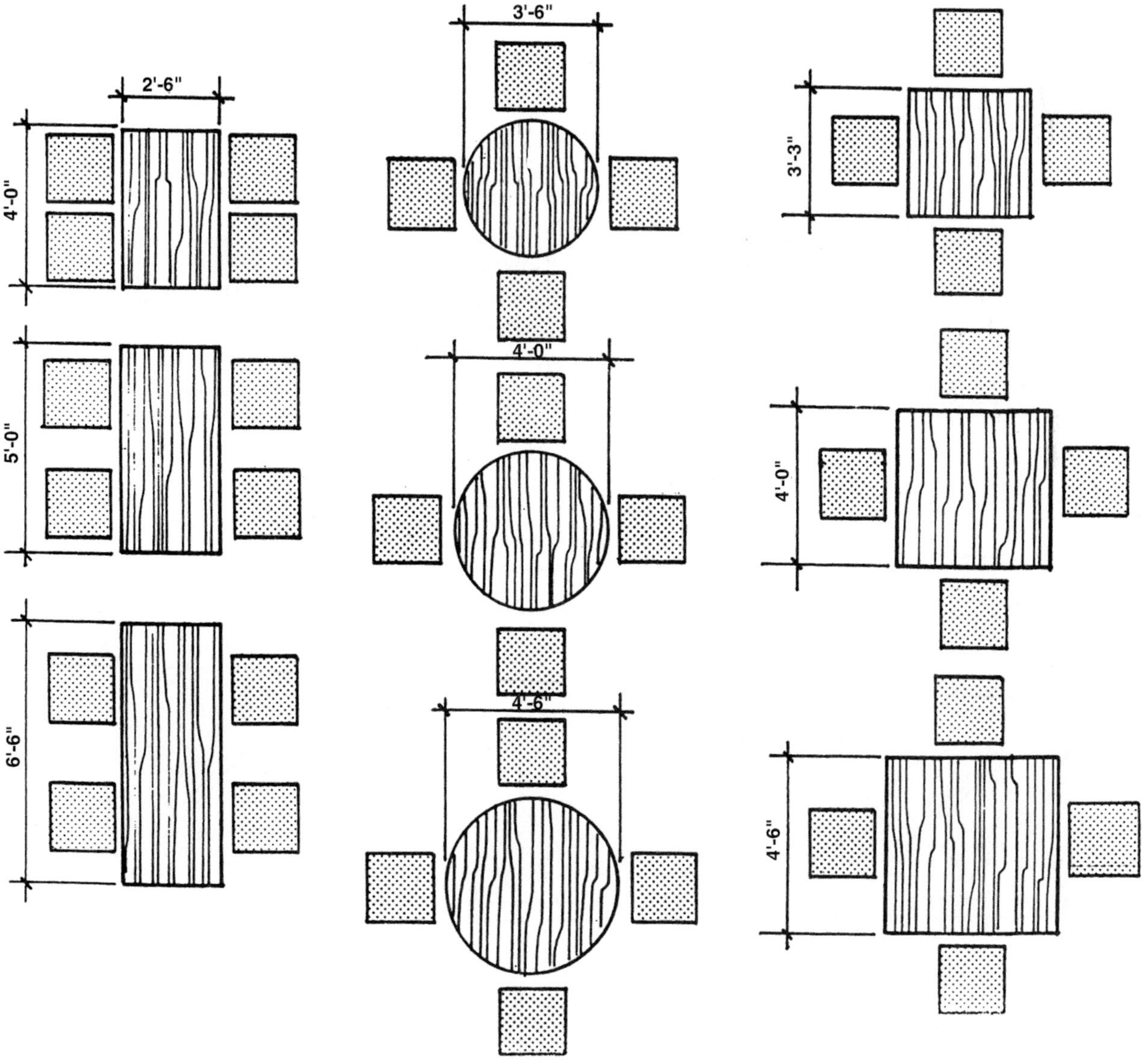

Fig. 4. Seating for four

RESTAURANTS
Types and Sizes of Table Arrangements

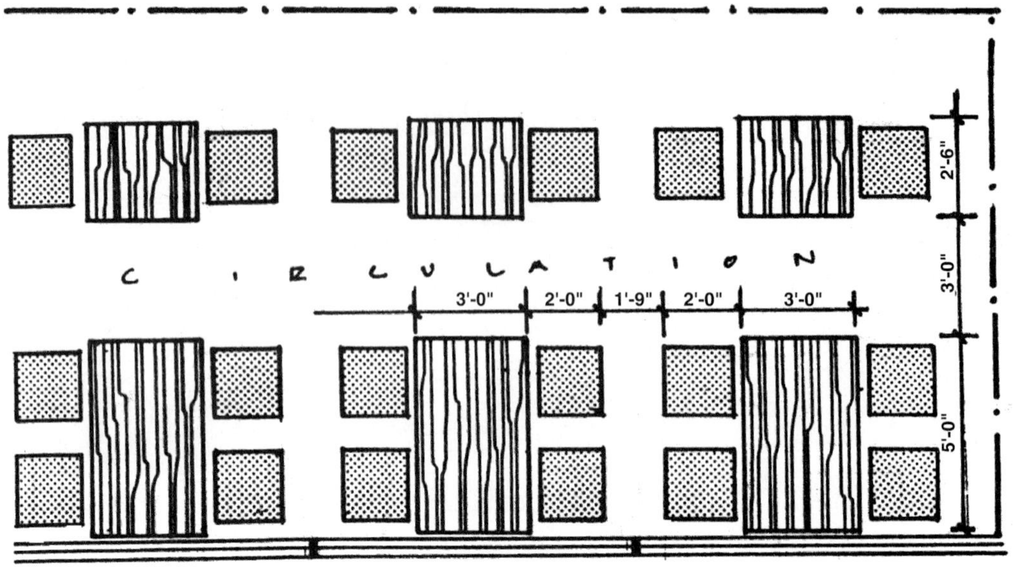

Fig. 5 13 ft × 27 ft, 351 ft², seats 18

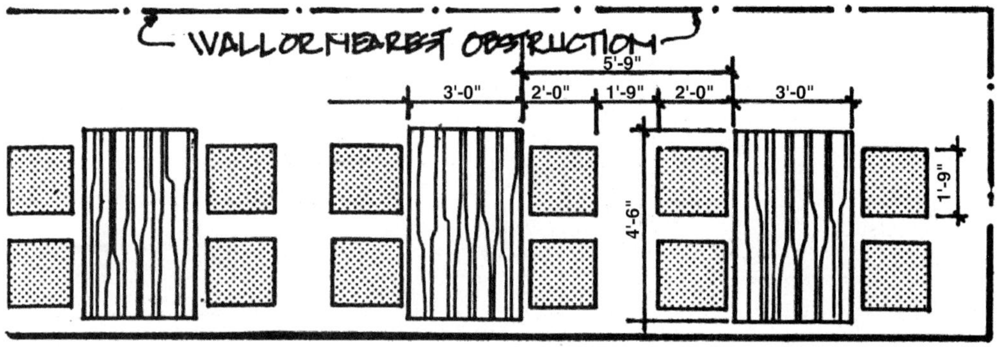

Fig. 6 8 ft × 27 ft, 216 ft², seats 12

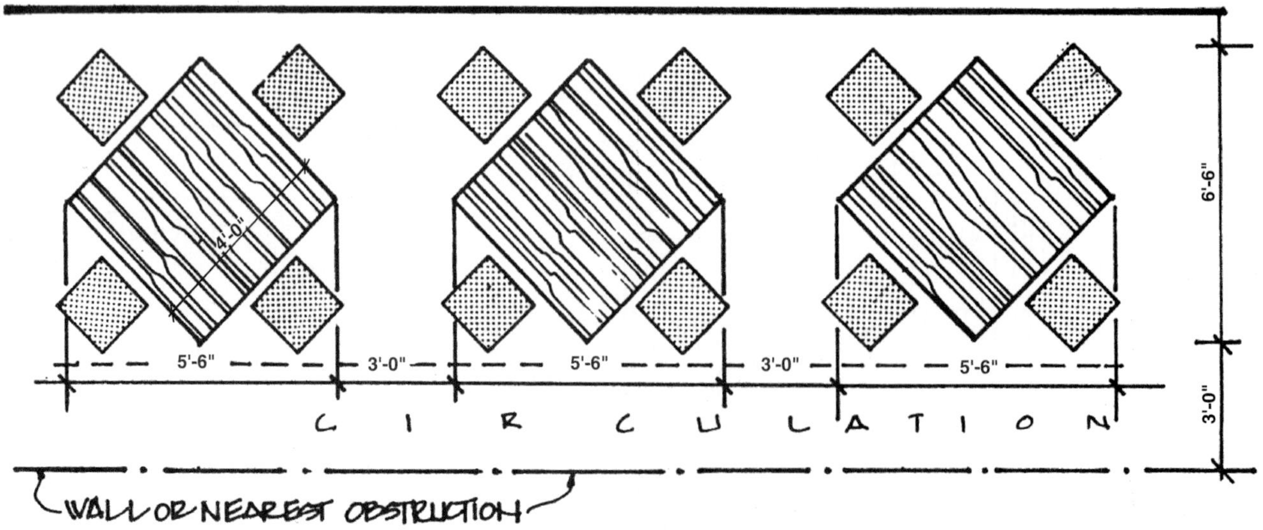

Fig. 7 33 ft × 11 ft, 363 ft², seats 12

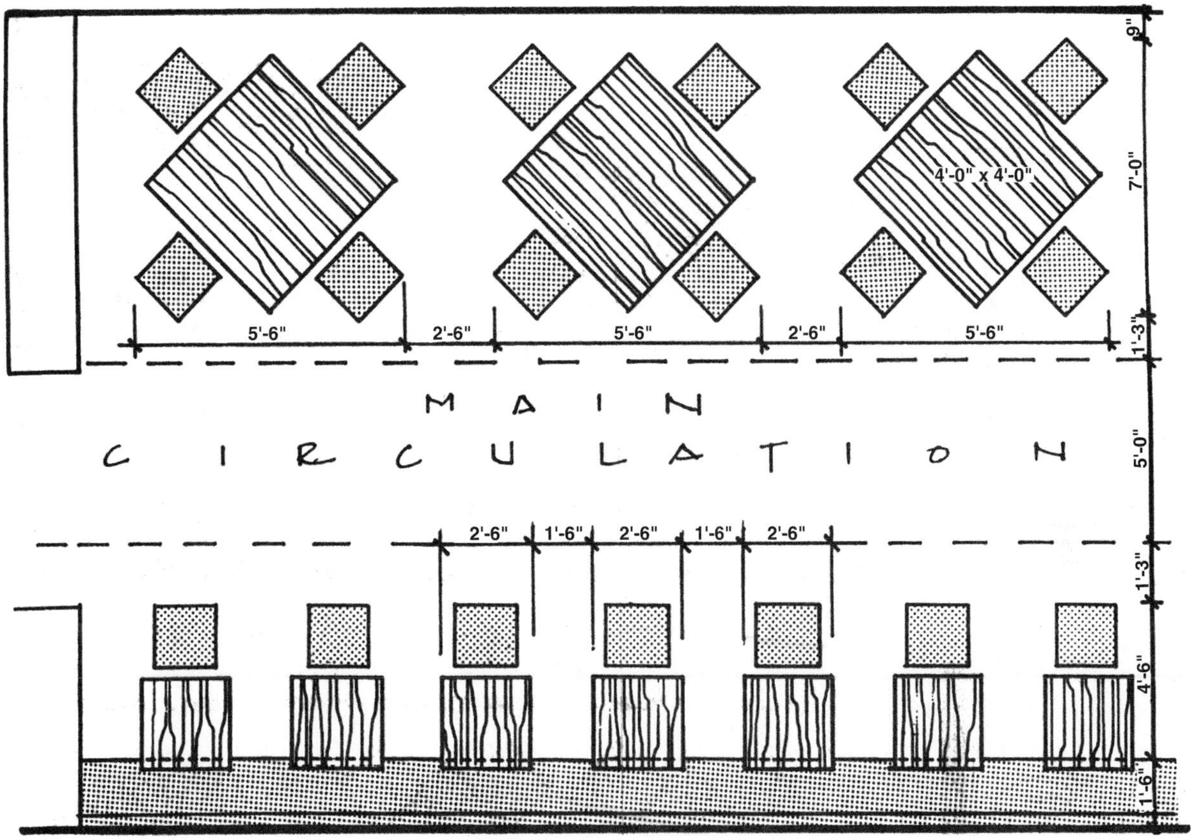

Fig. 8 33 ft × 22 ft, 726 ft^2, seats 26

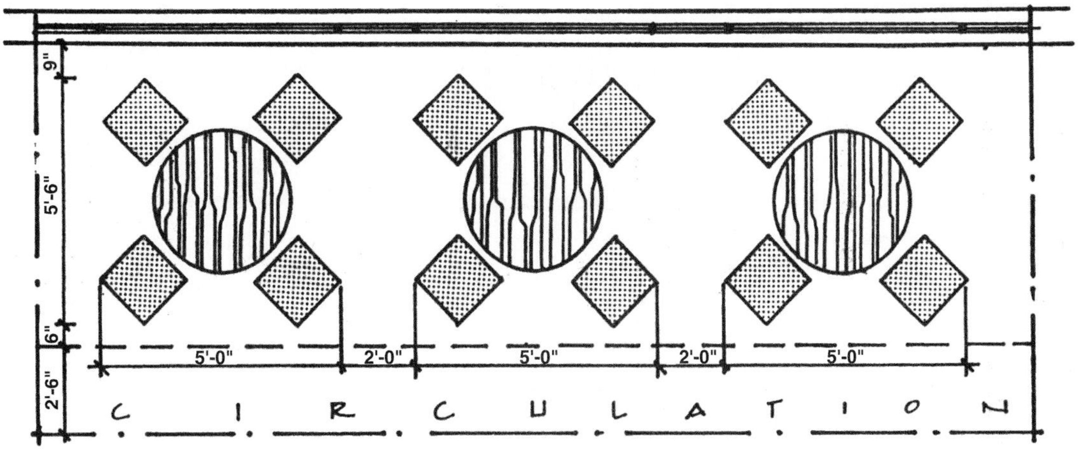

Fig. 9 11 ft × 28 ft, 308 ft^2, seats 12

RESTAURANTS
Tables: Design Criteria

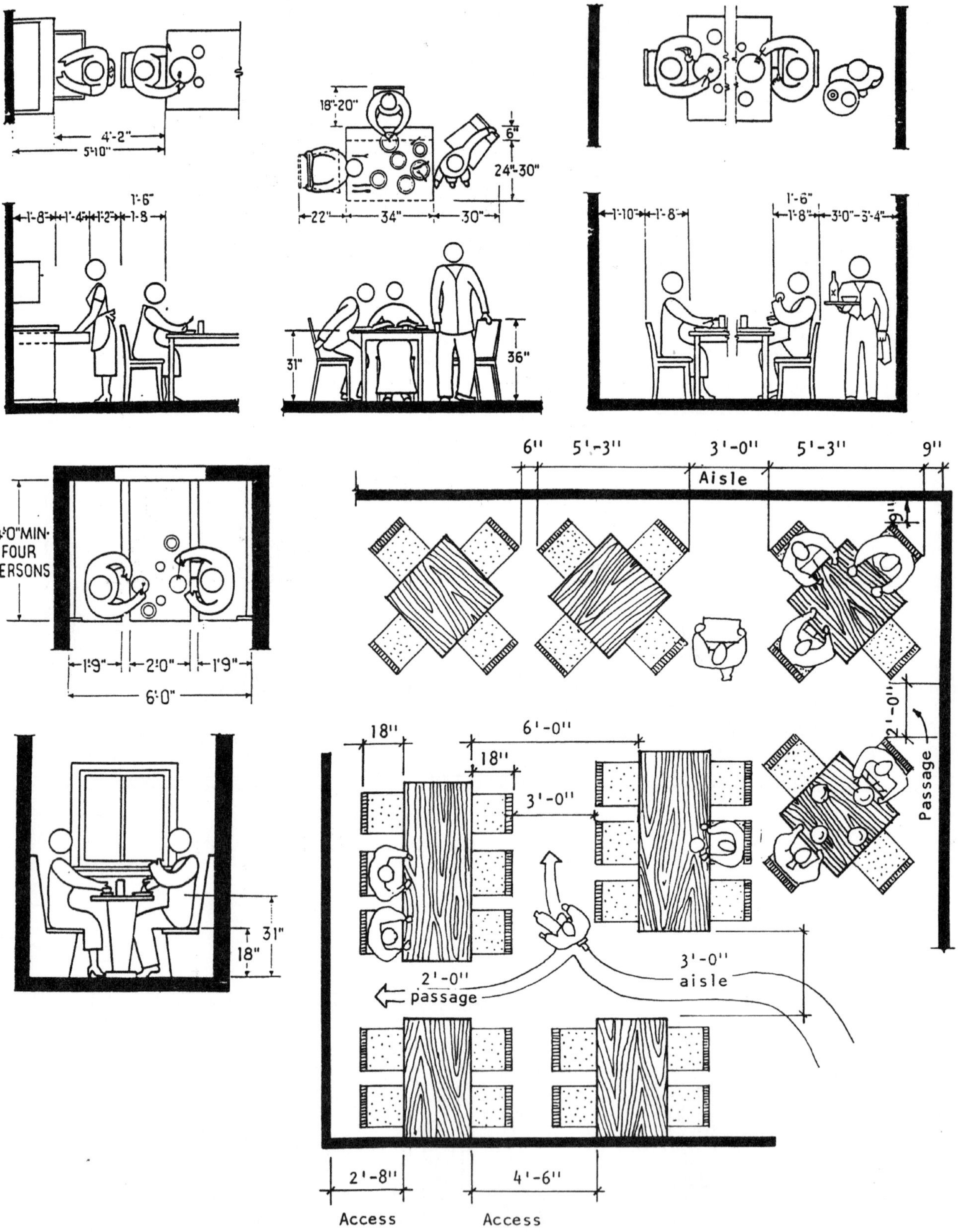

Fig. 10 These drawings highlight several critical dimensions that the designer must consider. Aisle circulation must be adequate in width; other clearances to consider include chair depth from edge of table and clearance between chairs. While laying out chair and table arrangements, a designer must anticipate the potential conflict between a patron leaving a seat and a tray-carrying waiter

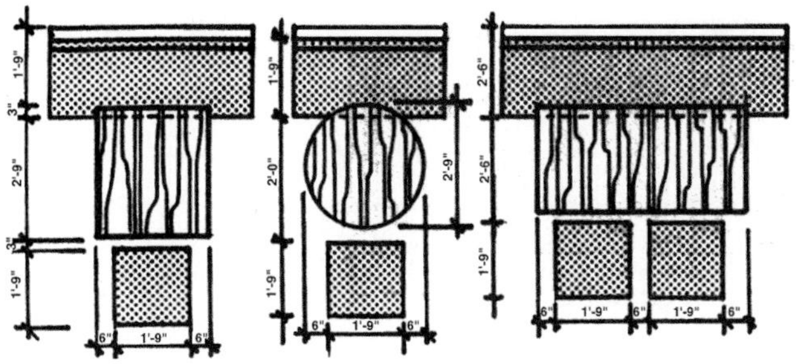

Fig. 11 Mixed banquette seating

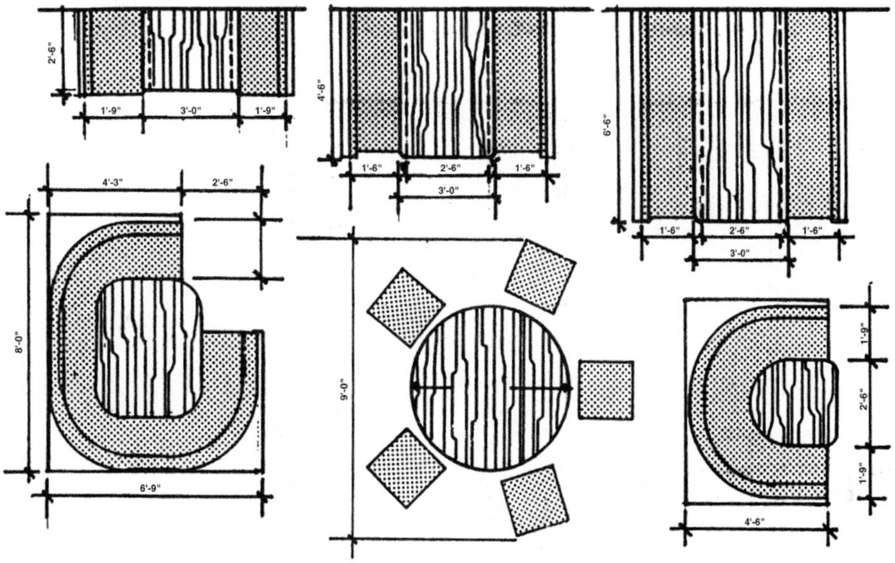

Fig. 12 Banquettes for two, four, and six persons

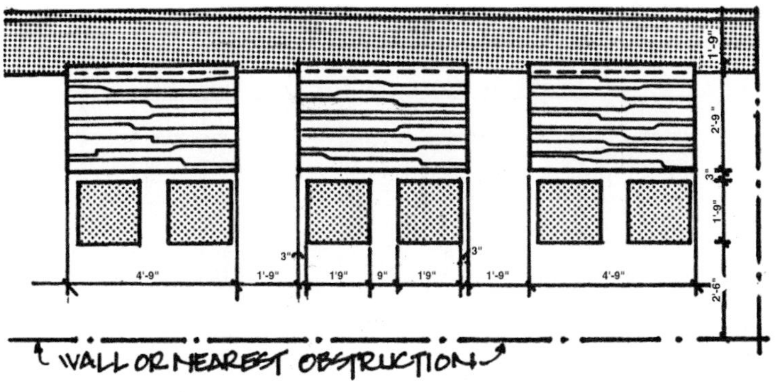

Fig. 13 21 ft × 19 ft, 189 ft^2, seats 12

RESTAURANTS

Types and Sizes of Booth Arrangements

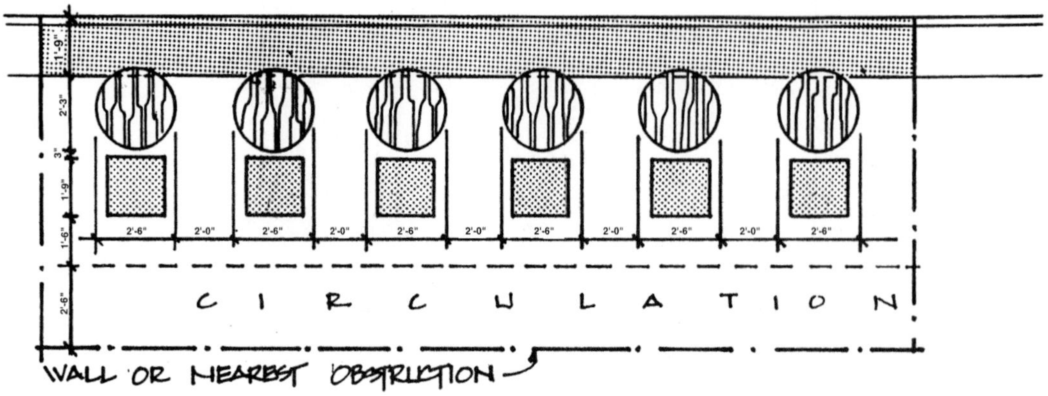

Fig. 14 27 ft × 10 ft, 270 ft², seats 12

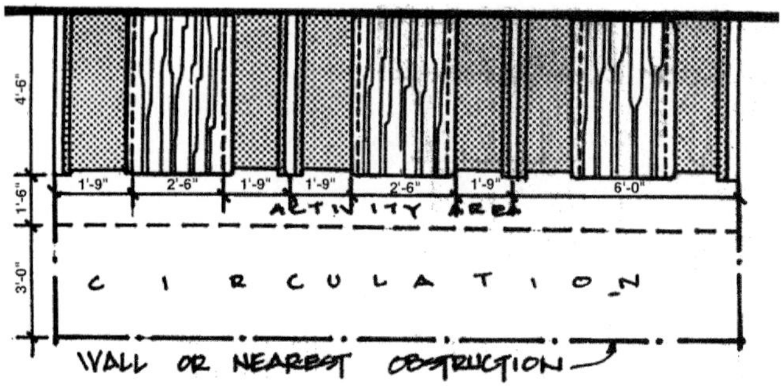

Fig. 15 19 ft × 9 ft, 171 ft², seats 12

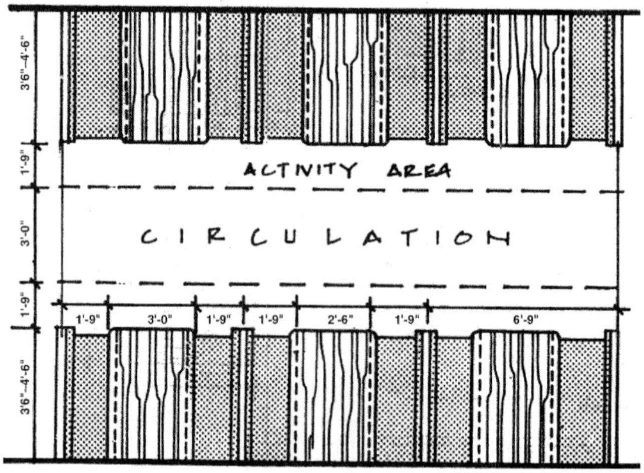

Fig. 16 19 ft × 15 ft, 285 ft², seats 24

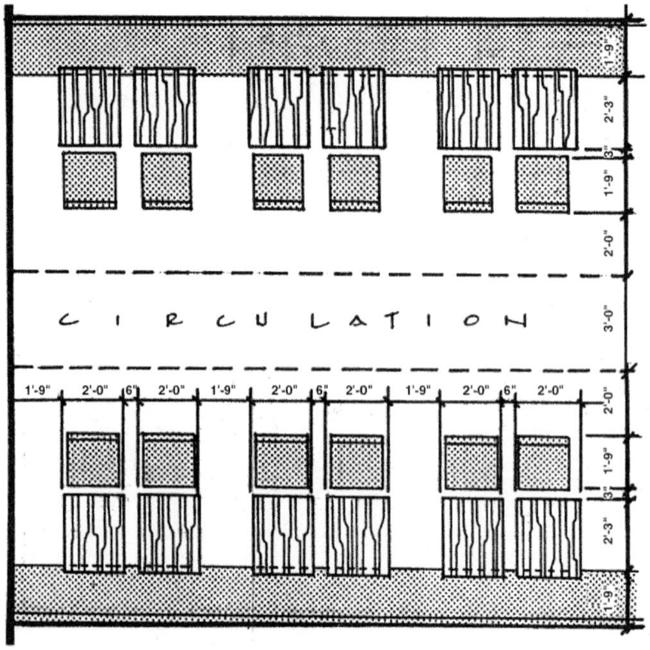

Fig. 17 21 ft × 19 ft, 400 ft², seats 24

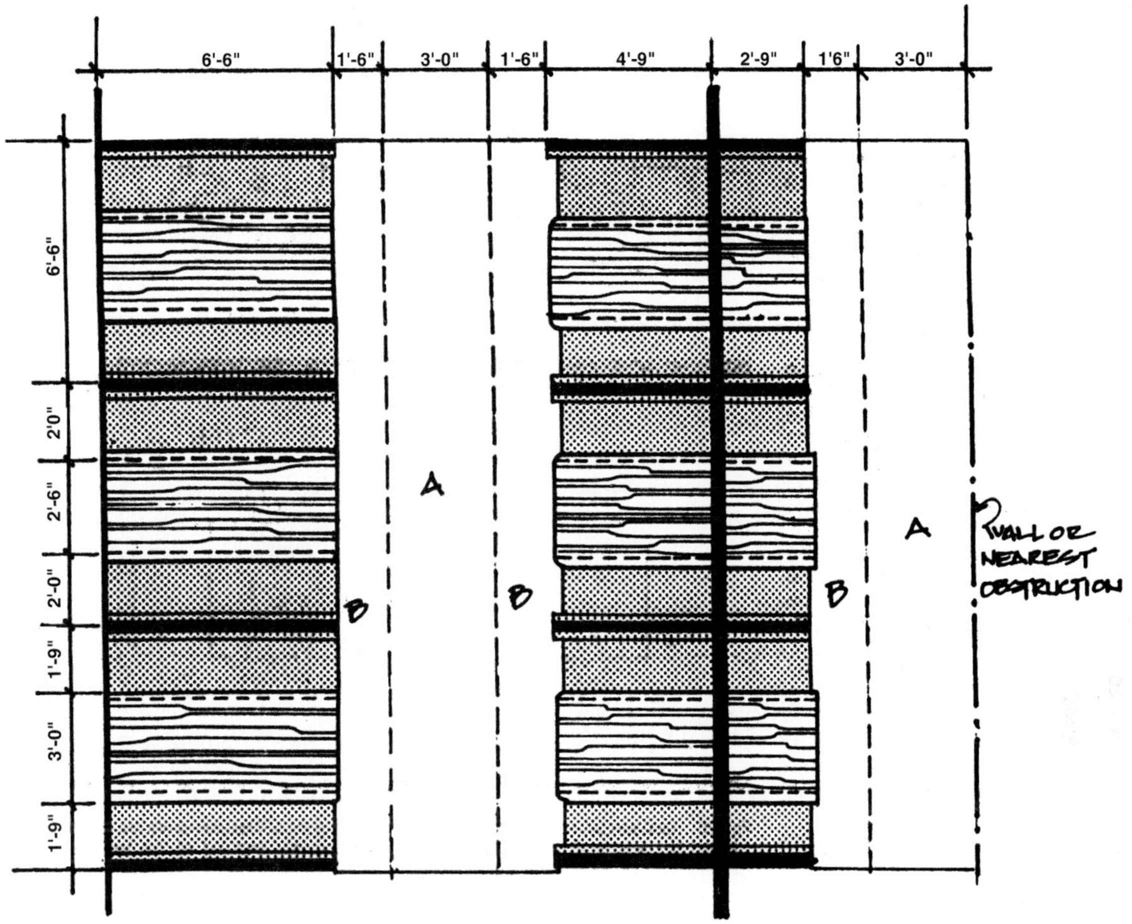

Fig. 18 24 ft × 20 ft, 480 ft², seats 36. A = main circulation, B = activity zone

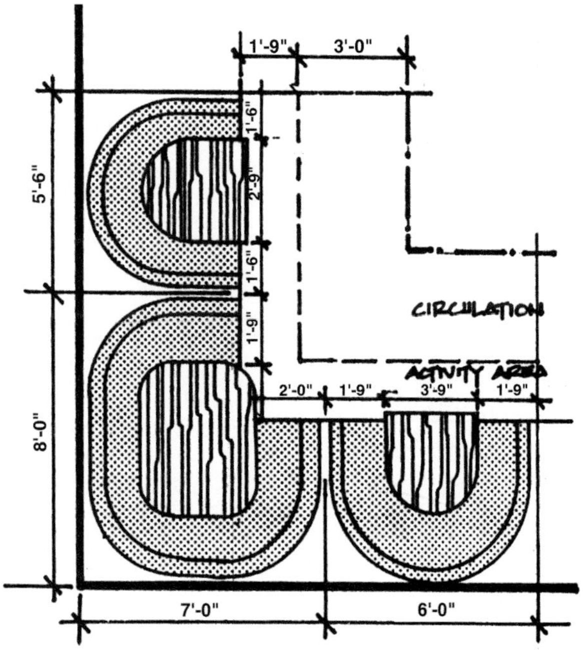

Fig. 19 13 ft × 13 ft, 169 ft², seats 16

RESTAURANTS
Dining Room Seating

Restaurant and Dining Room Seating

Dispersed seating suitable for guests with restricted mobility should be available in restaurants, coffee shops, and dining facilities. As a guide, the Uniform Federal Accessibility Standards (UFAS) require a minimum of 5 percent of restaurant seating to be accessible. Accessible aisles should connect the entrance to these locations, public rest rooms, and self-service areas such as salad bars, condiment stands, or buffet tables. Comfortable seating for waiting should be available to customers near the entrance.

A variety of accessible seating should be available, suitable for large and small dining groups. Small tables may not be accessible to guests in wheelchairs because of the restricted knee space. Therefore, a party of one or two may require a table usually set up for four. Restaurants or coffee shops with built-in seating, such as booths or banquettes, should also provide some chairs for guests who have difficulty getting into and out of bench seating. These chairs can be removed to seat guests in wheelchairs. Where seating areas are raised on platforms, accessible seating and similar services should be available on the main-floor level, or a ramp to the upper level should be provided.

Aisles serving accessible seating should be at least 3 ft 0 in wide, which typically requires a 6 ft 0 in clearance between parallel tables, or 4 ft 6 in between rotated tables. (See Fig. 21). Aisle widths should also provide room for customers to be seated at tables. At least a 2 ft 6 in clear space should be available behind each seating location. This space allows chairs to be withdrawn from the table and staff to assist guests in repositioning chairs close to the table.

For wheelchair seating, a 3 ft 0 in to 3 ft 6 in aisle is necessary, depending on the width of the knee space. (See Fig. 25.) Wheelchairs positioned at tables project approximately 5 in farther into aisles than most chairs. To allow guest with restricted mobility to turn around, seating arrangments should also include a 5 ft 0 in-diameter circle to T-shaped clear area at dead-end aisles.

Dining Tables and Chairs

Accessible seating locations should allow guests with restricted mobility to dine with ambulatory customers. Tables should provide knee space for customers in wheelchairs, and dining chairs should be coordinated to provide comfortable seating at the same table height.

Dining room chairs should be stable to maintain balance as guests seat themselves, and they should be comfortable to sit in during dinner. Chairs should be light and easy to reposition. The seat should have a slight slant to the rear to transfer body weight to the back of the chair. However, an exaggerated incline makes it difficult to rise. The seat should be approximately 16 in deep and at least 16 in wide to allow space for customers to reposition themselves during the meal. Padding or cushions on the chair seat should be firm, and the chair back should also be slightly inclined to the rear. To help guests sit and rise, dining chairs should have armrests 7 to 8 in above the front edge of the seat. (See Fig. 22.) Supports or cross-bracing should not interfere with kick-space below the seat, so the feet can be positioned to rise. The front edge of the chair seat should be low enough to allow the feet to rest on the floor, but not so low that it is difficult to rise. This is determined by the lower leg length (popliteal height), which varies between 15 and 20 in for most adults.

The height of the chair seat should be 10½ to 11½ in below the top of the table. Common seat heights vary between 14 and 18 in. Because the height of wheelchair seats is typically 19 in, a relatively high chair seat is necessary to coordinate with the table height. A chair with an 18-in-high seat is comfortable for most ambulatory guests and closely approximates the height of a wheelchair seat.

Dining room tables should have a stable surface at a convenient height and knee space and legroom below the tabletop for customers in wheelchairs. Narrow table configurations allow face-to-face seating, which reduces the distance between diners, making conversation easier and table lighting more effective. For safety, the corners and edges of the top should be rounded.

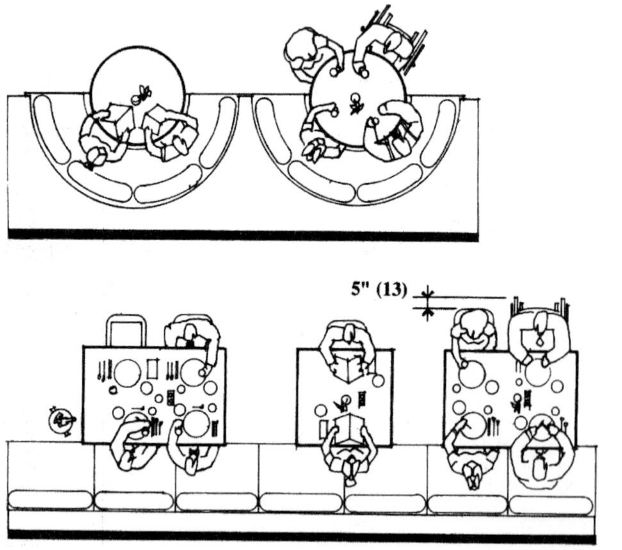

Fig. 20 Restaurants or coffee shops with fixed seating should include some movable seating for guests in wheelchairs and guests who have difficulty getting into and out of the bench seating. Number in parentheses is dimension in centimeters

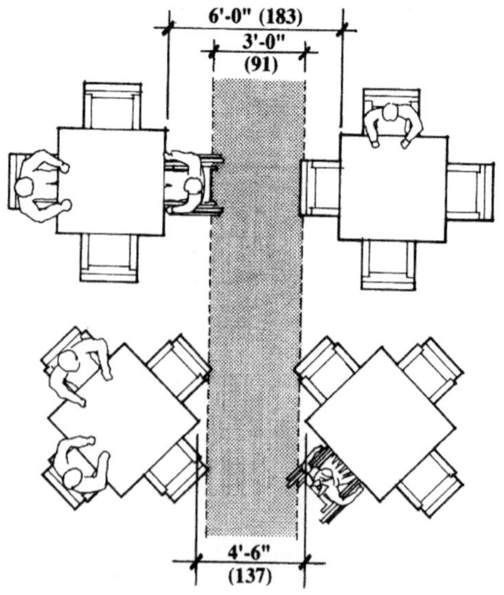

Fig. 21 Aisles serving accessible seating should provide a path at least 3 ft 0 in wide for passage and clear space for guests to seat themselves at tables. Numbers in parentheses are dimensions in centimeters

Full-height wheelchair knee space is 2 ft 6 in, which requires tabletops to be at least 2 ft 7 in above the floor—too high for most seating. Many wheelchairs now provide adjustable or two-tier armrests, which allow customers to sit close to tables in a knee space only 2 ft 3 in high. To provide this knee space, the tabletop (without an apron) should be 2 ft 4½ in to 2 ft 5 in above the floor. This is 11 to 11½ in above the chair seat, 10½ to 11 in above the seat of wheelchairs, and convenient for both. This knee space also permits the armrests of chairs to pass below the tabletop so seated customers can draw close. This combination of tables and chairs is suitable for the majority of wheelchair users and most ambulatory guests. (See Fig. 23.)

Foot room is important for customers with wheelchairs or leg braces. The footrests of wheelchairs are 2½ to 3 in above the ground and angled slightly forward, which requires 1 ft 7 in of foot room, measured from the edge of the tabletop. The outside width of footrests is only 1 ft 6 in, but 2 ft 6 in of side-to-side clearance is necessary to maneuver into position beneath the table. To provide knee space, table legs should be at least 2 ft 6 in apart, and the tabletop, for face-to-face seating, should be 3 ft 6 in wide. Pedestal-base tables should have low, tapered bases and a minimum diameter of 3 ft 6 in, although 4 ft 0 in is preferred.

A portable raised leaf should be available to modify tables for customers in wheelchairs with high armrests. The leaf should be approximately the size of a place setting, 1 ft 4 in by 2 ft 0 in, and secured to the underside of the of an accessible table with clamps. The raised leaf should project 6 in beyond the edge of the table and provide 2 ft 6 in clearance above the floor. (See Fig. 24.)

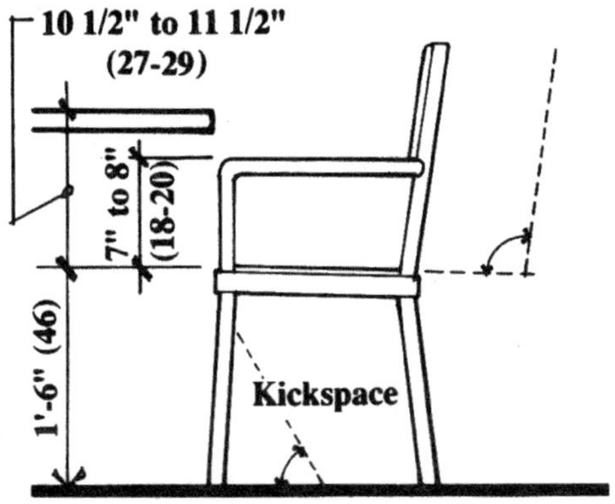

Fig. 22 Dining room chairs should have a seat 10½ to 11½ in below the top of the table and armrests 7 to 8 in above the seat. To coordinate with an accessible table, the seat height should be 18 in. Numbers in parentheses are dimensions in centimeters

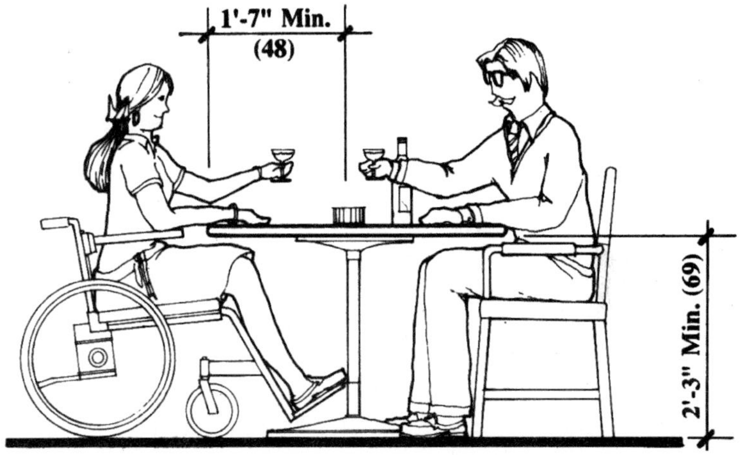

Fig. 23 Accessible tables should provide knee space at least 2 ft 3 in high by 2 ft 6 in wide with 1 ft 7 in of foot room. To increase the knee space height, a raised portable leaf can be provided. (See Fig. 24.) Numbers in parentheses are dimensions in centimeters

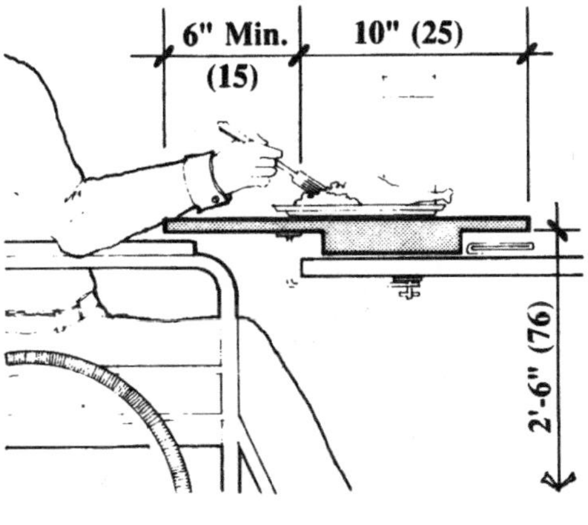

Kneespace Width	Clearance
2'-6" (minimum)	3'-6"
3'-0" or greater	3'-0"

Fig. 24 A portable raised leaf can be provided for accessible tables to accommodate customers in wheelchairs with high armrests. Numbers in parentheses are dimensions in centimeters

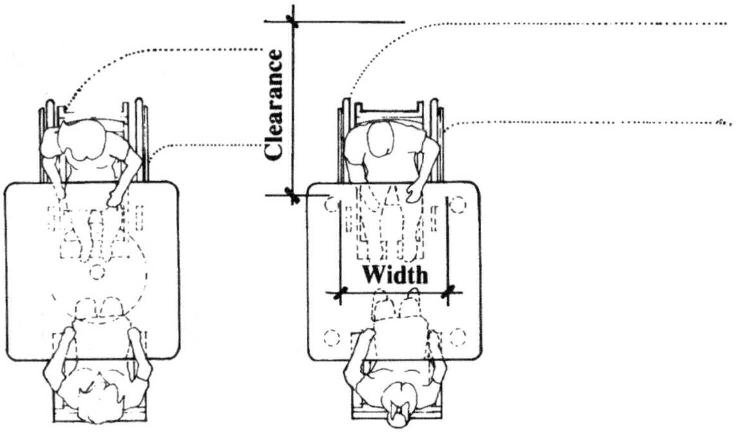

Fig. 25 The necessary maneuvering room required to access a knee space depends on its width

RESTAURANTS
Hostess Station

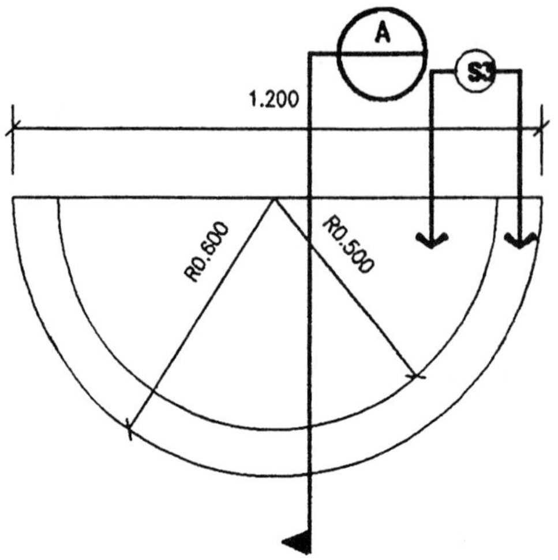

PLAN VIEW

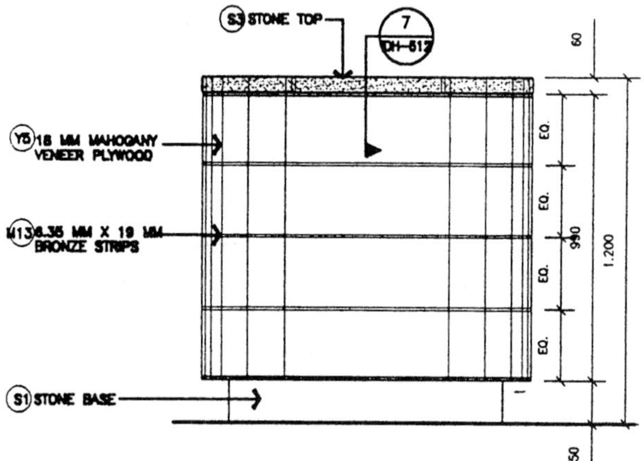

FRONT ELEVATION

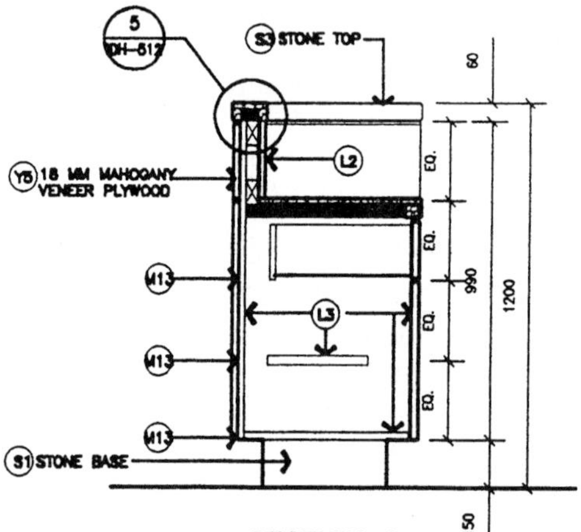

SECTION A

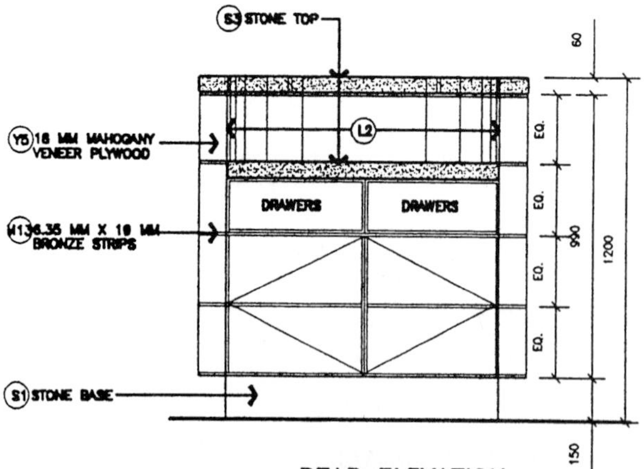

REAR ELEVATION

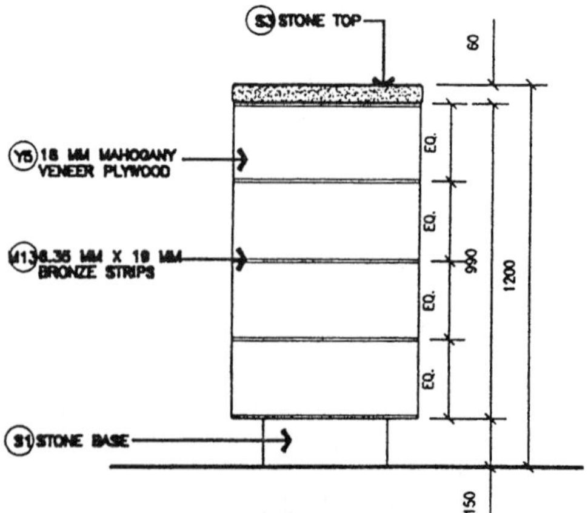

SIDE ELEVATION

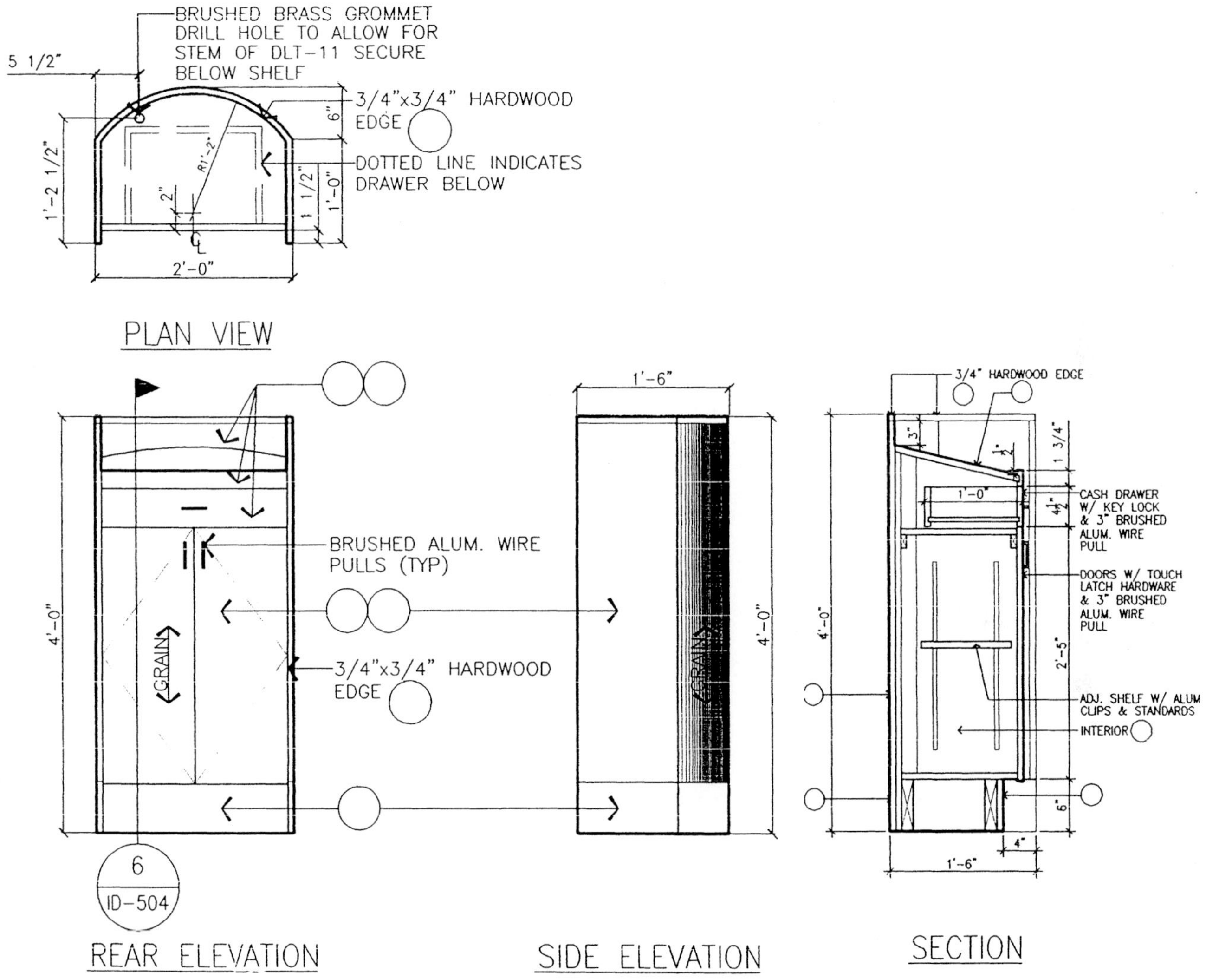
BRUSHED BRASS GROMMET DRILL HOLE TO ALLOW FOR STEM OF DLT-11 SECURE BELOW SHELF
5 1/2"
3/4"x3/4" HARDWOOD EDGE
6"
DOTTED LINE INDICATES DRAWER BELOW
1'-2 1/2"
2"
1 1/2"
1'-0"
2'-0"
PLAN VIEW
BRUSHED ALUM. WIRE PULLS (TYP)
3/4"x3/4" HARDWOOD EDGE
GRAIN
4'-0"
6
ID-504
REAR ELEVATION
1'-6"
4'-0"
SIDE ELEVATION
3/4" HARDWOOD EDGE
CASH DRAWER W/ KEY LOCK & 3" BRUSHED ALUM. WIRE PULL
1'-0"
DOORS W/ TOUCH LATCH HARDWARE & 3" BRUSHED ALUM. WIRE PULL
ADJ. SHELF W/ ALUM CLIPS & STANDARDS
INTERIOR
4'-0"
2'-5"
1 3/4"
6"
4"
1'-6"
SECTION

RESTAURANTS
Cashier's Station

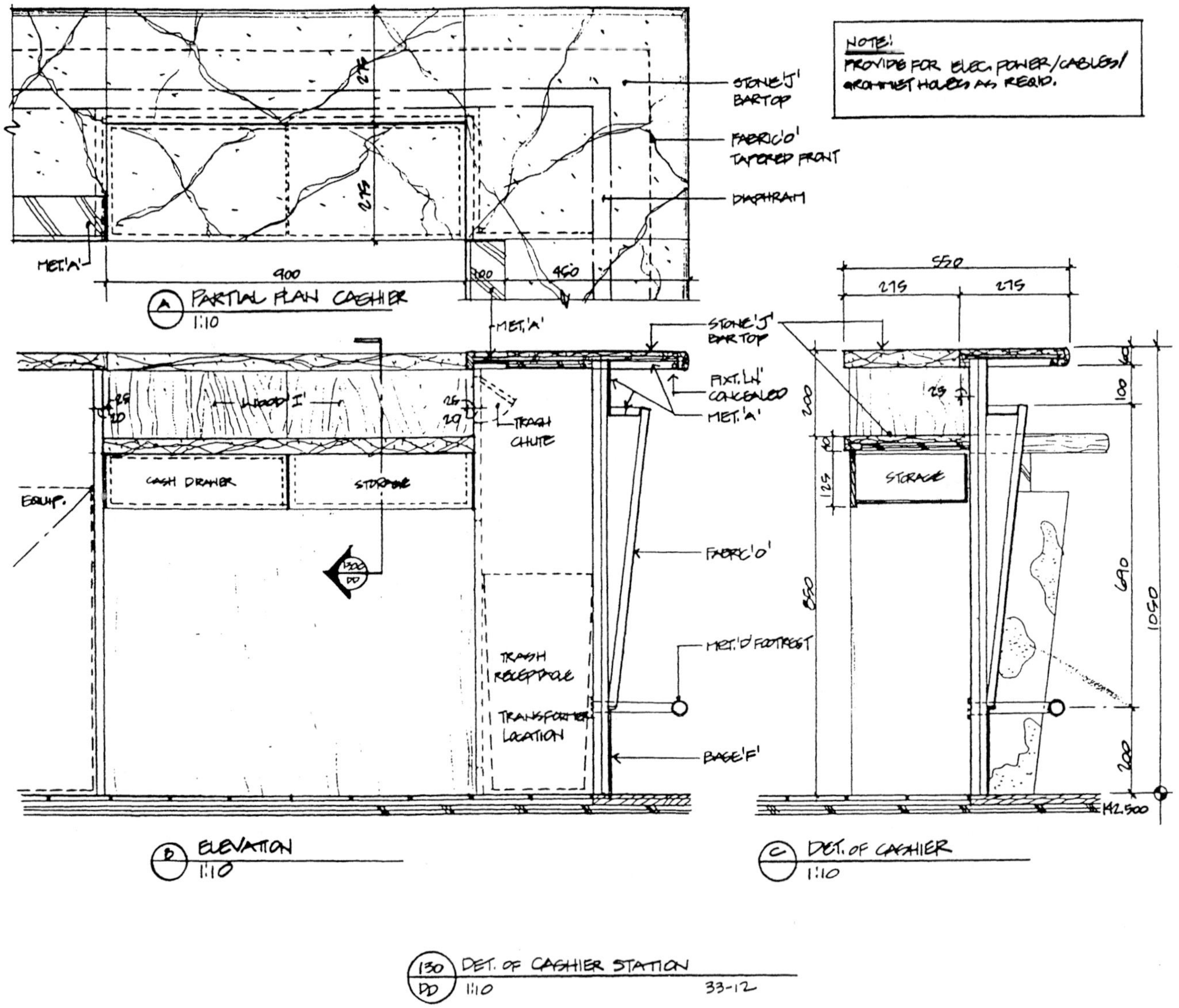
NOTE:
PROVIDE FOR ELEC. POWER/CABLES/ GROMMET HOLES AS REQ'D.
STONE 'J' BARTOP
FABRIC 'O' TAPERED FRONT
DIAPHRAM
MET. 'A'
900
200
460
A PARTIAL PLAN CASHIER
1:10
STONE 'J' BAR TOP
FIXT. 'LN' CONCEALED
MET. 'A'
WOOD 'I'
TRASH CHUTE
CASH DRAWER
STORAGE
EQUIP.
FABRIC 'O'
MET. 'D' FOOTREST
TRASH RECEPTACLE
TRANSFORMER LOCATION
BASE 'F'
550
275
275
100
690
1050
200
142.500
B ELEVATION
1:10
C DET. OF CASHIER
1:10
130 DD DET. OF CASHIER STATION
1:10
33-12

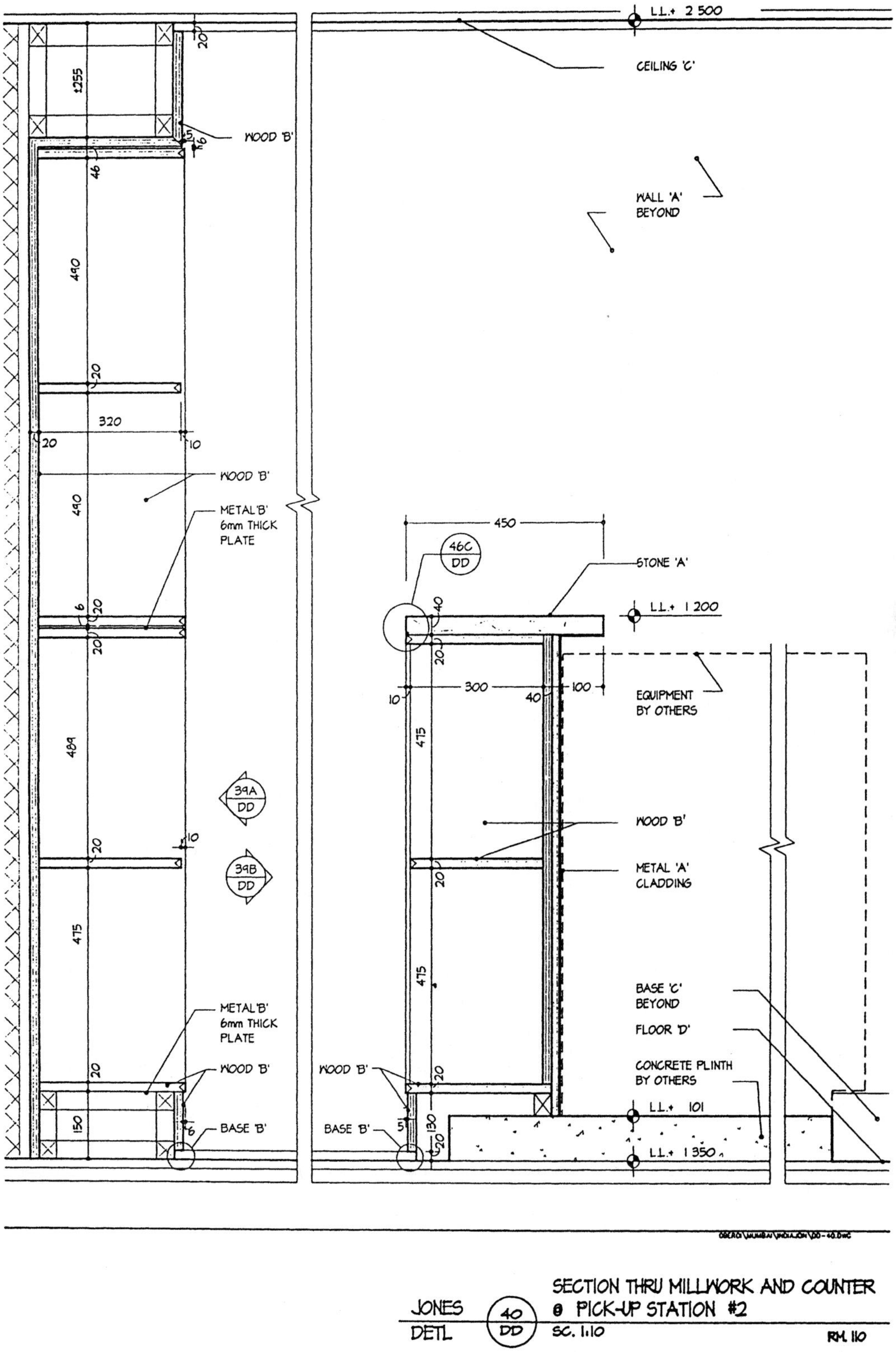
L.L.+ 2 500
CEILING 'C'
WOOD 'B'
WALL 'A' BEYOND
320
WOOD 'B'
METAL 'B' 6mm THICK PLATE
450
46C DD
STONE 'A'
L.L.+ 1 200
300
100
EQUIPMENT BY OTHERS
39A DD
39B DD
WOOD 'B'
METAL 'A' CLADDING
BASE 'C' BEYOND
FLOOR 'D'
METAL 'B' 6mm THICK PLATE
WOOD 'B'
CONCRETE PLINTH BY OTHERS
L.L.+ 101
BASE 'B'
L.L.+ 1 350
SECTION THRU MILLWORK AND COUNTER
@ PICK-UP STATION #2
JONES
DETL
40 DD
SC. 1:10
RM. 110

RESTAURANTS
Banquettes: Design Criteria

Figure 26 shows the basic dimensions for the design of banquette seating. The lack of armrests makes it difficult to define seat boundaries. The user, therefore, tends to establish a territory by assuming a desired sitting posture and placing personal articles—such as a briefcase, purse, or package—next to him or her. Since the nature of this type of seating can permit some form of body contact, hidden dimensions and personal space also play an important part in how close the users sharing the banquette will sit.

Because of the many hidden psychological factors involved, the actual efficiency of this seating type in terms of capacity is questionable. Figure 27 indicates two possible seating situations, each dictated by the anthropometrics involved. One arrangment is based on the premise that the user's elbows will be extended, possibly in conjunction with some activity, such as reading, or simply as an attempt to stake out additional territory, as would be the case in the strategic positioning of some personal article on the seat. In this situation it

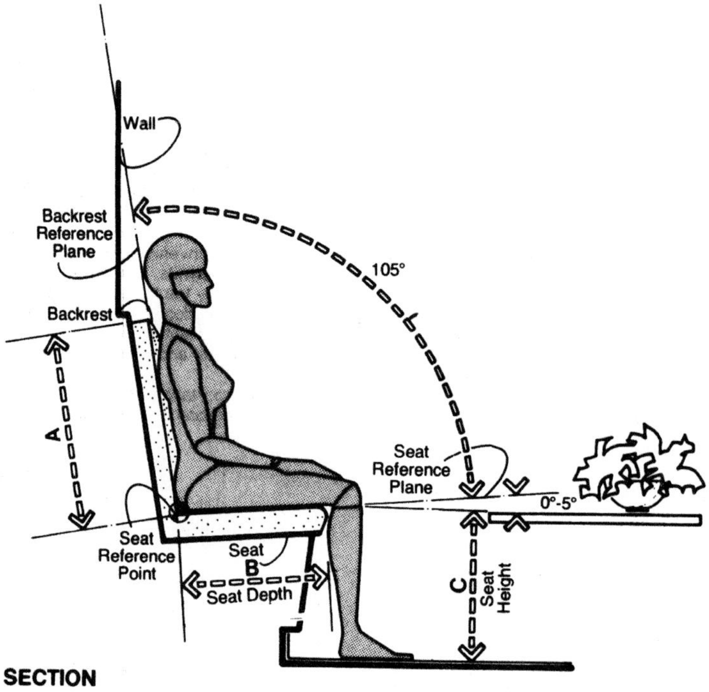

	in	cm
A	18–24	45.7–61.0
B	15.5–16	39.4–40.6
C	16–17	40.6–43.2
D	30	76.2
E	24	61.0

Fig. 26 Banquette seating

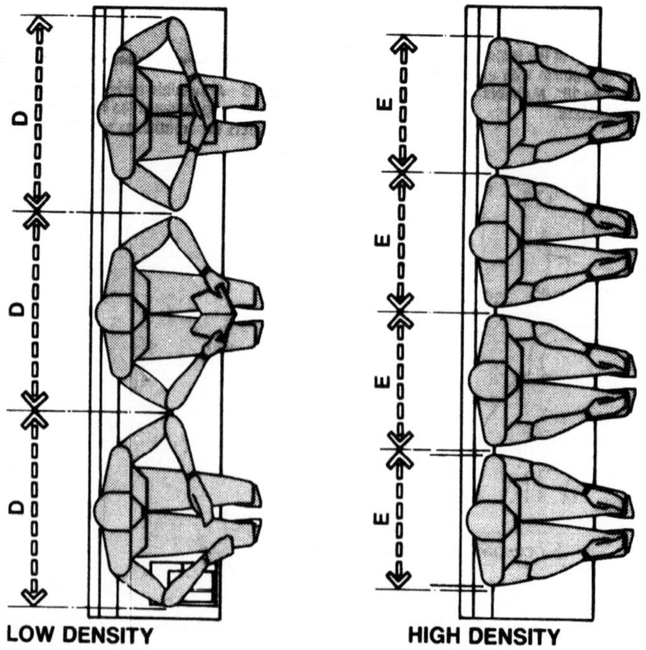

Fig. 27 Banquette seating

would be reasonable to assume that each user would take up about 30 in, or 76.2 cm, of space. The other diagram shows a more compact seating arrangement. Figure 26 shows a section through a typical banquette.

Banquette seating provides the designer with one of the few opportunities to custom design restaurant seating. While there can be a great variety of aesthetic solutions achieved through use of various materials, ergonomic considerations must be analyzed carefully. Specific attention should be given to depth of seat, slope of seat and back, height of back, and relationship of seat height to table height.

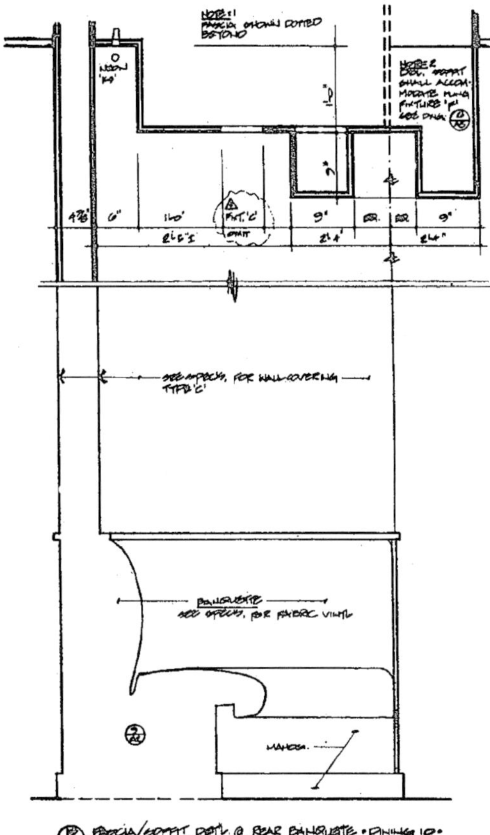

FASCIA/SOFFIT DETL. @ REAR BANQUETTE • DINING 10•

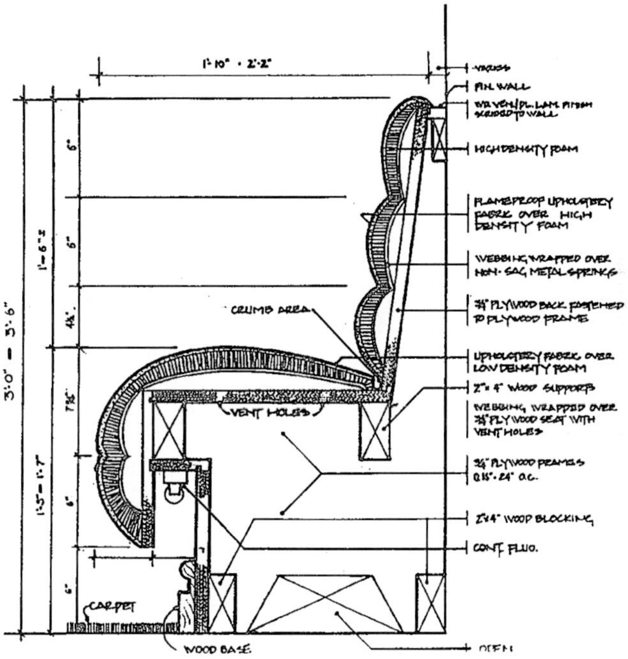

TYPICAL BANQUETTE DETAIL
SCALE 1½" = 1'-0"

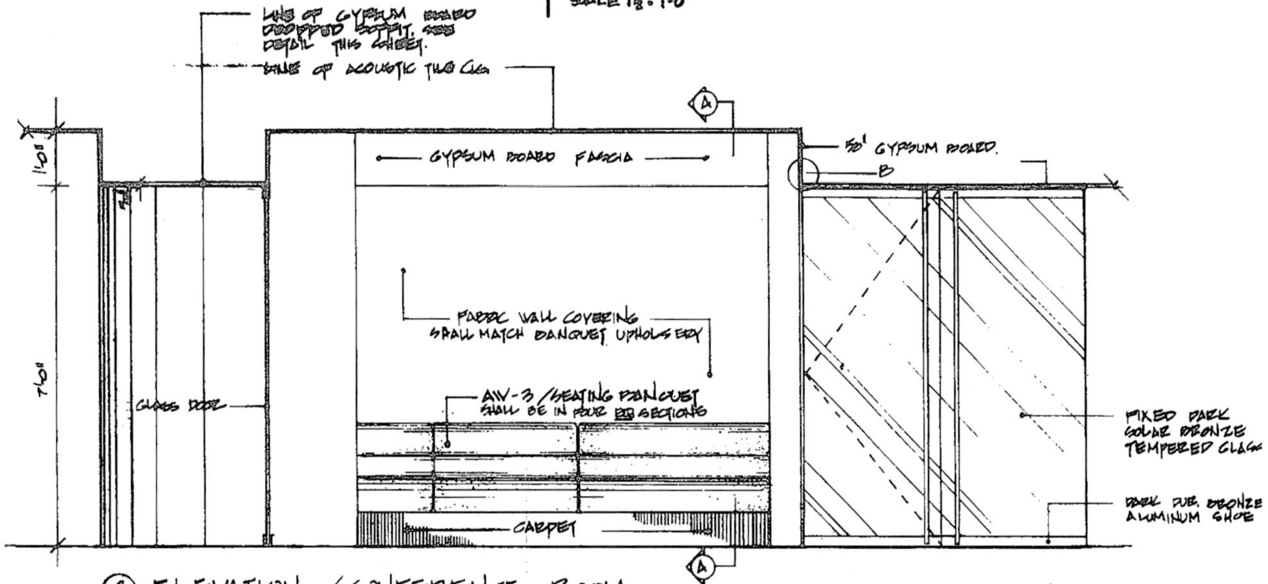

④ ELEVATION / CONFERENCE ROOM

RESTAURANTS

Banquette/Bench Seating Details

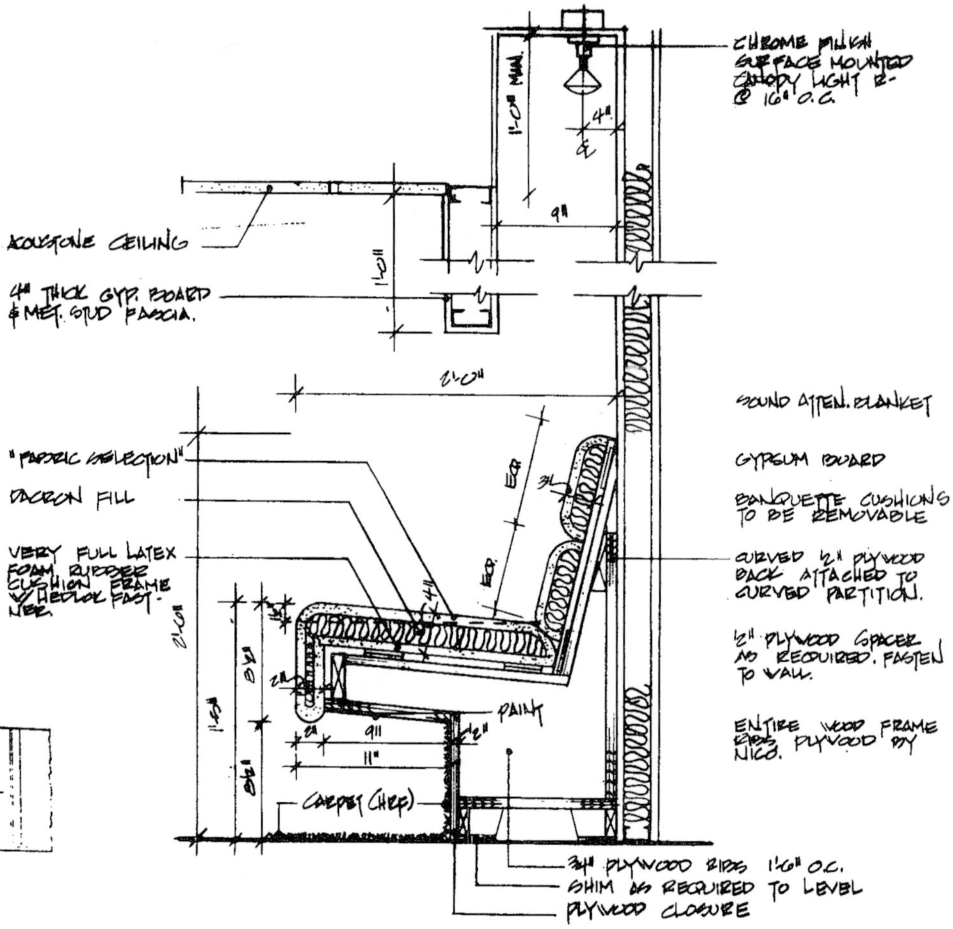

④ AW-3 / SECTION THRU BANQUETTE
SCALE 1/2" = 1'-0"

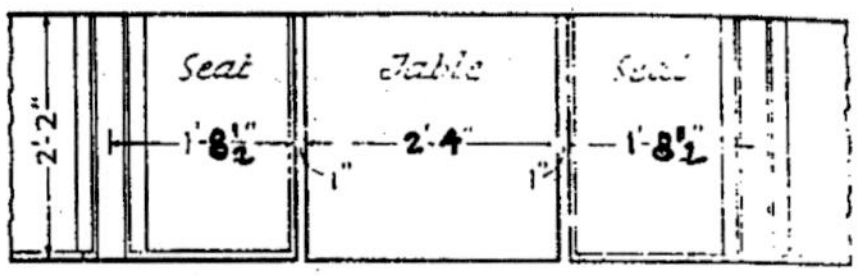

PLAN of SEATS 3/8" scale

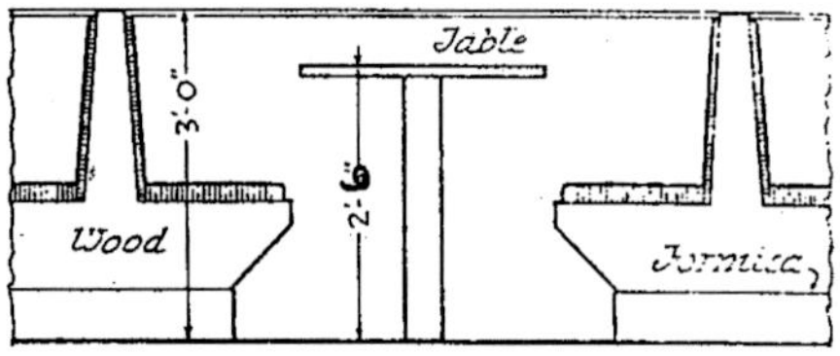

ELEVATION of SEATS

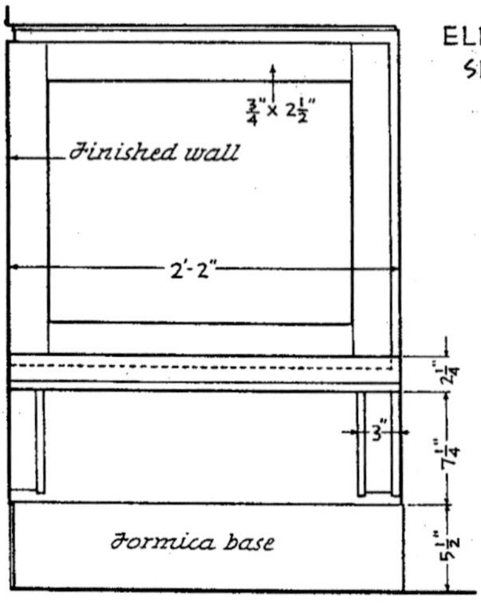

ELEVATION of SEAT BACK
1" scale

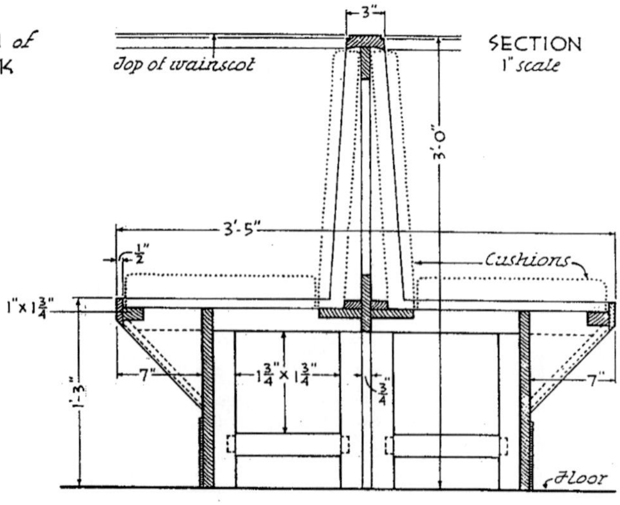

SECTION
1" scale

RESTAURANTS

Banquette/Bench Seating Details

Banquette seating can be detailed relatively simply, as Figs. 28 to 30 suggest. The simplest banquette may take the form of a plywood seating platform with a removable seat cushion or a box cushion seat and back support. Such seating is appropriate in fast-food or quick-turnover restaurant operations.

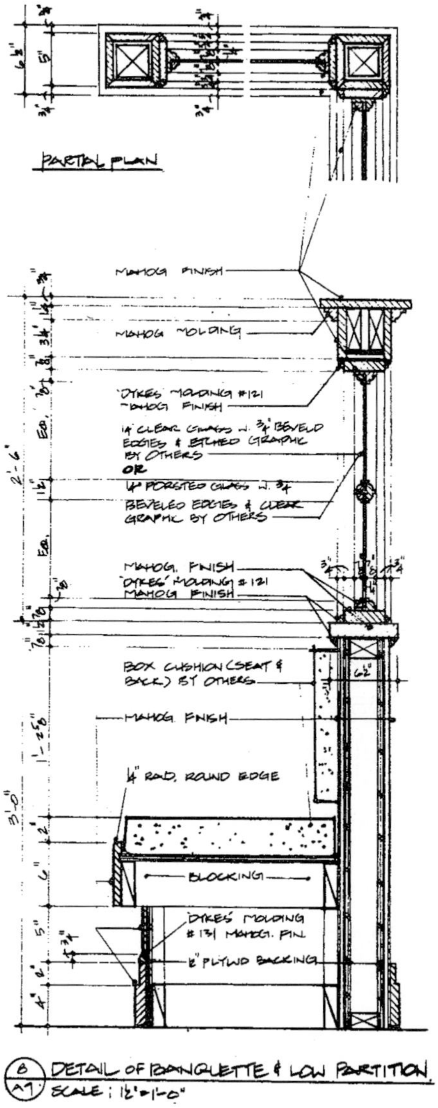

Fig. 28

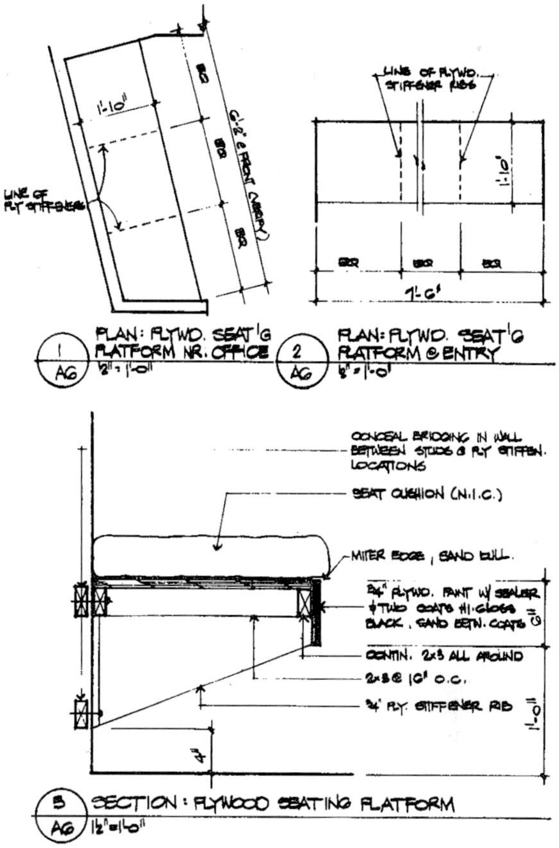

Fig. 29

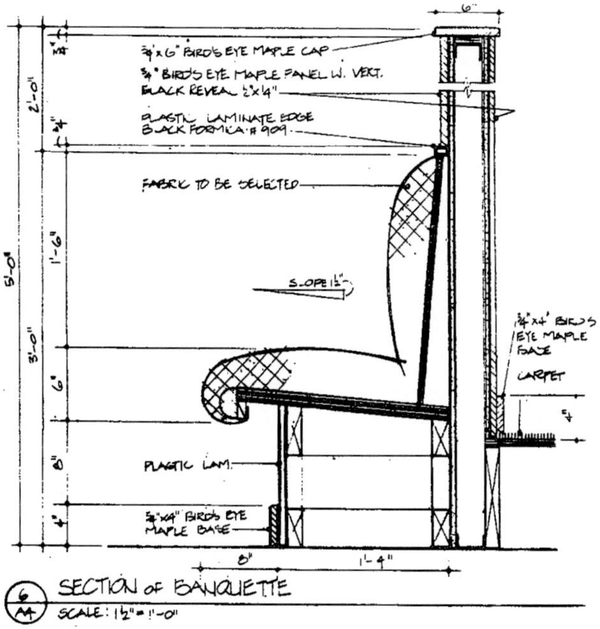

Fig. 30

RESTAURANTS
Booths

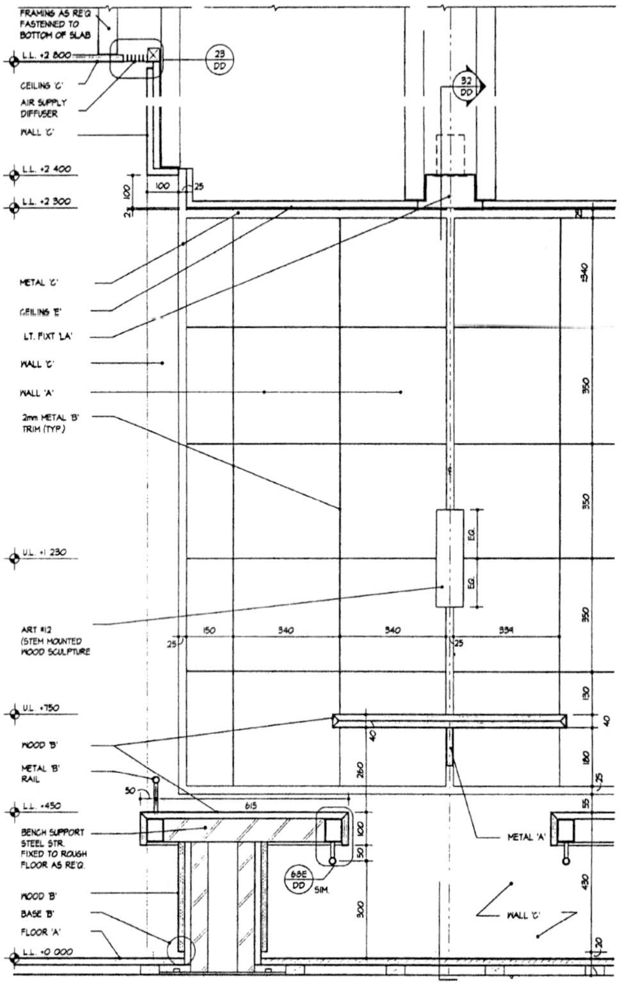

JONES DETL (33 DD) DETAIL SECTION THRU BOOTH DINING SC. 1:10 RM. 104

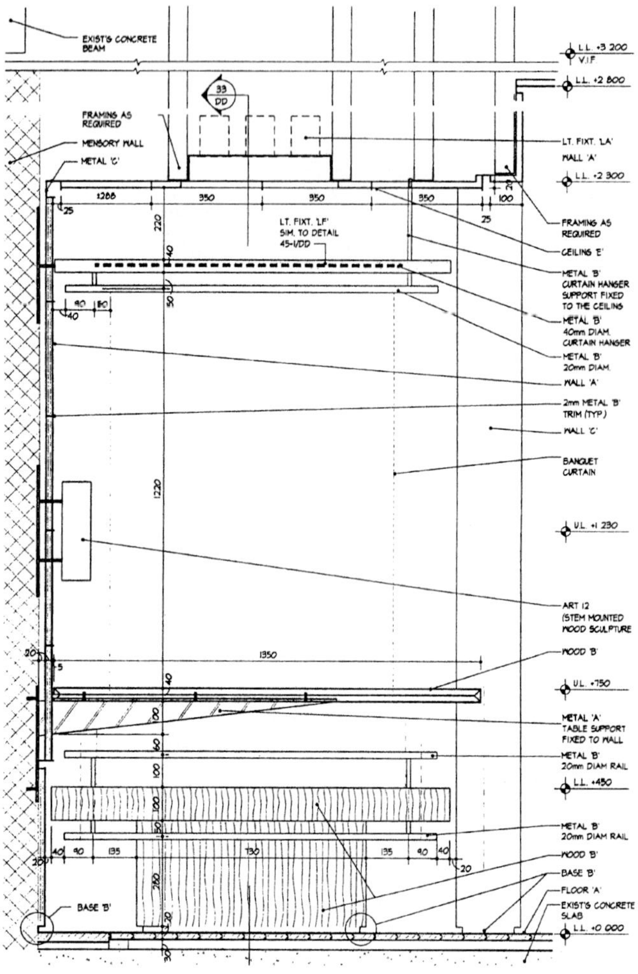

JONES DETL (32 DD) DETAIL SECTION THRU BOOTH DINING SC. 1:10 RM. 104

LUNCH COUNTERS: DESIGN CRITERIA

Figure 31 shows some of the basic clearances required for a typical counter: 36 in, or 91.4 cm, for work space behind the counter; 18 to 24 in, or 45.7 to 61 cm, for the countertop; and 60 to 66 in, or 152.4 to 167.6 cm, between the front face of the counter and the nearest obstruction. Figure 32 shows a section through the counter and back counter. Most counters are about 42 in, or 106.7 cm, in height. The clearance from the top of the seat to the underside of the countertop and the depth of the countertop overhang are extremely important. Buttock-knee length and thigh clearance are the key anthropometric measurements to consider for proper body fit. Footrest heights should take into consideration popliteal height. In most cases this is ignored, and 42-in counters are provided with 7-in, or 17.8-cm, footrests that are 23 in, or 58.4 cm, below the seat surface, which cannot work. The popliteal height of the larger user, based on 99th-percentile data, is only about 20 in, or 50.8 cm. Therefore, the feet dangle unsupported several inches above the footrest and the body is deprived of any stability. The footrest shown in Fig. 32, although higher, only serves a portion of the seated users and is intended primarily for standing patrons. The most logical solution is a separate footrest, integral with the stool.

	in	cm
A	60–66	152.4–167.6
B	18–24	45.7–61.0
C	36	91.4
D	24	61.0
E	12–18	30.5–45.7
F	35–36	88.9–91.4
G	42	106.7
H	30–31	76.2–78.7
I	11–12	27.9–30.5
J	10	25.4
K	12–13	30.5–33.0

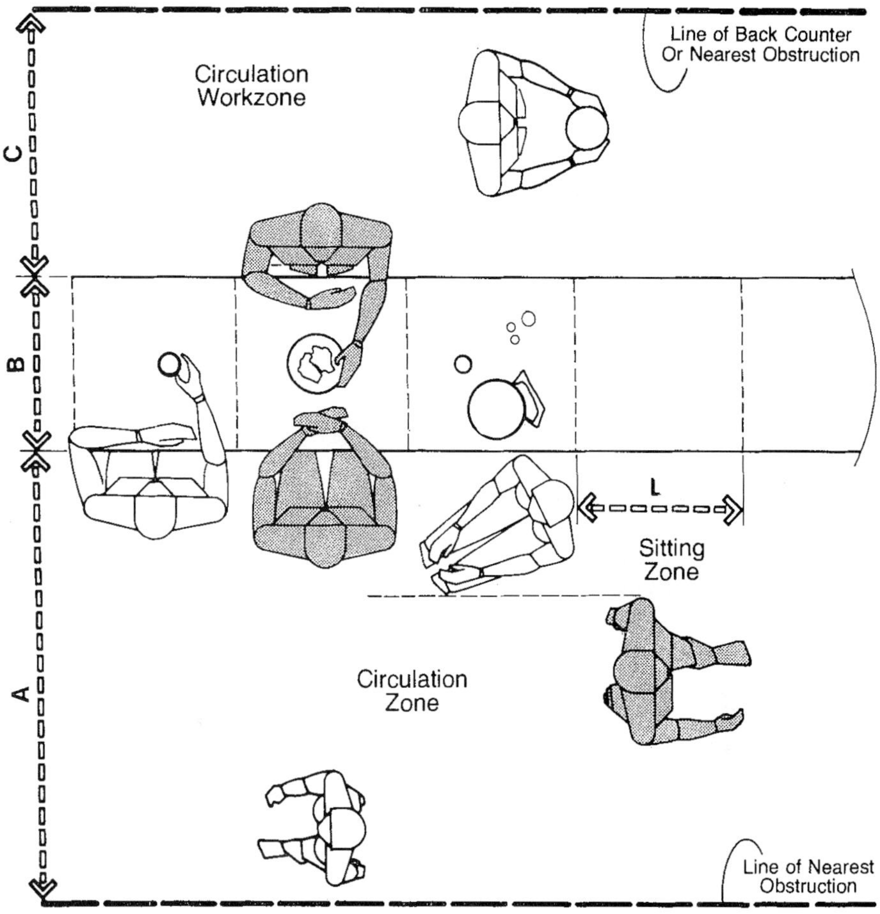

Fig. 31 Lunch counter

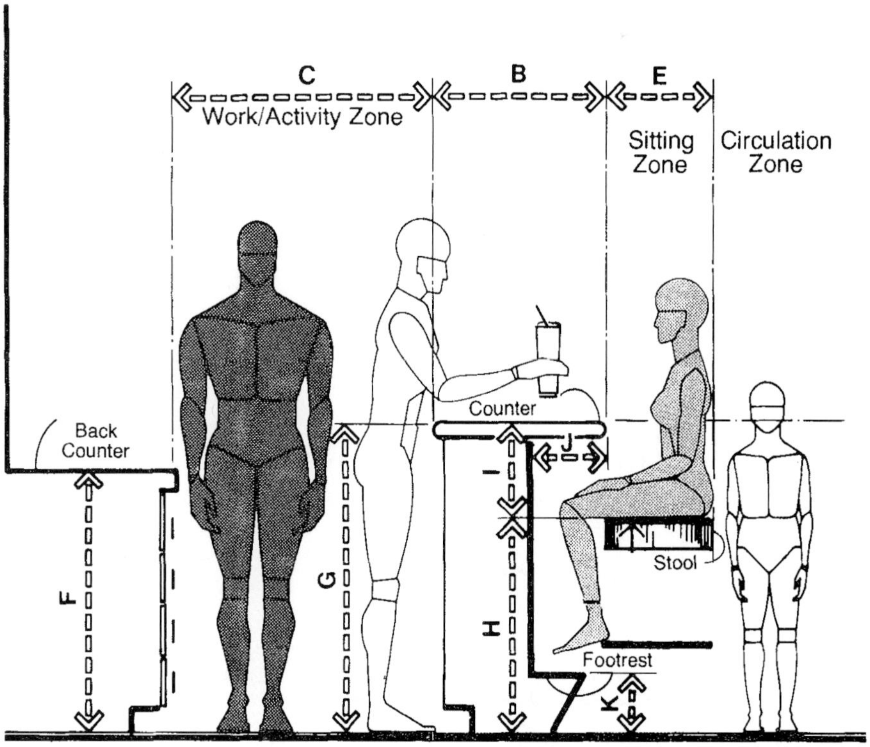

Fig. 32 Lunch counter

RESTAURANTS
Miscellaneous Counter Details

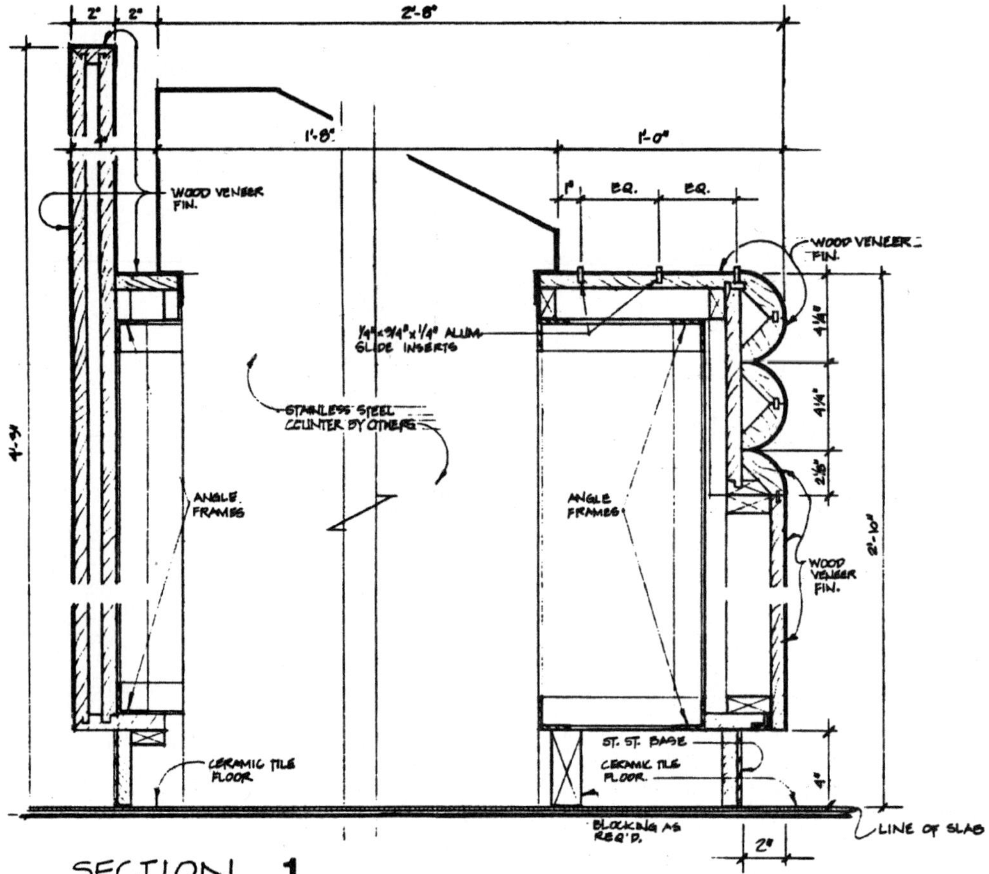

SECTION 1

SCALE 3" = 1'-0"

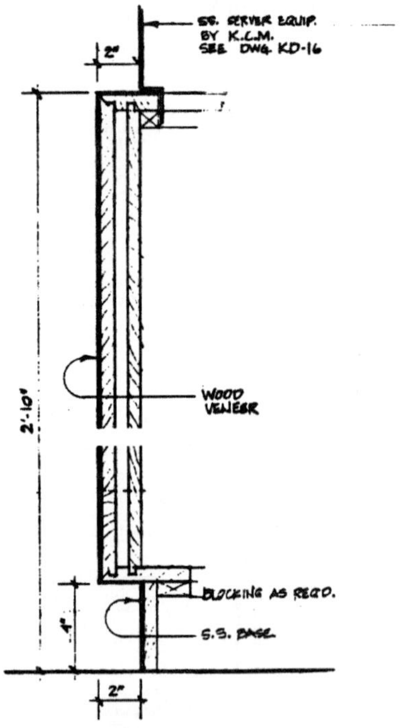

SECTION 2

SCALE: 3" = 1'-0"

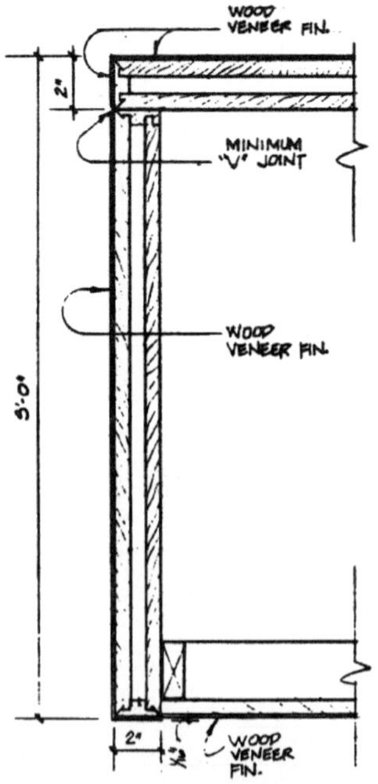

PLAN SECTION 3

SCALE: 3" = 1'-0"

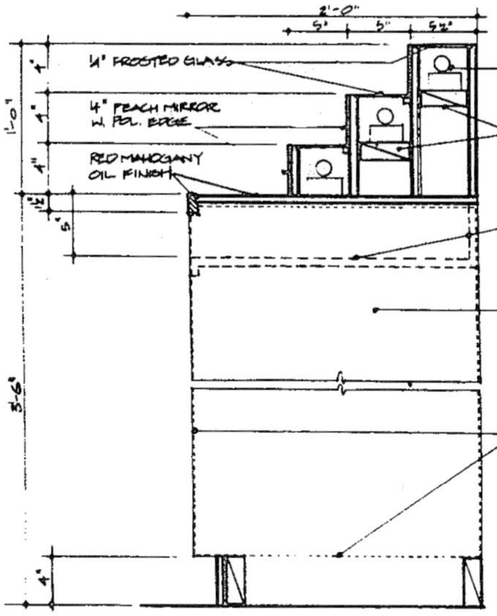

3/A9 SECT. of BACK BAR COUNTER W. LIQUER DISPLAY
SCALE: 1½"=1'-0"

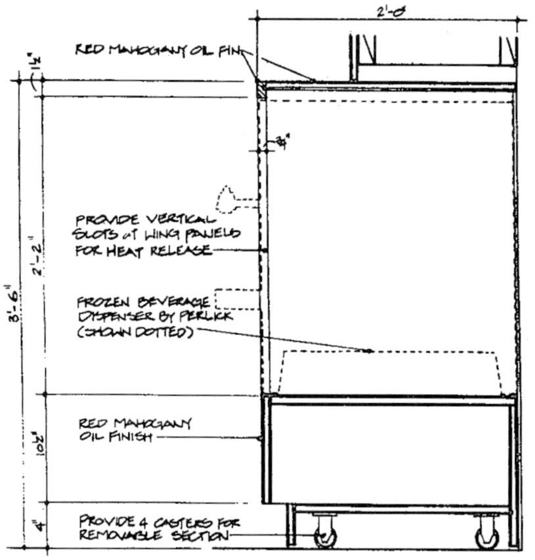

4/A9 SECT. of CABINET for FROZEN BEVERAGE DISPENSER
SCALE: 1½"=1'-0"

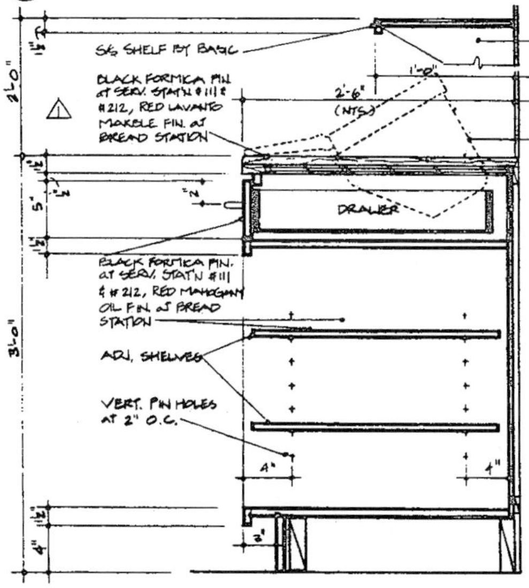

8/A9 CABINET DETAIL at SERVICE STATIONS # 111 & 212, BREAD ST'N # 113
SCALE: 1½"=1'-0"

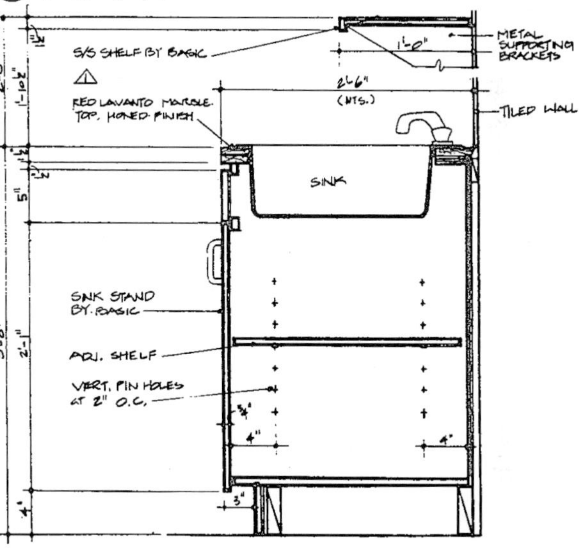

9/A9 CABINET DETAIL at KITCHEN #112
SCALE: 1½"=1'-0"

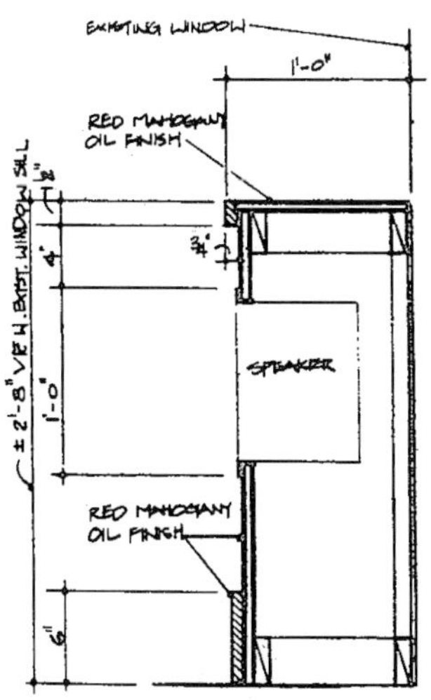

13/A9 DET. of WINDOW SILL CABINET
SCALE: 1½"=1'-0"

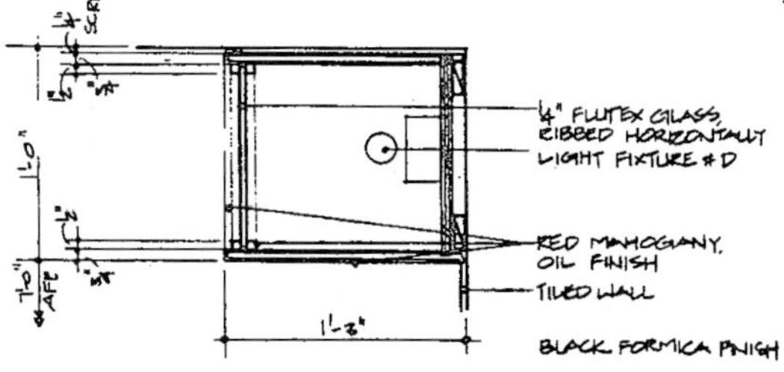

14/A9 LIGHT/CAB. ABOVE COUNTER at KITCHEN #112
SCALE: 1½"=1'-0"

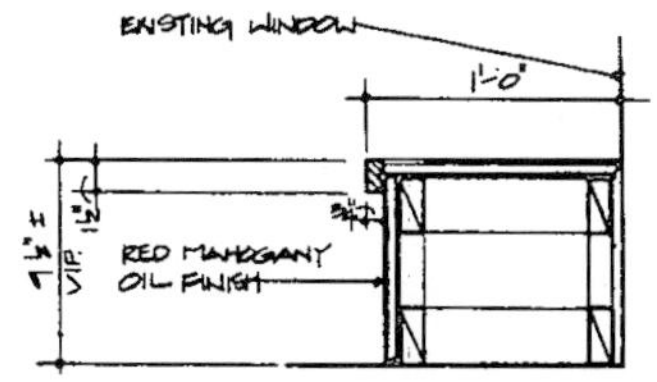

15/A9 DET. of LOW WINDOW SILL CAB. at DINING #101
SCALE: 1½"=1'-0" (SIM. DET. at VIP DINING #211)

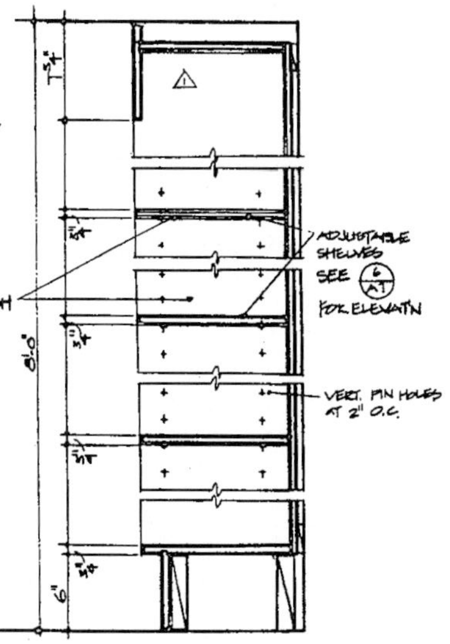

16/A9 CABINET DET. of GLASS STORAGE
SCALE: 1½"=1'-0"

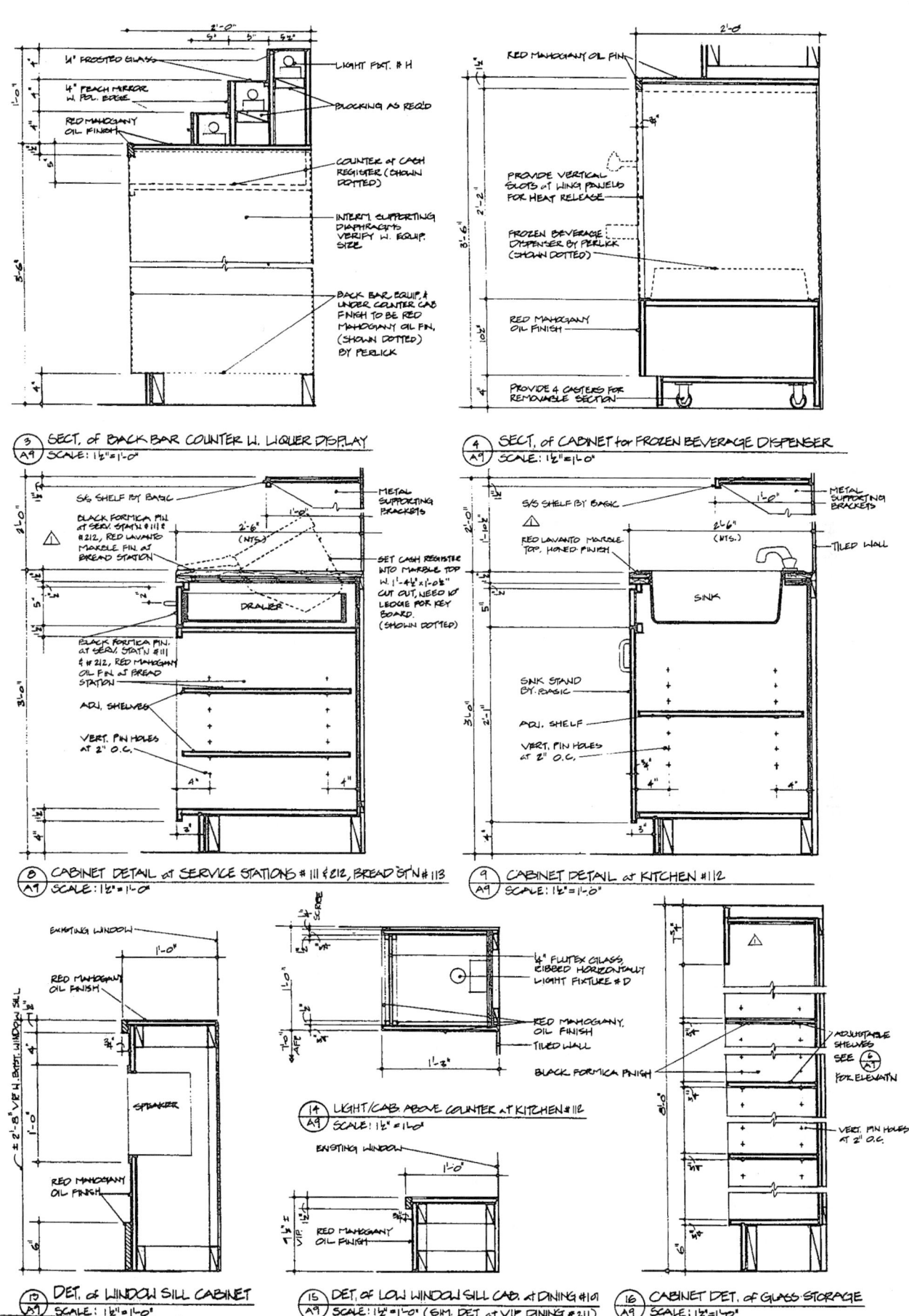

RESTAURANTS

Miscellaneous Counter Details

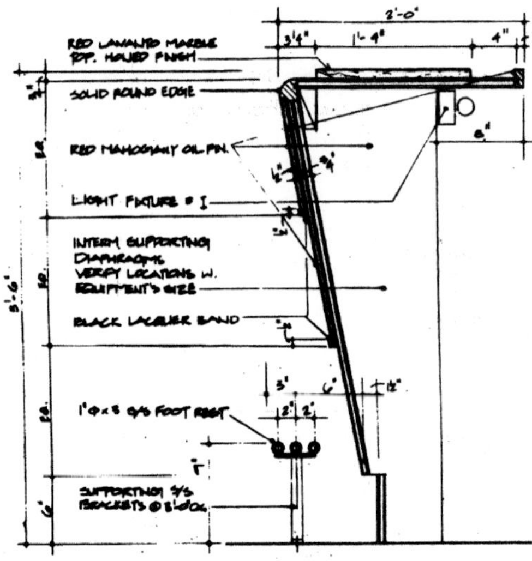

1/A9 SECT. of FRONT BAR COUNTER
SCALE: 1½" = 1'-0"

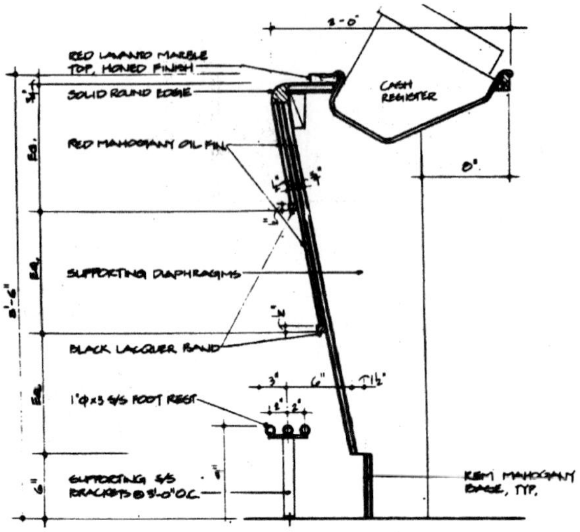

2/A9 SECT. of CASH REGISTER COUNTER at BAR # 108
SCALE: 1½" = 1'-0"

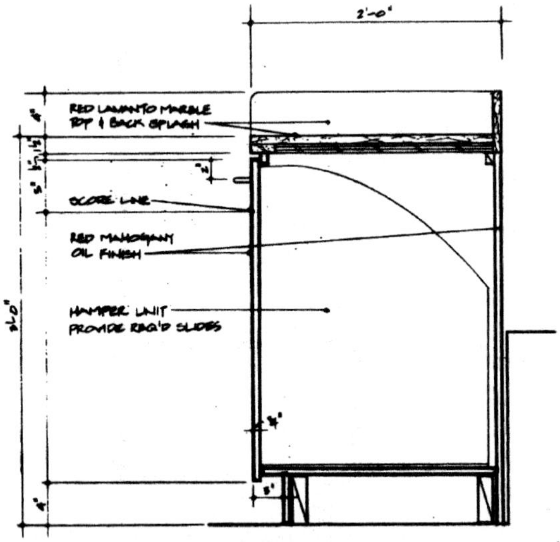

6/A9 CAB. DETAIL of HAMPER UNIT at SERVICE STATION # 108
SCALE: 1½" = 1'-0"

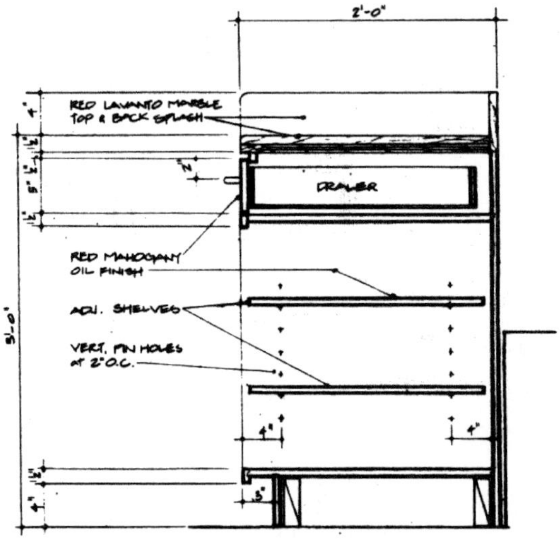

7/A9 CABINET DETAIL at SERVICE STATION # 108
SCALE: 1½" = 1'-0"

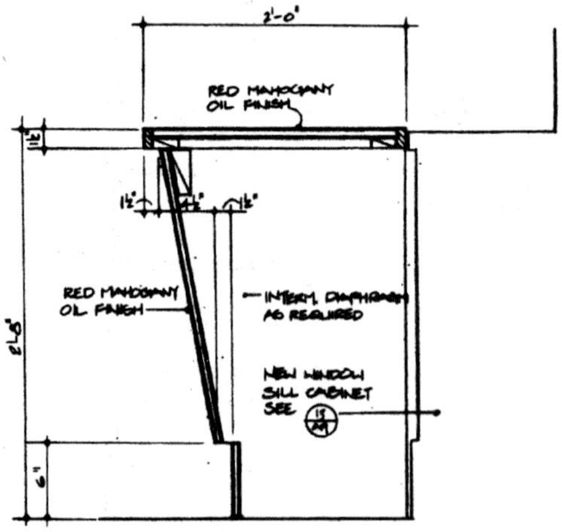

12/A9 DETAIL of FLORAL CABINET
SCALE: 1½" = 1'-0"

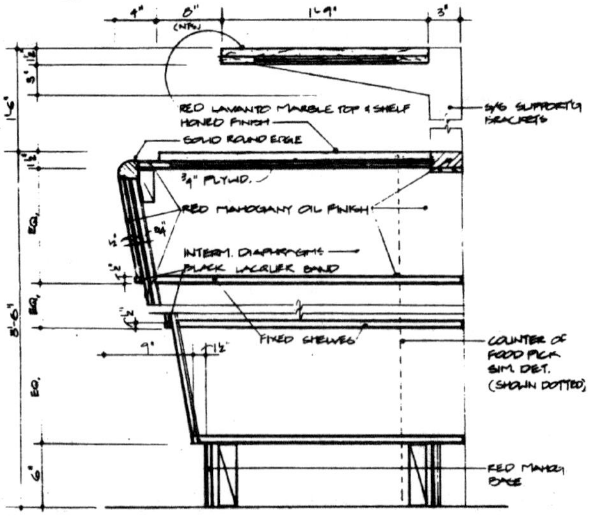

5/A9 SECT. of COUNTER at ESPRESSO & ANTIPASTO # 109
SCALE: 1½" = 1'-0"

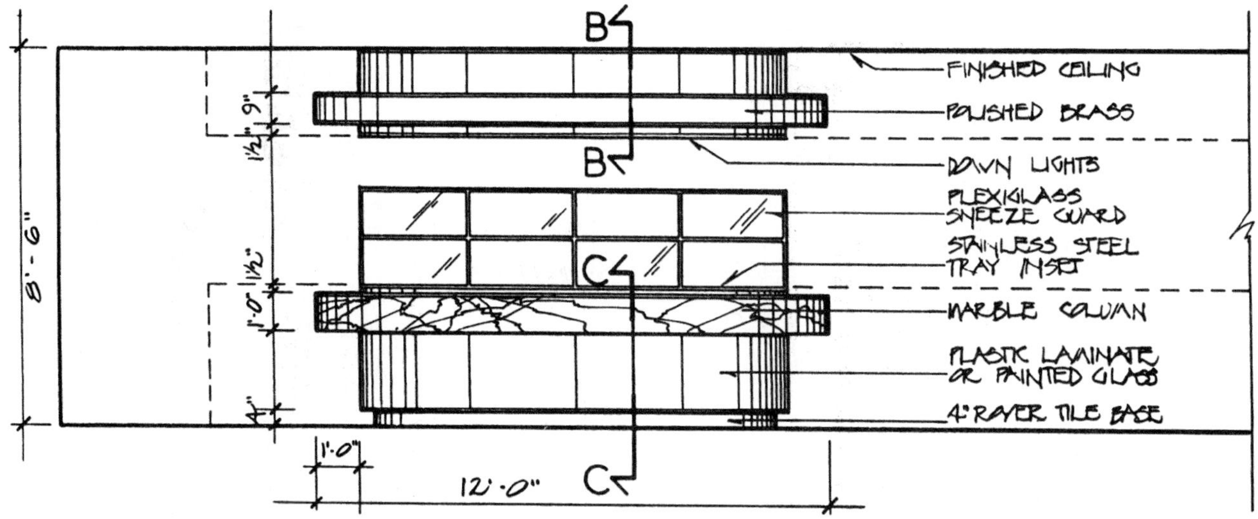

A ELEVATION OF SERVING ISLAND

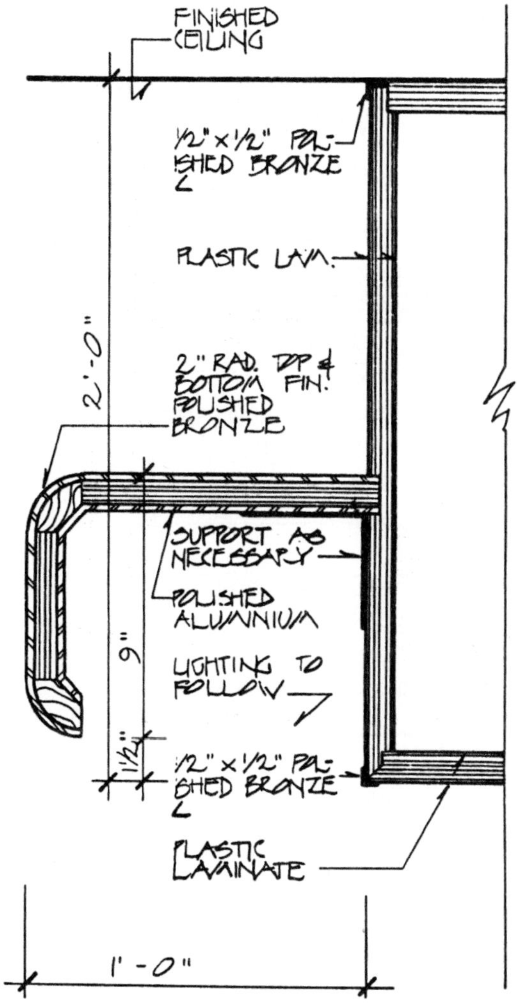

BB SECTION THRU HOOD

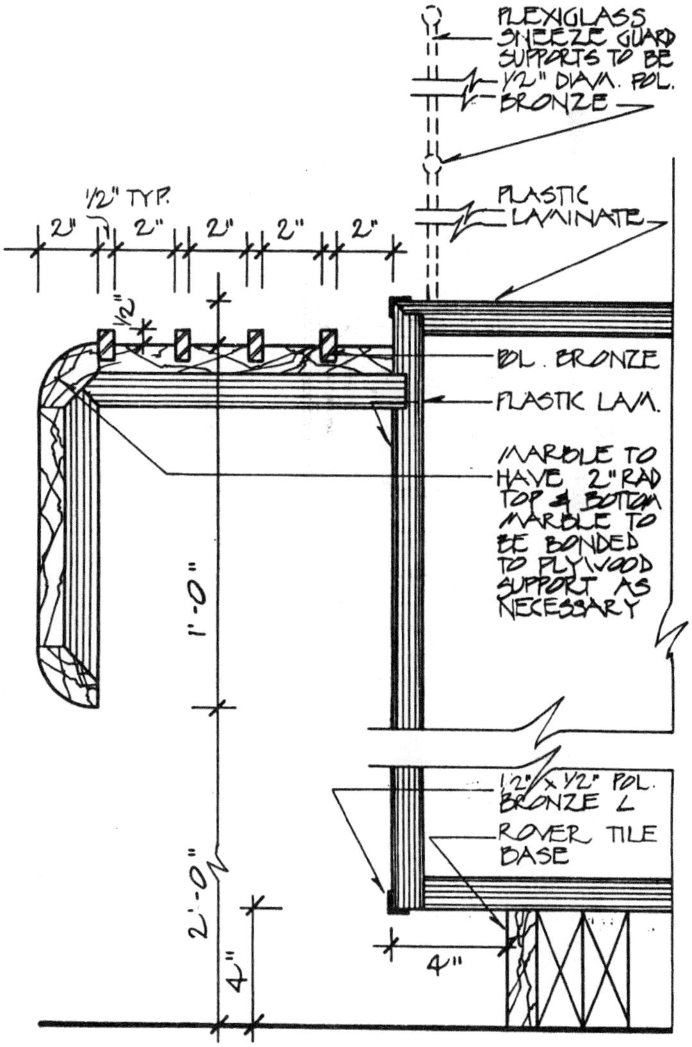

CC SECTION THRU SERVING COUNTER

RESTAURANTS

Waiter Station/Host Counter Details

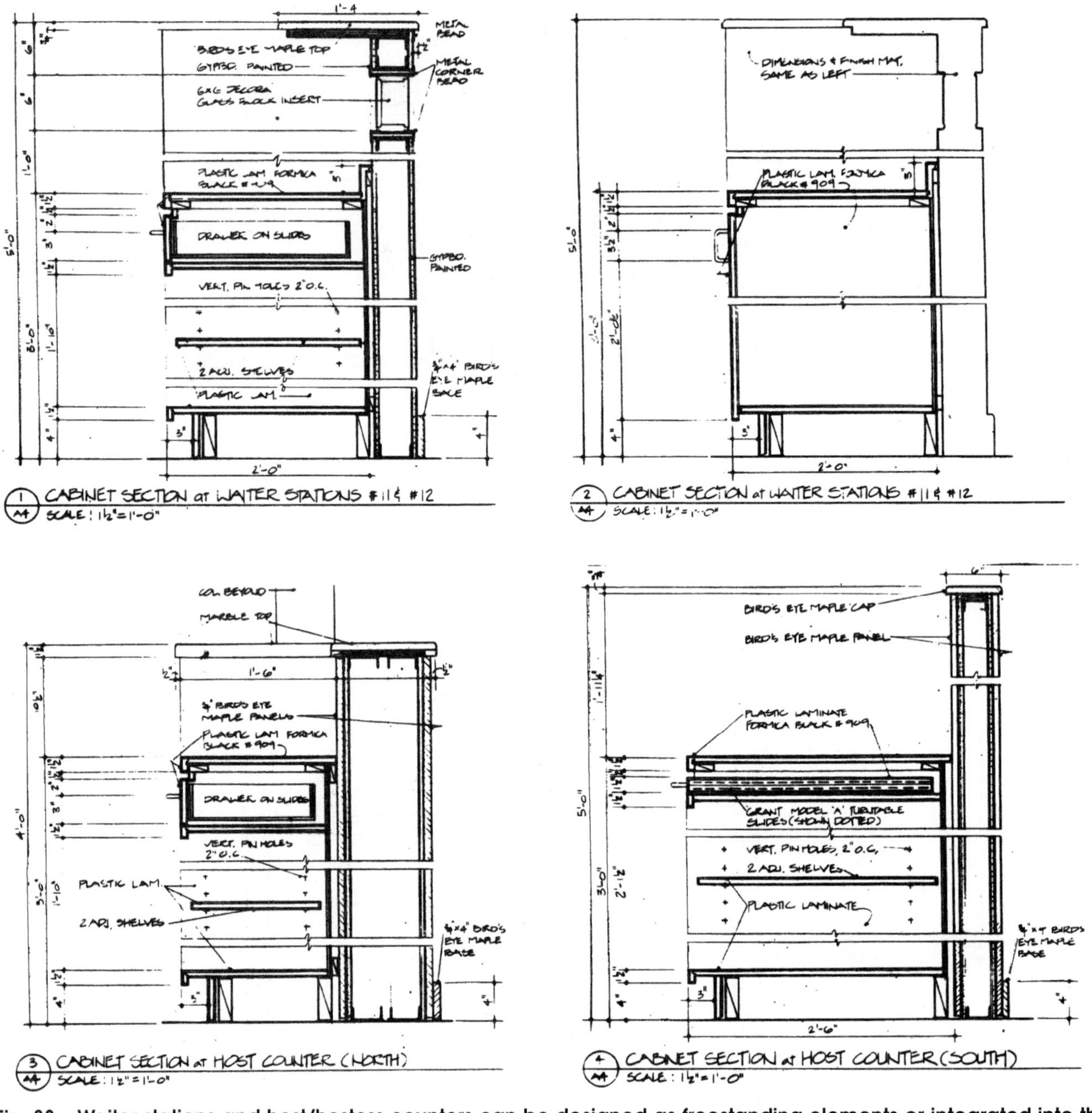

Fig. 33 Waiter stations and host/hostess counters can be designed as freestanding elements or integrated into the interior architecture, as shown by these details. Special attention must be given to specific drawer and storage requirements

RESTAURANTS
Waiter Station/Host Counter Details

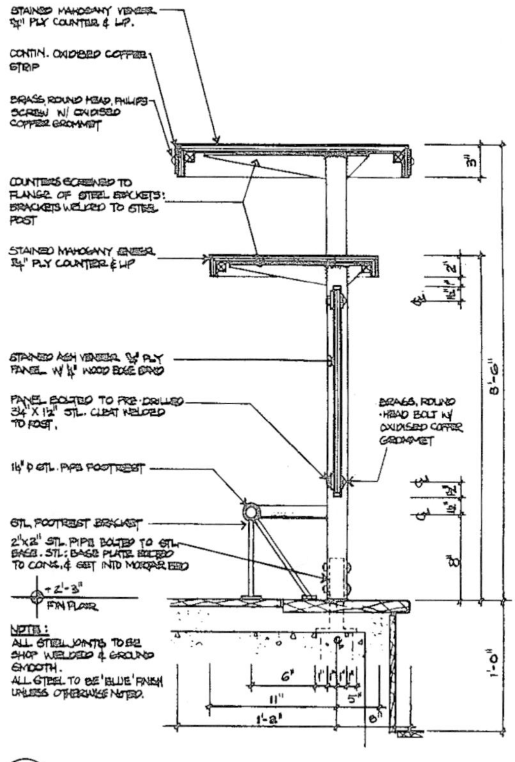

5 / A15 DETAIL OF LUNCH COUNTER
1½" = 1'-0"

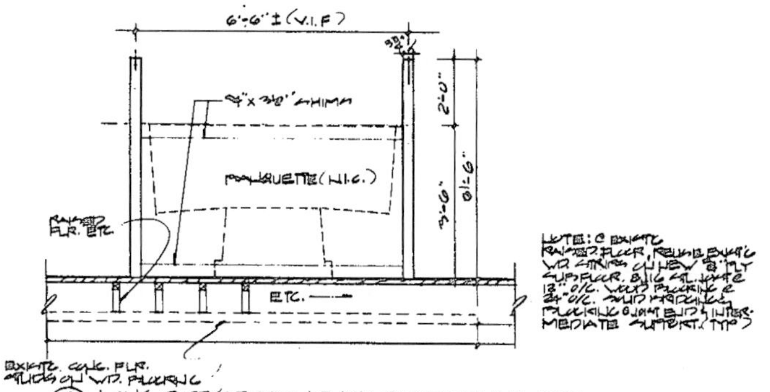

6 / AB LONG PART/SECTION THRU RAISED DINING AREA
½" = 1'-0"

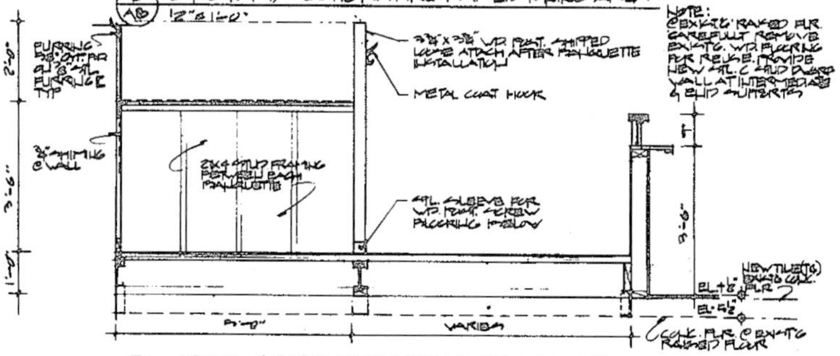

6 / AB CROSS SECTION THRU RAISED DINING AREA
½" = 1'-0"

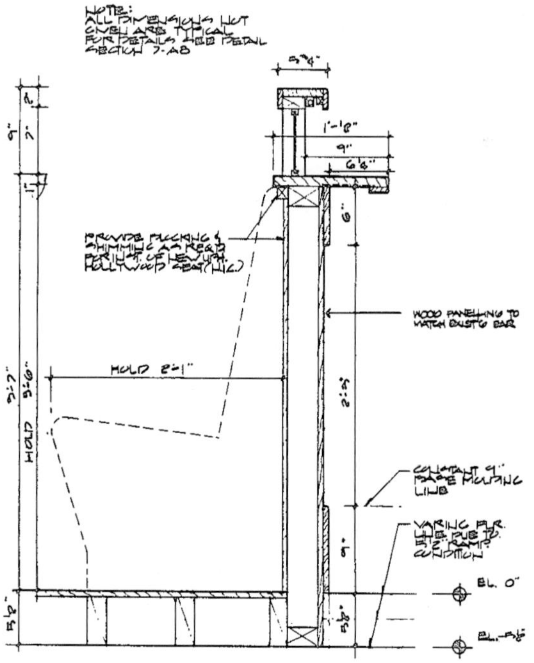

10 / AB SECTION @ CURVED SEAT IN SHUFFLE BD. AREA
1½" = 1'-0"

RESTAURANTS

Wheelchair Accessibility to Self-Service Areas

Self-Service Areas

Salad bars, buffet lines, condiment stands, and other self-service areas should be accessible. Cafeteria or food-service lines should have a minimum width of 3 ft 0 in, but a width of 3 ft 6 in is recommended to permit ambulatory customers to pass customers in wheelchairs.

The tray slide should be 2 ft 10 in above the floor, the maximum height for customers in wheelchairs and convenient for ambulatory guests. The tray slide should be continuous, if possible, from the entrance to the cashier. Tray slides restrict access to the counters and therefore should not be wider than necessary (1 ft 0 in recommended). In this instance, the reach of a customer in a wheelchair is extended if the wheelchair can be angled or positioned perpendicular to the tray slide. This is possible if the lower face of the counter is recessed to provide low knee space. (See Fig. 34.)

For guests with a limited range of motion, food, beverages, utensils, or other items should be displayed near the edge of the counter where they are easier to see and reach. When duplicate items are displayed, a vertical rather than horizontal arrangement allows customers to select items at the most convenient height. Self-service systems, such as beverage or ice dispensers, should be easy to operate without fine hand function. Instructions and price information should be prominently displayed in large, clear lettering.

Salad bars and buffets should provide a 3 ft 0 in wide clear space for access on all sides and plate slides, or areas to temporarily set plates, at a maximum height of 2 ft 10 in. This permits customers to serve themselves with one hand, without simultaneously balancing the plate or bowl. Knee space 2 ft 3 in high below the counter or table allows front wheelchair approach, to increase customers' forward reach. Condiments should be located as low and close to the edge of the counter or table as practical. A tilted mirror above the food display at salad bars also aids customers in wheelchairs and children. (See Fig. 35.) For some customers with restricted mobility, poor balance, or limited hand function, it is more difficult to carry a plate. Therefore, trays should be available at both salad bars and buffets.

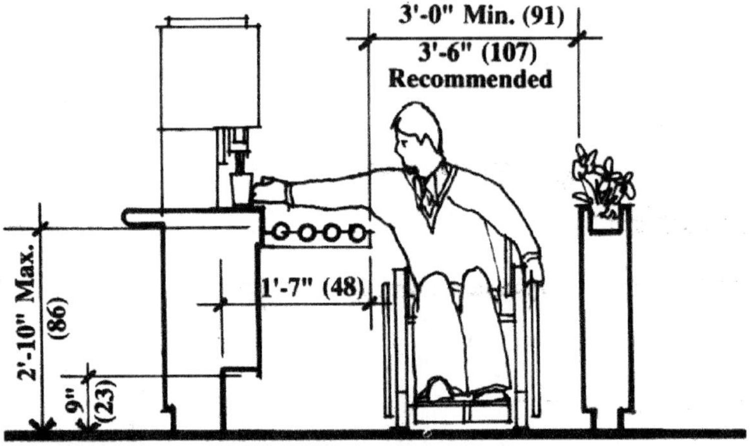

Fig. 34 Cafeteria lines should be wide enough to accommodate guests in wheelchairs. Food and beverages should be within a convenient vertical and horizontal reach. Numbers in parentheses are dimensions in centimeters

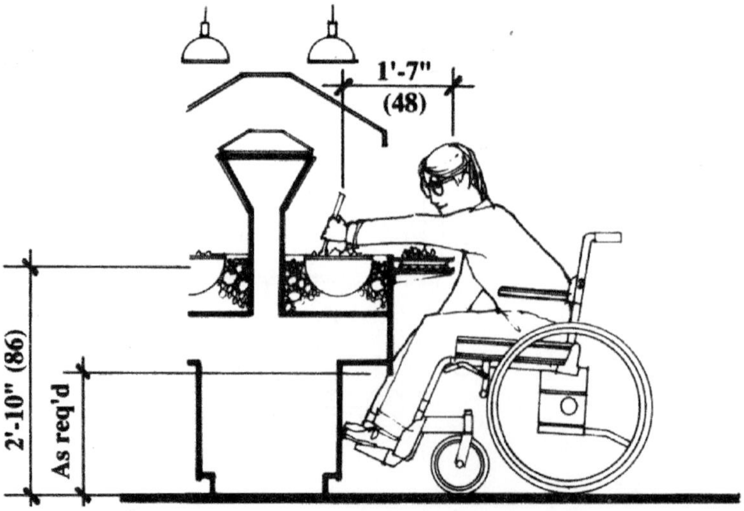

Fig. 35 A plate slide is recommended at salad bars and a knee space at the counter. A mirror surface above the bar is a further aid to guests in wheelchairs. Numbers in parentheses are dimensions in centimeters

RESTAURANTS

Cafeteria Counter Plans, Elevations, and Details

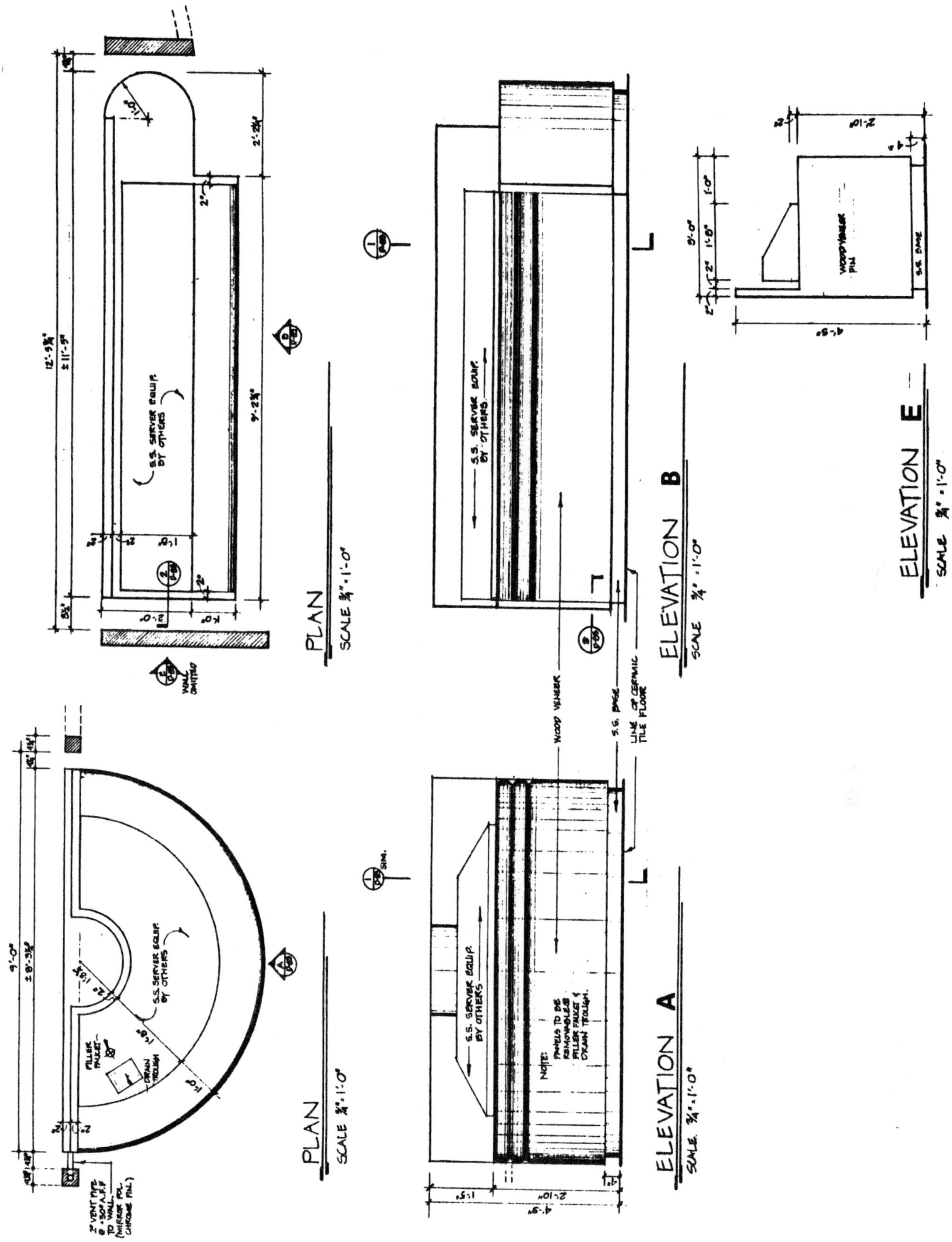

RESTAURANTS

Lunch Counters: Cashier Station

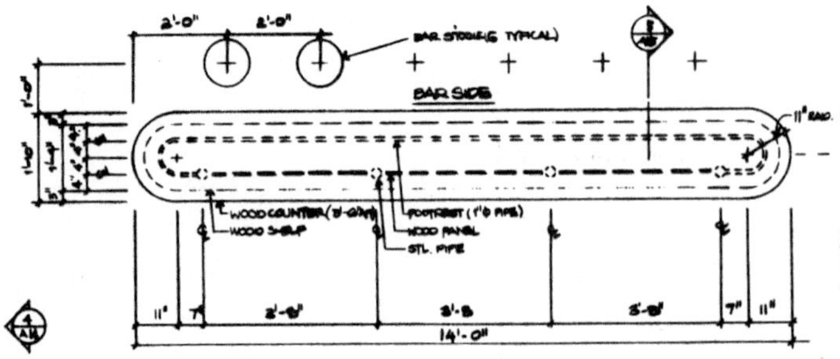

6/A14 PLAN OF LUNCH COUNTER ½" = 1'-0"

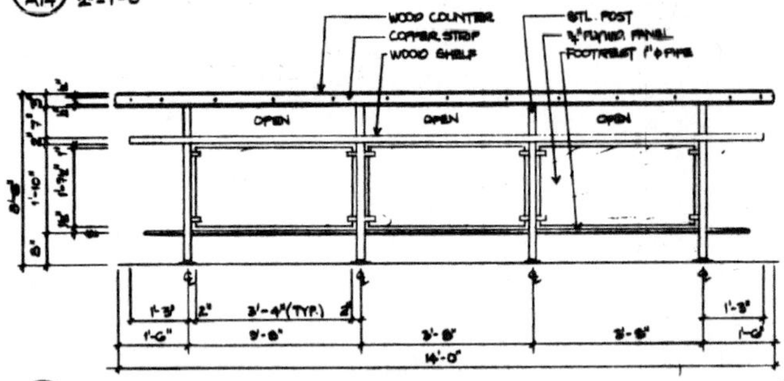

7/A14 ELEVATION OF LUNCH COUNTER FROM DINING ROOM ½" = 1'-0"

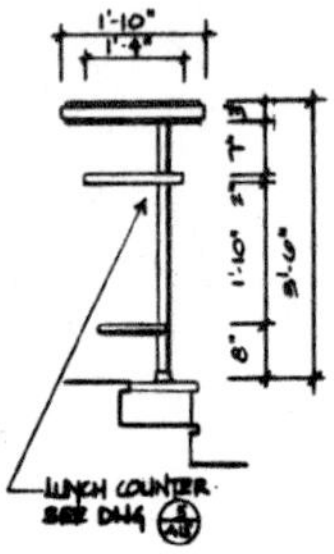

8/A14 SIDE ELEVATION OF LUNCH COUNTER ½" = 1'-0"

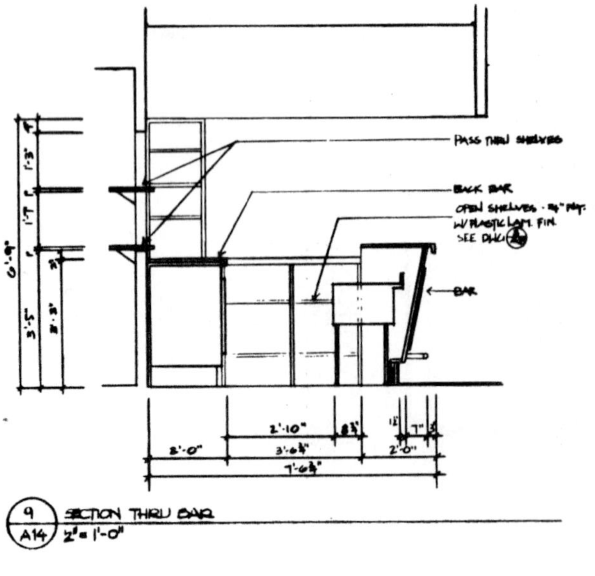

9/A14 SECTION THRU BAR ½" = 1'-0"

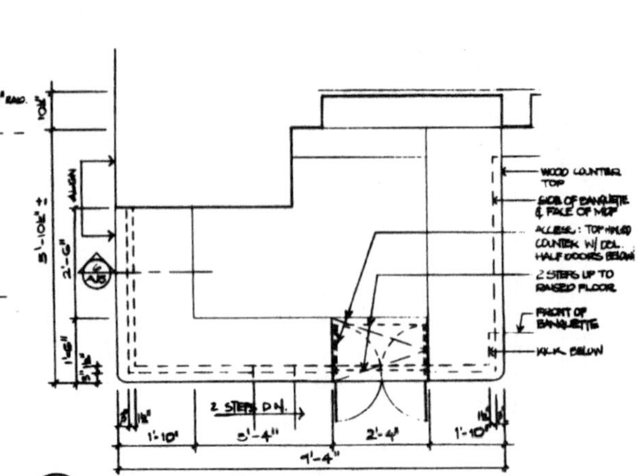

10/A14 PLAN OF CASHIERS STATION ½" = 1'-0"

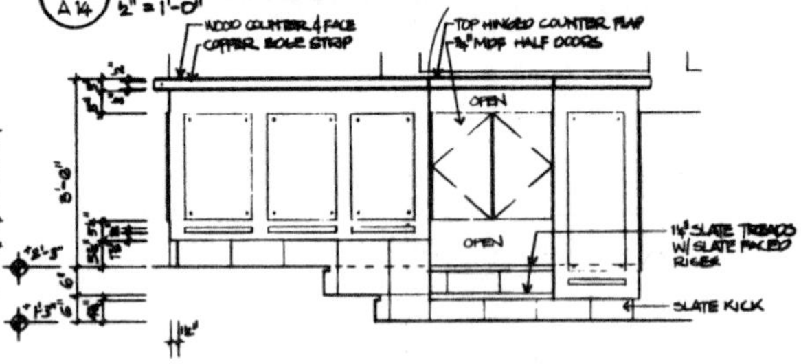

11/A14 SOUTH ELEVATION OF CASHIERS STATION ½" = 1'-0"

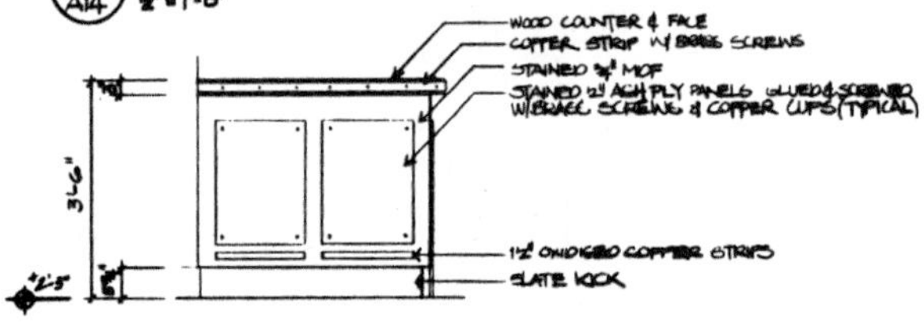

12/A14 WEST ELEVATION OF CASHIER STATION ½" = 1'-0"

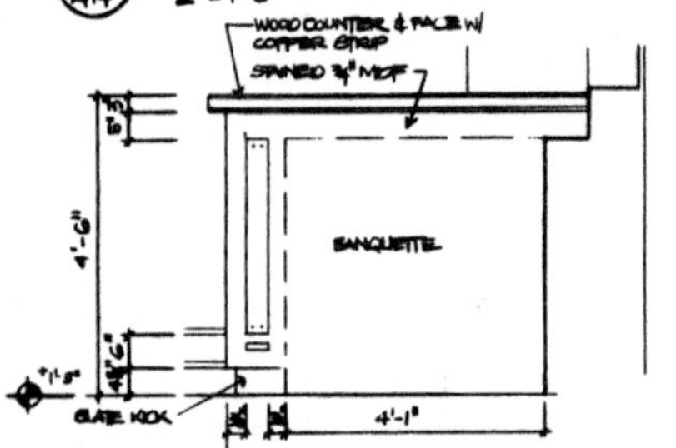

13/A14 EAST ELEVATION OF CASHIER STATION ½" = 1'-0"

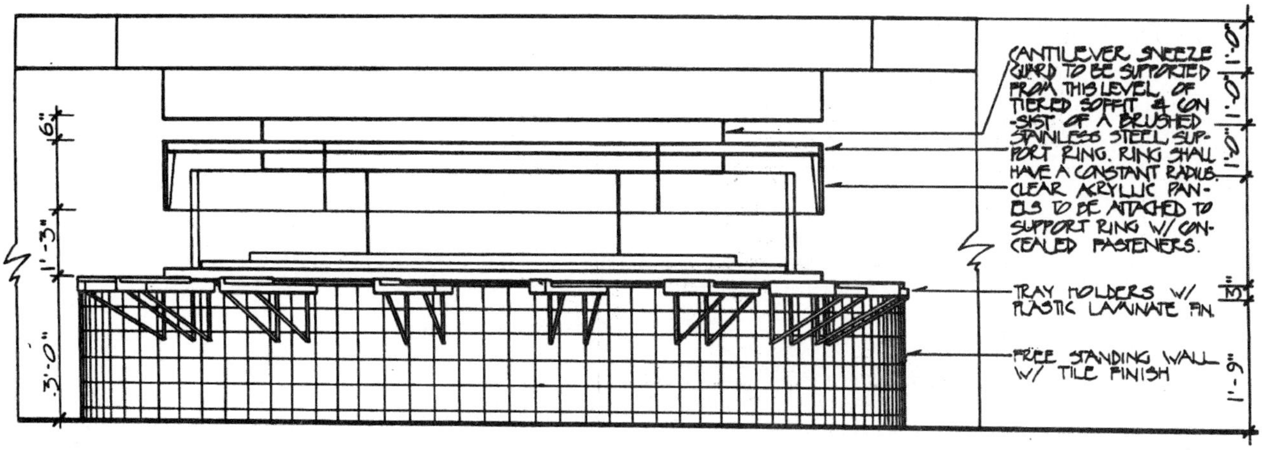

A ELEVATION OF TYPICAL 'ROTARY SERVING' UNIT

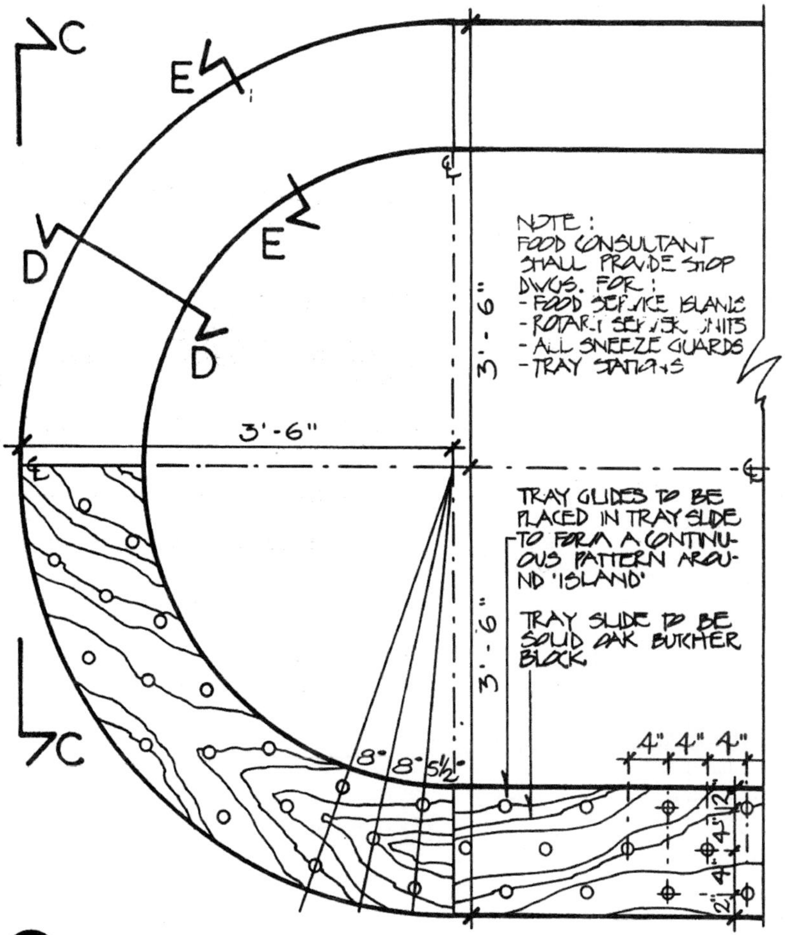

B PARTIAL PLAN OF TYPICAL 'ISLAND'

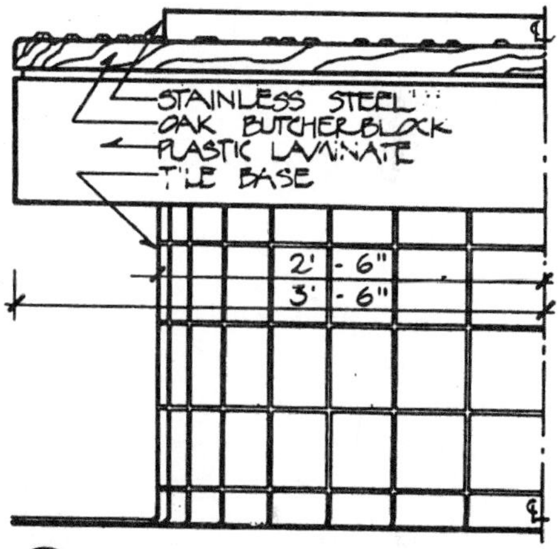

C PARTIAL ELEVATION

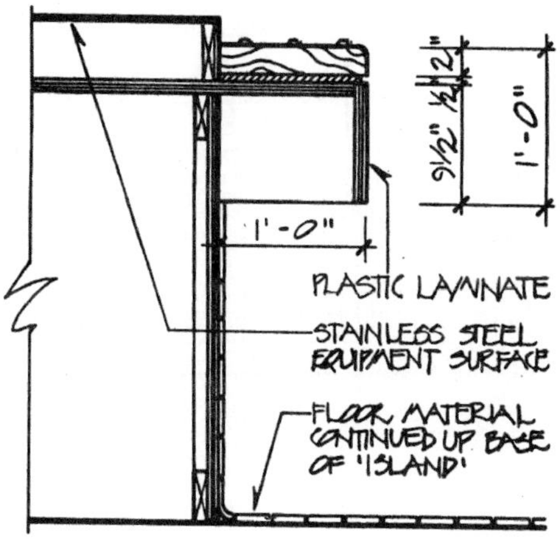

DD SECTION OF TRAY SLIDE

RESTAURANTS
Cafeteria/Servery Counter Details

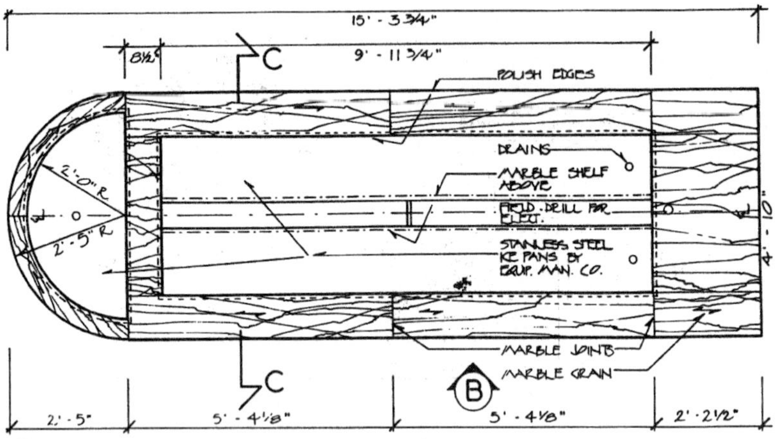

A PLAN AT MARBLE COUNTER

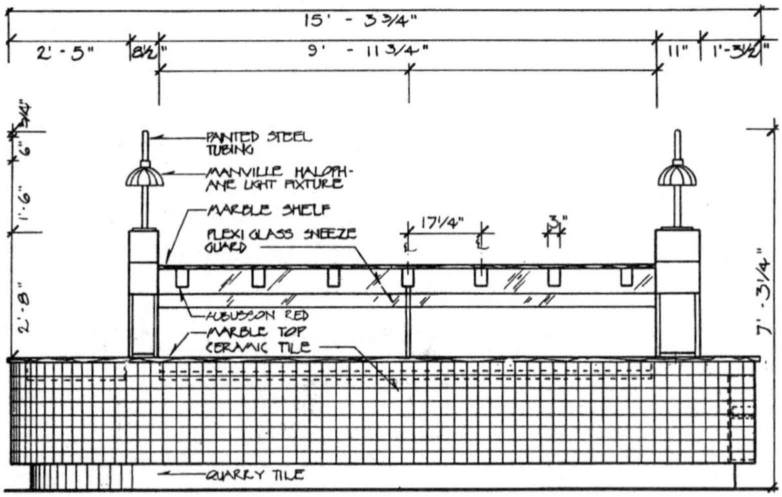

B ELEVATION

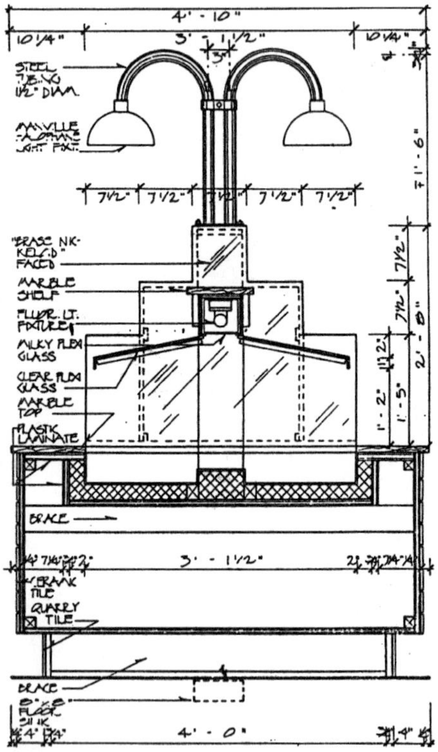

C SECTION

RESTAURANTS

Cafeteria/Servery Counter Details

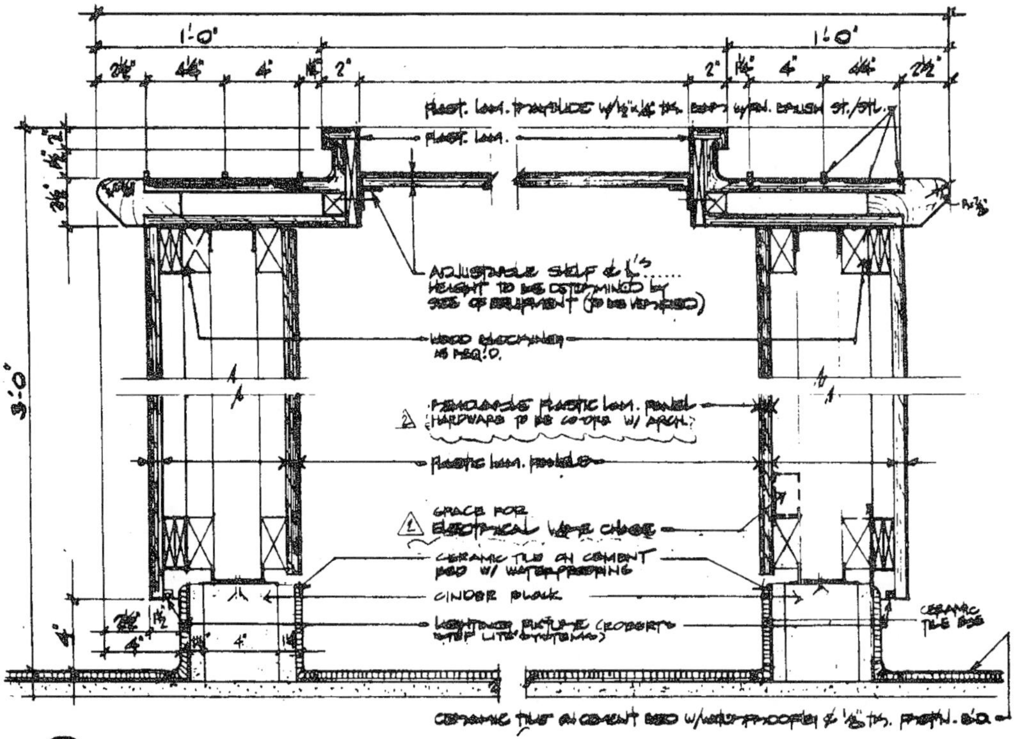

① SECTION THROUGH CASHIER'S COUNTER
3" = 1'-0"

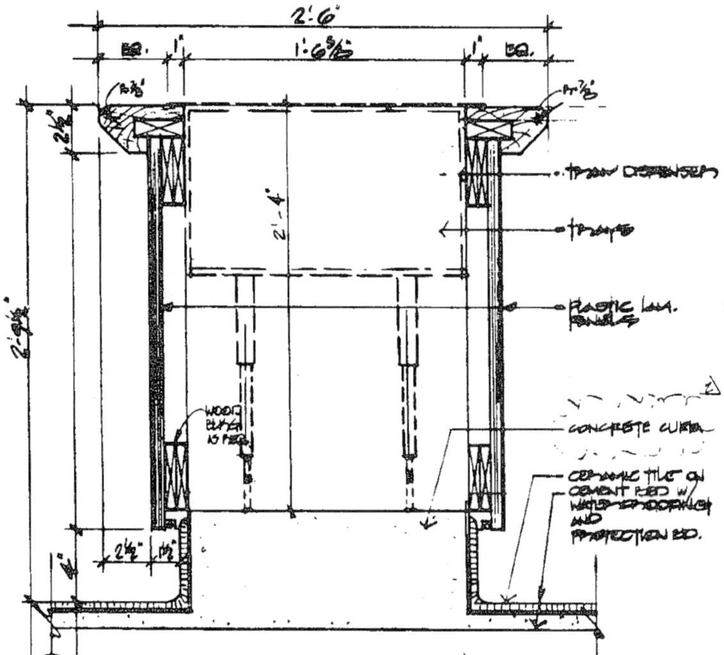

② SECTION THROUGH TRAY PICK-UP COUNTER

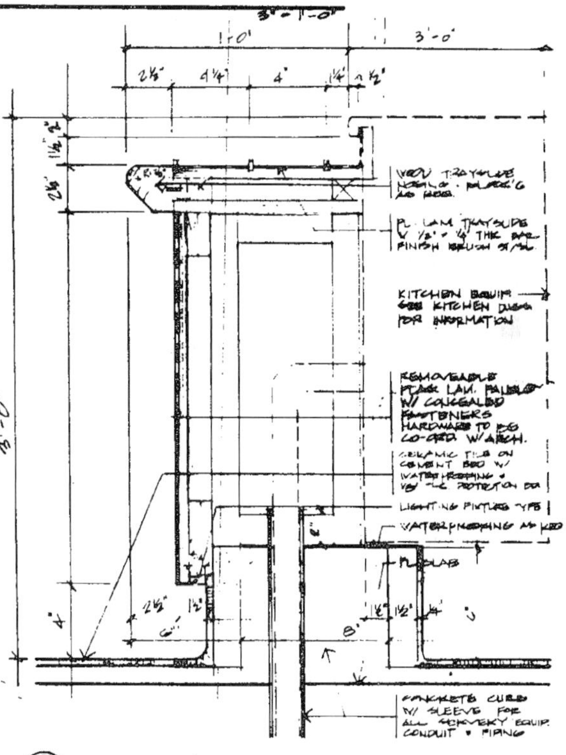

③ SECTION DETAIL - SERVERY TRAYSLIDE
SCALE 3" = 1'-0"

RESTAURANTS

Cafeteria/Servery Counter Details

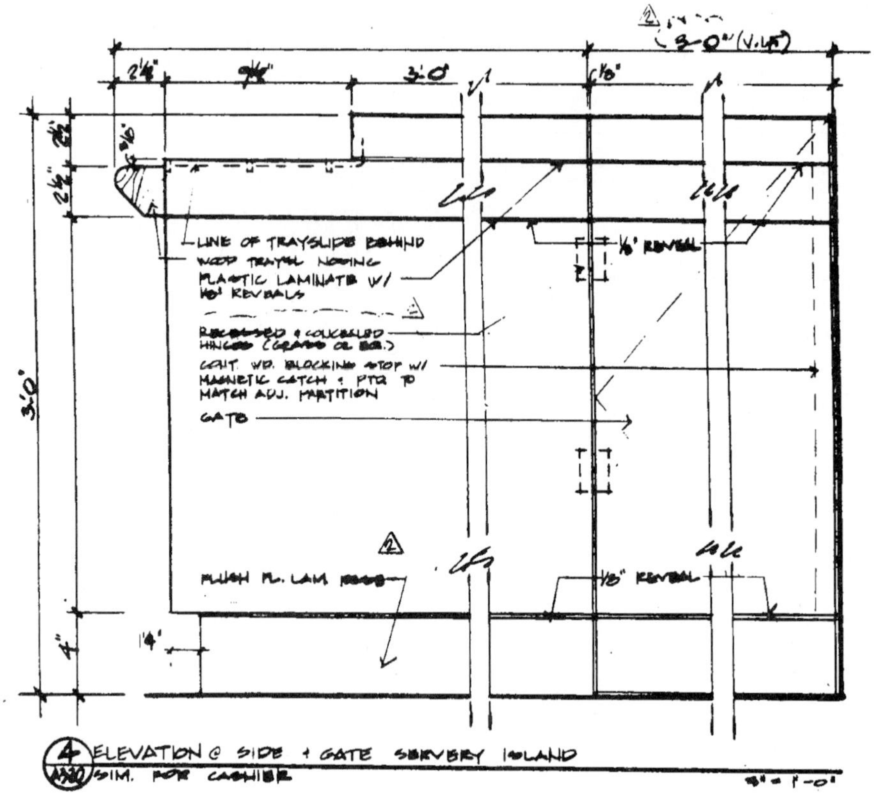

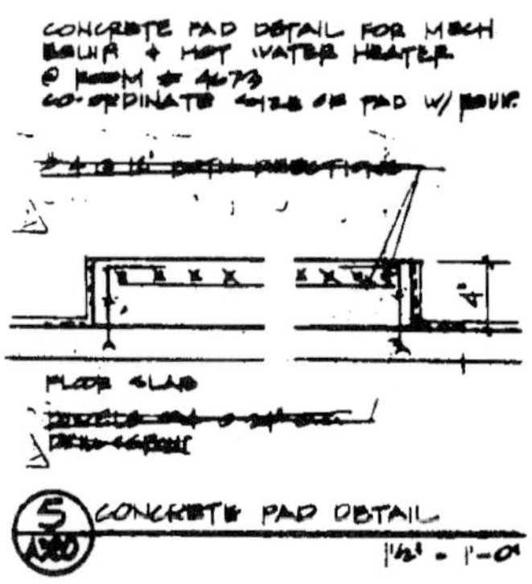

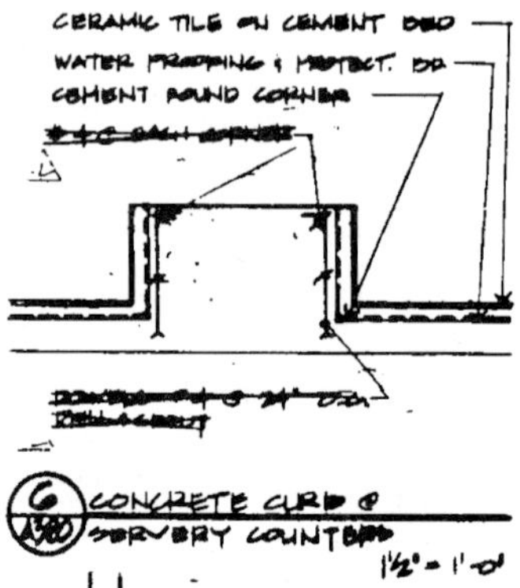

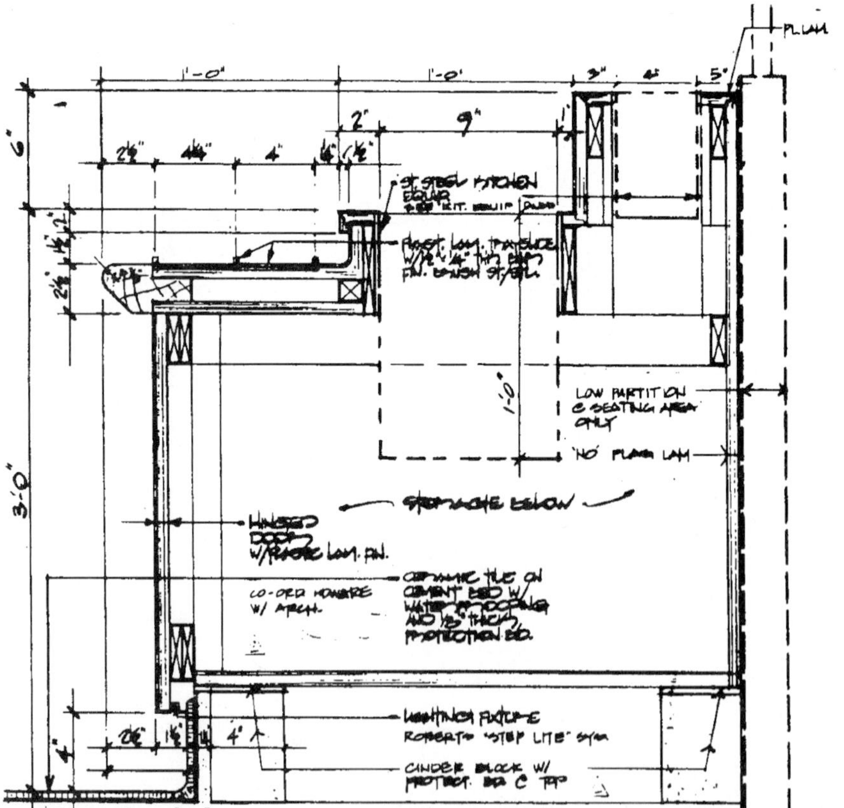

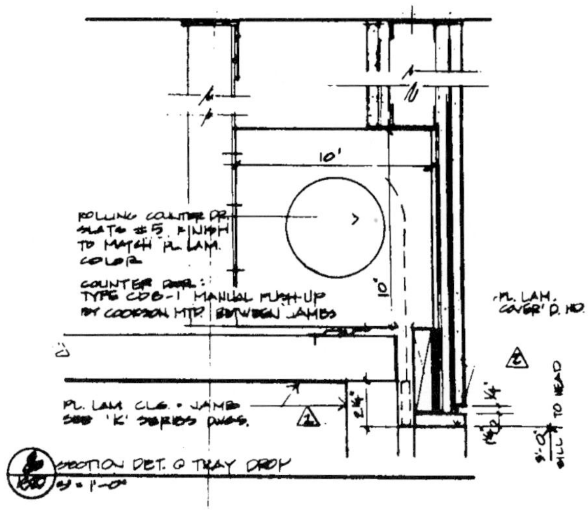
ROLLING COUNTER DR. SLATS #5 FINISH TO MATCH PL. LAM. COLOR
COUNTER DR.: TYPE CDB-1 MANUAL PUSH-UP BY COOKSON MTD. BETWEEN JAMBS
PL. LAM. COVER'D. HD.
PL. LAM. CLG. + JAMB SEE 'K' SERIES DWGS.
10'
SECTION DET. @ TRAY DROP

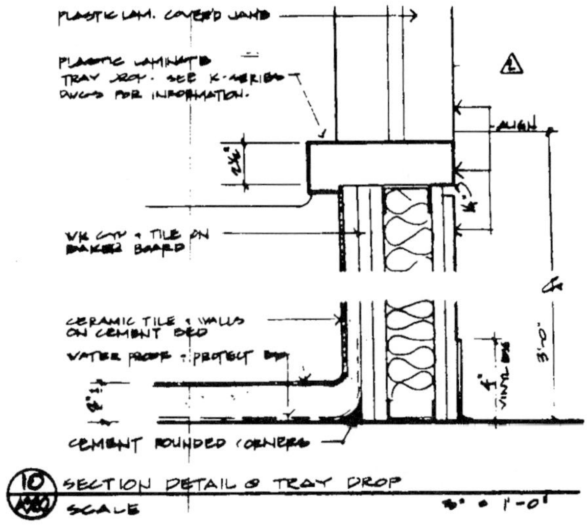
PLASTIC LAM. COVER'D JAMB
PLASTIC LAMINATE TRAY DROP - SEE K-SERIES DWGS FOR INFORMATION.
ALIGN
CERAMIC TILE & WALLS ON CEMENT BED
WATER PROOF + PROTECT
CEMENT ROUNDED CORNERS
3'-0"
SECTION DETAIL @ TRAY DROP
SCALE

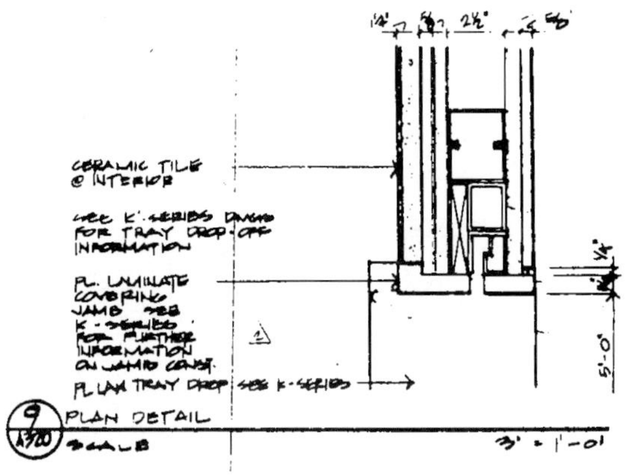
CERAMIC TILE @ INTERIOR
SEE K-SERIES DWGS FOR TRAY DROP-OFF INFORMATION
PL. LAMINATE COVERING JAMB SEE K-SERIES FOR FURTHER INFORMATION ON JAMB CONST.
PL. LAM TRAY DROP SEE K-SERIES
5'-0"
PLAN DETAIL
SCALE

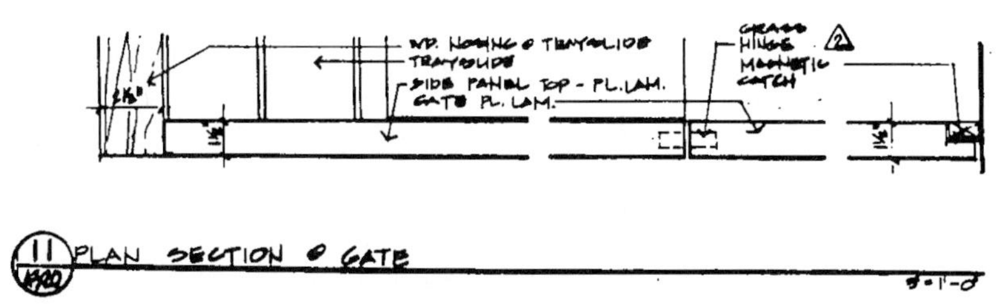
WD. NOSING @ TRAYSLIDE
TRAYSLIDE
SIDE PANEL TOP - PL. LAM.
GATE PL. LAM.
GRASS HINGE
MAGNETIC CATCH
PLAN SECTION @ GATE

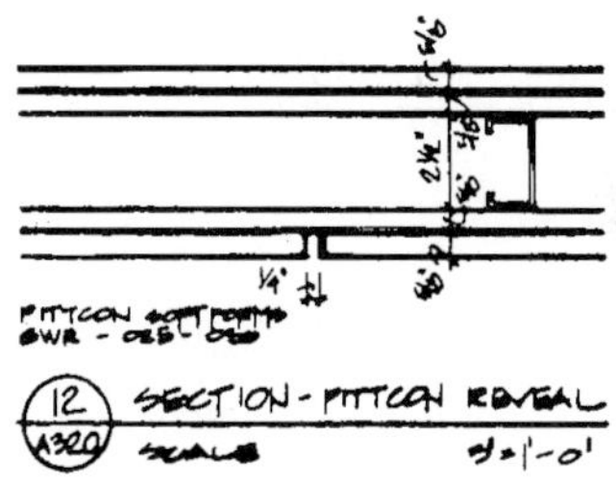
SECTION - FITTCON REVEAL
SCALE

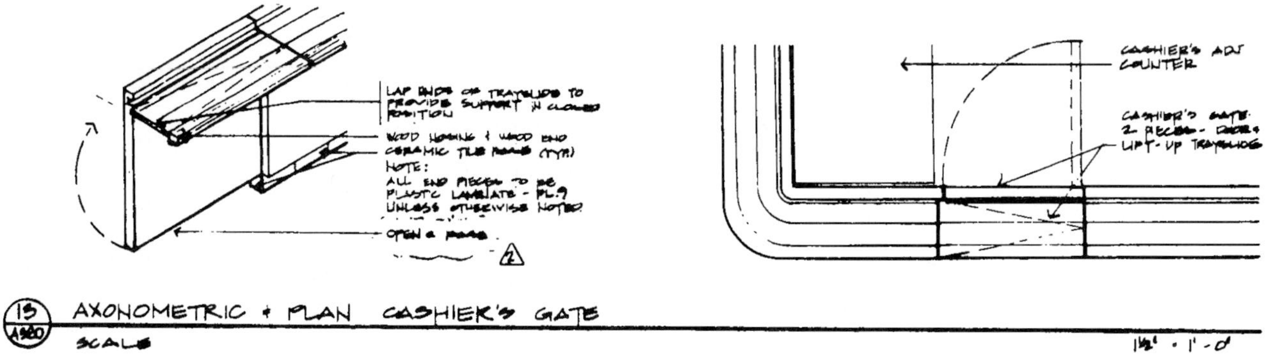
LAP ENDS OF TRAYSLIDE TO PROVIDE SUPPORT IN CLOSED POSITION
WOOD NOSING & WOOD END CERAMIC TILE BASE (TYP)
NOTE: ALL END PIECES TO BE PLASTIC LAMINATE - PL.9 UNLESS OTHERWISE NOTED
OPEN & BASE
CASHIER'S ADJ COUNTER
CASHIER'S GATE. 2 PIECES - DOORS LIFT-UP TRAYSLIDE
AXONOMETRIC + PLAN CASHIER'S GATE
SCALE

RESTAURANTS

Service Counter, Host Cabinet, Waiter's Station, and Trash Counter

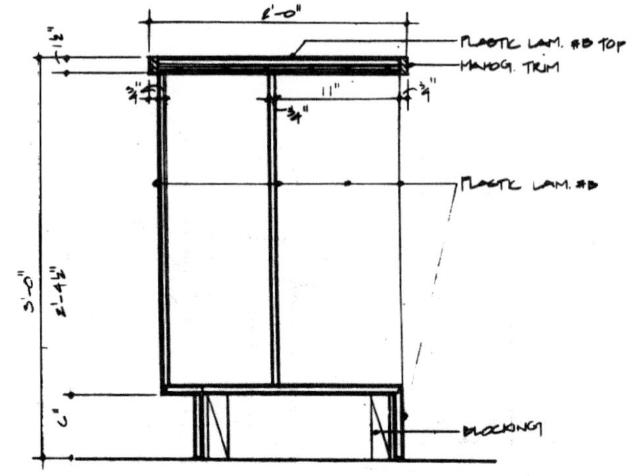

5 / A11 SECTION thru SERVICE COUNTER
SCALE 1½"=1'-0"

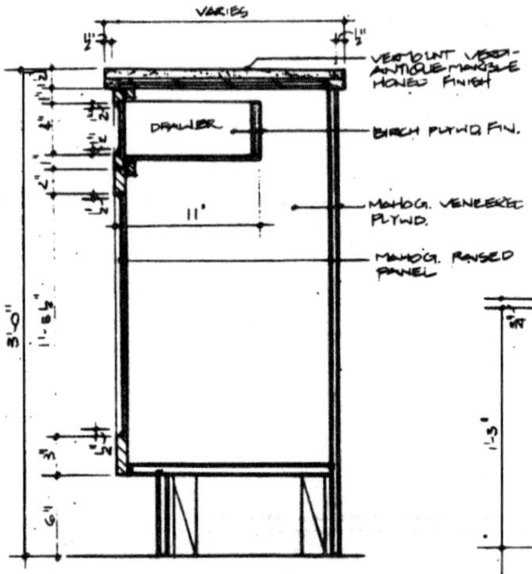

16 / A11 SECT. of HOST CABINET
SCALE: 1½"=1'-0"

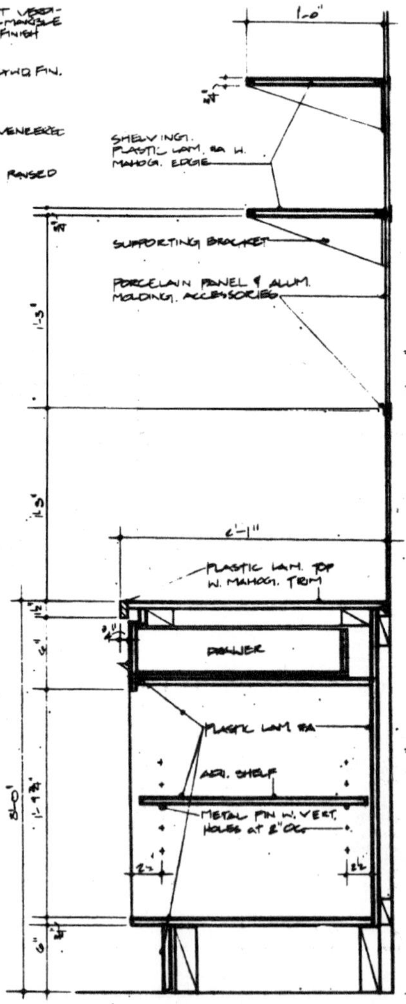

18 / A11 TYP. WAITER'S STATION CABINET
SCALE: 1½"=1'-0"

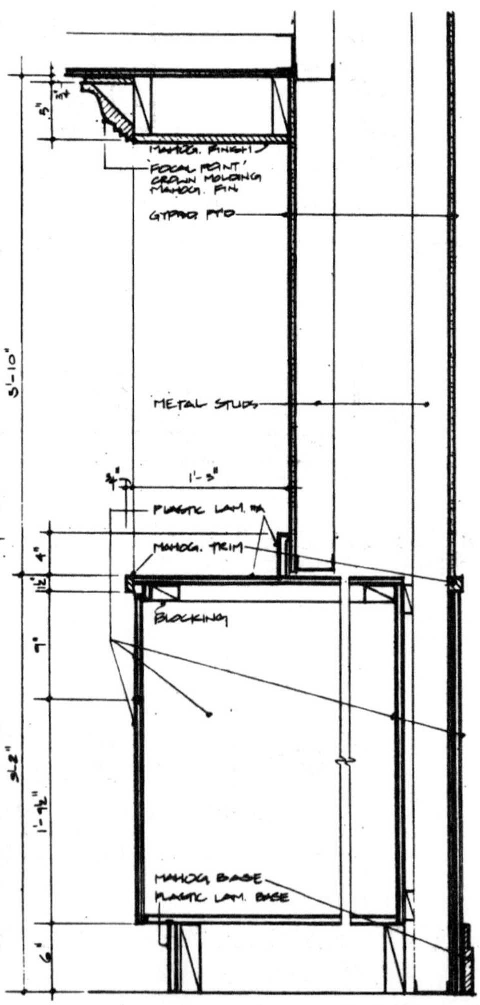

19 / A11 SECT. of TRASH COUNTER CABINET
SCALE: 1½"=1'-0"

RESTAURANTS
Display Cabinet

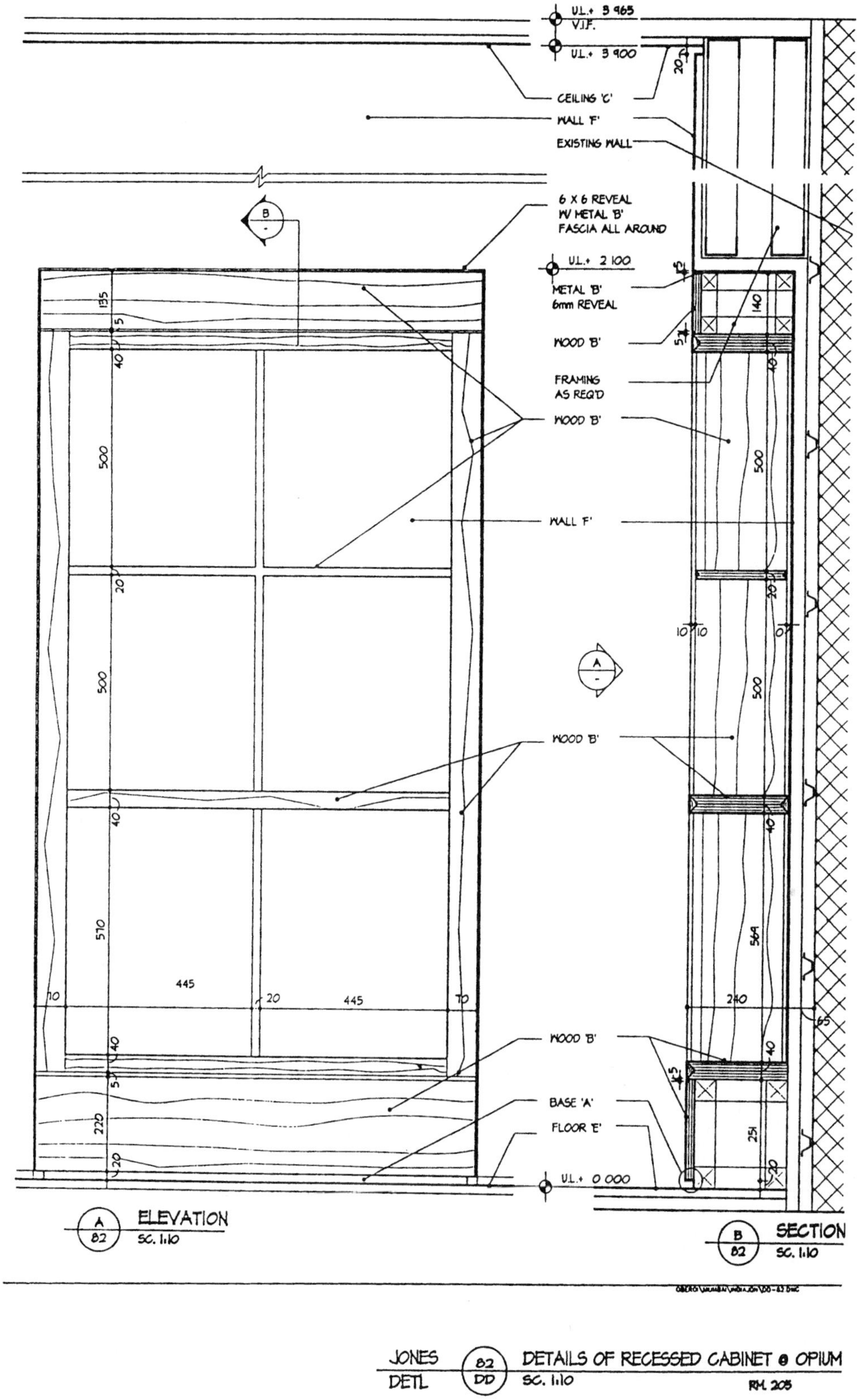
U.L.+ 3 965
V.I.F.
U.L.+ 3 900
CEILING 'C'
WALL 'F'
EXISTING WALL
6 X 6 REVEAL
W/ METAL 'B'
FASCIA ALL AROUND
U.L.+ 2 100
METAL 'B'
6mm REVEAL
WOOD 'B'
FRAMING
AS REQ'D
WOOD 'B'
WALL 'F'
WOOD 'B'
WOOD 'B'
BASE 'A'
FLOOR 'E'
U.L.+ 0 000
A 82 ELEVATION SC. 1:10
B 82 SECTION SC. 1:10
JONES
DETL
82 DD
DETAILS OF RECESSED CABINET @ OPIUM
SC. 1:10
RM. 205

RESTAURANTS
Service Stations

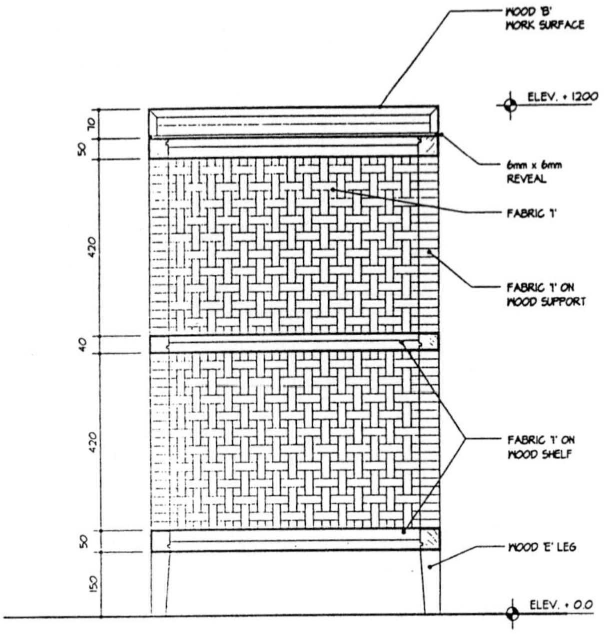

JONES | 110 DD | DETAIL. SECTION THRU SERVICE STATION T-7
DETL | | SC. 1:10 RM. 108/117

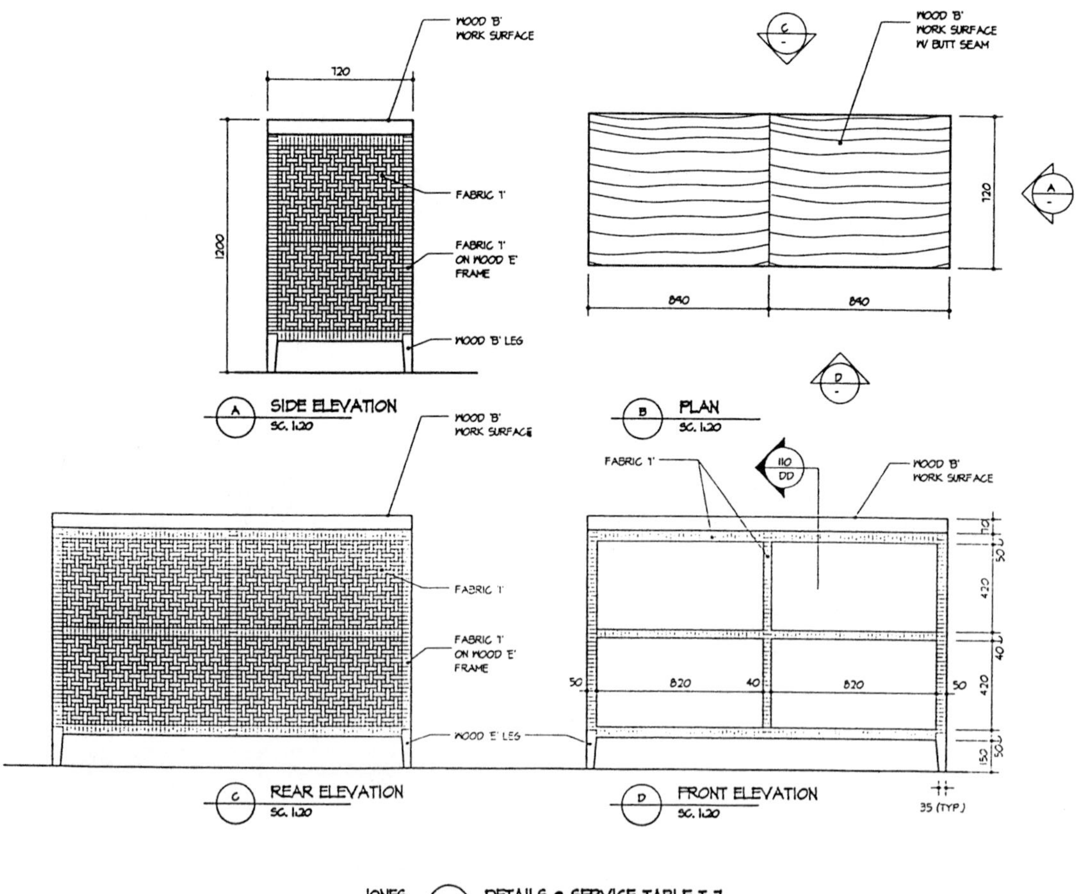

JONES | 104 DD | DETAILS @ SERVICE TABLE T-7
DETL | | 1:20 RM. 102/104

RESTAURANTS

Condiment Cabinet and Dining Room Server

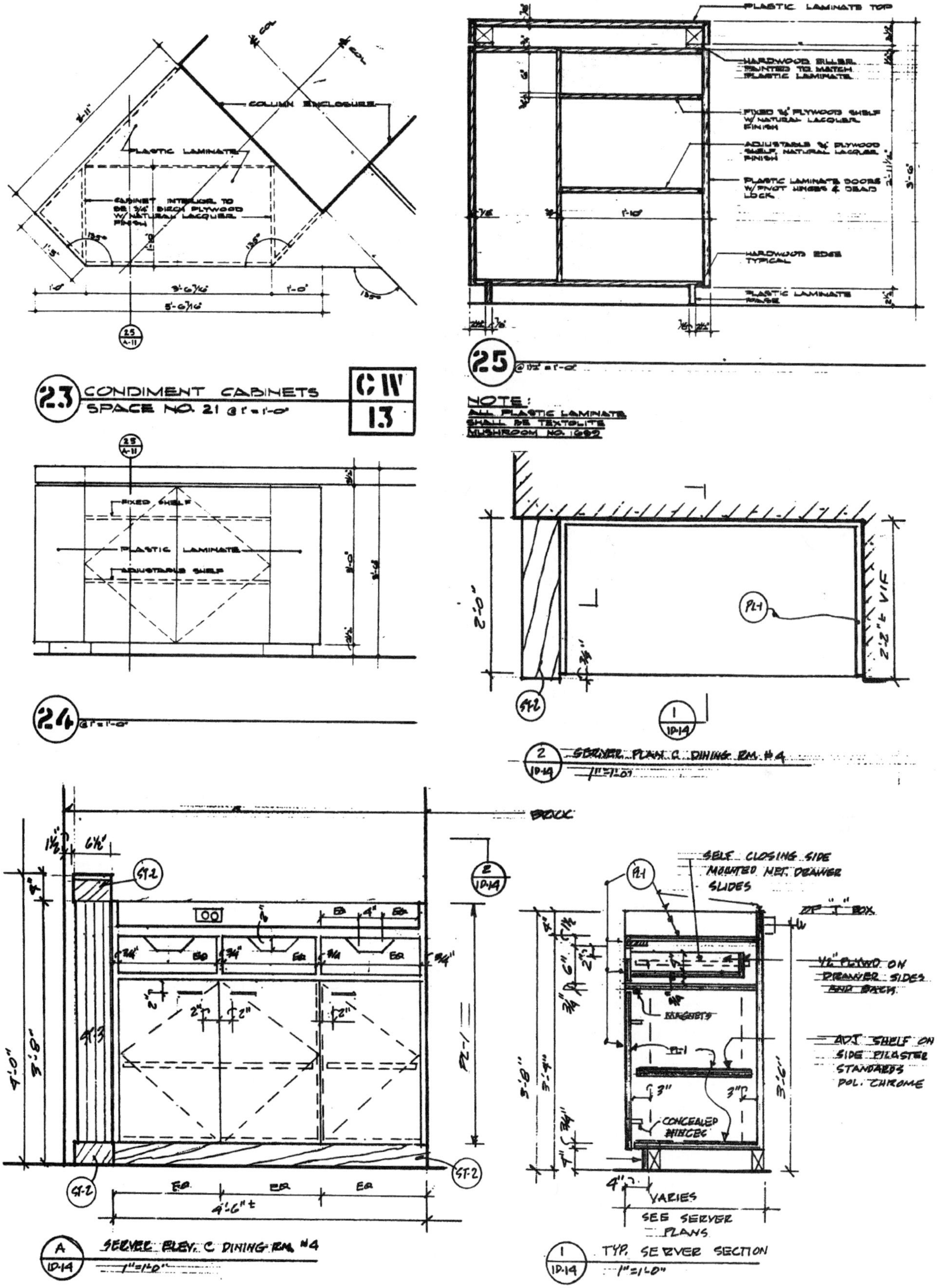

RESTAURANTS

Salad Bar/Serving Counter

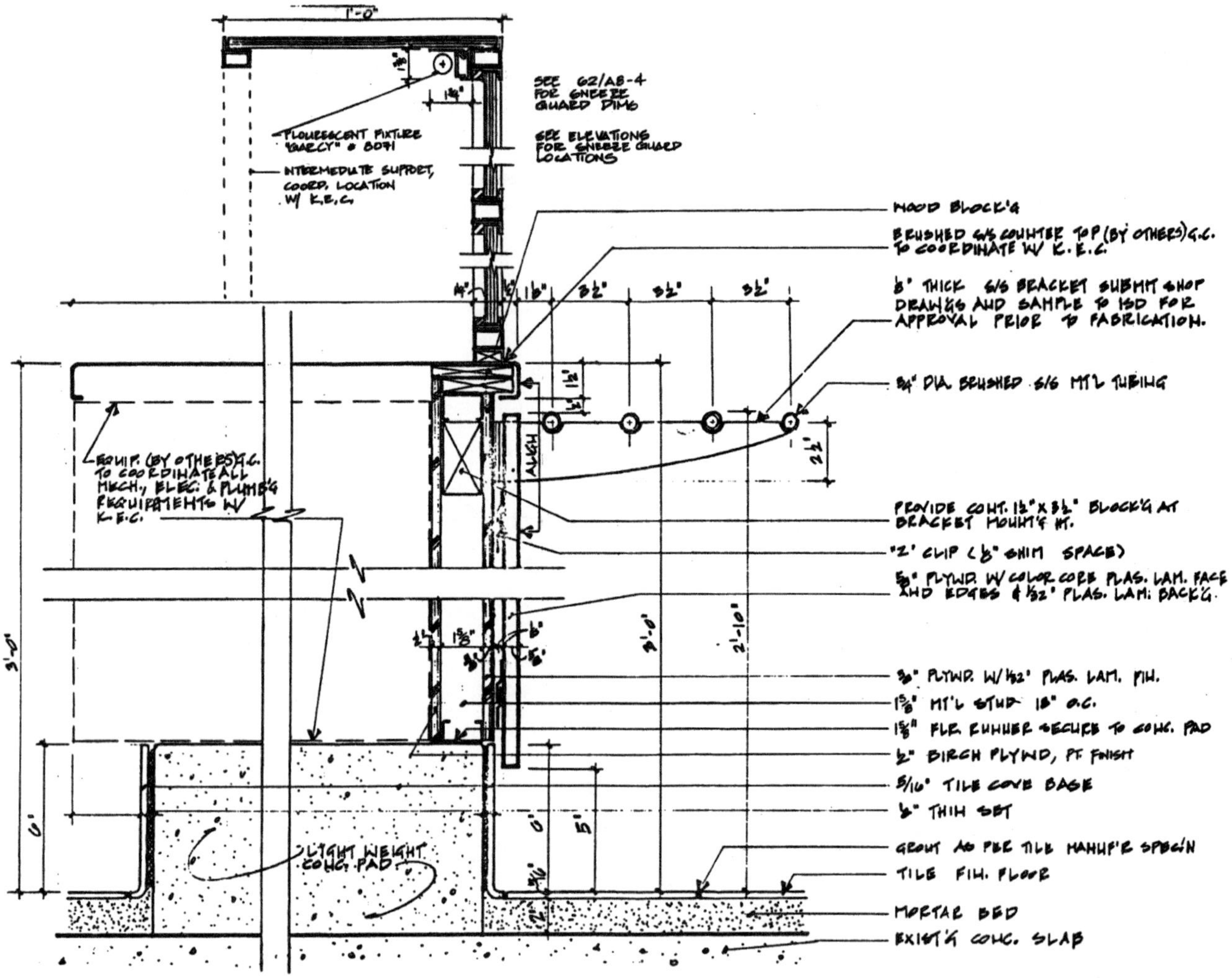
1'-0"
SEE 62/AB-4 FOR SNEEZE GUARD DIMS
FLOURESCENT FIXTURE "MARCY" # 8071
SEE ELEVATIONS FOR SNEEZE GUARD LOCATIONS
INTERMEDIATE SUPPORT, COORD. LOCATION W/ K.E.C.
WOOD BLOCK'G
BRUSHED S/S COUNTER TOP (BY OTHERS) G.C. TO COORDINATE W/ K.E.C.
1/8" THICK S/S BRACKET SUBMIT SHOP DRAW'GS AND SAMPLE TO ISD FOR APPROVAL PRIOR TO FABRICATION.
3/4" DIA. BRUSHED S/S MT'L TUBING
EQUIP. (BY OTHERS) G.C. TO COORDINATE ALL MECH., ELEC. & PLUMB'G REQUIREMENTS W/ K.E.C.
PROVIDE CONT. 1½" X 3½" BLOCK'G AT BRACKET MOUNT'G HT.
"Z" CLIP (1/8" SHIM SPACE)
5/8" PLYWD. W/ COLOR CORE PLAS. LAM. FACE AND EDGES & 1/32" PLAS. LAM. BACK'G.
3/8" PLYWD. W/ 1/32" PLAS. LAM. FIN.
1 5/8" MT'L STUD 16" O.C.
1 5/8" FLR. RUNNER SECURE TO CONC. PAD
1/2" BIRCH PLYWD, PT. FINISH
5/16" TILE COVE BASE
1/8" THIN SET
GROUT AS PER TILE MANUF'R SPEC'N
TILE FIN. FLOOR
MORTAR BED
EXIST'G CONC. SLAB
LIGHT WEIGHT CONC. PAD
3'-0"
3'-0"
2'-10"

RESTAURANTS

Tray Pick-Up Details and Condiment Counter Details

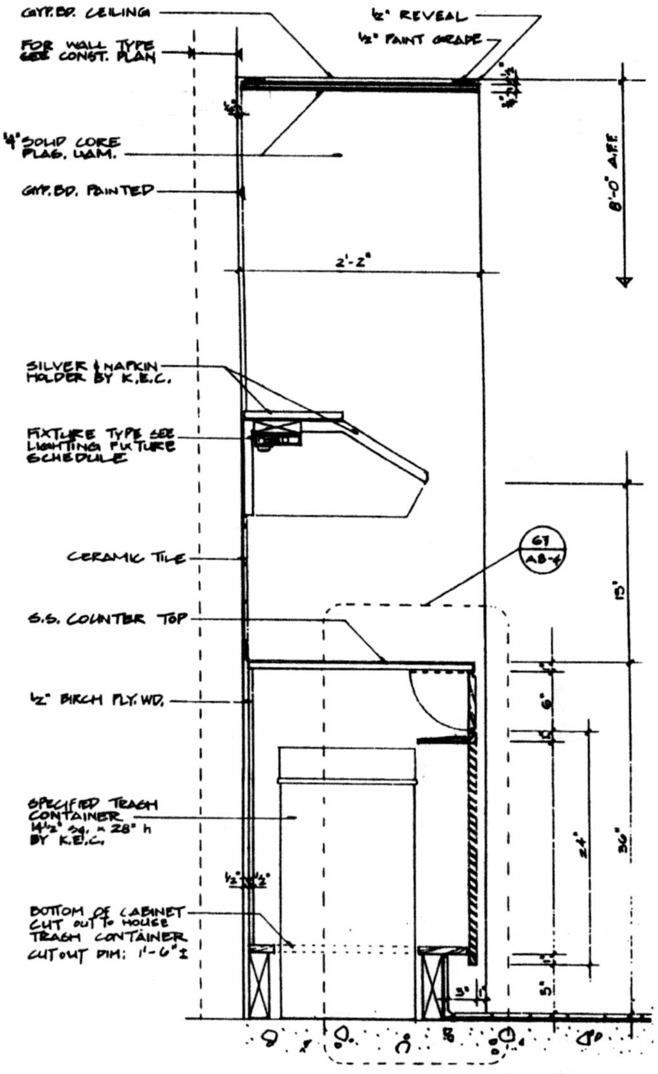

Condiment counter

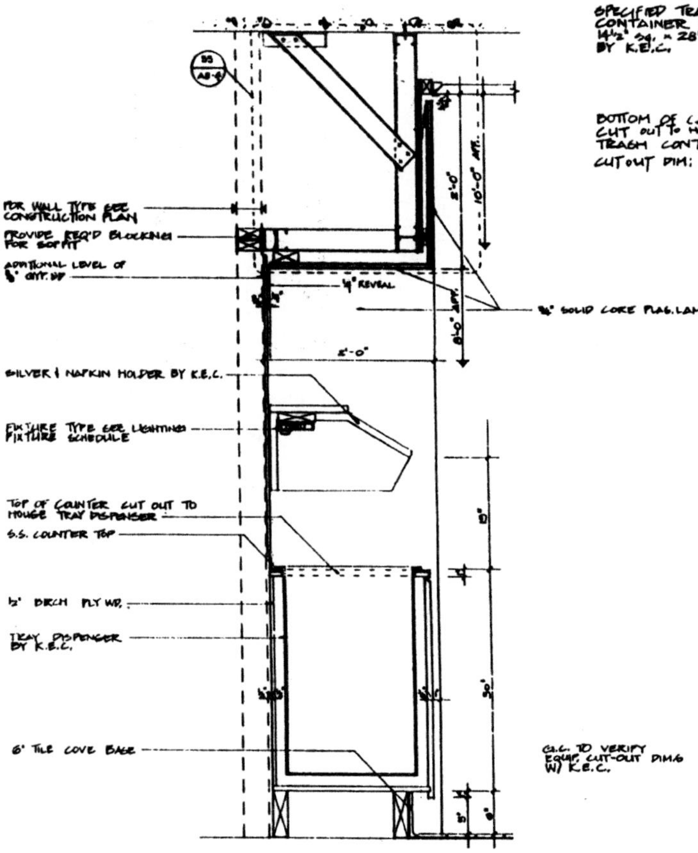

Section at tray pick-up

RESTAURANTS

Condiment Counter Details

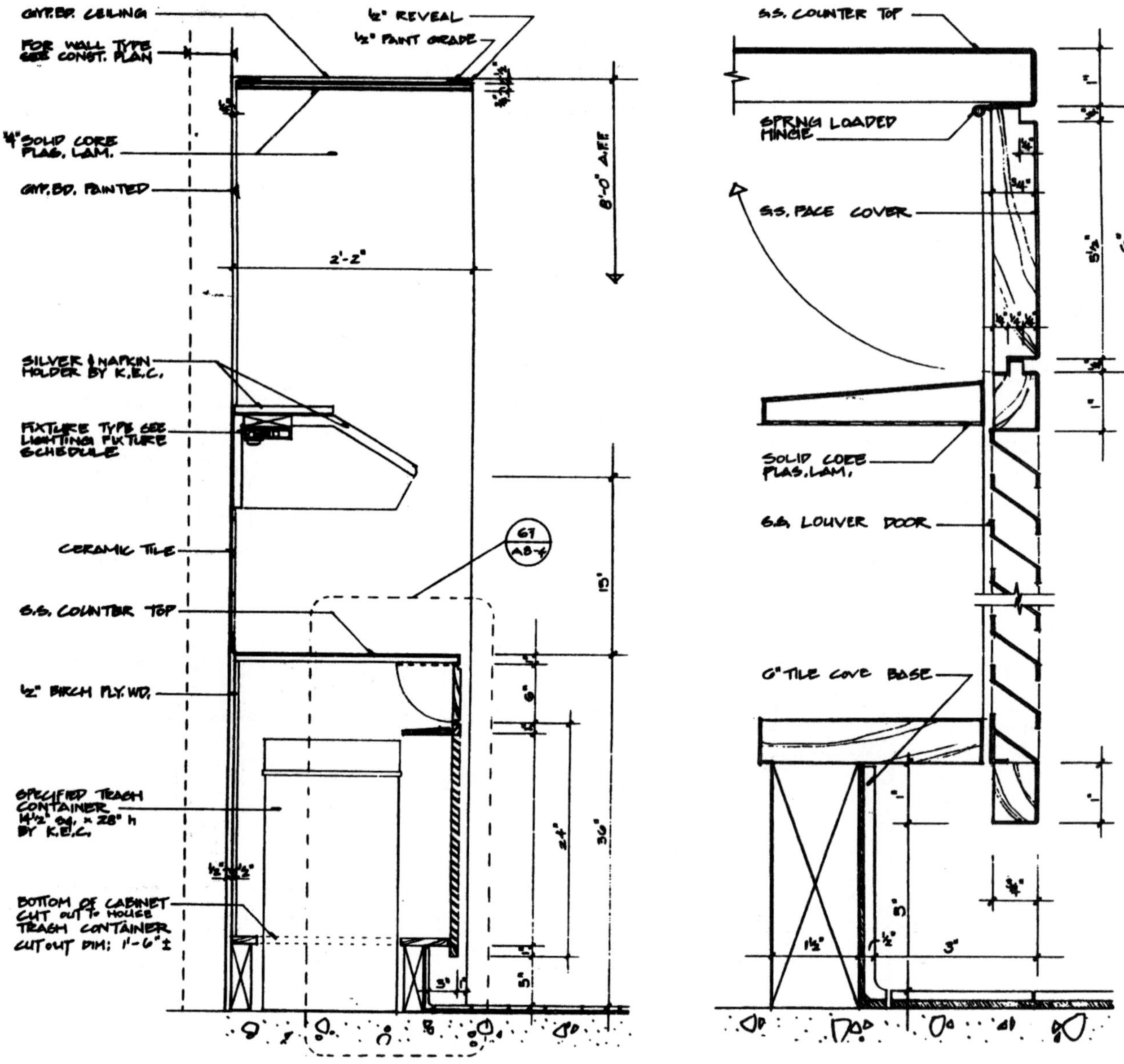

DETAIL SECTION AT
CONDIMENT COUNTER

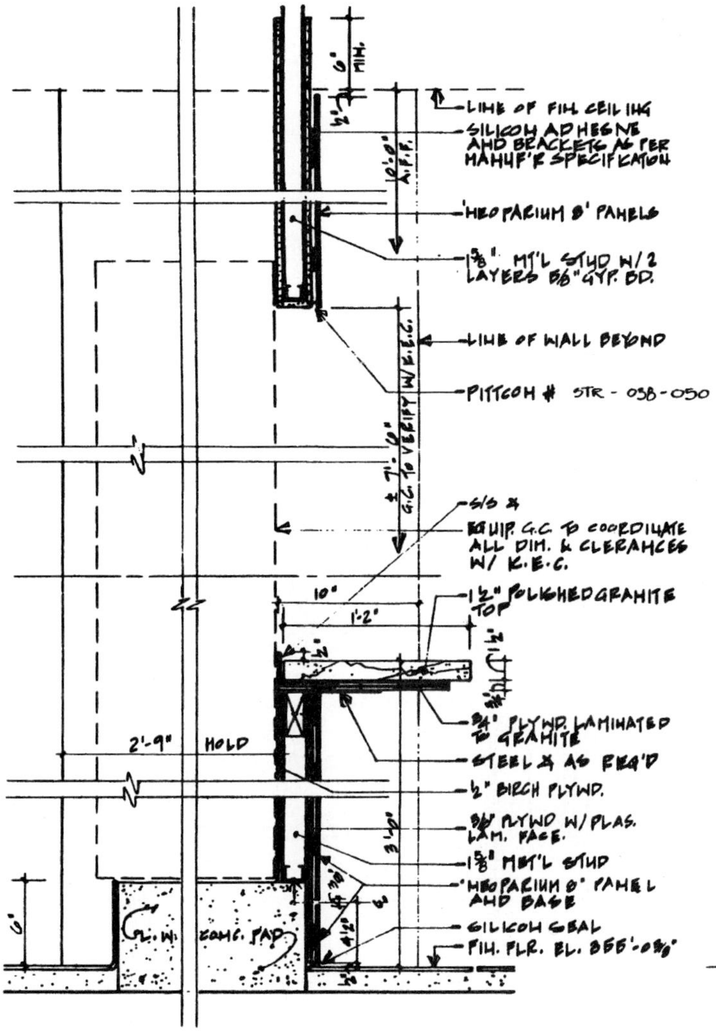

SECTION AT STONE COUNTERS

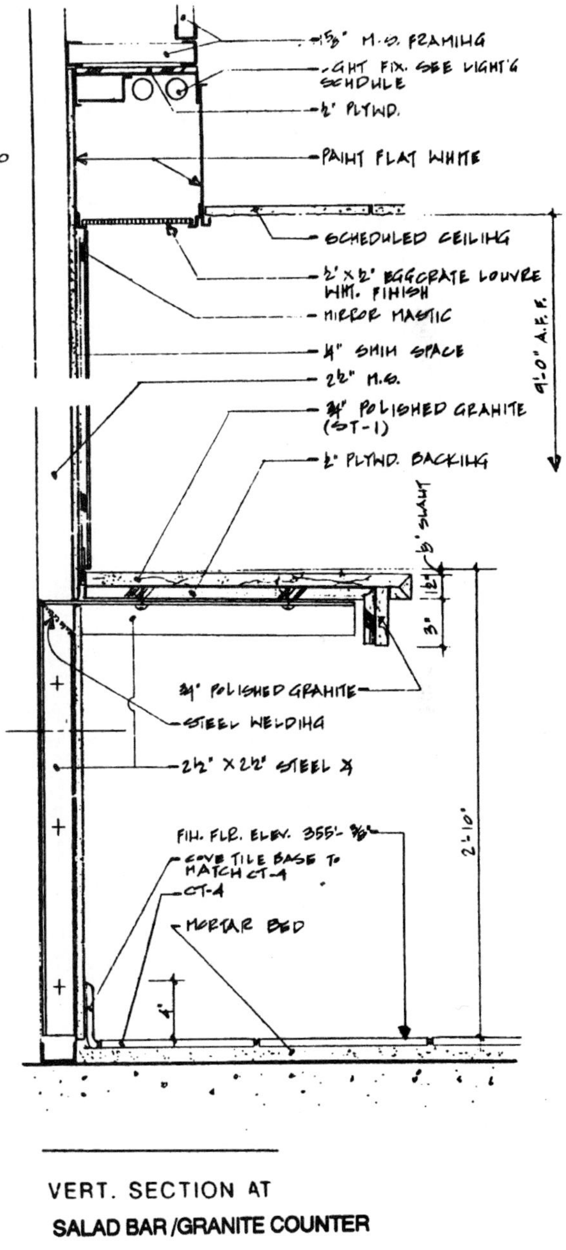

VERT. SECTION AT
SALAD BAR /GRANITE COUNTER

RESTAURANTS
Salad Bar Details

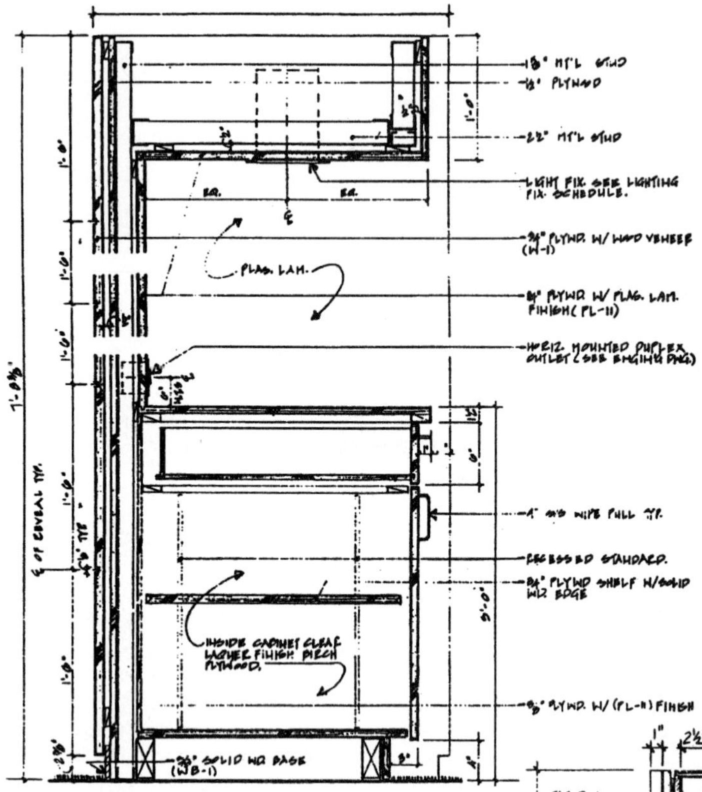

VERT. SECTION THROUGH CABINET AT SALAD BAR

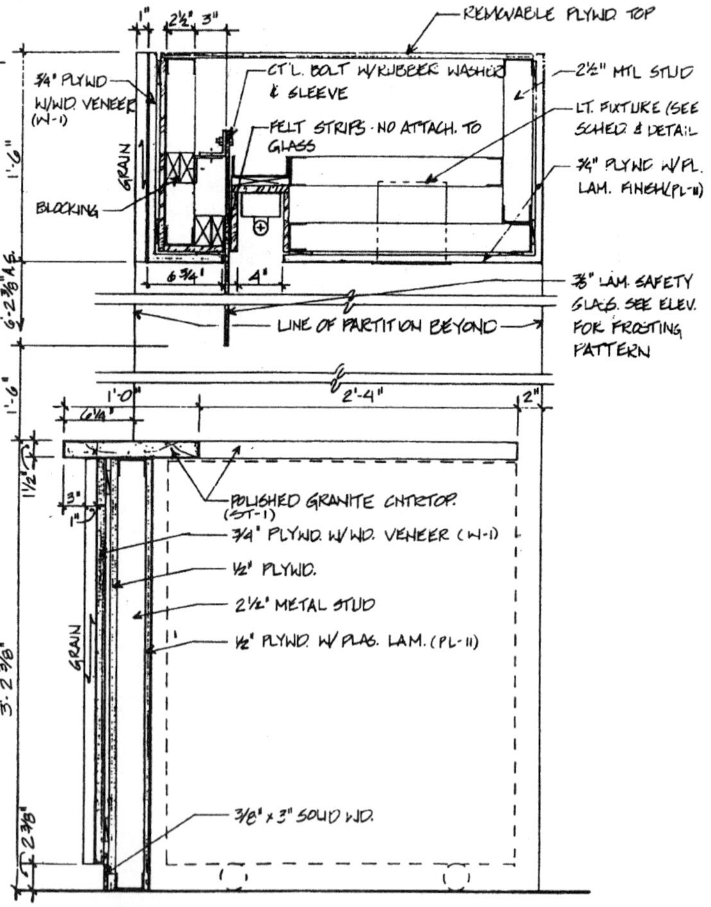

VERT. SECTION AT CENTER OF SALAD BAR & PROTECTIVE GLASS GUARD

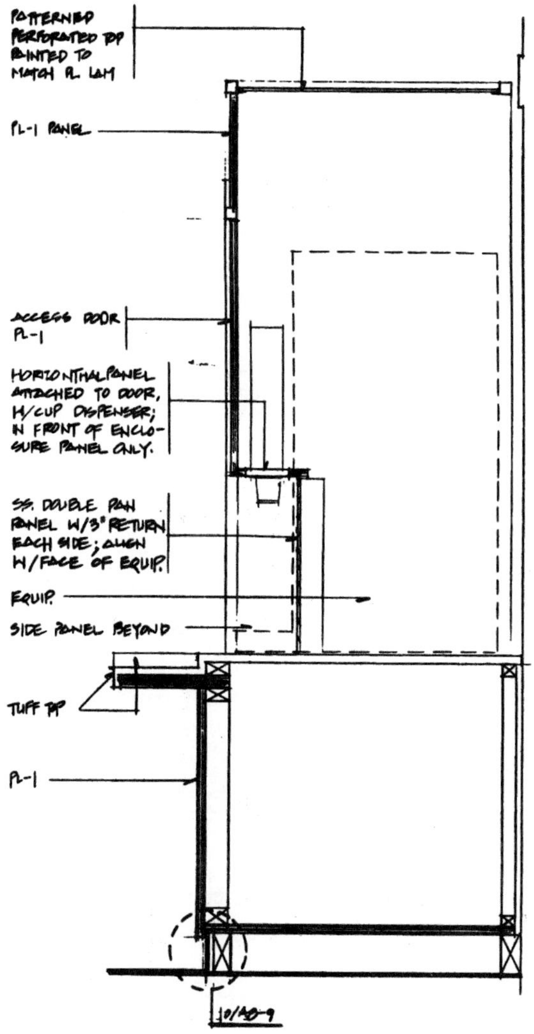

COLD BEVERAGE & DESSERT STAND

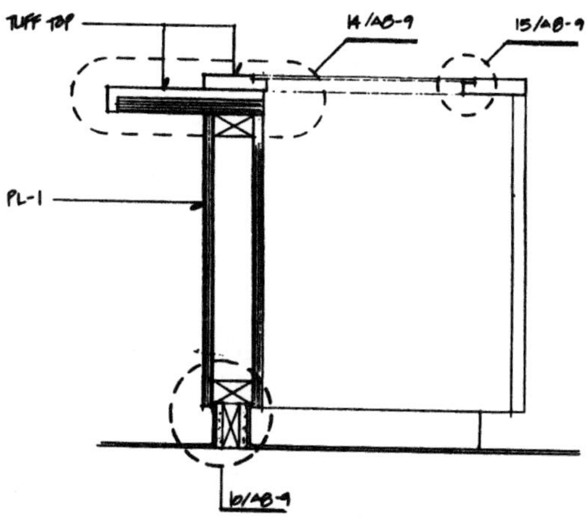

HOT FOOD STAND

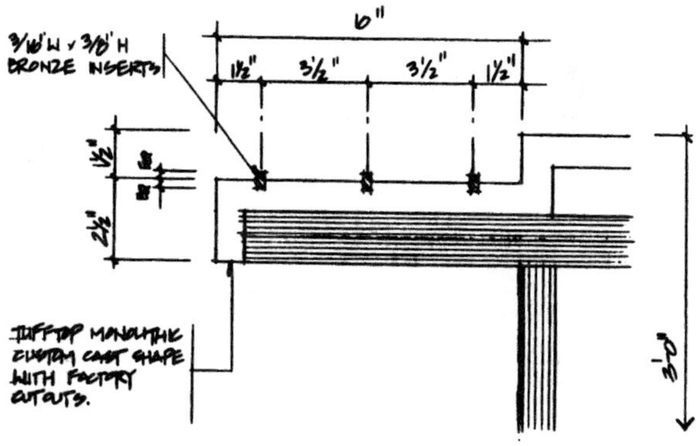

TRAY SLIDE

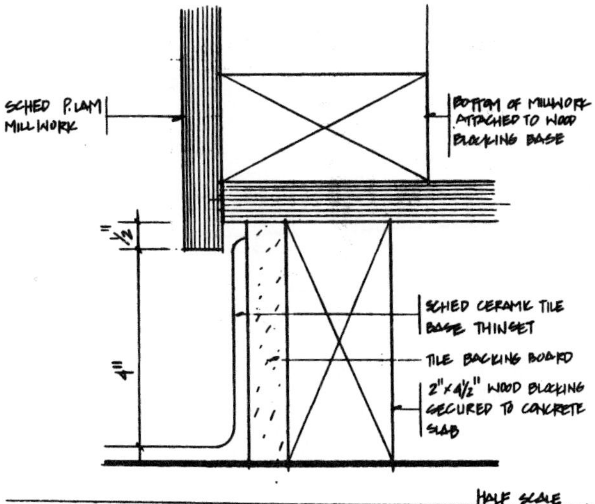

TYPICAL BASE DETAIL @ SERVERY MILLWORK | 10

BARS
Bar Section Details

The distance between bar and backbar should allow adequate work space. A minimum of 36 in, or 90 cm, should provide space for one bartender to serve and another to circulate behind. Maximum body depth and maximum body breadth are the primary anthropometric considerations in establishing clearance. A one-bartender operation would require a 30-in, or 75-cm, clearance. (See Fig. 1.)

In regard to bar stools, clearance between the stool seats is more critical than center line spacing, and it should allow patrons of larger body size a comfortable side approach and departure from the stool without body contact with the next person. A 12-in, or 30-cm wide stool on 24-in, or 61-cm, centers (which is quite common) will allow only less than 5 percent of male users access to the stool without dis-

	in	cm
A	54	137.2
B	18–24	45.7–61.0
C	24	61.0
D	30	76.2
E	16–18	40.6–45.7
F	24–30	61.0–76.2
G	30–36	76.2–91.4
H	28–38	71.1–96.5
I	100–128	254.0–325.1
J	42–45	106.7–114.3
K	11–12	27.9–30.5
L	6–7	15.2–17.8
M	7–9	17.8–22.9
N	6–9	15.2–22.9
O	22–26	55.9–66.0
P	60–69	152.4–175.3
Q	36–42	91.4–106.7

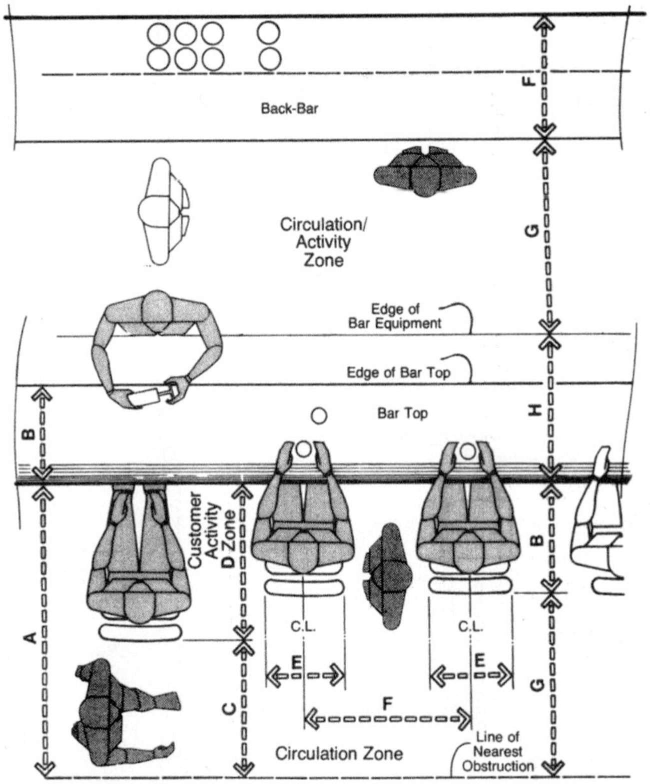

BAR AND BACK-BAR

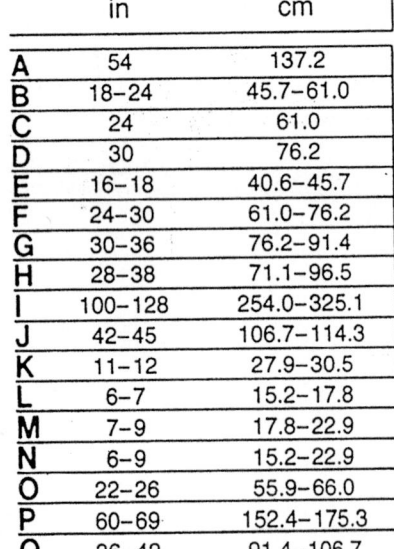

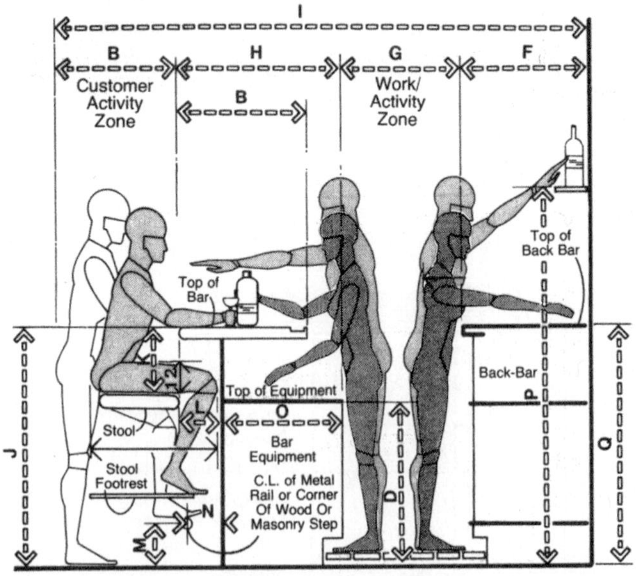

BAR / SECTION

Fig. 1

turbing the next patron, while a 30-in, or 75-cm, spacing will accommodate 95 percent of the users. The tradeoff, however, would be the loss of two seats for every 120 in, or 300 cm, of bar length. A spacing of 12-in stools on 28-in, or 70-cm, centers is suggested as a compromise. The ultimate decision is an individual one and must reconcile human factors with economic viability.

To ensure proper circulation and interface, adequate clearances in front of the bar are illustrated in Fig. 2. A customer activity zone of 18 to 24 in, or 45.7 to 61.0 cm, should be provided to allow for seating, standing, and access, in addition to a general circulation zone of at least 30 in, or 76.2 cm. If a supplementary drinking surface or shelf is provided, a smaller activity zone of 18 in is suggested in front of the shelf. The shelf can be 10 to 12 in, or 25.4 to 30.5 cm, deep. Figure 3 shows suggested clearances for 18- or 24-in cocktail tables.

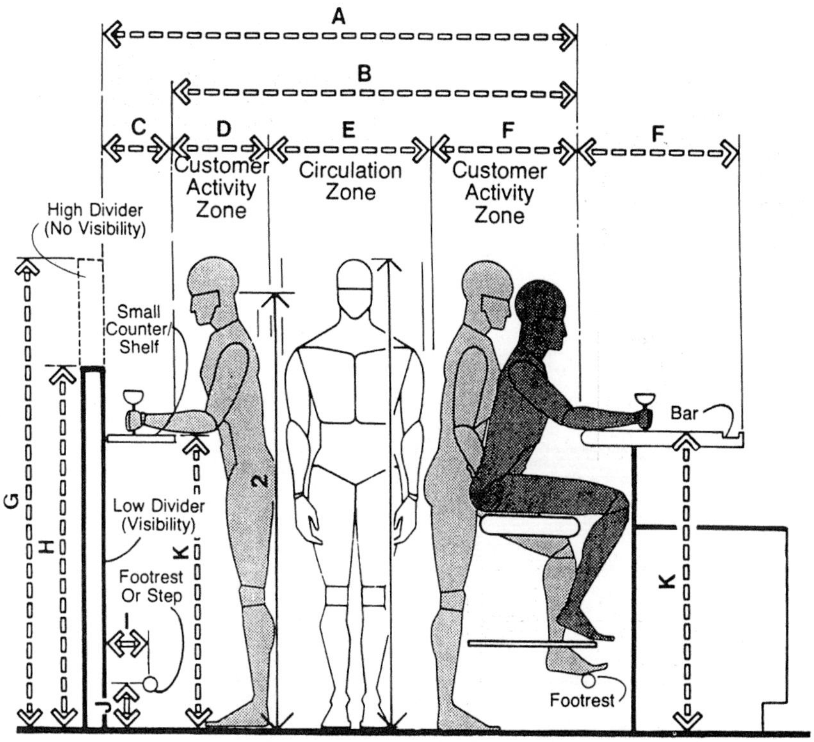

Fig. 2 Bar/clearances, public side

	in	cm
A	76–84	193.0–213.4
B	66–72	167.6–182.9
C	10–12	25.4–30.5
D	18	45.7
E	30	76.2
F	18–24	45.7–61.0
G	76	193.0
H	54–56	137.2–142.2
I	6–9	15.2–22.9
J	7–9	17.8–22.9
K	42–45	106.7–114.3
L	24	61.0
M	29–33	73.7–83.8
N	32–36	81.3–91.4

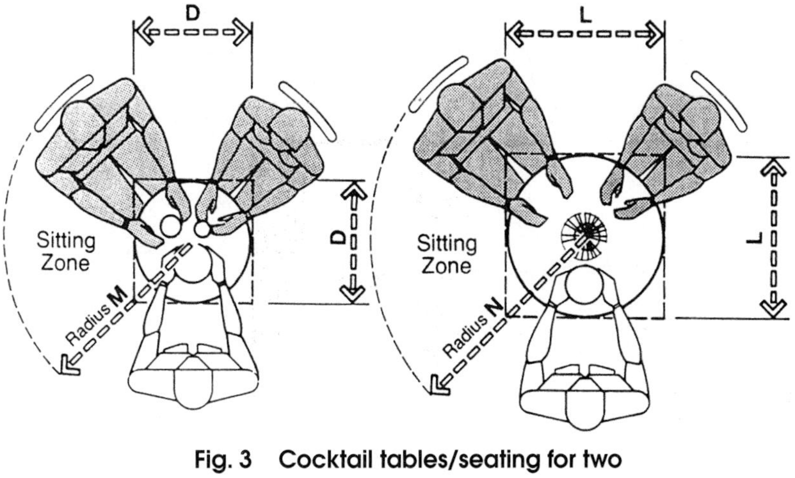

Fig. 3 Cocktail tables/seating for two

BARS

Bar Shapes: Planning Criteria

Bar shapes, seating capacities, overall dimensions, and footprints of bar areas vary greatly. Figures 4 to 22 show examples of bar designs drawn at a scale of ¼ in = 1 ft 0 in. Careful study of these designs would suggest that seating width, spacing, and circulation areas must be given special attention.

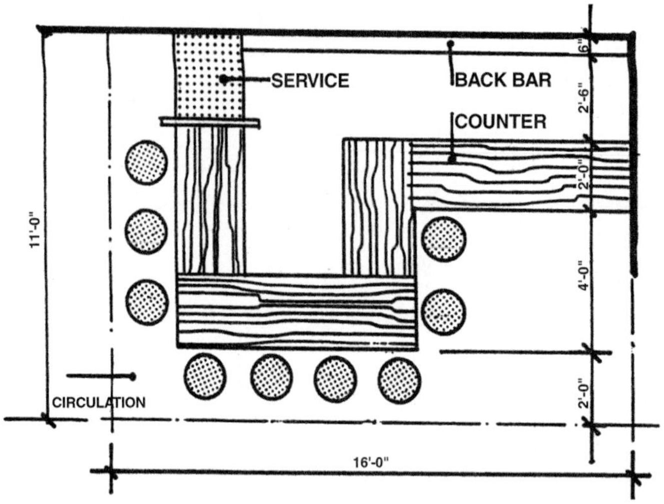

Fig. 4 U shape: 16 ft × 11 ft, 176 ft², seats nine

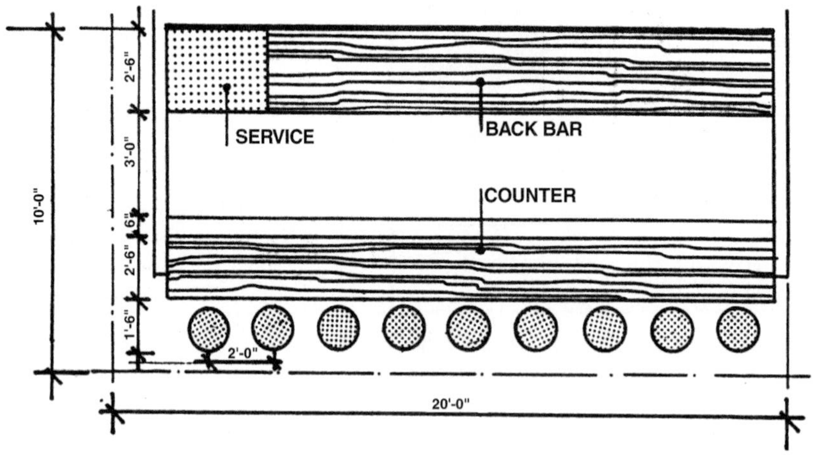

Fig. 5 Straight/enclosed: 20 ft × 10 ft, 200 ft², seats nine

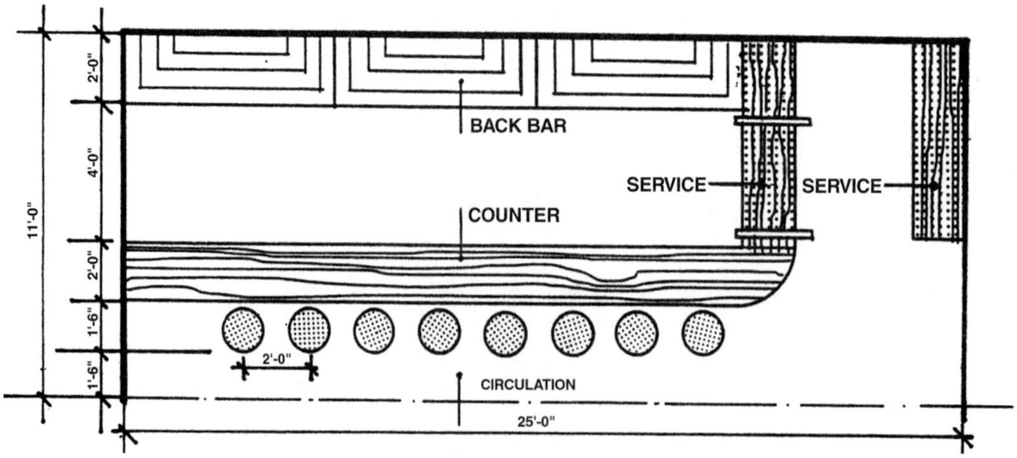

Fig. 6 Straight bar: 25 ft × 10 ft, 250 ft², seats eight

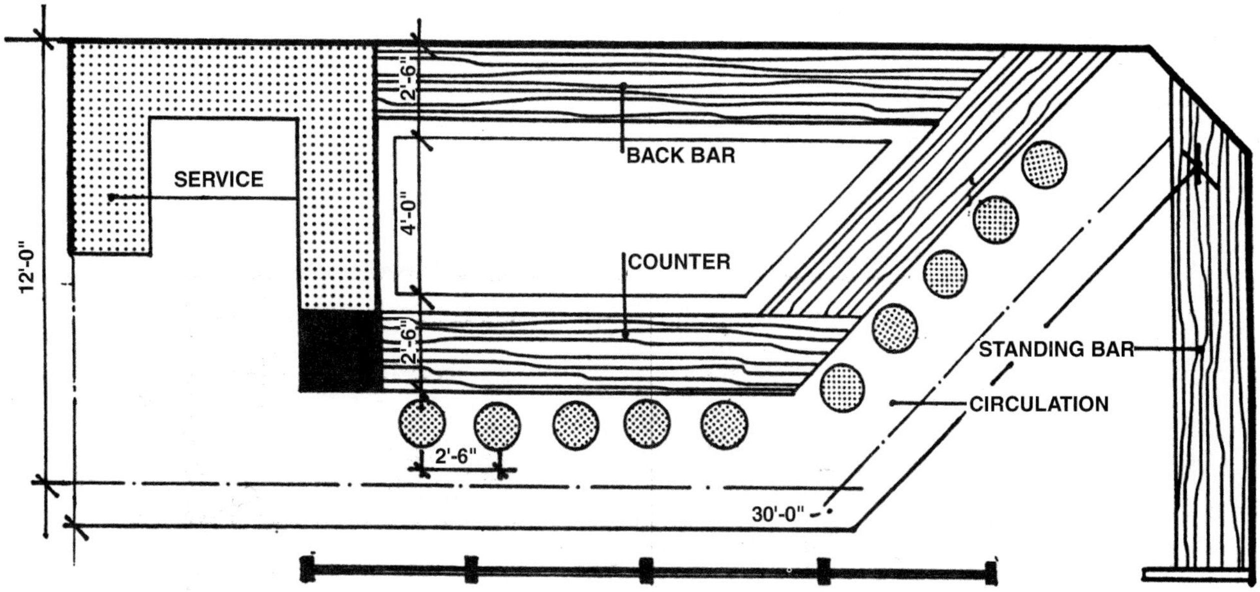

Fig. 7 Angular: 30 ft × 12 ft, 320 ft², seats 10

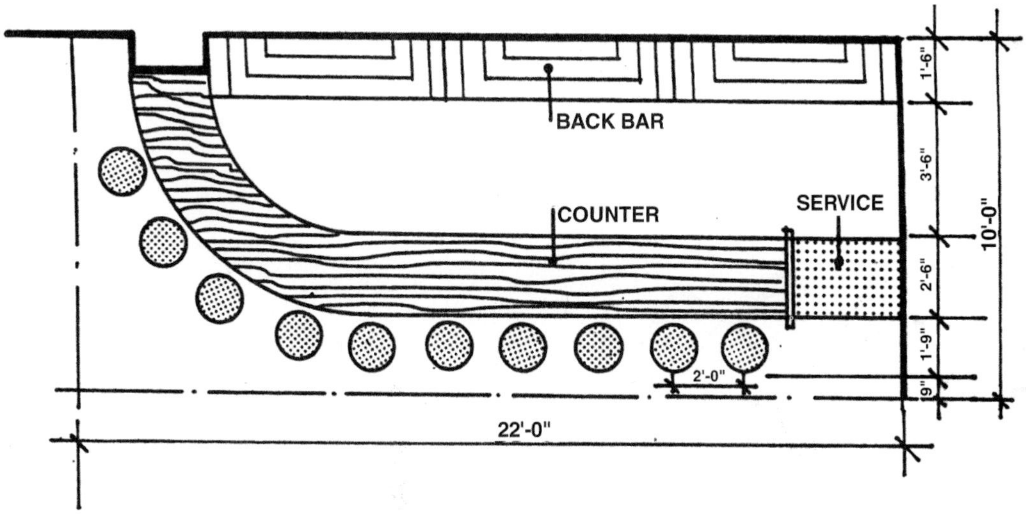

Fig. 8 Enclosed/rounded end: 22 ft × 9 ft, 198 ft², seats 10

BARS

Bar Shapes: Planning Criteria

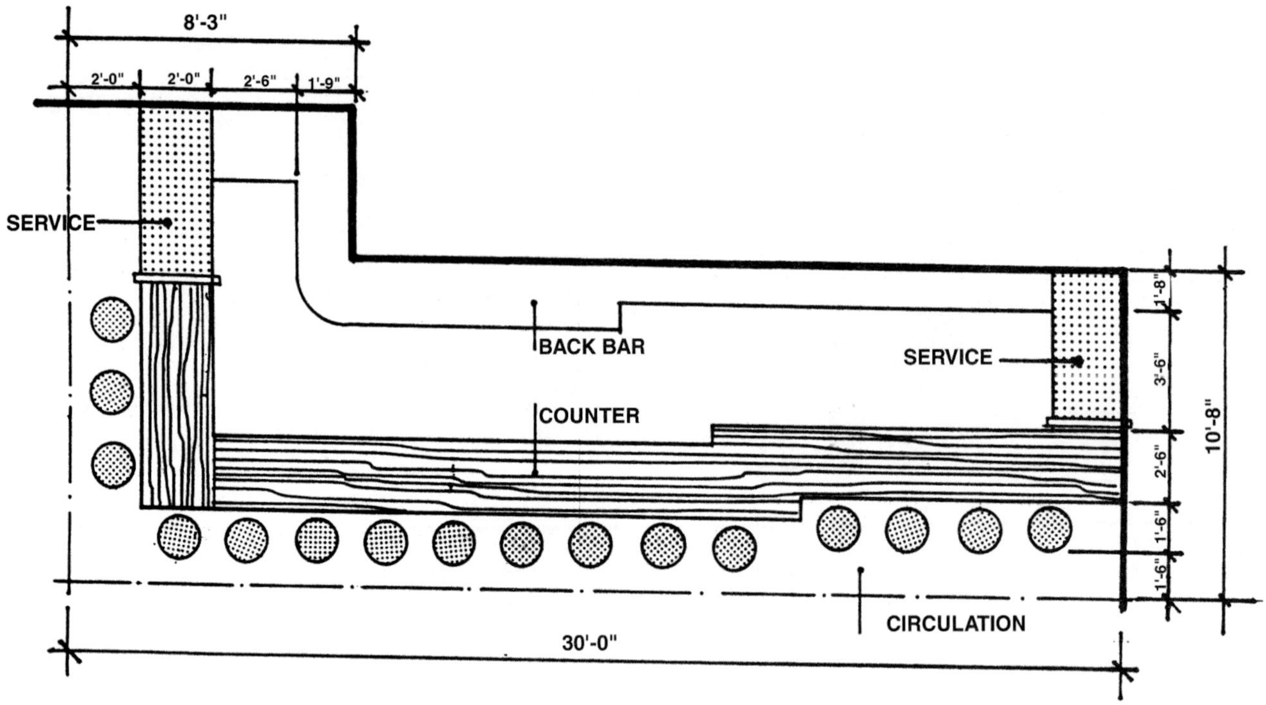

Fig. 9 L shape: 30 ft × 13 ft, 390 ft², seats 15

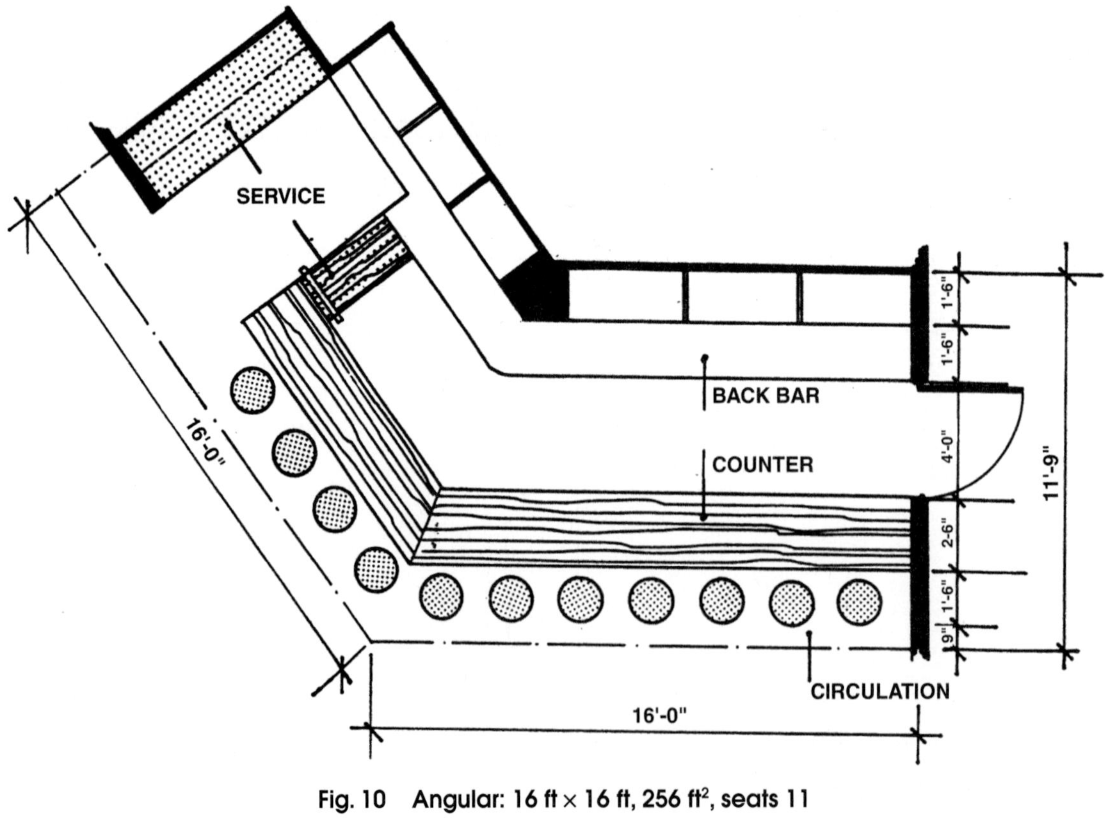

Fig. 10 Angular: 16 ft × 16 ft, 256 ft², seats 11

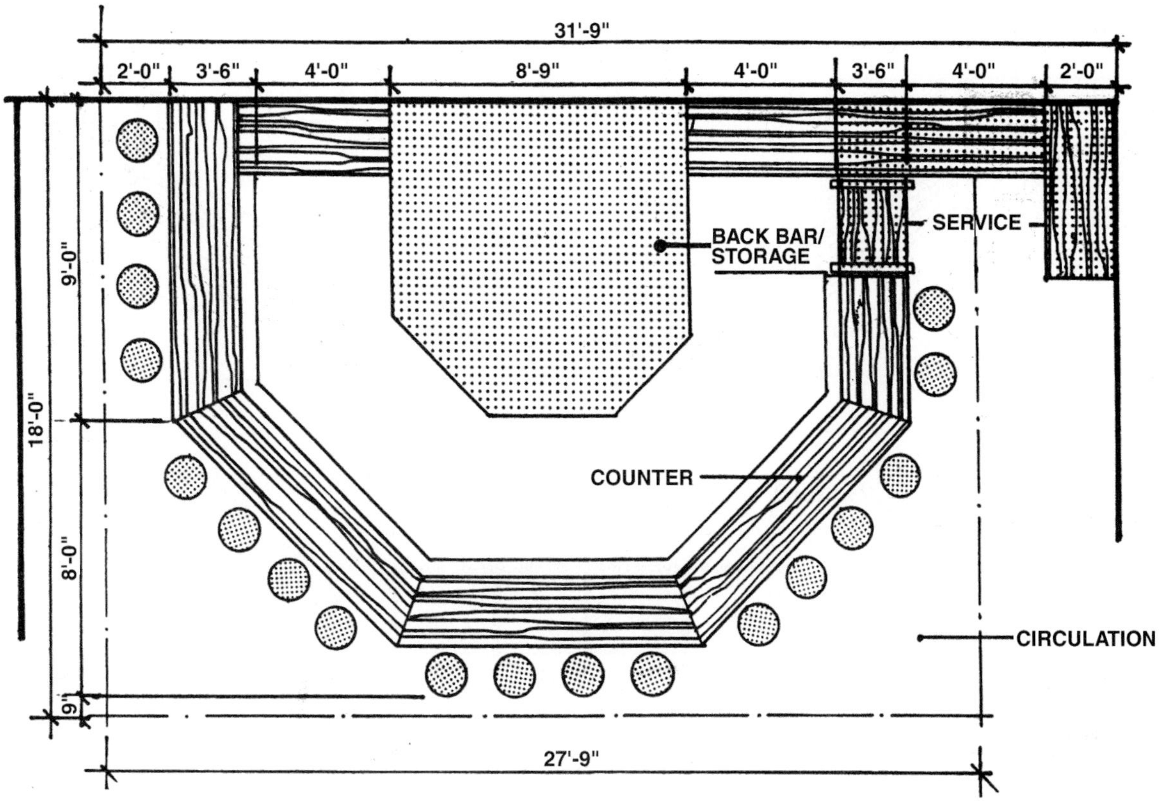

Fig. 11 Octagon/partial: 26 ft × 18 ft, 468 ft², seats 16

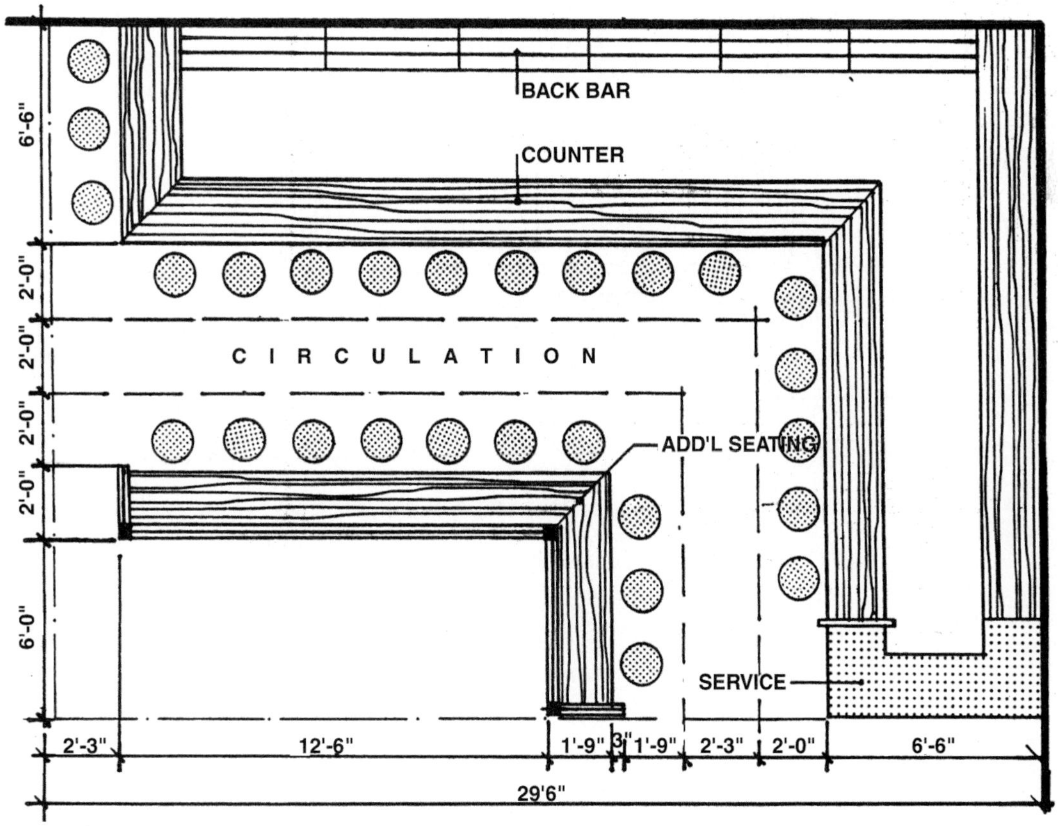

Fig. 12 L shape: 27 ft × 20 ft, 510 ft². Bar seating, 17; additional seating, 10

BARS

Bar Shapes: Planning Criteria

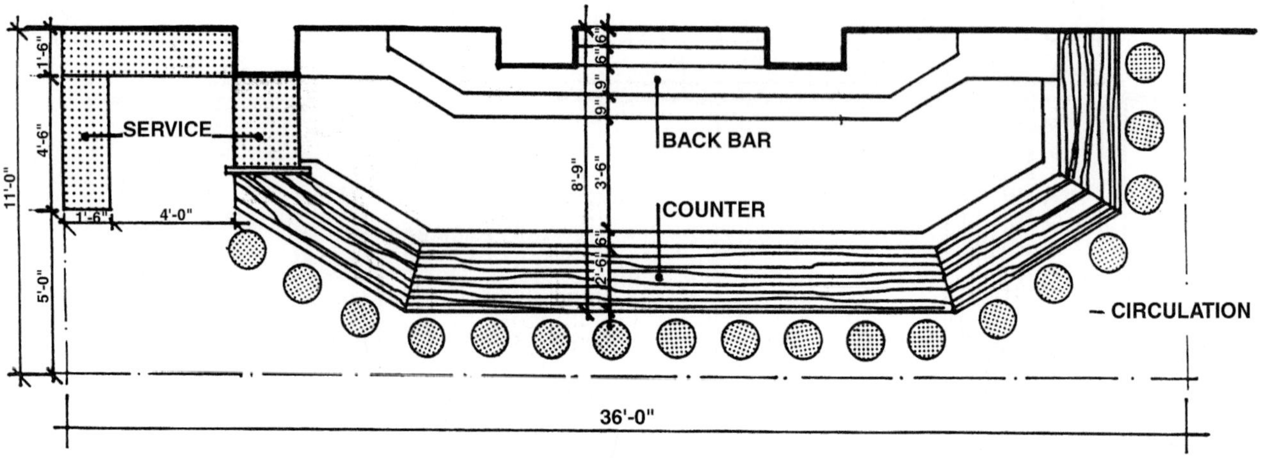

Fig. 13 Polygon: 36 ft × 11 ft, 396 ft², seats 18

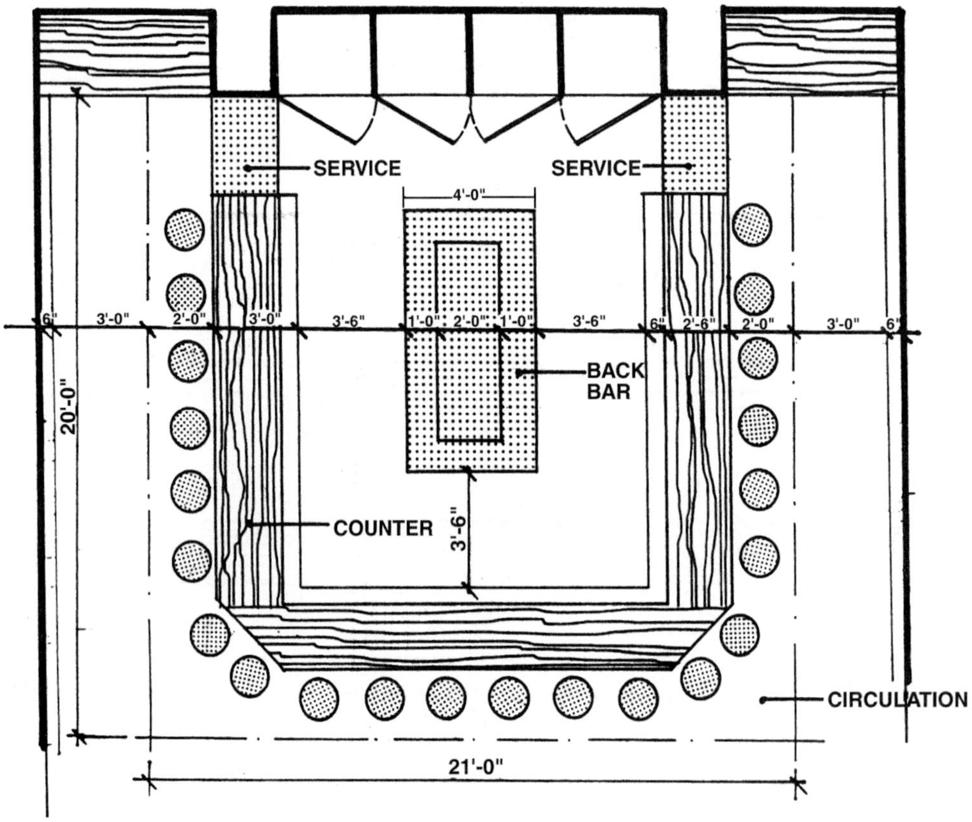

Fig. 14 U shape: 21 ft × 20 ft, 420 ft², seats 22

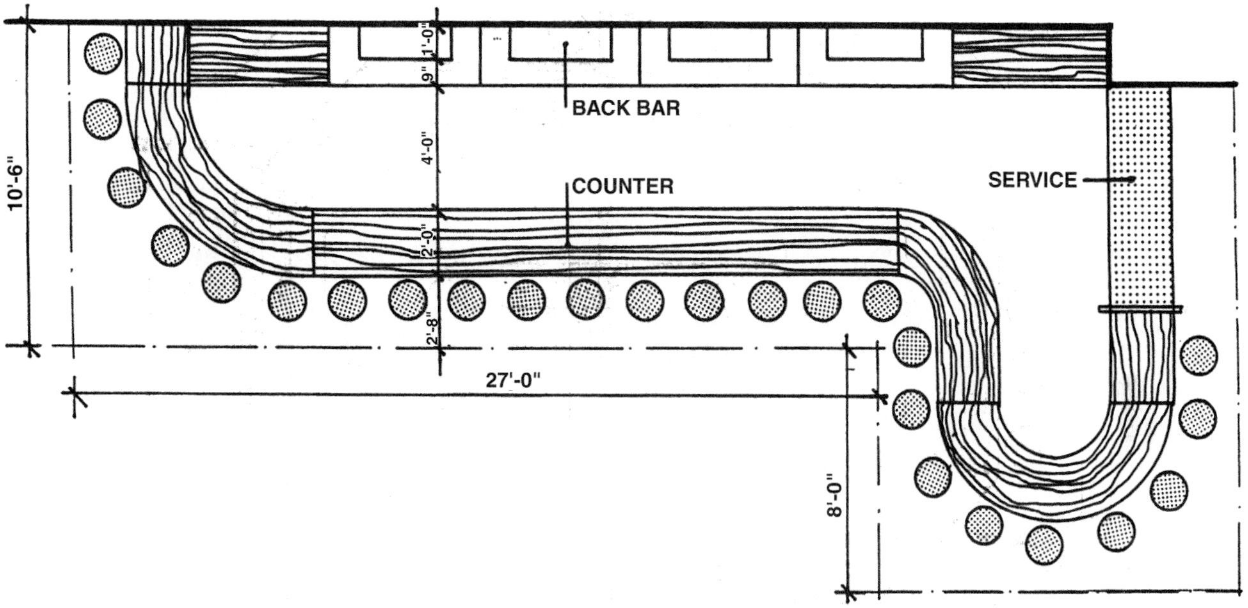

Fig. 15 Curvilinear bar: 500 ft², seats 25

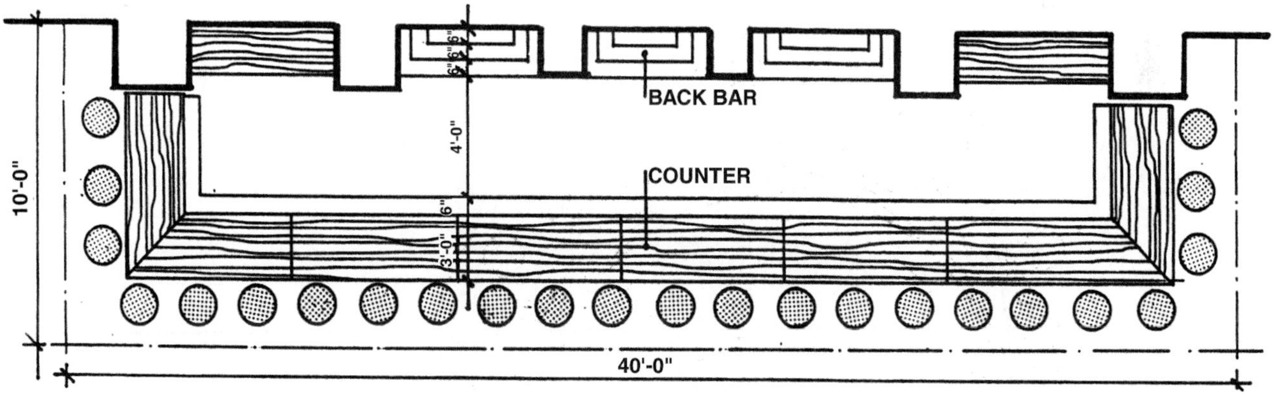

Fig. 16 Straight bar: 40 ft × 10 ft, 400 ft², seats 24

BARS
Bar Shapes: Planning Criteria

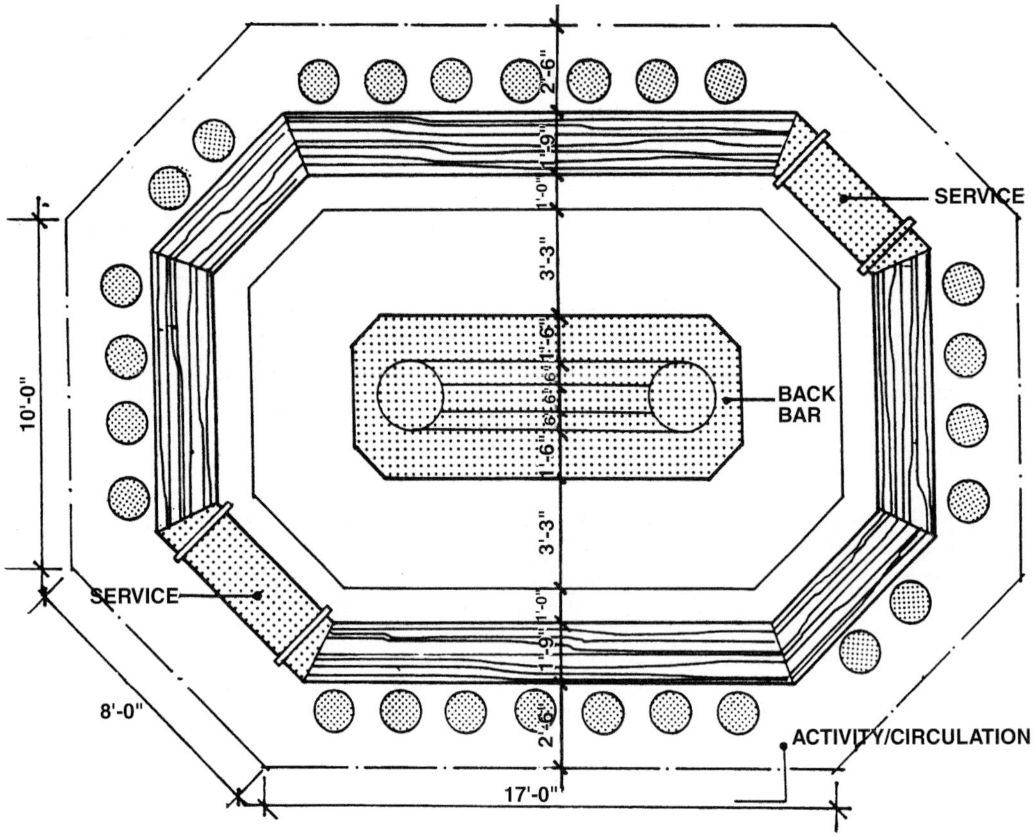

Fig. 17 Octagon/freestanding: 28 ft × 21 ft, 558 ft²

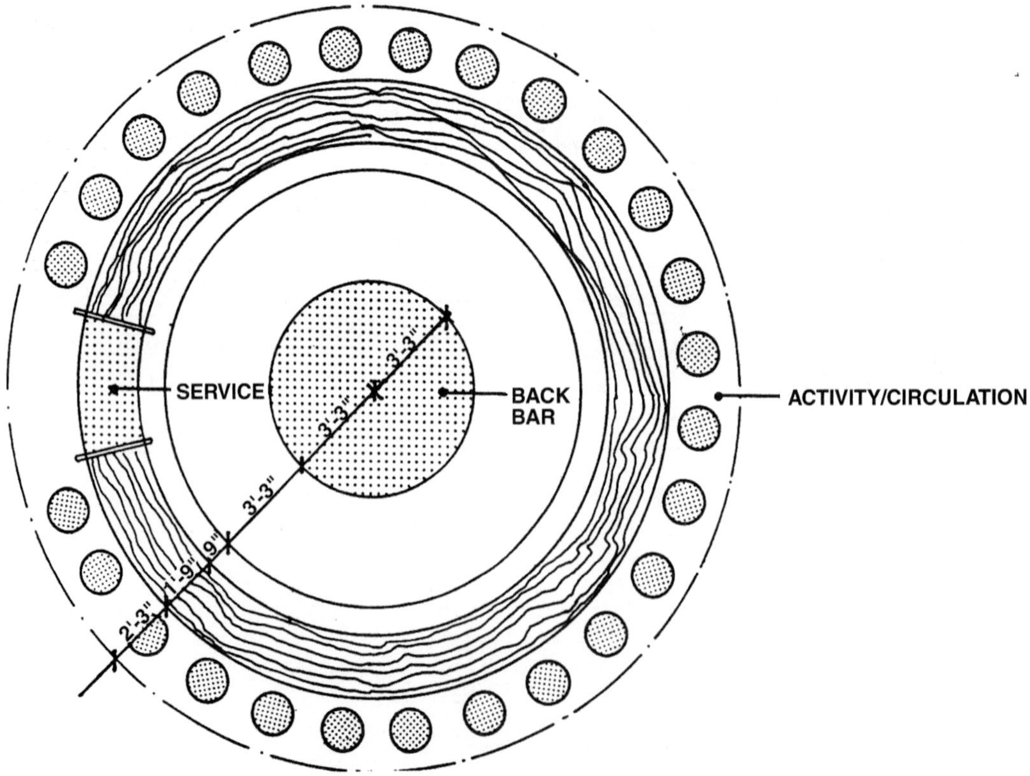

Fig. 18 Circular/freestanding: 22 ft × 22 ft, 334 ft², seats 26

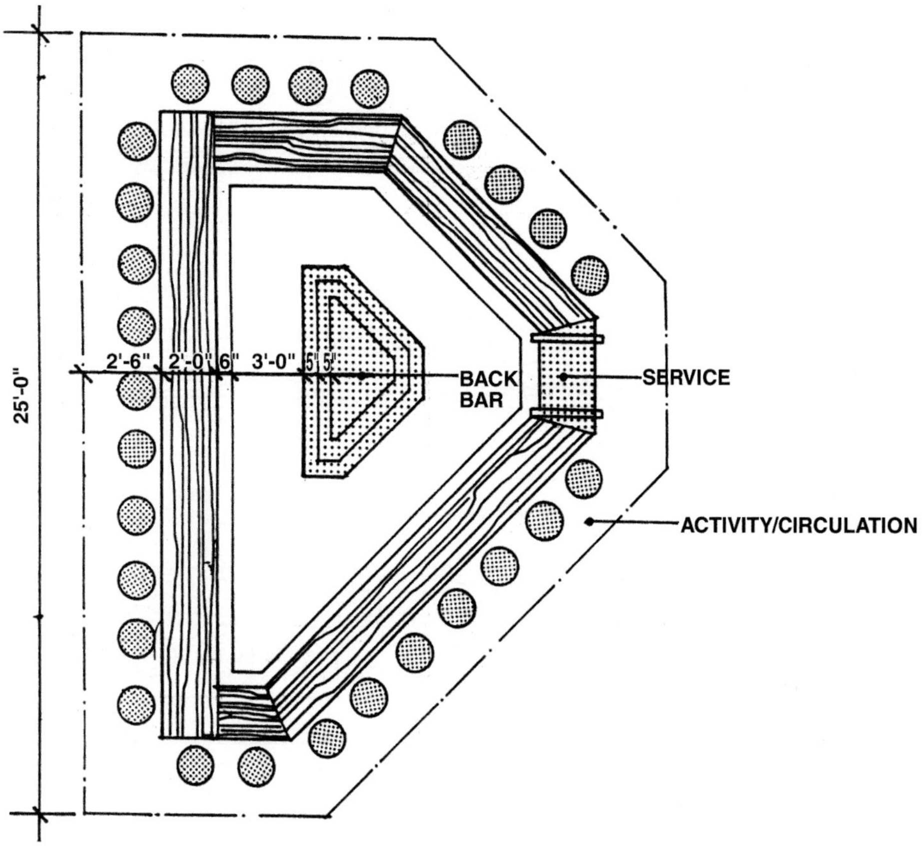

Fig. 19 Polygon irregular: 20 ft × 25 ft, 360 ft², seats 27

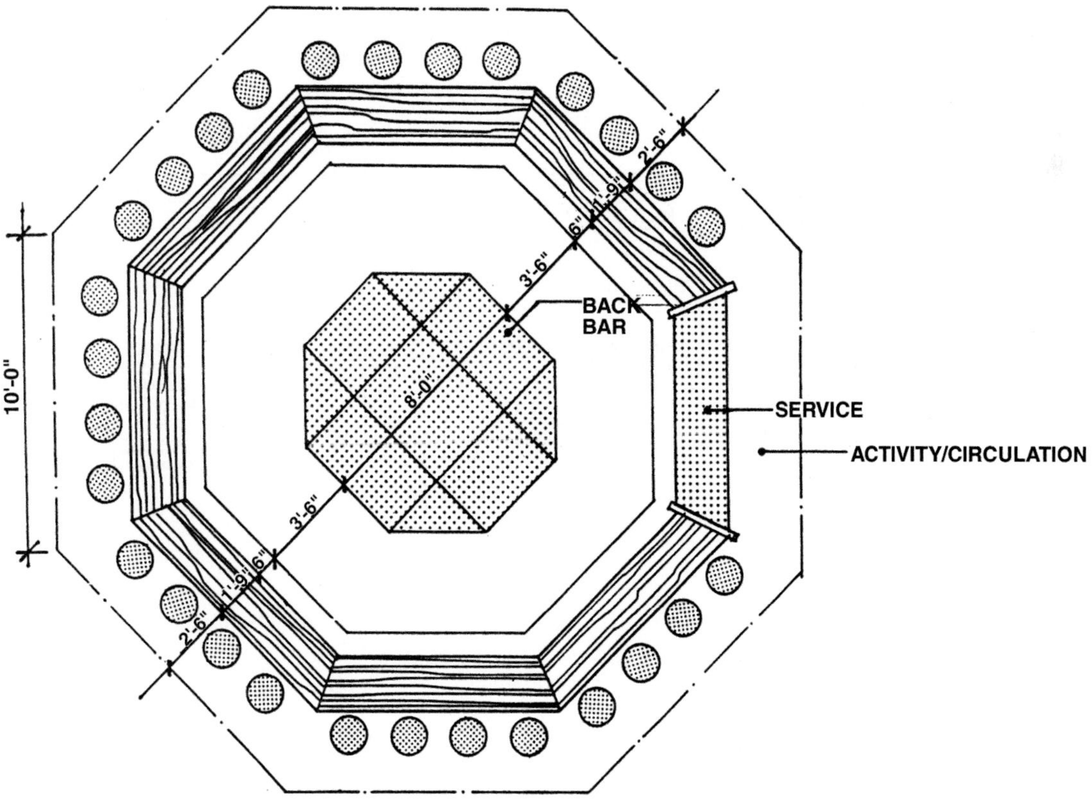

Fig. 20 Octagon: 25 ft × 25 ft, 429 ft², seats 28

BARS

Bar Shapes: Planning Criteria

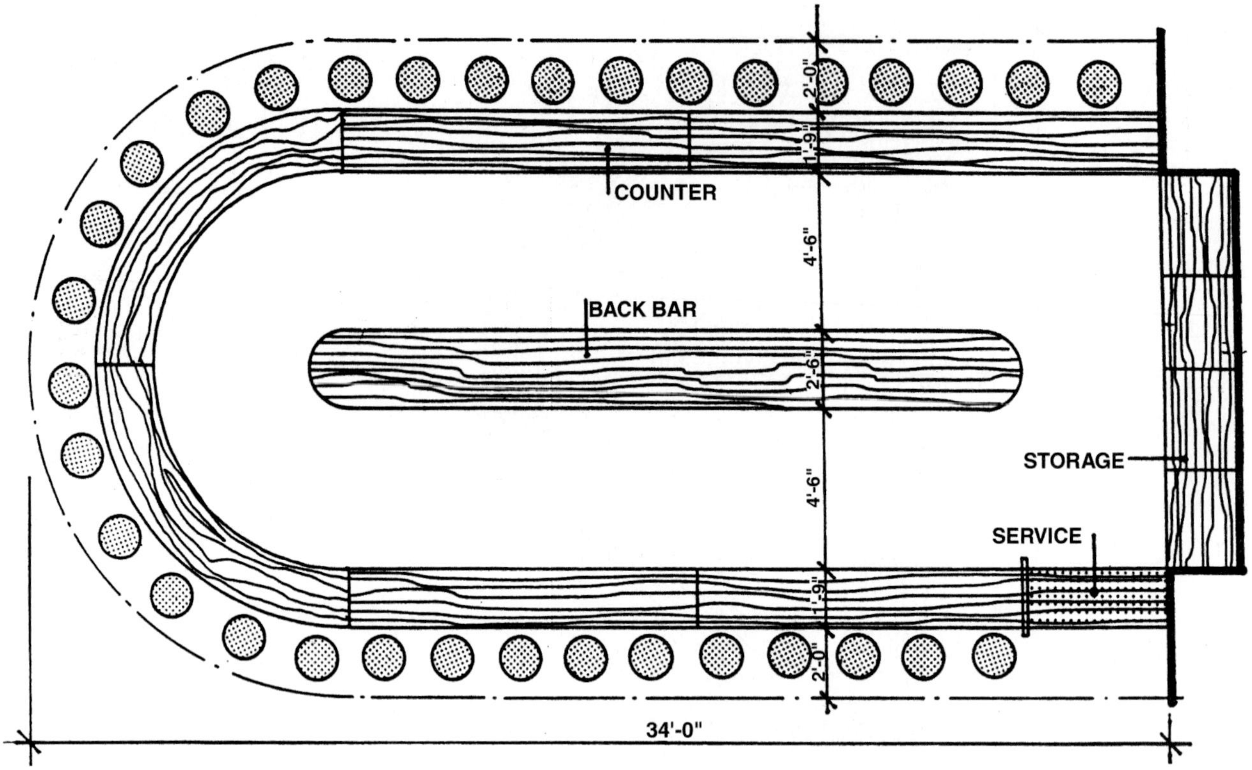

Fig. 21 Horseshoe/oval end: 34 ft × 19 ft, 546 ft², seats 34

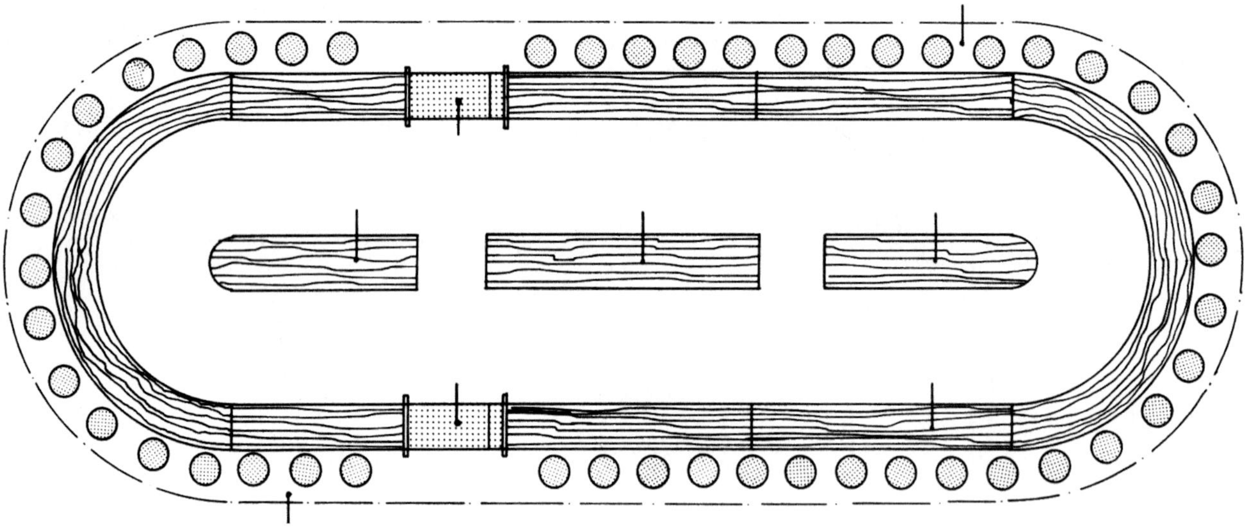

Fig. 22 Racetrack: 50 ft × 19 ft, 750 ft², seats 48

The detailing of bars and backbars can vary from the very simple and basic to the complicated and intricate. Figures 23 to 40 provide the designer with selected examples of working drawings from some of the most experienced restaurant and hospitality design firms in the world. Careful review of these drawings would suggest that overall dimensions and clearances vary from detail to detail. In that regard, individual requirements based on bar type and the hospitality area serviced must be given careful consideration. In addition, local building codes and health codes must be consulted.

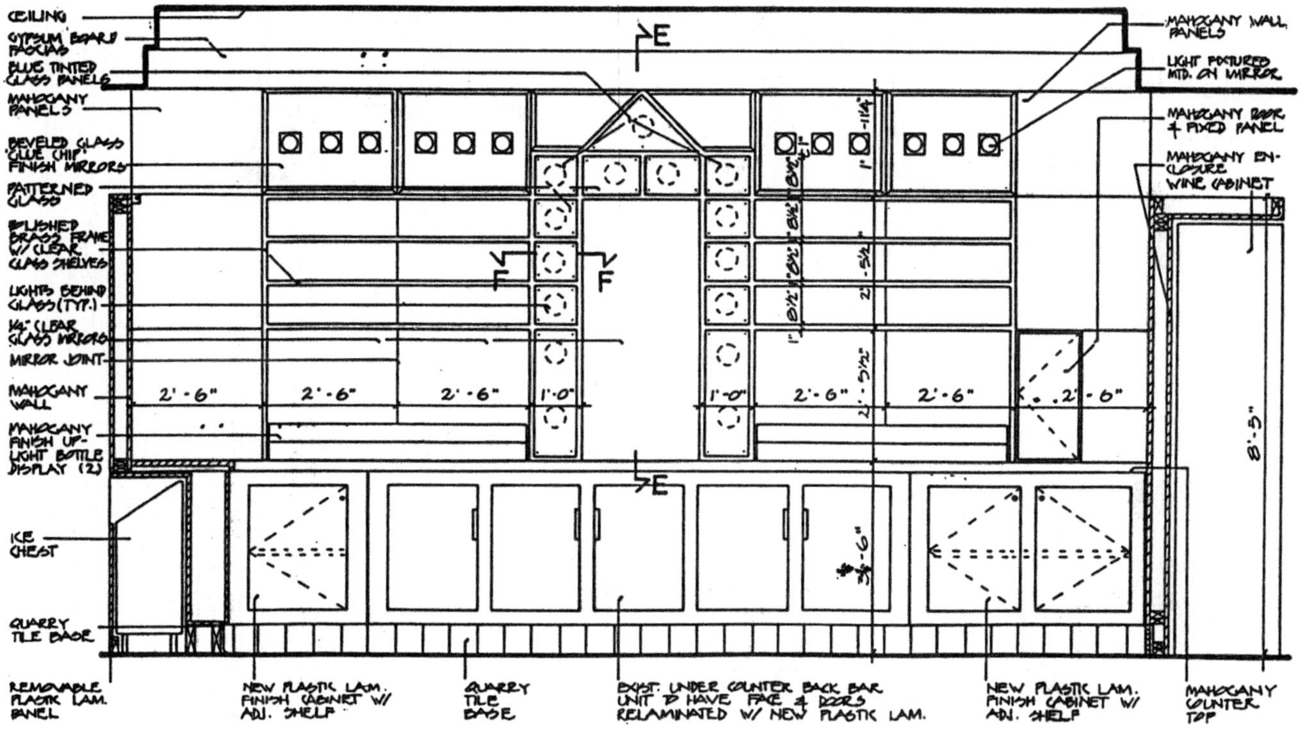

Fig. 23

BARS

Bar Plans, Elevations, and Sections

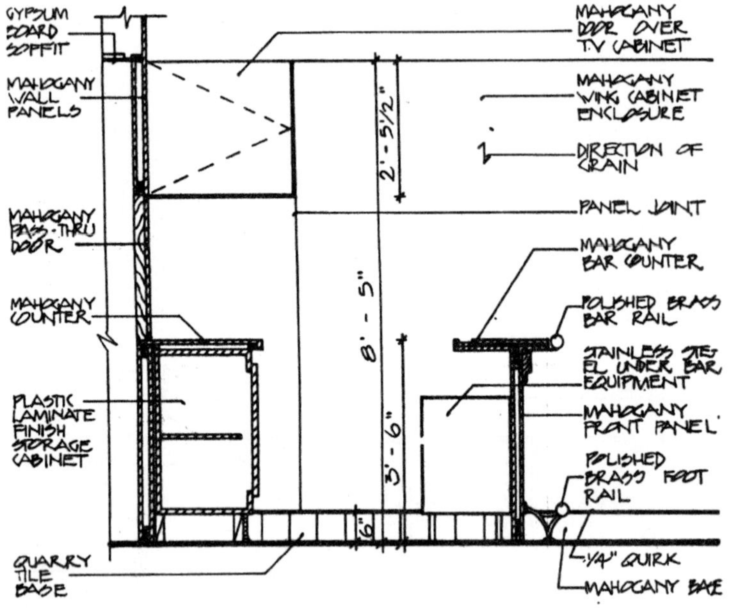
GYPSUM BOARD SOFFIT
MAHOGANY WALL PANELS
MAHOGANY PASS-THRU DOOR
MAHOGANY COUNTER
PLASTIC LAMINATE FINISH STORAGE CABINET
QUARRY TILE BASE
MAHOGANY DOOR OVER T.V. CABINET
MAHOGANY WING CABINET ENCLOSURE
DIRECTION OF GRAIN
PANEL JOINT
MAHOGANY BAR COUNTER
POLISHED BRASS BAR RAIL
STAINLESS STEEL UNDER BAR EQUIPMENT
MAHOGANY FRONT PANEL
POLISHED BRASS FOOT RAIL
1/4" QUIRK
MAHOGANY BASE
2' - 5 1/2"
8' - 5"
3' - 6"
6"

DD SECTION

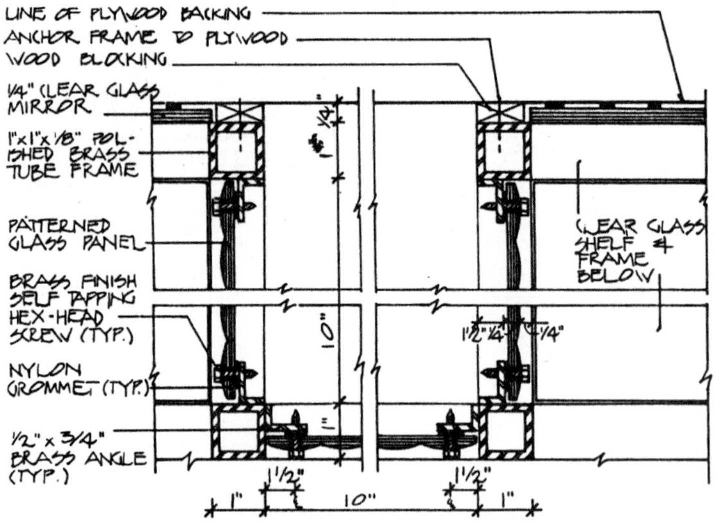
LINE OF PLYWOOD BACKING
ANCHOR FRAME TO PLYWOOD
WOOD BLOCKING
1/4" CLEAR GLASS MIRROR
1"x1"x1/8" POLISHED BRASS TUBE FRAME
PATTERNED GLASS PANEL
BRASS FINISH SELF TAPPING HEX-HEAD SCREW (TYP.)
NYLON GROMMET (TYP.)
1/2" x 3/4" BRASS ANGLE (TYP.)
CLEAR GLASS SHELF & FRAME BELOW
10"
1"
1 1/2"
1/4"
1 1/2"
10"
1"

FF SECTION

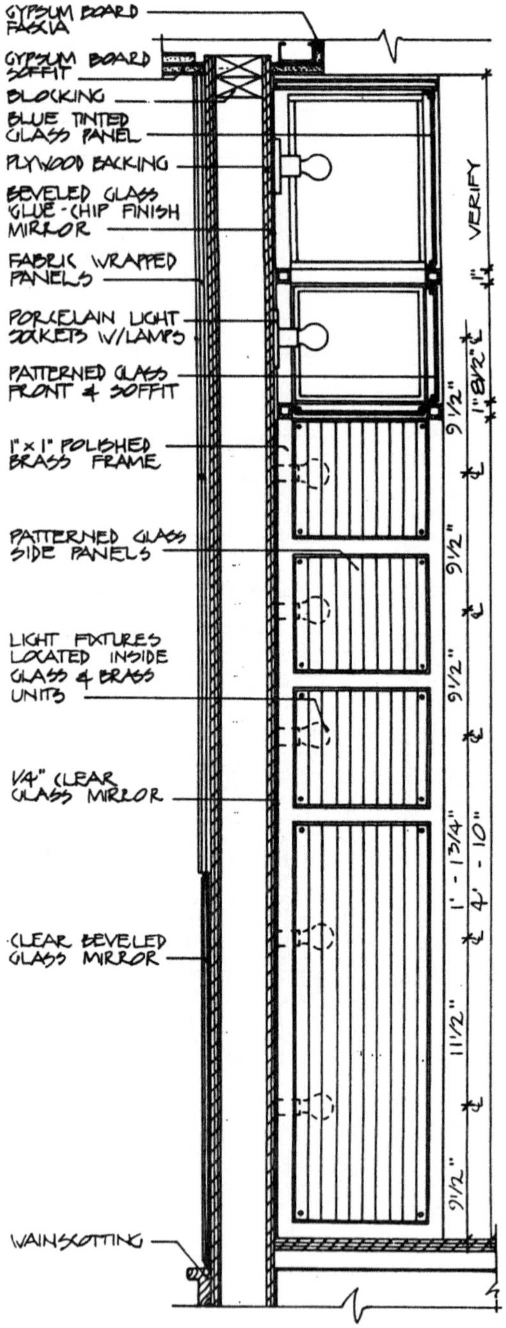
GYPSUM BOARD FASCIA
GYPSUM BOARD SOFFIT
BLOCKING
BLUE TINTED GLASS PANEL
PLYWOOD BACKING
BEVELED GLASS GLUE-CHIP FINISH MIRROR
FABRIC WRAPPED PANELS
PORCELAIN LIGHT SOCKETS W/LAMPS
PATTERNED GLASS FRONT & SOFFIT
1" x 1" POLISHED BRASS FRAME
PATTERNED GLASS SIDE PANELS
LIGHT FIXTURES LOCATED INSIDE GLASS & BRASS UNITS
1/4" CLEAR GLASS MIRROR
CLEAR BEVELED GLASS MIRROR
WAINSCOTTING
VERIFY
1"
8 1/2"
1"
9 1/2"
9 1/2"
9 1/2"
1' - 1 3/4"
4' - 10"
11 1/2"
9 1/2"

EE SECTION

Fig. 23 *(Continued)*

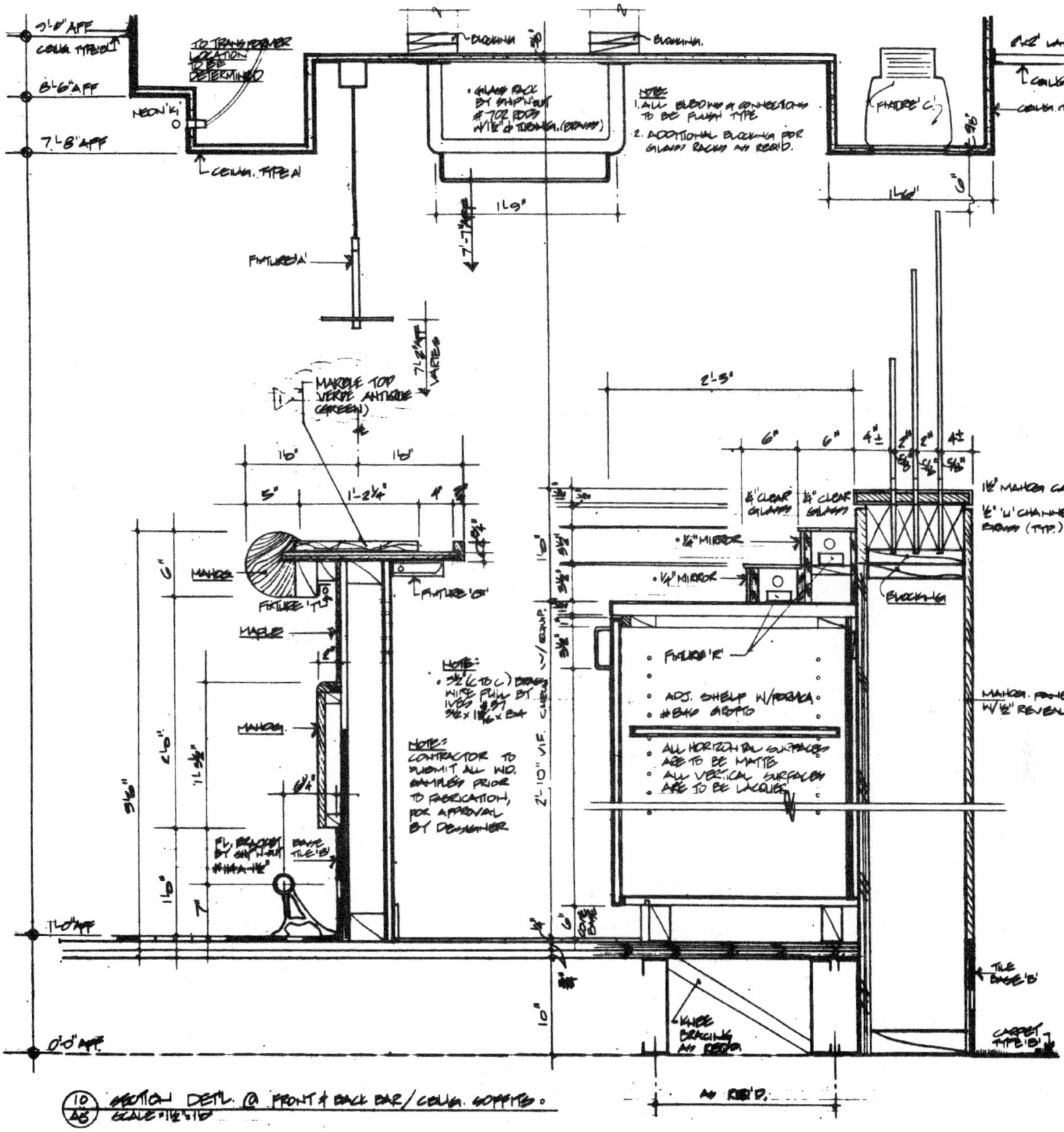

Fig. 24

BARS

Bar Plans, Elevations, and Sections

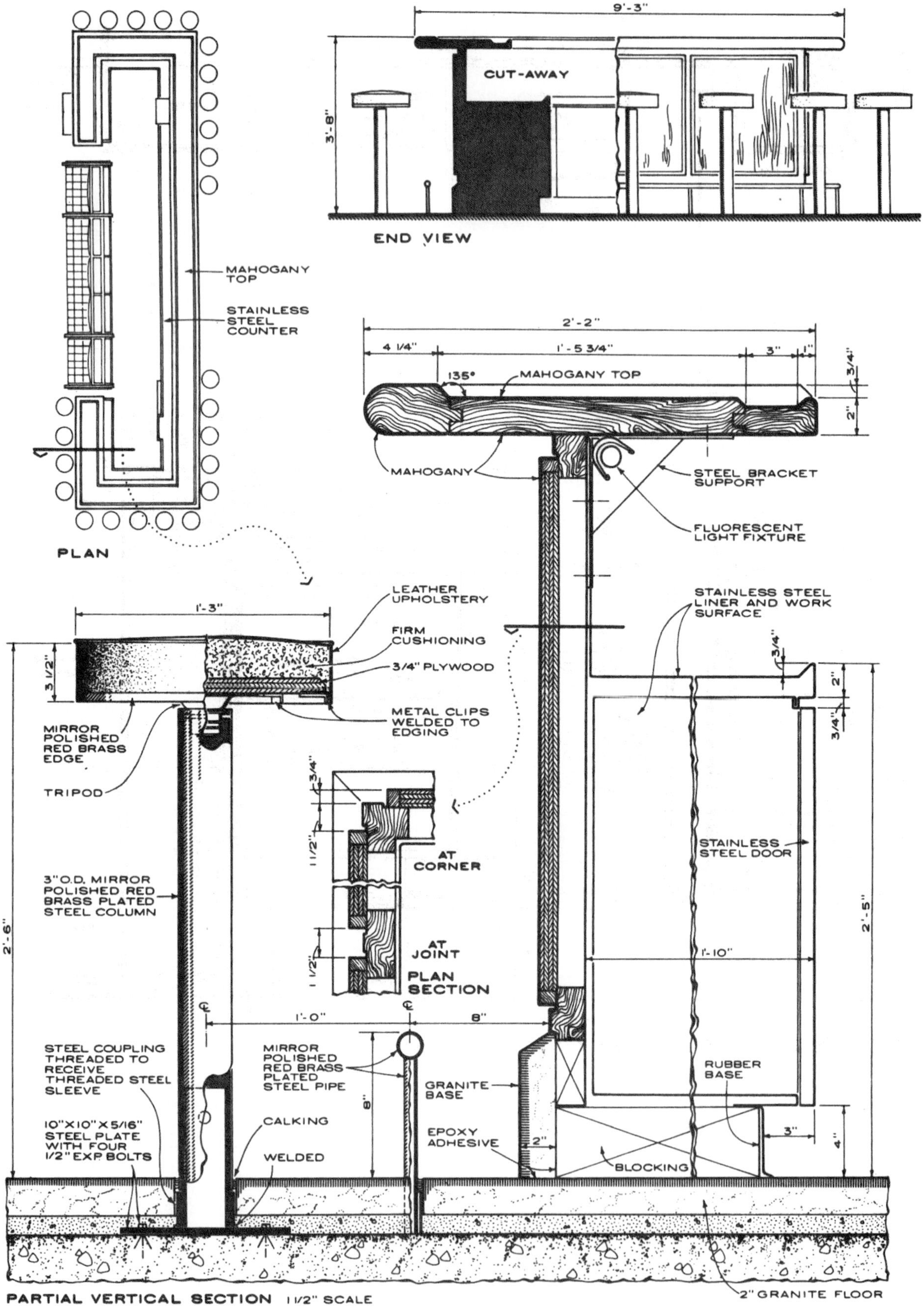
9'-3"
CUT-AWAY
3'-8"
END VIEW
MAHOGANY TOP
STAINLESS STEEL COUNTER
PLAN
2'-2"
4 1/4"
1'-5 3/4"
3"
1"
135°
MAHOGANY TOP
3/4"
2"
MAHOGANY
STEEL BRACKET SUPPORT
FLUORESCENT LIGHT FIXTURE
LEATHER UPHOLSTERY
FIRM CUSHIONING
3/4" PLYWOOD
METAL CLIPS WELDED TO EDGING
1'-3"
3 1/2"
MIRROR POLISHED RED BRASS EDGE
TRIPOD
STAINLESS STEEL LINER AND WORK SURFACE
3/4"
2"
3/4"
AT CORNER
1 1/2"
AT JOINT
1 1/2"
PLAN SECTION
STAINLESS STEEL DOOR
2'-5"
3"O.D. MIRROR POLISHED RED BRASS PLATED STEEL COLUMN
2'-6"
1'-10"
1'-0"
8"
STEEL COUPLING THREADED TO RECEIVE THREADED STEEL SLEEVE
MIRROR POLISHED RED BRASS PLATED STEEL PIPE
GRANITE BASE
RUBBER BASE
8"
10"X10"X5/16" STEEL PLATE WITH FOUR 1/2" EXP. BOLTS
CALKING
WELDED
EPOXY ADHESIVE
2"
BLOCKING
3"
4"
2" GRANITE FLOOR
PARTIAL VERTICAL SECTION 1 1/2" SCALE

Fig. 25

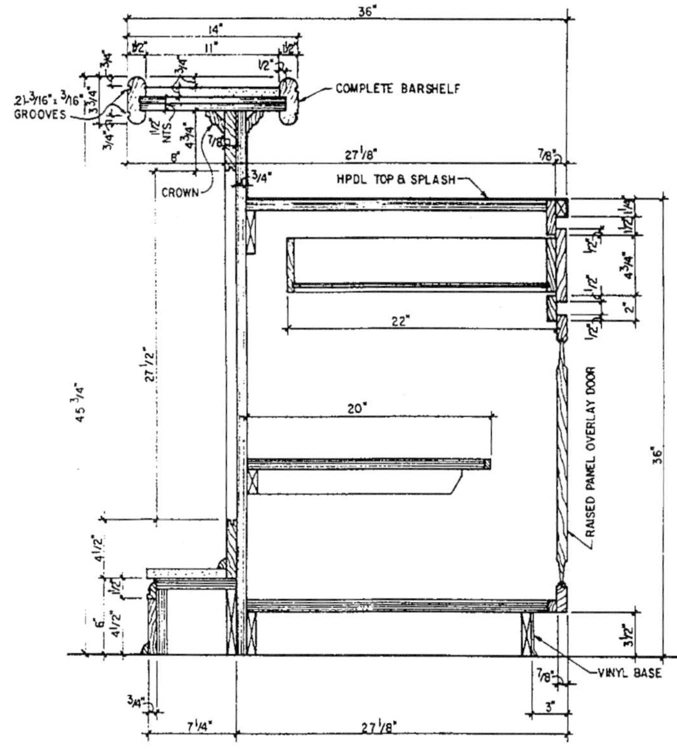

SECTION THRU BAR CABINET

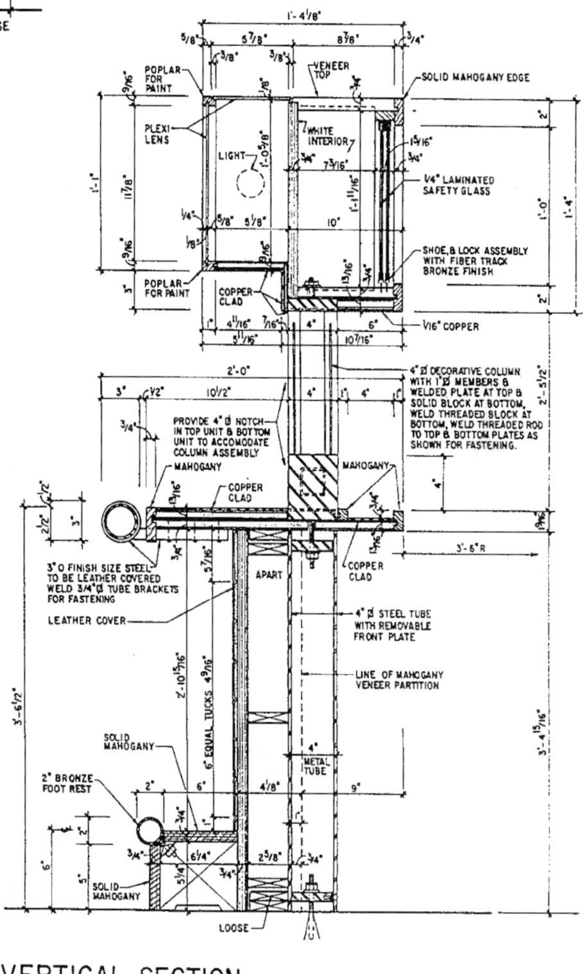

VERTICAL SECTION
AT METAL POST AND LIGHT BOX

Fig. 26

BARS

Bar Plans, Elevations, and Sections

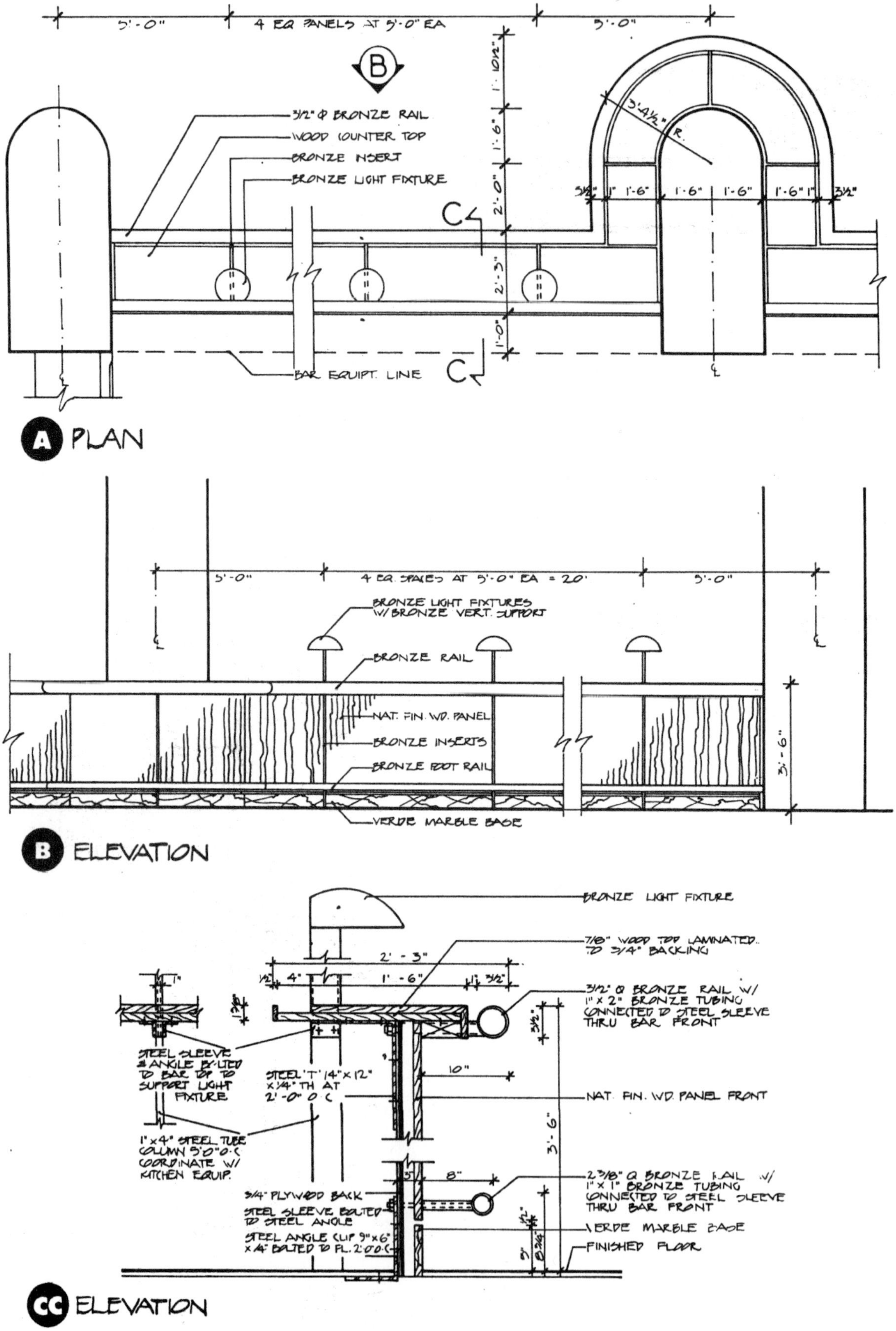

Fig. 27

BARS
Bar Plans, Elevations, and Sections

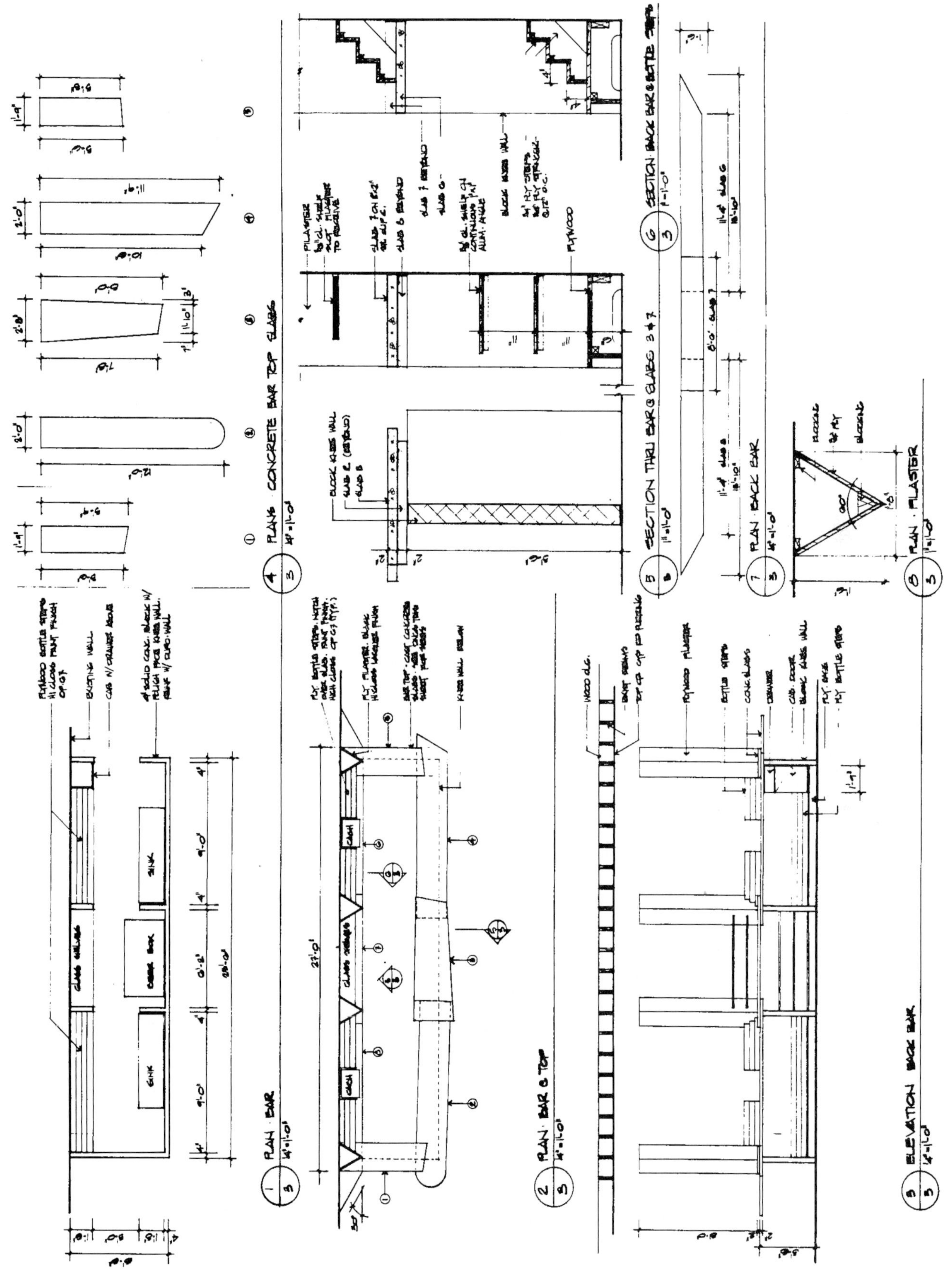

Fig. 28

BARS

Bar Plans, Elevations, and Sections

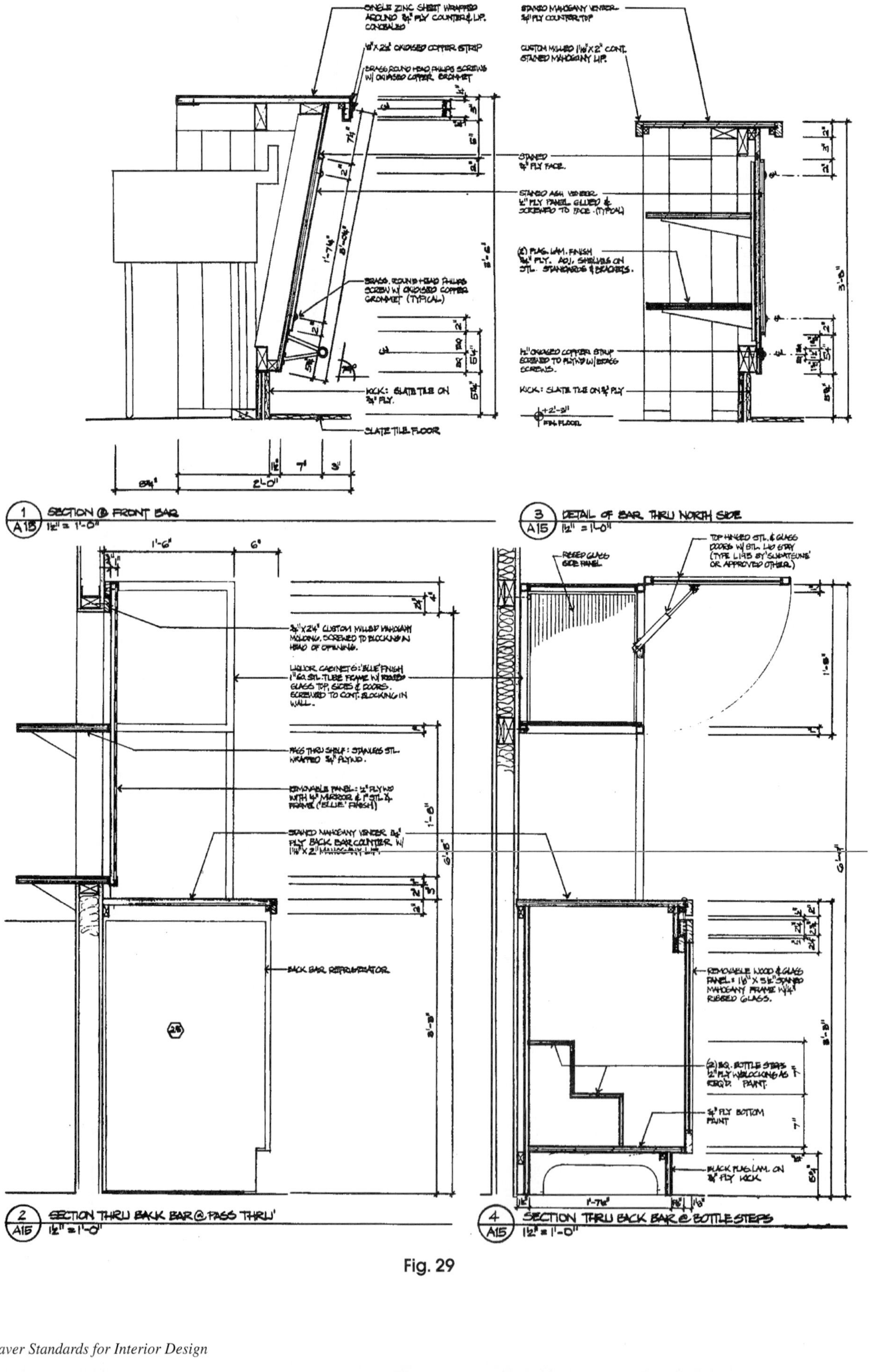

Fig. 29

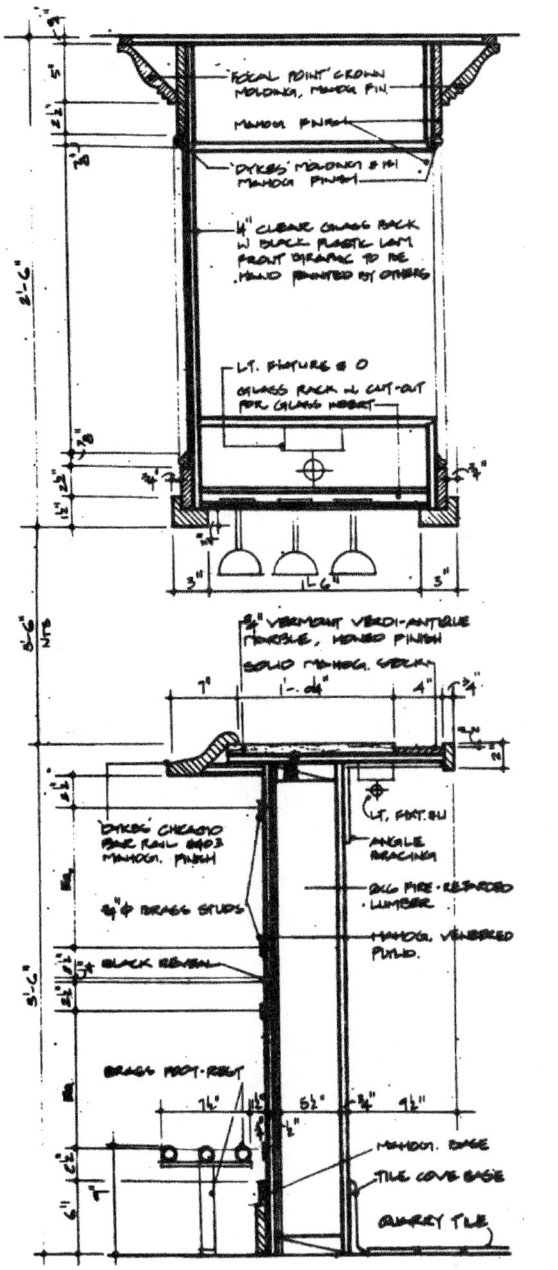

9 / A9 DETAILS of BAR COUNTER & GLASS RACK
SCALE: 1½"=1'-0"

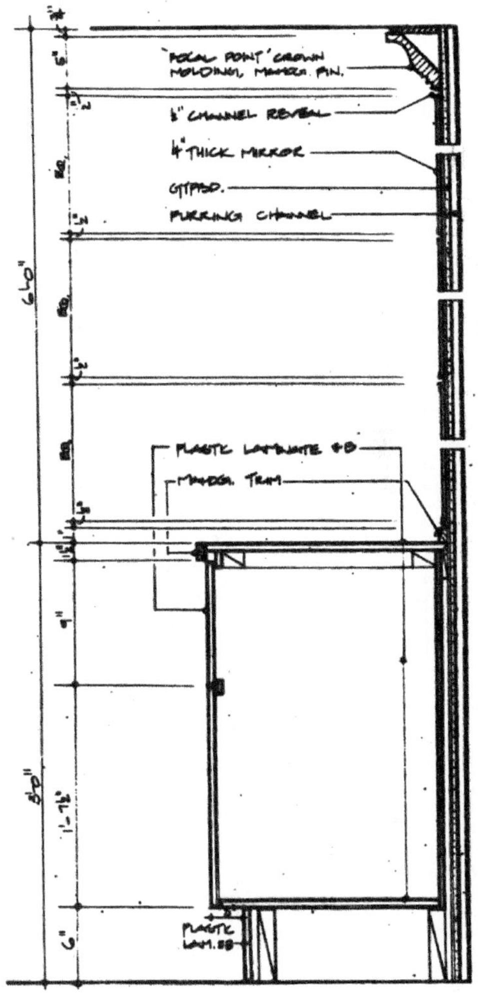

10 / A9 SECTION of SERVING COUNTER #104
SCALE: 1½"=1'-0"

Fig. 30

BARS

Bar Plans, Elevations, and Sections

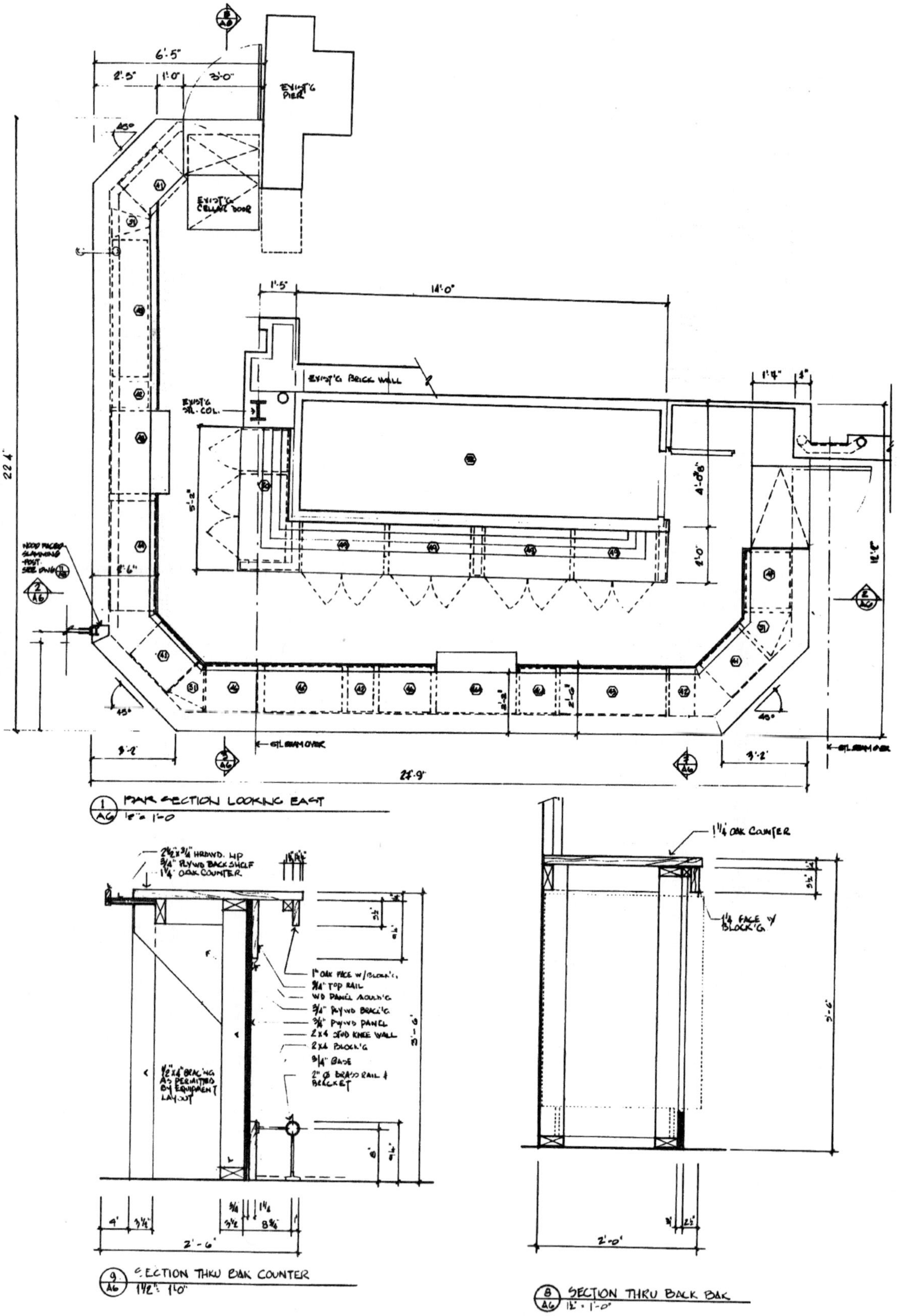

Fig. 31

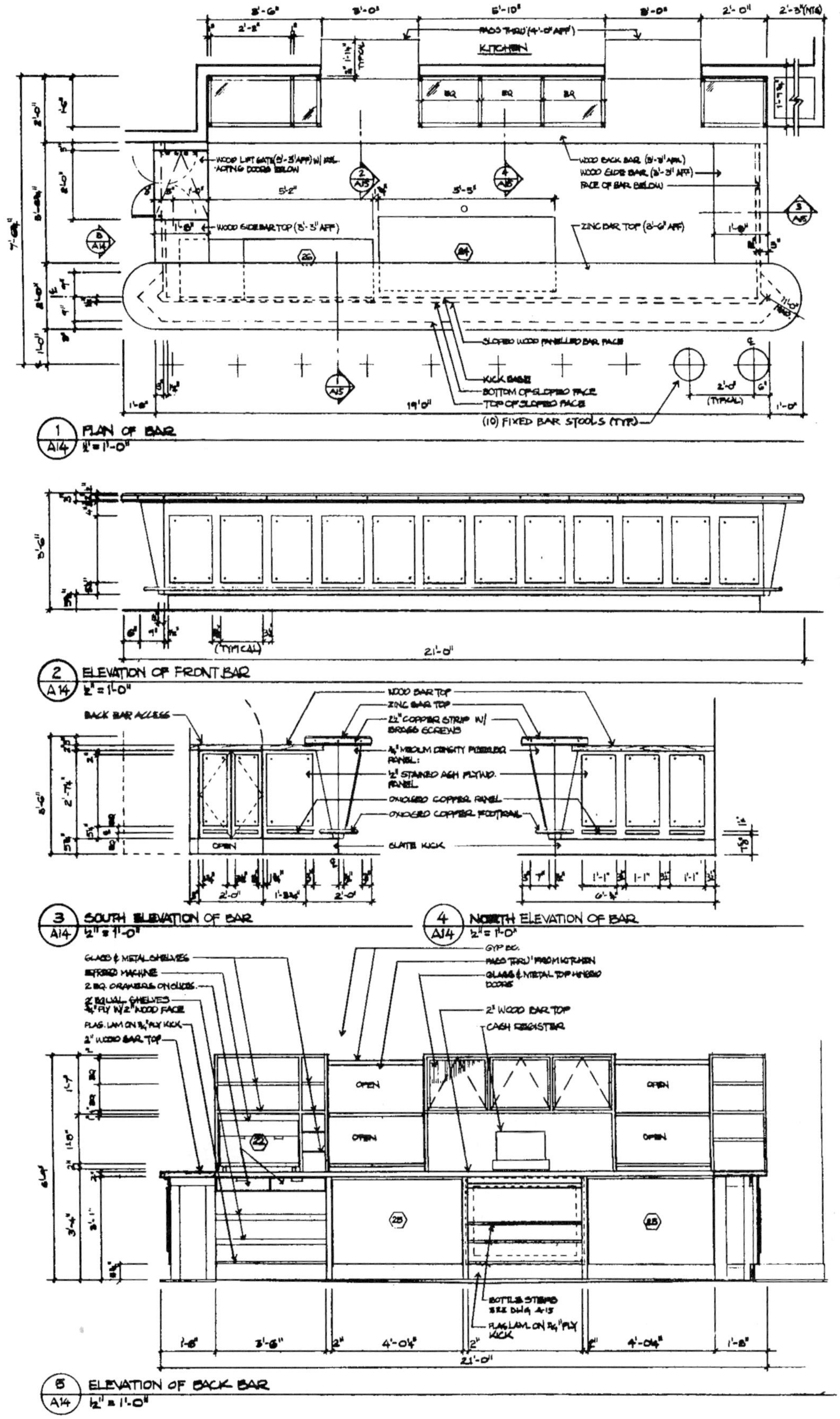
KITCHEN
(10) FIXED BAR STOOLS (TYP)
1 PLAN OF BAR
A14
2 ELEVATION OF FRONT BAR
A14
21'-0"
3 SOUTH ELEVATION OF BAR
A14
4 NORTH ELEVATION OF BAR
A14
5 ELEVATION OF BACK BAR
A14
21'-0"

Fig. 32

BARS
Bar Section Details

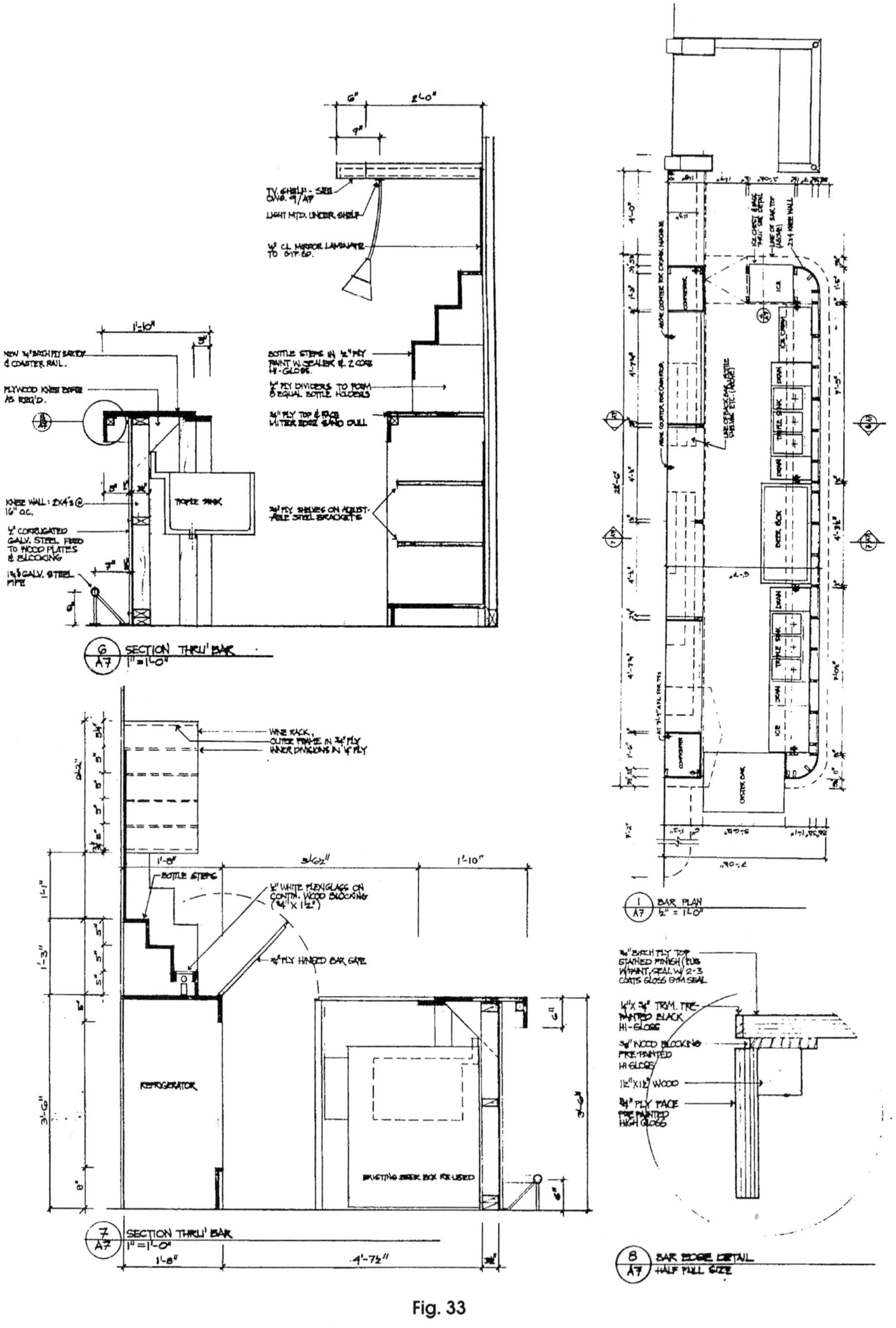

Fig. 33

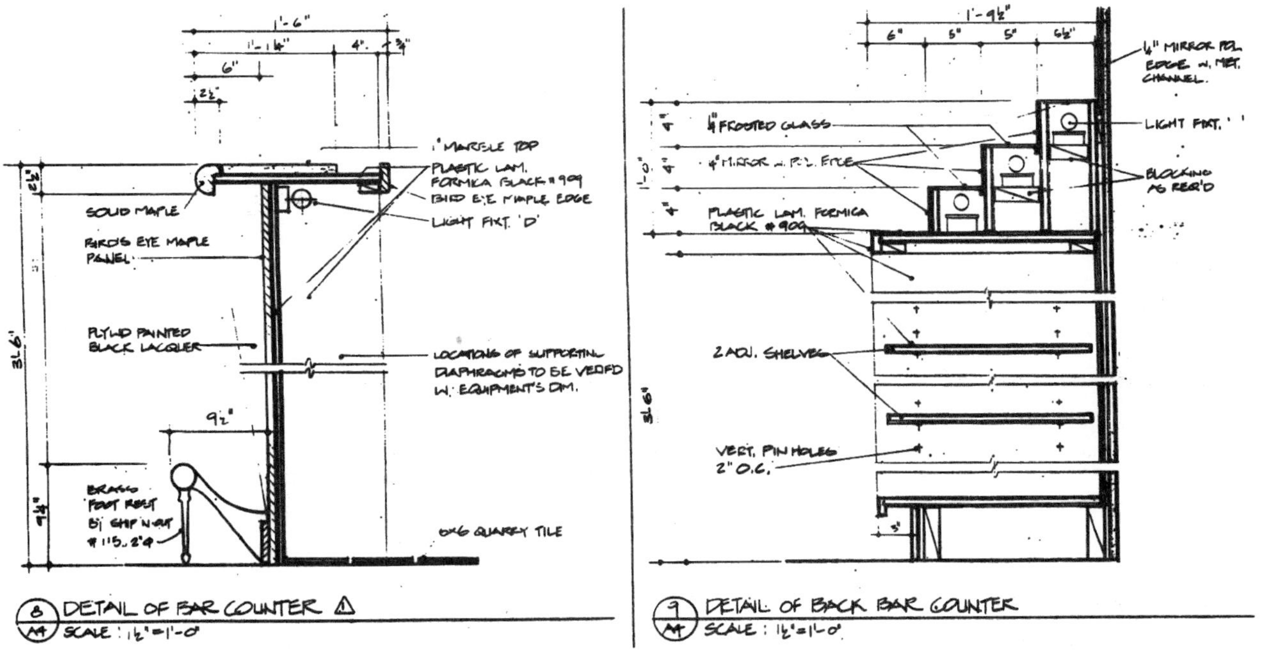
1" MARBLE TOP
PLASTIC LAM. FORMICA BLACK # 909
BIRD EYE MAPLE EDGE
LIGHT FIXT. 'D'
SOLID MAPLE
BIRD'S EYE MAPLE PANEL
PLYWD PAINTED BLACK LACQUER
LOCATIONS OF SUPPORTING DIAPHRAGMS TO BE VERIFD W. EQUIPMENT'S DIM.
BRASS FOOT REST
6x6 QUARRY TILE
DETAIL OF BAR COUNTER
SCALE : 1½"=1'-0"
¼" MIRROR POL. EDGE W. MET. CHANNEL.
LIGHT FIXT.
BLOCKING AS REQ'D
¼" FROSTED GLASS
¼" MIRROR W. POL. EDGE
PLASTIC LAM. FORMICA BLACK # 909
2 ADJ. SHELVES
VERT. PIN HOLES 2" O.C.
DETAIL OF BACK BAR COUNTER
SCALE : 1½"=1'-0"

Fig. 34

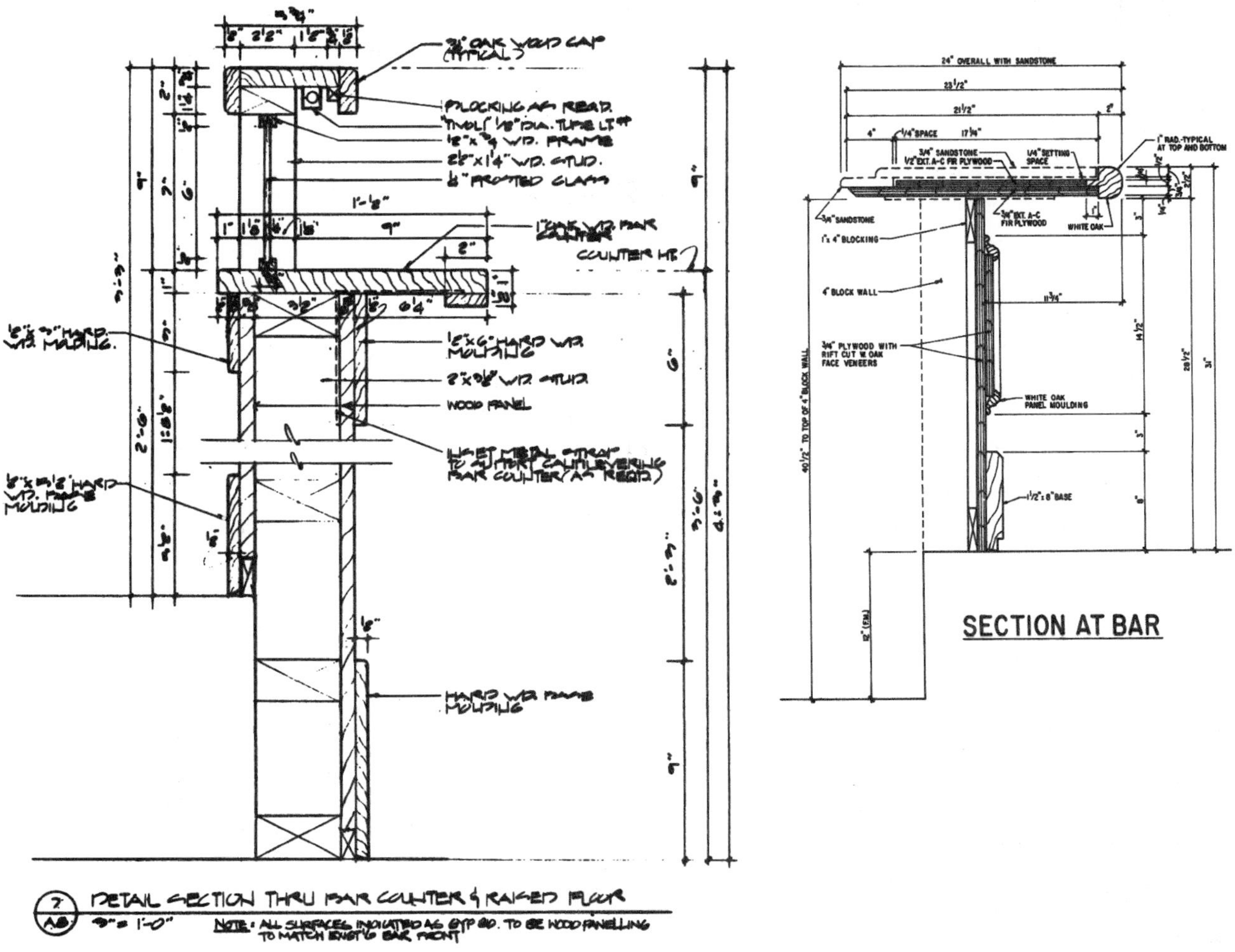
3/4" OAK WOOD CAP (TYPICAL)
BLOCKING AS REQ'D
¼" FROSTED GLASS
COUNTER HT.
WOOD PANEL
HARD WD. FRAME MOULDING
DETAIL SECTION THRU BAR COUNTER & RAISED FLOOR
NOTE: ALL SURFACES INDICATED AS TYP. TO BE WOOD PANELLING TO MATCH EXIST'G BAR FRONT
24" OVERALL WITH SANDSTONE
1/4" SPACE
3/4" SANDSTONE
1/2" EXT. A-C FIR PLYWOOD
1/4" SETTING SPACE
1" RAD.-TYPICAL AT TOP AND BOTTOM
3/4" EXT. A-C FIR PLYWOOD
WHITE OAK
1 x 4" BLOCKING
4" BLOCK WALL
3/4" PLYWOOD WITH RIFT CUT W. OAK FACE VENEERS
WHITE OAK PANEL MOULDING
1/2 x 8" BASE
SECTION AT BAR

Fig. 35

BARS

Bar Section Details

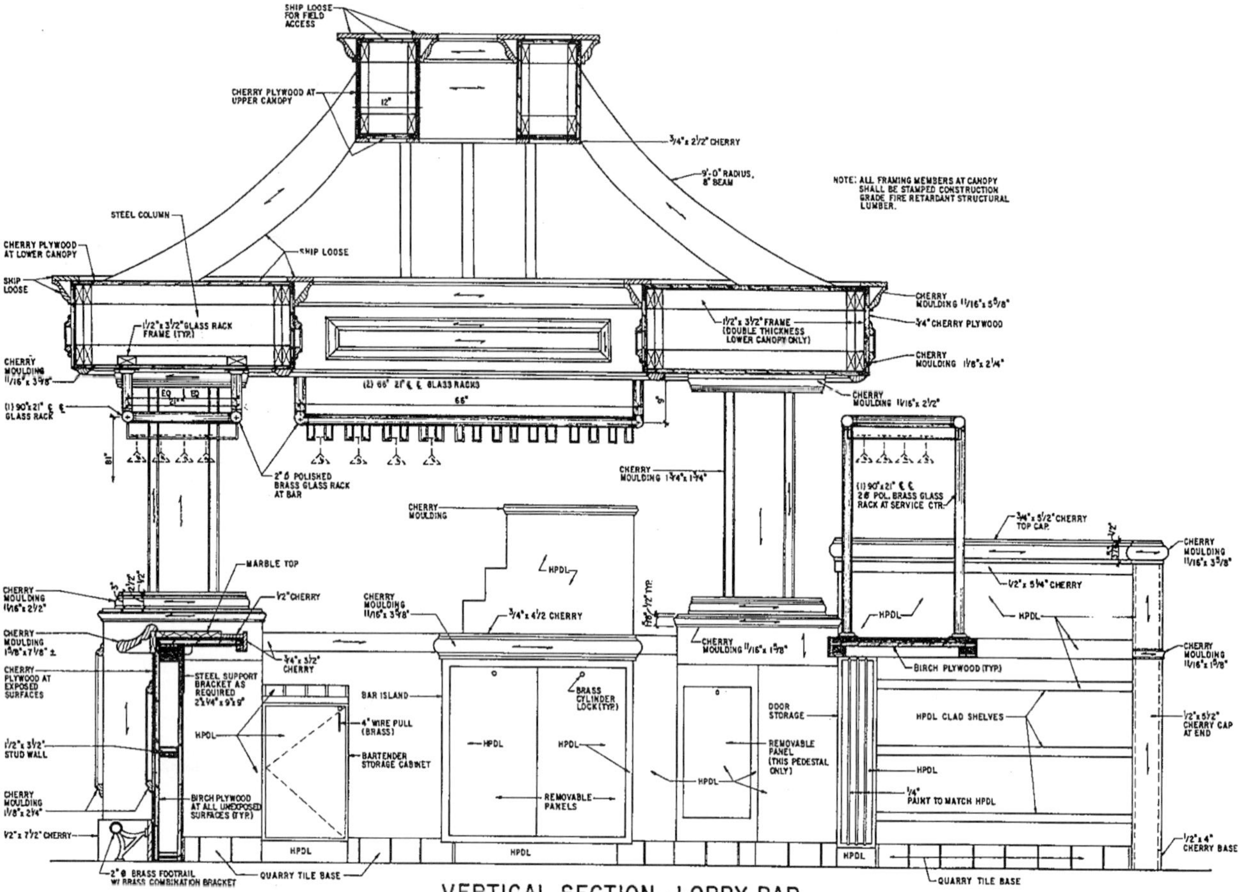

VERTICAL SECTION- LOBBY BAR

Fig. 36

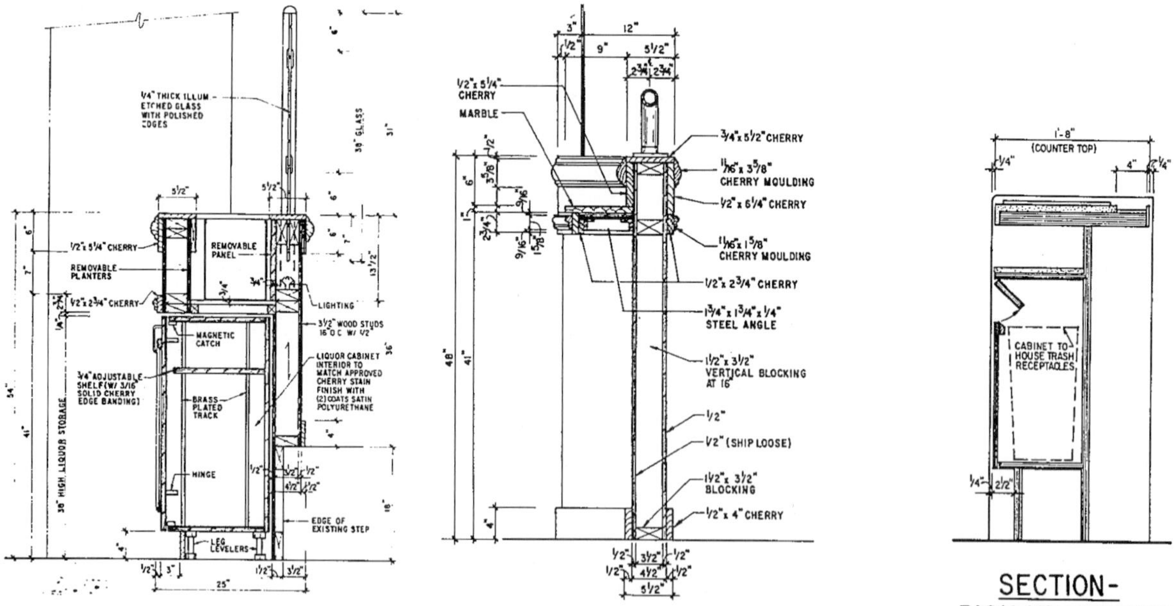

VERTICAL SECTION LIQUOR STORAGE UNIT

VERTICAL SECTION- DRINK RAIL

SECTION- PICK UP STATION

Fig. 37

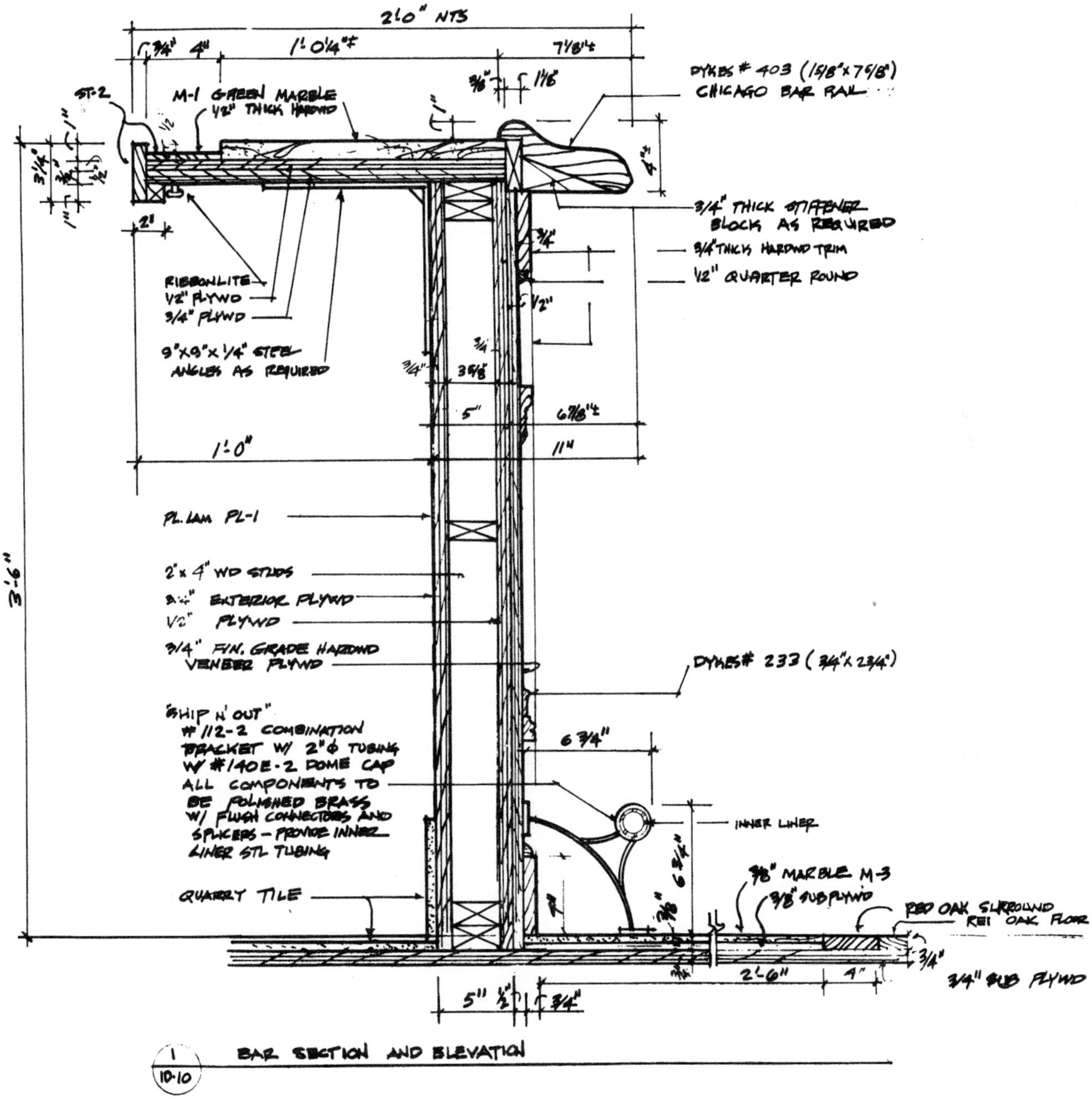
2'-0" NTS
DYKES # 403 (1 5/8" x 7 5/8")
CHICAGO BAR RAIL
M-1 GREEN MARBLE
1/2" THICK HARDWD
ST-2
3/4" THICK STIFFENER
BLOCK AS REQUIRED
3/4" THICK HARDWD TRIM
1/2" QUARTER ROUND
RIBBONLITE
1/2" PLYWD
3/4" PLYWD
9"x9"x1/4" STEEL
ANGLES AS REQUIRED
PL. LAM PL-1
2"x 4" WD STUDS
3/4" EXTERIOR PLYWD
1/2" PLYWD
3/4" FIN. GRADE HARDWD
VENEER PLYWD
DYKES# 233 (3/4"x 2 3/4")
"SHIP N' OUT"
#112-2 COMBINATION
BRACKET W/ 2"φ TUBING
W/ #140E-2 DOME CAP
ALL COMPONENTS TO
BE POLISHED BRASS
W/ FLUSH CONNECTORS AND
SPLICERS - PROVIDE INNER
LINER STL TUBING
INNER LINER
QUARRY TILE
3/8" MARBLE M-3
3/8" SUB PLYWD
RED OAK SURROUND
RED OAK FLOOR
3/4" SUB PLYWD
3'-6"
1'-0"
BAR SECTION AND ELEVATION
1
10-10

Fig. 38

BARS

Bar Section Details

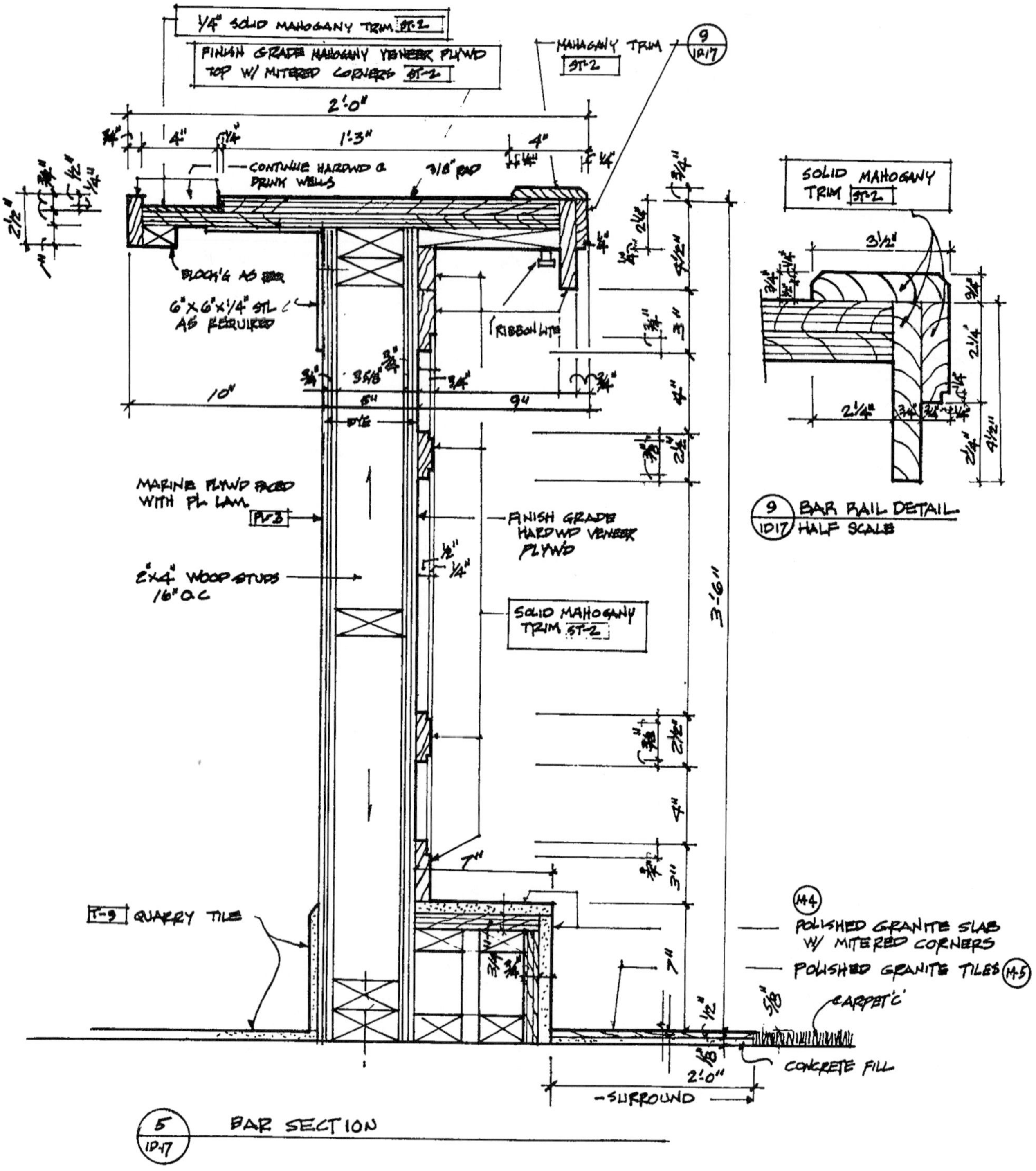
1/4" SOLID MAHOGANY TRIM ST-2
FINISH GRADE MAHOGANY VENEER PLYWD TOP W/ MITERED CORNERS ST-2
MAHAGANY TRIM ST-2
2'-0"
1'-3"
CONTINUE HARDWD @ DRINK WELLS
3/8" RAD
BLOCK'G AS REQ
6"x6"x1/4" STL AS REQUIRED
RIBBON LITE
10"
MARINE PLYWD FACED WITH PL LAM PL-3
2x4" WOOD STUDS 16" O.C
FINISH GRADE HARDWD VENEER PLYWD
SOLID MAHOGANY TRIM ST-2
3'-6"
T-9 QUARRY TILE
M-4
POLISHED GRANITE SLAB W/ MITERED CORNERS
POLISHED GRANITE TILES M-5
CARPET 'C'
CONCRETE FILL
2'-0"
SURROUND
5 1D-17 BAR SECTION
SOLID MAHOGANY TRIM ST-2
3 1/2"
9 1D17 BAR RAIL DETAIL HALF SCALE

Fig. 39

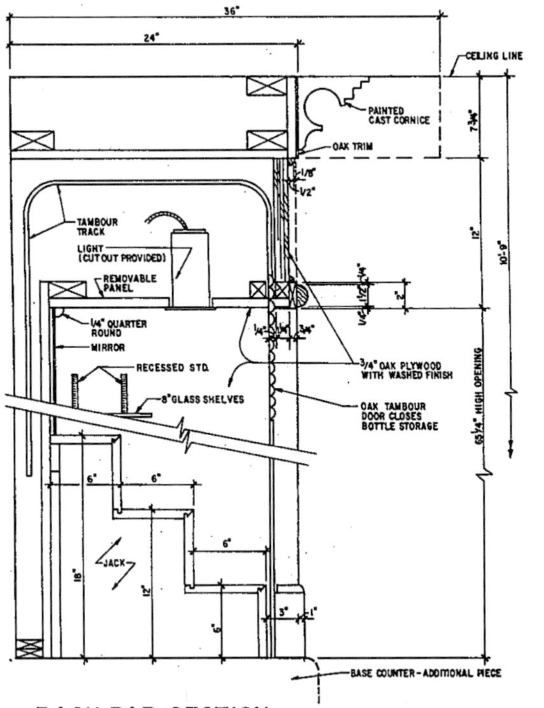

BACK BAR SECTION

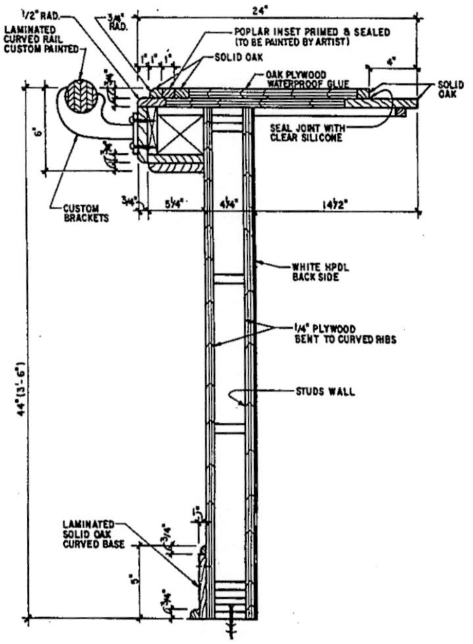

SECTION AT CURVED BAR

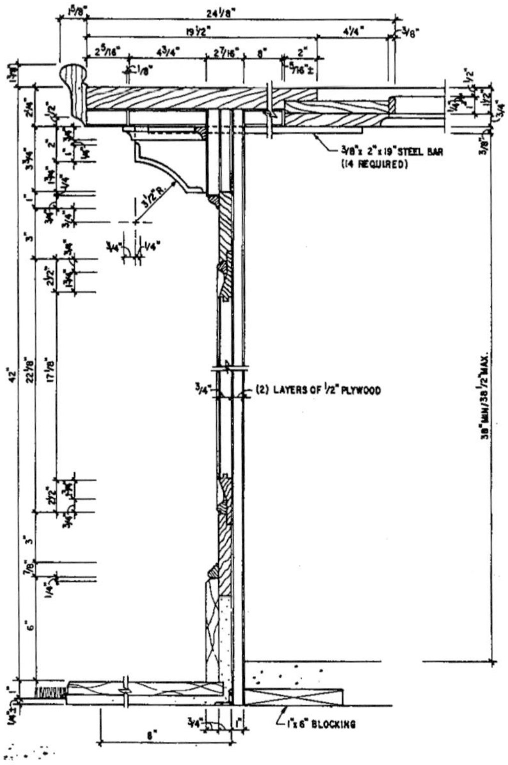

VERTICAL SECTION AT BAR

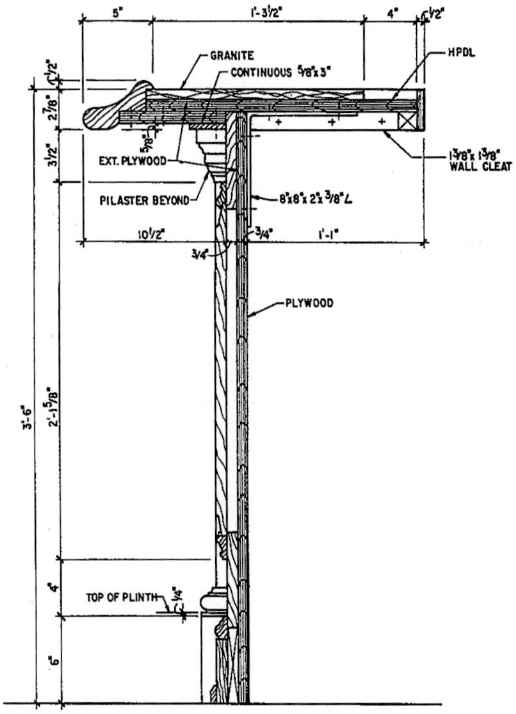

SECTION AT BAR

Fig. 40

BARS
Bar Section Details

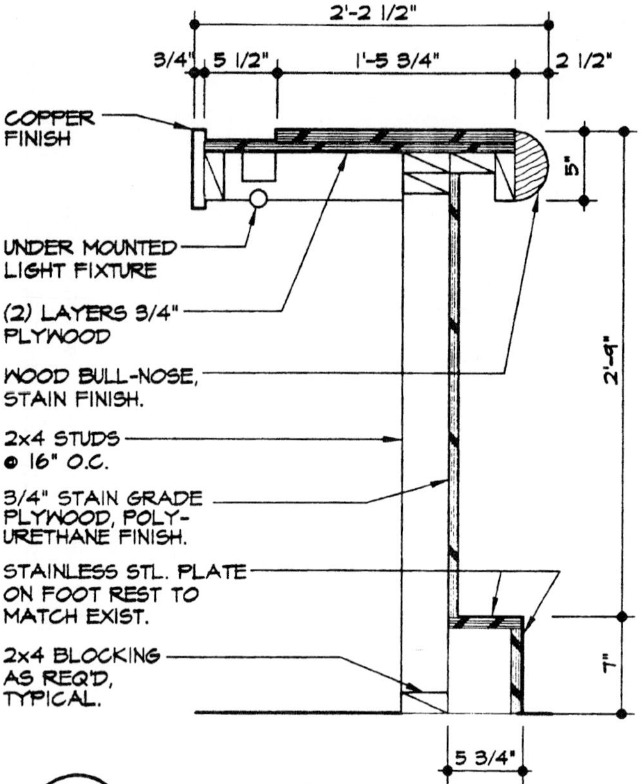

4 SECTION - NEW BAR
A4 1"=1'-0"

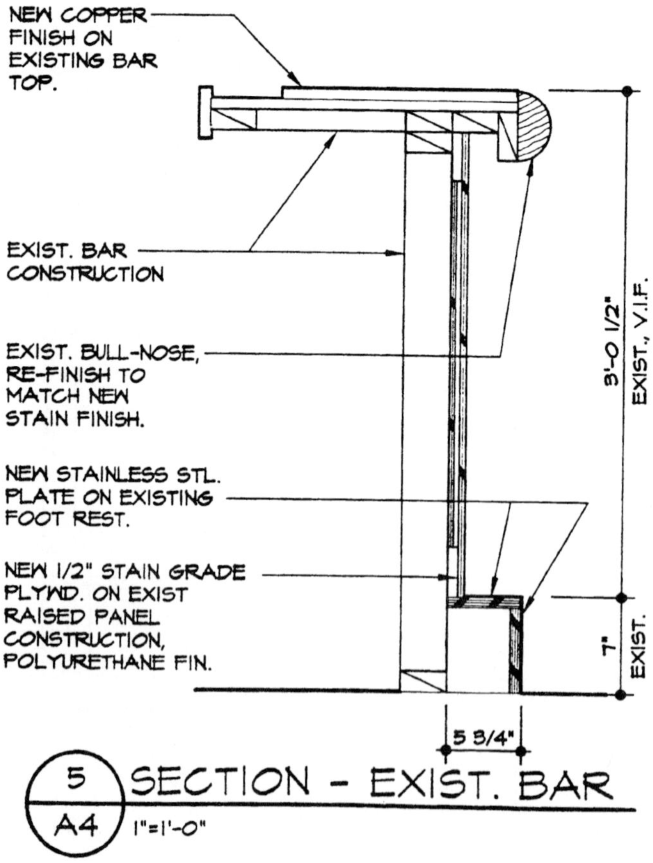

5 SECTION - EXIST. BAR
A4 1"=1'-0"

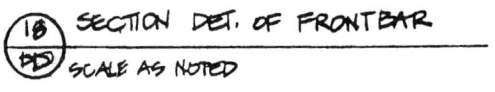

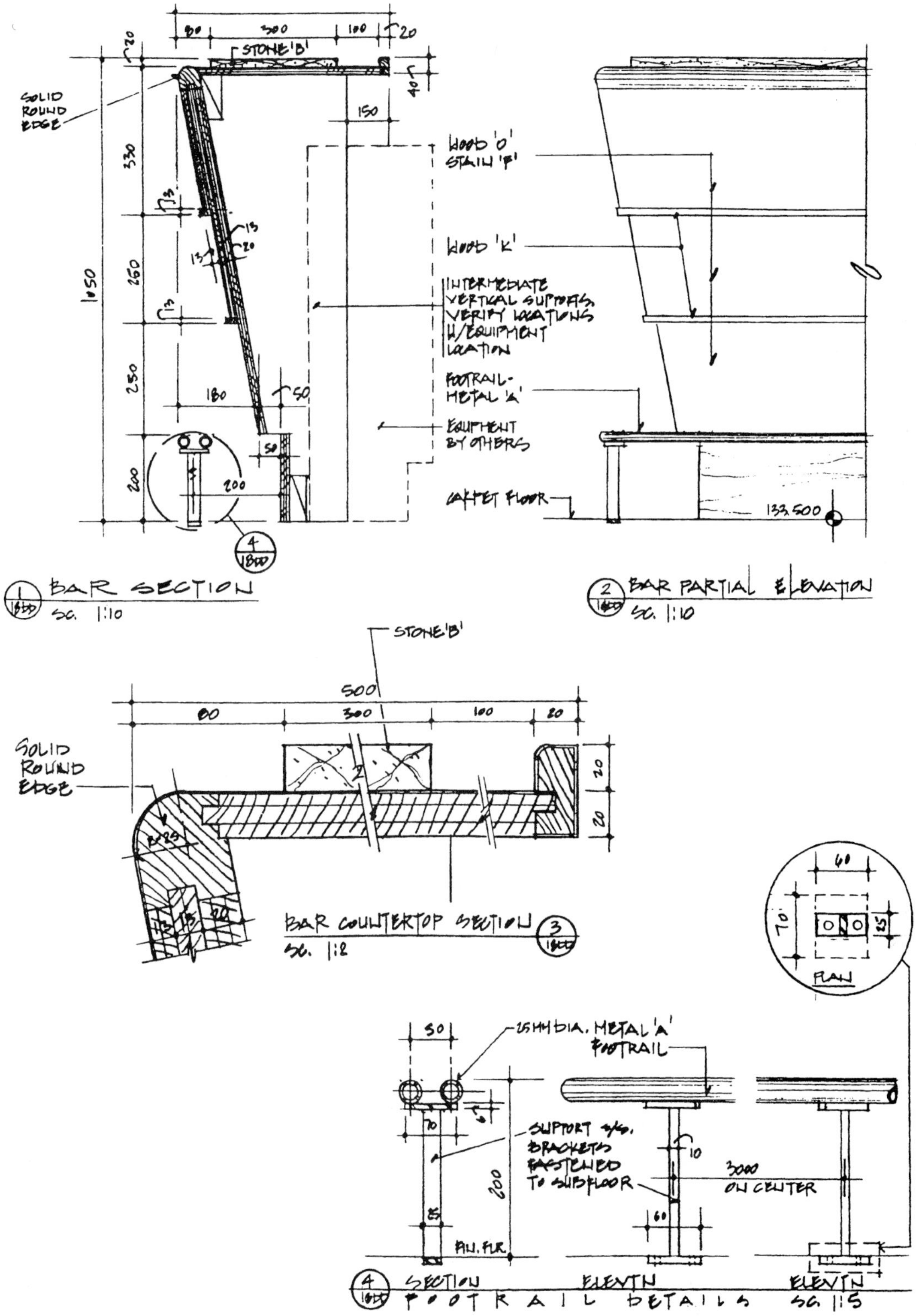
STONE 'B'
SOLID ROUND EDGE
WOOD 'O' STAIN 'F'
WOOD 'K'
INTERMEDIATE VERTICAL SUPPORTS, VERIFY LOCATIONS W/EQUIPMENT LOCATION
FOOTRAIL-METAL 'A'
EQUIPMENT BY OTHERS
CARPET FLOOR
BAR SECTION
SC. 1:10
BAR PARTIAL ELEVATION
SC. 1:10
BAR COUNTERTOP SECTION
SC. 1:2
25MM DIA. METAL 'A' FOOTRAIL
SUPPORT S/S. BRACKETS FASTENED TO SUBFLOOR
3000 ON CENTER
FIN. FLR.
PLAN
SECTION
ELEV'N
FOOTRAIL DETAILS
SC. 1:5

SECTION DET. OF FRONTBAR
SCALE AS NOTED

BARS

Island Bar

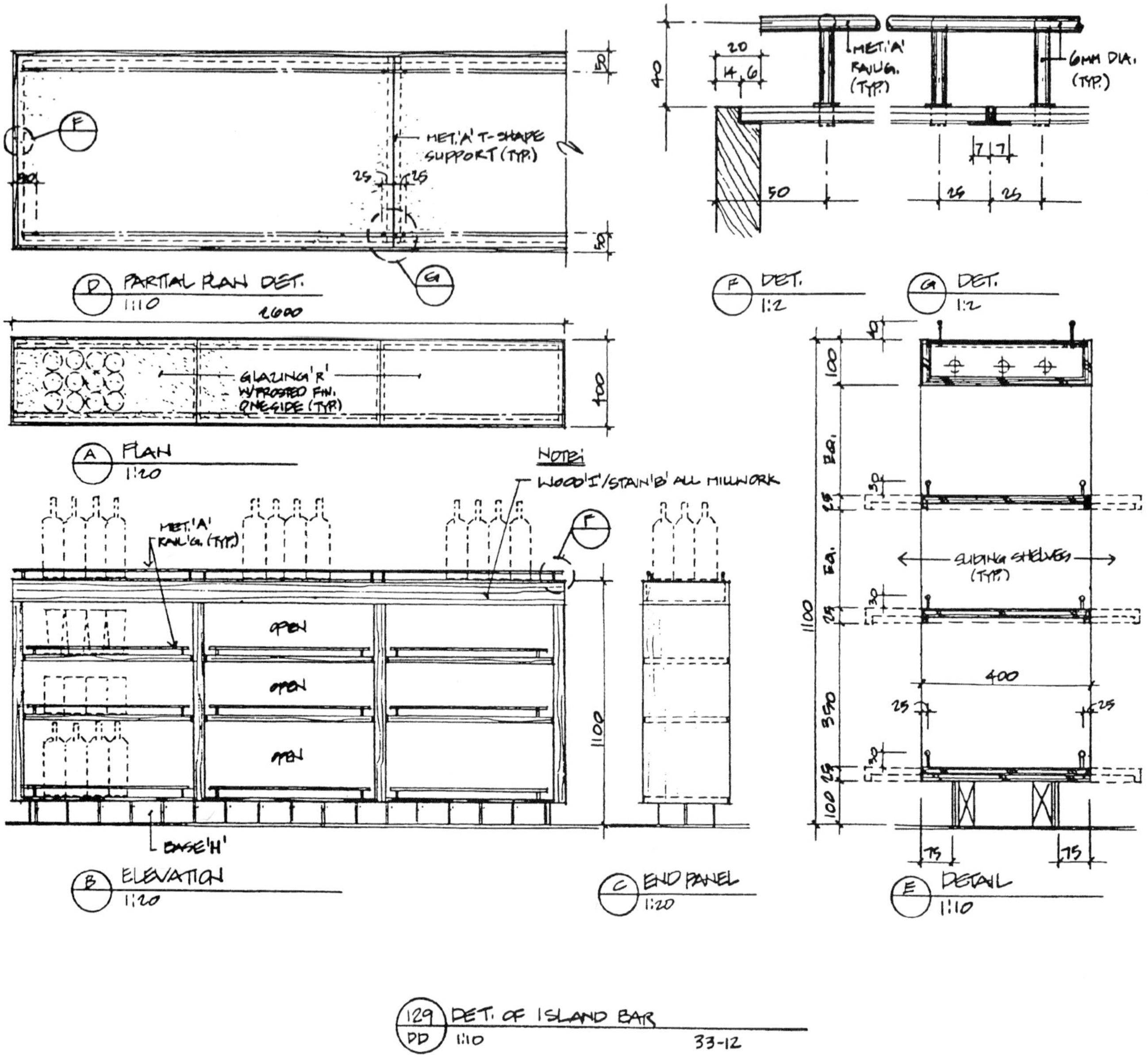

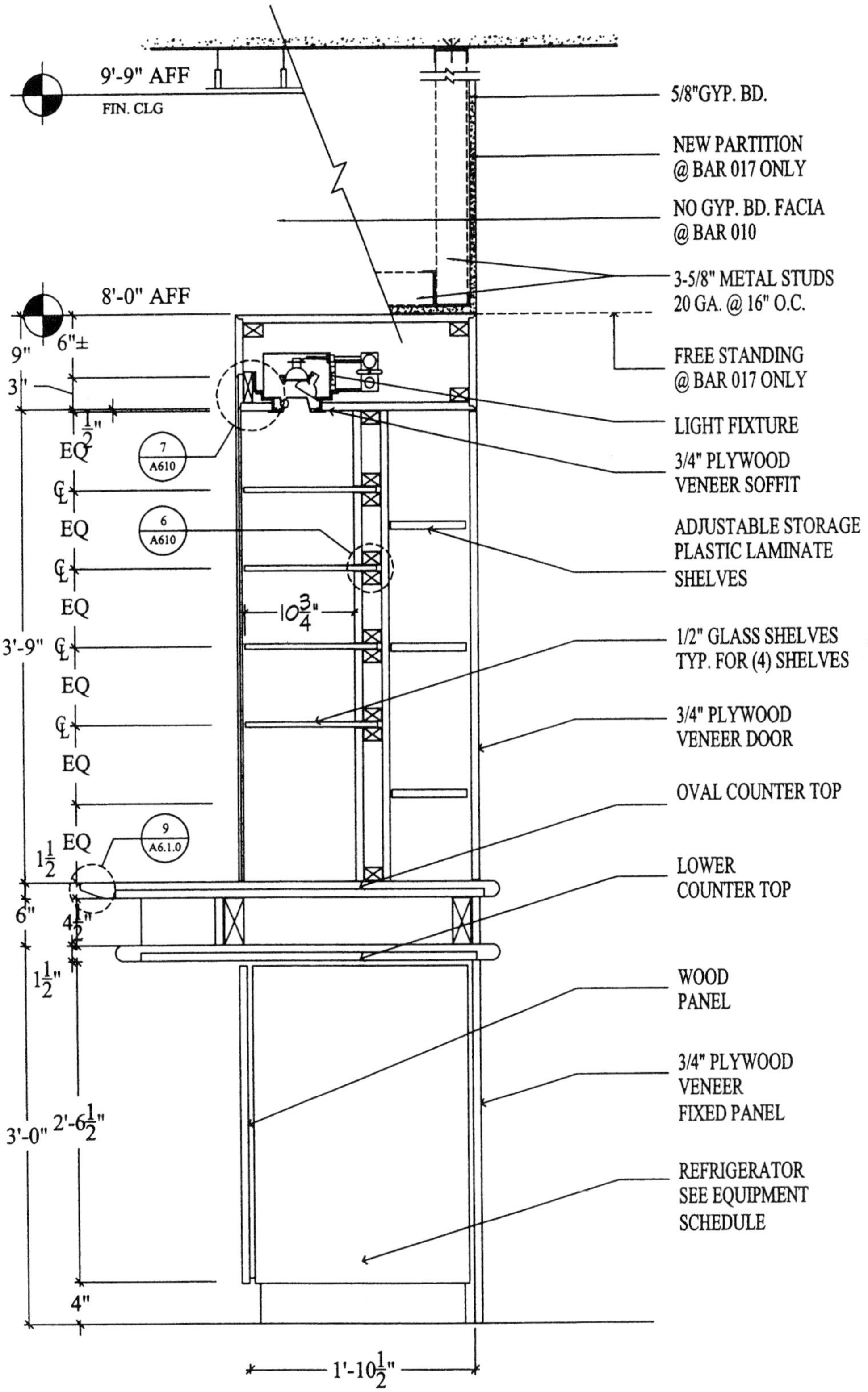
9'-9" AFF
FIN. CLG
8'-0" AFF
5/8"GYP. BD.
NEW PARTITION @BAR 017 ONLY
NO GYP. BD. FACIA @BAR 010
3-5/8" METAL STUDS 20 GA. @ 16" O.C.
FREE STANDING @BAR 017 ONLY
LIGHT FIXTURE
3/4" PLYWOOD VENEER SOFFIT
ADJUSTABLE STORAGE PLASTIC LAMINATE SHELVES
1/2" GLASS SHELVES TYP. FOR (4) SHELVES
3/4" PLYWOOD VENEER DOOR
OVAL COUNTER TOP
LOWER COUNTER TOP
WOOD PANEL
3/4" PLYWOOD VENEER FIXED PANEL
REFRIGERATOR SEE EQUIPMENT SCHEDULE
7 A610
6 A610
9 A6.1.0
EQ
3'-9"
3'-0"
2'-6½"
1'-10½"
10¾"
9"
6"±
6"
4½"
1½"
4"

16 BAR @ REFRIGERATOR AND SHELVES

3/4"=1'-0"

BARS
Backbar Details

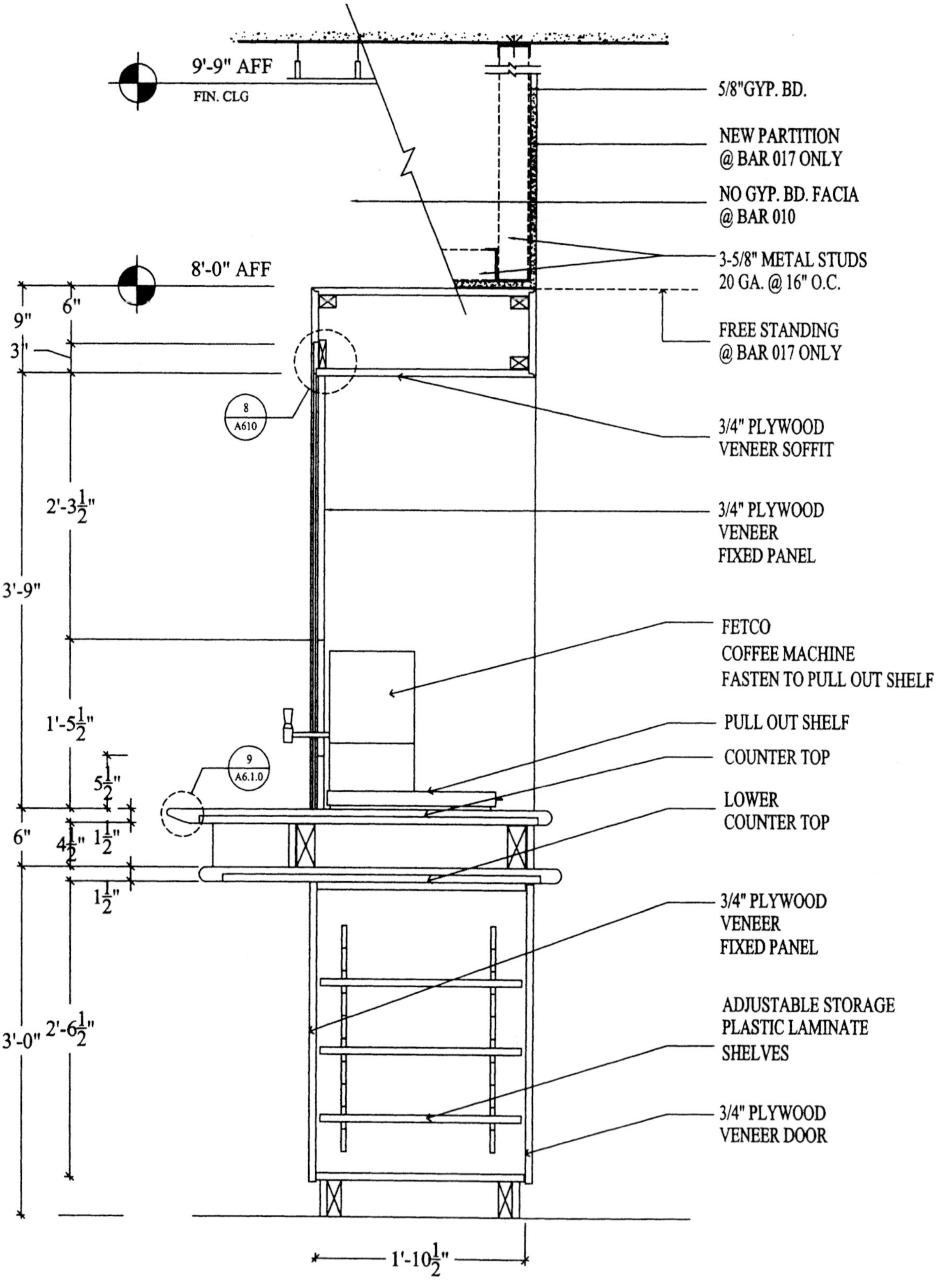
9'-9" AFF
FIN. CLG
8'-0" AFF
5/8"GYP. BD.
NEW PARTITION
@ BAR 017 ONLY
NO GYP. BD. FACIA
@ BAR 010
3-5/8" METAL STUDS
20 GA. @ 16" O.C.
FREE STANDING
@ BAR 017 ONLY
3/4" PLYWOOD
VENEER SOFFIT
3/4" PLYWOOD
VENEER
FIXED PANEL
FETCO
COFFEE MACHINE
FASTEN TO PULL OUT SHELF
PULL OUT SHELF
COUNTER TOP
LOWER
COUNTER TOP
3/4" PLYWOOD
VENEER
FIXED PANEL
ADJUSTABLE STORAGE
PLASTIC LAMINATE
SHELVES
3/4" PLYWOOD
VENEER DOOR
8
A610
9
A6.1.0
9"
6"
3"
2'-3 1/2"
3'-9"
1'-5 1/2"
5 1/2"
6"
4 1/2"
1 1/2"
1 1/2"
3'-0"
2'-6 1/2"
1'-10 1/2"

18 BAR @ SHELVES

3/4"=1'-0"

BARS

Bar Plan and Details

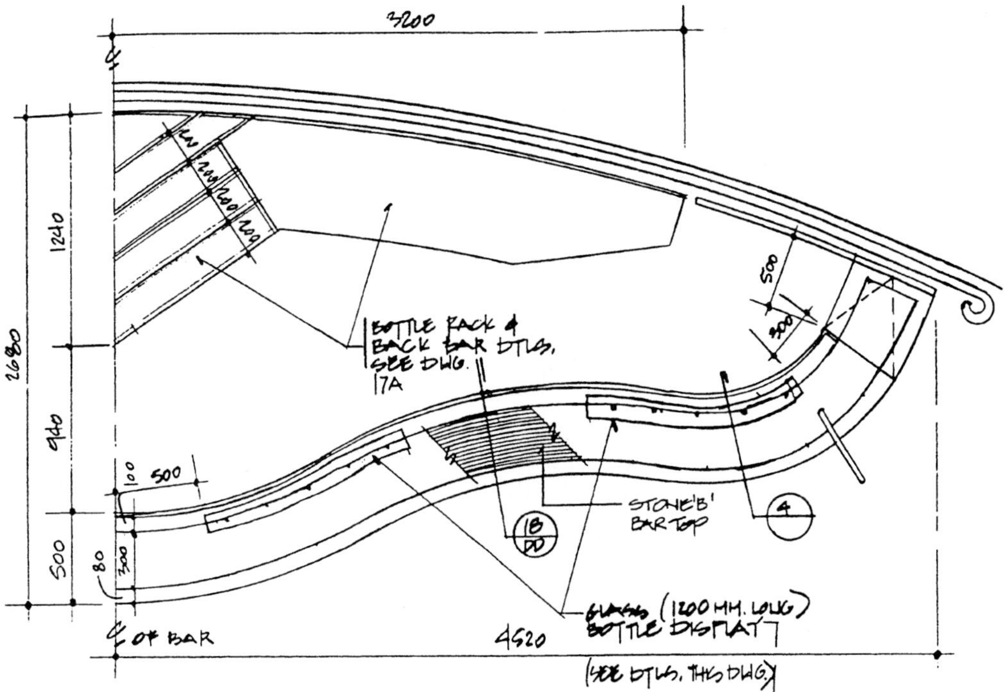

1/1600 PLAN OF BAR
SC. 1:30

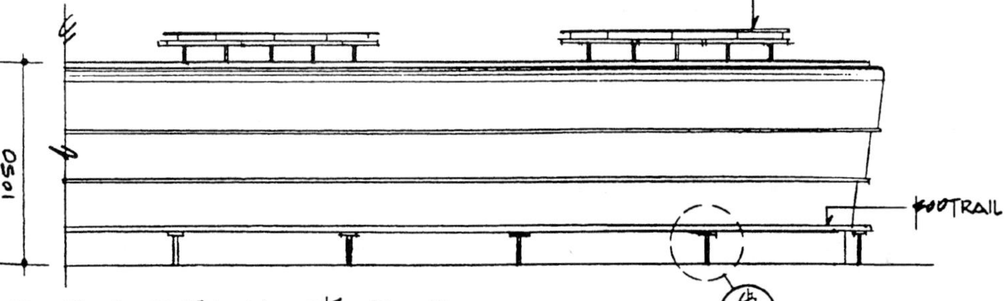

2/1600 ELEVATION OF BAR
SC. 1:30

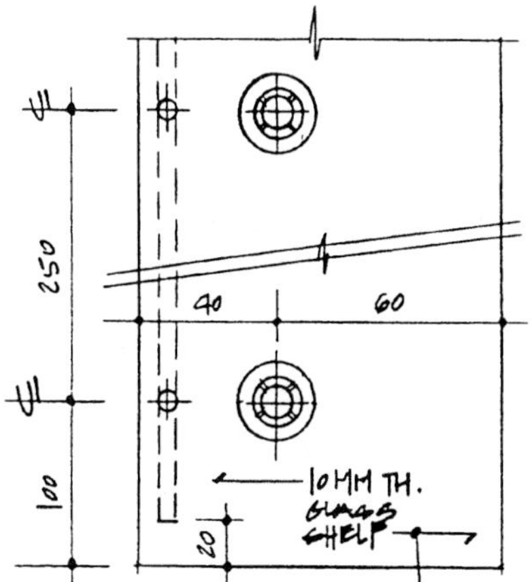

3/1600 BOTTLE DISPLAY - PLAN
SC. 1:2

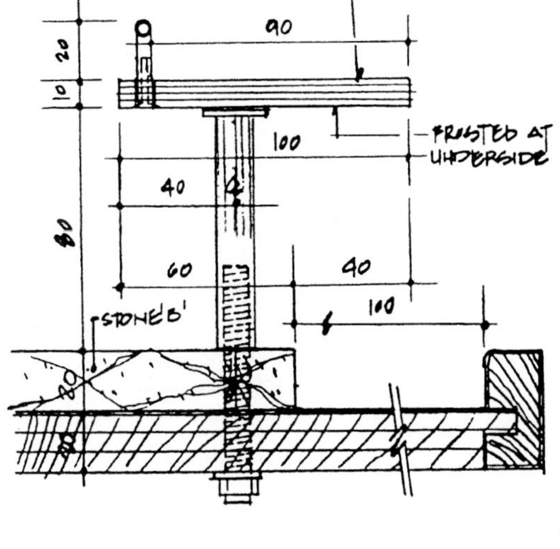

4/1600 BOTTLE DISPLAY - SECTION
SC. 1:1

BARS

Bar Elevation and Details

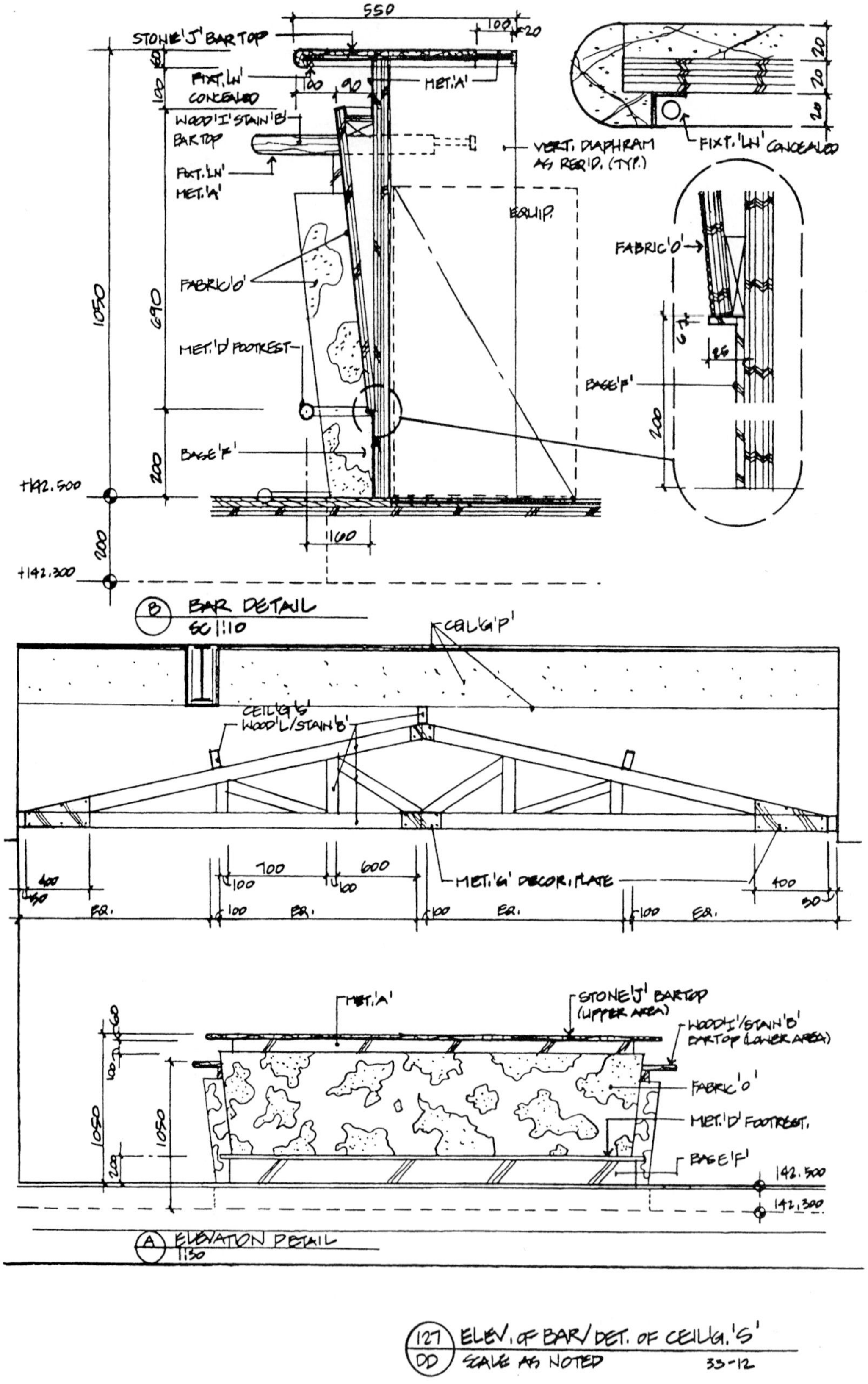

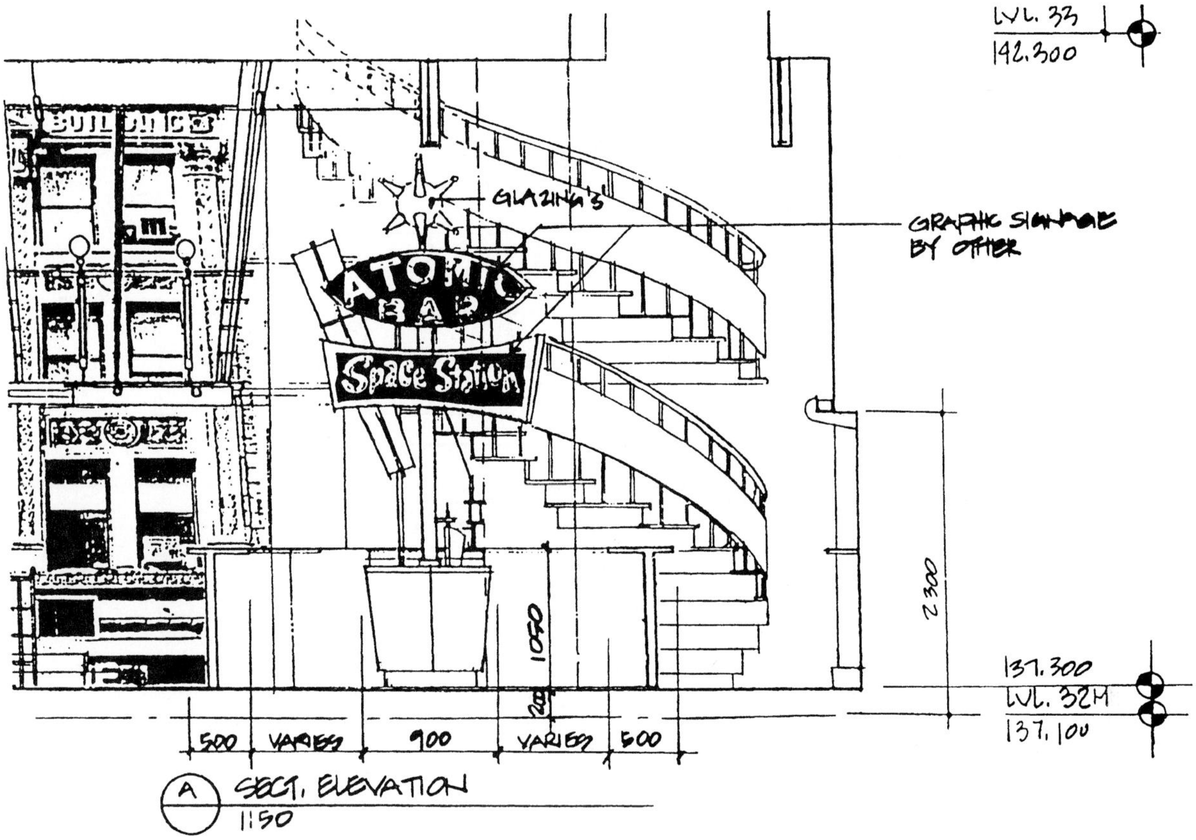
LVL. 33
142.300
GLAZING 'S'
GRAPHIC SIGNAGE BY OTHER
ATOMIC BAR
Space Station
2300
1050
200
137.300
LVL. 32M
137.100
500
VARIES
900
VARIES
500
A SECT. ELEVATION
1:50

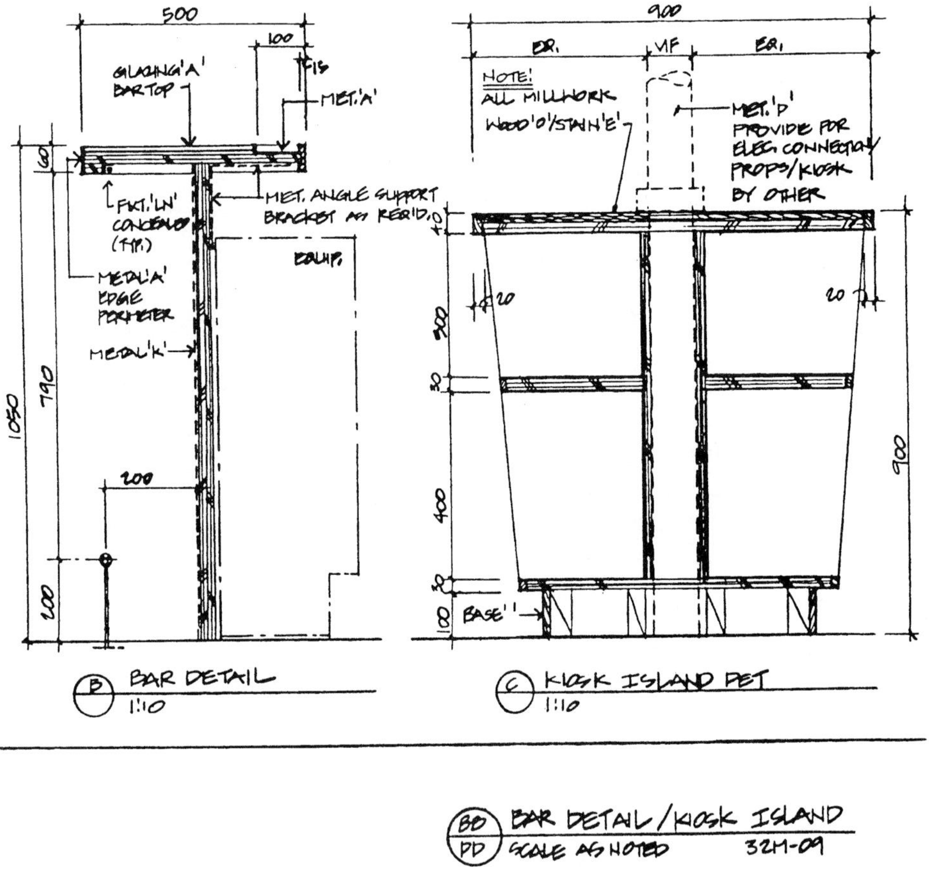
500
100
15
GLAZING 'A' BARTOP
MET. 'A'
60
FIXT. 'LN' CONCEALED (TYP.)
MET. ANGLE SUPPORT BRACKET AS REQ'D.
EQUIP.
METAL 'A' EDGE PERIMETER
METAL 'K'
1050
790
200
200
B BAR DETAIL
1:10
900
EQ.
V.F.
EQ.
NOTE: ALL MILLWORK WOOD 'O'/STAIN 'E'
MET. 'P' PROVIDE FOR ELEC. CONNECTION/ PROPS/KIOSK BY OTHER
20
20
300
30
400
30
100
BASE '1'
900
C KIOSK ISLAND DET
1:10
BD PD BAR DETAIL/KIOSK ISLAND
SCALE AS NOTED
32M-09

BARS

Bar Elevation and Details

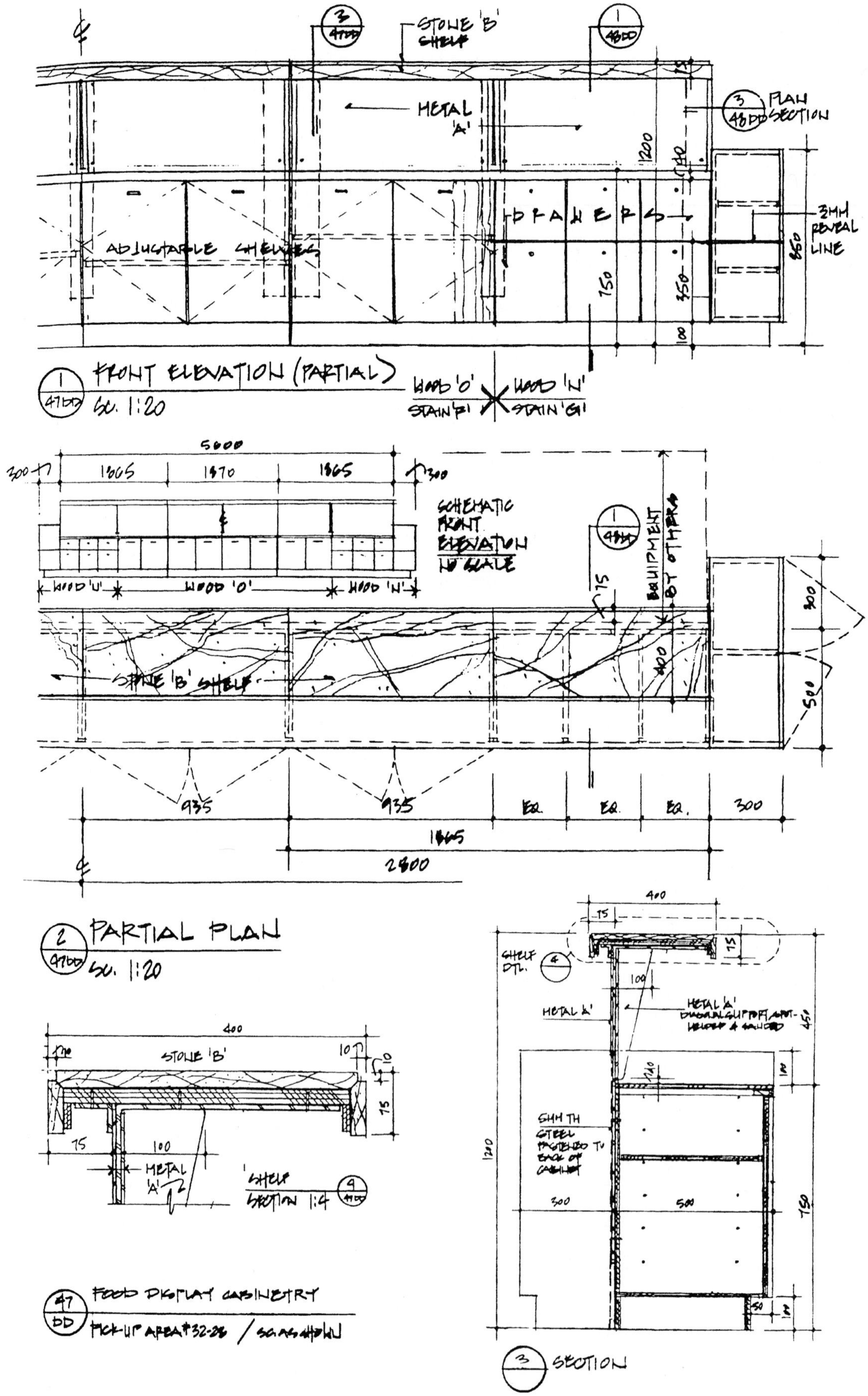

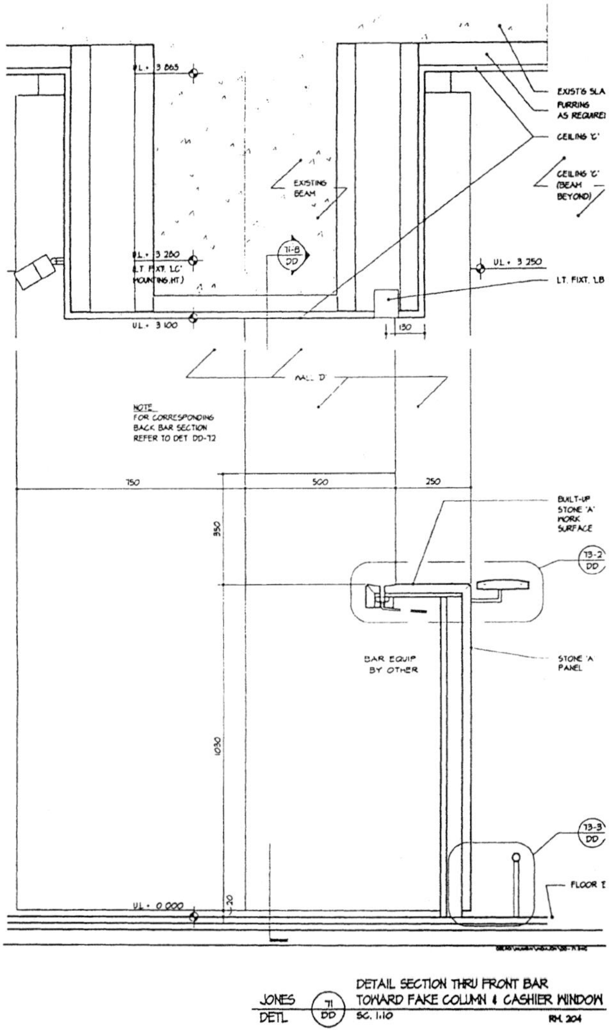
EXIST'G SLA
FURRING
AS REQUIRE
CEILING 'C'
CEILING 'C'
(BEAM
BEYOND)
EXISTING
BEAM
UL + 3 865
UL + 3 280
LT. FIXT. 'LC'
MOUNTING HT.)
UL + 3 250
LT. FIXT. 'LB
71-B
DD
UL + 3 100
130
WALL 'D'
NOTE
FOR CORRESPONDING
BACK BAR SECTION
REFER TO DET. DD-72
750
500
250
350
1030
20
BUILT-UP
STONE 'A'
WORK
SURFACE
73-2
DD
BAR EQUIP
BY OTHER
STONE 'A
PANEL
73-3
DD
FLOOR 'E
UL + 0.000
DETAIL SECTION THRU FRONT BAR
TOWARD FAKE COLUMN & CASHIER WINDOW
JONES
DETL
71
DD
SC. 1:10
RM. 204

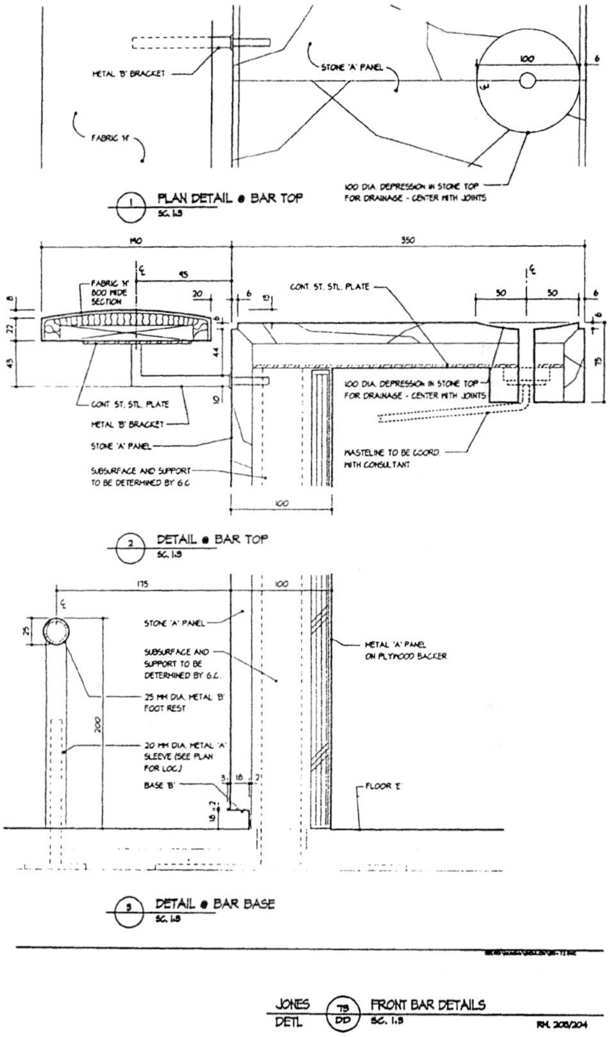
METAL 'B' BRACKET
STONE 'A' PANEL
FABRIC 'H'
100
6
100 DIA. DEPRESSION IN STONE TOP
FOR DRAINAGE - CENTER WITH JOINTS
1
PLAN DETAIL @ BAR TOP
SC. 1:5
140
350
FABRIC 'H'
800 WIDE
SECTION
95
20
6
CONT. ST. STL. PLATE
50
50
8
22
43
44
10
75
CONT. ST. STL. PLATE
METAL 'B' BRACKET
STONE 'A' PANEL
SUBSURFACE AND SUPPORT
TO BE DETERMINED BY G.C
100 DIA. DEPRESSION IN STONE TOP
FOR DRAINAGE - CENTER WITH JOINTS
WASTELINE TO BE COORD.
WITH CONSULTANT
100
2
DETAIL @ BAR TOP
SC. 1:5
175
100
25
STONE 'A' PANEL
SUBSURFACE AND
SUPPORT TO BE
DETERMINED BY G.C.
25 MM DIA. METAL 'B'
FOOT REST
200
20 MM DIA. METAL 'A'
SLEEVE (SEE PLAN
FOR LOC.)
BASE 'B'
3
18
2
METAL 'A' PANEL
ON PLYWOOD BACKER
FLOOR 'E'
3
DETAIL @ BAR BASE
SC. 1:5
JONES
DETL
73
DD
FRONT BAR DETAILS
SC. 1:5
RM. 203/204

HOTELS
Guest Room Plans

It is interesting to note how trends in hotel design have headed off in two directions, especially in regard to the design of rooms. On one hand, an effort is being made to provide more luxurious multipurpose rooms and suites. The hotel room as office away from work or as fantasy sleeping/relaxation environment often results in rooms with work areas, living rooms, and hot tubs, just to name a few of the more popular amenities. On the other hand, there is a trend toward economy accommodations. Hotel rooms are being designed as a place to rest and sleep, a place to feel comfortable and safe at a reasonable cost. Accordingly, these rooms use less floor area and provide fewer secondary or frill items. With both of these approaches, however, designers must ensure that the room or suite layouts are accessible to the physically challenged. In that regard, various room layouts and bathroom plans are provided in this section that address this issue. (See Figs. 1 to 4.)

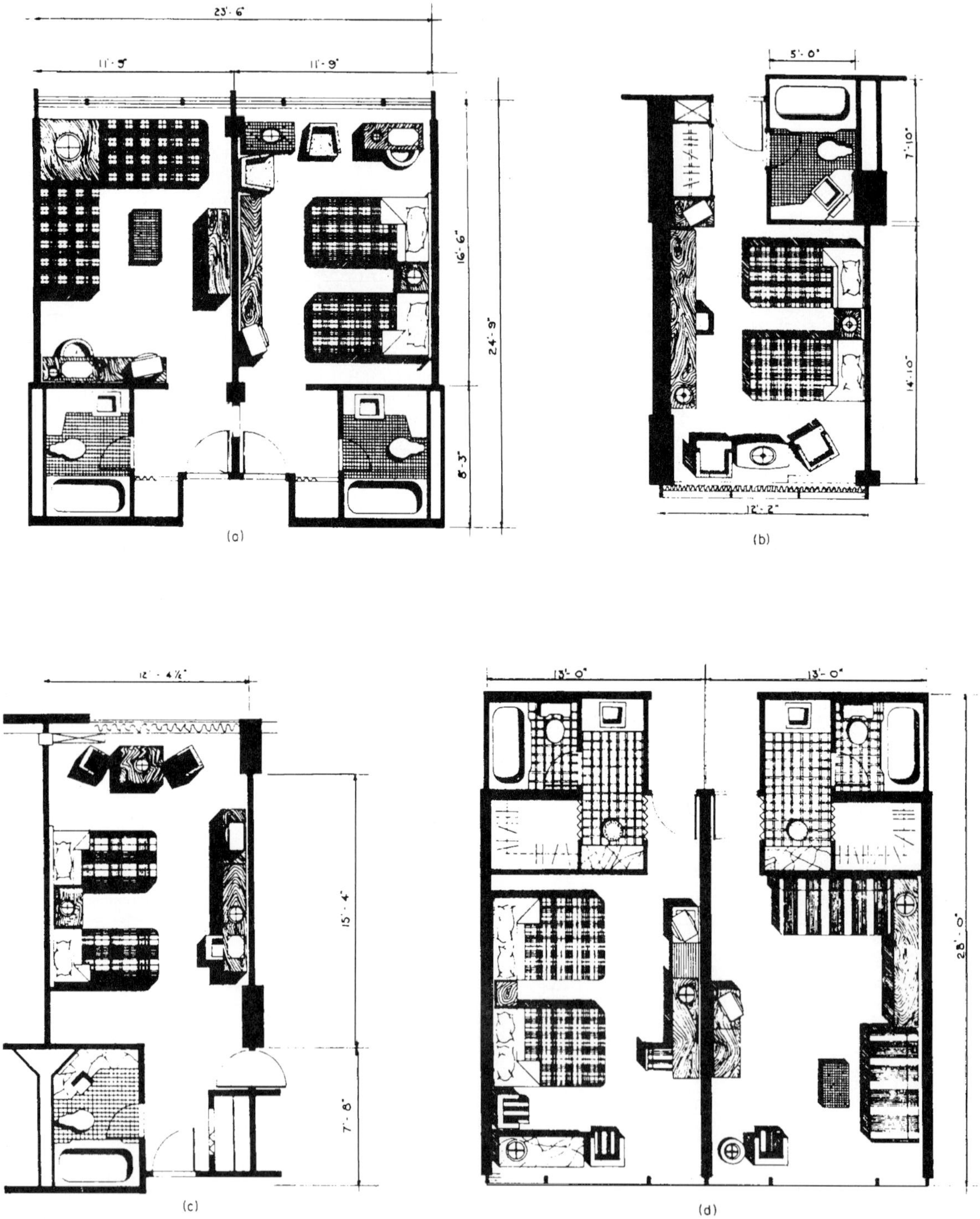

Fig. 1 (*a*) Uris Brothers Hotel, New York; (*b*) Americana Hotel, New York, typical tower room; (*c*) Loews N.Y. Motel, typical room; (*d*) Causeway Inn, Tampa, Florida

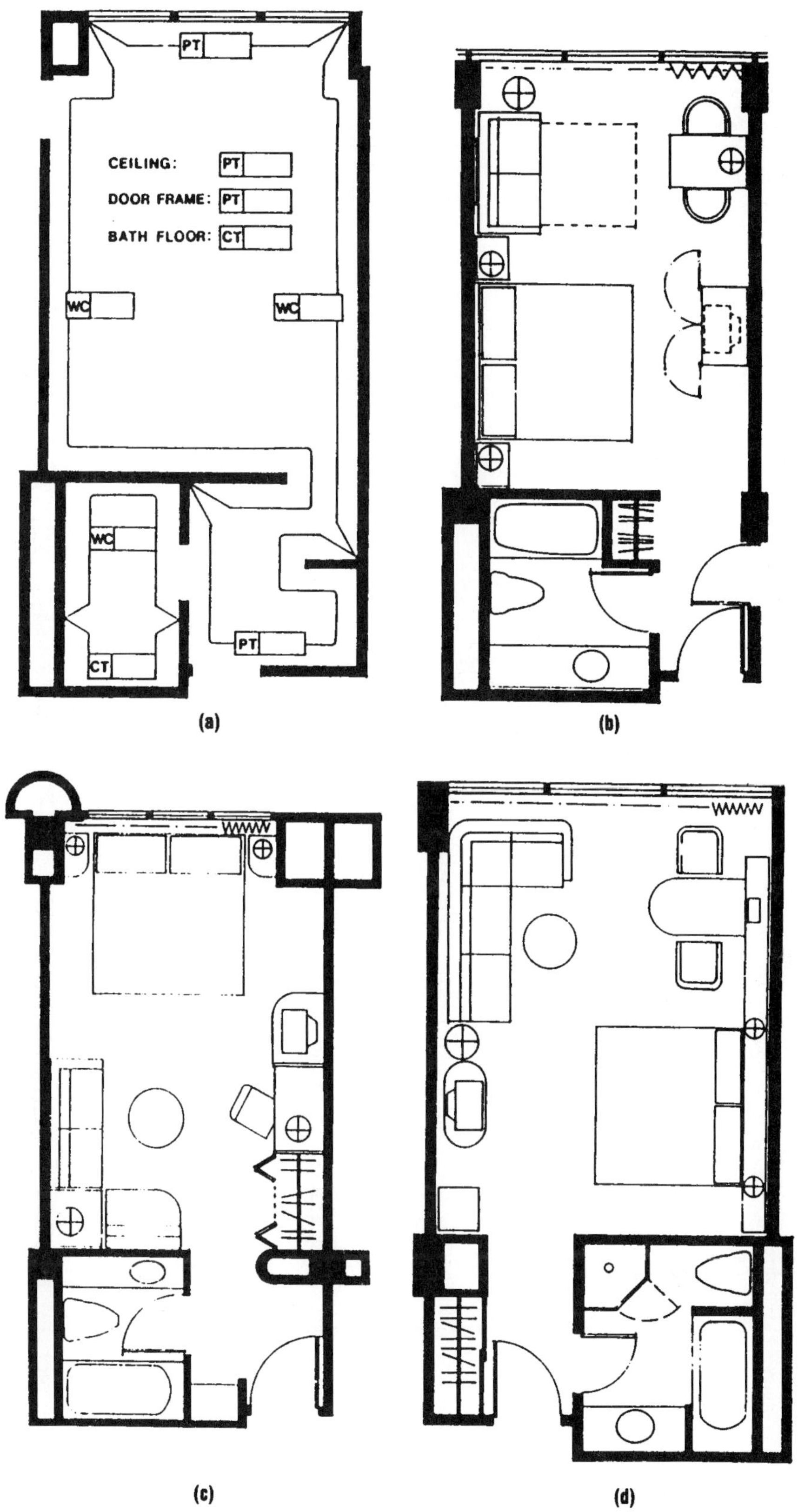

Fig. 2 Guest room plans. (*a*) Typical double-double finishes plan: vinyl wallcovering (WC), paint (P), carpet (C), ceramic tile (CT), identified and keyed to legend. (*b*) King-studio (Holiday Inn): standard layout with armoire unit and large lounge area including a convertible sofa. (*c*) Reversed layout (Sheraton, Washington, D.C.): unusual room with bed placed in front of window and lounge area near bathroom. (*d*) Luxury king room (Sheraton Grande, Los Angeles): oversized room with shelf/ledge in place of headboard, large desk surface, and lounge area; four-fixture bathroom

HOTELS
Guest Room Plans

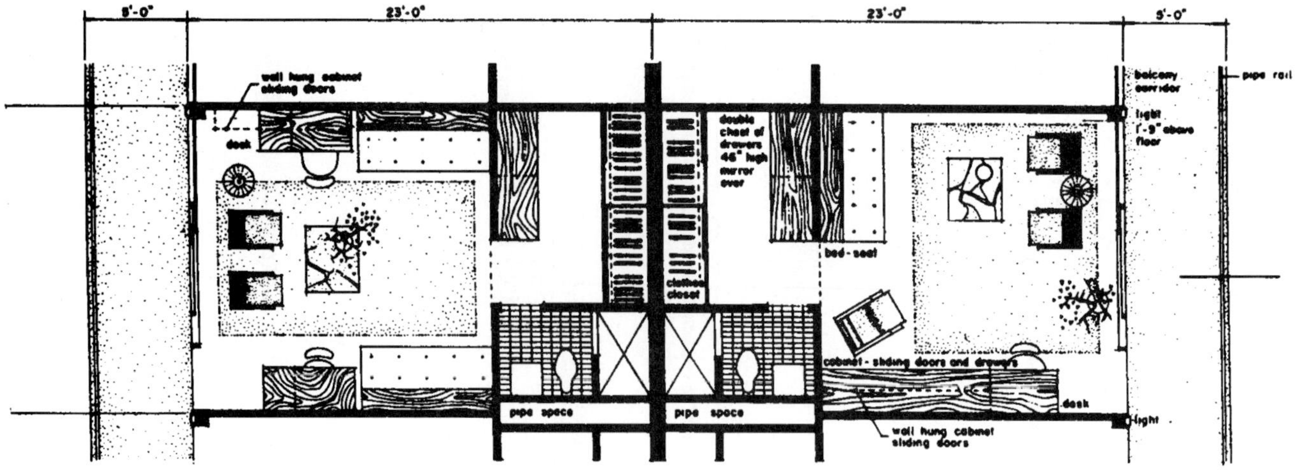

Fig. 3 Motel rooms—exterior entrance

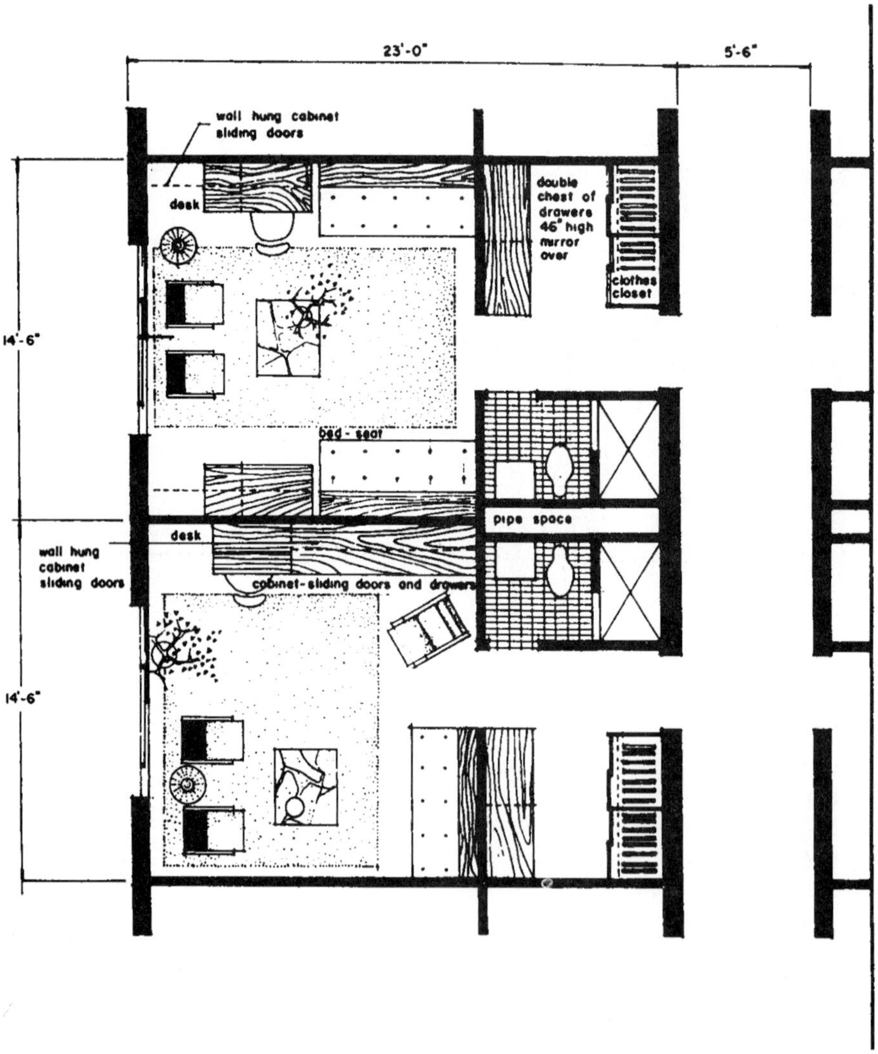

Fig. 4 Motel rooms—interior corridor

Accessible guest rooms have design features and floor plans that provide the maneuvering clearances for guests with limited mobility. Figures 5 to 9 show sample plans of guest rooms and bathrooms with the required:

- Widths and clearances at the entry, connecting, closet, and bathroom doors
- Maneuvering space in front of the closet, in the sleeping area, and within the bathroom
- Clearances to use and transfer to fixtures in the bathroom
- Clearances to open dresser drawers, to maneuver into knee space at the desk, and to access the bed, bedside table, windows, blinds, and thermostat

Clearances may depend on the design of specific furnishings. The width of the access aisle at the bed is determined by the design of the bedside table. Access to dressers is determined by the width of the drawer. The maneuvering space to turn into the desk is determined by the width of the knee space.

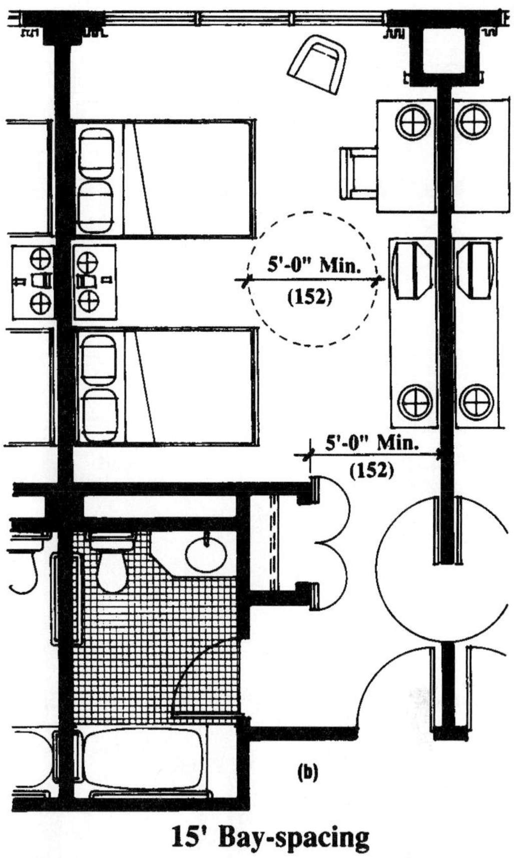

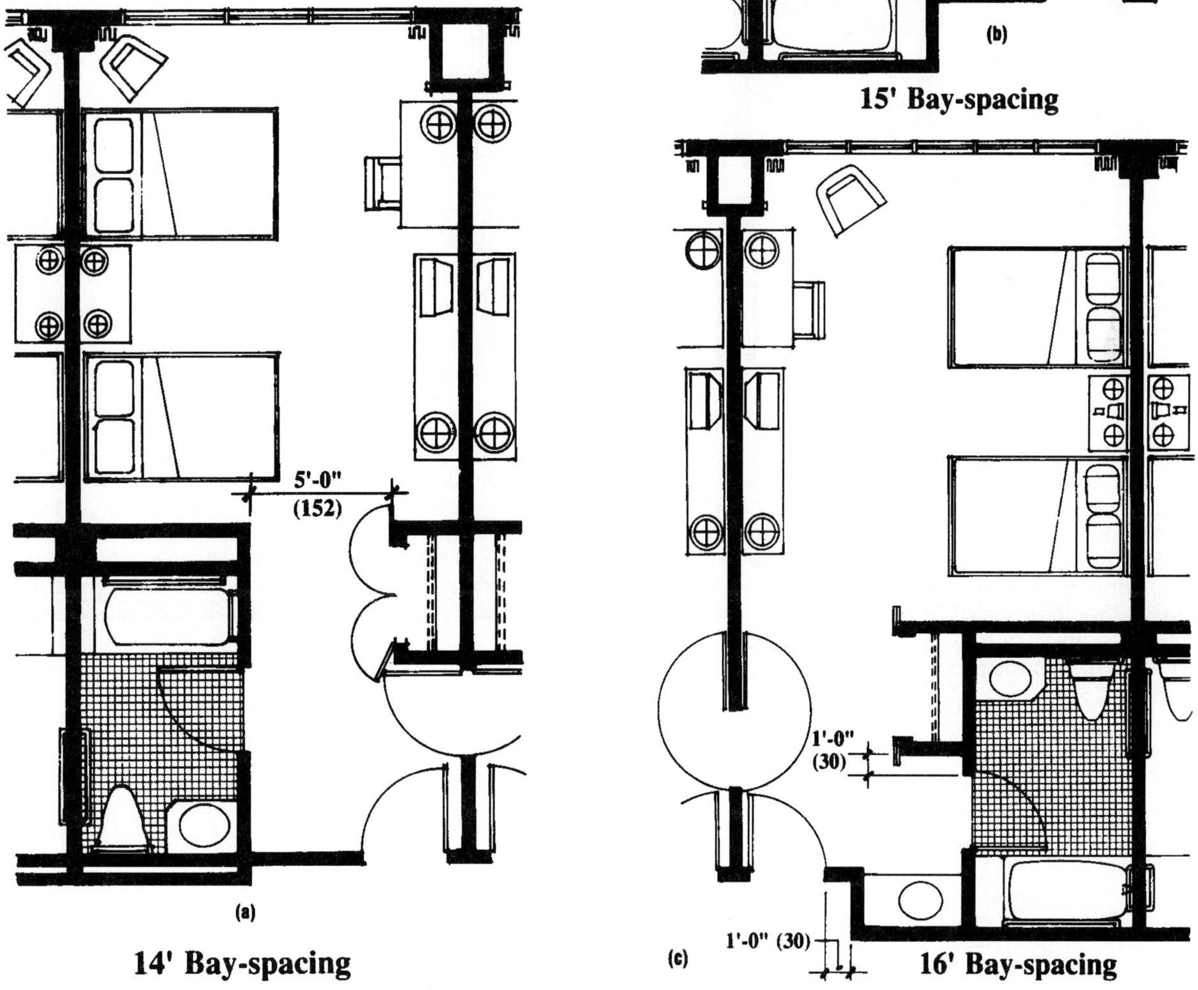

Fig. 5 Bay spacings of (*a*) 14 ft, (*b*) 15 ft, and (*c*) 16 ft can easily accommodate guests with restricted mobility

HOTELS

Accessible Guest Room Plans

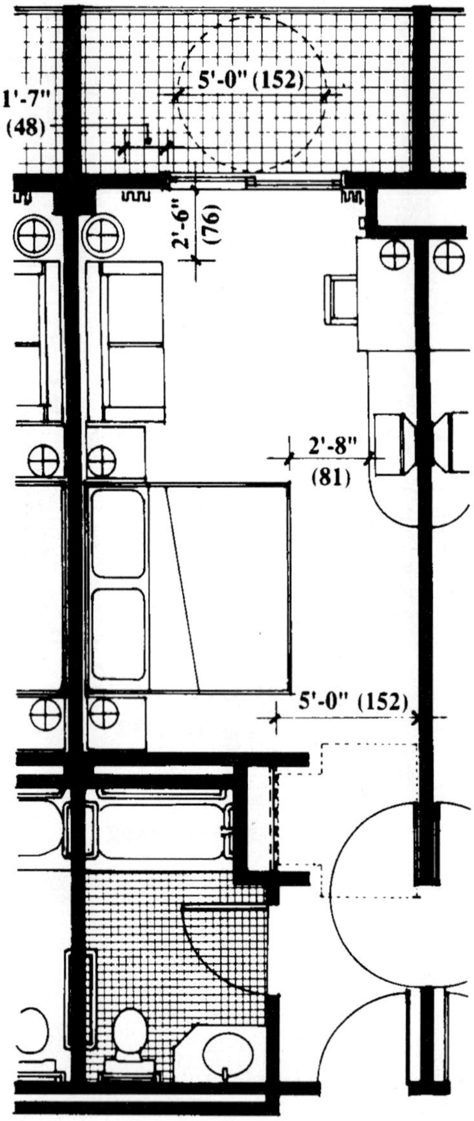

12' Bay-spacing

Fig. 6 This alternative 12 ft 0 in bay-spacing design requires the dresser to be offset from the foot of the bed. The bathroom wall is stepped back to provide clearances for the bathroom door and connecting door. The heating/cooling unit projects into the room to allow access to the thermostat. If balconies are provided, a minimum depth of 5 ft 0 in is recommended to allow guests with wheelchairs to turn around

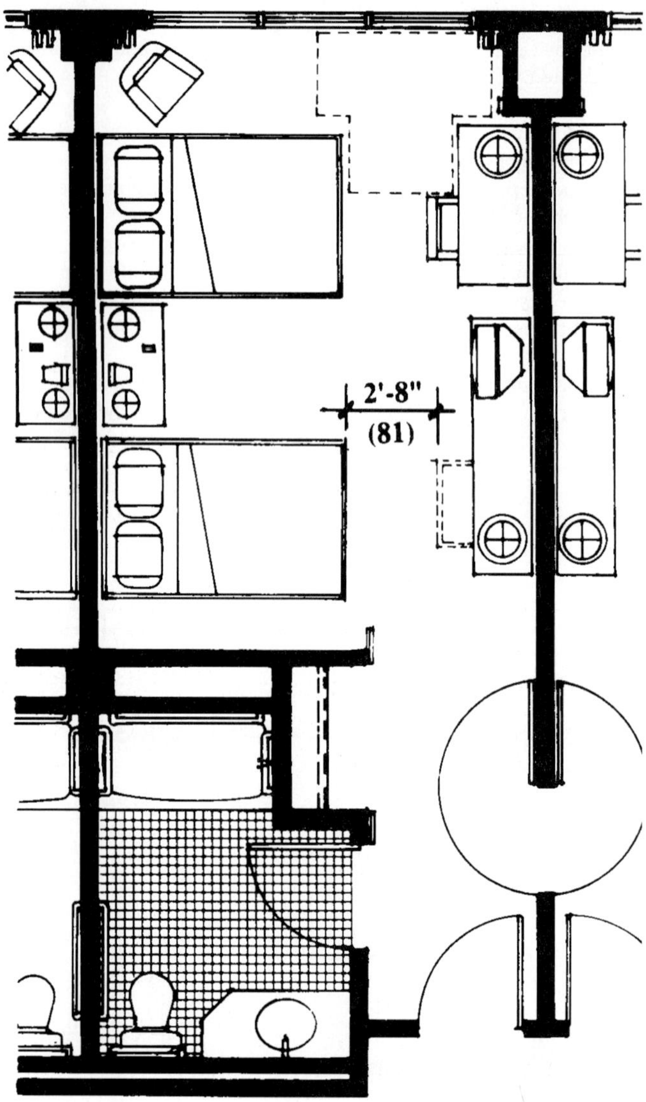

13' Bay-spacing

Fig. 7 A 13 ft 0 in bay spacing provides room for wheelchair clearances, including a turning space in front of the closet and at the foot of the beds, an access aisle between the beds, a T-turnaround at the window aisle for access to temperature controls and blinds and drapes, door clearances, and a bathroom that meets ANSI standards

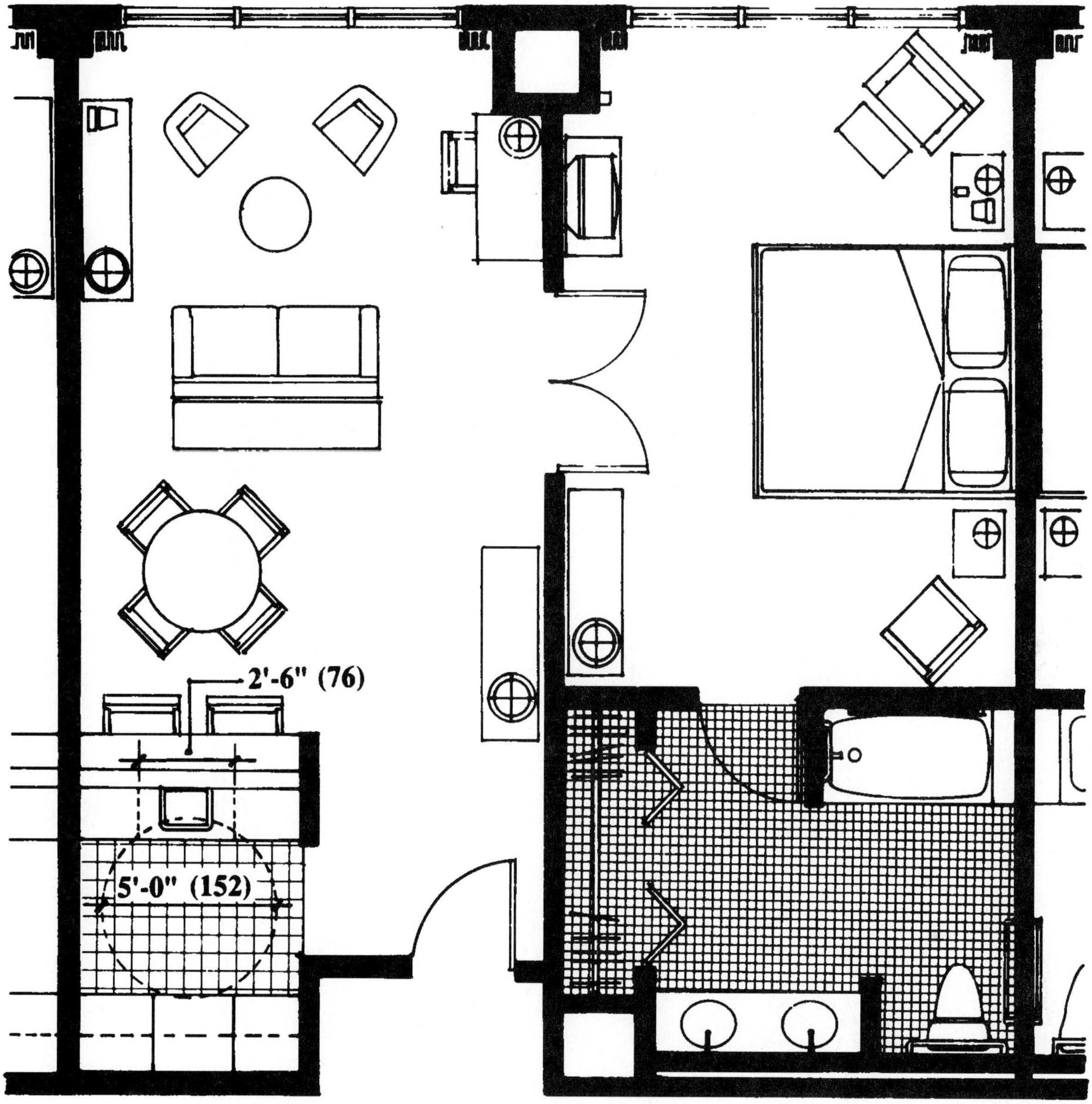

Suite with 14' Bay-spacing

Fig. 8 Accessible suites should meet the same requirements for accessible guest rooms and guest baths. Because suites are usually more generous in terms of space, providing accessibility is less difficult. If a small kitchenette is included, a knee space 2 ft 3 in high should be provided below the sink. A countertop height of 2 ft 10 in (2 in lower than standard) is suitable for both ambulatory guests and guests in wheelchairs. A pull-out lapboard at a height of 2 ft 6 in provides a work space for guests in wheelchairs. The kitchenette should include a 5 ft 0 in turning space

HOTELS
1-Bedroom Accessible Suite

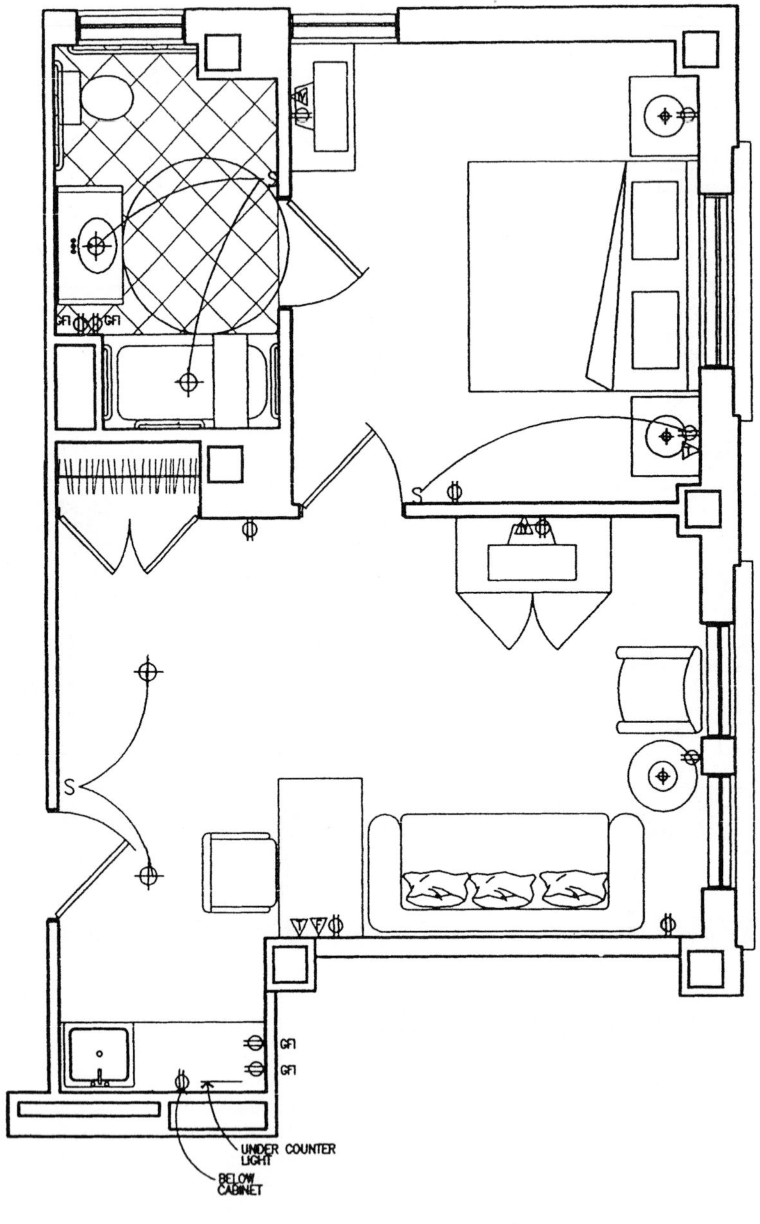

Accessible Suite Floor Plan

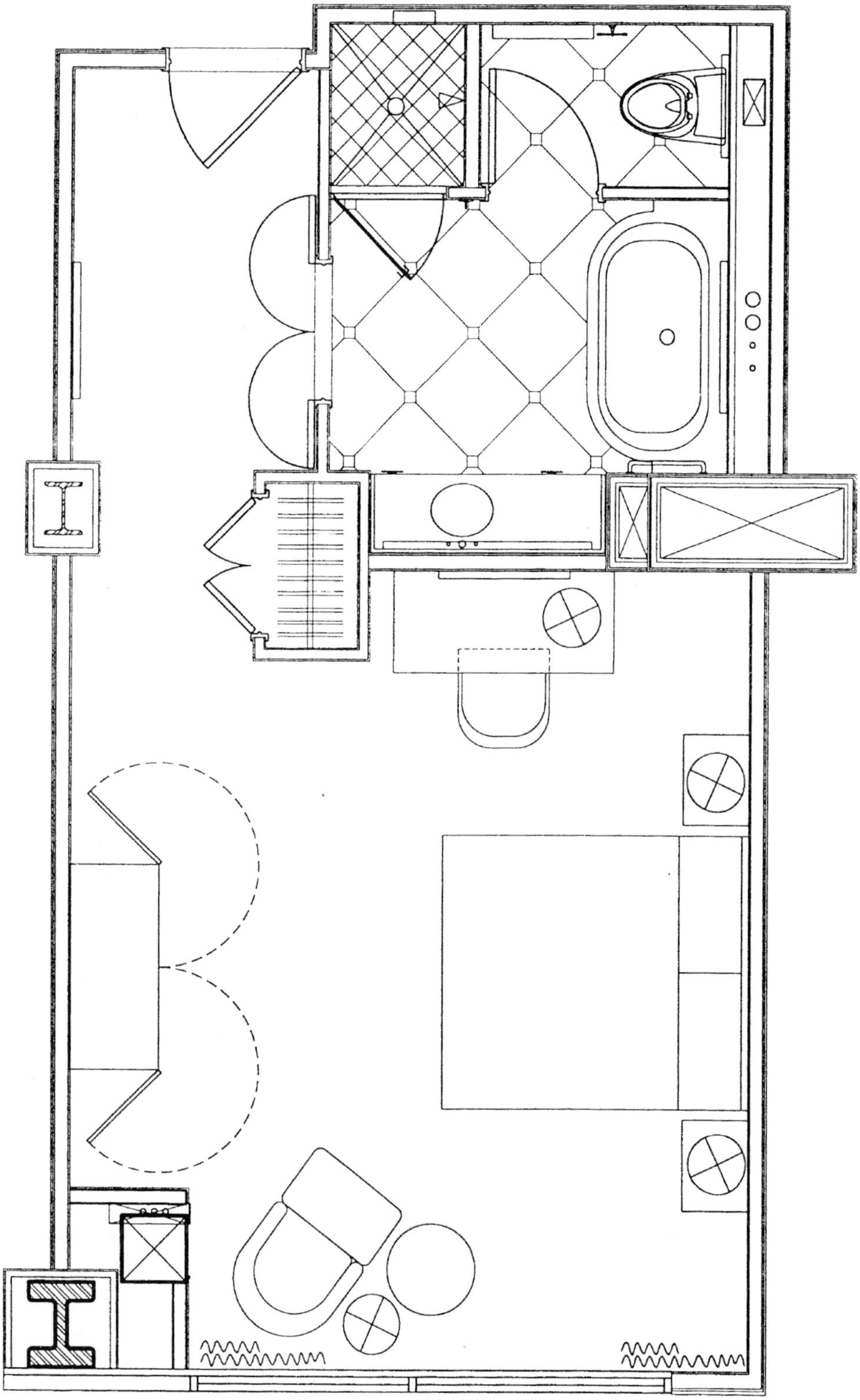

1 **ROOM TYPE: KING ROOM**
SCALE: 1/4" = 1'-0"

HOTELS
Guest Room/Single King

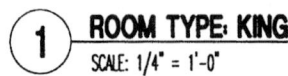

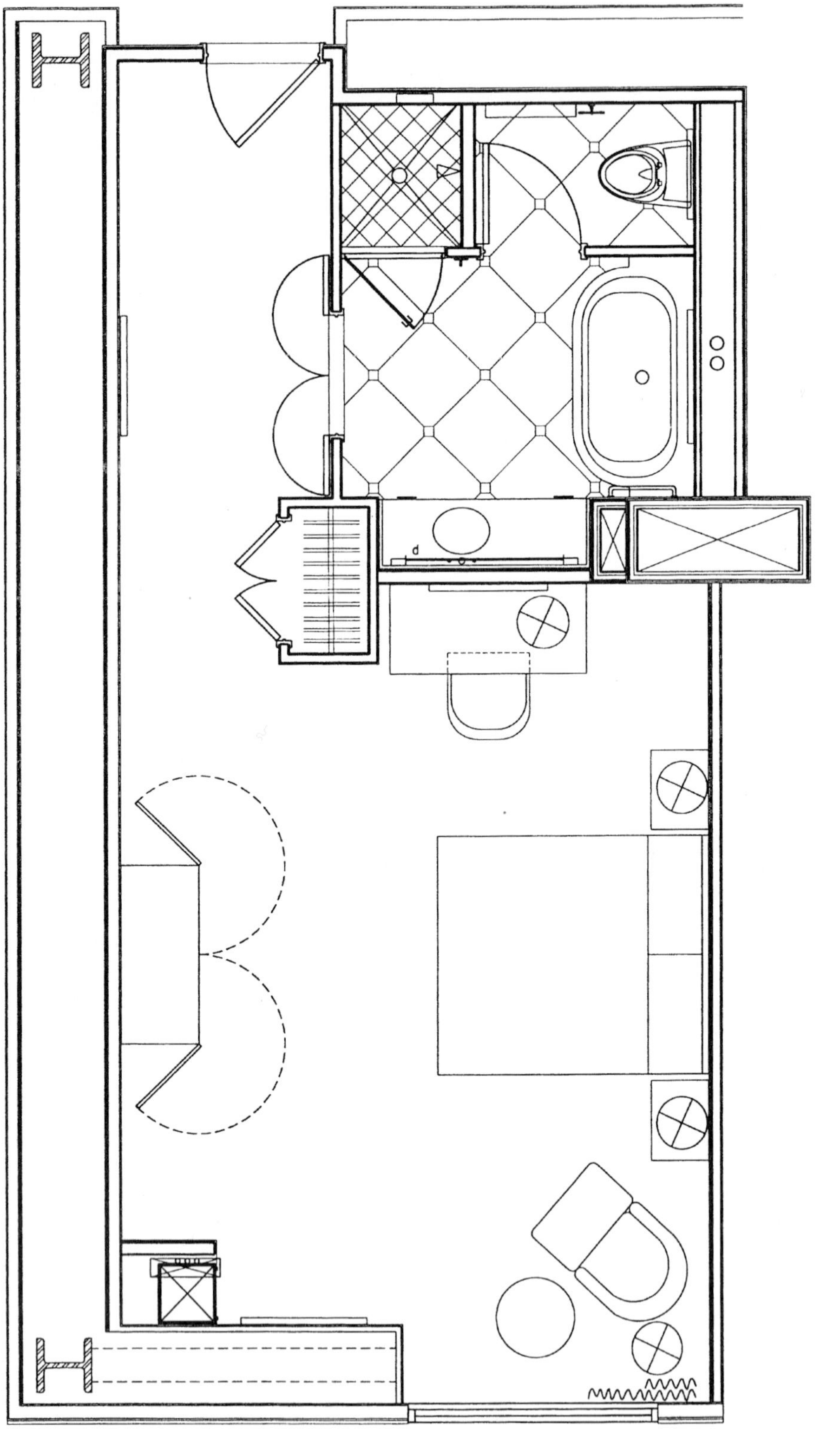

1 ROOM TYPE: KING
SCALE: 1/4" = 1'-0"

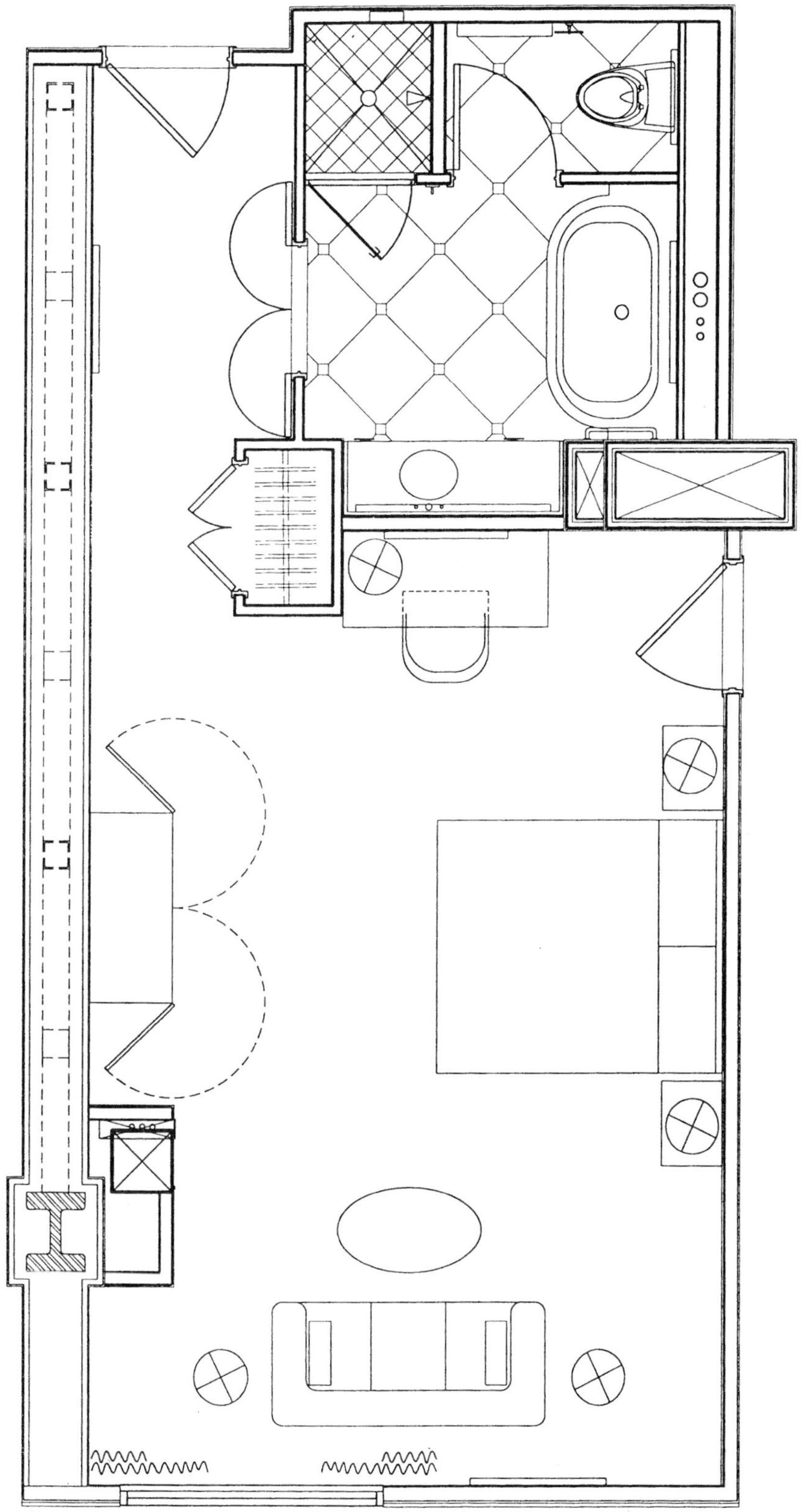

1 ROOM TYPE: EXTENDED KING ROOM
SCALE: 1/4" = 1'-0"

HOTELS
Guest Room/Single King

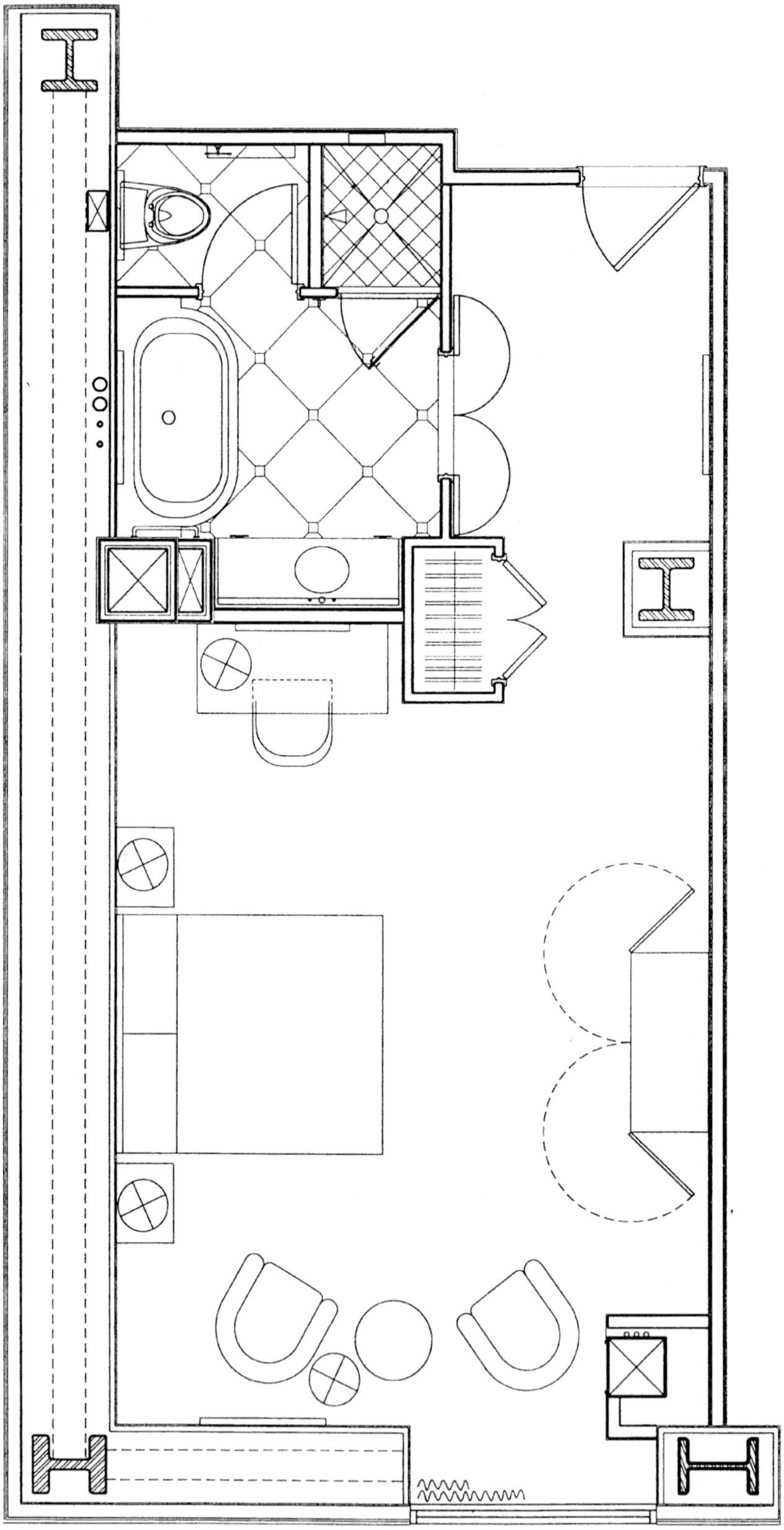

1 **ROOM TYPE: KING ROOM**
SCALE: 1/4" = 1'-0"

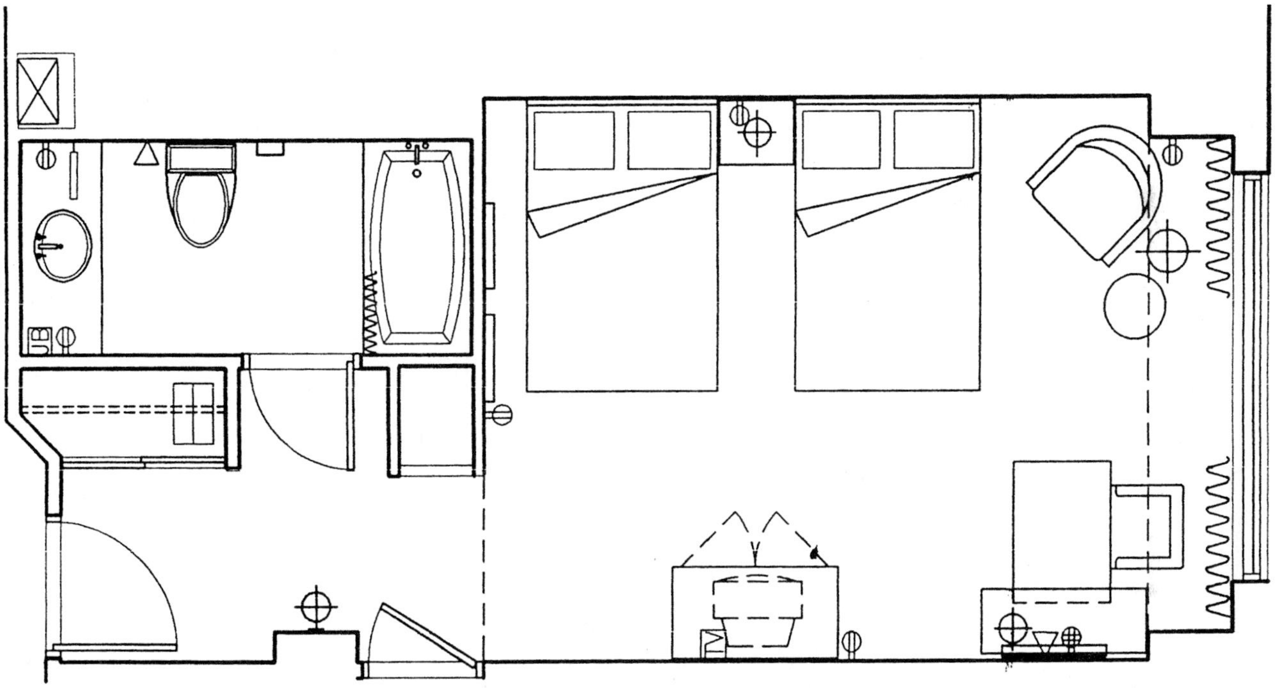

Typical "Double/Double" Floor Plan

HOTELS
One-Bedroom Suite

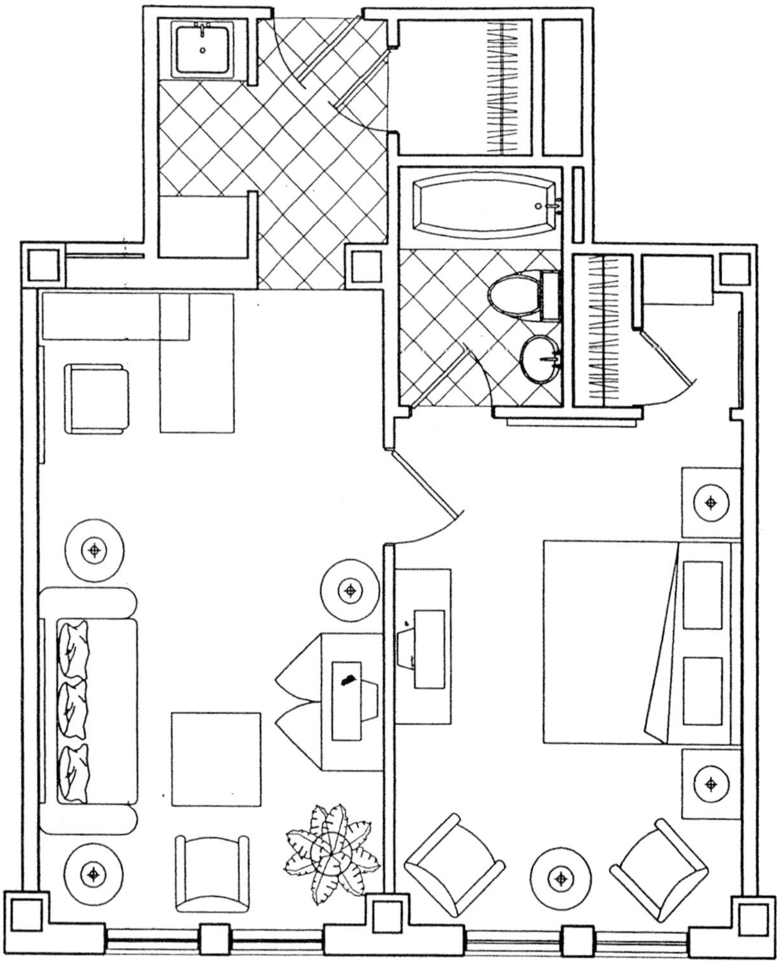

One Bedroom Suite Floor Plan

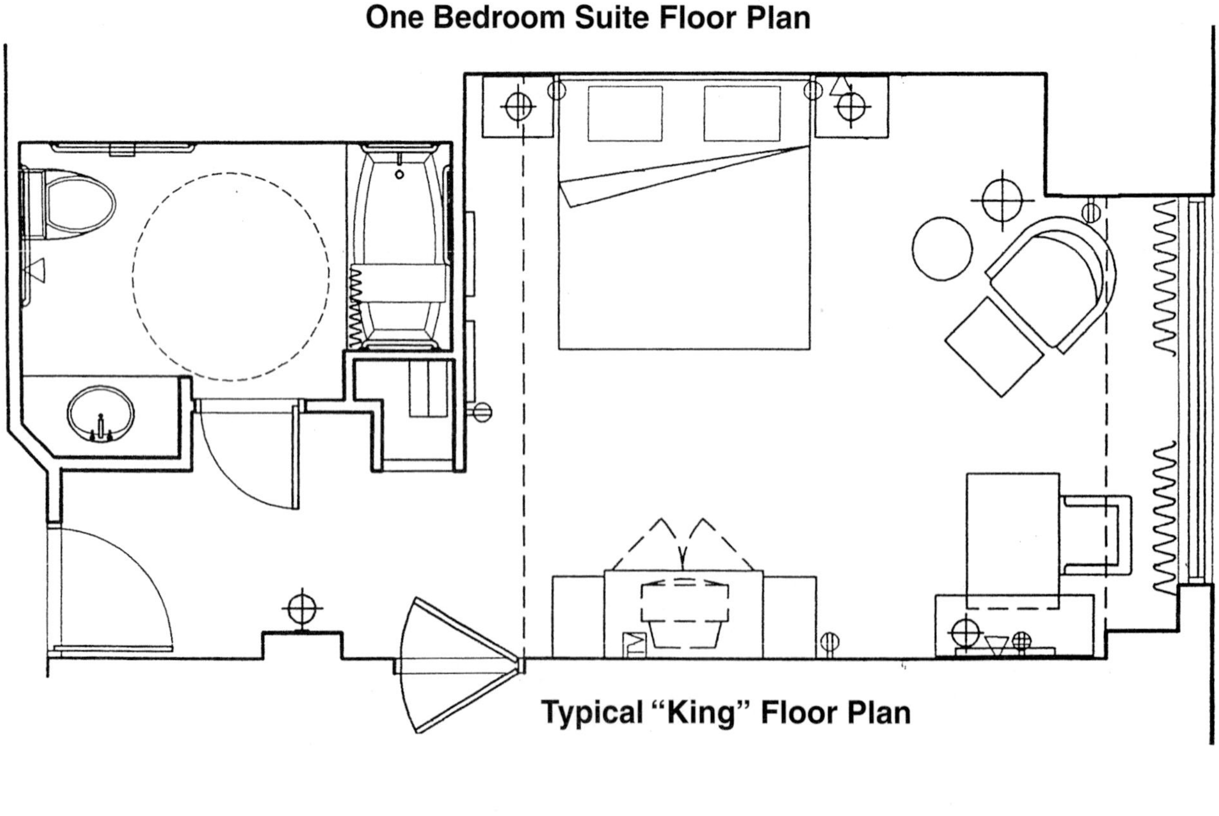

Typical "King" Floor Plan

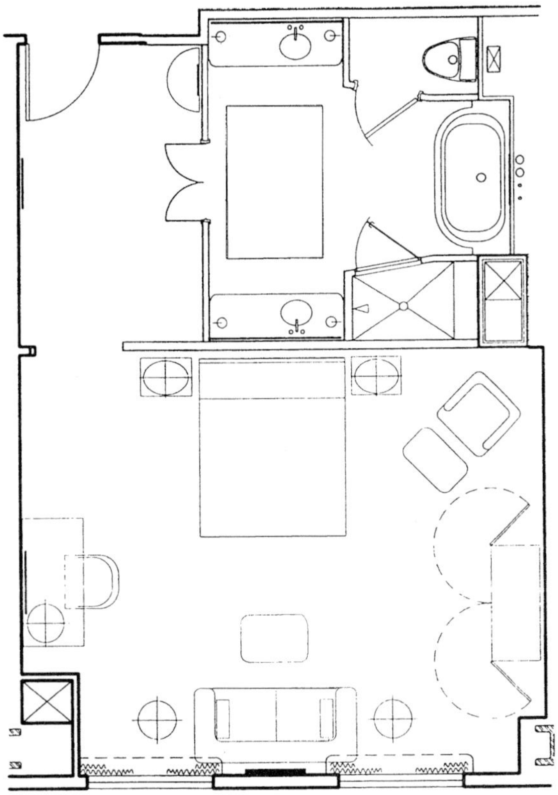

King Parlor Room

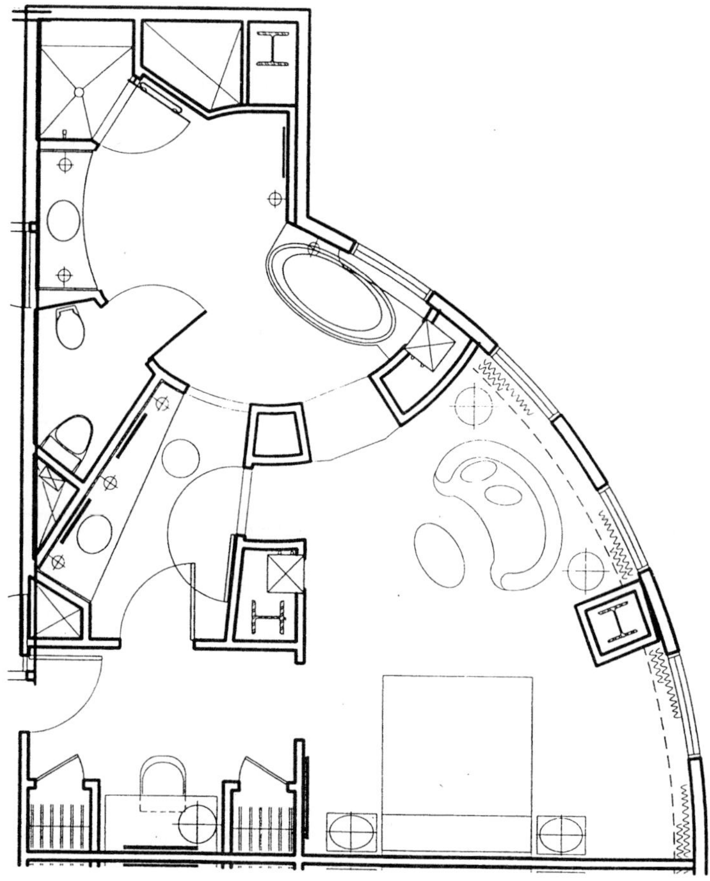

King Parlor Room

HOTELS
Luxury Suite

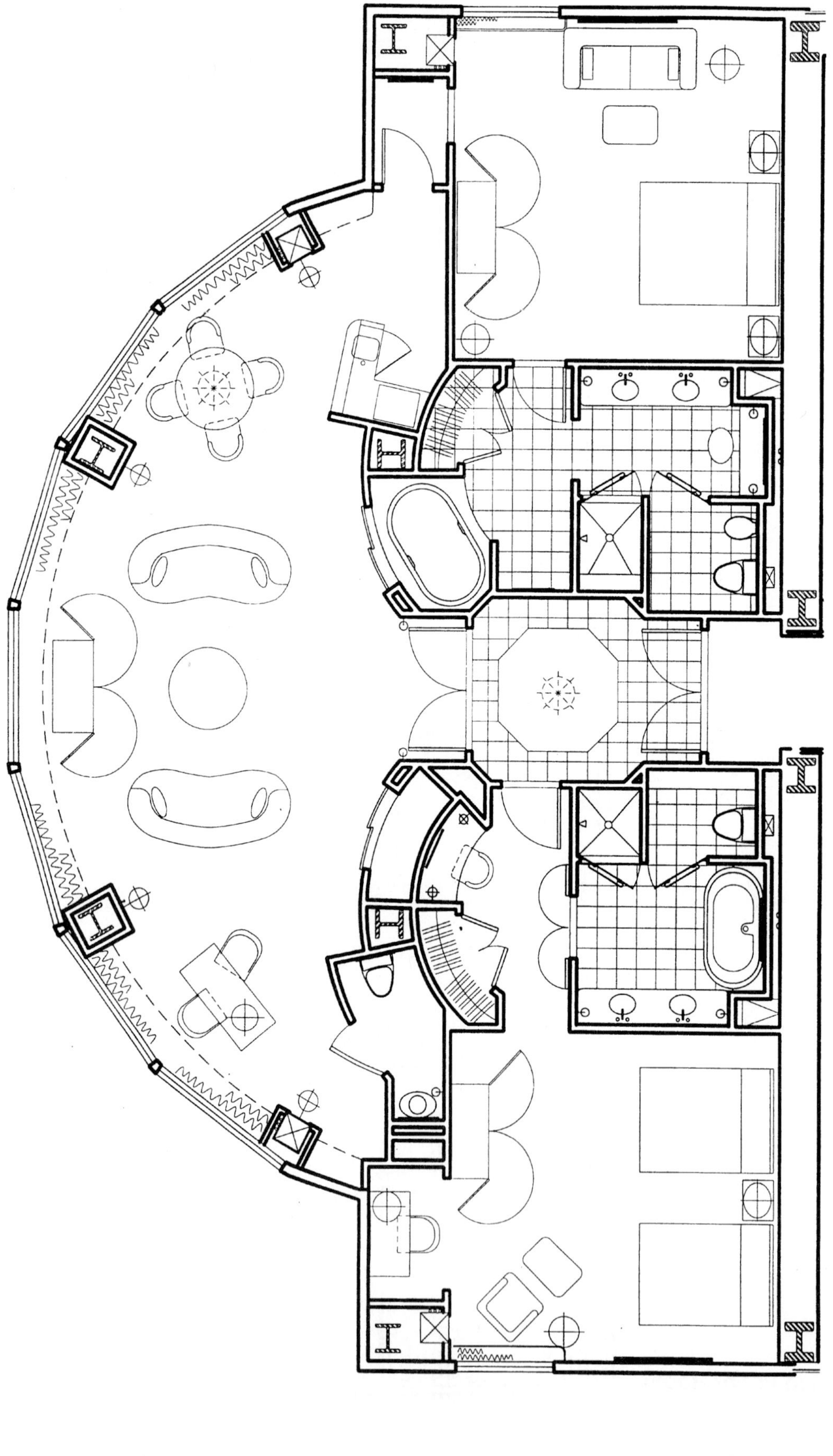

1 **DOUBLE QUEEN ROOM SUITE**
SCALE: 3/16" = 1'-0"

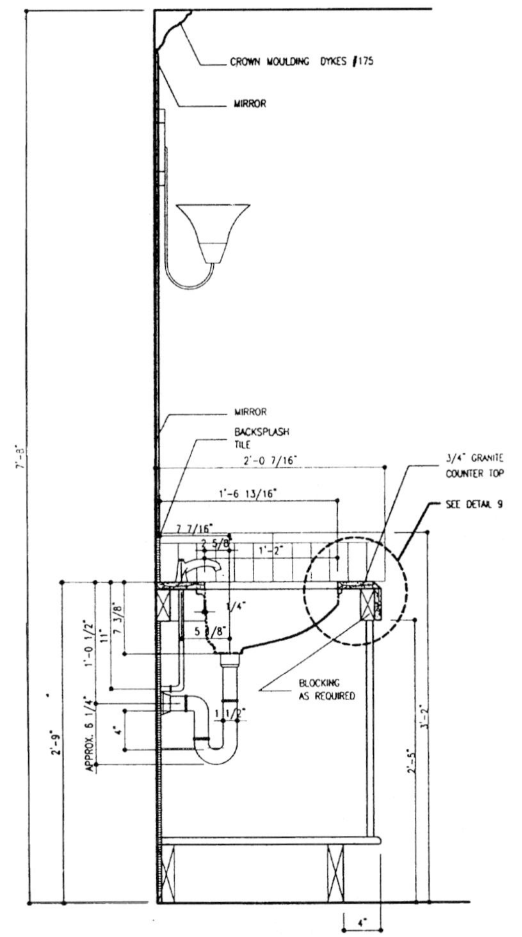

2 **VANITY COUNTER DETAIL**
SCALE: 1"=1'-0"

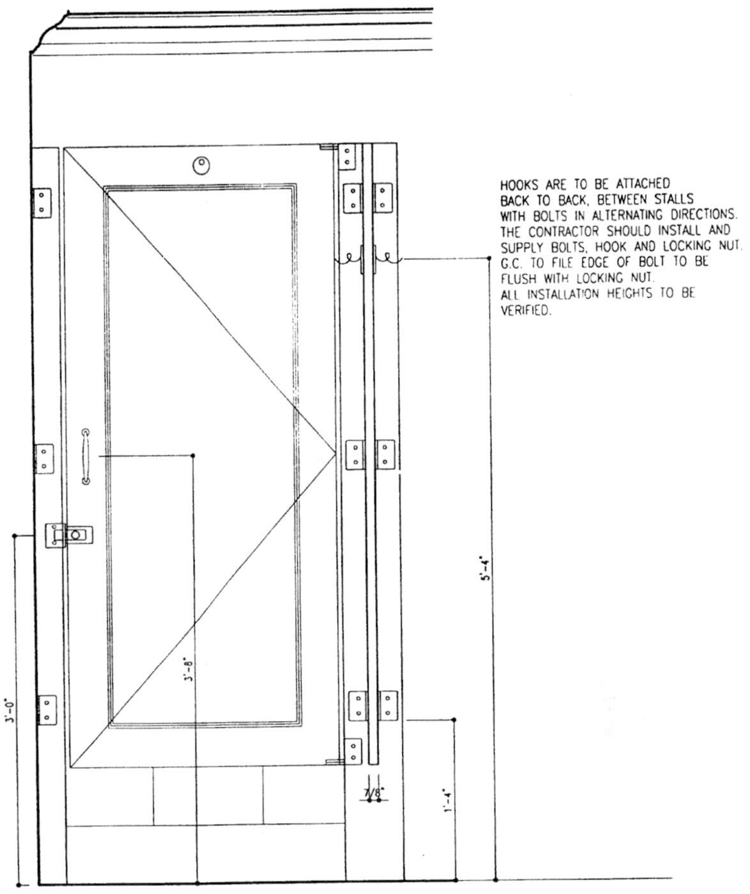

4 **TYP. STALL DETAIL (INT.)**
SCALE: 1"=1'-0"

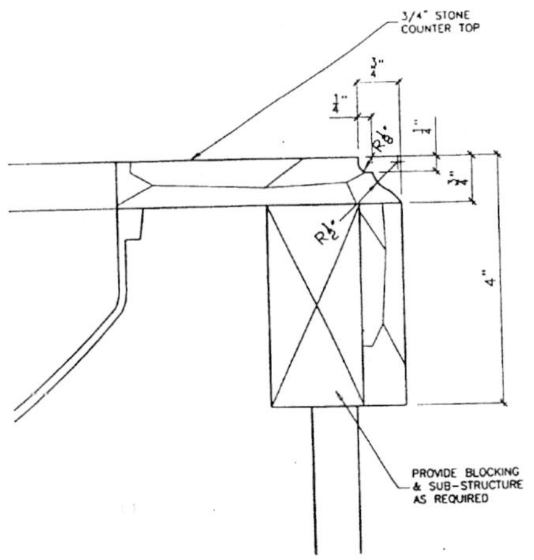

9 **DETAIL**
SCALE: 6" = 1'-0"

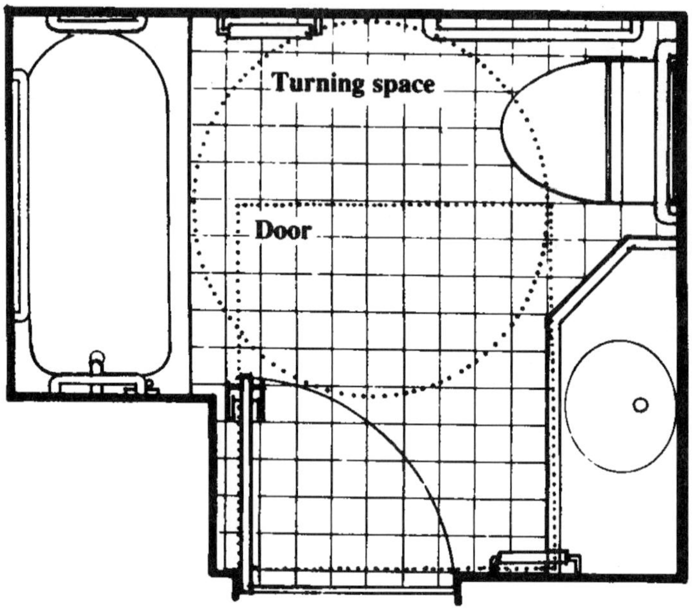

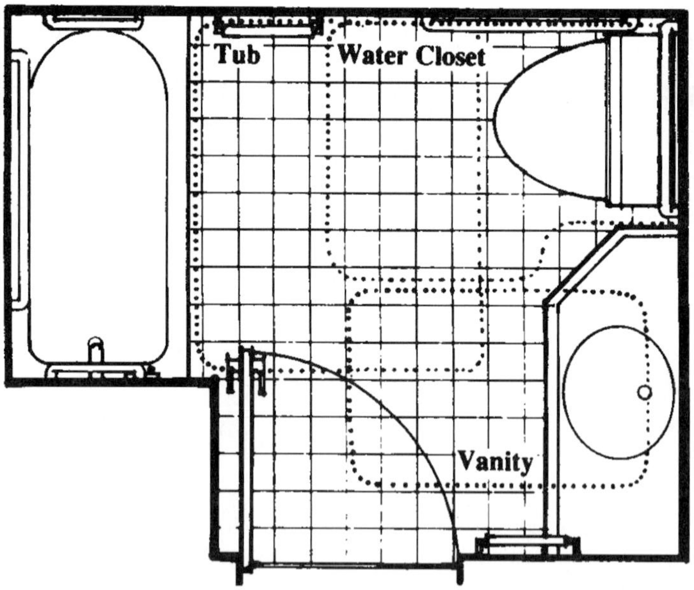

Fig. 9 These two diagrams illustrate the same bathroom plan with the required clearances for door operation and turning space and access to each fixture, including the tub/shower, vanity, and water closet. Clearances for maneuvering space, door operation, and individual fixtures can overlap. Because of the vertical characteristics of wheelchairs, clearances can include toe space (9 in high) below water closet and knee space (2 ft 3 in high) below vanities

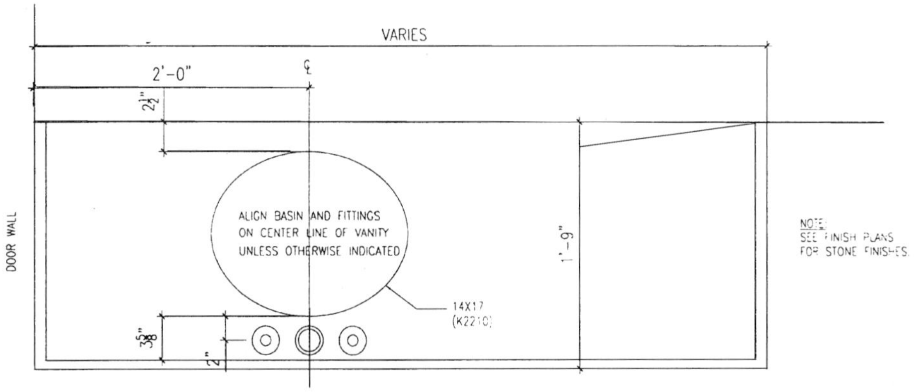

5 VANITY PLAN
SCALE: 1 1/2"=1'-0"

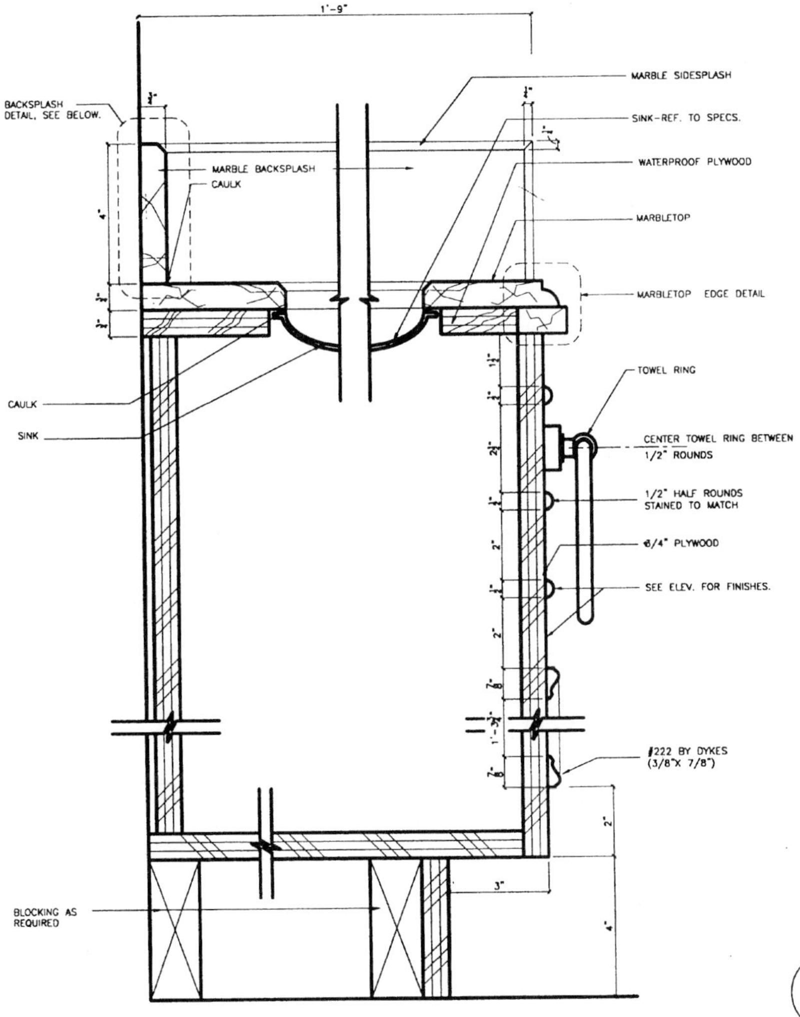

4 TYPICAL VANITY DETAIL
SCALE:

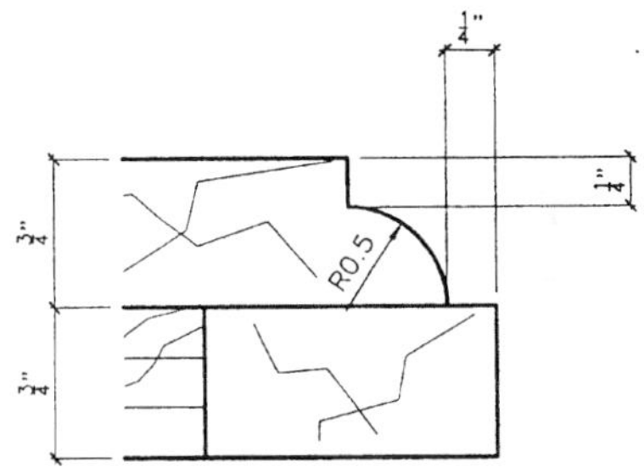

7 COUNTER EDGE DETAIL
SCALE: FULL SIZE

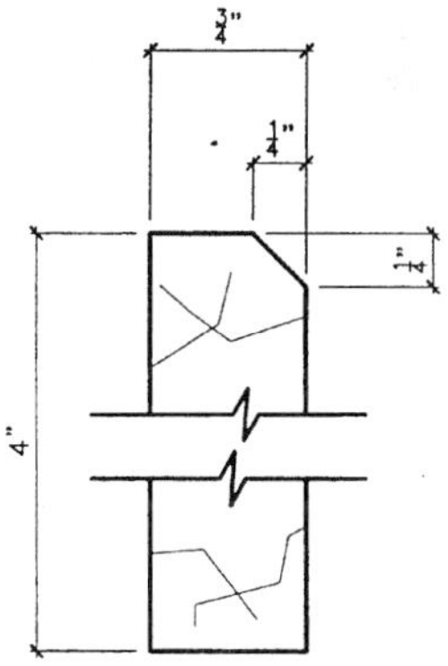

6 BACKSPLASH DETAIL
SCALE: FULL SIZE

HOTELS
Spa Shower Room/Elevations

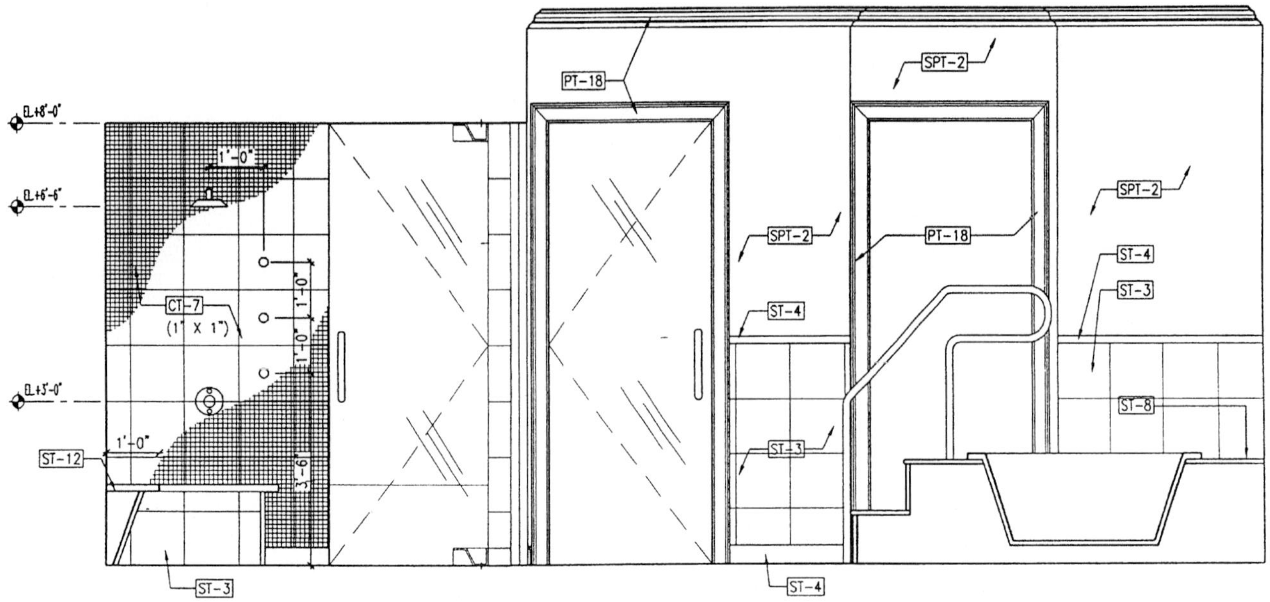

6 SPA SHOWER ROOM/ TUB AREA (GOLD)
SCALE: 1/2" = 1'-0"

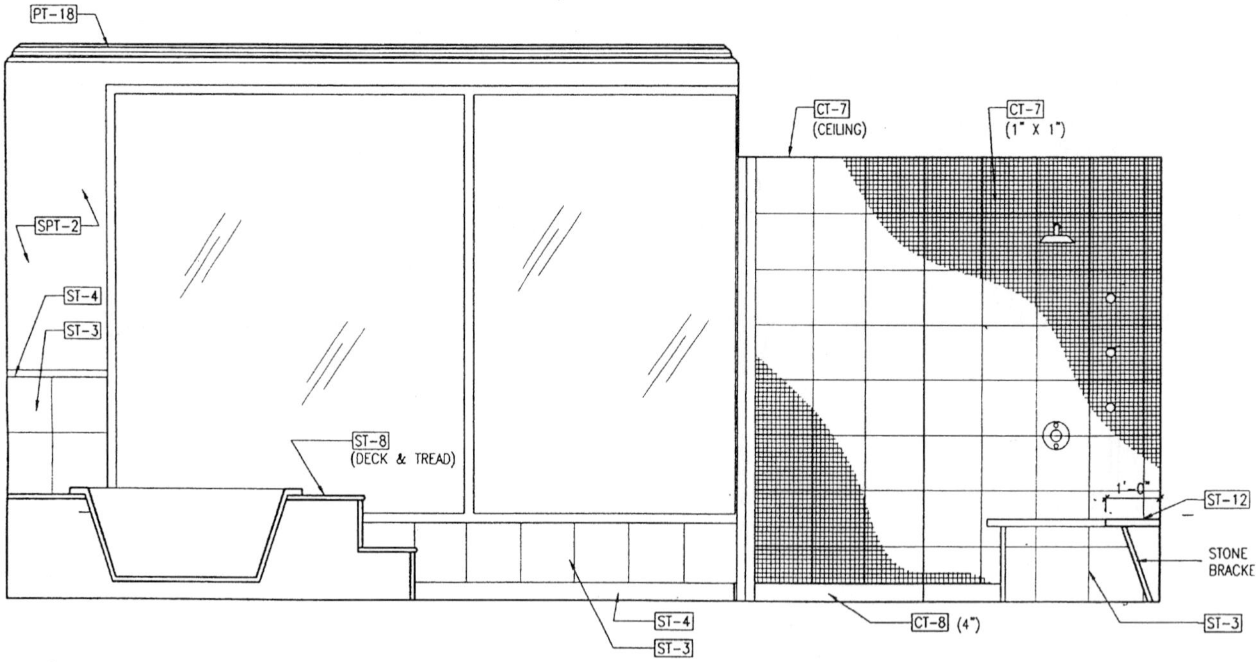

7 SPA SHOWER ROOM/TUB AREA (GOLD)
SCALE: 1/2" = 1'-0"

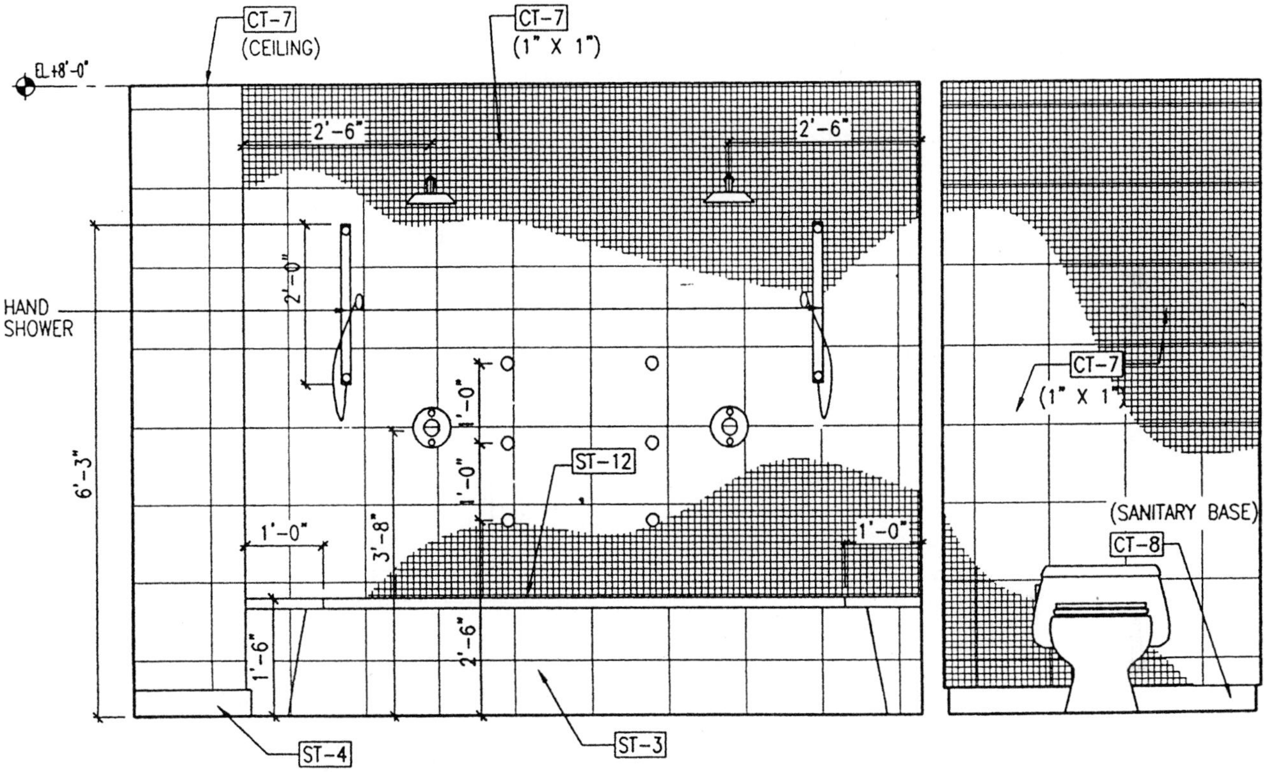

8 SPA SHOWER ROOM/TUB AREA (GOLD)
SCALE: 1/2" = 1'-0"

HOTELS

Tub and Shower Details

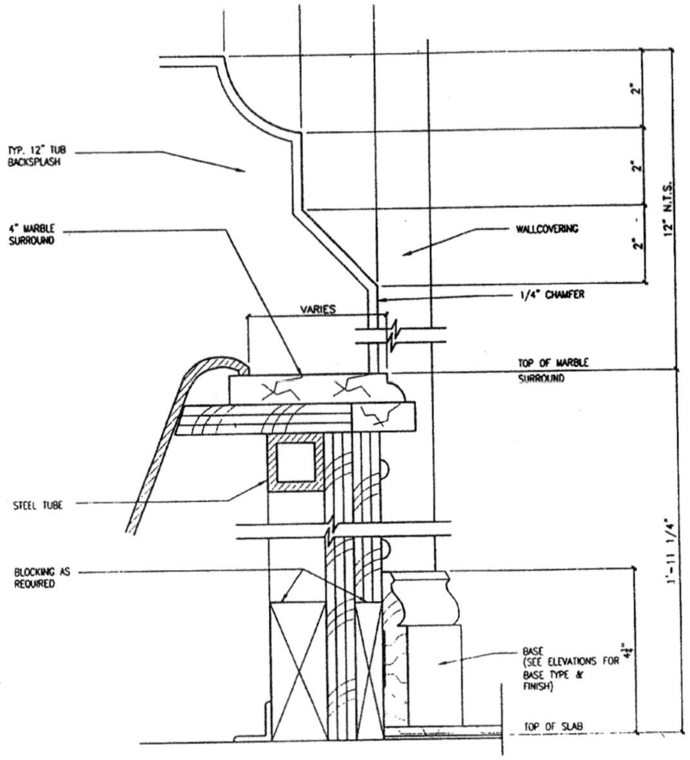

8 SECTION AT BATHTUB (@ 4/5/7 BAY ONLY)
SCALE: HALF SIZE

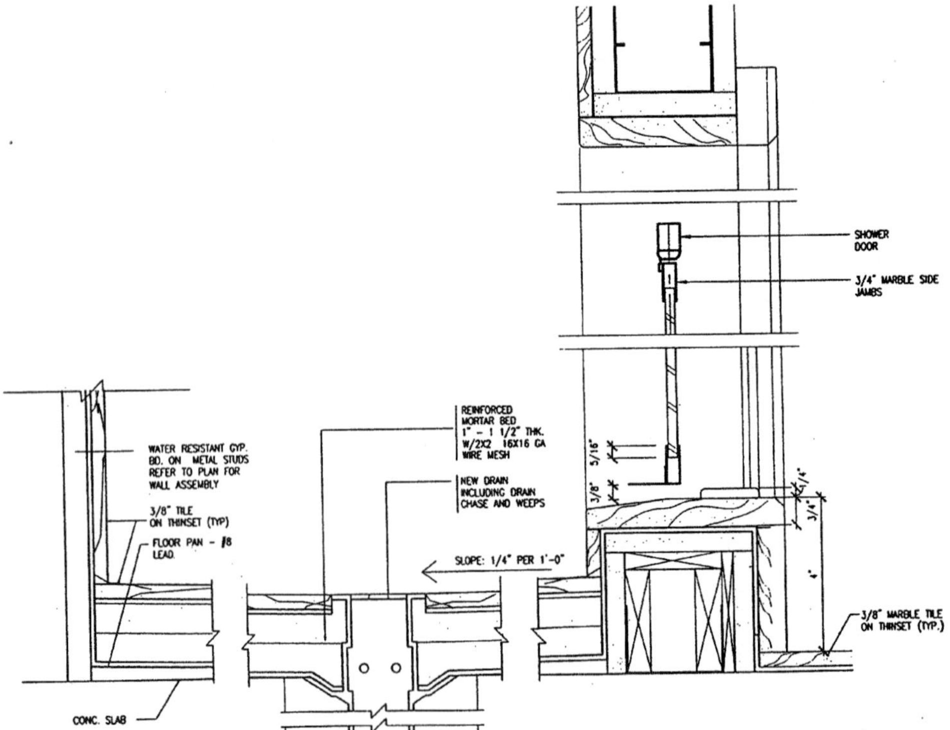

9 TYPICAL SHOWER CURB DETAIL
SCALE: HALF SIZE

HOTELS

Hotel Room Bar/Plan and Sections

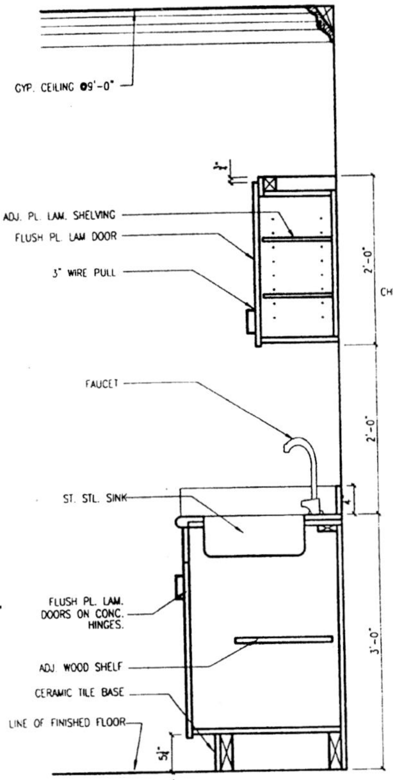

1 SECTION @ KITCHEN
SCALE: 3/4" = 1'-0"

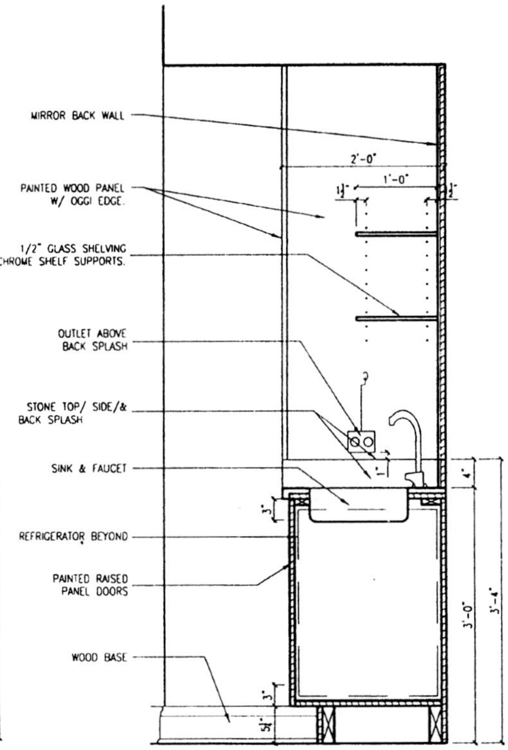

2 SECTION THRU BAR
SCALE: 3/4" = 1'-0"

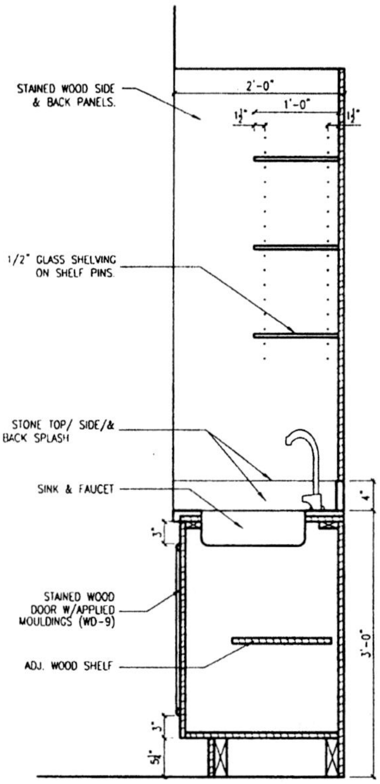

3 SECTION THRU BACK BAR
SCALE: 3/4" = 1'-0"

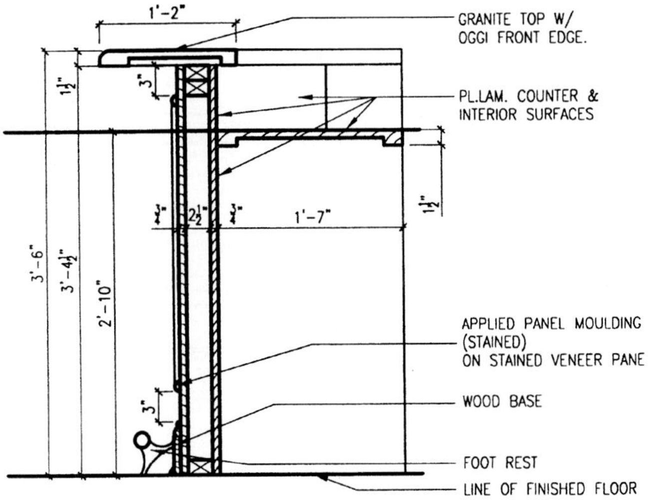

4 BAR SECTION
SCALE: 3/4" = 1'-0"

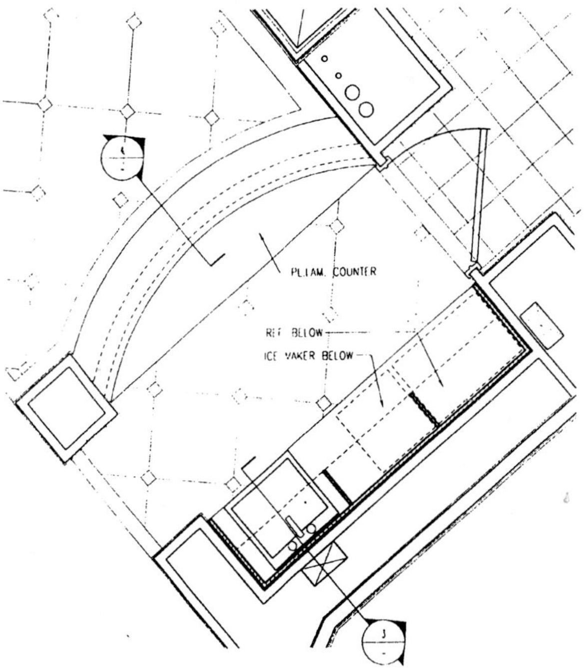

4A BAR PLAN
SCALE 1/2" = 1"

HOTELS

Registration Desk

The hotel registration desk serves as both a symbol of hospitality for the arriving guest and the operational nerve center for the hotel. With the advent of electronic check-in procedures, credit cards, and computer-aided management, the registration desk has become a sophisticated electronic workstation not unlike a trading table or an airline reservations desk. At the same time, this electronic data processing capability is meant to be maintained at low visibility for reasons of hotel image and confidentiality. Accordingly, the designer must be able to project the appropriate hospitality image while at the same time integrating all of the required technologies. Figures 10 to 13 show examples of architectural working drawings and details that meet many of these requirements.

The design of a front desk or registration desk can take many forms and be constructed with a variety of materials. Regardless of the design vocabulary used or architectural style, certain important design considerations must be observed.

1. The number of persons actively staffing the counterlike facility will dictate both the width and overall depth of the front desk. It is suggested that between 5 and 7 ft be allocated per staff workstation and that one workstation be allocated for every 125 to 150 rooms. For every additional 125 to 150 rooms, an additional workstation should be provided. Peak check-in/check-out loads could require even more staff workstations.

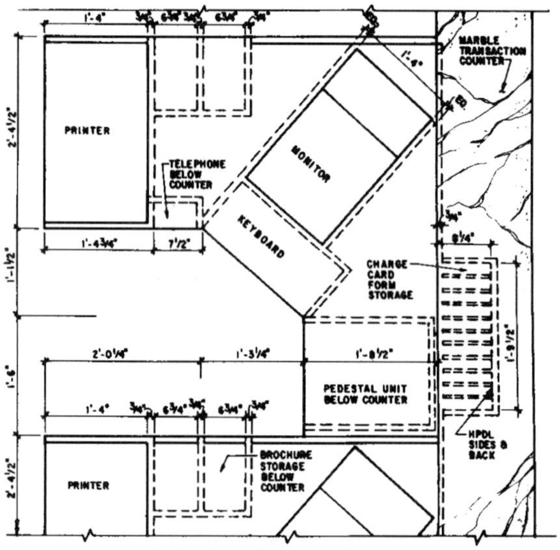

ENLARGED PARTIAL PLAN REGISTRATION COUNTER

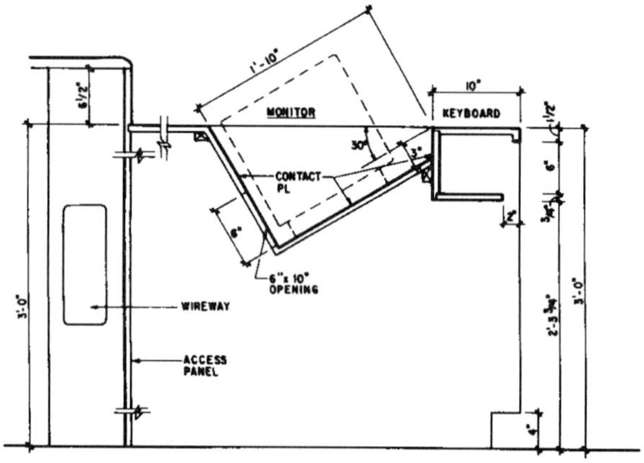

SECTION AT REGISTRATION DESK

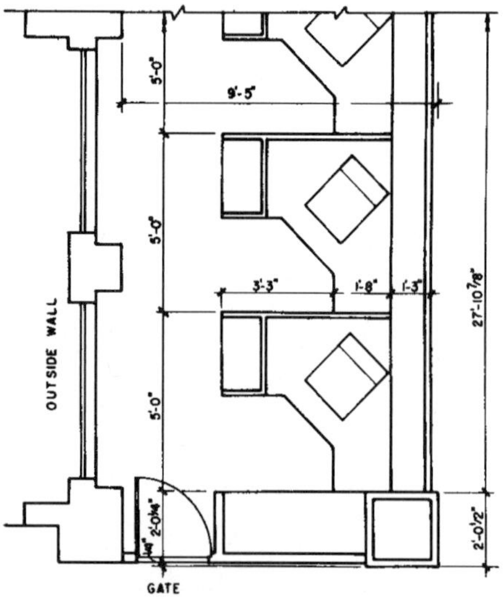

PARTIAL PLAN REGISTRATION COUNTER

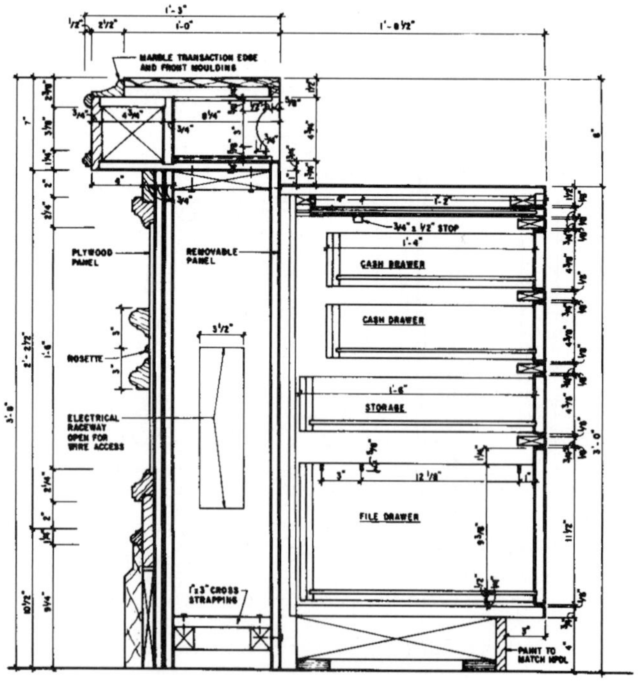

SECTION AT COUNTER

Fig. 10

2. The front desk should be easily accessible from and to the main hotel entrance. "Easily accessible" strongly implies clear visibility.
3. Elevators servicing the hotel guest rooms should be readily visible from the front desk. This is not always feasible in extremely large hotels.
4. The front desk should be designed in such a way as to take into consideration the various users it will accommodate. Special attention should be given to the fact that hotel guests may be physically challenged or chairbound. The overall height, writing surfaces, and overhangs should be designed to accommodate a hotel guest seated in a wheelchair.
5. The basic front desk design should avoid, wherever possible, visual obstructions that block sight lines or create blind spots. Accordingly, columns and high walls should be avoided.

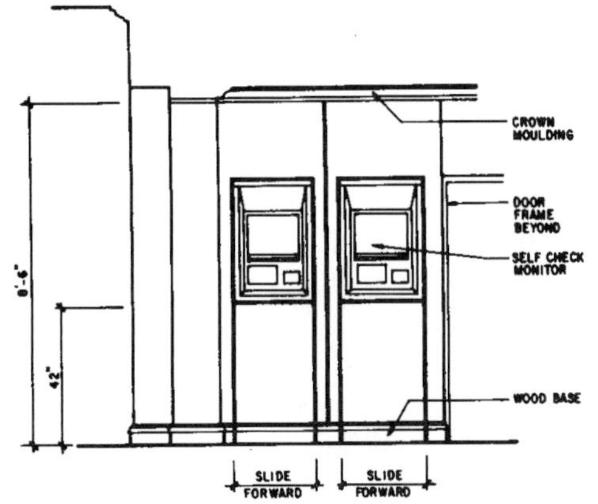

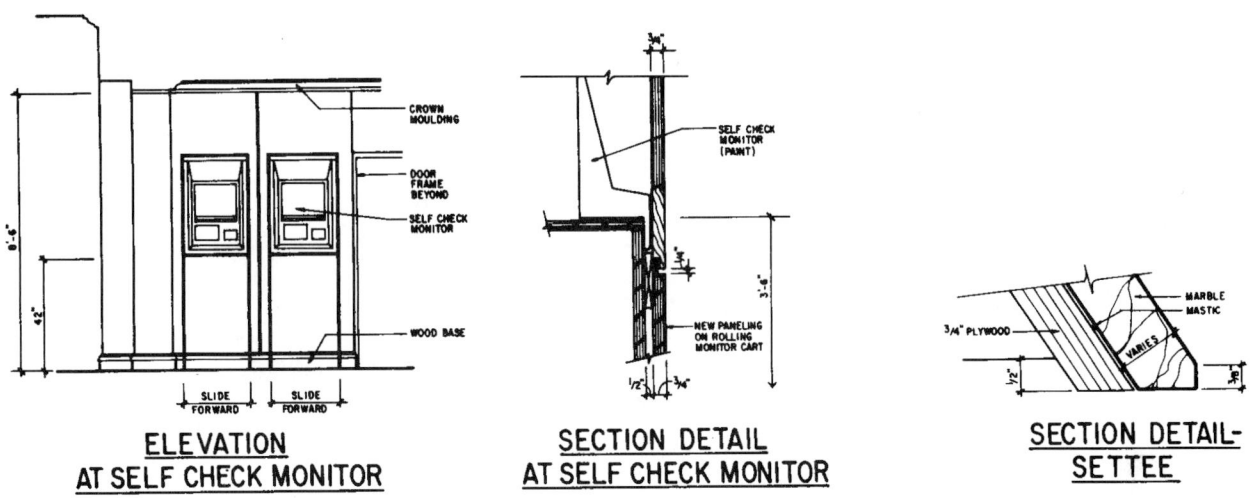

ELEVATION AT SELF CHECK MONITOR

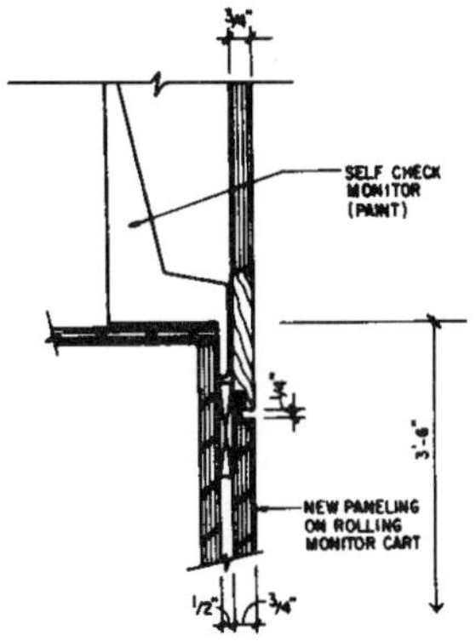

SECTION DETAIL AT SELF CHECK MONITOR

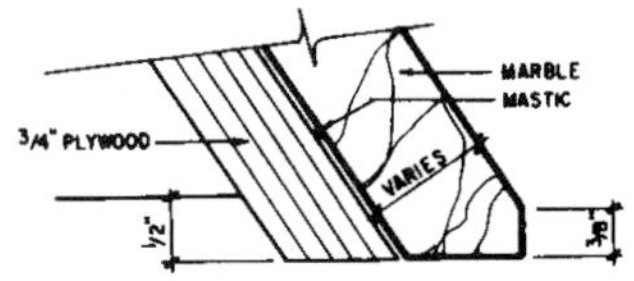

SECTION DETAIL-SETTEE

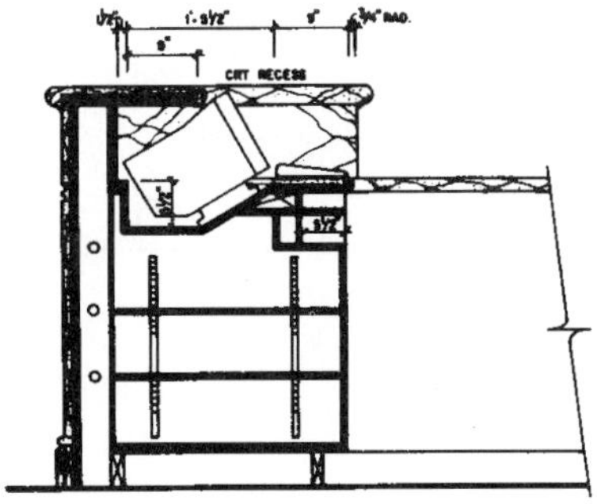

ELEVATION/SECTION-REGISTRATION COUNTER

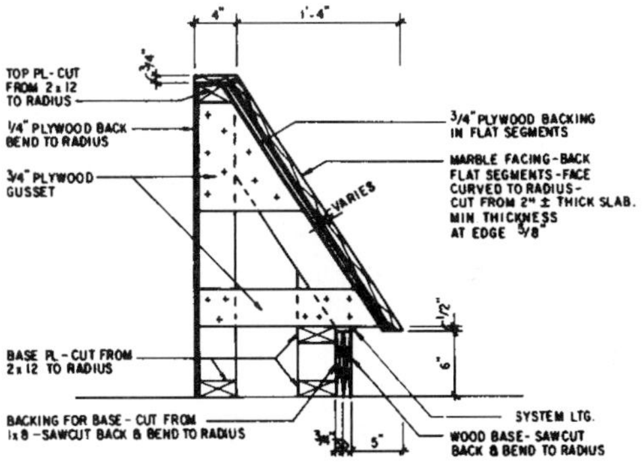

SECTION-CIRCULAR SETTEE BACK

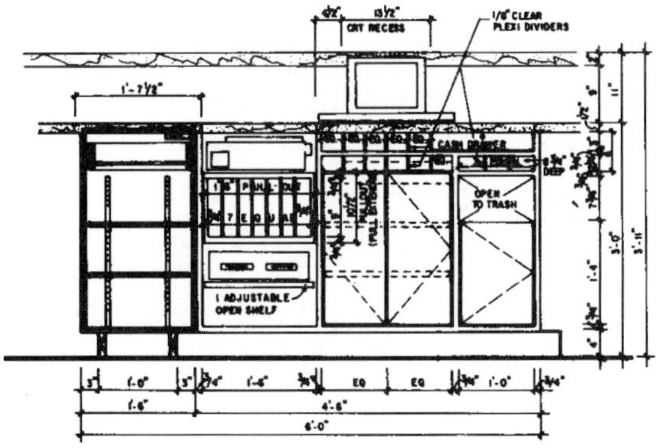

ELEVATION-REGISTRATION COUNTER

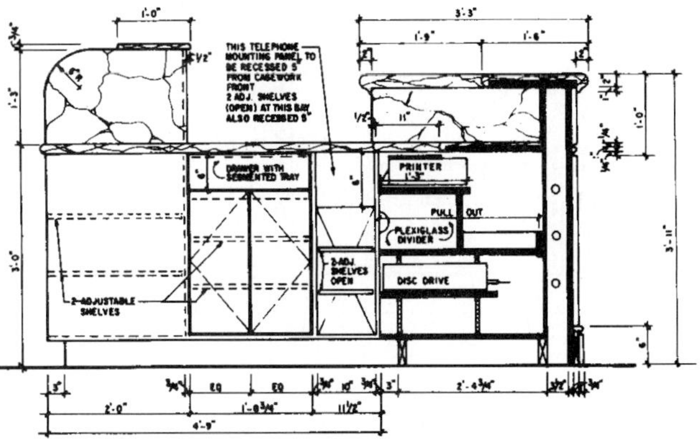

ELEVATION/SECTION-REGISTRATION COUNTER

Fig. 11

HOTELS
Registration Desk

6. Equipment and custom elements that are typically incorporated within the front desk include computer monitors/CRTs with keyboards and printer, room racks, reservation racks, information racks, room status displays, mail drawers, key drawers, alpha guest listings, message-waiting display, credit card imprinters, fax and telex, guest/employee paging system, automatic wake-up system, electric receptacles, cable chases, alarm systems, and file and cash drawers.

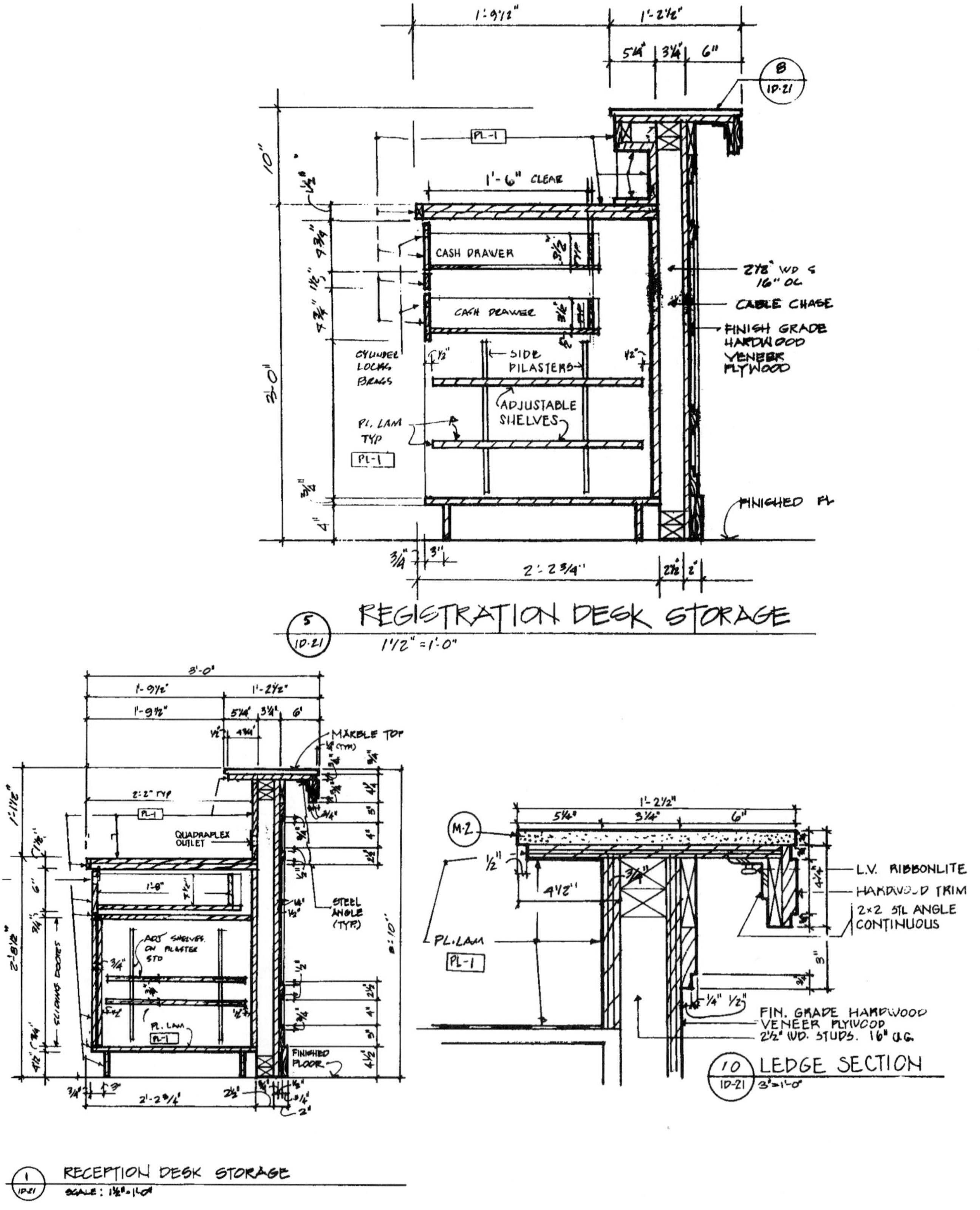

Fig. 12

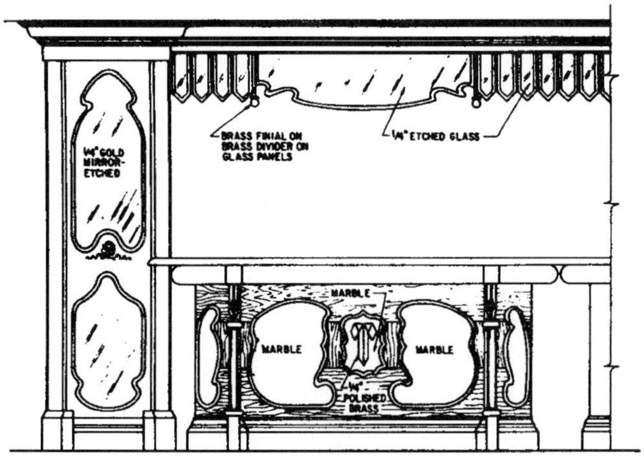

PARTIAL ELEVATION-FRONT DESK
TROPICANA HOTEL

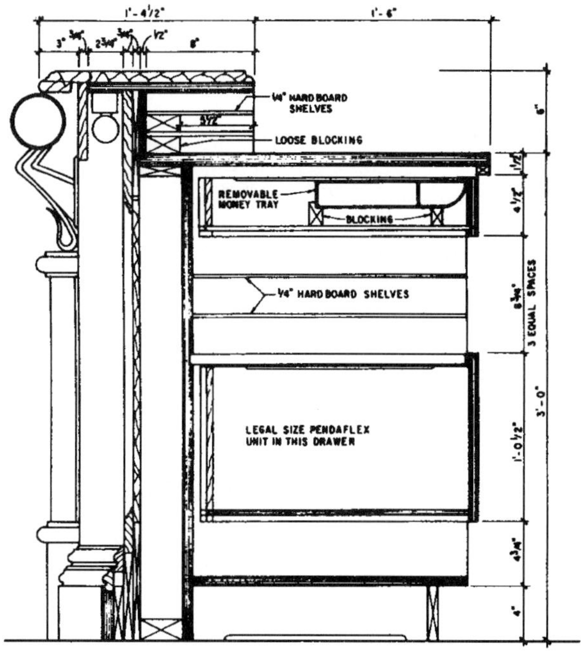

VERTICAL SECTION
REGISTRATION DESK TROPICANA HOTEL

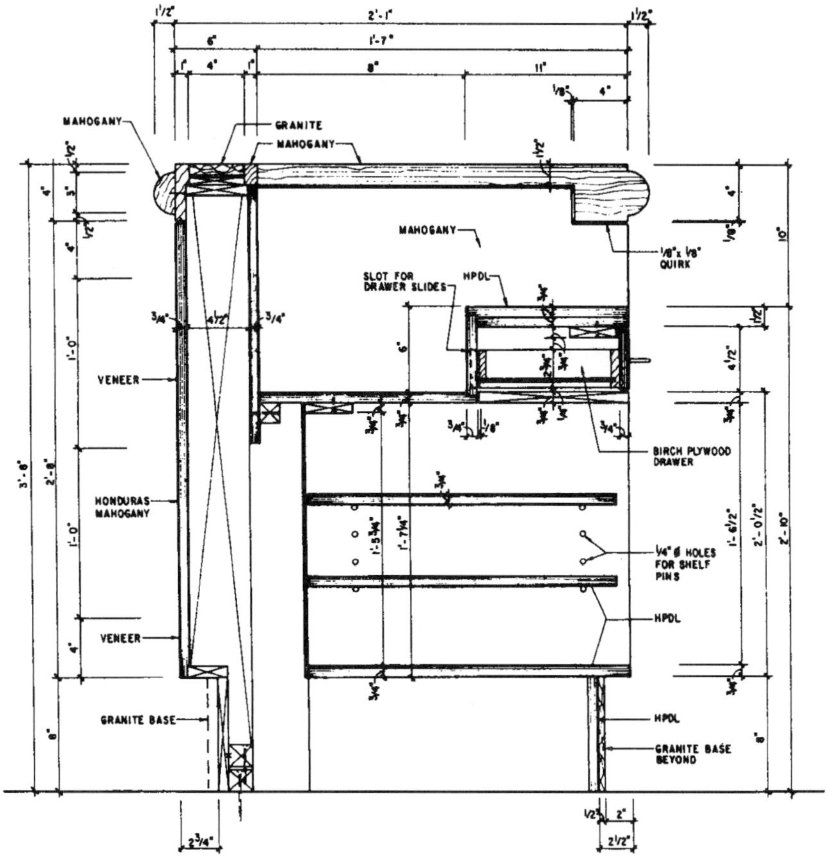

VERTICAL SECTION AT RECEPTION DESK

Fig. 13

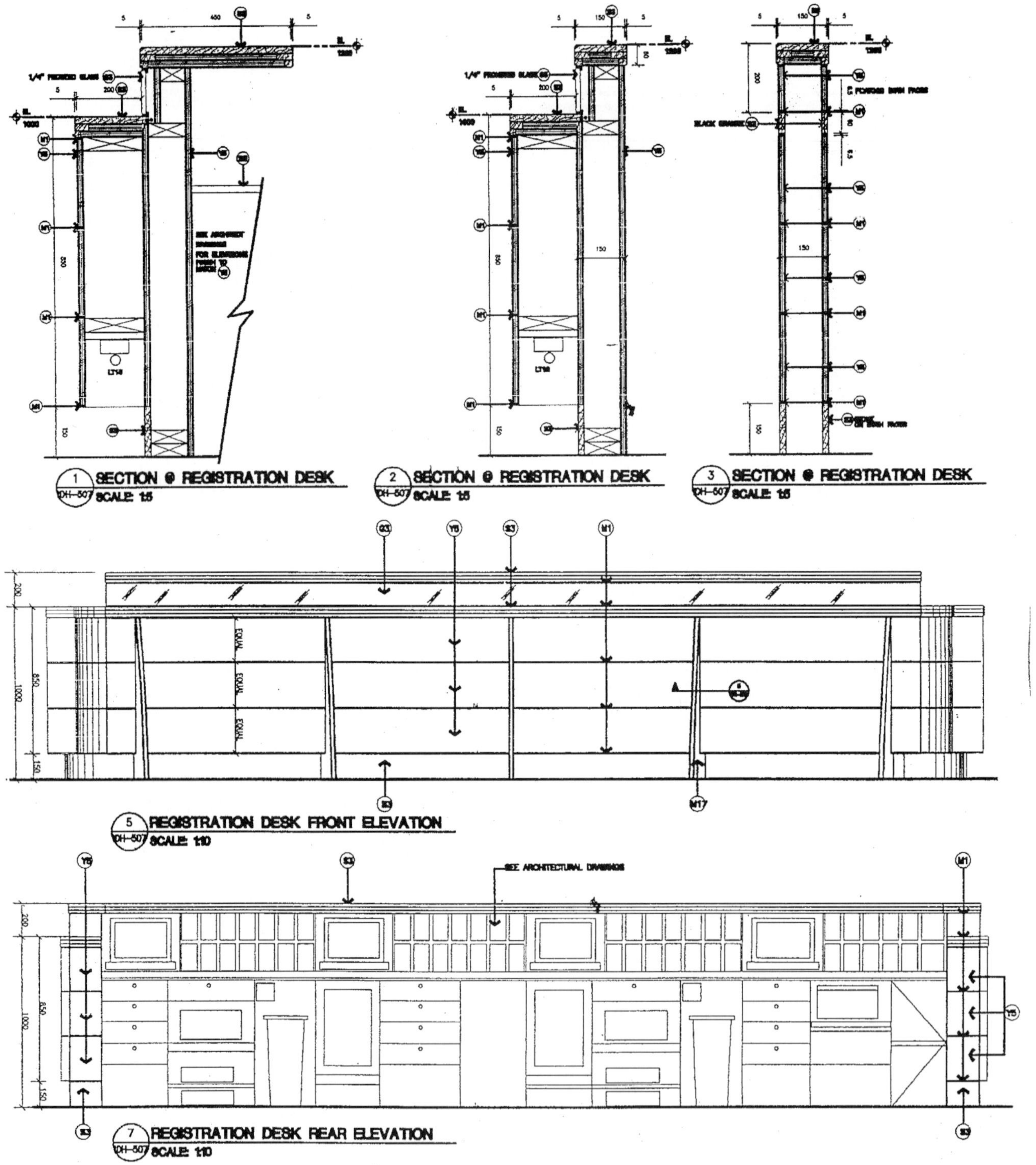

Registration Desk Details

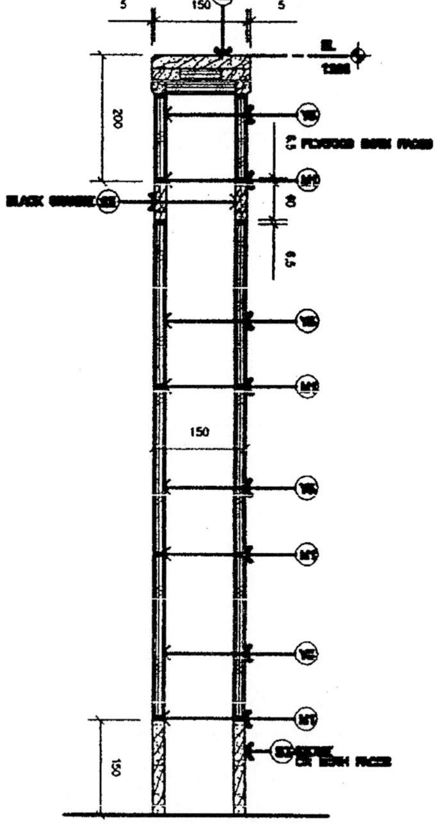

3 DH-507 **SECTION @ REGISTRATION DESK**
SCALE: 1:5

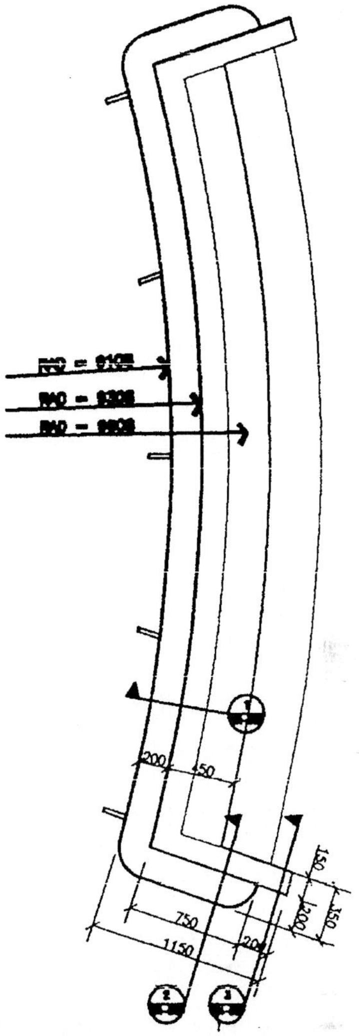

4 DH-507 **REGISTRATION DESK PLAN**
SCALE: 1:20

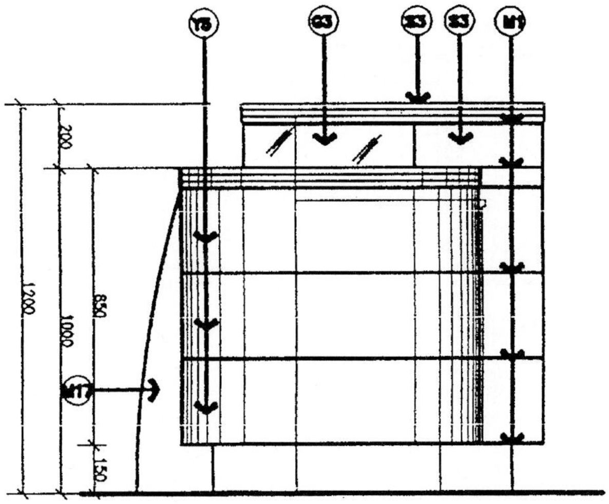

8 DH-507 **REGISTRATION DESK END ELEVATION**
SCALE: 1:10

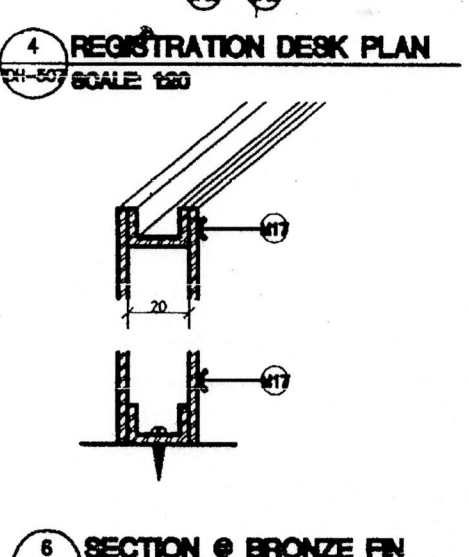

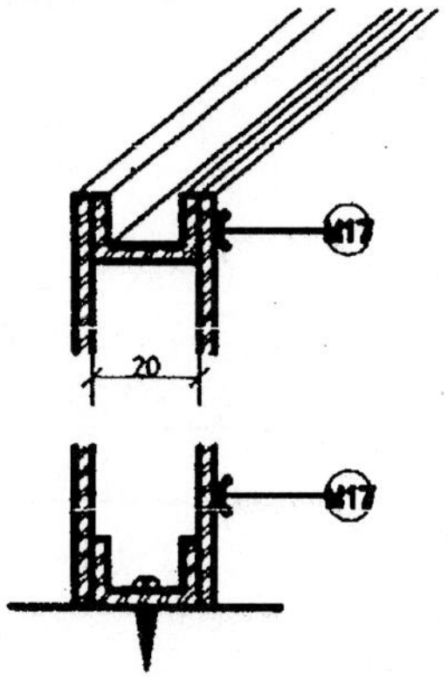

6 DH-507 **SECTION @ BRONZE FIN**
SCALE: 1:1

HOTELS

Registration Desks/Plan and Section

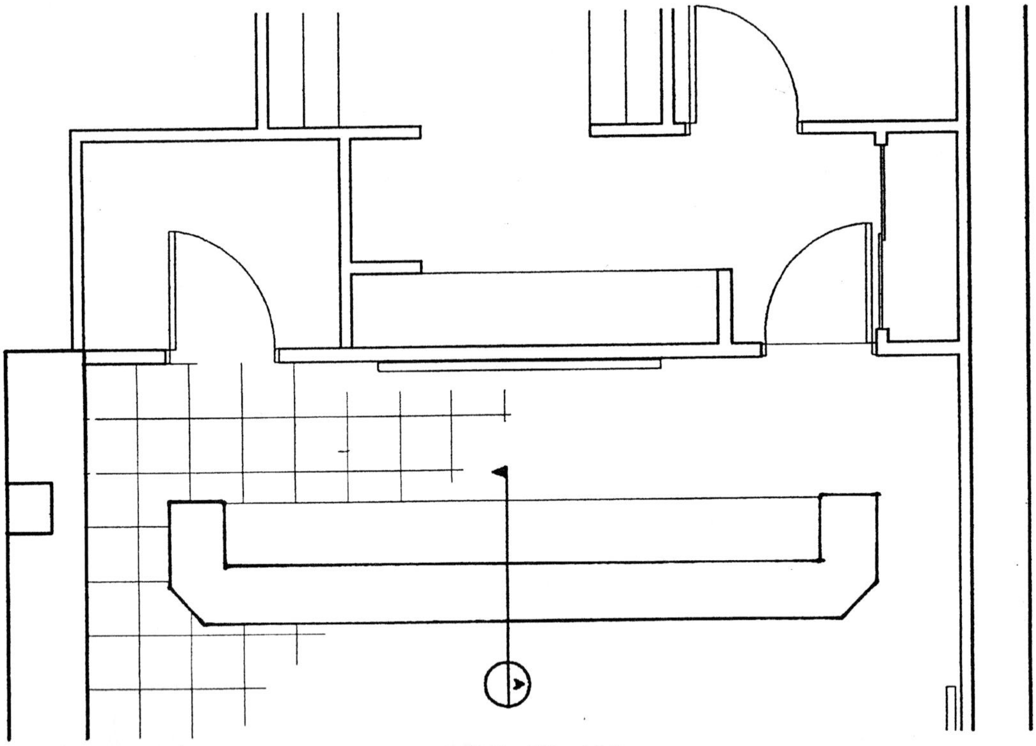

REGISTRATION DESK-FLOOR PLAN

SCALE: 1/4"= 1'-0"

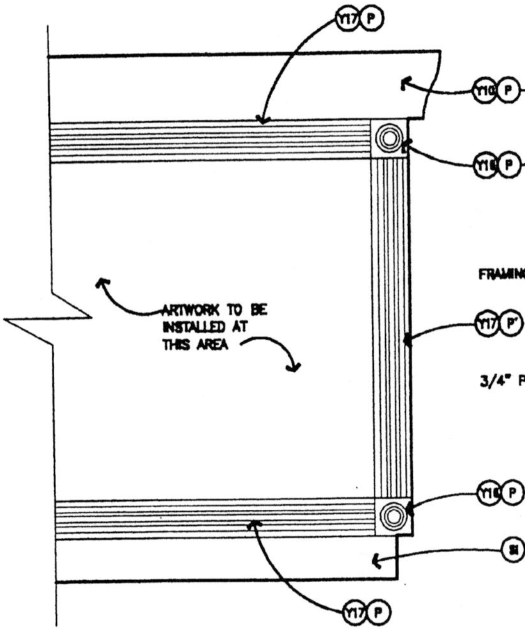

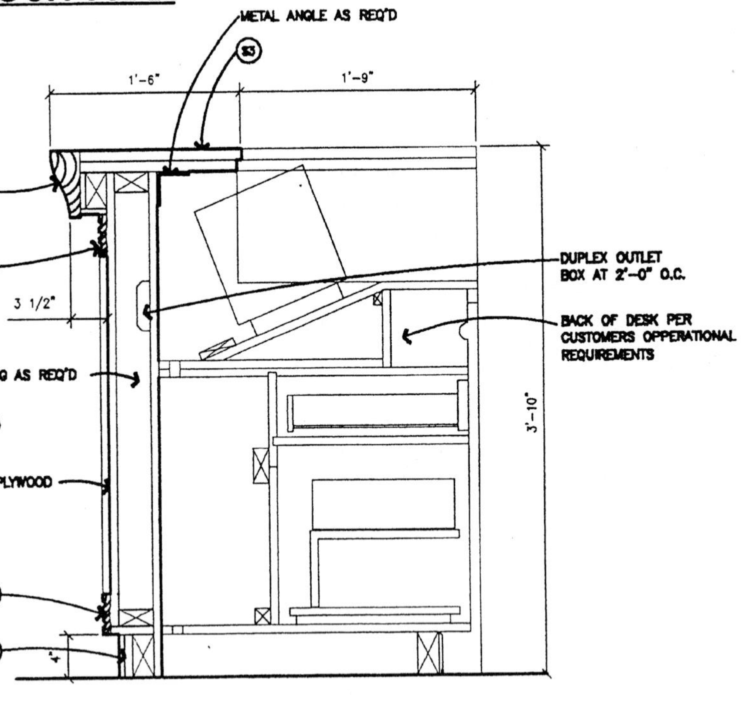

FRONT ELEVATION

SCALE: 1"= 1'-0"

(A) SECTION AT REGISTRATION DESK

SCALE: 1"= 1'-0"

6 ID-311 RECEPTION DESK-SIDE ELEVATION
1/4" =1'-0

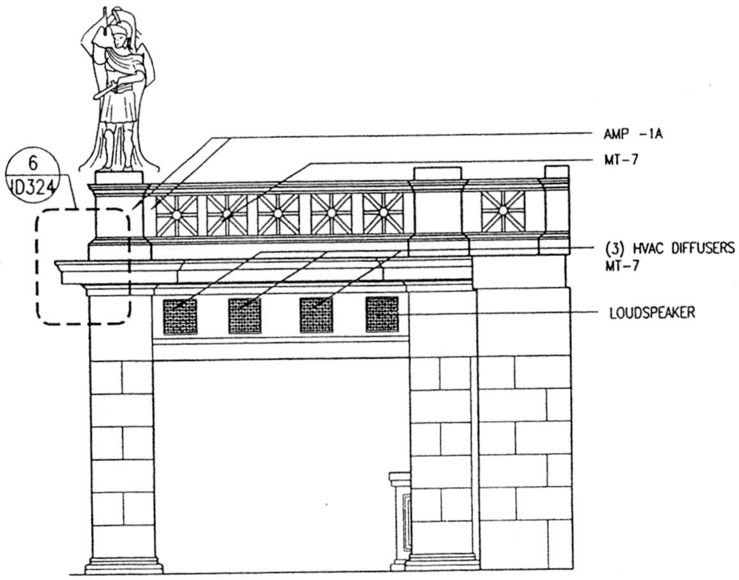

5 ID-311 RECEPTION DESK-SIDE ELEVATION
1/4" =1'-0

HOTELS

Registration Desks/Sections and Elevations

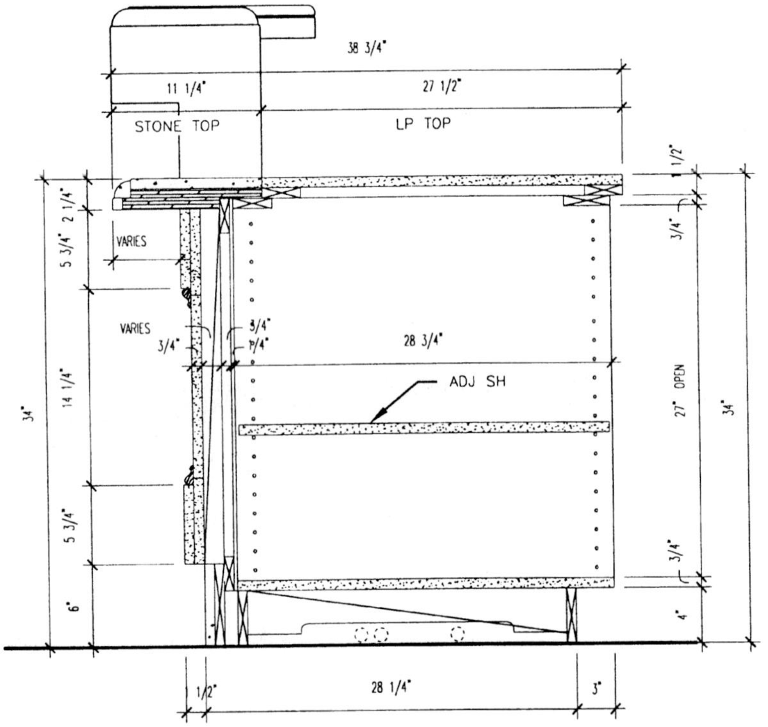

1. Section at Handicap Counter

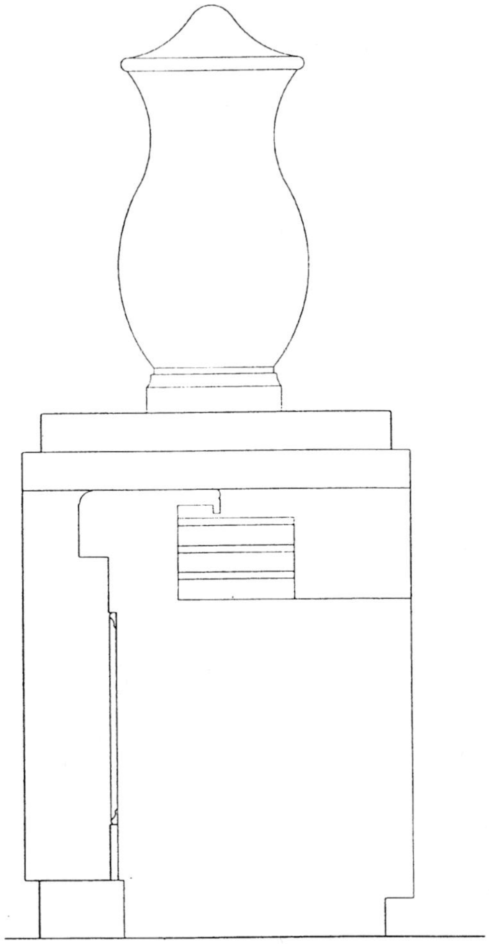

2. Section Through Front Desk

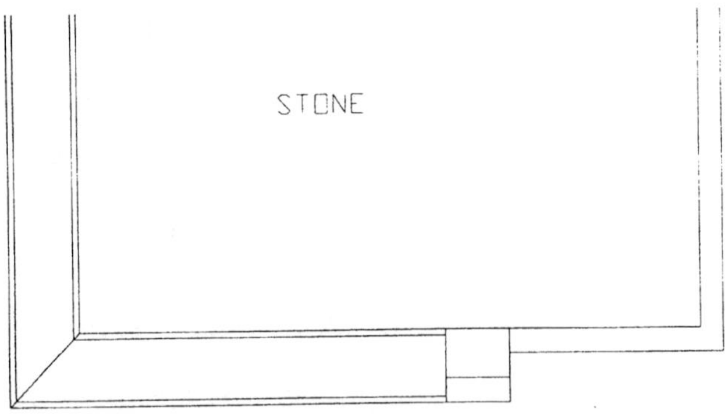

3. Plan of Stone Transaction Counter at Handicap Portion

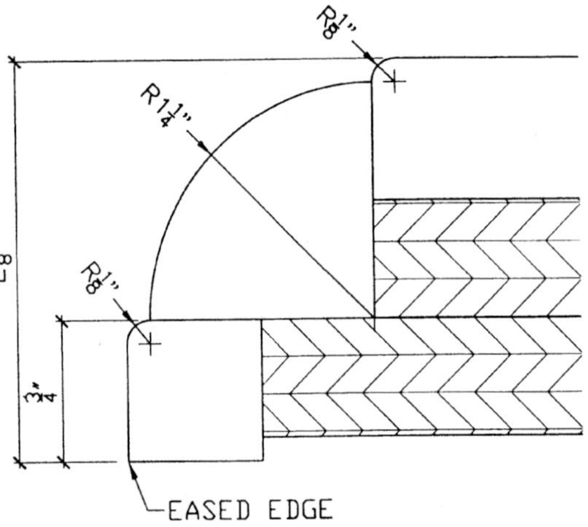

4. Detail Handicap Stone Counter

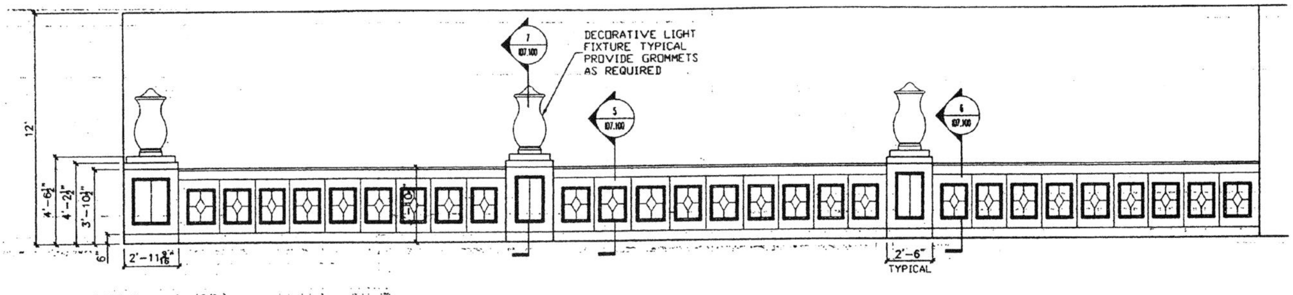

(1) FRONT DESK STRETCHED OUT ELEVATION
1/4" = 1'-0"

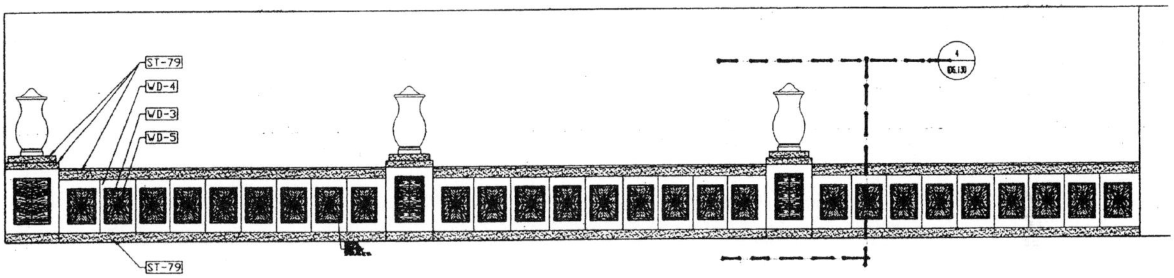

(2) FRONT DESK STRETCHED OUT FINISH ELEVATION
1/4" = 1'-0"

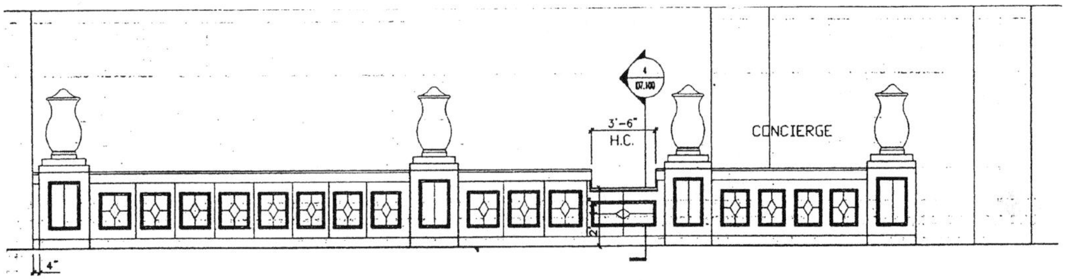

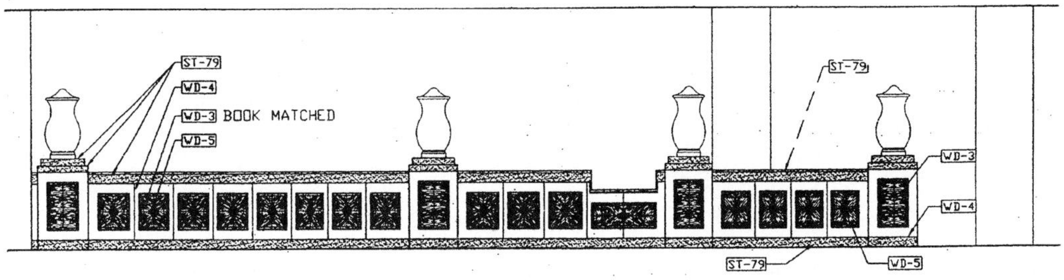

HOTELS
Registration Desks/Sections

GENERAL NOTES:

STONE TRANSACTION
COUNTER TO BE SEGMENTED

WOOD TO MATCH BBGM/I SAMPLE
SUBMIT SAMPLES FOR APPROVAL
PRIOR TO FABRICATION

BOOK MATCH TO MATCH BBGM/I SAMPLE
CONTRACTOR TO SUBMIT SAMPLES FOR
APPROVAL PRIOR TO FABRICATION. TYPICAL
FOR FRONT DESK, VIP FRONT DESK, VIP
BUFFET, BELL DESK

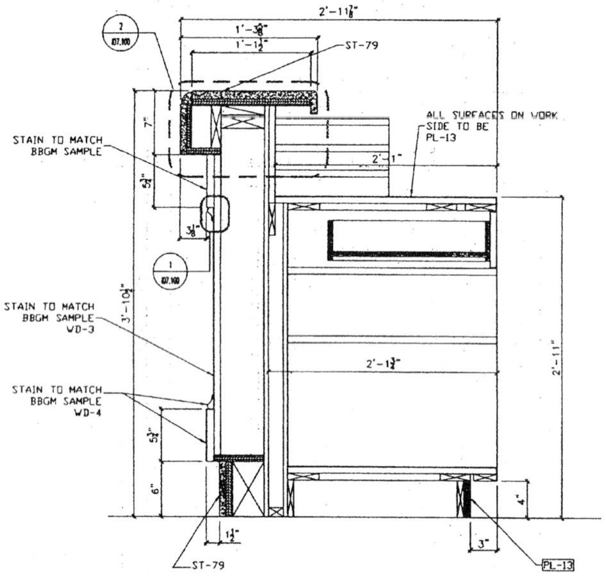

6 SECTION THROUGH FRONT DESK
1 1/2" = 1'-0"

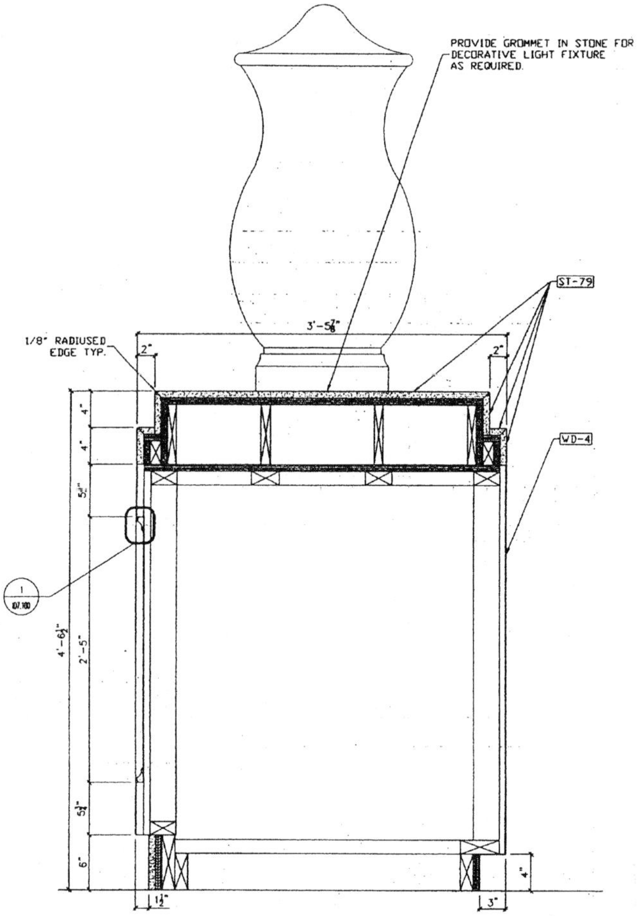

7 SECTION THROUGH LANTERN COUNTER
1 1/2" = 1'-0"

1 PANEL MOULDING DETAIL
FULL SCALE

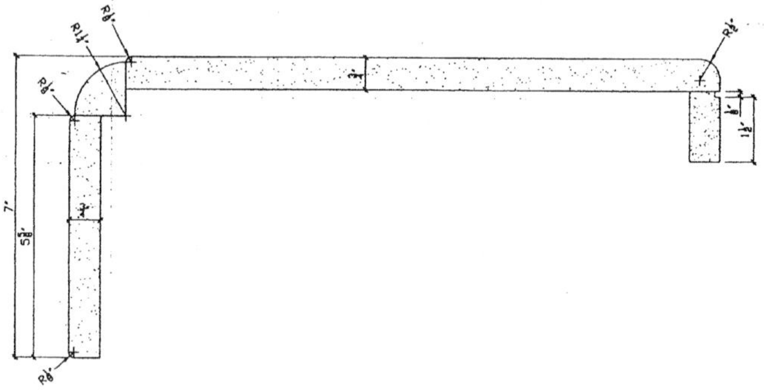

2 DETAIL STONE TRANSACTION COUNTER
6" = 1'-0"

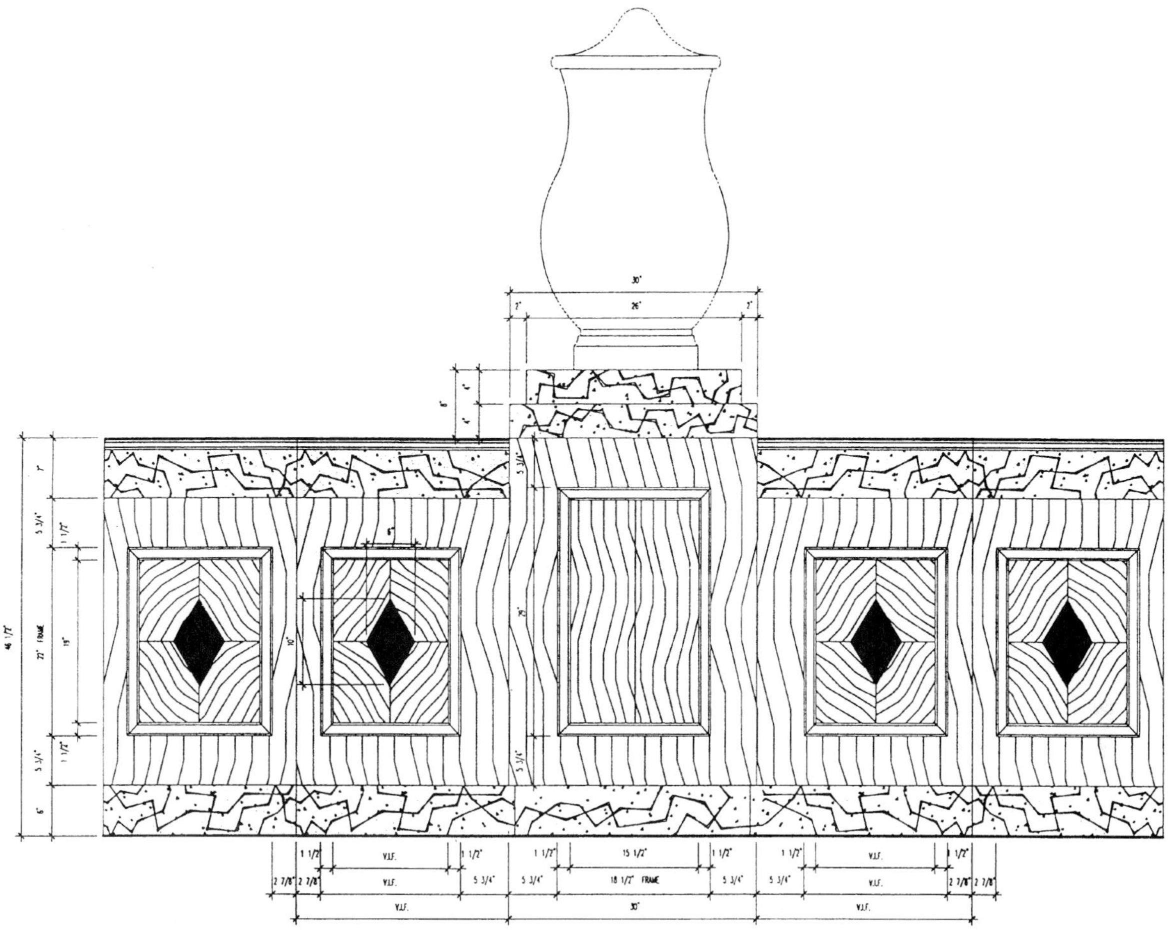

1. Enlarged Elevation of Customer Side of Front Registration Desk

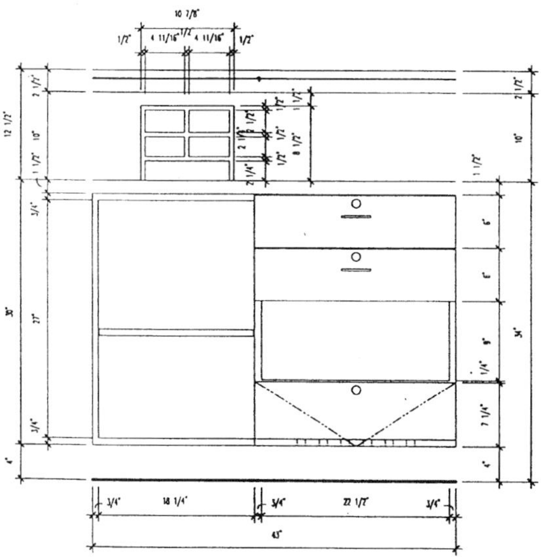

2. Enlarged Elevation of Work Side Middle at Front Desk

HOTELS

Registration Desks/Elevations

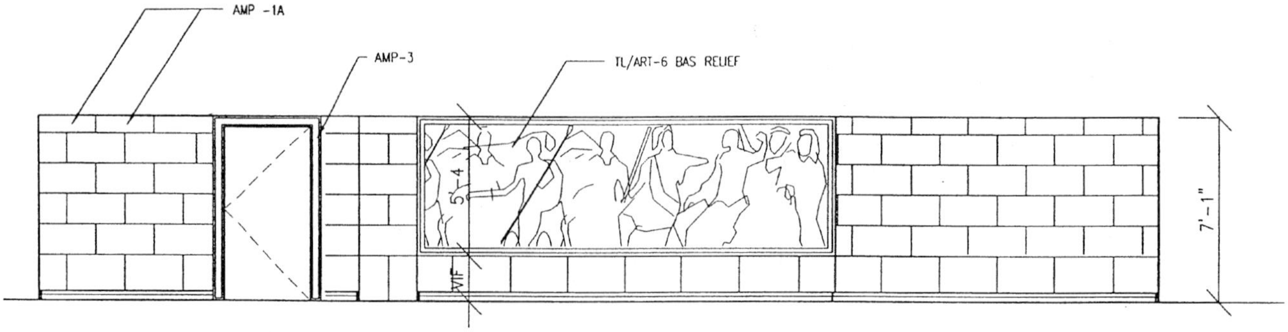

1 ID311.1 **INFORMATION DESK-BACK WALL ELEVATION**
1/4" =1'-0

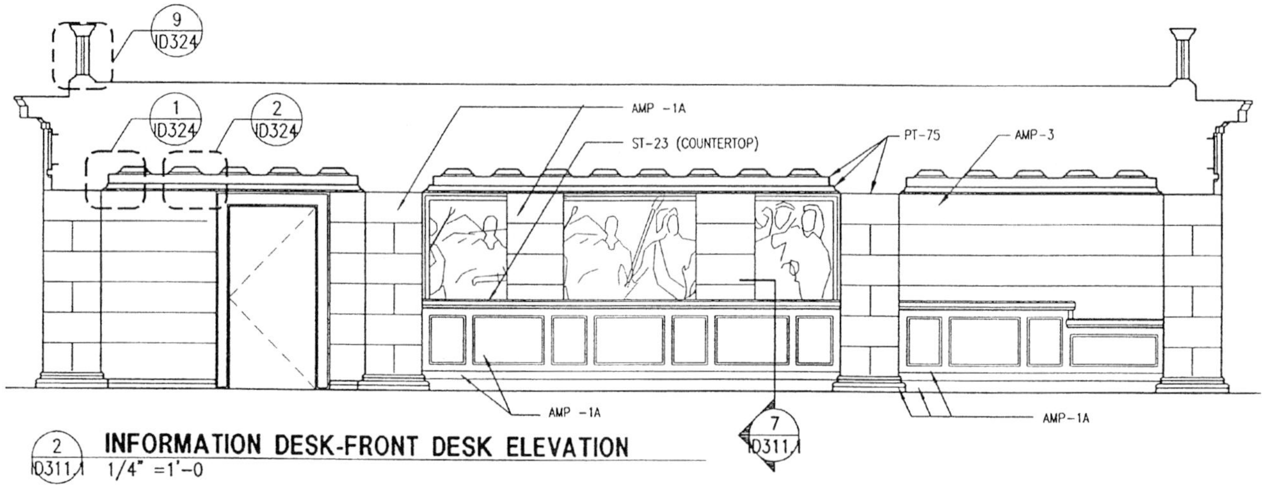

2 ID311.1 **INFORMATION DESK-FRONT DESK ELEVATION**
1/4" =1'-0

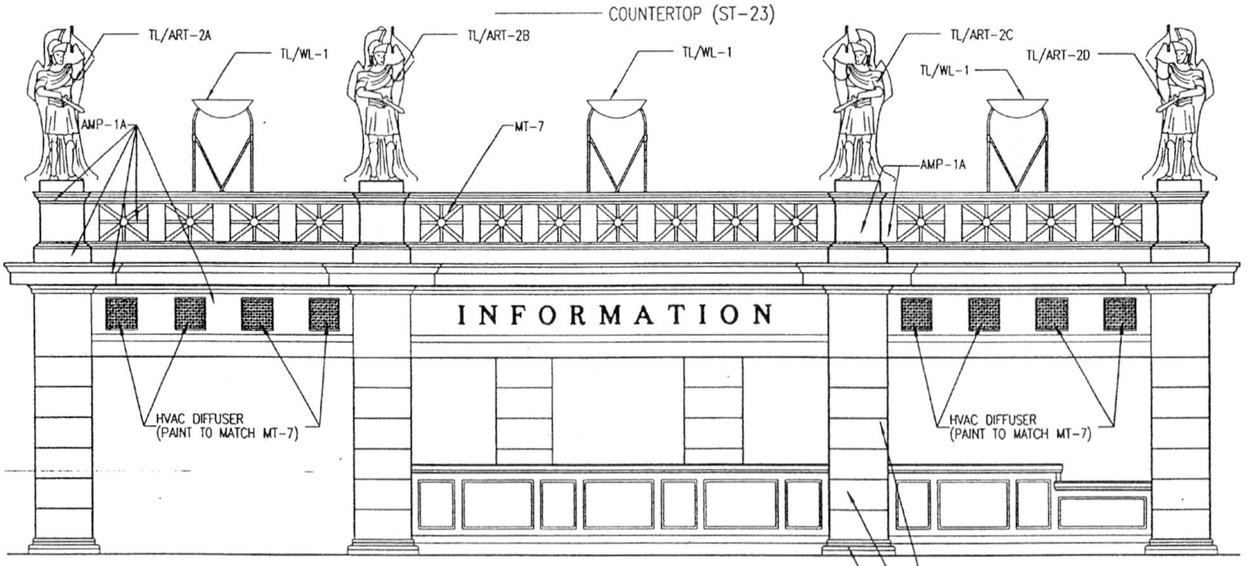

3 ID311.1 **INFORMATION DESK-CANOPY ELEVATION**
1/4" =1'-0

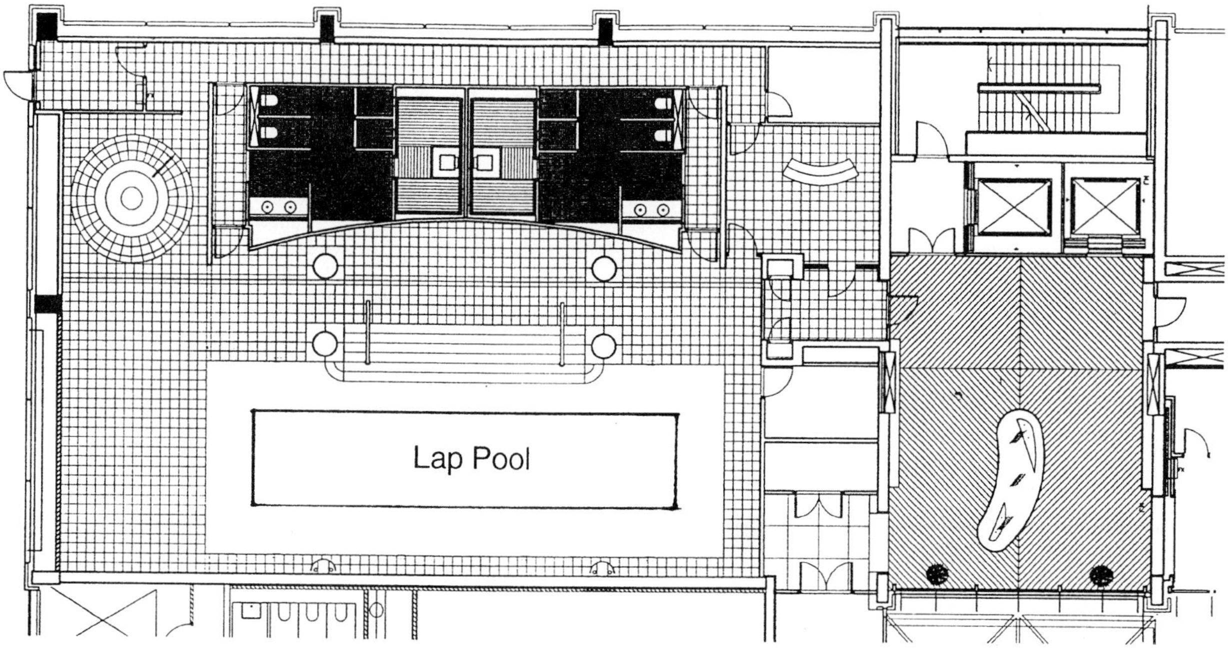

Hotel Pool And Gymnasium Area

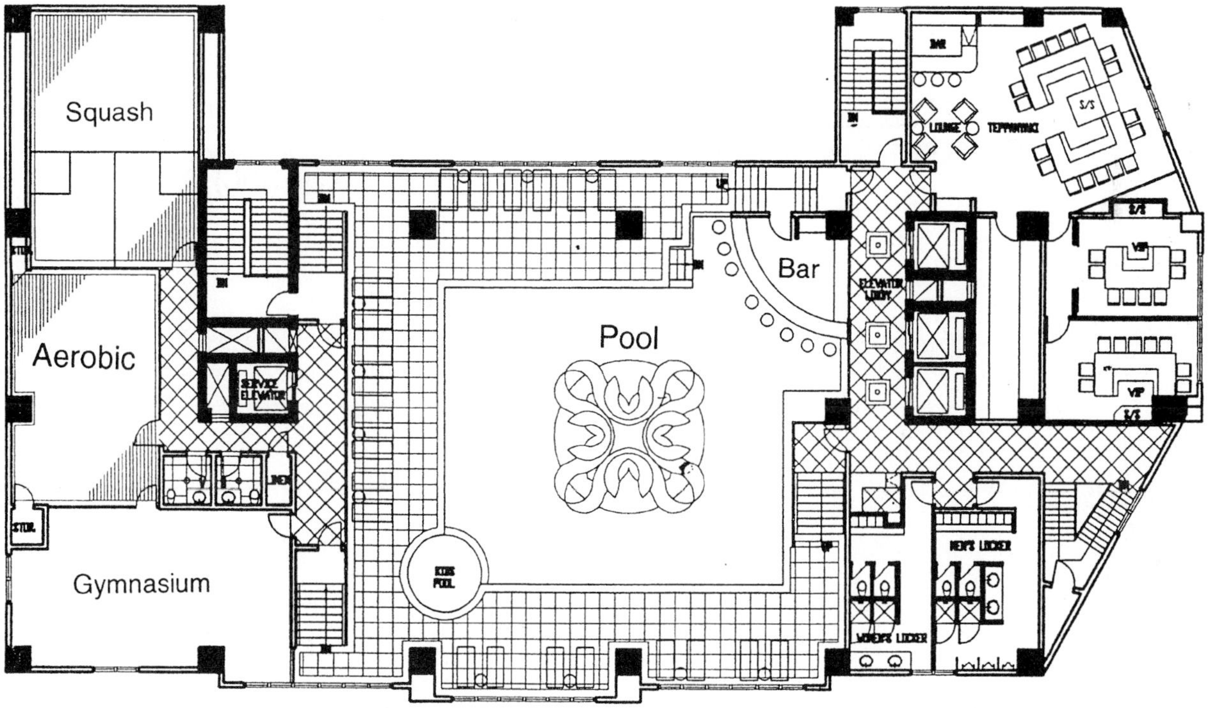

Hotel Pool And Gymnasium Area

HOTELS
Telephone Counter Details

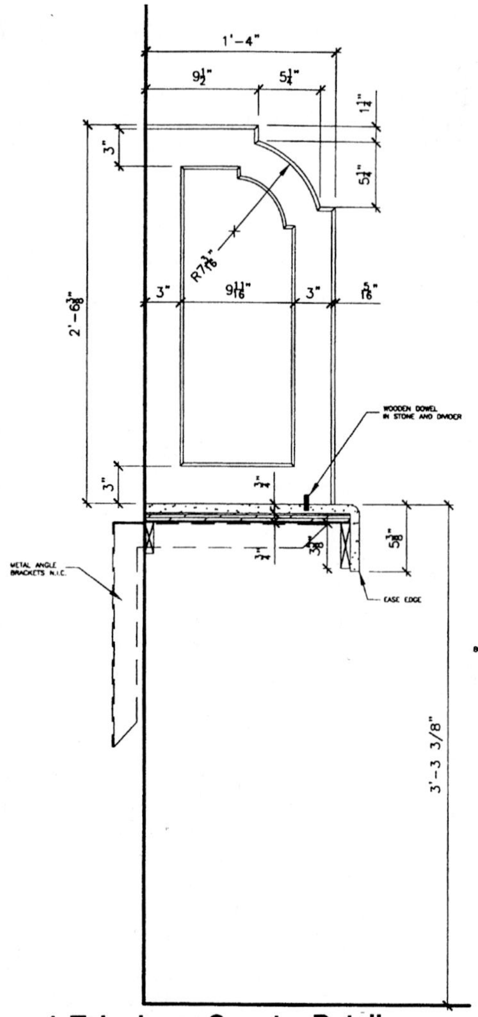

1. Telephone Counter Detail

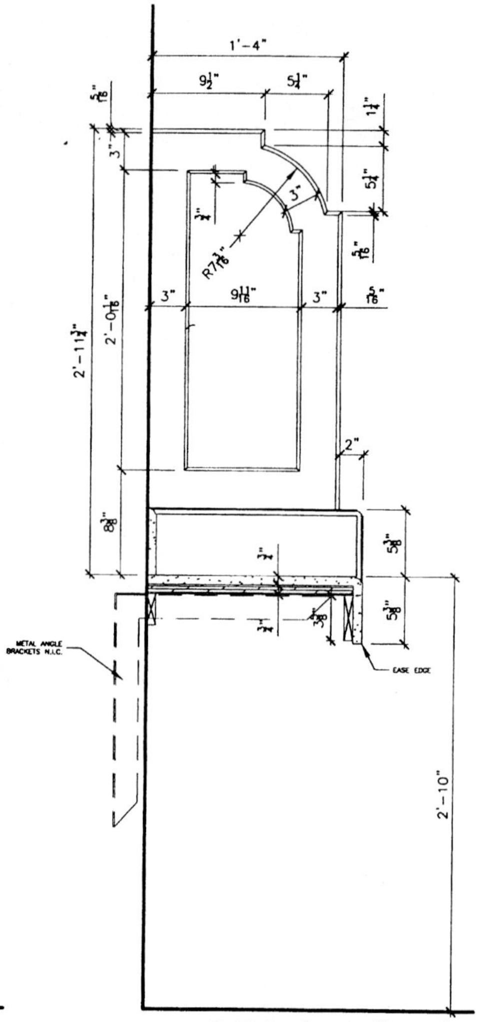

2. Telephone Counter Detail (HDC)

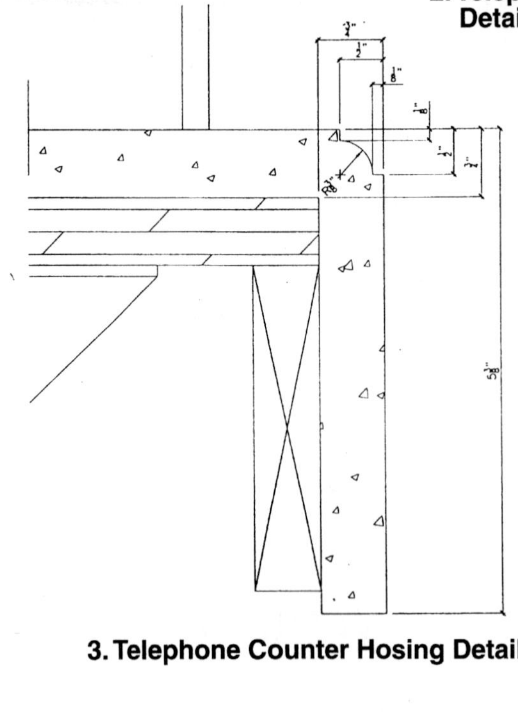

3. Telephone Counter Hosing Detail

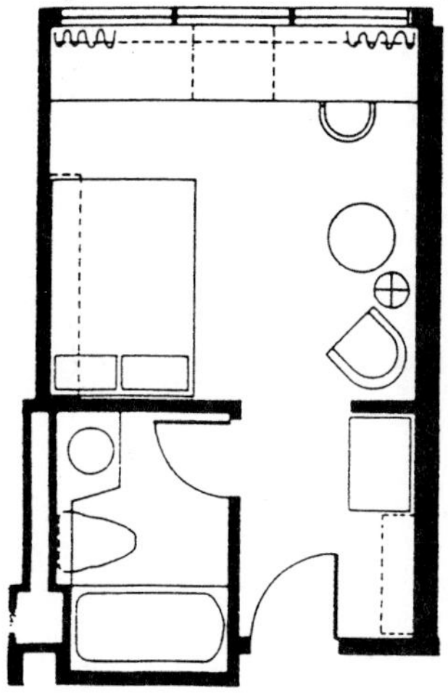

Typical Room/210 S.F.

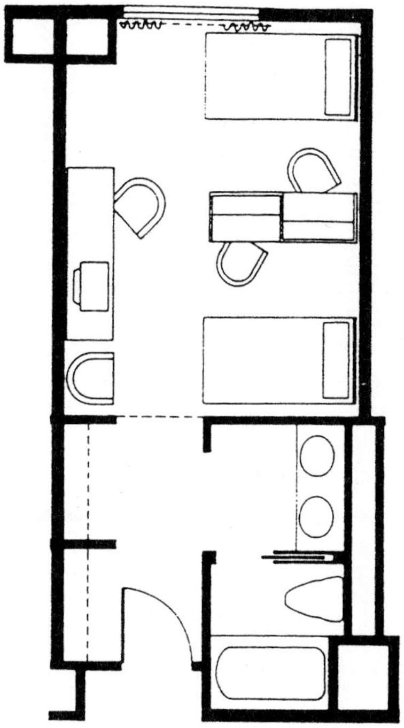

Typical Room/339 S.F.

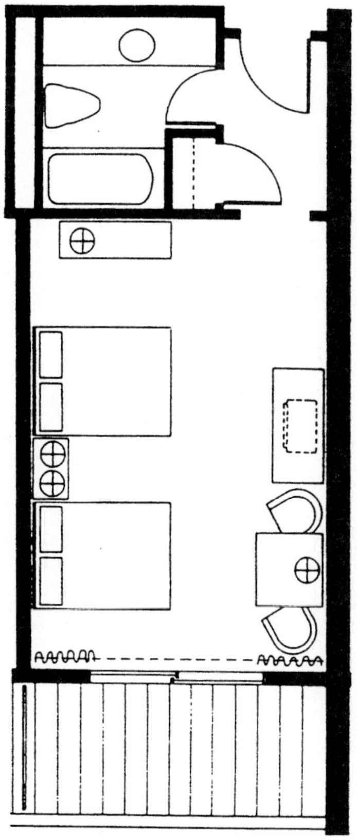

Typical Room/336 S.F.

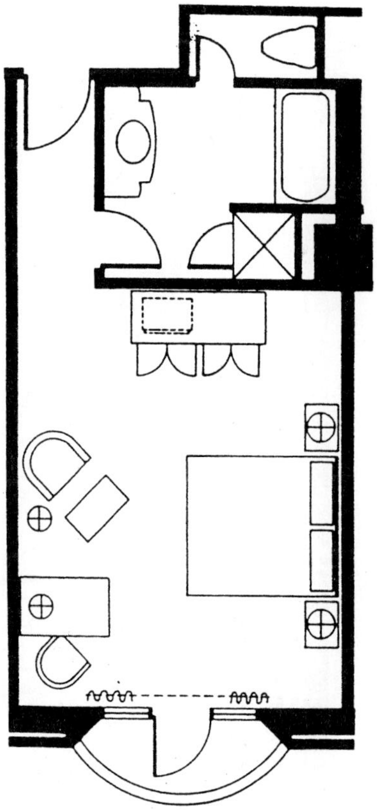

Typical Room/396 S.F.

CONFERENCE CENTERS

Guest Suites

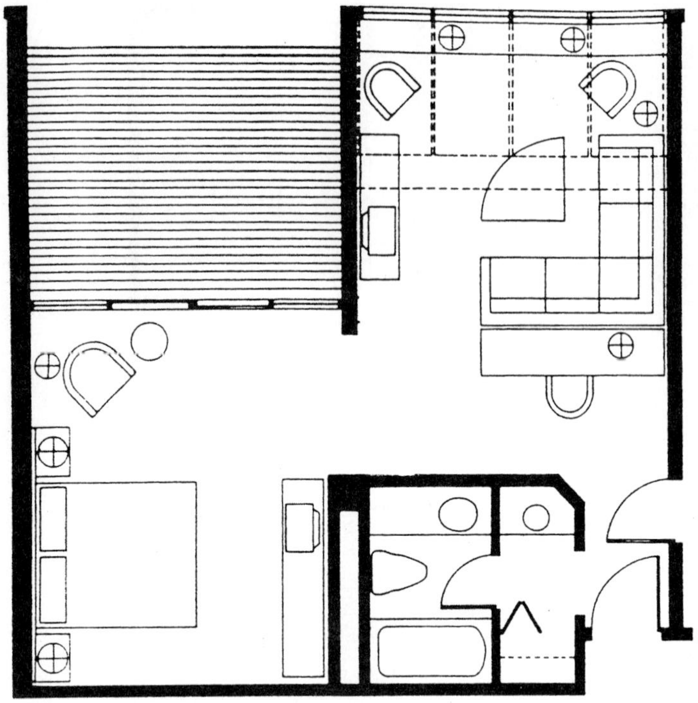

Typical Suite/550 S.F.

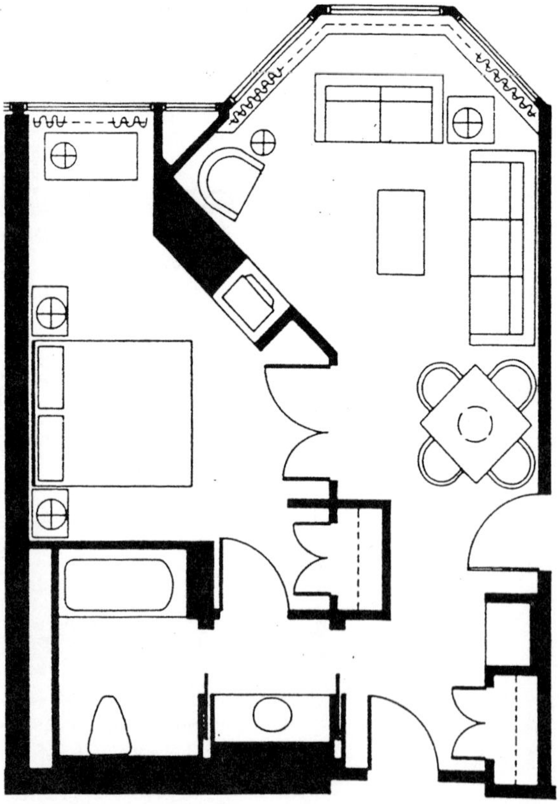

Typical Suite/510 S.F.

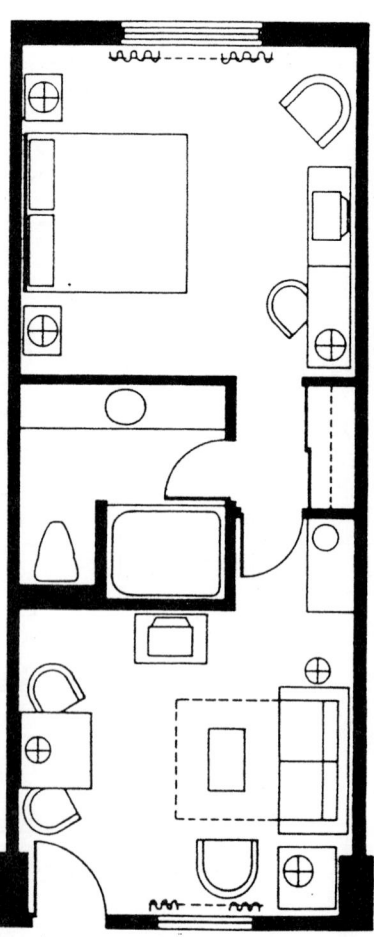

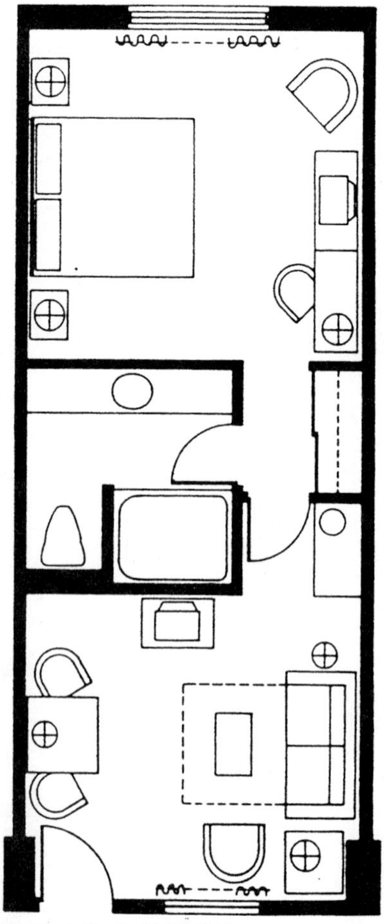

Typical Suite/518 S.F.

Conference Room Audiovisual and Electrical Layout

The plan illustrates a standard conference room, including separate lighting controls at front and rear; dual floor boxes for power, data, audiovisuals, and telephone; a combination of fluorescent and incandescent downlights, including wall washers on the tackable side wall; and a rear-projection room.

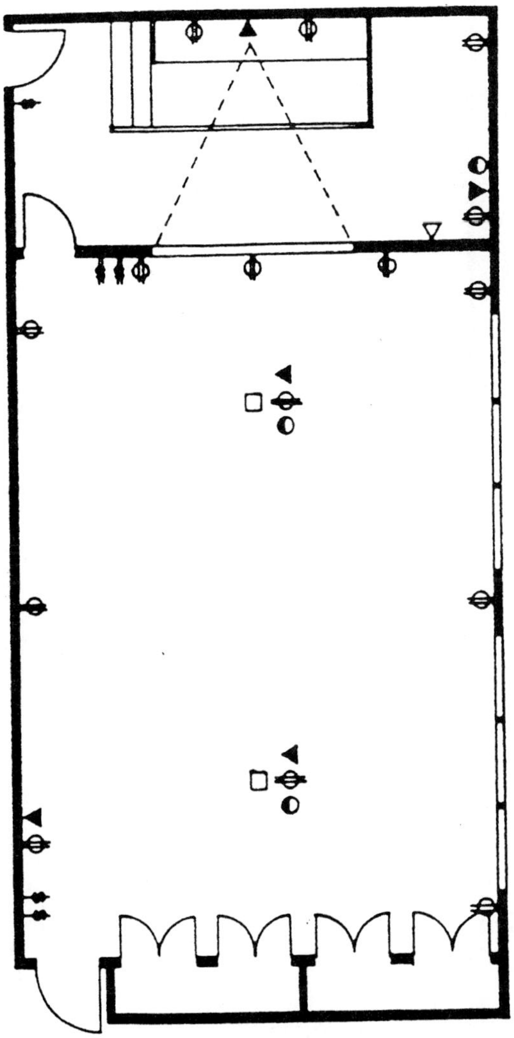

ELECTRICAL PLAN

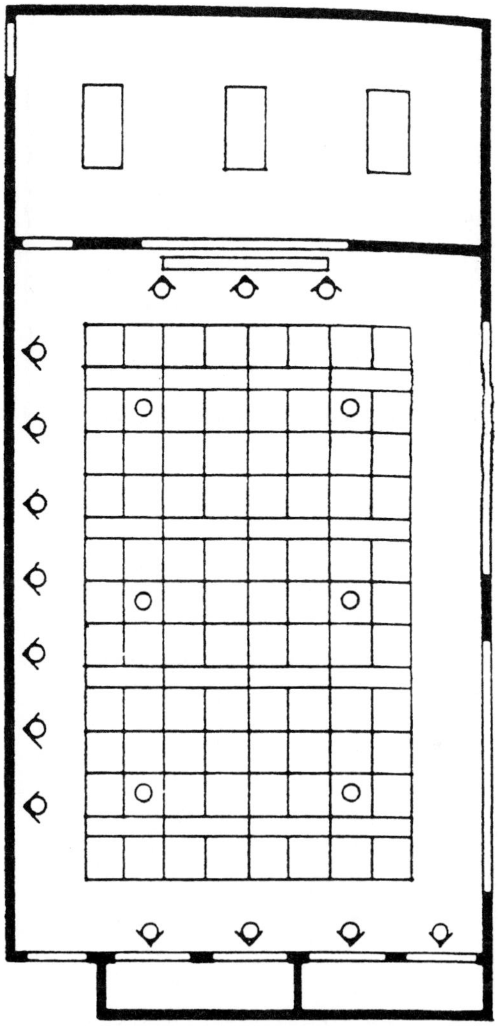

REFLECTED CEILING PLAN

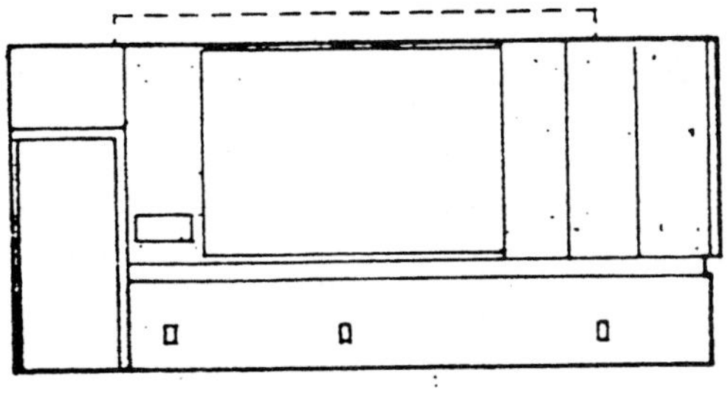

FRONT ELEVATION

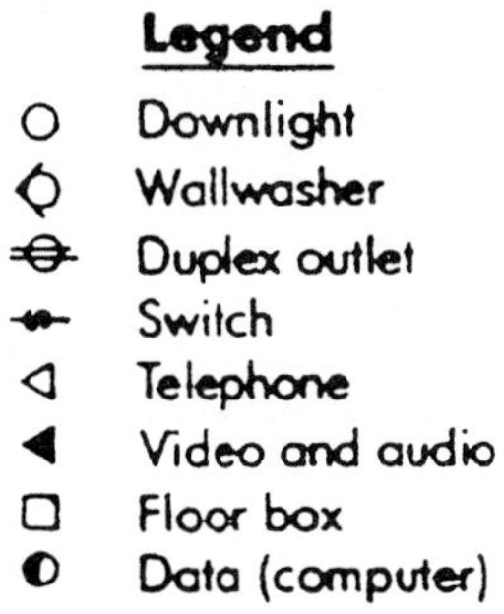

CONFERENCE CENTERS
Conference Room Layouts

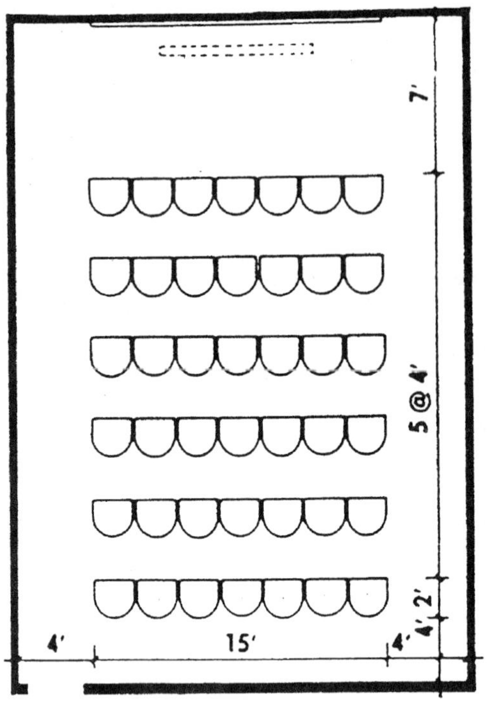

760 S.F./42 Persons

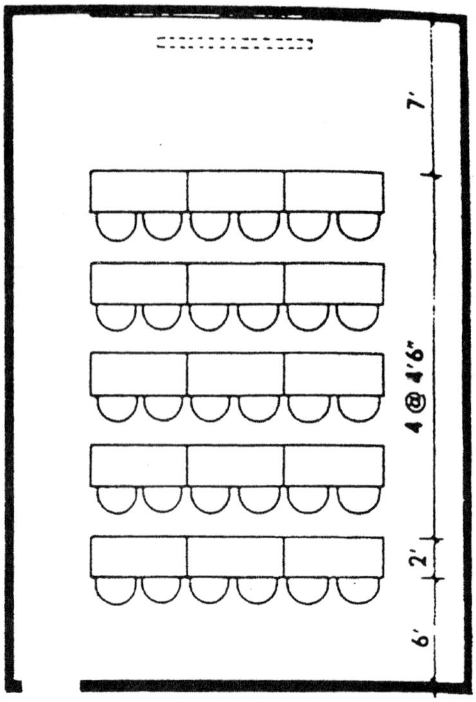

760 S.F./30 Persons

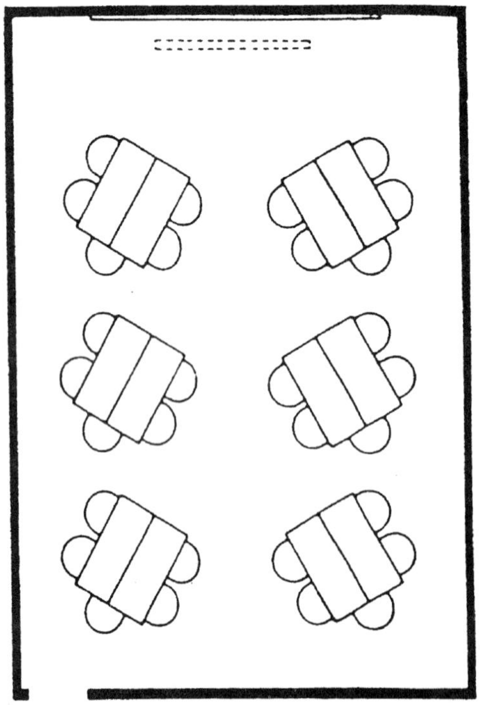

760 S.F./30 Persons

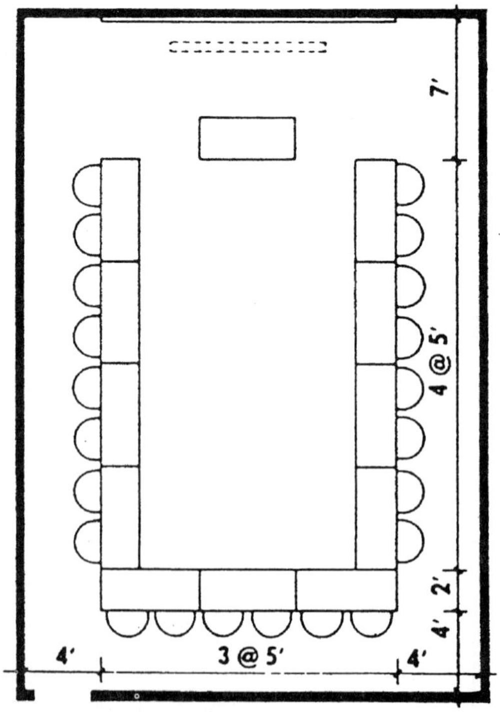

760 S.F./22 Persons

Special-purpose rooms offer less flexibility but may be essential for particular instructional objectives. Many centers provide amphitheaters—either gently curved or horseshoe-shaped—to enhance participation among the attendees.

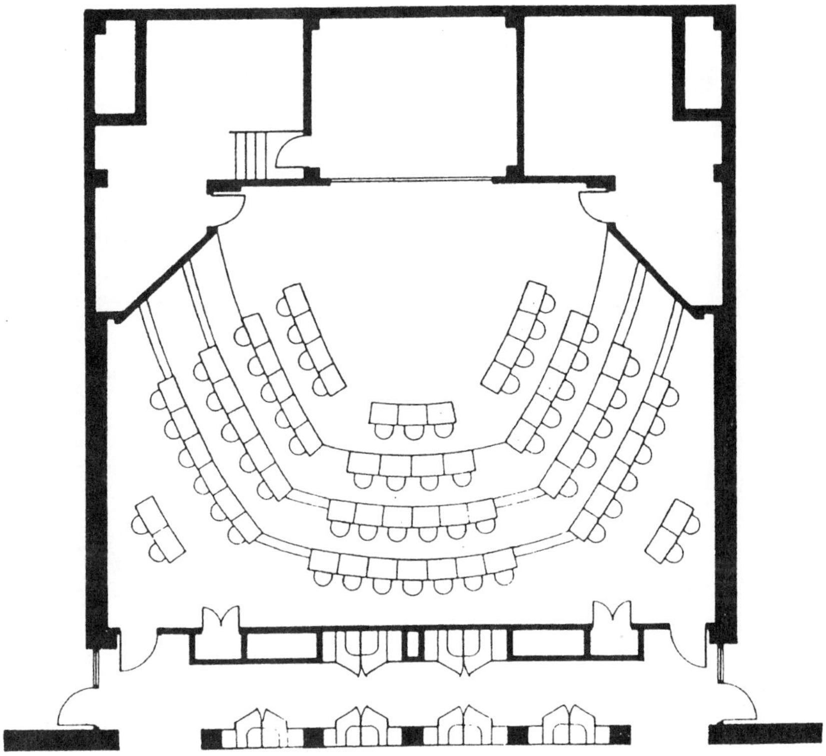

2450 S.F./64 Persons

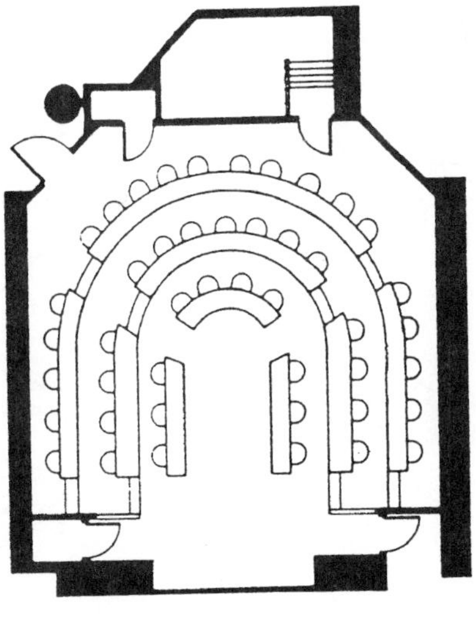

1080 S.F./45 Persons

CONFERENCE CENTERS
Lecture Hall

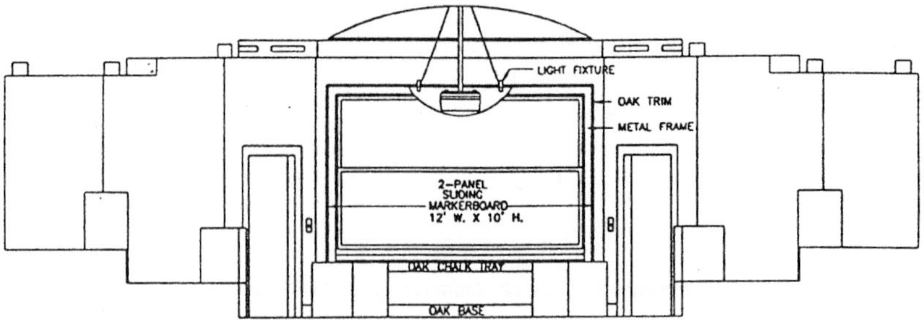

Front Elevation of Lecture Hall

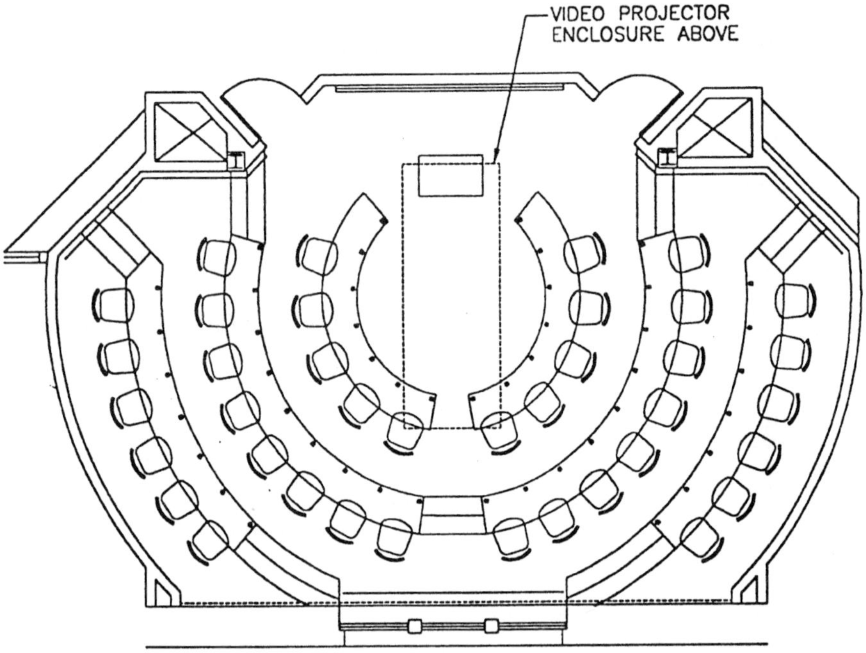

Plan of Lecture Hall

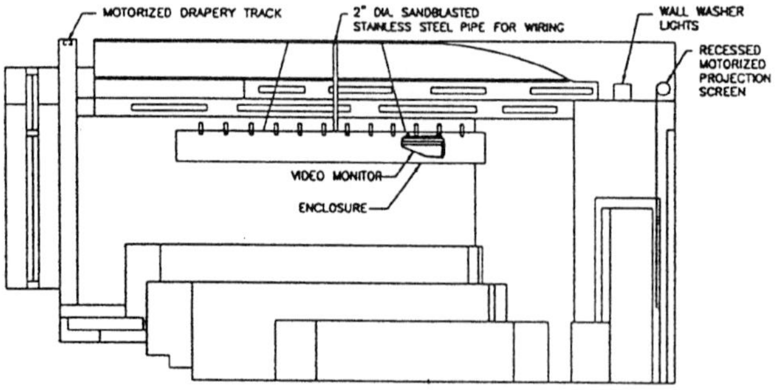

Section Through Lecture Hall

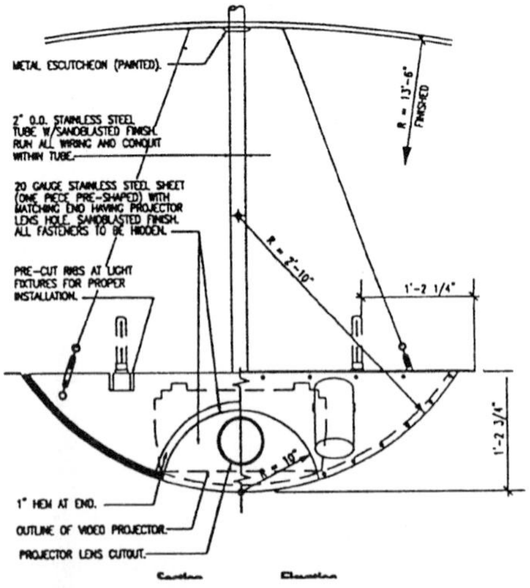

Detail of Video Projector Enclosure

RETAIL SPACES

The essential function of retail spaces is to display and sell merchandise. The design of these spaces involves the manipulation and coordination of architectural, interior design, and merchandising elements as necessary to meet the programmatic needs of the client. It is critical that the space in which the customer and store personnel function is of the highest quality. Ensuring this quality requires a knowledge of the planning and design of the various interior components that constitute the building blocks of retail spaces.

Figure 1 shows the clearances involved for a 42-in, or 106.7-cm, high counter to service a seated user. By filling the recess with an additional display, however, the counter can also be used exclusively as a typical sales counter. It should be noted, however, that, although sometimes used for special display situations, such a counter height is not recommended. Both the customer and the sales clerk of smaller body size would find coping with such a height uncomfortable anthropometrically, particularly when one considers that the counter would be higher than the elbow height of slightly more than 5 percent of the population. From a merchandising viewpoint, where customer convenience is of paramount importance, it would be unwise to exceed 39 to 40 in, or 99 to 101.6 cm, as a counter height. In addition, the smaller sales clerk forced to tend such a counter for extended periods of time could be subjected to severe backaches and pains. Getting on and off a high stool for elderly and disabled people or those of smaller body size can be not only difficult, but hazardous. Figure 2 illustrates the clearances for a typical sales counter.

	in	cm
A	26–30	66.0–76.2
B	18–24	45.7–61.0
C	42	106.7
D	28	71.1
E	84–112	213.4–284.5
F	18	45.7
G	18–24	45.7–61.0
H	30–48	76.2–121.9
I	18–22	45.7–55.9
J	35–38	88.9–96.5
K	72	182.9

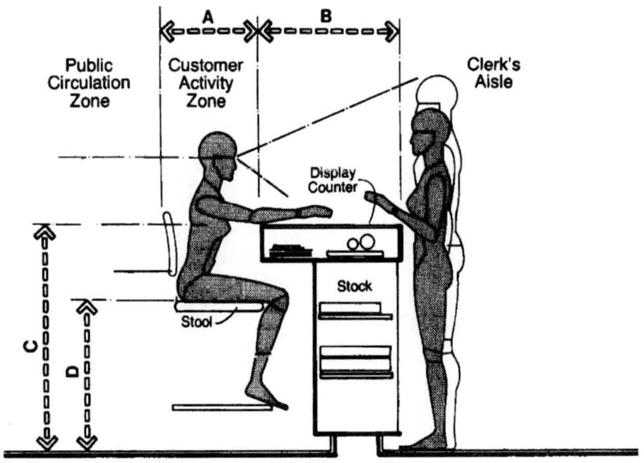

Fig. 1 Seated customer/high counter height

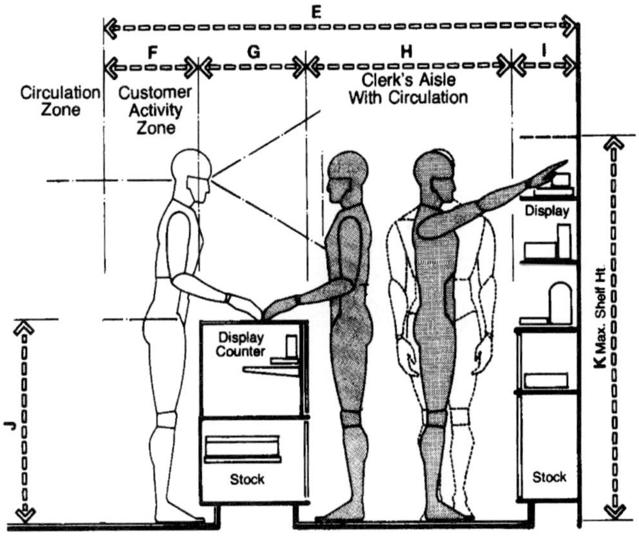

Fig. 2 Typical sales area/standing customer

SHOPS
Planning Data

Figure 3 shows the clearances required for a medium-height display counter. The suggested seat height of 21 to 22 in, or 53.3 to 55.8 cm, requires a footrest for the seated customer. The counter height shown will allow the display to be viewed by both the seated customer and the standing sales clerk. The customer activity zone allows adequate space for the chair. Knee height, buttock-knee length, popliteal height, and eye height sitting are all significant human dimensions to consider in the design of counters to be used by a seated customer.

Figure 4 shows a low 30-in, or 76.2-cm, display counter also for use by a seated customer. The anthropometric considerations are the same. Although the counter height is responsive to the anthropometric requirements of the seated customer, it is less than ideal for the standing clerk. For the standing user's optimum comfort, the counter height should be about 2 or 3 in, or 5 to 7.6 cm, below elbow height. This will allow a person to handle objects comfortably on the counter surface or use the counter as support for his or her arms. The 30-in height is too low to permit such use.

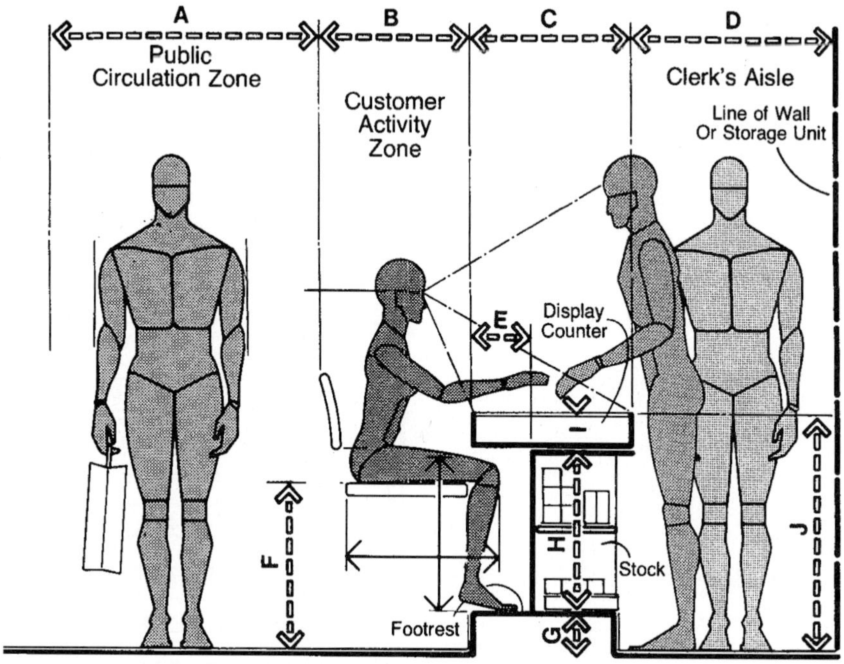

Fig. 3 Seated customer/desirable counter height

	in	cm
A	36	91.4
B	26–30	66.0–76.2
C	18–24	45.7–61.0
D	30 min.	76.2 min.
E	10	25.4
F	21–22	53.3–55.9
G	5	12.7
H	23–25	58.4–63.5
I	4–6	10.2–15.2
J	34–36	86.4–91.4
K	30	76.2
L	16–17	40.6–43.2

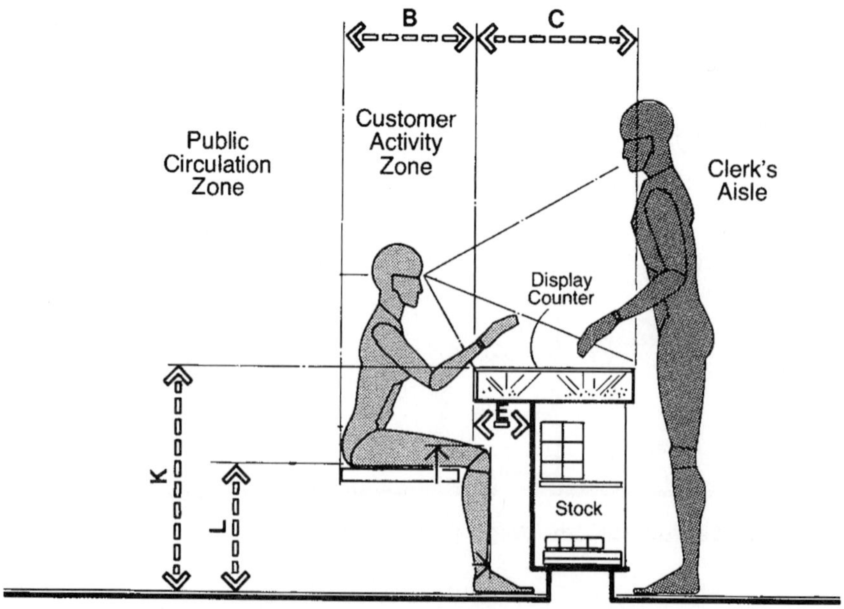

Fig. 4 Seated customer/low counter height

Shelving is probably used more than any other single interior component for the storage and/or display of merchandise. Not only must the merchandise be within reach anthropometrically, but it must be fairly visible as well. The heights established must therefore be responsive to vertical grip reach dimensions as well as to eye height. In establishing height limits, the body size data of the smaller person should be used. Since, in retail spaces, departments may cater exclusively to members of one sex or the other, two sets of data are presented. One is based on the body size of the smaller female and the other on the body size of the smaller male. The suggested heights reflect a compromise between reach requirements and visibility requirements. (See Fig. 5.)

Figure 6 illustrates the clearances involved in hanging-type merchandise cases. Rod heights should be related not only to human reach limitations, but in certain cases to the sizes of the merchandise displayed. There is usually no conflict in respect to garments.

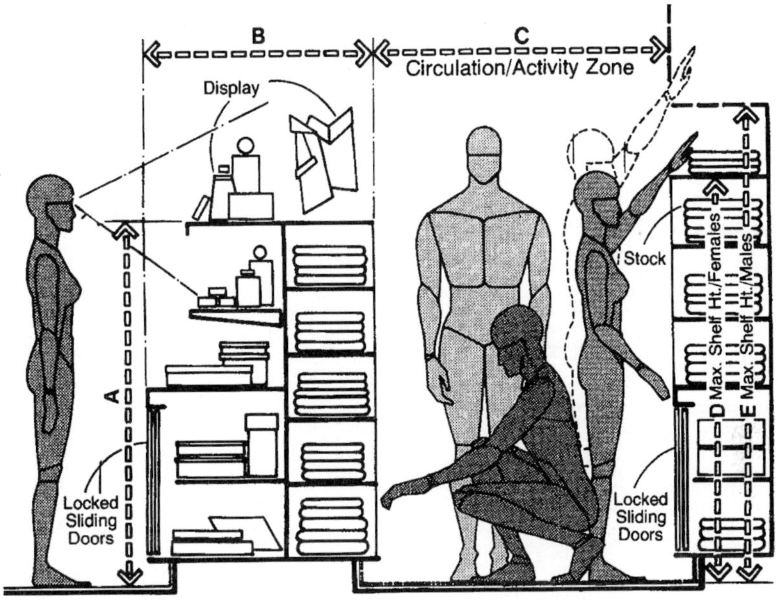

Fig. 5 Typical merchandise cases

	in	cm
A	48 max.	121.9 max.
B	30–36	76.2–91.4
C	51 min.	129.5 min.
D	66	167.6
E	72	182.9
F	84–96	213.4–243.8
G	20–26	50.8–66.0
H	28–30	71.1–76.2
I	18–24	45.7–61.0
J	18 min.	45.7 min.
K	72 max.	182.9 max.
L	4	10.2
M	42	106.7
N	26 min.	66.0 min.

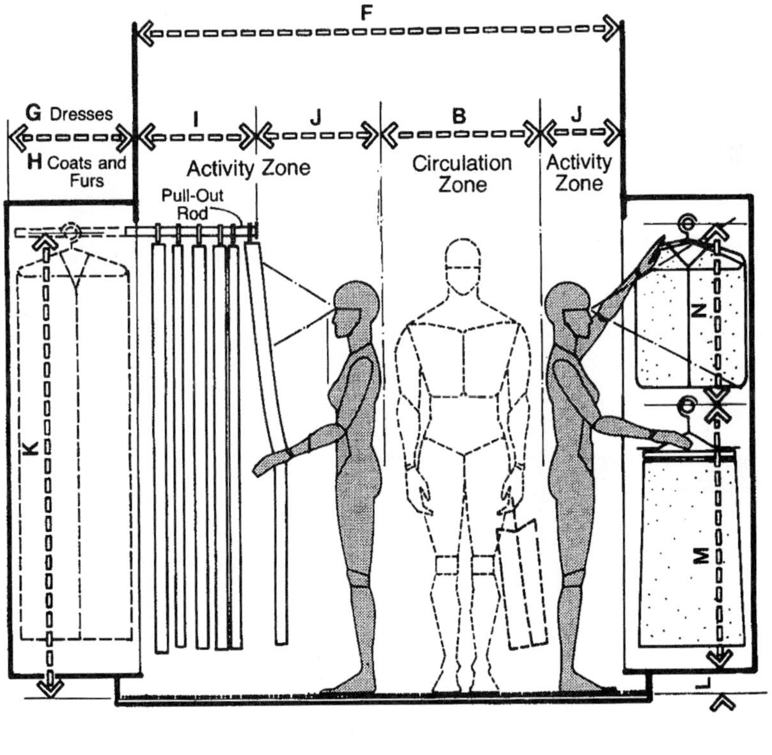

Fig. 6 Hanging merchandise cases

SHOPS
Storefronts

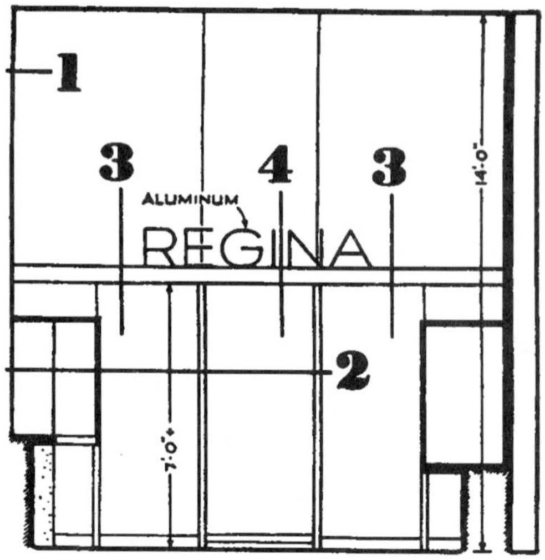
1
3
4
3
ALUMINUM
REGINA
2
14'-0"
7'-0"+

Section 3/16" SCALE

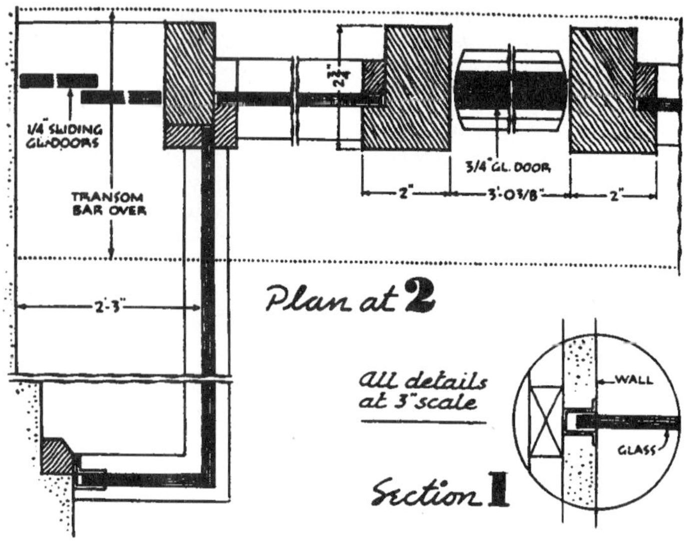
1/4" SLIDING GL. DOORS
TRANSOM BAR OVER
2'-3"
3/4" GL. DOOR
2"
3'-0 3/8"
2"
Plan at 2
All details at 3" scale
WALL
GLASS
Section 1

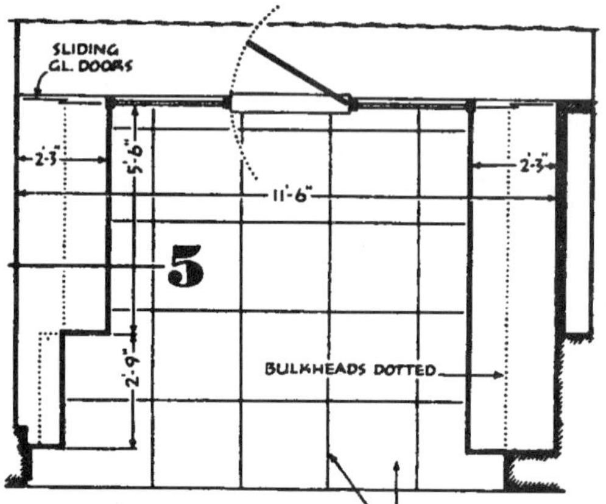
SLIDING GL. DOORS
2'-3"
5'-6"
11'-6"
2'-3"
5
2'-9"
BULKHEADS DOTTED
CERAMIC TILE FLOOR WIDE CEMENT JOINTS

Plan 3/16" SCALE

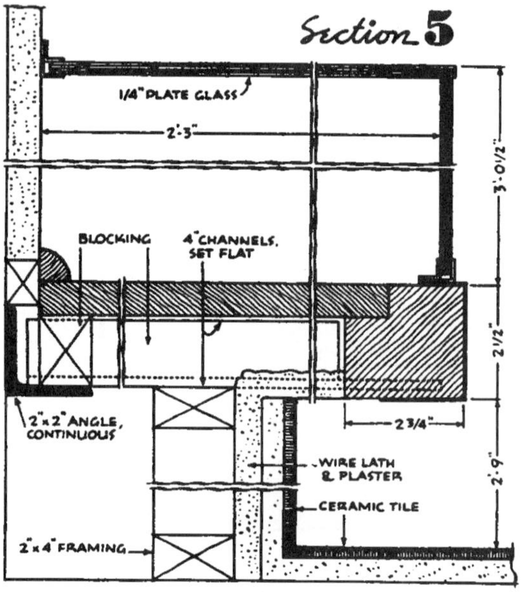
Section 5
1/4" PLATE GLASS
2'-3"
3'-0 1/2"
BLOCKING
4" CHANNELS, SET FLAT
2 1/2"
2"x2" ANGLE, CONTINUOUS
2 3/4"
WIRE LATH & PLASTER
CERAMIC TILE
2'-9"
2"x4" FRAMING

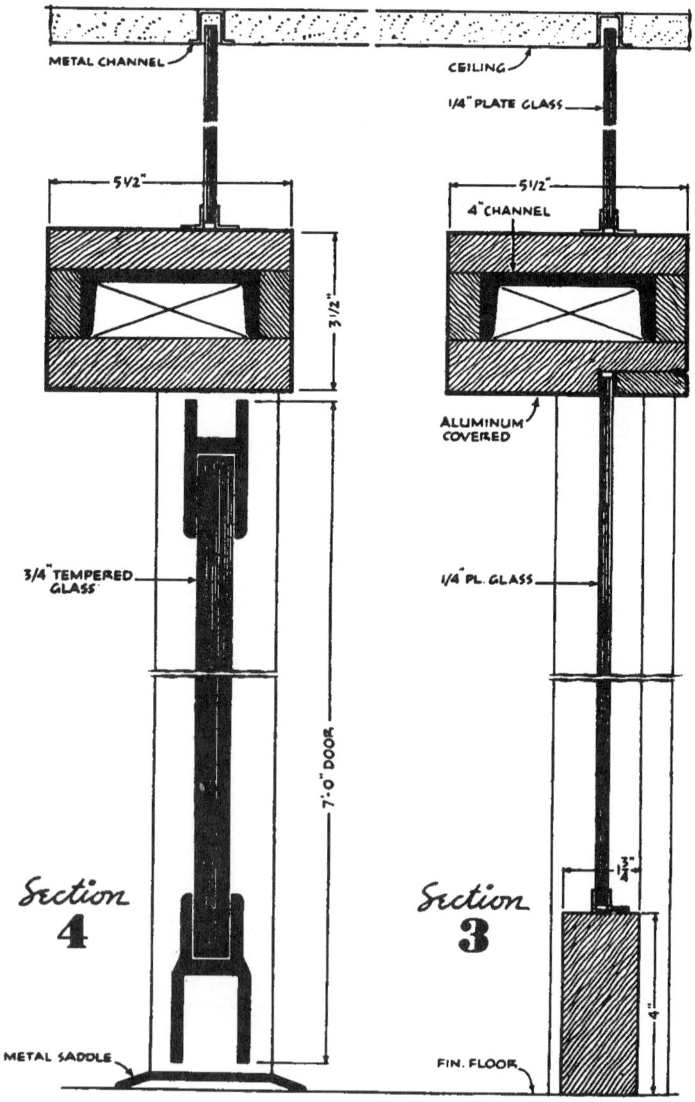
METAL CHANNEL
CEILING
1/4" PLATE GLASS
5 1/2"
5 1/2"
4" CHANNEL
3 1/2"
ALUMINUM COVERED
3/4" TEMPERED GLASS
1/4" PL. GLASS
7'-0" DOOR
Section 4
Section 3
METAL SADDLE
FIN. FLOOR
4"

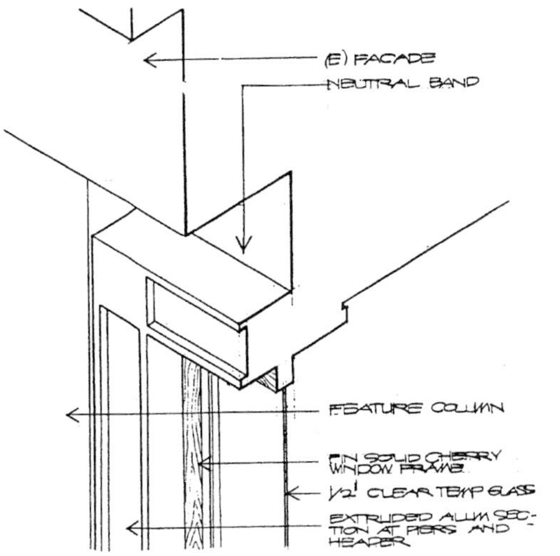

1 Pier Head Axonometric
Scale 1 1/2" = 1'-0"

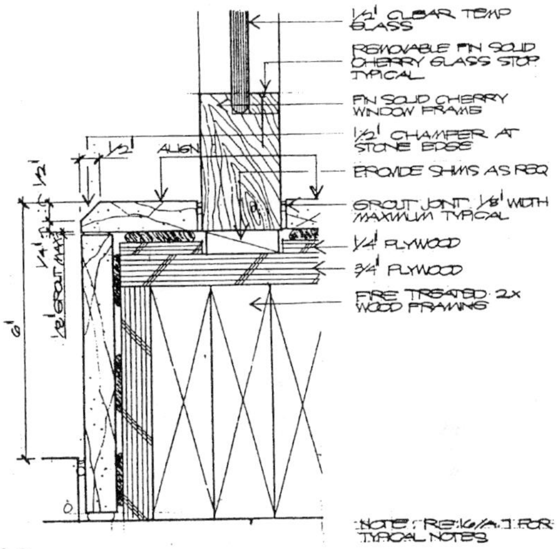

19 Detail at Base
Scale: 1/2" = 1"

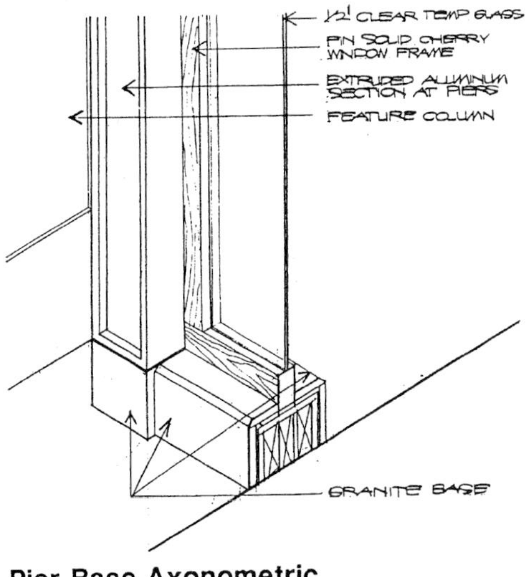

6 Pier Base Axonometric
Scale 1 1/2" = 1'-0"

SHOPS
Storefronts

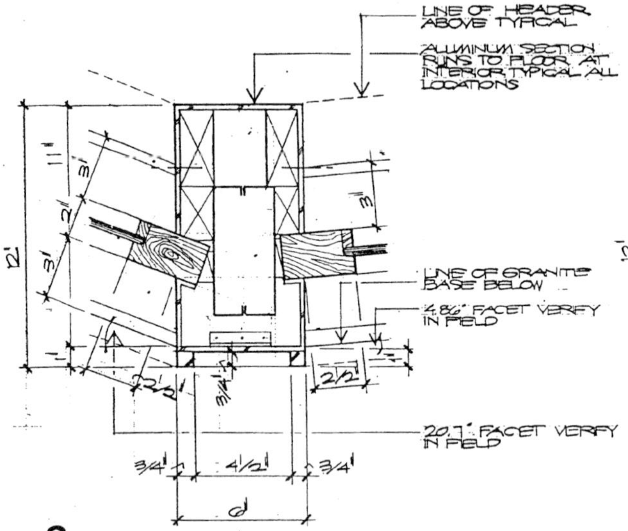

2 Plan Detail Note: See Detail 5/A.7 Typical Notes
Scale: 3" = 1'-0"

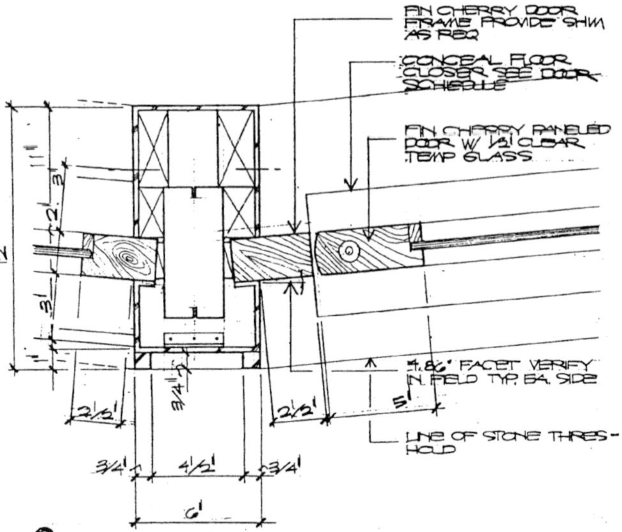

3 Door Jamb Note: See Detail 5/A.7 Typical Notes
Scale: 3" = 1'-0"

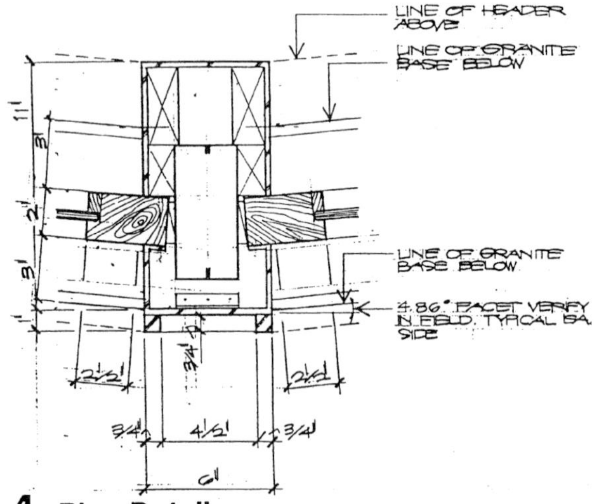

4 Plan Detail Note: See Detail 5/A.7 Typical Notes
Scale: 3" = 1'-0"

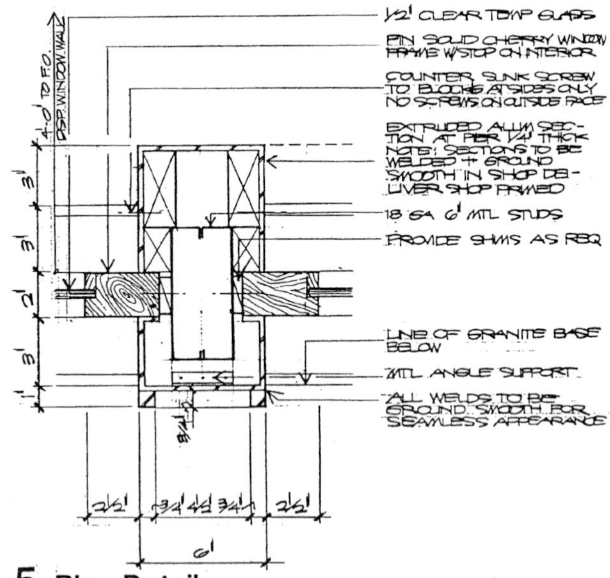

5 Plan Detail
Scale: 3" = 1'-0"

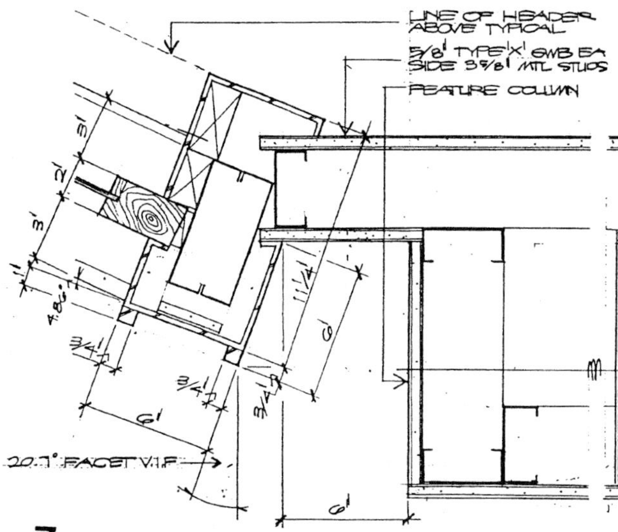

7 Plan Detail Note: See Detail 5/A.7 Typical Notes
Scale: 3" = 1'-0"

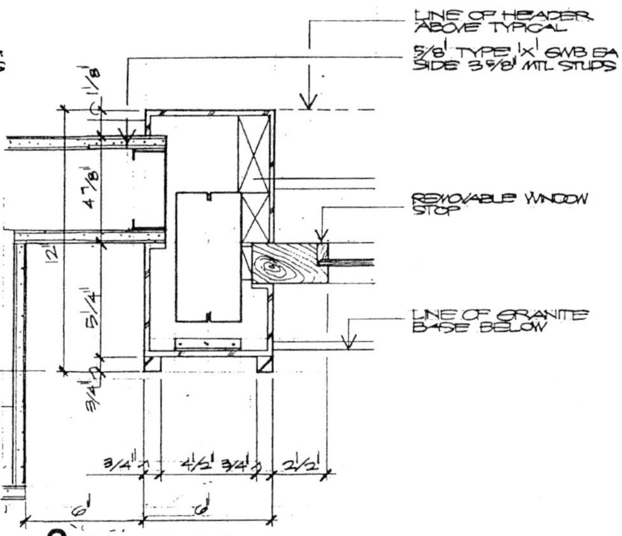

8 Plan Detail Note: See Detail 5/A.7 Typical Notes
Scale: 3" = 1'-0"

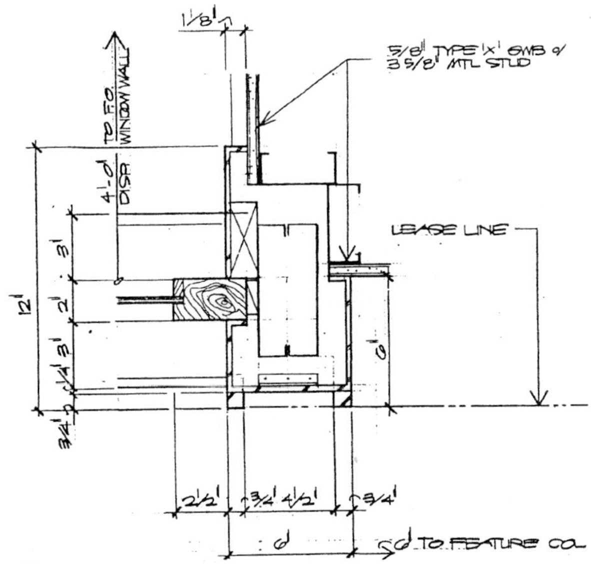

9 Plan Detail Note: See Detail 5/A.7 Typical Notes
Scale: 3" = 1'-0"

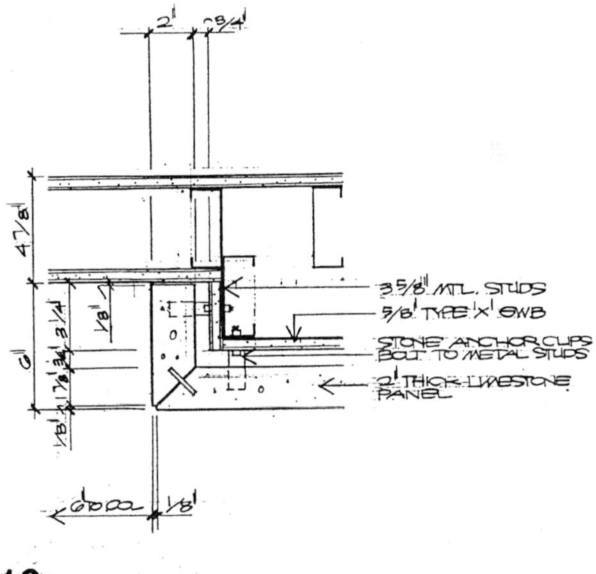

10 Plan Detail
Scale: 3" = 1'-0"

SHOPS
Storefronts

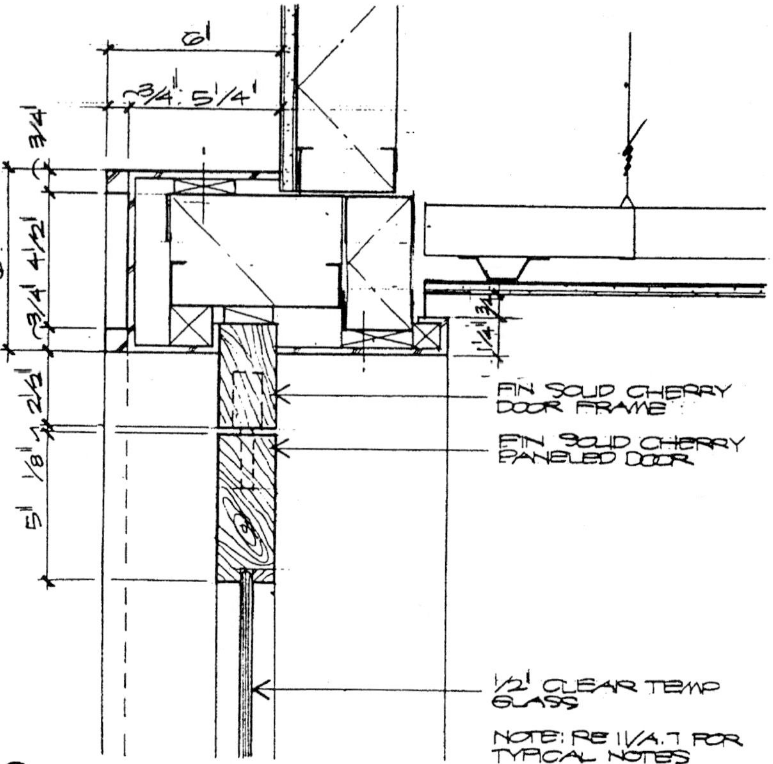

12 Door Head

Scale: 3" = 1'-0"

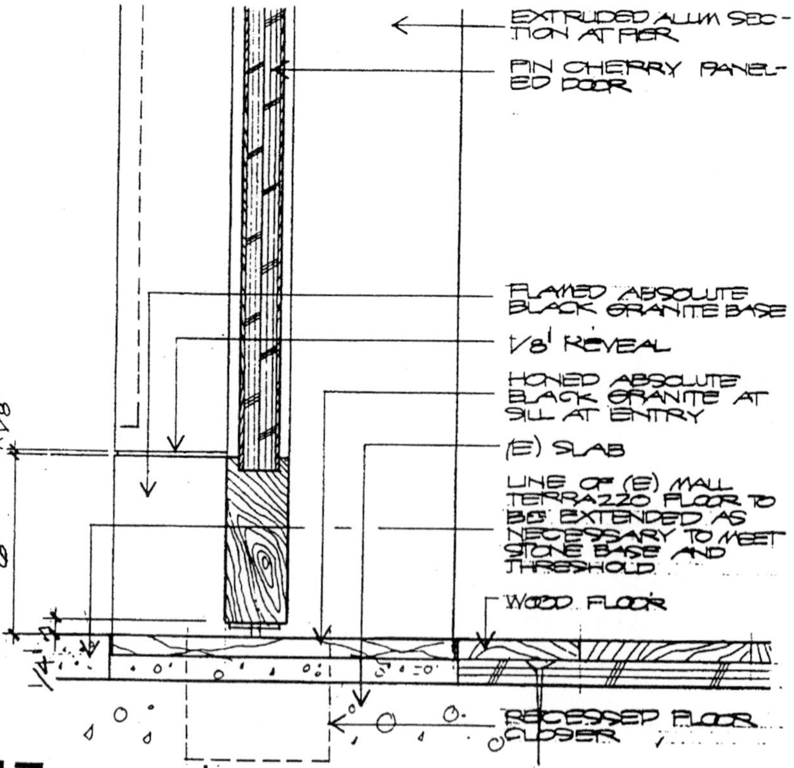

17 Door Sill

Scale: 3" = 1'-0"

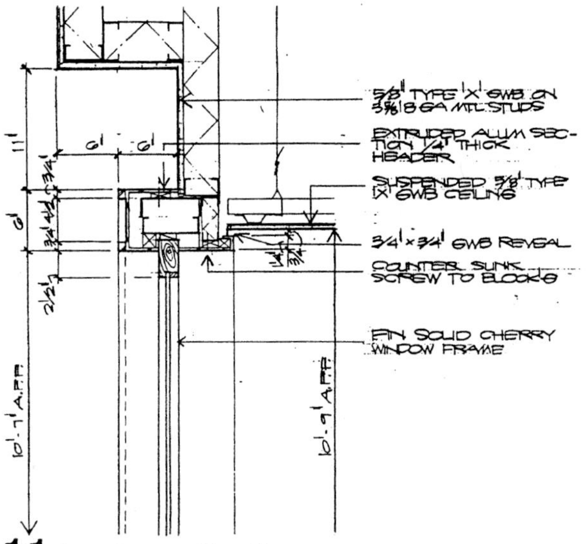

11 Section at Head
Scale 1 1/2" = 1'-0"

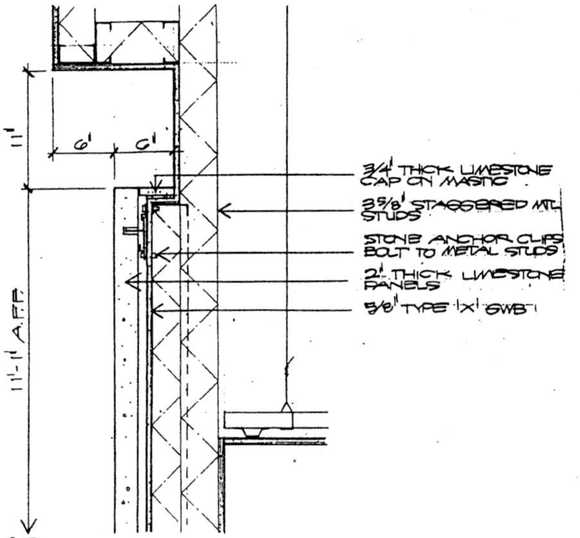

13 Section at Head
Scale 1 1/2" = 1'-0"

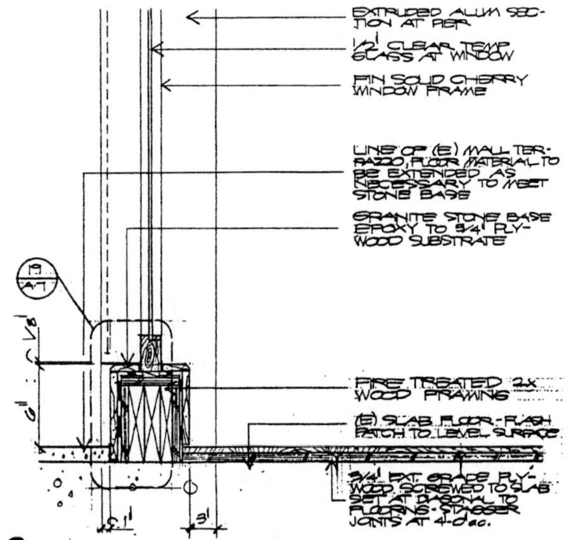

16 Section at Base
Scale 1 1/2" = 1'-0"

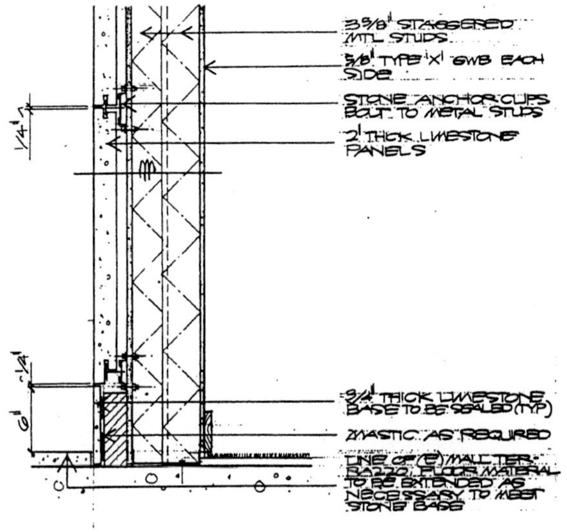

18 Section at Base
Scale 1 1/2" = 1'-0"

SHOPS
Storefronts

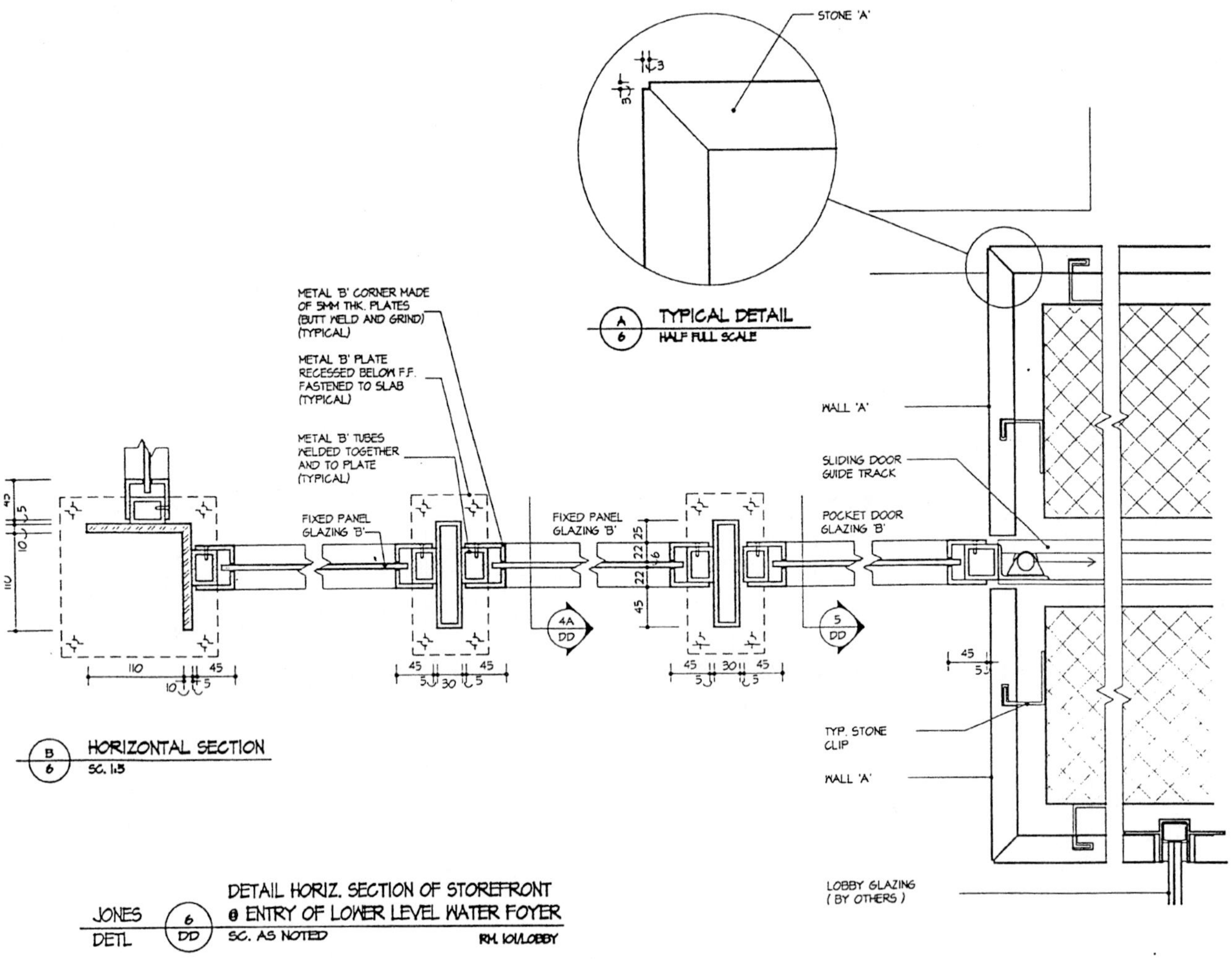
STONE 'A'
TYPICAL DETAIL
HALF FULL SCALE
METAL 'B' CORNER MADE OF 5MM THK. PLATES (BUTT WELD AND GRIND) (TYPICAL)
METAL 'B' PLATE RECESSED BELOW F.F. FASTENED TO SLAB (TYPICAL)
METAL 'B' TUBES WELDED TOGETHER AND TO PLATE (TYPICAL)
FIXED PANEL GLAZING 'B'
FIXED PANEL GLAZING 'B'
WALL 'A'
SLIDING DOOR GUIDE TRACK
POCKET DOOR GLAZING 'B'
TYP. STONE CLIP
WALL 'A'
LOBBY GLAZING (BY OTHERS)
HORIZONTAL SECTION
SC. 1:5
DETAIL HORIZ. SECTION OF STOREFRONT @ ENTRY OF LOWER LEVEL WATER FOYER
SC. AS NOTED
JONES
DETL
RM. 101/LOBBY

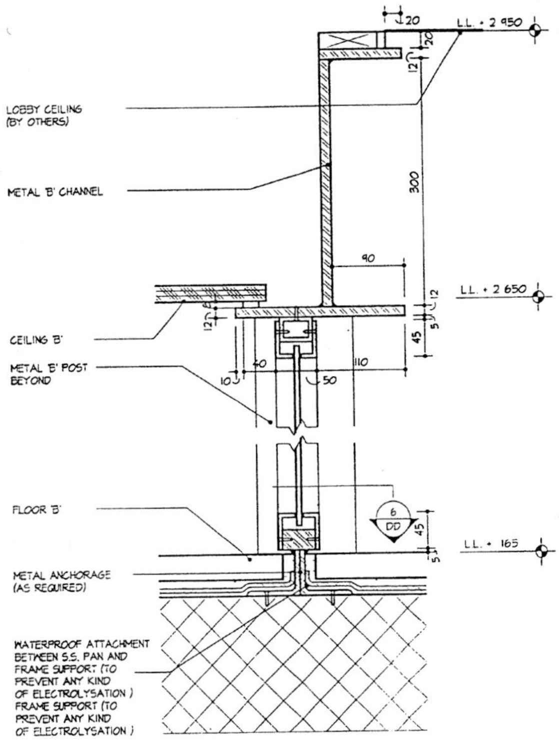

A 4 DETAIL SECTION
SC. 1:5

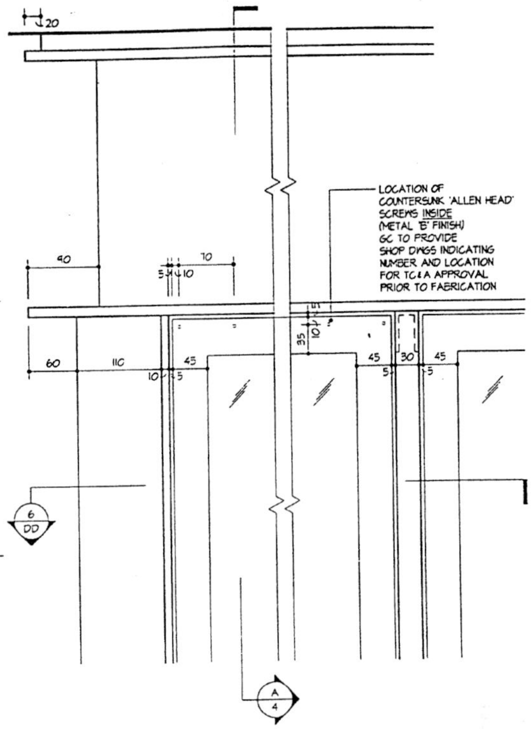

B 4 PARTIAL ELEVATION
SC. 1:5

DETAIL SECTION OF STOREFRONT
@ ENTRY OF LOWER LEVEL WATER FOYER
JONES DETL 4 DD SC. 1:5 R.M. IOVLOBE

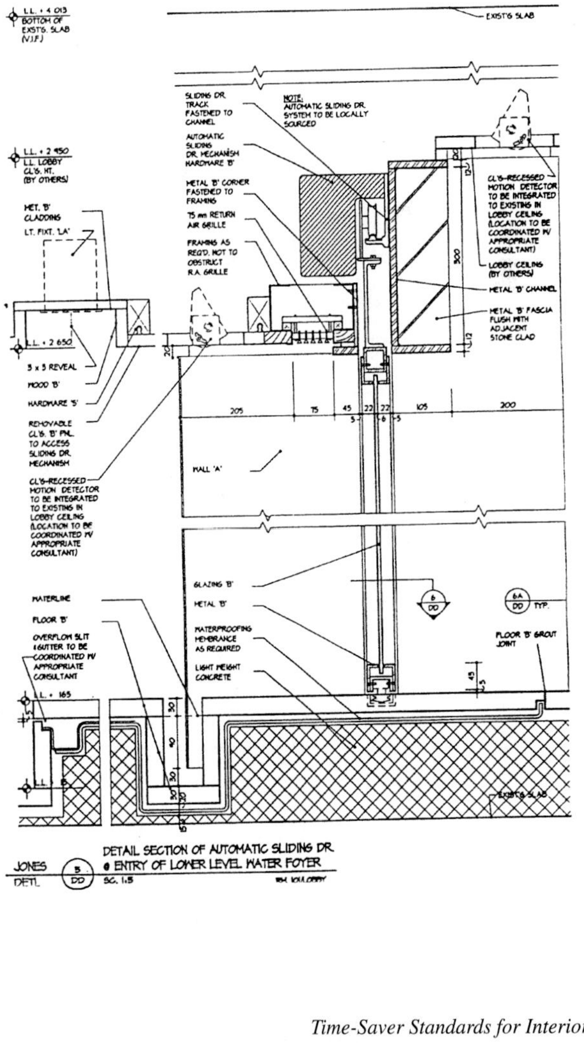

DETAIL SECTION OF AUTOMATIC SLIDING DR.
@ ENTRY OF LOWER LEVEL WATER FOYER
JONES DETL 5 DD SC. 1:5

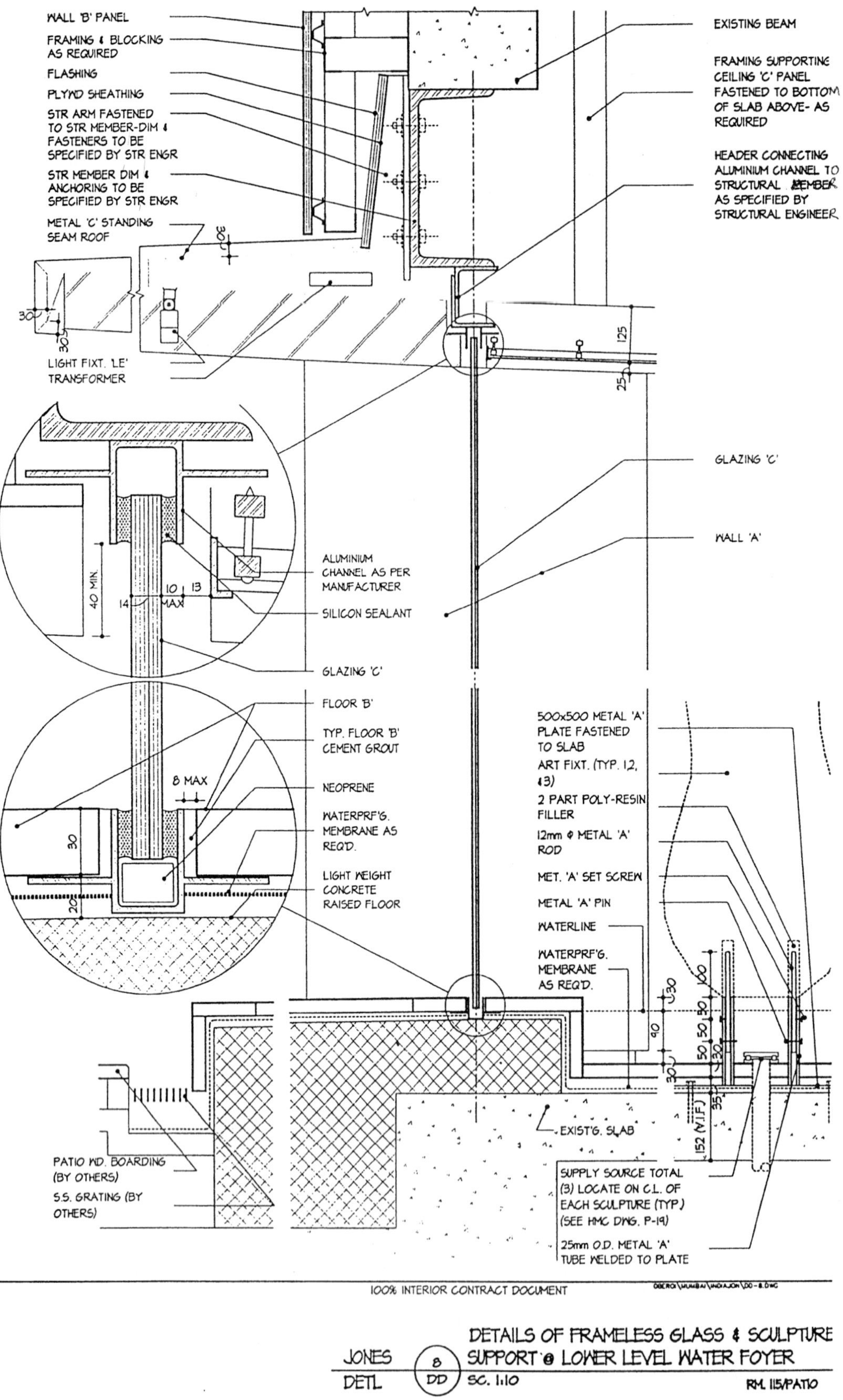
WALL 'B' PANEL
FRAMING & BLOCKING AS REQUIRED
FLASHING
PLYWD SHEATHING
STR ARM FASTENED TO STR MEMBER-DIM & FASTENERS TO BE SPECIFIED BY STR ENGR
STR MEMBER DIM & ANCHORING TO BE SPECIFIED BY STR ENGR
METAL 'C' STANDING SEAM ROOF
LIGHT FIXT. 'LE'
TRANSFORMER
EXISTING BEAM
FRAMING SUPPORTING CEILING 'C' PANEL FASTENED TO BOTTOM OF SLAB ABOVE- AS REQUIRED
HEADER CONNECTING ALUMINIUM CHANNEL TO STRUCTURAL MEMBER AS SPECIFIED BY STRUCTURAL ENGINEER
GLAZING 'C'
WALL 'A'
ALUMINIUM CHANNEL AS PER MANUFACTURER
SILICON SEALANT
GLAZING 'C'
40 MIN.
FLOOR 'B'
TYP. FLOOR 'B' CEMENT GROUT
NEOPRENE
8 MAX
WATERPRF'G. MEMBRANE AS REQ'D.
LIGHT WEIGHT CONCRETE RAISED FLOOR
500x500 METAL 'A' PLATE FASTENED TO SLAB
ART FIXT. (TYP. 1,2, & 3)
2 PART POLY-RESIN FILLER
12mm ϕ METAL 'A' ROD
MET. 'A' SET SCREW
METAL 'A' PIN
WATERLINE
WATERPRF'G. MEMBRANE AS REQ'D.
EXIST'G. SLAB
152 (V.I.F.)
PATIO WD. BOARDING (BY OTHERS)
S.S. GRATING (BY OTHERS)
SUPPLY SOURCE TOTAL (3) LOCATE ON C.L. OF EACH SCULPTURE (TYP.) (SEE HMC DWG. P-19)
25mm O.D. METAL 'A' TUBE WELDED TO PLATE
100% INTERIOR CONTRACT DOCUMENT
DETAILS OF FRAMELESS GLASS & SCULPTURE SUPPORT @ LOWER LEVEL WATER FOYER
JONES
DETL
8
DD
SC. 1:10
RM. 115/PATIO

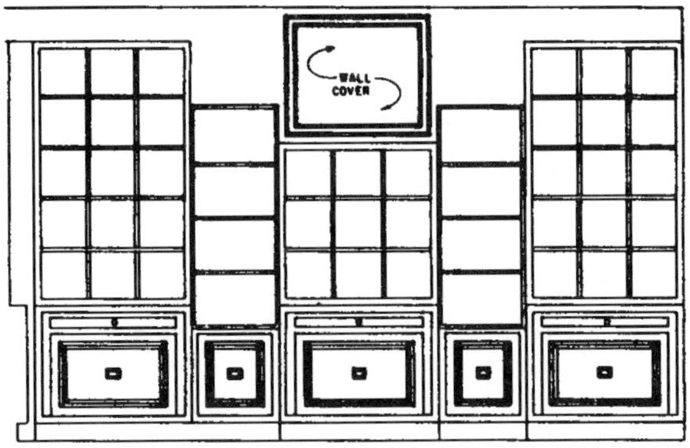

ELEVATION-SHIRT DISPLAY CASE

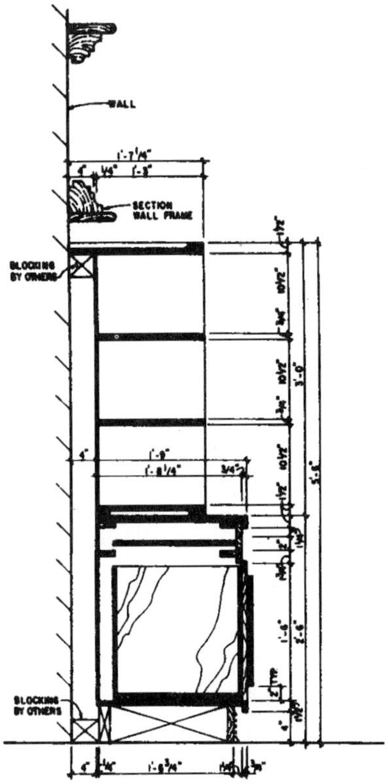

VERTICAL SECTION
SHIRT DISPLAY

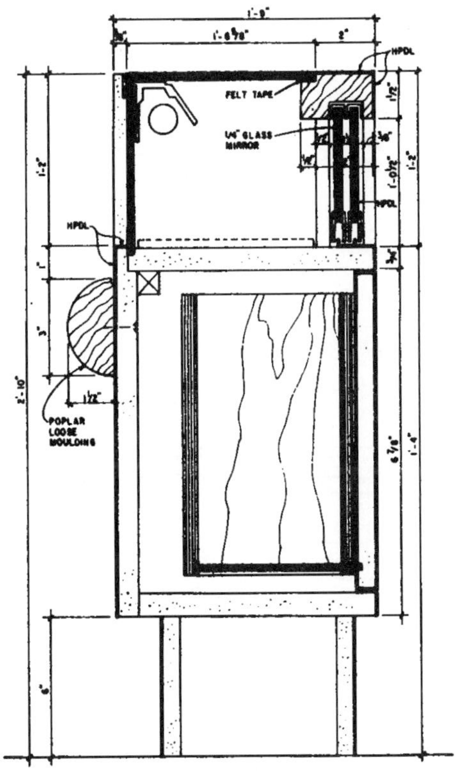

VERTICAL SECTION
JEWELRY SHOWCASE

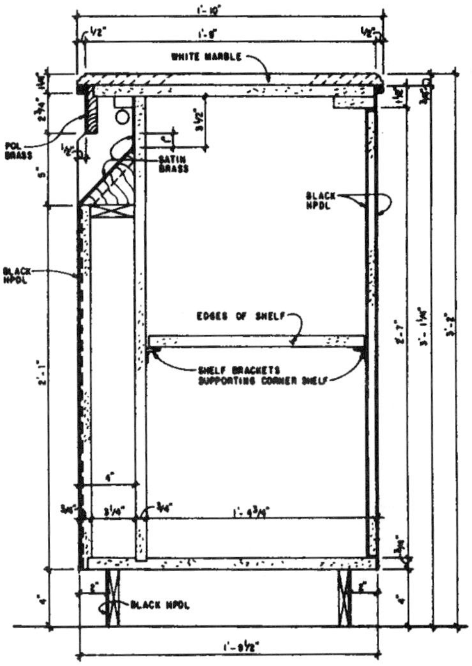

VERTICAL SECTION
COSMETIC DISPLAY

SHOPS
Display Cases

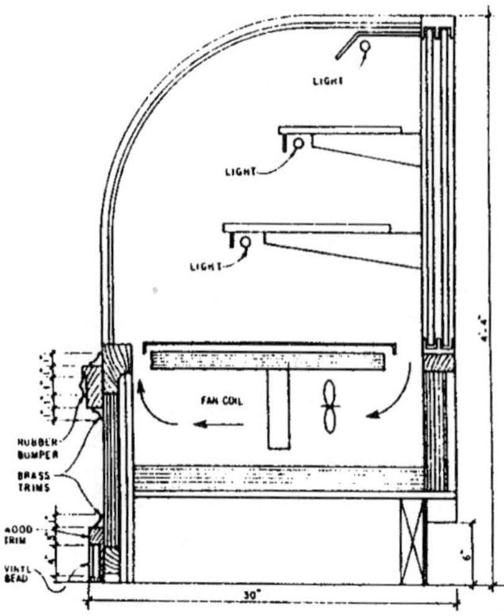

REFRIGERATED CASE

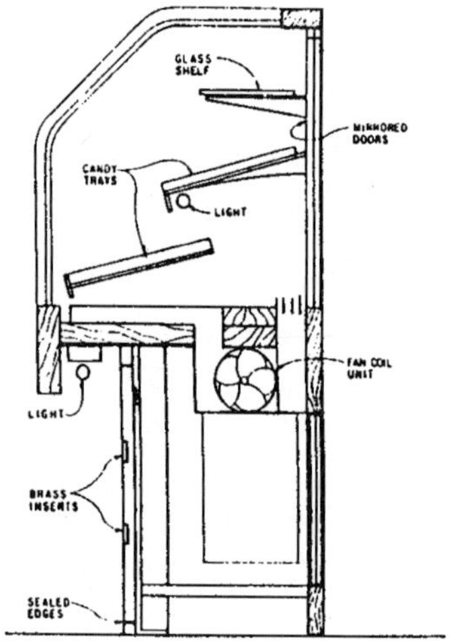

REFRIGERATED CASE

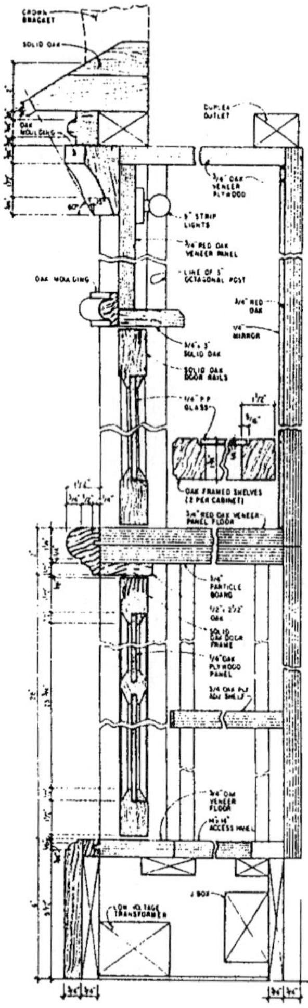

CROSS SECTION-DISPLAY CABINET

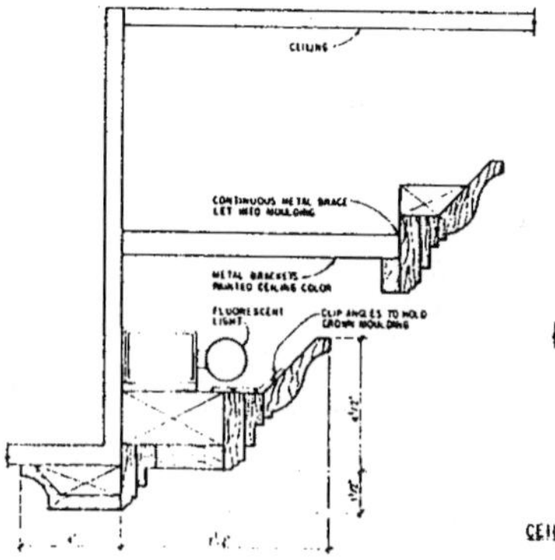

CEILING MOULDING

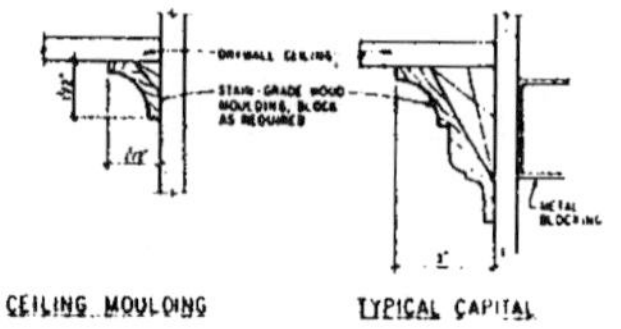

TYPICAL TRIM

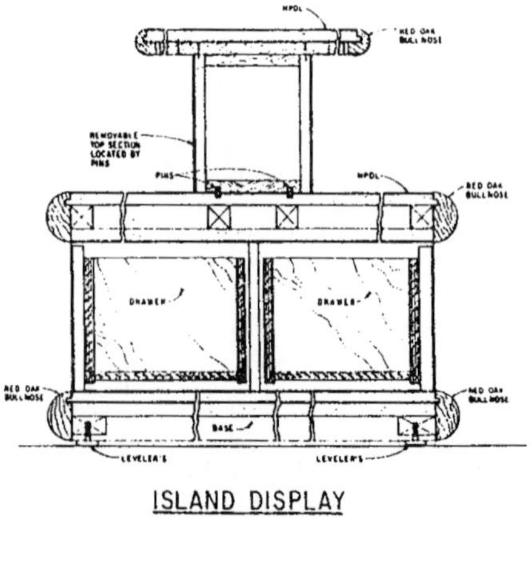

ISLAND DISPLAY

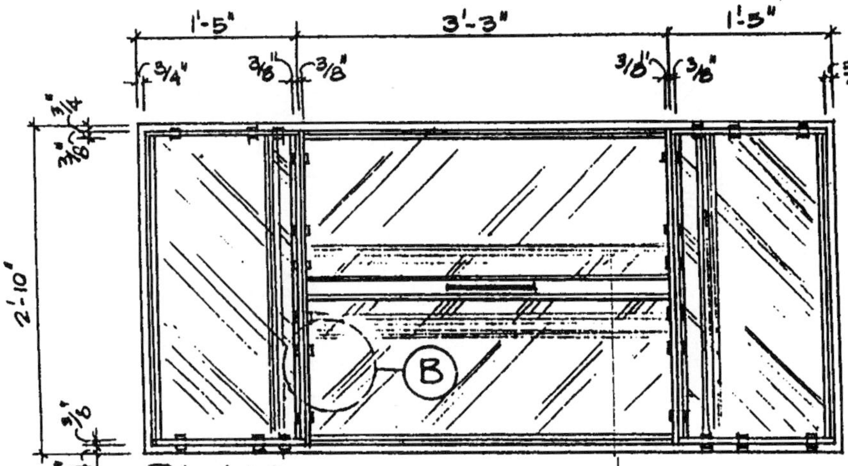

SIGN HOLDER
(2) 1/4" TH. PLEXI PANELS CEMENTED TO 1/4" TH. CENTER PANEL W/ 1/8" X 1/2" PEXI BAND ON THREE SIDES (TOP OPEN)
1/2" TH. PLYWD. CENTER DIVIDER PL. LAM. FIN. ALL SIDES
5/8" X 2' X 5 1/8" QUIRK P.T.M. PL. LAM.
PLAN
SC: 3/4" = 1'-0"
DETAIL D
SC: 3" = 1'-0"
PLEXI GLASS SIGN HOLDERS
1" RADIUS CORNERS
1 1/2" PLYWD. PANEL, PL. LAM. FIN. ALL SIDES
3/8" CL. PLEXI GL. SHELVES W/ CLIPS
3/8" CLEAR PLEXI PANELS
3/4" PLYWD. BASE PL. LAM. FIN. ALL SIDES, WOOD BLOCK'G. AS REQ'D.
PART FRONT ELEV.
SCALE: 3/4" = 1'-0"
VERTICAL SECTION
SCALE: 3/4" = 1'-0"
F.C. TO PROVIDE FINGER CUT-OUT IN EACH SIGN HOLDER
1/4" THK. PLEXI PANEL CEMENTED TO 3/8" PANEL W/ 1/8" X 1/2" PLEXI BAND ON (3) SIDES
3/8" CL. PLEXI SHELVES ON CL. ALLIGATOR CLIPS
CLEAR PLEXI ALLIGATOR CLIP
3/8" TH. CLEAR PLEXI PANELS
ALLIGATOR CLIP
3/8" CL. PLEXI GL. SHELF
EDGE OF 3/8" CL. PLEXI PANEL
DETAIL A
SC: 3" = 1'-0"
DETAIL B
SC: 3" = 1'-0"
DETAIL C
SC: 3" = 1'-0"

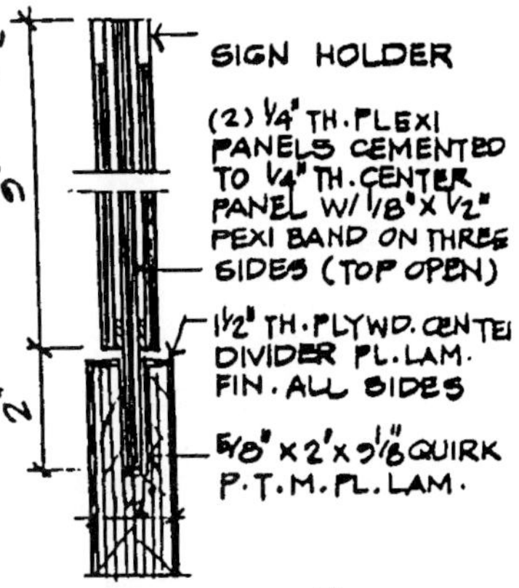

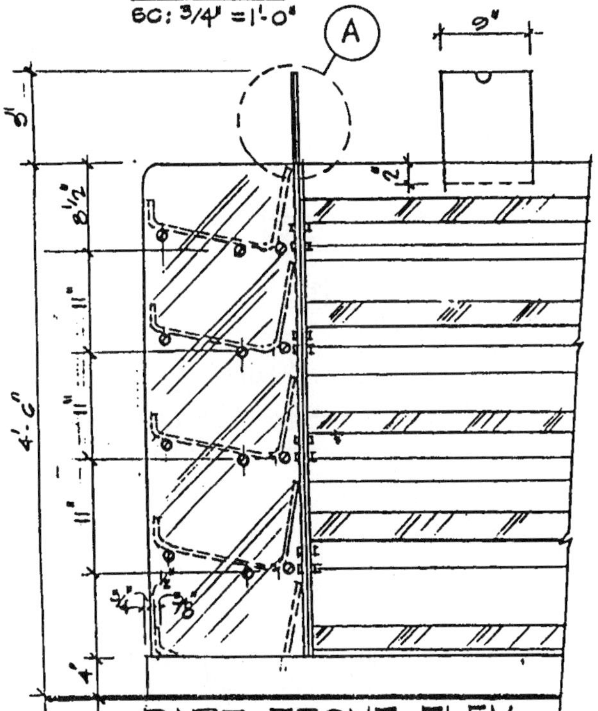

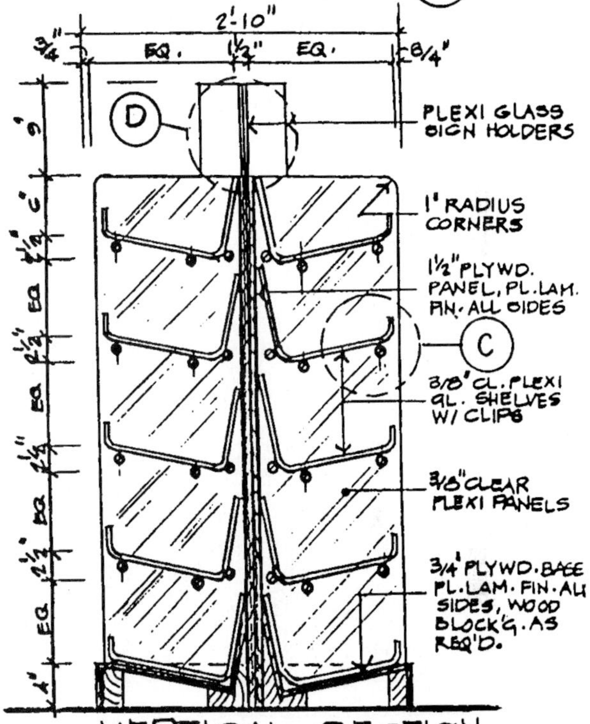

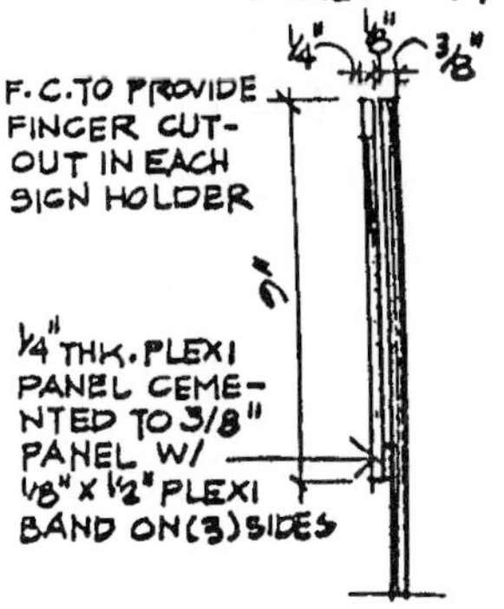

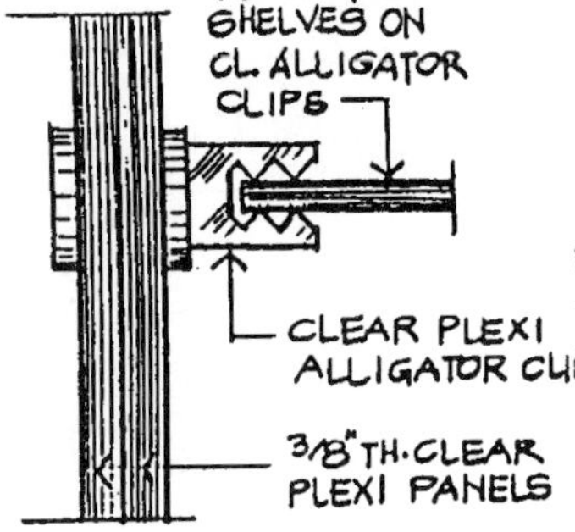

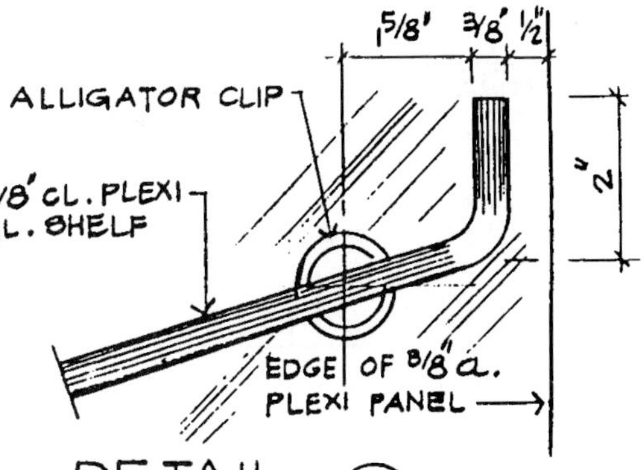

SHOPS
Display Cases

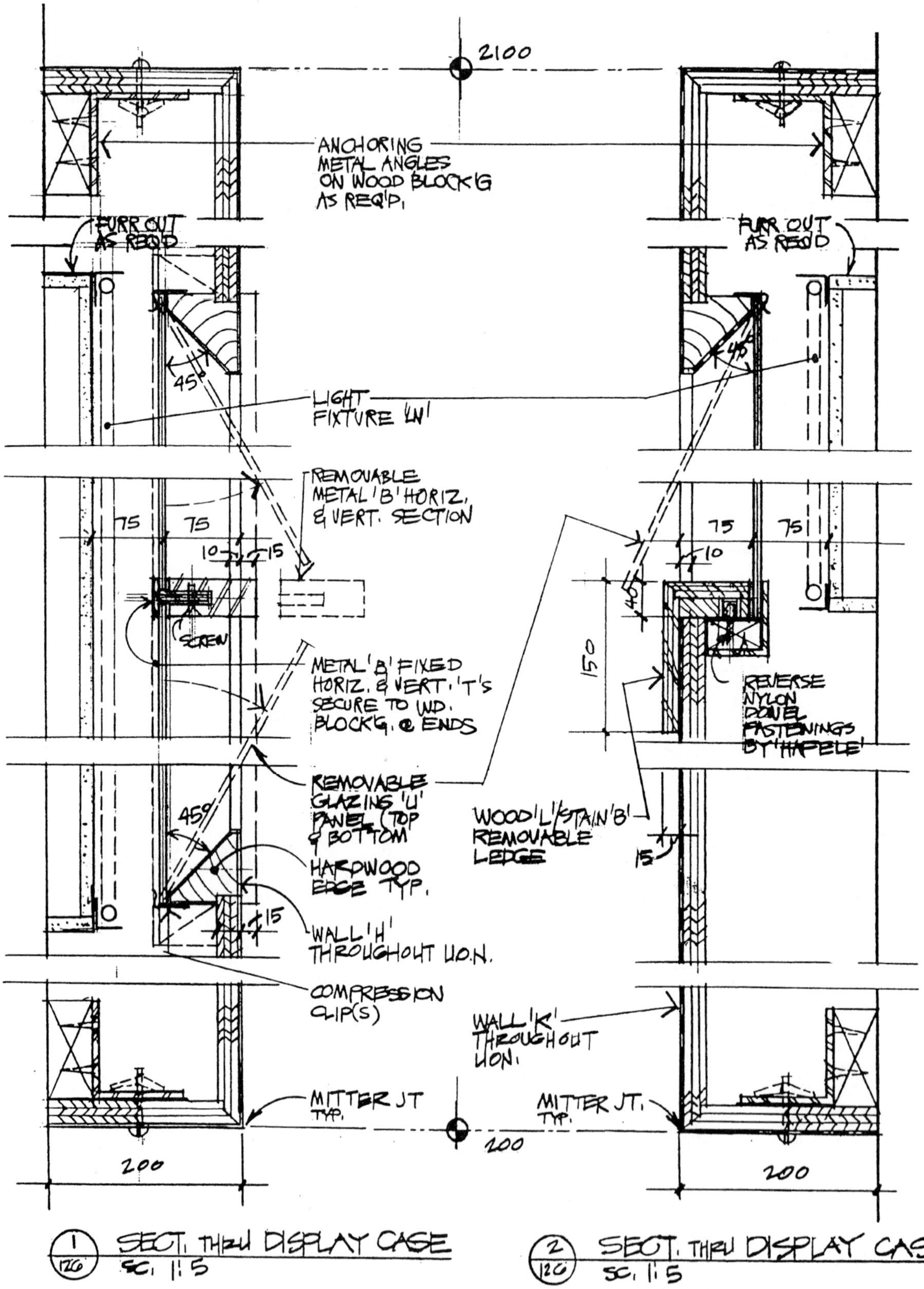
2100
ANCHORING METAL ANGLES ON WOOD BLOCK'G AS REQ'D.
FURR OUT AS REQ'D
FURR OUT AS REQ'D
45°
45°
LIGHT FIXTURE 'LN'
REMOVABLE METAL 'B' HORIZ. & VERT. SECTION
75
75
75
75
10
15
10
SCREW
40
150
METAL 'B' FIXED HORIZ. & VERT. 'T's SECURE TO WD. BLOCK'G. @ ENDS
REVERSE NYLON DOWEL FASTENINGS BY 'HAFELE'
REMOVABLE GLAZING 'U' PANEL (TOP & BOTTOM
WOOD 'L' STAIN 'B' REMOVABLE LEDGE
45°
15
HARDWOOD EDGE TYP.
15
WALL 'H' THROUGHOUT U.O.N.
COMPRESSION CLIP(S)
WALL 'K' THROUGHOUT U.O.N.
MITTER JT TYP.
MITTER JT. TYP.
200
200
200
1/126 SECT. THRU DISPLAY CASE SC. 1:5
2/126 SECT. THRU DISPLAY CASE SC. 1:5

126/DD SECT. DETS. THRU DECOR. WALL SC. 1:5

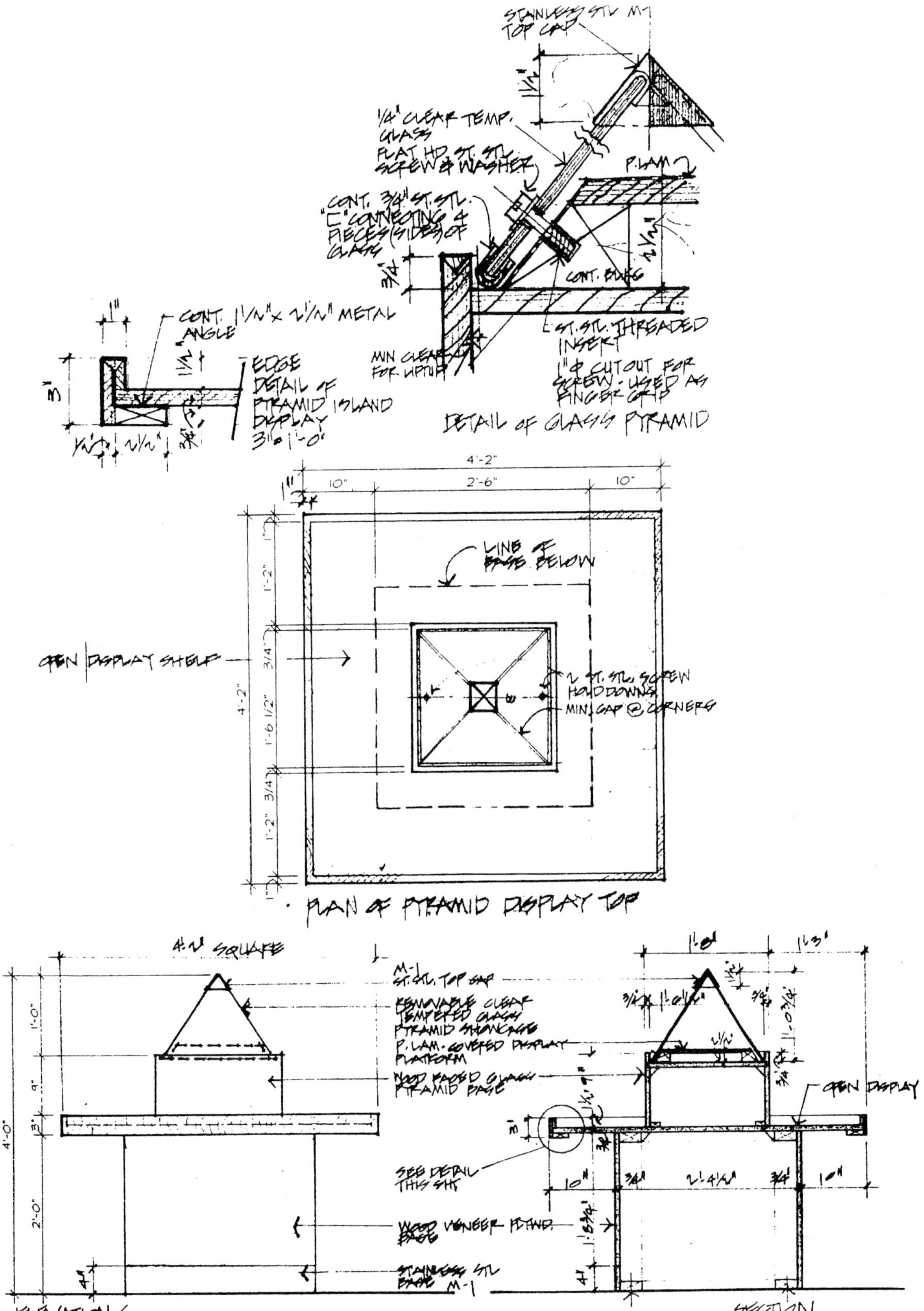
STAINLESS STL M-1 TOP CAP
1/4" CLEAR TEMP. GLASS
FLAT HD ST. STL SCREW & WASHER
P.LAM
CONT. 3/4" ST. STL. "C" CONNECTING 4 PIECES (SIDES) OF GLASS
CONT. BLKG
ST. STL. THREADED INSERT
1" Φ CUTOUT FOR SCREW - USED AS FINGER GRIP
MIN CLEAR FOR LIFTUP
DETAIL OF GLASS PYRAMID
CONT. 1 1/4" x 2 1/4" METAL ANGLE
EDGE DETAIL OF PYRAMID ISLAND DISPLAY 3" = 1'-0"
4'-2"
10"
2'-6"
10"
LINE OF BASE BELOW
OPEN DISPLAY SHELF
2 ST. STL. SCREW HOLDDOWNS
MIN. GAP @ CORNERS
1'-2"
3/4"
1'-6 1/2"
PLAN OF PYRAMID DISPLAY TOP
4'-2" SQUARE
M-1 ST. STL. TOP CAP
REMOVABLE CLEAR TEMPERED GLASS PYRAMID SHOWCASE
P. LAM. COVERED DISPLAY PLATFORM
WOOD FACED GLASS PYRAMID BASE
SEE DETAIL THIS SHT
WOOD VENEER PLYWD. BASE
STAINLESS STL BASE M-1
OPEN DISPLAY
1'-0"
4'-0"
2'-0"
ELEVATION/ ALL 4 SIDES EQUAL
SECTION

2 A402 PYRAMID CABINET DETAILS 1" = 1'-0"

SHOPS

Display Cases

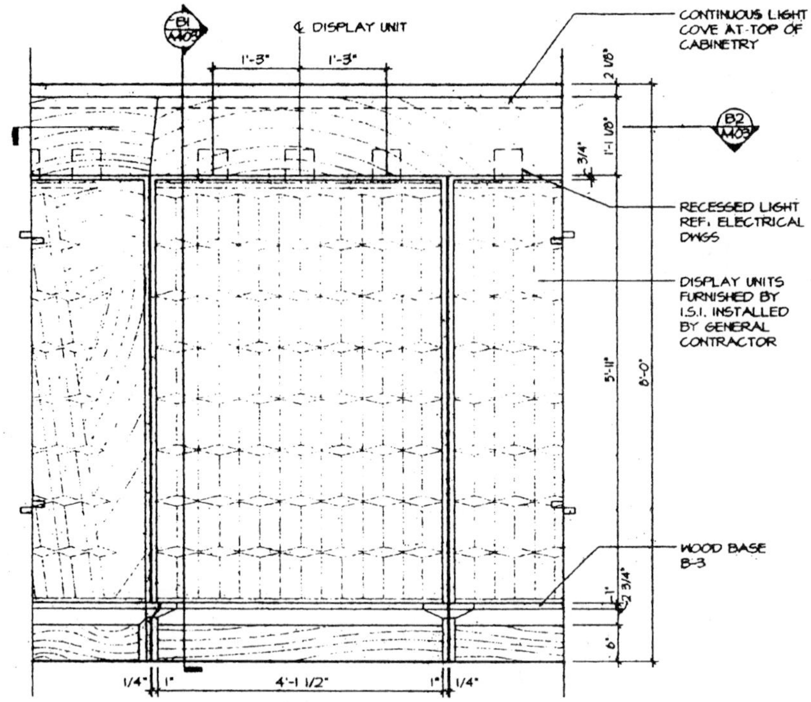

B DISPLAY CABINET ELEVATION
A403 3/4" = 1'-0"

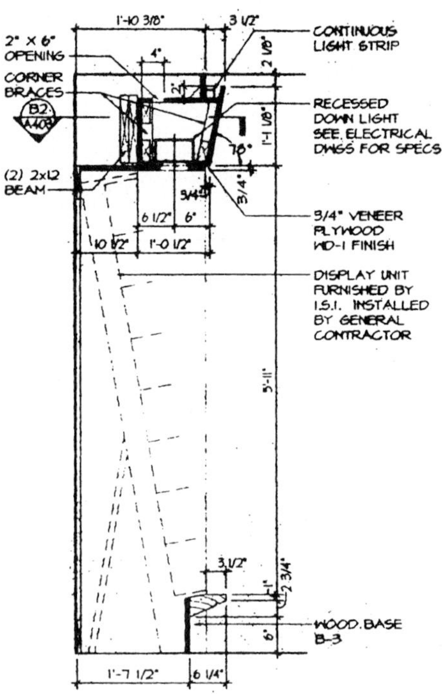

B1 SECTION
A403 3/4" = 1'-0"

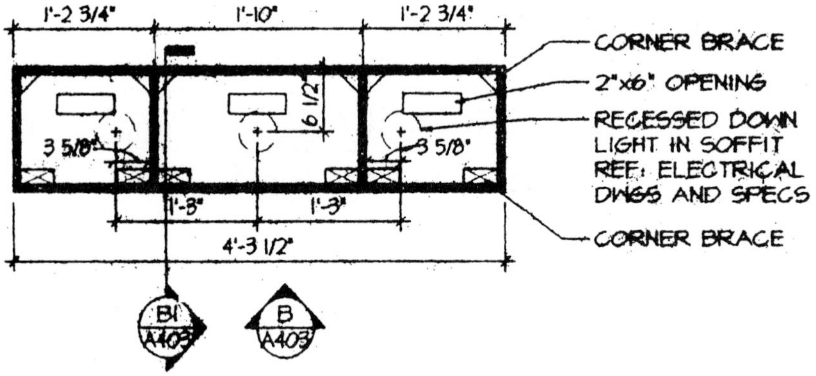

B2 SOFFIT @ DISPLAY CABINET
A403 3/4" = 1'-0"

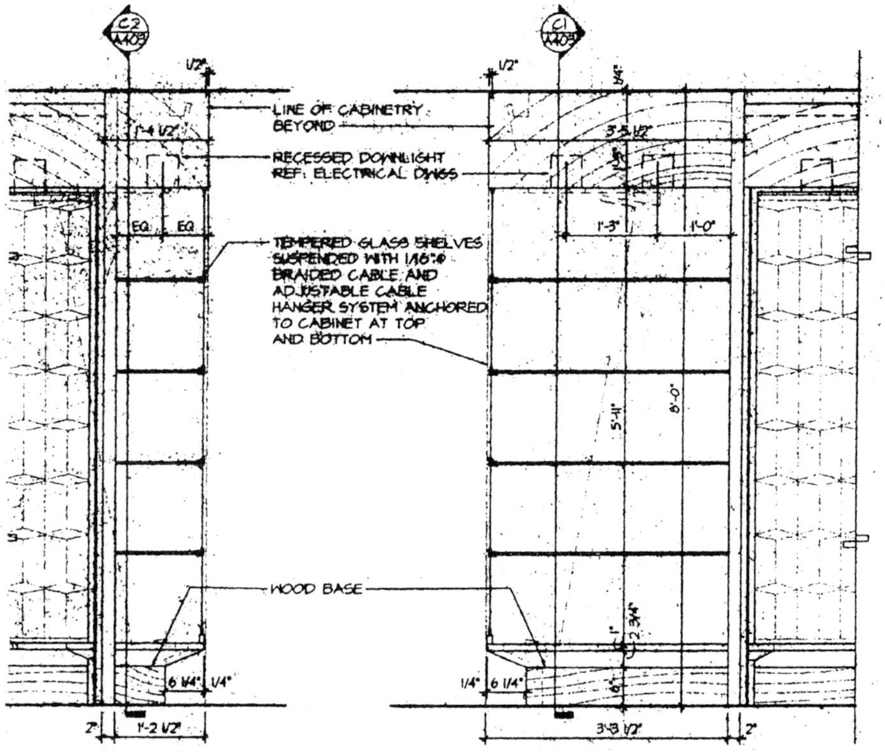
C2
A403
C1
A403
LINE OF CABINETRY BEYOND
RECESSED DOWNLIGHT REF: ELECTRICAL DWGS
TEMPERED GLASS SHELVES SUSPENDED WITH 1/16"Φ BRAIDED CABLE AND ADJUSTABLE CABLE HANGER SYSTEM ANCHORED TO CABINET AT TOP AND BOTTOM
WOOD BASE
EQ
EQ
1'-3"
1'-0"
5'-11"
8'-0"
6 1/4"
1/4"
1'-2 1/2"
3'-3 1/2"
2"

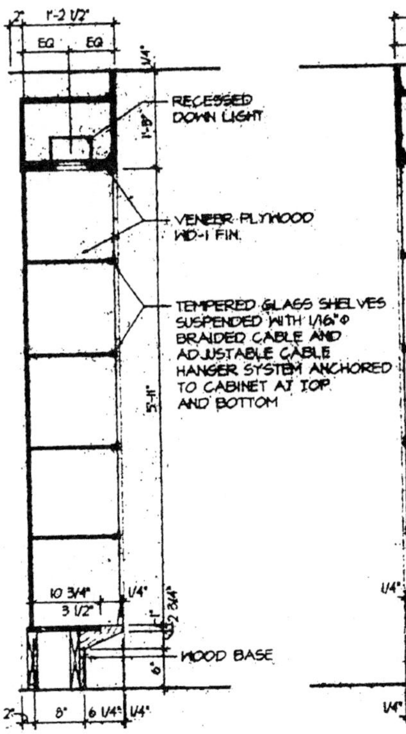
C
A403
CORNER CABINET ELEVATION
3/4" = 1'-0"

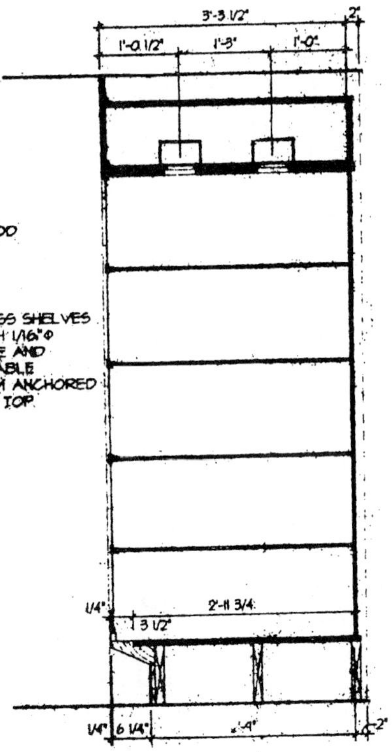
1'-2 1/2"
EQ
EQ
3'-3 1/2"
1'-0 1/2"
1'-3"
1'-0"
RECESSED DOWN LIGHT
VENEER PLYWOOD WD-1 FIN.
TEMPERED GLASS SHELVES SUSPENDED WITH 1/16"Φ BRAIDED CABLE AND ADJUSTABLE CABLE HANGER SYSTEM ANCHORED TO CABINET AT TOP AND BOTTOM
5'-11"
10 3/4"
3 1/2"
2'-11 3/4"
WOOD BASE
8"
6 1/4"
1/4"
2"
C1
A403
SECTION
3/4" = 1'-0"
C2
A403
SECTION
3/4" = 1'-0"

SHOPS
Display Cases

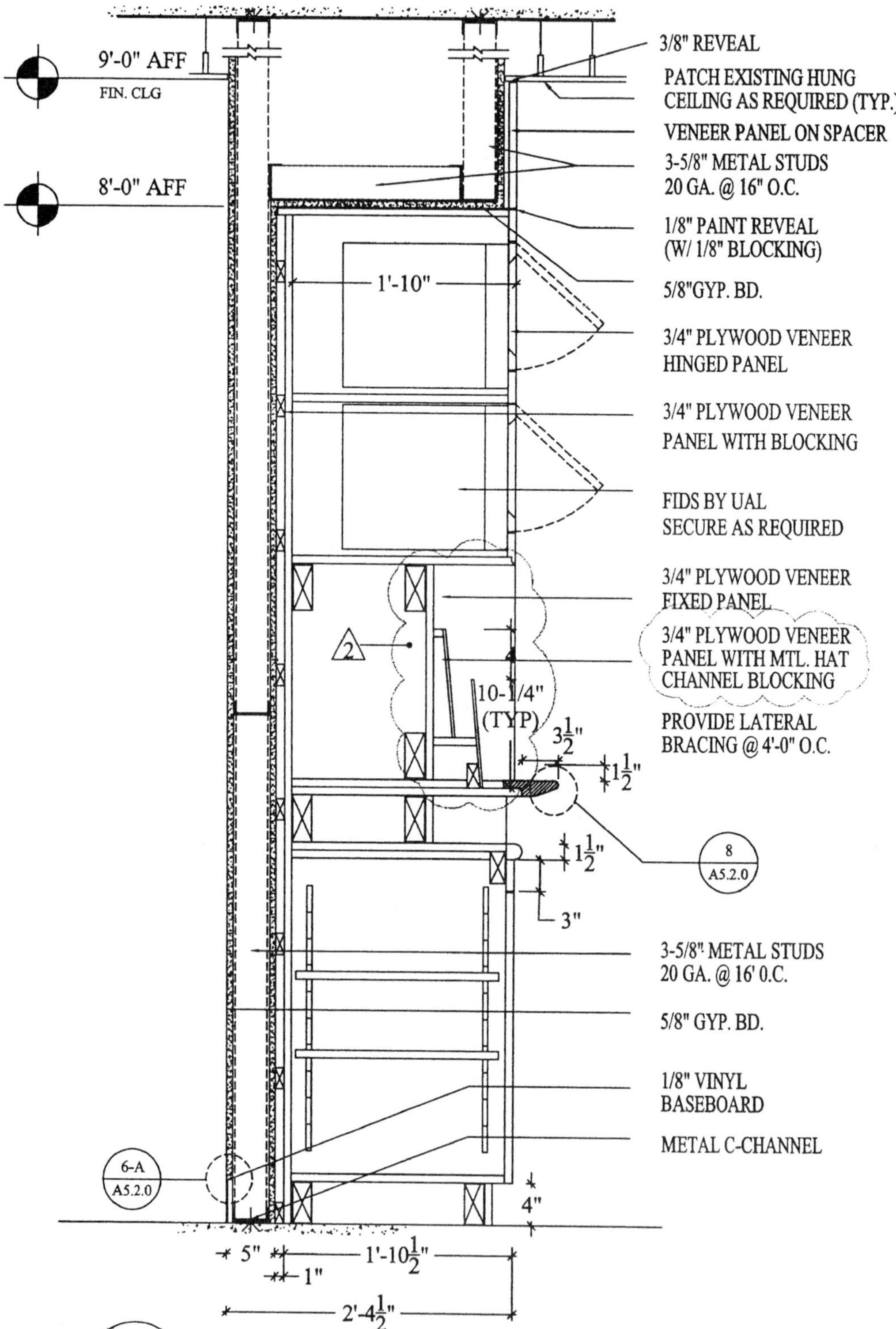
9'-0" AFF
FIN. CLG
8'-0" AFF
3/8" REVEAL
PATCH EXISTING HUNG CEILING AS REQUIRED (TYP.)
VENEER PANEL ON SPACER
3-5/8" METAL STUDS 20 GA. @ 16" O.C.
1/8" PAINT REVEAL (W/ 1/8" BLOCKING)
5/8"GYP. BD.
1'-10"
3/4" PLYWOOD VENEER HINGED PANEL
3/4" PLYWOOD VENEER PANEL WITH BLOCKING
FIDS BY UAL SECURE AS REQUIRED
3/4" PLYWOOD VENEER FIXED PANEL
3/4" PLYWOOD VENEER PANEL WITH MTL. HAT CHANNEL BLOCKING
PROVIDE LATERAL BRACING @ 4'-0" O.C.
10-1/4" (TYP)
3 1/2"
1 1/2"
1 1/2"
3"
8
A5.2.0
3-5/8" METAL STUDS 20 GA. @ 16' O.C.
5/8" GYP. BD.
1/8" VINYL BASEBOARD
METAL C-CHANNEL
6-A
A5.2.0
4"
5"
1"
1'-10 1/2"
2'-4 1/2"

9 FIDS/ MAGAZINES
3/4"=1'-0"

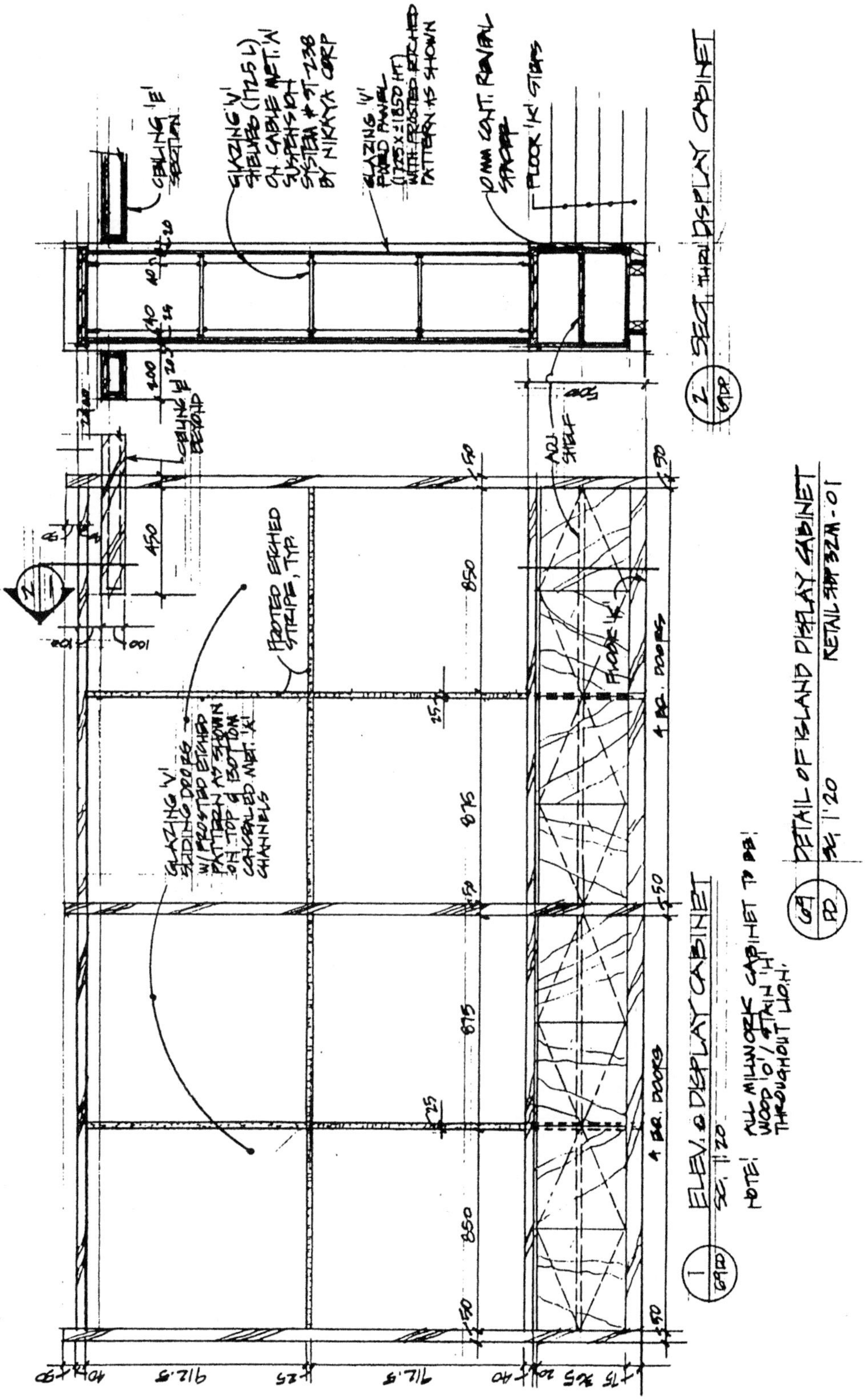

ELEV. @ DISPLAY CABINET
SECT. THRU DISPLAY CABINET
DETAIL OF ISLAND DISPLAY CABINET
FROSTED ETCHED STRIPE, TYP
4 PR. DOORS

SHOPS

Display Island

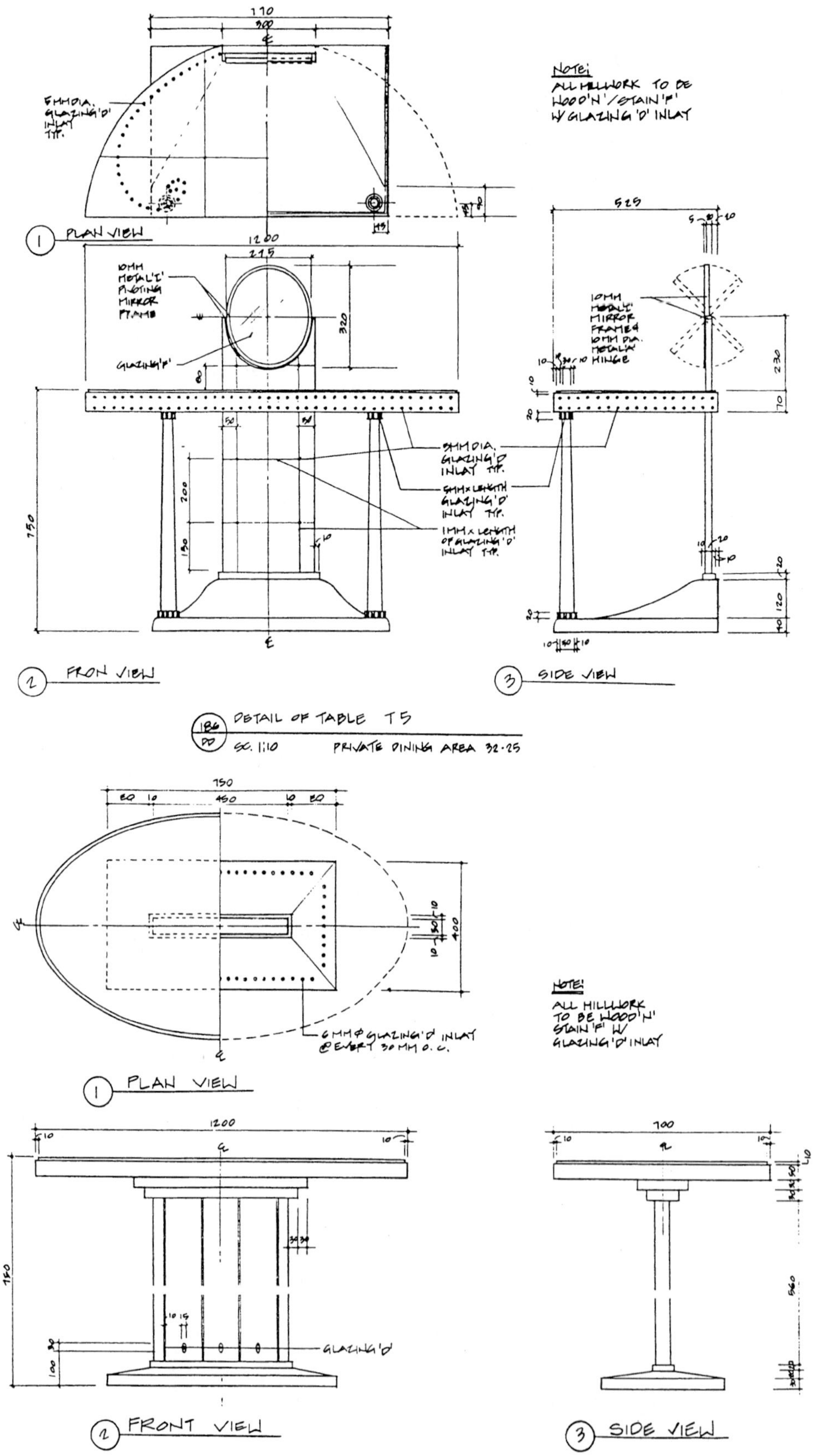

① PLAN VIEW

NOTE:
ALL MILLWORK TO BE
WOOD 'N' / STAIN 'F'
W/ GLAZING 'D' INLAY

② FRON VIEW

③ SIDE VIEW

⑱⑥/DD DETAIL OF TABLE T5
SC. 1:10 PRIVATE DINING AREA 32.25

① PLAN VIEW

NOTE:
ALL MILLWORK
TO BE WOOD 'N'
STAIN 'F' W/
GLAZING 'D' INLAY

② FRONT VIEW

③ SIDE VIEW

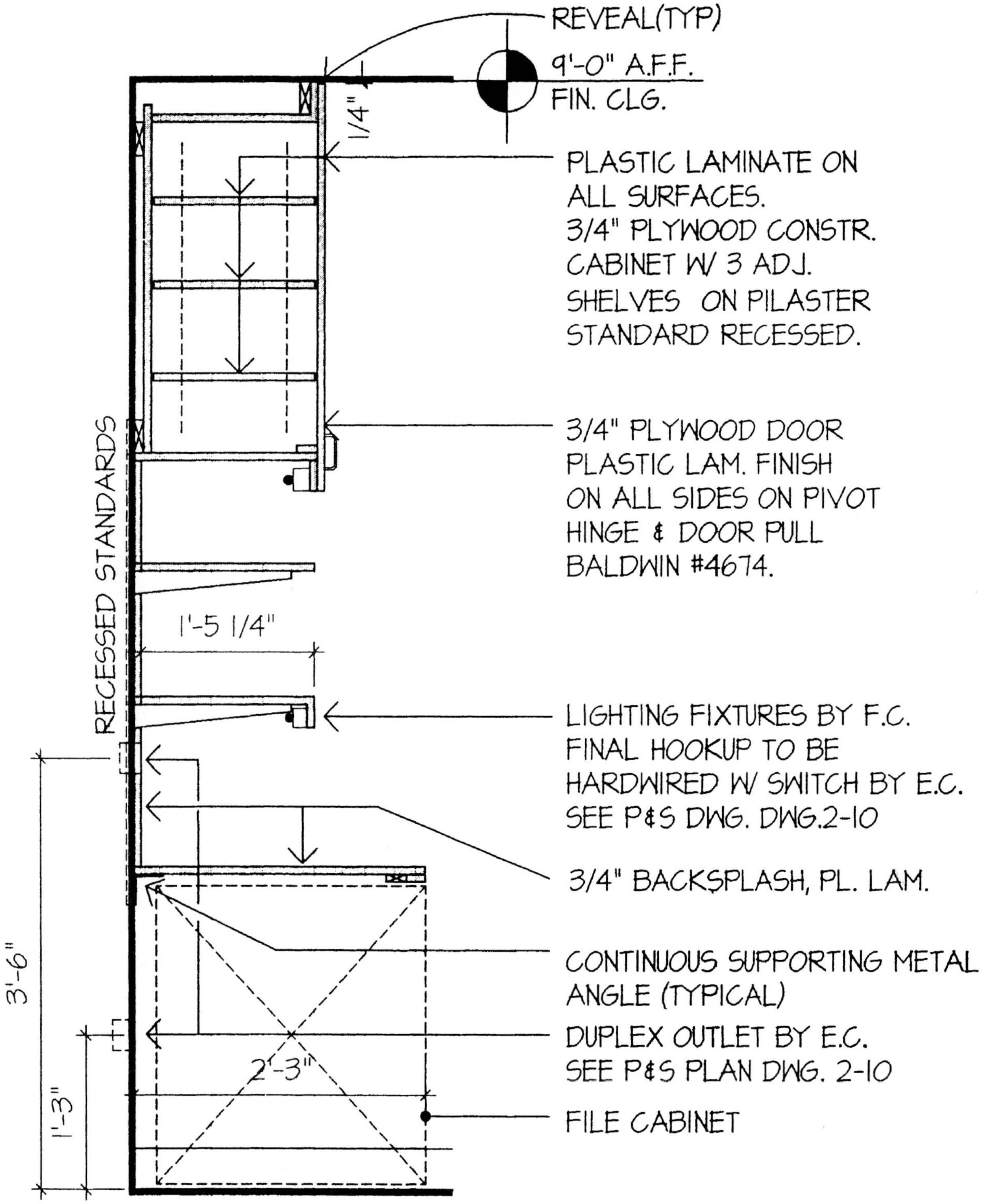
REVEAL(TYP)
9'-0" A.F.F.
FIN. CLG.
1/4"
PLASTIC LAMINATE ON ALL SURFACES. 3/4" PLYWOOD CONSTR. CABINET W/ 3 ADJ. SHELVES ON PILASTER STANDARD RECESSED.
3/4" PLYWOOD DOOR PLASTIC LAM. FINISH ON ALL SIDES ON PIVOT HINGE & DOOR PULL BALDWIN #4674.
RECESSED STANDARDS
1'-5 1/4"
LIGHTING FIXTURES BY F.C. FINAL HOOKUP TO BE HARDWIRED W/ SWITCH BY E.C. SEE P&S DWG. DWG.2-10
3/4" BACKSPLASH, PL. LAM.
CONTINUOUS SUPPORTING METAL ANGLE (TYPICAL)
DUPLEX OUTLET BY E.C. SEE P&S PLAN DWG. 2-10
FILE CABINET
3'-6"
1'-3"
2'-3"

OFFICE
G SECTION
SCALE: 3/4" = 1'-0"

SHOPS
Display Cases/Wall

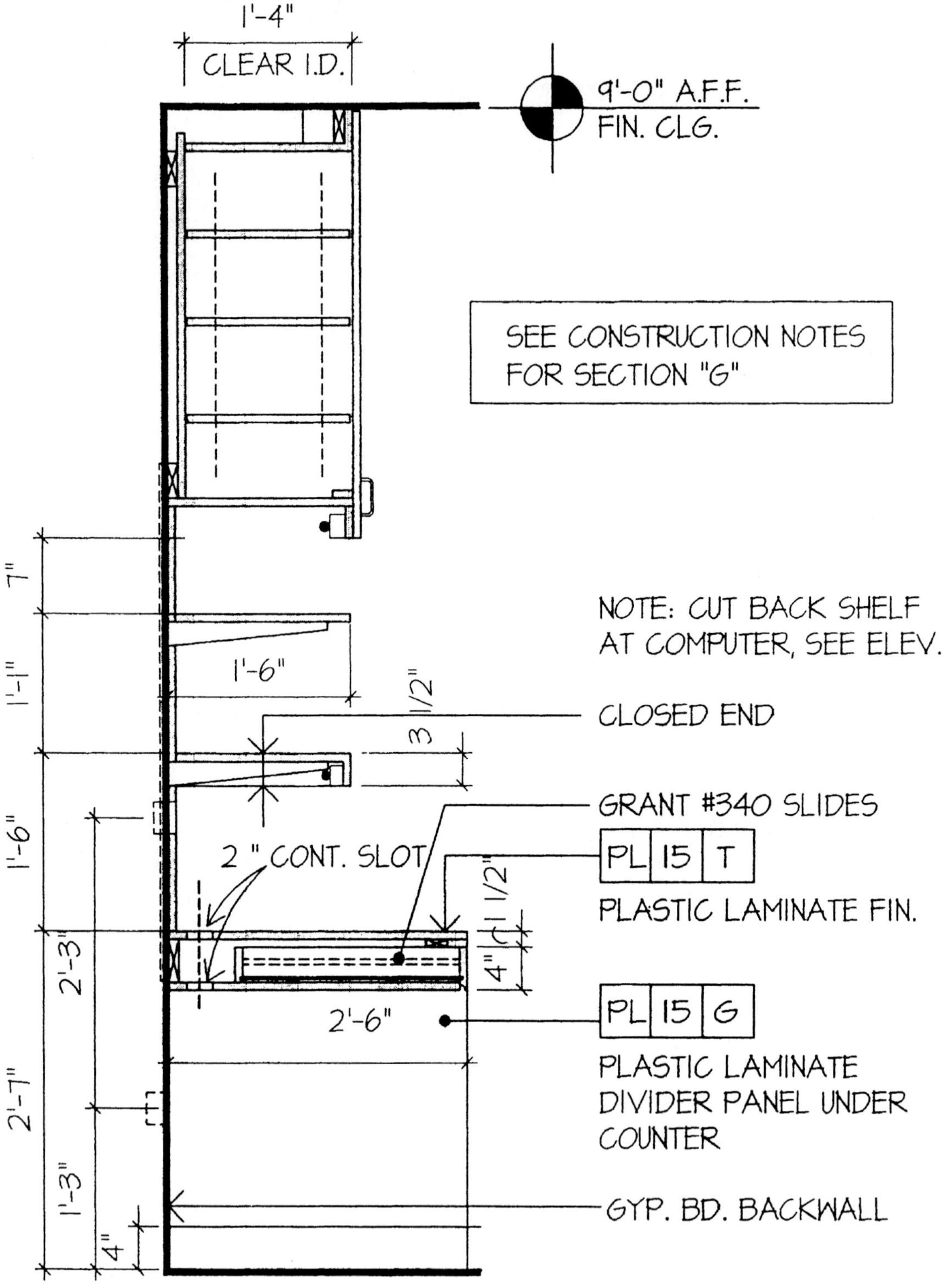

OFFICE
SECTION H
SCALE: 3/4" = 1'-0"

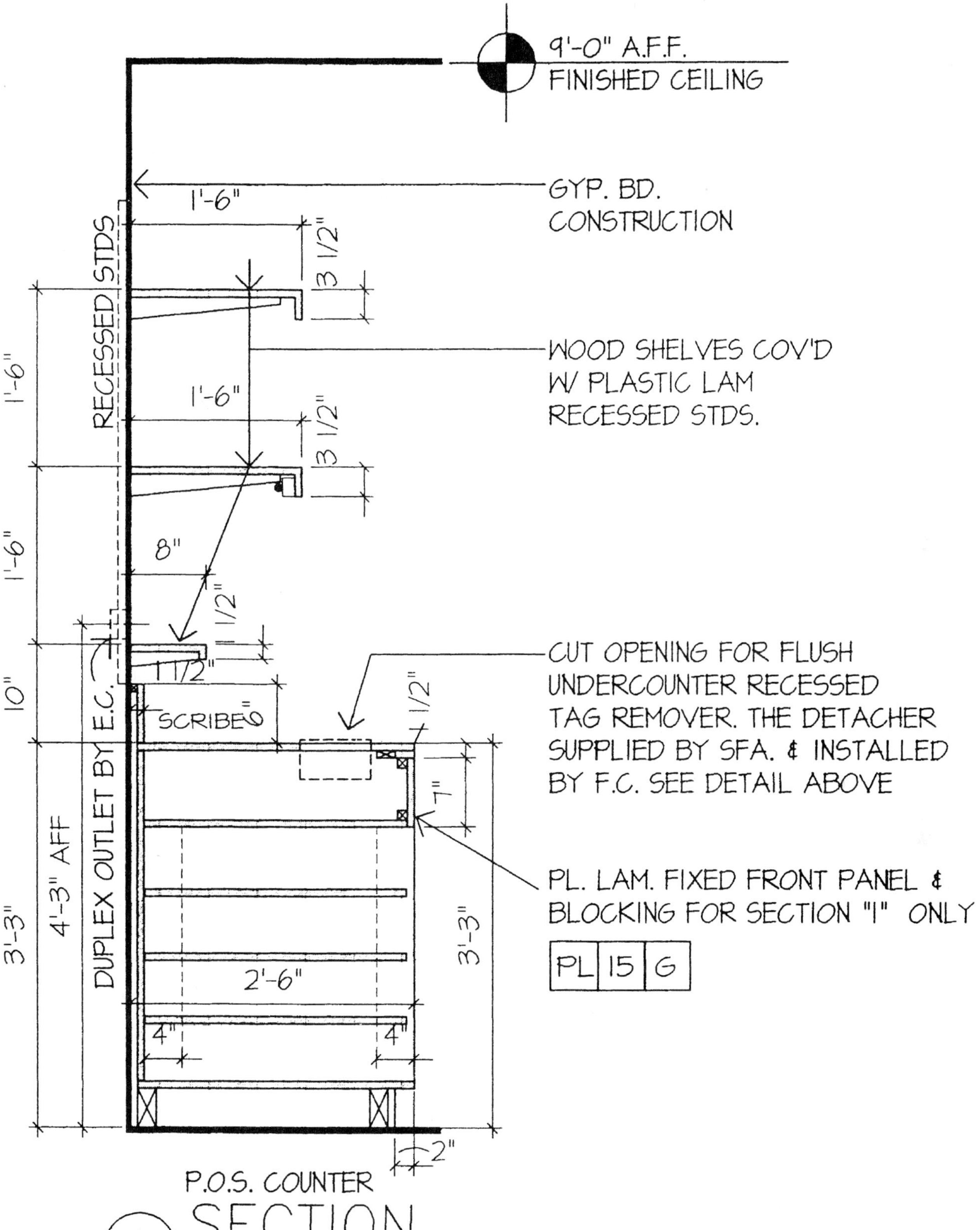
9'-0" A.F.F.
FINISHED CEILING
GYP. BD.
CONSTRUCTION
WOOD SHELVES COV'D
W/ PLASTIC LAM
RECESSED STDS.
CUT OPENING FOR FLUSH
UNDERCOUNTER RECESSED
TAG REMOVER. THE DETACHER
SUPPLIED BY SFA. & INSTALLED
BY F.C. SEE DETAIL ABOVE
PL. LAM. FIXED FRONT PANEL &
BLOCKING FOR SECTION "1" ONLY
PL 15 G
RECESSED STDS
DUPLEX OUTLET BY E.C.
4'-3" AFF
SCRIBE
1'-6"
3 1/2"
8"
1 1/2"
10"
3'-3"
2'-6"
4"
7"
2"

P.O.S. COUNTER
1 SECTION
SCALE: 3/4" = 1'-0"

SHOPS
Display Cases/Wall

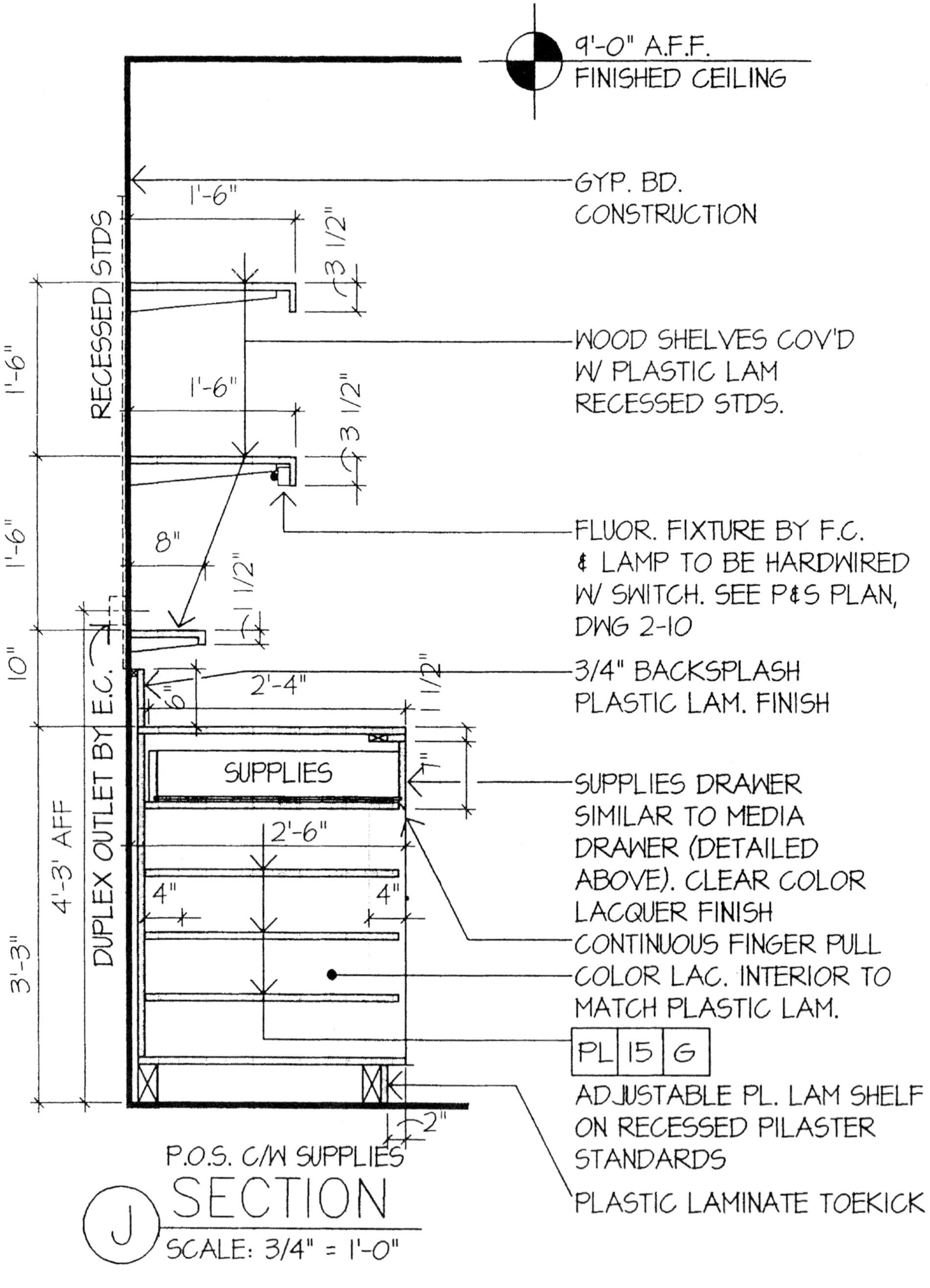
9'-0" A.F.F.
FINISHED CEILING
GYP. BD. CONSTRUCTION
1'-6"
3 1/2"
RECESSED STDS
WOOD SHELVES COV'D W/ PLASTIC LAM RECESSED STDS.
1'-6"
FLUOR. FIXTURE BY F.C. & LAMP TO BE HARDWIRED W/ SWITCH. SEE P&S PLAN, DWG 2-10
8"
1 1/2"
10"
3/4" BACKSPLASH PLASTIC LAM. FINISH
2'-4"
6"
SUPPLIES
SUPPLIES DRAWER SIMILAR TO MEDIA DRAWER (DETAILED ABOVE). CLEAR COLOR LACQUER FINISH
7"
2'-6"
4"
4"
CONTINUOUS FINGER PULL
COLOR LAC. INTERIOR TO MATCH PLASTIC LAM.
PL 15 G
ADJUSTABLE PL. LAM SHELF ON RECESSED PILASTER STANDARDS
PLASTIC LAMINATE TOEKICK
DUPLEX OUTLET BY E.C.
4'-3' AFF
3'-3"
2"
P.O.S. C/W SUPPLIES
J
SECTION
SCALE: 3/4" = 1'-0"

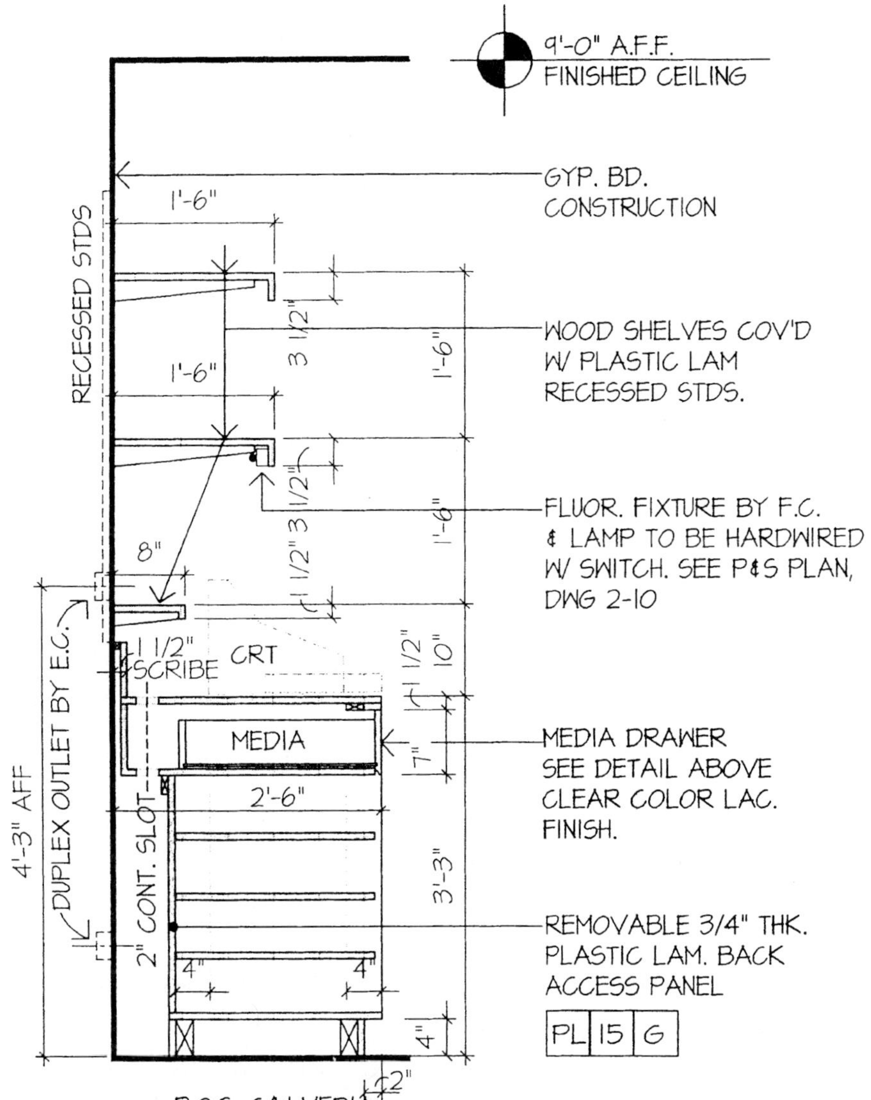

9'-0" A.F.F.
FINISHED CEILING
GYP. BD.
CONSTRUCTION
RECESSED STDS
1'-6"
3 1/2"
1'-6"
WOOD SHELVES COV'D
W/ PLASTIC LAM
RECESSED STDS.
FLUOR. FIXTURE BY F.C.
¢ LAMP TO BE HARDWIRED
W/ SWITCH. SEE P¢S PLAN,
DWG 2-10
8"
1 1/2"
SCRIBE
CRT
10"
MEDIA
MEDIA DRAWER
SEE DETAIL ABOVE
CLEAR COLOR LAC.
FINISH.
7"
2'-6"
3'-3"
4'-3" AFF
DUPLEX OUTLET BY E.C.
2" CONT. SLOT
REMOVABLE 3/4" THK.
PLASTIC LAM. BACK
ACCESS PANEL
PL 15 G
4"
2"
P.O.S. C/W MEDIA
K SECTION
SCALE: 3/4" = 1'-0"
1'-2"
6"
1 1/2"
5'-10" AFF
P.O.S. HANGING
L SECTION
SCALE: 3/4" = 1'-0"

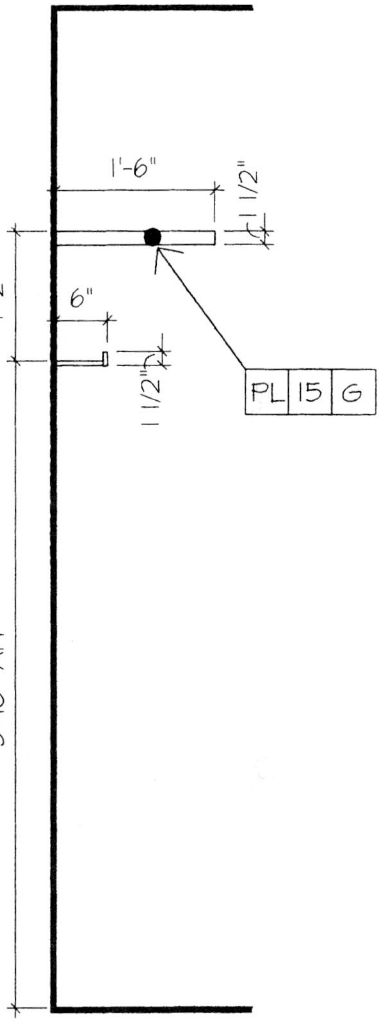

SHOPS
Sales Counter

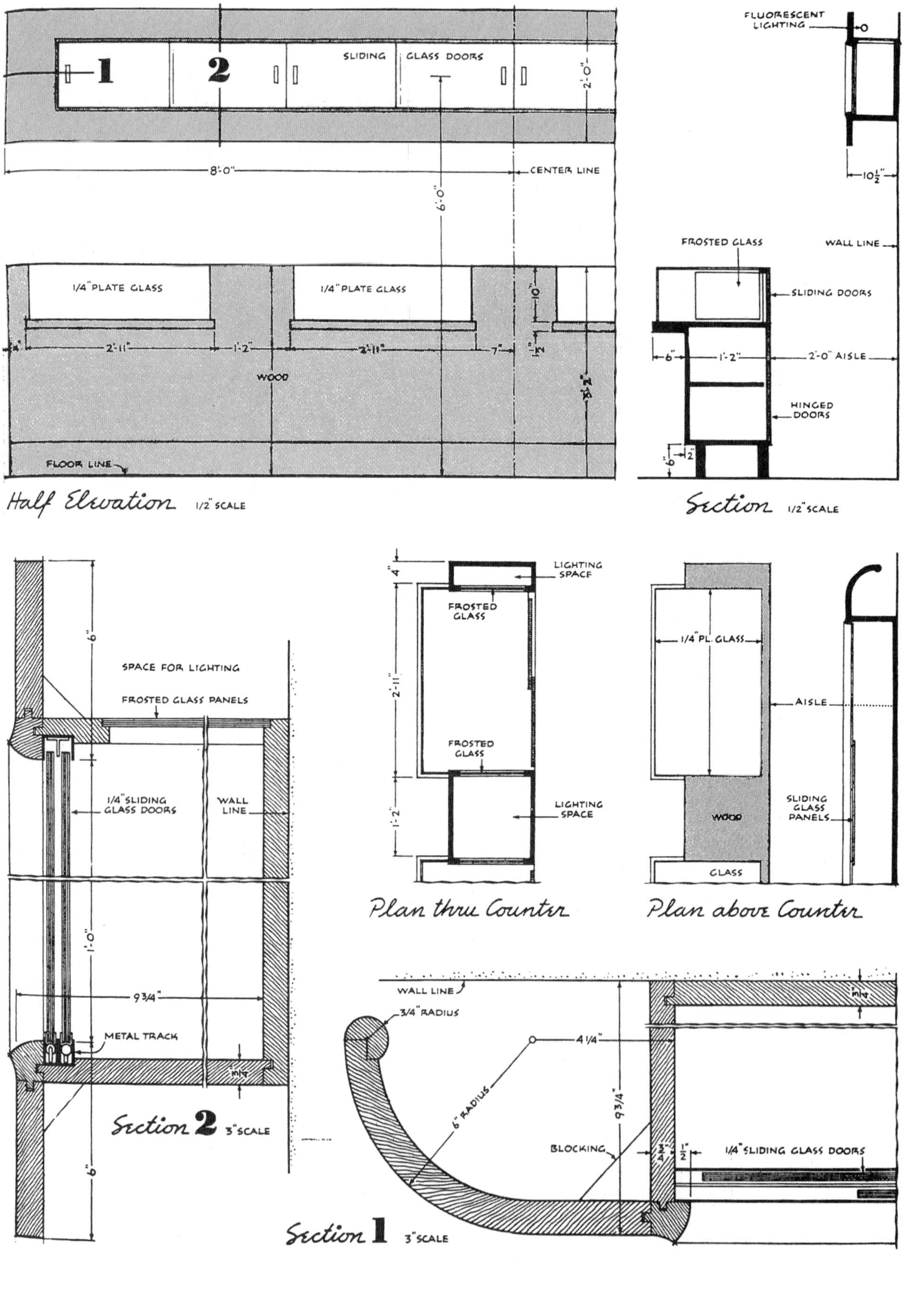

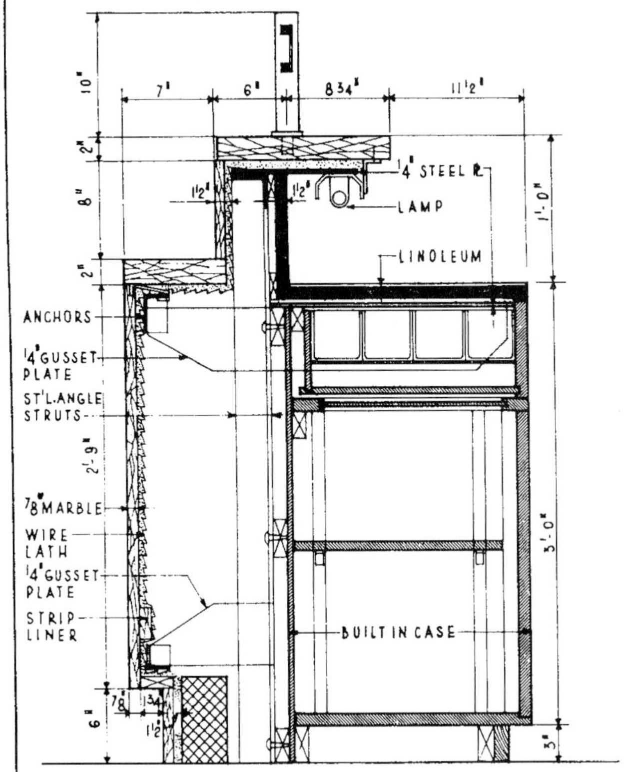

COUNTER WITH VERTICAL FRONT
3/4" = 1'-0"

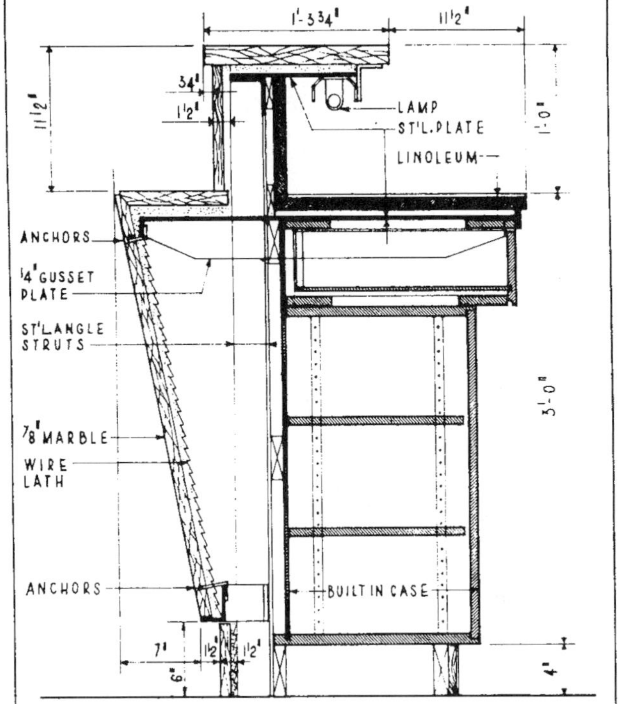

COUNTER WITH SLOPING FRONT
3/4" = 1'-0"

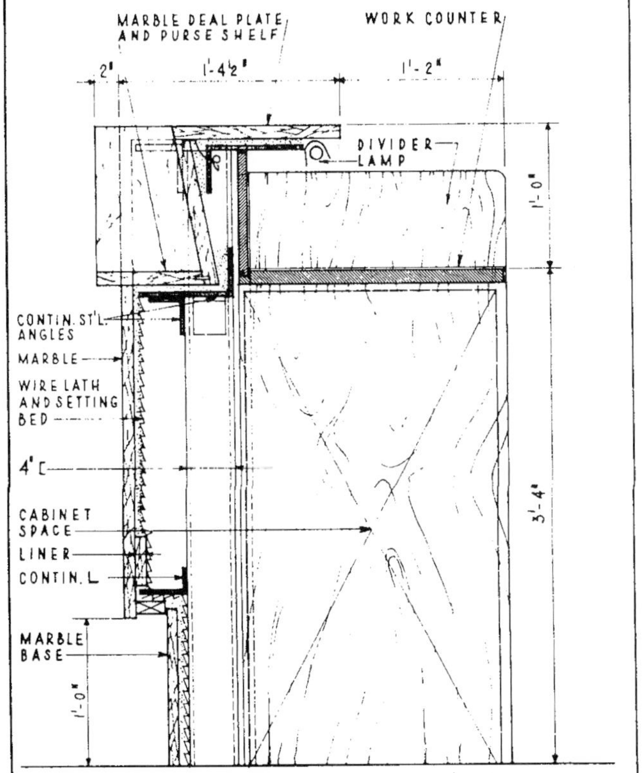

COUNTER WITH RECESSED PURSE SHELF
3/4" = 1'-0"

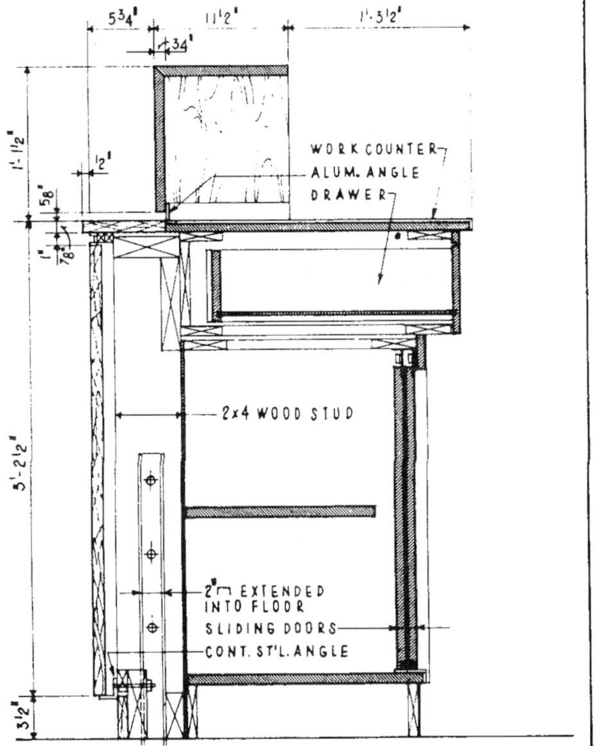

COUNTER ON WOOD FRAMING
3/4" = 1'-0"

SHOPS

Counter Details

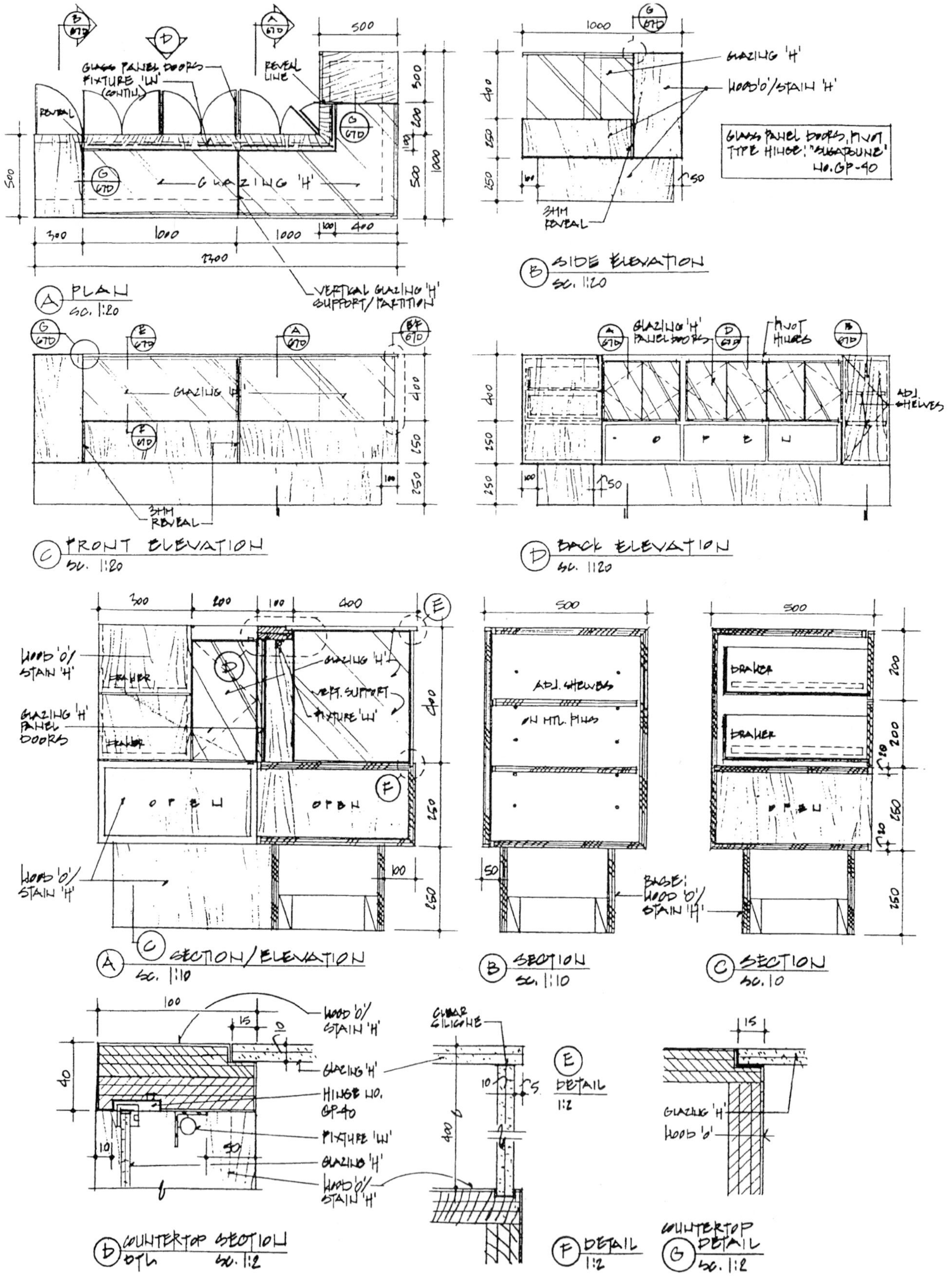

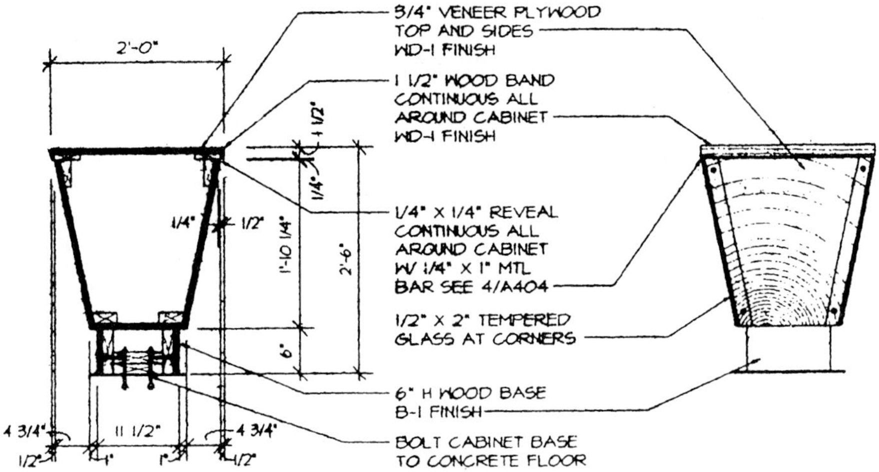

2'-0"
3/4" VENEER PLYWOOD TOP AND SIDES WD-1 FINISH
1 1/2" WOOD BAND CONTINUOUS ALL AROUND CABINET WD-1 FINISH
1/4" X 1/4" REVEAL CONTINUOUS ALL AROUND CABINET W/ 1/4" X 1" MTL BAR SEE 4/A404
1/2" X 2" TEMPERED GLASS AT CORNERS
6" H WOOD BASE B-1 FINISH
BOLT CABINET BASE TO CONCRETE FLOOR
1 1/2"
1/4"
1/2"
1'-10 1/4"
2'-6"
6"
4 3/4"
11 1/2"
1"
1/2"
1 A404 TYPICAL DISPLAY PEDESTAL
3/4" = 1'-0"
4'-0"Φ
3/4" VENEER PLYWOOD TOP WD-1 FINISH
1 1/2" WOOD BAND CONTINUOUS ALL AROUND CABINET WD-1 FINISH
1/4" X 1/4" REVEAL CONTINUOUS ALL AROUND CABINET W/ 1/4" X 1" MTL BAR SEE 4/A404
1/4" VENEER PLYWOOD OVER 1/4" PLYWOOD - BEND TO RADIUS (WD-1 FIN.)
6" H WOOD BASE B-1 FINISH
BOLT CABINET BASE TO CONCRETE FLOOR
2'-11 1/2"Φ
2 A404 FREESTANDING DISPLAY PEDESTAL
3/4" = 1'-0"

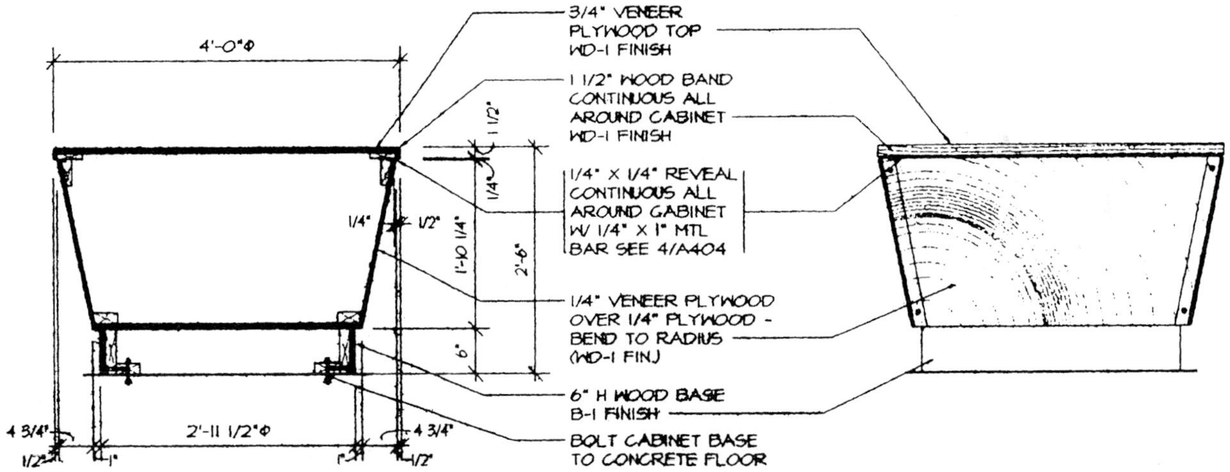

SHOPS

Pedestal and Cabinets

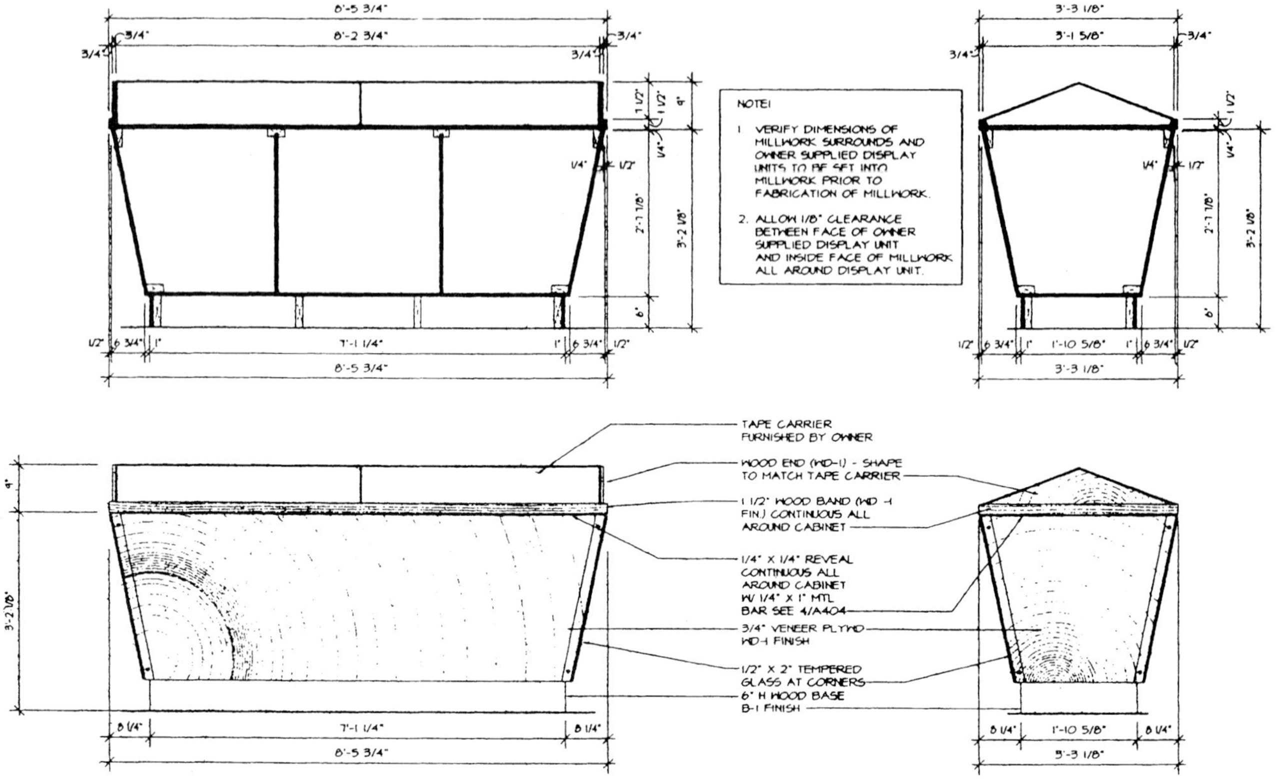

3/A404 FREESTANDING ISLAND CABINET
3/4" = 1'-0"

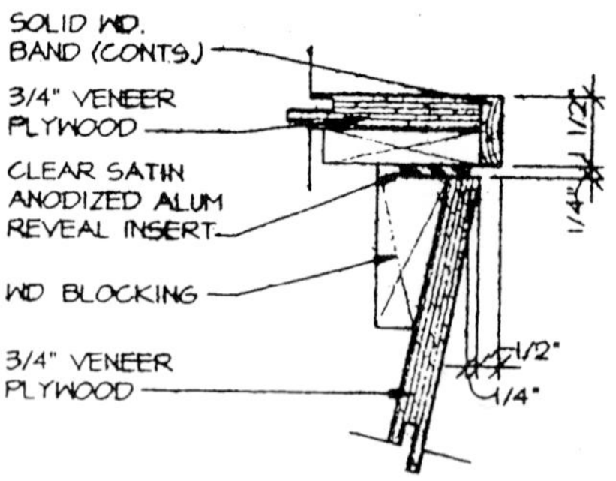

4/A404 TYPICAL REVEAL DETAIL
3" = 1'-0"

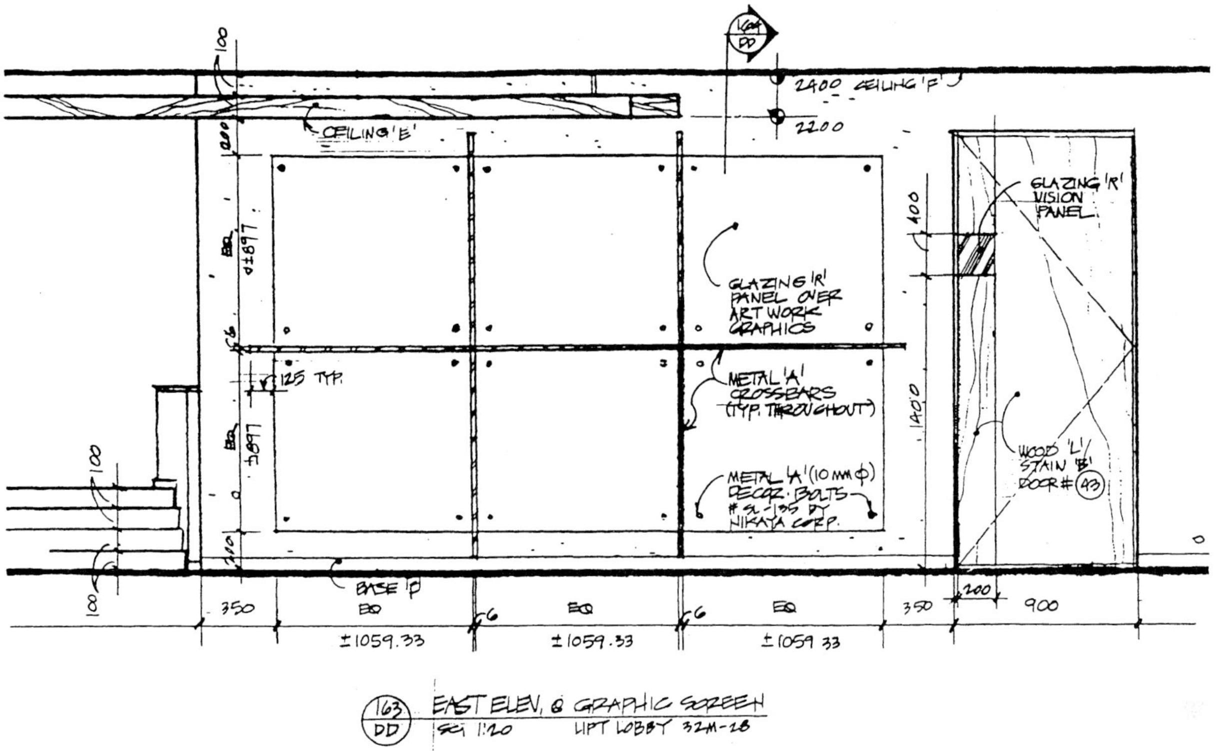
2400 CEILING 'F'
2200
CEILING 'E'
GLAZING 'R' PANEL OVER ART WORK GRAPHICS
METAL 'A' CROSSBARS (TYP. THROUGHOUT)
METAL 'A' (10 MM Φ) DECOR. BOLTS # SL-135 BY NIKAYA CORP.
GLAZING 'R' VISION PANEL
WOOD 'L' STAIN 'B' DOOR # 43
125 TYP.
BASE 'P'
350
EQ
±1059.33
900
EAST ELEV. @ GRAPHIC SCREEN
SC. 1:20
LIFT LOBBY 32M-28

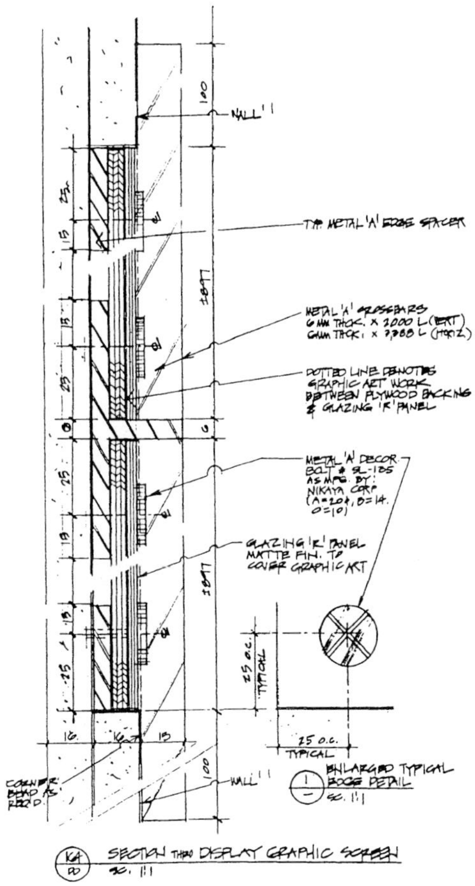
WALL 'I'
TYP. METAL 'A' EDGE SPACER
METAL 'A' CROSSBARS
DOTTED LINE DENOTES GRAPHIC ART WORK BETWEEN PLYWOOD BACKING & GLAZING 'R' PANEL
METAL 'A' DECOR BOLT # SL-135 AS MFG. BY: NIKAYA CORP.
GLAZING 'R' PANEL MATTE FIN. TO COVER GRAPHIC ART
25 O.C. TYPICAL
ENLARGED TYPICAL EDGE DETAIL
SC. 1:1
CORNER BEAD AS REQ'D.
SECTION THRU DISPLAY GRAPHIC SCREEN
SC. 1:1

SHOPS

Column Details

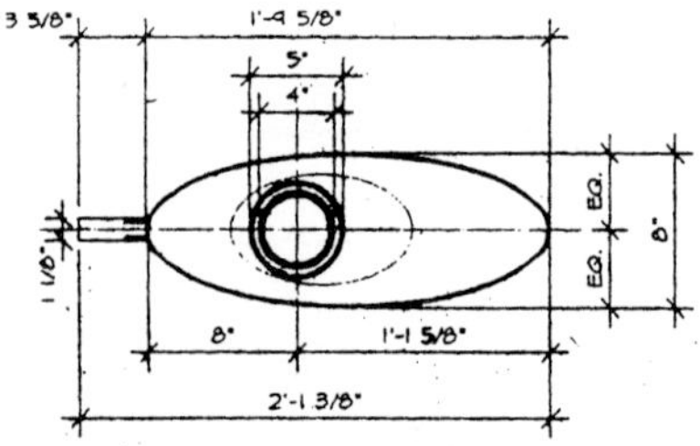

3 DETAIL @COL.TOP
A611 SCALE: 1 1/2" = 1'-0"

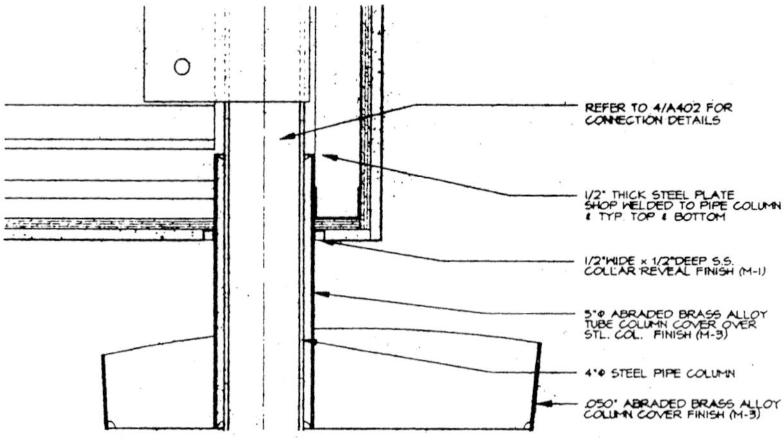

6 DETAIL @COL.TOP
A611 SCALE: 3"=1'-0"

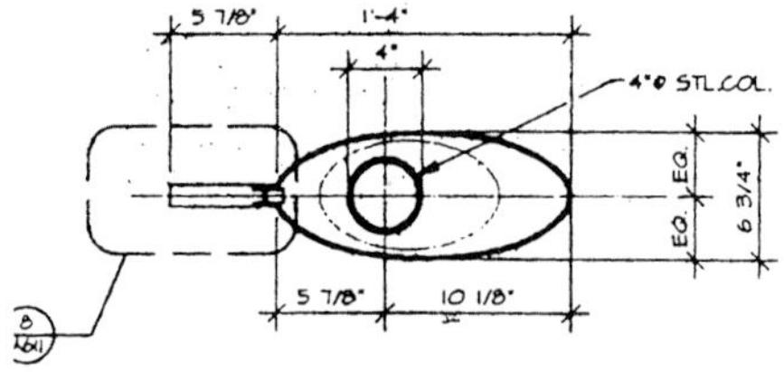

4 DETAIL @COL.MID.PT.
A611 SCALE: 1 1/2" = 1'-0"

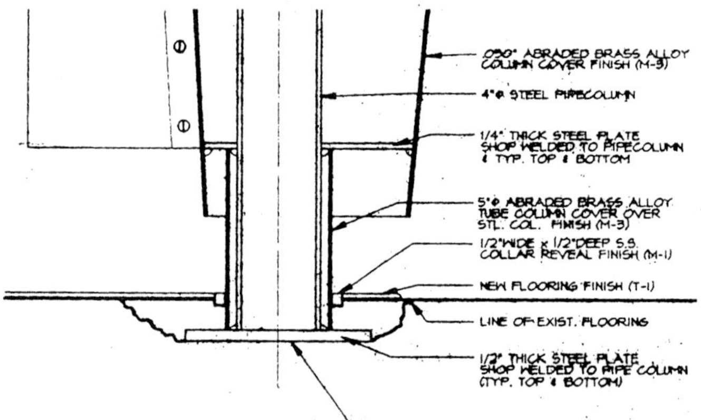

7 DETAIL @COL.BAS.
A611 SCALE: 3"=1'-0"

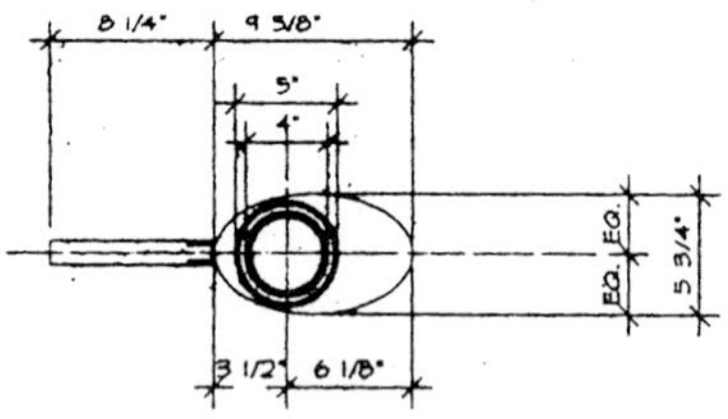

5 DETAIL @COL.BOTTOM
A611 SCALE: 1 1/2" = 1'-0"

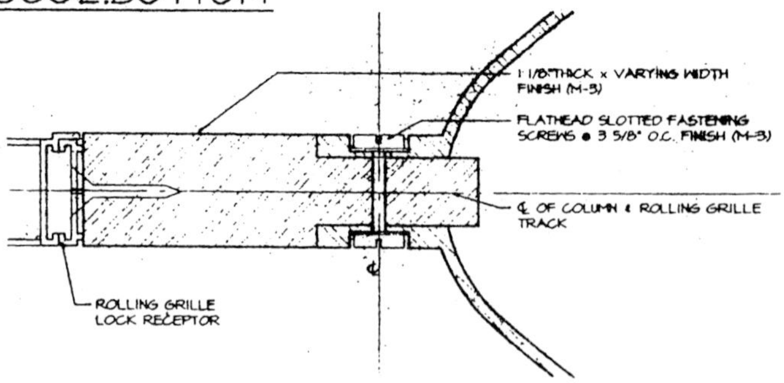

8 FIN DETAIL
A611 SCALE: FULL

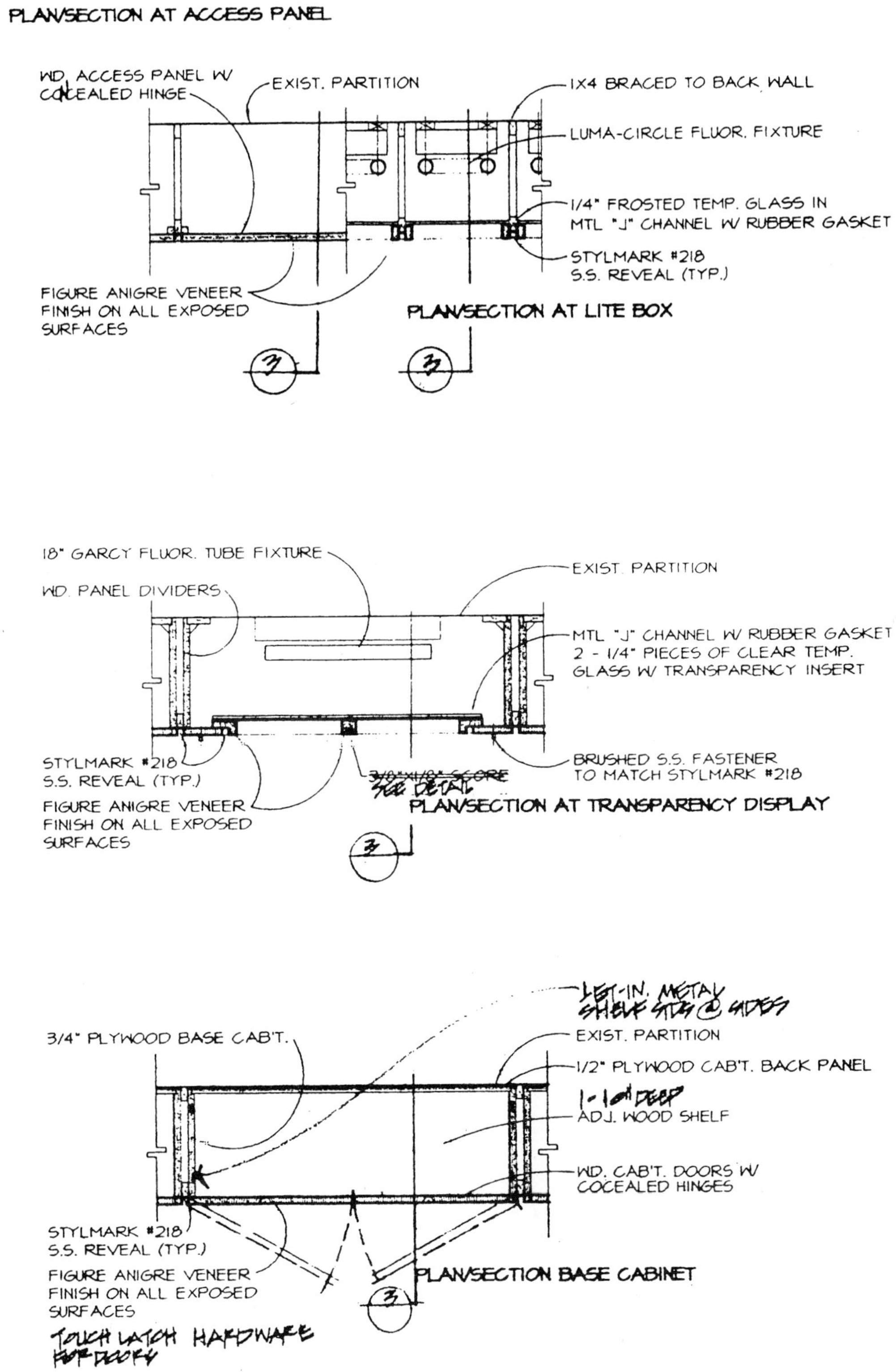
PLAN/SECTION AT ACCESS PANEL
WD. ACCESS PANEL W/ COCEALED HINGE
EXIST. PARTITION
1X4 BRACED TO BACK WALL
LUMA-CIRCLE FLUOR. FIXTURE
1/4" FROSTED TEMP. GLASS IN MTL "J" CHANNEL W/ RUBBER GASKET
STYLMARK #218 S.S. REVEAL (TYP.)
FIGURE ANIGRE VENEER FINISH ON ALL EXPOSED SURFACES
PLAN/SECTION AT LITE BOX
3
3
18" GARCY FLUOR. TUBE FIXTURE
WD. PANEL DIVIDERS
EXIST. PARTITION
MTL "J" CHANNEL W/ RUBBER GASKET
2 - 1/4" PIECES OF CLEAR TEMP. GLASS W/ TRANSPARENCY INSERT
STYLMARK #218 S.S. REVEAL (TYP.)
BRUSHED S.S. FASTENER TO MATCH STYLMARK #218
FIGURE ANIGRE VENEER FINISH ON ALL EXPOSED SURFACES
PLAN/SECTION AT TRANSPARENCY DISPLAY
3
LET-IN. METAL SHELF STDS @ SIDES
3/4" PLYWOOD BASE CAB'T.
EXIST. PARTITION
1/2" PLYWOOD CAB'T. BACK PANEL
ADJ. WOOD SHELF
WD. CAB'T. DOORS W/ COCEALED HINGES
STYLMARK #218 S.S. REVEAL (TYP.)
FIGURE ANIGRE VENEER FINISH ON ALL EXPOSED SURFACES
TOUCH LATCH HARDWARE FOR DOORS
PLAN/SECTION BASE CABINET
3

1 TYPICAL WALL CABINET DETAILS
A402 1" = 1'-0"

SHOPS

Wall Cabinet Details/Light Box

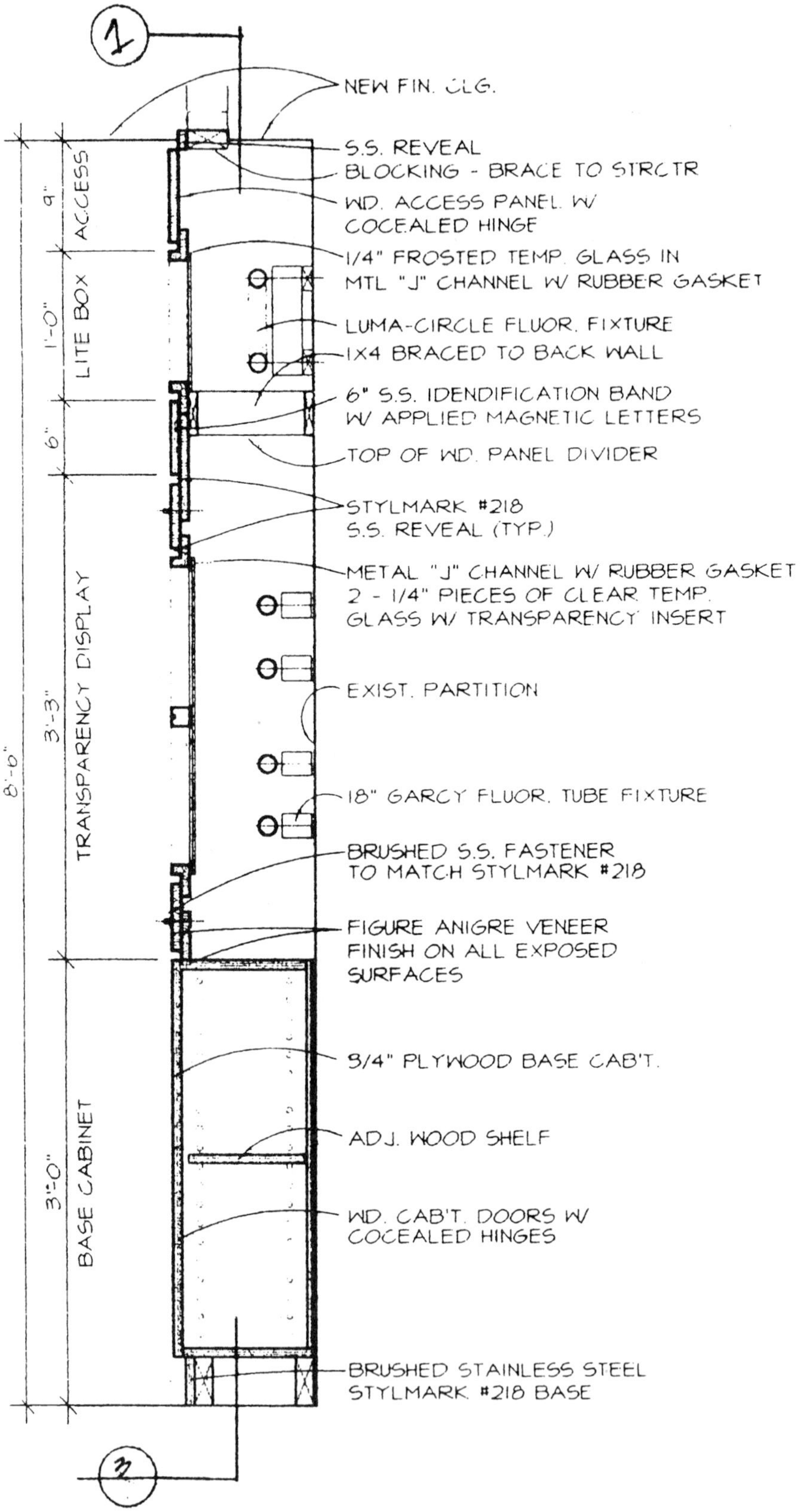
1
NEW FIN. CLG.
S.S. REVEAL
BLOCKING - BRACE TO STRCTR
WD. ACCESS PANEL W/
COCEALED HINGE
1/4" FROSTED TEMP. GLASS IN
MTL "J" CHANNEL W/ RUBBER GASKET
LUMA-CIRCLE FLUOR. FIXTURE
1X4 BRACED TO BACK WALL
6" S.S. IDENDIFICATION BAND
W/ APPLIED MAGNETIC LETTERS
TOP OF WD. PANEL DIVIDER
STYLMARK #218
S.S. REVEAL (TYP.)
METAL "J" CHANNEL W/ RUBBER GASKET
2 - 1/4" PIECES OF CLEAR TEMP.
GLASS W/ TRANSPARENCY INSERT
EXIST. PARTITION
18" GARCY FLUOR. TUBE FIXTURE
BRUSHED S.S. FASTENER
TO MATCH STYLMARK #218
FIGURE ANIGRE VENEER
FINISH ON ALL EXPOSED
SURFACES
3/4" PLYWOOD BASE CAB'T.
ADJ. WOOD SHELF
WD. CAB'T. DOORS W/
COCEALED HINGES
BRUSHED STAINLESS STEEL
STYLMARK #218 BASE
9"
ACCESS
1'-0"
LITE BOX
6"
3'-3"
TRANSPARENCY DISPLAY
8'-6"
3'-0"
BASE CABINET
2

1 A402 TYPICAL WALL CABINET DETAILS

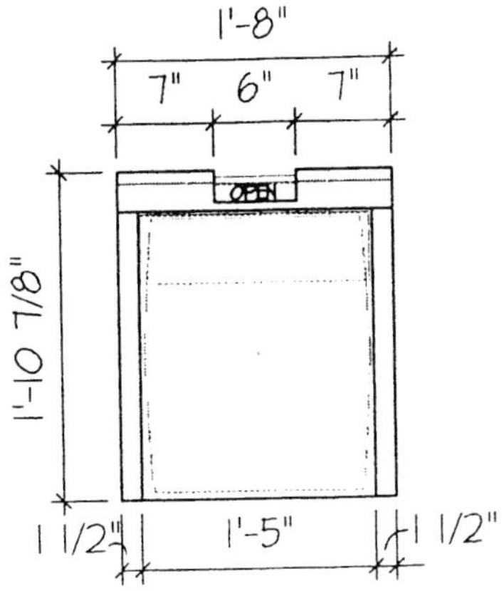

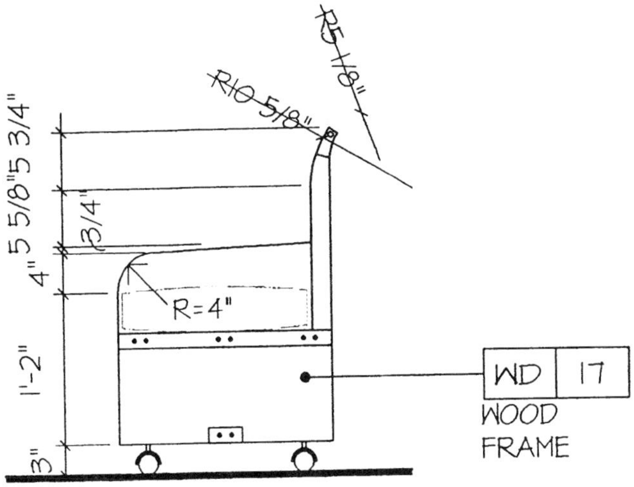

CHAIR PLAN

SCALE: 3/4" = 1'-0"

SIDE ELEV.

SCALE: 3/4" = 1'-0"

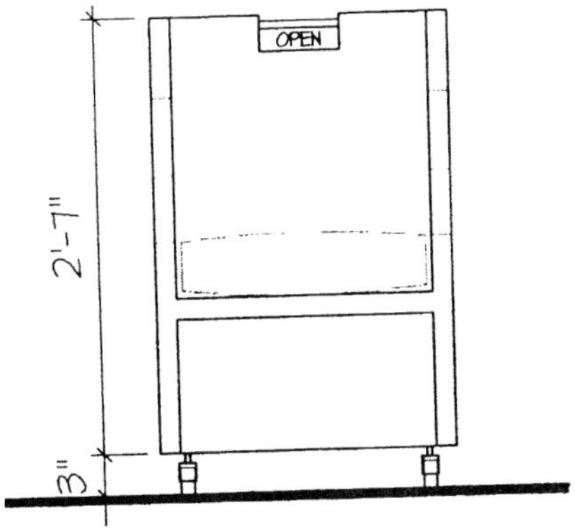

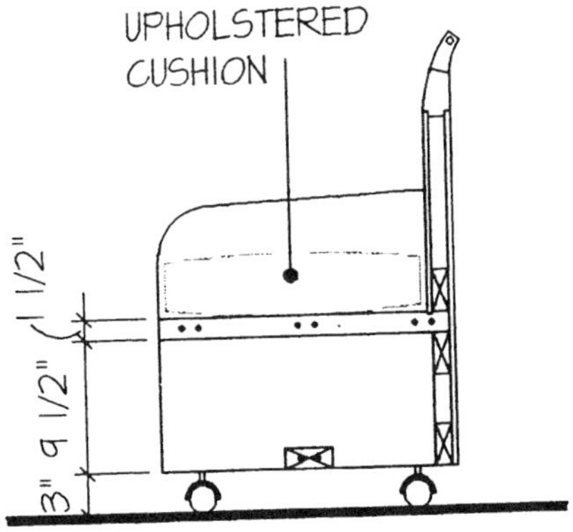

FRONT ELEV.

SCALE: 3/4" = 1'-0"

SECTION

SCALE: 3/4" = 1'-0"

CHAIR UPHOLSTERY:
CLARENCE HOUSE
(212)752-2890
ATTEN: JOHN HOWARD
ITEM # 10369/36-50"WIDE
4 WEEKS LEAD TIME
$16.00 PER YARD
FLAMEPROOF & SCOTCHGUARDED
ALLOW 2 WEEKS ADDITONAL
LEAD TIME

SHOPS

Upholstered Seating/Stool

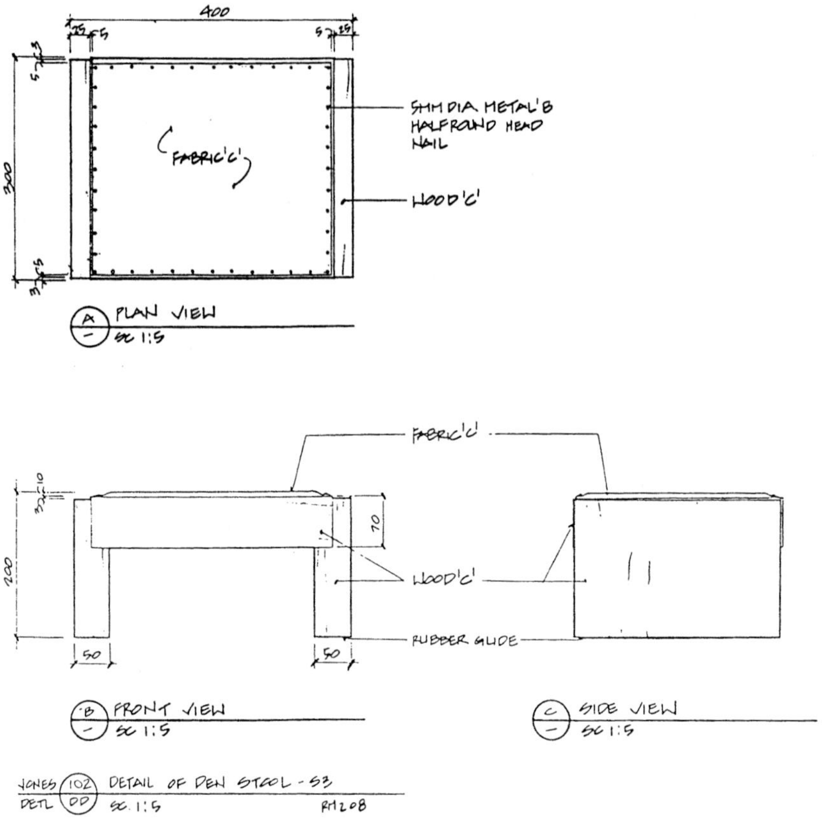

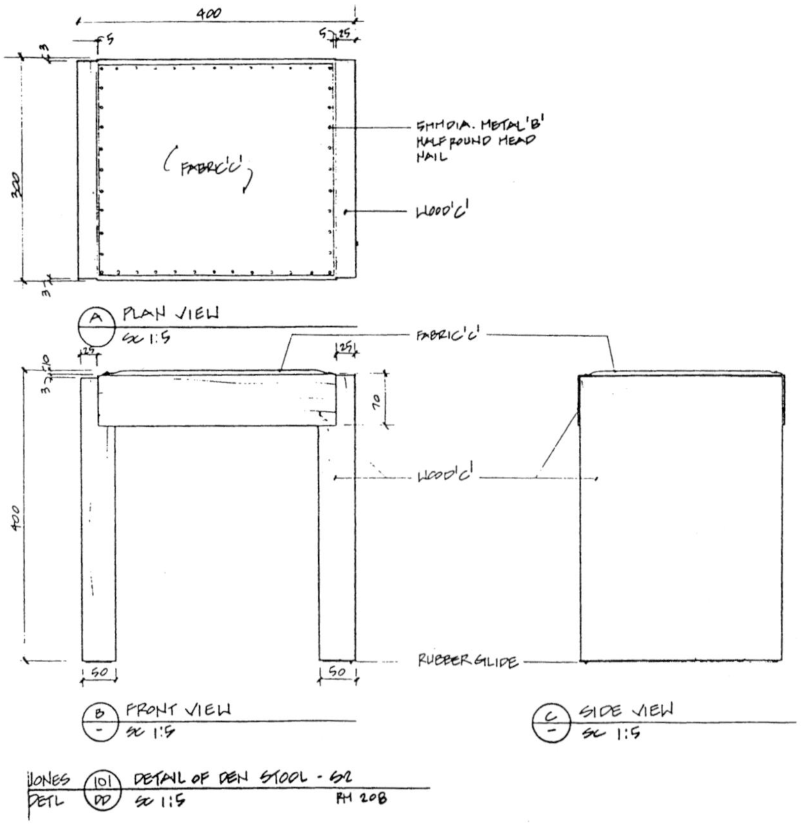

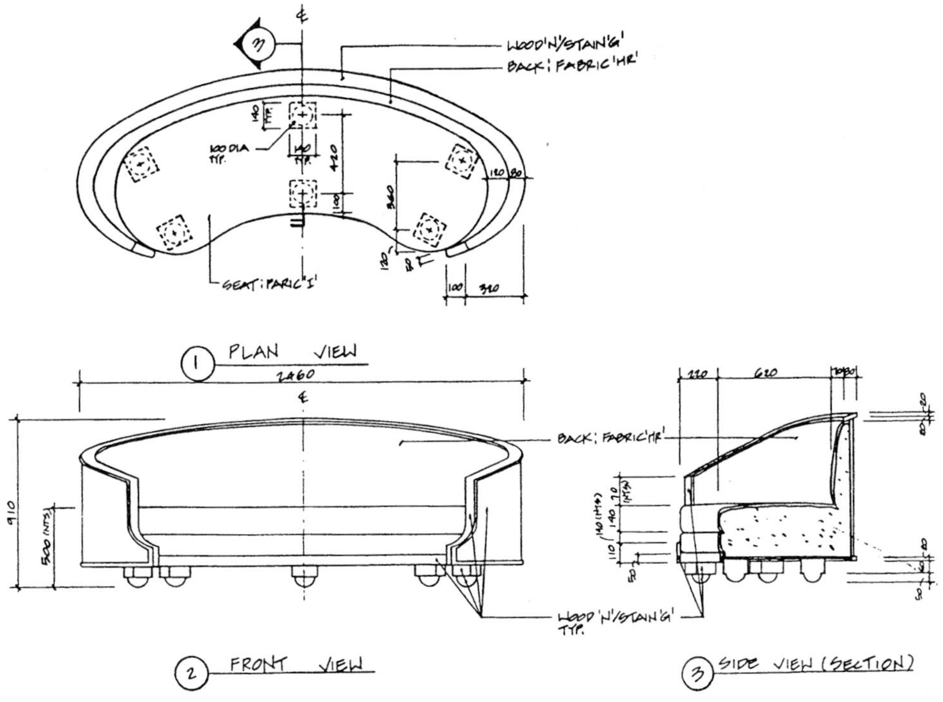

171/DD DETAIL OF SOFA C3
SC. 1:20 DINING QUARTER 32ND FL.

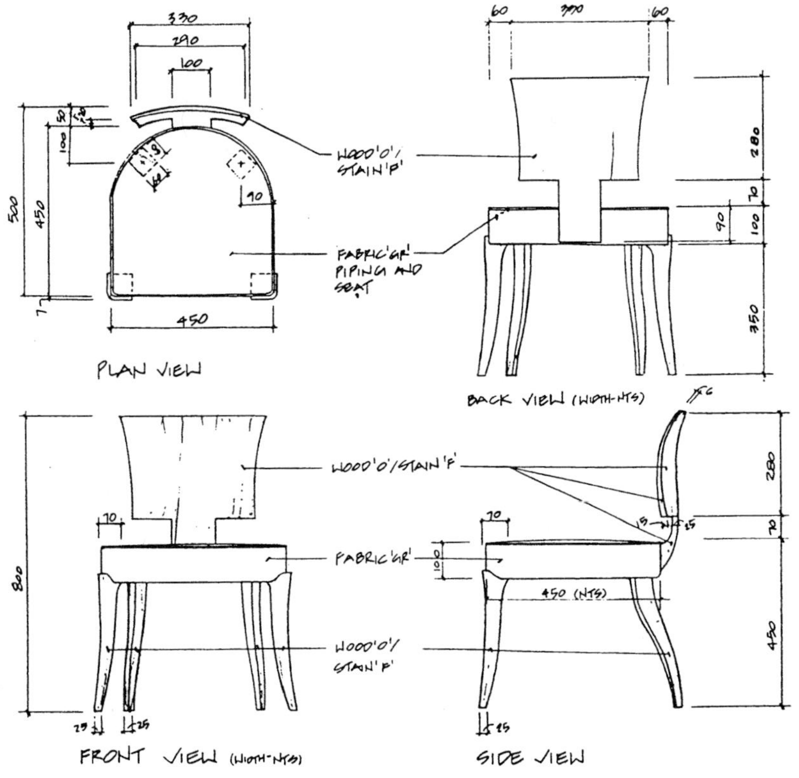

172/DD DETAIL OF CHAIR C4
SC. 1:10 DINING QUARTER 32ND FL

DEPARTMENT STORES

Fashion and Fine Jewelry Back Island Details

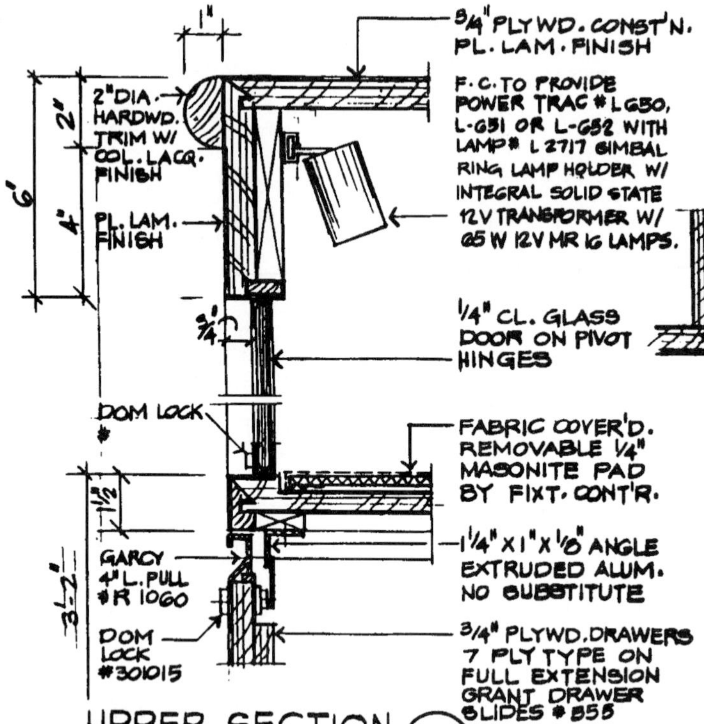

UPPER SECTION (A)
SCALE: 3" = 1'-0".

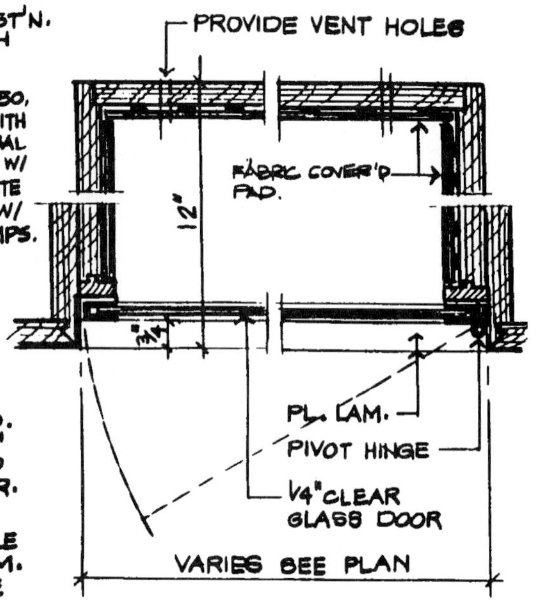

PLAN SECTION (B)
SCALE: 3" = 1'-0".

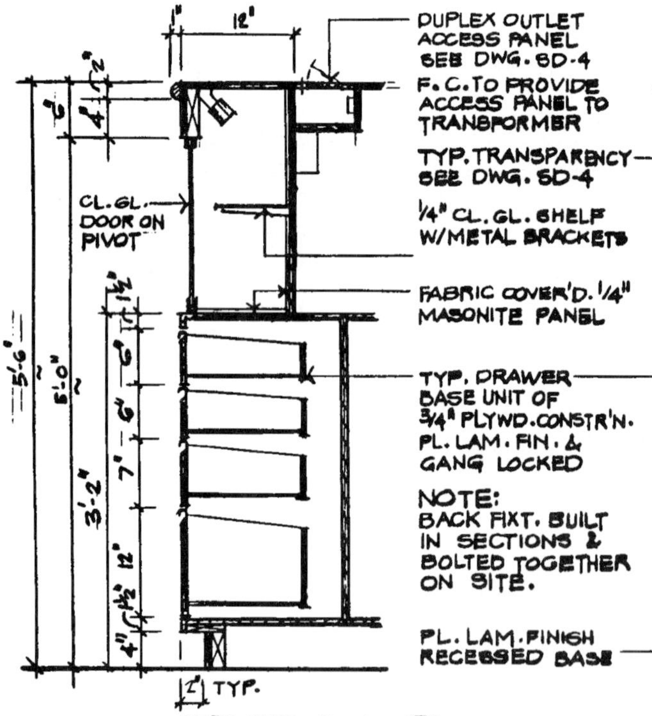

SECTION (1)
SCALE: 3/4" = 1'-0"

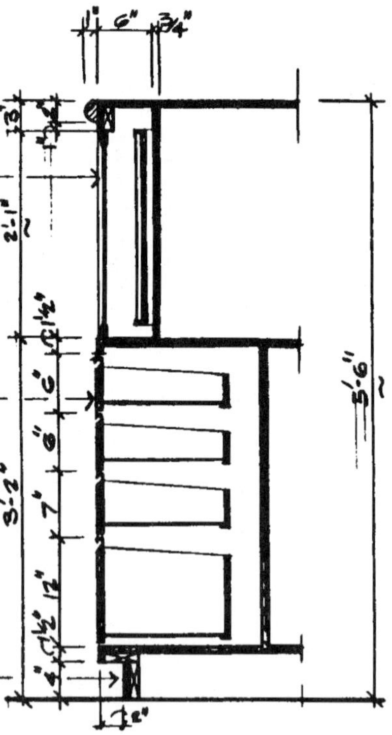

SECTION (2)
SCALE: 3/4" = 1'-0"

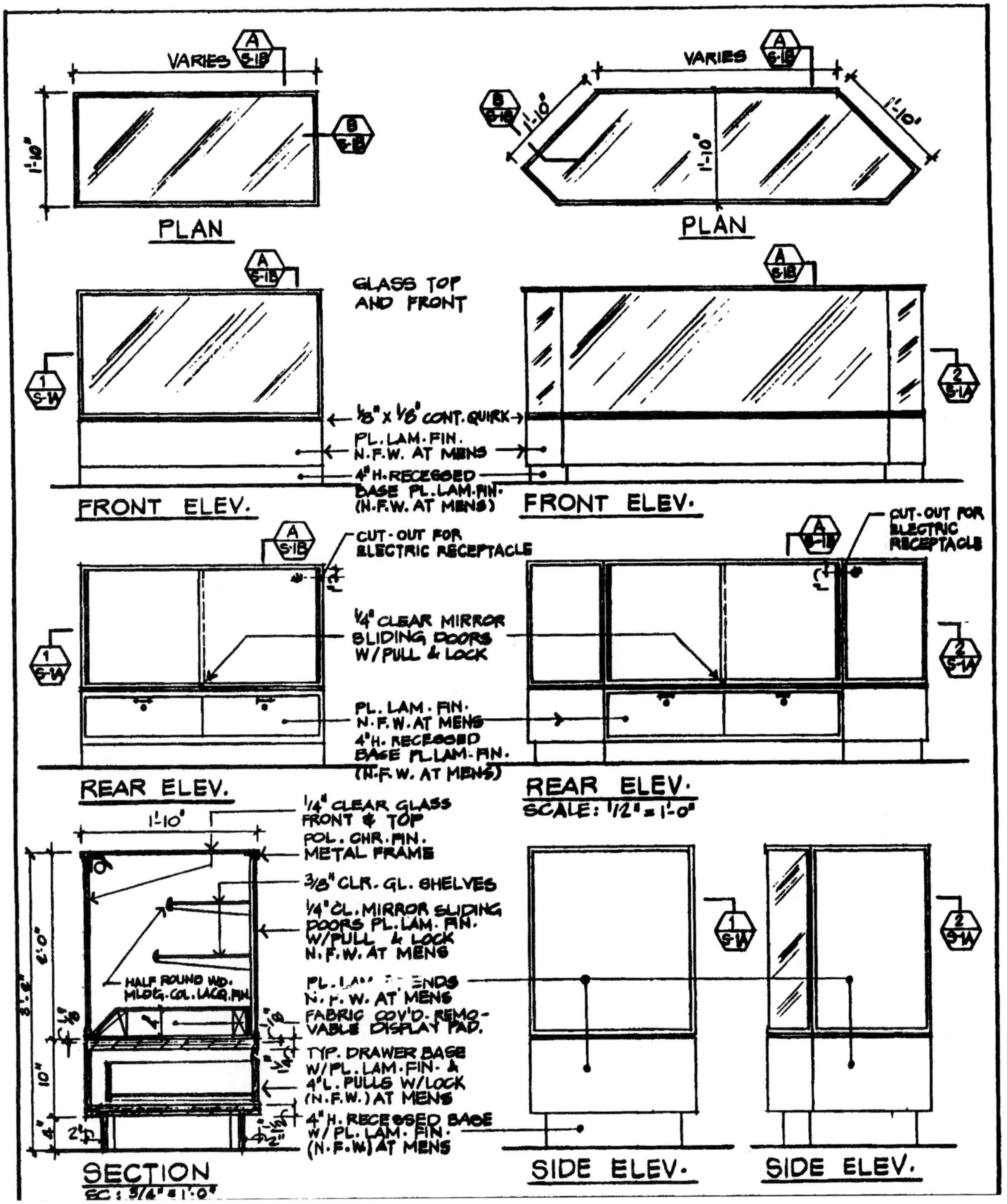
VARIES
1'-10"
PLAN
1'-10"
PLAN
GLASS TOP AND FRONT
1/8" x 1/8" CONT. QUIRK
PL. LAM. FIN. N.F.W. AT MENS
4" H. RECESSED BASE PL. LAM. FIN. (N.F.W. AT MENS)
FRONT ELEV.
FRONT ELEV.
CUT-OUT FOR ELECTRIC RECEPTACLE
1/4" CLEAR MIRROR SLIDING DOORS W/PULL & LOCK
PL. LAM. FIN. N.F.W. AT MENS
4" H. RECESSED BASE PL. LAM. FIN. (N.F.W. AT MENS)
REAR ELEV.
REAR ELEV.
SCALE: 1/2" = 1'-0"
1/4" CLEAR GLASS FRONT & TOP
POL. CHR. FIN. METAL FRAME
3/8" CLR. GL. SHELVES
1/4" CL. MIRROR SLIDING DOORS PL. LAM. FIN. W/PULL & LOCK N.F.W. AT MENS
HALF ROUND WD. MLDG. COL. LACQ. FIN.
N.F.W. AT MENS
FABRIC COV'D. REMOVABLE DISPLAY PAD.
TYP. DRAWER BASE W/PL. LAM. FIN. & 4" L. PULLS W/LOCK (N.F.W.) AT MENS
4" H. RECESSED BASE W/PL. LAM. FIN. (N.F.W.) AT MENS
SECTION
SIDE ELEV.
SIDE ELEV.

DEPARTMENT STORES

Showcase for Men's Cosmetics and Fragrances

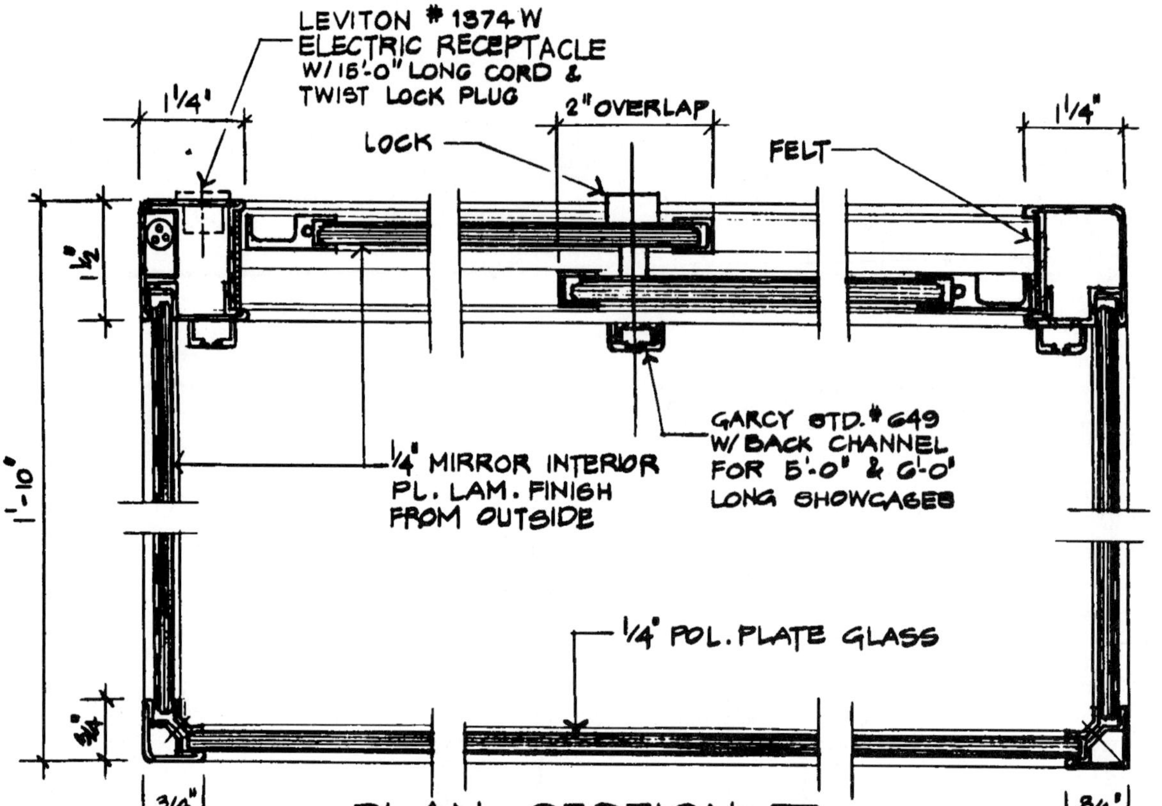

PLAN SECTION 1
SCALE: HALF FULL SIZE.

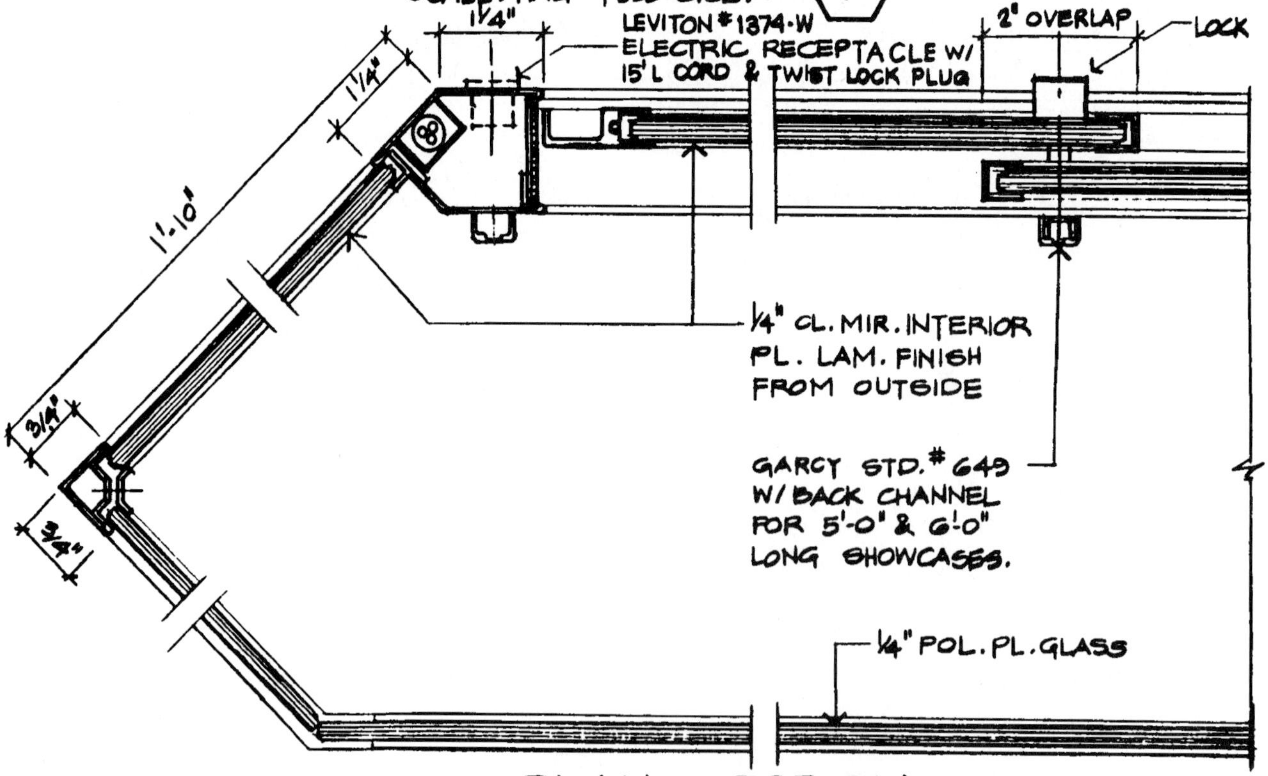

PLAN SECTION 2
SCALE: HALF FULL SIZE.

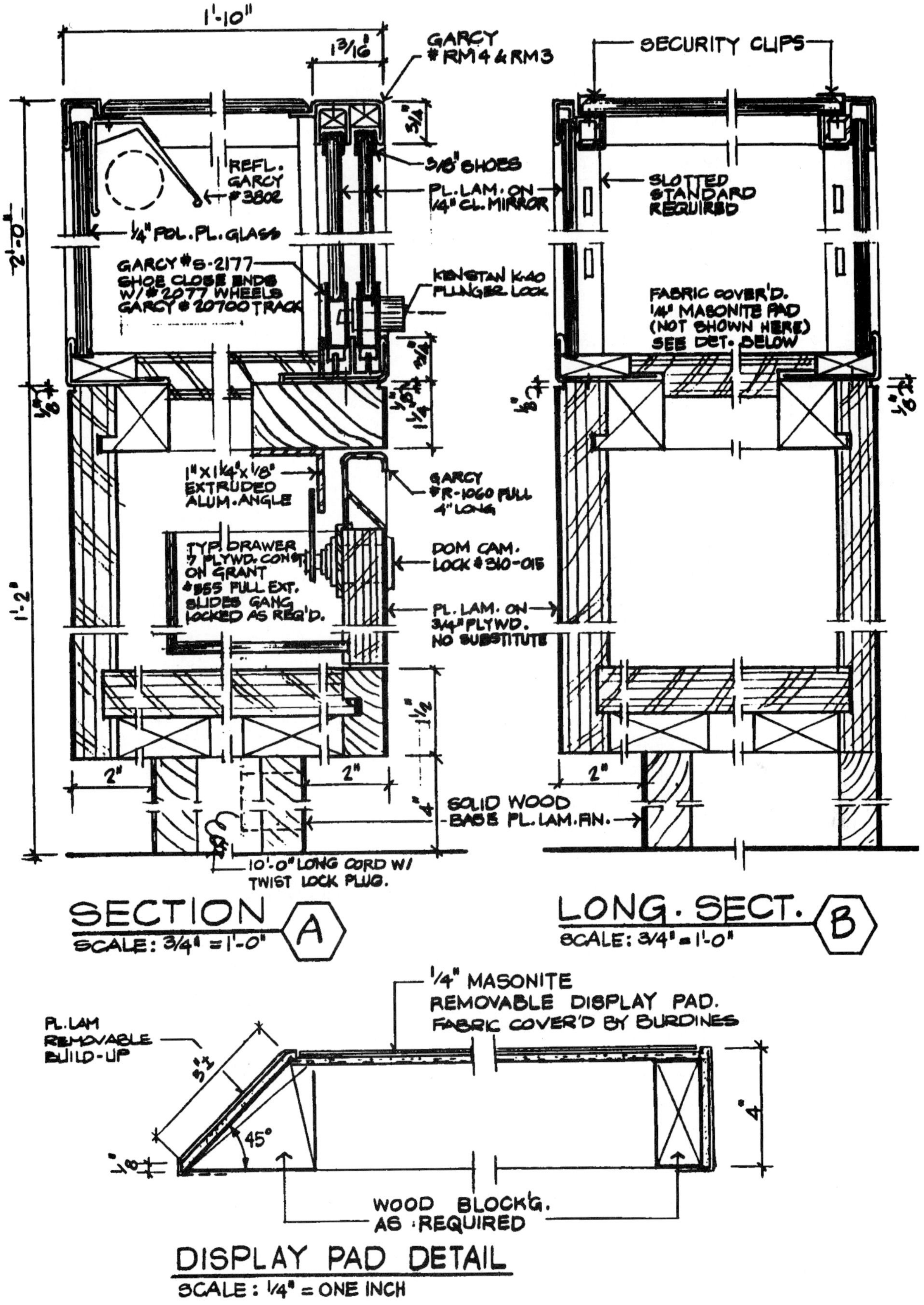
1'-10"
13/16"
GARCY #RM4 & RM3
3/16" SHOES
REFL. GARCY #3802
1/4" POL. PL. GLASS
PL. LAM. ON 1/4" CL. MIRROR
GARCY #S-2177 SHOE CLOSE ENDS W/#2077 WHEELS GARCY #20700 TRACK
KENSTAN K-40 PLUNGER LOCK
1"X1 1/4"X1/8" EXTRUDED ALUM. ANGLE
GARCY #R-1060 PULL 4" LONG
TYP. DRAWER 1/2" PLYWD. CONST. ON GRANT #355 FULL EXT. SLIDES GANG LOCKED AS REQ'D.
DOM CAM. LOCK #310-015
PL. LAM. ON 3/4" PLYWD. NO SUBSTITUTE
SOLID WOOD BASE PL. LAM. FIN.
10'-0" LONG CORD W/ TWIST LOCK PLUG.
2'-0"
1'-2"
2"
SECURITY CLIPS
SLOTTED STANDARD REQUIRED
FABRIC COVER'D. 1/4" MASONITE PAD (NOT SHOWN HERE) SEE DET. BELOW
SECTION A
SCALE: 3/4" = 1'-0"
LONG. SECT. B
SCALE: 3/4" = 1'-0"
1/4" MASONITE REMOVABLE DISPLAY PAD. FABRIC COVER'D BY BURDINES
PL. LAM REMOVABLE BUILD-UP
45°
4"
WOOD BLOCK'G. AS REQUIRED
DISPLAY PAD DETAIL
SCALE: 1/4" = ONE INCH

DEPARTMENT STORES

Display Case/Freestanding

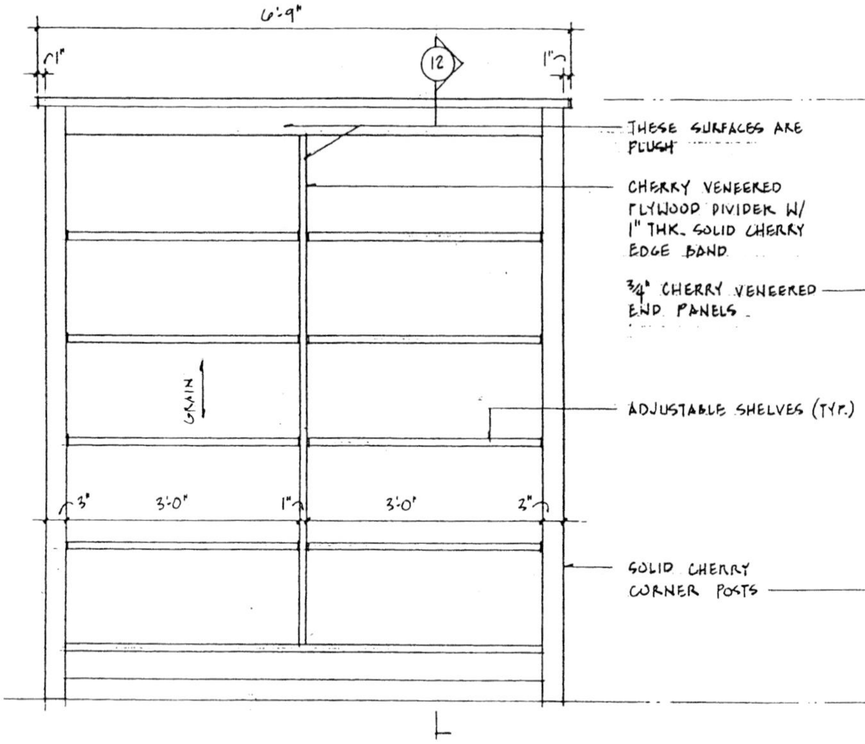

1 Front Elev. - Cab. F 6

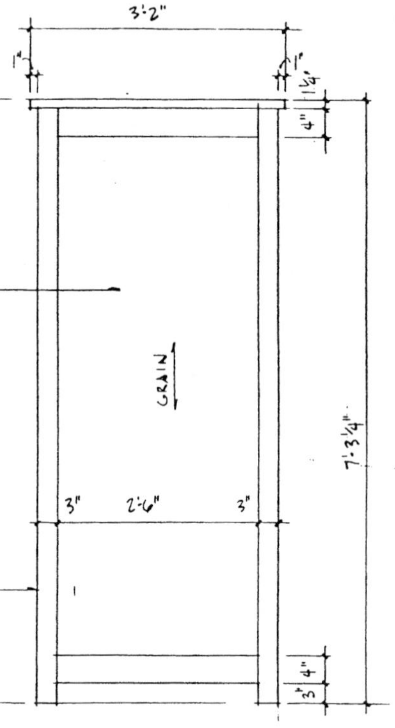

2 Side Elev.- Cab. F 6

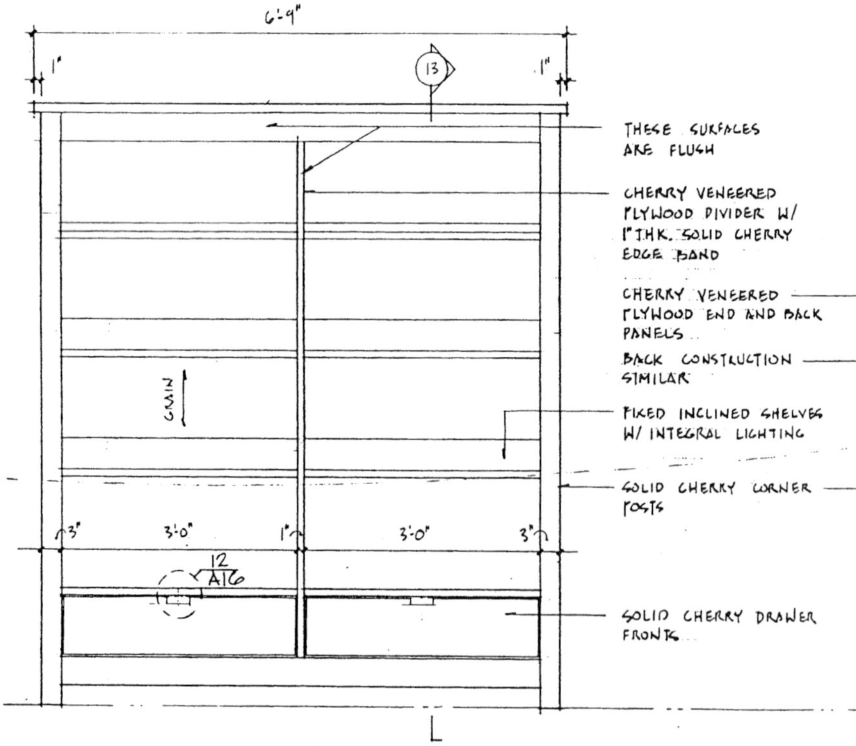

3 Front Elev. - Cab. D 6

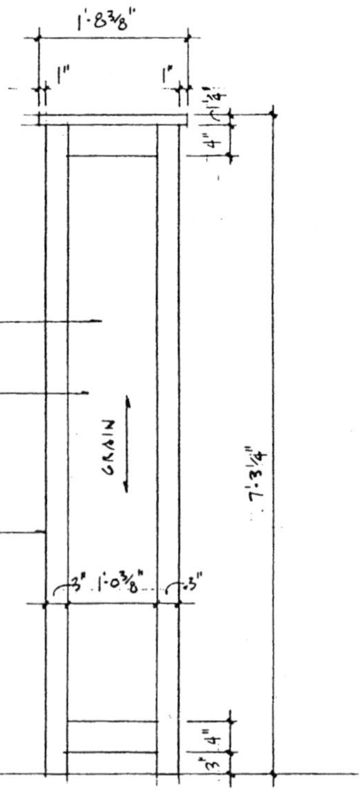

4 Side Elev.- Cab. D 6

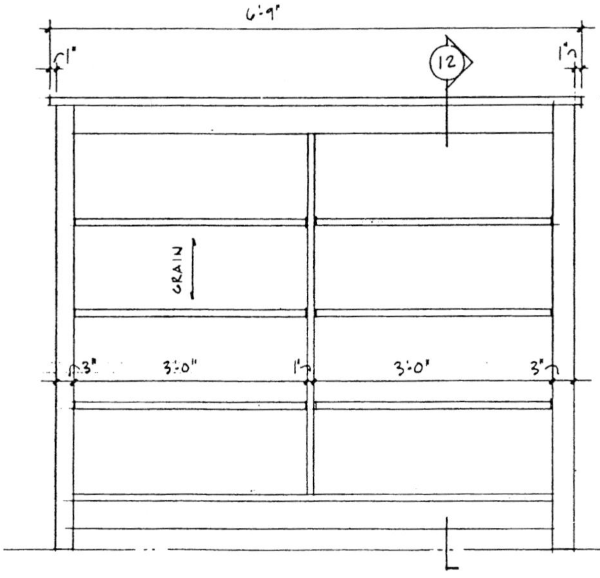

6 Front Elev. - Cab's. F 7

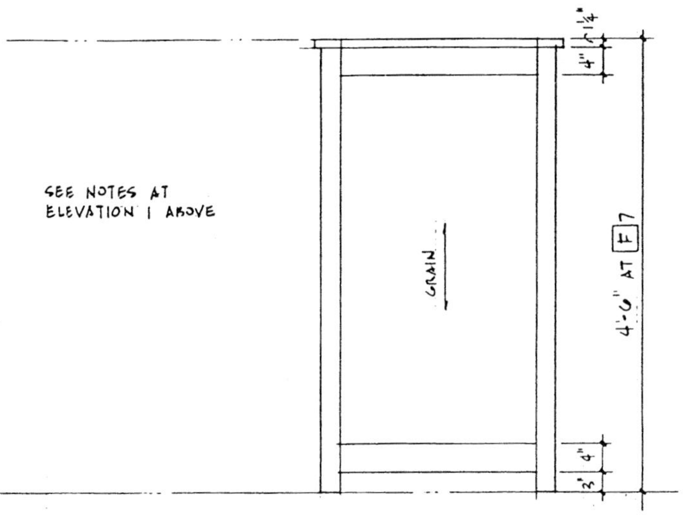

7 Side Elev. - Cab's. F 7

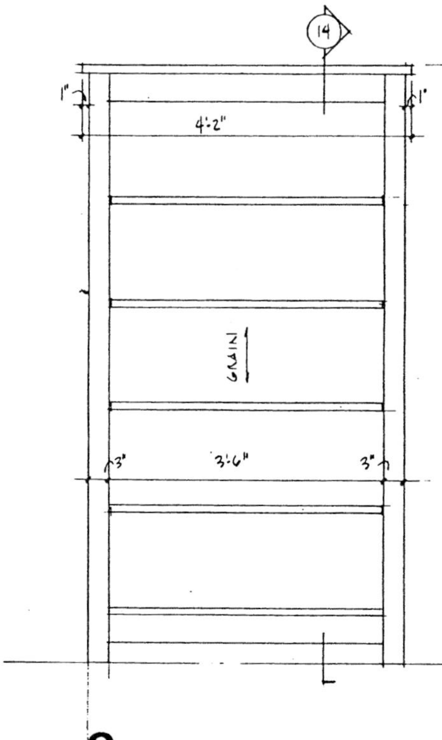

8 Front Elev. - Cab. S 3.5

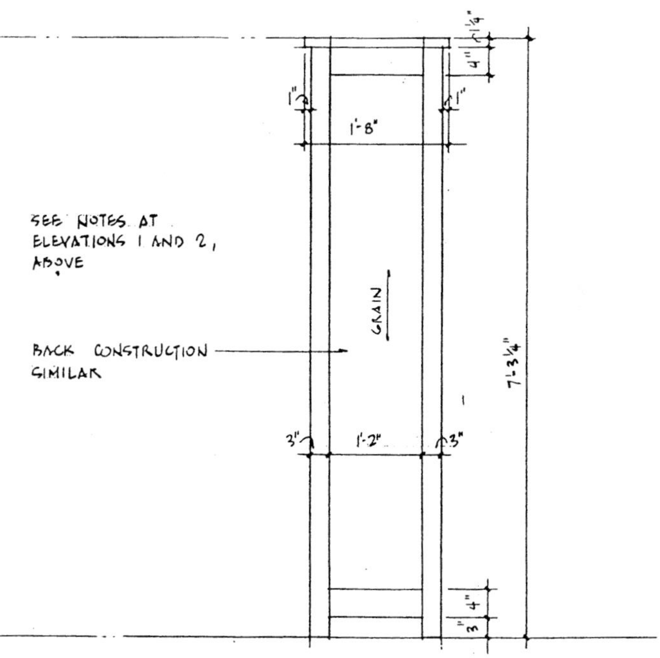

9 Side Elev.- Cab. S 3.5

DEPARTMENT STORES
Display Case/Freestanding

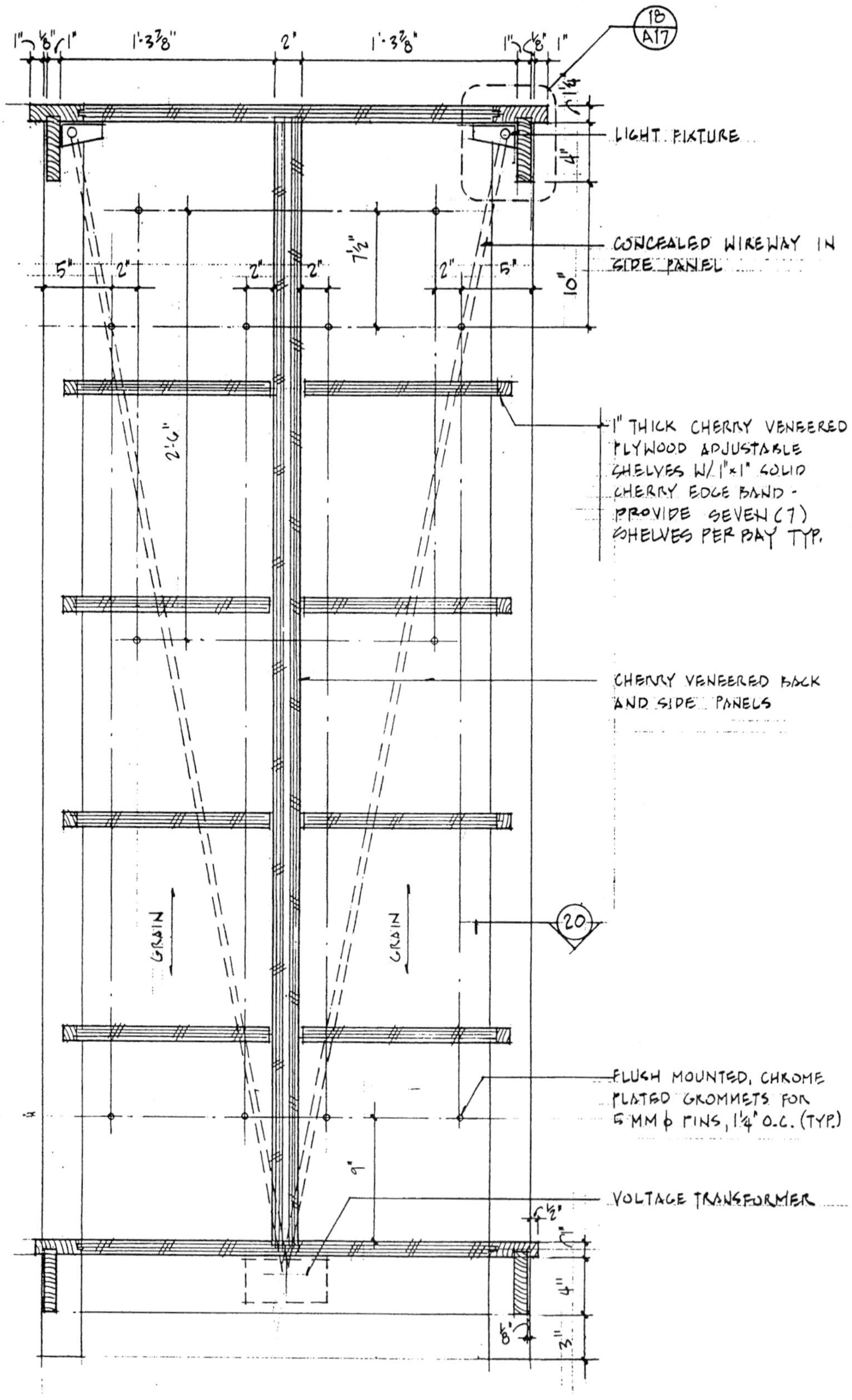

12 Section - Cab's. F6, F7

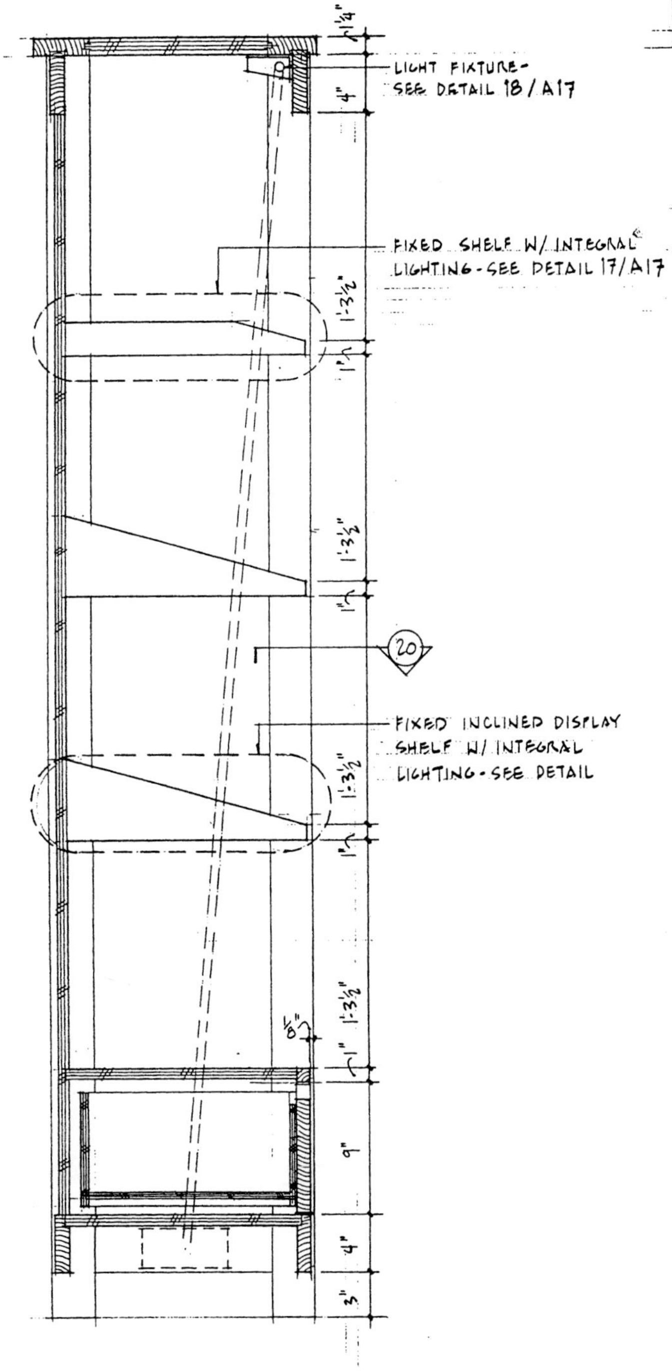
LIGHT FIXTURE-
SEE DETAIL 18 / A17
FIXED SHELF W/ INTEGRAL
LIGHTING - SEE DETAIL 17/A17
FIXED INCLINED DISPLAY
SHELF W/ INTEGRAL
LIGHTING - SEE DETAIL
20

13 Section - Cab. D 6

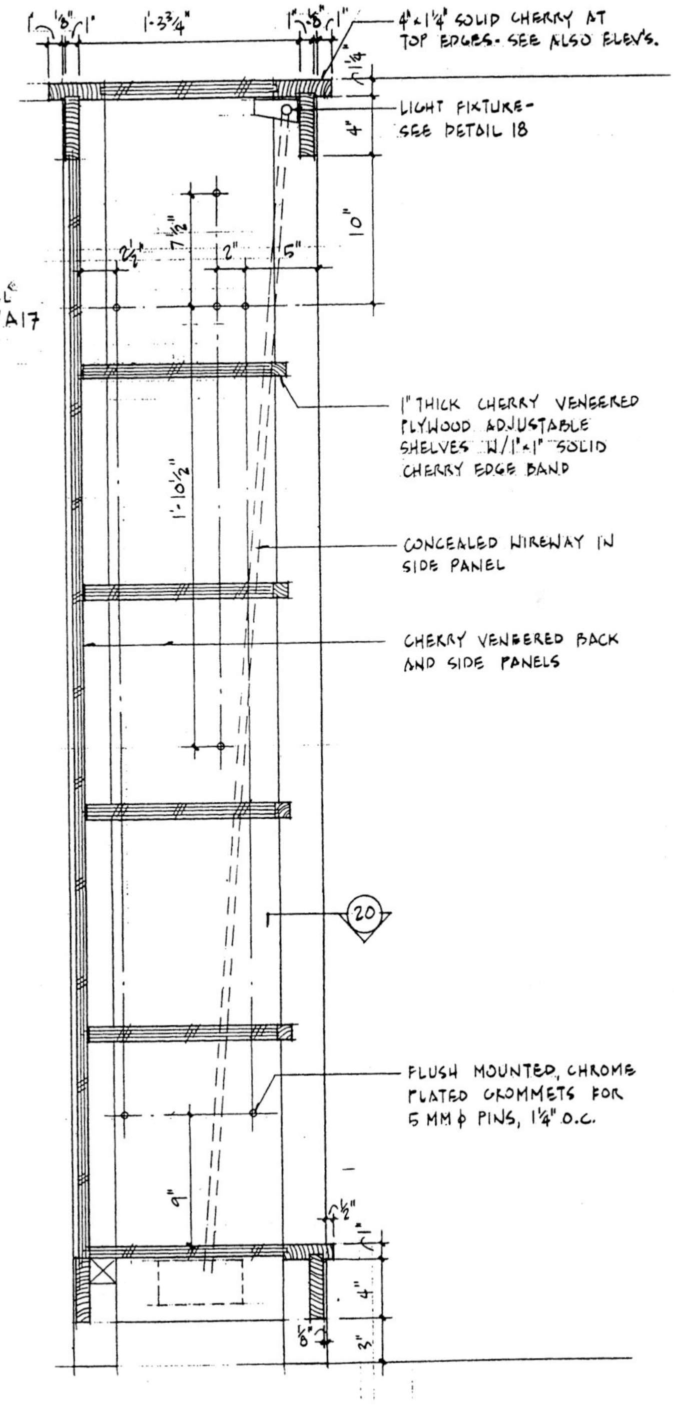
4"x1¼" SOLID CHERRY AT
TOP EDGES - SEE ALSO ELEV'S.
LIGHT FIXTURE-
SEE DETAIL 18
1" THICK CHERRY VENEERED
PLYWOOD ADJUSTABLE
SHELVES W/1"x1" SOLID
CHERRY EDGE BAND
CONCEALED WIREWAY IN
SIDE PANEL
CHERRY VENEERED BACK
AND SIDE PANELS
20
FLUSH MOUNTED, CHROME
PLATED GROMMETS FOR
5 MM ϕ PINS, 1¼" O.C.

14 Section - Cab. S 3.5

DEPARTMENT STORES
Display Case/Freestanding

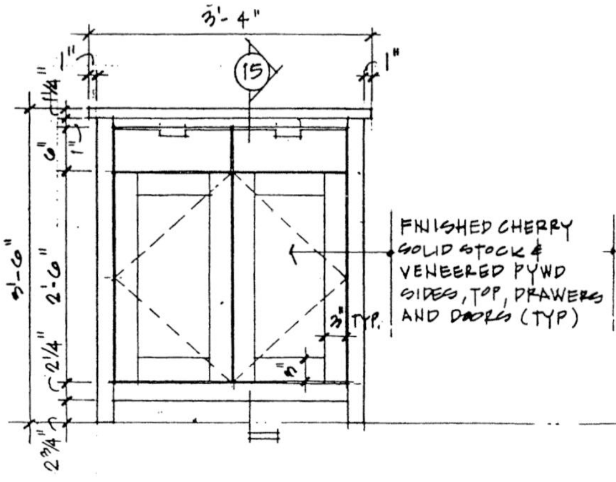

10 Front Elev. - Cab. A 2.5

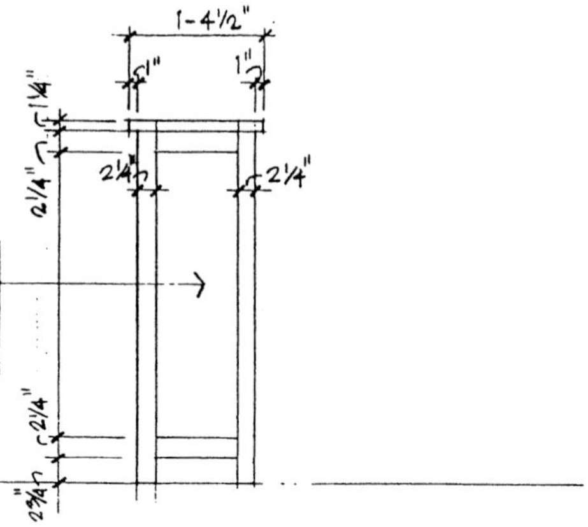

11 Side Elev.- Cab. A 2.5

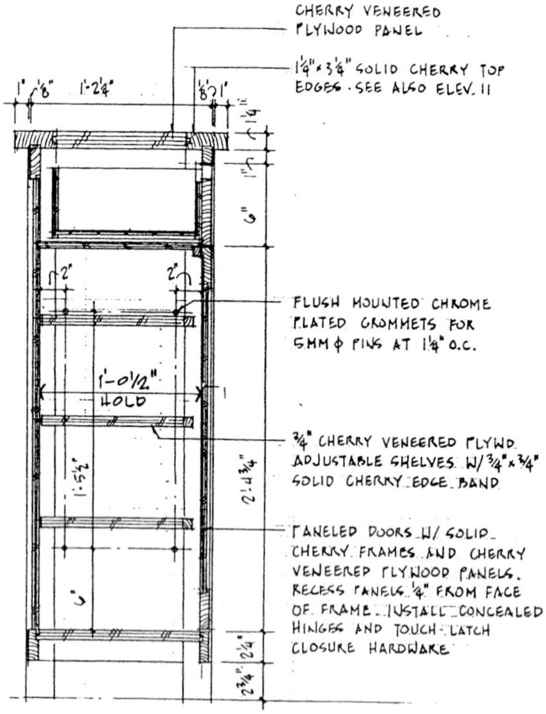

15 Section - Cab. A 2.5

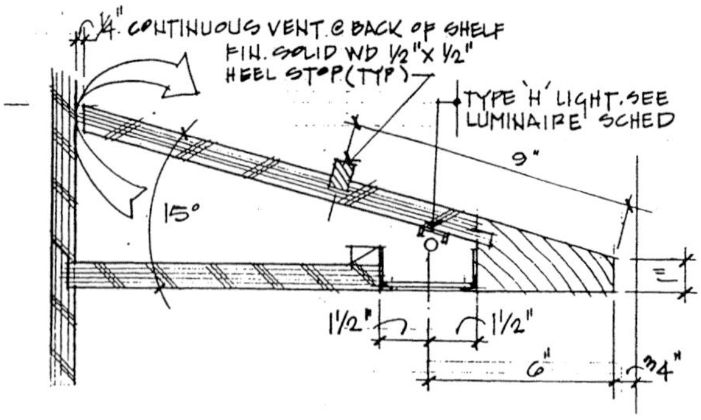

16 Section at Shelf
SCALE: 3" = 1'-0"

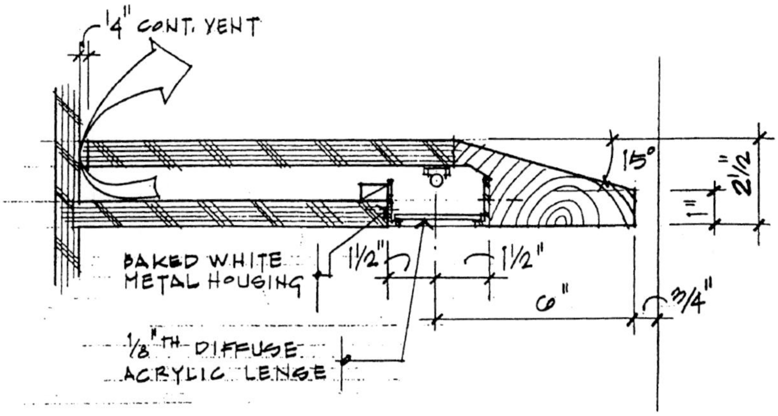

17 Section at Shelf

SCALE: 3" = 1'-0"

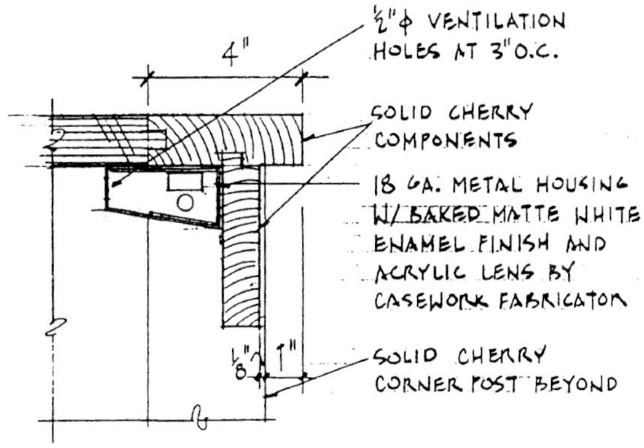

18 Section Detail at Light

SCALE: 3" = 1'-0"

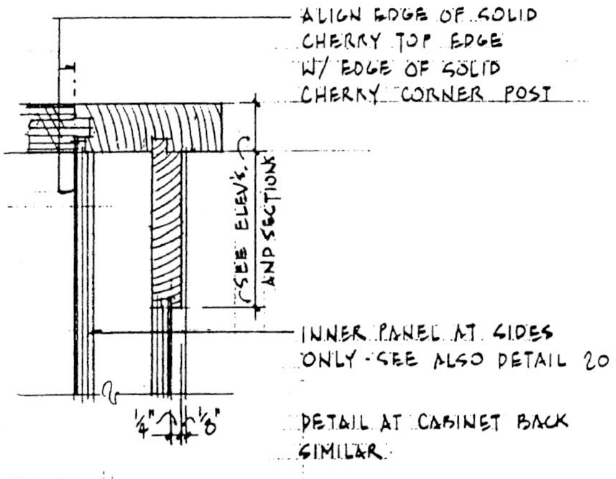

19 Section Detail at End

SCALE: 3" = 1'-0"

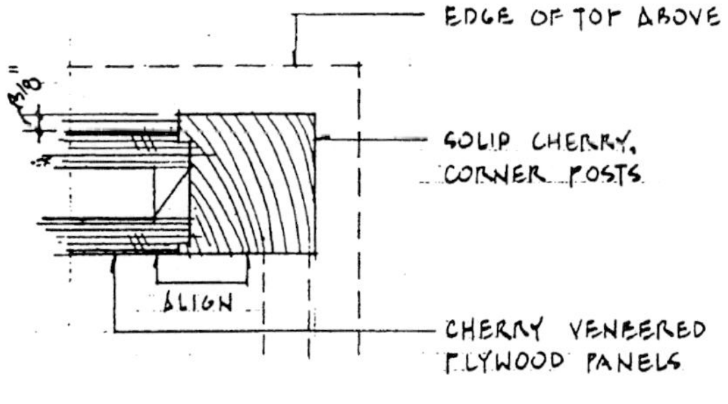

20 Plan Detail at Corner

SCALE: 3" = 1'-0"

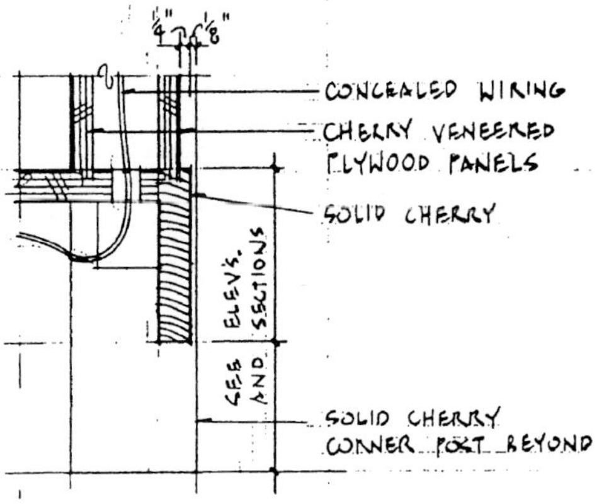

21 Section Detail at Base

SCALE: 3" = 1'-0"

DEPARTMENT STORES

Display Case/Handbags

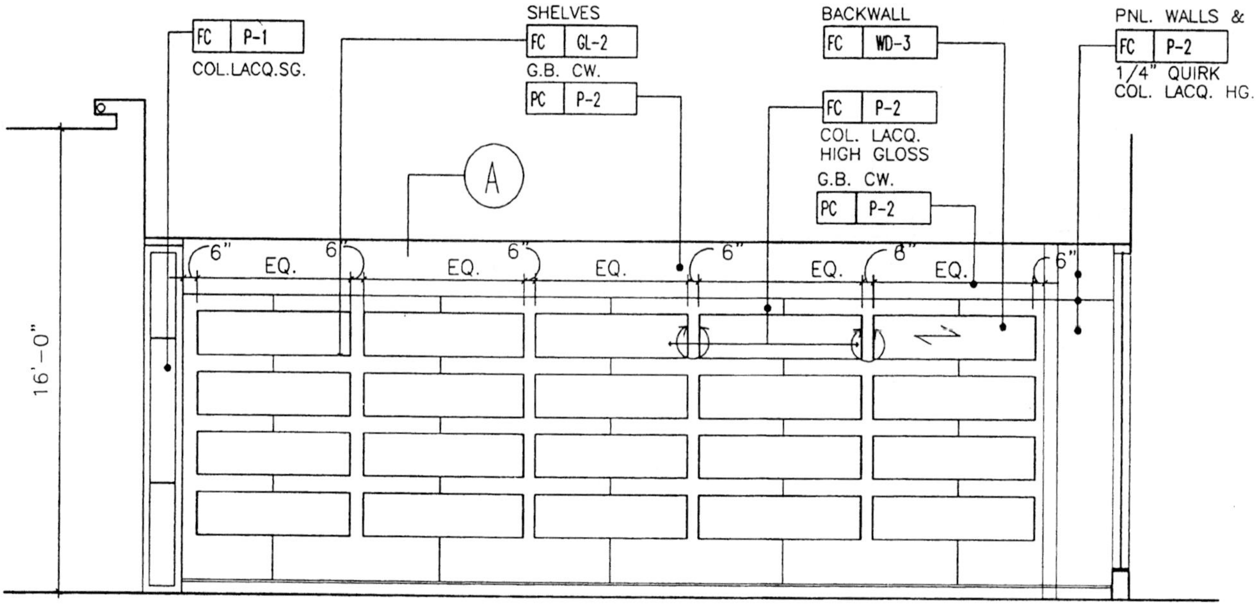

39 CONTEMPORARY HANDBAGS

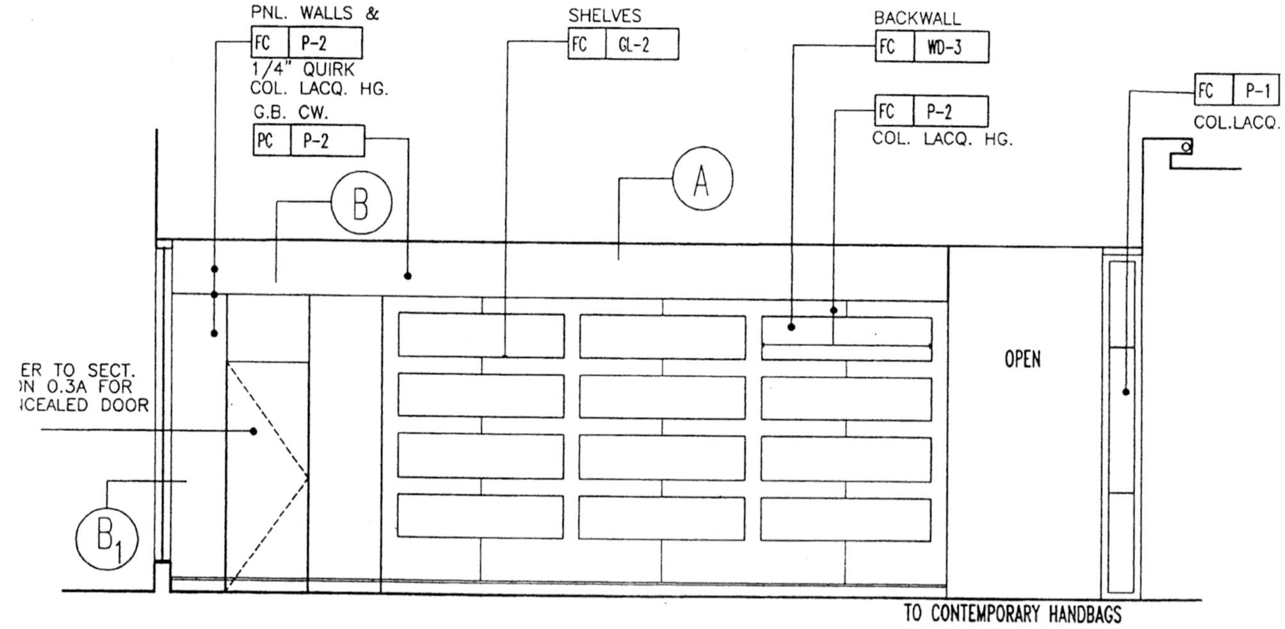

41

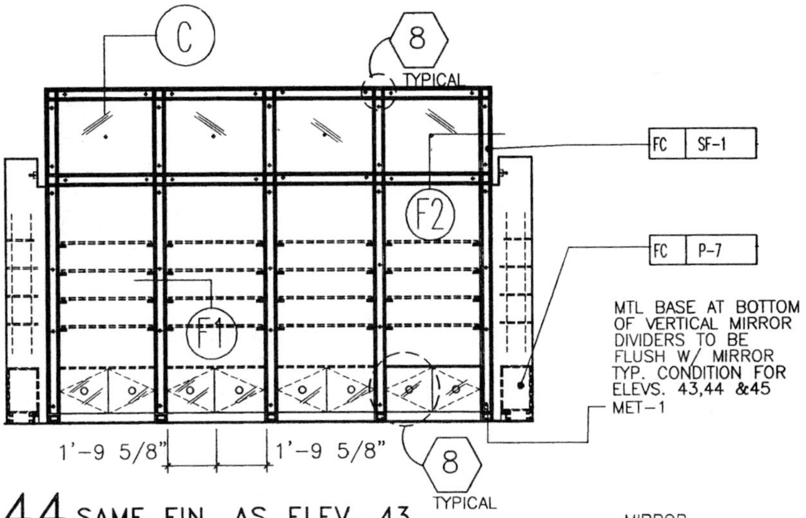

C
8
TYPICAL
FC SF-1
F2
FC P-7
F1
MTL BASE AT BOTTOM OF VERTICAL MIRROR DIVIDERS TO BE FLUSH W/ MIRROR TYP. CONDITION FOR ELEVS. 43,44 &45
MET-1
1'-9 5/8"
1'-9 5/8"
8
TYPICAL
44 SAME FIN. AS ELEV. 43
FC SP-1
COL.LACQ.SG.
F2
FC P-1
COL. LACQ. HG.
WD. BASE
PC PRIME
PC P-1
TYPICAL SG.
SC-421
42 & 46
SECURE MIRROR W/ DECORATIVE ROSSETTE MET-5
MIRROR
FC MIR-1
BACKWALL & RETURNS
PC WC-12
C
OPEN
EQ.
EQ.
3"EQ.
BACKWALL & RETURNS
PC WC-1
SHELVES
FC GL-5
GLASS
F2
PULLS
FC MET-2
F1
FC P-7
TO CONTEMPORARY HANDBAGS
BUNKERS
FC MIR-2
BUNKER TOPS
FC MIR-1
MTL BASE
FC MET-2
FRAMES
43 EVENING HANDBAGS
FC P-1
COL. LACQ. SEMI-GLOSS
PC P-3
PC P-3
D
PC P-3
OPEN
SHELVES
FC P-3
COL LACQ.
FC LUC-1
BUNKERS
FC P-3
COL LACQ. HIGH GLOSS
TO CONTEMPORARY HANDBAGS
47 DESIGNER HANDBAGS

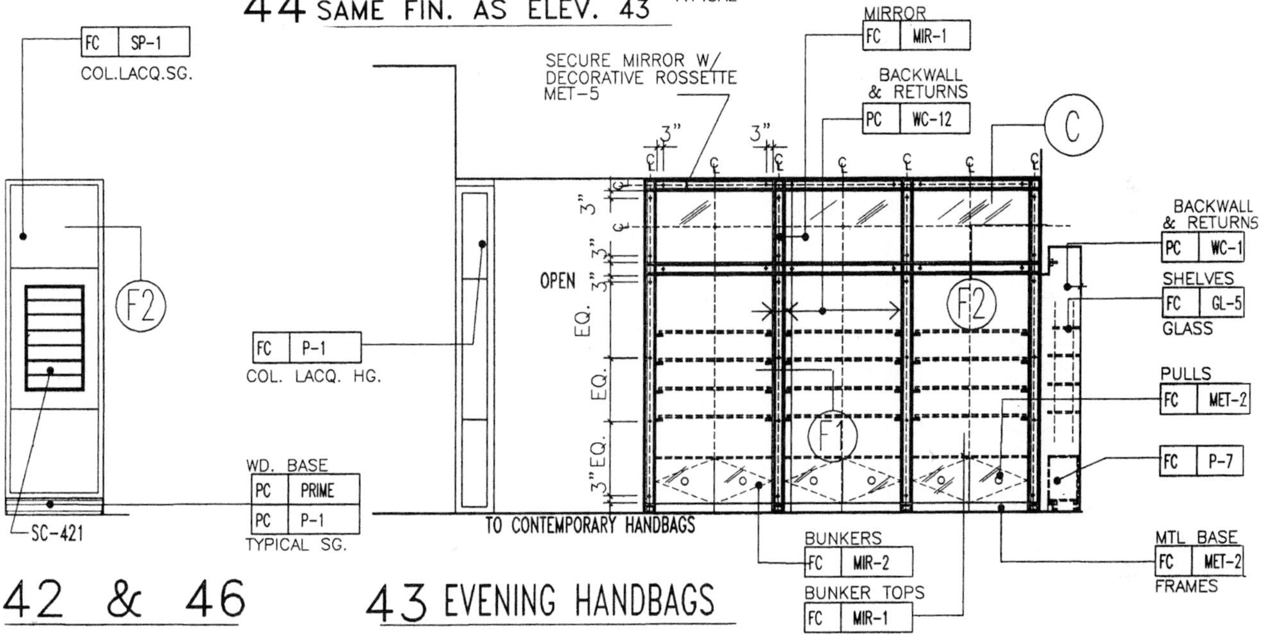

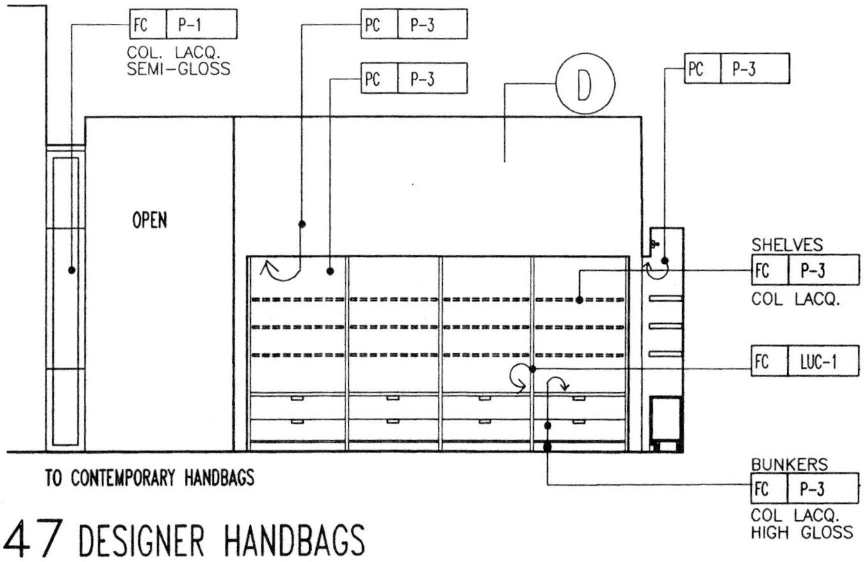

DEPARTMENT STORES
Display Case/Handbags

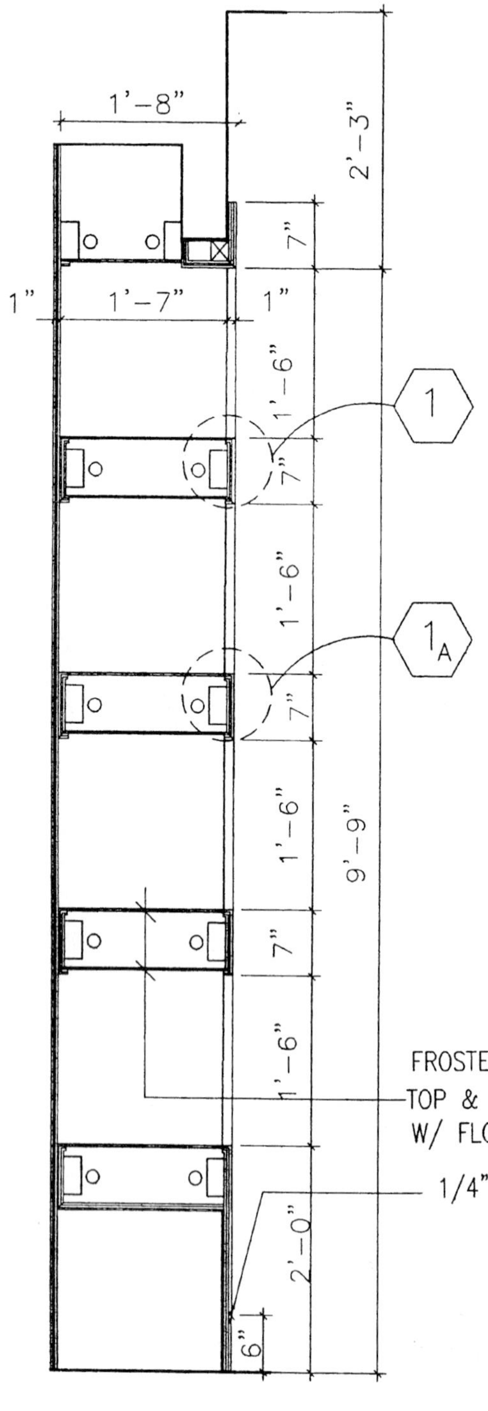

SECTION **A**
3/4"=1'-0"

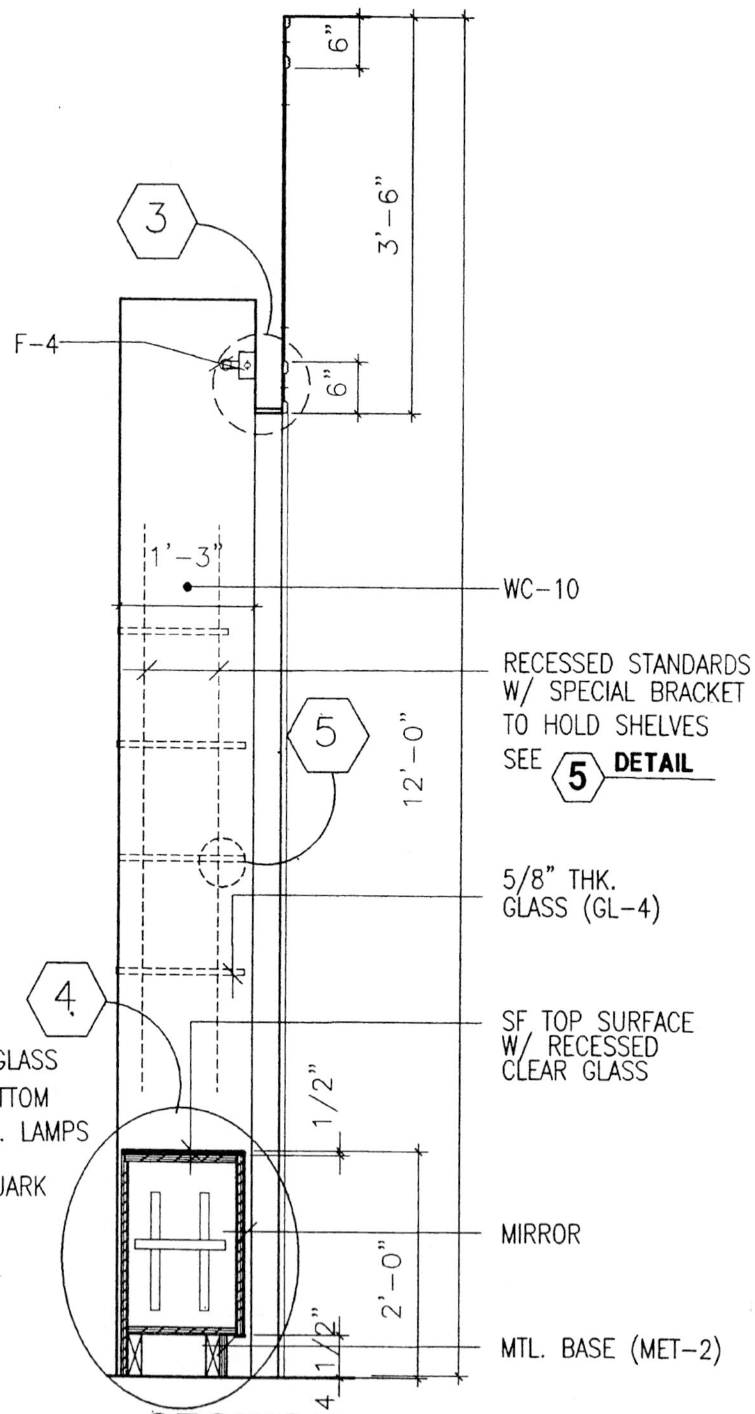

SECTION **C**
3/4"=1'-0"

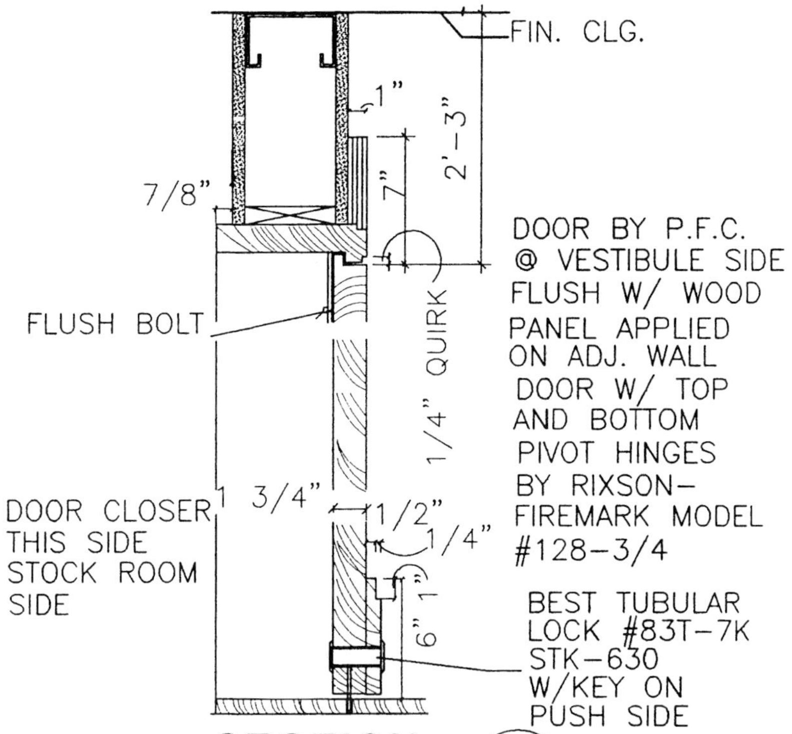
FIN. CLG.
1"
7"
2'-3"
7/8"
DOOR BY P.F.C.
@ VESTIBULE SIDE
FLUSH W/ WOOD
PANEL APPLIED
ON ADJ. WALL
DOOR W/ TOP
AND BOTTOM
PIVOT HINGES
BY RIXSON-
FIREMARK MODEL
#128-3/4
FLUSH BOLT
1/4" QUIRK
DOOR CLOSER
THIS SIDE
STOCK ROOM
SIDE
1 3/4"
1/2"
1/4"
1"
6"
BEST TUBULAR
LOCK #83T-7K
STK-630
W/KEY ON
PUSH SIDE

SECTION B

1 1/2=1'-0"

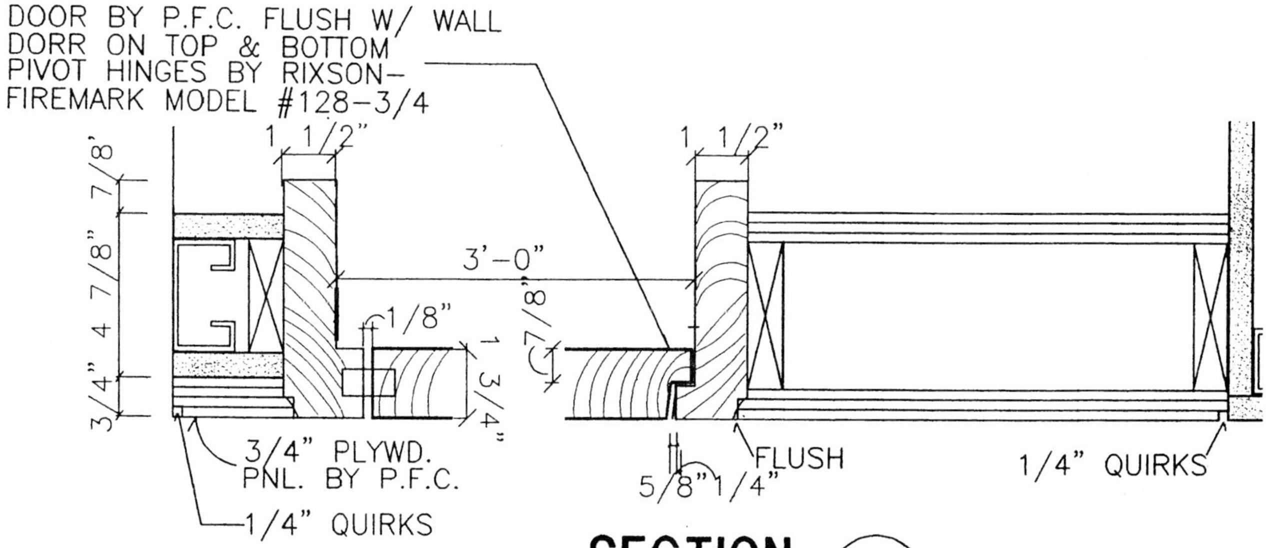
DOOR BY P.F.C. FLUSH W/ WALL
DORR ON TOP & BOTTOM
PIVOT HINGES BY RIXSON-
FIREMARK MODEL #128-3/4
1 1/2"
1 1/2"
7/8"
4 7/8"
3/4"
3'-0"
1/8"
7/8"
1 3/4"
3/4" PLYWD.
PNL. BY P.F.C.
1/4" QUIRKS
FLUSH
5/8"
1/4"
1/4" QUIRKS

SECTION B1

3"=1'-0"

DEPARTMENT STORES
Display Case/Handbags

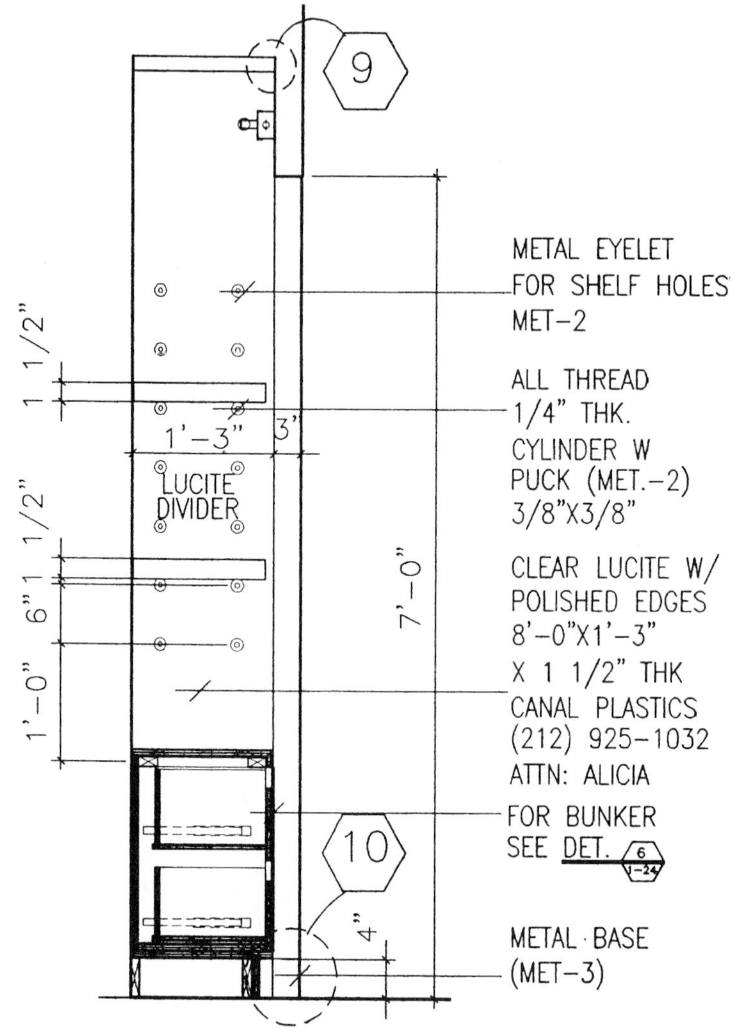

SECTION D
3/4"=1'-0"

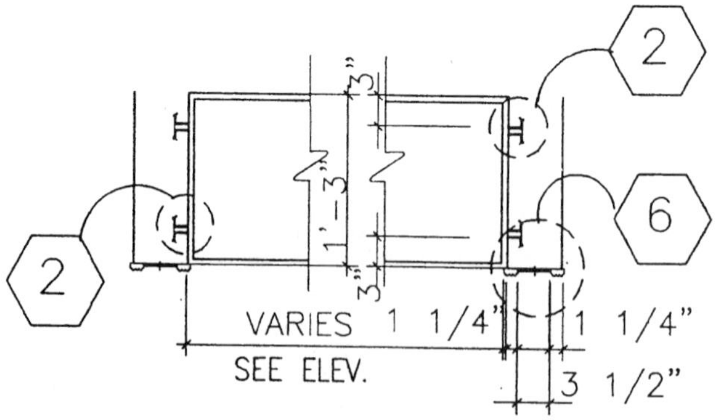

PLAN-SECTION F1
3/4"=1'-0"

DEPARTMENT STORES
Display Case/Handbags

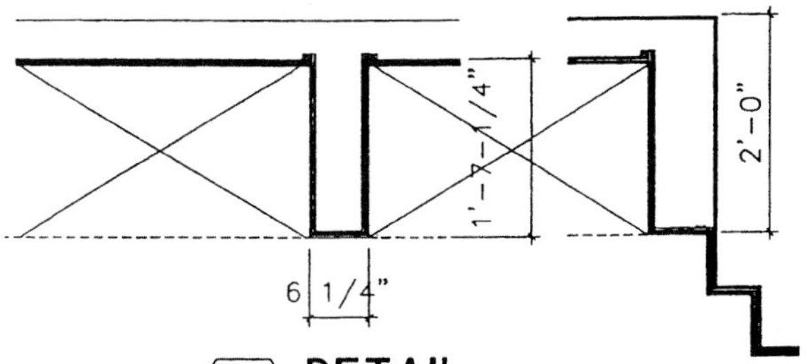

1 DETAIL
3/4"=1'-0"

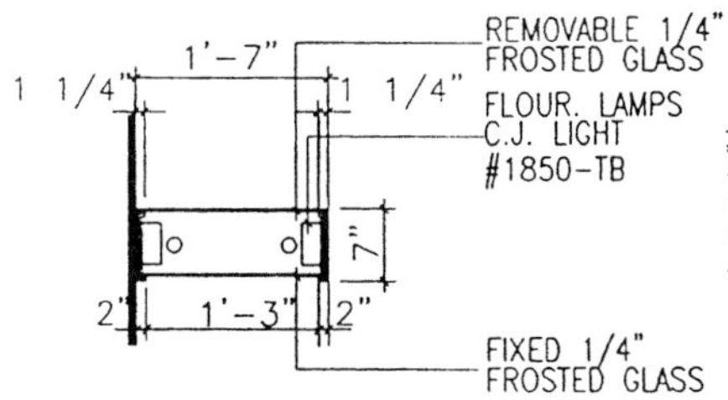

1A DETAIL
3/4"=1'-0"

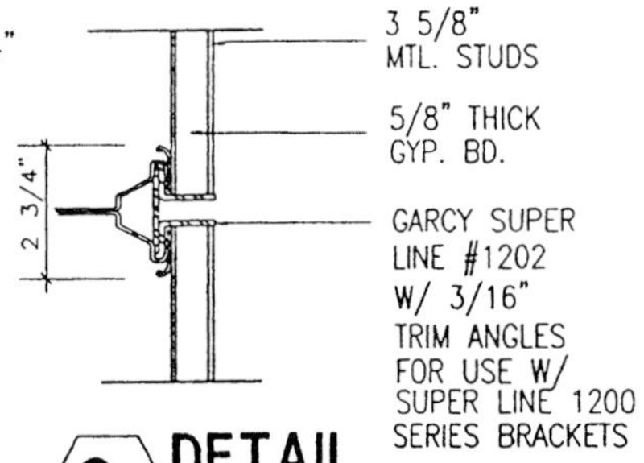

2 DETAIL
3"=1'-0"

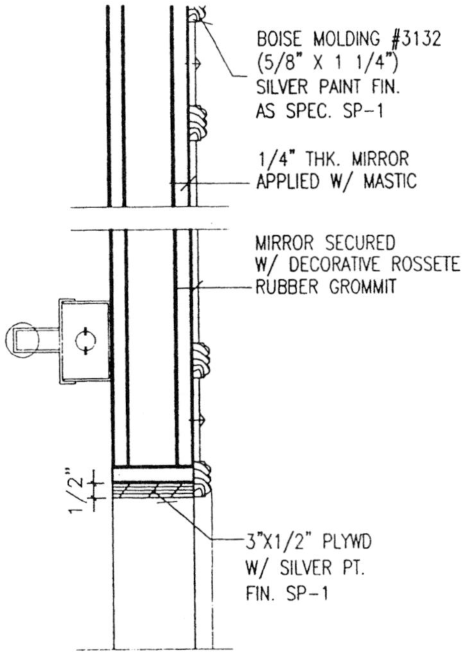

3 DETAIL
3"=1'-0"

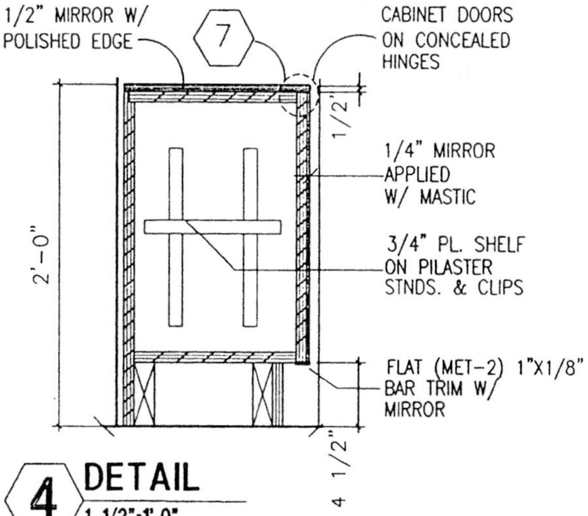

4 DETAIL
1 1/2"=1'-0"

DEPARTMENT STORES
Display Case/Handbags

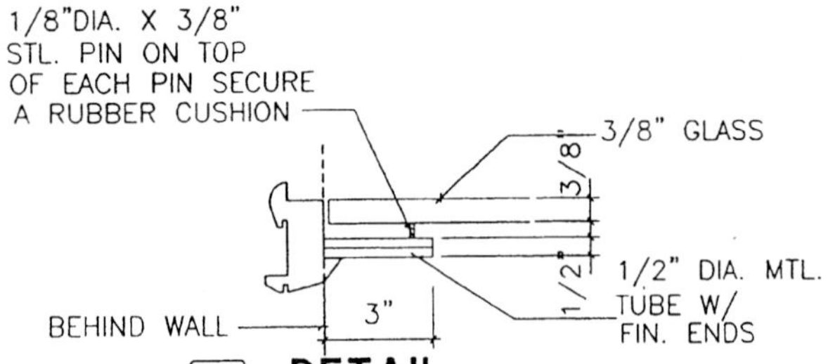

5 DETAIL
3"=1'-0"

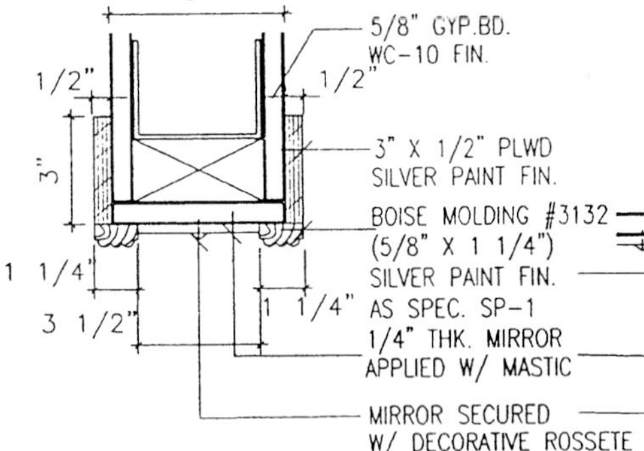

6 DETAIL
3"=1'-0"

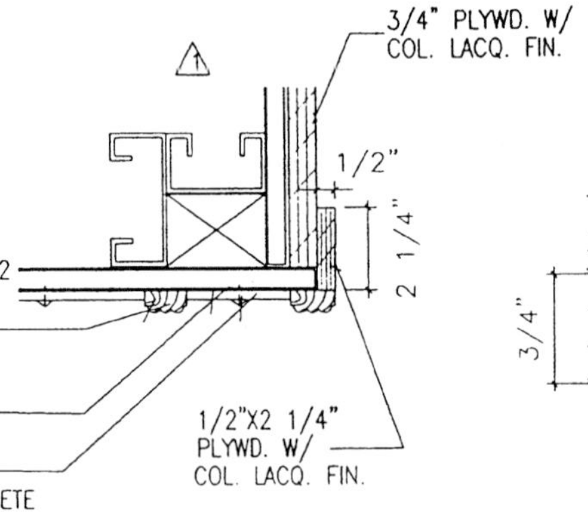

F2 DETAIL
3"=1'-0"

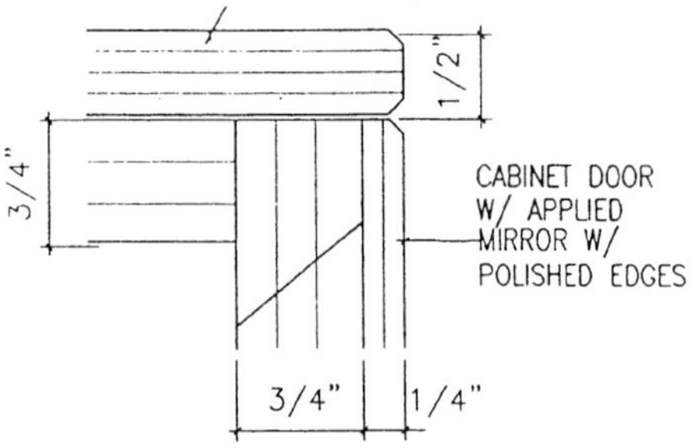

7 DETAIL
FULL SCALE

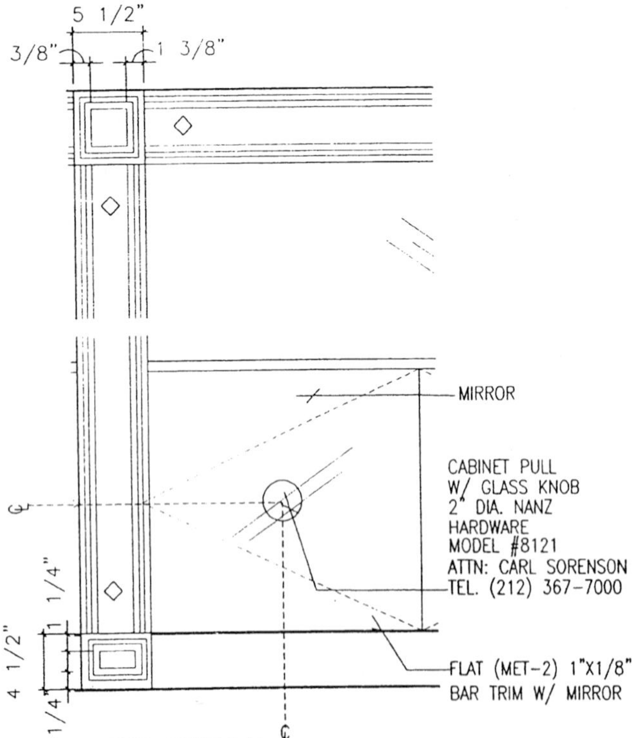

8 DETAIL
1 1/2"=1'-0"

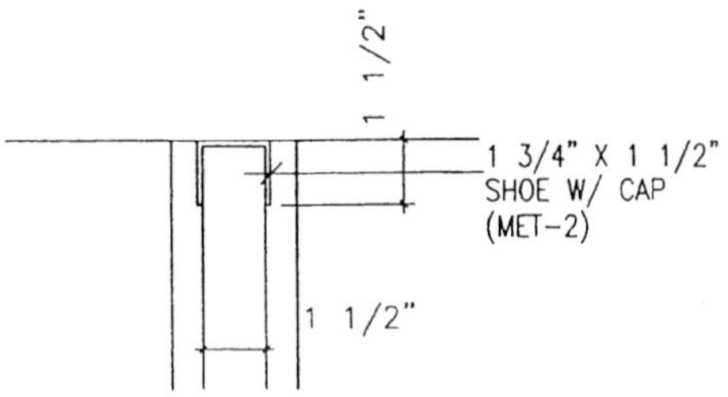

9 DETAIL
3"=1'-0"

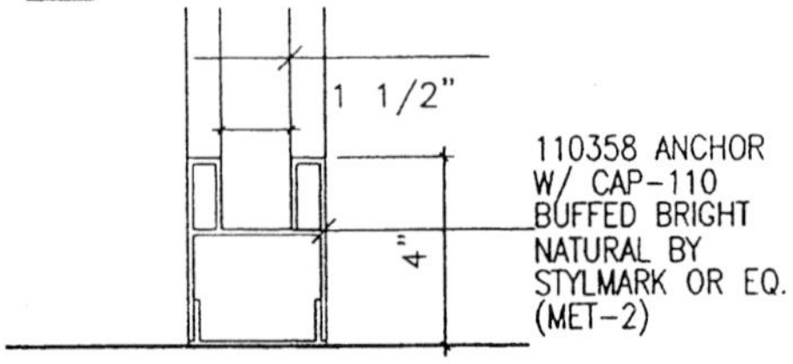

10 DETAIL
3"=1'-0"

DEPARTMENT STORES
Display Case/Shirts

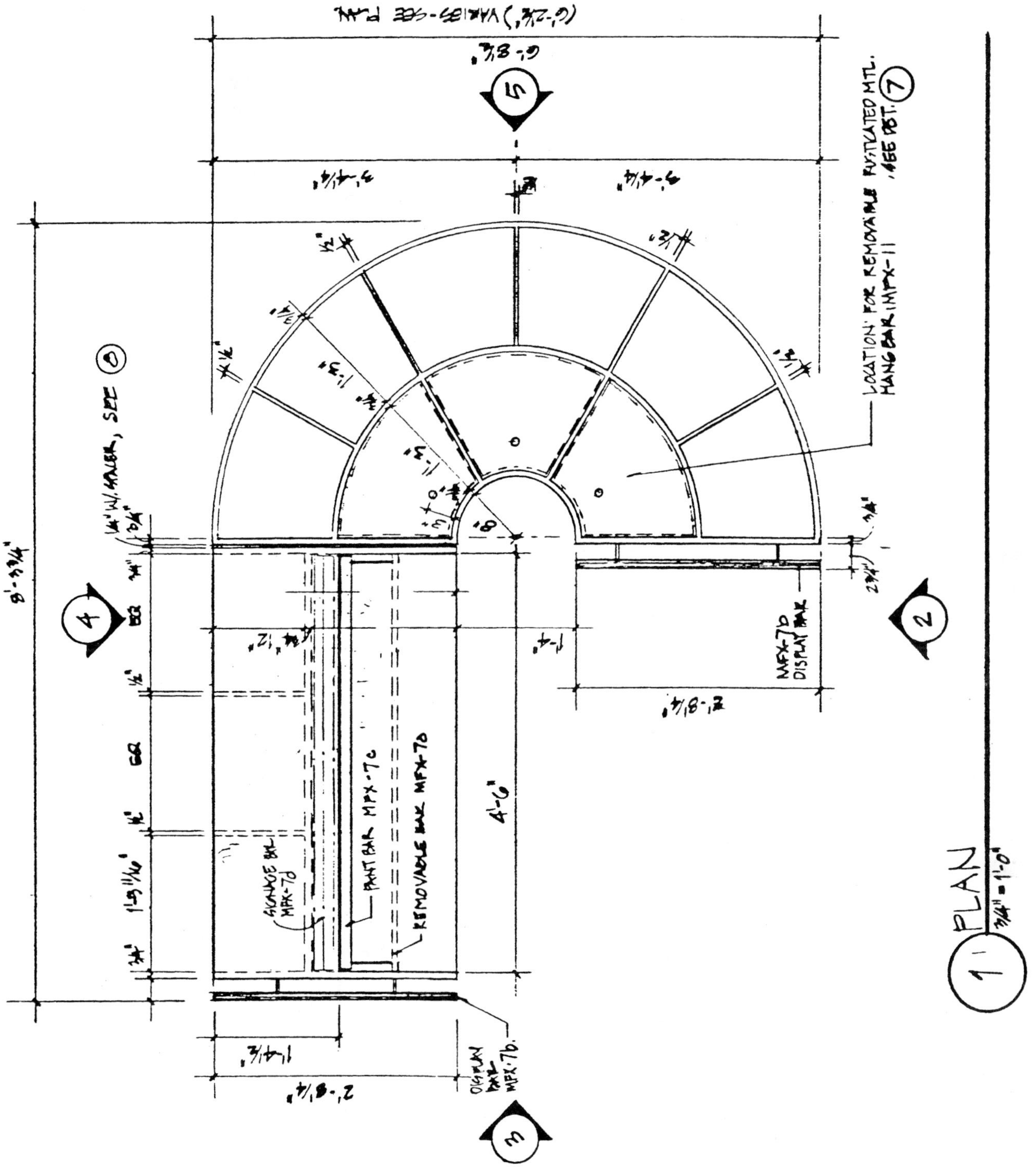

DEPARTMENT STORES

Display Case/Shirts

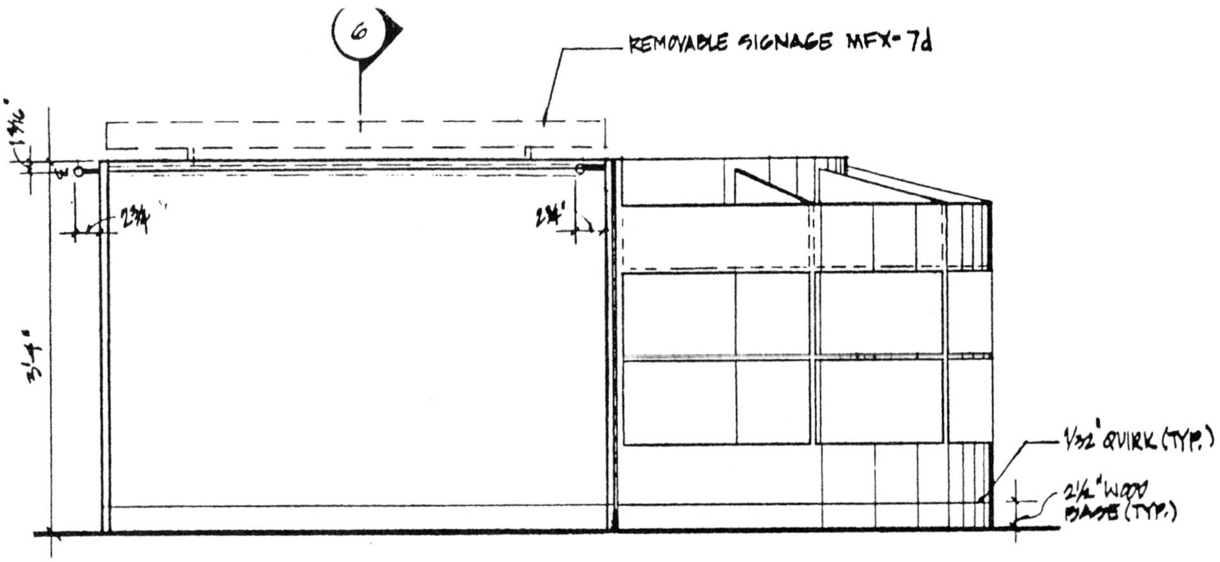

2 ELEVATION 3/4" = 1'-0"

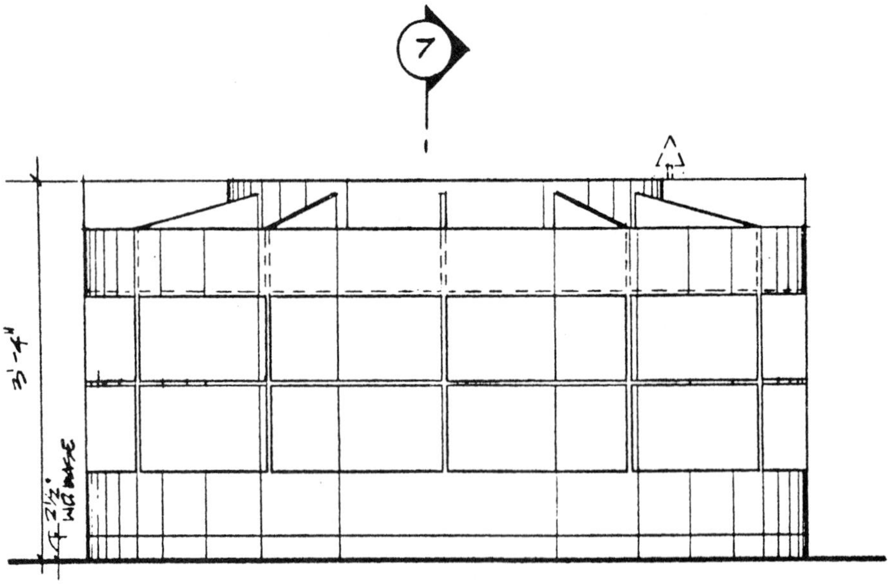

5 ELEVATION 3/4" = 1'-0"

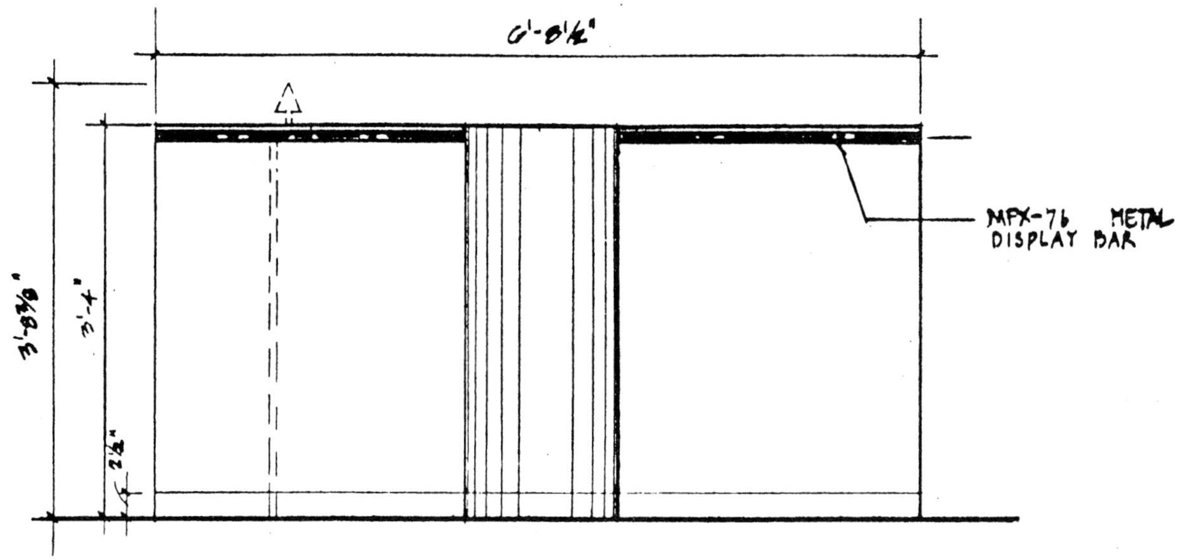
6'-8½"
MFX-76 METAL DISPLAY BAR
3'-8⅜"
3'-4"
2½"
3 ELEVATION
¾"=1'-0"

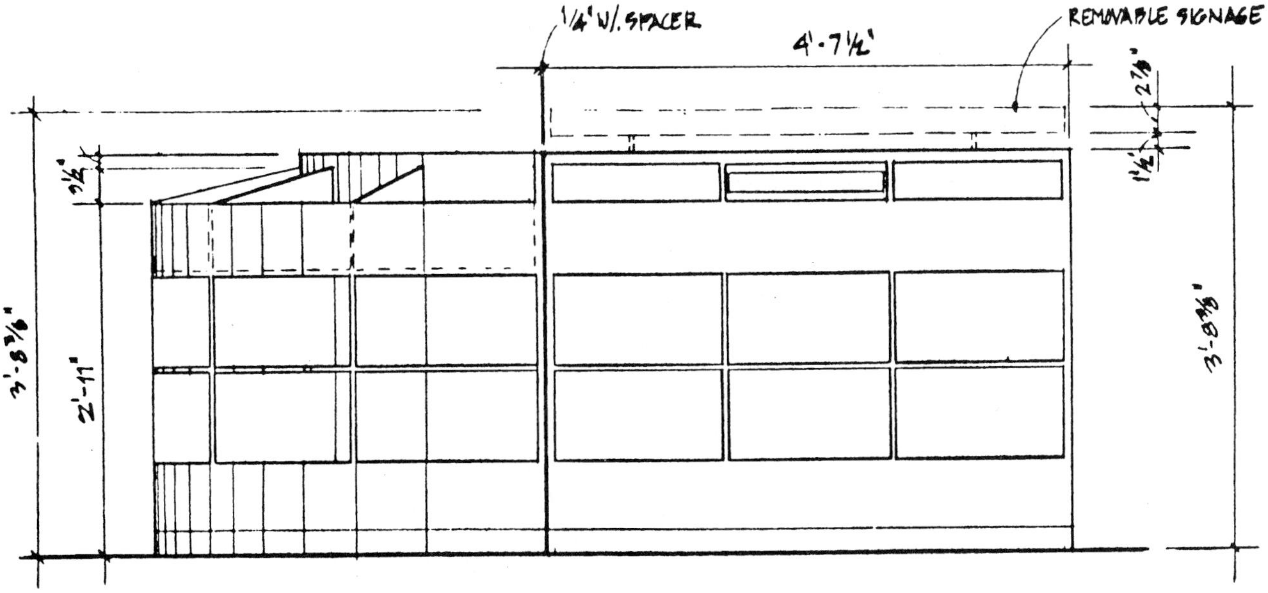
¼" W/. SPACER
4'-7½"
REMOVABLE SIGNAGE
2⅞"
1½"
3'-8⅜"
2'-11"
4 ELEVATION
¾"=1'-0"

DEPARTMENT STORES

Display Case/Shirts

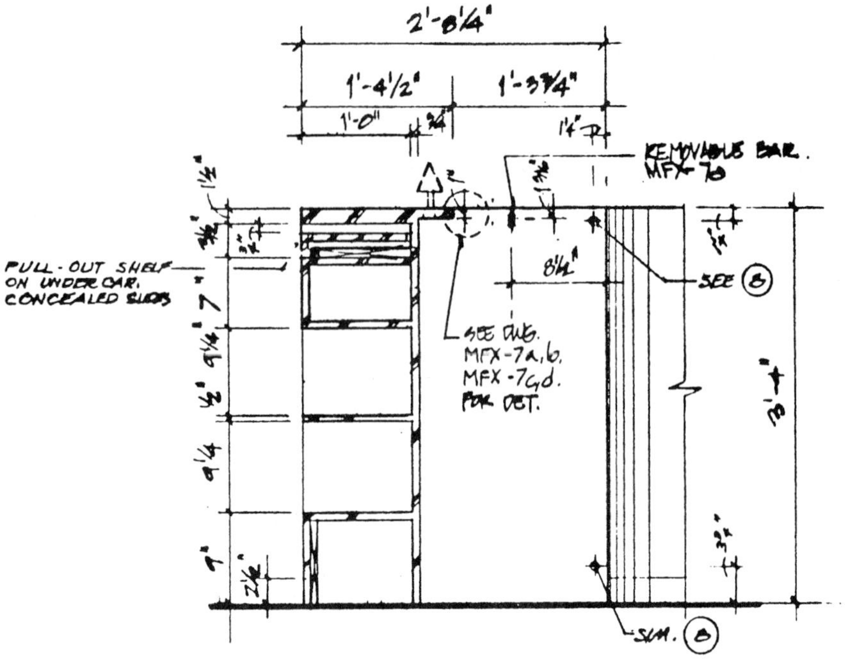

6 SECTION
3/4" = 1'-0"

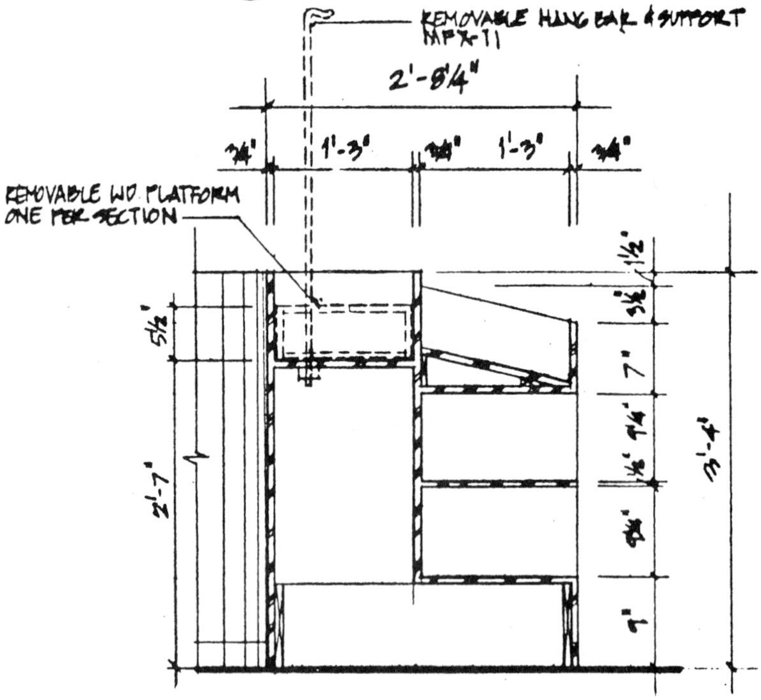

7 SECTION
3/4" = 1'-0"

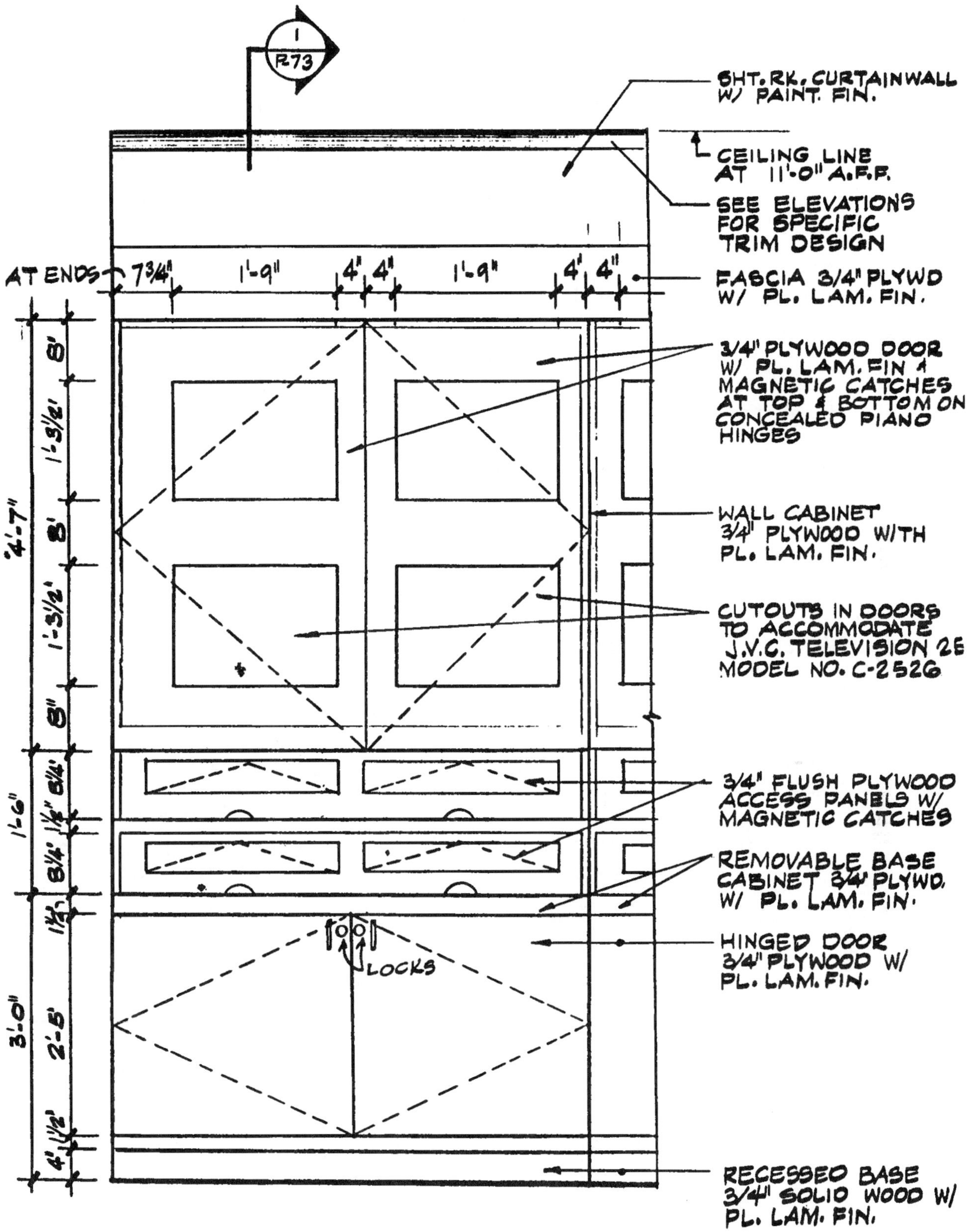
1
R73
SHT. RK. CURTAINWALL W/ PAINT. FIN.
CEILING LINE AT 11'-0" A.F.F.
SEE ELEVATIONS FOR SPECIFIC TRIM DESIGN
AT ENDS 7¾" 1'-9" 4" 4" 1'-9" 4" 4"
FASCIA 3/4" PLYWD W/ PL. LAM. FIN.
3/4" PLYWOOD DOOR W/ PL. LAM. FIN & MAGNETIC CATCHES AT TOP & BOTTOM ON CONCEALED PIANO HINGES
WALL CABINET 3/4" PLYWOOD WITH PL. LAM. FIN.
CUTOUTS IN DOORS TO ACCOMMODATE J.V.C. TELEVISION 25 MODEL NO. C-2526
3/4" FLUSH PLYWOOD ACCESS PANELS W/ MAGNETIC CATCHES
REMOVABLE BASE CABINET 3/4" PLYWD. W/ PL. LAM. FIN.
HINGED DOOR 3/4" PLYWOOD W/ PL. LAM. FIN.
LOCKS
RECESSED BASE 3/4" SOLID WOOD W/ PL. LAM. FIN.
4'-7"
8"
1'-3½"
8"
1'-3½"
8"
1'-6"
8¼"
1½"
8¼"
1½"
3'-0"
2'-5"
1½"
4"

ELEVATION
SCALE: 3/4" = 1'-0"

DEPARTMENT STORES
Television Cabinet Details

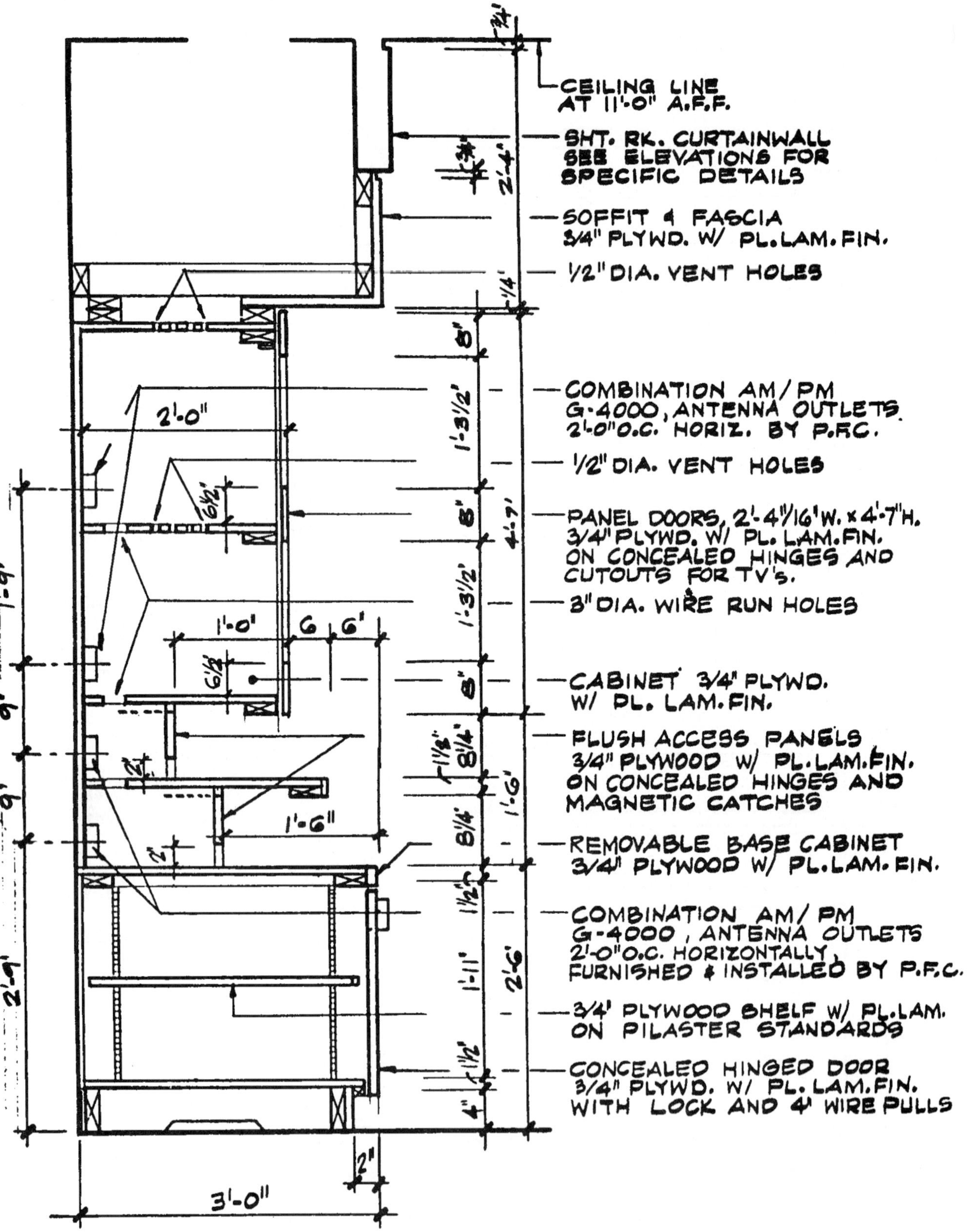
CEILING LINE AT 11'-0" A.F.F.
SHT. RK. CURTAINWALL SEE ELEVATIONS FOR SPECIFIC DETAILS
SOFFIT & FASCIA 3/4" PLYWD. W/ PL.LAM.FIN.
1/2" DIA. VENT HOLES
COMBINATION AM/PM G-4000, ANTENNA OUTLETS 2'-0" O.C. HORIZ. BY P.F.C.
1/2" DIA. VENT HOLES
PANEL DOORS, 2'-4 1/16"W. x 4'-7"H. 3/4" PLYWD. W/ PL. LAM.FIN. ON CONCEALED HINGES AND CUTOUTS FOR TV's.
3" DIA. WIRE RUN HOLES
CABINET 3/4" PLYWD. W/ PL. LAM. FIN.
FLUSH ACCESS PANELS 3/4" PLYWOOD W/ PL.LAM.FIN. ON CONCEALED HINGES AND MAGNETIC CATCHES
REMOVABLE BASE CABINET 3/4" PLYWOOD W/ PL.LAM. FIN.
COMBINATION AM/PM G-4000, ANTENNA OUTLETS 2'-0" O.C. HORIZONTALLY, FURNISHED & INSTALLED BY P.F.C.
3/4" PLYWOOD SHELF W/ PL.LAM. ON PILASTER STANDARDS
CONCEALED HINGED DOOR 3/4" PLYWD. W/ PL. LAM.FIN. WITH LOCK AND 4" WIRE PULLS
2'-0"
1'-0"
6
6"
1'-6"
3'-0"
2"
2'-4"
8"
1'-3 1/2"
4'-7"
2'-6"
1'-11"
1'-9"
9"
2'-9"

SECTION ①
SCALE: 3/4"=1'-0"

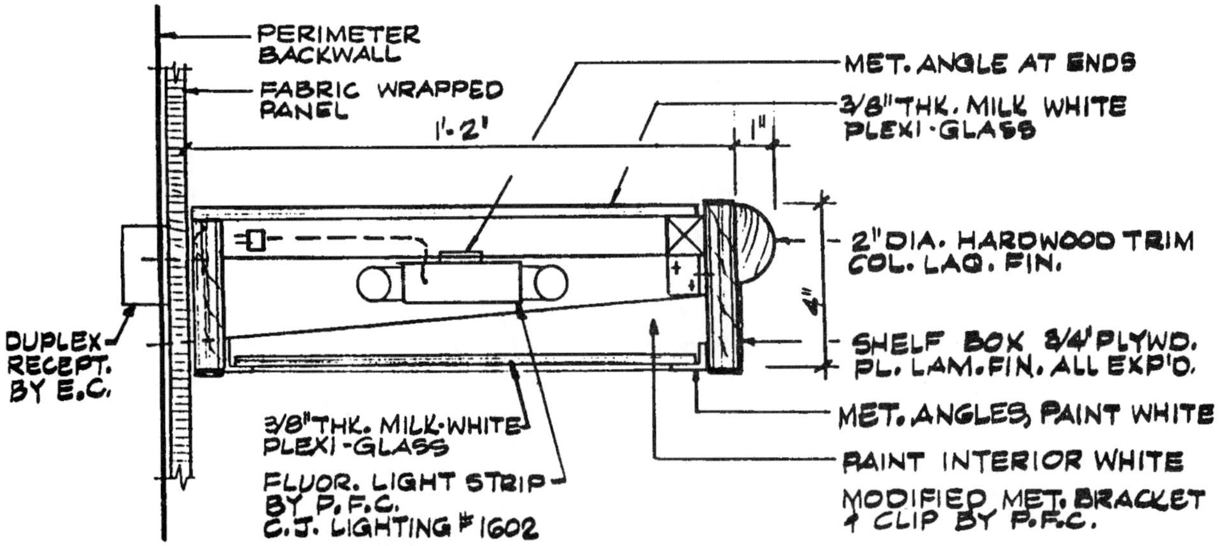

PERIMETER BACKWALL
FABRIC WRAPPED PANEL
1'-2"
1"
MET. ANGLE AT ENDS
3/8" THK. MILK WHITE PLEXI-GLASS
2" DIA. HARDWOOD TRIM COL. LAQ. FIN.
4"
SHELF BOX 3/4" PLYWD. PL. LAM. FIN. ALL EXP'D.
MET. ANGLES, PAINT WHITE
PAINT INTERIOR WHITE
MODIFIED MET. BRACKET & CLIP BY P.F.C.
DUPLEX RECEPT. BY E.C.
3/8" THK. MILK-WHITE PLEXI-GLASS
FLUOR. LIGHT STRIP BY P.F.C. C.J. LIGHTING #1602
SHELF DETAIL
A
SCALE: 3"=1'-0"
1"
4'-1"
1"
DUPLEX RECEPTACLE 1 PER SHELF BY E.C.
PERIMETER BACKWALL
REMOVABLE PADS W/ FABRIC COV'G BY P.F.C.
FLUOR. LIGHT STRIP BY PERIM. FIXT. CONTR.
1'-2"
METAL ANGLES AT ENDS
MODIFIED METAL BRACKET AT ENDS W/ SHELF CLIPS BY P.F.C.
1"
BULLNOSE TRIM 2" DIA. HARDWOOD
SHELF BOX, 3/4" PLYWD. PL. LAM. FIN.
PLAN SECTION @ SHELF
B
SCALE: 1 1/2"=1'-0"
4'-3"
3/4'
3/4"
A
2'-1"
1'-3"
REMOVABLE PADS W FABRIC COV'G
MILK WHITE PLEXI AT SHELF
SHELF BOX
MILK WHITE PLEXI AT BASE CABINET
BASE CABINET
PLAN WHERE SHELVES ABUTT
SCALE: 3/4"=1'-0"

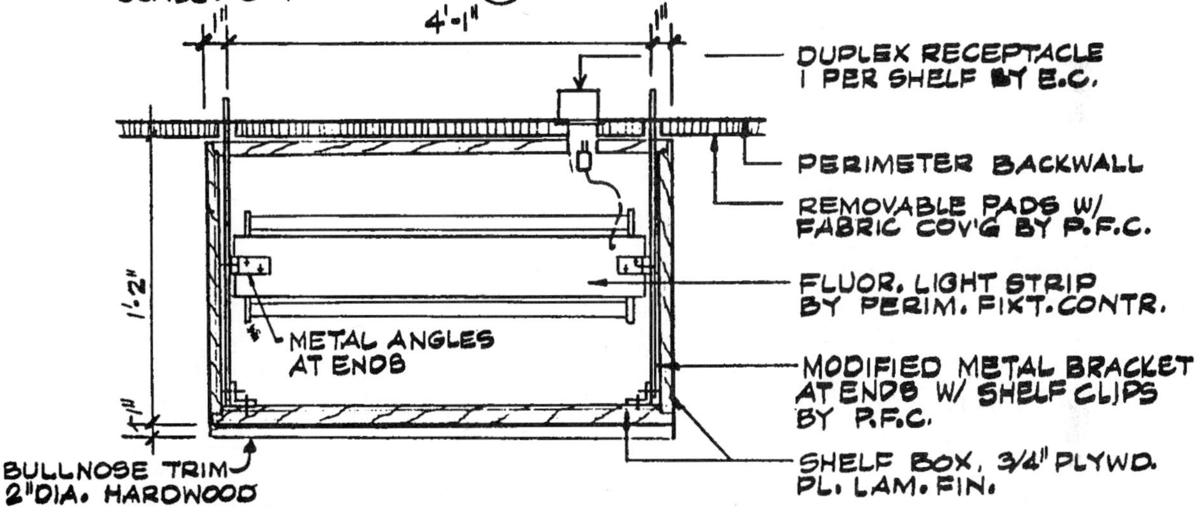

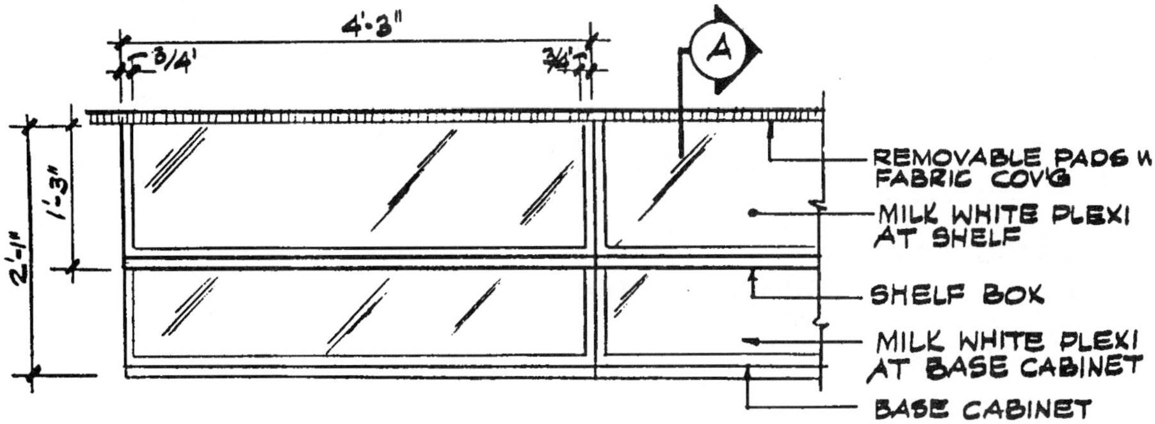

DEPARTMENT STORES
Shelving Details

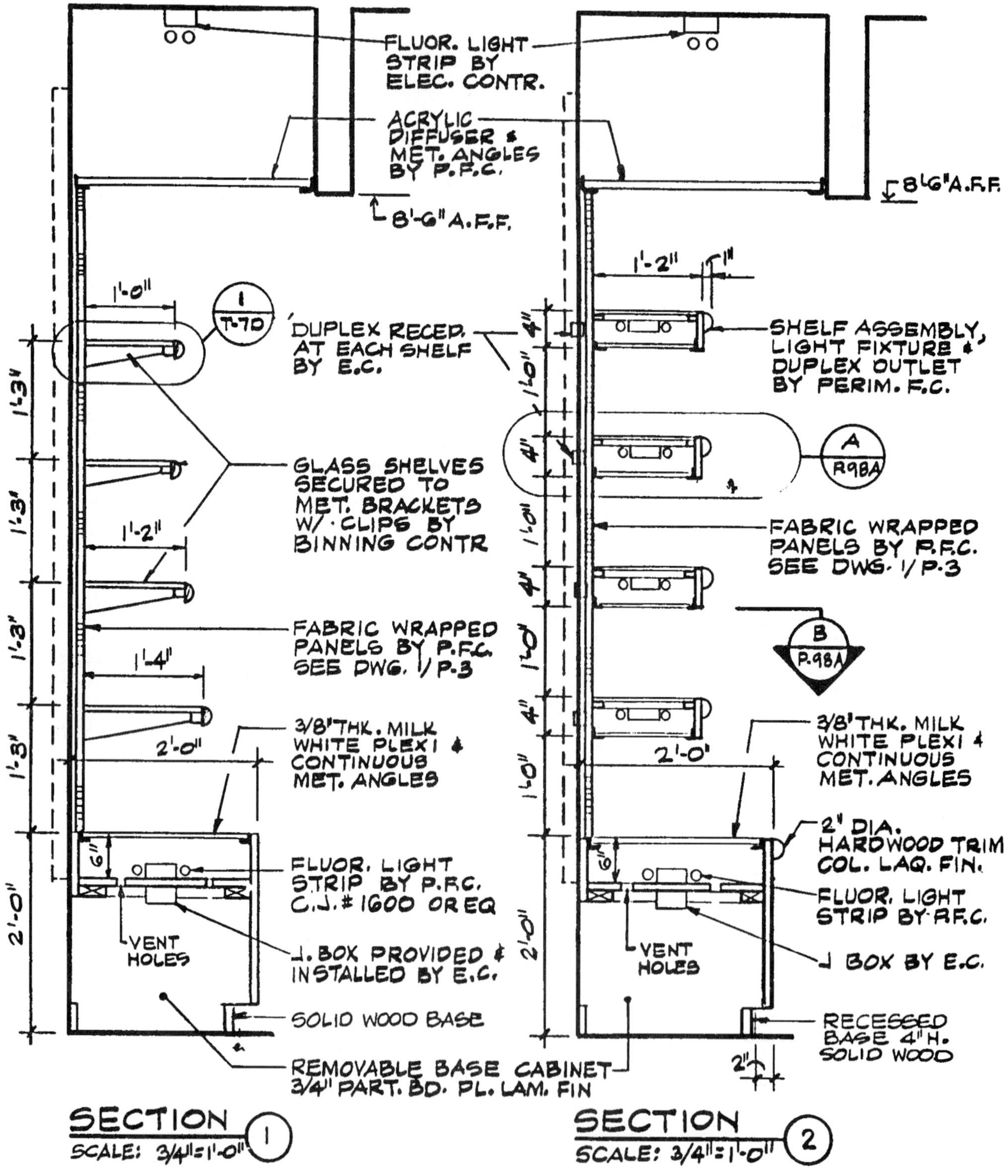
FLUOR. LIGHT STRIP BY ELEC. CONTR.
ACRYLIC DIFFUSER & MET. ANGLES BY P.F.C.
8'-6" A.F.F.
1'-0"
1 T-70
DUPLEX RECEP. AT EACH SHELF BY E.C.
GLASS SHELVES SECURED TO MET. BRACKETS W/ CLIPS BY BINNING CONTR
1'-2"
FABRIC WRAPPED PANELS BY P.F.C. SEE DWG. 1/P-3
1'-4"
3/8" THK. MILK WHITE PLEXI & CONTINUOUS MET. ANGLES
2'-0"
1'-3"
6"
FLUOR. LIGHT STRIP BY P.F.C. C.J. # 1600 OR EQ
VENT HOLES
J. BOX PROVIDED & INSTALLED BY E.C.
SOLID WOOD BASE
REMOVABLE BASE CABINET 3/4" PART. BD. PL. LAM. FIN
SECTION 1
SCALE: 3/4"=1'-0"
1'-2"
1"
4"
1'-0"
SHELF ASSEMBLY, LIGHT FIXTURE & DUPLEX OUTLET BY PERIM. F.C.
A R98A
FABRIC WRAPPED PANELS BY P.F.C. SEE DWG. 1/P-3
B P-98A
3/8" THK. MILK WHITE PLEXI & CONTINUOUS MET. ANGLES
2" DIA. HARDWOOD TRIM COL. LAQ. FIN.
FLUOR. LIGHT STRIP BY P.F.C.
J BOX BY E.C.
RECESSED BASE 4" H. SOLID WOOD
2"
SECTION 2
SCALE: 3/4"=1'-0"

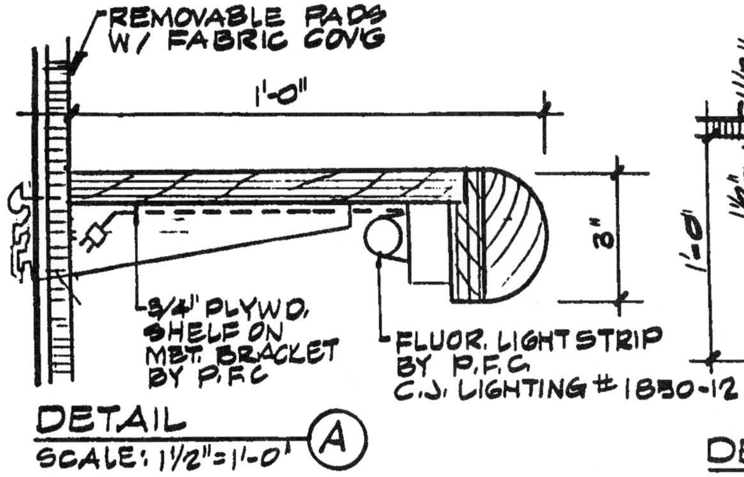
REMOVABLE PADS W/ FABRIC COV'G
1'-0"
3"
3/4" PLYWD. SHELF ON MET. BRACKET BY P.F.C
FLUOR. LIGHT STRIP BY P.F.C. C.J. LIGHTING #1830-12
DETAIL A
SCALE: 1 1/2"=1'-0"

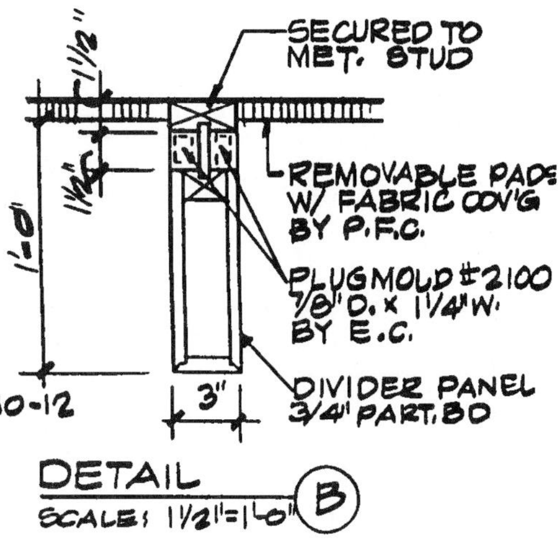
SECURED TO MET. STUD
1 1/2"
1'-0"
REMOVABLE PADS W/ FABRIC COV'G BY P.F.C.
PLUGMOLD #2100 7/8"D. x 1 1/4"W. BY E.C.
DIVIDER PANEL 3/4" PART. BD
3"
DETAIL B
SCALE: 1 1/2"=1'-0"

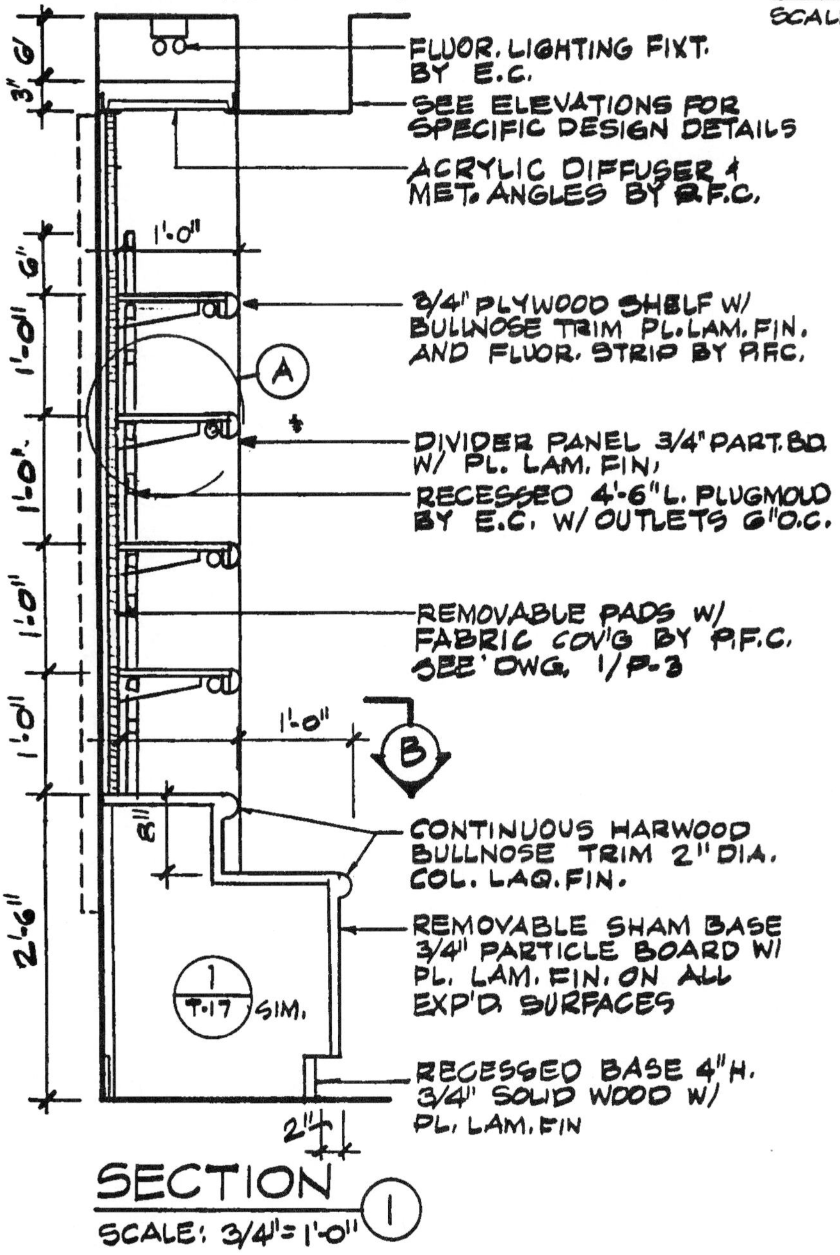
FLUOR. LIGHTING FIXT. BY E.C.
SEE ELEVATIONS FOR SPECIFIC DESIGN DETAILS
ACRYLIC DIFFUSER & MET. ANGLES BY P.F.C.
3/4" PLYWOOD SHELF W/ BULLNOSE TRIM PL. LAM. FIN. AND FLUOR. STRIP BY P.F.C.
DIVIDER PANEL 3/4" PART. BD. W/ PL. LAM. FIN.
RECESSED 4'-6" L. PLUGMOLD BY E.C. W/ OUTLETS 6" O.C.
REMOVABLE PADS W/ FABRIC COV'G BY P.F.C. SEE DWG. 1/P-3
CONTINUOUS HARWOOD BULLNOSE TRIM 2" DIA. COL. LAQ. FIN.
REMOVABLE SHAM BASE 3/4" PARTICLE BOARD W/ PL. LAM. FIN. ON ALL EXP'D SURFACES
RECESSED BASE 4"H. 3/4" SOLID WOOD W/ PL. LAM. FIN
1'-0"
1 T-17 SIM.
2'-6"
2"
SECTION 1
SCALE: 3/4"=1'-0"

DEPARTMENT STORES

Triple Mirror Details

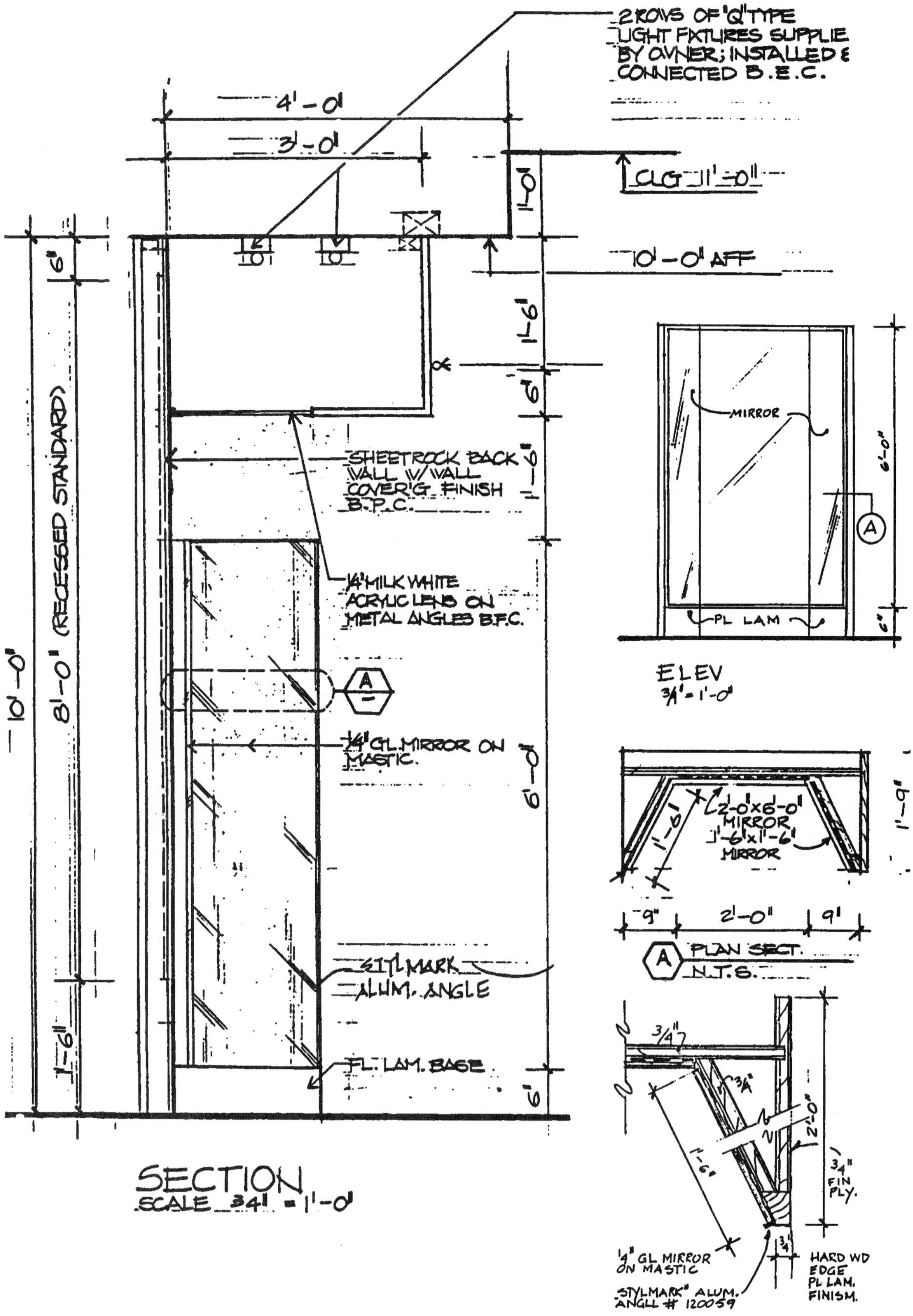
2 ROWS OF 'Q' TYPE LIGHT FIXTURES SUPPLIE BY OWNER; INSTALLED & CONNECTED B.E.C.
4'-0"
3'-0"
CLG 11'-0"
10'-0" AFF
10'-0"
8'-0" (RECESSED STANDARD)
6"
1'-6"
6"
1'-6"
6'-0"
6"
1'-6"
SHEETROCK BACK WALL W/ WALL COVER'G FINISH B.P.C.
1/4" MILK WHITE ACRYLIC LENS ON METAL ANGLES B.F.C.
1/4" GL. MIRROR ON MASTIC.
STYLMARK ALUM. ANGLE
PL. LAM. BASE
SECTION
SCALE 3/4" = 1'-0"
MIRROR
A
PL LAM
6'-0"
6"
ELEV
3/4" = 1'-0"
2'-0" x 6'-0" MIRROR
1'-6" x 1'-6" MIRROR
1'-6"
1'-9"
9"
2'-0"
9"
A PLAN SECT.
N.T.S.
3/4"
3/4"
2'-0"
1'-6"
3/4" FIN PLY.
3/4"
1/4" GL MIRROR ON MASTIC
"STYLMARK" ALUM. ANGLE # 120059
HARD WD EDGE PL LAM. FINISH.

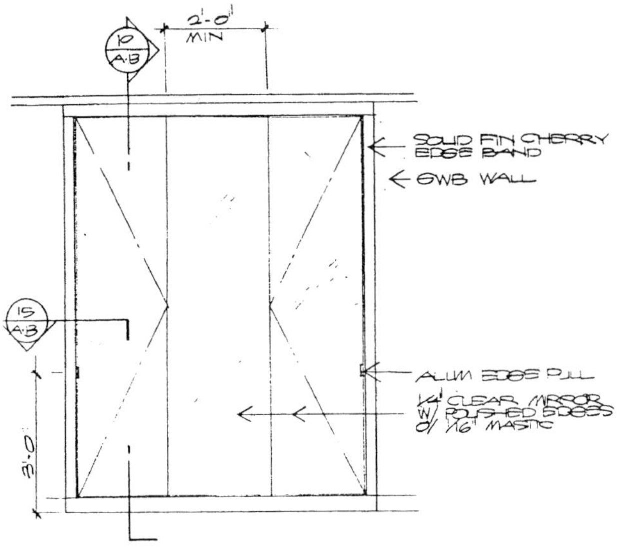

9 Elevation at Adj. 3-Way Mirror
Scale: 1/2" = 1'-0"

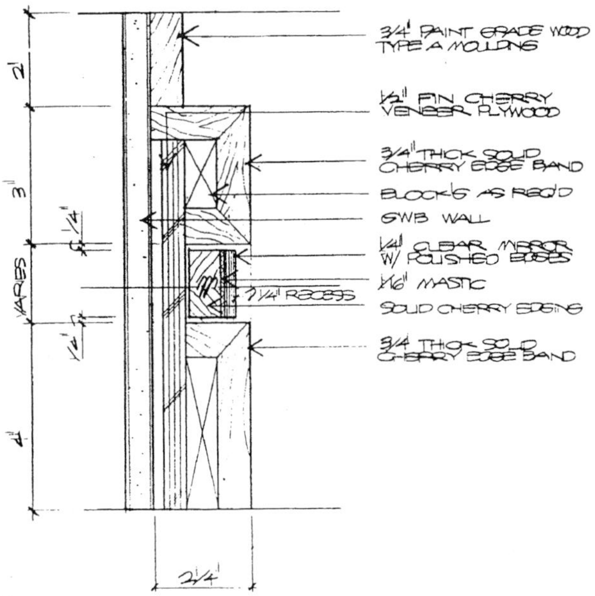

10 Section at Adj. 3-Way Mirror
Scale: 1/2" = 1"

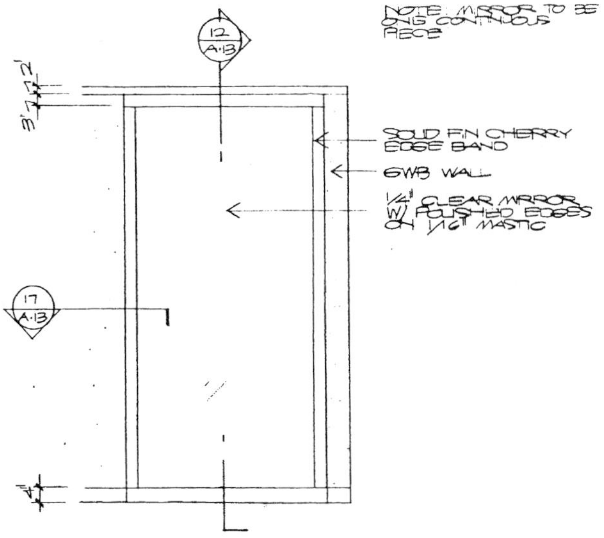

11 Elevation at Mirror
Scale: 1/2" = 1'-0"

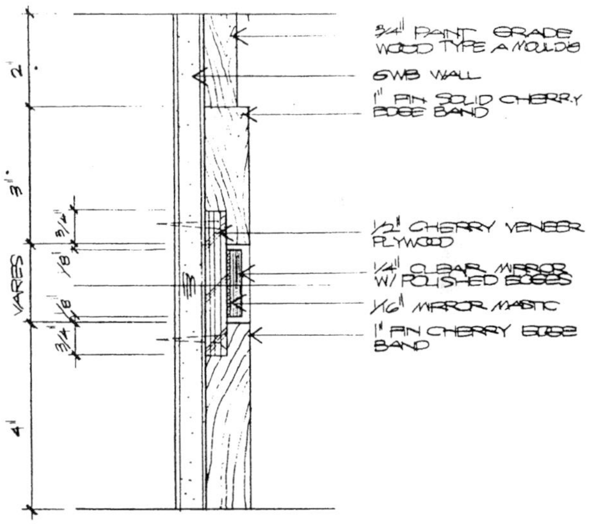

12 Section at Mirror
Scale: 1/2" = 1"

DEPARTMENT STORES
Mirror/Three-Way

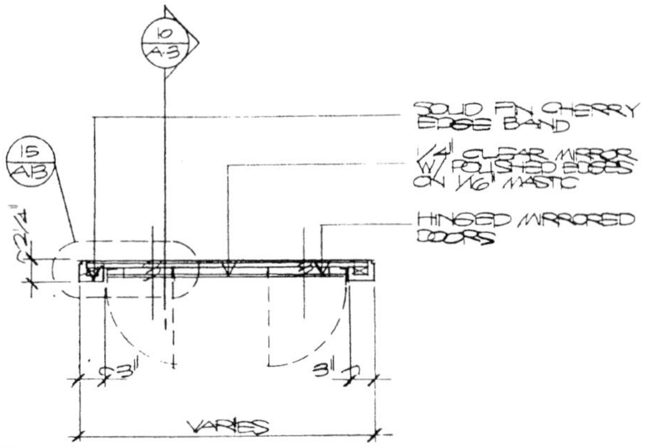

14 Plan at Adj. 3-Way Mirror
Scale: 1" = 1'-0"

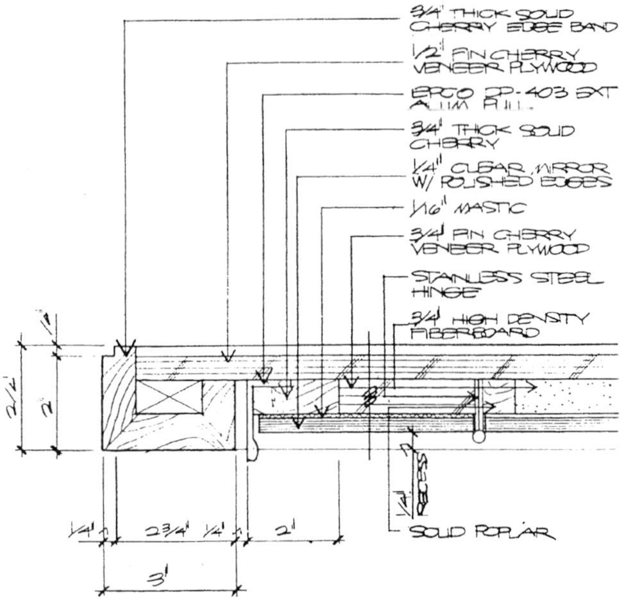

15 Plan Detail
Scale: 1/2" = 1"

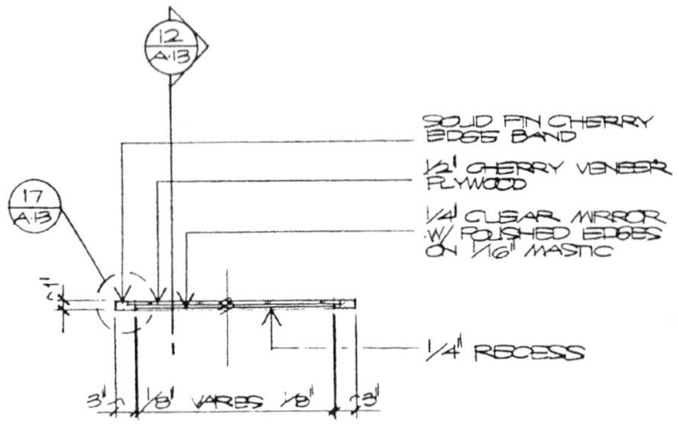

16 Plan at Mirror
Scale: 1" = 1'-0"

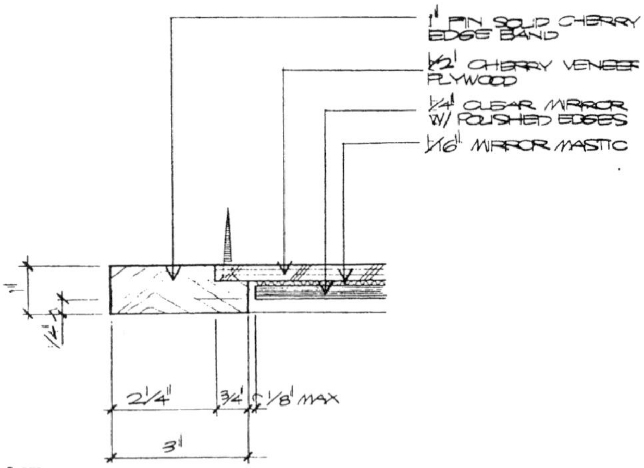

17 Plan Detail
Scale: 1/2" = 1"

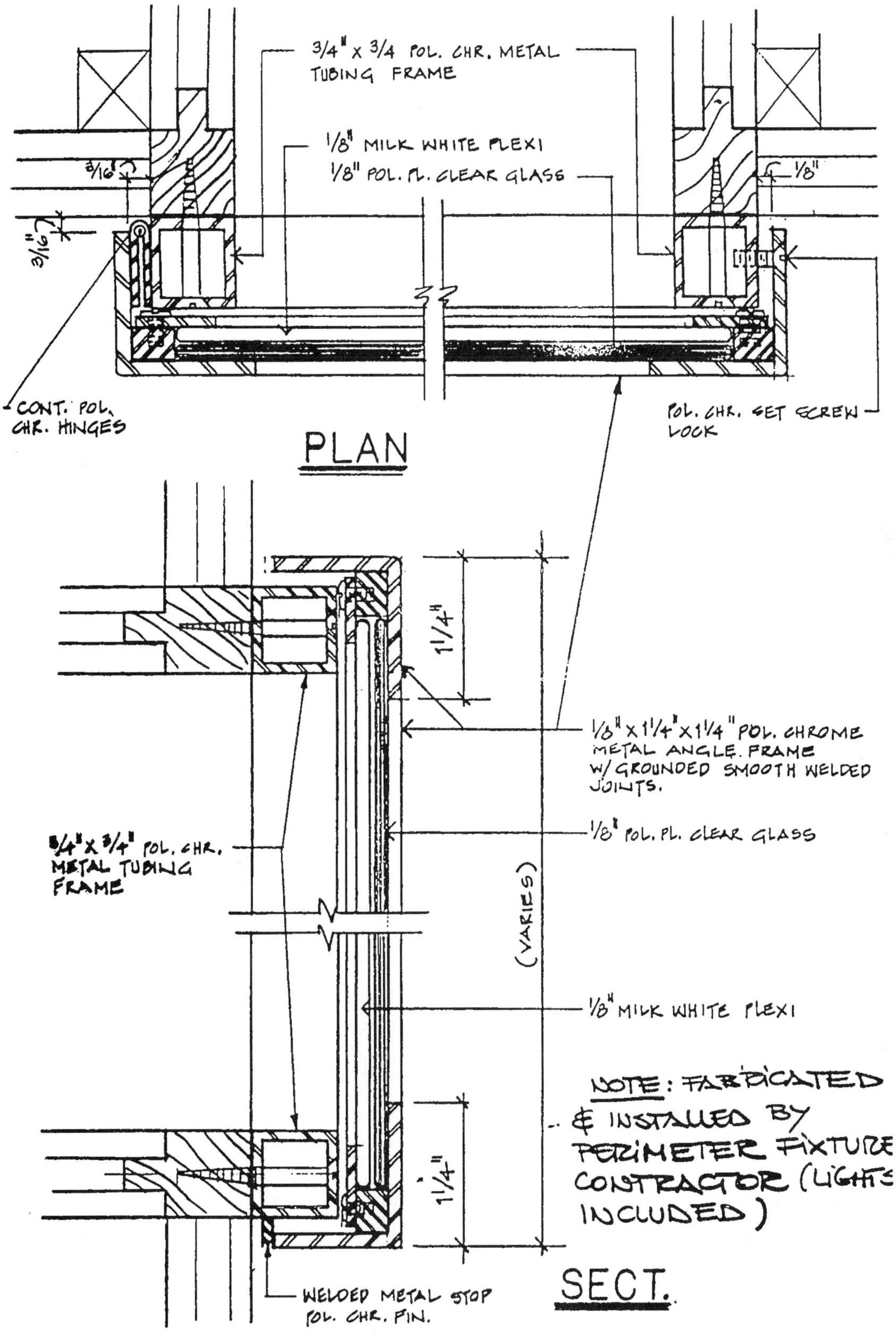
3/4" x 3/4 POL. CHR. METAL TUBING FRAME
1/8" MILK WHITE PLEXI
1/8" POL. PL. CLEAR GLASS
3/16"
3/16"
1/8"
CONT. POL. CHR. HINGES
POL. CHR. SET SCREW LOCK
PLAN
1 1/4"
1/8" x 1 1/4" x 1 1/4" POL. CHROME METAL ANGLE FRAME W/ GROUNDED SMOOTH WELDED JOINTS.
1/8" POL. PL. CLEAR GLASS
3/4" x 3/4" POL. CHR. METAL TUBING FRAME
(VARIES)
1/8" MILK WHITE PLEXI
NOTE: FABRICATED & INSTALLED BY PERIMETER FIXTURE CONTRACTOR (LIGHTS INCLUDED)
1 1/4"
WELDED METAL STOP POL. CHR. FIN.
SECT.

TYPICAL TRANSPARENCY DETAIL

DEPARTMENT STORES

Feature Wall Lighting

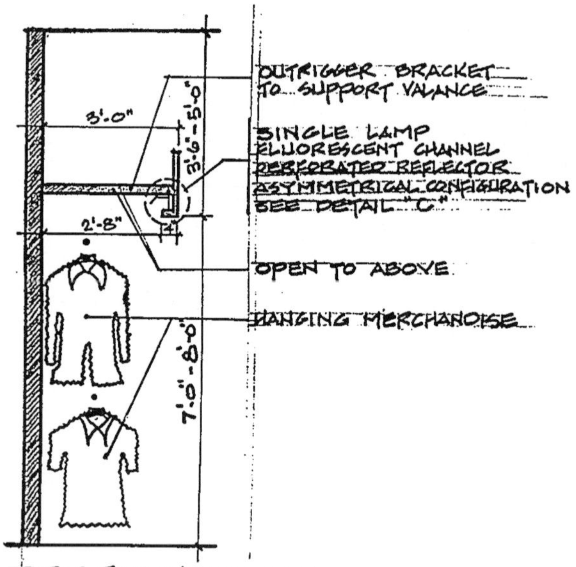

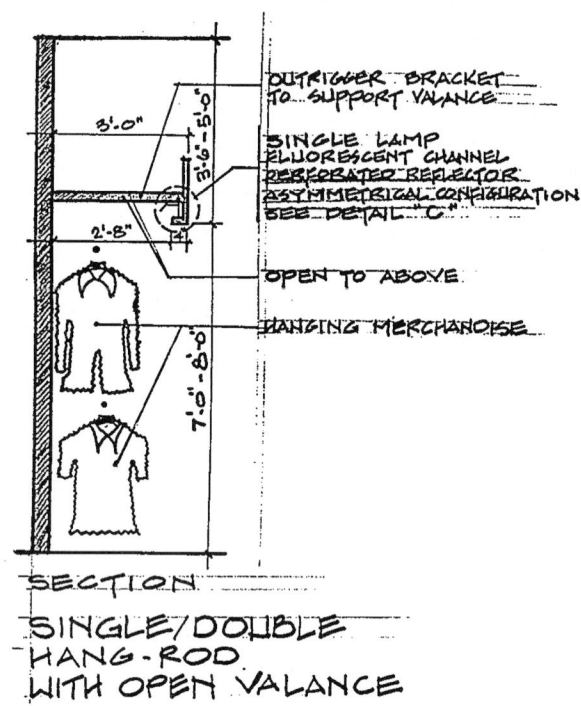

SECTION
SINGLE/DOUBLE HANG-ROD WITH OPEN VALANCE

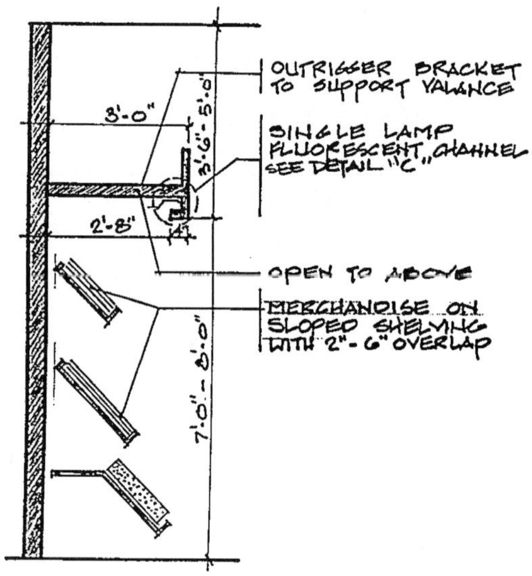

SECTION
SLOPED SHELVING WITH OPEN VALANCE

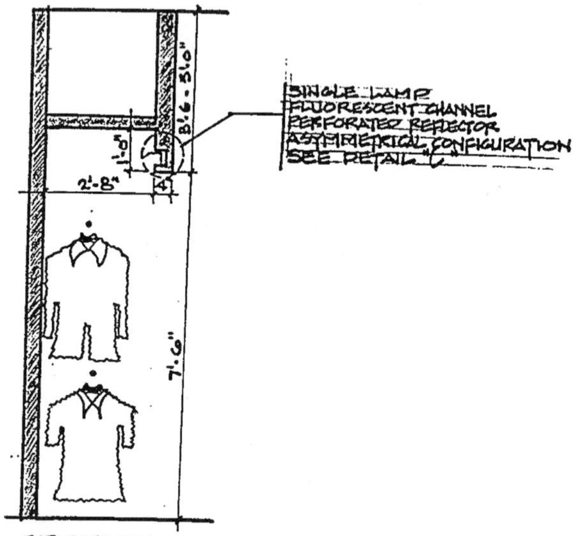

SECTION
SINGLE/DOUBLE HANG-ROD

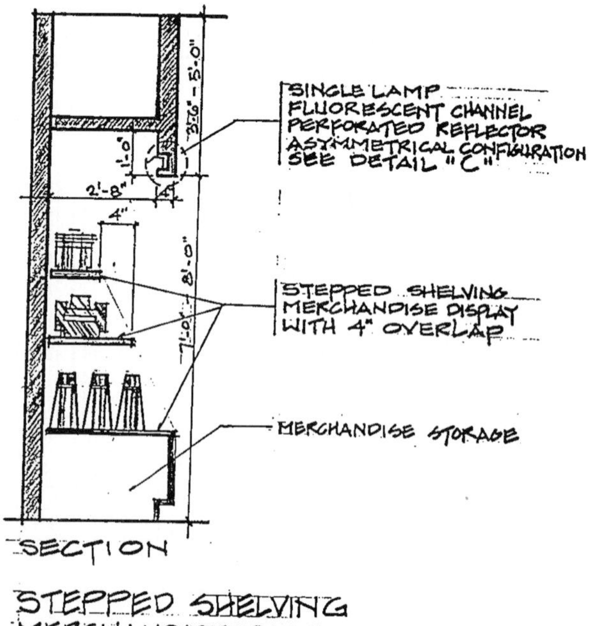

SECTION
STEPPED SHELVING MERCHANDISE DISPLAY

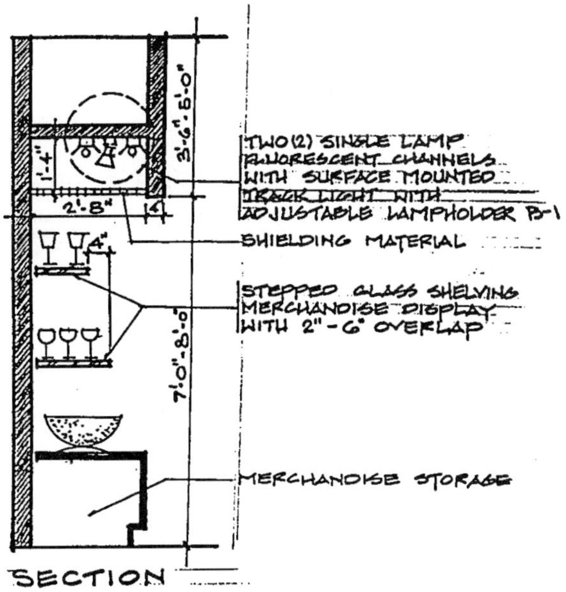

SECTION

STEPPED SHELVING MERCHANDISE DISPLAY

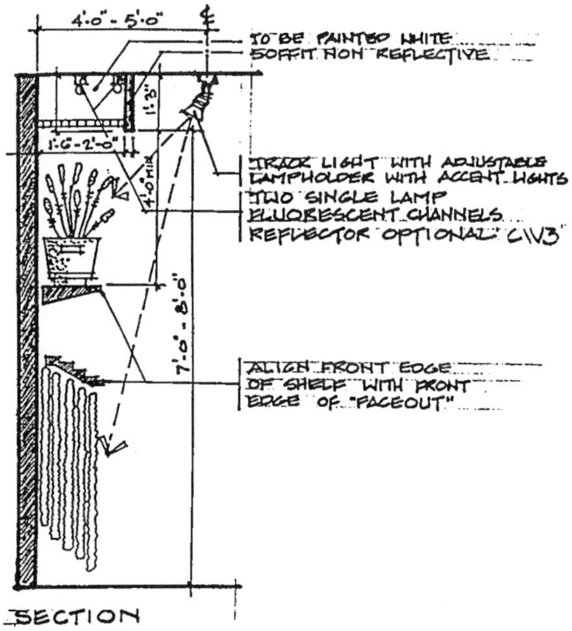

SECTION

FEATURE WALL DISPLAY WITH ILLUMINATED SOFFIT AND ACCENT LIGHT

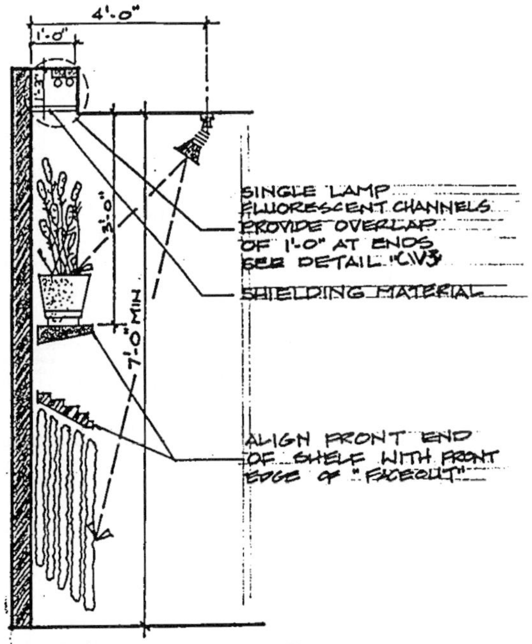

SECTION

FEATURE WALL DISPLAY WITH RECESSED COVE IN SOFFIT AND TRACK LIGHT

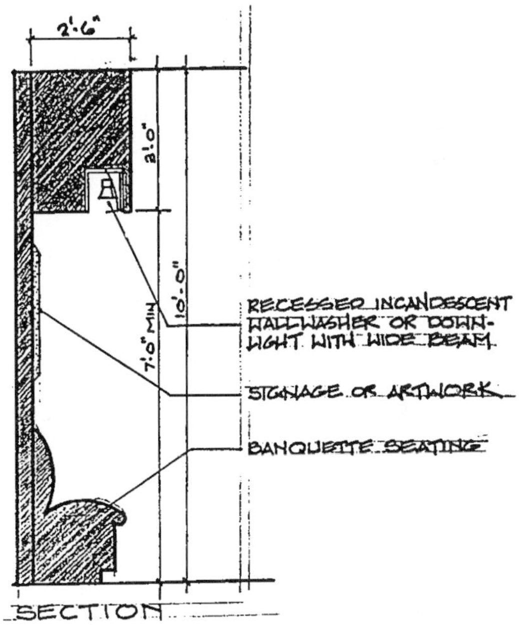

SECTION

FEATURE WALL DISPLAY DROPPED SOFFIT ABOVE BANQUETTE SEATING

DEPARTMENT STORES

Feature Wall Lighting

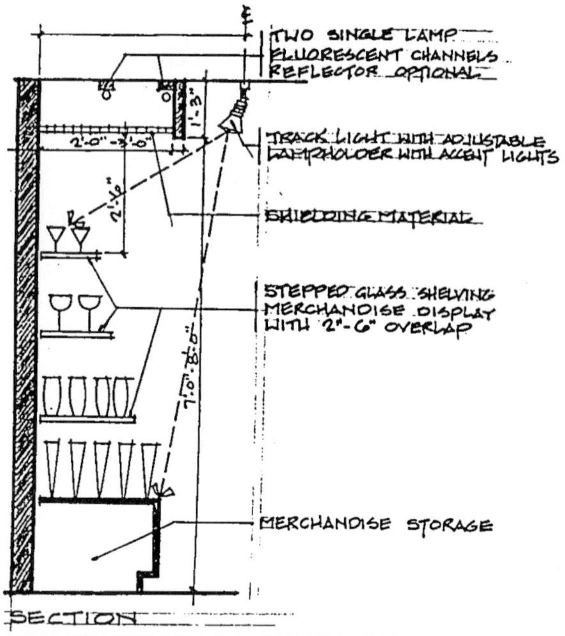

FEATURE WALL DISPLAY WITH ILLUMINATED SOFFIT AND ACCENT LIGHT

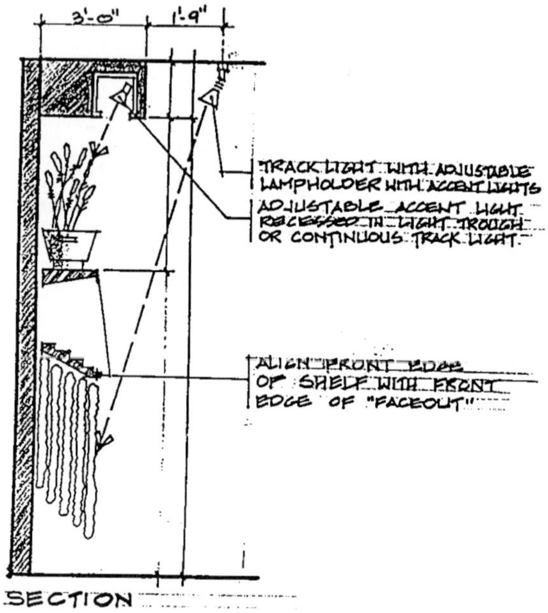

FEATURE WALL DISPLAY WITH RECESSED LIGHT TROUGH AND ACCENT LIGHT

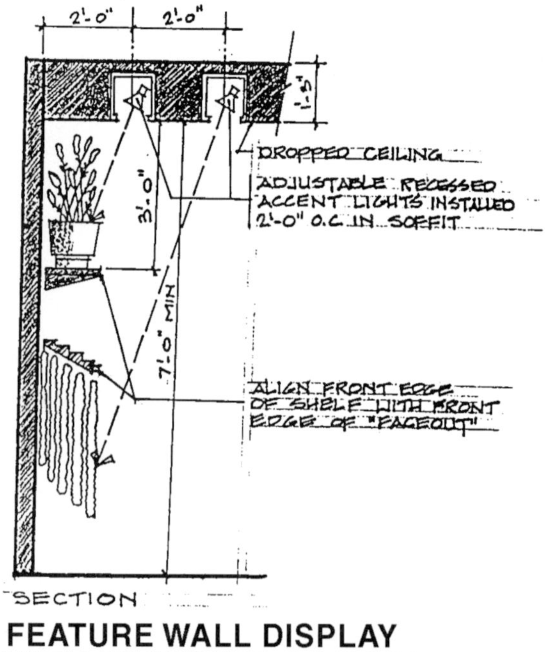

FEATURE WALL DISPLAY WITH RECESSED ACCENT LIGHT IN DROPPED CEILING

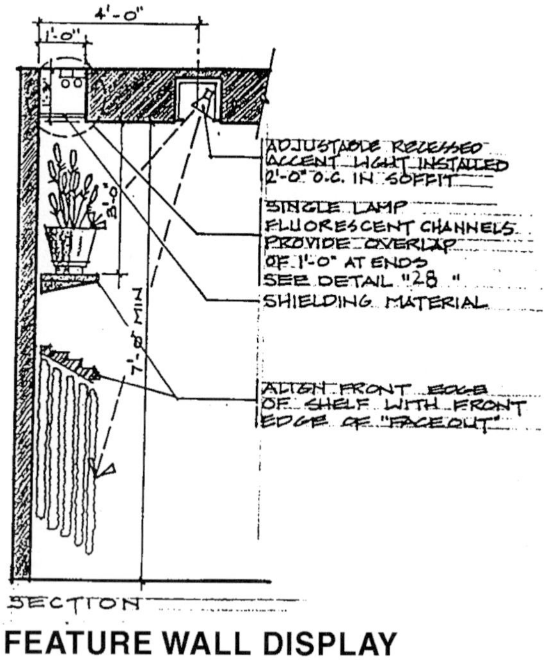

FEATURE WALL DISPLAY WITH RECESSED COVE IN SOFFIT AND ACCENT LIGHT

DEPARTMENT STORES
Display Case/Vitrine Section

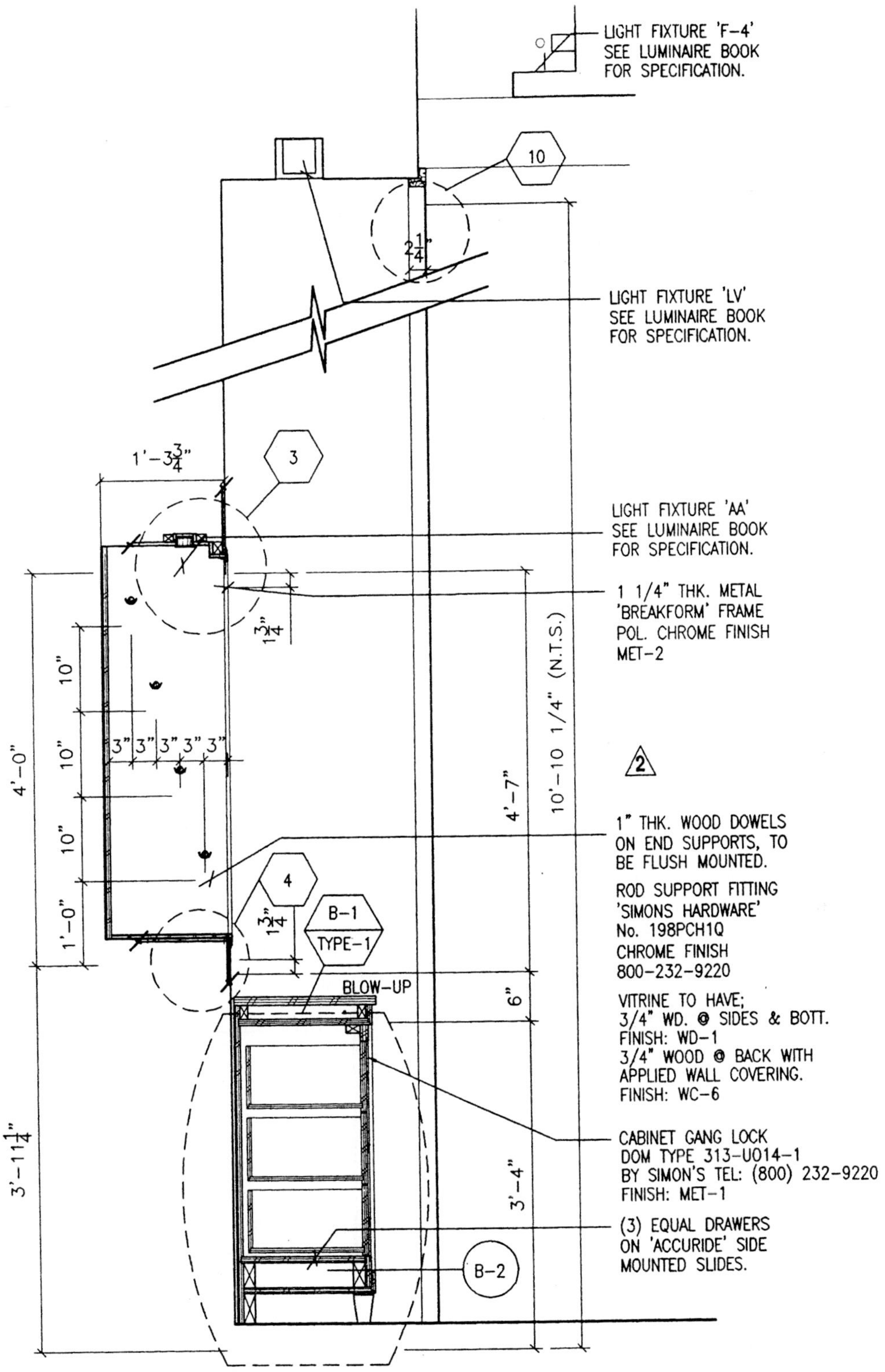

B-1 **SECTION**
SCALE: 3/4"=1'-0"

DEPARTMENT STORES
Display Case/Vitrine Section

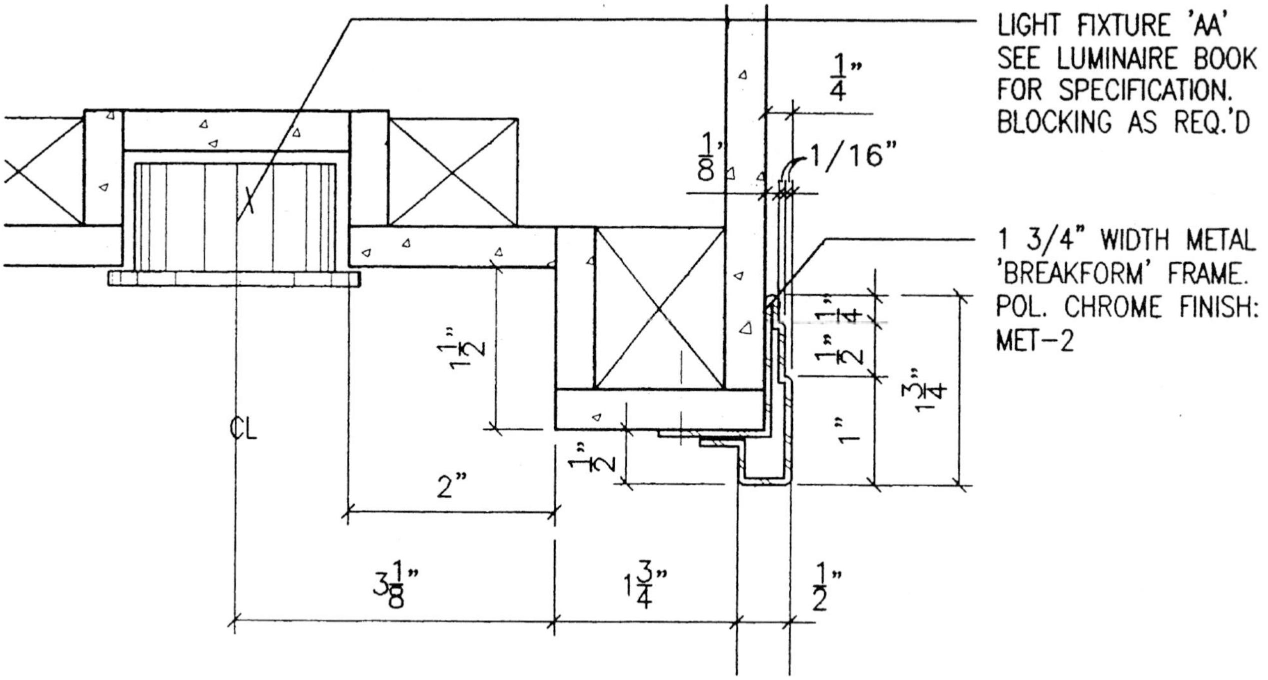

3 VITRINE DETAIL TOP
SCALE: HALF SCALE

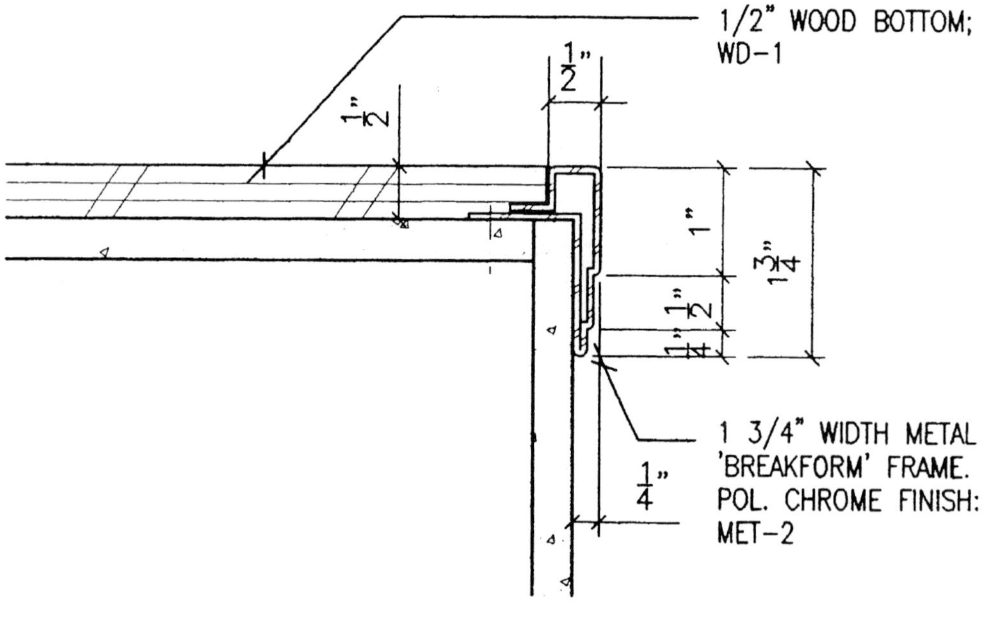

4 VITRINE DETAIL BOTTOM
SCALE: HALF SCALE

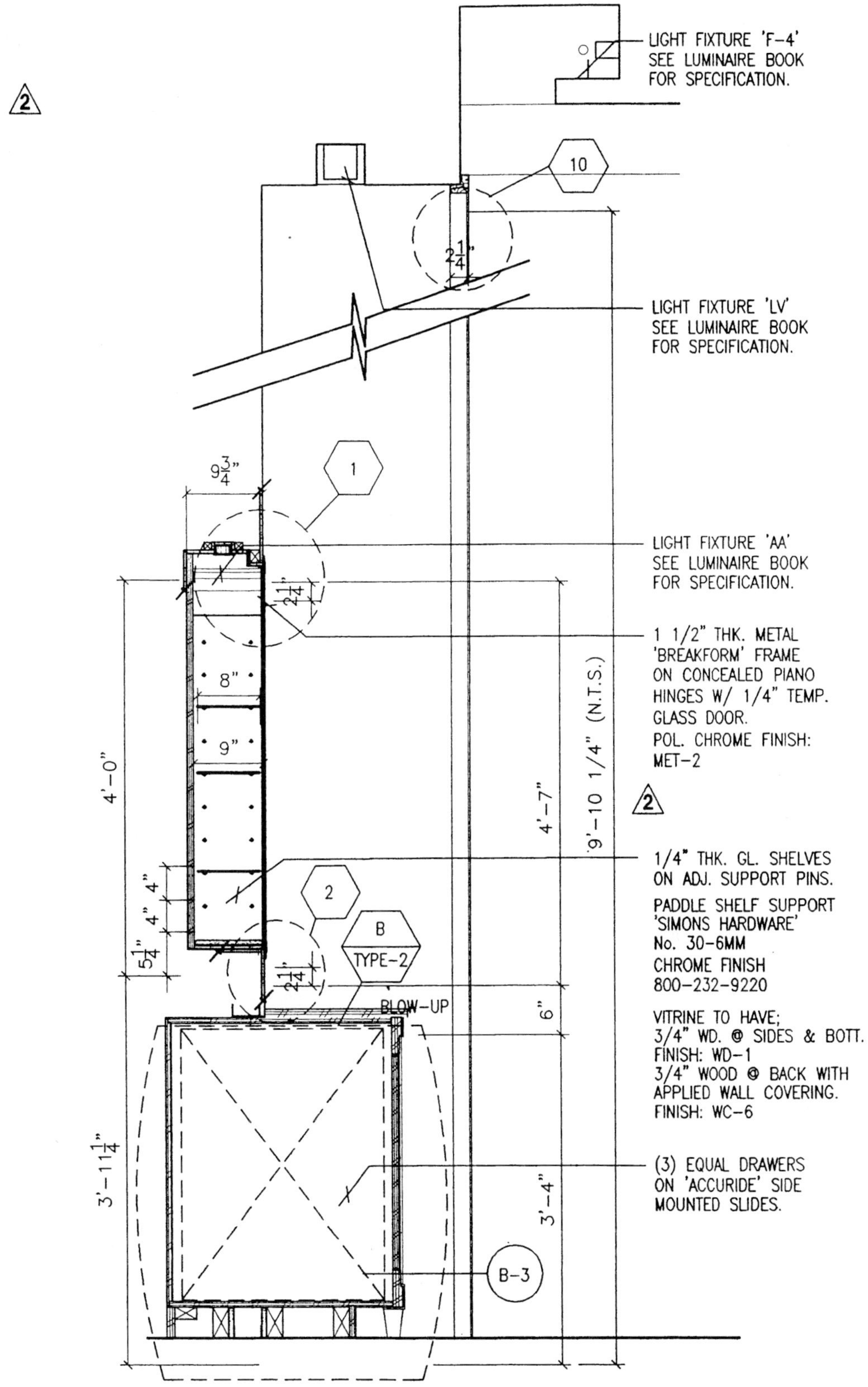
2
LIGHT FIXTURE 'F-4'
SEE LUMINAIRE BOOK
FOR SPECIFICATION.
10
2 1/4"
LIGHT FIXTURE 'LV'
SEE LUMINAIRE BOOK
FOR SPECIFICATION.
9 3/4"
1
LIGHT FIXTURE 'AA'
SEE LUMINAIRE BOOK
FOR SPECIFICATION.
2 1/4"
1 1/2" THK. METAL
'BREAKFORM' FRAME
ON CONCEALED PIANO
HINGES W/ 1/4" TEMP.
GLASS DOOR.
POL. CHROME FINISH:
MET-2
8"
9"
4'-0"
4'-7"
9'-10 1/4" (N.T.S.)
2
1/4" THK. GL. SHELVES
ON ADJ. SUPPORT PINS.
PADDLE SHELF SUPPORT
'SIMONS HARDWARE'
No. 30-6MM
CHROME FINISH
800-232-9220
4"
4"
5 1/4"
2
B
TYPE-2
BLOW-UP
2 1/4"
6"
VITRINE TO HAVE;
3/4" WD. @ SIDES & BOTT.
FINISH: WD-1
3/4" WOOD @ BACK WITH
APPLIED WALL COVERING.
FINISH: WC-6
3'-11 1/4"
3'-4"
(3) EQUAL DRAWERS
ON 'ACCURIDE' SIDE
MOUNTED SLIDES.
B-3

B **SECTION**
SCALE: 3/4"=1'-0"

DEPARTMENT STORES

Display Case/Vitrine Section

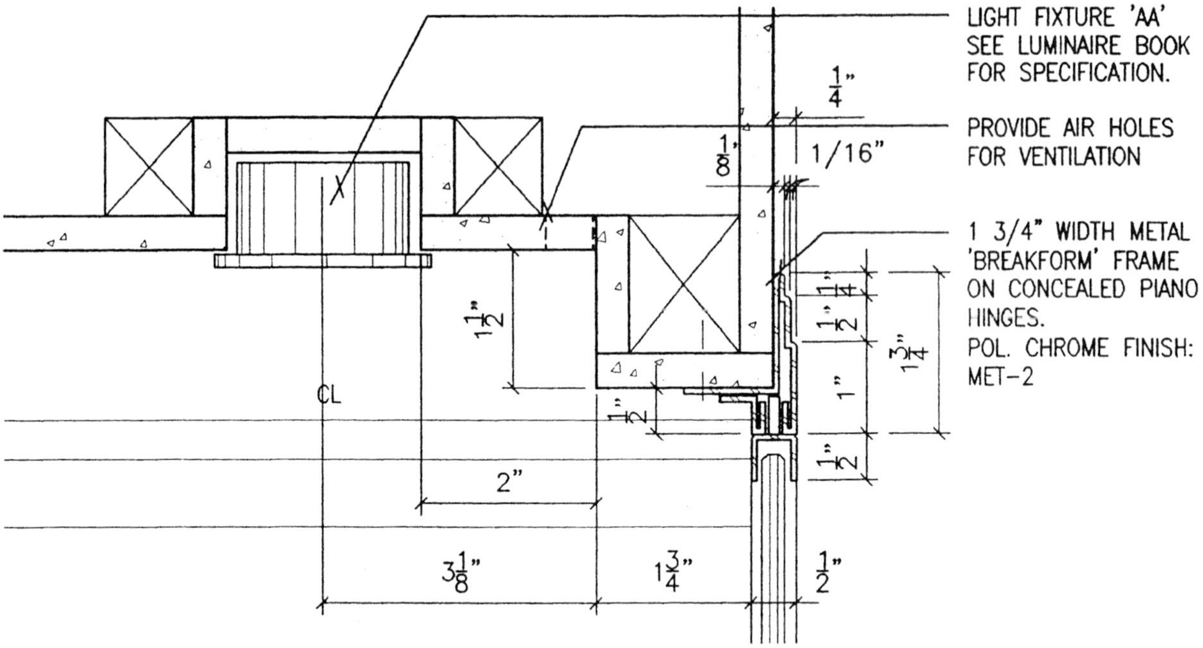

VITRINE DETAIL TOP

(1) SCALE: HALF SCALE

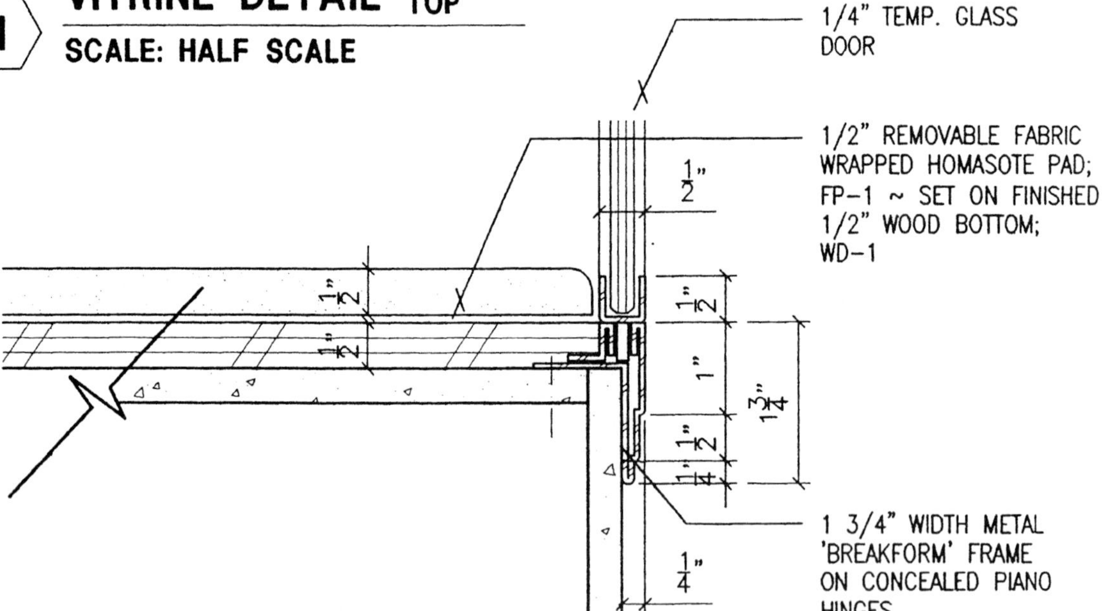

VITRINE DETAIL BOTTOM

(2) SCALE: HALF SCALE

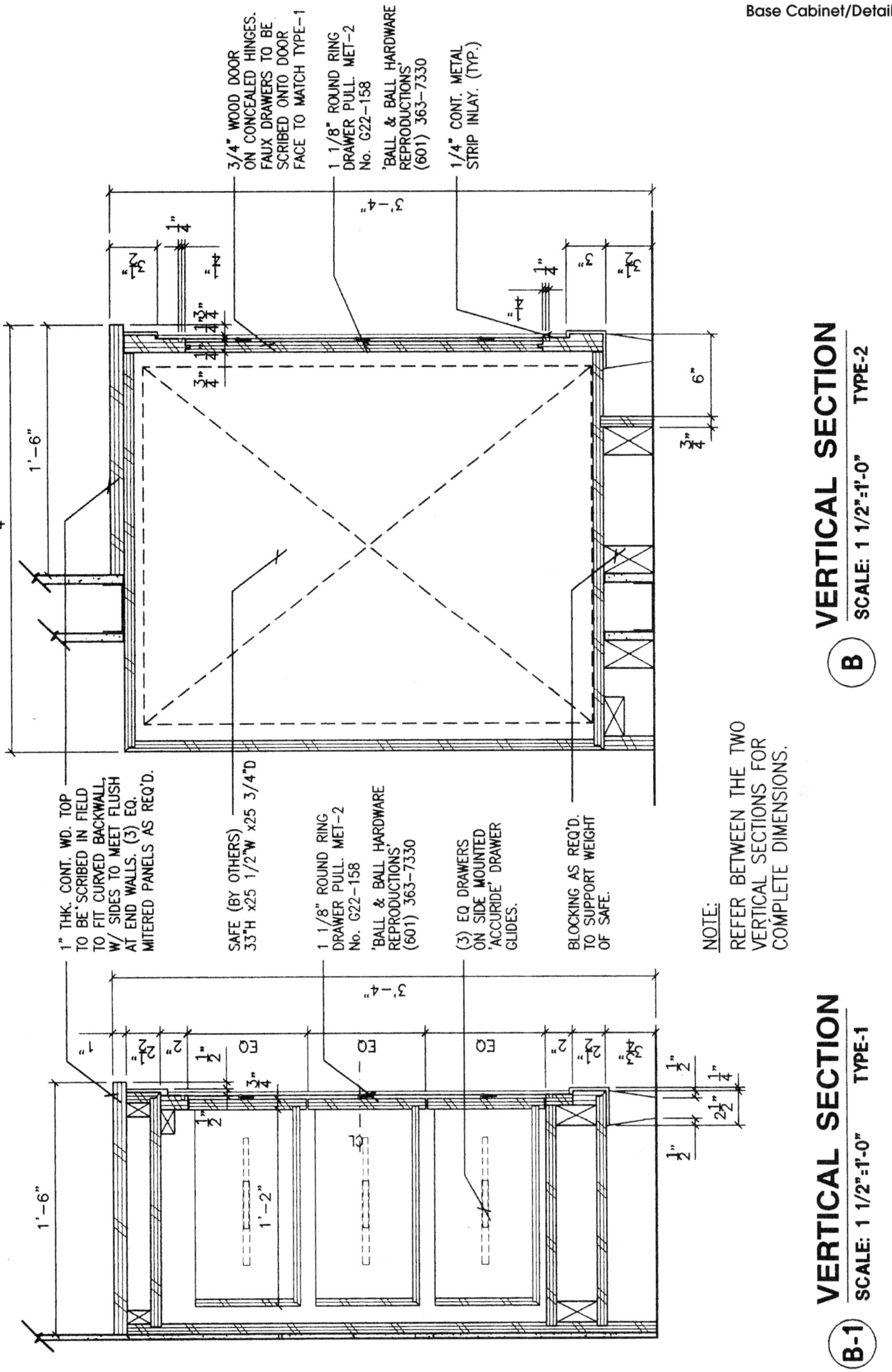

B-1 VERTICAL SECTION
SCALE: 1 1/2"=1'-0" TYPE-1

B VERTICAL SECTION
SCALE: 1 1/2"=1'-0" TYPE-2

DEPARTMENT STORES
Base Cabinet/Plan Section

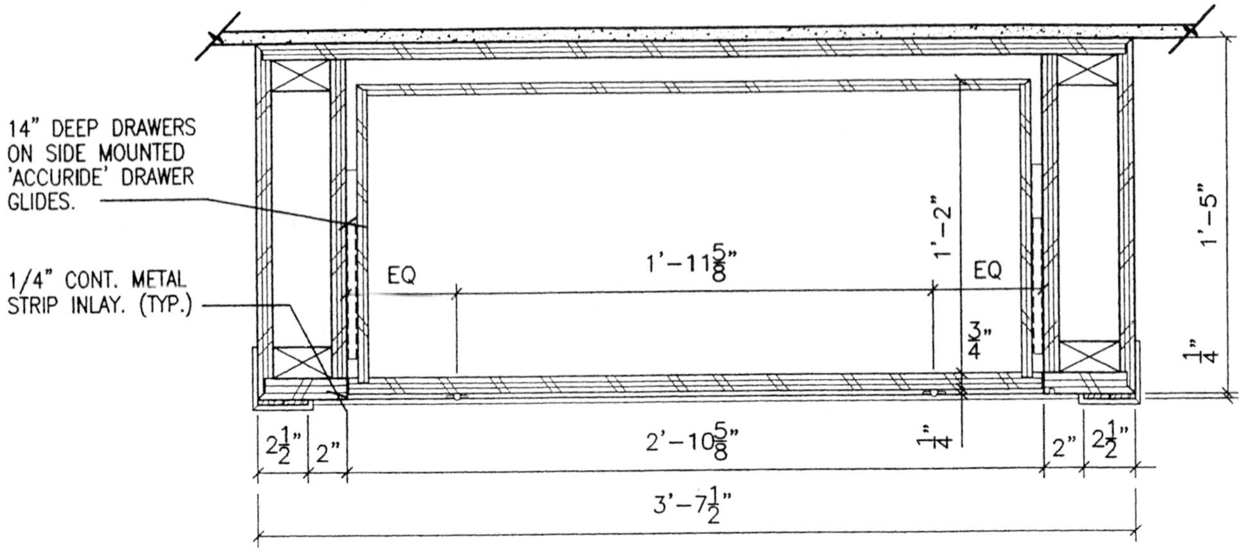

B-2 **PLAN SECTION**
SCALE: 1 1/2":1'-0" TYPE-1

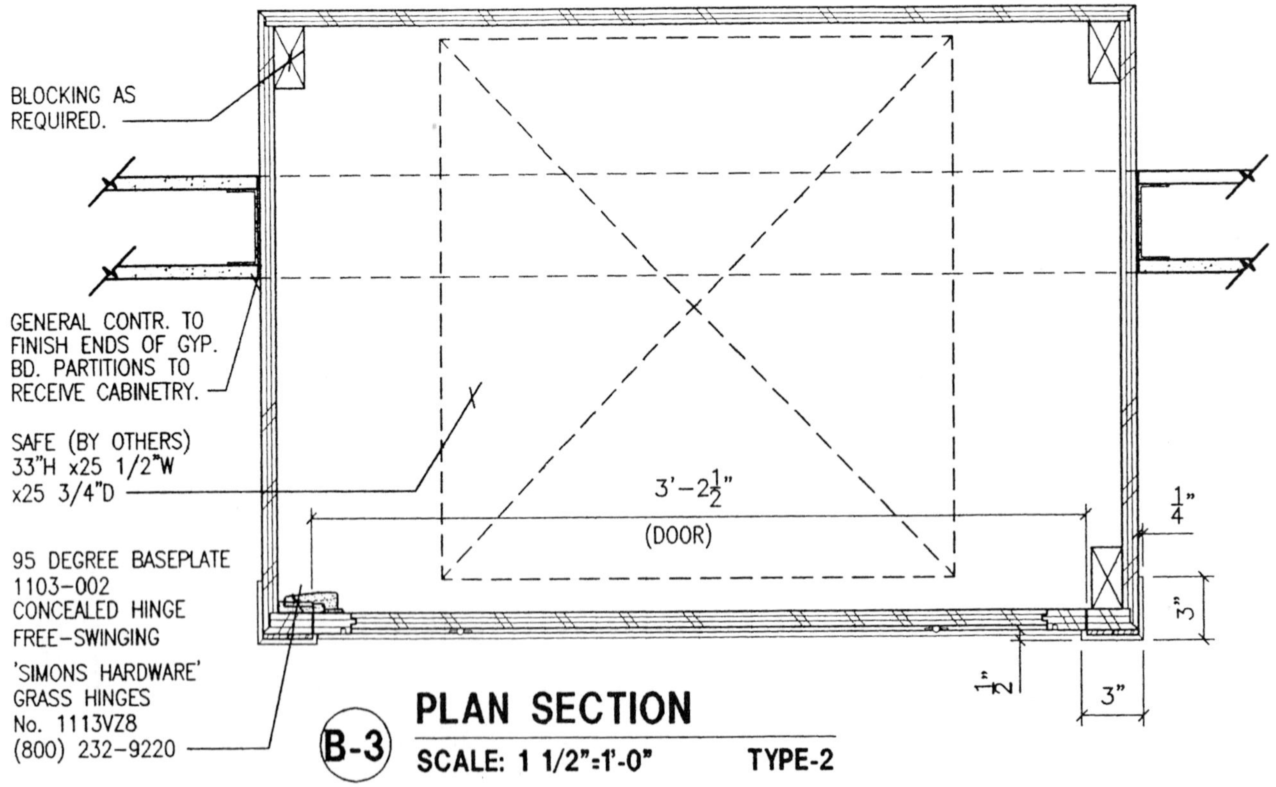

B-3 **PLAN SECTION**
SCALE: 1 1/2":1'-0" TYPE-2

DEPARTMENT STORES

Wall Paneling/Elevation and Details

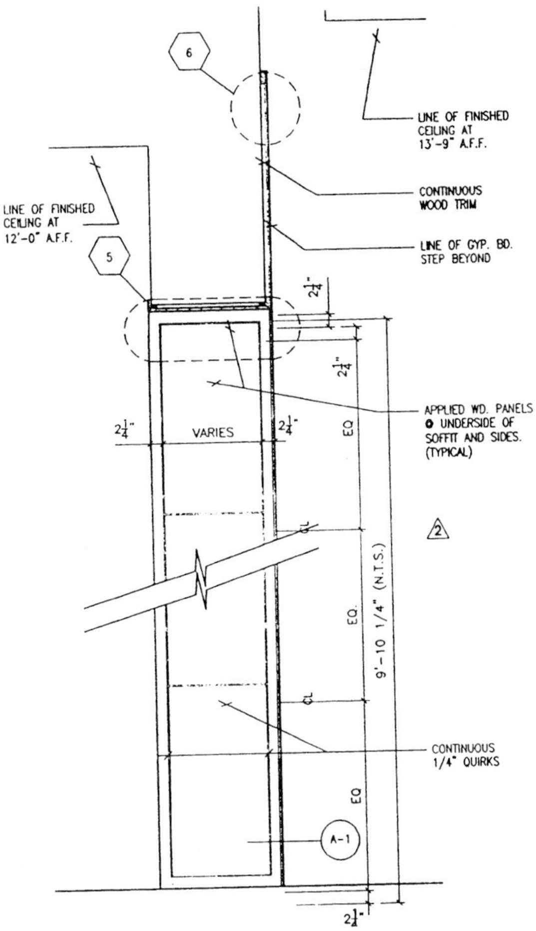

D SECTION
SCALE: 3/4"=1'-0"

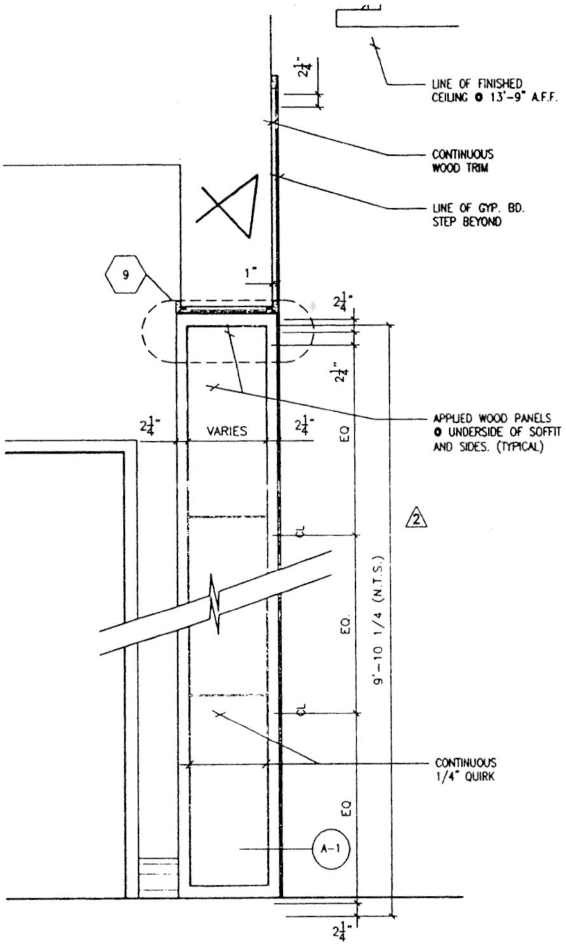

A SECTION
SCALE: 3/4"=1'-0"

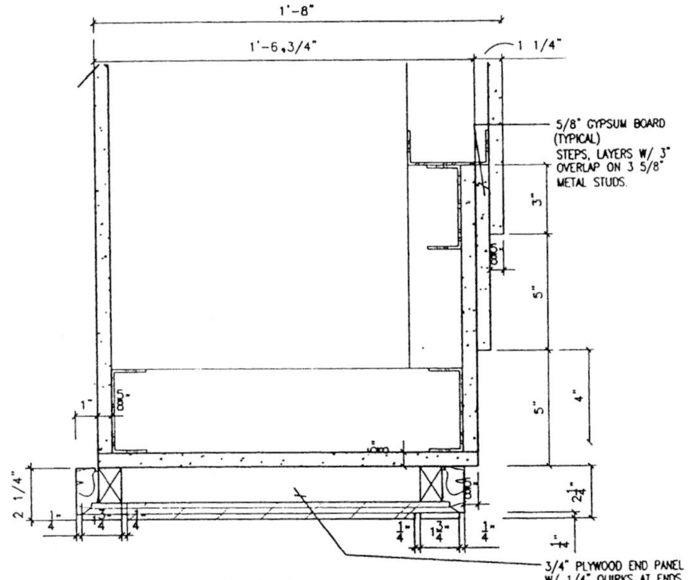

A-1 PLAN SECTION
SCALE: 3"=1'-0"

DEPARTMENT STORES
Wall Paneling/Details

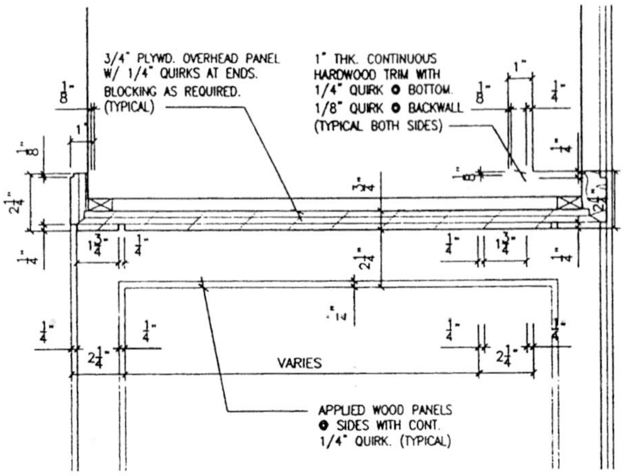

5 **TRIM DETAIL** @ CEILING
SCALE: 3"=1'-0"

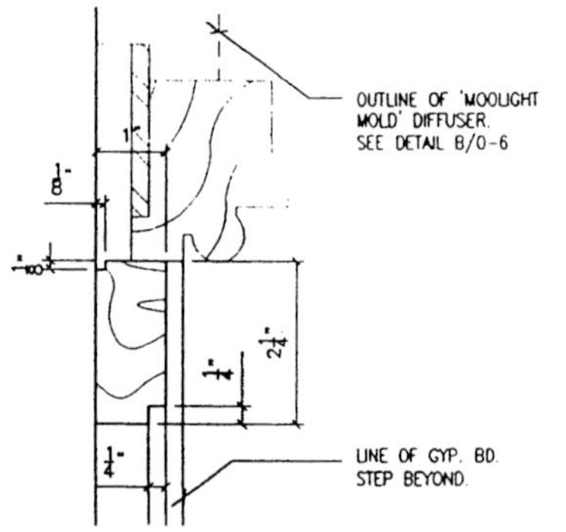

6 **TRIM DETAIL** TOP
SCALE: HALF SCALE

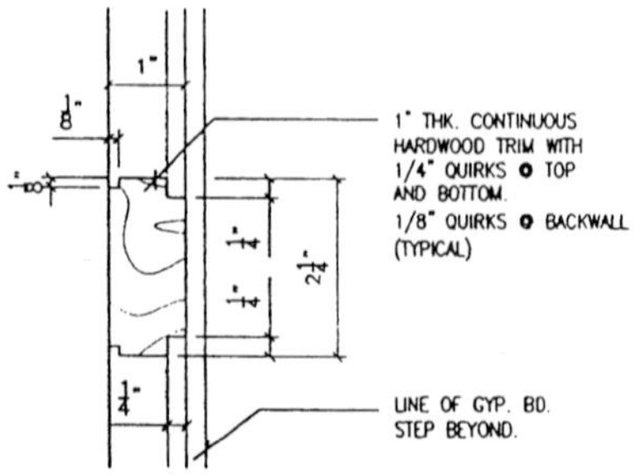

7 **TRIM DETAIL** MIDDLE
SCALE: HALF SCALE

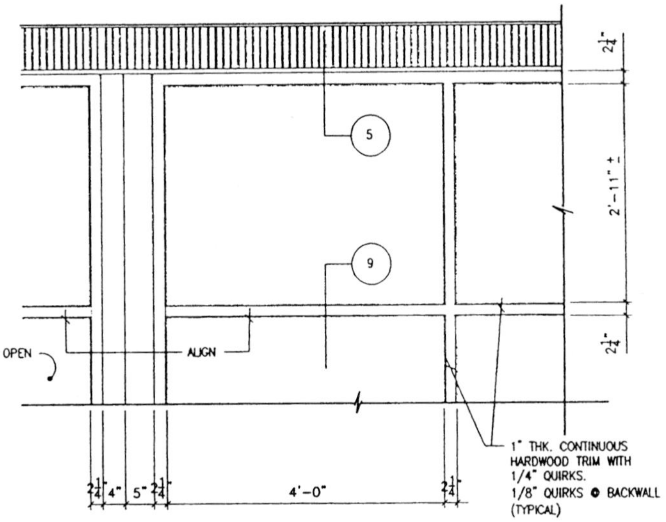

8 **PANEL TRIM DETAIL**
SCALE: 3/4"=1'-0"

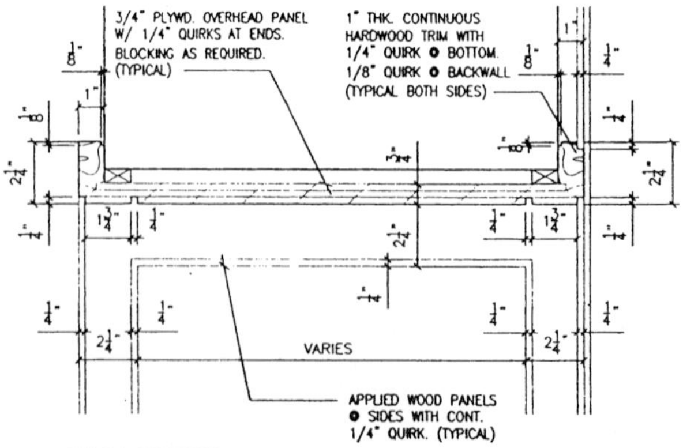

9 **TRIM DETAIL** @ CEILING
SCALE: 3"=1'-0"

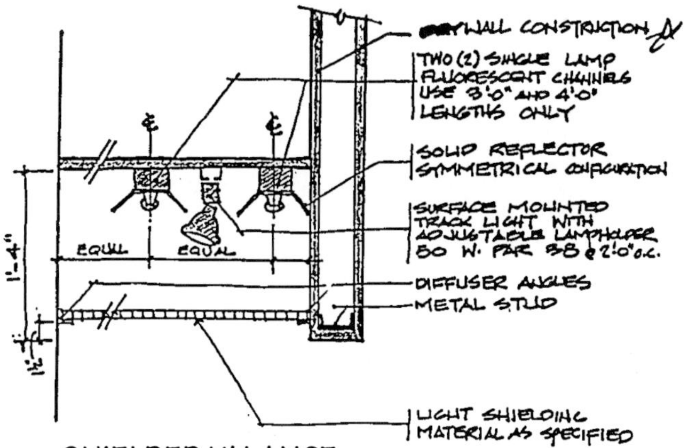

SHIELDED VALANCE
WITH TWO (2) SINGLE
LAMP FLUORESCENT
CHANNELS AND TRACK
LIGHT WITH INCANDESCENT
"CURTAIN WALL" TYPE

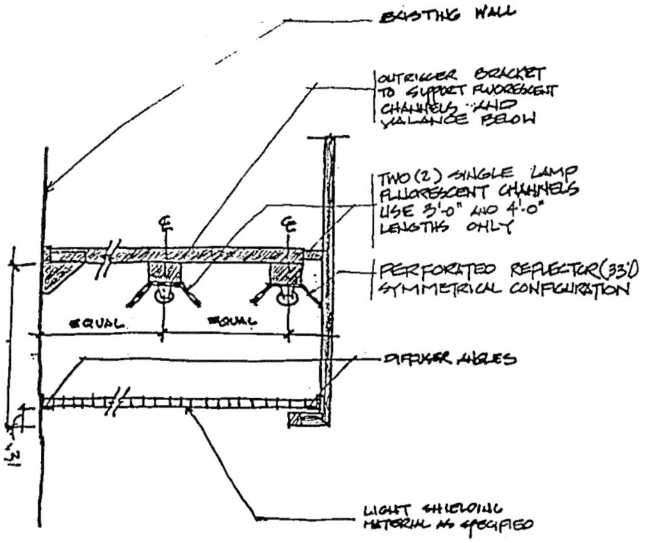

SHIELDED VALANCE
WITH TWO (2) SINGLE
LAMP FLUORESCENT CHANNELS

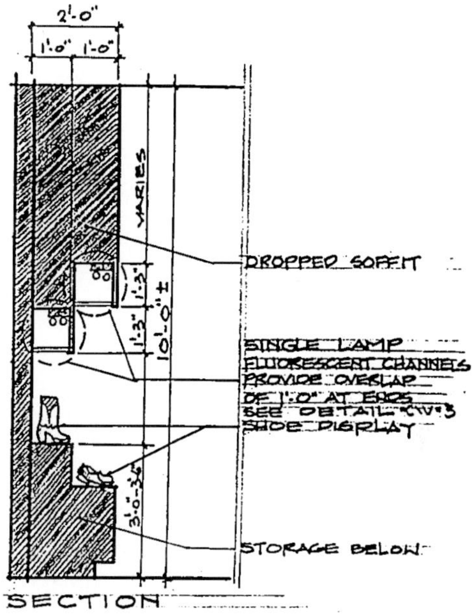

FEATURE WALL DISPLAY
WITH DOUBLE COVE
IN SOFFIT

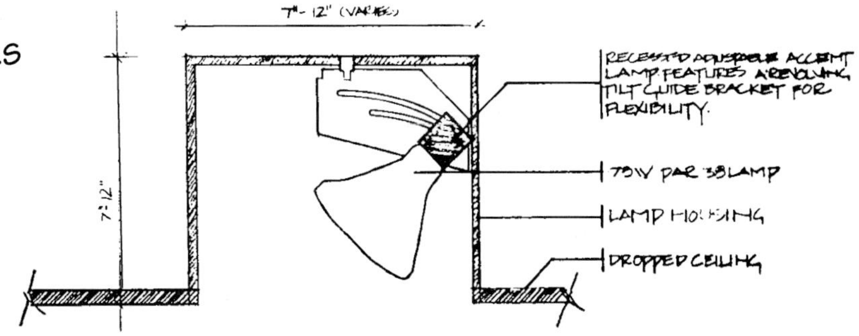

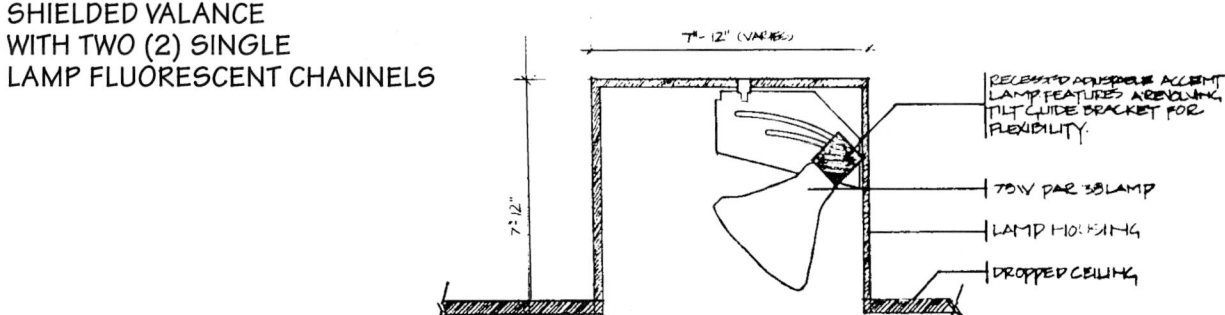

RECESSED ADJUSTABLE
ACCENT LIGHT

DEPARTMENT STORES

Valance and Cove Lighting Details

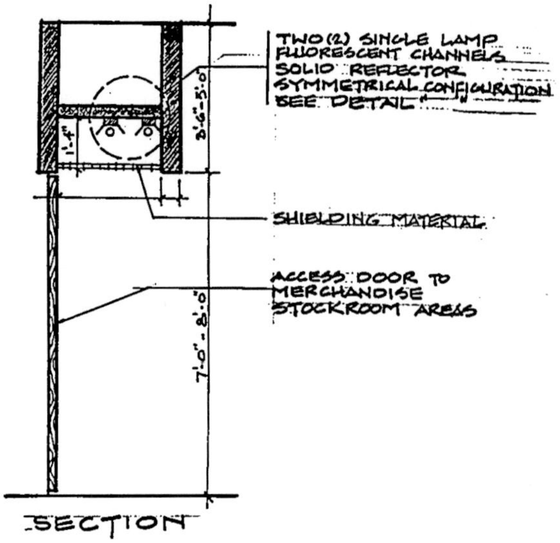

ACCESS DOOR THRU
MERCHANDISE DISPLAY
"CURTAIN WALL"

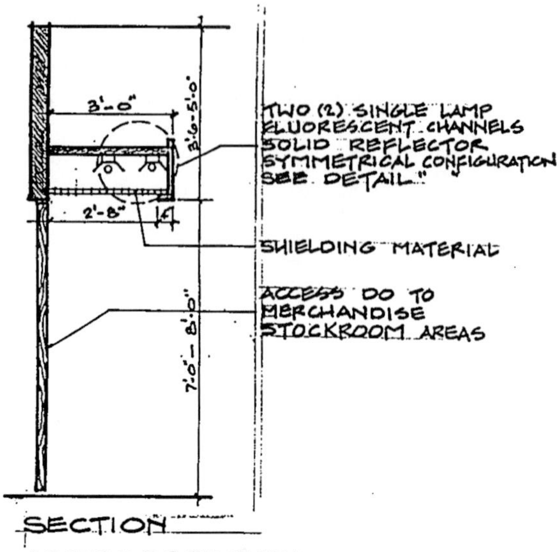

ACCESS DOOR THRU
MERCHANDISE DISPLAY
"OPEN VALANCE"

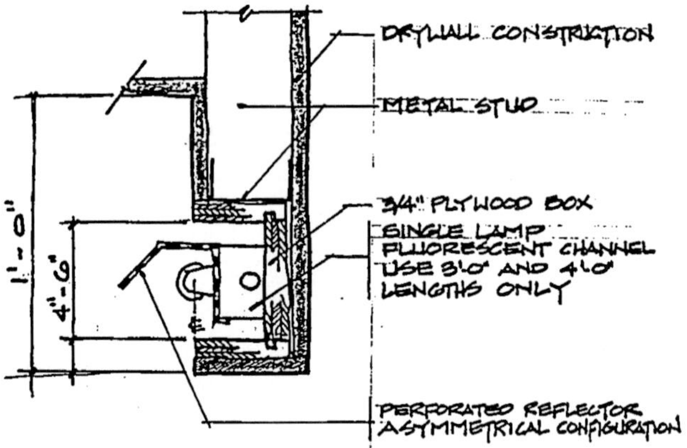

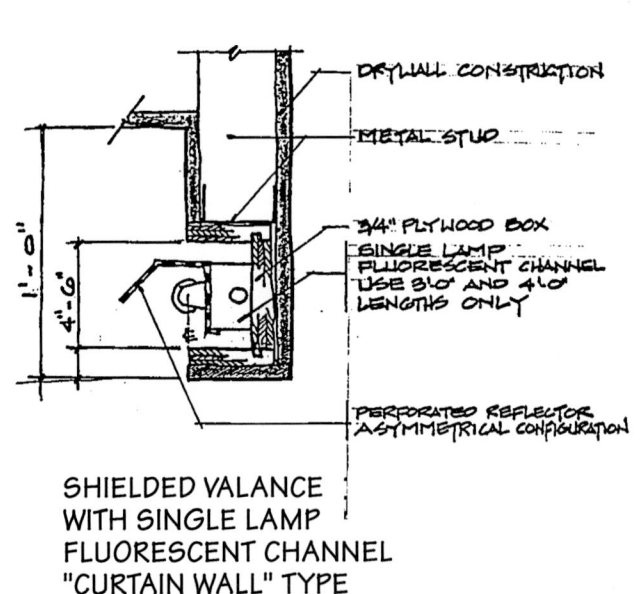

SHIELDED VALANCE
WITH SINGLE LAMP
FLUORESCENT CHANNEL
"CURTAIN WALL" TYPE

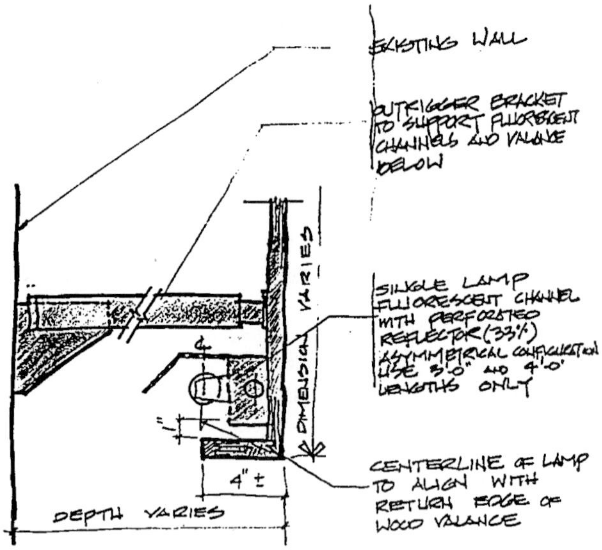

VALANCE WITH
SINGLE LAMP
FLUORESCENT CHANNEL

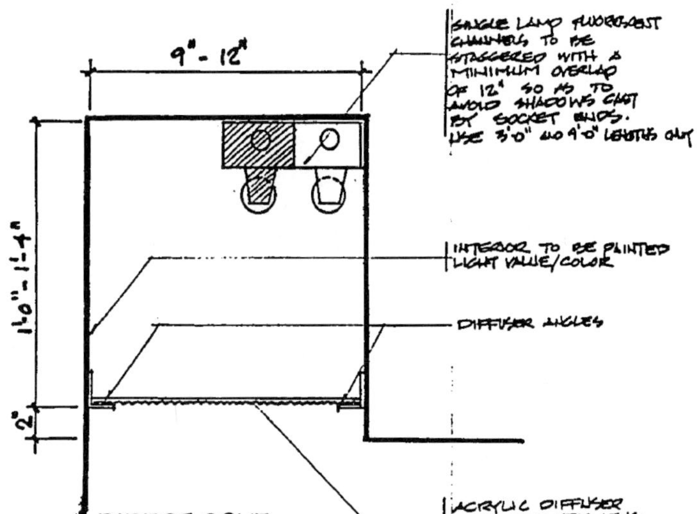

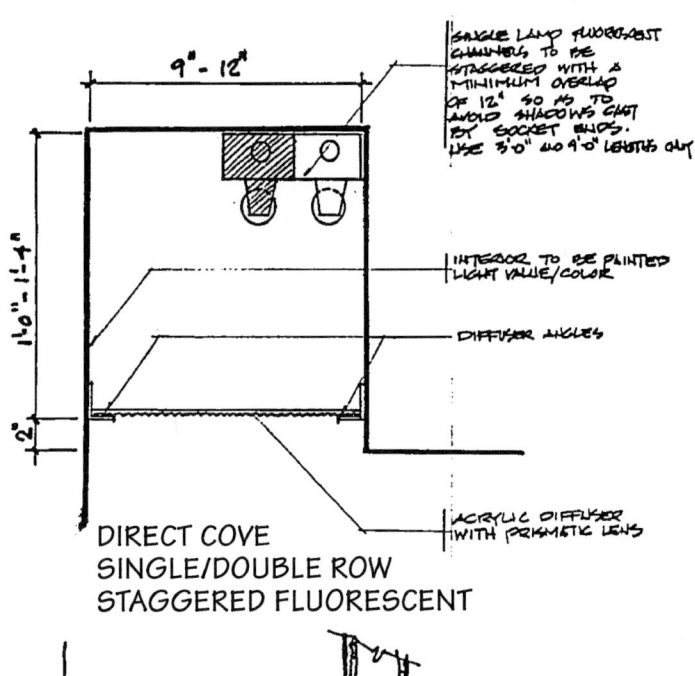

DIRECT COVE
SINGLE/DOUBLE ROW
STAGGERED FLUORESCENT

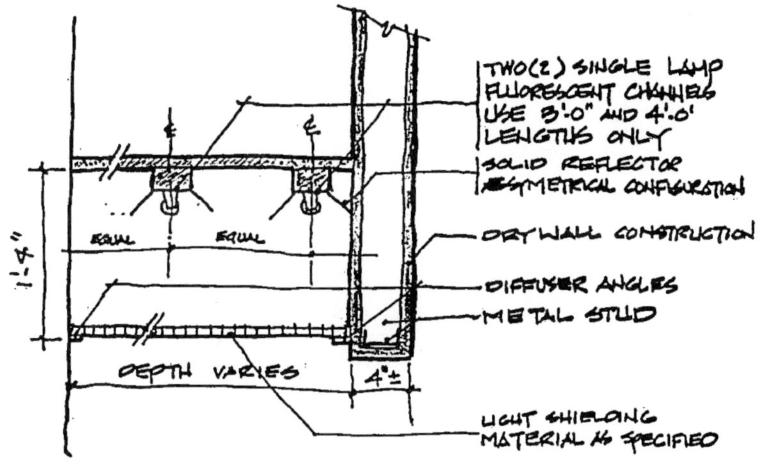

SHIELDED VALANCE
WITH TWO (2) SINGLE
LAMP FLUORESCENT CHANNELS
"CURTAIN WALL" TYPE

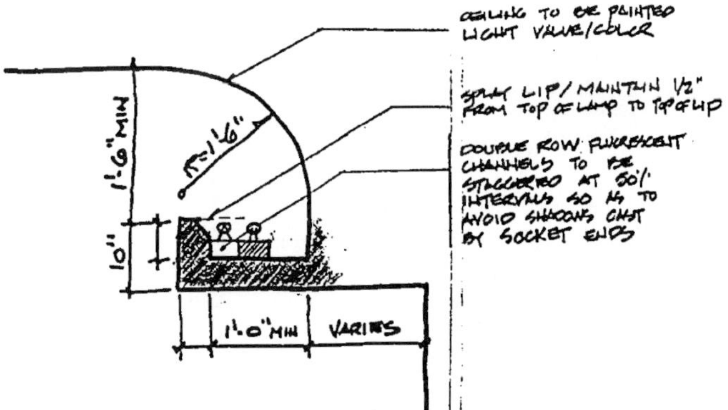

INDIRECT/CURVED COVE
DOUBLE ROW FLUORESCENT

DEPARTMENT STORES
Wall Display Systems

WATERFALL
Average Quantity of
Garments Per Post: 48

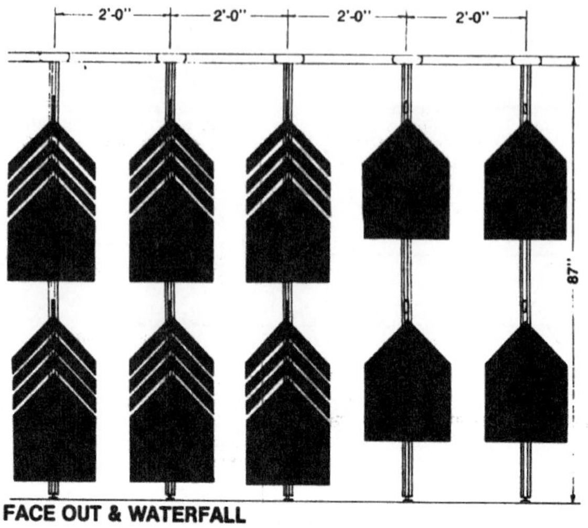

FACE OUT & WATERFALL

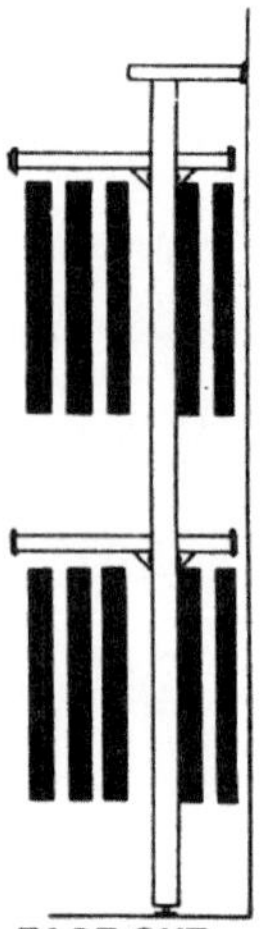

FACE OUT
Average Quantity of
Garments Per Post: 46

POST FACE OUT WITH STRAIGHT HANGING
Average Quantity of
Garments Per 4'-0" Section: 94

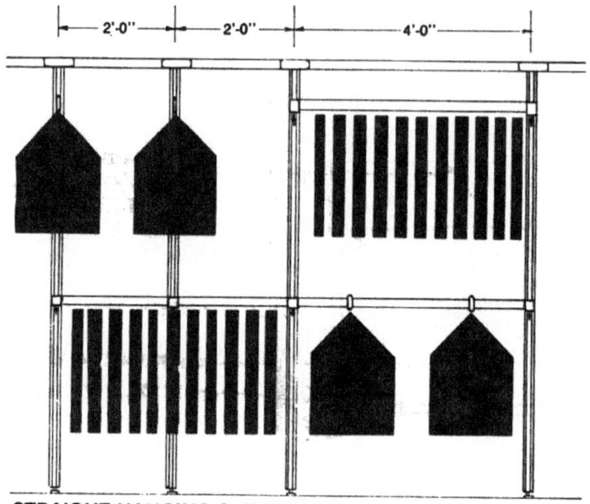

STRAIGHT HANGING & FACE OUT

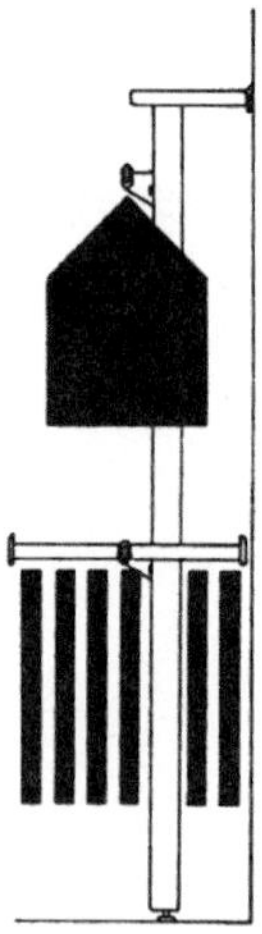

STRAIGHT WITH HANGRAIL FACE OUT
Average Quantity of Garments
Per 4'-0" Section: 96

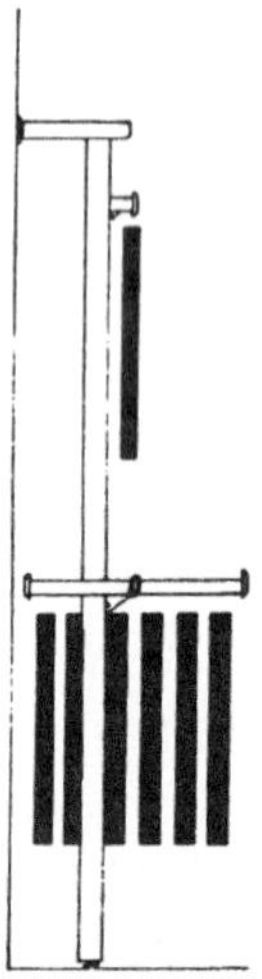

FACE OUT WITH DISPLAY
Average Quantity of Garments
Per 4'-0" Section: 49

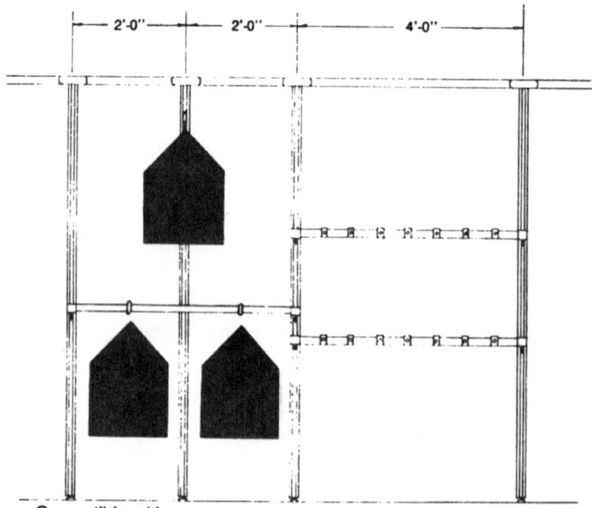

- Compatible with universal ½" slotting
- Unique new oval hangrail

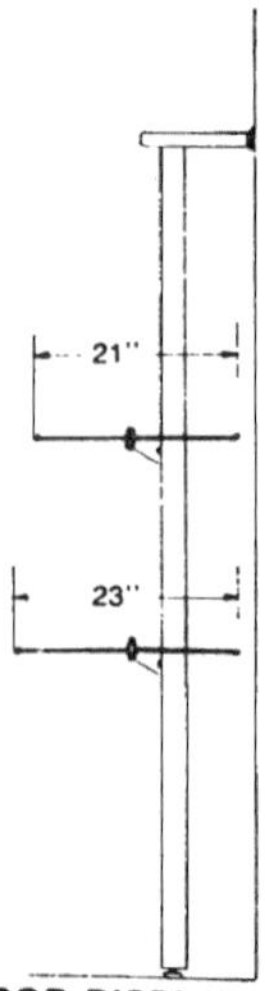

ROD DISPLAYS
6 or 7 Rods Per
4'-0" Section

- Design continuity from wall to floor carries theme throughout the department or the store
- Designed for high volume merchandising
- Flexible merchandising
- Designed to be compatible with other Pam International Systems

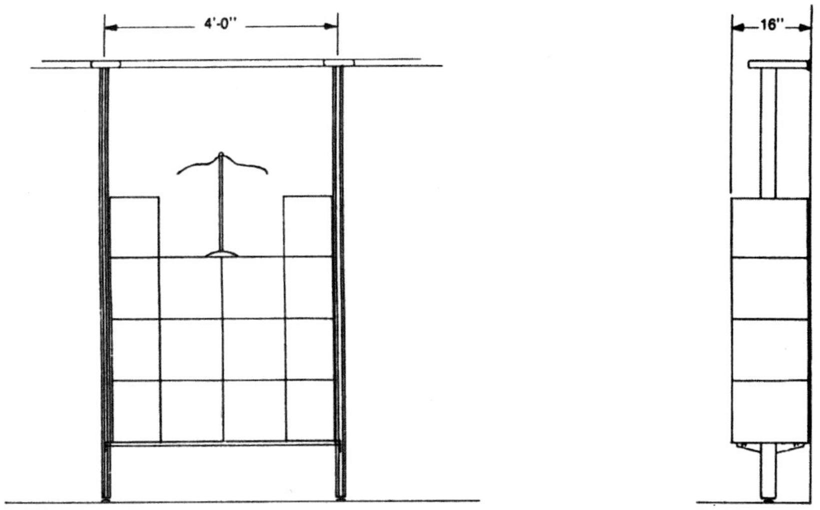

BINNING SYSTEM

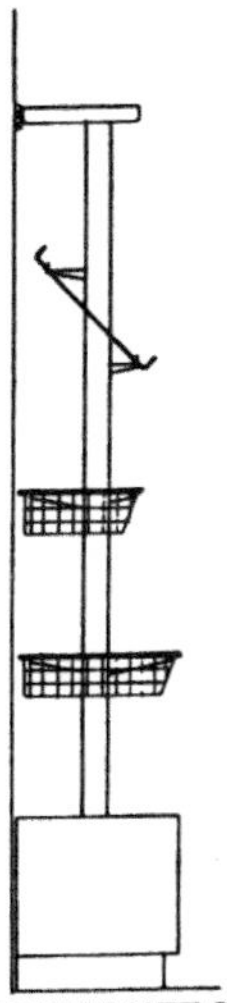

MULTI-NET SYSTEM

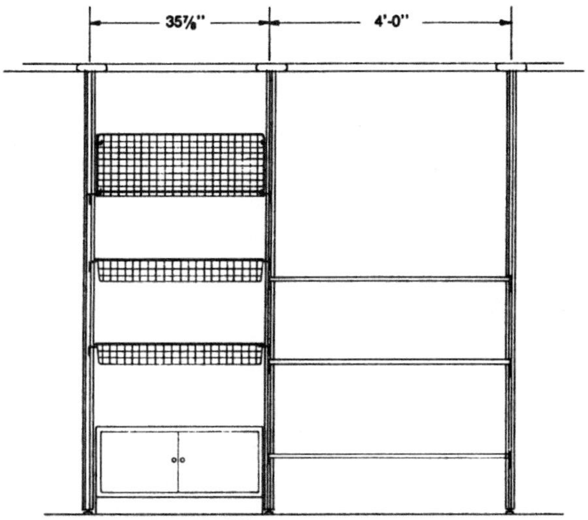

BASKETS & SHELVES

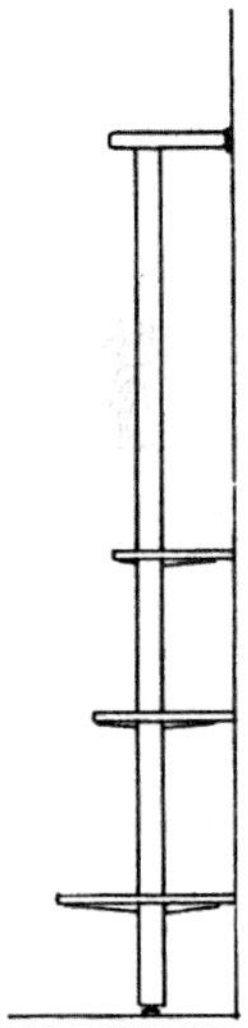

WOOD OR GLASS SHELVES

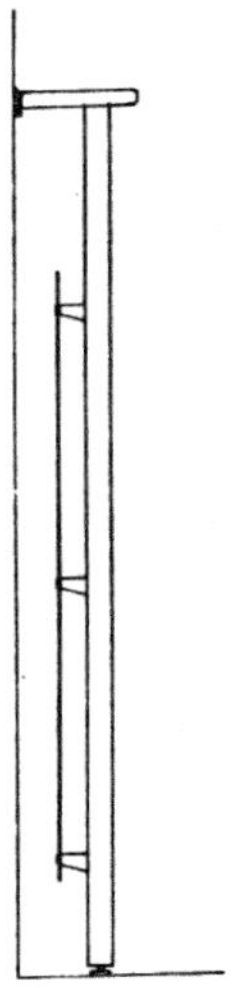

MULTI-NET PANELS

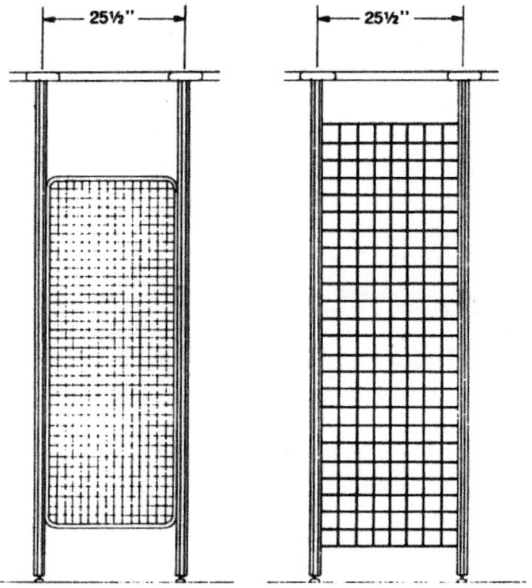

MESH PANEL SYSTEMS

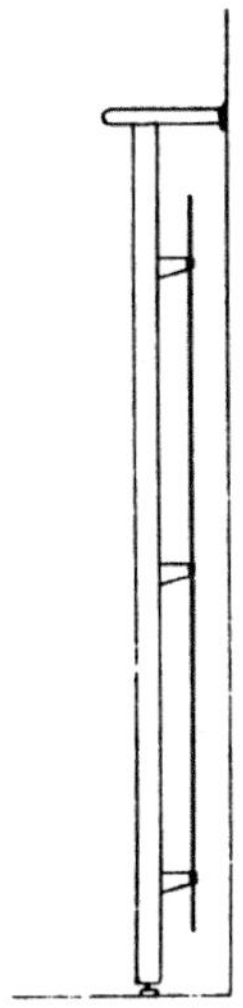

GRID WALL PANELS

- All Multiples/Systems 2™ upright posts are engineered with easily changeable post covers (Pat. Pend.)
- All metal components are coated with a durable, long lasting, baked on epoxy powder finish.

DEPARTMENT STORES
Rack Display Systems

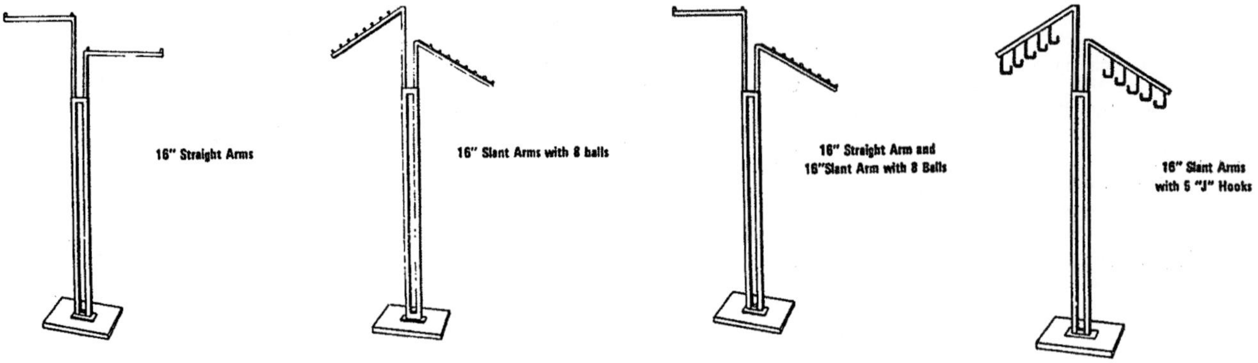

Two-arm costumers

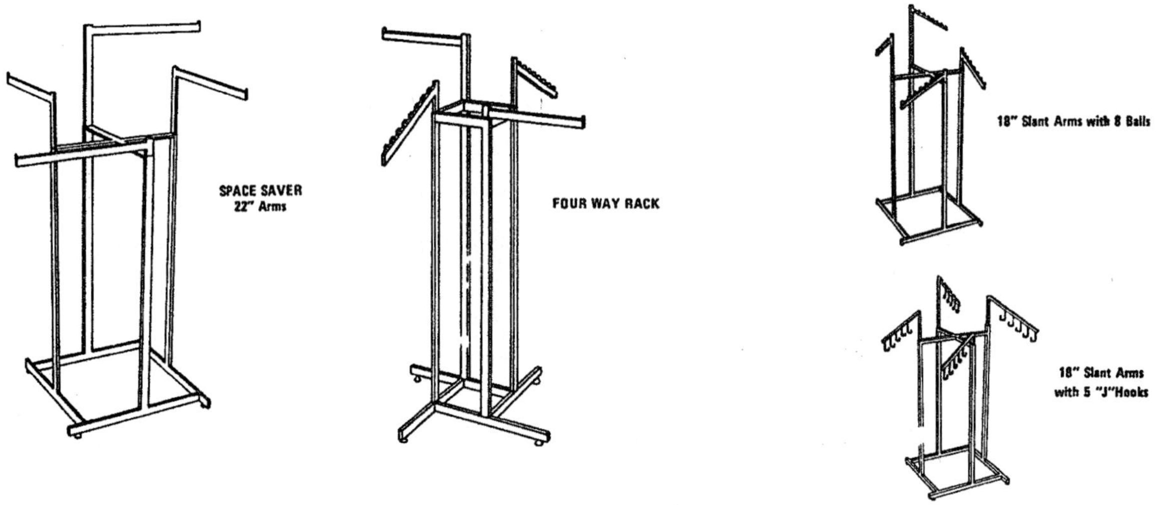

Four-way racks

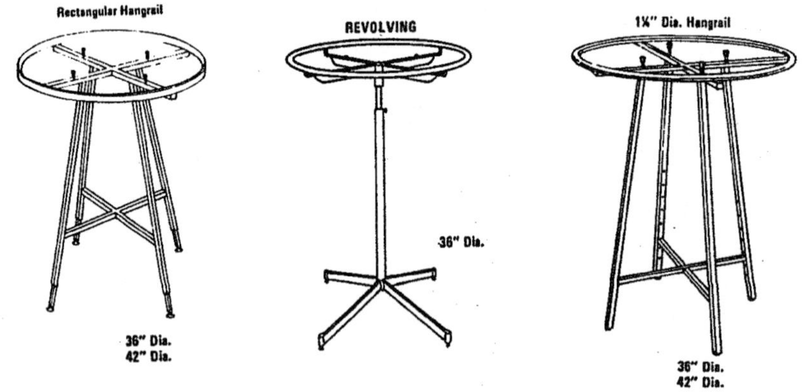

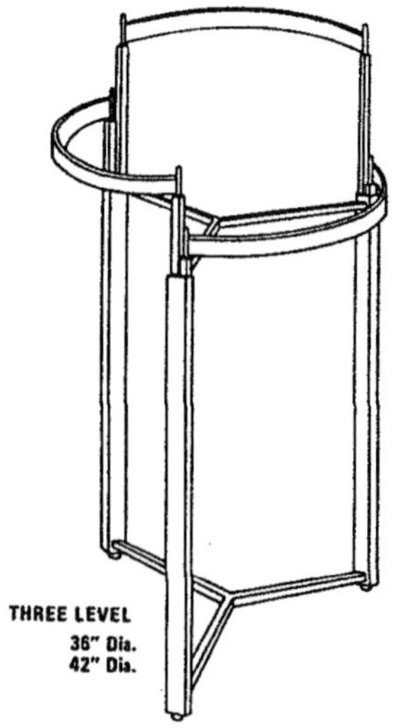

Circular racks

DEPARTMENT STORES
Rack Display Systems

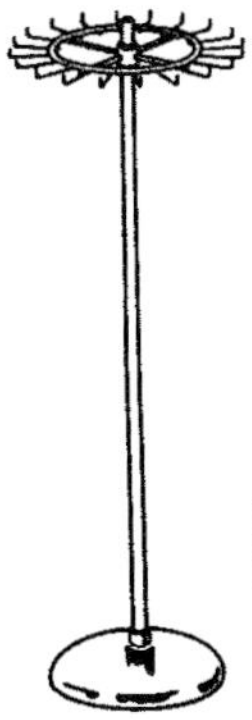

Single Tier Revolving Belt Rack

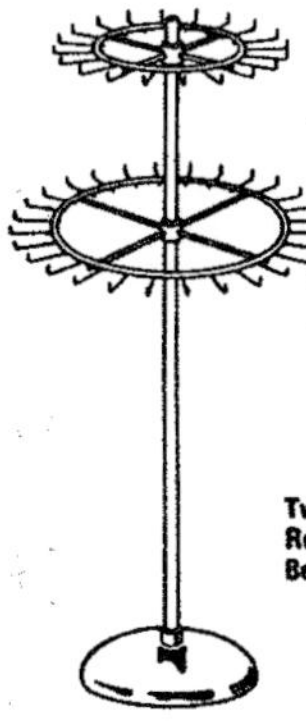

Two Tier Revolving Belt Rack

Specialty racks

OUTRIGGER
All Chrome Wall Fin

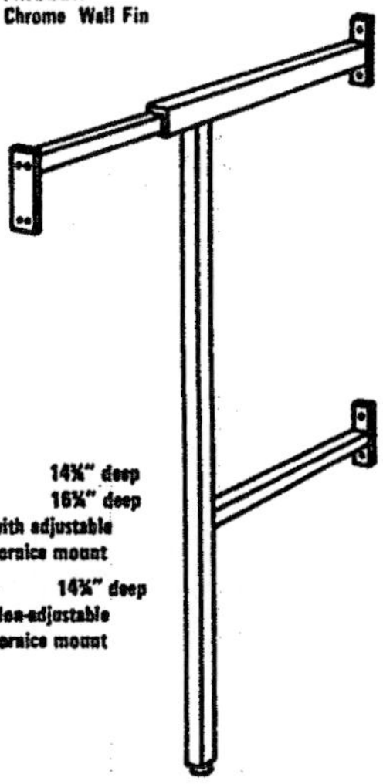

14¾" deep
16¾" deep
with adjustable cornice mount
14¾" deep
Non-adjustable cornice mount

14¾" deep
16¾" deep

Outriggers, wall fins

60" Long

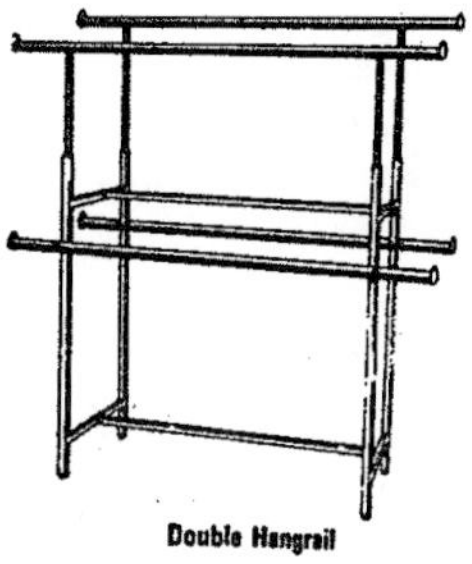

Double Hangrail

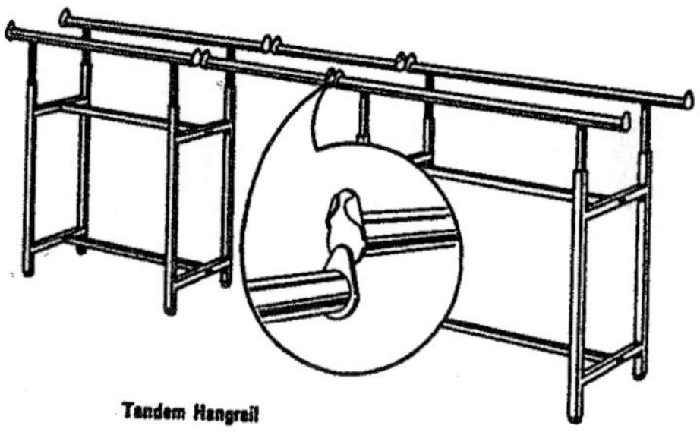

Tandem Hangrail

Rectangular racks

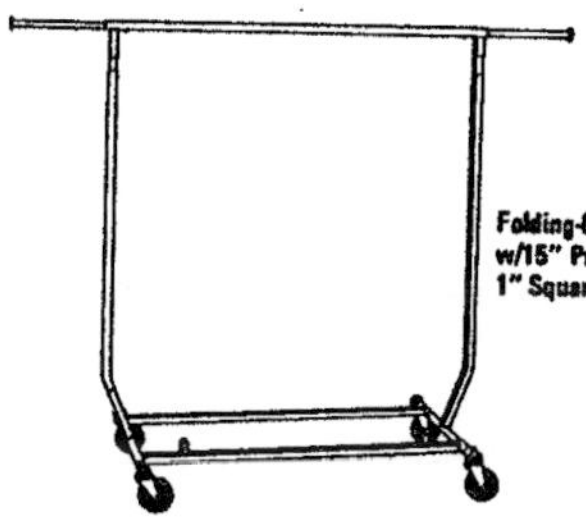

Folding-60" long
w/15" Pullouts
1" Square Tubing

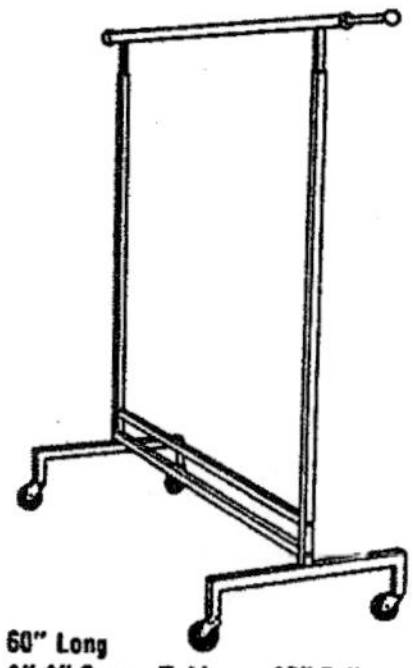

60" Long
All 1" Square Tubing 12" Pullout

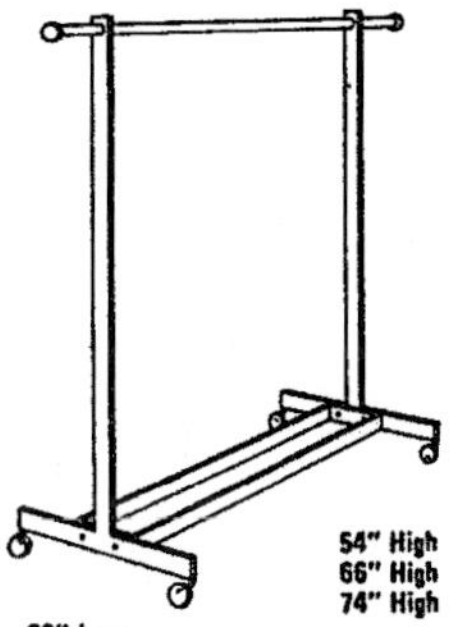

54" High
66" High
74" High
60" Long
All Rectangular Tubing 1¼" Hangrail

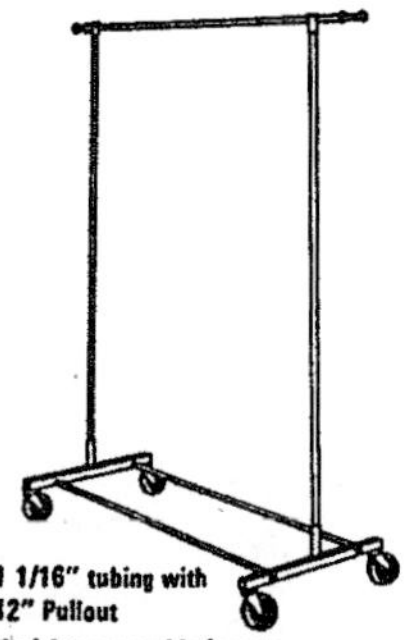

1 1/16" tubing with
12" Pullout
Uprights removable for storage.
60" Long

Rolling racks

DEPARTMENT STORES
Display Systems Standards

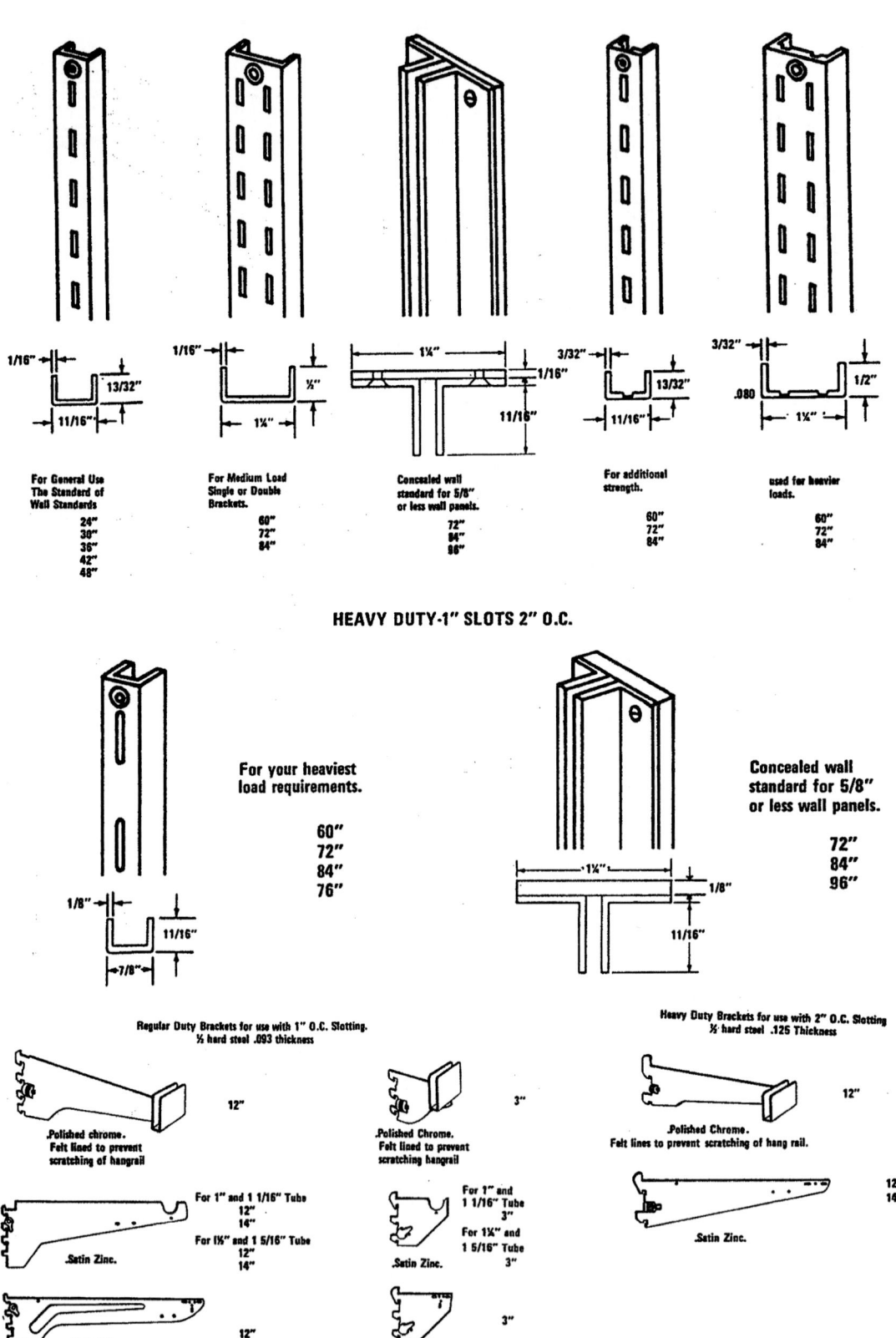

MEDIUM DUTY-½" SLOTS 1" O.C.

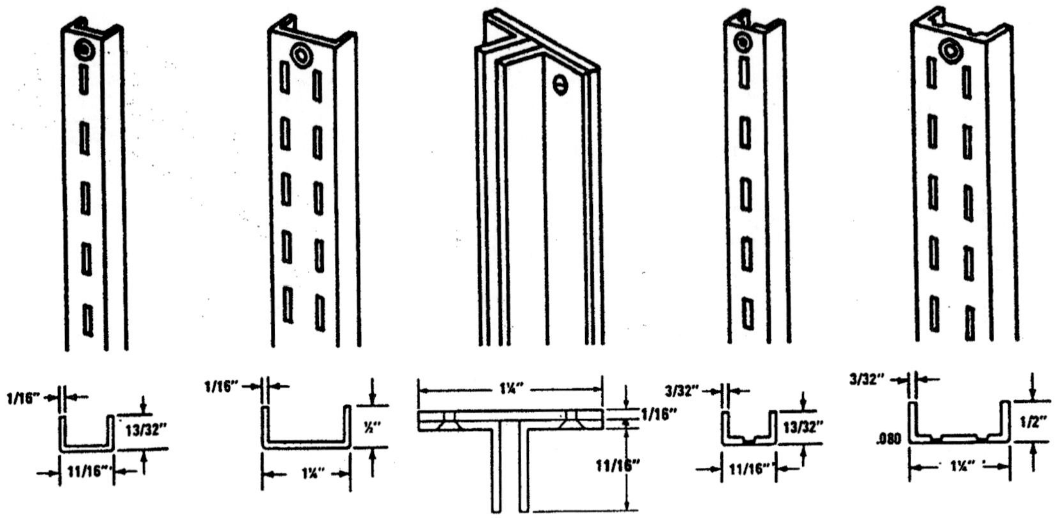

For General Use The Standard of Wall Standards
24"
30"
36"
42"
48"

For Medium Load Single or Double Brackets.
60"
72"
84"

Concealed wall standard for 5/8" or less wall panels.
72"
84"
96"

For additional strength.
60"
72"
84"

used for heavier loads.
60"
72"
84"

HEAVY DUTY-1" SLOTS 2" O.C.

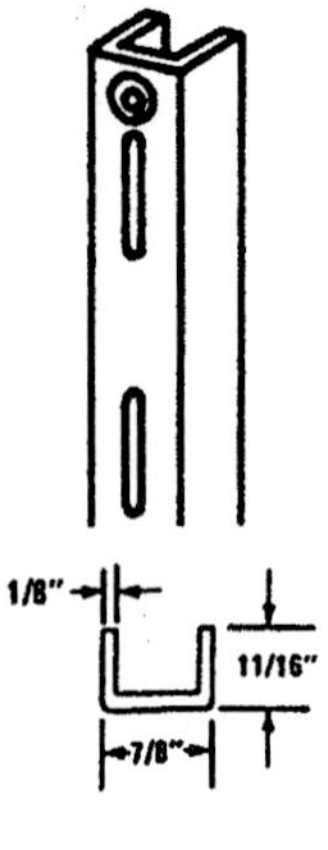

For your heaviest load requirements.
60"
72"
84"
76"

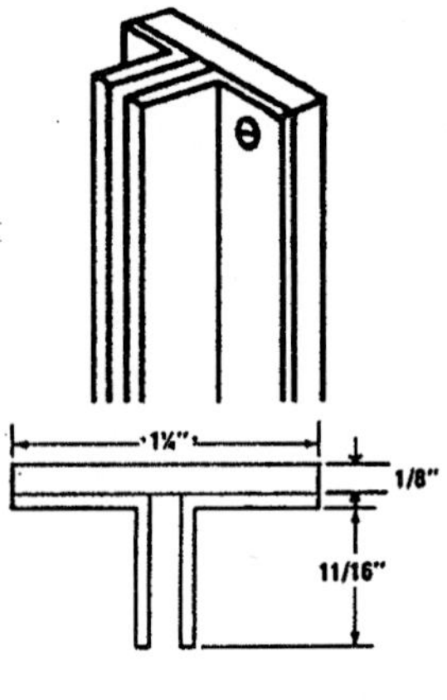

Concealed wall standard for 5/8" or less wall panels.
72"
84"
96"

Regular Duty Brackets for use with 1" O.C. Slotting.
½ hard steel .093 thickness

12"
Polished chrome. Felt lined to prevent scratching of hangrail

3"
Polished Chrome. Felt lined to prevent scratching hangrail

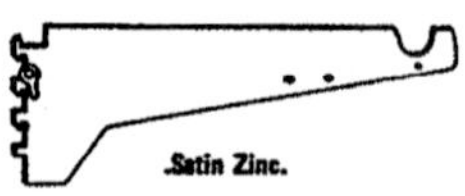
For 1" and 1 1/16" Tube
12"
14"
For 1½" and 1 5/16" Tube
12"
14"
Satin Zinc.

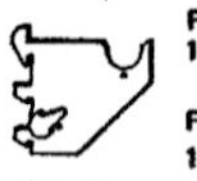
For 1" and 1 1/16" Tube
3"
For 1¼" and 1 5/16" Tube
3"
Satin Zinc.

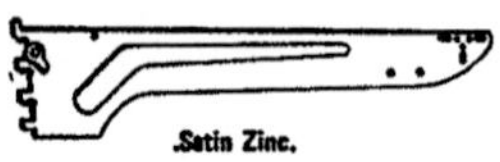
12"
14"
Satin Zinc.

3"
Satin Zinc.

Heavy Duty Brackets for use with 2" O.C. Slotting
½ hard steel .125 Thickness

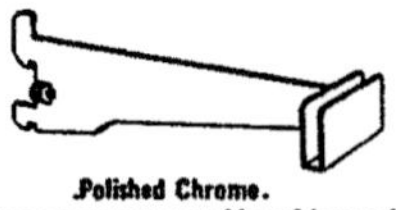
12"
Polished Chrome. Felt lines to prevent scratching of hang rail.

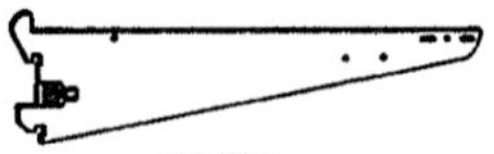
12"
14"
Satin Zinc.

Universal Standards (Regular)

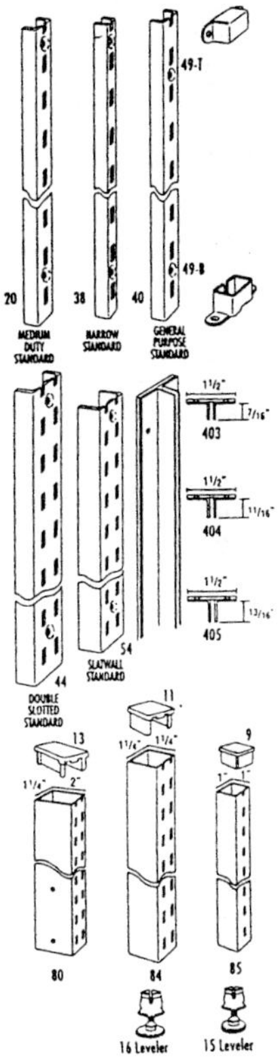

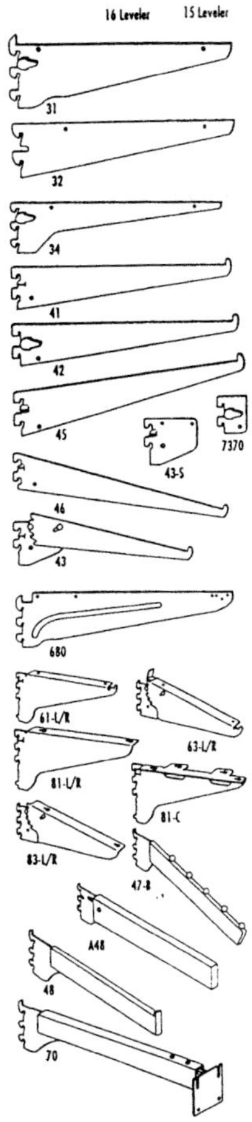

Universal Standards & Brackets (Heavy Duty)

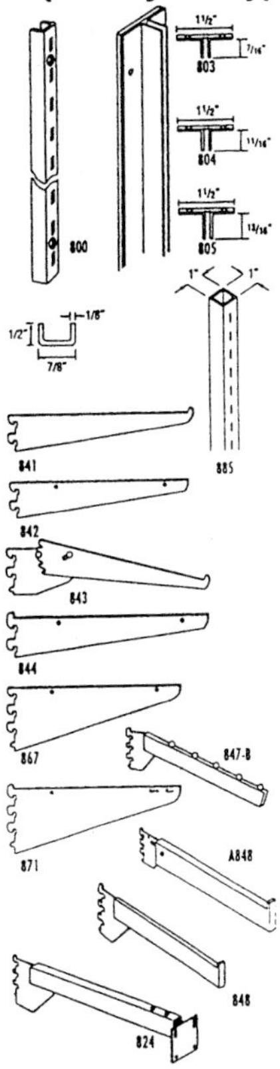

Hangrod & Accessories

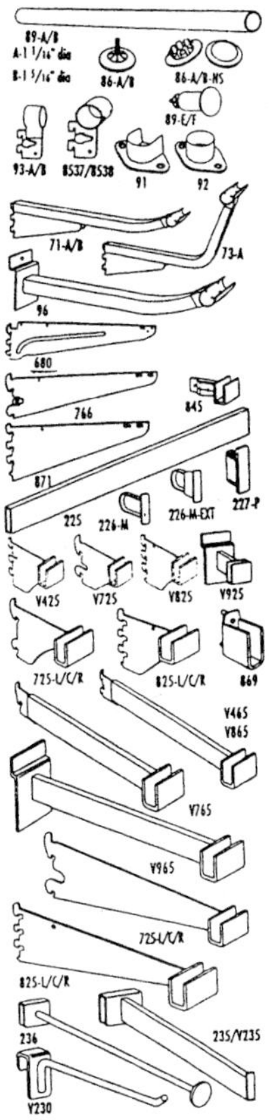

Universal Standards & Brackets (Heavy Duty)

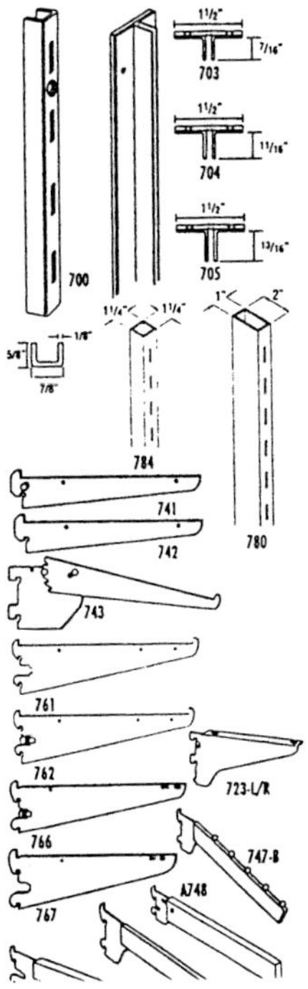

Pegboard Hardware

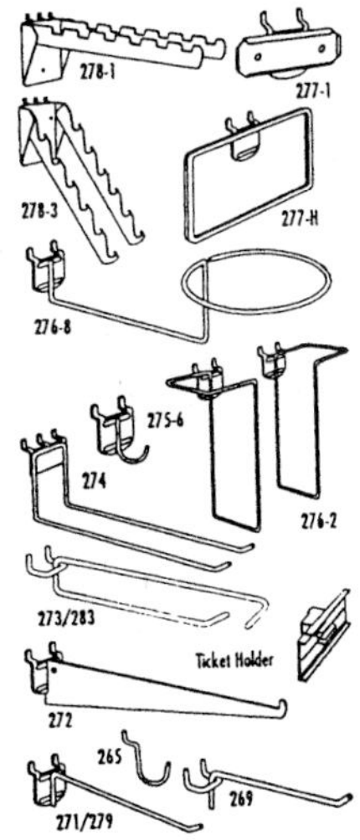

Grid Hardware

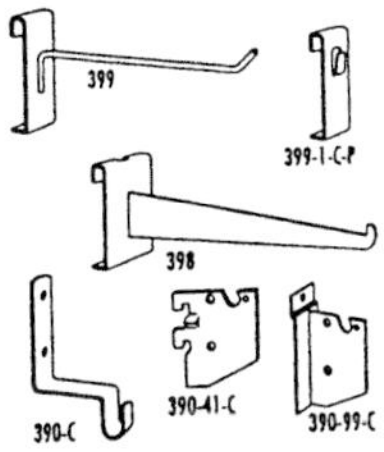

Merchandise Bar & Accessories

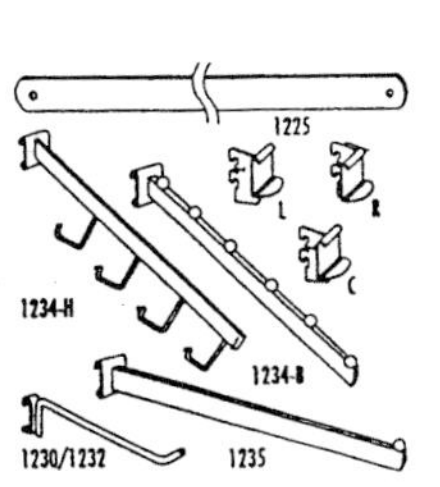

Slatwall Hardware

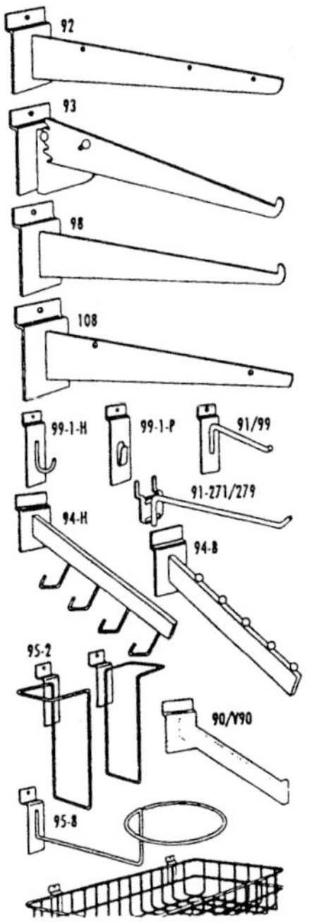

DEPARTMENT STORES

Cash Wrap Counter/Elevations

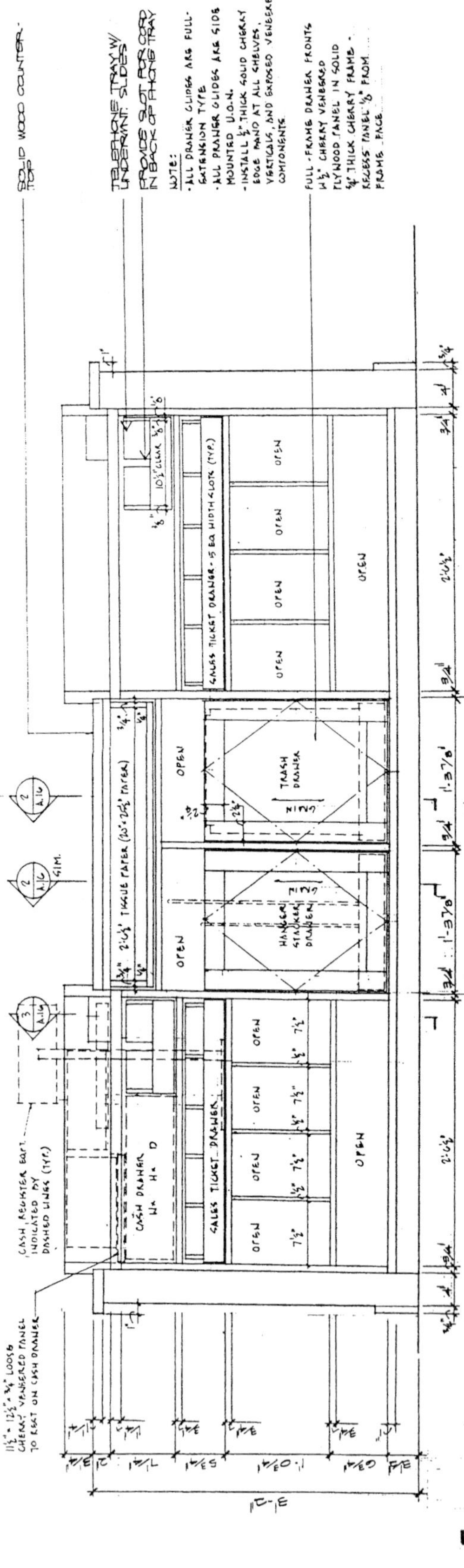

5 Back Elevation at Cashwrap

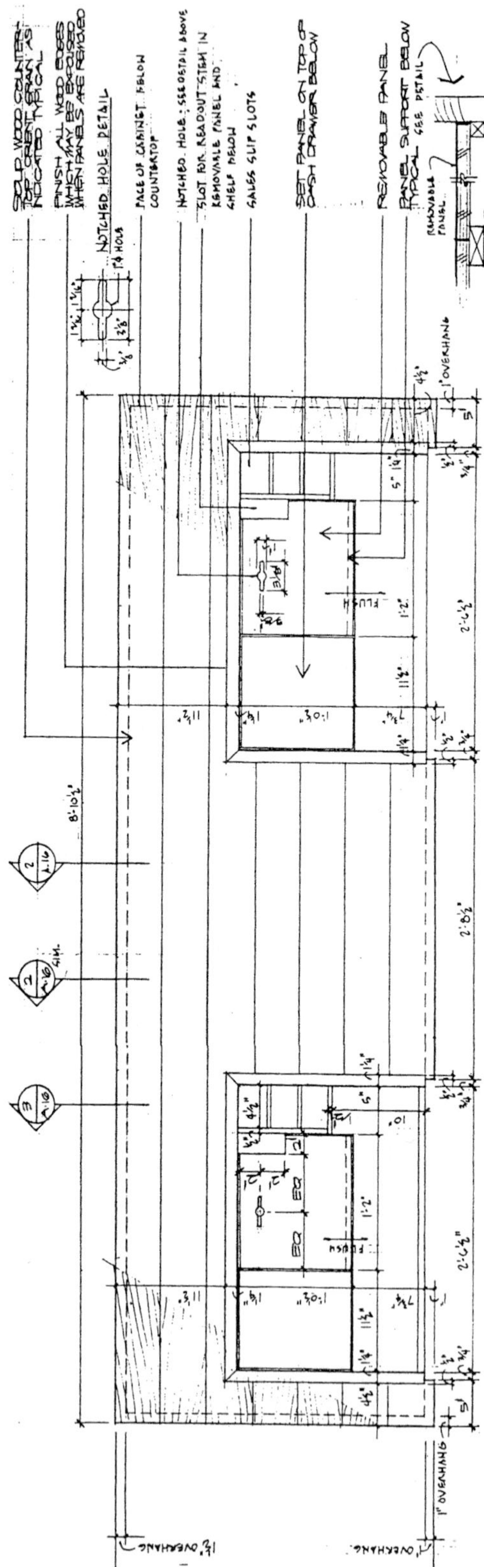

6 Plan at Cashwrap

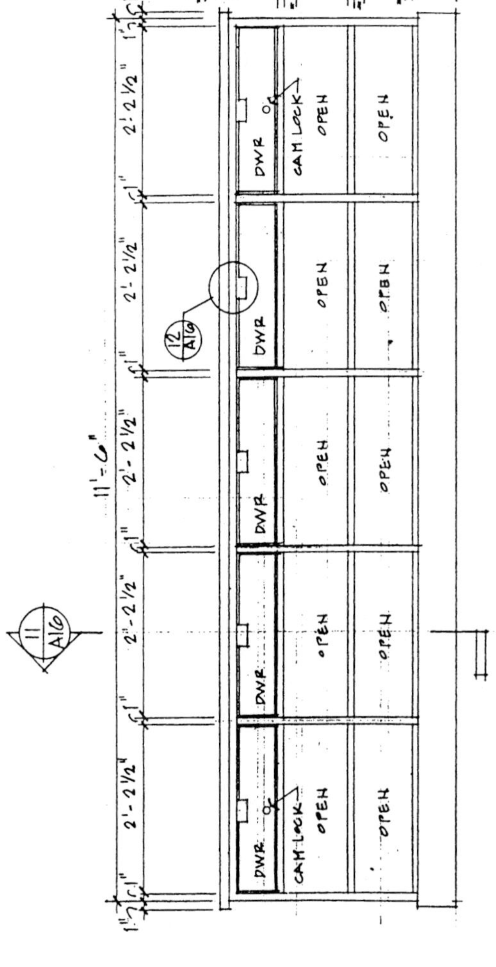

7 Front View Back of Cash B 11.5

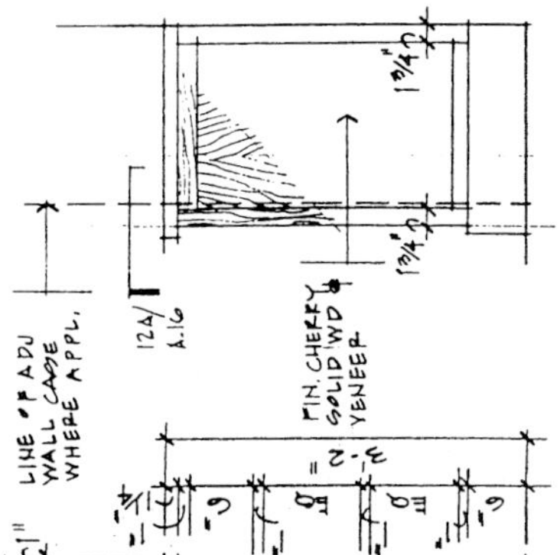

7a Side View

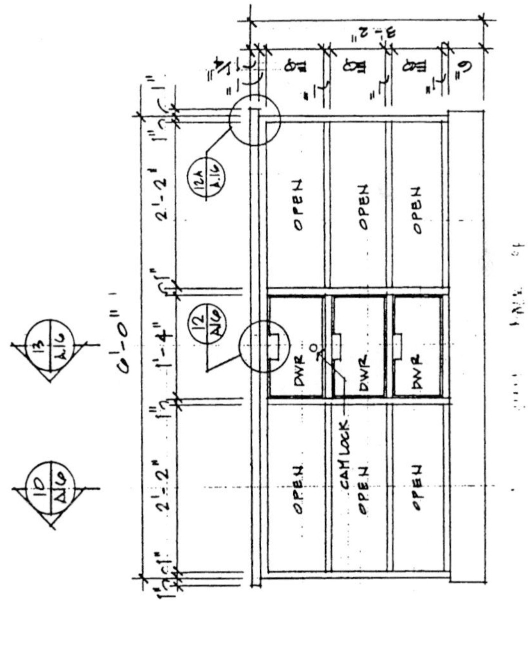

8 Front View Back of Cash B 6

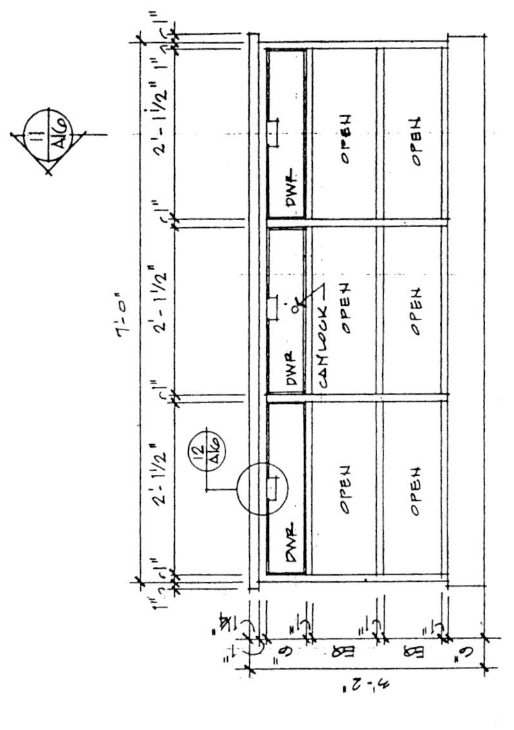

9 Front View Back of Cash B 7

DEPARTMENT STORES

Cash Wrap Counter/Sections and Elevation

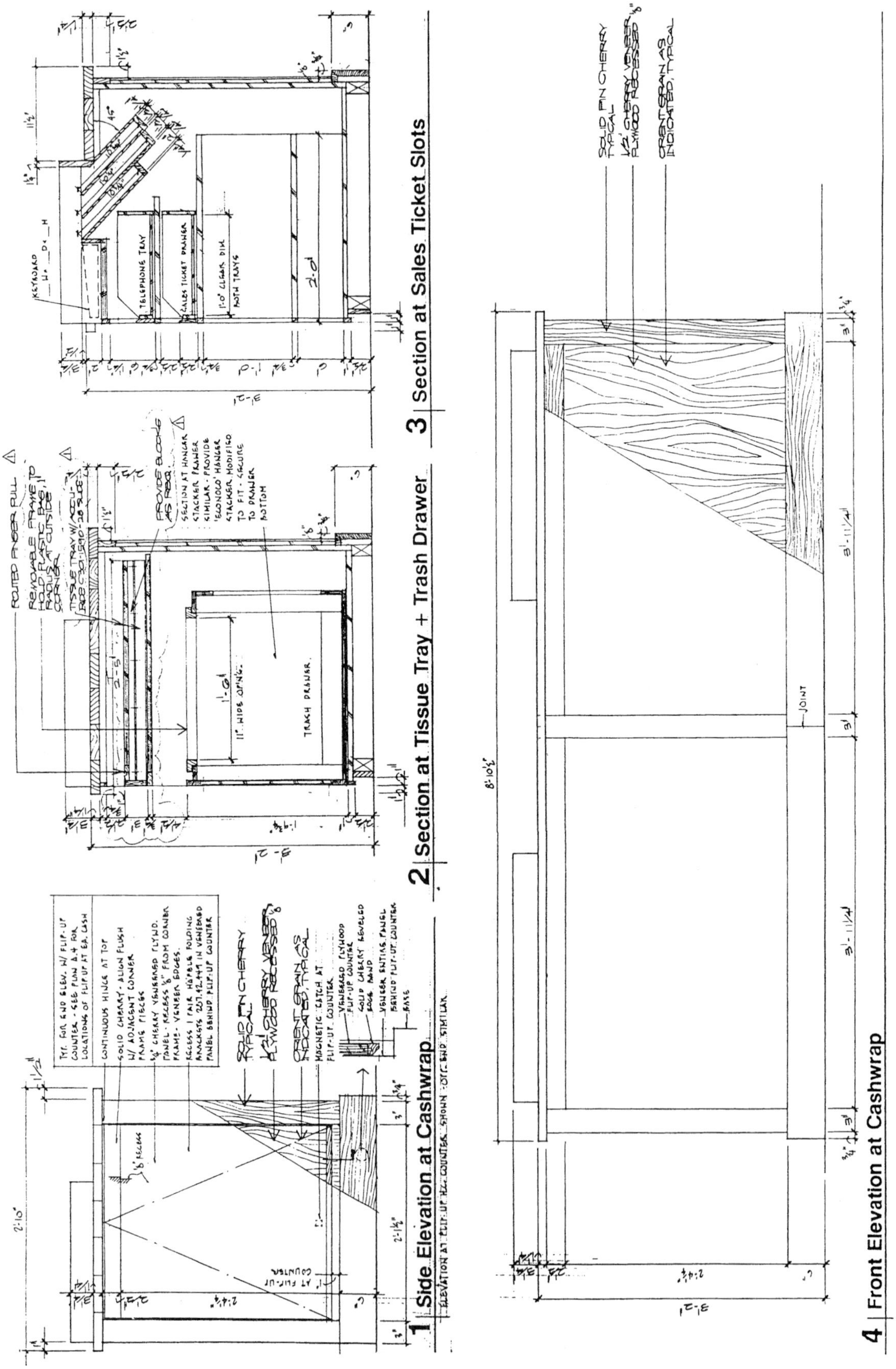

1 Side Elevation at Cashwrap

2 Section at Tissue Tray + Trash Drawer

3 Section at Sales Ticket Slots

4 Front Elevation at Cashwrap

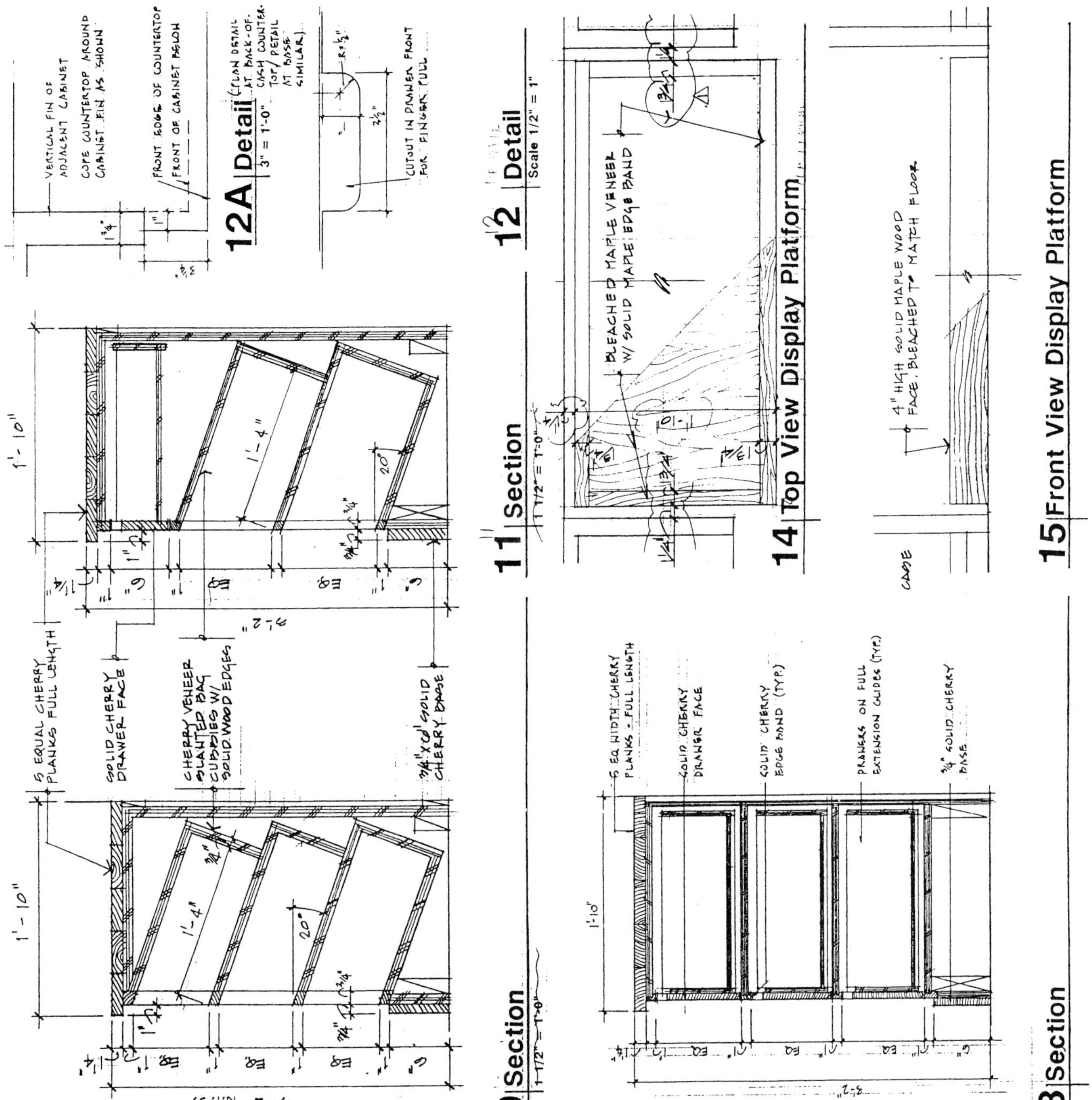
VERTICAL FIN OF ADJACENT CABINET
COPE COUNTERTOP AROUND CABINET FIN AS SHOWN
FRONT EDGE OF COUNTERTOP
FRONT OF CABINET BELOW
12A Detail 3" = 1'-0"
(PLAN DETAIL AT BACK-OF-CASH COUNTER-TOP / DETAIL AT BASE SIMILAR)
CUTOUT IN DRAWER FRONT FOR FINGER PULL
12 Detail Scale 1/2" = 1"
BLEACHED MAPLE VENEER W/ SOLID MAPLE EDGE BAND
14 Top View Display Platform
4" HIGH SOLID MAPLE WOOD FACE; BLEACHED TO MATCH FLOOR
15 Front View Display Platform
1'-10"
1'-4"
20°
11 Section 1 1/2" = 1'-0"
5 EQUAL CHERRY PLANKS FULL LENGTH
SOLID CHERRY DRAWER FACE
CHERRY VENEER SLANTED BAG CUBBIES W/ SOLID WOOD EDGES
3/4" x 6" SOLID CHERRY BASE
3'-2" N.T.S.
10 Section 1 1/2" = 1'-0"
5 EQ. WIDTH CHERRY PLANKS - FULL LENGTH
SOLID CHERRY DRAWER FACE
SOLID CHERRY EDGE BAND (TYP.)
DRAWERS ON FULL EXTENSION GLIDES (TYP.)
3/4" SOLID CHERRY BASE
13 Section

DEPARTMENT STORES

Cash Wrap Counter/Plan and Section

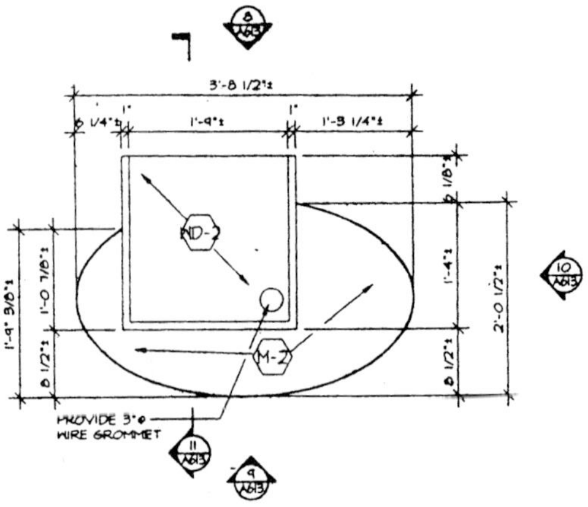

7 PLAN CASH WRAP 'B'
A613 SCALE: 1" =1'-0"
ARCHITECT TO PROVIDE FULL SCALE TEMPLATE OF COUNTER

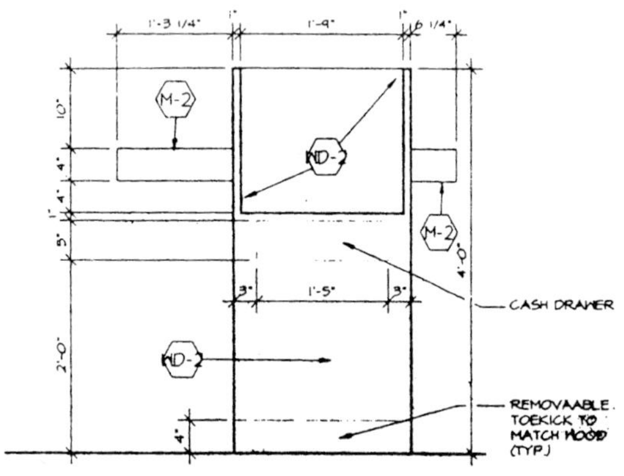

8 FRONT ELEVATION
A613 SCALE: 1" =1'-0"
CABINET TO BE ANCHORED TO FLOOR

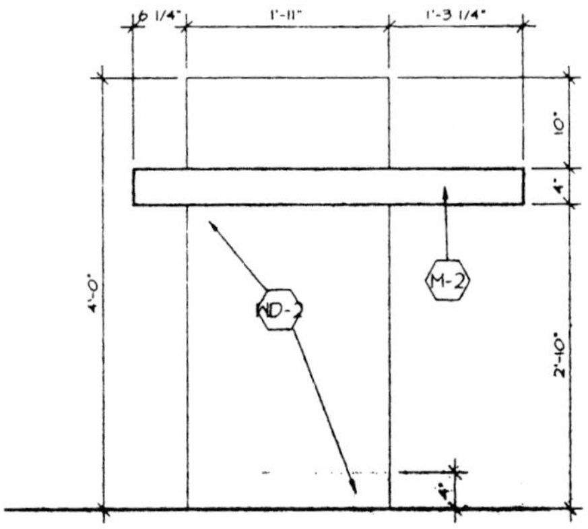

9 BACK ELEVATION
A613 SCALE: 1" =1'-0"

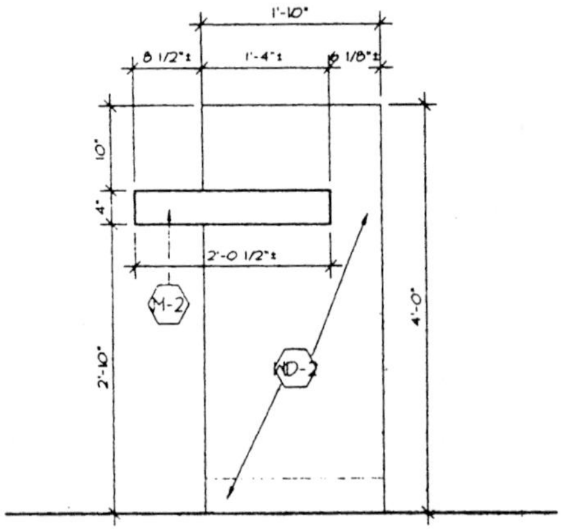

10 SIDE ELEVATION
A613 SCALE: 1" =1'-0"

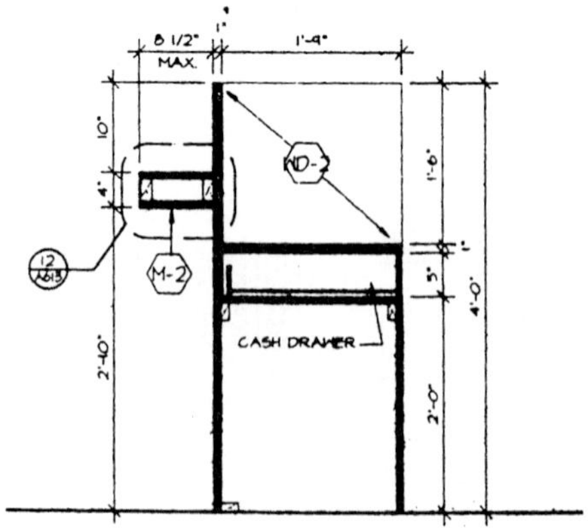

11 SECTION
A613 SCALE: 1" =1'-0"

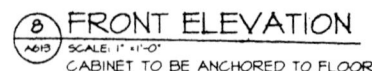

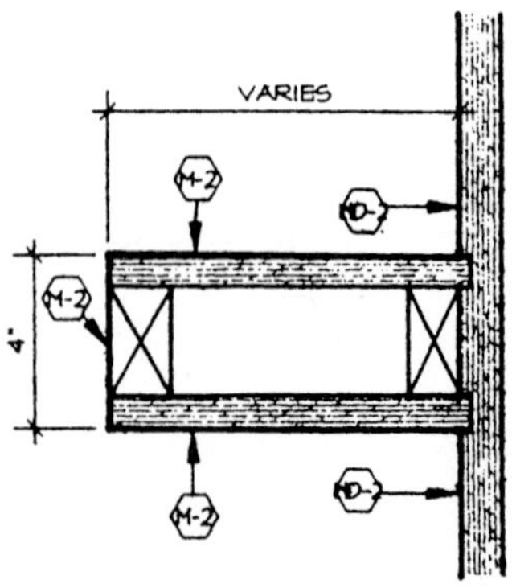

12 DETAIL
A613 SCALE: 3" =1'-0"

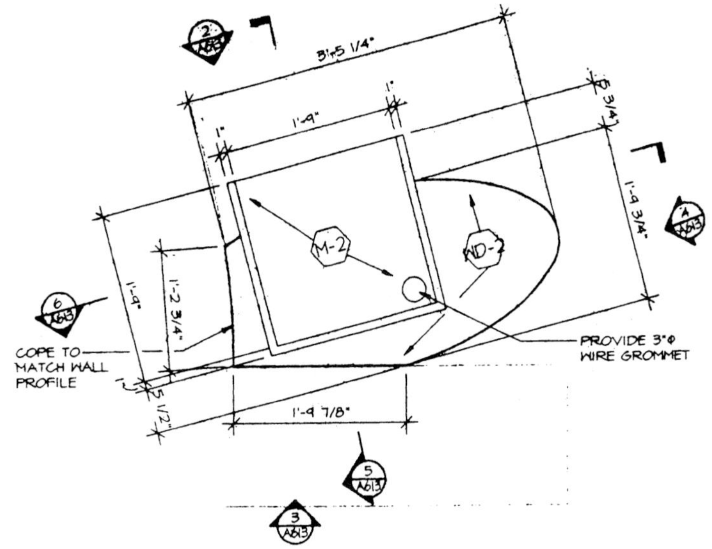

1 A613 PLAN CASH WRAP 'A'
SCALE: 1" = 1'-0"
ARCHITECT TO PROVIDE FULL SCALE TEMPLATE OF COUNTER

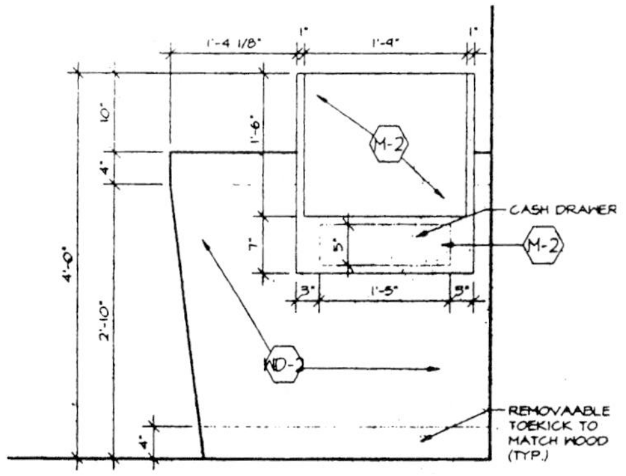

2 A613 FRONT ELEVATION
SCALE: 1" = 1'-0"
CABINET TO BE ANCHORED TO FLOOR & WALL

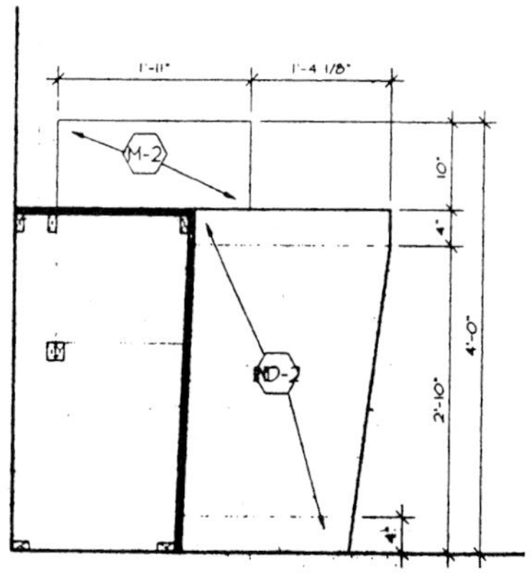

3 A613 BACK ELEVATION
SCALE: 1" = 1'-0"

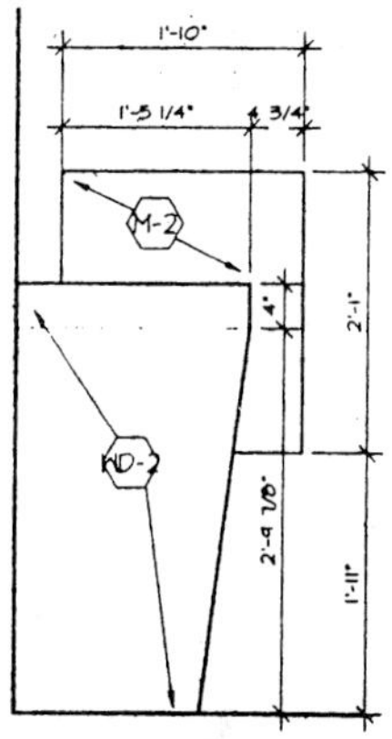

4 A613 SIDE ELEVATION
SCALE: 1" = 1'-0"

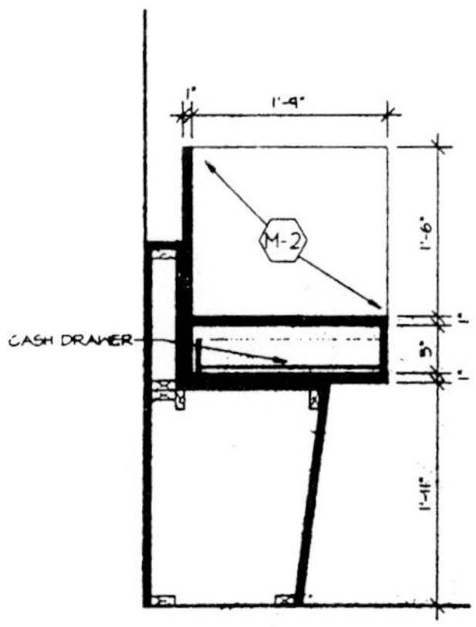

5 A613 SECTION
SCALE: 1" = 1'-0"

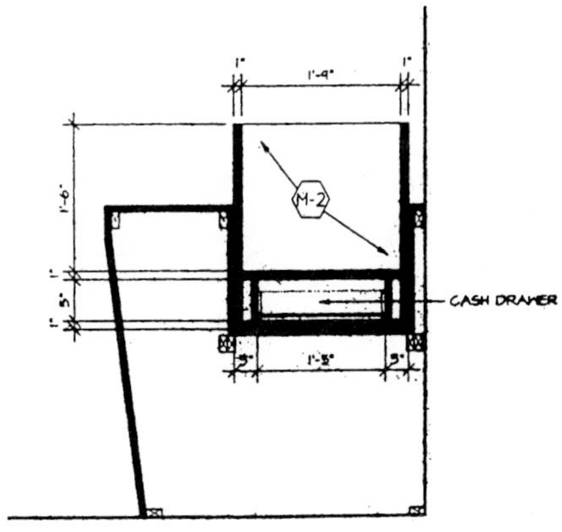

6 A613 SECTION
SCALE: 1" = 1'-0"

DEPARTMENT STORES

Cash Wrap Counter/Plan

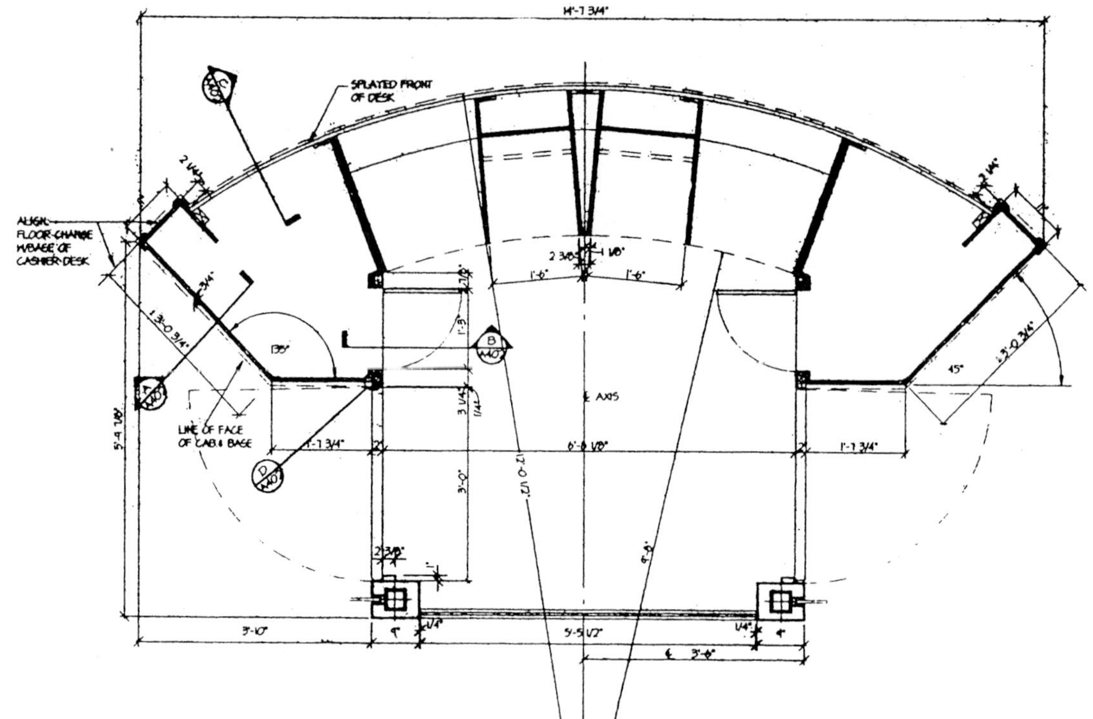

1 CASHWRAP CONSTRUCTION PLAN
A-402 3/4" = 1'-0"

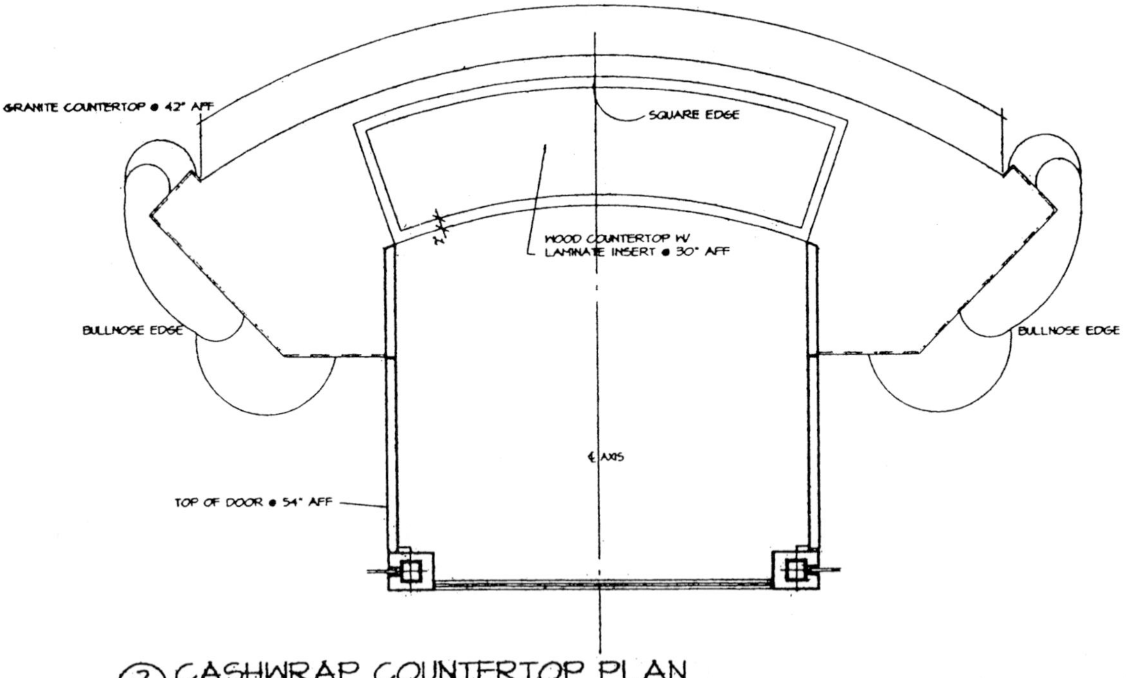

2 CASHWRAP COUNTERTOP PLAN
A-402 3/4" = 1'-0"

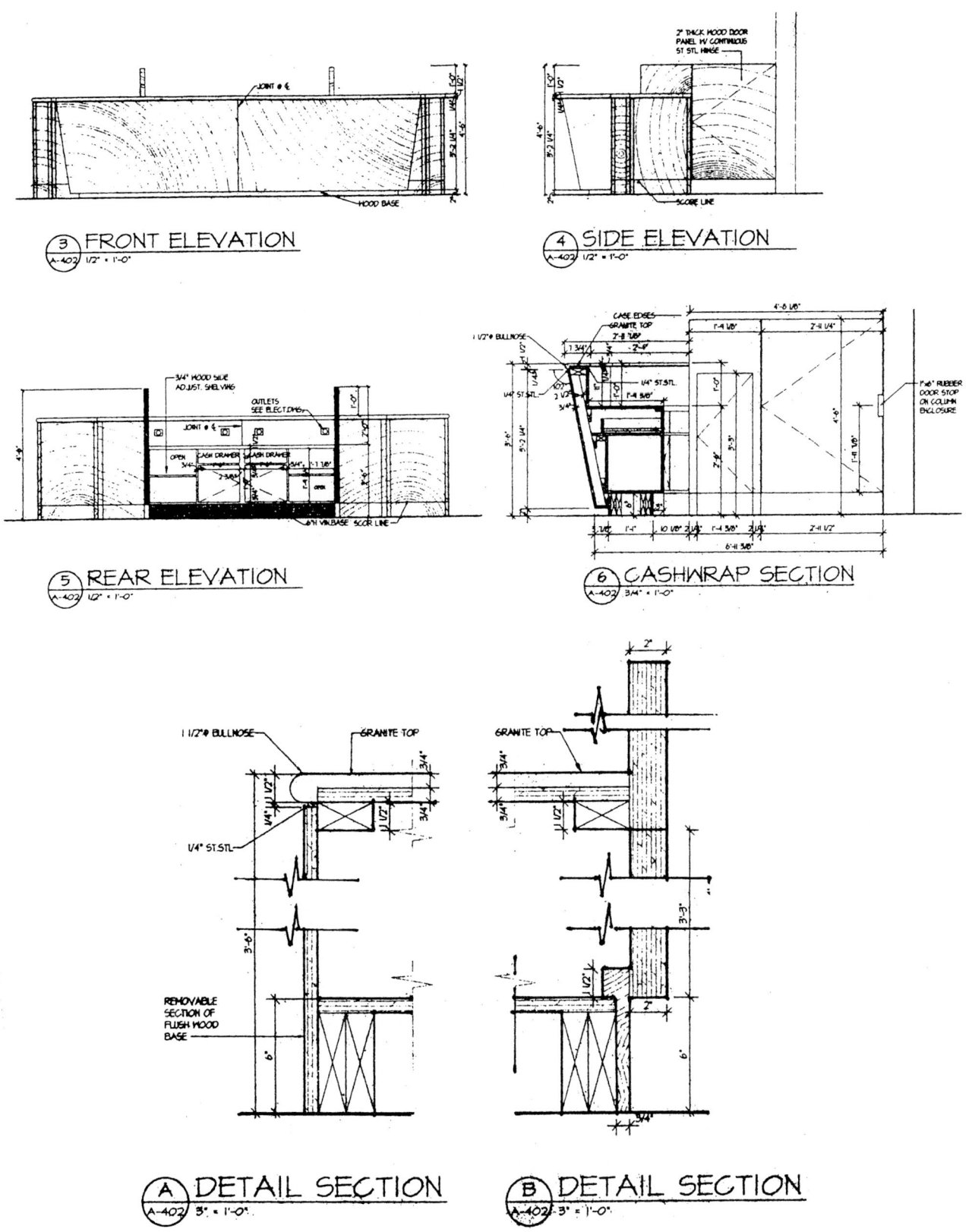

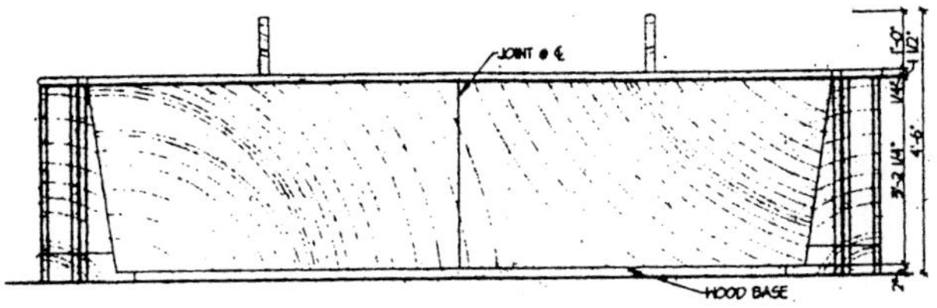

3 FRONT ELEVATION
A-402 1/2" = 1'-0"

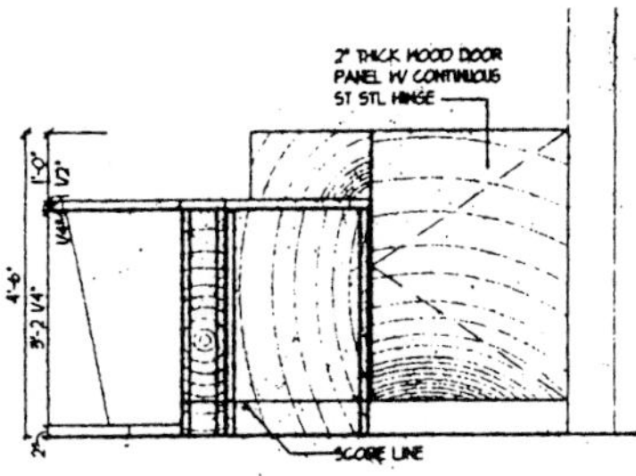

4 SIDE ELEVATION
A-402 1/2" = 1'-0"

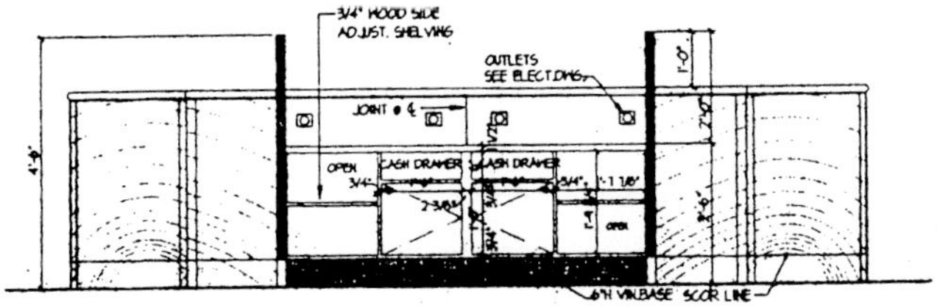

5 REAR ELEVATION
A-402 1/2" = 1'-0"

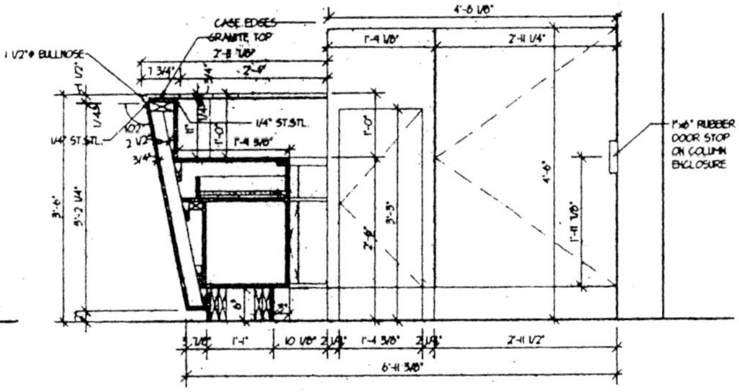

6 CASHWRAP SECTION
A-402 3/4" = 1'-0"

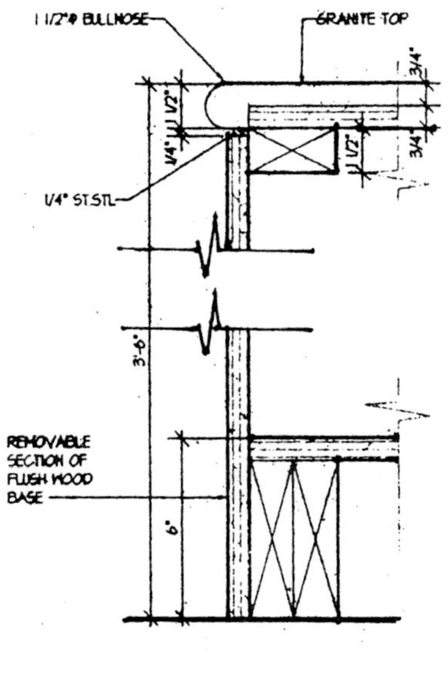

A DETAIL SECTION
A-402 3" = 1'-0"

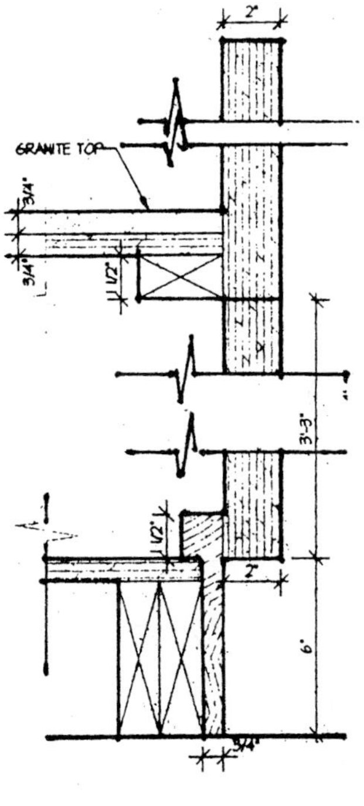

B DETAIL SECTION
A-402 3" = 1'-0"

DEPARTMENT STORES
Cash Wrap Counter/Details

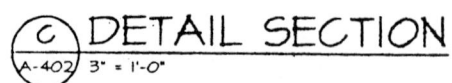

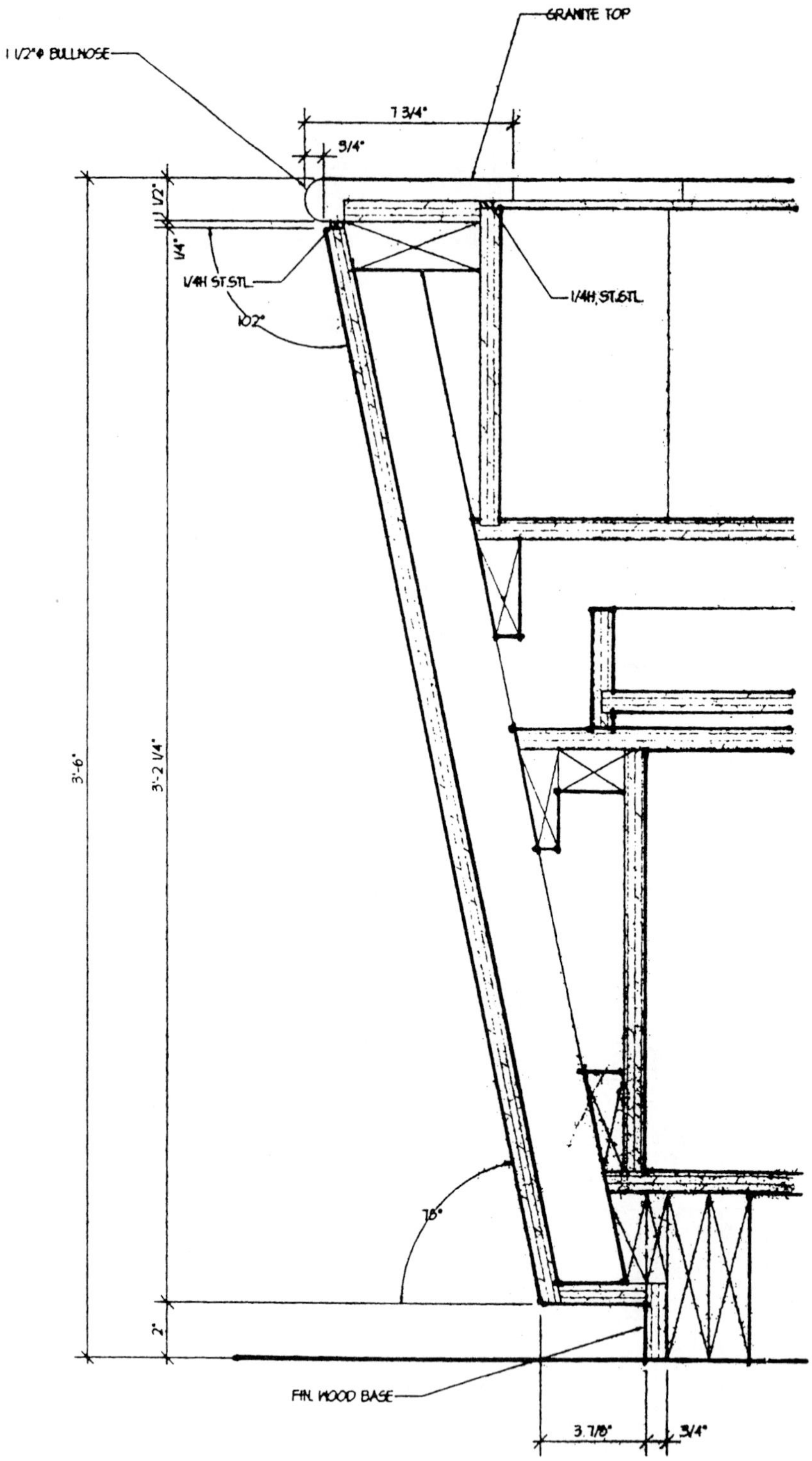

C
A-402
DETAIL SECTION
3" = 1'-0"

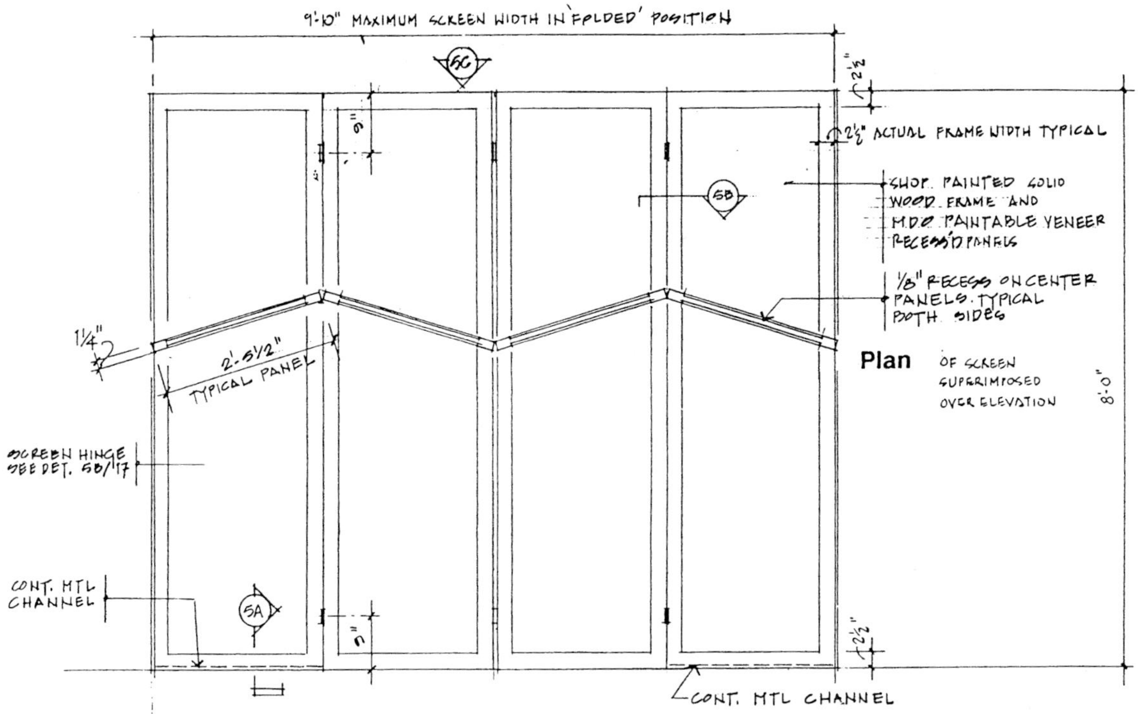

5 Elevation and Plan - Screen [S]

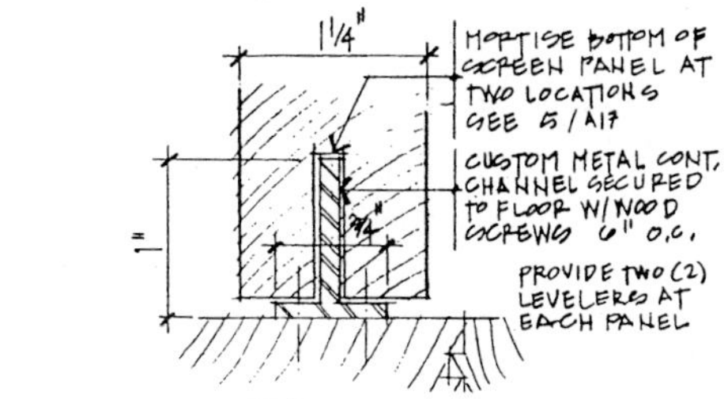

5A Detail - Screen
SC FULL

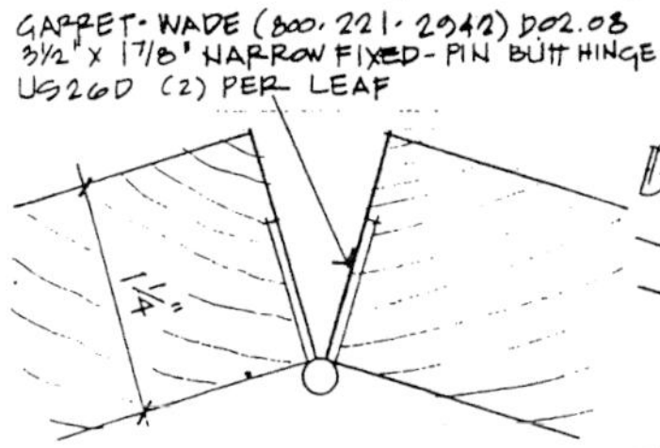

5B Detail - Screen
SC FULL

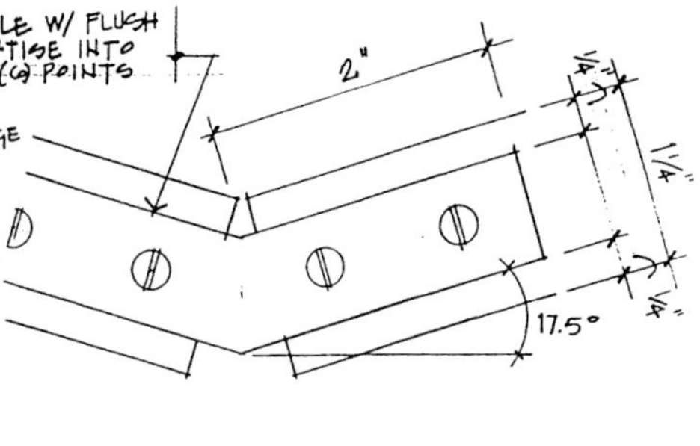

5C Detail - Screen
SC. FULL

DEPARTMENT STORES
Fitting Room/Plan

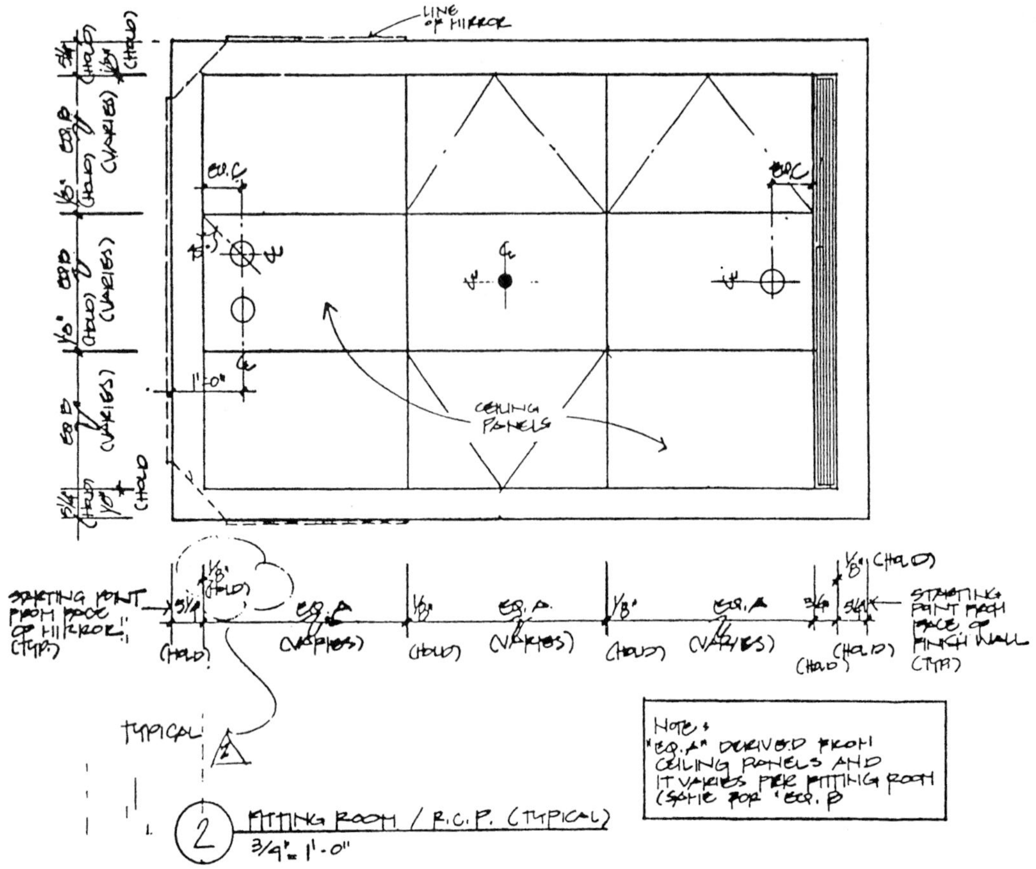

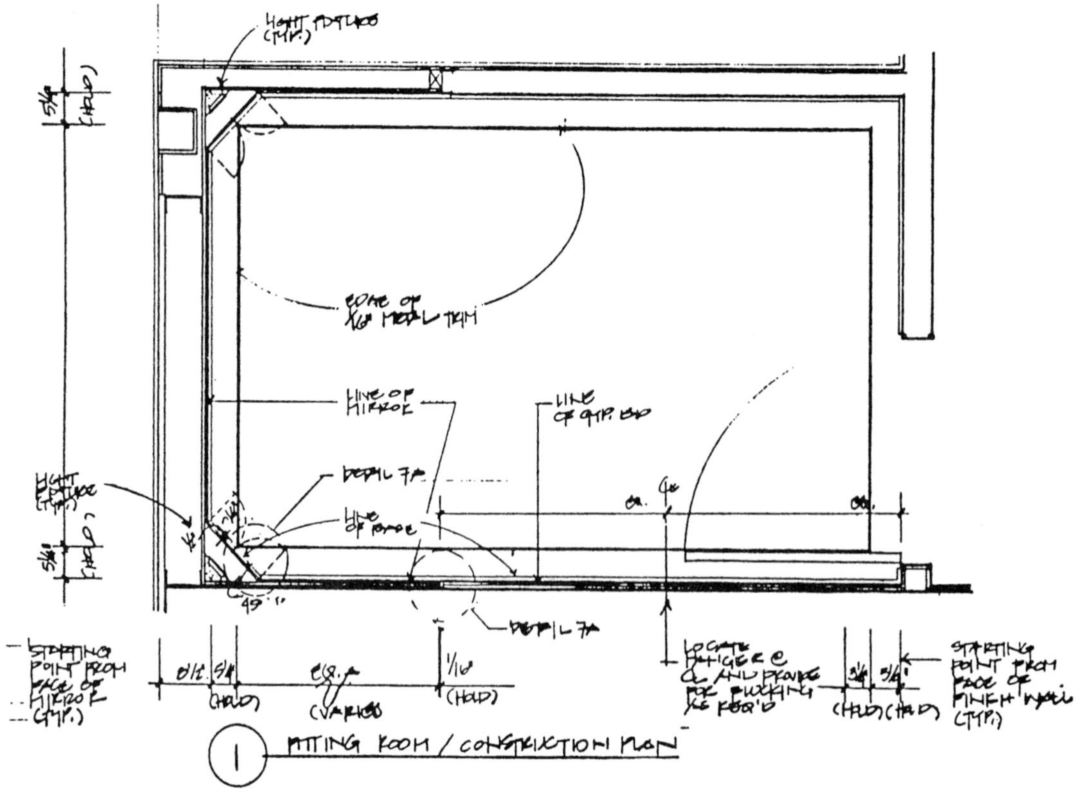

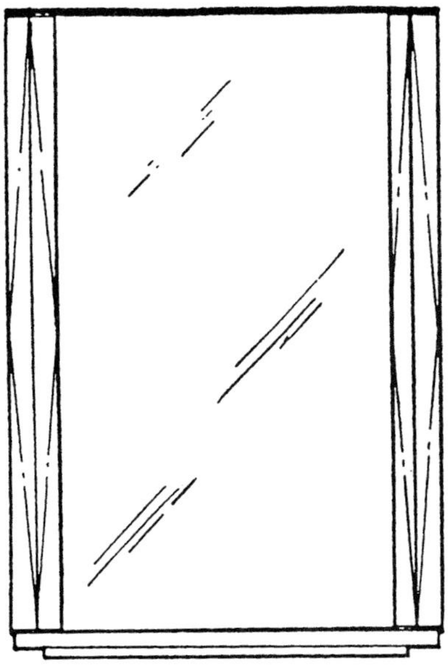

3 ELEVATION : NORTH
1/2" = 1'-0"

4 ELEVATION : EAST
1/2" = 1'-0"

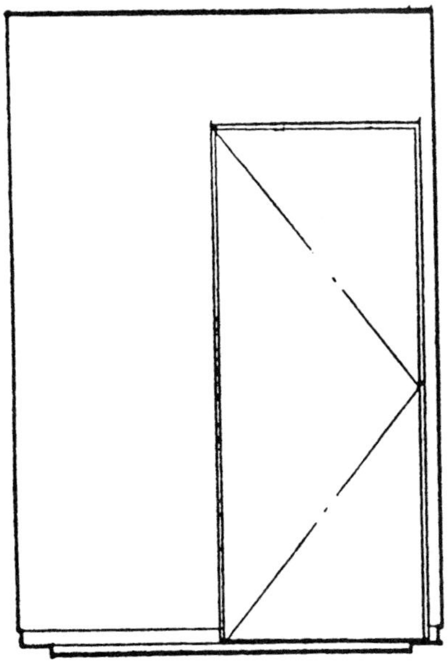

5 ELEVATION : SOUTH
1/2" = 1'-0"

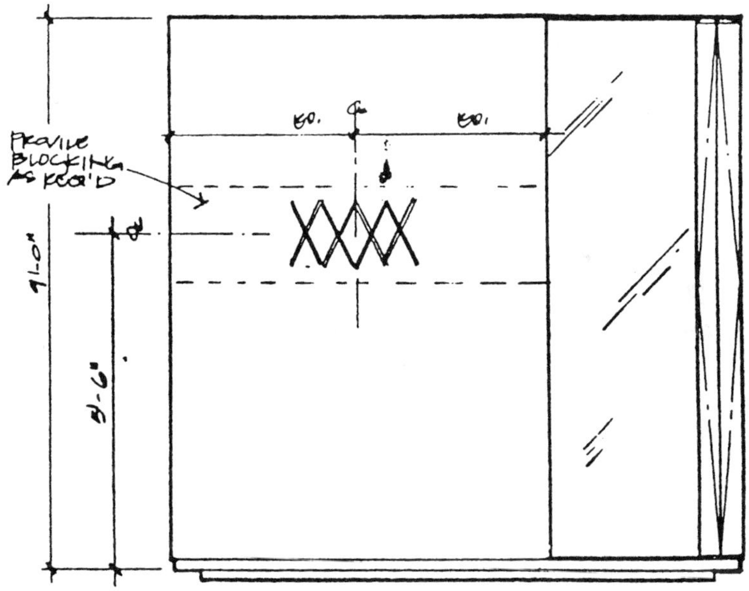

6 ELEVATION : WEST
1/2" = 1'-0"

DEPARTMENT STORES
Fitting Room/Details

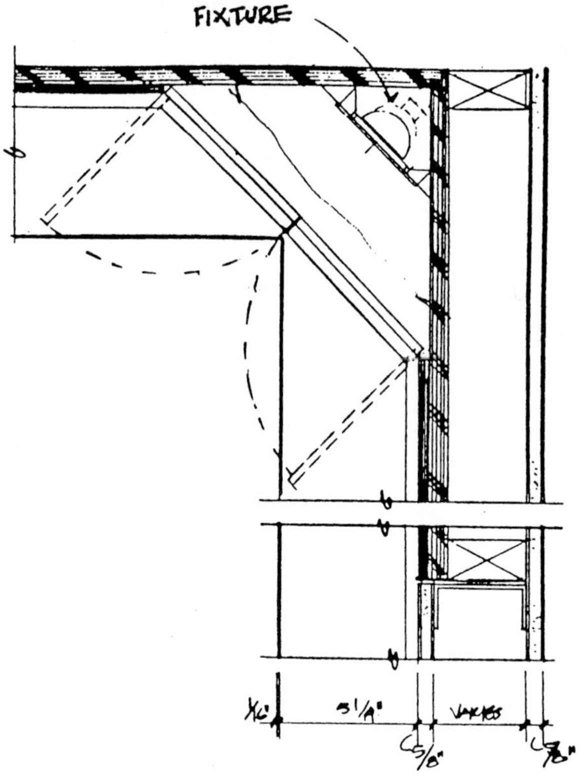

7 DETAIL 3"=1'-0"

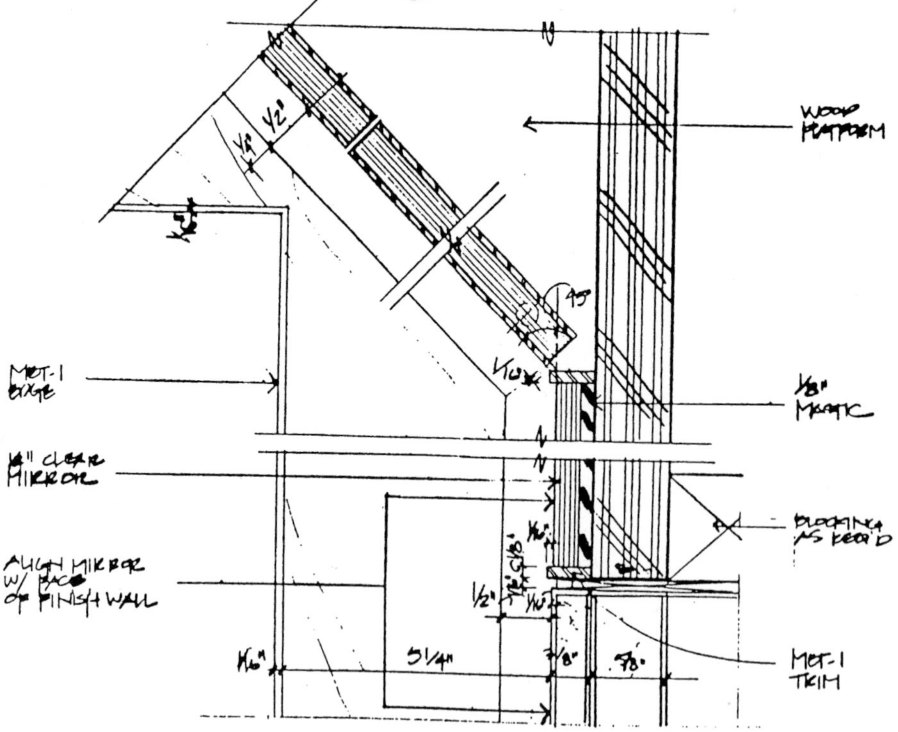

7A DETAIL N.S.

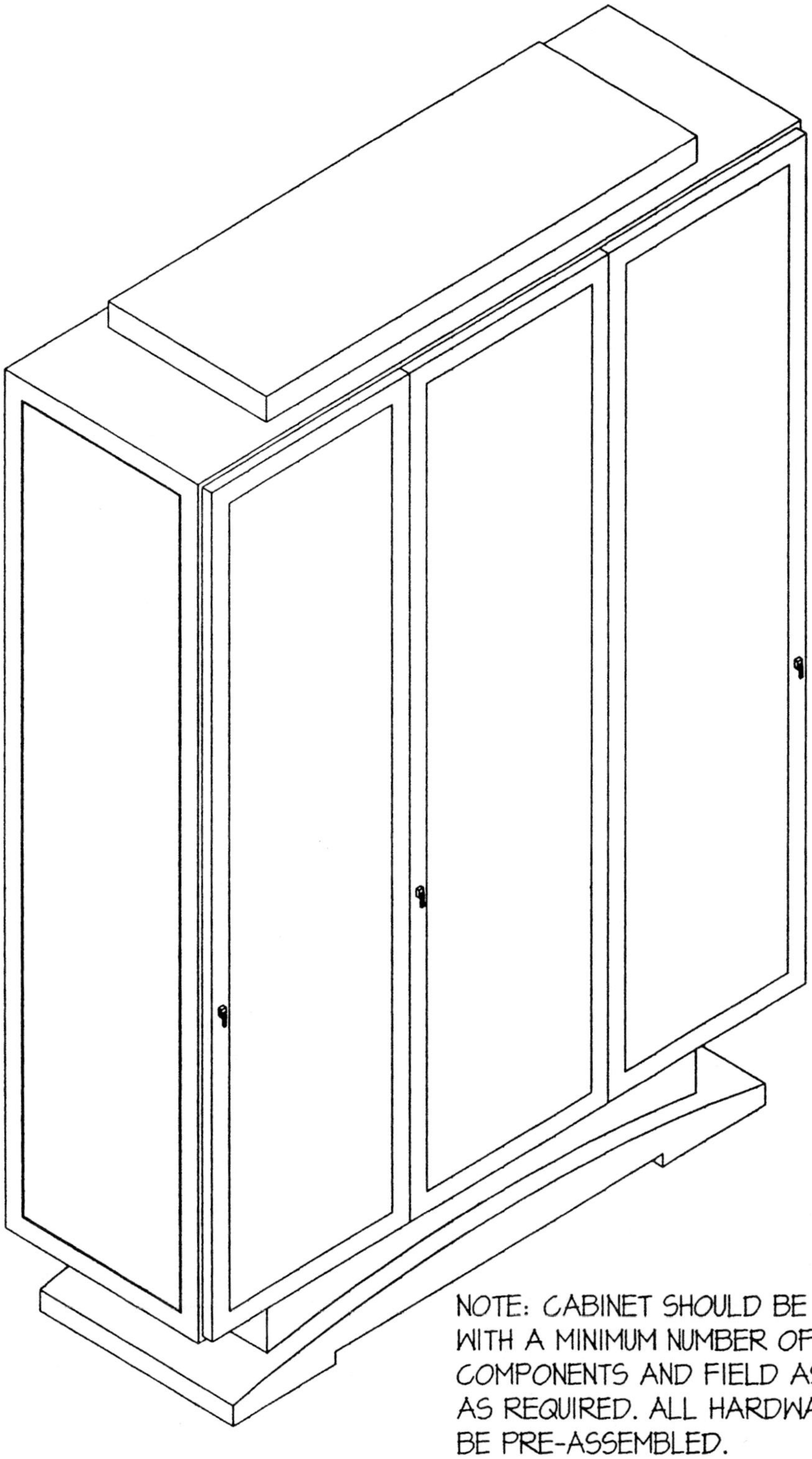

NOTE: CABINET SHOULD BE FABRICATED WITH A MINIMUM NUMBER OF COMPONENTS AND FIELD ASSEMBLED AS REQUIRED. ALL HARDWARE SHOULD BE PRE-ASSEMBLED.

ISOMETRIC

SCALE: 3/4" = 1'-0"

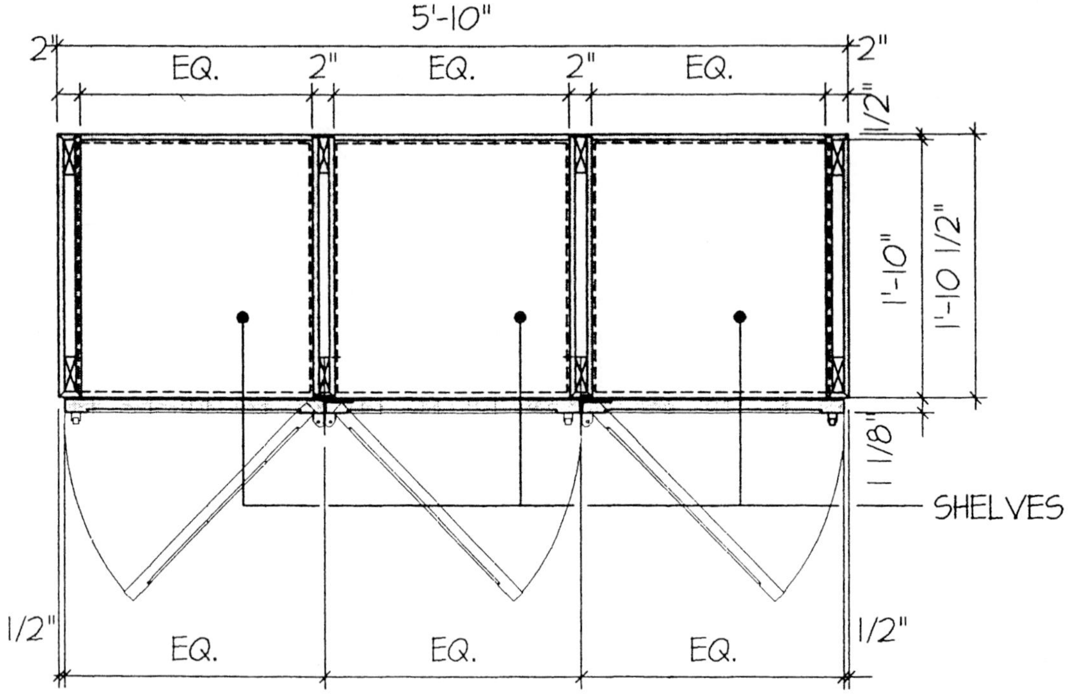

ARMOIRE PLAN

SCALE: 3/4" = 1'-0"

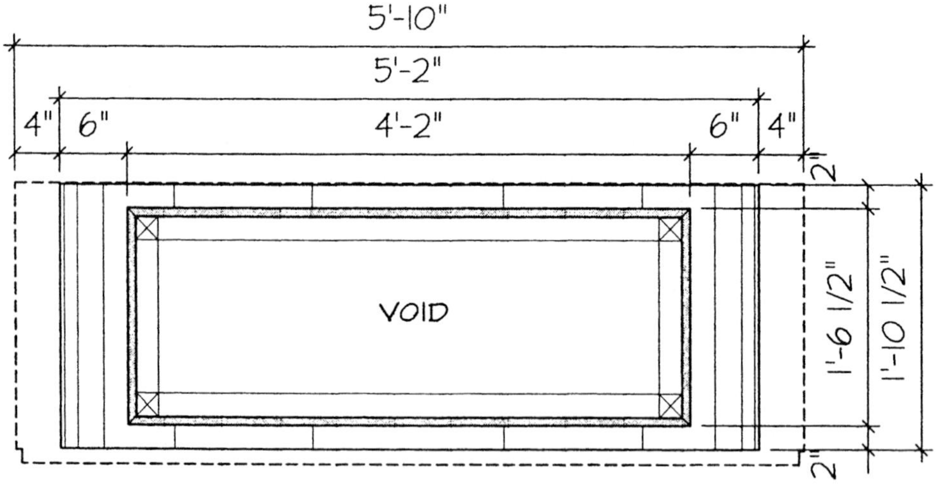

ARMOIRE PLAN

SCALE: 3/4" = 1'-0"

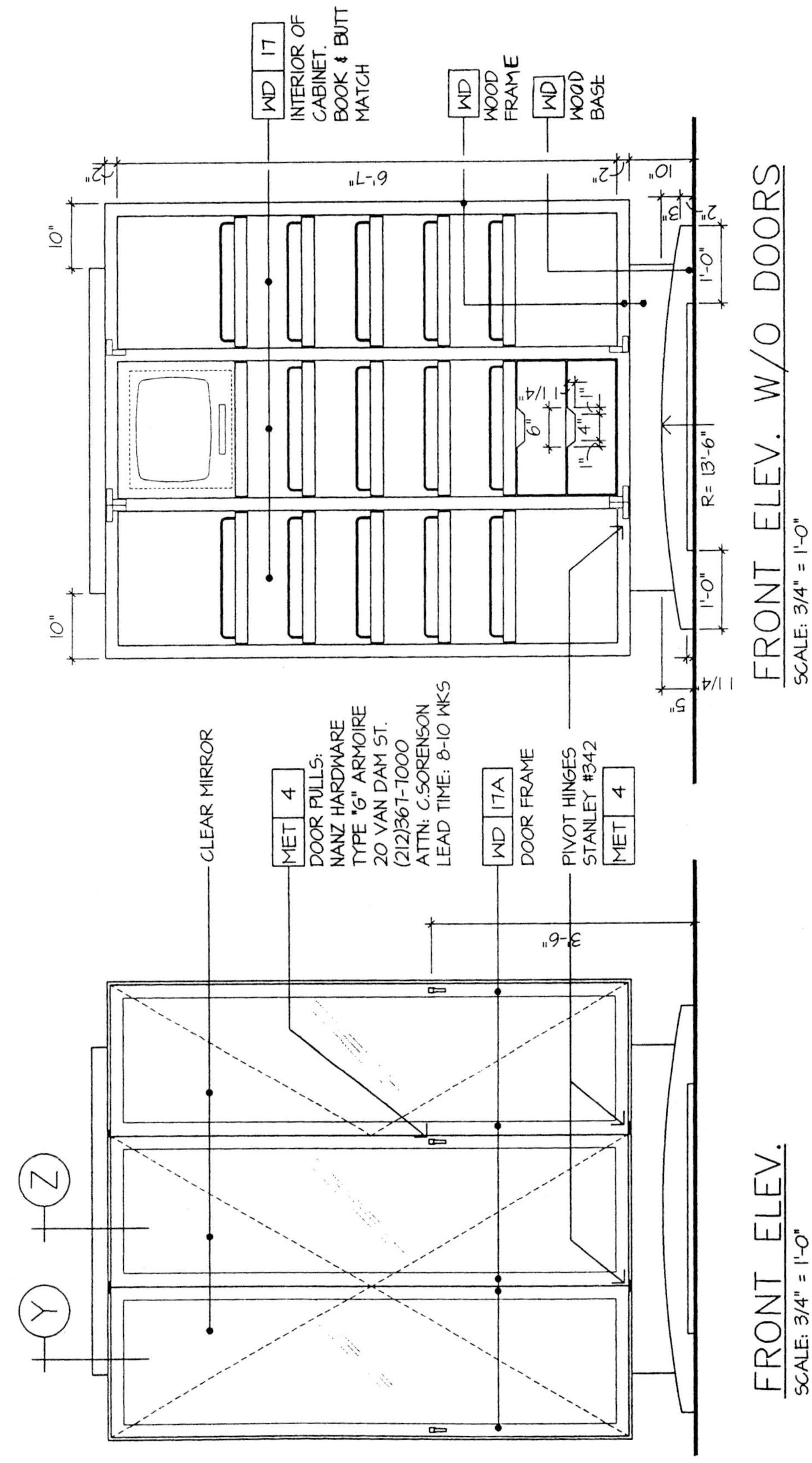
WD 17
INTERIOR OF CABINET. BOOK & BUTT MATCH
WD
WOOD FRAME
WD
WOOD BASE
6'-7"
R= 13'-6"
1'-0"
10"
FRONT ELEV. W/O DOORS
SCALE: 3/4" = 1'-0"
CLEAR MIRROR
MET 4
DOOR PULLS:
NANZ HARDWARE
TYPE "G" ARMOIRE
20 VAN DAM ST.
(212)367-7000
ATTN: C.SORENSON
LEAD TIME: 8-10 WKS
WD 17A
DOOR FRAME
PIVOT HINGES
STANLEY #342
MET 4
3'-6"
Y
Z
FRONT ELEV.
SCALE: 3/4" = 1'-0"

DEPARTMENT STORES
Armoire/Elevation and Section

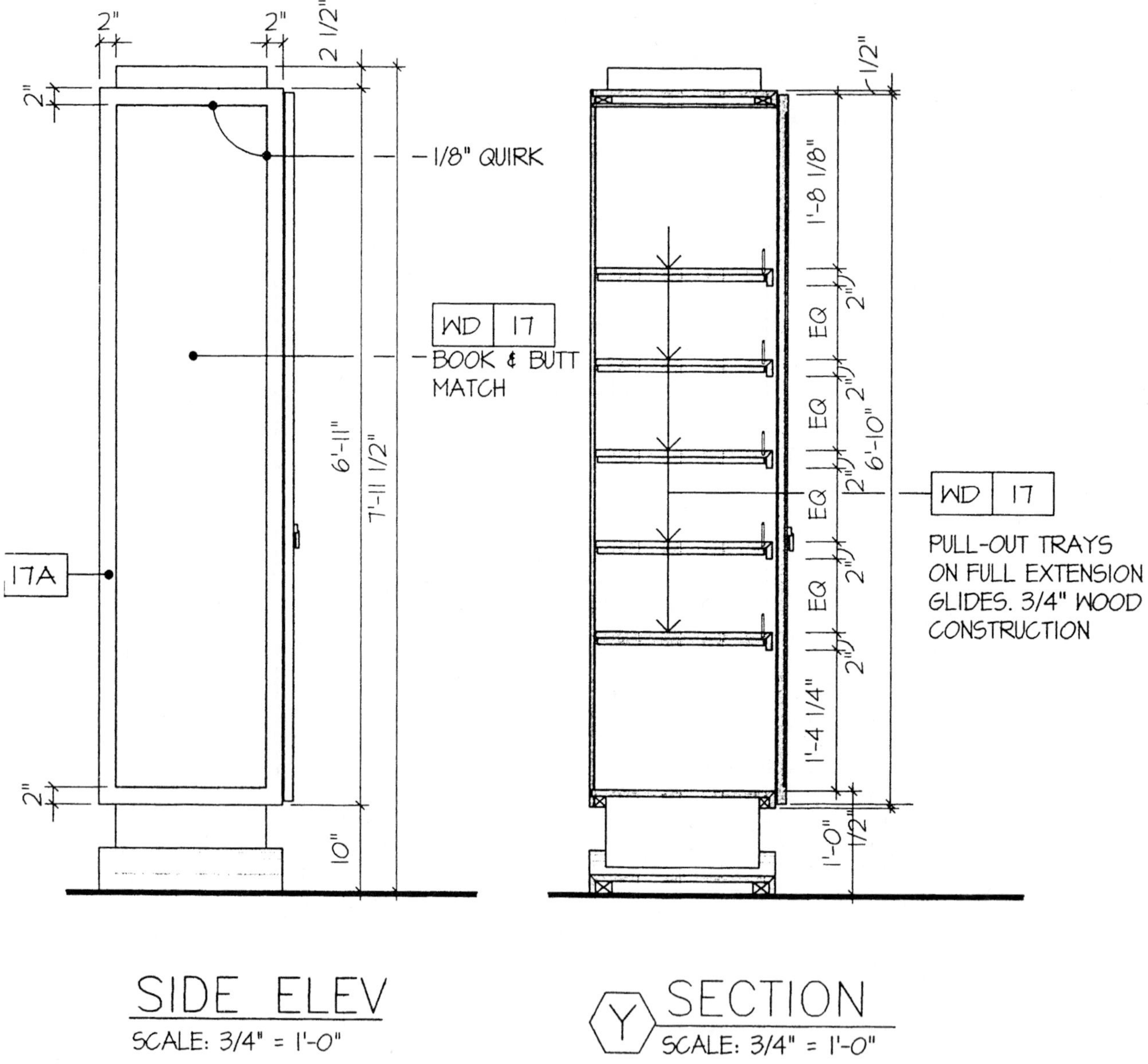

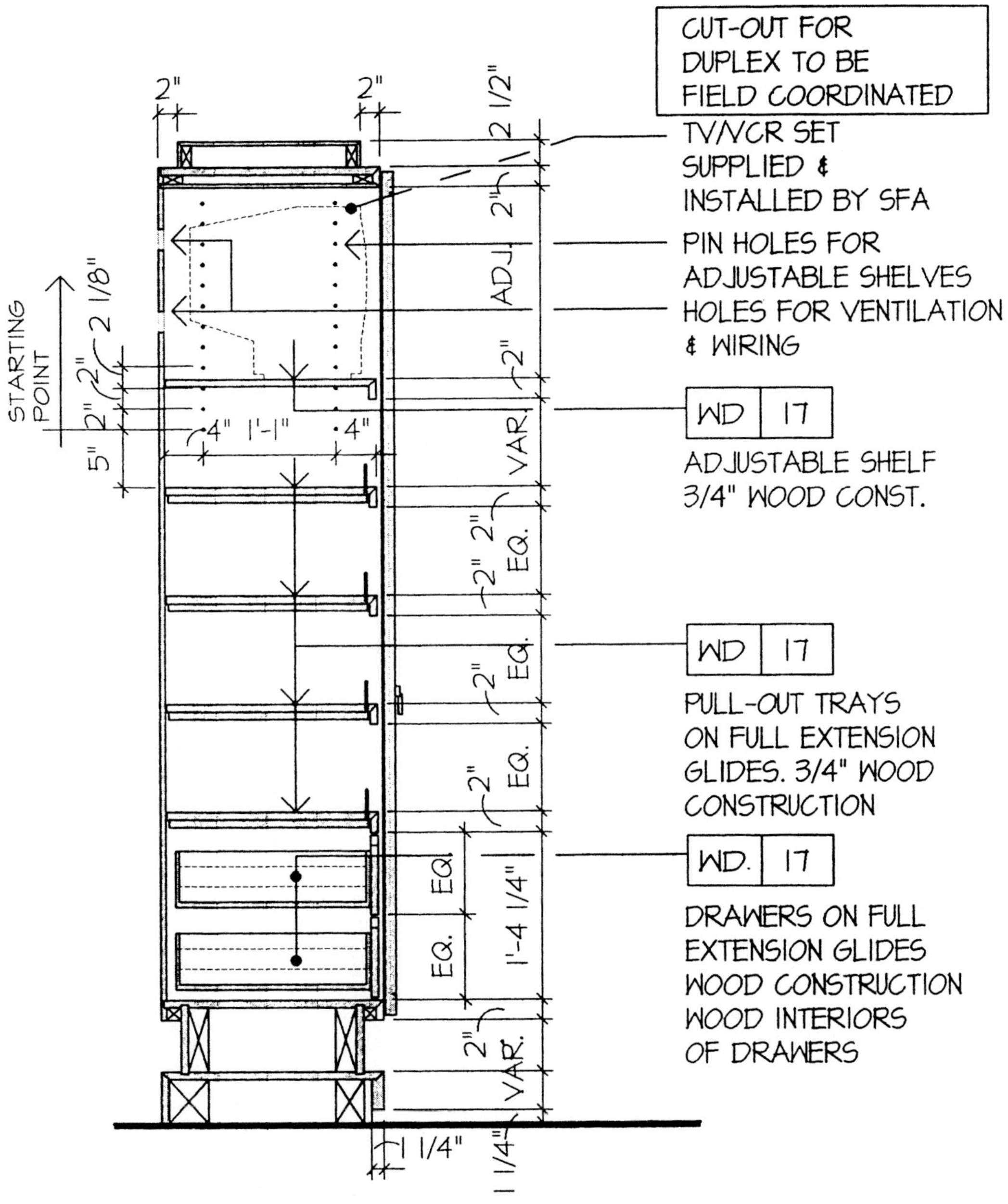
CUT-OUT FOR DUPLEX TO BE FIELD COORDINATED
TV/VCR SET SUPPLIED & INSTALLED BY SFA
PIN HOLES FOR ADJUSTABLE SHELVES
HOLES FOR VENTILATION & WIRING
WD 17
ADJUSTABLE SHELF 3/4" WOOD CONST.
WD 17
PULL-OUT TRAYS ON FULL EXTENSION GLIDES. 3/4" WOOD CONSTRUCTION
WD. 17
DRAWERS ON FULL EXTENSION GLIDES WOOD CONSTRUCTION WOOD INTERIORS OF DRAWERS
STARTING POINT
2"
2"
2 1/2"
2"
ADJ.
2 1/8"
2"
VAR.
EQ.
1'-4 1/4"
1 1/4"
4"
1'-1"
5"

Z SECTION
SCALE: 3/4" = 1'-0"

DEPARTMENT STORES
Armoire/Elevation and Section

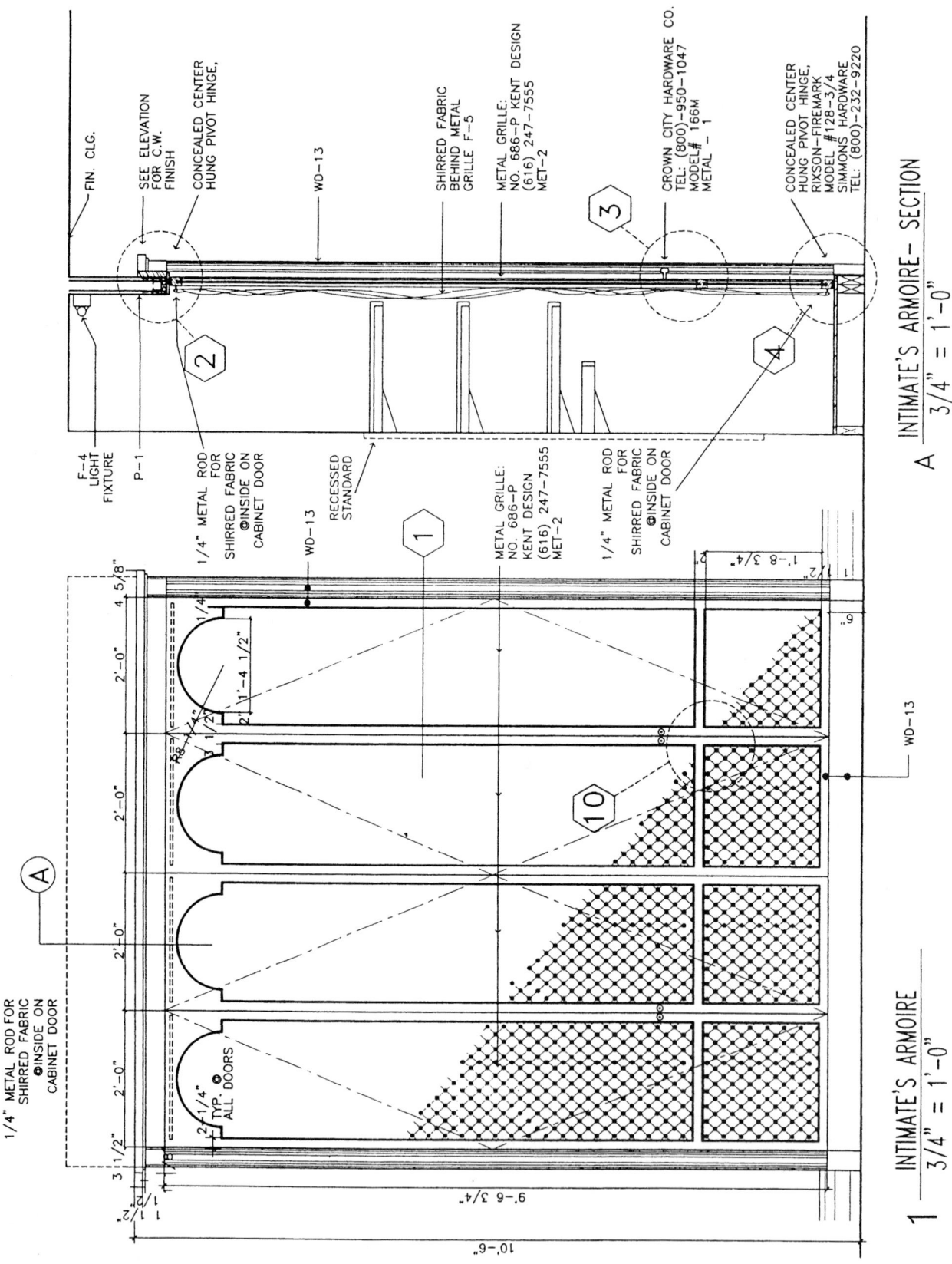

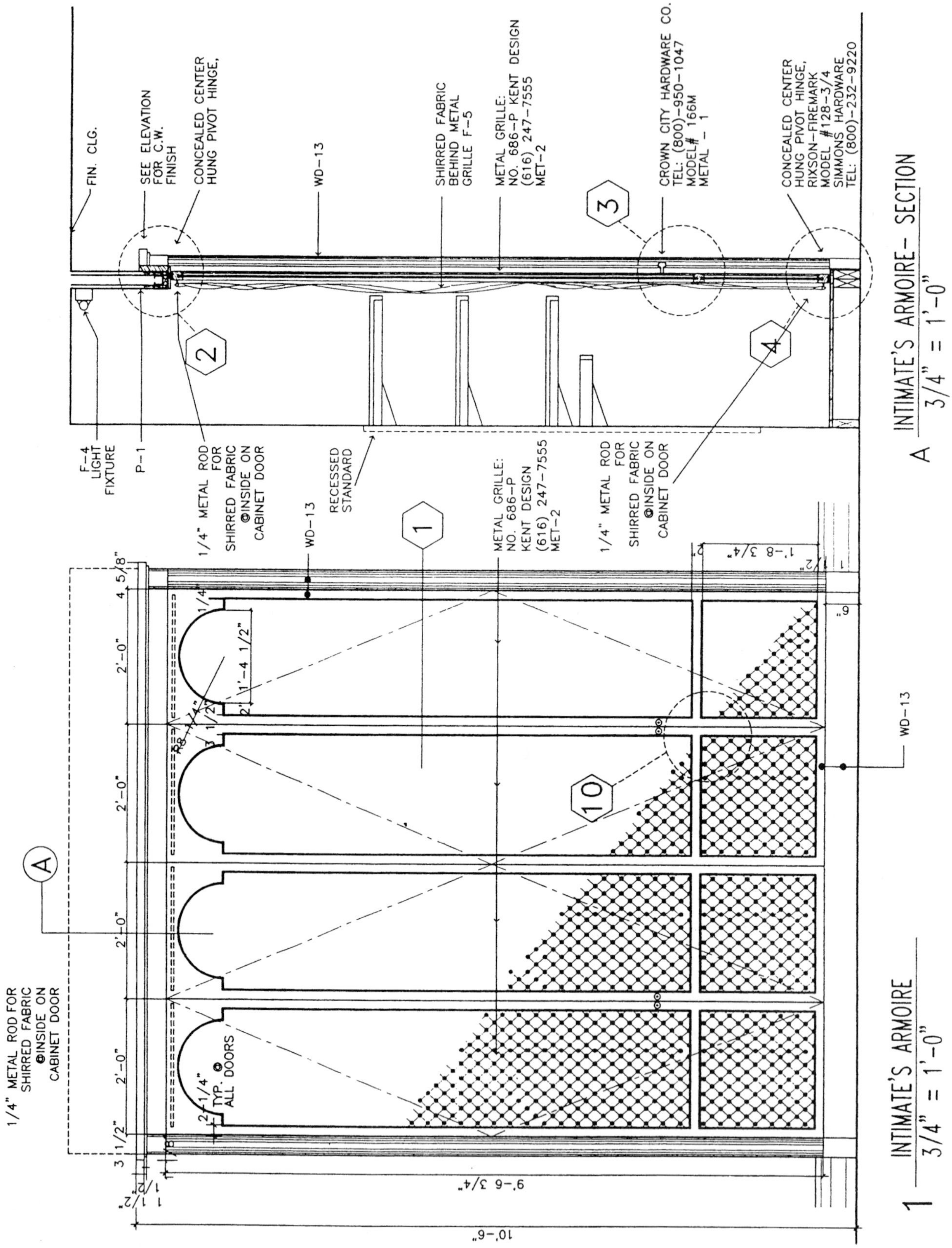
FIN. CLG.
SEE ELEVATION FOR C.W. FINISH
CONCEALED CENTER HUNG PIVOT HINGE,
WD-13
SHIRRED FABRIC BEHIND METAL GRILLE F-5
METAL GRILLE: NO. 686-P KENT DESIGN (616) 247-7555 MET-2
CROWN CITY HARDWARE CO. TEL: (800)-950-1047 MODEL# 166M METAL - 1
CONCEALED CENTER HUNG PIVOT HINGE, RIXSON-FIREMARK MODEL #128-3/4 SIMMONS HARDWARE TEL: (800)-232-9220
F-4 LIGHT FIXTURE
P-1
1/4" METAL ROD FOR SHIRRED FABRIC @INSIDE ON CABINET DOOR
RECESSED STANDARD
WD-13
METAL GRILLE: NO. 686-P KENT DESIGN (616) 247-7555 MET-2
1/4" METAL ROD FOR SHIRRED FABRIC @INSIDE ON CABINET DOOR
A INTIMATE'S ARMOIRE- SECTION 3/4" = 1'-0"
1/4" METAL ROD FOR SHIRRED FABRIC @INSIDE ON CABINET DOOR
TYP. @ ALL DOORS
WD-13
1'-8 3/4"
9'-6 3/4"
10'-6"
1 INTIMATE'S ARMOIRE 3/4" = 1'-0"

DEPARTMENT STORES

Armoire/Elevation and Section

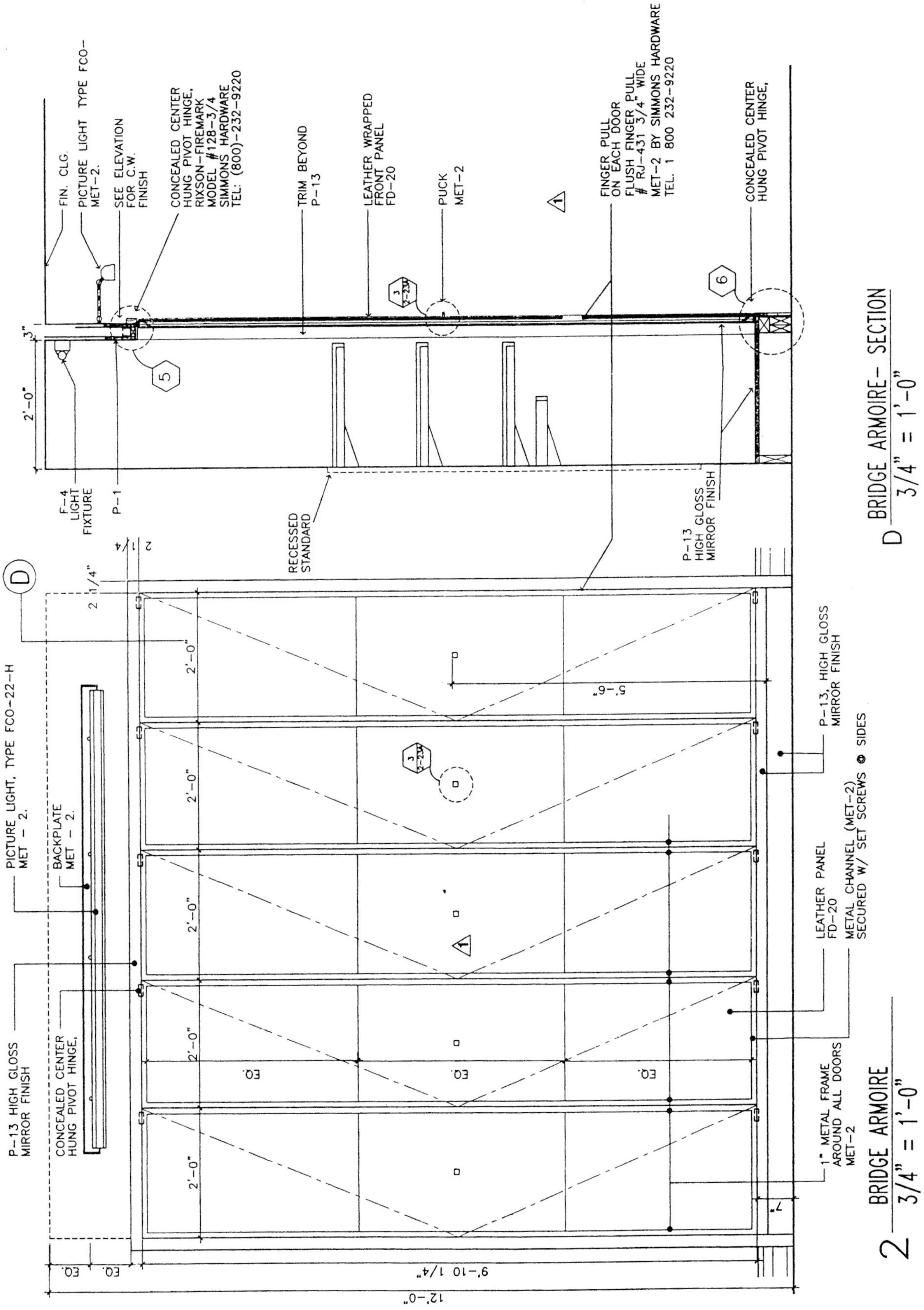
FIN. CLG.
PICTURE LIGHT TYPE FCO-MET-2.
SEE ELEVATION FOR C.W. FINISH
CONCEALED CENTER HUNG PIVOT HINGE, RIXSON-FIREMARK MODEL #128-3/4 SIMMONS HARDWARE TEL: (800)-232-9220
TRIM BEYOND P-13
LEATHER WRAPPED FRONT PANEL FD-20
PUCK MET-2
FINGER PULL ON EACH DOOR FLUSH FINGER PULL # RJ-431 3/4" WIDE MET-2 BY SIMMONS HARDWARE TEL. 1 800 232-9220
CONCEALED CENTER HUNG PIVOT HINGE,
F-4 LIGHT FIXTURE
P-1
RECESSED STANDARD
P-13 HIGH GLOSS MIRROR FINISH
D BRIDGE ARMOIRE- SECTION 3/4" = 1'-0"
PICTURE LIGHT, TYPE FCO-22-H MET - 2.
BACKPLATE MET - 2.
P-13 HIGH GLOSS MIRROR FINISH
CONCEALED CENTER HUNG PIVOT HINGE,
P-13, HIGH GLOSS MIRROR FINISH
LEATHER PANEL FD-20
METAL CHANNEL (MET-2) SECURED W/ SET SCREWS @ SIDES
1" METAL FRAME AROUND ALL DOORS MET-2
2 BRIDGE ARMOIRE 3/4" = 1'-0"
2'-0"
5'-6"
EQ.
9'-10 1/4"
12'-0"

DEPARTMENT STORES

Armoire/Elevation and Section

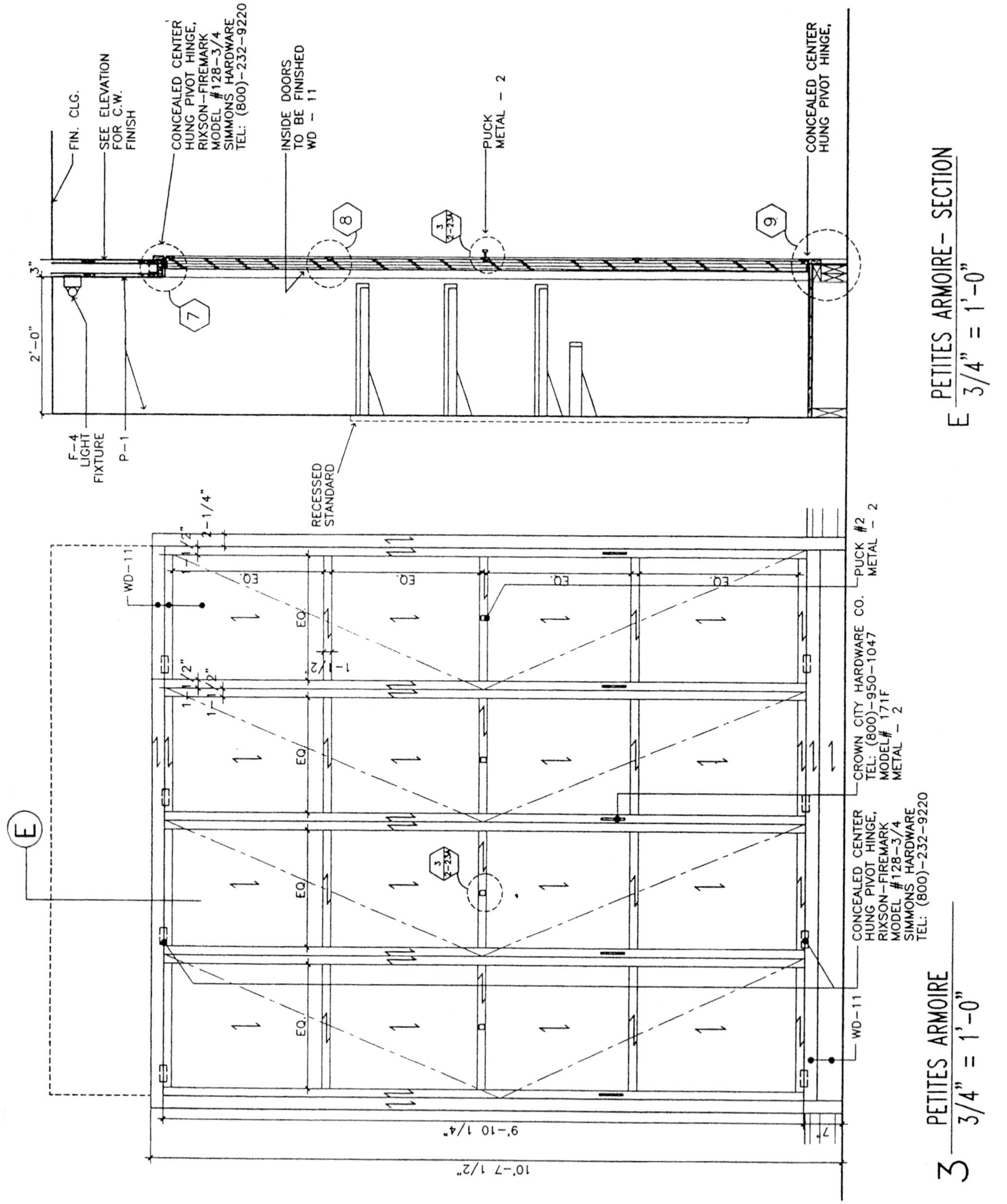
FIN. CLG.
SEE ELEVATION FOR C.W. FINISH
CONCEALED CENTER HUNG PIVOT HINGE, RIXSON–FIREMARK MODEL #128–3/4 SIMMONS HARDWARE TEL: (800)–232–9220
INSIDE DOORS TO BE FINISHED WD – 11
PUCK METAL – 2
CONCEALED CENTER HUNG PIVOT HINGE,
F–4 LIGHT FIXTURE
P–1
2'–0"
3"
RECESSED STANDARD
E PETITES ARMOIRE– SECTION 3/4" = 1'–0"
WD–11
PUCK #2 METAL – 2
CROWN CITY HARDWARE CO. TEL: (800)–950–1047 MODEL# 171F METAL – 2
CONCEALED CENTER HUNG PIVOT HINGE, RIXSON–FIREMARK MODEL #128–3/4 SIMMONS HARDWARE TEL: (800)–232–9220
WD–11
EQ.
9'–10 1/4"
10'–7 1/2"
3 PETITES ARMOIRE 3/4" = 1'–0"

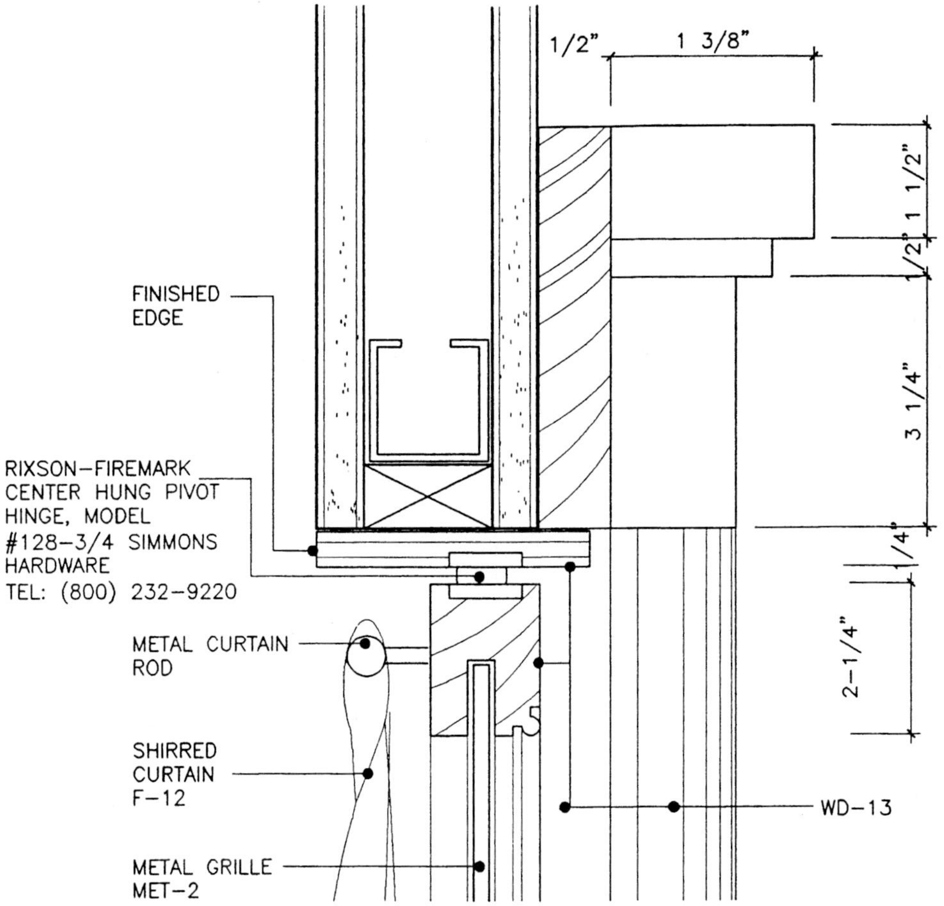

SECTION - DETAIL 2
SCALE: HALF

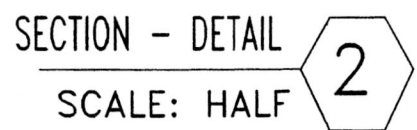

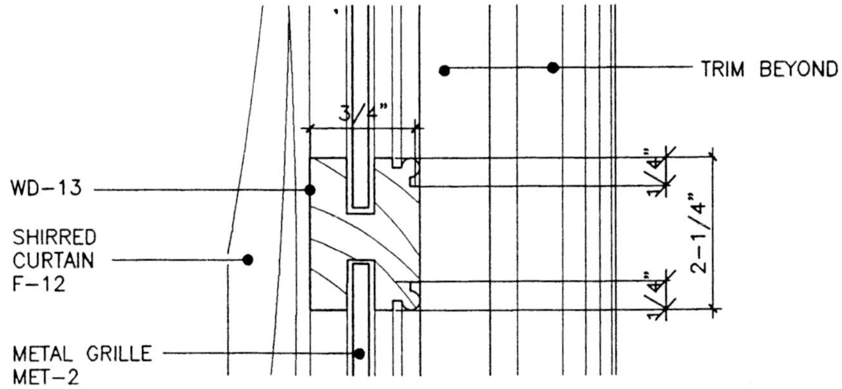

SECTION - DETAIL 3
SCALE: HALF

DEPARTMENT STORES

Armoire/Sections and Details

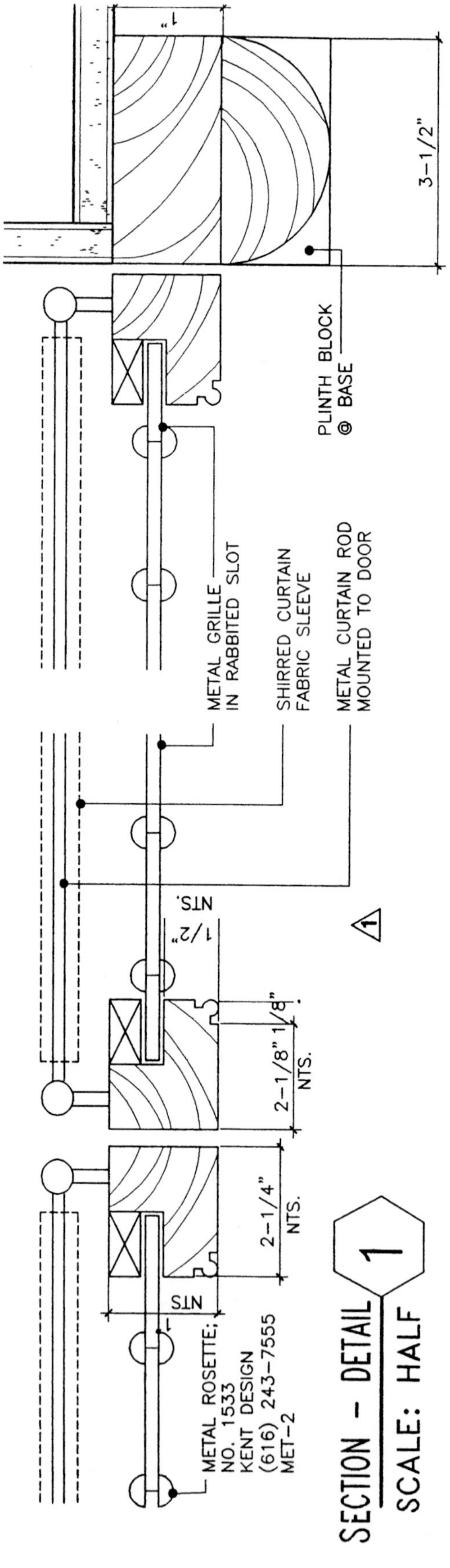

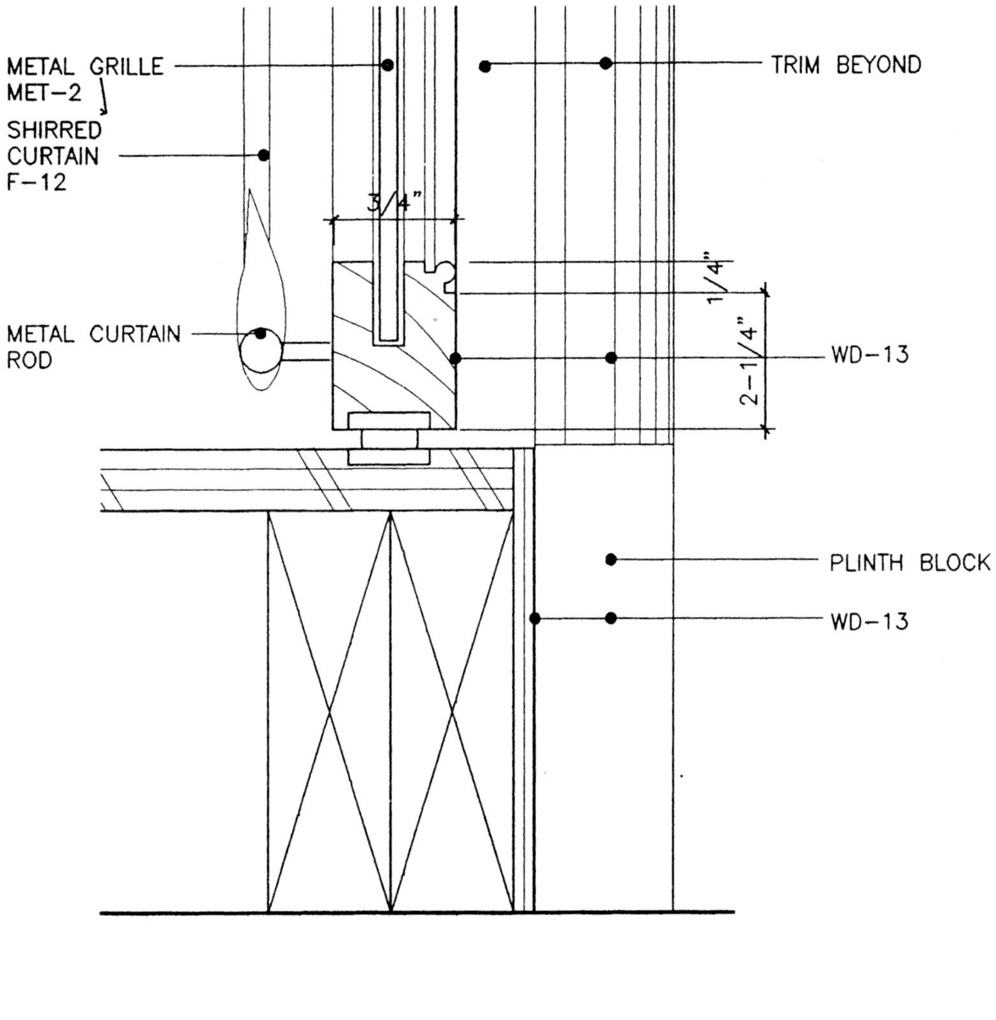

SECTION - DETAIL
SCALE: HALF
4

DEPARTMENT STORES
Armoire/Sections and Details

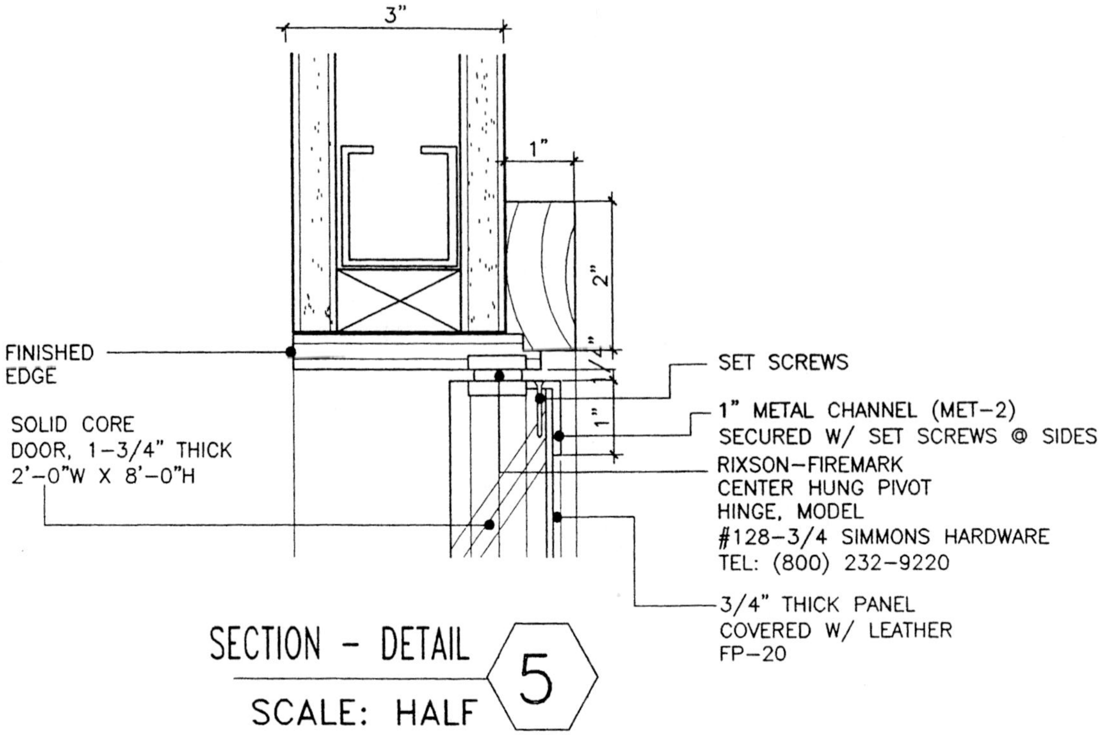

SECTION - DETAIL 5
SCALE: HALF

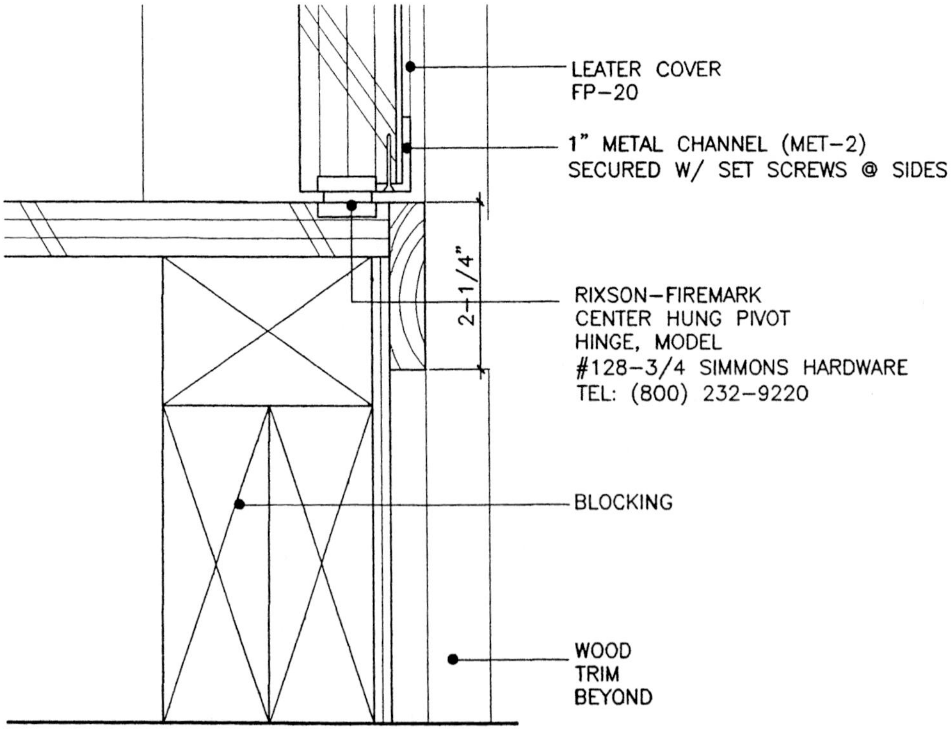

SECTION - DETAIL 6
SCALE: HALF

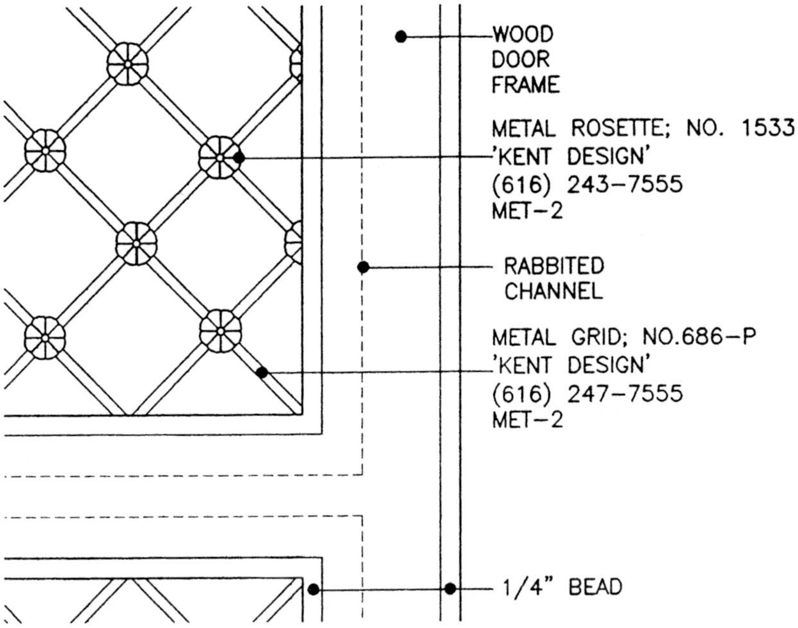
WOOD
DOOR
FRAME
METAL ROSETTE; NO. 1533
'KENT DESIGN'
(616) 243-7555
MET-2
RABBITED
CHANNEL
METAL GRID; NO.686-P
'KENT DESIGN'
(616) 247-7555
MET-2
1/4" BEAD
DETAIL
SCALE: HALF
10

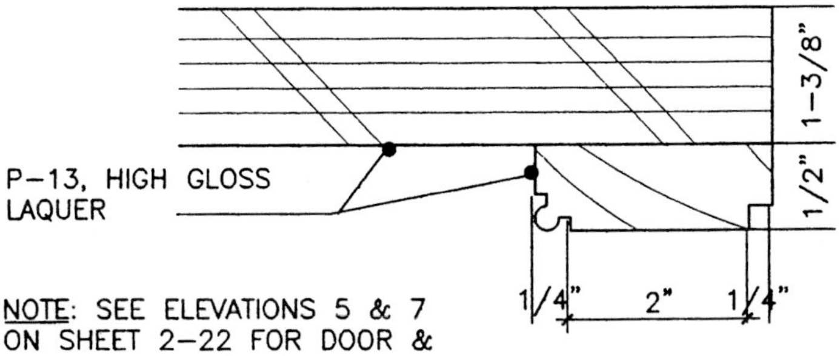
1-3/8"
1/2"
P-13, HIGH GLOSS
LAQUER
1/4"
2"
1/4"
NOTE: SEE ELEVATIONS 5 & 7
ON SHEET 2-22 FOR DOOR &
PANEL ELEVATIONS
SECTION @ FAUX PANEL & DOOR 202
SCALE: HALF
11

HEALTH CARE SPACES

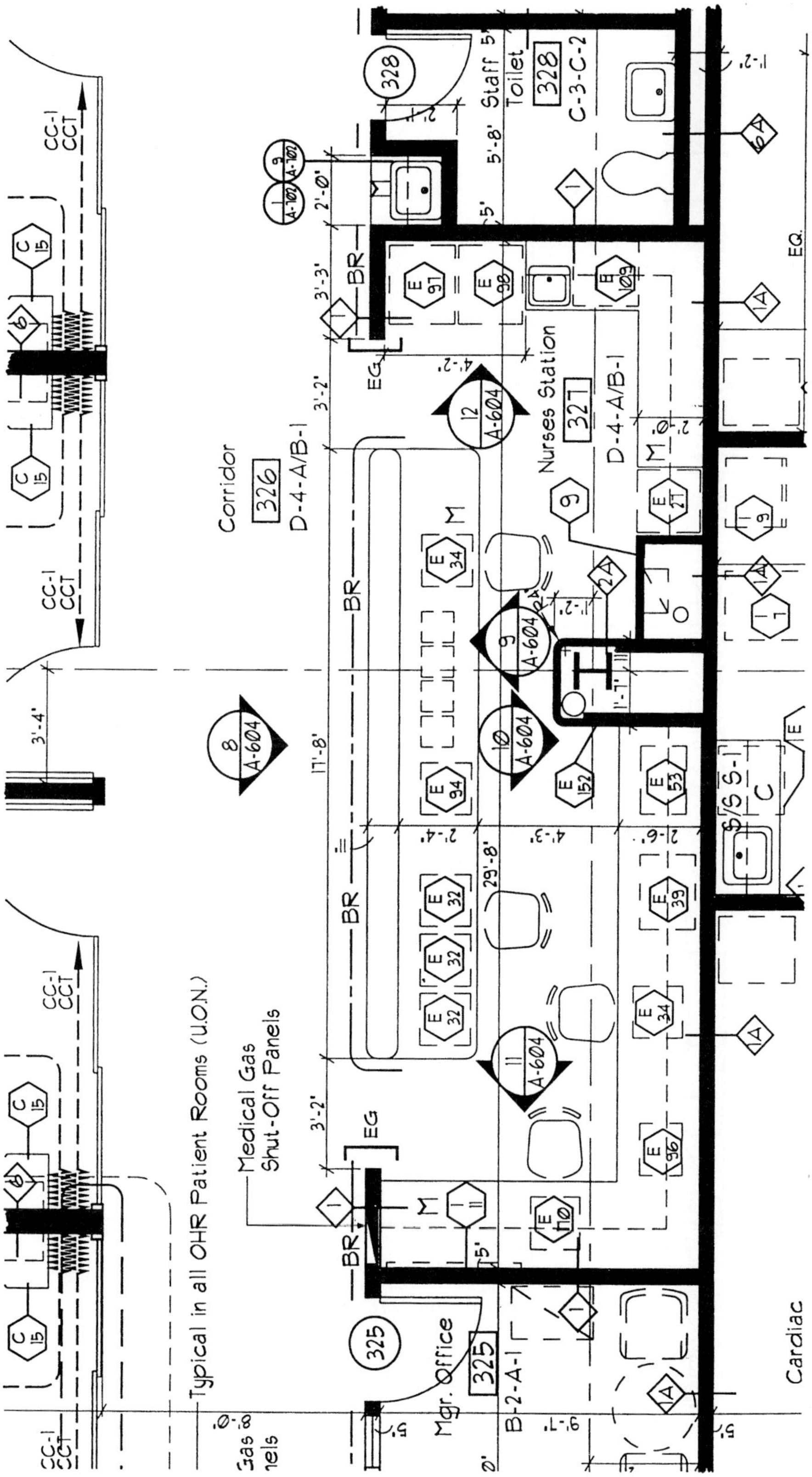

Plan / Typical Nurses' Station

NURSES' STATIONS
Elevations

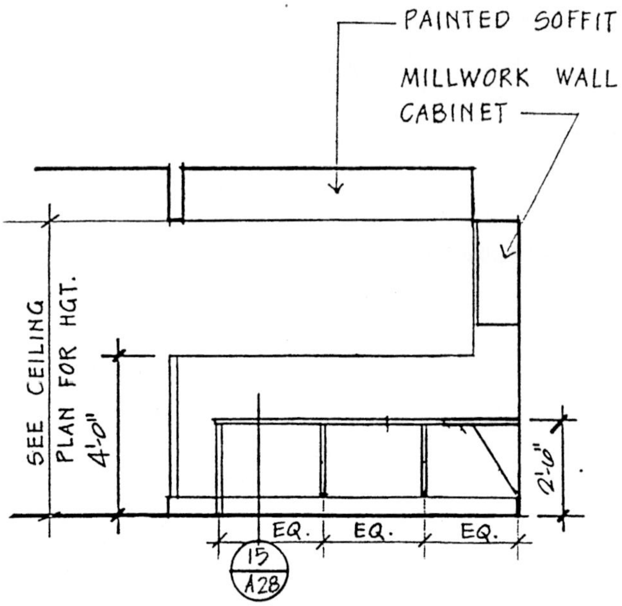

17
A25
NURSE - 144

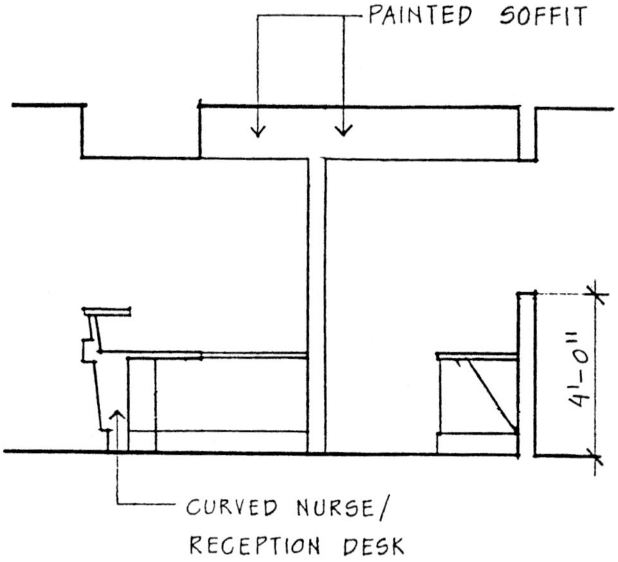

18
A25
NURSE - 144

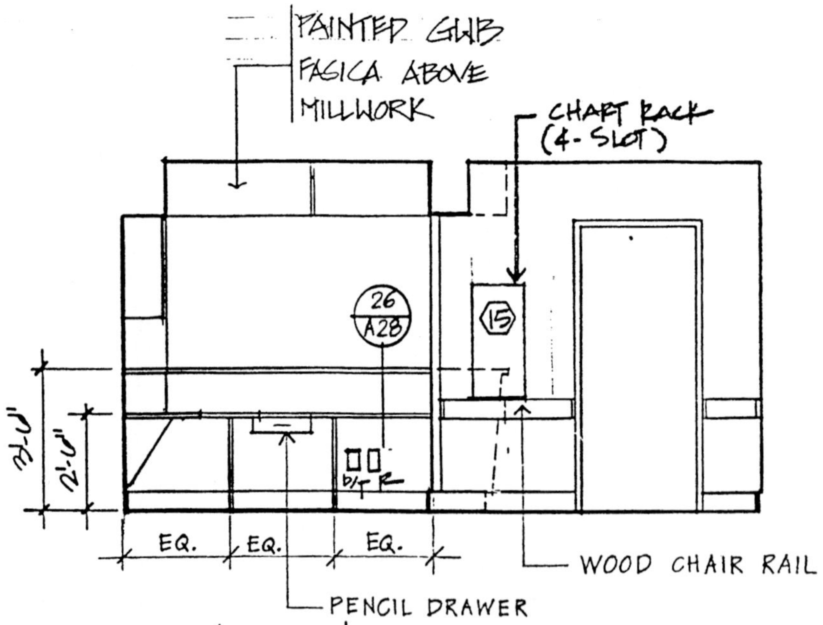

19
A25
NURSE & CORR - 144, 149

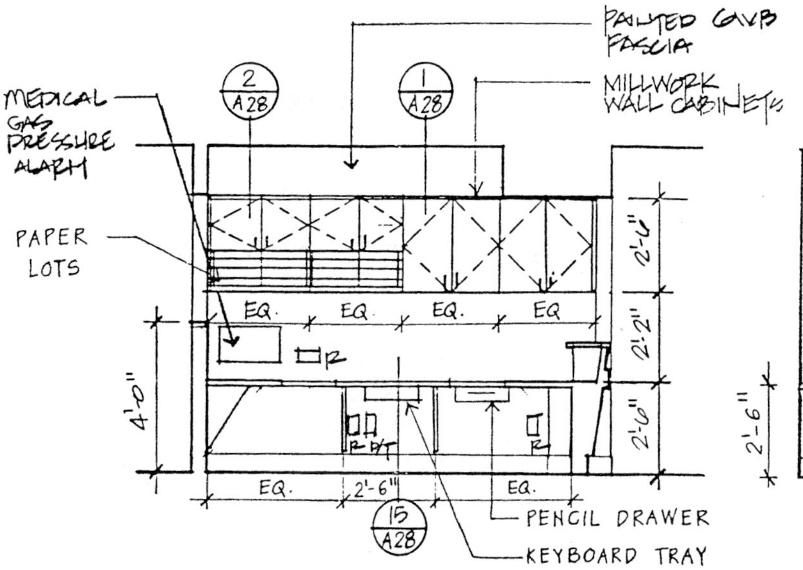

20 A25 NURSE - 144

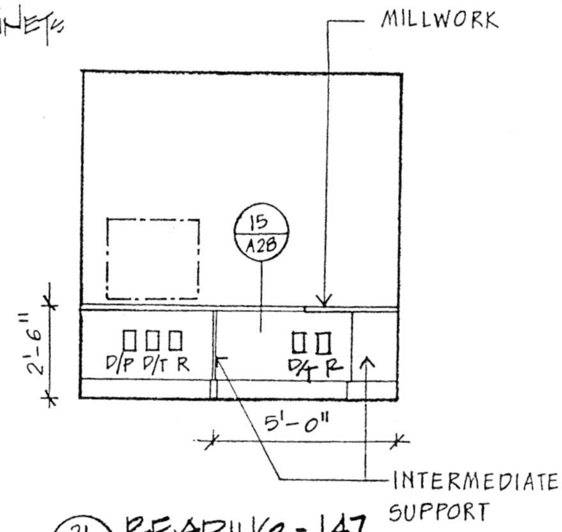

21 A25 READING - 147

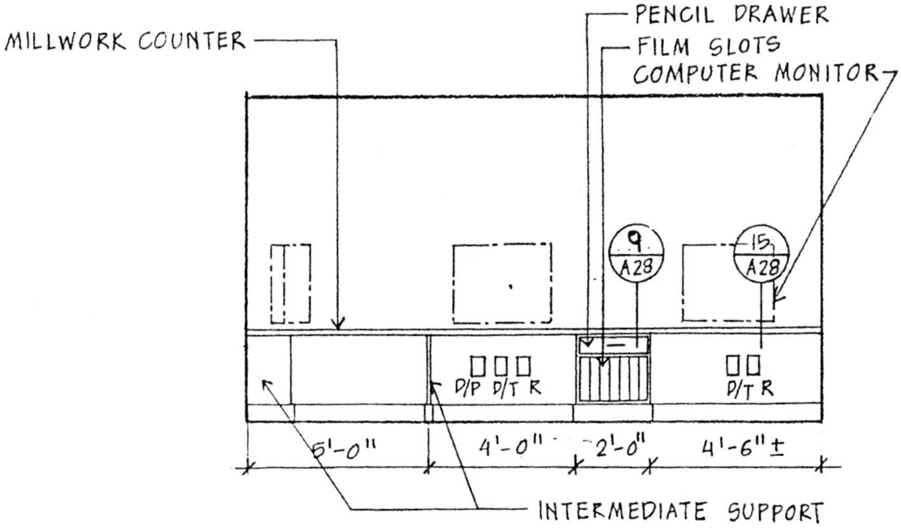

22 A25 READING - 147

NURSES' STATIONS
Counter Sections and Details

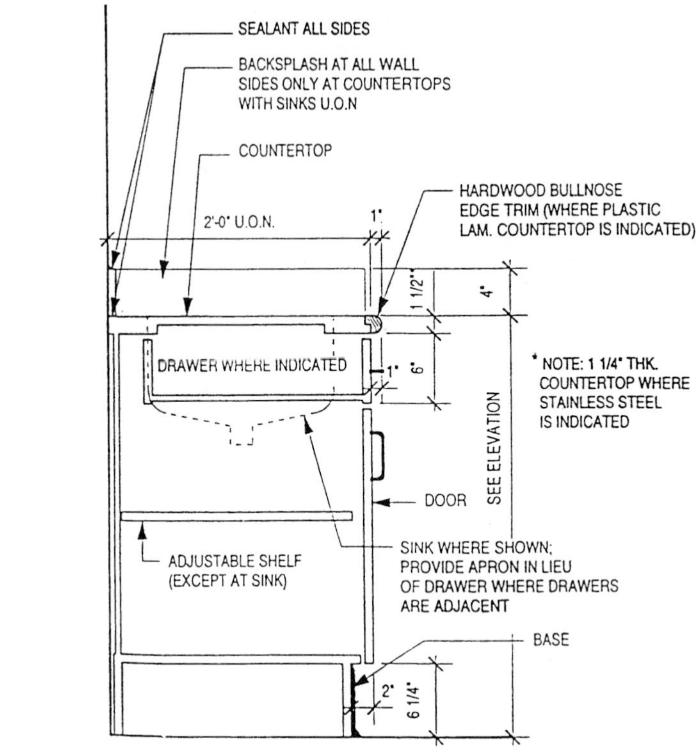
SEALANT ALL SIDES
BACKSPLASH AT ALL WALL SIDES ONLY AT COUNTERTOPS WITH SINKS U.O.N
COUNTERTOP
HARDWOOD BULLNOSE EDGE TRIM (WHERE PLASTIC LAM. COUNTERTOP IS INDICATED)
2'-0" U.O.N.
1"
1 1/2"
4"
DRAWER WHERE INDICATED
1"
6"
* NOTE: 1 1/4" THK. COUNTERTOP WHERE STAINLESS STEEL IS INDICATED
SEE ELEVATION
DOOR
ADJUSTABLE SHELF (EXCEPT AT SINK)
SINK WHERE SHOWN; PROVIDE APRON IN LIEU OF DRAWER WHERE DRAWERS ARE ADJACENT
BASE
2"
6 1/4"

14 BASE CABINET

1" = 1'-0"

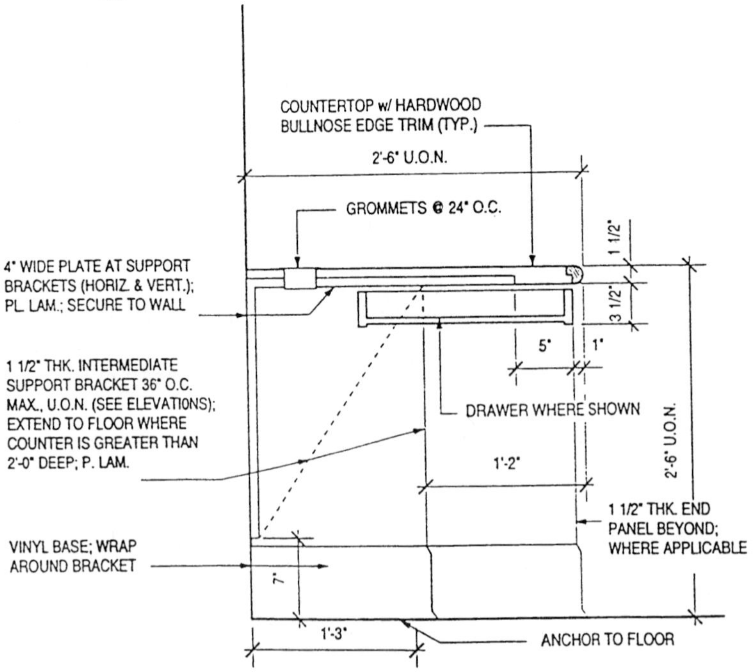
COUNTERTOP w/ HARDWOOD BULLNOSE EDGE TRIM (TYP.)
2'-6" U.O.N.
GROMMETS @ 24" O.C.
1 1/2"
4" WIDE PLATE AT SUPPORT BRACKETS (HORIZ. & VERT.); PL. LAM.; SECURE TO WALL
3 1/2"
5"
1"
1 1/2" THK. INTERMEDIATE SUPPORT BRACKET 36" O.C. MAX., U.O.N. (SEE ELEVATIONS); EXTEND TO FLOOR WHERE COUNTER IS GREATER THAN 2'-0" DEEP; P. LAM.
DRAWER WHERE SHOWN
2'-6" U.O.N.
1'-2"
1 1/2" THK. END PANEL BEYOND; WHERE APPLICABLE
VINYL BASE; WRAP AROUND BRACKET
7"
1'-3"
ANCHOR TO FLOOR

15 COUNTERTOP

1" = 1'-0"

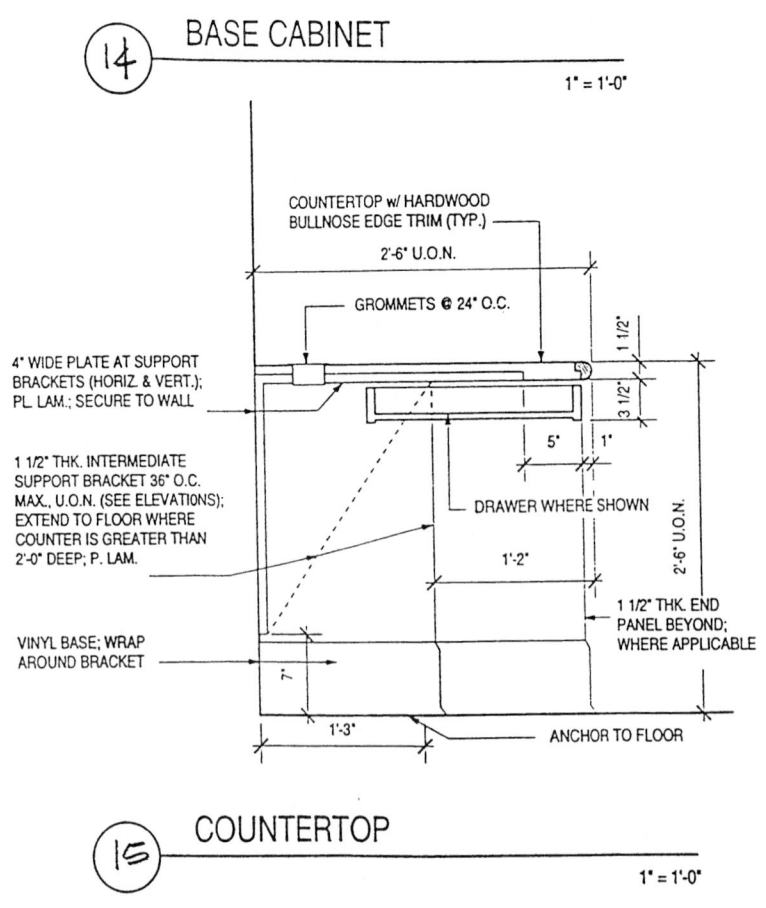

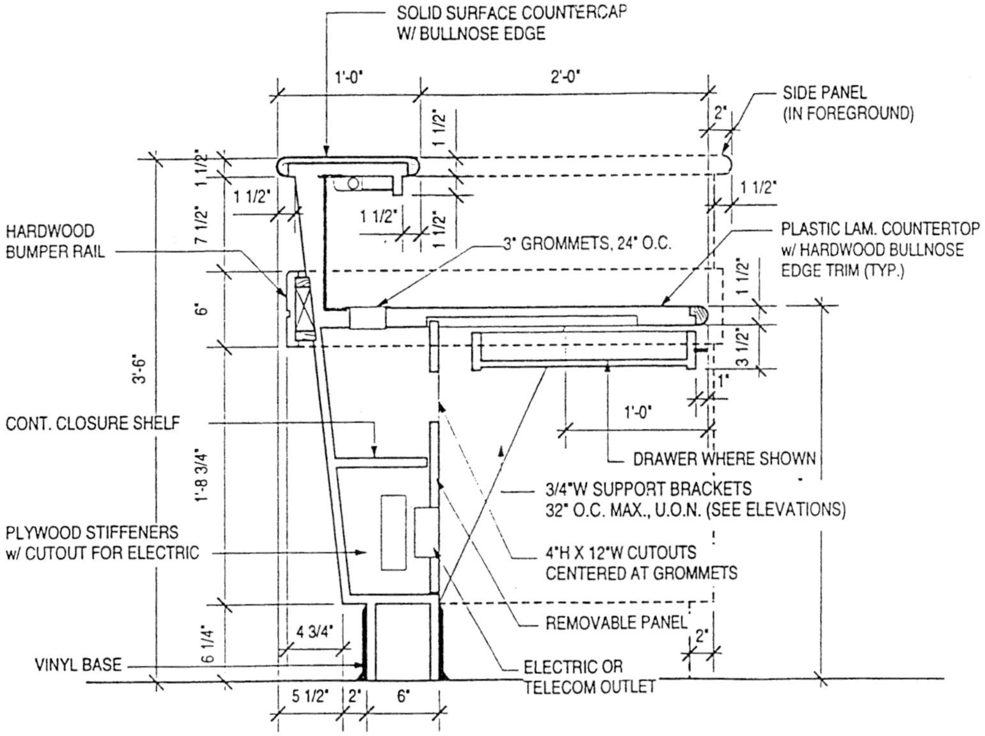

ANGIO RECEPTION DESK

23

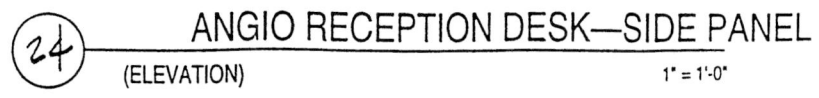

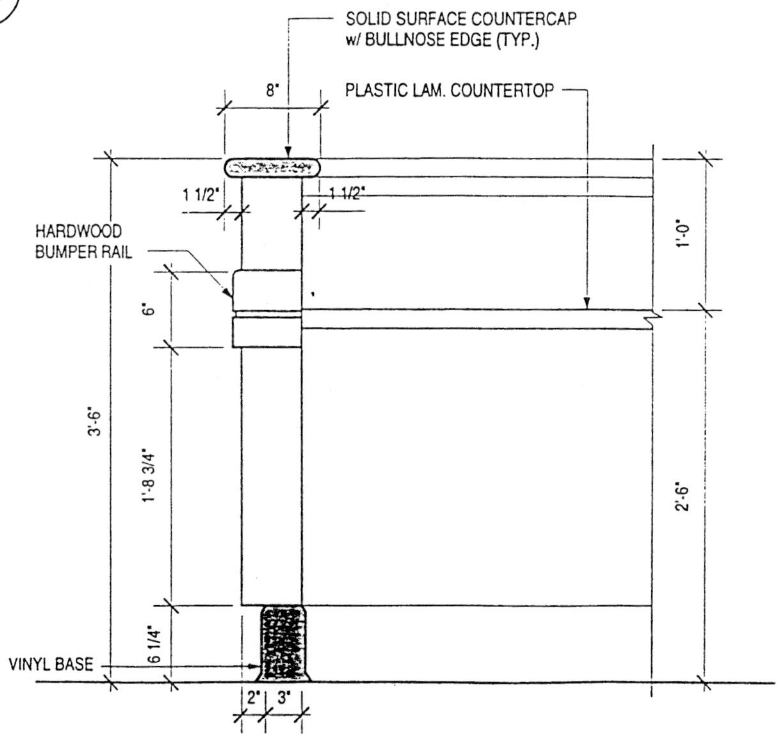

ANGIO RECEPTION DESK—SIDE PANEL

24

(ELEVATION) 1" = 1'-0"

NURSES' STATIONS
Counter Sections and Details

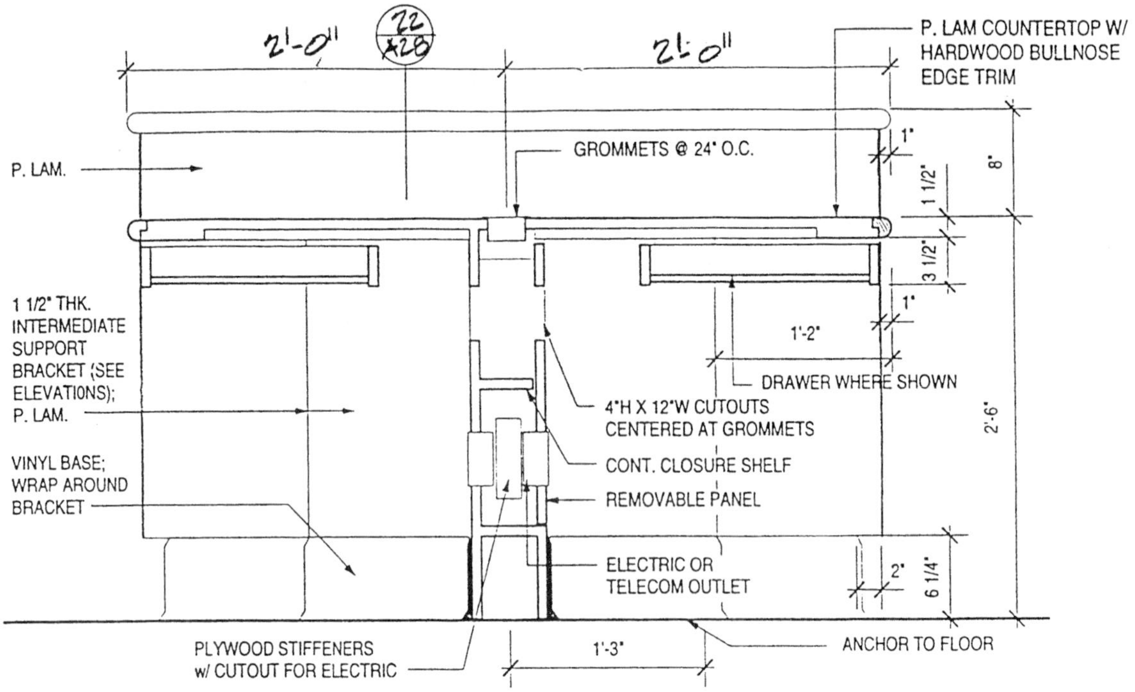

21 ANGIO NURSES STATION COUNTERTOP

1" = 1'-0"

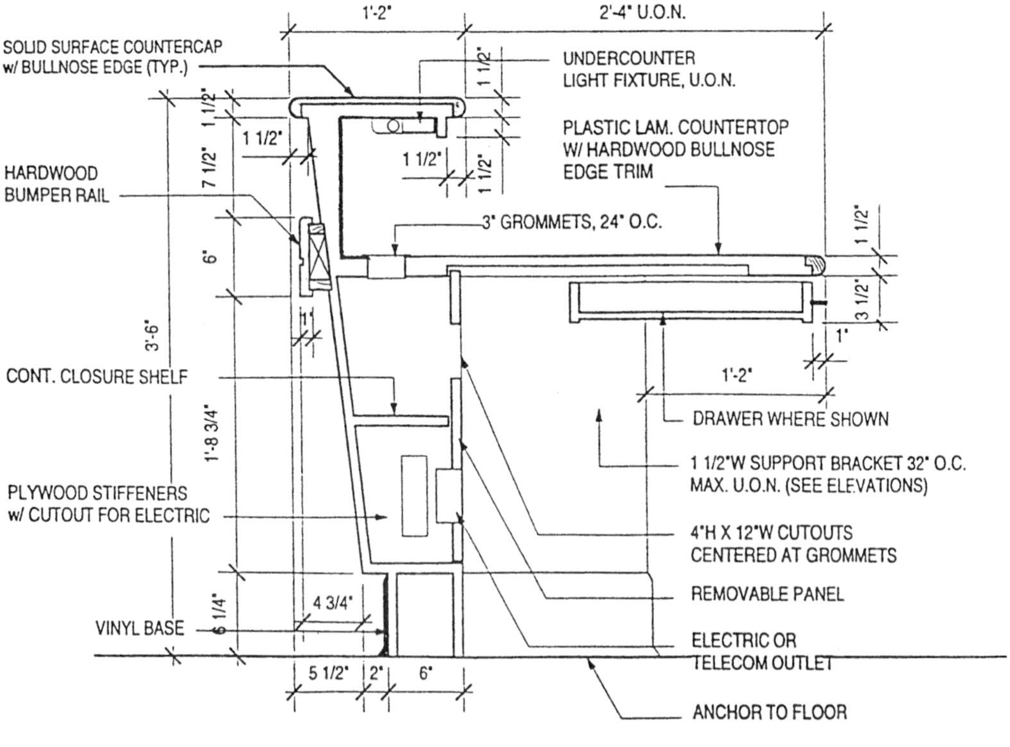

26 RECEPTION DESK—HIGH SECTION

1" = 1'-0"

COUNTERTOP
8"
SOLID SURFACE CAP
w/ BULLNOSE EDGE
6"
HARDWOOD
BUMPER RAIL
1 1/2"
1 1/2"
BASE
CABINET
2'-6"
1'-8 3/4"
2'-10 1/2"
6 1/4"
VINYL BASE
3"
2"

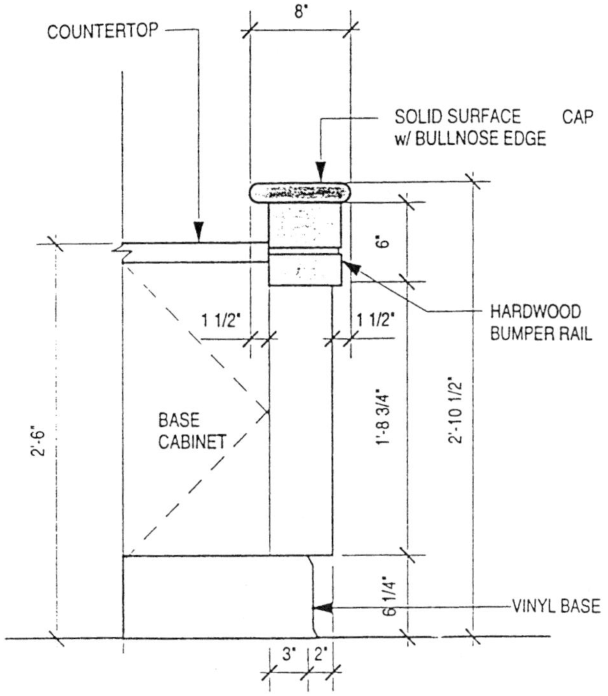

25
ANGIO BASE CABINET—SIDE PANEL
(ELEVATION)
1" = 1'-0"

HIGH COUNTERCAP
(WHERE INDICATED)
HARDWOOD VENEER
W/ HARDWOOD
BULLNOSE EDGE
HARDWOOD
BUMPER RAIL
6"
2'-11 1/4"
1"
1 1/2"
3 1/2"
1"
1'-2"
6"
2'-9"
1'-8 3/4"
6 1/4"
SIDE PANEL
(IN FOREGROUND)
2"
4 3/4"
2"
6"

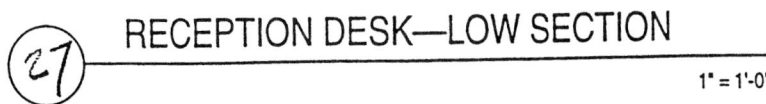

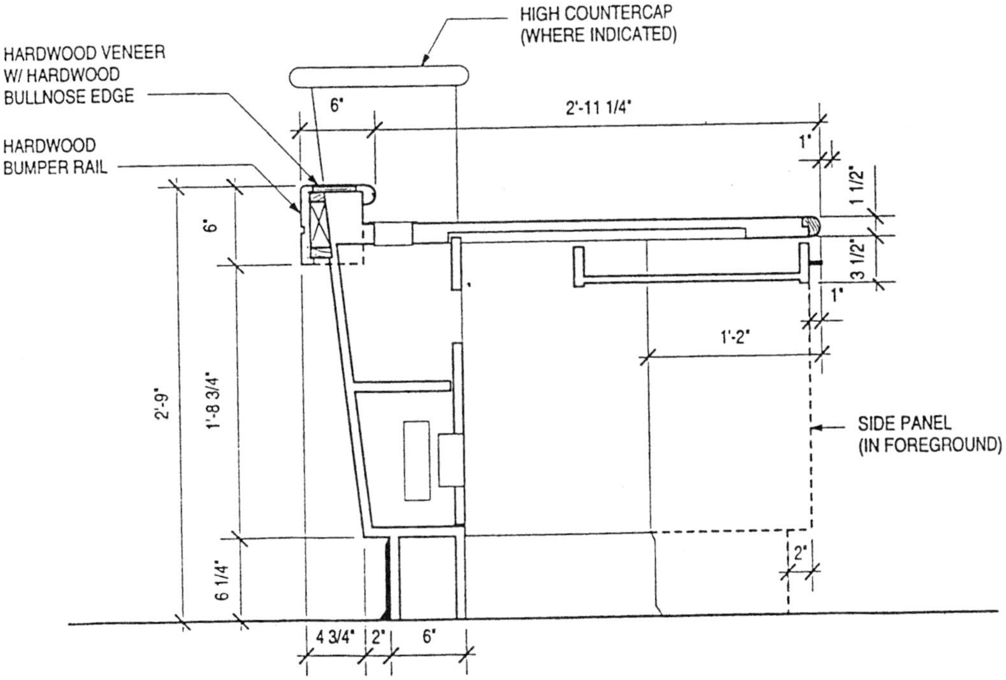

27
RECEPTION DESK—LOW SECTION
1" = 1'-0"

NURSES' STATIONS
Counter Sections and Details

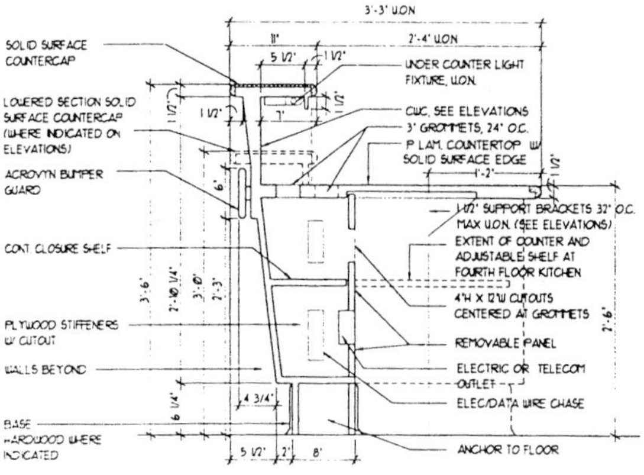

(15) STATION & RECEPTION DESKS
1" = 1'-0"

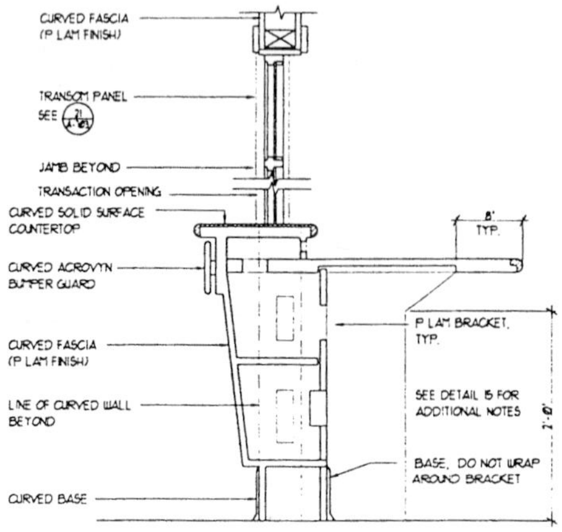

(16) SECTION @ THIRD FLOOR RECEPTION DESK
1" = 1'-0"

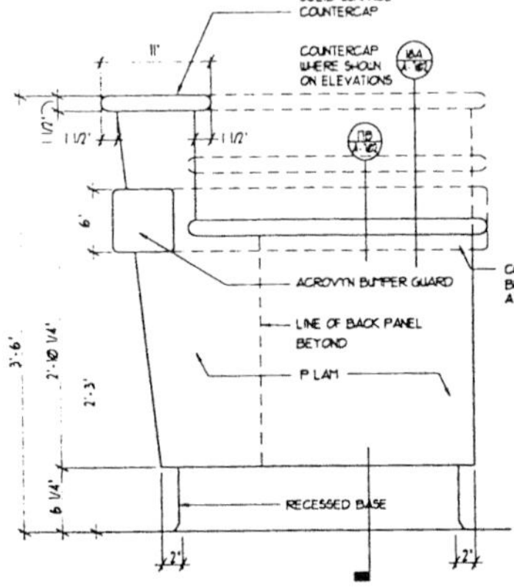

(17A) SIDE ELEV. HALF RETURN
1" = 1'-0"

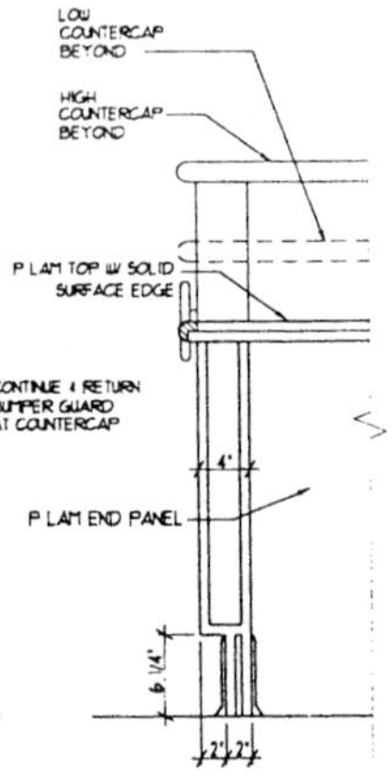

(17B) SECTION @ SIDE ELEV
1" = 1'-0"

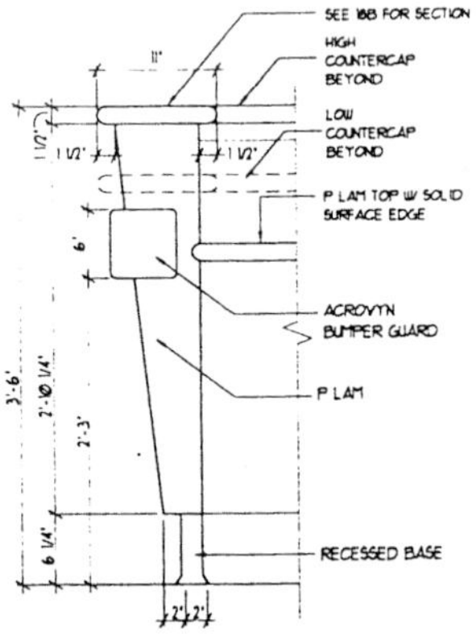

(18A) BACK ELEV. FULL RETURN
1" = 1'-0"

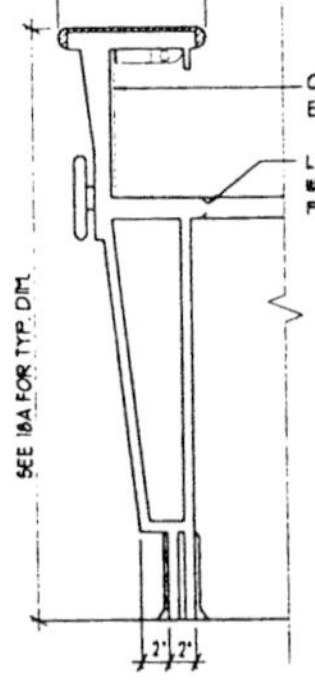

(18B) SECTION @ FULL RETURN
1" = 1'-0"

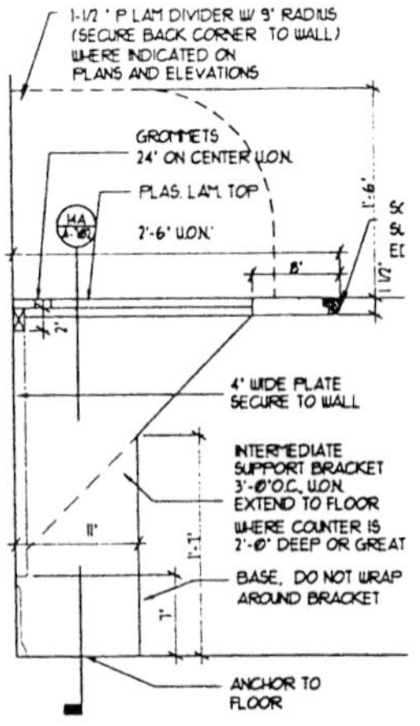

(19) COUNTERTOP
1" = 1'-0"

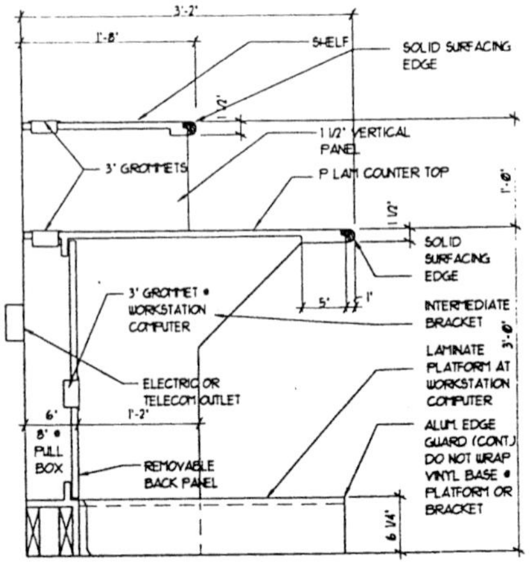

(20) WORK STATION
1" = 1'-0"

NURSES' STATIONS
Counter Sections and Details

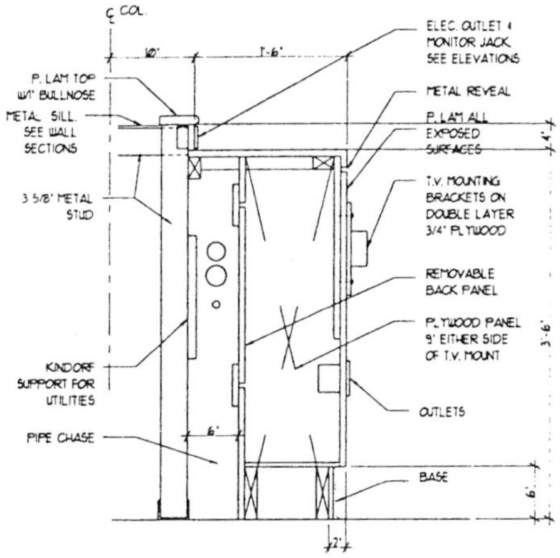

21 SECTION THROUGH RENAL DIALYSIS HEADWALL 1" = 1'-0"

22 NOT USED

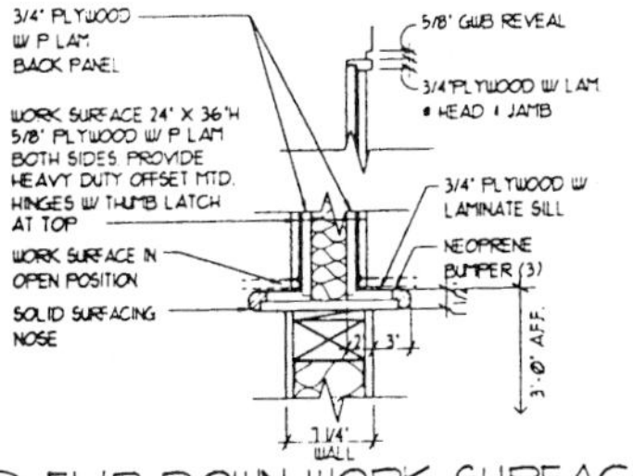

23 FLIP DOWN WORK SURFACE 1" = 1'-0"

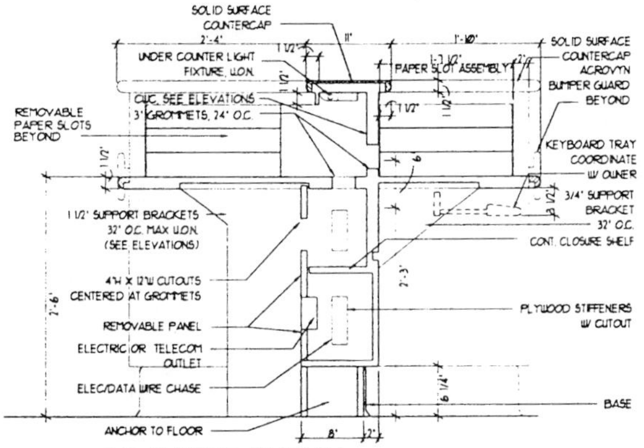

24 O.R. NURSES STATION 1" = 1'-0"

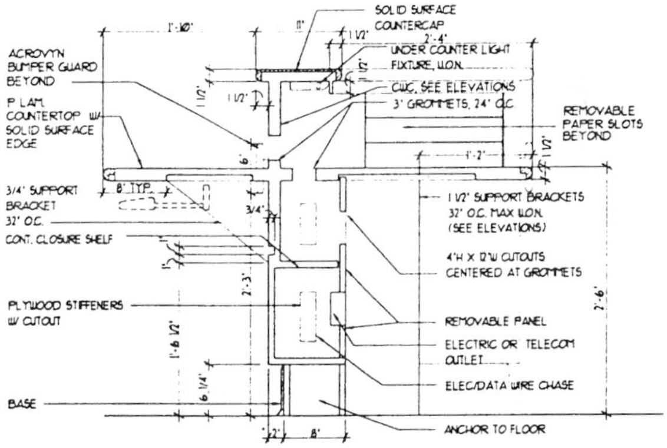

24A O.R. NURSES STATION 1" = 1'-0"

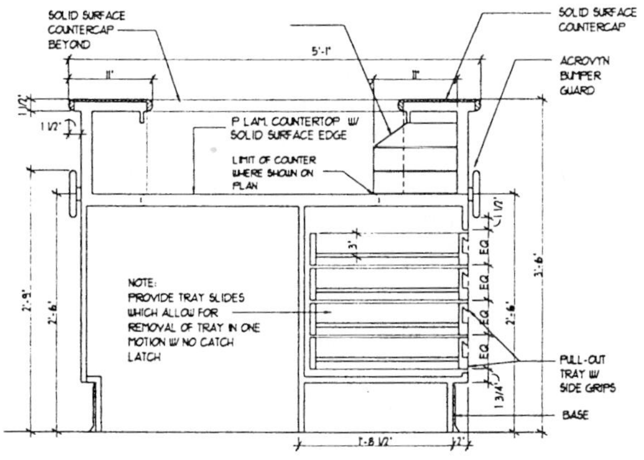

24B O.R. NURSES STATION 1" = 1'-0"

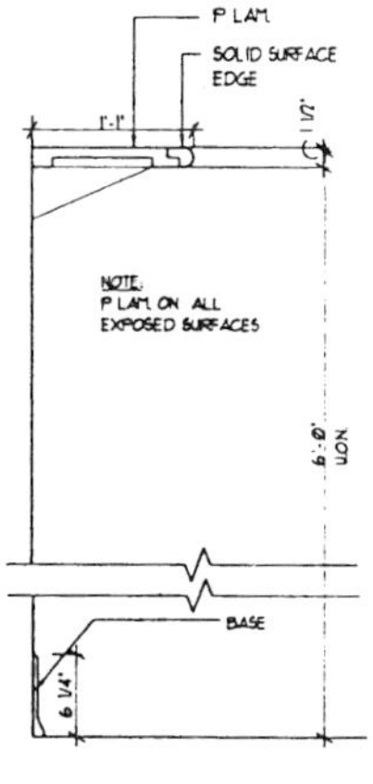

25 SHELF 1" = 1'-0"

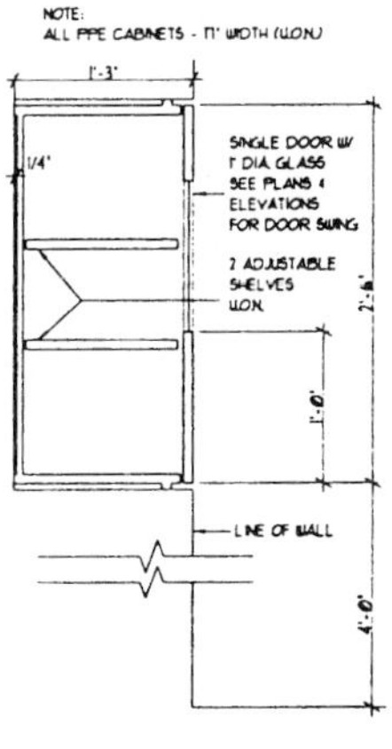

25A PPE CABINET 1" = 1'-0"

EXAMINATION ROOMS
Plans

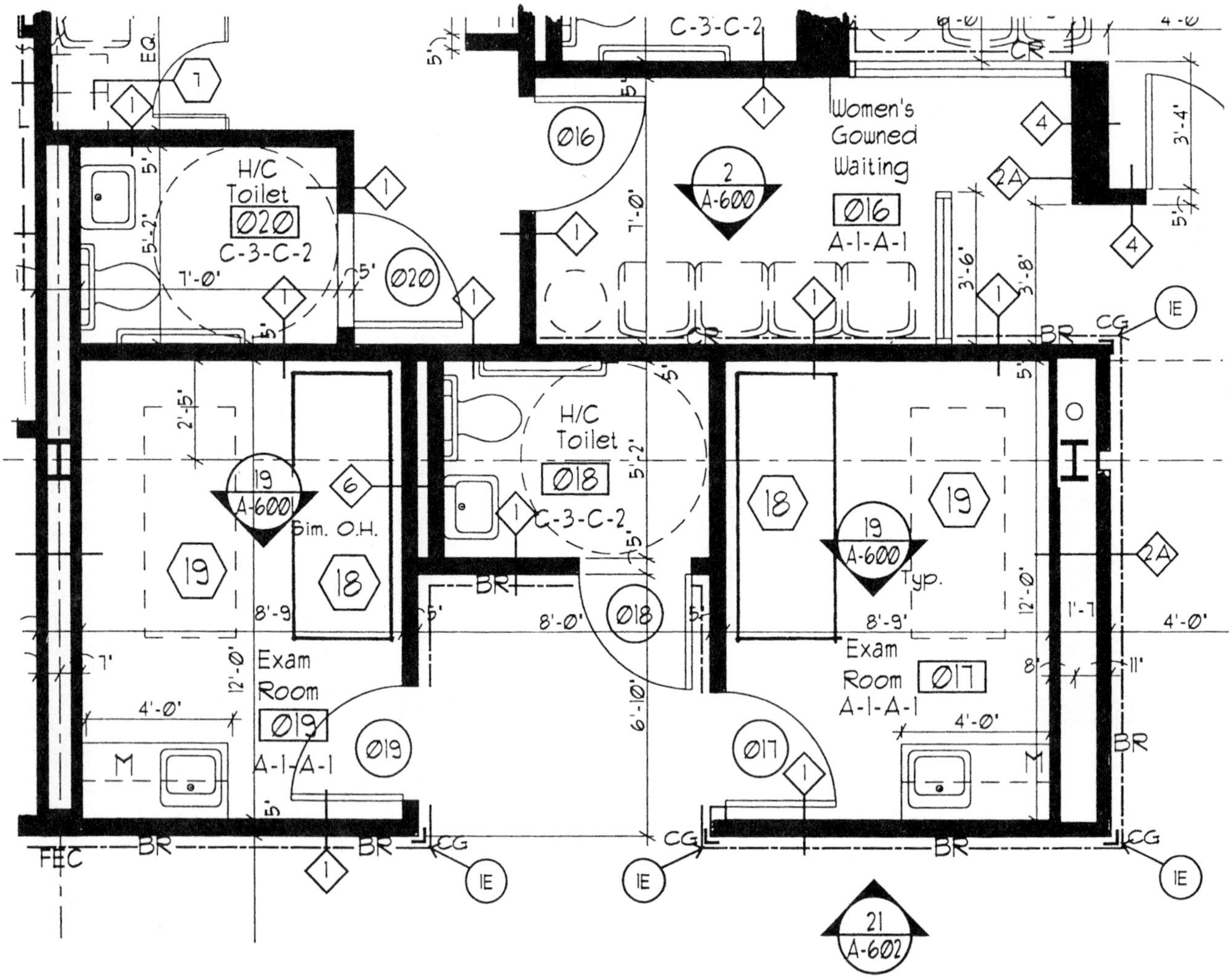

Plan / 2-Room Examination Suite

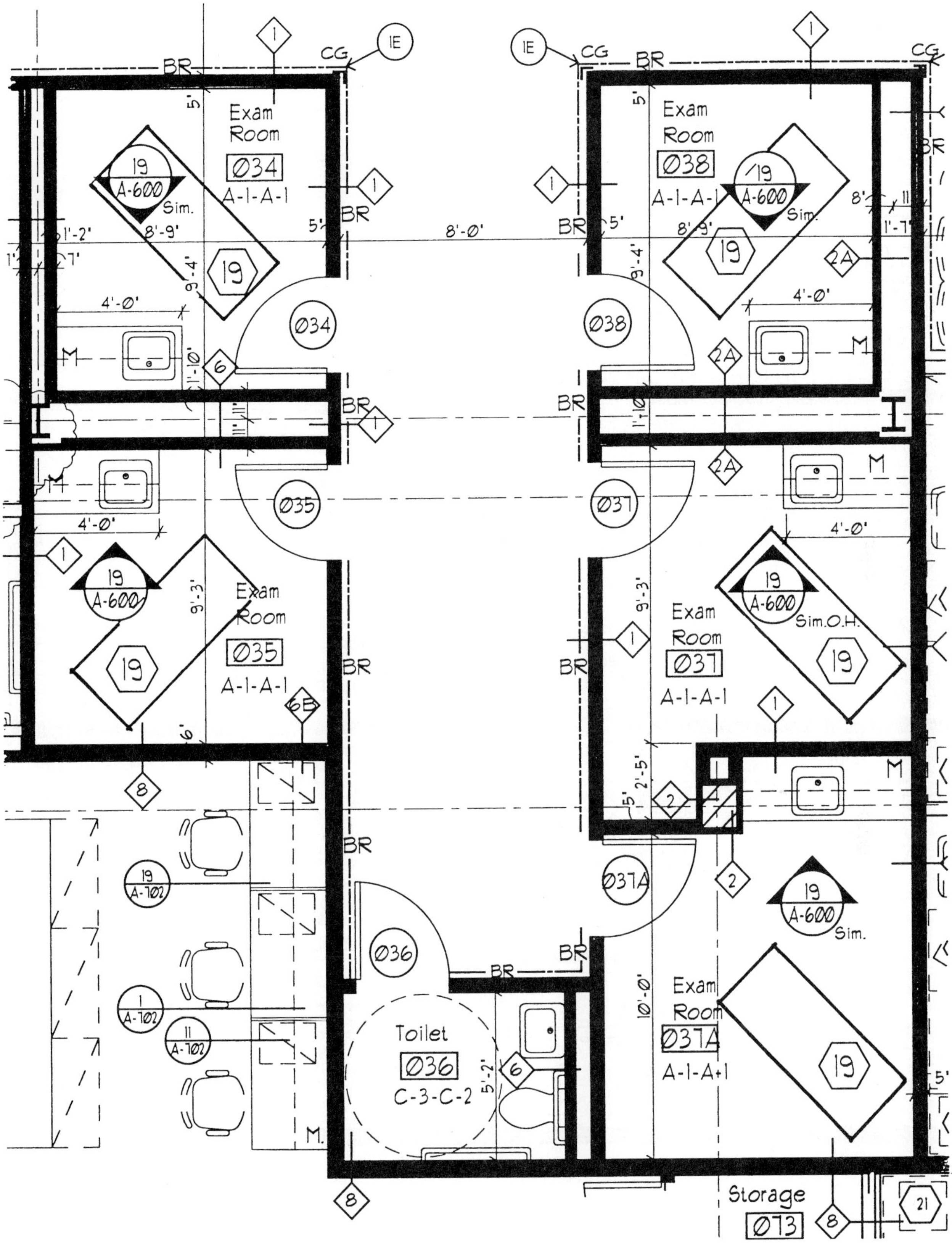

Plan / 5-Room Examination Suite

EXAMINATION ROOMS
Plans

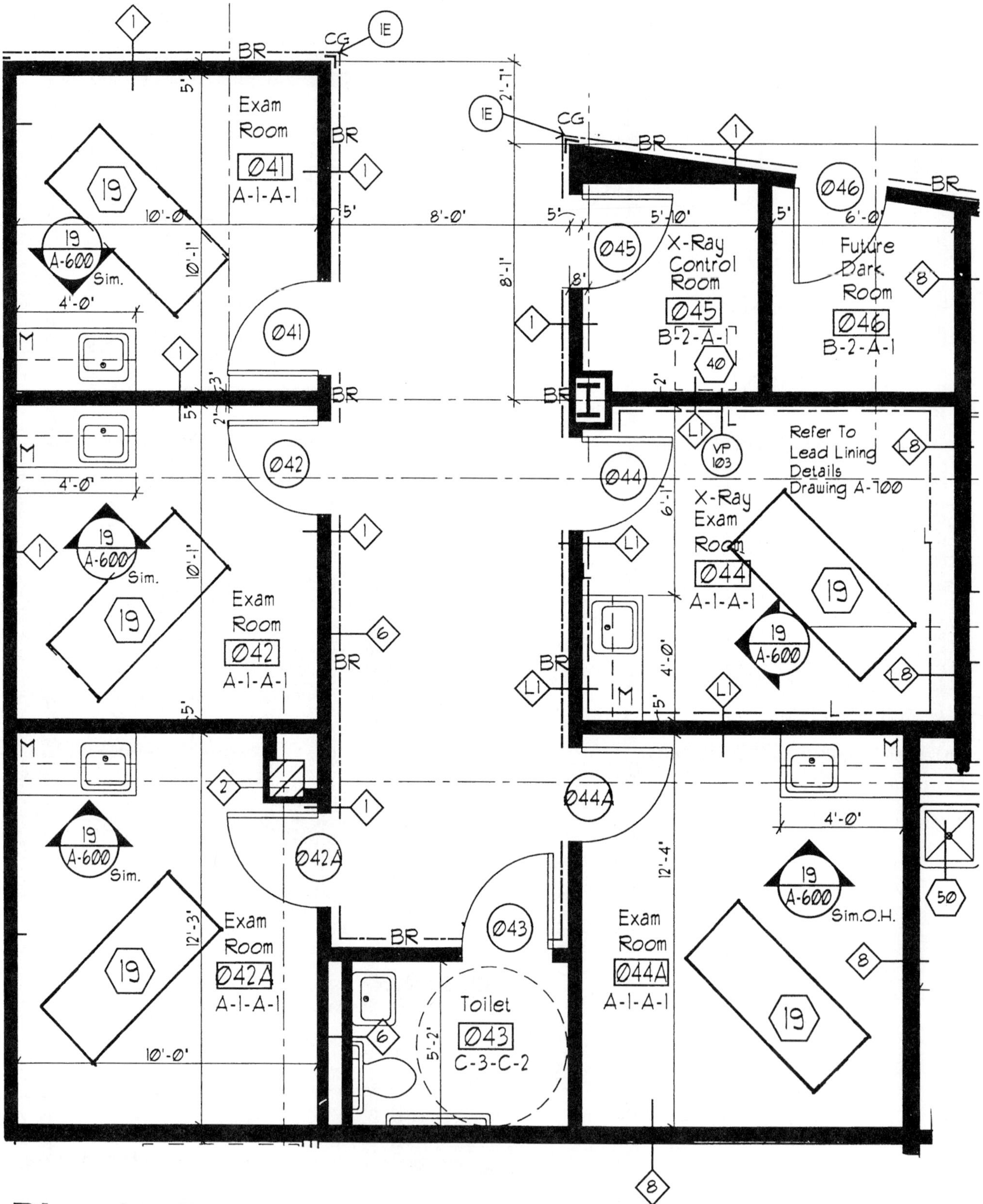

Plan / 5-Room Examination Suite

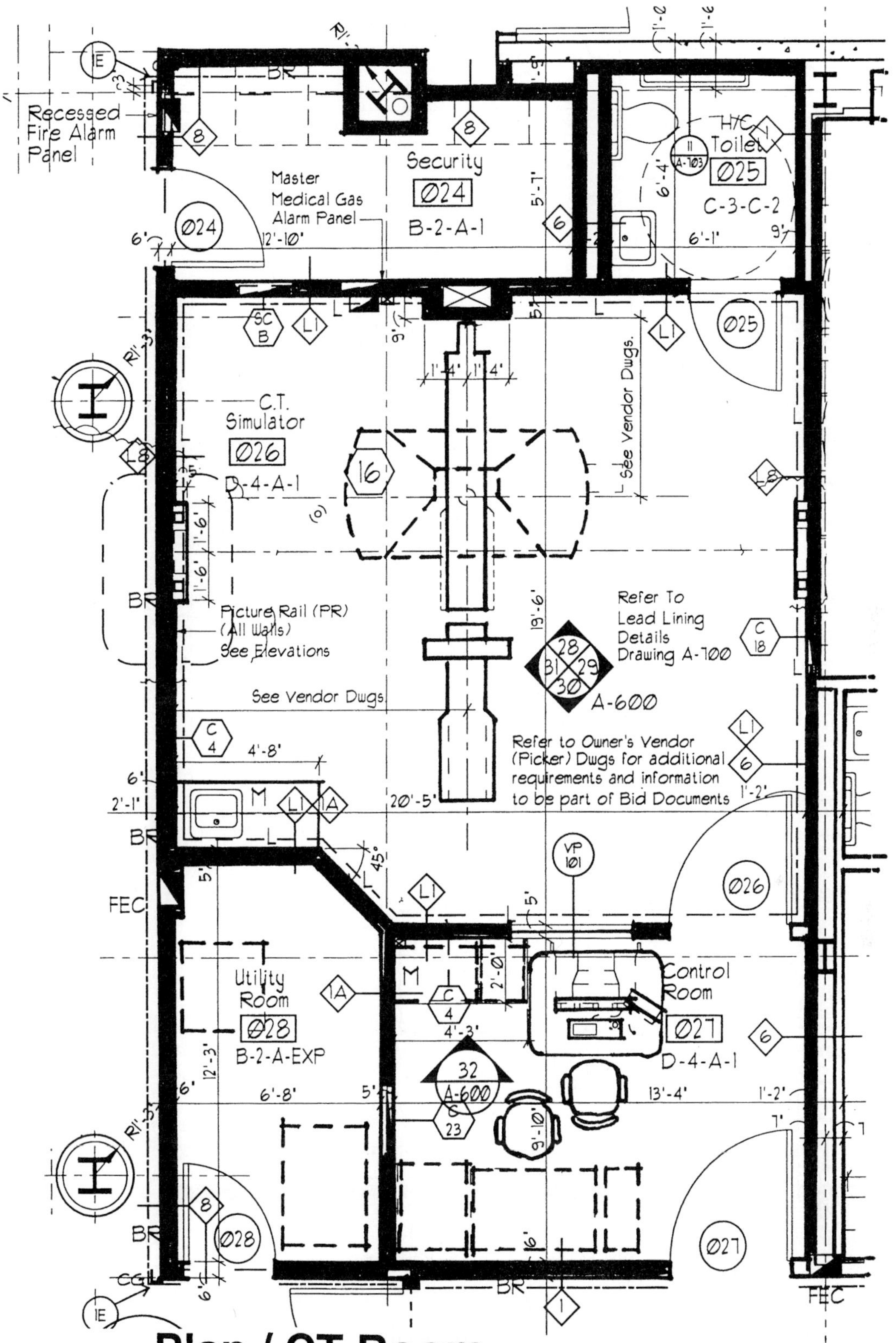
Recessed Fire Alarm Panel
Master Medical Gas Alarm Panel
Security
Ø24
B-2-A-1
H/C Toilet
Ø25
C-3-C-2
C.T. Simulator
Ø26
D-4-A-1
See Vendor Dwgs.
Picture Rail (PR) (All Walls) See Elevations
Refer To Lead Lining Details Drawing A-7ØØ
A-6ØØ
Refer to Owner's Vendor (Picker) Dwgs for additional requirements and information to be part of Bid Documents
Utility Room
Ø28
B-2-A-EXP
Control Room
Ø27
D-4-A-1
FEC
BR

Plan / CT Room

X-RAY ROOMS AND CT SUITES

Plans

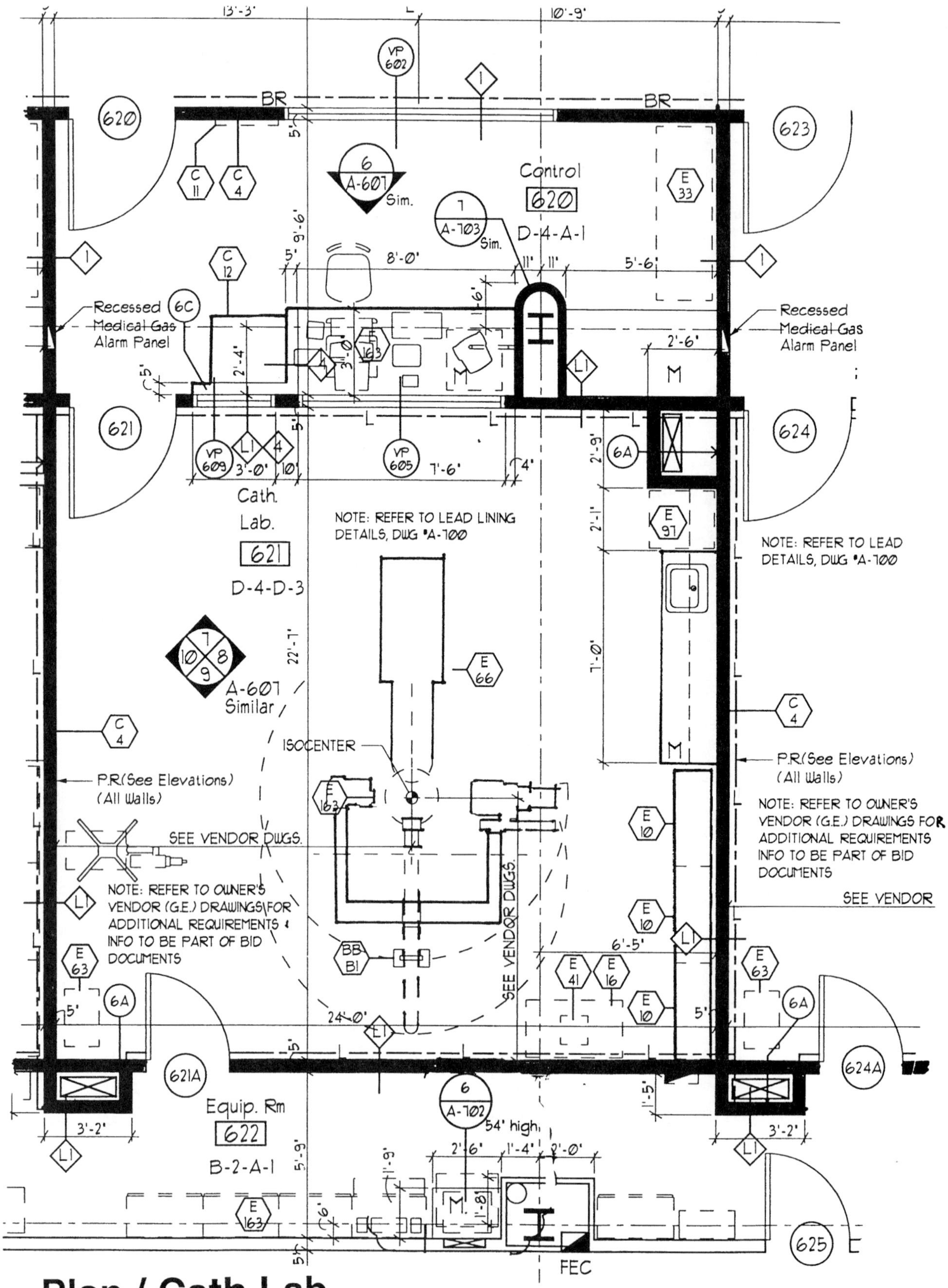

Plan / Cath Lab

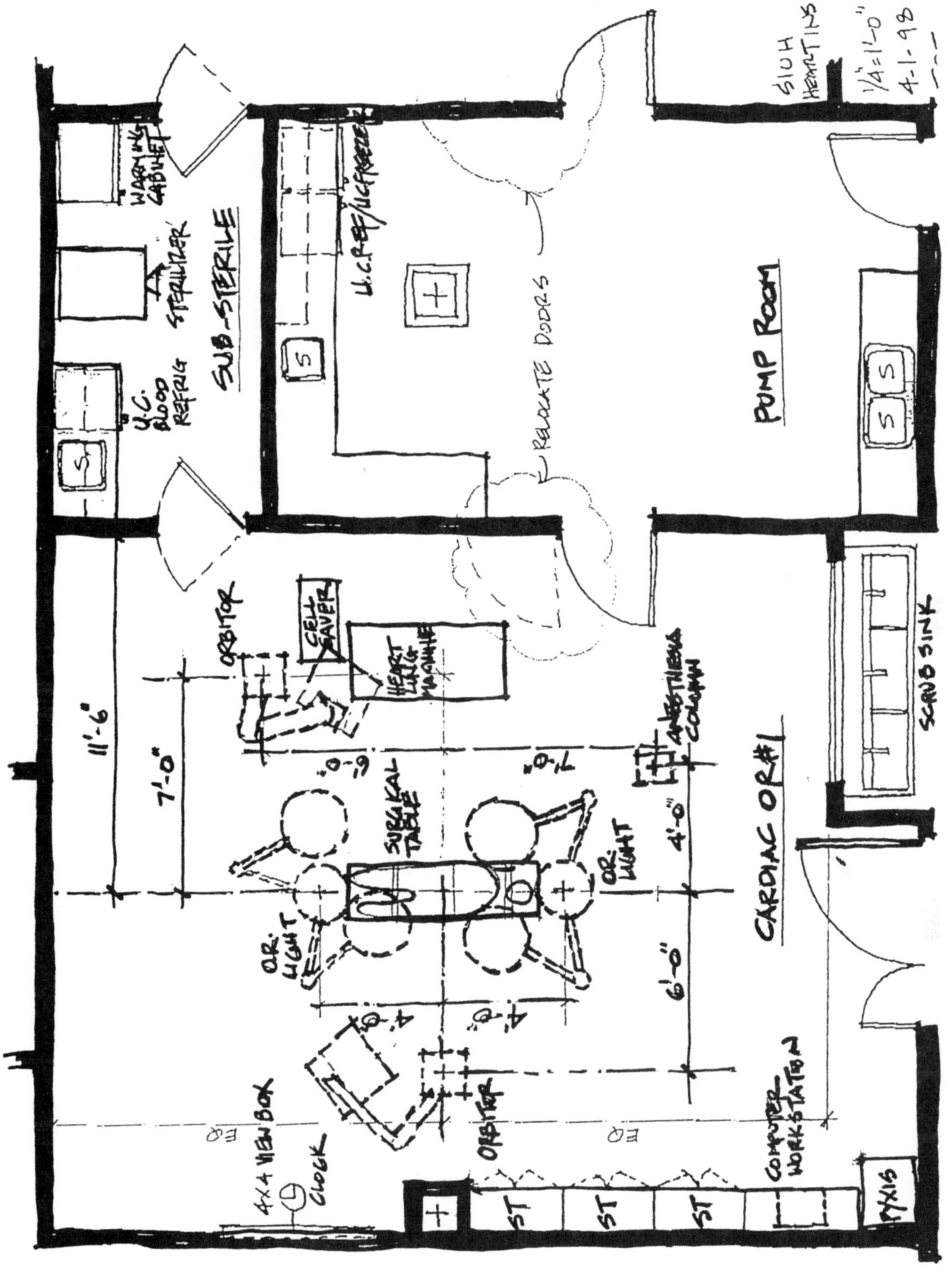

Plan / Cardiac Operating Room

OPERATING/SURGICAL SUITE

Section/Elevation/Cardiac Operating Room

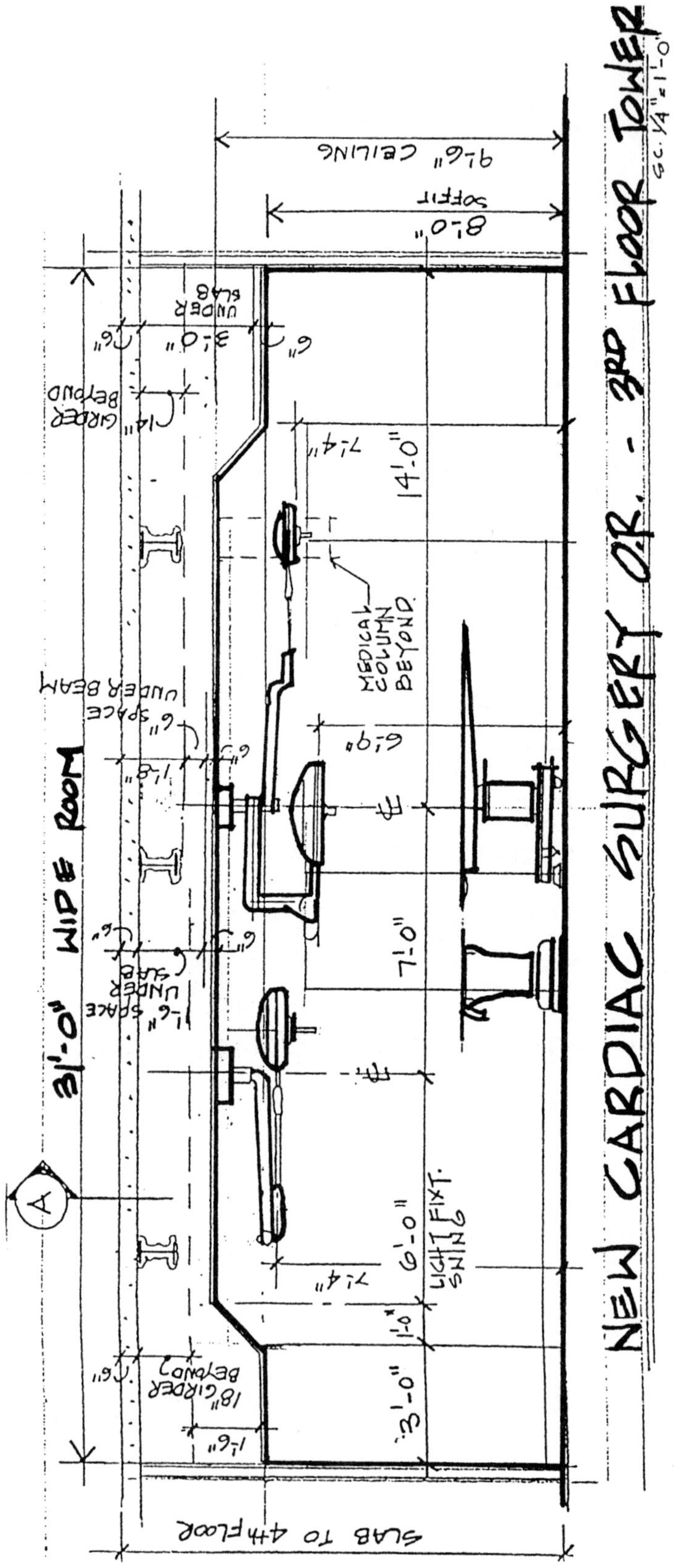

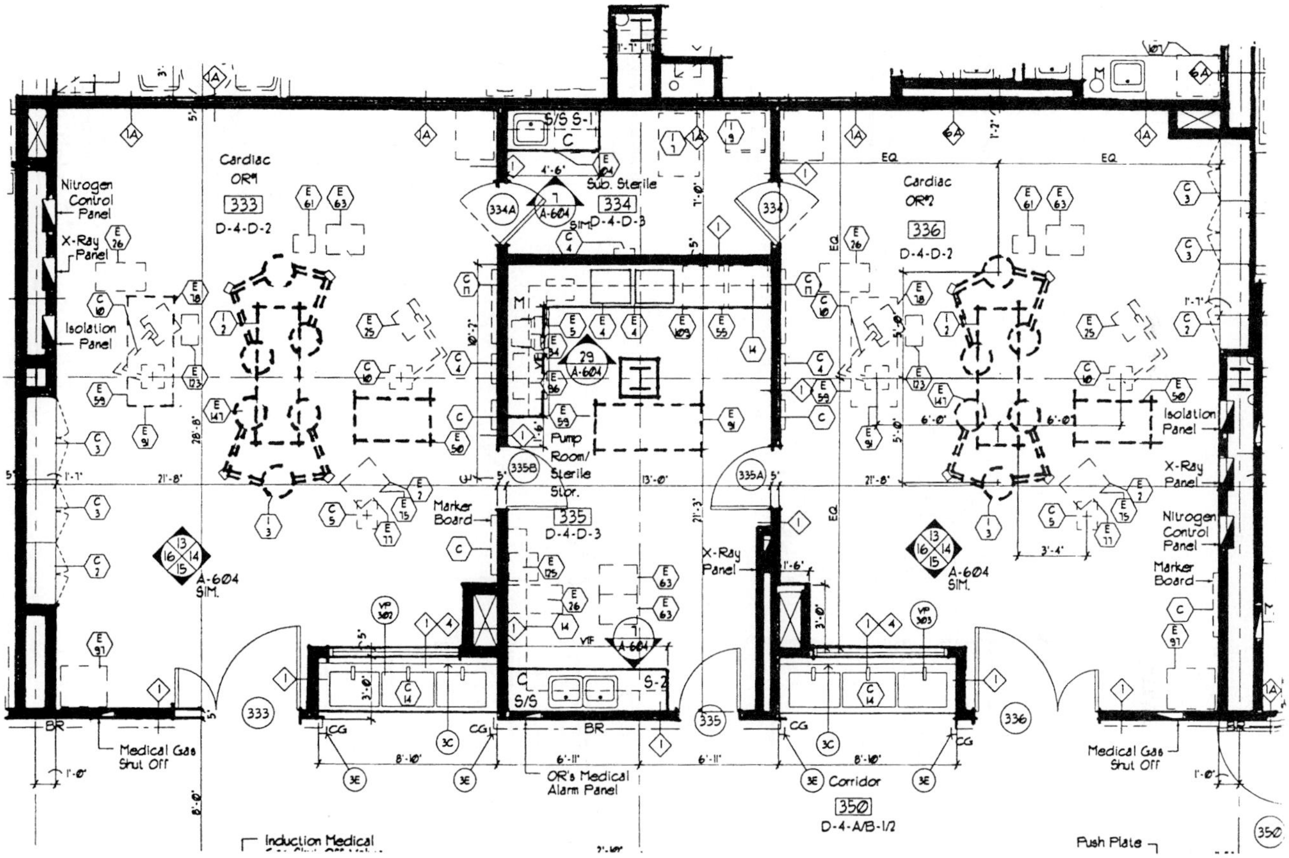

Plan / Double Cardiac Operating Room

PATIENT ROOMS

Plans/Critical Care Unit-Burn Center

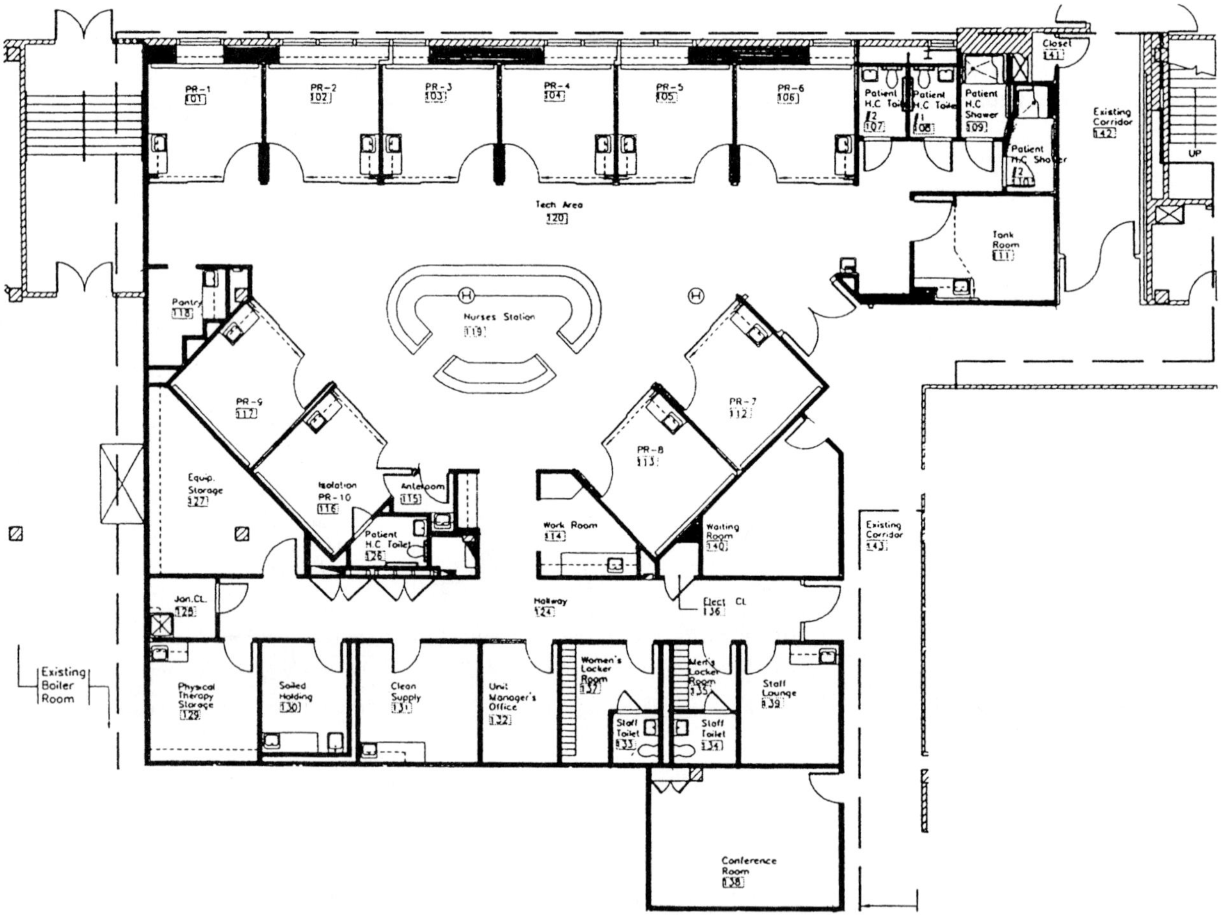

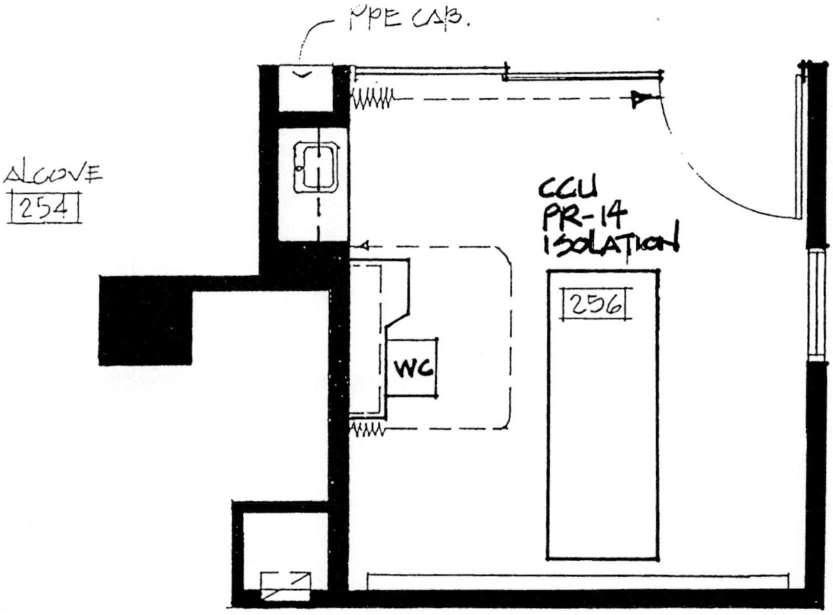

1 C.C.U. ISOLATION (PR-14) #256
(2ND FLOOR) 1/4" = 1'-0"

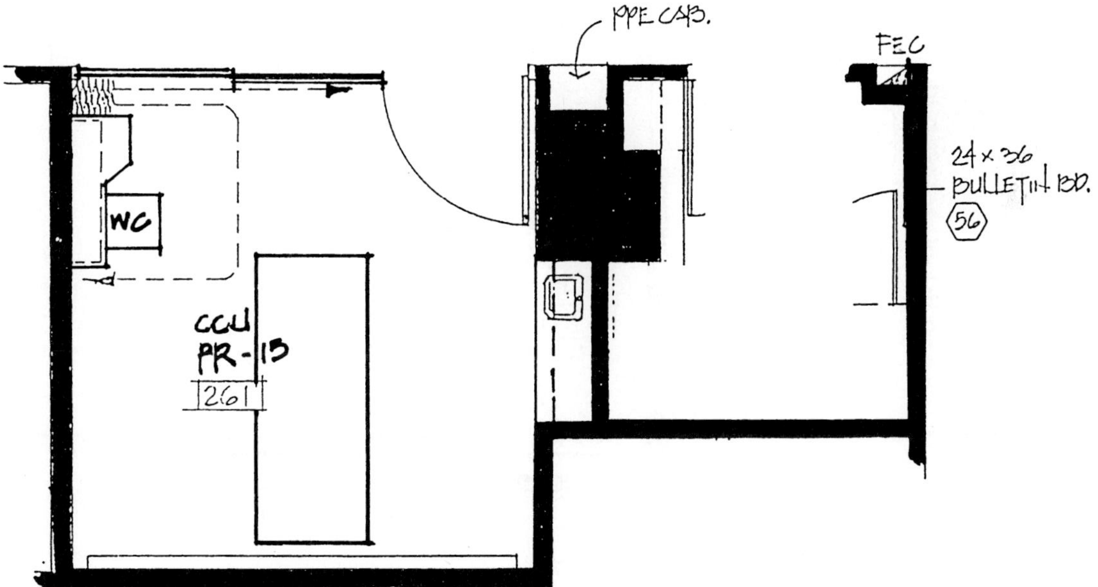

2 C.C.U. ISOLATION (PR-15) #261
(2ND FLOOR) 1/4" = 1'-0"

PATIENT ROOMS

Plans/CCU—Isolation

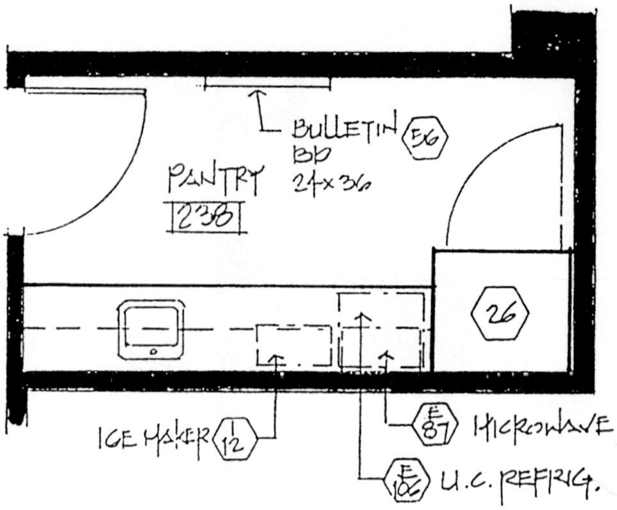

5 PANTRY #238
(2ND FLOOR)
1/4" = 1'-0"

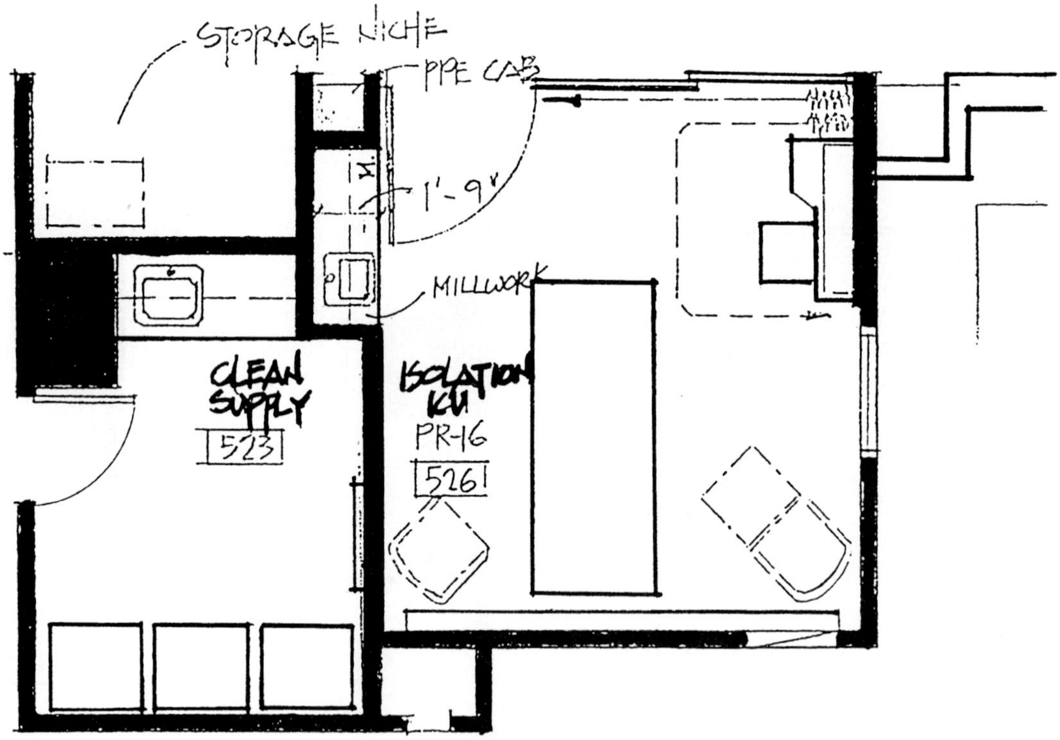

1 CLEAN SUPPLY & ISOLATION - 526
(5TH FLOOR)
1/4" = 1'-0"

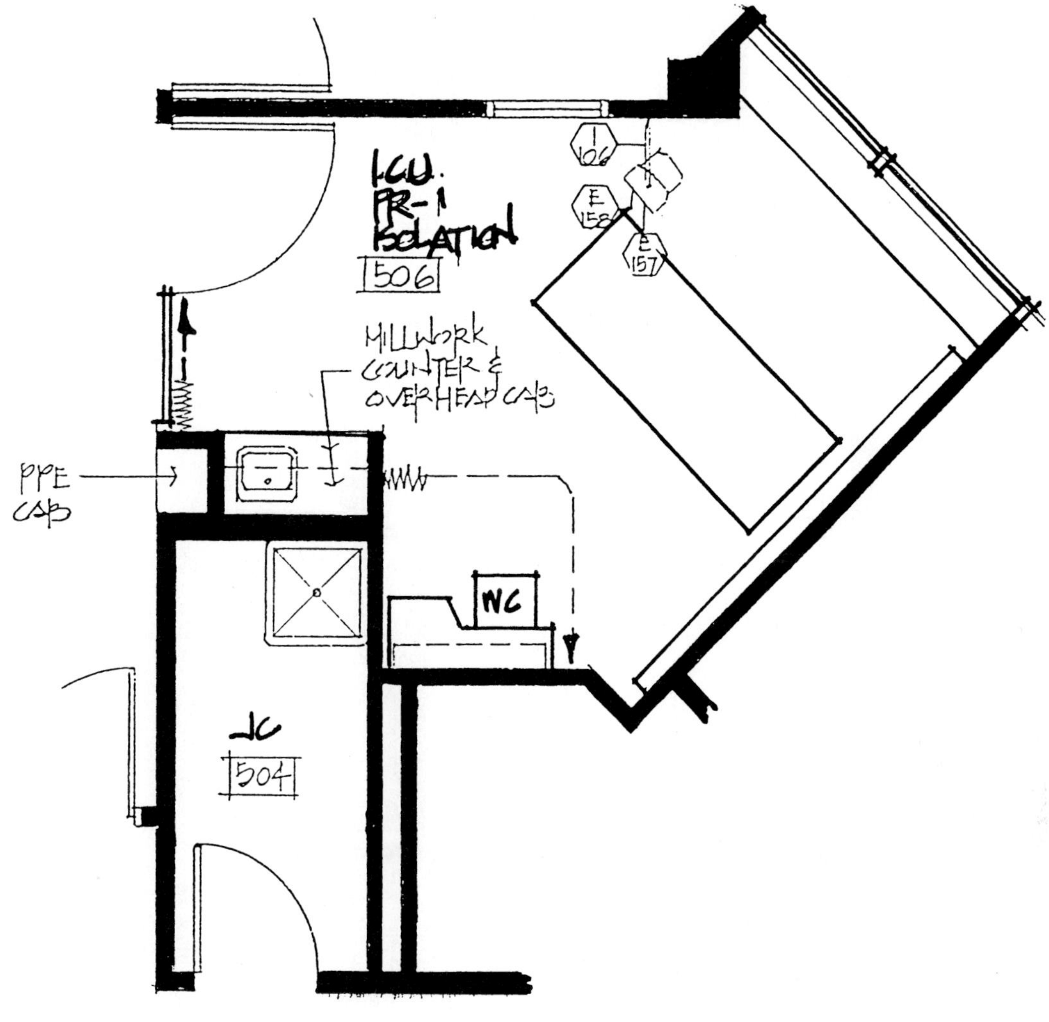

2 ICU ISOLATION (PR-1) #506
(5TH FLOOR) 1/4" = 1'-0"

PATIENT ROOMS

Plans/Intensive Care—Isolation

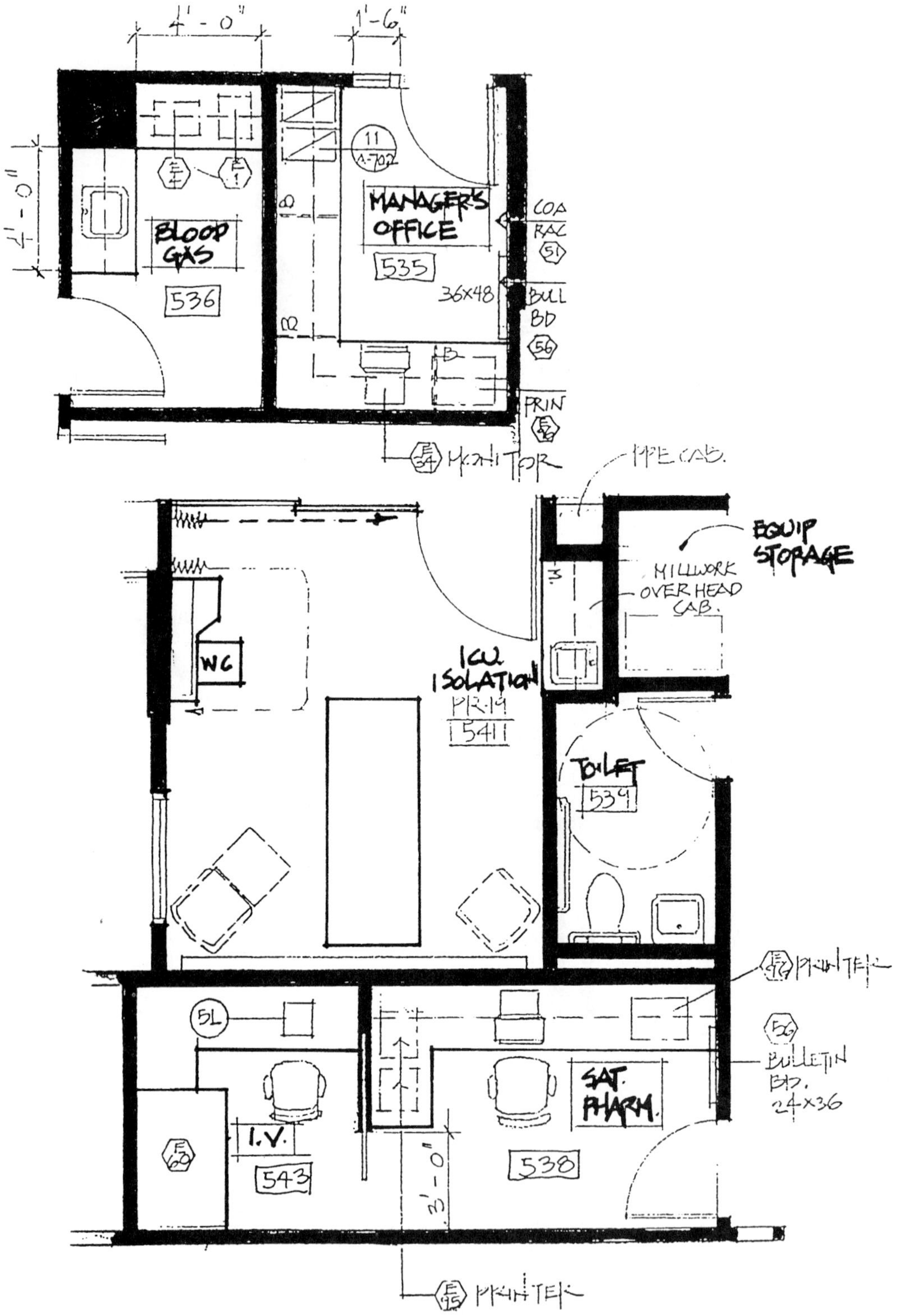

4 I.C.U. ISOLATION PR & MANAG. OFF (5TH FLOOR) / SAT. PHARM. / BLOOD GAS

1/4" = 1'-0"

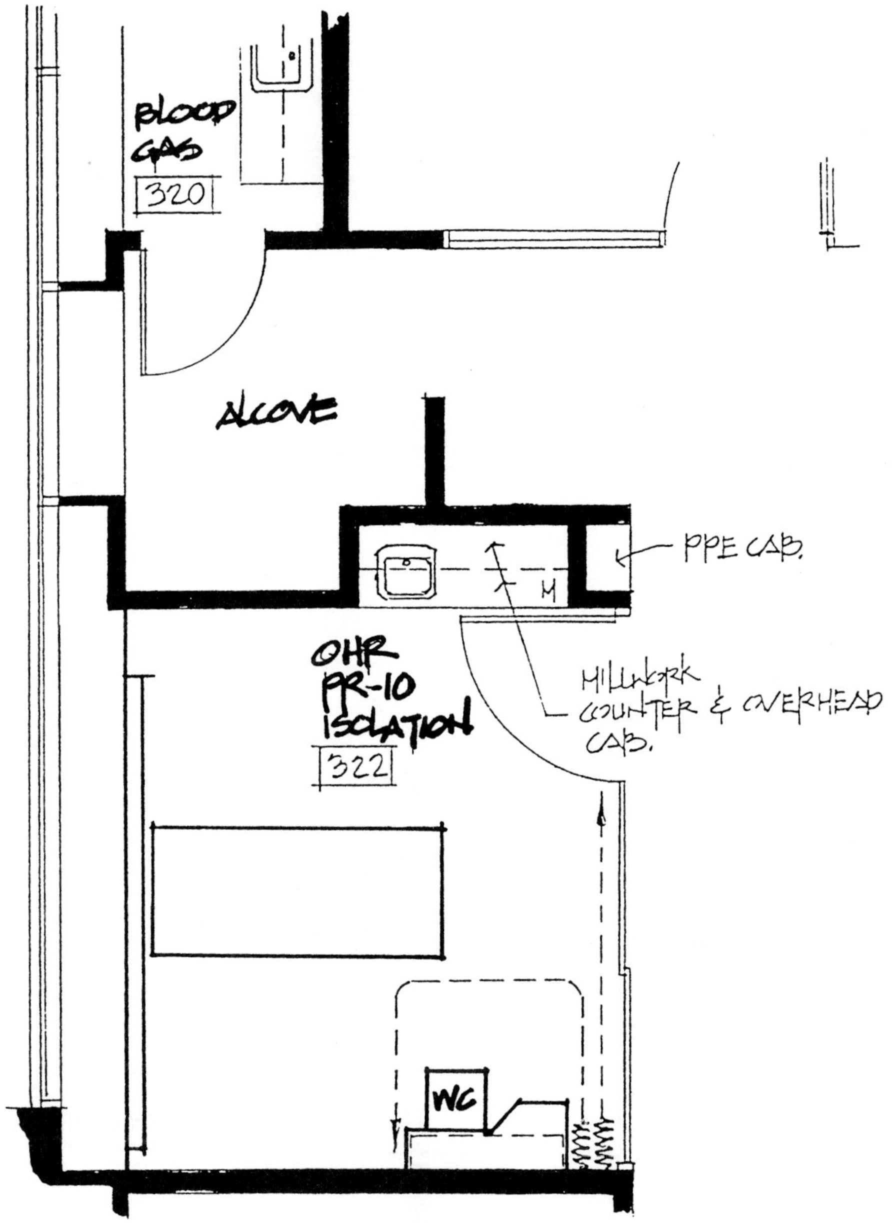

1 OHR ISOLATION (PR-10) #322
(3RD FLOOR) 1/4" = 1'-0"

PATIENT ROOMS
Plans/CCU—Related Offices

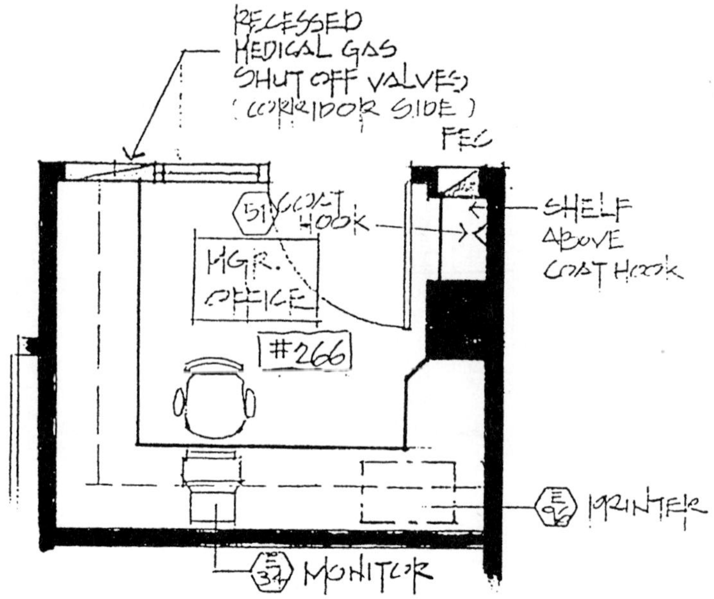

3 C.C.U. MANAG. OFFICE
(2ND FLOOR)
1/4" = 1'-0"

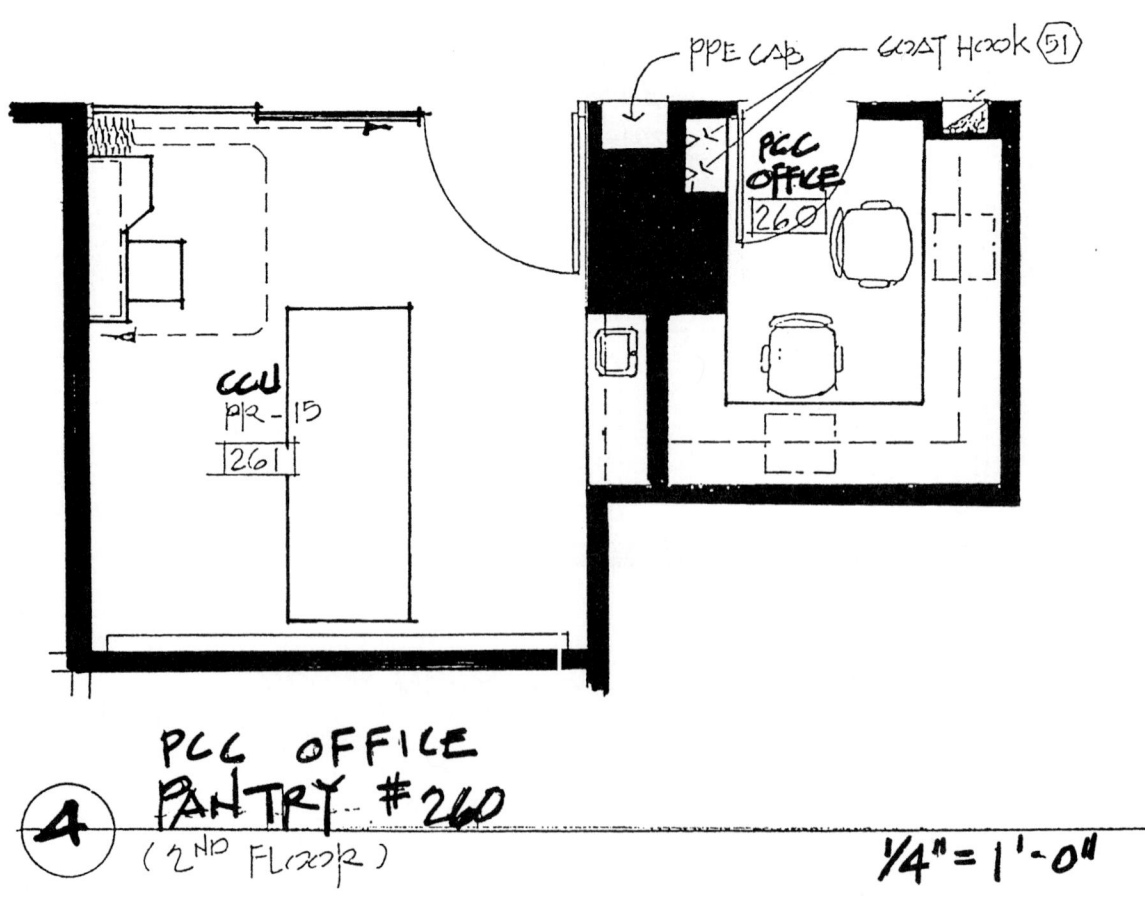

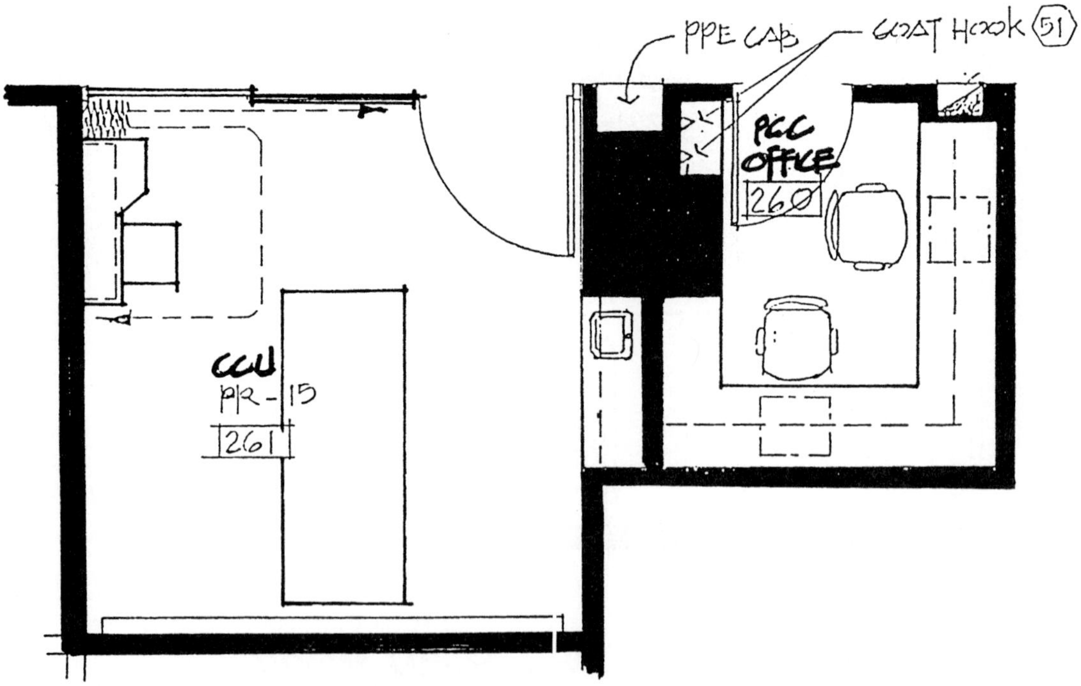

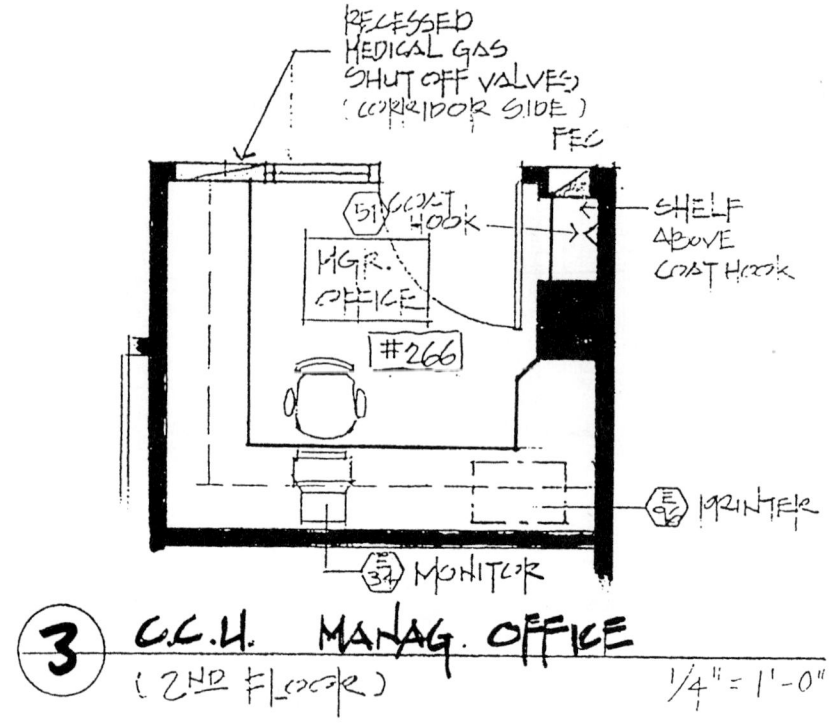

4 PCC OFFICE PANTRY #260
(2ND FLOOR)
1/4" = 1'-0"

PATIENT ROOMS

Plans/Elevations/Typical Patient Rooms

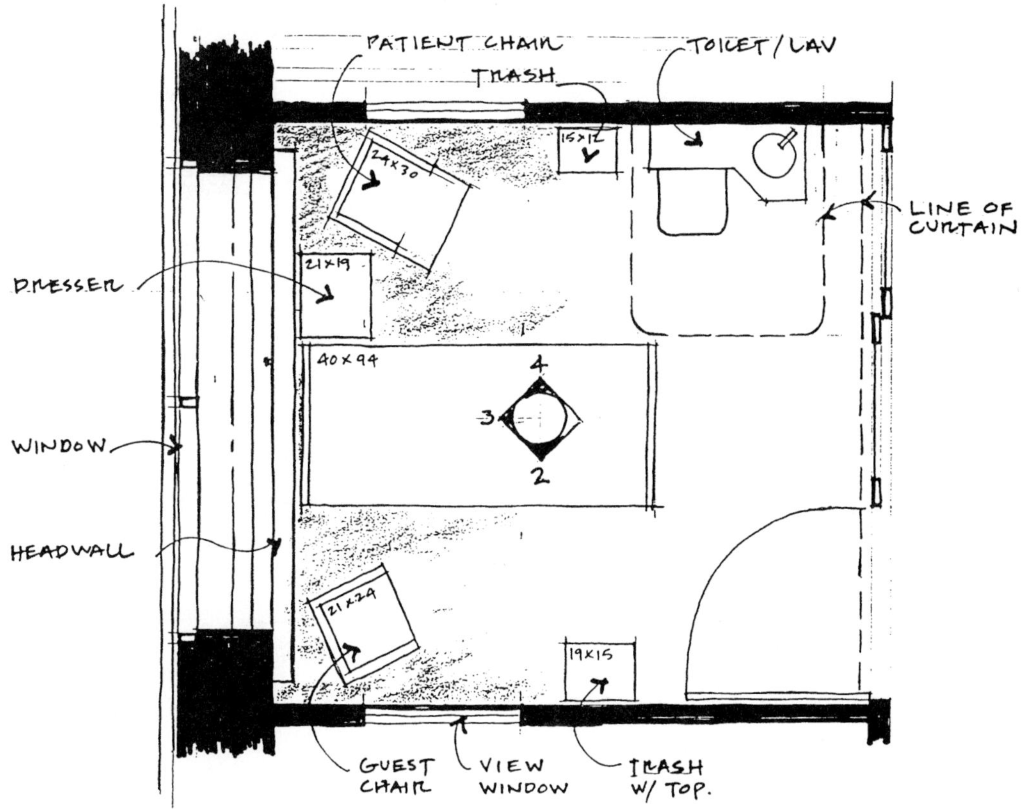

PLAN
1/2"=1'-0"

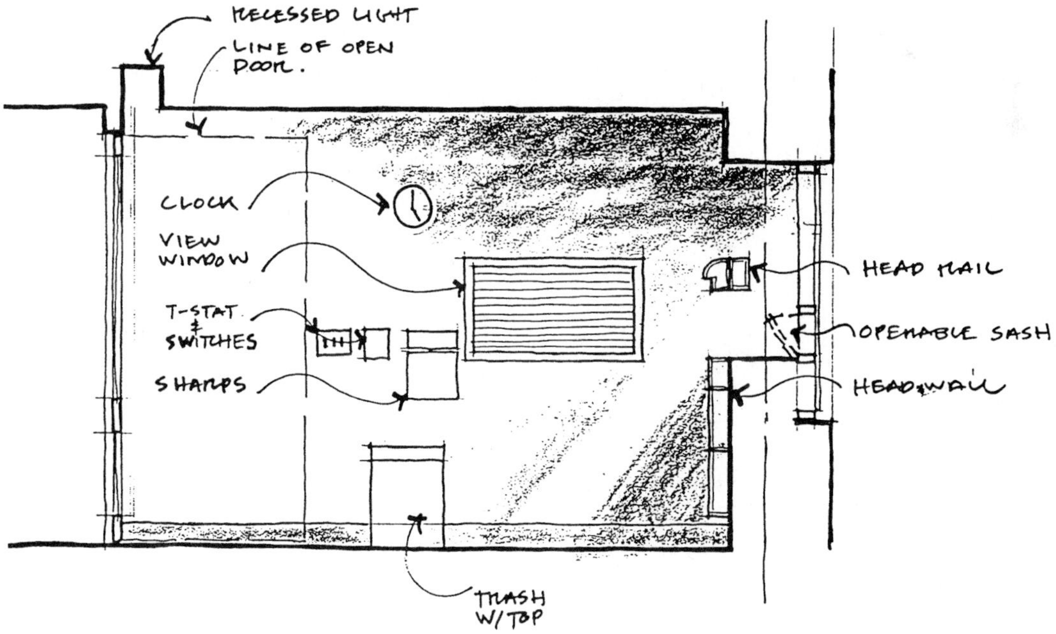

ELEVATION 2
1/2"=1'-0"

PATIENT ROOMS
Elevations/Intensive Care—Isolation

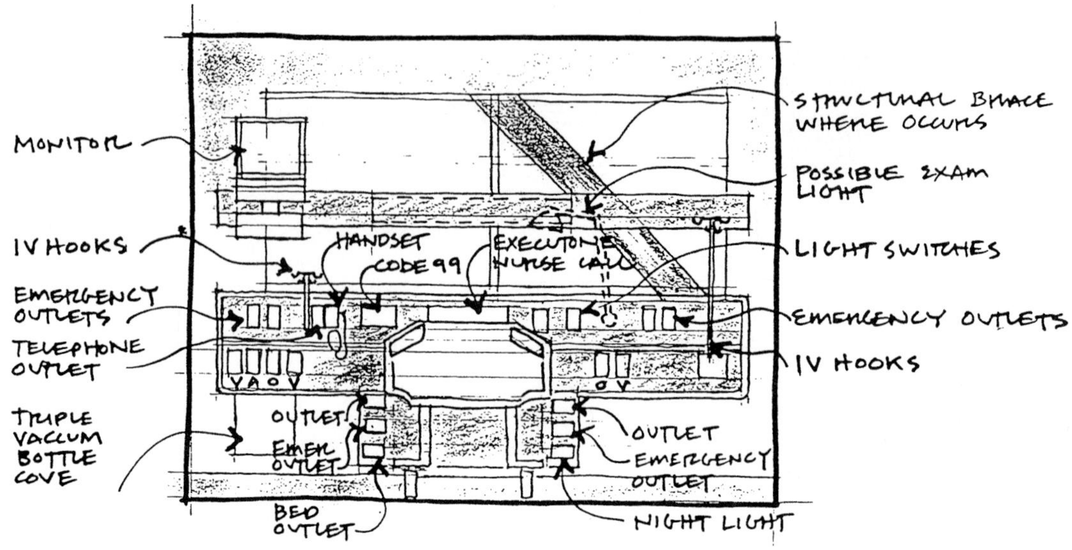

ELEVATION 3
1/2"=1'0"

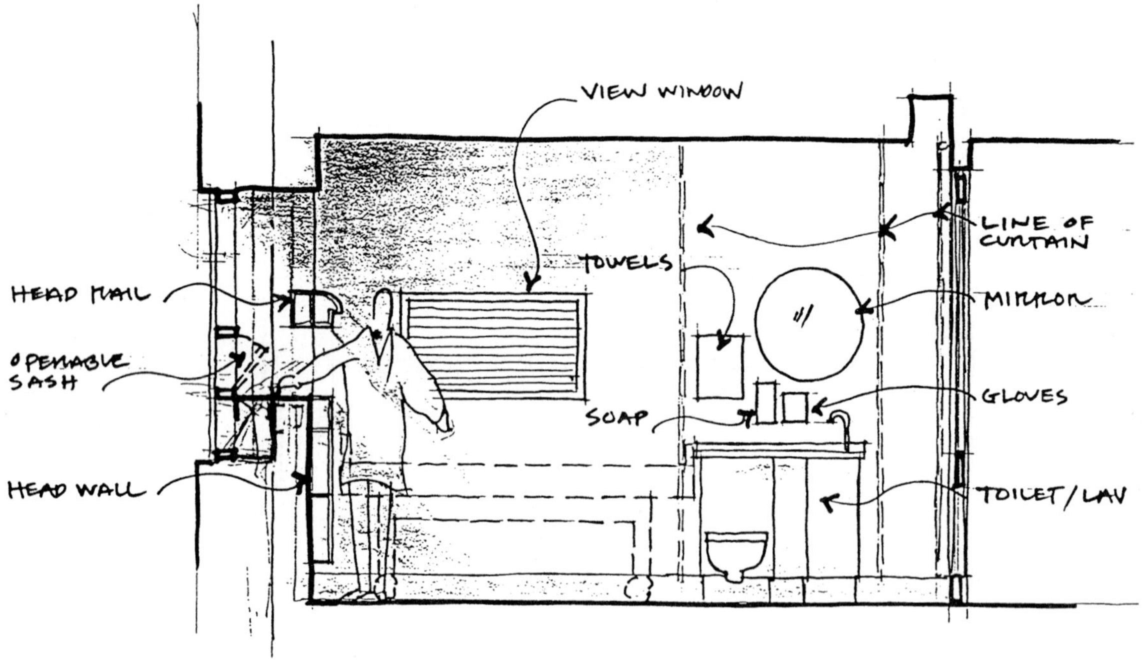

ELEVATION 4
1/2"=1'0"

PATIENT ROOMS

Plans/Two-Bed Induction Room and Related Areas

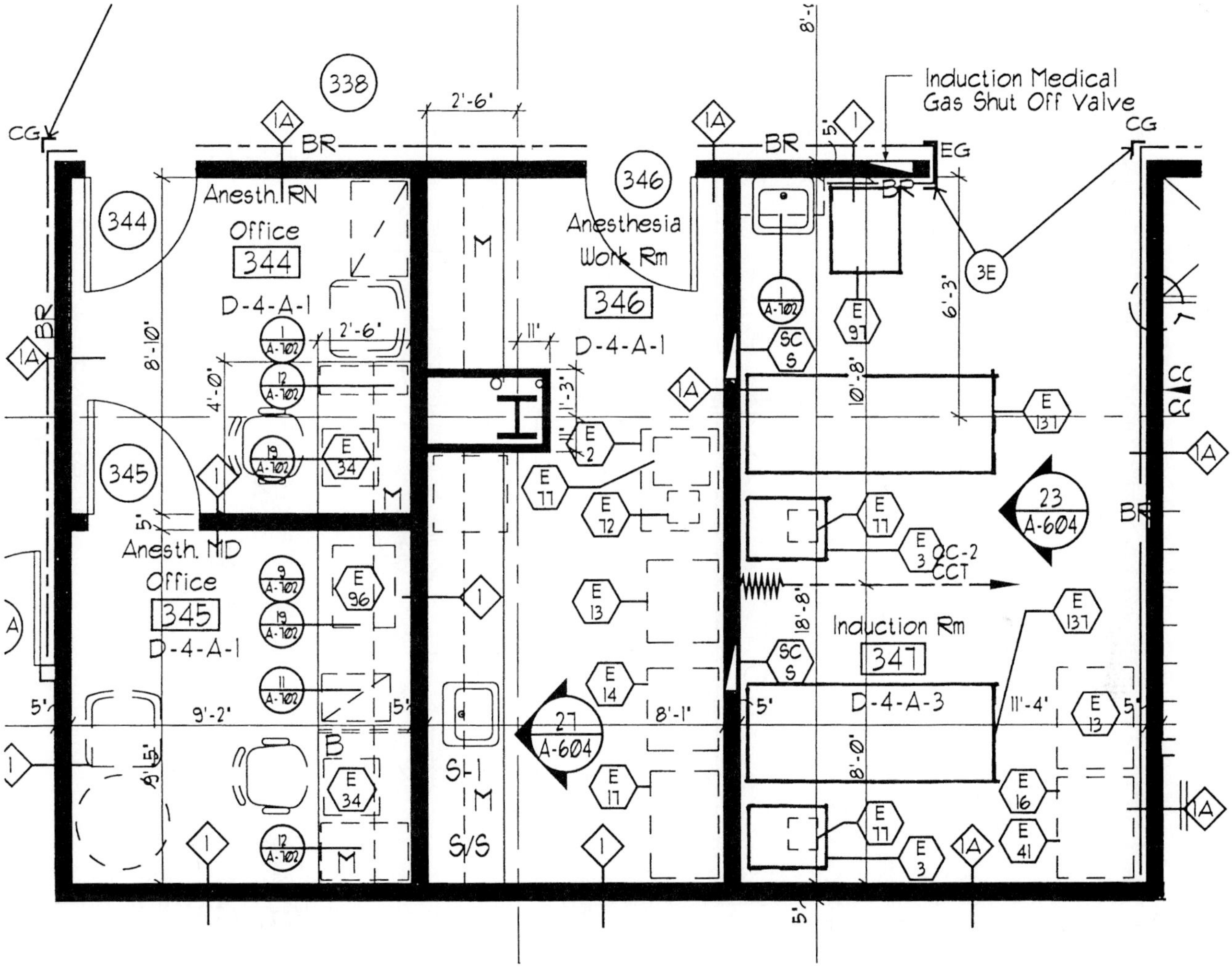

PATIENT ROOMS

Plans/Double Isolation Room

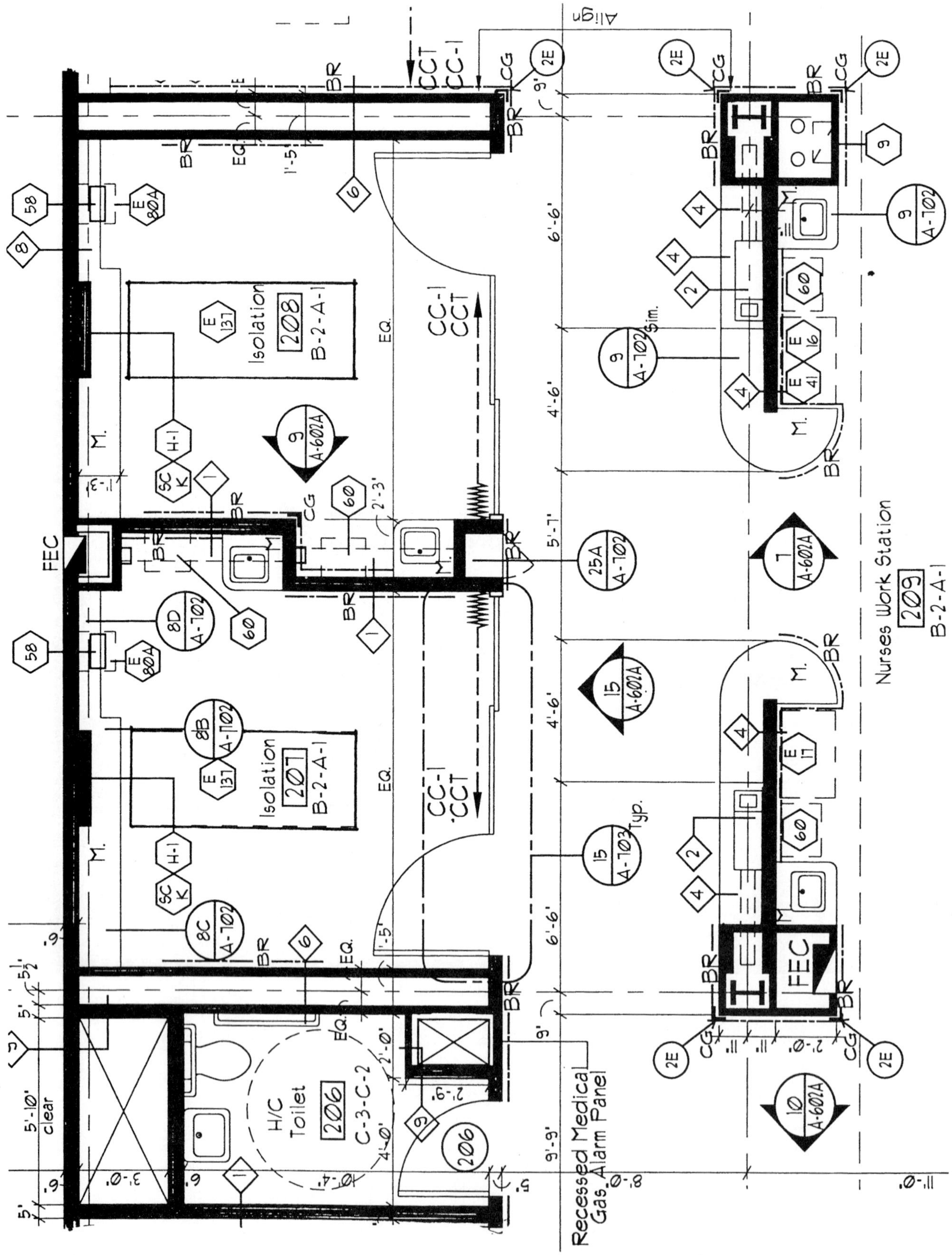

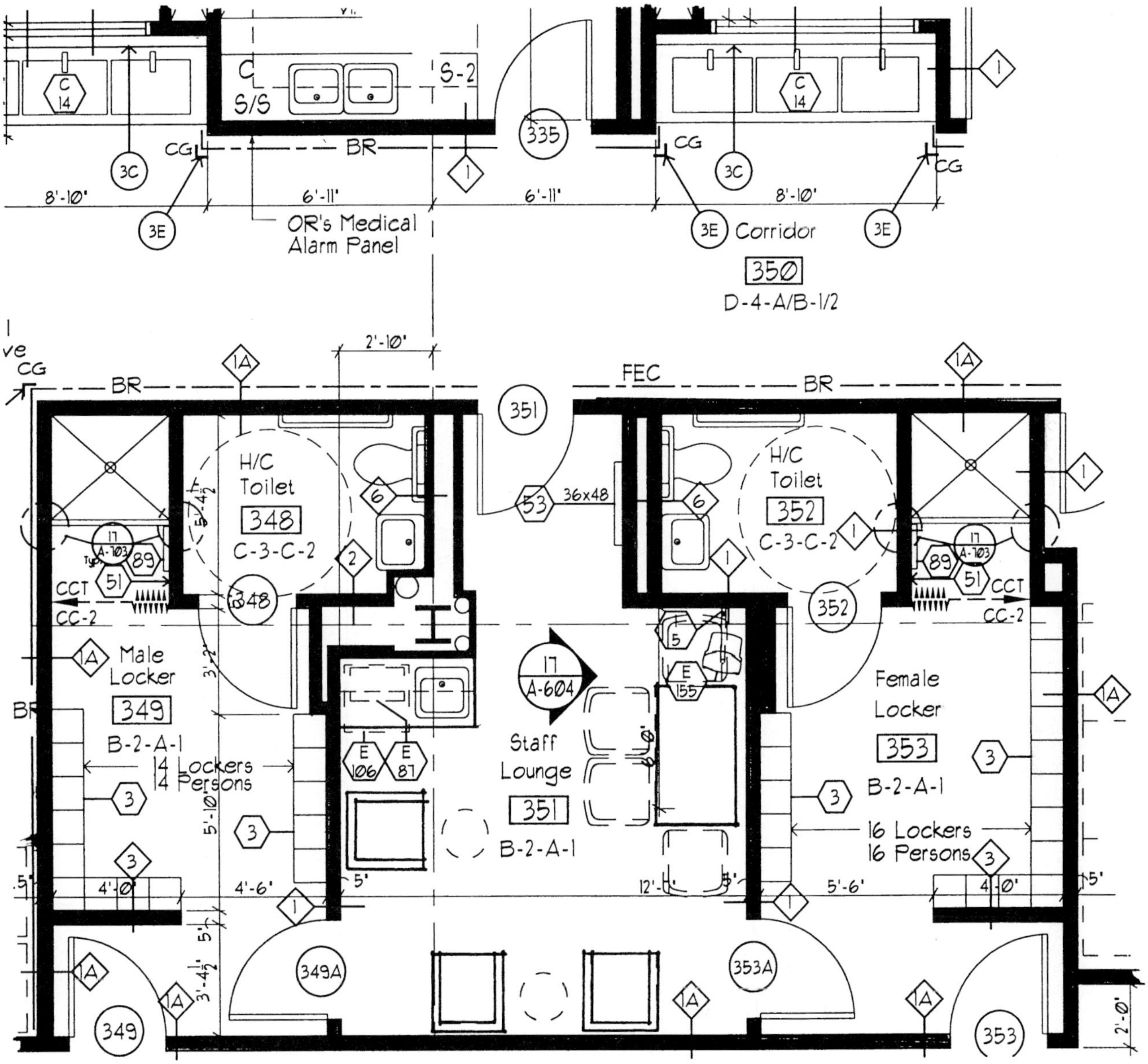
S/S
S-2
BR
CG
3C
3E
8'-10'
6'-11'
6'-11'
8'-10'
OR's Medical Alarm Panel
335
Corridor
350
D-4-A/B-1/2
2'-10'
FEC
BR
351
H/C Toilet
348
C-3-C-2
H/C Toilet
352
C-3-C-2
36x48
CCT
CC-2
Male Locker
349
B-2-A-1
14 Lockers
14 Persons
Staff Lounge
351
B-2-A-1
Female Locker
353
B-2-A-1
16 Lockers
16 Persons
349A
353A
349
353
A-604
A-103

ASSISTED LIVING FACILITIES
Private Patient Room

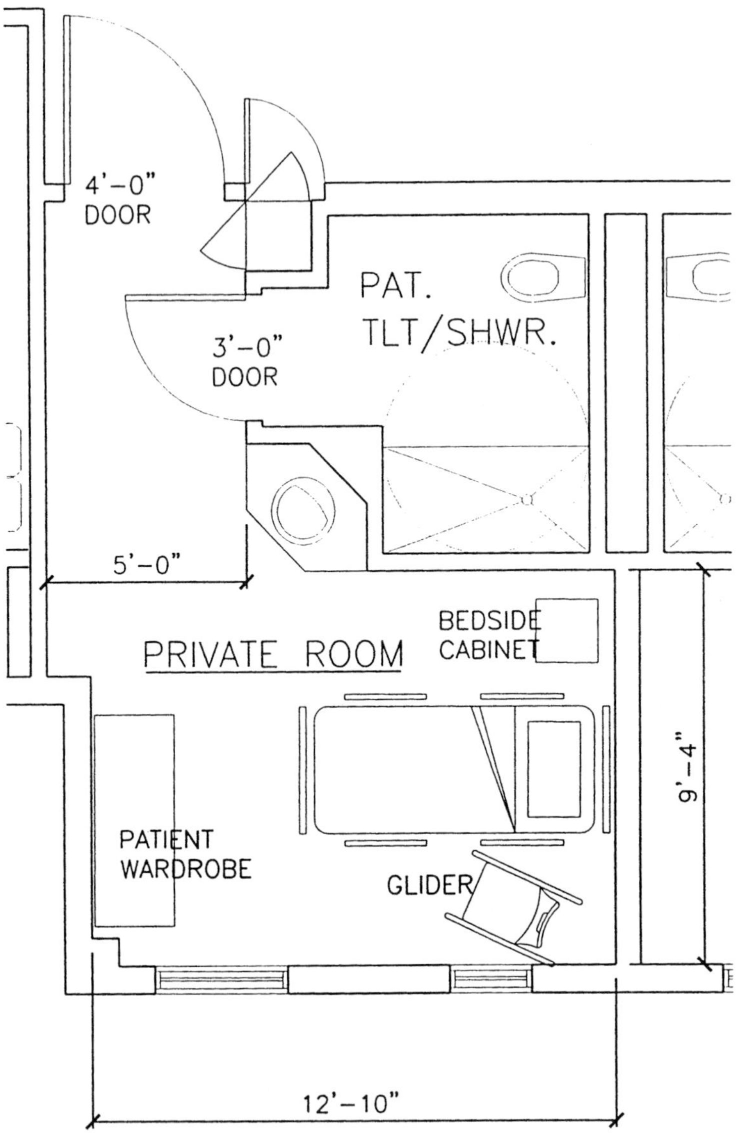

SKILLED NURSING/ SUBACUTE CARE PRIVATE PATIENT ROOM

SCALE: 1/4"=1'-0"

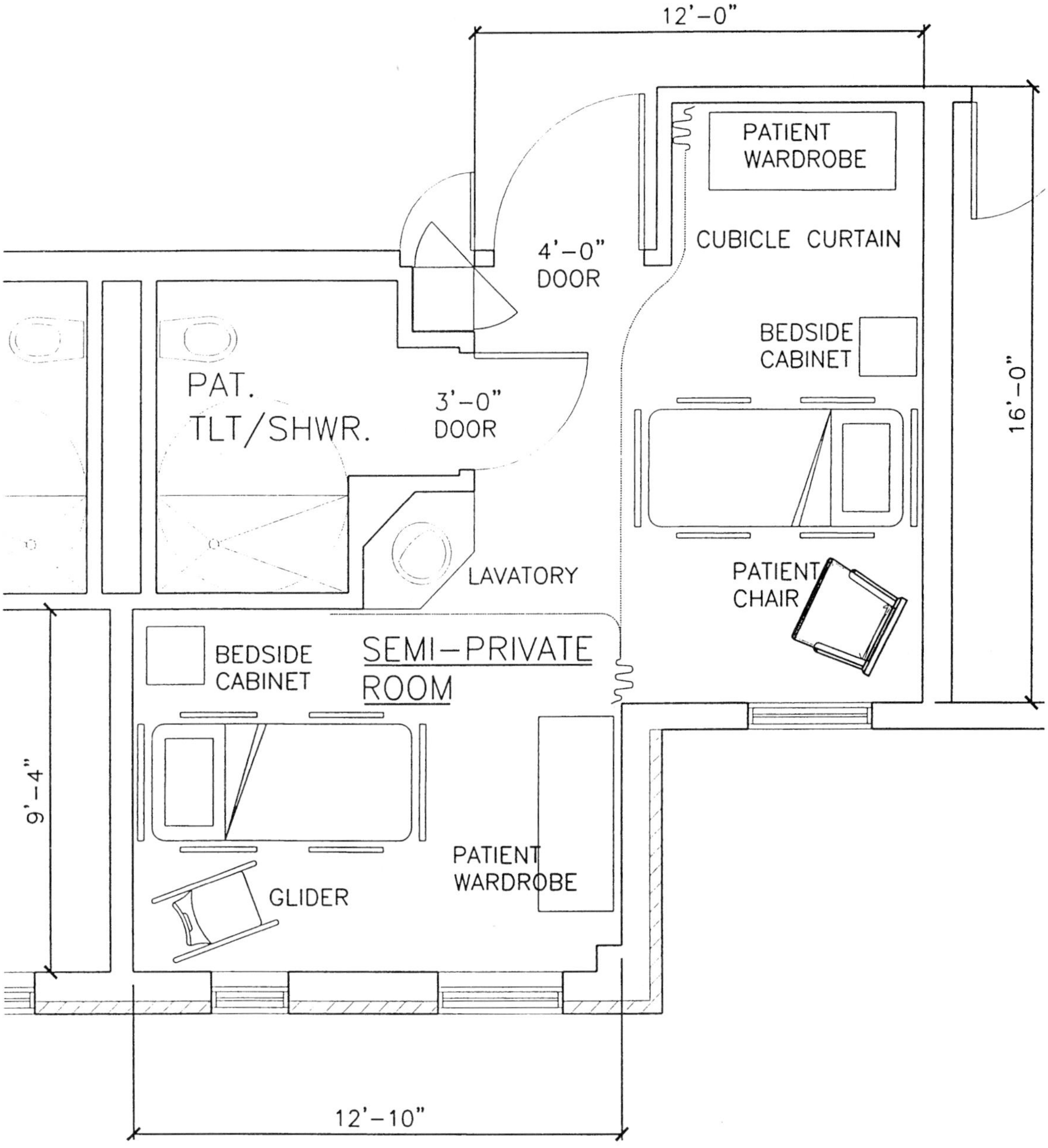

SKILLED NURSING/SUBACUTE CARE SEMIPRIVATE PATIENT ROOM

SCALE: 1/4"=1'-0"

ASSISTED LIVING FACILITIES
Patient Room Elevations

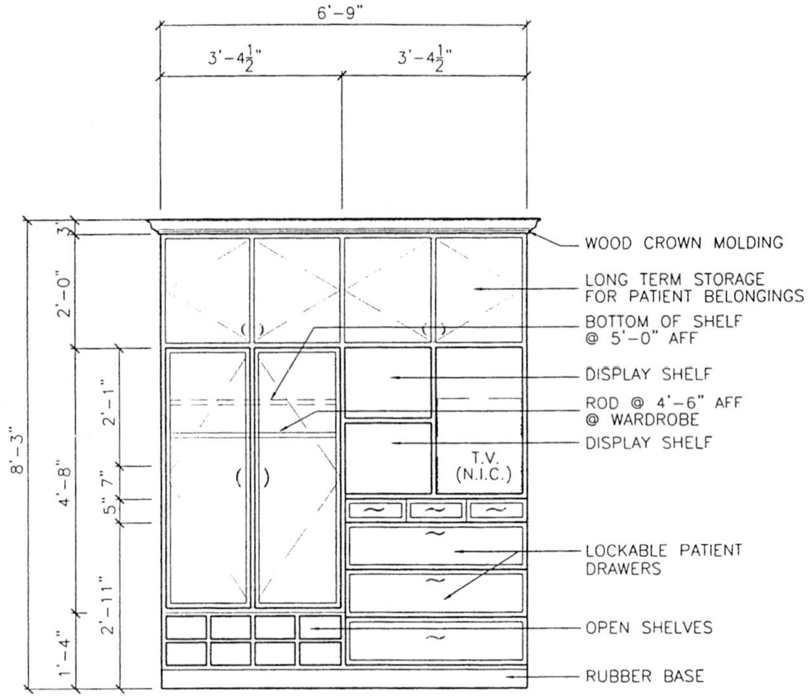

NOTE: ALL CABINETS THIS ELEVATION REVEAL OVERLAY STYLE-CLAD W/PLASTIC LAMINATE

SKILLED NURSING/SUBACUTE CARE PATIENT WARDROBE ELEVATION

SCALE: 3/8"=1'-0"

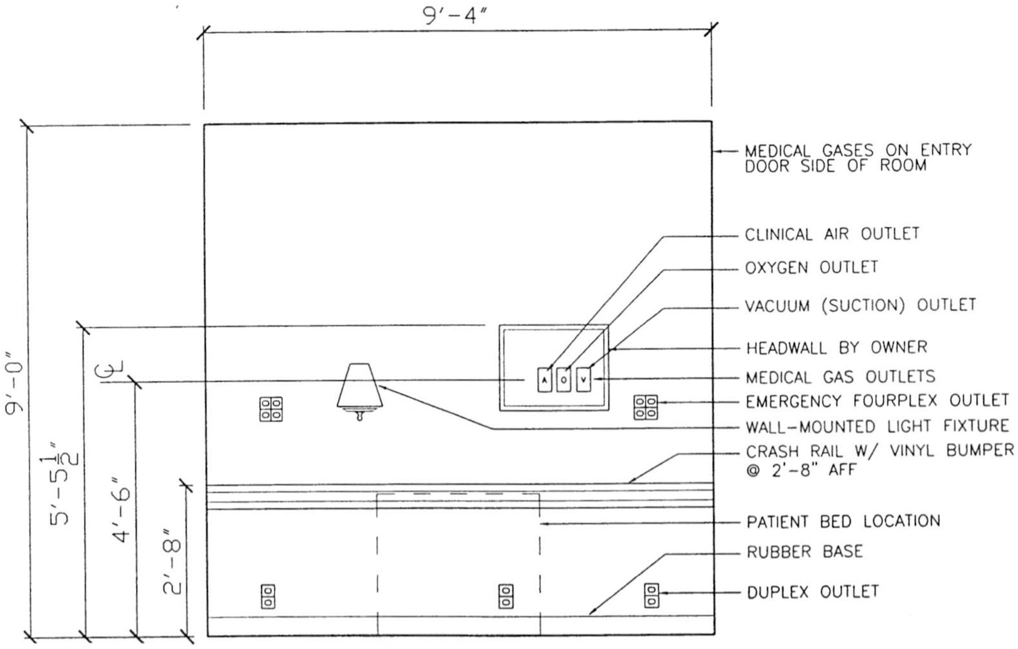

HEADWALL ELEVATION @ SKILLED NURSING/SUBACUTE PATIENT ROOM

SCALE: 3/8"=1'-0"

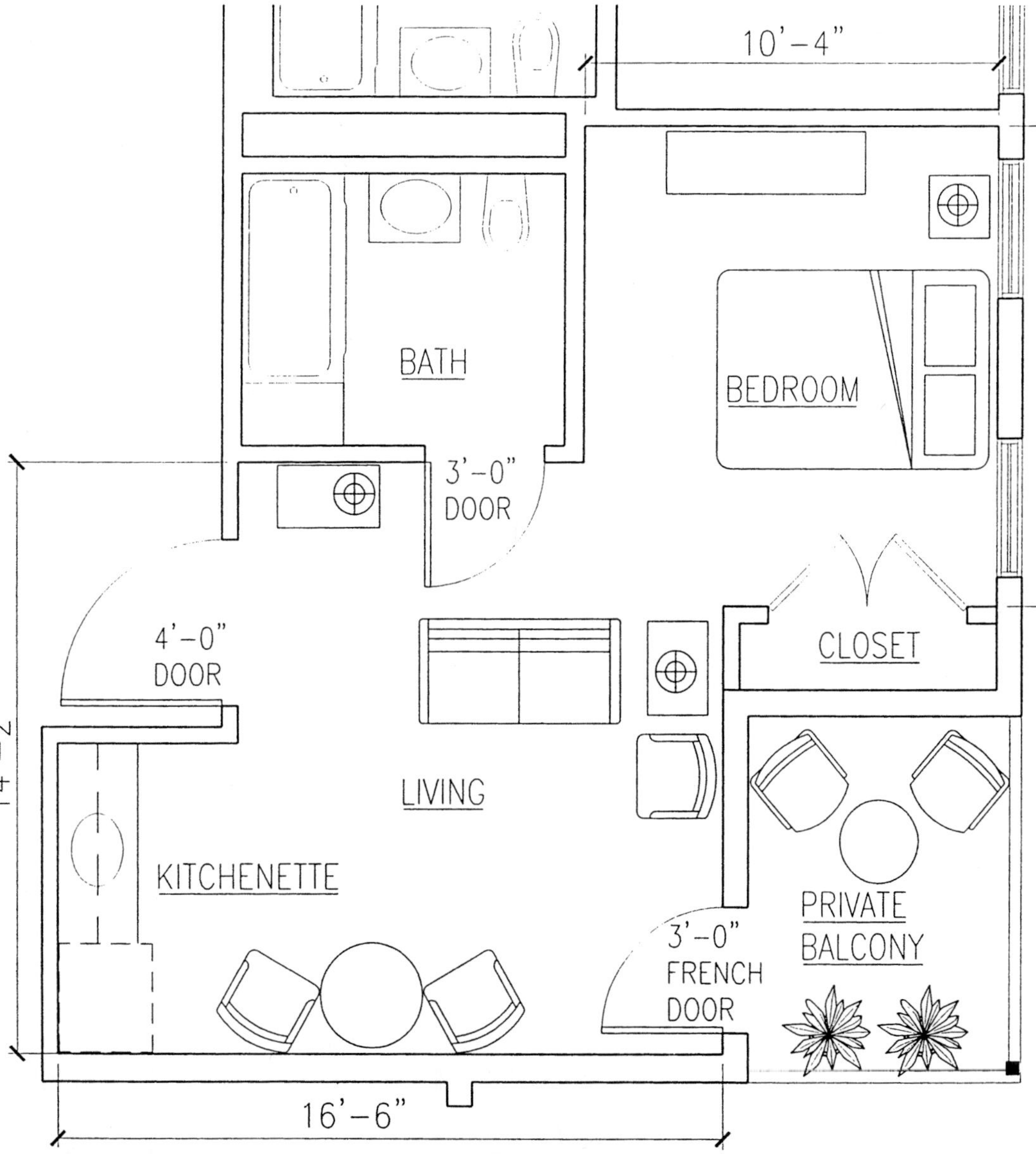

ASSISTED LIVING APARTMENT

SCALE: 1/4=1'-0"

ASSISTED LIVING FACILITIES
Bathroom and Kitchenette Elevations

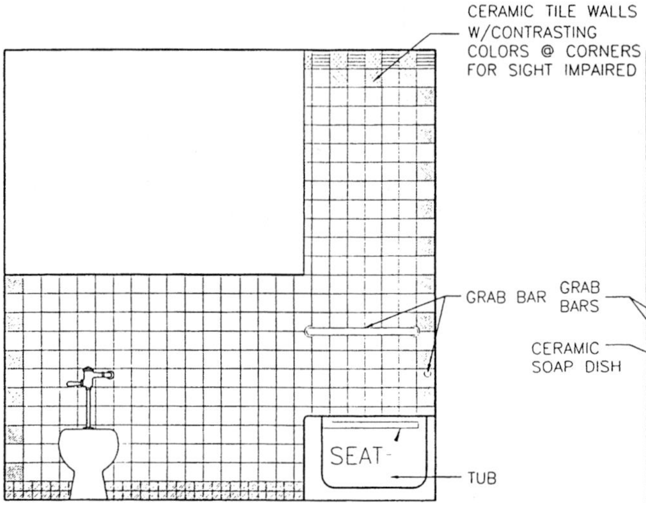

ASSISTED LIVING APARTMENT TOILET ELEVATION

SCALE: 3/8"=1'–0" (HANDICAP ACCESSIBLE)

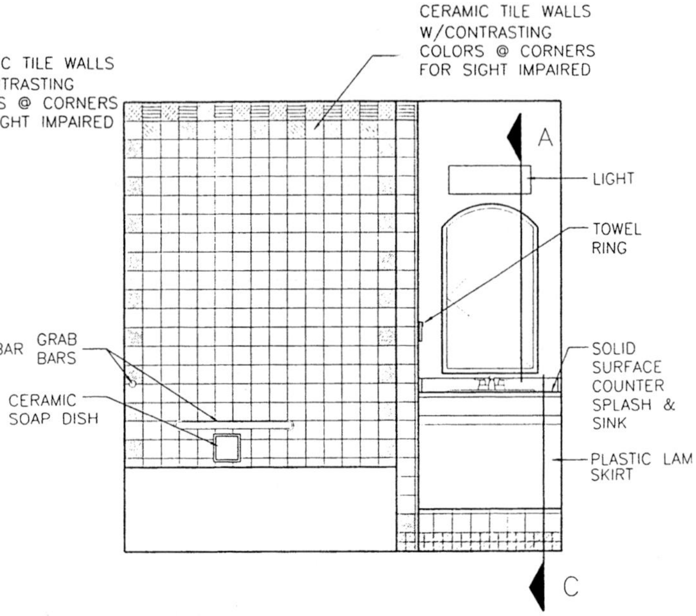

ASSISTED LIVING APARTMENT TOILET ELEVATION

SCALE: 3/8"=1'–0" (HANDICAP ACCESSIBLE)

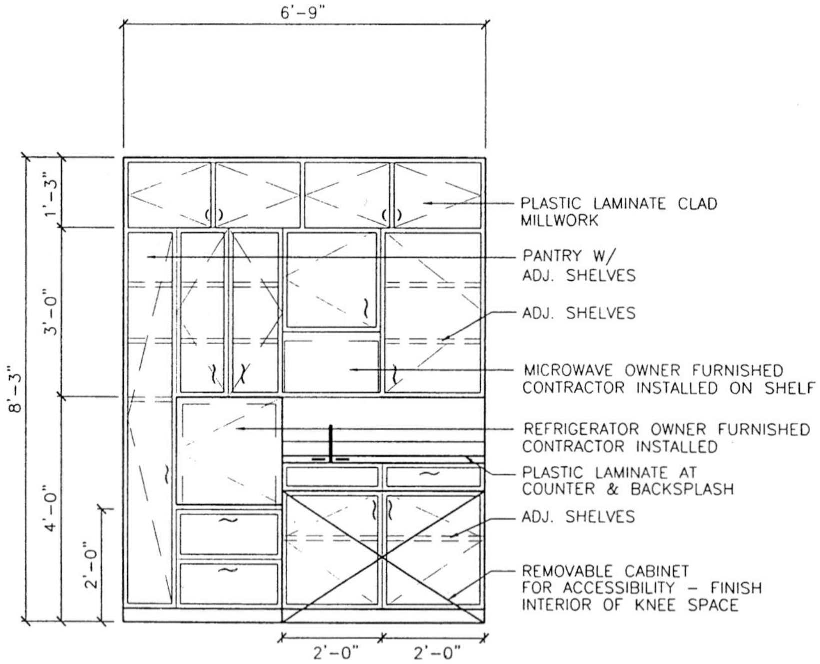

HANDICAP ACCESSIBLE

NOTE: ALL CABINETS THIS ELEVATION REVEAL OVERLAY STYLE-CLAD W/PLASTIC LAMINATE

ASSISTED LIVING KITCHENETTE

SCALE: 3/8"=1'–0"

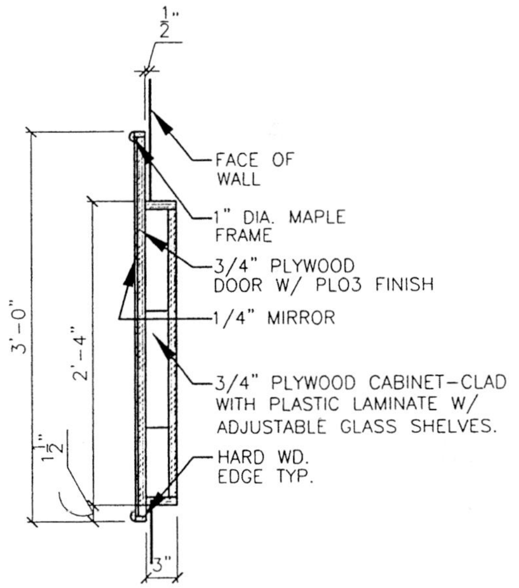

A SECTION @ PATIENT CABINET
SCALE: 3/4=1'-0"

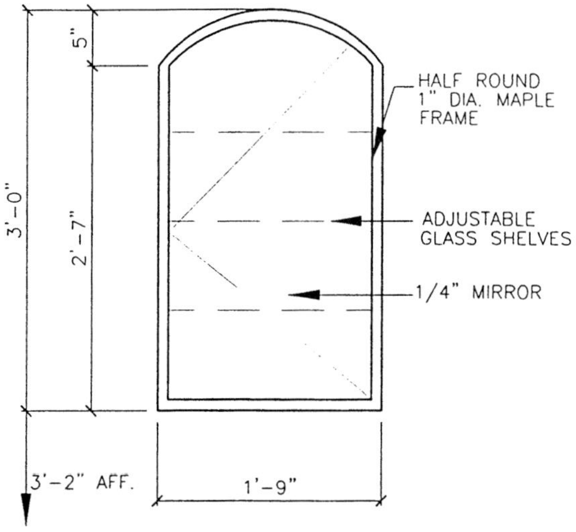

B ELEVATION @ HANDICAP CAB (CC)
SCALE: 3/4=1'-0"

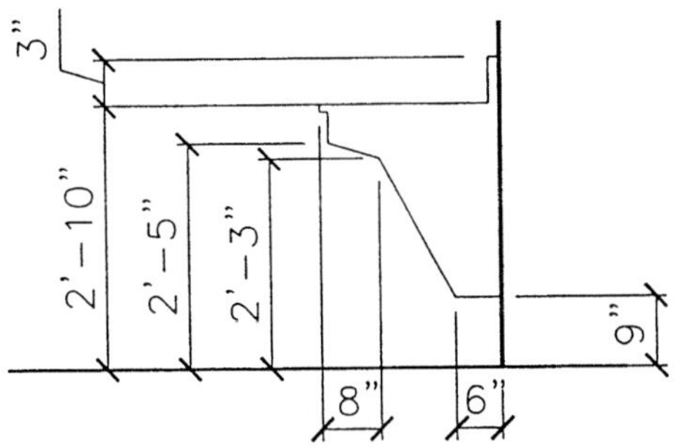

C H.C. ACCESSIBLE UNDER LAVATORIES
N.T.S.

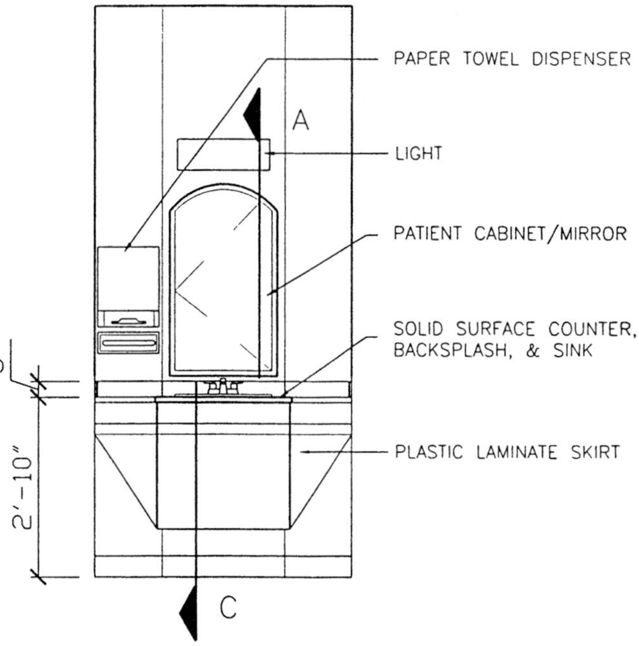

PATIENT ROOM LAVATORY ELEVATION
SCALE: 3/8"=1'-0"

ASSISTED LIVING FACILITIES
Dining/Activity Room

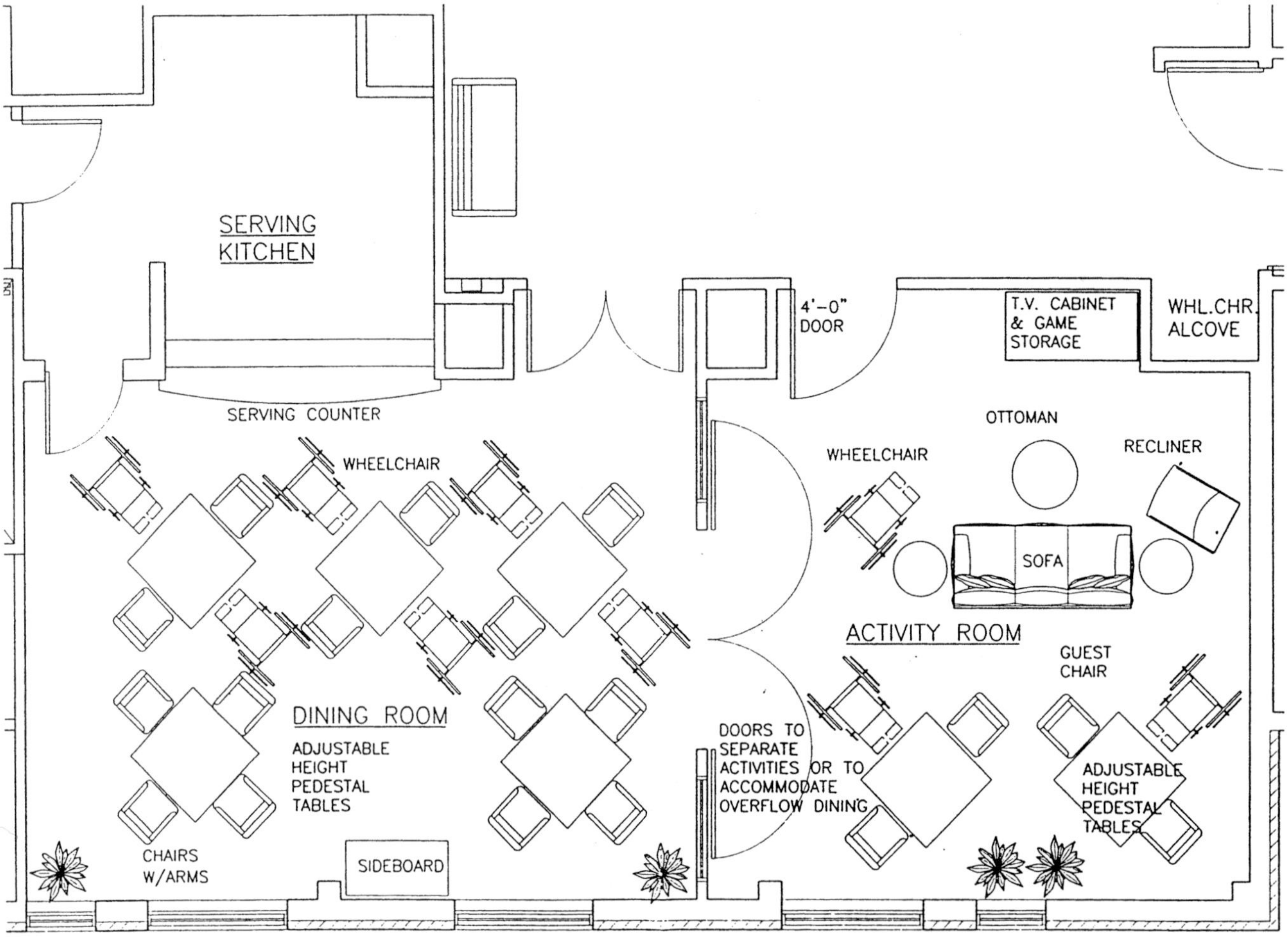

DINING/ACTIVITY ROOM
SKILLED NURSING

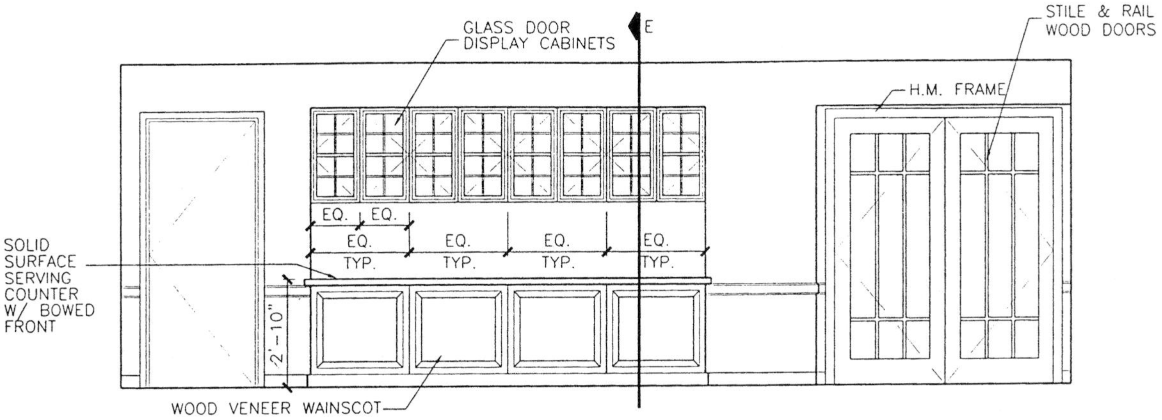

SUBACUTE DINING ROOM ELEVATION

SCALE: 1/4"=1'-0"

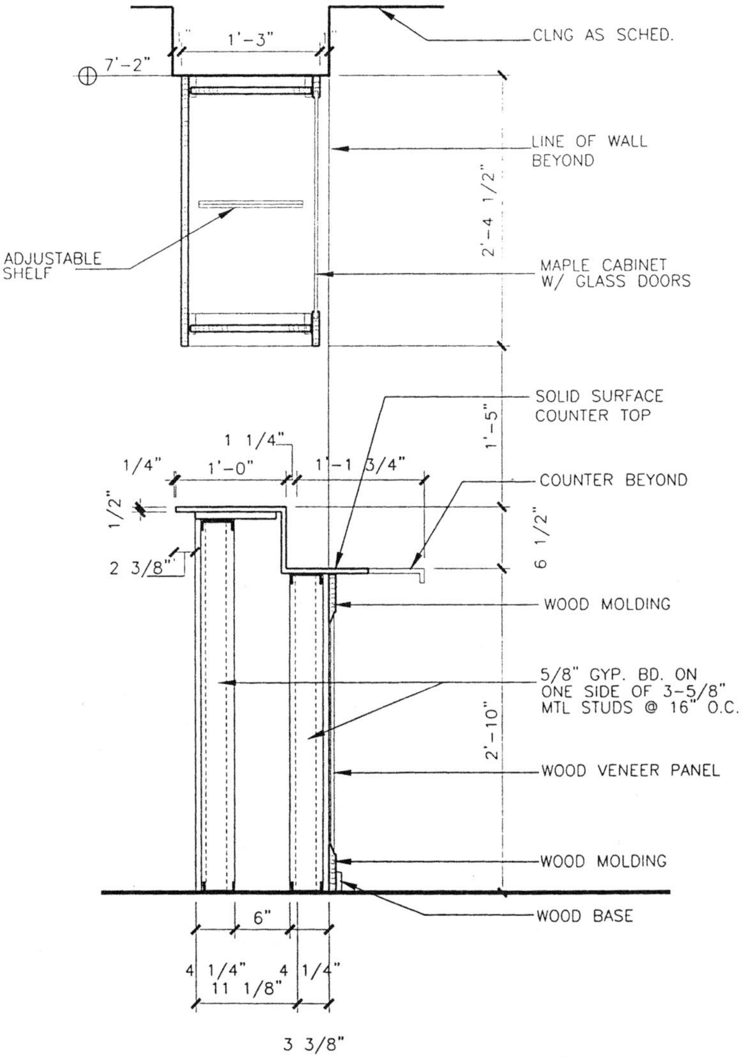

E SECTION @ DINING ROOM COUNTER

SCALE: 3/4"=1'-0"

ASSISTED LIVING FACILITIES
Stair Rail Elevation and Section

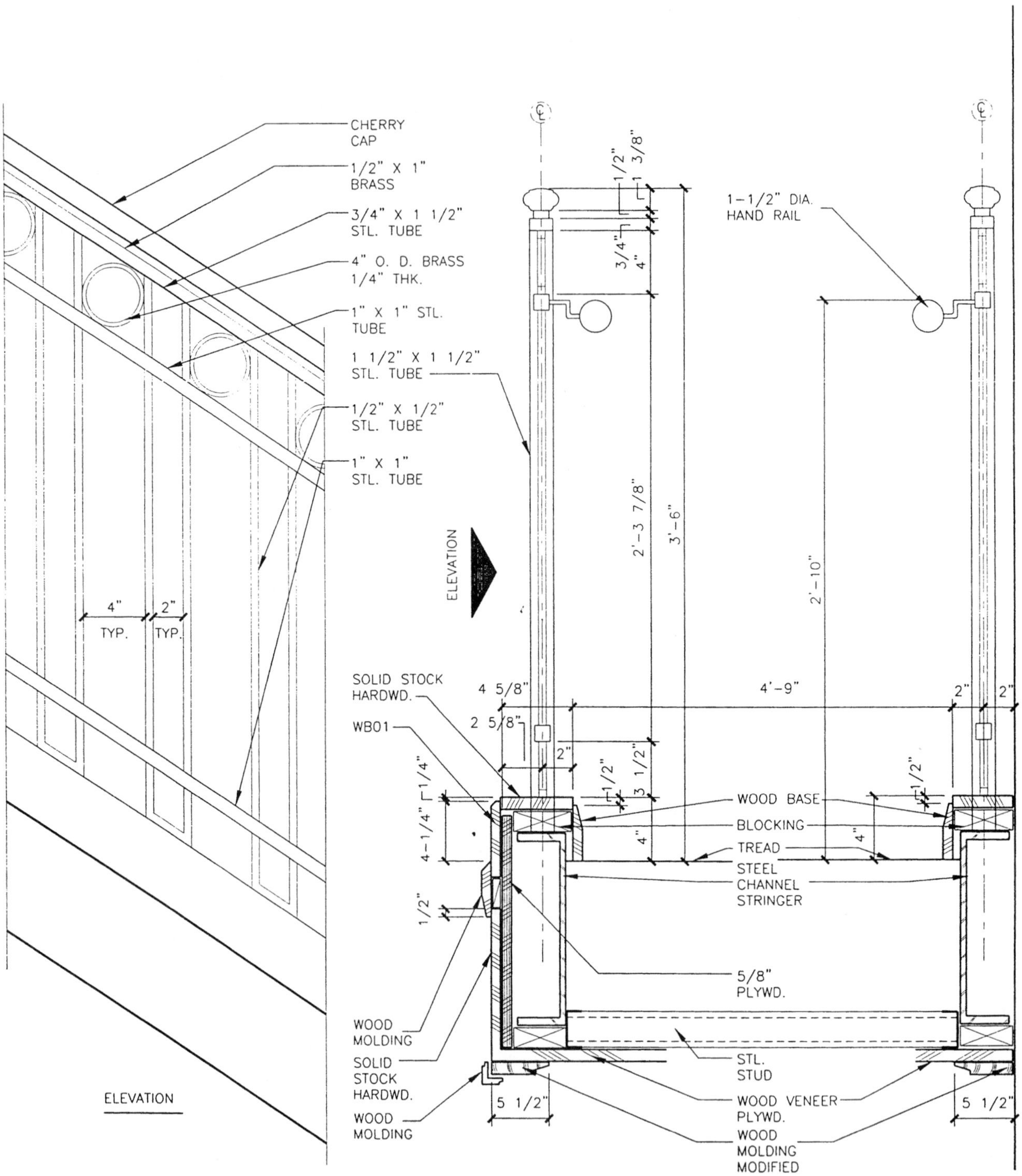

STAIR RAIL ELEVATION AND SECTION AT GRAND STAIR

SCALE: 1'-1/2"=1'-0"

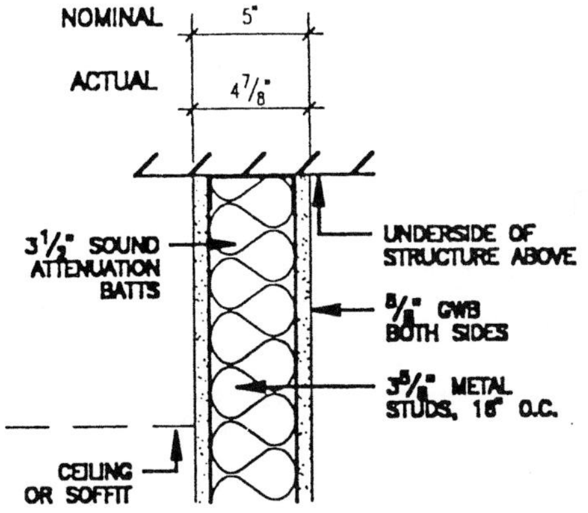

1 GWB FULL HEIGHT

1A 1HR FIRE RATED

L1 LEAD LINED

(7'-0" HIGH ROOM SIDE) LEAD LINING

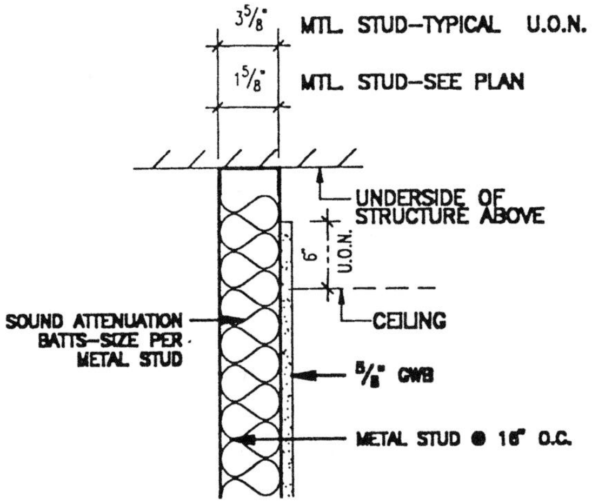

2 FURRED WALL

2A GWB FULL HEIGHT

(TO UNDERSIDE OF STRUCT ABOVE)

L2 LEAD LINED

(7'-0" HIGH ROOM SIDE) LEAD LINING

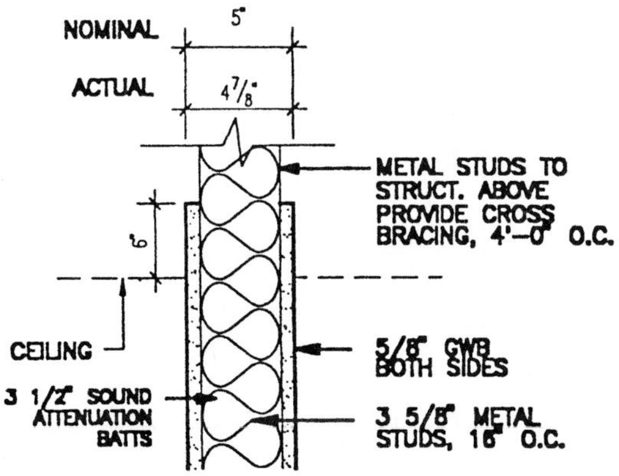

3 ABOVE CEILING

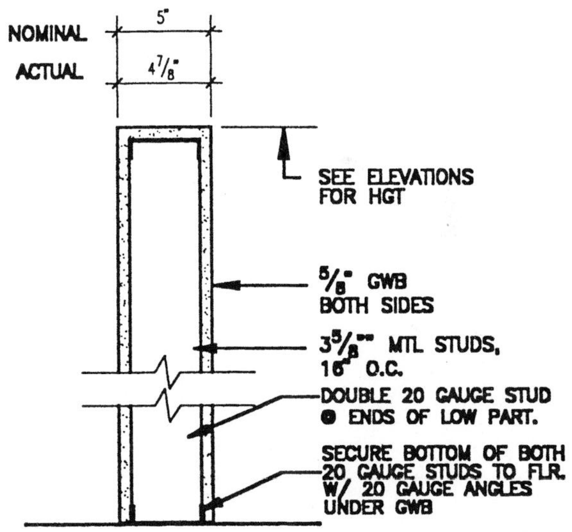

4 LOW PARTITION

SPECIAL DOORS AND PARTITIONS

Partition Types

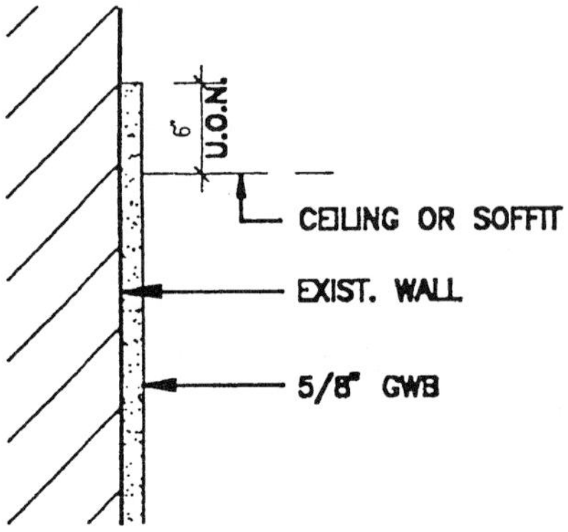

5 GWB LAMINATE

L5 LEAD LINED
(7'-0" HIGH ROOM SIDE) LEAD LINING

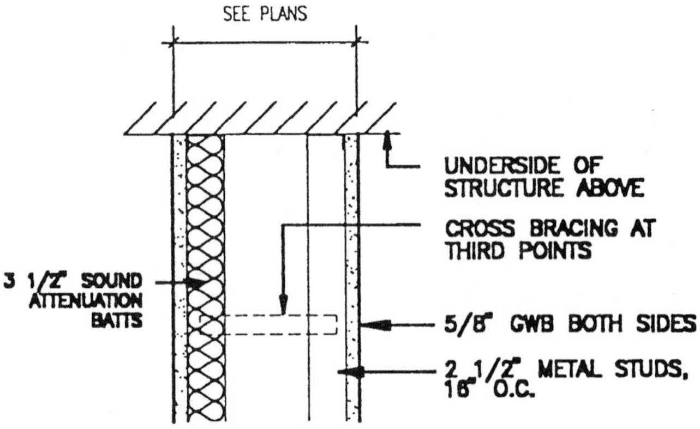

6 CHASE WALL

6A 1HR FIRE RATED

L6 LEAD LINED
(7'-0" HIGH ROOM SIDE) LEAD LINING

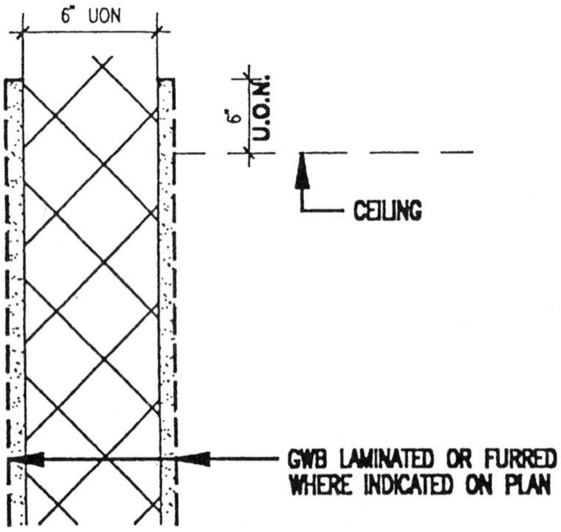

7 CMU WALL FULL HEIGHT

2 HOUR, FIRE RATED
WHERE INDICATED

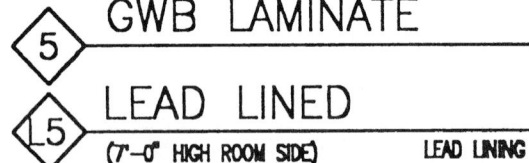

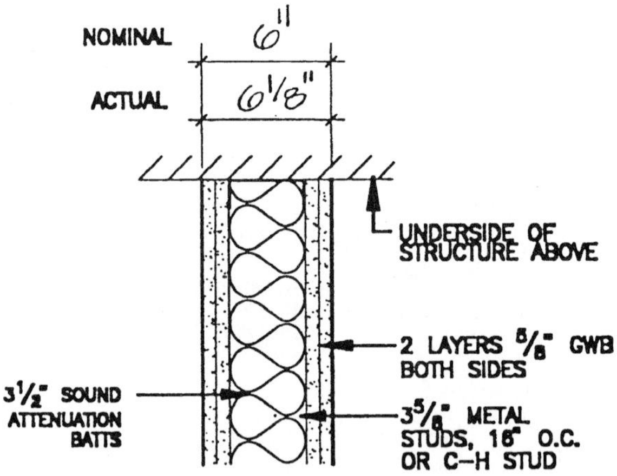

8 2 HOUR, FIRE RATED

L8 2 HOUR, FIRE RATED
(7'-0" HIGH LEAD LINING
ROOM SIDE)

SPECIAL DOORS AND PARTITIONS

Lead-lined Partitions

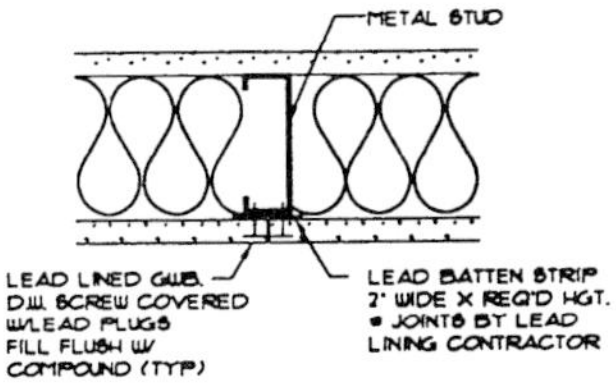

(1) LEAD BATTEN STRIP(TYP.)
3"=1'-0"

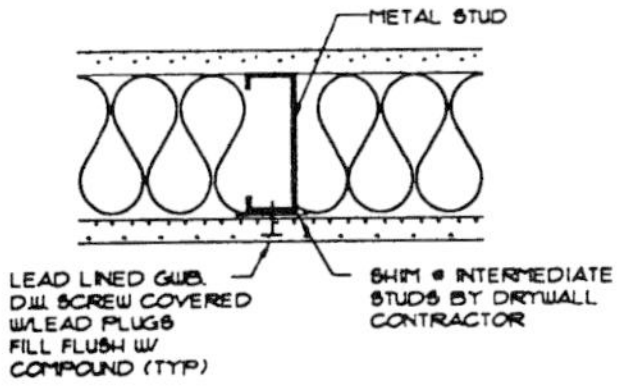

(2) LEAD LINED SHIMS(TYP.)
3"=1'-0"

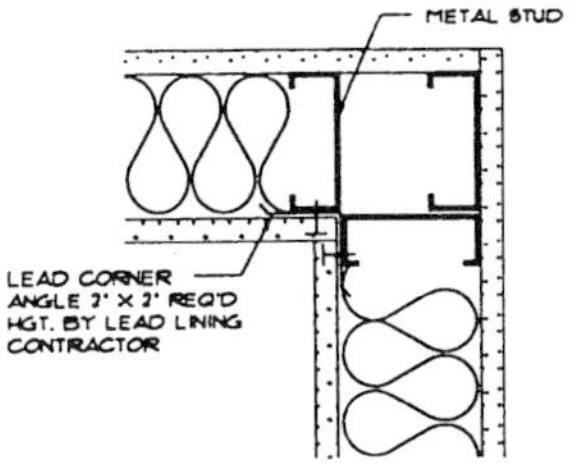

(3) LEAD LINED INSIDE CORNER(TYP.)
3" = 1'-0"

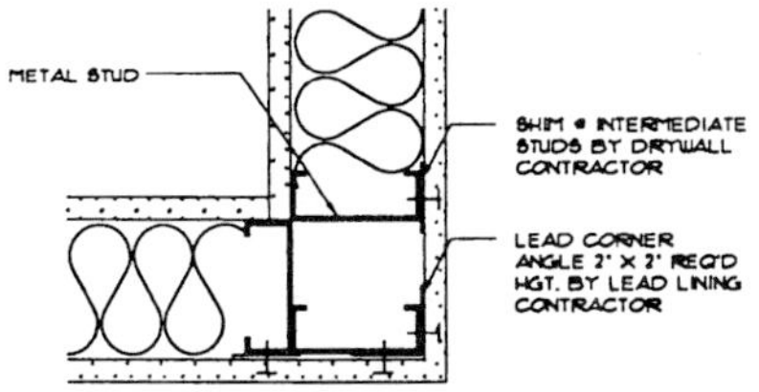

(4) LEAD LINED OUTSIDE CORNER(TYP.)
3" = 1'-0"

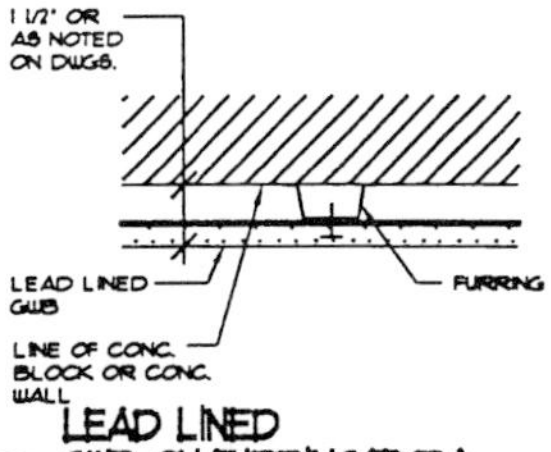

(5) LEAD LINED GWB ON FURRING(TYP.)
3" = 1'-0"

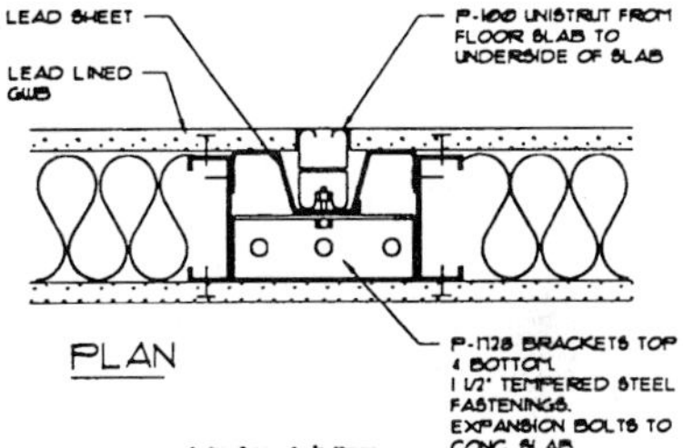

(6) LEAD LINED UNISTRUT SUPPORT(TYP.)
3" = 1'-0"

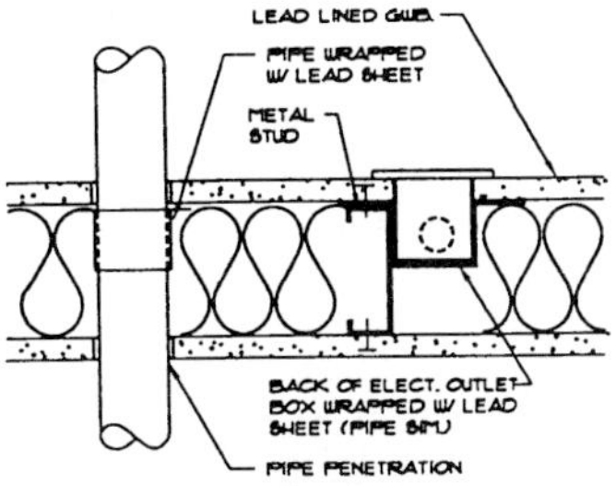

(7) LEAD LINED PLUMB. AND ELECT. PENETRATIONS(TYP.)
3" = 1'-0"

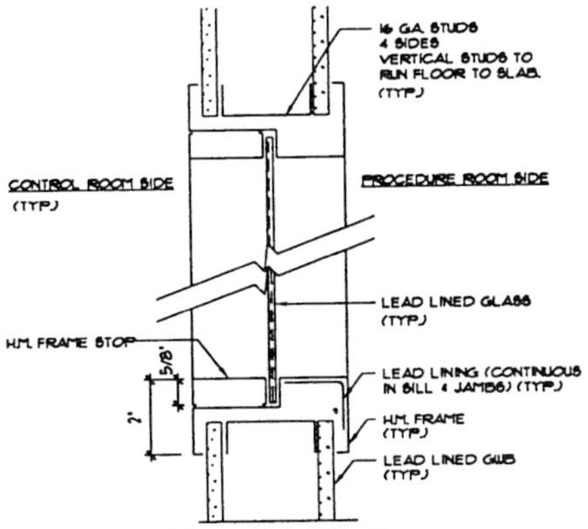

(8) LEAD LINED VIEW WINDOW
NOT TO SCALE

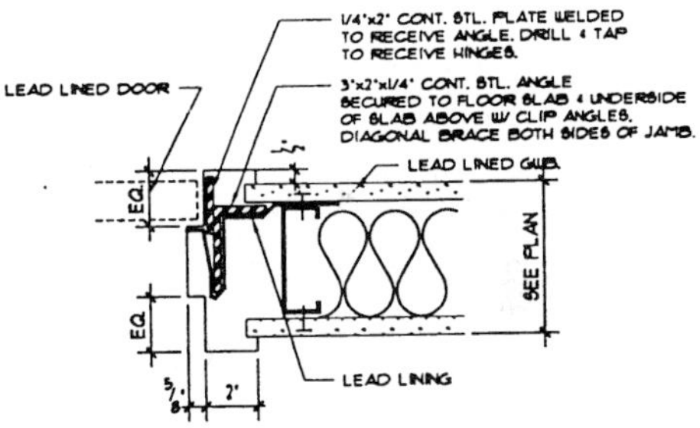

(9) LEAD LINED DOOR JAMB(TYP.)
3" = 1'-0"

LEAD LINING NOTES:

1. GWB shall be 5/8" thick with lead lining up to 7'-0" AFF.
2. Lead thickness indicated on partition types shall be 1.5mm(1/16" nominal) unless otherwise noted.
3. Standard 5/8" GWB is to be provided from 7'-0" AFF to underside of structure. See architectural dwg. for partition types, rating, etc.
4. --L--- on plan indicates Lead Lining.

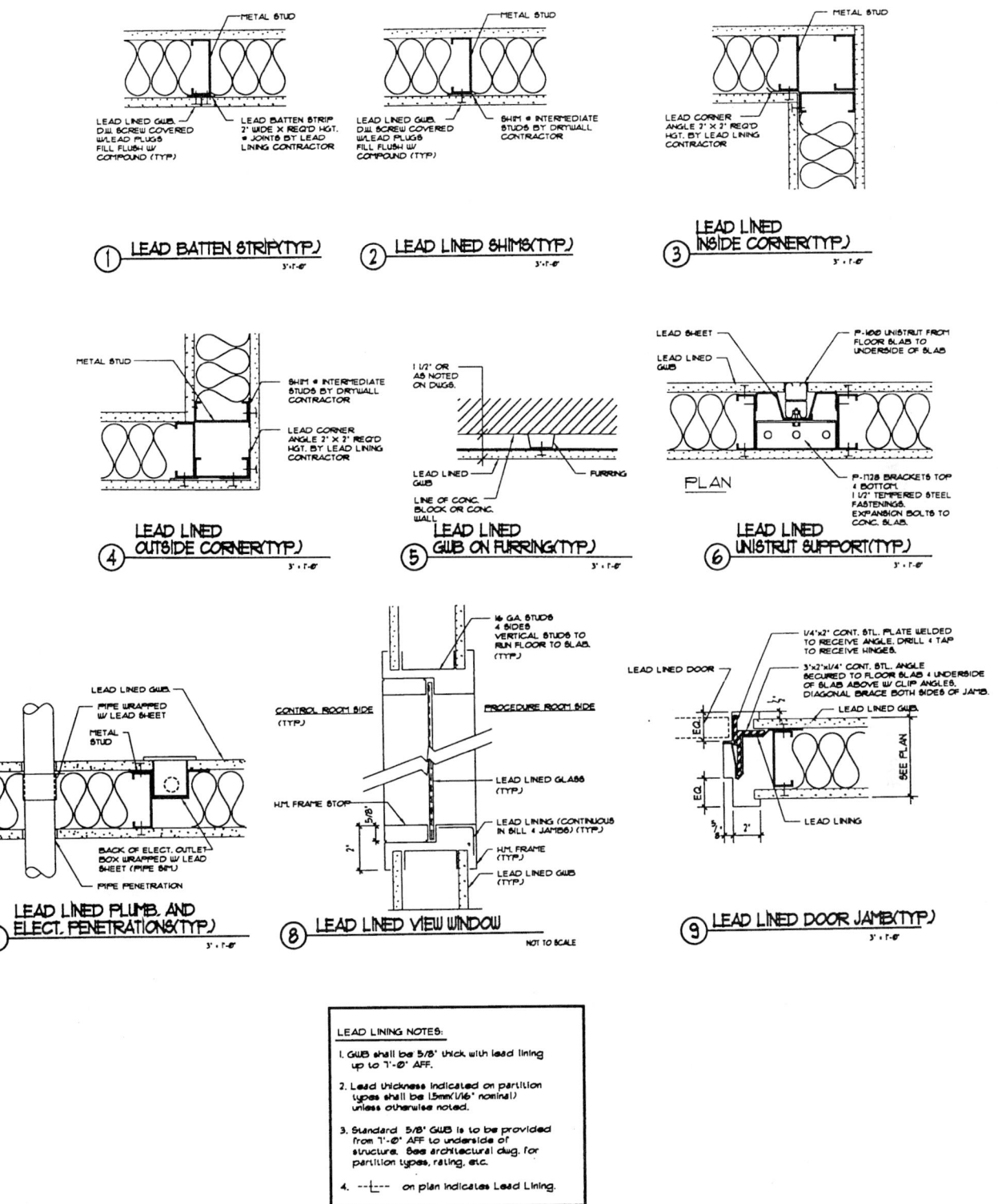

SPECIAL DOORS AND PARTITIONS

Details/Patient Room Doors

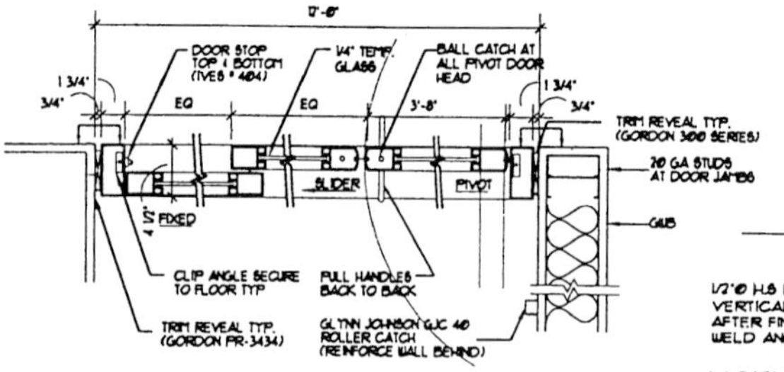

(15) PATIENT ROOM DOOR - PLAN
1 1/2" = 1'-0"

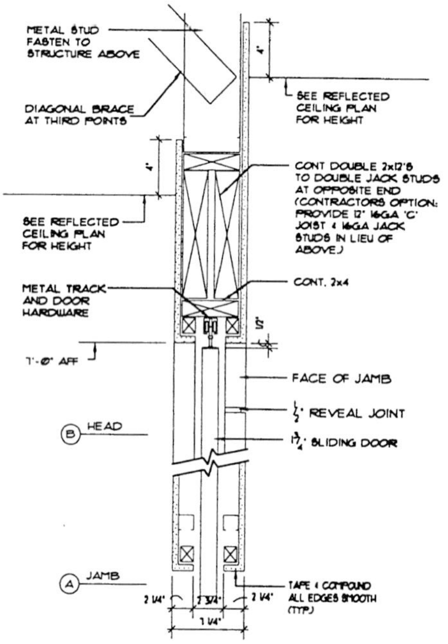

(13) SLIDING DOORS
ALUM. GRILLE SIMILAR
1 1/2" = 1'-0"

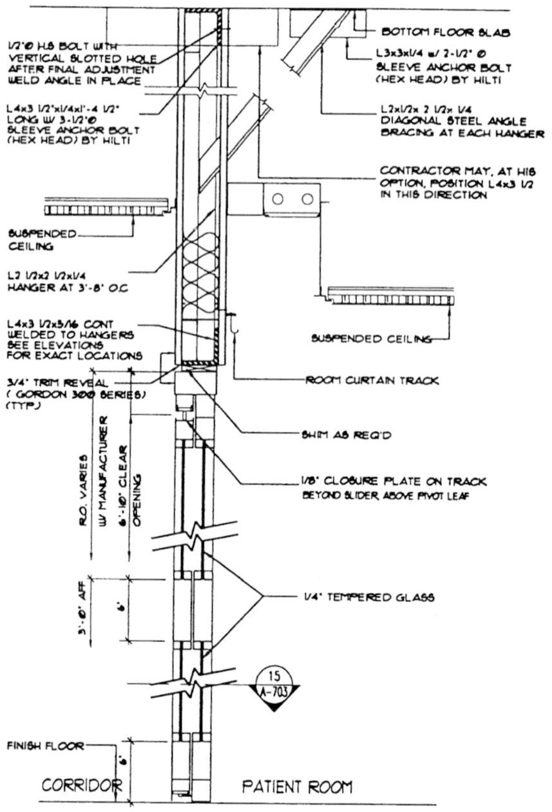

(14) PATIENT ROOM DOOR - SECTION
1 1/2" = 1'-0"

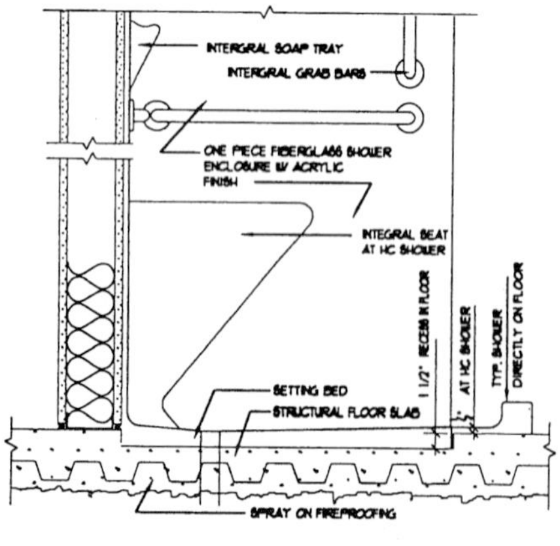

(16) ONE PIECE ACRYLIC SHOWER MODULE
1 1/2" = 1'-0"

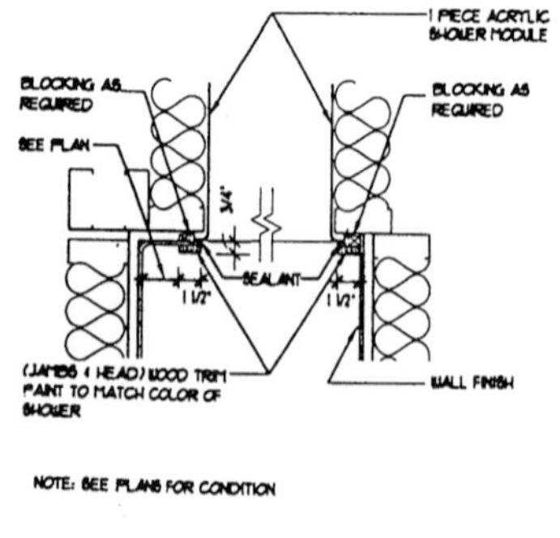

(17) DETAIL TRIM @ SHOWER MODULE
1 1/2" = 1'-0"

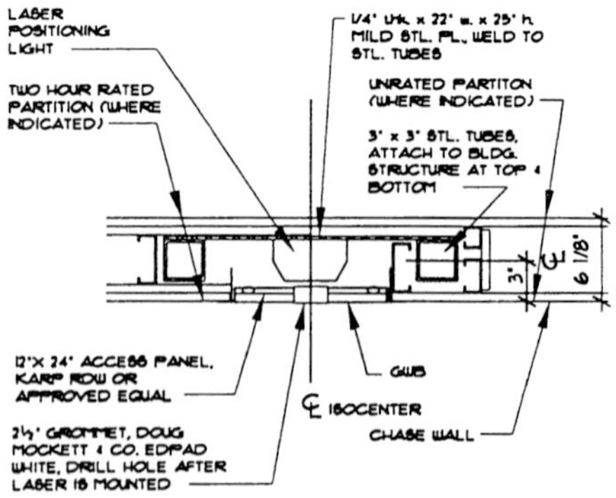

(18) LASER POSITIONING LIGHT
1 1/2" = 1'-0"

SPECIAL DOORS AND PARTITIONS
Details/Radiator Enclosures

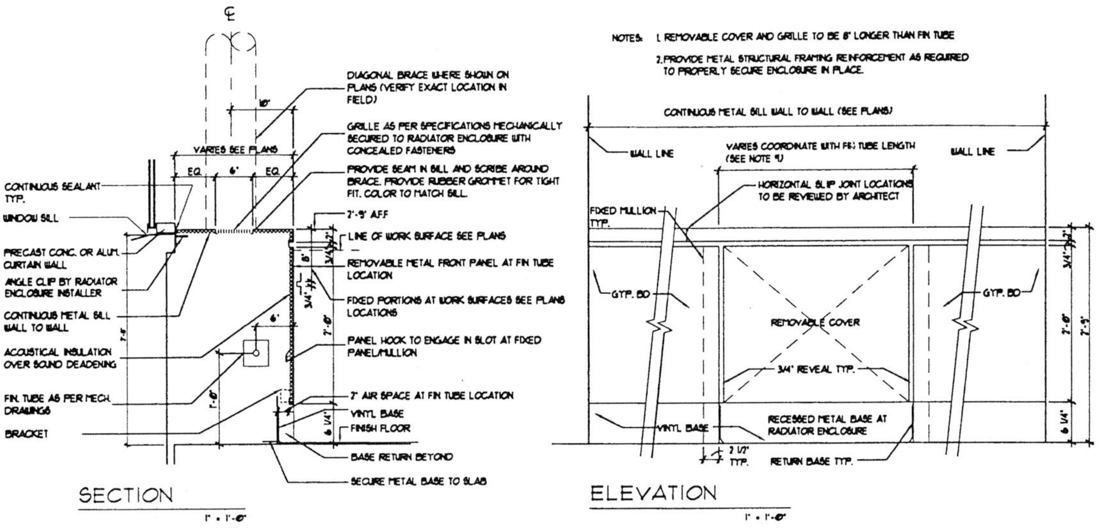

9 TYPICAL METAL WINDOW SILL / RADIATOR ENCLOSURE

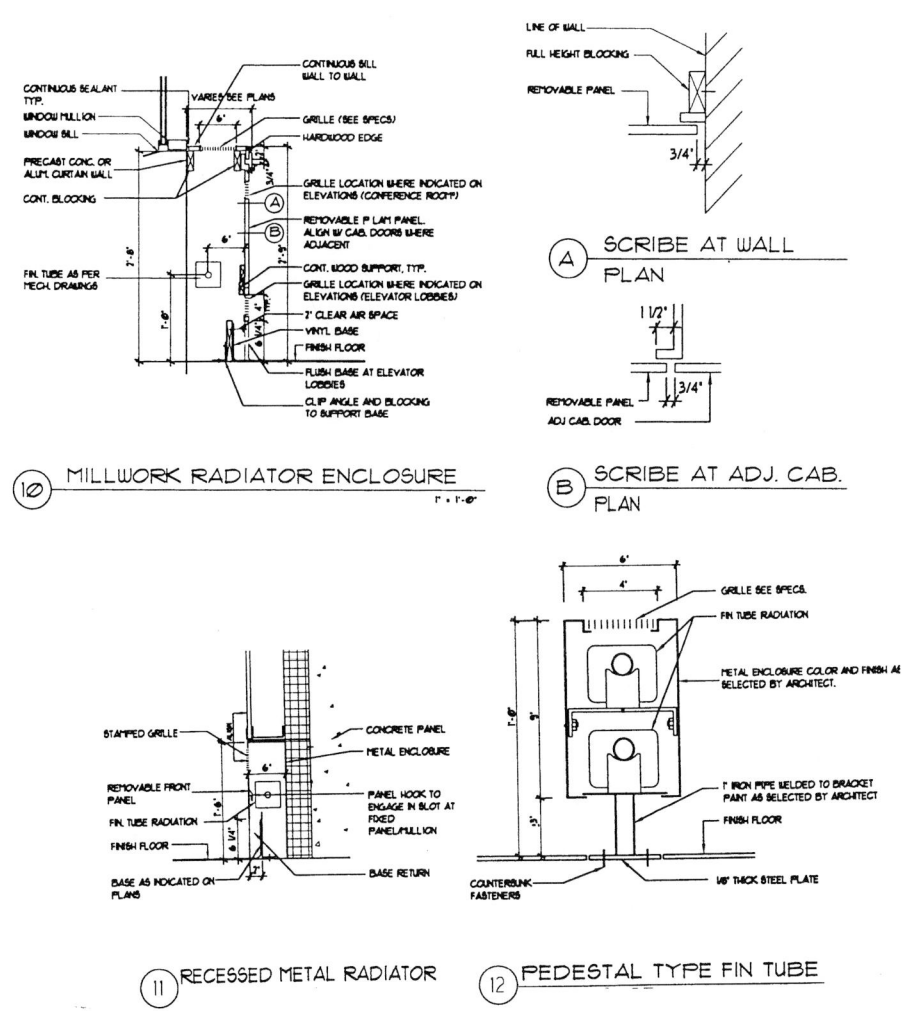

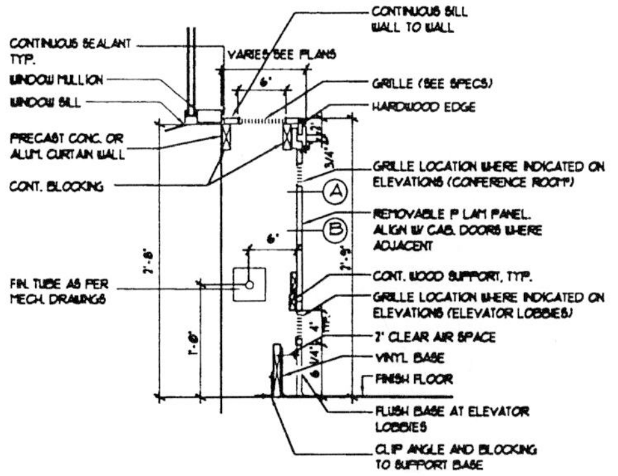

10 MILLWORK RADIATOR ENCLOSURE
1" = 1'-0"

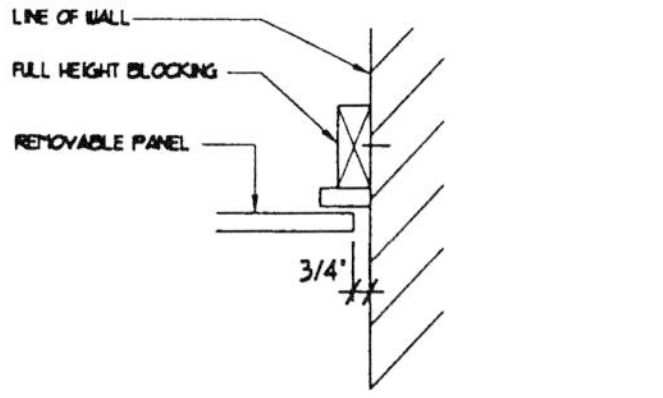

A SCRIBE AT WALL
PLAN

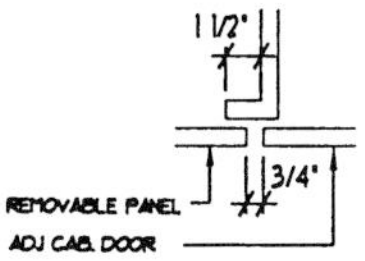

B SCRIBE AT ADJ. CAB.
PLAN

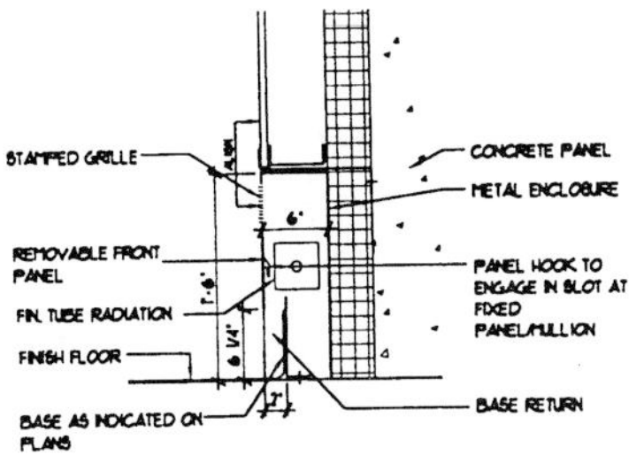

11 RECESSED METAL RADIATOR

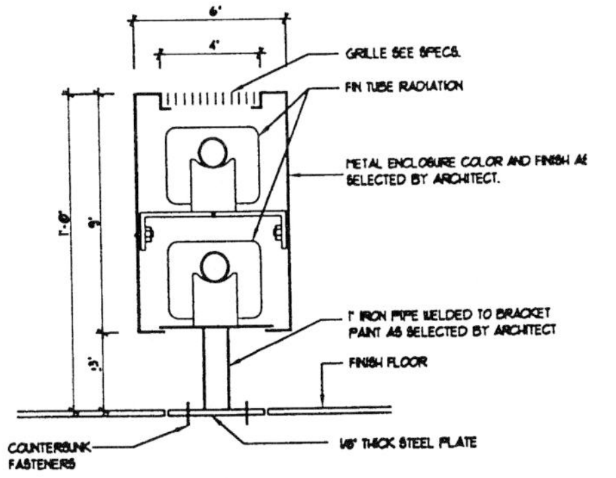

12 PEDESTAL TYPE FIN TUBE

HEALTH CARE SPECIALTIES
Details and Sections/Hospital Equipment

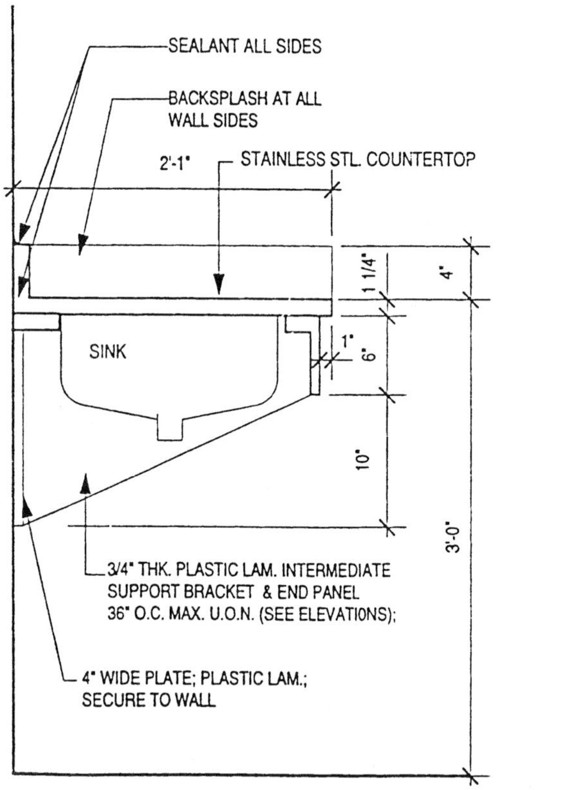

16 SOILED UTILITY COUNTERTOP

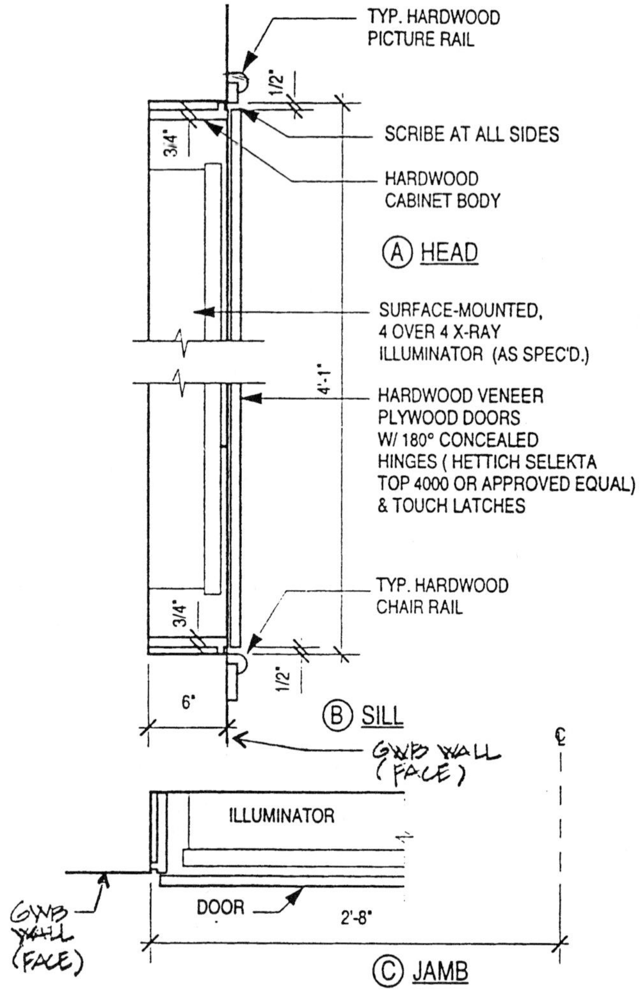

17 ILLUMINATOR CABINET

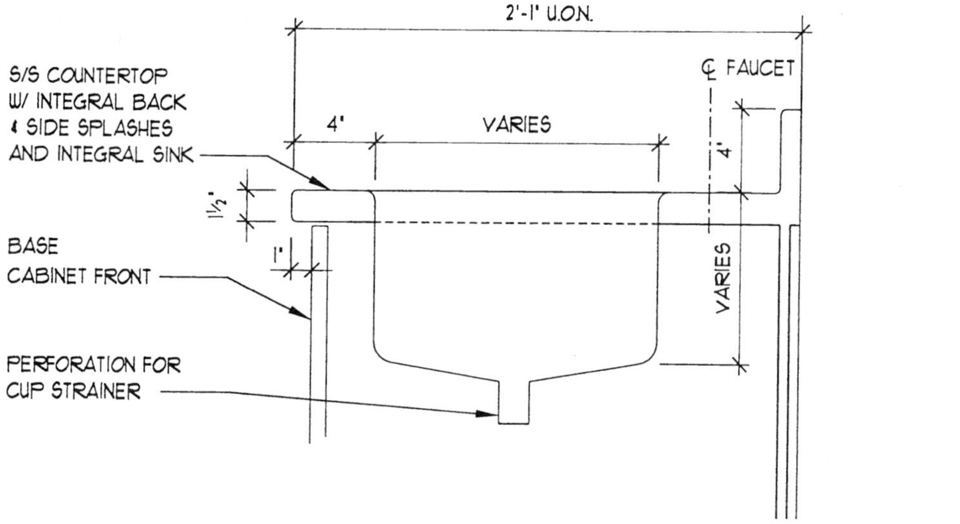

(23) STAINLESS STEEL (S/S) COUNTERTOPS

1½" = 1'-0"

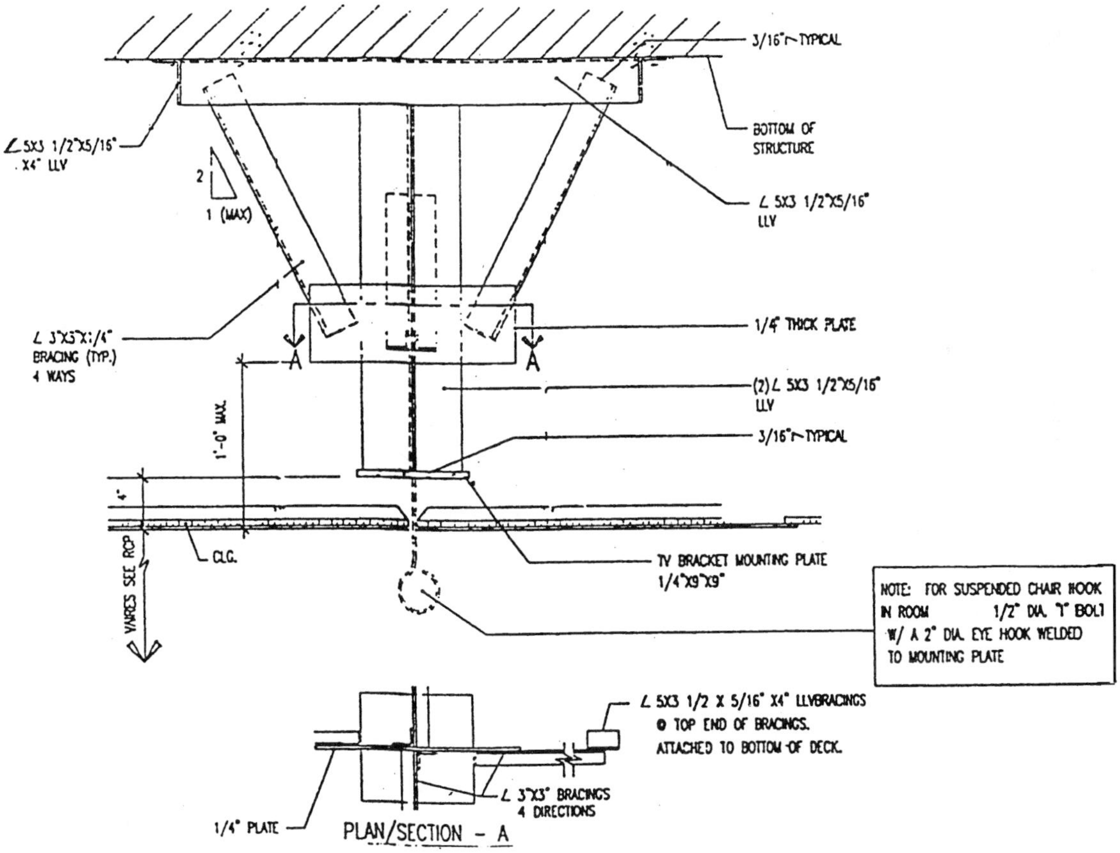

(24) CHAIR SUPPORT DETAIL

NOT TO SCALE

HEALTH CARE SPECIALTIES
Details and Sections/Hospital Equipment

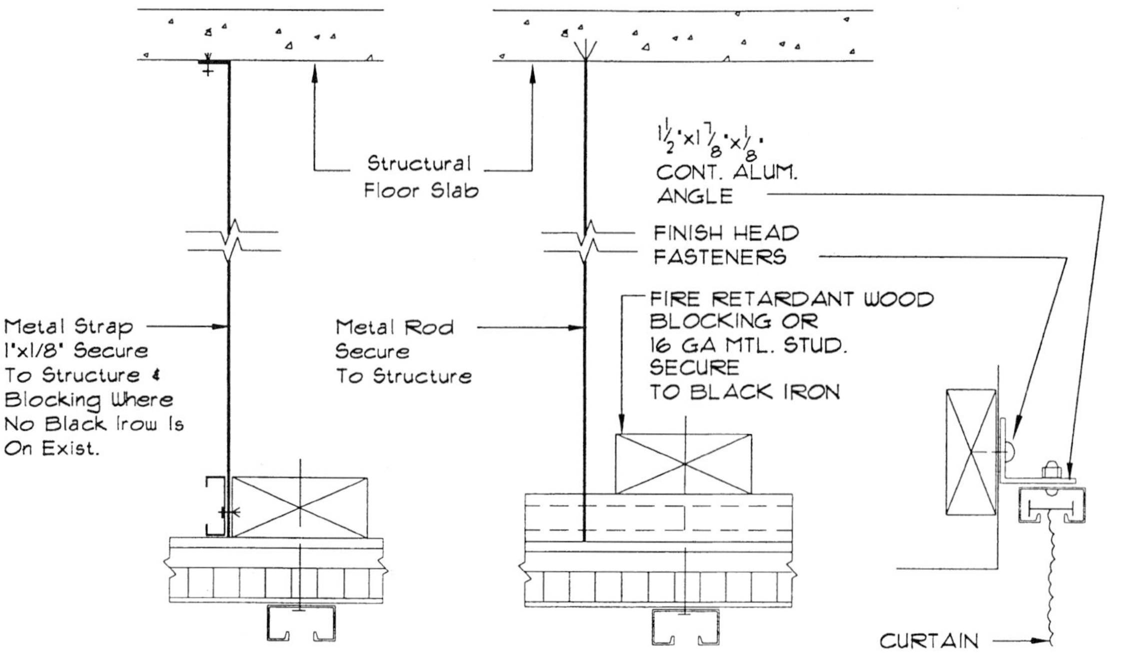

16 TYP. CURTAIN/I.V. TRACK

1 1/2" = 1'-0"

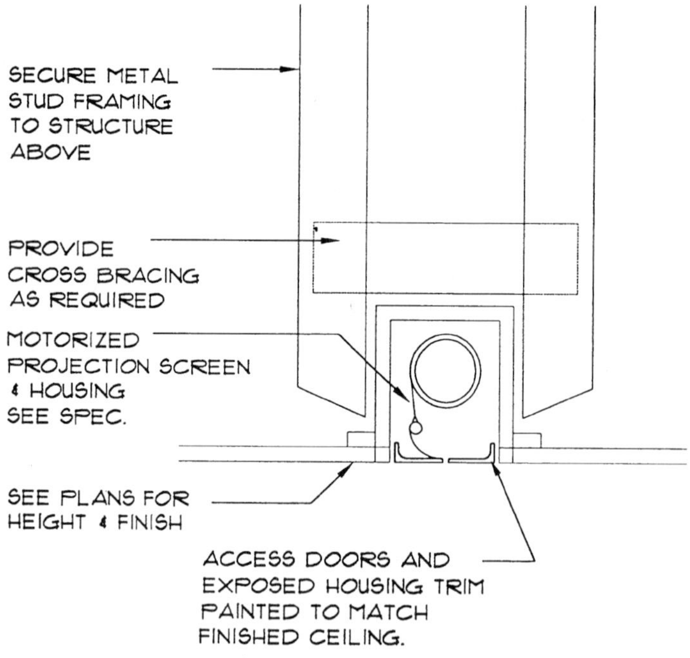

17 CEILING @ PROJECTION SCREEN

1-1/2" = 1'-0"

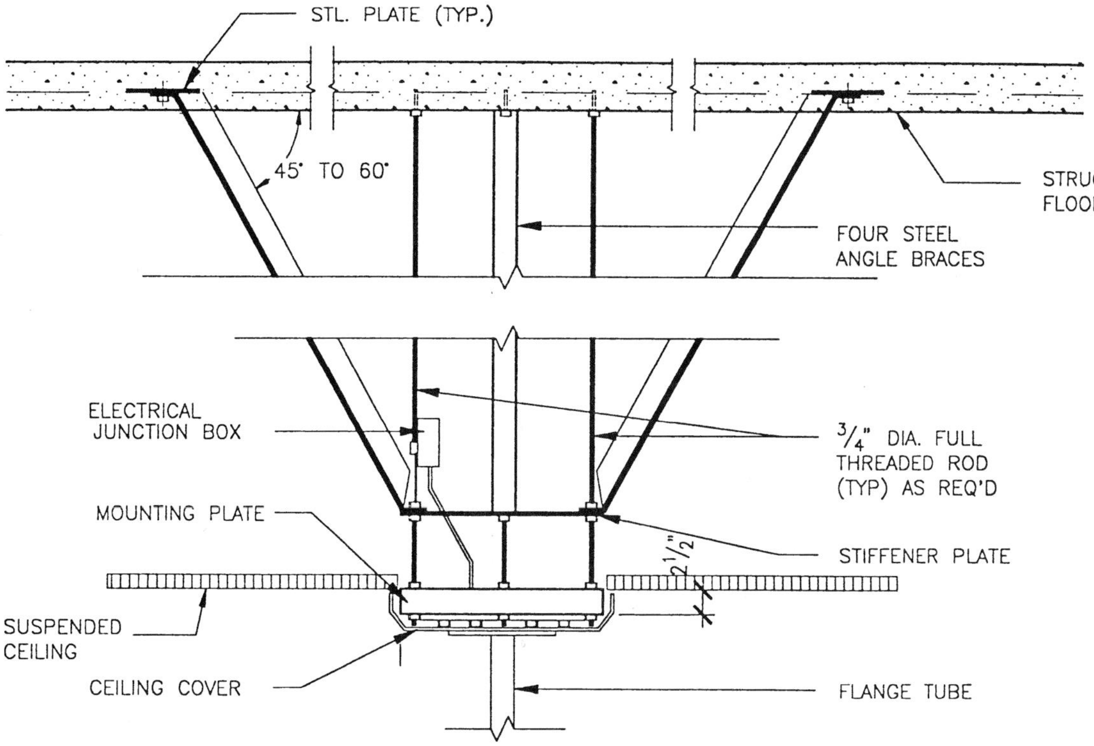
STL. PLATE (TYP.)
45° TO 60°
STRUCTURAL FLOOR SLAB
FOUR STEEL ANGLE BRACES
ELECTRICAL JUNCTION BOX
3/4" DIA. FULL THREADED ROD (TYP) AS REQ'D
MOUNTING PLATE
2 1/2"
STIFFENER PLATE
SUSPENDED CEILING
CEILING COVER
FLANGE TUBE

15 SURGICAL LIGHT SUPPORT

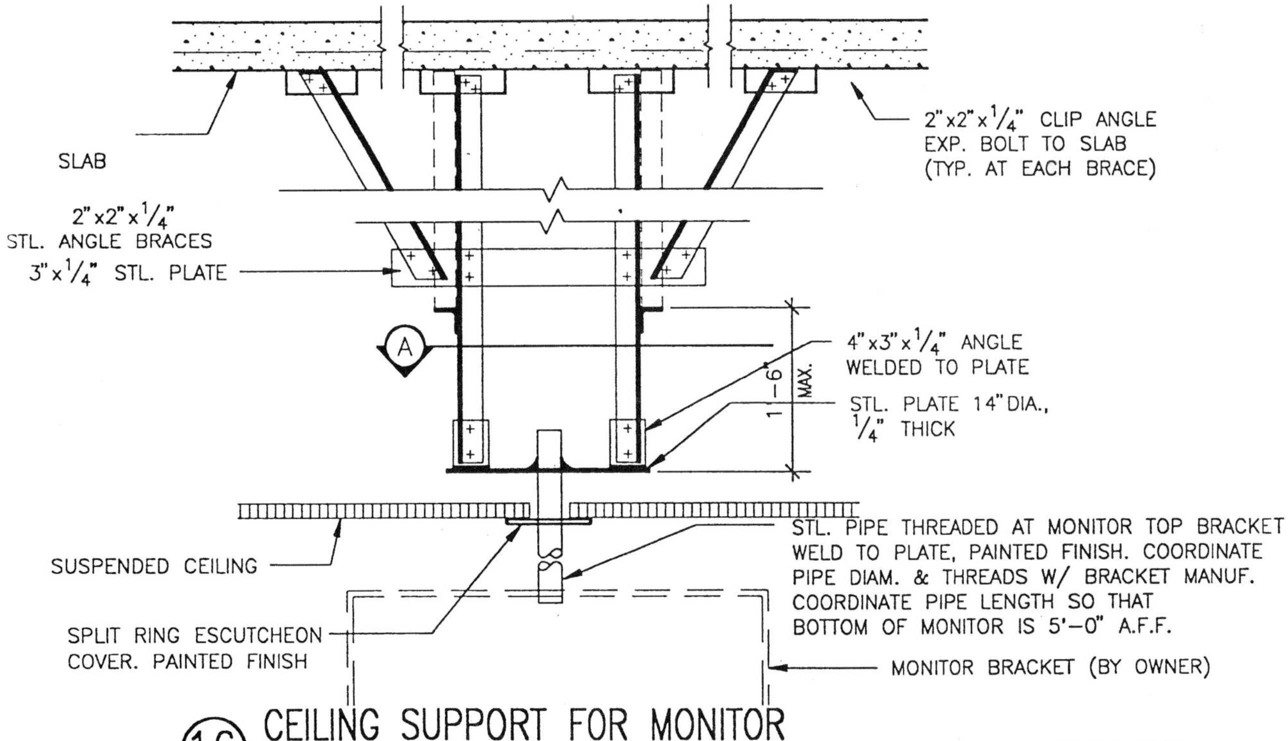
SLAB
2"x2"x1/4" CLIP ANGLE EXP. BOLT TO SLAB (TYP. AT EACH BRACE)
2"x2"x1/4" STL. ANGLE BRACES
3"x1/4" STL. PLATE
A
4"x3"x1/4" ANGLE WELDED TO PLATE
1'-6" MAX.
STL. PLATE 14" DIA., 1/4" THICK
SUSPENDED CEILING
STL. PIPE THREADED AT MONITOR TOP BRACKET WELD TO PLATE, PAINTED FINISH. COORDINATE PIPE DIAM. & THREADS W/ BRACKET MANUF. COORDINATE PIPE LENGTH SO THAT BOTTOM OF MONITOR IS 5'-0" A.F.F.
SPLIT RING ESCUTCHEON COVER. PAINTED FINISH
MONITOR BRACKET (BY OWNER)

16 CEILING SUPPORT FOR MONITOR

HEALTH CARE SPECIALTIES
Elevations/Equipment and Accessories

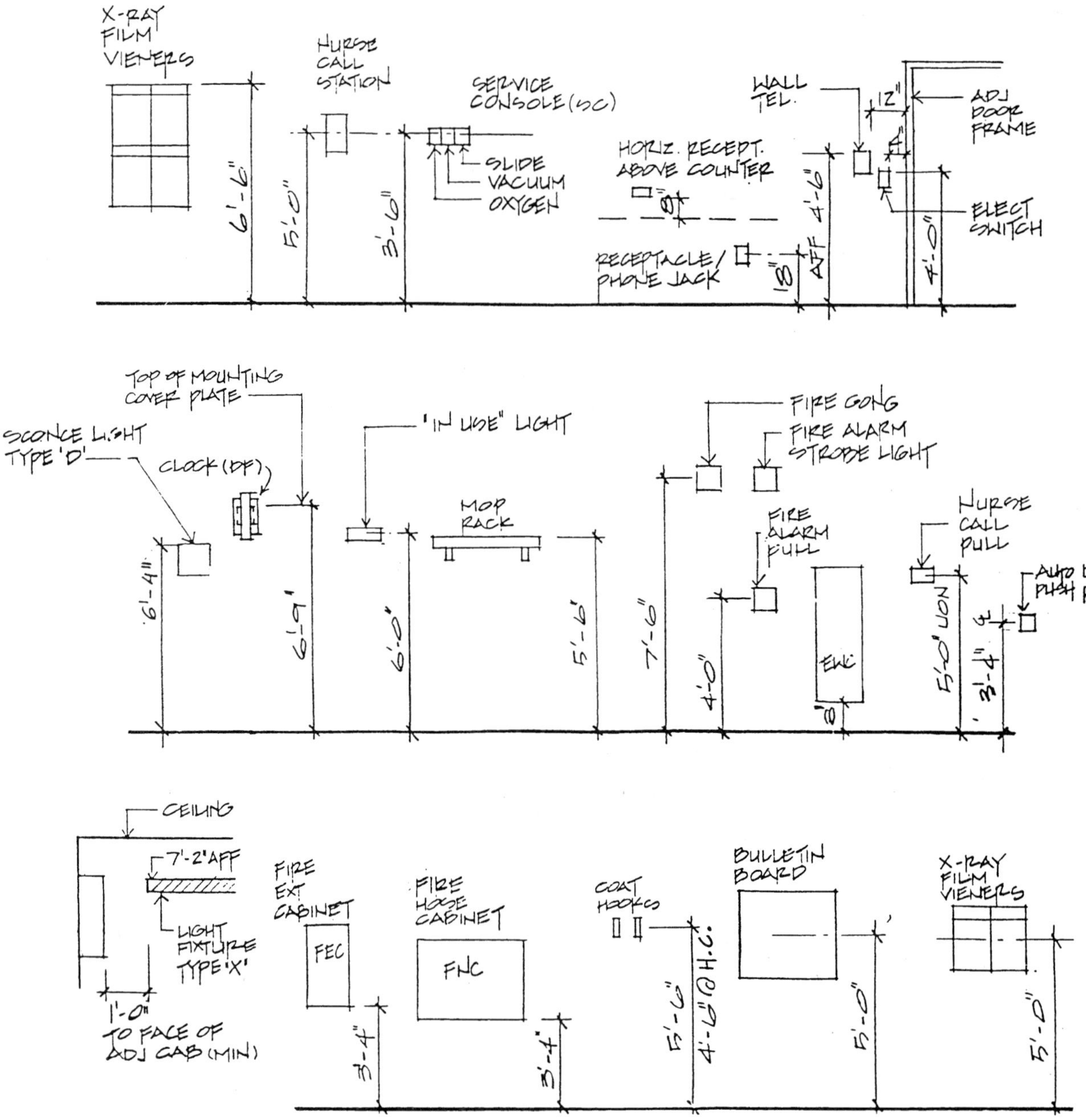

(23/A25) MISC. EQUIPMENT & ACCESSORY ITEMS

(TYPICAL ELEVATIONS) ALL HEIGHTS TYPICAL UNLESS OTHERWISE NOTED (U.O.N)

BANKING SPACES

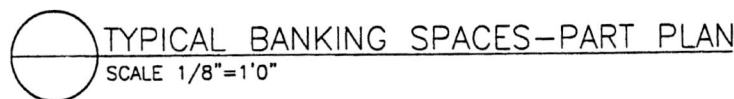

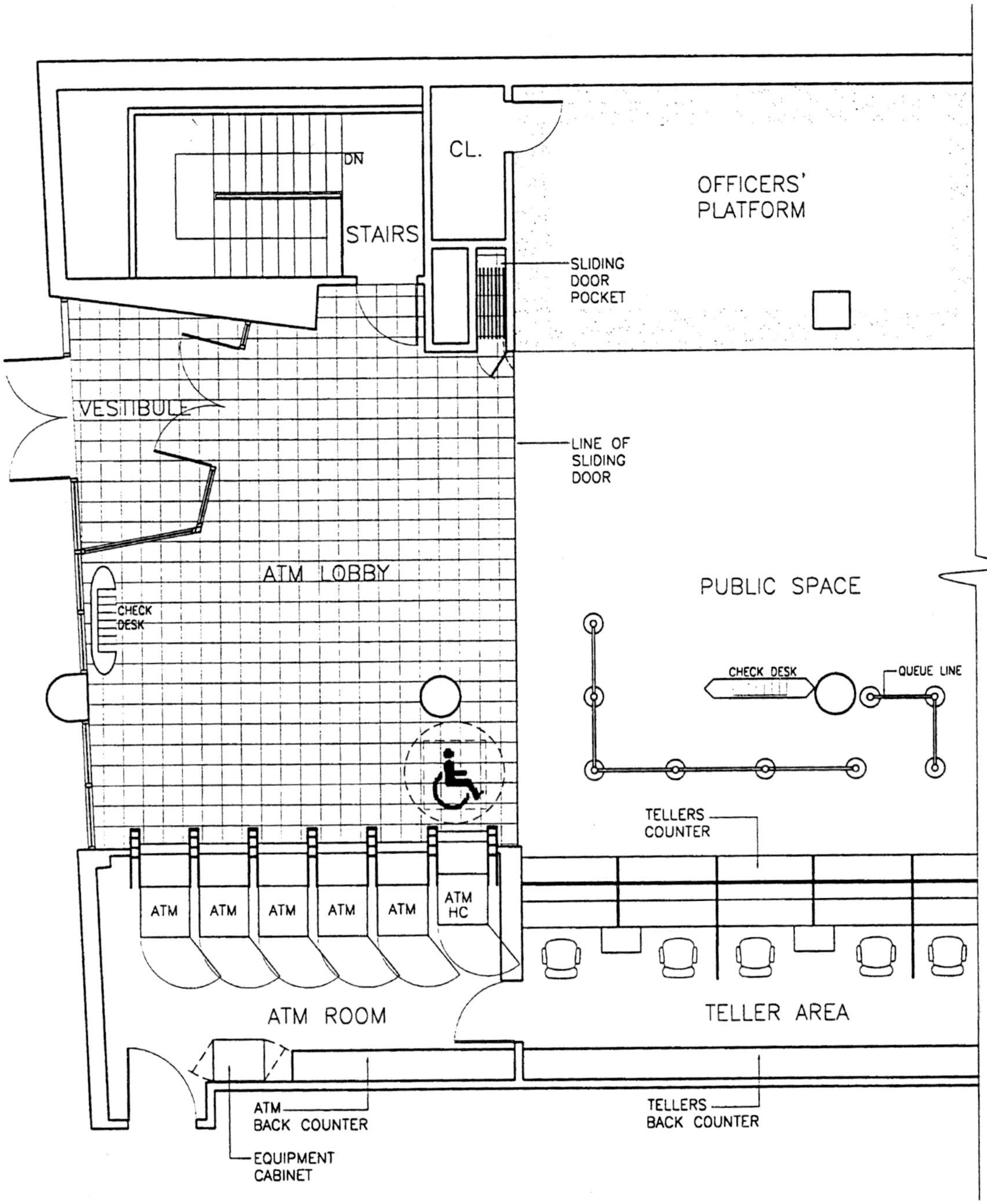

TYPICAL BANKING SPACES–PART PLAN
SCALE 1/8"=1'0"

BRANCH BANKS
Typical Spaces/Teller's Areas

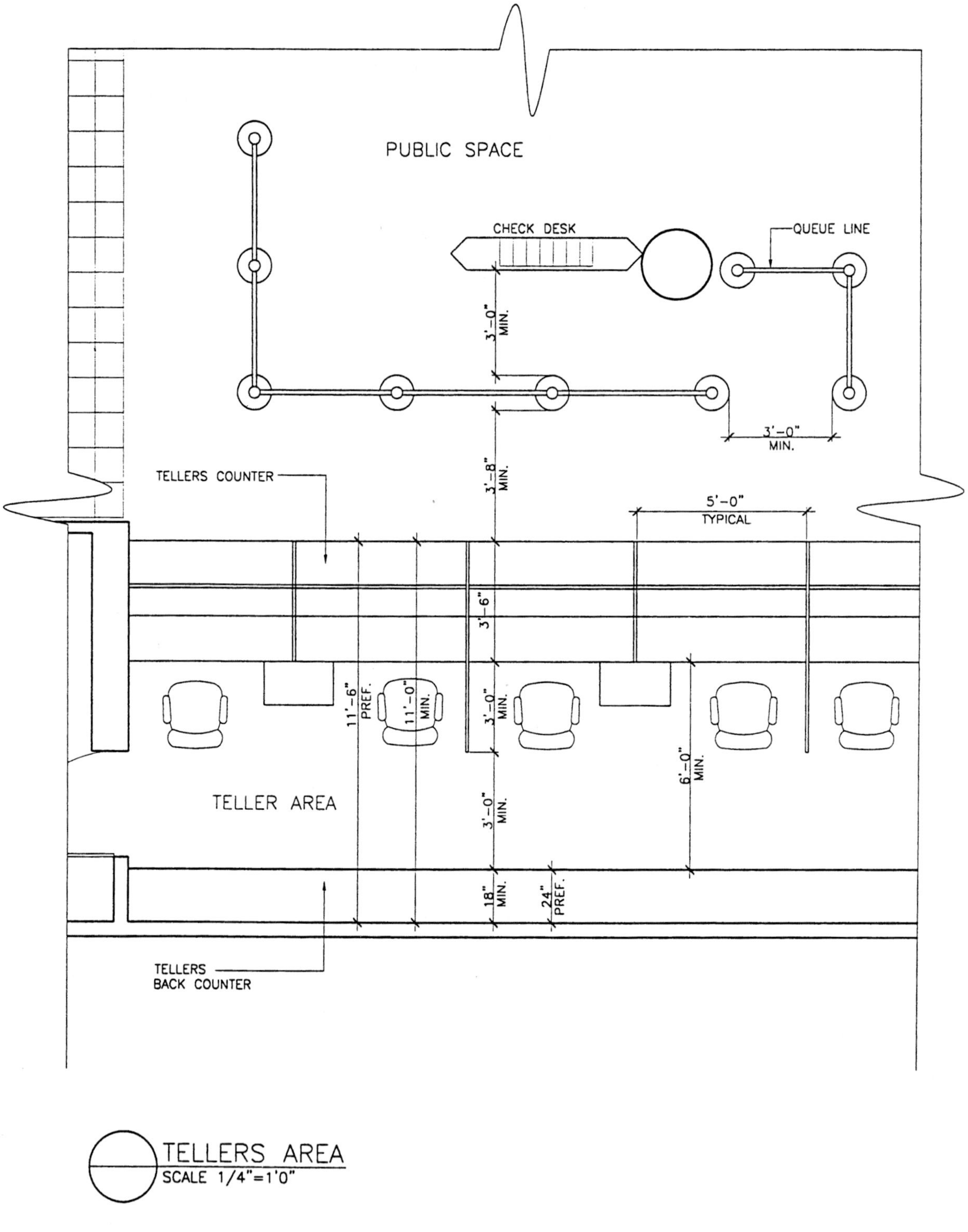

BRANCH BANKS
Typical Spaces/ATM Room and Lobby

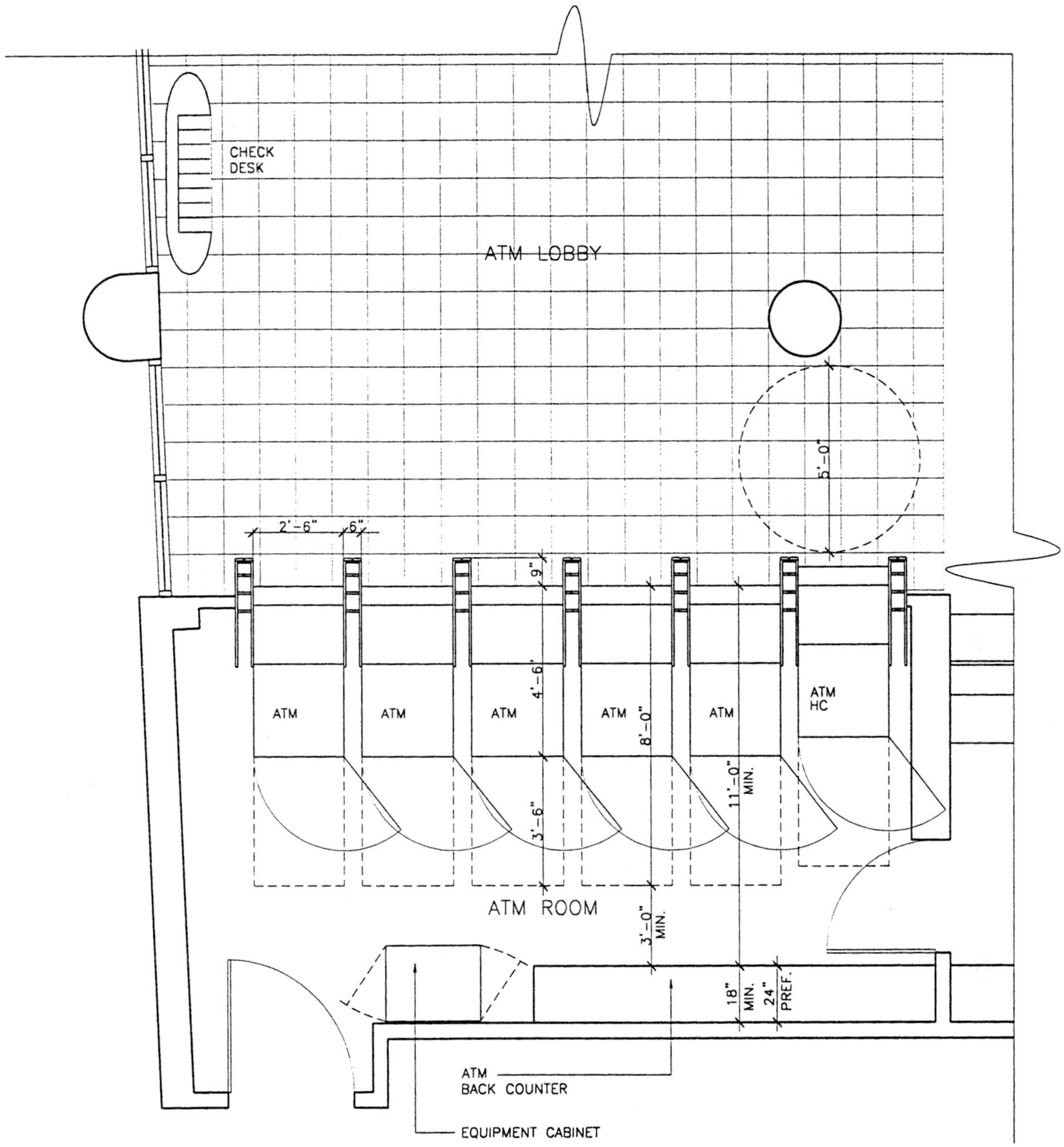

ATM ROOM/LOBBY
SCALE 1/4"=1'0"

BRANCH BANKS

Check Writing Desk/Freestanding Plan Section

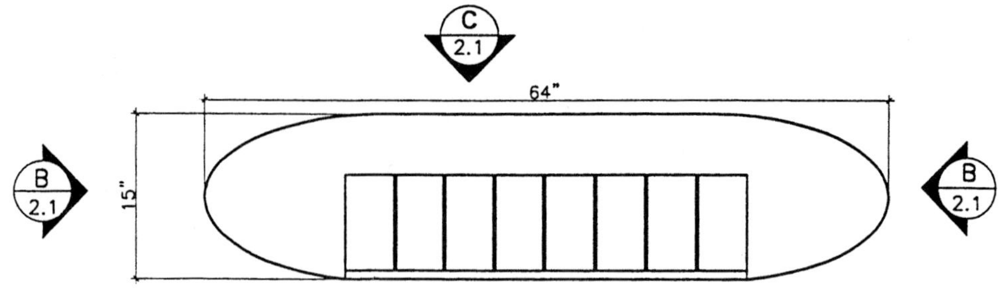

1 / 2.0 CHECKDESK PLAN
SCALE 3/4"=1'-0"

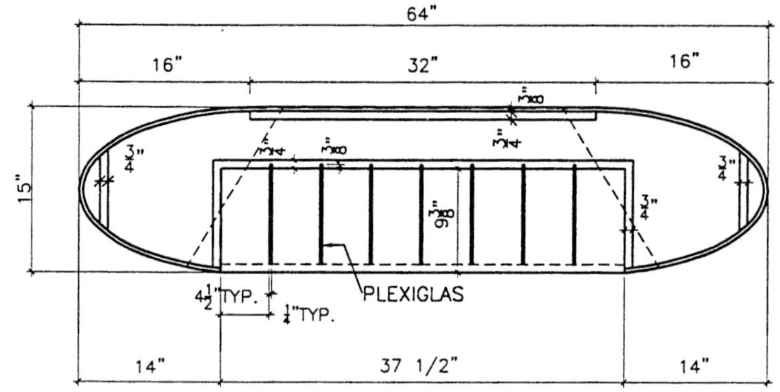

2 / 2.0 CHECKDESK TOP PLAN SECTION
SCALE 3/4"=1'-0"

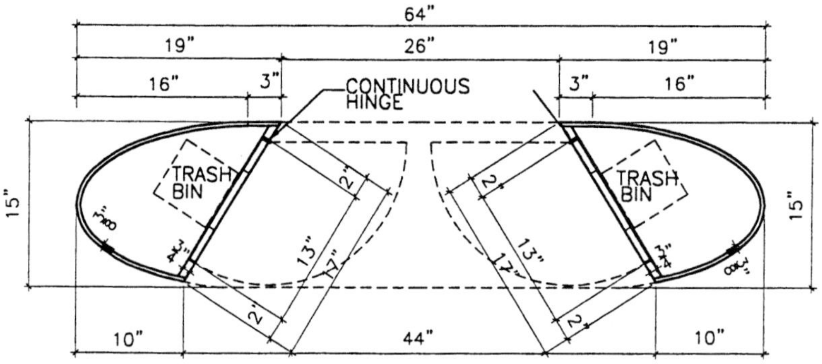

3 / 2.0 CHECKDESK MID PLAN SECTION
SCALE 3/4"=1'-0"

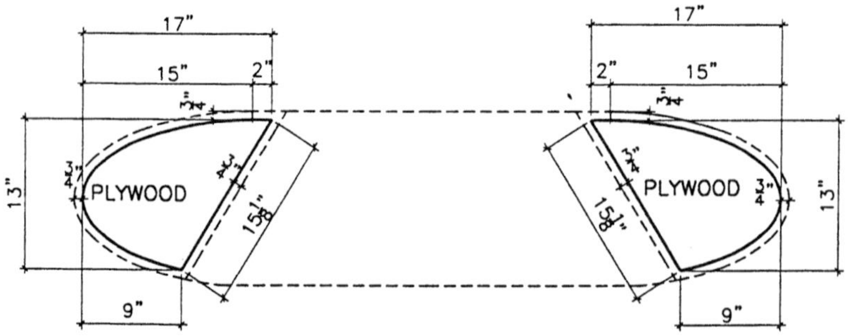

4 / 2.0 CHECKDESK LOWER PLAN SECTION
SCALE 3/4"=1'-0"

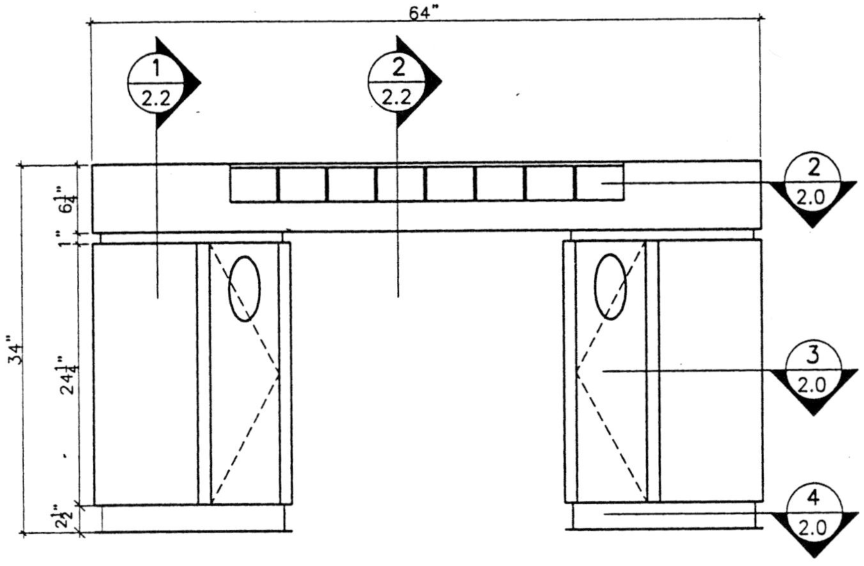

A 2.1 CHECKDESK FRONT ELEVATION
SCALE 3/4"=1'-0"

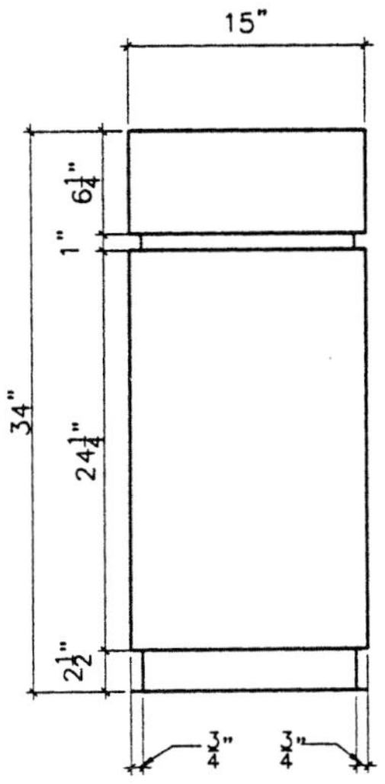

B 2.1 SIDE ELEVATION
SCALE 3/4"=1'-0"

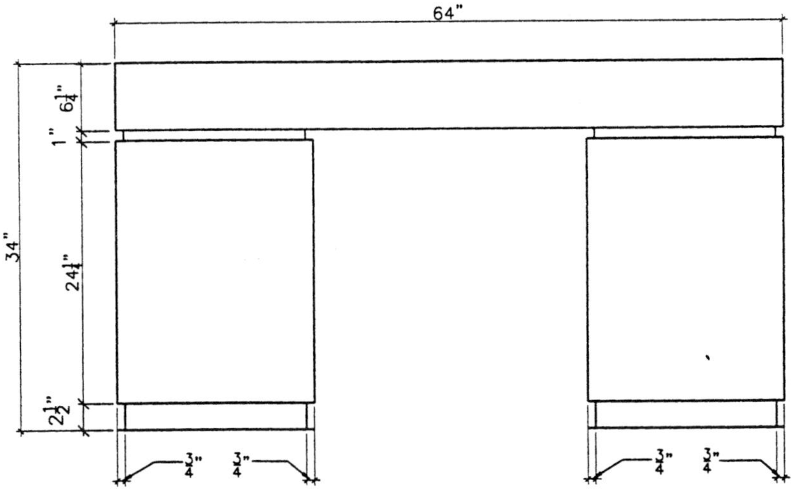

C 2.1 CHECKDESK REAR ELEVATION
SCALE 3/4"=1'-0"

BRANCH BANKS

Check Writing Desk/Freestanding/Sections and Elevations

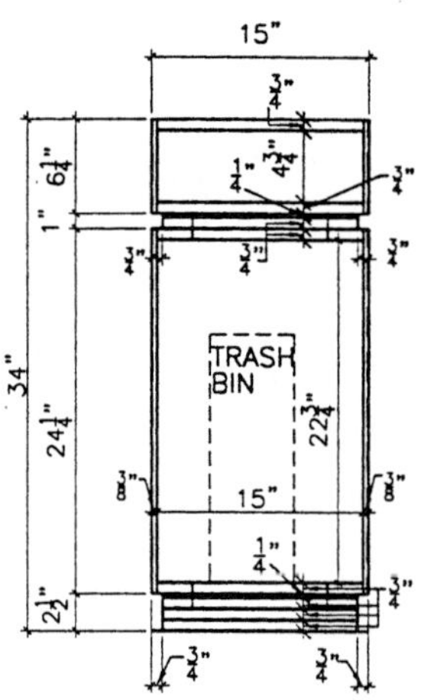

1 / 2.2 CHECKDESK VERTICAL SECTION
SCALE 3/4"=1'-0"

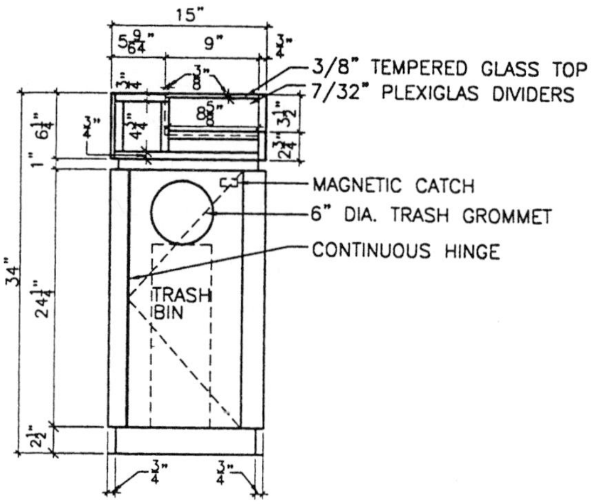

2 / 2.2 CHECKDESK VERTICAL SECTION
SCALE 3/4"=1'-0"

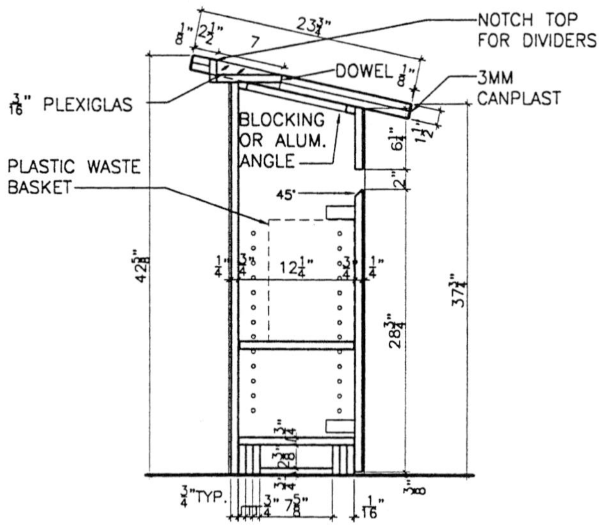

1 / 2.3 CHECKDESK VERTICAL SECTION
SCALE 3/4"=1'-0"

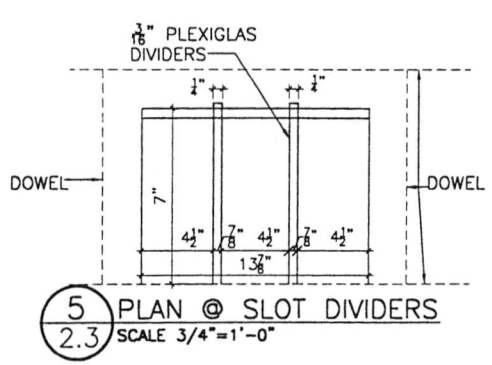

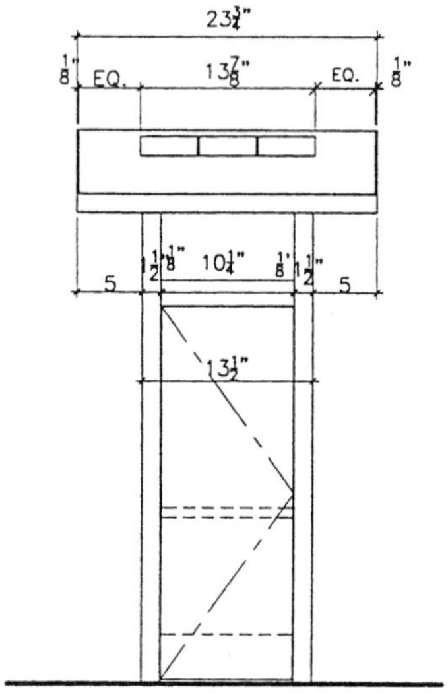

2 / 2.3 CHECKDESK ELEVATION
SCALE 3/4"=1'-0"

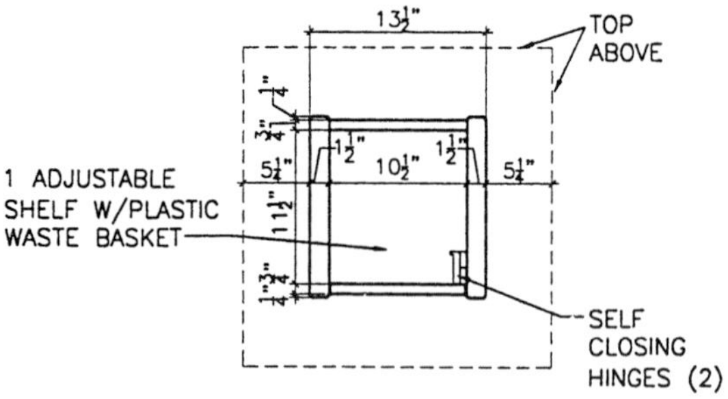

3 / 2.3 CHECKDESK PLAN SECTION
SCALE 3/4"=1'-0"

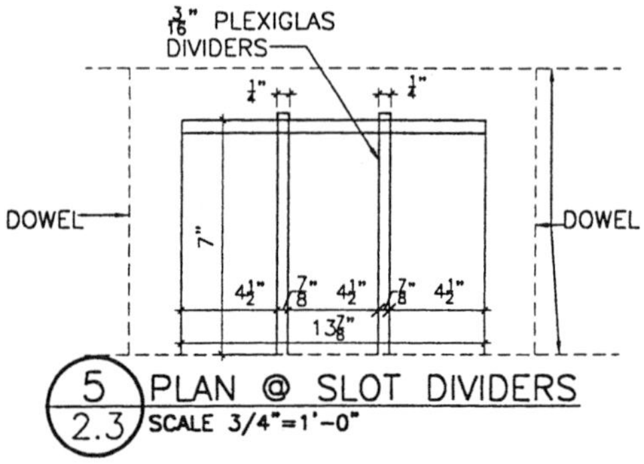

5 / 2.3 PLAN @ SLOT DIVIDERS
SCALE 3/4"=1'-0"

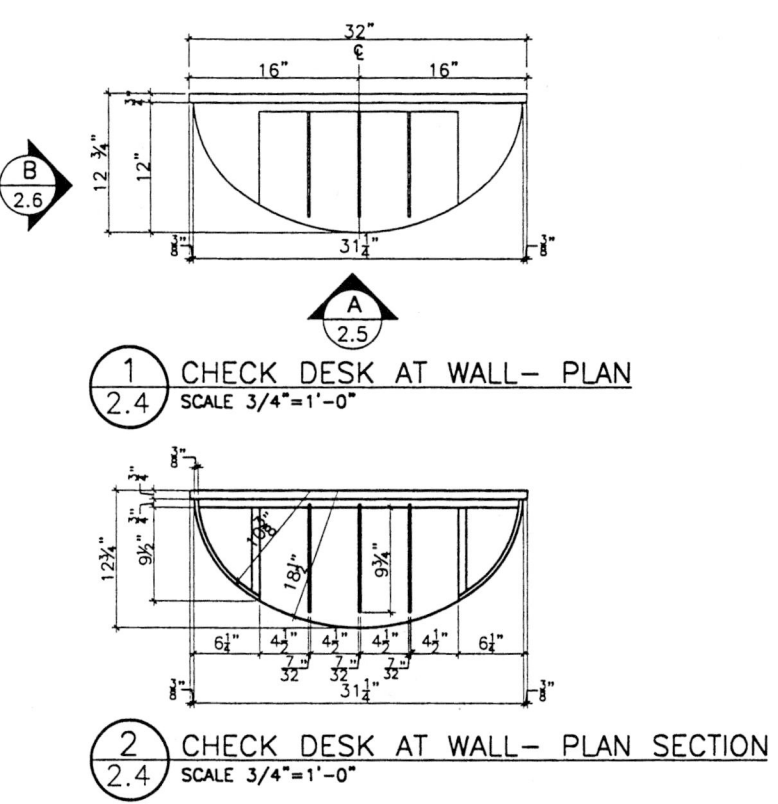

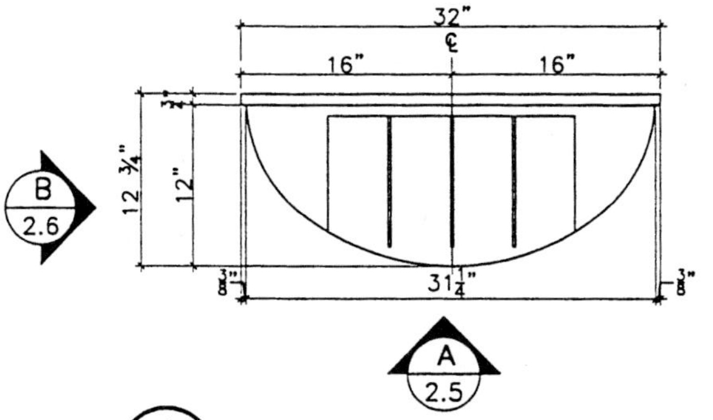

1 / 2.4 CHECK DESK AT WALL– PLAN
SCALE 3/4"=1'-0"

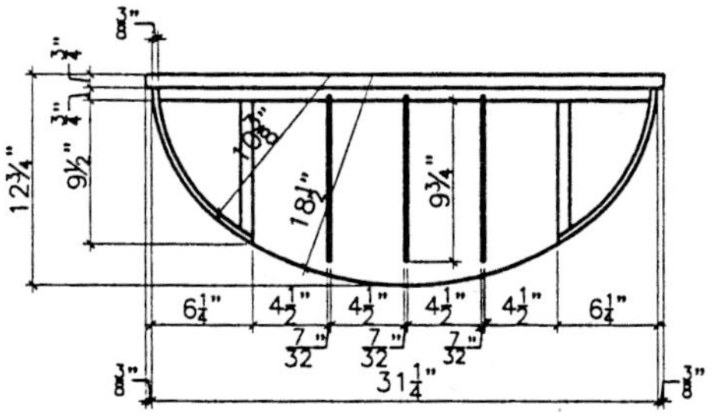

2 / 2.4 CHECK DESK AT WALL– PLAN SECTION
SCALE 3/4"=1'-0"

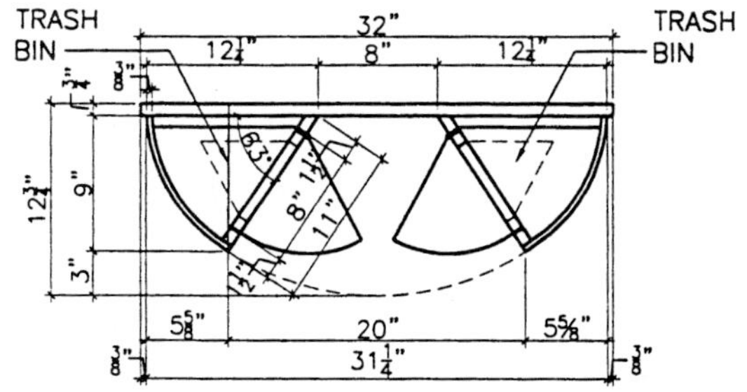

3 / 2.4 CHECK DESK AT WALL– PLAN SECTION
SCALE 3/4"=1'-0"

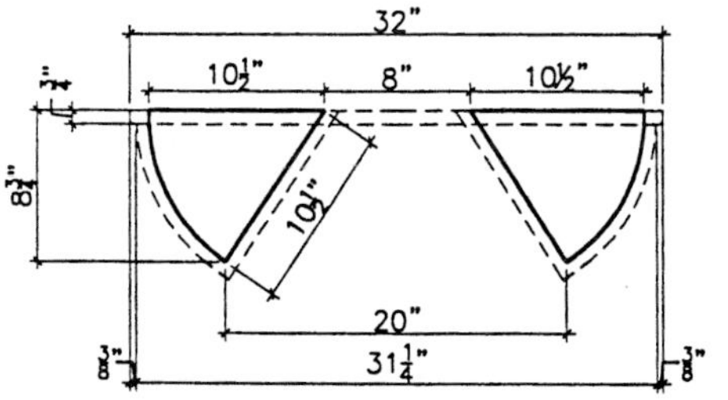

4 / 2.4 CHECK DESK AT WALL– PLAN SECTION
SCALE 3/4"=1'-0"

BRANCH BANKS

Check Writing Desk/At Wall/Elevations

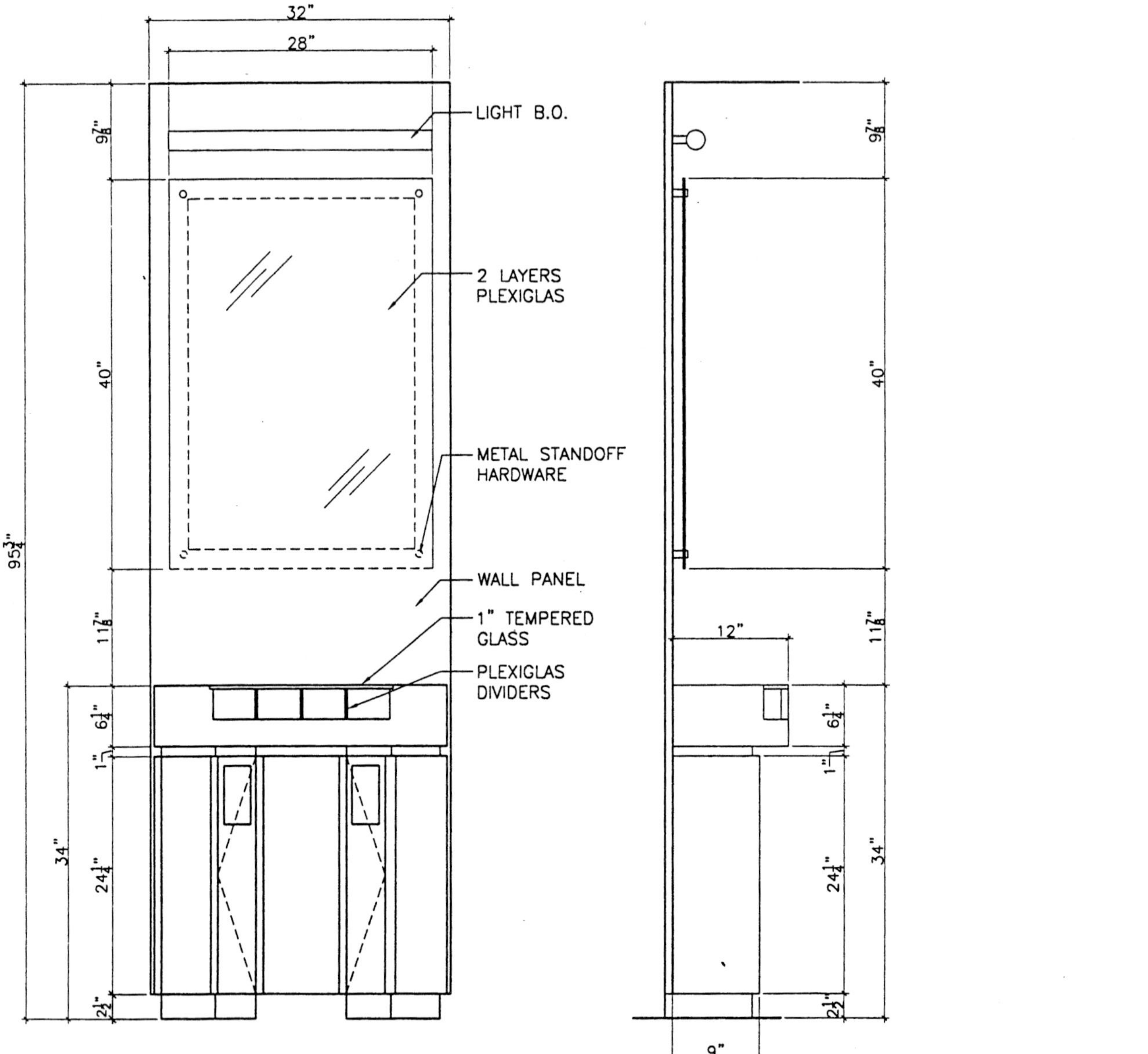

A 2.5 CHECK DESK AT WALL–ELEVATION
SCALE 3/4"=1'–0"

B 2.6 CHECK DESK AT WALL–ELEVATION
SCALE 3/4"=1'–0"

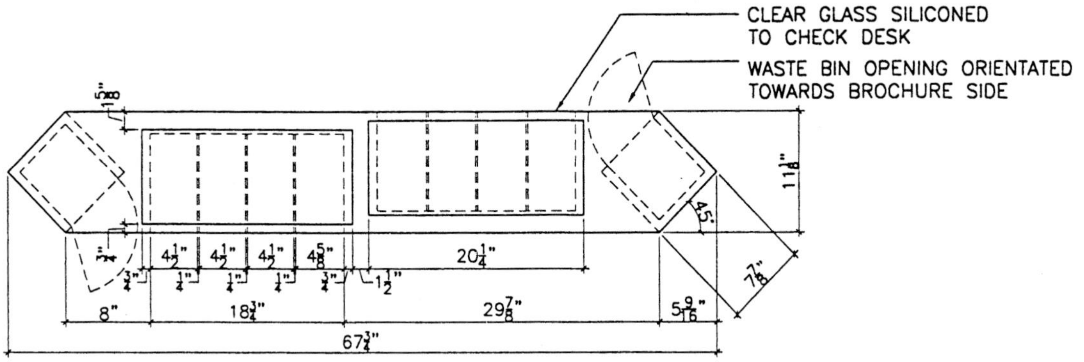

1 / 2.7 CHECK DESK LINEAR TWO SIDED– PLAN
SCALE 3/4"=1'-0"

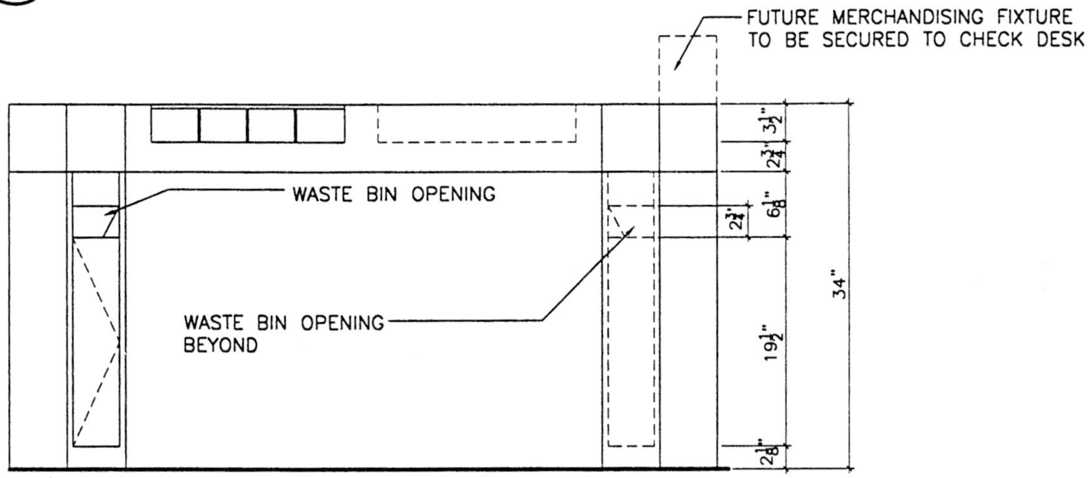

A / 2.7 CHECK DESK LINEAR TWO SIDED– FRONT ELEVATION
SCALE 3/4"=1'-0"

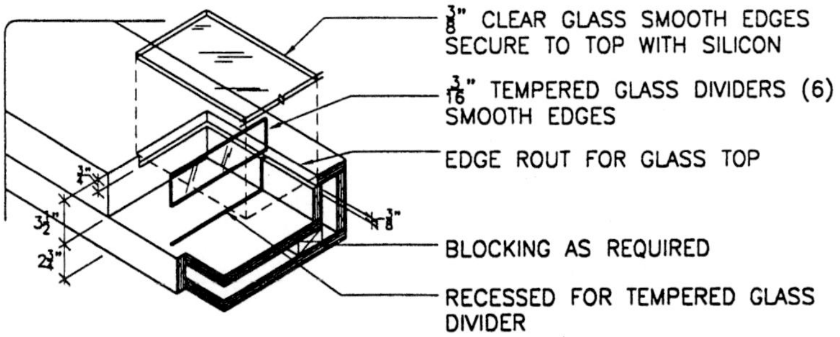

2 / 2.7 CHECK DESK LINEAR TWO SIDED– ISOMETRIC NTS

BRANCH BANKS
Check Writing Desk

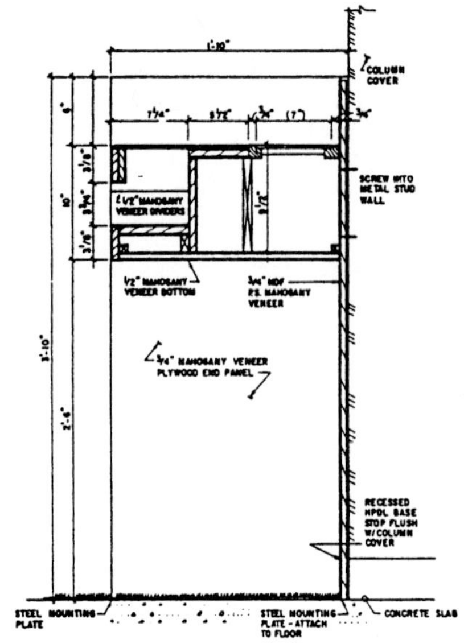

VERTICAL SECTION AT CHECK STAND

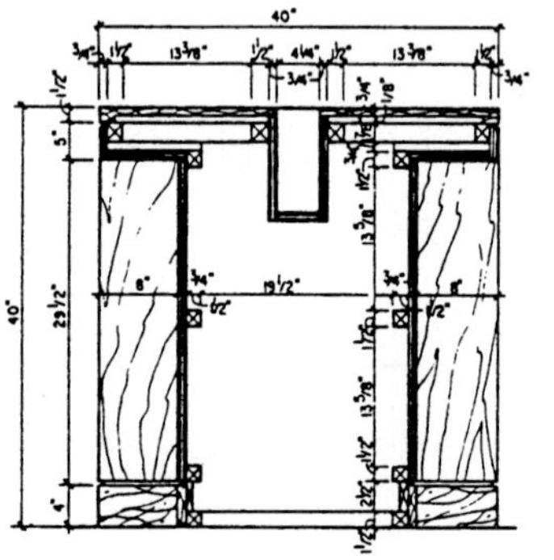

VERTICAL SECTION AT CHECK DESK

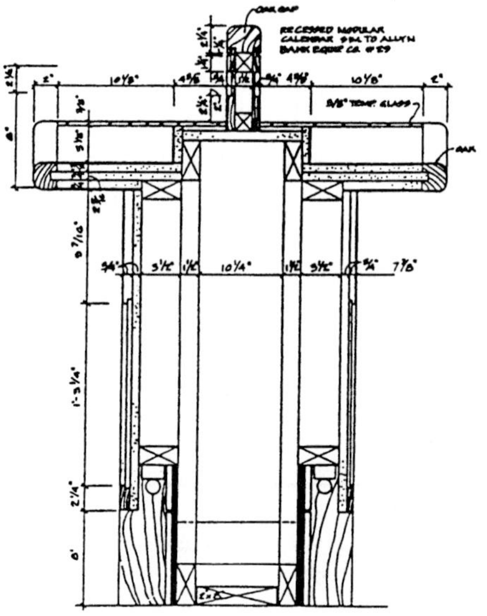

SECTION AT CHECK DESK

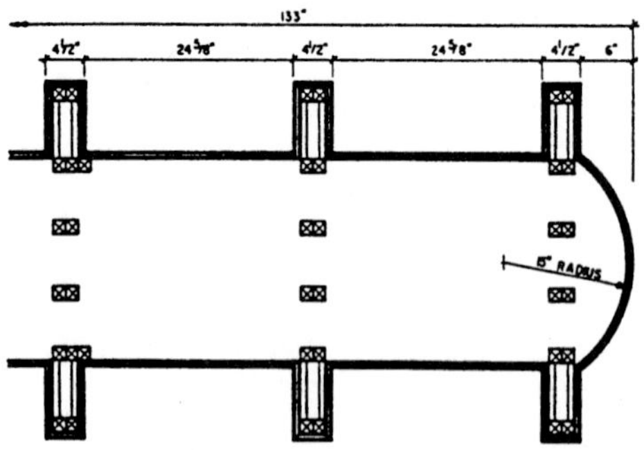

HALF PLAN THRU CHECK DESK

BRANCH BANKS

Single Teller's Station/Plan Section

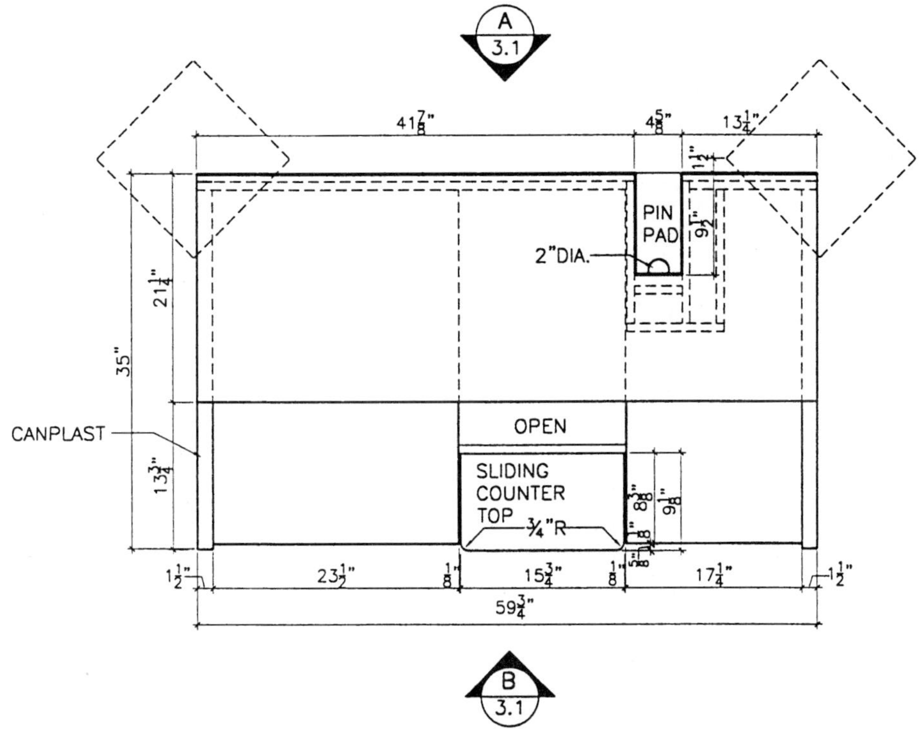

1/3.0 SINGLE TELLER STATION—PLAN SECTION
SCALE 3/4"=1'-0"

BRANCH BANKS
Single Teller's Station/Elevations

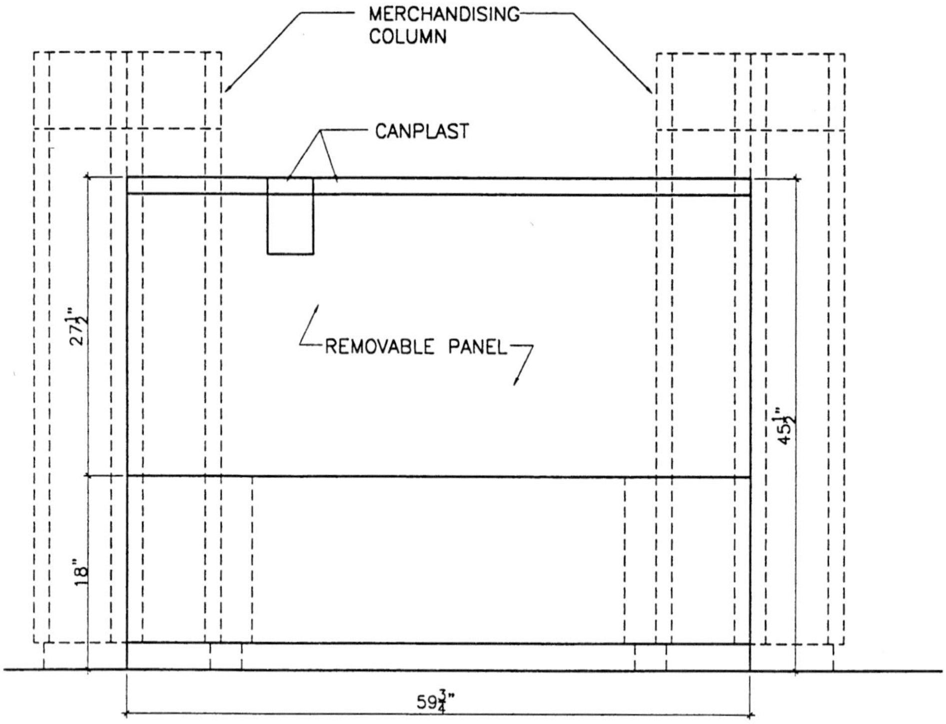

A/3.1 SINGLE TELLER STATION–ELEVATION
SCALE 3/4"=1'-0"

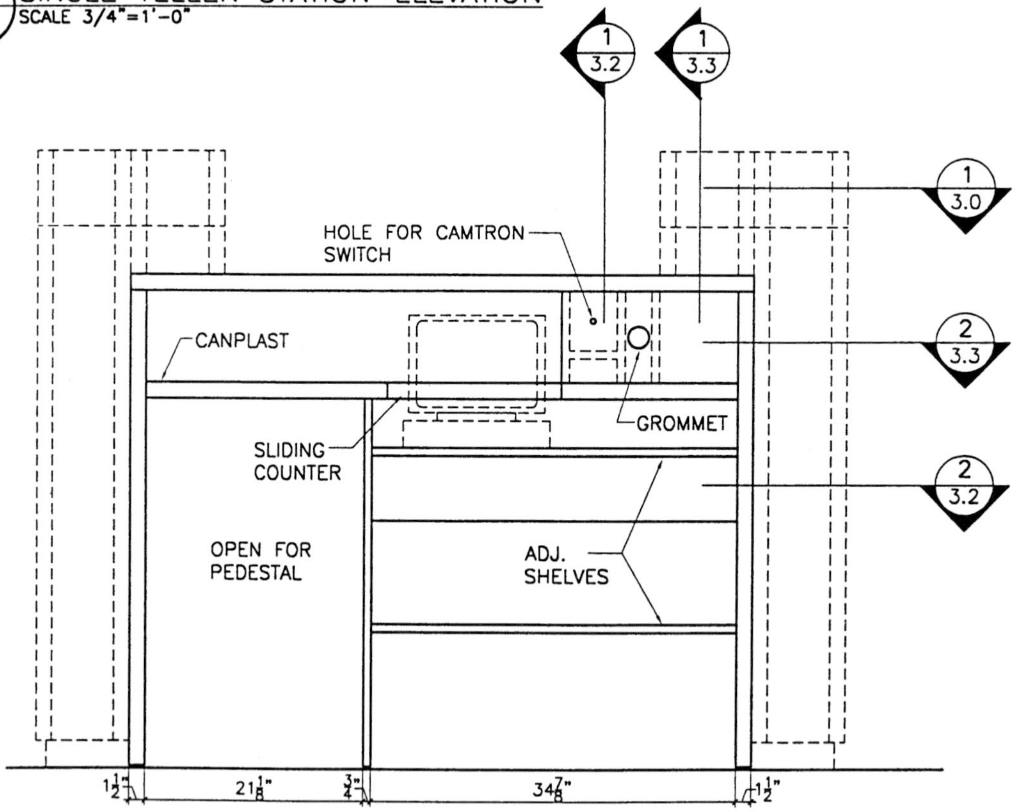

B/3.1 SINGLE TELLER STATION–ELEVATION
SCALE 3/4"=1'-0"

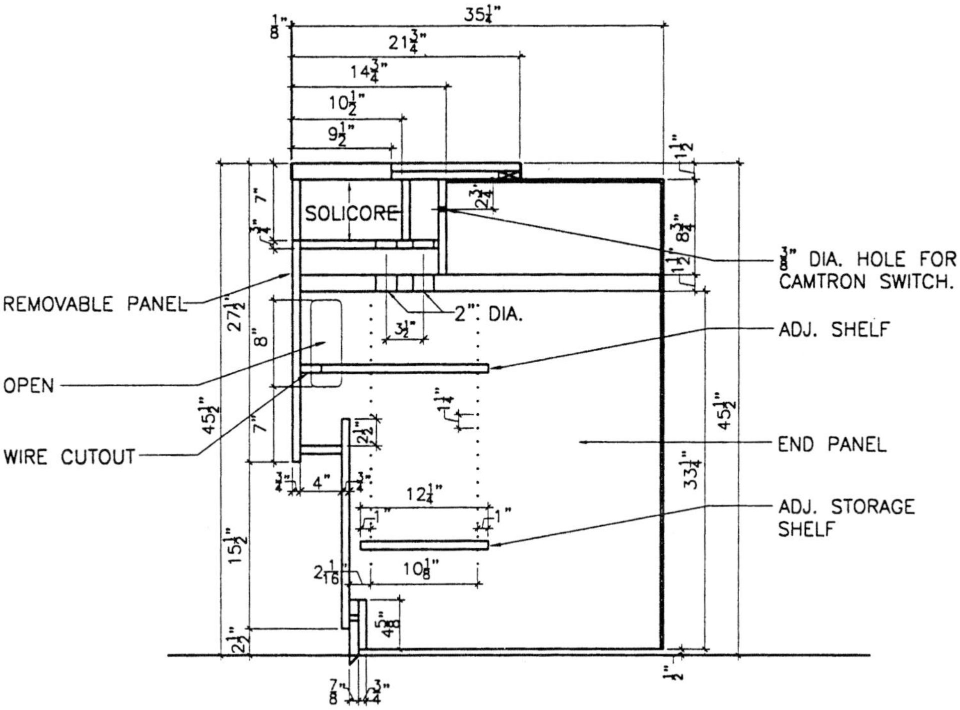

1 / 3.2 SINGLE TELLER STATION– VERTICAL SECTION
SCALE 3/4"=1'-0"

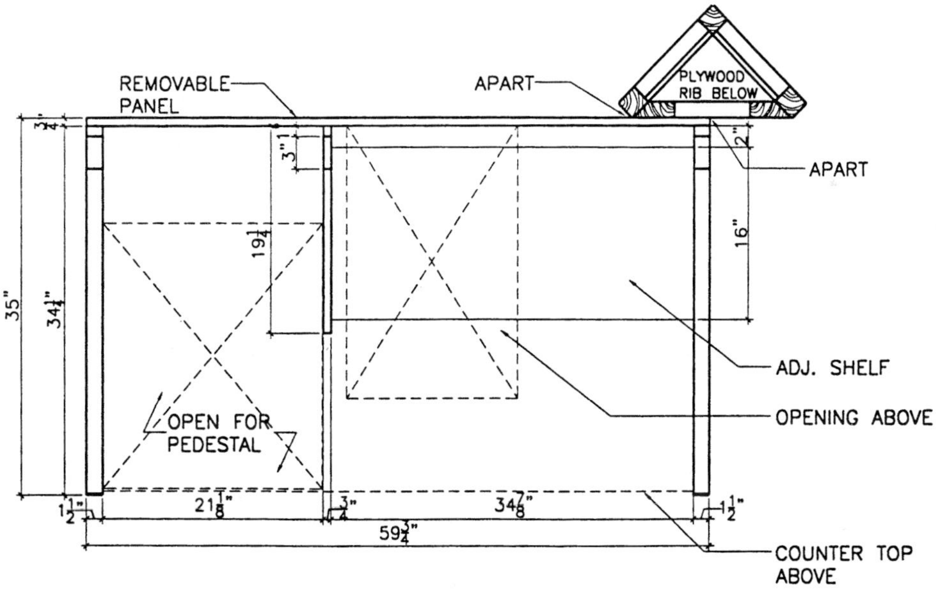

2 / 3.2 SINGLE TELLER STATION–PLAN SECTION
SCALE 3/4"=1'-0"

BRANCH BANKS
Single Teller's Station/Sections

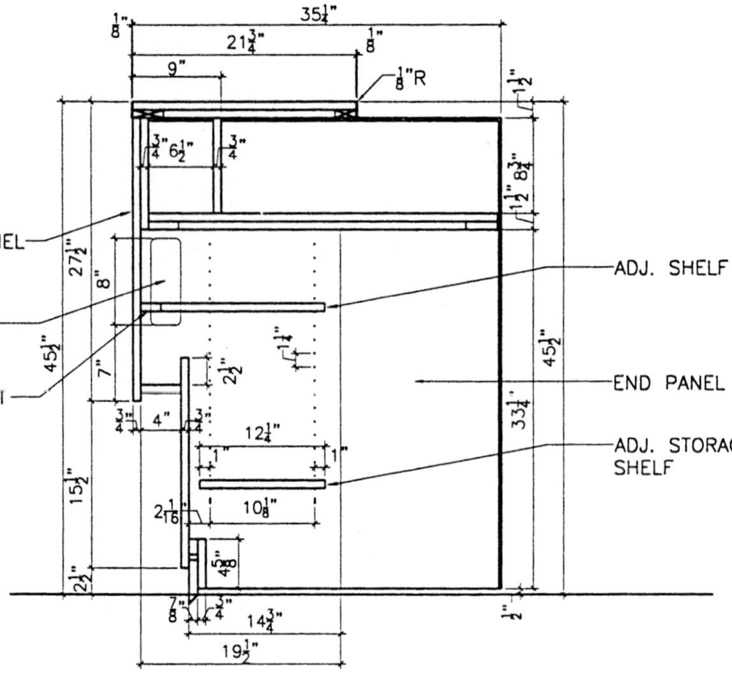

1/3.3 SINGLE TELLER STATION– VERTICAL SECTION
SCALE 3/4"=1'-0"

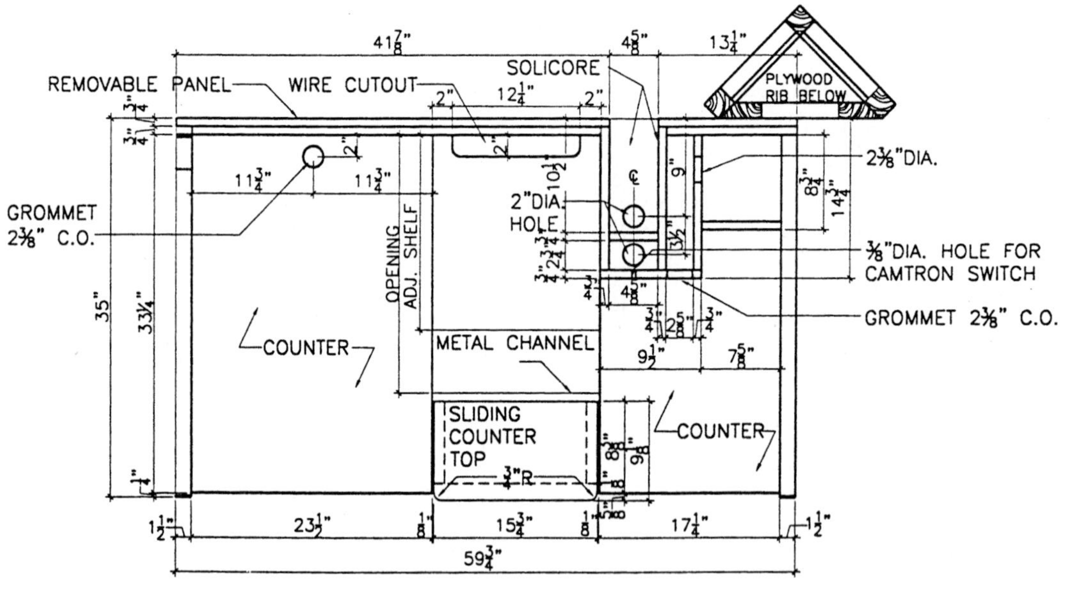

2/3.3 SINGLE TELLER STATION–PLAN SECTION
SCALE: 3/4"=1'-0"

BRANCH BANKS

Double Teller's Station/Plan Section

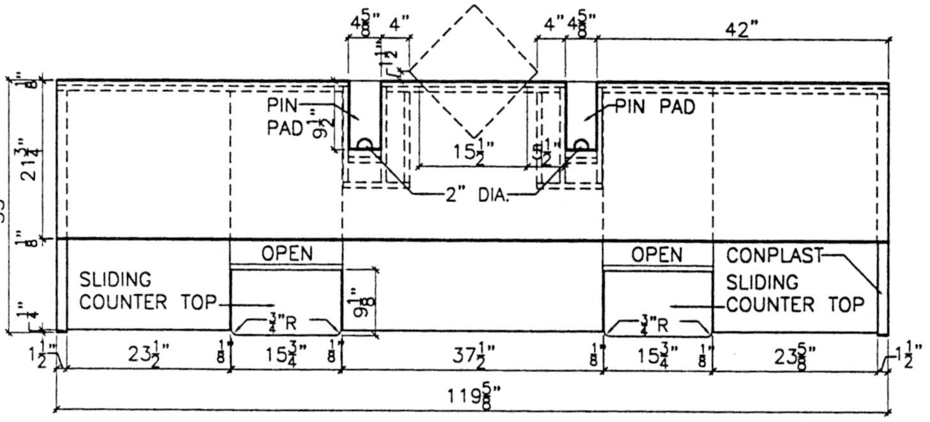

1 / 3.4 DOUBLE TELLER STATION–PLAN SECTION
SCALE 1/2"=1'0"

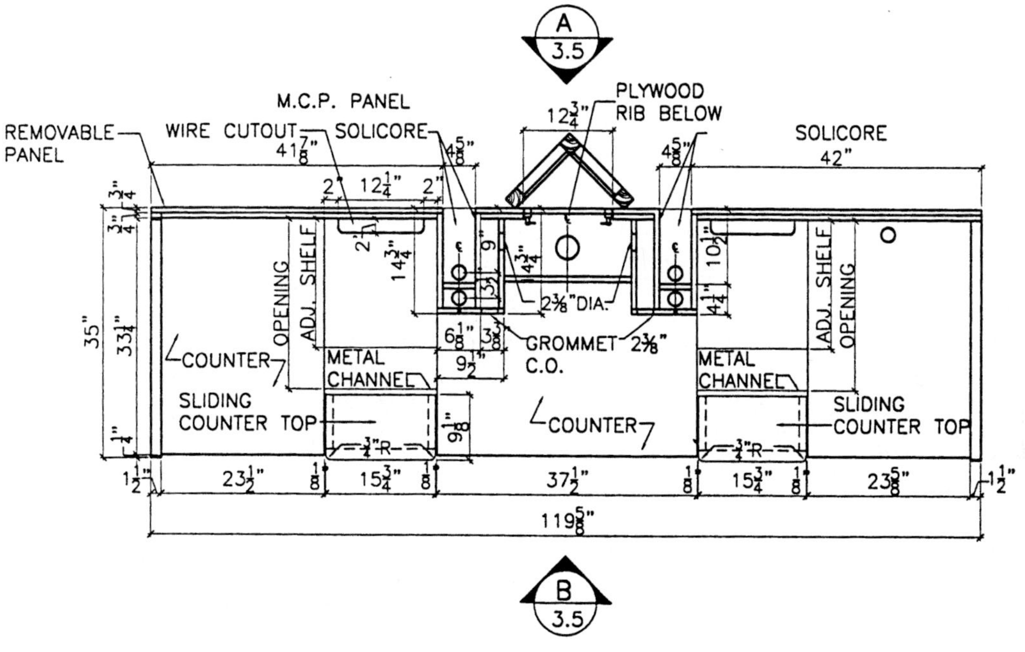

2 / 3.4 DOUBLE TELLER STATION–PLAN SECTION
SCALE 1/2"=1'0"

BRANCH BANKS

Double Teller's Station/Elevations

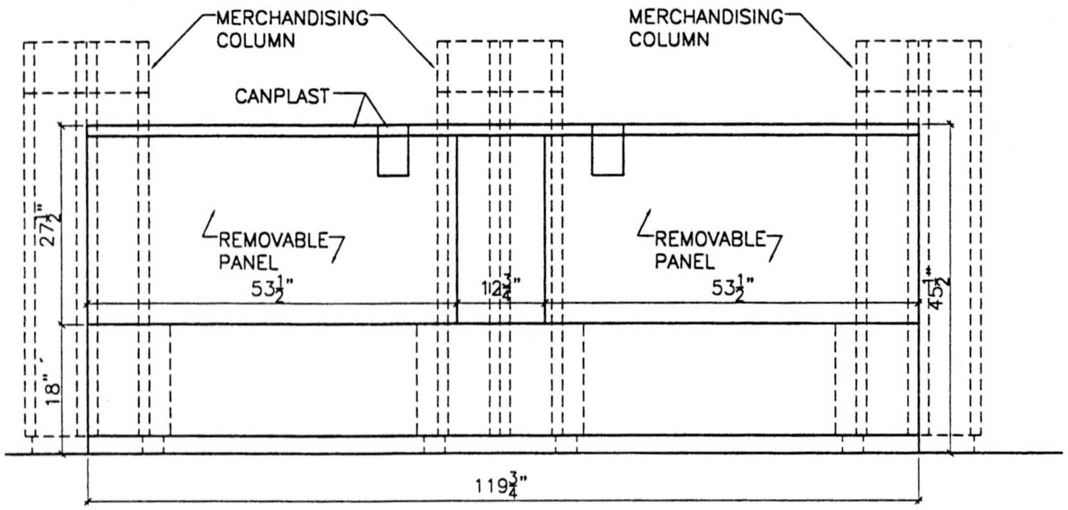

A/3.5 DOUBLE TELLER STATION–ELEVATION
SCALE 1/2"=1'0"

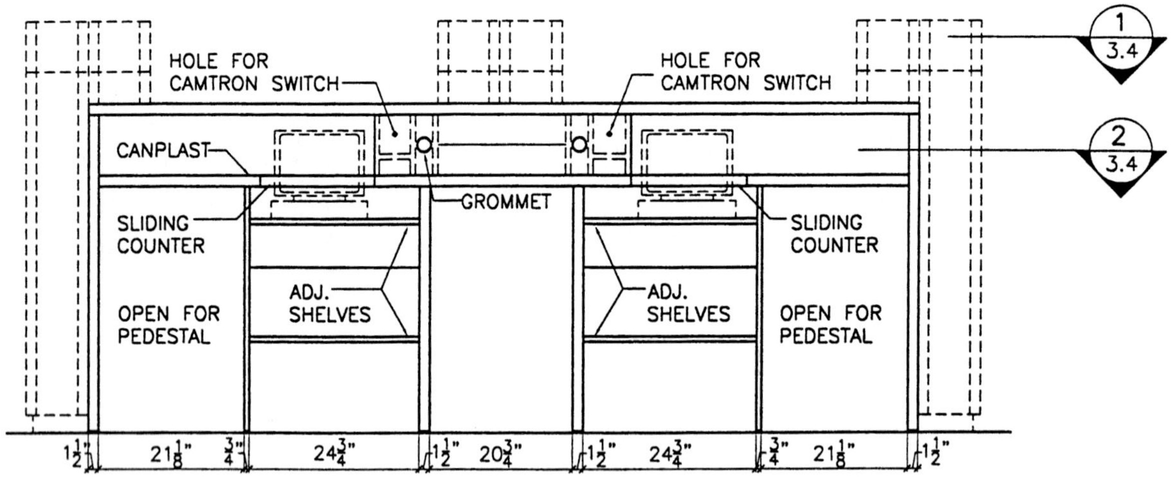

B/3.5 DOUBLE TELLER STATION–ELEVATION
SCALE 1/2"=1'0"

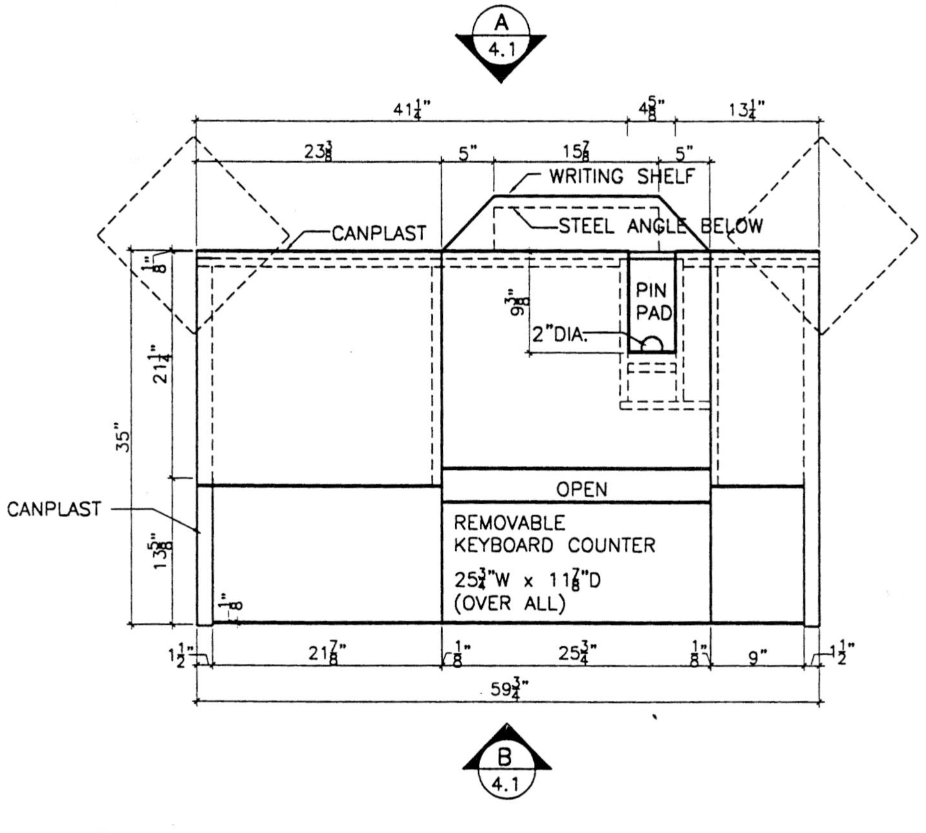

1 / 4.0 SINGLE HANDICAPPED TELLER STATION–PLAN SECTION
SCALE 3/4"=1'-0"

BRANCH BANKS

Single Accessible Teller's Station/Elevations

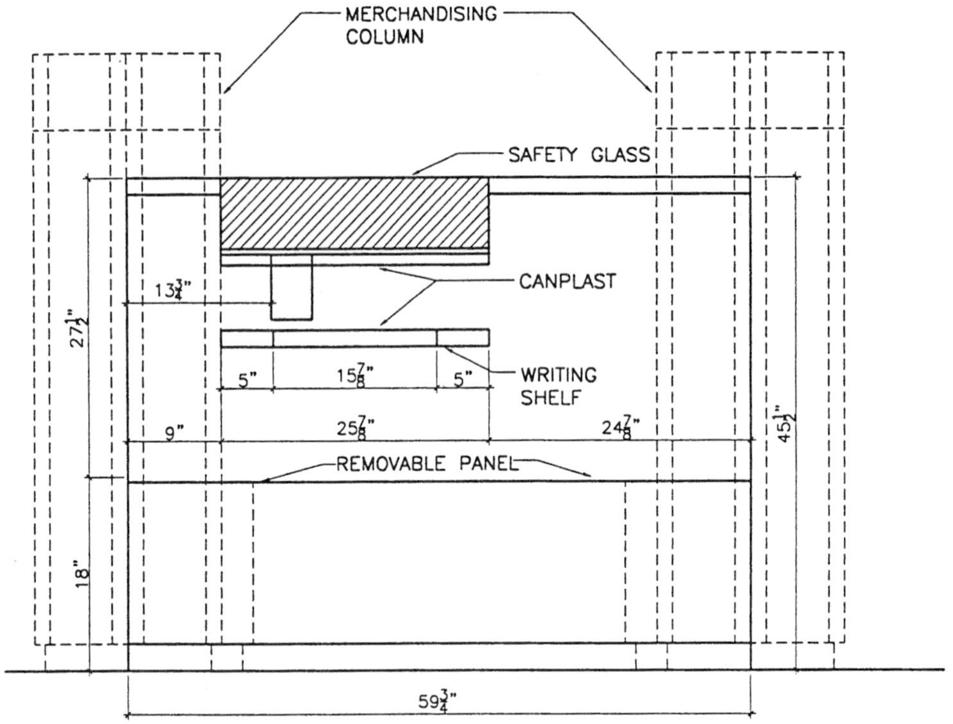

A / 4.1 SINGLE HANDICAPPED TELLER STATION– ELEVATION
SCALE 3/4"=1'-0"

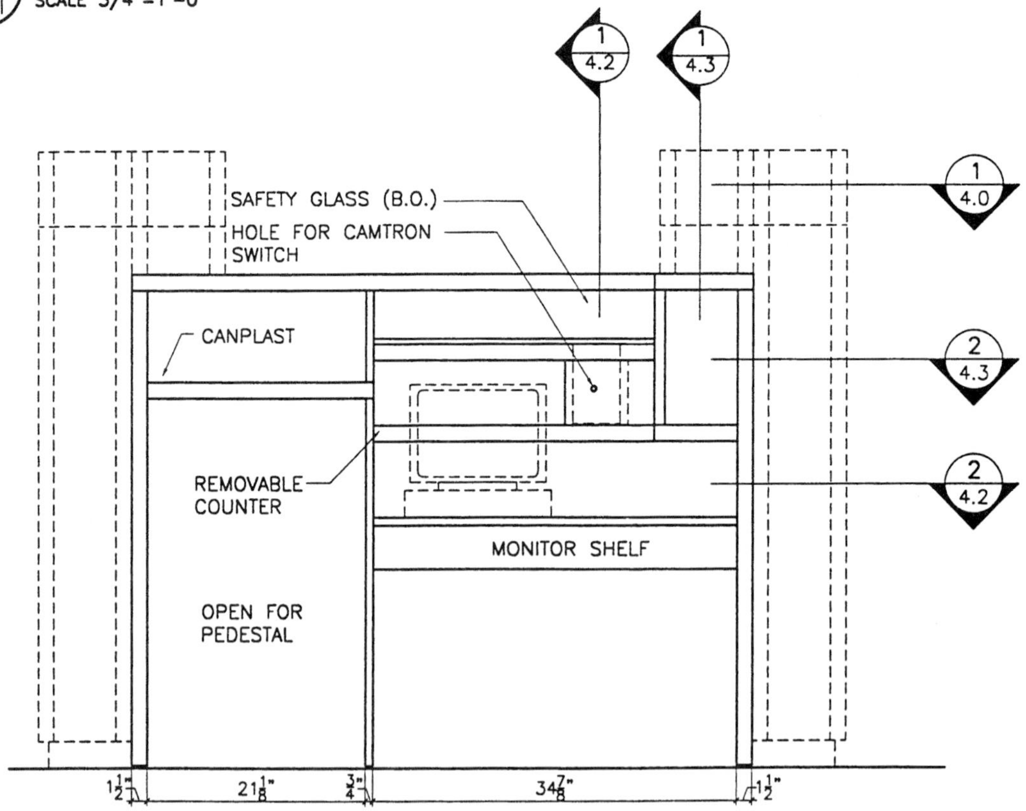

B / 4.1 SINGLE HANDICAPPED TELLER STATION– ELEVATION
SCALE 3/4"=1'-0"

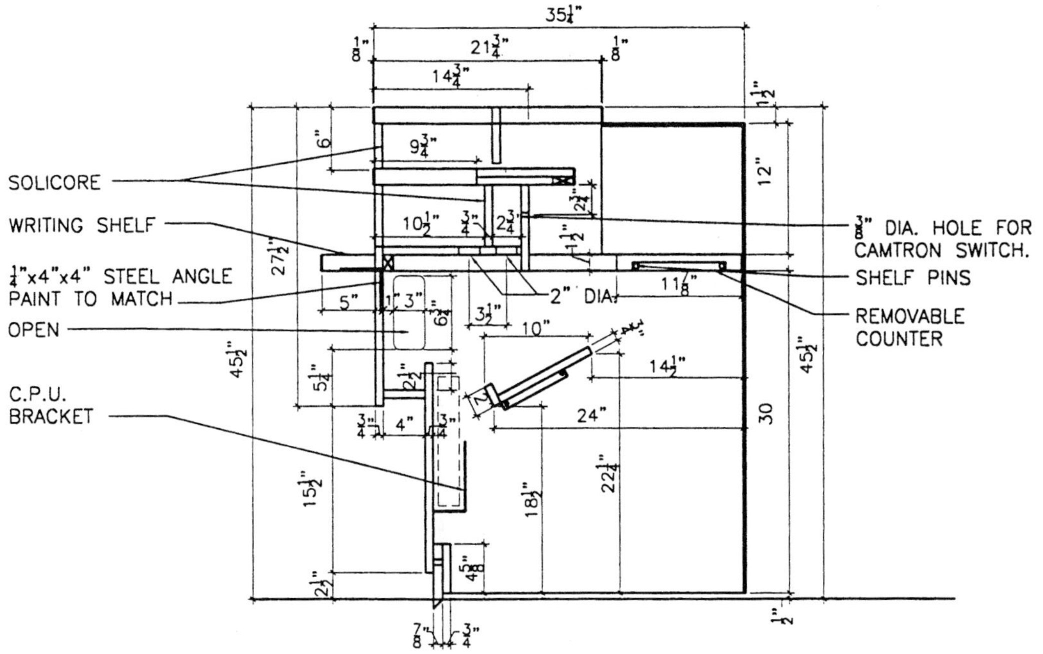

1 / 4.2 SINGLE HANDICAPPED TELLER STATION– VERTICAL SECTION
SCALE 3/4"=1'-0"

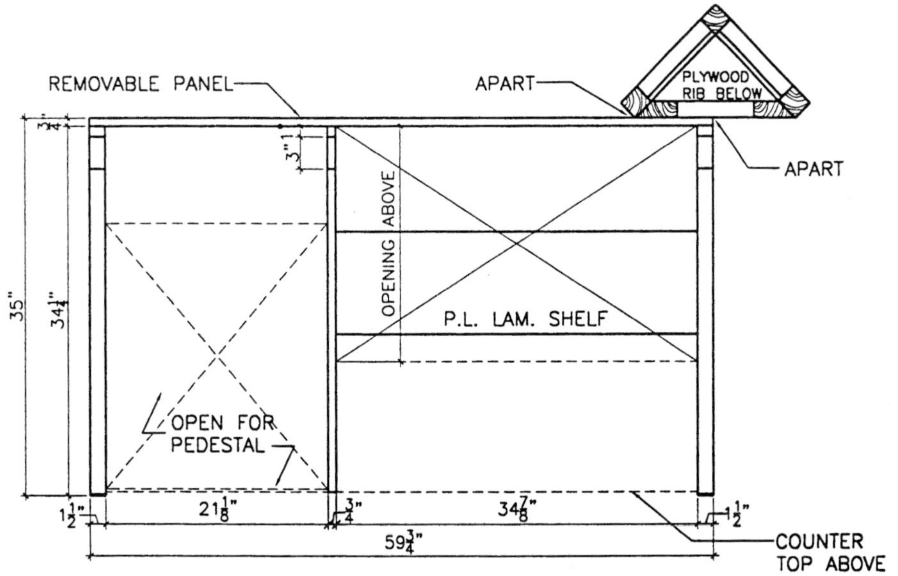

2 / 4.2 SINGLE HANDICAPPED TELLER STATION–PLAN SECTION
SCALE 3/4"=1'-0"

BRANCH BANKS

Single Accessible Teller's Station/Sections

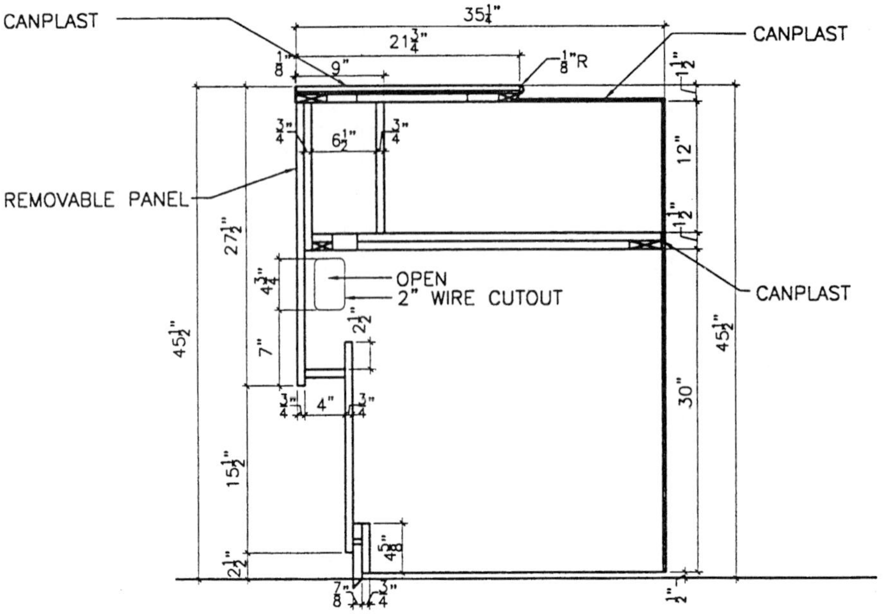

1 / 4.3 SINGLE HANDICAPPED TELLER STATION– VERTICAL SECTION

SCALE 3/4"=1'-0"

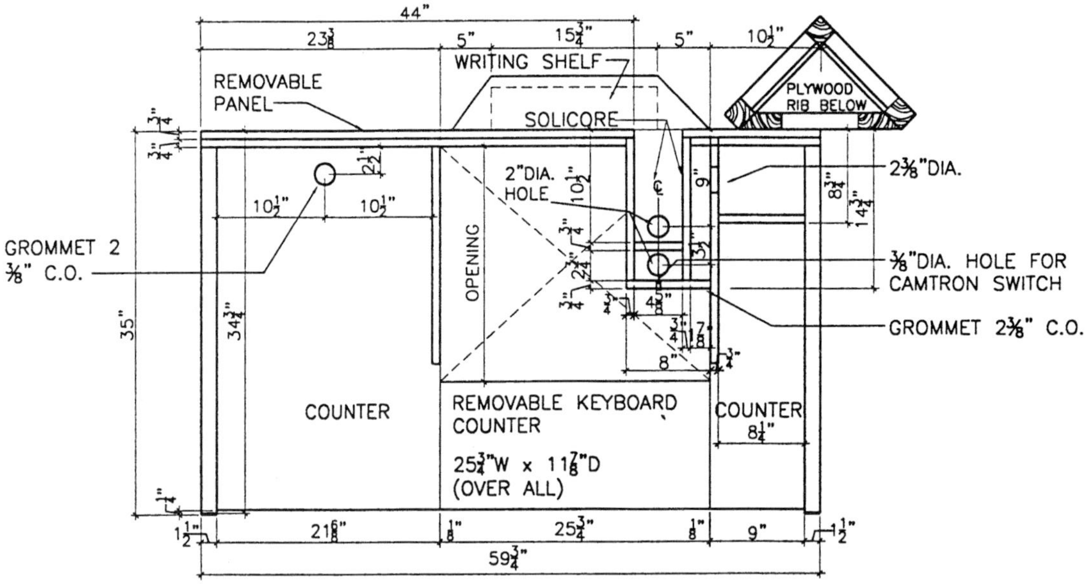

2 / 4.3 SINGLE HANDICAPPED TELLER STATION–PLAN SECTION

SCALE 3/4"=1'-0"

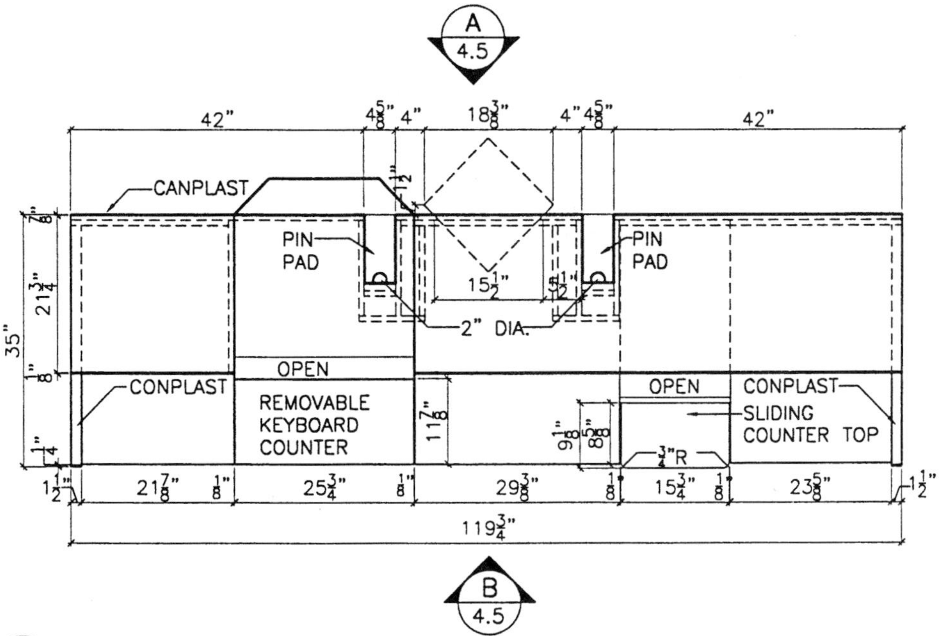

1 / 4.4 DOUBLE HANDICAPPED TELLER STATION– PLAN SECTION
SCALE 1/2"=1'-0"

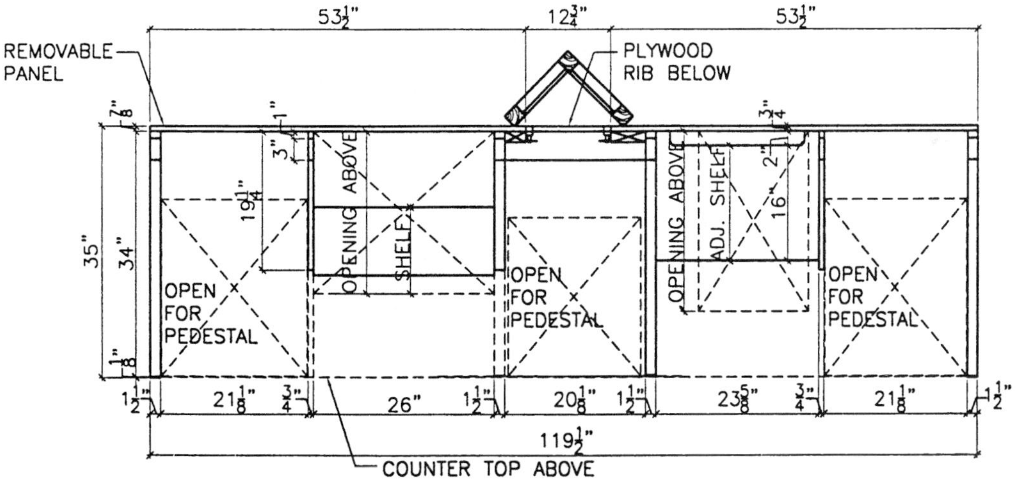

2 / 4.4 DOUBLE HANDICAPPED TELLER STATION– PLAN SECTION
SCALE 1/2"=1'-0"

BRANCH BANKS
Double Accessible Teller's Station/Elevations

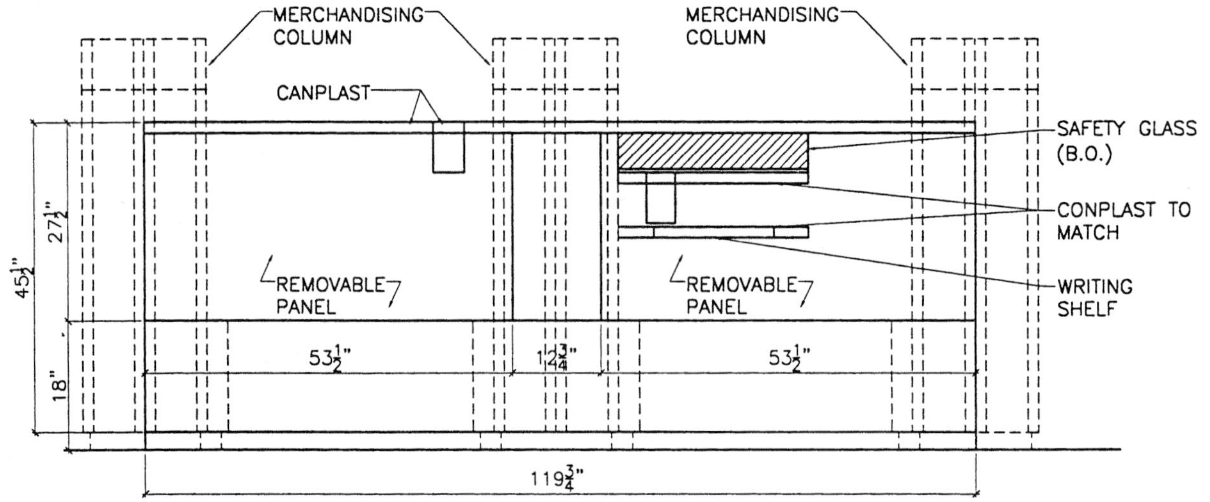

A 4.5 DOUBLE HANDICAPPED TELLER STATION– ELEVATION
SCALE 1/2"=1'-0"

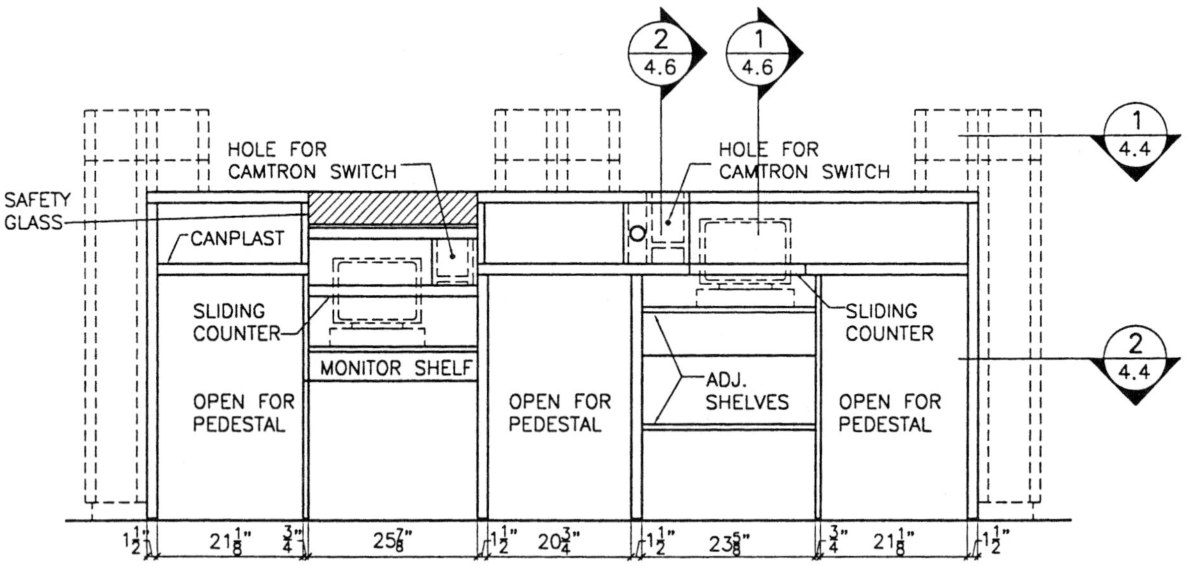

B 4.5 DOUBLE HANDICAPPED TELLER STATION– ELEVATION
SCALE 1/2"=1'-0"

BRANCH BANKS

Double Accessible Teller's Station/Sections

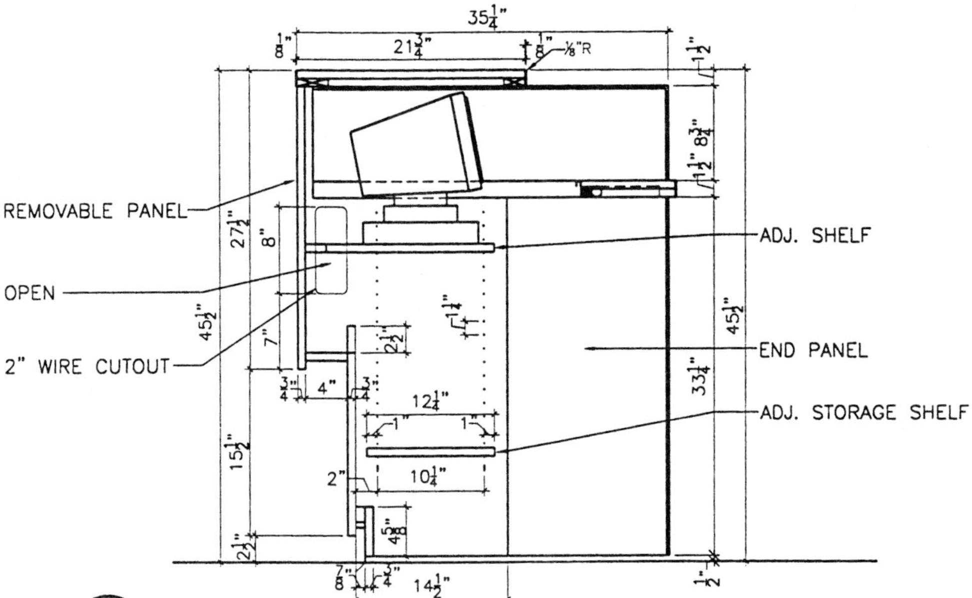

1 / 4.6 DOUBLE HANDICAPPED TELLER STATION—VERTICAL SECTION
SCALE 3/4"=1'-0"

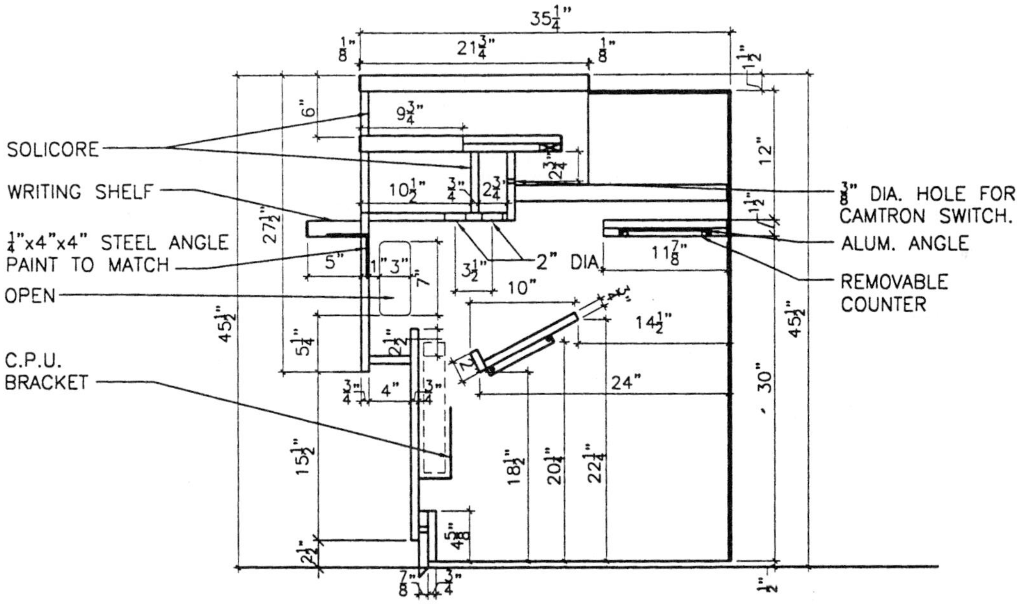

2 / 4.6 DOUBLE HANDICAPPED TELLER STATION—VERTICAL SECTION
SCALE 3/4"=1'-0"

BRANCH BANKS
Teller's Stations

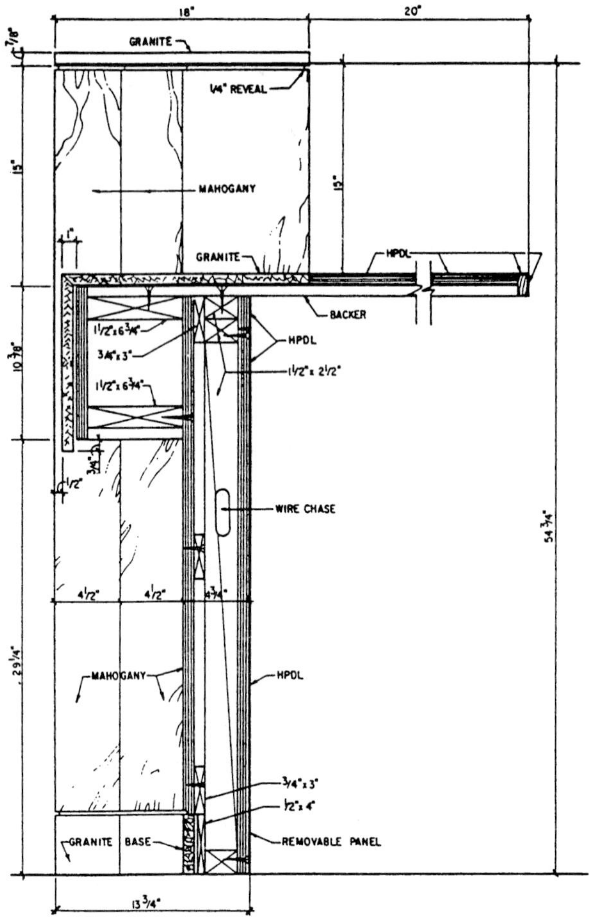

VERTICAL SECTION-TELLERS UNITS

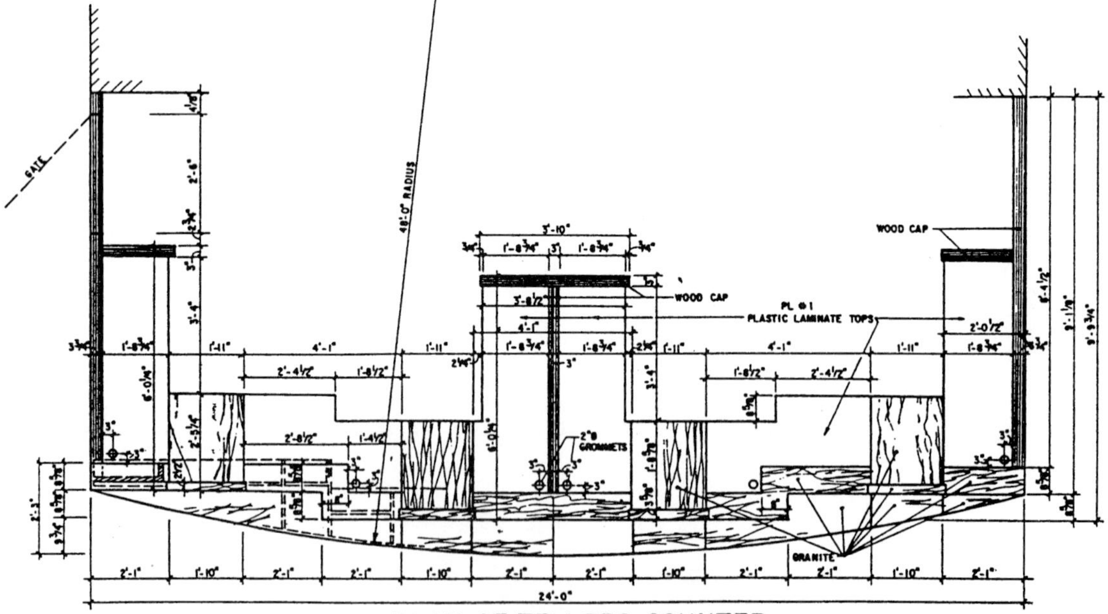

PLAN OF TELLERS COUNTER

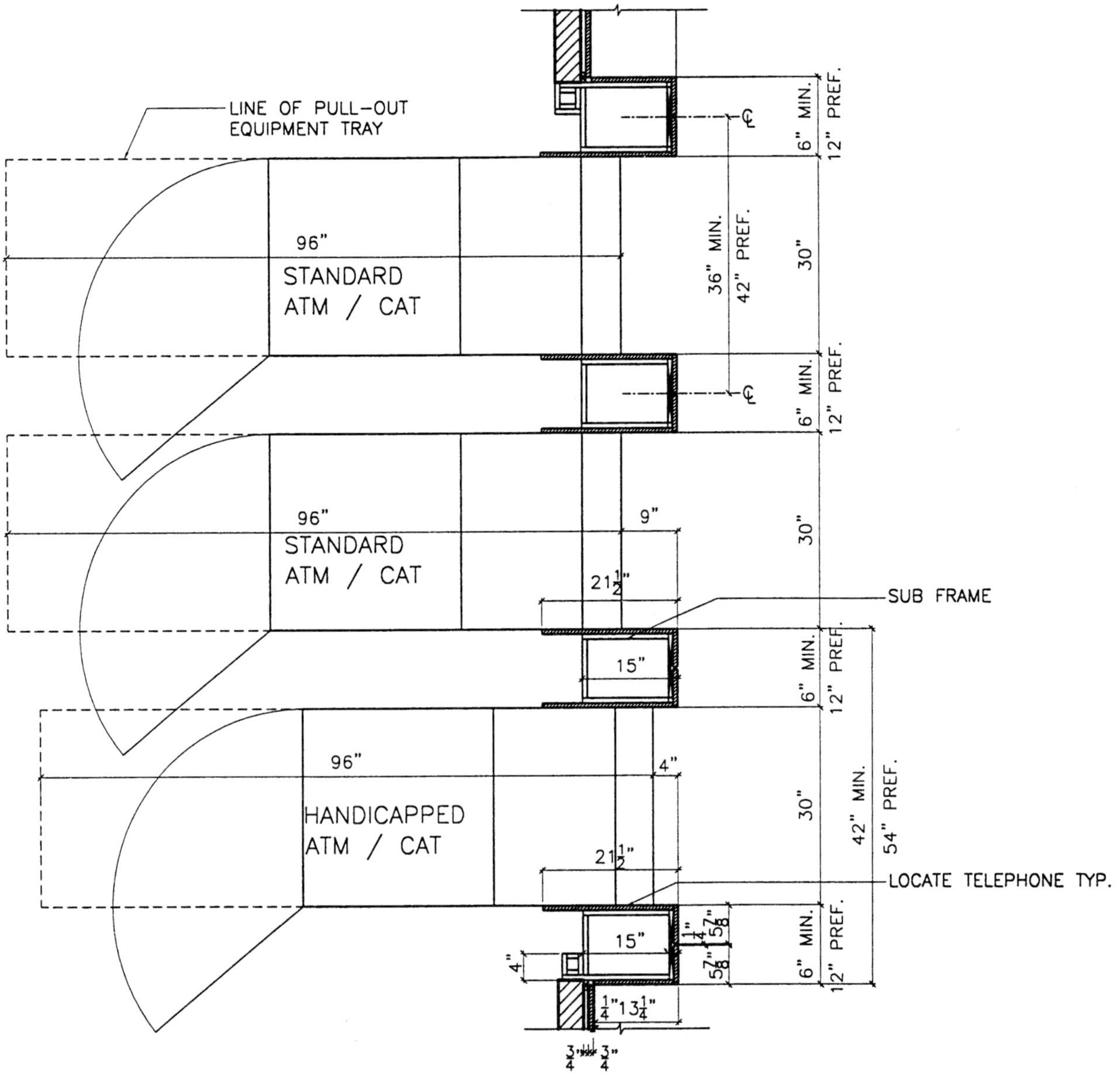

1 / 5.0 ATM LAYOUT–LOWER PLAN SECTION
SCALE 1/2"=1'0"

BRANCH BANKS
ATM Unit/Plan Sections

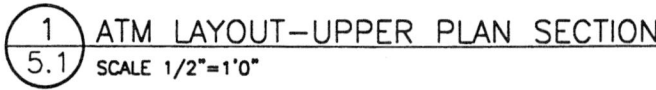

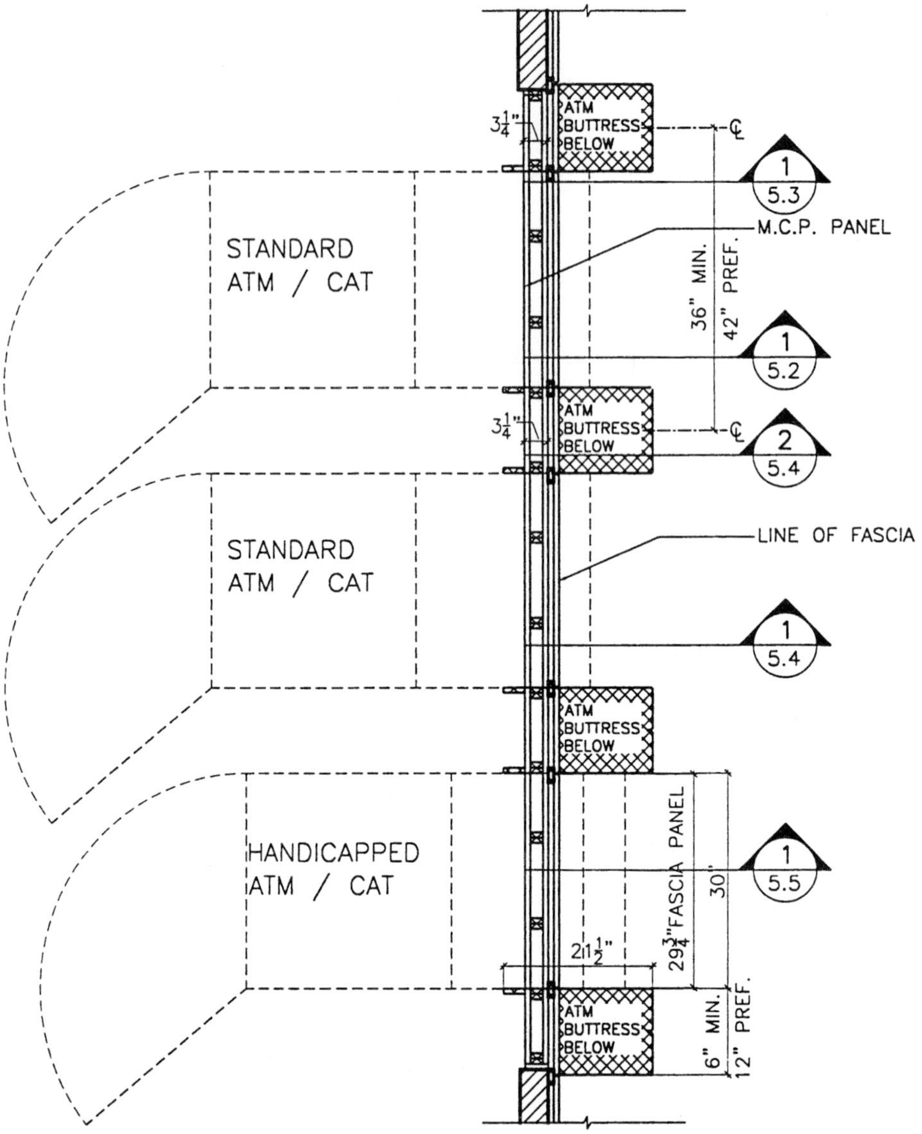

1/5.1 ATM LAYOUT—UPPER PLAN SECTION
SCALE 1/2"=1'0"

BRANCH BANKS
ATM Unit/ADA Vertical Section

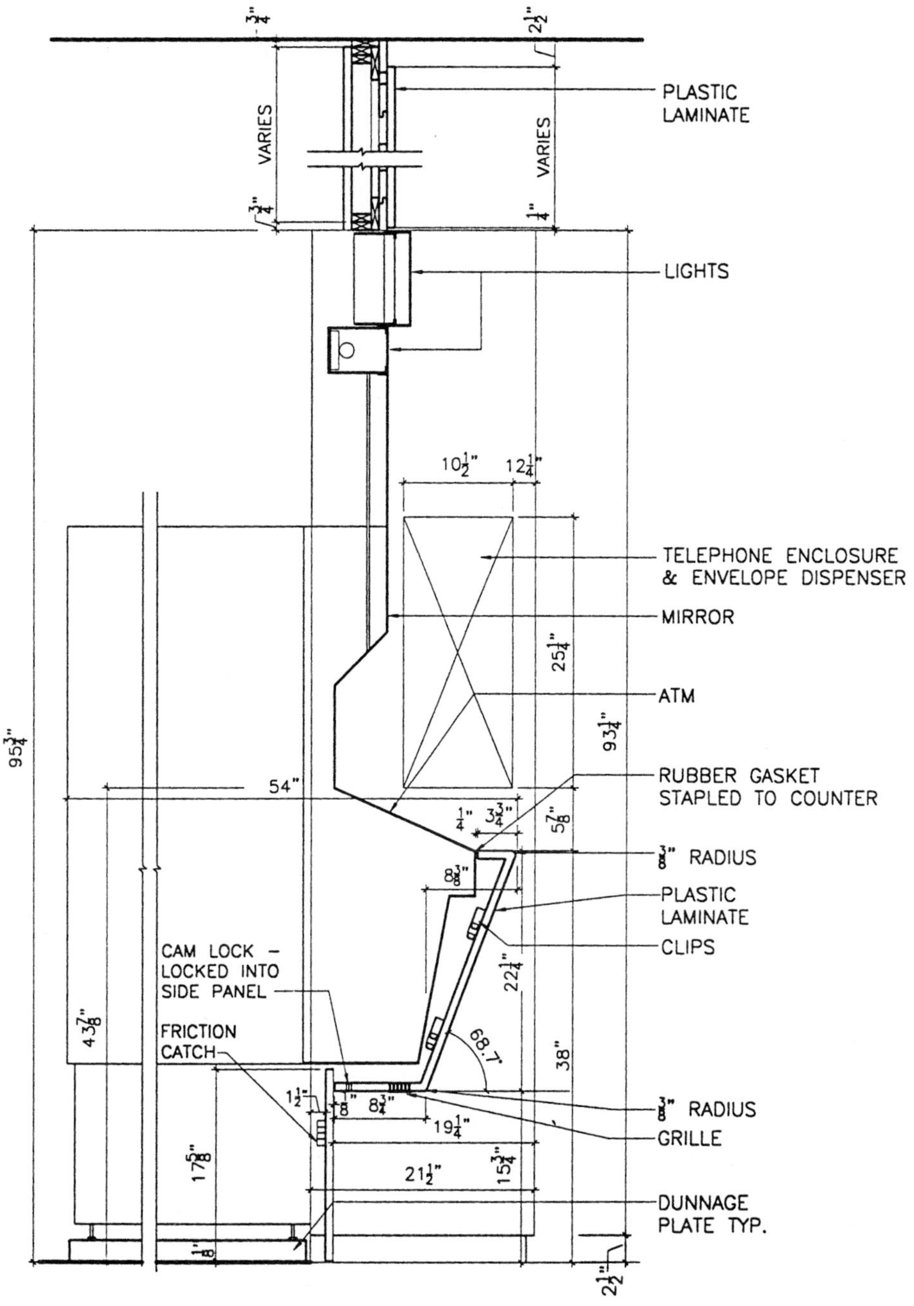

1 / 5.2 STANDARD ATM–VERTICAL SECTION
SCALE 3/4"=1'-0"

BRANCH BANKS

ATM Unit/Longitudinal Section

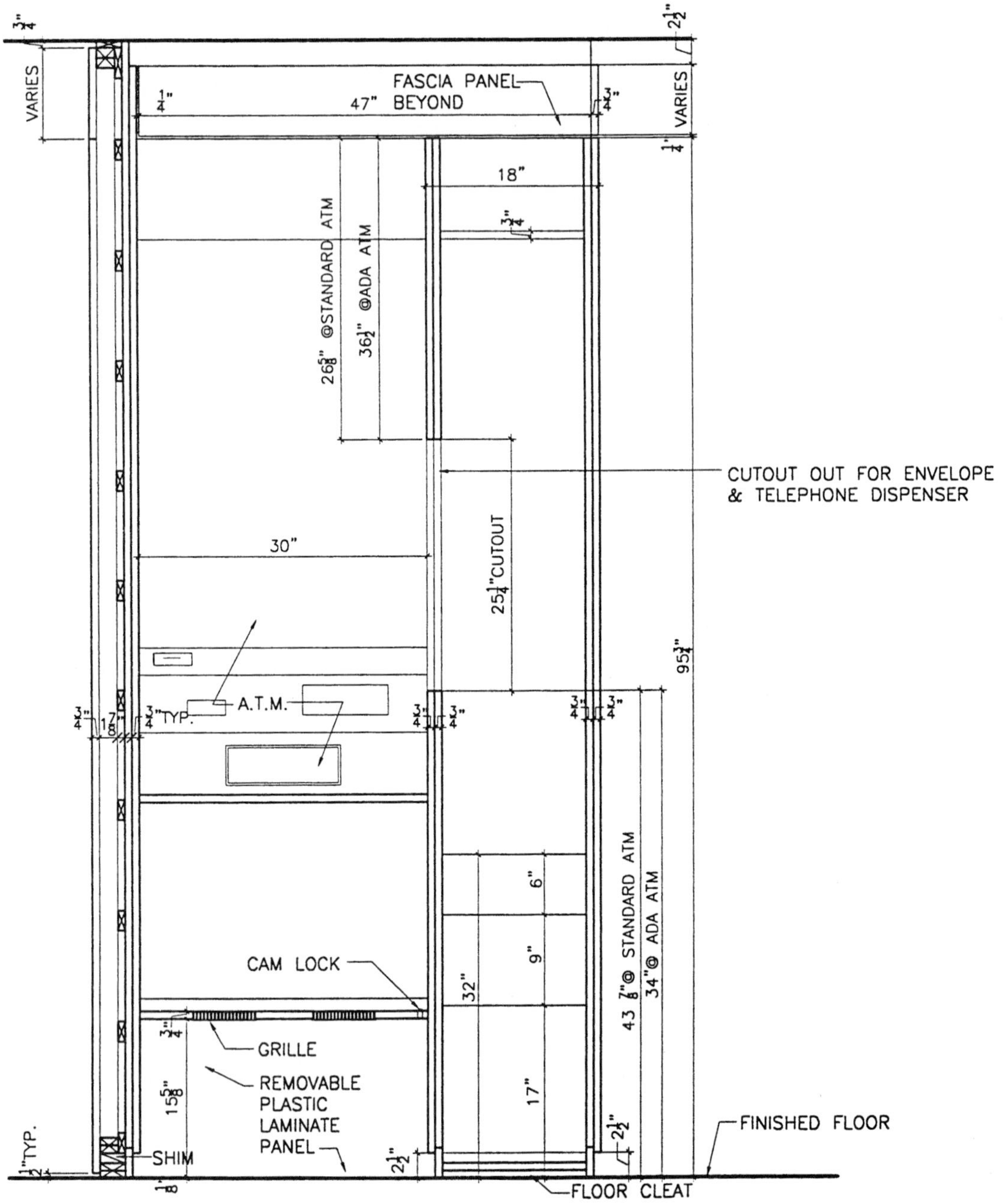

1 / 5.3 STANDARD ATM—LONGITUDINAL SECTION

SCALE 3/4"=1'-0"

BRANCH BANKS

ATM Unit/ADA Vertical Section

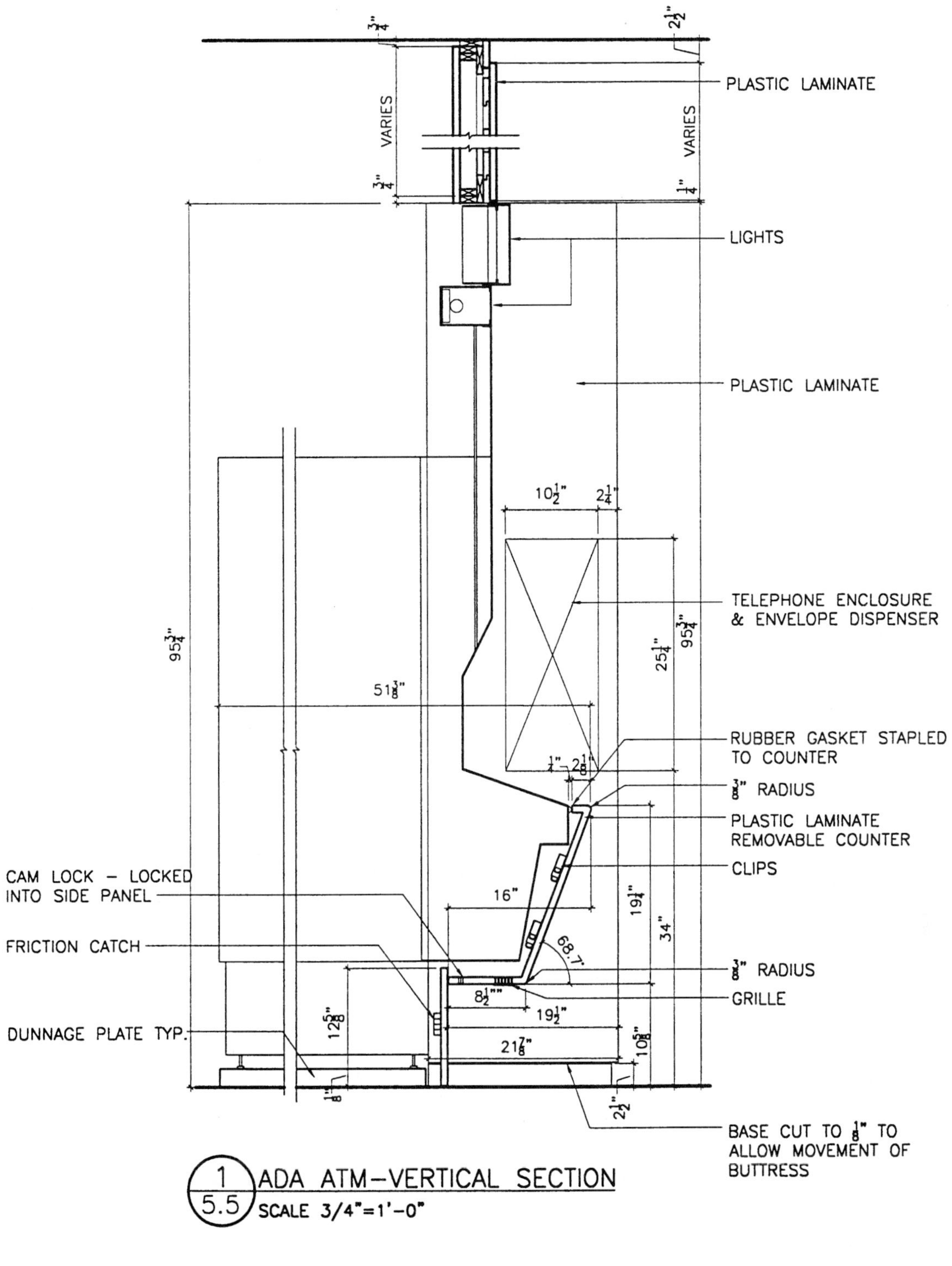

1 / 5.5 ADA ATM–VERTICAL SECTION
SCALE 3/4"=1'–0"

BRANCH BANKS

ATM Unit/ADA Vertical Section

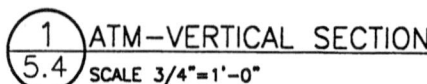

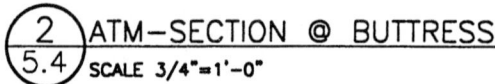

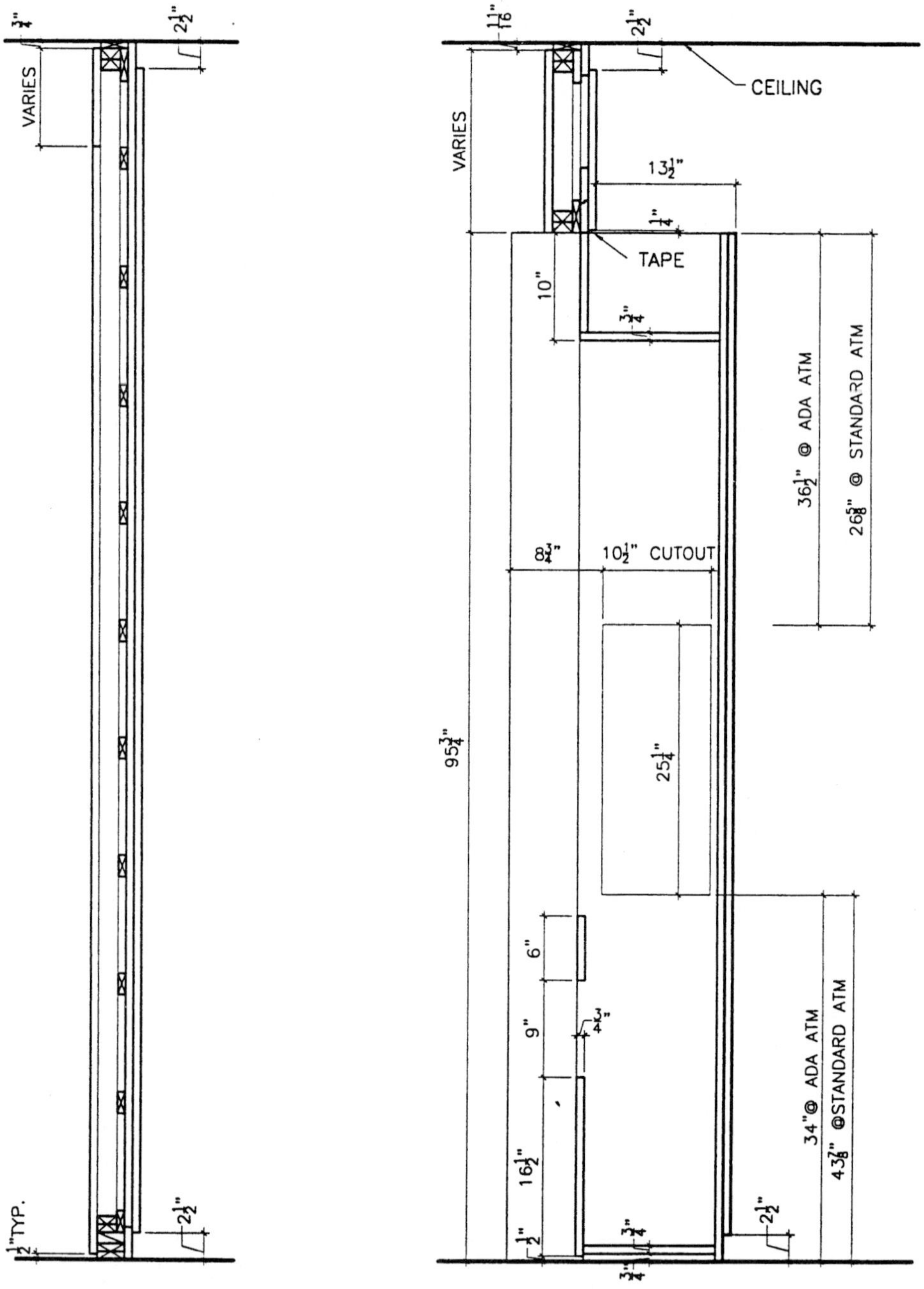

1/5.4 ATM–VERTICAL SECTION
SCALE 3/4"=1'-0"

2/5.4 ATM–SECTION @ BUTTRESS
SCALE 3/4"=1'-0"

BRANCH BANKS

Lottery Machine

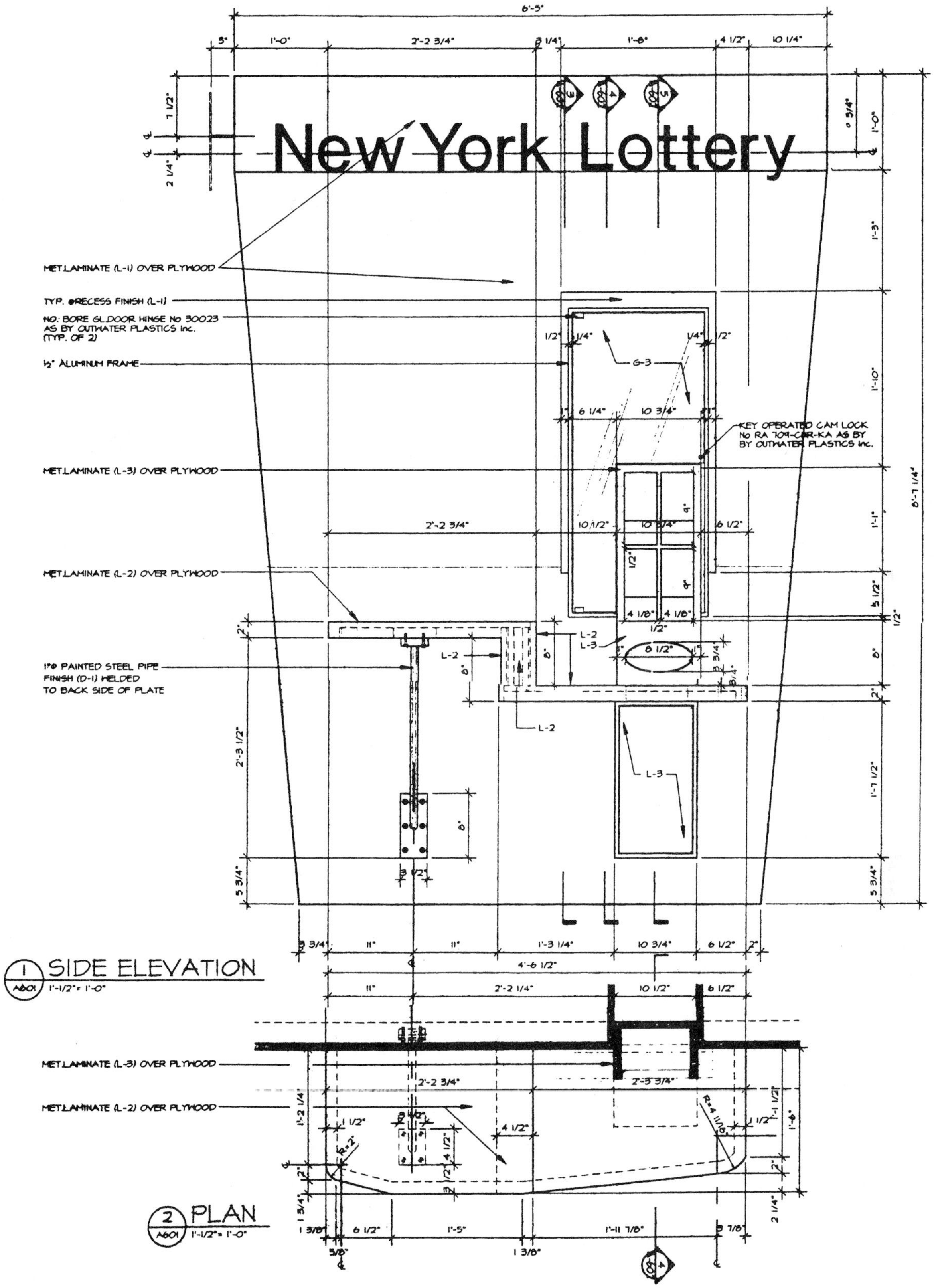

NOTE: ALL LAMINATE JOINTS AT OUTSIDE EDGES SHALL BE MITERED.
ALL EDGES OF SEAMS IN FINISH L-3 (ALUM. FOOTPLATE) SHALL

BRANCH BANKS
Lottery Machine

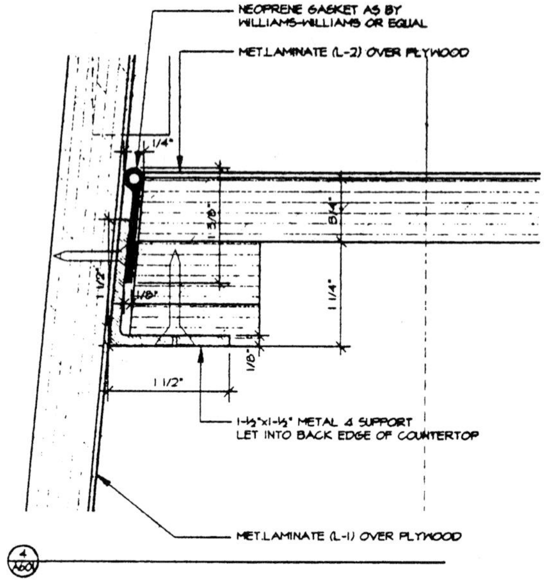

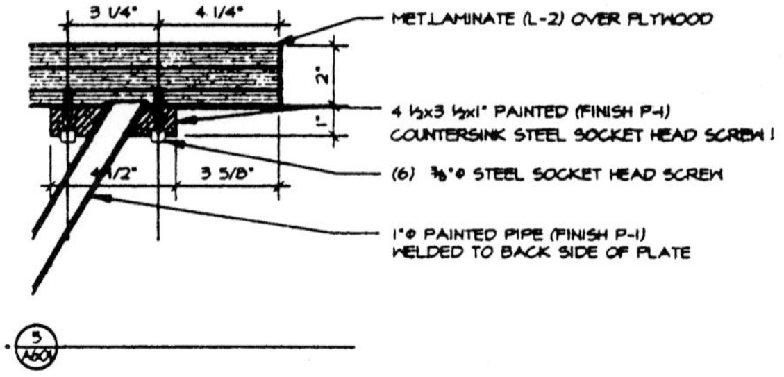

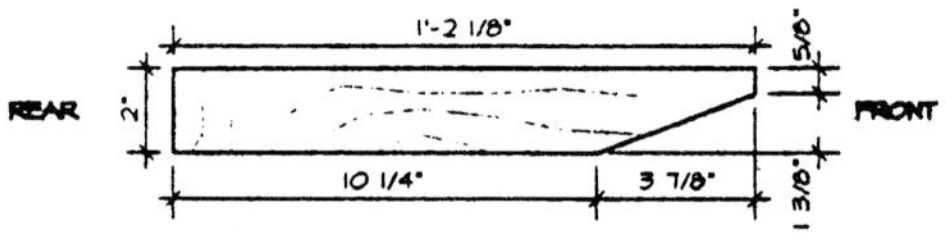

PLAN VIEW
6 WASTE BASKET RETAINER
A601 3"=1'-0"
TYPICAL OF 2

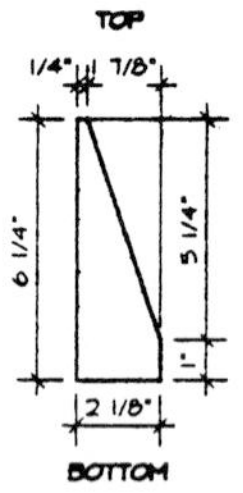

SECTION VIEW OF ANGLED
7 WOOD BLOCK WASTE RECEPTACLE
A601 3"=1'-0"
TYPICAL OF 3

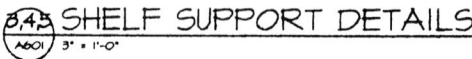

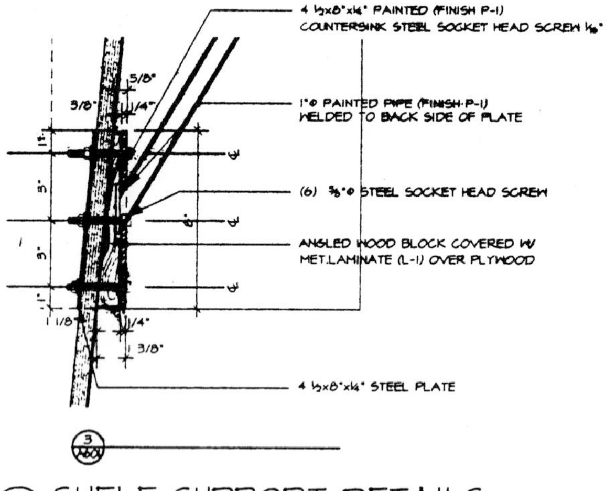

3,4,5 SHELF SUPPORT DETAILS
A601 3" = 1'-0"

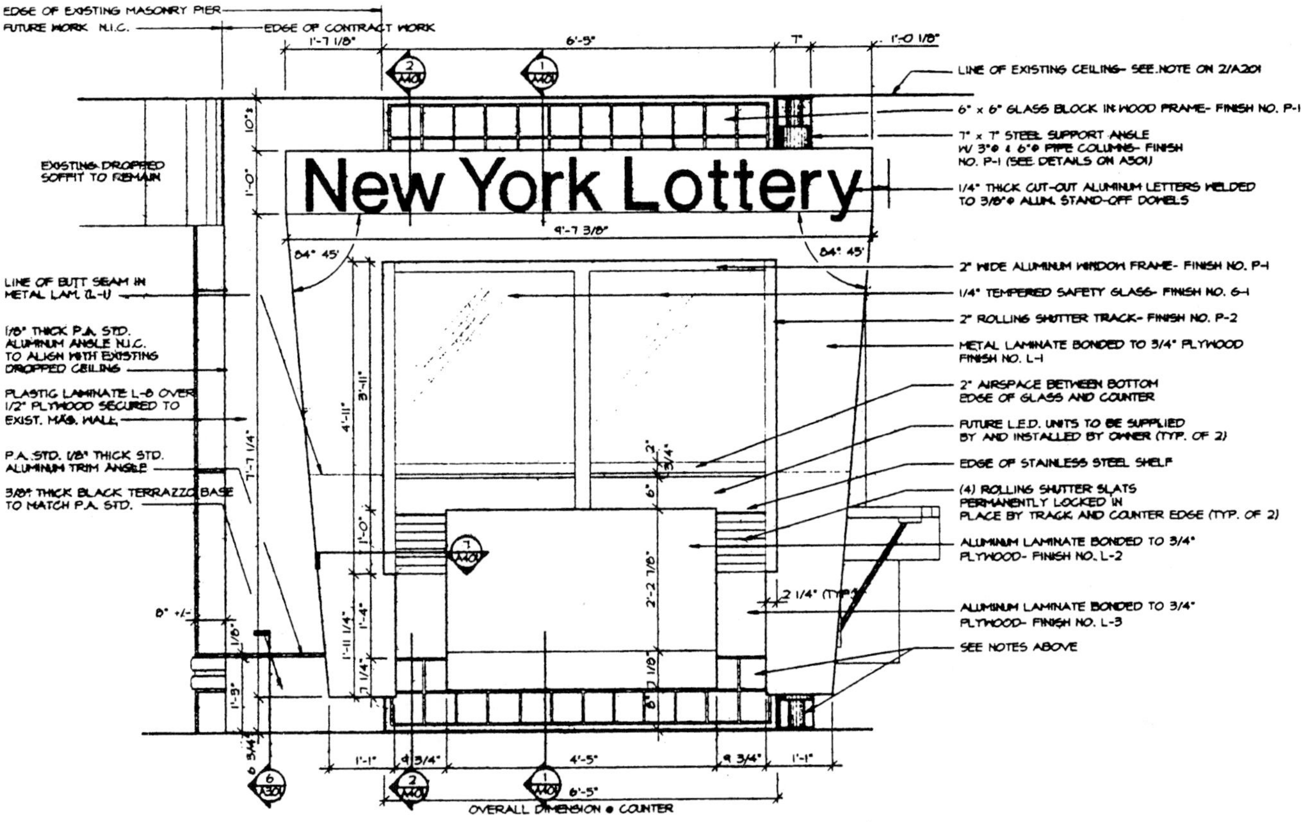
EDGE OF EXISTING MASONRY PIER
FUTURE WORK N.I.C.
EDGE OF CONTRACT WORK
LINE OF EXISTING CEILING- SEE NOTE ON 2/A201
6" x 6" GLASS BLOCK IN WOOD FRAME- FINISH NO. P-1
7" x 7" STEEL SUPPORT ANGLE W/ 3"ø & 6"ø PIPE COLUMNS- FINISH NO. P-1 (SEE DETAILS ON A501)
EXISTING DROPPED SOFFIT TO REMAIN
New York Lottery
1/4" THICK CUT-OUT ALUMINUM LETTERS WELDED TO 3/8"ø ALUM. STAND-OFF DOWELS
2" WIDE ALUMINUM WINDOW FRAME- FINISH NO. P-1
1/4" TEMPERED SAFETY GLASS- FINISH NO. G-1
2" ROLLING SHUTTER TRACK- FINISH NO. P-2
METAL LAMINATE BONDED TO 3/4" PLYWOOD FINISH NO. L-1
LINE OF BUTT SEAM IN METAL LAM. (L-1)
1/8" THICK P.A. STD. ALUMINUM ANGLE N.I.C. TO ALIGN WITH EXISTING DROPPED CEILING
PLASTIC LAMINATE L-8 OVER 1/2" PLYWOOD SECURED TO EXIST. MAS. WALL
P.A. STD. 1/8" THICK STD. ALUMINUM TRIM ANGLE
3/8" THICK BLACK TERRAZZO BASE TO MATCH P.A. STD.
2" AIRSPACE BETWEEN BOTTOM EDGE OF GLASS AND COUNTER
FUTURE L.E.D. UNITS TO BE SUPPLIED BY AND INSTALLED BY OWNER (TYP. OF 2)
EDGE OF STAINLESS STEEL SHELF
(4) ROLLING SHUTTER SLATS PERMANENTLY LOCKED IN PLACE BY TRACK AND COUNTER EDGE (TYP. OF 2)
ALUMINUM LAMINATE BONDED TO 3/4" PLYWOOD- FINISH NO. L-2
ALUMINUM LAMINATE BONDED TO 3/4" PLYWOOD- FINISH NO. L-3
SEE NOTES ABOVE
OVERALL DIMENSION @ COUNTER

FRONT ELEVATION (SHUTTER OPEN)
1/A301 3/4"=1'-0"

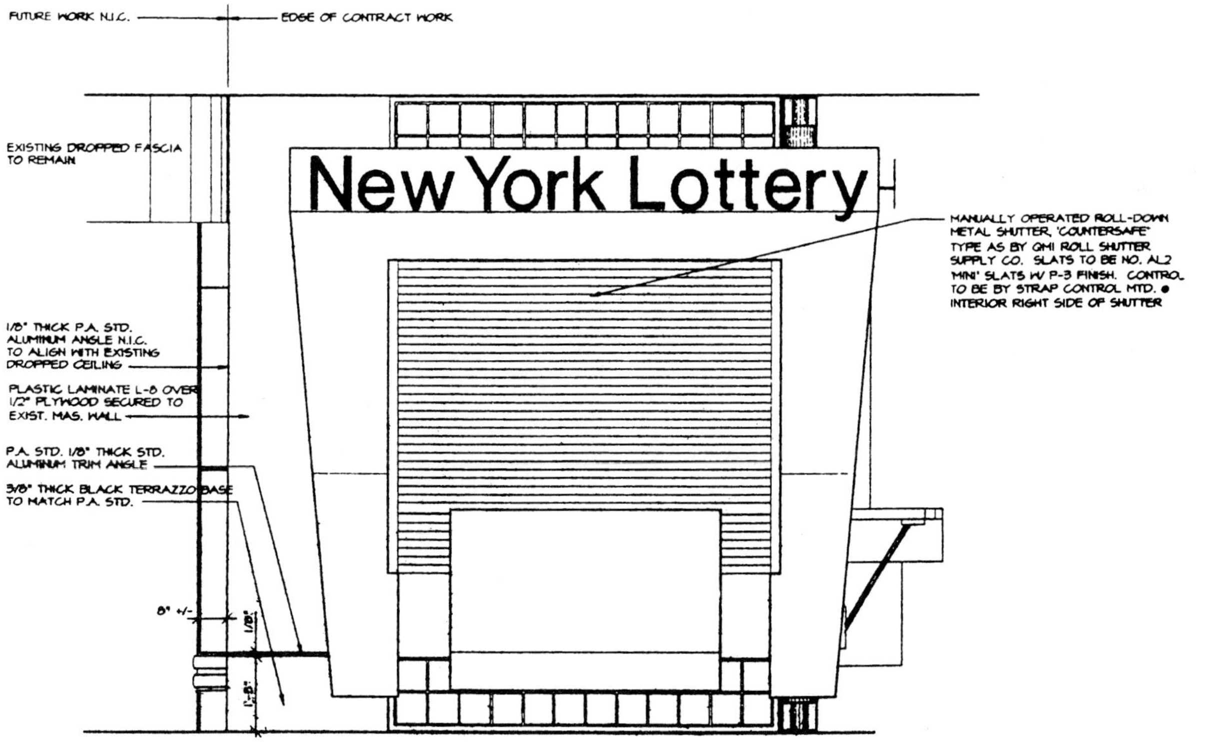
FUTURE WORK N.I.C.
EDGE OF CONTRACT WORK
EXISTING DROPPED FASCIA TO REMAIN
New York Lottery
MANUALLY OPERATED ROLL-DOWN METAL SHUTTER, 'COUNTERSAFE' TYPE AS BY QMI ROLL SHUTTER SUPPLY CO. SLATS TO BE NO. AL2 'MINI' SLATS W/ P-3 FINISH. CONTROL TO BE BY STRAP CONTROL MTD. @ INTERIOR RIGHT SIDE OF SHUTTER
1/8" THICK P.A. STD. ALUMINUM ANGLE N.I.C. TO ALIGN WITH EXISTING DROPPED CEILING
PLASTIC LAMINATE L-8 OVER 1/2" PLYWOOD SECURED TO EXIST. MAS. WALL
P.A. STD. 1/8" THICK STD. ALUMINUM TRIM ANGLE
3/8" THICK BLACK TERRAZZO BASE TO MATCH P.A. STD.

FRONT ELEVATION (SHUTTER CLOSED)
2/A301 3/4"=1'-0"

BRANCH BANKS
Lottery Machine

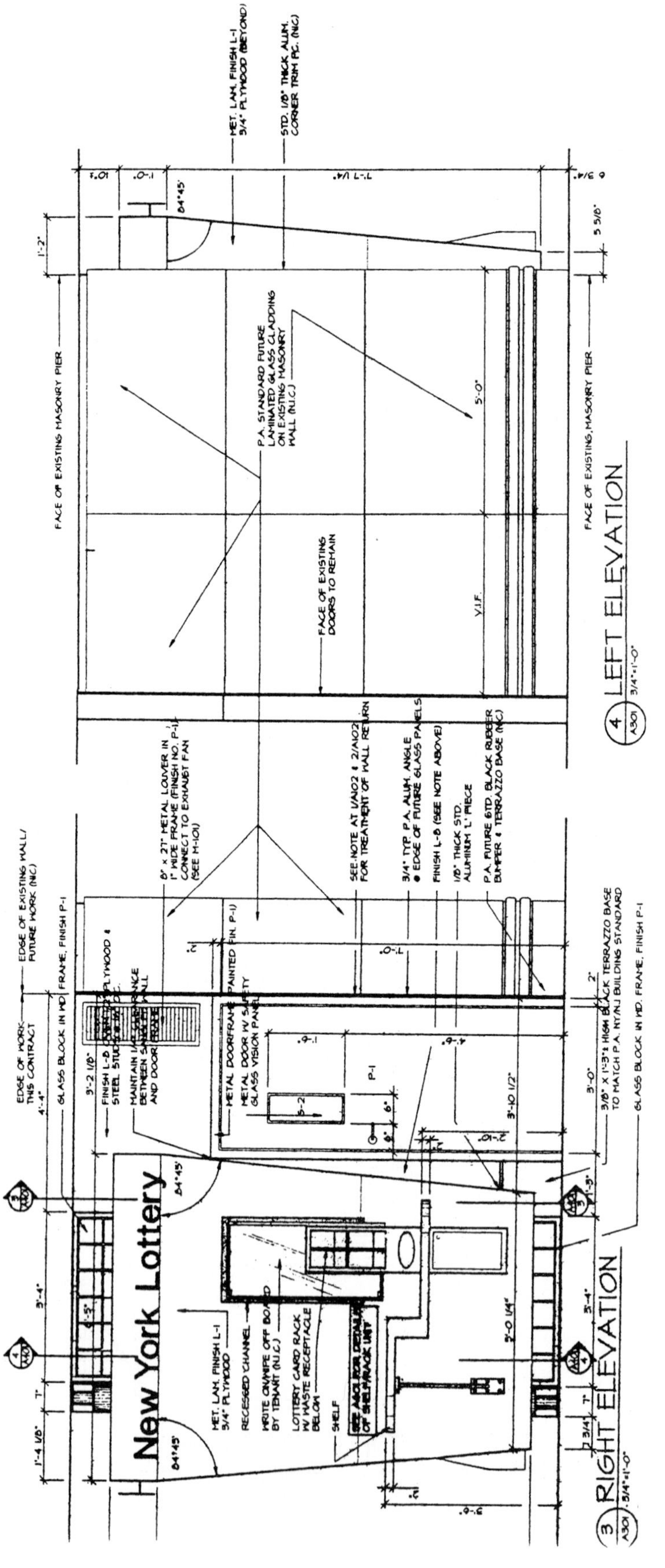

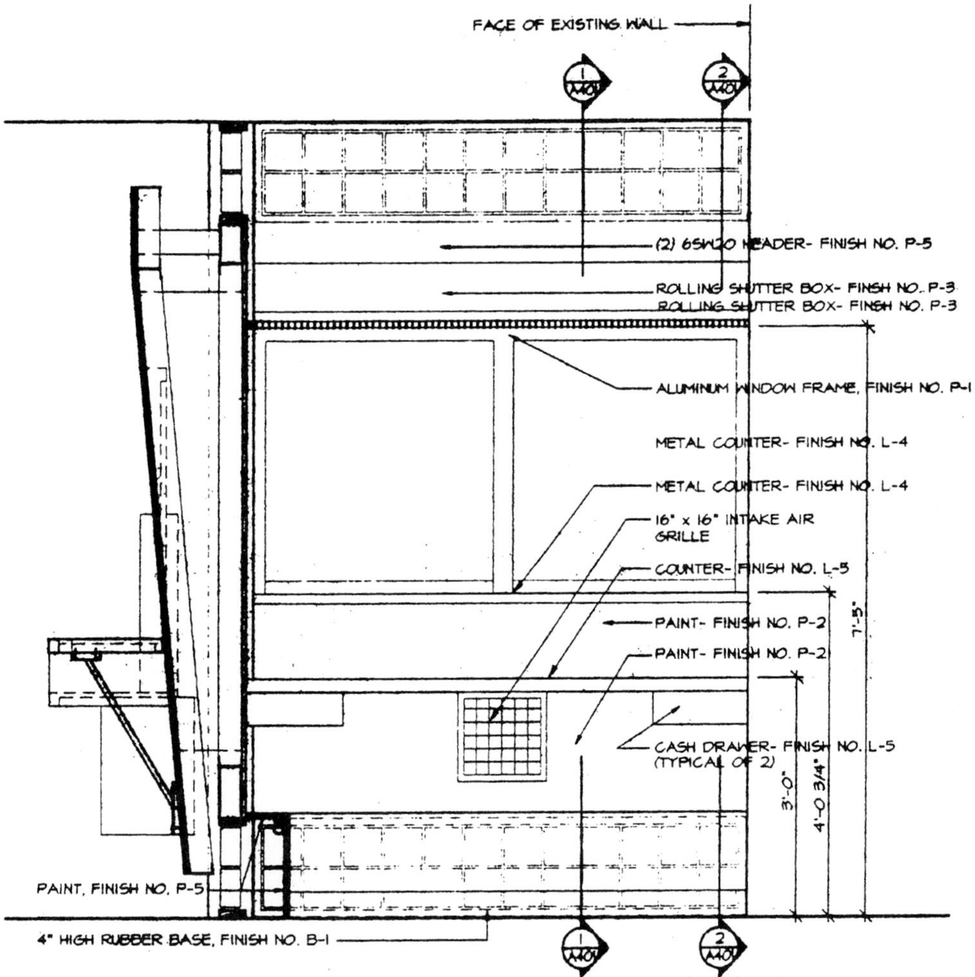

FACE OF EXISTING WALL
(2) 6SW20 HEADER- FINISH NO. P-5
ROLLING SHUTTER BOX- FINISH NO. P-3
ROLLING SHUTTER BOX- FINISH NO. P-3
ALUMINUM WINDOW FRAME, FINISH NO. P-1
METAL COUNTER- FINISH NO. L-4
METAL COUNTER- FINISH NO. L-4
16" x 16" INTAKE AIR GRILLE
COUNTER- FINISH NO. L-5
PAINT- FINISH NO. P-2
PAINT- FINISH NO. P-2
CASH DRAWER- FINISH NO. L-5 (TYPICAL OF 2)
7'-5"
4'-0 3/4"
3'-0"
PAINT, FINISH NO. P-5
4" HIGH RUBBER BASE, FINISH NO. B-1
5 A301 INTERIOR ELEVATION OF COUNTER
3/4"=1'-0"
FACE OF EXIST. OR NEW WALL
1/4" STAINLESS STEEL DIVIDER AS PER PA NY/NJ STANDARDS
1/8" WIDE SEALANT
1/4" PLYWOOD BACKUP
1/8" THINSET SETTING BED
3/8" PRECAST TERRAZZO BASE AS PER PA NY/NJ STANDARDS
1/8" (TYPICAL)
℄ JOINT
ALIGN
1'-3"
EXISTING PAVERS IN CONCOURSE
6 A301 TYP. TERRAZZO BASE
3"=1'-0"

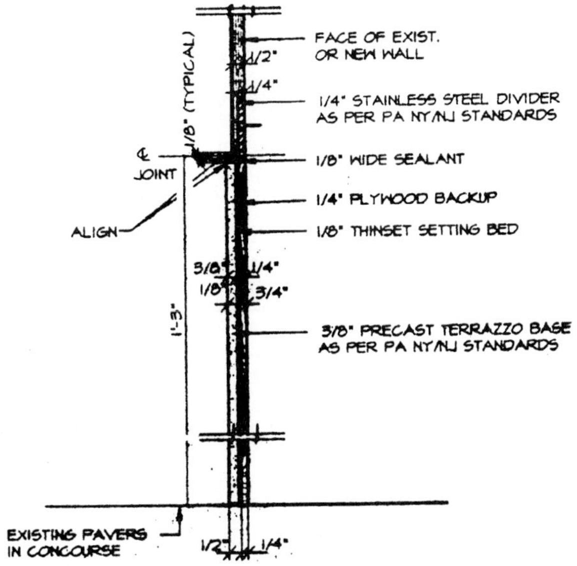

PUBLIC REST ROOMS, TOILETS, AND COATROOMS

Table 1 Minimum number of plumbing fixtures required by building occupancy type*

Type of building occupancy	Type of fixture					
	Water closets	Urinals	Lavatories	Bathtubs or showers	Drinking fountains	Other fixtures
Assembly—places of worship†	1 for ea. sex for ea. 150 persons	Urinals may be provided in toilet rooms in lieu of water closets but for not more than ½ of the required number of water closets	1			
Assembly—other than places of worship (including but not limited to auditoriums, theaters, convention halls) and all spaces classified as F-4	No. of persons / No of fixtures for each sex 1-100 1 101-200 2 201-300 3 301-400 4 Over 400, add 1 fixture for ea. sex for ea. additional 200 persons	Urinals may be provided in toilet rooms in lieu of water closets but for not more than ½ of the required number of water closets	No. of persons / No. of fixtures 1-200 1 201-400 2 401-750 3 Over 750, add 1 fixture for ea. 500 persons		1 for ea. 1,000 persons except that there shall be at least 1 fixture at each assembly floor level or tier	Where motion picture projection booths contain more than 2 projectors, at least 1 water closet and 1 lavatory shall be provided on the same level and within 20 ft. of the booth
Dormitories — school or labor, also institutional	1 for ea. sex for ea. 8 persons	Urinals may be provided in toilet rooms in lieu of water closets but for not more than ½ of the required number of water closets	1 for ea. 12 persons	1 for ea. 8 persons; for women's dormitories, 1 bathtub shall be substituted for 1 shower at the ratio of 1 for ea. 30 women		Laundry trays — 1 for ea. 50 persons
Single room occupancies for sleeping accommodations only	1 for ea. 6 persons		1 for ea. 6 persons	1 for ea. 6 persons		
Dwellings — one- and two-family	1 for each dwelling unit		1 for each dwelling unit	1 for each dwelling unit		Kitchen sink — 1 for each dwelling unit
Public buildings, offices, business mercantile, storage; warehouses, factories and institutional employees‡	No. of persons each sex / No. of fixtures 1-15 1 16-35 2 36-55 3 56-80 4 81-110 5 111-150 6 1 fixture for ea. additional 40 persons	Urinals may be provided in toilet rooms in lieu of water closets but for not more than ½ of the required number of water closets when more than 35 persons	No. of persons / No. of fixtures 1-20 1 21-40 2 41-60 3 61-90 4 91-125 5 1 fixture for ea. additional 45 persons		1 for ea. 75 persons	
Public bathing	1 fixture for ea. sex for ea. 30 persons	Urinals may be provided in toilet rooms in lieu of water closets but for not more than ½ of the required number of water closets	1/60	1/40		
Schools: Elementary Secondary	1 fixture for ea. sex for ea. 35 students	Urinals may be provided in toilet rooms in lieu of water closets but for not more than ½ of the required number of water closets	1/50 pupils 1/50 pupils Over 300 pupils: 1/100 pupils	In gym or pool shower rooms, ⅓ pupils of a largest class using pool at any one time	1/50 persons but at least 1 per floor	
Workers' portable facilities	1/30 workers	1/30 workers			At least 1 per floor equivalent for ea. 100 workmen	
Industrial — foundries only	No. of persons / No. of fixtures 1-10 1 11-25 2 26-50 3 51-80 4 81-125 5 1 additional fixture for each additional 45 persons	Where more than 10 men are employed: No. of men / No. of urinals 11-29 1 30-79 2 1 additional fixture for each additional 80 males Urinals may be provided in toilet rooms in lieu of water closets but for not more than ½ of the required number of water closets	No. of persons / No. of fixtures 1-8 1 9-16 2 17-30 3 31-45 4 46-65 5 1 additional fixture for each additional 25 persons	1 shower for each 15 persons exposed to excessive heat or occupational hazard from poisonous, infectious, or irritating material	1 for ea. 75 persons	
					Other fixtures	
Kitchens for public or employees dining			1 lavatory for the personal use of kitchen employees		One machine or a 3-compartment sink for the effective washing and sanitizing of all cutlery, dishes and glasses before re-use	
Dwellings — multiple or apartment	1 for each dwelling unit or apartment		1 for each dwelling unit or apartment	1 for each dwelling unit or apartment	Kitchen sink — 1 for each dwelling unit or apartment. Within each dwelling unit, not designed for use by transients, one laundry tray or automatic laundry washing machine; or in a readily accessible location within a general laundry room. 1 two-compartment tray for each 10 dwelling units or 1 automatic laundry washing machine for each 20 dwelling units.	

*The population used in determining the number of fixtures required shall be based on the number of people to occupy the space but in no case shall the population be less than that determined by allowing 125 sq. ft. of net floor area per person.

†Such facilities may be in adjacent buildings under the same ownership or control, and shall be accessible during periods when the assembly space is occupied.

‡Facilities for employees in a storage building or warehouse may be located in an adjacent building, under the same ownership, where the maximum distance of travel from the working space to the toilet facilities does not exceed 500 ft. horizontally.

REST ROOMS AND TOILETS

Plumbing Fixture and Accessory Heights

While Fig. 1 provides specific vertical dimensions of both plumbing fixtures and accessories, the designer is cautioned that every plumbing fixture and accessory must be carefully analyzed in light of the users to be served. Plumbing contractors will follow the manufacturer's recommendations or their own standards unless the designer provides this information on the working drawings. In large-scale projects, it is suggested that the designer carefully provide all fixture mounting heights on all interior elevations or on a separate diagramatic drawing, such as is shown in Fig. 1.

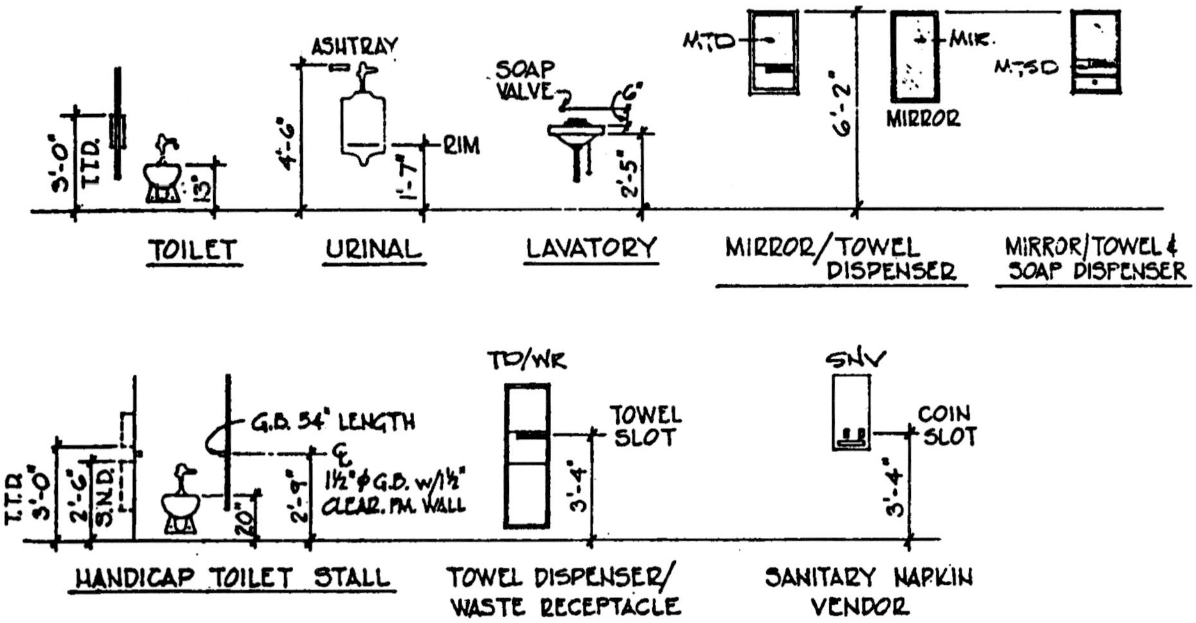

Fig. 1 Fixture heights

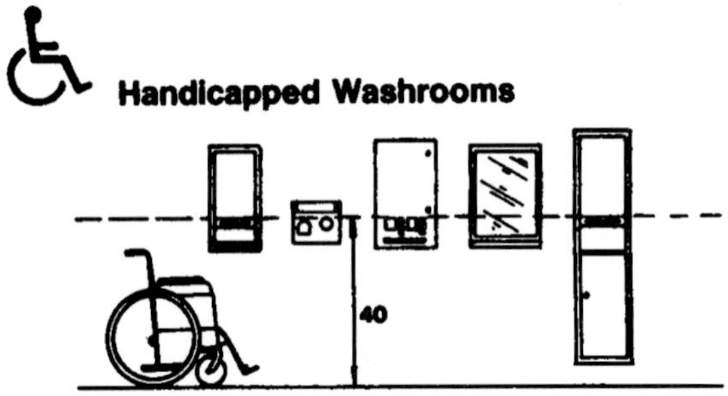

Fig. 2 Suggested mounting heights for various bathroom accessories

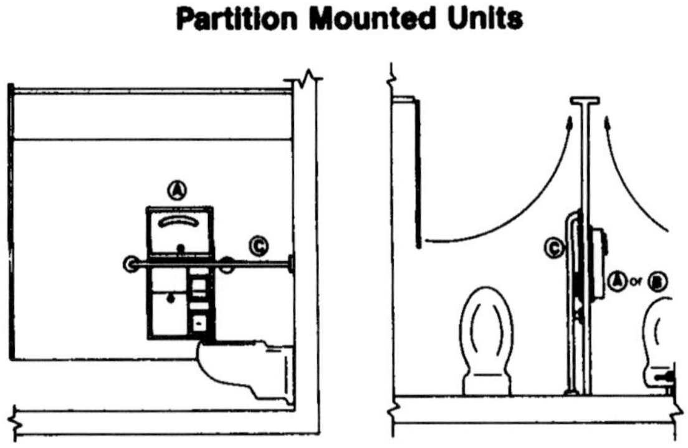

Fig. 3 Typical back-to-back male/female washroom stalls using partition-mounted units to accommodate a handicapped stall and one standard stall. If room permits, grab bars should be placed on all three sides, resulting in a U-shaped configuration. Most codes require toilet stall doors to open outward

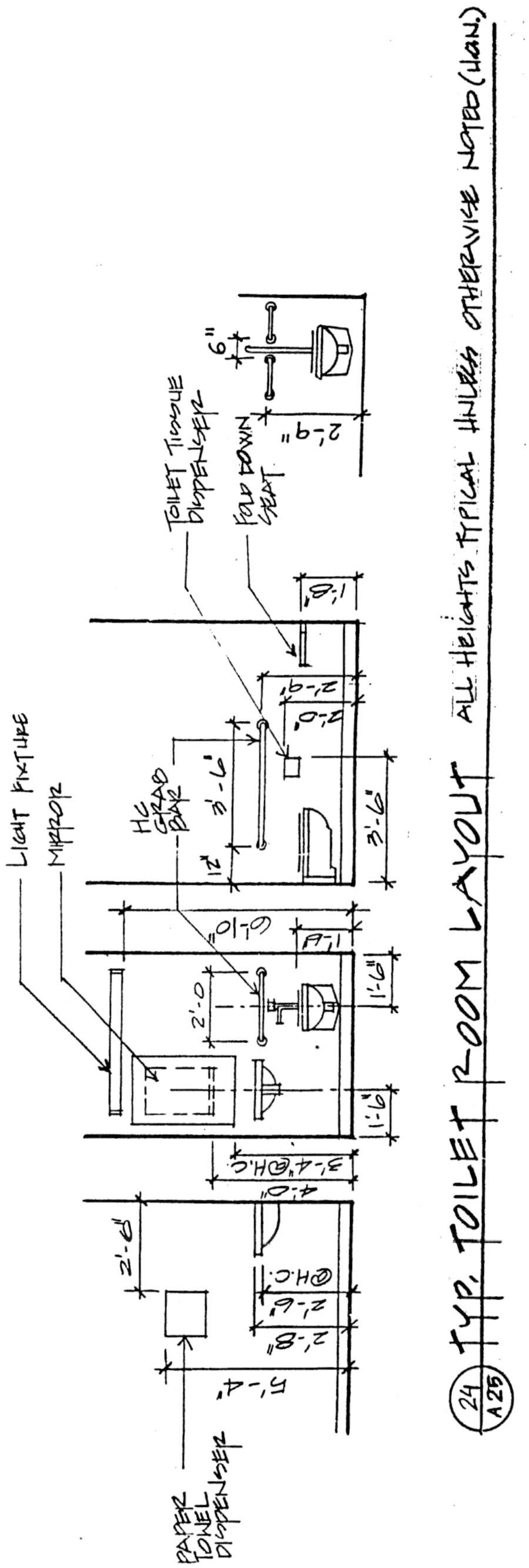
24
A25
TYP. TOILET ROOM LAYOUT
ALL HEIGHTS TYPICAL UNLESS OTHERWISE NOTED
LIGHT FIXTURE
MIRROR
HC GRAB BAR
TOILET TISSUE DISPENSER
FOLD DOWN SEAT
PAPER TOWEL DISPENSER
5'-4"
2'-8"
2'-6"
@H.C.
4'-0"
3'-4"@H.C.
2'-6"
1'-6"
2'-0"
6'-10"
12"
3'-6"
2'-0"
2'-9"
1'-8"
6"

REST ROOMS AND TOILETS

Plumbing Fixture and Accessory Heights

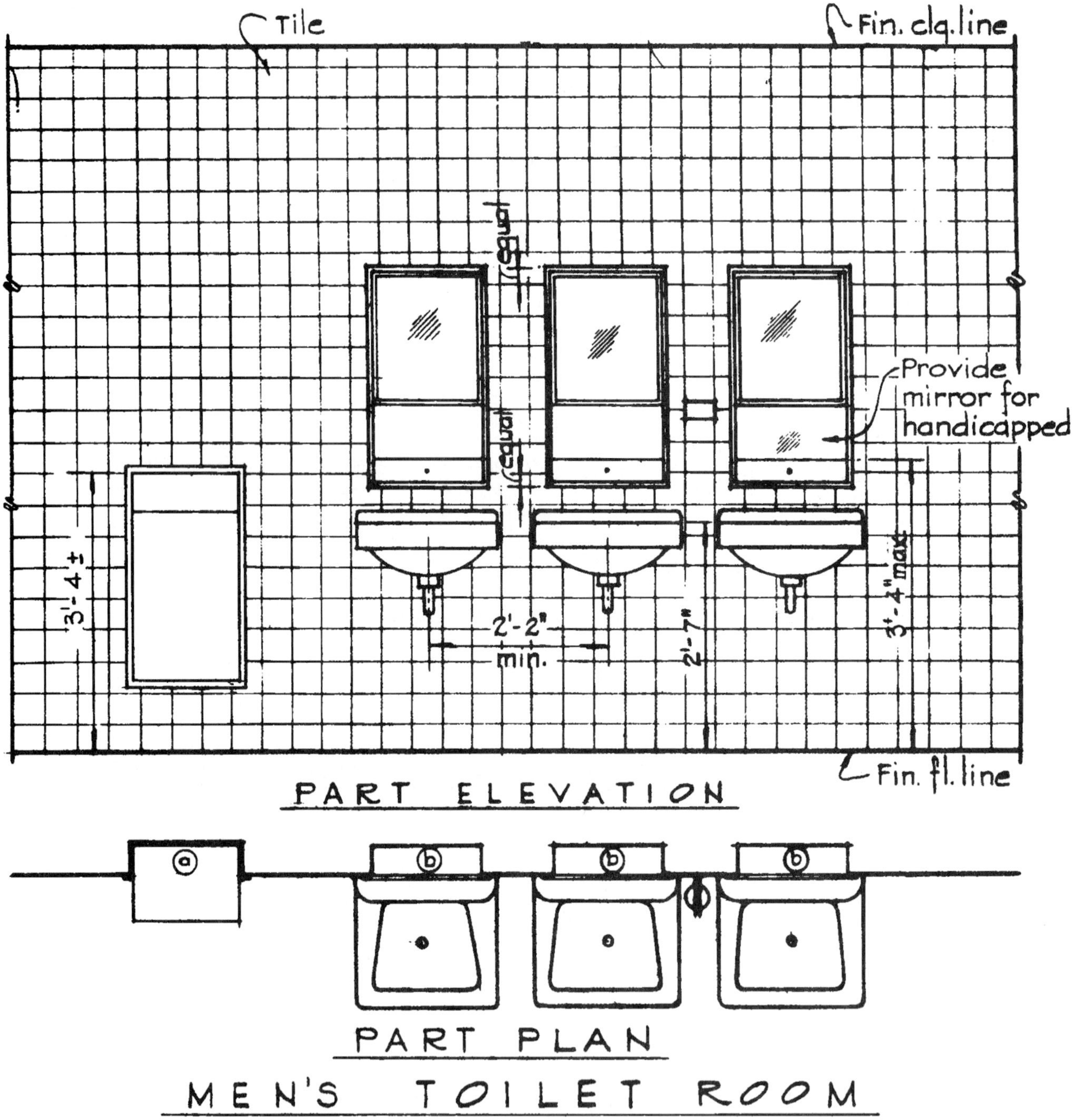

Fig. 4 This drawing of a part plan and part elevation of a men's toilet room demonstrates how mounting heights of plumbing fixtures and accessories are indicated. In addition, spacing of plumbing fixtures is indicated by use of a horizontal dimension from centerline to centerline of the lavatories. Many designers prefer to show horizontal dimensions on the plan. a = recessed waste receptacle, b = recessed towel dispenser and soap dispenser with shelf

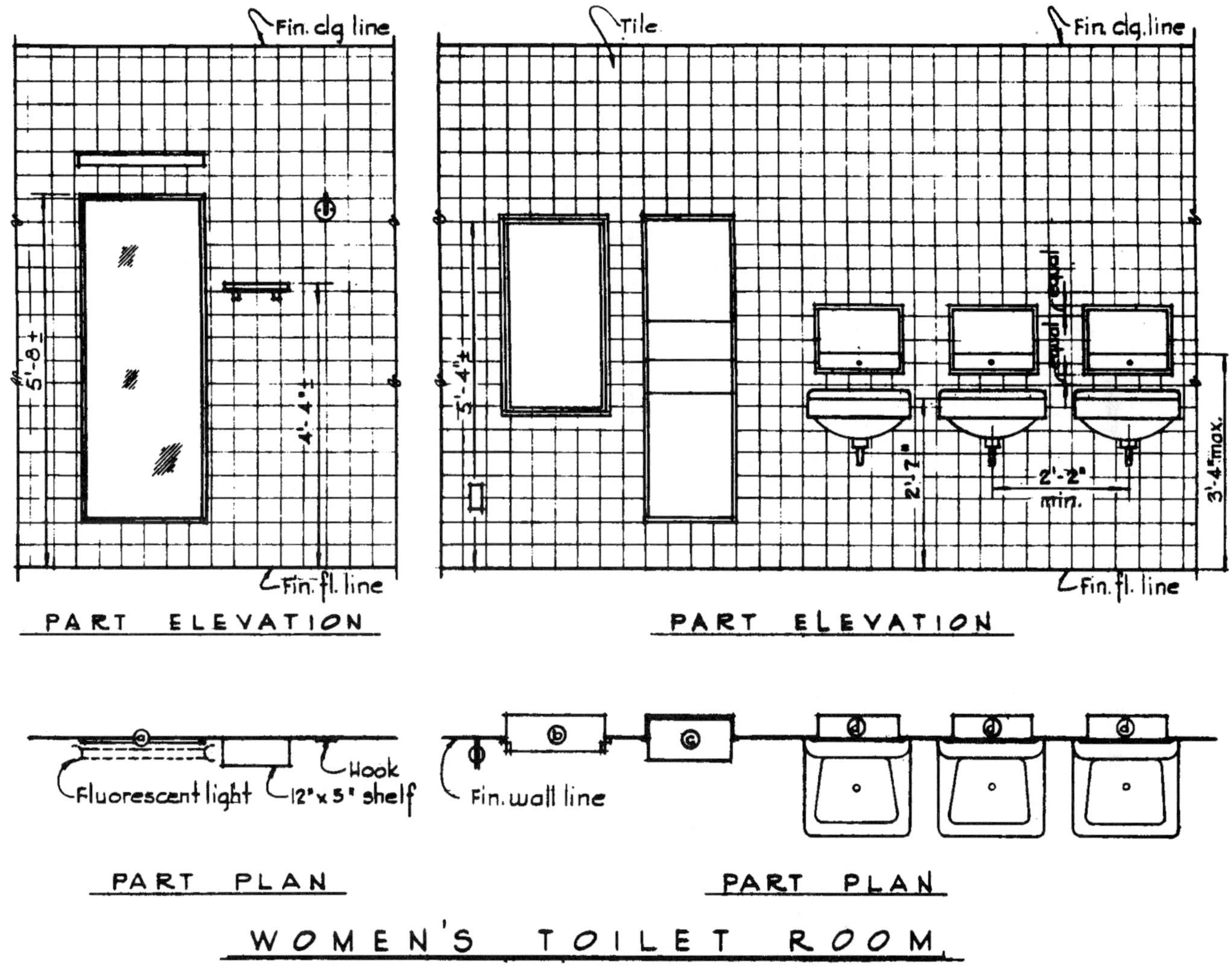

Fig. 5 Mounting heights or vertical dimensions are always taken from the finished floor. When installing accessories on tile walls, the tile module and dimensions should be taken into consideration. a = full length mirror, b = recessed feminine napkin dispenser, c = recessed towel cabinet and waste receptacle, d = recessed soap dispenser with shelf

REST ROOMS AND TOILETS
Plumbing Fixture and Accessory Heights

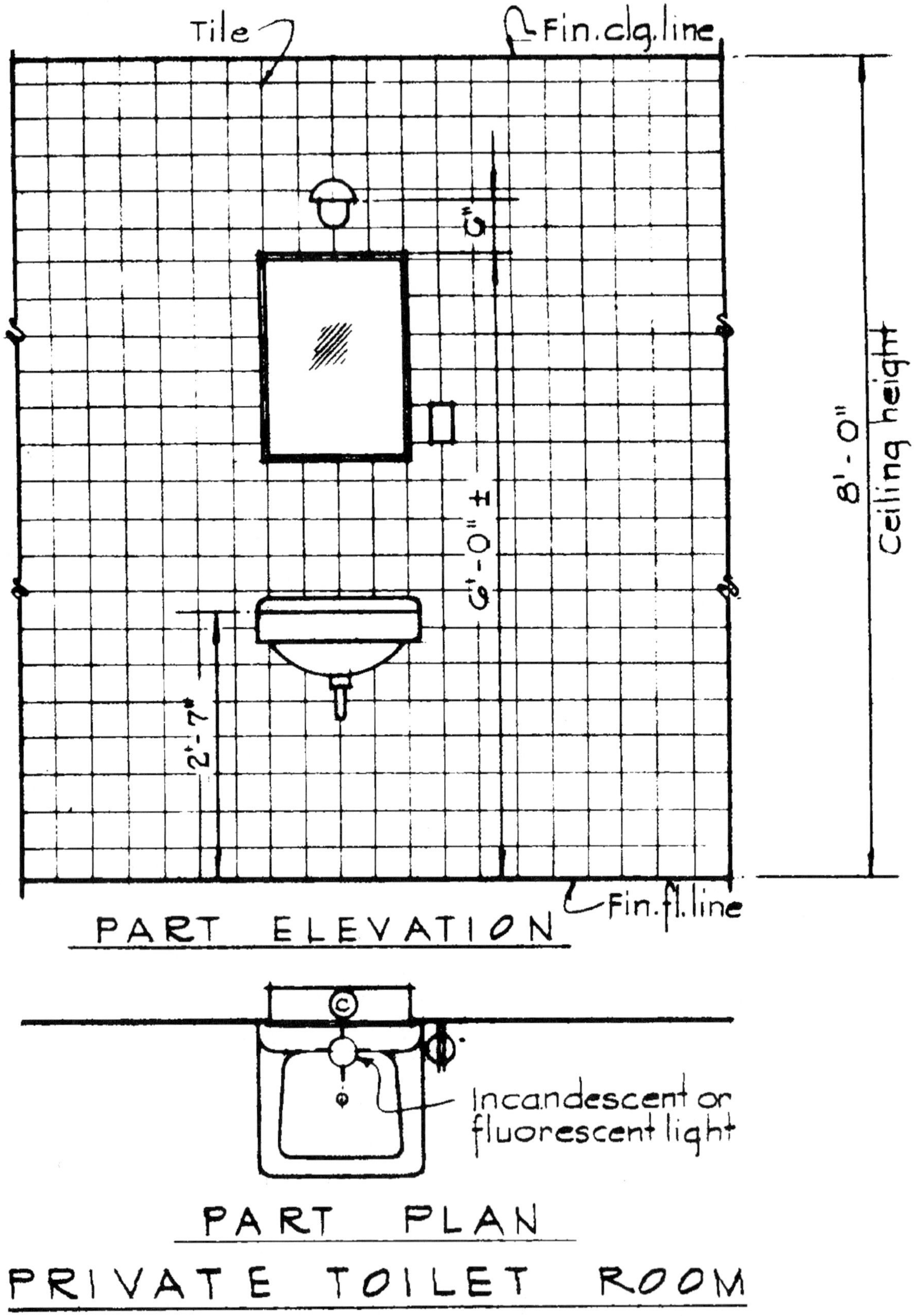

Fig. 6 The mounting heights of plumbing fixtures and accessories for a private toilet are, in many instances, determined by the physical characteristics of the primary user. A person 6 ft 6 in tall might require the mounting height of a lavatory, mirror, or shower head to be higher than usual. Note that any electrical outlets near a lavatory or shower must be specified with a ground fault interrupter. c = first aid cabinet and medicine cabinet

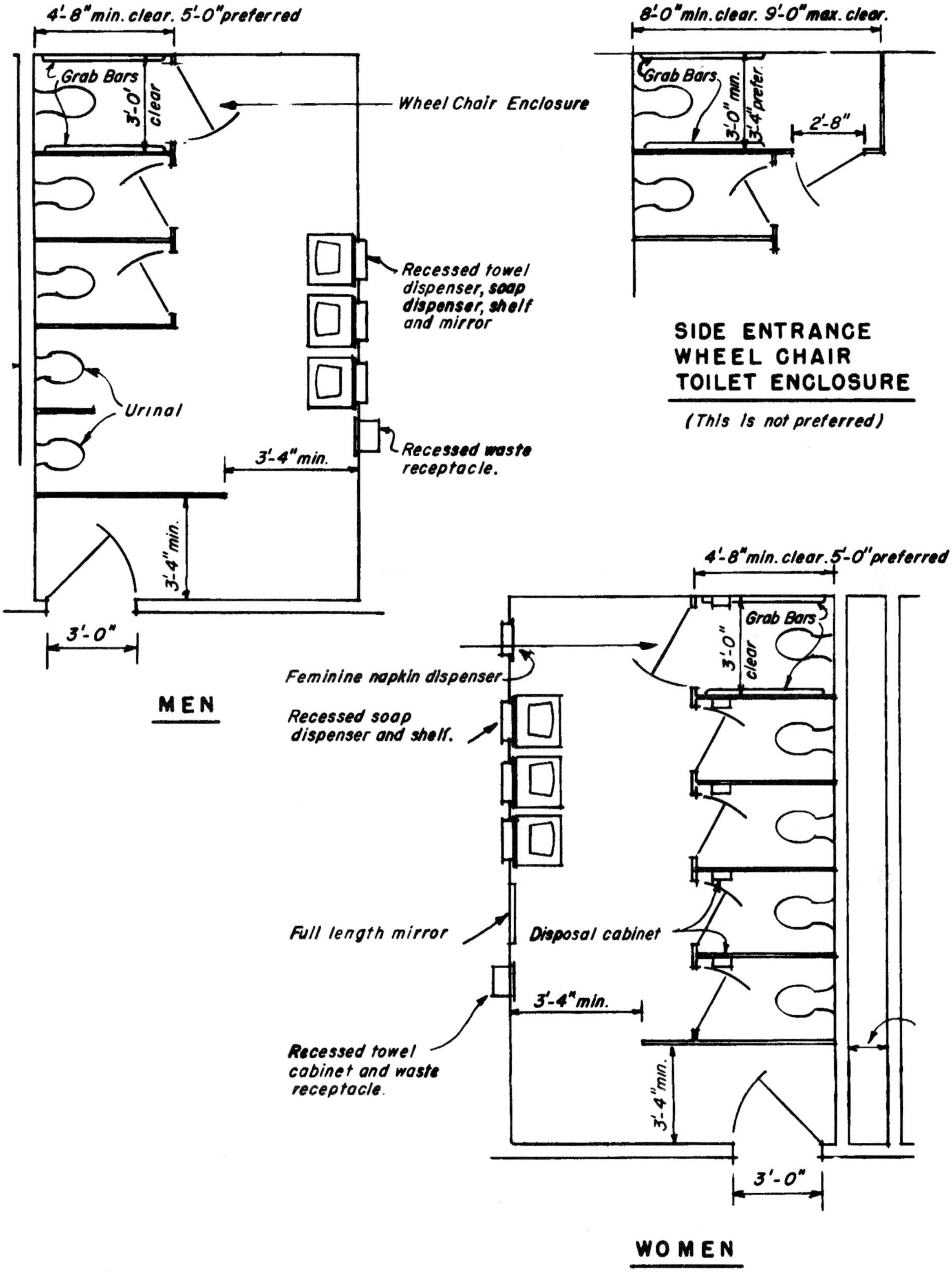

Fig. 7 These drawings show minimum dimensions both for toilet enclosures and between partitions and walls. These layouts are recommendations provided by the General Services Administration, but they may not be in conformity with other codes or desired bathroom layouts, especially in regard to accessibility. Remember, too, that codes provide minimum, not optimal, standards

REST ROOMS AND TOILETS
Plans and Elevations

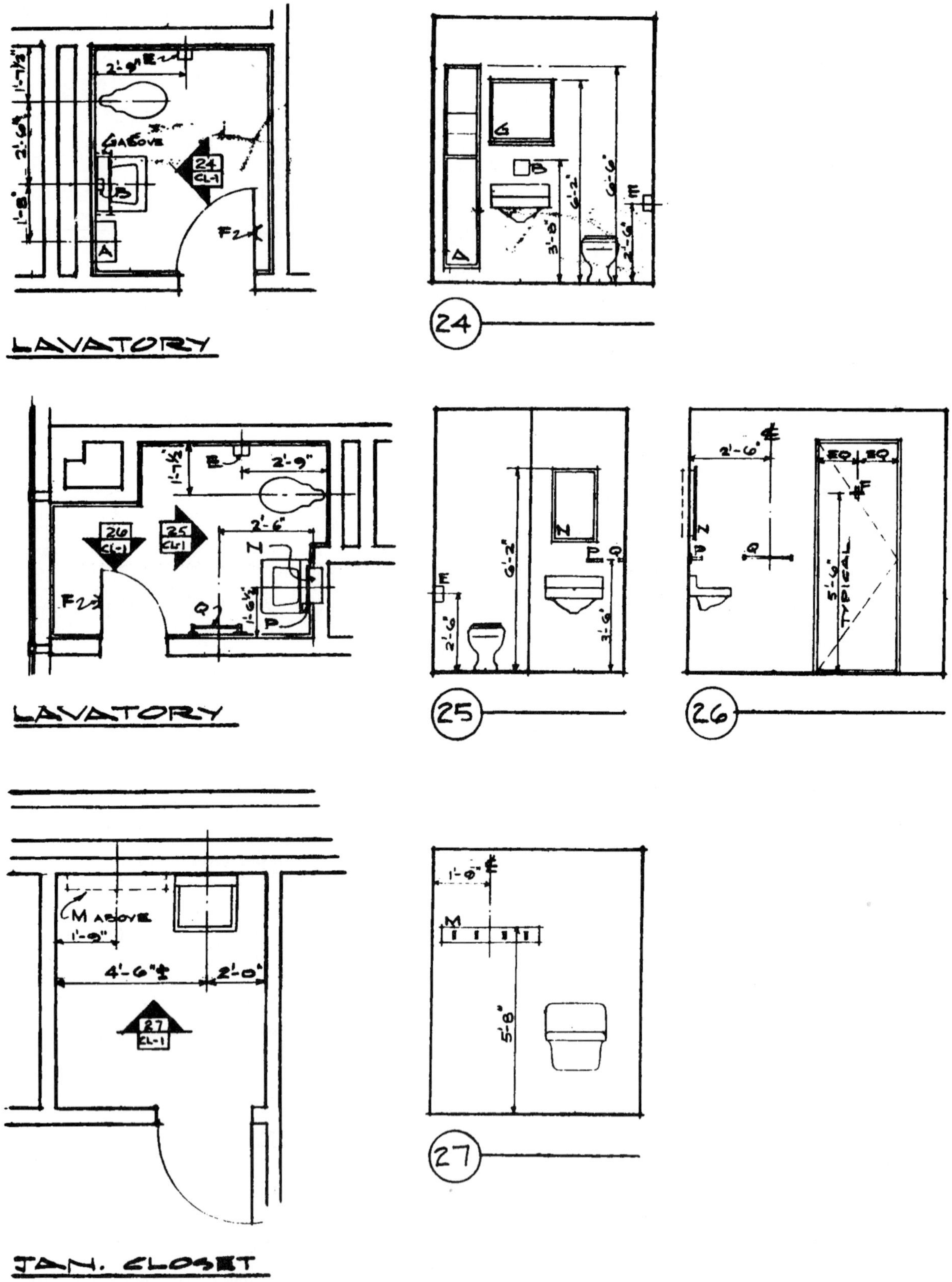

Fig. 8 These working drawings provide both vertical and horizontal dimensions for placement of plumbing fixtures and accessories. Note that accessories are identified or called out through the use of letters, which would be coordinated with either a legend or a schedule

REST ROOMS AND TOILETS

Plans

In multiple-fixtured public toilets, at least one water closet and lavatory must be designed to conform to barrier-free or accessibility standards.

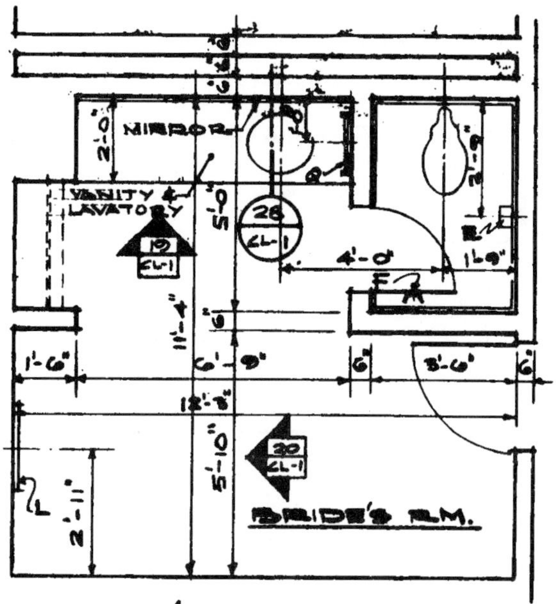

BRIDE'S ROOM
LAVATORY

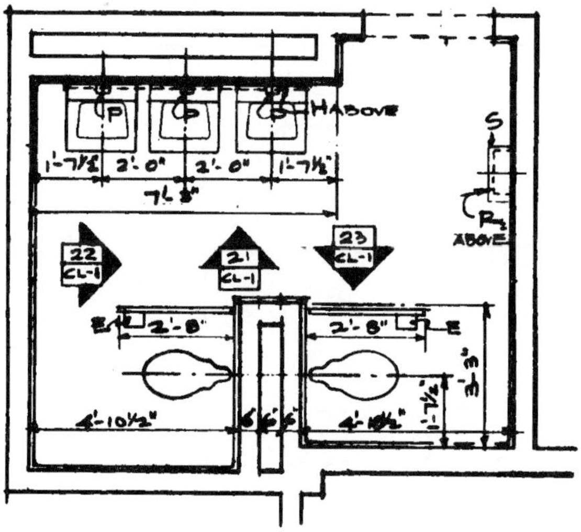

LAVATORY

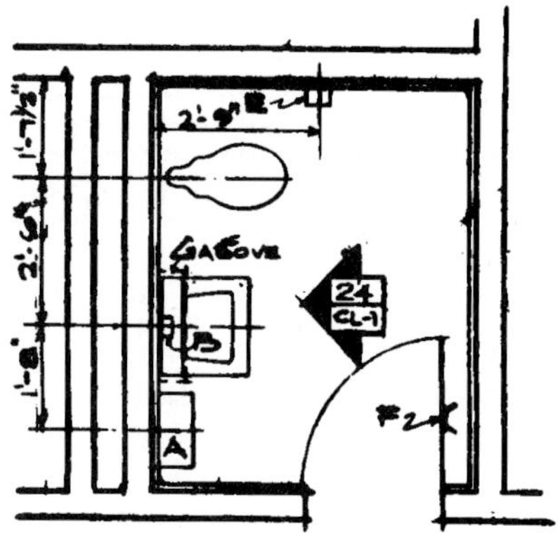

LAVATORY

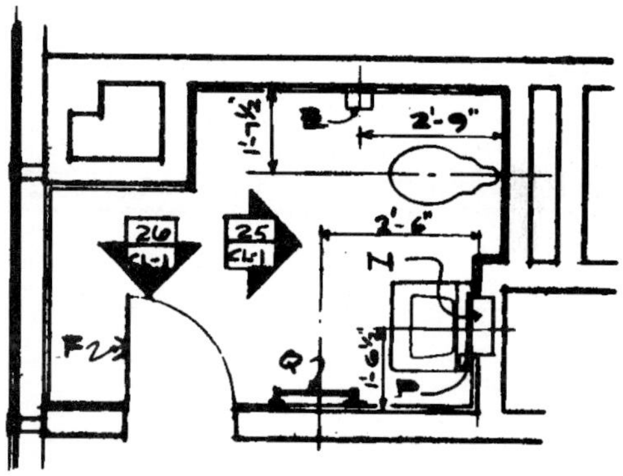

LAVATORY

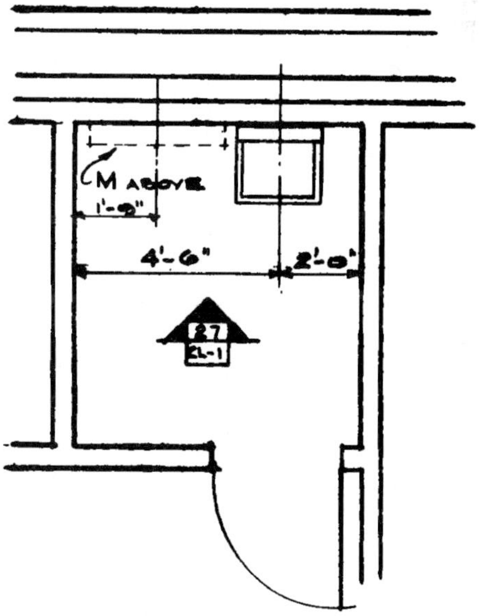

JAN. CLOSET

REST ROOMS AND TOILETS
Plans and Elevations

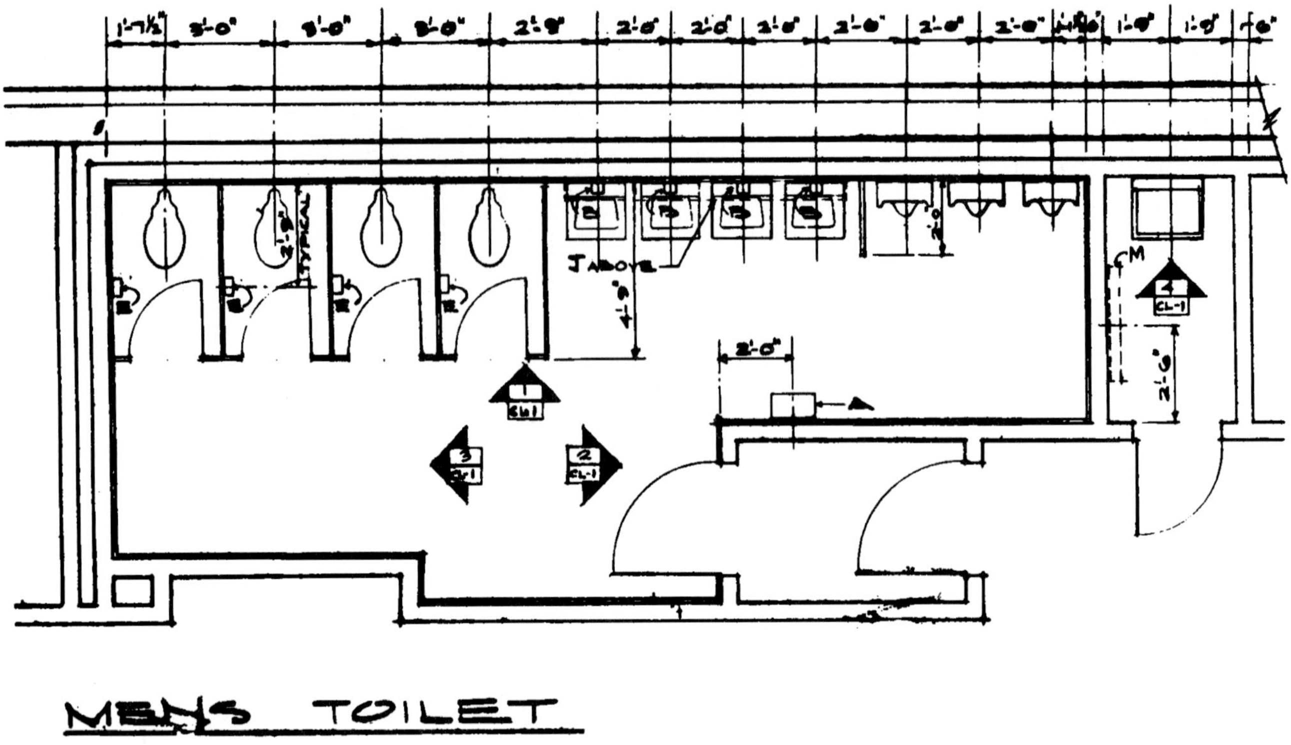

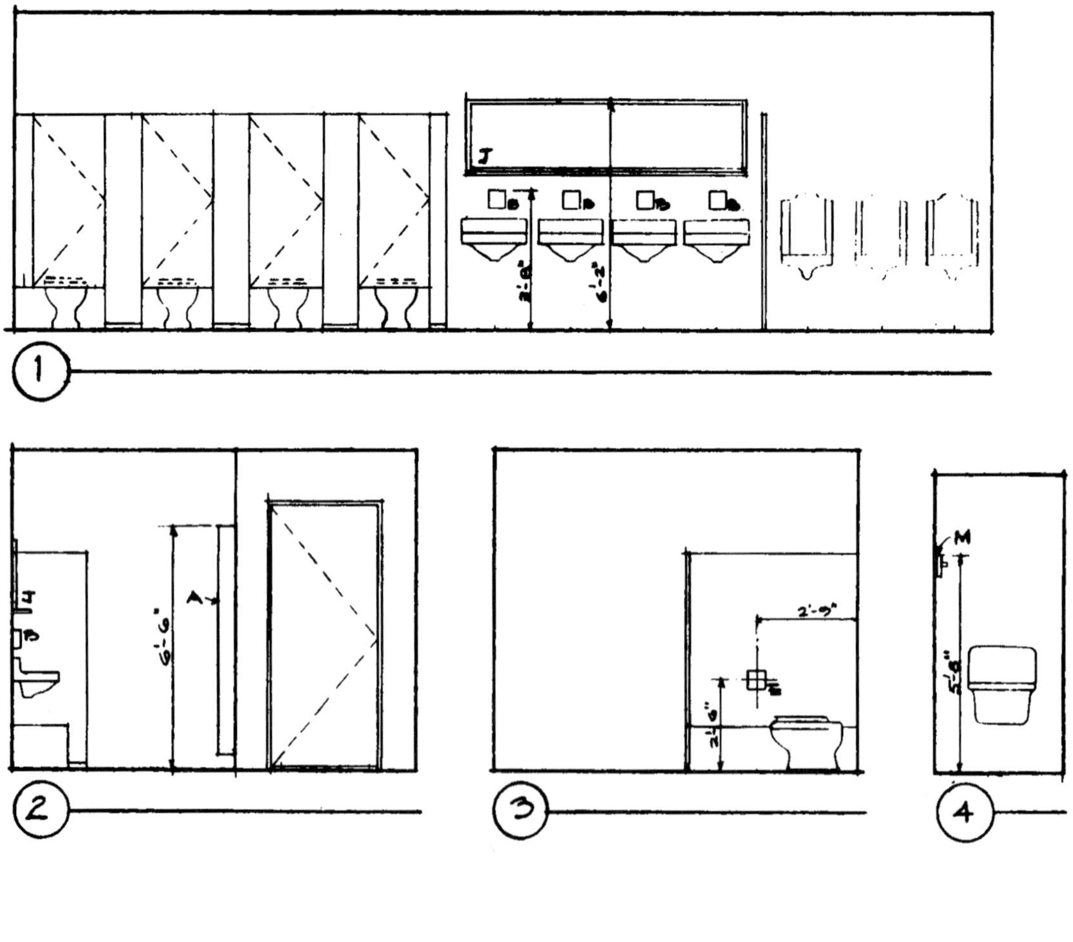

The women's room shown in Fig. 9 requires approximately 250 ft^2 for the toilet area and about the same for the vanity area. Wall elevations for the two areas are shown in Fig. 10. The designer should carefully analyze the number of lavatories and water closets specified for a given facility. Research suggests that most fixture counts provided by city or state codes are too low and do not adequately reflect the amount of time that women require. As a result, it is not unusual to see long lines in front of women's rooms, particularly those that service places of public assembly. Note that the plan in Fig. 9 provides supplemental vanity or counter surfaces.

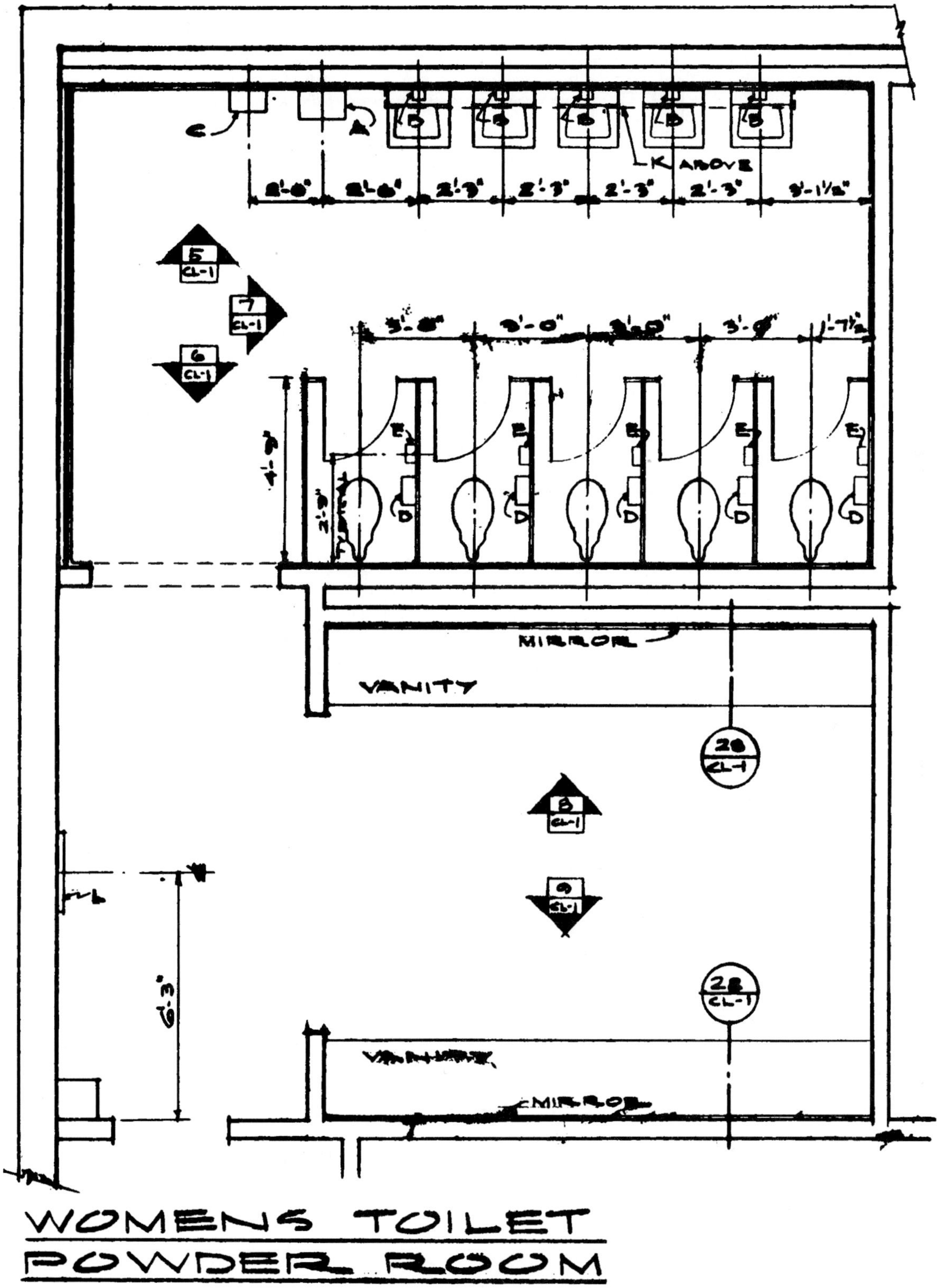

Fig. 9

REST ROOMS AND TOILETS

Plans and Elevations

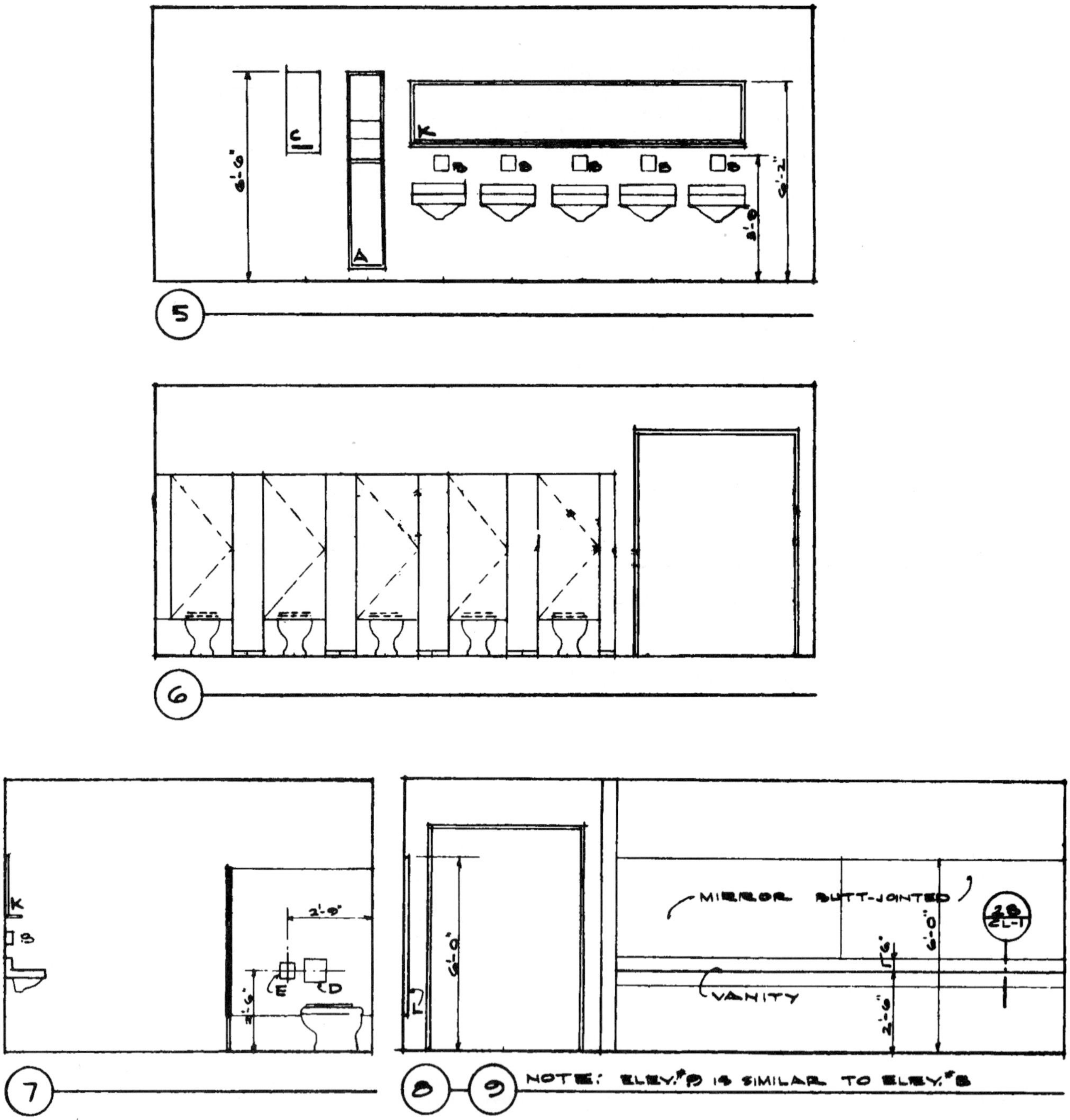

Fig. 10 Wall elevations for the women's room plan in Fig. 9

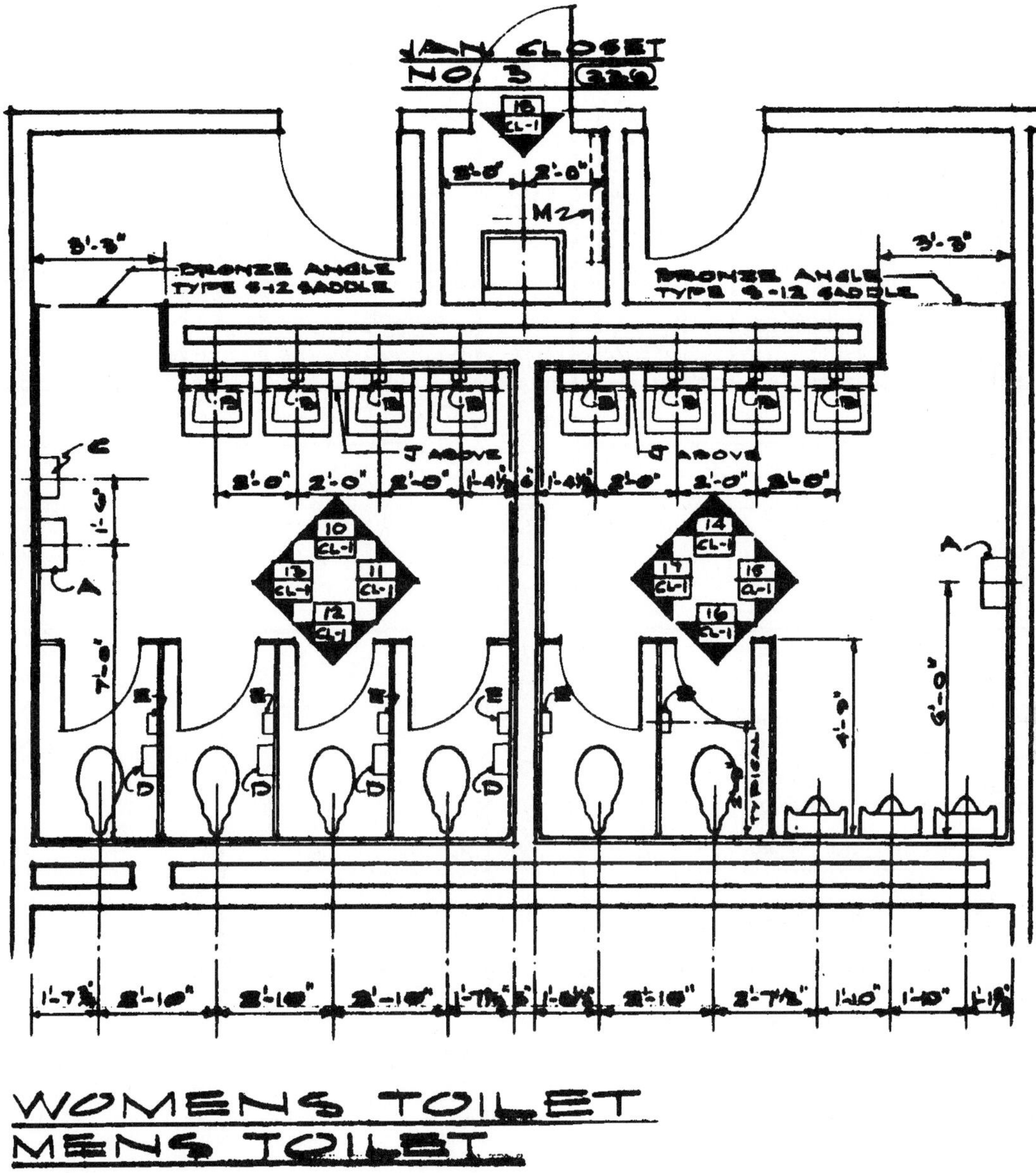

Fig. 11 This men's room and women's room complex, including a janitor's closet, requires slightly more than 400 ft^2 of floor area. Corresponding wall elevations are shown in Fig. 12

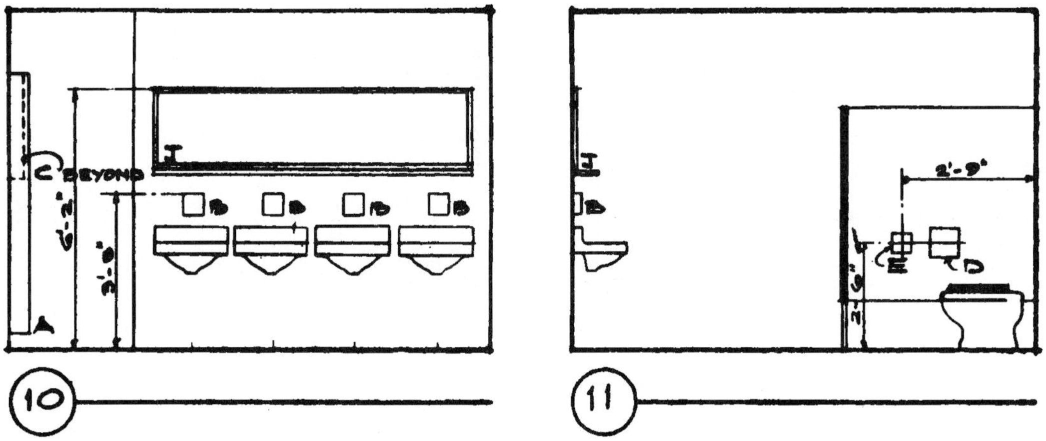

Fig. 12 Wall elevations for the men's room and women's room complex shown in Fig. 11

REST ROOMS AND TOILETS
Plans and Elevations

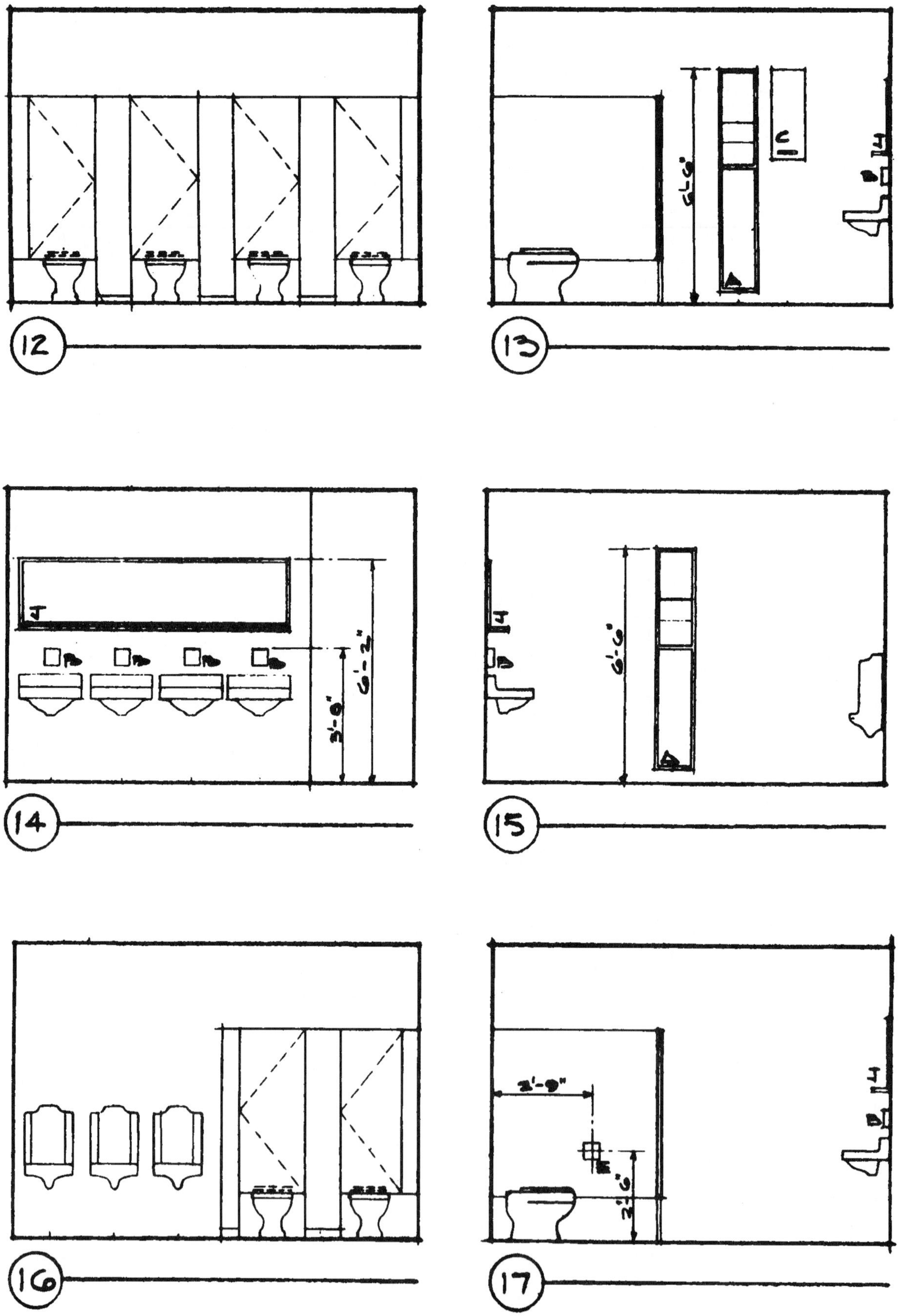

Fig. 12 ***(Continued)***

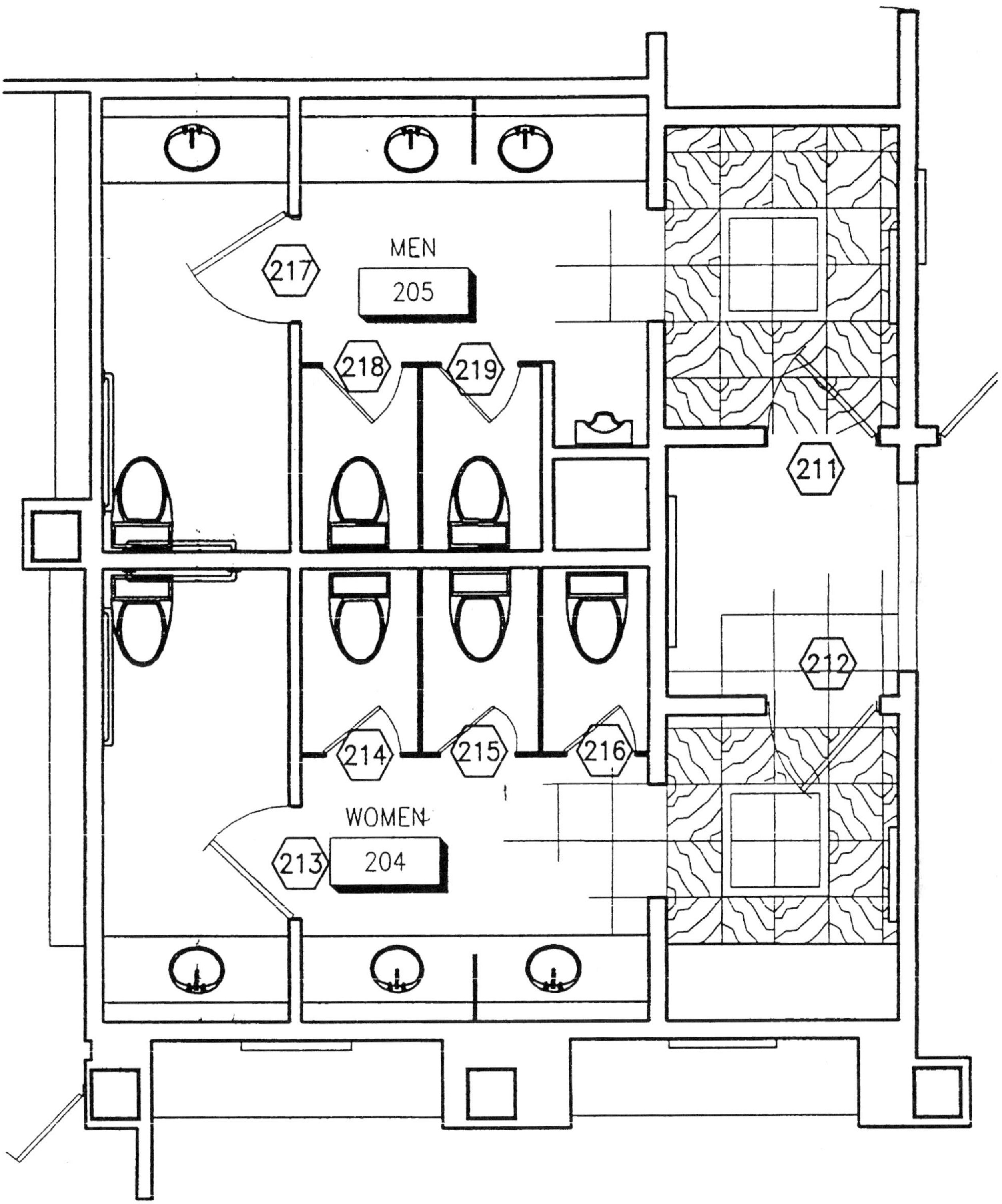

Typical Public Rest Rooms

REST ROOMS AND TOILETS
Plans and Elevations

men's toilet

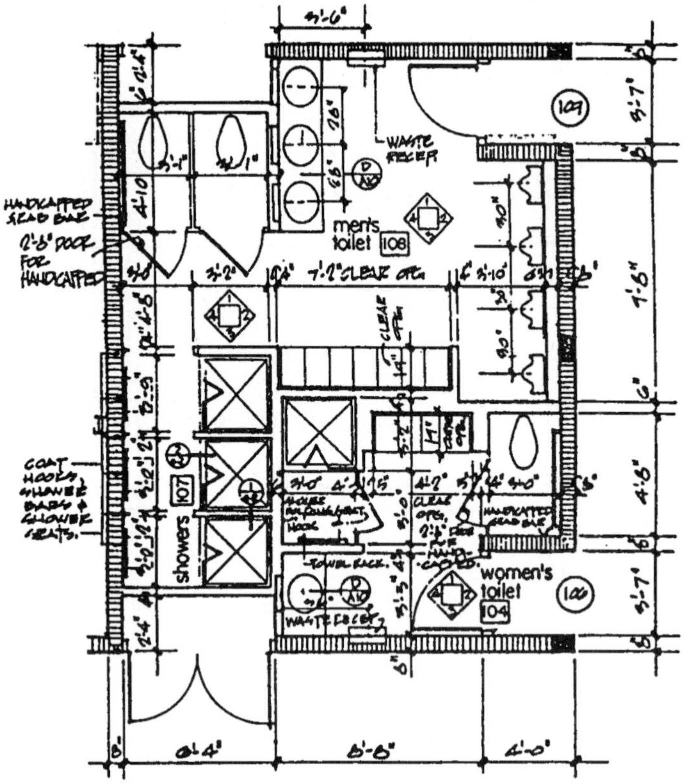

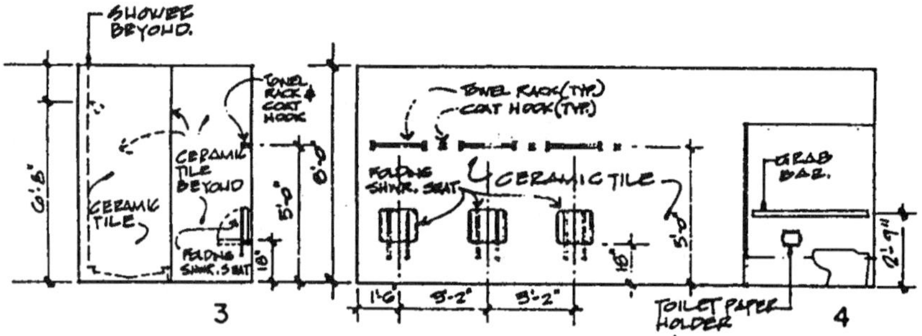

showers

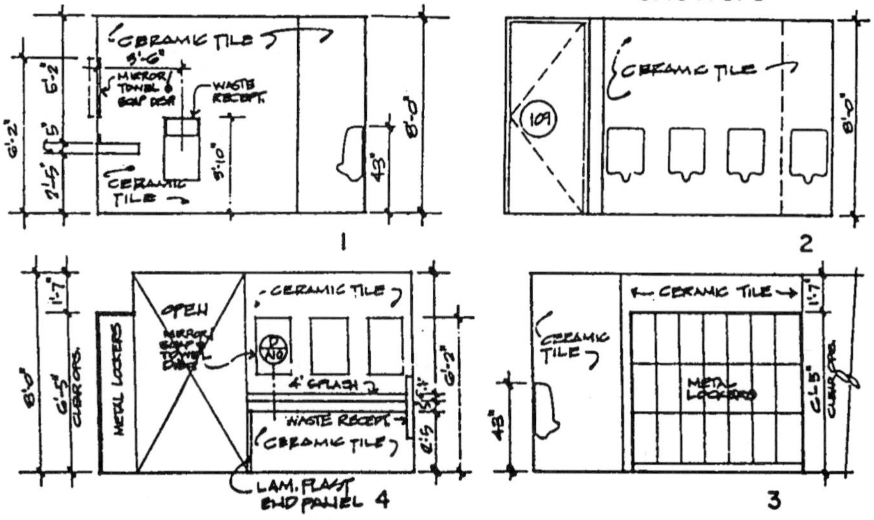

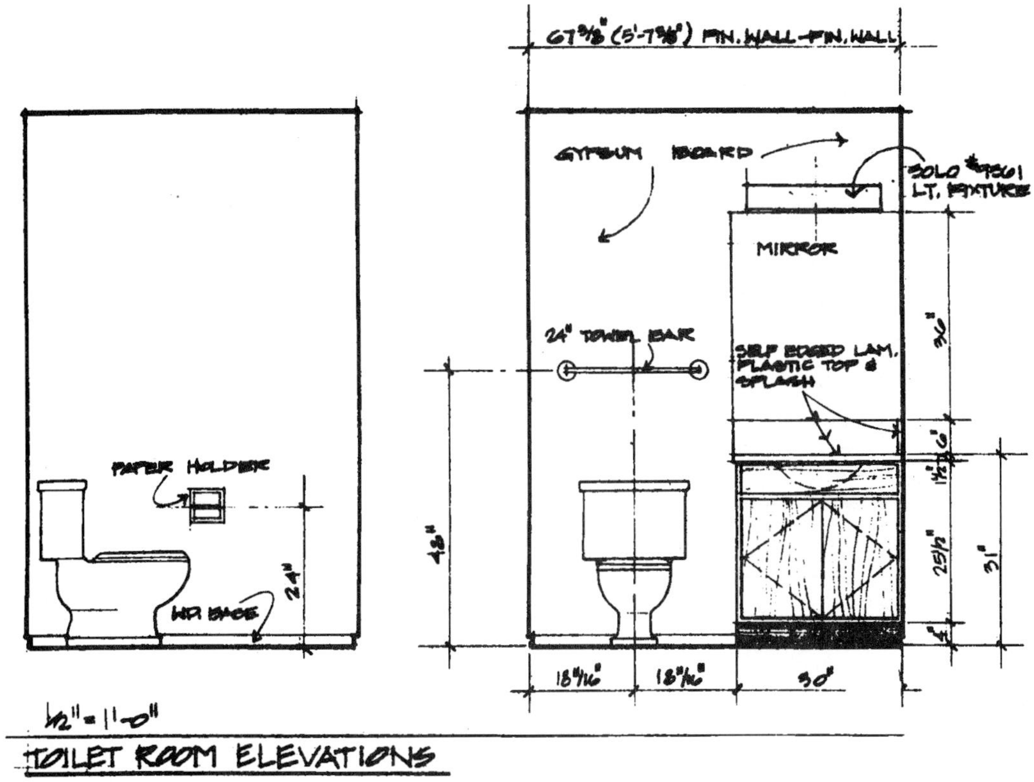

Fig. 13 Detailed large-scale wall elevations such as this are required to show materials, accessory mounting heights, the coordination and placement of plumbing fixtures, and even manufacturers' model numbers

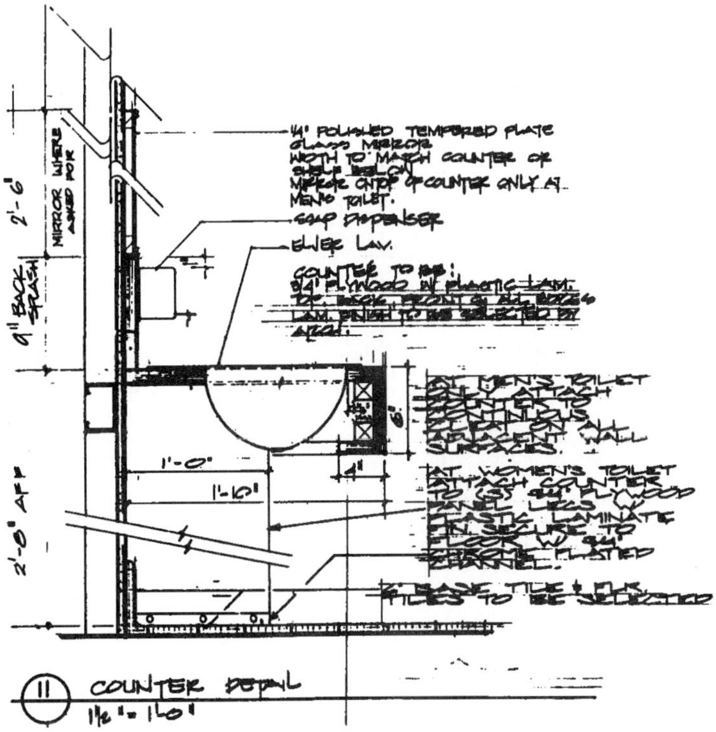

Fig. 14 The large-scale counter detail shown here provides all the information needed to construct this essential bathroom element. Not only are the construction details carefully defined and described, but all the other design relationships are clearly shown. Note the relationships of the mirror, soap dispenser, and lavatory to the plastic laminate counter. Other lavatory counter details are shown in Figs. 15 to 18

REST ROOMS AND TOILETS
Lavatory Counter Details

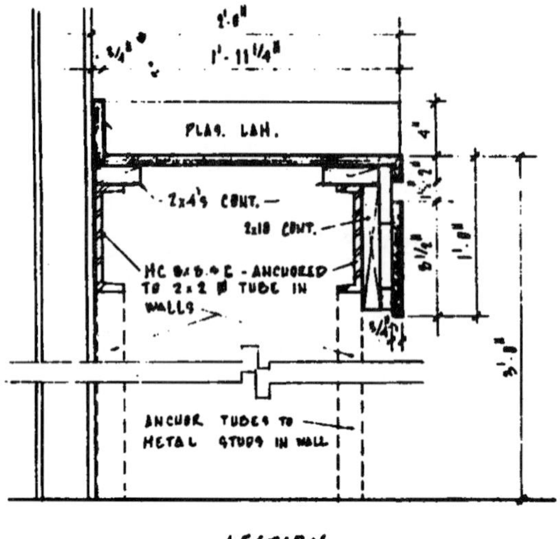

SECTION

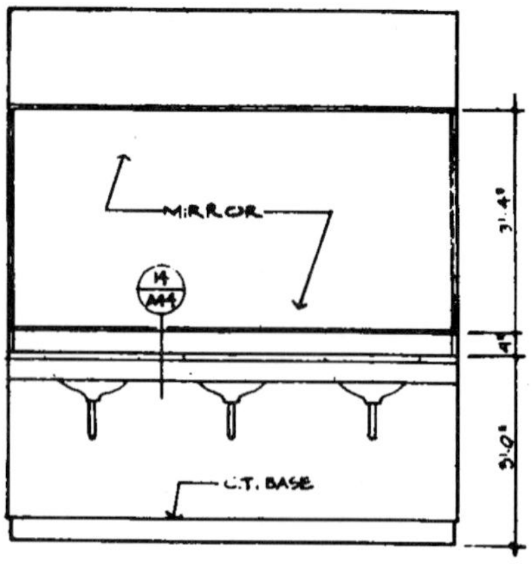

TOILET LAVATORY-TYP.

SEE FLOOR PLAN FOR LOCATION AT SILOS
TOILETS - 103, 104, 132, 196, 216, 297

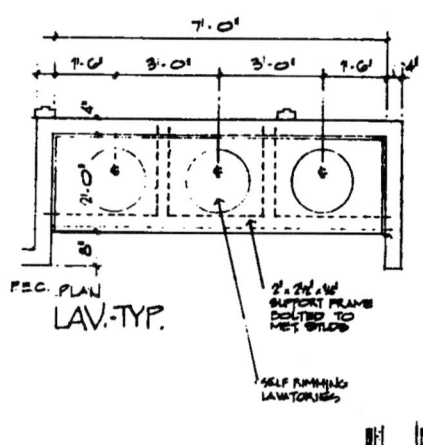

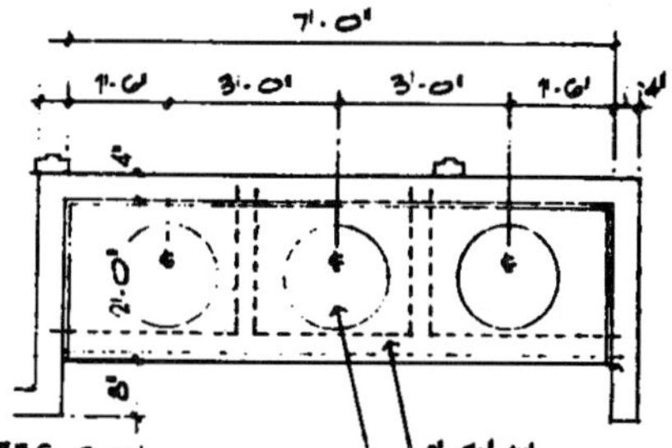

F.E.C. PLAN
LAV.-TYP.

2" x 2 1/2" x 1/4" SUPPORT FRAME BOLTED TO MET. STUDS

SELF RIMMING LAVATORIES

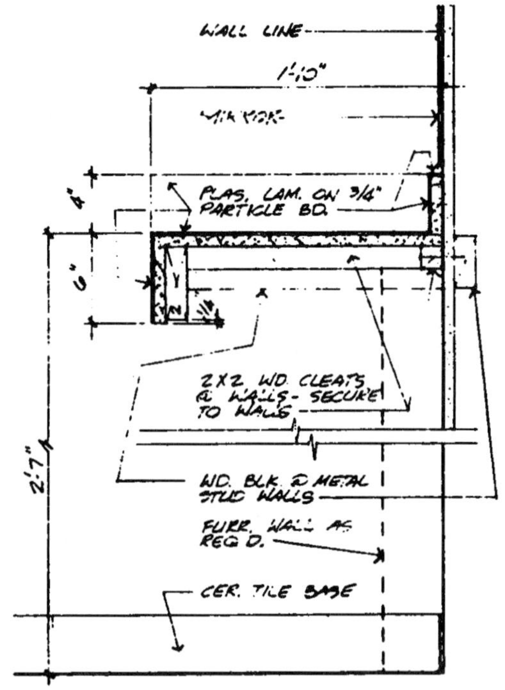

SECTION - LAV. COUNTER

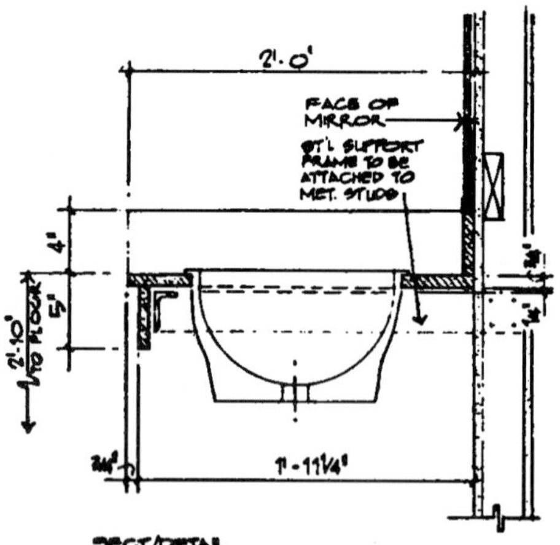

SECT./DETAIL
SILO LAVATORIES

Fig. 15

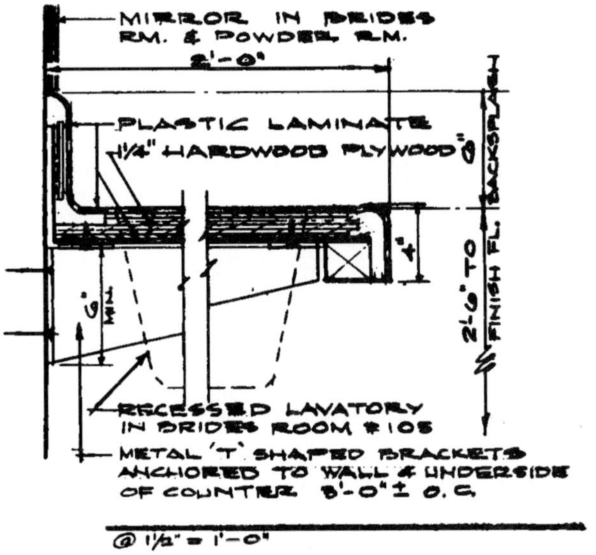
MIRROR IN BRIDES RM. & POWDER RM.
2'-0"
PLASTIC LAMINATE
1 1/4" HARDWOOD PLYWOOD
6" BACKSPLASH
4"
6" MIN.
2'-6" TO FINISH FL.
RECESSED LAVATORY IN BRIDES ROOM #105
METAL 'T' SHAPED BRACKETS ANCHORED TO WALL & UNDERSIDE OF COUNTER 3'-0" ± O.C.
@ 1 1/2" = 1'-0"

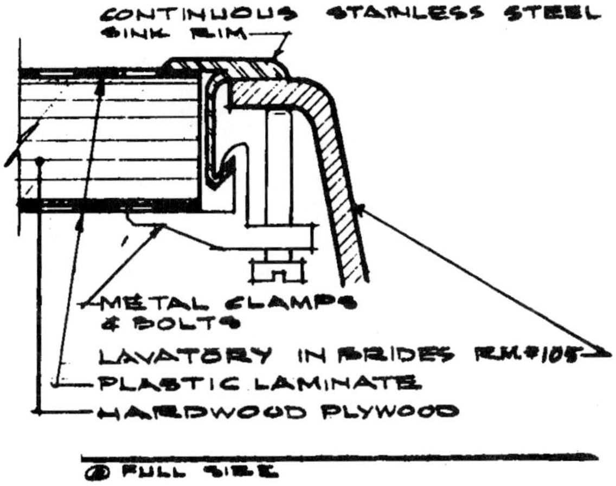
CONTINUOUS STAINLESS STEEL SINK RIM
METAL CLAMPS & BOLTS
LAVATORY IN BRIDES RM.#105
PLASTIC LAMINATE
HARDWOOD PLYWOOD
@ FULL SIZE

VANITY DETAILS

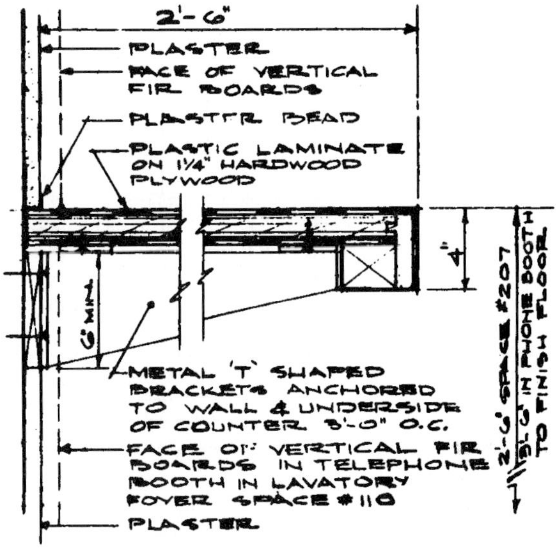
2'-6"
PLASTER
FACE OF VERTICAL FIR BOARDS
PLASTER BEAD
PLASTIC LAMINATE ON 1/4" HARDWOOD PLYWOOD
4"
6" MIN.
METAL 'T' SHAPED BRACKETS ANCHORED TO WALL & UNDERSIDE OF COUNTER 3'-0" O.C.
FACE OF VERTICAL FIR BOARDS IN TELEPHONE BOOTH IN LAVATORY FOYER SPACE #110
PLASTER
2'-6" SPACE #207
3'-0" IN PHONE BOOTH TO FINISH FLOOR

COUNTER DETAILS
@ 1/2" = 1'-0"

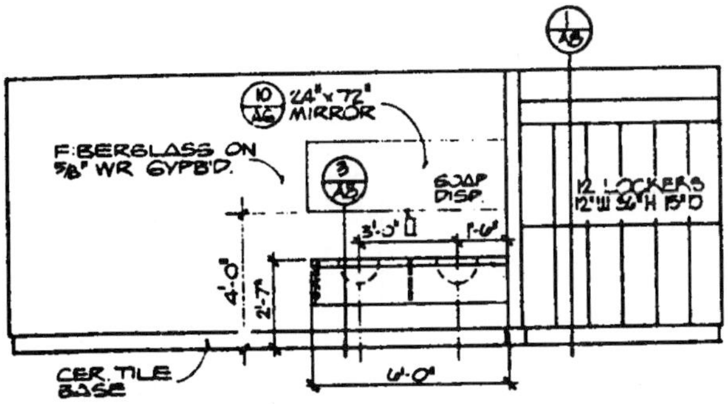
1 A6
10 A6 24"x72" MIRROR
FIBERGLASS ON 5/8" WR GYPB'D.
3 A6
SOAP DISP.
12 LOCKERS 12"W 36"H 15"D
3'-0"
1'-6"
4'-0"
2'-7"
6'-0"
CER. TILE BASE

223-224 - WEST

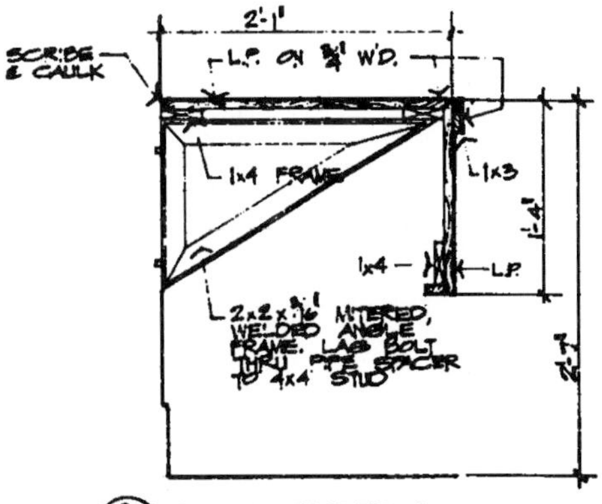
2'-1"
SCRIBE & CAULK
L.P. ON 3/4" W'D.
1x4 FRAME
1x3
1'-4"
1x4
L.P.
2x2x3/16 MITERED, WELDED ANGLE FRAME. LAG BOLT THRU PIPE SPACER TO 4x4 STUD

3 A6 LAVATORY

Fig. 16

REST ROOMS AND TOILETS
Lavatory Counter Details

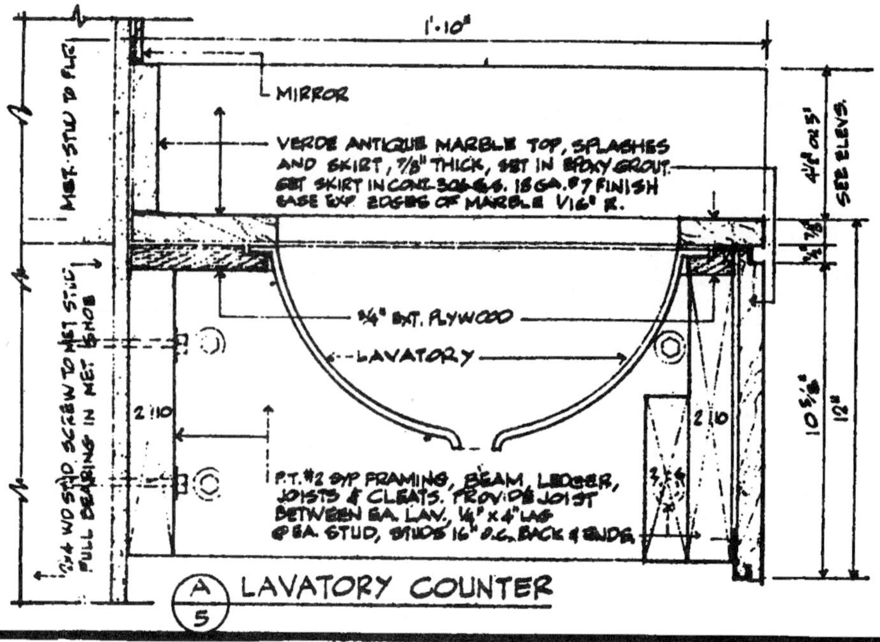
1'-10"
MIRROR
VERDE ANTIQUE MARBLE TOP, SPLASHES AND SKIRT, 7/8" THICK, SET IN EPOXY GROUT. SET SKIRT IN CONT. 3x6x6. 18 GA. #7 FINISH EASE EXP. EDGES OF MARBLE 1/16" R.
3/4" EXT. PLYWOOD
LAVATORY
P.T. #2 SYP FRAMING, BEAM, LEDGER, JOISTS & CLEATS. PROVIDE JOIST BETWEEN EA. LAV. 1/4" x 4" LAG @ EA. STUD, STUDS 16" O.C. BACK & ENDS.
MET. STUD TO FLR.
2x4 WD STUD SCREW TO MET STUD FULL BEARING IN MET SHOE
2x10
2x10
3x4
10 5/8"
12"
SEE ELEVS.
LAVATORY COUNTER
A
5

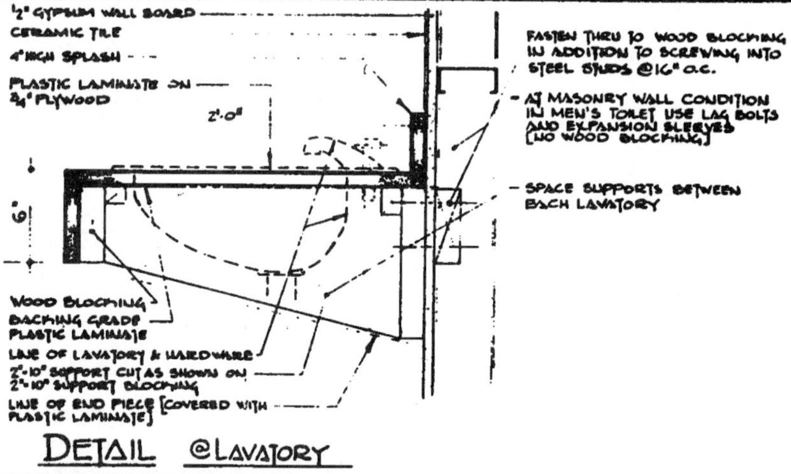
1/2" GYPSUM WALL BOARD
CERAMIC TILE
4" HIGH SPLASH
PLASTIC LAMINATE ON 3/4" PLYWOOD
2'-0"
6"
FASTEN THRU TO WOOD BLOCKING IN ADDITION TO SCREWING INTO STEEL STUDS @ 16" O.C.
AT MASONRY WALL CONDITION IN MEN'S TOILET USE LAG BOLTS AND EXPANSION SLEEVES (NO WOOD BLOCKING)
SPACE SUPPORTS BETWEEN EACH LAVATORY
WOOD BLOCKING
BACKING GRADE PLASTIC LAMINATE
LINE OF LAVATORY & HARDWARE
2'-10" SUPPORT CUT AS SHOWN ON 2x10" SUPPORT BLOCKING
LINE OF END PIECE (COVERED WITH PLASTIC LAMINATE)
DETAIL @LAVATORY

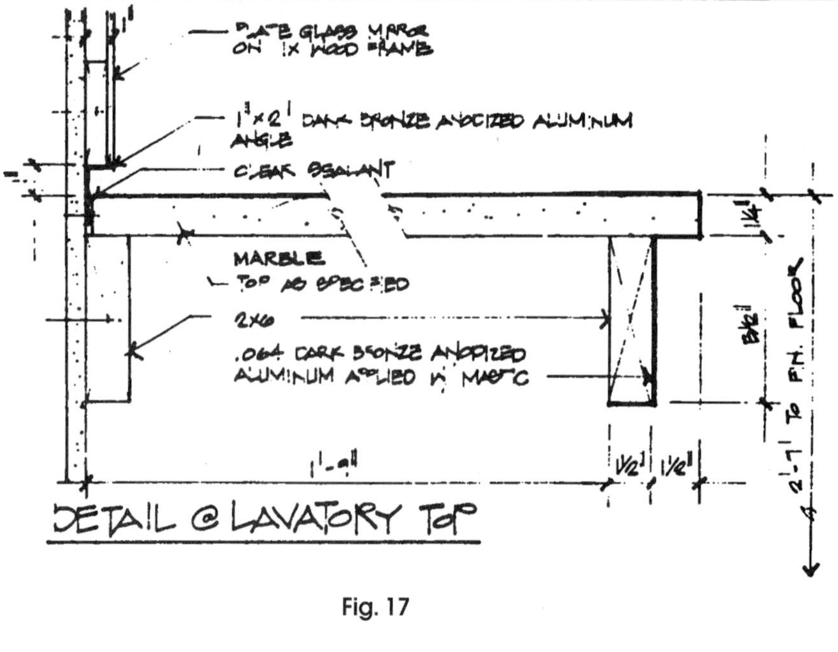
PLATE GLASS MIRROR ON 1x WOOD FRAME
1 1/2 x 2 DARK BRONZE ANODIZED ALUMINUM ANGLE
CLEAR SEALANT
MARBLE TOP AS SPECIFIED
2x6
.064 DARK BRONZE ANODIZED ALUMINUM APPLIED W/ MASTIC
1 1/4"
1'-8"
1 1/2"
1 1/2"
2'-7" TO FIN. FLOOR
DETAIL @ LAVATORY TOP

Fig. 17

REST ROOMS AND TOILETS

Lavatory Counter Details

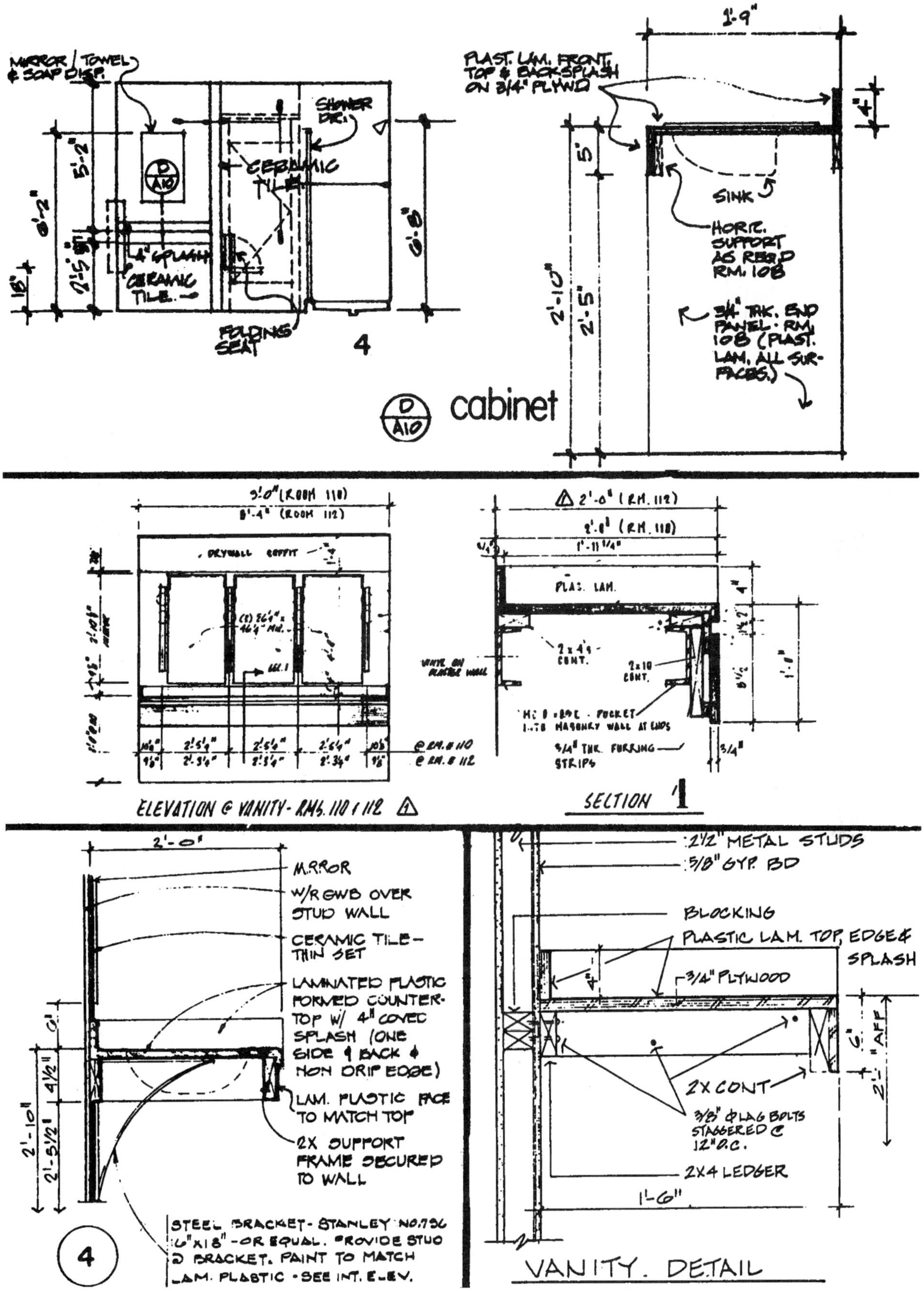

Fig. 18

REST ROOMS AND TOILETS
Lavatory Cabinet Details

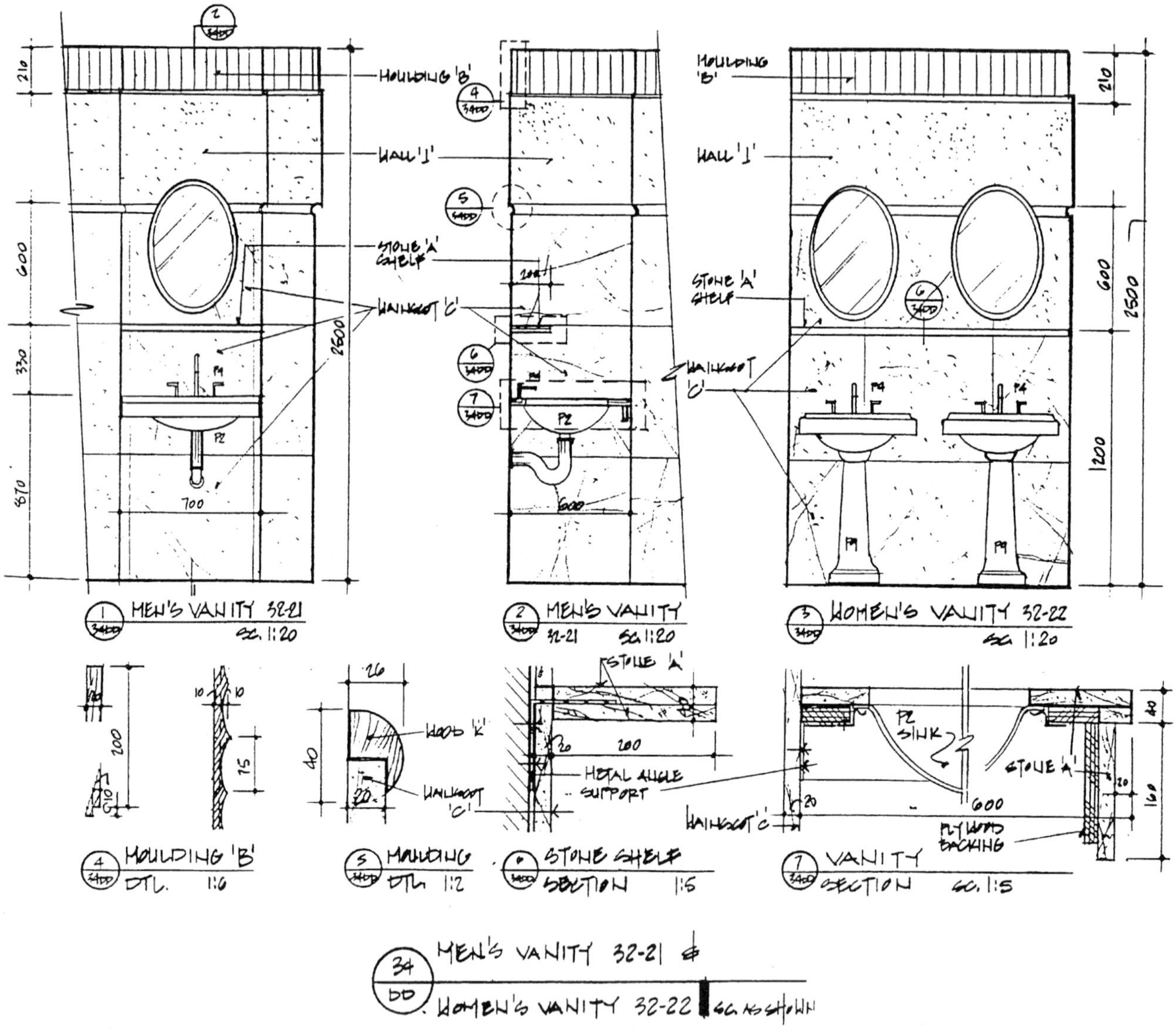

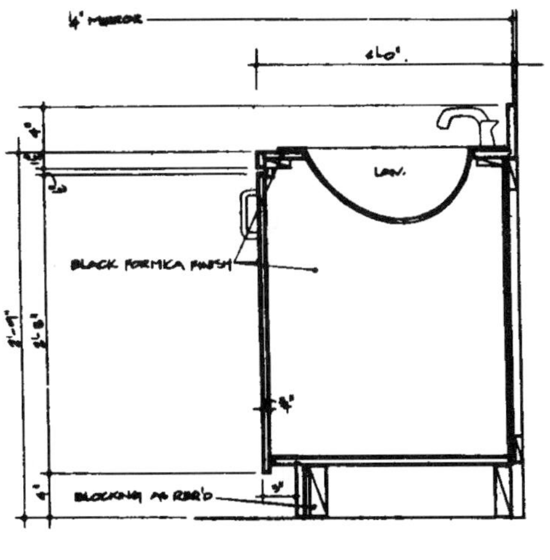

CABINET DETAIL at POWDER ROOM
SCALE: 1½" = 1'-0"

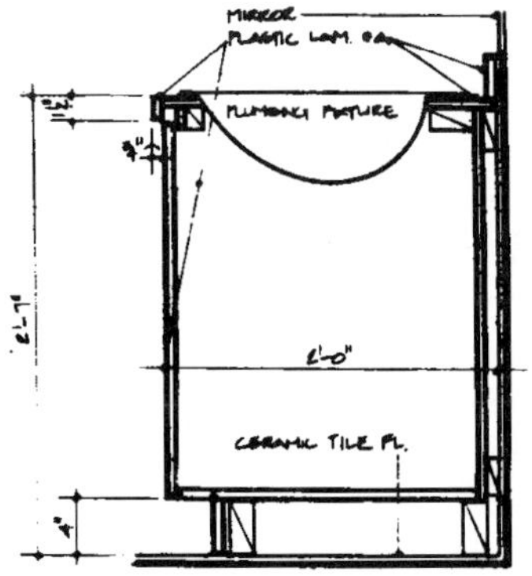

DET. OF BATHRM. CABINET
SCALE: 1½" = 1'-0"

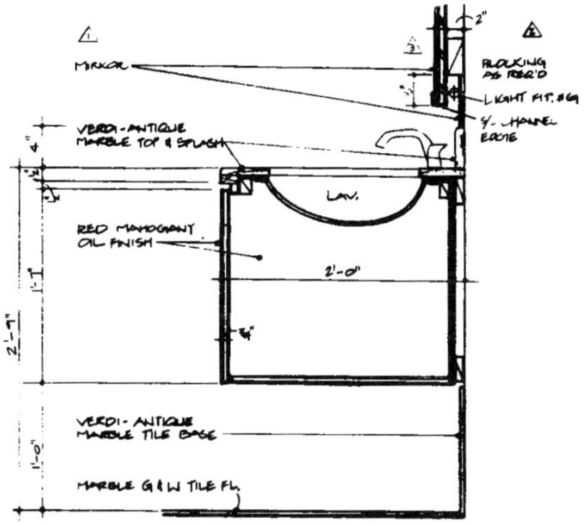

CABINET DETAIL at WOMEN
SCALE: 1½" = 1'-0"

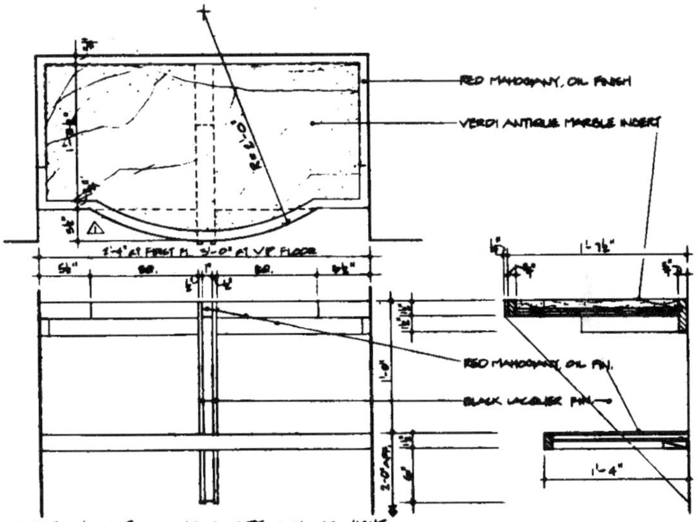

PLAN, ELEV. & SECT. of SHELF at TELEPHONE NICHE
SCALE: 1½" = 1'-0"

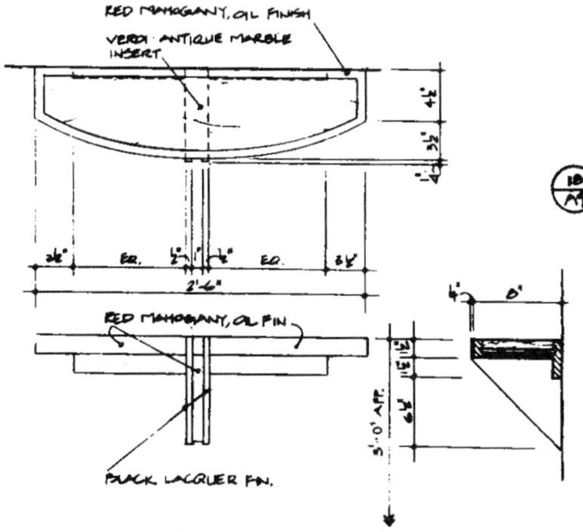

PLAN, ELEV. & SECT. of SHELF at WOMEN
SCALE: 1½" = 1'-0"

Fig. 19 Elegantly detailed lavatory cabinets are shown here. Note the use of an exposed oil-finished red mahogany frame or edge surrounding a verdi antique marble top. Complementary telephone shelf details in plan, elevation, and large-scale detail are also shown

REST ROOMS AND TOILETS
Vanity Plans

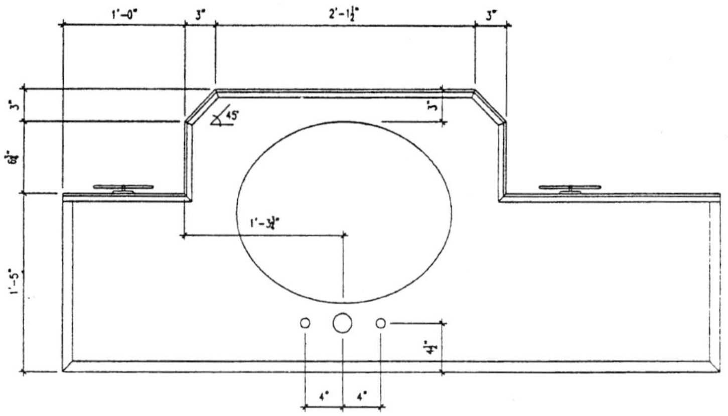

1 VANITY PLAN (4/5/7 BAY ONLY)
SCALE: 1 1/2"=1'-0"

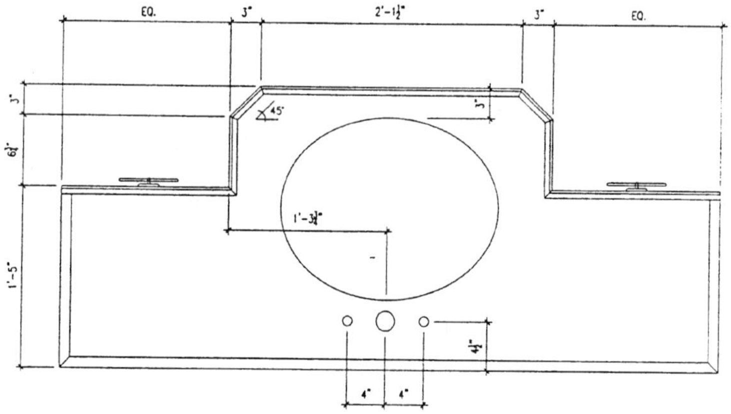

2 VANITY PLAN (4/5/7 BAY ONLY)
SCALE: 1 1/2"=1'-0"

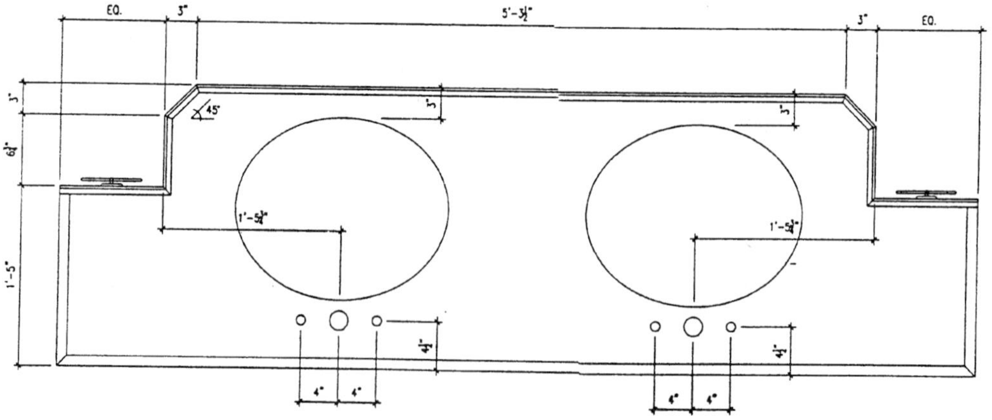

3 VANITY PLAN (4/5/7 BAY ONLY)
SCALE: 1 1/2"=1'-0"

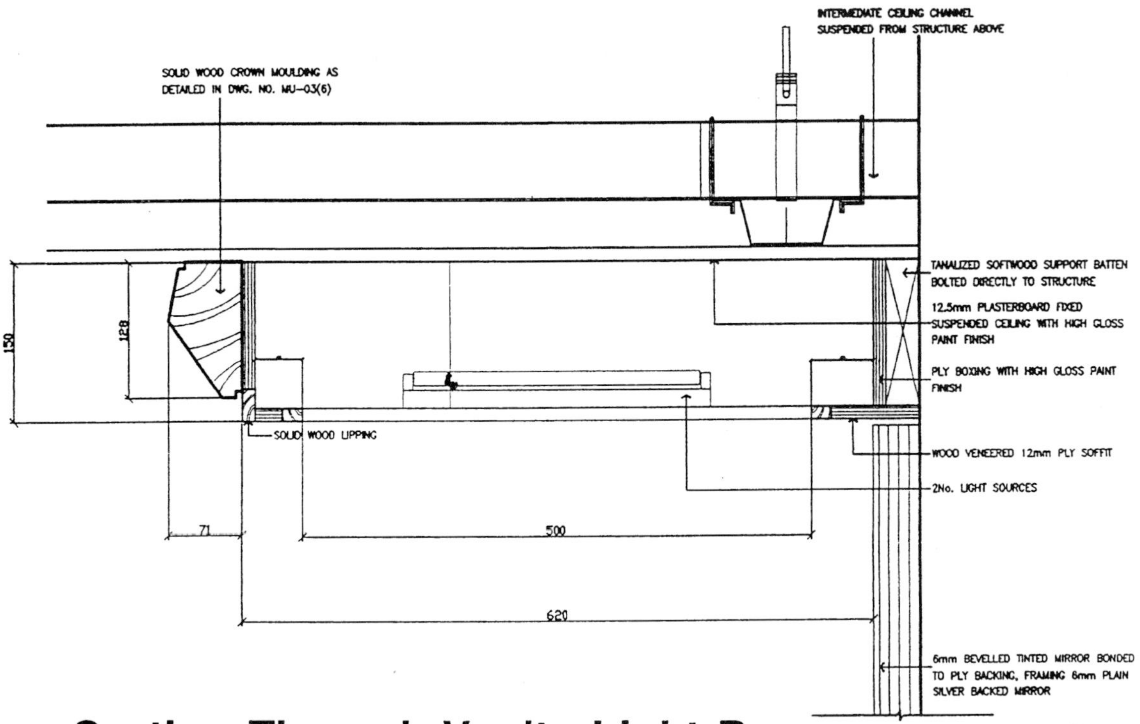

Section Through Vanity Light Box

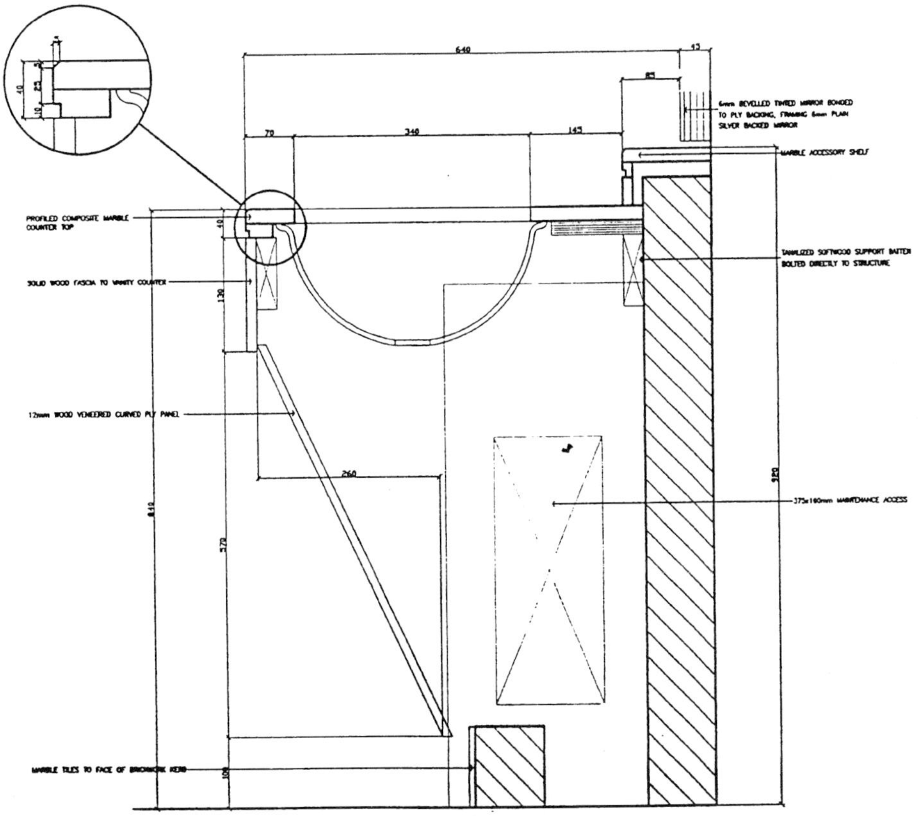

Section Through Vanity Counter

REST ROOMS AND TOILETS

Barrier-Free Bars

Grab Bars Comply with Barrier-Free Design Codes

- Constructed of satin-finish stainless steel tubing in 1¼- and 1½-in (30- and 40-mm) diameters; concealed or exposed mounting.
- Peened nonslip gripping surface available on all series. Add suffix .99 to model number.
- Bar 18-gauge (1.2-mm), type-304 stainless steel.
- Bar passes through flange and is heliarc welded to form single structural unit.
- Comply with structural strength requirements: grab bars that provide 1½-in (40-mm) clearance from the wall can support loads in excess of 900 lb (408 kg) when properly installed, meeting ADA Accessibility Guidelines in USA.
- Mandrel bending process ensures uniform bar diameter around curves.
- All joints and supports are contour cut and welded.
- Concealed anchors and fasteners available as an optional accessory.

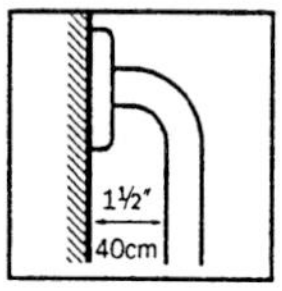

Clearance between wall and grab bar

GRAB BAR CONFIGURATIONS CLASSIC SERIES: RED

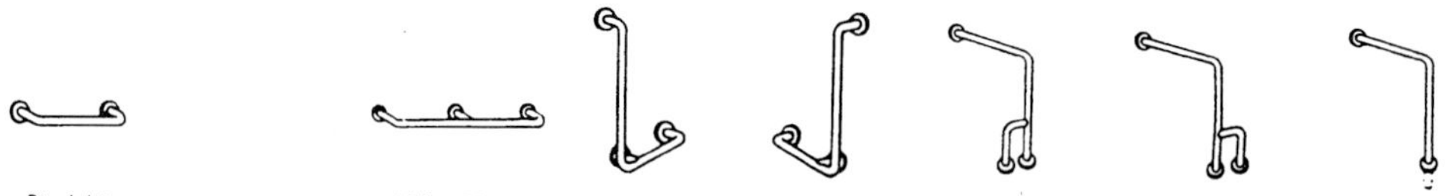

Straight

48″ (122cm) Horizontal

16″ W x 32″ H (41 x 81cm)

90° Angle

90° Angle

33″ H x 30″ D (84 x 76cm)

Wall To Floor With Outrigger

Wall To Floor With Outrigger

Wall To Floor With Socket

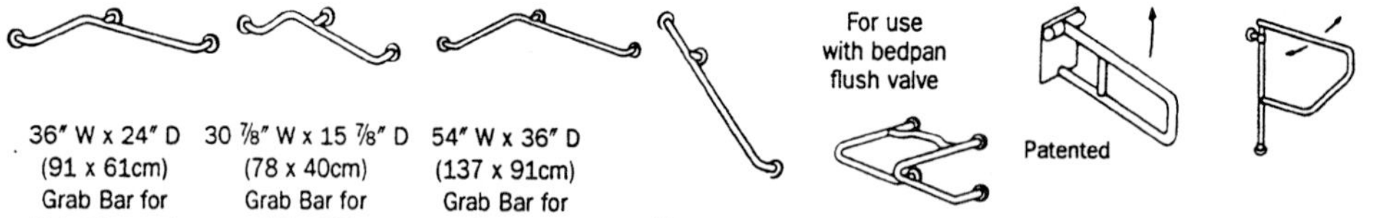

36″ W x 24″ D (91 x 61cm) Grab Bar for Tub/Shower/ Toilet Compartment

30 ⅞″ W x 15 ⅞″ D (78 x 40cm) Grab Bar for 36″ x 36″ (91 x 91cm) Shower Stall

54″ W x 36″ D (137 x 91cm) Grab Bar for Toilet Compartment/ Tub/Shower

55 ½″ (141cm) Wheelchair Toilet Comp.

24″ W x 16″ H x 24″ D (61 x 41 x 61cm) Straddle

29″ (74cm) Swing Up (Wall Mounted)

33 ⅛″ H x 27 ⅞″ D (84 x 71cm) Swing Away (Floor Mounted)

†OPTIONAL MOUNTING DEVICES
Order for each Series using part numbers listed below. See descriptions above.

FLOOR-TO-CEILING ANCHORED

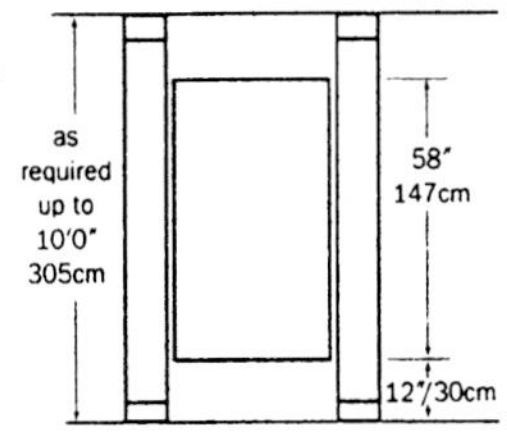

Recommended for installations where abusive treatment is expected and maximum support and vandal-resistance is critical. Furnished with sleeve anchors that require minimum 2" (51mm) penetration into 3" (76mm) thick structural concrete floor and threaded rods for attachment to structural ceiling support furnished by others. (1086 Floor-to-Ceiling Anchored DuraLine Series pictured.)

DESCRIPTION	SERIES NO.
Solid Phenolic	1086, 1186

BARRIER-FREE

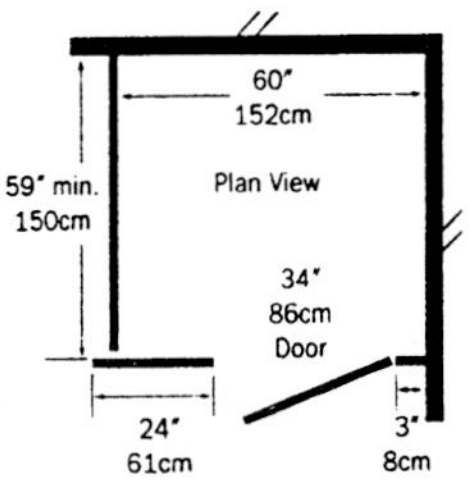

Recommended for barrier-free access code compliance. Layouts available from Bobrick for TrimLine, Classic, Designer, FRP, and DuraLine Series Ceiling Hung, Floor Anchored, Overhead Braced, and Floor-to-Ceiling Anchored installation with either front or side entry. Furnished with black vinyl-coated aluminum handle and an international handicap symbol. (1041 Barrier-Free Floor-Anchored Designer Series pictured.) Plan view shown meets ANSI A117.1 -1992 Toilet Stall Size and Arrangement (section 4.17.3).

COMBAT SERIES

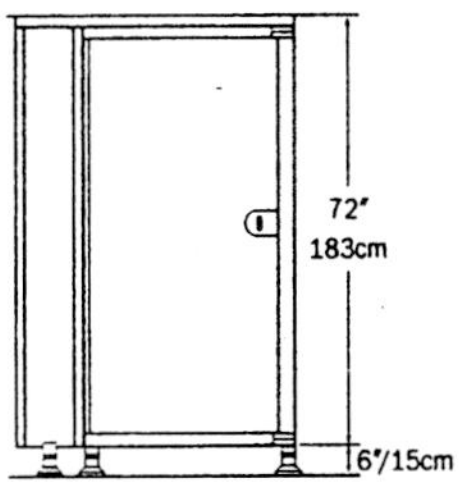

Provides outstanding design with unmatched durability. Extruded aluminum framing is inherently strong; unique black nylon floor supports provide anchoring for panels and doors and serve as door pivot hinges. Textured FRP panel and door surfaces are graffiti-, scratch- and dent-resistant. Combat Series partitions are ideal for educational, recreational and transportation facilities and for renovation projects where previously installed metal partitions have failed to withstand heavy use and vandalism.

DESCRIPTION	SERIES NO.
FRP Surfaces	1350

TYPICAL INSTALLATION DETAILS

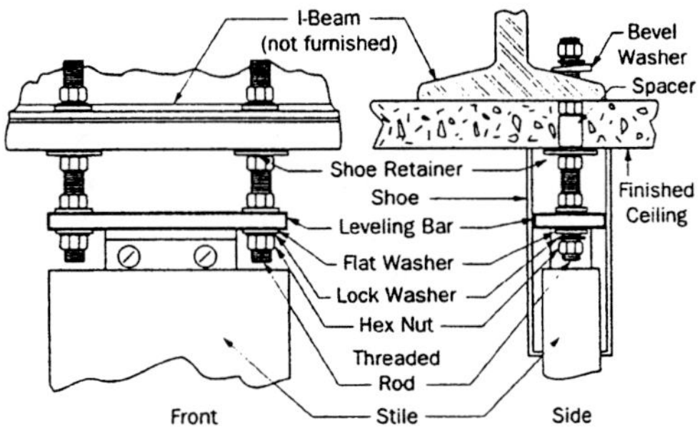

CEILING HUNG

Requires structural support in ceiling furnished by others. Note: structural member in ceiling must run in same direction as stile to provide rigidity and support. Please refer to Bobrick Advisory Bulletin TB-32 for Recommended Mounting Systems for Ceiling-Hung Partitions.

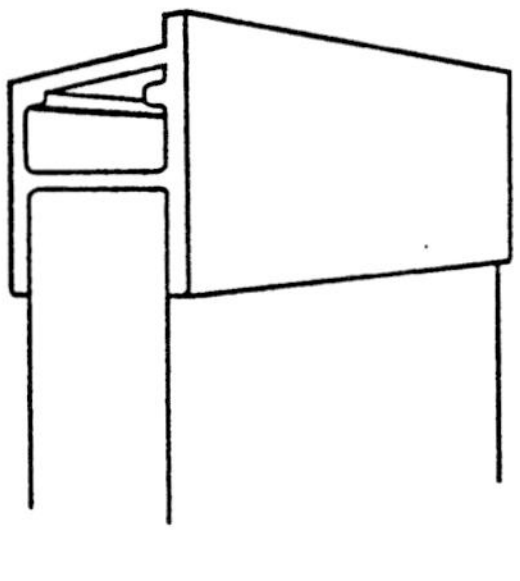

OVERHEAD BRACED

Headrail provides additional support, securing top of stiles to wall. Satin-finish aluminum headrail has raised front edge, anti-grip feature to discourage swinging and chinning. Headrail is enclosed at top and all ends are capped to prevent hiding contraband; stiles anchor to floor as shown in drawing.

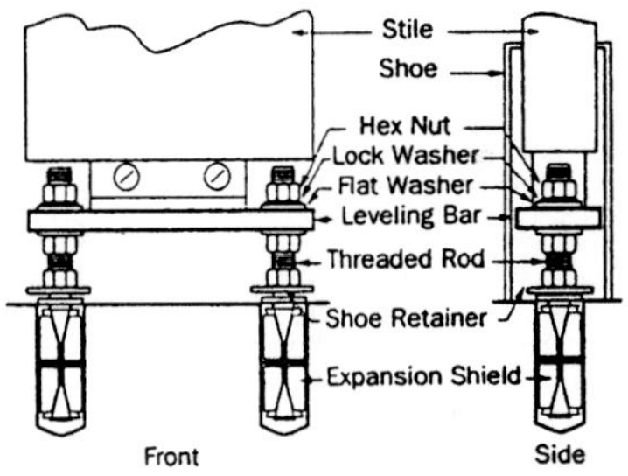

FLOOR ANCHORED

Furnished with sleeve anchors that require minimum 2" (51mm) penetration into 3" (76mm) thick structural concrete floor. Please refer to Bobrick Advisory Bulletin TB-46 for Recommended Mounting Systems for Floor-Anchored Partitions.

REST ROOMS AND TOILETS

Toilet Partitions and Accessories

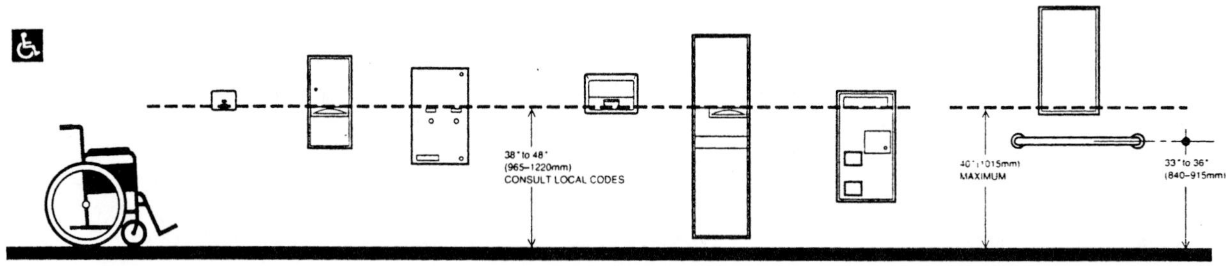

CEILING HUNG

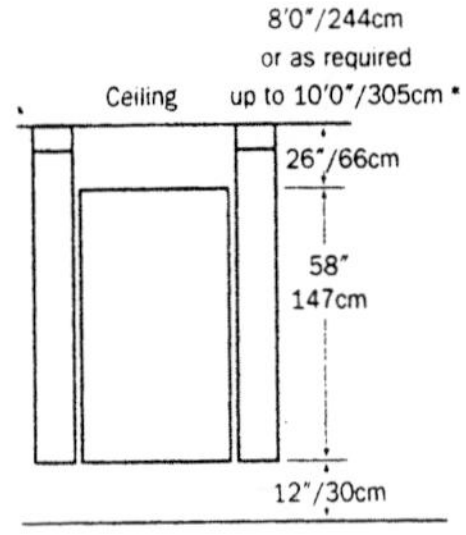

Provides clean, open design at the floor. Maintenance is improved and operating costs are reduced by providing clear area for easy floor access. Furnished with threaded rods for attachment to structural ceiling support furnished by others. (1038 Ceiling-Hung TrimLine Series pictured.)

DESCRIPTION	SERIES NO.
Stainless Steel Edge	1038
Laminated Plastic Edge	1048, 1548*
Solid Phenolic	1088, 1188
FRP Surfaces	1848

*Maximum 9'0" (275cm) ceiling for 1548.

FLOOR ANCHORED

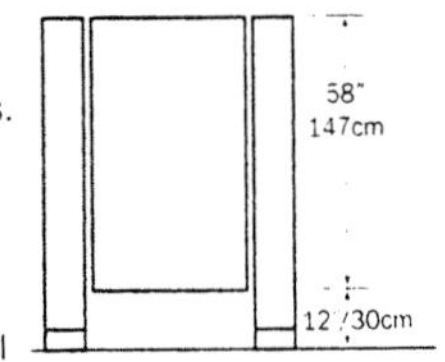

Recommended for high ceiling washrooms, provides a clean line across top of partitions. Furnished with sleeve anchors that require minimum 2" (51mm) penetration into 3" (76mm) thick structural concrete floor. (1041 Floor-Anchored Designer Series pictured.)

DESCRIPTION	SERIES NO.
Stainless Steel Edge	1031
Laminated Plastic Edge	1041, 1541
Solid Phenolic	1081, 1181
FRP Surfaces	1841

OVERHEAD BRACED

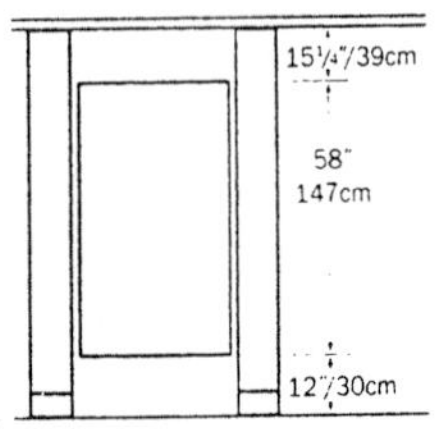

Recommended for installations where there are lightweight concrete floors, structural concrete floors less than 3" thick or plywood floors. Overhead bracing provides additional rigidity. Furnished with sleeve anchors that require minimum 2" (51mm) penetration into 3" (76mm) thick structural concrete floor. (1082 Overhead-Braced DuraLine Series pictured.)

DESCRIPTION	SERIES NO.
Stainless Steel Edge	1032
Laminated Plastic Edge	1042, 1542
Solid Phenolic	1082, 1182
FRP Surfaces	1842

TYPICAL LAYOUTS

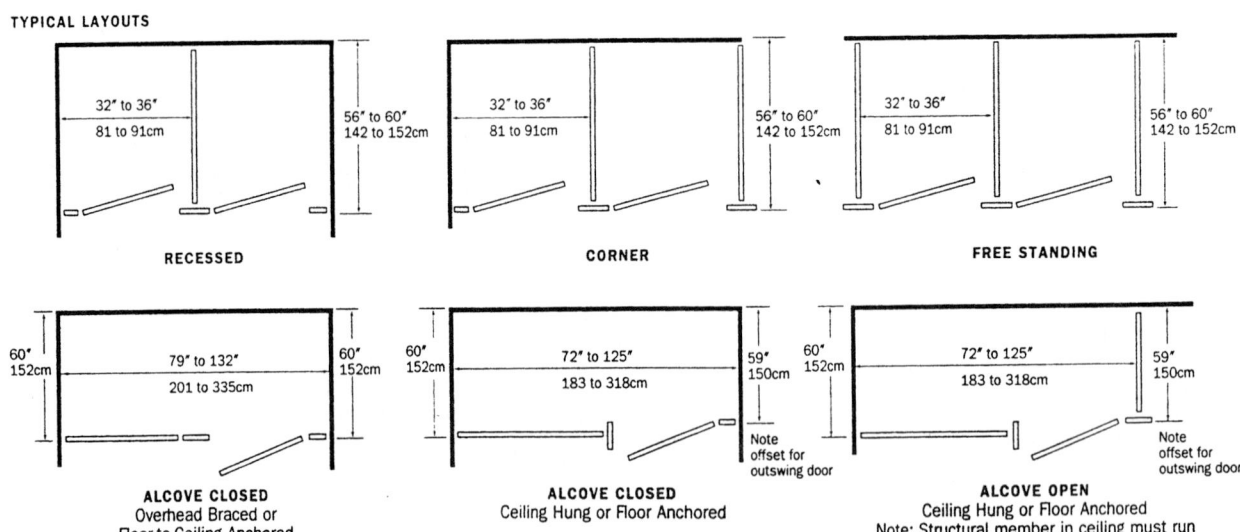

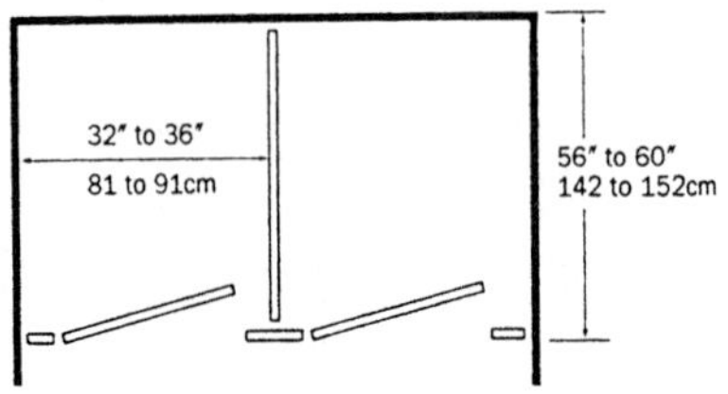

RECESSED

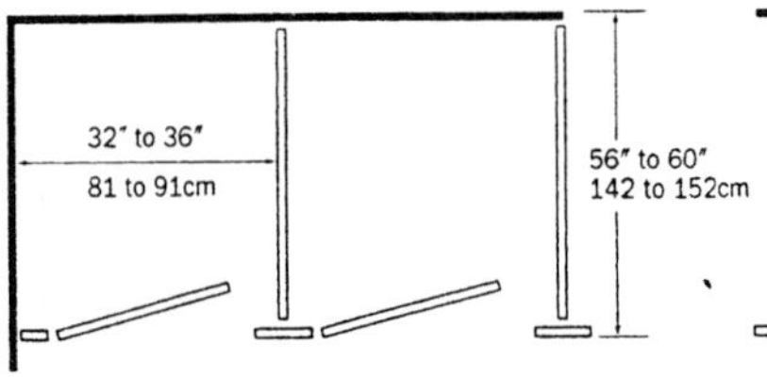

CORNER

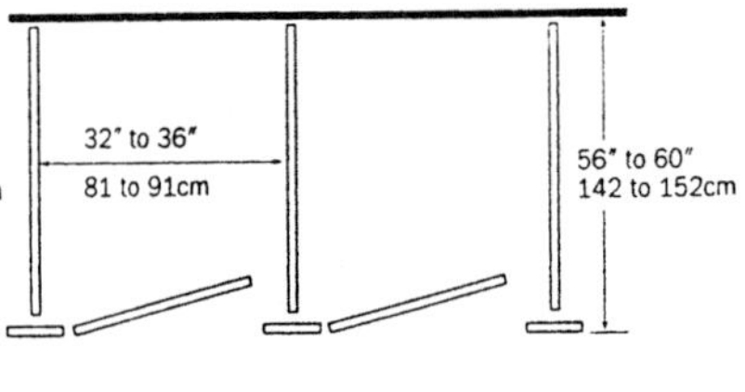

FREE STANDING

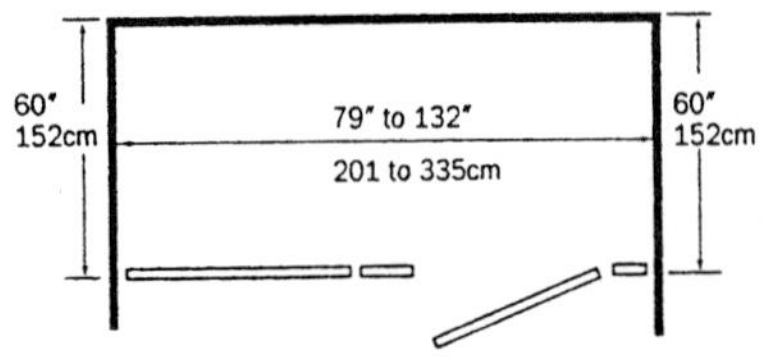

ALCOVE CLOSED
Overhead Braced or
Floor-to-Ceiling Anchored

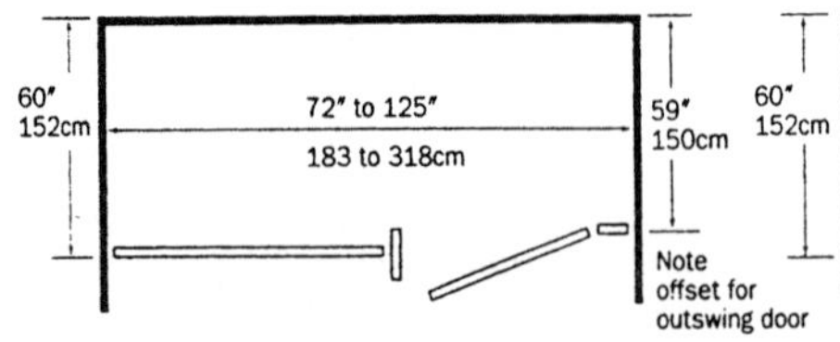

ALCOVE CLOSED
Ceiling Hung or Floor Anchored

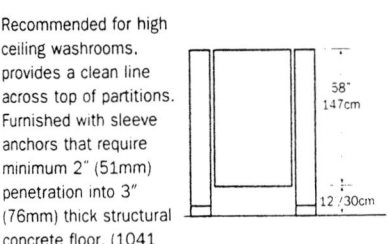

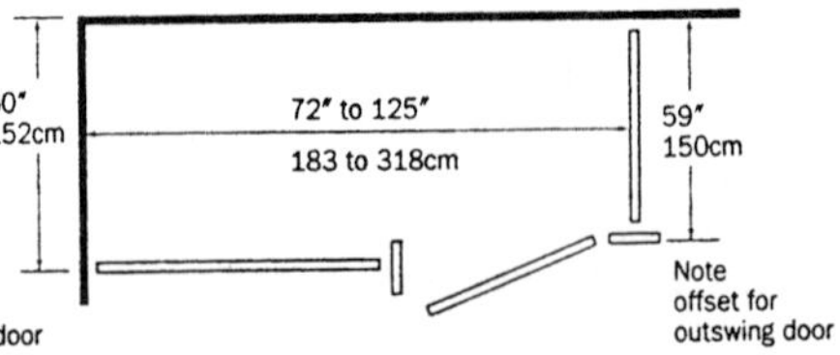

ALCOVE OPEN
Ceiling Hung or Floor Anchored
Note: Structural member in ceiling must run in same direction as stile.

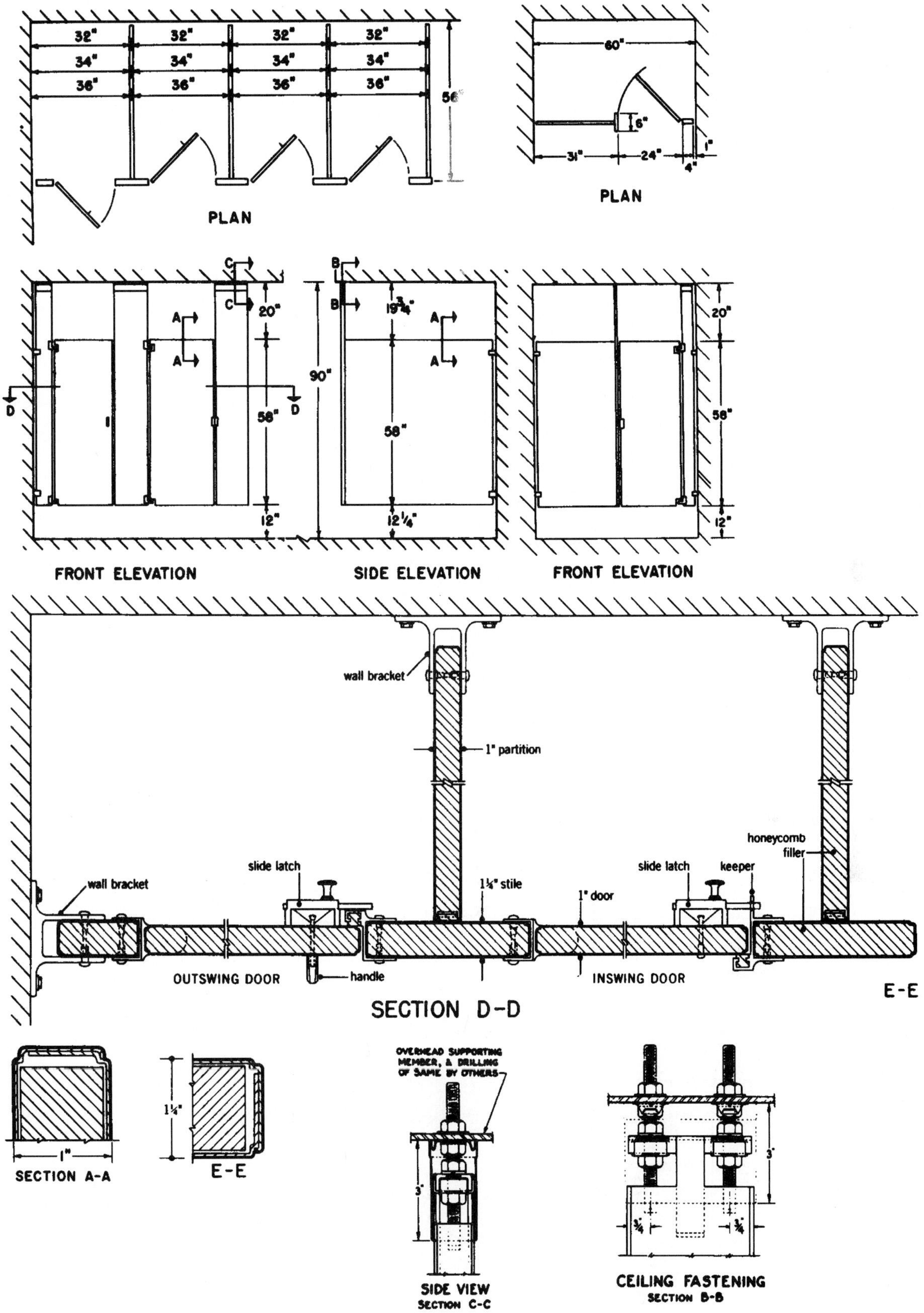
32"
34"
36"
56"
PLAN
60"
6"
31"
24"
1"
4"
PLAN
C
C
A
A
D
D
20"
58"
12"
90"
B
B
19¾"
58"
12¼"
20"
58"
12"
FRONT ELEVATION
SIDE ELEVATION
FRONT ELEVATION
wall bracket
1" partition
honeycomb filler
slide latch
1¼" stile
1" door
slide latch
keeper
wall bracket
OUTSWING DOOR
handle
INSWING DOOR
E-E
SECTION D-D
1"
SECTION A-A
1¼"
E-E
OVERHEAD SUPPORTING MEMBER, & DRILLING OF SAME BY OTHERS
3"
SIDE VIEW
SECTION C-C
3"
¾"
¾"
CEILING FASTENING
SECTION B-B

Fig. 20

REST ROOMS AND TOILETS

Toilet Stall Details

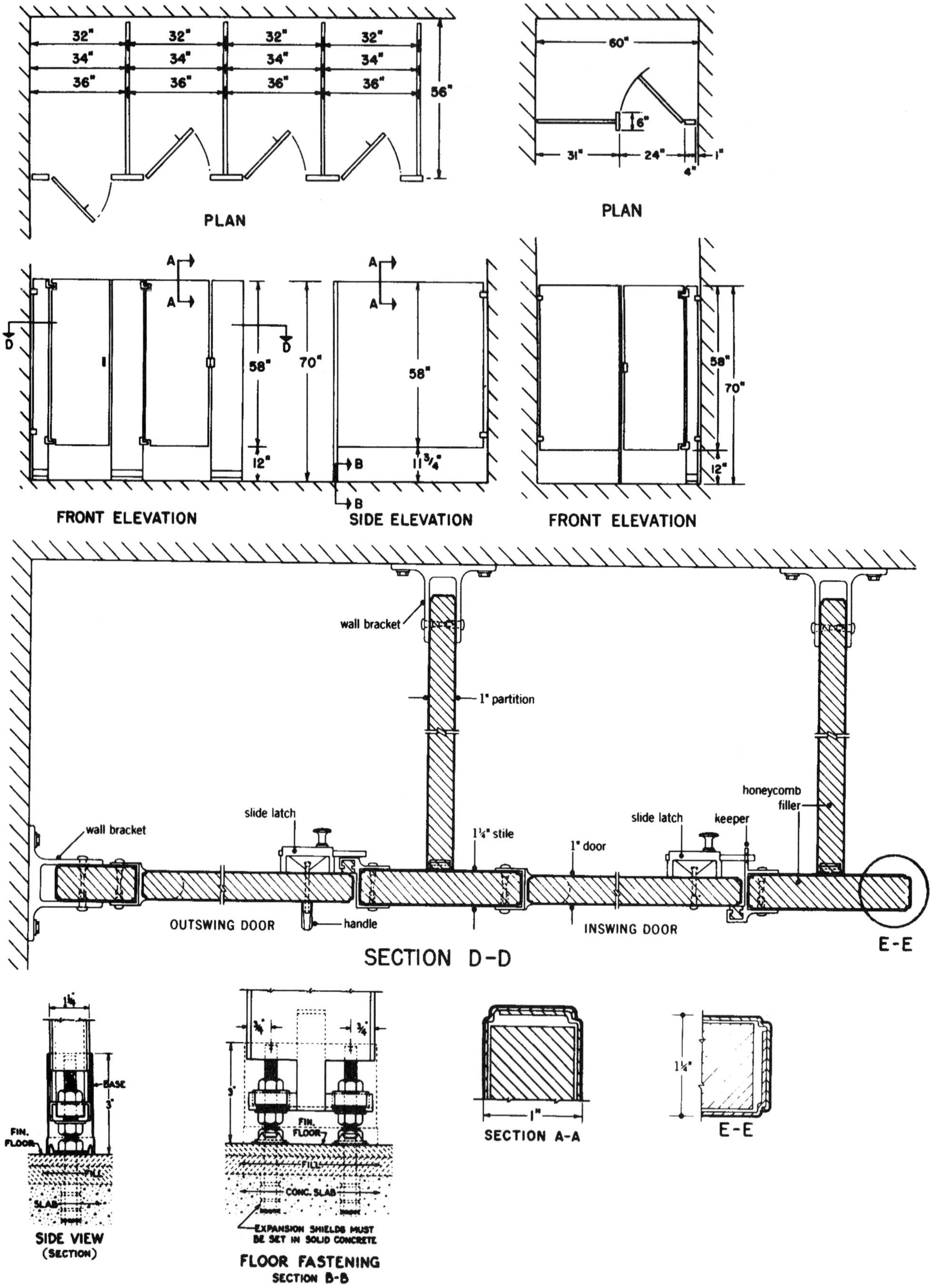

Fig. 21

REST ROOMS AND TOILETS
Wheel Chair-Accessible Design

The design data contained on the following pages are intended to illustrate functional accessibility concepts. Some examples illustrate minimum federal requirements, while others are culled from among the various state standards. Designers are cautioned to consult local standards in their respective jurisdictions.

The current minimum federal standard is ANSI A117.1-1986, published by the American National Standards Institute, Inc. It specifies a stall typified by detail a/3. This "front transfer" type stall requires a water closet mounted at 1 ft 8 in a.f.f., preferably wall hung. Stall doors must be outswinging.

Because a significant portion of people using wheelchairs cannot transfer in this manner, the side transfer stall (b/3) has been developed. Clear stall dimensions and seat heights vary somewhat with jurisdiction. Most standards that address side transfer stalls require lower seat heights with 15- to 17-in mounting heights being typical.

We recommend locking devices for doors that do not require twisting and grasping motions, avoidance of foot-operated flush valves, installation of ceiling or wall-hung partitions as practical, and avoidance of curtains in lieu of doors.

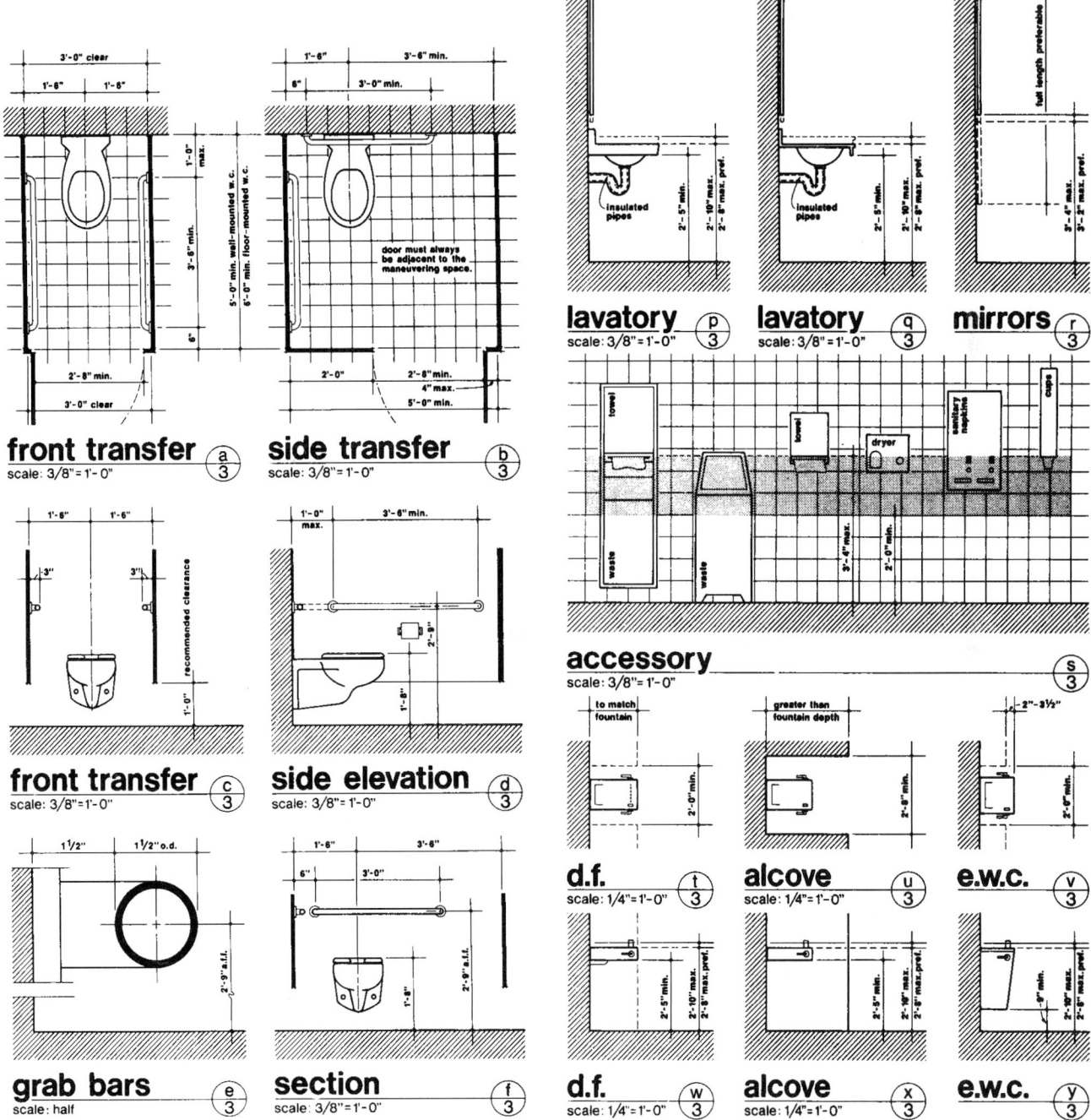

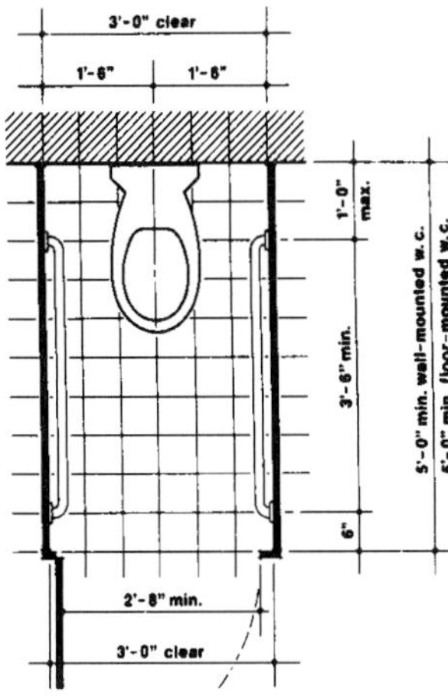

front transfer (a/3)
scale: 3/8" = 1'-0"

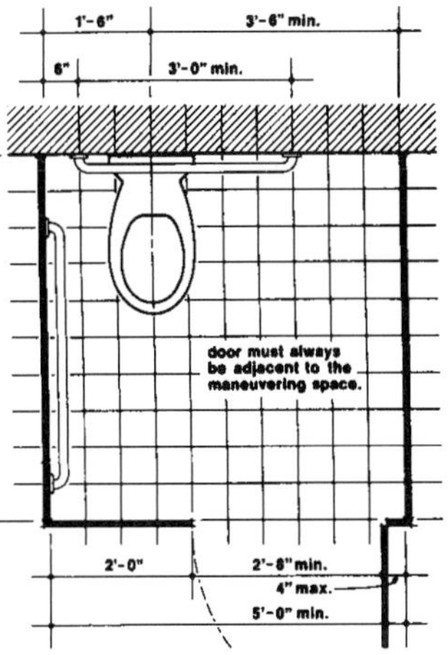

side transfer (b/3)
scale: 3/8" = 1'-0"

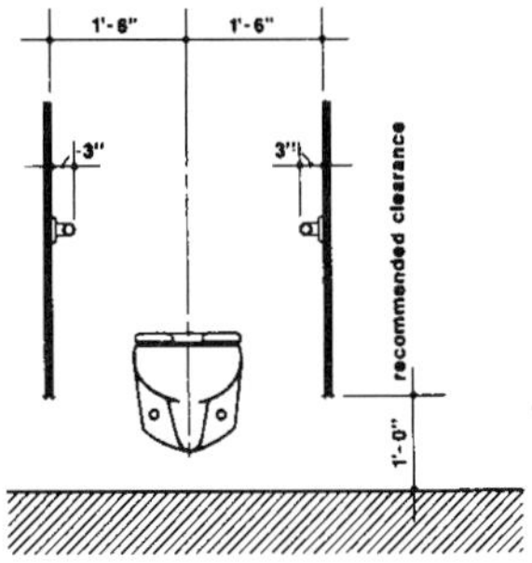

front transfer (c/3)
scale: 3/8" = 1'-0"

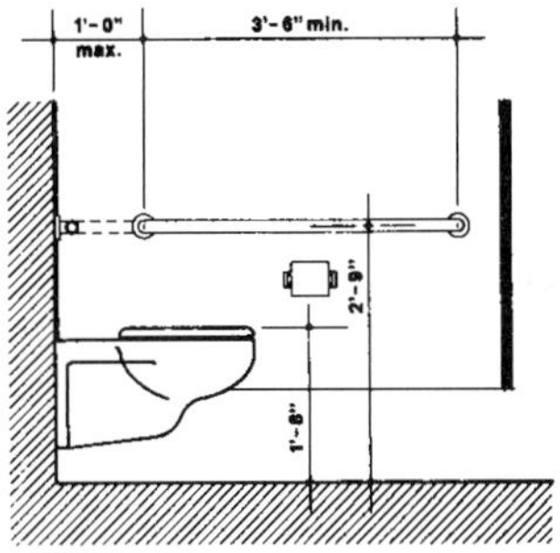

side elevation (d/3)
scale: 3/8" = 1'-0"

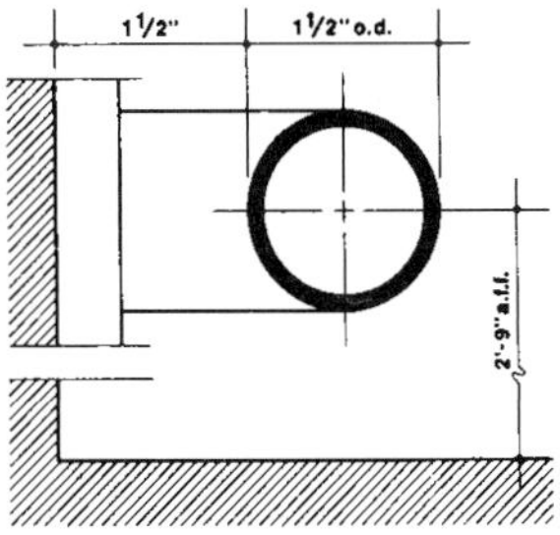

grab bars (e/3)
scale: half

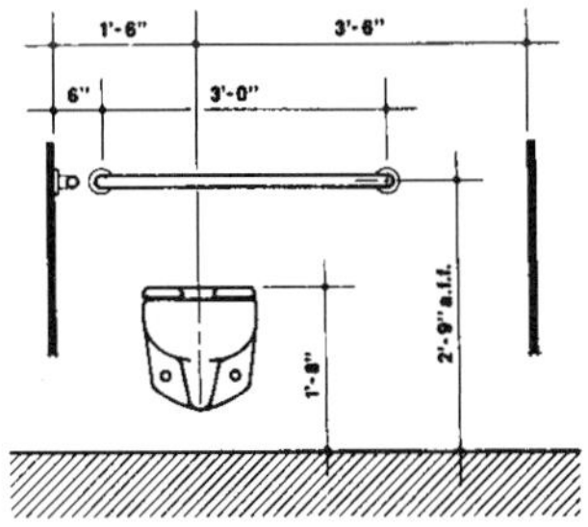

section (f/3)
scale: 3/8" = 1'-0"

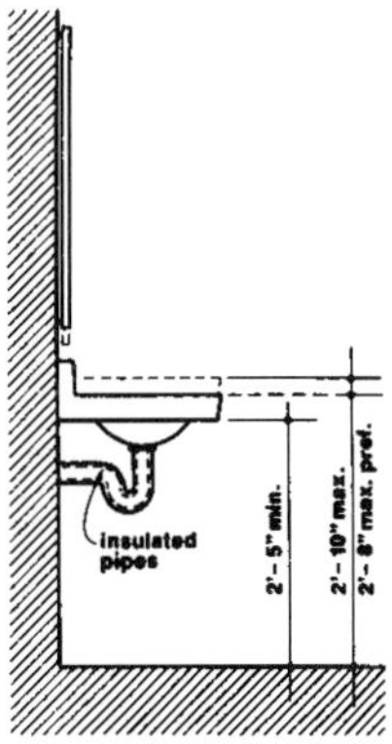

lavatory (p/3)
scale: 3/8" = 1'-0"

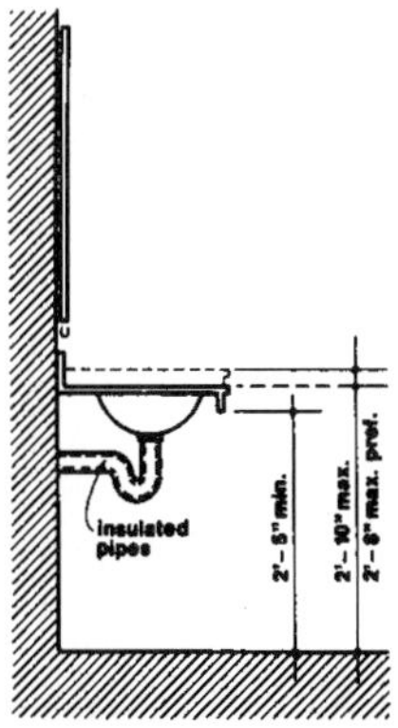

lavatory (q/3)
scale: 3/8" = 1'-0"

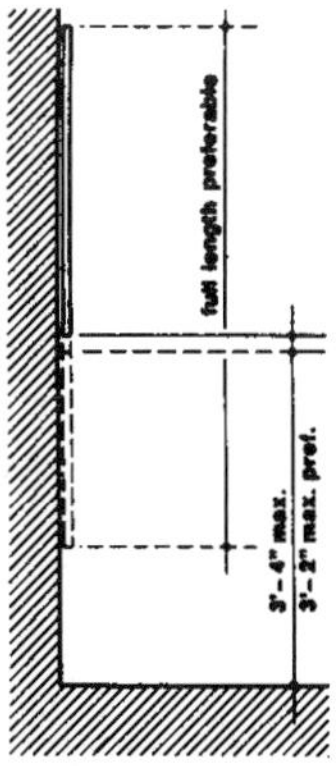

mirrors (r/3)

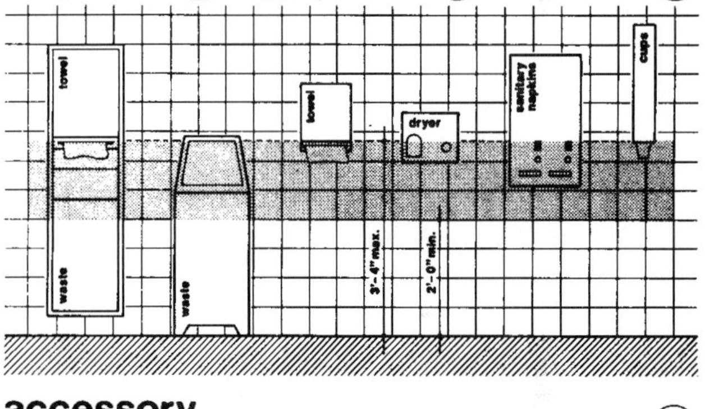

accessory (s/3)
scale: 3/8" = 1'-0"

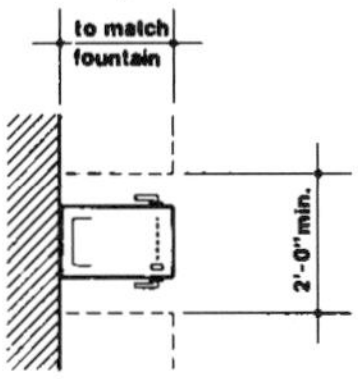

d.f. (t/3)
scale: 1/4" = 1'-0"

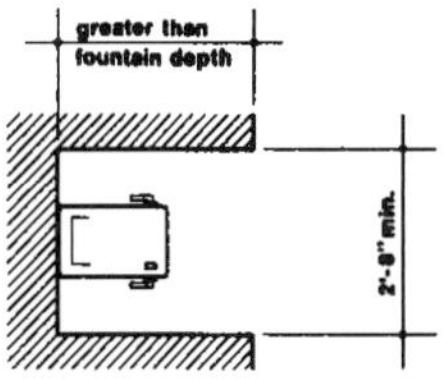

alcove (u/3)
scale: 1/4" = 1'-0"

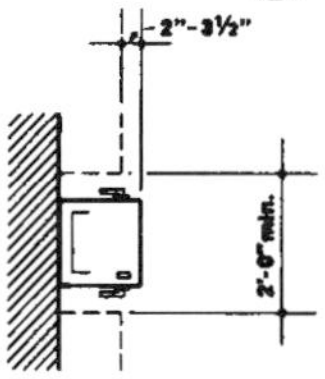

e.w.c. (v/3)

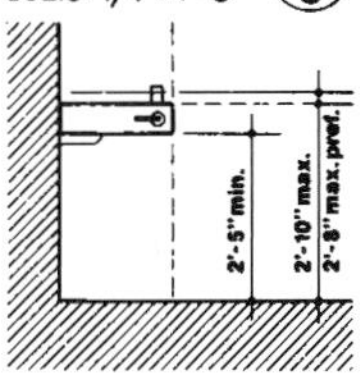

d.f. (w/3)
scale: 1/4" = 1'-0"

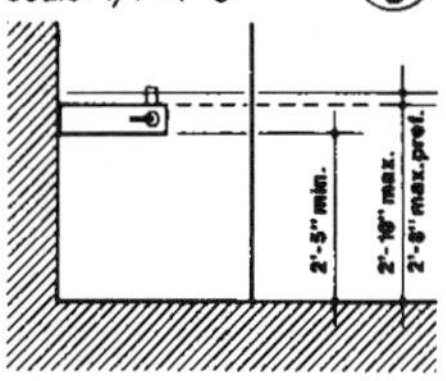

alcove (x/3)
scale: 1/4" = 1'-0"

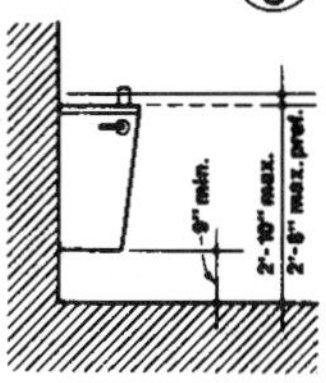

e.w.c. (y/3)

REST ROOMS AND TOILETS
Wheel Chair-Accessible Design

Federal standards mandate grab bars of 1½-in o.d. The bars must be securely mounted 1½-in clear from the wall or partition. This mounting distance is critical, as it provides a cradle for a forearm during transfer or if a user loses her or his grip.

Lavatories need not be specialized designs to be accessible. Utilization of clearances shown will do much to make lavatories accessible. Because persons with loss of sensation in their legs cannot feel pain (and because they heal at a slower rate), hot water lines and drains must be insulated. Also, under several state codes, faucets are required to be lever, blade, or multiarm handle operated.

Single lever controls are preferable. Spring-operated faucets must have time delay devices.

At least one mirror must be located with the reflecting surface mounted at 3 ft 4 in a.f.f. (3 ft 2 in or lower preferable). Where possible, full-length mirrors are preferable.

At least one of each type of toilet accessory must also be located at 3 ft 4 in a.f.f. or less. Note that this dimension is measured to the highest control required for operation. Controls that require twisting and grasping motions should be avoided.

Because people that use wheelchairs require increased fluid intake, drinking fountains become more than convenience items. While there is not space here to address all configurations, the following concerns are typical to all: controls should be operable without the need for precise grasping; the faucet should not direct spray away from the user and must be located as near the front edge as practical; the units must be free of sharp edges and corners and overhead obstructions.

Urinals, if provided, should have elongated bowls with the opening of the basin located at 19 in a.f.f. or less, or mounted level with the main floor. Many state standards specify maximum mounting heights of 15 to 16 in a.f.f. These lower dimensions are preferable.

The toilet room itself should provide a clear floor area with minimum dimensions of 60 in × 60 in to facilitate maneuvering wheelchairs. Additionally, provide a minimum of 3 ft 6 in clearance in front of accessible toilet stalls to facilitate entry.

Similarly, adequate clearances must be provided at entrances. The spaces shown in details l/3 to o/3 represent typical dimensions specified in state codes. Note, however, that federal and many state standards require 12-in clear jamb areas adjoining both sides of all doors. A clearance of 18 in or more on the strike side of a door is more effective. In vestibules having doors in series, there must be space for a wheelchair to clear one door prior to opening another.

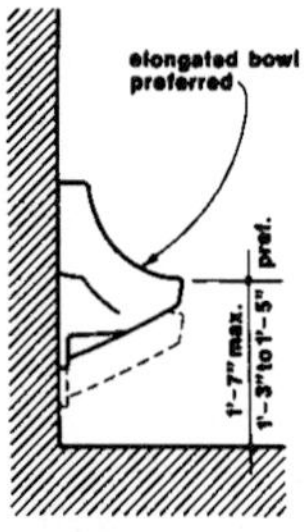

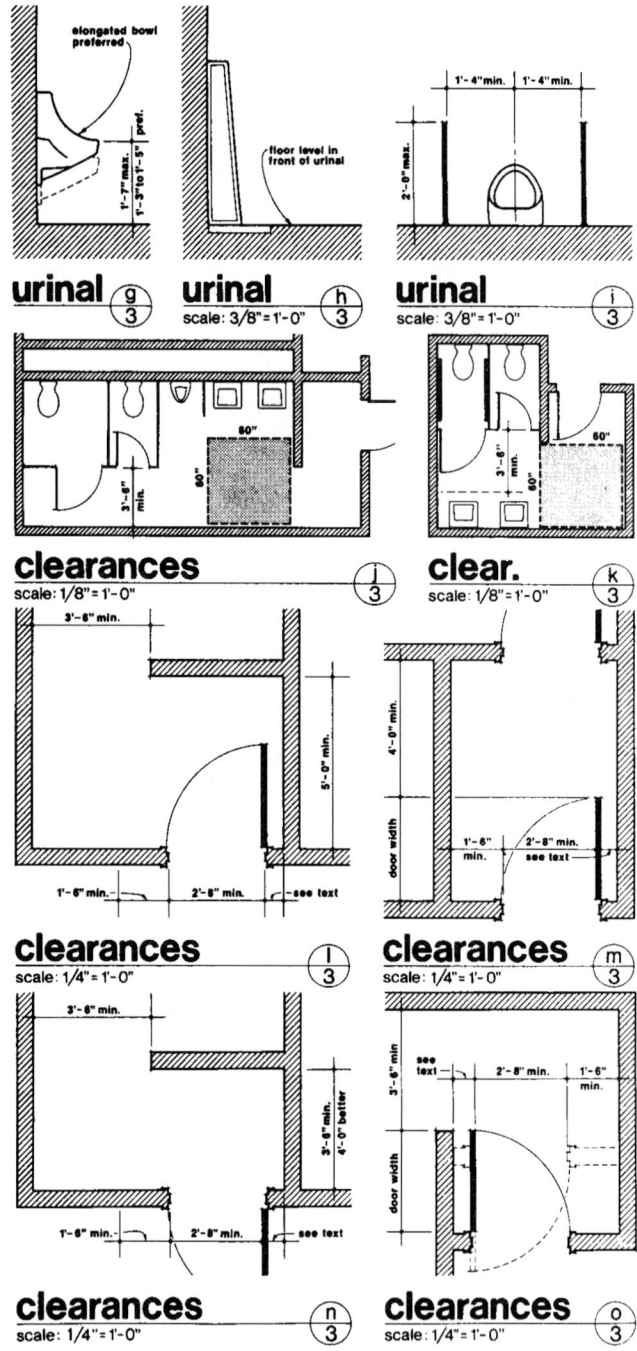

urinal g/3

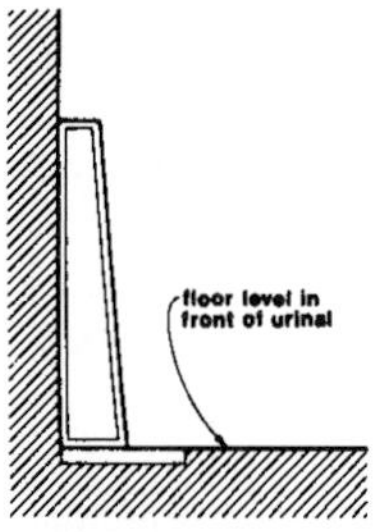

urinal h/3
scale: 3/8" = 1'-0"

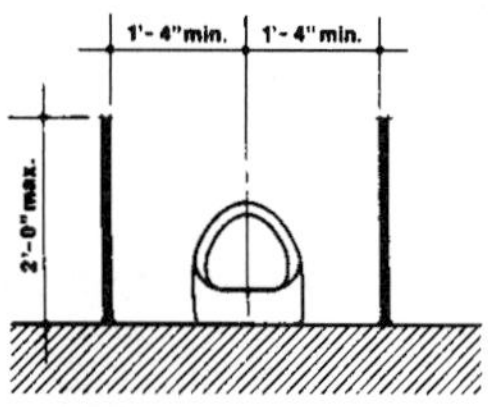

urinal i/3
scale: 3/8" = 1'-0"

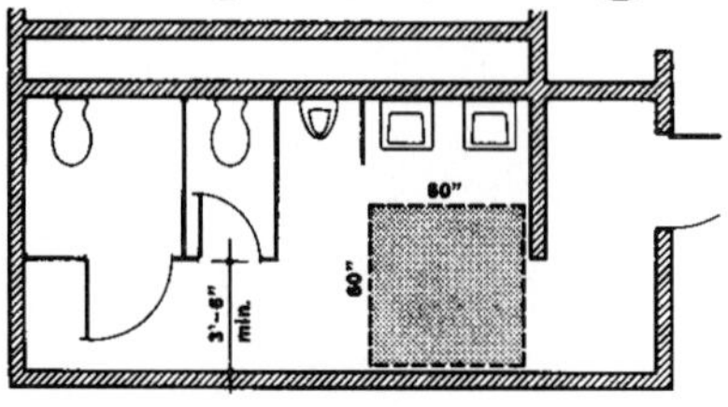

clearances j/3
scale: 1/8" = 1'-0"

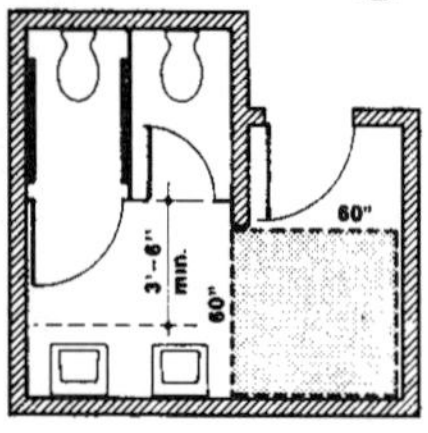

clear. k/3
scale: 1/8" = 1'-0"

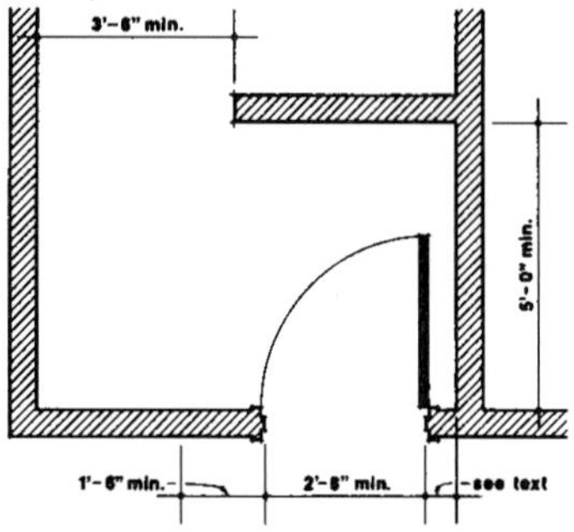

clearances l/3
scale: 1/4" = 1'-0"

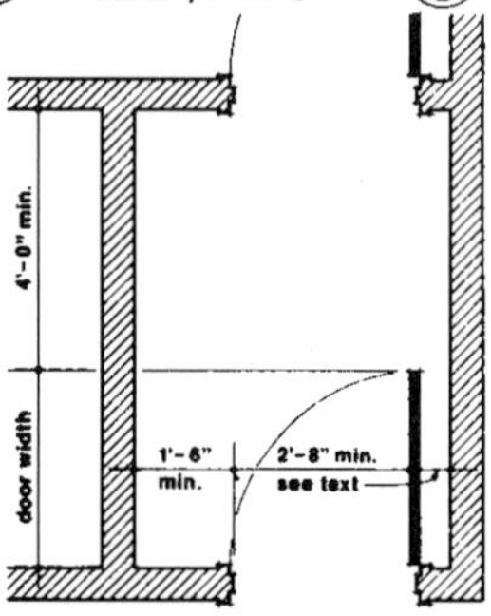

clearances m/3
scale: 1/4" = 1'-0"

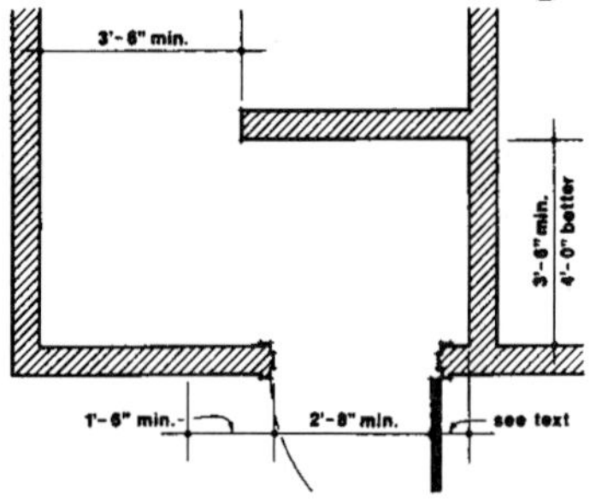

clearances n/3
scale: 1/4" = 1'-0"

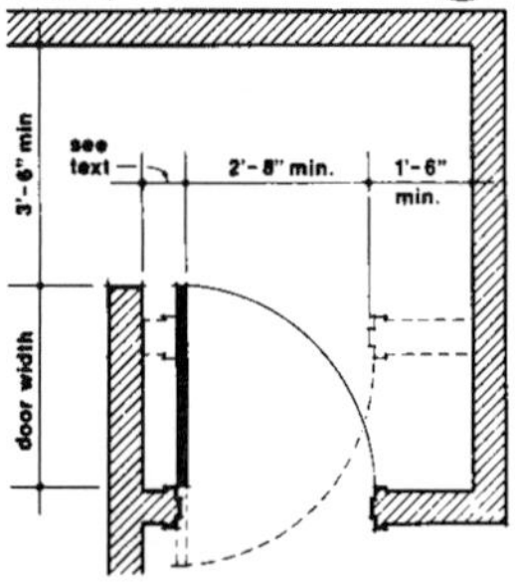

clearances o/3
scale: 1/4" = 1'-0"

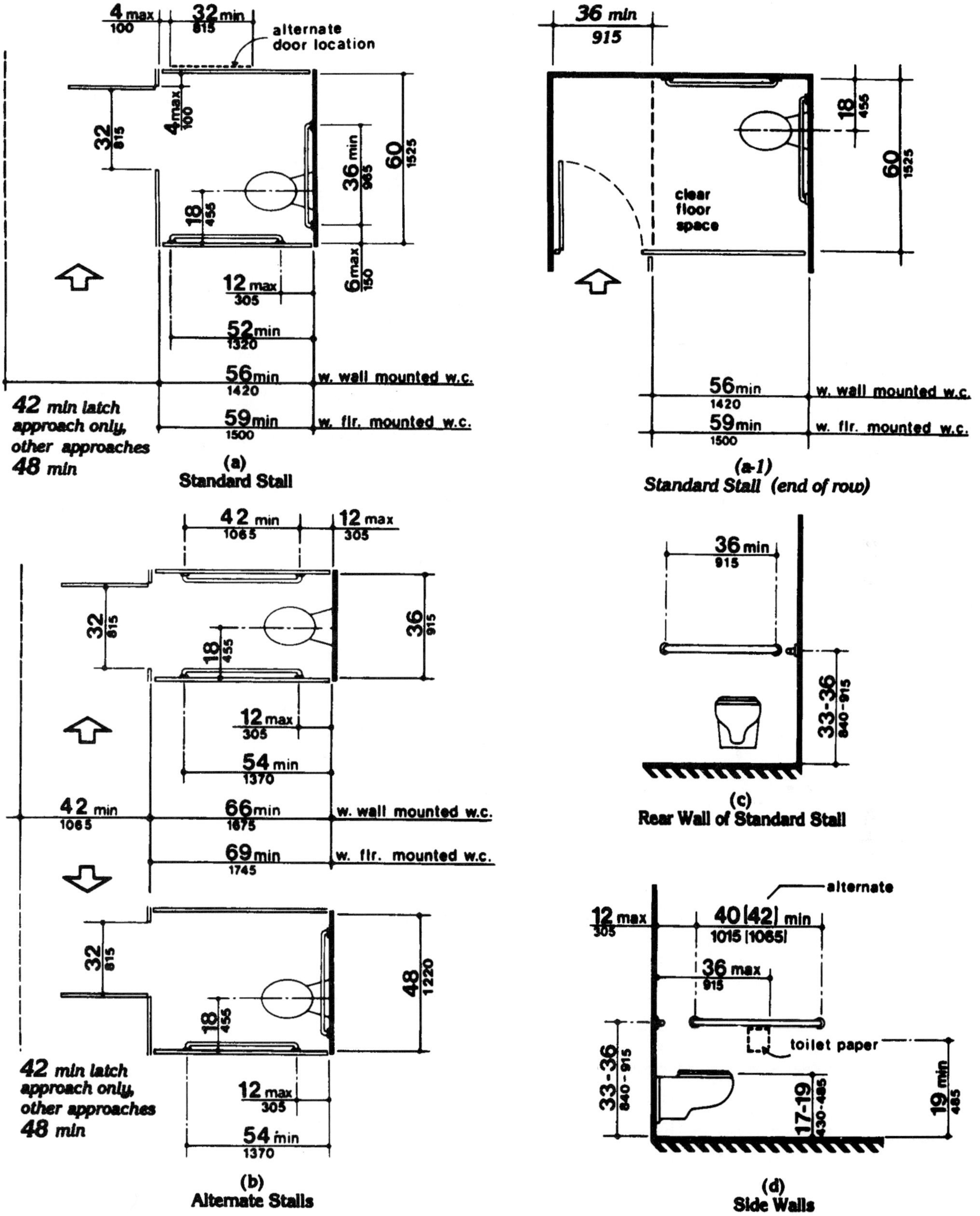

Fig. 22 Toilet stalls

REST ROOMS AND TOILETS

Barrier-Free Toilet Planning Standards

Wheelchair Maneuverability Drawing Template

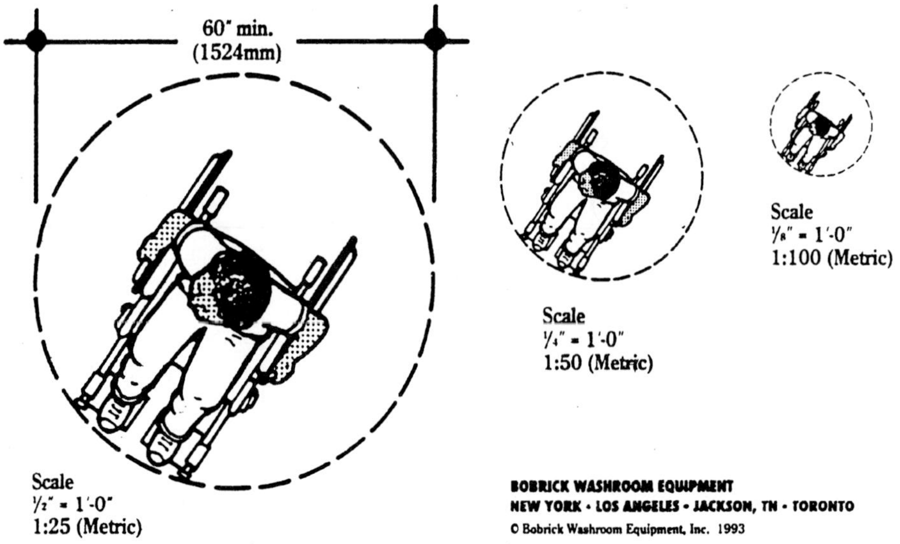

Children's Reach Ranges

Note: Refer to these charts to find the best locations within the given overall ADAAG ranges that are most appropriate for the specific children's age group for which you are designing.

Forward or Side Reach	Ages 3 and 4	Ages 5 through 8	Ages 9 through 12
High (maximum)	36" (915mm)	40" (1015mm)	44" (1120mm)
Low (minimum)	20" (510mm)	18" (455mm)	16" (405mm)

Specifications for Water Closets Serving Children Ages 3 through 12

	Ages 3 and 4	Ages 5 through 8	Ages 9 through 12
Water Closet Centerline	12" (305mm)	12" to 15" (305 to 380mm)	15" to 18" (330 to 455mm)
Toilet Seat Height	11" to 12" (280 to 305mm)	12" to 15" (305 to 380mm)	15" to 17" (380 to 430mm)
Grab Bar Height	18" to 20" (455 to 510mm)	20" to 25" (510 to 635mm)	25" to 27" (635 to 685mm)
Toilet Tissue Dispenser Height	14" (355mm)	14" to 17" (355 to 430mm)	17" to 19" (430 to 485mm)

Bobrick's Recommended Mounting Heights for Washroom Accessories.

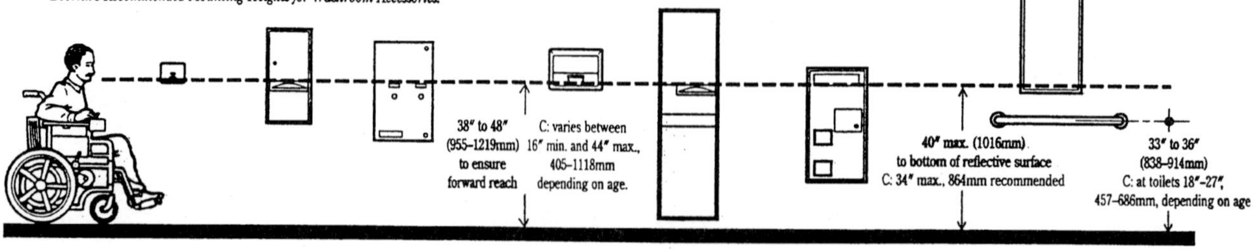

REST ROOMS AND TOILETS

Barrier-Free Toilet Planning Standards

Wheelchair Turning Space for 180° Turns.

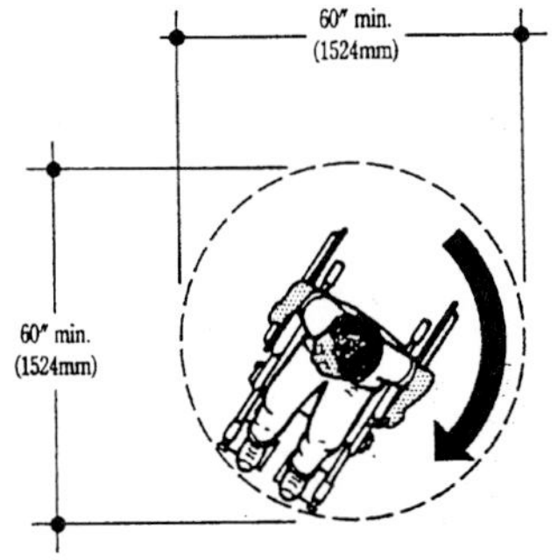

60" (1524mm) Diameter Turning Space.

Scale: 1/4" = 1'- 0"

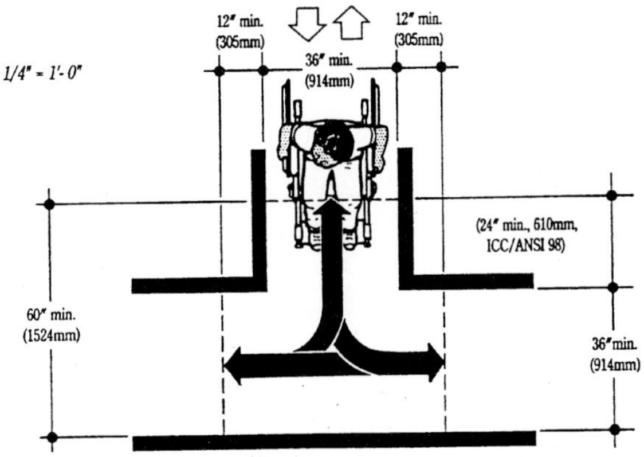

T-Shaped Turning Space.

Scale: 1/4" = 1'- 0"

Washroom Entrance and Exit Maneuvering Clearances.

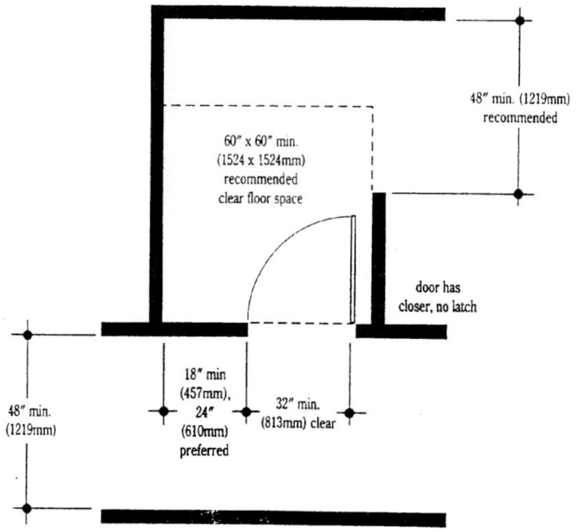

Single Door.

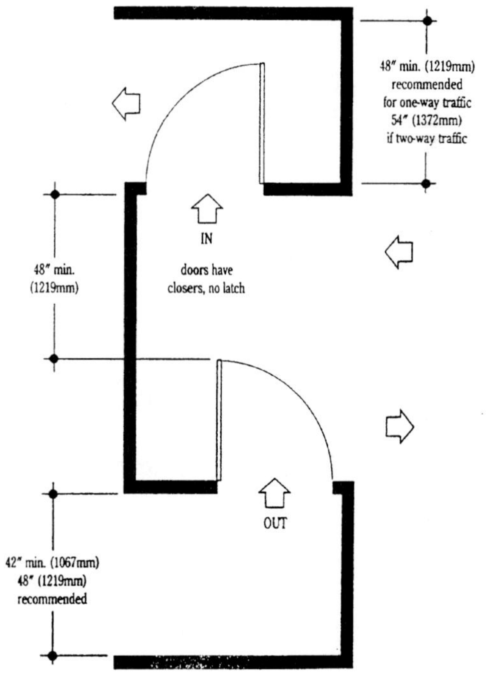

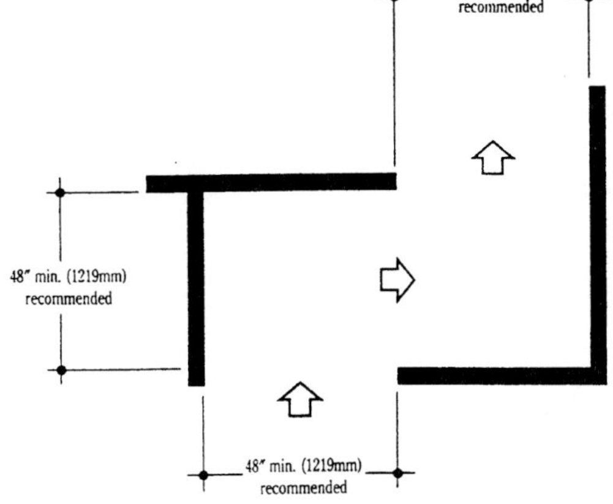

Open Vestibule.

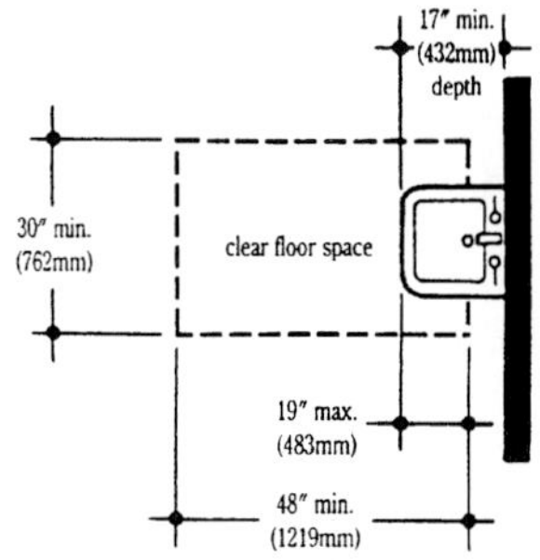

Clear Floor Space at Lavatory.

REST ROOMS AND TOILETS

Barrier-Free Lavatory and Toilet Compartment Clearances

Lavatory Clearances.

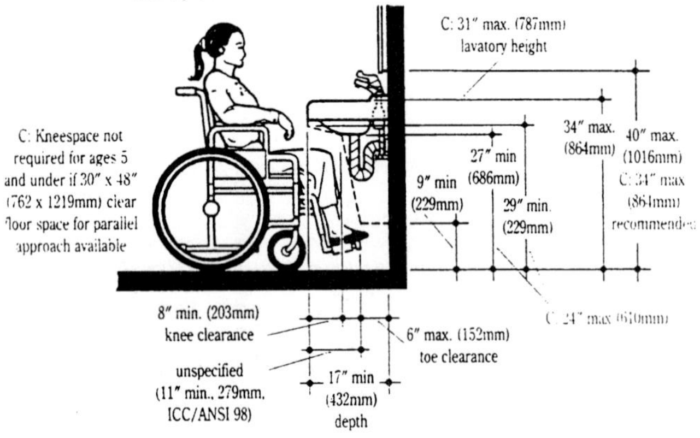

Knee and Toe Clearance at Lavatory.

(a)

Protective Panel Under Lavatory.

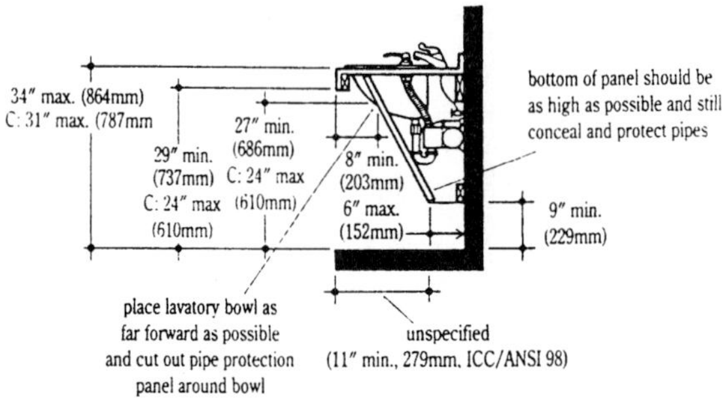

(b)

TOILET COMPARTMENTS ARE A MAJOR SERVICE AMENITY IN ALL PUBLIC WASHROOMS.

Wheelchair Transfers to Toilet.

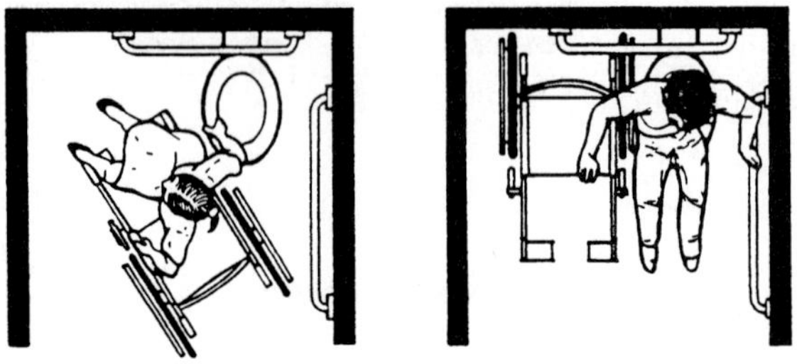

Reverse Diagonal Approach. *Side Approach.*

(c)

Standard Compartment (ICC/ANSI 98 Wheelchair Accessible Compartment).

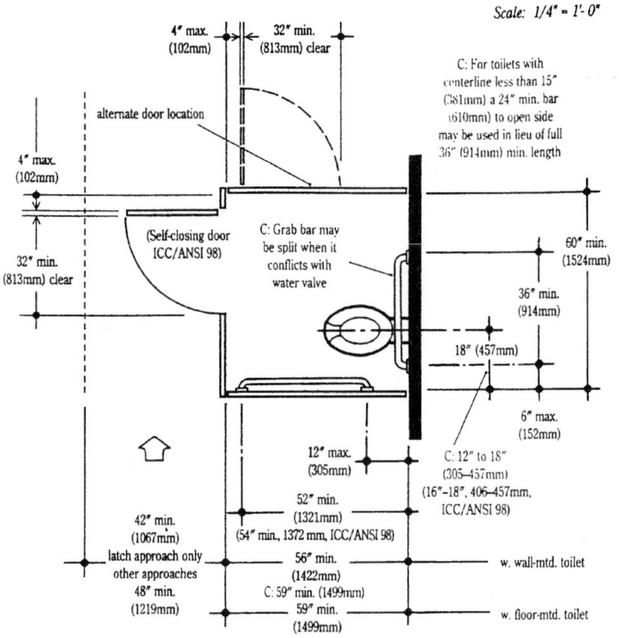

(d)

Standard Alcove (End of Row) Compartment (ICC/ANSI 98 Wheelchair Accessible Compartment).

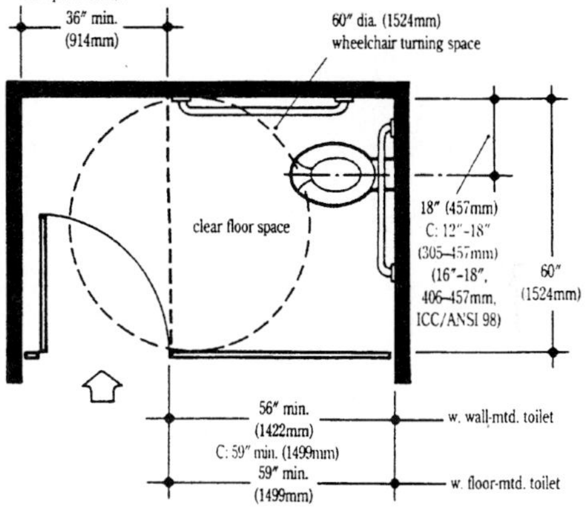

(e)

Alternative Compartment 36" (914mm) Wide (No ICC/ANSI 98 equivalent).

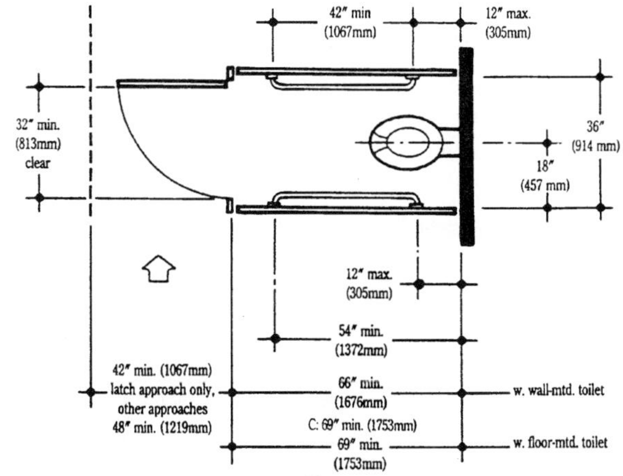

(f)

Alternate 48" Min. (1219 mm) Wide Compartment (No ICC/ANSI equivalent).

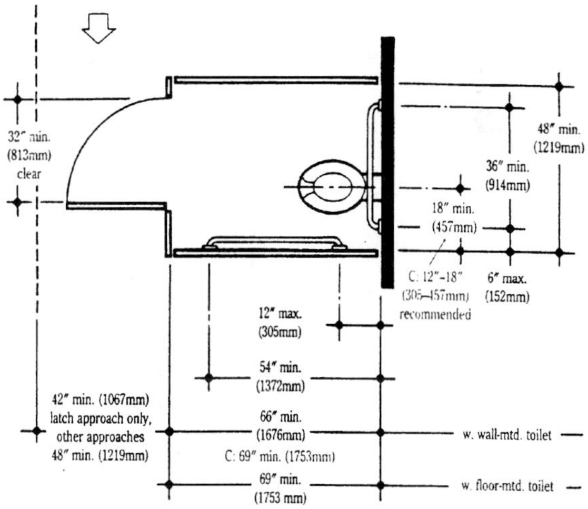

(g)

REST ROOMS AND TOILETS

Barrier-Free Public Rest Room Floor Plans

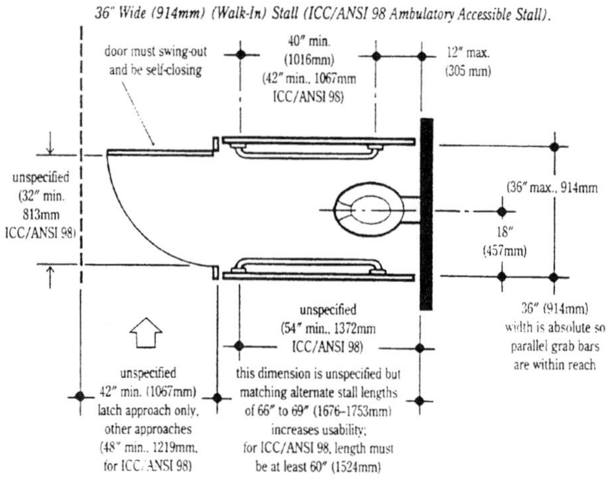

(h)

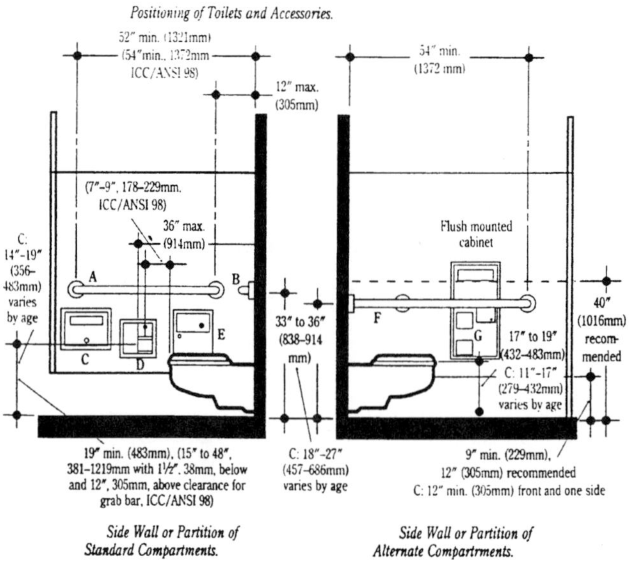

(i)

BARRIER-FREE PUBLIC REST ROOM FLOOR PLANS

Design Solutions for Large Public Washrooms

When designing large washrooms with multiple compartments and lavatories, follow this simple check list:

- Entrances and exits are properly laid out for universal access.
- Passageways and access aisles are at least 48 in (1067 mm) wide.
- There is 80 in (2032 mm) minimum clear height throughout all circulation routes, passageways, and access aisles.
- Wheelchair turning spaces are provided wherever required.
- Accessories are fully recessed into the walls wherever possible.
- Each type of accessory meets or exceeds ADAAG specifications.
- 30 in × 48 in (760 × 1219 mm) minimum clear floor space is provided for each accessory.
- Lavatories, urinals, and toilet compartments meet or exceed ADAAG specifications.
- If there are six or more toilet compartments, there is a 36-in (914-mm) compartment similar to the alternate compartment 36 in (914 mm) wide in addition to the standard accessible compartment.

The following three plans illustrate barrier-free washrooms with suggested universal-design features that meet or exceed ADAAG specifications.

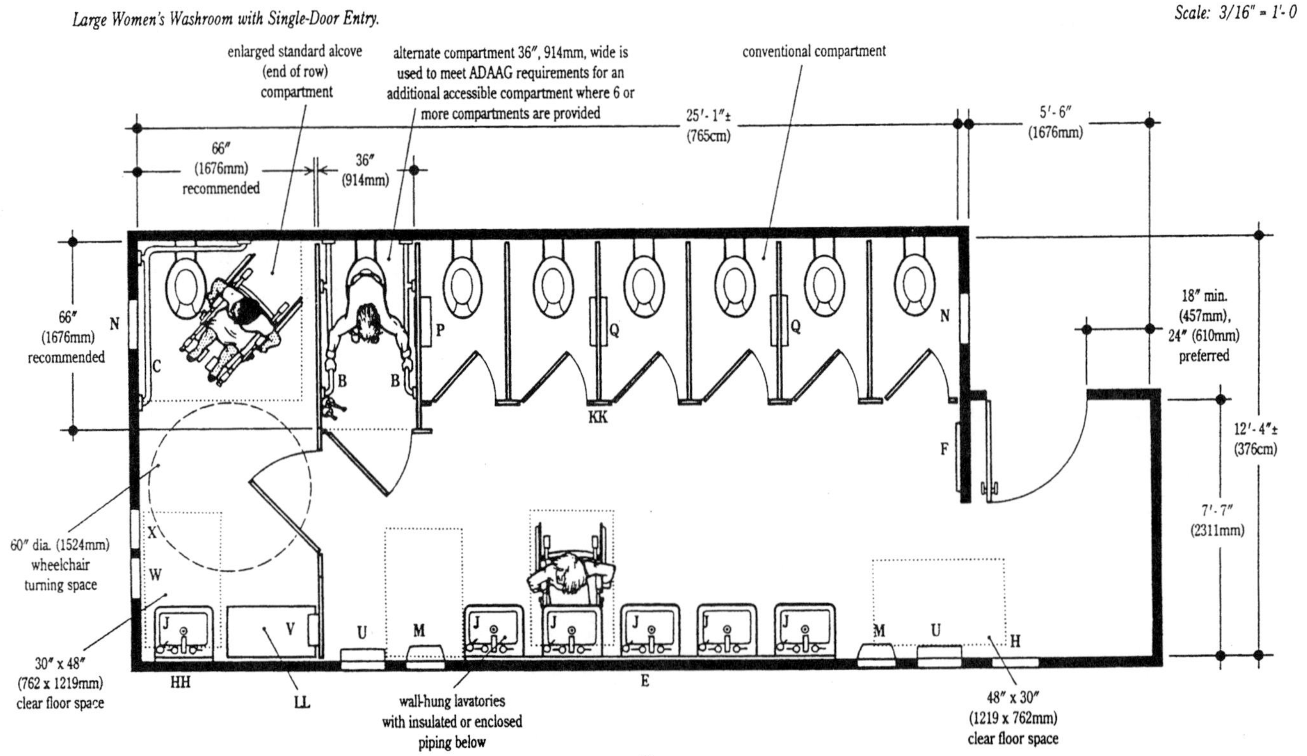

(j)

REST ROOMS AND TOILETS

Barrier-Free Public Rest Room Floor Plans

Large Women's Washroom with Open Vestibule.

Drawings not to scale.

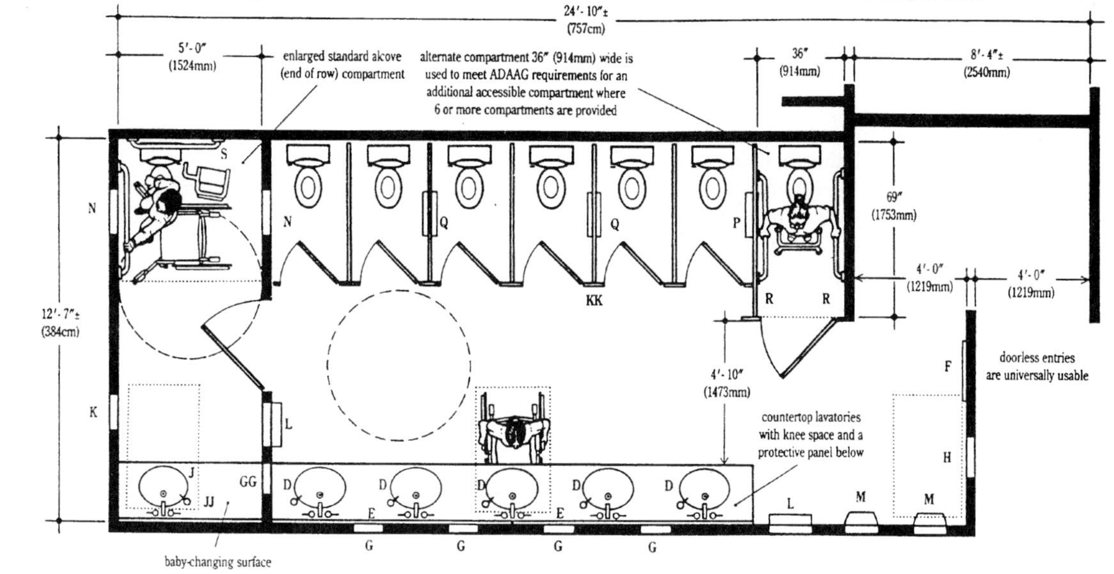

(k)

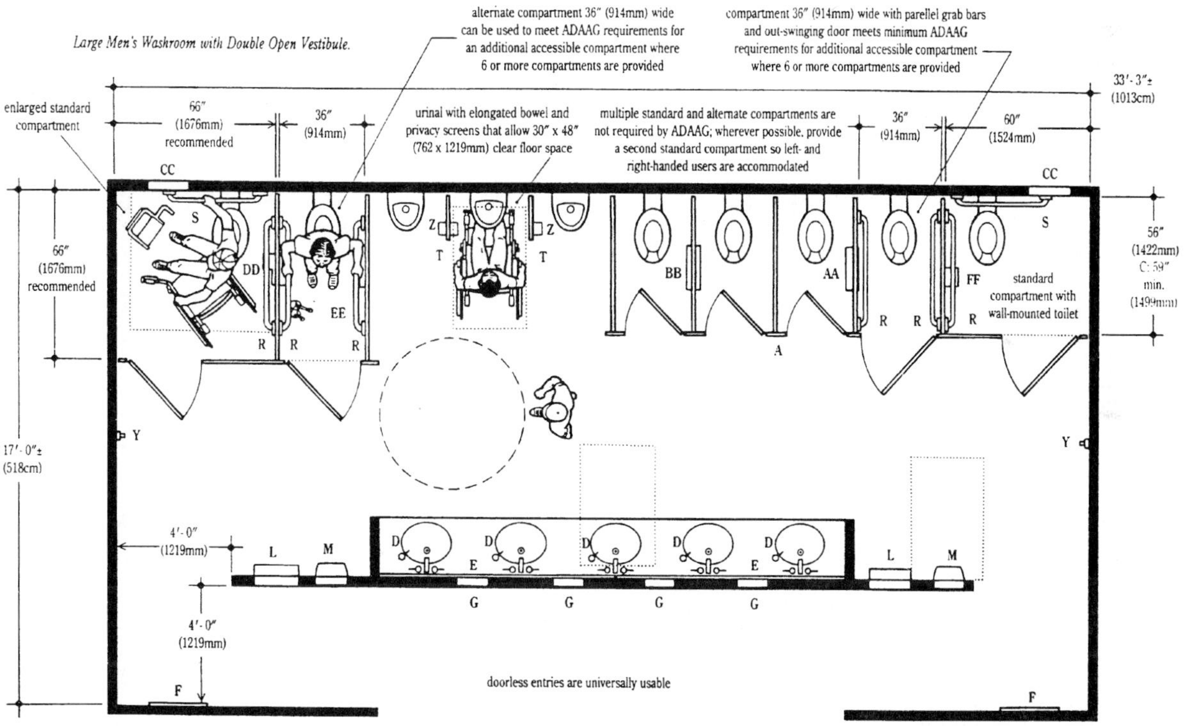

LEGEND

- A 1041 Series Floor-Anchored Laminated Plastic Toilet Compartments.
- B B-5893 Horizontal Side-Wall Grab Bar, 54" (1372mm) Long.
- C B-5837 Horizontal Two-Wall Grab Bar, 36" x 54" (914 x 1372mm).
- D B-922 Lavatory-Mounted Soap Dispensers with Under-the-Counter Soap Reservoir.
- E B-290 Series Mirror.
- F B-290 Series Full-Length Mirror, 24" W x 60" H (610 x 1524mm).
- G B-318 Recessed Paper Towel Dispenser.
- H B-3500X2 Recessed Sanitary Napkin/Tampon Vendor.
- J B-822 Lavatory-Mounted Soap Dispenser.
- K B-369 Recessed Paper Towel Dispenser and Waste Receptacle.
- L B-3644 Recessed Waste Receptacle.
- M B-750 Recessed AutoPilot No-Touch Hand Dryer.
- N B-3574 Recessed Toilet-Seat-Cover Dispenser, Sanitary Napkin Disposal, Toilet Tissue Dispenser with Theft-Resistant Spindle.
- P B-3571 Partition-Mounted Toilet-Seat-Cover Dispenser, Sanitary Napkin Disposal, Toilet Tissue Dispenser with Theft-Resistant Spindle (serves two compartments).
- Q B-357 Partition-Mounted Toilet-Seat-Cover Dispenser, Sanitary Napkin Disposal, Toilet Tissue Dispenser with Theft-Resistant Spindle (serves two compartments).
- R B-5806 x 42 Horizontal Grab Bar.
- S B-5806 x 36 Horizontal Grab Bar.
- T 1045 Series Wall-Hung Urinal Screen.
- U B-3944 Recessed Paper Towel Dispenser and Waste Receptacle.
- V B-262 Surface-Mounted Paper Towel Dispenser.
- W B-362 Recessed Paper Towel Dispenser.
- X B-525 Recessed Waste Receptacle.
- Y B-6877 Door Bumper.
- Z B-240 Surface-Mounted Ashtray.
- AA B-3471 Partition-Mounted Toilet-Seat-Cover Dispenser, Toilet Tissue Dispenser with Theft-Resistant Spindle (serves two compartments).
- BB B-347 Partition-Mounted Toilet-Seat-Cover Dispenser, Toilet Tissue Dispenser with Theft-Resistant Spindle (serves two compartments).
- CC B-301 Recessed Toilet-Seat-Cover Dispenser (mounts below grab bar).
- DD B-386 Partition-Mounted Toilet Tissue Dispenser (mounts below grab bar, serves two compartments).
- EE B-221 Surface-Mounted Toilet-Seat-Cover Dispenser (mounts below grab bar).
- FF B-2888 Surface-Mounted Toilet Tissue Dispenser (mounts below grab bar).
- GG B-359 Recessed Paper Towel Dispenser.
- HH B-290 Series Mirror, 24" W x 36" H (610 x 914mm).
- JJ B-290 Series Wall-to-Wall Mirror.
- KK 1042 Series Overhead-Braced Laminated Plastic Toilet Compartments.
- LL B-2210 Surface-Mounted Diaper Changing Station

(l)

REST ROOMS AND TOILETS

Barrier-Free Public Rest Room Floor Plans

Design Solutions for Small Public Washrooms and Individual Toilet Rooms

Small Public Washrooms

These require one standard 60 in (1524 mm) wide toilet compartment because it is the most universally usable. Minimum 60 in (1524 mm) diameter or T-shaped turning spaces are also required, as well as a barrier-free lavatory, accessories, and access aisles that meet ADAAG specifications. Entry doors should swing into vestibules, not directly into corridors, access aisles, or clear floor spaces required by lavatories and other washroom equipment.

Individual Toilet Rooms

Under ADAAG, the minimum size of individual toilet rooms is determined by combining the clear floor spaces required for each feature or fixture, the turning space, and maneuvering clearances at doors. In-swinging entry doors must not swing into any clear floor space required for lavatories and other washroom equipment. Outswinging entry doors may be used only if they swing into another room, such as a patient's room or a private office, vestibule, or alcove, but never into a corridor. Locating the lavatory next to the toilet will eliminate the option of a parallel approach to the toilet by people using wheelchairs; therefore, to maximize usability, design individual toilet rooms so there is a minimum clearance of 60 in (1524 mm) from side wall of toilet to the adjacent lavatory, or locate lavatory on a different wall altogether. This 60 in (1524 mm) minimum dimension is a requirement in the ICC/ANSI 98 Standard. Additionally, the clear floor space required for toilets not located in compartments is larger than those in the ADAAG. In ICC/ANSI 98 no fixture can obstruct the 60 in × 56 in (1524–1422 mm) minimum clear floor space for toilets. These differences may result in larger minimum room sizes when following the ICC/ANSI 98 Standard than may result from ADAAG specifications. Drawings in this section reflect these differences. Because individual toilet rooms provide privacy for a physically disabled person who needs the help of an attendant (or even a child who needs the help of a parent), especially when they are of the opposite sex, it may be useful to provide this type of unisex or family toilet room in addition to multicompartment washrooms in many large public buildings.

As in all barrier-free facilities, small public washrooms and individual toilet rooms should meet or exceed ADAAG specifications for entrance and exit, lavatories, toilets, grab bars, accessories, controls, and operating mechanisms.

Small Barrier-Free Public Washrooms.

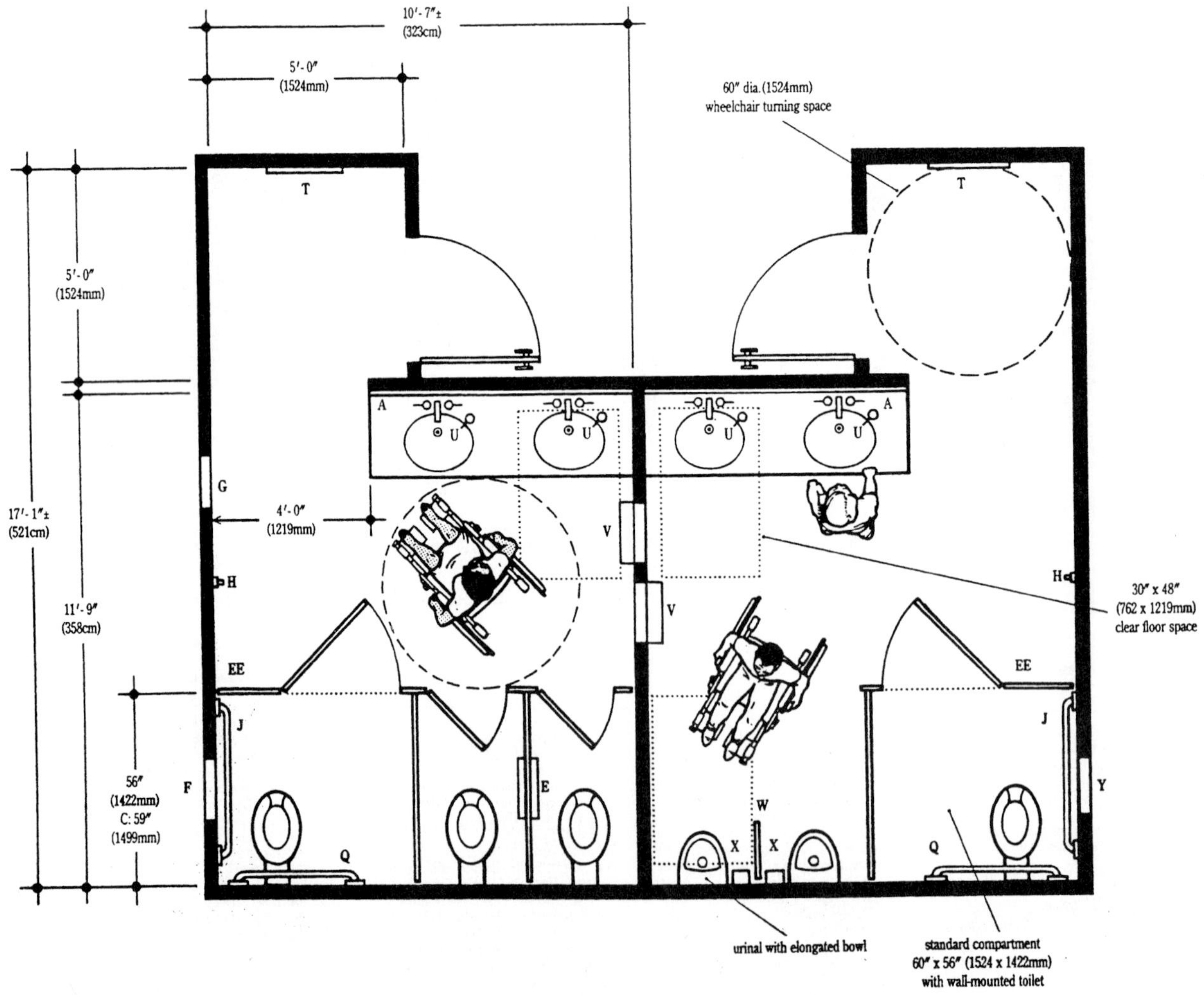

(m)

REST ROOMS AND TOILETS

Barrier-Free Public Rest Room Floor Plans

Small Public Washroom with Single Compartment.

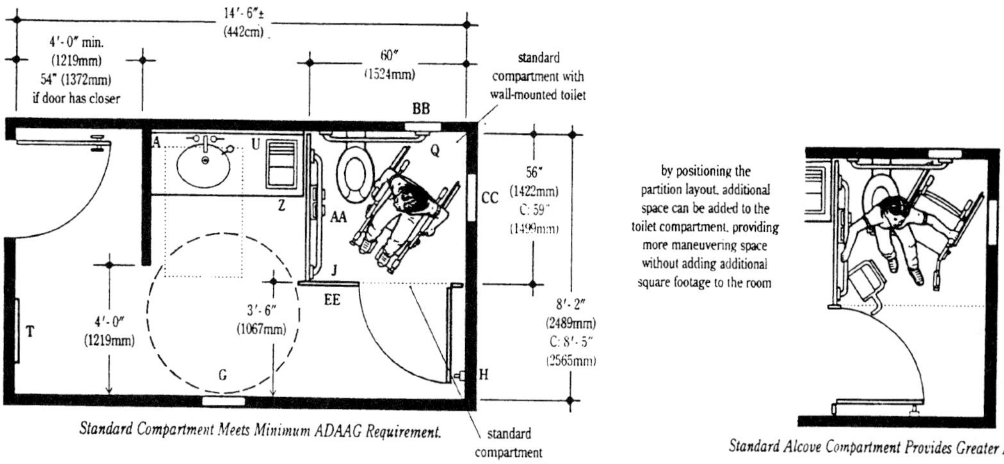

Standard Compartment Meets Minimum ADAAG Requirement.

Standard Alcove Compartment Provides Greater Accessibility.

(n)

Small Public Washroom Provides Standard Compartment and Alternate Compartment 36" (914mm) Wide.

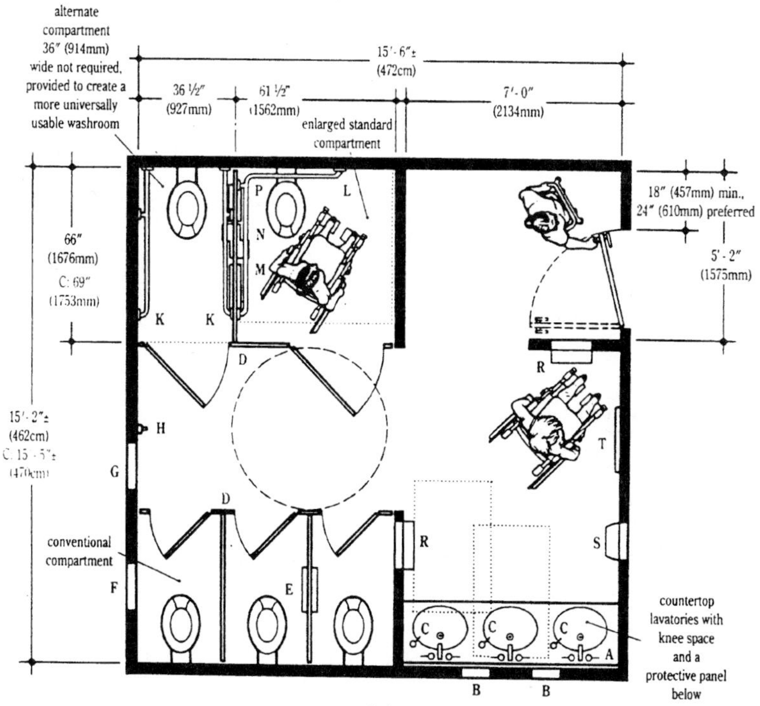

(o)

LEGEND

- A *B-290 Series Wall-to-Wall Mirror.*
- B *B-318 Recessed Paper Towel Dispenser.*
- C *B-922 Lavatory-Mounted Soap Dispenser with Under-the-Counter Soap Reservoir.*
- D *1042 Series Overhead-Braced Laminated Plastic Toilet Compartments.*
- E *B-357 Partition-Mounted Toilet-Seat-Cover Dispenser, Sanitary Napkin Disposal, Toilet Tissue Dispenser with Theft-Resistant Spindle (serves two compartments).*
- F *B-3574 Recessed Toilet-Seat-Cover Dispenser, Sanitary Napkin Disposal, Toilet Tissue Dispenser with Theft-Resistant Spindle.*
- G *B-3500X2 Recessed Sanitary Napkin/Tampon Vendor.*
- H *B-6877 Door Bumper.*
- J *B-5806 x 42 Horizontal Grab Bar.*
- K *B-5893 Horizontal Side-Wall Grab Bar, 54" (1372mm) Long.*
- L *B-5837 Horizontal Two-Wall Grab Bar, 36" x 54" (914 x 1372mm).*
- M *B-304 Partition-Mounted Toilet-Seat-Cover Dispenser (mounts below grab bar, serves two compartments).*
- N *B-386 Partition-Mounted Toilet Tissue Dispenser (mounts below grab bar, serves two compartments).*
- P *B-354 Partition-Mounted Sanitary Napkin Disposal (mounts below grab bar, serves two compartments).*
- Q *B-5806 x 36 Horizontal Grab Bar.*
- R *B-3644 Recessed Waste Receptacle.*
- S *B-750 Recessed AutoPilot No-Touch Hand Dryer.*
- T *B-290 Series Full-Length Mirror, 24" W x 60" H (610 x 1524mm).*
- U *B-822 Lavatory-Mounted Soap Dispenser.*
- V *B-3944 Recessed Paper Towel Dispenser and Waste Receptacle.*
- W *1045 Series Wall-Hung Urinal Screen.*
- X *B-240 Surface-Mounted Ashtray.*
- Y *B-3474 Recessed Toilet-Seat-Cover Dispenser, Toilet Tissue Dispenser with Theft-Resistant Spindle.*
- Z *B-528 Combination Paper Towel Dispenser and Waste-Disposal Door.*
- AA *B-2740 Surface-Mounted Toilet Tissue Dispenser, no controlled delivery (mounts below grab bar).*
- BB *B-353 Recessed Sanitary Napkin Disposal (mounts below grab bar).*
- CC *B-301 Recessed Toilet-Seat-Cover Dispenser.*
- DD *B-369 Recessed Paper Towel Dispenser and Waste Receptacle.*
- EE *1041 Series Floor-Anchored Laminated Plastic Toilet Compartments.*
- FF *B-290 Series Mirror, 18" W x 36" H (457 x 914mm).*

REST ROOMS AND TOILETS
Barrier-Free Public Rest Room Floor Plans

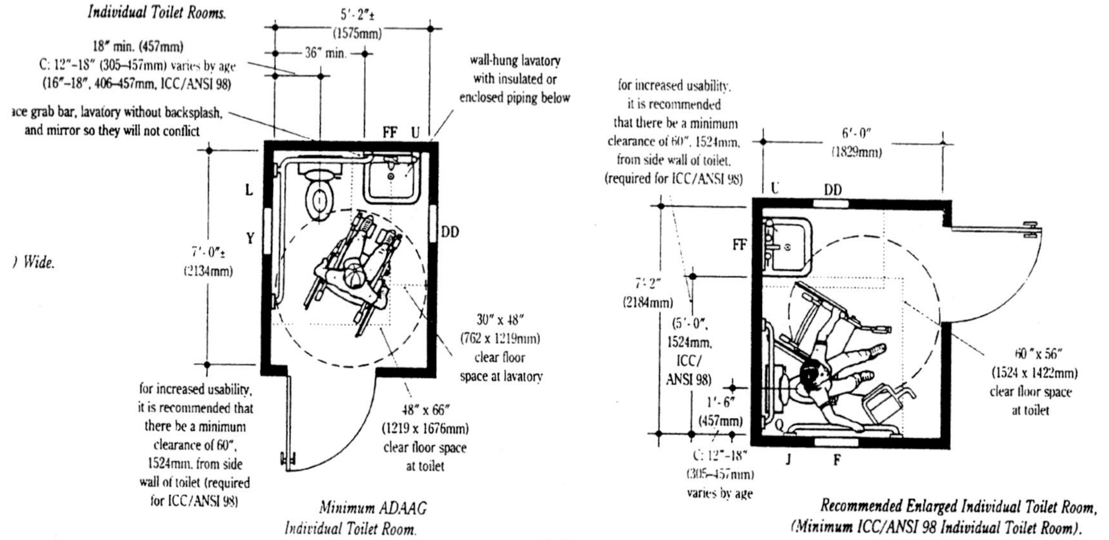

(p)

LEGEND

- **A** *B-290 Series Wall-to-Wall Mirror.*
- **B** *B-318 Recessed Paper Towel Dispenser.*
- **C** *B-922 Lavatory-Mounted Soap Dispenser with Under-the-Counter Soap Reservoir.*
- **D** *1642 Series Overhead-Braced Laminated Plastic Toilet Compartments.*
- **E** *B-357 Partition-Mounted Toilet-Seat-Cover Dispenser, Sanitary Napkin Disposal, Toilet Tissue Dispenser with Theft-Resistant Spindle (serves two compartments).*
- **F** *B-3574 Recessed Toilet-Seat-Cover Dispenser, Sanitary Napkin Disposal, Toilet Tissue Dispenser with Theft-Resistant Spindle.*
- **G** *B-3500X2 Recessed Sanitary Napkin/Tampon Vendor.*
- **H** *B-6877 Door Bumper.*
- **J** *B-5806 x 42 Horizontal Grab Bar.*
- **K** *B-5893 Horizontal Side-Wall Grab Bar, 54" (1372mm) Long.*
- **L** *B-5837 Horizontal Two-Wall Grab Bar, 36" x 54" (914 x 1372mm).*
- **M** *B-304 Partition-Mounted Toilet-Seat-Cover Dispenser (mounts below grab bar, serves two compartments).*
- **N** *B-386 Partition-Mounted Toilet Tissue Dispenser (mounts below grab bar, serves two compartments).*
- **P** *B-354 Partition-Mounted Sanitary Napkin Disposal (mounts below grab bar, serves two compartments).*
- **Q** *B-5806 x 36 Horizontal Grab Bar.*
- **R** *B-3644 Recessed Waste Receptacle.*
- **S** *B-750 Recessed AutoPilot No-Touch Hand Dryer.*
- **T** *B-290 Series Full-Length Mirror, 24" W x 60" H (610 x 1524mm).*
- **U** *B-822 Lavatory-Mounted Soap Dispenser.*
- **V** *B-3944 Recessed Paper Towel Dispenser and Waste Receptacle.*
- **W** *1045 Series Wall-Hung Urinal Screen.*
- **X** *B-240 Surface-Mounted Ashtray.*
- **Y** *B-3474 Recessed Toilet-Seat-Cover Dispenser, Toilet Tissue Dispenser with Theft-Resistant Spindle.*
- **Z** *B-528 Combination Paper Towel Dispenser and Waste-Disposal Door.*
- **AA** *B-2740 Surface-Mounted Toilet Tissue Dispenser, no controlled delivery (mounts below grab bar).*
- **BB** *B-353 Recessed Sanitary Napkin Disposal (mounts below grab bar).*
- **CC** *B-301 Recessed Toilet-Seat-Cover Dispenser.*
- **DD** *B-369 Recessed Paper Towel Dispenser and Waste Receptacle.*
- **EE** *1041 Series Floor-Anchored Laminated Plastic Toilet Compartments.*
- **FF** *B-290 Series Mirror, 18" W x 36" H (457 x 914mm).*

REST ROOMS AND TOILETS

Barrier-Free Shower Stall Plans and Elevations

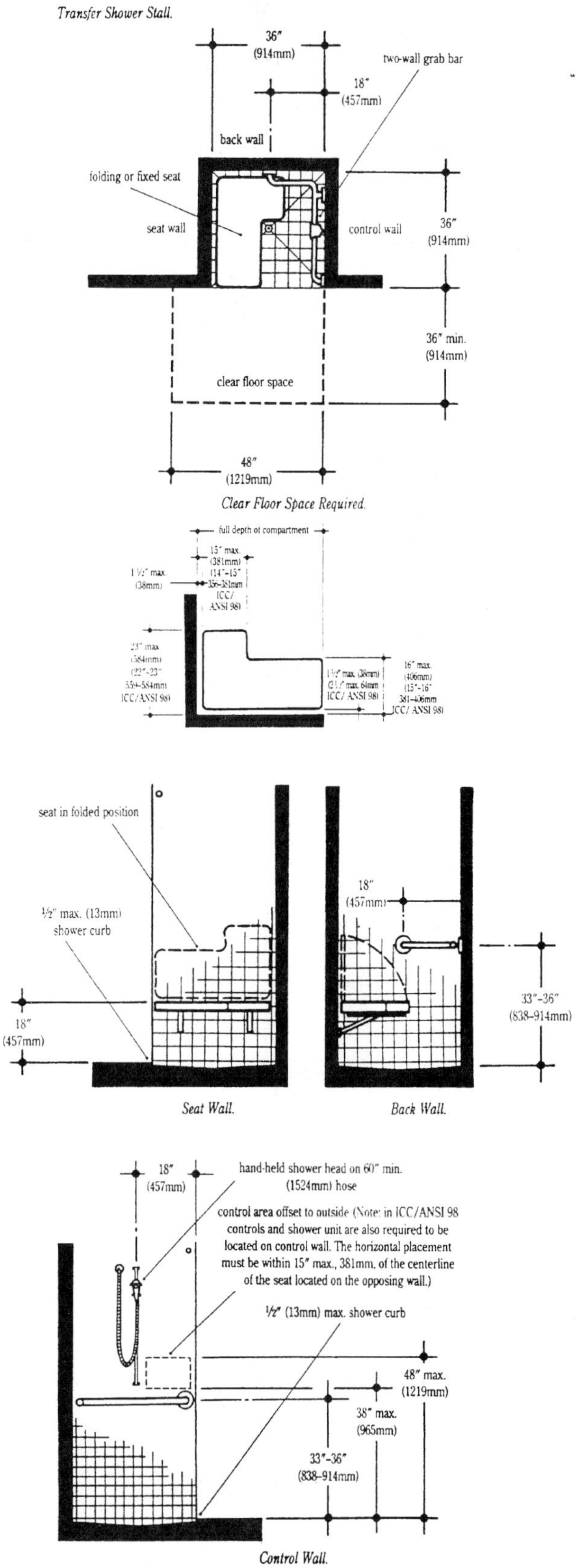

(q)

60" (1524mm) Wide Shower Stalls.

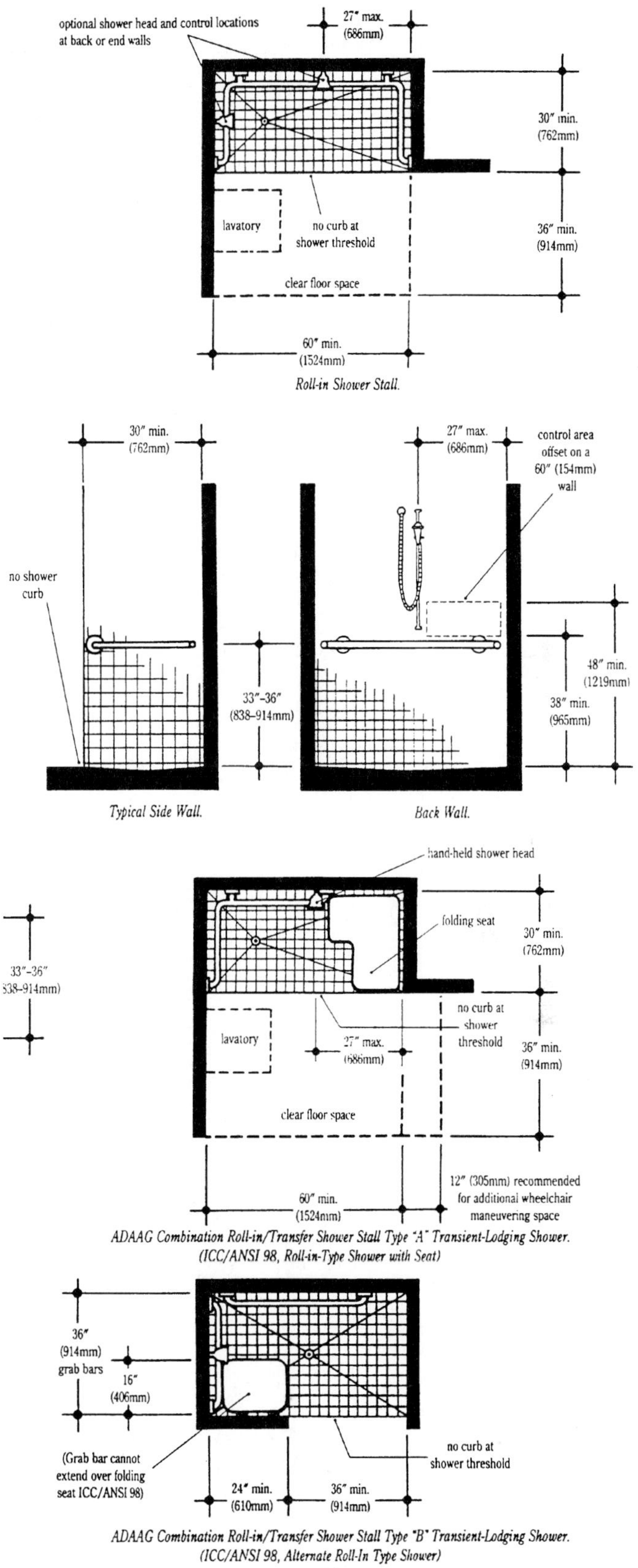

(r)

REST ROOMS AND TOILETS

Barrier-Free Bathtub Plans and Elevations

Bathtub with Portable Seat in Tub.

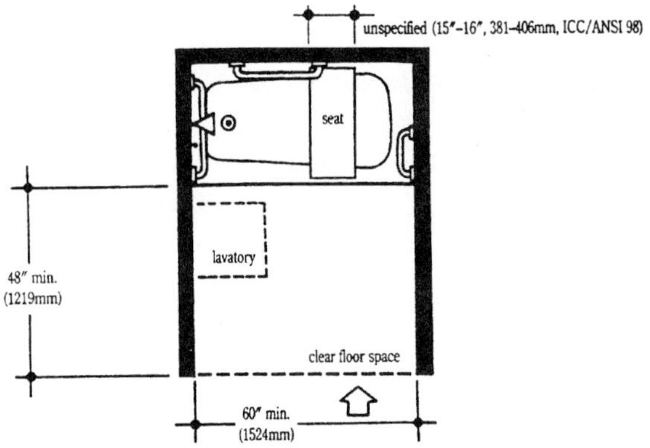

Clear Floor Space Required for Forward Approach.

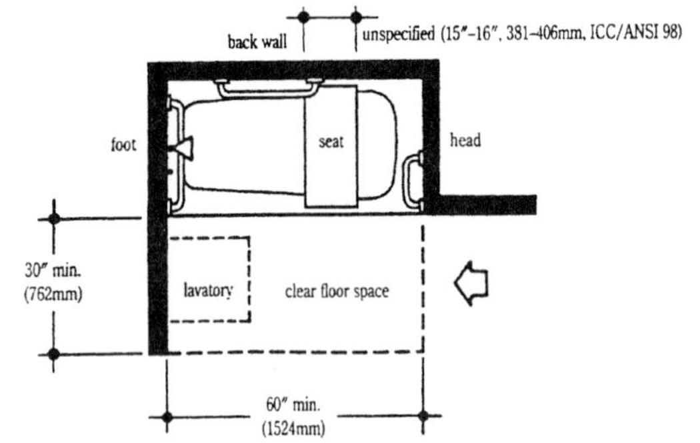

Clear Floor Space Required for Side Approach.

Drawings not to scale.

Bathtub with Integral Seat at Head of Tub.

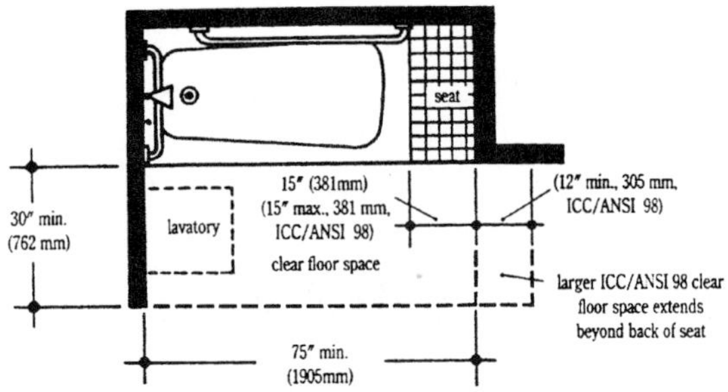

Clear Floor Space Required for Side Approach.

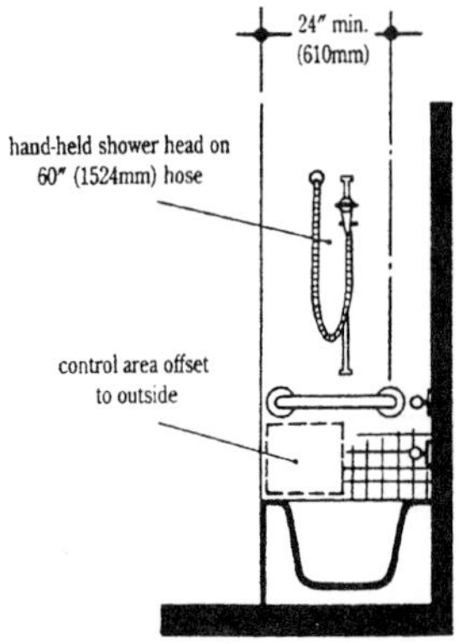

Foot of Tub.

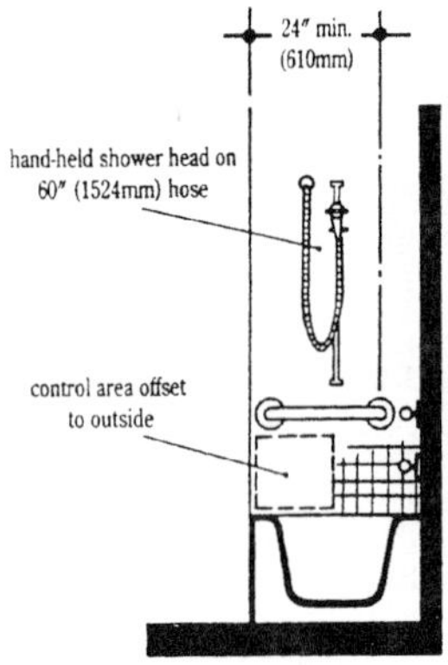

Foot of Tub.

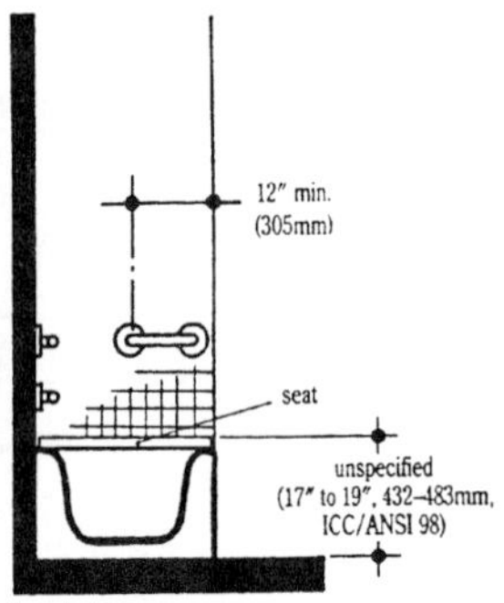

Head of Tub.

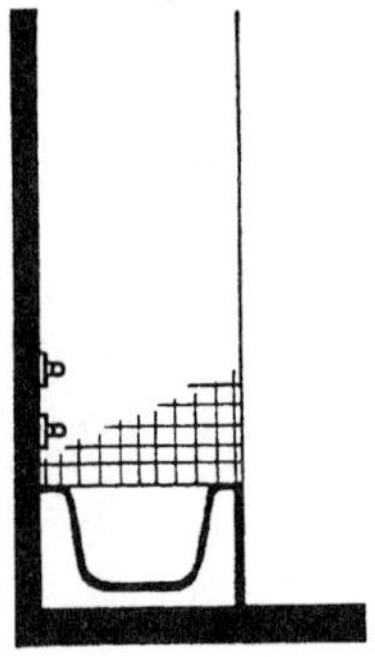

Head of Tub.

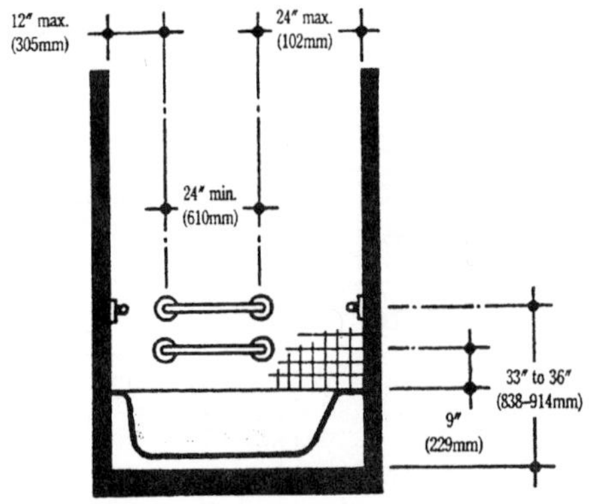

Back Wall.

(s)

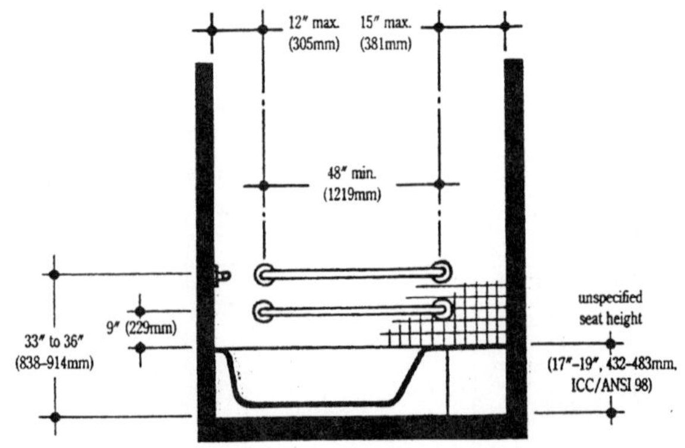

Back Wall.

(t)

Design Solutions for Bathrooms with Shower Stalls

Bathtub with Transfer Shower Stall.

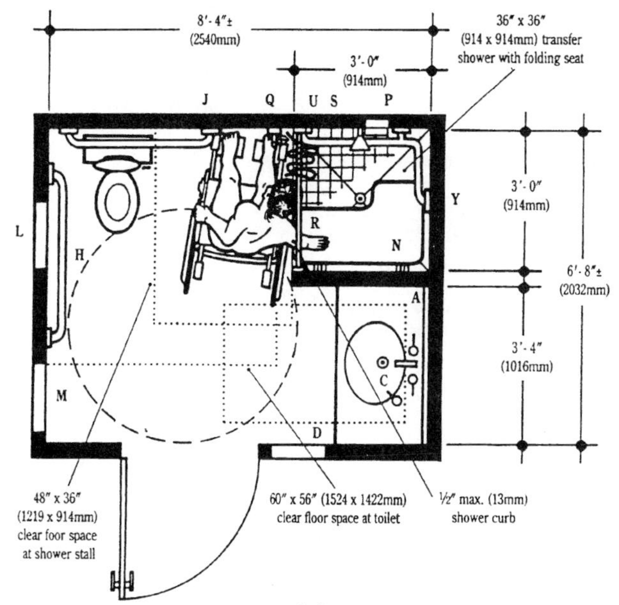

(u)

Bathroom with Wet-Area Shower Stall.

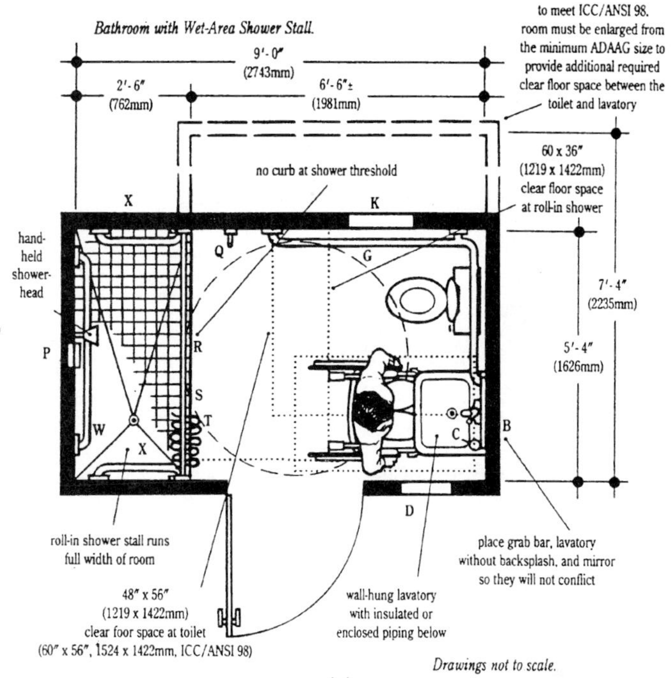

Drawings not to scale.

(v)

Bathroom with Enlarged Roll-in Shower Stall.

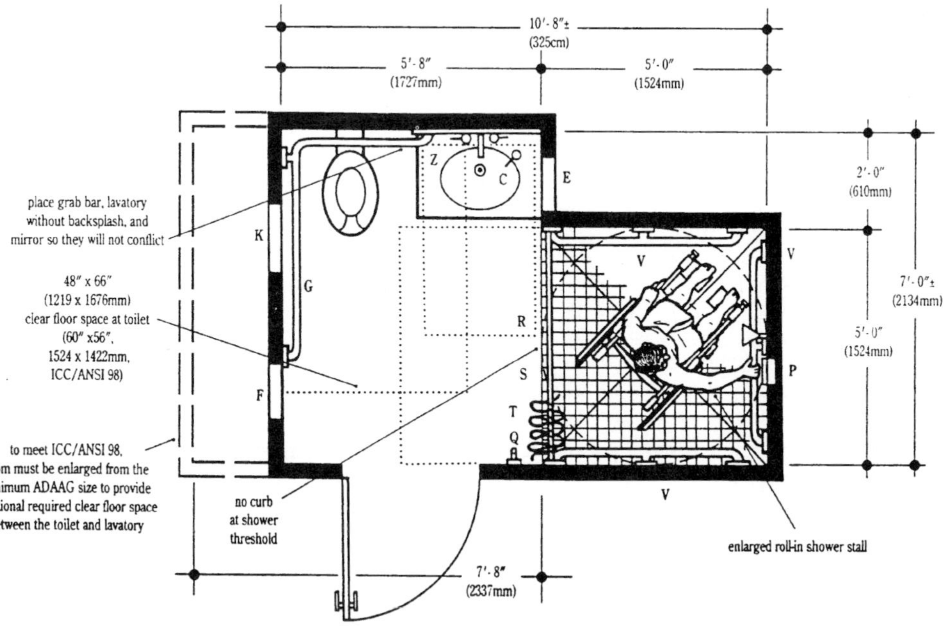

(w)

LEGEND

- A *B-290 Series Wall-to-Wall Mirror.*
- B *B-290 Series Mirror, 18" W x 36" H (457 x 914mm).*
- C *B-822 Lavatory-Mounted Soap Dispenser.*
- D *B-369 Recessed Paper Towel Dispenser and Waste Receptacle.*
- E *B-359 Recessed Paper Towel Dispenser.*
- F *B-525 Recessed Waste Receptacle.*
- G *B-5837 Horizontal Two-Wall Grab Bar, 36" x 54" (914 x 1372mm).*
- H *B-5806 x 42 Horizontal Grab Bar.*
- J *B-5806 x 36 Horizontal Grab Bar.*
- K *B-3474 Recessed Toilet-Seat-Cover Dispenser, Toilet Tissue Dispenser with Theft-Resistant Spindle.*
- L *B-3574 Recessed Toilet-Seat-Cover Dispenser, Sanitary Napkin Disposal, Toilet Tissue Dispenser with Theft-Resistant Spindle.*
- M *B-3500X2 Recessed Sanitary Napkin/Tampon Vendor.*
- N *B-517 Folding Shower Seat, Padded Seat, Right-Hand Seat.*
- P *B-6617 Recessed Soap Dish.*
- Q *B-2116 Single Robe/Clothes Hook with Concealed Mounting.*
- R *B-6107 Shower Curtain Rod.*
- S *204-1 Shower Curtain Hooks.*
- T *204-3 Vinyl Shower Curtain, 70" W x 72" H (1778 x 1829mm).*
- U *204-2 Vinyl Shower Curtain, 42" W x 72" H (1067 x 1829mm).*
- V *B-58061.99 x 48 Horizontal Grab Bar with Peened Grip.*
- W *B-5806.99 x 48 Horizontal Grab Bar with Peened Grip.*
- X *B-5806.99 x 24 Horizontal Grab Bar with Peened Grip.*
- Y *B-5861.99 Shower Grab Bar with Peened Grip, 15 ⅞" x 30 ⅞" (403 x 784mm).*
- Z *B-290 Series Mirror, 33" W x 36" H (838 x 914mm).*

REST ROOMS AND TOILETS

Barrier-Free Bathroom Plan with Shower Stall

Bathroom with Wet-Area Roll-in/Transfer Shower Stall.

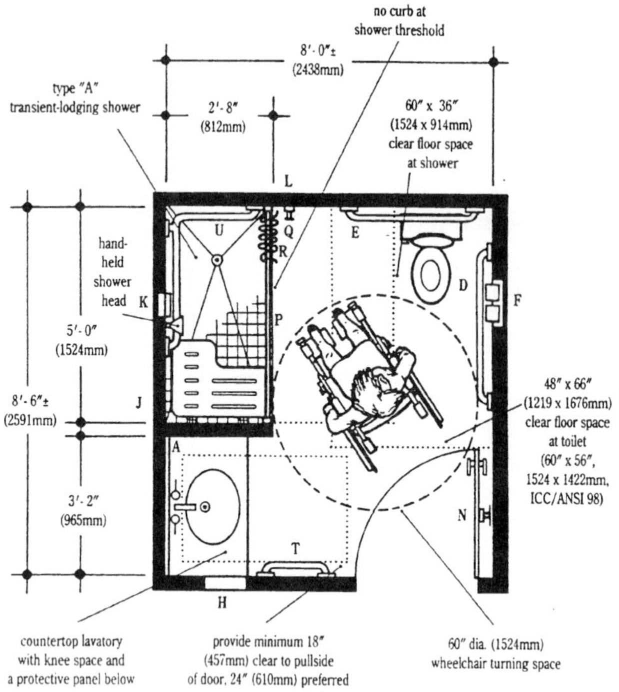

(x)

Bathroom with Enlarged Roll-in/Transfer Shower Stall.

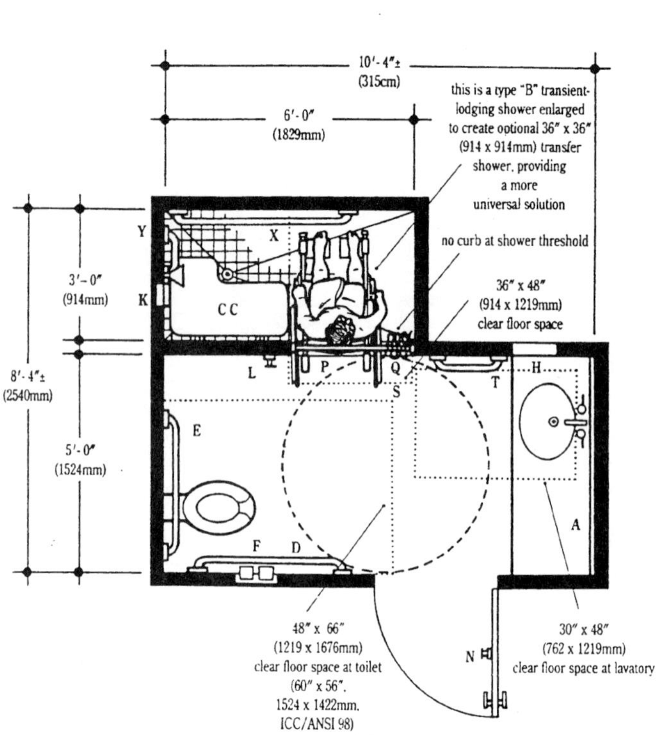

(y)

Scale: 1/4 = 1'-0"

Design Solutions for Bathrooms with Tub/Shower Units

Bathroom with Combination Tub/Shower Unit and In-Tub Seat.

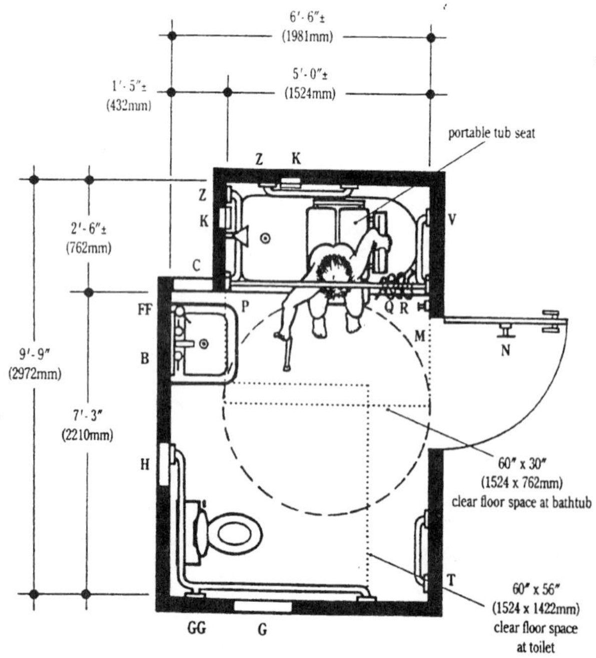

(z)

Bathroom with Combination Tub/Shower Unit and Integral Seat.

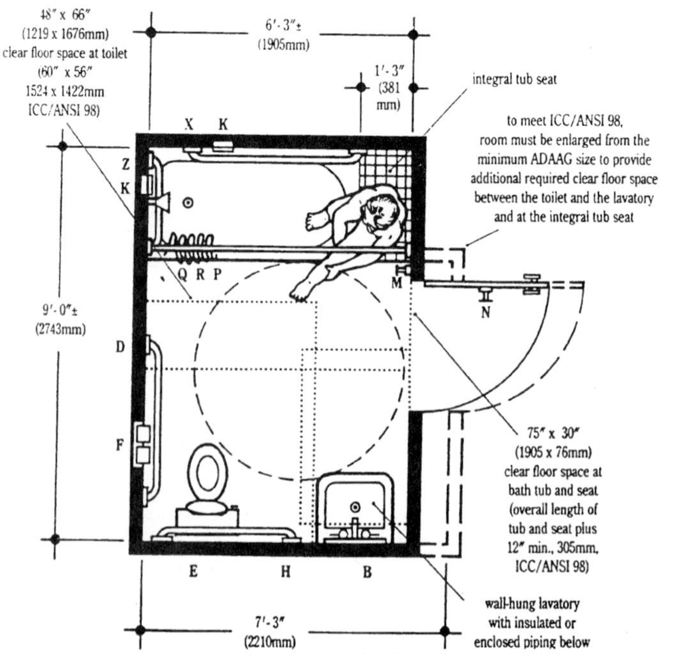

(aa)

Design Solutions for Multiple Shower Stalls and Dressing Compartments

Multiple Shower Installation with Enlarged Roll-in Shower Stall and Dressing Compartment.

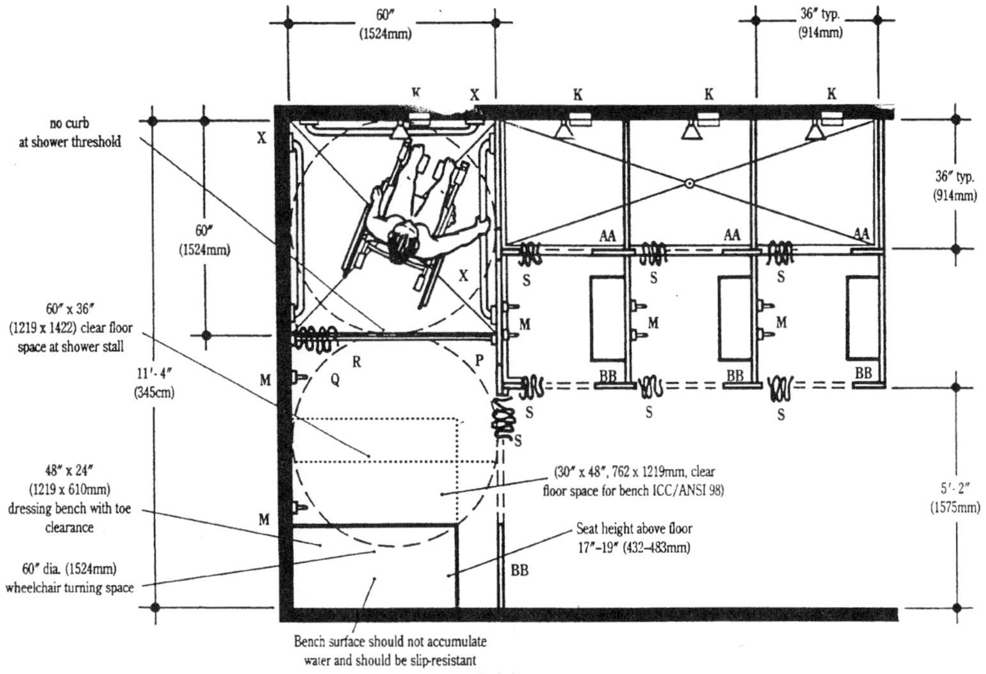

(bb)

Multiple Shower Installation with Transfer Shower Stall and Dressing Compartment.

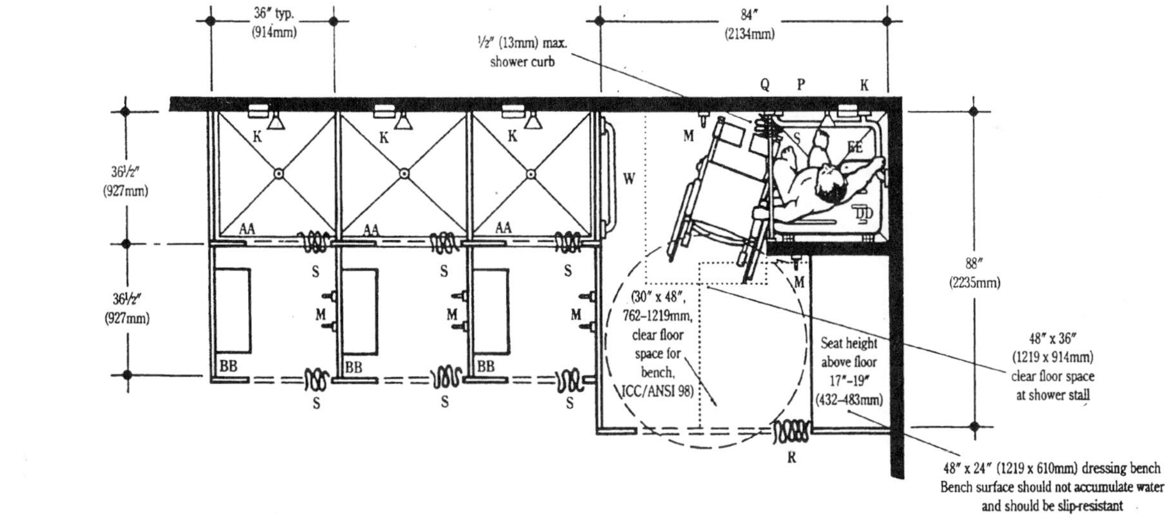

(cc)

LEGEND

- A *B-290 Series Wall-to-Wall Mirror.*
- B *B-290 Series Mirror, 18" W x 36" H (457 x 914mm).*
- C *B-369 Recessed Paper Towel Dispenser and Waste Receptacle.*
- D *B-5806 x 42 Horizontal Grab Bar.*
- E *B-5806 x 36 Horizontal Grab Bar.*
- F *B-6977 Recessed Toilet Paper Holder for Two Rolls.*
- G *B-3574 Recessed Toilet-Seat-Cover Dispenser, Sanitary Napkin Disposal, Toilet Tissue Dispenser with Theft-Resistant Spindle.*
- H *B-355 Recessed Facial Tissue Dispenser.*
- J *B-5181 Reversible Folding Shower Seat, Solid Phenolic, Left-Hand Seat.*
- K *B-6617 Recessed Soap Dish.*
- L *B-76717 Single Robe/Clothes Hook.*
- M *B-2116 Single Robe/Clothes Hook with Concealed Mounting.*
- N *B-76727 Double Robe/Clothes Hook.*
- P *B-6107 Shower Curtain Rod.*
- Q *204-1 Shower Curtain Hooks.*
- R *204-3 Vinyl Shower Curtain, 70" W x 72" H (1778 x 1829mm).*
- S *204-2 Vinyl Shower Curtain, 42" W x 72" H (1067 x 1829mm).*
- T *B-5806 x 18 Horizontal Grab Bar used as towel bar.*
- U *B-58616.99 Shower Grab Bar with Peened Grip, 24" x 36" (610 x 914mm).*
- V *B-5806.99 x 18 Horizontal Grab Bar with Peened Grip.*
- W *B-5806.99 x 30 Horizontal Grab Bar with Peened Grip.*
- X *B-5806.99 x 48 Horizontal Grab Bar with Peened Grip.*
- Y *B-5806.99 x 12 Grab Bar with Peened Grip.*
- Z *B-5806.99 x 24 Horizontal Grab Bar with Peened Grip.*
- AA *1082 Series Solid Phenolic Shower Dividers with Shower Curtain Track in underside of headrail.*
- BB *1082 Series Solid Phenolic Dressing Compartments with Bench, Curtain Track in underside of headrail.*
- CC *B-518 Folding Shower Seat, Padded Seat, Left-Hand Seat.*
- DD *B-5181 Reversible Folding Shower Seat, Solid Phenolic, Right-Hand Seat.*
- EE *B-5861.99 Shower Grab Bar with Peened Grip, 15 ⅞" x 30 ⅞" (403 x 784mm).*
- FF *B-822 Lavatory-Mounted Soap Dispenser.*
- GG *B-5837 Horizontal Two-Wall Grab Bar, 36" x 54" (914 x 1372mm).*

REST ROOMS AND TOILETS

Barrier-Free Toilet Plans and Elevation

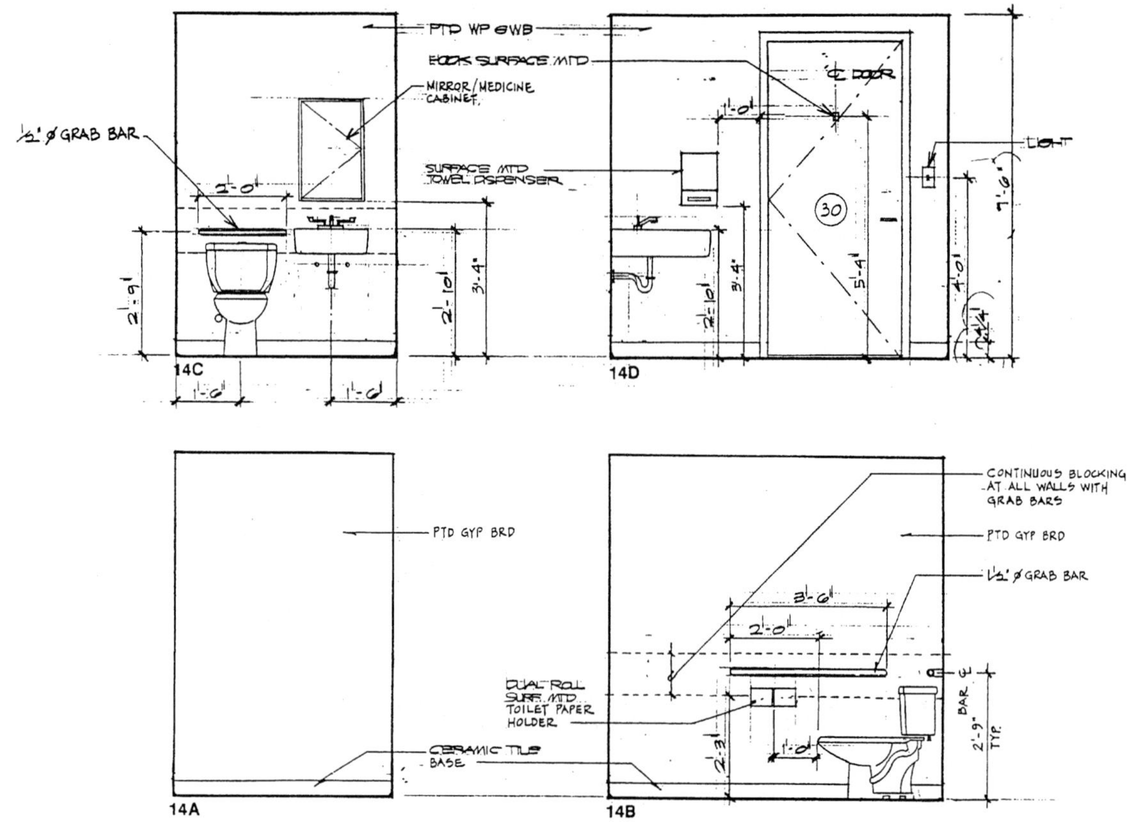

14 Typical Handicap Accessible Toilet Room D.A. Toilet

SCALE: ½" = 1'-0"

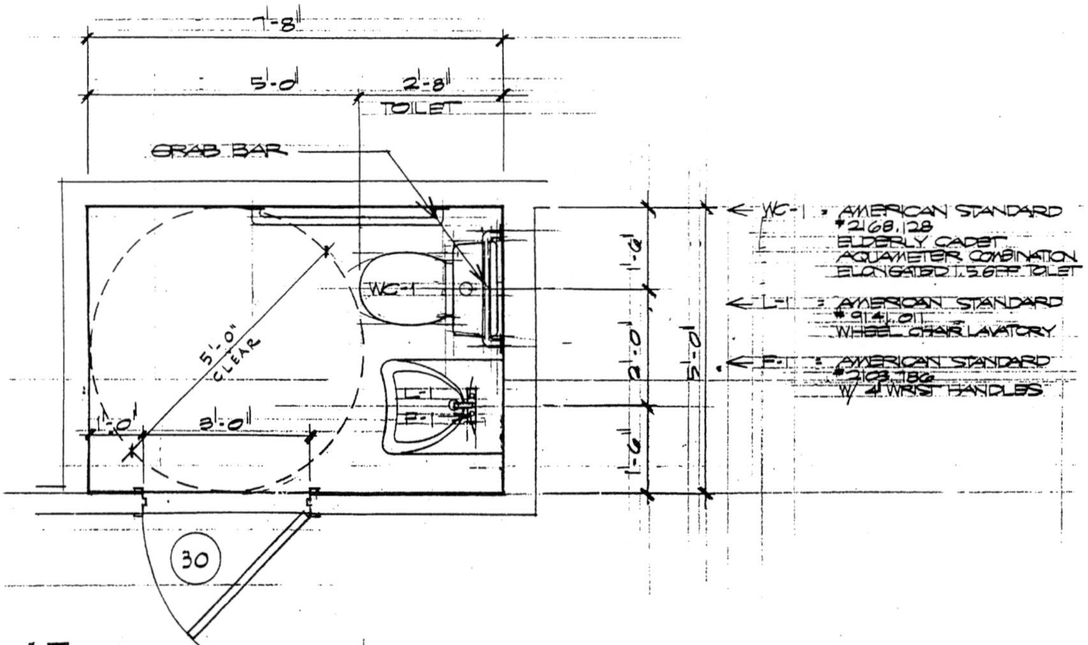

15 Plan D.A. Toilet No.1

SCALE: ½" = 1'-0"   Layout Typical for Toilet D.A. No. 2

In Figs. 23 to 29, various generic toilet accessories and grab bar configurations are illustrated. While most manufacturers have similar accessories and grab bars within their catalogs, overall dimensions and methods of installation vary greatly. Placement of accessories in relationship to plumbing fixtures, door swings, and interior circulation is to be carefully studied by the designer.

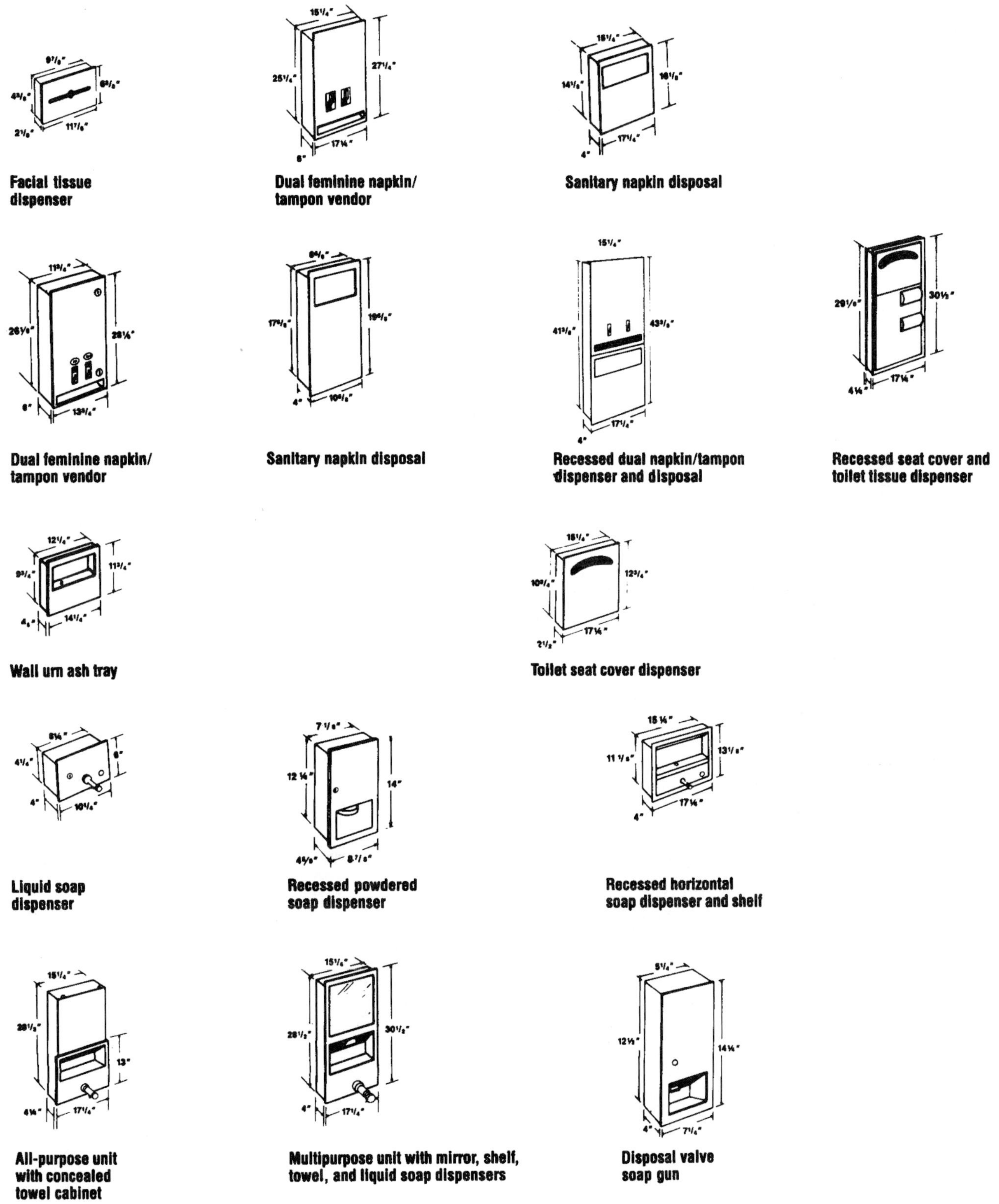
Facial tissue dispenser
Dual feminine napkin/ tampon vendor
Sanitary napkin disposal
Dual feminine napkin/ tampon vendor
Sanitary napkin disposal
Recessed dual napkin/tampon dispenser and disposal
Recessed seat cover and toilet tissue dispenser
Wall urn ash tray
Toilet seat cover dispenser
Liquid soap dispenser
Recessed powdered soap dispenser
Recessed horizontal soap dispenser and shelf
All-purpose unit with concealed towel cabinet
Multipurpose unit with mirror, shelf, towel, and liquid soap dispensers
Disposal valve soap gun

Fig. 23

REST ROOMS AND TOILETS

Toilet Accessories

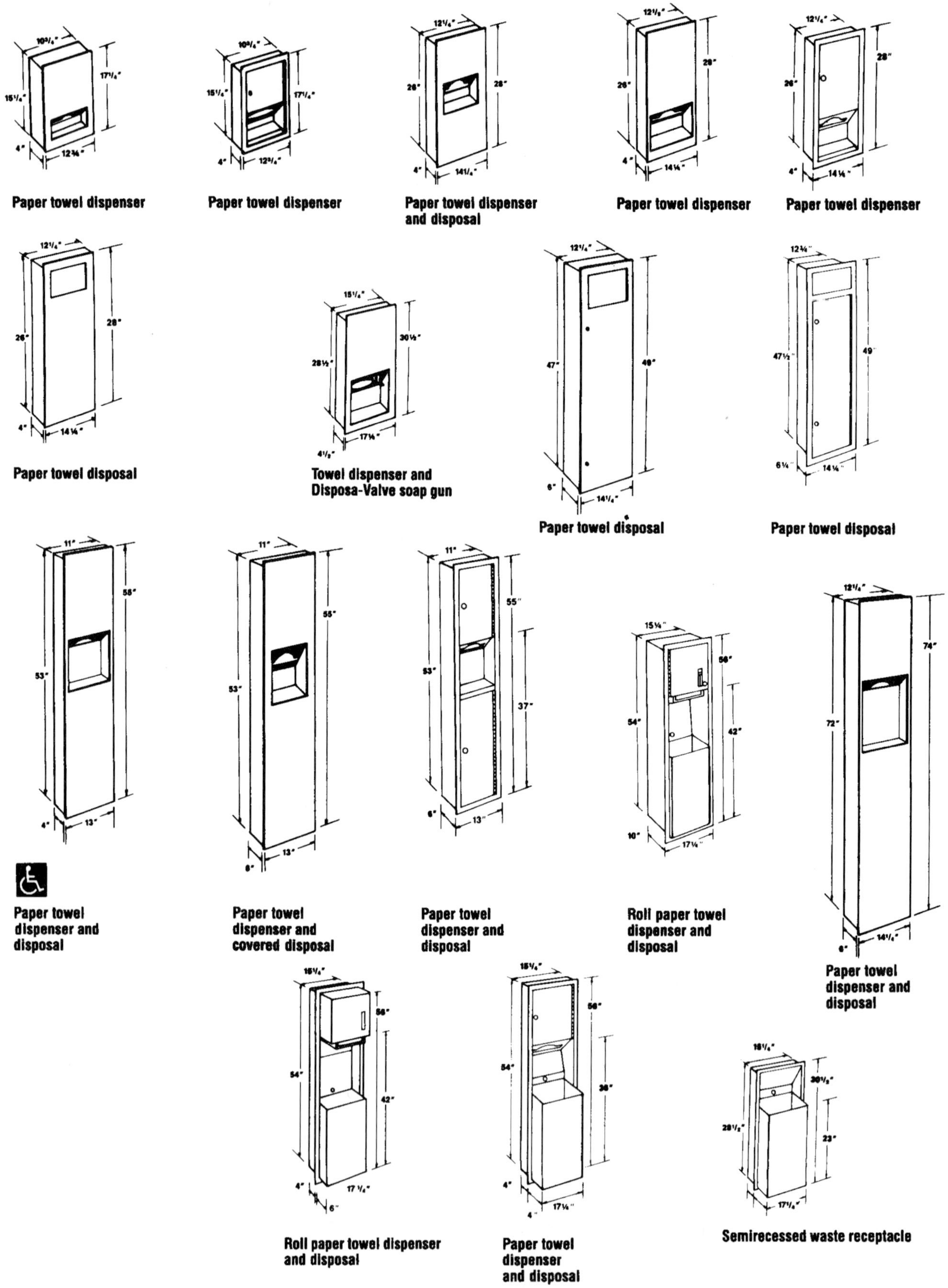
Paper towel dispenser
Paper towel dispenser
Paper towel dispenser and disposal
Paper towel dispenser
Paper towel dispenser
Paper towel disposal
Towel dispenser and Disposa-Valve soap gun
Paper towel disposal
Paper towel disposal
Paper towel dispenser and disposal
Paper towel dispenser and covered disposal
Paper towel dispenser and disposal
Roll paper towel dispenser and disposal
Paper towel dispenser and disposal
Roll paper towel dispenser and disposal
Paper towel dispenser and disposal
Semirecessed waste receptacle

Fig. 24

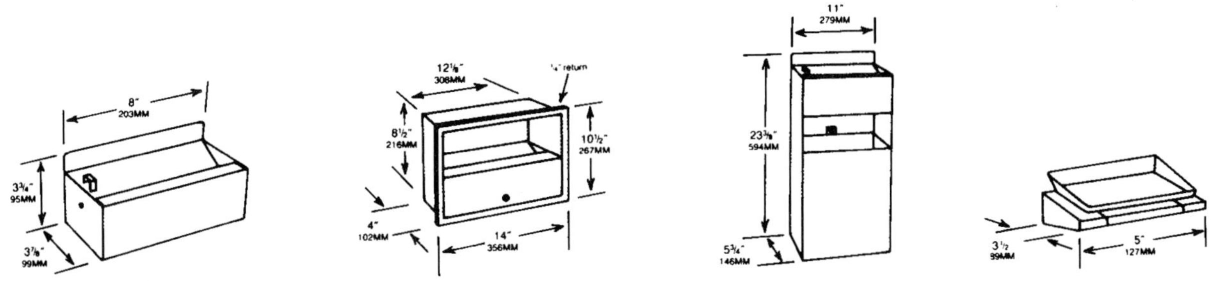

Ash trays

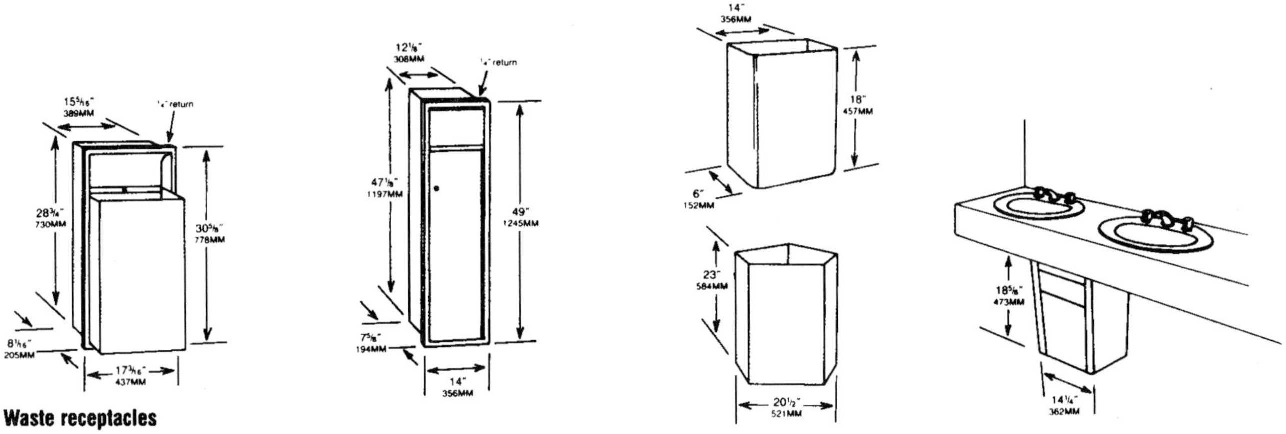

Waste receptacles

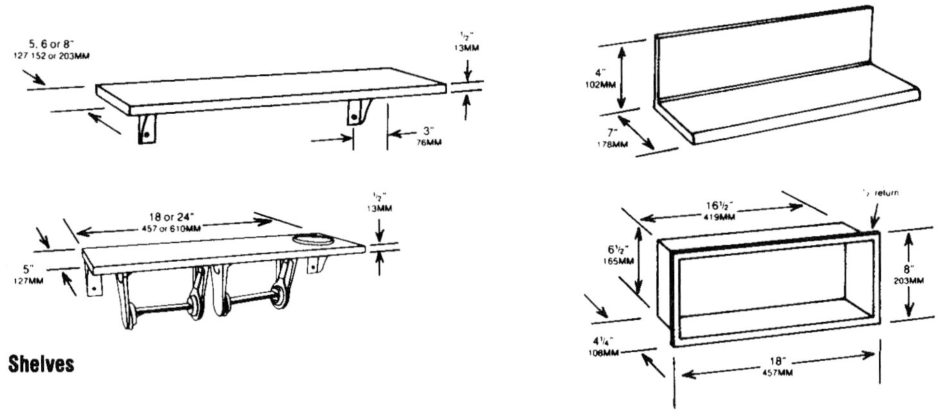

Shelves

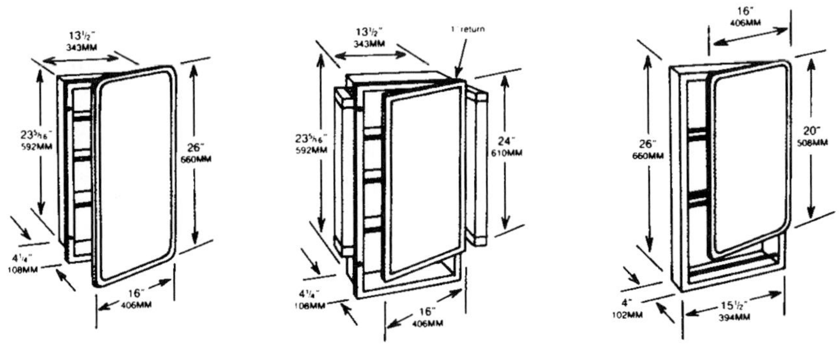

Medicine cabinets

Fig. 25

REST ROOMS AND TOILETS
Toilet Accessories

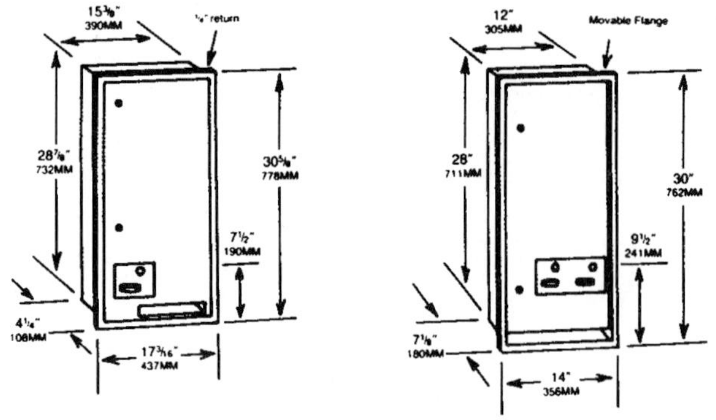

Sanitary napkin dispensers

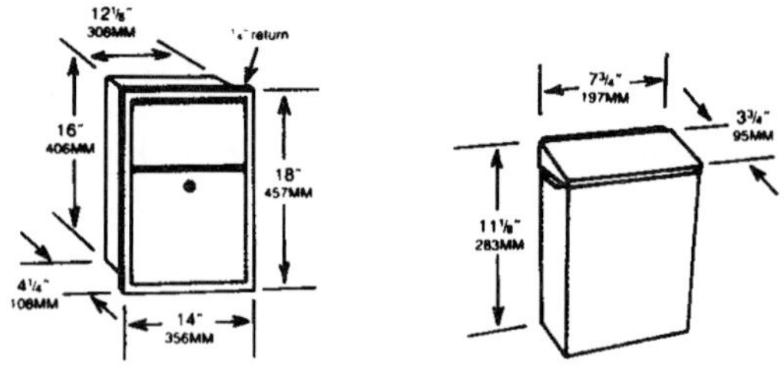

Sanitary napkin disposals

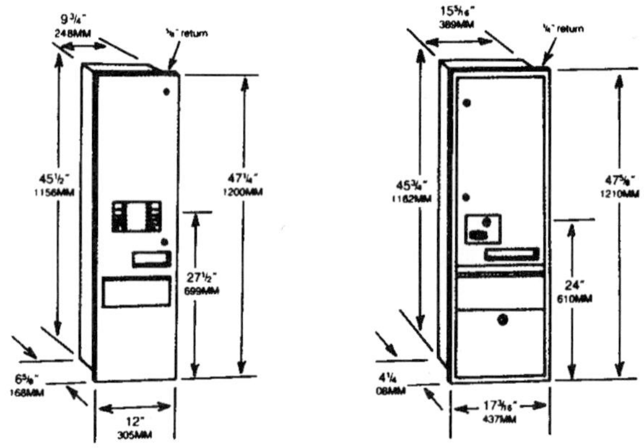

Combined sanitary napkin dispenser and disposal

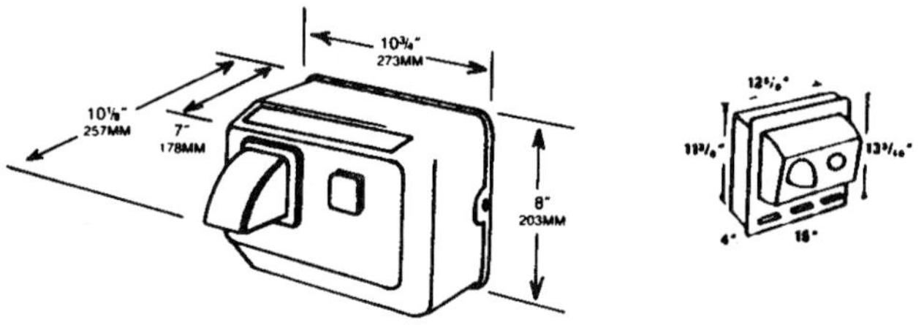

Hand and hair dryers

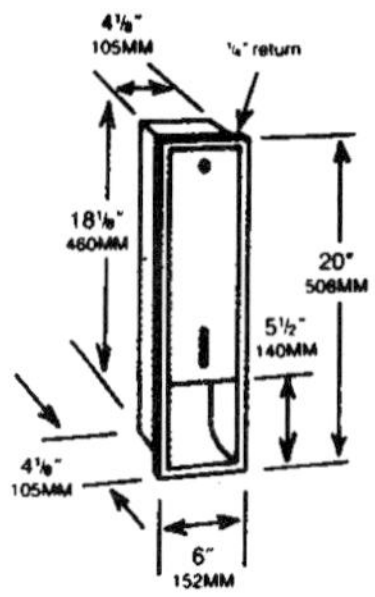

Paper cup dispenser

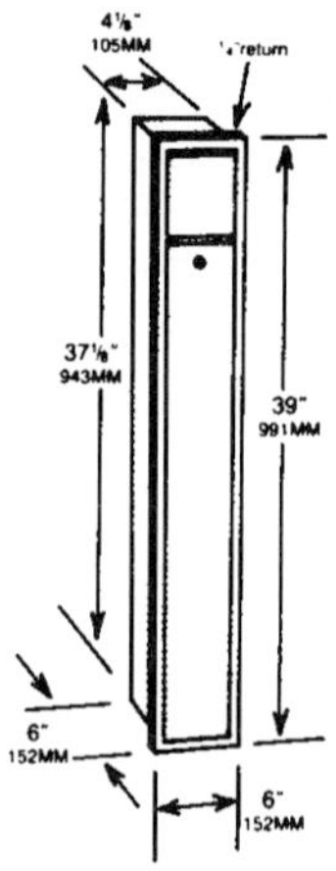

Paper cup disposal

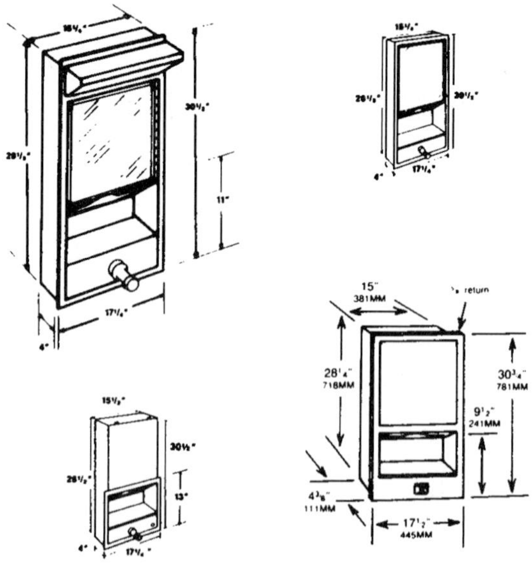

Multipurpose cabinet

Fig. 26

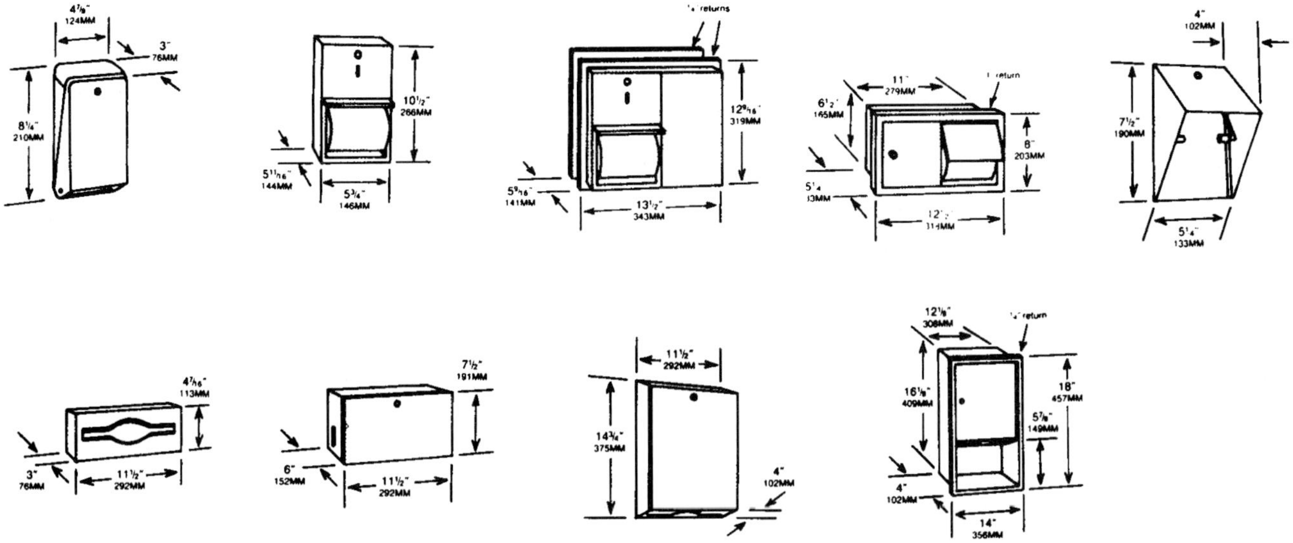

Toilet tissue dispensers

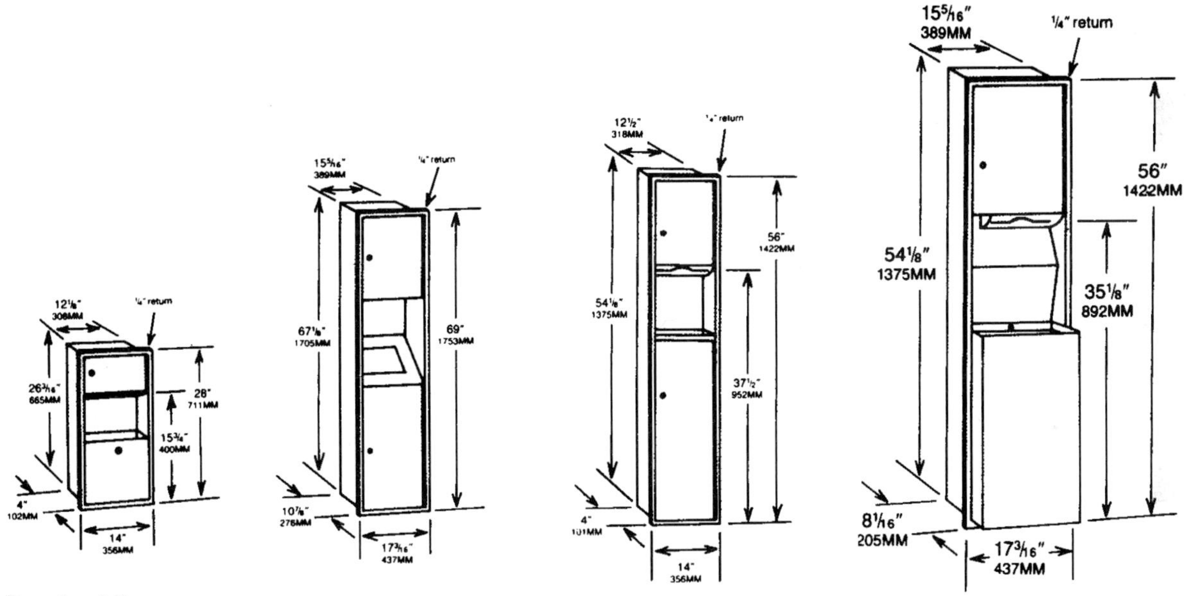

Paper towel dispensers

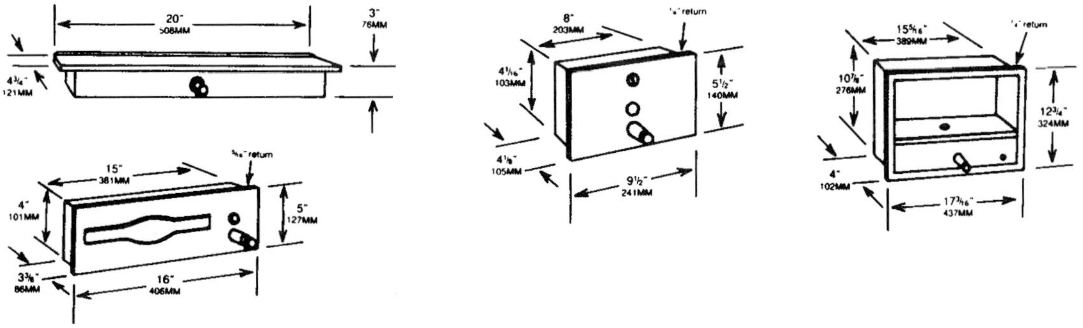

Soap dispensers

Fig. 27

REST ROOMS AND TOILETS

Grab Bar Configurations

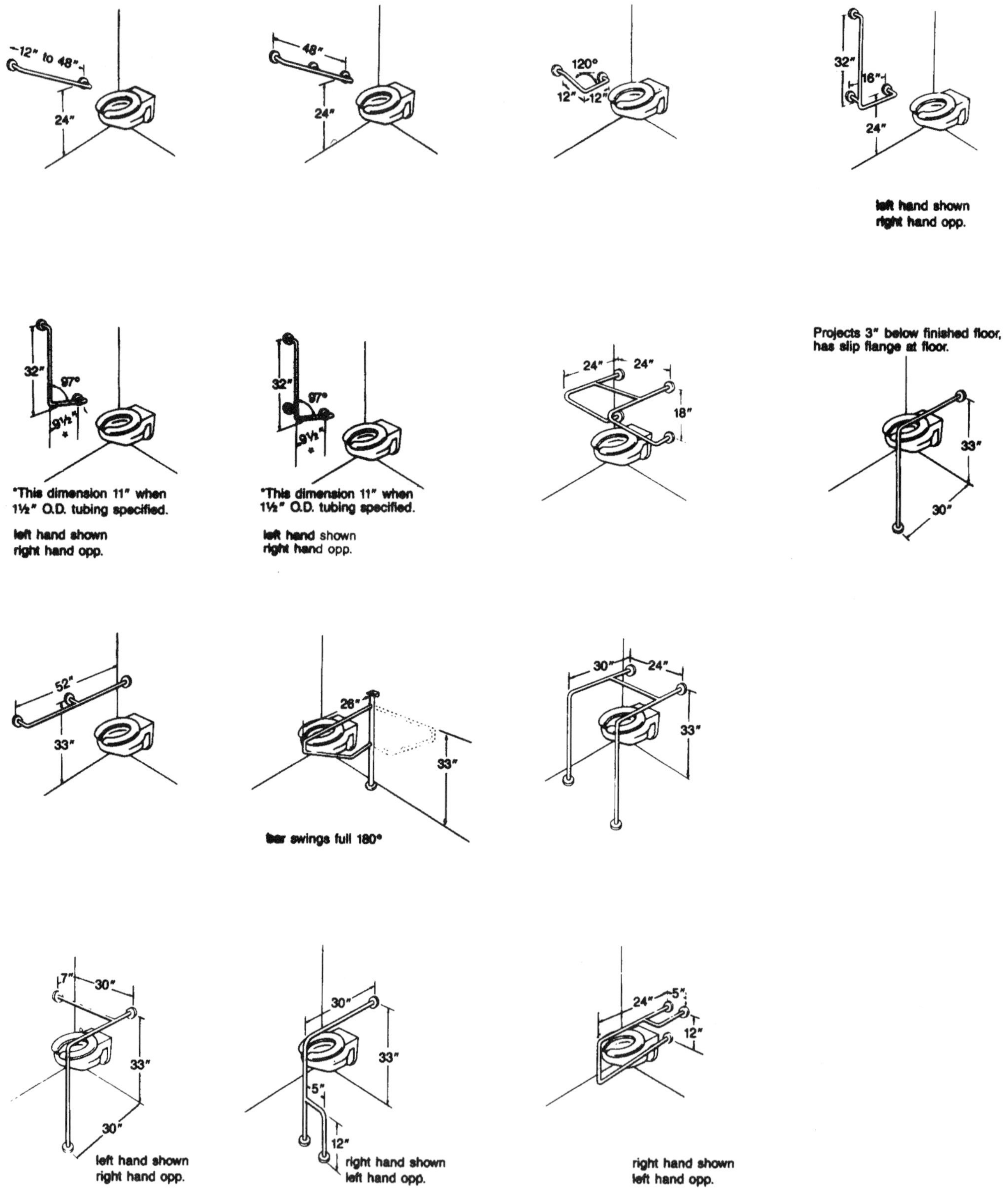

Fig. 28

REST ROOMS AND TOILETS
Grab Bar Configurations

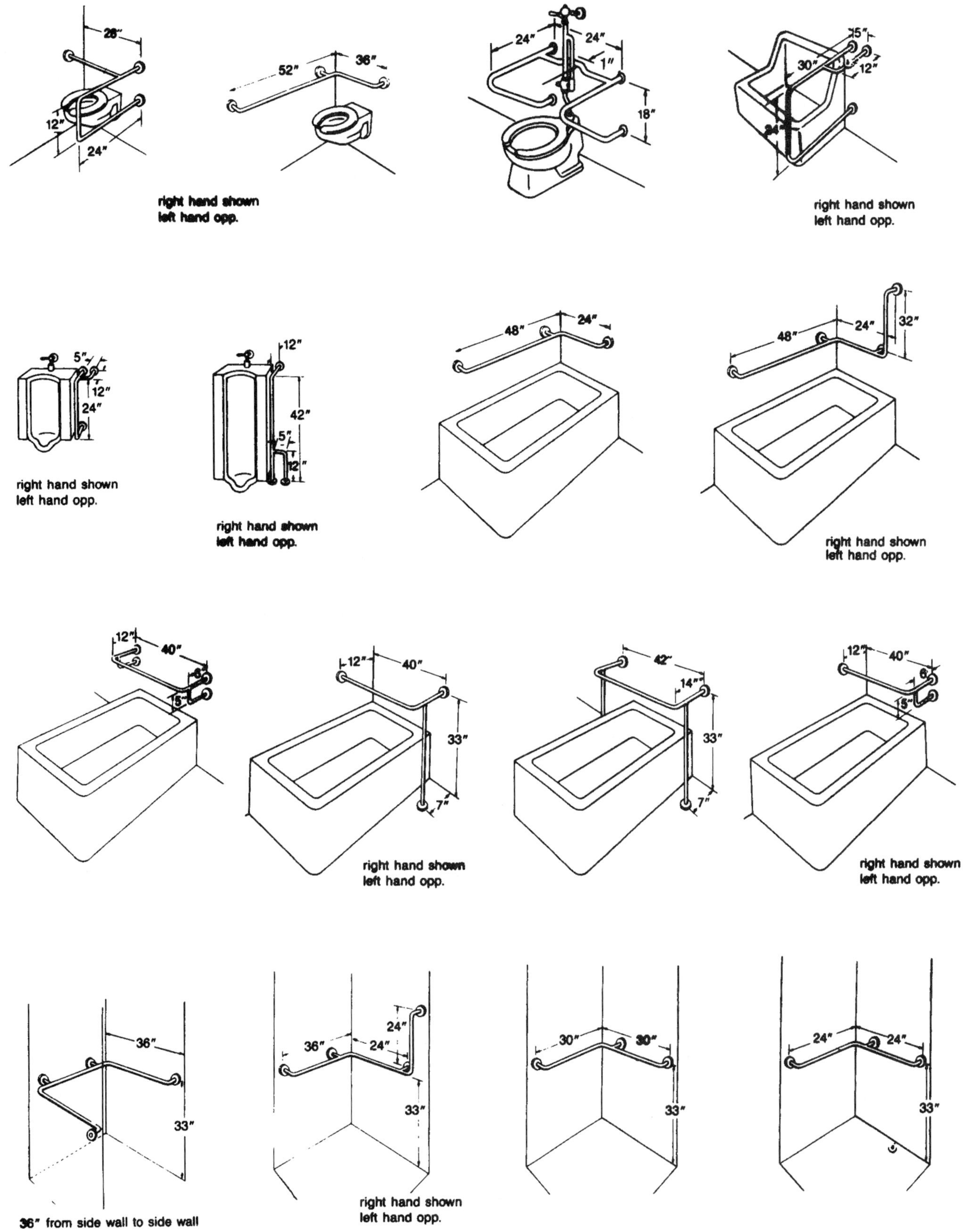

Fig. 29

Table 1 Floor area requirements for public coatrooms

Number of coats (capacity)	Floor area (with attendant) Min	Floor area (with attendant) Max	Floor area (without attendant)		Floor area (electric conveyor)	
50	35	50	40	60	N/A	N/A
100	65	85	80	100	80	100
150	90	120	110	145	110	125
200	125	150	150	180	140	150
250	150	190	180	230	100	110
300	180	225	215	270	125	140
350	200	260	240	300	135	150
400	225	275	270	330	150	160
450	260	320	310	370	160	175
500	300	365	425	430	175	190
750	450	500	540	600	250	275
1000	600	650	720	780	325	350
1500	800	900	950	1080	450	480
2000	1000	1250	1200	1500	600	675
3000	1600	1850	1900	2200	1000	1150

Note: The above floor areas are approximate and should only be used for preliminary space planning requirements.

Since the number of coats per linear foot of hanging can vary from 4 to 8, the floor area can vary dramatically. A lightweight overcoat, for example, can measure 1–1.5 inches in width. A medium weight to heavyweight coat might measure from 2 to 4 inches. A fur coat might require a minimum of 4–6 in. The designer must consider the overall size of coatroom based upon the following critical factors: (1) geographic location/climate; (2) attendants required or not required; (3) aisle clearance; (4) peak entry/exit loads for coat retrieval; (5) assumed garment thickness or garments per linear foot; (6) linear feet of counter surface and overhead shelving; and (7) other storage components, i.e., hats, umbrellas, briefcases, packages, etc.

COATROOMS

FLOOR AREA REQUIREMENTS

Coatrooms typically fall into two categories: those that are self-service and those that are controlled by one or more attendants. The latter category of coatroom can be more compact because only one, or perhaps two, attendants have access to the coats. A self-service coatroom must have more space between rows of coats so that several persons can enter and get their coats.

Self-service coatrooms are susceptible to theft of property, particularly expensive outerwear. Therefore, it is desirable that these coatrooms be visible to someone at all times, such as a maitre d' in a restaurant or a receptionist in an office. In those situations where a supervised self-service coatroom is inappropriate or cannot be provided, self-service keyed locks offer a viable alternative. In addition to being able to provide secure coat storage, lockers can also store briefcases, packages, or other encumbrances.

TYPES OF CHECKROOM SYSTEMS

Three basic types of manufactured or prefabricated coat storage units are shown in Figs. 1 to 3. Exact coat storage capacities are provided by the manufacturer. All units can be customized to suit various room configurations. Note the adjoining counter space to speed operations. Coat capacities relative to length are listed in Table 2.

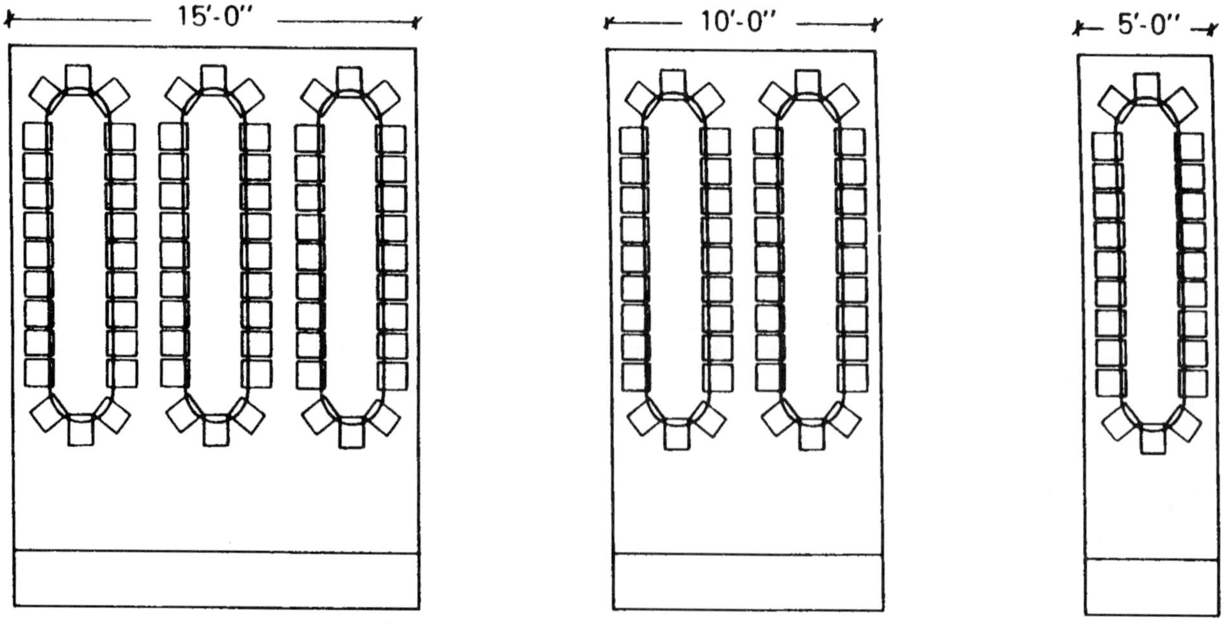

Fig. 1 Electric carousel coat storage

COATROOMS

Types of Checkroom Systems

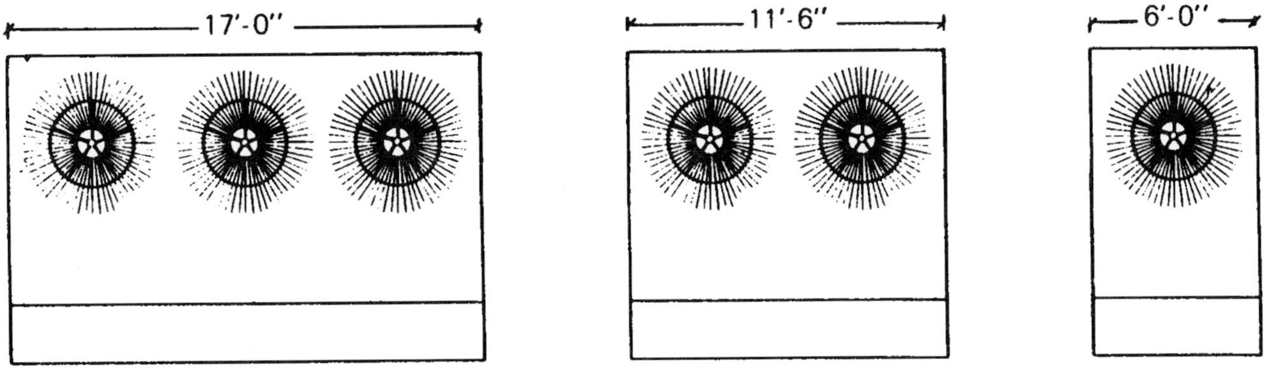

Fig. 2 Rotating reels coat storage

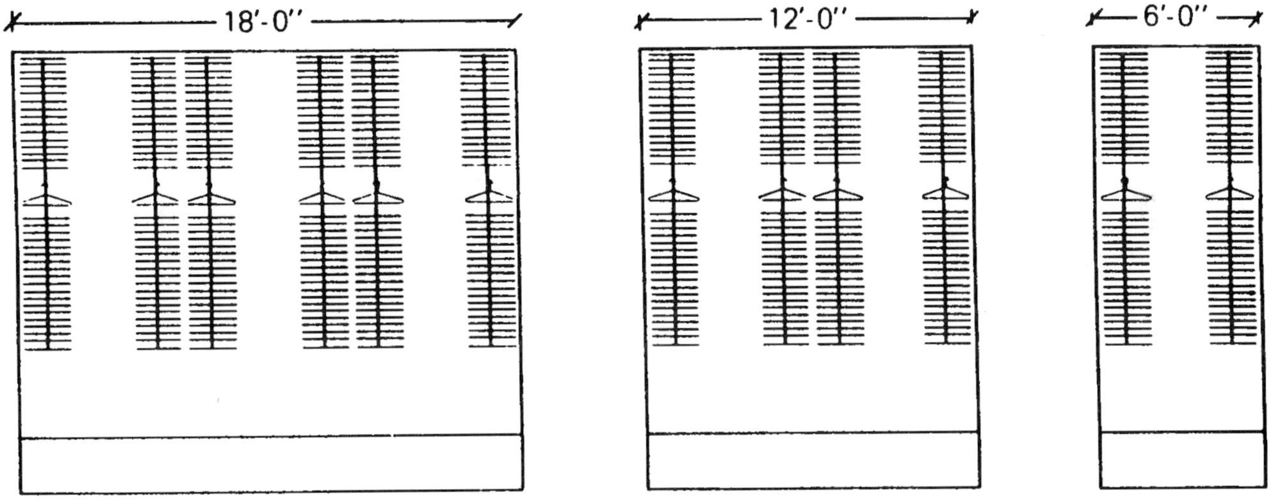

Fig. 3 Stationary coat storage

COATROOMS
Electric Checkroom Systems

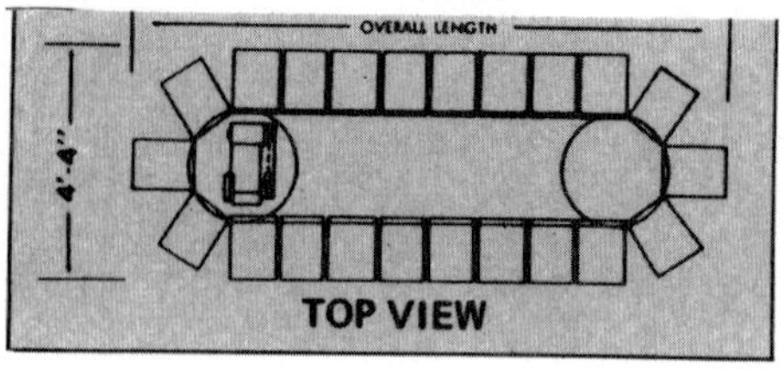

Fig. 4

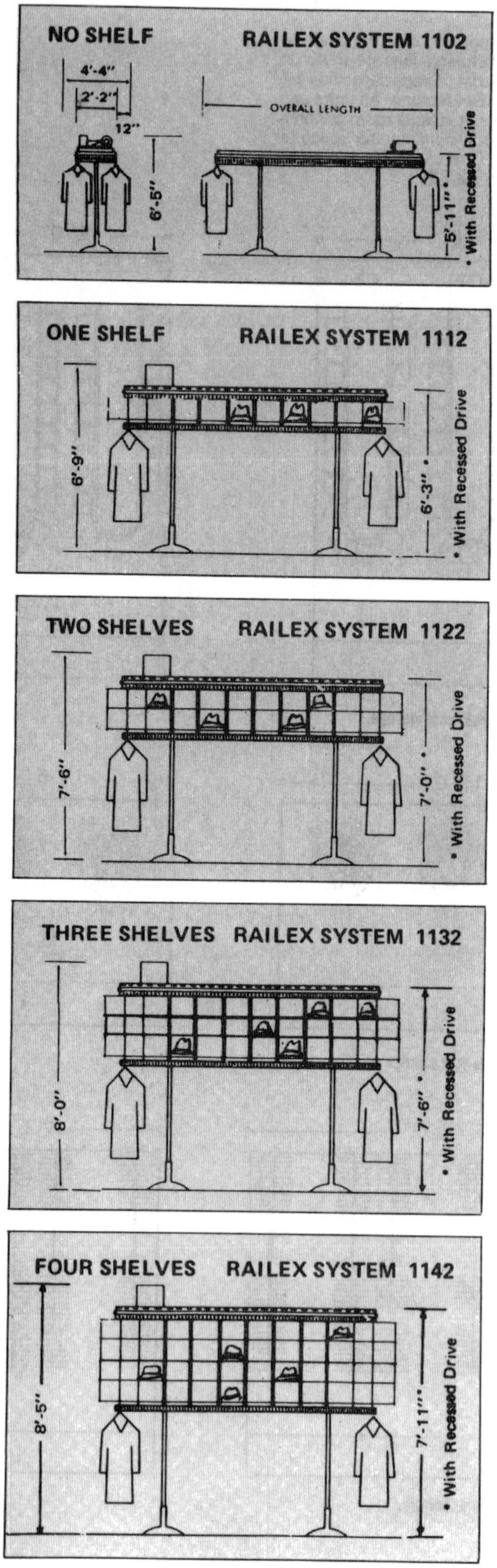

Fig. 5

Table 2

Overall length with garments*	Length of hanging capacity	Coat capacity: no. of slots†
7′ 5″	13′ 0″	144
7′11½″	14′ 1″	156
8′ 6″	15′ 2″	168
9′ 1″	16′ 3″	180
9′ 7″	17′ 4″	192
10′ 1½″	18′ 5″	204
10′ 8″	19′ 6″	216
11′ 2½″	20′ 7″	228
11′ 9″	21′ 8″	240
12′ 3½″	22′ 9″	252
12′10″	23′10″	264
13′ 4½″	24′11″	276
13′11″	26′ 0″	288
14′ 5½″	27′ 1″	300
15′ 0″	28′ 2″	312
15′ 6½″	29′ 3″	324
16′ 1″	30′ 4″	336
16′ 7½″	31′ 5″	348
17′ 2″	32′ 6″	360
17′ 8½″	33′ 7″	372
18′ 3″	34′ 8″	384
18′ 9½″	35′ 9″	396
19′ 4″	36′10″	408
19′10½″	37′11″	420
20′ 5″	39′ 0″	432
20′11½″	40′ 1″	444
21′ 6″	41′ 2″	456
22′ 0½″	42′ 3″	468
22′ 7″	43′ 4″	480
23′ 1½″	44′ 5″	492
23′ 8″	45′ 6″	504
24′ 2½″	46′ 7″	516
24′ 9″	47′ 8″	528
25′ 3½″	48′ 9″	540
25′10″	49′10″	552
26′ 4½″	50′11″	564
26′11″	52′ 0″	576
27′ 5½″	53′ 1″	588
28′ 0″	54′ 2″	600

*Add 4″ minimum clearance to each end and each side when adjacent to walls, columns, obstructions, or other machines.

†This provides 1.1″ per coat. In areas or facilities where bulky coats are customary, the actual capacity may be reduced one-third.

COATROOMS
Stationary Checkroom Systems

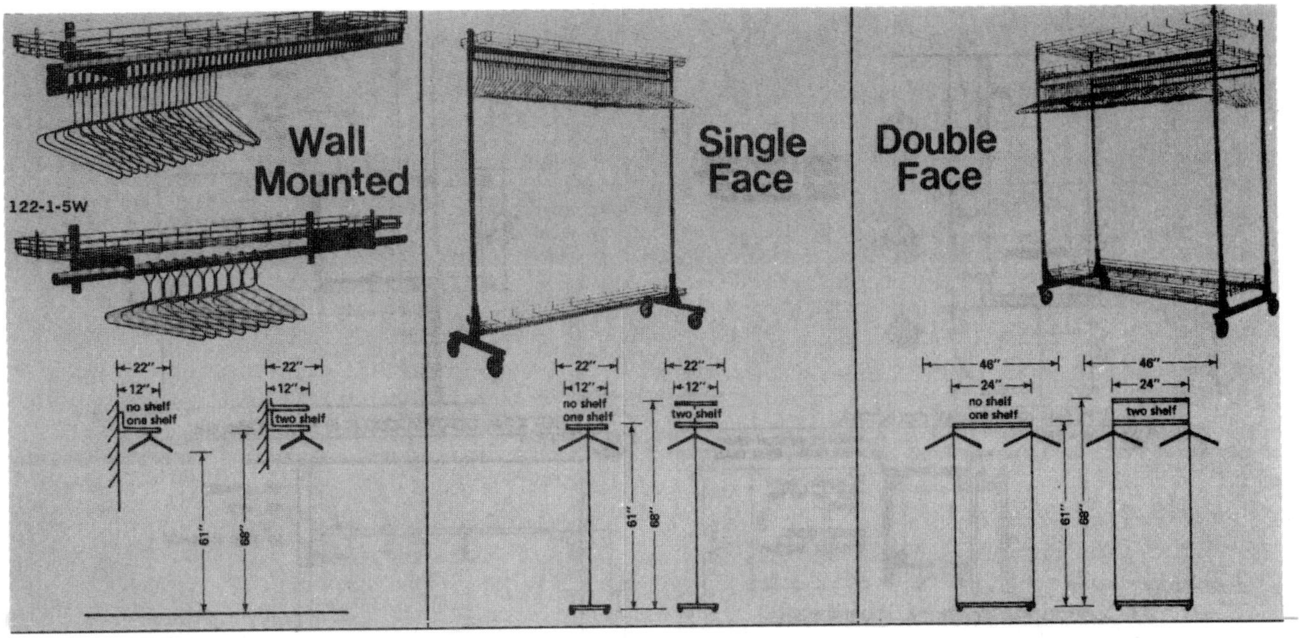

	Length	Number of Coats	Number of Shelves
Wall Mounted	3'-0"	36	0 1 2
	4'-0"	48	0 1 2
	5'-0"	60	0 1 2
Single Face	3'-4"	36	0 1 2
	4'-4"	48	0 1 2
	5'-4"	60	0 1 2
Double Face	3'-4"	72	0 1 2
	4'-4"	96	0 1 2
	5'-4"	120	0 1 2

COATROOMS

Coartoom Plans, Elevations, and Sections

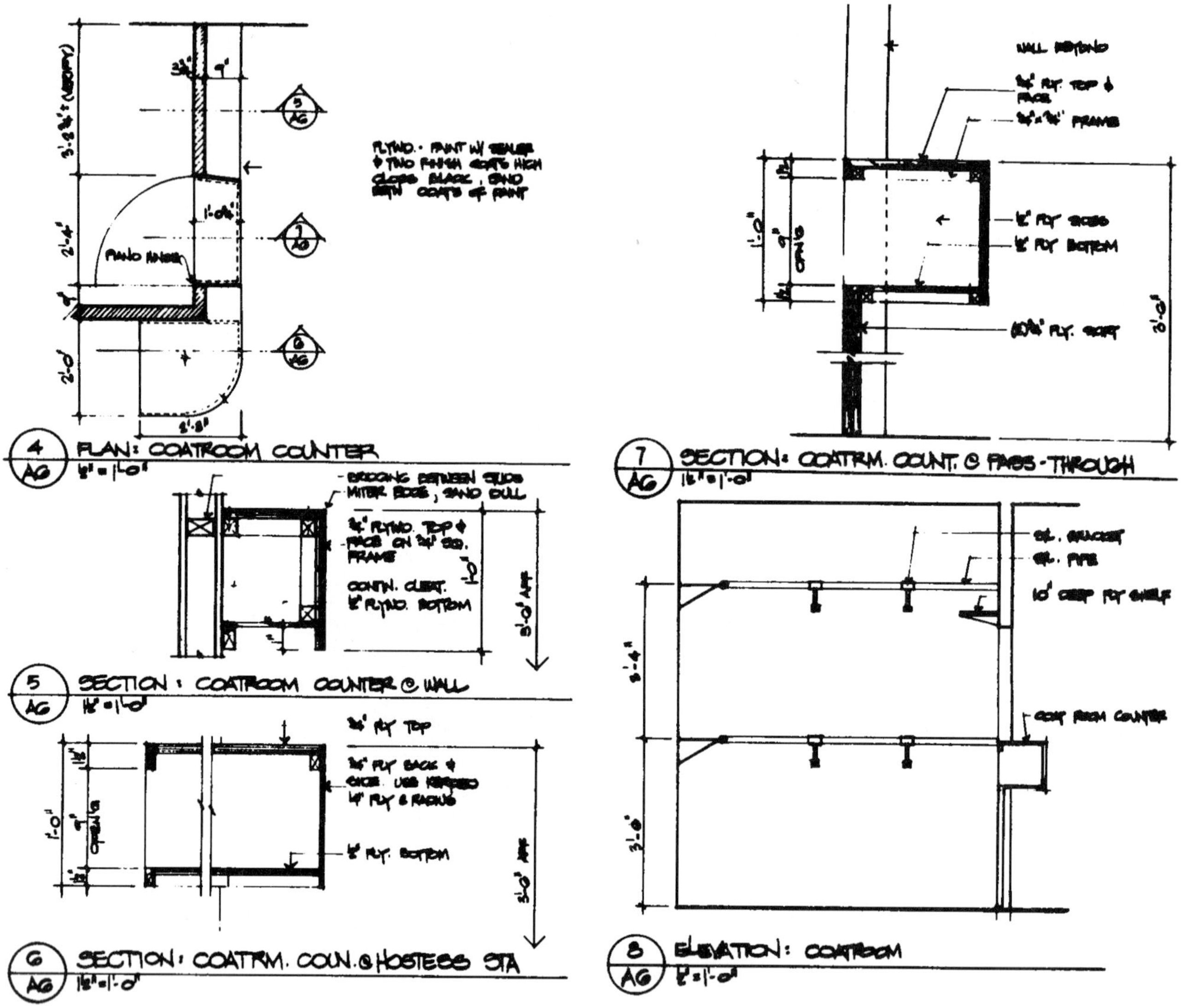

Fig. 6 A typical coatroom configuration will often consist of a counter with an access door plus the required shelves and hang rods. The overall size of the coatroom will vary with the number and types of coats to be stored. In high-volume coatroom situations, the design should provide appropriate counter space for those persons working behind the counter

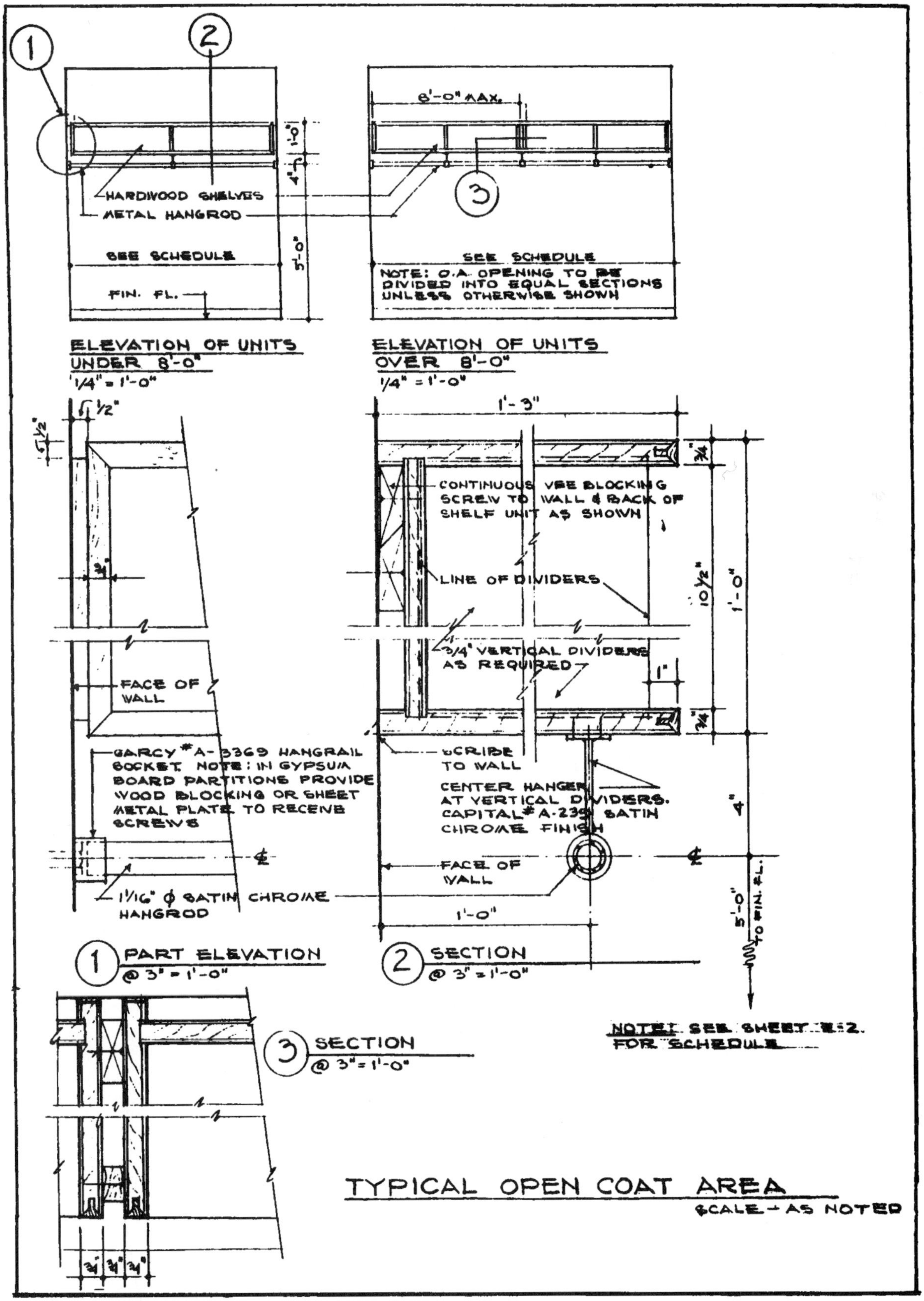
HARDWOOD SHELVES
METAL HANGROD
SEE SCHEDULE
FIN. FL.
1'-0"
4"
5'-0"
8'-0" MAX.
SEE SCHEDULE
NOTE: O.A. OPENING TO BE DIVIDED INTO EQUAL SECTIONS UNLESS OTHERWISE SHOWN
ELEVATION OF UNITS UNDER 8'-0"
1/4" = 1'-0"
ELEVATION OF UNITS OVER 8'-0"
1/4" = 1'-0"
1/2"
1'-3"
CONTINUOUS VEE BLOCKING SCREW TO WALL & BACK OF SHELF UNIT AS SHOWN
LINE OF DIVIDERS
3/4" VERTICAL DIVIDERS AS REQUIRED
FACE OF WALL
10 1/2"
1'-0"
GARCY #A-3369 HANGRAIL SOCKET. NOTE: IN GYPSUM BOARD PARTITIONS PROVIDE WOOD BLOCKING OR SHEET METAL PLATE TO RECEIVE SCREWS
SCRIBE TO WALL
CENTER HANGER AT VERTICAL DIVIDERS. CAPITAL #A-239 SATIN CHROME FINISH
FACE OF WALL
1 1/16" ϕ SATIN CHROME HANGROD
1'-0"
5'-0" TO FIN. FL.
PART ELEVATION
@ 3" = 1'-0"
SECTION
@ 3" = 1'-0"
SECTION
@ 3" = 1'-0"
NOTE: SEE SHEET E-2. FOR SCHEDULE
TYPICAL OPEN COAT AREA
SCALE - AS NOTED

2
CONSTRUCTION DETAILS AND FINISHES

PARTITIONS AND WALL FINISHES

Selecting the appropriate partition or wall type is both a science and an art. In fact, there are so many options available to the designer that it is not unusual to refer to the partition or wall as a system, a combination of framing, sheathing, and finish elements, all working together to meet aesthetic, functional, code, and economic requirements.

In that regard, this section explores the great variety of wall and partition types, examining all of their characteristics with the exception of load-bearing capacity and cost of labor and materials. With respect to load-bearing or structural capacities, while many of the wall and partition types are able to carry superimposed loads, it is not the intent of this book to discuss structural issues. With respect to cost, too many factors and variables make this a topic that is difficult to analyze with any precision.

Information on both traditional and contemporary partitions and wall types is provided. Many traditional materials and methods of construction, such as solid gypsum plaster and plaster on clay tile, are cited, thus providing information to the designer who is redesigning or altering older structures.

A large portion of this section is devoted to the detailing of contemporary partition systems. In addition to providing examples of partition types, these pages place great emphasis on the detailing of unusual interface conditions that many designers often leave to the contractor to work out in the field. It should be noted that most, if not all, of these details have been selected from the working drawings of outstanding architectural and interior design firms.

While general information has also been provided about acoustics, sound transmission, and fire ratings of various walls and partitions, the designer is cautioned to verify all such information with manufacturers' certified test results, as well as with those building and fire codes having jurisdiction. It also should be noted that while test results may demonstrate a certain fire rating or sound transmission classification, it is important to determine if the results have been accepted by the local building or fire department.

It is often necessary to apply a finish to a wall or partition. Again, both traditional and contemporary methods to apply wood paneling, ceramic tile, and stone are clearly illustrated through the use of architectural details.

Finally, walls and partitions must ultimately meet floors and ceilings, and, of course, have doors and openings penetrate them. While some examples are provided in this section, the designer will also find important information in the sections entitled "Floors and Floor Finishes," "Doors," and "Ceilings," which follow.

PARTITIONS AND WALL FINISHES
Partition and Wall Types

DRAWING AND DESCRIPTION		FIRE-RATING	SOIL AND DAMAGE RESISTANCE	ACOUSTICS	REMARKS	COST COMPARISON
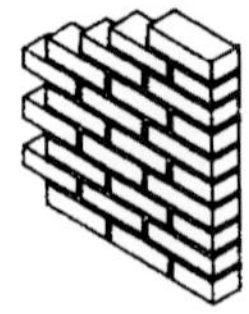	4 inch face brick, tooled joints; Actual thickness, 3⅝ inches; Weight, 40 lbs. per square foot of wall surface	Incombustible, with one hour fire-rating	Good	Very good; transmission loss, 45 decibels	Low maintenance, but limited flexibility; a good-looking wall, but poor light reflection	installation cost maintenance and insurance cost for 20 years
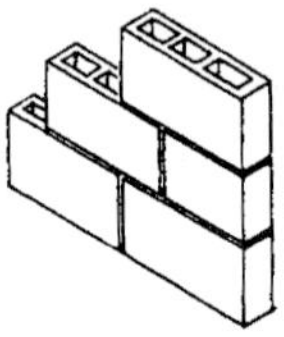	4 inch concrete block, tooled joints, two coats of paint on each side; Actual thickness, 3⅝ inches; Weight, 30 lbs. per square foot	Incombustible, with one hour fire-rating	Good	Good; transmission loss, 40 decibels	Inexpensive; attractive if constructed neatly; frequently used for corridors, gyms, assembly rooms, etc.; no flexibility	
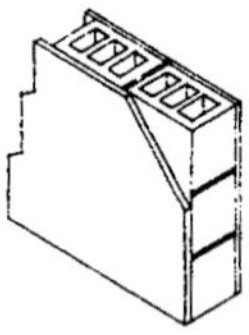	4 inch cinder block, ¾ inch layer of plaster on each side, 2 coats of paint on each side; Actual thickness, 5¼ inches; Weight, 30 lbs. per square foot	Incombustible, with two hour fire-rating	Poor	Good; transmission loss, 43 decibels	A smooth, dense finish; a good light reflector if painted a light color; no flexibility	
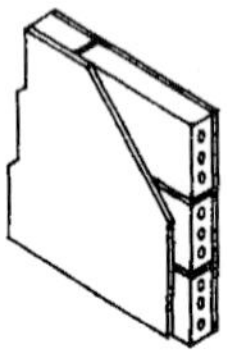	3 inch cinder block, ¾ inch layer of plaster on each side, 2 coats of paint on each side; Thickness, 4½ inches; Weight, 21 lbs. per square foot	Incombustible, with two hour fire-rating	Poor	Good; transmission loss, 39 decibels	A smooth, dense finish; a good light reflector if painted a light color; no flexibility	
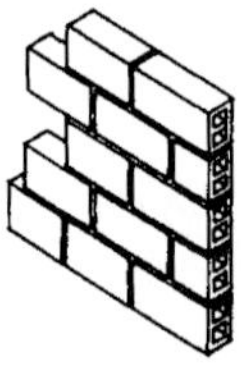	4 inch structural facing tile, glazed on each side; Actual thickness, 3¾ inches; Weight, 40 lbs. per square foot	Incombustible, with a fire-rating of less than one hour	Very good	Good; transmission loss, 35 decibels	Used well in classrooms, corridors, also in toilets and showers; care must be taken with the design to avoid bright reflectivity; no flexibility	
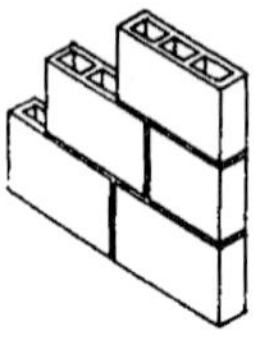	4 inch concrete block, 2 coats of vinyl plastic spray over entire surface of each side; Actual thickness, 3¾ inches; Weight, 38 lbs. per square foot	Incombustible, with one hour fire-rating	Good	Good; transmission loss, 40 decibels	Sleek finish, but no flexibility	
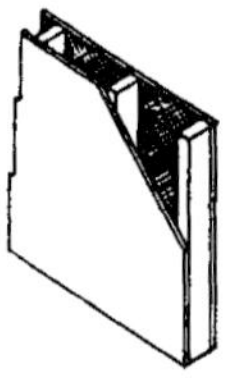	2 by 4 inch wood studs, spaced 16 inches apart; metal lath and plaster, 2 coats of paint on each side; Thickness, 4¾ inches; Weight, 20 lbs. per square foot	Combustible	Poor	Good; transmission loss, 39 decibels	Good light reflector, not much flexibility	

PARTITIONS AND WALL FINISHES

Partition and Wall Types

W-1
WOOD STUDS - 16" O.C. 3/8" 3-PLY PLYWOOD NAILED BOTH SIDES

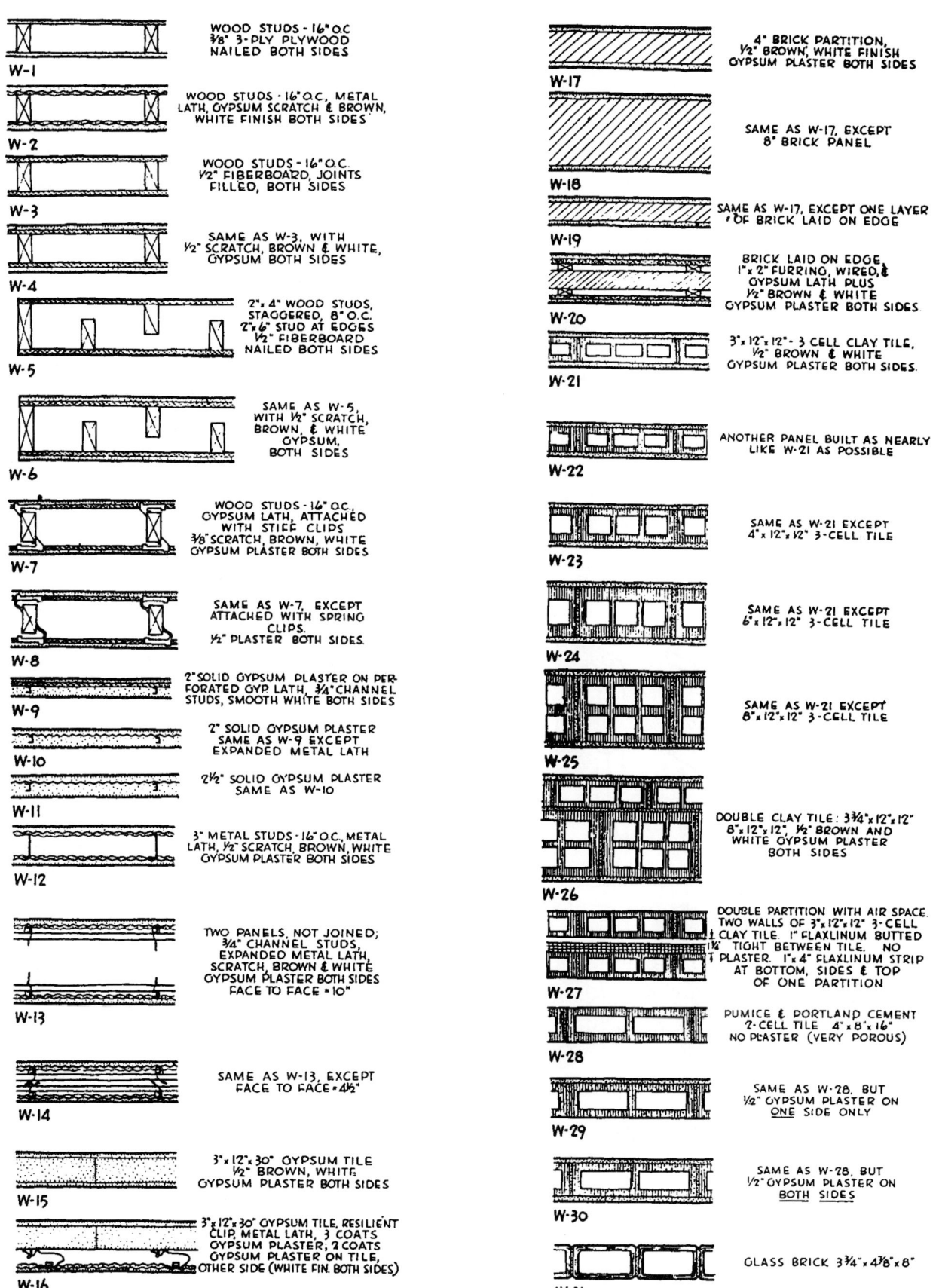

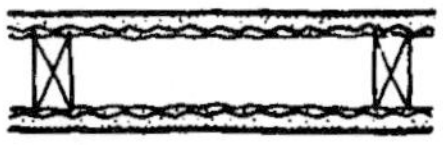
W-2
WOOD STUDS - 16" O.C., METAL LATH, GYPSUM SCRATCH & BROWN, WHITE FINISH BOTH SIDES

W-3
WOOD STUDS - 16" O.C. 1/2" FIBERBOARD, JOINTS FILLED, BOTH SIDES

W-4
SAME AS W-3, WITH 1/2" SCRATCH, BROWN & WHITE, GYPSUM BOTH SIDES

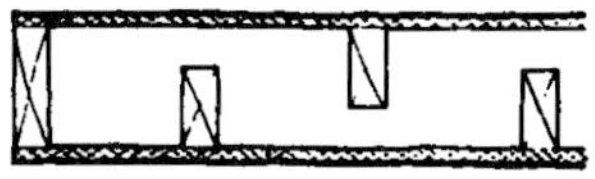
W-5
2" x 4" WOOD STUDS, STAGGERED, 8" O.C. 2" x 6" STUD AT EDGES 1/2" FIBERBOARD NAILED BOTH SIDES

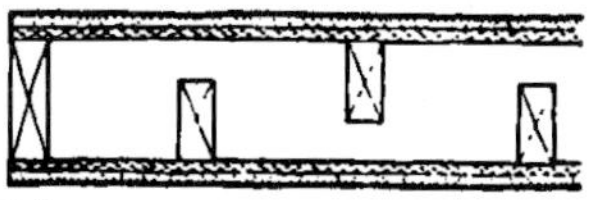
W-6
SAME AS W-5, WITH 1/2" SCRATCH, BROWN, & WHITE GYPSUM, BOTH SIDES

W-7
WOOD STUDS - 16" O.C., GYPSUM LATH, ATTACHED WITH STIFF CLIPS 3/8" SCRATCH, BROWN, WHITE GYPSUM PLASTER BOTH SIDES

W-8
SAME AS W-7, EXCEPT ATTACHED WITH SPRING CLIPS. 1/2" PLASTER BOTH SIDES.

W-9
2" SOLID GYPSUM PLASTER ON PERFORATED GYP. LATH, 3/4" CHANNEL STUDS, SMOOTH WHITE BOTH SIDES

W-10
2" SOLID GYPSUM PLASTER SAME AS W-9 EXCEPT EXPANDED METAL LATH

W-11
2 1/2" SOLID GYPSUM PLASTER SAME AS W-10

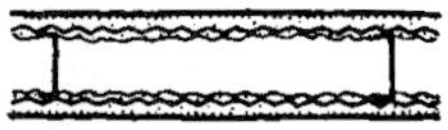
W-12
3" METAL STUDS - 16" O.C., METAL LATH, 1/2" SCRATCH, BROWN, WHITE GYPSUM PLASTER BOTH SIDES

W-13
TWO PANELS, NOT JOINED; 3/4" CHANNEL STUDS, EXPANDED METAL LATH, SCRATCH, BROWN & WHITE GYPSUM PLASTER BOTH SIDES FACE TO FACE = 10"

W-14
SAME AS W-13, EXCEPT FACE TO FACE = 4 1/2"

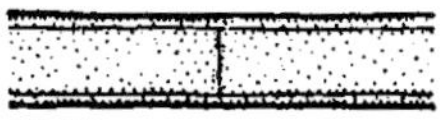
W-15
3" x 12" x 30" GYPSUM TILE 1/2" BROWN, WHITE GYPSUM PLASTER BOTH SIDES

W-16
3" x 12" x 30" GYPSUM TILE, RESILIENT CLIP, METAL LATH, 3 COATS GYPSUM PLASTER; 2 COATS GYPSUM PLASTER ON TILE, OTHER SIDE (WHITE FIN. BOTH SIDES)

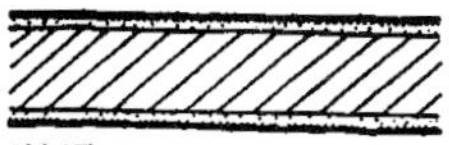
W-17
4" BRICK PARTITION, 1/2" BROWN, WHITE FINISH GYPSUM PLASTER BOTH SIDES

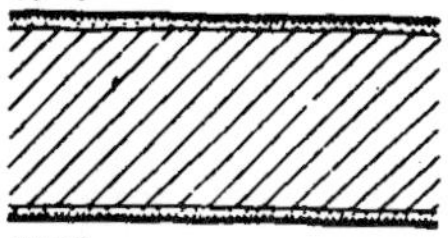
W-18
SAME AS W-17, EXCEPT 8" BRICK PANEL

W-19
SAME AS W-17, EXCEPT ONE LAYER OF BRICK LAID ON EDGE

W-20
BRICK LAID ON EDGE, 1" x 2" FURRING, WIRED, & GYPSUM LATH PLUS 1/2" BROWN & WHITE GYPSUM PLASTER BOTH SIDES

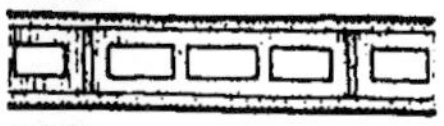
W-21
3" x 12" x 12" - 3 CELL CLAY TILE, 1/2" BROWN & WHITE GYPSUM PLASTER BOTH SIDES.

W-22
ANOTHER PANEL BUILT AS NEARLY LIKE W-21 AS POSSIBLE

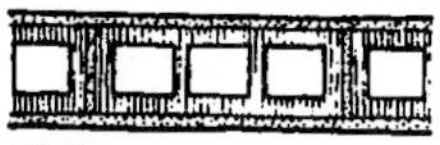
W-23
SAME AS W-21 EXCEPT 4" x 12" x 12" 3-CELL TILE

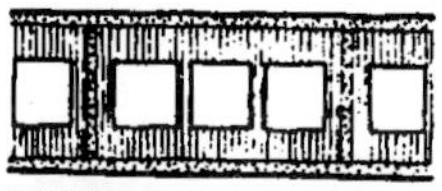
W-24
SAME AS W-21 EXCEPT 6" x 12" x 12" 3-CELL TILE

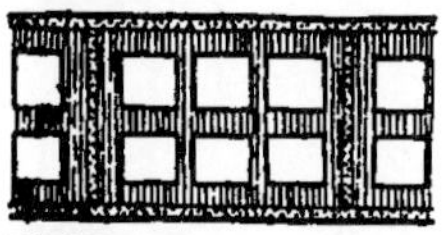
W-25
SAME AS W-21 EXCEPT 8" x 12" x 12" 3-CELL TILE

W-26
DOUBLE CLAY TILE: 3 3/4" x 12" x 12" 8" x 12" x 12", 1/2" BROWN AND WHITE GYPSUM PLASTER BOTH SIDES

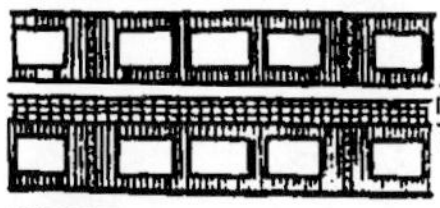
W-27
DOUBLE PARTITION WITH AIR SPACE. TWO WALLS OF 3" x 12" x 12" 3-CELL CLAY TILE. 1" FLAXLINUM BUTTED TIGHT BETWEEN TILE. NO PLASTER. 1" x 4" FLAXLINUM STRIP AT BOTTOM, SIDES & TOP OF ONE PARTITION

W-28
PUMICE & PORTLAND CEMENT 2-CELL TILE 4" x 8" x 16" NO PLASTER (VERY POROUS)

W-29
SAME AS W-28, BUT 1/2" GYPSUM PLASTER ON ONE SIDE ONLY

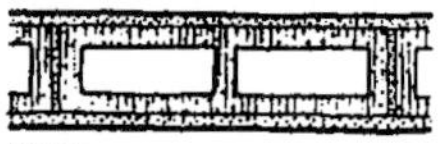
W-30
SAME AS W-28, BUT 1/2" GYPSUM PLASTER ON BOTH SIDES

W-31
GLASS BRICK 3 3/4" x 4 7/8" x 8"

PARTITIONS AND WALL FINISHES

Types of Masonry Walls and Piers

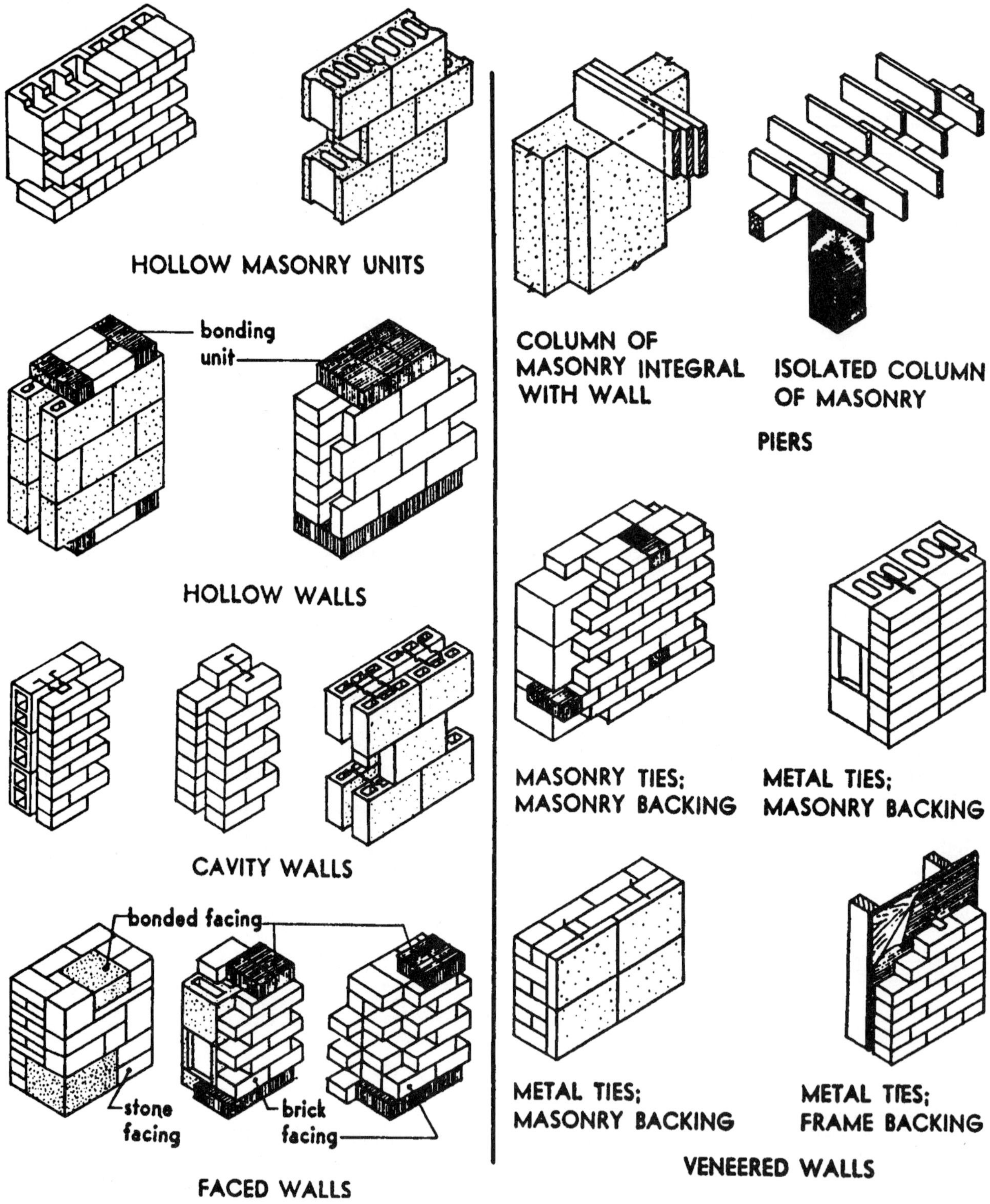

PARTITIONS AND WALL FINISHES

Types of Masonry Walls and Piers

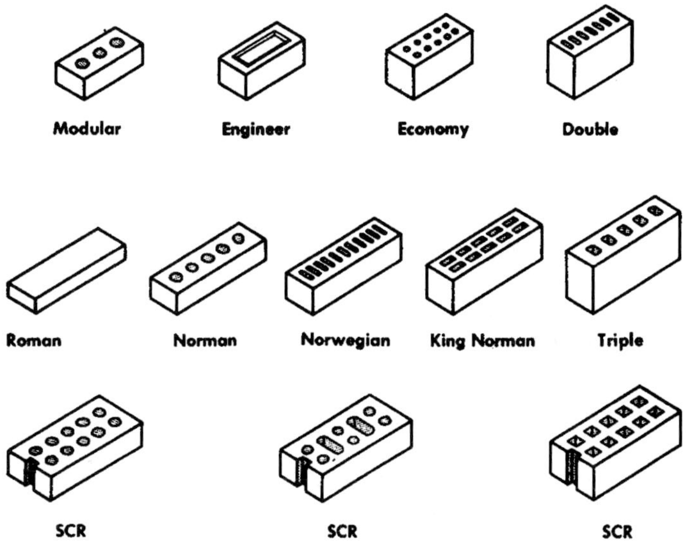

Fig. 1 Typical clay brick

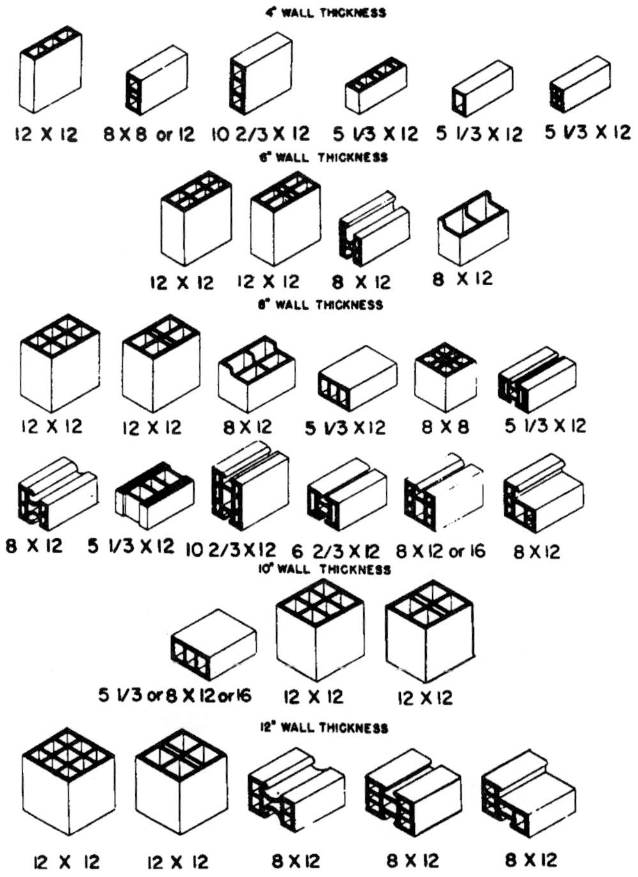

Fig. 2 Structural clay tile

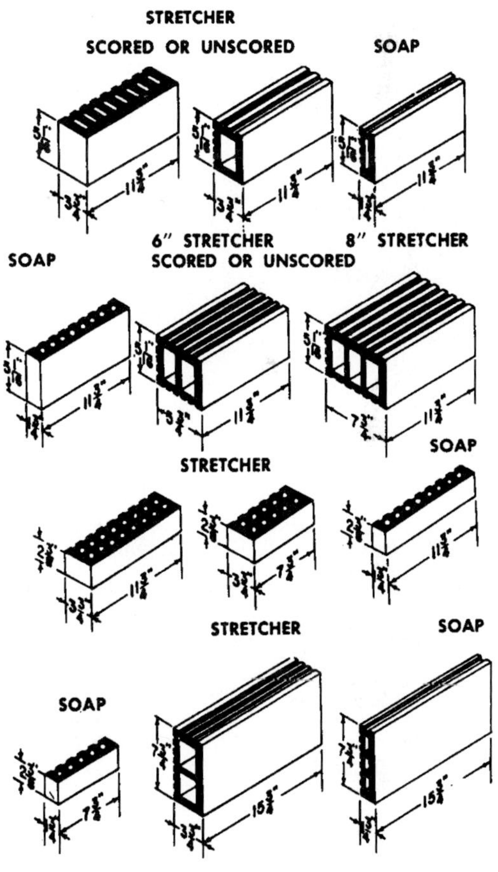

Fig. 3 Structural facing tile

PARTITIONS AND WALL FINISHES

Types of Masonry

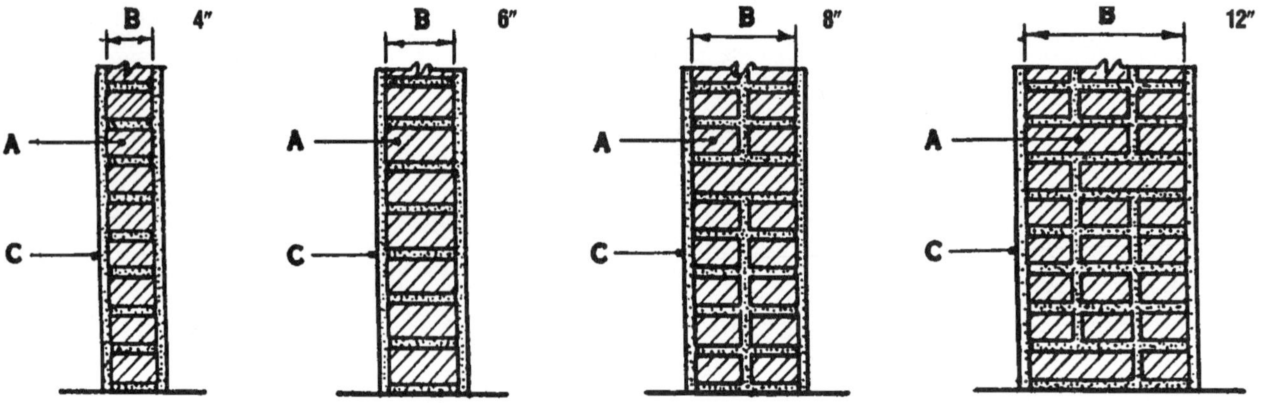

Fig. 4 Solid brick: bearing or nonbearing (sections). A = brick; B = nominal wall thickness; C = finish

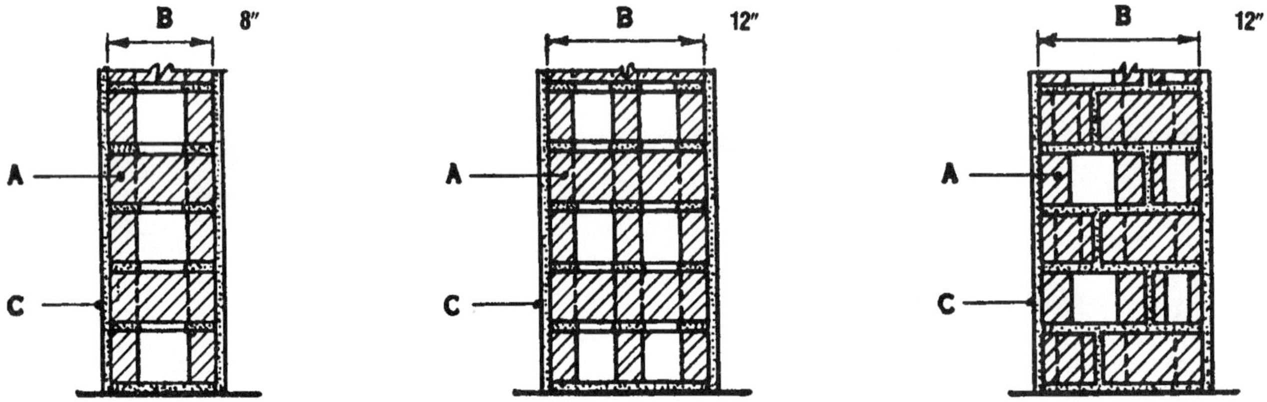

Fig. 5 Hollow brick units: bearing or nonbearing (sections). A = brick; B = nominal wall thickness; C = finish

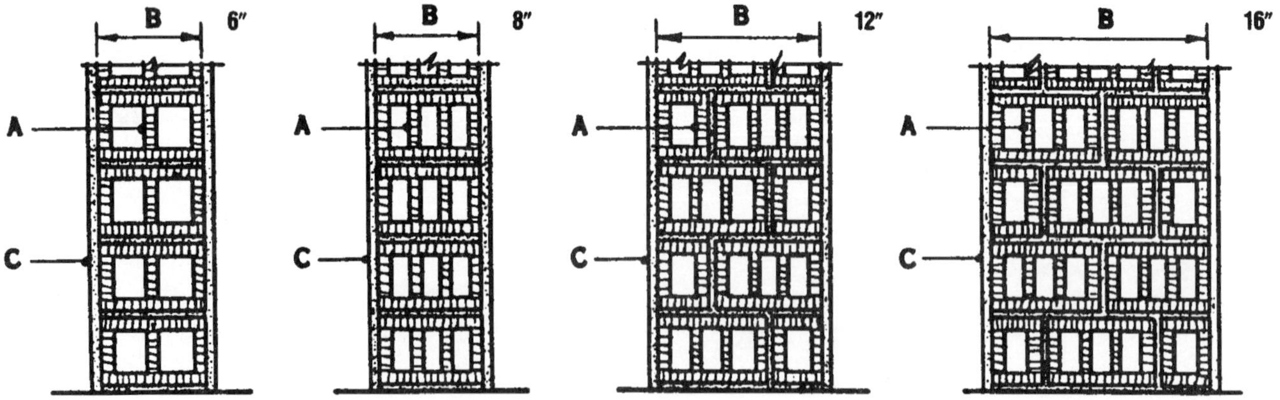

Fig. 6 Structural clay tile: bearing (sections). A = structural clay tile; B = nominal wall thickness; C = finish

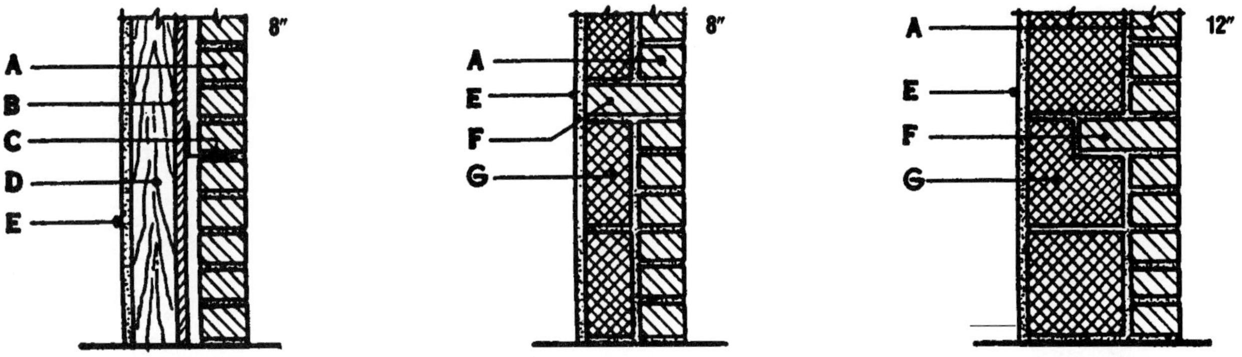

Fig. 7 Faced or veneered construction: bearing (sections). A = brick; B = sheathing; C = corrosion-resistant metal ties spaced 24 in on centers, vertically and horizontally; D = wood or steel studs; E = plaster or gypsum wallboard; F = masonry bond; G = masonry backing unit

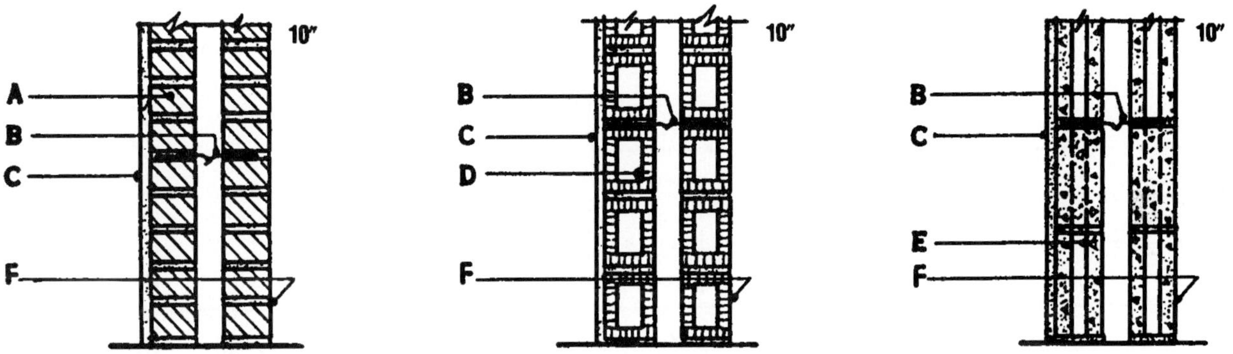

Fig. 8 Cavity type: bearing (sections). A = clay brick; B = corrosion-resistant metal ties spaced to provide one tie to each 3 ft^2 of wall surface; C = gypsum plaster; D = structural clay load-bearing tile; E = concrete masonry units of load-bearing grade; F = exterior face of wall

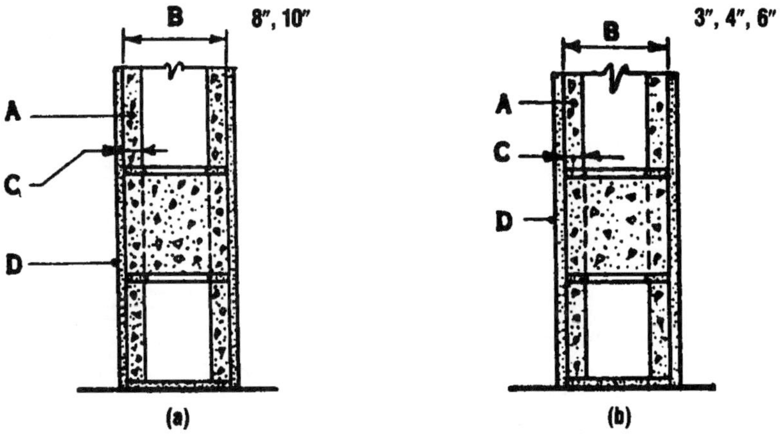

Fig. 9 Hollow concrete masonry units (sections): (*a*) bearing; (*b*) nonbearing. A = concrete masonry units conforming to ASTM, *Standard Specifications for Hollow Load-Bearing Concrete Masonry Units;* B = nominal wall thickness; C = nominal shell thickness; D = gypsum plaster

PARTITIONS AND WALL FINISHES

Types of Masonry

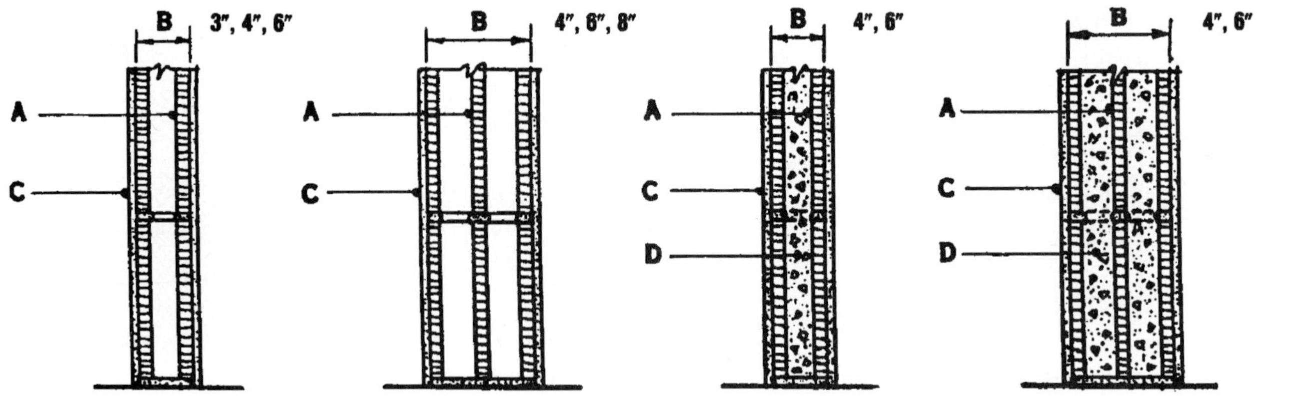

Fig. 10 Structural clay tile: nonbearing (sections). A = structural clay tile; B = nominal wall thickness; C = finish; D = fill

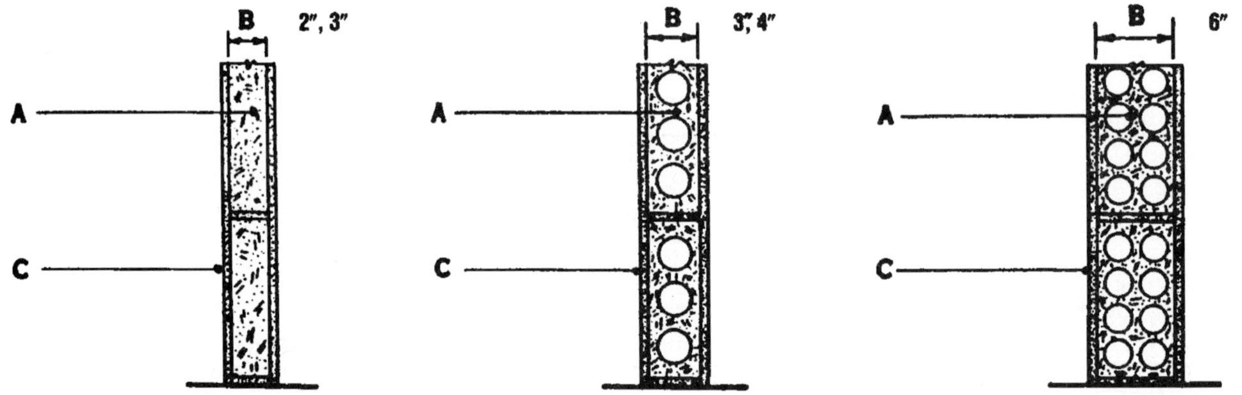

Fig. 11 Gypsum tile or block: nonbearing (sections). A = gypsum block; B = nominal wall thickness; C = finish

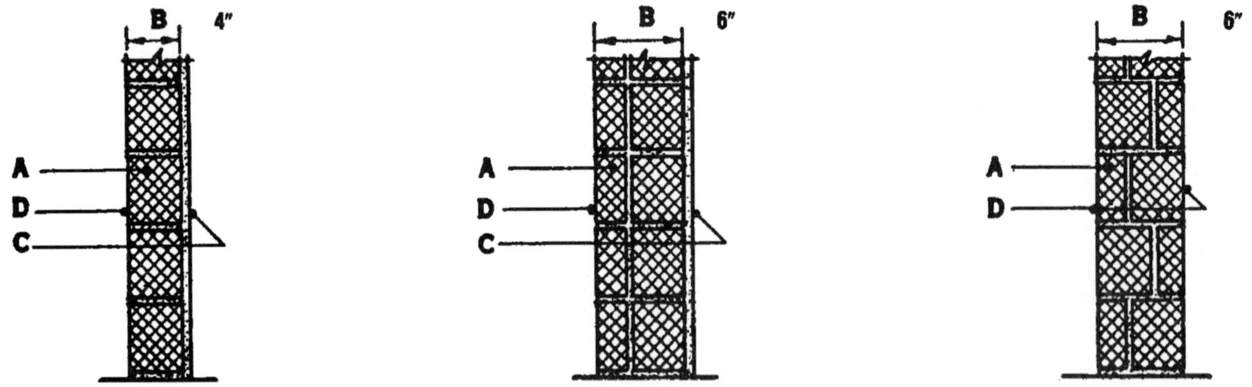

Fig. 12 Structural clay facing tile: nonbearing (sections). A = clay tile; B = nominal wall thickness; C = plaster; D = glazed or smooth-surfaced side of tile

PARTITIONS AND WALL FINISHES
Brick Types and Bonds

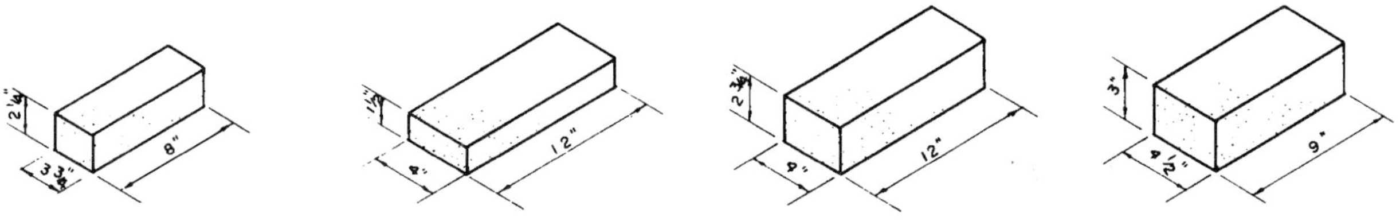

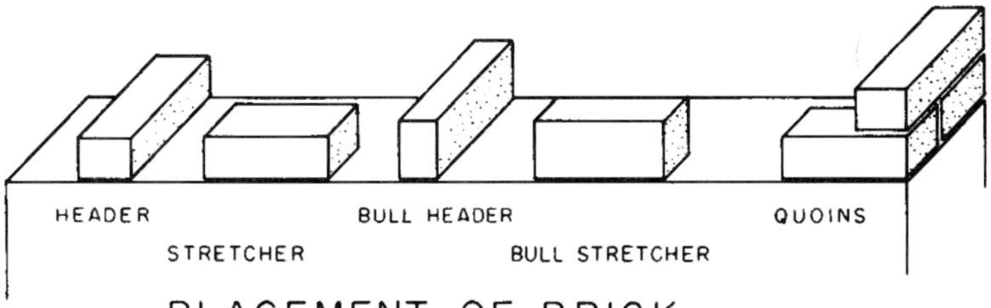

PLACEMENT OF BRICK

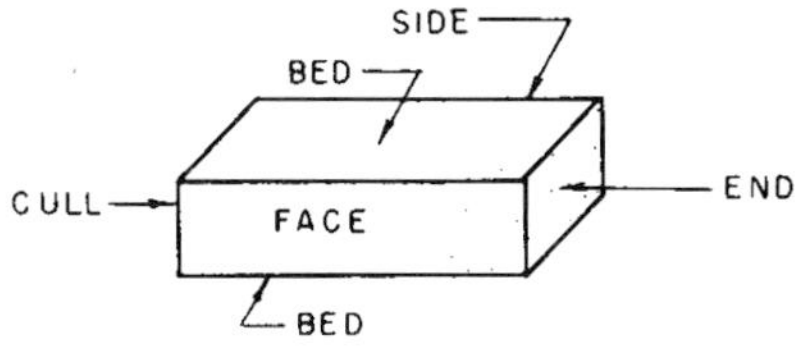

SIX FACES OF BRICK

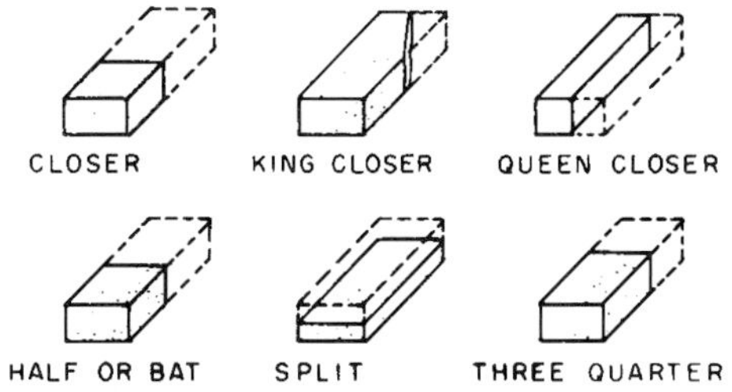

METHODS OF CUTTING BRICK

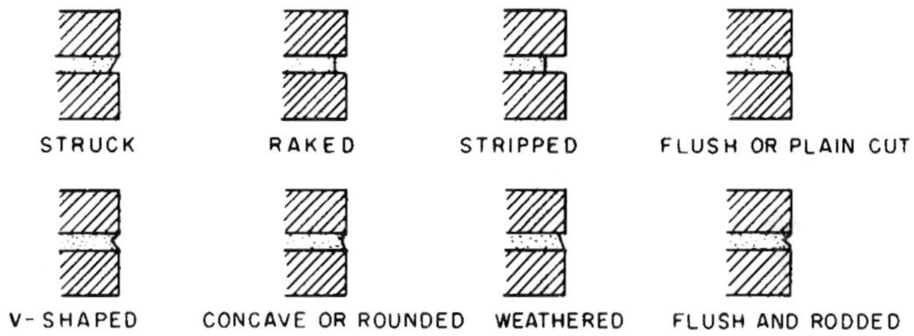

BRICK JOINTS

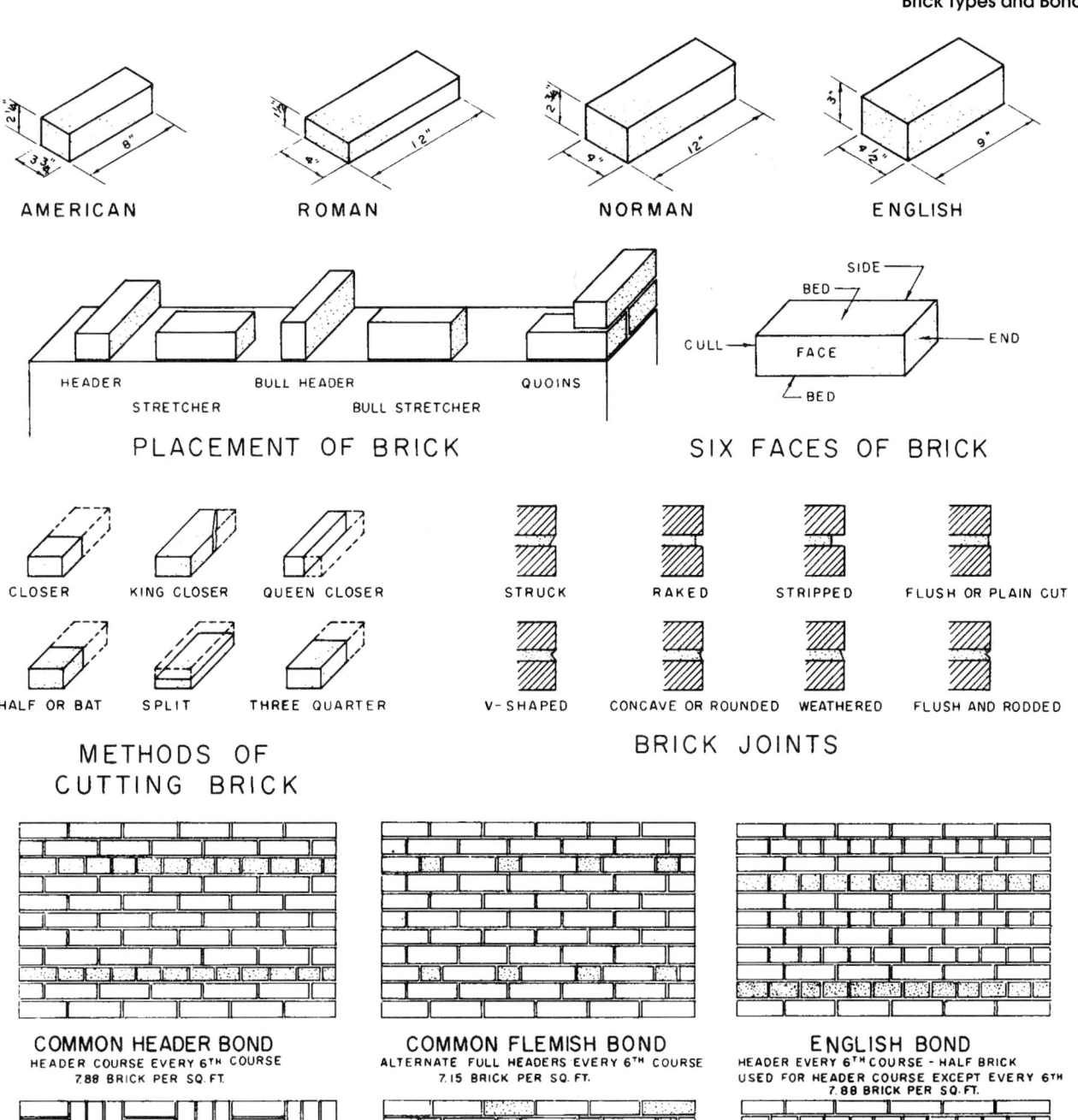

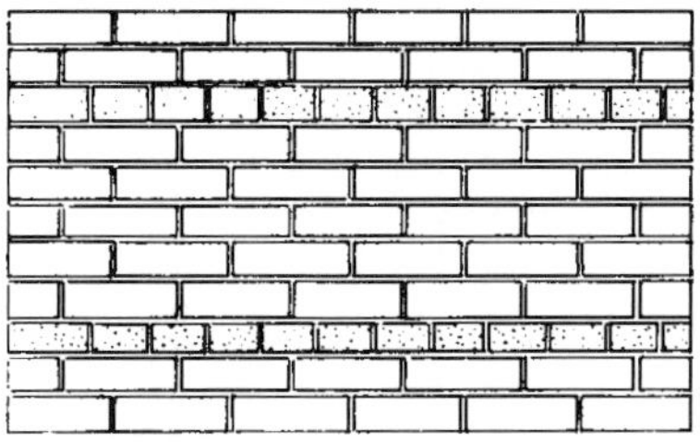
COMMON HEADER BOND
HEADER COURSE EVERY 6TH COURSE
7.88 BRICK PER SQ. FT.

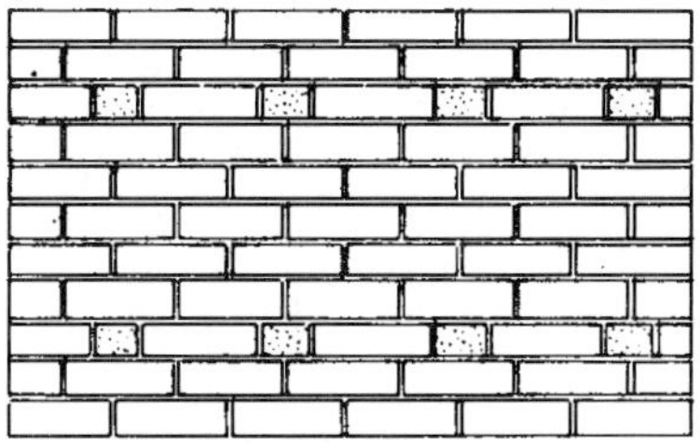
COMMON FLEMISH BOND
ALTERNATE FULL HEADERS EVERY 6TH COURSE
7.15 BRICK PER SQ. FT.

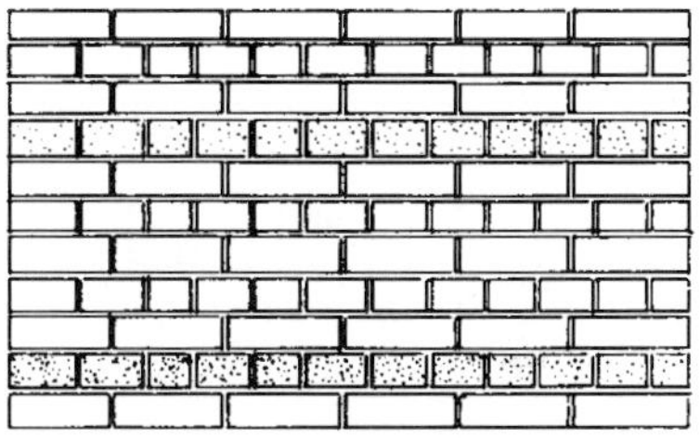
ENGLISH BOND
HEADER EVERY 6TH COURSE - HALF BRICK USED FOR HEADER COURSE EXCEPT EVERY 6TH
7.88 BRICK PER SQ. FT.

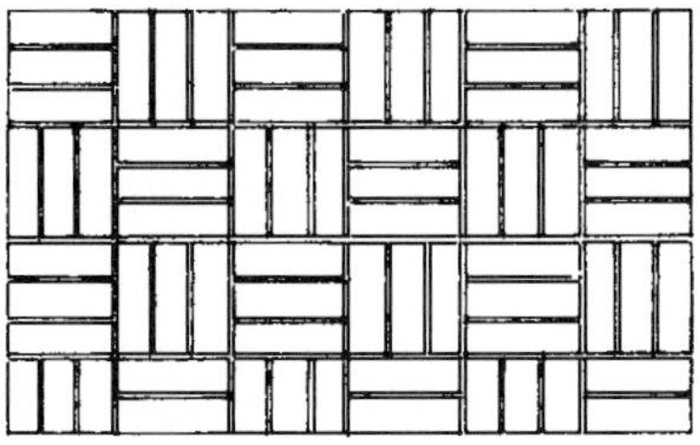
BASKET PATTERN
6.75 BRICK PER SQ. FT.

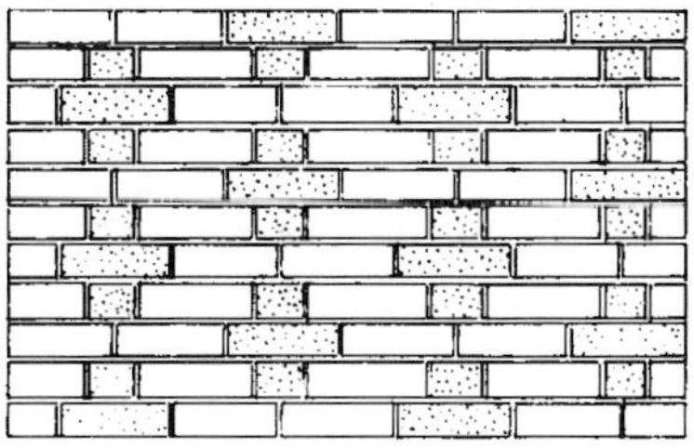
FLEMISH CROSS BOND
ALTERNATE FULL HEADER EVERY 6TH COURSE
7.15 BRICK PER SQ. FT.

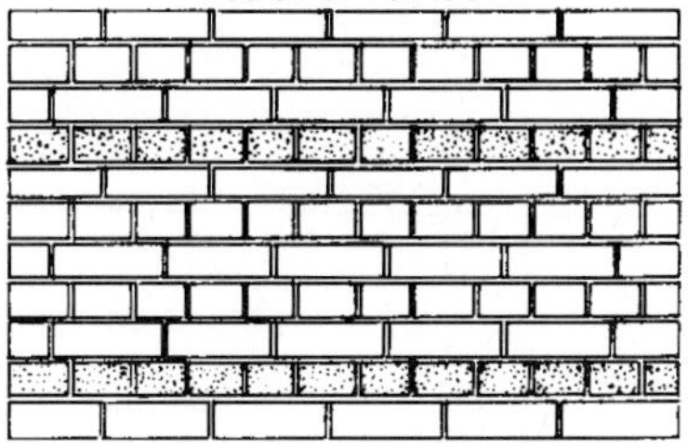
ENGLISH CROSS BOND
CONTINUOUS FULL HEADERS EVERY 6TH COURSE
7.88 BRICK PER SQ. FT.

PARTITIONS AND WALL FINISHES
Masonry Walls

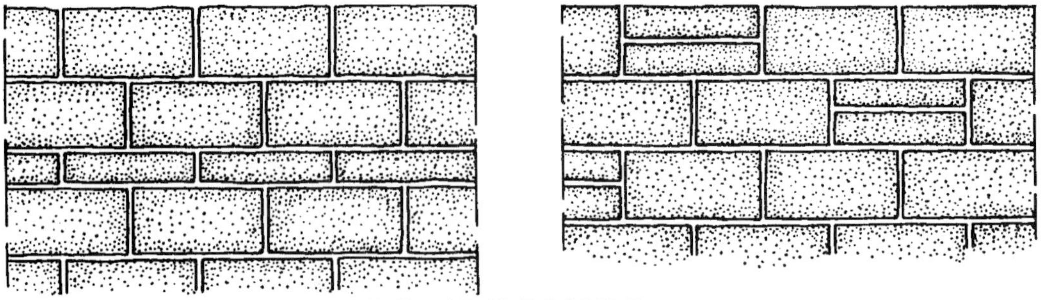

Full and Half-Height Units

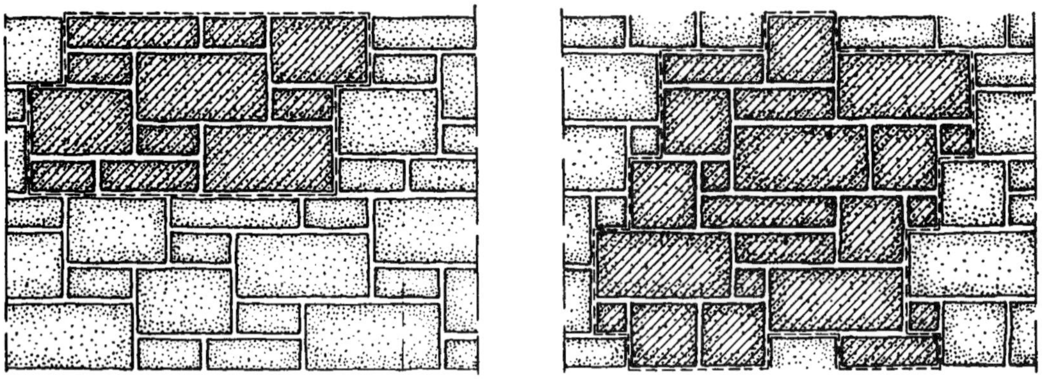

Full, Half and Fractional Size Units

Fig. 13 Designs of standard-size hollow concrete-masonry units

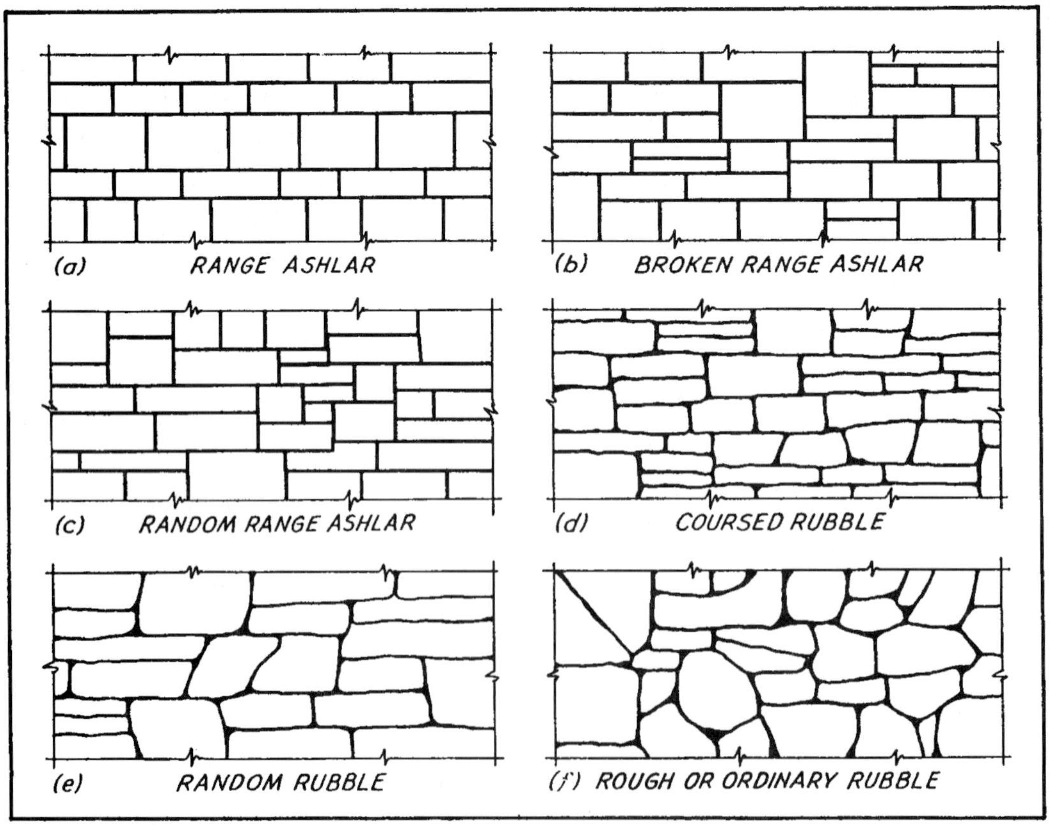

Fig. 14 Stone ashlar and rubble masonry

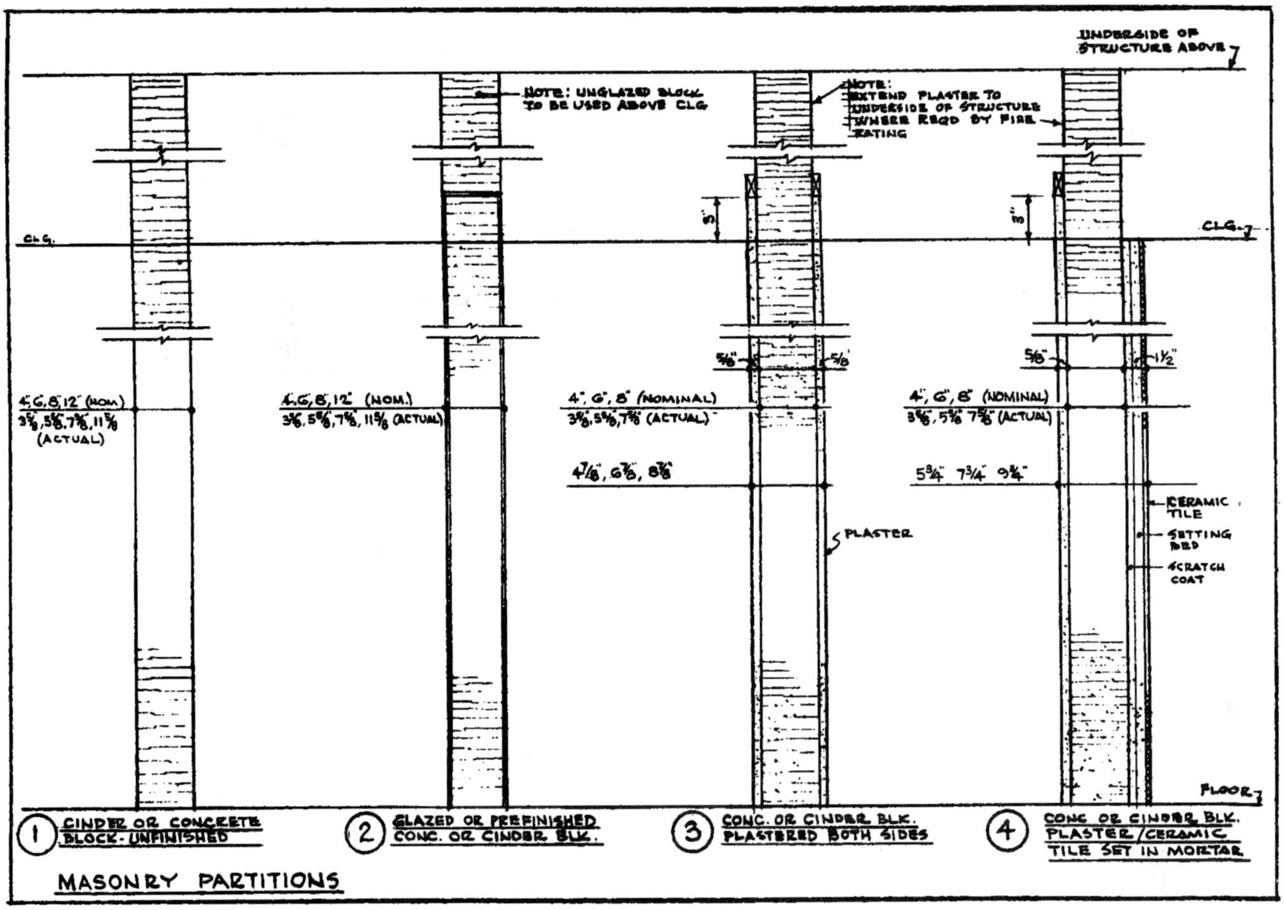
UNDERSIDE OF STRUCTURE ABOVE
NOTE: UNGLAZED BLOCK TO BE USED ABOVE CLG.
NOTE: EXTEND PLASTER TO UNDERSIDE OF STRUCTURE WHERE REQ'D BY FIRE RATING
CLG.
4,6,8,12" (NOM.)
3⅝,5⅝,7⅝,11⅝ (ACTUAL)
4,6,8,12" (NOM.)
3⅝,5⅝,7⅝,11⅝ (ACTUAL)
4", 6", 8" (NOMINAL)
3⅝,5⅝,7⅝ (ACTUAL)
4⅞, 6⅞, 8⅞
4", 6", 8" (NOMINAL)
3⅝, 5⅝ 7⅝ (ACTUAL)
5¾ 7¾ 9¾
⅝
⅝
⅝
1½"
PLASTER
CERAMIC TILE
SETTING BED
SCRATCH COAT
FLOOR
1 CINDER OR CONCRETE BLOCK-UNFINISHED
2 GLAZED OR PREFINISHED CONC. OR CINDER BLK.
3 CONC. OR CINDER BLK. PLASTERED BOTH SIDES
4 CONC OR CINDER BLK. PLASTER/CERAMIC TILE SET IN MORTAR
MASONRY PARTITIONS

TYPICAL SIZES AND SHAPES OF CONCRETE BLOCK

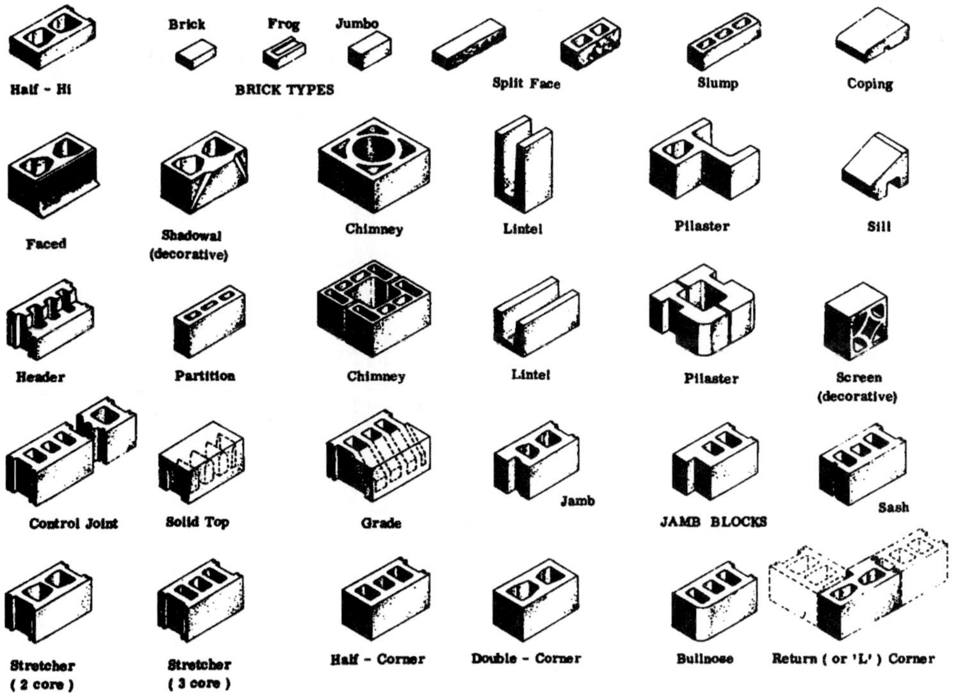
Half - Hi
Brick
Frog
Jumbo
BRICK TYPES
Split Face
Slump
Coping
Faced
Shadowal (decorative)
Chimney
Lintel
Pilaster
Sill
Header
Partition
Chimney
Lintel
Pilaster
Screen (decorative)
Control Joint
Solid Top
Grade
Jamb
JAMB BLOCKS
Sash
Stretcher (2 core)
Stretcher (3 core)
Half - Corner
Double - Corner
Bullnose
Return (or 'L') Corner

PARTITIONS AND WALL FINISHES

Metal Stud and Gypsum Board

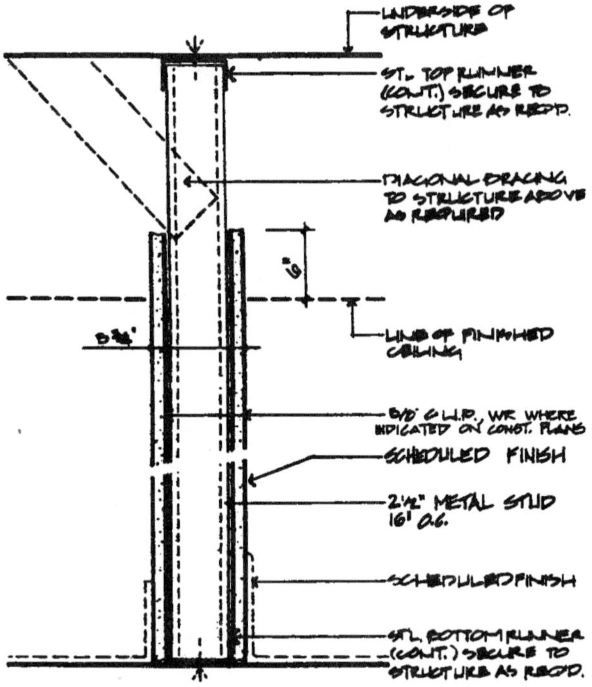

Metal stud and gypsum board: braced to slab

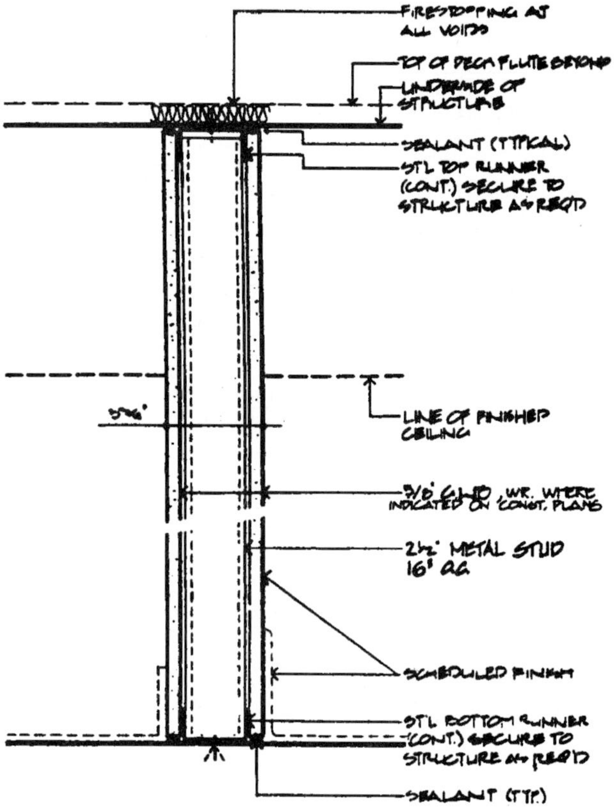

Metal stud and gypsum board partition: floor to slab

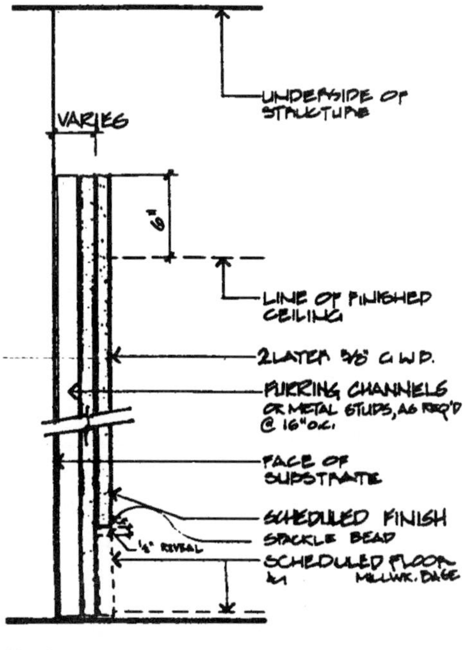

Metal channels and gypsum board: wall furring

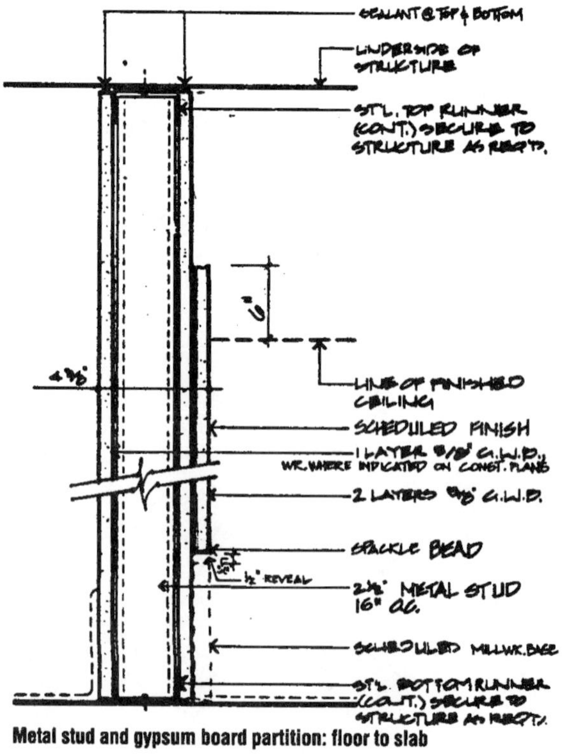

Metal stud and gypsum board partition: floor to slab

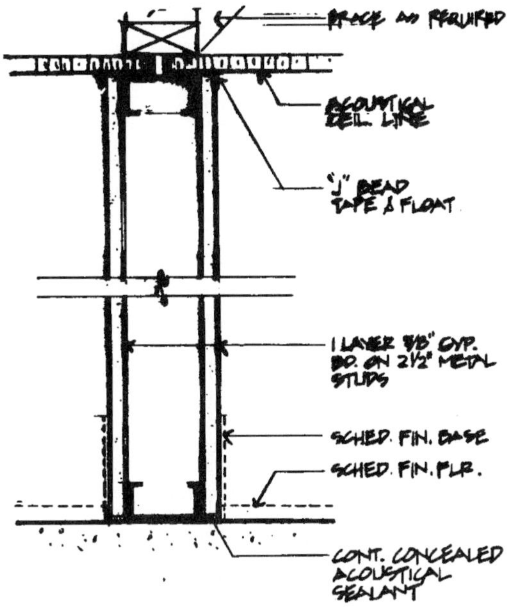

Metal stud and gypsum board: underside of ceiling

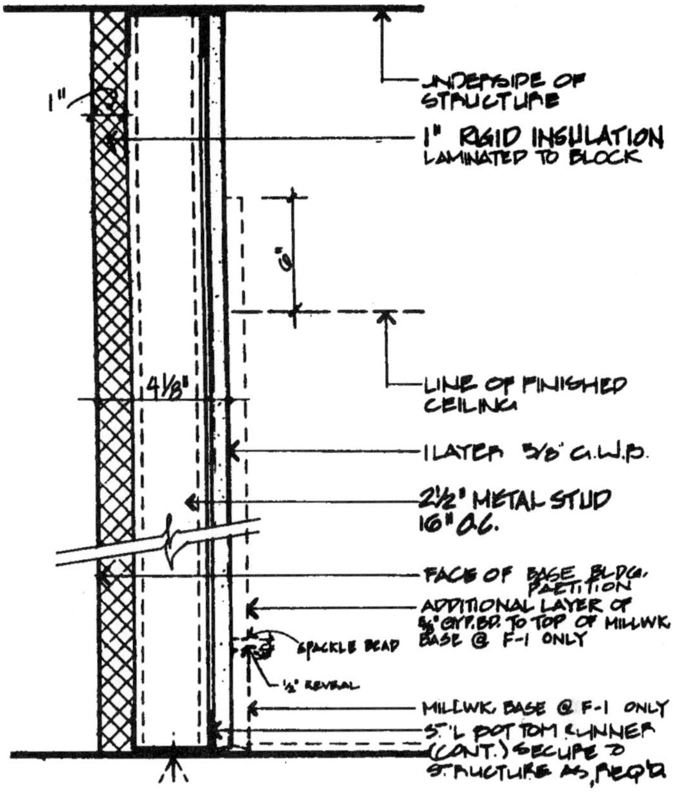

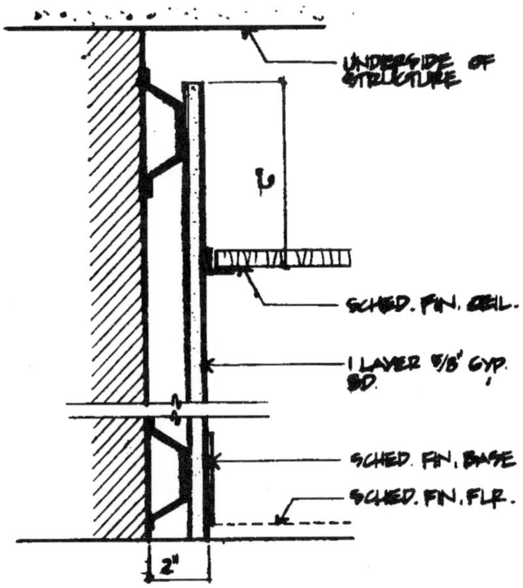

Metal channels and gypsum board: wall furring

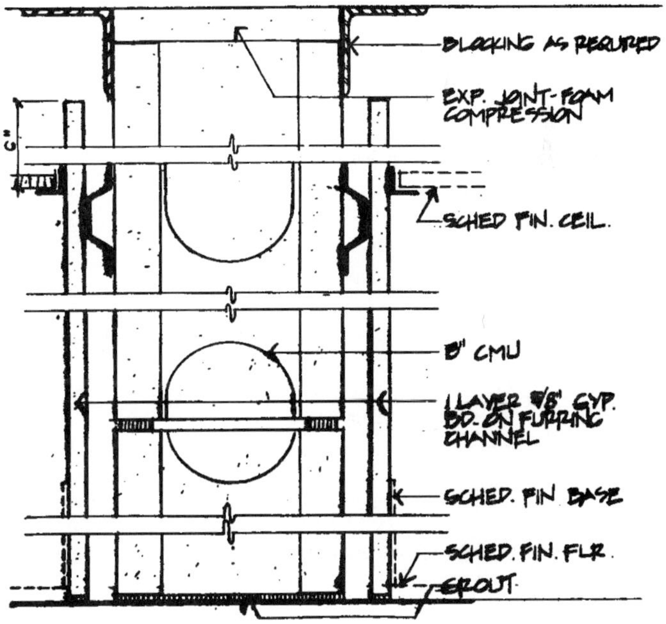

PARTITIONS AND WALL FINISHES

Metal Stud and Gypsum Board

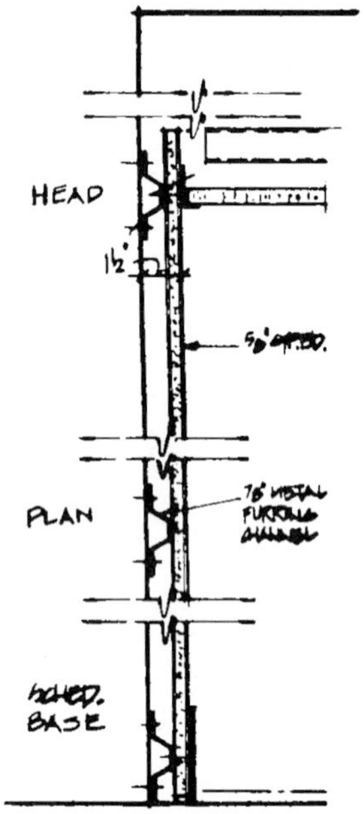

FUR-OUT GYPSUM B'D ON METAL FURRING CHANNEL

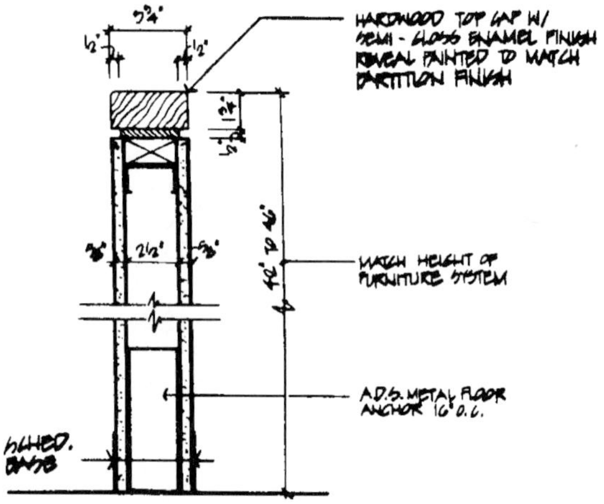

SECTION @ LOW PARTITION

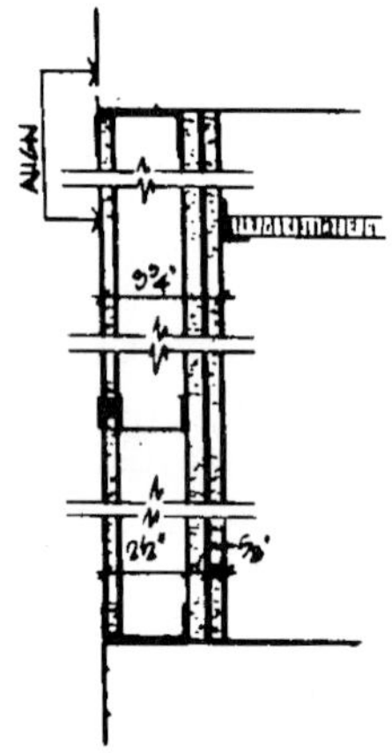

SHAFT WALL TWO HOUR FIRE RATED PARTITION

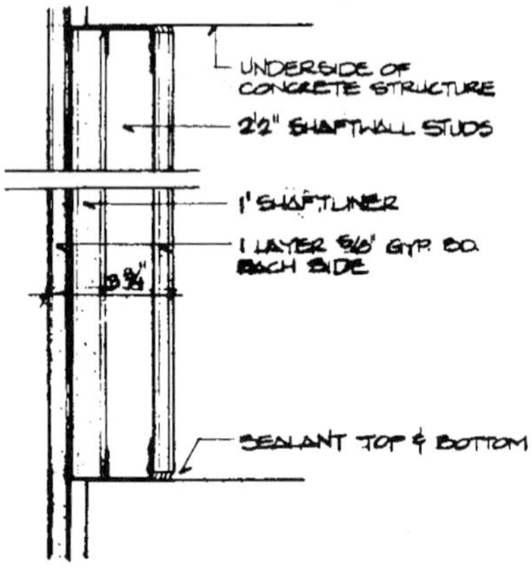

Metal stud and gypsum board: shaftwall

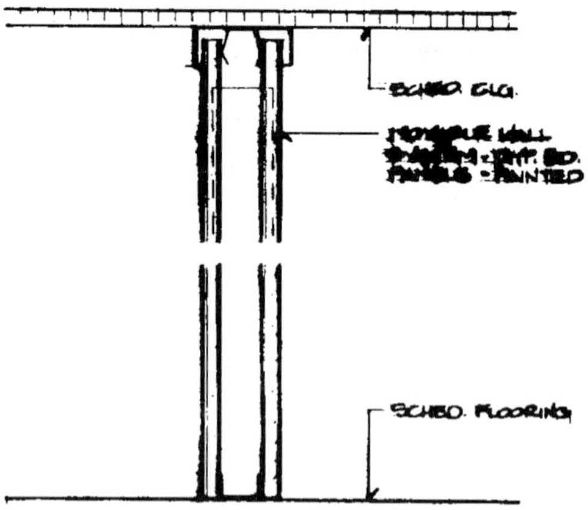

Metal stud and gypsum board: movable

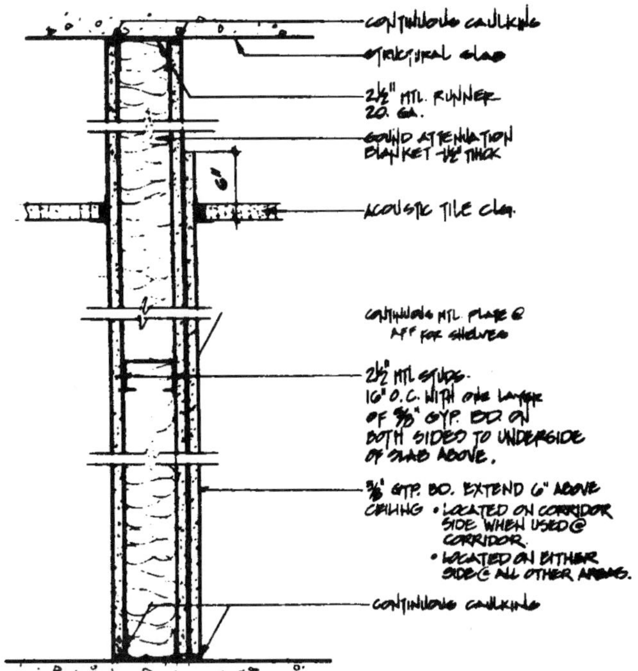
CONTINUOUS CAULKING
STRUCTURAL SLAB
2½" MTL. RUNNER 20 GA.
SOUND ATTENUATION BLANKET-1½" THICK
6"
ACOUSTIC TILE CLG.
CONTINUOUS MTL. PLATE @ AFF FOR SHELVES
2½" MTL STUDS. 16" O.C. WITH ONE LAYER OF 5/8" GYP. BD ON BOTH SIDES TO UNDERSIDE OF SLAB ABOVE.
5/8" GYP. BD. EXTEND 6" ABOVE CEILING
• LOCATED ON CORRIDOR SIDE WHEN USED @ CORRIDOR.
• LOCATED ON EITHER SIDE @ ALL OTHER AREAS.
CONTINUOUS CAULKING
1 TYPE 1 (TYPICAL PARTITION)

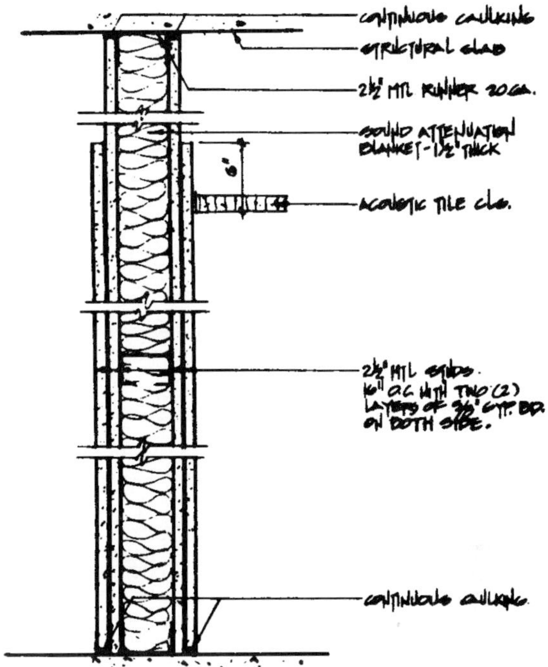
CONTINUOUS CAULKING
STRUCTURAL SLAB
2½" MTL RUNNER 20 GA.
SOUND ATTENUATION BLANKET-1½" THICK
6"
ACOUSTIC TILE CLG.
2½" MTL STUDS. 16" O.C. WITH TWO (2) LAYERS OF 5/8" GYP BD. ON BOTH SIDE.
CONTINUOUS CAULKING
2 TYPE 2 (4-LAYER ACOUSTICAL PARTITION)

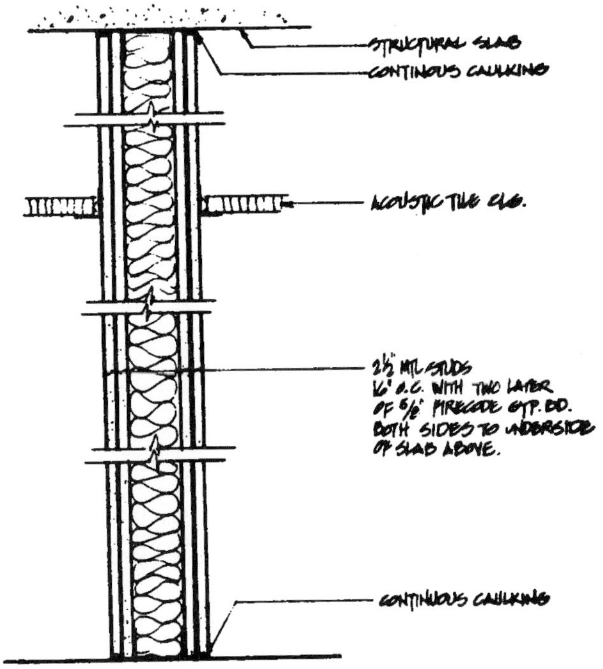
STRUCTURAL SLAB
CONTINOUS CAULKING
ACOUSTIC TILE CLG.
2½" MTL STUDS 16" O.C. WITH TWO LAYER OF 5/8" FIRECODE GYP. BD. BOTH SIDES TO UNDERSIDE OF SLAB ABOVE.
CONTINUOUS CAULKING
3 TYPE 3 (2-HOUR FIRE-RATED PARTITION)

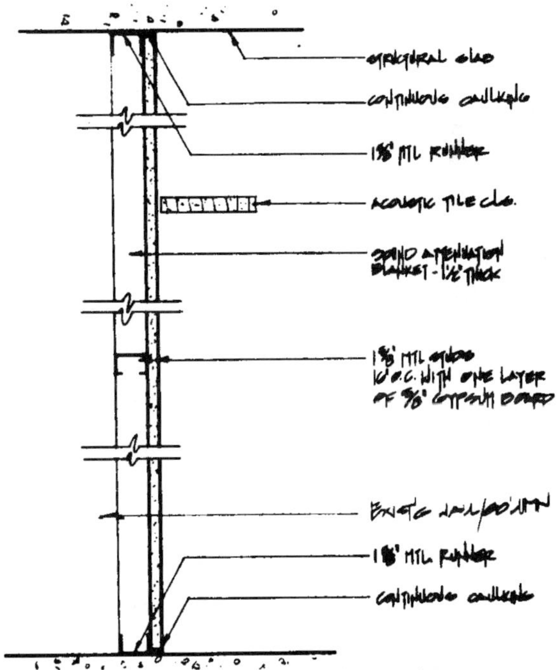
STRUCTURAL SLAB
CONTINUOUS CAULKING
1⅝" MTL RUNNER
ACOUSTIC TILE CLG.
SOUND ATTENUATION BLANKET-1½" THICK
1⅝" MTL STUDS 16" O.C. WITH ONE LAYER OF 5/8" GYPSUM BOARD
1⅝" MTL RUNNER
CONTINUOUS CAULKING
4 TYPE 4 - EXIST'G WALL/COL. FURRED OUT

PARTITIONS AND WALL FINISHES

Metal Stud and Gypsum Board

PARTITION TYPES AND DIMENSIONING SYSTEM

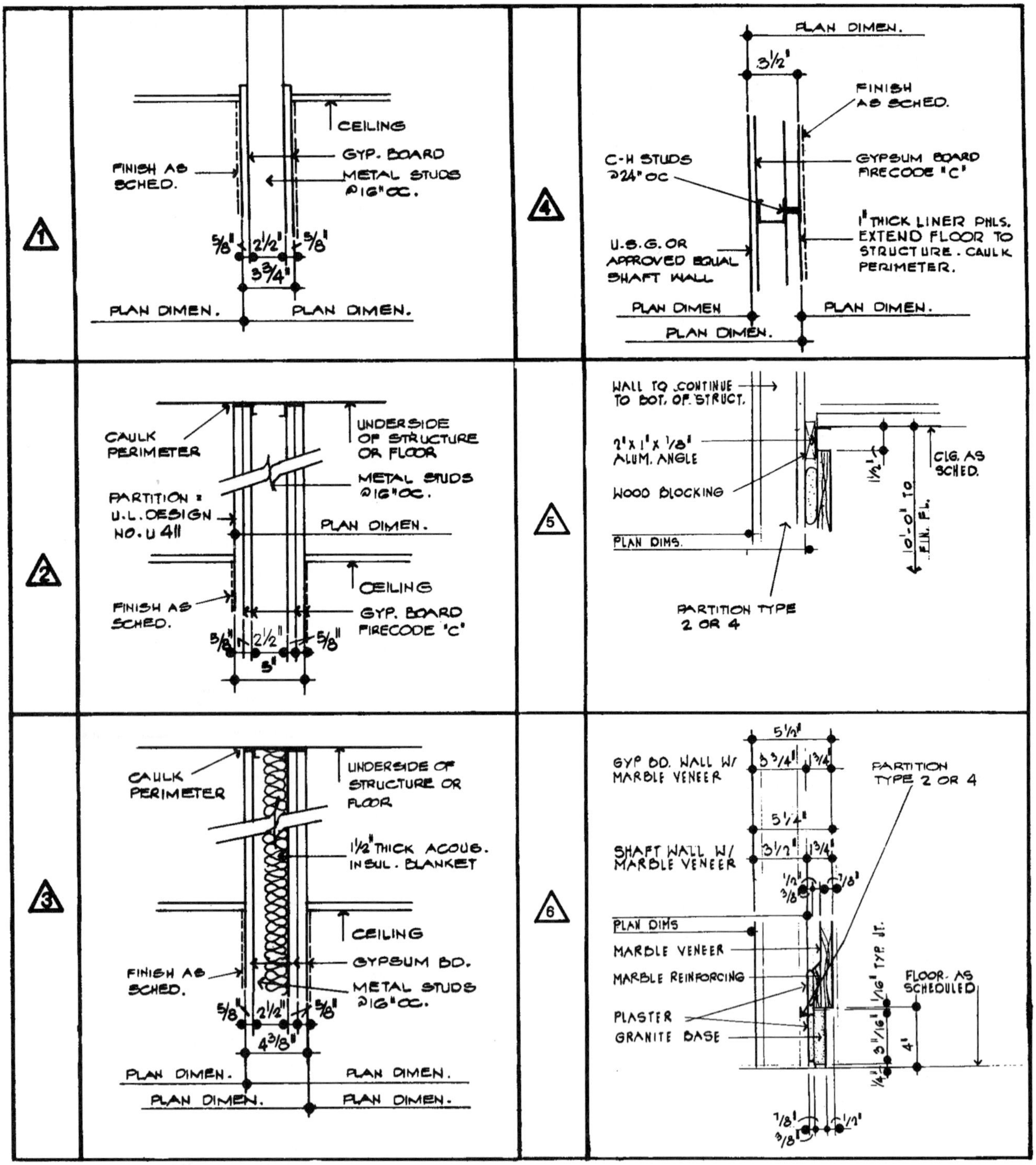

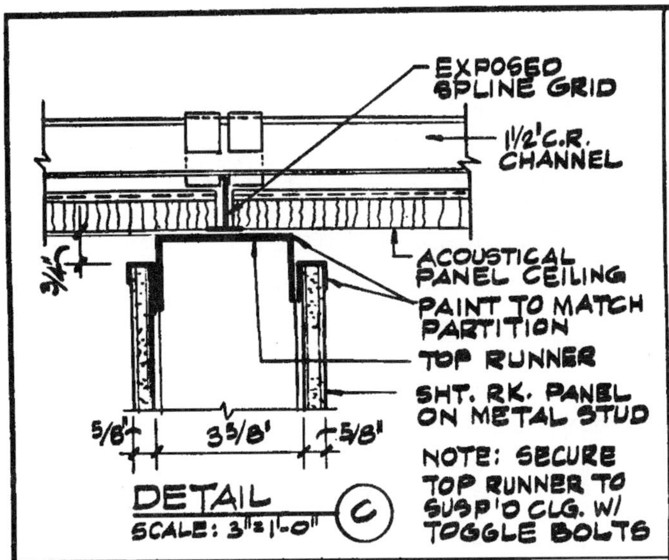
EXPOSED SPLINE GRID
1/2" C.R. CHANNEL
ACOUSTICAL PANEL CEILING
PAINT TO MATCH PARTITION
TOP RUNNER
SHT. RK. PANEL ON METAL STUD
3/4"
5/8"
3 5/8"
5/8"
NOTE: SECURE TOP RUNNER TO SUSP'D CLG. W/ TOGGLE BOLTS
DETAIL C
SCALE: 3"=1'-0"

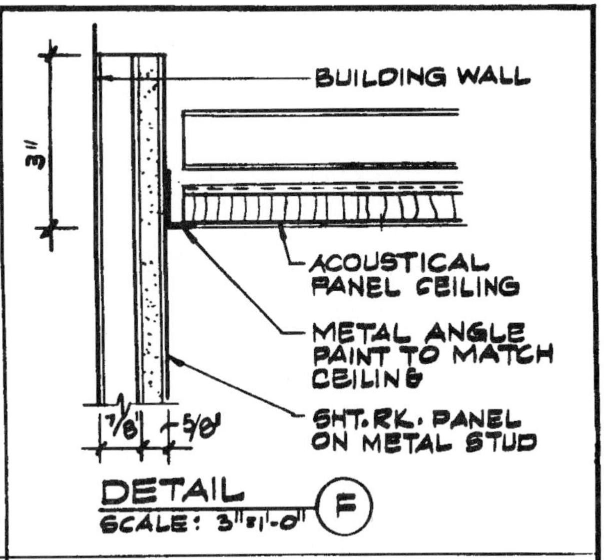
BUILDING WALL
3"
ACOUSTICAL PANEL CEILING
METAL ANGLE PAINT TO MATCH CEILING
SHT. RK. PANEL ON METAL STUD
7/8"
5/8"
DETAIL F
SCALE: 3"=1'-0"

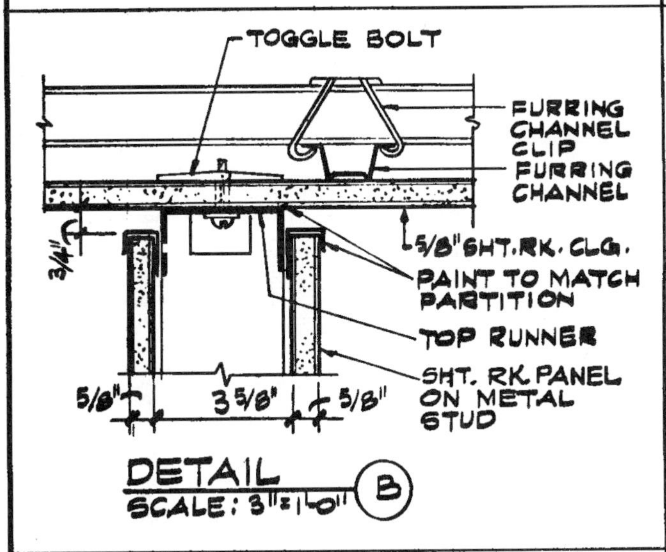
TOGGLE BOLT
FURRING CHANNEL CLIP
FURRING CHANNEL
5/8" SHT. RK. CLG.
PAINT TO MATCH PARTITION
TOP RUNNER
SHT. RK. PANEL ON METAL STUD
3/4"
5/8"
3 5/8"
5/8"
DETAIL B
SCALE: 3"=1'-0"

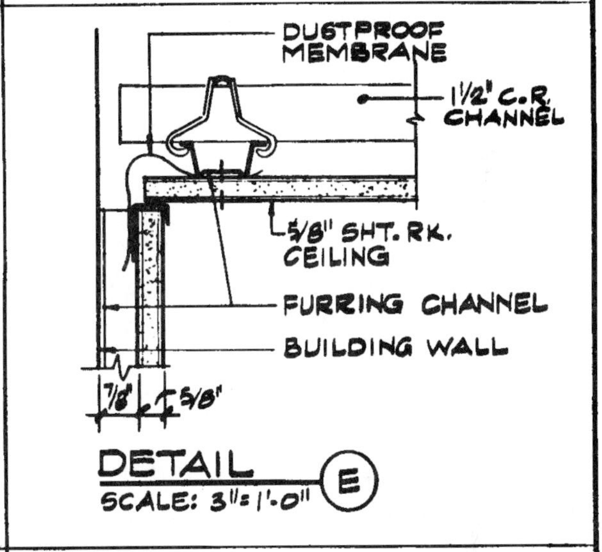
DUSTPROOF MEMBRANE
1/2" C.R. CHANNEL
5/8" SHT. RK. CEILING
FURRING CHANNEL
BUILDING WALL
7/8"
5/8"
DETAIL E
SCALE: 3"=1'-0"

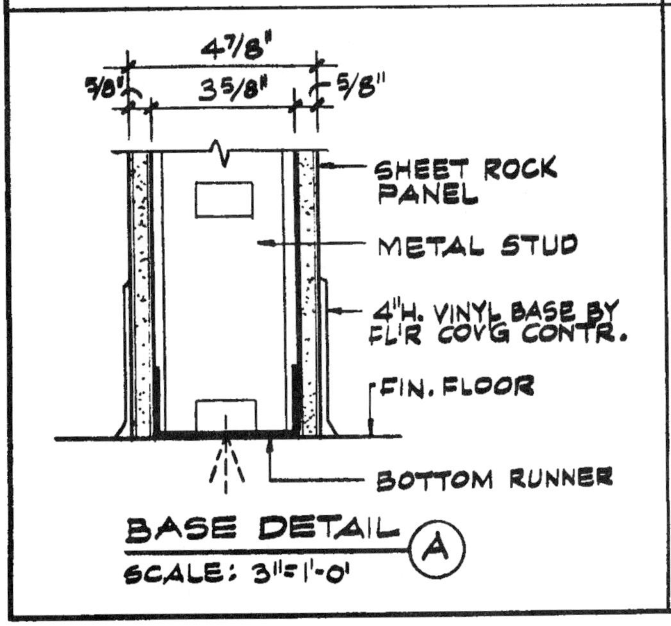
4 7/8"
5/8"
3 5/8"
5/8"
SHEET ROCK PANEL
METAL STUD
4"H. VINYL BASE BY FL'R COV'G CONTR.
FIN. FLOOR
BOTTOM RUNNER
BASE DETAIL A
SCALE: 3"=1'-0"

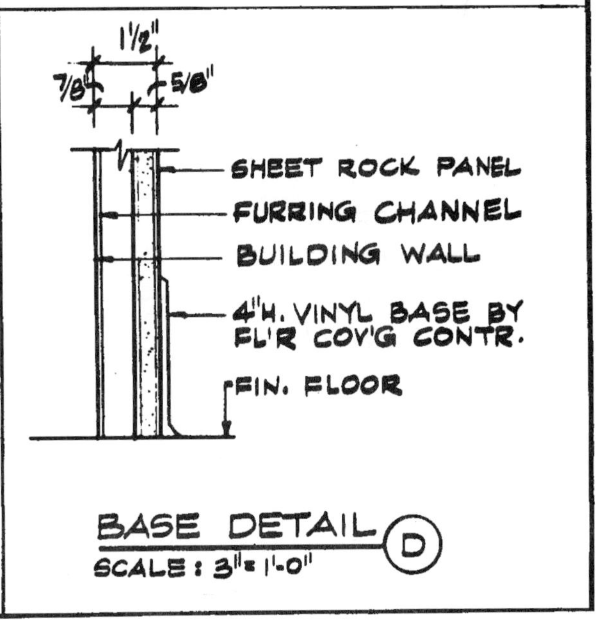
1 1/2"
7/8"
5/8"
SHEET ROCK PANEL
FURRING CHANNEL
BUILDING WALL
4"H. VINYL BASE BY FL'R COV'G CONTR.
FIN. FLOOR
BASE DETAIL D
SCALE: 3"=1'-0"

PARTITIONS AND WALL FINISHES

Metal Stud and Gypsum Board Details

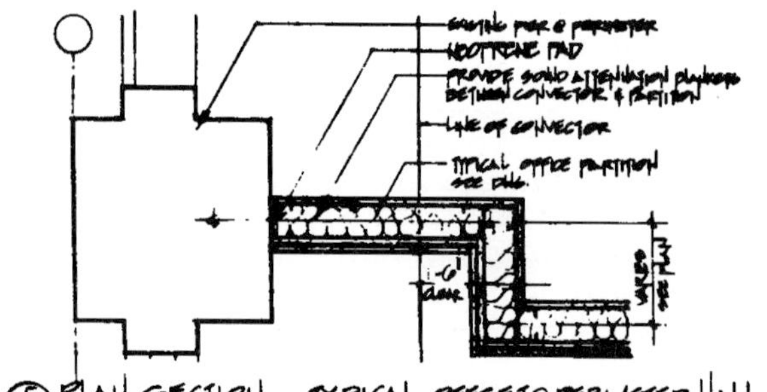

5 PLAN-SECTION - TYPICAL OFFSET @ PERIMETER WALL

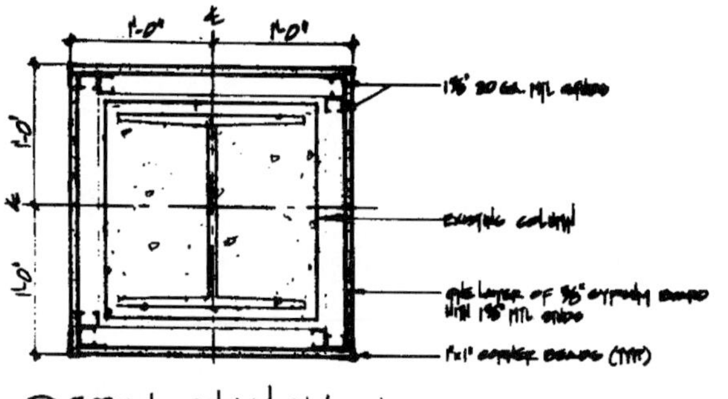

6 TYPICAL COLUMN ENCLOSURE

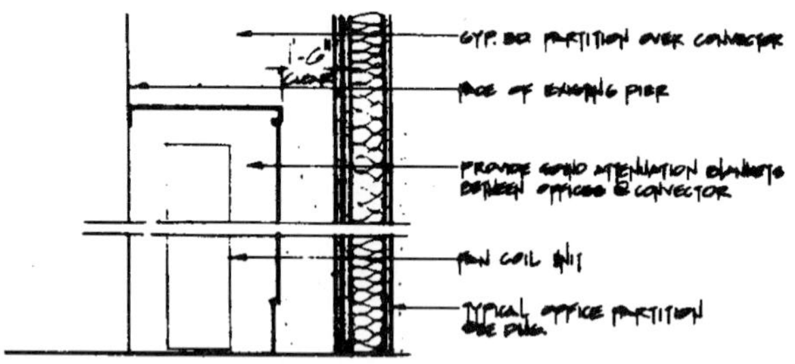

8 VERT-SECTION THROUGH TYP. OFFSET @ PERIMETER WALL

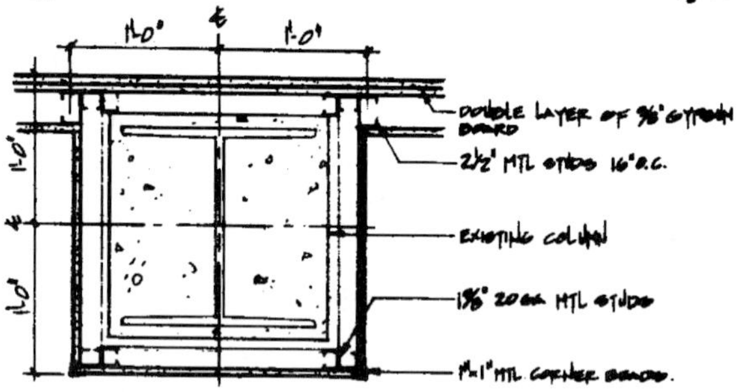

9 COLUMN ENCLOSURE WITH ADJOINING PARTITIONS

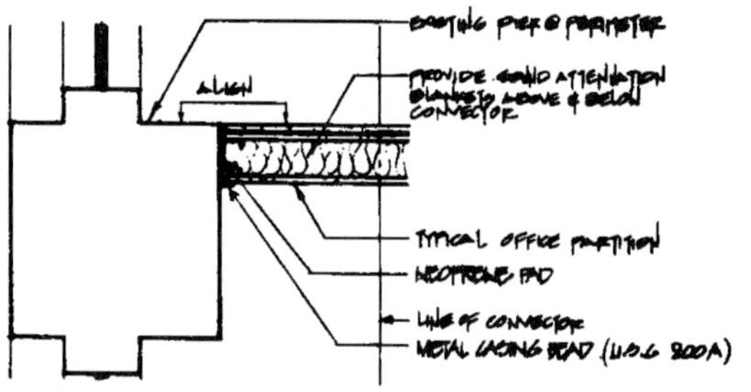

7 PLAN-SECTION-PARTITION ALIGNED W/ PIER

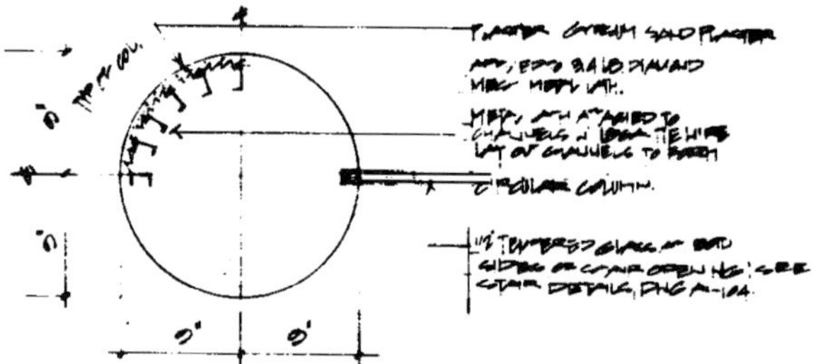

14 CYLINDRICAL COLUMN DETAIL

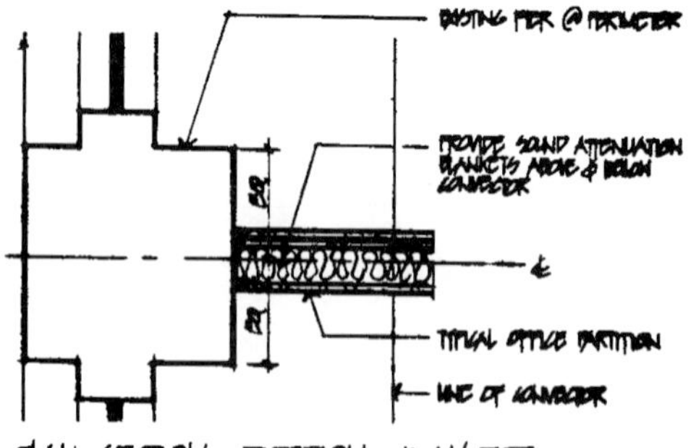

10 PLAN-SECTION - PARTITION ℄ W/ PIER

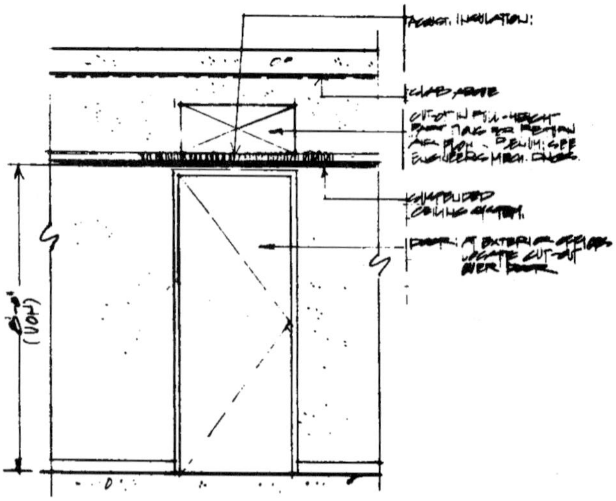

3 TYP. DETAIL OF RETURN AIR CUT-OUT IN FULL HT. PARTITIONS

PARTITIONS AND WALL FINISHES

Metal Stud and Gypsum Board Partition Sections

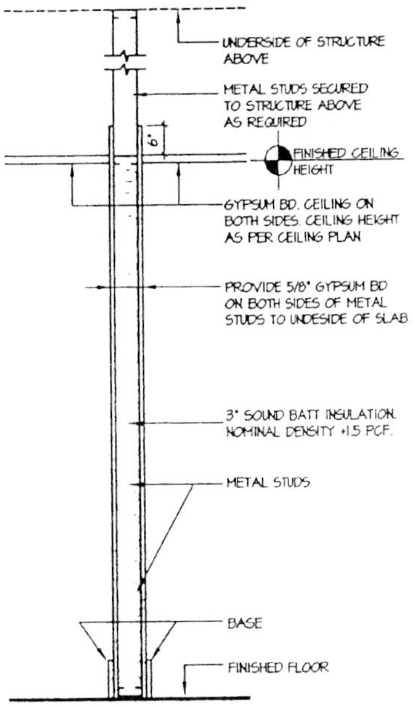

Ⓐ AS DRAWN GYPSUM BD. ON BOTH SIDES OF STUD

Ⓐ1 CAVITY WALL AS Ⓐ EXCEPT: GYPSUM BD. WALL & CEILNG ONE SIDE NO GYPSUM BD. ON OTHER SIDE

Ⓐ2 CAVITY WALL AS Ⓐ EXCEPT: COORDINATE WITH OWNERS INTERIOR DESIGN DRAWINGS FOR INFORMATION RELATING TO OTHER SIDE OF WALL AND CEILING.

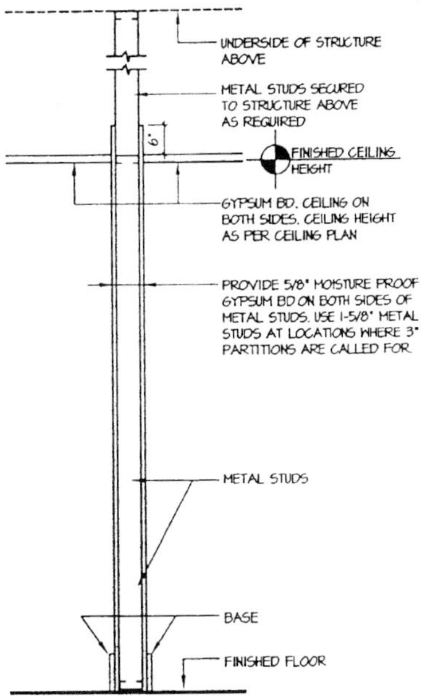

Ⓑ AS DRAWN GYPSUM BD. ON BOTH SIDES OF STUD

Ⓑ1 CAVITY WALL AS Ⓑ EXCEPT: GYPSUM BD. WALL & CEILNG ONE SIDE NO GYPSUM BD. ON OTHER SIDE

Ⓑ2 CAVITY WALL AS Ⓑ EXCEPT: COORDINATE WITH OWNERS INTERIOR DESIGN DRAWINGS FOR INFORMATION RELATING TO OTHER SIDE OF WALL AND CEILING.

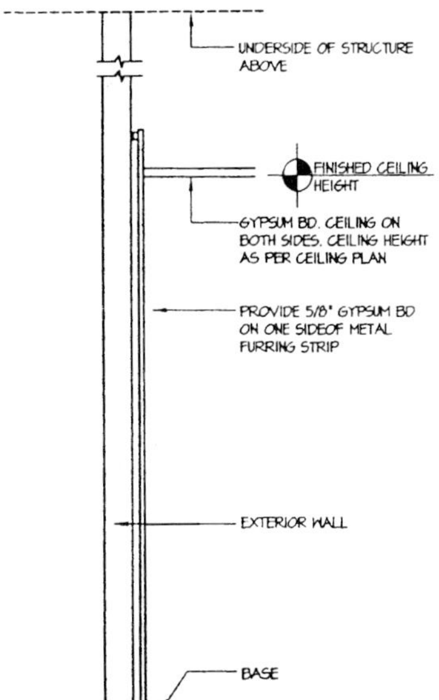

Ⓒ

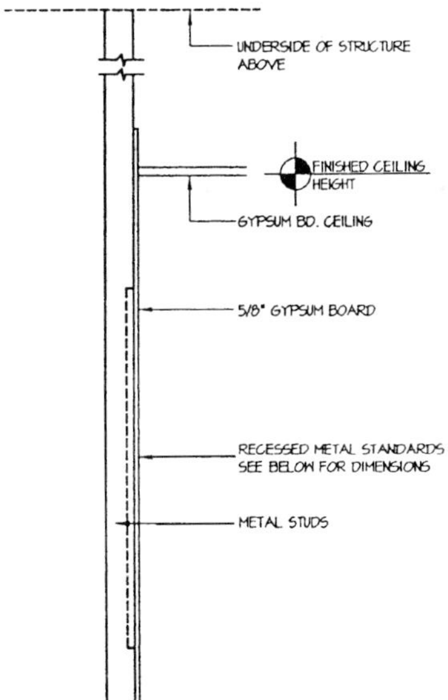

Ⓔ GARCY STANDARDS # 1483 MOUNTED 1'-6" A.F.F. X 6'-0" LONG (NOT USED)

Ⓕ GARCY STANDARDS # 1483 MOUNTED 3'-4" A.F.F. X 4'-0" LONG

Ⓖ GARCY STANDARDS # 1483 MOUNTED 2'-6" A.F.F. X 3'-6" LONG

PARTITIONS AND WALL FINISHES

Metal Stud and Gypsum Board Partition Sections

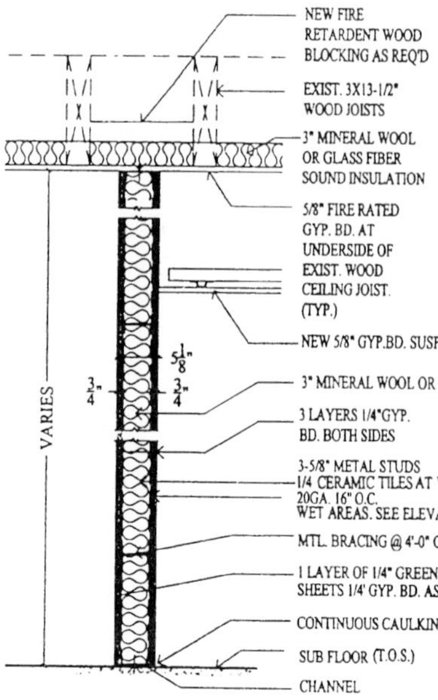

4 CURVED WALL PARTITION

4A SAME AS TYPE 4. W/ NO INSULATION

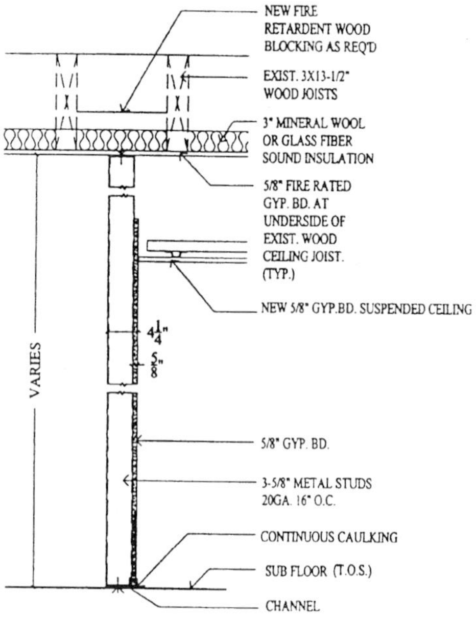

5 PARTITION

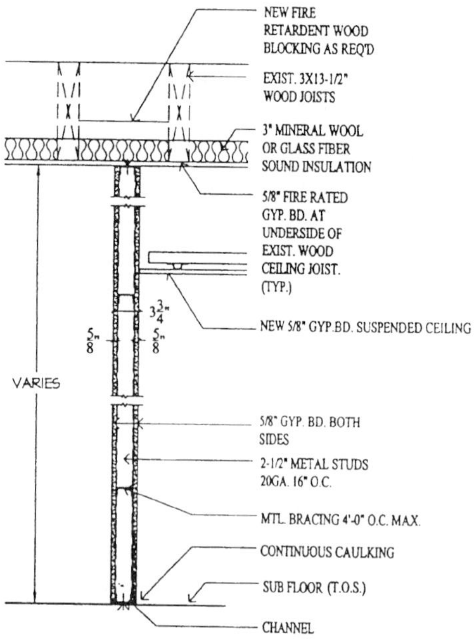

6 PARTITION

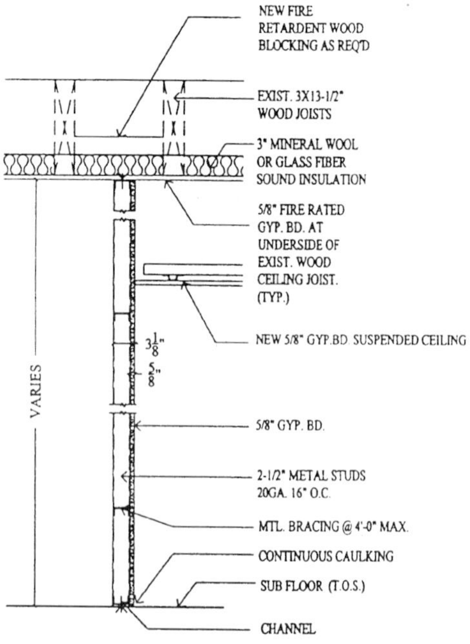

7 PARTITION

PARTITIONS AND WALL FINISHES

Metal Stud and Gypsum Board Partition Sections

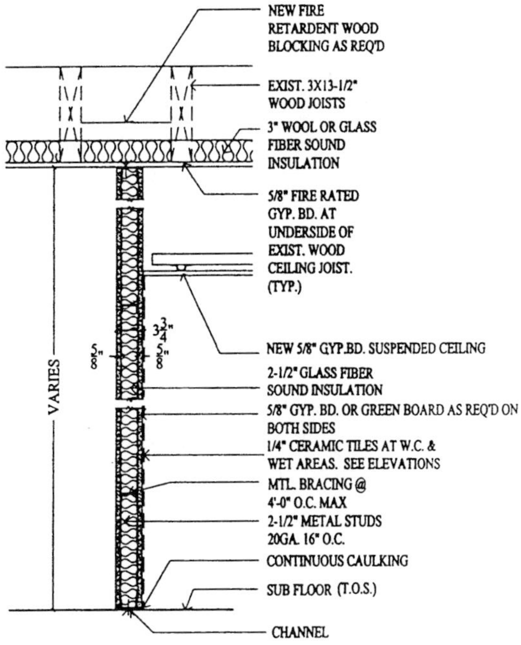

8 PARTITION

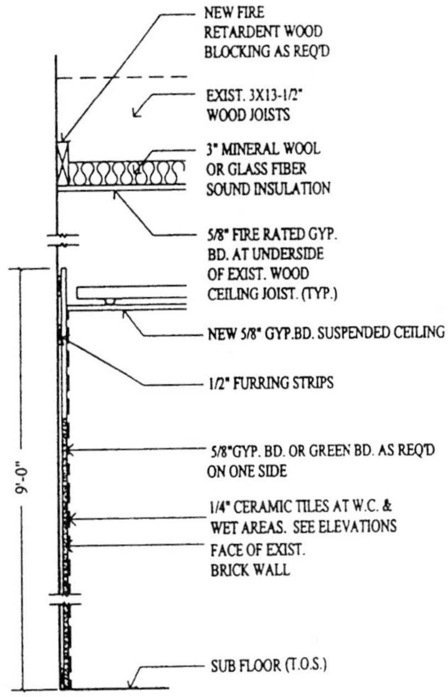

9 PARTITION

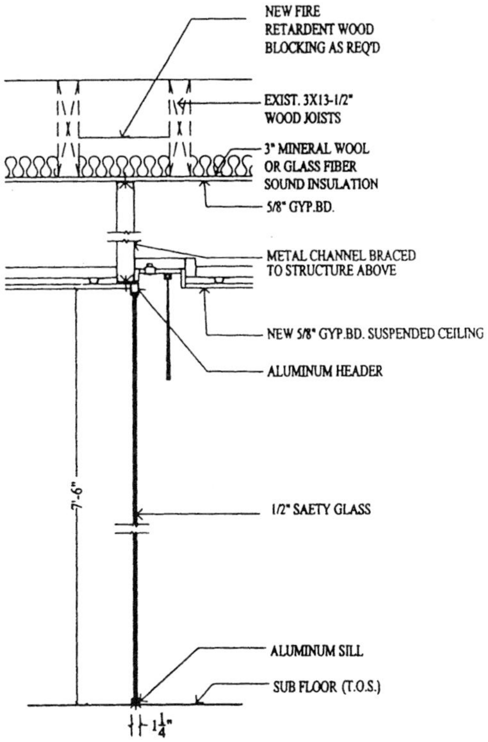

11 PARTITION

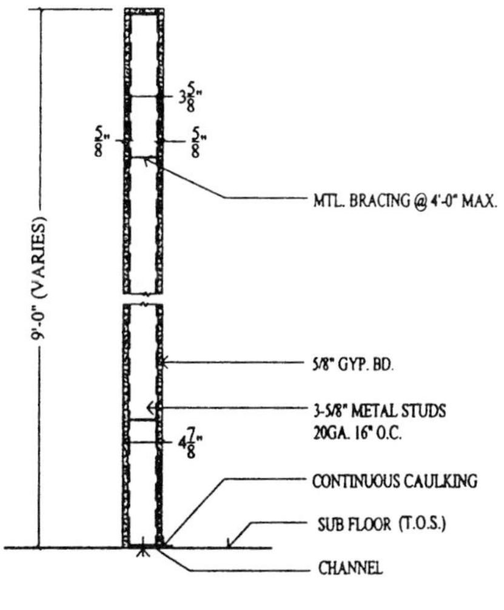

10 PARTITION FREE STANDING

PARTITIONS AND WALL FINISHES
Metal Stud and Gypsum Board Partition Sections

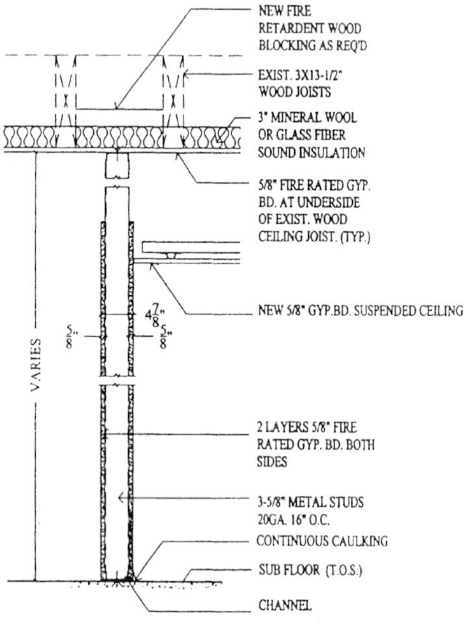

1 PARTITION

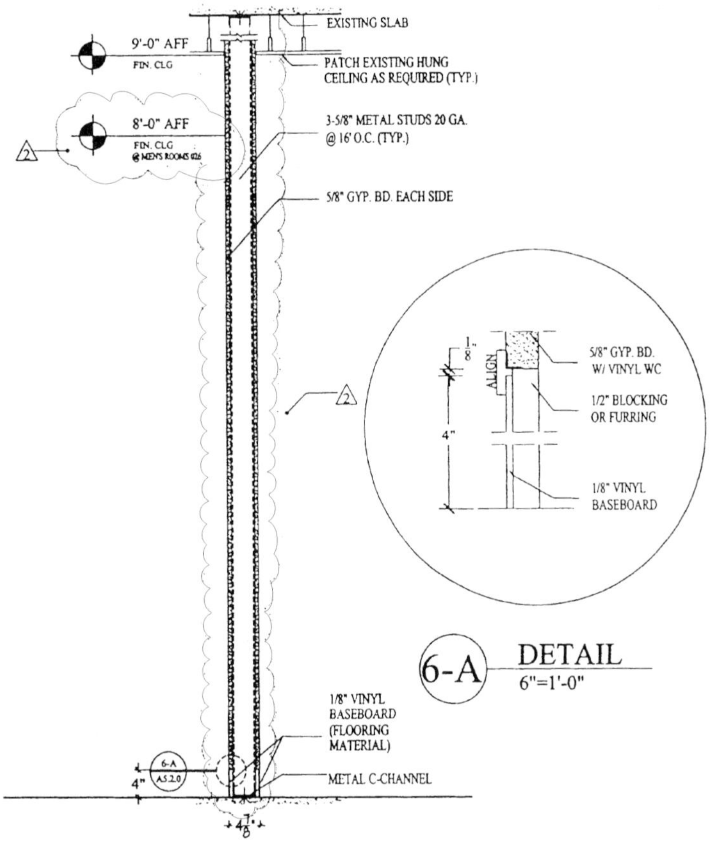

6 CORRIDOR (TYP.)
3/4"=1'-0"

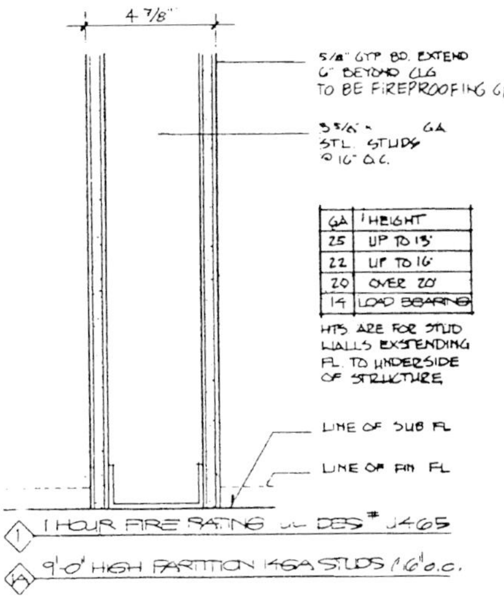

GA	HEIGHT
25	UP TO 13'
22	UP TO 16'
20	OVER 20'
14	LOAD BEARING

HTS ARE FOR STUD WALLS EXTENDING FL. TO UNDERSIDE OF STRUCTURE

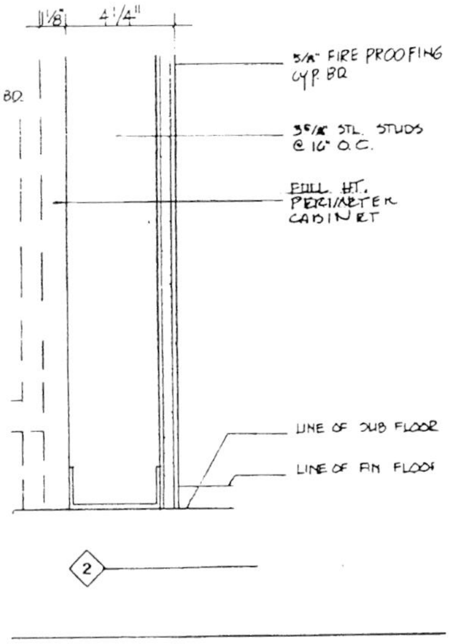

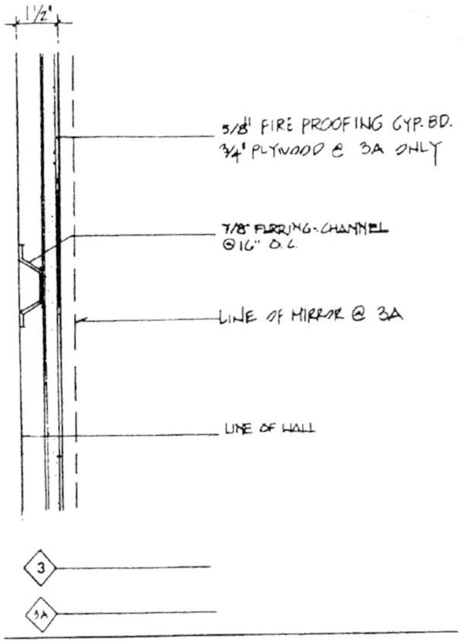

1 Partition Types

Scale: 3" = 1'-0"

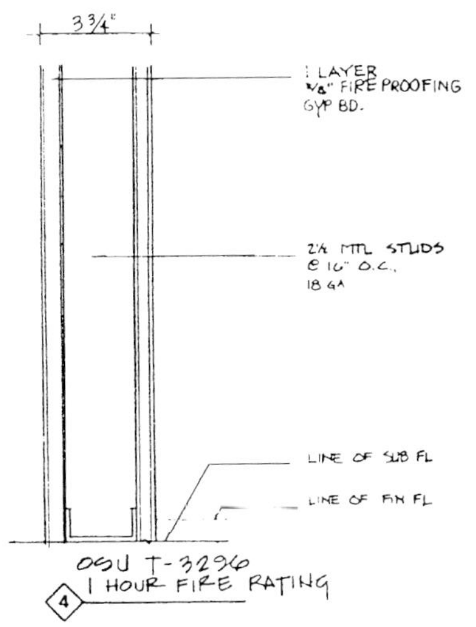

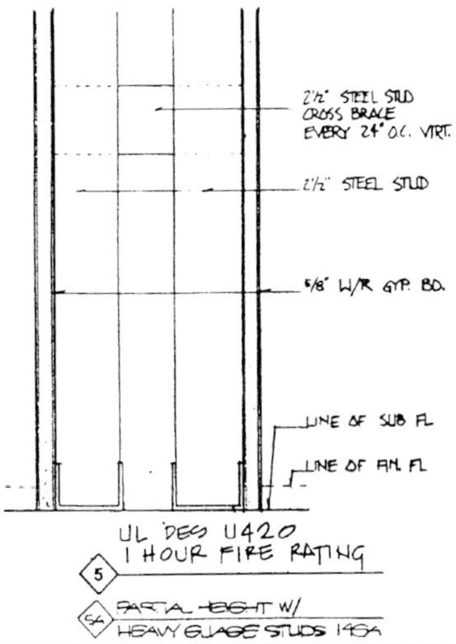

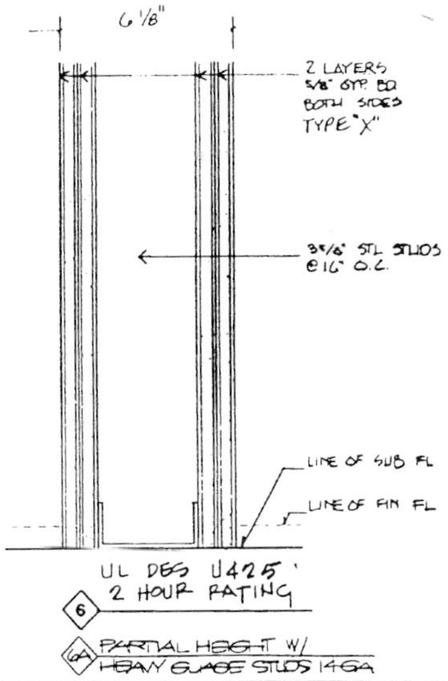

PARTITIONS AND WALL FINISHES

Metal Stud and Gypsum Board Corner and End Conditions

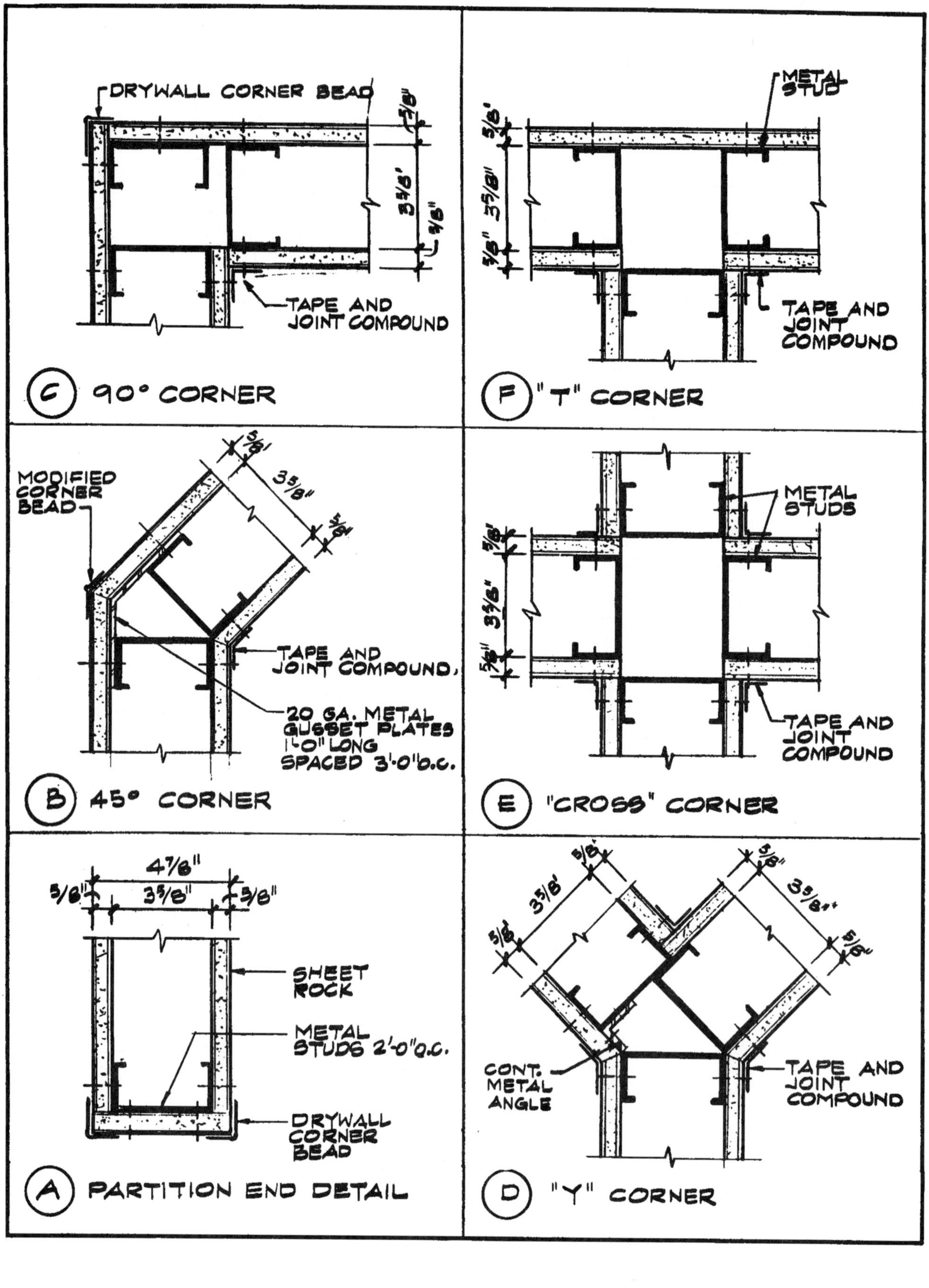

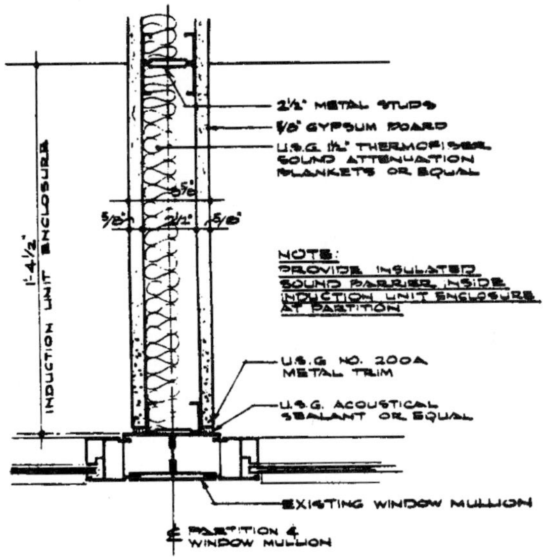

Metal stud and gypsum board: partition to mullion detail

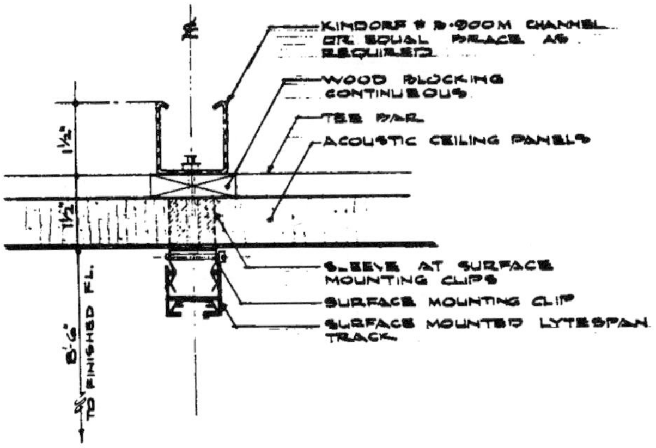

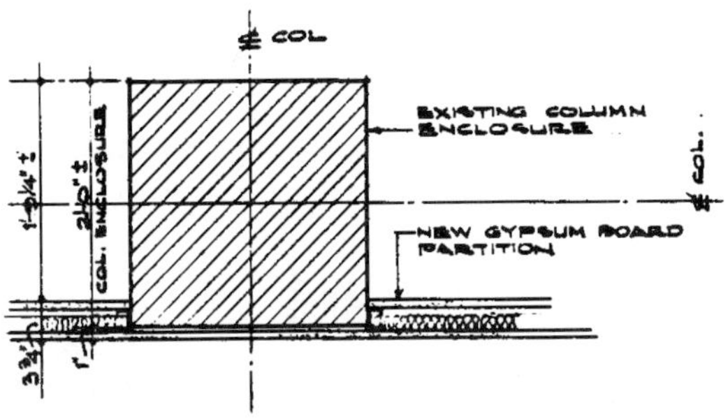

Metal stud and gypsum board: partition to column detail

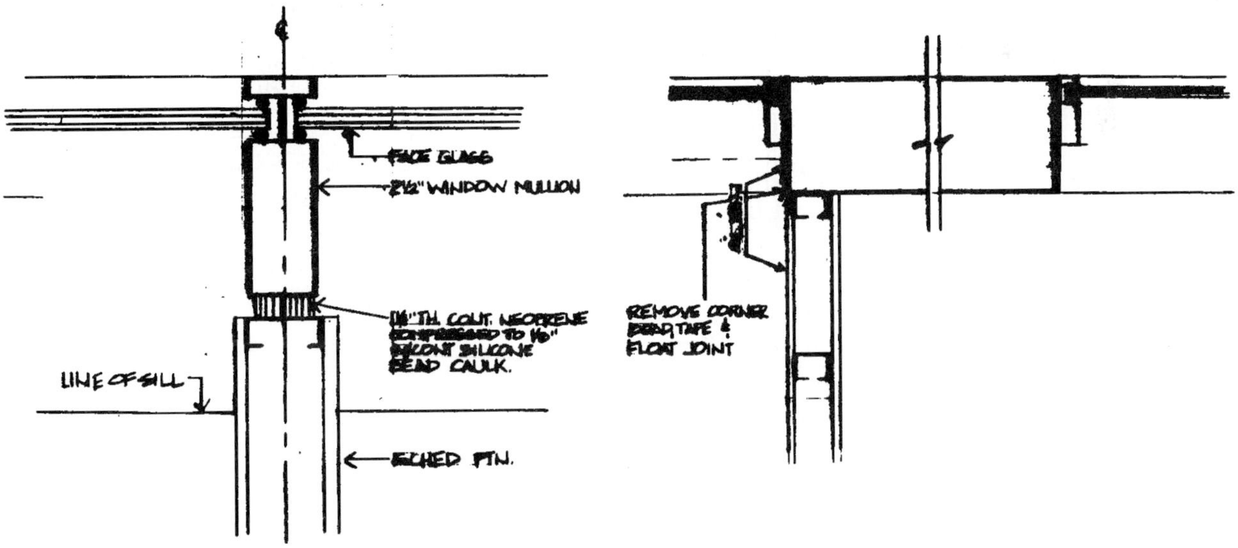

Metal stud and gypsum board: partition to mullion detail

PARTITIONS AND WALL FINISHES

Metal Stud and Gypsum Board: Column Enclosures and Fireproofing

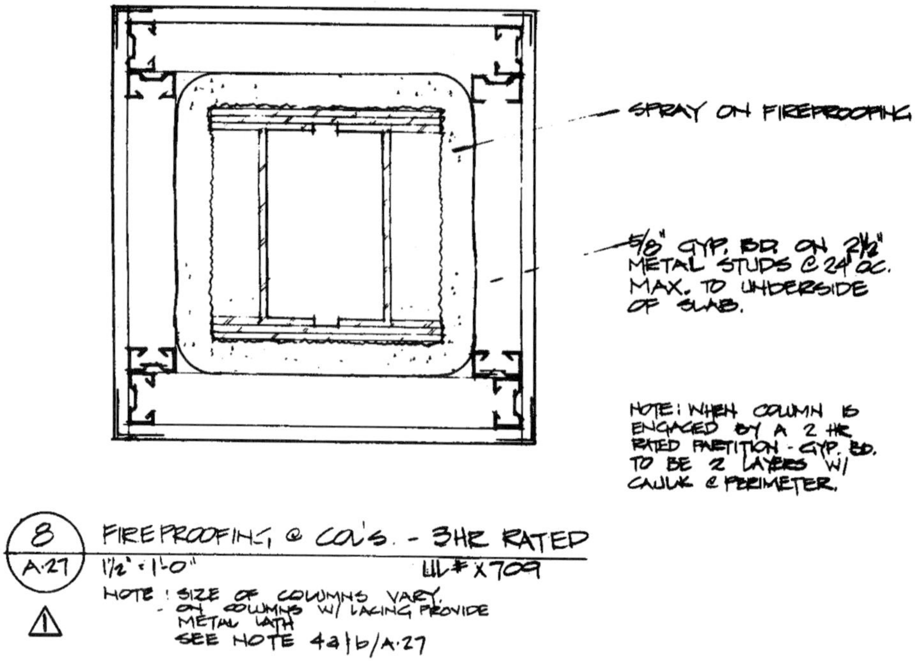

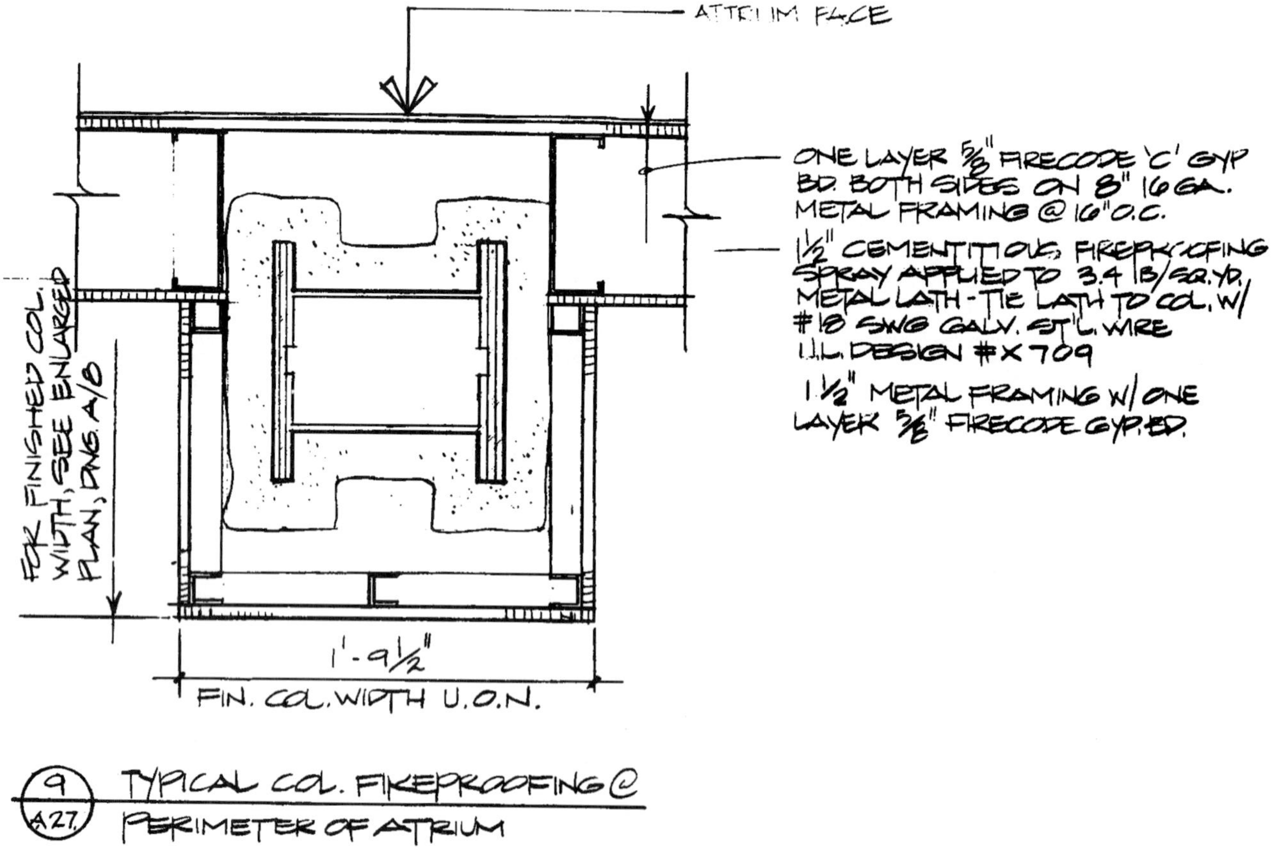

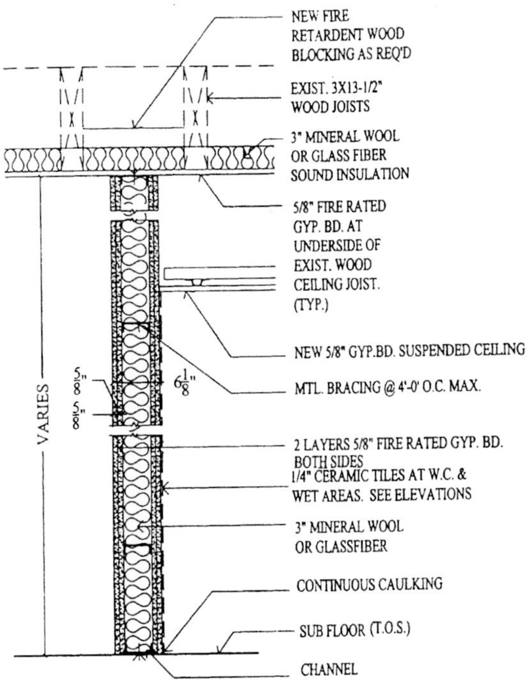

3 2 HR FIRE RATED PARTITION

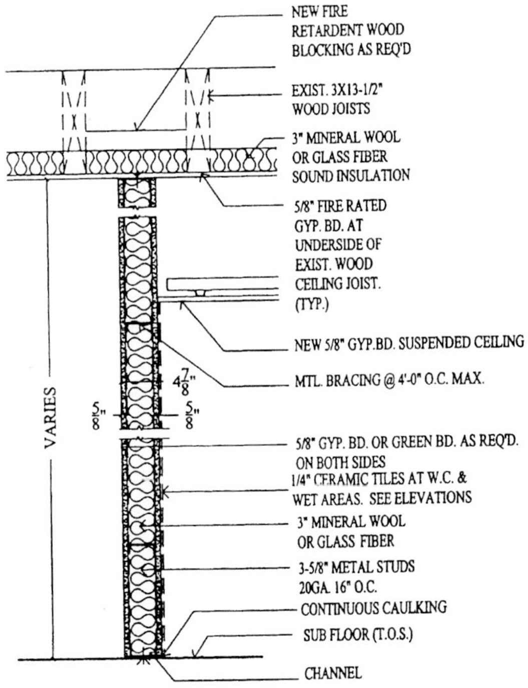

2 PARTITION

NEW FIRE
RETARDENT WOOD
BLOCKING AS REQ'D

EXIST. 3X13-1/2"
WOOD JOISTS

3" MINERAL WOOL
OR GLASS FIBER
SOUND INSULATION

5/8" FIRE RATED
GYP. BD. AT
UNDERSIDE OF
EXIST. WOOD
CEILING JOIST.
(TYP.)

NEW 5/8" GYP.BD. SUSPENDED CEILING

MTL. BRACING @ 4'-0' O.C. MAX.

2 LAYERS 5/8" FIRE RATED GYP. BD.
BOTH SIDES
1/4" CERAMIC TILES AT W.C. &
WET AREAS. SEE ELEVATIONS

3" MINERAL WOOL
OR GLASSFIBER

CONTINUOUS CAULKING

SUB FLOOR (T.O.S.)

CHANNEL

VARIES

$6\frac{1}{8}$"

$\frac{5}{8}$" $\frac{5}{8}$"

③ 2 HR FIRE RATED PARTITION

NEW FIRE
RETARDENT WOOD
BLOCKING AS REQ'D

EXIST. 3X13-1/2"
WOOD JOISTS

3" MINERAL WOOL
OR GLASS FIBER
SOUND INSULATION

5/8" FIRE RATED
GYP. BD. AT
UNDERSIDE OF
EXIST. WOOD
CEILING JOIST.
(TYP.)

NEW 5/8" GYP.BD. SUSPENDED CEILING

MTL. BRACING @ 4'-0' O.C. MAX.

5/8" GYP. BD. OR GREEN BD. AS REQ'D.
ON BOTH SIDES
1/4" CERAMIC TILES AT W.C. &
WET AREAS. SEE ELEVATIONS

3" MINERAL WOOL
OR GLASS FIBER

3-5/8" METAL STUDS
20GA. 16" O.C.

CONTINUOUS CAULKING

SUB FLOOR (T.O.S.)

CHANNEL

VARIES

$4\frac{7}{8}$"

$\frac{5}{8}$" $\frac{5}{8}$"

PARTITIONS AND WALL FINISHES

Metal Stud and Gypsum Board Fire-Rated and Lead-Lined Partitions

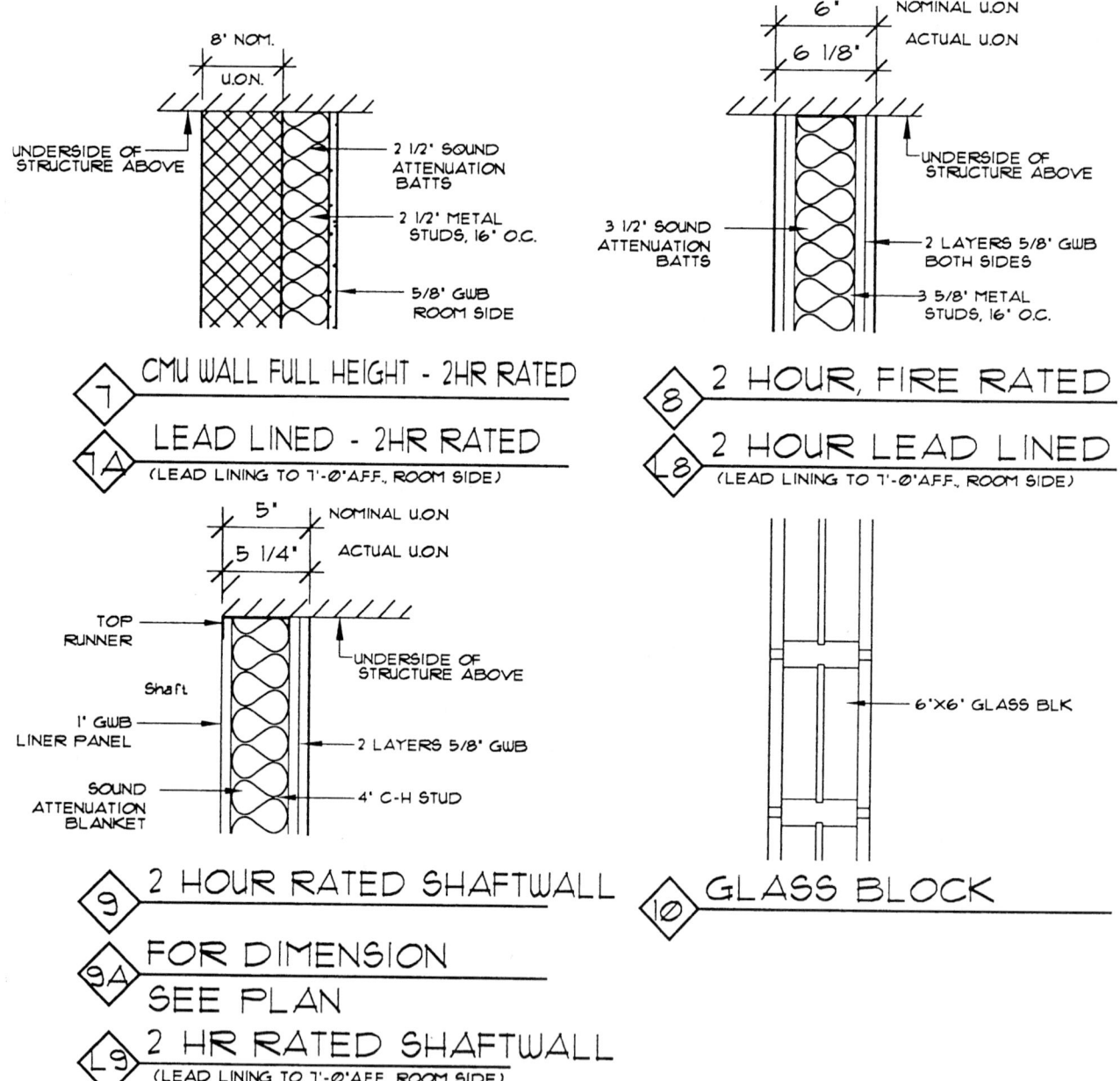

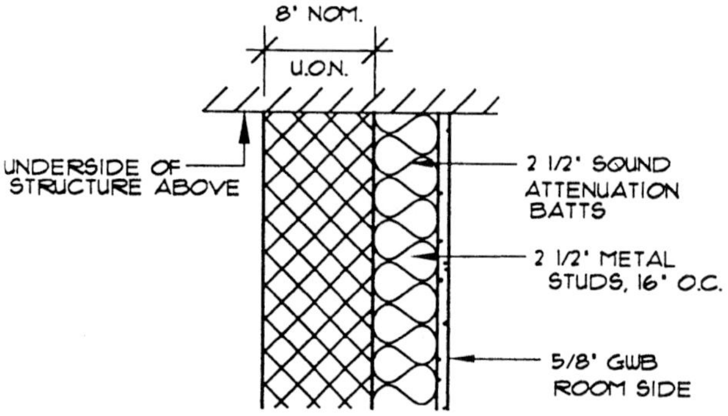

7 CMU WALL FULL HEIGHT - 2HR RATED

7A LEAD LINED - 2HR RATED

(LEAD LINING TO 7'-0"A.F.F., ROOM SIDE)

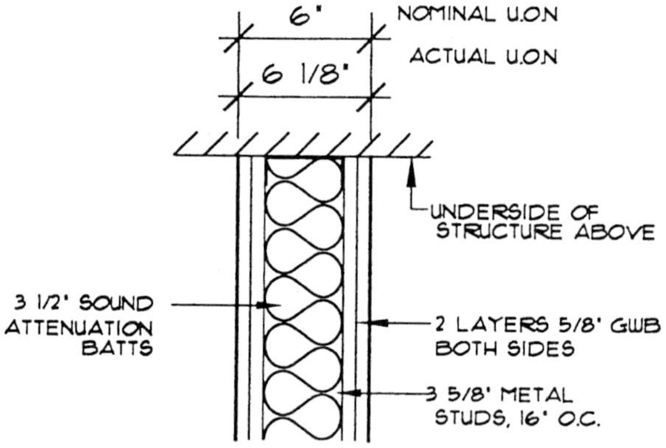

8 2 HOUR, FIRE RATED

L8 2 HOUR LEAD LINED

(LEAD LINING TO 7'-0"A.F.F., ROOM SIDE)

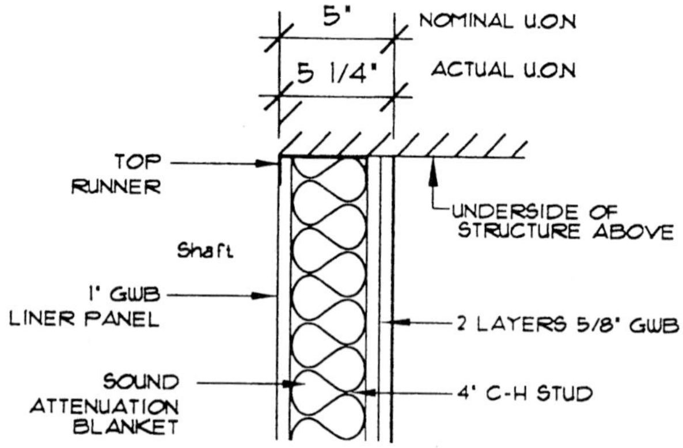

9 2 HOUR RATED SHAFTWALL

9A FOR DIMENSION SEE PLAN

L9 2 HR RATED SHAFTWALL

(LEAD LINING TO 7'-0"A.F.F., ROOM SIDE)

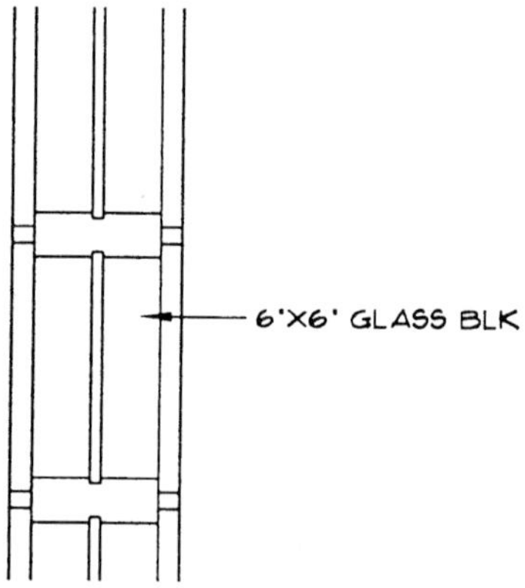

10 GLASS BLOCK

The resistance of a building element, such as a wall, to the passage of airborne sound is rated by its *sound transmission class* (STC). Thus, the higher the number, the better the sound barrier. The approximate effectiveness of walls with varying STC numbers is shown in the following tabulation:

STC no.	*Effectiveness*
25	Normal speech can be understood quite easily
35	Loud speech audible but not intelligible
45	Must strain to hear loud speech
48	Some loud speech barely audible
50	Loud speech not audible

Sound travels readily through the air and also through some materials. When airborne sound strikes a conventional wall, the studs act as sound conductors unless they are separated in some way from the covering material.

Wall Construction

As the preceding STC tabulation shows, a wall providing sufficient resistance to airborne sound transfer likely has an STC rating of 45 or greater. Thus, in construction of such a wall between the rooms of a house, its cost as related to the STC rating should be considered. As shown in Fig. 15, details A, with gypsum wallboard, and B, with plastered wall, are those commonly used for partition walls. However, the hypothetical rating of 45 cannot be obtained in this construction.

Good STC ratings can be obtained in a wood-frame wall by using the combination of materials shown in Fig. 15D and E. One-half-inch sound-deadening board nailed to the studs, followed by a lamination of ½-in gypsum wallboard, will provide an STC value of 46 at a relatively low cost. A slightly better rating can be obtained by using ⅝-in gypsum wallboard rather than ½-in. A very satisfactory STC rating of 52 can be obtained by using resilient clips to fasten gypsum backer boards to the studs, followed by adhesive-laminated ½-in fiberboard (Fig. 15E). This method further isolates the wall covering from the framing.

A similar isolation system consists of resilient channels nailed horizontally to 2- by 4-in studs spaced 16 in on center. Channels are spaced 24 in apart vertically and ⅝-in gypsum wallboard is screwed to the channels. An STC rating of 47 is thus obtained at a moderately low cost.

Thus, use of a double wall, which may consist of a 2 by 6 or wider plate and staggered 2- by 4-in studs, is sometimes desirable. One-half-inch gypsum wallboard on each side of this wall (Fig. 16A) results in an STC value of 45. However, two layers of ⅝-in gypsum wallboard add little, if any, additional sound-transfer resistance (Fig. 16B). When 1½-in blanket insulation is added to this construction (Fig. 16C), the STC rating increases to 49. This insulation may be installed as shown or placed between studs on one wall. A single wall with 3½ in of insulation will show a marked improvement over an open stud space and is low in cost.

The use of ½-in sound-deadening board and a lamination of gypsum wallboard in the double wall will result in an STC rating of 50 (Fig. 16D). The addition of blanket insulation to this combination will likely provide an even higher value, perhaps 53 or 54.

PARTITIONS AND WALL FINISHES
Sound Insulation and Transmission

WALL DETAIL	DESCRIPTION	STC RATING
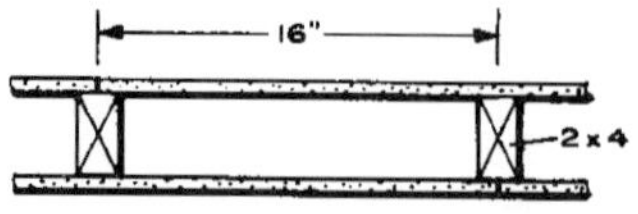 A	½" GYPSUM WALLBOARD ⅝" GYPSUM WALLBOARD	32 37
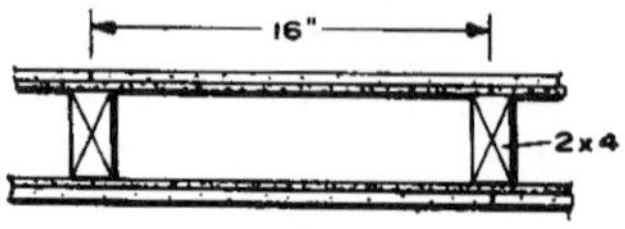 B	⅜" GYPSUM LATH (NAILED) PLUS ½" GYPSUM PLASTER WITH WHITECOAT FINISH (EACH SIDE)	39
 C	8" CONCRETE BLOCK	45
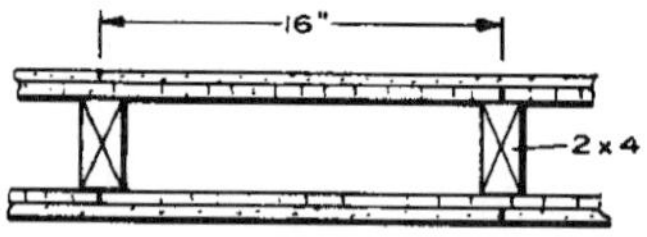 D	½" SOUND DEADENING BOARD (NAILED) ½" GYPSUM WALLBOARD (LAMINATED) (EACH SIDE)	46
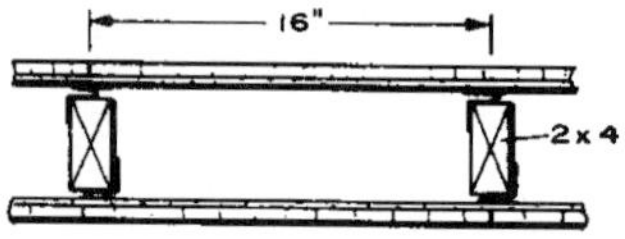 E	RESILIENT CLIPS TO ⅜" GYPSUM BACKER BOARD ½" FIBERBOARD (LAMINATED) (EACH SIDE)	52

Fig. 15 Sound insulation of single walls

WALL DETAIL	DESCRIPTION	STC RATING
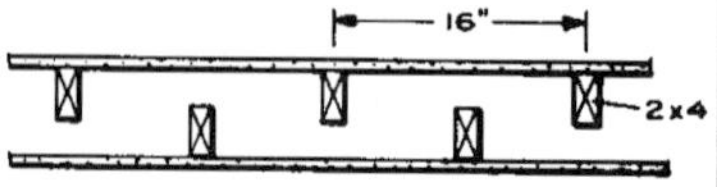 A	½" GYPSUM WALLBOARD	45
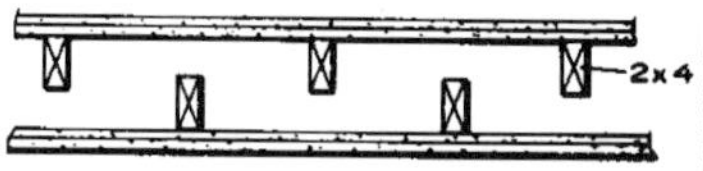 B	⅝" GYPSUM WALLBOARD (DOUBLE LAYER EACH SIDE)	45
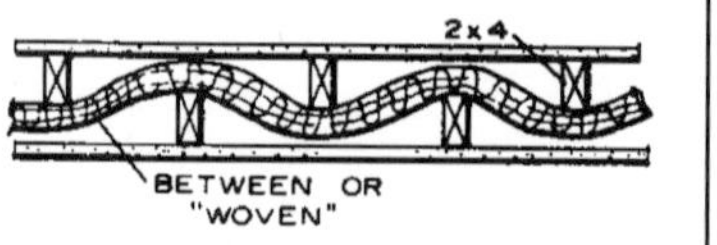 C	½" GYPSUM WALLBOARD 1½" FIBROUS INSULATION	49
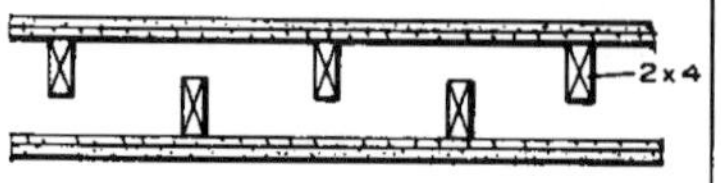 D	½" SOUND DEADENING BOARD (NAILED) ½" GYPSUM WALLBOARD (LAMINATED)	50

Fig. 16 Sound insulation of double walls

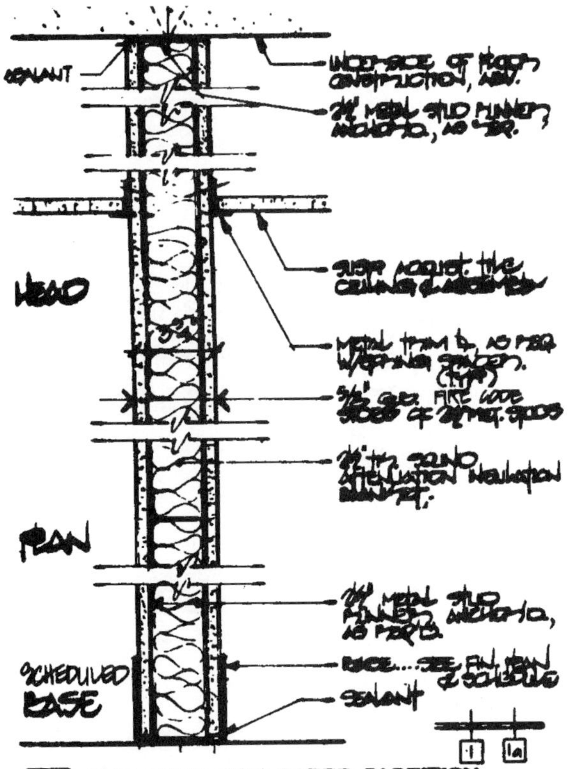

1 ONE HOUR FIRE RATED PARTITION

1a SAME AS 1 BUT WITH SOUND ATTENUATION BLANKET

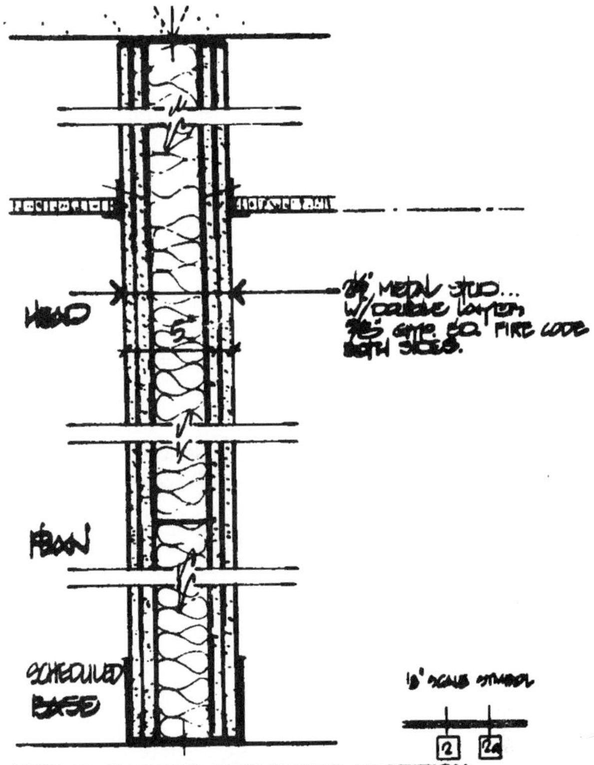

2 TWO HOUR FIRE RATED PARTITION

2a SAME AS 2 BUT WITH SOUND ATTENUATION BLANKET

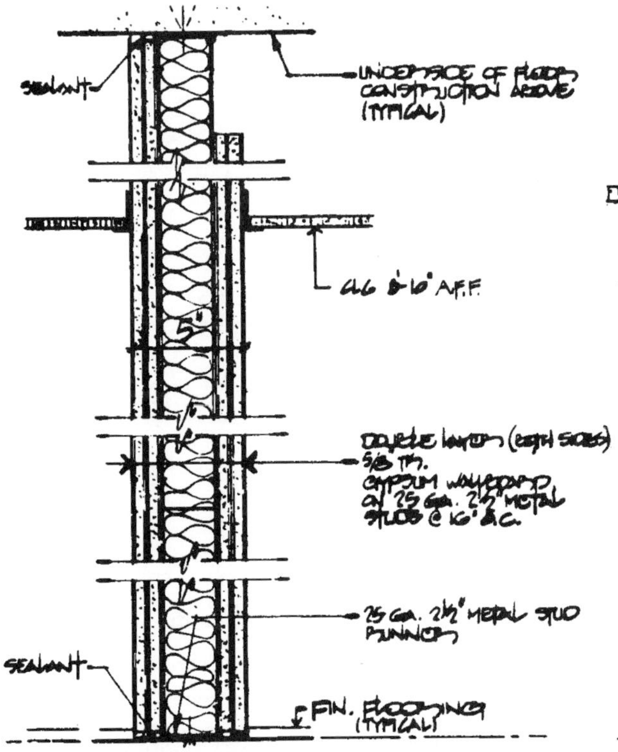

3a SOUND PARTITION / "CLASS A" /

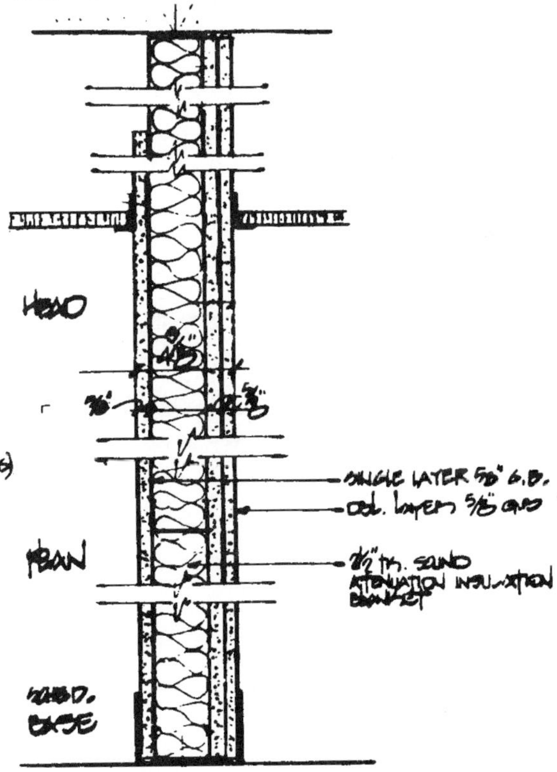

4a SOUND PARTITION / "CLASS B" /

PARTITIONS AND WALL FINISHES

Acoustical and Fire-Rated Metal Stud and Gypsum Board

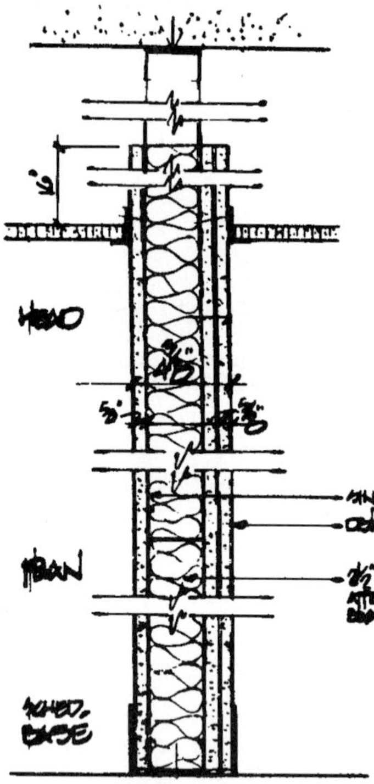

5 DRYWALL PARTITION. USE TO ALIGN WITH PARTITION [2] @ NON-FIRE RATED AREA

5a SAME AS [5] BUT WITH SOUND ATTENUATION BLANKET USE TO ALIGN WITH PARTITION [2a] & [3a] @ NON-FIRE RATED AREA

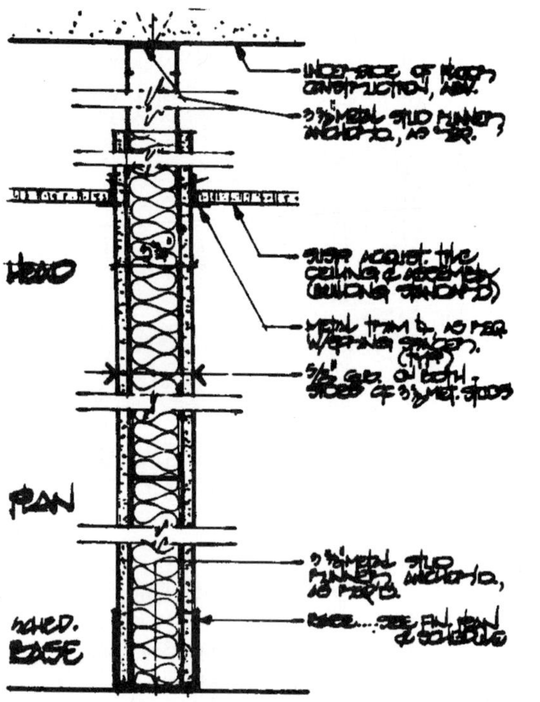

6 DRYWALL PARTITION TO 6" ABOVE CEILING

6a SAME AS [6] BUT WITH SOUND ATTENUATION BLANKET /"CLASS C"/

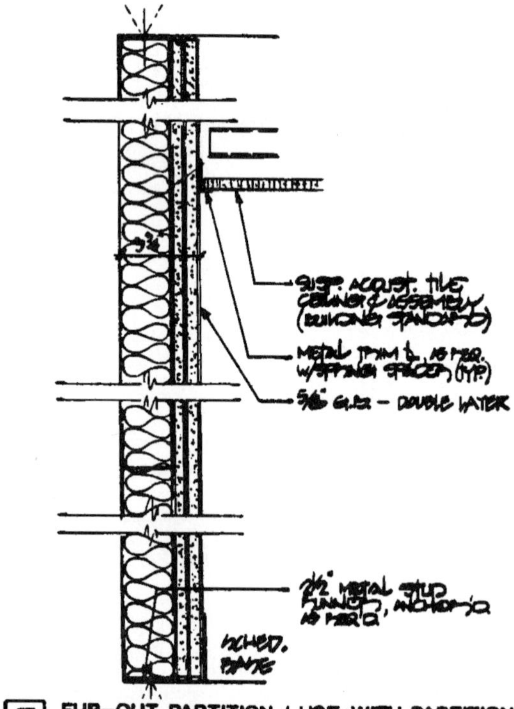

7 FUR-OUT PARTITION / USE WITH PARTITIONS [2] @ COLUMN ENCLOSURE

7a SAME AS [7] BUT WITH SOUND ATTENUATION BLANKET

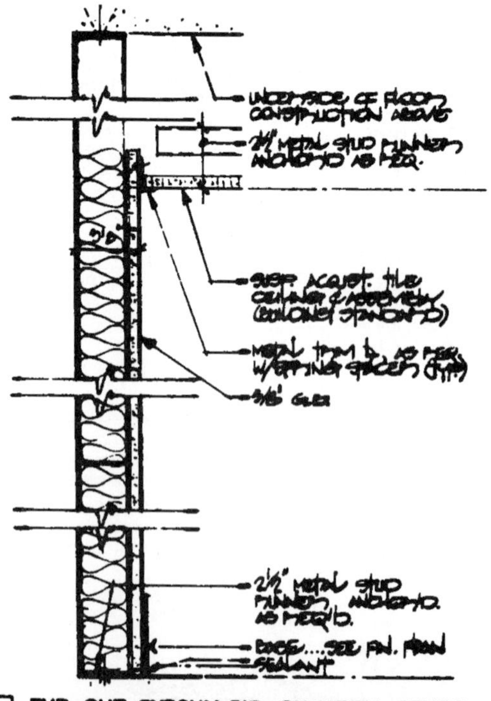

8 FUR-OUT GYPSUM B'D. ON METAL STUDS. CHASE PARTITION & COLUMN ENCLOSURE

8a SAME AS [8] BUT WITH SOUND ATTENUATION BLANKET

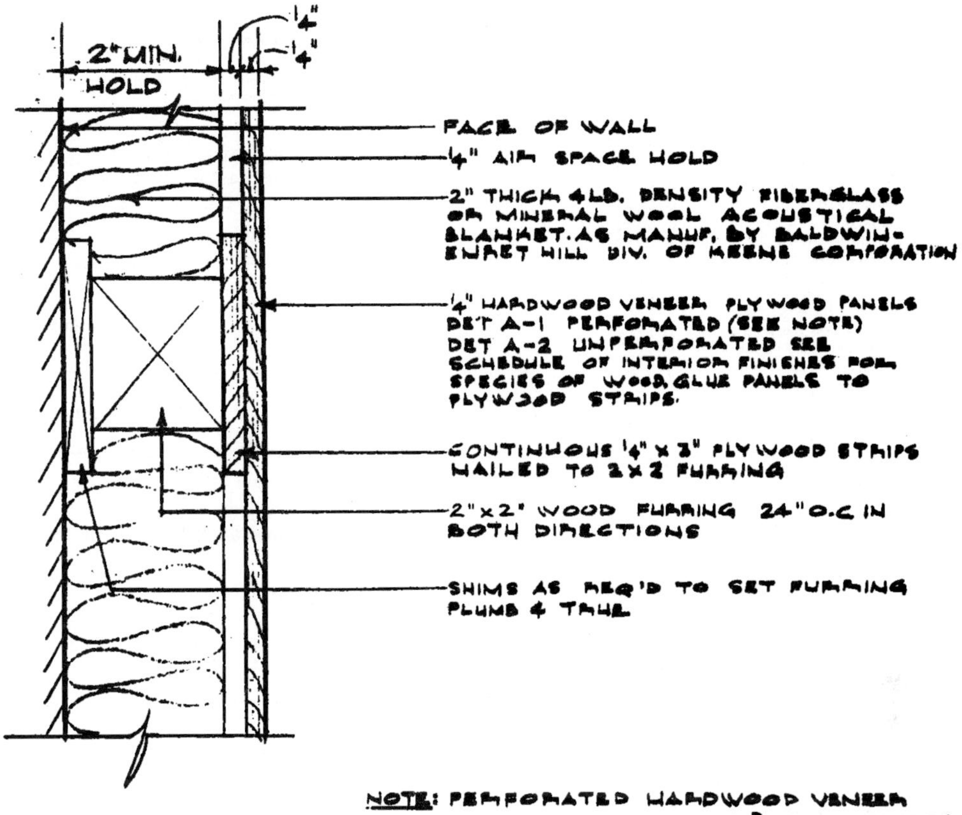

NOTE: PERFORATED HARDWOOD VENEER PANELS SHALL HAVE 3/16" DIA. HOLES 1/2" O.C. HOLES SHALL BE DRILLED NOT PUNCHED OPEN AREA TO BE AT LEAST 11%

(A-1) PERFORATED HARDWOOD VENEER PLYWOOD FINISH

(A-2) UNPERFORATED HARDWOOD VENEER PLYWOOD FINISH

ACOUSTIC WALL TREATMENT DETAILS

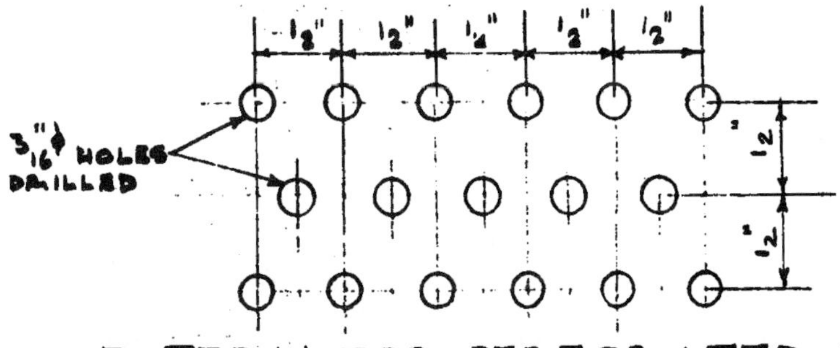

PATTERN FOR PERFORATED PLYWOOD

PARTITIONS AND WALL FINISHES
Wood Frame Partition Systems for Sound Control

PARTITION SYSTEM	WALL NUMBER	WALL FACE	STC
single stud walls Basic construction is 2" x 4" studs 16" o.c. with double top plate and single or double bottom plate. Faces are 5/8" thick fire resistive type gypsum board applied, taped and finished in accordance with manufacturer's recommendations. Resilient channels are applied to studs 24" o.c. as shown with a 1/2"x3" gypsum nailing strip at the bottom. Absorptive material is paper-backed glass fiber or mineral wool batts stapled in the stud space as illustrated. Sound deadening board is sound-rated organic fiber board with a 15-18 pcf density. 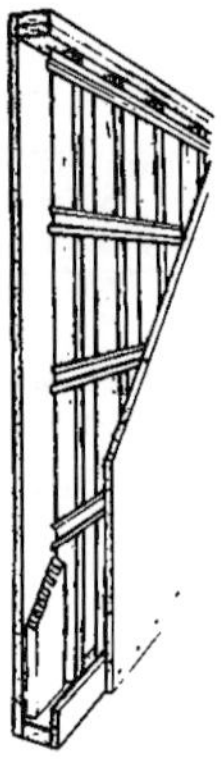 **no. 3**	1	Single gypsum board each side, applied with screws; no resilient channels	34
	2	Single gypsum board laminated and nailed[2] over sound board each side; no channels	45
	3	Single gypsum board applied with screws 1 side; opposite side on resilient channels	50
	4	Single gypsum board laminated and nailed[2] over sound board, opposite side on resilient channels	52
	5	Single gypsum board on resilient channels each side	53
	6	Double ½" gypsum board, base sheet vertical; face sheet horizontal; applied on resilient channels one side	59
double stud walls with a common plate basic construction is a double row of 2"x3" or 2"x4" studs, each row 16" o.c. and each row aligned with an opposite edge of the 2"x6" top and bottom plates. The rows of studs are offset 2" to 8" to prevent any chance contact. Other details and materials are as described for single stud walls.  **no. 11**	7	Single gypsum board each side, applied with screws (2x3 studs—16" o.c.); no resilient channels	49
	8	Single gypsum board laminated and nailed[2] over sound deadening board each side (2x4 studs—16" o.c.); no resilient channels	49
	9	Single gypsum board nailed one side. Single gypsum on resilient channels opposite	50
	10	Single gypsum board laminated and nailed[2] over sound deadening board 1 side. Single gypsum board on resilient channels opposite (2x3 studs—16" o.c.)	53
	11	Double gypsum board (½" over ⅝") nailed one side; single gypsum board on resilient channels opposite (2x4 studs—24" o.c.)	56
double stud walls on separate plates Basic construction is a double wall of 2"x3" studs on separate plates about 1" apart. Studs of each frame are 16" o.c. with the studs in one frame offset 2" to 8" from those of the other. Other details and materials are as described for single stud walls. 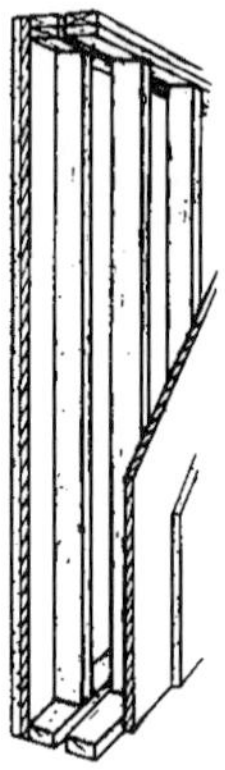 **no. 13**	12	Single gypsum board each side applied with screws	51
	13	Single gypsum board laminated and nailed[2] over sound board each side	53
	14	Same as wall 13	60
	15	Single gypsum board laminated and nailed[2] over sound board 1 side; single gypsum board on resilient channels opposite	58
	16	Double gypsum board; nailed each side	51
	17	Double gypsum board each side; outer layer laminated and nailed[2]; base layer nailed	59
	18	Double gypsum board laminated and nailed[2] one side. Single gypsum board on resilient channels opposite	57

[1] Design No. 5—1 Hr. combustible (bearing wall) Underwriters' Lab. Inc. (10)
[2] Face laminated vertically with three 6-inch wide strips of construction adhesive and nailed with about half the usual number of nails.

PARTITIONS AND WALL FINISHES

Wood Frame Partition Systems for Sound Control

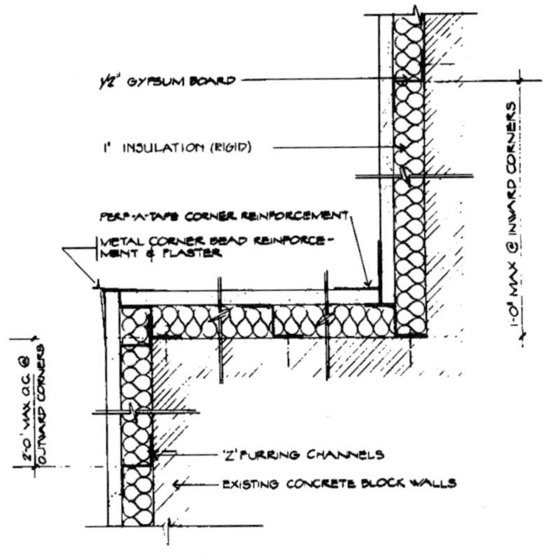

1 OUTWARD & INWARD CORNER DETAIL (TYPICAL)
SCALE: 1/2" = 1'-0"

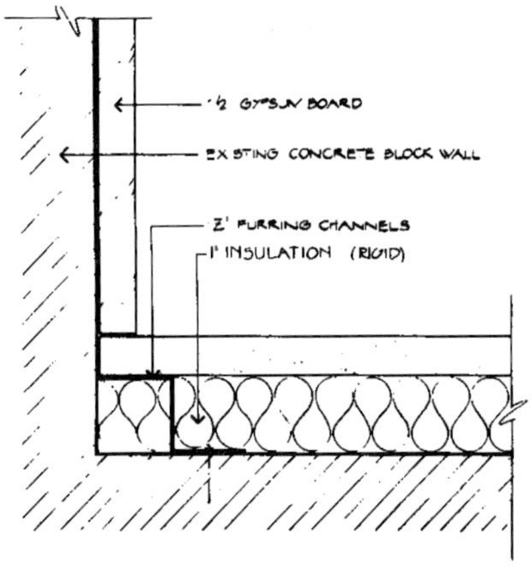

4 FURRING AT INTERIOR CORNERS
FULL SCALE

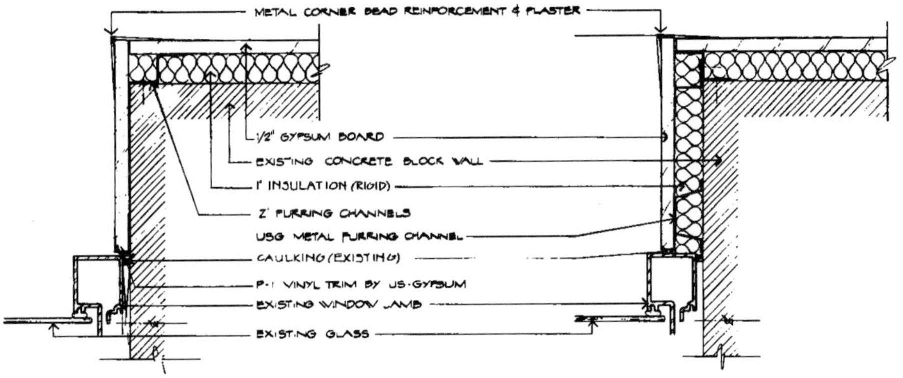

NOTE: THE ABOVE DETAILS ARE SOLUTIONS FOR THE SAME CONDITION

2 FURRING AT WINDOW JAMB
SCALE: 1/2" = 1'-0"

3 FURRING AT WINDOW JAMB
SCALE: 1/2" = 1'-0"

Metal "Z" furring and gypsum board: exterior walls

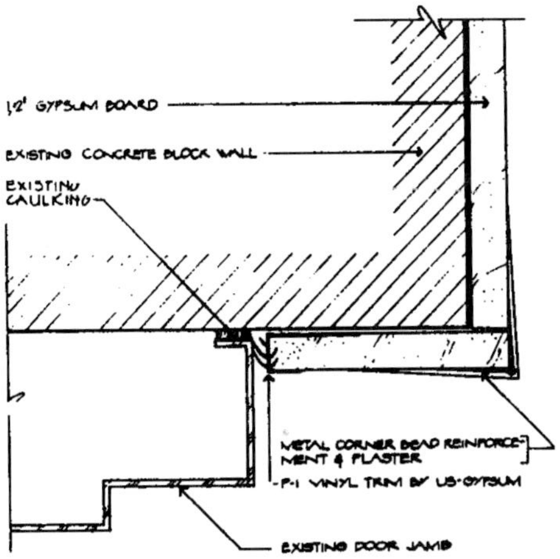

5 FURRING AT DOOR JAMB (TYPICAL @ INTERIOR WALLS)
FULL SCALE

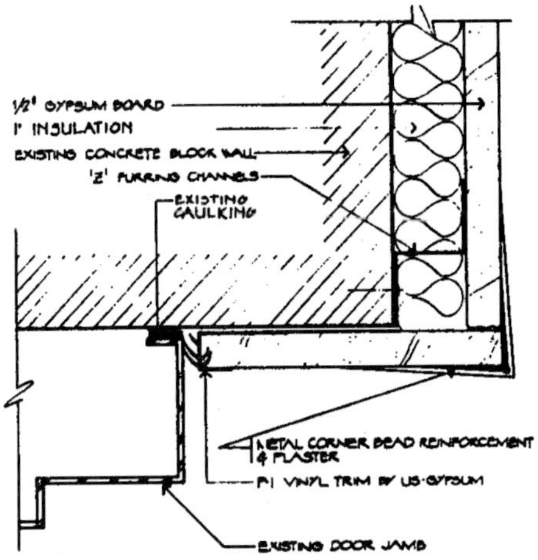

6 FURRING AT DOOR JAMB (TYPICAL @ EXTERIOR WALLS)
FULL SCALE

Metal "Z" furring and gypsum board: door jamb details

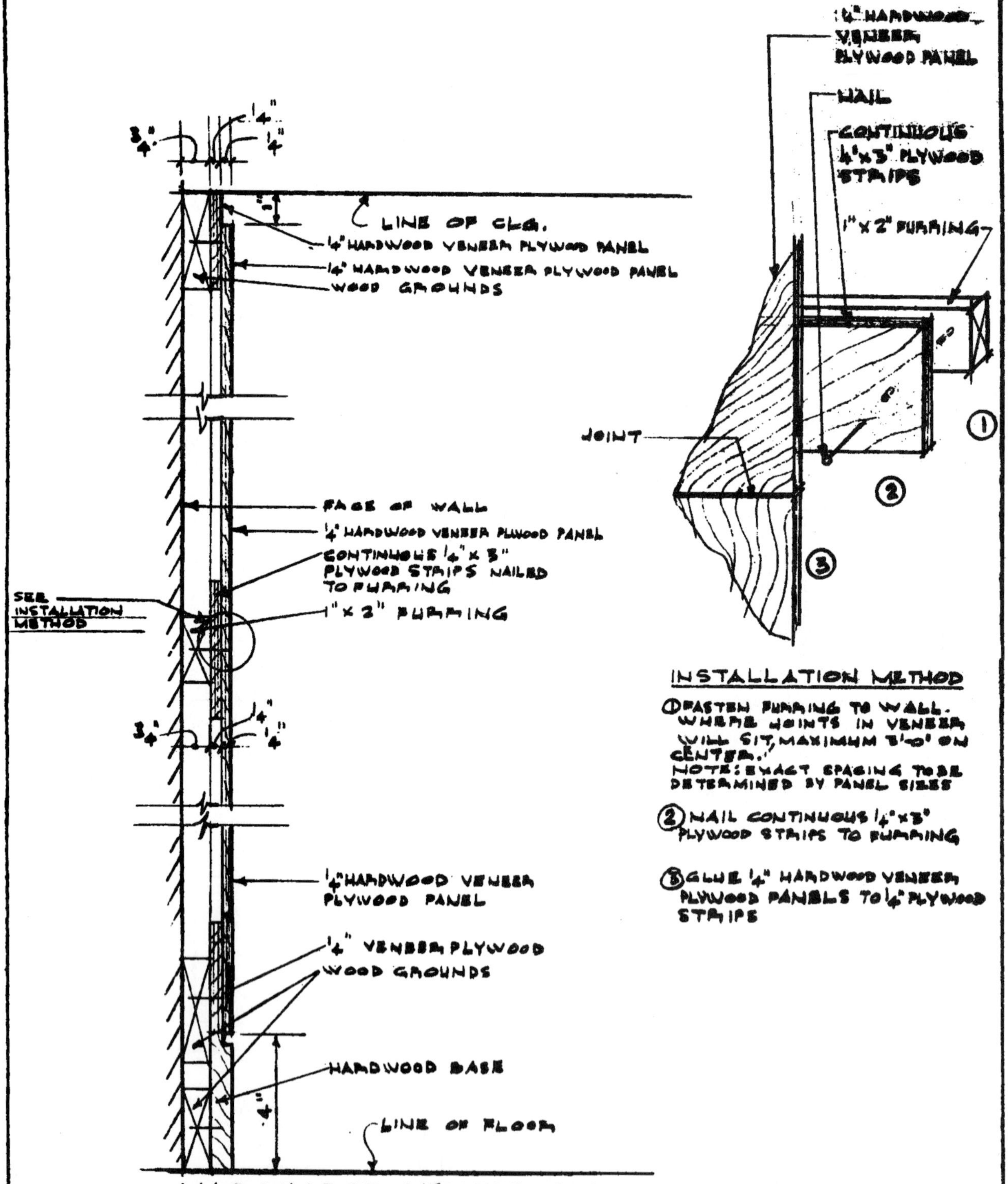
1/4" HARDWOOD VENEER PLYWOOD PANEL
NAIL
CONTINUOUS 1/4"x3" PLYWOOD STRIPS
1"x2" FURRING
JOINT
LINE OF CLG.
1/4" HARDWOOD VENEER PLYWOOD PANEL
1/4" HARDWOOD VENEER PLYWOOD PANEL
WOOD GROUNDS
FACE OF WALL
1/4" HARDWOOD VENEER PLYWOOD PANEL
CONTINUOUS 1/4"x3" PLYWOOD STRIPS NAILED TO FURRING
SEE INSTALLATION METHOD
1"x2" FURRING
1/4" HARDWOOD VENEER PLYWOOD PANEL
1/4" VENEER PLYWOOD
WOOD GROUNDS
HARDWOOD BASE
LINE OF FLOOR
INSTALLATION METHOD
1 FASTEN FURRING TO WALL. WHERE JOINTS IN VENEER WILL SIT, MAXIMUM 3'-0" ON CENTER.
NOTE: EXACT SPACING TO BE DETERMINED BY PANEL SIZES
2 NAIL CONTINUOUS 1/4"x3" PLYWOOD STRIPS TO FURRING
3 GLUE 1/4" HARDWOOD VENEER PLYWOOD PANELS TO 1/4" PLYWOOD STRIPS

HARDWOOD VENEER PLYWOOD PANEL
SCALE: 3"=1'-0"

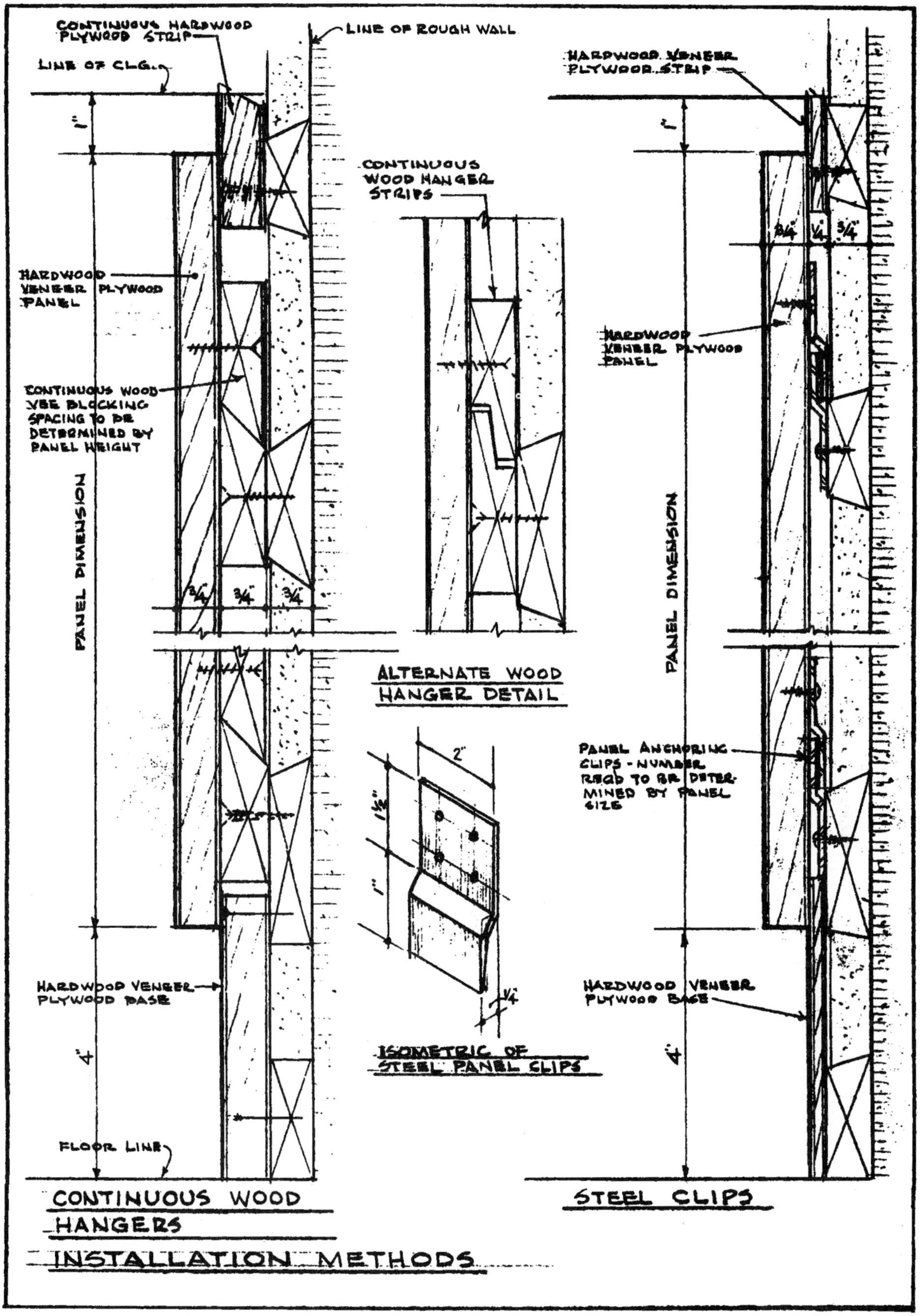
CONTINUOUS HARDWOOD PLYWOOD STRIP
LINE OF ROUGH WALL
LINE OF CLG.
1"
HARDWOOD VENEER PLYWOOD PANEL
CONTINUOUS WOOD VEE BLOCKING SPACING TO BE DETERMINED BY PANEL HEIGHT
PANEL DIMENSION
3/4"
3/4"
3/4"
HARDWOOD VENEER PLYWOOD BASE
4"
FLOOR LINE
CONTINUOUS WOOD HANGERS
CONTINUOUS WOOD HANGER STRIPS
ALTERNATE WOOD HANGER DETAIL
2"
1 1/4"
1"
1/4"
ISOMETRIC OF STEEL PANEL CLIPS
HARDWOOD VENEER PLYWOOD STRIP
1"
3/4"
1/4"
3/4"
HARDWOOD VENEER PLYWOOD PANEL
PANEL DIMENSION
PANEL ANCHORING CLIPS - NUMBER REQD TO BE DETERMINED BY PANEL SIZE
HARDWOOD VENEER PLYWOOD BASE
4"
STEEL CLIPS
INSTALLATION METHODS

PARTITIONS AND WALL FINISHES

Wood Wall Paneling Details and Conditions

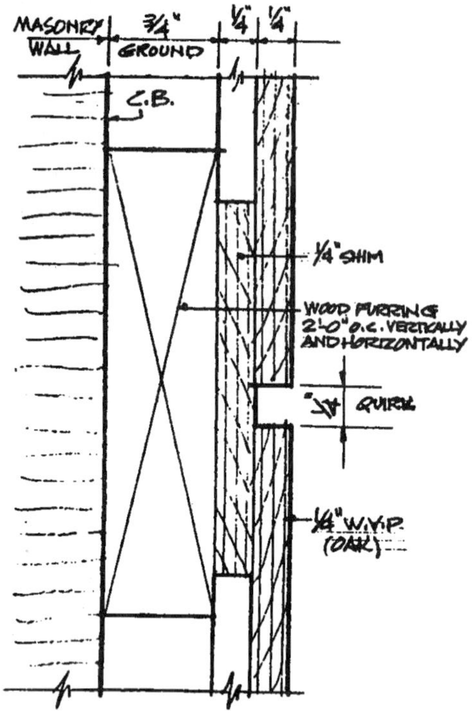

2A TYPICAL JOINT FOR W.V.P. WALLS

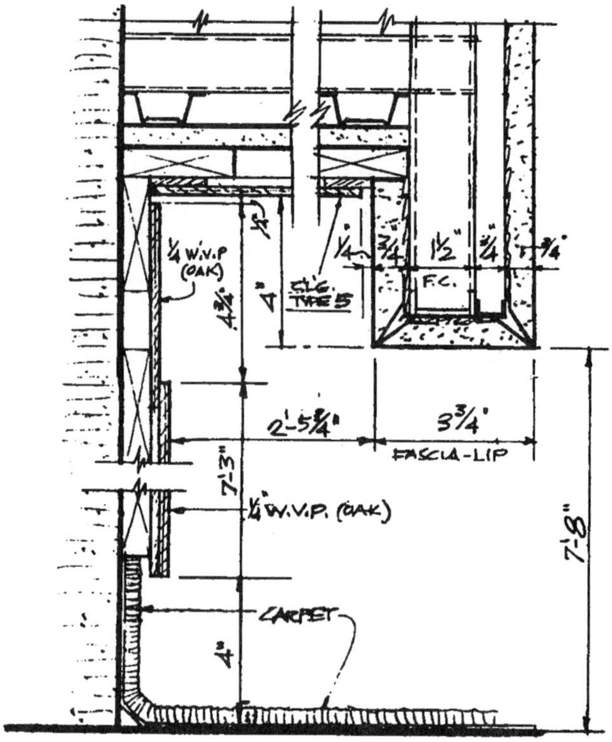

2B (TYPE 5) WALL/CEILING/FASCIA INTERSECTIONS IN SANTURRY/FOYER

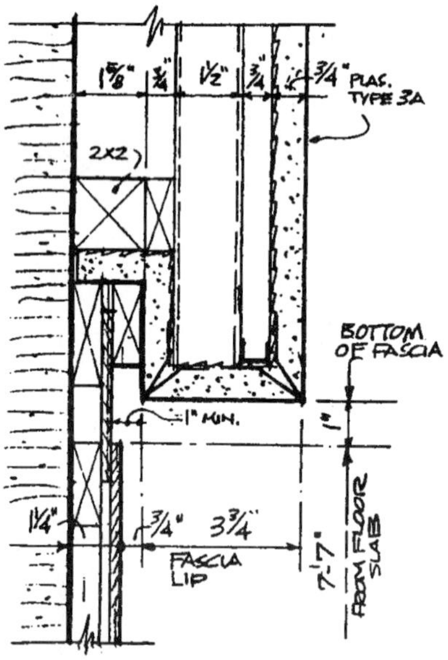

2C WALL/FASCIA INTERSECTION (WITH NO SOFFIT)

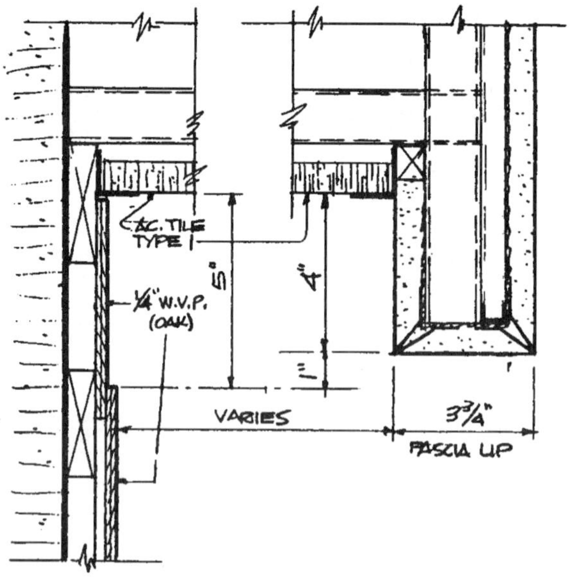

2D (TYPE 1) W.V.P. WALL / AC. TILE CEILING/ FASCIA INTERSECTIONS

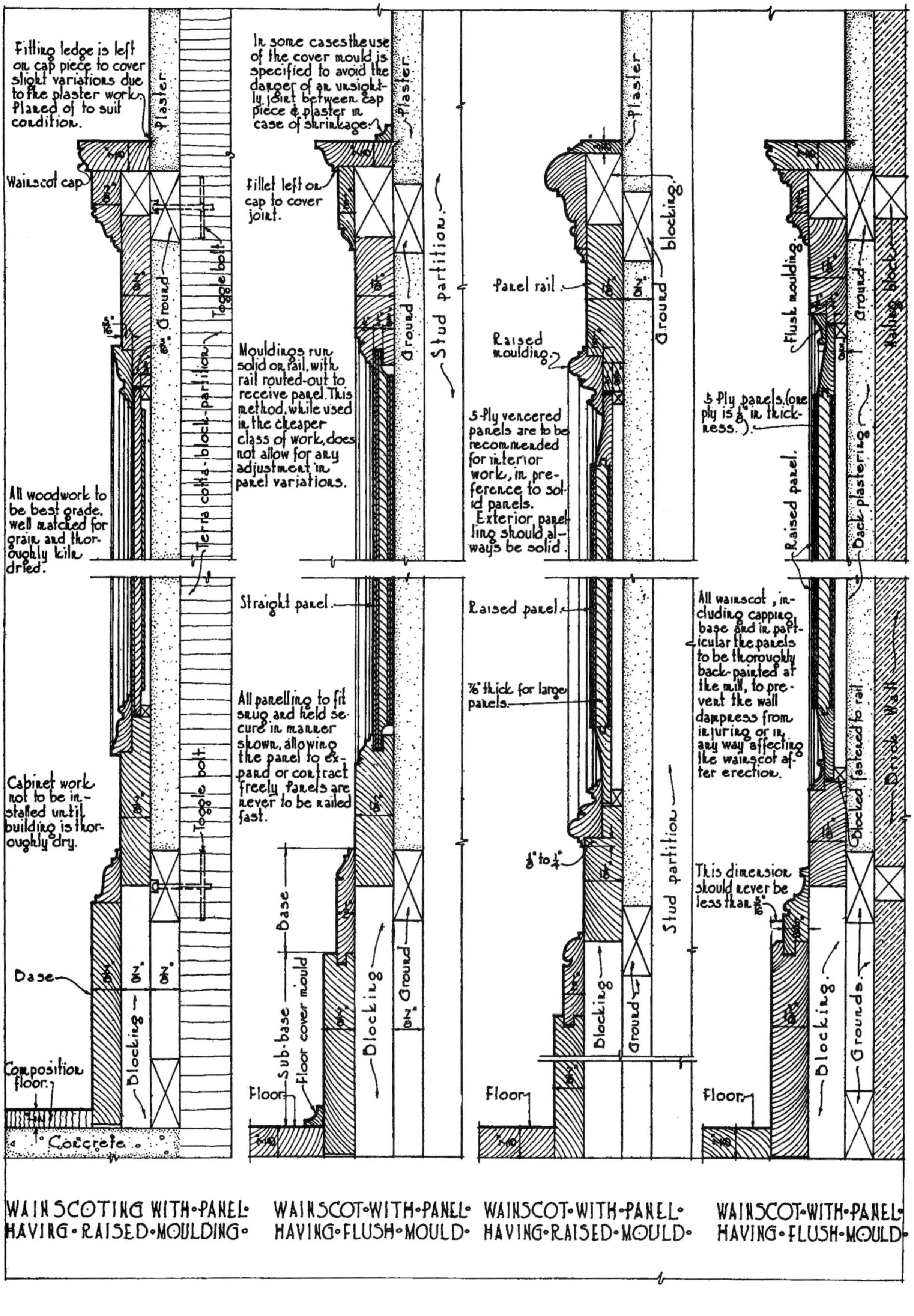
Fitting ledge is left on cap piece to cover slight variations due to the plaster work. Planed of to suit condition.
Plaster
Wainscot cap
Ground
Toggle bolt
Terra cotta-block-partition
All woodwork to be best grade, well matched for grain and thoroughly kiln dried.
Cabinet work not to be installed until building is thoroughly dry.
Toggle bolt
Base
Blocking
Composition floor.
Concrete
In some cases the use of the cover mould is specified to avoid the danger of an unsightly joint between cap piece & plaster in case of shrinkage.
Fillet left on cap to cover joint.
Stud partition
Ground
Mouldings run solid on rail, with rail routed-out to receive panel. This method, while used in the cheaper class of work, does not allow for any adjustment in panel variations.
Straight panel
All panelling to fit snug and held secure in manner shown, allowing the panel to expand or contract freely. Panels are never to be nailed fast.
Base
Sub-base
Floor cover mould
Floor
Blocking
Ground
Panel rail
Raised moulding
5-Ply veneered panels are to be recommended for interior work, in preference to solid panels. Exterior panelling should always be solid.
blocking
Ground
Raised panel
7/8" thick for large panels.
1/8" to 1/4"
Stud partition
Blocking
Ground
Floor
Flush moulding
Ground
Nailing block
5 Ply panels (one ply is 1/8" in thickness.)
Raised panel
Back plastering
All wainscot, including capping base and in particular the panels to be thoroughly back-painted at the mill, to prevent the wall dampness from injuring or in any way affecting the wainscot after erection.
Blocked fastened to rail
Brick Wall
This dimension should never be less than 5/8"
Blocking
Grounds
Floor
WAINSCOTING WITH PANEL HAVING RAISED MOULDING
WAINSCOT WITH PANEL HAVING FLUSH MOULD
WAINSCOT WITH PANEL HAVING RAISED MOULD
WAINSCOT WITH PANEL HAVING FLUSH MOULD

PARTITIONS AND WALL FINISHES

Wall Paneling Elevation

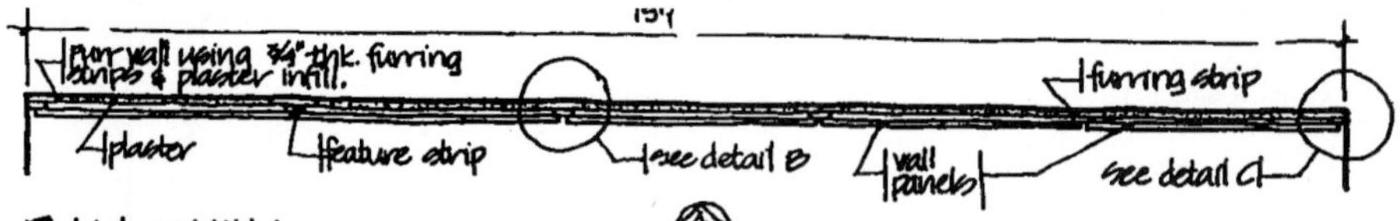

PLAN OF WALL
SCALE 1/2"=1'-0"

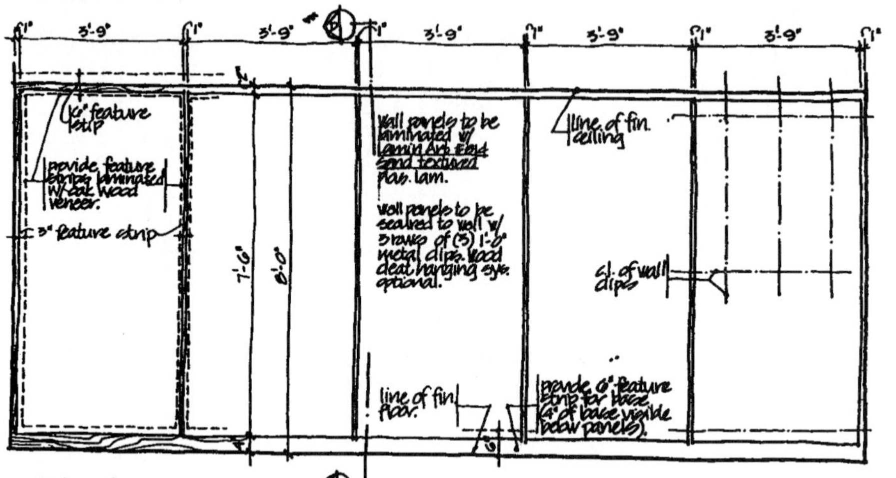

WALL ELEVATION A
SCALE 1/2"=1'-0"

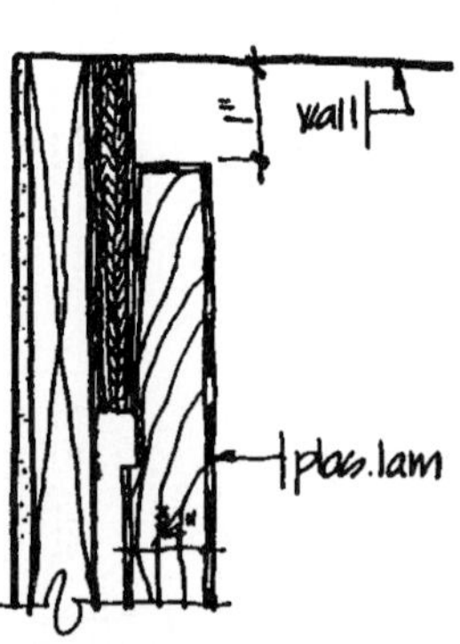

CORNER DETAIL C
1/2 FULL SCALE

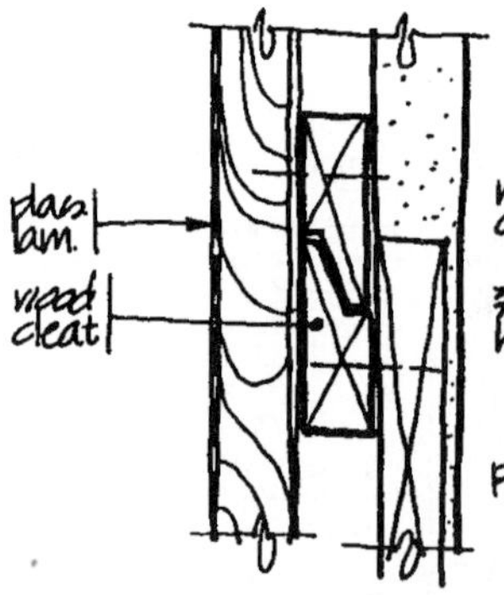

DETAIL/OPTIONAL WOOD CLEAT HANGING SYS.
1/2 FULL SCALE

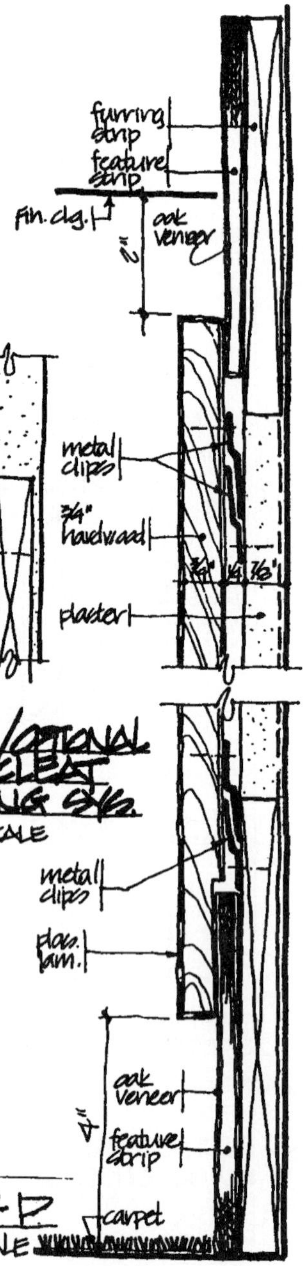

SECTION D-D
SCALE: 1/2 FULL SCALE

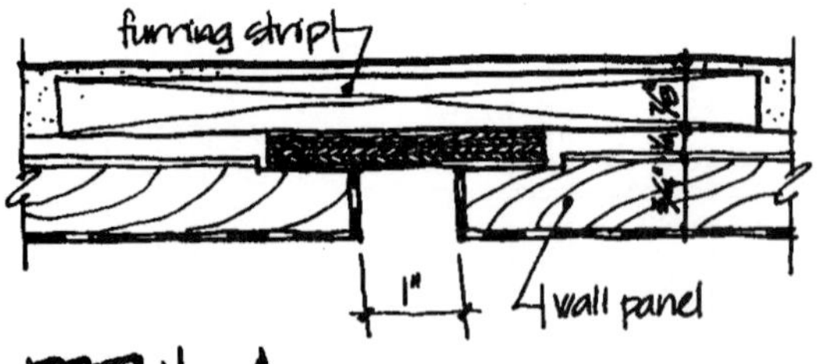

DETAIL A
1/2 FULL SCALE

Wood Studs or Furring

Cement Mortar

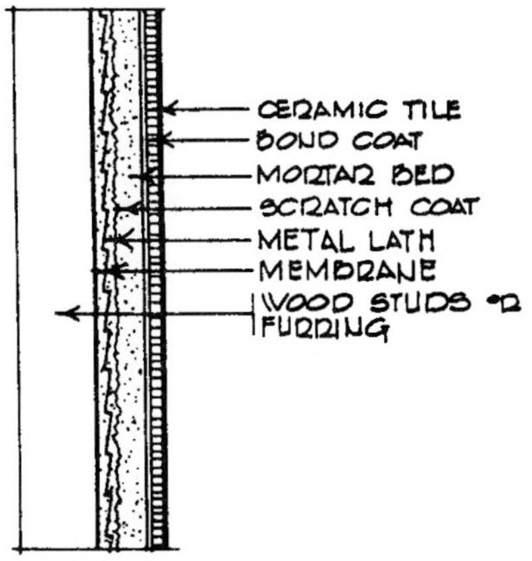

Recommended uses

- over dry, well-braced wood studs or furring
- preferred method of installation over wood studs in showers and tub enclosures

Metal Studs

Cement Mortar

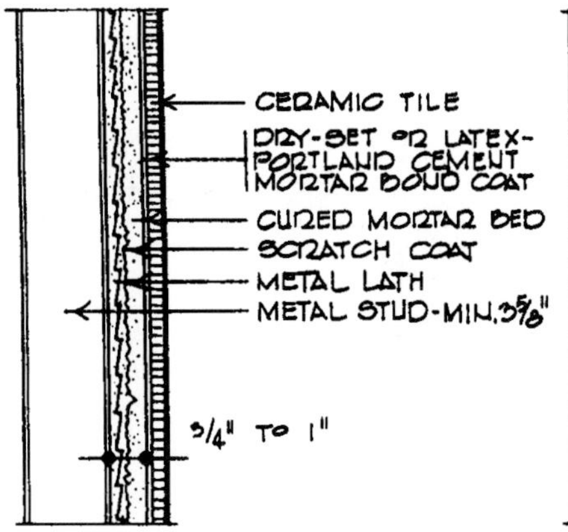

Recommended use

- over metal studs

Gypsum Board
Organic Adhesive

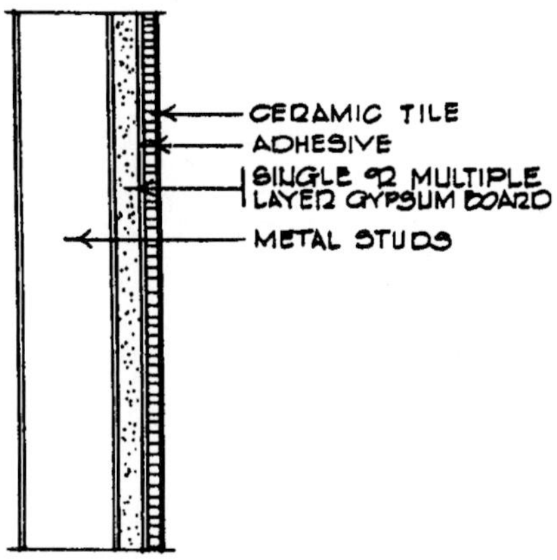

Recommended uses

- over gypsum board screwed to metal studs, single or double layer installed in accordance with GA-216
- where a gypsum board, non-load-bearing partition is desired with durable, low-maintenance finish
- for fire-resistant, sound-insulated, ceramic-tiled walls (fire-resistance and sound-insulation ratings calculated on partitions before tiling)
- for dry areas in schools, institutions, and commercial buildings

Wood or Metal Studs

Gypsum Board
Dry-Set Mortar or Latex Portland Cement Mortar

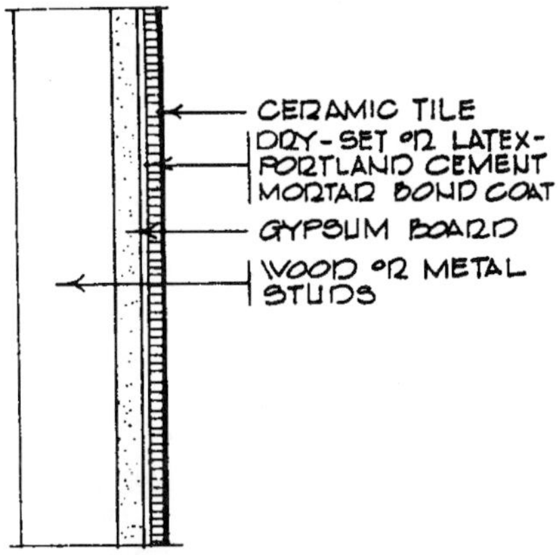

Recommended uses

- dry interiors over gypsum wall board
- for dry areas in schools, institutions, and commercial buildings

Glass Mesh Mortar Unit

Dry-Set Mortar or Latex Portland Cement Mortar

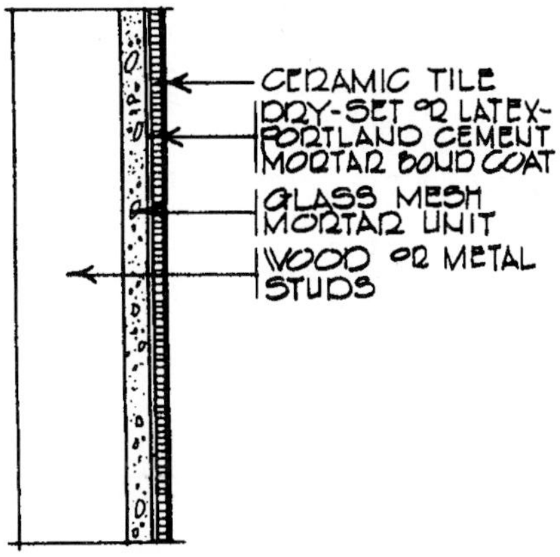

Recommended uses

- in wet areas
- over dry, well-braced wood studs or furring
- over well-braced metal studs

PARTITIONS AND WALL FINISHES
Ceramic Tile Wall Finishes

Masonry

Cement Mortar

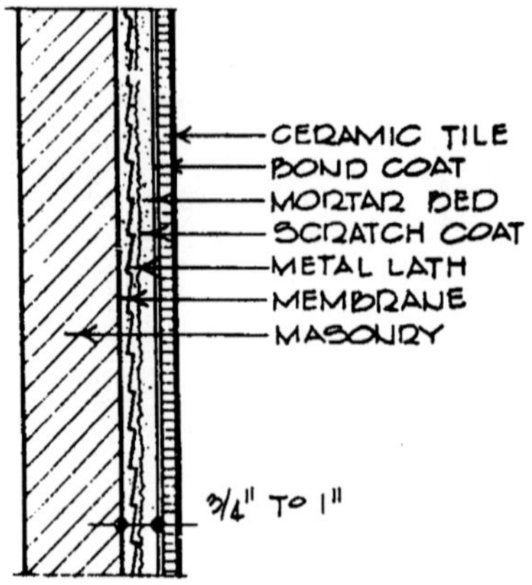

Recommended use
- over masonry or concrete on exteriors

Dry-Set Mortar or Latex-Portland Cement Mortar

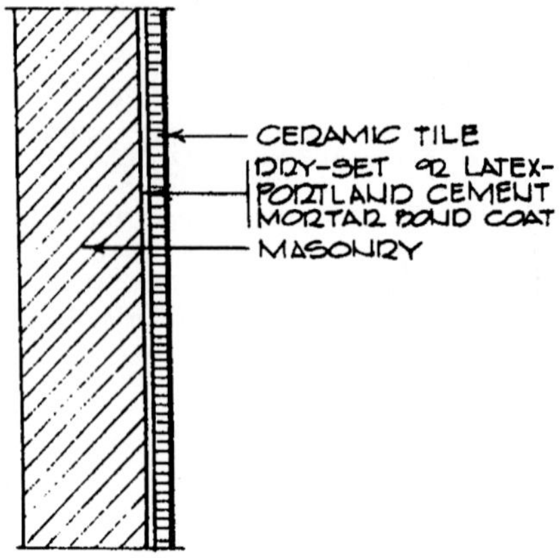

Recommended use
- over clean, sound, dimensionally stable masonry or concrete

Masonry or Concrete

Cement Mortar Bonded

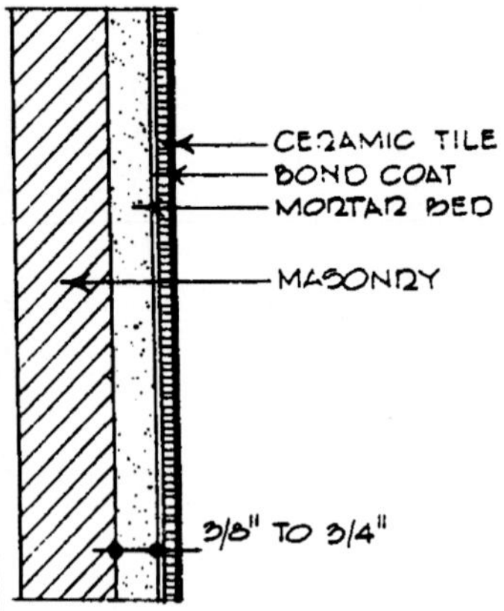

Recommended use
- over clean sound, dimensionally stable masonry or concrete

Cement Mortar

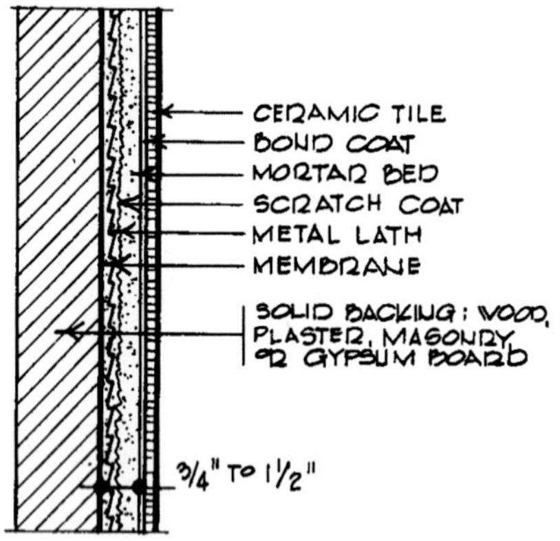

Recommended uses
- over masonry, plaster, or other solid backing that provides firm anchorage for metal lath
- ideal for remodeling or on surfaces that present bonding problems

One Coat Method

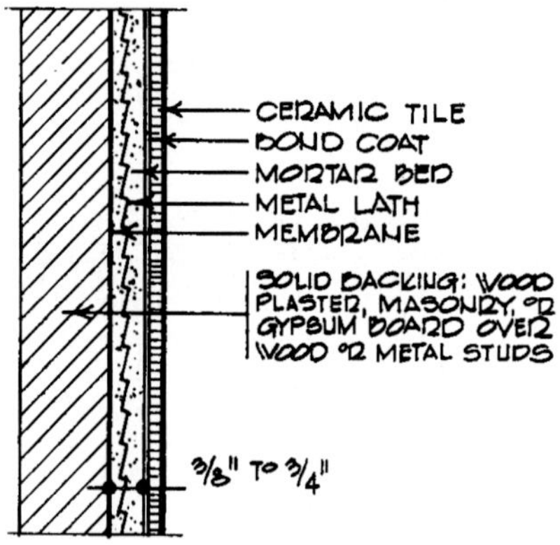

Recommended uses
- over masonry, plaster, or other solid backing that provides firm anchorage for metal lath
- ideal for remodeling or on surfaces that present bonding problems
- ideal for remodeling where space limitations exist
- preferred method of applying tile over gypsum plaster or gypsum board in showers and tub enclosures

Solid Backing

Organic Adhesive

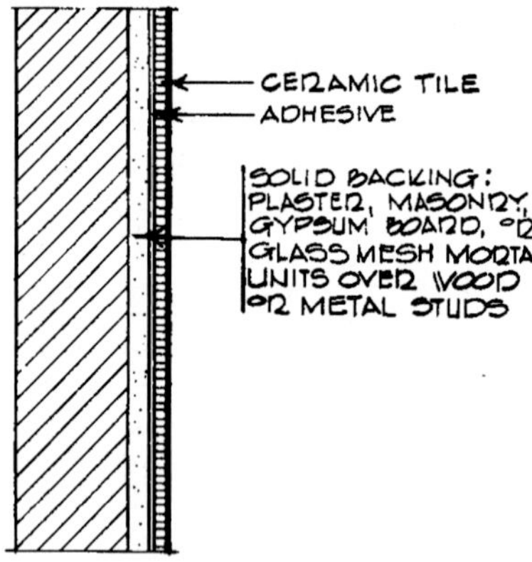

Recommended use
- interiors over gypsum board, plaster, dimensionally stable masonry, or other smooth surfaces

PARTITIONS AND WALL FINISHES
Ceramic Tile Wall Finishes

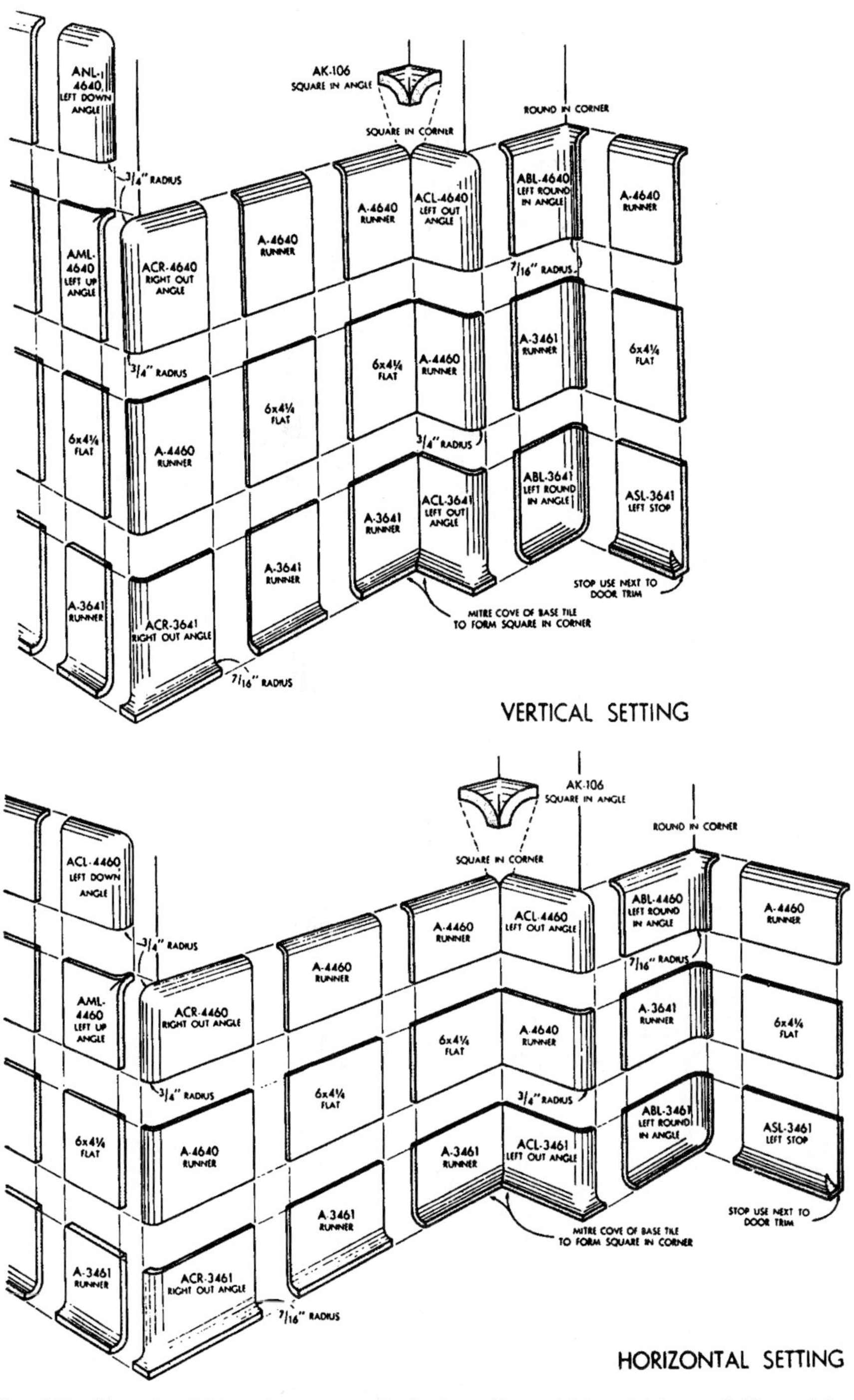

Fig. 17 Standard trim shapes and designations (6 by 4¼ in wall tile set in conventional mortar bed)

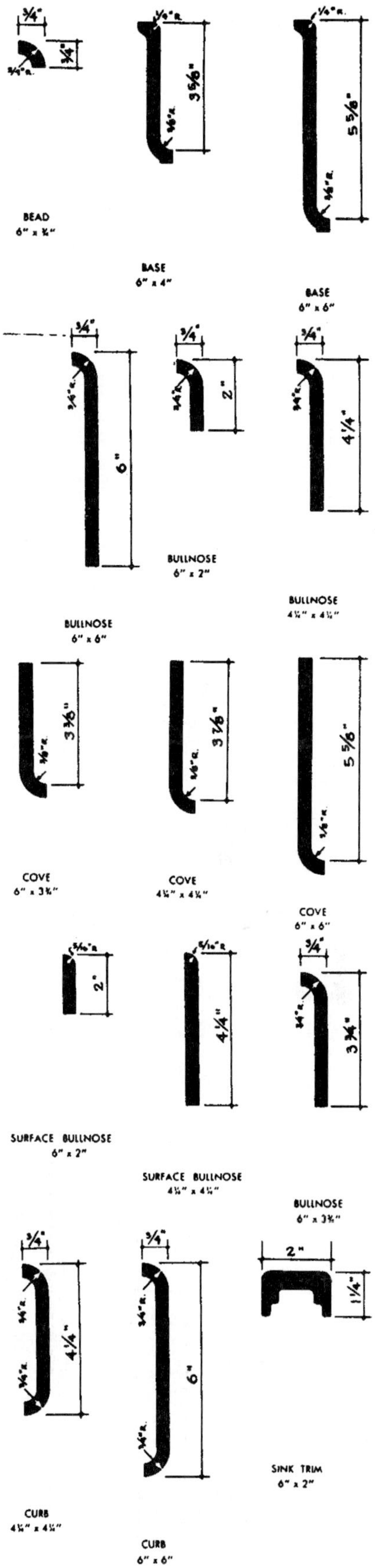

Fig. 18 Standard trim shapes and sizes

PARTITIONS AND WALL FINISHES

Marble Veneer Wall Finishes

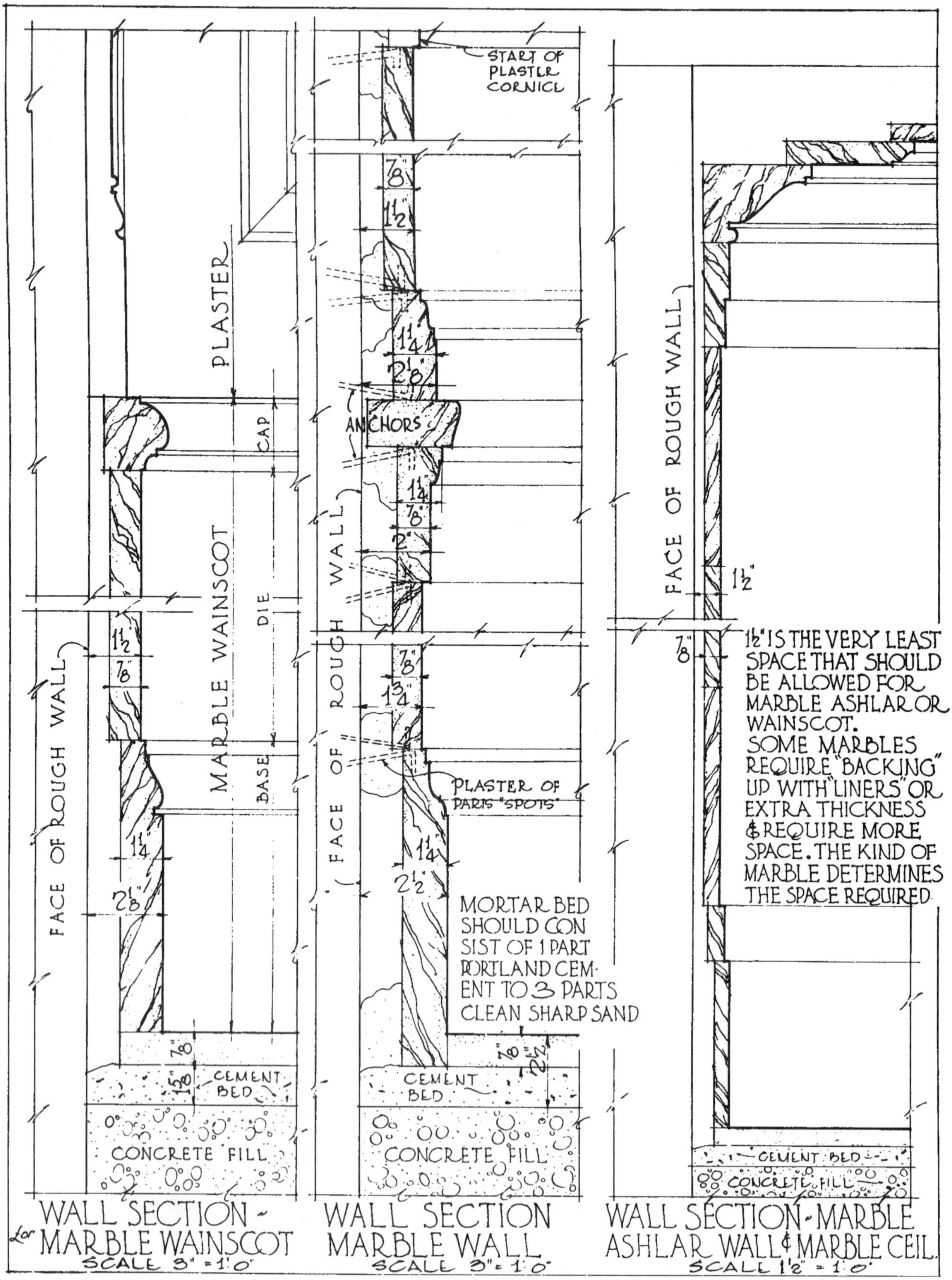

Fig. 19 Marble treatment for walls and wainscots

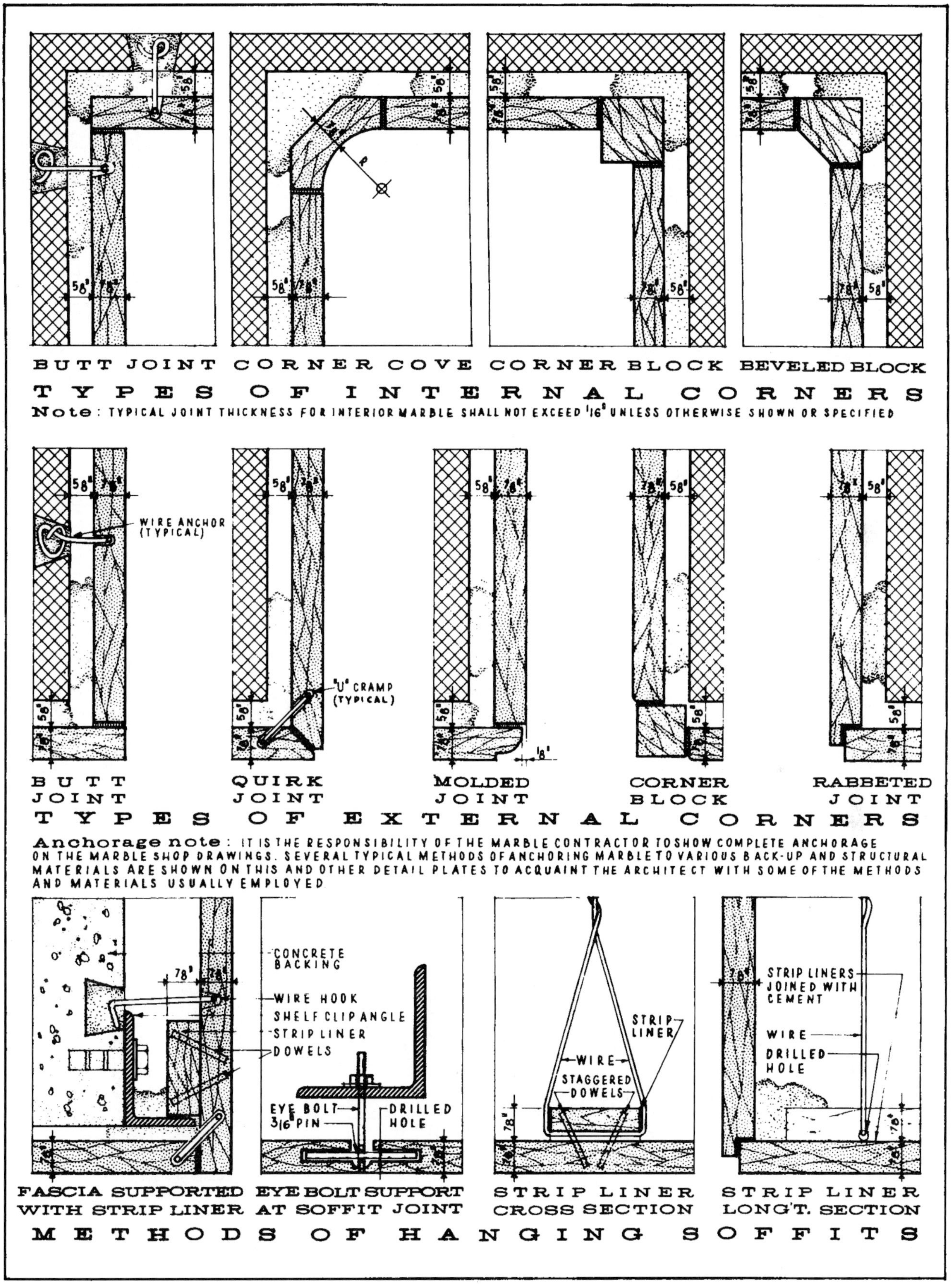
BUTT JOINT
CORNER COVE
CORNER BLOCK
BEVELED BLOCK
TYPES OF INTERNAL CORNERS
Note: TYPICAL JOINT THICKNESS FOR INTERIOR MARBLE SHALL NOT EXCEED 1/16" UNLESS OTHERWISE SHOWN OR SPECIFIED
WIRE ANCHOR (TYPICAL)
"U" CRAMP (TYPICAL)
BUTT JOINT
QUIRK JOINT
MOLDED JOINT
CORNER BLOCK
RABBETED JOINT
TYPES OF EXTERNAL CORNERS
Anchorage note: IT IS THE RESPONSIBILITY OF THE MARBLE CONTRACTOR TO SHOW COMPLETE ANCHORAGE ON THE MARBLE SHOP DRAWINGS. SEVERAL TYPICAL METHODS OF ANCHORING MARBLE TO VARIOUS BACK-UP AND STRUCTURAL MATERIALS ARE SHOWN ON THIS AND OTHER DETAIL PLATES TO ACQUAINT THE ARCHITECT WITH SOME OF THE METHODS AND MATERIALS USUALLY EMPLOYED
CONCRETE BACKING
WIRE HOOK
SHELF CLIP ANGLE
STRIP LINER
DOWELS
EYE BOLT
3/16" PIN
DRILLED HOLE
STRIP LINER
WIRE
STAGGERED DOWELS
STRIP LINERS JOINED WITH CEMENT
WIRE
DRILLED HOLE
FASCIA SUPPORTED WITH STRIP LINER
EYE BOLT SUPPORT AT SOFFIT JOINT
STRIP LINER CROSS SECTION
STRIP LINER LONG'T. SECTION
METHODS OF HANGING SOFFITS

Fig. 20 Anchorage details

PARTITIONS AND WALL FINISHES
Marble and Travertine Veneer Wall Finishes

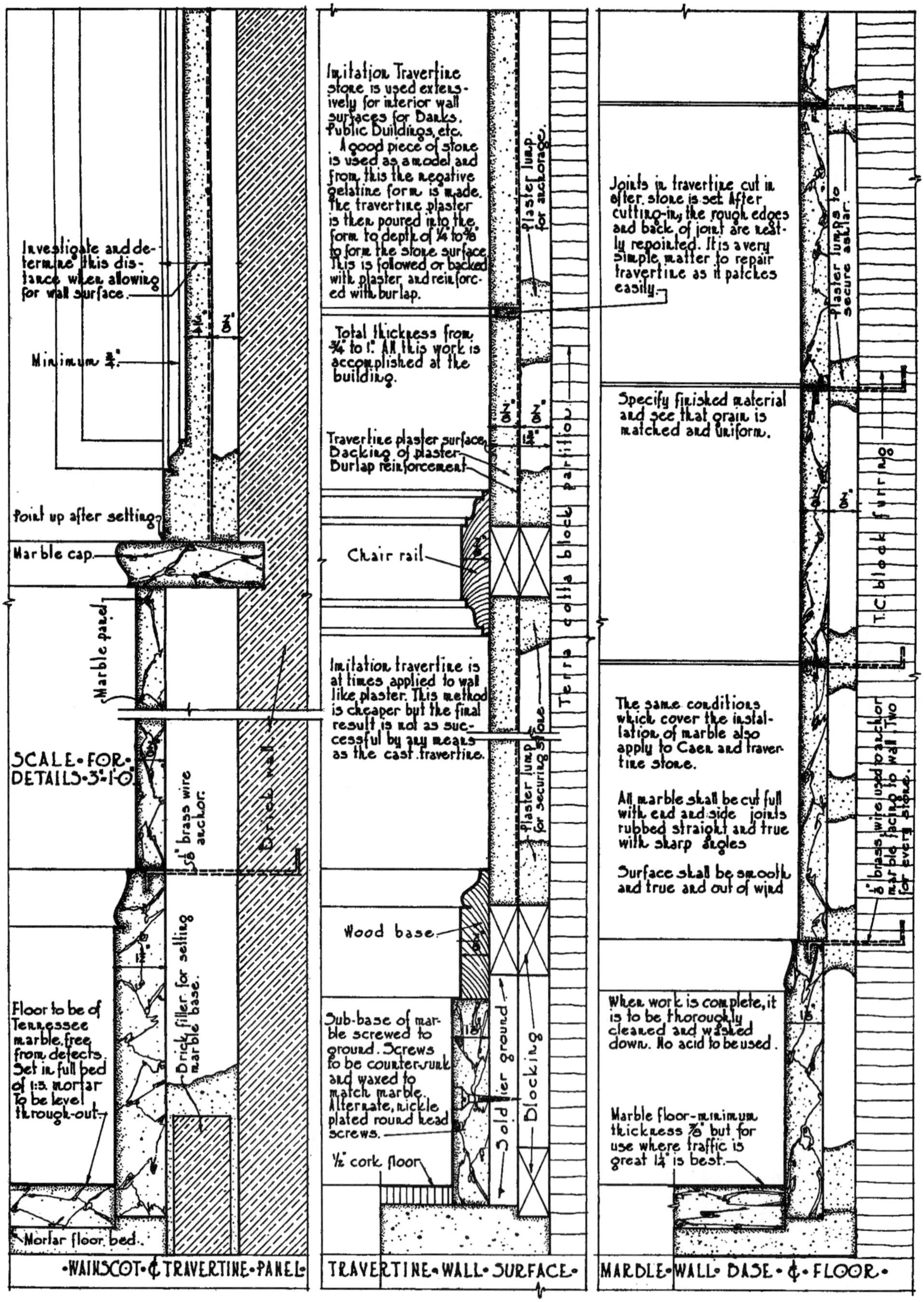
Investigate and determine this distance when allowing for wall surface.
Minimum ¾"
Point up after setting
Marble cap
Marble panel
SCALE•FOR•DETAILS•3"-1'-0"
⅝" brass wire anchor.
Brick wall
Brick filler for setting marble base.
Floor to be of Tennessee marble, free from defects. Set in full bed of 1:3 mortar To be level through-out.
Mortar floor bed.
•WAINSCOT•& TRAVERTINE•PANEL•
Imitation Travertine stone is used extensively for interior wall surfaces for Banks, Public Buildings, etc.
A good piece of stone is used as a model and from this the negative gelatine form is made. The travertine plaster is then poured into the form to depth of ¼ to ⅜ to form the stone surface. This is followed or backed with plaster and reinforced with burlap.
Total thickness from ¾" to 1". All this work is accomplished at the building.
Travertine plaster surface
Backing of plaster
Burlap reinforcement
Chair rail
Imitation travertine is at times applied to wall like plaster. This method is cheaper but the final result is not as successful by any means as the cast travertine.
Wood base
Sub-base of marble screwed to ground. Screws to be counter-sunk and waxed to match marble. Alternate, nickle plated round head screws.
½" cork floor
Plaster lump for anchorage.
Plaster lump for securing stone
Terra cotta block partition
Soldier ground
Blocking
TRAVERTINE•WALL•SURFACE•
Joints in travertine cut in after stone is set. After cutting-in, the rough edges and back of joint are neatly repointed. It is a very simple matter to repair travertine as it patches easily.
Specify finished material and see that grain is matched and uniform.
The same conditions which cover the installation of marble also apply to Caen and travertine stone.
All marble shall be cut full with end and side joints rubbed straight and true with sharp angles
Surface shall be smooth and true and out of wind
When work is complete, it is to be thoroughly cleaned and washed down. No acid to be used.
Marble floor-minimum thickness ⅞" but for use where traffic is great 1¼" is best.
Plaster lumps to secure ashlar.
T.C. block furring
⅛" brass wire used to anchor marble facing to wall Two for every stone.
MARBLE•WALL•BASE•&•FLOOR•

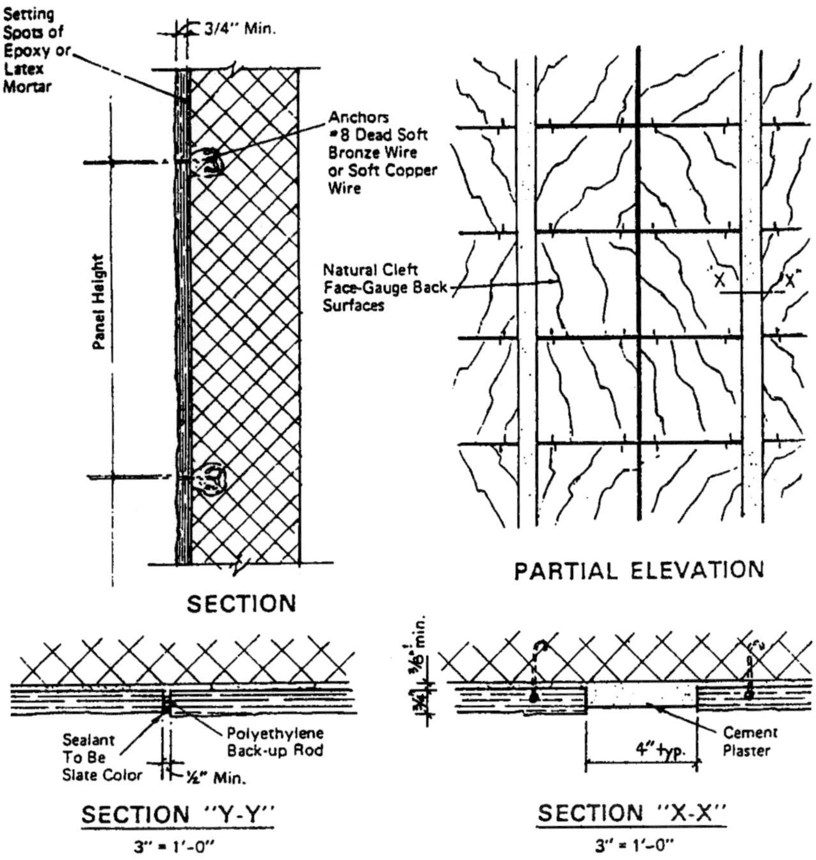

Fig. 21 Slate panel veneer

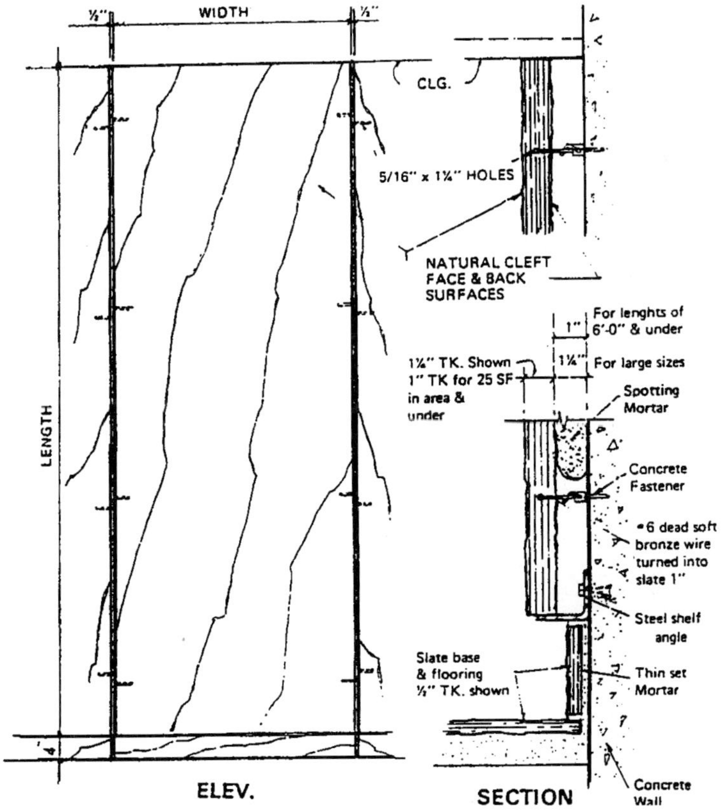

Fig. 22 Slate panels applied to concrete wall

PARTITIONS AND WALL FINISHES

Reception and Pass-Through Windows

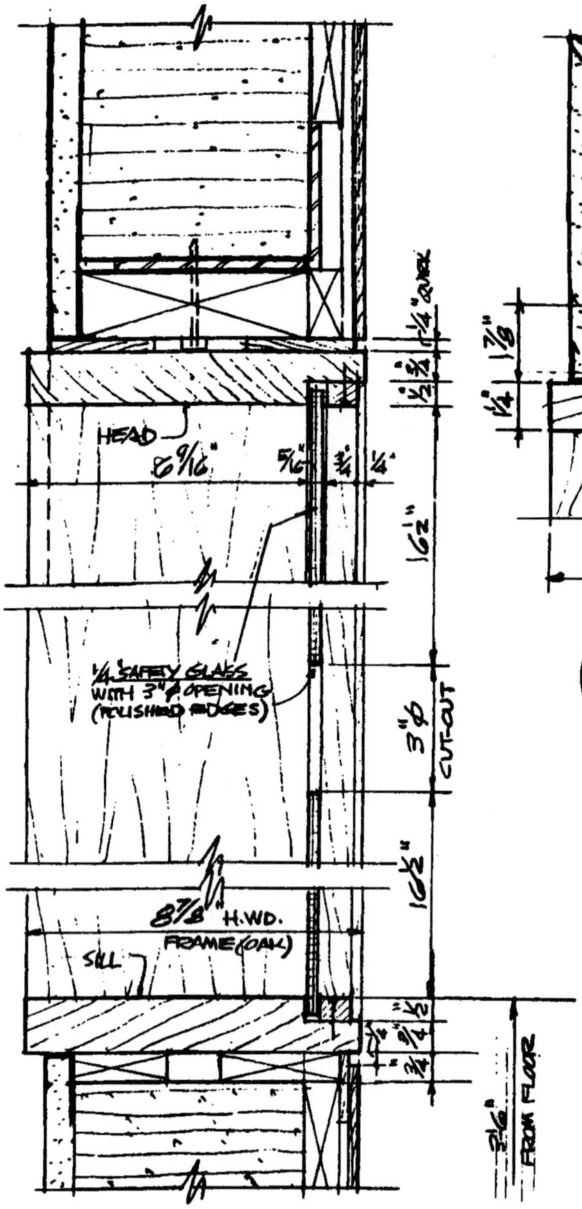

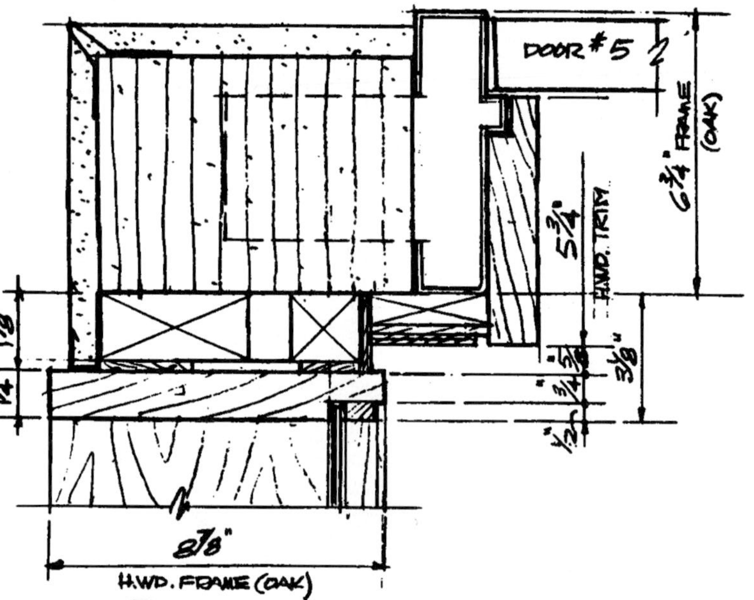

2A JAMB DETAIL AT INTERSECTION-CORNER AT DOOR #5

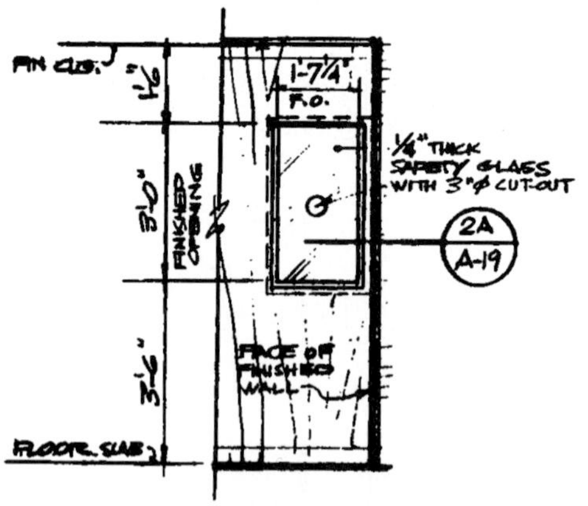

ELEVATION OF LOBBY CONTROL WINDOW

2 VERTICAL SECTION THRU LOBBY CONTROL WINDOW

No. of Block for 100 Sq. Ft. Panel

Block Sizes (Nominal)	6″	8″	12″	4″x 8″	6″x 8″
No. of Block	400	225	100	450	300

Cu. Ft. of Mortar* for 100 Sq. Ft. Panel

Block Sizes (Nominal)	6″	8″	12″	4″x 8″	6″x 8″
Premiere Series Glass Block (3⅞″)	5.4	4.0	2.7	6.1	4.7
VISTABRIK® Solid Glass Block (3″)	—	2.3**	—	—	—
Thinline™ Series Glass Block (3⅛″)	4.3	3.3	—	4.9	3.8

*Based on a ¼″ exposed mortar joint.
**Based on a ⅜″ exposed mortar joint.

Glossary of Terms (Detail Drawings pages 12-17)

BLDG - Building
CMU - Concrete Masonry Unit (concrete block)
CONT STL - Continuous Steel (used to reinforce wall)
ELEV - Elevation (view of side of building)
GYP SD - Gypsum Board
HM - Hollow Metal (door frame)
INT - Interior
MAX HT - Maximum Height (for Pittsburgh Corning Glass Block panel 20′/6m)
SILL - Bottom of Panel
TYP - Typical (detail)
CLG - Ceiling
CONC - Concrete
EIFS - Exterior Insulation Finishing System
EXT - Exterior
HEAD - Top of Panel
HORIZ - Horizontal
JAMB - Side of Panel
PLAN - View of building from above, typically the floor
STL - Steel
WD - Wood

Materials shown other than glass block are for illustration purpose *only* as examples of typical construction details.

Inside Radius Minimums for Curved Panel Construction

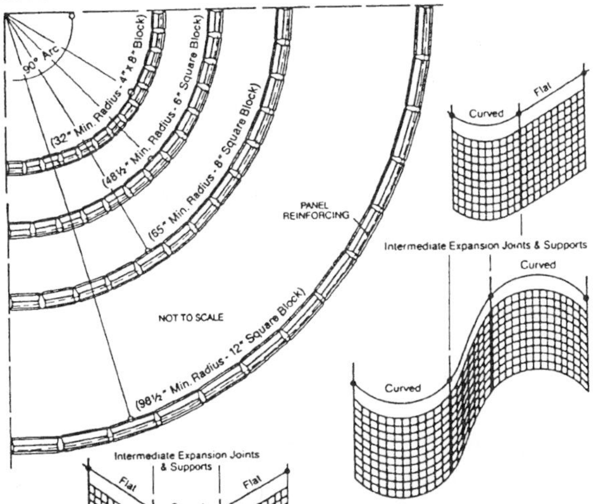

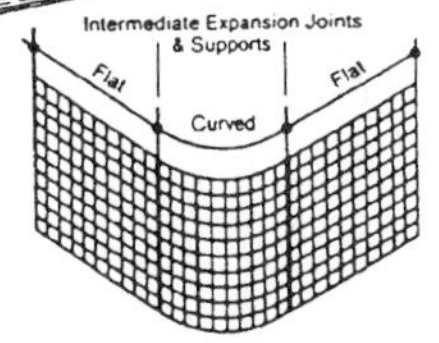

NOTES:
1. It is suggested that curved areas be separated from flat areas by intermediate expansion joints and supports, as indicated in these drawings.
2. When straight, ladder-type reinforcing is used on curved walls, the innermost parallel wire may be cut periodically and bent to accommodate the curvature of the wall.

Radius Minimums for Curved Panel Construction

Block Size	Inside Radius, Inches	Number of Blocks in 90° Arc	Joint Thickness In Inches	
			Inside	Outside
4″x 8″	32	13	⅛	⅝
6″x 6″	48½	13	⅛	⅝
8″x 8″	65	13	⅛	⅝
12″x 12″	98½	13	⅛	⅝

EndBlock™ Finishing Unit		HEDRON® Corner Unit		TRIDRON 45° Block® Unit	ENCURVE® Finishing Unit	ARQUE™ Block Unit
DECORA® Pattern 8″ High 6 lbs 2.72 (kg) *Premiere Series*	**DECORA® Pattern Thinline™ Series** 8″ High 2.8 lbs 1.26 (kg) Thinline™ Series Only	**DECORA® Pattern** 6″ High 4.3 lbs 1.95 (kg) *Premiere Series*	**DECORA® Pattern** 8″ High 6 lbs 2.72 (kg)	**DECORA® Pattern** 8″ High 2.9 lbs 1.28 (kg) *Premiere Series*	**DECORA® Pattern** 8″ High 5.7 lbs 2.57 (kg) *Premiere Series*	**DECORA® Pattern** 8″ High 5.4 lbs. 2.43 (kg) *Premiere Series*

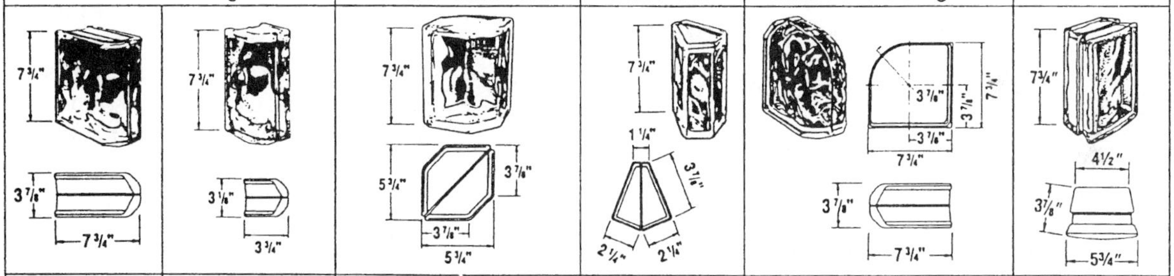

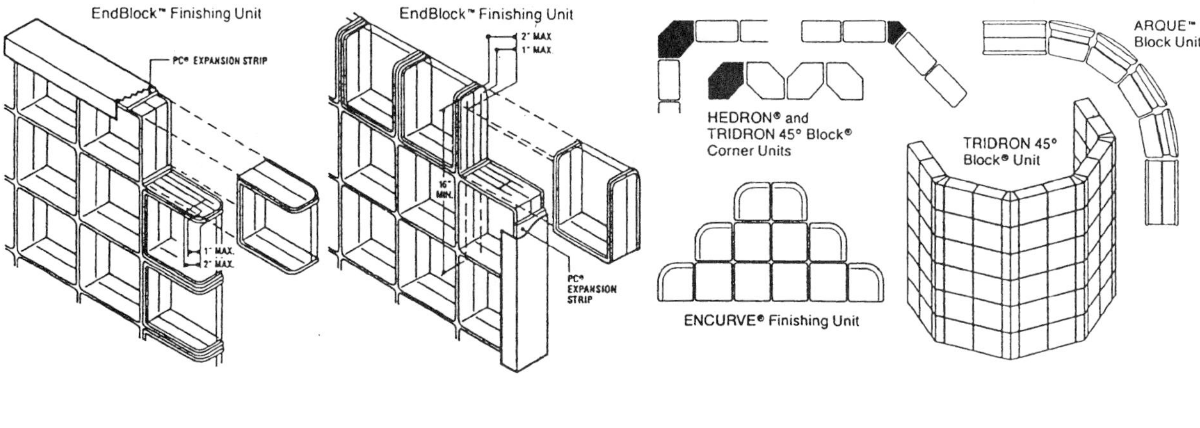

PARTITIONS AND WALL FINISHES

Glass Block Partition Details

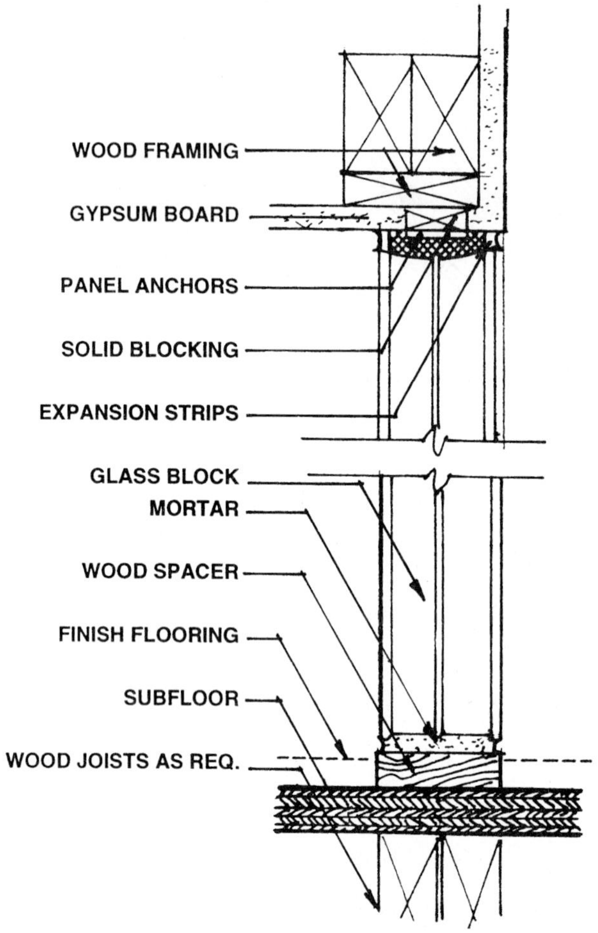

VERTICAL SECTION

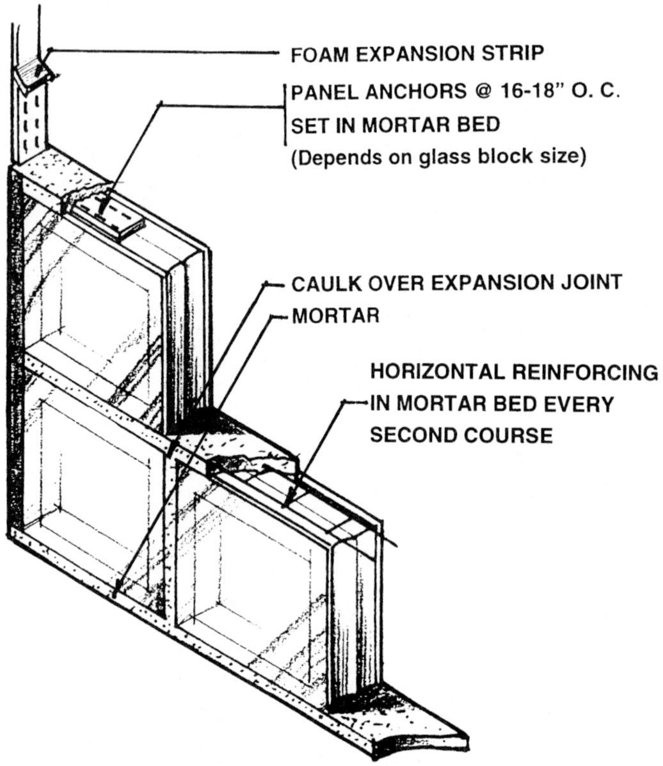

ISOMETRIC OF PANEL ASSEMBLY

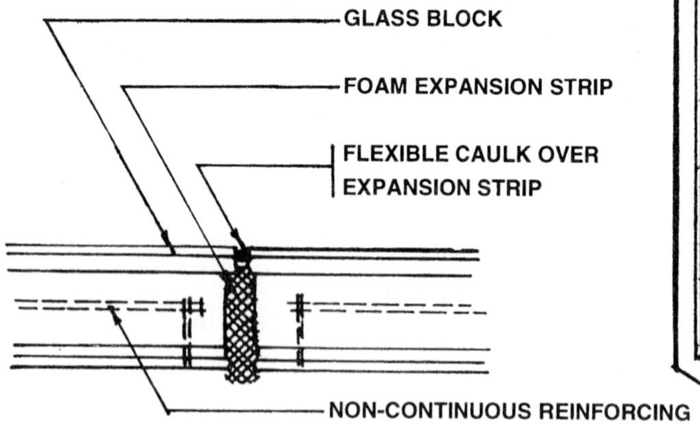

TYPICAL EXPANSION JOINT

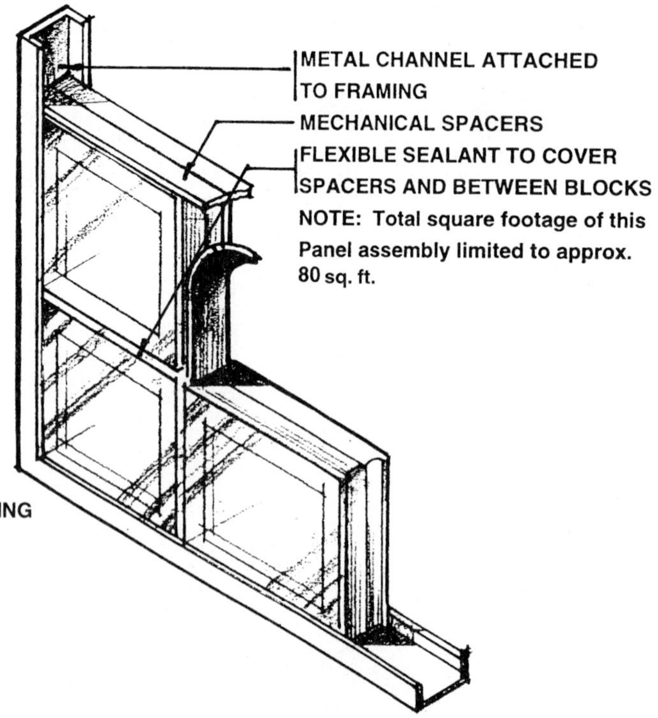

ALT. PANEL ASSEMBLY

Panel Anchor Construction

PC® Panel Anchor
Sealant
Lintel Plate
PC® Expansion Strip
Lintel Plate
Sealant
SEE NOTE
PC® Expansion Strip
PC® Panel Anchor
Pittsburgh Corning Glass Block Unit
NOTE: This dimension is determined by the anticipated deflection of the structural member above the glass block.
Sealant
PC® Expansion Strip
PC® Panel Anchor
1/4" Exp. Bolts Two Per Anchor
PC® Panel Reinforcing
Pittsburgh Corning Glass Block Unit
Mortar
PC® Panel Reinforcing
Mortar
Asphalt Emulsion
Wall framing shown here for illustrative purposes only. Wall framing can be concrete, masonry, wood, steel or any other structural surround.

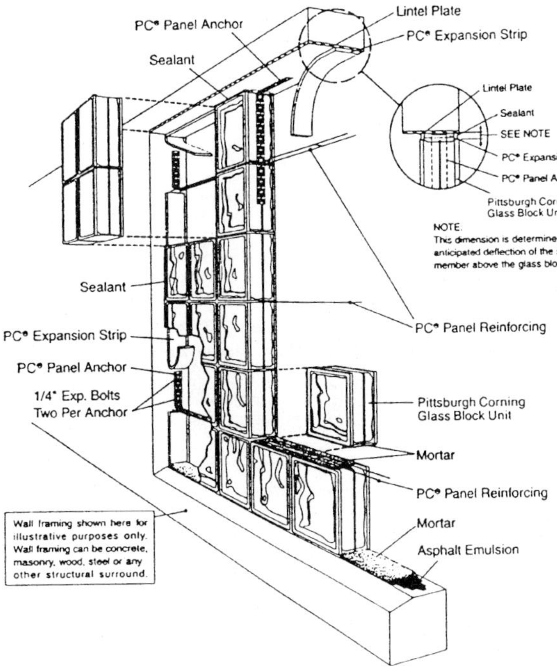

Channel-Type Restraint Construction

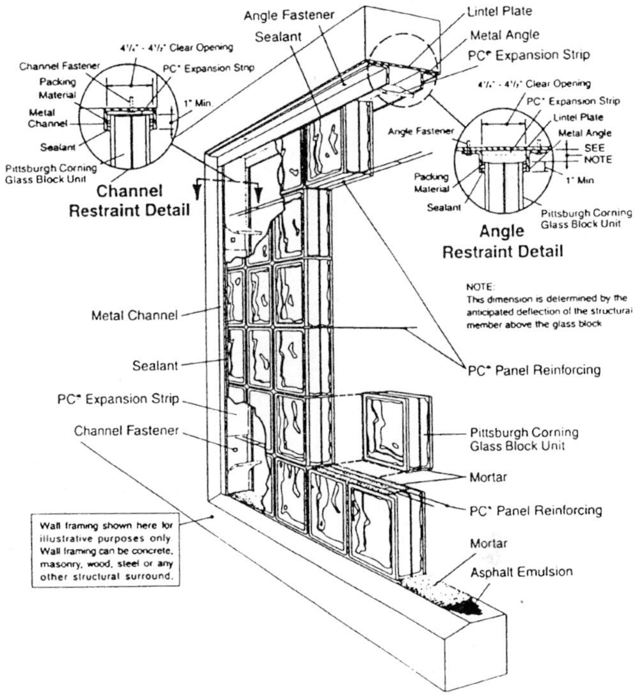

PARTITIONS AND WALL FINISHES
Glass Block Head and Jamb Details

Typical Head Details
Exterior Openings

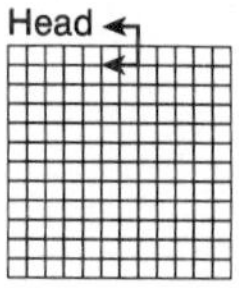

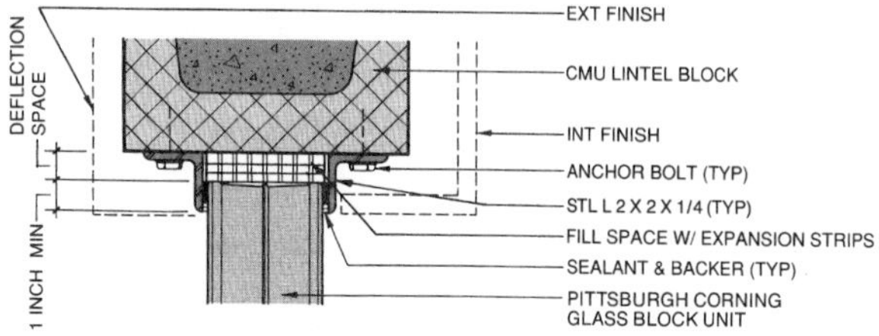

Head - Glass Block in CMU Wall (PCD 004) Fire Rated

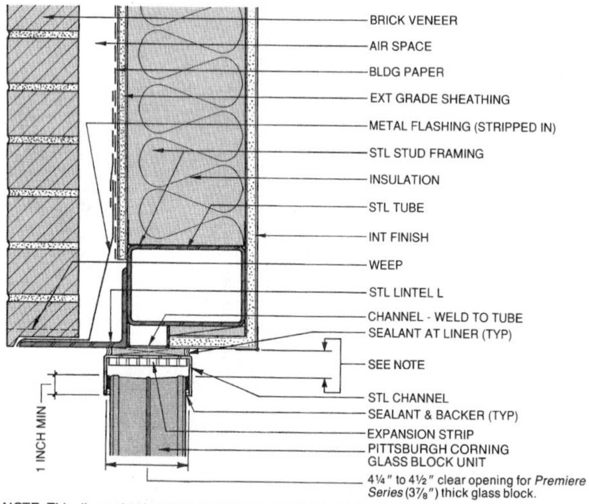

NOTE: This dimension is determined by the anticipated deflection of the structural member above the glass block.

Head - Glass Block in Steel Stud Wall With Brick Veneer (PCD 061)

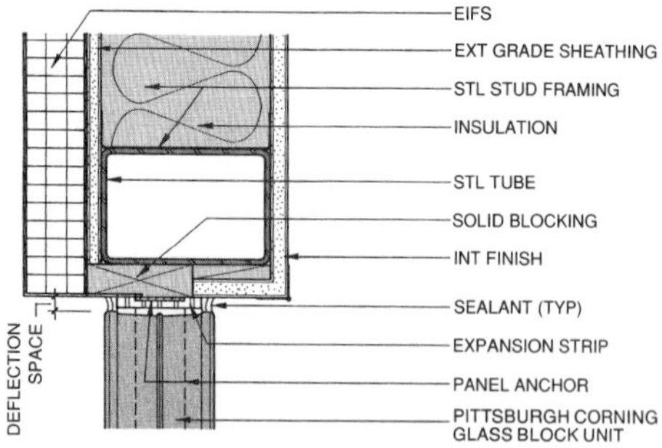

Head - Glass Block in Steel Stud Wall With Synthetic Plaster Finish (PCD 031)

Typical Jamb Details
Exterior Openings

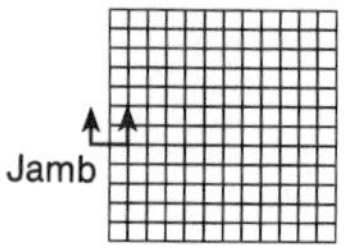

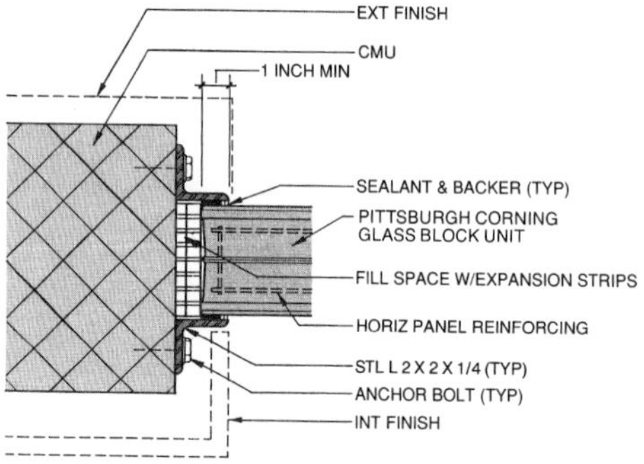

Jamb - Glass Block in CMU Wall (PCD 005) Fire Rated

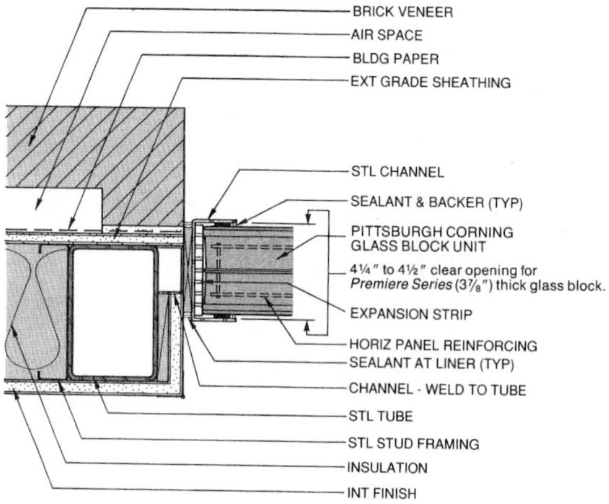

Jamb - Glass Block in Steel Stud Wall With Brick Veneer (PCD 062)

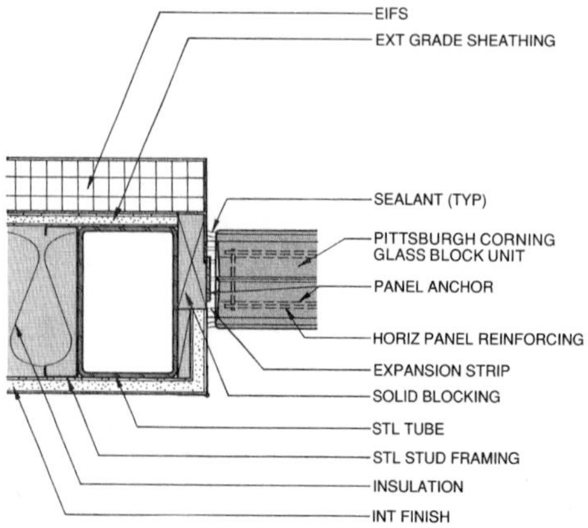

Jamb - Glass Block in Steel Stud Wall With Synthetic Plaster Finish (PCD 032)

Typical Sill Details

Exterior Openings

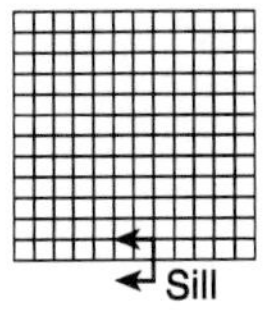

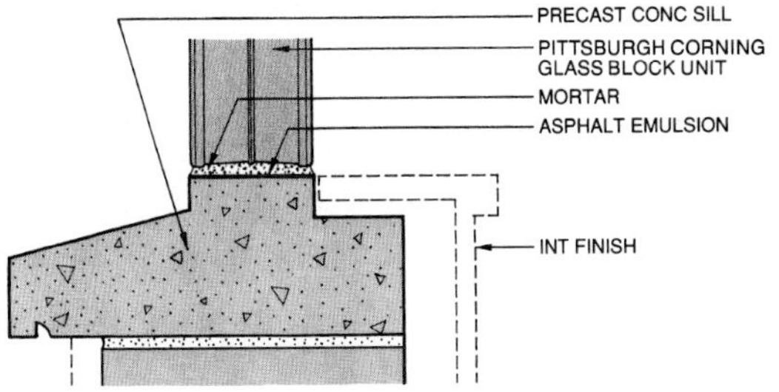

Sill - Glass Block in CMU Wall (PCD 006) Fire Rated

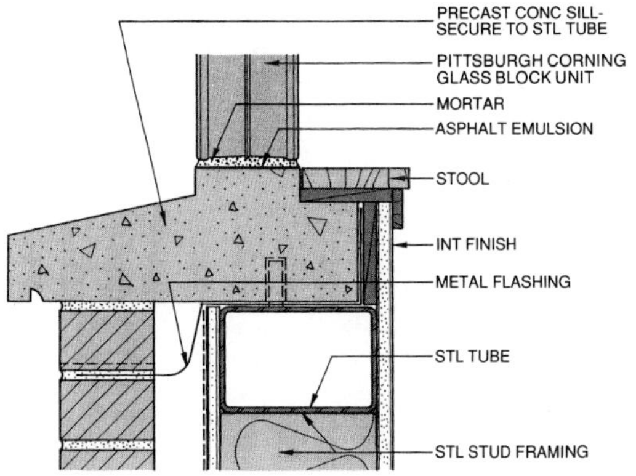

Sill - Glass Block in Steel Stud Wall With Brick Veneer (PCD 063)

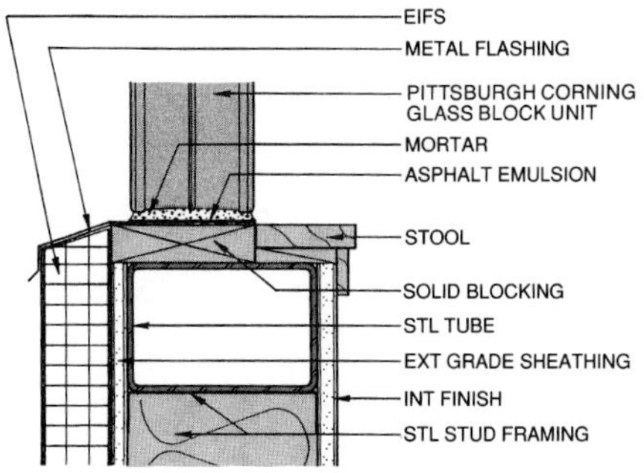

Sill - Glass Block in Steel Stud Wall With Synthetic Plaster Finish (PCD 033)

Typical Mortared Stiffener Details

250 Sq. Ft. Panels

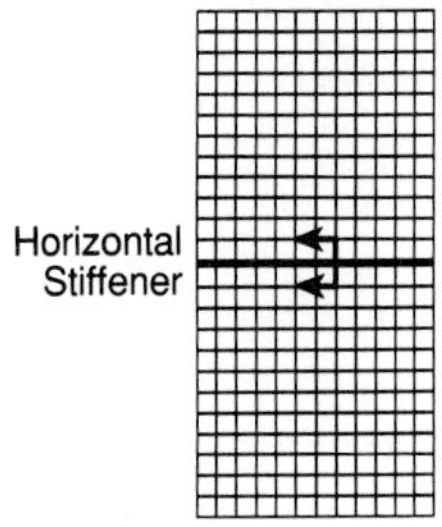

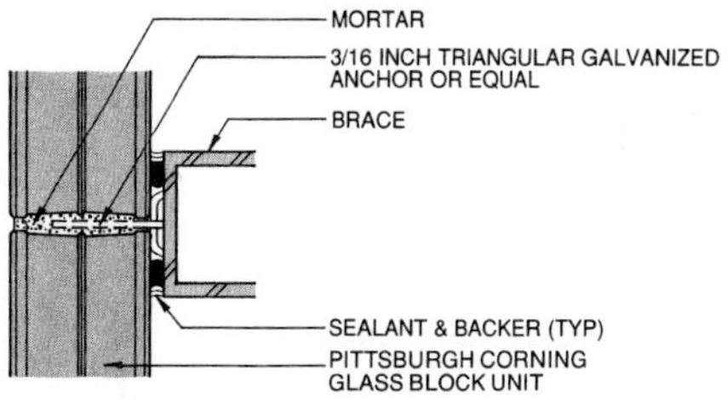

Intermediate Horizontal Brace in Glass Block Panel (PCD 089)

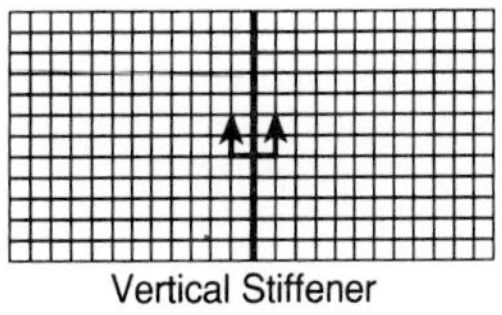

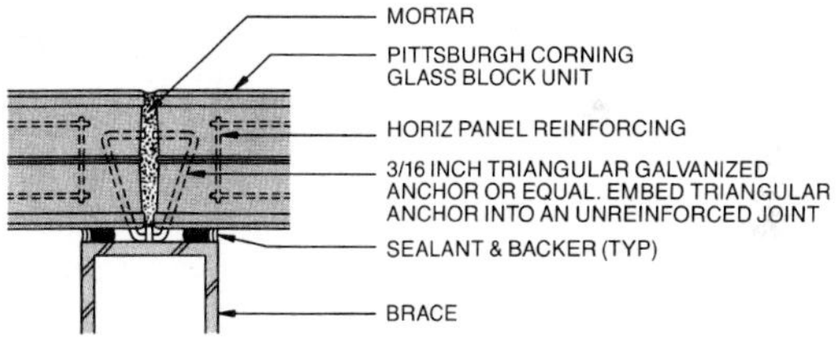

Intermediate Vertical Brace in Glass Block Panel (PCD 088)

Solid Glass Block Details

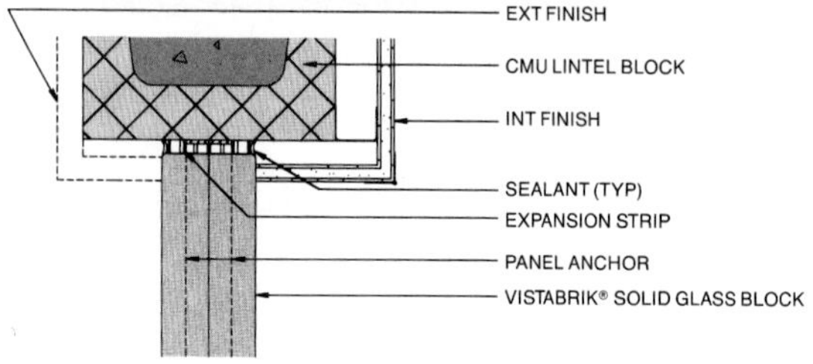

Head — Solid Glass Block in CMU Wall (PCD 037)

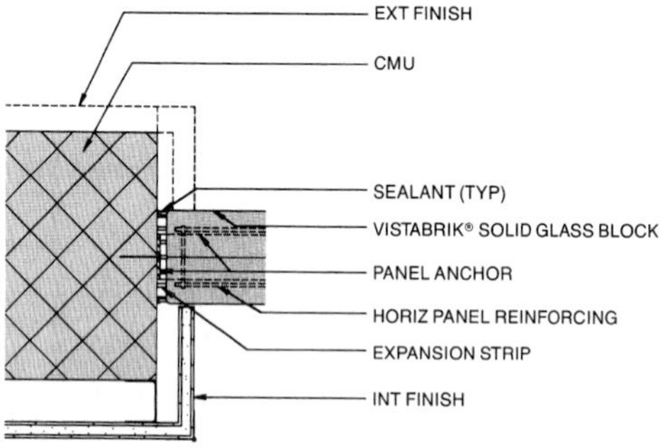

Jamb — Solid Glass Block in CMU Wall (PCD 038)

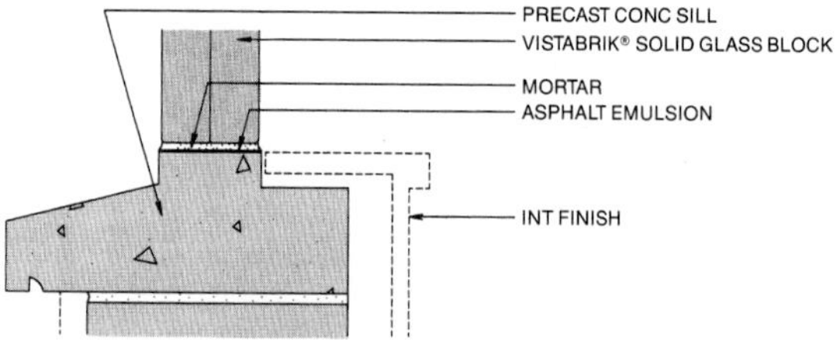

Sill — Solid Glass Block in CMU Wall (PCD 039)

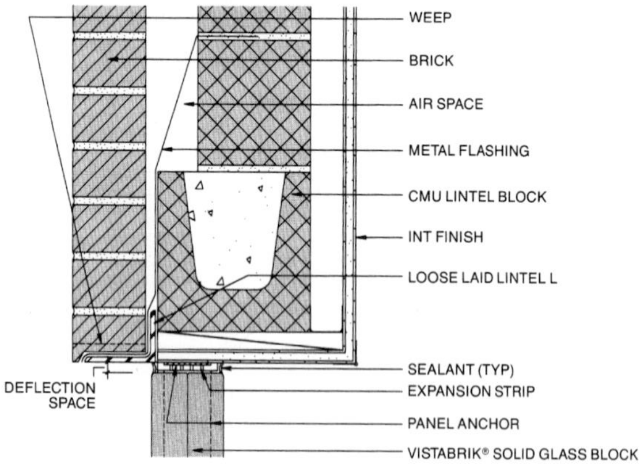

Head — Solid Glass Block in Brick Masonry Cavity Wall (PCD 040)

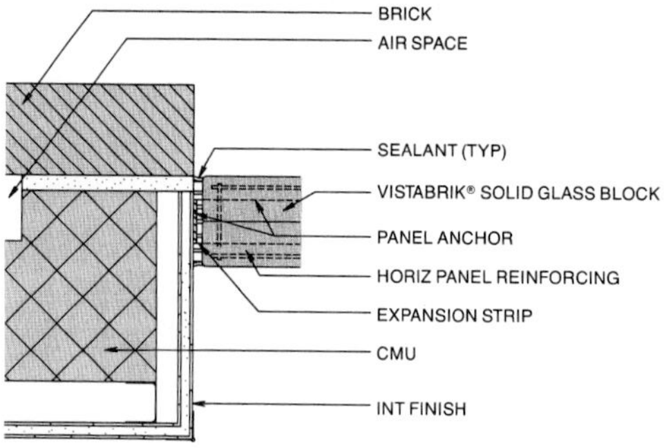

Jamb — Solid Glass Block in Brick Masonry Cavity Wall (PCD 041)

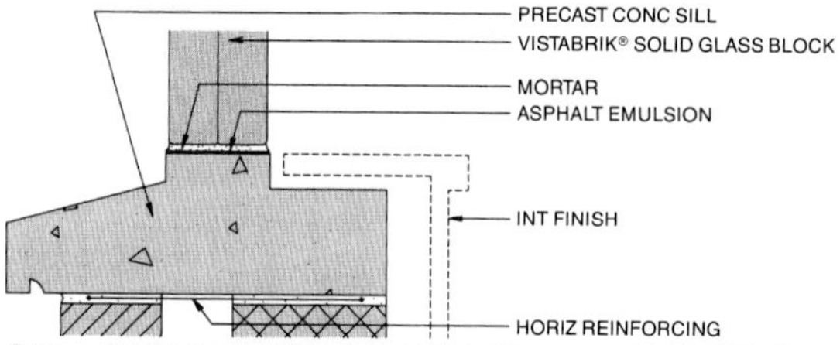

Sill — Solid Glass Block in Brick Masonry Cavity Wall (PCD 042)

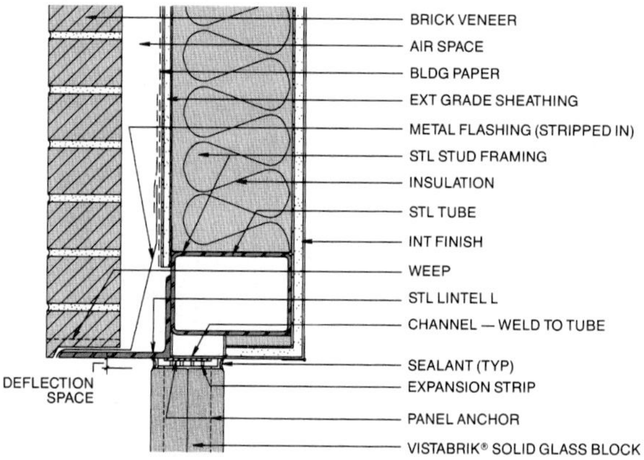

Head — Solid Glass Block in Steel Stud Wall With Brick Veneer (PCD 043)

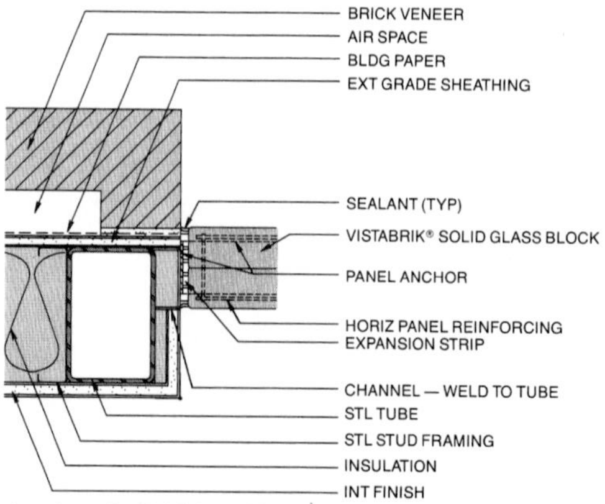

Jamb — Solid Glass Block in Steel Stud Wall With Brick Veneer (PCD 044)

Miscellaneous Interior Details

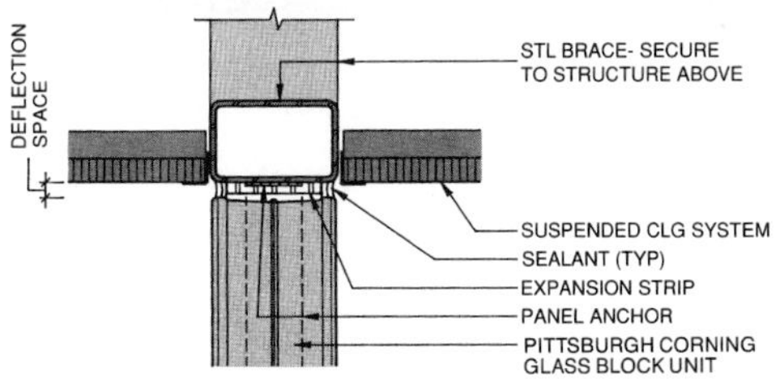

Head - Glass Block at Suspended Ceiling (PCD 148)

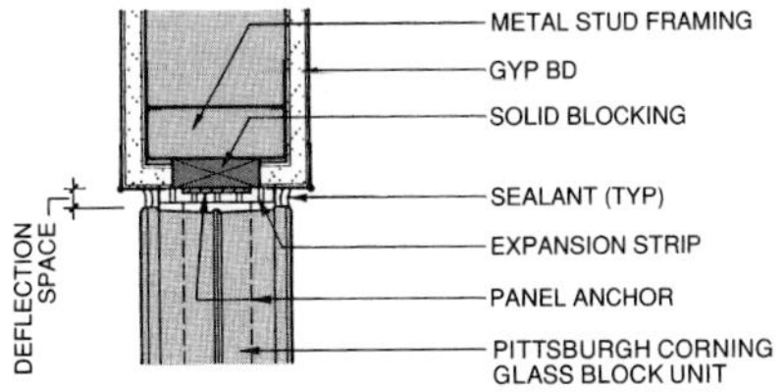

Head - Glass Block in Partition (PCD 149)

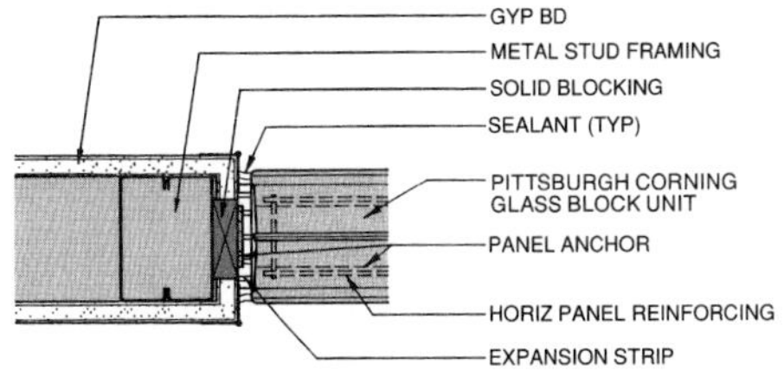

Jamb - Glass Block in Partition (PCD 150)

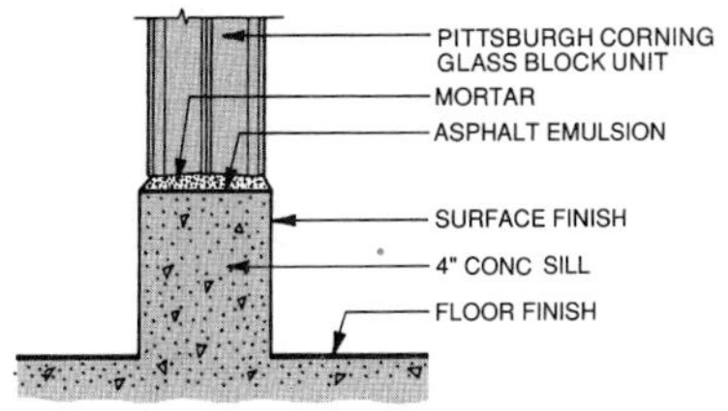

Sill - Interior Concrete Floor Slab

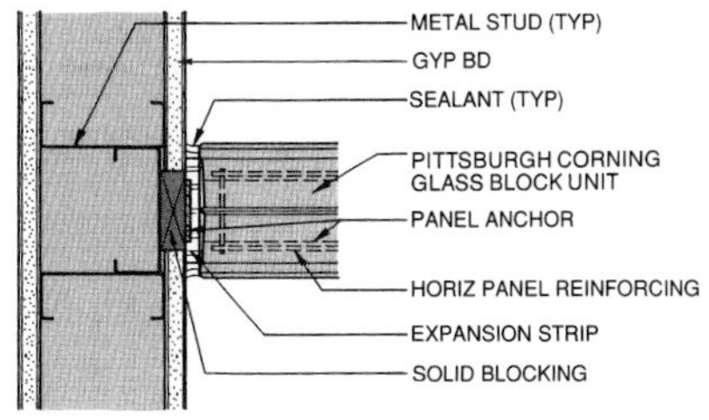

Jamb - Glass Block Perpendicular to Partition (PCD 151)

Finishing Units Details

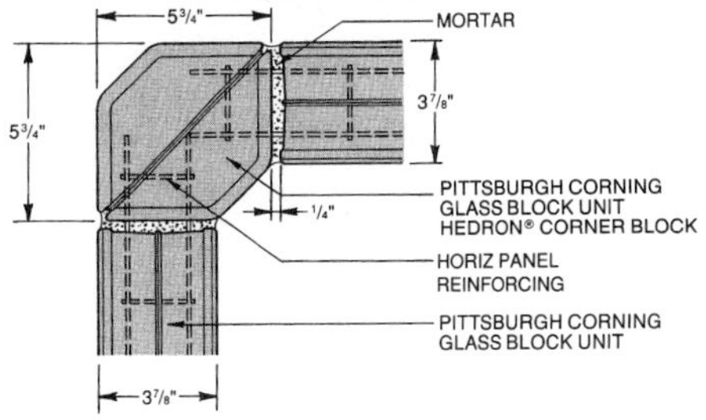

Glass Block at Corner - Plan (PCD 155)

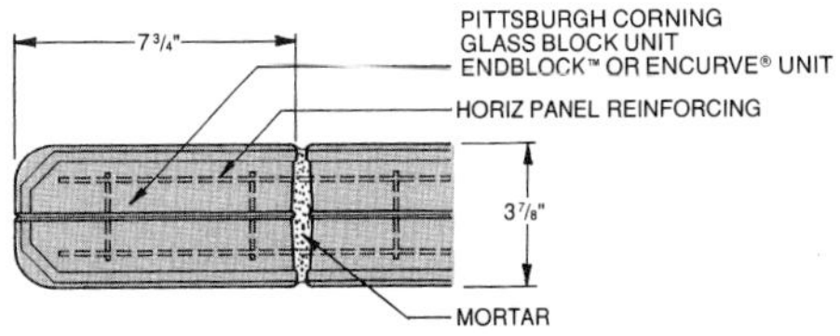

EndBlock™ or ENCURVE® Finishing Block - Plan (PCD 156)

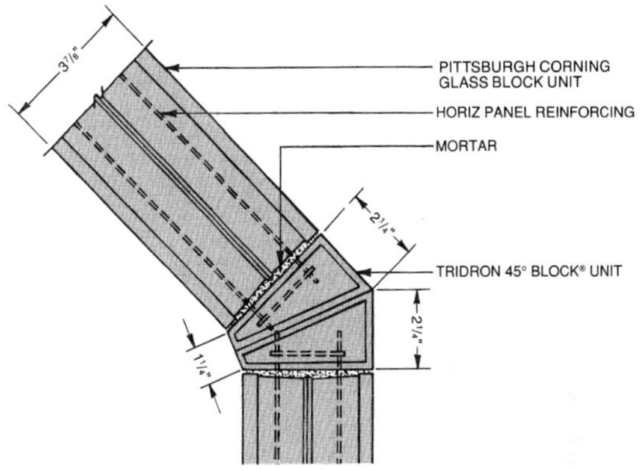

TRIDRON 45° Block® Unit - Plan

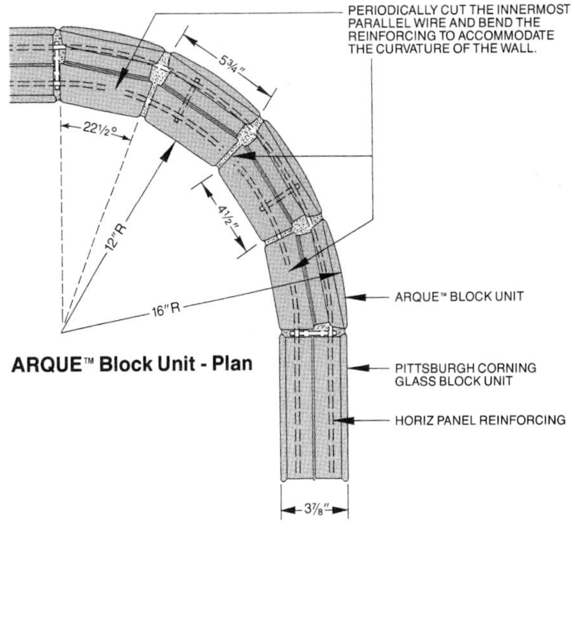

ARQUE™ Block Unit - Plan

PARTITIONS AND WALL FINISHES
Glass Block Miscellaneous Details

Typical Shelf Angle Details
Continuous Panels ≤144 Sq. Ft. Each

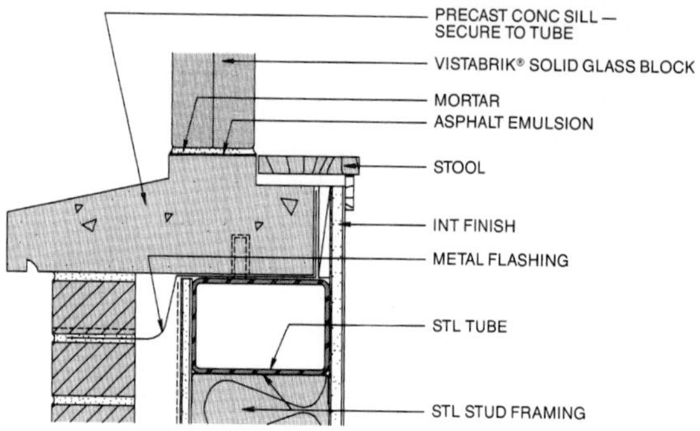

Sill — Solid Glass Block in Steel Stud Wall With Brick Veneer (PCD 045)

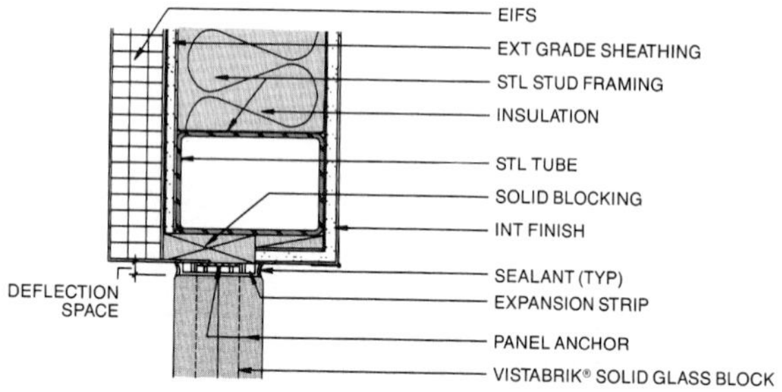

Head — Solid Glass Block in Steel Stud Wall With Synthetic Plaster Finish (PCD 049)

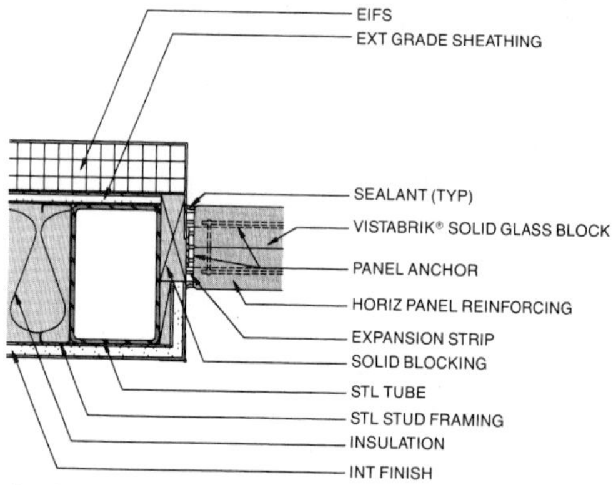

Jamb — Solid Glass Block in Steel Stud Wall With Synthetic Plaster Finish (PCD 050)

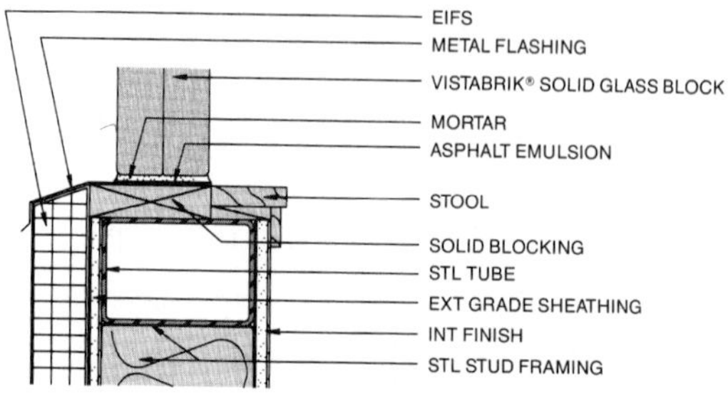

Sill — Solid Glass Block in Steel Stud Wall With Synthetic Plaster Finish (PCD 051)

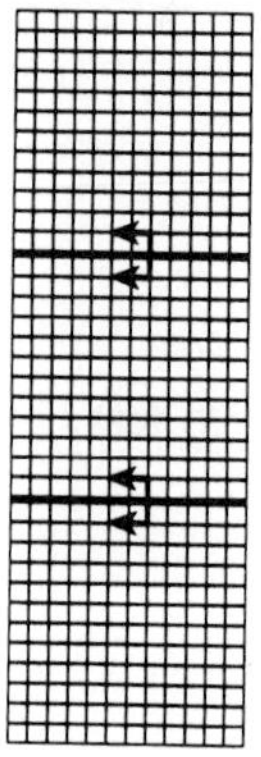

Horizontal Stiffener

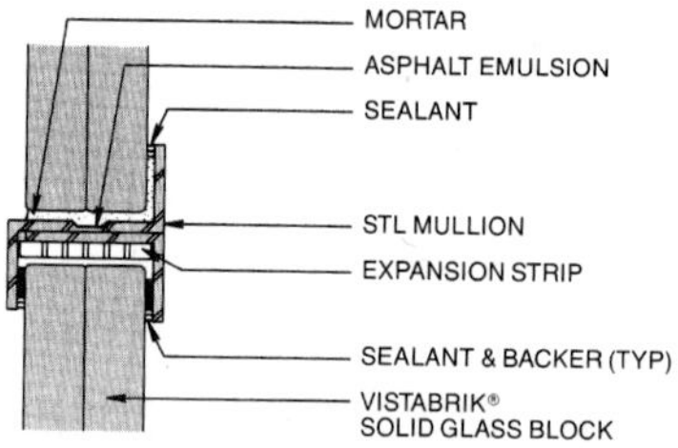

Intermediate Horizontal Support in Multiple Vertical Panels (PCD 130)

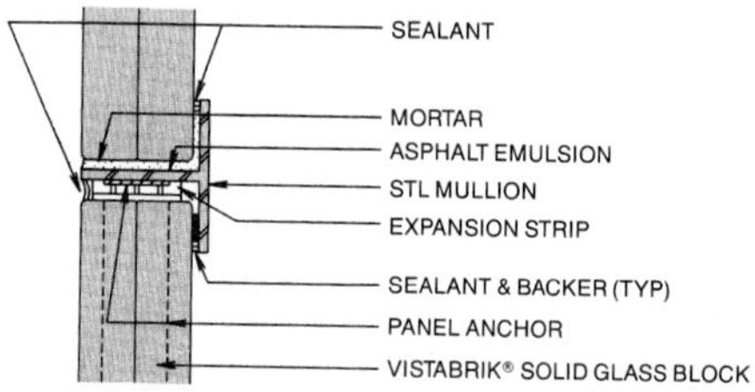

Intermediate Horizontal Support in Multiple Vertical Panels (PCD 131)

Typical Stiffener Details
Continuous Panels ≤144 Sq. Ft. Each

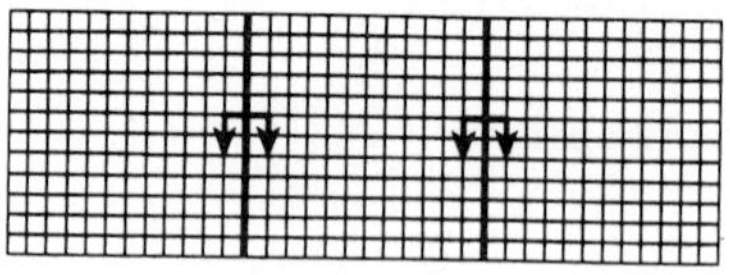

Vertical Stiffener

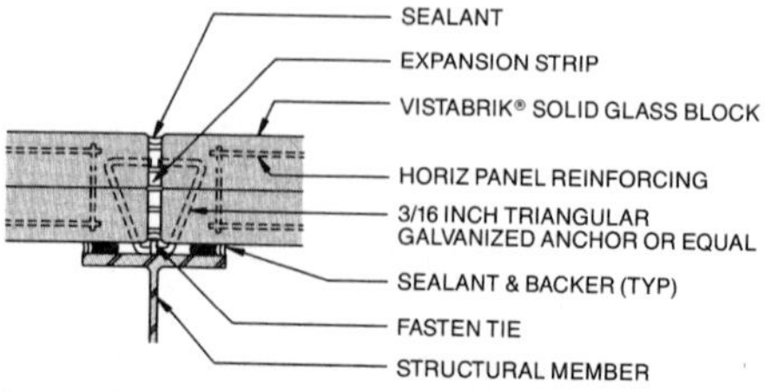

Intermediate Vertical Support in Multiple Horizontal Panels (PCD 133)

Typical Stiffener Details

Continuous Panels ≤144 Sq. Ft. Each

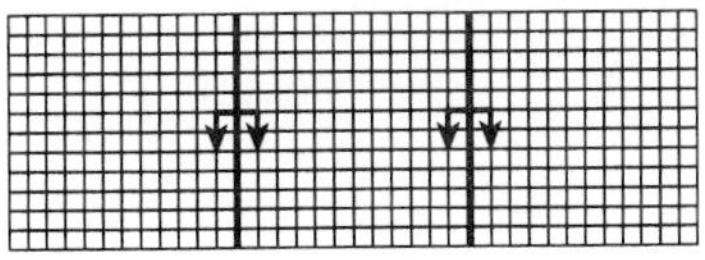

Vertical Stiffener

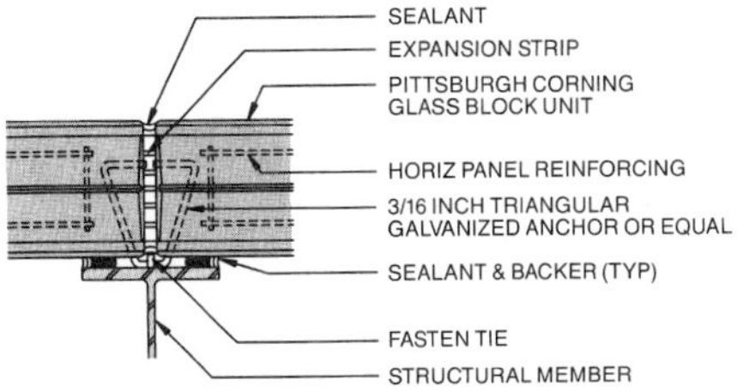

Intermediate Vertical Support in Multiple Horizontal Panels (PCD 132A)

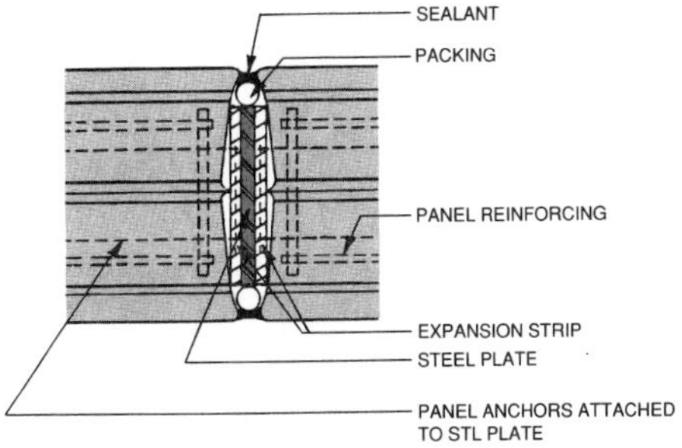

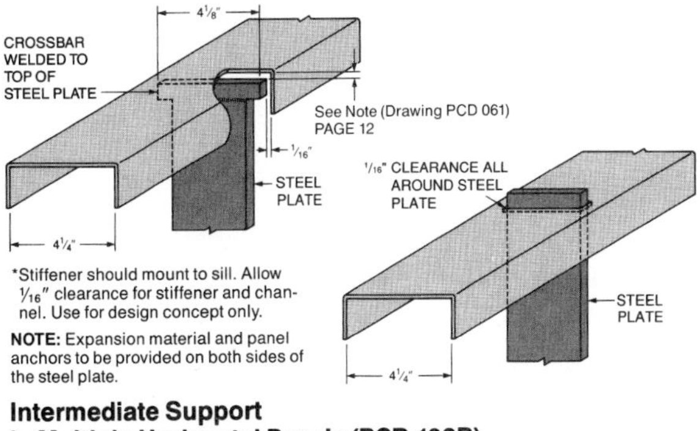

*Stiffener should mount to sill. Allow 1/16" clearance for stiffener and channel. Use for design concept only.

NOTE: Expansion material and panel anchors to be provided on both sides of the steel plate.

Intermediate Support in Multiple Horizontal Panels (PCD 132B)

NOTE: Panels with an expansion joint stiffener incorporating a vertical hidden plate should be limited to a maximum 10′ in height.

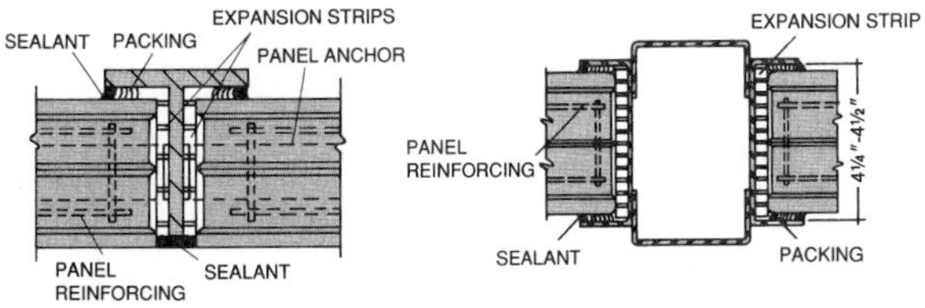

Intermediate Support in Multiple Horizontal Panels (PCD 132C & D)

Typical Shelf Angle Details

Continuous Panels ≤144 Sq. Ft. Each

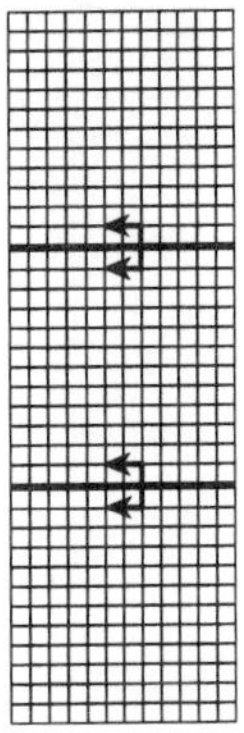

Horizontal Stiffener

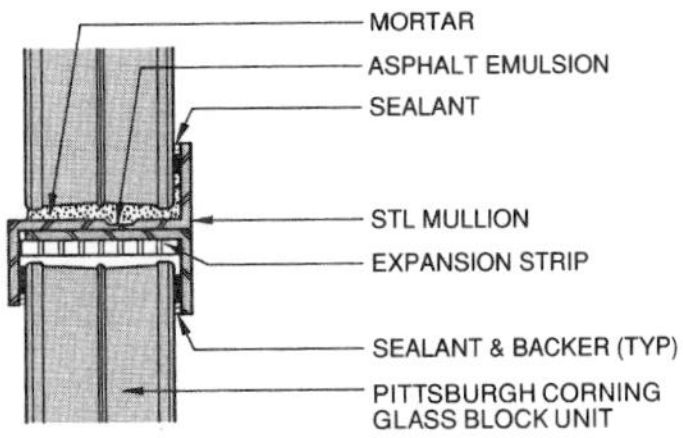

Intermediate Horizontal Support in Multiple Vertical Panels (PCD 128)

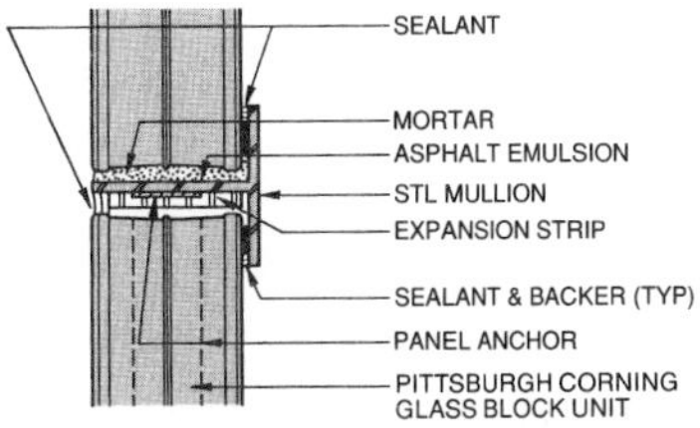

Intermediate Horizontal Support in Multiple Vertical Panels (PCD 129)

Hollow Metal Door Frame Details

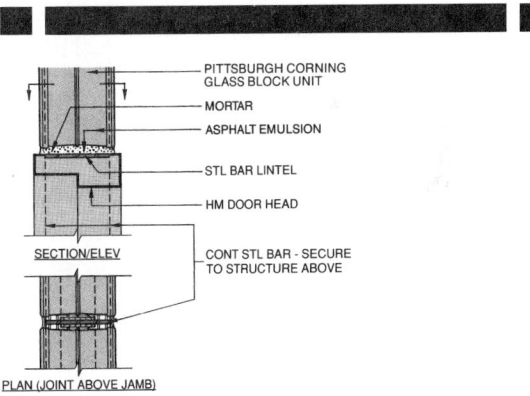

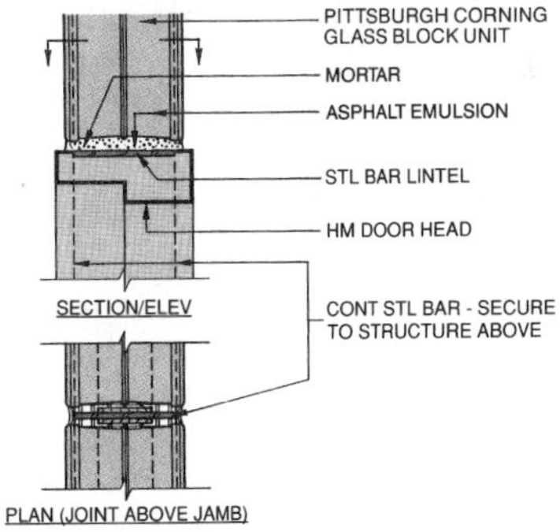

Head - Hollow Metal Door Frame at Glass Block (PCD 153)

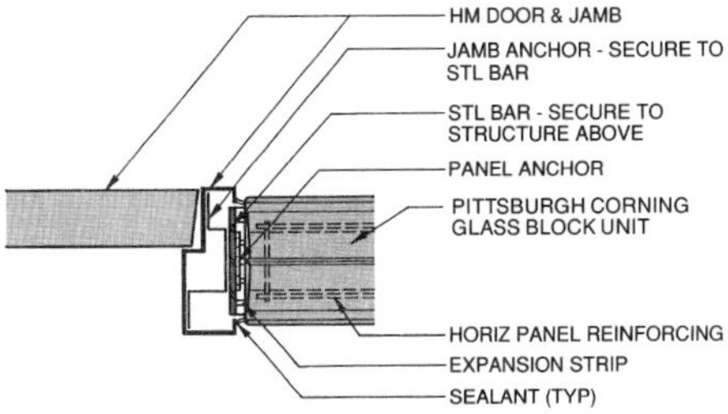

Jamb - Hollow Metal Door Frame at Glass Block (PCD 154)

PARTITIONS AND WALL FINISHES
Glass Block Miscellaneous Details

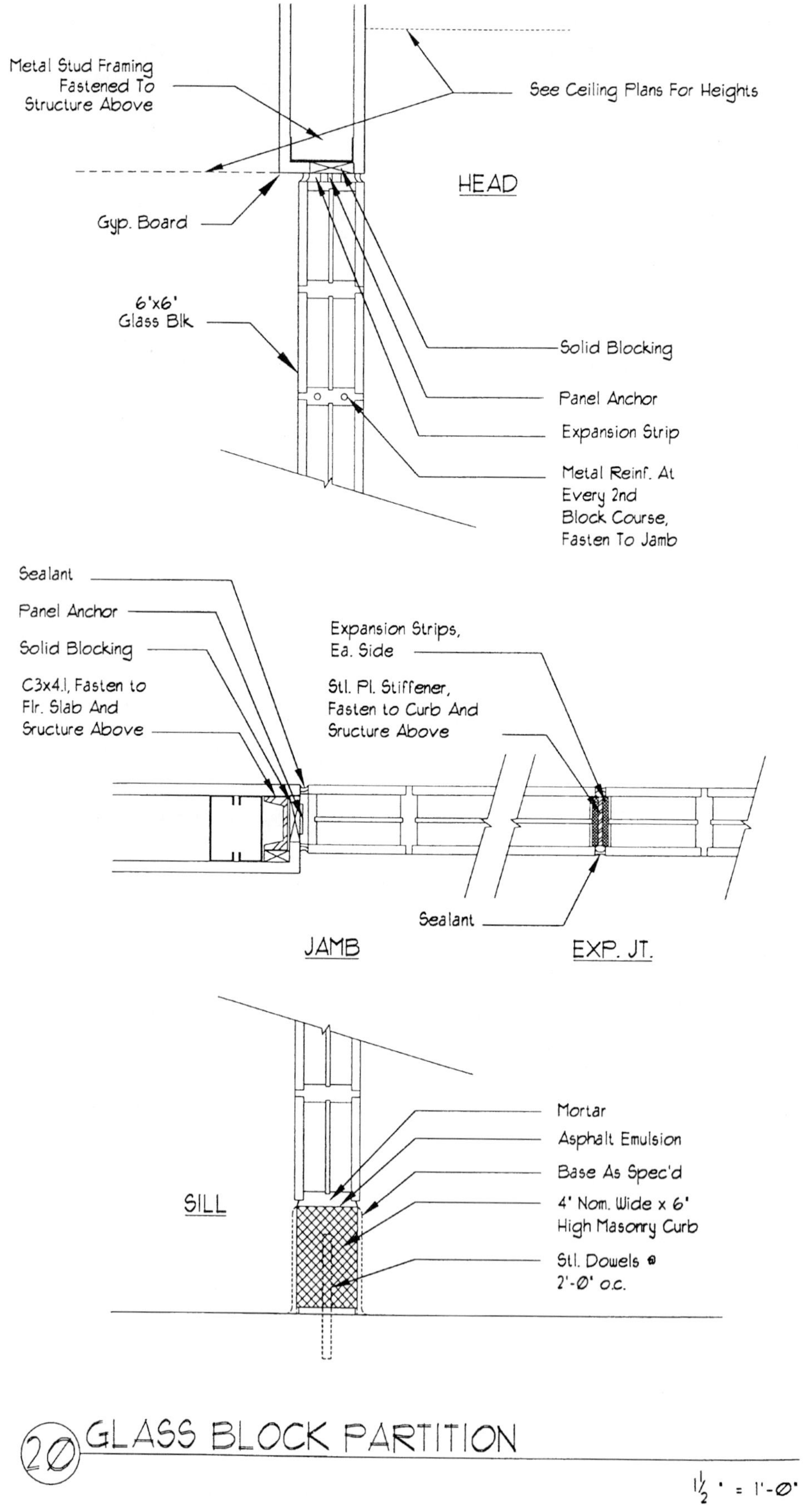

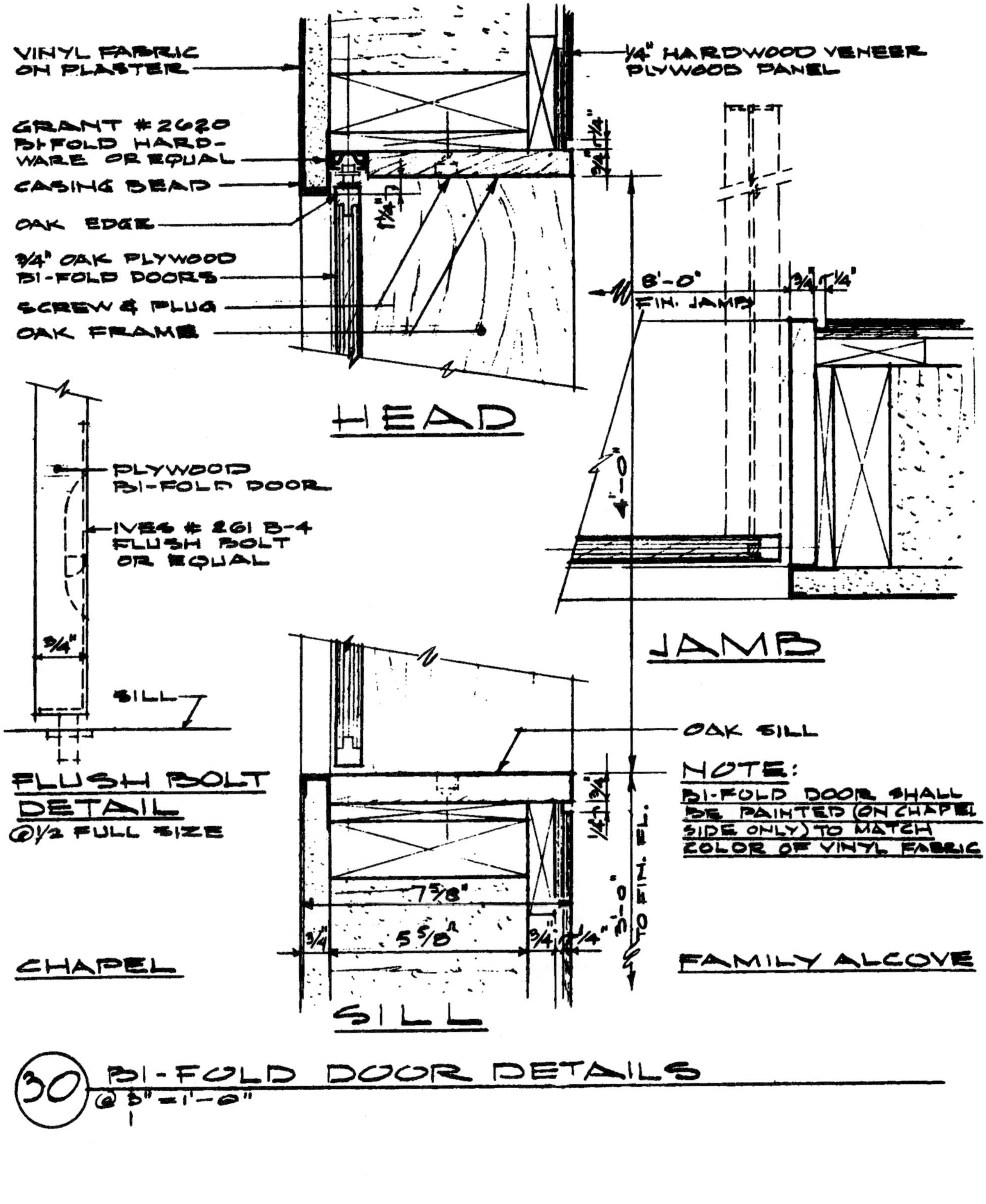
VINYL FABRIC ON PLASTER
1/4" HARDWOOD VENEER PLYWOOD PANEL
GRANT #2620 BI-FOLD HARDWARE OR EQUAL
CASING BEAD
OAK EDGE
3/4" OAK PLYWOOD BI-FOLD DOORS
SCREW & PLUG
OAK FRAME
HEAD
8'-0" FIN. JAMB
3/4 1/4
4'-0"
JAMB
PLYWOOD BI-FOLD DOOR
IVES # 261 B-4 FLUSH BOLT OR EQUAL
3/4"
SILL
FLUSH BOLT DETAIL
@1/2 FULL SIZE
OAK SILL
NOTE:
BI-FOLD DOOR SHALL BE PAINTED (ON CHAPEL SIDE ONLY) TO MATCH COLOR OF VINYL FABRIC
7 5/8"
3/4 5 5/8" 3/4 1/4"
0'-0" TO FIN. FL.
CHAPEL
FAMILY ALCOVE
SILL
30 BI-FOLD DOOR DETAILS
@ 3"=1'-0"

PARTITIONS AND WALL FINISHES

Column Fireproofing Details

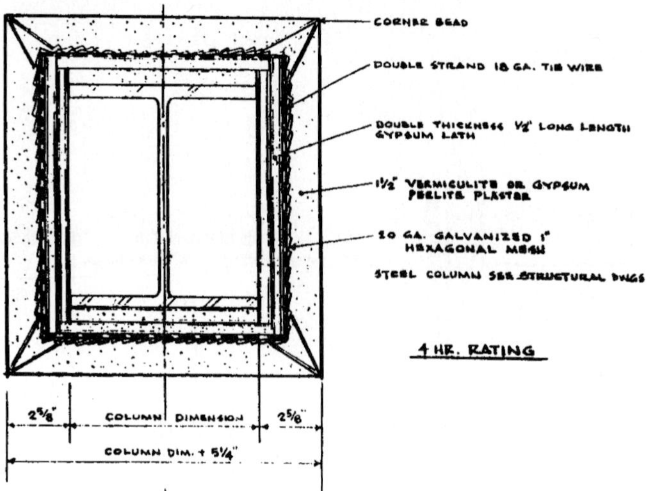

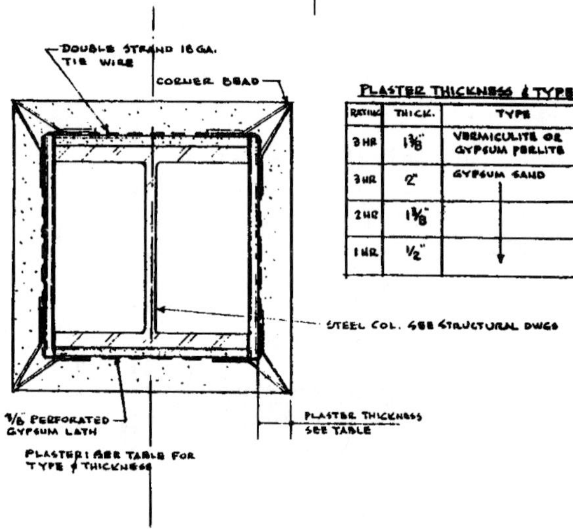

PLASTER THICKNESS & TYPE

RATING	THICK.	TYPE
3 HR	1⅜"	VERMICULITE OR GYPSUM PERLITE
3 HR	2"	GYPSUM SAND
2 HR	1⅜"	↓
1 HR	½"	↓

GYPSUM LATH & PLASTER FIREPROOFING

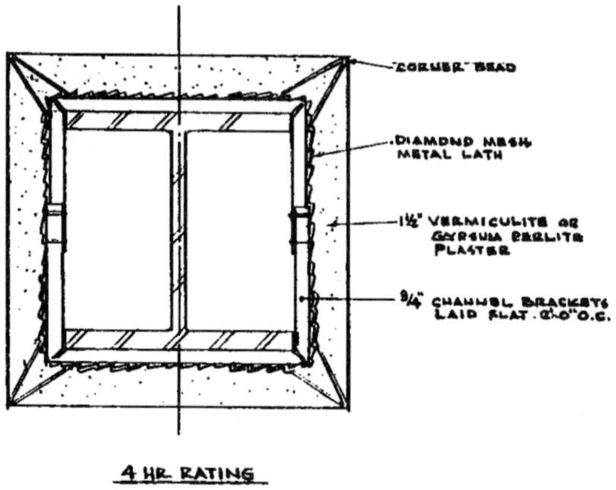

METAL LATH & PLASTER FIREPROOFING

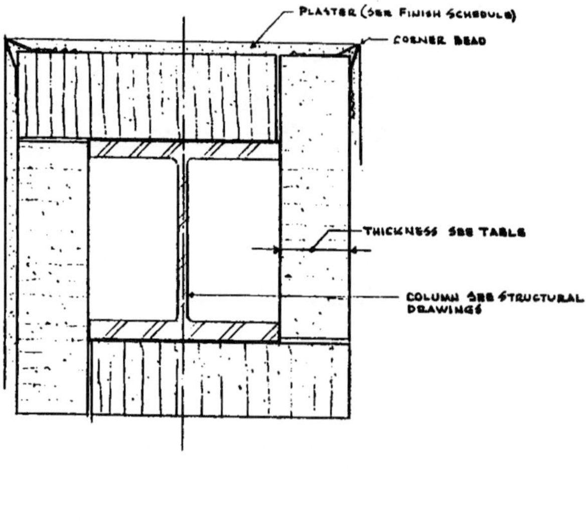

MATERIAL	THICKNESS IN INCHES			
	1 HR	2 HR	3 HR	4 HR
BRICK (BURNED CLAY OR SHALE)	2¼"	2¼"	3¾"	3¾"
BRICK (SAND LIME)	2¼"	2¼"	3¾"	3¾"
CONCRETE BLOCK, BRICK, OR TILE EXCEPT CINDER CONCRETE UNITS	2¼"	2¼"	3¾"	3¾"
HOLLOW CINDER OR CONCRETE BLOCK & TILE HAVING A COMPRESSIVE STRENGTH OF AT LEAST 700#/SQ.IN. OF GROSS AREA	1½"	2"	2"	2½"
SOLID GYPSUM BLOCK PROVIDED THAT TO OBTAIN 4-HR RATING, BLOCKS SHALL BE PLASTERED WITH AT LEAST ½" GYPSUM PLASTER	1"	1½"	2"	2"
HOLLOW OR SOLID BURNED CLAY TILE OR COMBINATION OF TILE & CONCRETE	1½"	2"	2"	2½"
HOLLOW GYPSUM BLOCK, PROVIDED THAT TO OBTAIN A 4 HR. RATING, BLOCKS SHALL BE PLASTERED WITH AT LEAST ½" GYPSUM PLASTER	3"	3"	3"	3"

MASONRY FIREPROOFING

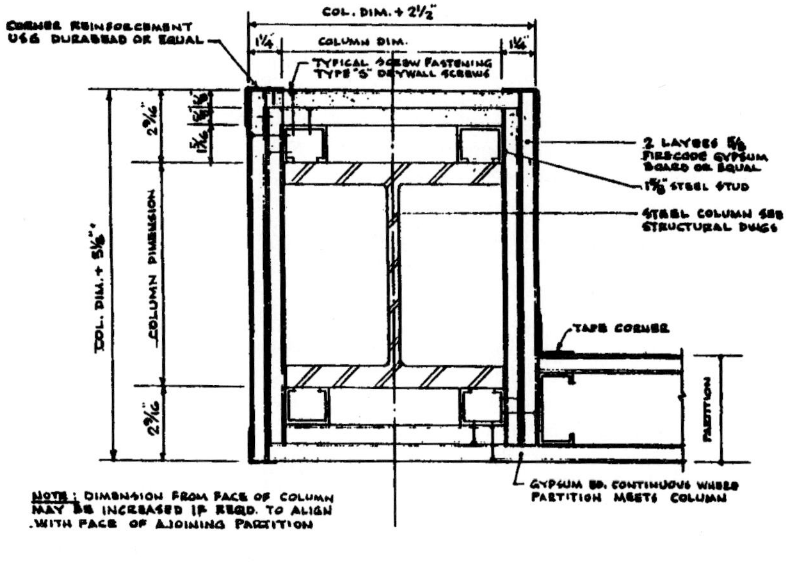

GYPSUM BOARD FIREPROOFING — 2 HR. RATING

FOR 3 HR. RATING ADD 1 ADDITIONAL LAYER OF 5/8" FIRECODE GYPSUM BOARD
1 1/2 HR RATING 3 LAYERS OF GYPSUM BD. (STANDARD)
1 HR. RATING 2 " " " " "
SCALE: 3"=1'-0"

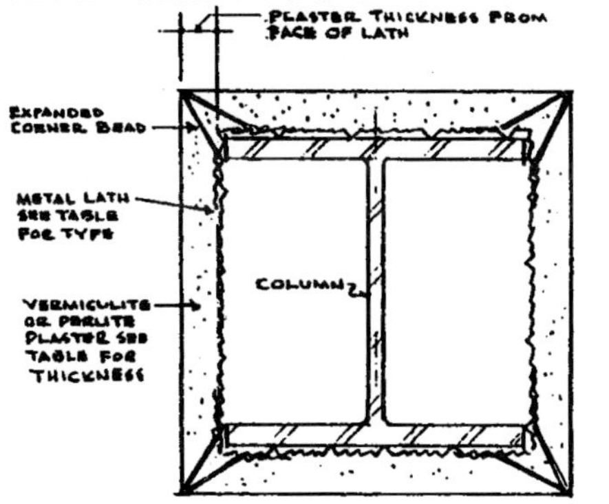

RATING	PLASTER THICK.	LATH
1 HR.	5/8"	3.4# DIAMOND MESH METAL LATH
2 HR.	1"	3.4# SELF FURRING DIAMOND MESH METAL LATH
3 HR.	1 3/8"	
4 HR.	1 3/4"	

NOTE: N.Y.C. CODE - 4 HR RATING MAY BE OBTAINED WITH 1" VERMICULITE PLASTER ON S.F. LATH & BACKFILL OF LOOSE VERMICULITE

VERMICULITE OR GYPSUM PERLITE FIREPROOFING

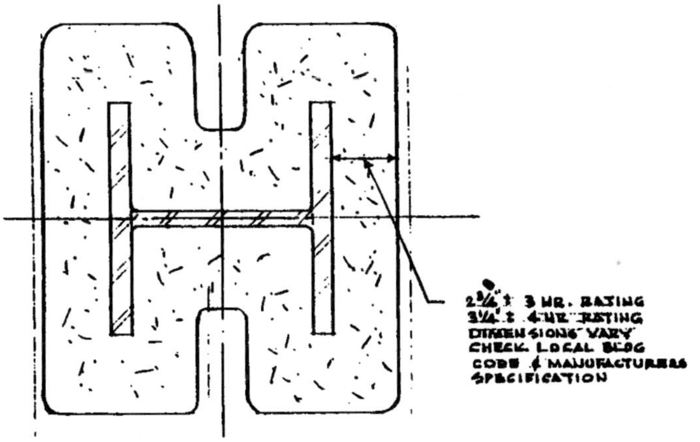

SPRAYED ON FIREPROOFING

FLOORS AND FLOOR FINISHES

The designer must be familiar with the great variety of floor types, finishes, and patterns in order to specify and detail architectural flooring properly. While some examples of "soft finishes" such as carpeting and resilient flooring are shown, this section explores in depth the installation and detailing of "hard" or architectural finishes.

It is important for the designer to research the various characteristics of the floor finish being specified. While aesthetics and color are obviously important considerations, the designer must also analyze other factors. Among these factors are wear resistance and durability, soil resistance, maintenance, resiliency, flammability, costs of installation, and life cycle cost. Once these factors have been analyzed, the final specification and detailing of the architectural finish must be developed.

Examples of standard patterns are provided, but the designer must become familiar with the infinite number of pattern possibilities. The inherent limitations of materials control their sizes and thicknesses. The patterns of certain materials are dictated by both the thickness of the material and the weight or "dead load" of the material superimposed on the structure. For example, a large pattern of marble or granite will necessitate a slab of material that will weigh much more per square foot than that of a smaller pattern. This greater weight might have structural consequences, as well as make floor transitions more significant.

Transitions between flooring materials, particularly under doors or at entrances, and transitions between flooring and walls are some of the key material interfaces that have to be detailed. Again, this section provides such information using both traditional and contemporary approaches.

Finally, a portion of this section is devoted to the detailing of raised computer room floors. While not traditionally a floor finish, raised computer room floors seem appropriate for this section. While generic architectural details are provided, the designer should always develop final details in conjunction with the manufacturer(s) being specified.

FLOORS AND FLOOR FINISHES

Typical Characteristics of Floor Finishes

DRAWING AND DESCRIPTION		WEAR RESISTANCE	SOIL RESISTANCE, CLEANING AND MAINTENANCE	RESILIENCY	REMARKS	COST COMPARISON
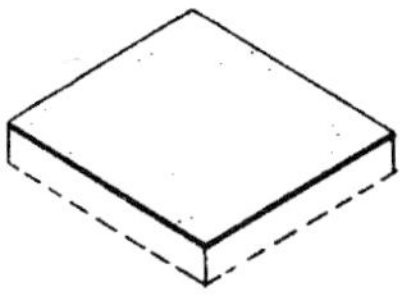	1/8 inch hardened cement finish on concrete slab	Good	Poor; frequent cleaning needed; must be refinished every ten years	Very hard	Cement base costs little, is too hard a floor to be comfortable; infrequently used in classrooms, sometimes used in corridors, shops and inexpensive toilet rooms	installation cost maintenance and insurance cost for 20 years
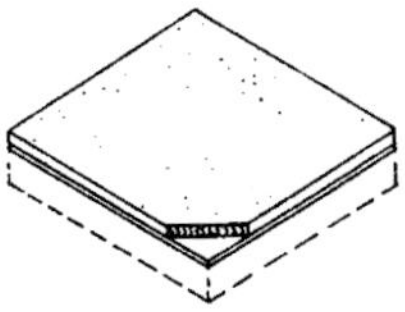	3/4 inch terrazzo finish, with 3/4 inch cement underbed on a concrete slab	Very good	Very good; needs cleaning once a week with detergent and water	Very hard	Terrazzo base is easy to clean and sanitary, but not resilient and sometimes noisy; seldom used in classrooms, often used in corridors, vestibules, toilets and shower rooms	
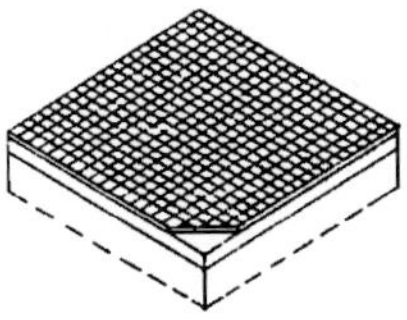	Ceramic mosaic tile, 3/4 inch setting bed on concrete slab	Very good	Very good	Very hard	Used in toilet rooms, showers, food service areas, but seldom used in classrooms	
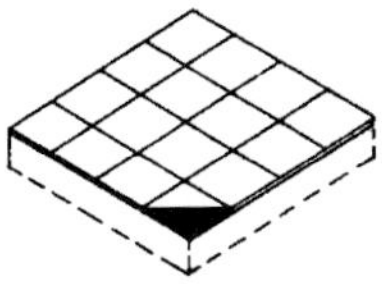	1/8 inch asphalt tile finish installed in mastic on concrete slab	Poor, usually needs replacing every ten years	Fair; must be cleaned and waxed once a week	Fair	Low first cost; finish requires careful maintenance	
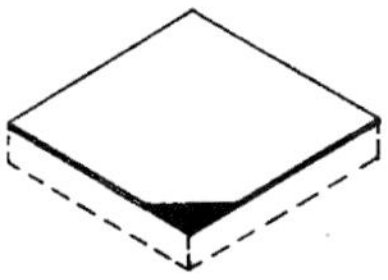	1/8 inch linoleum finish installed in mastic on concrete slab	Good	Fair; must be cleaned and waxed once a week	Fair	Serviceable; a sanitary floor for classrooms, corridors, assembly and administration rooms	
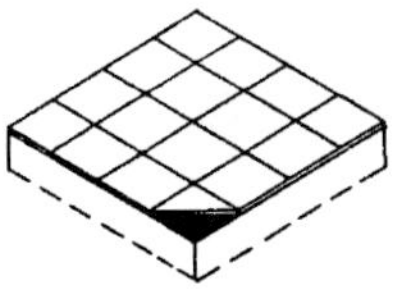	1/8 inch cork tile floor installed in mastic on concrete slab	Good	Fair; needs frequent cleaning and waxing	Very good	Used primarily in libraries and kindergartens; floor is subject to indentations by chair legs; acoustically good	
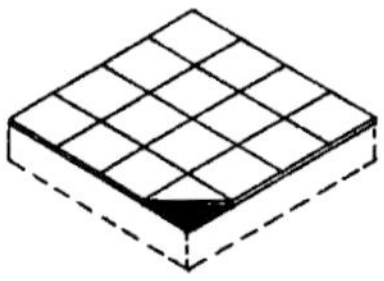	1/8 inch rubber tile finish installed in mastic on concrete slab	Good	Fair; needs cleaning and waxing once a week	Very good	Subject to slight indentation by chair legs	
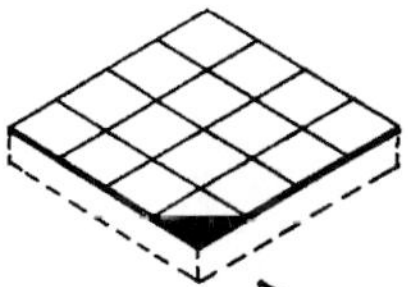	1/8 inch vinyl tile finish installed in mastic on concrete slab	Good	Fair; needs a weekly cleaning and waxing	Very good	Subject to indentation	
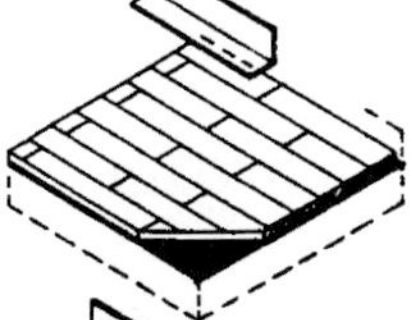	25/32 inch maple strip flooring set in 1/8 inch hot asphalt mastic on concrete slab	Very good	Good; requires monthly cleaning with steelwool and a wax finish	Fair	Steel angles necessary to cover expansion joint; used in gymnasiums and playrooms; not suitable for damp areas or climates	
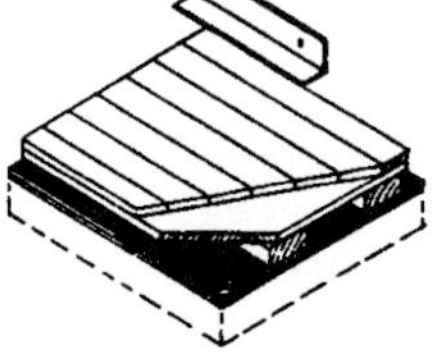	25/32 inch maple finish; 1 by 4 inch cypress subfloor laid diagonally; 2 by 6 inch cypress sleepers, 12 inches apart, set in two 1/8 inch layers of hot asphalt mastic	Very good	Good; requires a monthly cleaning with steelwool and a wax finish; sand and re-finish every 2 years	Excellent	A deluxe gymnasium floor	

FLOORS AND FLOOR FINISHES

Floor Construction Details

2"x 8" JOISTS - 16" O.C., 13/16" OAK FLOORING, SUB-FLOOR, METAL LATH, 1/2" GYPSUM PLASTER

F-1

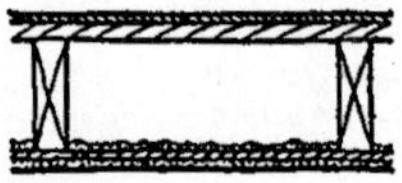

1 3/8" HARD WOOD FLOOR, SUB-FLOOR, 2"x 6" WOOD JOISTS, WOOD LATH, 1/2". PLASTER

F-2

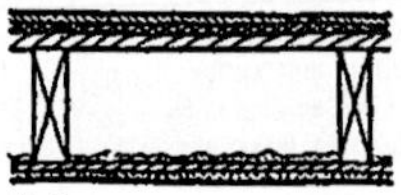

SAME AS F-2, EXCEPT 1/2" FIBERBOARD BETWEEN ROUGH & FINISH FLOOR

F-3

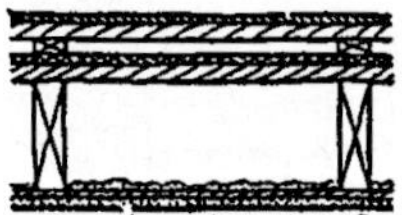

3/8" HARDWOOD FLOOR, SUB-FLOOR, 3/4"x 2" NAILING STRIPS (SEE NOTE) 1/2" FIBERBOARD, SUB-FLOOR, 2"x 6" WOOD JOISTS, WOOD LATH, 1/2" PLASTER.

NOTE - ROUGH & FINISH FLOOR NAILED TO NAILERS; NAILERS NOT NAILED THROUGH FIBERBOARD: MERELY RESTING THEREON.

F-4

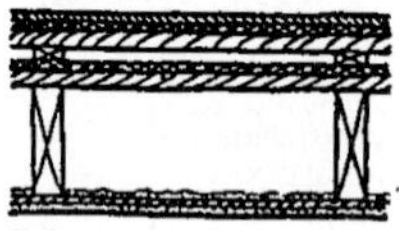

SAME AS F-4, EXCEPT 1/2" FIBERBOARD BETWEEN ROUGH & FINISH FLOOR

F-5

3/8" HARD WOOD FLOOR, SUB-FLOOR, 2"x 6" WOOD JOISTS - 16" O.C. SUSPENDED CEILING - 2"x 4" JOISTS - 16" O.C. 1/2" FIBERBOARD, 1/2" PLASTER

NOTE - COMMON END SUPPORT FOR BOTH JOIST SYSTEMS; NO INTERMEDIATE CONNECTIONS BETWEEN 2x6s & 2x4s.

F-6

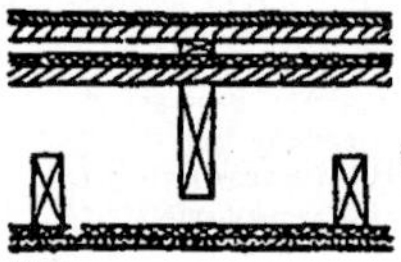

SAME AS F-6, EXCEPT 1/2" FIBERBOARD ON PRIMARY SUB-FLOOR. 3/4"x 2" NAILERS (SEE NOTE WITH F-4) PLUS ROUGH & FINISH FLOOR.

F-7

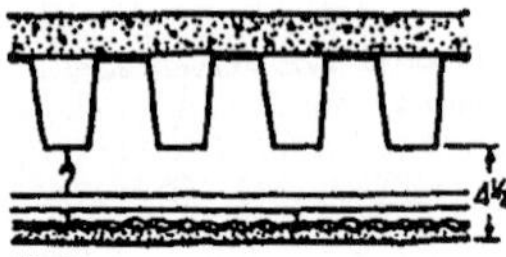

2" CONCRETE FILL, STEEL FLOOR SECTION, SUSPENDED METAL LATH, 1/2" PLASTER

F-8

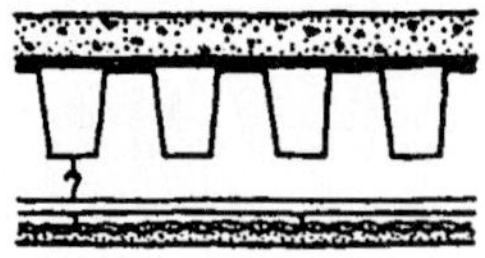

SAME AS F-8, EXCEPT 1/2" EMULSIFIED ASPHALT APPLIED BEFORE 2" CONCRETE FILL.

F-9

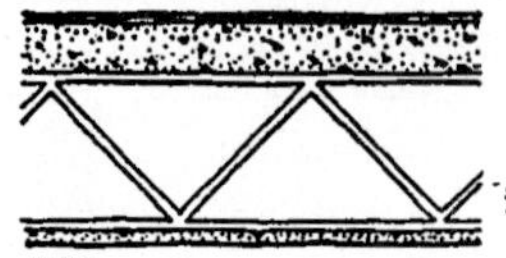

BATTLESHIP LINOLEUM, 2 1/2" CONCRETE FILL ON HIGH-RIB METAL LATH, 8" MAC-MAR JOISTS, HIGH-RIB METAL LATH, 3 COATS GYPSUM PLASTER

F-10

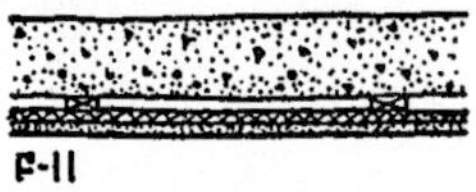

4" REINF CONCRETE SLAB, 3/4"x 2" FURRING, 1/2" FIBERBOARD LATH, 1/2" GYPSUM PLASTER.

F-11

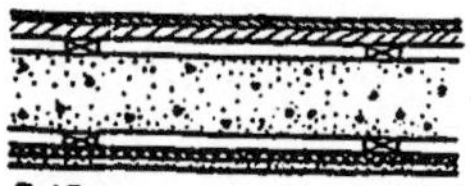

SAME AS F-11, EXCEPT 3/4"x 2" SLEEPERS PLUS ROUGH & FINISH FLOOR ADDED, TOP

F-12

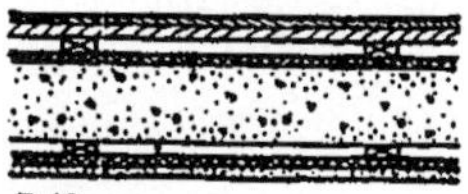

SAME AS F-12, EXCEPT 1/2" FIBERBOARD PLACED UNDER SLEEPERS

F-13

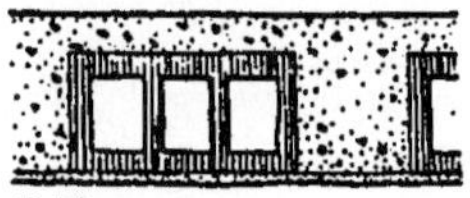

8" COMBINATION FLOOR, 6"x 12"x 12" 3-CELL TILE, 1/2" TWO-COAT GYPSUM PLASTER CEILING

F-14

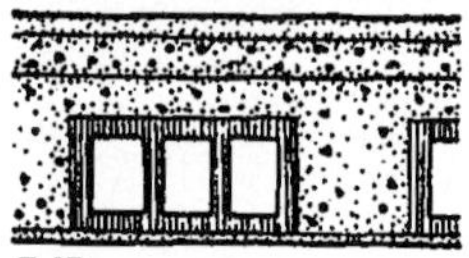

SAME AS F-14, EXCEPT 2" CINDER CONCRETE FILL PLUS 1" CEMENT TOPPING ADDED FOR FLOOR

F-15

6" COMBINATION FLOOR, 4"x 12"x 12" 3-CELL TILE, 3/4"x 2" FURRING - 16" O.C., 1/2" FIBERBOARD LATH, 1/2" GYPSUM PLASTER

F-16

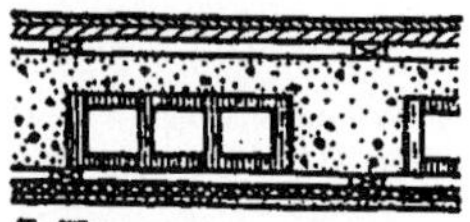

SAME AS F-16, EXCEPT 3/4"x 2" SLEEPERS PLUS ROUGH & FINISH FLOOR ADDED, TOP

F-17

SAME AS F-17, EXCEPT 1/2" FIBERBOARD PLACED UNDER SLEEPERS

F-18

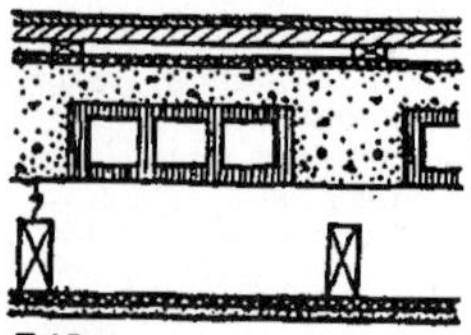

FINISH & ROUGH FLOOR ON 3/4"x 2" SLEEPERS - 16" O.C. RESTING ON 1/2" FIBERBOARD, 6" COMBINATION FLOOR, 4"x 12"x 12" 3-CELL TILE, SUSPENDED 2"x 4" JOISTS, PLUS 1/2" FIBERBOARD LATH, 1/2" GYPSUM PLASTER

F-19

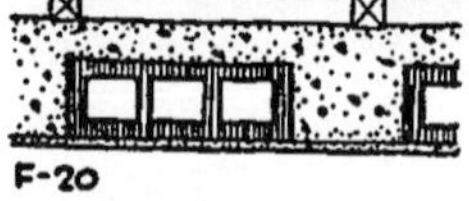

13/16" OAK FLOORING NAILED TO 2"x 2" SLEEPERS - 16" O.C., SLEEPERS GROUTED ON 6" COMBINATION FLOOR (SIMILAR TO F-19), 1/2" TWO-COAT GYPSUM PLASTER CEILING

F-20

SAME AS F-20, EXCEPT 2"x 2" SLEEPERS CARRIED ON RESILIENT STEEL CLIPS

F-21

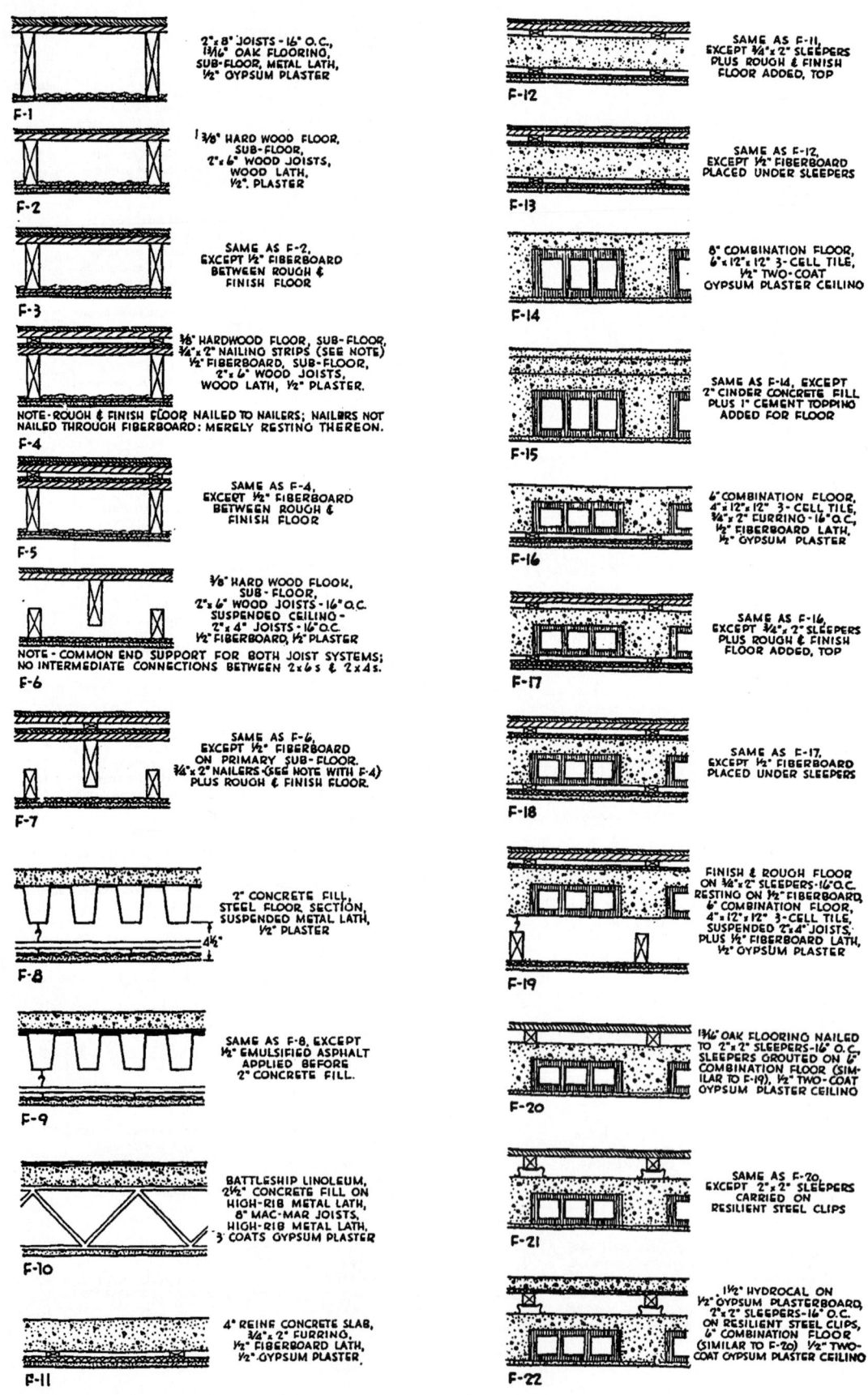

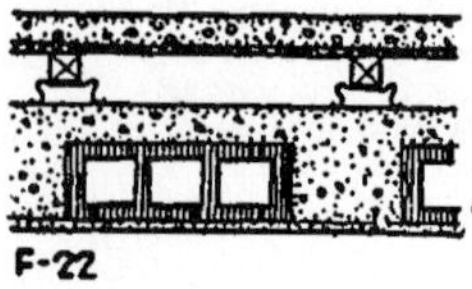

1 1/2" HYDROCAL ON 1/2" GYPSUM PLASTERBOARD, 2"x 2" SLEEPERS - 16" O.C. ON RESILIENT STEEL CLIPS, 6" COMBINATION FLOOR (SIMILAR TO F-20) 1/2" TWO-COAT GYPSUM PLASTER CEILING

F-22

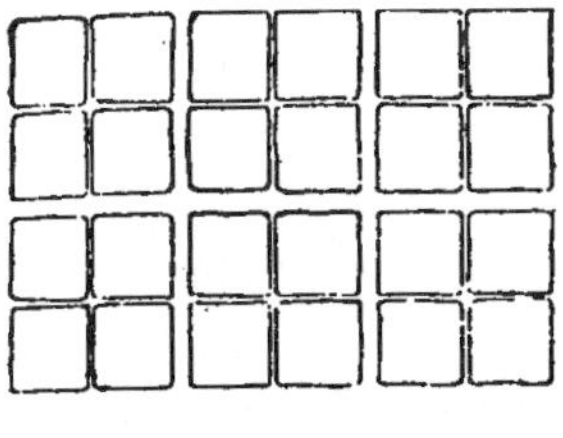

By groups of four squares as a unit separated by wider joints, the scale is increased.

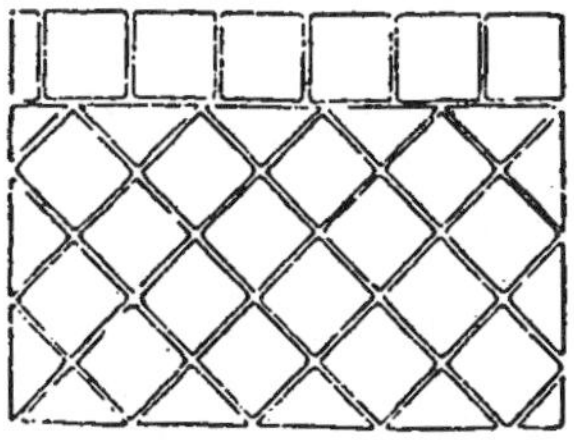

A diagonal pattern of square tiles is emphasized by a border.

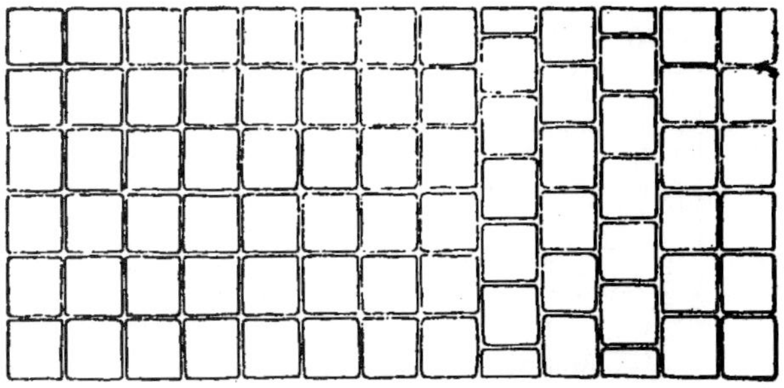

By a few rows of broken joints, an effect of border is produced in a field of square tiles.

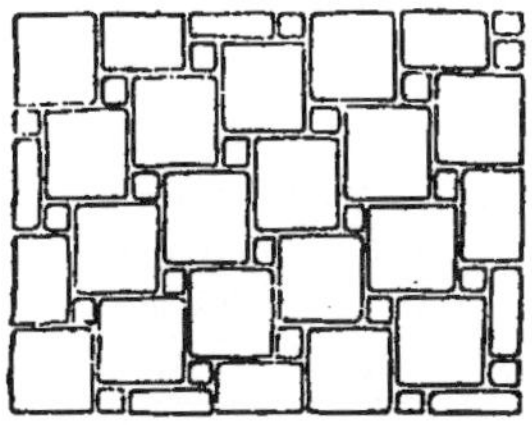

When the small squares are less than one-quarter of the area of the large squares, the pattern runs off at the side.

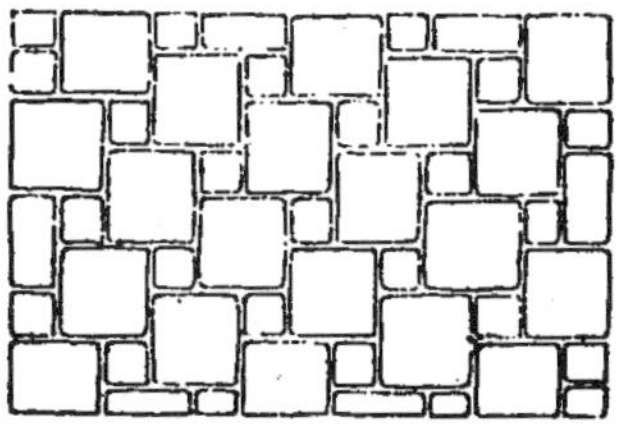

When the small squares are one quarter of the area of the large squares, the pattern has more repose.

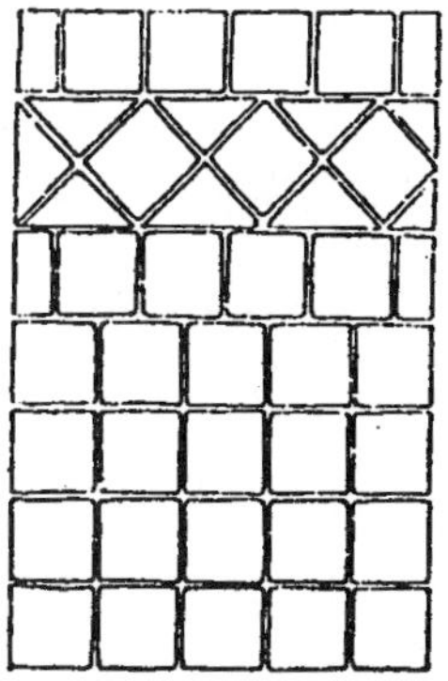

By breaking joints in one course, the border is made wide.

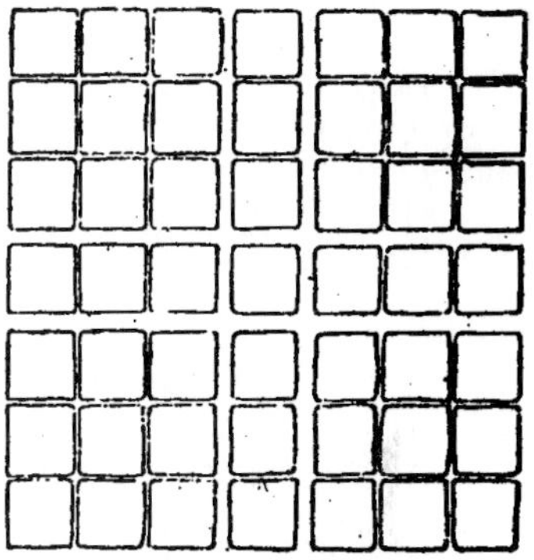

An arrangement adapted to large rooms.

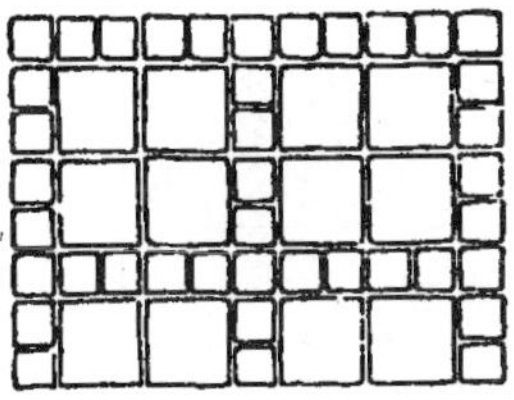

Another way to increase the scale with small tiles.

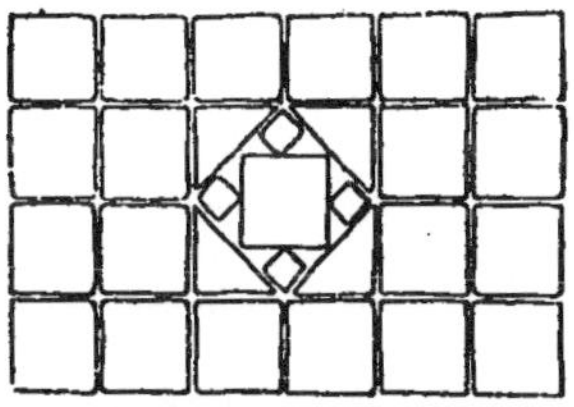

A decorative pattern that can be made on the job.

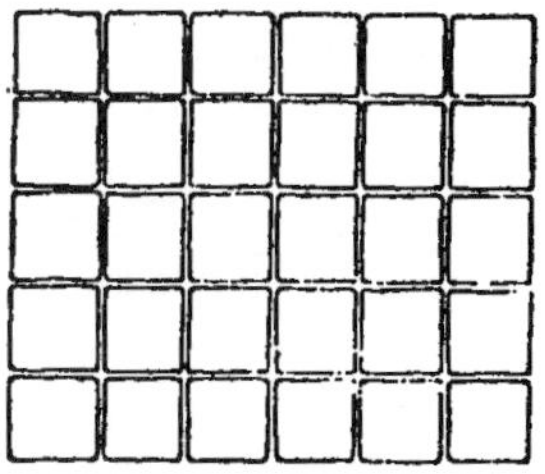

The simplest floor of square tiles is interesting if the joints are in scale.

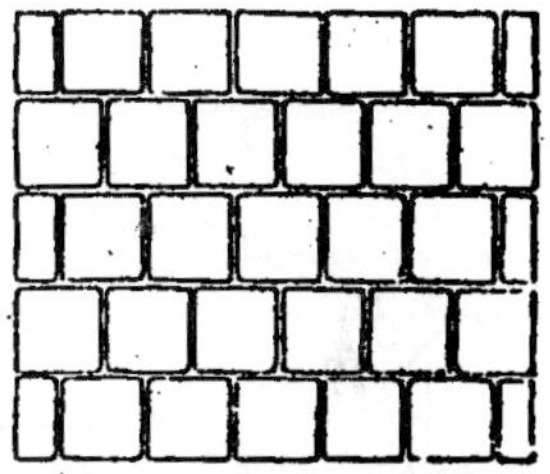

When square tiles are laid with broken joints, long lines in one direction are the result.

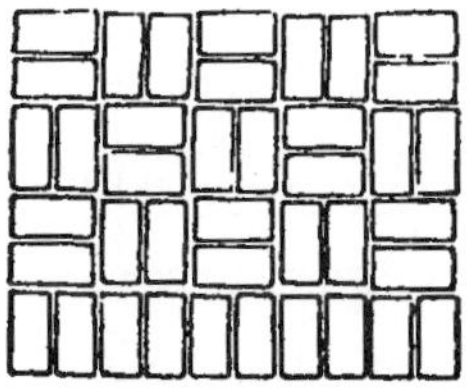

When double squares are laid "basket pattern," the necessary allowance for joints adds interest.

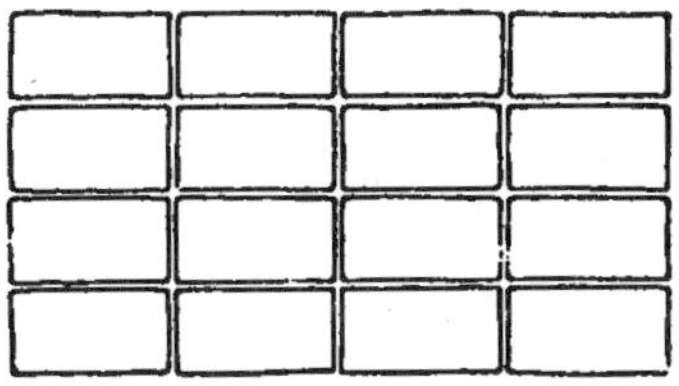

A good pattern for corridors.

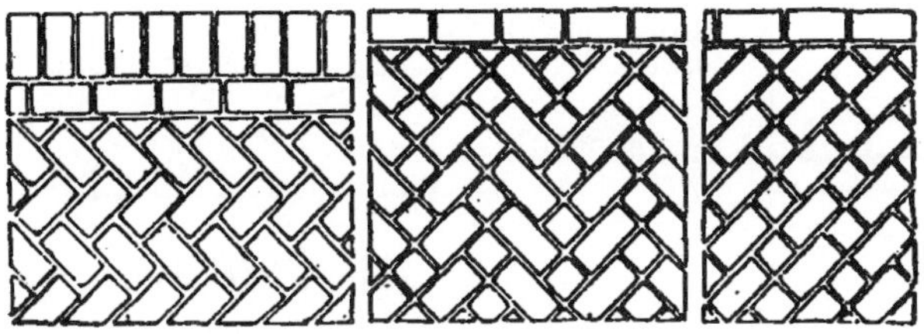

Varieties of "herringbone."

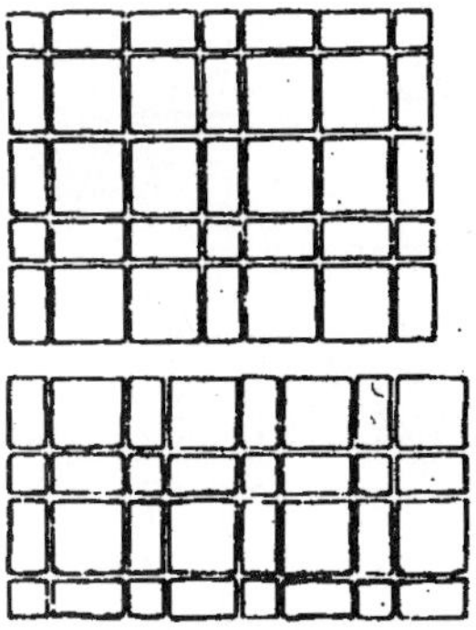

Two combinations suggesting plaids.

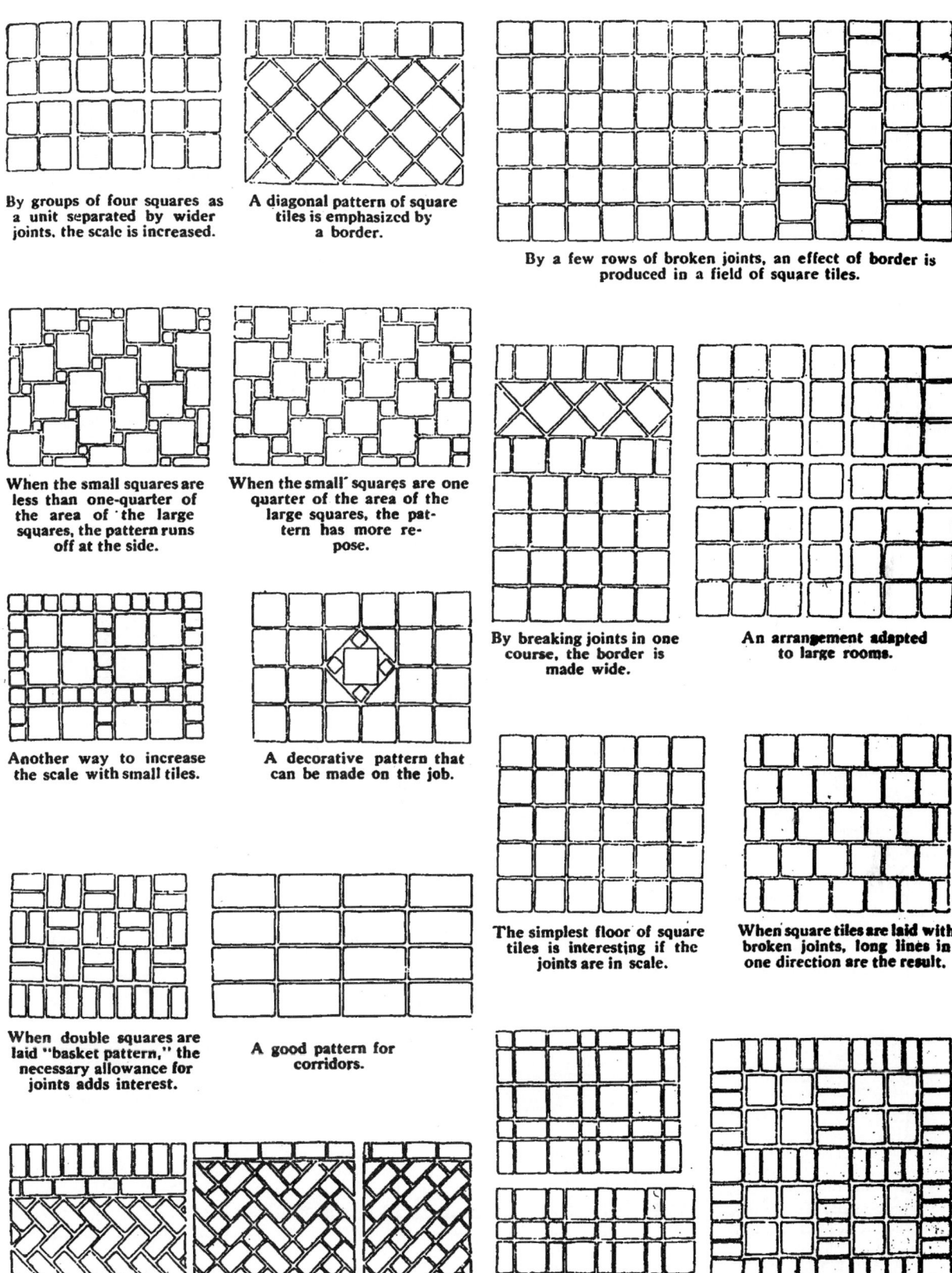

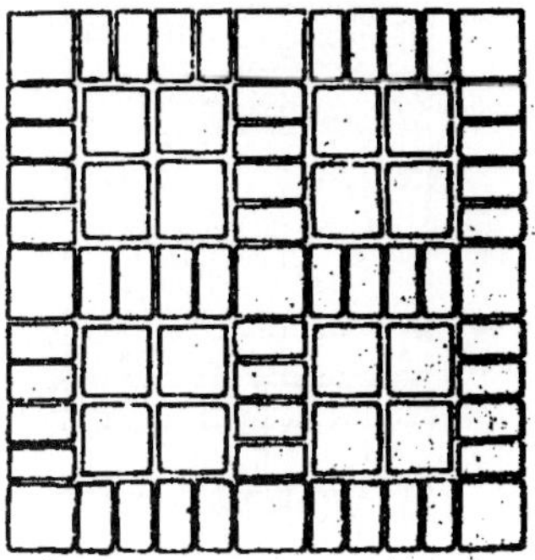

A simple device for a panel or a floor for a large room.

FLOORS AND FLOOR FINISHES
Marble Floor Patterns and Details

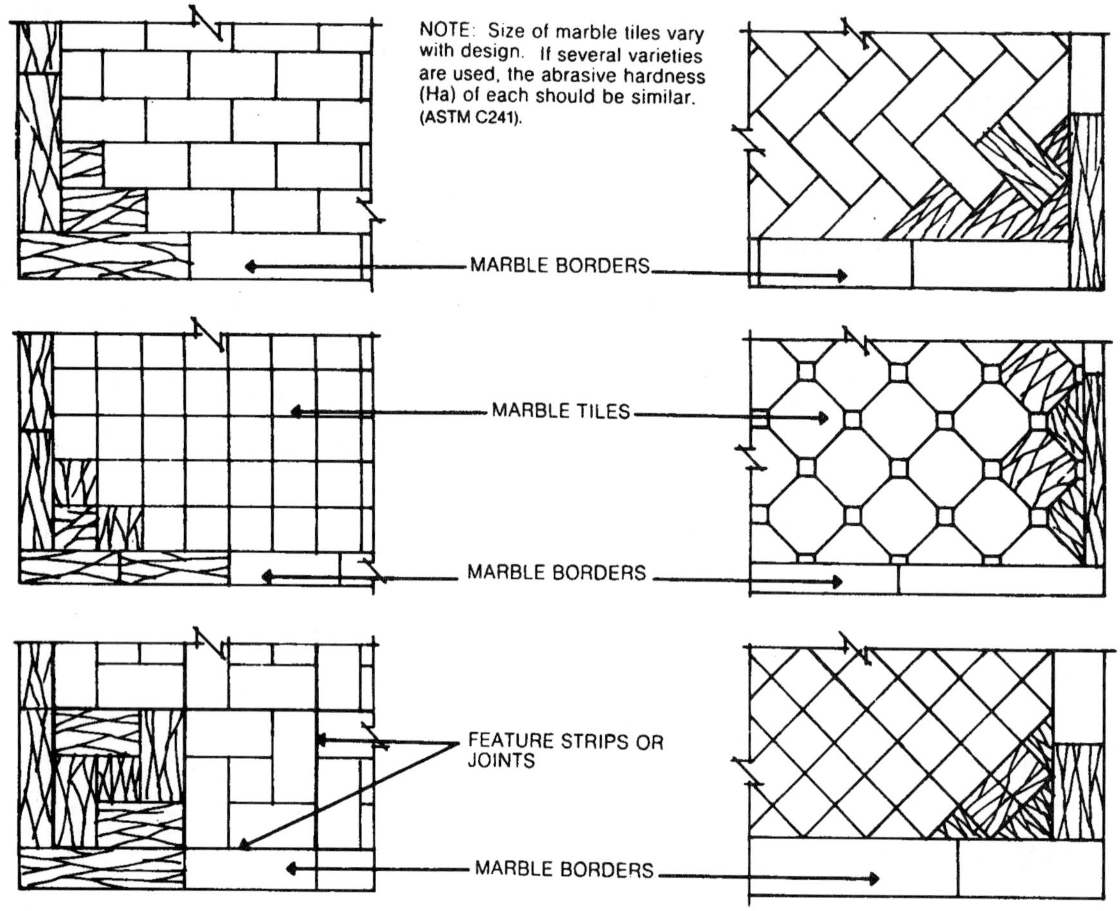

TYPICAL MARBLE FLOORING DESIGNS 3/8"=1'-0"

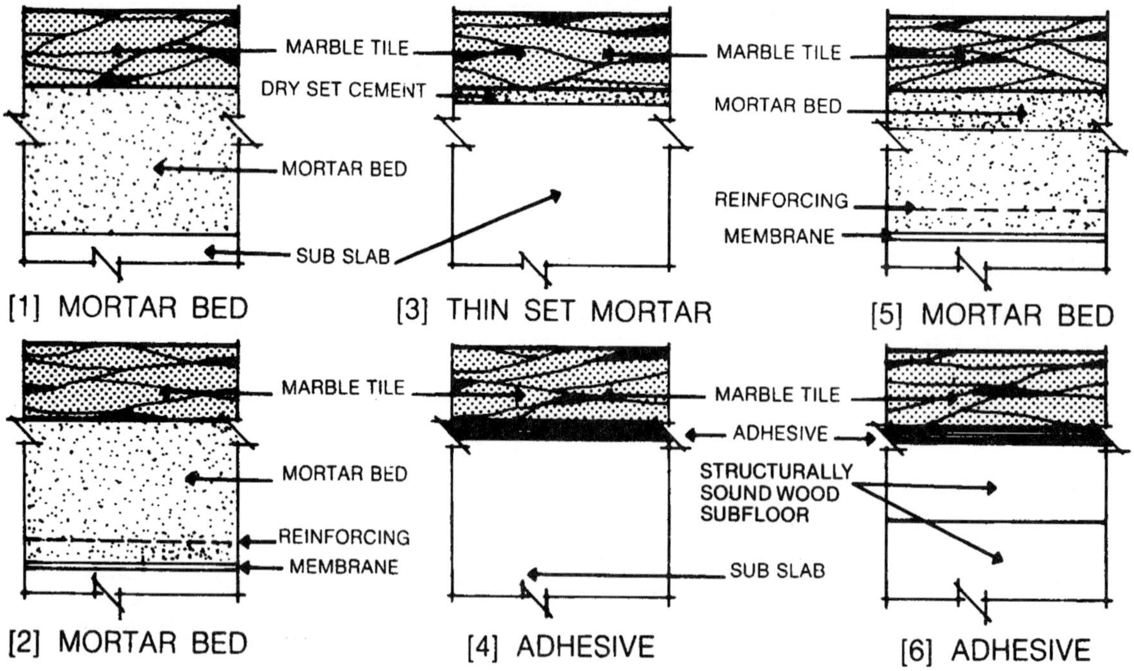

METHODS OF INSTALLATION HALF SIZE

Fig. 1 Marble flooring details

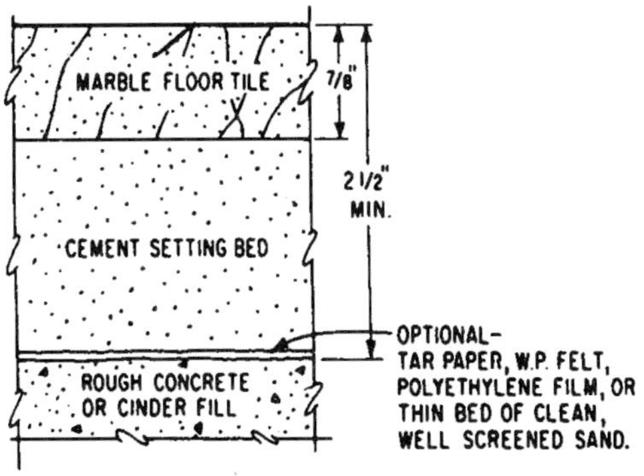

a. Standard floor tile, preferred method

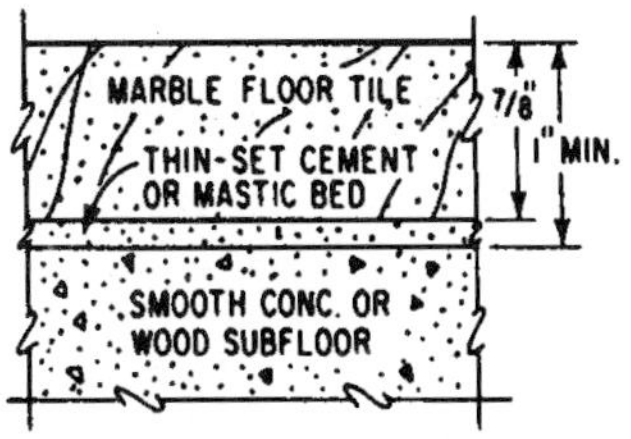

b. Standard floor tile, thin-set method

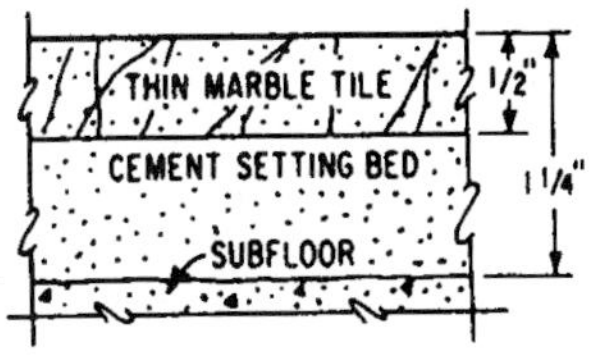

c. Thin marble tile, preferred method

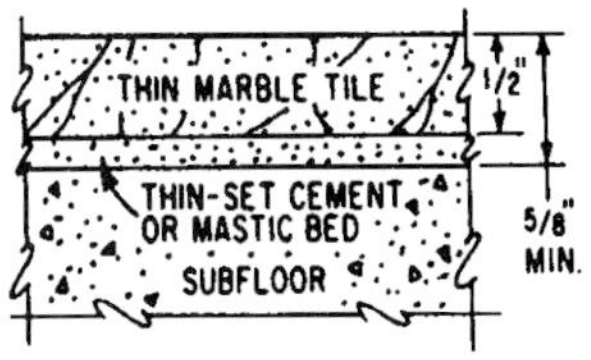

d. Thin marble tile, thin-set method

Fig. 2 Marble floor setting methods

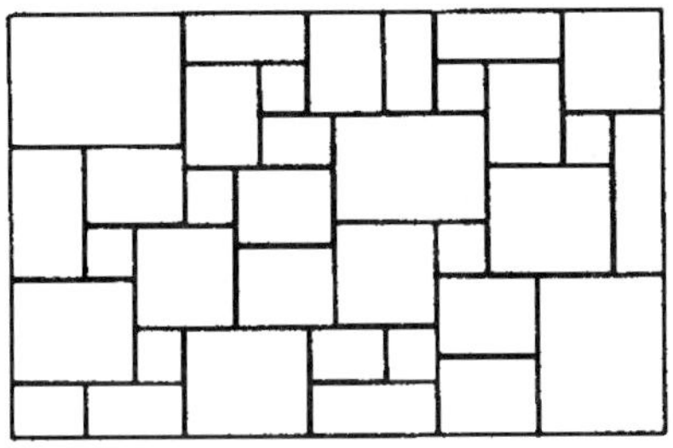

a. Random rectangular

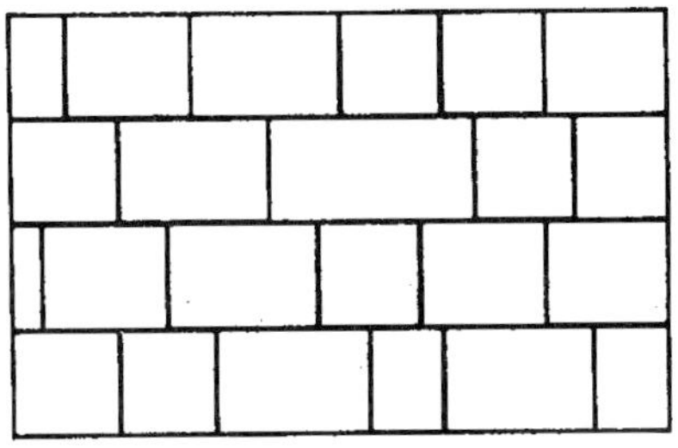

b. Coursed

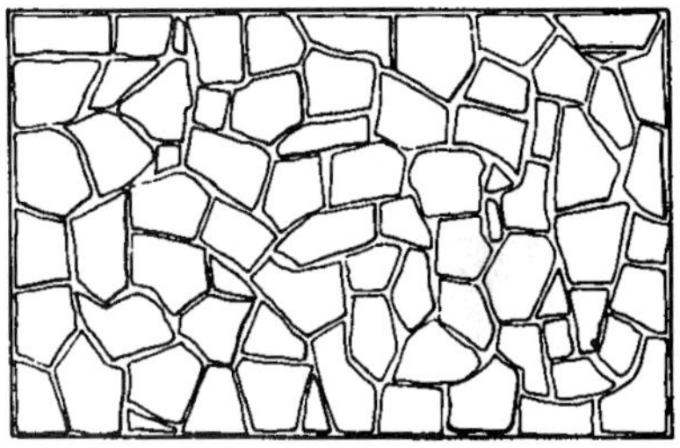

c. Irregular or mosaic

Fig. 3 Flagging patterns

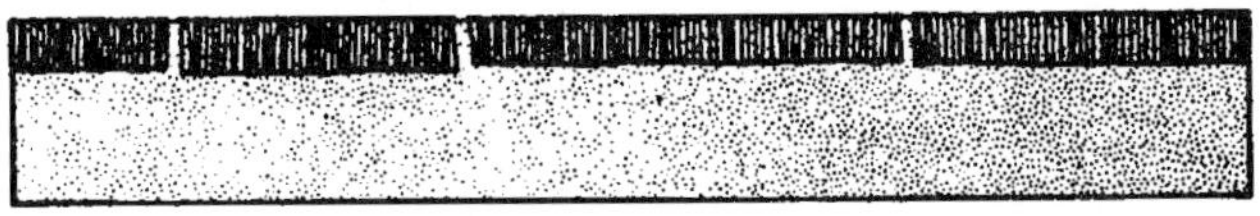

Flagging 1 to 1½ in.
Sand bed 4 in.

a. On sand bed

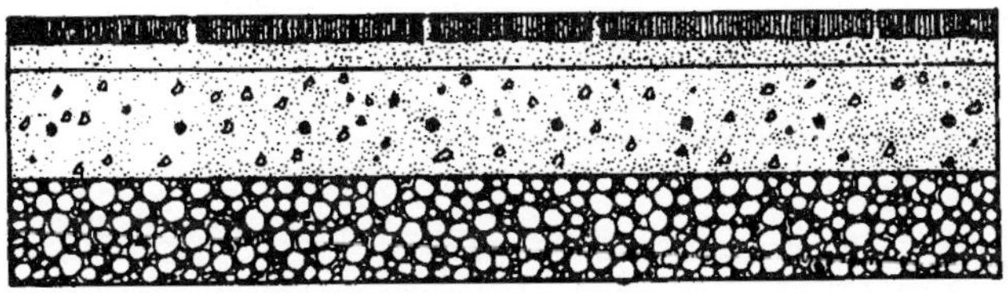

Flagging ¾ to 1 in.
Setting bed 1 to 1½ in.
Reinforced concrete slab 4 in.
Gravel or cinders 4 in.

b. On concrete slab on grade

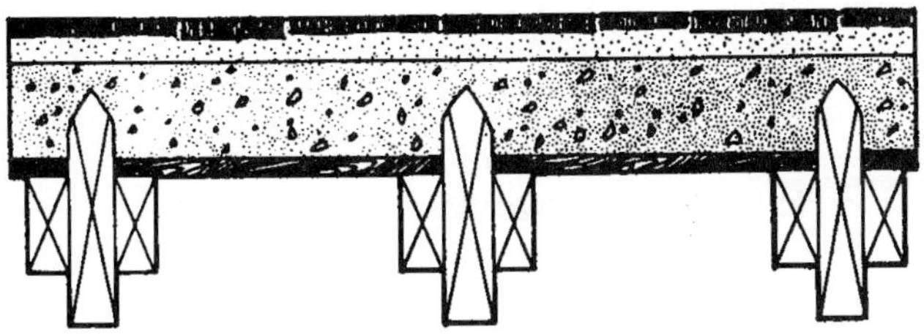

Flagging ¾ to 1 in.
Setting bed 1 to 1½ in.
Reinforced concrete slab 4 in.
Wood subfloor ¾ in.

c. On wood joist construction

Fig. 4 Flagstone setting methods

FLOORS AND FLOOR FINISHES

Saddles/Floor Transitions

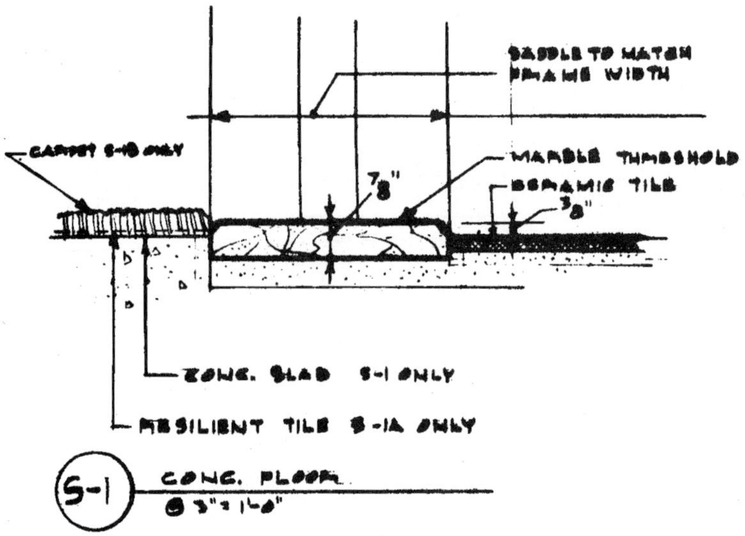

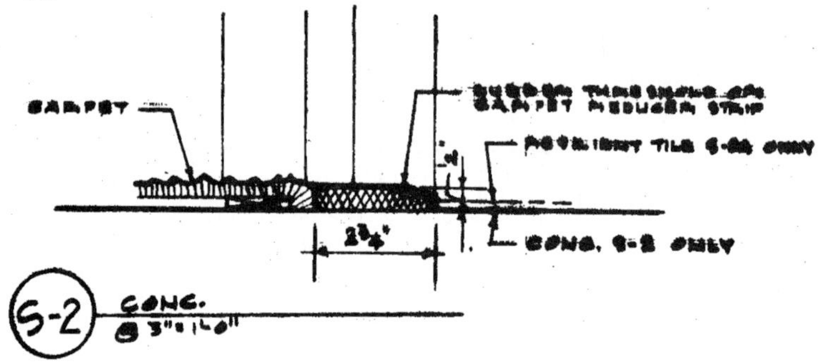

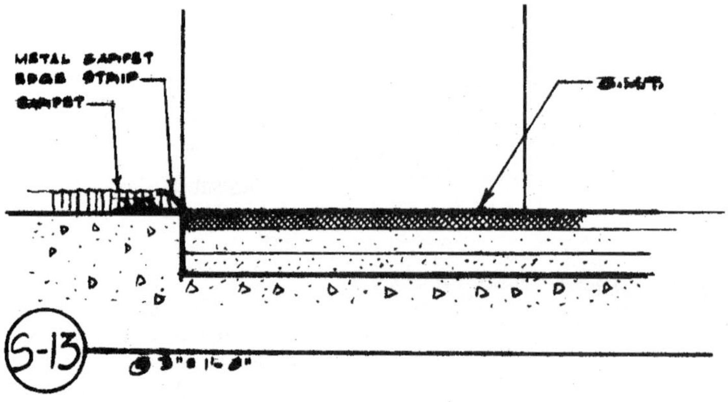

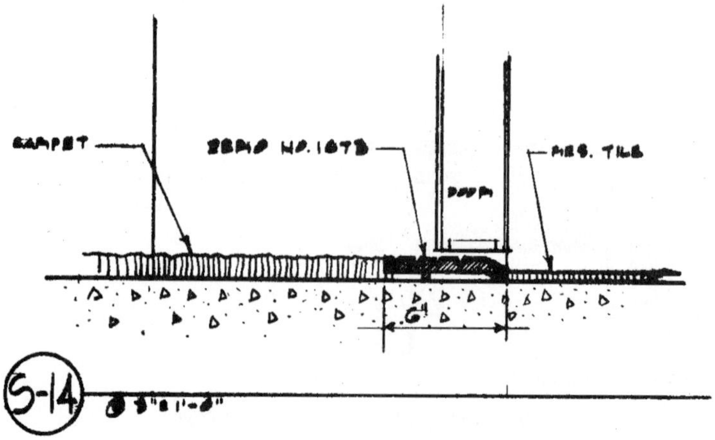

FLOORS AND FLOOR FINISHES
Saddles/Floor Transitions

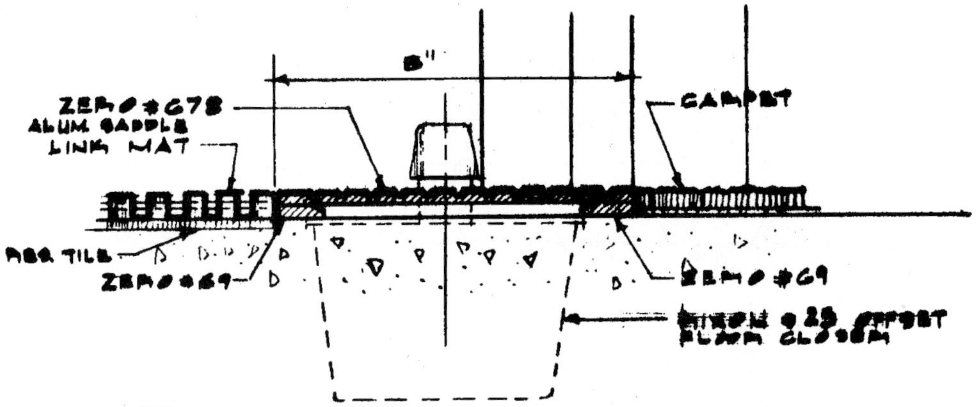

S-4 @ 3"=1'-0"
NOTE: SEE DETAIL # IN THIS SHEET

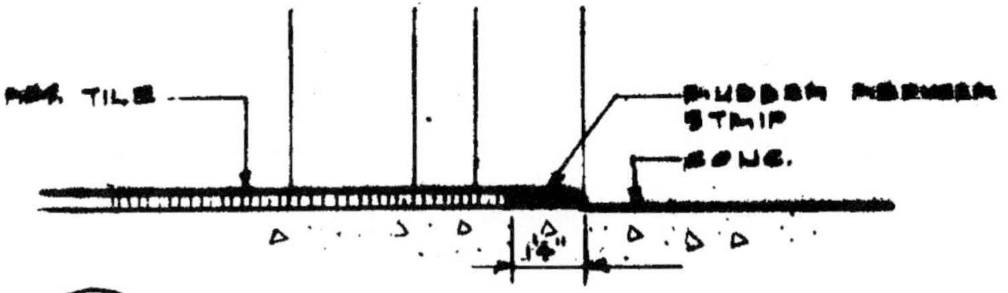

S-6 @ 3"=1'-0"

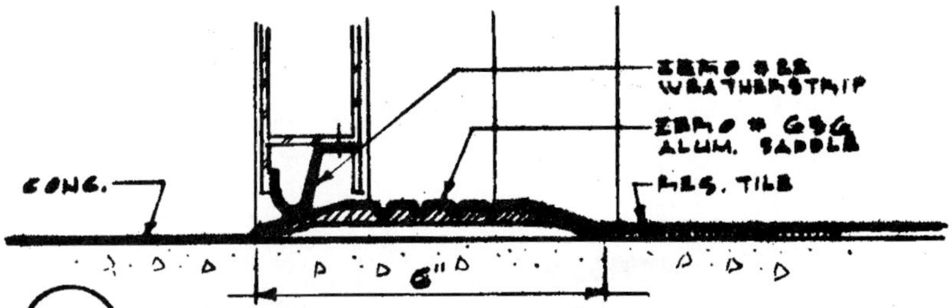

S-7 RES. TILE
@ 3"=1'-0"

S-7A CONC. OR QUARRY TILE
@ 3"=1'-0"

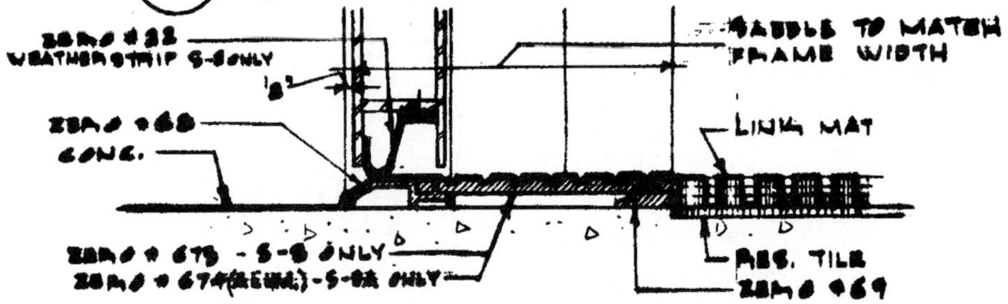

S-8 @ 3"=1'-0"

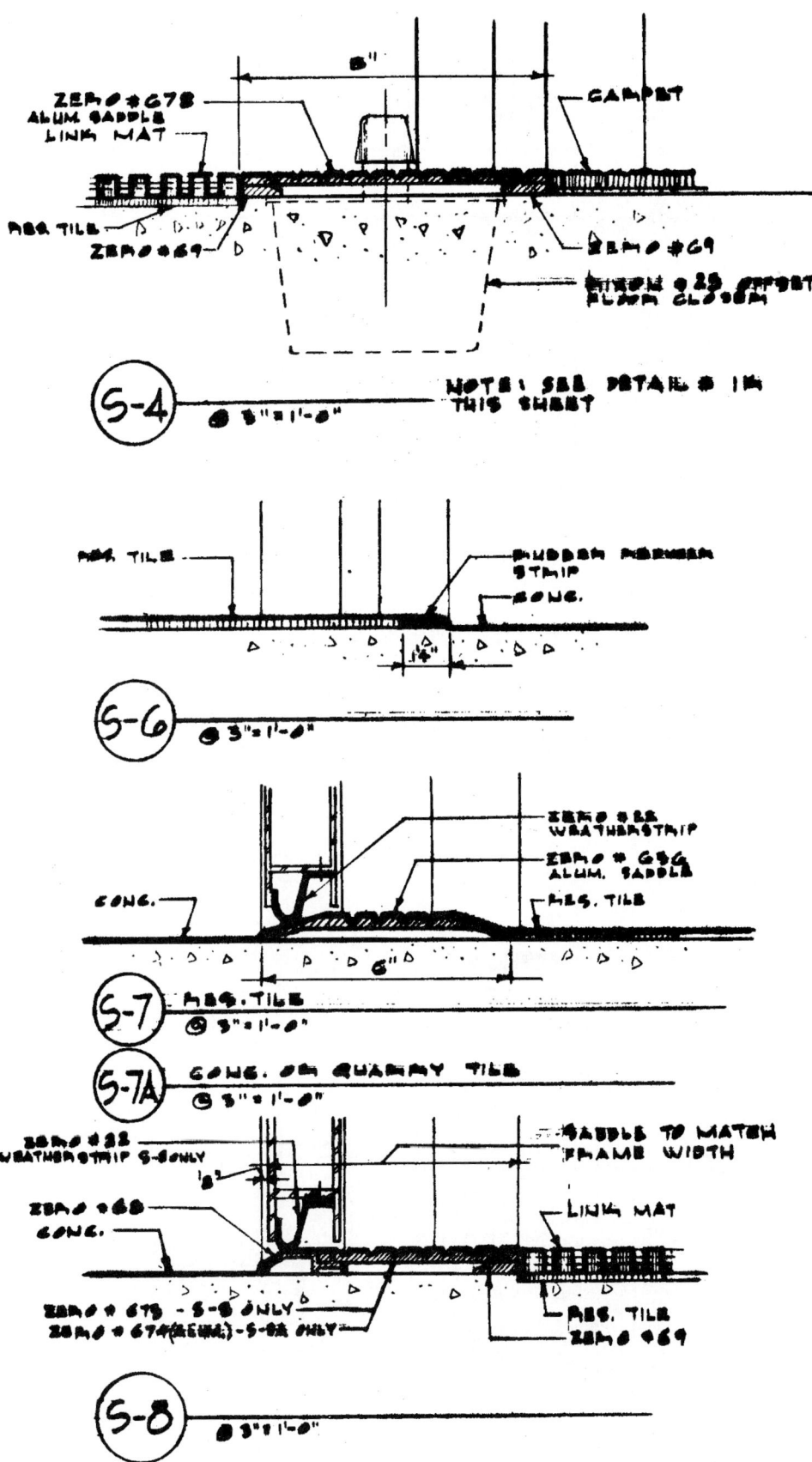

FLOORS AND FLOOR FINISHES

Saddles/Floor Transitions

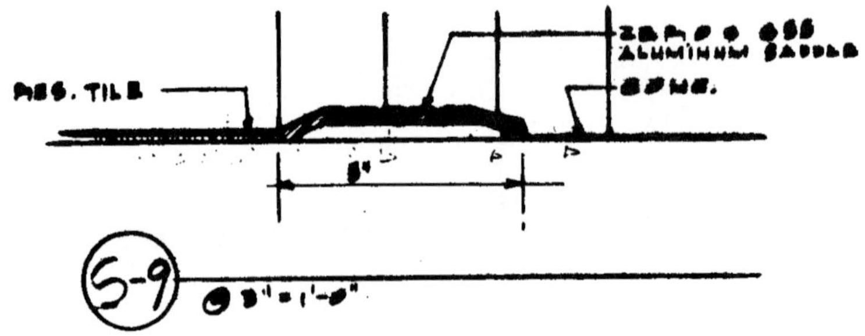

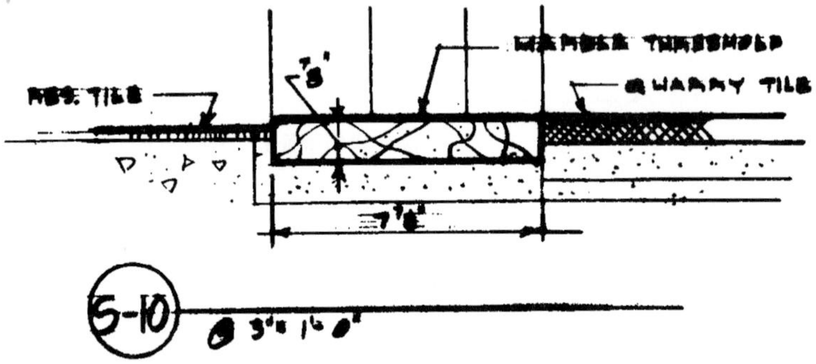

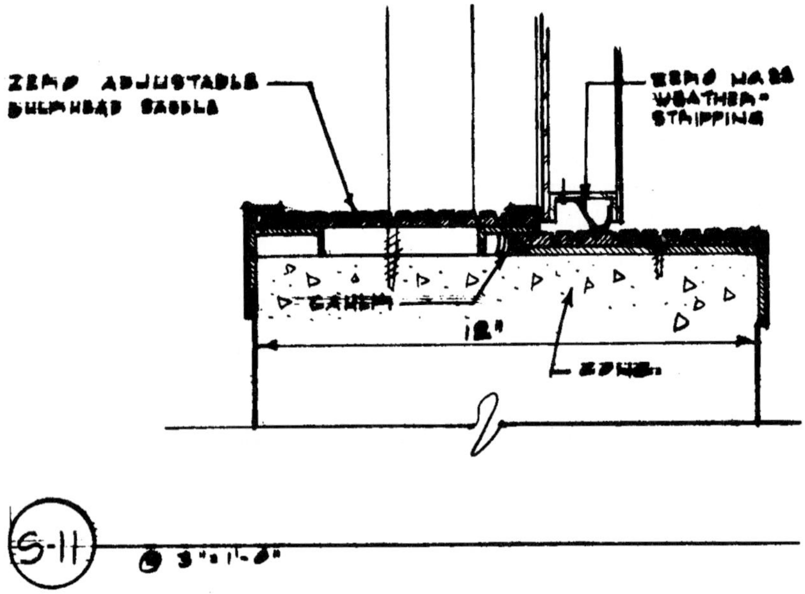

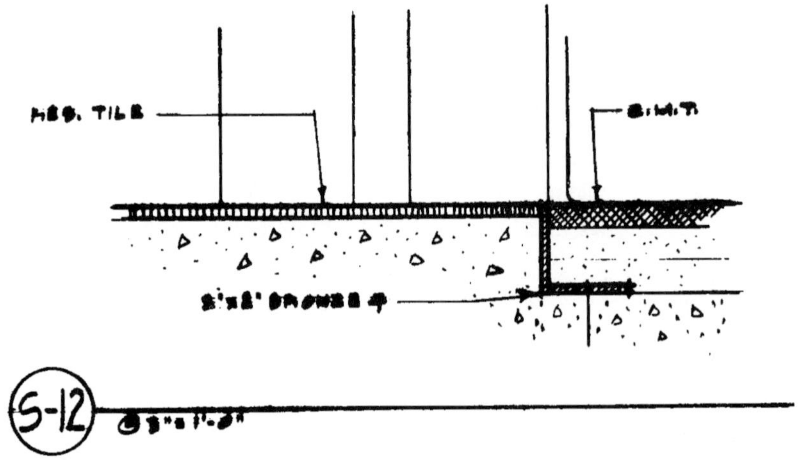

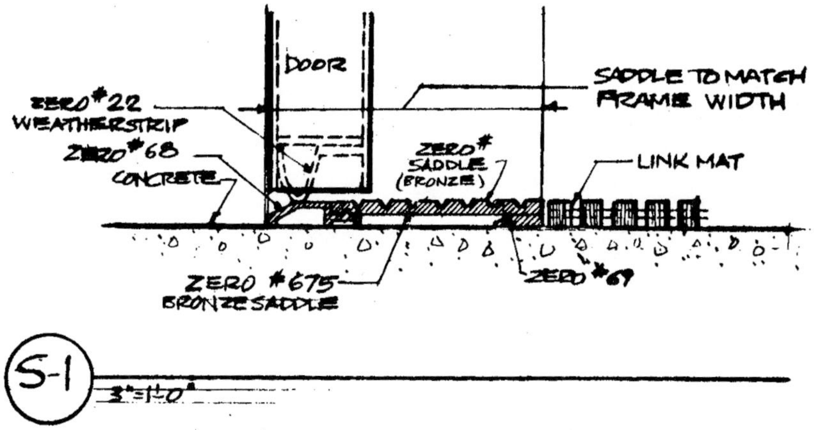
DOOR
SADDLE TO MATCH FRAME WIDTH
ZERO #22 WEATHERSTRIP
ZERO #68
CONCRETE
ZERO # SADDLE (BRONZE)
LINK MAT
ZERO #675 BRONZE SADDLE
ZERO #69
S-1
3"=1'-0"

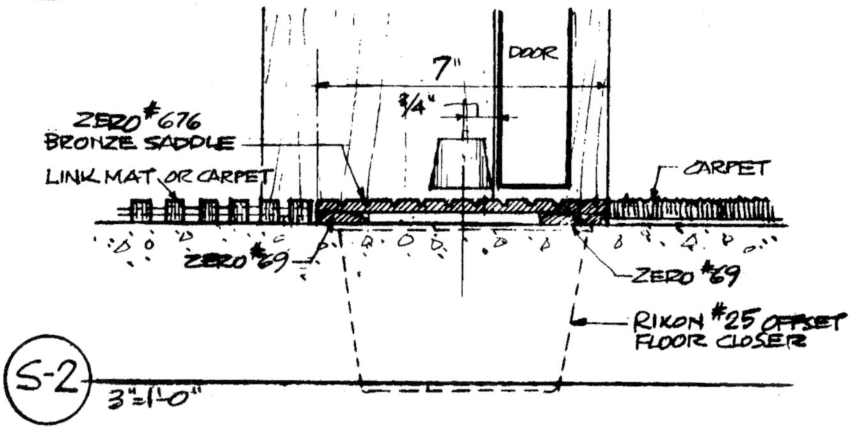
DOOR
7"
3/4"
ZERO #676 BRONZE SADDLE
LINK MAT OR CARPET
CARPET
ZERO #69
ZERO #69
RIKON #25 OFFSET FLOOR CLOSER
S-2
3"=1'-0"

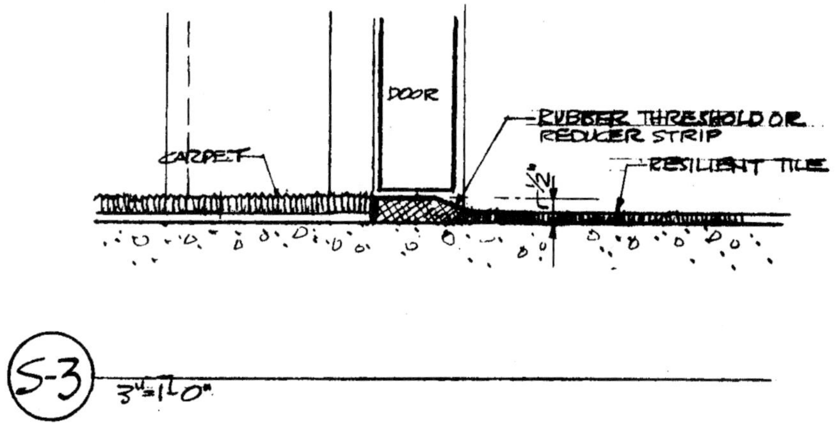
DOOR
RUBBER THRESHOLD OR REDUCER STRIP
RESILIENT TILE
CARPET
1/2"
S-3
3"=1'-0"

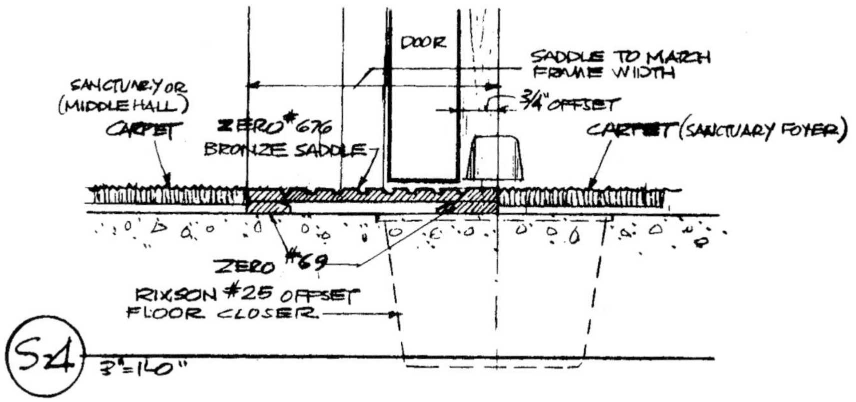
DOOR
SADDLE TO MATCH FRAME WIDTH
3/4" OFFSET
SANCTUARY OR (MIDDLE HALL) CARPET
ZERO #676 BRONZE SADDLE
CARPET (SANCTUARY FOYER)
ZERO #69
RIXSON #25 OFFSET FLOOR CLOSER
S-4
3"=1'-0"

FLOORS AND FLOOR FINISHES

Door Saddles

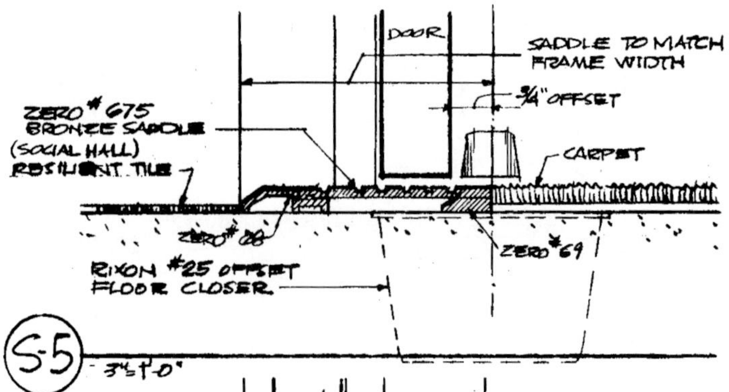

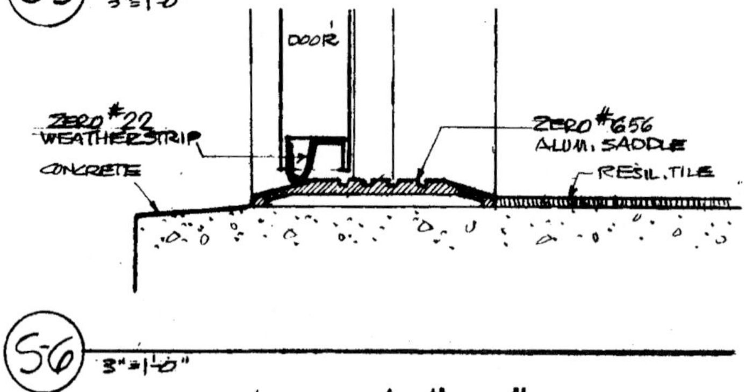

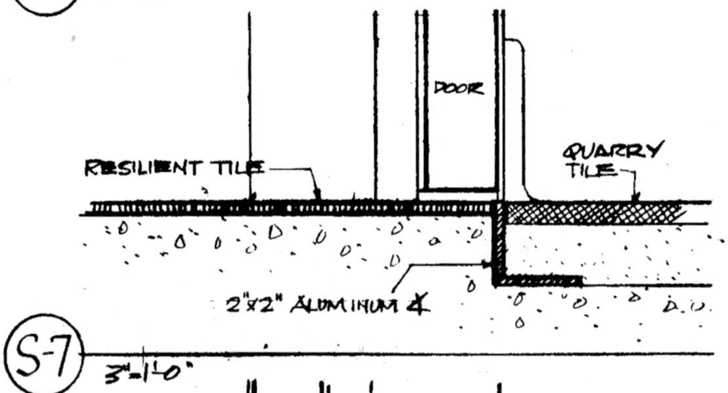

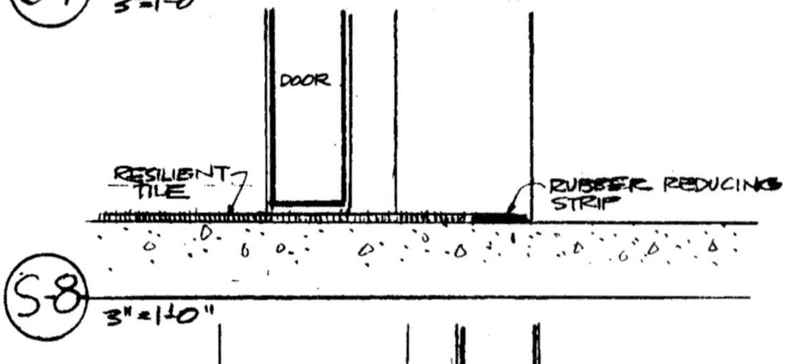

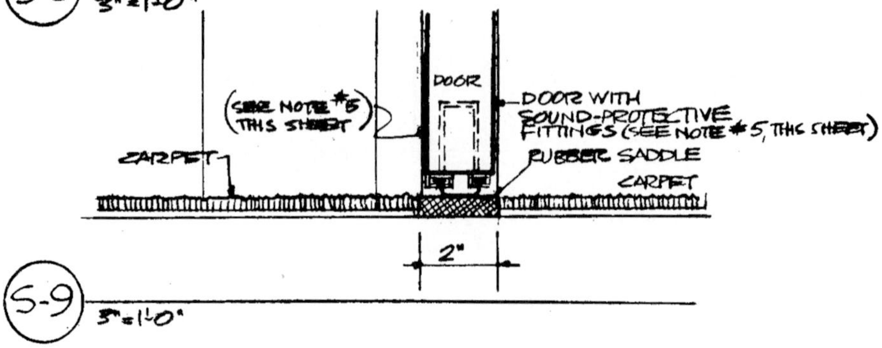

FLOORS AND FLOOR FINISHES

Saddles/Floor Transitions

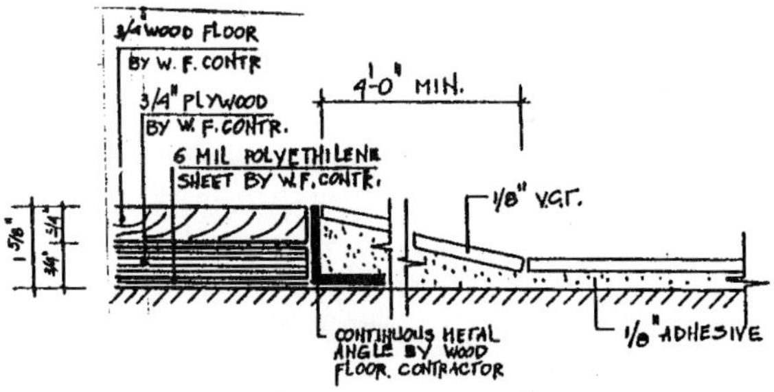

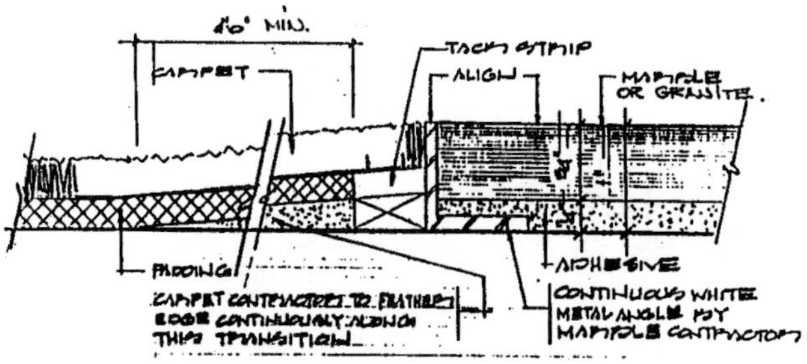

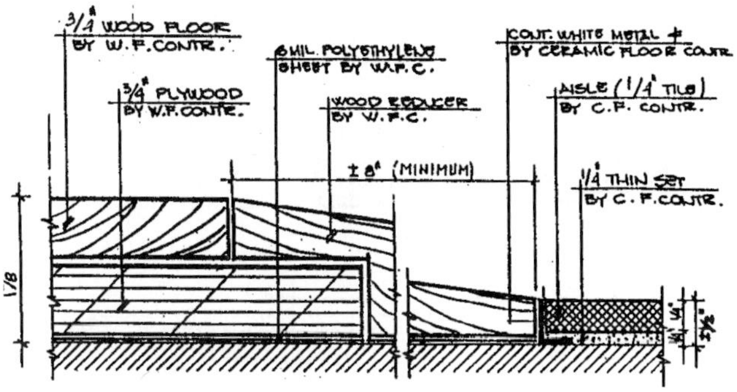

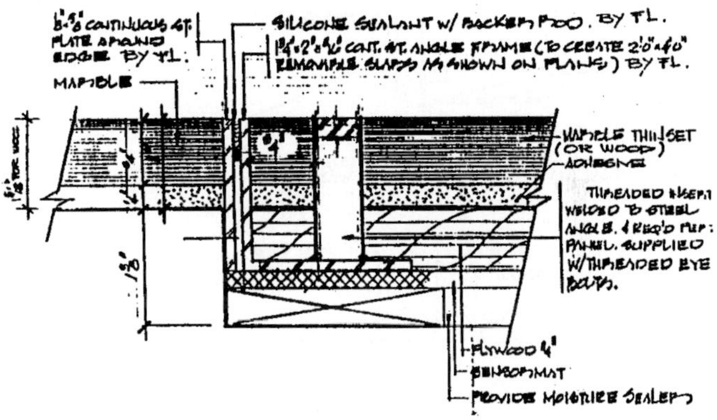

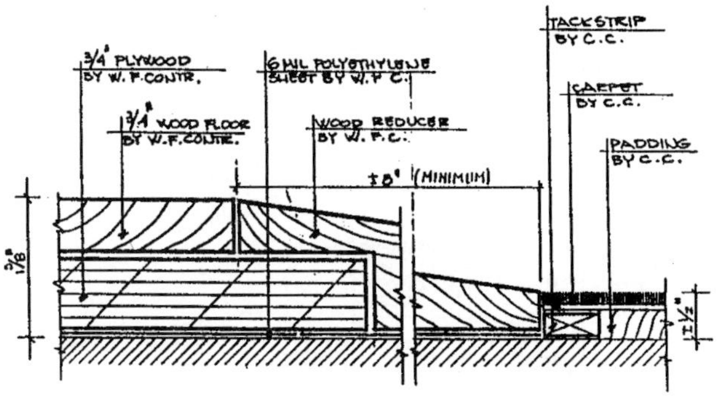

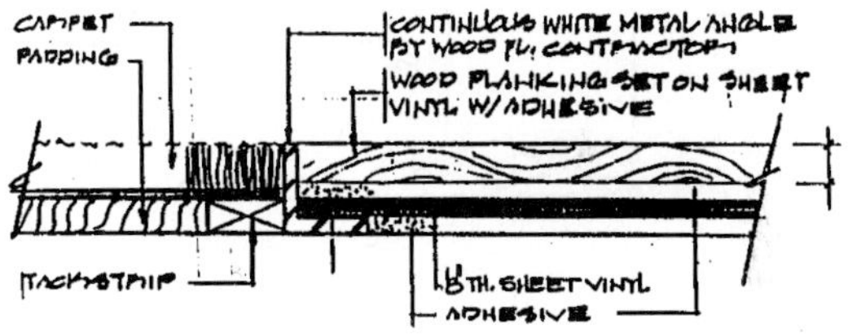

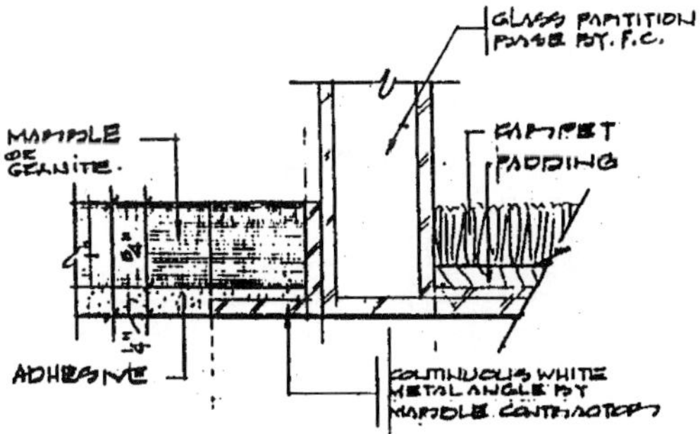

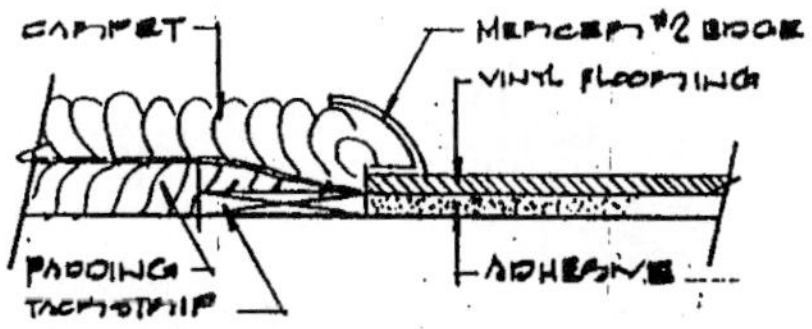

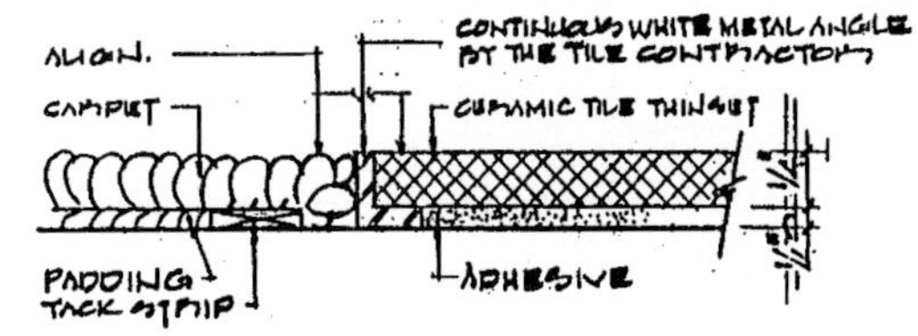

FLOORS AND FLOOR FINISHES
Saddles/Floor Transitions

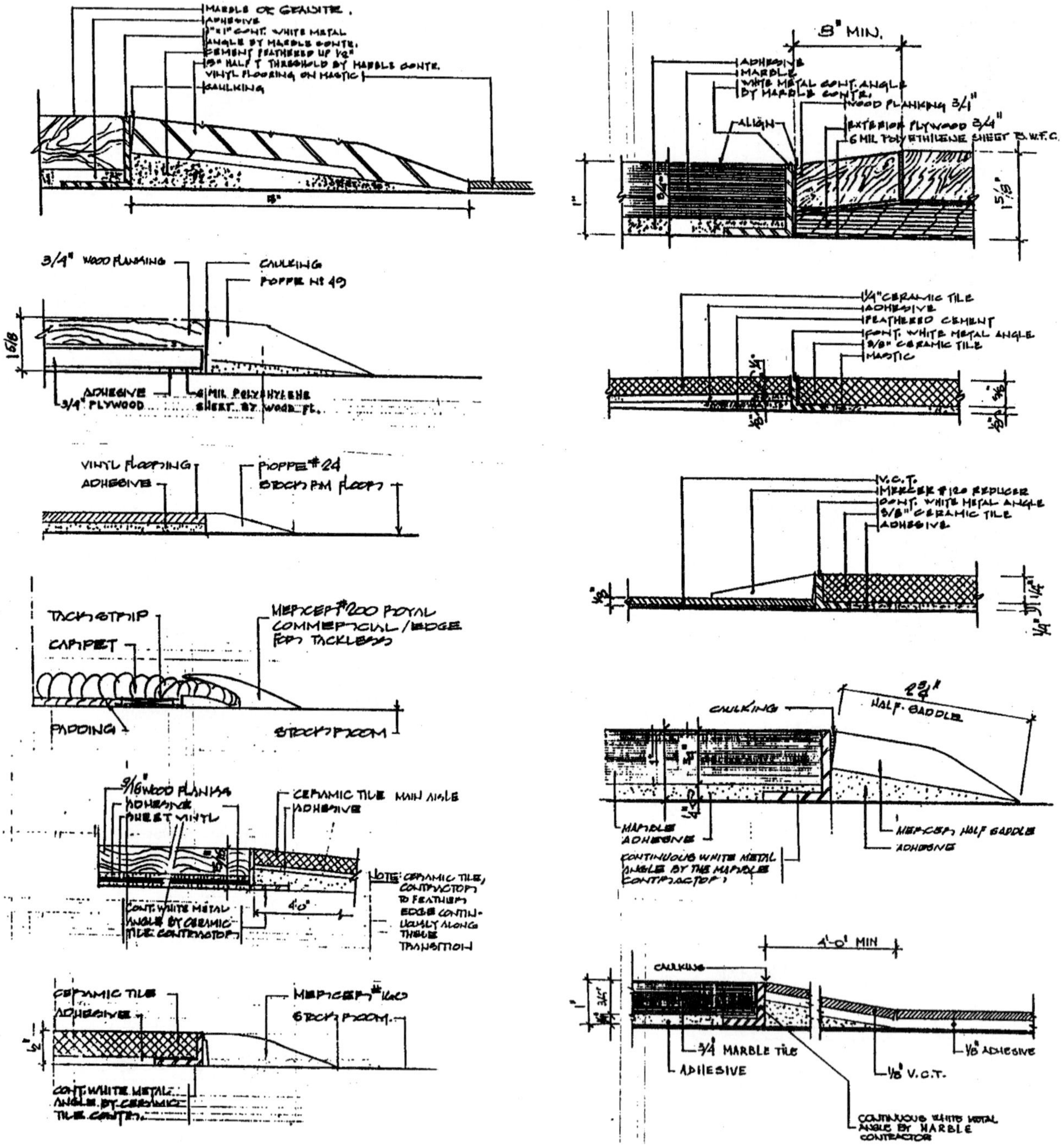

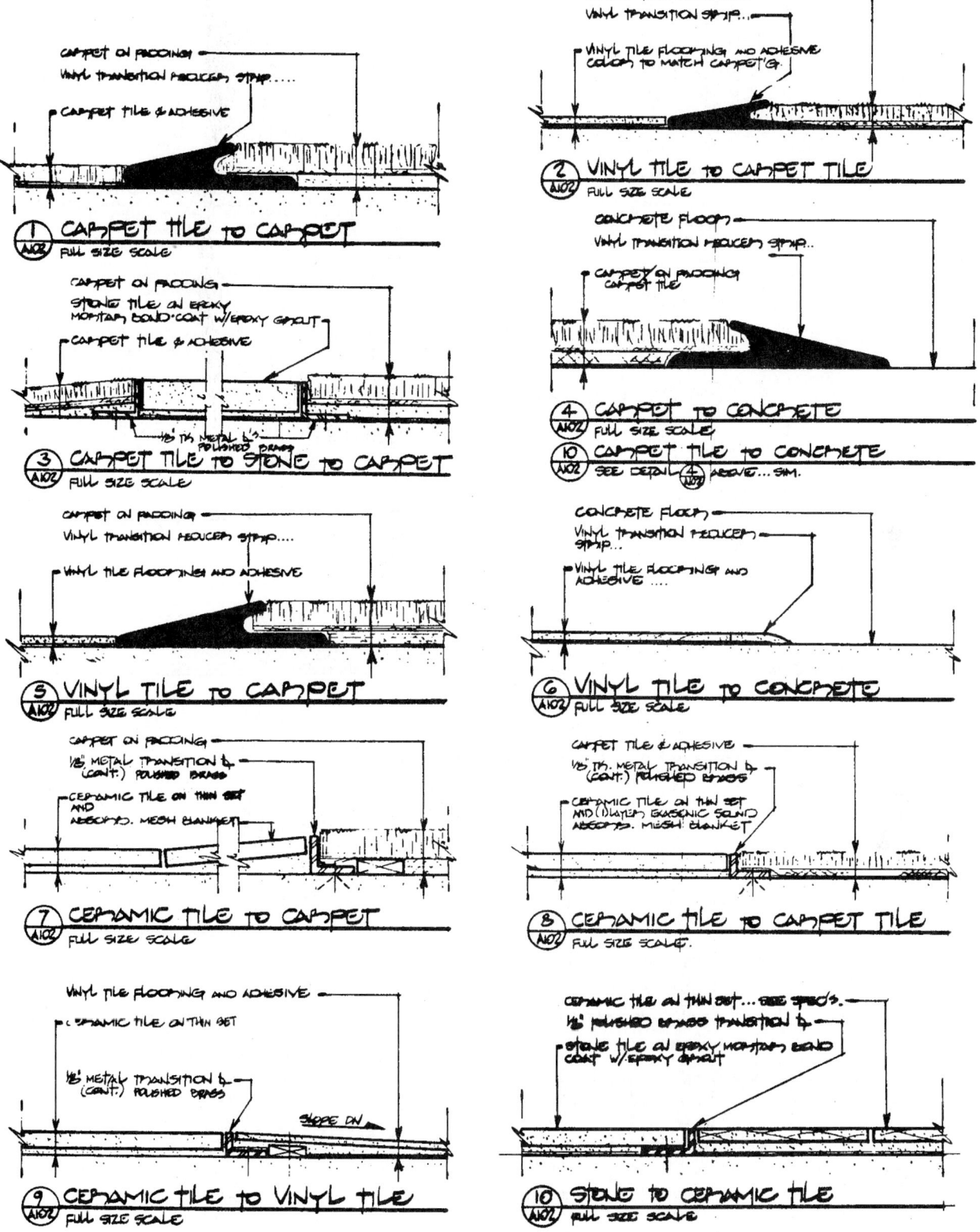

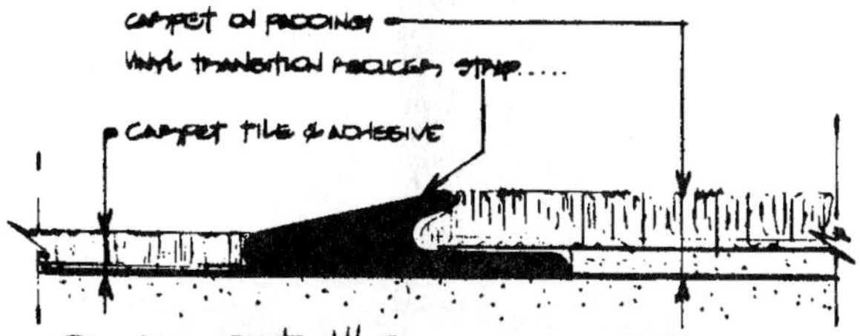

1 CARPET TILE TO CARPET
A102 FULL SIZE SCALE

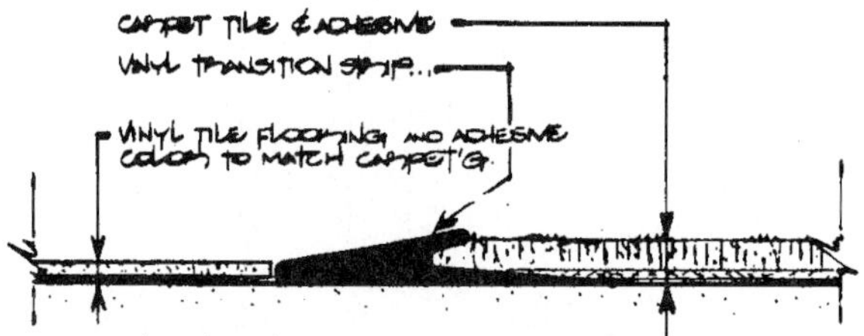

2 VINYL TILE TO CARPET TILE
A102 FULL SIZE SCALE

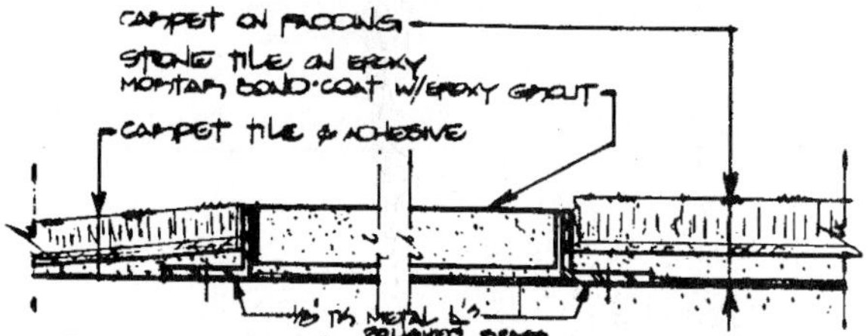

3 CARPET TILE TO STONE TO CARPET
A102 FULL SIZE SCALE

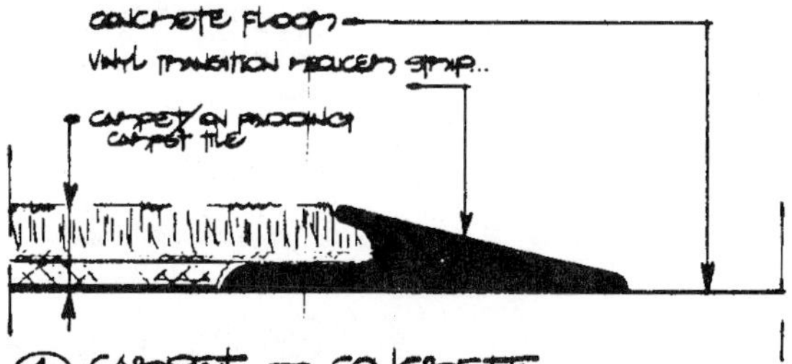

4 CARPET TO CONCRETE
A102 FULL SIZE SCALE

10 CARPET TILE TO CONCRETE
A102 SEE DETAIL 4/A102 ABOVE... SIM.

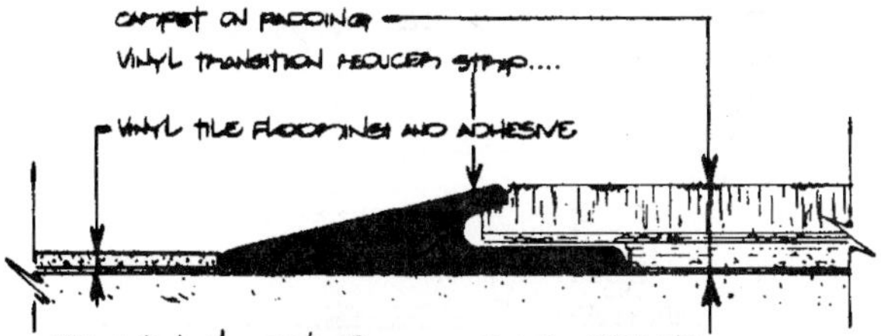

5 VINYL TILE TO CARPET
A102 FULL SIZE SCALE

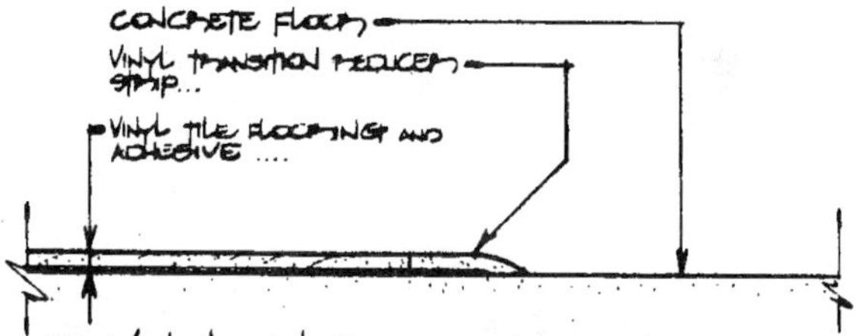

6 VINYL TILE TO CONCRETE
A102 FULL SIZE SCALE

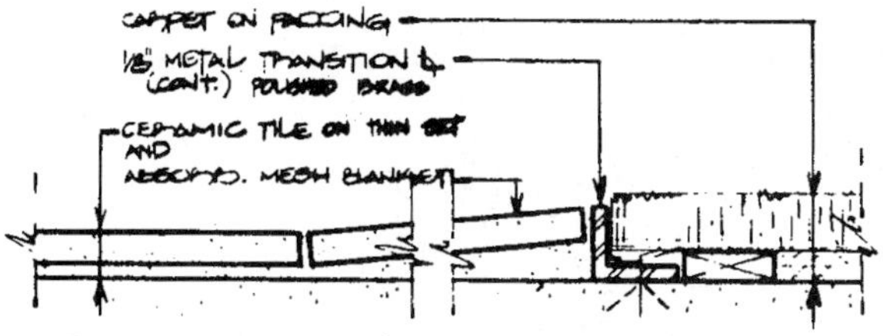

7 CERAMIC TILE TO CARPET
A102 FULL SIZE SCALE

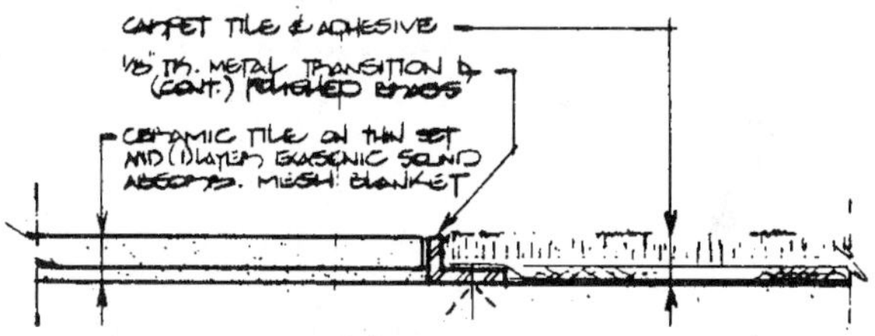

8 CERAMIC TILE TO CARPET TILE
A102 FULL SIZE SCALE.

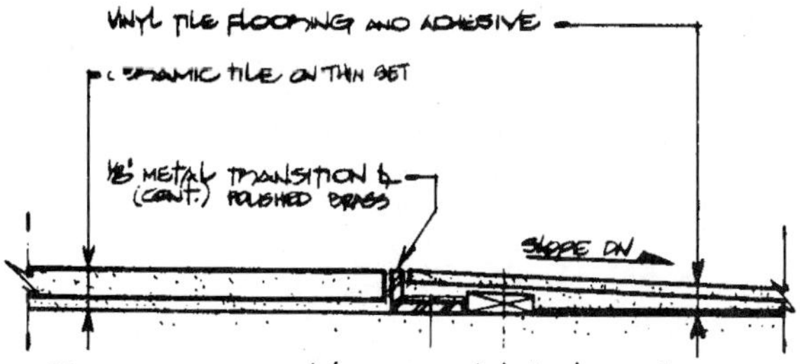

9 CERAMIC TILE TO VINYL TILE
A102 FULL SIZE SCALE

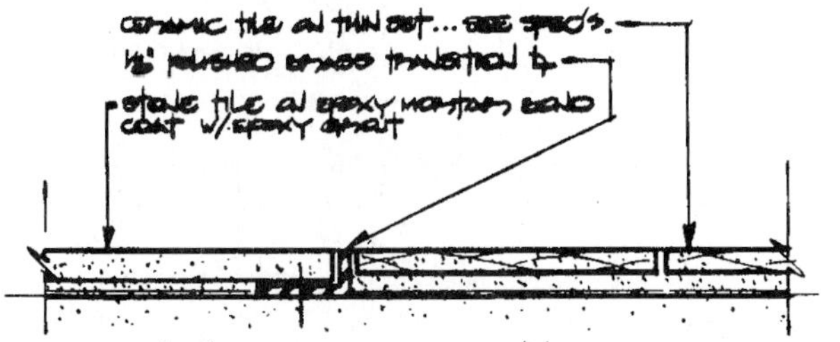

10 STONE TO CERAMIC TILE
A102 FULL SIZE SCALE

FLOORS AND FLOOR FINISHES

Floor Finish Transition Details

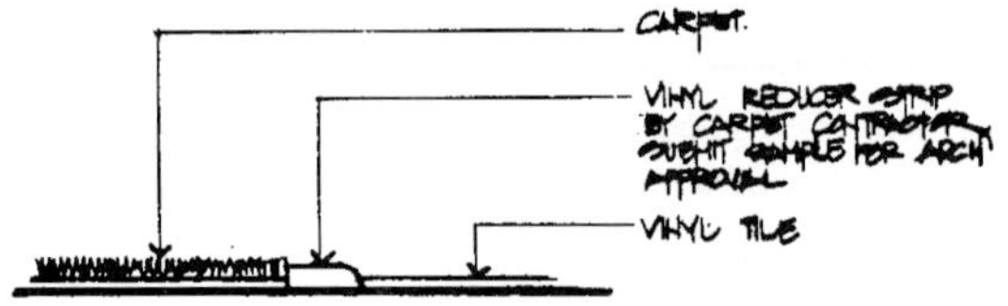

2 SECTION @ FLOOR TRANSITION/ CARPET/VAT
NTS

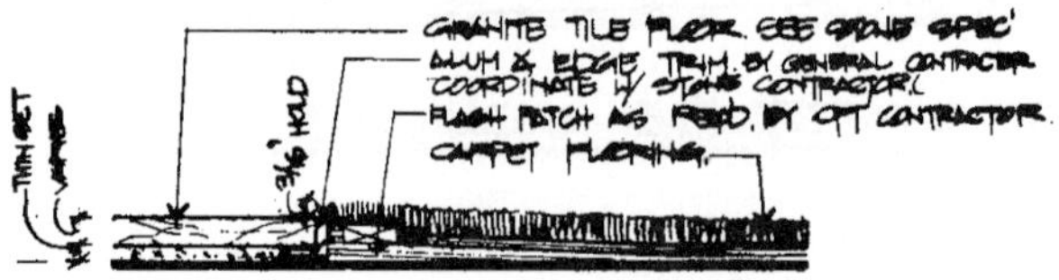

1 SECTION @ FLOOR TRANSITION. STONE/CPT'
1/2 F.S.

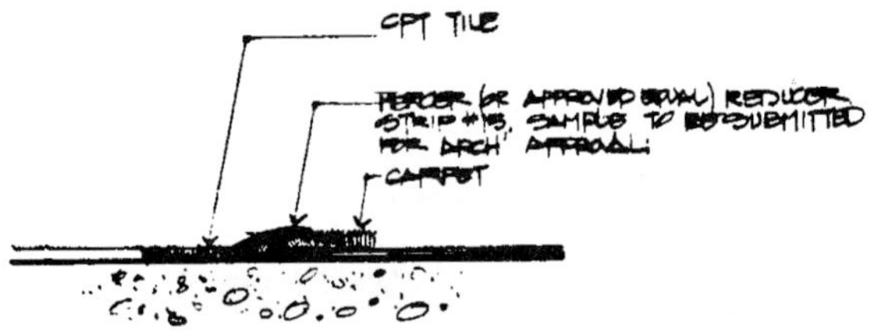

4 SECTION @ FLOOR TRANSITION CPT'TILE/CPT'
NTS

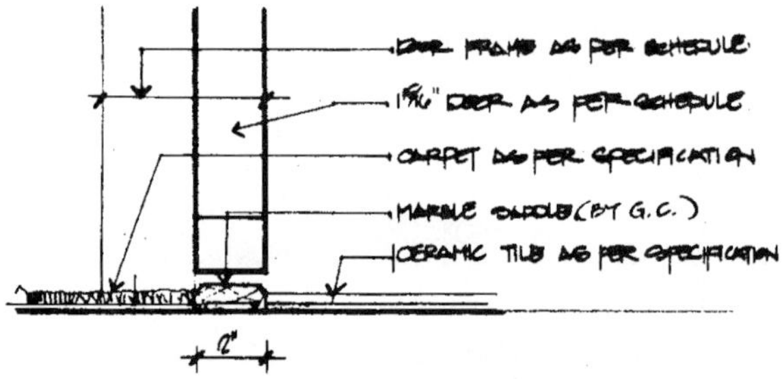

3 SECT @ FLOOR TRANSITION: CPT/C.TILE.
3"=1'-0"

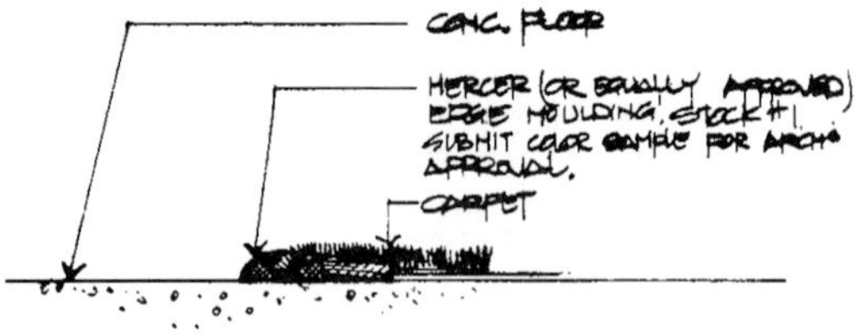

6 SECT @ FLOOR TRANSITION. CPT/CONC.
NTS

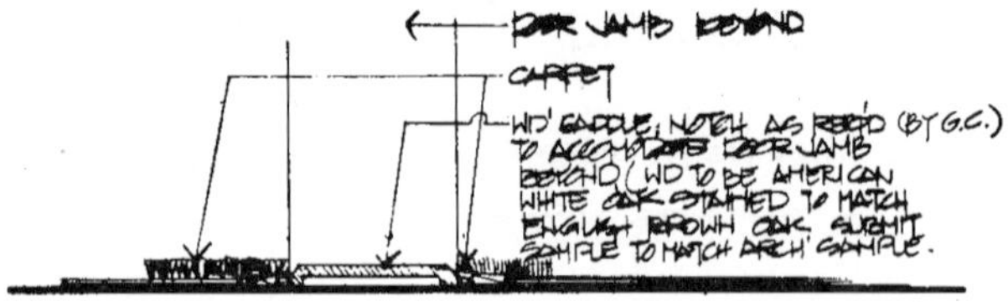

5 SECT @ WD SADDLE.
NTS

FLOORS AND FLOOR FINISHES
Edgings, Tile/Carpet Joiners, and Reducer Strips

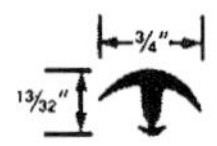

Vinyl Snap Down Divider
- 3/4" wide removable section for joining carpets

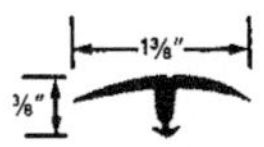

Vinyl Snap Down Divider
- 1 3/8" wide removable section for joining carpets

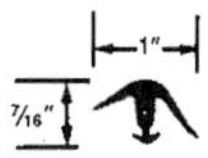

Vinyl Snap Down Edging
- 1" wide removable section for joining carpet to tile

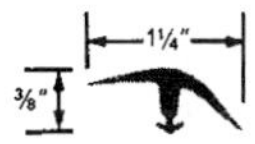

Vinyl Snap Down Edging
- 1 1/4" wide removable section for joining carpet to tile

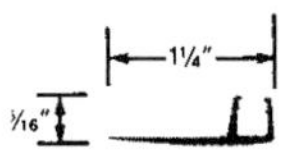

Vinyl Single Flange Track

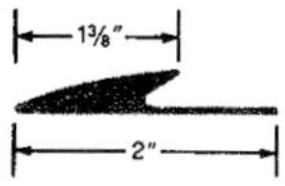

Vinyl 5/16" Glue Down Reducer
- 1/4" butting gauge undercut
- Long flange, smooth taper

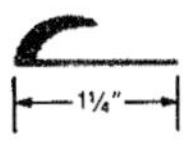

Vinyl Custom Edge
- For sponge backs
- General purpose edge and cap

Vinyl 1/4" Square Cove Cap
- Undercut 1/4"
- Cap for coved carpets and wall paneling

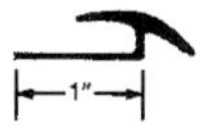

Vinyl Tile Carpet Joiner
- Provides smooth carpet/tile transition

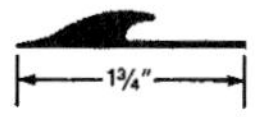

Vinyl 3/16" Glue Down Reducer
- Undercut, flange, and transition combined
- Undercut 3/16" smooth transition

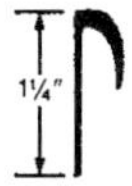

Vinyl Carpet Cove Cap
- Trim for coved carpet
- Undercut 3/16" (flexible)

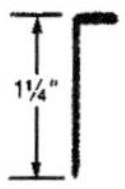

Vinyl 9/32" Cap
- For capping coved carpets, ceramics, and paneling

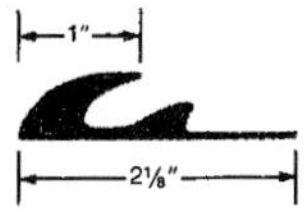

Vinyl Tackless Carpet Bar
- 1/4" butting edge to accept tackless strip
- Deep undercut

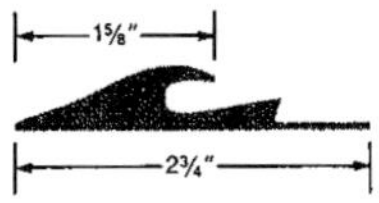

Vinyl Tackless Carpet Bar Reducer
- 1/4" butting edge to accept tackless strip

Vinyl 1/8" Square Cove Cap
- Undercut 1/8"
- Cap for coved sheet vinyl

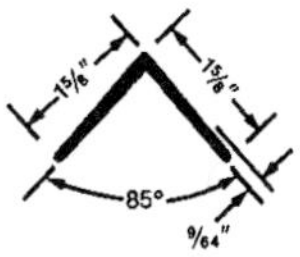

Vinyl Corner Guard
- Protects corners and columns from bumps, abrasion, wear

Vinyl Fillet Strip
- Superb backing for flashing up the wall
- Black only

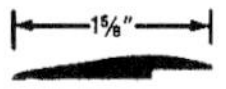

Vinyl Underslung Reducer
- Binder-bar type edging for resilient flooring
- Undercut .105" for use with 1/16" to 1/8" material

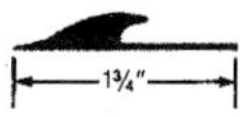

Vinyl 1/4" Glue Down Reducer
- 1/4" butting gauge undercut
- Long flange, smooth taper

Vinyl 1/16" Tile Reducer
- Beveled edge for resilient flooring material
- 1/16" (.063") butting gauge

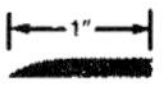

Vinyl 3/32" Tile Reducer
- Beveled edge for resilient flooring material
- 3/32" (.094") butting gauge

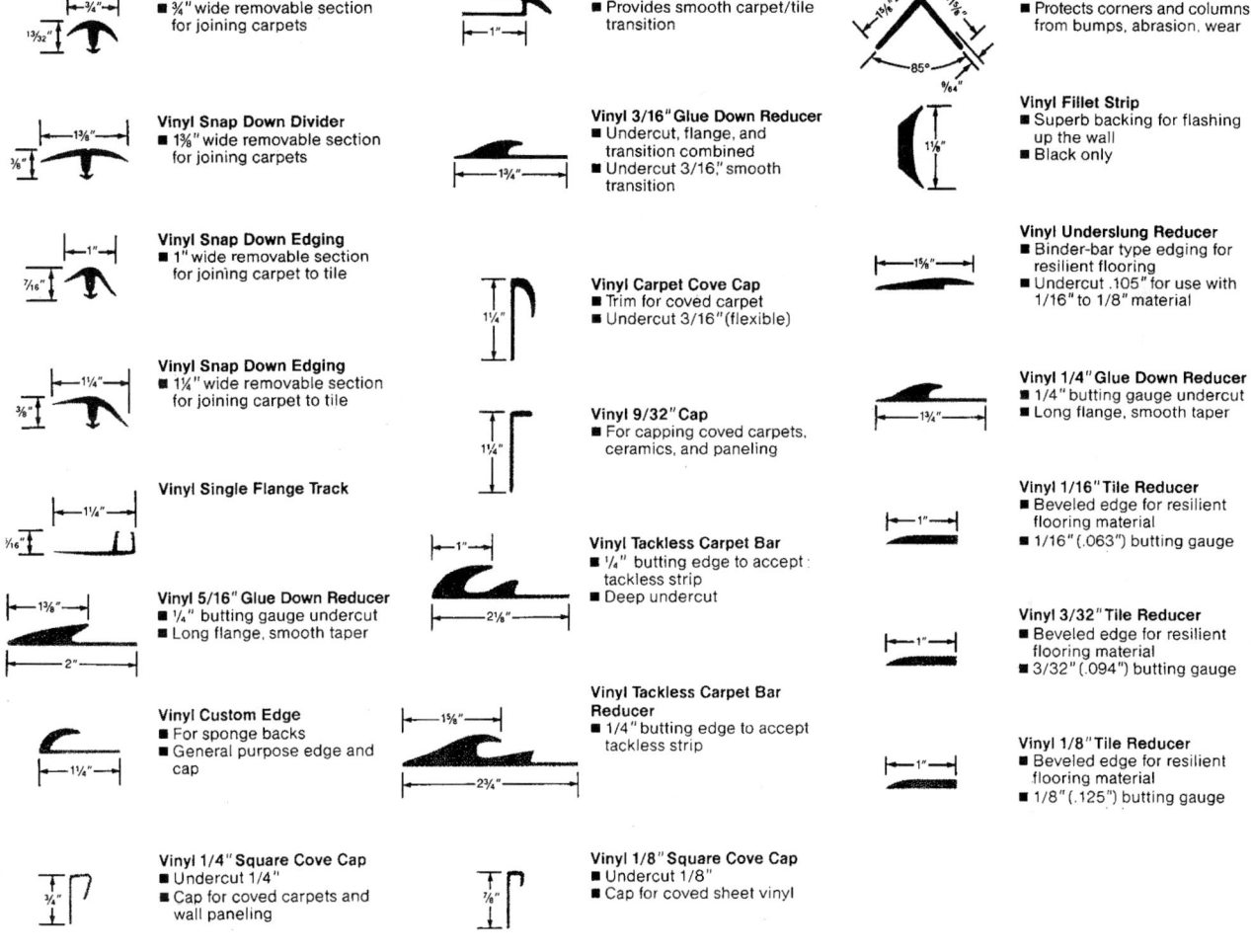

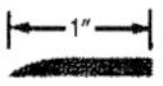

Vinyl 1/8" Tile Reducer
- Beveled edge for resilient flooring material
- 1/8" (.125") butting gauge

FLOORS AND FLOOR FINISHES

Base Details

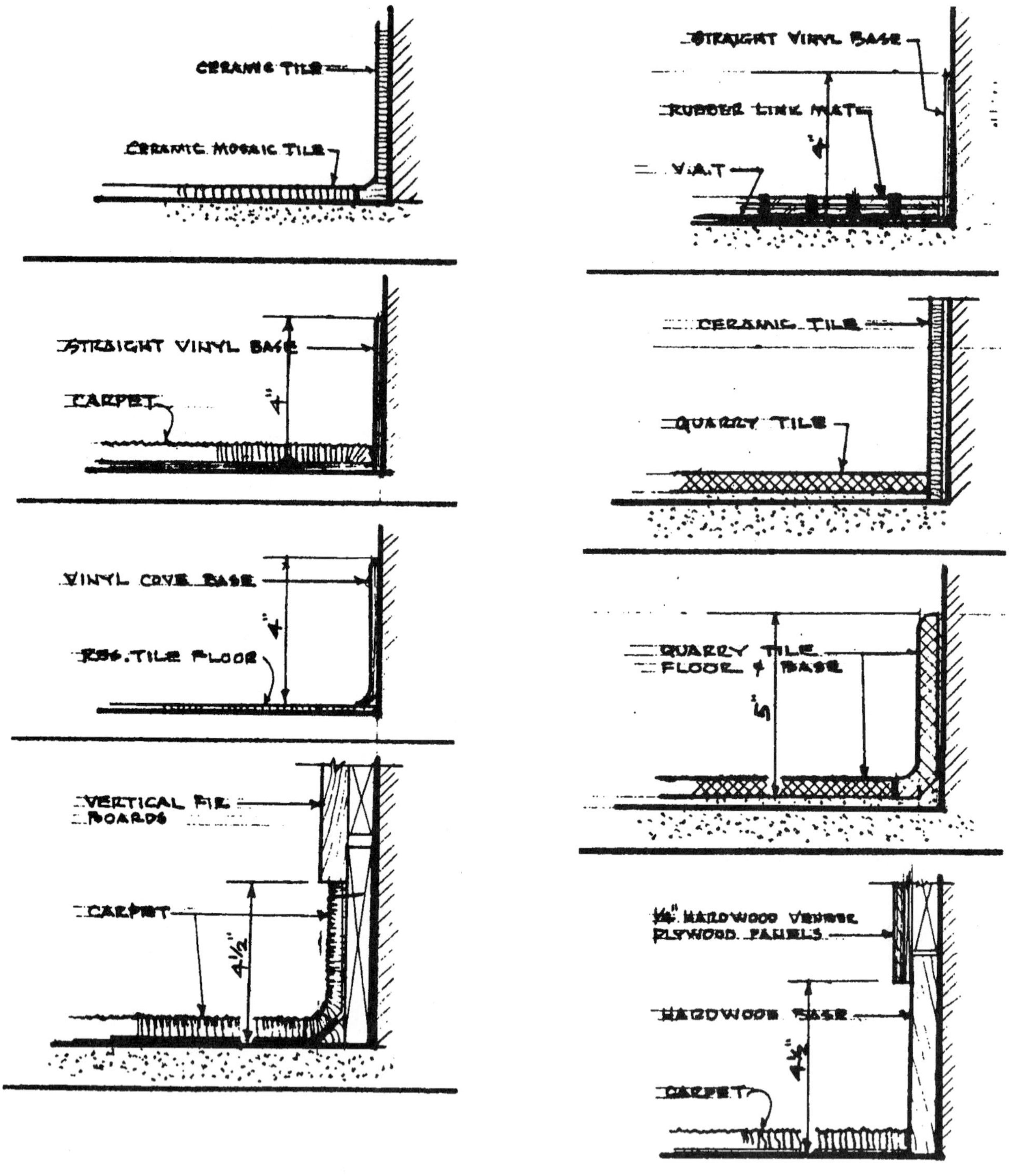

BASE TYPES

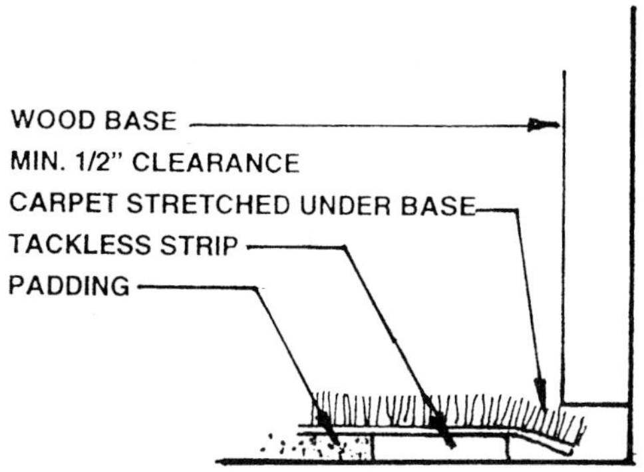

STRETCHED CARPET

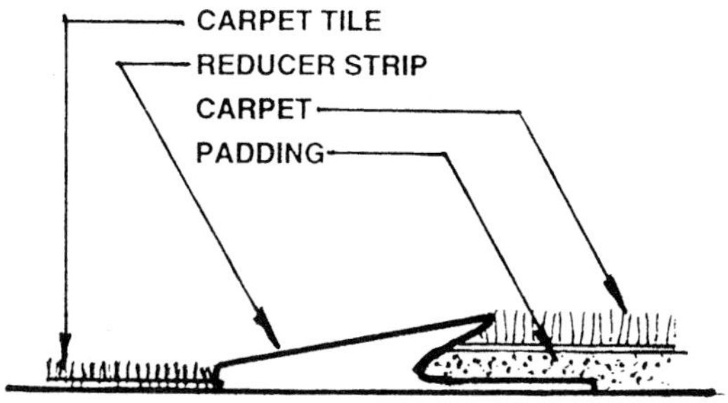

CARPET OVER PADDING
TO CARPET TILE

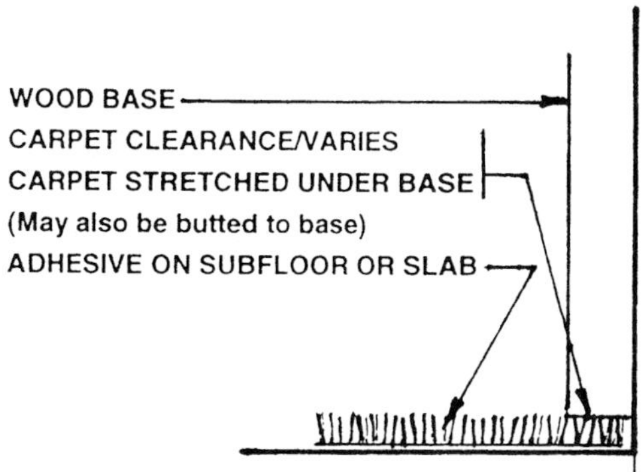

GLUED DOWN CARPET

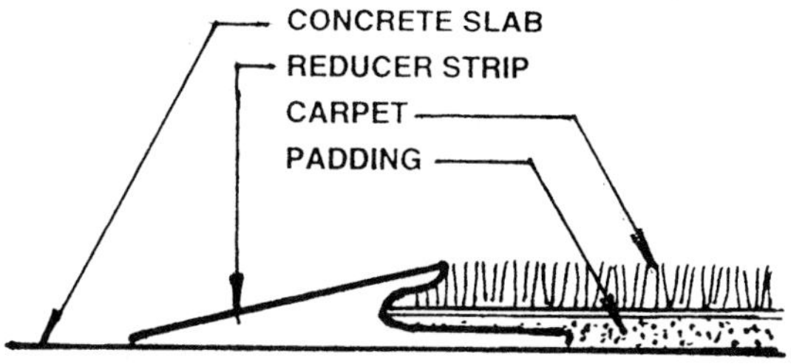

CARPET OVER PADDING
TO CONCRETE SLAB

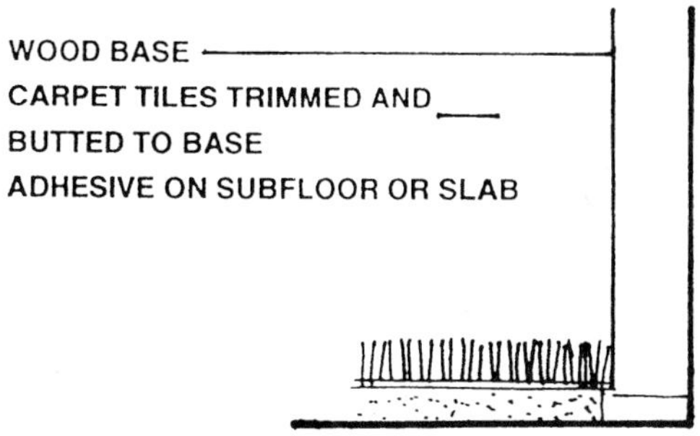

CARPET TILES

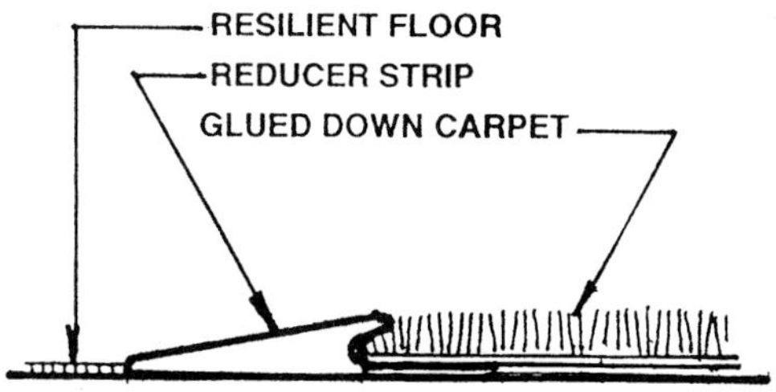

GLUED DOWN CARPET
TO RESILIENT FLOORING

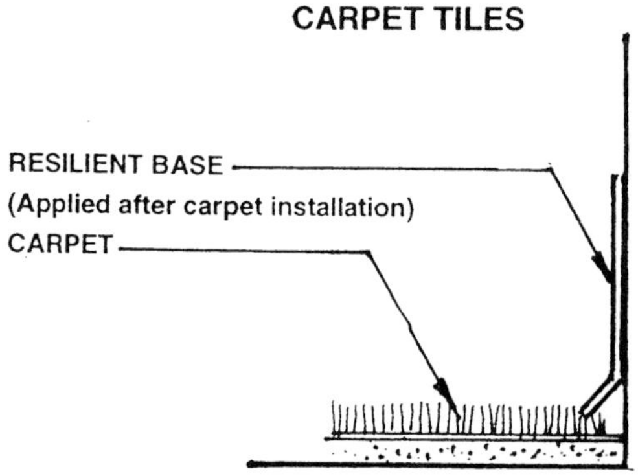

RESILIENT BASE

FLOORS AND FLOOR FINISHES
Floor Transition Details

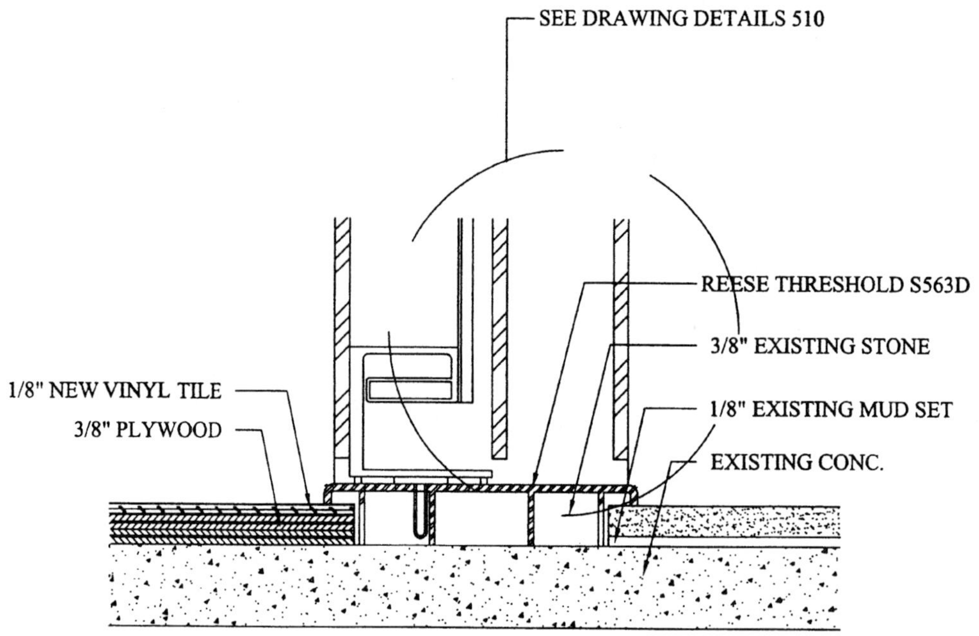

FLOOR DETAIL (EXISTING CONC. TO NEW VINYL TILE)
SCALE 6" : 1'-0"

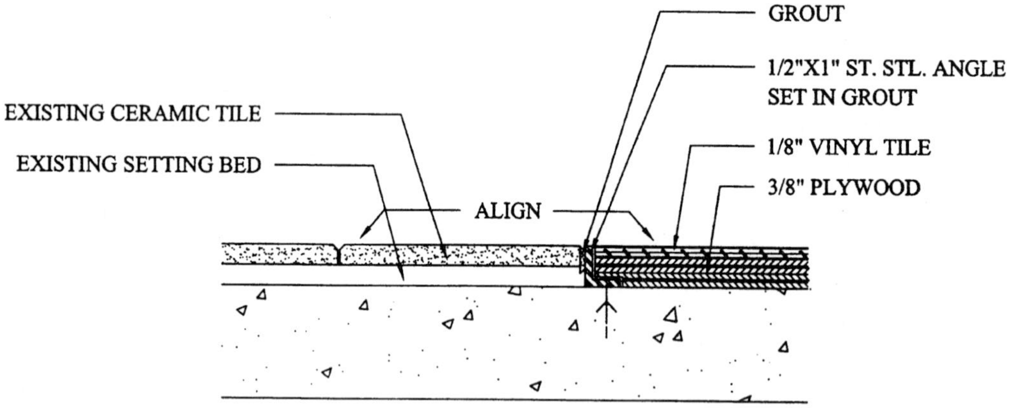

FLOOR DETAIL (EXISTING TILE TO VINYL TILE)
SCALE 6" : 1'-0"

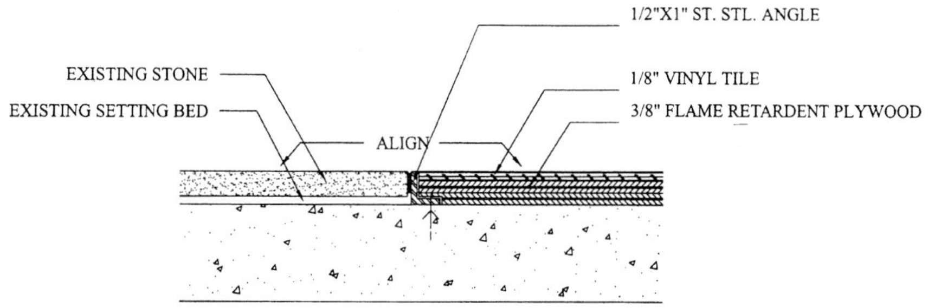

FLOOR DETAIL (EXISTING STONE TO NEW VINYL TILE)
SCALE 6 " : 1'-0"

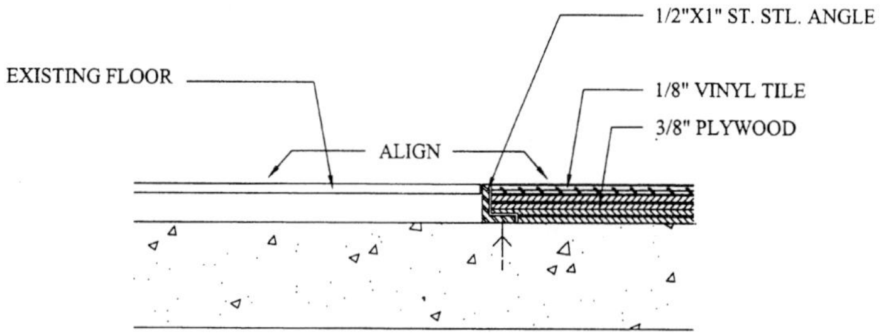

FLOOR DETAIL (EXISTING VINYL TO NEW VINYL TILE)
SCALE 6" : 1'-0"

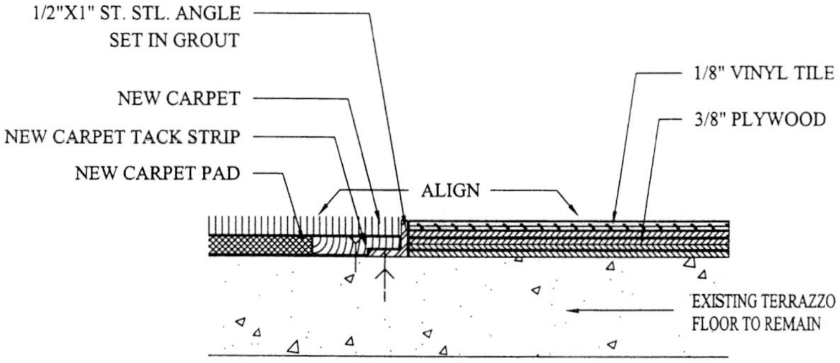

FLOOR DETAIL (NEW CARPET TO NEW VINYL TILE)
SCALE 6" : 1'-0"

FLOORS AND FLOOR FINISHES

Baseboards

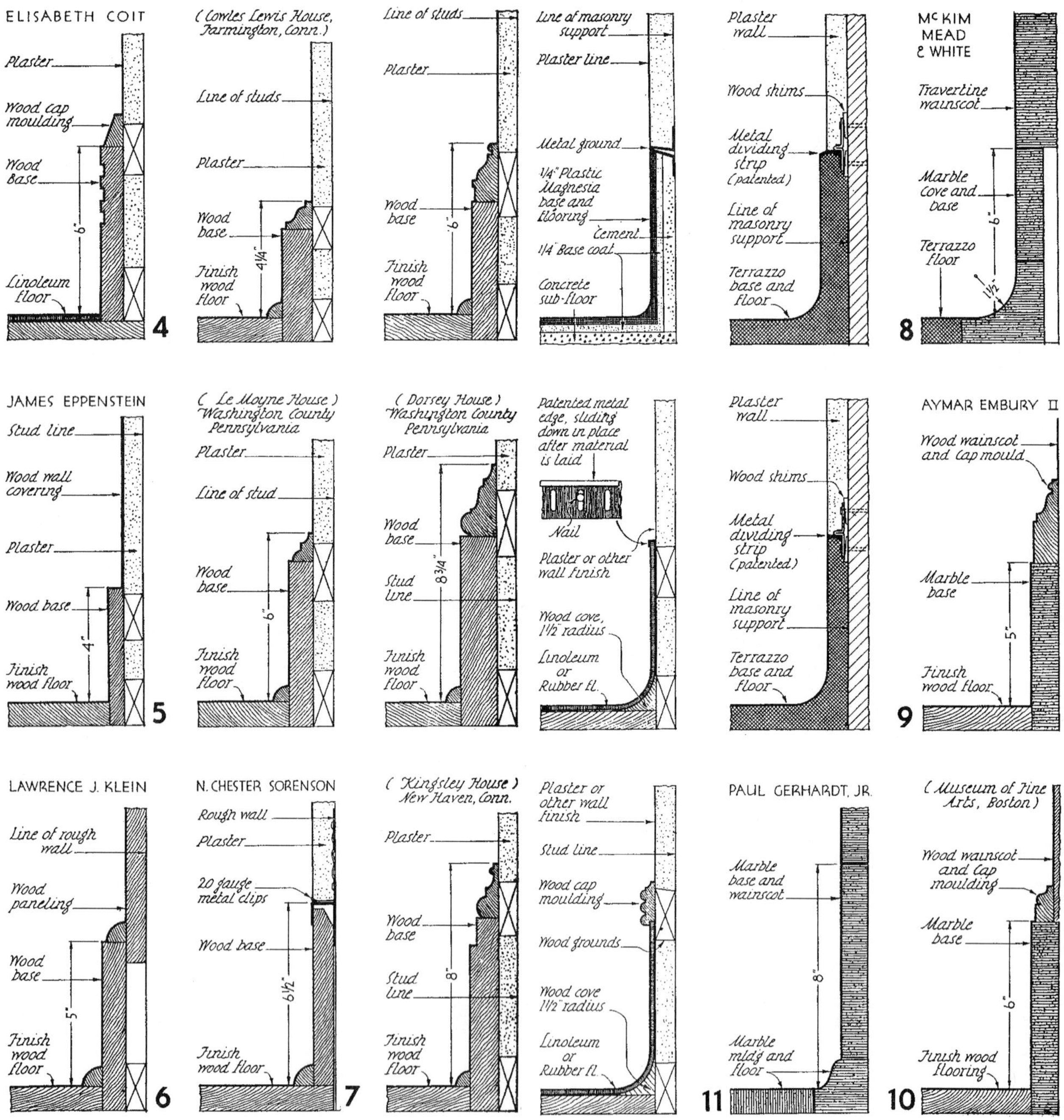

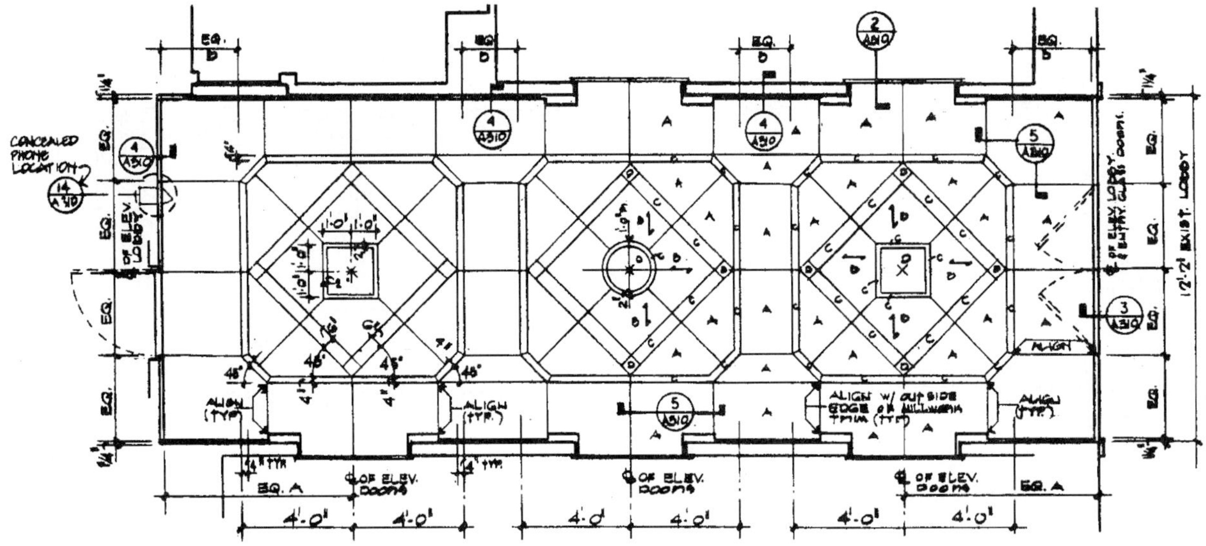

COLORS SEE SPEC. ON DWG A-310
A - VERDE AVER POLISHED
B - CIPPOLINO POLISHED
C - ANDES BLACK GRANITE POLISHED
D - ROSSO LEVANTO POLISHED WITHOUT GREEN

1/A310 STONE FLOORING PATTERN DETAIL TYP. FLOORS 37TH THRU 45TH FL.
1/4" = 1'-0"

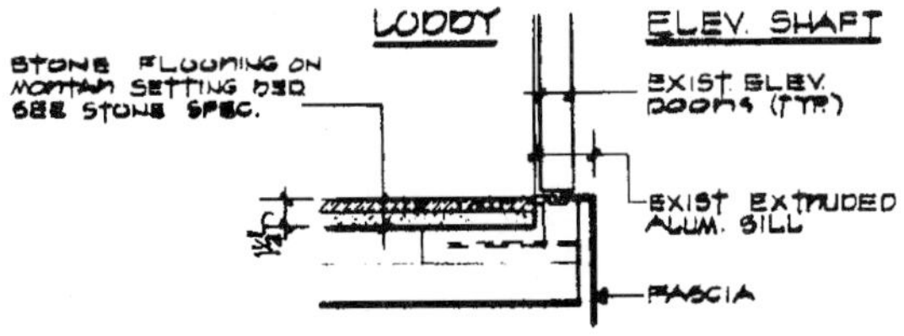

2/A310 STONE DET. @ ELEV. DOOR SILL
1 1/2" = 1'-0"

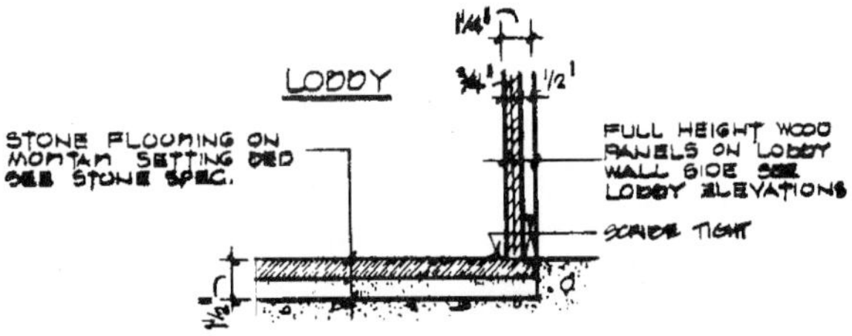

4/A310 TYP. STONE FLOORING DET. @ LOBBY PANEL WALL
3" = 1'-0"

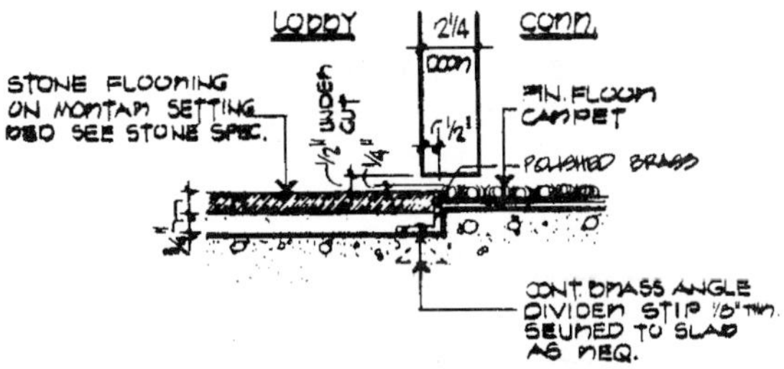

3/A310 STONE FLOORING DET. @ ENTRY DOORS
3" = 1'-0"

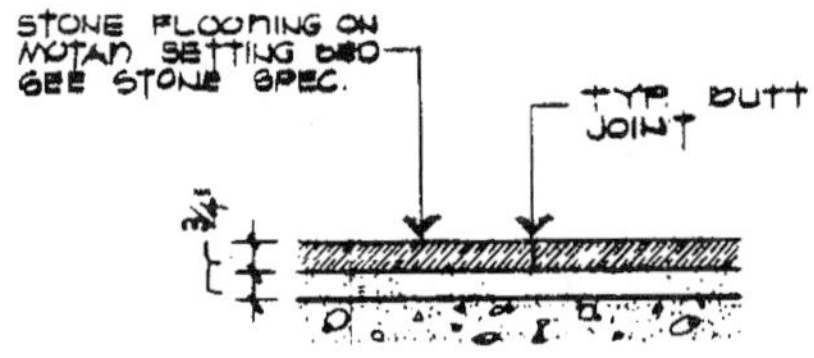

5/A310 TYP. STONE BUTT JOINT DETAIL
3" = 1'-0"

FLOORS AND FLOOR FINISHES

Terrazzo Floor Construction Details

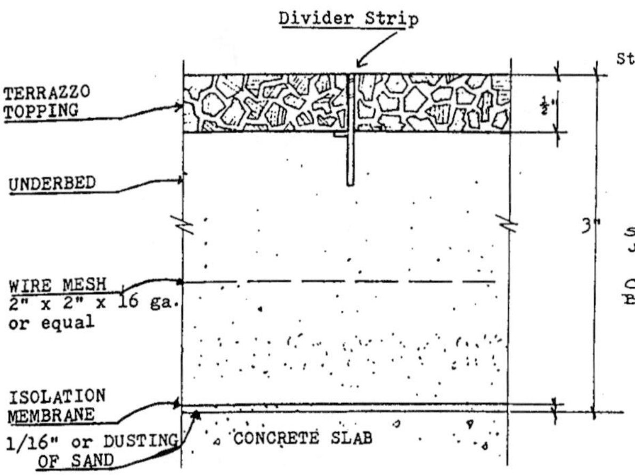

SAND CUSHION TERRAZZO

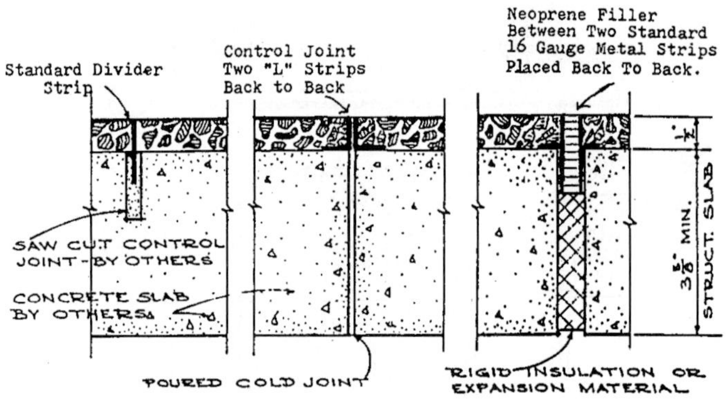

Monolithic Terrazzo

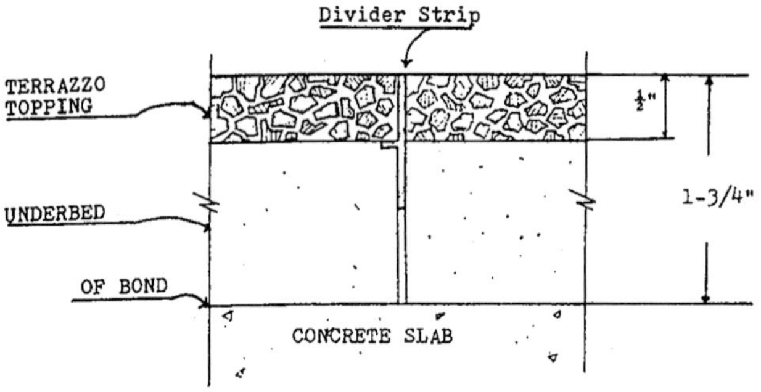

BONDED TO CONCRETE

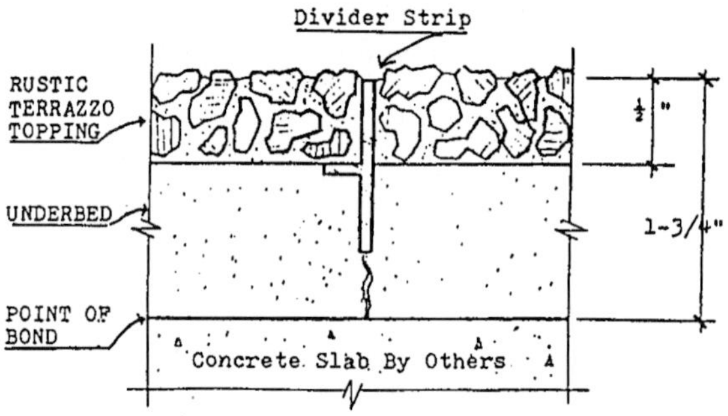

RUSTIC TERRAZZO
Bonded to Concrete

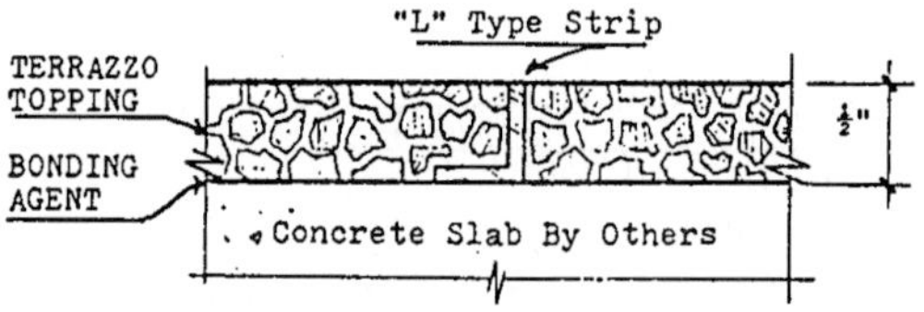

BONDED TO CONCRETE

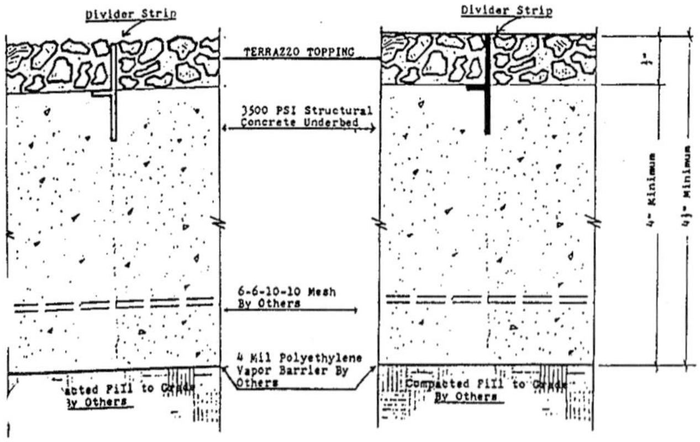

RUSTIC TERRAZZO
FULL SIZE

POLISHED TERRAZZO
FULL SIZE

STRUCTURAL TERRAZZO SYSTEMS

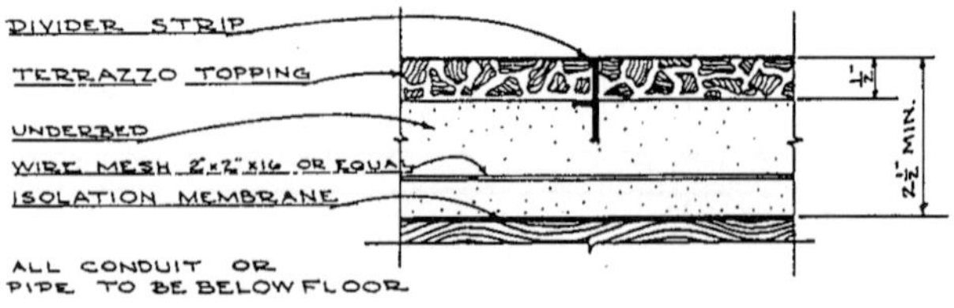

Terrazzo Over Wood

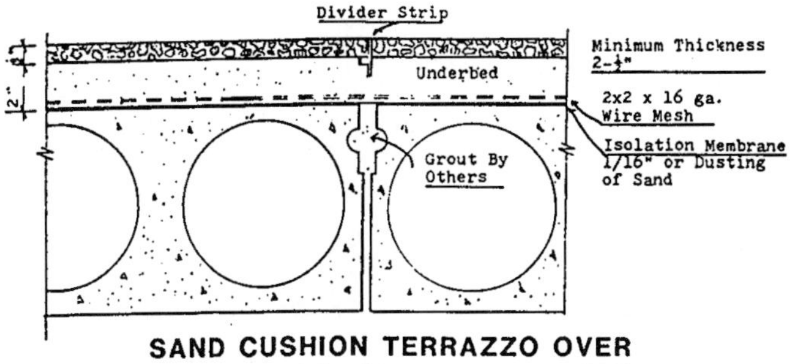

SAND CUSHION TERRAZZO OVER PRECAST CONCRETE TYPE DECK

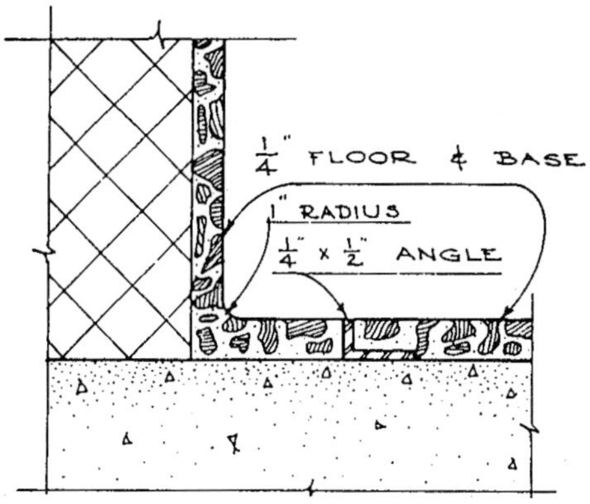

EPOXY, POLYESTER, TERRAZZO FLOOR & BASE

Fig.5

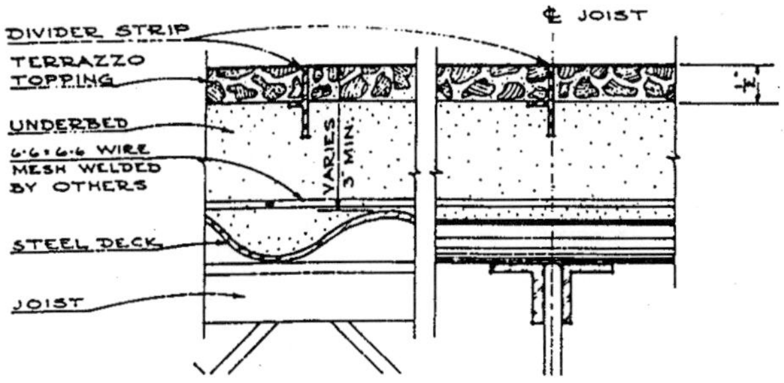

TERRAZZO OVER CORRUGATED METAL TYPE FLOOR

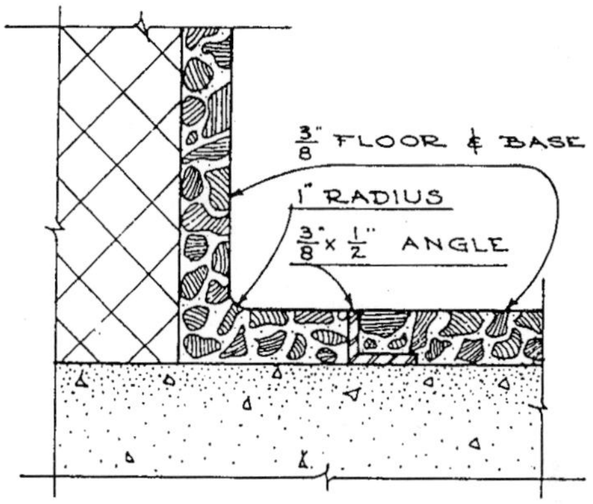

POLYACRYLATE TERRAZZO FLOOR & BASE

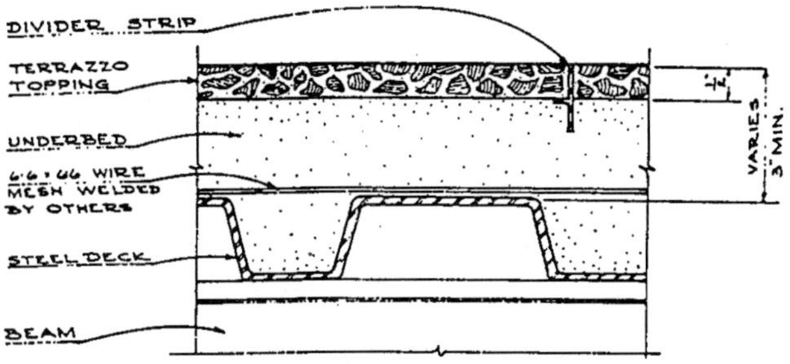

TERRAZZO OVER CELL TYPE FLOOR

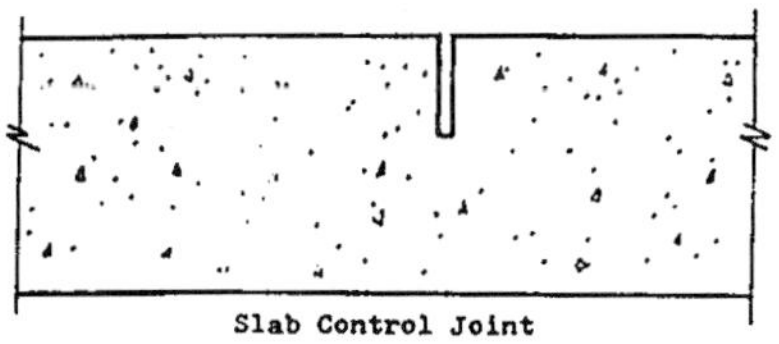

Slab Control Joint

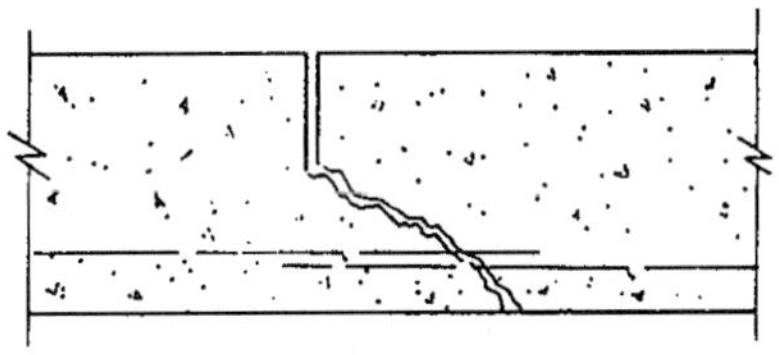

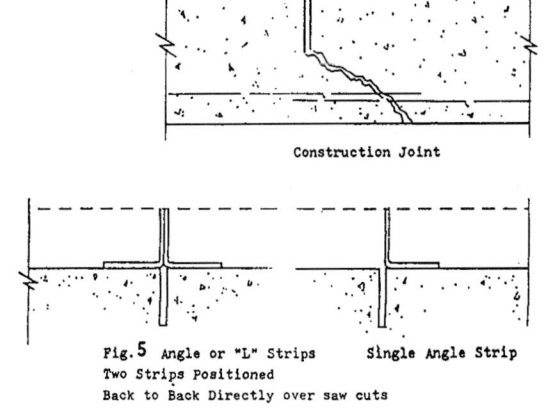

Construction Joint

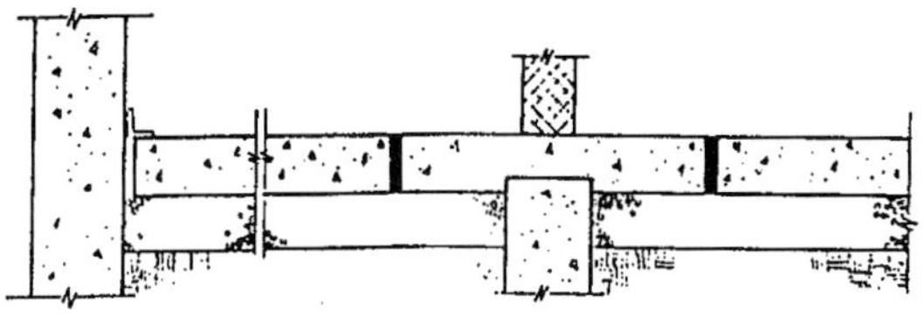

Isolation Joint

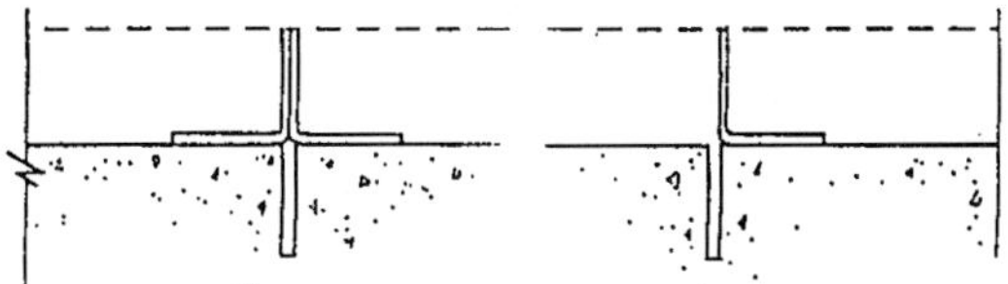

Fig.5 Angle or "L" Strips Two Strips Positioned Back to Back Directly over saw cuts

Single Angle Strip

FLOORS AND FLOOR FINISHES

Terrazzo Base Details

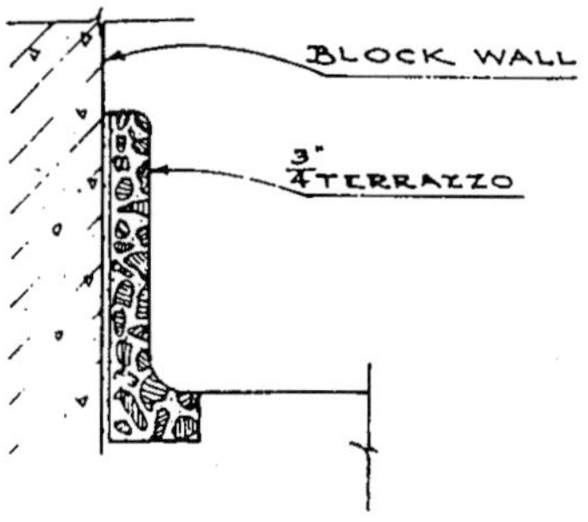

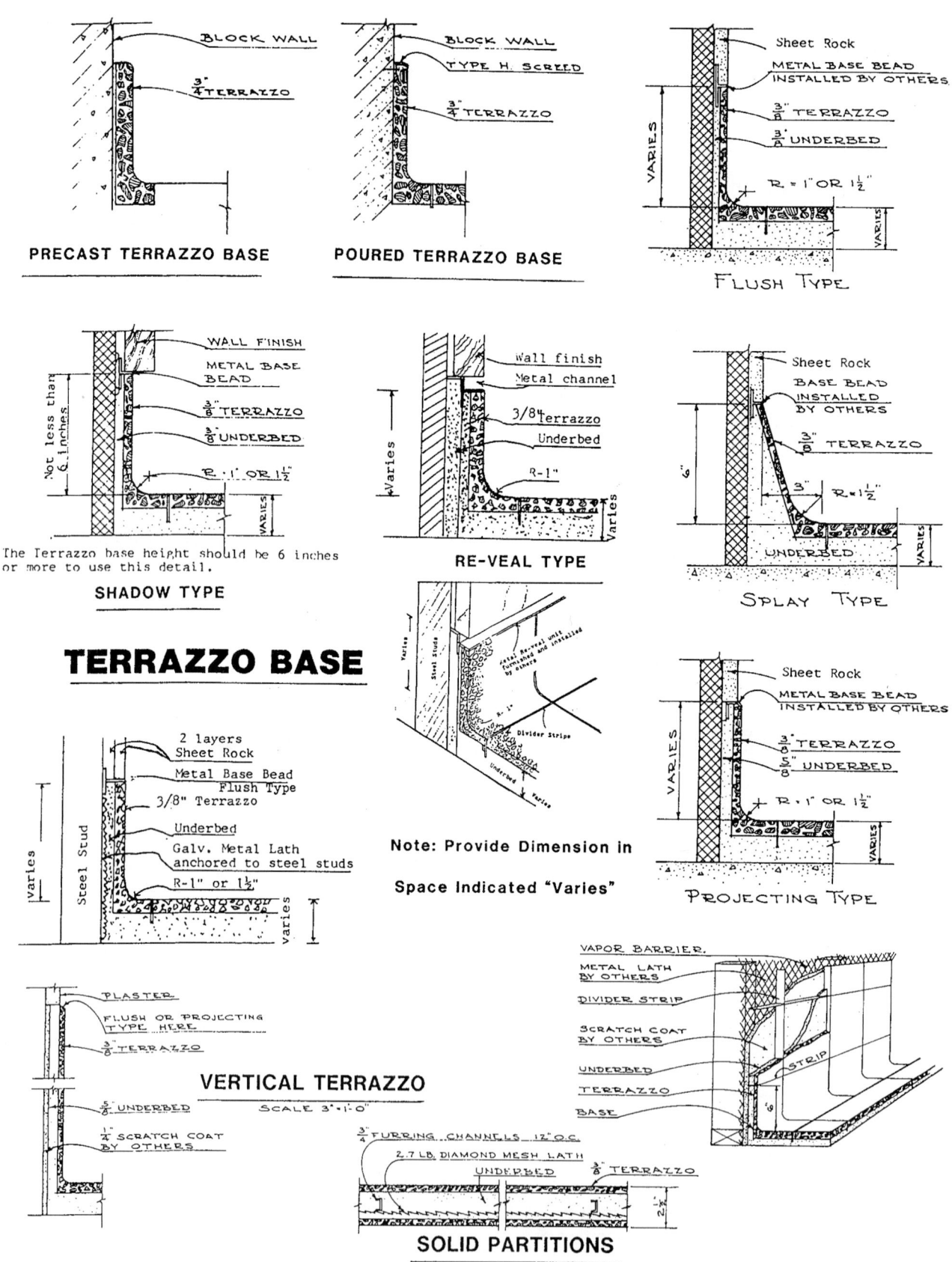

PRECAST TERRAZZO BASE

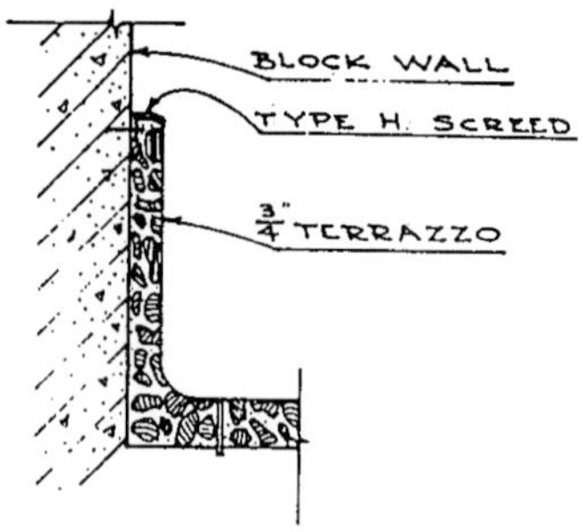

POURED TERRAZZO BASE

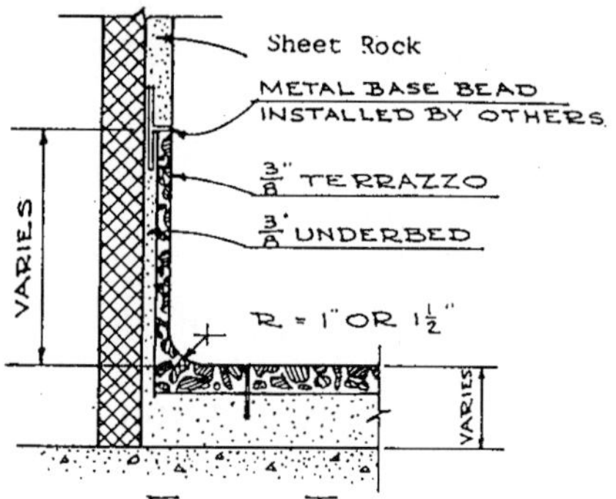

FLUSH TYPE

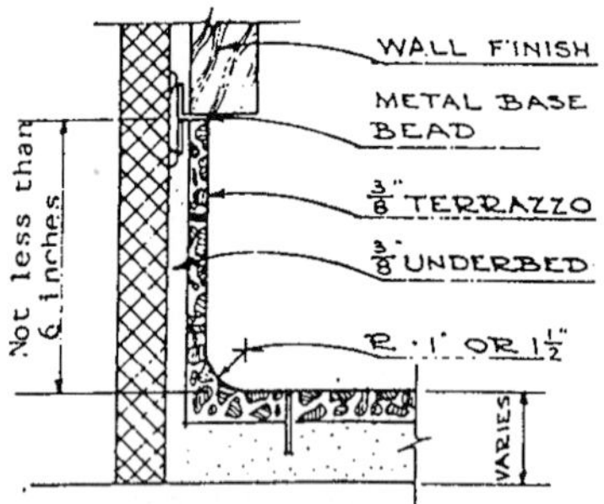

The Terrazzo base height should be 6 inches or more to use this detail.

SHADOW TYPE

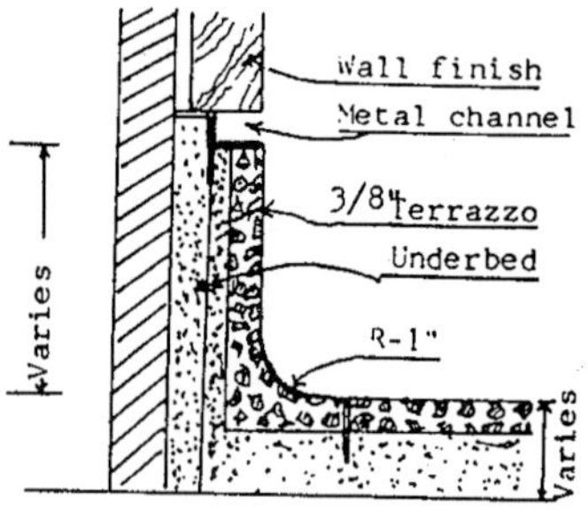

RE-VEAL TYPE

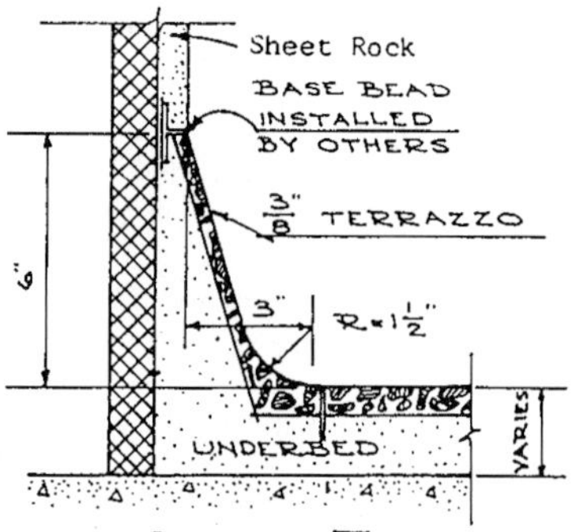

SPLAY TYPE

TERRAZZO BASE

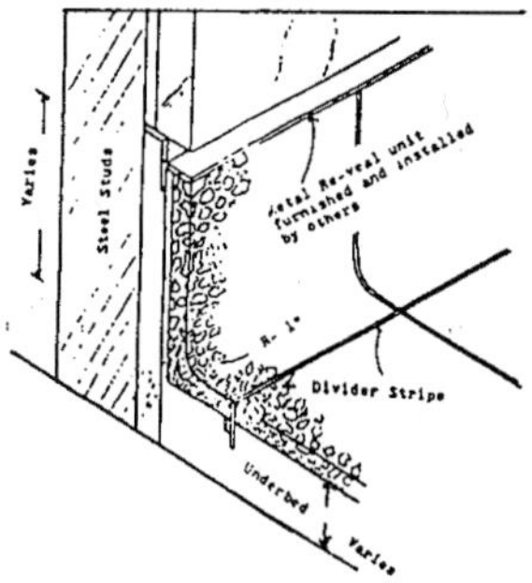

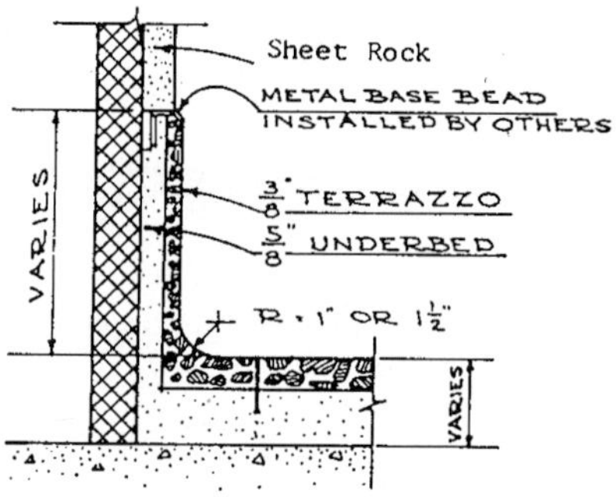

PROJECTING TYPE

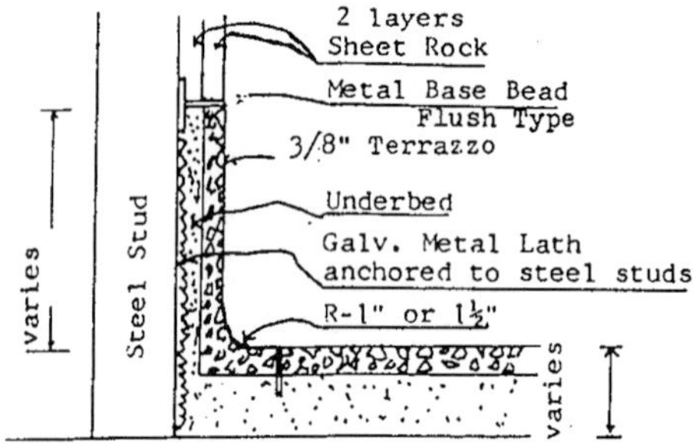

Note: Provide Dimension in Space Indicated "Varies"

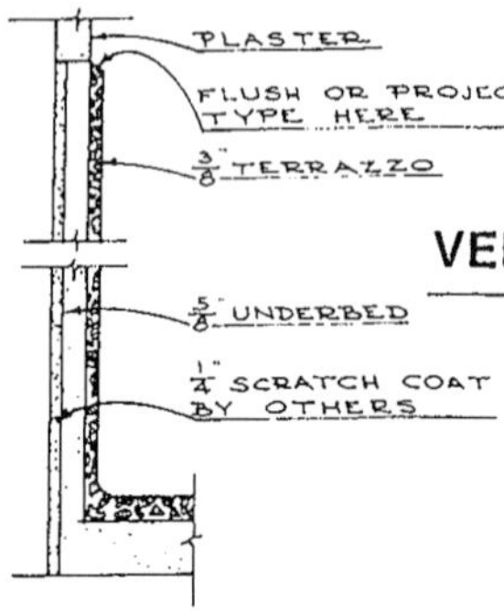

VERTICAL TERRAZZO

SCALE 3"=1'-0"

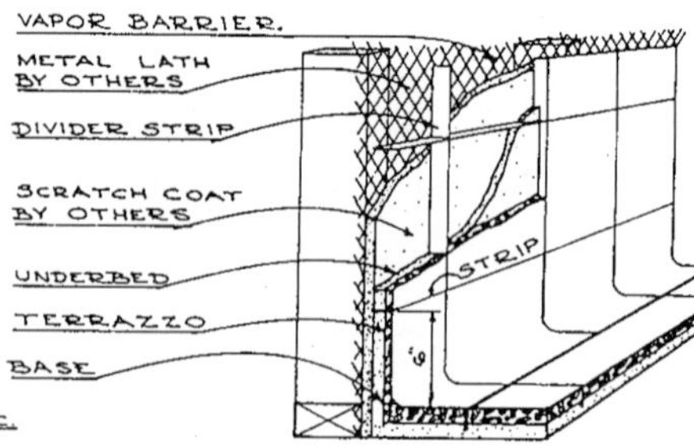

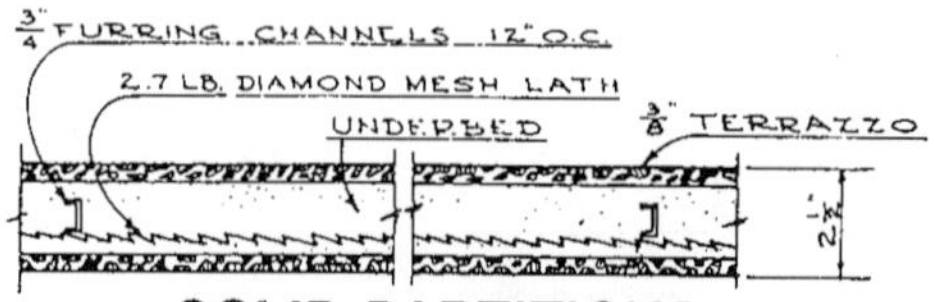

SOLID PARTITIONS

SCALE 3"=1'0"

The edges of terrazzo at a wall may be trimmed with any base material, but are most often finished with a terrazzo base. Base is available precast, or it may be poured in place with the same material used for the body of the floor. It is difficult to grind the top edge of poured-in-place base because of the proximity of finish wall materials. A metal base cap is usually used to eliminate the need for grinding the base top. A divider strip should be located between the main floor and the flush precast or poured base.

Where terrazzo meets other flooring it is best if the two materials are flush. A terrazzo divider strip can serve as a transition between the two surfaces. If the terrazzo is not flush with the adjacent flooring, its edge may be treated similar to that of tile or masonry.

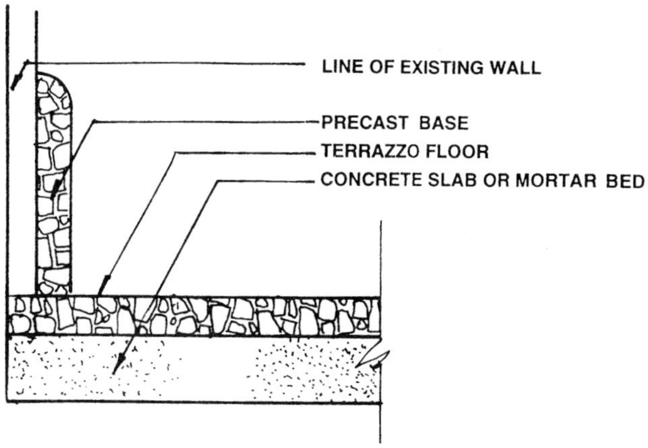

TERRAZZO BASE/ PRECAST

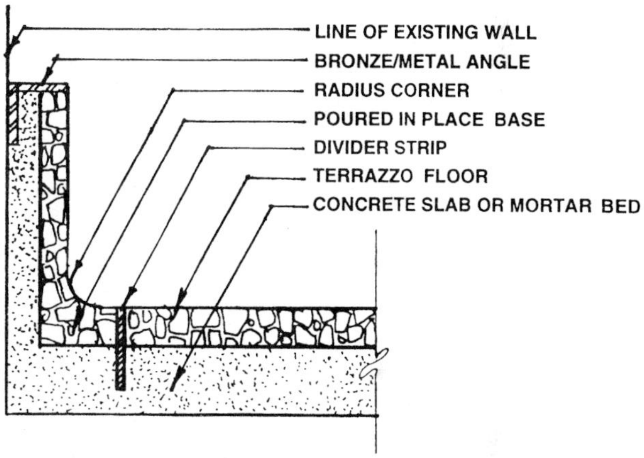

TERRAZZO BASE/
POURED IN PLACE ON CONCRETE SLAB

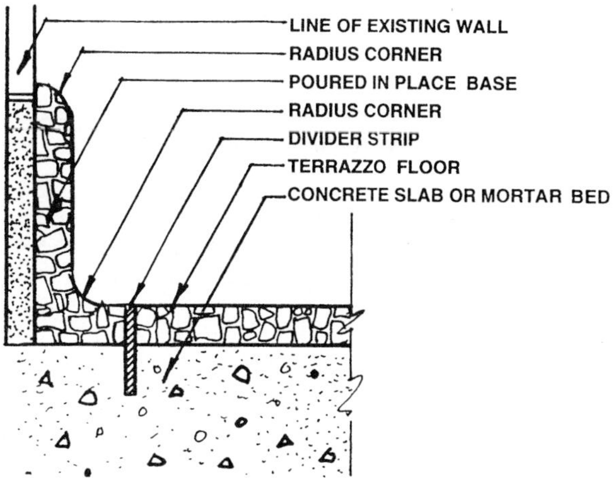

TERRAZZO BASE/
POURED IN PLACE ON MORTAR BED

Terrazzo floors are made of stone or marble chips bound together by a cement matrix. The finished surface is generally polished It is most typical to provide a terrazzo floor with a terrazzo base, although other materials maybe utilized. A terrazzo base may be either poured in place or precast. Due to the difficulty of finishing the top edge of a poured in place base, a metal screed or base cap may be used to cover the edge.

There are four general types of terrazzo floors: Standard, Venetian, Palladiana, and Rustic.

Standard is considered the most common type of terrazzo floor, consisting of relatively small #1 and #2 size chips.

Venetian is made up of larger #3-#8 size chips, with #1 and #2 chips being used as a filler.

Palladiana is made up of random slabs of marble ranging in size from 2-14" maximum.

The matrix consists of a uniformly textured terrazzo where the chips are exposed due to the depression of the matrix. The grinding of the surface is minimized.

The stone chips used in terrazzo consist of stones that are capable of being polished, including marble and onyx, while granite, quartz and silica are used for rustic floors.

The matrix generally consists of portland cement and chemical binders, with either white or gray cement being utilized. Color pigments are also added depending on desired overall effect and color desired.

Various types of divider strips are available for both poured in place and pre cast terrazzo. Divider strips come in thicknesses varying from 1/8" to 1/2" thick and may be anywhere from 3/4" to 1 1/2" deep. Brass, bronze, zinc, stainless steel, and plastic are common finishes.

Best design practice dictates that terrazzo flooring and other dissimilar materials always meet flush with each other, although slight variations in height may be treated with various transition strips.

FLOORS AND FLOOR FINISHES

Terrazzo Floor Details

The most durable terrazzo floors are installed over a mortar base. The mortar base adds strength and helps to isolate the terrazzo topping from the structure and minimize cracking. The mortar base can be applied directly to a concrete slab or over a thin sand cushion, further isolating the terrazzo from the structure. Over a wood subfloor, a mortar base provides stiffness and a cementitious surface to which the terrazzo topping can adhere. A mortar base installed over a sand cushion or wood structure needs reinforcement, but no reinforcement is required when the mortar is directly on a concrete slab.

To apply the terrazzo, a thin (¼ to ⅝ in) mixture of terrazzo is placed on the mortar base or concrete subfloor and is compressed with a roller to force out excess water and cement. The compressed wet surface is troweled flat and even with the tops of the divider strips. The cured terrazzo is machine ground to achieve a smooth, polished finish. A clear sealer is applied to prevent the cement matrix from staining or absorbing moisture (the marble or granite aggregate is not porous and will not absorb the sealer).

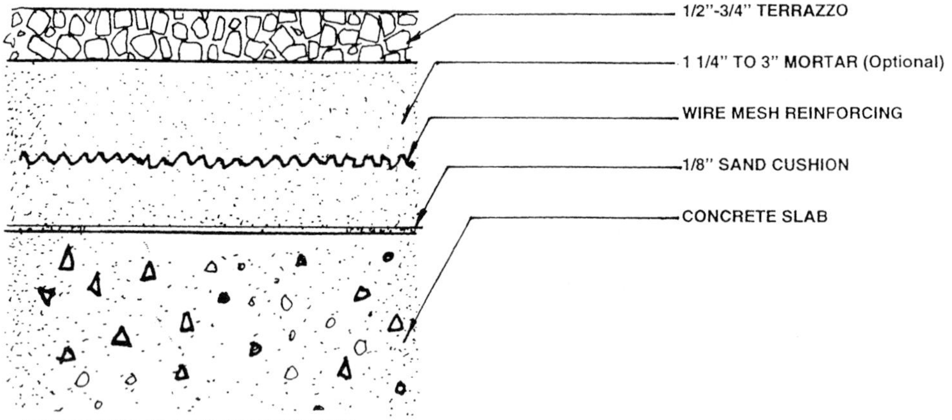

TERRAZZO FLOOR ON MORTAR BED OVER CONCRETE SLAB

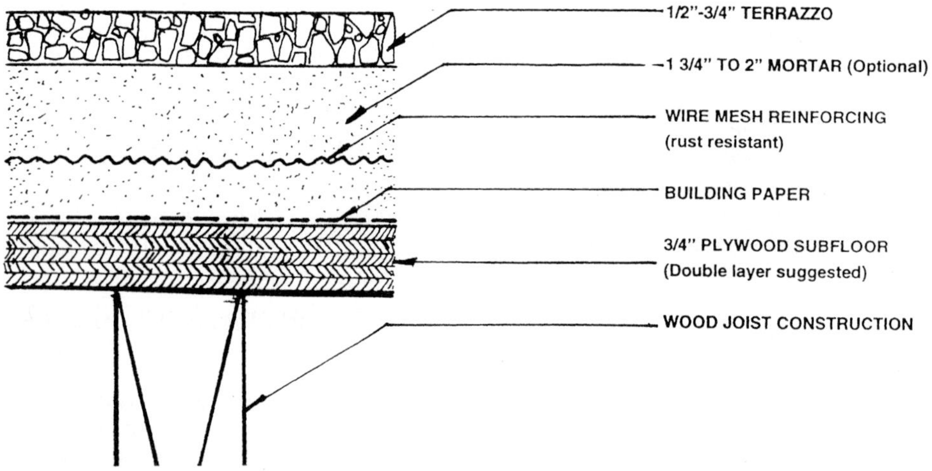

TERRAZZO FLOOR ON MORTAR BED OVER FRAME CONSTRUCTION

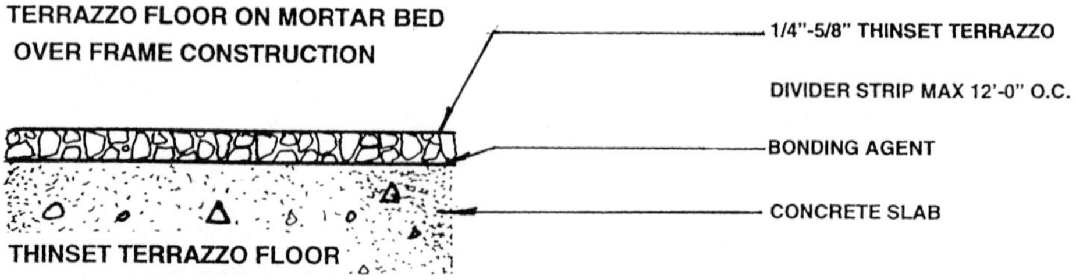

THINSET TERRAZZO FLOOR ON CONCRETE SLAB

Best practice indicates that terrazzo floors should be installed over a mortar bed rather than directly over a concrete slab. This type of installation is stronger and tends to prevent cracks from developing. Height, weight, and cost considerations may mitigate against that approach.When installing a terrazzo floor overframe construction, the designer is urged to use a double layer of 3/4" plywood whenever possible, and to reduce the on center spacing of floor joists. This takes into consideration the weight of the material as well as the deflection and vibration of the floor system which could cause undesired cracking.

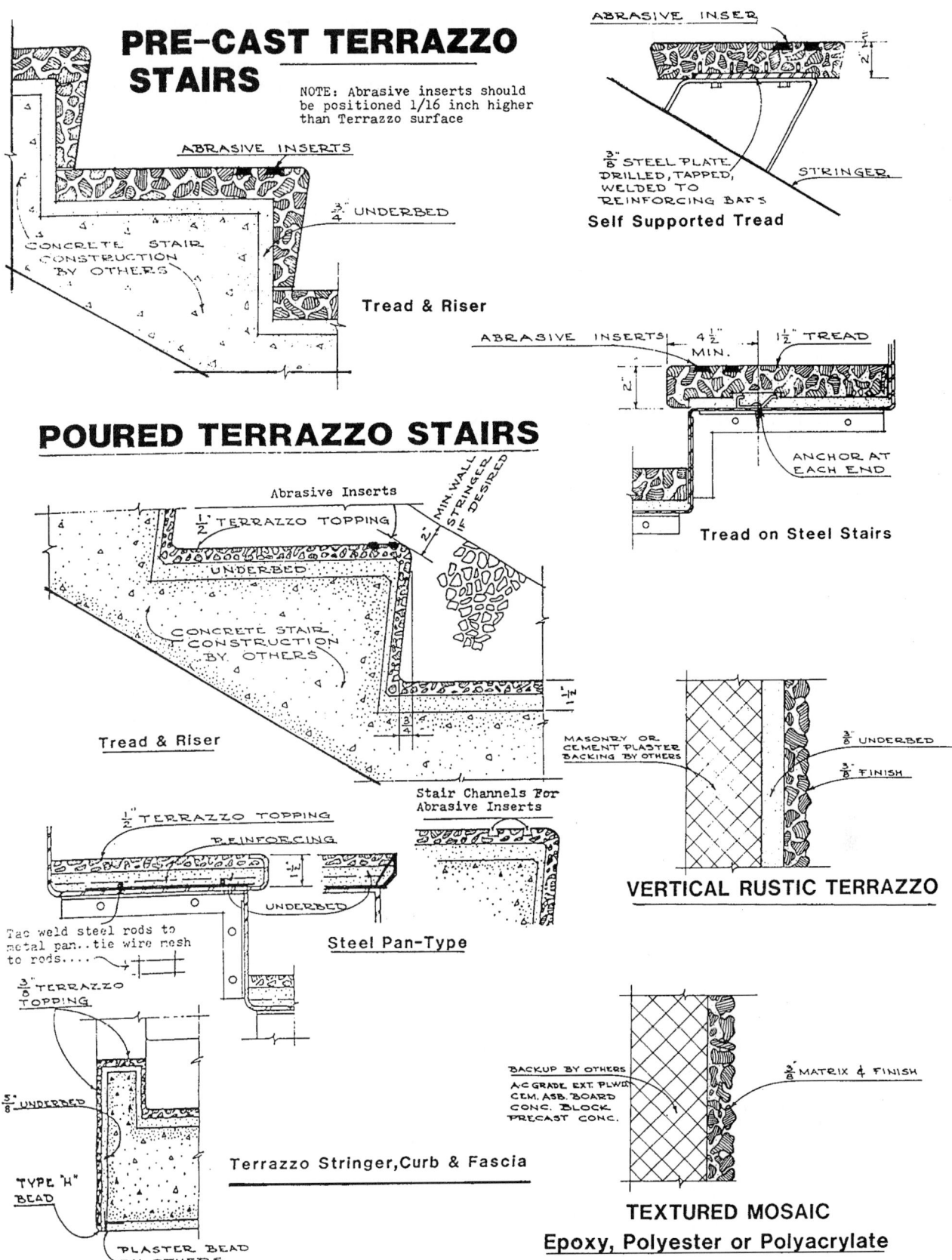

PRE-CAST TERRAZZO STAIRS
NOTE: Abrasive inserts should be positioned 1/16 inch higher than Terrazzo surface
ABRASIVE INSERTS
3/4" UNDERBED
CONCRETE STAIR CONSTRUCTION BY OTHERS
Tread & Riser
ABRASIVE INSER
3/8" STEEL PLATE DRILLED, TAPPED, WELDED TO REINFORCING BARS
STRINGER
Self Supported Tread
ABRASIVE INSERTS
4 1/2" MIN.
1 1/2" TREAD
ANCHOR AT EACH END
Tread on Steel Stairs
POURED TERRAZZO STAIRS
Abrasive Inserts
1/2" TERRAZZO TOPPING
MIN. WALL STRINGER IF DESIRED
UNDERBED
CONCRETE STAIR CONSTRUCTION BY OTHERS
Tread & Riser
1/2" TERRAZZO TOPPING
REINFORCING
UNDERBED
Tac weld steel rods to metal pan..tie wire mesh to rods....
Steel Pan-Type
Stair Channels For Abrasive Inserts
MASONRY OR CEMENT PLASTER BACKING BY OTHERS
3/8" UNDERBED
3/8" FINISH
VERTICAL RUSTIC TERRAZZO
3/8" TERRAZZO TOPPING
5/8" UNDERBED
TYPE "H" BEAD
PLASTER BEAD BY OTHERS
Terrazzo Stringer, Curb & Fascia
BACKUP BY OTHERS
A-C GRADE EXT. PLWD.
CEM. ASB. BOARD
CONC. BLOCK
PRECAST CONC.
3/8" MATRIX & FINISH
TEXTURED MOSAIC
Epoxy, Polyester or Polyacrylate

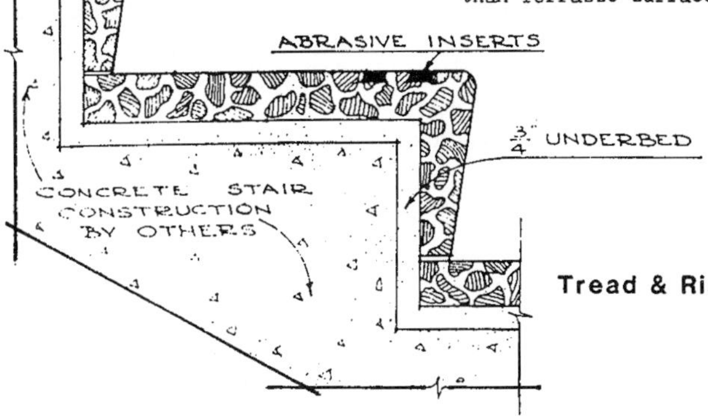

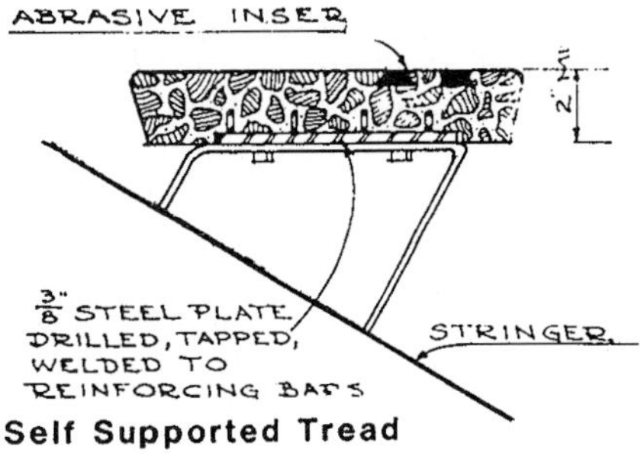

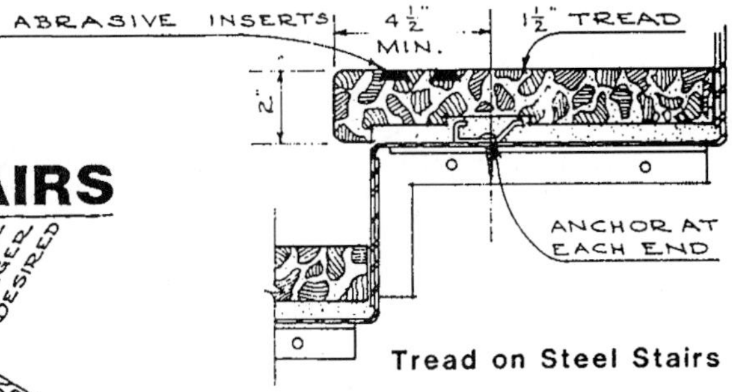

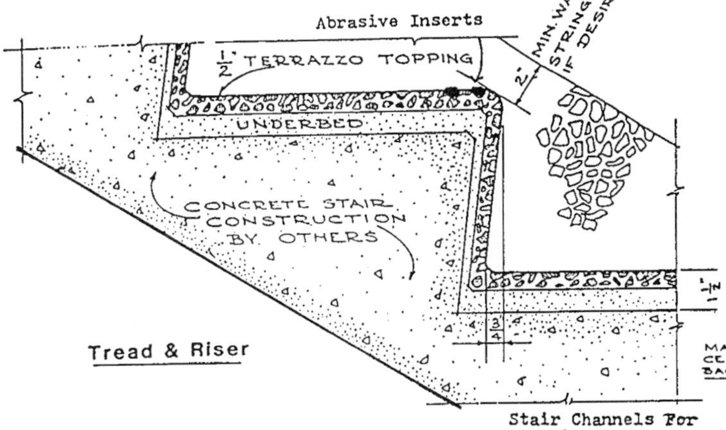

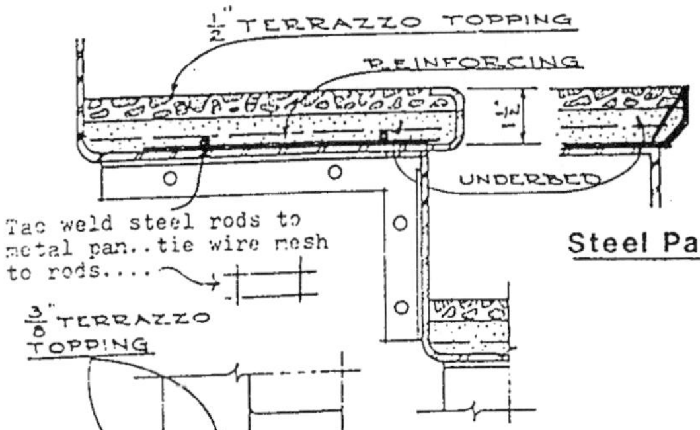

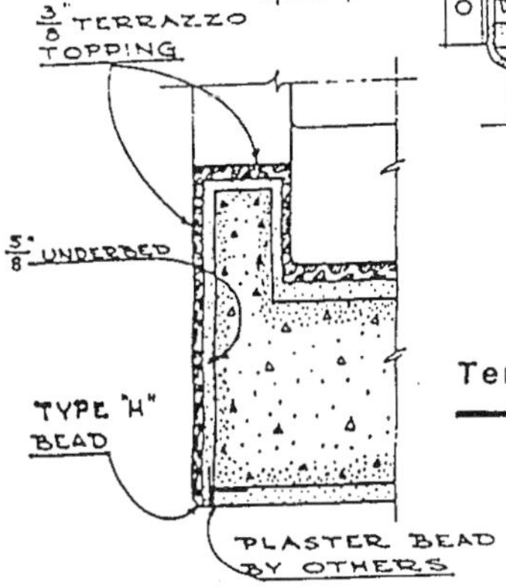

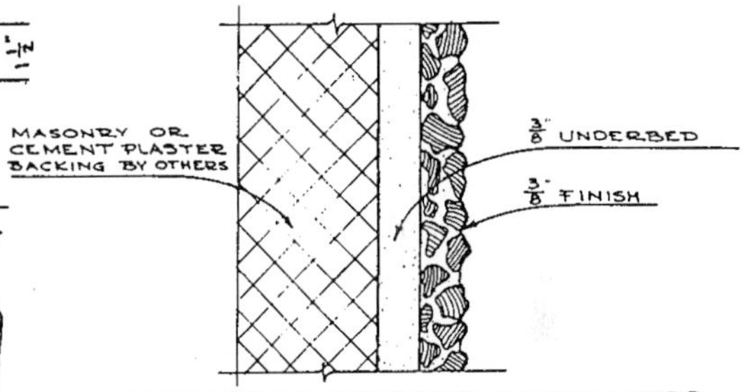

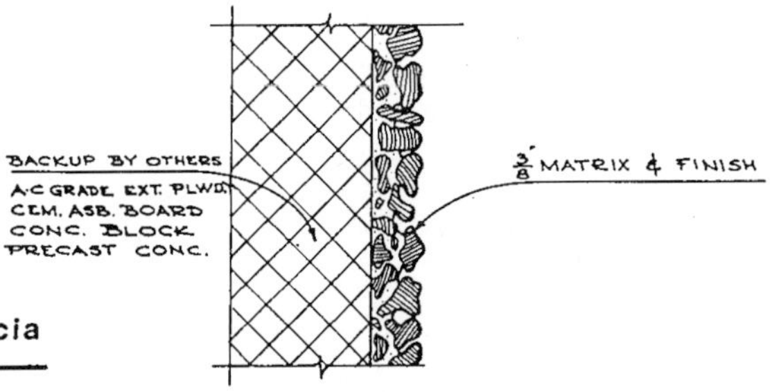

FLOORS AND FLOOR FINISHES

Wood Strip Floor Construction Details

Perhaps the most widely used pattern is a ²⁵⁄₃₂- by 2¼-in *strip flooring.* These strips are laid lengthwise in a room and normally at right angles to the floor joists. Some type of a subfloor of diagonal boards or plywood is normally used under the finish floor. Strip flooring of this type is tongued-and-grooved and end-matched (Fig. 5). Strips are random length and may vary from 2 to 16 ft or more. End-matched strip flooring in ²⁵⁄₃₂-in thickness is generally hollow backed (Fig. 5*A*). The face is slightly wider than the bottom so that tight joints result when flooring is laid. The tongue fits tightly into the groove to prevent movement and floor squeaks. All of these details are designed to provide beautiful finished floors that require a minimum of maintenance.

Another matched pattern may be obtained in ⅜- by 2-in size (Fig. 5*B*). This is commonly used for remodeling work or when subfloor is edge-blocked or thick enough to provide very little deflection under loads.

Square-edged strip flooring (Fig. 5*C*) might also be used occasionally. It is usually ⅜ by 2 in in size and is laid up over a substantial subfloor. Facenailing is required for this type.

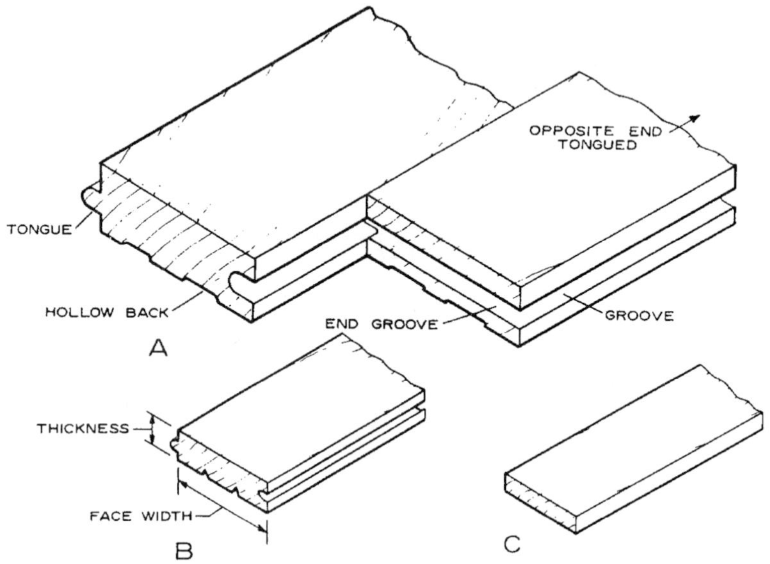

Fig. 5 Types of strip flooring: *A*, side- and end-matched—²⁵⁄₃₂-in; *B*, thin flooring strips—matched; *C*, thin flooring strips—square-edged

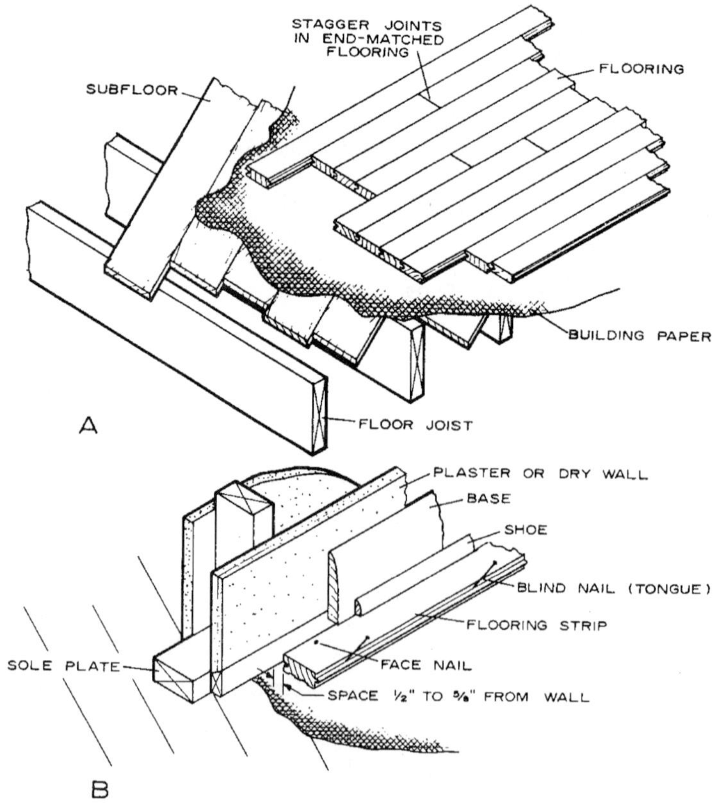

Fig. 6 Application of strip flooring: *A*, general application; *B*, starting strip

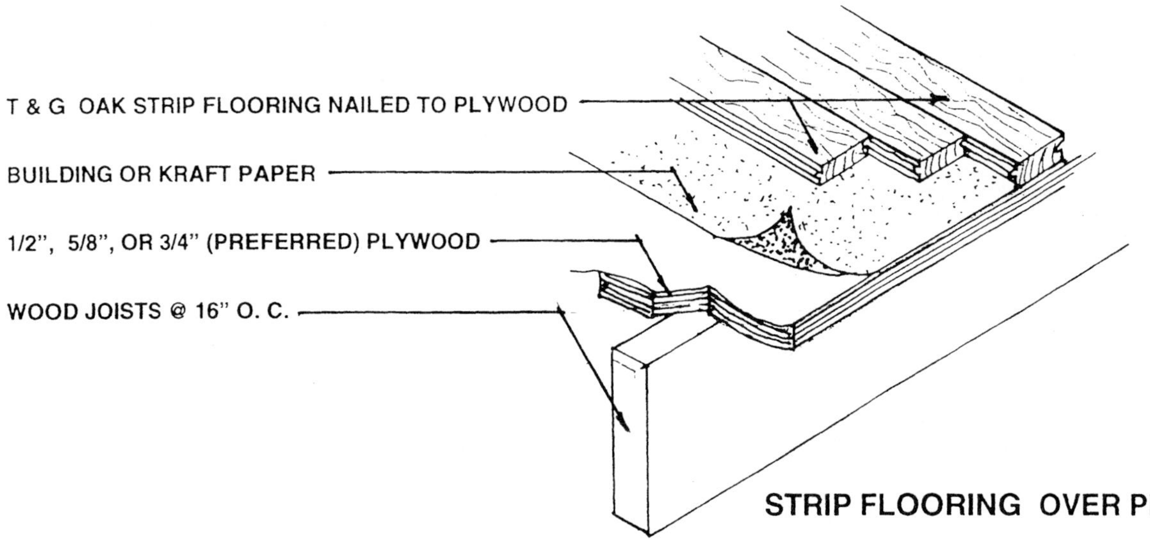

STRIP FLOORING OVER PLYWOOD

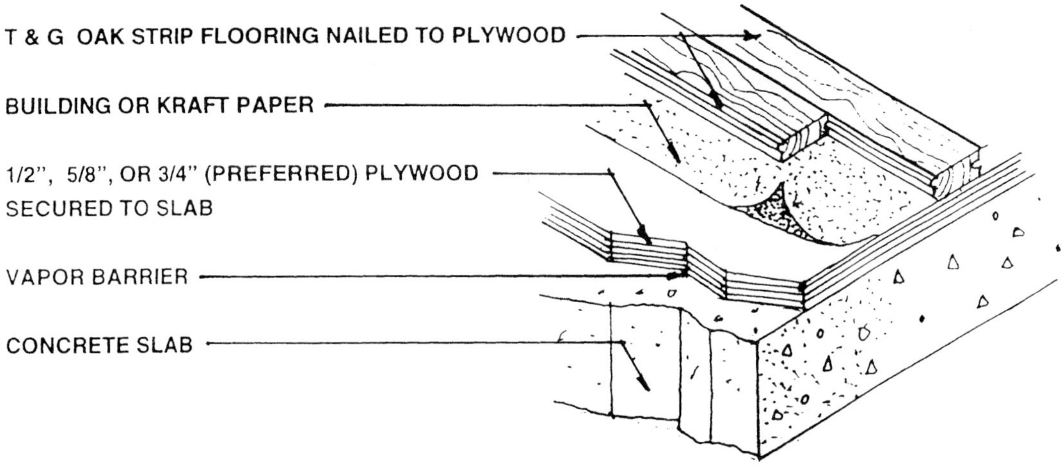

STRIP FLOORING ON CONCRETE SLAB/PLYWOOD SUBFLOOR

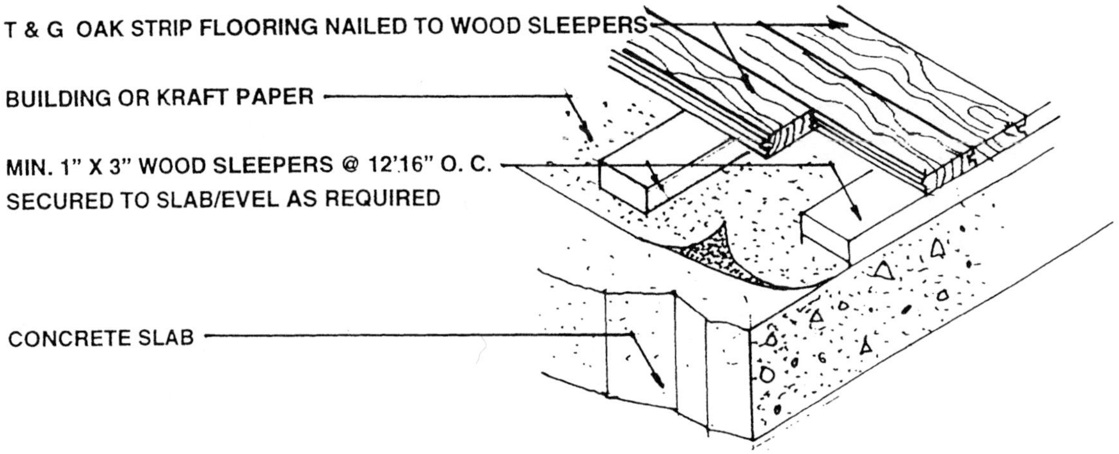

STRIP FLOORING ON CONCRETE SLAB/WOOD SLEEPERS

FLOORS AND FLOOR FINISHES

Wood Athletic Floor Details

Sleeper System

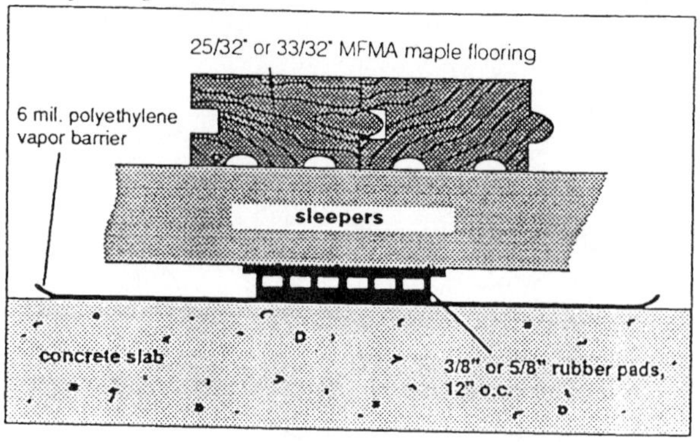

Sleeper with Plywood System

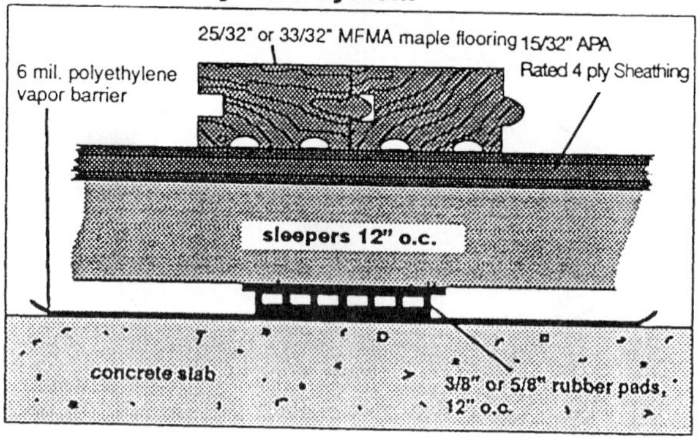

Double Plywood System

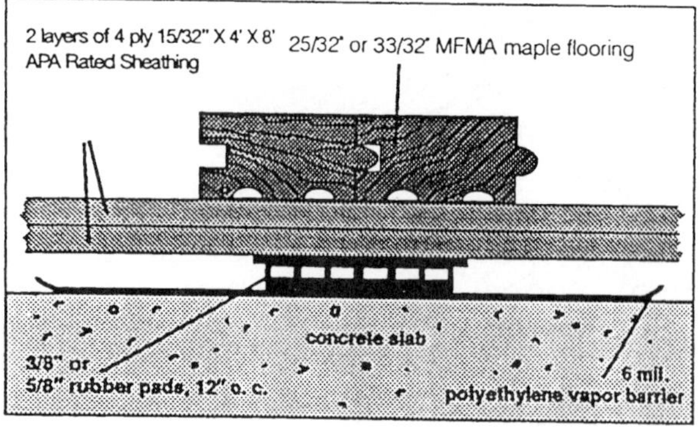

Clip Over Tongue

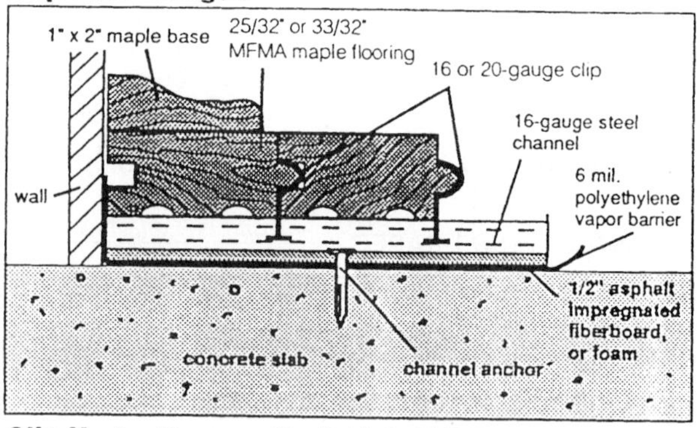

Clip Under Tongue (Available in 33/32" x 2-1/4" only.)

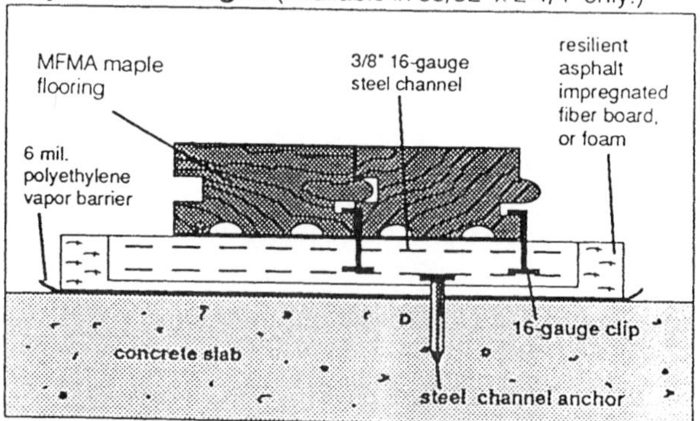

Backwards-Clip (Available in 27/32" x 2-1/4" only.)

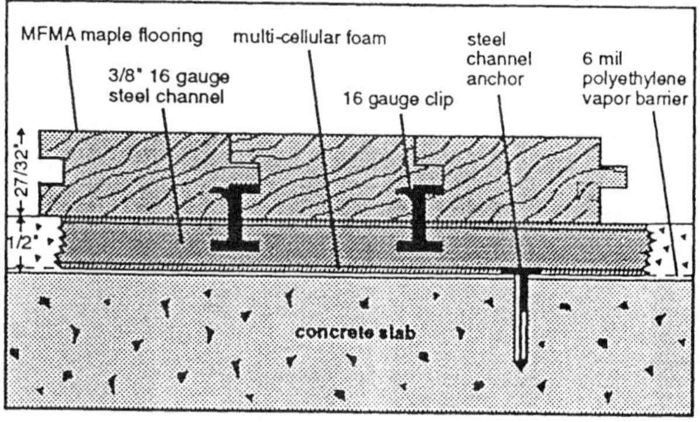

Nail-in-channel System

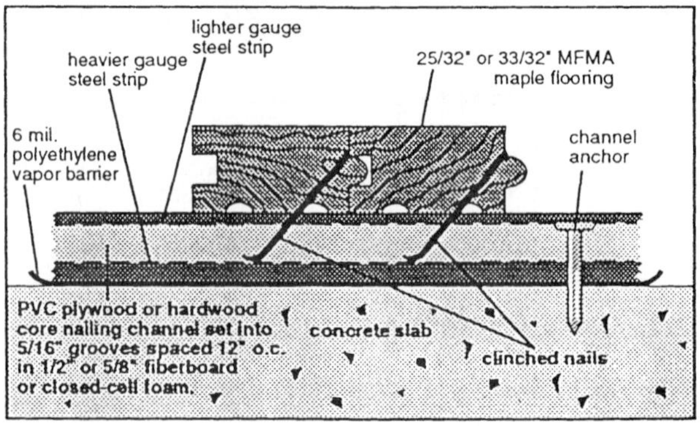

FLOORS AND FLOOR FINISHES
Wood Parquet Floor Patterns

	PRODUCT DESCRIPTION AND PATTERN	*PANEL SIZE	GRADE	*SPECIES
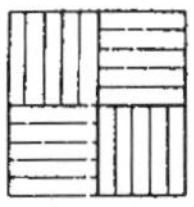	STANDARD Pattern Unfinished—paper-faced	5/16" x 19" x 19" 16 equal alternating squares 5/16" x 12" x 12" 4 equal alternating squares	Select & Better Rustic	Cherry, Maple, Red Oak, White Oak, Cedar, Pecan, Walnut, Rhodesian Teak, Angelique (Guiana Teak)
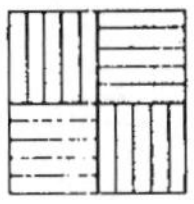	STANDARD Pattern Unfinished—WebBack or Mesh-Back	5/16" x 19" x 19" 16 equal alternating squares 5/16" x 11" x 11" 4 equal alternating squares	Select & Better Rustic Select & Better (Par & Better) Rustic	Red Oak, White Oak, Pecan Pecan Red and White Oak
	STANDARD Pattern Unfinished—WebBack (For Industrial Use)	5/16" x 19" x 19" 16 equal alternating squares 9/16" x 19" x 19" 16 equal alternating squares	Select & Better (Par & Better) Select Rustic & Better Rustic	Maple, Red Oak White Oak Pecan
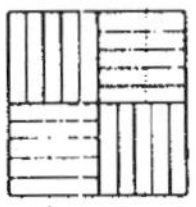	STANDARD Pattern Unfinished WebBack (For Industrial Use)	11/16" x 11" x 11" 4 equal alternating squares ¾" x 12-11/16" x 12-11/16" 4 equal alternating squares	Select & Better (Par & Better) Select & Better (Rustic & Better)	Red Oak, Maple White Oak
	STANDARD Pattern Factory-Finished and Unfinished (Available in various colors)	5/16" x 6-11/32" x 6-11/32" 5/16" x 2" x 12" (slats) 5/16" x 6" x 6" 5/16" x 6¾" x 6¾" 5/16" x 6½" x 6½" individual unit	Select & Better Natural & Better Fireside Rustic Cabin & Better Cabin	Oak, Walnut Pecan, Maple White Oak, Ash
	STANDARD Pattern Factory-Finished Foam-Back Tile	5/16" x 6½" x 6½" individual units . . . ⅛" foam, 2 lb. density	Natural & Better Cabin & Better Cabin	Oak, Pecan Maple
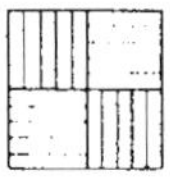	ANTIQUE TEXTURED (Factory-Finished and Unfinished)—Kerfsawn Various colors available	5/16" x 6" x 6" individual squares 5/16" x 6¾" x 6¾" individual squares 5/16" x 6½" x 6½" individual squares 5/16" x 11" x 11" 4 equal alternating squares	Select Natural & Better Select & Better (Par & Better) Rustic Fireside	Red Oak & White Oak Red Oak & White Oak
	ANTIQUE TEXTURED (Factory-Finished and Unfinished)—Wire brushed Various colors available	5/16" x 6¾" x 6¾" 5/16" x 6½" x 6½" individual squares	Natural & Better Cabin	Oak
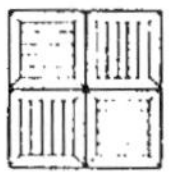	MONTICELLO Pattern Unfinished—Paper-Faced— Pre-Finished, Mesh-Back	5/16" x 6" x 6" individual squares used with 5/16" x ⅞" x 8" pickets 5/16" x 13¼" x 13¼" 4 equal alternating squares 5/16" x 13⅛" x 13⅛" (Factory Finished)	Select & Better (Par & Better) Rustic Natural & Better	Angelique (Guiana Teak) Red Oak, White Oak Black Walnut Ash, Maple
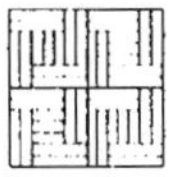	HADDON HALL Pattern Unfinished—Paper-Faced— Pre-Finished, Mesh-Back	5/16" x 14¼" x 14¼" 5/16" x 13¼" x 13¼" 4 equal squares 5/16" x 13⅛" x 13⅛" (Factory Finished)	Select & Better (Par & Better) Rustic Natural & Better	Angelique (Guiana Teak) Red Oak, White Oak Black Walnut
	HERRINGBONE Pattern Unfinished—Paper-Faced	5/16" x 2" x 12" individual slats 5/16" x 14⅛" x 18⅛" (Approximate overall) 2 - "V" shape courses wide and 11 slats long	Select & Better (Par & Better)	Angelique (Guiana Teak) Red Oak, White Oak Black Walnut
	SAXONY Pattern Unfinished—Paper-Faced	5/16" x 19" x 19" 4 equal squares on diagonal and 8 equal half squares	Select & Better (Par & Better)	Angelique (Guiana Teak) Red Oak, White Oak
	CANTERBURY Pattern Unfinished—Paper-Faced Pre-Finished, Mesh-Back	5/16" x 13¼" x 13¼" 4 equal alternating squares with diagonal center slats 5/16" x 13⅛ x 13⅛"	Select & Better (Par & Better) Natural & Better	Angelique (Guiana Teak) Red Oak, White Oak Black Walnut
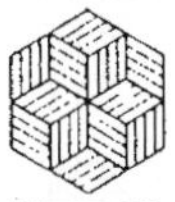	RHOMBS Pattern Unfinished—Paper-Faced	Hexagonal Shape 5/16" x 15⅛" x 15⅛" 12 equal Rhomboids	Select & Better (Par & Better) Rustic	Red Oak & White Oak Angelique (Guiana Teak) Black Walnut
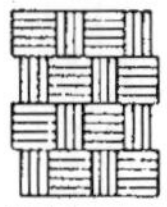	BASKET WEAVE Pattern Unfinished—Paper-Faced	5/16" x 15-1/5" x 19" 4 runs of 3 slats and 5 slats alternating	Select & Better (Par & Better)	Angelique (Guiana Teak) Red Oak, White Oak Black Walnut
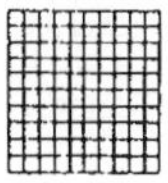	ITALIAN & DOMINO Pattern Unfinished—Paper-Faced	5/16" x 19" x 19" 400 equal size pieces butt-jointed	Select & Better (Par & Better)	Black Walnut Angelique (Guiana Teak) Maple, Red Oak White Oak

FLOORS AND FLOOR FINISHES

Wood Floor Patterns

Pattern #1
Same length of any size

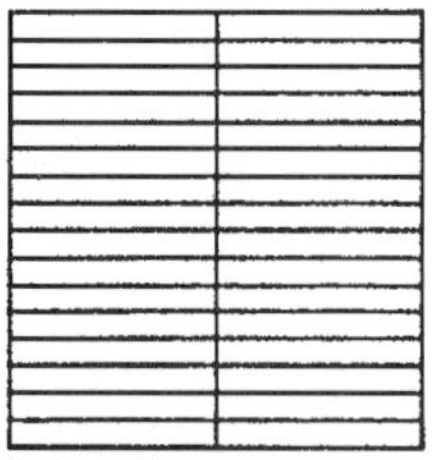
Pattern #2
Same length of any size

Pattern #3
Same length of any size

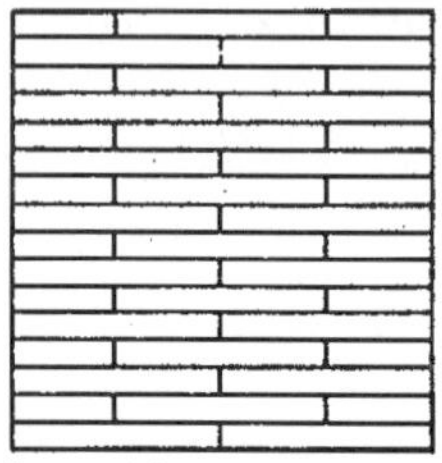
Pattern #4
Same length of any size

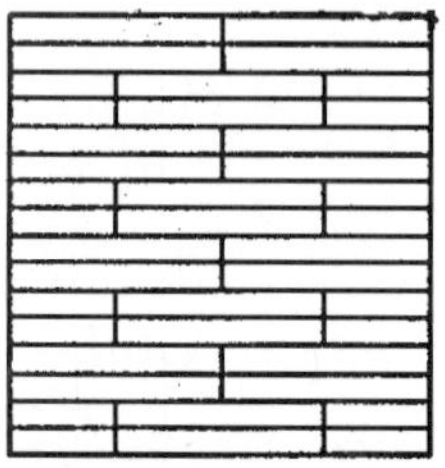
Pattern #5
Same length of any size

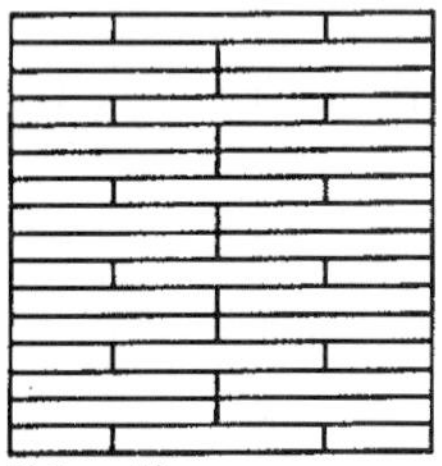
Pattern #6
Same length of any size

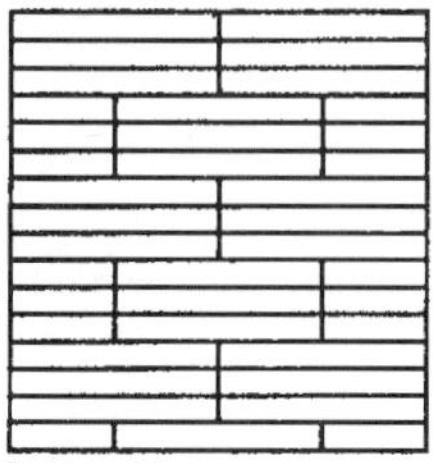
Pattern #7
Same length of any size

Pattern #8
Same length of any size

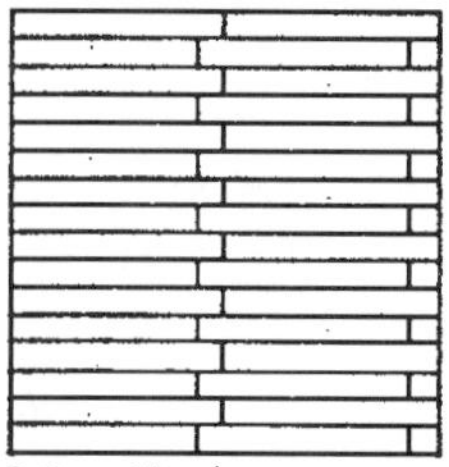
Pattern #9
Same length of any size

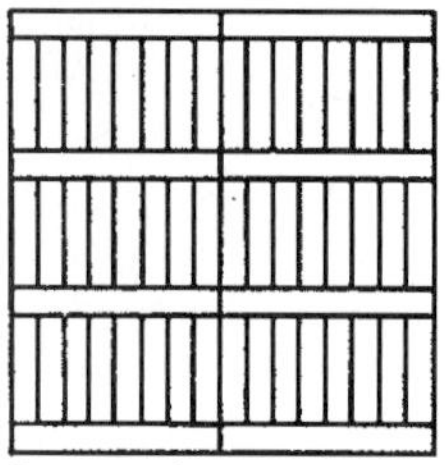
Pattern #10
36" and 18" lengths

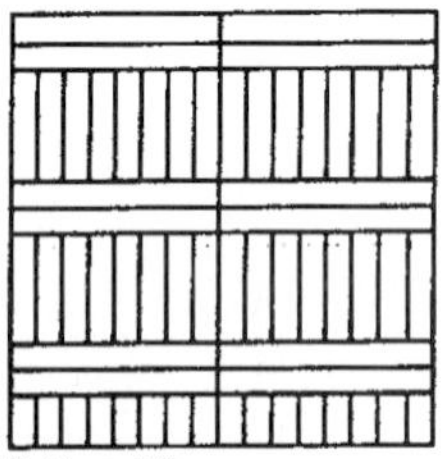
Pattern #11
36" and 18" lengths

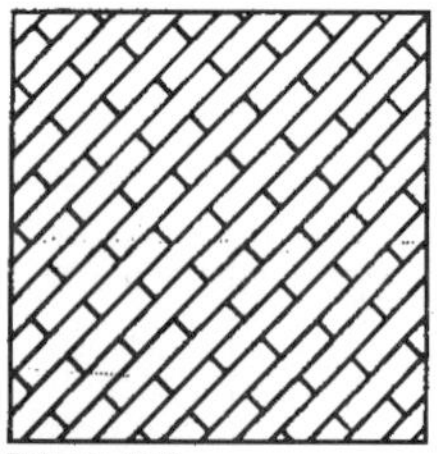
Pattern #12
Same length of any size

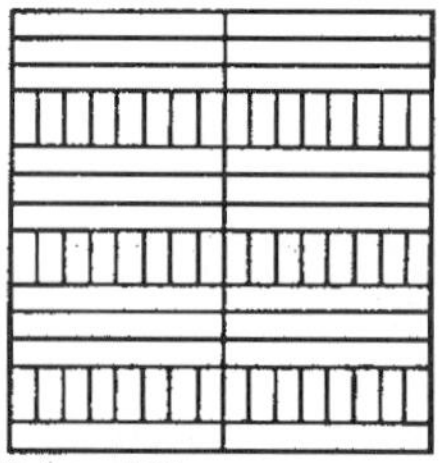
Pattern #13
36" and 9" lengths

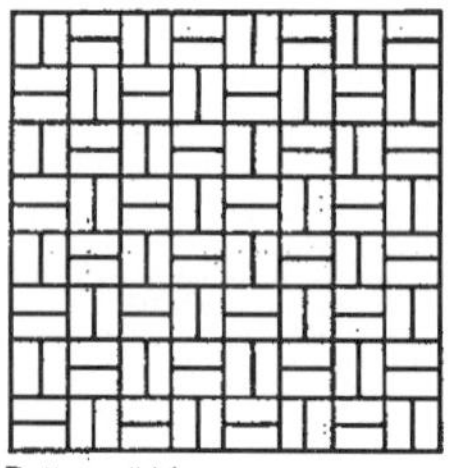
Pattern #14
9" lengths

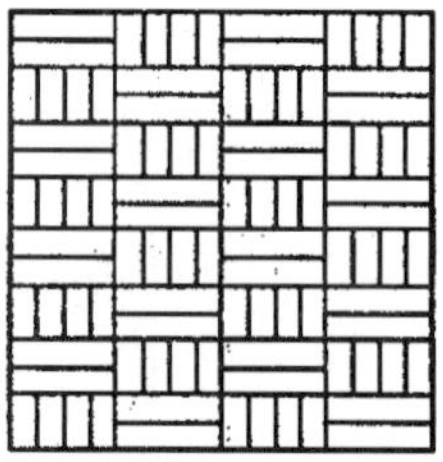
Pattern #15
18" and 9" lengths

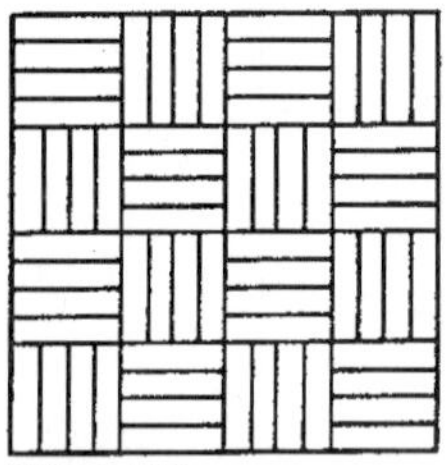
Pattern #16
18" lengths

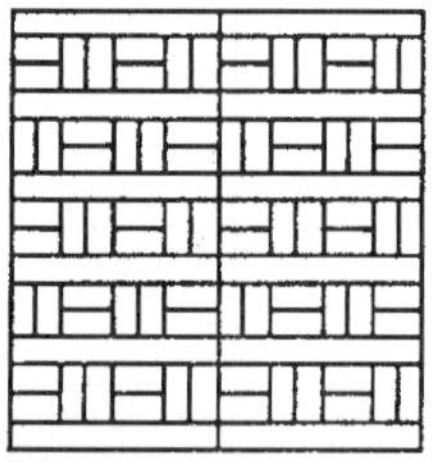
Pattern #17
36" and 9" lengths

Pattern #18
9" lengths

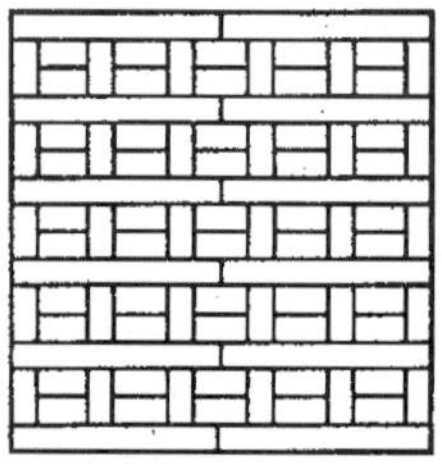
Pattern #19
36" and 9" lengths

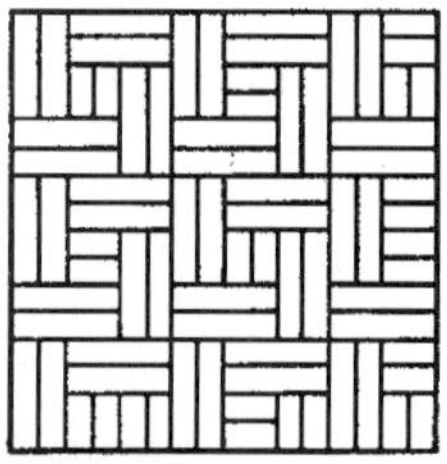
Pattern #20
18" and 9" lengths

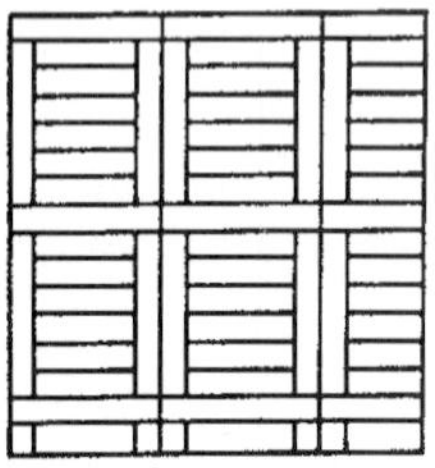
Pattern #21
36" and 27" lengths

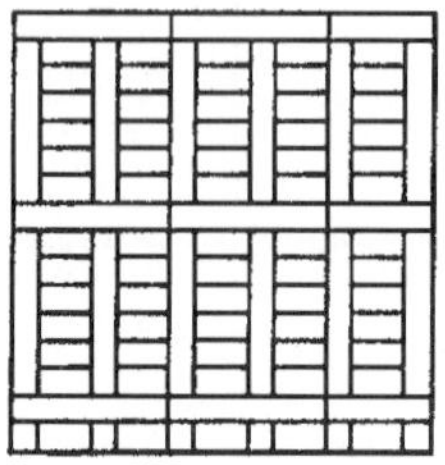
Pattern #22
27" and 9" lengths

Pattern #23
Same length of any size

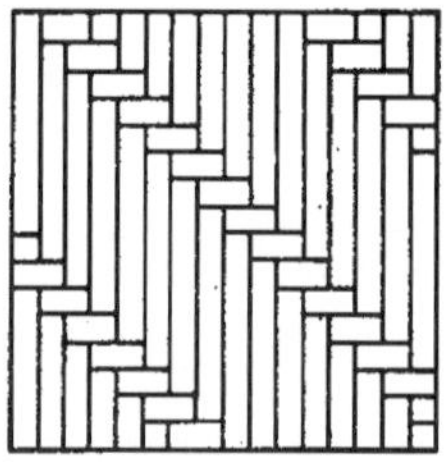
Pattern #24
36" and 9" lengths

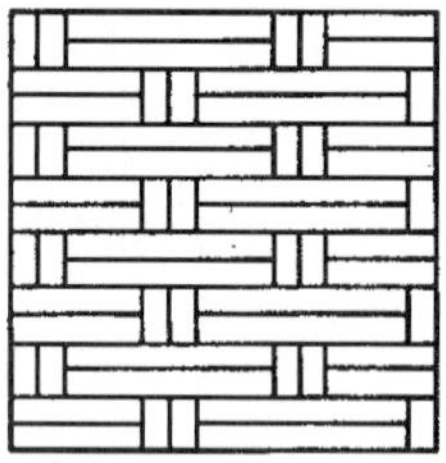
Pattern #25
36" and 9" lengths

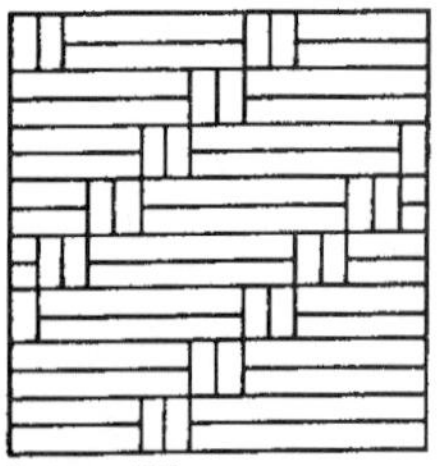
Pattern #26
36" and 9" lengths

Pattern #27
18" and 9" lengths

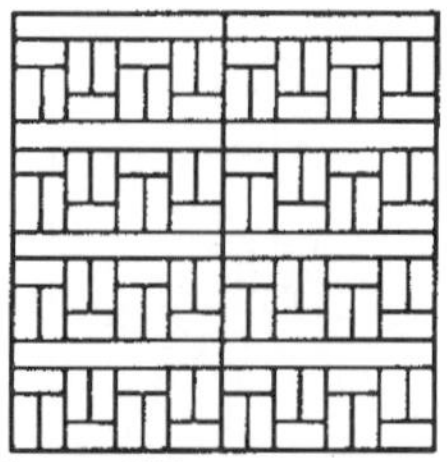
Pattern #28
36" and 9" lengths

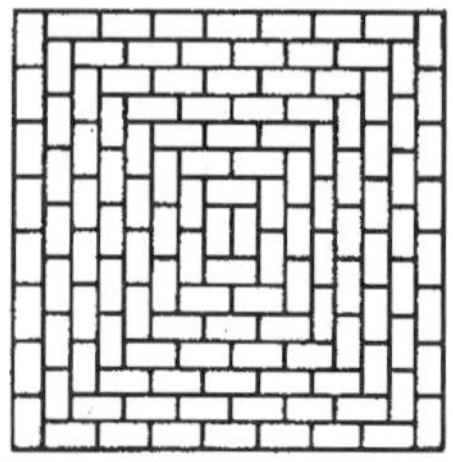
Pattern #29
9" lengths

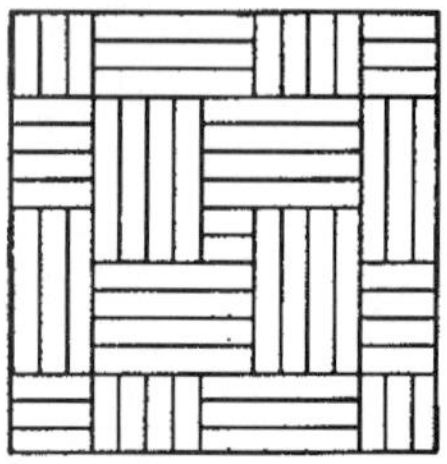
Pattern #31
27" and 9" lengths

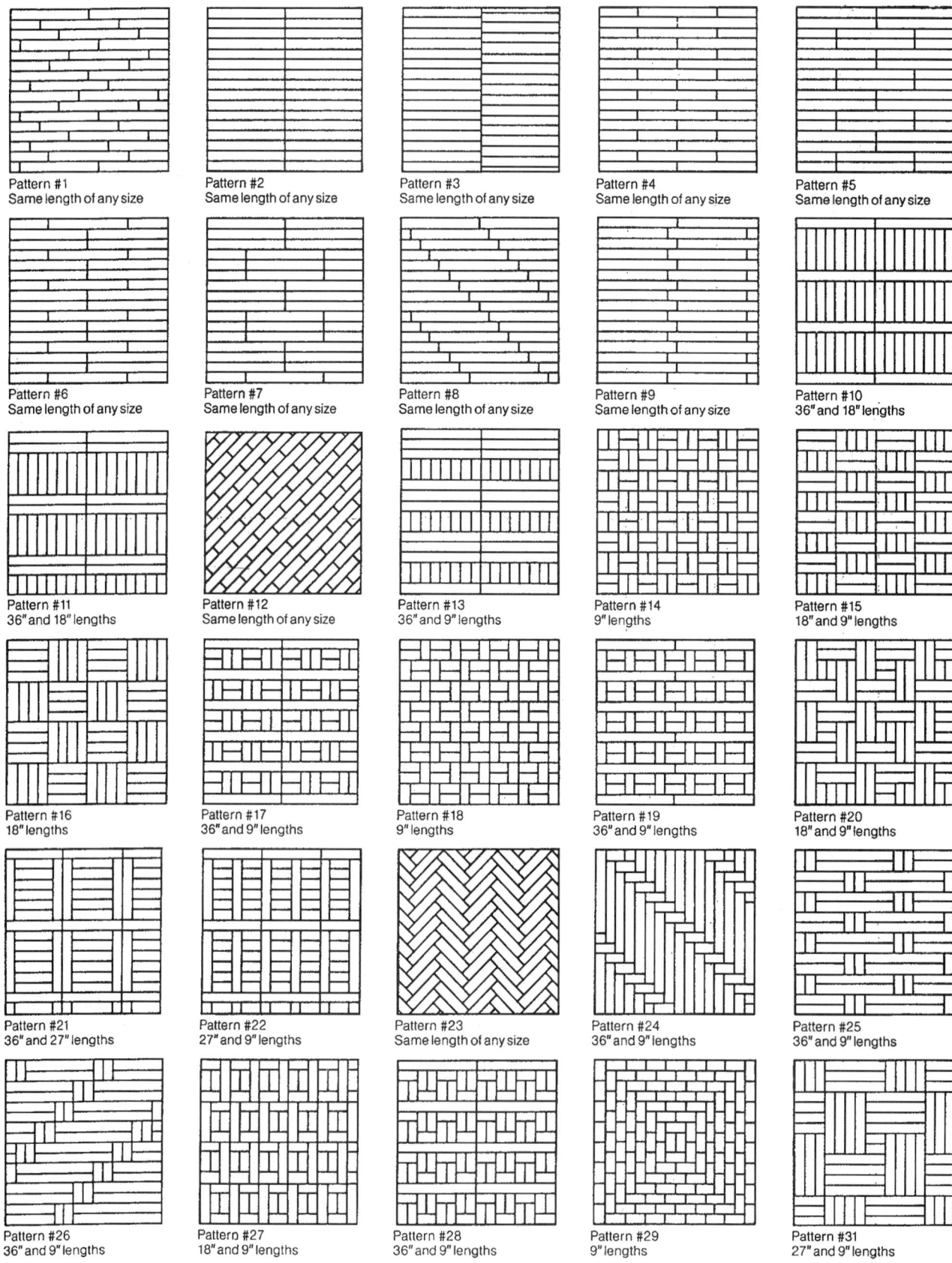

FLOORS AND FLOOR FINISHES

Wood Parquet and Plank Floor Patterns

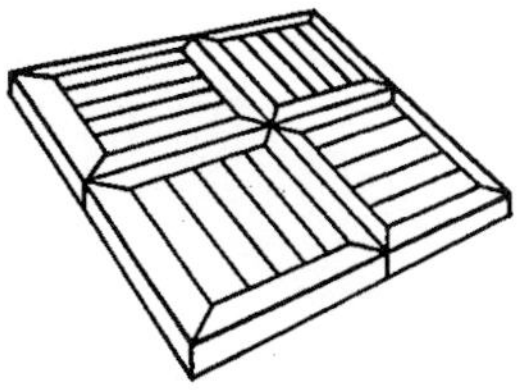

5/16" x 13-1/4" x 13-1/4"

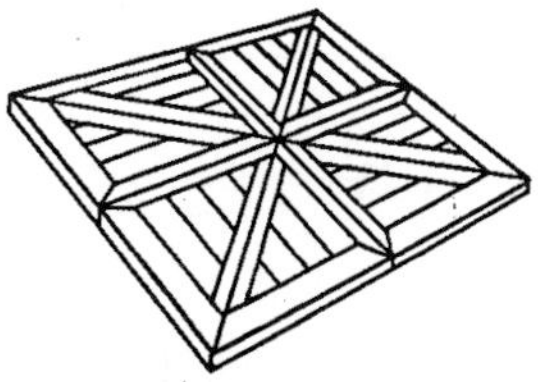

5/16" x 13-1/4" x 13-1/4"

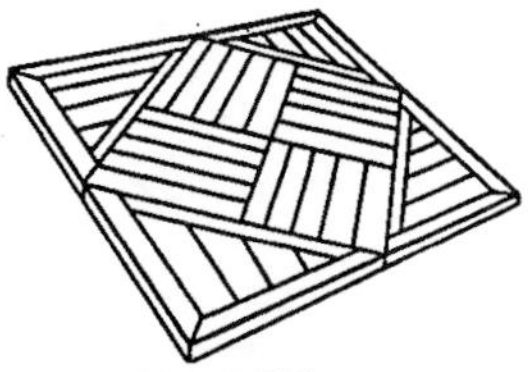

5/16" x 13-7/16" x 13-7/16"

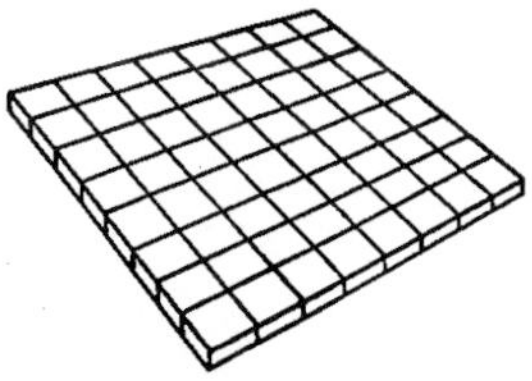

5/16" x 18" x 18"

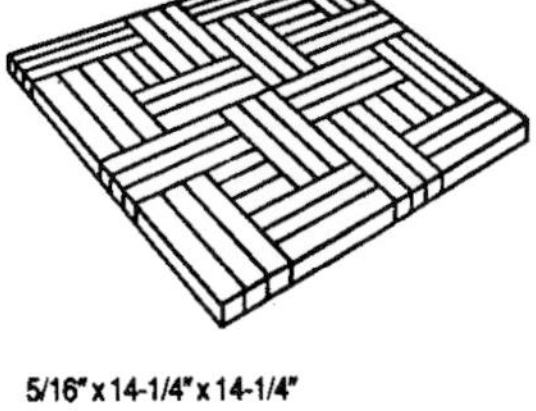

5/16" x 14-1/4" x 14-1/4"

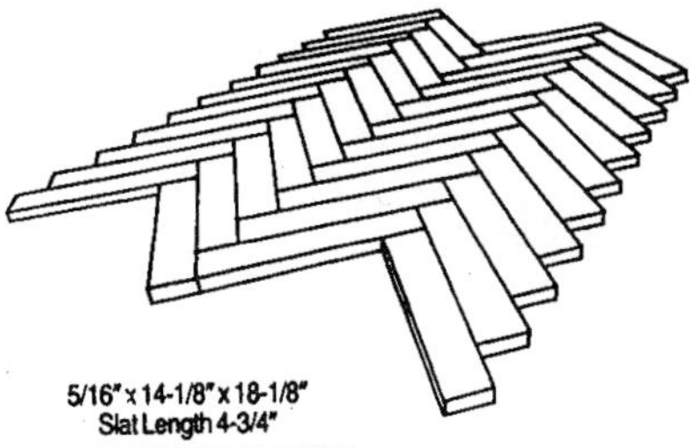

5/16" x 14-1/8" x 18-1/8"
Slat Length 4-3/4"

5/16" x 16-1/4" x 18-1/8"
Slat Length 5-1/2"

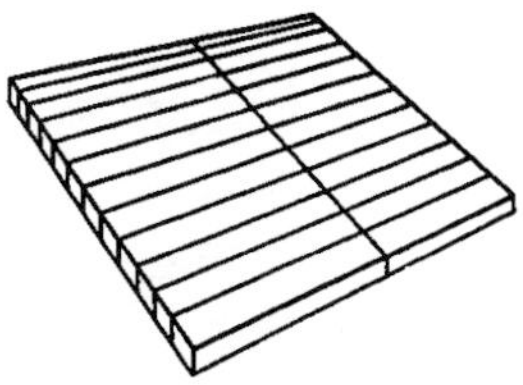

5/16" x 19" x 19"

5/16" x 11" x 11"

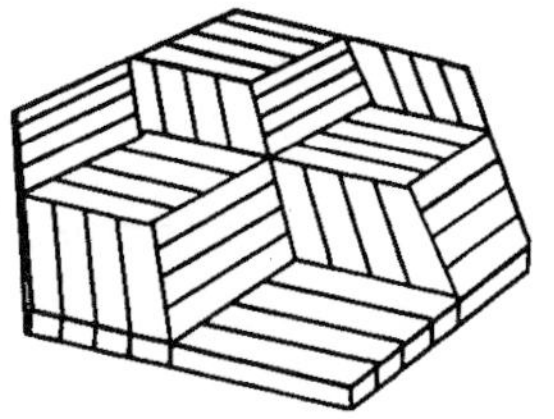

5/16" x 15-1/8" x 15-1/8"

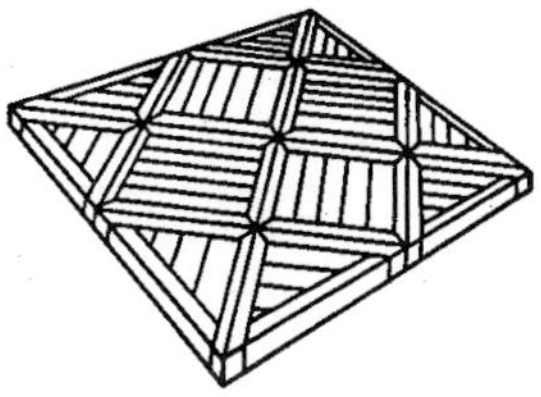

5/16" x 19" x 19"

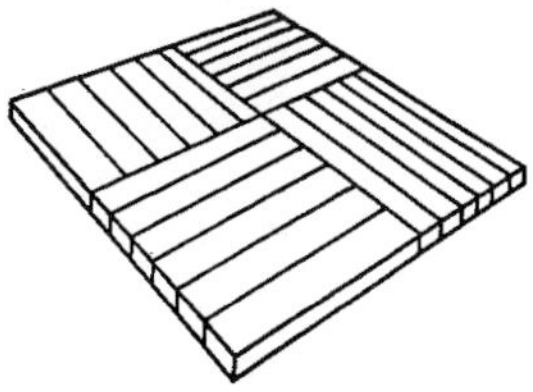

5/16" x 19" x 19"

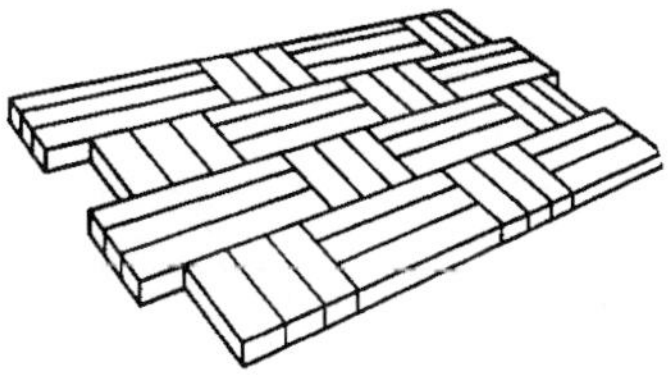

5/16" x 11" x 16-1/2"

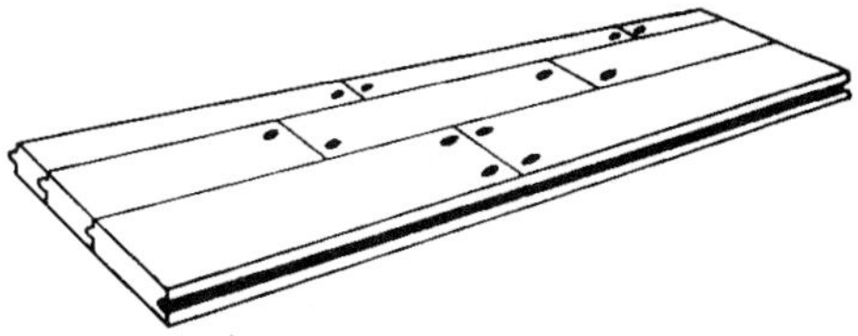

3/4" x 3", 5", & 7"

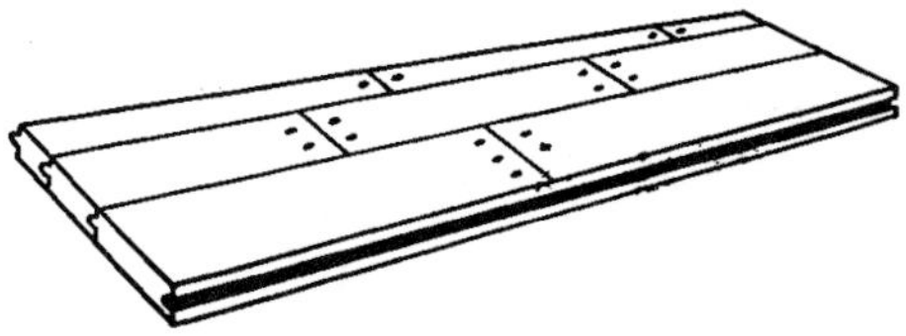

3/4" x 3", 5", & 7"

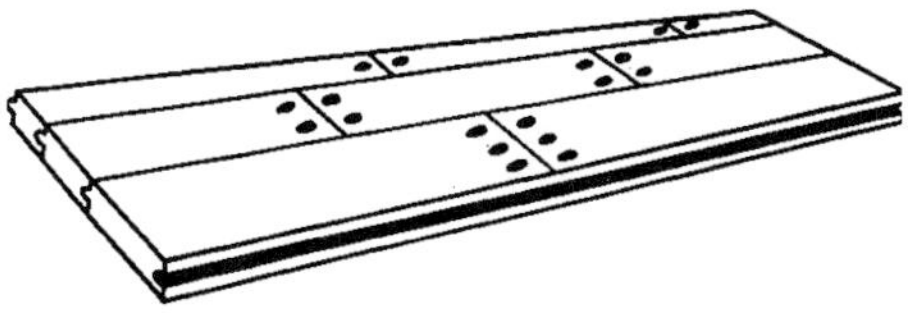

3/4" x 3", 5", & 7""

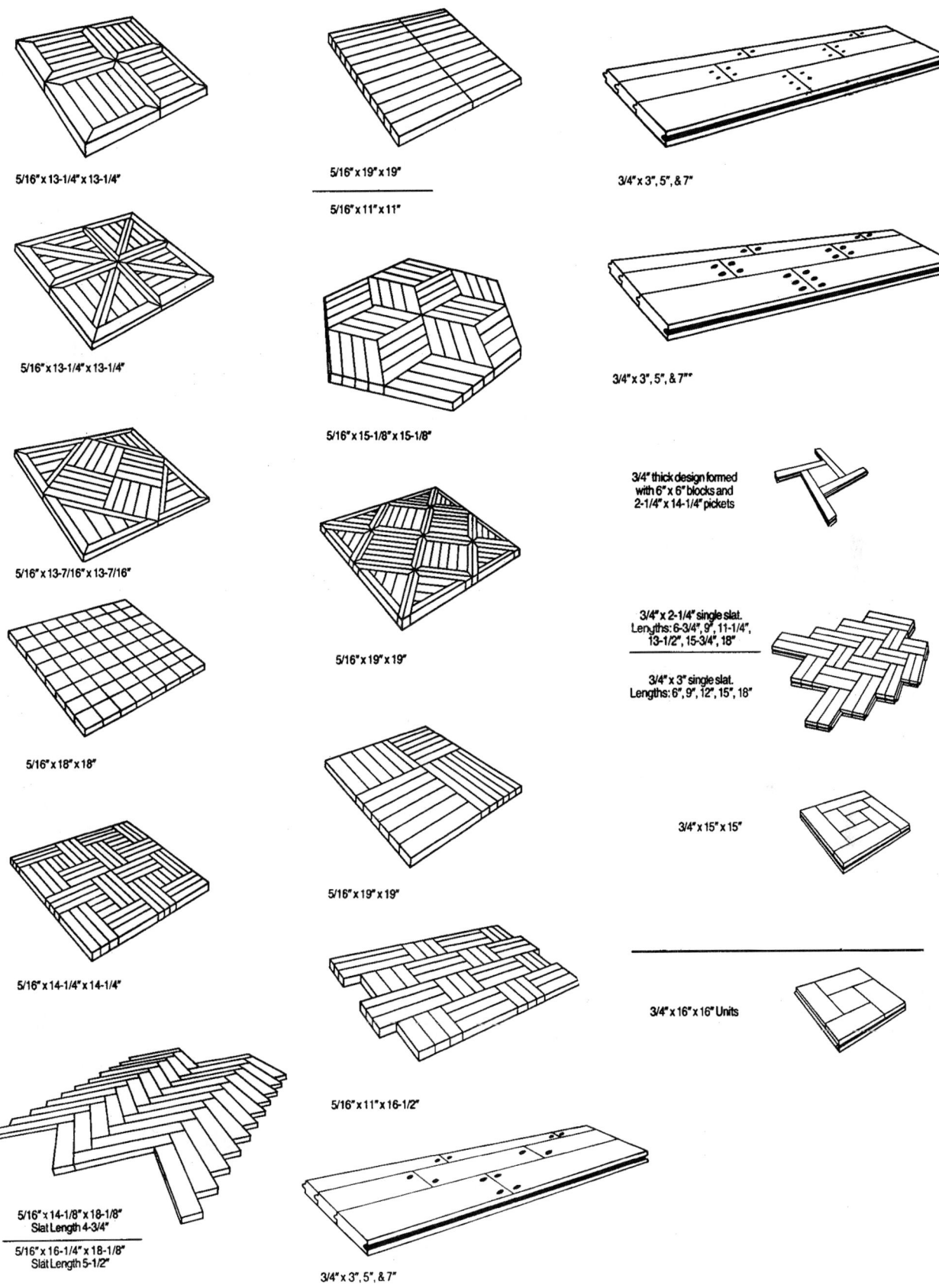

3/4" thick design formed with 6" x 6" blocks and 2-1/4" x 14-1/4" pickets

3/4" x 2-1/4" single slat.
Lengths: 6-3/4", 9", 11-1/4", 13-1/2", 15-3/4", 18"

3/4" x 3" single slat.
Lengths: 6", 9", 12", 15", 18"

3/4" x 15" x 15"

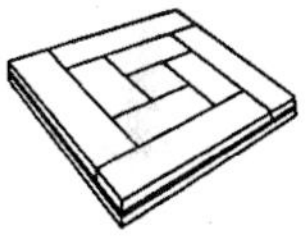

3/4" x 16" x 16" Units

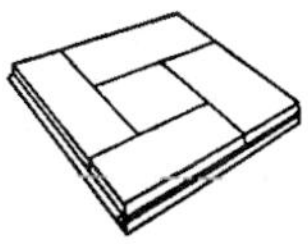

FLOORS AND FLOOR FINISHES

Wood on Concrete Slab Floor Construction Details

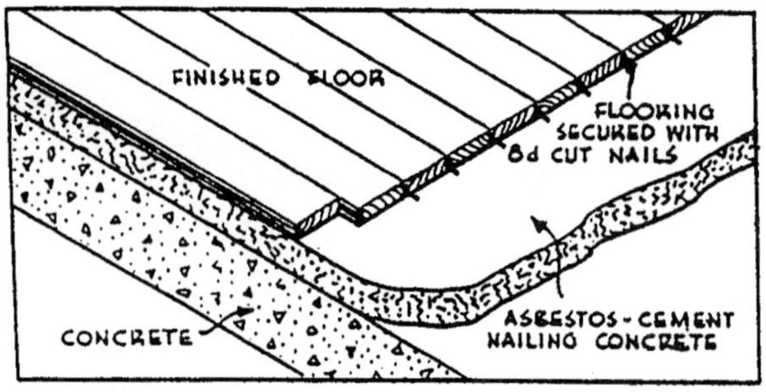

WOOD FLOOR OVER CONCRETE WITH UNDERLAYER OF NAILING CONCRETE

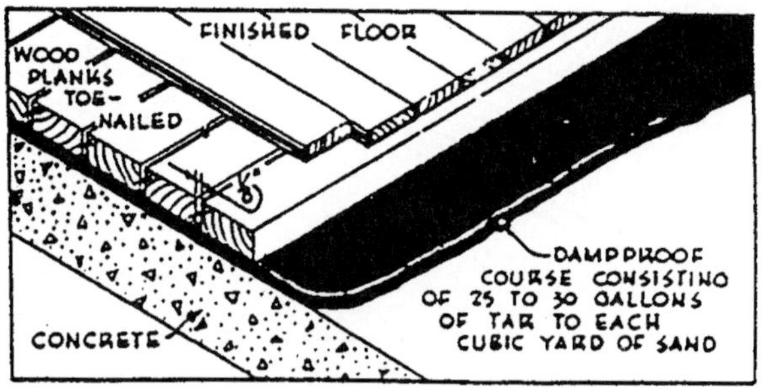

WOOD FLOOR OVER CONCRETE

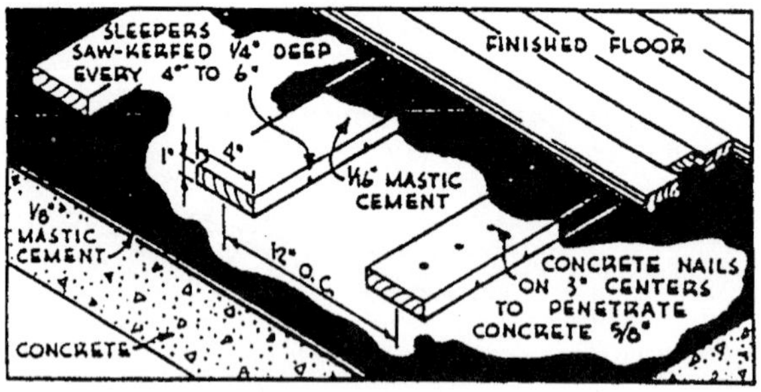

FINISHED FLOOR DIRECTLY ON SLEEPERS SET IN MASTIC CEMENT & NAILED TO CONCRETE

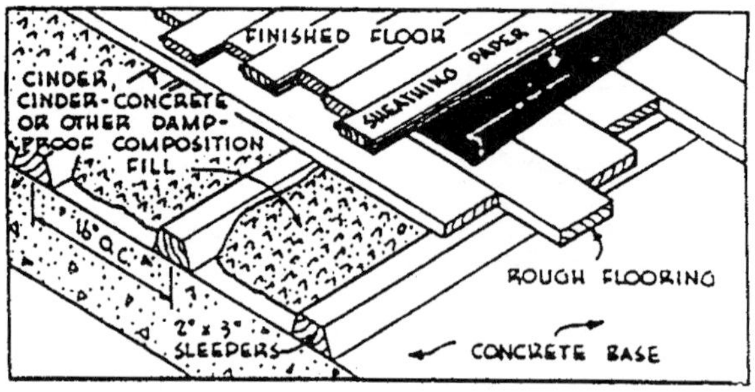

WOOD FLOOR OVER CONCRETE WITH SUB-BASE OF SLEEPERS & SLEEPER FILL

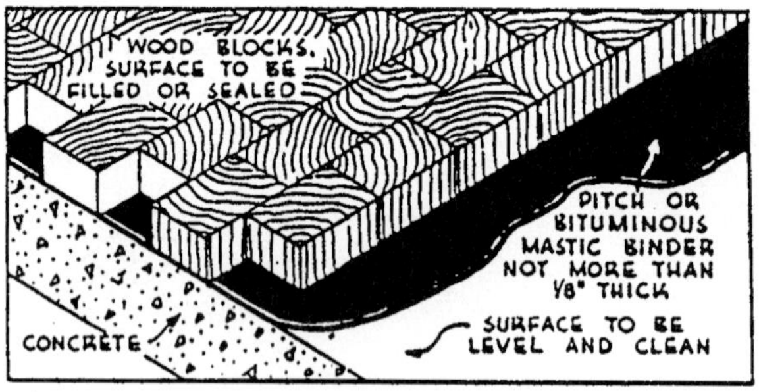

WOOD BLOCK FLOOR OVER CONCRETE

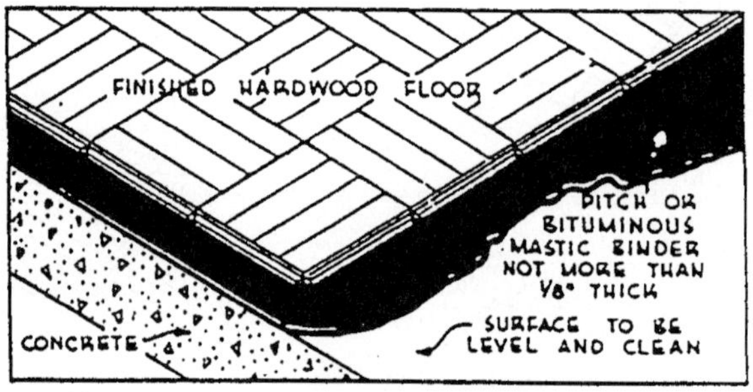

WOOD FLOOR OVER CONCRETE IN MASTIC

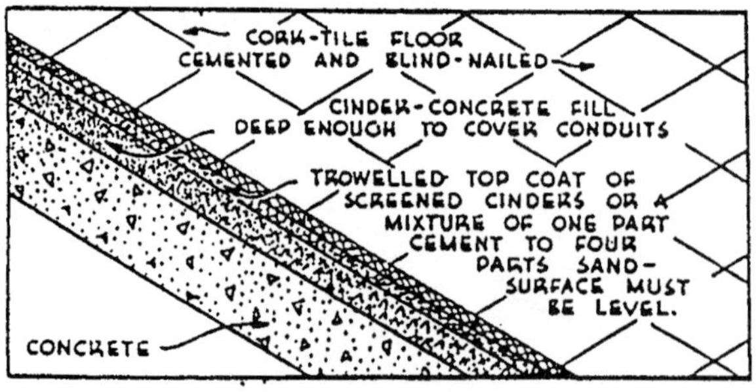

CORK TILE FLOOR OVER CONCRETE

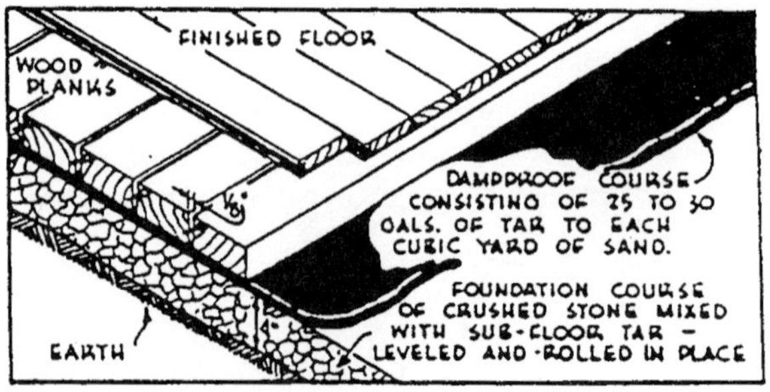

WOOD FLOOR APPLIED OVER EARTH

Sound insulation between an upper floor and the ceiling of a lower floor not only involves resistance of airborne sounds but also that of impact noises. Thus, impact noise control must be considered as well as the STC value. Impact noise is caused by an object striking or sliding along a wall or floor surface, such as by dropped objects, footsteps, or moving furniture. It may also be caused by the vibration of a dishwasher, bathtub, food-disposal apparatus, or other equipment. In all instances, the floor is set into vibration by the impact or contact and sound is radiated from both sides of the floor.

A method of measuring impact noise has been developed and is commonly expressed as the *impact noise ratings* (*INR*). The greater the positive value of the INR, the more resistant is the floor to impact noise transfer. For example, an INR of –2 is better than one of –17, and one of +5 INR is a further improvement in resistance to impact noise transfer.

Figure 7 shows STC and approximate INR(db) values for several types of floor constructions. Figure 7*A*, perhaps a minimum floor assembly with tongued-and-grooved floor and ⅜-in gypsum board ceiling, has an STC value of 30 and an approximate INR value of –18. This is improved somewhat by the construction shown in Fig. 7*B*, and still further by the combination of materials in Fig. 7*C*.

The value of isolating the ceiling joists from a gypsum lath and plaster ceiling by means of spring clips is illustrated in Fig. 8*A*. An STC value of 52 and an approximate INR value of –2 result.

Foam-rubber padding and carpeting improve both the STC and the INR values. The STC value increases from 31 to 45 and the approximate INR from –17 to +5 (Fig. 8*B* and *C*). This can likely be further improved by using an isolated ceiling finish with spring clips. The use of sound-deadening board and a lamination of gypsum board for the ceiling would also improve resistance to sound transfer.

An economical construction similar to (but an improvement over) Fig. 8*C*, with an STC value of 48 and an approximate INR of +18, consists of the following: (a) a pad and carpet over ⅝-in tongued-and-grooved plywood underlayment, (b) 3-in fiberglass insulating batts between joists, (c) resilient channels spaced 24 in apart, across the bottom of the joists, and (d) ⅝-in gypsum board screwed to the bottom of the channels and finished with taped joints.

The use of separate floor joists with staggered ceiling joists below provides reasonable values but adds a good deal to construction costs. Separate joists with insulation between and a soundboard between subfloor and finish provide an STC rating of 53 and an approximate INR value of –3.

		ESTIMATED VALUES	
DETAIL	DESCRIPTION	STC RATING	APPROX. INR
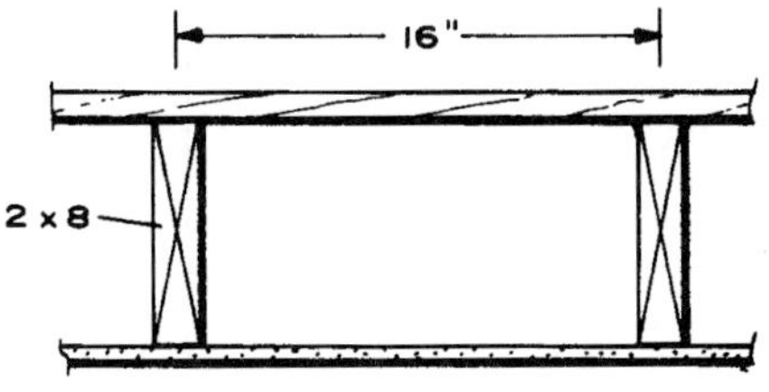 A	FLOOR 7/8" T. & G. FLOORING CEILING 3/8" GYPSUM BOARD	30	-18
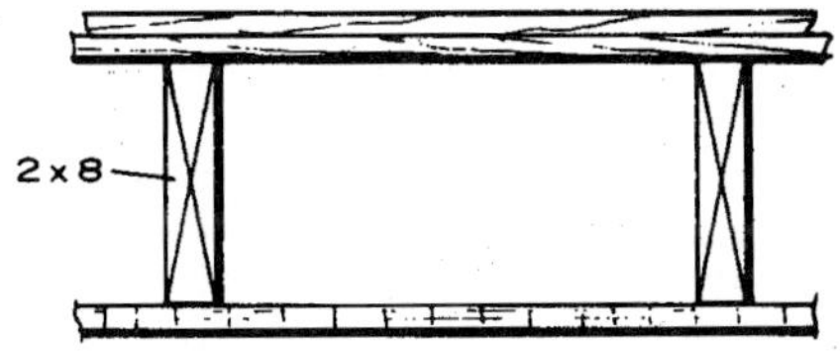 B	FLOOR 3/4" SUBFLOOR 3/4" FINISH FLOOR CEILING 3/4" FIBERBOARD	42	-12
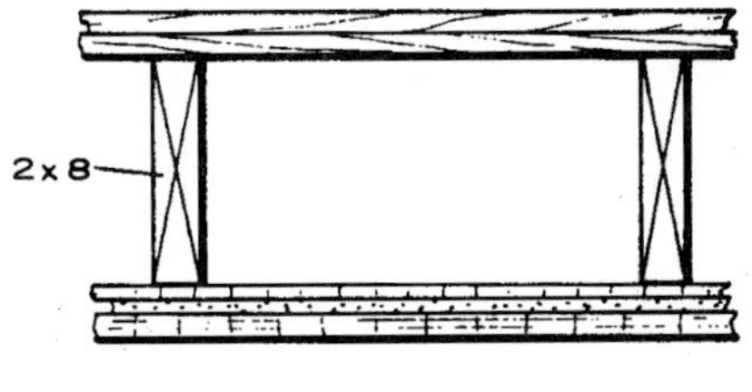 C	FLOOR 3/4" SUBFLOOR 3/4" FINISH FLOOR CEILING 1/2" FIBERBOARD LATH 1/2" GYPSUM PLASTER 3/4" FIBERBOARD	45	-4

Fig. 7 Relative impact and sound transfer in floor-ceiling combinations (2- by 8-in joists)

FLOORS AND FLOOR FINISHES

Floor Construction Sound Insulation

Sound Absorption

Design of the "quiet" house can incorporate another system of sound insulation, namely, sound absorption. Sound-absorbing materials can minimize the amount of noise by stopping the reflection of sound back into a room. Sound-absorbing materials do not necessarily have resistance to airborne sounds. Perhaps the most commonly used sound-absorbing material is acoustic tile. Wood fiber or similar materials are used in the manufacture of the tile, which is usually processed to provide some fire resistance and designed with numerous tiny sound traps on the tile surfaces. These may consist of tiny drilled or punched holes, fissured surfaces, or a combination of both.

Acoustic tile is most often used in the ceiling and areas where it is not subjected to excessive mechanical damage, such as above a wall wainscoting. It is normally manufactured in sizes from 12 by 12 to 12 by 48 in. Thicknesses vary from ½ to ¾ in, and the tile is usually factory finished ready for application. Paint or other finishes which fill or cover the tiny holes or fissures for trapping sound will greatly reduce its efficiency.

Acoustic tile may be applied by a number of methods—to existing ceilings or any smooth surface with a mastic adhesive designed specifically for this purpose, or to furring strips nailed to the underside of the ceiling joists. Nailing or stapling tile is the normal application method in this system. It is also used with a mechanical suspension system involving small "H," "Z," or "T" members. Manufacturers' recommendations should be followed in application and finishing.

		ESTIMATED VALUES	
DETAIL	DESCRIPTION	STC RATING	APPROX. INR
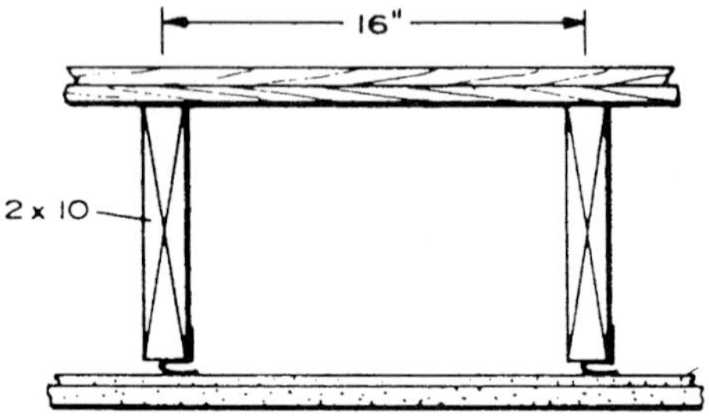 A	FLOOR ¾" SUBFLOOR (BUILDING PAPER) ¾" FINISH FLOOR CEILING GYPSUM LATH AND SPRING CLIPS ½" GYPSUM PLASTER	52	-2
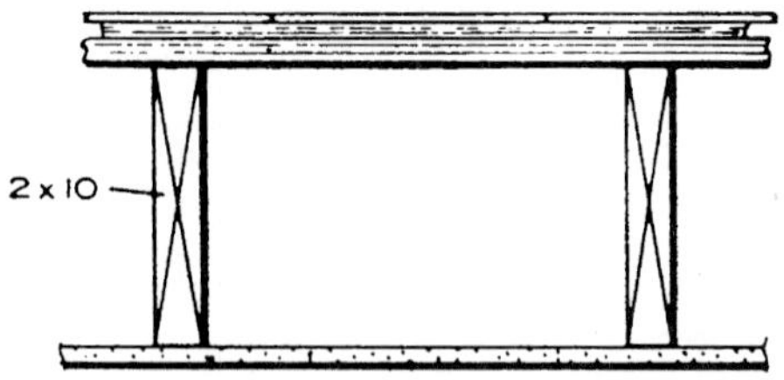 B	FLOOR ⅝" PLYWOOD SUBFLOOR ½" PLYWOOD UNDERLAYMENT ⅛" VINYL-ASBESTOS TILE CEILING ½" GYPSUM WALLBOARD	31	-17
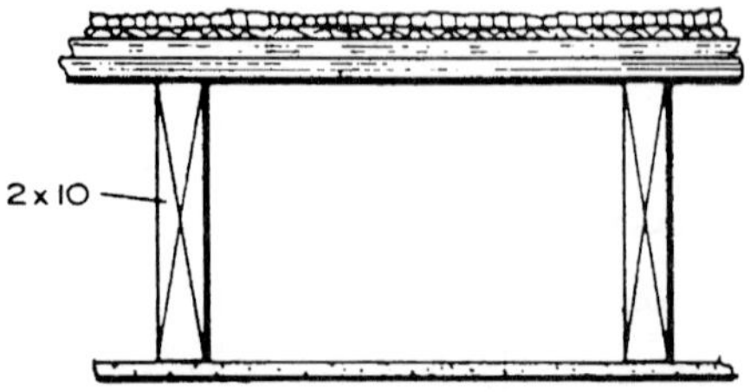 C	FLOOR 5/8" PLYWOOD SUBFLOOR ½" PLYWOOD UNDERLAYMENT FOAM RUBBER PAD ⅜" NYLON CARPET CEILING ½" GYPSUM WALLBOARD	45	+5

Fig. 8 Relative impact and sound transfer in floor-ceiling combinations (2- by 10-in joists)

conventional wood floor joist systems for sound control

conventional

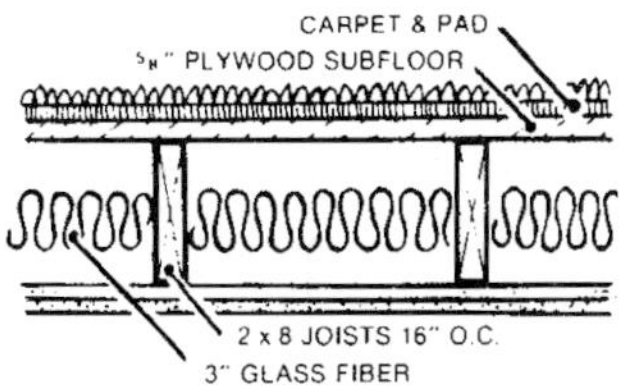

FLOOR NO. 3

The basic construction is illustrated by floor No. 3 although floors 4 and 5 have 2"x10" joists and ½" subfloor. Except in floor No. 1, the ceiling is fire-resistive type gypsum board applied with screws to resilient channels 24" o.c. Standard carpet is 44-ounce (sq. yd.) gropoint over 40-ounce hair pad.

FLOOR NUMBER	FLOOR COVERING
1	⅛" vinyl asbestos tile on ⅜" plywood underlayment
2	.075" vinyl sheet on ⅜" plywood underlayment
3	Carpet and pad directly over subfloor
4	25/32" oak strip floor over subfloor
5	Carpet and pad added to No. 4

conventional
With Floated Floor Over

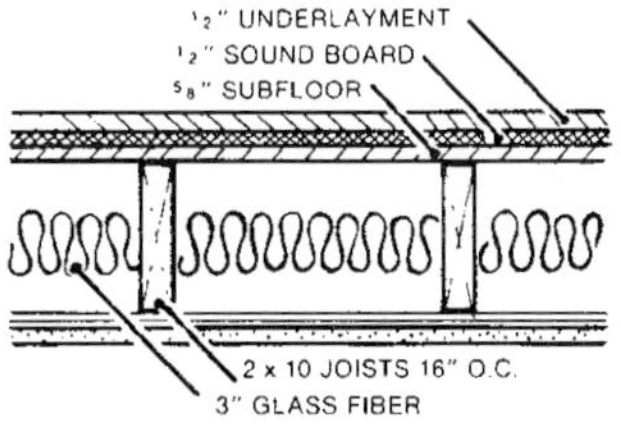

FLOOR NO. 8

The basic construction is illustrated. Sound deadening board (15-18 p.c.f.) is laid over a ⅝" plywood subfloor, with or without stapling, and ½" T&G underlayment grade plywood glued over the sound board. The ceiling is ⅝" fire-resistive type gypsum board on resilient channels; absorptive material is 3-inch thick glass fiber batts

FLOOR NUMBER	FLOOR COVERING
6	Wood block (5/16") laminated to underlayment
7	Carpet and pad
8	Vinyl flooring laminated to underlayment applied over sound board with 4-inch circular globs of glue
9	Vinyl covering like 8 with sleepers glued between sound board and underlayment
10	Oak strip flooring (25/32") nailed to 2x3 sleepers glued over sound board strips 1⅞" glass fiber between sleepers
11	Vinyl flooring (0.07") on ⅝" T&G plywood underlayment glued to 2x2 sleepers glued to subfloor 16" o.c. Sand fill over subfloor to depth of sleepers (1½"). Balance as in basic construction

conventional
With lightweight Concrete or Gypsum Cement Added

FLOOR NO. 14

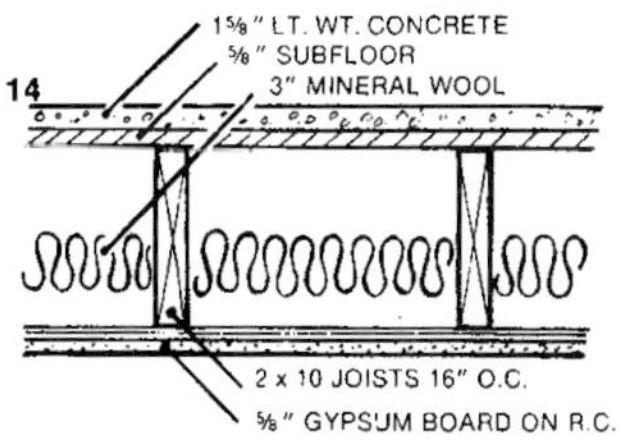

The basic construction is illustrated by floor No. 14. The floor topping is 1⅝" thick cellular (foamed) concrete (100 p.c.f.). Ceilings are fire-resistive type gypsum board on resilient channels, 24 inches o.c. Absorptive material is 3" thick mineral wool batts. Floor coverings for impact tests are 44-ounce carpet over 40-ounce hair pad or vinyl floor covering, approximately 0.07 inches thick. Note variations from basic construction drawn in plans 12-16.

FLOOR NUMBER	FLOOR COVERING
12	Ceiling nailed to joists; no absorptive material; with carpet and pad..
13	Ceiling nailed to joists; 3" glass fiber with carpet and pad..
14	**Basic construction**—(no floor covering) with carpet and pad..
15	Add ½" sound board between concrete and subfloor with vinyl tile.. with carpet and pad..
16	Basic construction—but with ¾" thick gypsum concrete in place of 1⅝" thick cellular concrete; ½" gypsum ceiling without floor covering..

The improved resistance to airborne sound transmission gained by isolating the ceiling with resilient channels and adding absorptive material is evident by comparing floors 2 to 5 with No. 1. A 10-point increase in STC reduces the loudness of transmitted noise by one-half. Improved resistance to impact noise transmission is gained by adding carpet and pad as is evident by comparing floor No. 3 with No. 2 or floor No. 5 with 4. An IIC of 51 is often recommended as an acceptable level of impact insulation.

FLOORS AND FLOOR FINISHES

Resilient Base Details

Standard toe base

No-toe base: Adds a decorative touch to carpeted interiors.

Butt toe base: Engineered to butt precisely to ⅛-in floor coverings.

Long toe base: For special applications. Features a longer toe extending 1 in to cover wide irregularities between floor and wall.

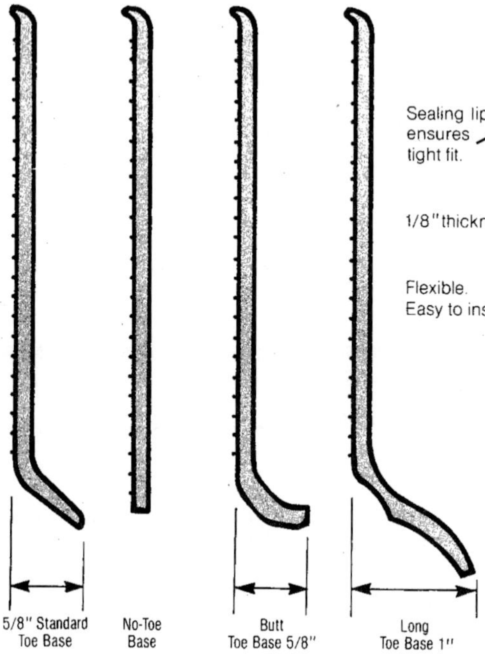

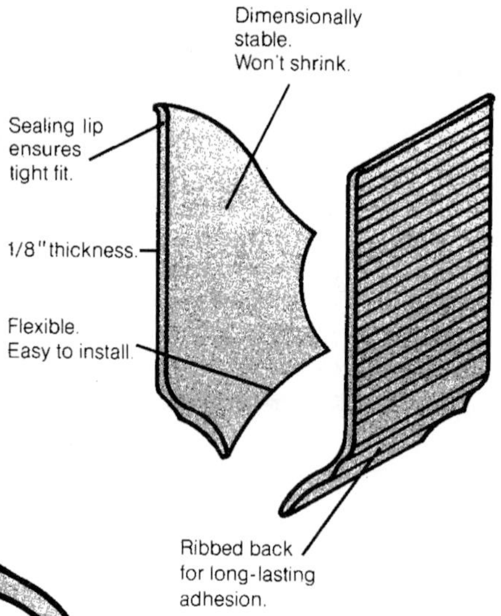

Table 1 Cove base specifications

Type	Sizes available		
Standard toe base	2½"	4"	6"
No-toe base	2½"	4"	6"
Butt toe base		4"	6"
Long toe base		4"	

Length: 48"

Table 2 Corner specifications

Type	Length of return	Sizes available		
Inside/outside	2¼"	2½"	4"	6"
Underlap outside	3" (with underlap)		4"	
No-toe outside	2¼"	2½"	4"	
Long toe outside	2¼"		4"	

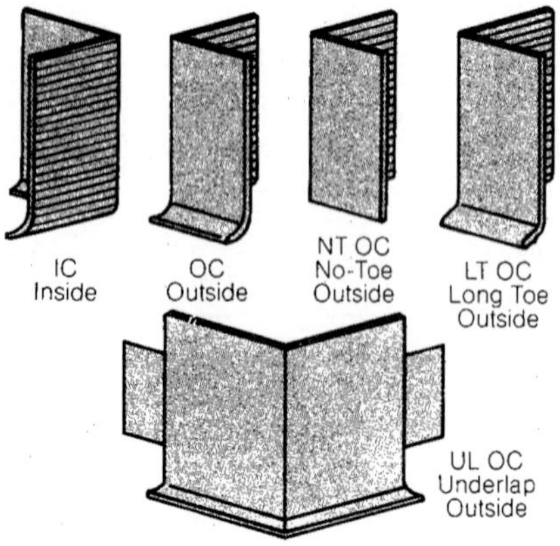

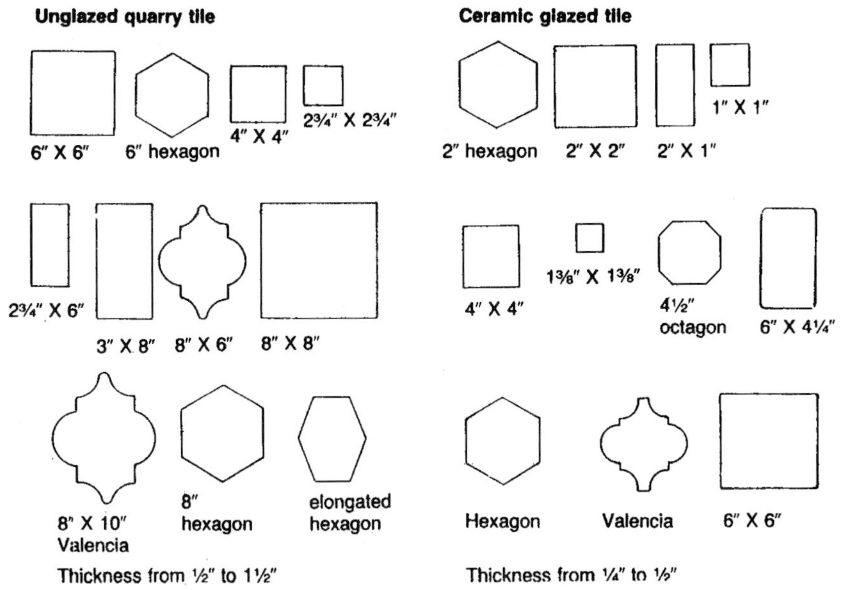

Fig. 9 Ceramic tile shapes

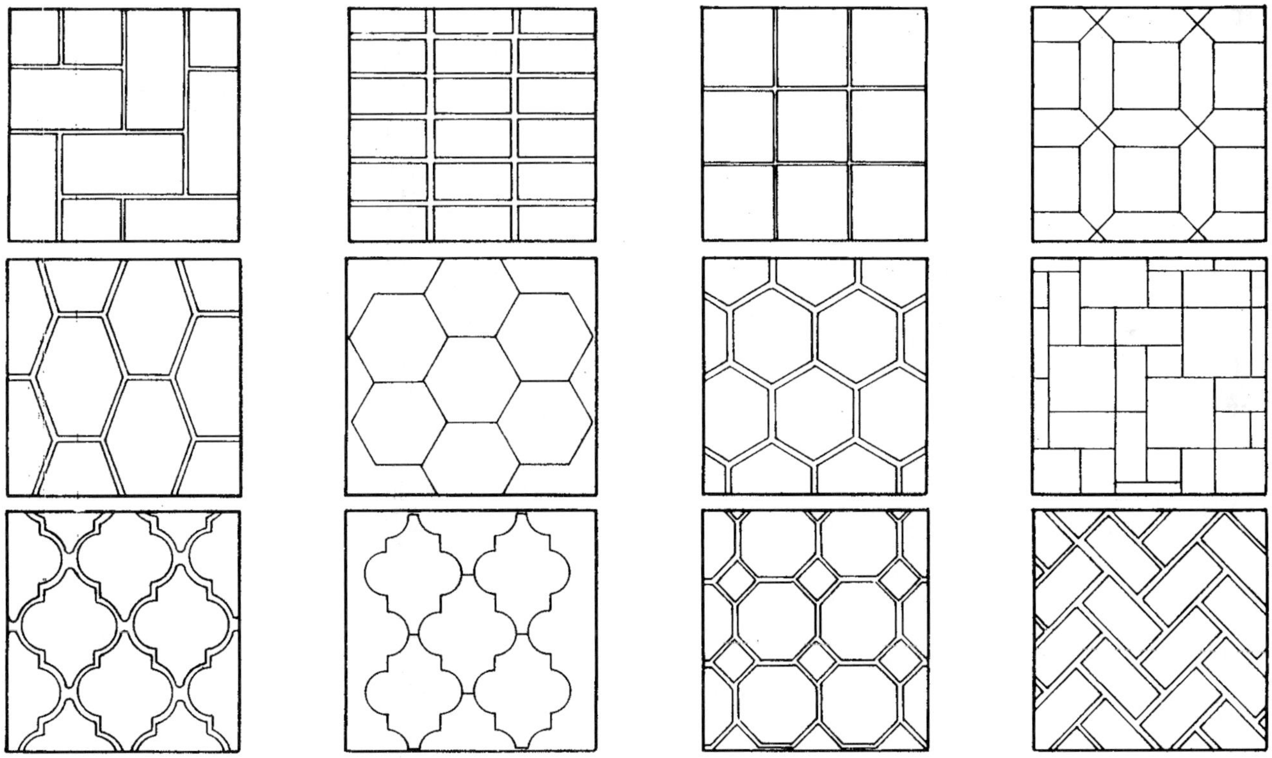

Fig. 10 Ceramic tile patterns

FLOORS AND FLOOR FINISHES

Ceramic Tile Patterns

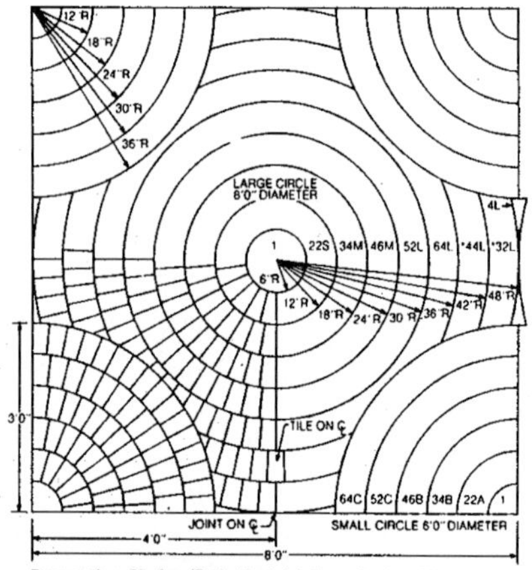

Serpentine Circles (8 Ft. Module) Quantity for 100 sq. feet: 3.2 pcs. circle; 70 pcs. small wedge: 256 pcs. medium wedge: 500 pcs. large wedge

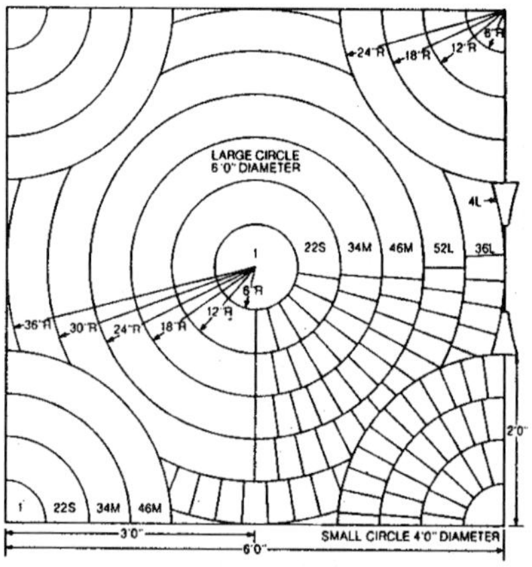

Serpentine Circles (6 Ft. Module) Quantity for 100 sq. feet: 5.7 pcs. circle; 126 pcs. small wedge: 460 pcs. medium wedge: 280 pcs. large wedge

Meandering Serpentine Quantity for 100 sq. feet: 3 pcs. circle; 58 pcs. small wedge: 220 pcs. medium wedge: 610 pcs. large wedge

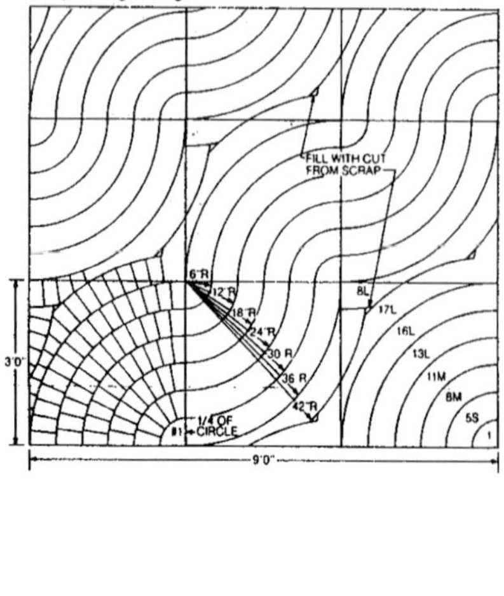

Serpentine Fan Quantity for 100 sq. feet: 106 pcs. small wedge; 290 pcs. medium wedge; 484 pcs. large wedge

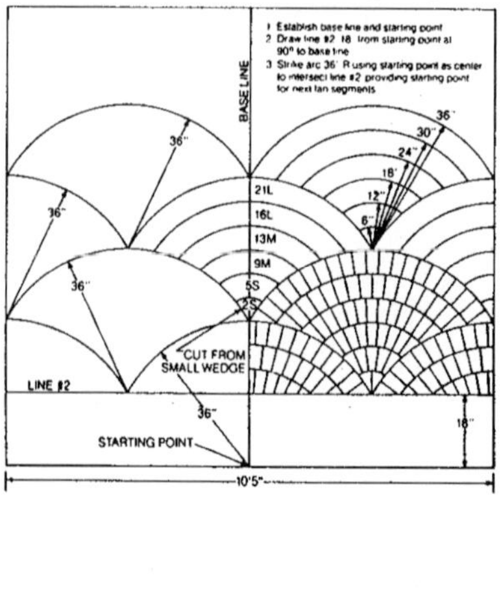

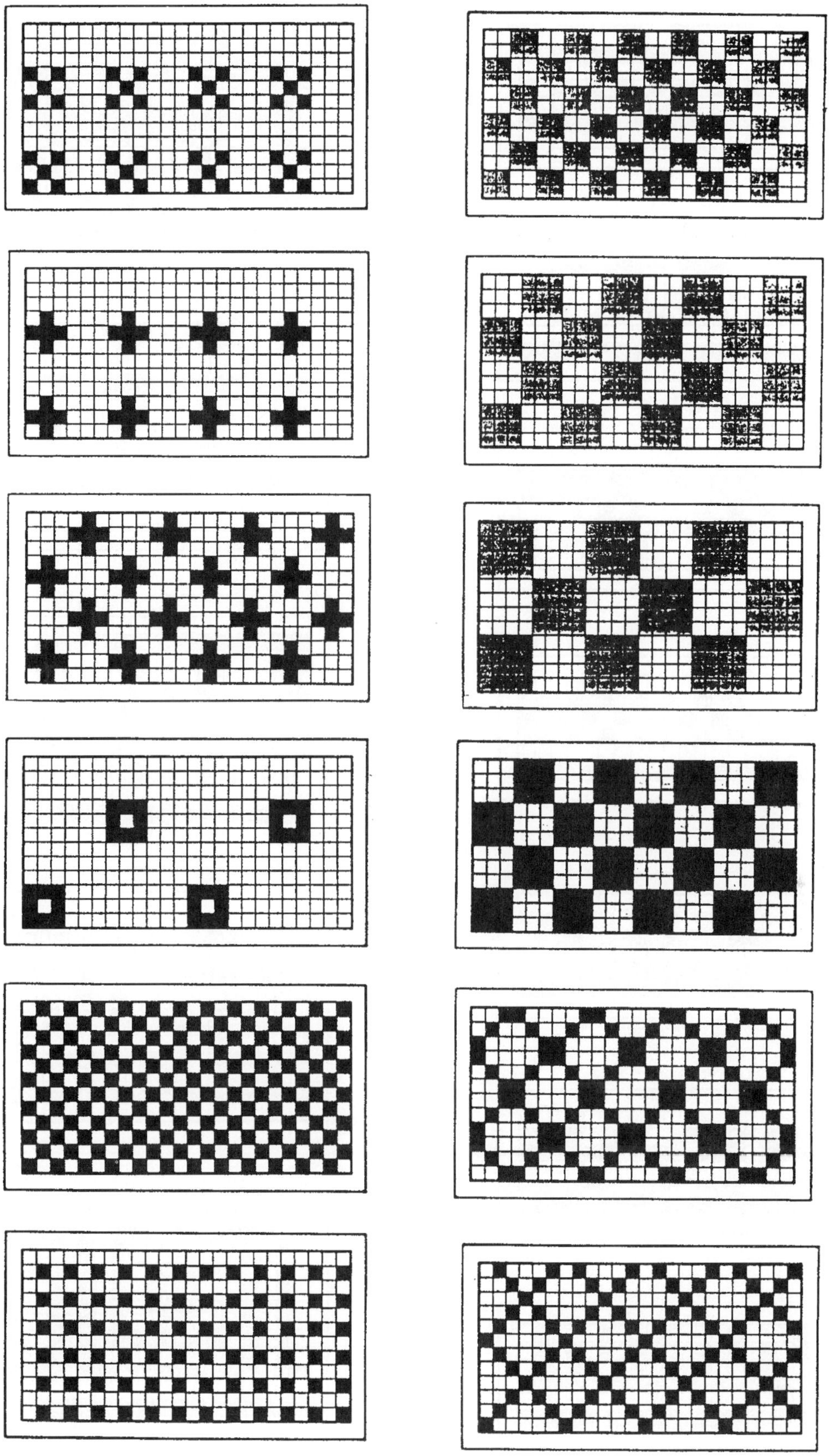

Fig. 11 1 × 1 overall patterns

FLOORS AND FLOOR FINISHES

Ceramic Tile Patterns

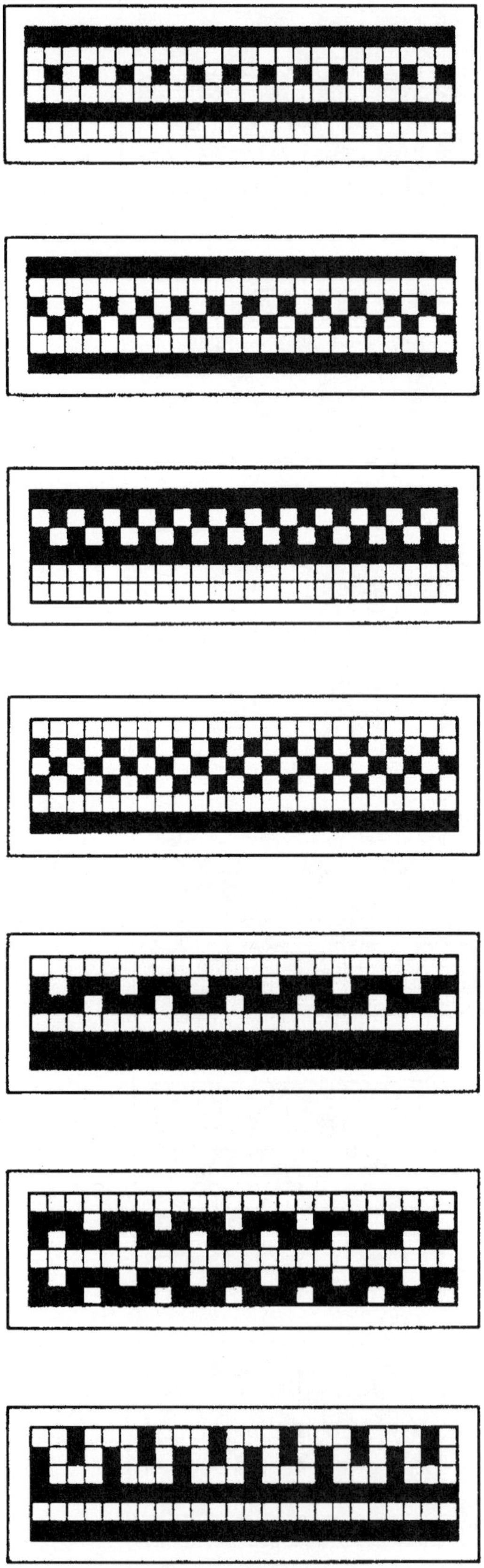

Fig. 12 1 × 1 six-inch borders

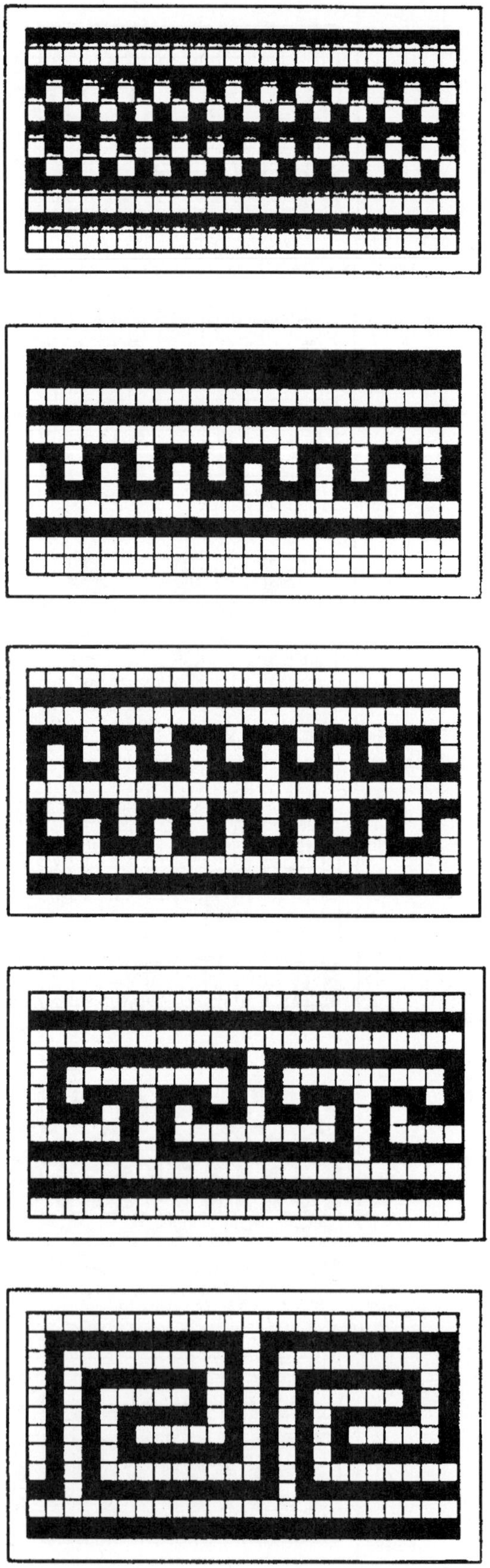

Fig. 13 1 × 1 twelve-inch borders

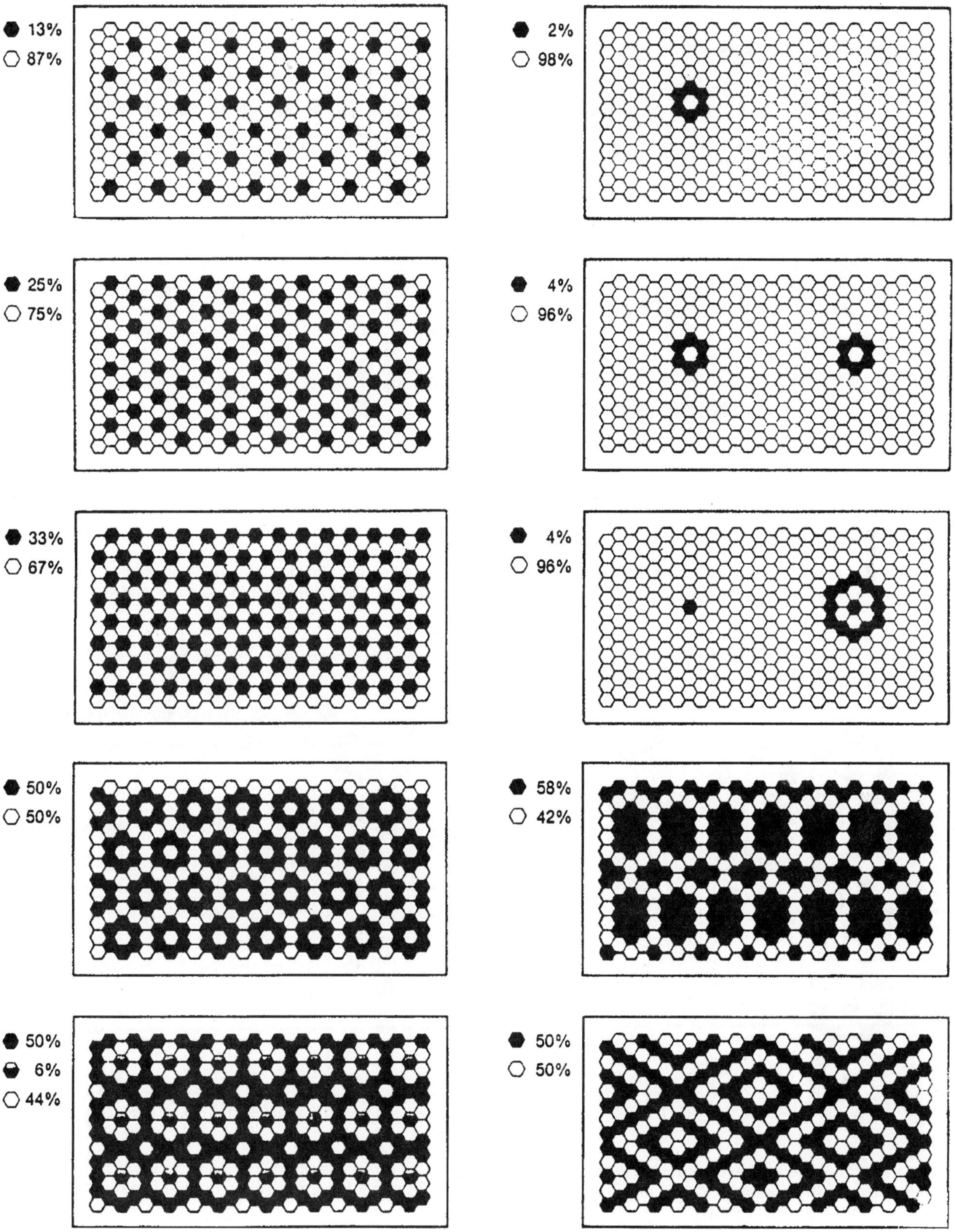

Fig. 14 1-in hex overall patterns. All patterns master-set 12″ × 24″ sheets

FLOORS AND FLOOR FINISHES

Ceramic Tile Patterns

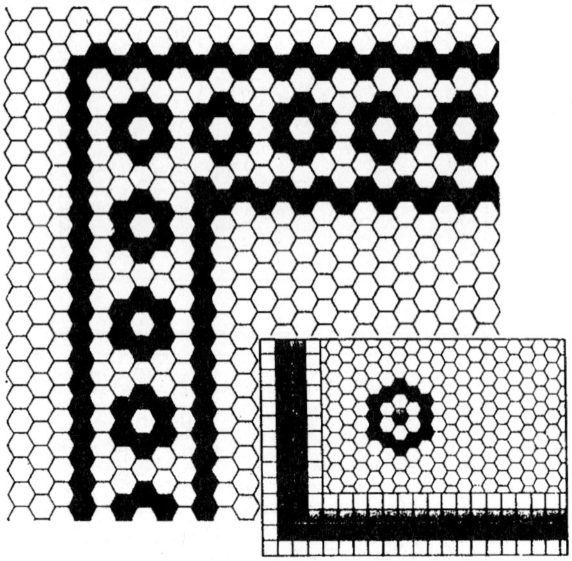

1″ Square Border with Hexagon Field

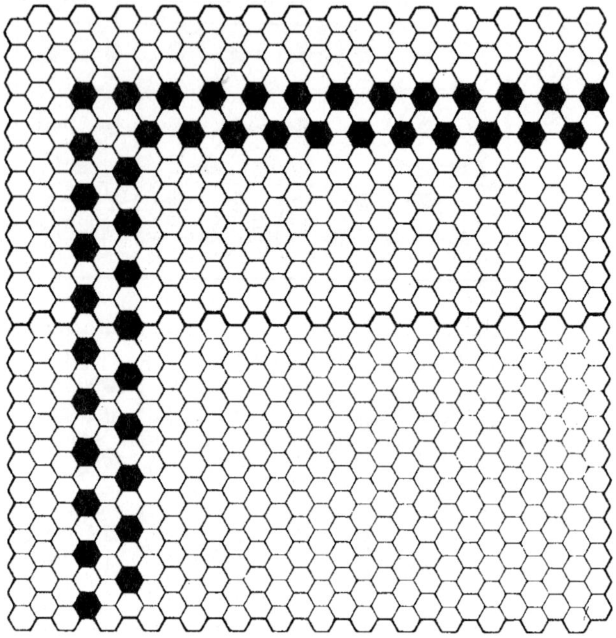

Due to the complexity of mounting 1″ Hexagon border pattern corners which require a number of special sheets on smaller jobs, a premium charge is made. To avoid this, it is suggested that on smaller jobs the border be formed using 1″ squares with a hexagon field.

If a Hexagon border is required, you must provide a plan of the area with dimensions because the Hexagon configuration precludes interchanging sheets. We will provide specific sheets for those areas and setting plans.

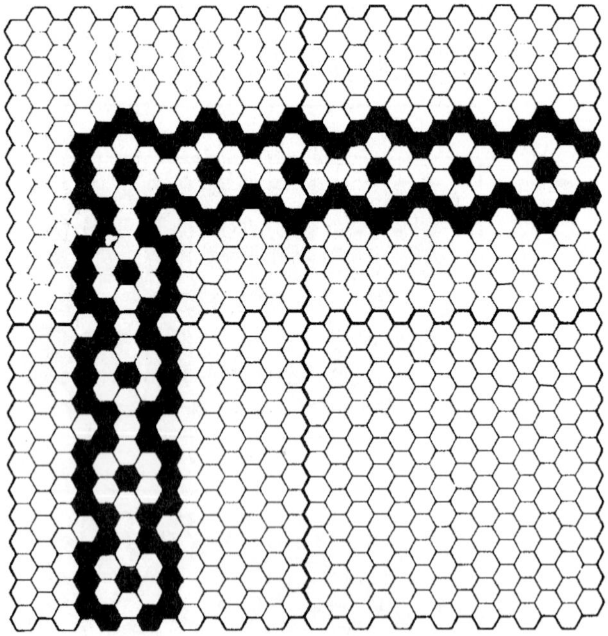

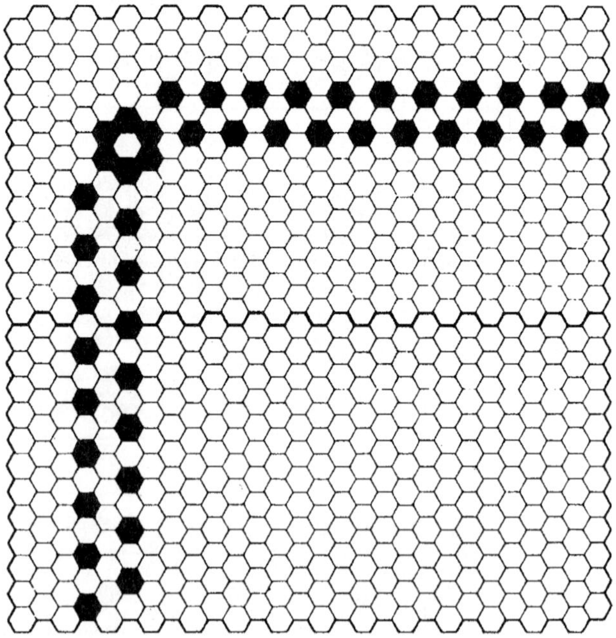

Note that on three of these border patterns a full sheet is used for the corner. Some designs, however, will require a half sheet for the corner as shown in SB-1404. In this case a right and left corner will be on one sheet and the sheet is cut in half before placement.

Fig. 15 1-in hex border patterns. All patterns master-set 12 in × 24 in sheets

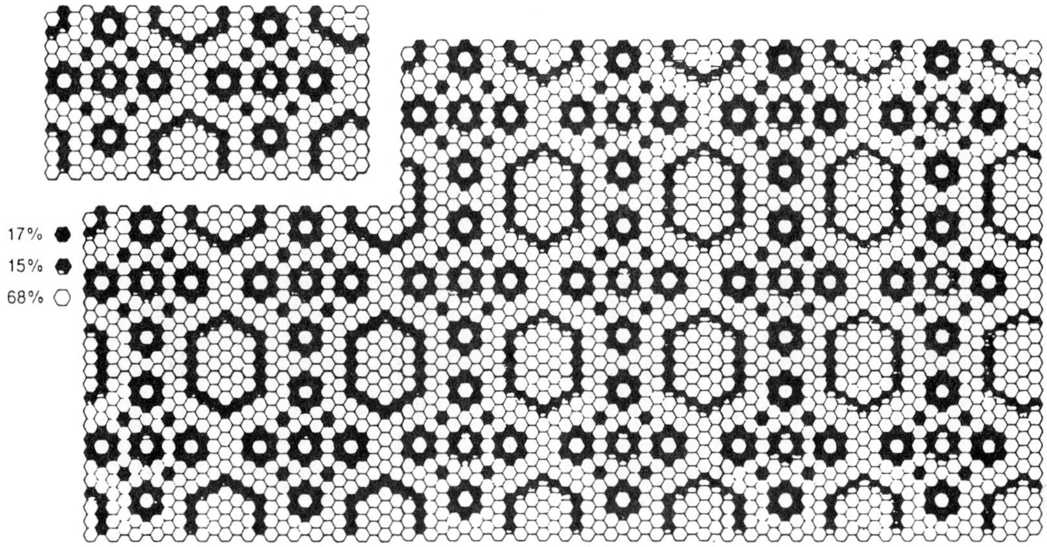

Single sheet repeat pattern. Repeat for overall pattern.

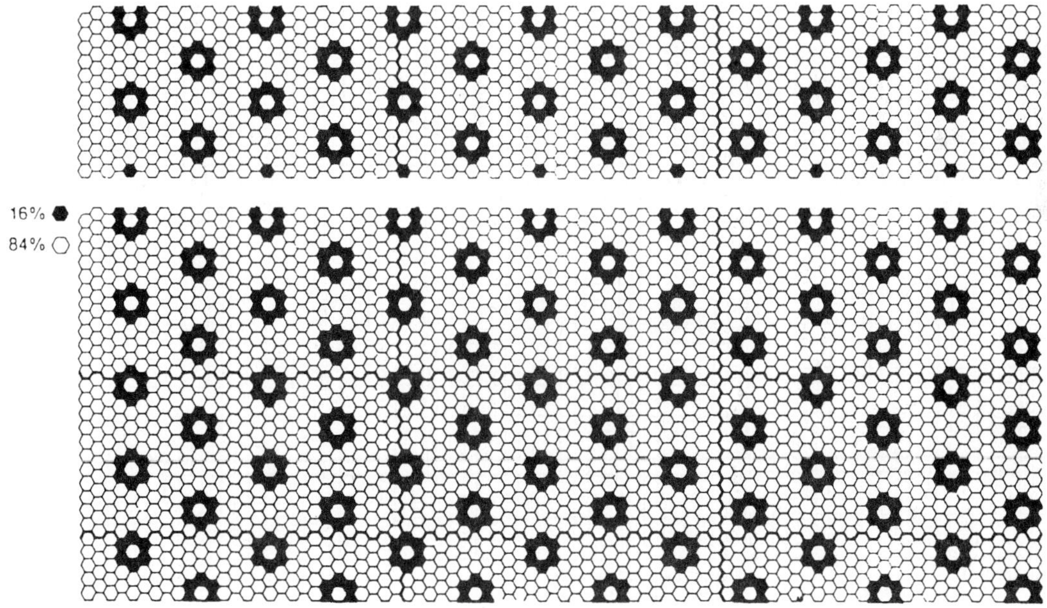

Three sheet repeat pattern. Three different sheets complete the pattern, then repeat throughout.

Fig. 16 1-in hex overall patterns. All patterns master-set 12 in × 24 in sheets

FLOORS AND FLOOR FINISHES

Basic Quarry Tile Patterns

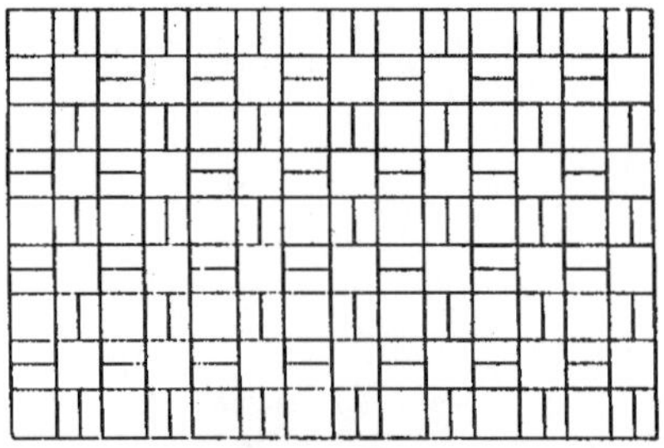

QP-6101 ALTERNATING CHECKERBOARD
Shown: 3⅞" × 8" (50%), 8" × 8" (50%)

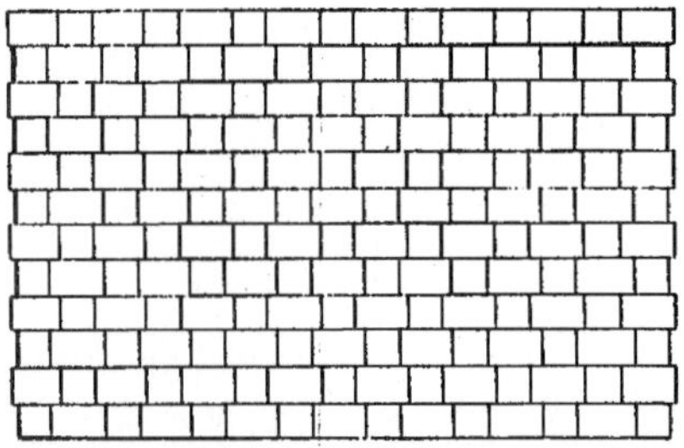

QP-6102 FLEMISH BOND
Shown: 6" × 6" (40%), 6" × 9" (60%)
Also Use: 3⅞" × 3⅞", 3⅞" × 8", or 6" × 6", 6" × 12⅛"

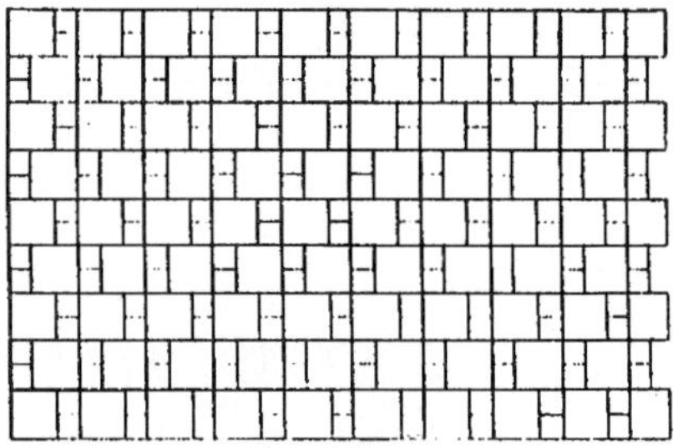

QP-6103 FLEMISH SQUARE BOND
Shown: 3⅞" × 3⅞" (33⅓%), 8" × 8" (66⅔%)

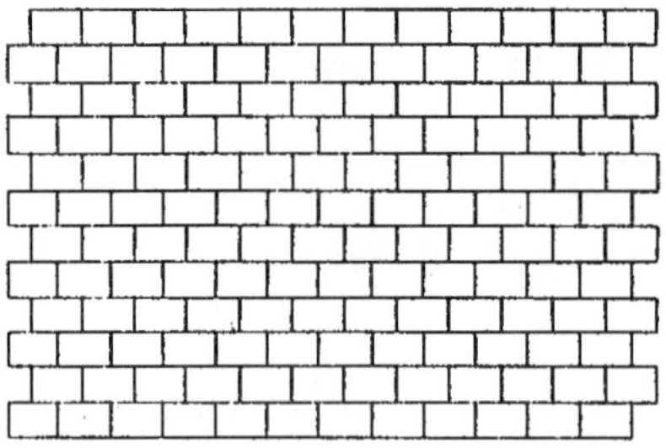

QP-6104 BROKEN JOINT
Shown: 6" × 9" (100%)
Also Use: 3⅞" × 8" or 6" × 12⅛"

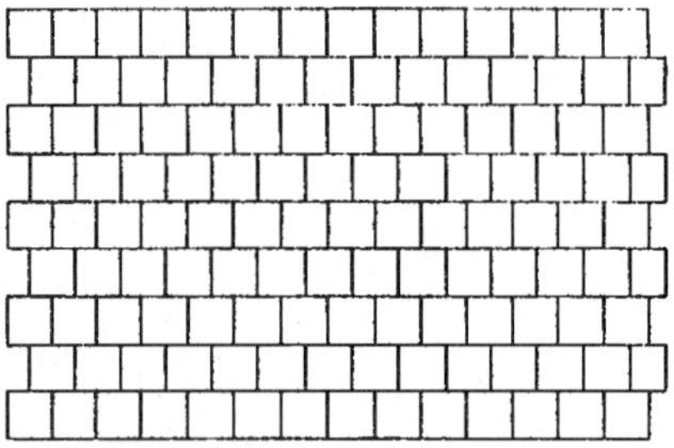

QP-6105 BROKEN JOINT SQUARE
Shown: 8" × 8" (100%)
Also Use: 6" × 6"

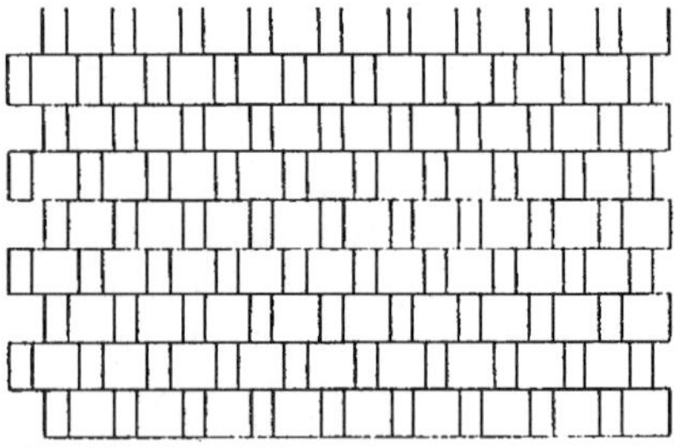

QP-6106 BARRED SQUARE
Shown: 3⅞" × 8" (33⅓%), 8" × 8" (66⅔%)

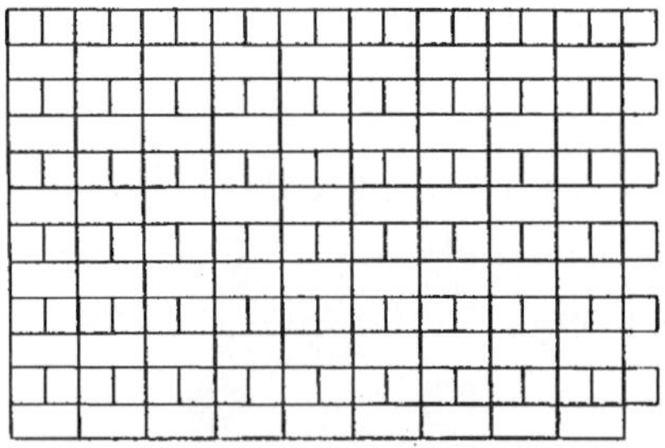

QP-6107 ALTERNATING STRIPE VARIATION
Shown: 6" × 6" (50%), 6" × 12⅛" (50%)
Also Use: 3⅞" × 3⅞", 3⅞" × 8"

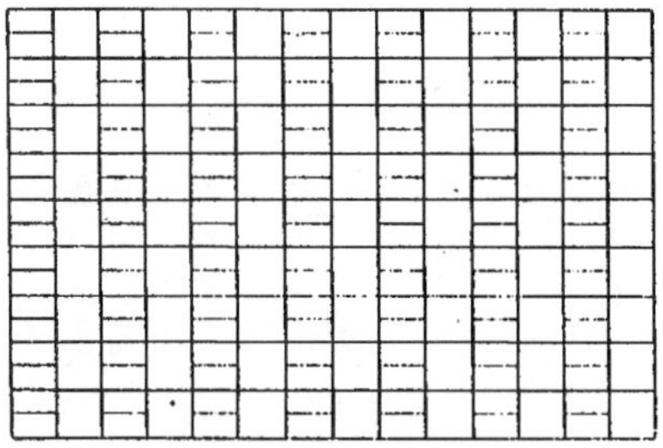

QP-6108 ALTERNATING STRIPE
Shown: 3⅞" × 8" (50%), 8" × 8" (50%)

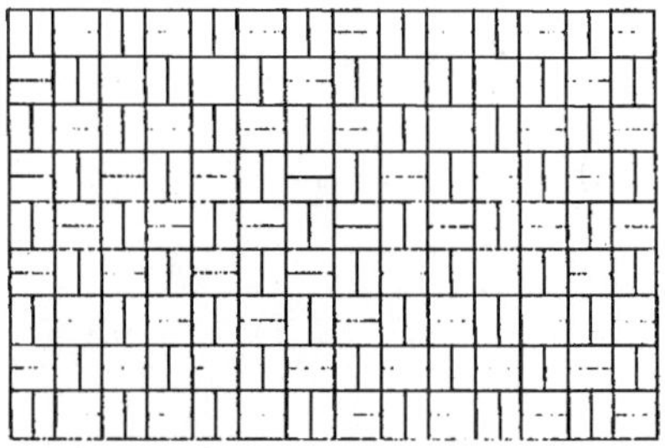

QP-6109 BASKETWEAVE
Shown: 3⅞" × 8" (100%)
Also Use: 6" × 12⅛"

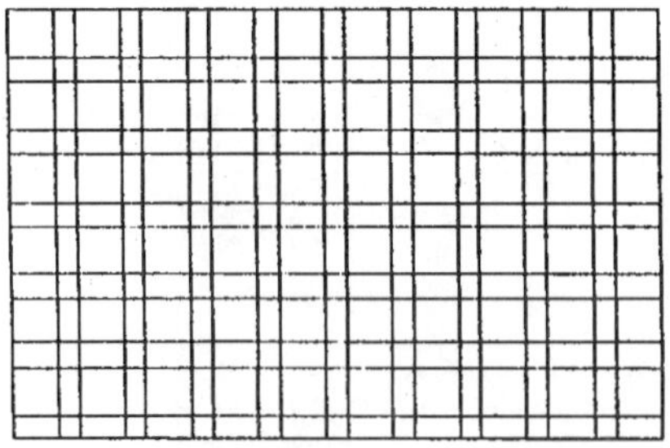

QP-6110 FORMAL RANDOM
Shown: 3⅞" × 3⅞" (11.2%), 3⅞" × 8" (44.4%), 8" × 8" (44.4%)

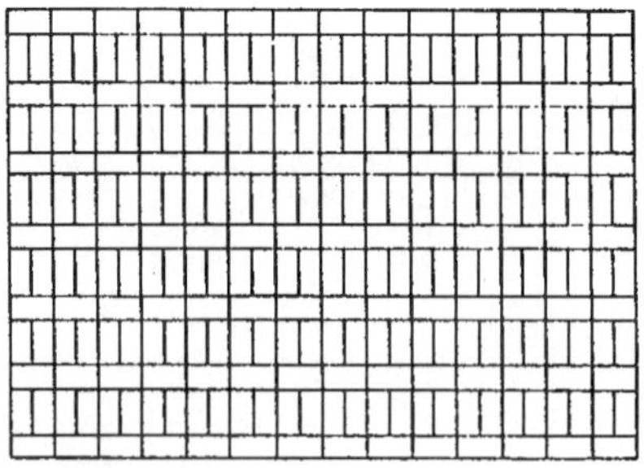

QP-6111 RAILROAD BOND
Shown: 3⅞" × 8" (100%)
Also Use: 6" × 12⅛"

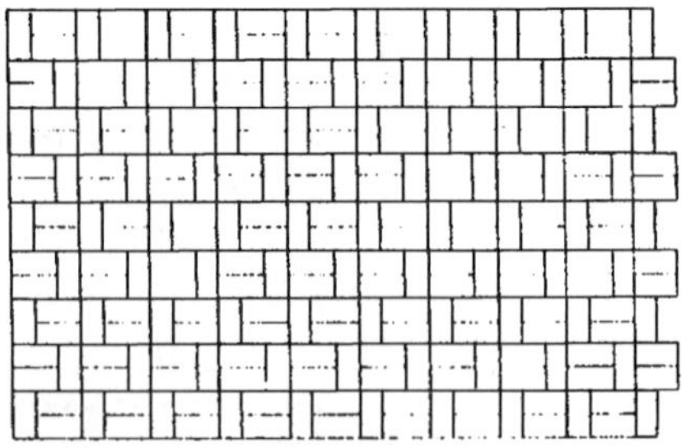

QP-6112 BASKETWEAVE VARIATION
Shown: 3⅞" × 8" (100%)
Also Use: 6" × 12⅛"

FLOORS AND FLOOR FINISHES
Basic Quarry Tile Patterns

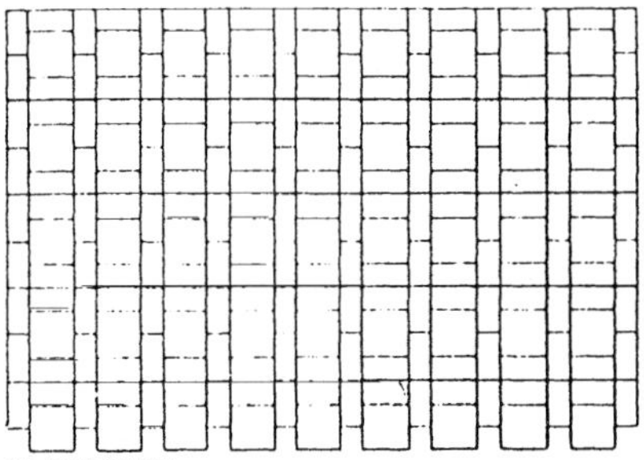

QP-6221 SPIRAL
Shown: 3⅞" × 8" (66⅔%), 8" × 8" (33⅓%)

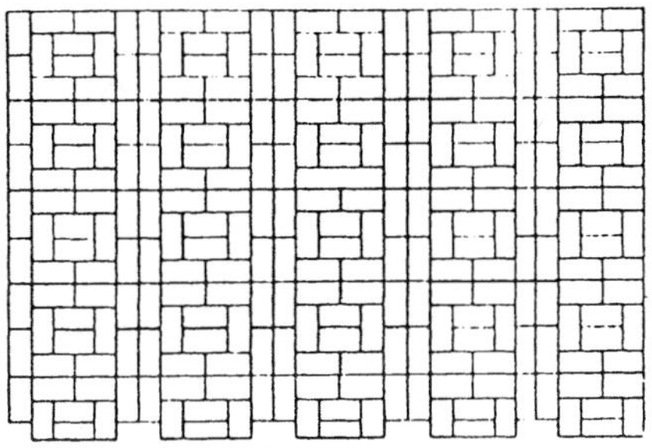

QP-6222 INTERLOCKING SPIRAL
Shown: 3⅞" × 8" (100%)
Also Use: 6" × 12⅛"

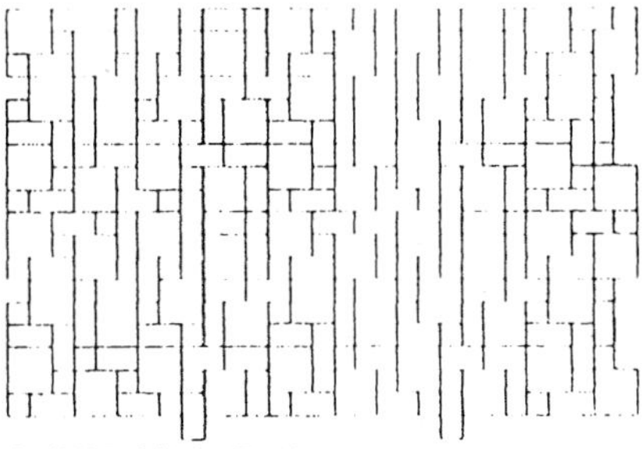

QP-6223 BLOCK RANDOM
Shown: 3⅞" × 3⅞" (15%), 3⅞" × 8" (41%)
8" × 8" (44%)

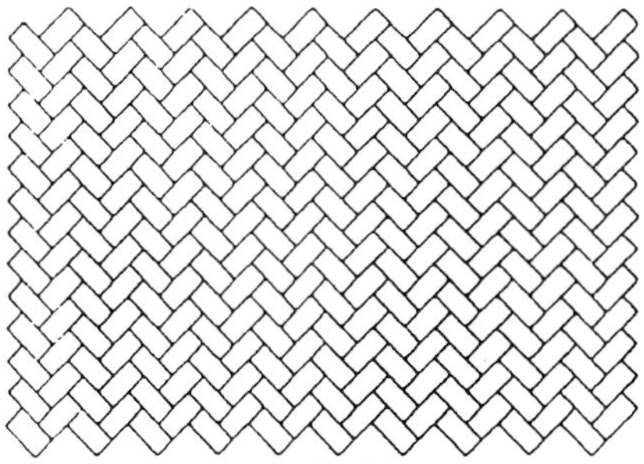

QP-6224 VERTICAL HERRINGBONE
Shown: 3⅞" × 8" (100%)
Also Use: 6" × 12⅛"

QP-6225 PINWHEEL
Shown: 3⅞" × 3⅞" (11.1%), 3⅞" × 8" (88.9%)
Also Use: 6" × 6", 6" × 12⅛"

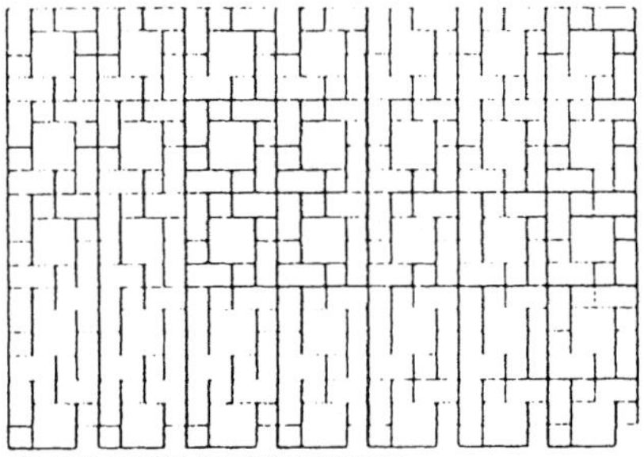

QP-6226 BLOCK RANDOM SQUARE
Shown: 3⅞" × 3⅞" (25%), 3⅞" × 8" (50%)
8" × 8" (25%)

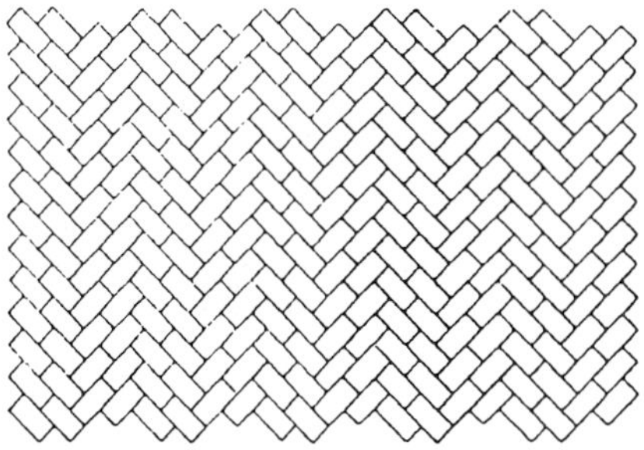

QP-6227 DOUBLE HERRINGBONE
Shown: 3⅞" × 8" (100%)
Also Use: 6" × 12⅛"

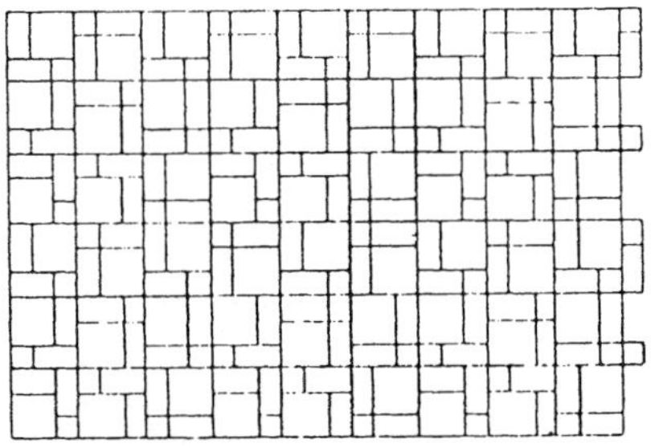

QP-6228 BLOCK RANDOM VARIATION
Shown: 3⅞" × 3⅞" (11.2%), 3⅞" × 8" (44.4%),
8" × 8" (44.4%)

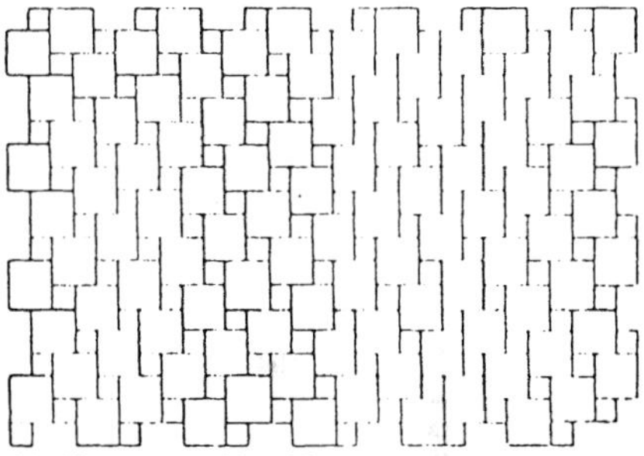

QP-6229 RANDOM SQUARE
Shown: 3⅞" × 3⅞" (19½%), 8" × 8" (80½%)

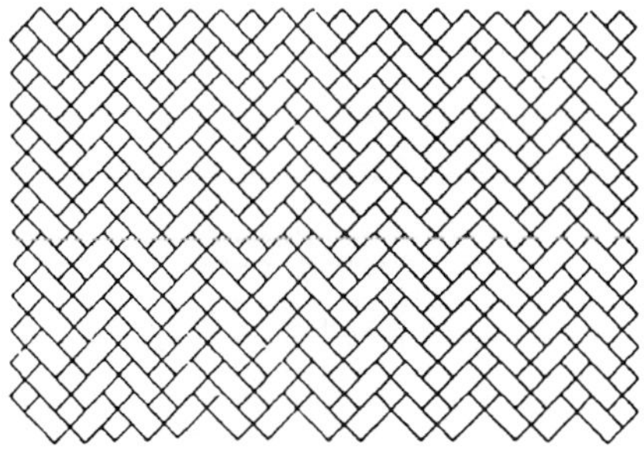

QP-6230 DIAMOND HERRINGBONE
Shown: 3⅞" × 3⅞" (33⅓%), 3⅞" × 8" (66⅔%)
Also Use: 6" × 6", 6" × 12⅛"

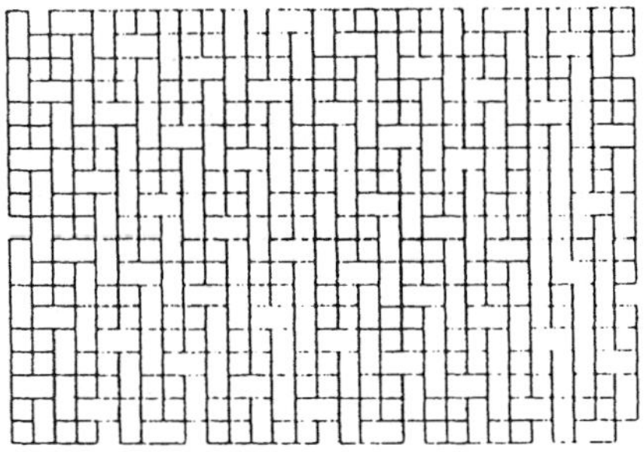

QP-6231 RAMBLING SQUARES
Shown: 3⅞" × 3⅞" (40%), 3⅞" × 8" (60%)
Also Use: 6" × 6", 6" × 12⅛"

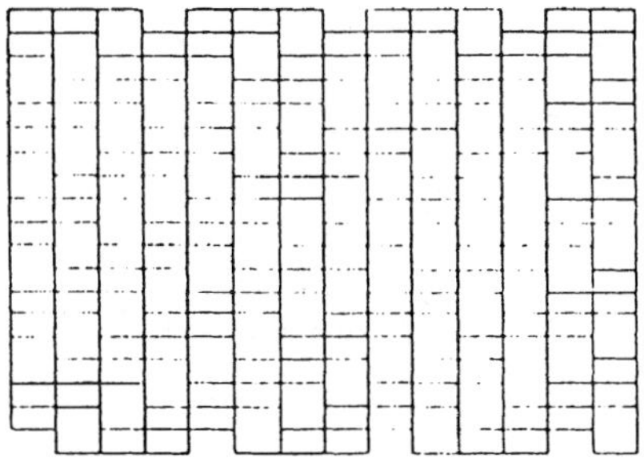

QP-6232 DIAGONAL STRIPE
Shown: 3⅞" × 8" (50%), 8" × 8" (50%)

FLOORS AND FLOOR FINISHES

Floor Construction Details: Ceramic Tile on Wood and Concrete Subfloors

FLOORS

Wood Subfloor

Cement Mortar

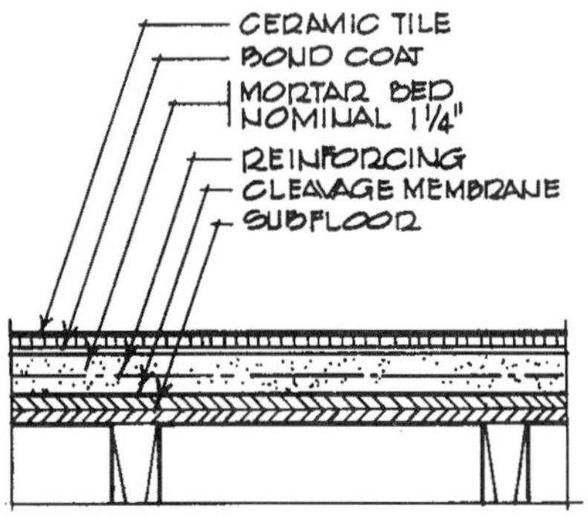

Recommended use

- over all wood floors that are structurally sound

Organic Adhesive

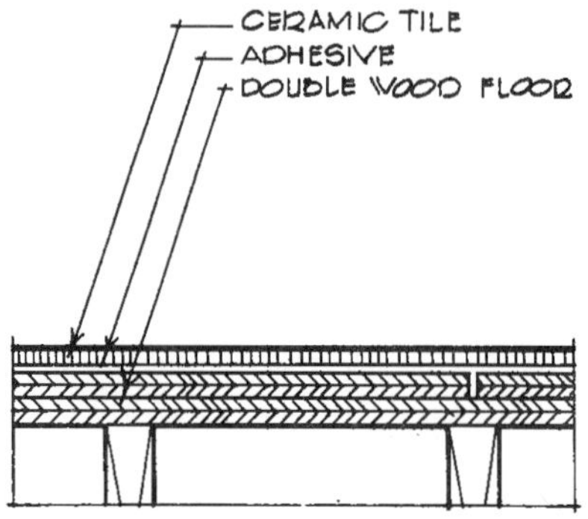

Recommended use

- over wood floors exposed to residential traffic only

Wood Subfloor

Epoxy Mortar and Grout

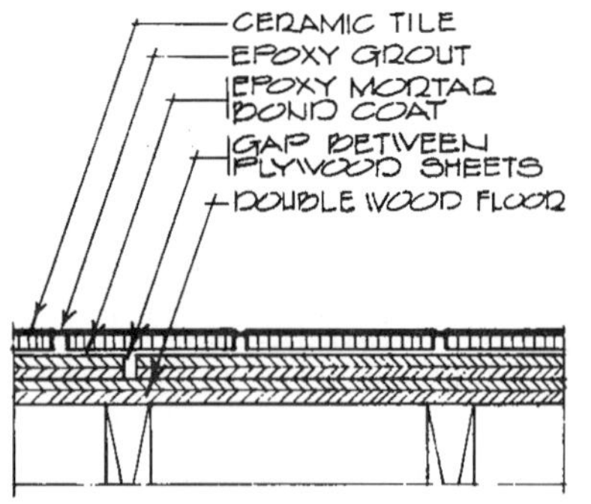

Recommended uses

- over wood floors where resistance to foot traffic in better residential, normal commercial, and light institutional use is desired with thin-set construction
- where water, chemical, and stain resistance is desired
- for tilework exposed to prolonged high temperatures, use high temperature, chemical resistant epoxy mortar, and grout

Glass Mesh Mortar Units

Dry-Set Mortar or Latex-Portland Cement

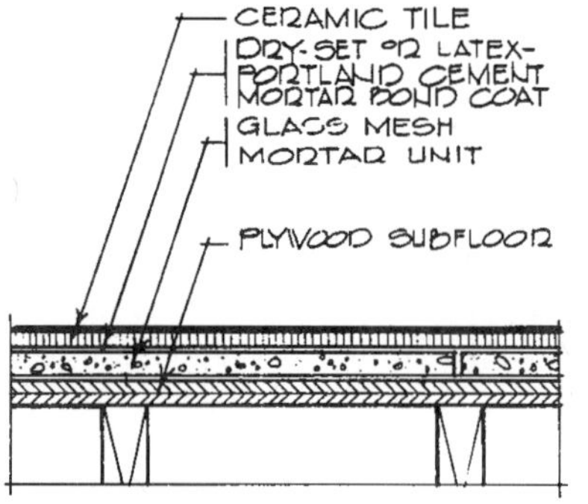

Recommended uses

- over structurally sound plywood where lightweight construction is a factor
- where water resistance is desired
- eliminates necessity of recessing subfloor to accommodate portland cement mortar bed

STAIRS

Cement Mortar

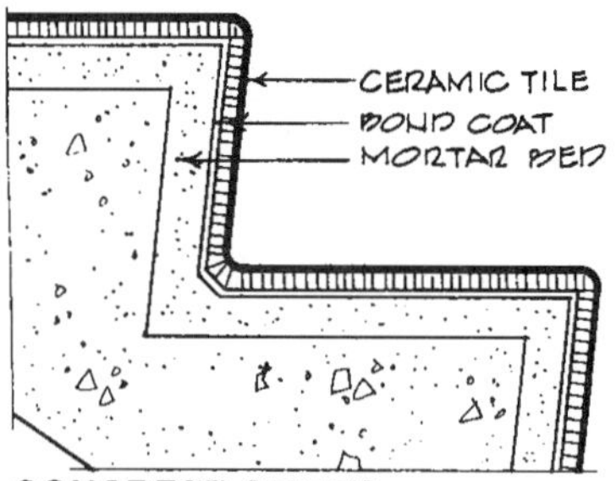

CONCRETE STAIRS

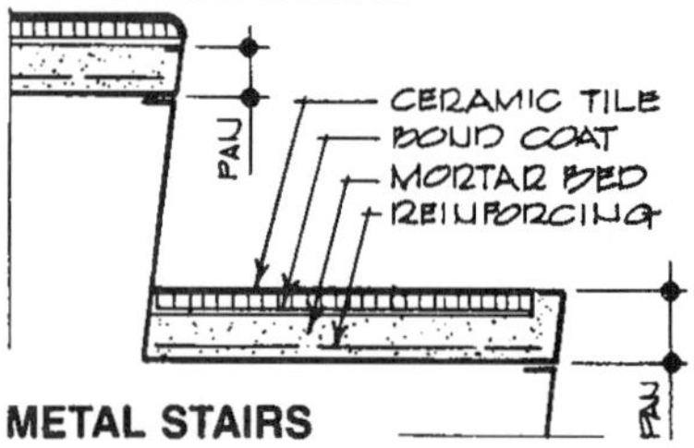

METAL STAIRS

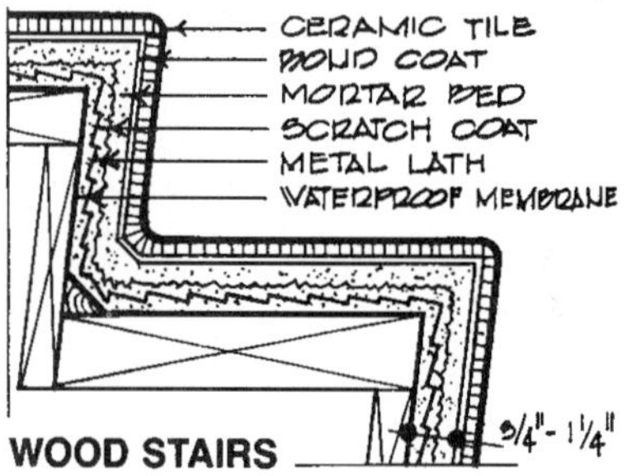

WOOD STAIRS

CEILINGS, SOFFITS

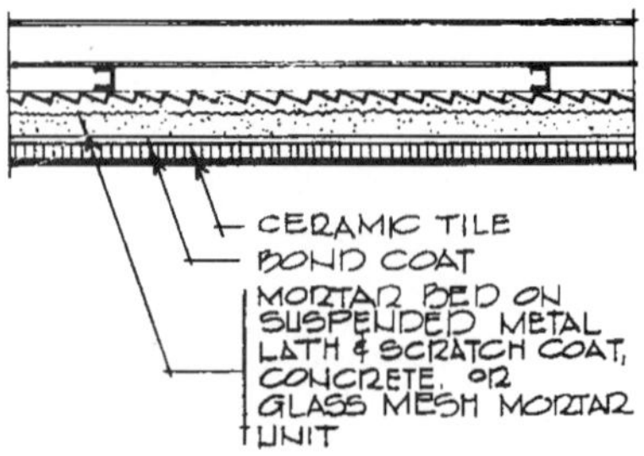

Recommended uses

- over a mortar bed
- over glass mesh mortar units
- over clean, sound, dimensionally stable concrete
- over metal lath attached directly to the bottom of wood joists or trusses; spacing not to exceed 16" on center

CONCRETE SUBFLOOR

Cement Mortar Cleavage Membrane

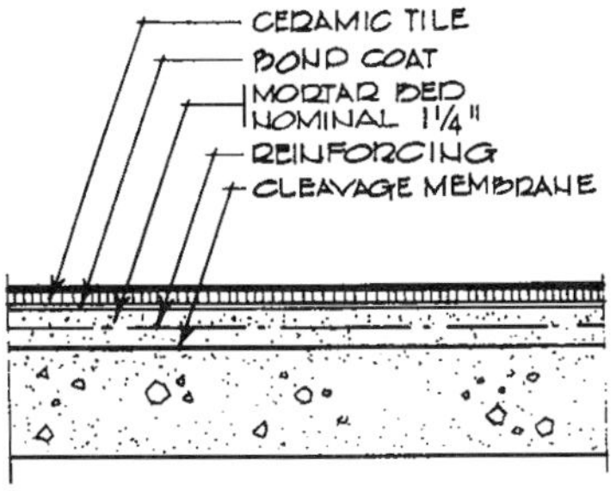

Recommended use

■ over structural floors subject to bending and deflection

Requirements

■ reinforcing mesh mandatory

■ motor bed thickness to be uniform, nominal 1¼" thick

Cement Mortar, Bonded

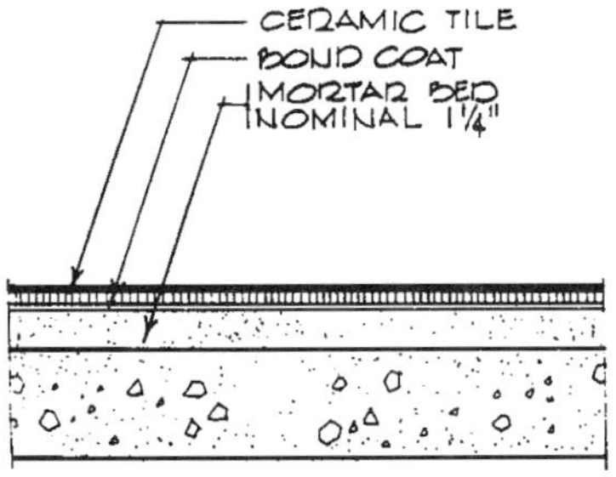

Recommended uses

■ on slab-on-grade construction where no bending stresses occur

■ on properly cured structural slabs where deflection does not exceed 1/360 of span

■ on properly cured structural slabs of limited area

Dry-Set Mortar or Latex-Portland Cement Mortar

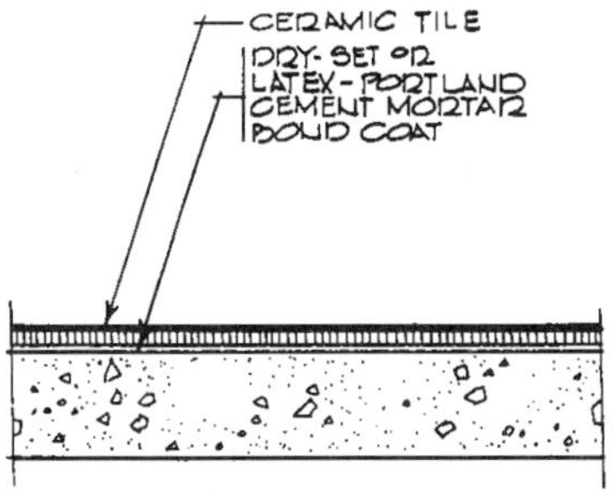

Recommended uses

■ on plane, clean concrete

■ on slab-on-grade construction where no bending stresses occur

Cement Mortar Epoxy or Furan Grout

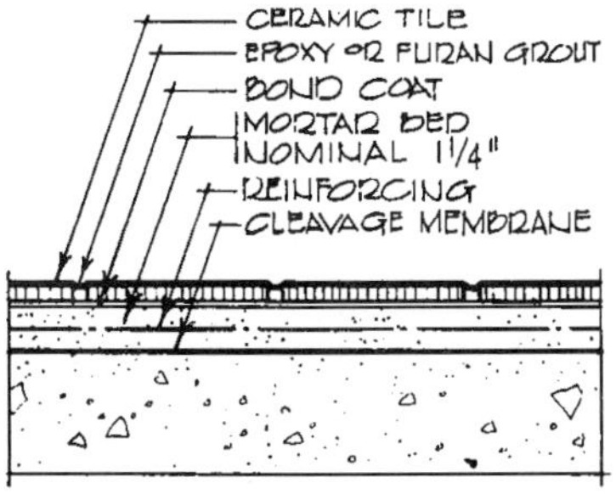

Recommended uses

■ with tile set by Method F111 requiring good stain resistance and resistance to erosion caused by occasional contact with mild chemicals such as found in commercial dining areas, photographic dark rooms, public toilets, public foyers, etc.

■ for use with quarry tile and paver tile

Dry-Set Mortar, Epoxy or Furan Grout

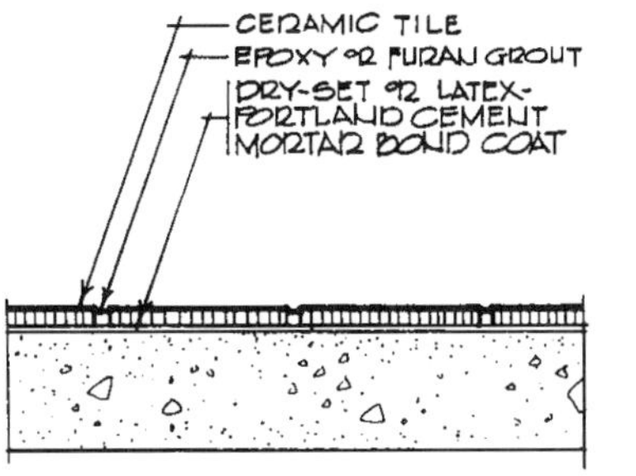

Recommended uses

■ with tile set by Method F112 or Method F113 requiring good stain resistance and resistance to erosion caused by occasional contact with mild chemicals such as found in commercial dining areas, photographic dark rooms, public toilets, public foyers, etc.

■ for use with quarry tile and paver tile

Organic Adhesive or Epoxy Adhesive

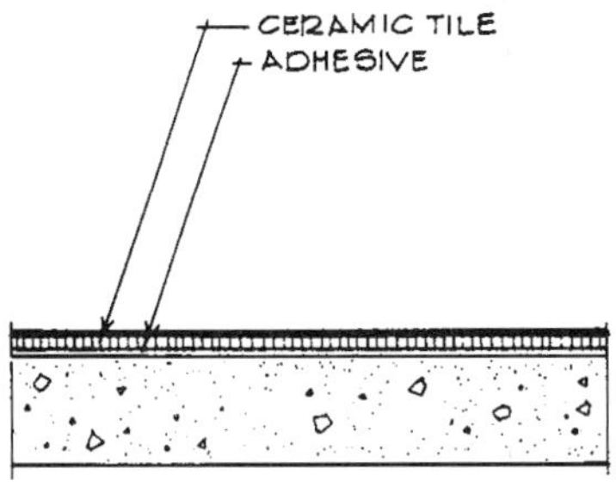

Recommended use

■ for use over concrete floors in residential construction only; for heavier service select Method F113

WATERPROOF MEMBRANE

Cement Mortar Bed

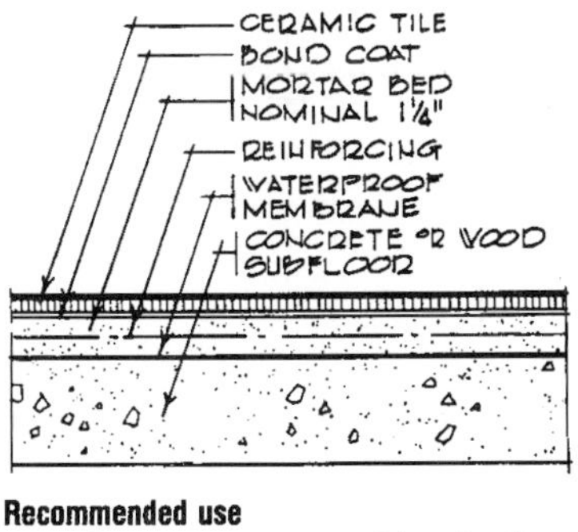

Recommended use

■ wherever a waterproof interior floor is required in conjunction with ceramic tile installed on a portland cement mortar bed

Thin-Set

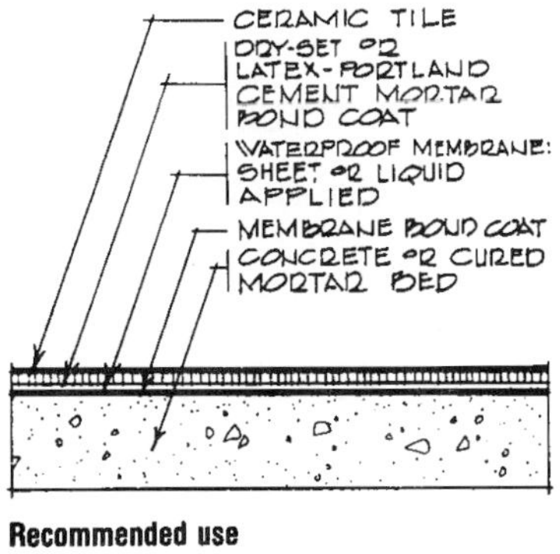

Recommended use

■ wherever a waterproof interior floor is required in conjunction with ceramic tile installed in a thin-set method

FLOORS AND FLOOR FINISHES

Ceramic Tile on Concrete Slab Floor Construction Details

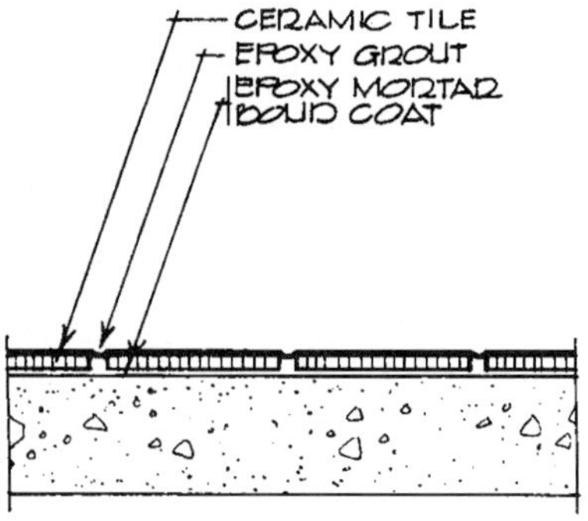

Recommended uses

- for setting and grouting ceramic mosaics, quarry tile, and paver tile
- where moderate chemical exposure and severe cleaning methods are used, such as in commercial kitchens, dairies, breweries, food processing plants, etc.
- for tilework exposed to prolonged high temperatures, use high-temperature, chemical-resistant epoxy mortar and grout

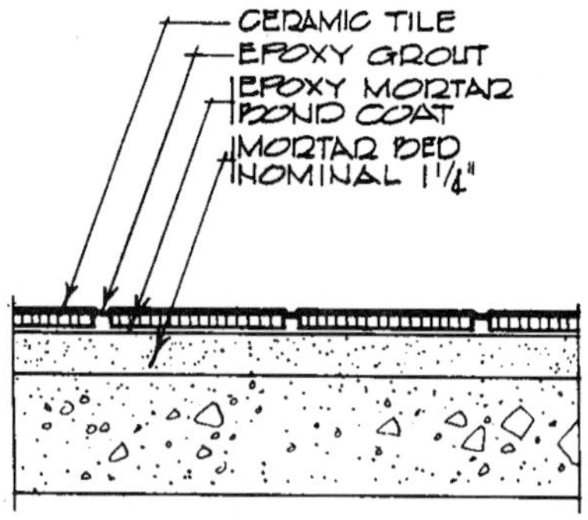

Recommended uses

- where leveling of subfloor is required
- for setting and grouting ceramic mosaics, quarry tile, and paver tile
- where moderate chemical exposure and severe cleaning methods are used, such as in commerical kitchens, dairies, breweries, food processing plants, etc.
- for tilework exposed to prolonged high temperatures, use high-temperature chemical resistant epoxy mortar and grout

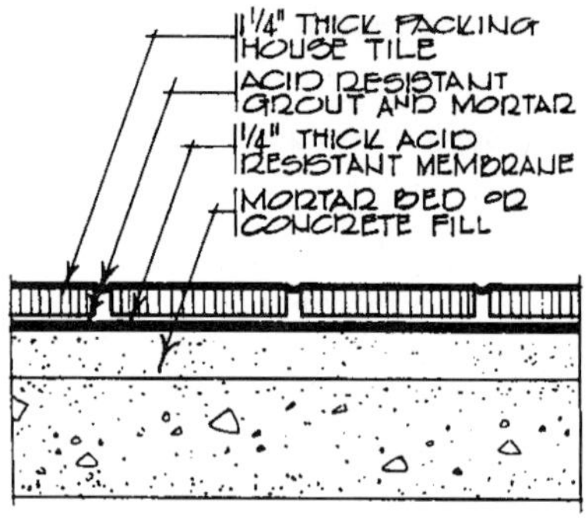

Recommended use

- for setting 1¼" thick packing house tile in areas of continuous or severe chemical exposure where special protection against leakage or damage to concrete subfloor is required

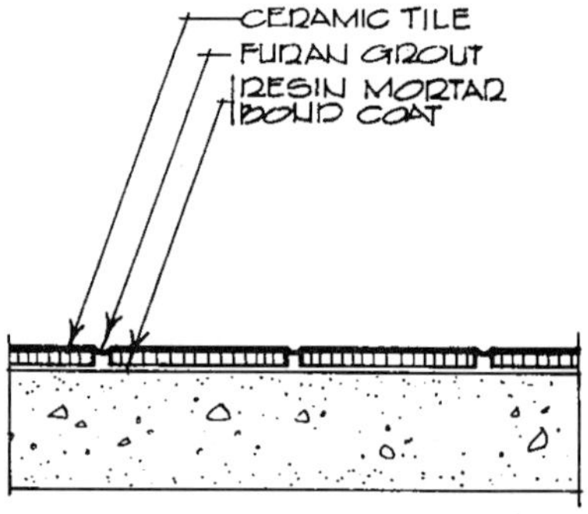

Recommended uses

- for setting and grouting quarry tile and paver tile
- in kitchens, chemical plants, etc.

EXPANSION JOINTS
Vertical and Horizontal

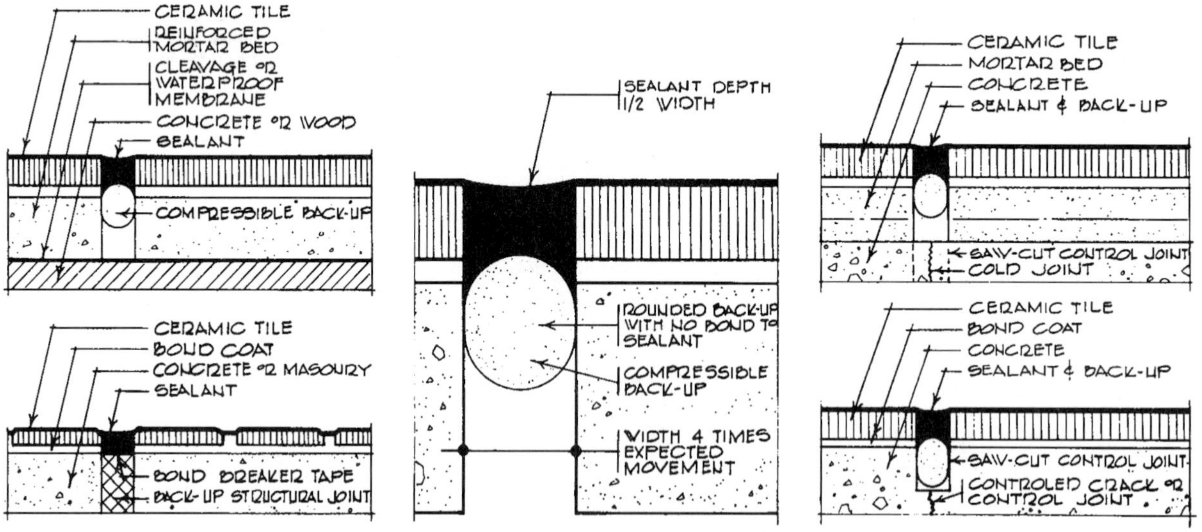

Use these details for control, contraction, and isolation joints

FLOORS AND FLOOR FINISHES

Raised Computer Room Floors

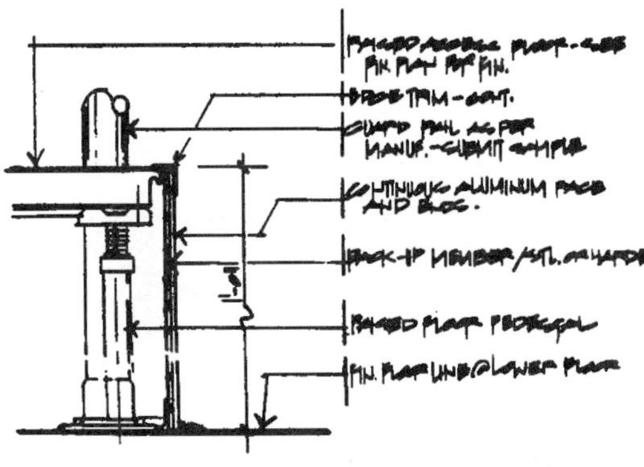

1 SECTION-DET. END PANEL 3"=1'-0"

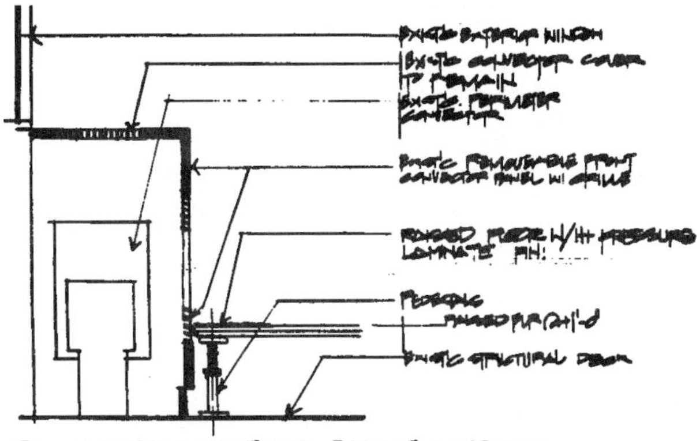

2 RAISED FLOOR EDGE DETAIL @ CONVECTORS

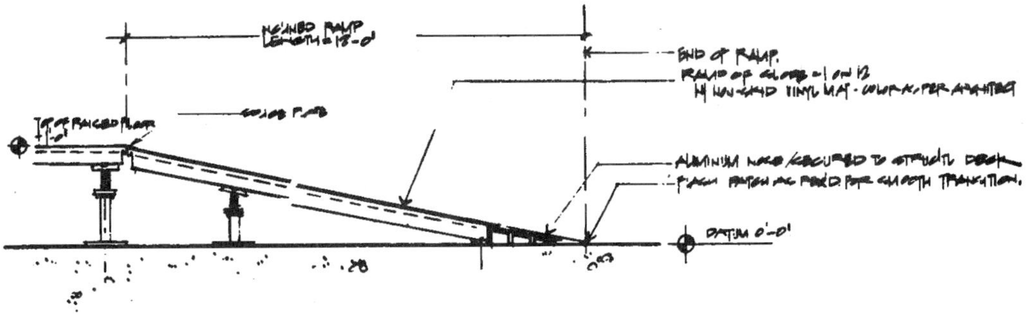

3 RAISED FLOOR RAMP SECTION

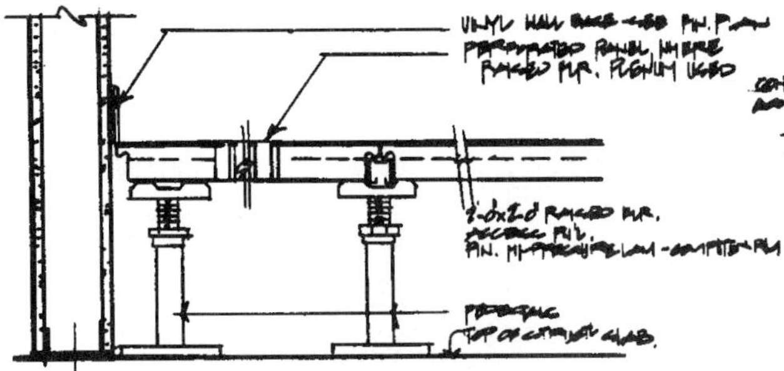

4 SECTION-DET. AT PERIMETER WALL 3"=1'-0"

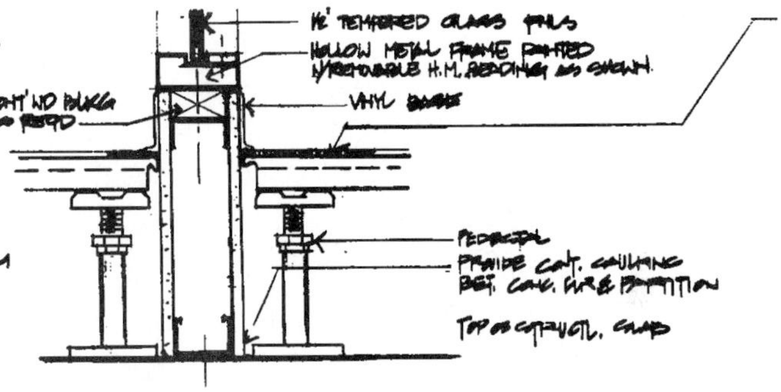

5 DETAIL THRU RATED WALL 3"=1'-0"

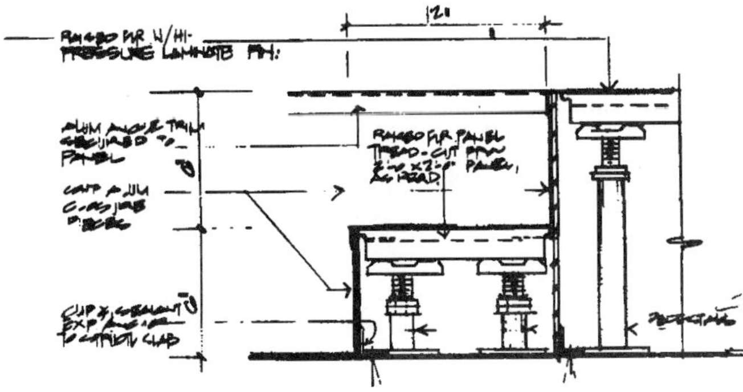

6 SECTION THRU STAIR 3"=1'-0"

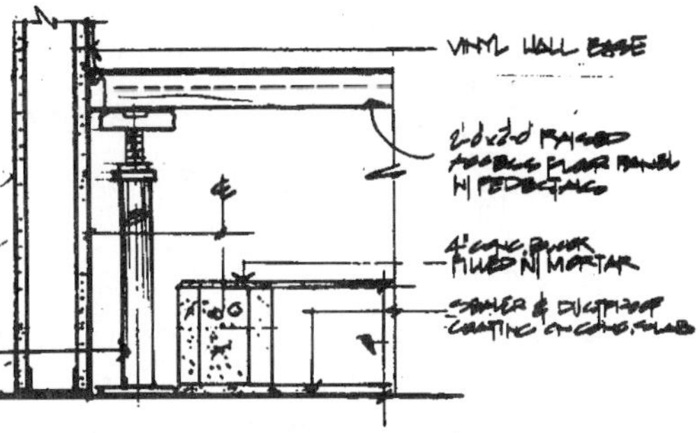

7 CONCRETE BLOCK CURB DETAIL 3"=1'-0"

FLOORS AND FLOOR FINISHES
Raised Computer Room Floors

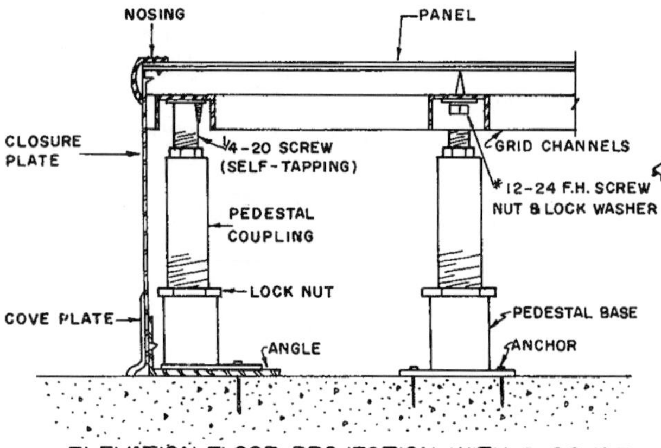

ELEVATION FLOOR PROJECTION WITH CLOSURE PLATE AND NOSING

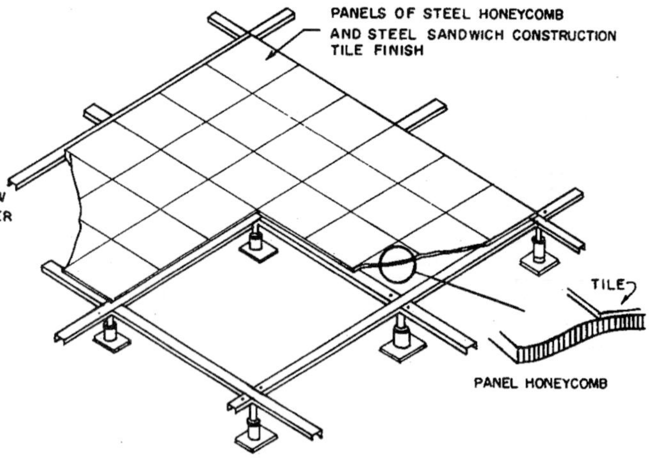

TYPICAL ELEVATED FLOOR

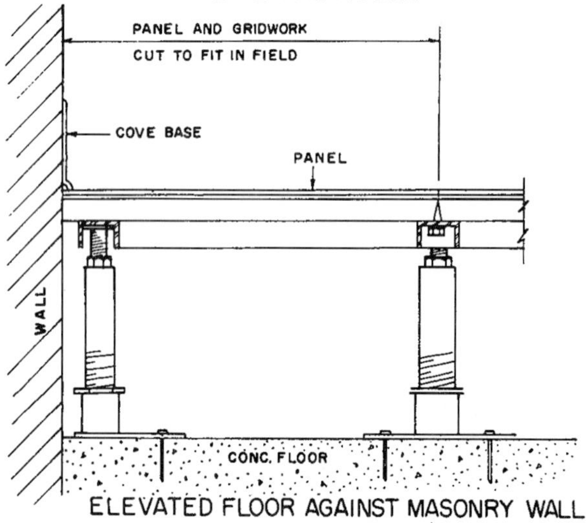

ELEVATED FLOOR AGAINST MASONRY WALL

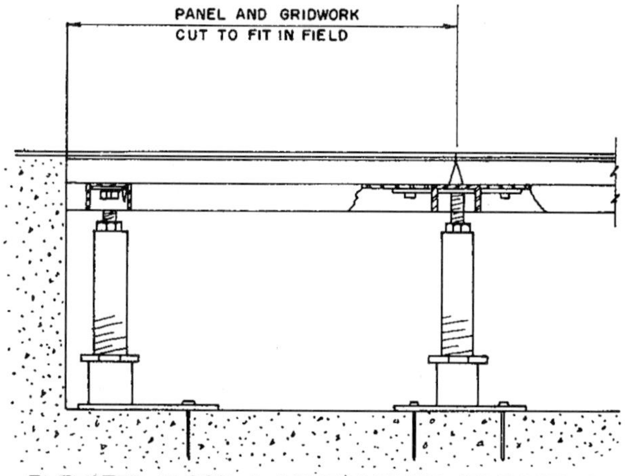

ELEVATED FLOOR-A CONTINUATION OF EXISTING FLOOR

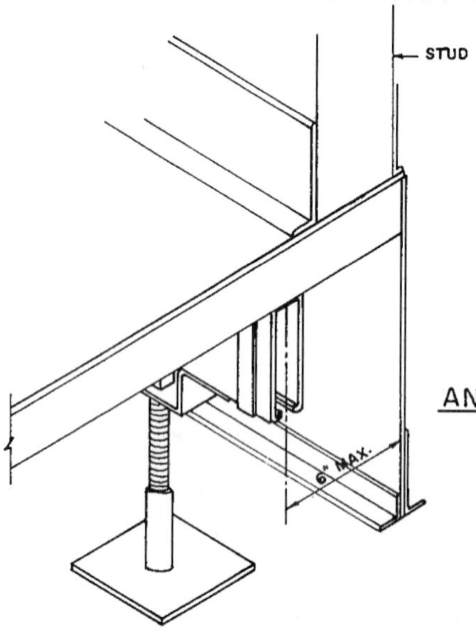

PARTITION EDGE OF ELEVATED FLOOR

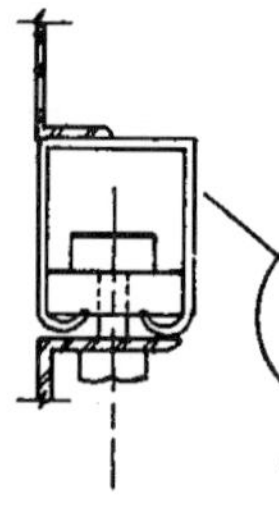

ANGLE CLIP

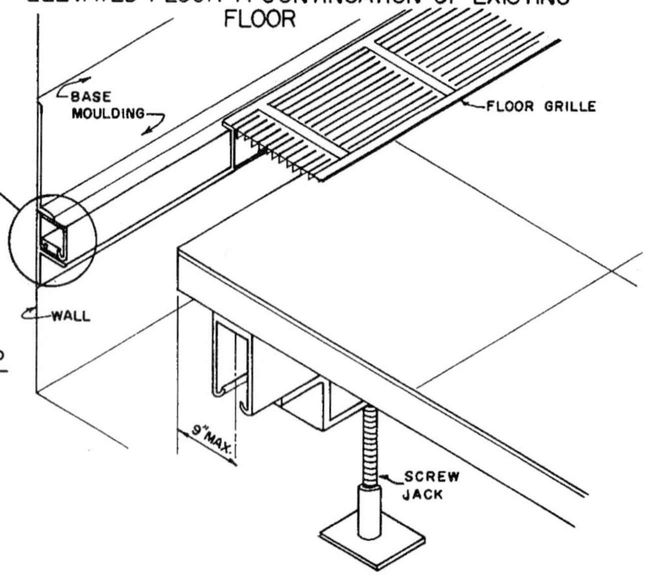

AIR GRILLE

DOORS

HOLLOW METAL DOOR CONSTRUCTION

The design, specification, and detailing of a door can have serious consequences for functional considerations such as accessibility and sound transmission. The door is also one of the most important architectural elements with respect to design image and aesthetics. A door can be a major part of design expression: a monumental door to a church or synagogue, the main entrance to a residence, the doors to a corporate board room—all of these doors have symbolic importance.

Doors come in a variety of standard heights, widths, and thicknesses, yet they may also be custom designed, assume a variety of shapes and forms, and be constructed with a variety of materials. The design, specification, and detailing of a door is, in fact, a rather complex task.

A door is typically set within a frame or jamb, but may also be installed within a wall without a frame or jamb. The frame/jamb interface between door and wall partition is another area requiring special attention by the designer.

The design of a door is never complete without the specification of hardware. Hinges, locksets, closers, stops, and thresholds are but a few of the hardware elements that a designer must consider.

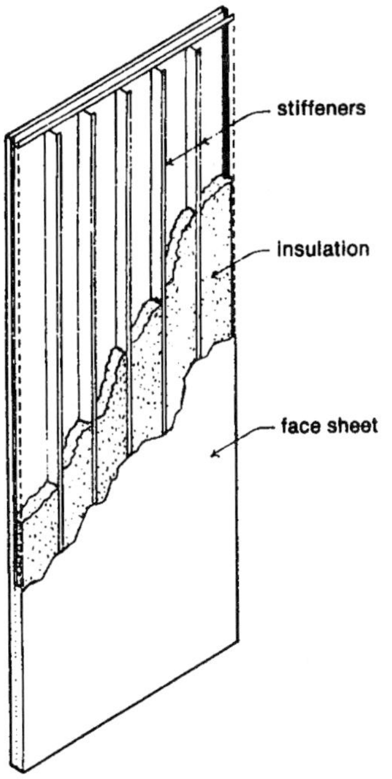

STEEL STIFFENERS

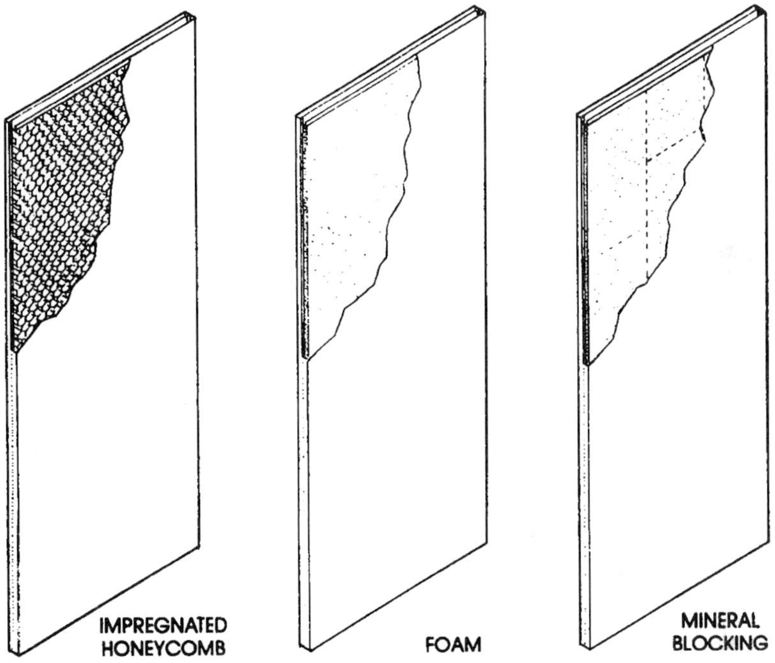

LAMINATED CONSTRUCTIONS

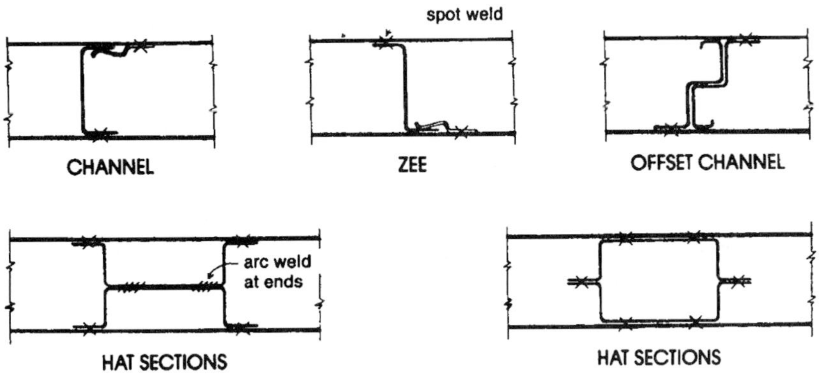

REPRESENTATIVE STIFFENER SECTIONS
Other sections used by some manufacturers

DOORS

Hollow Metal Door Construction

This section on doors provides the designer with extensive information on door types, materials, door frames, and materials and methods of door construction and installation. Details show doors and frames installed in all types of walls and partitions, including wood and metal stud, masonry, concrete, and glass.

Of special interest to the designer are examples of less standard door types such as elevator doors, sliding pocket doors, and fabric-covered doors. The majority of the details in this section are taken from the actual working drawings of successfully executed projects.

Panel Construction

There are two basic types of panel construction:

Steel stiffened: Face sheets supported by steel stiffeners, which are channels, Z-shaped sections, hat-shaped sections, or similar members, positioned vertically. Sheets are attached to these members by spot welding.

Laminated core: Sandwich construction employing a core of impregnated kraft paper honeycomb, plastic foam, or structural mineral blocking, to which the steel face sheets are laminated, using a structural adhesive.

Types of Construction

The four basic types of construction for hollow metal swing doors are illustrated and identified in Fig. 1. The type usually specified in commercial work is the continuously welded edge seam construction. Type A, and it is this type which is the basis of NAAMM Standard HMMA 861.

Most custom hollow metal doors are of the full flush type with continuously welded edges (Type A). When glazed openings, recessed panels, or louvers are to be provided, they are built into the door during fabrication, rather than being cut out of a flush panel door by field modification.

Fire-rated doors may differ in certain details of construction; see NAAMM Standard HMMA 850, Fire-Rated Hollow Metal Doors and Frames.

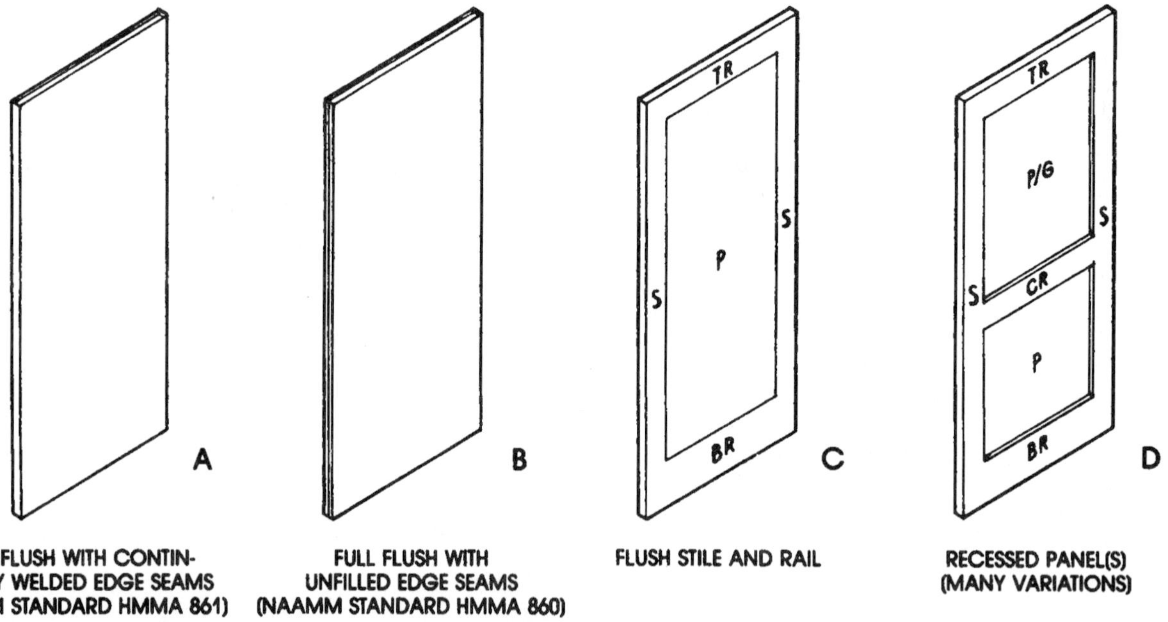

Fig. 1 The top edge of Types A and B doors may have only an inverted channel (standard construction) or may have an additional closing channel. Types C and D have tubular rails and stiles, with no edge seams. S = stile (hinge stile is stile at edge where hinges or pivots are located, lock stile is stile in which a lock or latch is installed, and meeting stile is stile adjacent to another door, in a pair of doors); TR = top rail; CR = center rail; BR = bottom rail; P = panel; P/G = panel or glass

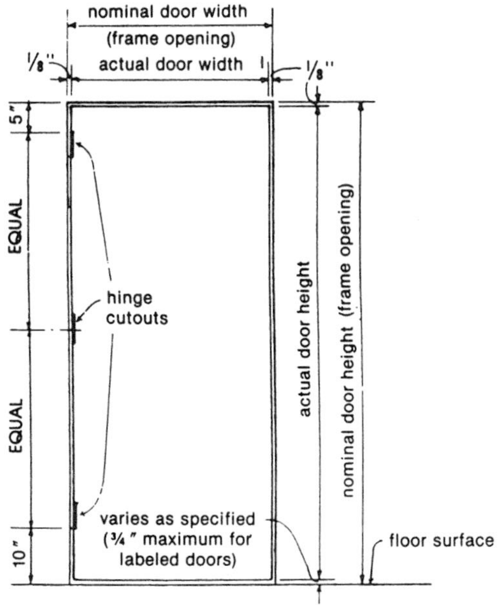

DIMENSIONS AND HINGE LOCATIONS

Hinge locations shown represent the industry standard, but may be altered to suit requirements.

MOST COMMON SIZES FOR 1¾-INCH THICK DOORS*

Width of Opening	Height of Opening				
2'0"	6'8"	7'0"	7'2"	7'10"	8'0"
2'4"	6'8"	7'0"	7'2"	7'10"	8'0"
2'6"	6'8"	7'0"	7'2"	7'10"	8'0"
2'8"	6'8"	7'0"	7'2"	7'10"	8'0"
3'0"	6'8"	7'0"	7'2"	7'10"	8'0"
3'4"	6'8"	7'0"	7'2"	7'10"	8'0"
3'6"	6'8"	7'0"	7'2"	7'10"	8'0"
3'8"	6'8"	7'0"	7'2"	7'10"	8'0"
4'0"	6'8"	7'0"	7'2"	7'10"	8'0"

*Sizes shown are for single doors only; for pairs of doors, use twice the width indicated.

OTHER DOOR SIZES: The sizes listed are those most commonly used, but custom hollow metal doors are available in any width, height and thickness desired. It is not uncommon to supply them in widths of 5' or more and/or heights of 10' or more. Standard doors, on the other hand, are generally available from inventory only in the most commonly used sizes.

LISTING DESIGNATION: Always preface the door listing with "SGL" or "PR," followed by the designation of the opening size. For example, a single flush door for a 4'0" × 8'0" frame opening is listed SGL 4080F, and a pair of flush doors for an 8'0" × 8'0" frame opening is listed as PR 8080F.

REPRESENTATIVE DOOR DESIGNS

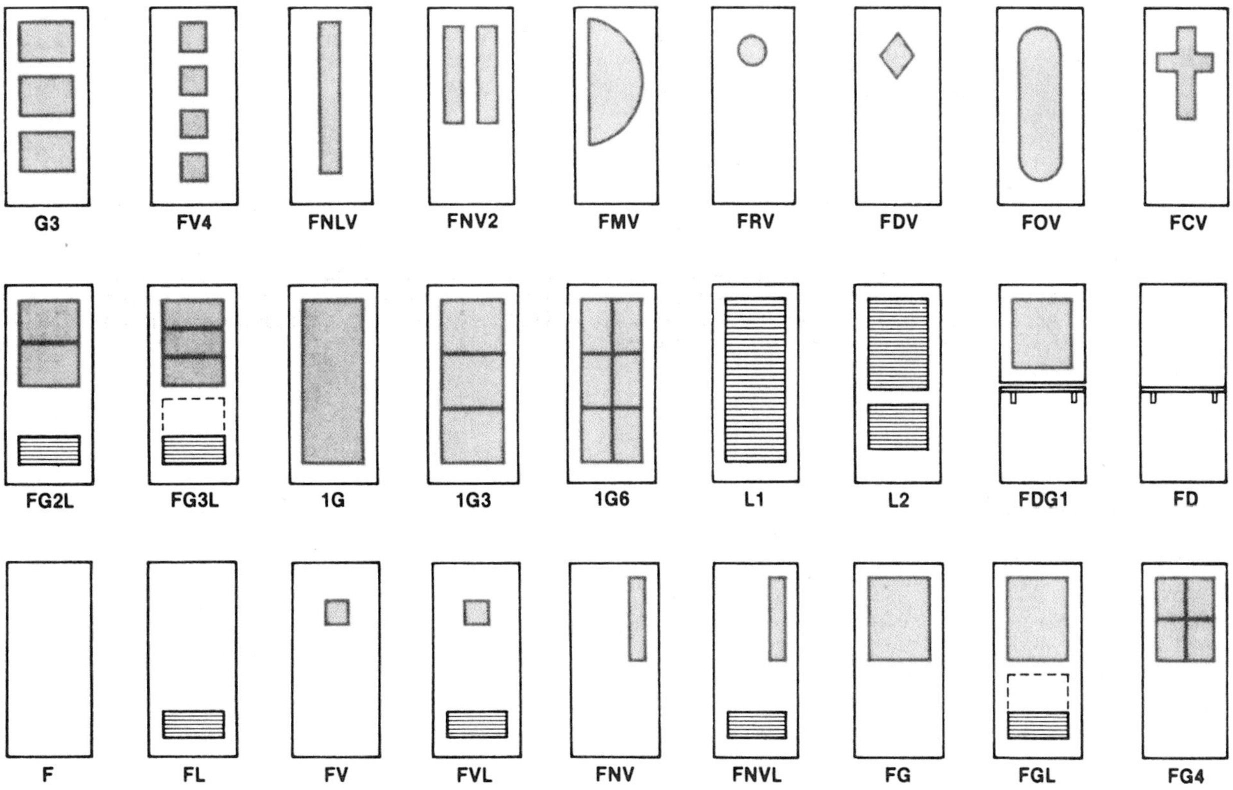

NOTE: Some manufacturers may use differing designations for some designs

___ 2. Recommended Locations ___ 3. Door Hand Conventions

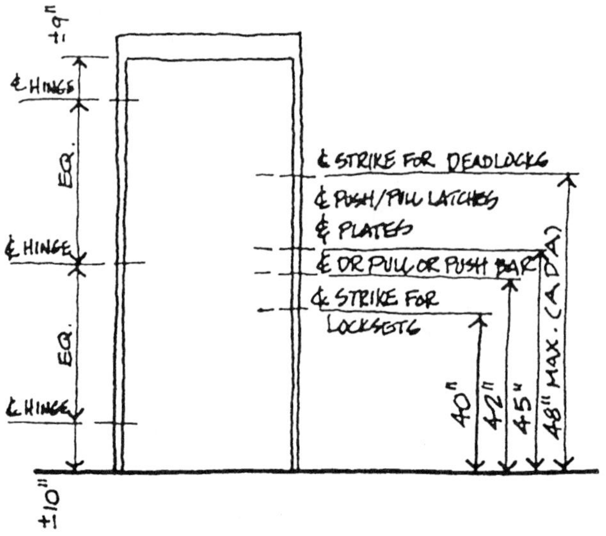

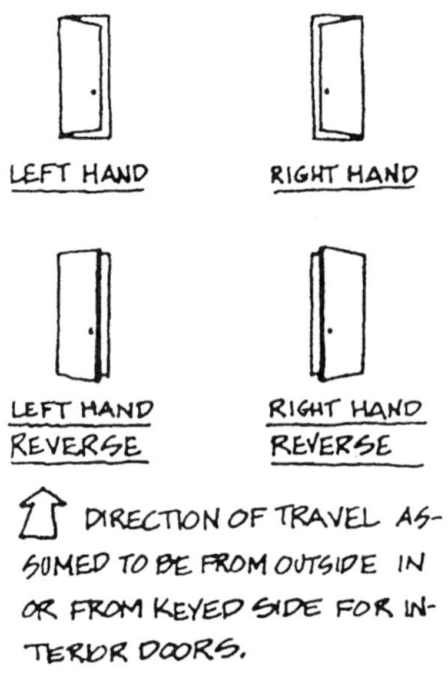

Hardware Locations

Door Hand Conventions

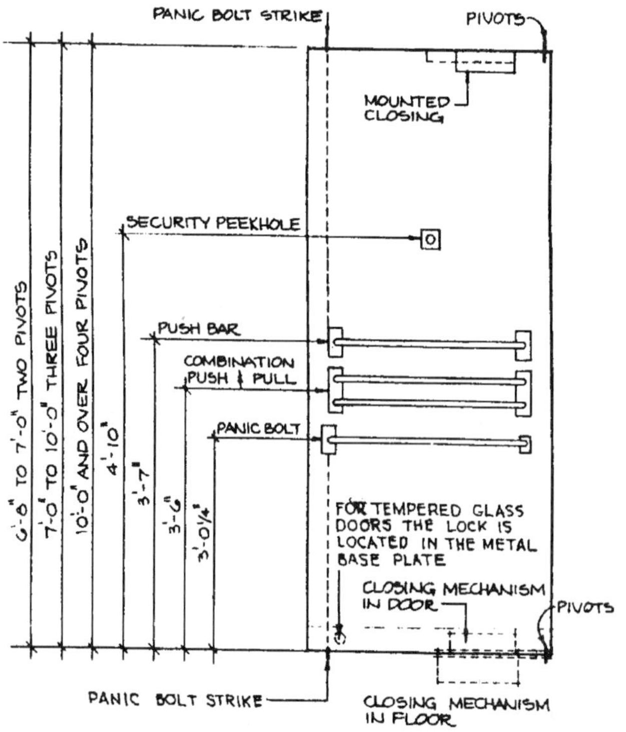

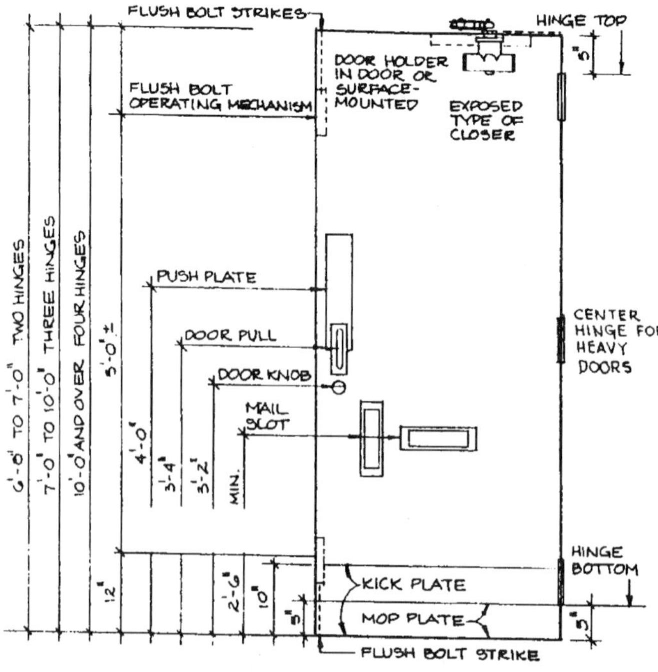

FINISH HARDWARE LOCATION FOR ALL TYPES OF DOORS

TYPICAL HARDWARE PREPARATION

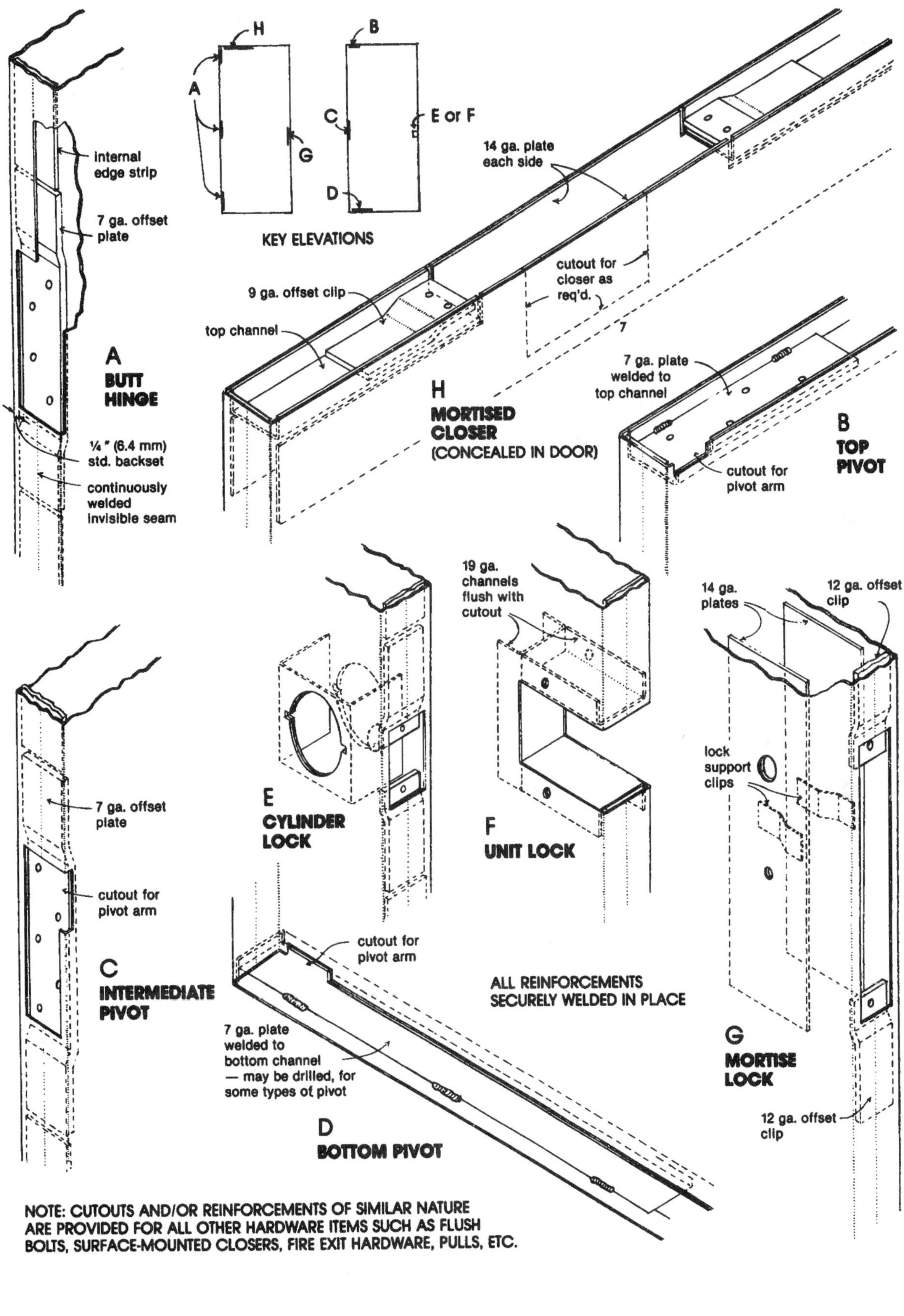

NOTE: CUTOUTS AND/OR REINFORCEMENTS OF SIMILAR NATURE ARE PROVIDED FOR ALL OTHER HARDWARE ITEMS SUCH AS FLUSH BOLTS, SURFACE-MOUNTED CLOSERS, FIRE EXIT HARDWARE, PULLS, ETC.

DOORS
Hollow Metal Door Schedules

DOOR SCHEDULE

Column numbers are for 14 ← reference here only

1	2	3	4				5	6		7	8	9	10	11			12	13	14
Opening Number	DOOR											FRAME					Fire Rating	Hard-Ware Set	Remarks
	Type	Mat'l.	Nominal Size*				Sill Detail	Louver		Glass *	Spec'l. Detail	Type	Mat'l.	Sections					
			No.	Width	Height	Thkns.		W	H					Jamb	Head	Sill			
101	F	HM	1	3-0	7-0	1 3/4	24/17	—	—	—		1	HM	1/17	1/17	—	—	1	
102	1G	AL	2	6-0	8-0	1 3/4	25/17	—	—	TEMP	—	2	AL	6/17	6/17	—	—	8	Contin. aluminum threshold
103	FGL	WD	1	3-0	7-0	1 3/4	25/17	—	—	1/4" TEMP	28/17	1	HM	1/17	1/17	—	—	4	
104	FG	HM	1	3-0	7-0	1 3/4	24/17	—	—	1/4" WIRE	—	1	HM	6/17	6/17	—	C	6	
105	FV	HM	3	4-0	7-0	1 3/4	24/17	—	—	1/4" TEMP	—	5	HM	2/17	2/17	—	—	1	Mullions 16/17
106	F	HM	2	7-0	7-0	1 3/4	29/17	—	—	—	—	2	HM	1/17	1/17	—	A	5	
107	FL	HM	1	3-0	7-0	1 3/4	24/17	23	12	—	—	3	HM	1/17	1/17	—	—	7	Transom bar 16/17
108	F	WD*	1	2-10	7-0	1 3/4	24/17	—	—	—	28/17	1	HM	3/17	3/17	—	—	4	Plastic faced door
109	—	—	—	—	—	—	—	—	—	—	—	1	HM	5/17	5/17	—	—	—	Cased opening
110	FGL	HM	1	3-0	7-0	1 3/4	26/17	23	20	1/4" TEMP	—	4	HM	1/17	1/17	25, 19/17	—	1	Side light mullion 16/17
111	F	HM	1	3-0	7-0	1 3/4	24/17	—	—	—	31/17	1	HM	8/17	8/17	—	—	2	Sound retardant

*Use metric units if desired; 1 inch = 25.4 mm, 1 foot = 0.305 m.

1. **Opening Number**
Number all openings individually, with the numbering system reflecting floor numbers if practicable.

2. **Door Type**
Use alphabetical designation for types, as shown on elevation views on facing page. Elevations should show door configurations and all features such as louvers, vision lights, etc. Do not use one elevation with dash lines to indicate variations.

3. **Door Material**
Designate material from which door is made: HM = hollow metal; AL = aluminum; WD = wood. * indicates special facing as noted in Remarks column. Type of core construction should be stated in the specifications.

4. **Nominal Size**
List number of doors per framed opening, plus width, height and thickness of door. State head and jamb clearances in specifications, using Hollow Metal Manufacturers Association recommended standards unless special conditions require otherwise.

5. **Sill Detail**
Reference sill detail, which shows sill clearance, threshold if any, and any special condition. Reference number shows detail number first, followed by sheet number.

6. **Louver**
Note width and height (in inches) of louver panel. Louver types may be either specified or shown in detail drawings.

7. **Glass**
Note thickness and type of glass to be used in glazed opening.

8. **Special Detail**
Reference detail(s) showing special features such as astragal (on pair), dutch door shelf, flush transom panel or other.

9. **Frame Type**
Use numerical designation for type, as shown on elevation views on facing page.

10. **Frame Material**
Designate material from which frame is made, using same symbols as for door materials.

11. **Frame Sections**
Reference details, showing frame sections at head and jamb, and details of such members as transom bars, mullions and other special features.

12. **Fire Rating**
State fire rating, if any, required for opening.

13. **Hardware Set**
State applicable hardware set number as described in specifications.

14. **Remarks**
Note here any special characteristics or required features of the opening, to insure that the contractor or supplier will be properly informed.

DOOR TYPES:

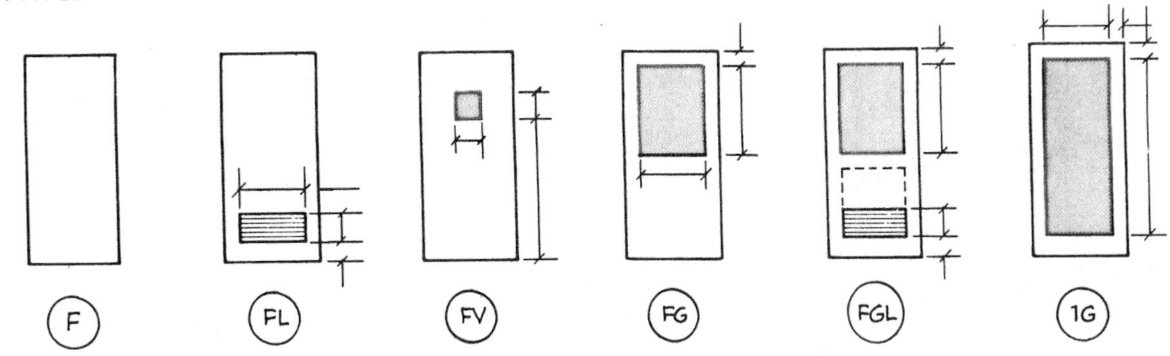

FRAME TYPES:

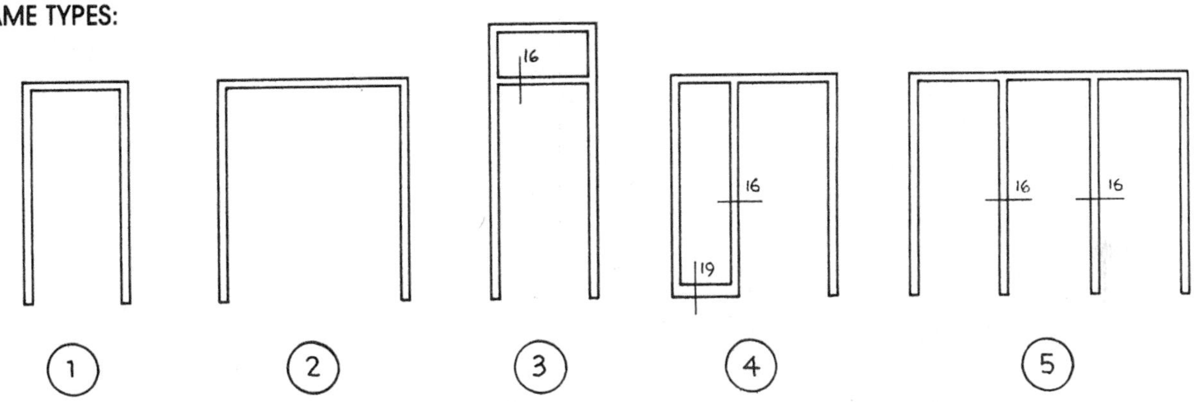

DETAILS:

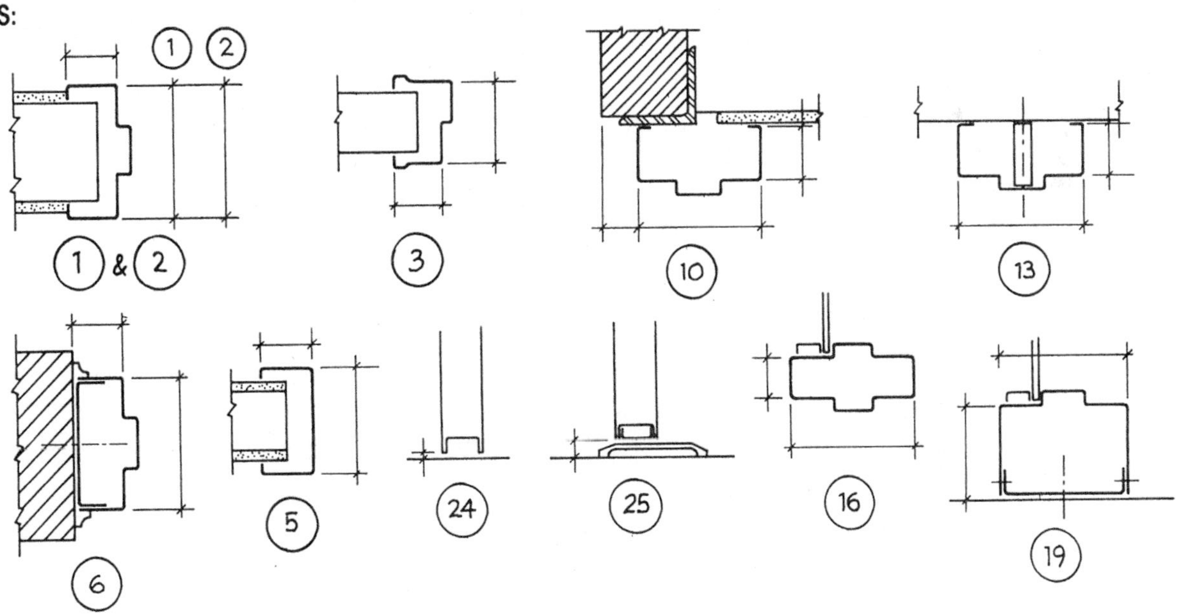

DOORS

Hollow Metal Door Schedules

DOOR SCHEDULE

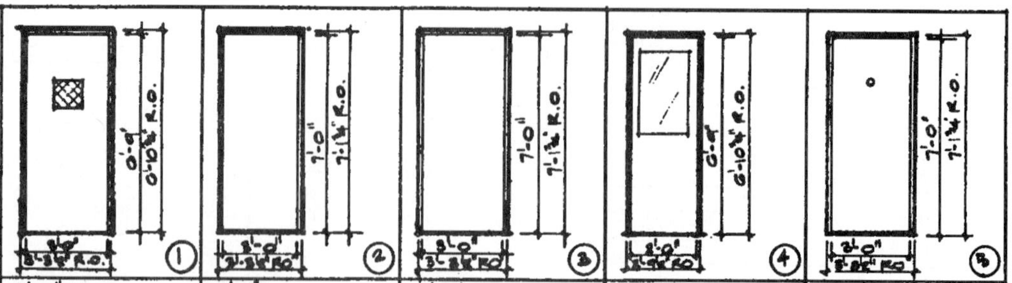

SYMBOL	1	2	3	4	5
SIZE	3'-0" x	3'-0" x	3'-0" x	2'-6" x	3'-0" x
LOCATION	CELLAR EXITS	CELLAR • BOILER RM	CELLAR	CELL. APRT. / COURTYD.	APARTMENT ENTRY
TYPE	FLUSH, INSULATED	FLUSH	FLUSH	FLUSH	FLUSH
MATERIAL	HOLL. MET., 1/4" WIRE GLASS	HOLLOW METAL	HOLLOW METAL	HOLL. MET. / INSUL. GLASS	HOLLOW METAL
SADDLE	STEEL			STEEL	
REMARKS	1 1/2 HR. F.P.S.C.	1 1/2 HR. F.P.S.C.			1 1/2 HR. F.P.S.C., STC-35 W/FEETPOLE. MEA # 187.72

NOTES:

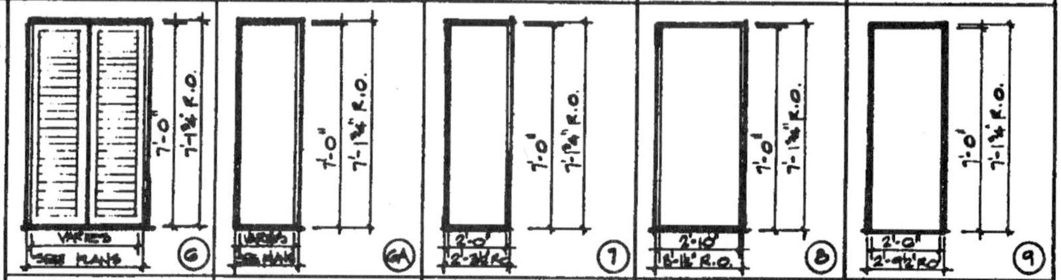

SYMBOL	6	6A	7	8	9
SIZE	VARIES	VARIES	2'-0" x	2'-10" x	2'-6" x
LOCATION	CLOSETS	CLOSETS	BATHROOMS	BATHRMS @ GRND. FLOOR	BEDROOMS
TYPE	BI-FOLD W/ LOUVERS	FLUSH	FLUSH	FLUSH	FLUSH
MATERIAL	WOOD	WOOD	WOOD	WOOD	WOOD
SADDLE			MARBLE	MARBLE	
REMARKS	UNDERCUT 1"	UNDERCUT 1"	UNDERCUT 1/2"	TO COMPLY W/L.L. 58 UNDERCUT 1/2"	

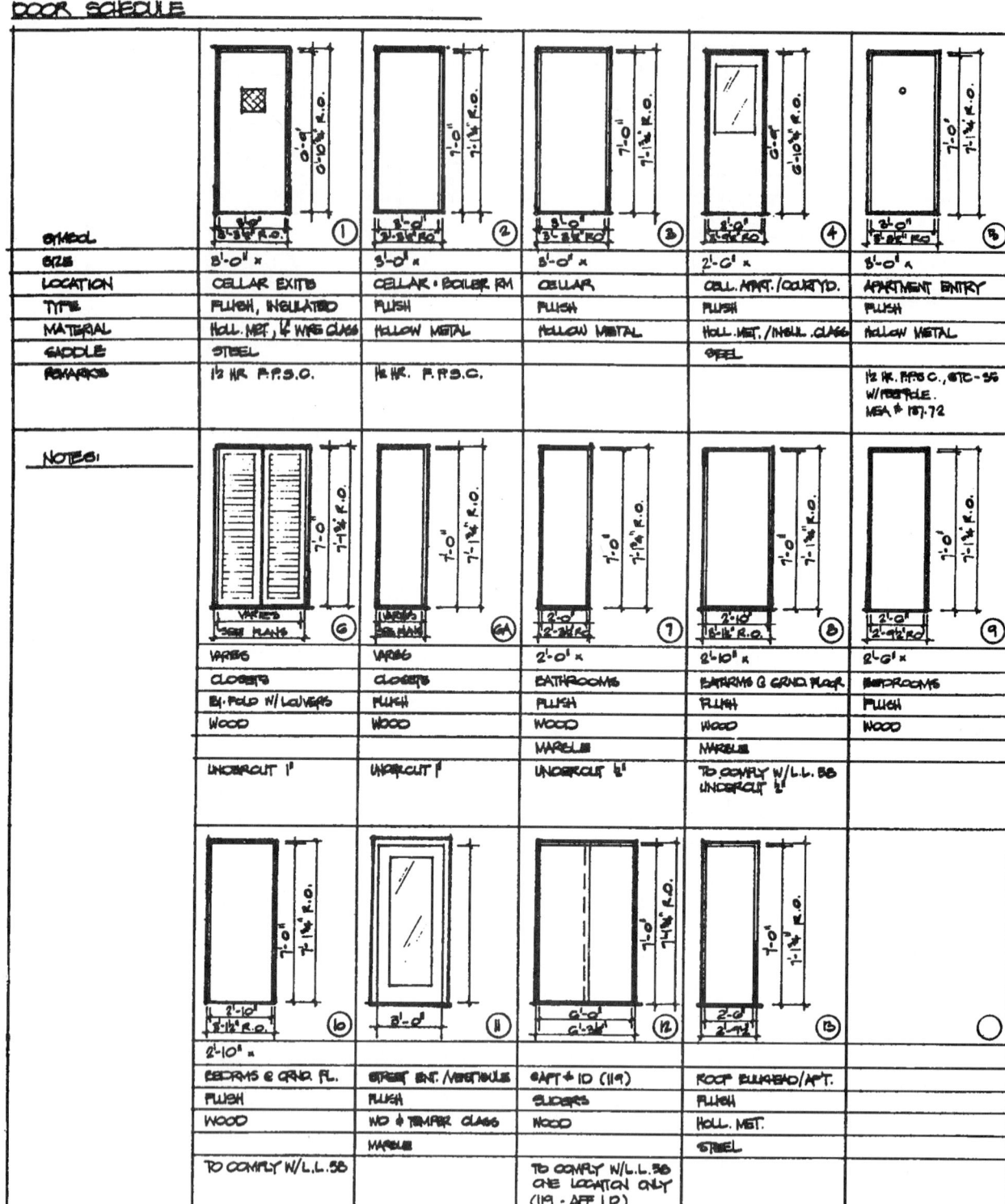

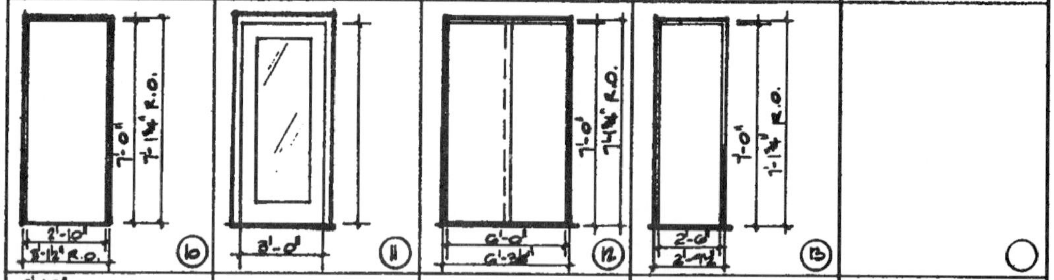

SYMBOL	10	11	12	13	
SIZE	2'-10" x				
LOCATION	BEDRMS @ GRND. FL.	STREET ENT. / VESTIBULE	APT 4 10 (119)	ROOF BULKHEAD/APT.	
TYPE	FLUSH	FLUSH	SLIDERS	FLUSH	
MATERIAL	WOOD	WD & TEMPER GLASS	WOOD	HOLL. MET.	
SADDLE		MARBLE		STEEL	
REMARKS	TO COMPLY W/L.L.58		TO COMPLY W/L.L.58 ONE LOCATION ONLY (119 - APT 1D)		

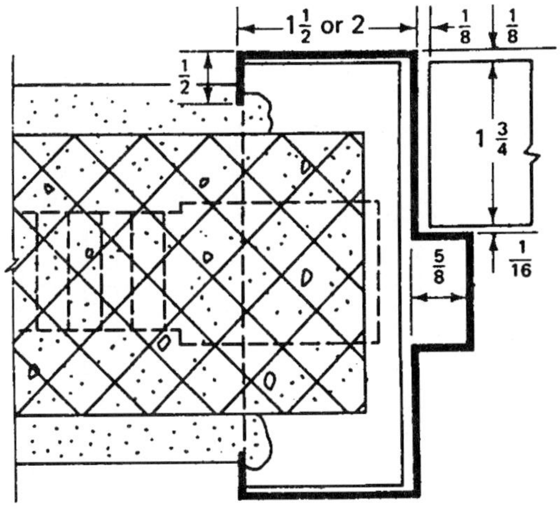

(a) Masonry with plaster, one or both sides

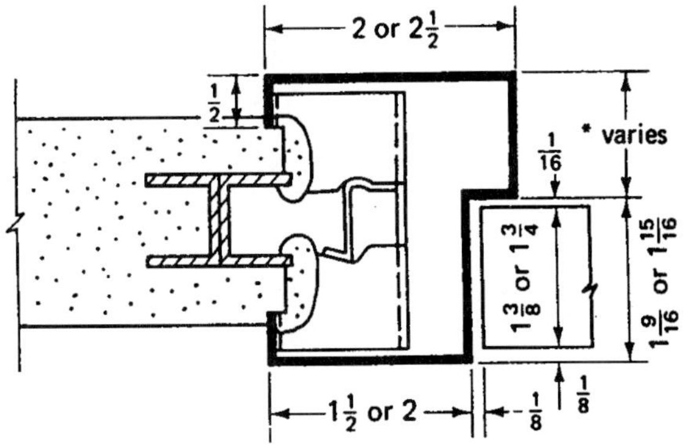

(b) Two-inch plaster wall

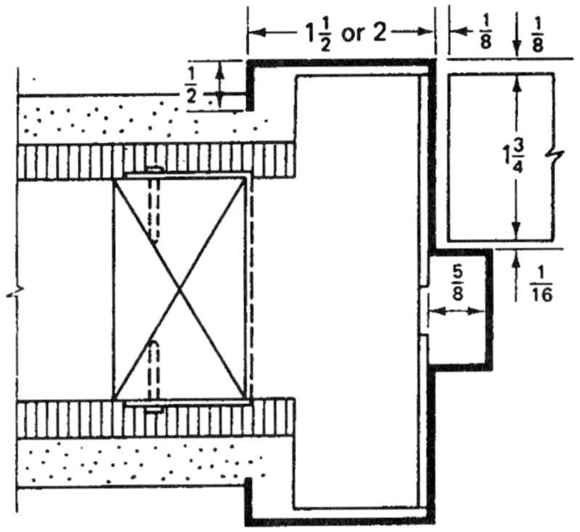

(c) Wood stud and plaster

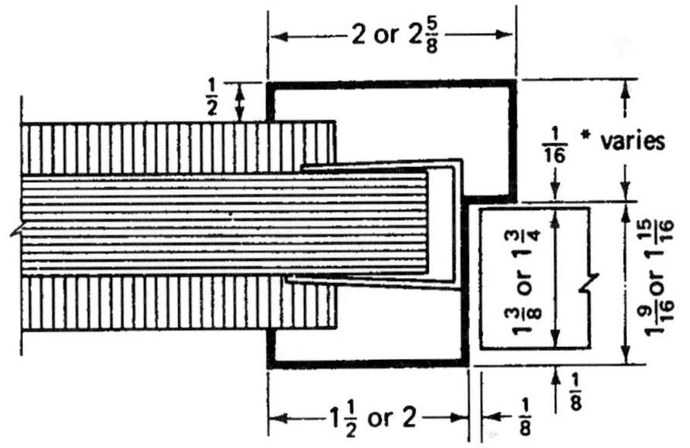

(d) Two-inch solid dry wall

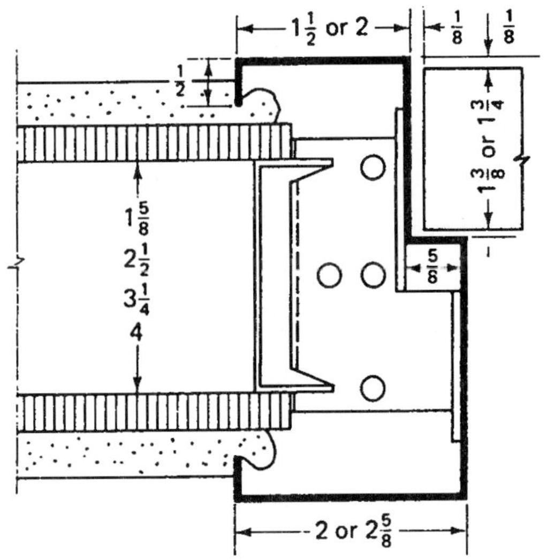

(e) Steel stud and plaster

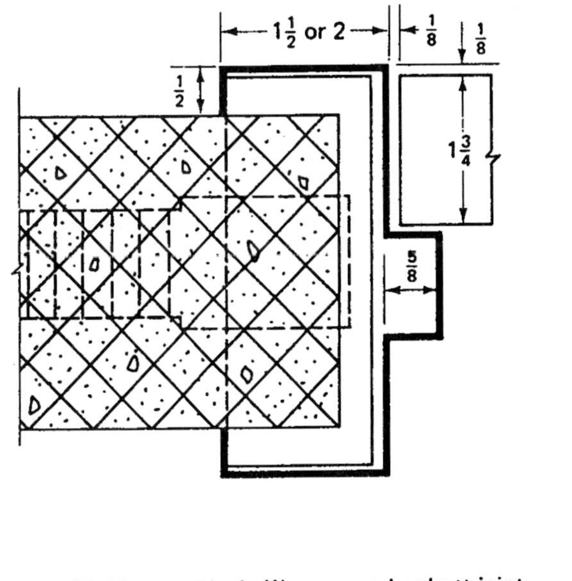

(f) Masonry block. Wrap-around or butt joint

Fig. 2 Typical jamb installations

DOORS

Hollow Metal Door Frames

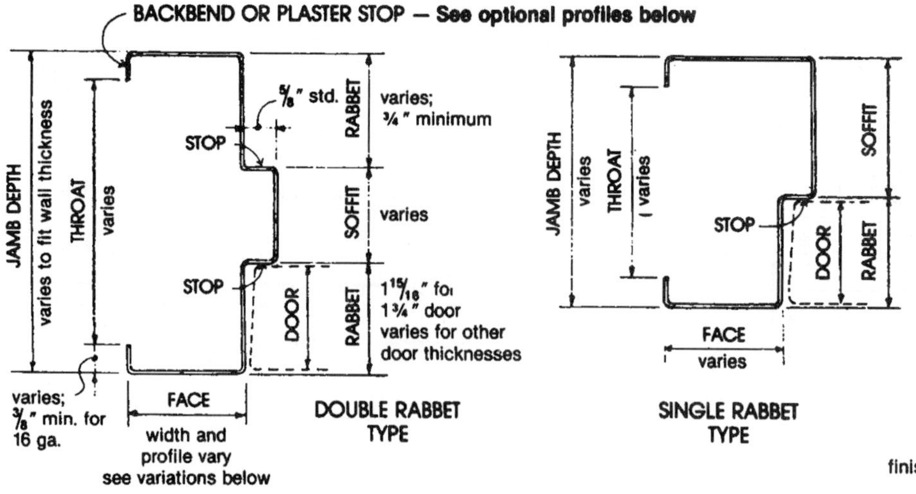

BASIC DOOR FRAME PROFILES AND THEIR PARTS

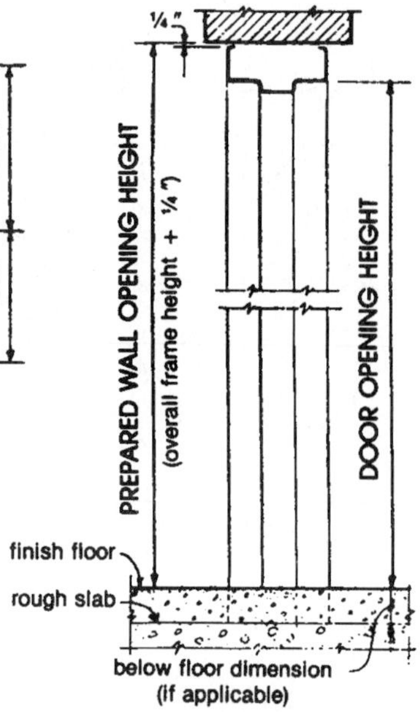

VERTICAL FRAME DIMENSIONS

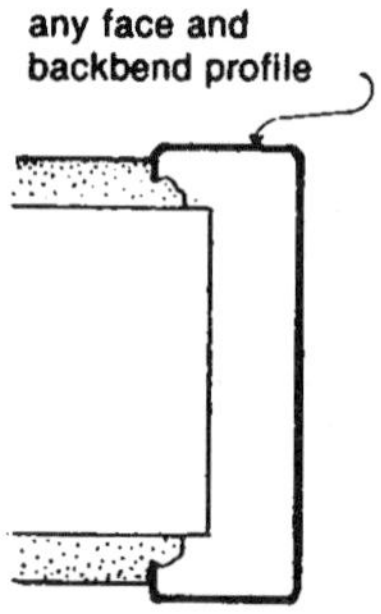

CASED OPENING
BLANK JAMB

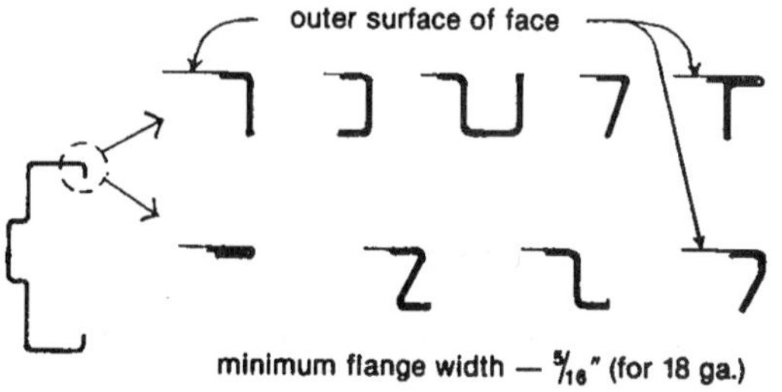

BACKBENDS NEED NOT BE THE SAME ON OPPOSITE TRIM FACES — ANY COMBINATION MAY BE USED

TYPICAL BACKBEND or PLASTER STOP PROFILES

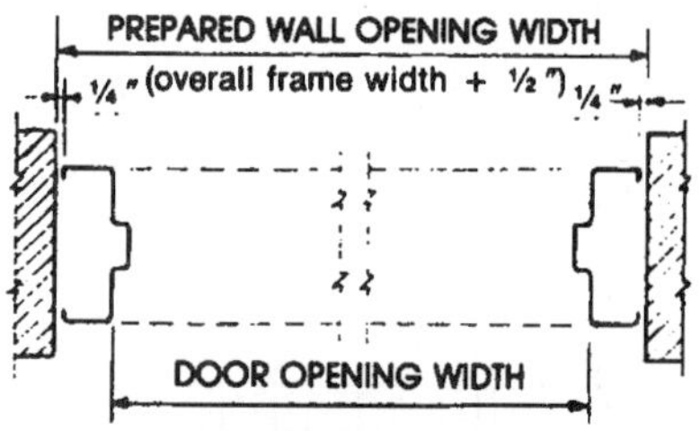

HORIZONTAL FRAME DIMENSIONS

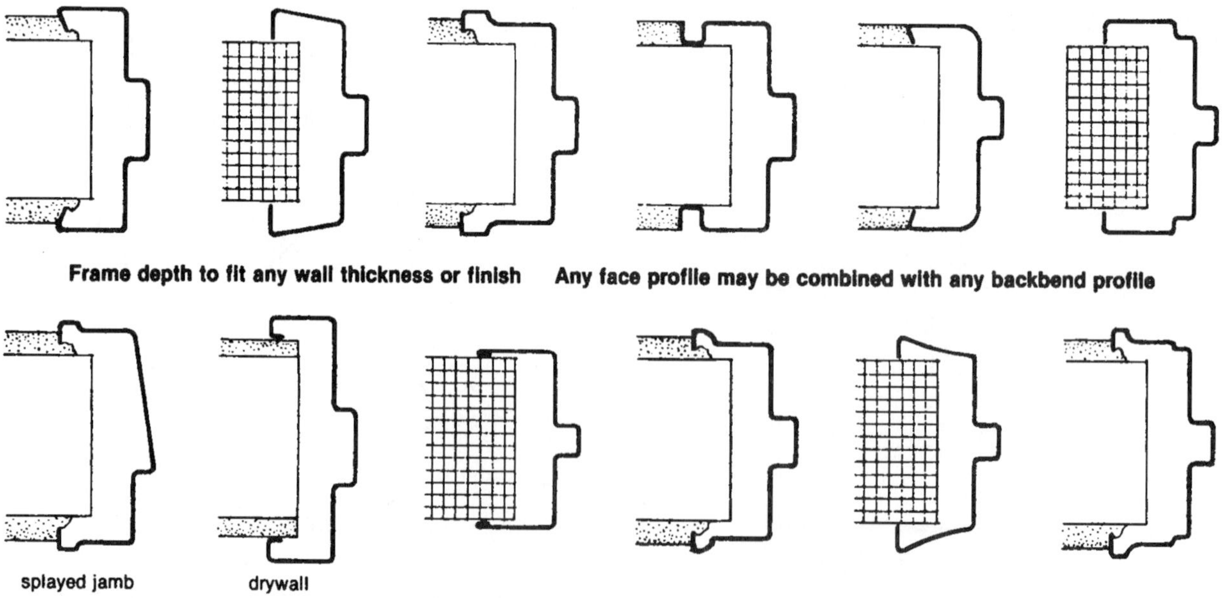

REPRESENTATIVE FRAME PROFILES

DOORS
Hollow Metal Door Frames

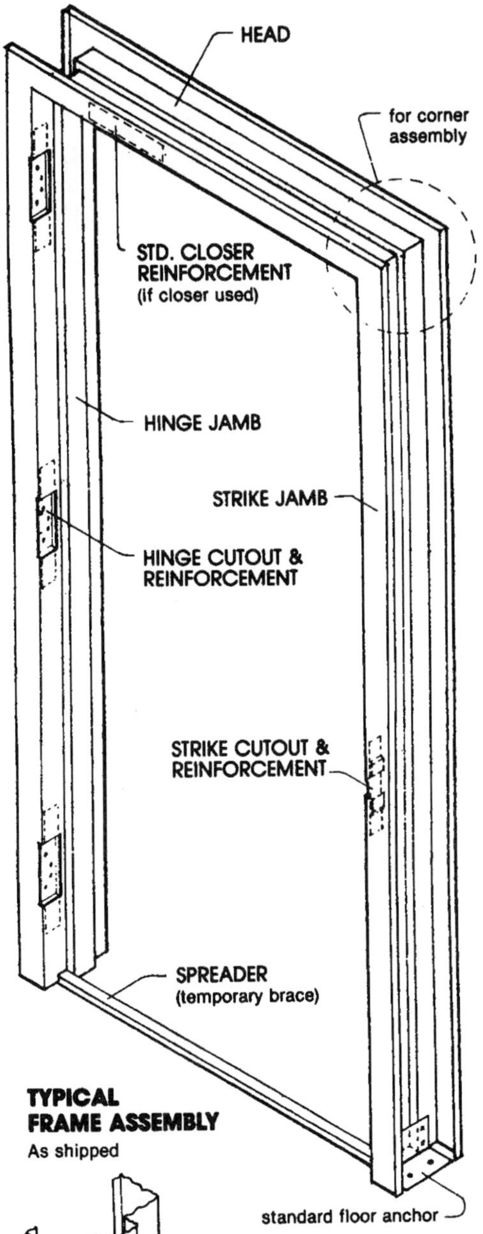

TYPICAL FRAME ASSEMBLY
As shipped

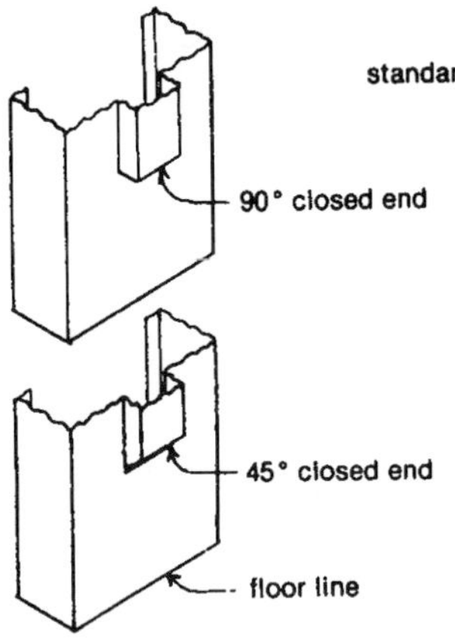

CUTOFF (SANITARY) STOPS

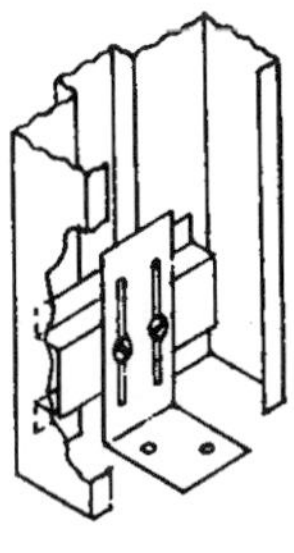

ADJUSTABLE FLOOR ANCHOR

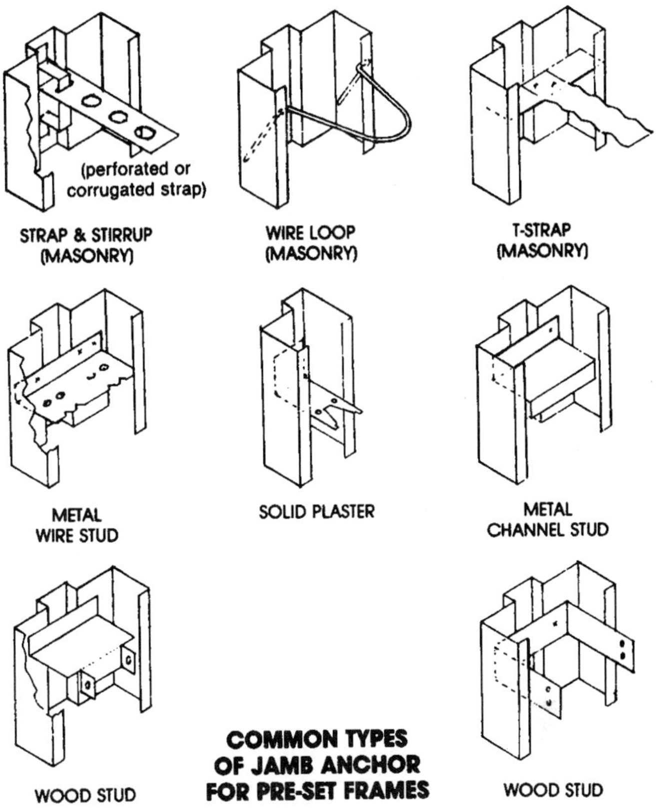

COMMON TYPES OF JAMB ANCHOR FOR PRE-SET FRAMES

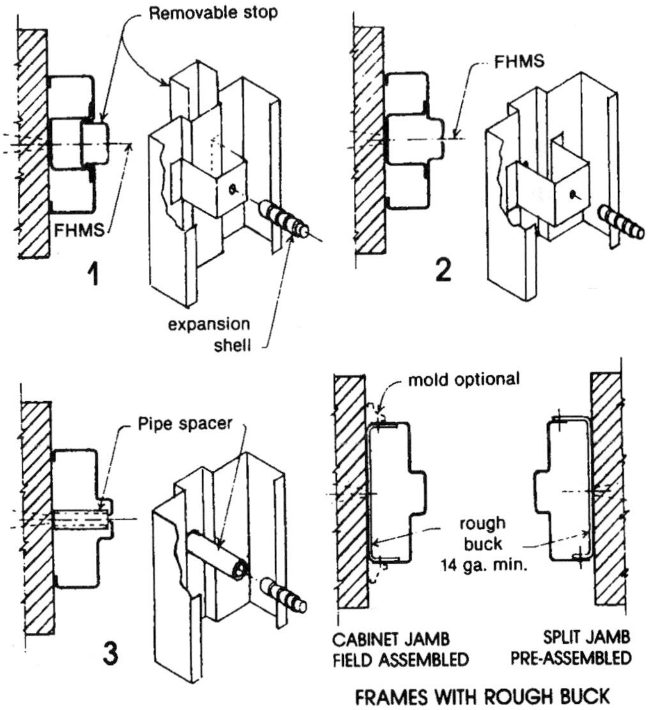

FRAMES WITH ROUGH BUCK

ANCHORAGE OF FRAMES IN PREPARED OPENINGS

DOORS

Hollow Metal Door Frames

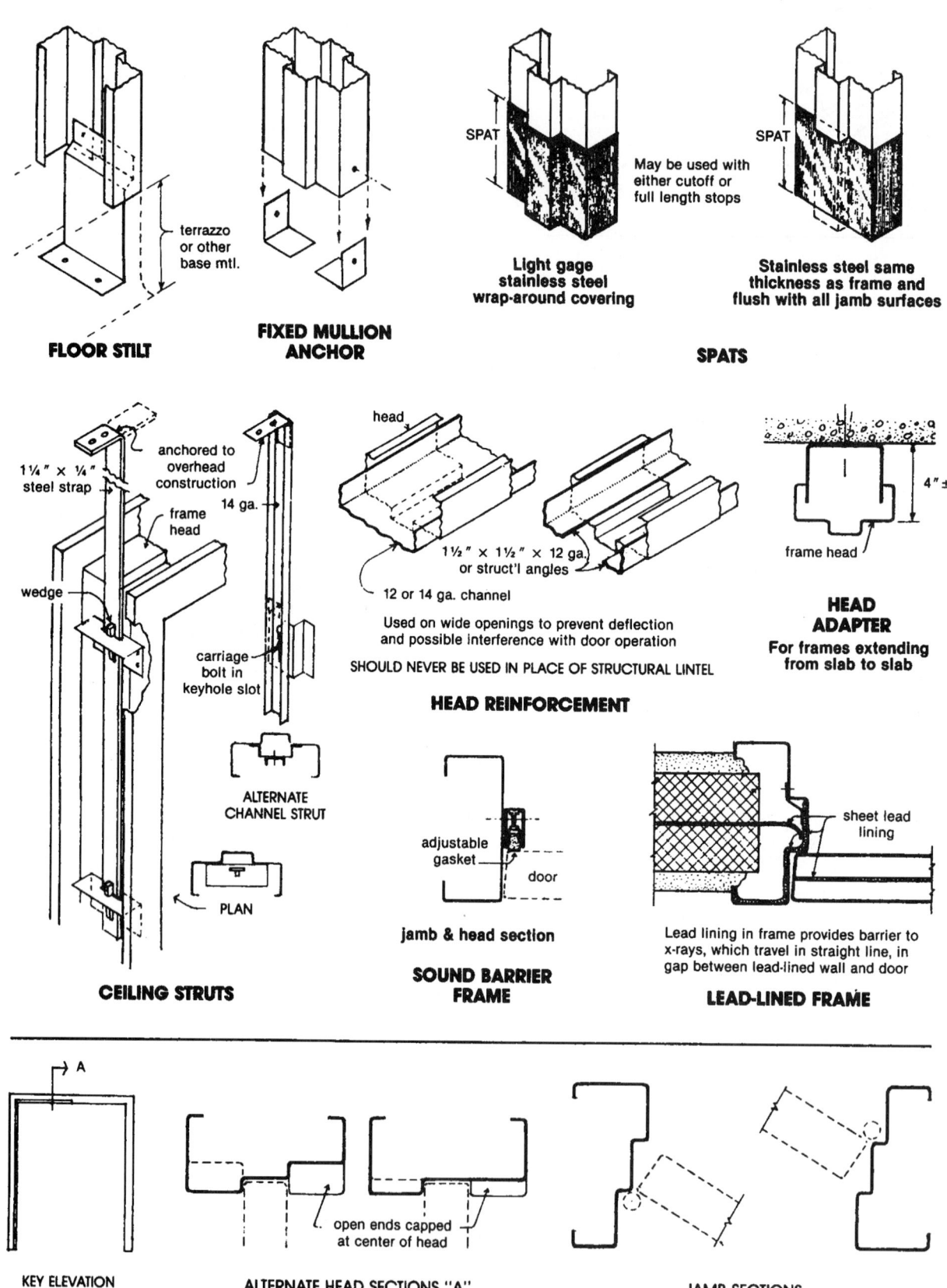

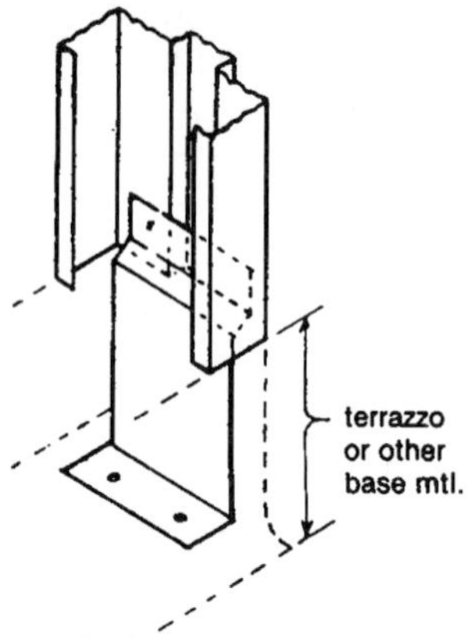

FLOOR STILT

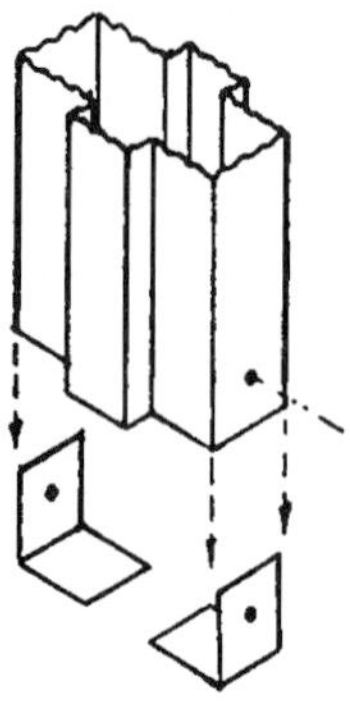

FIXED MULLION ANCHOR

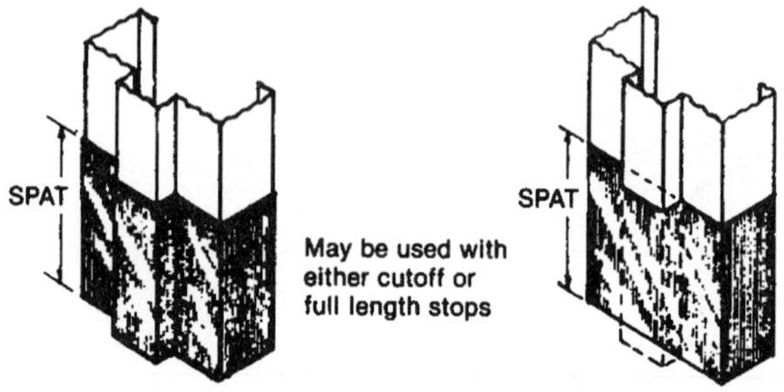

Light gage stainless steel wrap-around covering

Stainless steel same thickness as frame and flush with all jamb surfaces

SPATS

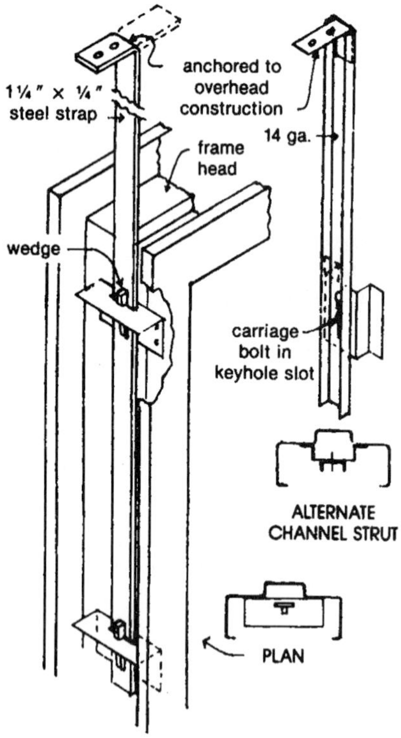

CEILING STRUTS

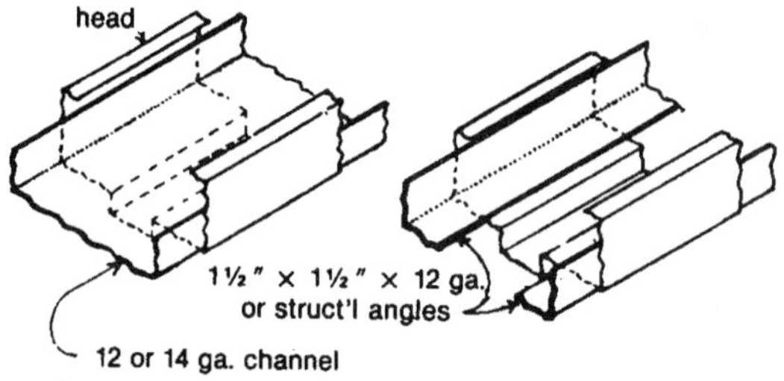

Used on wide openings to prevent deflection and possible interference with door operation

SHOULD NEVER BE USED IN PLACE OF STRUCTURAL LINTEL

HEAD REINFORCEMENT

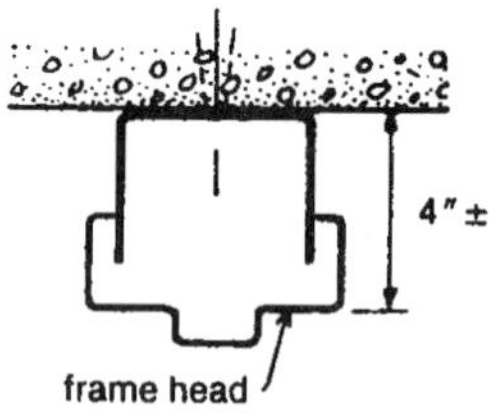

HEAD ADAPTER

For frames extending from slab to slab

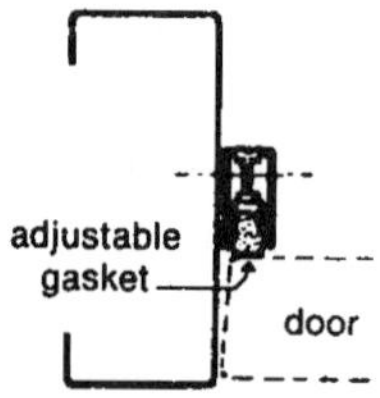

jamb & head section

SOUND BARRIER FRAME

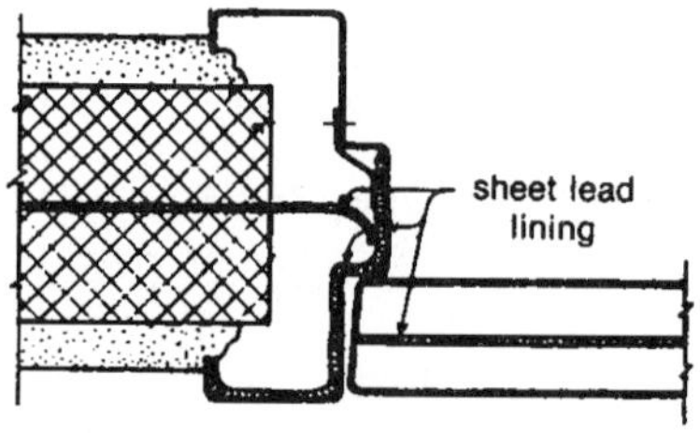

Lead lining in frame provides barrier to x-rays, which travel in straight line, in gap between lead-lined wall and door

LEAD-LINED FRAME

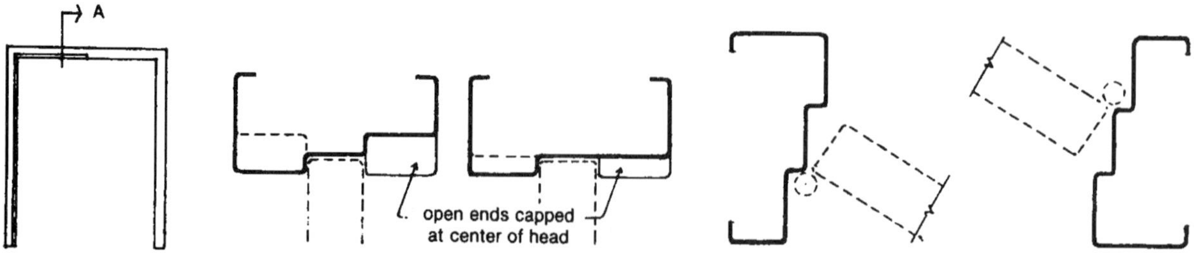

KEY ELEVATION

ALTERNATE HEAD SECTIONS "A"

JAMB SECTIONS

DETAILS OF DOUBLE EGRESS FRAME

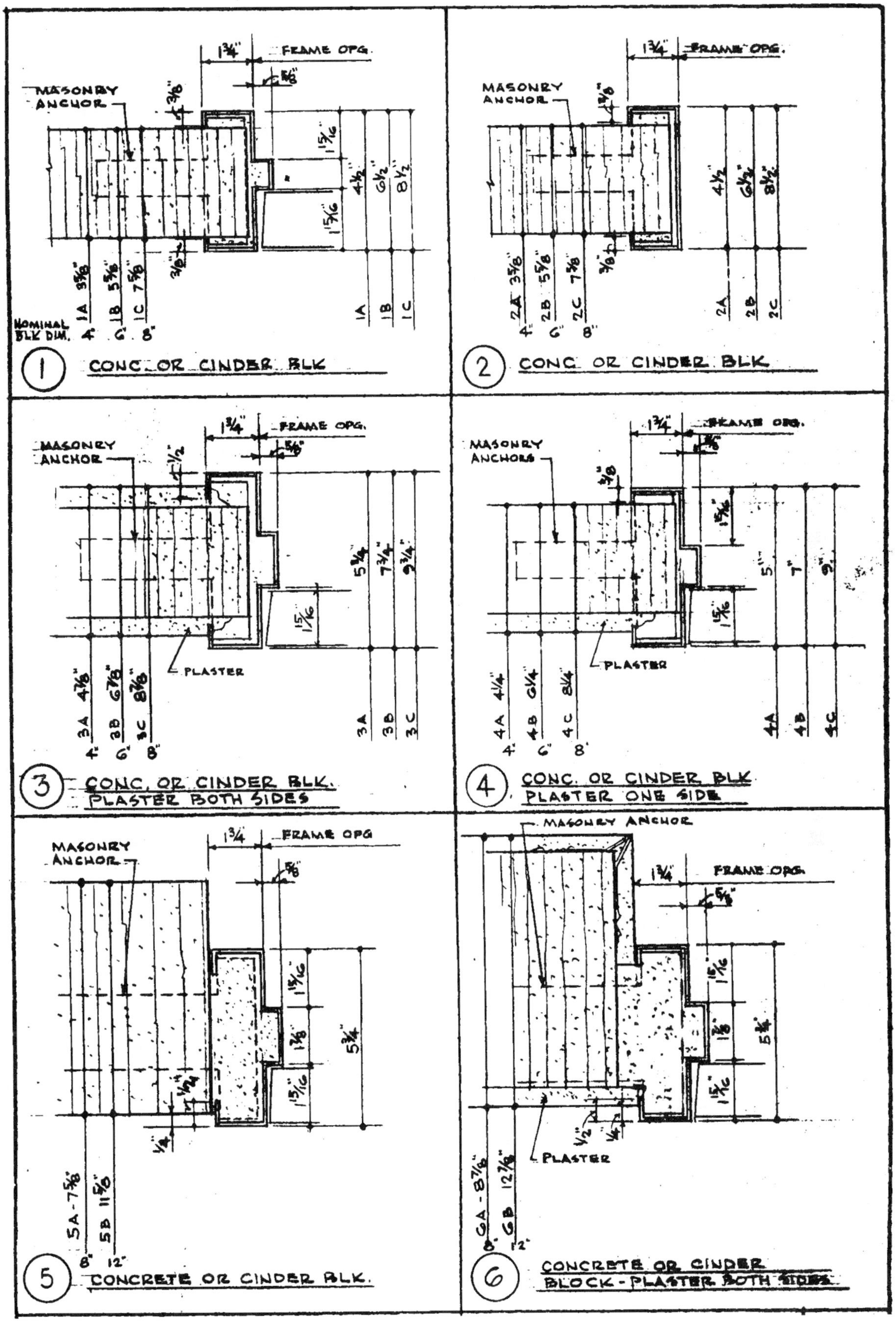
MASONRY ANCHOR
FRAME OPG.
1 CONC. OR CINDER BLK
NOMINAL BLK DIM.
2 CONC. OR CINDER BLK
PLASTER
3 CONC. OR CINDER BLK. PLASTER BOTH SIDES
4 CONC. OR CINDER BLK PLASTER ONE SIDE
5 CONCRETE OR CINDER BLK.
6 CONCRETE OR CINDER BLOCK - PLASTER BOTH SIDES

DOORS

Hollow Metal Door Frames

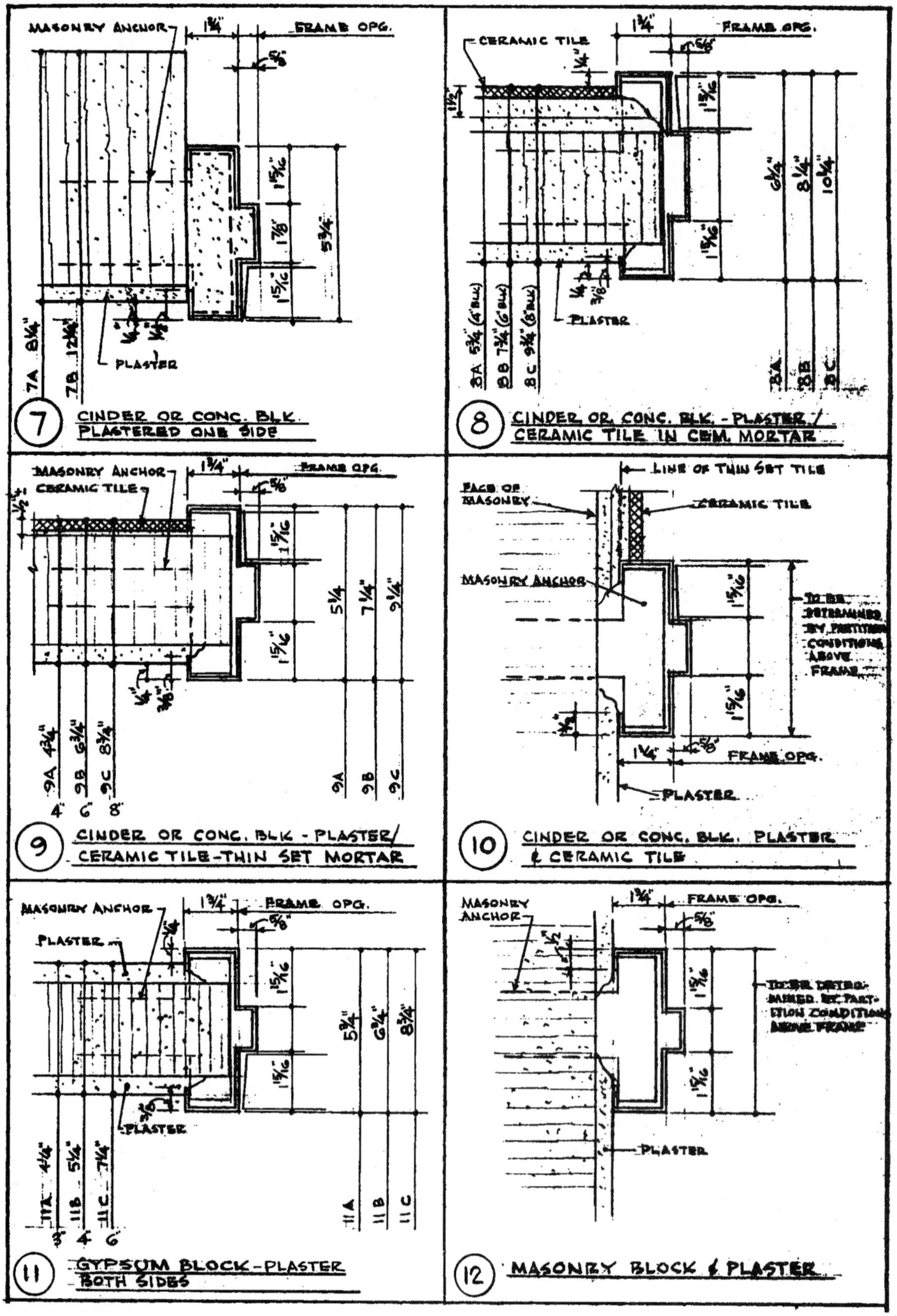

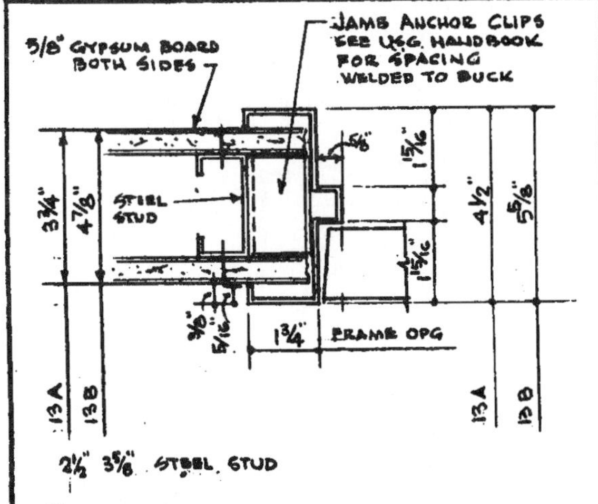

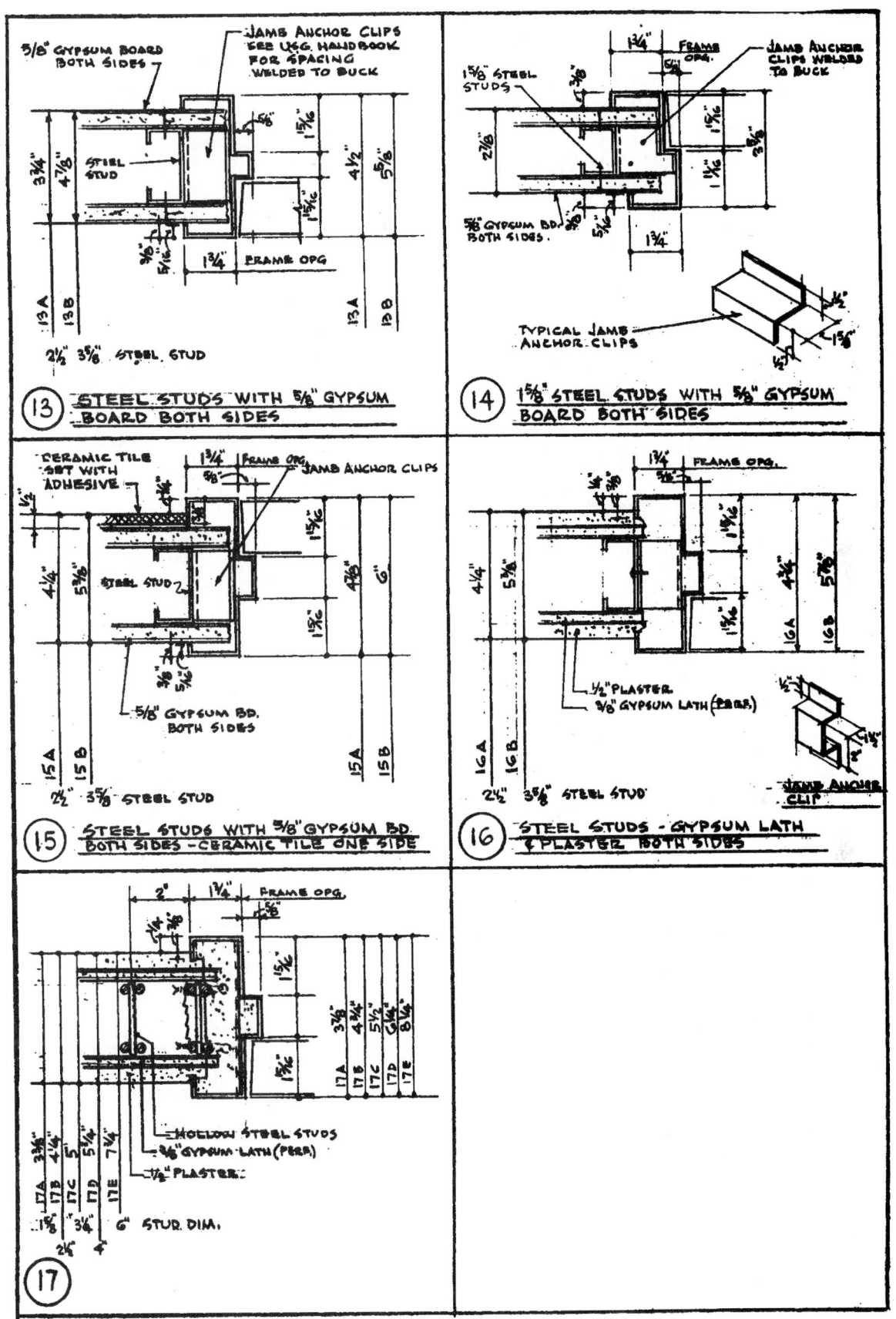

(13) STEEL STUDS WITH 5/8" GYPSUM BOARD BOTH SIDES

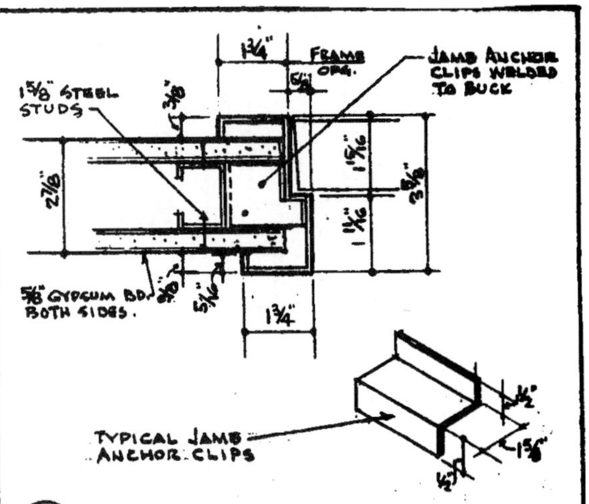

(14) 1⅝" STEEL STUDS WITH 5/8" GYPSUM BOARD BOTH SIDES

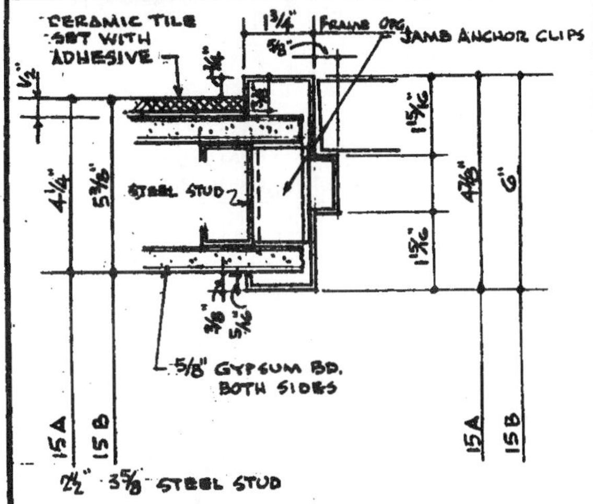

(15) STEEL STUDS WITH 5/8" GYPSUM BD. BOTH SIDES – CERAMIC TILE ONE SIDE

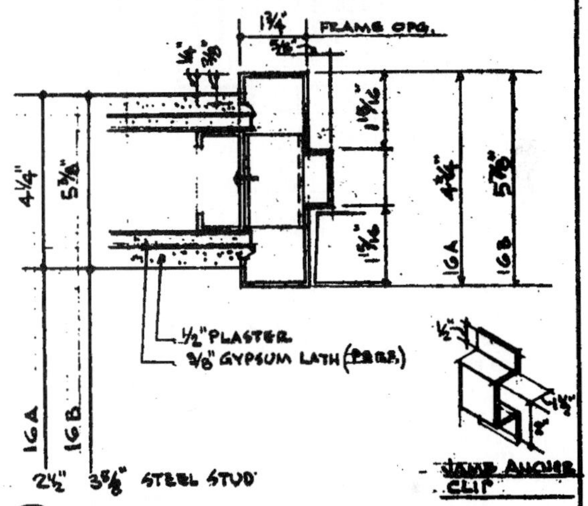

(16) STEEL STUDS – GYPSUM LATH & PLASTER BOTH SIDES

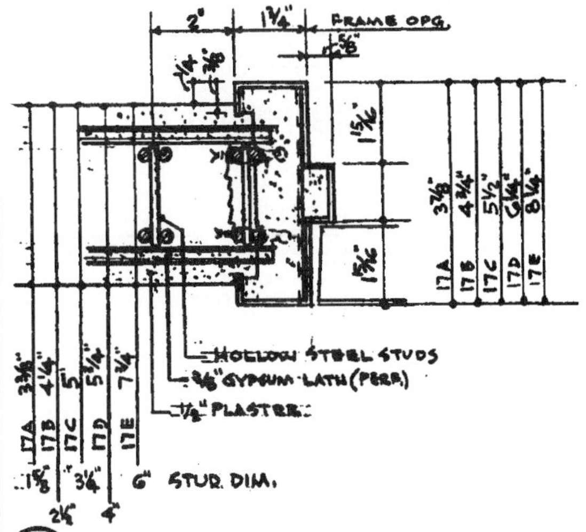

(17)

DOORS

Hollow Metal Door Frames

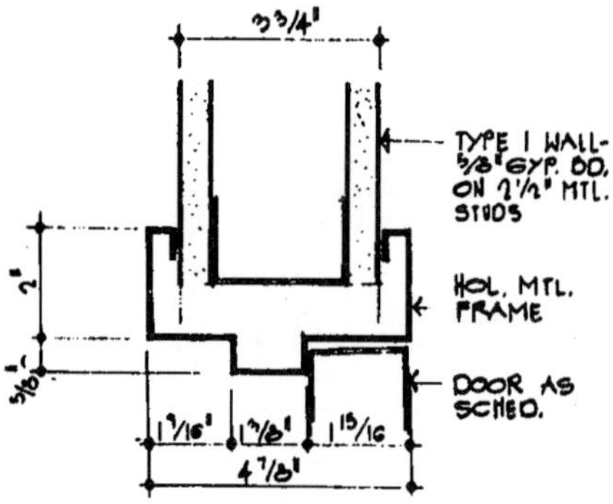

HEAD/JAMB

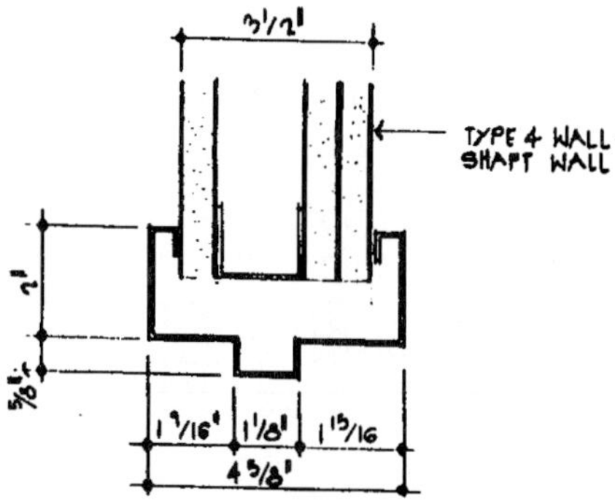

HEAD/JAMB

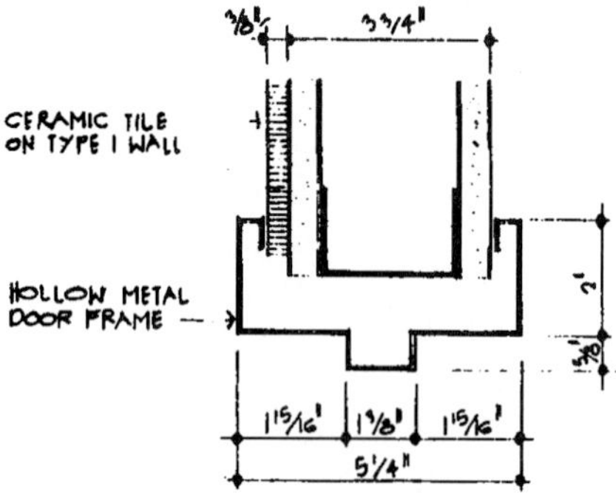

HEAD/JAMB

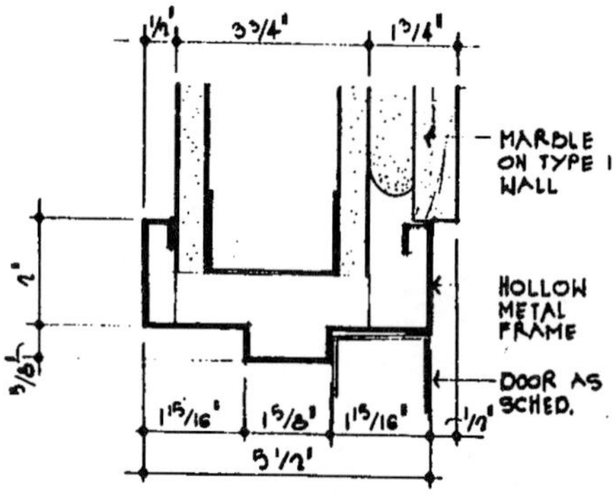

JAMB

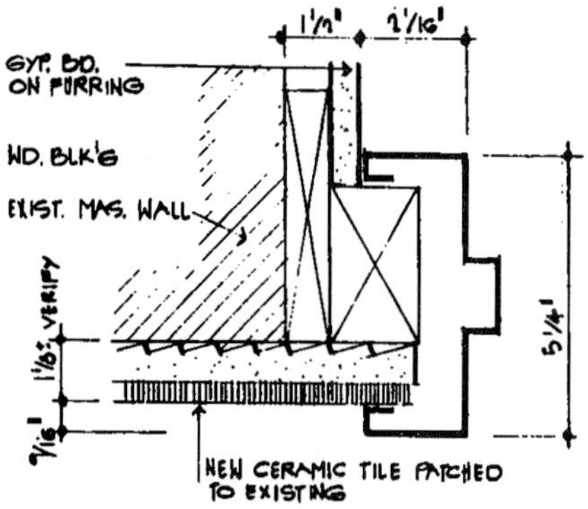

JAMB

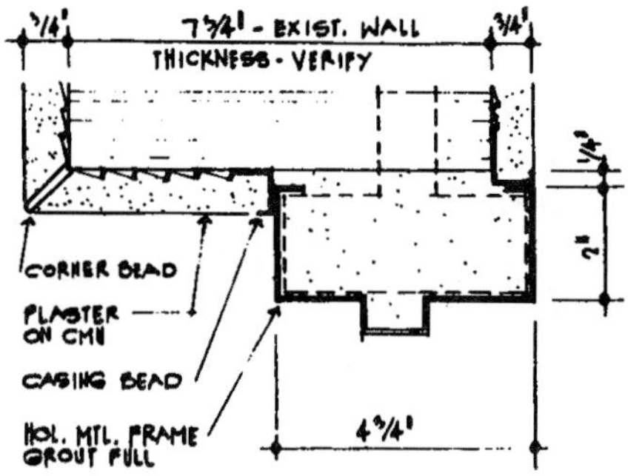

JAMB/HEAD

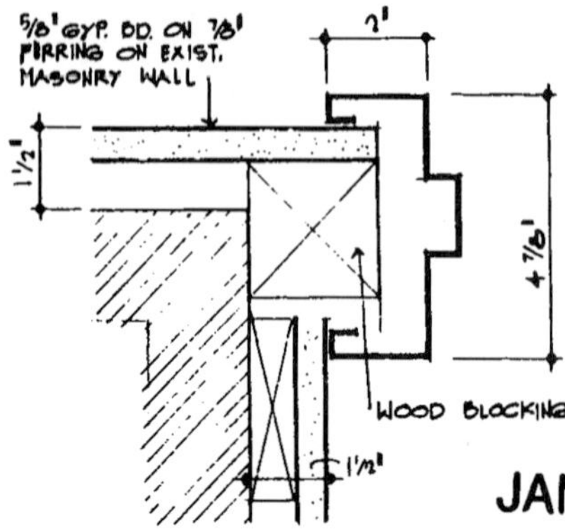

JAMB

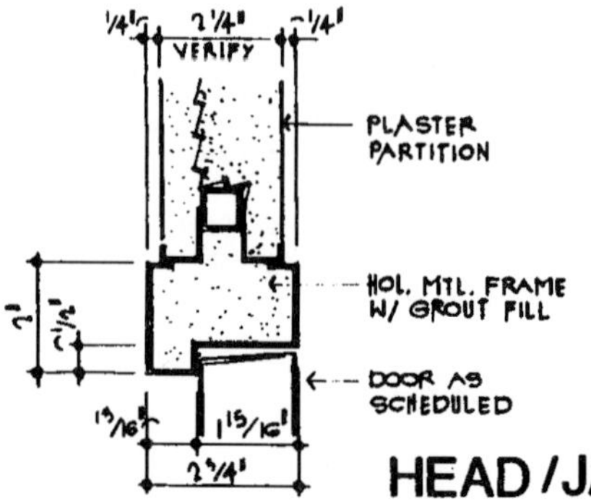

HEAD / JAMB

DOORS
Hollow Metal Door Frames

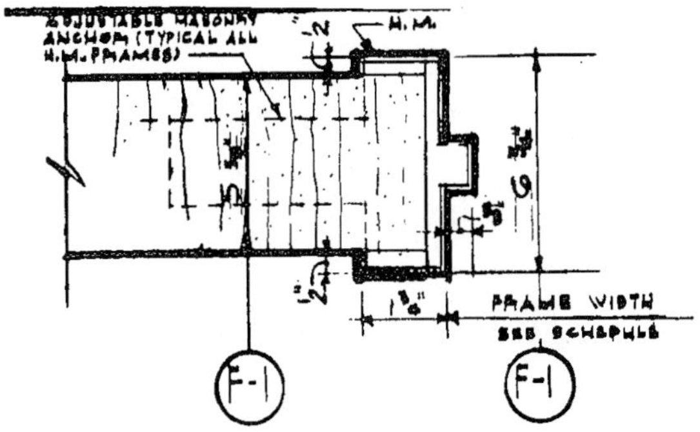

F-1 UNFINISHED MASONRY BLOCK @ 3"=1'-0"

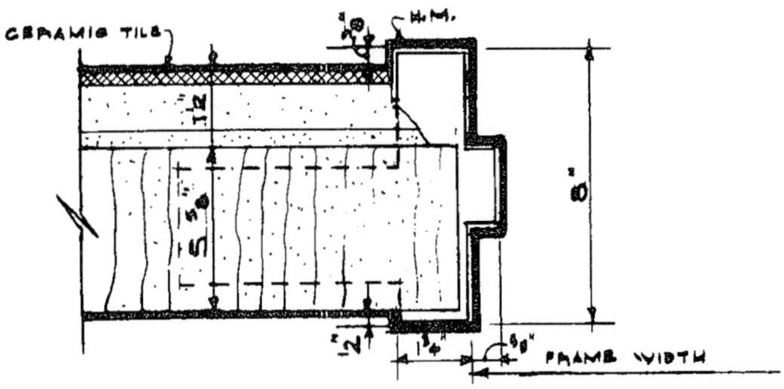

F-2 MASONRY BLK.- CERAMIC TILE ONE SIDE @ 3"=1'-0"

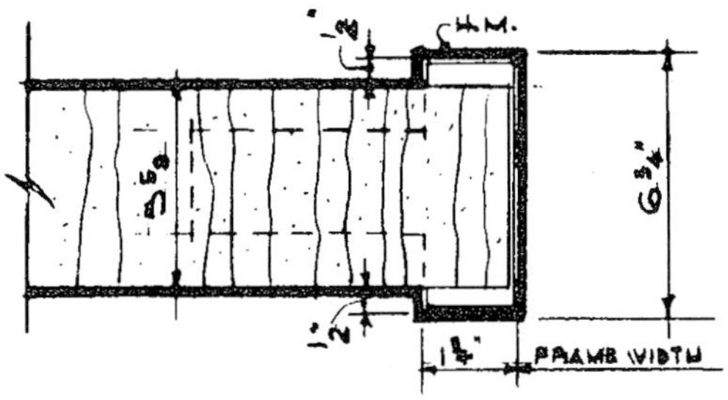

F-3 TRIMMED OPG. MASONRY BLOCK @ 3"=1'-0"

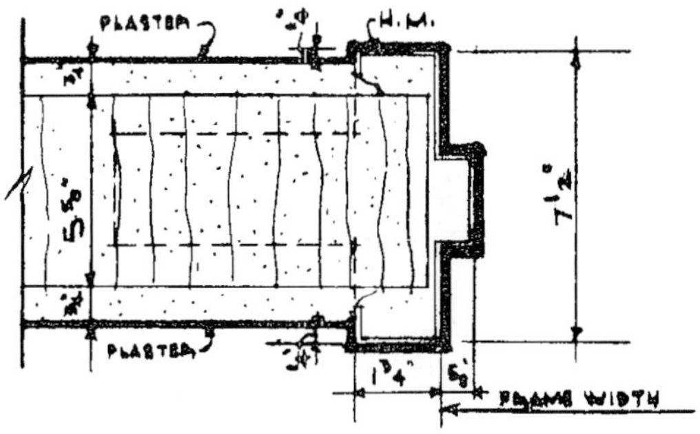

F-4 MASONRY BLK. PLASTER BOTH SIDES @ 3"=1'-0"

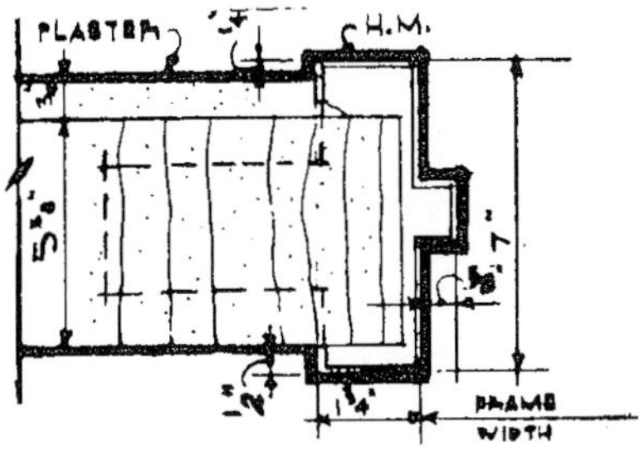

F-5 MASONRY BLK. PLASTER ONE SIDE @ 3"=1'-0"

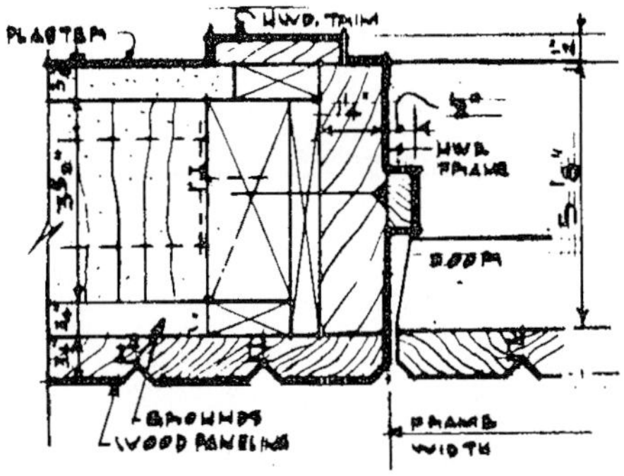

F-6 HARDWOOD FRAME @ 3"=1'-0"

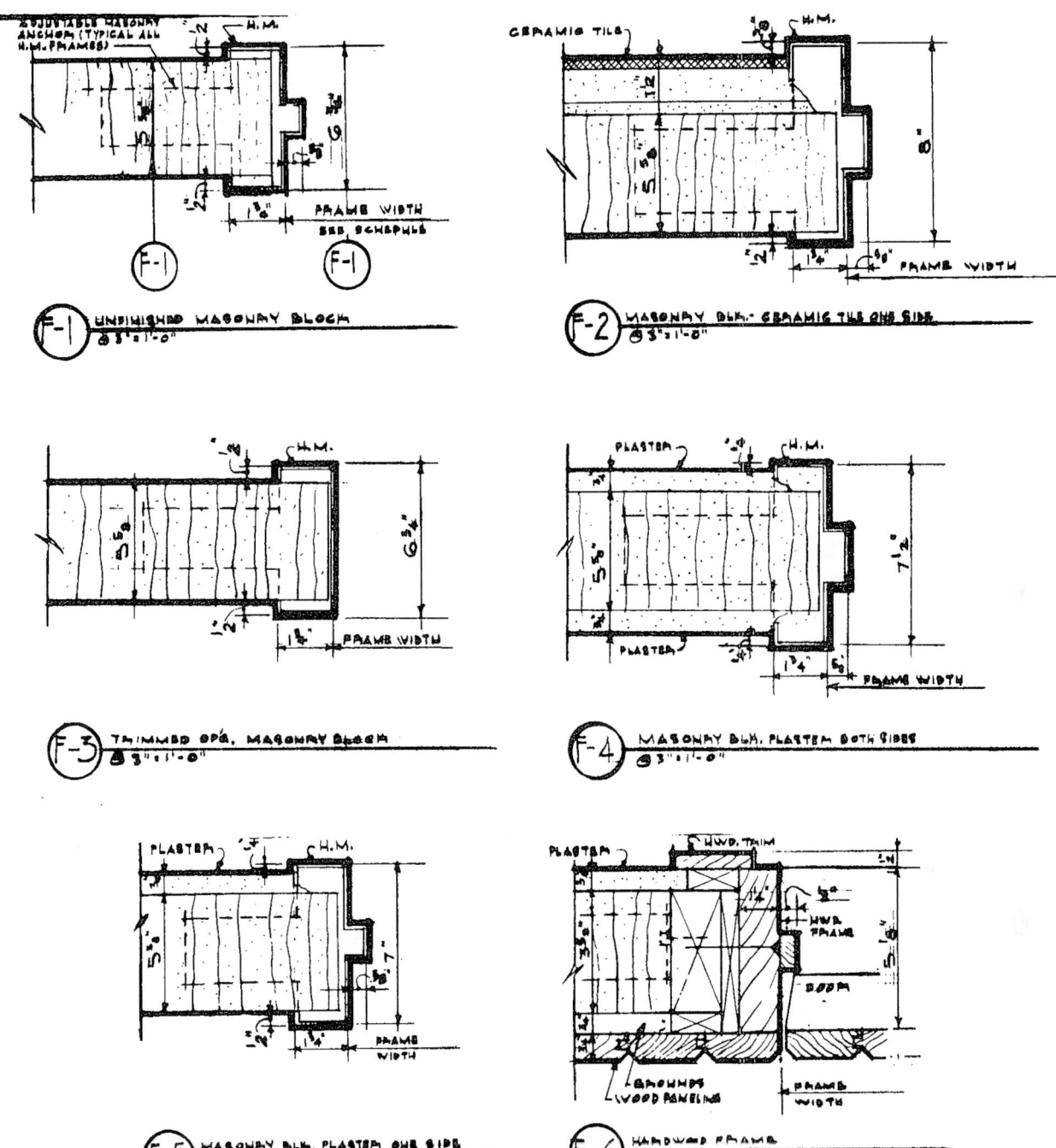

DOORS

Hollow Metal Door Frames

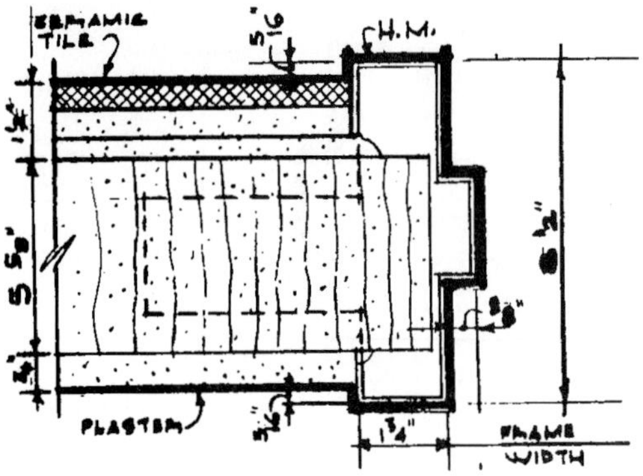

F-7 MASONRY DIM. CERAMIC TILE & PLASTER
@ 3" = 1'-0"

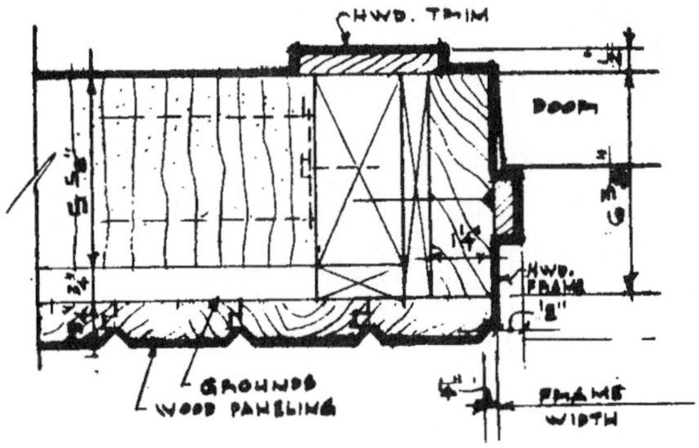

F-8 HARDWOOD FRAME
@ 3" = 1'-0"

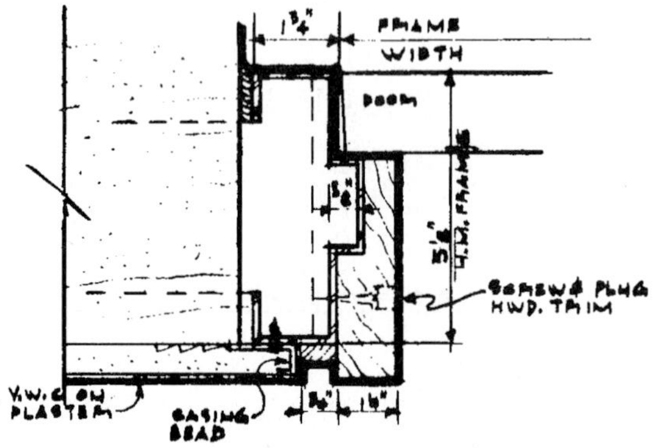

F-9 H.M. FRAME – HWD. COVERING
@ 3" = 1'-0"

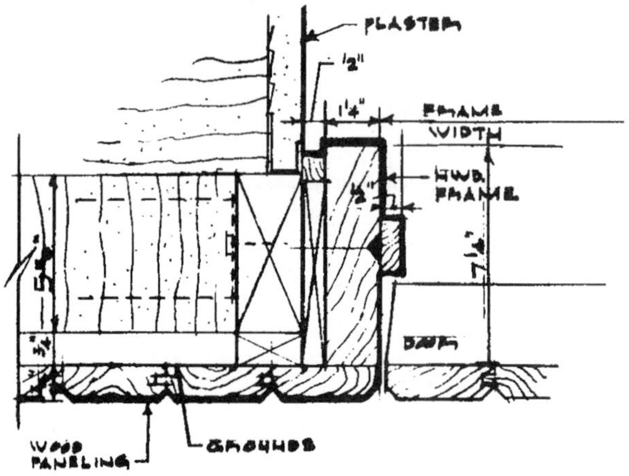

F-10 HARDWOOD FRAME
@ 3" = 1'-0"

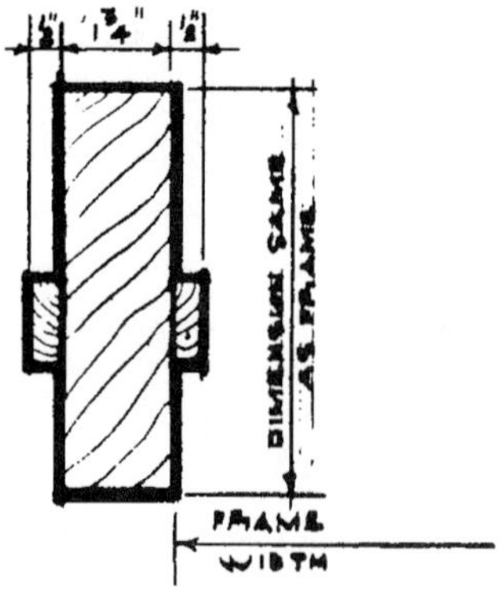

F-11 TYPICAL HARDWOOD MULLION
@ 3" = 1'-0"

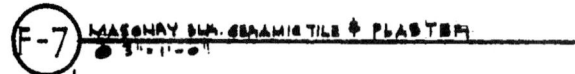

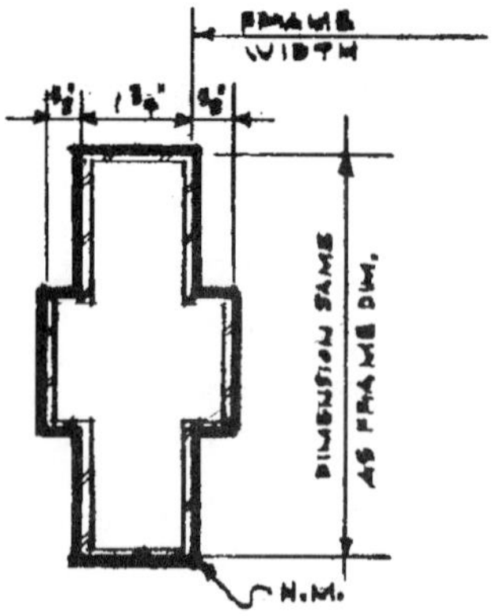

F-12 TYPICAL H.M. MULLION
@ 3" = 1'-0"

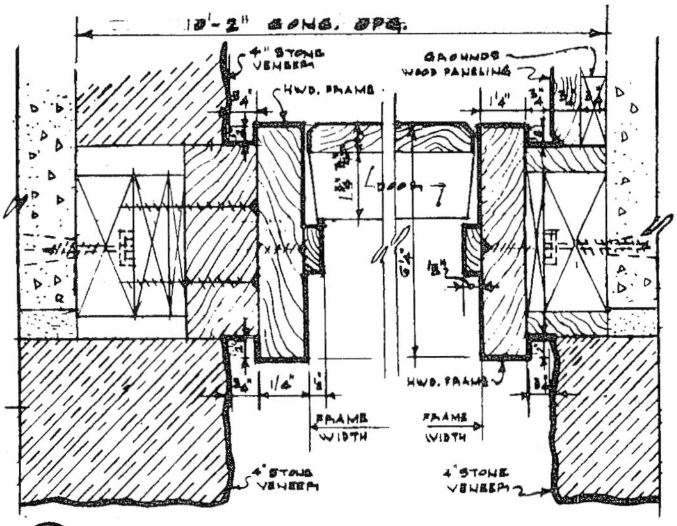

F-13 HARDWOOD FRAME
@ 3"=1'-0"

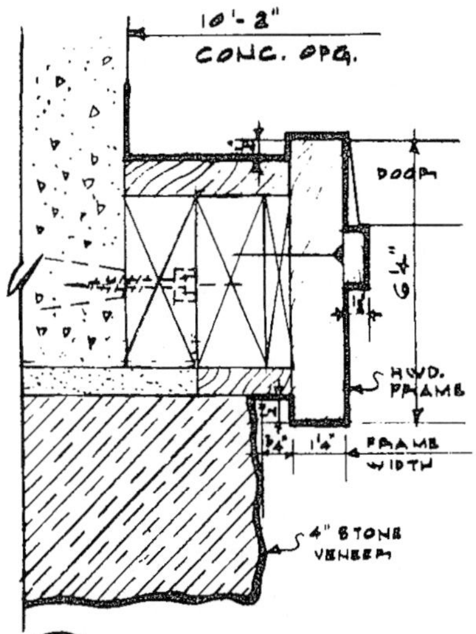

F-14 HARDWOOD FRAME
@ 3"=1'-0"

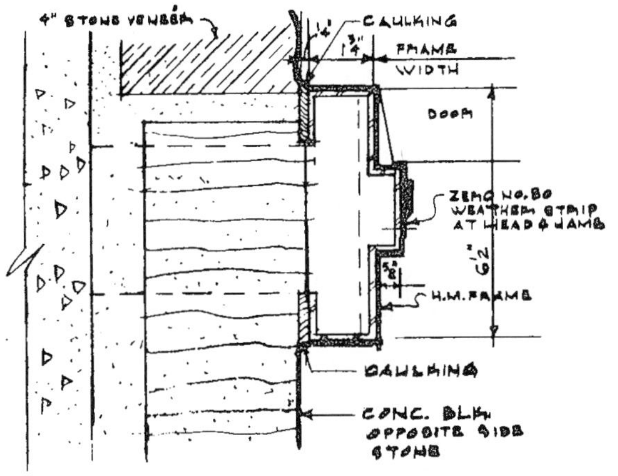

F-15 EXTERIOR HOLLOW METAL FRAME
@ 3"=1'-0"

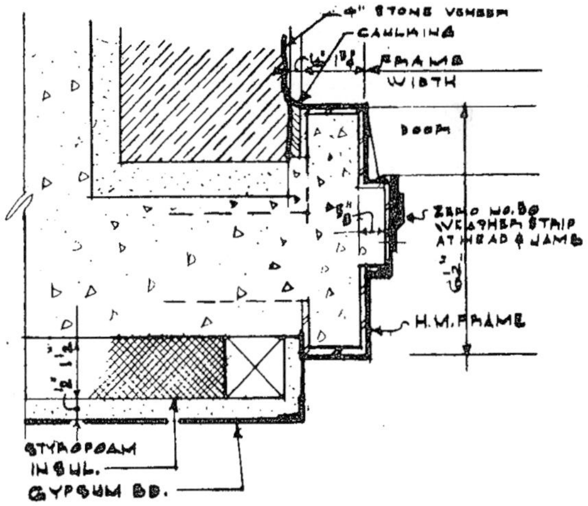

F-16 EXTERIOR HOLLOW METAL FRAME
@ 3"=1'-0"

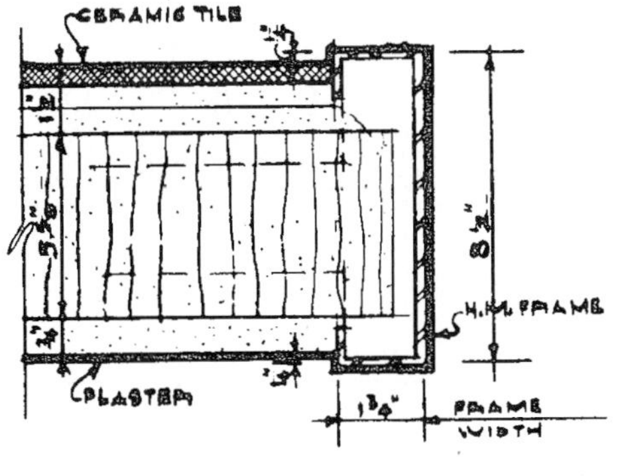

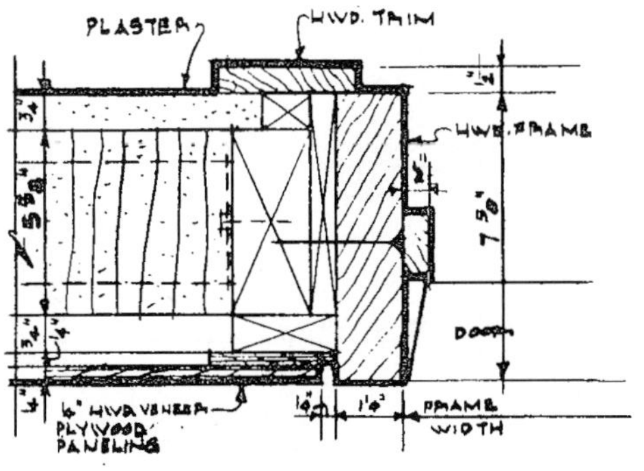

F-18 HARDWOOD FRAME
@ 3"=1'-0"

F-17 TRIMMED OPG. MASONRY BLK. CERAMIC TILE
& PLASTER @ 3"=1'-0"

DOORS

Hollow Metal and Wood Door Frames

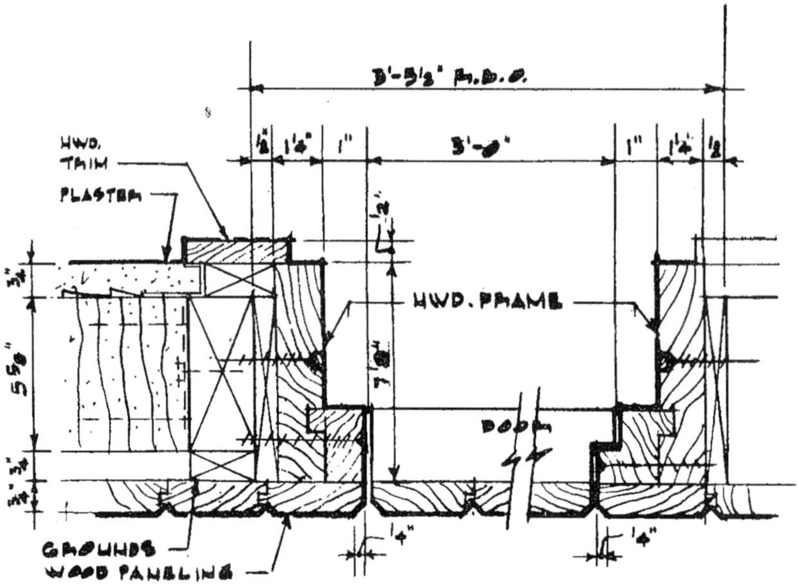

(F-25) HARDWOOD FRAME
@ 3" = 1'-0"

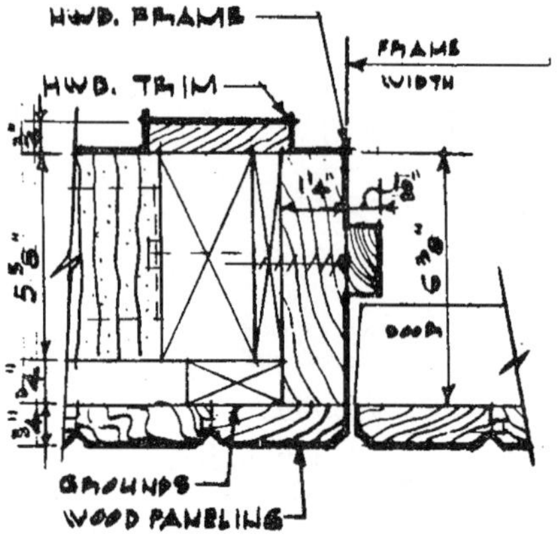

(F-26) HARDWOOD FRAME
@ 3" = 1'-0"

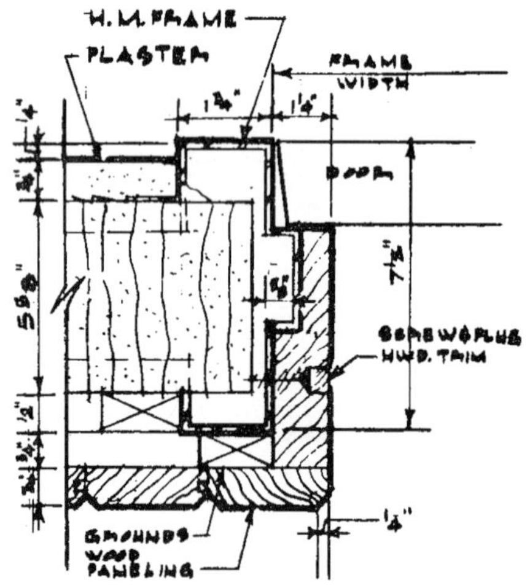

(F-27) H.M. FRAME – HWD. COVERING
@ 3" = 1'-0"

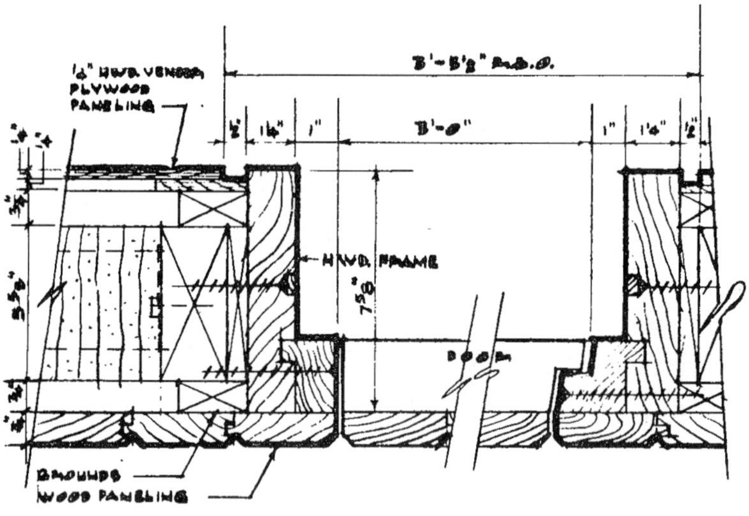

(F-28) HARDWOOD FRAME
@ 3" = 1'-0"

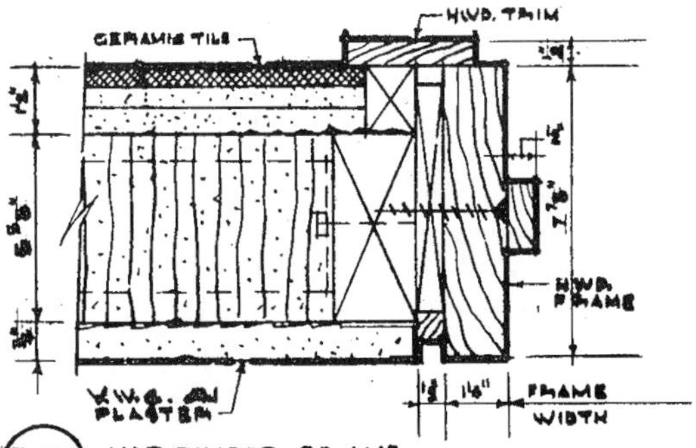

F-29 HARDWOOD FRAME @ 3"=1'-0"

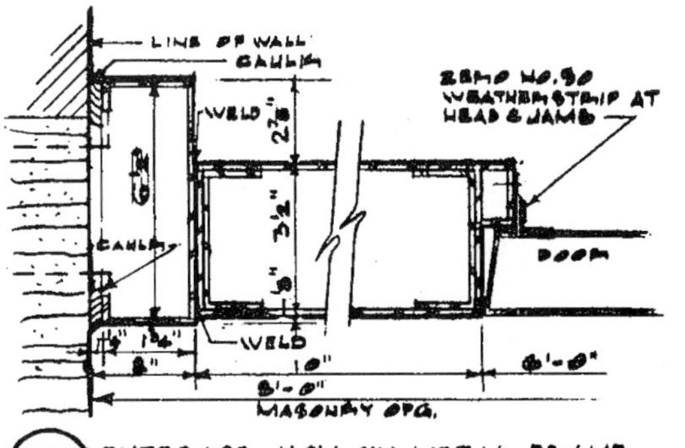

F-30 EXTERIOR HOLLOW METAL FRAME @ 3"=1'-0"

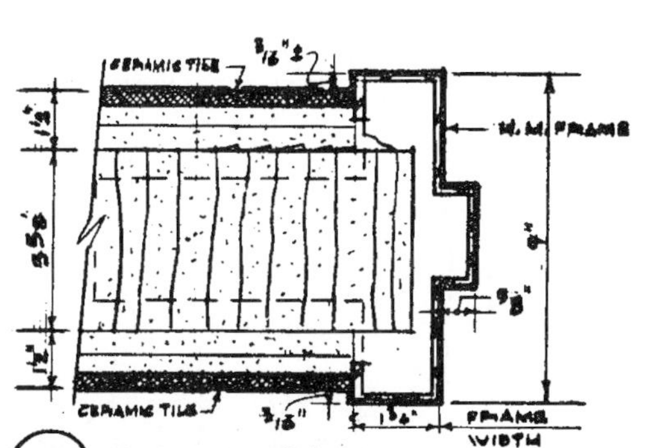

F-31 HOLLOW METAL FRAME @ 3"=1'-0"

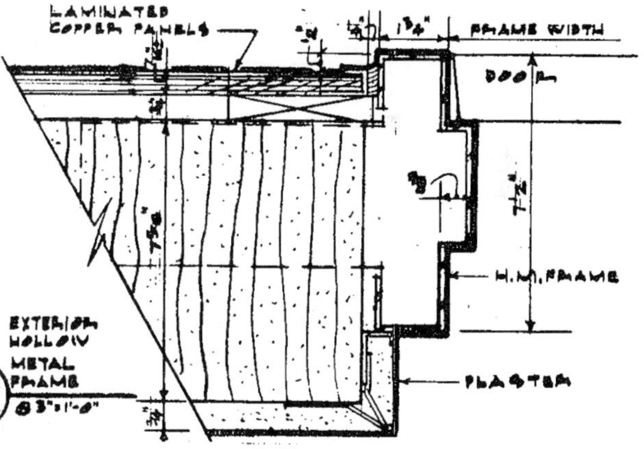

F-32 EXTERIOR HOLLOW METAL FRAME @ 3"=1'-0"

DOORS

Hollow Metal and Wood Door Types

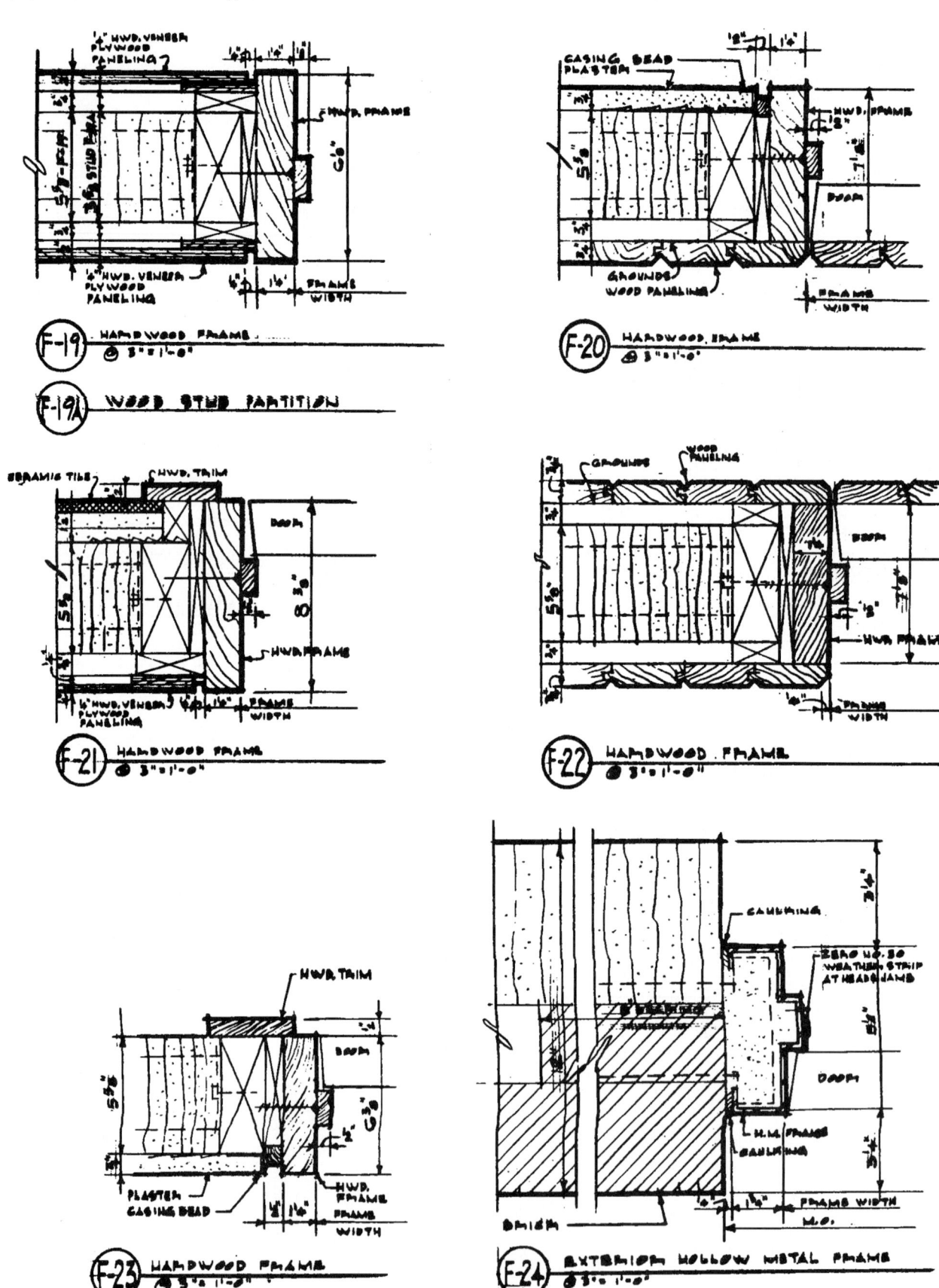

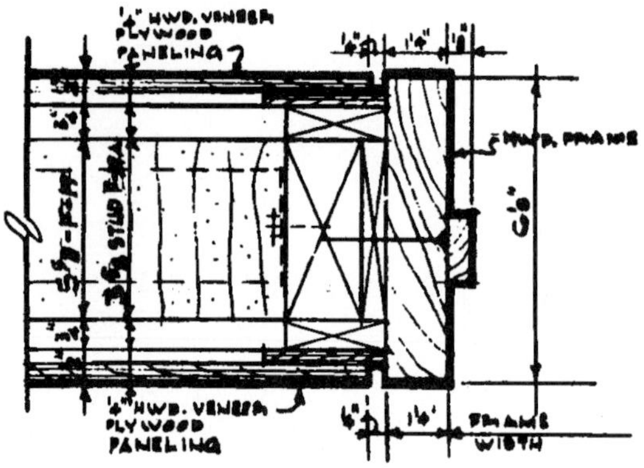

F-19 HARDWOOD FRAME @ 3"=1'-0"

F-19A WOOD STUD PARTITION

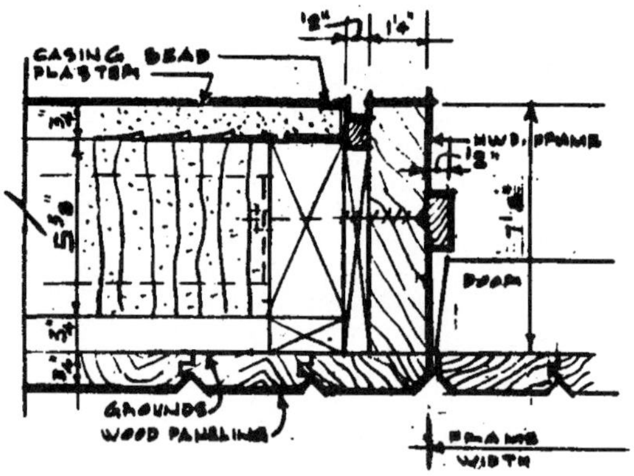

F-20 HARDWOOD FRAME @ 3"=1'-0"

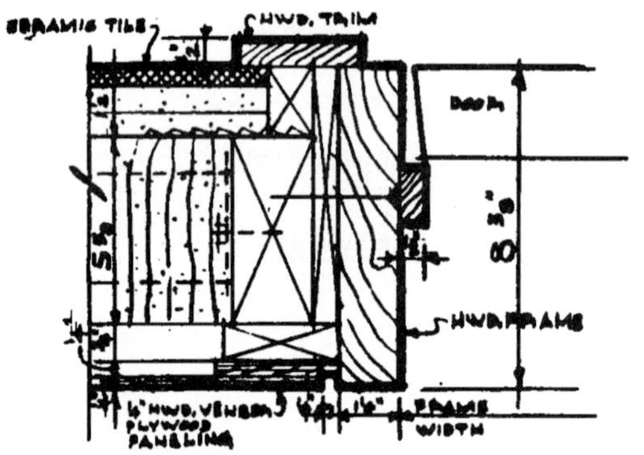

F-21 HARDWOOD FRAME @ 3"=1'-0"

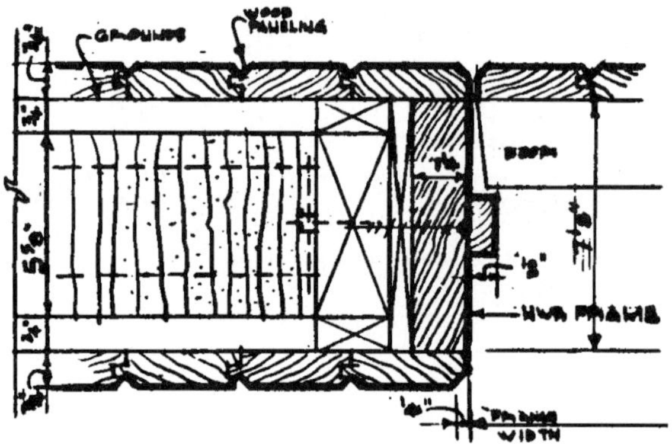

F-22 HARDWOOD FRAME @ 3"=1'-0"

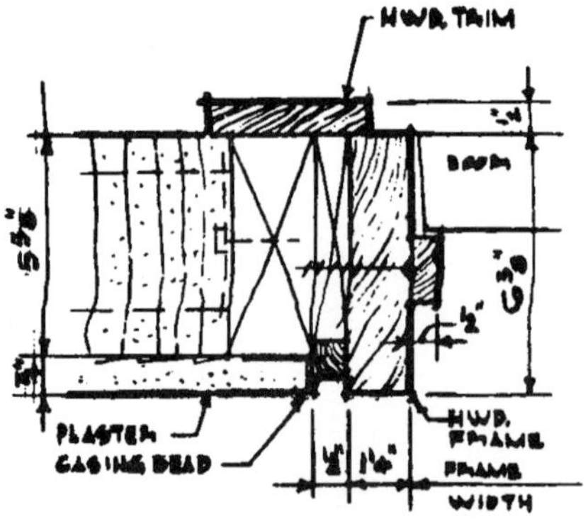

F-23 HARDWOOD FRAME @ 3"=1'-0"

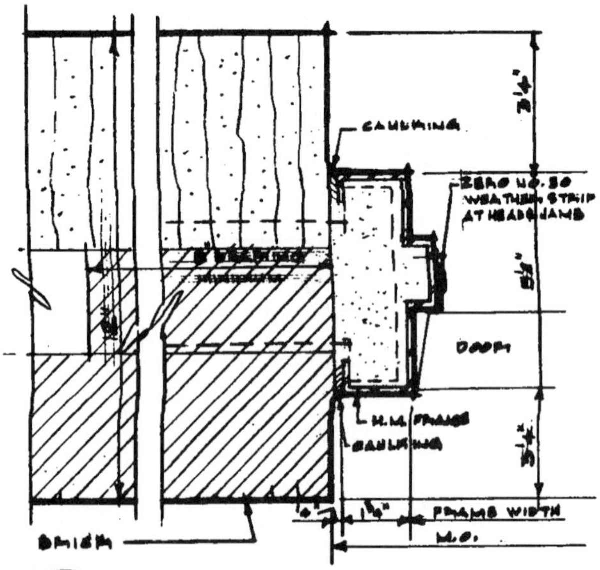

F-24 EXTERIOR HOLLOW METAL FRAME @ 3"=1'-0"

DOORS

Door Types

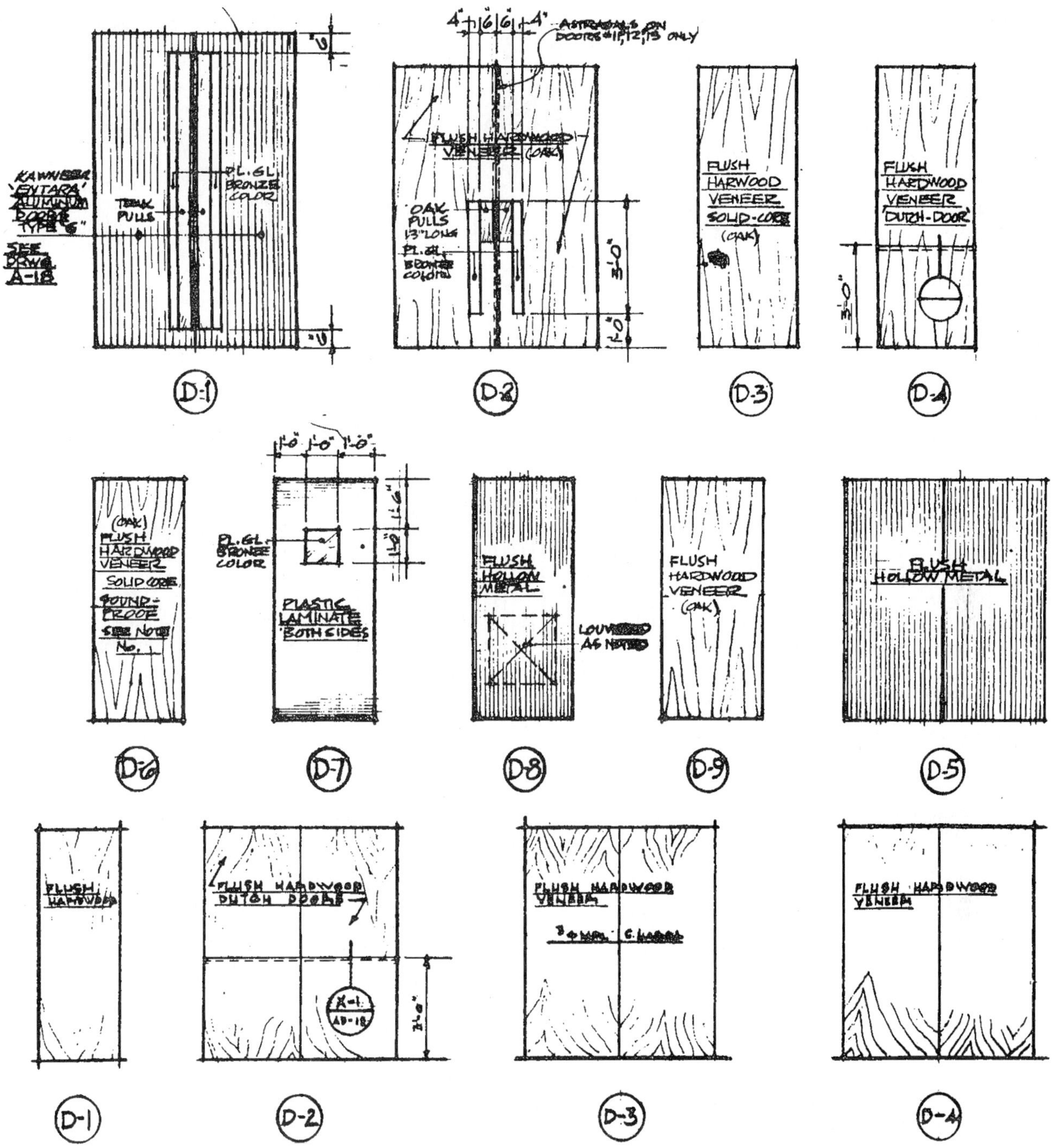

DOORS

Door Types

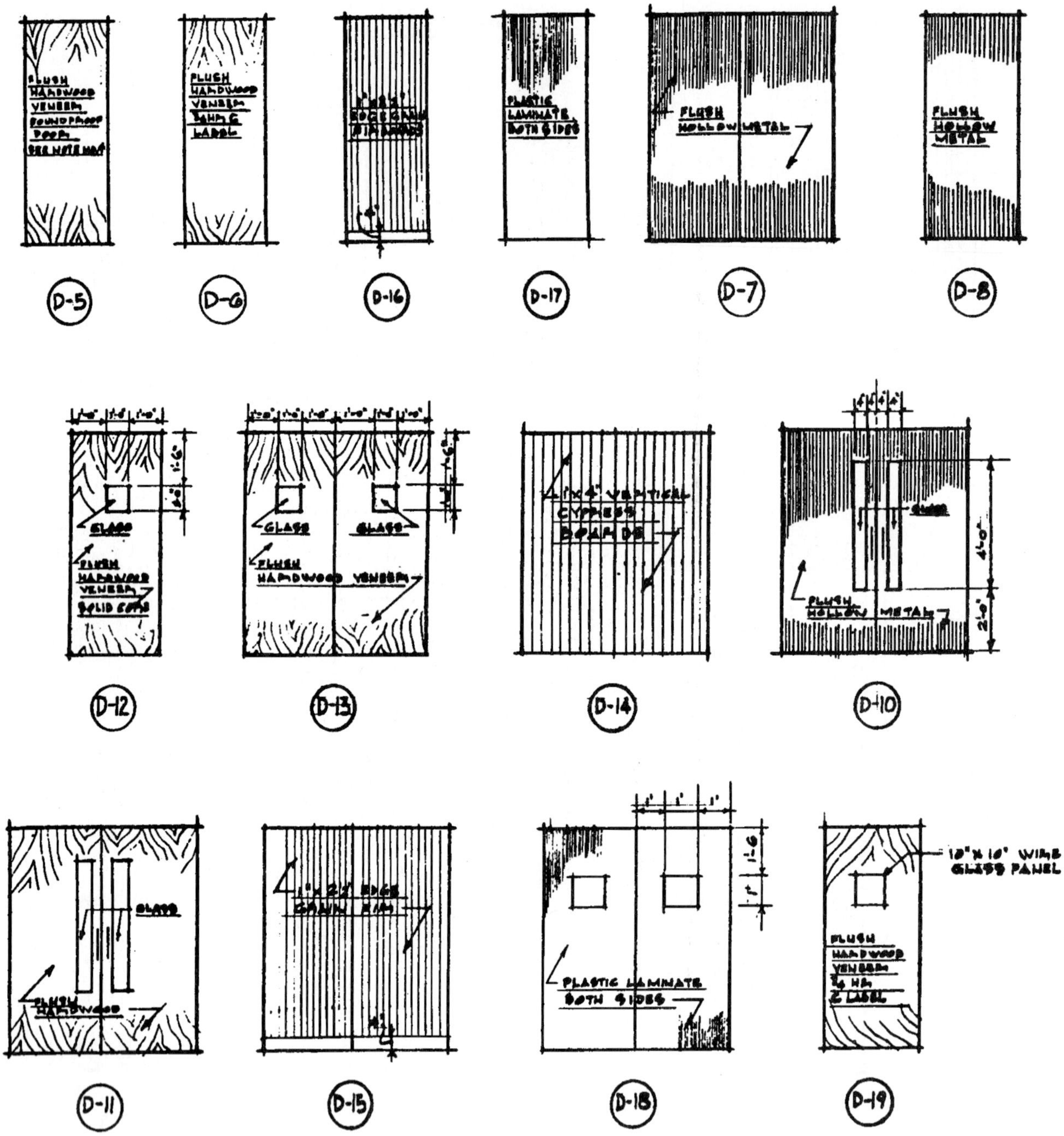

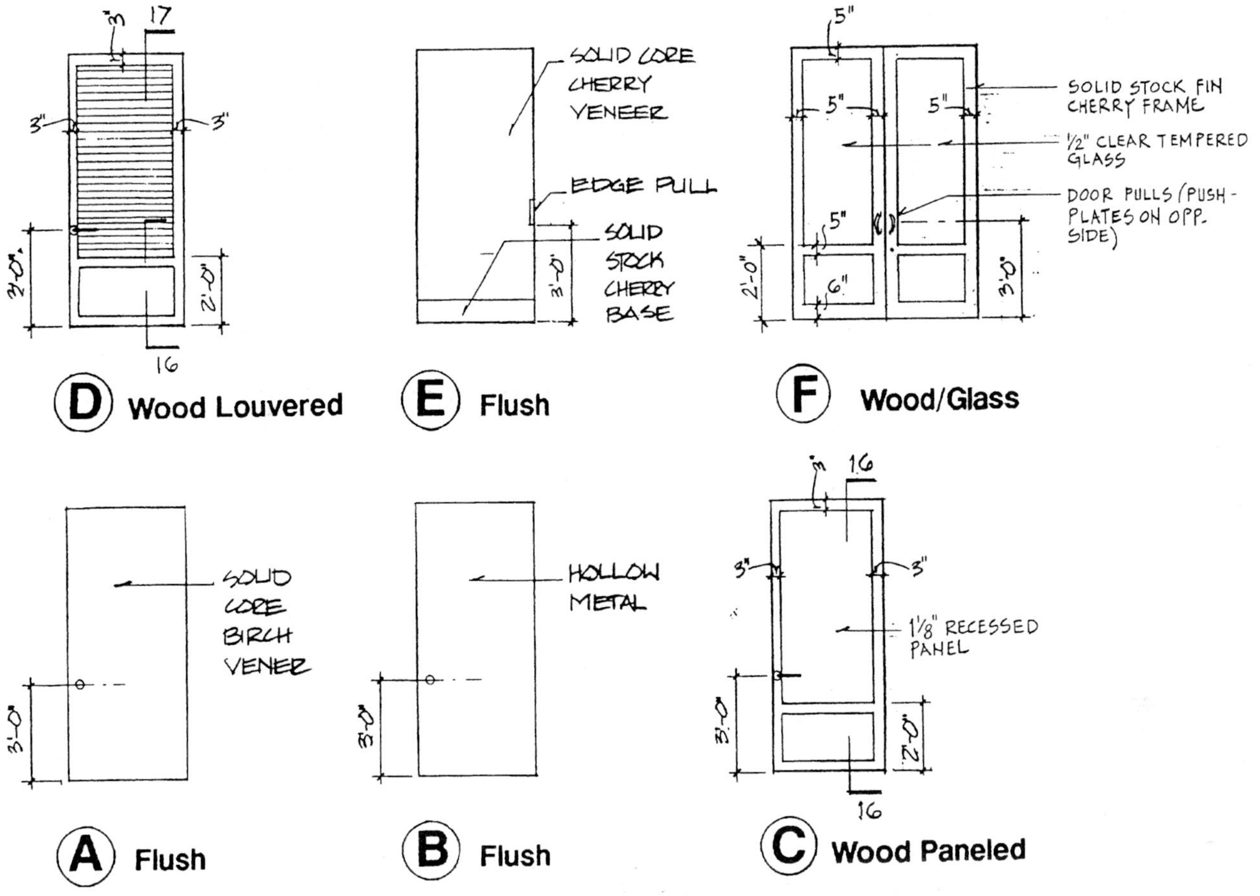

14 | Door Types

No Scale

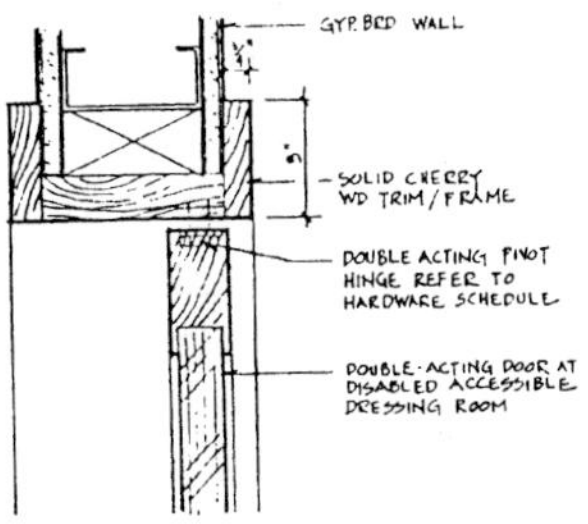

13 | Head

3" = 1'-0"

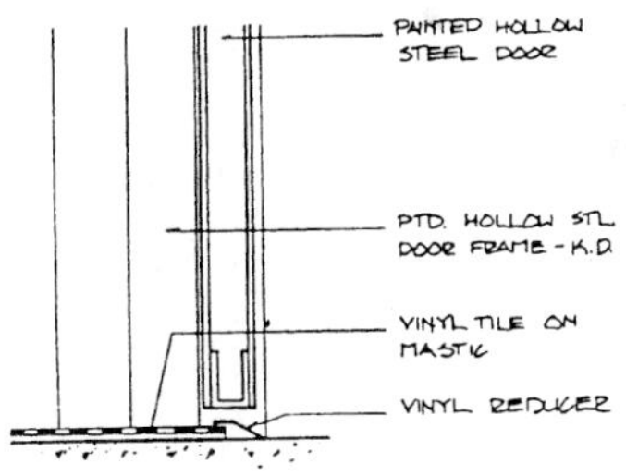

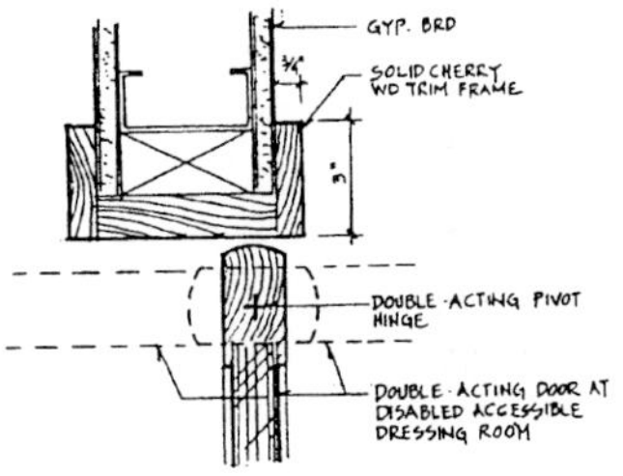

15 | Jamb

3" = 1'-0"

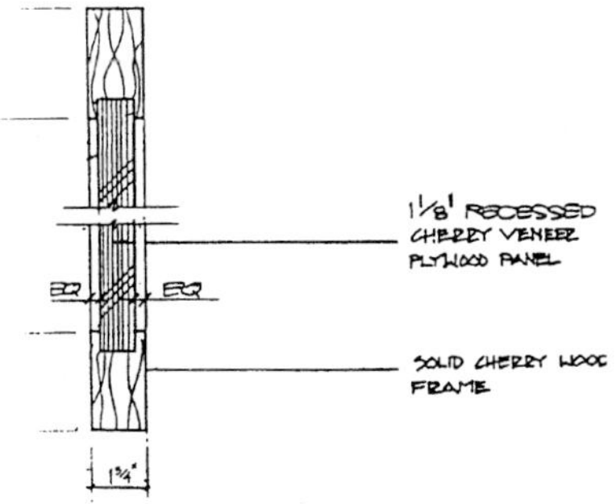

16 | SECT: Wood Paneled Door

3" = 1'-0"

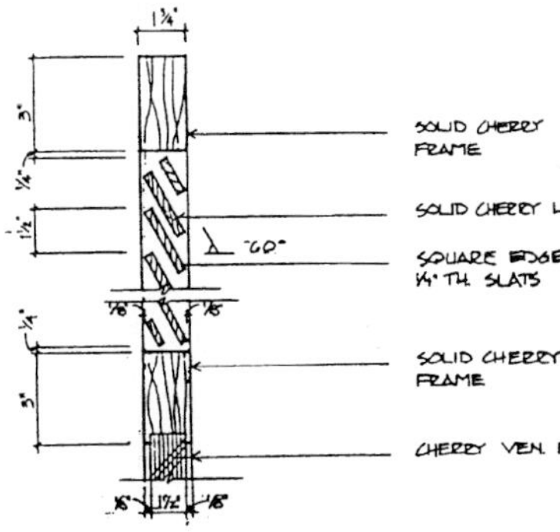

17 | SECT: Wood Louvered Door

3" = 1'-0"

DOORS
Door Types and Details

DOOR TYPES

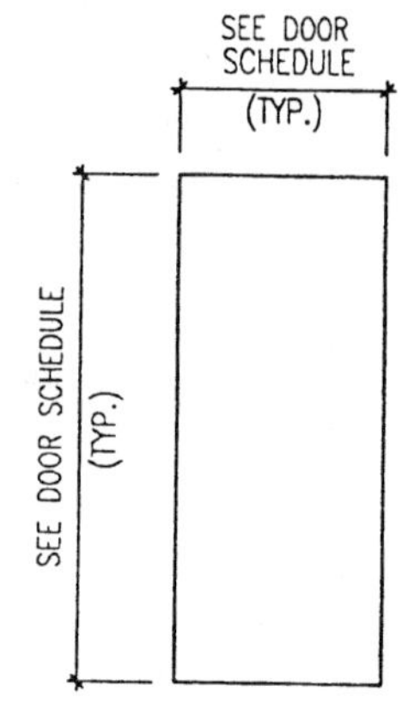

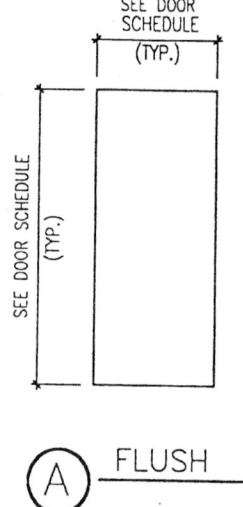

(A) FLUSH

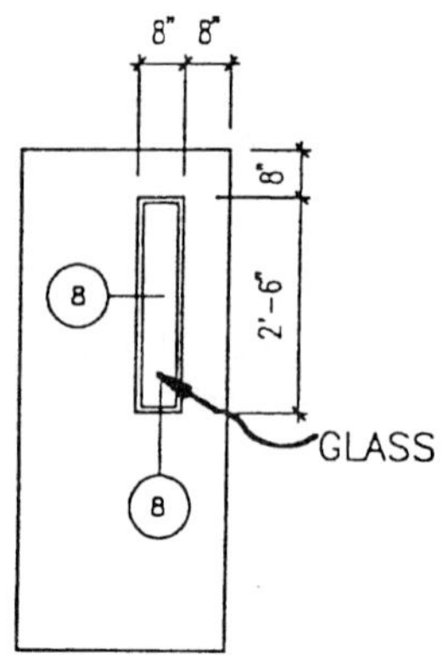

(B) VISION PANEL

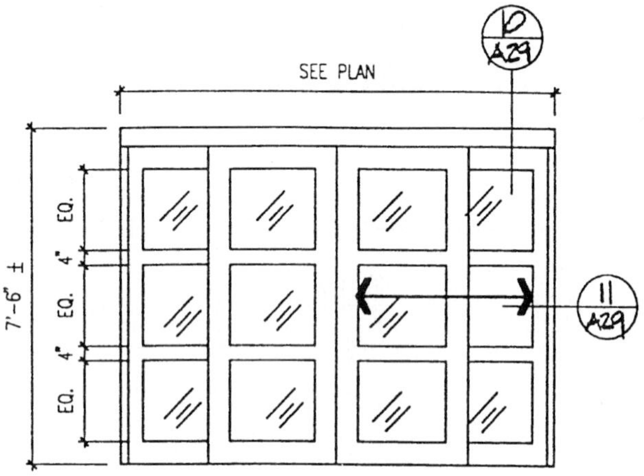

(C) BI–PARTING AUTO–SLIDING ALUM & GLASS DOOR

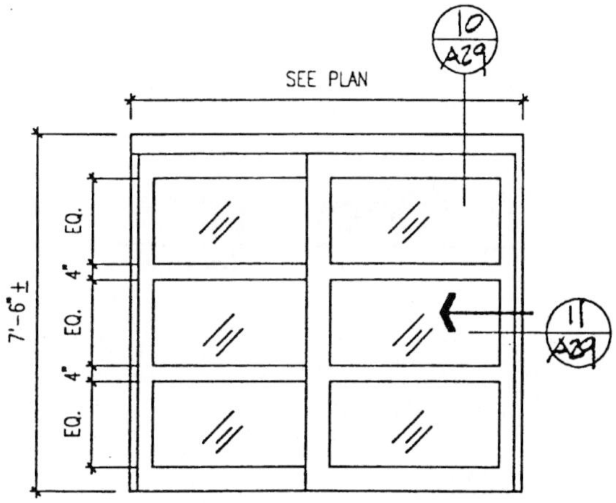

(D) SINGLE AUTO–SLIDING ALUM & GLASS DOOR

NOTE: SEE ARCHITECTURAL ELEVATIONS FOR GLASS TYPES

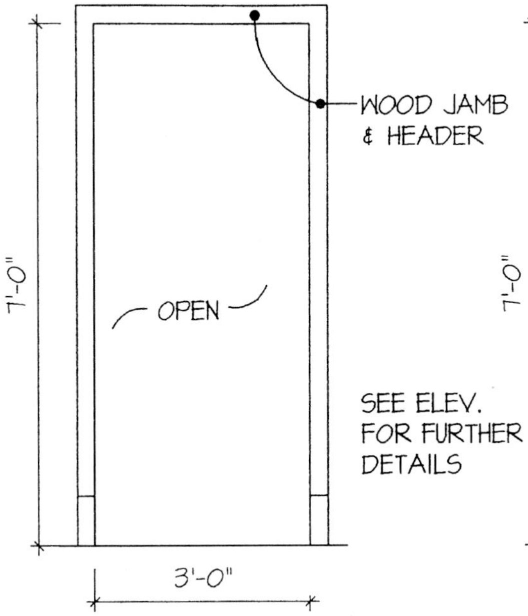

WOOD JAMB
& HEADER
7'-0"
OPEN
SEE ELEV.
FOR FURTHER
DETAILS
3'-0"
TYPE 2
SCALE 1/2'=1'-0"
WOOD JAMB
& HEADER
7'-0"
LOCK SET
3'-2"
SEE ELEV.
FOR FURTHER
DETAILS
1'-6"
1'-6"
TYPE 3
SCALE 1/2'=1'-0"
DECORATIVE
GLASS TRANSOM
WOOD JAMB
& HEADER
WOOD DOOR
W/ 1/8" QUIRK
DIAMOND
PATTERN
7'-0"
LOCK SET
3'-2"
SEE ELEV.
FOR FURTHER
DETAILS
3'-0"
TYPE 4
SCALE 1/2'=1'-0"
WOOD JAMB
& HEADER
FLUSH WOOD
DOOR
7'-0"
LOCK SET
3'-2"
SEE ELEV.
FOR FURTHER
DETAILS
3'-0"
TYPE 5
SCALE 1/2'=1'-0"

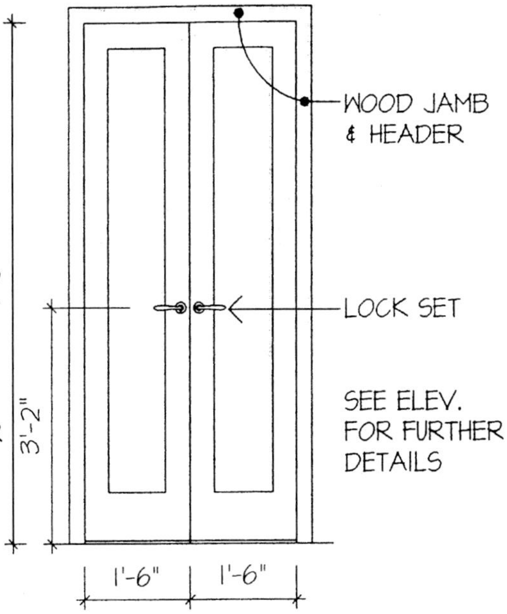

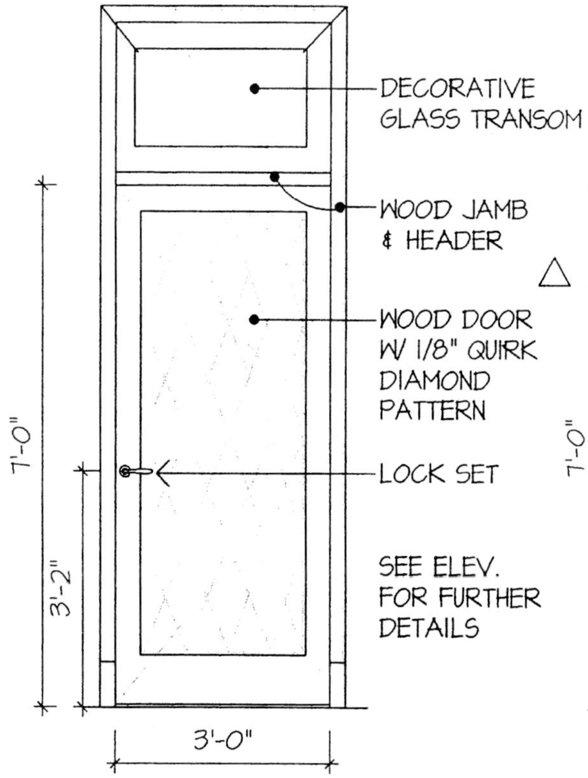

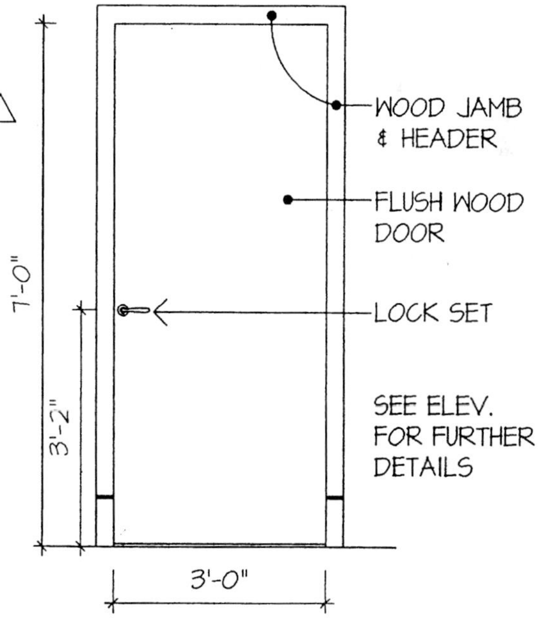

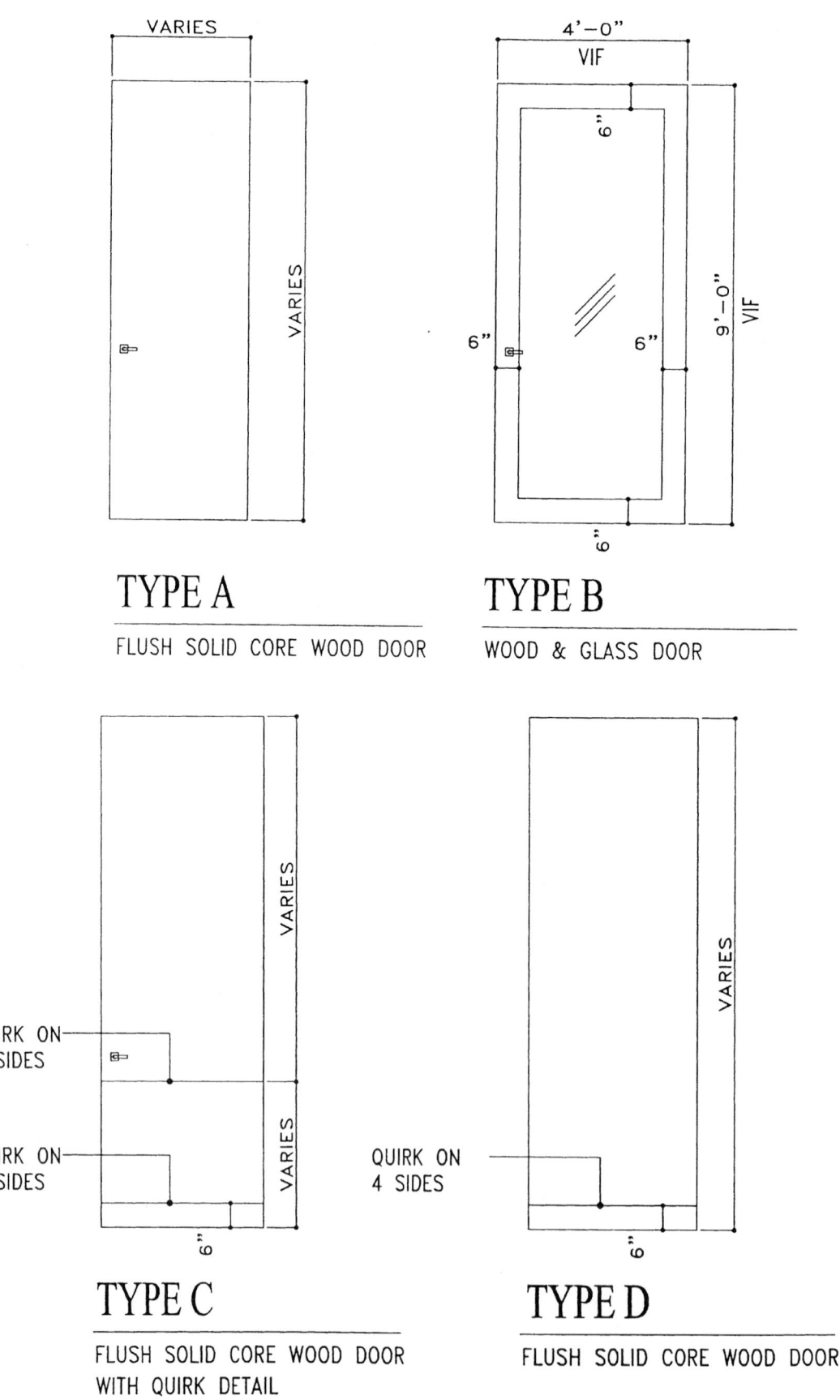

DOORS
Door Types and Details

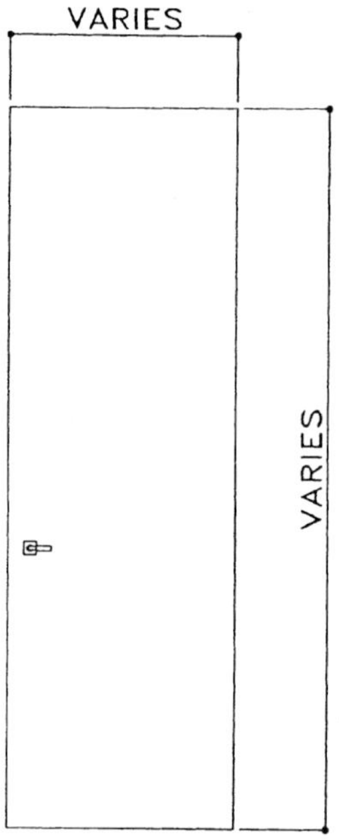

TYPE A

FLUSH SOLID CORE WOOD DOOR

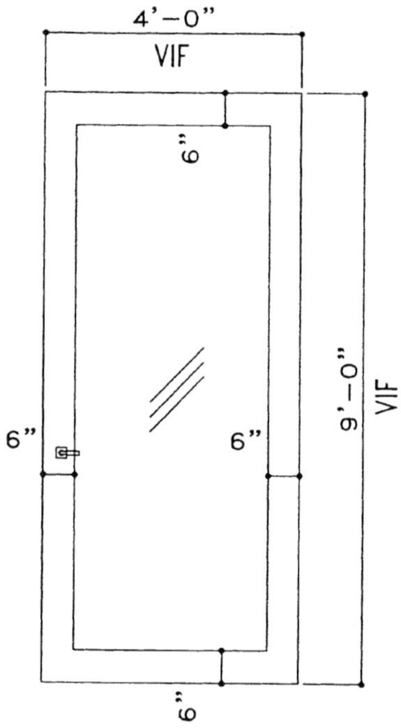

TYPE B

WOOD & GLASS DOOR

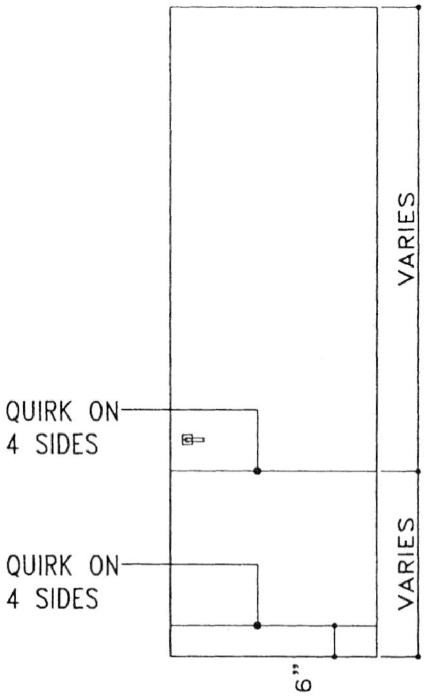

TYPE C

FLUSH SOLID CORE WOOD DOOR
WITH QUIRK DETAIL

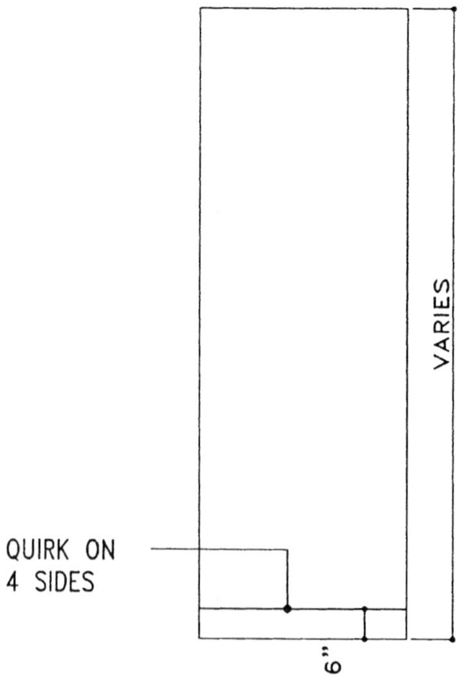

TYPE D

FLUSH SOLID CORE WOOD DOOR

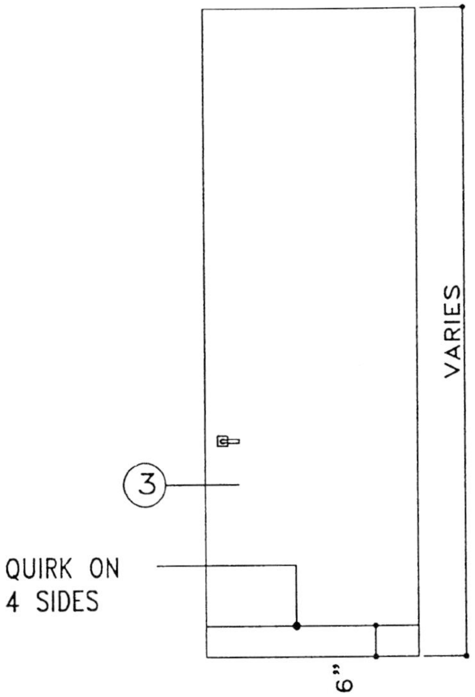

TYPE E

FLUSH SOLID CORE WOOD DOOR
CUSTOM MITRED EDGE DETAIL
ONE SIDE ONLY

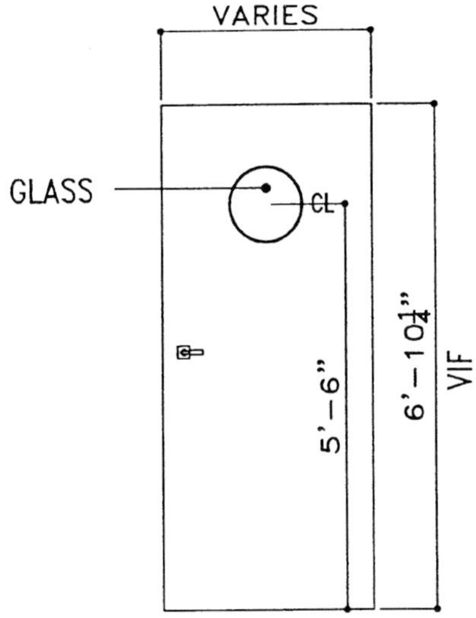

TYPE F

STAINLESS STEEL CLAD
SOLID CORE DOOR

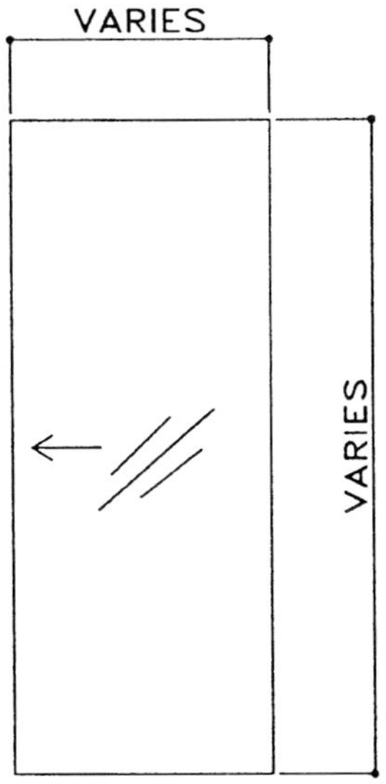

TYPE G

FRAMELESS GLASS DOOR

DOORS

Hollow Metal Door Hardware: Hinges

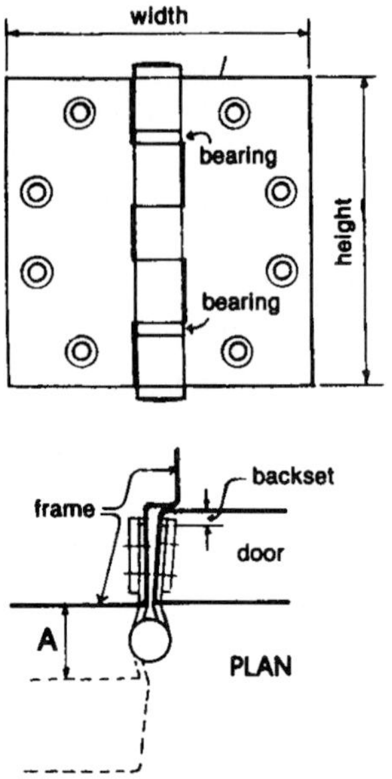

FULL MORTISE BUTT HINGE

Two equal square-edged leaves, one mortised into door edge, the other into frame rabbet.
Two bearings, as shown, on regular weight hinges, four on heavy weight.

Typical Uses:

By far the most common type of hinge for both interior and exterior hollow metal and wood swing doors, in all types of buildings.

Usual Sizes (see NOTE below):

heights — 4½"; 5" for doors over 36" w.
widths — 4½" for 1¾" door and 1½" trim clearance (dimension A); 5" (or more) for thicker doors or larger clearances.

HALF MORTISE BUTT HINGE

One square-edged leaf mortised into door edge; the other leaf, bevel-edged, mounted on face of frame.

Typical Uses:

Used with hollow metal or kalamein doors in structural channel frames, usually in industrial type buildings.

Usual Sizes:

4½", 5" and 6" heights.

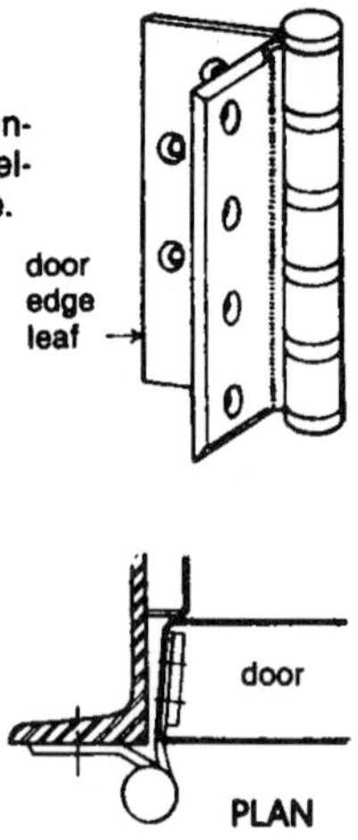

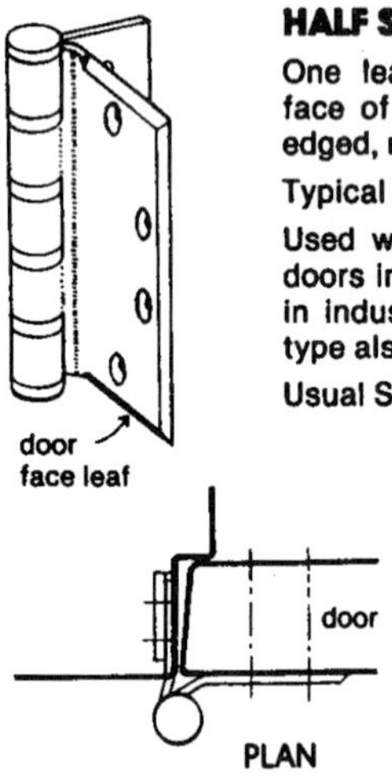

HALF SURFACE BUTT HINGE

One leaf, bevel-edged, mounted on face of door; the other leaf, square-edged, mortised into frame rabbet.

Typical Uses:

Used with hollow metal or kalamein doors in hollow metal frames, usually in industrial buildings. Heavy weight type also used on lead-lined doors.

Usual Sizes: 4½", 5" and 6" heights.

FULL SURFACE BUTT HINGE

Two bevel-edged leaves of differing widths, one surface-mounted on door face, the other on frame face.

Typical Uses:

Used with hollow metal or kalamein doors in structural channel frames, in industrial buildings. Heavy weight type may be used on lead-lined doors.

Usual Sizes: 4½", 5" and 6" heights.

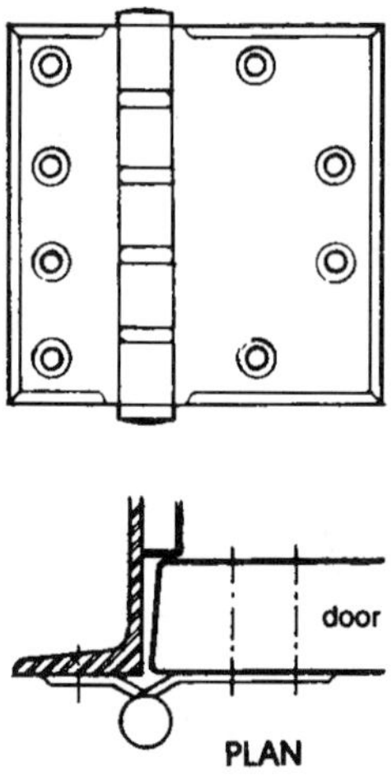

NOTE: Anchor hinges and pivot hinges should be specified for heavy doors and doors with high frequency use, such as entrances to large department stores, office buildings, theaters, banks and schools, or to toilet rooms in schools and airport buildings. Regular weight hinges may be specified for doors with average and low frequency uses such as corridor doors in public buildings and doors in residential buildings.

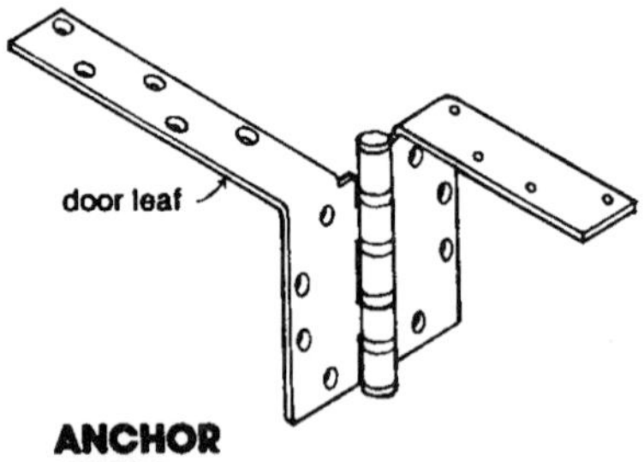

ANCHOR HINGE

Heavy weight hinge with each leaf extended at its top edge and bent to form a flange that fastens to top edge of door and to frame head rabbet. May be used as top hinge on heavy doors and doors having high frequency usage.

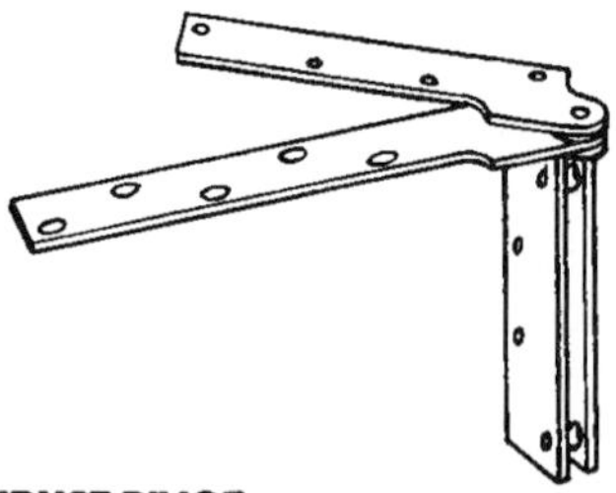

THRUST PIVOT UNIT AND HINGE SET

Pivot unit for top of door, with both jamb and top plates for both door and frame. Used, with conventional butt hinges, on wide doors that may be subjected to abnormal abuse. The hinge is almost invisible when door is closed.

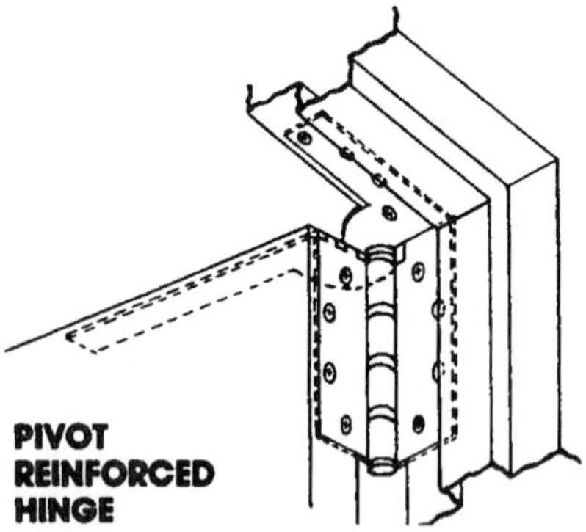

PIVOT REINFORCED HINGE

Heavy weight hinge with added pivot on the same pin. Leaves of pivot are interlocked with hinge leaves. Used with conventional butt hinges on doors subject to abnormal abuse, particularly with overhead closers.

HOSPITAL "SWING CLEAR" TYPES

These hinges have their pins located approximately 2" beyond the door edge, providing an unobstructed clear frame opening width when the door is open 90°.

They are used on hospital corridor doors to patients' rooms, operating rooms, emergency rooms, or wherever a completely clear opening is required in hospitals, institutional or public buildings.

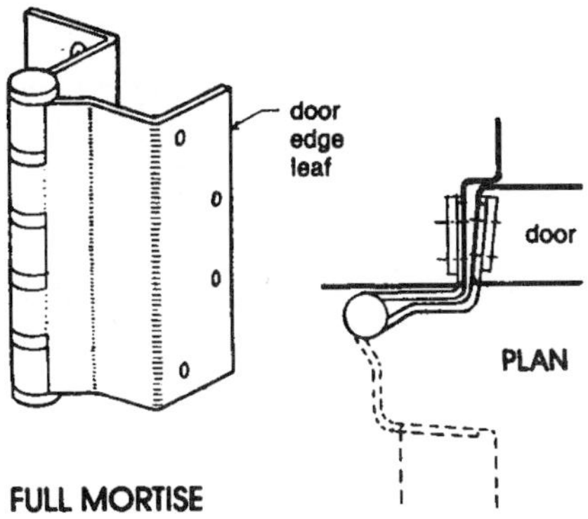

FULL MORTISE

Both leaves bent; one mortised into frame rabbet, the other into door edge.

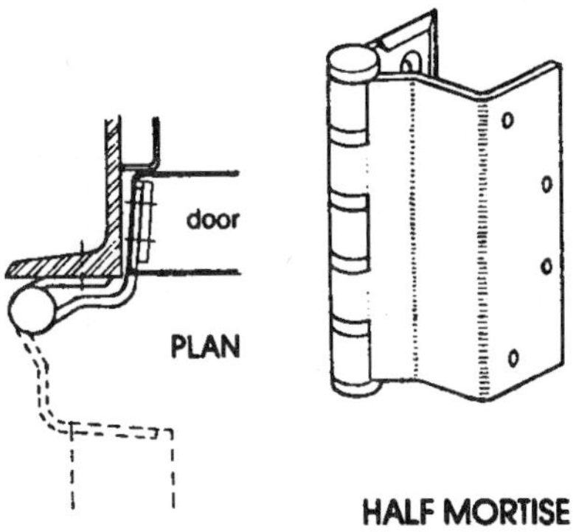

HALF MORTISE

One bent leaf mortised into edge of door, one flat, bevel-edged leaf surface-mounted on frame face.

Swing clear hinges are available only in heavy weight

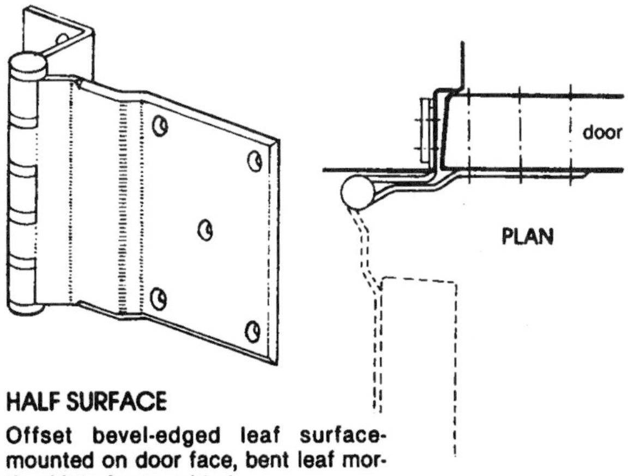

HALF SURFACE

Offset bevel-edged leaf surface-mounted on door face, bent leaf mortised into frame rabbet.

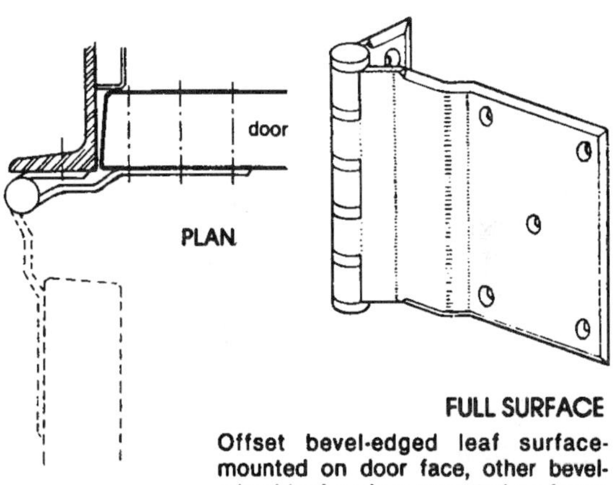

FULL SURFACE

Offset bevel-edged leaf surface-mounted on door face, other bevel-edged leaf surface-mounted on frame face.

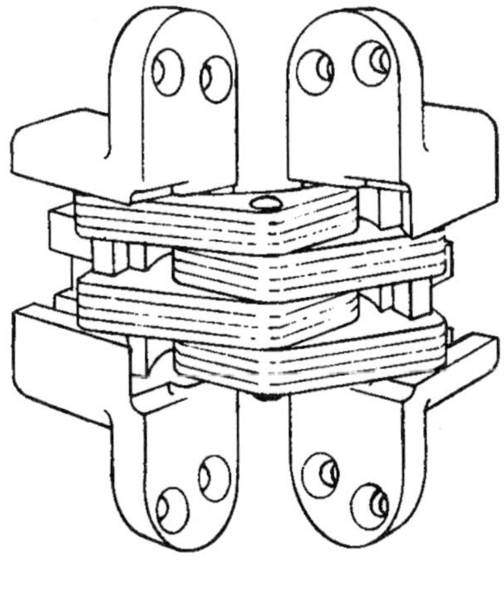

Full mortised, centered on door thickness. Hinge is completely concealed when door is closed.

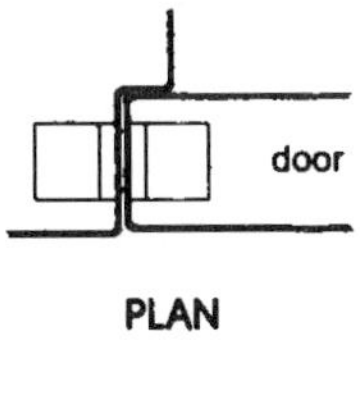

INVISIBLE HINGE

Full mortised; door leaf usually centered on door thickness. When door is closed, only the knuckle is visible.

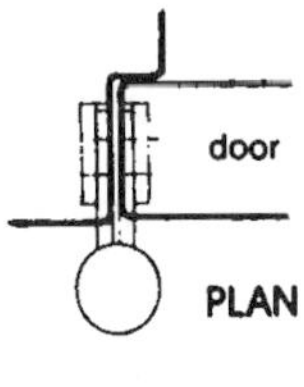

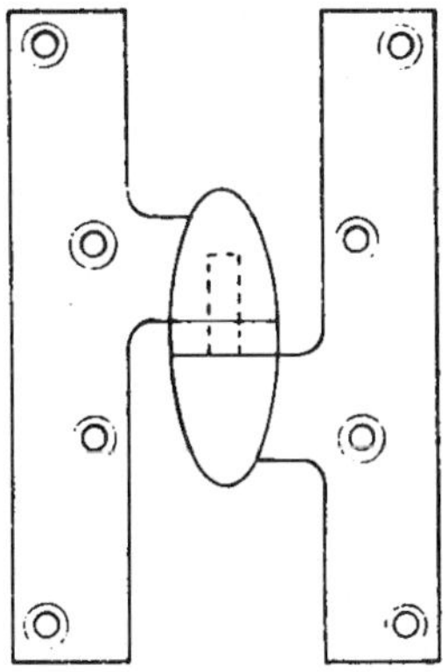

OLIVE KNUCKLE HINGE
(PAUMELLE HINGE SIMILAR)

DOORS

Hollow Metal Door Hardware: Pivots

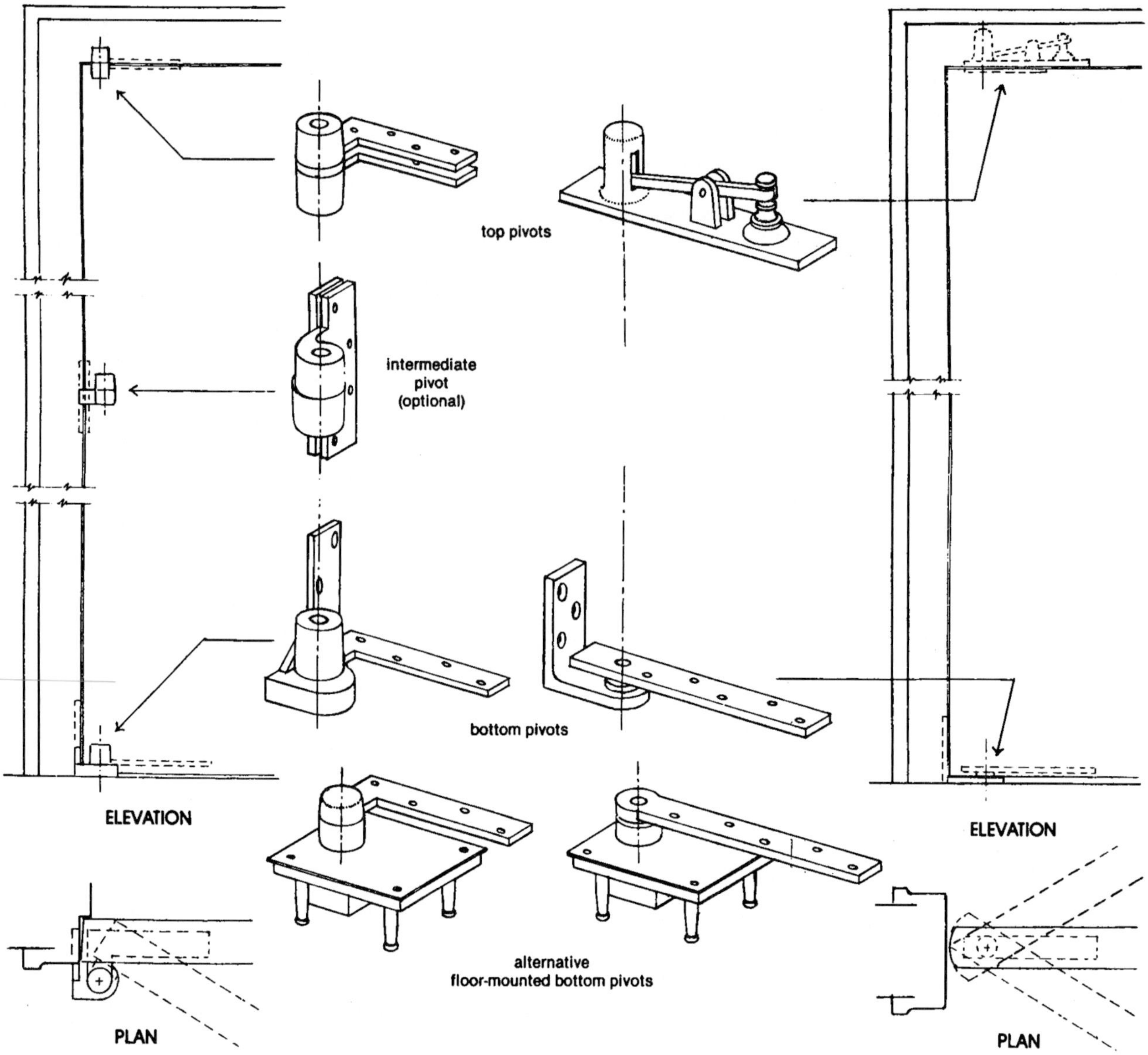

OFFSET TYPE

Used on single-acting doors only. Need for intermediate pivot depends upon the size, weight and usage of door; recommendation of hardware manufacturer should be followed. Pivot knuckles visible when door is closed.

CENTER TYPE

Used at top and bottom of double-acting doors only. Pivots are completely invisible when door is closed.

Pivots are stronger and more durable than hinges and are better able to withstand the racking stresses to which doors are subjected. Their use is generally recommended on oversize doors, on heavy doors such as lead-lined doors, and on entrance doors to public buildings such as schools, theaters, banks, stores, and office buildings.

NOTE: Because of adjustments that must be made during the installation of doors with bottom pivots, it is recommended that reinforcements be furnished in blank and that drilling and tapping be done in the field by the contractor.

LOCKS, LATCHES, AND DEADLOCKS

The selection of the proper lock type is very important. The types shown here are those most commonly used, but are by no means the only types available. Their names serve to identify either the type of lock construction or the type of installation. Mortise locks provide the greatest variety of lock functions, the best security, and excellent durability. Another popular type, with rugged construction and easily operated, is the preassembled lock, which is completely assembled at the factory. It does not have as many lock functions as the mortise lock, but can have a separate deadbolt. The bored lock is the least secured type and is not available with a separate deadbolt in the lock.

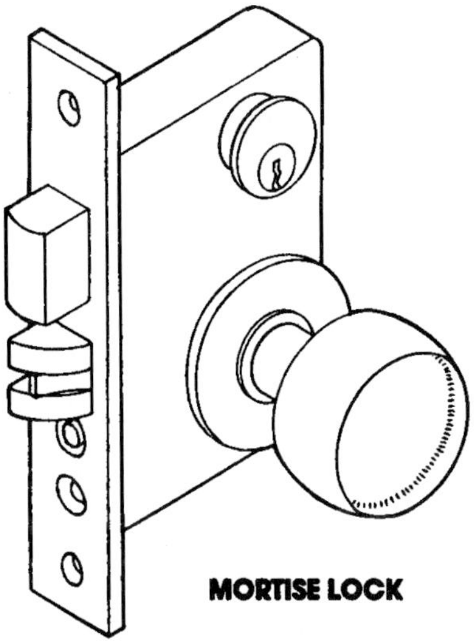

MORTISE LOCK

The mortise lock is so named because it is installed in a prepared recess (mortise) in the door. Working parts are contained in a rectangular case with holes for cylinder and knob spindle. Anti-friction split bolts are available for smooth retraction of the lock bolt. Lock front may be armored to protect against burglars getting at cylinder screws and lock fasteners. Lever handles may be used if desired, and trim may be either sectional or full plate.

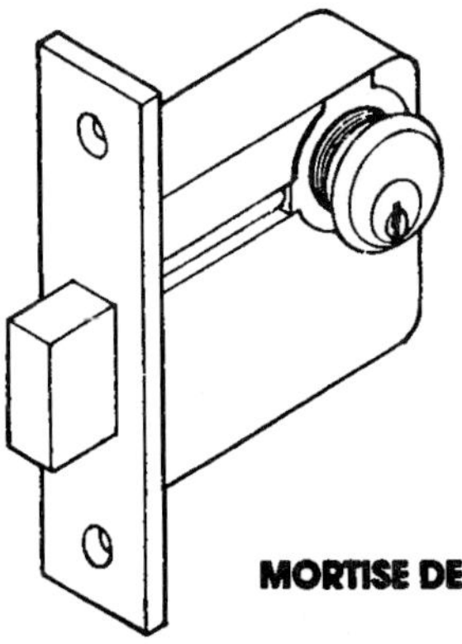

MORTISE DEADLOCK

This is a mortise lock with a deadlock only. (A deadlock is a lock bolt which has no bevel or spring action, and is operated by a key or thumb turn.) It is often used for locking a door having push or pull plates or for providing added security on doors with cylindrical locks.

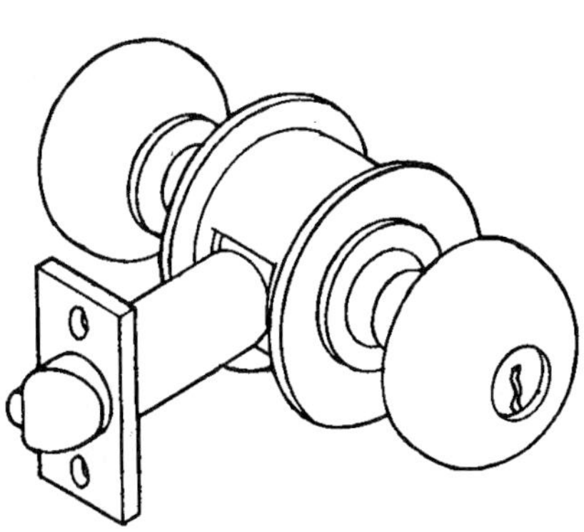

BORED (CYLINDRICAL) LOCK

This type of lock uses the key-in-the-knob principle. It is installed in a door having one hole bored through the thickness of the door and another bored in from the edge. The assembly must be tight on the door, without excessive play, to avoid binding.

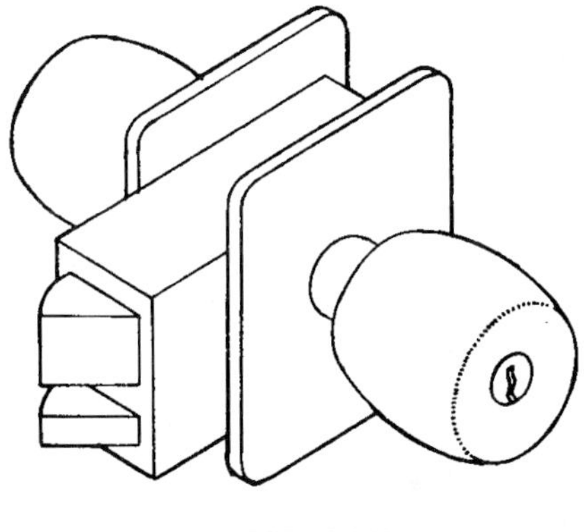

UNIT LOCK

This lock is preassembled in the factory and consists of a one-piece extruded or cast brass frame within which all parts are contained. It is installed in a rectangular reinforced notch cut in the door edge. Lever handles may be used in plaoe of knobs.

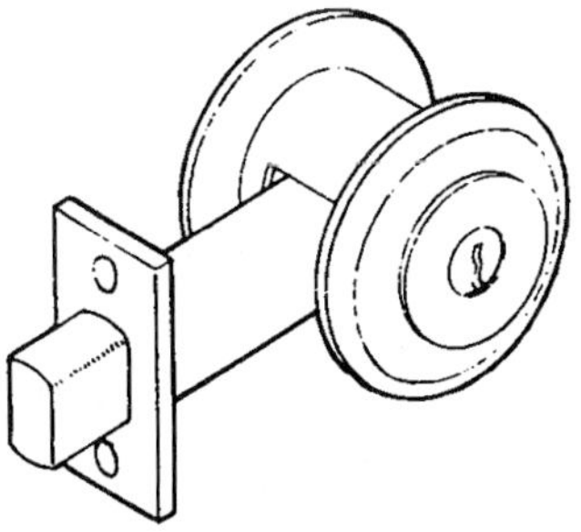

BORED (CYLINDRICAL) DEADLOCK

This is a cylindrical type of lock having a deadbolt only. It fits into the same type of cylindrical cutout as that required for the bored lock.

DOORS

Hollow Metal Door Hardware: Overhead Closers

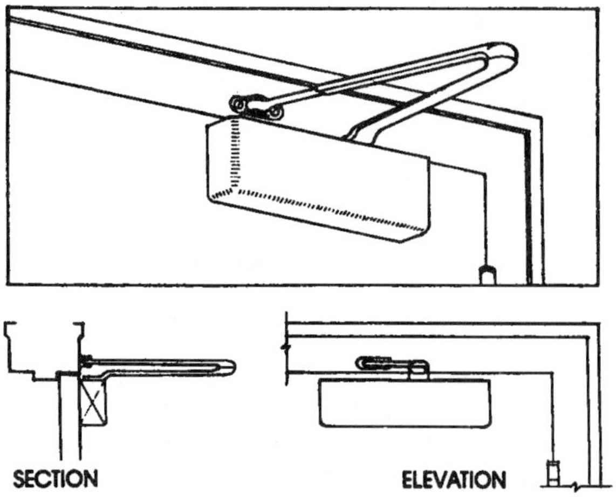

Fig. 3 Surface mounted, on hinge face of door

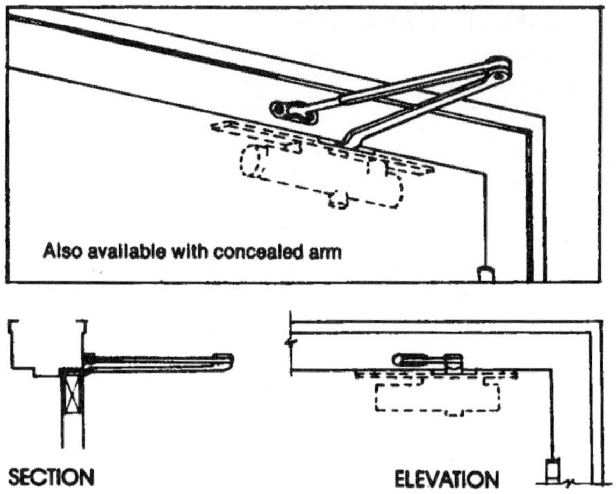

Fig. 4 Concealed in door, with exposed arm

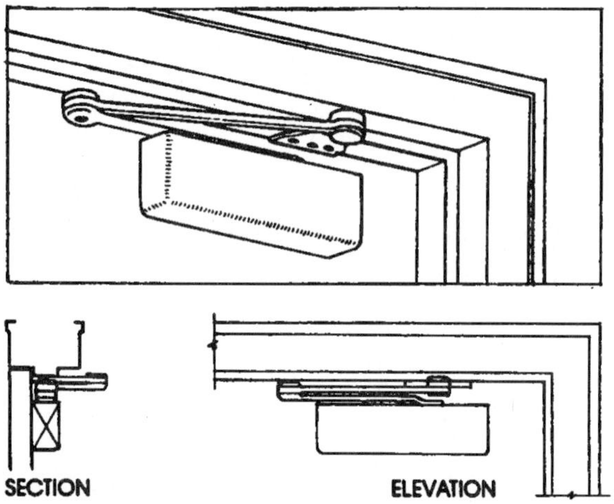

Fig. 5 Surface mounted, on stop face of door

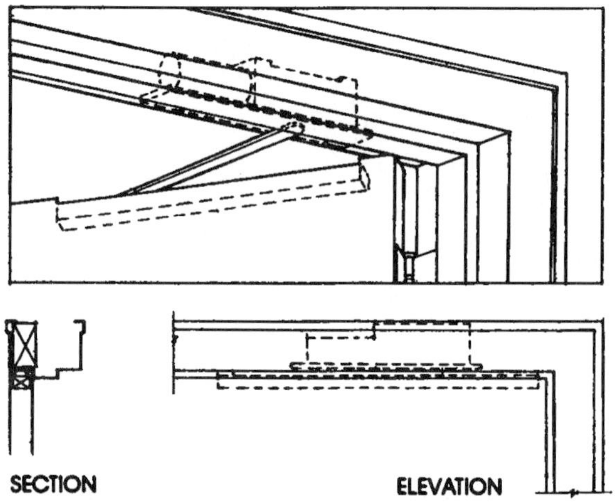

Fig. 6 Concealed in head, with concealed arm

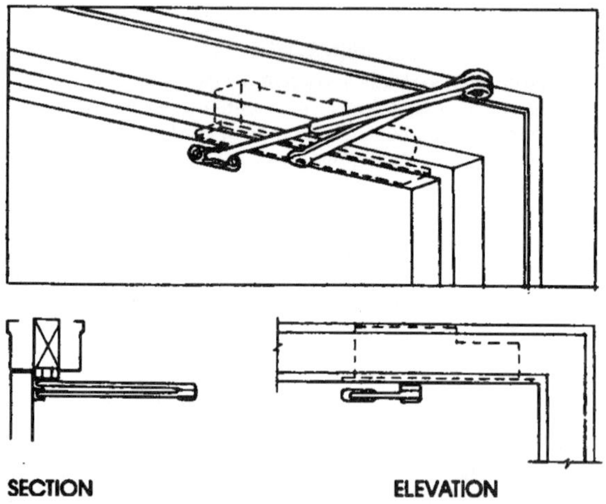

Fig. 7 Concealed in head, with exposed arm

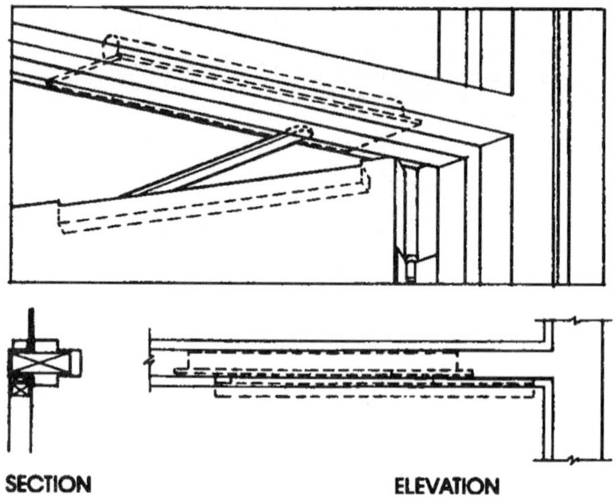

Fig. 8 Concealed in transom bar

Overhead and Floor Closers

Overhead closers (Figs. 3 to 8) are hydraulic devices, containing a piston, fluid chambers, and a spring. When the door is opened, the piston is pulled back, the spring is compressed, and the fluid is moved from one side of the piston to the other. With release of the door a reverse action takes place, closing the door. Closing speed is controlled by an adjustable valve or valves. Overhead closers may be installed on either single- or double-acting doors.

Floor closers, generally more durable than overhead closers, provide concealed closing mechanisms often appropriate for doors having a high frequency of use. As shown, the type of closer used depends on whether the door is hung on hinges, offset pivots, or center pivots.

Both overhead and floor closers are available in a range of sizes for various door sizes, locations, and job conditions. The manufacturer's recommendations should always be followed in determining which size and type should be used.

Where surface-mounted closers are specified, internal reinforcement plates shall be provided in the door and frame by the manufacturer. Drilling and tapping for the closer shall be done in the field by the installer. Only after the door is installed and adjusted can the closer be mounted for proper operation. If drilling and tapping have been done at the factory, the necessary field adjustments become difficult if not impossible.

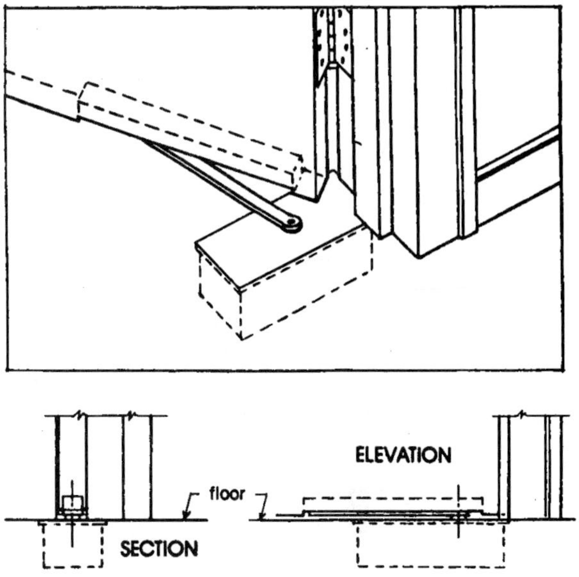

FOR HINGED DOORS

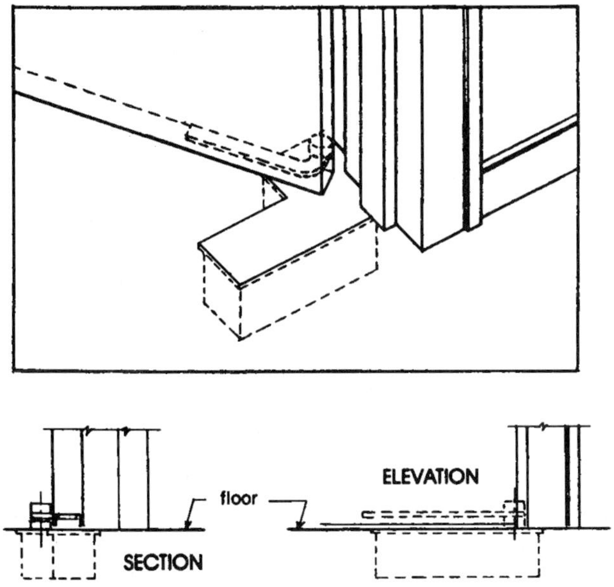

FOR OFFSET PIVOTED DOORS

single acting

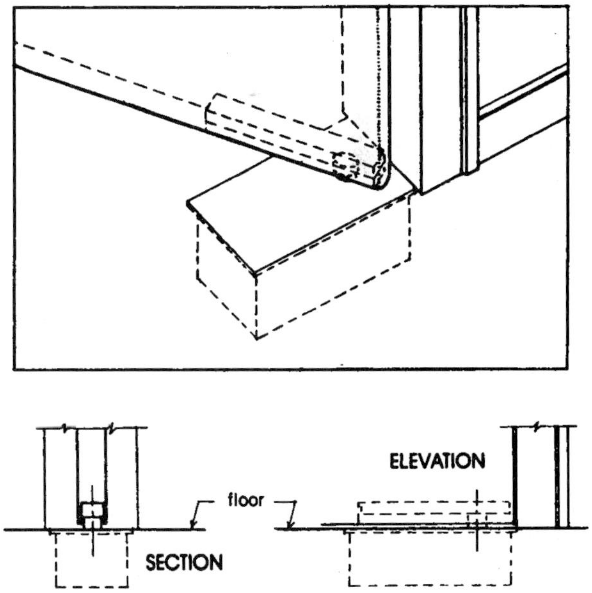

FOR CENTER PIVOTED DOORS

either single or double-acting

DOORS

Hollow Metal Door Hardware: Panic and Fire Exit Hardware

Types of Installation

Panic hardware is tested and labeled for casualty only; fire exit hardware, for both casualty and fire resistance. Only the latter may be used where fire-rated doors are required. Both types are always releasable from the inside by depressing the crash bar. The mortise type (Fig. 9) and the concealed vertical rod type (Fig. 10) are the least conspicuous, and either of these types is readily applicable to custom hollow metal doors.

Rim and mortise types are used on

- Single door
- Active door of pair
- Both doors of pair with mullion

Vertical rod types are used on

- Single door
- Active door of pair
- Both doors of pair

Where rim type (Fig. 11) or exposed vertical rod (Fig. 12) exit devices are specified, internal reinforcement plates shall be provided in the door and frame by the manufacturer. Drilling and tapping for trim and mounting plates shall be done in the field by the installer. The hardware can then be more readily adjusted for best operation.

In preparing the door for a lock, the drilling of three bolt holes (½ in diameter or less) and/or the drilling and tapping for sectional or full trim plates shall be done in the field by the installer and not at the factory. After the lock is installed and adjusted, the trim plate can be applied to suit the final position of the latching device. If through-bolt holes or tapped holes are provided at the factory, this adjustment becomes difficult, if not impossible.

The manufacturer shall drill for all function holes—cylinder, turn piece, and knob.

Door Coordinators

Coordinators (Figs. 13 and 14) are used on pairs of doors having overlapping astragals and closers. When both leaves are open, the coordinator holds the active leaf open until the inactive leaf is closed, preventing interferences of the astragal.

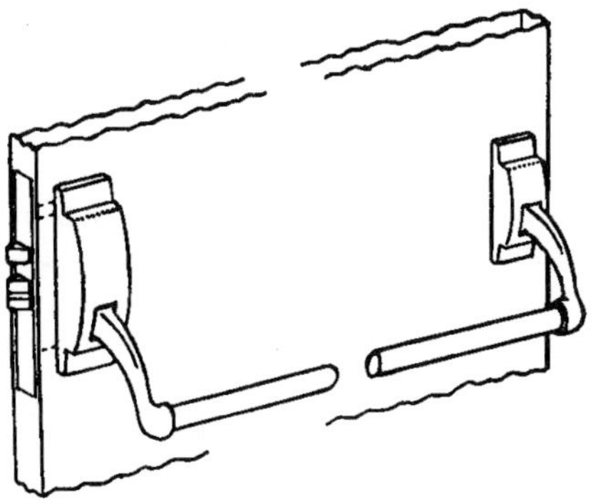

Fig. 9 Mortise-type exit device

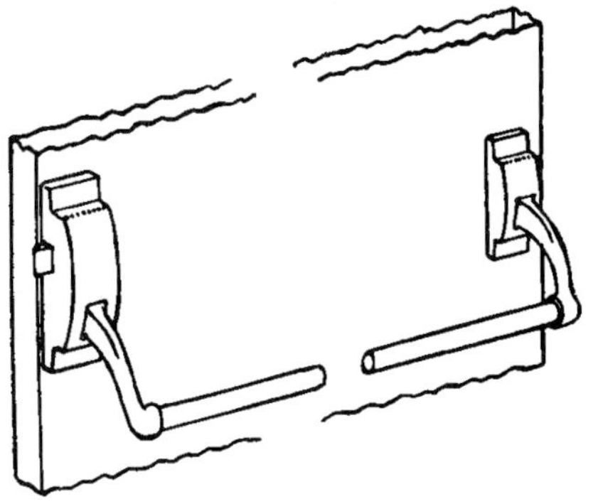

Fig. 11 Rim-type exit device

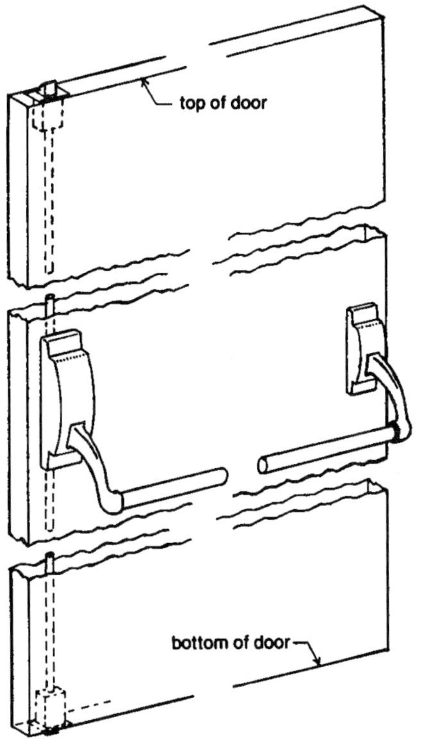

Fig. 10 Concealed vertical rod-type exit

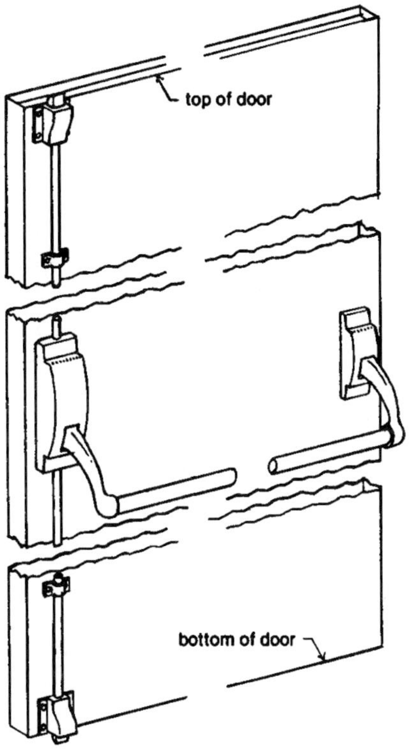

Fig. 12 Exposed vertical rod-type exit device

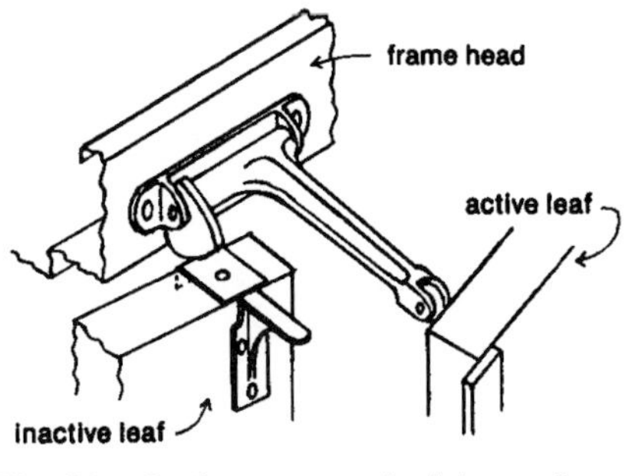

Fig. 13 Surface-mounted-type door and coordinator

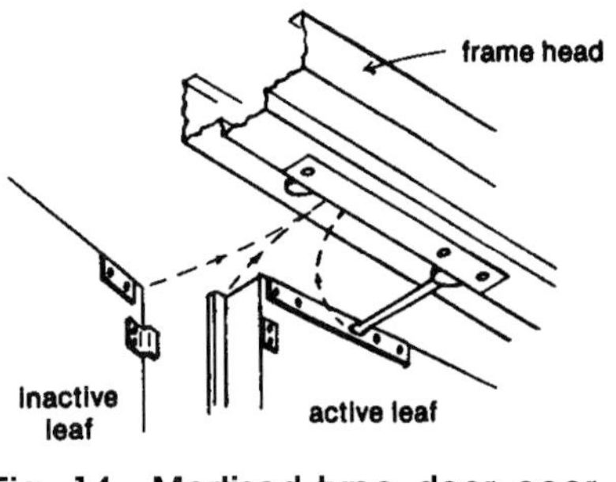

Fig. 14 Mortised-type door coordinator

DOORS

Hollow Metal Door Hardware: Flush Bolts

These bolts are installed on the inactive leaf of a pair of doors to secure it in the closed position to serve as a latching point for the active leaf. They may also be used as auxiliary locking devices for added security. Bolts may be either surface mounted or flush (concealed rod); only the latter type is illustrated in Fig. 15.

There are many variations of these flush bolts; only the more common types being shown in Fig. 15. Due to the variety of frame construction encountered, the selection of the most appropriate type of strike is particularly important, and clearance at the floor must be very carefully controlled to ensure proper engagement.

The manual type (Fig. 15*A*) requires hand operation of the operating lever for both latching and unlatching. The variable length of the extension rod, however, permits convenient location of the operating mechanism in the door edge. The self-latching types (Fig. 15*B* and *C*) latch automatically when the inactive leaf is closed, but must be unlatched manually. The automatic type (Fig. 15*D*) both latches and unlatches automatically when the inactive leaf is closed or opened.

None of these types of flush bolt should be used on doors that are intended to serve as emergency exists. NFPA pamphlet 80 should be consulted for the selection of bolts for fire-rated pairs of doors.

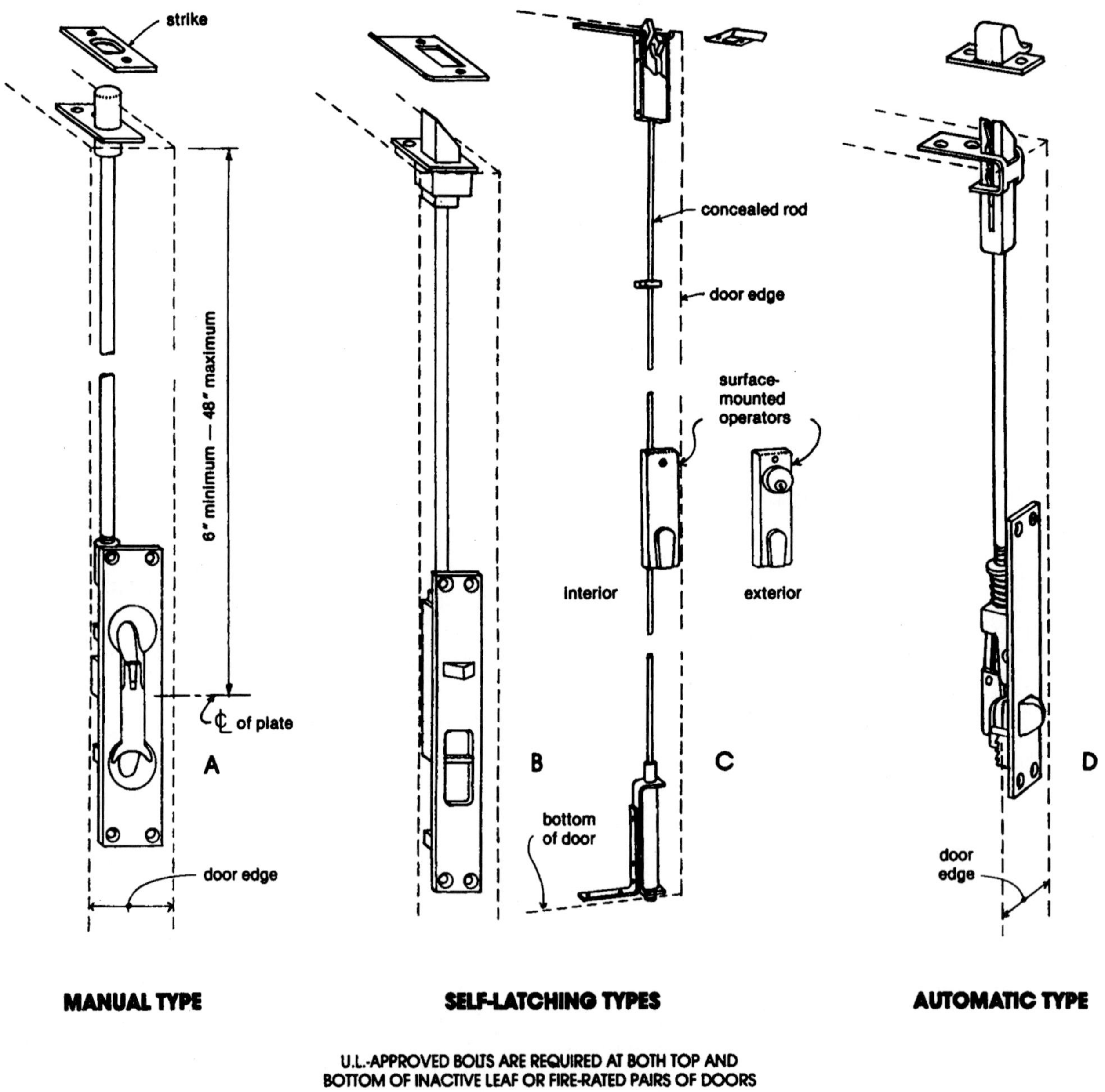

Fig. 15 Except for Type C, only top bolts are shown; bottom bolts are similar in all cases.

OVERHEAD DOOR HOLDERS

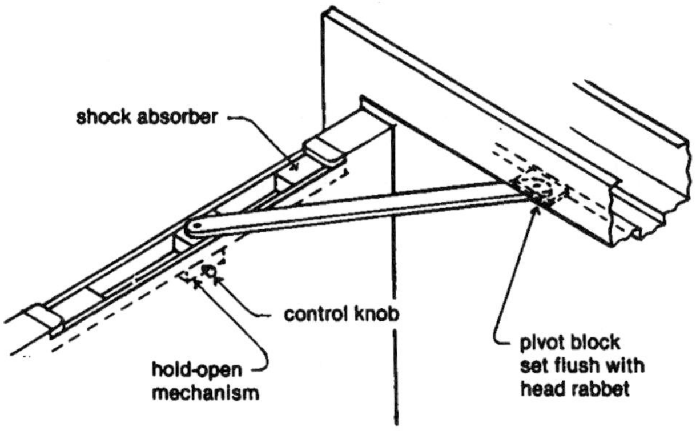

CONCEALED TYPE
For single-or double-acting doors

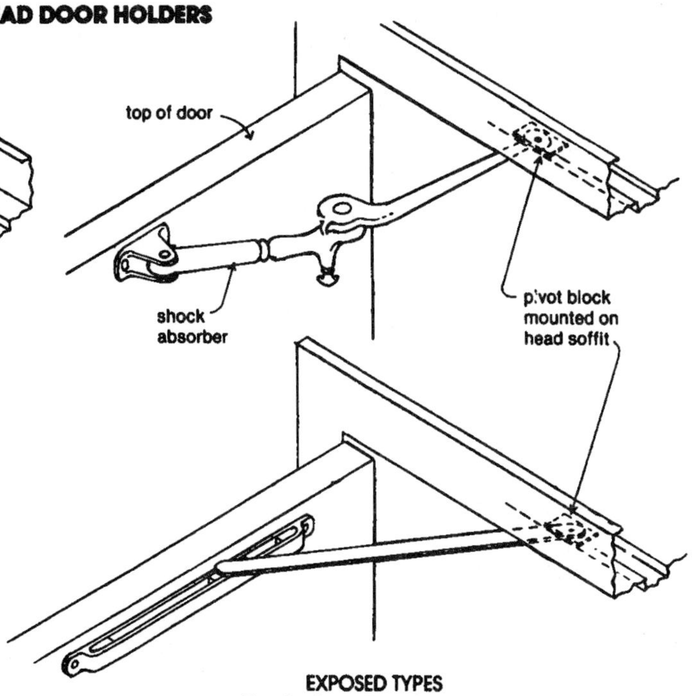

These are devices used to limit and control the swing of the door or hold it in the open position. By controlling the door action they serve to protect against damage to the door and/or hinges caused by abusive usage, and damage to the holder caused by violent opening of the door.

EXPOSED TYPES
For single-acting doors only

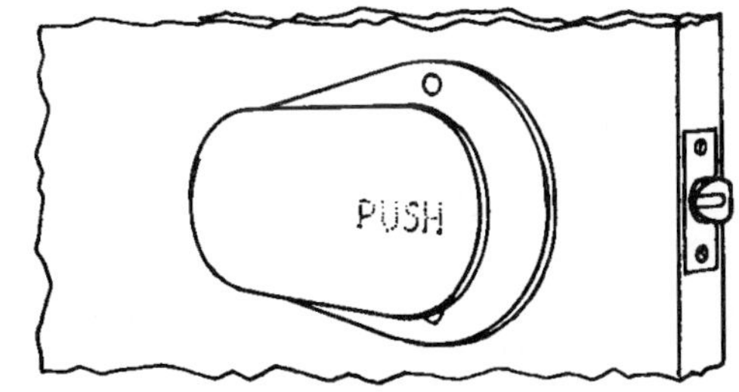

PUSH LEVER

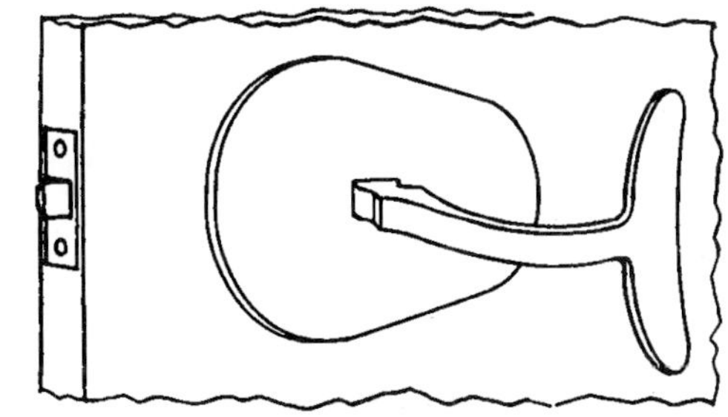

PULL LEVER ON OPPOSITE FACE

HOSPITAL DOOR LATCH

Designed primarily for use in hospitals, on corridor doors leading to patient rooms. May also be used on any door requiring push-pull operation, particularly by forearm or elbow, when hands are engaged in carrying objects.

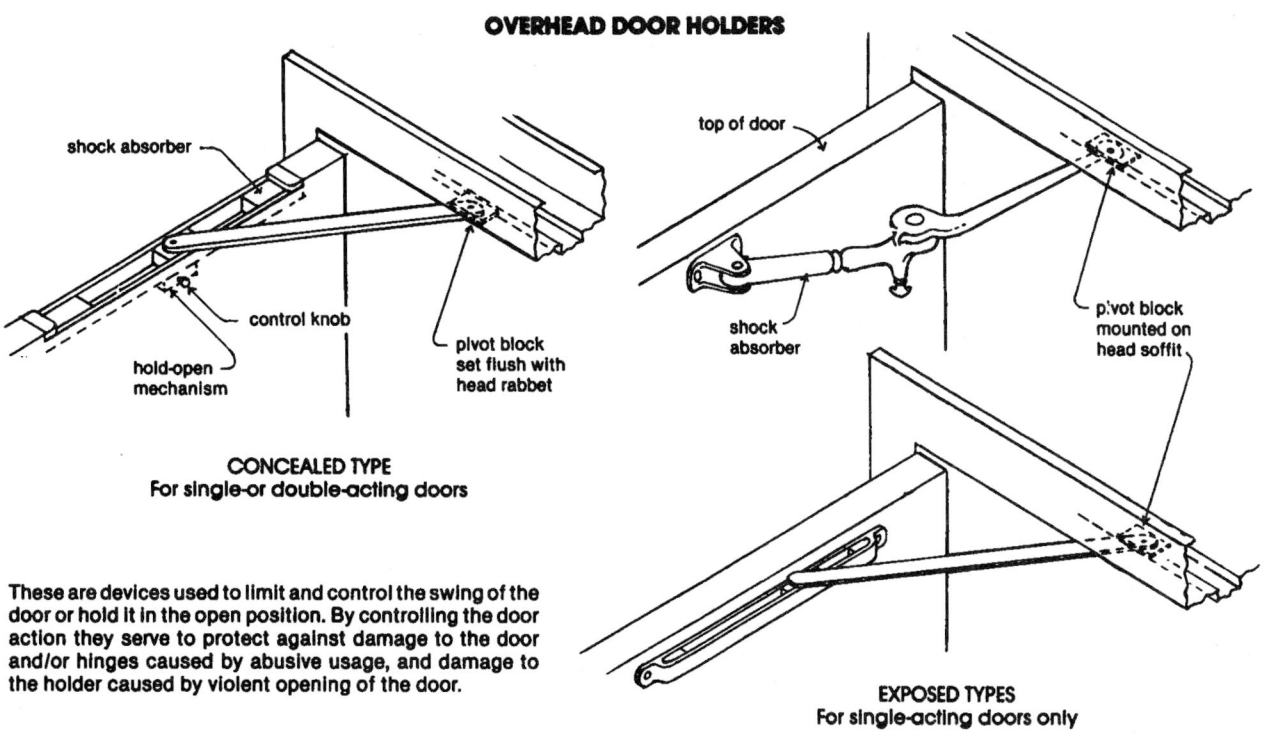

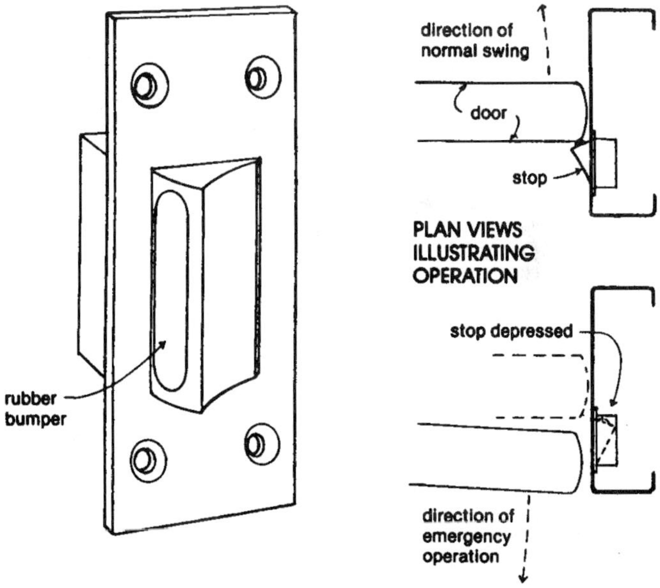

EMERGENCY DOOR STOP

Intended primarily for use in hospitals, on doors between patient rooms and toilets. This stop permits door to be opened from the stop side in the event that an incapacitated patient should block the normal swing by falling. Door must be hung on center (double-acting) pivots.

DOORS
Hardware Locations

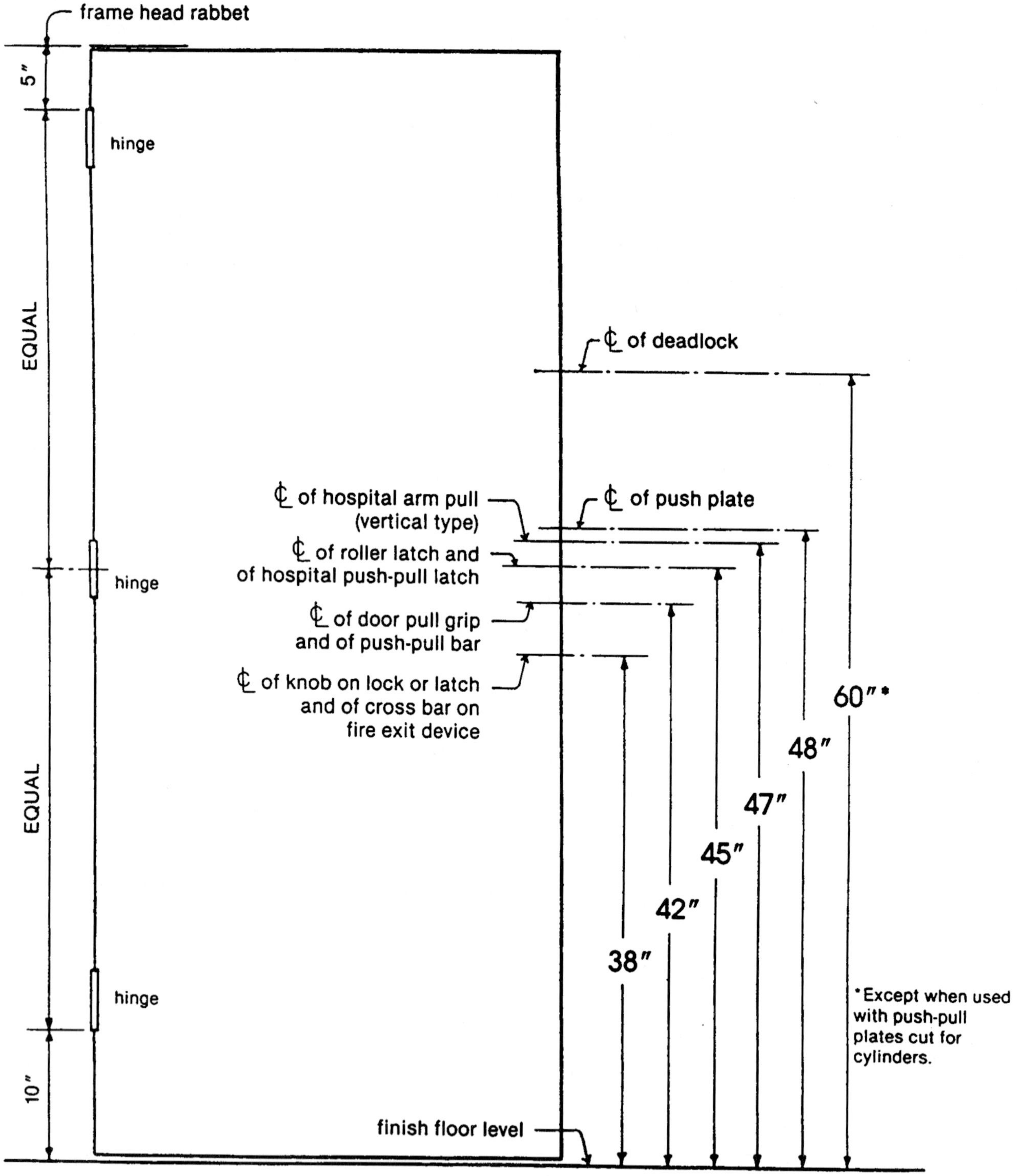

frame head rabbet
5″
hinge
EQUAL
hinge
EQUAL
hinge
10″
℄ of deadlock
℄ of hospital arm pull (vertical type)
℄ of push plate
℄ of roller latch and of hospital push-pull latch
℄ of door pull grip and of push-pull bar
℄ of knob on lock or latch and of cross bar on fire exit device
60″*
48″
47″
45″
42″
38″
*Except when used with push-pull plates cut for cylinders.
finish floor level

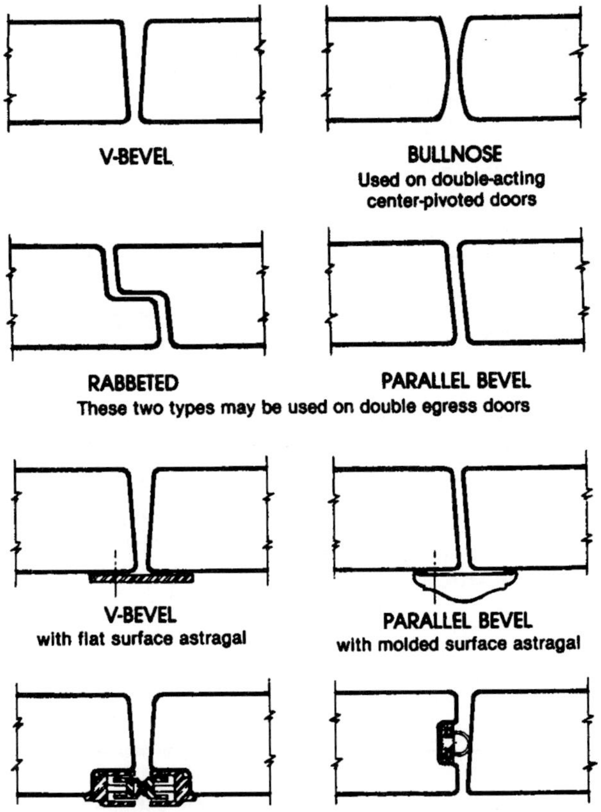

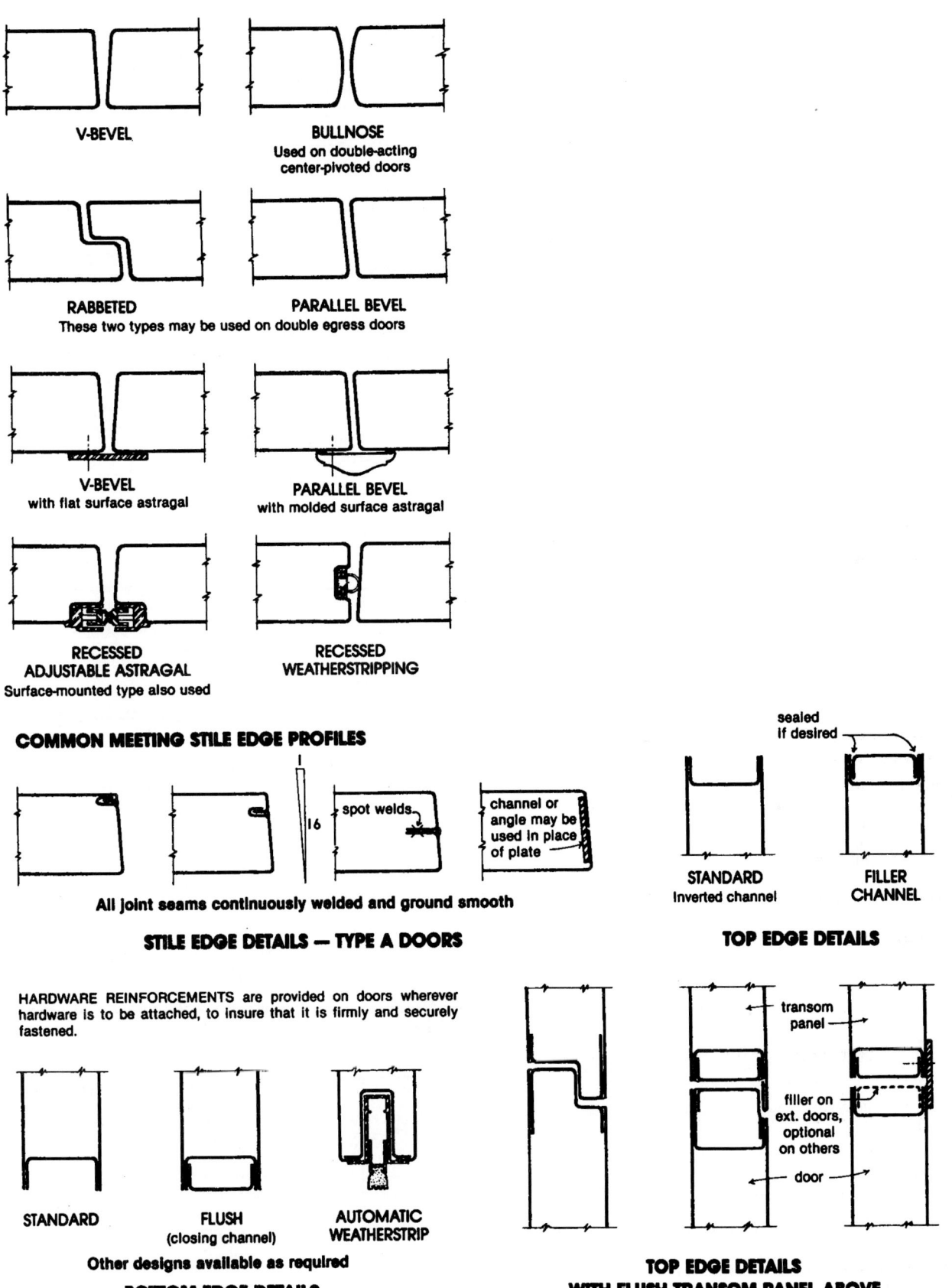

V-BEVEL

BULLNOSE
Used on double-acting center-pivoted doors

RABBETED

PARALLEL BEVEL

These two types may be used on double egress doors

V-BEVEL
with flat surface astragal

PARALLEL BEVEL
with molded surface astragal

RECESSED ADJUSTABLE ASTRAGAL
Surface-mounted type also used

RECESSED WEATHERSTRIPPING

COMMON MEETING STILE EDGE PROFILES

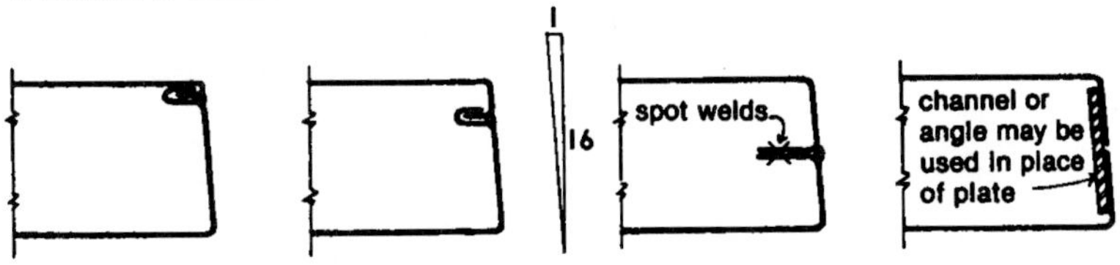

All joint seams continuously welded and ground smooth

STILE EDGE DETAILS — TYPE A DOORS

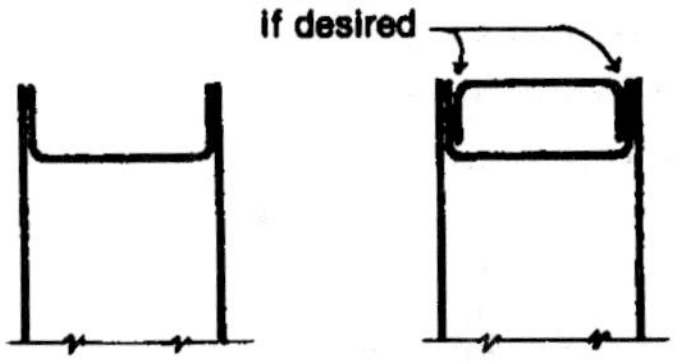

STANDARD
Inverted channel

FILLER CHANNEL

TOP EDGE DETAILS

HARDWARE REINFORCEMENTS are provided on doors wherever hardware is to be attached, to insure that it is firmly and securely fastened.

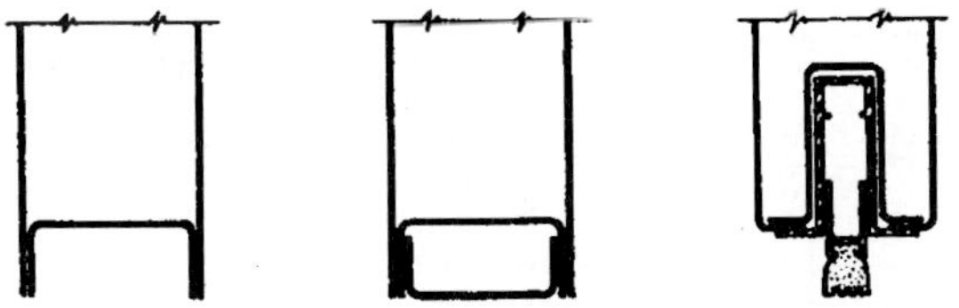

STANDARD

FLUSH
(closing channel)

AUTOMATIC WEATHERSTRIP

Other designs available as required

BOTTOM EDGE DETAILS

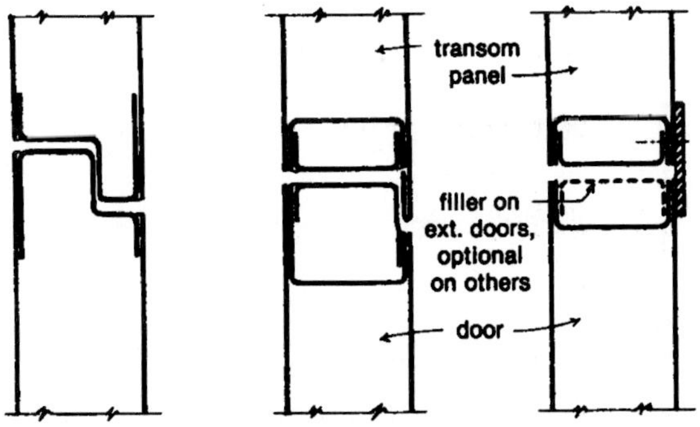

TOP EDGE DETAILS WITH FLUSH TRANSOM PANEL ABOVE

DOORS

Fire-Protected Wood Doors

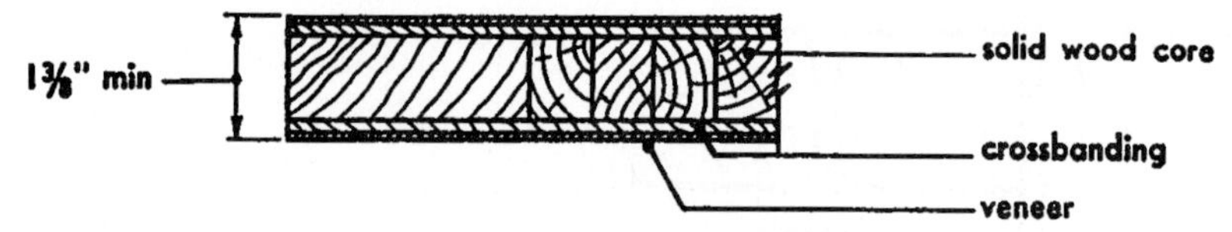
1⅜" min
solid wood core
crossbanding
veneer

SOLID WOOD CORE FLUSH DOORS

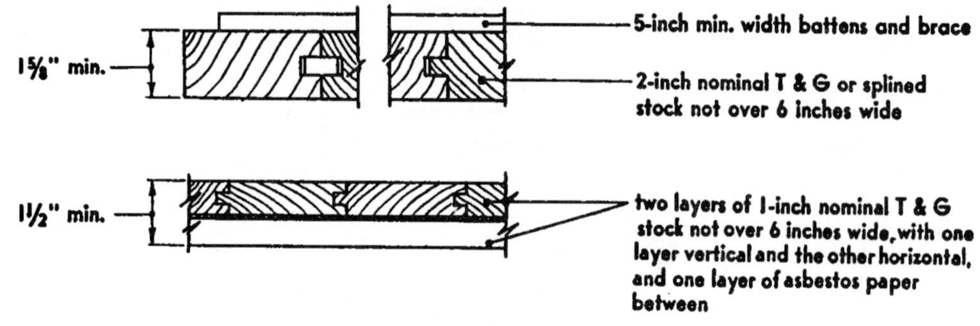
1⅝" min.
5-inch min. width battens and brace
2-inch nominal T & G or splined stock not over 6 inches wide
1½" min.
two layers of 1-inch nominal T & G stock not over 6 inches wide, with one layer vertical and the other horizontal, and one layer of asbestos paper between

BATTENED DOORS

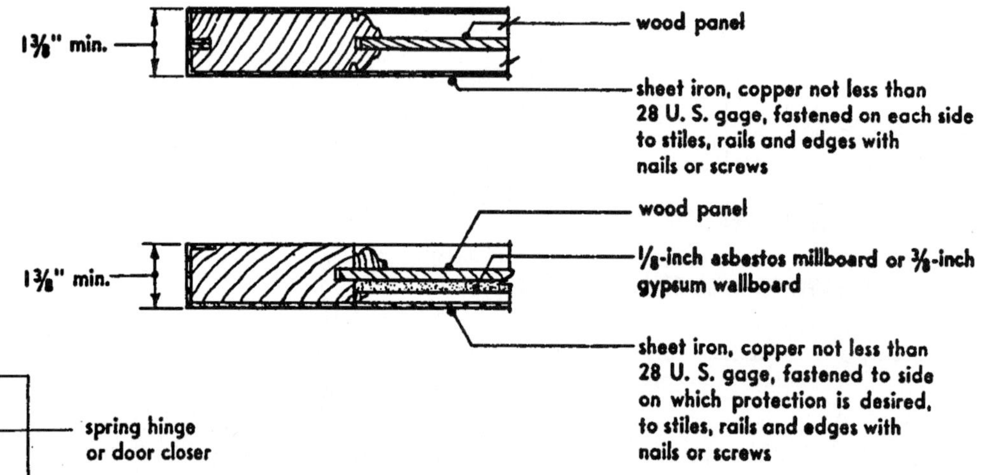
1⅜" min.
wood panel
sheet iron, copper not less than 28 U. S. gage, fastened on each side to stiles, rails and edges with nails or screws
wood panel
1⅜" min.
⅛-inch asbestos millboard or ⅜-inch gypsum wallboard
sheet iron, copper not less than 28 U. S. gage, fastened to side on which protection is desired, to stiles, rails and edges with nails or screws

PROTECTED PANEL DOORS

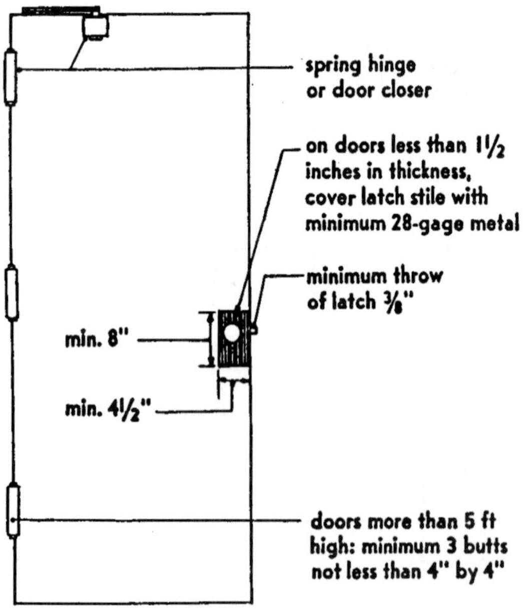
spring hinge or door closer
on doors less than 1½ inches in thickness, cover latch stile with minimum 28-gage metal
minimum throw of latch ⅜"
min. 8"
min. 4½"
doors more than 5 ft high: minimum 3 butts not less than 4" by 4"

HARDWARE

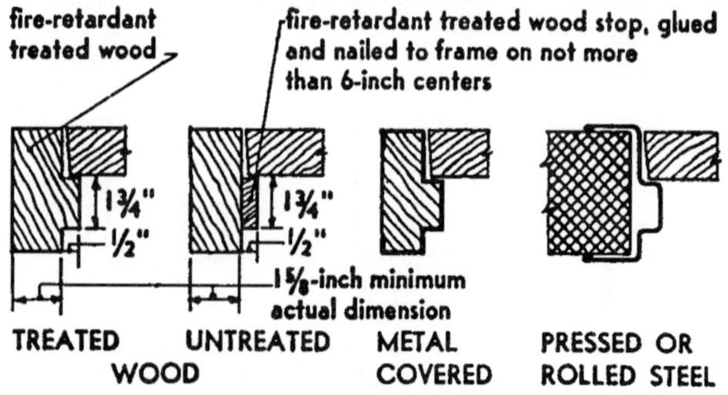
fire-retardant treated wood
fire-retardant treated wood stop, glued and nailed to frame on not more than 6-inch centers
1¾"
½"
1¾"
½"
1⅝-inch minimum actual dimension
TREATED
UNTREATED
WOOD
METAL COVERED
PRESSED OR ROLLED STEEL

FRAMES

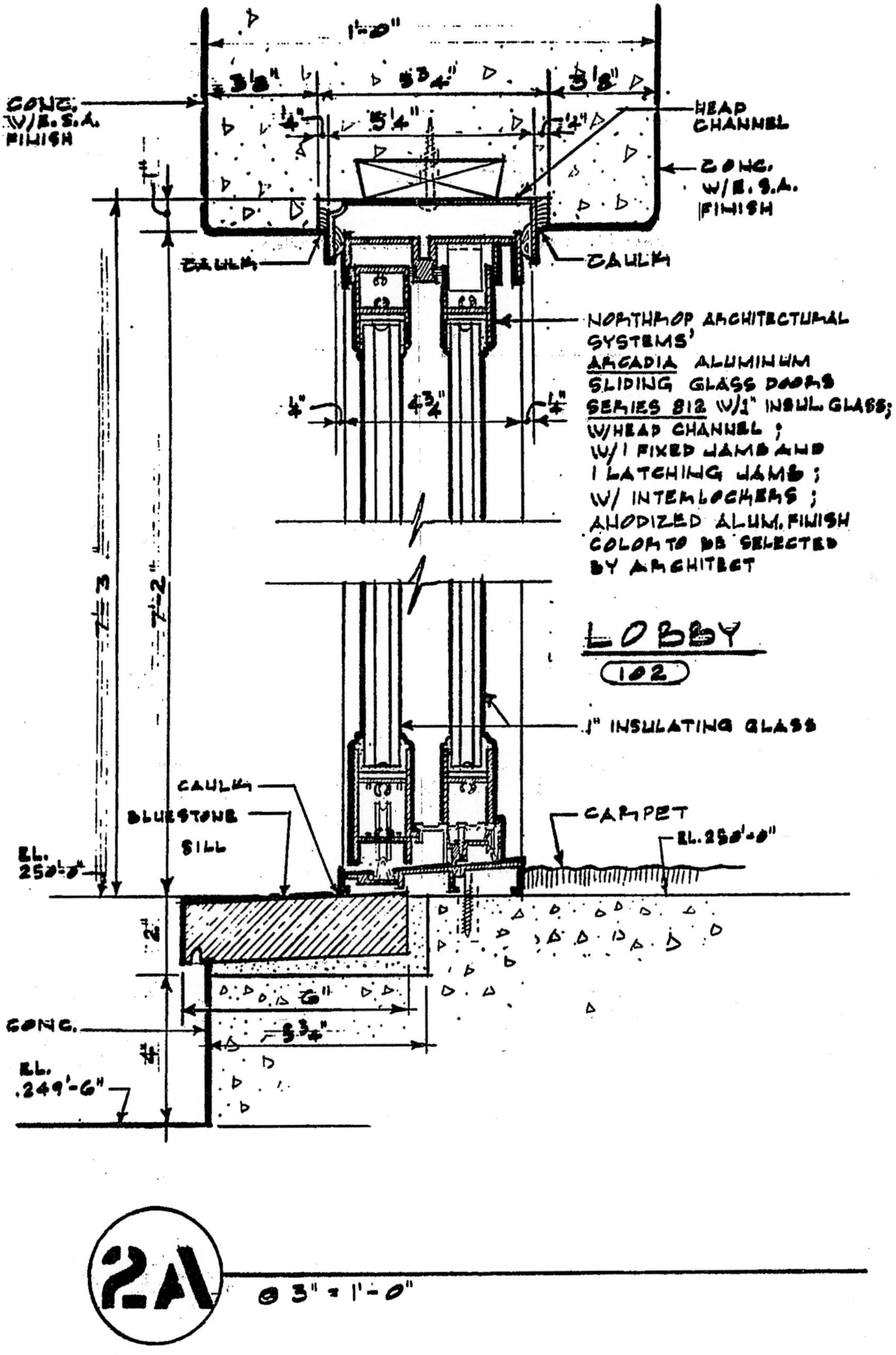
1'-0"
3 1/8"
5 3/4"
3 1/8"
1/4"
5 1/4"
1/4"
CONC. W/E.S.A. FINISH
HEAD CHANNEL
CONC. W/E.S.A. FINISH
CAULK
CAULK
NORTHROP ARCHITECTURAL SYSTEMS' ARCADIA ALUMINUM SLIDING GLASS DOORS SERIES 812 W/1" INSUL. GLASS; W/HEAD CHANNEL; W/1 FIXED JAMB AND 1 LATCHING JAMB; W/ INTERLOCKERS; ANODIZED ALUM. FINISH COLOR TO BE SELECTED BY ARCHITECT
1/4"
4 3/4"
1/4"
7'-3"
7'-2"
LOBBY
102
1" INSULATING GLASS
CAULK
BLUESTONE SILL
CARPET
EL. 250'-0"
EL. 250'-0"
2"
6"
3 3/4"
CONC.
EL. 249'-6"

2A
@ 3" = 1'-0"

DOORS
Thresholds

Thresholds are essential for nearly every type of door. Usually a standard section is satisfactory. Where conditions require, special sections may be designed.

Thresholds of plain surface, extruded or rolled.

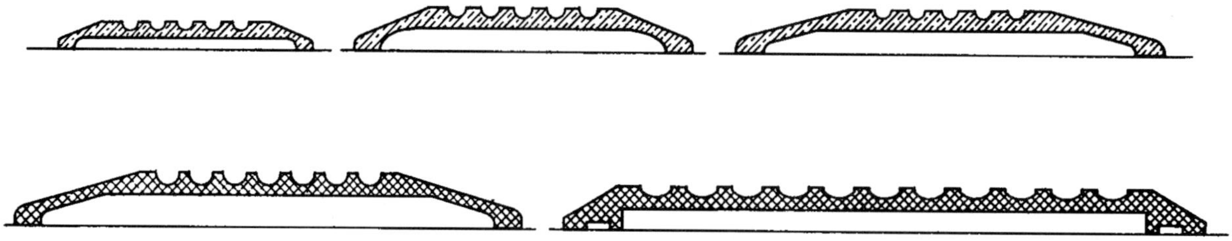

Thresholds with fluted surface, extruded or rolled.

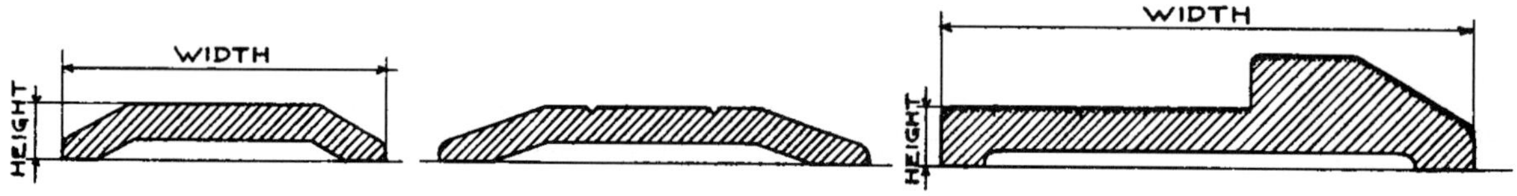

Thresholds cast with plain or abrasive surface.

Thresholds for weather strips.

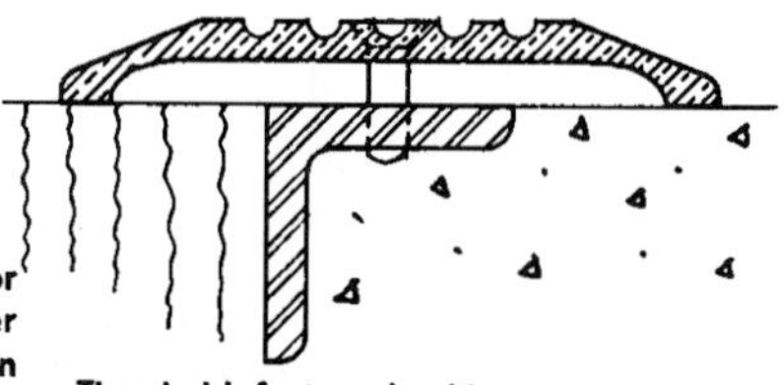

Threshold fastened with screws tapped to steel angle set in floor construction.

Holes for fastening not to exceed 12" o.c. for threshold less than 3" wide. For thresholds over 3" fastenings should not exceed 15" o.c. On wide sills holes may be staggered.

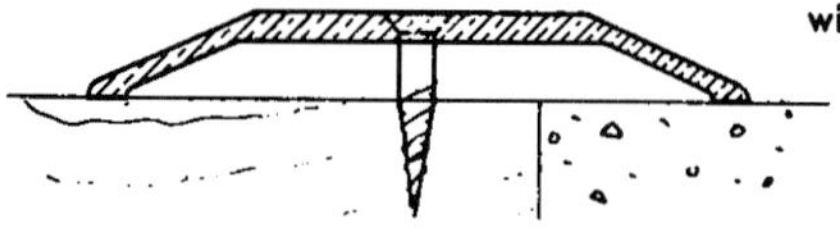

Threshold fastened to wood with wood screws.

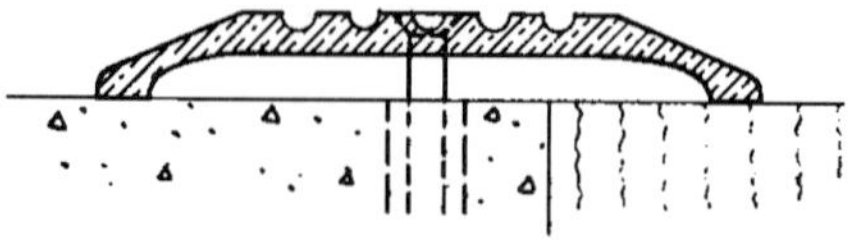

Threshold fastened with screw in fibre plug or expansive metal anchor. Floor may be cement, terrazzo or similar construction.

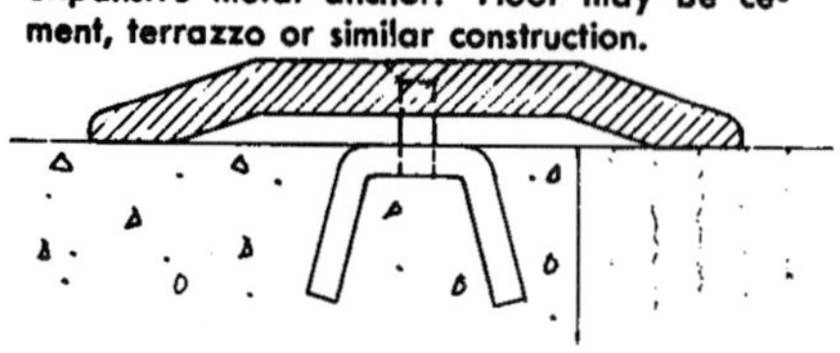

Threshold fastened with screws tapped to clips set in cement.

THRESHOLD SIZES AND METAL

FIG.	WIDTH	HEIGHT	CAST	STEEL	BRASS	BRONZE	ALUMINUM	NICKEL SILVER
14	2½"	¼"		o	o	o	o	o
15	3"	¼"		o	o	o	o	o
16	4"	½"		o	o	o	o	
17	3"	5/16"		o	o	o	o	
18	4"	½"		o	o	o	o	
19	5"	½"		o	o	o	o	
20	6"	5/8"			o	o	o	
21	7½"	½"					o	
22	3"	½"	o					
23	4"	½"	o					
24	5"	½"	o					
25	4 3/16"	5/8"			o	o	o	
26	4" 5" 6"	5/8"	o					

Cast metal may be iron, aluminum, bronze, or nickel silver, with or without abrasive surface.

These thresholds are representative of a great many sections produced in various metals, widths, heights, and types of surface. For other sections refer to manufacturers' catalogs.

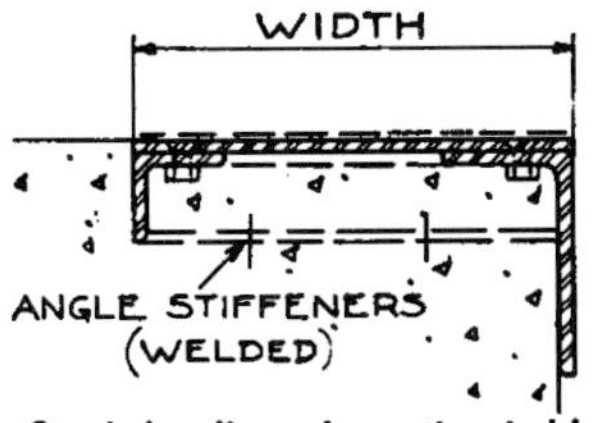

Steel loading door threshold anchored to concrete

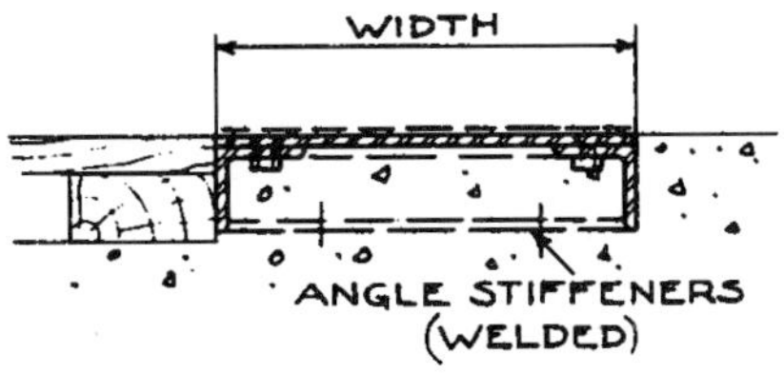

Steel shipping door threshold anchored to concrete

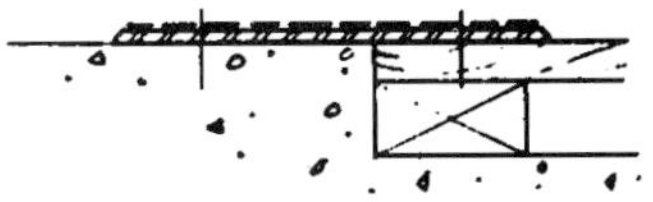

Steel shipping door threshold screwed to floor

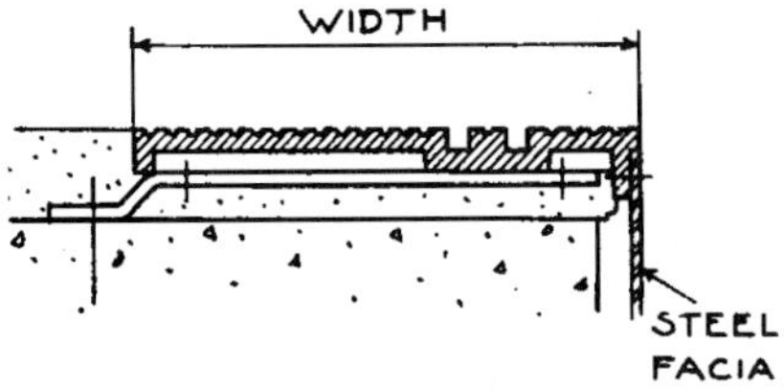

Elevator door threshold for double doors cast with grooves. Surface may be abrasive or plain of cast iron, aluminum or bronze.

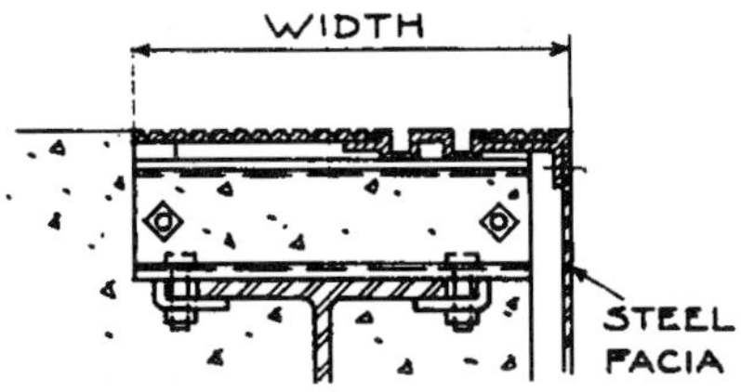

Elevator door threshold for double doors of rolled sections, steel, bronze or aluminum.

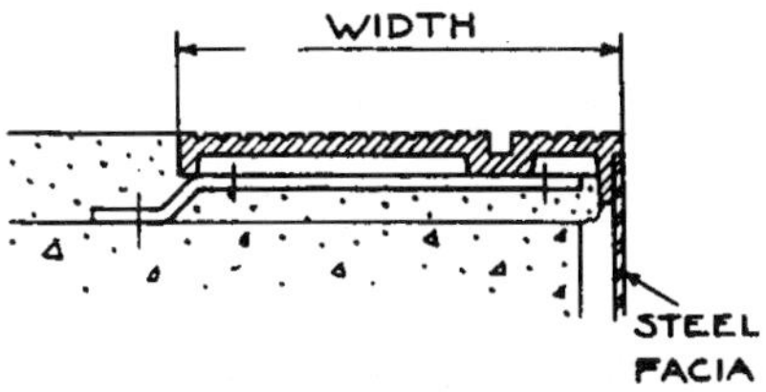

Elevator door threshold for single doors cast with grooves. Surface may be abrasive or plain of cast iron, aluminum or bronze.

Thresholds with concealed steel anchors are usually fastened to anchors with flat head machine screws, the anchors independently fastened to the floor construction.

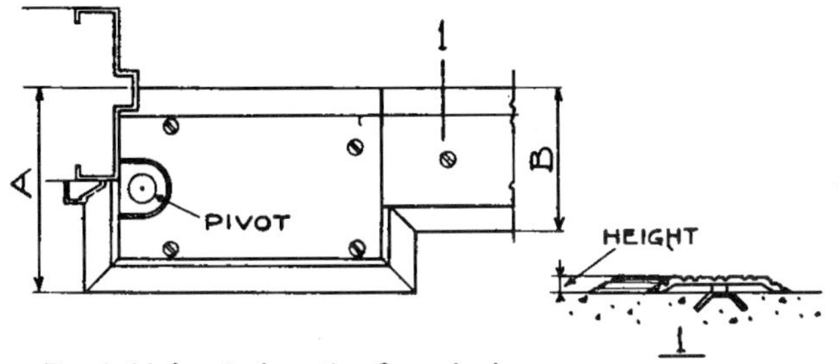

Threshold for single acting floor check.

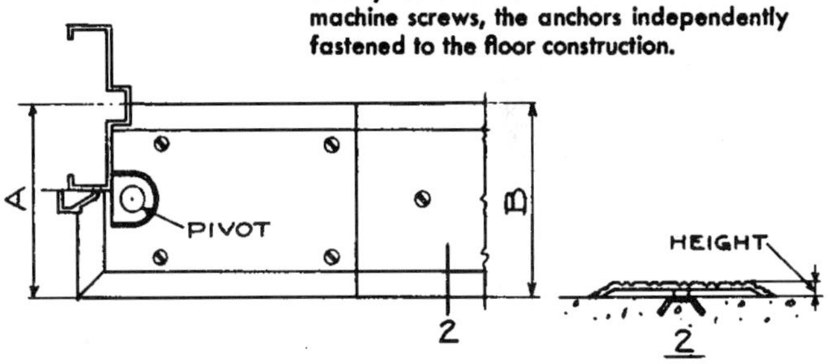

Threshold for single acting floor check.

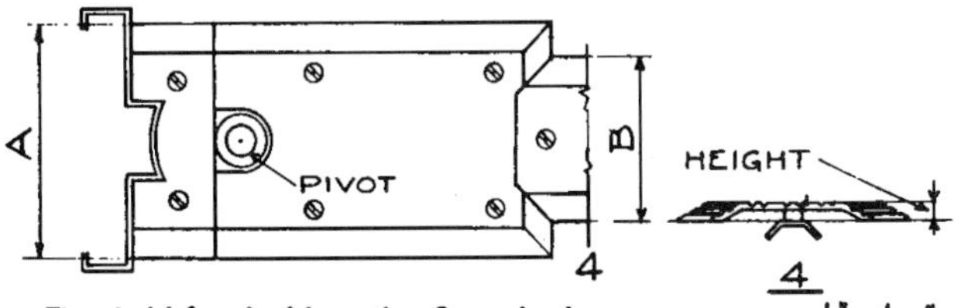

Threshold for double acting floor check.

SCALE $1\frac{1}{2}$" = 1'-0"

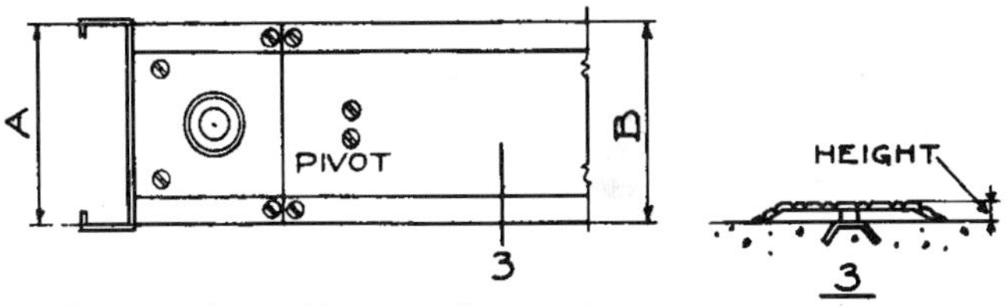

Threshold for double acting floor check.

Thresholds for floor checks may be obtained in the same metals and sections as standard thresholds or may be designed to fit special conditions.
All thresholds fitted to floor checks must be designed with removable cover plate.
Screw spacing must fit floor check.
Dimension "A" is determined by type of floor check, usually 5¾", 6¾" or 7¾".
Dimension "B" may be same as "A" or less as specified.

SPECIFY:
- Type, location
- Width, length
- Metal and finish
- Show detail of special requirements

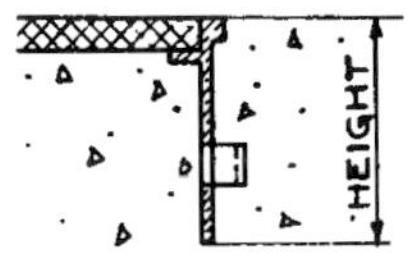

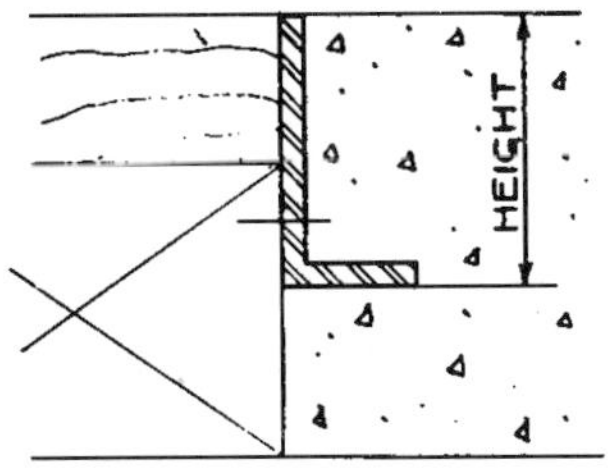

Joint strips, also called dividing strips or division bars, used for separation of floors of different materials, may be of steel or non-ferrous metals. They may be of angles or other sections with anchors attached, or of a patented design.

SCALE $\frac{1}{2}$" = 1"

Terrazzo strips for design or pattern work in terrazzo floors are not considered architectural metal.

DOORS

Thresholds and Edging Strips

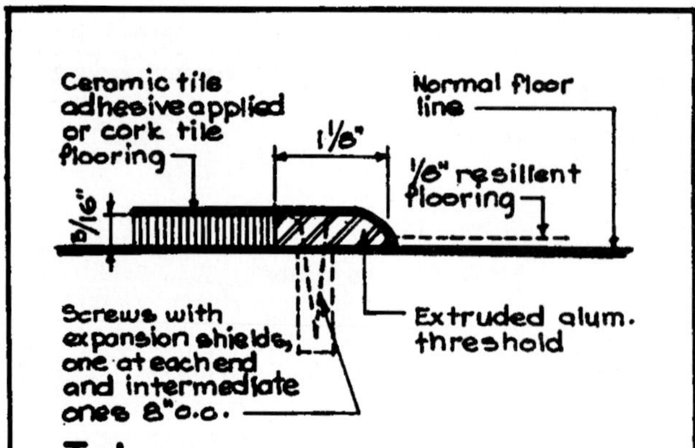

T-1

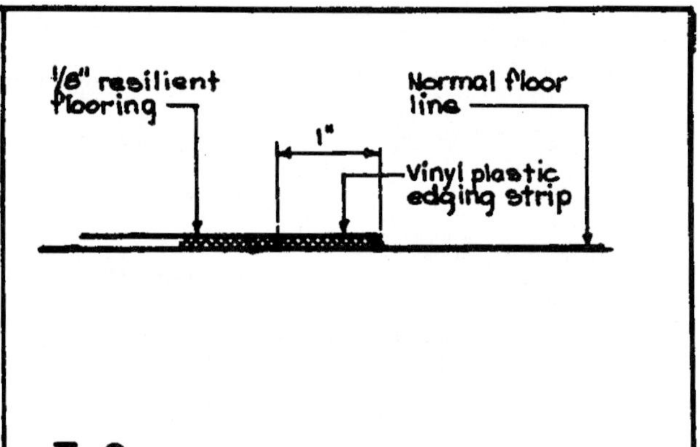

T-2

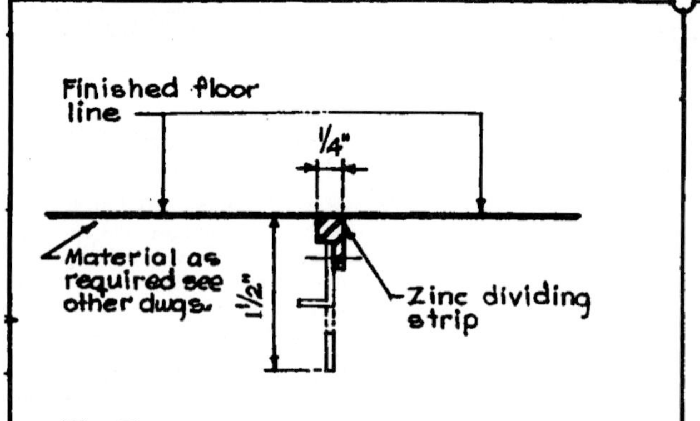

T-3

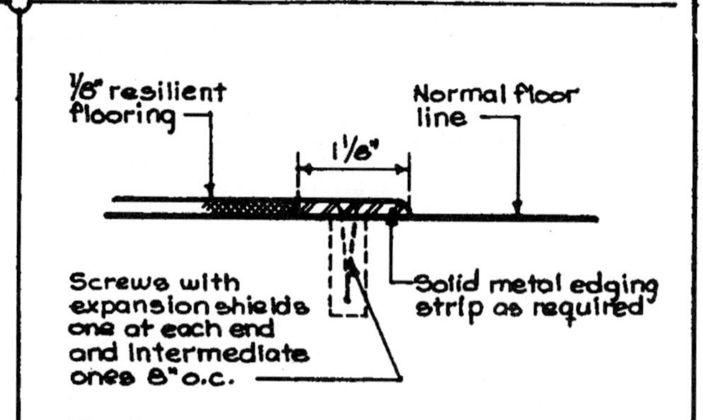

T-4

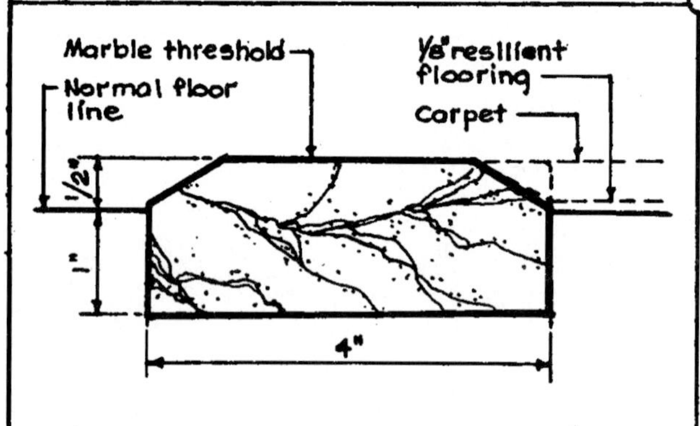

T-5

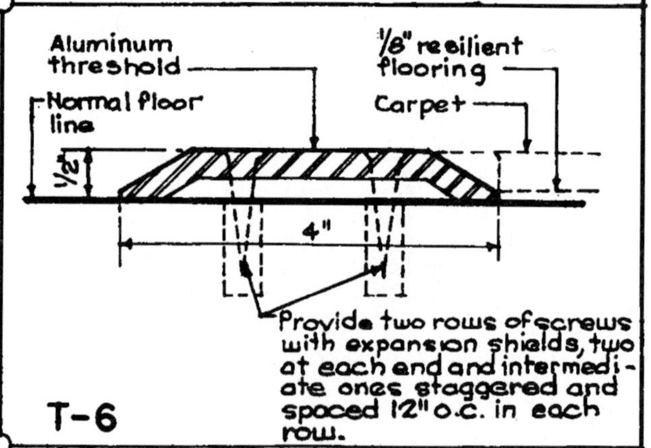

T-6

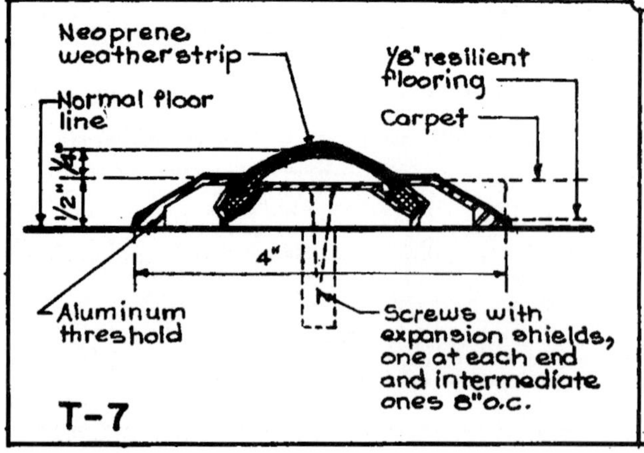

T-7

NOTES:

1. For door swing, see other drawings.
2. For schedule of floor finishes, see other drawings.
3. For gauges of metal see specifications.

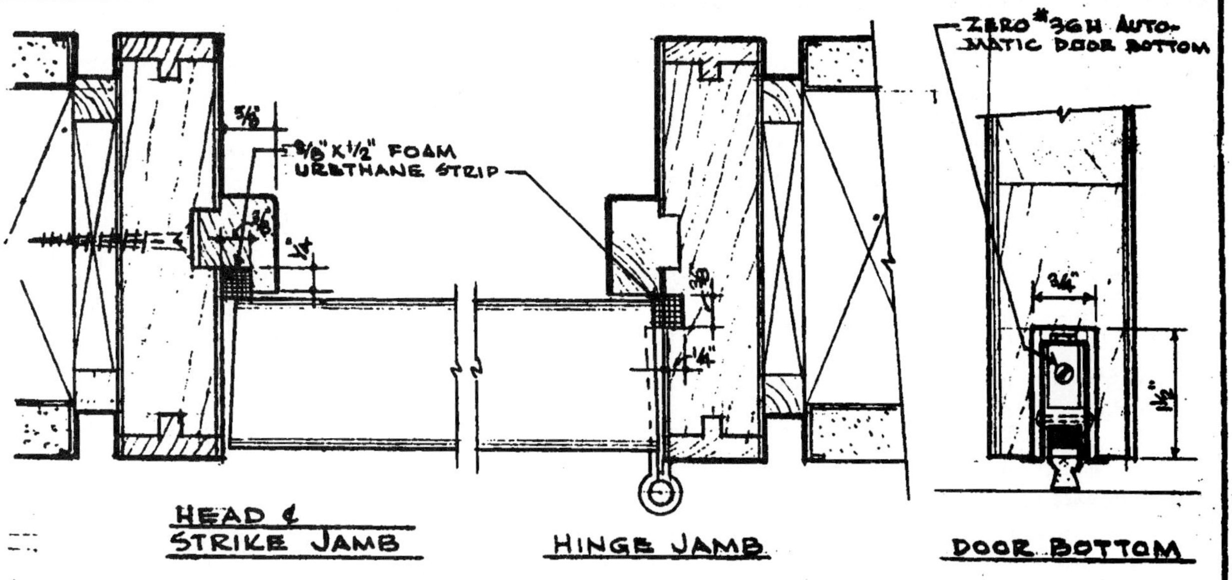

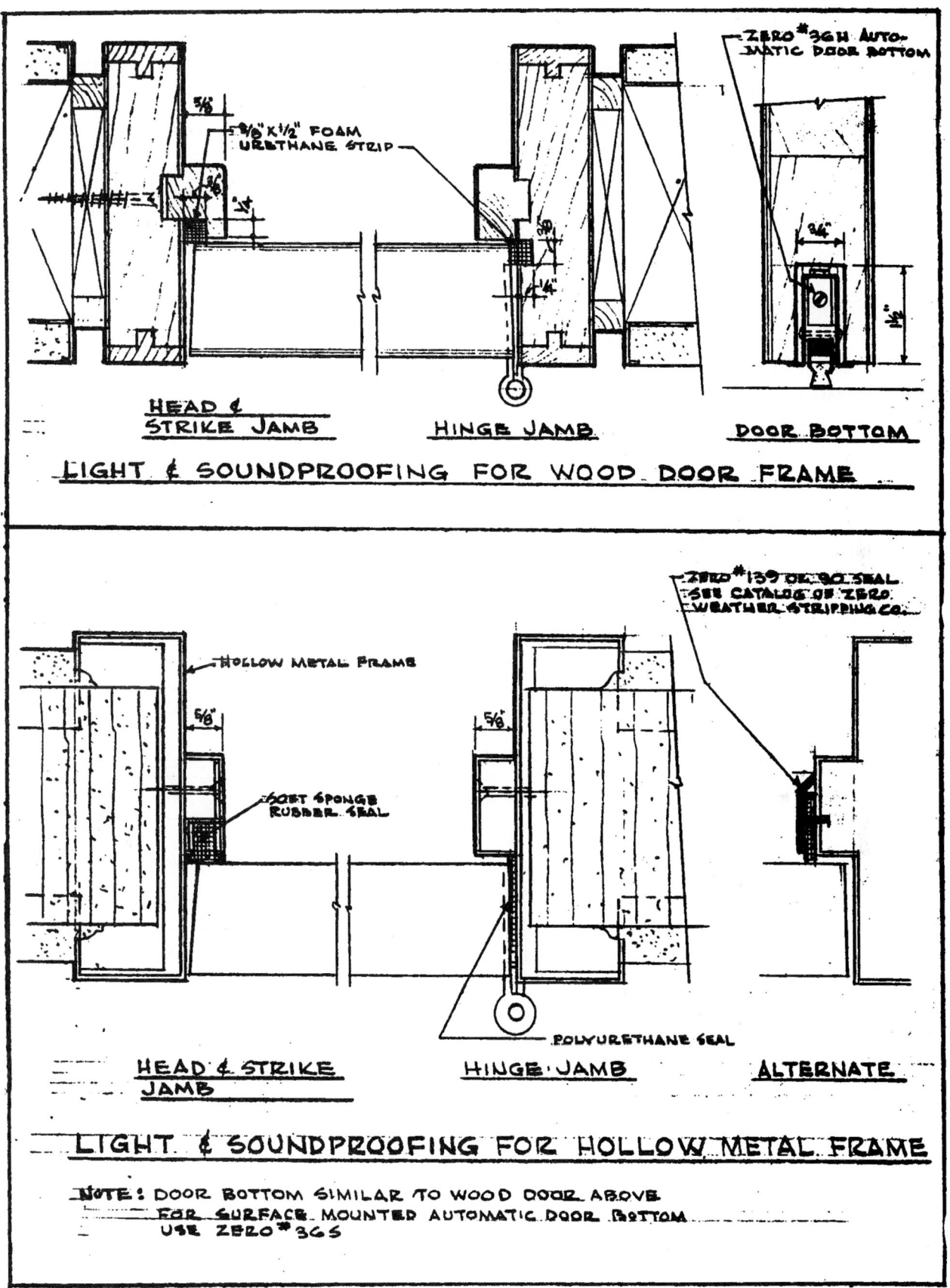

ZERO #36H AUTOMATIC DOOR BOTTOM
5/8"
3/8" X 1/2" FOAM URETHANE STRIP
HEAD & STRIKE JAMB
HINGE JAMB
DOOR BOTTOM
LIGHT & SOUNDPROOFING FOR WOOD DOOR FRAME
ZERO #139 OR 90 SEAL. SEE CATALOG OF ZERO WEATHER STRIPPING CO.
HOLLOW METAL FRAME
5/8"
SOFT SPONGE RUBBER SEAL
POLYURETHANE SEAL
HEAD & STRIKE JAMB
HINGE JAMB
ALTERNATE
LIGHT & SOUNDPROOFING FOR HOLLOW METAL FRAME
NOTE: DOOR BOTTOM SIMILAR TO WOOD DOOR ABOVE
FOR SURFACE MOUNTED AUTOMATIC DOOR BOTTOM
USE ZERO #365

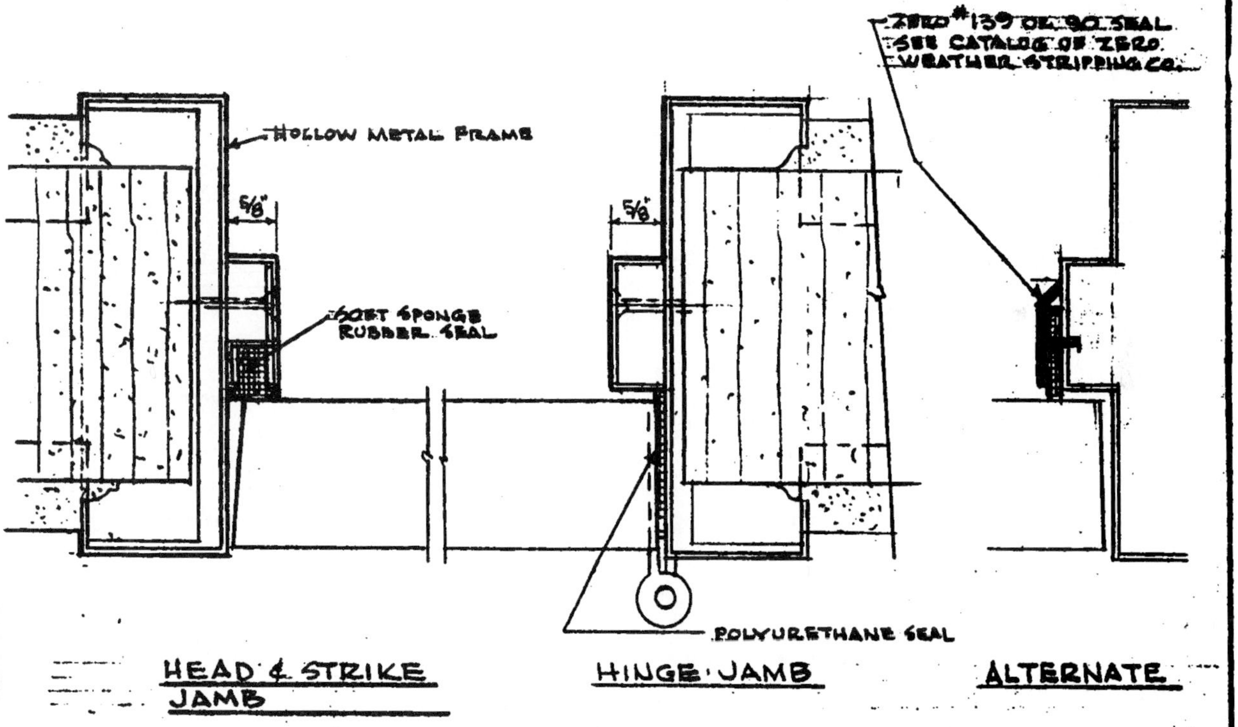

DOORS

Hollow Metal Door Frames

The prime functions of the door frame are to hold the door and its controls in the opening, and to trim the opening. But frames often serve other esthetic or functional purposes also, such as trimming a wall opening having no door, or enclosing glazed areas that provide through-wall visibility or admitting light and/or air. Hollow metal frames, which are strong, sturdy, and durable, serve all such functions economically.

The variety of configurations available in custom hollow metal frames is virtually unlimited. Illustrated in Fig. 16 are some of the more common and representative types.

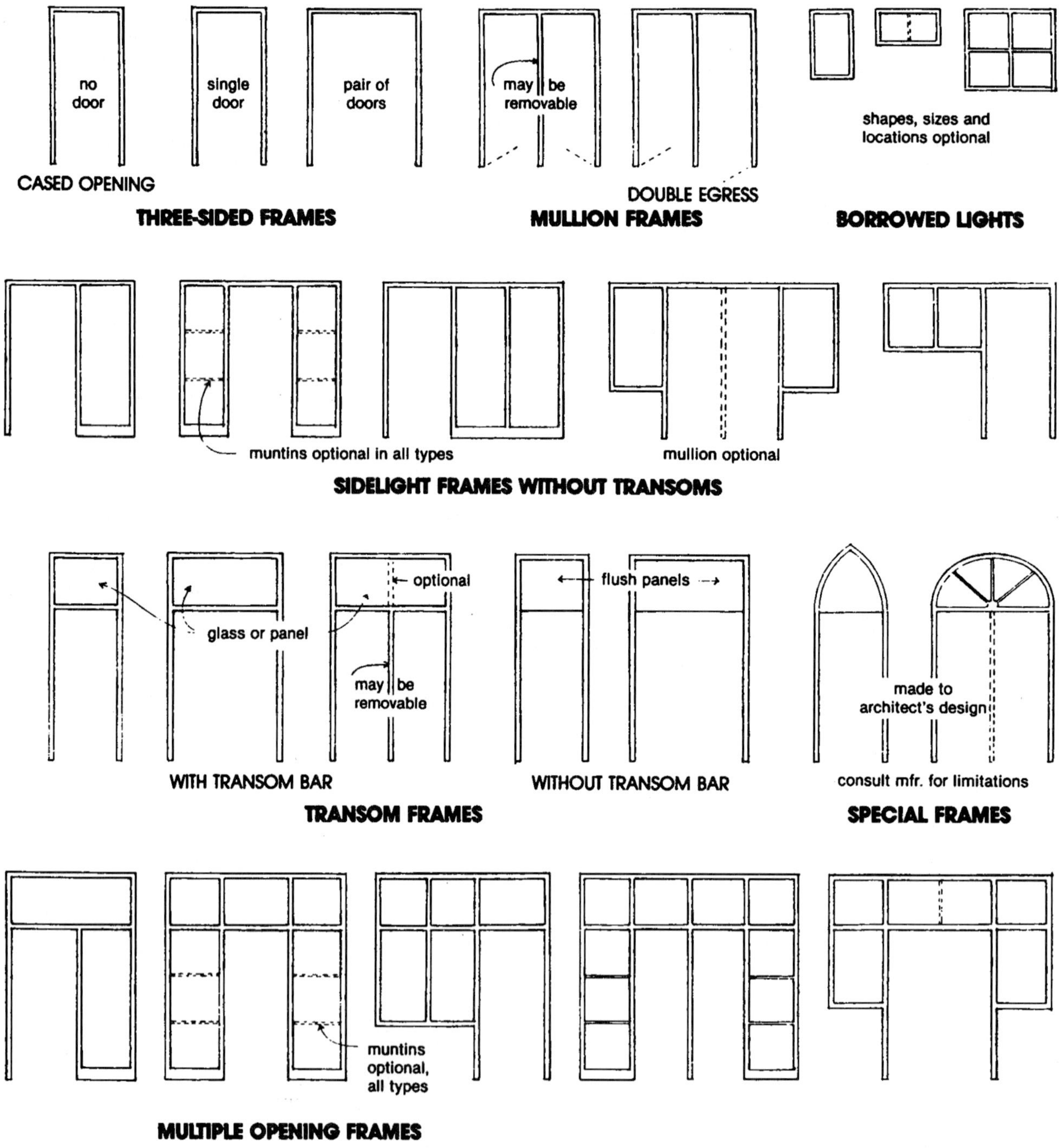

Fig. 16

DOORS
Frame Types

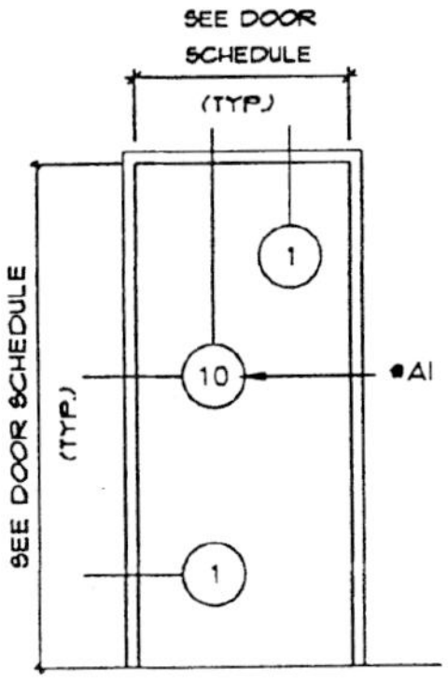

Ⓐ SINGLE / DOUBLE

Ⓐ1 TRIMMED OPENING

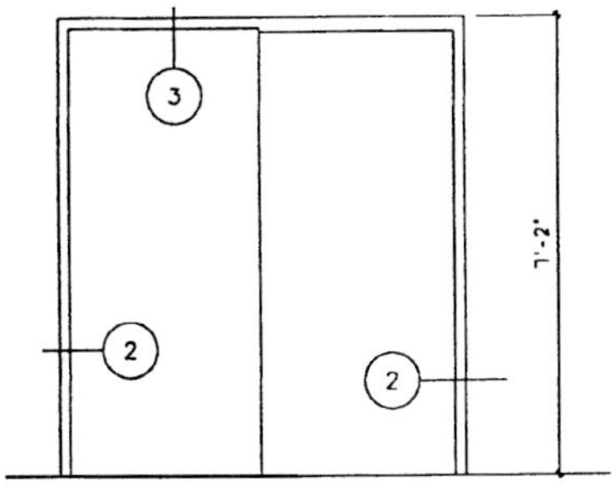

Ⓑ DOUBLE EGRESS

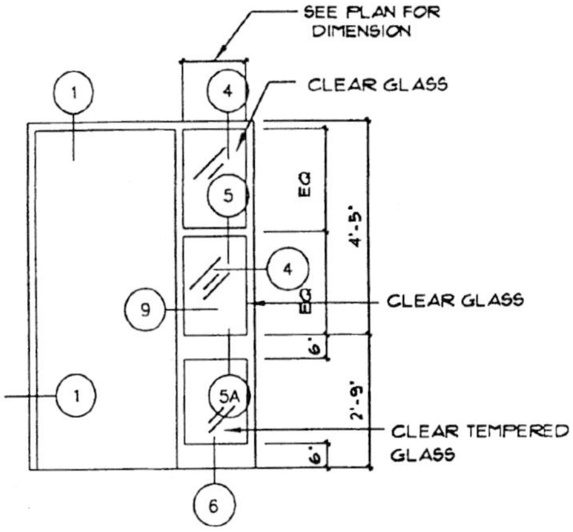

Ⓒ SINGLE W/ SIDELIGHT

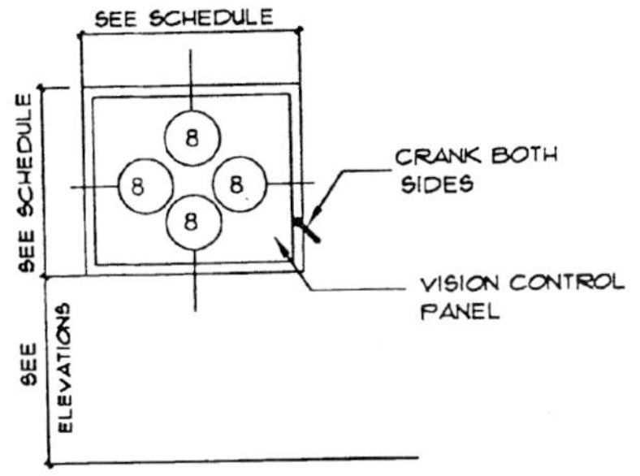

Ⓓ VISION CONTROL UNIT

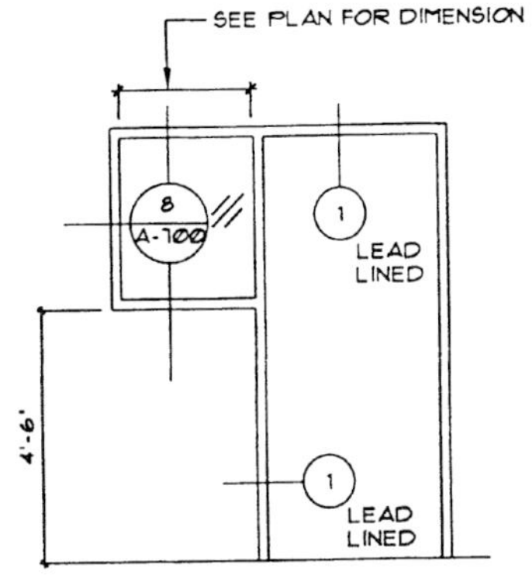

Ⓔ SINGLE W/ SIDELIGHT (LEAD LINED)

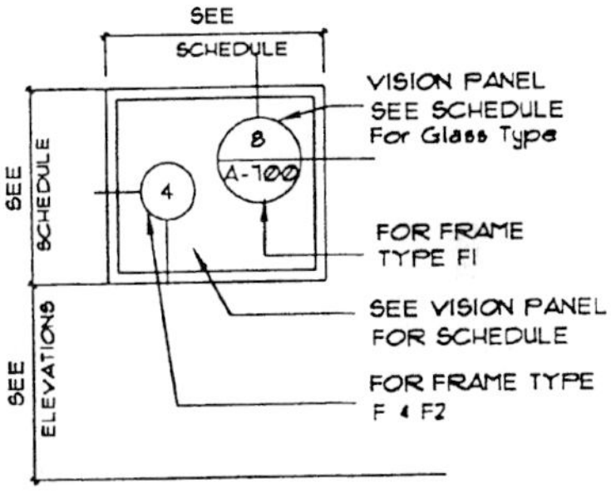

Ⓕ VISION PANEL

Ⓕ1 VISION PANEL (LEAD LINED)

Ⓕ2 ROUND VISION PANEL

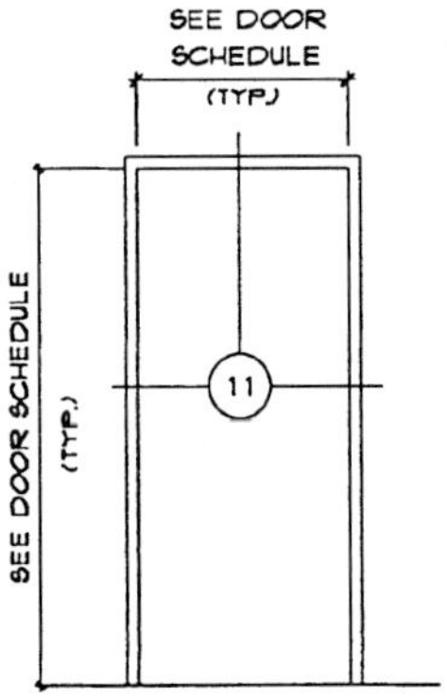

Ⓖ POCKET

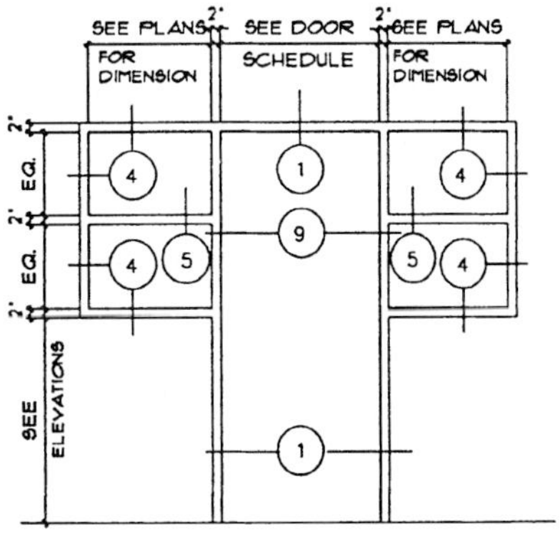

Ⓗ SINGLE W/ SIDELIGHTS

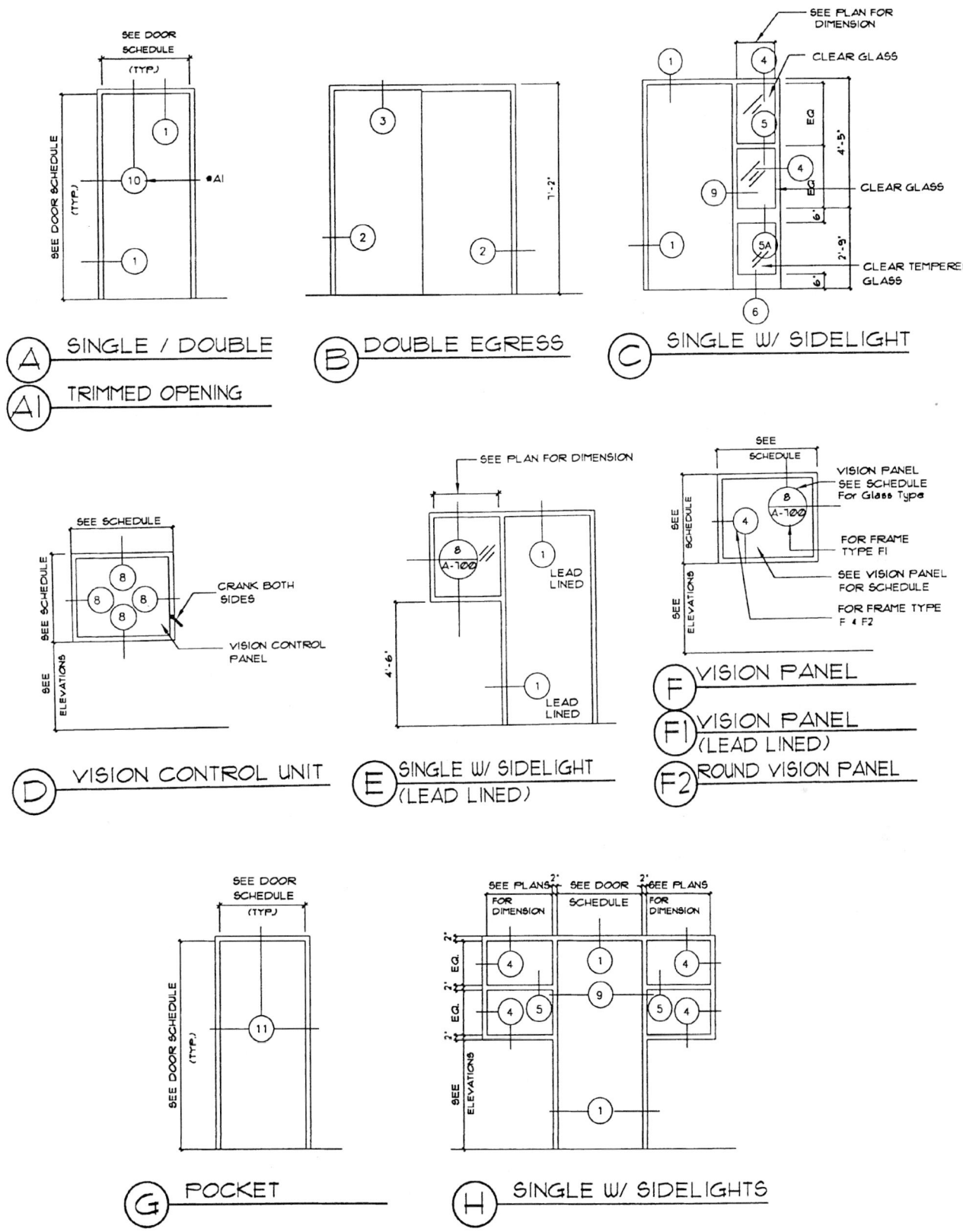

DOORS
Frame Types

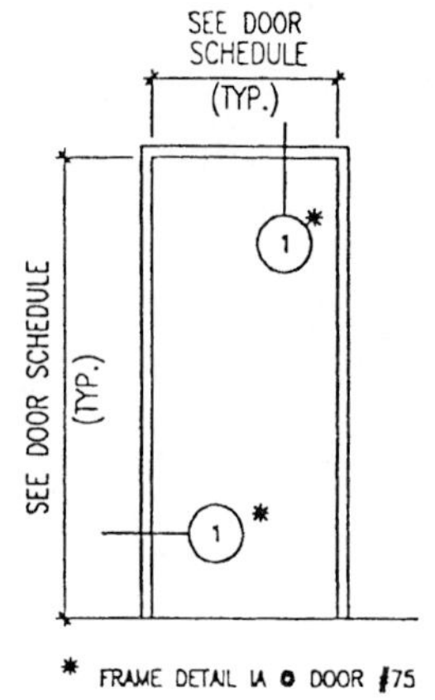

A SINGLE / DOUBLE

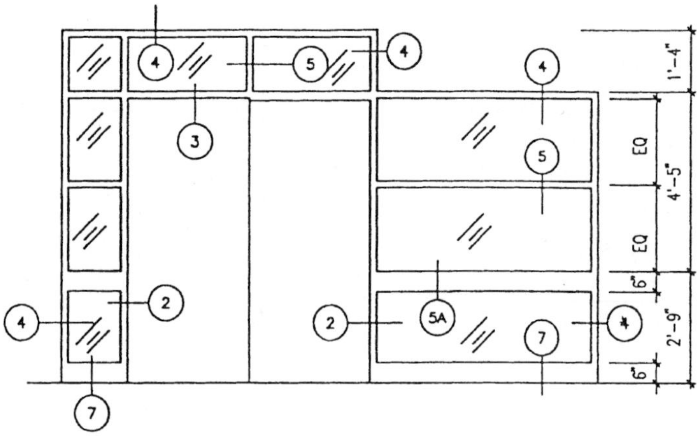

C DOUBLE EGRESS

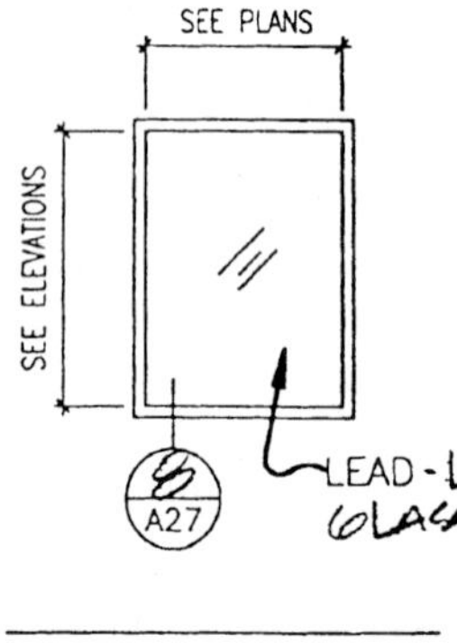

E VIEW WINDOW

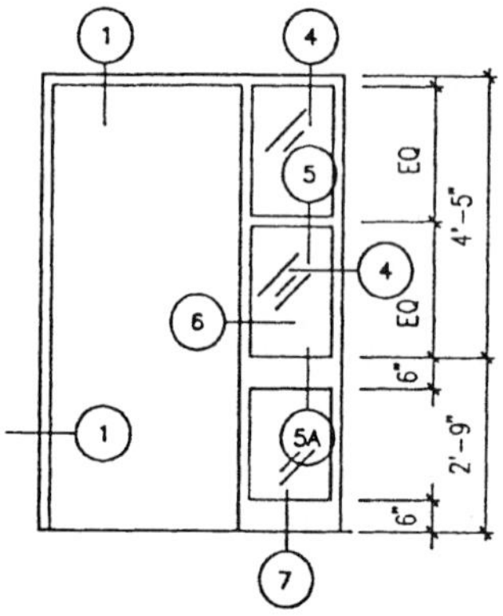

D SINGLE W/ SIDELIGHT

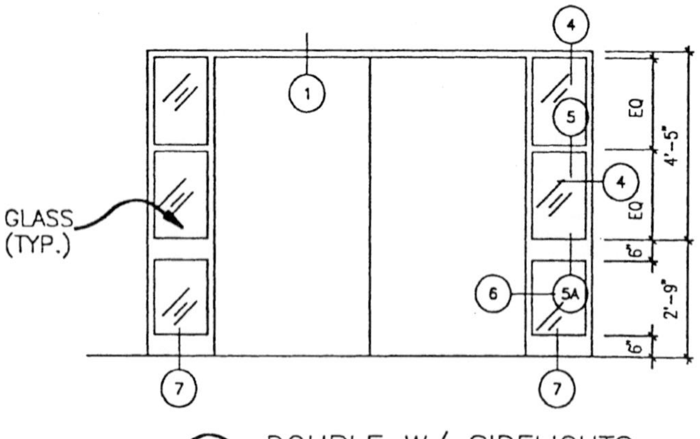

F DOUBLE W/ SIDELIGHTS

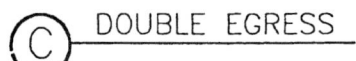

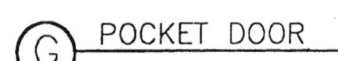

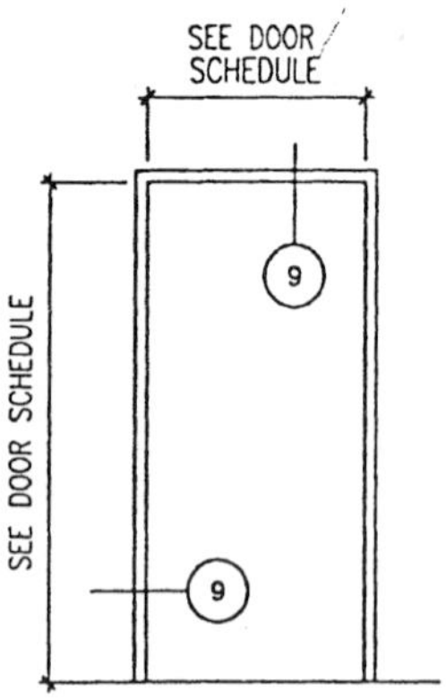

G POCKET DOOR

DOORS
Frame Types

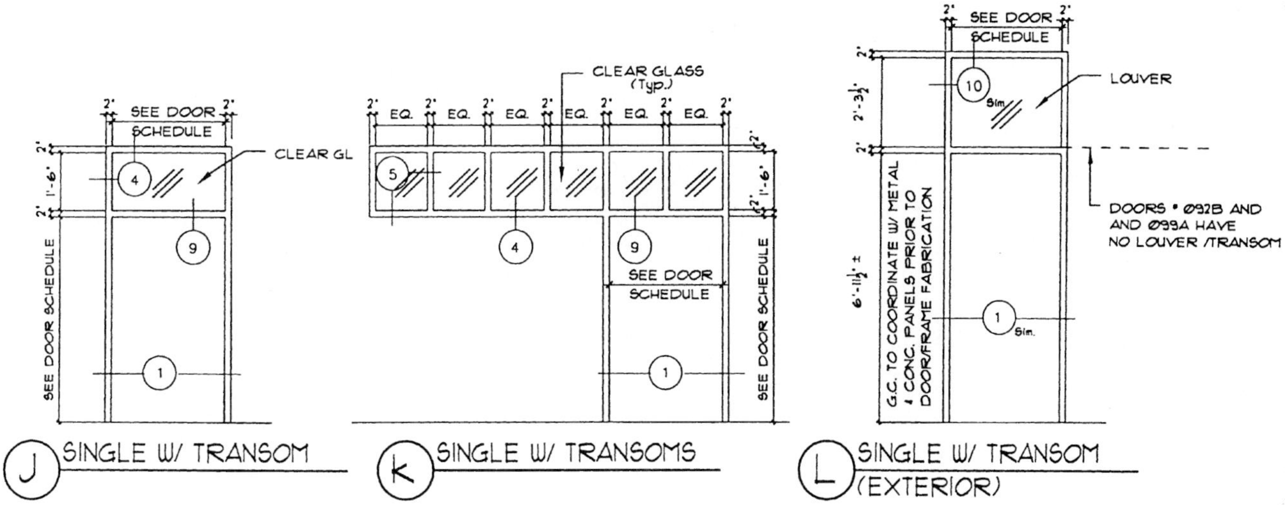

DOORS

Hollow Metal Frame Details

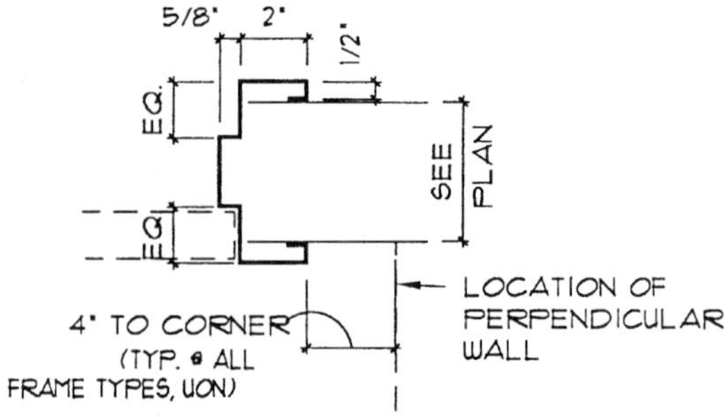

1 DOUBLE RABBET

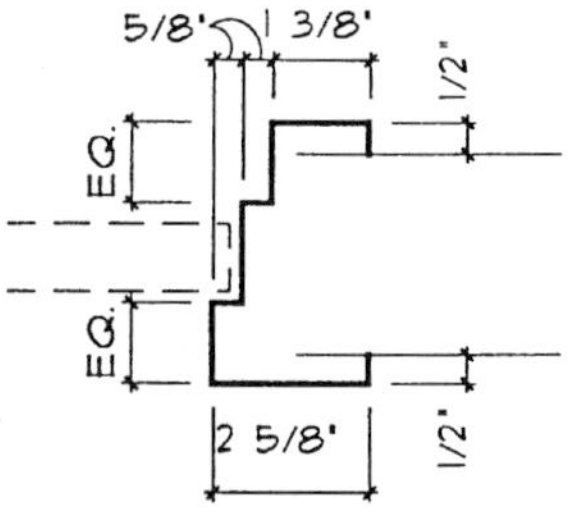

2 DOUBLE EGRESS

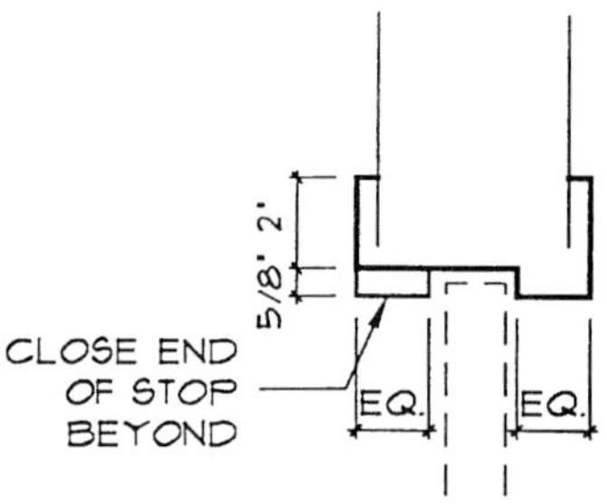

3 DOUBLE EGRESS

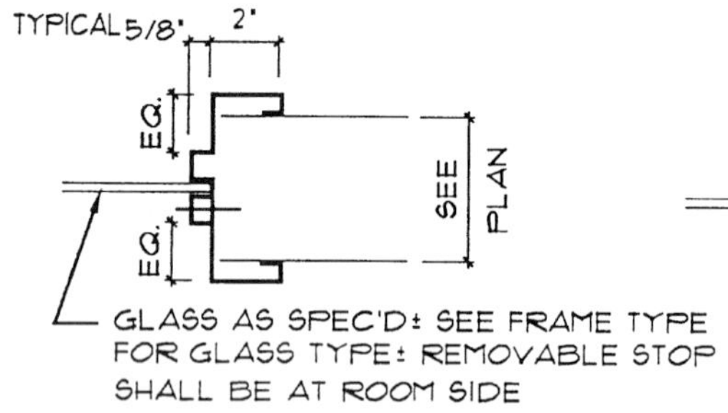

4 HEAD/JAMB/SILL

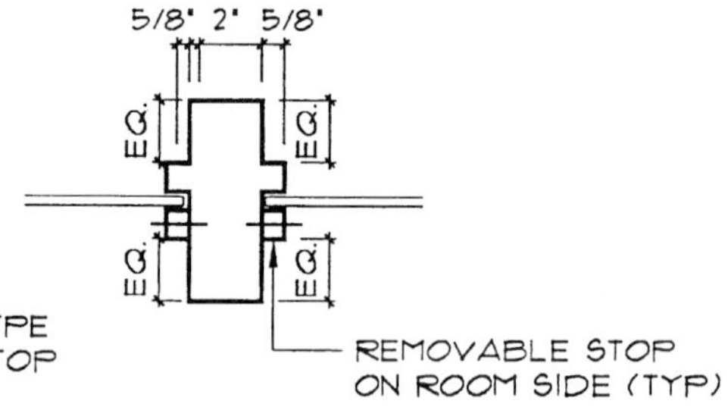

5 INTERMEDIATE

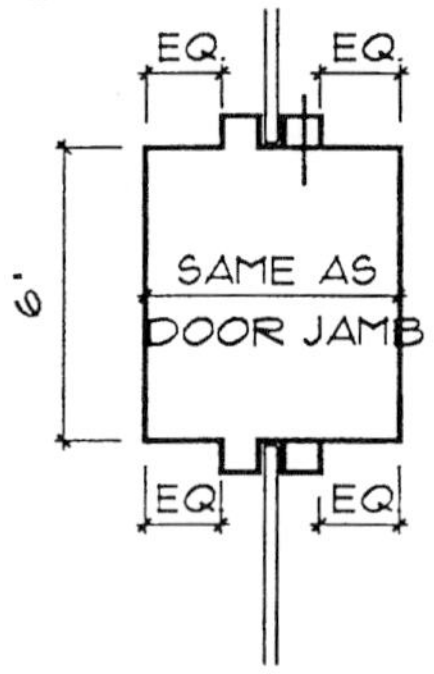

5A INTERMEDIATE

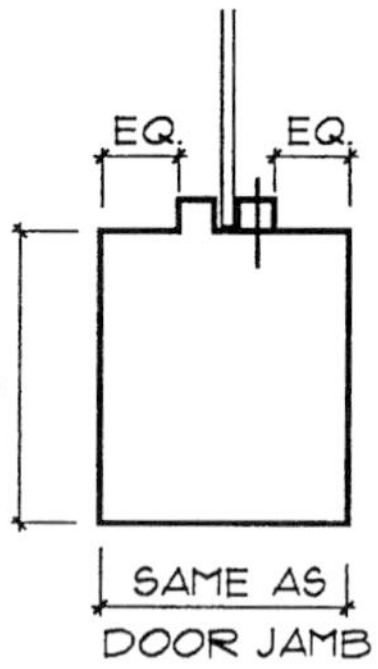

6 BASE

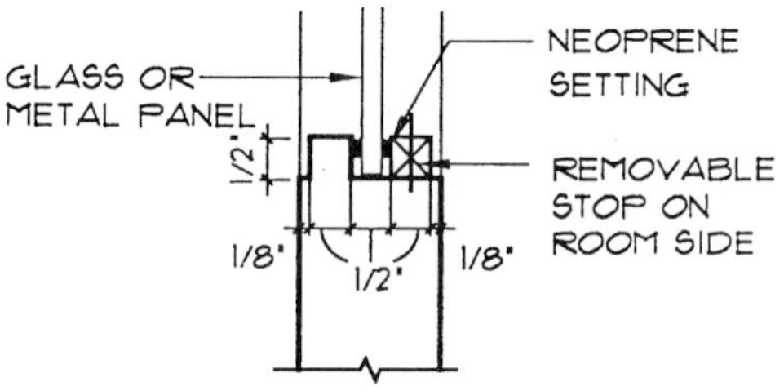

7 VISION WINDOW FRAME

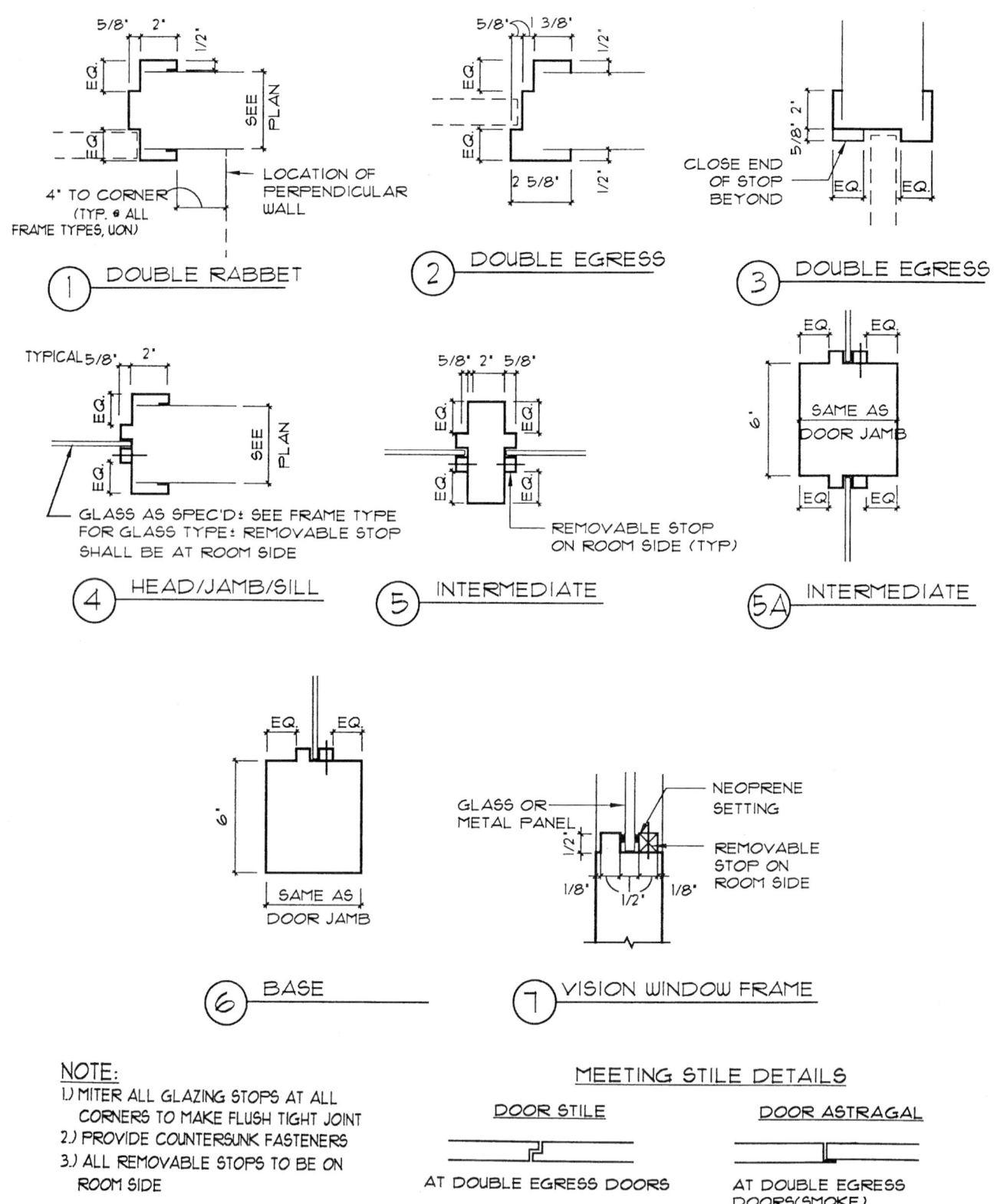

NOTE:
1.) MITER ALL GLAZING STOPS AT ALL CORNERS TO MAKE FLUSH TIGHT JOINT
2.) PROVIDE COUNTERSUNK FASTENERS
3.) ALL REMOVABLE STOPS TO BE ON ROOM SIDE

MEETING STILE DETAILS

DOOR STILE

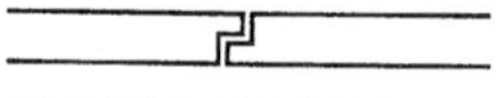

AT DOUBLE EGRESS DOORS

DOOR ASTRAGAL

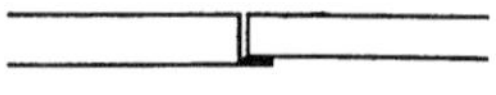

AT DOUBLE EGRESS DOORS(SMOKE)

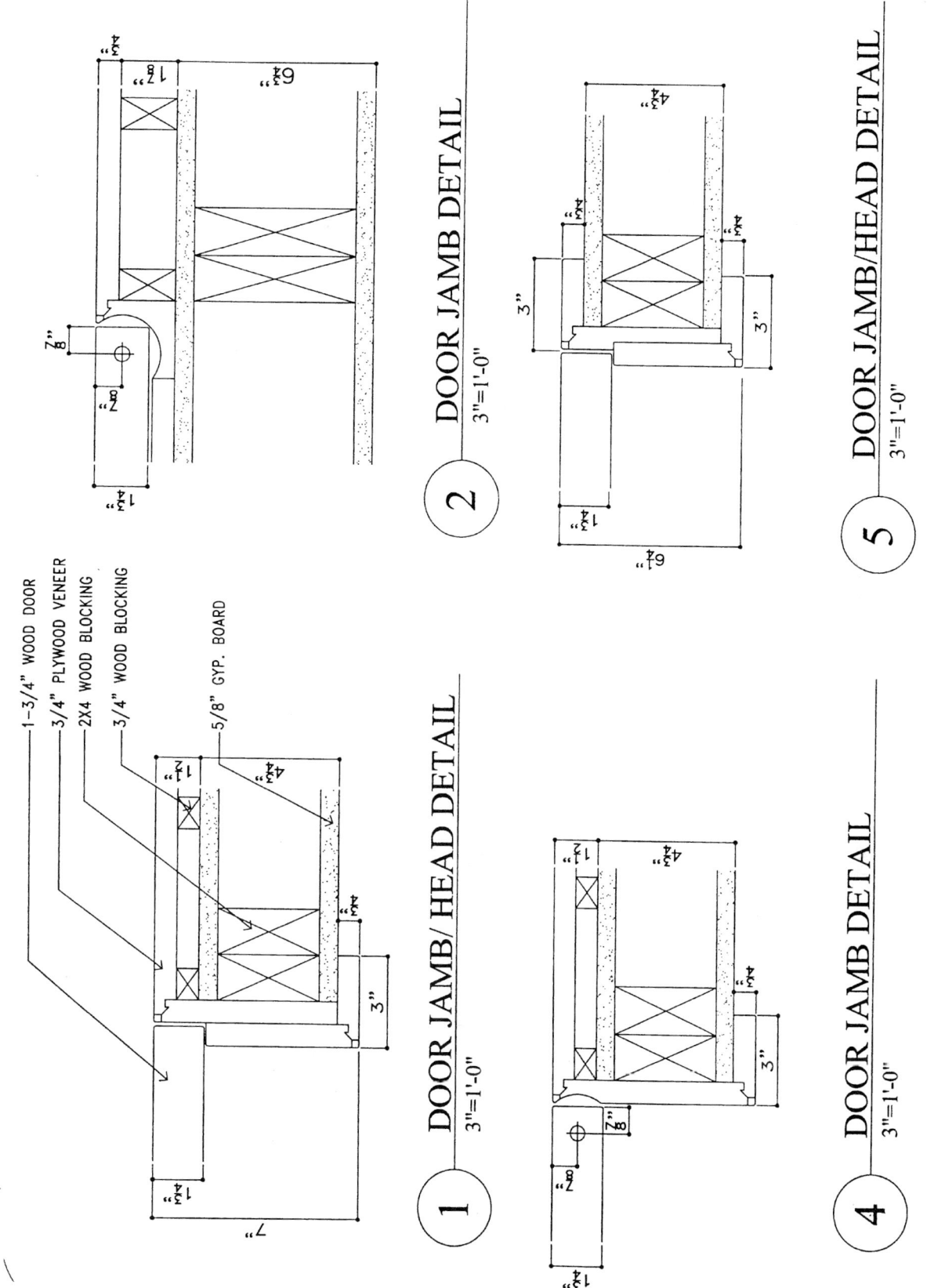

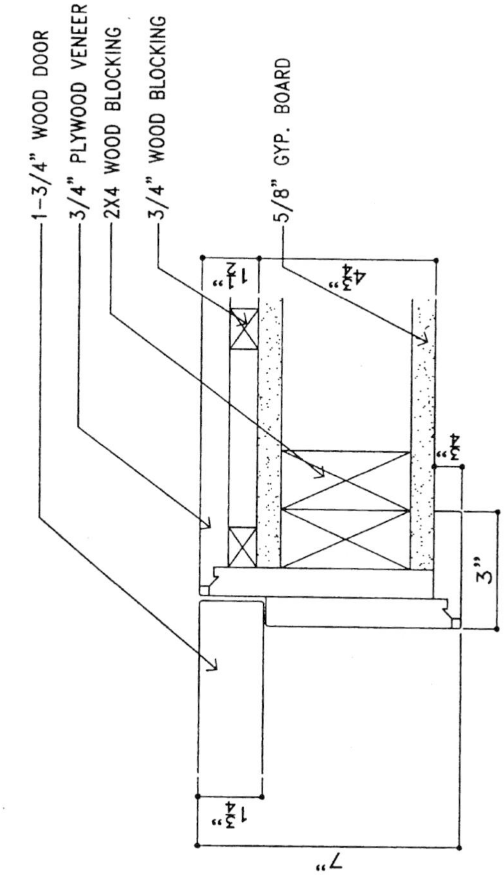

1 DOOR JAMB/ HEAD DETAIL
3"=1'-0"

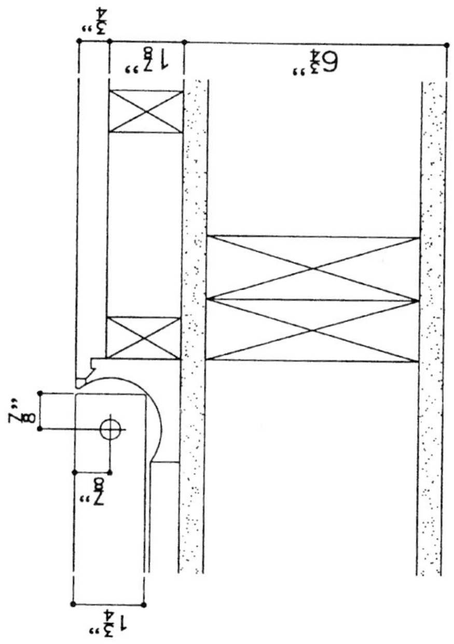

2 DOOR JAMB DETAIL
3"=1'-0"

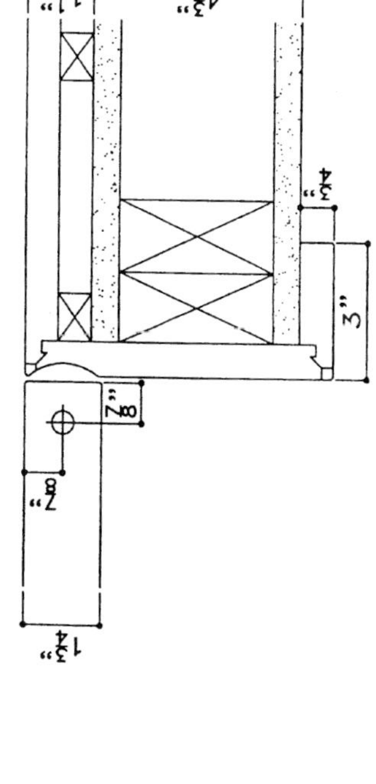

4 DOOR JAMB DETAIL
3"=1'-0"

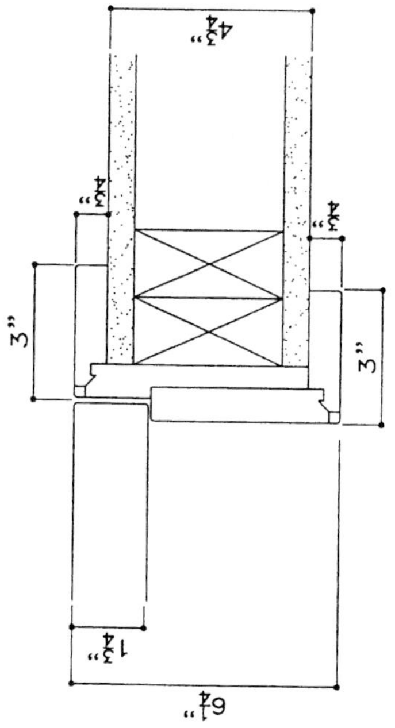

5 DOOR JAMB/HEAD DETAIL
3"=1'-0"

DOORS
Wood Door Jamb Details

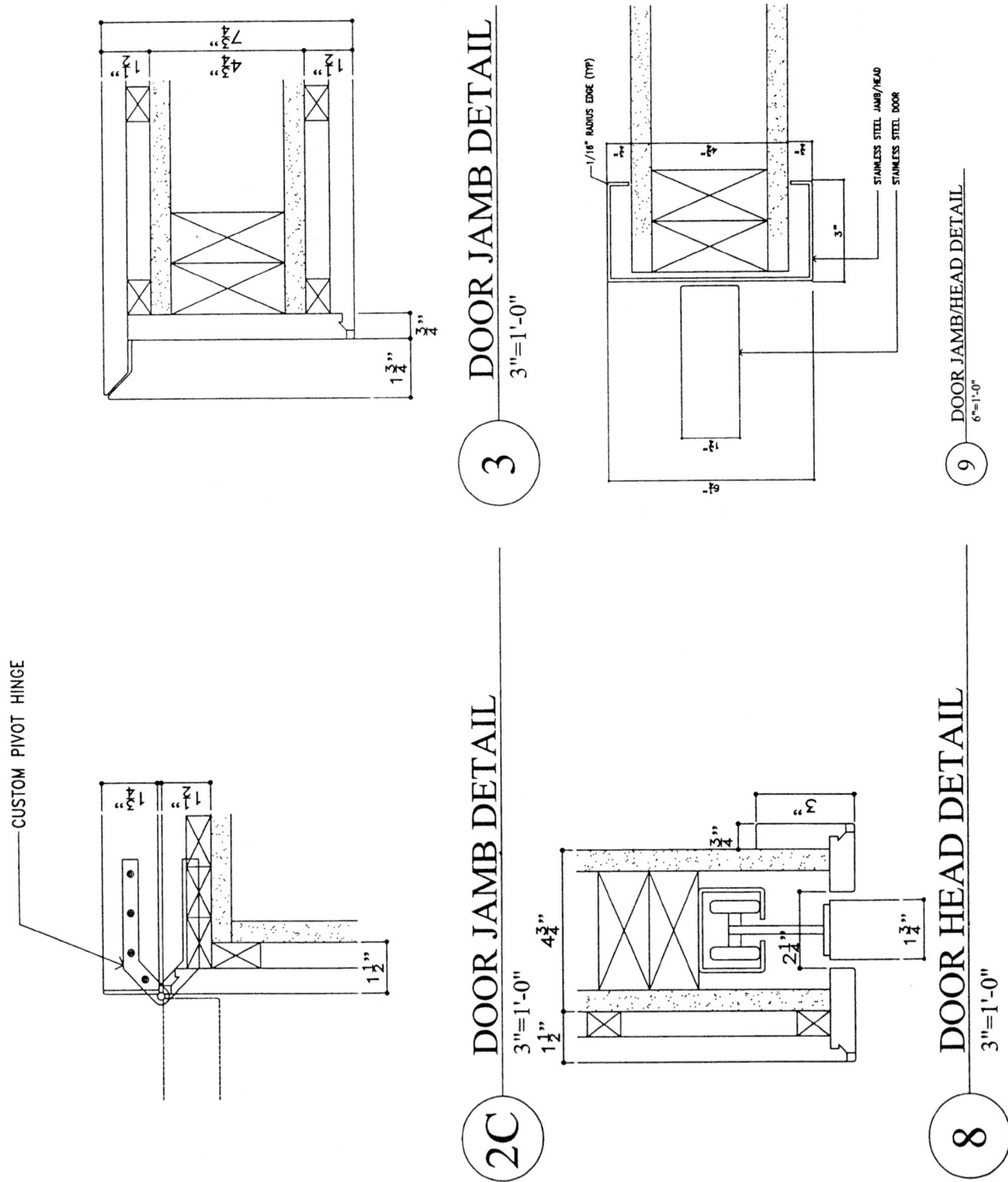

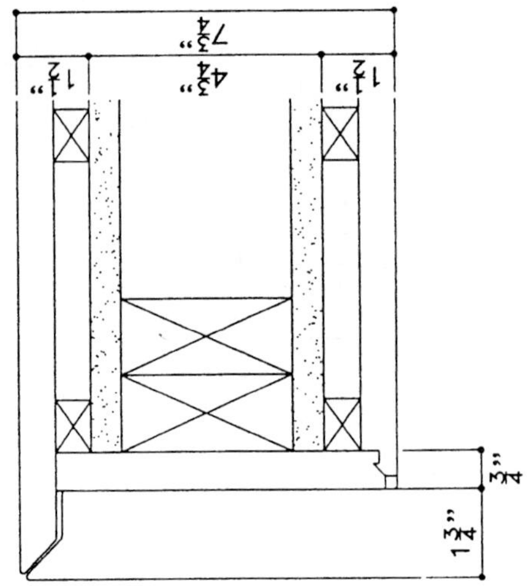

3 DOOR JAMB DETAIL
3"=1'-0"

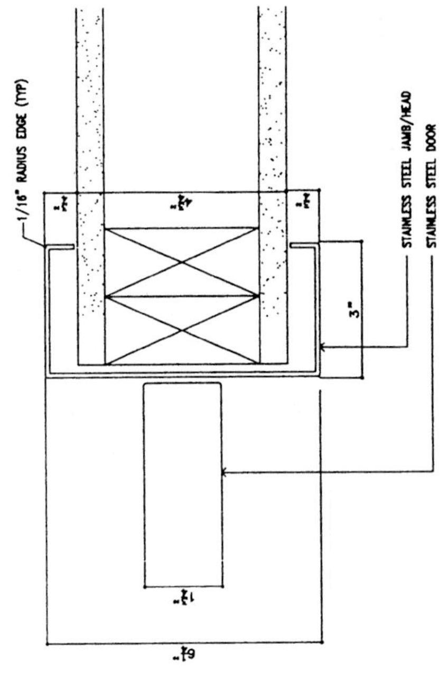

9 DOOR JAMB/HEAD DETAIL
6"=1'-0"

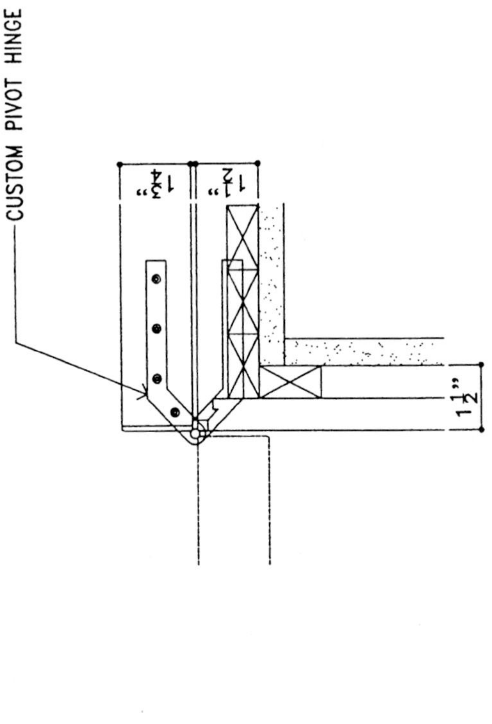

2C DOOR JAMB DETAIL
3"=1'-0"

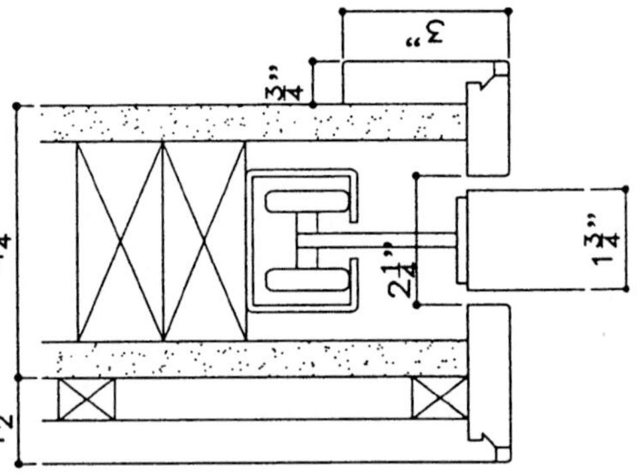

8 DOOR HEAD DETAIL
3"=1'-0"

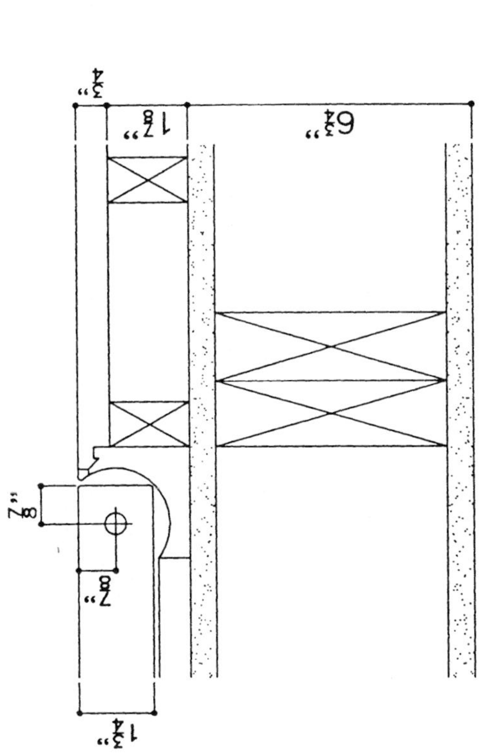

2A DOOR JAMB DETAIL
3"=1'-0"

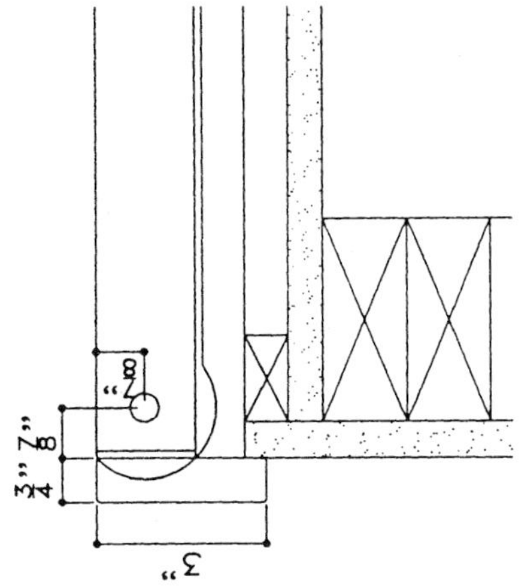

2B DOOR JAMB DETAIL
3"=1'-0"

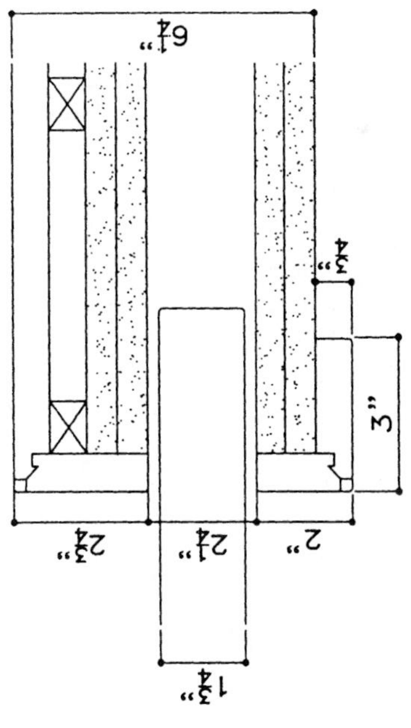

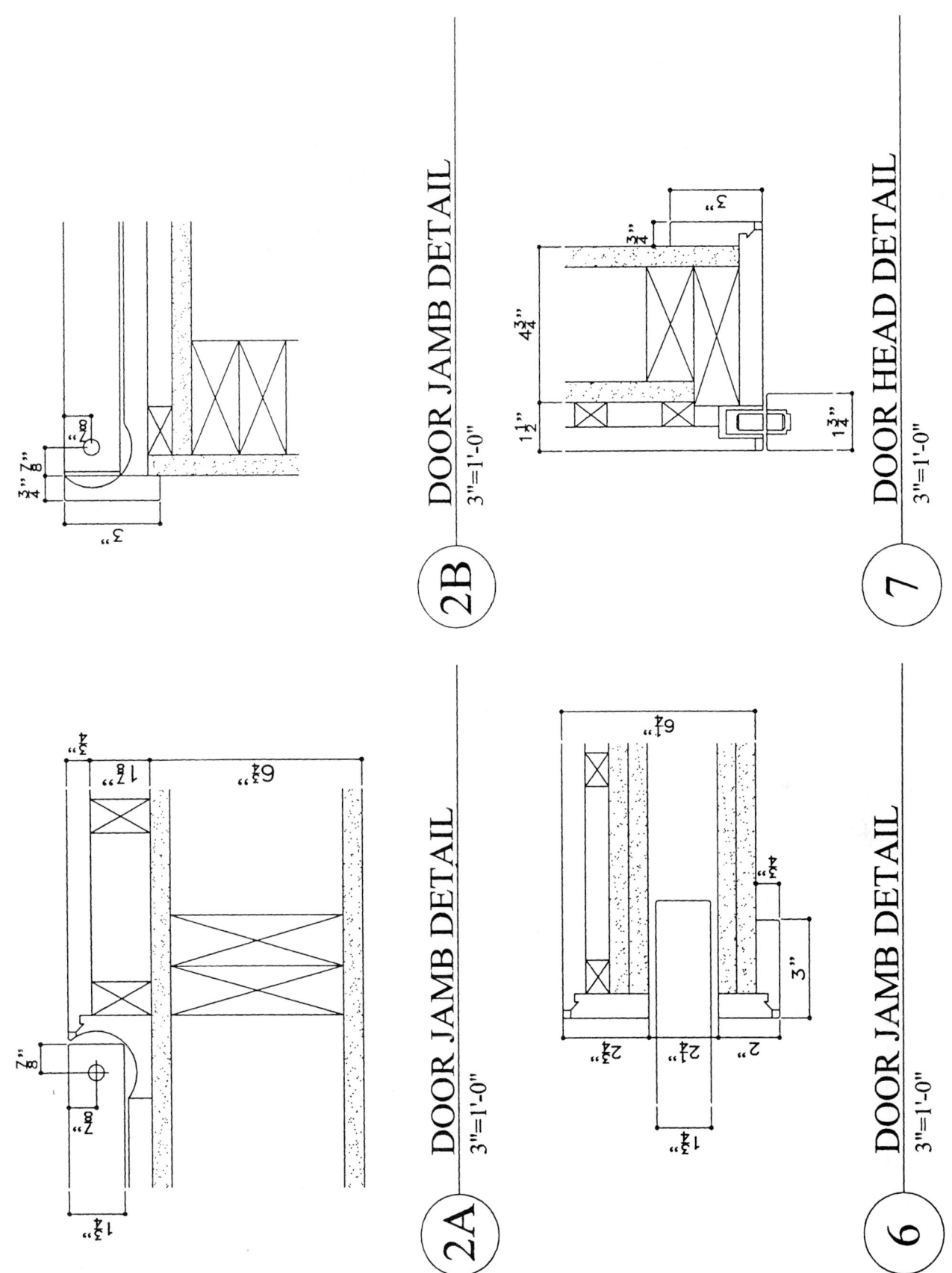

6 DOOR JAMB DETAIL
3"=1'-0"

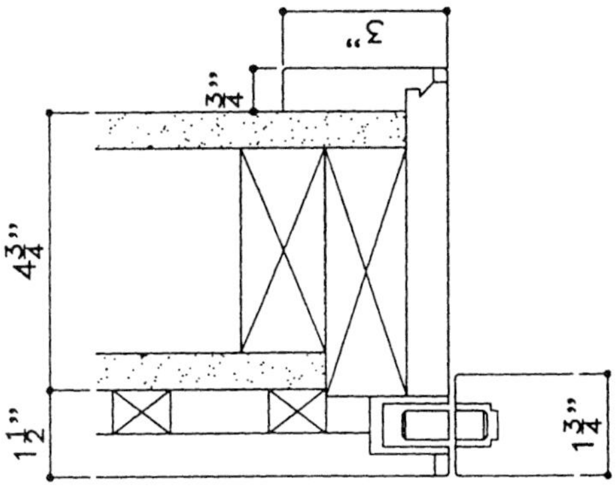

7 DOOR HEAD DETAIL
3"=1'-0"

DOORS

Hollow Metal Door and Frame Notes

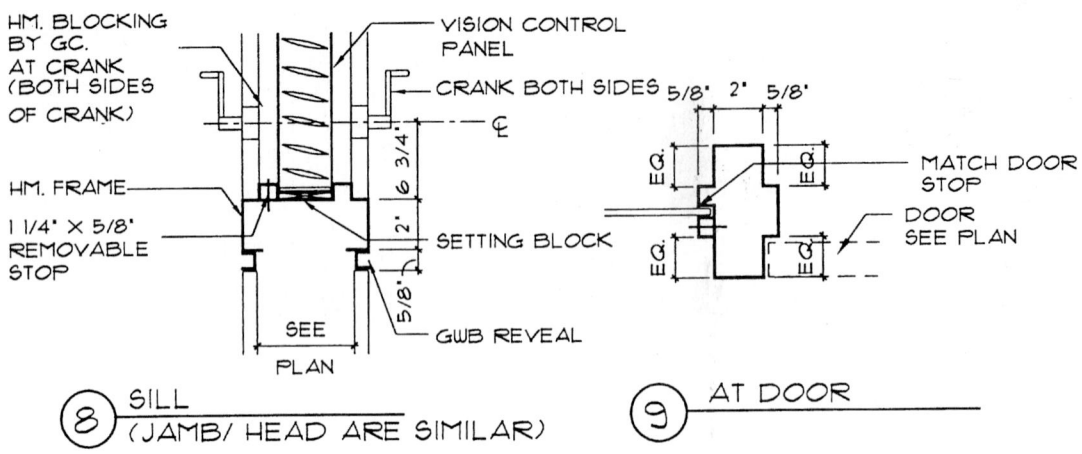

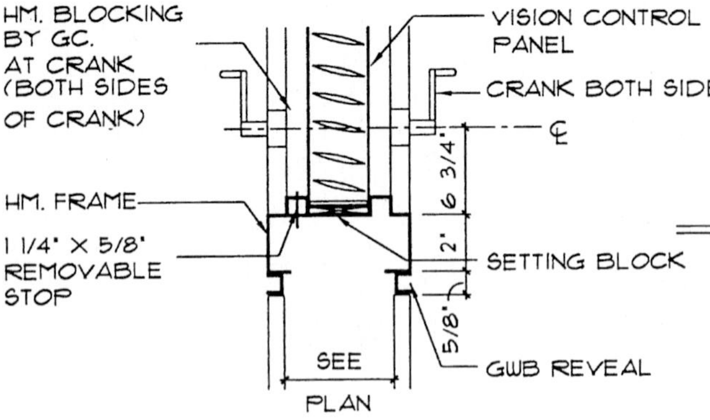

(8) SILL (JAMB/ HEAD ARE SIMILAR)

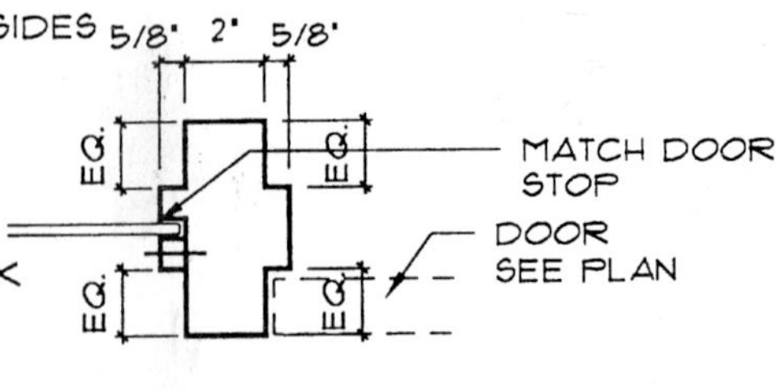

(9) AT DOOR

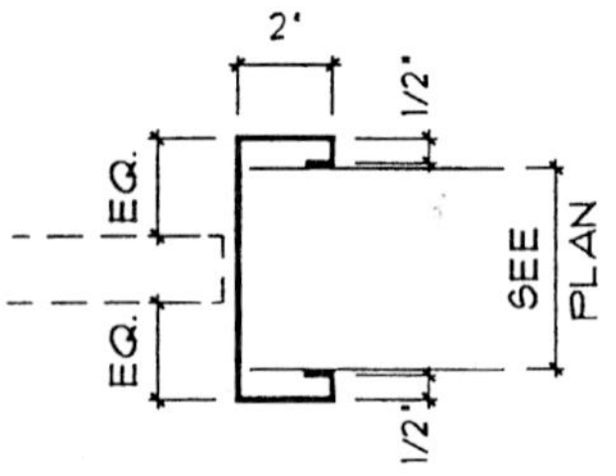

(10) TRIMMED OPENING

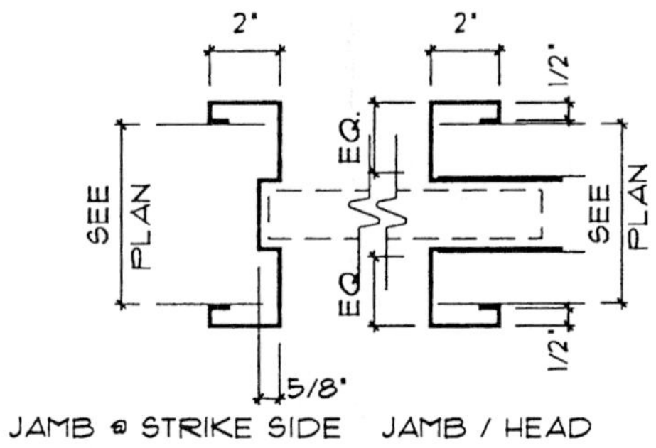

(11) SLIDING POCKET DOOR

DOOR & FRAME NOTES

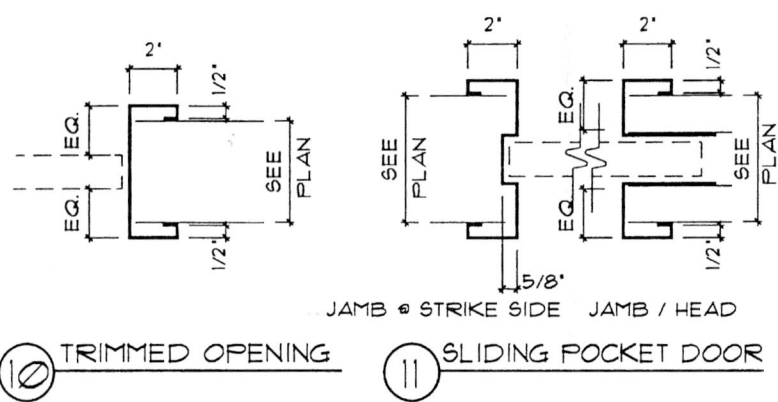

1. All doors except lead-lined to be 1 3/4" thick and 7'-0" high, unless otherwise noted.
2. All vision panels in rated doors (B or C label) to be 1/4" wire glass, square pattern horizontal & vertical, and 1/4" tempered glass at non-rated doors. Provide lead-lined glass at lead lined doors.
3. Where rated doors are indicated, door frame rating shall be equal to door rating.
4. Door width is indicated in inches. Two numbers separated by slash. Slash indicates double doors.
5. UL Labels: B Label = 1 1/2 hours
   C Label = 3/4 hour
6. Provide head reinf. for frames over 4'-0" wide.
7. All doors to be 3/4" undercut unless otherwise noted.
8. Provide interlock switch at all lead-lined doors. Provide "in-use" light over all doors leading into rooms with radio-graphic equipment , unless otherwise noted. Coordinate with equipment, hollow metal and hardware.
8. All rated doors to be B.S.A. or MEA approved.

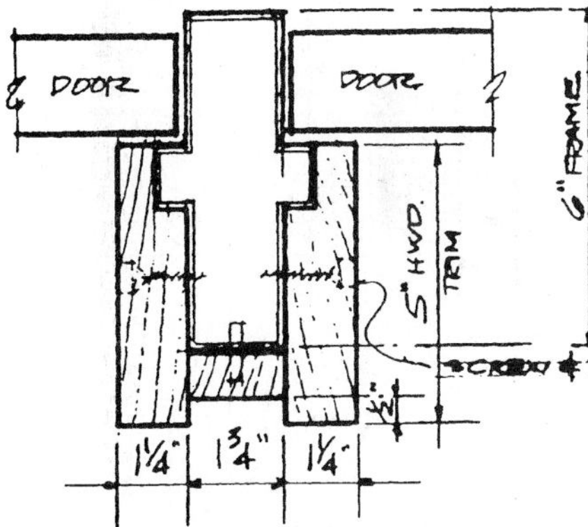

F-11A H.M. FRAME HWD. TRIM/ONE SIDE 3"=1'-0"

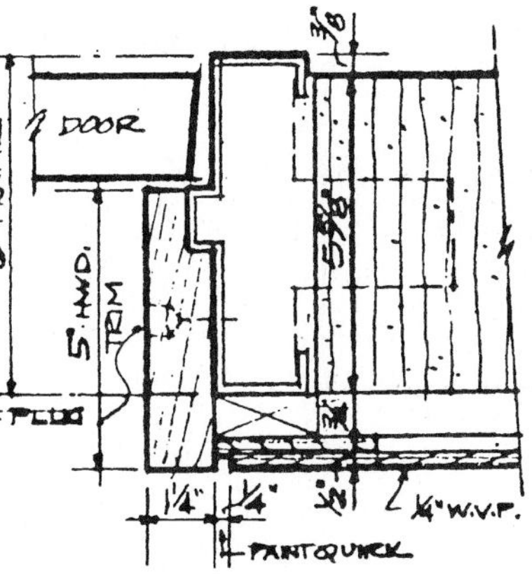

F-11 H.M. FRAME HWD. TRIM/ONE SIDE 3"=1'-0"

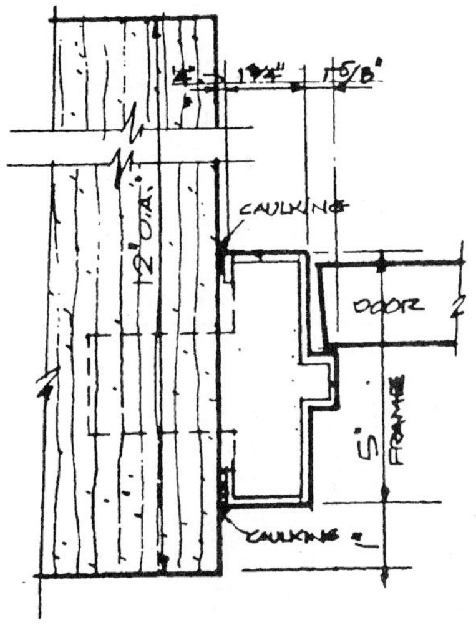

F-12 H.M. EXTERIOR FRAME 3"=1'-0"

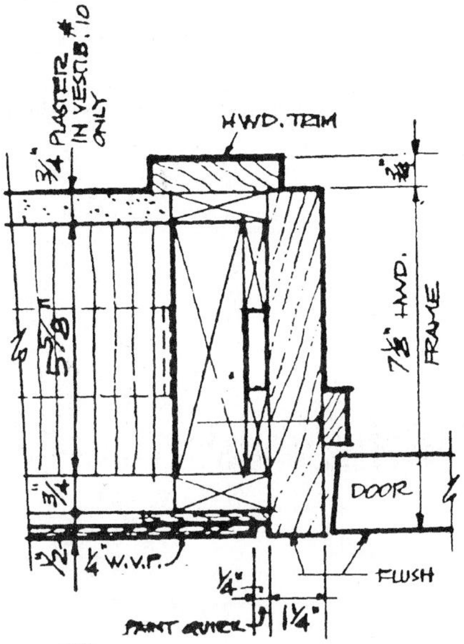

F-13 HARDWOOD FRAME 3"=1'-0"

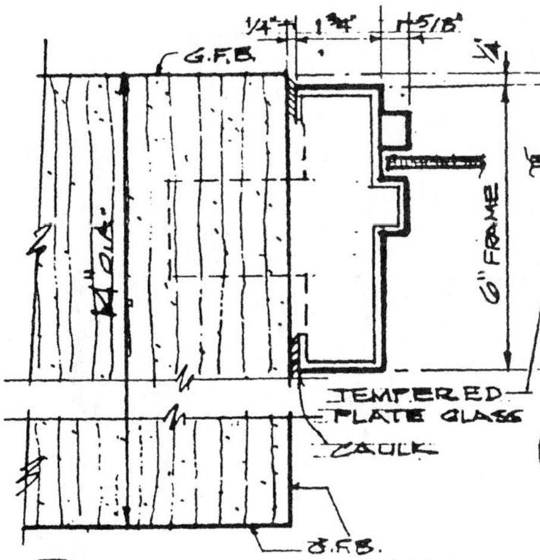

F-14 3"=1'-0" #24

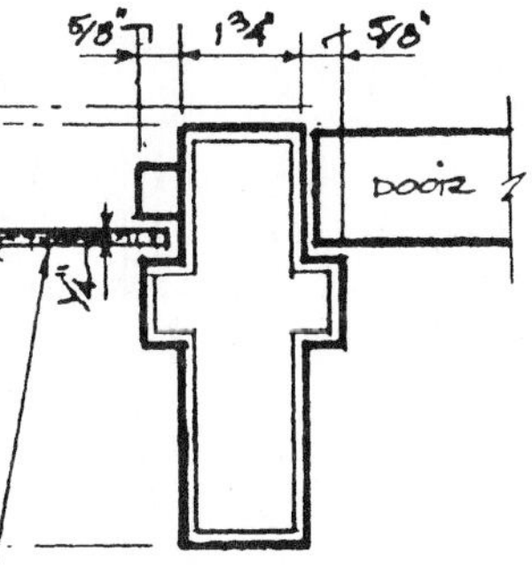

F-14A 3"=1'-0" #24

DOORS

Hollow Metal Door Frames

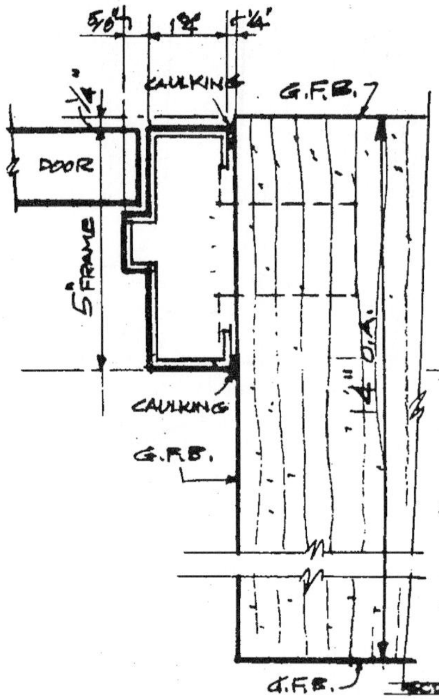

F-6 H.M. EXTERIOR FRAME
3"=1'-0"

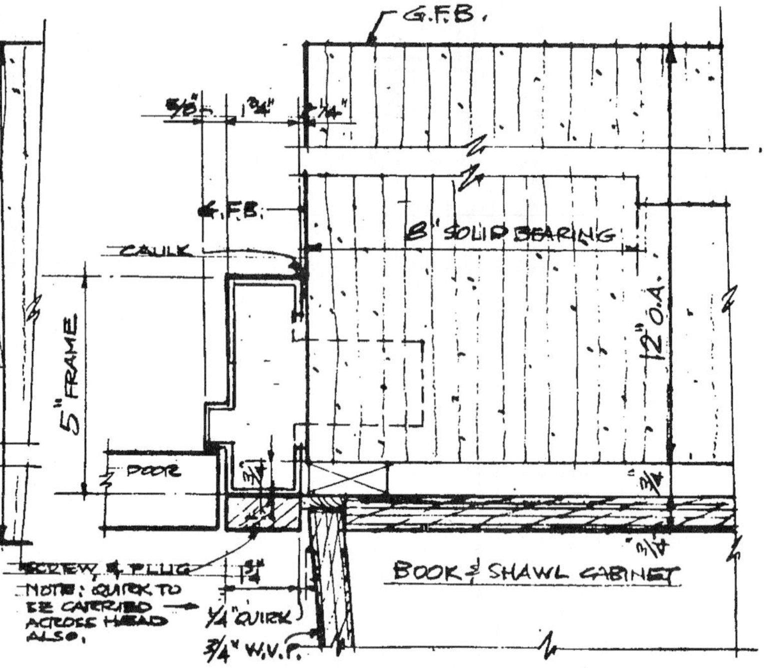

F-7 H.M. FRAME - HARDWOOD/ONE SIDE
3"=1'-0" SEE DETAIL 4/A-20 FOR DOOR #11

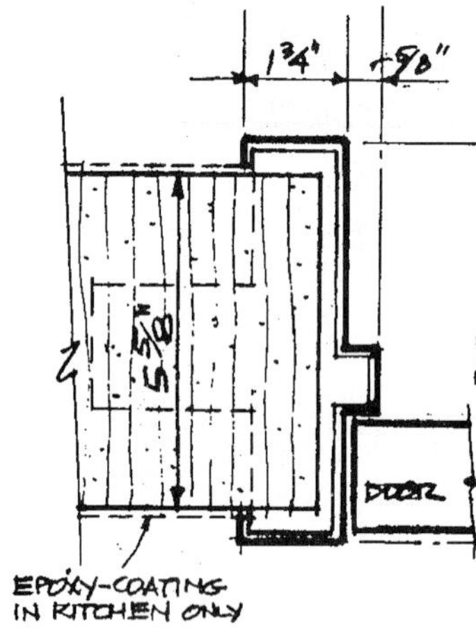

F-8 H.M. FRAME
3"=1'-0"

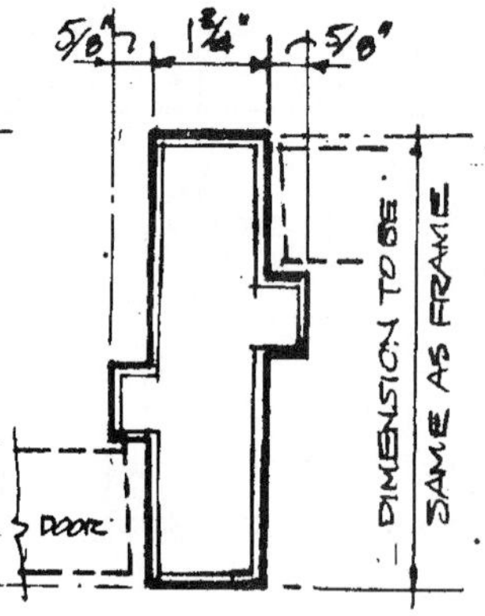

F-9 H.M. MULLION
3"=1'-0"

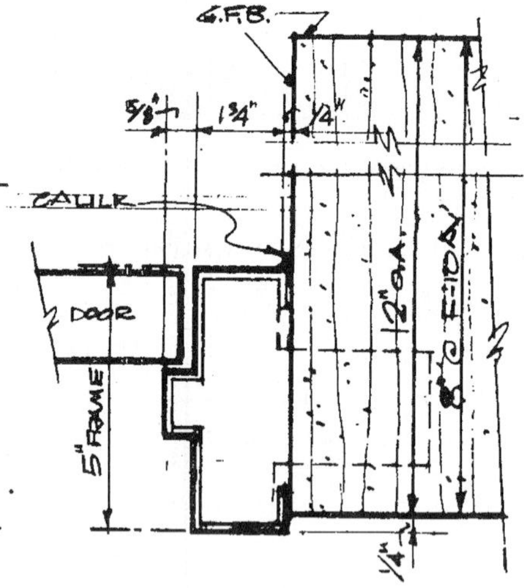

F-10 H.M. FRAME
3"=1'-0"

F10A H.M. FRAM.

	PARTICLE	STAVE	HOLLOW	ACOUSTICAL** STC 31′, 36′, 38′, & 40′	LEAD	STILE AND RAIL	
THICKNESS	1-3/8", 1-3/4"	1-3/8", 1-3/4", 2-1/4"	1-3/8", 1-3/4"	1-3/4"	1-3/4" — lead thickness to 3/8".	1-3/4", 2-1/4"	THICKNESS
MAX. SIZE	4′ 0" x 12′ 0"	4′ 0" x 12′ 0"	4′ 0" x 12′ 0"	4′ 0" x 10′ 0"	4′ 0" x 10′ 0"	4′ 0" x 12′ 0"	MAX. SIZE
CORE	Mat-formed particle board conforming to ANSI A208.1-1L1.	(21-27 pcf) Low density wood blocks bonded together. One species per core.	Resin impregnated honeycomb — 1/2" cell.	Special materials and assembly to meet ratings shown.	Divided core. Mat-formed particle board conforming to ANSI A208.1-1M3. Lead over 1/8" reinforced with lead plugs.	Stiles and rails: Low density wood blocks bonded together & to edgebands. Panels: Mill option, mat-formed particle board or edge-glued lumber core.	CORE
STILES	1-3/8" face matching or compatible to face veneer, mill option inner-ply. Glued to core. Maximum 5".	5/8" matching or compatible to face veneer. Glued to core.	1-1/8" 2 ply. Matching or compatible to face veneer, mill option inner-ply.	STC 31 — Stave 5/8", particle 1-3/8" matching or compatible to face veneer. Glued to core. STC 36, 38, 40 — 2". Face compatible outer-ply. Glued to core.	1-1/2" matching or compatible to face veneer. Glued to core.	5/8" Matching or compatible to face veneer. Glued to stile.	STILES
RAILS	1-3/8" mill option hardwood glued to core standard. Nominal 2-1/2", 5", 8" and 12" optional.		2-1/4" mill option hardwood.	STC 31 — 1-1/8" mill option hardwood glued to core. STC 36, 38, 40 — 3".	2-1/2" mill option hardwood glued to core.	1/2" edgeband compatible to face veneer. Glued to rail.	RAILS
FACES	All available domestic and foreign veneers. Medium density overlays. High pressure laminates.					All available 1/10" sliced hardwood veneers on stiles and rails. Standard veneers on panel faces.	FACES
CROSSBANDS	Min. 1/16" hardwood.					1/30" mill option hardwood.	CROSSBANDS
VENEER MATCHING	Virtually unlimited in standard veneers, end matching in door and transoms with wood grain plastics.					Limited veneer matching.	VENEER MATCHING
PREMACHINING	Prefitting, mortise for appropriate hardware. No preparation for surface mounted.						PREMACHINING
OPENINGS	Min. 5" margins edge of door and adjacent hardware cut-outs. Max. opening 40% of door area or 50% of height.					Min. 5" stiles, minimum 10" bottom rail, min. 5" top rail.	OPENINGS
SPECIAL DETAILS	Cut light openings.* Install metal and wood louvers, wood beads, and safety glazing. Standard beads or architect's detail at light and louver openings. Applied mouldings. Dutch doors and shelves.		Cut light openings.* Install metal and wood louvers, wood beads, and safety glazing. Standard beads or architect's detail at light and louver openings.	Cut light openings.* Safety glazing. Standard wood, acoustical and lead lined beads. No applied mouldings. No dutch doors.		Solid sticking or moulding per architect's detail. Wood louvers and safety glazing factory installed.	SPECIAL DETAILS
FINISHING	Gardall II, primed, painted, sealed, oiled or waxed as specified.						FINISHING
WARRANTY	Interior — Life of original installation. Exterior — 2 years.		Interior — 1 year. Exterior — Not recommended.	Interior — Life of original installation. Exterior — Not recommended.		Interior — 2 years. Exterior — Not recommended.	WARRANTY
STANDARDS	NWWDA I.S.-1 AWI Section 1300 PC Federal LLLD581 Type I & II, Class 1	NWWDA I.S.-1 AWI Section 1300 SLC Federal LLLD581 Type I & II, Class1	NWWDA I.S.-1	NWWDA I.S.-1 AWI Section 1300 SR — ASTM E90-70 Federal LLLD581 Type IV, Class 4	NWWDA I.S.-1 AWI-1300-LL and E413-73 Federal LLLD581, Type IV, Class 5	AWI Section 1400 Federal LLLD581, Type III	STANDARDS

*Footnote on openings — Minimum margins per AWI Section 1300. **No rating guaranteed on doors with lites or pairs.

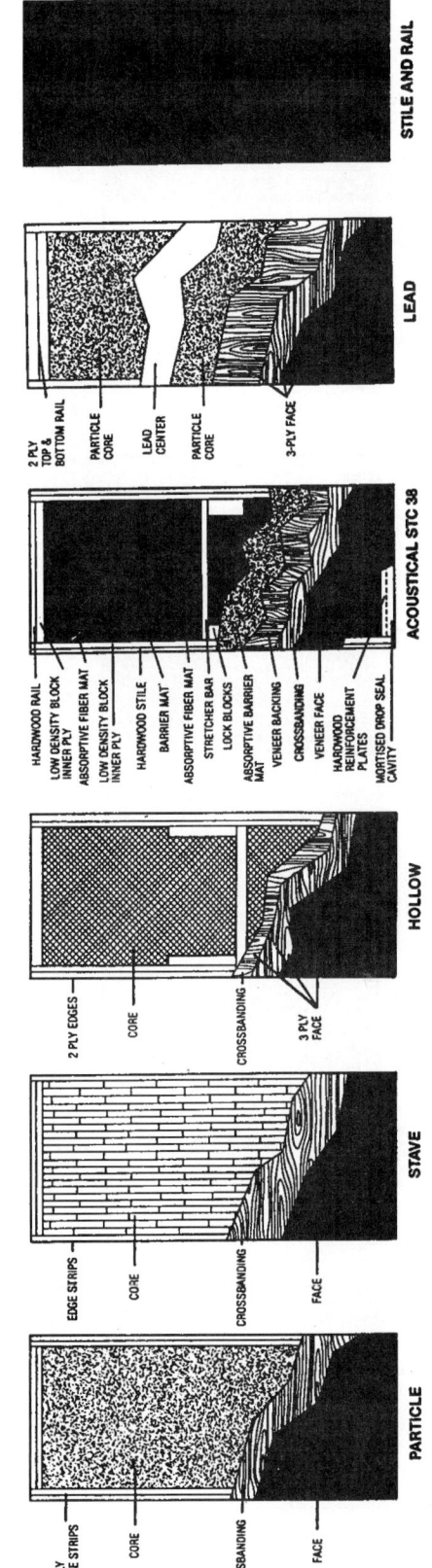

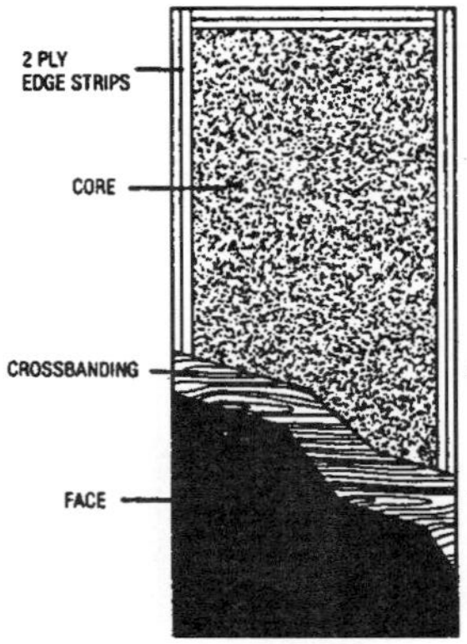

PARTICLE

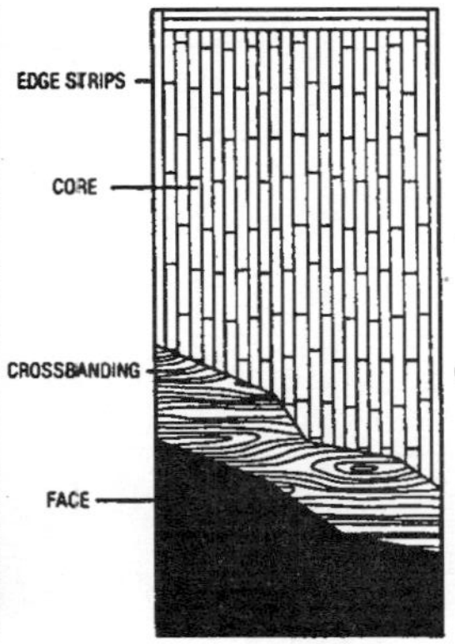

STAVE

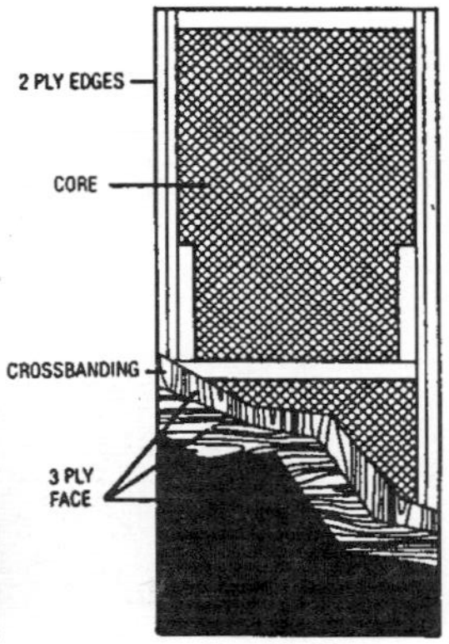

HOLLOW

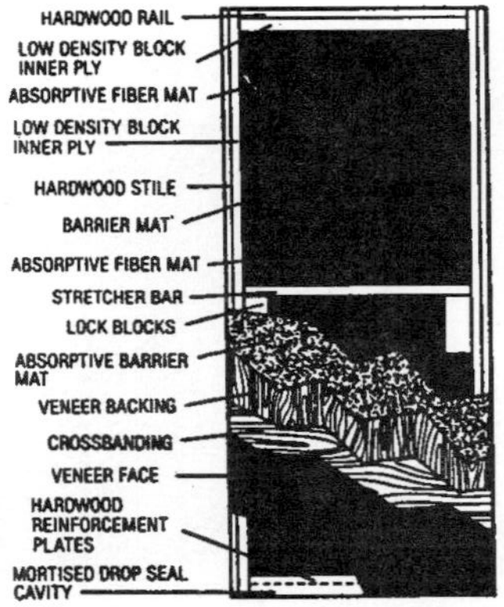

ACOUSTICAL STC 38

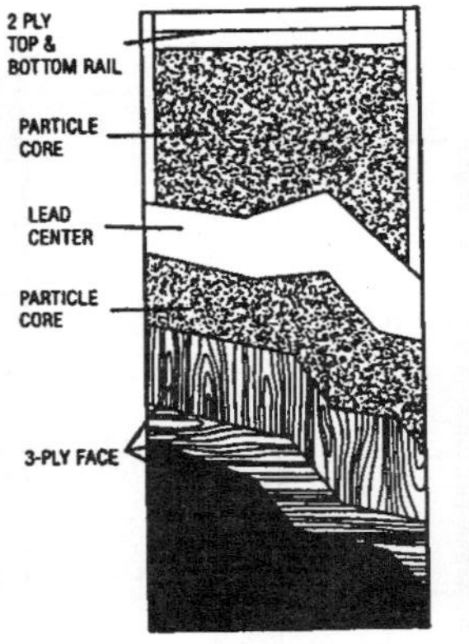

LEAD

STILE AND RAIL

DOORS

Sliding Doors and Handles

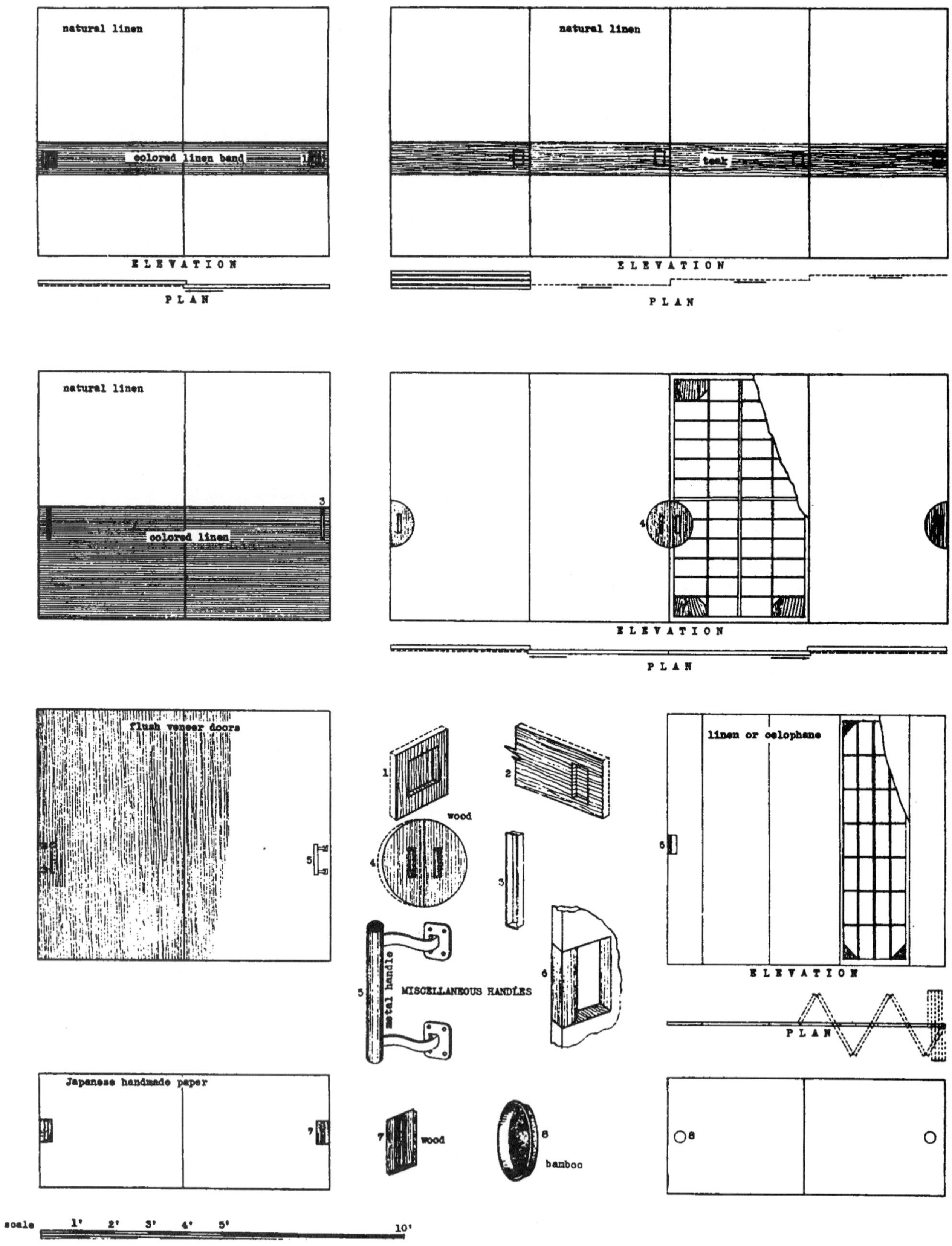

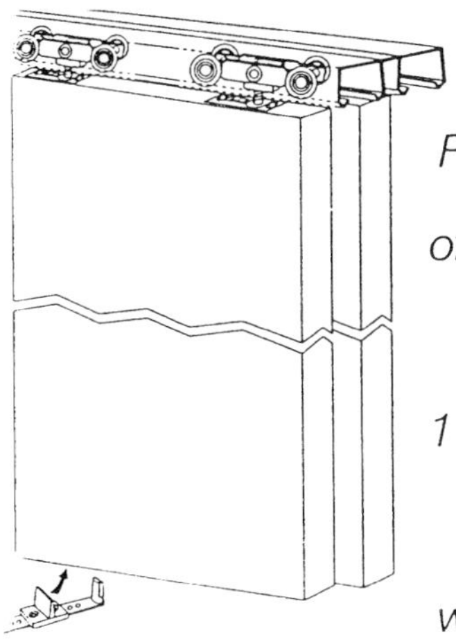

For installation of 2 by-passing doors, with 1 3/8" to 1 3/4" thick panels weighing up to 150 lbs. each.

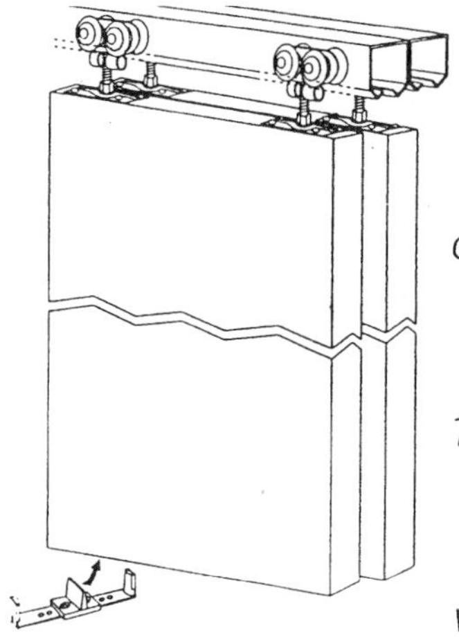

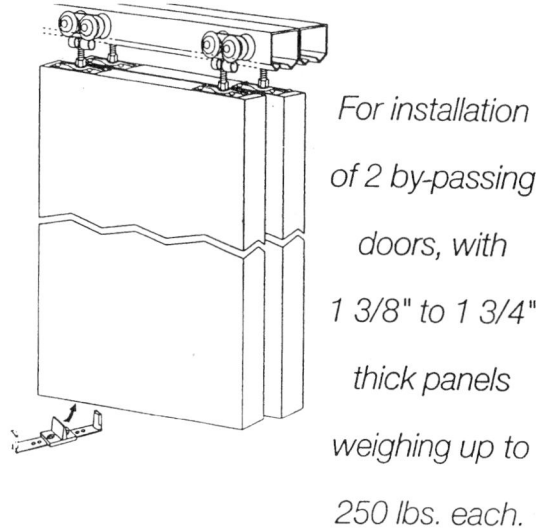

For installation of 2 by-passing doors, with 1 3/8" to 1 3/4" thick panels weighing up to 250 lbs. each.

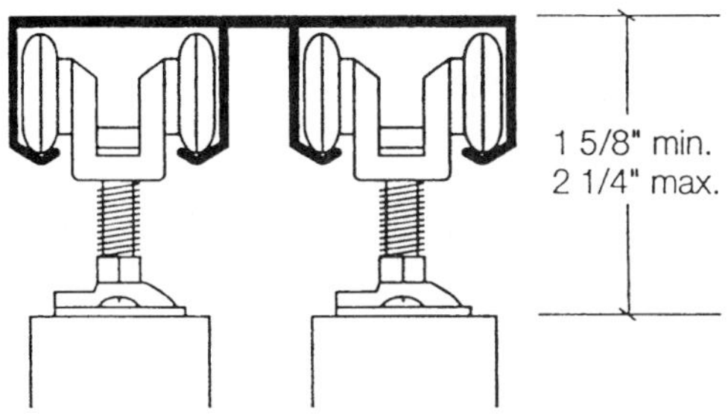

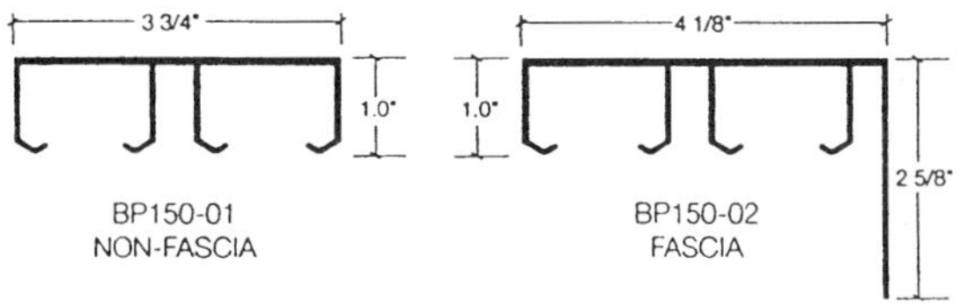

BP150-01
NON-FASCIA

BP150-02
FASCIA

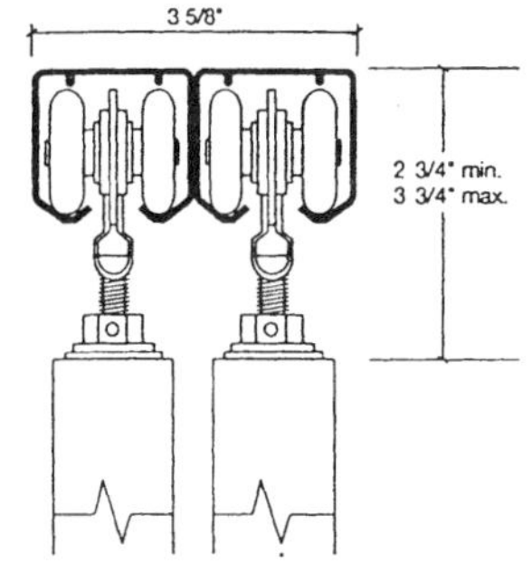

1 3/8" DOORS

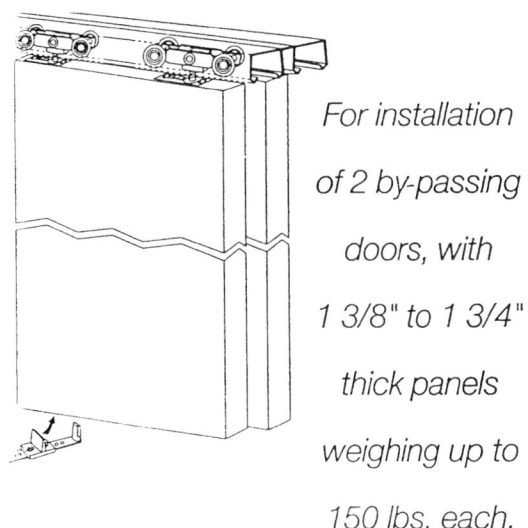

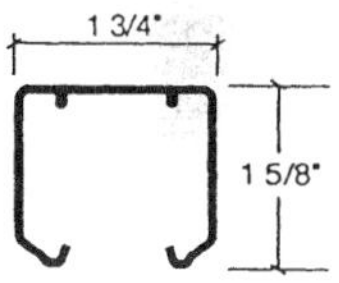

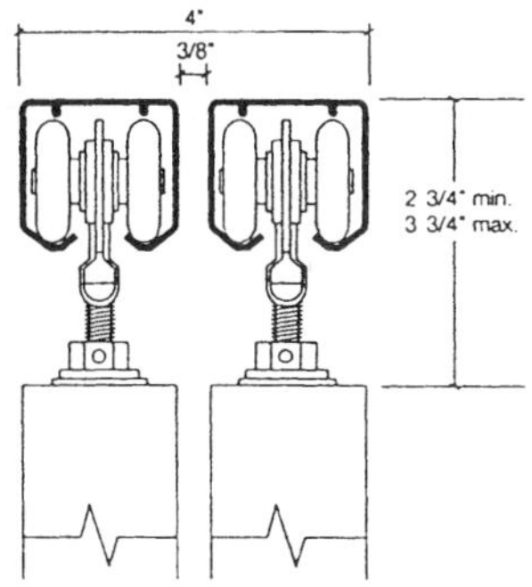

1 3/4" DOORS

To Determine Panel Width:
Panel Width = Known Finished Opening Width plus 1" per overlap, divide by number of panels
To Determine Opening Width:
Opening Width = Known Finished Panel Width multiplied by number of panels, less 1" per overlap,
Door Height = 2 1/8" less than finished opening height

To Determine Panel Width:
Panel Width = Known Finished Opening Width plus 1" per overlap, divide by number of panels
To Determine Opening Width:
Opening Width = Known Finished Panel Width multiplied by number of panels, less 1" per overlap,
Door Height = 3 1/4" less than finished opening height

DOORS
Door/Sliding

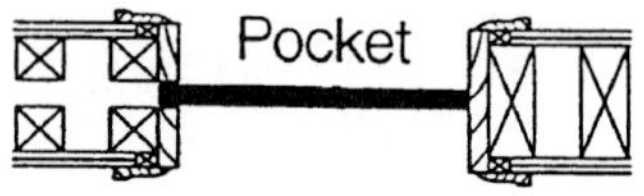

36" AND 48" OPENING

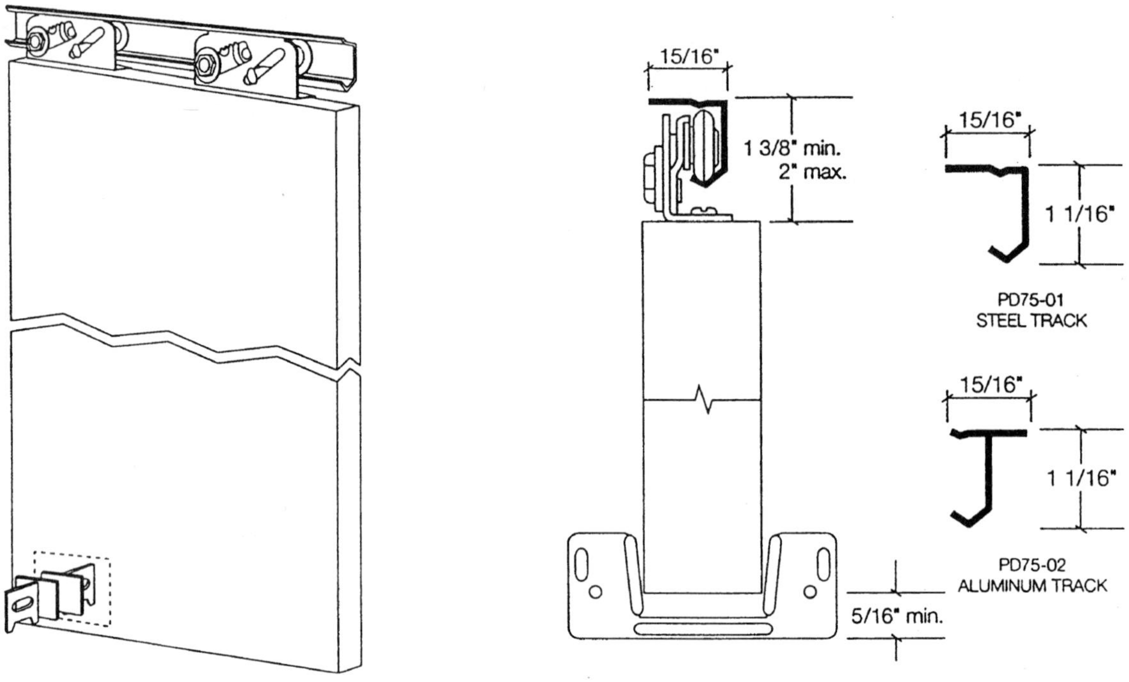

75 LB PANEL

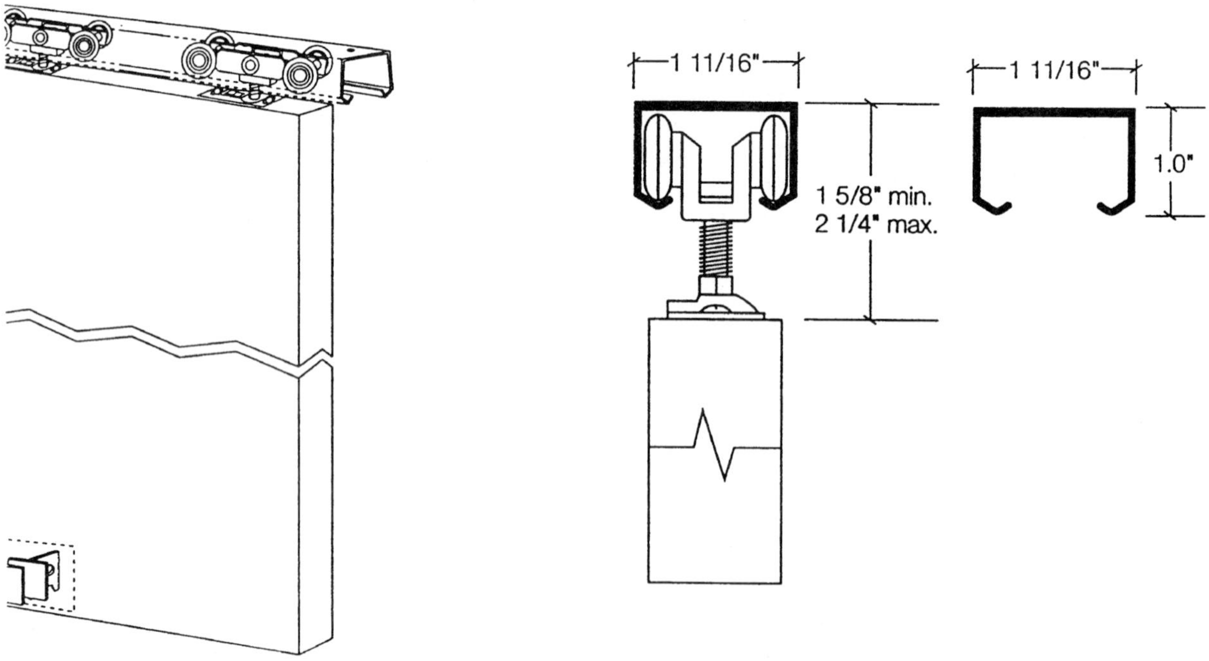

150 LB PANEL

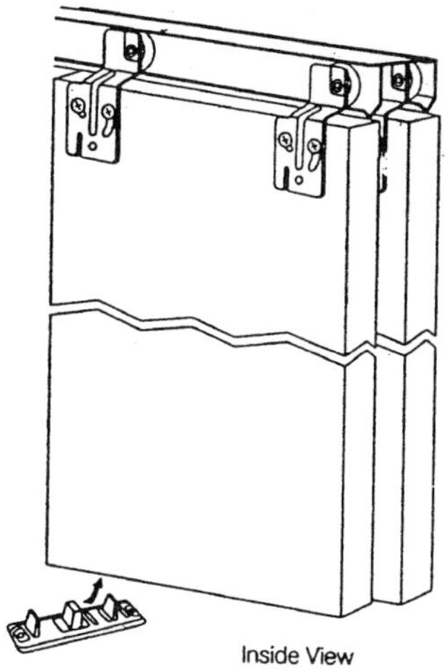

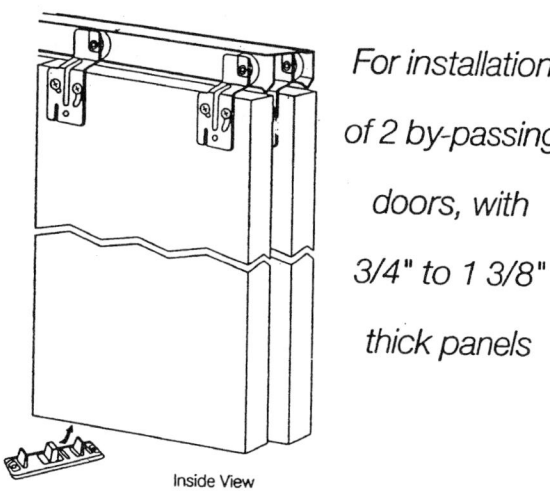

For installation of 2 by-passing doors, with 3/4" to 1 3/8" thick panels

60 LB PANEL

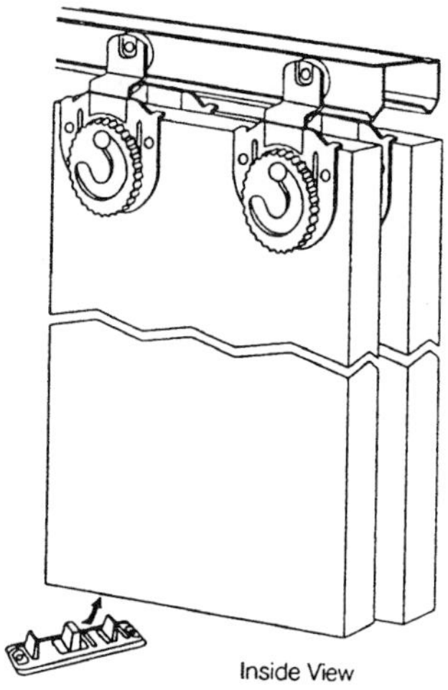

For installation of 2 by-passing doors, with 3/4" or 1 3/8" thick panels

60 LB PANEL

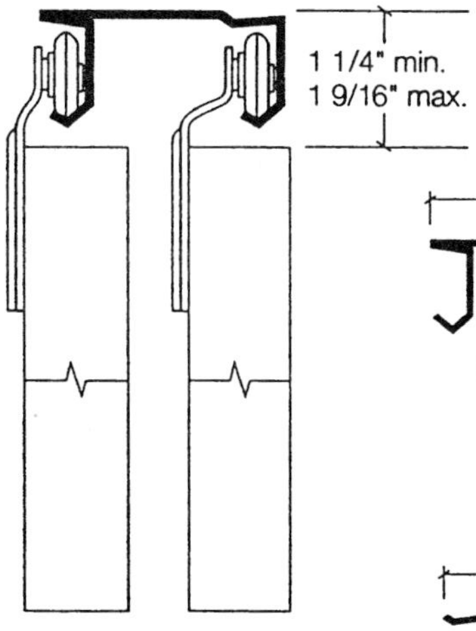

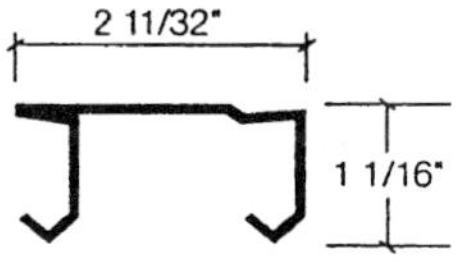

BP75-01
Steel

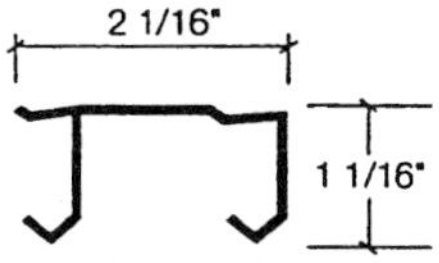

BP75-02, Aluminum
BP75-03, Steel

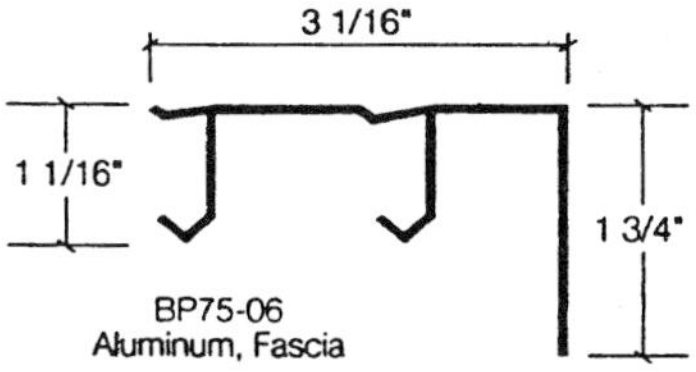

BP75-06
Aluminum, Fascia

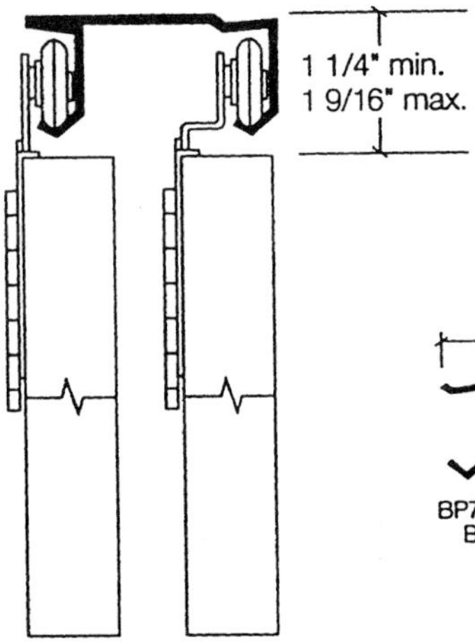

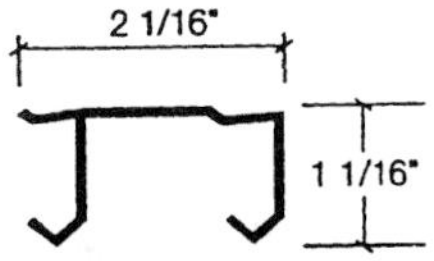

BP75-02, Aluminum
BP75-03, Steel

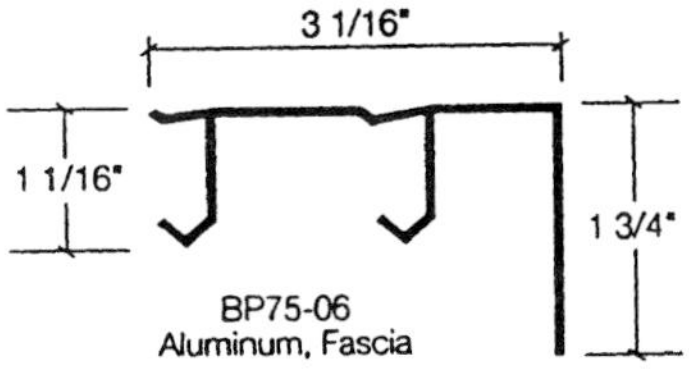

BP75-06
Aluminum, Fascia

DOORS
Door/Pocket

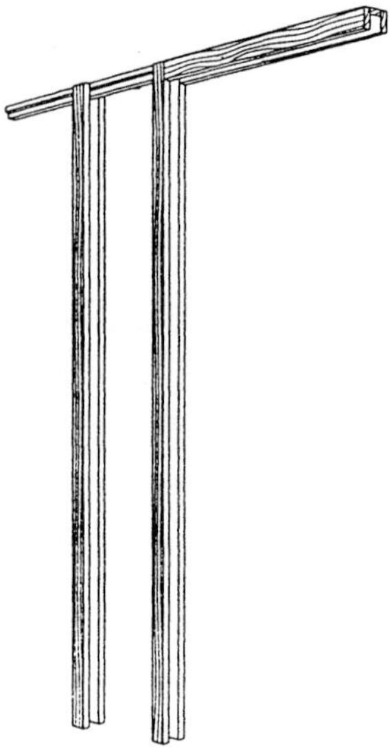

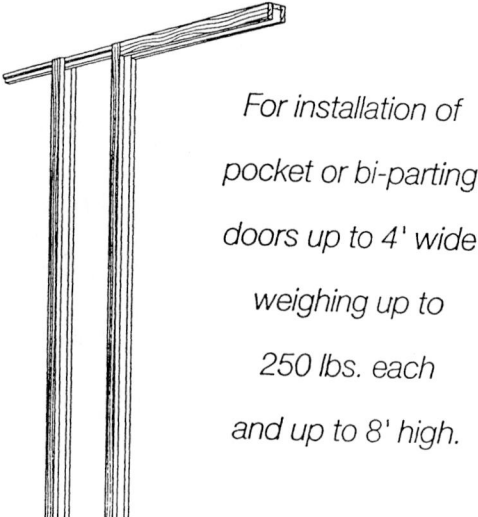

For installation of pocket or bi-parting doors up to 3' wide weighing up to 150 lbs. each and up to 8' high.

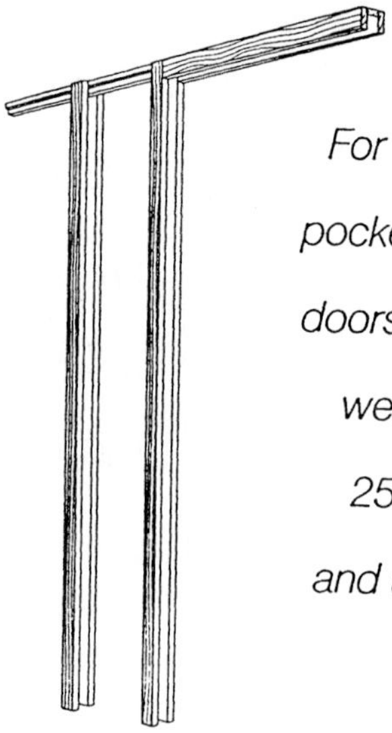

For installation of pocket or bi-parting doors up to 4' wide weighing up to 250 lbs. each and up to 8' high.

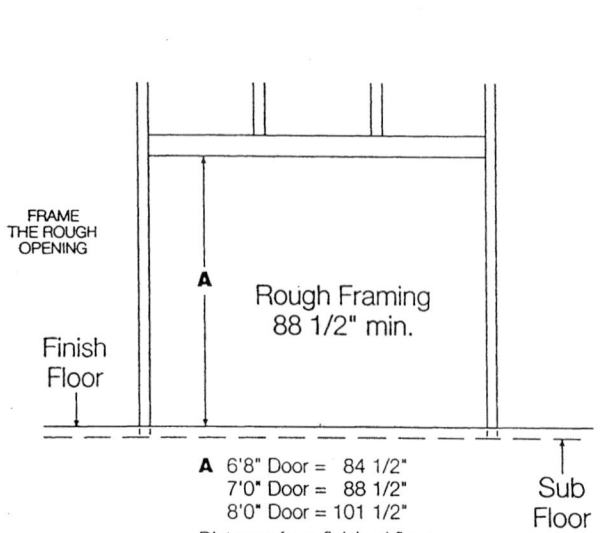

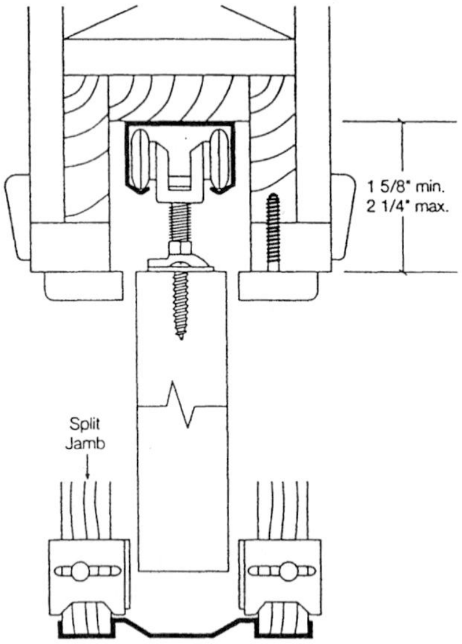

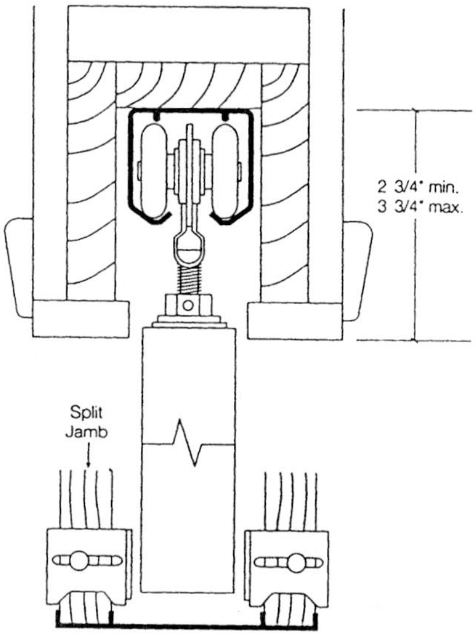

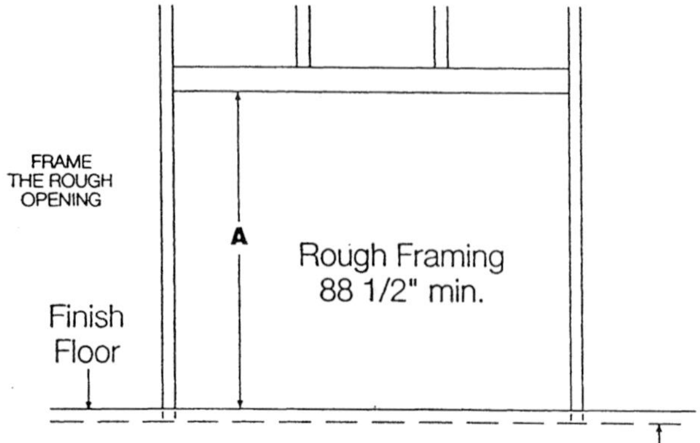

A 6'8" Door = 84 1/2"
7'0" Door = 88 1/2"
8'0" Door = 101 1/2"
Distance from finished floor to bottom of rough opening

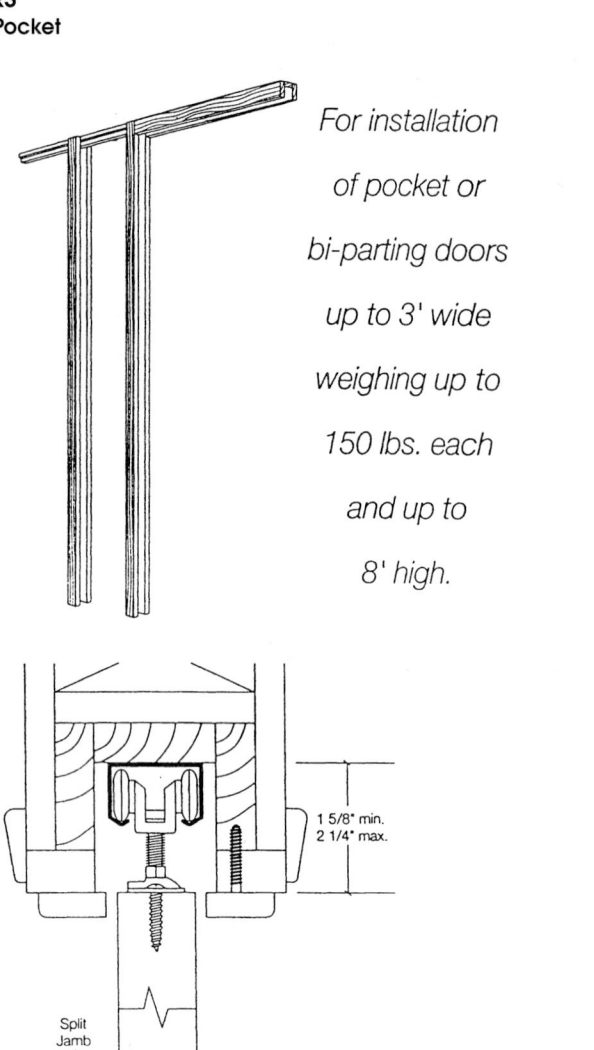

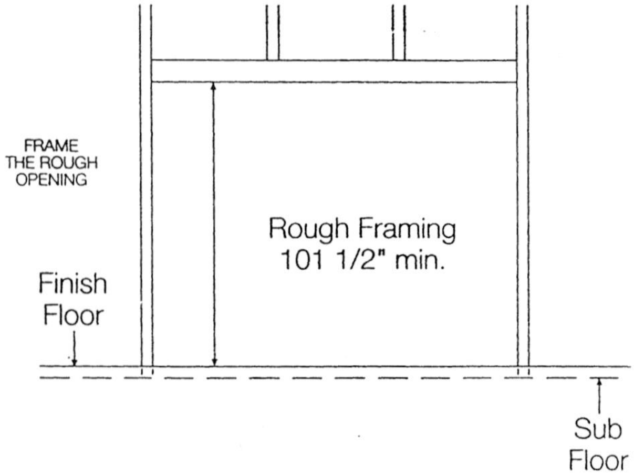

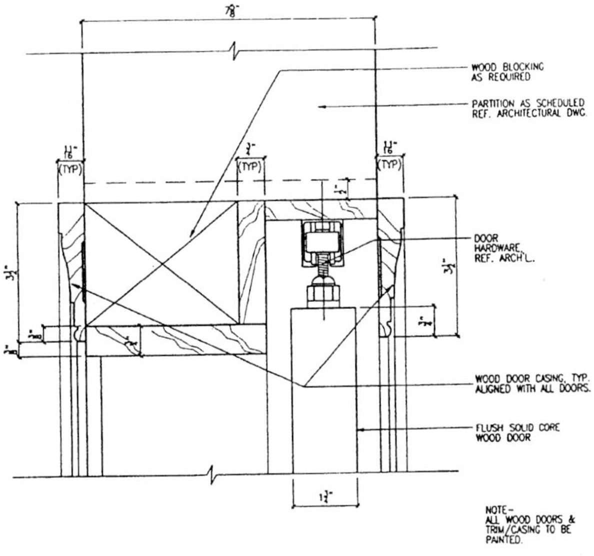

12 SLIDING DOOR HEAD DETAIL
SCALE: HALF FULL SCALE

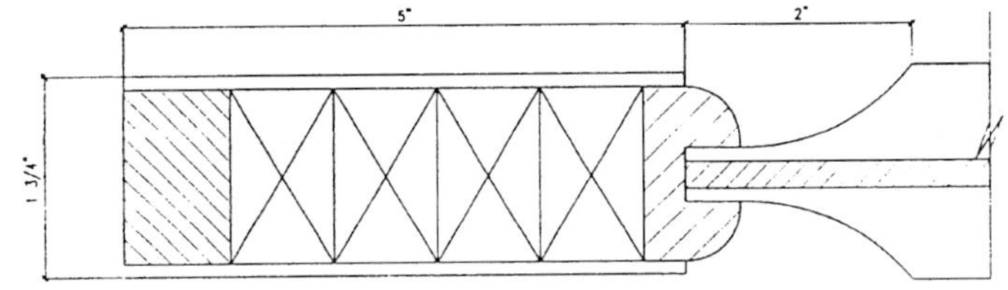

14 TYP. RAISED PANEL DOOR STYLE
SCALE: FULL SIZE

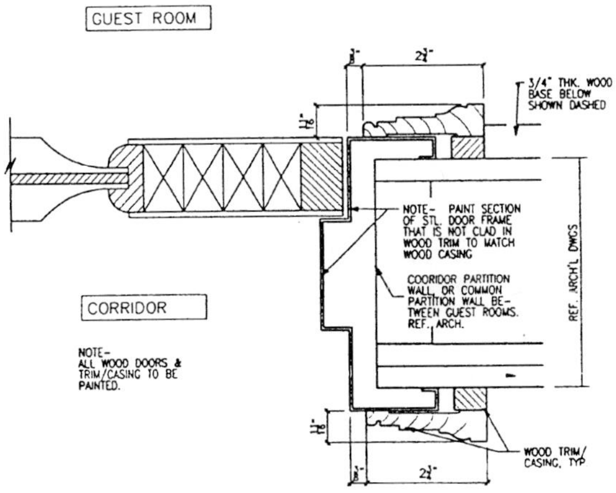

11 JAMB/HEAD DETAIL AT FIRE RATED DOORS
SCALE: HALF FULL SCALE

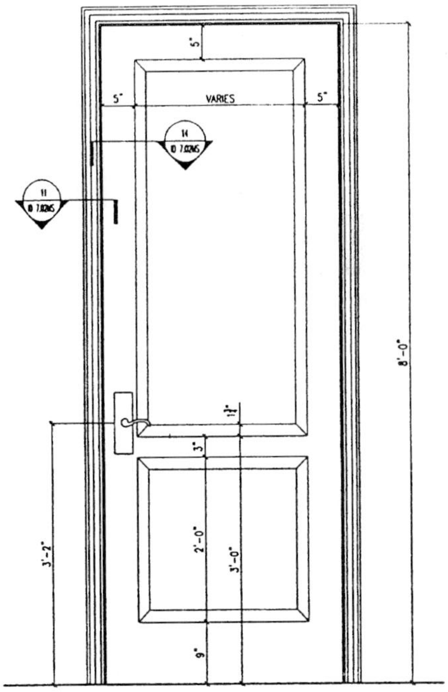

13 TYPICAL DOOR ELEVATION
SCALE: 1"=1'-0"

DOORS
Door Types

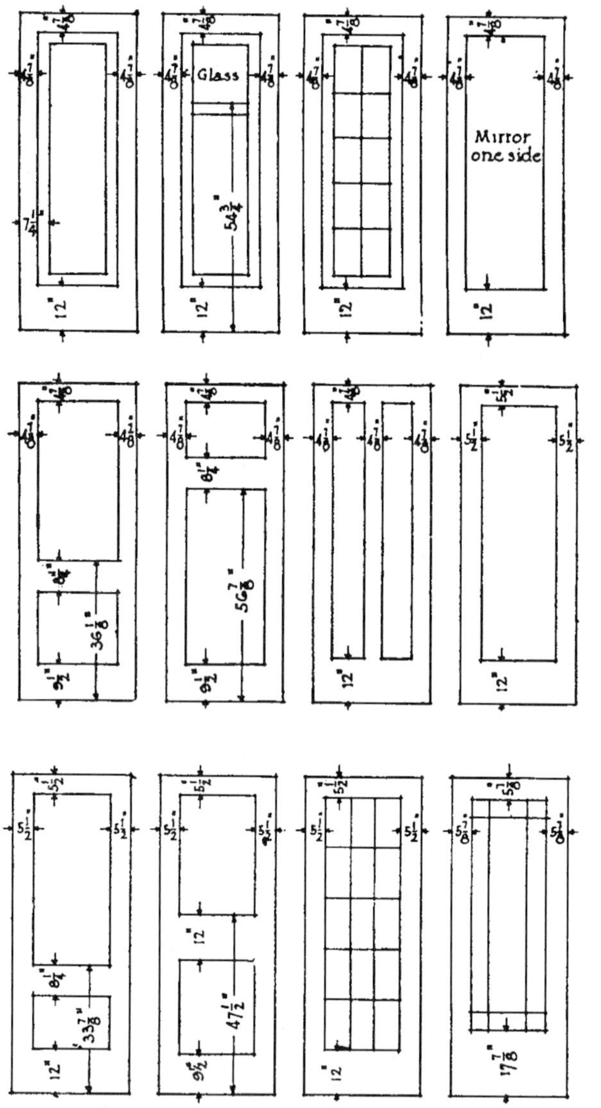

Fig. 17 Typical interior doors showing the dimensions of stiles and rails

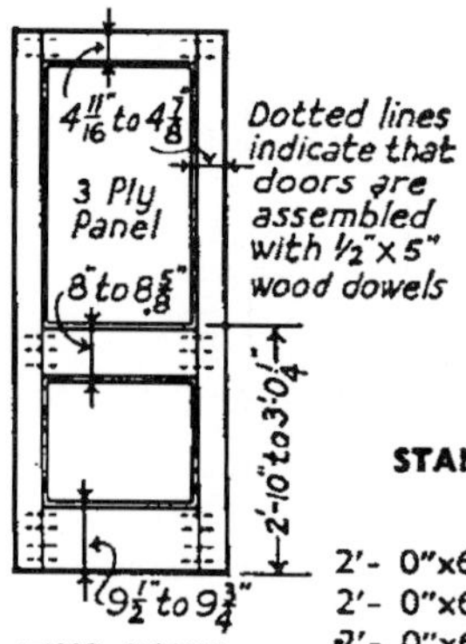

TWO PANEL

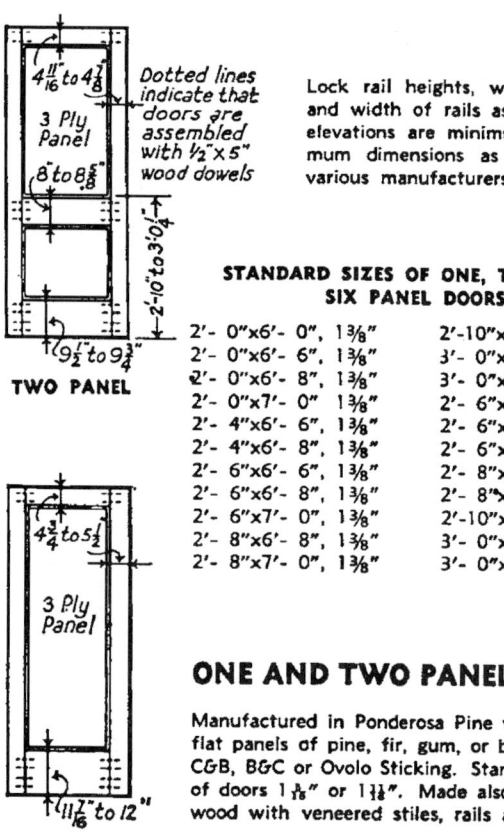

ONE PANEL

Lock rail heights, width of stiles, and width of rails as noted on all elevations are minimum and maximum dimensions as used by the various manufacturers.

STANDARD SIZES OF ONE, TWO, AND SIX PANEL DOORS

2'- 0"x6'- 0", 1⅜"	2'-10"x6'-10", 1⅜"
2'- 0"x6'- 6", 1⅜"	3'- 0"x6'- 8", 1⅜"
2'- 0"x6'- 8", 1⅜"	3'- 0"x7'- 0", 1⅜"
2'- 0"x7'- 0" 1⅜"	2'- 6"x6'- 6", 1¾"
2'- 4"x6'- 6", 1⅜"	2'- 6"x6'- 8", 1¾"
2'- 4"x6'- 8", 1⅜"	2'- 6"x7'- 0", 1¾"
2'- 6"x6'- 6", 1⅜"	2'- 8"x6'- 8", 1¾"
2'- 6"x6'- 8", 1⅜"	2'- 8"x7'- 0", 1¾"
2'- 6"x7'- 0", 1⅜"	2'-10"x6'-10", 1¾"
2'- 8"x6'- 8", 1⅜"	3'- 0"x6'- 8", 1¾"
2'- 8"x7'- 0", 1⅜"	3'- 0"x7'- 0", 1¾"

ONE AND TWO PANEL DESIGNS

Manufactured in Ponderosa Pine with laminated flat panels of pine, fir, gum, or birch. Moulded C&B, B&C or Ovolo Sticking. Standard thickness of doors 1⅜" or 1¾". Made also in any Hardwood with veneered stiles, rails and panels.

Fig. 18 Sizes of panelled interior doors

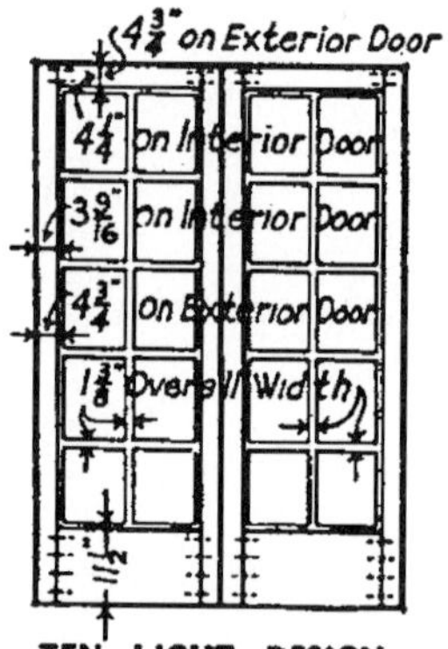

TEN LIGHT DESIGN

STANDARD SIZES

4'-0" opening, 2'-0"x6'-8" or 2'-0"x7'-0"
4'-8" opening, 2'-4"x6'-8" or 2'-4"x7'-0"
5'-0" opening, 2'-6"x6'-8" or 2'-6"x7'-0"
5'-4" opening, 2'-8"x6'-8" or 2'-8"x7'-0"

CASEMENT DESIGNS

Casement doors can also be divided into:

8 lights (2 wide—4 high) and
12 lights (3 wide—4 high).

Pairs of casement doors in openings less than 5'-0" wide have 3 9/16" stiles as shown while pairs in openings 5'-0" wide and wider have 4¼" stiles.

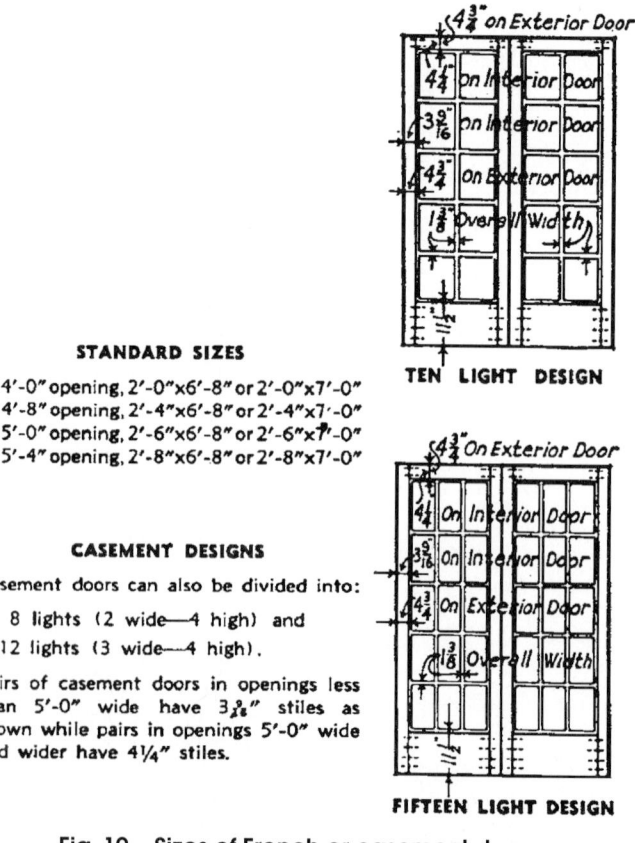

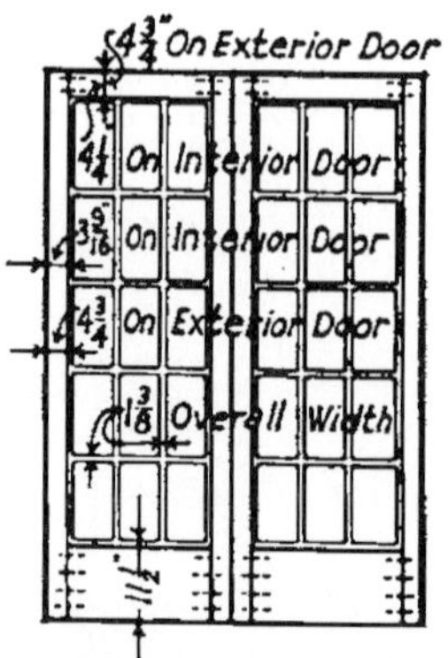

FIFTEEN LIGHT DESIGN

Fig. 19 Sizes of French or casement doors

DOORS

Door Types

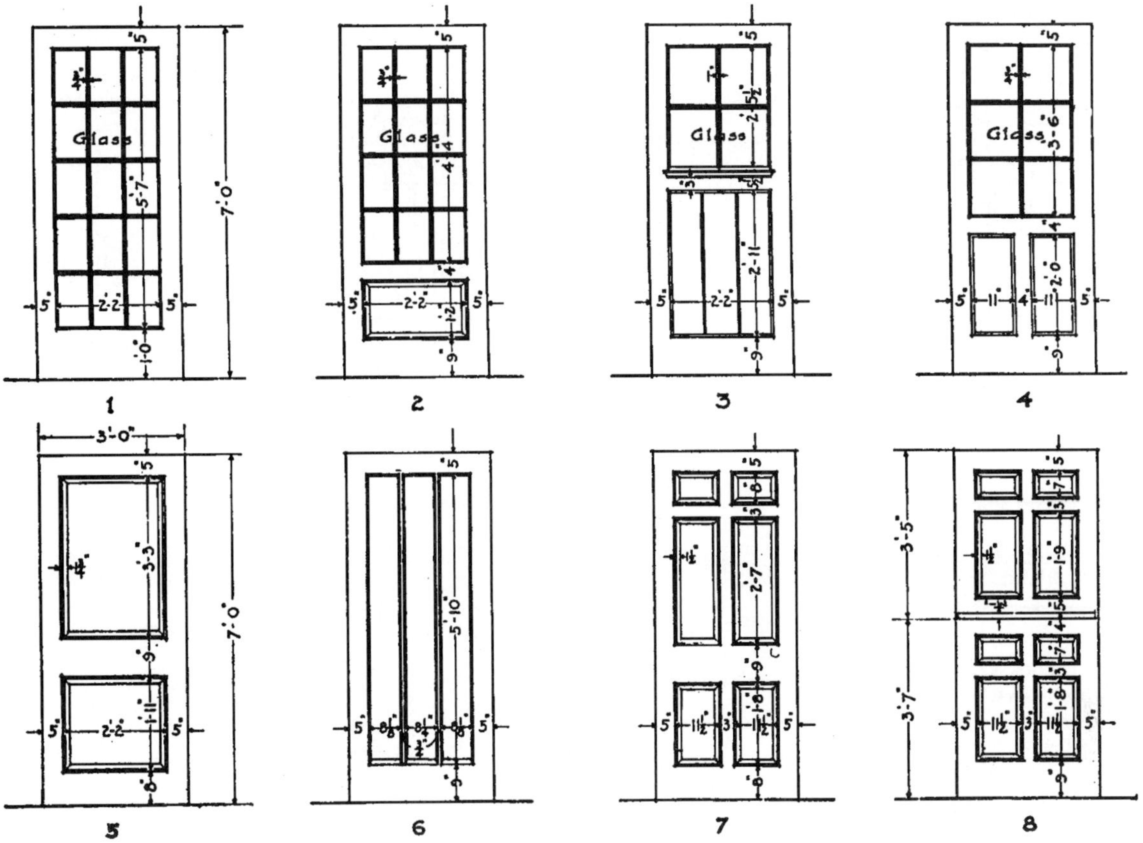

Fig. 20 Exterior wood doors

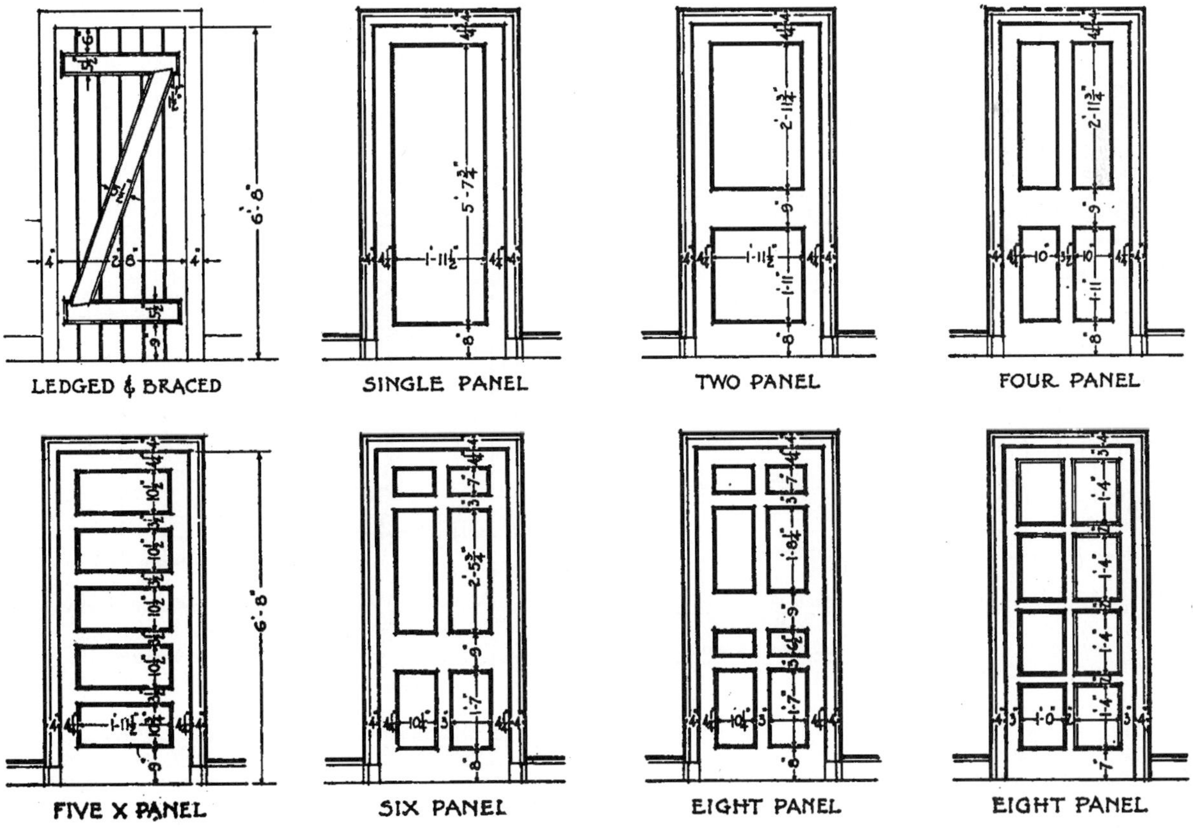

Fig. 21 Interior wood doors

DOORS

Wood Door Frames

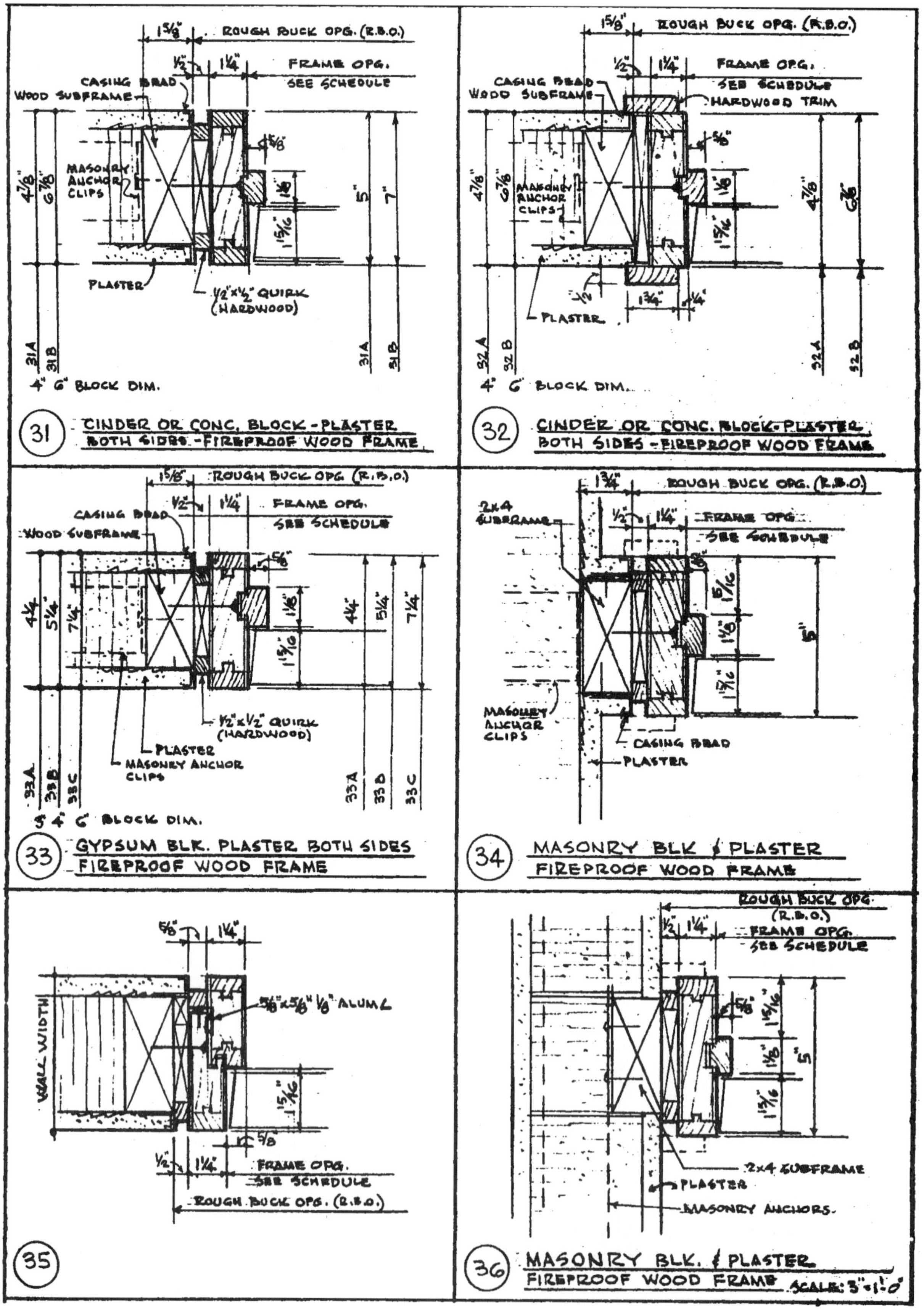

MASTER BATHROOM
MASTER BEDROOM
2'-4"
PLAN
TYP. TRIM AS PER SCHEDULE
4½"
4⅛"
3'-3¾"
6'-8" DOOR OPN'G
4⅛"
⅜"
2'-4" DOOR OPN'G
5¾"
9"
1'-9"
6"
TYP. BASE AS PER SCHEDULE
FIN. FLR.
28
ELEVATION
2"
2"
ALIGN
4¼"
BASE
DETAIL @ JAMB
F.S.

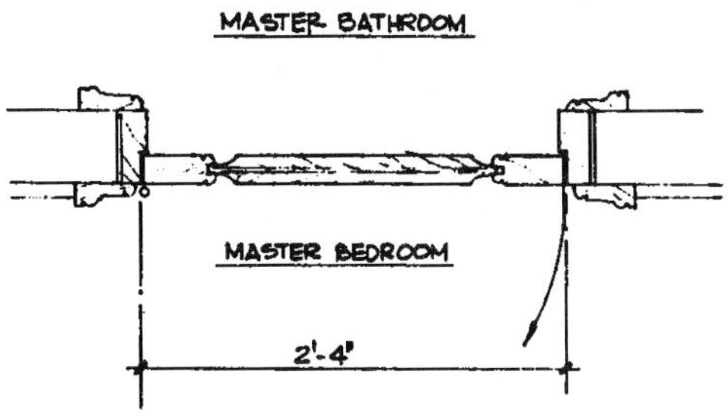

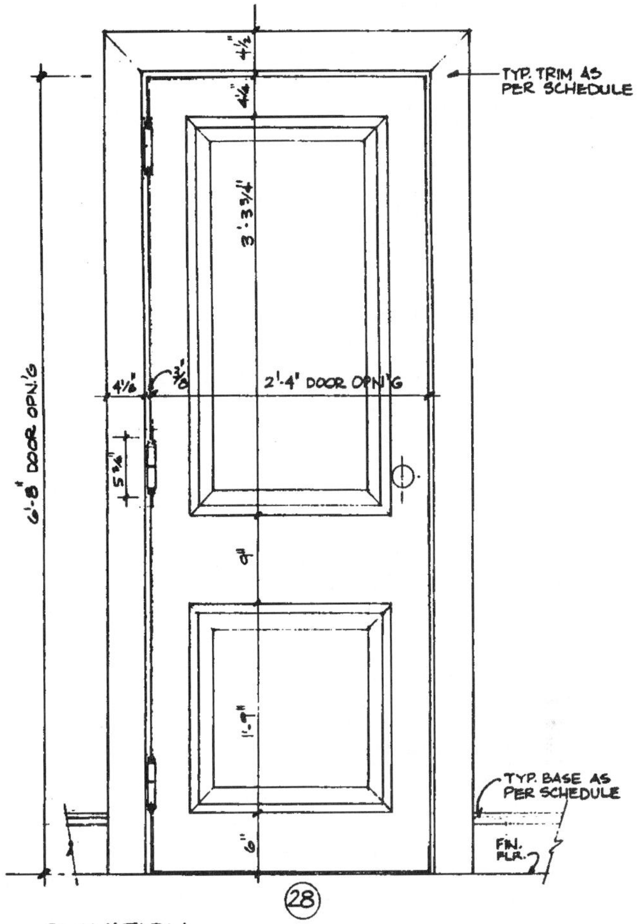

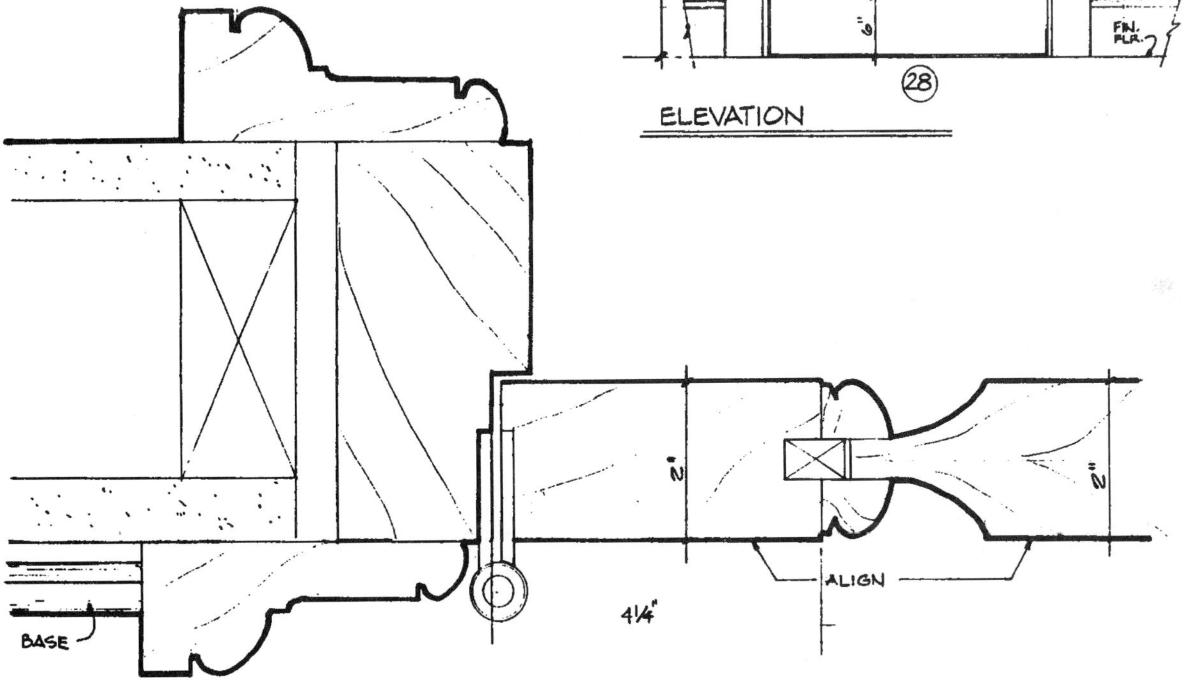

DOORS

Secret Door

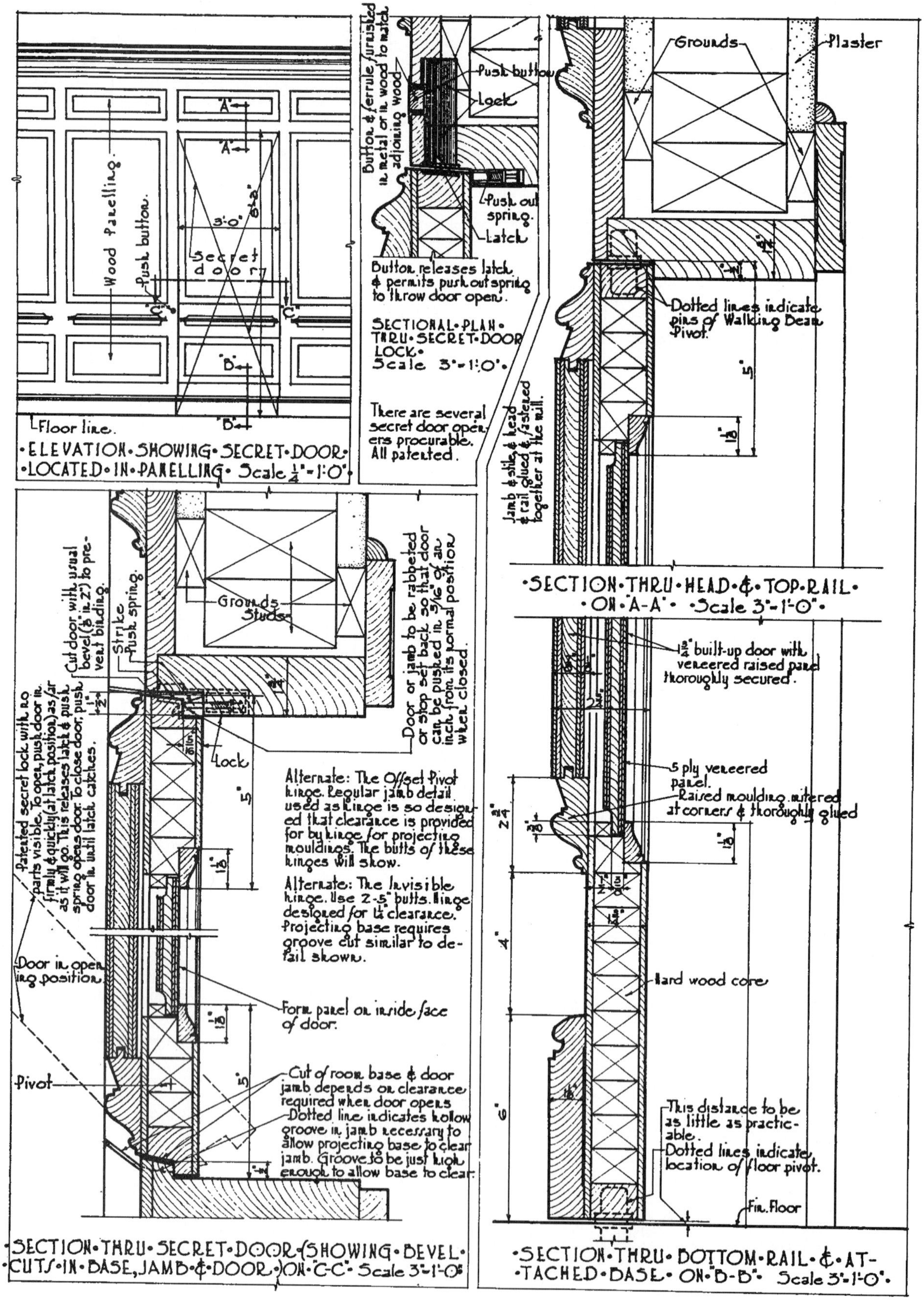
Wood Panelling
Push button
Secret door
3'-0"
"A"
"B"
"C"
Floor line.
•ELEVATION•SHOWING•SECRET•DOOR•
•LOCATED•IN•PANELLING• Scale 1/4"-1'-0"
Button & ferrule furnished in metal or in wood to match adjoining wood
Push button
Lock
Push out spring.
Latch
Button releases latch & permits push out spring to throw door open.
SECTIONAL•PLAN•THRU•SECRET•DOOR LOCK•
Scale 3"-1'-0".
There are several secret door openers procurable. All patented.
Grounds
Plaster
Dotted lines indicate pins of Walking Beam Pivot.
Jamb & stile & head & rail glued & fastened together at the mill.
•SECTION•THRU•HEAD•&•TOP•RAIL•
•ON•"A-A"• •Scale 3"-1'-0"•
1 3/4" built-up door with veneered raised panel thoroughly secured.
5 ply veneered panel.
Raised moulding mitered at corners & thoroughly glued
Hard wood core
This distance to be as little as practicable.
Dotted lines indicate location of floor pivot.
Fin. Floor
•SECTION•THRU•BOTTOM•RAIL•&•AT-
•TACHED•BASE• ON•"B-B"• Scale 3"-1'-0".
Cut door with usual bevel (1/8" in 2") to prevent binding.
Strike
Push spring.
Grounds
Studs
Door or jamb to be rabbeted or stop set back so that door can be pushed in 3/16 of an inch from its normal position when closed.
Lock
Patented secret lock with no parts visible. To open, push door in firmly & quickly (at latch position) as far as it will go. This releases latch & push spring opens door. To close door, push door in until latch catches.
Alternate: The Offset Pivot hinge. Regular jamb detail used as hinge is so designed that clearance is provided for by hinge for projecting mouldings. The butts of these hinges will show.
Alternate: The Invisible hinge. Use 2-5" butts. Hinge designed for 1/4" clearance. Projecting base requires groove cut similar to detail shown.
Door in opening position
Form panel on inside face of door.
Pivot
Cut of room base & door jamb depends on clearance required when door opens
Dotted line indicates hollow groove in jamb necessary to allow projecting base to clear jamb. Groove to be just high enough to allow base to clear.
•SECTION•THRU•SECRET•DOOR•(SHOWING•BEVEL•
•CUTS•IN•BASE,JAMB•&•DOOR•)ON•"C-C"• Scale 3"-1'-0"

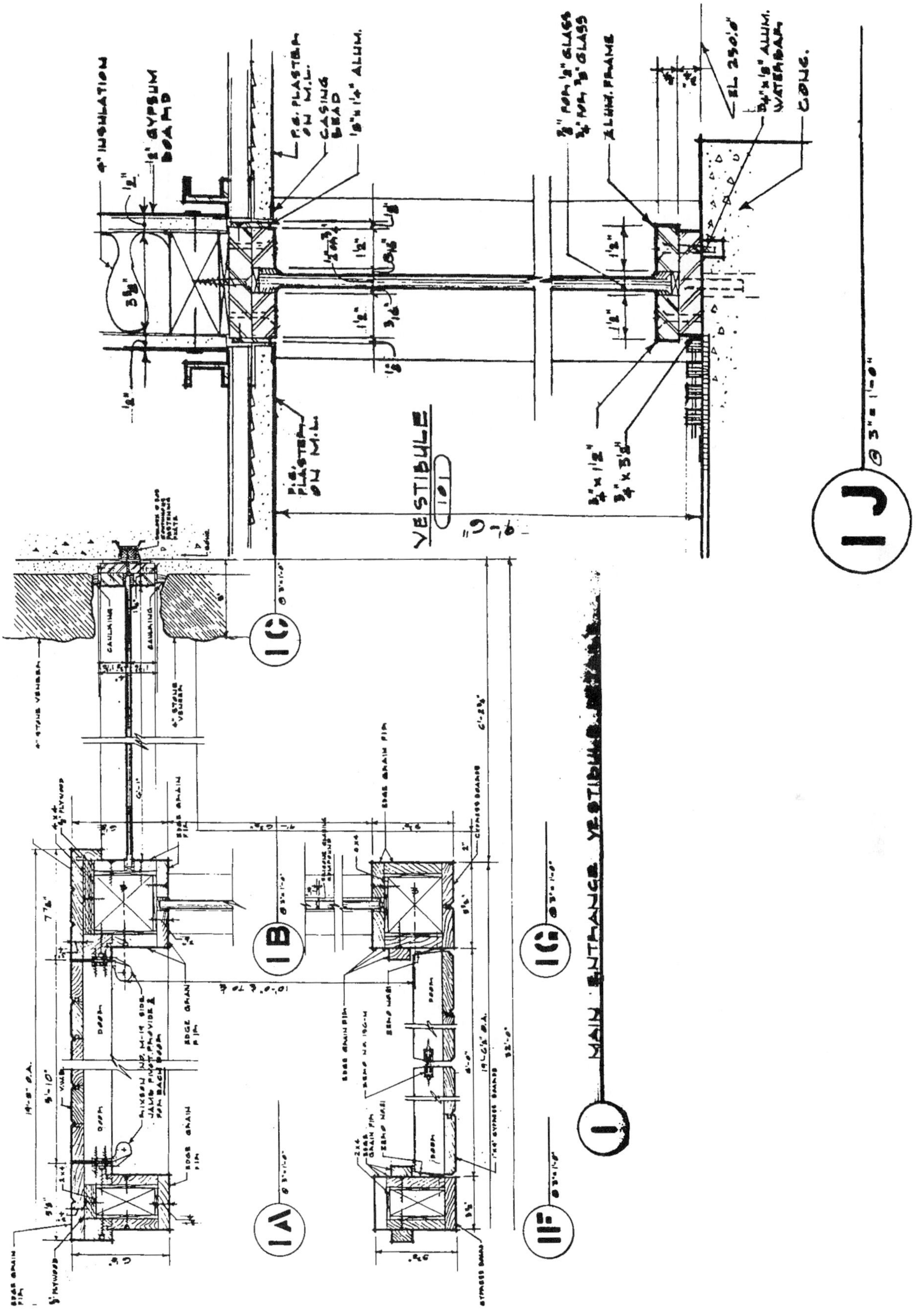
4" INSULATION
GYPSUM BOARD
P.G. PLASTER ON M.L.
CASING BEAD
ALUM. FRAME
CONC.
VESTIBULE
101
9'-6"
1J
@ 3" = 1'-0"
1C
1B
1G
1A
1F
1
MAIN ENTRANCE VESTIBULE DETAILS

DOORS

Exterior Wood Entrance Doors

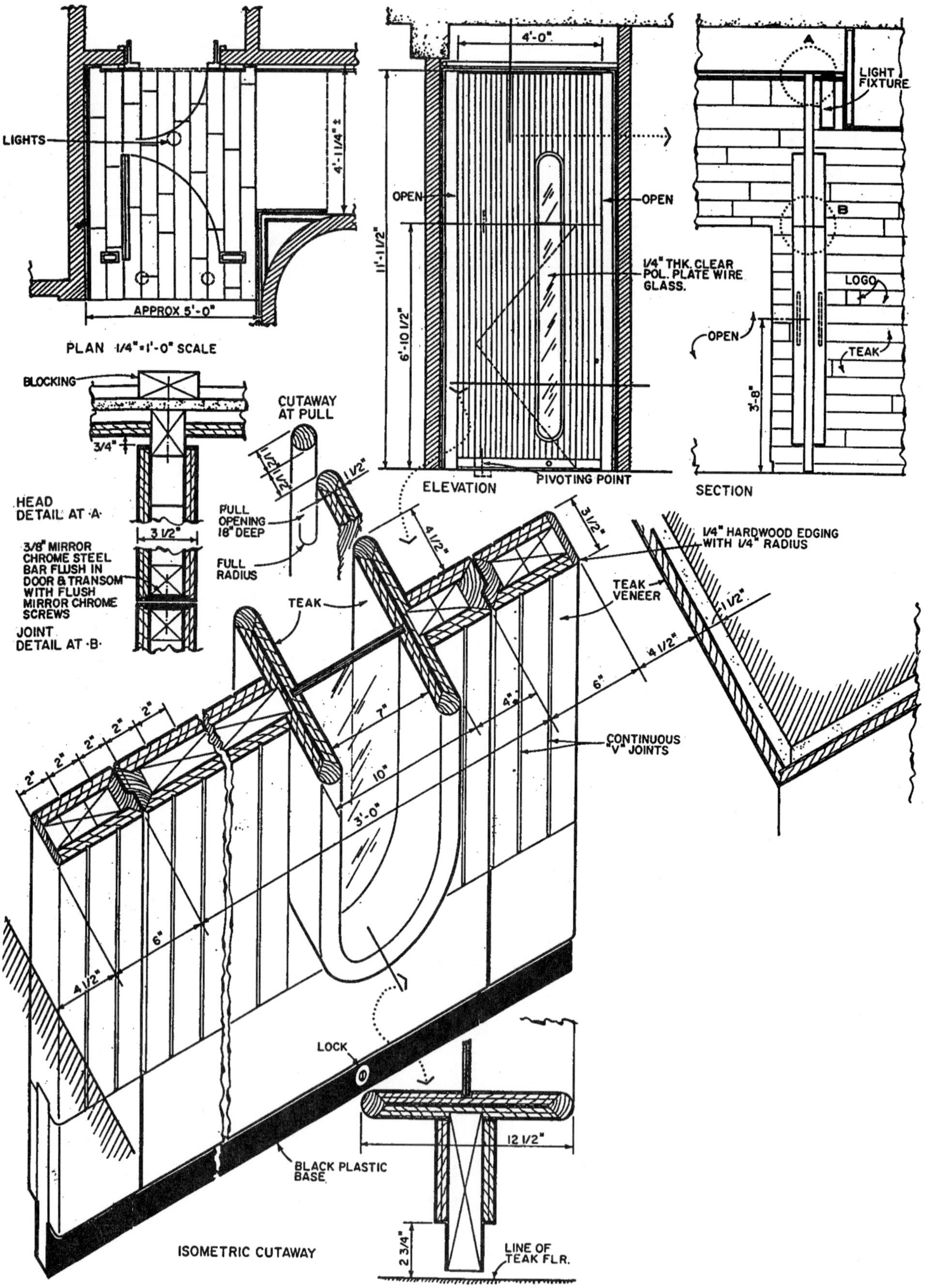

LIGHTS
4'-11 1/4" ±
APPROX 5'-0"
PLAN 1/4"=1'-0" SCALE
4'-0"
OPEN
OPEN
11'-11 1/2"
6'-10 1/2"
1/4" THK. CLEAR POL. PLATE WIRE GLASS.
ELEVATION
PIVOTING POINT
A
LIGHT FIXTURE
B
LOGO
OPEN
TEAK
3'-8"
SECTION
BLOCKING
3/4"
HEAD DETAIL AT A
3 1/2"
3/8" MIRROR CHROME STEEL BAR FLUSH IN DOOR & TRANSOM WITH FLUSH MIRROR CHROME SCREWS
JOINT DETAIL AT B
CUTAWAY AT PULL
2 1/2"
1 1/2"
PULL OPENING 18" DEEP
FULL RADIUS
TEAK
4 1/2"
3 1/2"
1/4" HARDWOOD EDGING WITH 1/4" RADIUS
TEAK VENEER
1 1/2"
4 1/2"
6"
4"
7"
10"
3'-0"
CONTINUOUS "V" JOINTS
2"
2"
2"
2"
2"
6"
4 1/2"
LOCK
BLACK PLASTIC BASE
12 1/2"
2 3/4"
LINE OF TEAK FLR.
ISOMETRIC CUTAWAY

DOORS

Miscellaneous Door Details

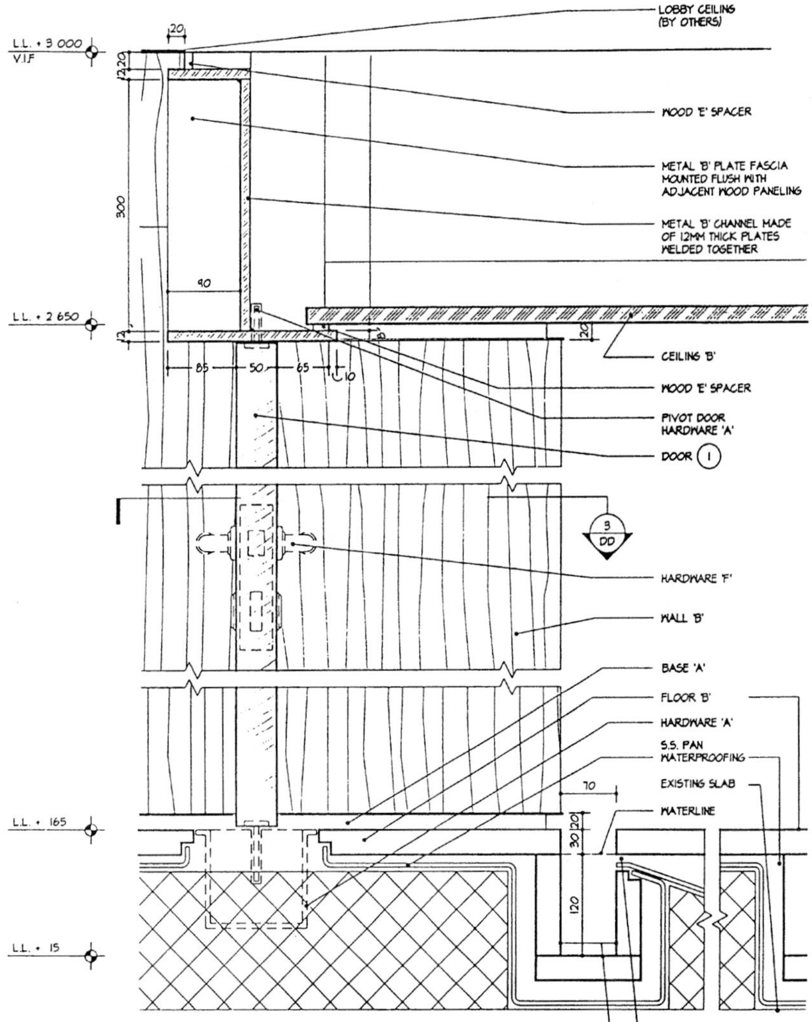

JONES (2/DD) DETAIL SECTION @ SIDE ENTRY OF LOWER LEVEL WATER FOYER
DETL SC. 1:5 RM. 101/LOBBY

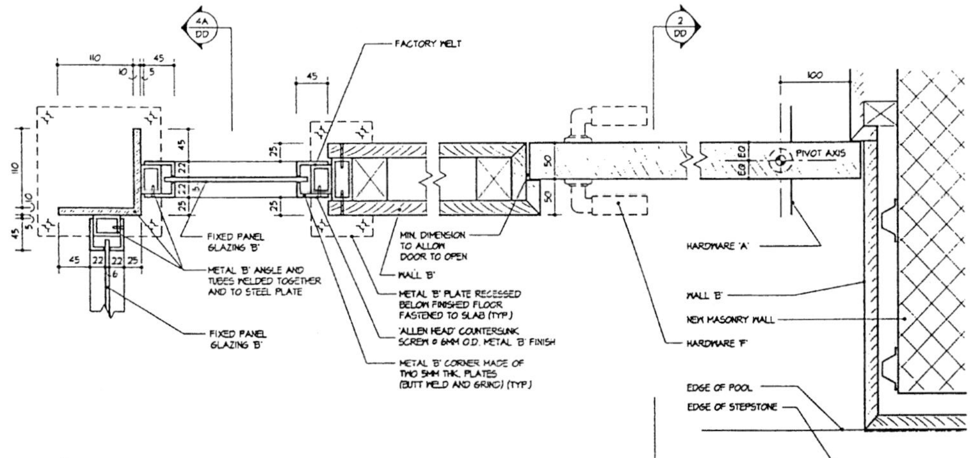

(A/3) PARTIAL PLAN @ PIVOT DOOR SC. 1:5

JONES (3/DD) DETAIL HORIZONTAL SECTION @ SIDE ENTRY OF LOWER LEVEL WATER FOYER
DETL SC. 1:5 RM. 101/LOE

DOORS

Miscellaneous Door Details

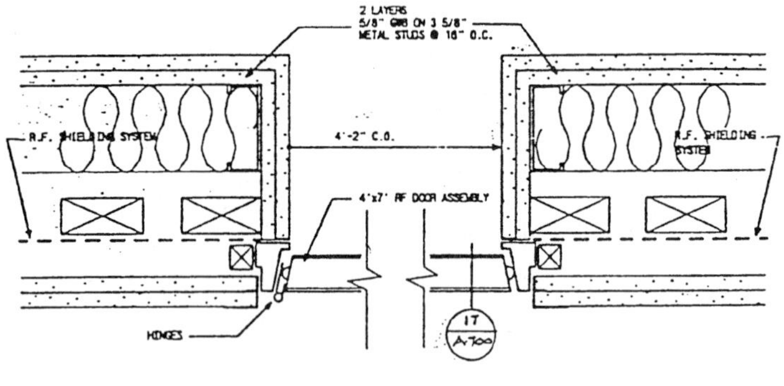

15 RF DOOR - PLAN

3" = 1'-0"

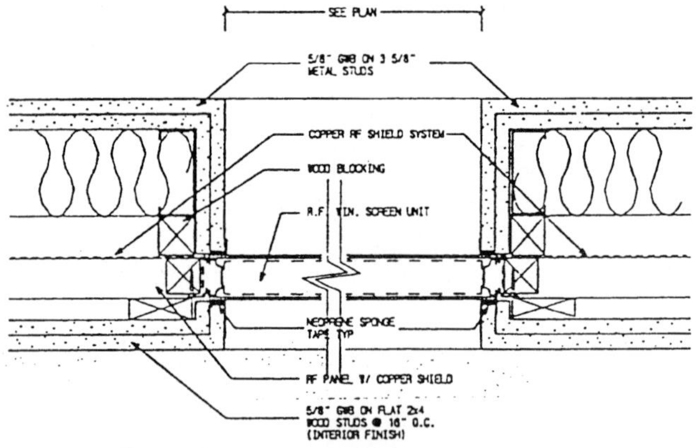

16 TYPICAL R.F. WINDOW JAMB

3" = 1'-0"

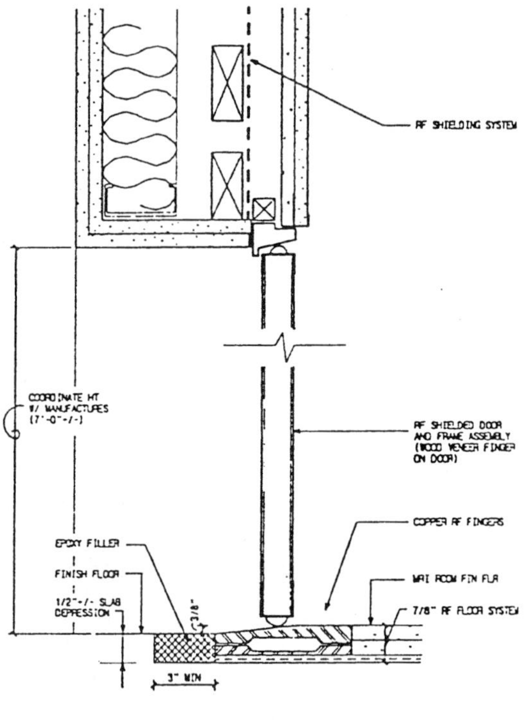

17 RF DOOR HEAD & SADDLE

3" = 1'-0"

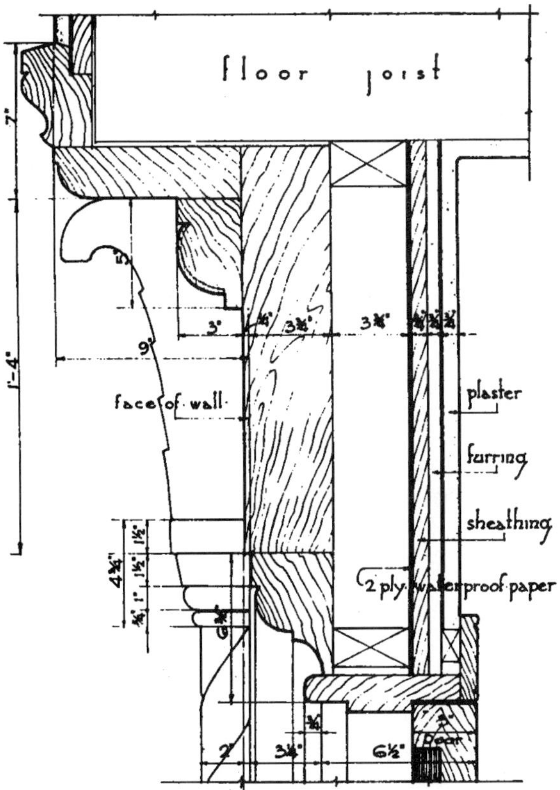

floor joist
face of wall
plaster
furring
sheathing
2 ply waterproof paper
Door
SECTION "A-A"
scale: 1½" = 1'-0"
stucco
Carved Wood Bracket
W.I. Lighting Fixture
Glazed Panel
Wood Door by Owner (See Detail)
fin. floor
Grade
stone step
ELEVATION
Scale: ⅜" = 1'-0"
SECTION "B-B"
scale: 1½" = 1'-0"
steel sash
plaster
furring
sheathing
2 ply waterproof paper
Screen
blocking
8" x 8" OAK
splayed
Note:
Old door by owner "built-in" to make a 3" door with battens in back.
Brick Fill

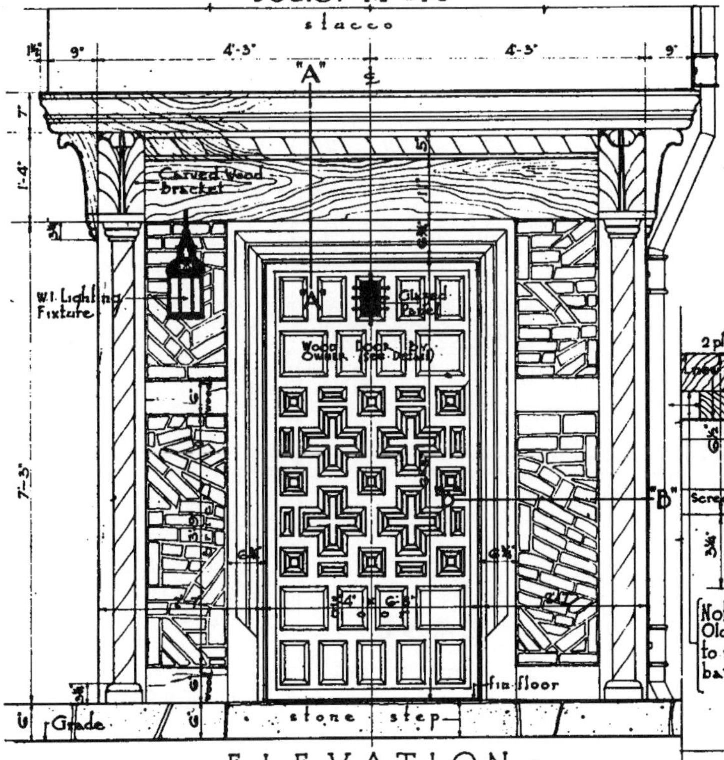

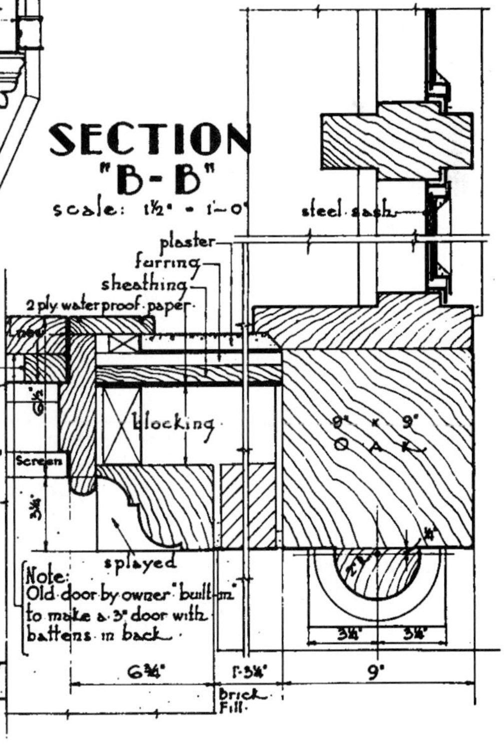

DOORS

Exterior Wood Entrance Doors

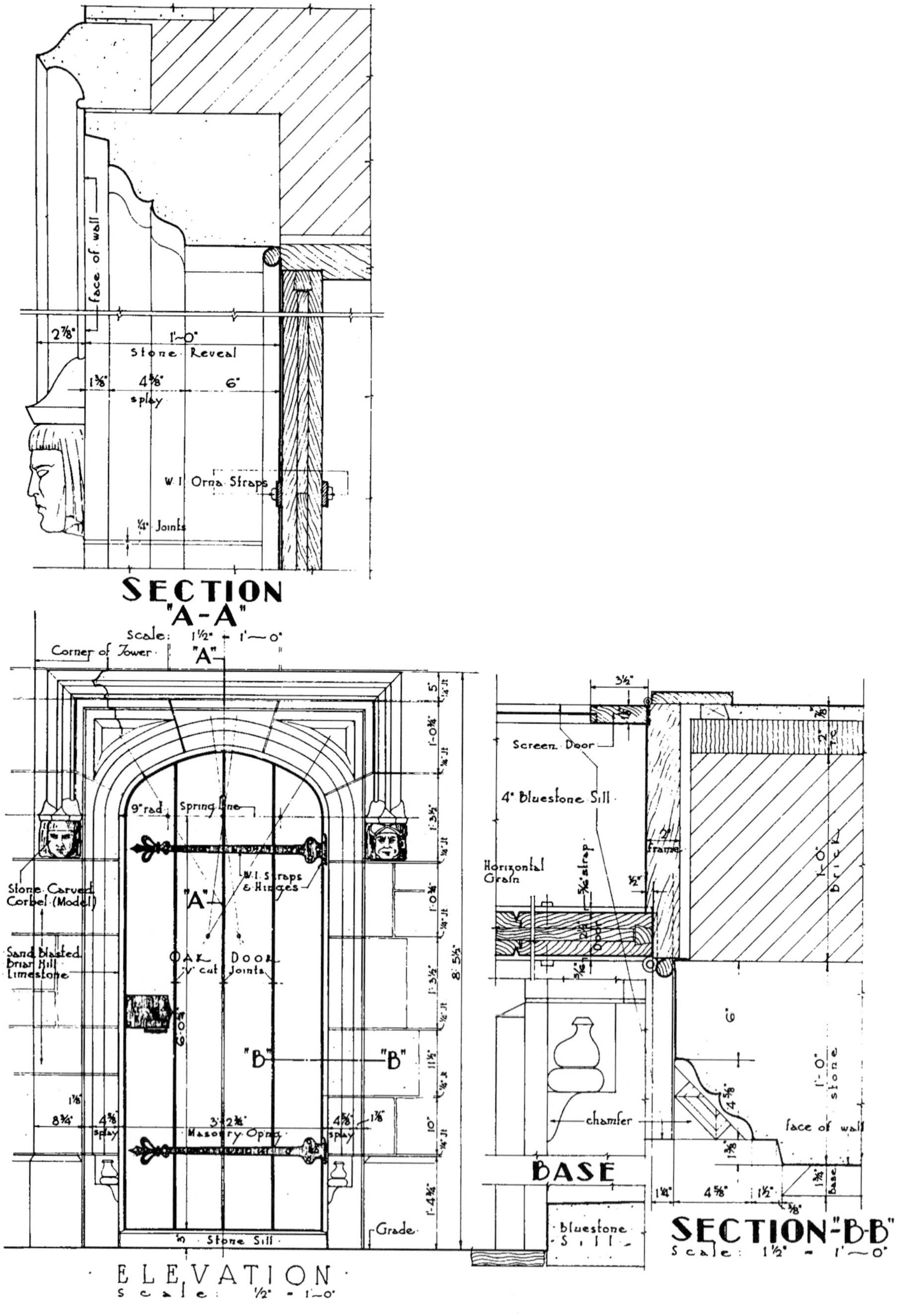

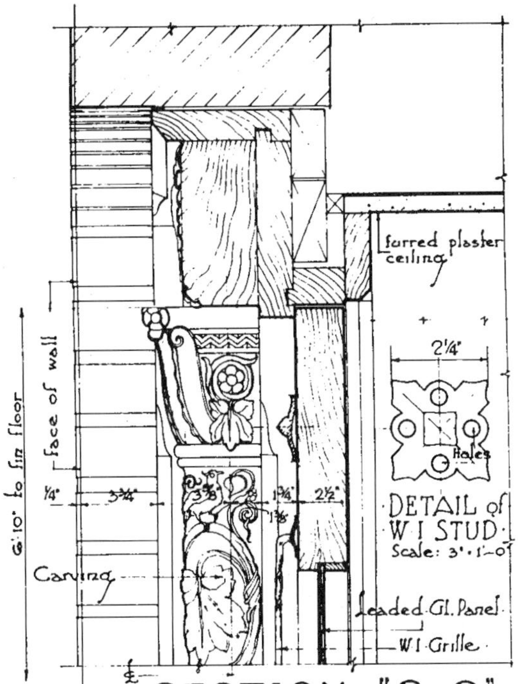

SECTION "C-C"
Scale: 1½" = 1'—0"

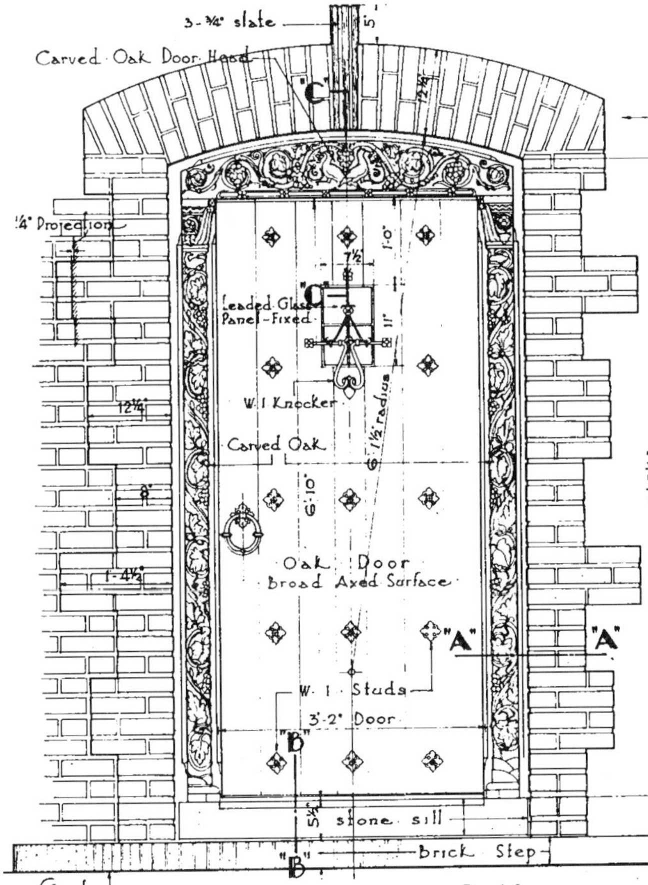

ELEVATION
Scale: ½" = 1'—0"

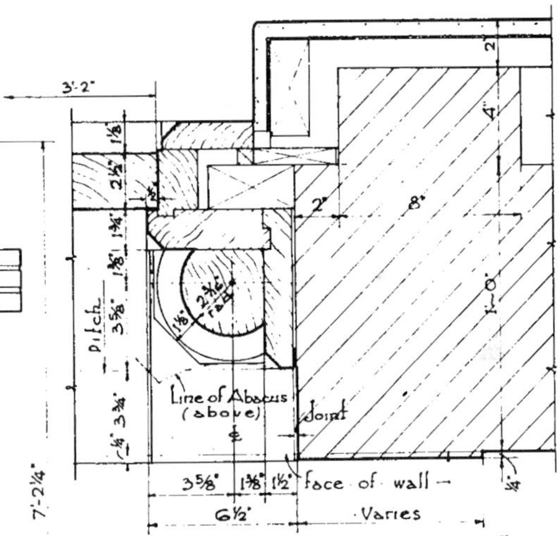

SECTION "A-A"
Scale: 1½" = 1'—0"

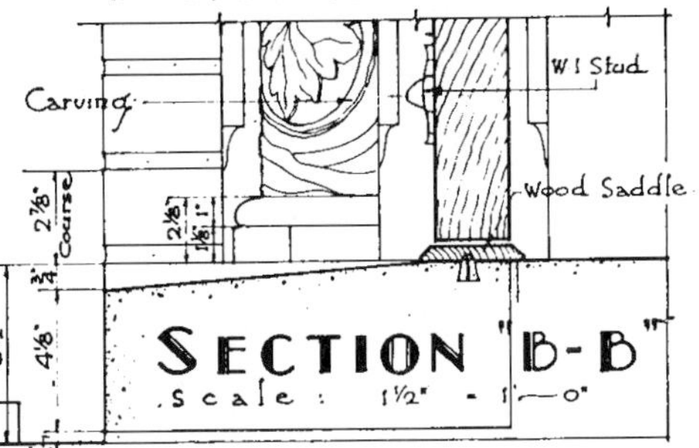

SECTION "B-B"
Scale: 1½" = 1'—0"

DOORS

Exterior Wood Entrance Doors

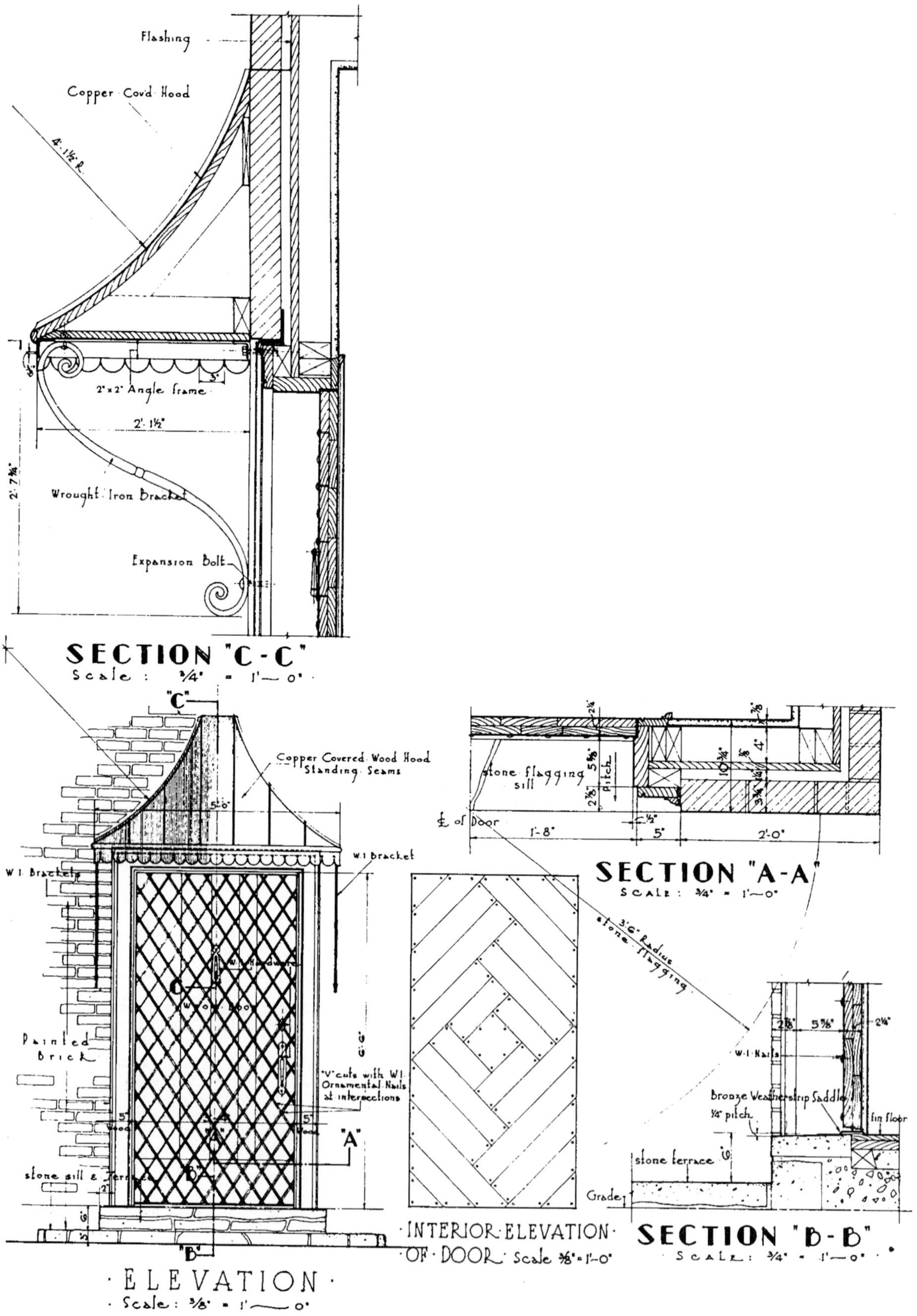
Flashing
Copper Cov'd Hood
4'-1½" R.
2"x2" Angle frame
2'-1½"
2'-7⅝"
Wrought Iron Bracket
Expansion Bolt
SECTION "C-C"
Scale: ¾" = 1'—0"
"C"
Copper Covered Wood Hood Standing Seams
5'-0"
W.I. Bracket
W.I. Brackets
Painted Brick
"V" cuts with W.I. Ornamental Nails at intersections
W.I. Door
stone sill & Terrace
"A"
"B"
· ELEVATION ·
Scale: ⅜" = 1'—0"
stone flagging sill
pitch
℄ of Door
1'-8"
5"
2'-0"
SECTION "A-A"
SCALE: ¾" = 1'—0"
3'-6" Radius stone flagging
INTERIOR ELEVATION OF DOOR Scale ⅜" = 1'-0"
W.I. Nails
Bronze Weatherstrip Saddle
¼" pitch
fin floor
stone terrace
Grade
SECTION "B-B"
SCALE: ¾" = 1'—0"

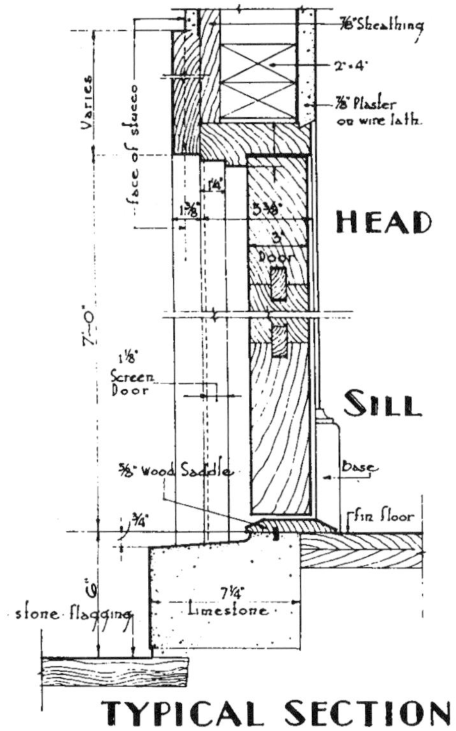

TYPICAL SECTION

SCALE: 1½" = 1'—0"

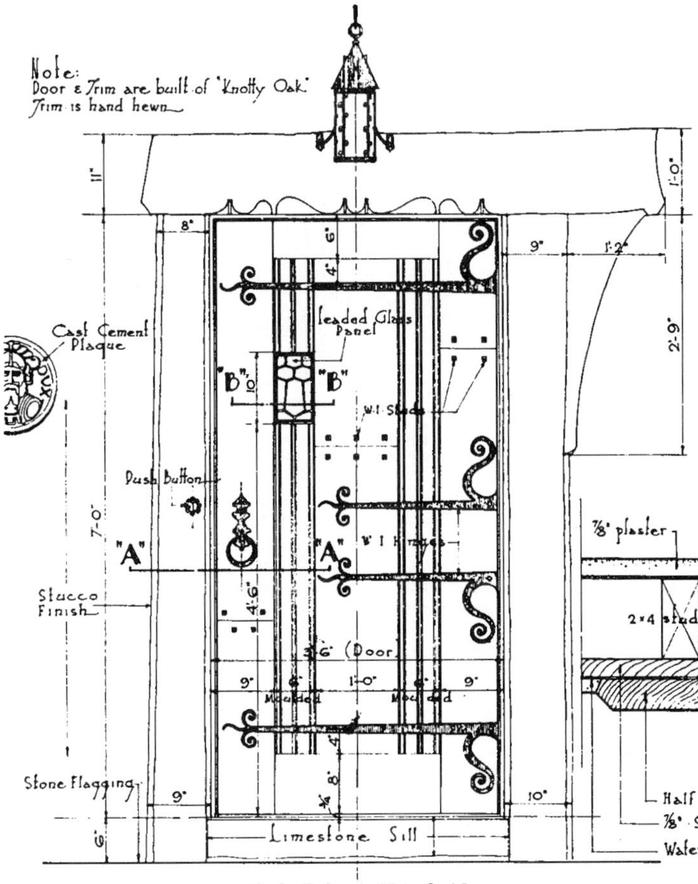

ELEVATION

SCALE: ½" = 1'—0"

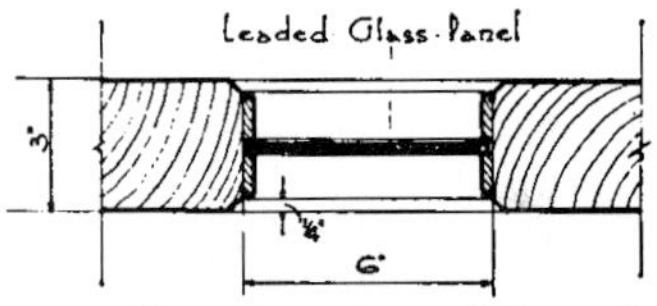

SECTION "B-B"

SCALE: 1½" = 1'—0"

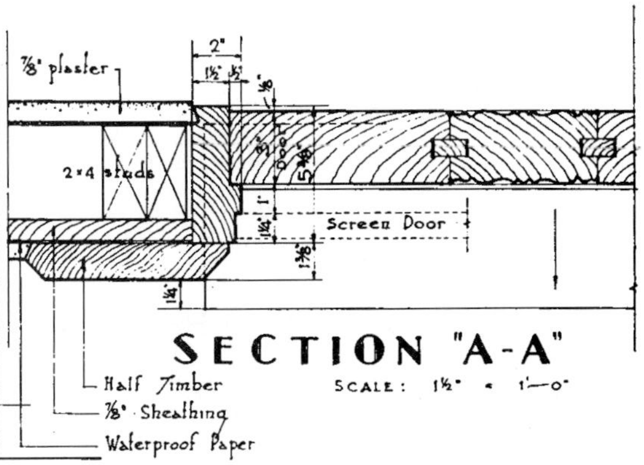

SECTION "A-A"

SCALE: 1½" = 1'—0"

DOORS

Exterior Wood Entrance Doors

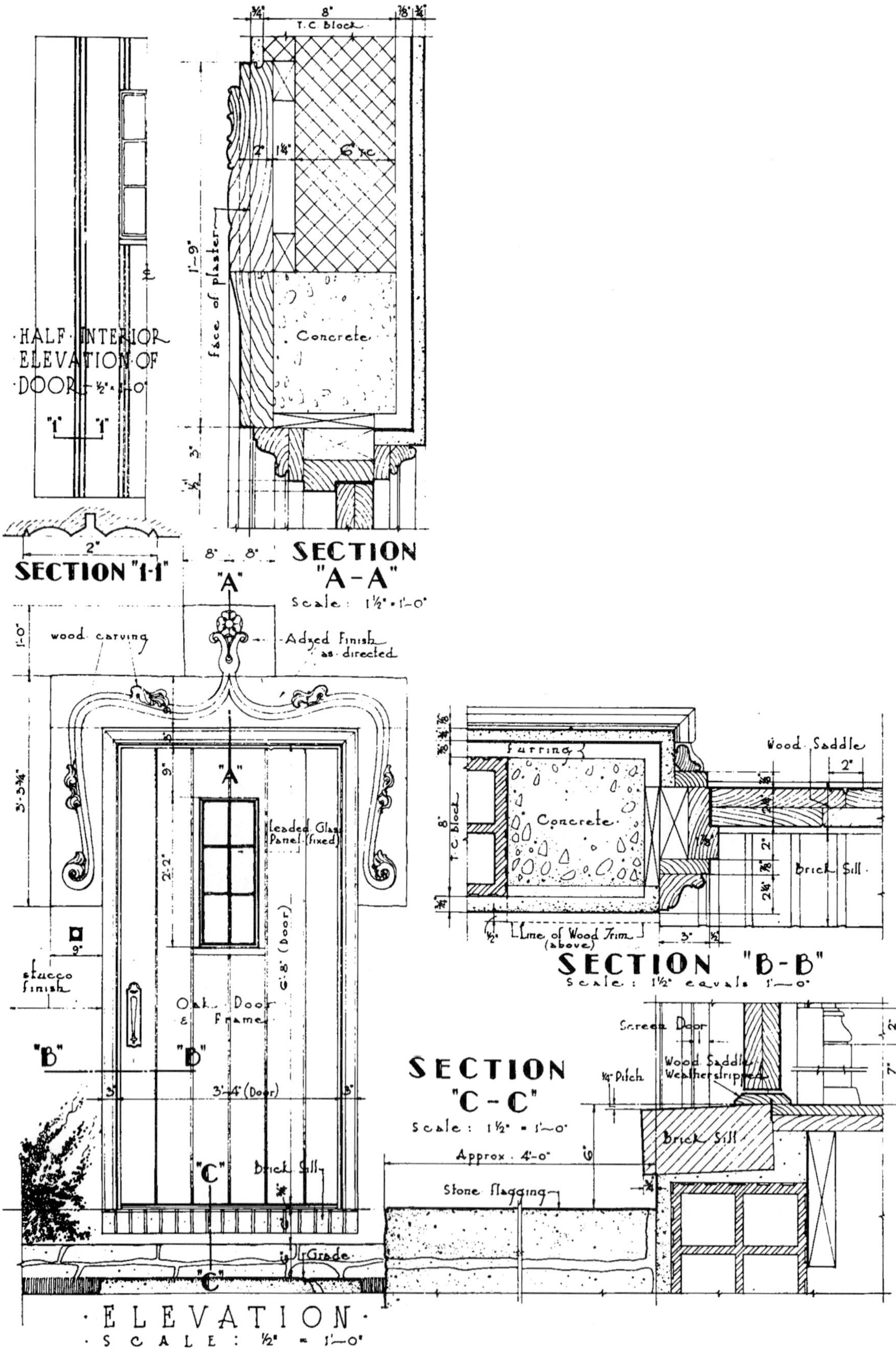

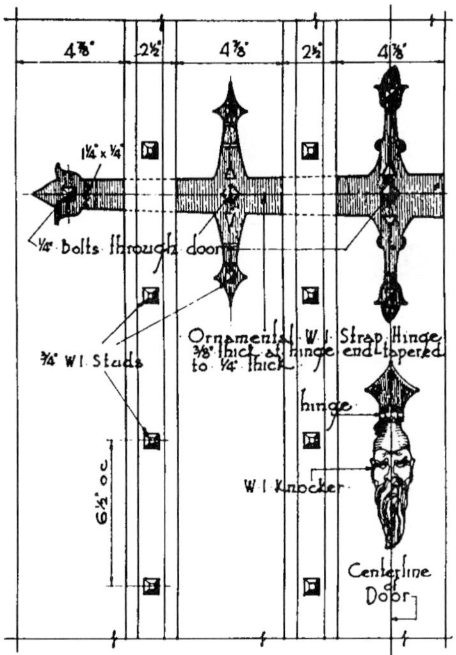

·1½"·SCALE·DETAIL·OF·W·I·
·STRAP·&·DOOR·KNOCKER·

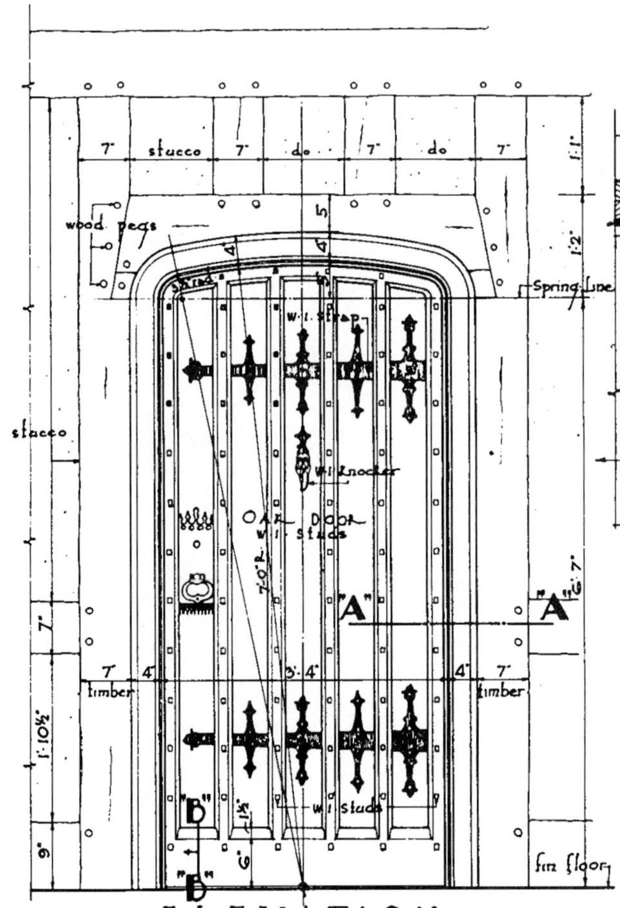

ELEVATION
Scale: ½" = 1'-0"

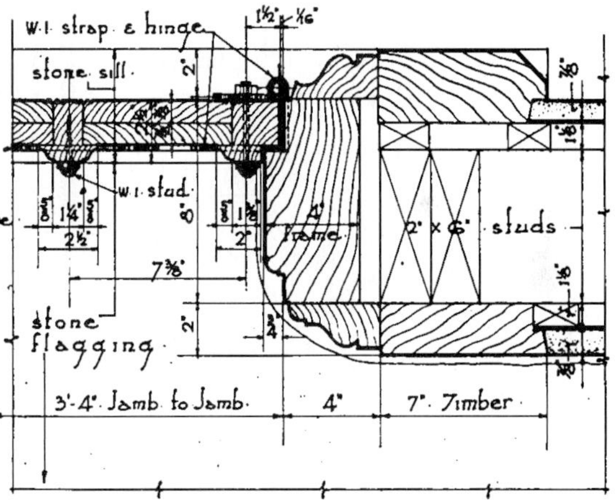

SECTION "A-A"
scale: 1½" = 1'-0"

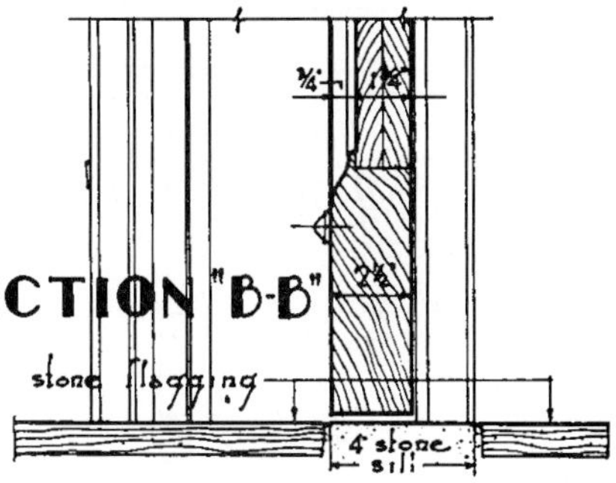

SECTION "B-B"

DOORS

Exterior Wood Entrance Doors

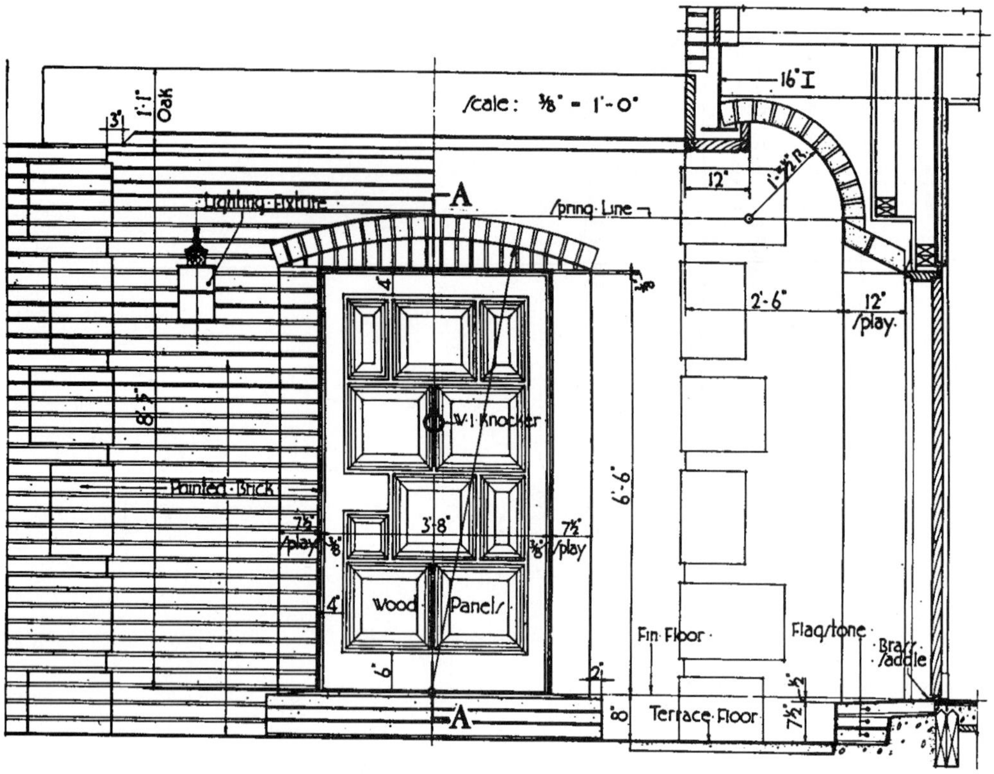

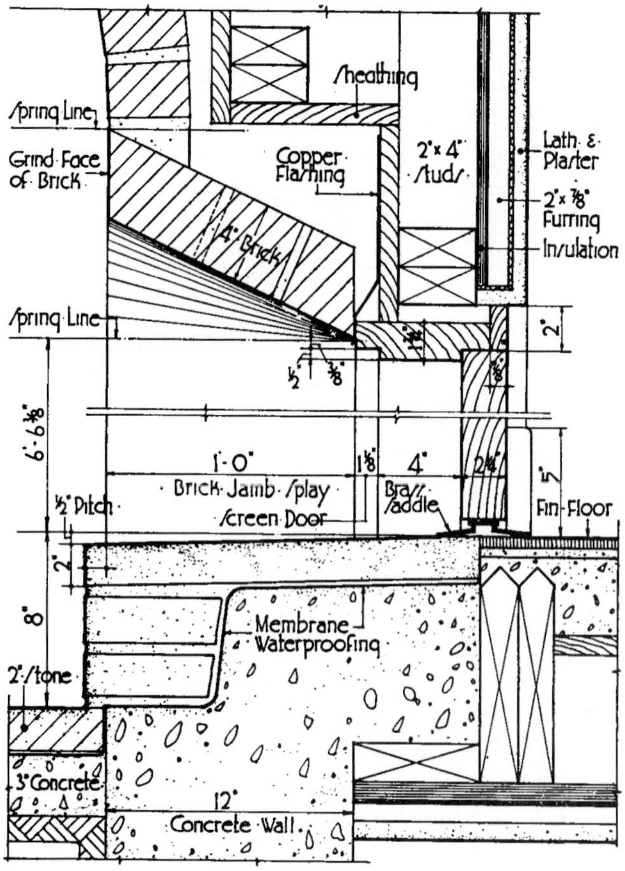

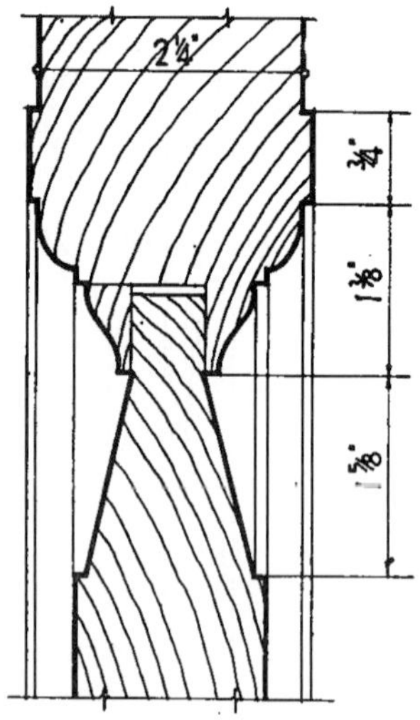

·DETAIL·OF·
·DOOR·PANEL
·Scale: Half - Full Size·

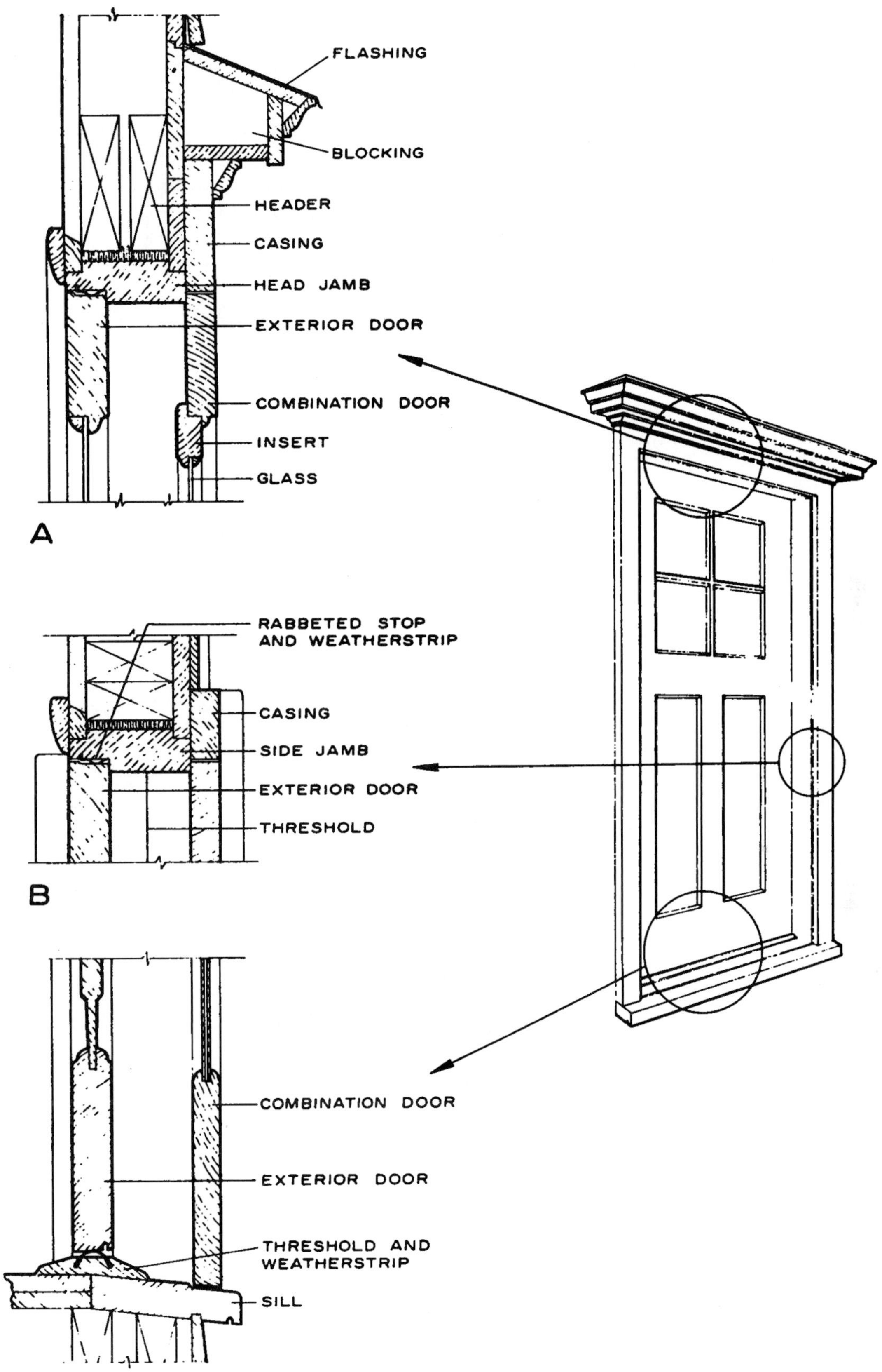

Fig. 23 Exterior door and frame. Exterior-door and combination-door (screen and storm) cross sections: *A*, head jamb; *B*, side jamb; *C*, sill

DOORS
Exterior Wood Entrance Doors

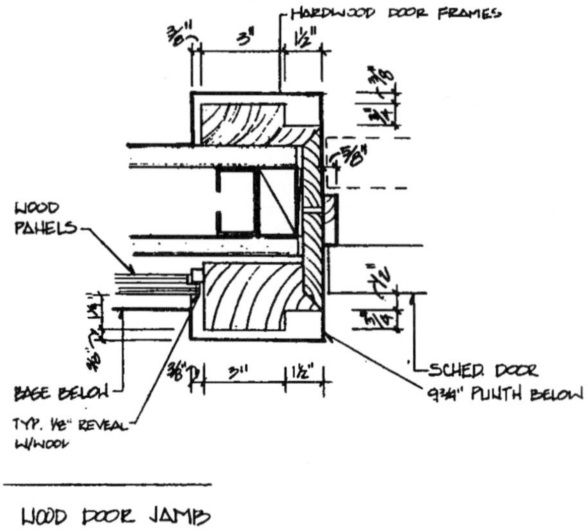

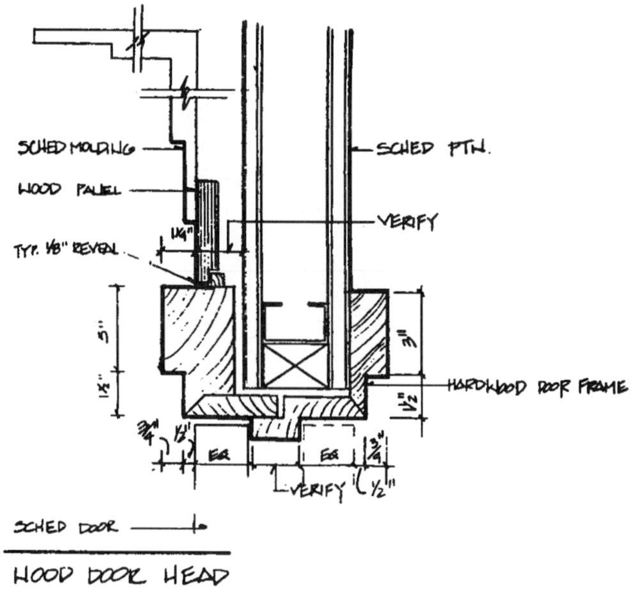

Wood clad metal door frames

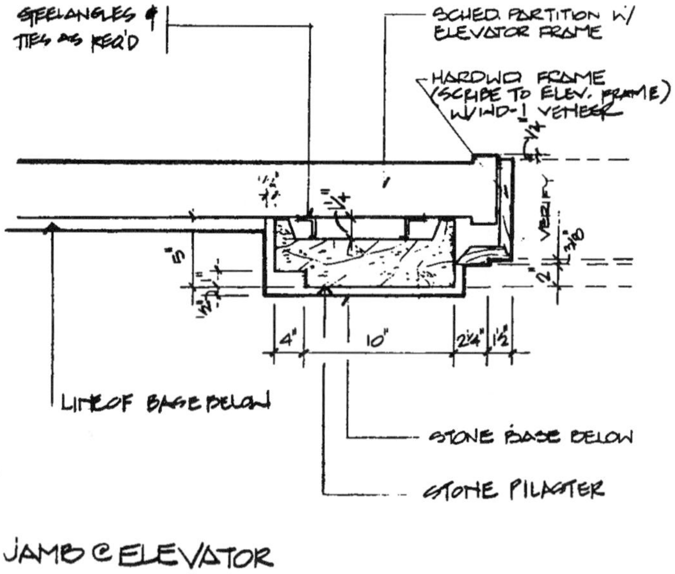

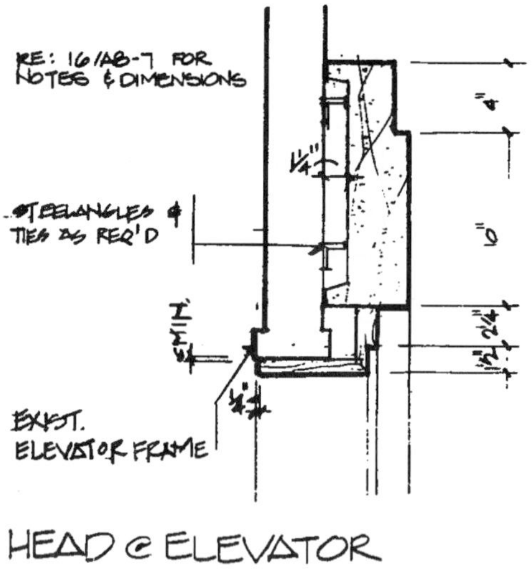

Marble jamb and head details at elevator

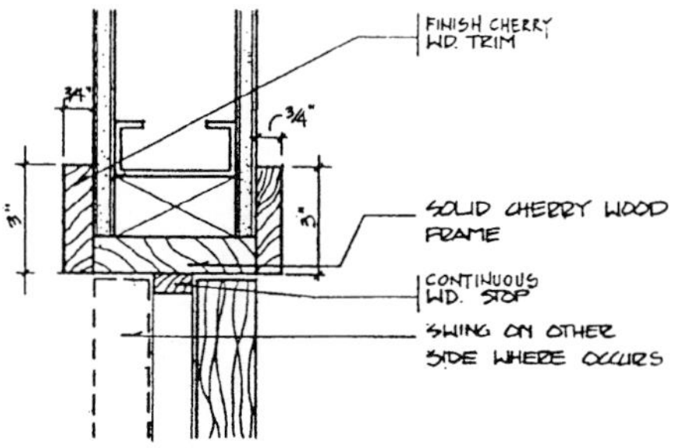

FINISH CHERRY WD. TRIM
SOLID CHERRY WOOD FRAME
CONTINUOUS WD. STOP
SWING ON OTHER SIDE WHERE OCCURS
1 Head/Jamb
3"=1'-0"
WD. TRIM OVER MTL DOOR FRAME
F.R. WD. GROUND
PAINTED HOLLOW METAL DOOR FRAME - K.D.
CLIP
3 Head/Jamb
3"=1'-0"
SOLID WD CHERRY LOUVERED DOOR
SWING ON OTHER SIDE WHERE OCCUR
1/2" UNDERCUT
CARPET & PAD
1/4" PLYWOOD
3/4" PLYWOOD
CONCRETE
2 Sill
(JAMBS AT DISABLED ACCESSIBLE D.R.S DO NOT HAVE STOP SEE DET. 13)
3"=1'-0"
H.M. DOOR
H.M. FRAME
VINYL TILE
VINYL TILE
4 Sill
3"=1'-0"
F.R. WD. GROUND
PTD. HOLLOW STL DOOR FRAME - K.D.
CLIP
5 Head/Jamb
3"=1'-0"
FIN. WD. CHERRY TRIM
INTEGRAL FIN WD STOP CHERRY
PTD WD TRIM
CHERRY FIN. WD PANELED DOOR
9A Head/Jamb
3"= 1'- 0"
PAINTED HOLLOW STEEL DOOR
CERAMIC TILE
Stock Room
3/4" WHITE CARRERA MARBLE SADDLE
SETTING BED W/ WIRE MESH
ADD STONE
VINYL TILE ON MASTIC
SONNEBORN LM 5000 WATERPROOF MEMBRANE
6 Sill
3"=1'-0"
Sales Floor
Stockroom #1
INTEGRAL FIN. WD. STOP
CHERRY FIN. WD PANELED DOOR
FINISH WD TRIM
PTD WD TRIM
FIN. FLR
TAPERED WD SADDLE
VINYL TILE ON MASTIC
9 Sill
3"= 1'- 0"

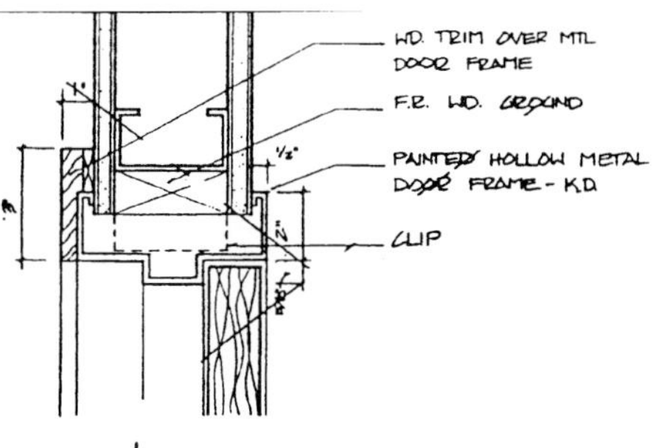

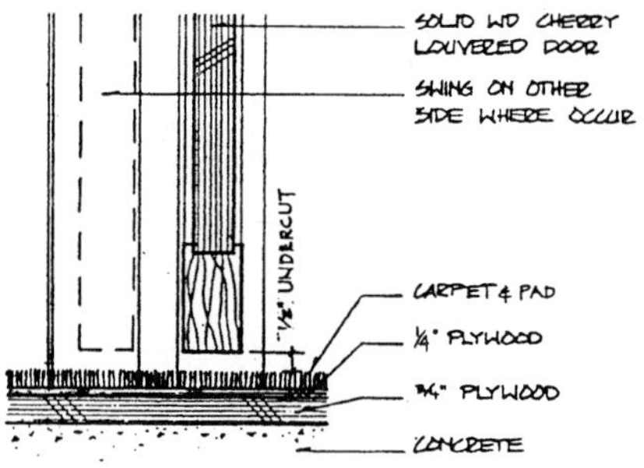

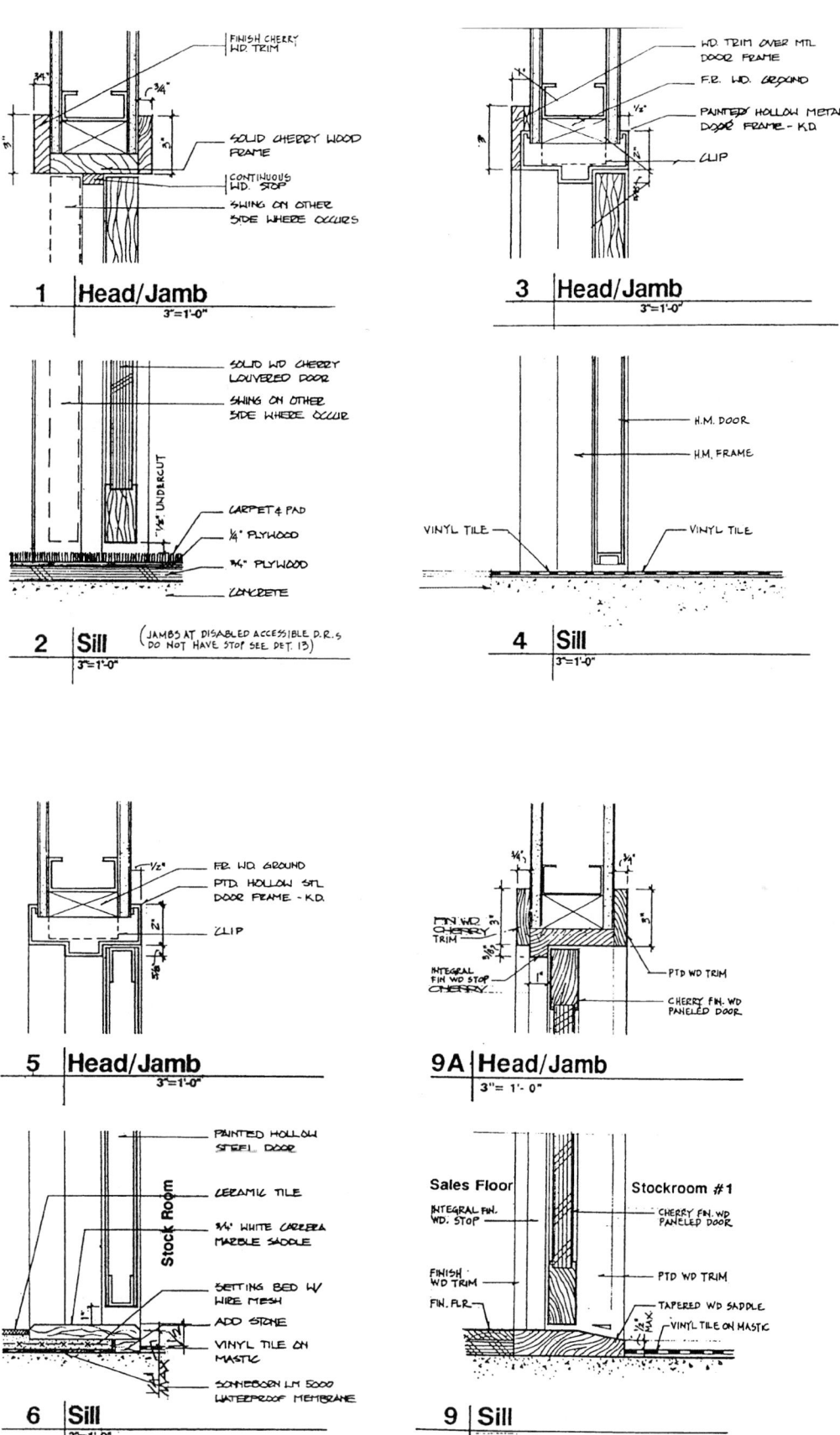

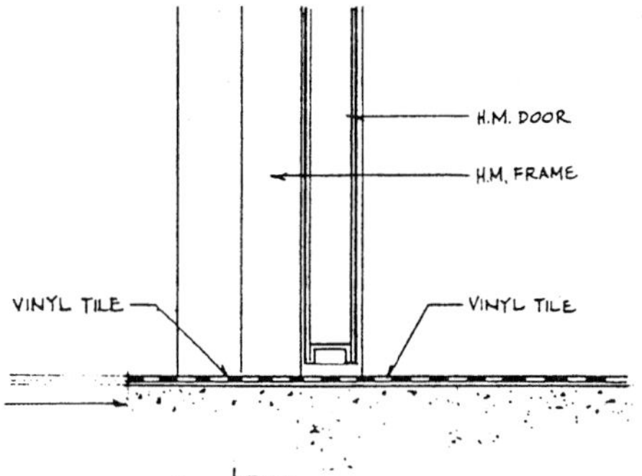

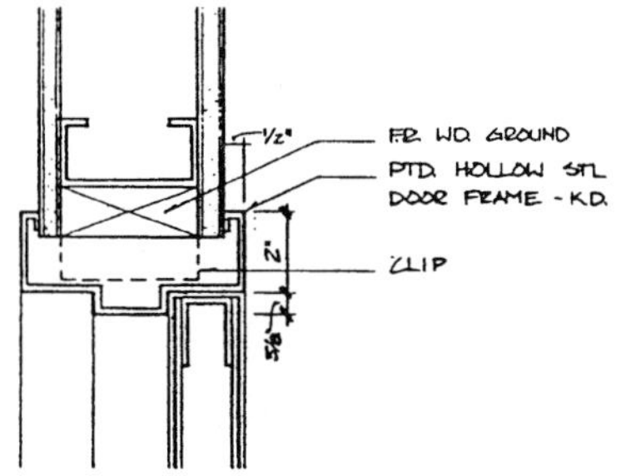

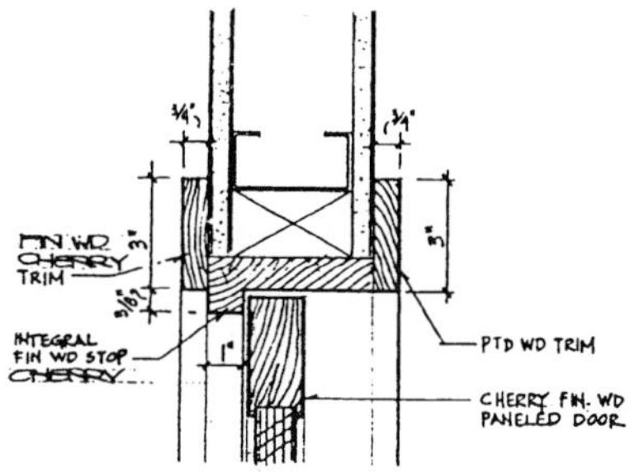

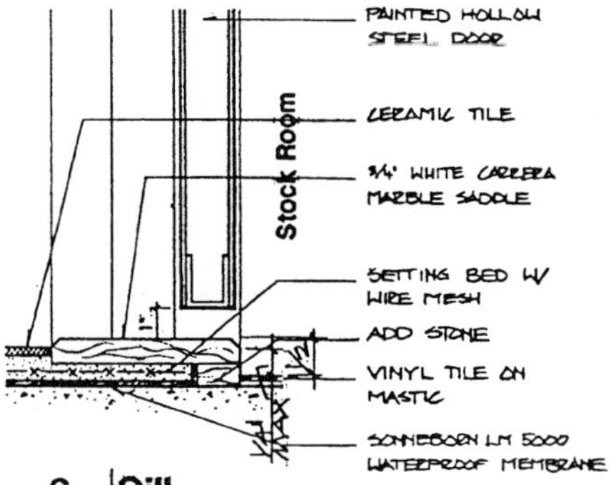

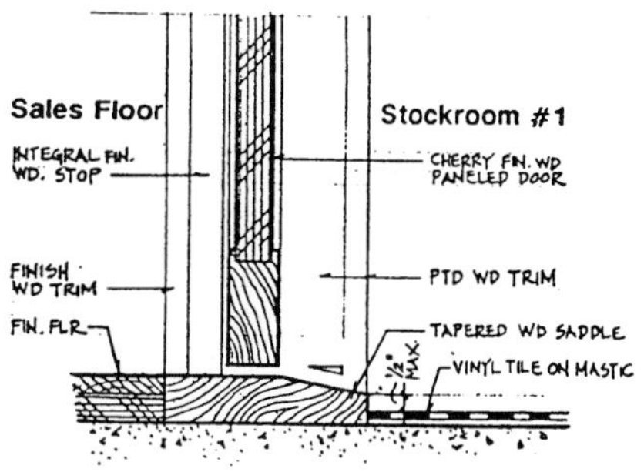

DOORS

Metal Door Frames

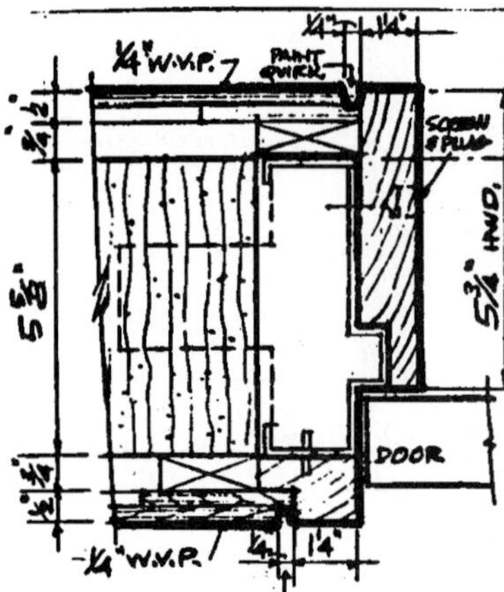

F-1 H.M. FRAME - HWD. TRIM 3"=1'-0"

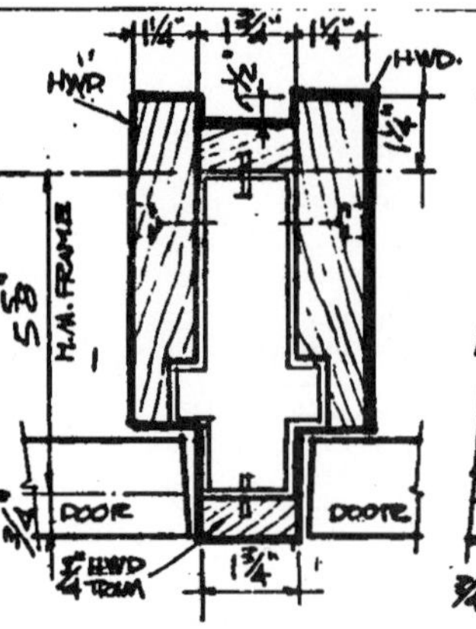

F-2 H.M. MULLION HWD. TRIM 3"=1'-0" (ALSO TYPICAL AS ASTRAGAL FOR CLASS "B" F.R.S.C. DOORS IN FIREWALL)

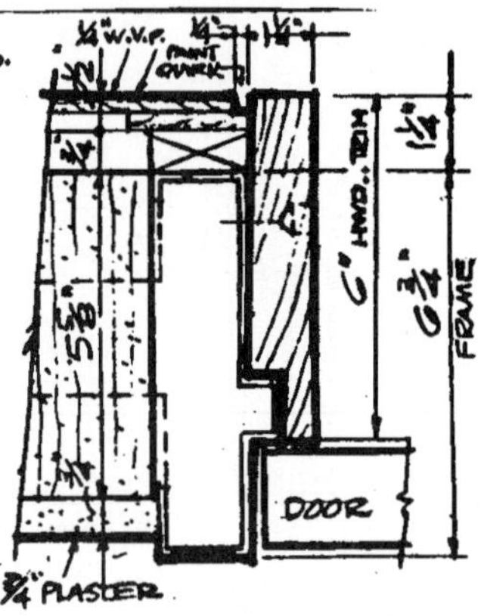

F-3 ONE-SIDE H.M. FRAME - HWD. TRIM 3"=1'-0"

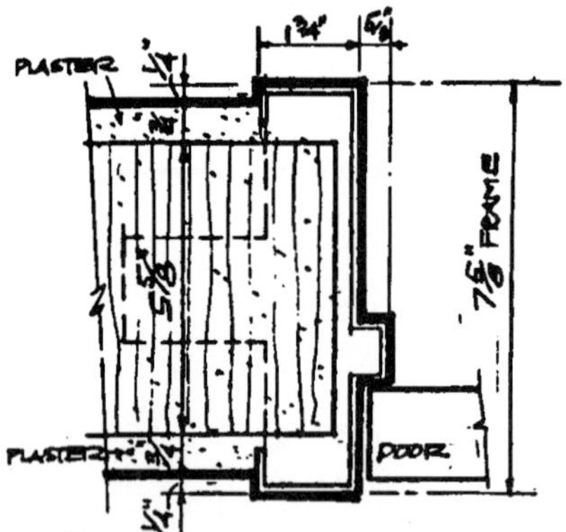

F-4 H.M. FRAME - PLAS./BOTH SIDES 3"=1'-0"

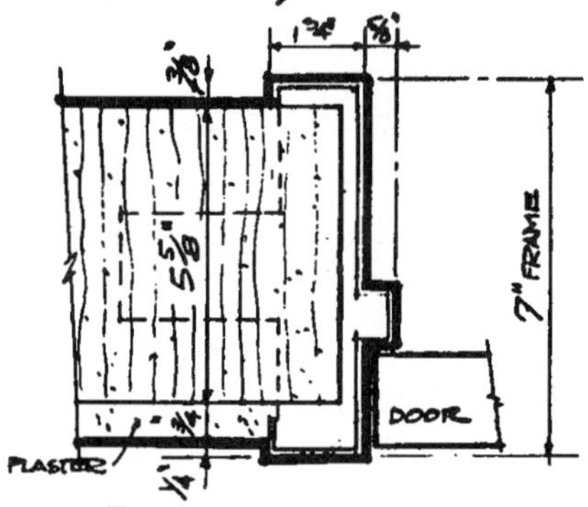

F-5 H.M. FRAME - PLAS./ONE SIDE 3"=1'-0"

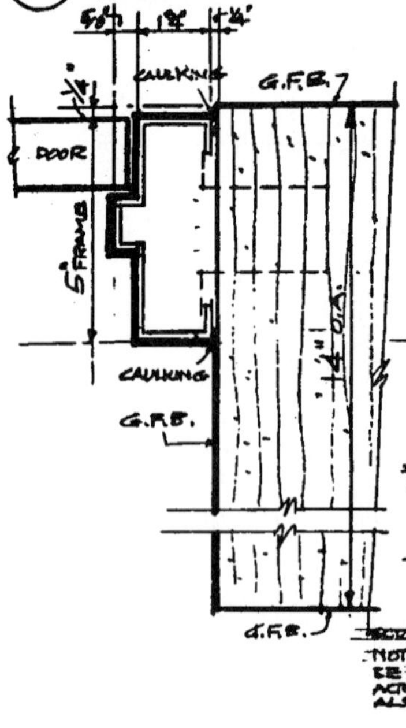

F-6 H.M. EXTERIOR FRAME 3"=1'-0"

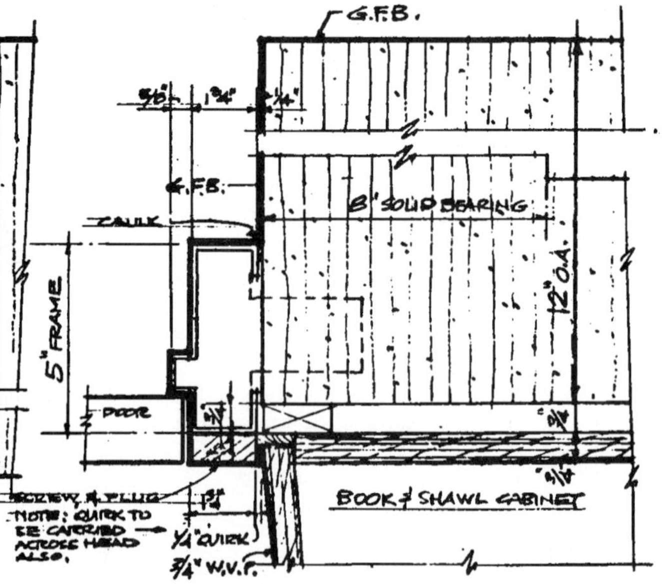

F-7 H.M. FRAME - HARDWOOD/ONE SIDE 3"=1'-0" SEE DETAIL 4/A-20 FOR DOOR #11

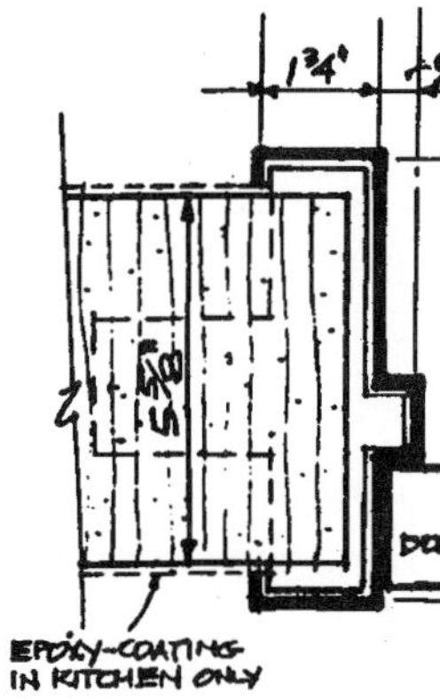

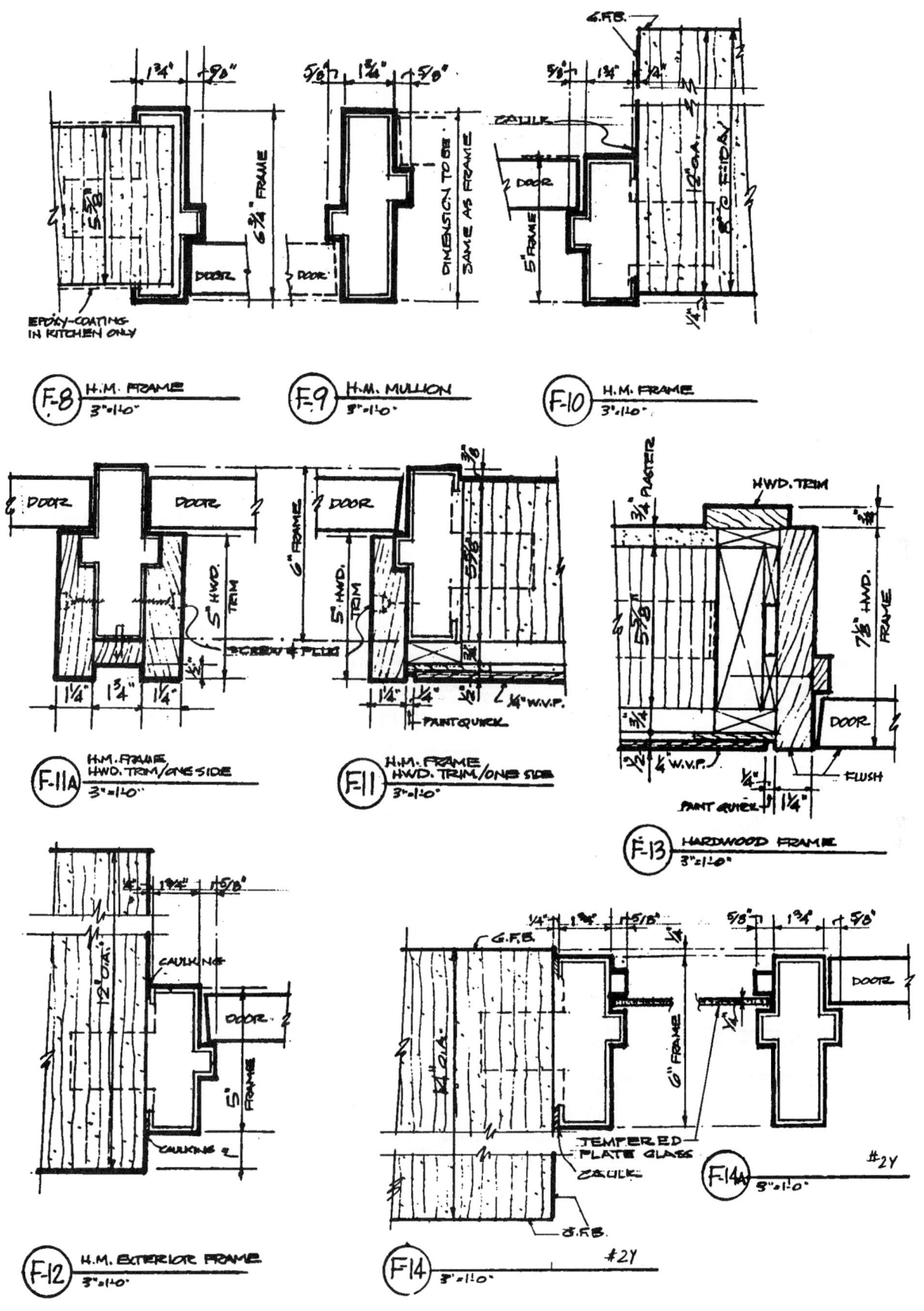

F-8 H.M. FRAME 3"=1'-0"

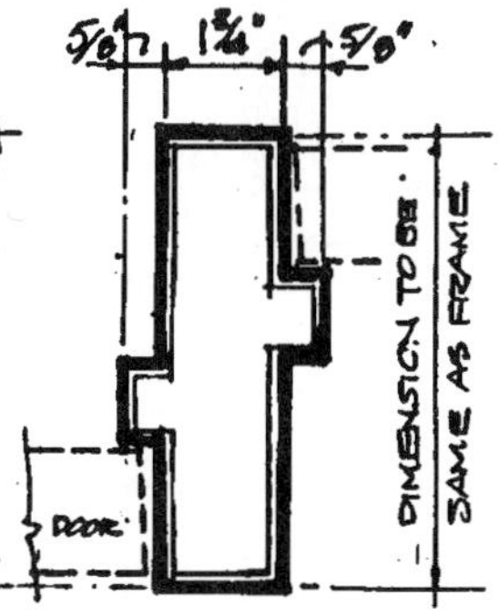

F-9 H.M. MULLION 3"=1'-0"

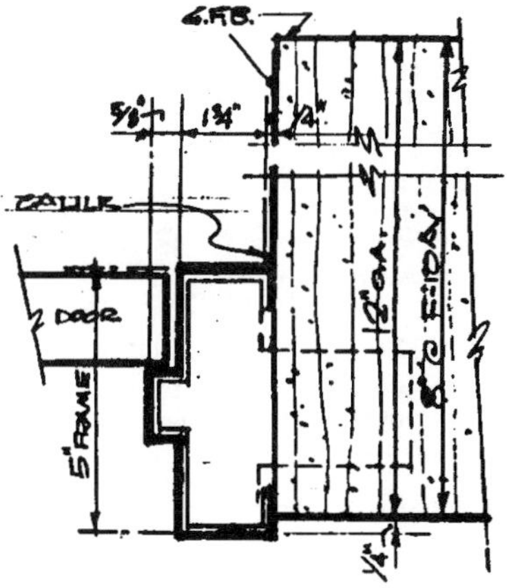

F-10 H.M. FRAME 3"=1'-0"

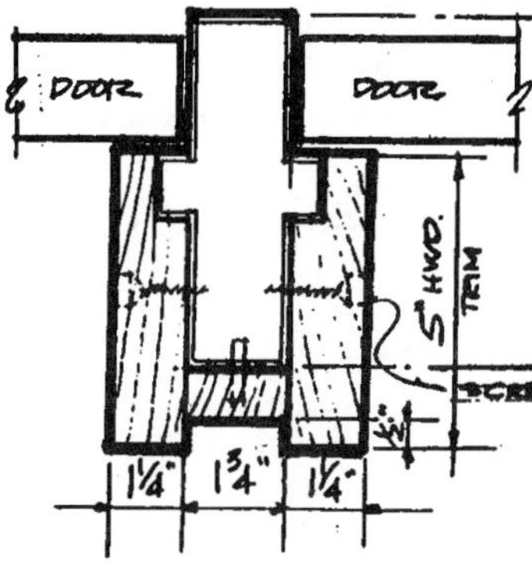

F-11A H.M. FRAME HWD. TRIM/ONE SIDE 3"=1'-0"

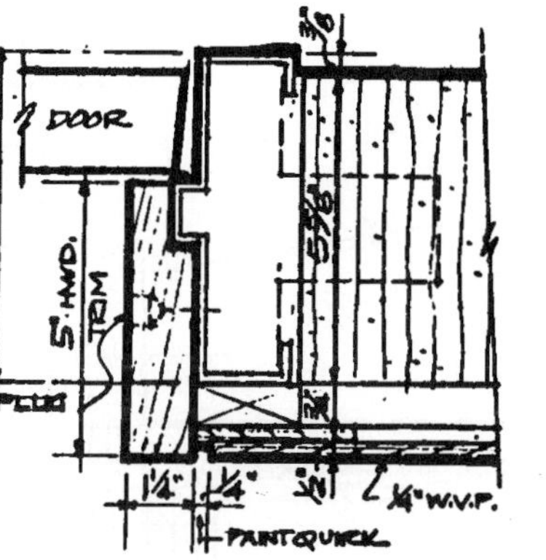

F-11 H.M. FRAME HWD. TRIM/ONE SIDE 3"=1'-0"

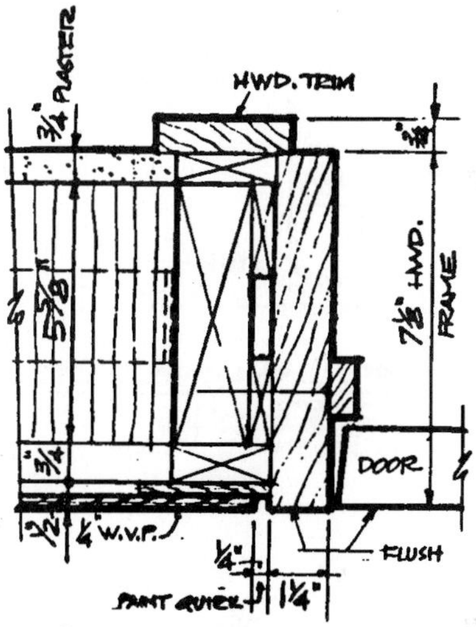

F-13 HARDWOOD FRAME 3"=1'-0"

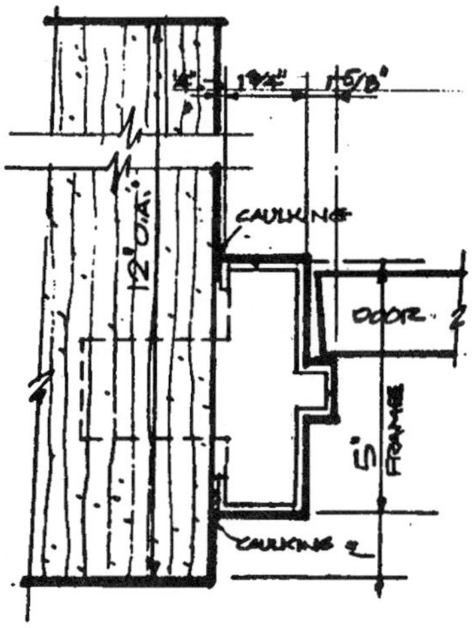

F-12 H.M. EXTERIOR FRAME 3"=1'-0"

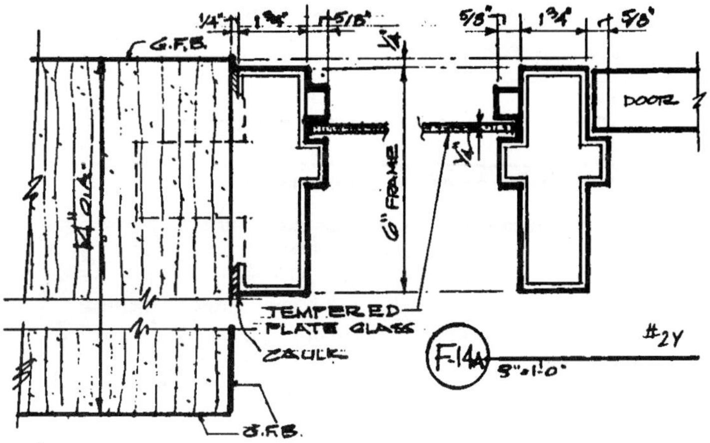

F-14A 3"=1'-0"

F-14 3"=1'-0" #2Y

DOORS
BiFold Doors

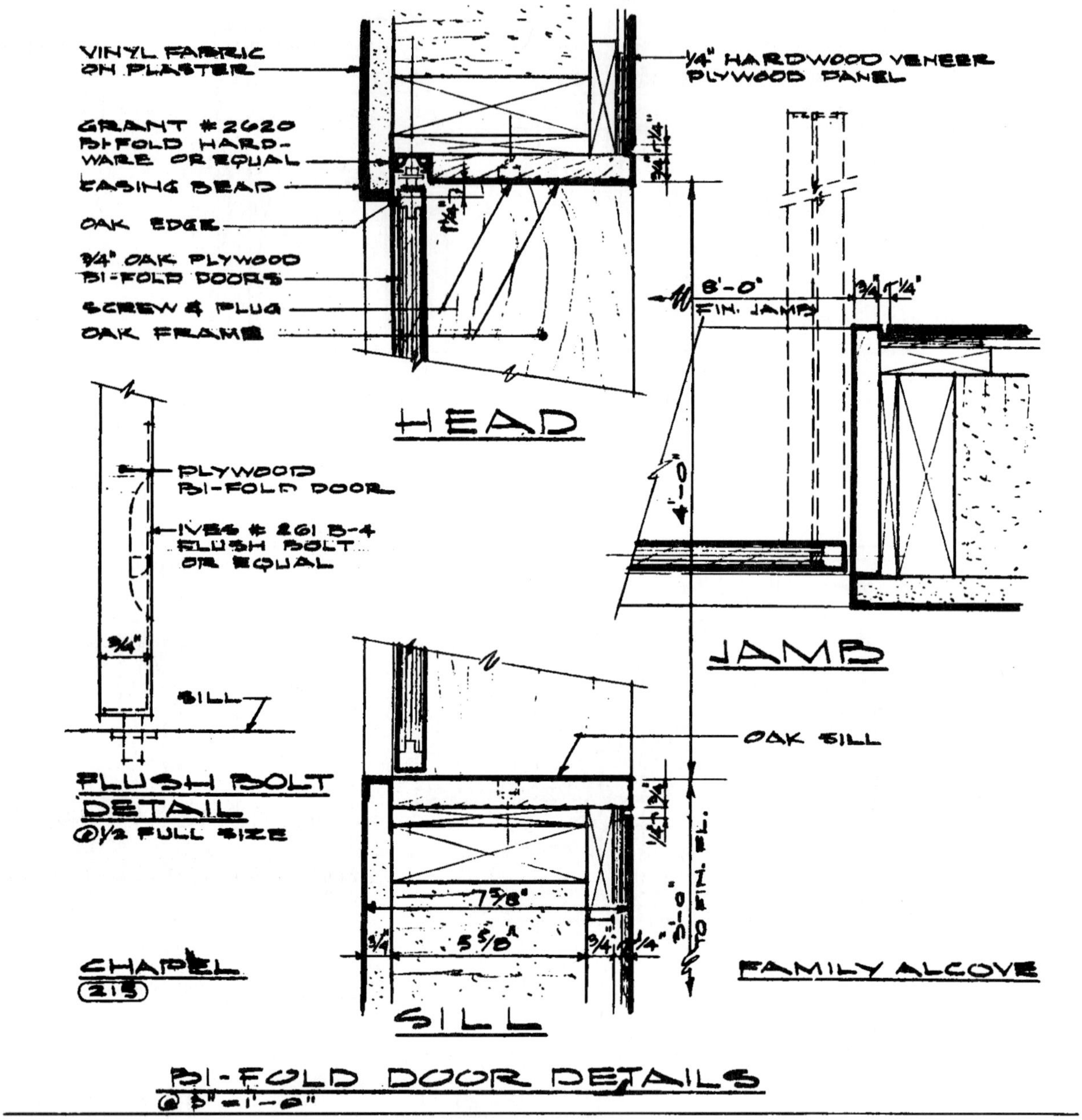
VINYL FABRIC ON PLASTER
1/4" HARDWOOD VENEER PLYWOOD PANEL
GRANT #2620 BI-FOLD HARDWARE OR EQUAL
CASING BEAD
OAK EDGE
3/4" OAK PLYWOOD BI-FOLD DOORS
SCREW & PLUG
OAK FRAME
HEAD
8'-0" FIN. JAMB
PLYWOOD BI-FOLD DOOR
IVES # 261 B-4 FLUSH BOLT OR EQUAL
SILL
FLUSH BOLT DETAIL
@1/2 FULL SIZE
JAMB
OAK SILL
7 5/8"
5 5/8"
CHAPEL
215
SILL
FAMILY ALCOVE
BI-FOLD DOOR DETAILS
@ 3"=1'-0"

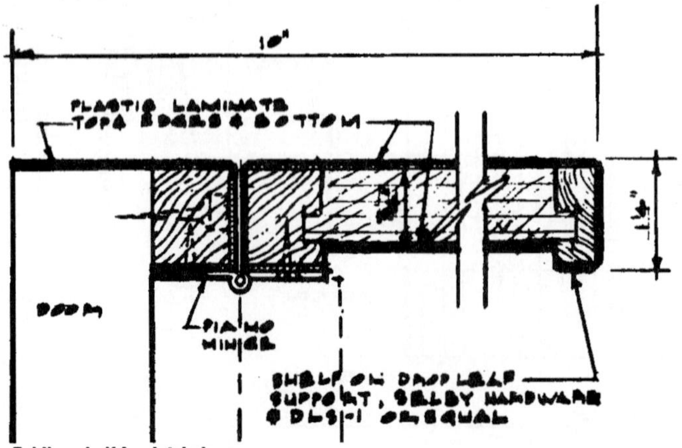
10"
PLASTIC LAMINATE TOP & EDGES & BOTTOM
ROOM
PIANO HINGE
SHELF ON DROP LEAF SUPPORT, SELBY HARDWARE # DLS-1 OR EQUAL

Folding shelf for dutch doors

DOORS

Sliding French Door

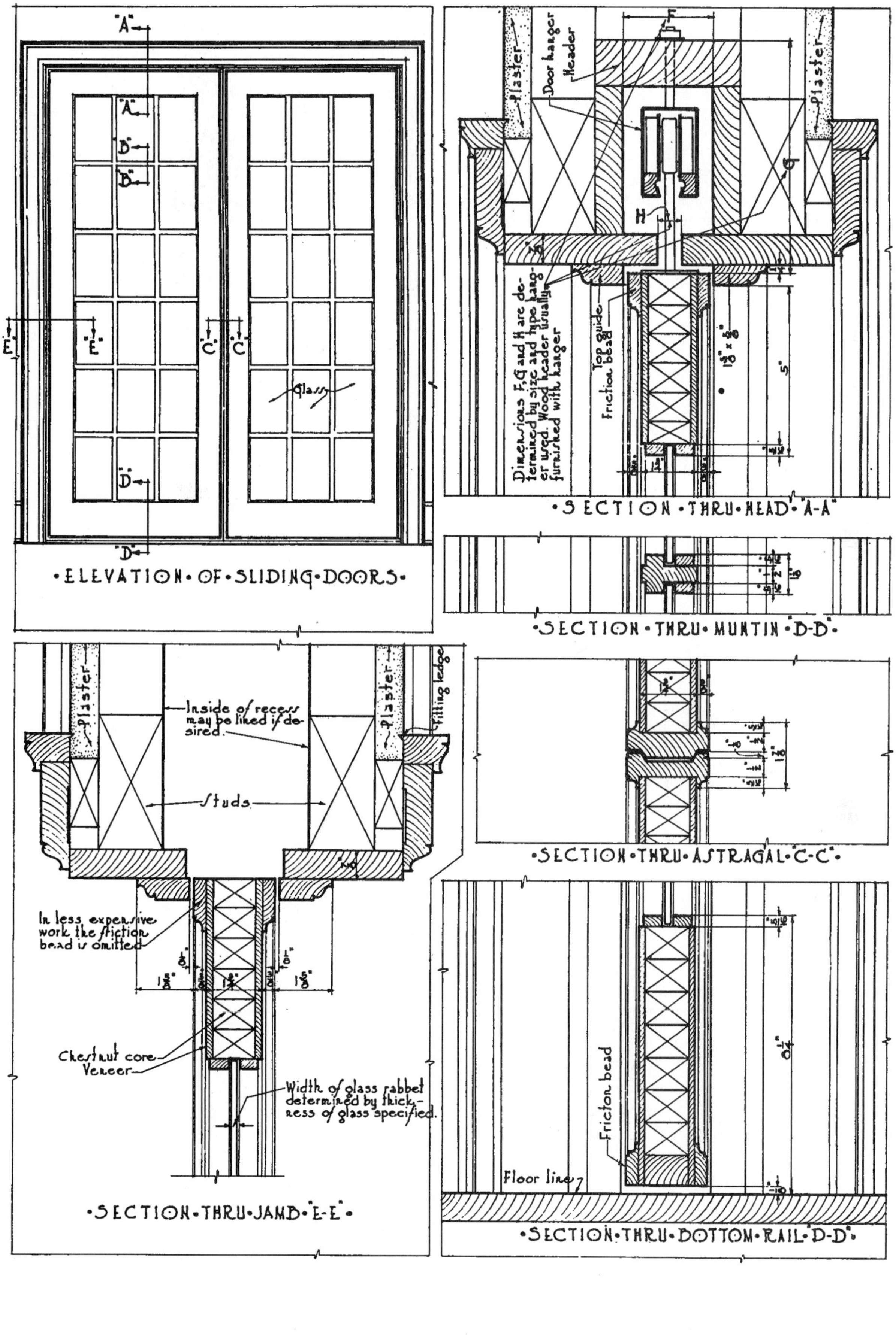

DOORS
Hardware

Hardware for doors may be obtained in a number of finishes, with brass, bronze, and nickel perhaps the most common. Door sets are usually classed as (a) entry lock for exterior doors, (b) bathroom set (inside lock control with safety slot for opening from the outside), (c) bedroom lock (keyed lock), and (d) passage set (without lock).

Hinges

Using three hinges for hanging 1¾-in exterior doors and two hinges for the lighter interior doors is common practice. There is some tendency for exterior doors to warp during the winter because of the difference in exposure on the opposite sides. The three hinges reduce this tendency. Three hinges are also useful on doors that lead to unheated attics and for wider and heavier doors that may be used within the house.

Loose-pin butt hinges should be used and must be of the proper size for the door they support. For 1¾-in-thick doors, use 4- by 4-in butts; for 1⅜-in doors, 3½- by 3½-in butts. After the door is fitted to the framed opening, with the proper clearances, hinge halves are fitted to the door. They are routed into the door edge with about a 3/16-in back distance (Fig. 26*A*). One hinge half should be set flush with the surface and must be fastened square with the edge of the door. Screws are included with each pair of hinges.

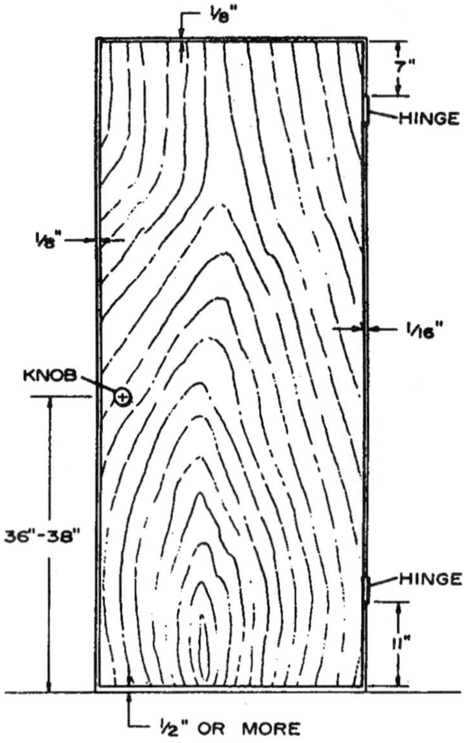

Fig. 24 Door clearances

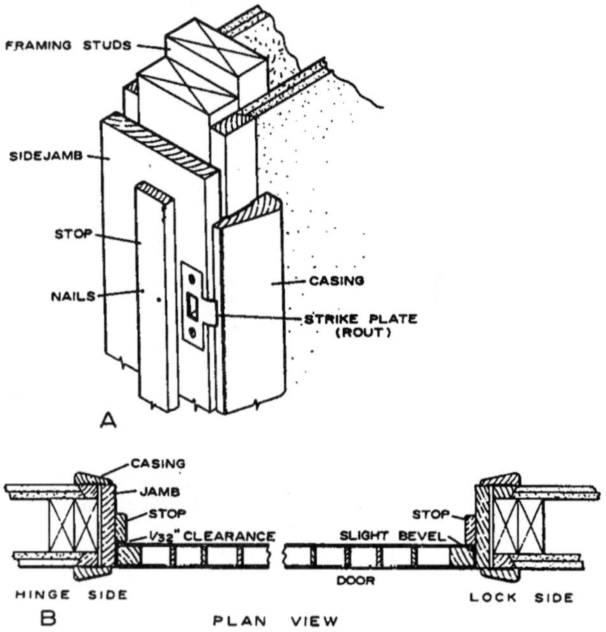

Fig. 25 Door details: *A*, installation of strike plate; *B*, location of stops

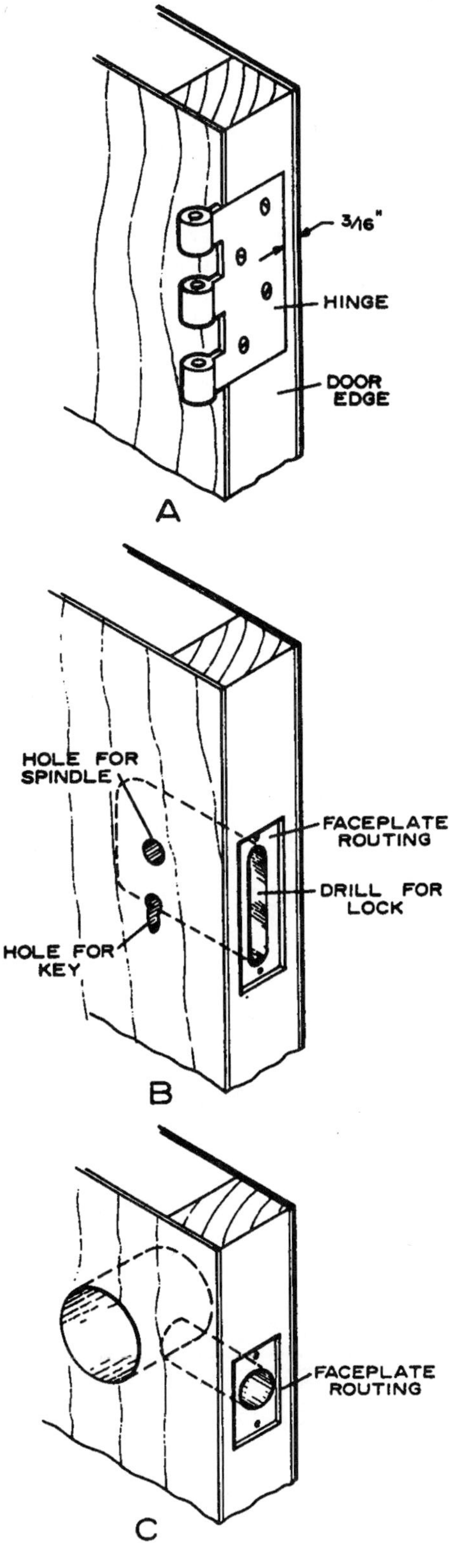

Fig. 26 Installation of door hardware: *A*, hinge; *B*, mortise lock; *C*, bored lock set

DOORS
Hand of Locks and Lock Functions

Locks not designated as reversible are made right-hand, left-hand, right-hand reverse bevel, or left-hand reverse bevel.

The hand of a lock is invariably determined from the outside of an entrance door or from the corridor or hall side of a room door. An easy method of determining the hand of a lock is to imagine oneself on that side of the opening from which the lock is controlled or operated by the key. Viewing the opening in this position, note which one of the following is true: (1) If the door swings in and is hinged at your right hand, the lock is right-hand; (2) if hinged at your left hand, the lock is left-hand; (3) if the door swings toward you and is hinged at your right, the lock is right-hand reverse bevel; (4) if hinged at your left hand, the lock is left-hand reverse bevel.

You may find that many locks are marked "reversible," meaning that they are interchangeably right- or left-hand, and in these instances no reference to hand or bevel of lock is necessary. These are locks which operate alike from both sides or locks which can be inverted in order to reverse the locking functions.

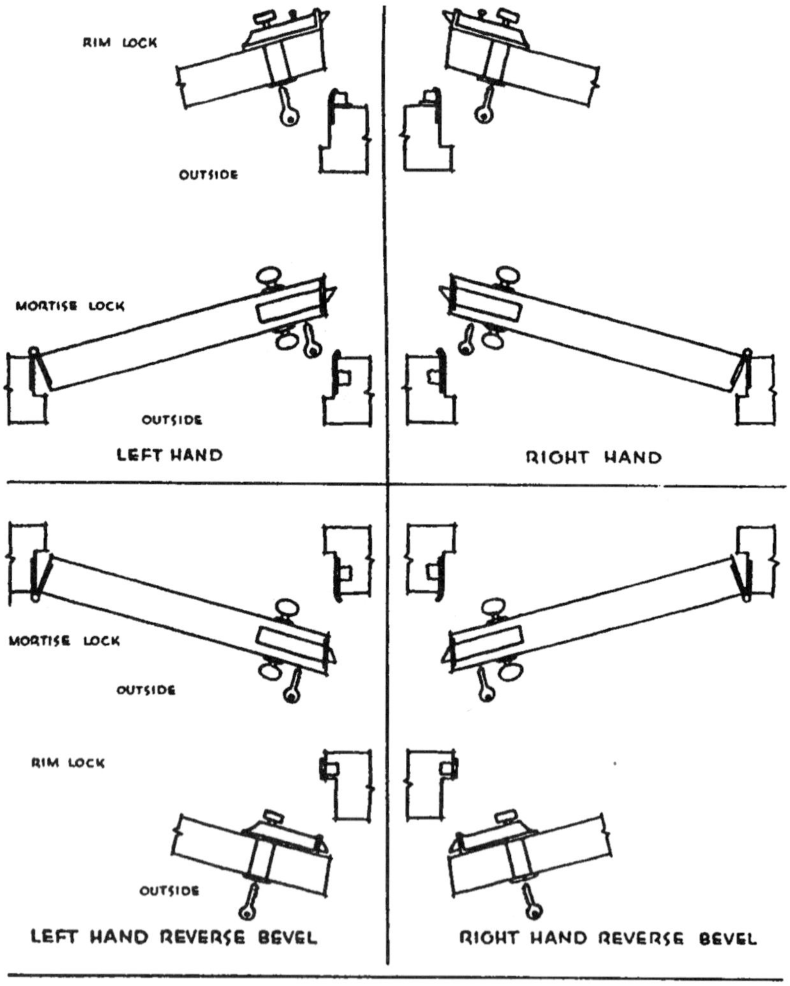

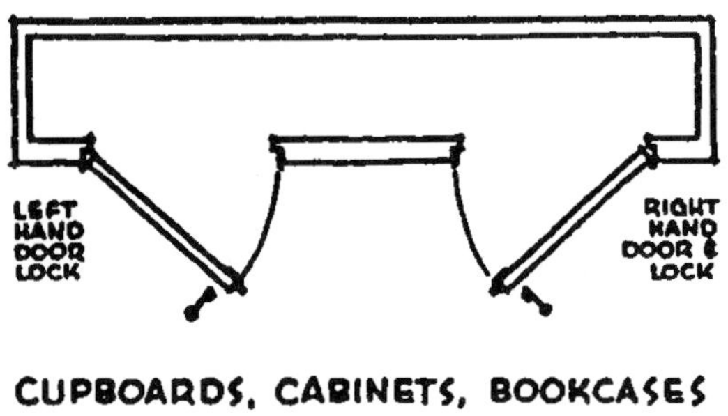

Determination of the hand of mortise or rim locks

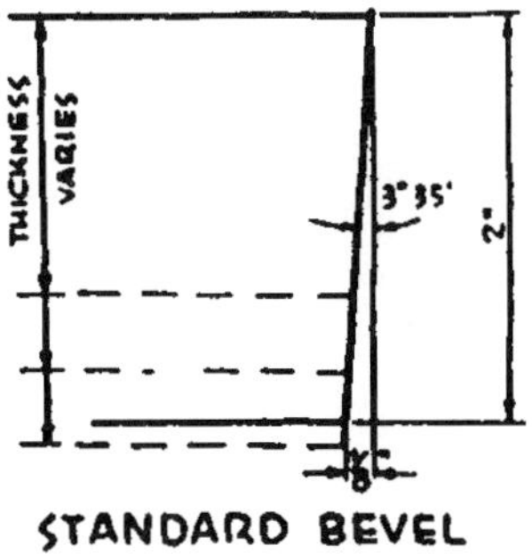

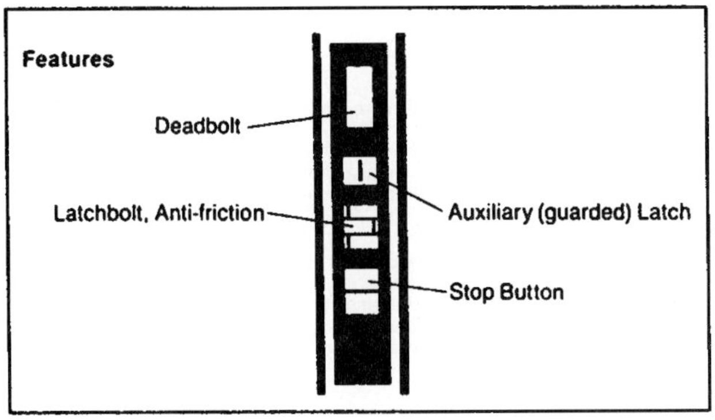

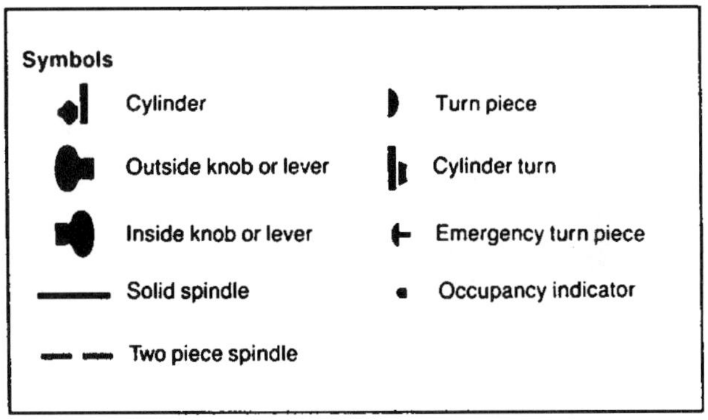

Features of and symbols for door hardware

DOORS
Lock Functions

OFFICE

For Inner Office and Area Entry Doors.
- Latchbolt retracted by lever or knob from either side unless outside is locked by stop button.
- When outside is locked, latchbolt is retracted by key outside and lever or knob inside.
- Auxiliary latch deadlocks latchbolt when door is closed.
- Latch holdback available.

APARTMENT ENTRANCE

For Apartment House or Office Building Entrance Doors
- Latchbolt retracted by lever or knob either side unless outside is locked by key from inside.
- When locked, latchbolt retracted by tenant key outside, lever or knob inside.
- Auxiliary latch deadlocks latchbolt when door is closed.

INSTITUTION

For Permanently Locked Passage Doors.
- Latchbolt retracted by key from either side.
- Both levers or knobs always inoperative.
- Auxiliary latch deadlocks latchbolt when door is closed.
- Latch holdback available.

STORE DOOR

For Store Entrance Doors.
- Latchbolt retracted by lever or knob from either side unless outside is locked by stop button.
- When locked latchbolt retracted by key outside and lever or knob inside.
- Deadbolt operated by key from either side.
- Auxiliary latch deadlocks latchbolt when door is closed.

STORE DOOR

For Storedoor, Storeroom or Utility Room Doors.
- Latchbolt retracted by lever or knob from either side.
- Deadbolt operated by key from either side.

CYLINDER X TURN PIECE

Deadlock
- Deadbolt operated by key outside and turn inside.

DOUBLE CYLINDER

Double Cylinder Deadlock
- Deadbolt operated by key from either side.
- Bolt automatically deadlocks when fully thrown.

CLASSROOM

Classroom Deadlock
- Deadbolt operated by key outside.
- Cylinder turn inside will retract deadbolt but will not project it.
- Bolt automatically deadlocks when fully thrown.

CYLINDER X BLANK

Deadlock
- Deadbolt operated by key from one side.
- No trim on opposite side.
- Bolt automatically deadlocks when fully thrown.

CLASSROOM
- Latchbolt retracted by lever or knob from either side unless outside is locked by key.
- Inside lever or knob always free for immediate exit.
- Auxiliary latch deadlocks latchbolt when door is closed.

STOREROOM
- Latchbolt retracted by lever or knob inside, by key outside.
- Outside lever or knob always inoperative. Knob is free spinning.
- Auxiliary latch deadlocks latchbolt when door is closed.
- Latch holdback available.

ENTRANCE

For Commercial and Residential Entry Doors
- Deadbolt and latchbolt retracted by lever or knob trim either side unless outside is locked by stop button.
- When locked, key outside and lever or knob inside retracts deadbolt and latchbolt simultaneously. Outside remains locked until stop button is reset to unlocked position.
- Deadbolt operated by key and turn piece. Throwing deadbolt automatically locks stop button.
- Auxiliary latch deadlocks latchbolt when door is closed and locked.

CONVALESCENT

For Convalescent or Bedroom Doors
- Latchbolt retracted by lever or knob from either side when unlocked.
- Deadbolt operated by key outside and turn piece inside.
- Throwing deadbolt disengages outside lever or knob.
- Turning inside lever or knob retracts deadbolt and latchbolt simultaneously for immediate exit and unlocks outside.

CLOSET

For Closet, Storeroom, or Utility Room Doors
- Latchbolt retracted by lever or knob from either side at all times.
- Deadbolt operated by key outside.

DORMITORY

For Dormitory or Bedroom Doors.
- Latchbolt retracted by lever or knob from either side at all times.
- Deadbolt is operated by key outside and by turn piece inside.

HOTEL

For Corridor Doors to Guest Rooms.
- Outside lever or knob always inoperative. Knob is free spinning.
- Latchbolt retracted by guest key outside except when deadbolt is thrown by turn piece inside.
- When thrown occupancy indicator is engaged, all keys inoperative except emergency or display keys.
- Turning inside lever or knob retracts deadbolt and latchbolt simultaneously. Aux. latch deadlocks latchbolt when door is closed.

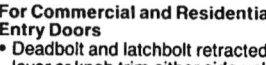

HOTEL

For Corridor Doors to Guest Rooms
- Same as 85P function except that visual "DO NOT DISTURB" plate replaces occupancy indicator button.

Available for 1¾" doors and escutcheon trim only.

Non-Keyed Locks

ANSI A156.2 Series 4000

No.	A. N. S. I. No.	Grade	Function
A10S C10S D10S F10N	F75	2 1 1 2	***Passage Latch:*** Both knobs always unlocked
D12D	F89	1	***Exit Lock:*** Unlocked by knob inside only. Outside knob always fixed.
A20S			***Closet Latch:*** Outside knob and inside thumbturn are always unlocked.
A25D D25D			***Exit Lock:*** Blank plate outside. Inside knob always unlocked. (Specify door thickness, 1⅜″ or 1¾″.)
A30D D30D F30N	F77	2 1 2	***Patio Lock:*** Push-button locking. Turning inside knob releases button. Closing door on A & D series also releases button.
A40S C40S D40S F40N	F76	2 1 1 2	***Bath/Bedroom Privacy Lock:*** Push-button locking. Can be opened from outside with small screwdriver or flat narrow tool. Turning inside knob releases push-button. Closing door on A, C and D series also releases button, preventing lock-out.
A43D	F79	2	***Communicating Lock:*** Turn button in outer knob locks and unlocks knob and inside thumbturn.
A44S D44S			***Hospital Privacy Lock:*** Push-button locking. Unlocked from outside by turning emergency turn-button. Rotating inside knob or closing door releases inside button.

Dummy Trim

No.	A. N. S. I. No.	Grade	Function
A170 D170 F170N			***Single Dummy Trim:*** Single dummy trim for one side of door. Used for door pull or as matching inactive trim.

Keyed Locks

ANSI A156.2 Series 4000

No.	A. N. S. I. No.	Grade	Function
F51N	F81	2	***Entrance Lock:*** Unlocked by key from outside when outer knob is locked by turn-button in inside knob. Inside knob always unlocked.
D50PD	F82	1	***Entrance/Office Lock:*** Push button locking. Pushing button locks outside lever until unlocked with key or by turning inside lever.
A53PD C53PD D53PD	F81 F82 F82	2 1 1	***Entrance Lock:*** Turn/Push button locking: Pushing and turning button locks outside knob requiring use of key until button is manually unlocked. Push button locking: Pushing button locks outside knob until unlocked by key or by turning inside knob.
A55PD D55PD	F92	2 1	***Service Station Lock:*** Unlocked by key from outside when outer knob is locked by universal button in inside knob. Closing door releases button. Outside knob may be fixed by rotating universal button.
D60PD	F88	1	***Vestibule Lock:*** Unlocked by key from outside when outside knob is locked by key in inside knob. Inside knob is always unlocked.
D66PD	F91	1	***Store Lock:*** Key in either knob locks or unlocks both knobs.
A70PD C70PD D70PD	F84	2 1 1	***Classroom Lock:*** Outside knob locked and unlocked by key. Inside knob always unlocked.
D72PD	F80	1	***Communicating Lock:*** Key in either knob locks or unlocks each knob independently.
A73PD D73PD	F90	2 1	***Dormitory Lock:*** Locked or unlocked by key from outside. Push-button locking from inside. Turning inside knob or closing door releases button.
D76PD	F85	1	***Classroom Hold-Back Lock:*** Outside knob locked or unlocked by key. Inside knob always unlocked. Latch may be locked in retracted position by key.

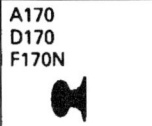

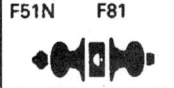

DOORS

Lock Functions

Keyed Locks — ANSI A156.2 Series 4000

Schlage Number	A. N. S. I. No.	Grade	Function
A79PD			***Communicating Lock:*** Locked or unlocked by key from outside. Blank plate inside.
A80PD C80PD D80PD F80N	F86	2 1 1 2	***Storeroom Lock:*** Outside knob fixed. Entrance by key only. Inside Knob always unlocked.
D82PD	F87	1	***Institution Lock:*** Both knobs fixed. Entrance by key in either knob.
A85PD D85PD	F93	2 1	***Hotel-Motel Lock:*** Outside knob fixed. Entrance by key only. Push-button in inside knob activates visual occupancy indicator, allowing only emergency masterkey to operate. Rotation of inside spanner-button provides lockout feature by keeping indicator thrown.

Deadbolt Locks — ANSI A 156.5

Schlage Number	A. N. S. I. No.	Grade	Function
B160N B460P B560	E2151	2 1 1	***Single Cylinder Deadbolt Lock:*** Deadbolt thrown or retracted by key from outside or by inside turn unit. Bolt automatically deadlocks when fully thrown.
B162N† B462P† B562†	E2141	2 1 1	***Double Cylinder Deadbolt Lock:*** Deadbolt thrown or retracted by key from either side.
B461P	E2161	1	***One-Way Deadbolt Lock:*** Deadbolt thrown or retracted by key only. Blank plate inside.
B463P	E2171	1	***Classroom Deadbolt Lock:*** Deadbolt thrown or retracted by key outside. Inside turn unit will retract bolt only.
B464P			***Cylinder Lock:*** Deadbolt thrown or retracted by key from one side. No inside trim.
B180 B480	E2191	2 1	***Door Bolt:*** Deadbolt thrown or retracted by turn unit only. No outside trim.

Deadlatch Locks — ANSI A156.5

Schlage Number	A. N. S. I. No.	Grade	Function
B250PD	E2121	1	***Night Latch:*** Deadlocking latchbolt retracted by key from outside or by inside turn unit. Rotating turn unit and activating hold-back feature keeps latch retracted.
B252PD†	E2111	1	***Double Cylinder Deadlatch:*** Deadlocking latchbolt retracted by key from either side. No hold-back feature.
B270D	E2181	1	***Exit Latch:*** Deadlocking latchbolt retracted by inside turn unit only. No outside trim. Rotating turn unit and activating hold-back feature keeps latch retracted.

Lever Functions

Schlage Number	A. N. S. I. No.	Grade	Function
B245S			***Lever Passage Latch:*** For use on passage, closet and doors that do not require locking. Rotating either lever retracts latchbolt. (Specify door hand.)
B281 B282			***Single Dummy Trim-Double Dummy Trim:*** For use on single or pairs of doors when fixed turn is required. (Specify door hand.)

Grip Handle Sets

Schlage Number	A. N. S. I. No.	Grade	Function
E51PD			***Entrance Lock:*** Unlocked by key from outside when thumb-piece is locked by inside turn-button.
F160N			***Entrance Lock:*** Deadbolt thrown or retracted by key from outside or by inside turn unit. Latch retracted by thumbpiece from outside or by inside knob.
F162N†			***Double Cylinder Entrance Lock:*** Deadbolt thrown or retracted by key from either side. Latch retracted by thumbpiece from outside or by inside knob.

†CAUTION: Double cylinder locks on residences and any door in any structure which is used for egress are a safety hazard in times of emergency and their use is not recommended. Installation should be in accordance with existing codes only.

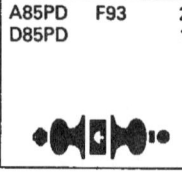

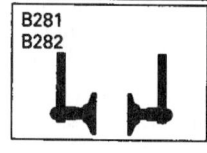

Dummy Trim

A. N. S. I. No. Grade

E193

Outside and Inside Dummy Trim: For use as door pull or as dummy trim on an inactive of pair of doors. Fixed thumbpiece and inside knob. Thru bolted dummy cylinder.

F193N

Outside and Inside Dymmy Trim: For use as door pull or as dummy trim on inactive leaf of pair of doors. Fixed thumbpiece and inside knob. Dummy cylinder with inside plate.

Interconnected Locks — *ANSI A156.12*

A. N. S. I. No. Grade

H110 F95 4

Entrance—Single Locking: Deadbolt thrown or retracted by key in upper lock from outside or by inside turn unit. Latchbolt retracted by knob from either side. Turning inside knob retracts deadbolt and latchbolt simultaneously for immediate exit.

H153 F97 4

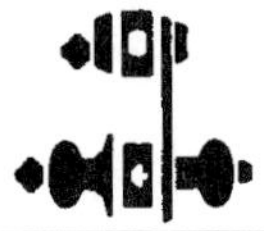

Entrance—Double Locking: Deadbolt thrown or retracted by key in upper lock from outside or by inside turn unit. Deadlatch retracted by key in outer knob when locked by pushing turn-button in inner knob. Outer knob may be fixed in locked position by rotating turn-button. Inside knob retracts deadbolt and deadlatch simultaneously for immediate exit.

H180

Storeroom Lock: Bolt may be operated by key from outside or by turn unit from inside. Bolt automatically deadlocks when fully thrown. Lock may be opened by key from outside. Inside knob will retract both latch and deadbolt. Latch automatically deadlocks when door is closed, inside knob always free for immediate exit. Outer knob always fixed.

H185 F100 4

Hotel-Motel Lock: Deadbolt thrown or retracted by key in upper lock from outside or by inside turn unit. Deadlatch retracted by key in outer fixed knob. Push-button in inner knob activates visual occupancy indicator, allowing only emergency masterkey to operate. Rotation of inside spanner-button provides lockout feature by keeping indicator thrown. Turning inside knob retracts deadbolt simultaneously for immediate exit.

Dummy Trim

A. N. S. I. No. Grade

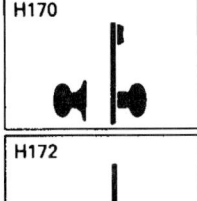

H170

Single Dummy Inside Trim: Snap-on rose and knob. Concealed mounting screws.

H172

Dummy Trim Inside and Outside: Snap-on rose and knobs thru-bolted.

Mortise Locks Non-Keyed — *ANSI A156.13 Series 1000*

A. N. S. I. No. Grade

L9010* F01 1

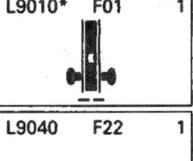

Passage Latch: Latch bolt retracted by lever or knob from either side at all times.

L9040 F22 1

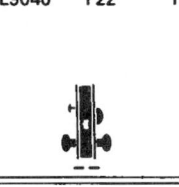

Bath/Bedroom Privacy Lock: Latchbolt retracted by lever or knob from either side unless outside is locked by inside turn piece. Operating inside lever or knob or closing door unlocks outside lever or knob. To unlock from outside, remove emergency button, insert turn piece (furnished) in access hole and rotate.

L0170

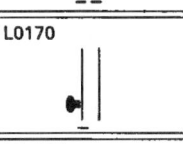

Single Dummy Trim: Lever or knob on both sides fixed by mounting bar.

L0172*

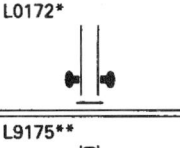

Pair Dummy Trim: Lever or knob on both sides fixed by mounting bar.

L9175**

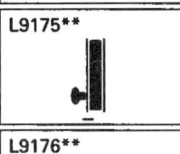

Single Dummy Trim: Lever or knob on one side fixed. Includes lock chassis and armor front.

L9176**

Pair Dummy Trim: Lever or knob both sides fixed. Includes lock chassis and armor front.

Keyed Locks

A. N. S. I. No. Grade

L9050* F04 1

Office and Inner Entry Lock: Latchbolt retracted by lever or knob from either side unless outside is made inoperative by key outside or by rotating inside turn piece. When outside is locked, latchbolt is retracted by key outside or by lever or knob inside. Outside lever or knob remains locked until thumbturn is returned to vertical or by counter clockwise rotation of key. Auxiliary latch deadlocks latchbolt when door is closed.

L9060* F09 1

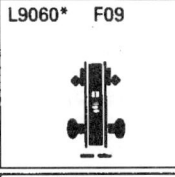

Apartment Entrance Lock: Latchbolt retracted by lever or knob from either side unless outside is locked by key from inside. When locked, latchbolt retracted by key outside or lever or knob inside. Auxiliary latch deadlocks when door is closed.

L9070* F05 1

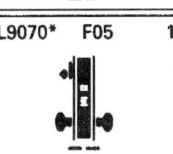

Classroom Lock: Latchbolt retracted by lever or knob from either side unless outside is locked by key. Unlocked from outside by key. Inside lever or knob always free for immediate exit. Auxiliary latch deadlocks latchbolt when door is closed.

**When armored front is required as strike for inactive door, specify L9177 for single or L9178 for pair of dummy trim. Specify door hand.

DOORS
Lock Functions

Keyed Locks

A. N. S. I. No. Grade

L9080 F07 1

Storeroom Lock: Latchbolt retracted by key outside or by lever or knob inside. Outside lever or knob always inoperative. Auxiliary latch deadlocks latchbolt when door is closed.

L9080EL

Storeroom Lock: Electrically locked. Outside lever or knob continuously locked by 24V AC or DC. Latchbolt retracted by key outside or by lever or knob inside. Switch or power failure allows outside lever or knob to retract latchbolt. Auxiliary latch deadlocks latchbolt when door is closed. Inside lever or knob always free for immediate exit.

L9080EU

Storeroom Lock: Electrically unlocked. Outside lever or knob unlocked by 24V AC or DC. Latchbolt retracted by key outside or lever or knob inside. Auxiliary latch deadlocks latchbolt when door is closed. Inside lever or knob always free for immediate exit.

L9082

Institution Lock: Latchbolt retracted by key from either side. Lever or knob on both sides always inoperative. Auxiliary latch deadlocks latchbolt when door is closed.

L9453 F20 1

Entrance Lock: Latchbolt retracted by lever or knob from either side unless outside is locked by 20° rotation of thumbturn. Deadbolt thrown or retracted by 90° rotation of thumbturn. When locked, key outside or lever or knob inside retracts deadbolt and latchbolt simultaneously. Outside lever or knob remains locked until thumbturn is restored to vertical position. Throwing deadbolt automatically locks outside lever or knob. Auxiliary latch deadlocks latchbolt when door is closed.

L9456 F13 1

Dormitory/Exit Lock: Latchbolt retracted by lever or knob from either side. Deadbolt thrown or retracted by key outside or inside thumbturn. Throwing deadbolt locks outside lever or knob. Rotating inside lever or knob simultaneously retracts deadbolt and latchbolt, and unlocks outside lever or knob.

L9465 1

Closet/Storeroom Lock: Latchbolt retracted by lever or knob from either side except when deadbolt is extended. Deadbolt extended or retracted by key outside.

L9466 F14 1

Store/Utility Room Lock: Latchbolt retracted by knob or lever from either side except when deadbolt extended. Deadbolt extended or retracted by key from either side.

L9473 F21 1

Dormitory/Bedroom Lock: Latchbolt retracted by knob or lever from either side except when deadbolt is extended. Deadbolt extended or retracted by key outside or thumbturn inside.

Keyed Locks

A. N. S. I. No. Grade

L9485

Hotel Lock: Latchbolt by key outside or by lever or knob inside. Outside lever or knob always fixed. Deadbolt thrown or retracted by inside thumbturn. When deadbolt is thrown, all keys become inoperative except emergency or display keys. Turning inside lever or knob retracts both deadbolt and latchbolt simultaneously. Auxiliary latch deadlocks latchbolt when door is closed.

L9486 F15 1

Hotel Lock: Latchbolt retracted by key outside or by lever or knob inside. Outside lever or knob always fixed. Deadbolt thrown or retracted by inside thumbturn. When deadbolt is thrown, "DO NOT DISTURB" plate is displayed—all keys become inoperative except emergency or display keys. Turning inside lever or knob retracts both deadbolt and latchbolt simultaneously. Auxiliary latch deadlocks latchbolt when door is closed.

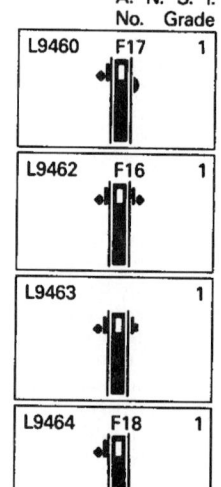

Deadlocks

A. N. S. I. No. Grade

L9460 F17 1

Cylinder X Thumbturn: Deadbolt thrown or retracted by key outside or thumbturn inside.

L9462 F16 1

Double Cylinder: Deadbolt operated by key from either side.

L9463 1

Classroom Lock: Deadbolt thrown or retracted by key from outside. Inside cylinder turn retracts deadbolt but cannot project it.

L9464 F18 1

Cylinder Lock: Deadbolt thrown or retracted by key from one side. No trim on opposite side.

CEILINGS

SUSPENSION SYSTEM TYPES

This section provides the designer with information on both suspended ceilings and ceilings directly attached to the structure above. It starts with a review of generic suspension systems and then provides details and discussion of the various suspended ceiling types.

Large-scale details show how, in addition to standard acoustical tiles, other ceiling materials such as plaster, metal panels, baffles, gypsum board, and wood can be attached to suspension systems. A variety of unusual conditions are also detailed, including curved and vaulted ceilings, wall conditions, light coves, and lighting fixture framing.

Acoustical Tile and Lay-in Panel Ceiling Suspension Systems

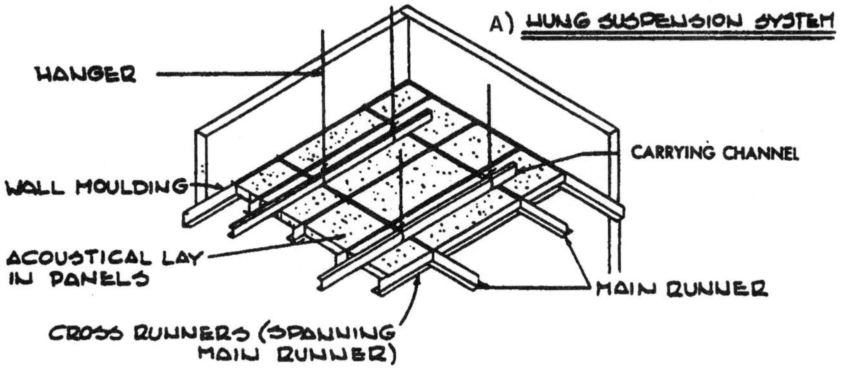

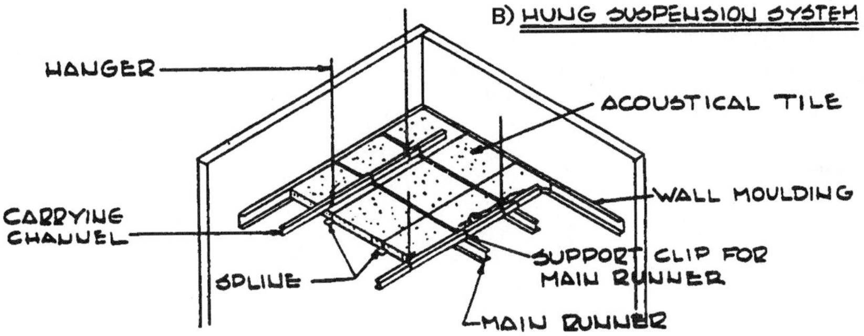

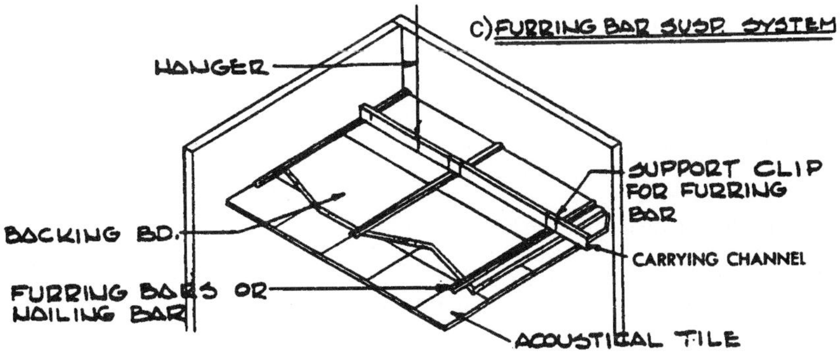

CEILINGS

Suspension System Types

The designer is cautioned that in many jurisdictions, suspension systems must attain a higher level of structural integrity than most other architectural elements. For example, wire hangers may not be an acceptable method of suspending channels from the structure above. Rather, steel rods of a minimum diameter or flat bar hangers of a minimum width and thickness may be required. Local or state codes should always be consulted prior to finalizing such details.

In many situations, the ceiling "skin" takes on further importance beyond aesthetic, acoustical, or visual requirements. It can also be used to complete an envelope that provides a fire-resistive rating to the structural members above. Again, it is necessary to thoroughly investigate the building and fire codes that might govern ceiling design.

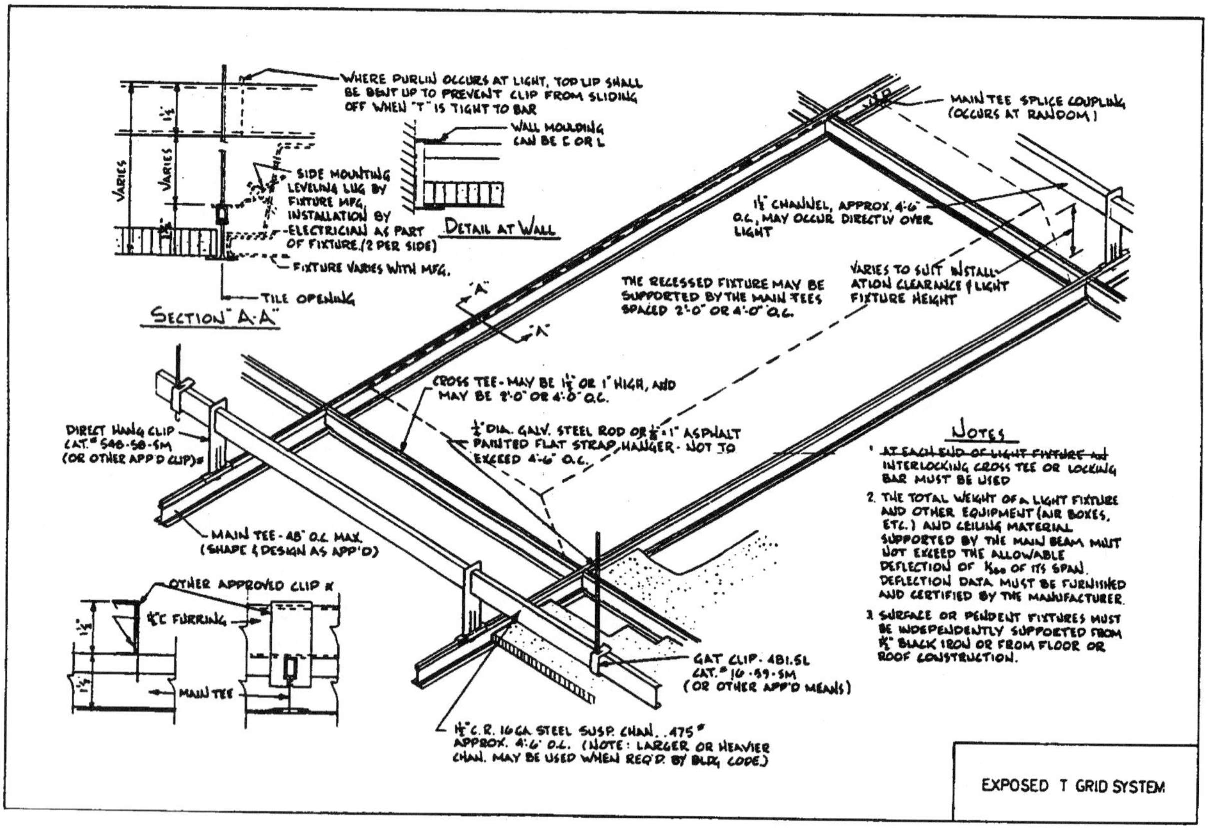

EXPOSED T GRID SYSTEM

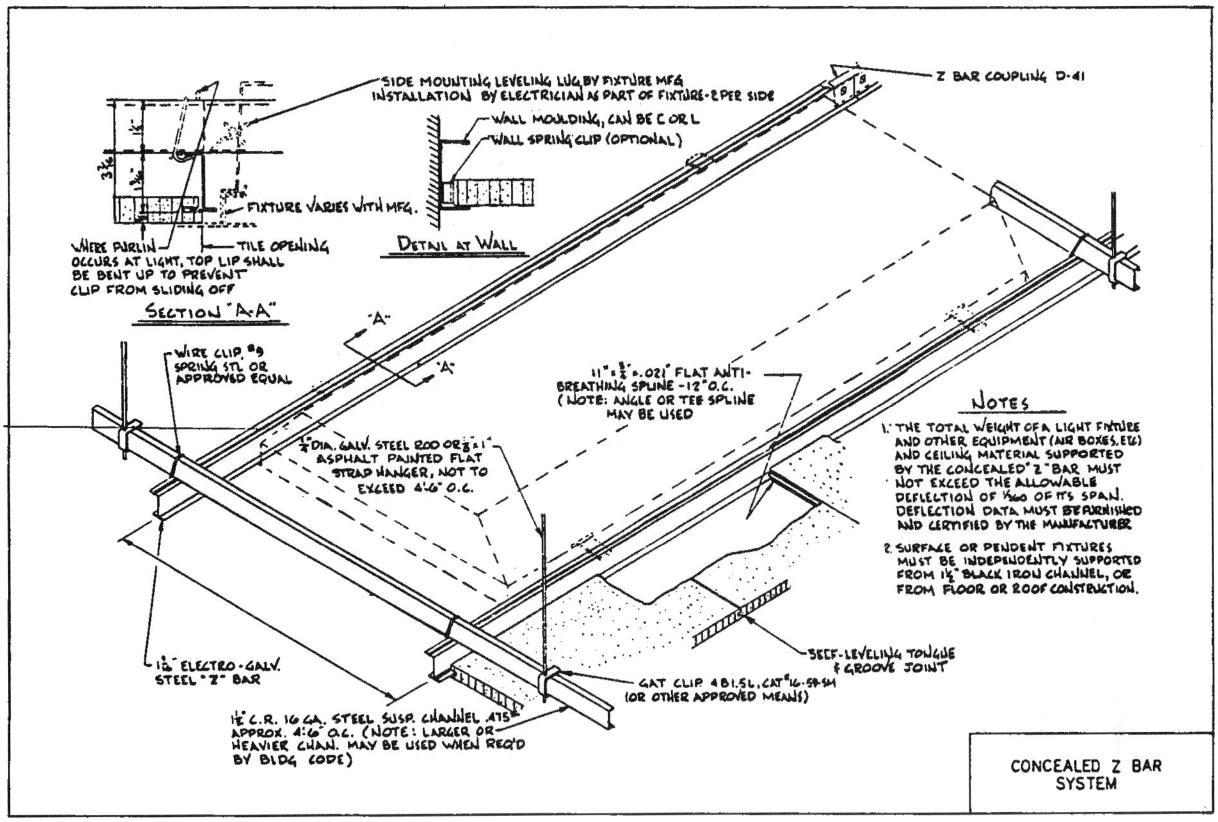
SIDE MOUNTING LEVELING LUG BY FIXTURE MFG INSTALLATION BY ELECTRICIAN AS PART OF FIXTURE - 2 PER SIDE
Z BAR COUPLING D-41
WALL MOULDING, CAN BE C OR L
WALL SPRING CLIP (OPTIONAL)
FIXTURE VARIES WITH MFG.
WHERE PURLIN OCCURS AT LIGHT, TOP LIP SHALL BE BENT UP TO PREVENT CLIP FROM SLIDING OFF
TILE OPENING
DETAIL AT WALL
SECTION "A-A"
"A"
WIRE CLIP, #9 SPRING STL OR APPROVED EQUAL
11" × 3/8" × .021" FLAT ANTI-BREATHING SPLINE - 12" O.C. (NOTE: ANGLE OR TEE SPLINE MAY BE USED
1/4" DIA. GALV. STEEL ROD OR 1/8" × 1" ASPHALT PAINTED FLAT STRAP HANGER, NOT TO EXCEED 4'-6" O.C.
NOTES
1. THE TOTAL WEIGHT OF A LIGHT FIXTURE AND OTHER EQUIPMENT (AIR BOXES, ETC) AND CEILING MATERIAL SUPPORTED BY THE CONCEALED "Z" BAR MUST NOT EXCEED THE ALLOWABLE DEFLECTION OF 1/360 OF ITS SPAN. DEFLECTION DATA MUST BE FURNISHED AND CERTIFIED BY THE MANUFACTURER
2. SURFACE OR PENDENT FIXTURES MUST BE INDEPENDENTLY SUPPORTED FROM 1 1/2" BLACK IRON CHANNEL, OR FROM FLOOR OR ROOF CONSTRUCTION.
SELF-LEVELING TONGUE & GROOVE JOINT
1 1/2" ELECTRO-GALV. STEEL "Z" BAR
GAT CLIP 4B1.5L, CAT#16-59-SM (OR OTHER APPROVED MEANS)
1 1/2" C.R. 16 GA. STEEL SUSP. CHANNEL .475# APPROX. 4'-6" O.C. (NOTE: LARGER OR HEAVIER CHAN. MAY BE USED WHEN REQ'D BY BLDG CODE)

CONCEALED Z BAR SYSTEM

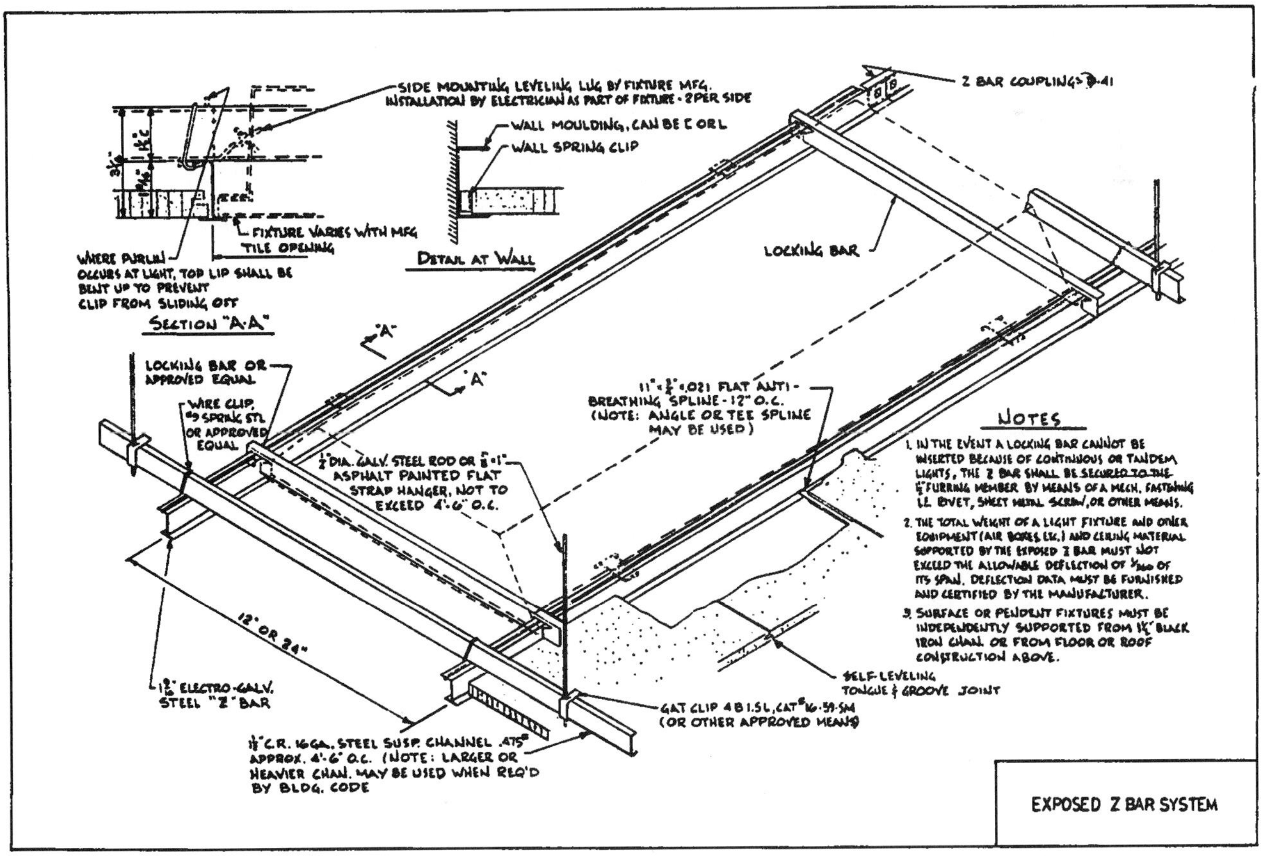
SIDE MOUNTING LEVELING LUG BY FIXTURE MFG. INSTALLATION BY ELECTRICIAN AS PART OF FIXTURE - 2 PER SIDE
Z BAR COUPLINGS D-41
WALL MOULDING, CAN BE C OR L
WALL SPRING CLIP
FIXTURE VARIES WITH MFG
TILE OPENING
WHERE PURLIN OCCURS AT LIGHT, TOP LIP SHALL BE BENT UP TO PREVENT CLIP FROM SLIDING OFF
DETAIL AT WALL
SECTION "A-A"
LOCKING BAR
"A"
LOCKING BAR OR APPROVED EQUAL
WIRE CLIP, #9 SPRING STL OR APPROVED EQUAL
11" × 3/8" × .021 FLAT ANTI-BREATHING SPLINE - 12" O.C. (NOTE: ANGLE OR TEE SPLINE MAY BE USED)
1/4" DIA. GALV. STEEL ROD OR 1/8" × 1" ASPHALT PAINTED FLAT STRAP HANGER, NOT TO EXCEED 4'-6" O.C.
NOTES
1. IN THE EVENT A LOCKING BAR CANNOT BE INSERTED BECAUSE OF CONTINUOUS OR TANDEM LIGHTS, THE Z BAR SHALL BE SECURED TO THE 3/4" FURRING MEMBER BY MEANS OF A MECH. FASTENING I.E. RIVET, SHEET METAL SCREW, OR OTHER MEANS.
2. THE TOTAL WEIGHT OF A LIGHT FIXTURE AND OTHER EQUIPMENT (AIR BOXES ETC.) AND CEILING MATERIAL SUPPORTED BY THE EXPOSED Z BAR MUST NOT EXCEED THE ALLOWABLE DEFLECTION OF 1/360 OF ITS SPAN. DEFLECTION DATA MUST BE FURNISHED AND CERTIFIED BY THE MANUFACTURER.
3. SURFACE OR PENDENT FIXTURES MUST BE INDEPENDENTLY SUPPORTED FROM 1 1/2" BLACK IRON CHAN. OR FROM FLOOR OR ROOF CONSTRUCTION ABOVE.
12" OR 24"
SELF-LEVELING TONGUE & GROOVE JOINT
1 1/2" ELECTRO-GALV. STEEL "Z" BAR
GAT CLIP 4B1.5L, CAT#16-59-SM (OR OTHER APPROVED MEANS)
1 1/2" C.R. 16GA. STEEL SUSP. CHANNEL .475# APPROX. 4'-6" O.C. (NOTE: LARGER OR HEAVIER CHAN. MAY BE USED WHEN REQ'D BY BLDG. CODE

EXPOSED Z BAR SYSTEM

CEILINGS
Flat Drywall

Flat Drywall Ceiling Notes

- Main tee and cross tee spacing is provided in the table on page 17
- See pages 18-19 for special requirements for fire rated assemblies.

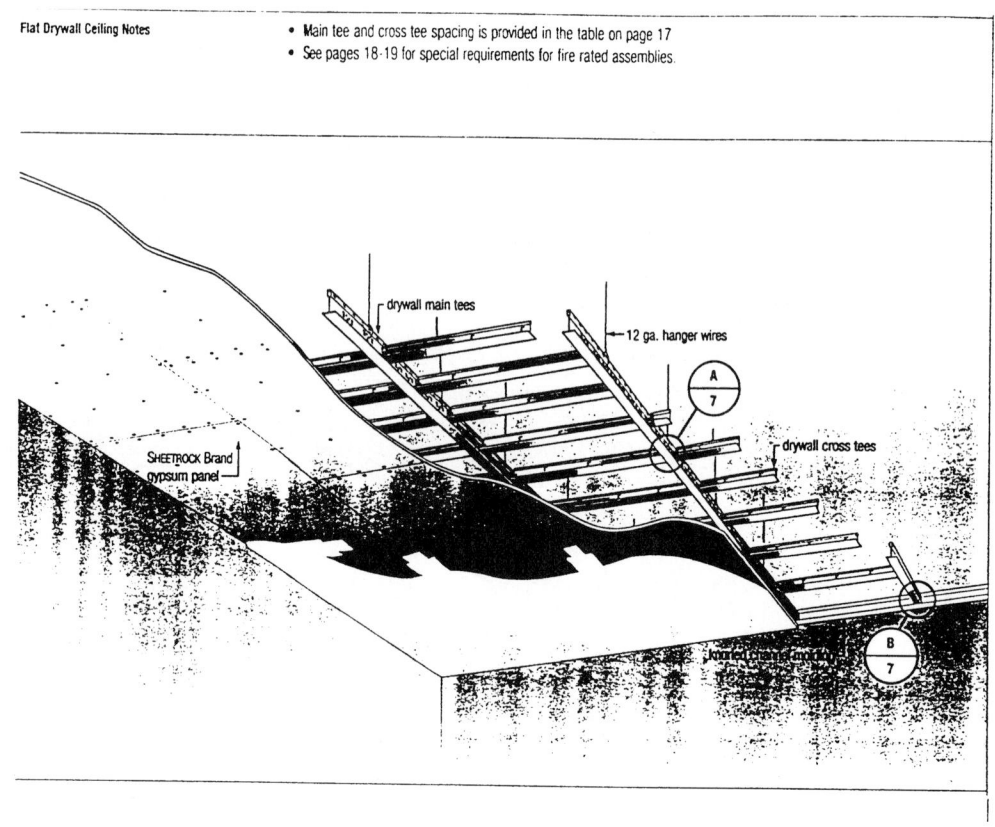

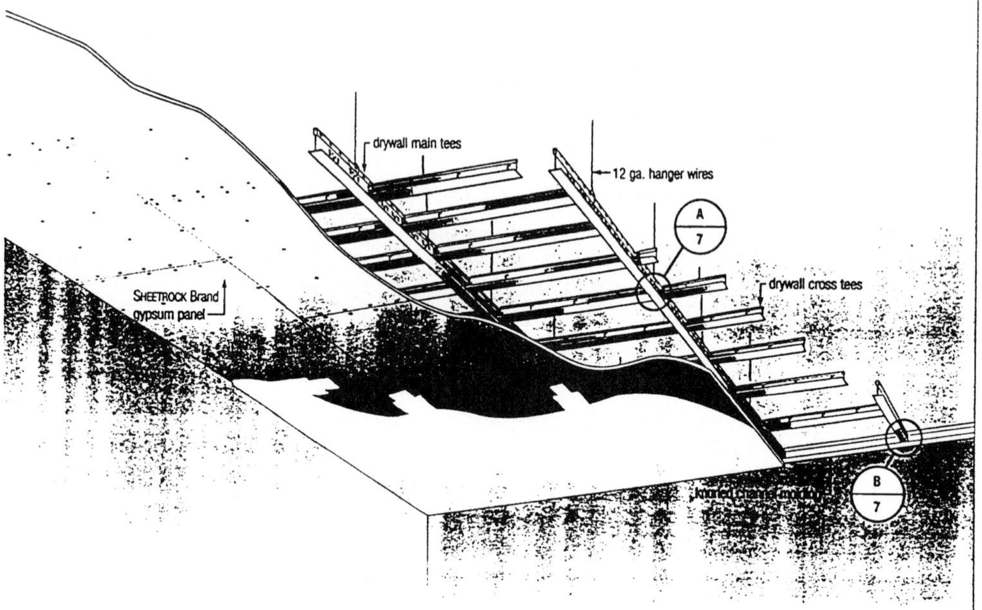

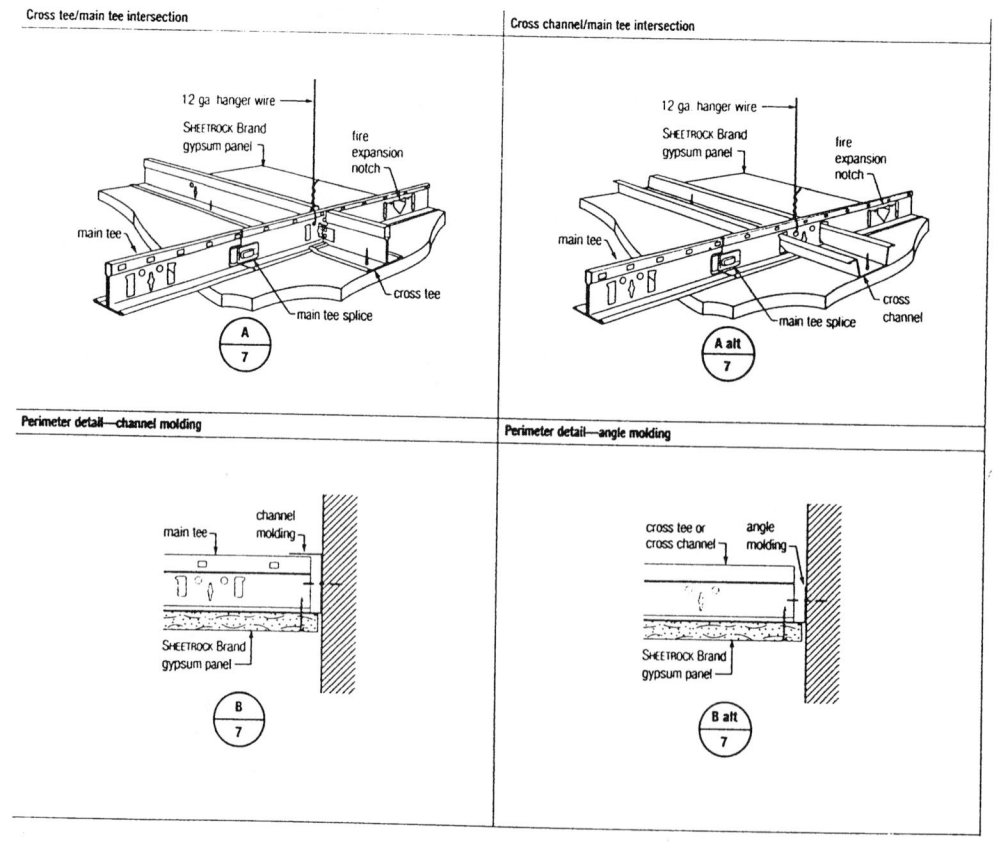

Cross tee/main tee intersection

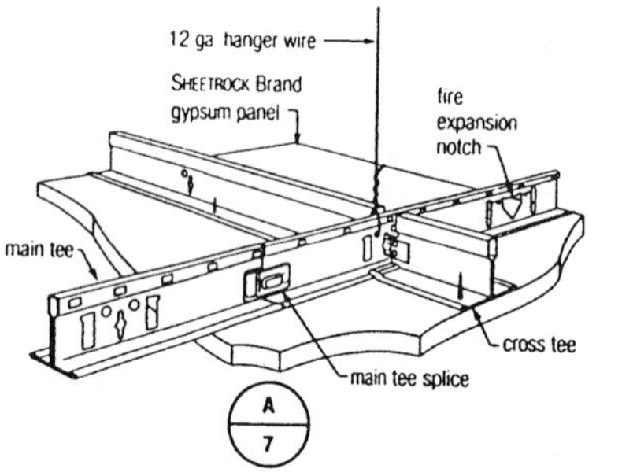

Cross channel/main tee intersection

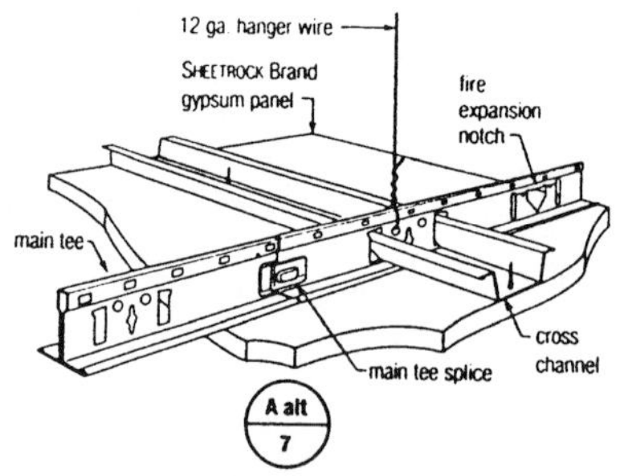

Perimeter detail—channel molding

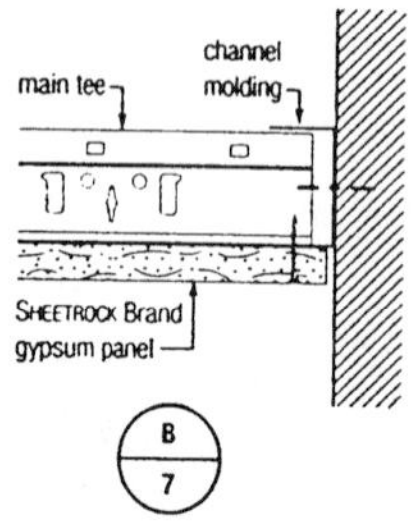

Perimeter detail—angle molding

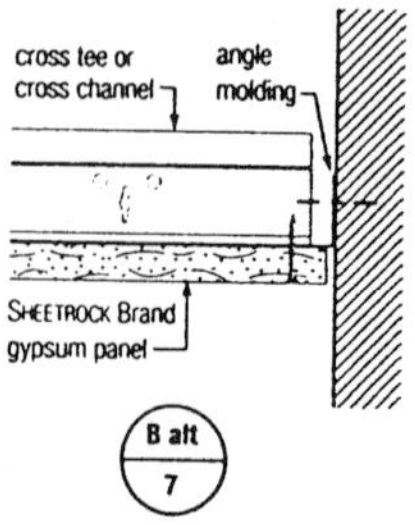

CEILINGS
Drywall to Acoustical

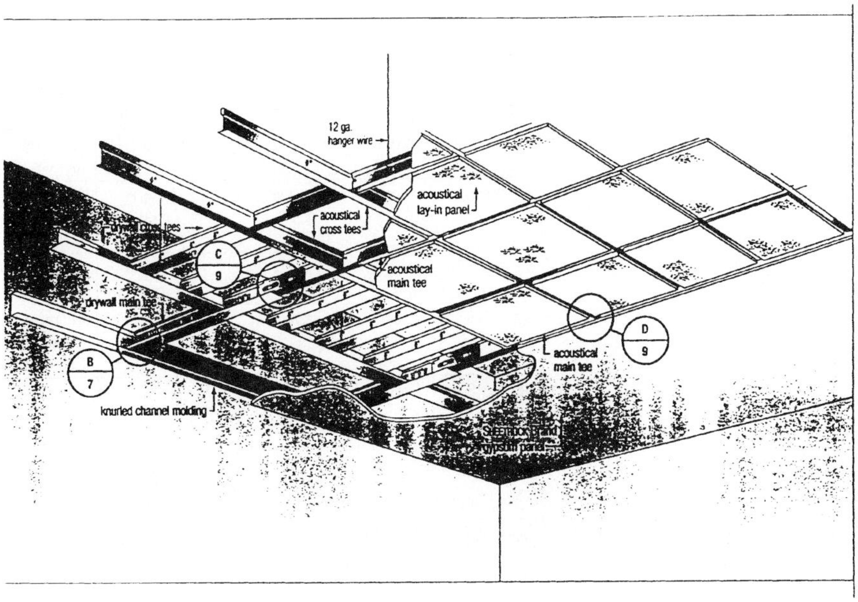

Plan view

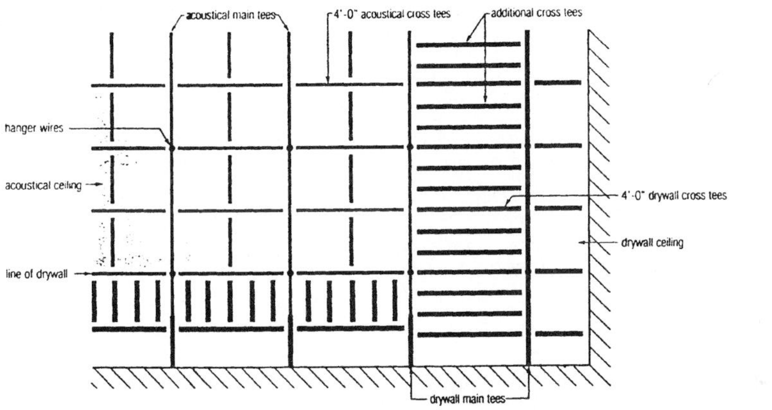

Drywall to acoustical transition—field cut connection

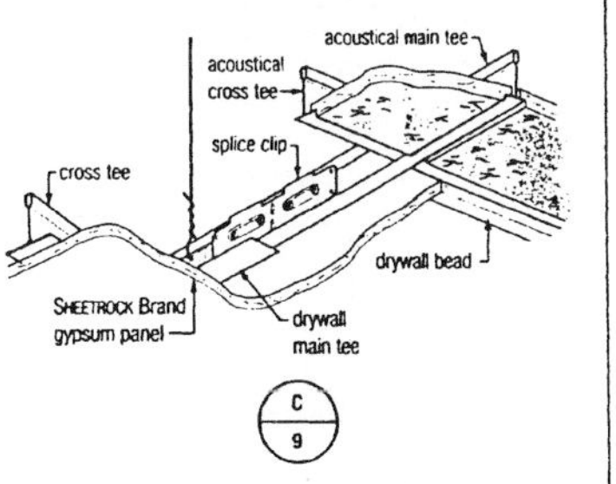

Drywall to acoustical transition

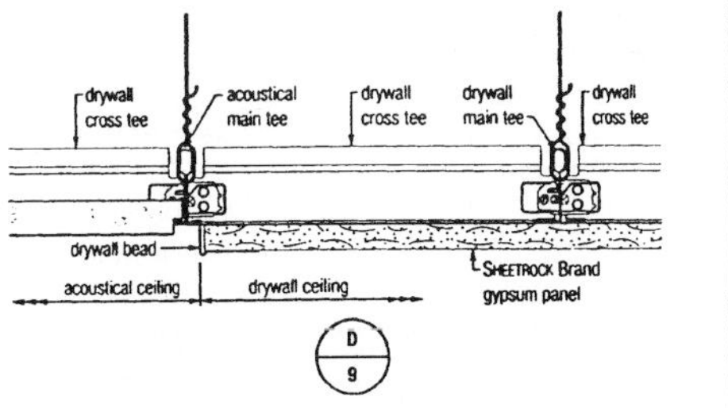

Drywall to acoustical transition—factory end connection

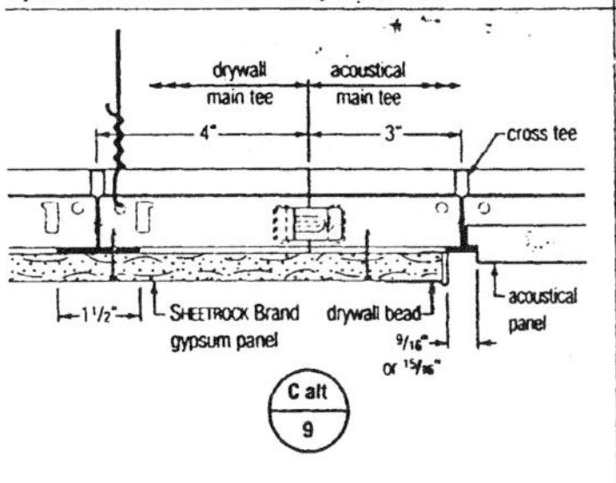

Flush transition

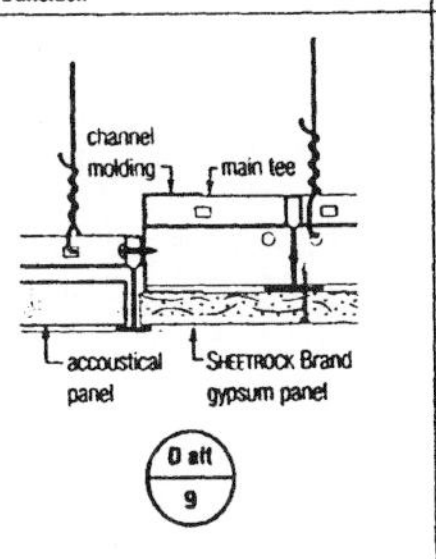

Standard offset

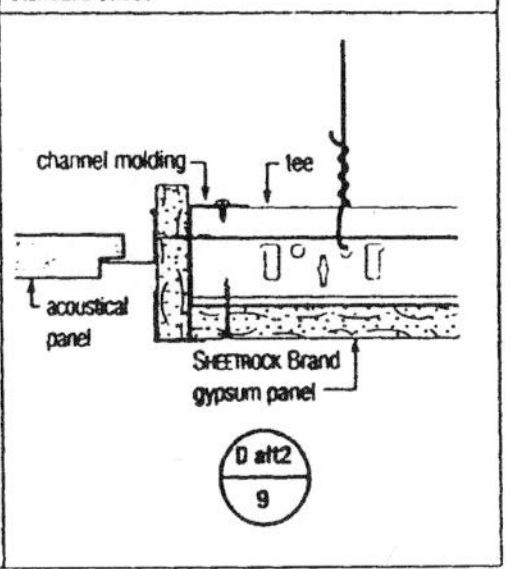

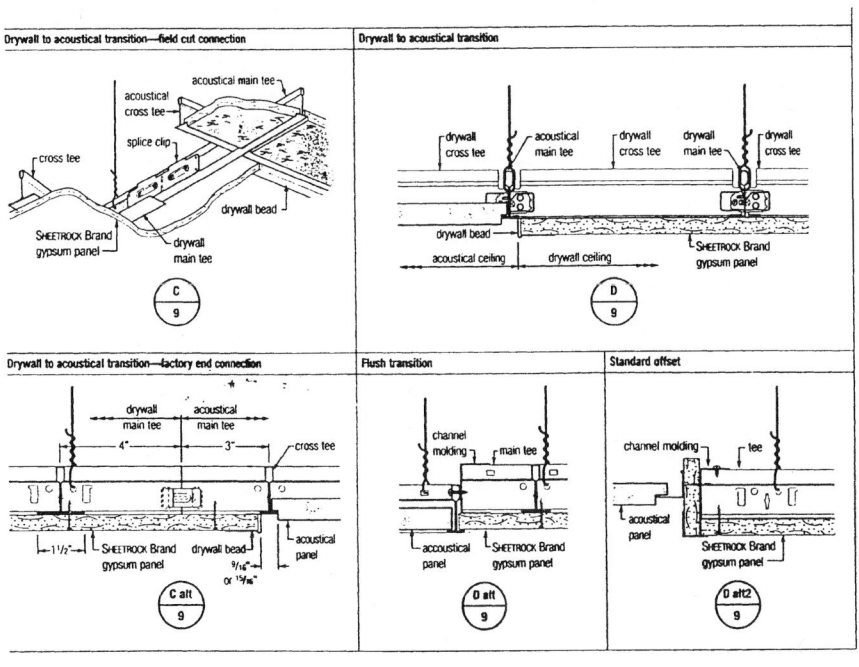

CEILINGS

Fire-Rated Assemblies

Roof/Ceiling Designs

	U.L. Design No.	Assembly Rating*	Board Thick.	Wallboard Core Type	Fixture Size (% of Fixtures)	Max. Duct Area per 100 sf	Assembly Constructions
Double Ceiling Roof Assemblies	P237	2 HR-U	1/2"	SHEETROCK Brand FIRECODE C	1x4 or 2x4 (24%)	576 sq. in.	Roof system on steel roof deck, min. fiber 8H3 or 10k1 min @ 72" o.c. max
	P239	1-1/2 HR-U	1/2"	SHEETROCK Brand FIRECODE C	1x4 or 2x4 (24%)	576 sq. in.	Roof covering on gypsum concrete over USG form board, subpurlins and 12J3 Joists w/ w6x16 beam.
	P241	2 HR-U	1/2"	SHEETROCK Brand FIRECODE C	1x4 or 2x4 (24%)	576 sq. in.	Roof covering over over insulating concrete on steel roof deck and 10J3 min joists @ 48" o.c.
Mineral and Fiber Board on Building Units or Precast Concrete	P501	1 and 2 HR-U	5/8"	SHEETROCK Brand FIRECODE C	N/A	N/A	Roof covering over mineral and fiber board on building or precast concrete units, 14J5 joists @ 48" o.c. max.
Gypsum Plank, Insulation Board	P506	1-1/2 HR-U	5/8"	SHEETROCK Brand FIRECODE C	2x4 (24%)	57 sq in	Roof covering over min & fiber bds. on gypsum planks, subpurlinsand 12 H5 joists @48" o.c. max.
	P508	1 HR-U	5/8"	SHEETROCK Brand FIRECODE C	2x4 (24%)	144 sq in	Roof covering over min & fiber bds (see alt) gyp wallbd., steel roof deck, 10J4 joists (min) @48" o.c.
Insulating Concrete	P507	1-1/2 HR-R 1 HR-U	5/8"	SHEETROCK Brand FIRECODE C	2x4 (24%)	57 sq in	Roof covering on foamed plastic insulation, Gypsum conc and form bds. on subpurlins and 10J4 Joists(min) @ 4'o.c.
	P509	1 HR-U	5/8"	SHEETROCK Brand FIRECODE C	2x4 (24%)	144 sq in	Roof covering on foamed plastic insulation, Gypsum conc. and form bds. on subpurlins and 10J4 Joists (min) @ 4'o.c.
Corrugated Steel Deck w/Insluated Board or Foam Plastic Insulation	P510	1 & 1-1/2 HR-U	1/2" & 5/8"	SHEETROCK Brand FIRECODE C	2x4 (24%)	57 sq in	Roof covering over insulation (see alt) on gypsum wallboard steel roof deck, 10J4 Joists (min) @ 72" o.c. max.
	P513	1-1/2 HR-U	5/8"	SHEETROCK Brand FIRECODE C	2x4 (24%)	144 sq in	Roof covering on insulating concrete and foamedplastic over corrugated steel deck, 10J4 steel joists @ 48" o.c.
	P514	2 HR-U	5/8"	SHEETROCK Brand FIRECODE C	2x4 (24%)	255 sq in	Roof covering over insulation (see ALT),gyp. wallboard and steel deck, 8H3 steel joists @ 48" o.c.
	P516	1 HR-R & U 1 HR-UB	5/8" (2 layers)	FIRECODE Core	NA	NA	Metal roof deck panels on Min. 8" deep C-or-Z-shaped purlins @ 60" max, glass fiber insulation between roof deck panels and steel roof purlins, W-shaped beam

Fire-Rated Butt Joint Cross Tee Spacing

Fire Rated ceilings require extra cross tees spaced 8" or less on either side of the butt joint.
Fire Rated assemblies require a hanger wire installed adjacent to fire relief notch.

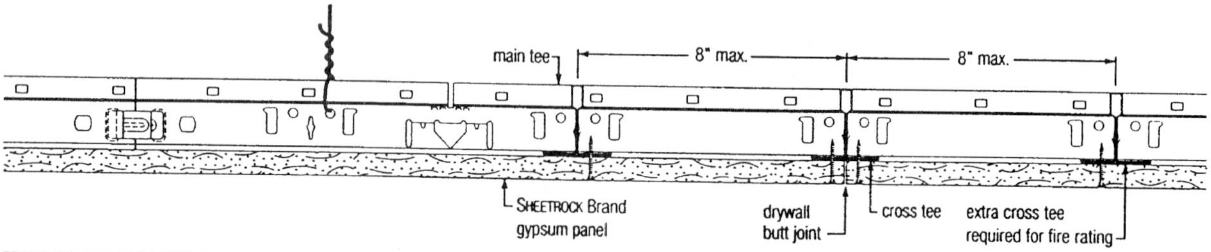

Fire-Rated Butt Joint Cross Channel Spacing

Fire Rated ceilings require extra cross channels spaced 8" or less on either side of the butt joint.
Fire Rated assemblies require a hanger wire installed adjacent to fire relief notch.

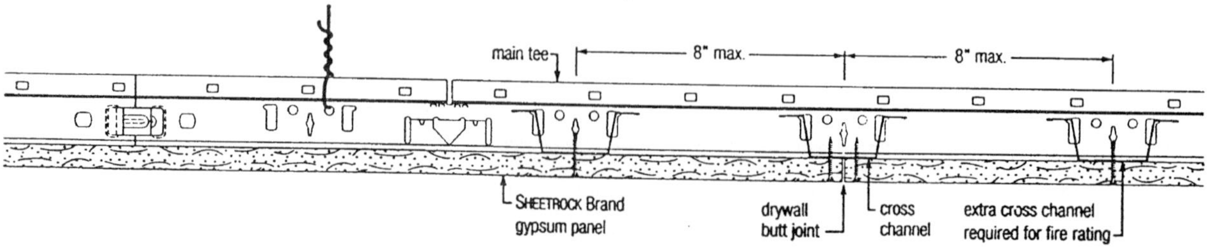

ASSEMBLY | **REMARKS**

GYPSUM BOARD, ATTACHED

DIRECT TO FRAMING

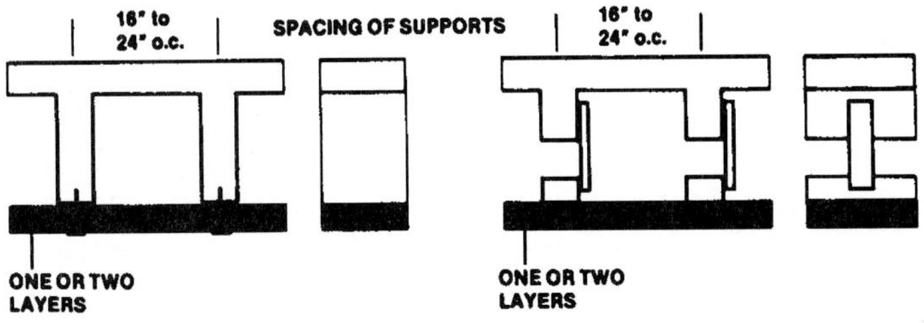

- secured directly to framing members or to solid furring.
- most widely used in residential and light commercial construction.
- two layers may be required for an improved fire resistance rating or for better resistance to sound transmission.
- directly affected by deflection and/or expansion/contraction in supporting framing.

FURRED-DOWN

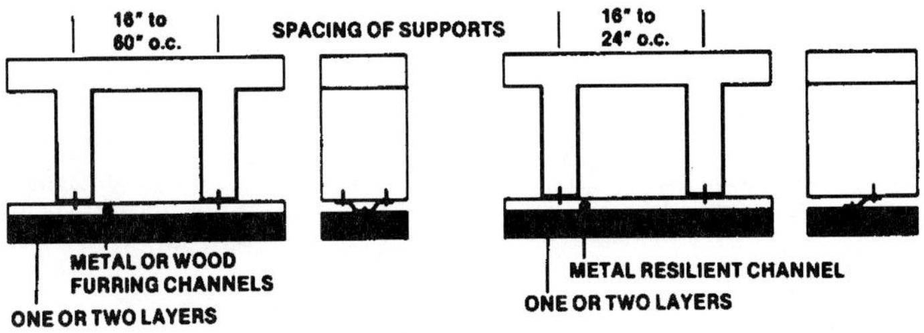

- hat-shaped or resilient channels may be used.
- furring will minimize effects of deflection and expansion/contraction in framing upon membrane.
- resilient channels also used to improve resistance to sound transmission.
- furring will also minimize effects of streaking due to temperature differential which may occur with direct attachment.

GYPSUM BOARD, SUSPENDED

PRIMARY SUPPORTS ONLY

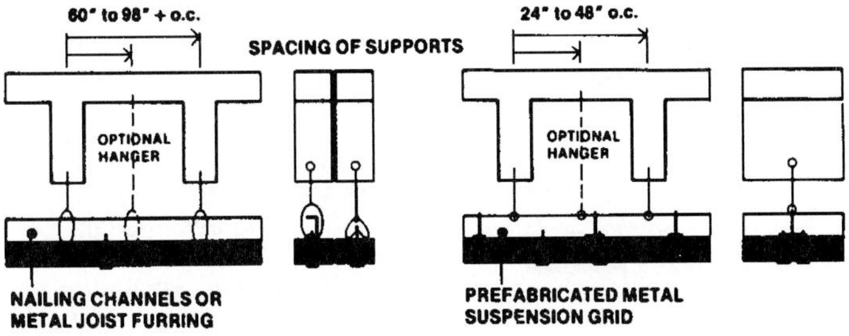

- when framing is spaced more than 24 inches on centers, or when a plenum space for mechanical/electrical service lines is required, a suspension/support system consisting of wood or metal sections or special nailing channels is generally provided.
- prefabricated metal suspension systems are available.

PRIMARY AND SECONDARY SUPPORTS

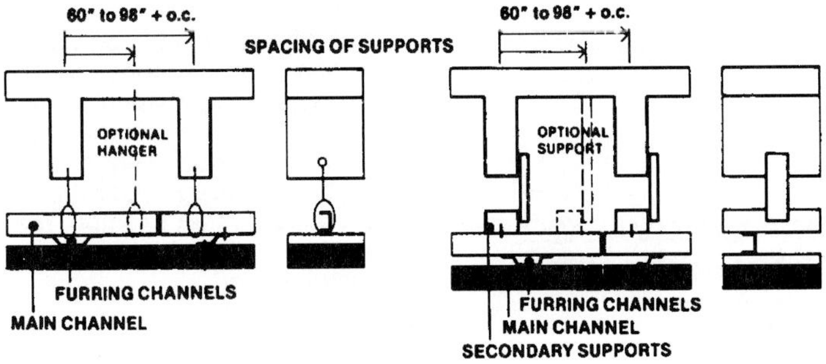

- primary suspension system may also include a secondary system of furring channels used to align the primary system and/or to provide resilient mounting of the membrane.
- it is a high cost assembly and not widely used.
- resilient furring channels generally used with wood framing.

CEILINGS
Plaster Suspended Ceilings

ASSEMBLY | **REMARKS**

PLASTER, ATTACHED

DIRECT TO FRAMING

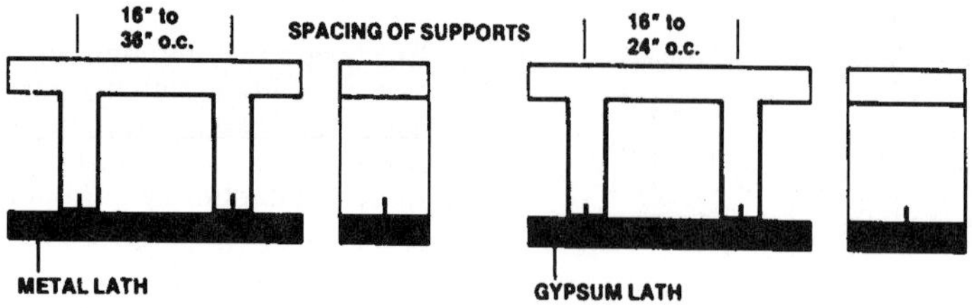

- metal or gypsum lath secured directly to framing.
- membrane will be directly affected by deflection and/or expansion/contraction in supporting framing.
- metal lath may be backed for machine application of plaster.
- fire resistance ratings for different assemblies have been established.

FURRED-DOWN

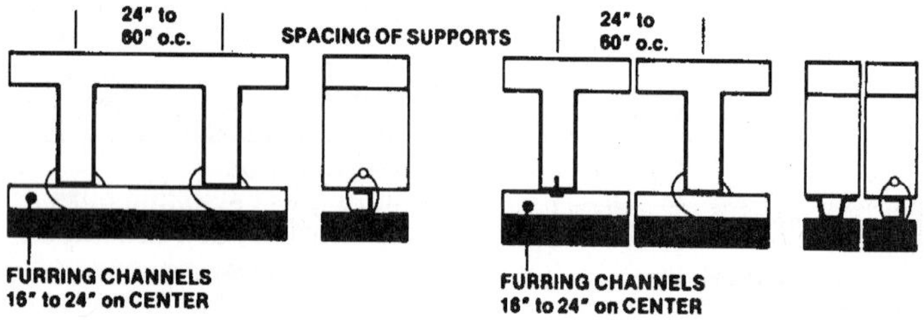

- furring channels secured to framing, lath supported by furring.
- furring will minimize effects of deflection and expansion/contraction upon membrane.
- large areas of membrane should have expansion joints and should not be restrained at the perimeter.
- corners of openings in gypsum lath membranes should have metal lath reinforcing.

PLASTER, SUSPENDED

PRIMARY SUPPORTS ONLY

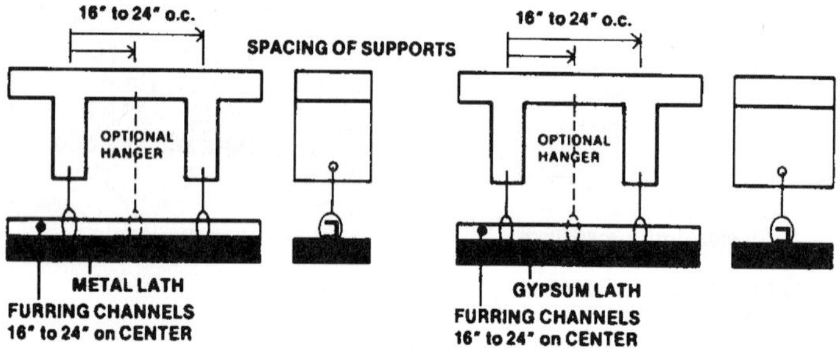

- suspended membrane with furring channels only is similar to furred membrane except that furring channels are suspended from, rather than directly attached to, framing members.
- suspension of membrane may be a requirement in some fire resistance rated floor or roof/ceiling assemblies.
- spacing of hangers is quite close and limits the size and/or extent of mechanical/electrical service lines in plenum space.

PRIMARY AND SECONDARY SUPPORTS

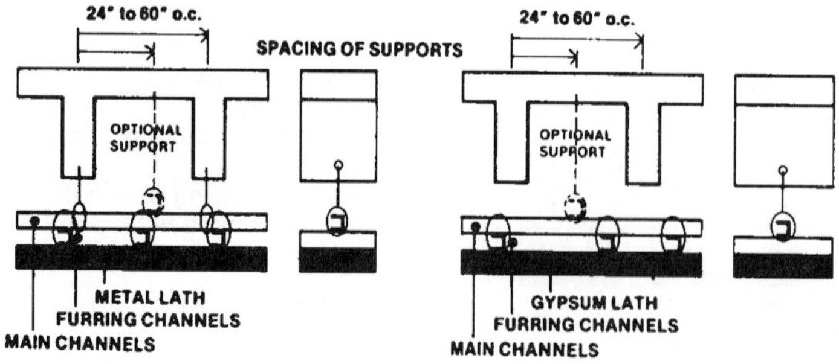

- when spacing of framing is wide and/or the number of hangers must be reduced, a primary support system consisting of main carrying channels may be used; the furring channels are then a secondary system, secured to such primary supports.
- for wide hanger spacing, metal joists instead of carrying channels may be used.

ASSEMBLY | **REMARKS**

EXPOSED GRID: FLAT UNITS

SQUARE EDGE

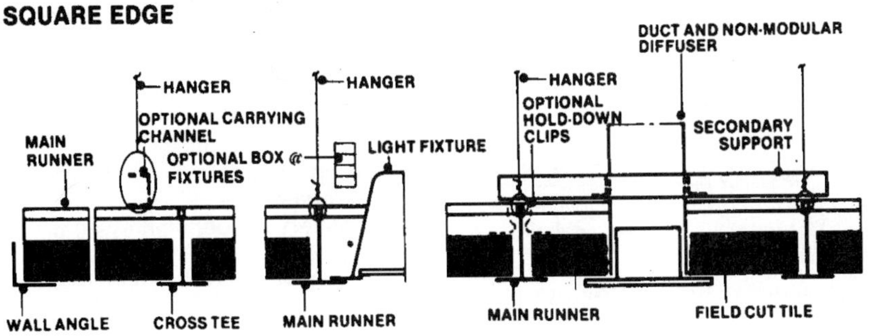

Remarks:

- lay-in panels should be secured in place by clips when assembly requires a fire resistance rating; also against uplift due to pressure differential.
- fixtures generally have to be boxed-in for fire resistance rating; fire dampers must be provided at all openings, such as diffusers.
- hangers secured to framing members, structural deck, or to secondary framing system.

RECESSED EDGE

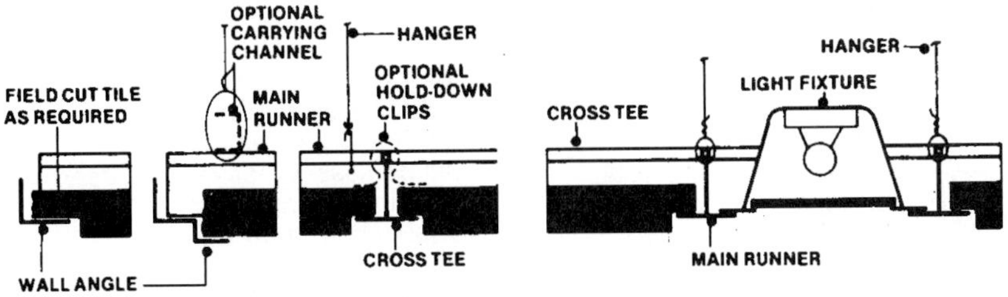

Remarks:

- clearance required for all lay-in panels for tilting them into place.
- suspension system used is the same as for square edge tile, but tile only available in 2x2 foot size.
- may be used in fire resistance-rated floor or roof/ceiling assemblies; clips to secure tiles in place and opening protection generally required.

EXPOSED GRID, SHAPED UNITS

INLAY PANELS, CORRUGATED, RIBBED

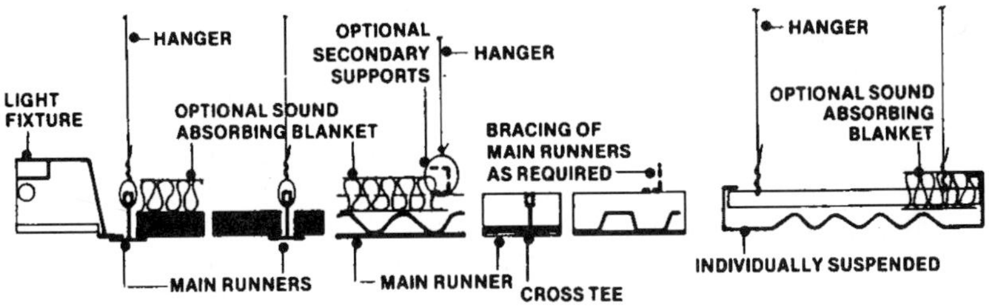

Remarks:

- metal panels generally perforated, with sound absorbing blankets.
- plastic panels generally solid; used in luminous ceiling installations.
- corrugated/ribbed metal or plastic panels generally used with main runners only.
- flat plastic panels generally either 2x4 or 2x2 feet in size, used with main runners and cross tees.

PRE-ASSEMBLED MODULES

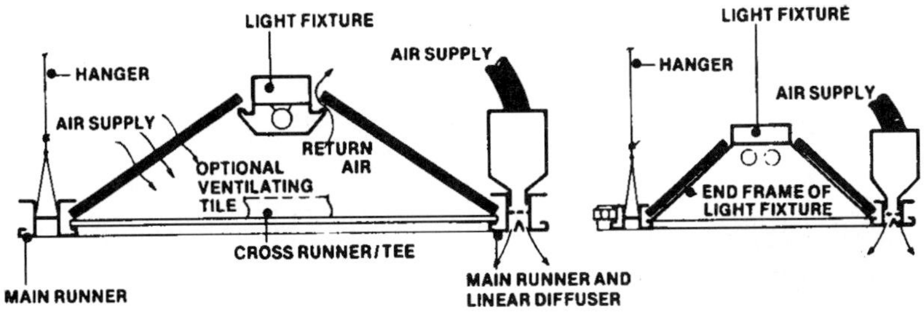

Remarks:

- flat pre-assembled modules are also available.
- when pressurized plenum and ventilating tile are used, air return must be ducted through plenum.
- with ventilating plenum, dirt streaking may result unless the membrane is made completely air tight.
- may be used in fire resistance-rated floor or roof/ceiling assemblies.

CEILINGS
Concealed Spline Suspended Ceilings

ASSEMBLY | **REMARKS**

CONCEALED GRID, SHAPED UNITS

METAL PAN TILE

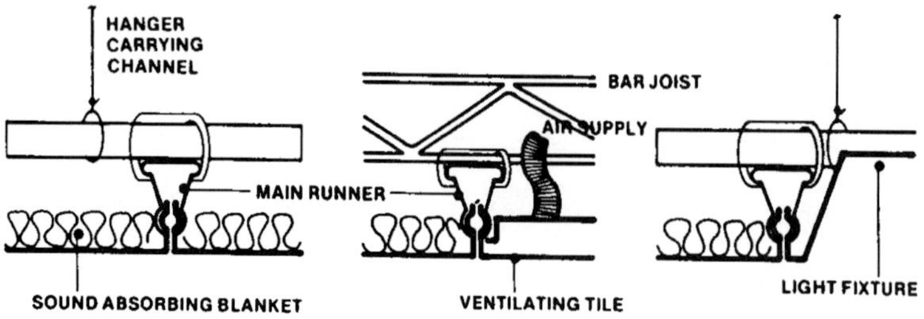

- tile may be repeatedly repainted without loss in sound absorbing characteristics.
- heating/cooling piping may be incorporated into the system.
- combination lighting/infra-red heating fixtures may be integrated into membrane.
- secondary suspension system generally required.
- tile may be used for supply/return air.

LINEAR PANELS

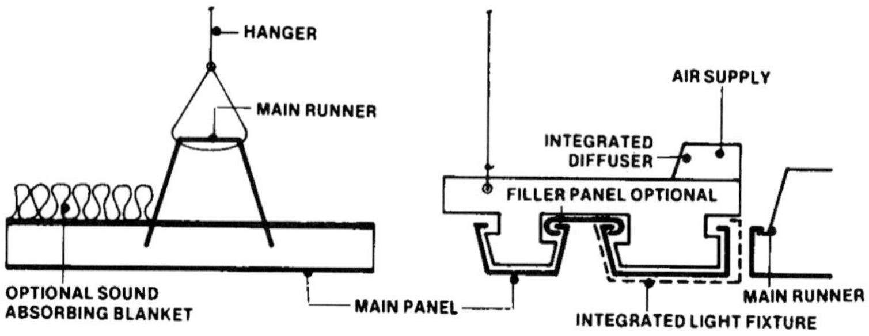

- formed prefinished metal panels in long lengths.
- air supply/return and lighting fixtures may be integrated into the system.
- may be used outdoors in protected locations, such as large soffits, canopies.
- some assemblies may be used as required components in fire resistance rated floor or roof/ceiling assemblies.
- membranes may be curved perpendicular to direction of panels.

BAFFLES

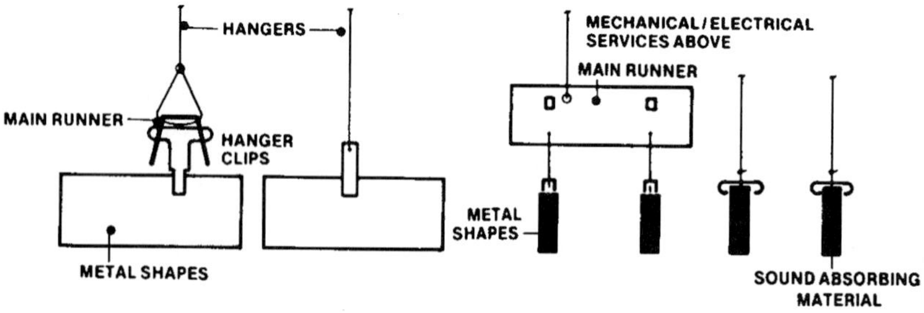

- baffles available in shaped metal, with or without sound absorbent material cores, or in faced sound absorbent material.
- various arrangements available, such as linear, radial, hexagonal.
- used to: provide additional sound absorption in selected locations; for visual interest, or to conceal mechanical/electrical services.

CONCEALED GRID, FLAT UNITS

KERFED EDGE

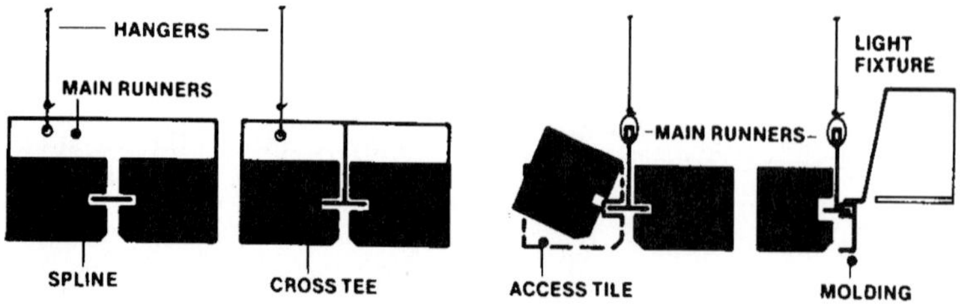

- tile, generally 12x12 inches in size with kerfed edges secured in place by main runners in one direction, and cross tees or splines in the other.
- secondary supports, such as carrying channels may be used to reduce spacing of hangers to framing system.
- may be used as component in fire resistance rated floor or roof/ceiling assemblies.
- special panels available to provide access to plenum.

CEILINGS

Acoustical Ceiling Edge Details

Special edge configurations are available for a variety of suspension systems. Consult Celotex for details.

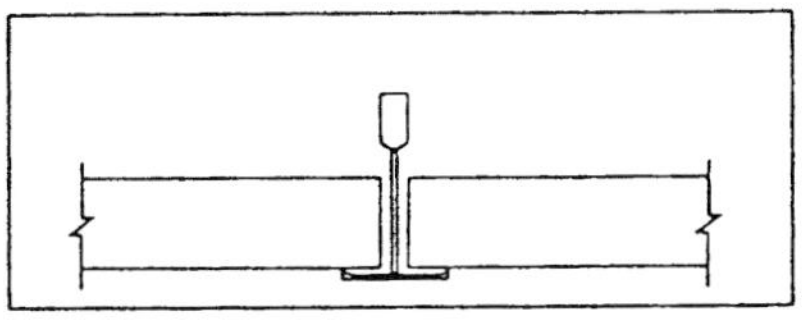

Trim Edge

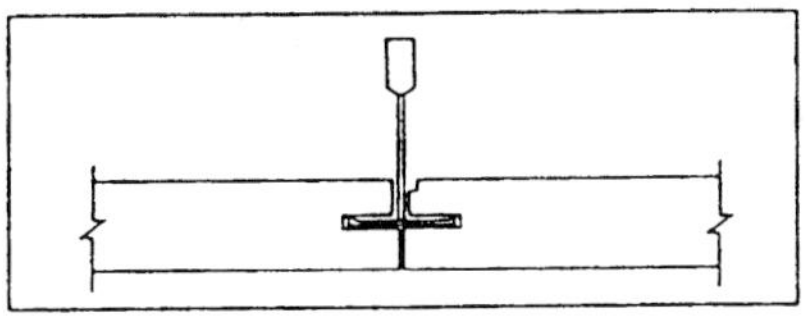

Square Edge – Kerfed and Back Cut

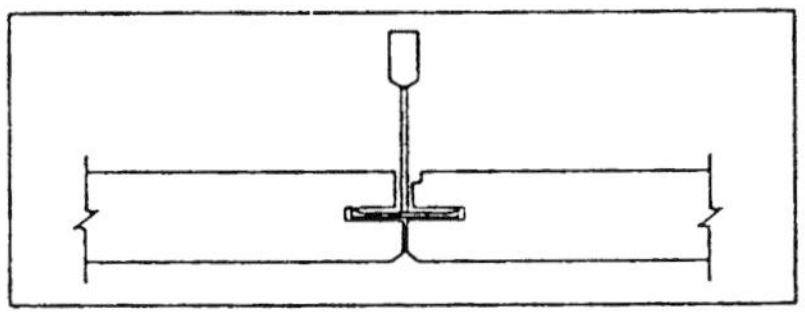

Bevel Edge – Kerfed and Back Cut

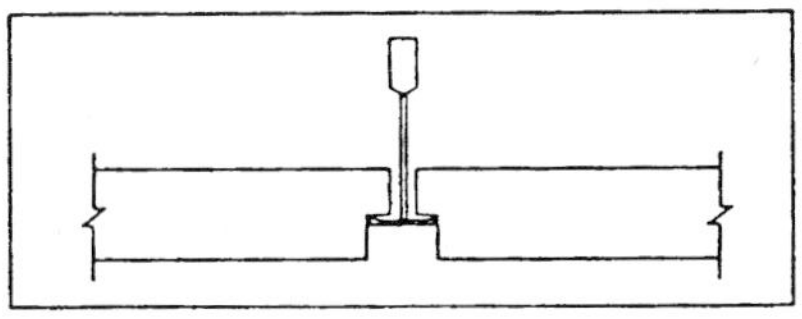

Narrow Reveal Edge – 9/16 Grid System (Tee)
Hytone/Celotone L'Anse Plant 2x2

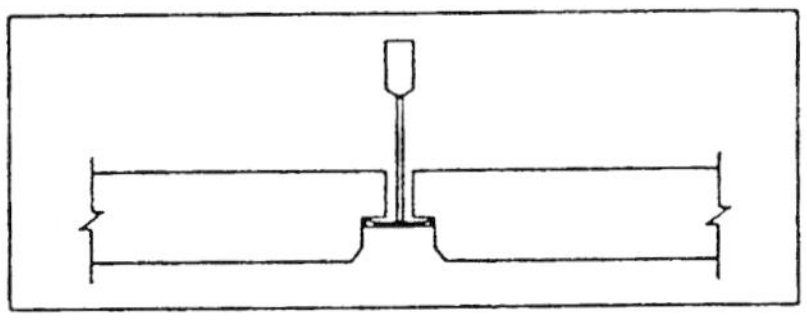

Narrow Reveal Edge – 9/16 Grid System (Tee)
Softone/Meridian Plant Hytone 2x2

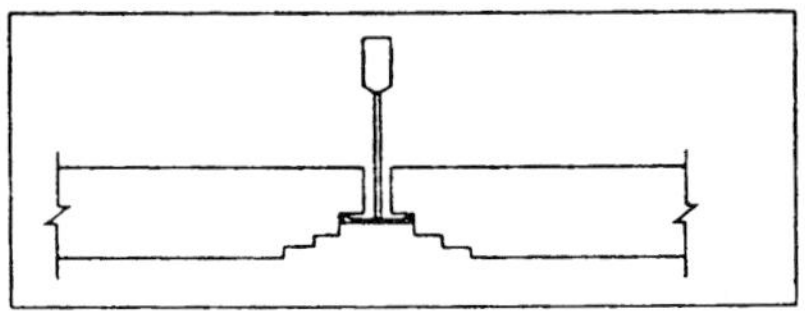

Tier Reveal Edge

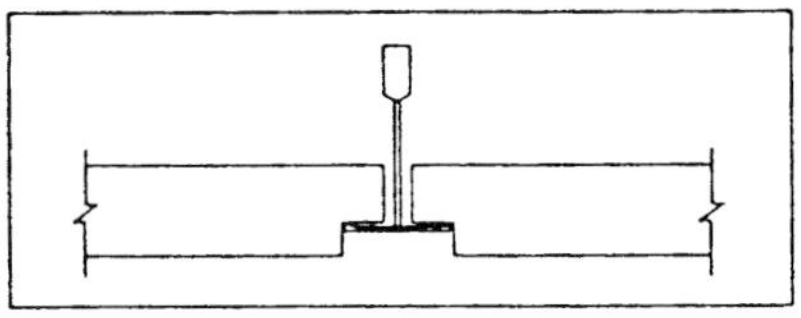

Reveal Edge – Celotone

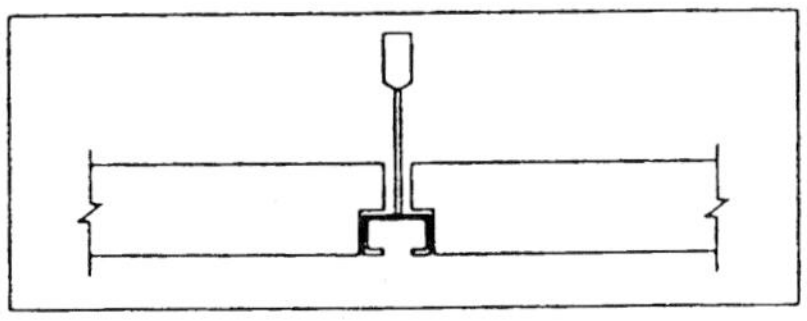

Narrow Reveal Edge – 9/16 Grid System (Screw Slot)
L'Anse Plant

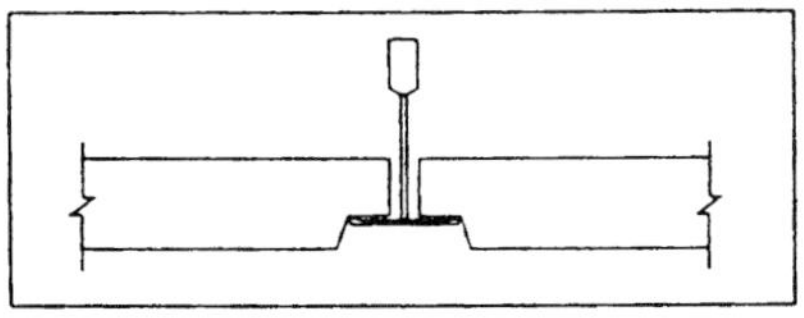

Reveal Edge

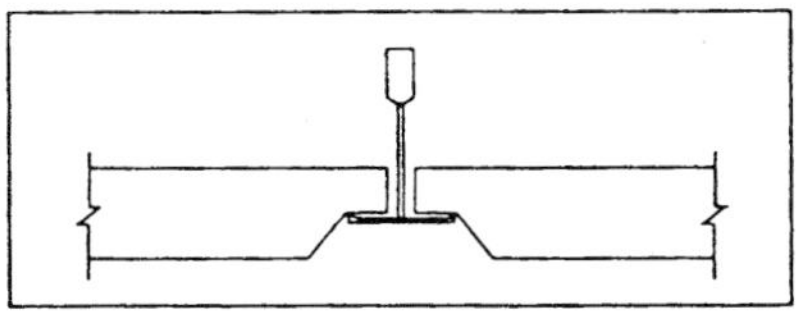

Tapered Reveal Edge

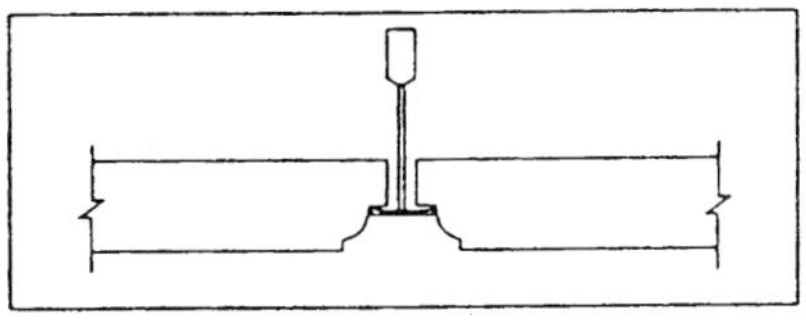

Radius Reveal Edge

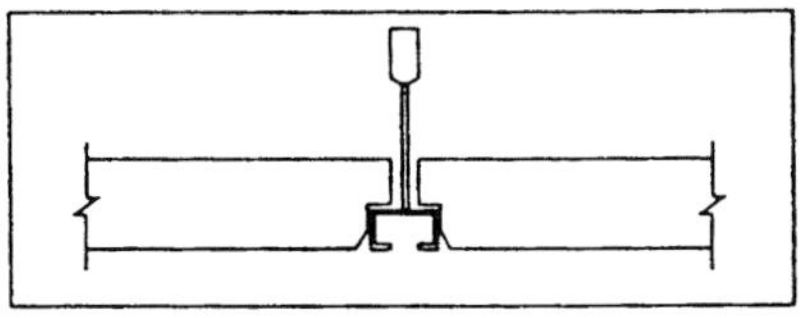

Narrow Reveal Edge – 9/16 Grid System (Screw Slot)
Cashmere at L'Anse & Meridian Plant 2x2

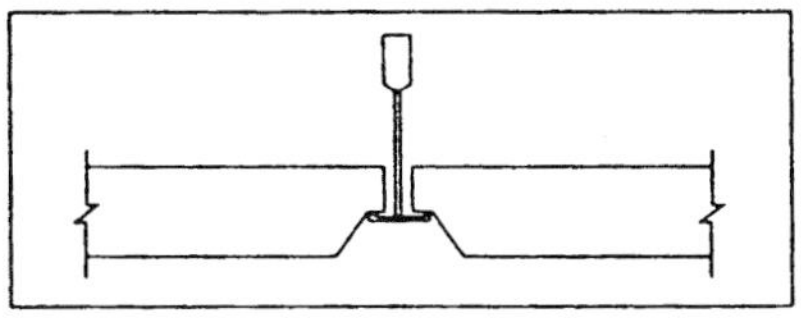

Bevel Reveal

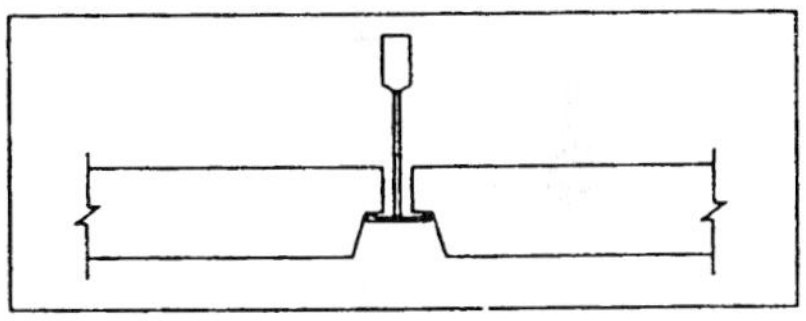

Narrow Reveal Edge 2x4 – Hytone, Softone

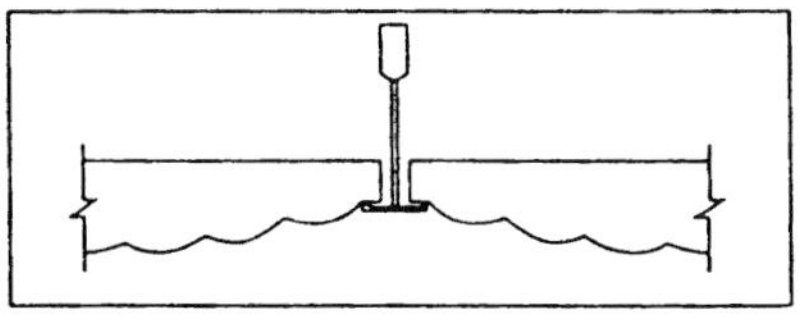

Classic Fluted Edge

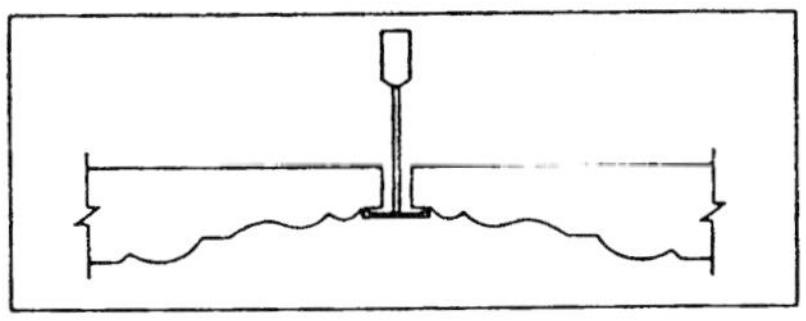

Ogee Edge

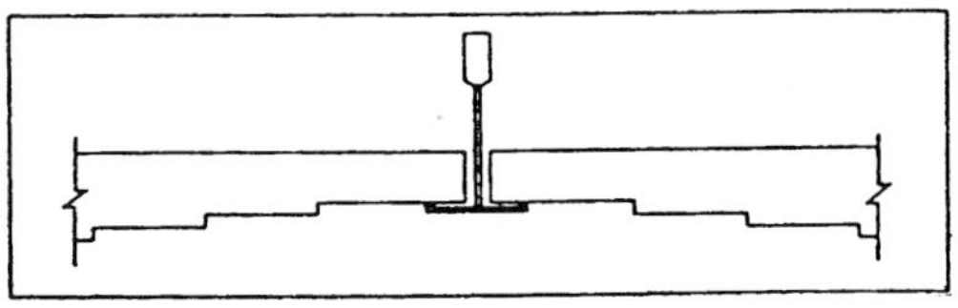

Neo Edge

CEILINGS

Suspended Ceiling Types

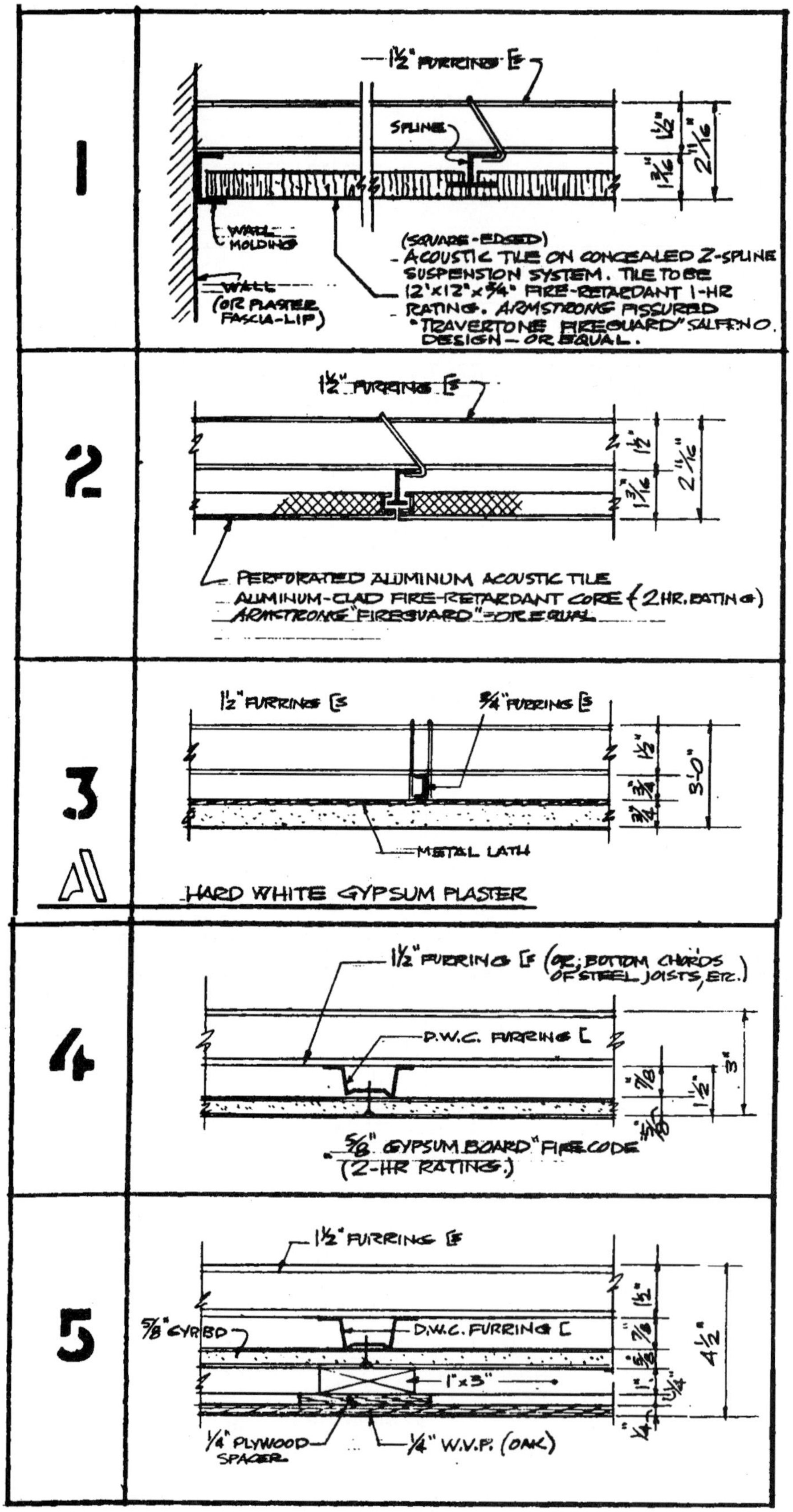

Concealed 2-spline system with acoustical tile

Concealed 2-spline system with aluminum-clad acoustical tile

Suspended plaster ceiling

Suspended ceiling with gypsum board

Suspended ceiling with plywood finish

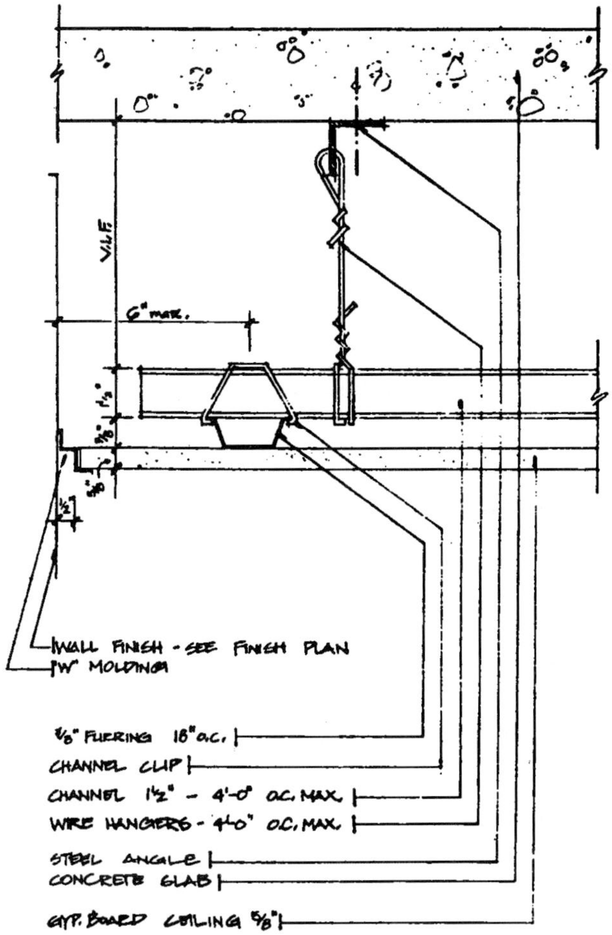

TYPICAL HUNG GYP.BOARD
CEILING DETAIL

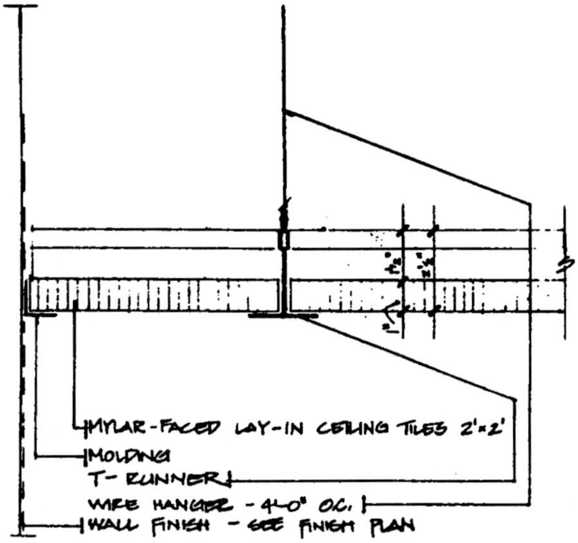

TYPICAL LAY-IN TILE
CEILING DETAIL

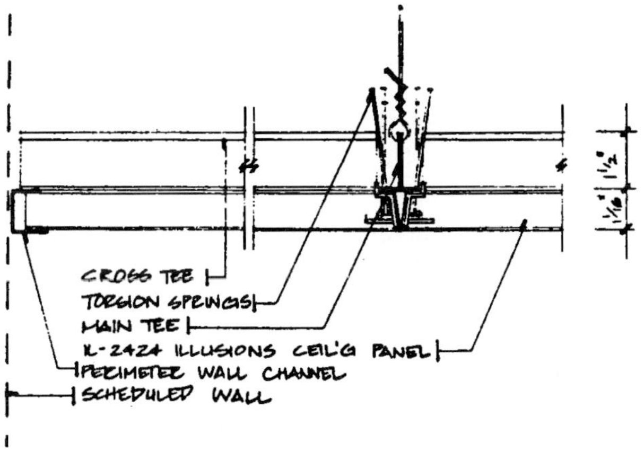

TYPICAL
CEILING DETAIL

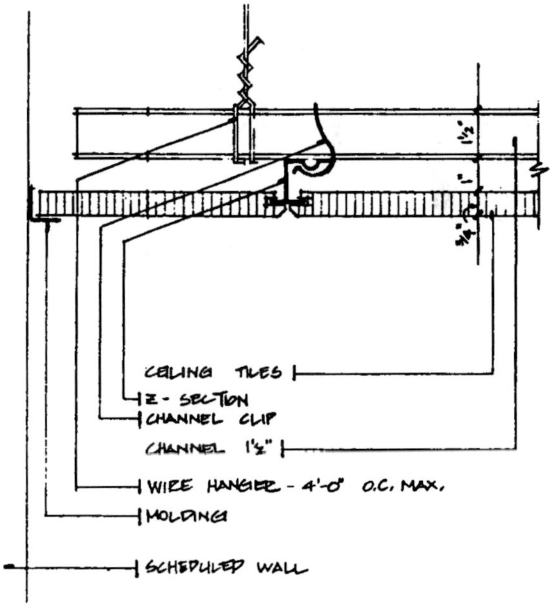

TYPICAL CONCEALED SPLINE
CEILING DETAIL

CEILINGS
Suspended Ceiling Details

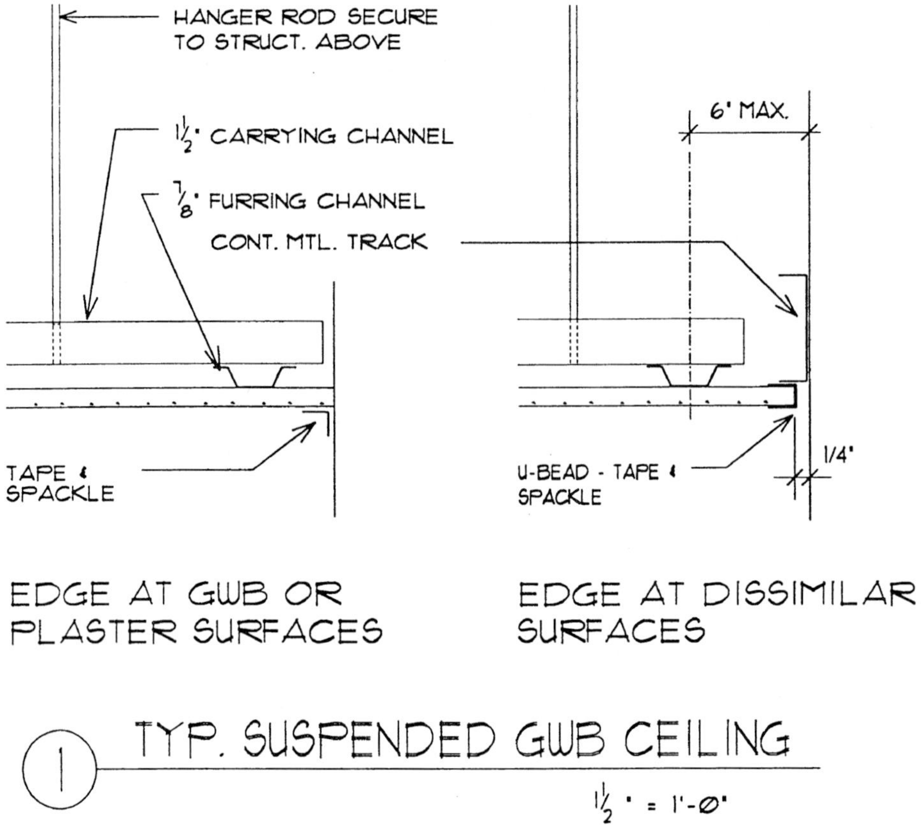
HANGER ROD SECURE TO STRUCT. ABOVE
1 1/2" CARRYING CHANNEL
7/8" FURRING CHANNEL
CONT. MTL. TRACK
6' MAX.
TAPE & SPACKLE
U-BEAD - TAPE & SPACKLE
1/4"
EDGE AT GWB OR PLASTER SURFACES
EDGE AT DISSIMILAR SURFACES
1
TYP. SUSPENDED GWB CEILING
1 1/2" = 1'-0"

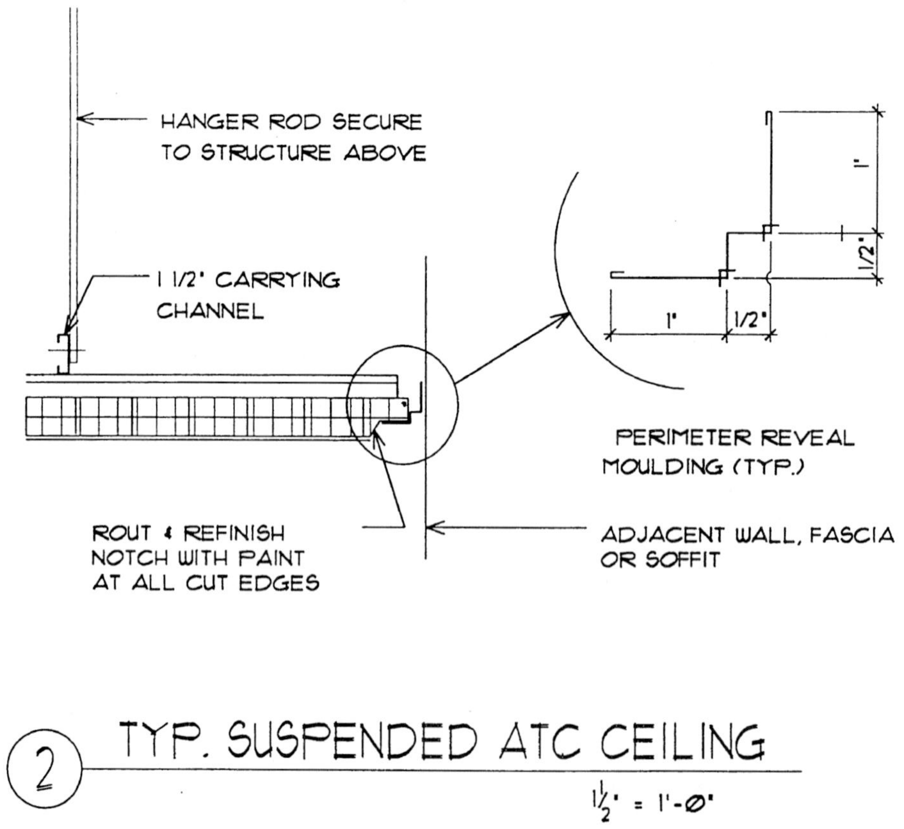
HANGER ROD SECURE TO STRUCTURE ABOVE
1 1/2" CARRYING CHANNEL
1"
1/2"
1"
1/2"
PERIMETER REVEAL MOULDING (TYP.)
ROUT & REFINISH NOTCH WITH PAINT AT ALL CUT EDGES
ADJACENT WALL, FASCIA OR SOFFIT
2
TYP. SUSPENDED ATC CEILING
1 1/2" = 1'-0"

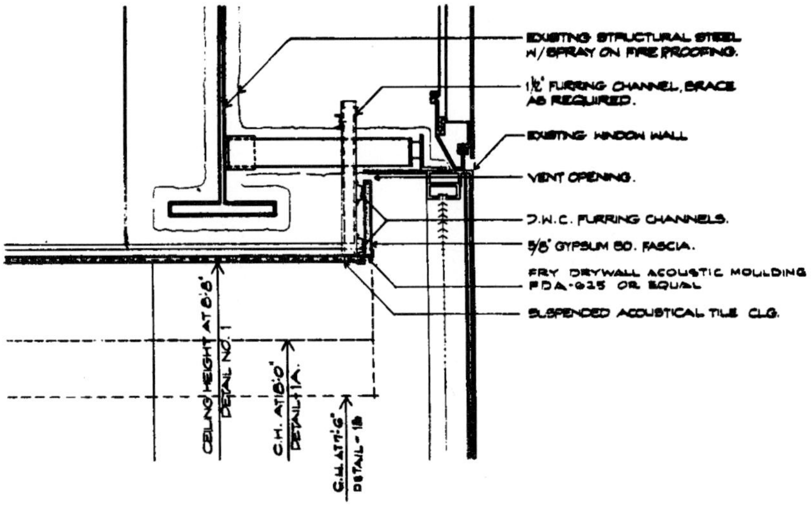
EXISTING STRUCTURAL STEEL W/SPRAY ON FIRE PROOFING.
1½" FURRING CHANNEL, BRACE AS REQUIRED.
EXISTING WINDOW WALL
VENT OPENING.
D.W.C. FURRING CHANNELS.
5/8" GYPSUM BD. FASCIA.
FRY DRYWALL ACOUSTIC MOULDING FDA-625 OR EQUAL
SUSPENDED ACOUSTICAL TILE CLG.
CEILING HEIGHT AT 8'-8" DETAIL NO. 1
C.H. AT 8'-0" DETAIL 1A
C.H. AT 7'-6" DETAIL-1B

1

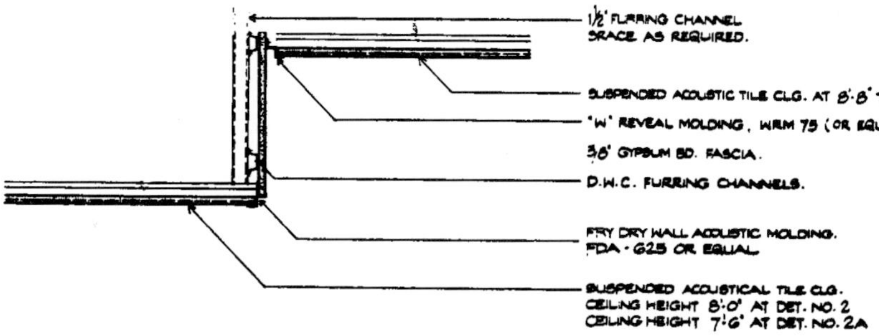
1½" FURRING CHANNEL BRACE AS REQUIRED.
SUSPENDED ACOUSTIC TILE CLG. AT 8'-8" TYP.
"W" REVEAL MOLDING, WRM 75 (OR EQUAL)
5/8" GYPSUM BD. FASCIA.
D.W.C. FURRING CHANNELS.
FRY DRY WALL ACOUSTIC MOLDING. FDA - 625 OR EQUAL
SUSPENDED ACOUSTICAL TILE CLG.
CEILING HEIGHT 8'-0" AT DET. NO. 2
CEILING HEIGHT 7'-6" AT DET. NO. 2A

2

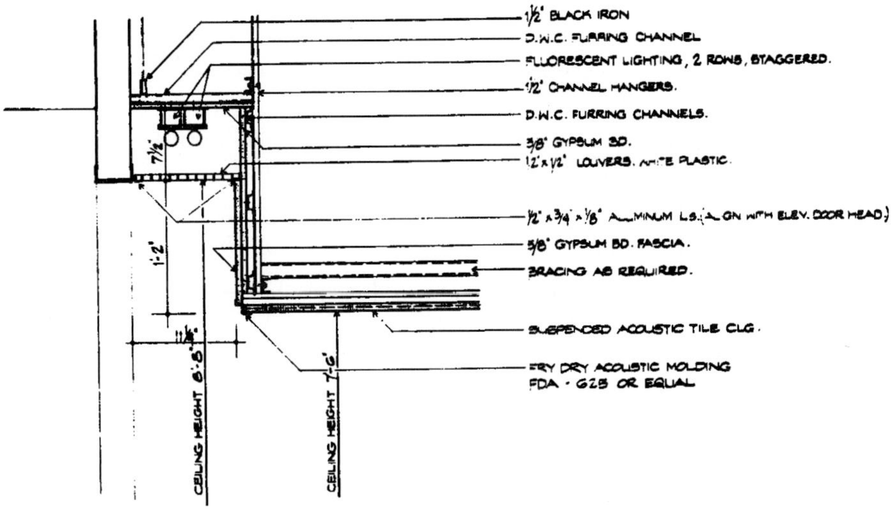
1½" BLACK IRON
D.W.C. FURRING CHANNEL
FLUORESCENT LIGHTING, 2 ROWS, STAGGERED.
½" CHANNEL HANGERS.
D.W.C. FURRING CHANNELS.
5/8" GYPSUM BD.
½" x ½" LOUVERS, WHITE PLASTIC.
½" x ¾" x ⅛" ALUMINUM L.S. (ALIGN WITH ELEV. DOOR HEAD)
5/8" GYPSUM BD. FASCIA.
BRACING AS REQUIRED.
SUSPENDED ACOUSTIC TILE CLG.
FRY DRY ACOUSTIC MOLDING FDA - 625 OR EQUAL
7½"
1'-2"
11⅝"
CEILING HEIGHT 8'-8"
CEILING HEIGHT 7'-6"

3

CEILINGS

Suspended Ceiling Details

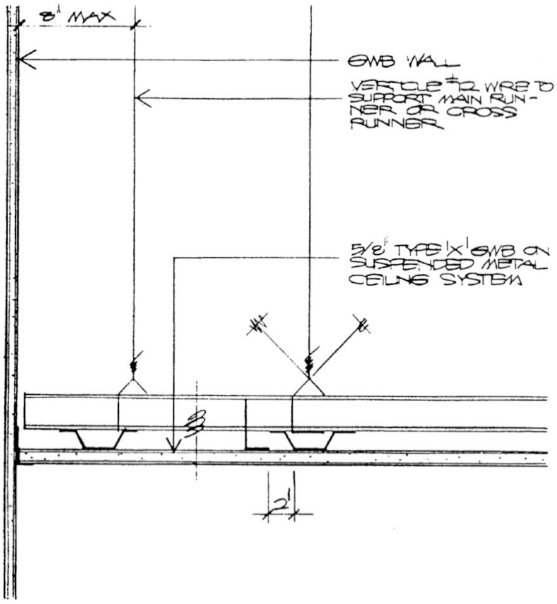

3 Section At Suspended GWB Ceiling
Scale: 3" = 1'-0"

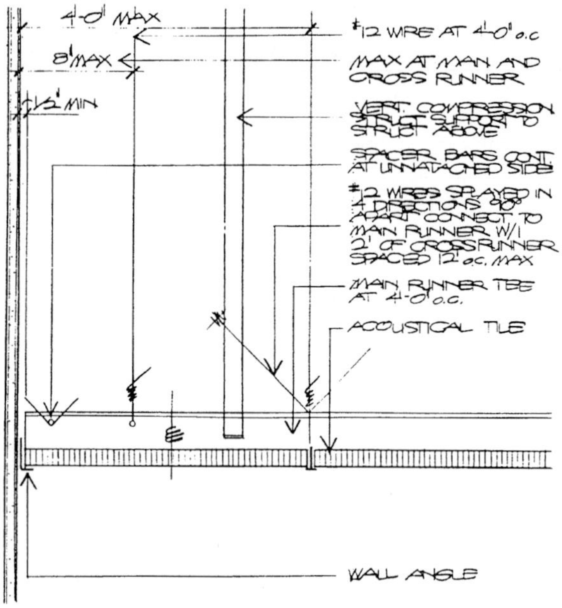

4 Section at Suspended Acoustical Ceiling
Scale: 3" = 1'-0"

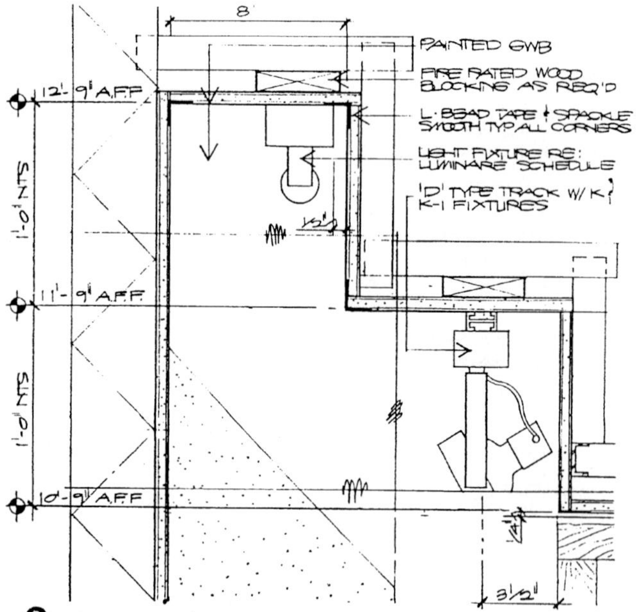

6 Section at Light Soffit
Scale: 3" = 1'-0"

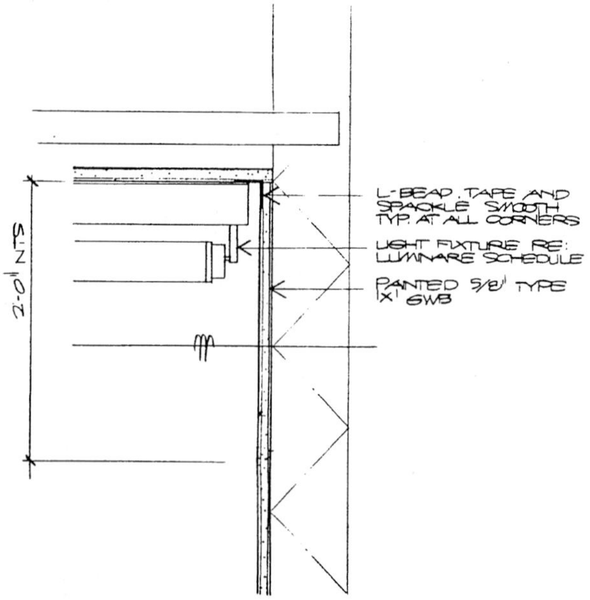

7 Section at Light Soffit
Scale: 3" = 1'-0"

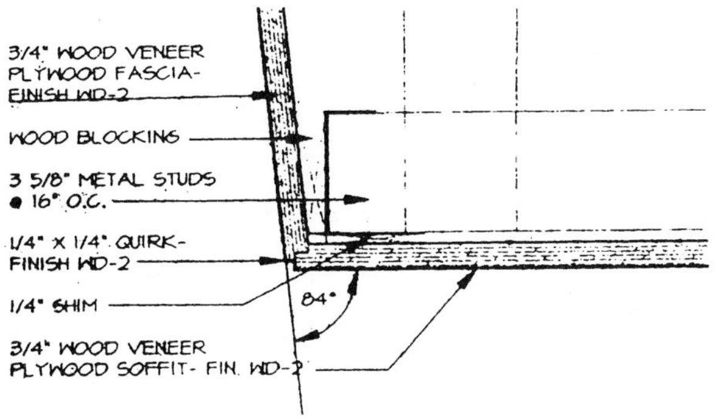

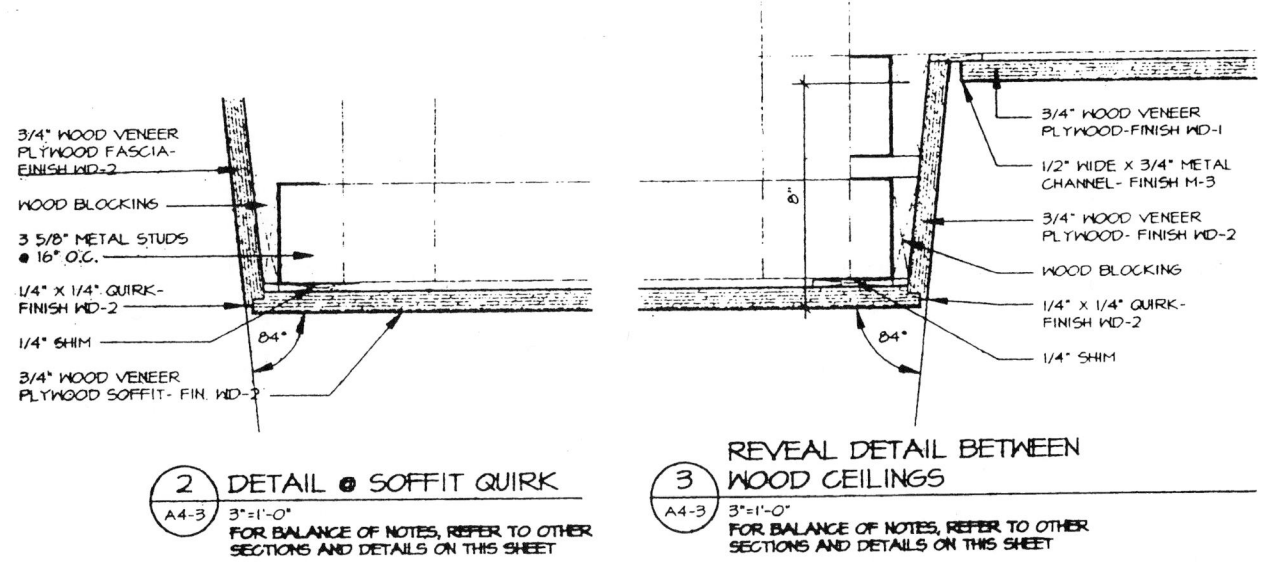

2 A4-3 DETAIL @ SOFFIT QUIRK
3"=1'-0"
FOR BALANCE OF NOTES, REFER TO OTHER SECTIONS AND DETAILS ON THIS SHEET

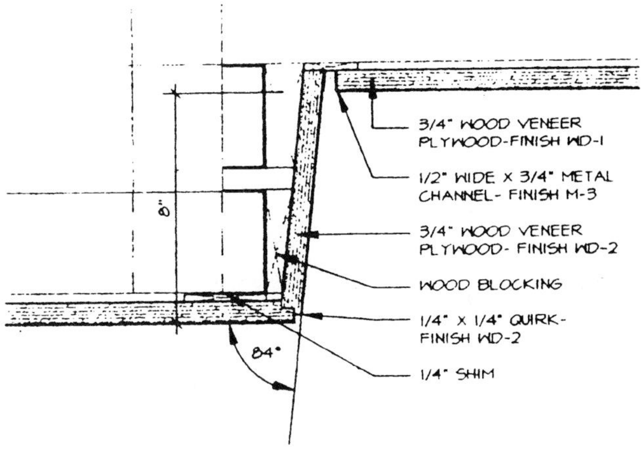

3 A4-3 REVEAL DETAIL BETWEEN WOOD CEILINGS
3"=1'-0"
FOR BALANCE OF NOTES, REFER TO OTHER SECTIONS AND DETAILS ON THIS SHEET

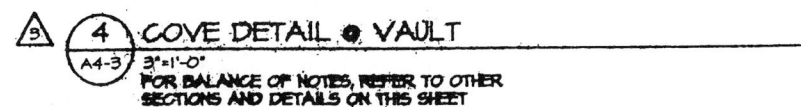

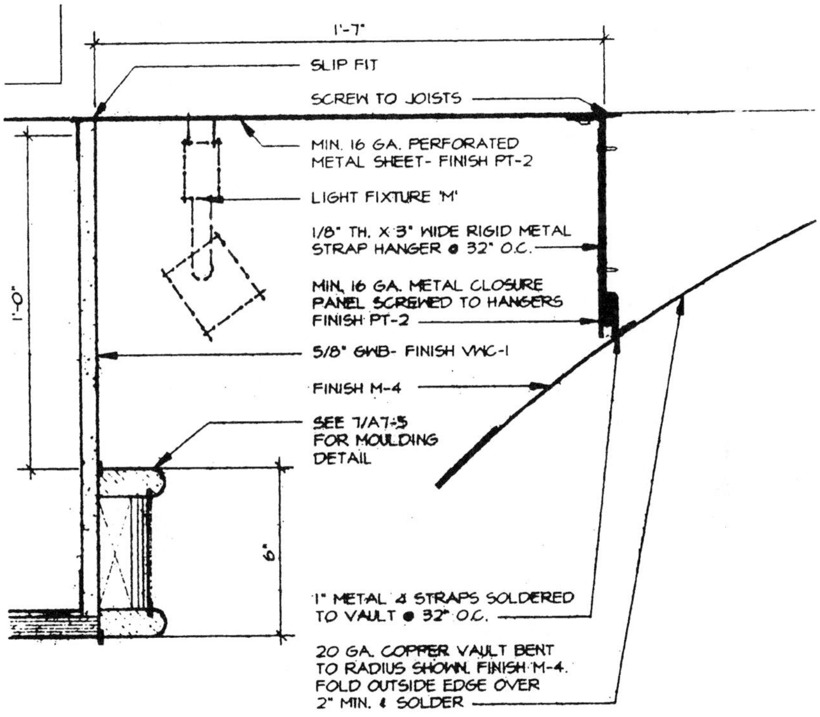

NOTES:
-PROVIDE NEOPRENE, FELT PAD OR ASPHALTUM BETWEEN COPPER VAULT AND OTHER METALS (I.E. EDGE BEAD, STUDS, ETC. TO PREVENT ELECTROLYTIC ACTION.
-PAINT ALL SCREWHEADS, WASHERS, & OTHER FASTENERS TO MATCH SURROUNDING FINISH

△3 4 A4-3 COVE DETAIL @ VAULT
3"=1'-0"
FOR BALANCE OF NOTES, REFER TO OTHER SECTIONS AND DETAILS ON THIS SHEET

CEILINGS

Curved Ceiling

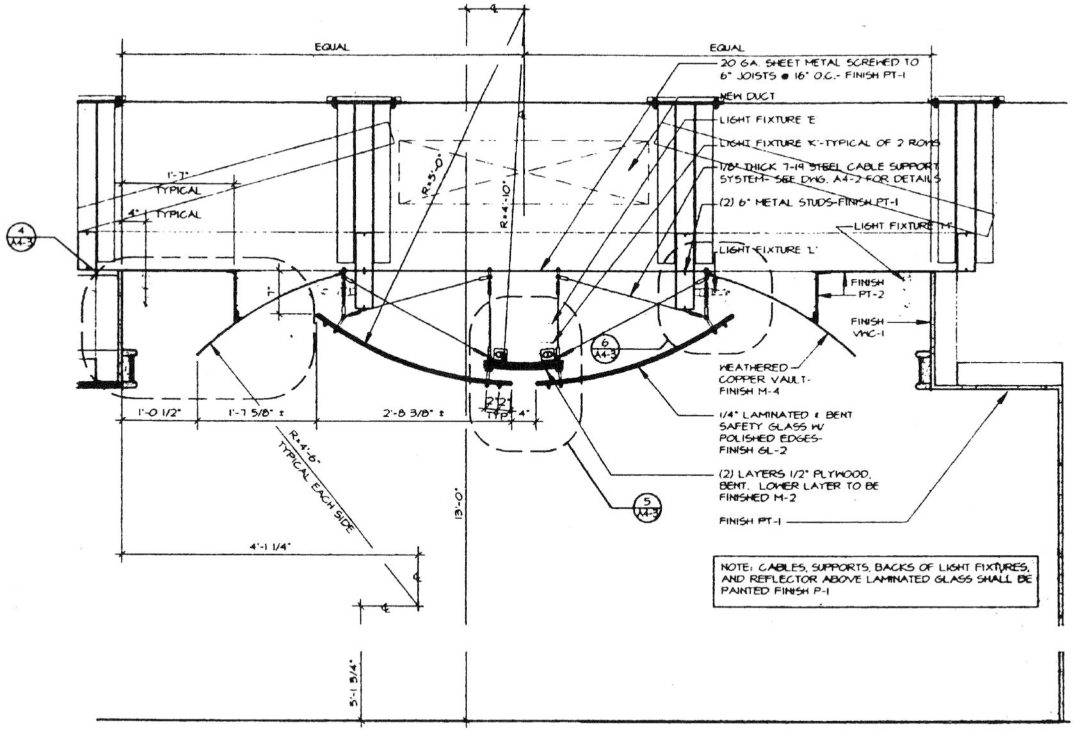
EQUAL
EQUAL
20 GA. SHEET METAL SCREWED TO 6" JOISTS @ 16" O.C.- FINISH PT-1
NEW DUCT
LIGHT FIXTURE 'E'
LIGHT FIXTURE 'K'-TYPICAL OF 2 ROWS
1/8" THICK 7-19 STEEL CABLE SUPPORT SYSTEM- SEE DWG. A4-2 FOR DETAILS
(2) 6" METAL STUDS-FINISH PT-1
LIGHT FIXTURE 'M'
LIGHT FIXTURE 'L'
1'-7"
TYPICAL
4"
TYPICAL
R=3'-0"
R=4'-10"
FINISH PT-2
FINISH VWC-1
WEATHERED COPPER VAULT- FINISH M-4
1/4" LAMINATED & BENT SAFETY GLASS W/ POLISHED EDGES- FINISH GL-2
(2) LAYERS 1/2" PLYWOOD, BENT. LOWER LAYER TO BE FINISHED M-2
FINISH PT-1
1'-0 1/2"
1'-7 5/8" ±
2'-8 3/8" ±
R=4'-6" TYPICAL EACH SIDE
4'-1 1/4"
13'-0"
5'-1 3/4"
NOTE: CABLES, SUPPORTS, BACKS OF LIGHT FIXTURES, AND REFLECTOR ABOVE LAMINATED GLASS SHALL BE PAINTED FINISH P-1

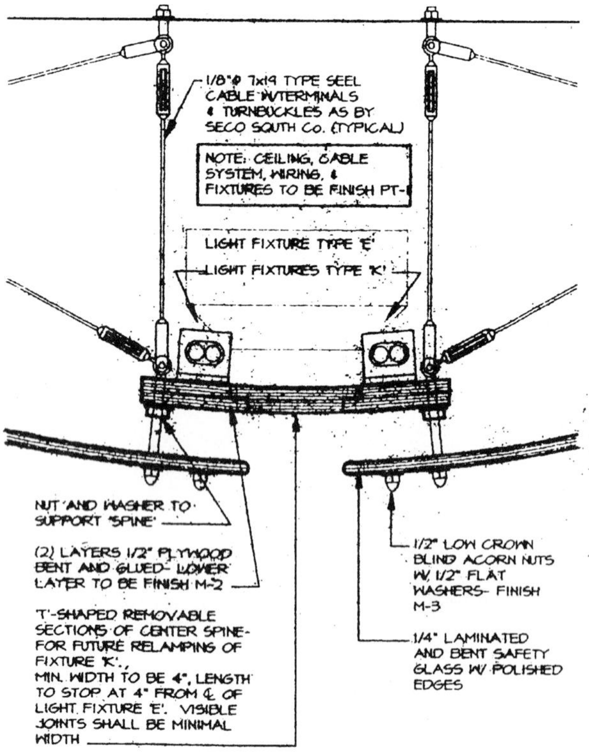
1/8"Ø 7x19 TYPE SEEL CABLE W/TERMINALS & TURNBUCKLES AS BY SECO SOUTH Co. (TYPICAL)
NOTE: CEILING, CABLE SYSTEM, WIRING, & FIXTURES TO BE FINISH PT-1
LIGHT FIXTURE TYPE 'E'
LIGHT FIXTURES TYPE 'K'
NUT AND WASHER TO SUPPORT 'SPINE'
(2) LAYERS 1/2" PLYWOOD BENT AND GLUED- LOWER LAYER TO BE FINISH M-2
'T'-SHAPED REMOVABLE SECTIONS OF CENTER SPINE- FOR FUTURE RELAMPING OF FIXTURE 'K'., MIN. WIDTH TO BE 4", LENGTH TO STOP AT 4" FROM ℄ OF LIGHT FIXTURE 'E'. VISIBLE JOINTS SHALL BE MINIMAL WIDTH
1/2" LOW CROWN BLIND ACORN NUTS W/ 1/2" FLAT WASHERS- FINISH M-3
1/4" LAMINATED AND BENT SAFETY GLASS W/ POLISHED EDGES

5 A4-3 DETAIL @ SPINE OF GLASS DIFFUSER 3"=1'-0"

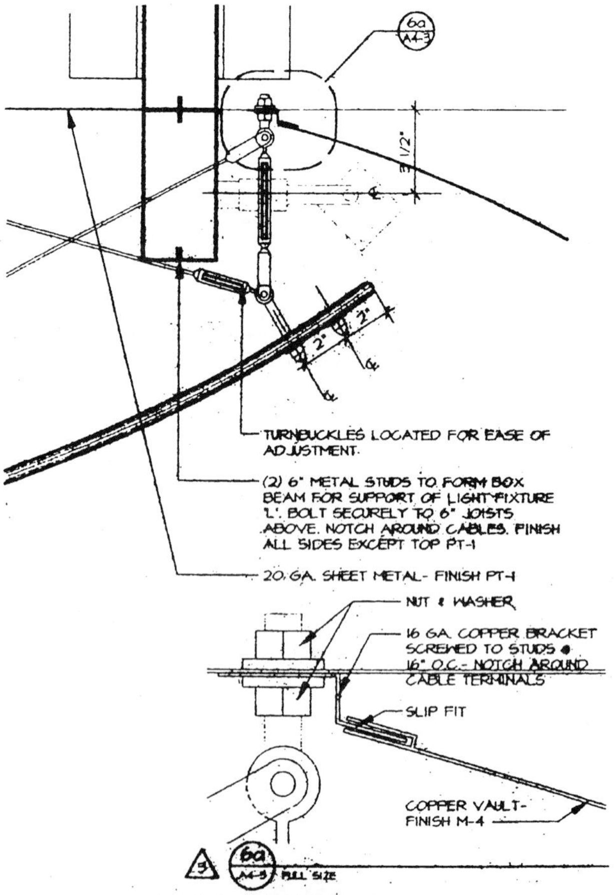
6a A4-3
1/2"
2"
2"
TURNBUCKLES LOCATED FOR EASE OF ADJUSTMENT.
(2) 6" METAL STUDS TO FORM BOX BEAM FOR SUPPORT OF LIGHT FIXTURE 'L'. BOLT SECURELY TO 6" JOISTS ABOVE. NOTCH AROUND CABLES. FINISH ALL SIDES EXCEPT TOP PT-1
20 GA. SHEET METAL- FINISH PT-1
NUT & WASHER
16 GA. COPPER BRACKET SCREWED TO STUDS @ 16" O.C.- NOTCH AROUND CABLE TERMINALS
SLIP FIT
COPPER VAULT- FINISH M-4
6a A4-3 FULL SIZE

6 A4-3 DETAIL @ EDGE OF GLASS DIFFUSER 3"=1'-0"

Vault Notes

- Hanger wires shall be spaced a maximum 48″ for Vaults main tees.
- Additional hanger wires or bracing may be necessary to stabilize curved ceilings during and after drywall attachment.
- At least 1 hanger wire is required within 8″ of a standard curved main tee splice.
- Hanger wires are required within 8″ on both sides of a modified Splice Clip attached to the nearest hanger holes.
- At least 1 hanger wire is required within 8″ of a Transition Clip.
- All drywall joints must be a minimum of 12″ from all main tee splices.
- In some instances, hanger wires, bracing and grid components have been omitted or truncated for clarity. For additional information, please contact technical services.

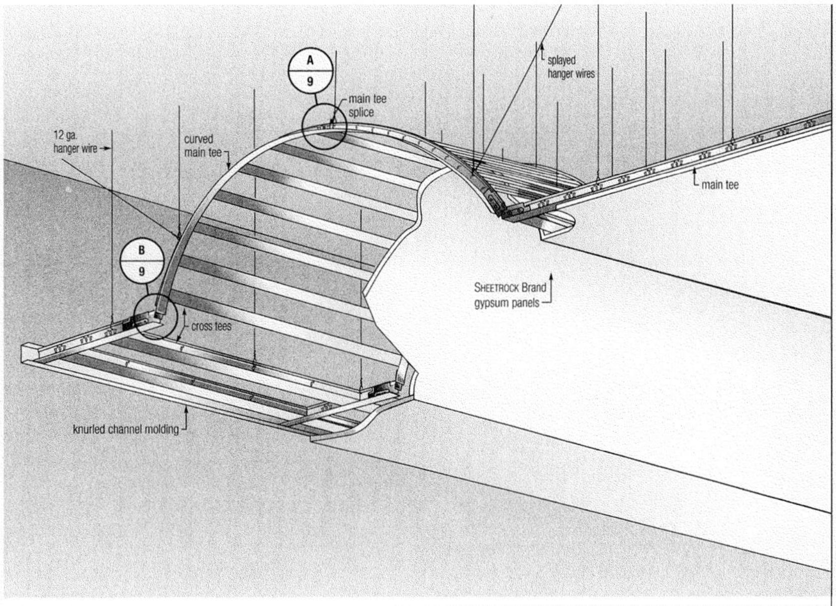

Vault to vault—factory end connection

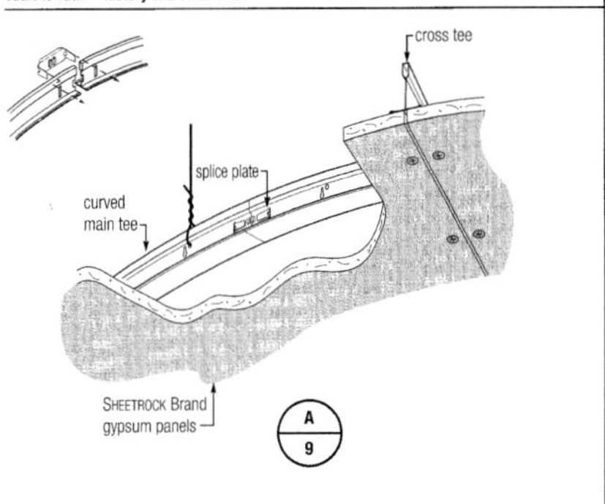

Vault to vault—field cut

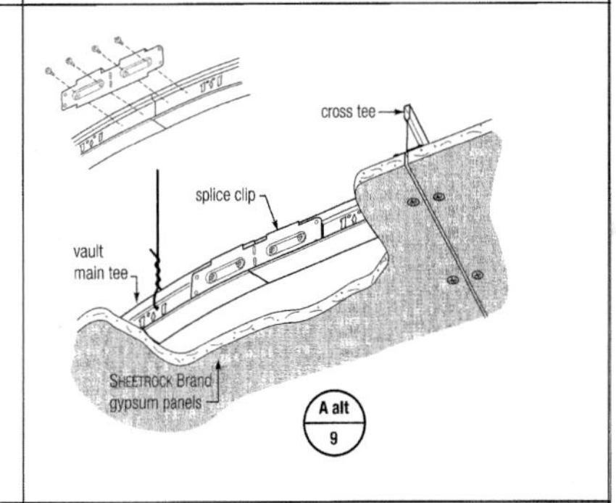

Flat to vault with greater than 90° angle

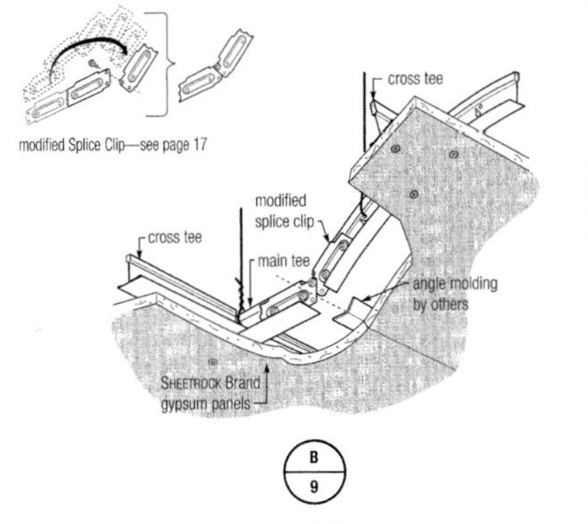

Flat to vault with 90° angle (not shown in preceeding perspective)

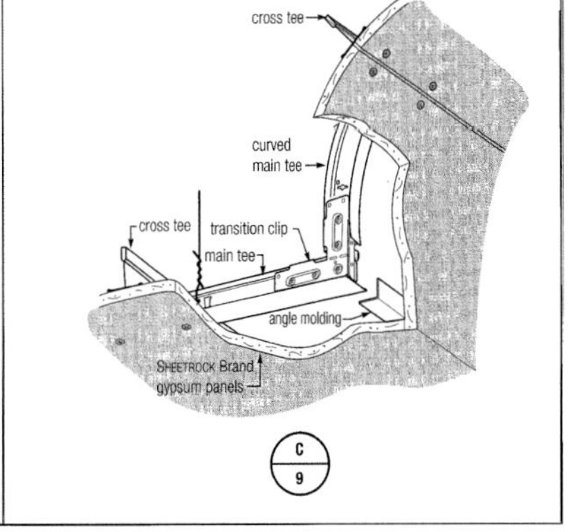

CEILINGS

Vault and Valley Drywall Ceilings

Vault and Valley Notes

- Hanger wires shall be spaced a maximum 48″ for Vaults main tees.
- Hanger wires shall be spaced a maximum 24″ for Valley main tees.
- Additional hanger wires or bracing may be necessary to stabilize curved ceilings during and after drywall attachment.
- At least 1 hanger wire is required within 8″ of a standard curved main tee splice.
- Hanger wires are required within 8″ on both sides of a modified Splice Clip attached to the nearest hanger holes.
- At least 1 hanger wire is required within 8″ of a Transition Clip.
- All drywall joints must be a minimum of 12″ from all main tee splices.
- In some instances, hanger wires, bracing and grid components have been omitted or truncated for clarity.
  For additional information, please contact technical services.

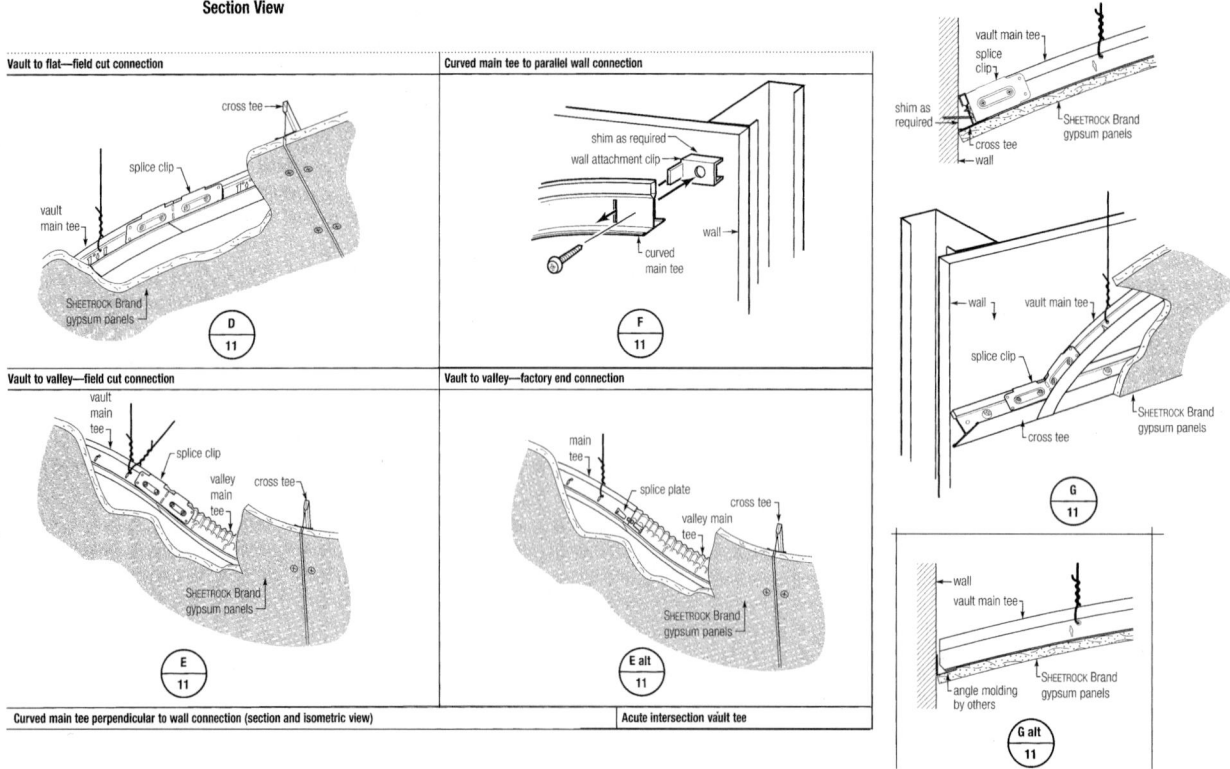

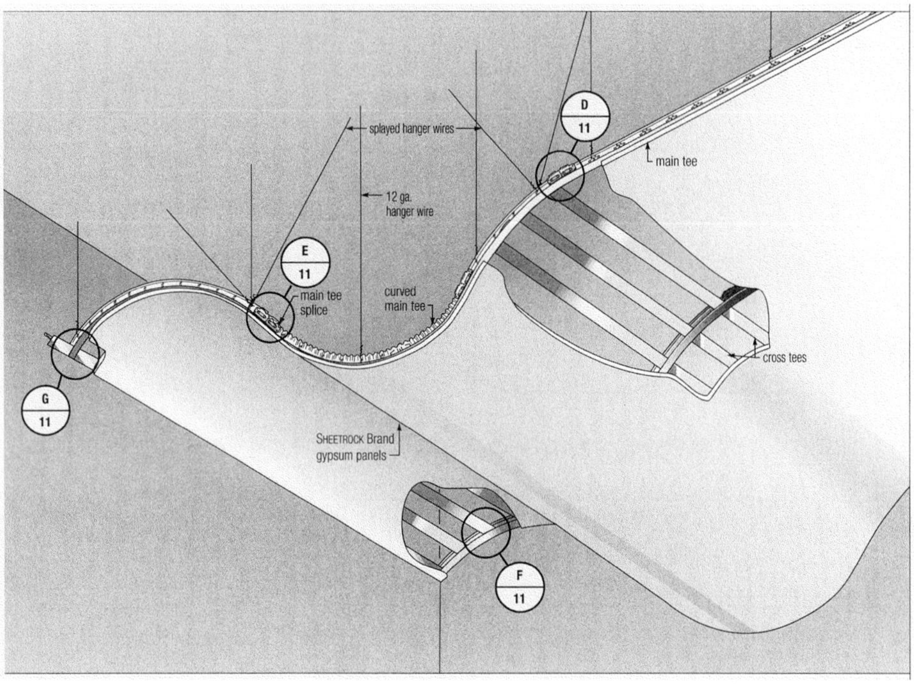

Section View

Vault to flat—field cut connection

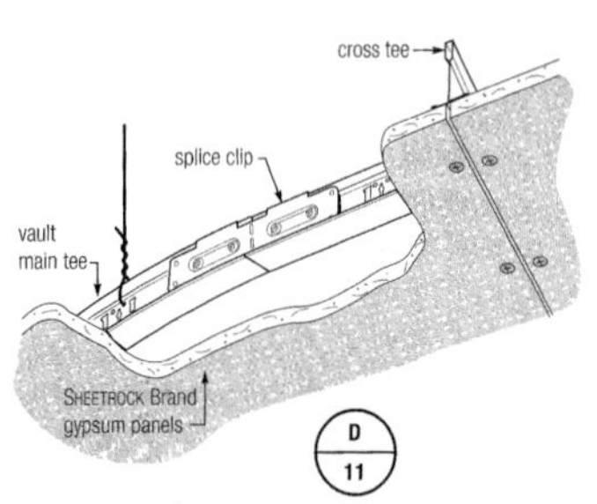

Curved main tee to parallel wall connection

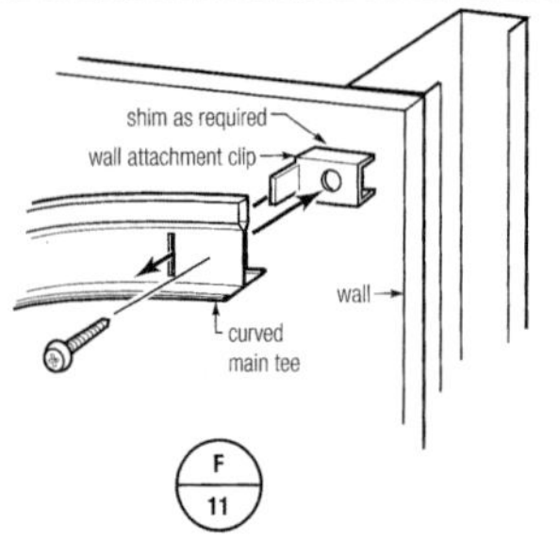

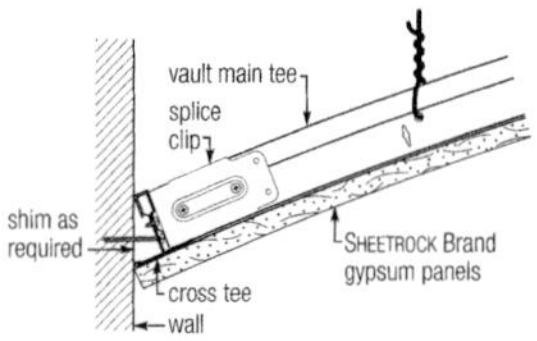

Vault to valley—field cut connection

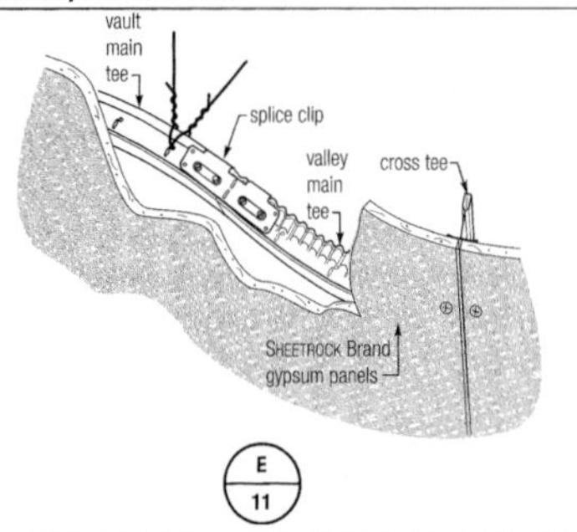

Vault to valley—factory end connection

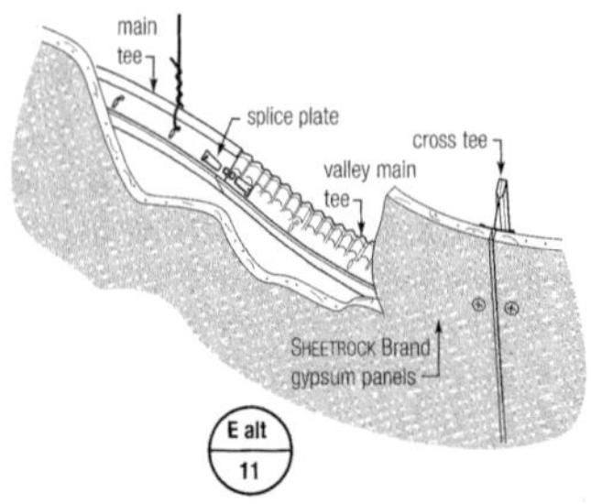

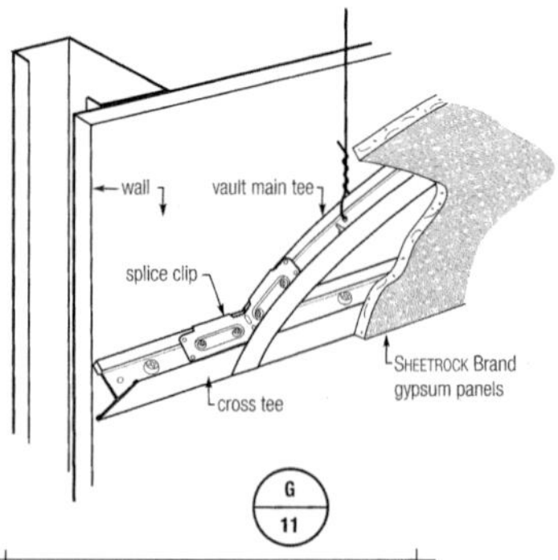

Curved main tee perpendicular to wall connection (section and isometric view)

Acute intersection vault tee

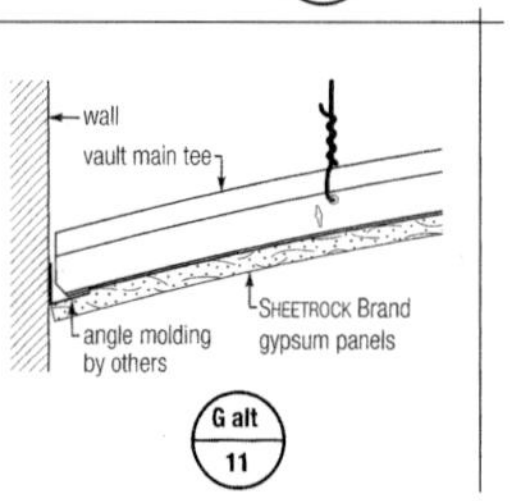

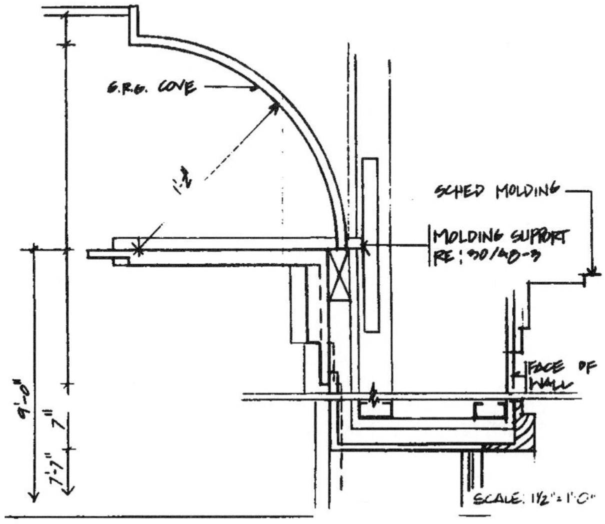

HEAD SECTION THRU PORTAL

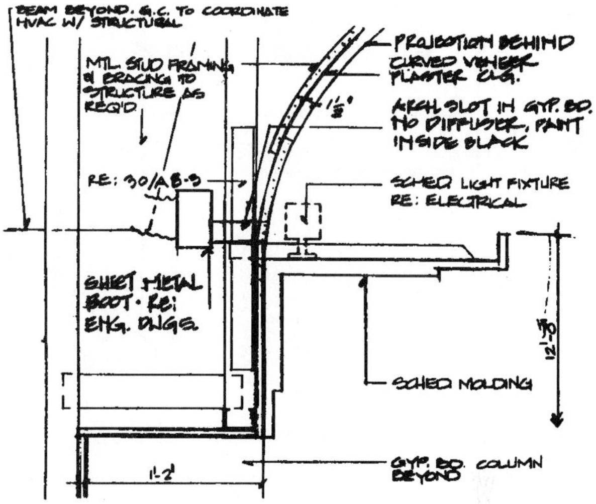

VAULTED CEILING WITH
MOULDING FRAMED
COVE LIGHT

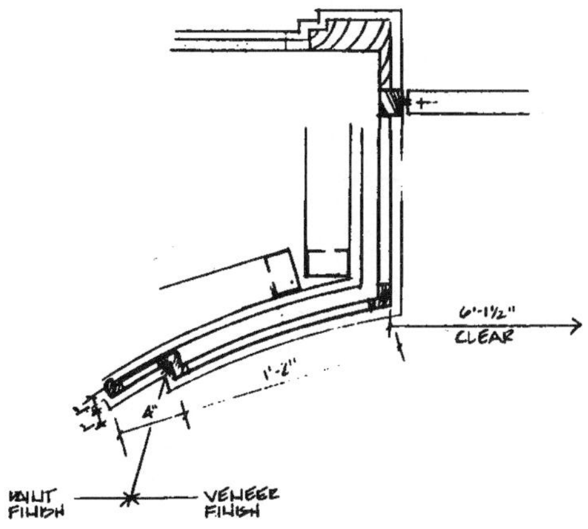

JAMB @ PORTAL

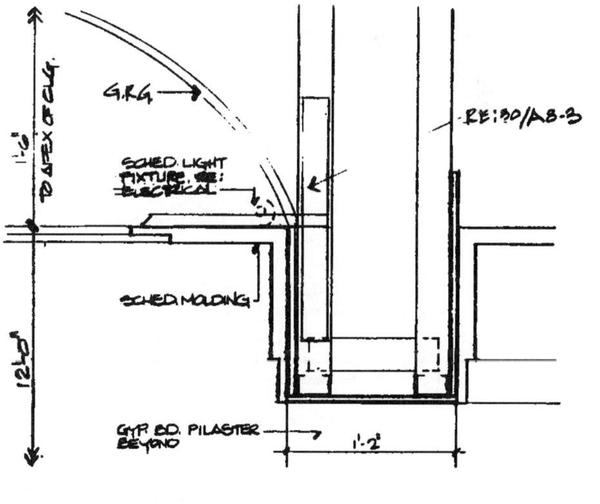

VAULTED CEILING WITH
MOULDING FRAMED BEAM

CEILINGS

Miscellaneous Details of Suspended Ceilings

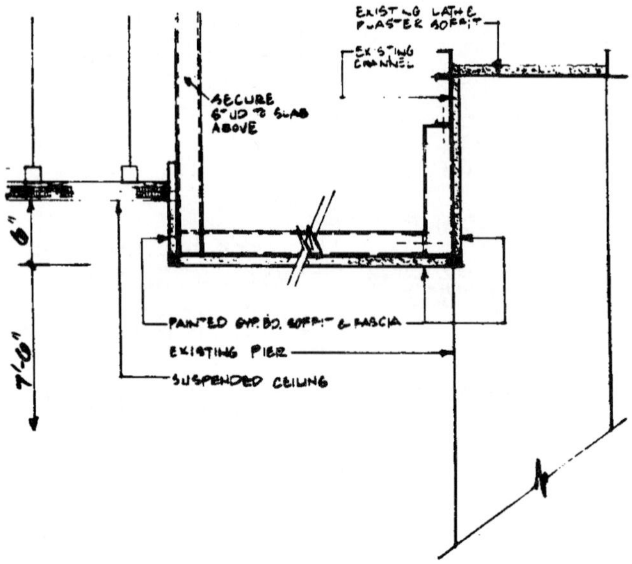

DETAIL - SOFFIT IN CAFETERIA AT WINDOW WALL

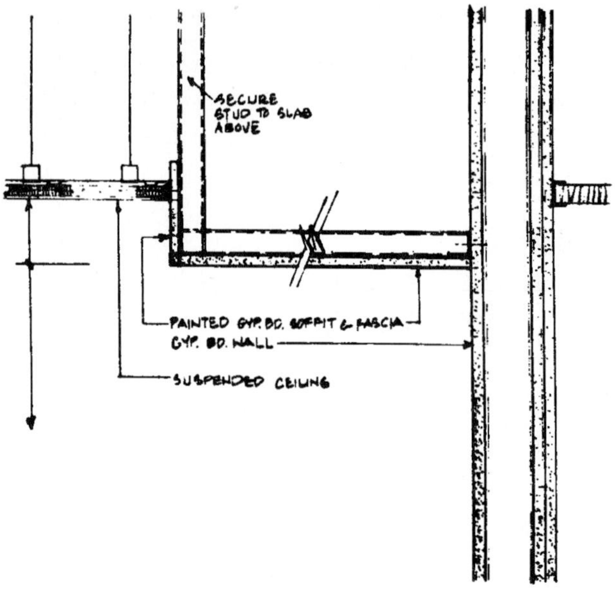

DETAIL - SOFFIT IN CAFETERIA

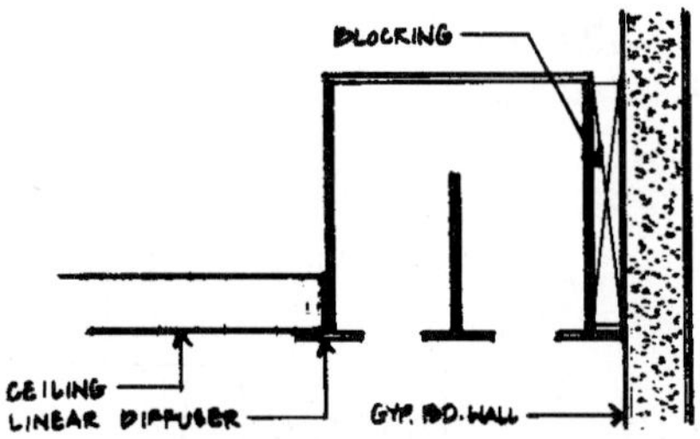

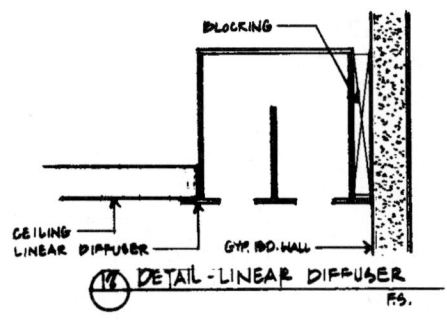

DETAIL - LINEAR DIFFUSER

F.S.

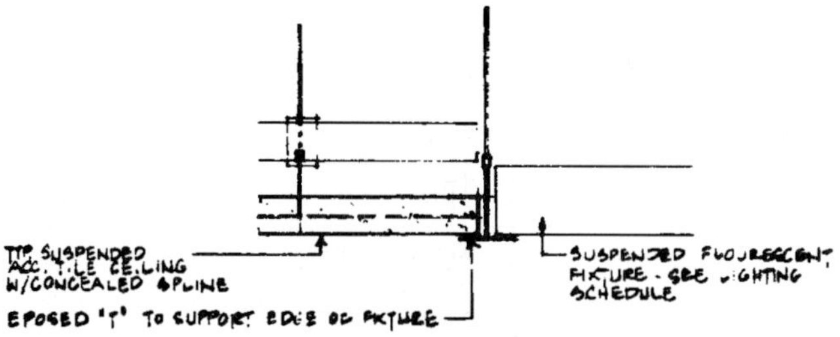

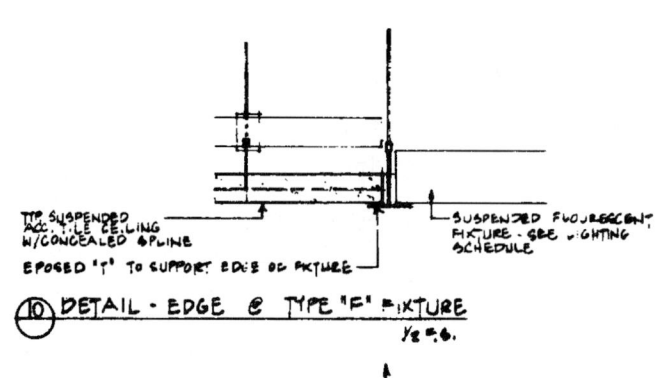

(10) DETAIL - EDGE @ TYPE "F" FIXTURE

1/2 F.S.

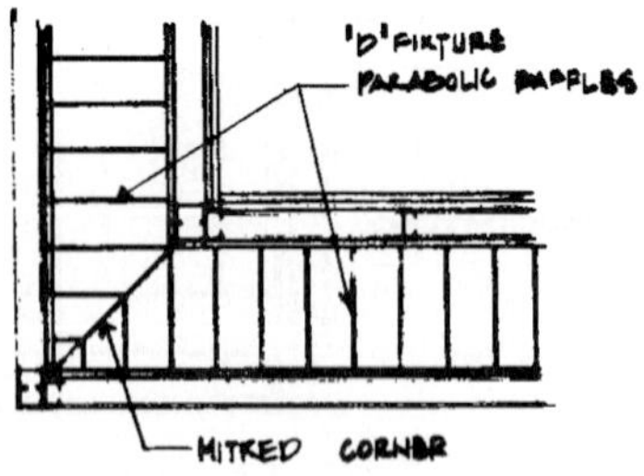

DETAIL - COVE AT MITRE CORNER

1" = 1'-0"

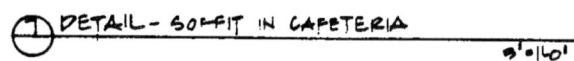

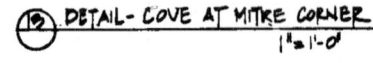

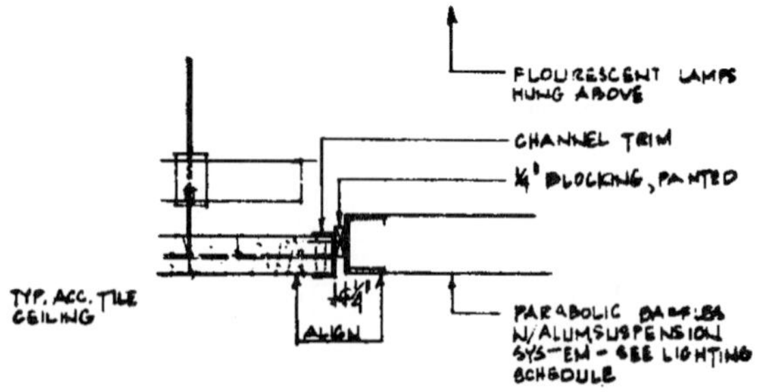

(11) DETAIL - EDGE @ TYPE 'P' FIXTURE

1/2 F.S.

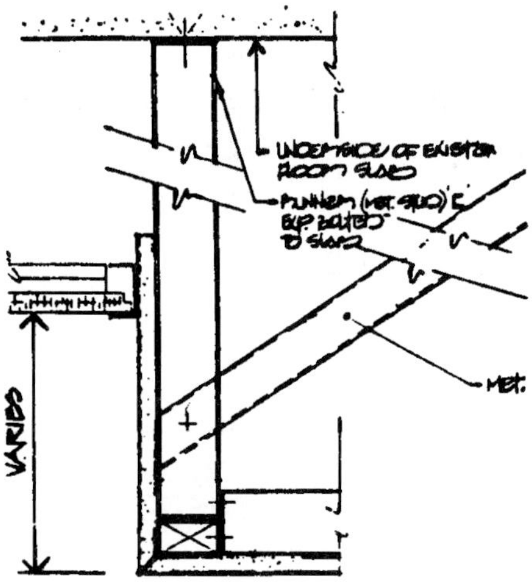

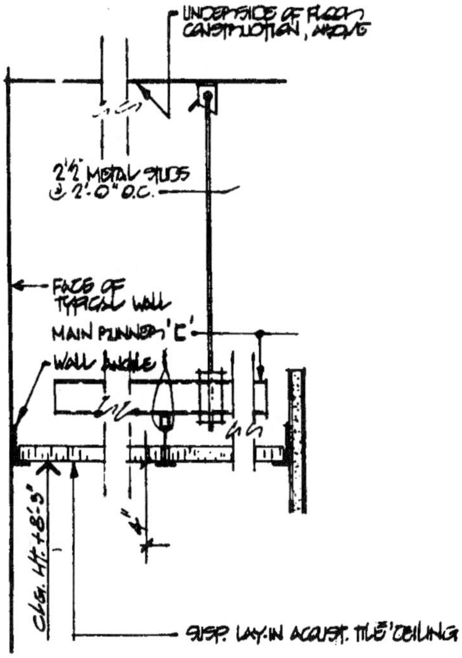

1 SECTION THRU SUSP. CLG.

2 EXPOSED 'T' GRID (2'x2')

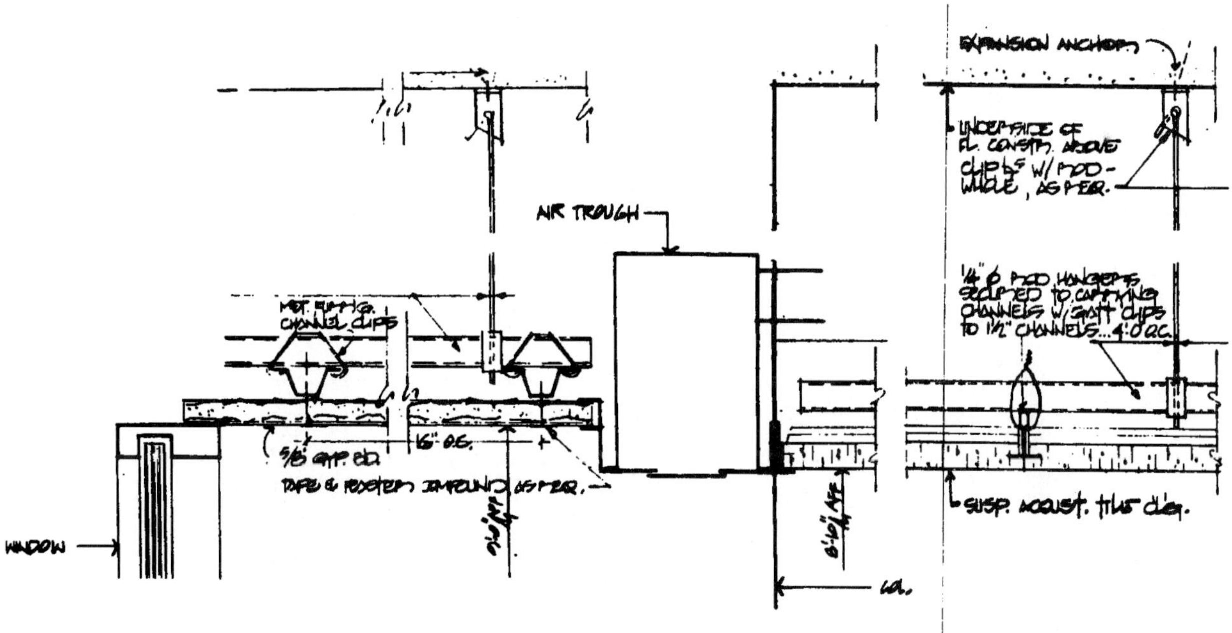

3 WINDOW HEAD - ALL FLOOR EXCEPT 2ND FL.

CEILINGS

Suspended Ceilings: Perimeters and Drops

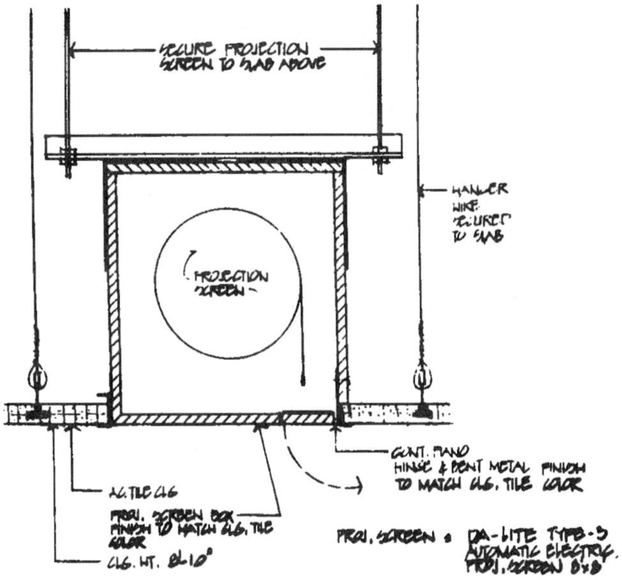

4 A-103 PROJECTION SCREEN

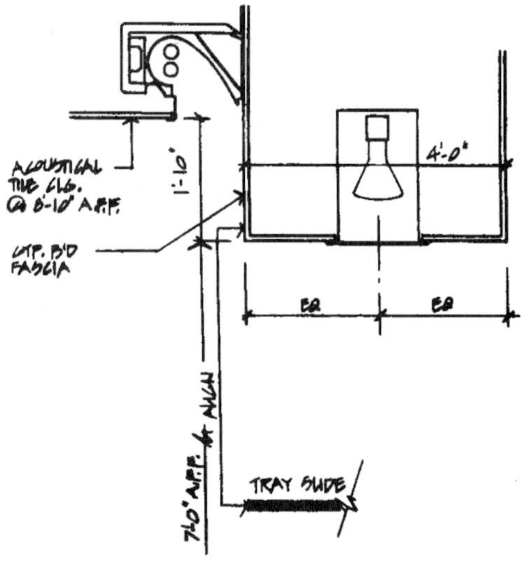

5 A-103 PERIMETER TROUGH SYSTEM @ SERVERY (PTS-4)

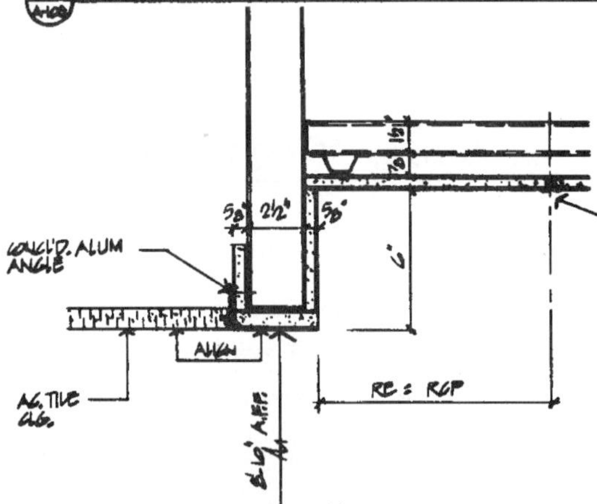

6 A-103 CONF. CNTR. CLG. - TYP.

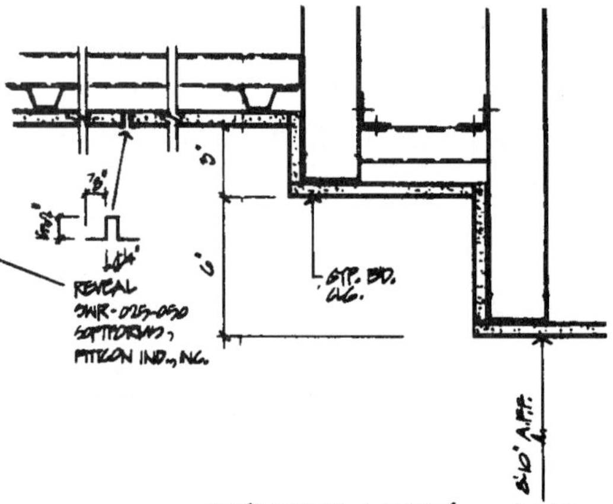

7 A-103 ELEVATOR LOBBY - SECT. REVEAL @ CLG.

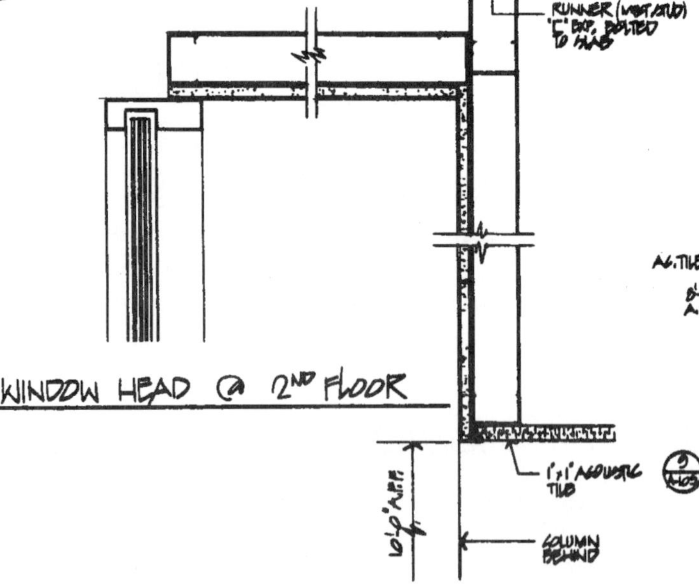

8 A-103 WINDOW HEAD @ 2ND FLOOR

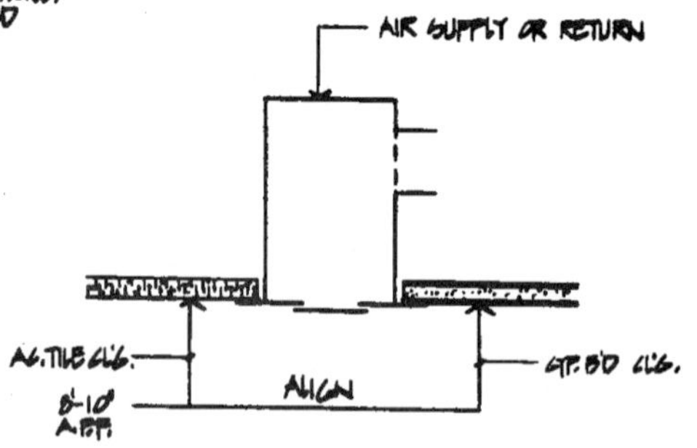

9 A-103 SECT. THRU TWO (2) DIFF. SUSP. CLG'S.

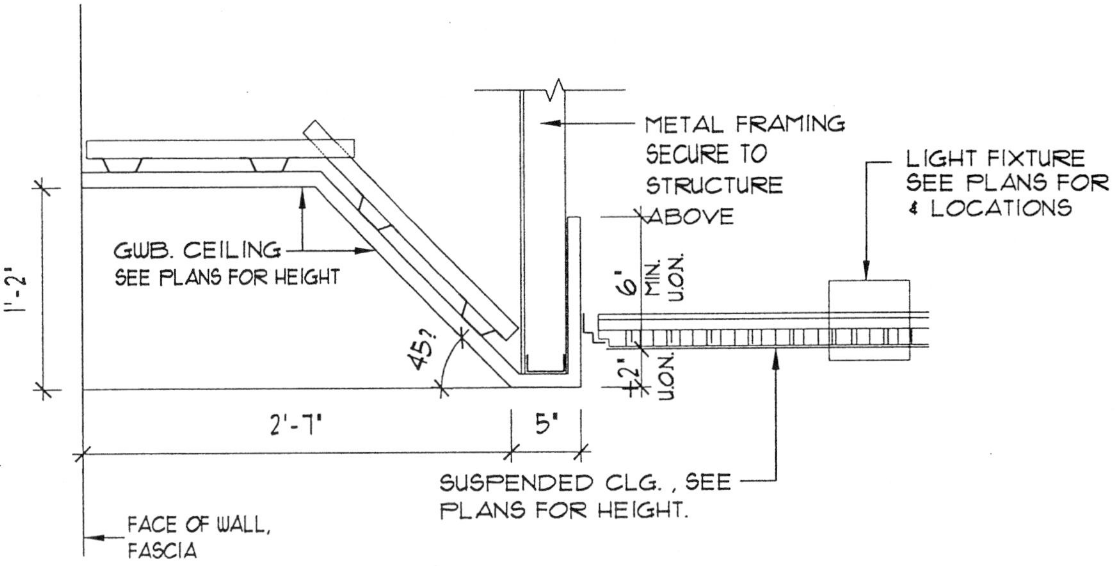

7 CORRIDOR DETAIL

1½" = 1'-0"

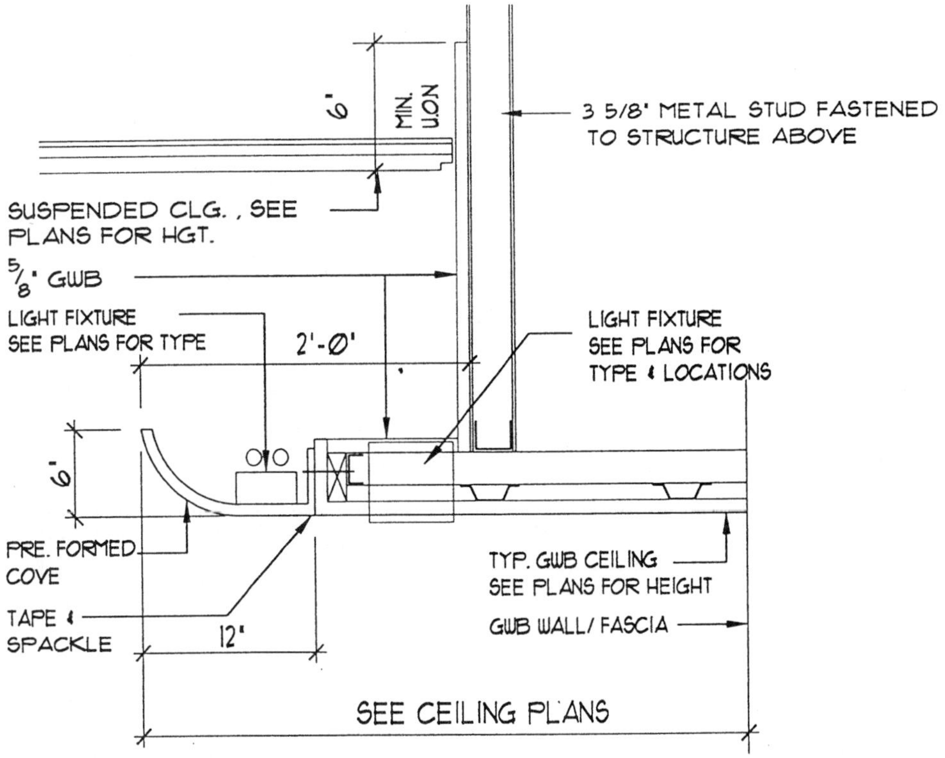

8 ELEVATOR LOBBY CEILING DETAIL

1" = 1'-0"

CEILINGS

Gypsum Board and Plaster Suspended Ceilings

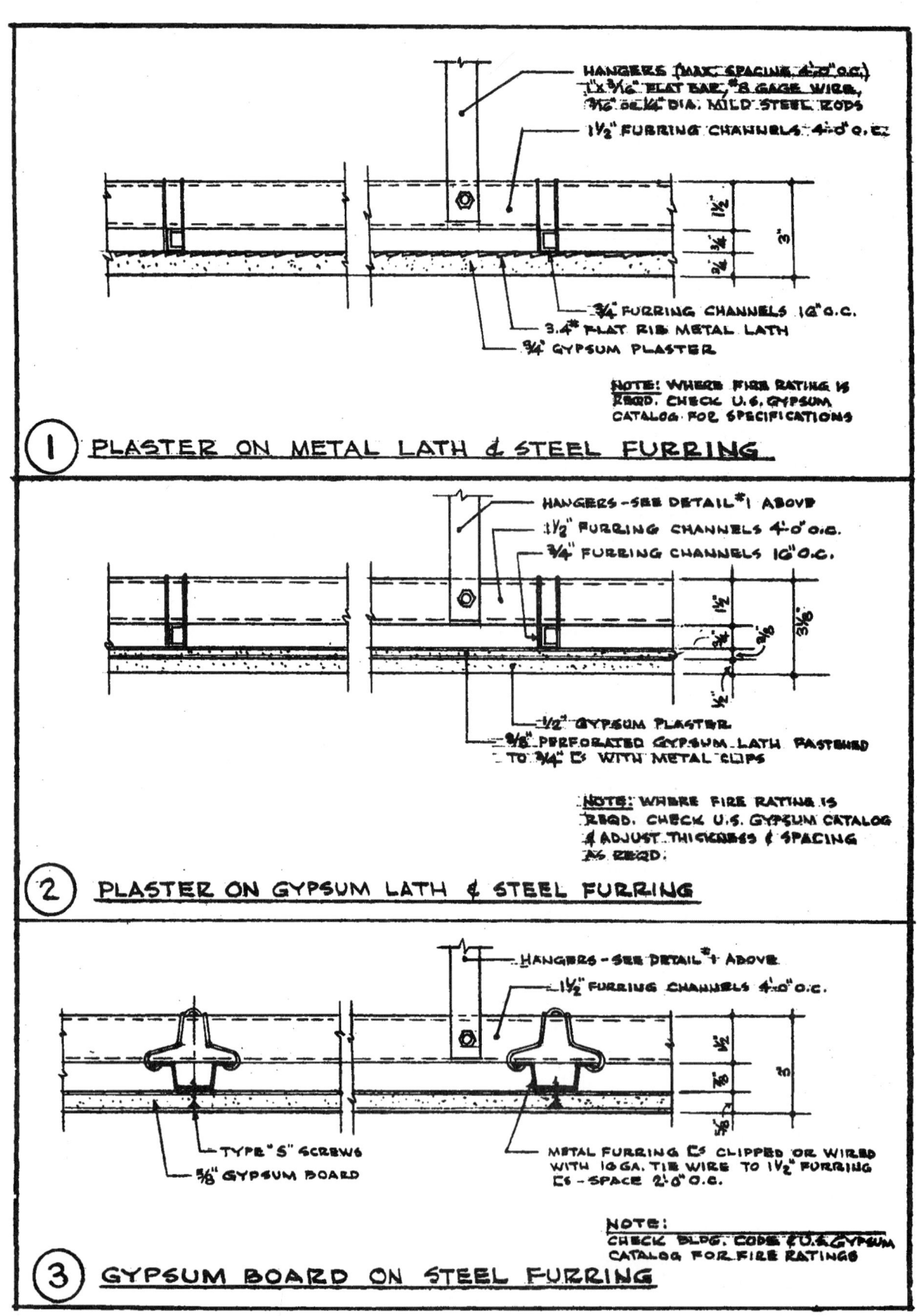

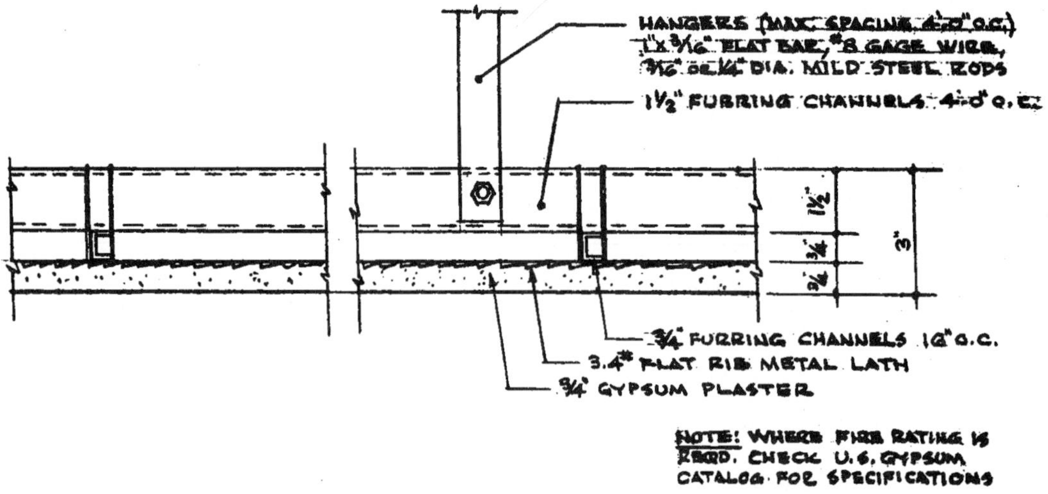

1 PLASTER ON METAL LATH & STEEL FURRING

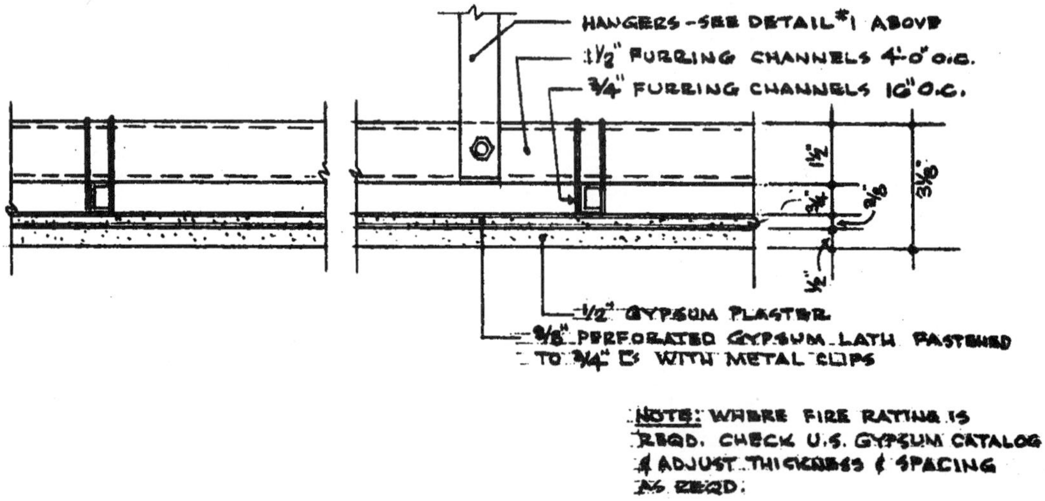

2 PLASTER ON GYPSUM LATH & STEEL FURRING

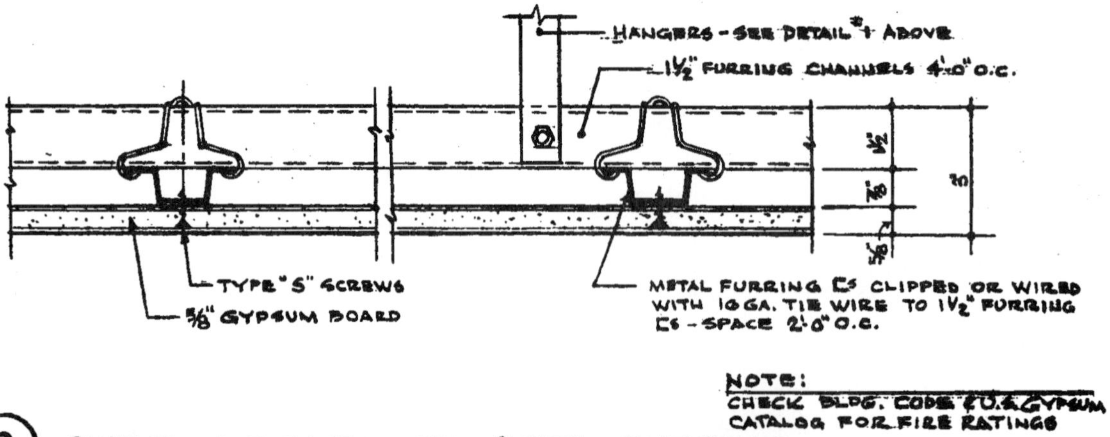

3 GYPSUM BOARD ON STEEL FURRING

CEILINGS
Soffit Details

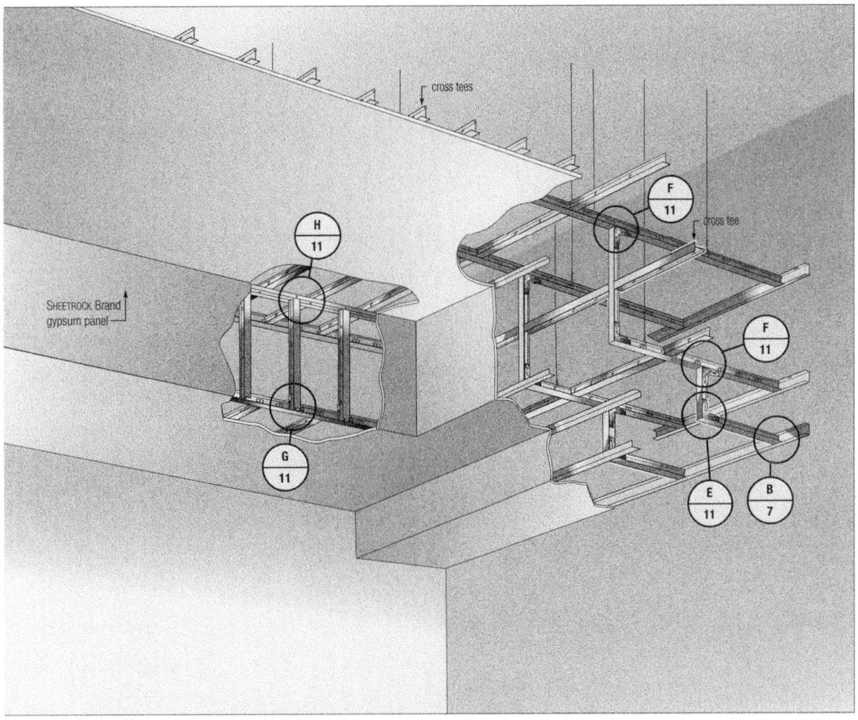

Soffit Notes

- In some instances, hanger wires, bracing, and grid components have been omitted or truncated for clarity. For additional information, please contact technical services.
- When constructing soffits, bracing of the drywall suspension and/or additional hanger wires may be necessary to ensure stability and structural performance during and after drywall attachment.
- The maximum vertical soffit height is 48″ with cross tees spaced 24″ on center. (Maximum unsupported drywall area 48″ x 24″). Intermediate cross tees are not necessary when soffit dimensions do not exceed 24″.
- When used in soffit construction, all Transition Clips are to have a minimum of 4 screws for attachment.

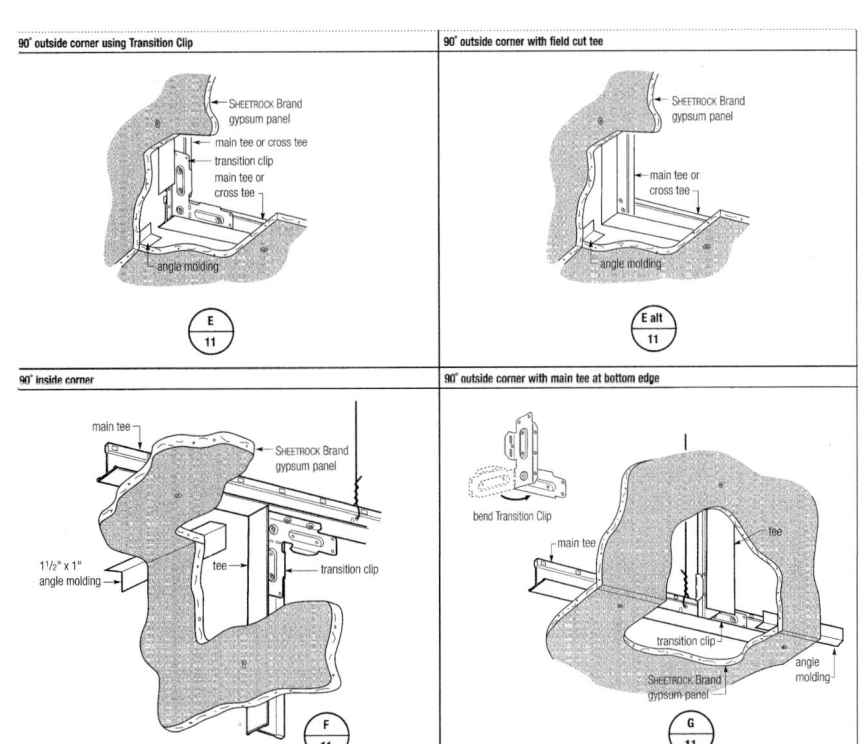

90° outside corner using Transition Clip

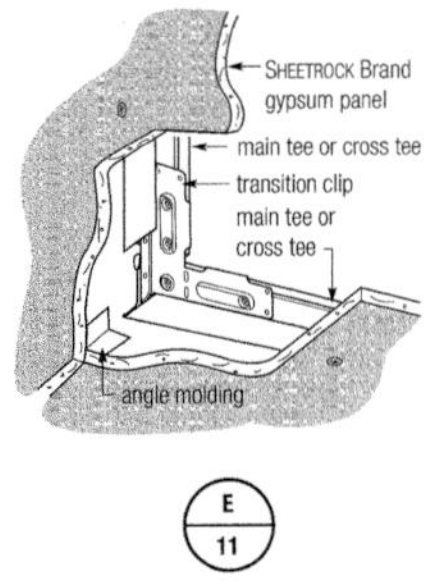

90° outside corner with field cut tee

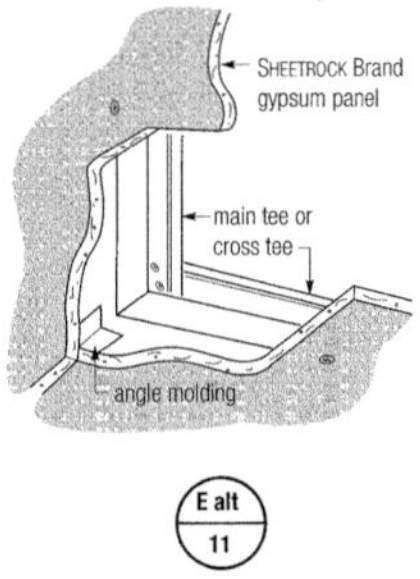

90° inside corner with channel molding at top edge

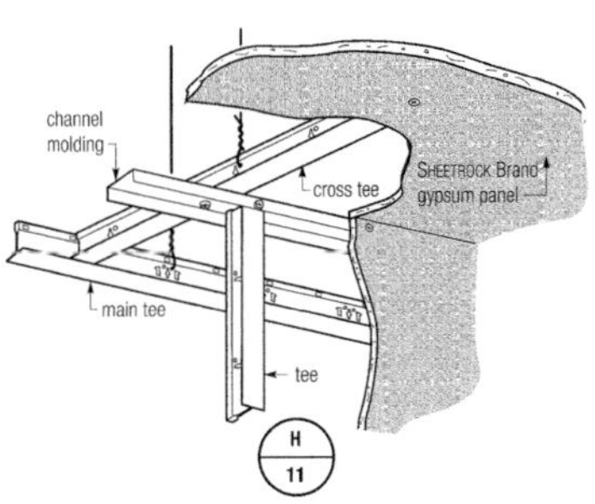

90° inside corner

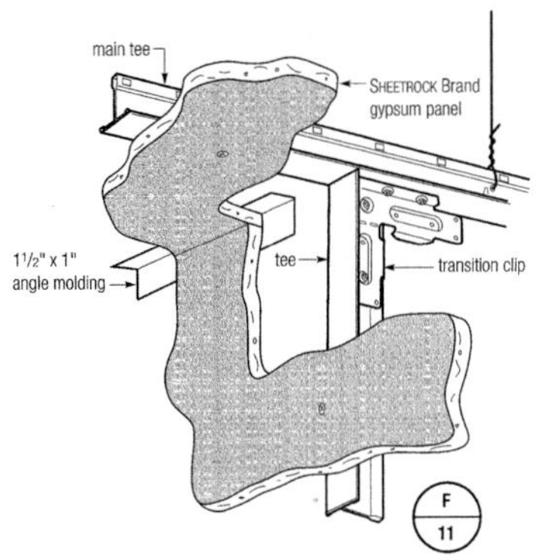

90° outside corner with main tee at bottom edge

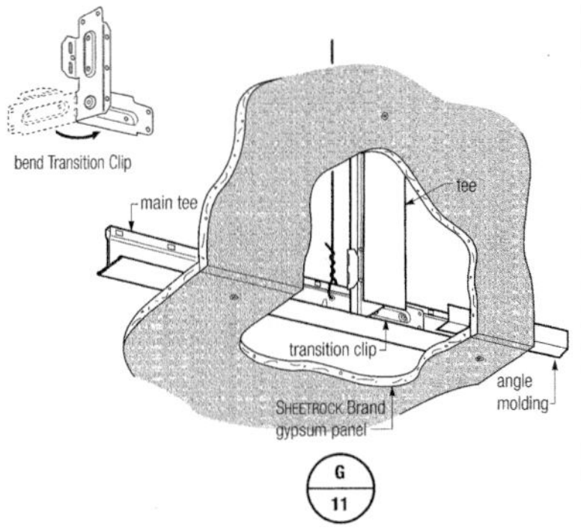

CEILINGS
Fascia Details

Fascia Ceiling Notes

- Main tee and cross tee spacing is provided in the table on page 19.
- Hanger wires must be placed within 12" of the fascia where main tees and cross tees intersect the fascia.
- Extra hanger wires may be required at the perimeter of fascia applications to ensure adequate support and stability, such as cross tees less than 12" in length.

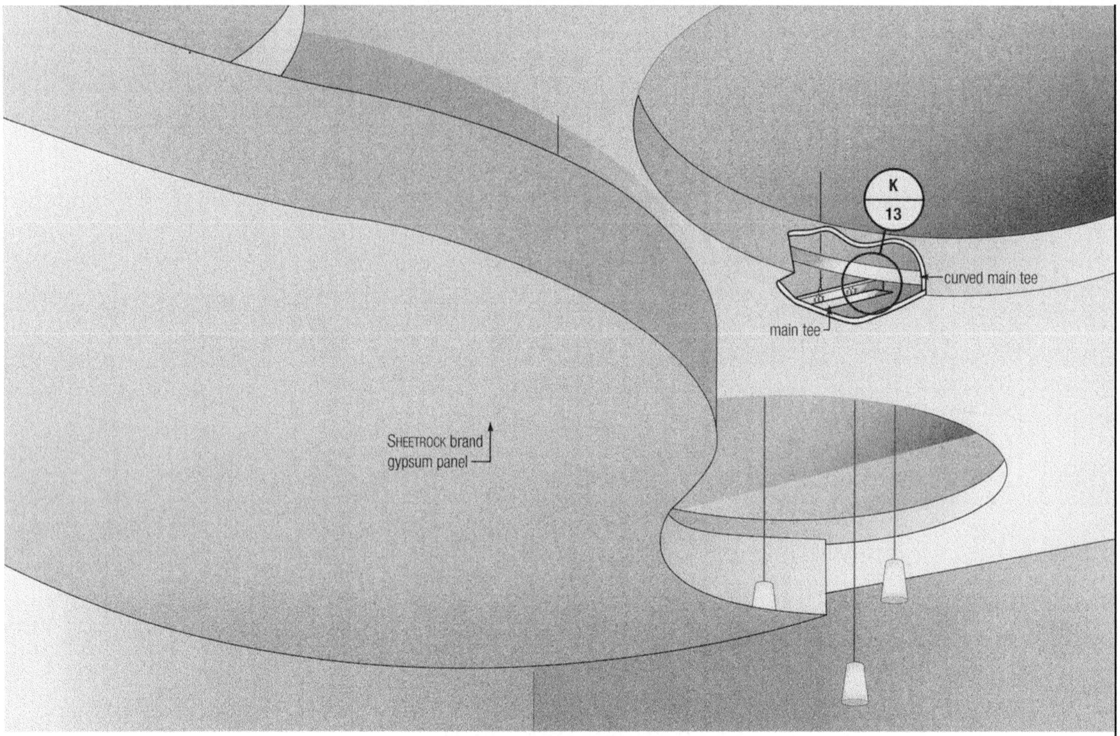

COMPASSO trim parallel to main or cross tee	COMPASSO trim perpendicular to main or cross tee
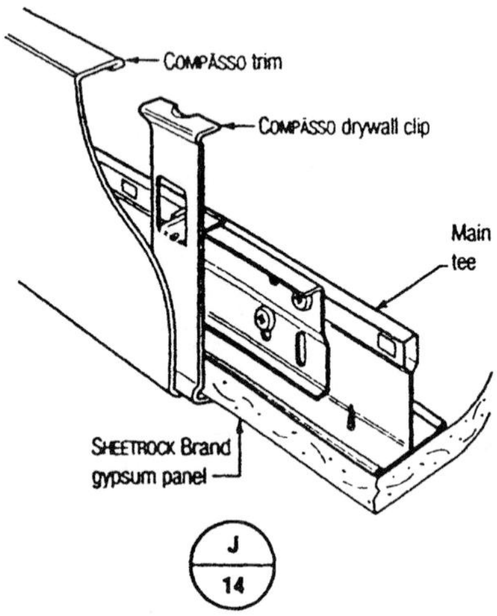	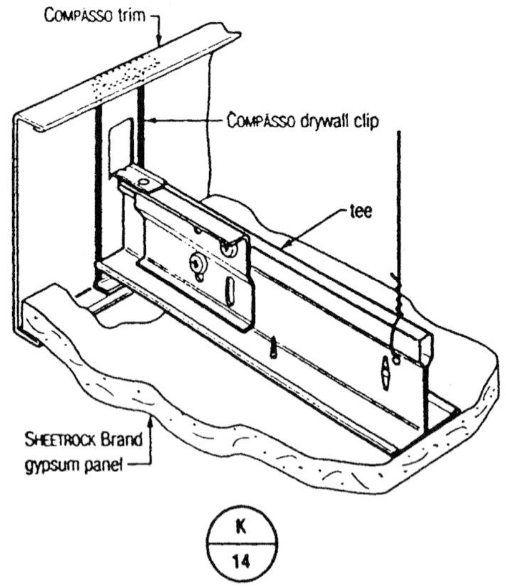

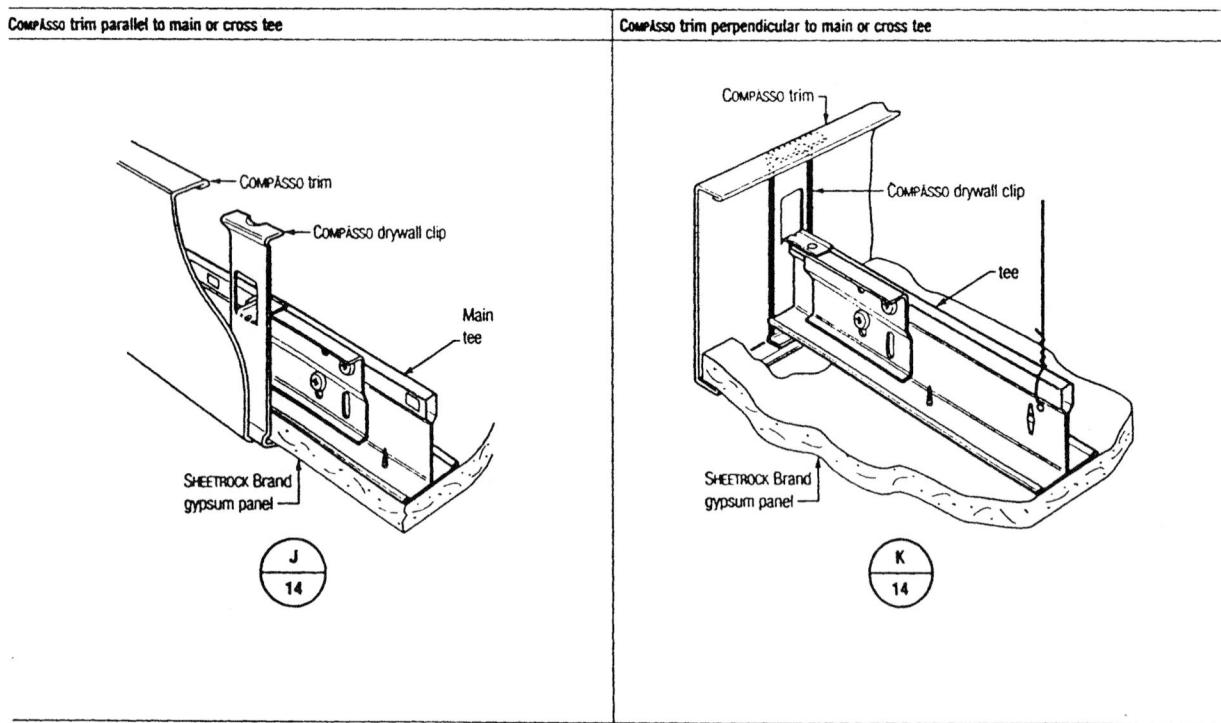

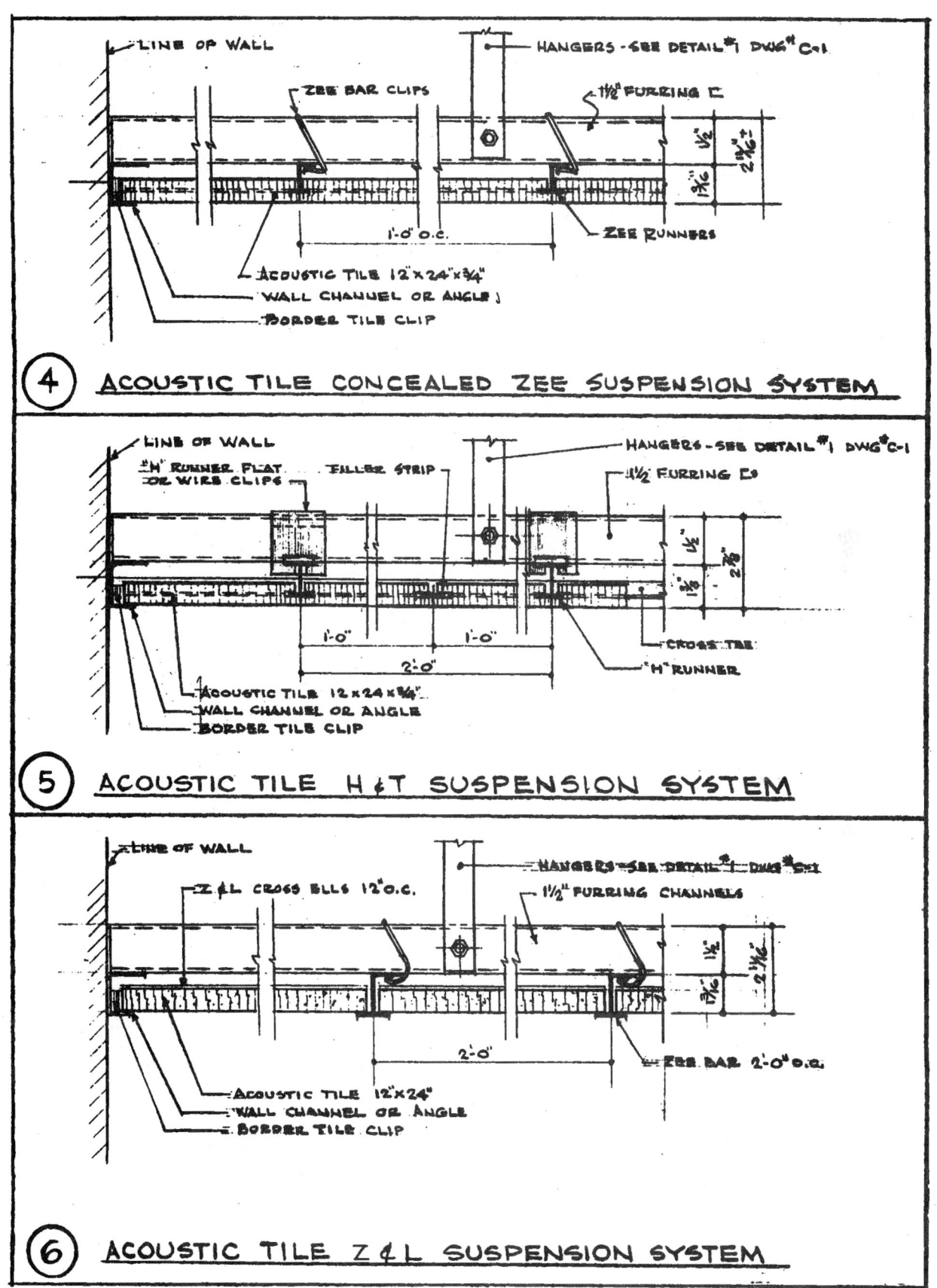

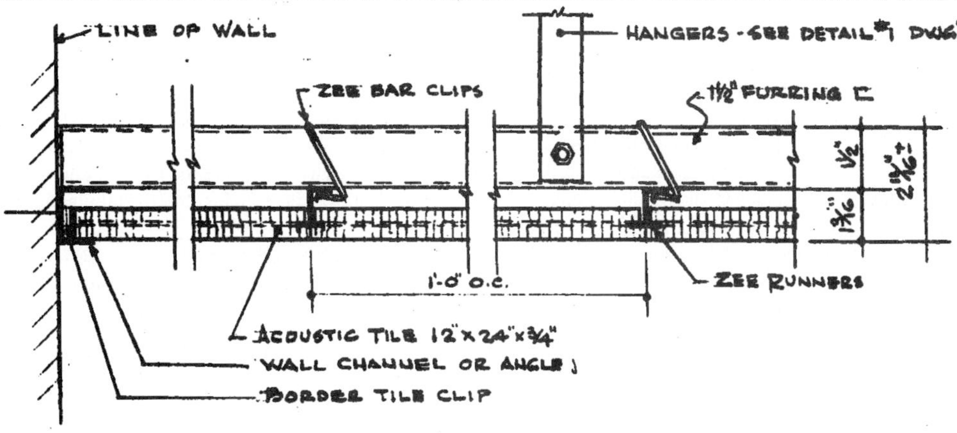

(4) ACOUSTIC TILE CONCEALED ZEE SUSPENSION SYSTEM

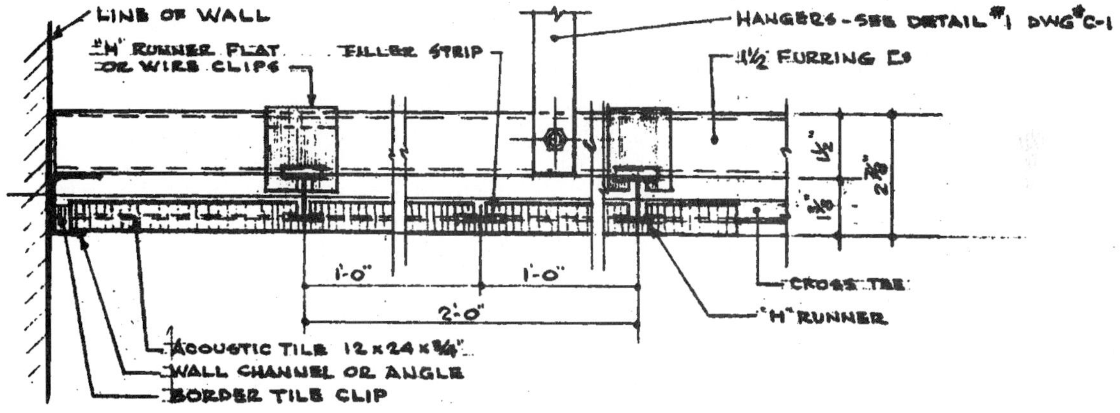

(5) ACOUSTIC TILE H & T SUSPENSION SYSTEM

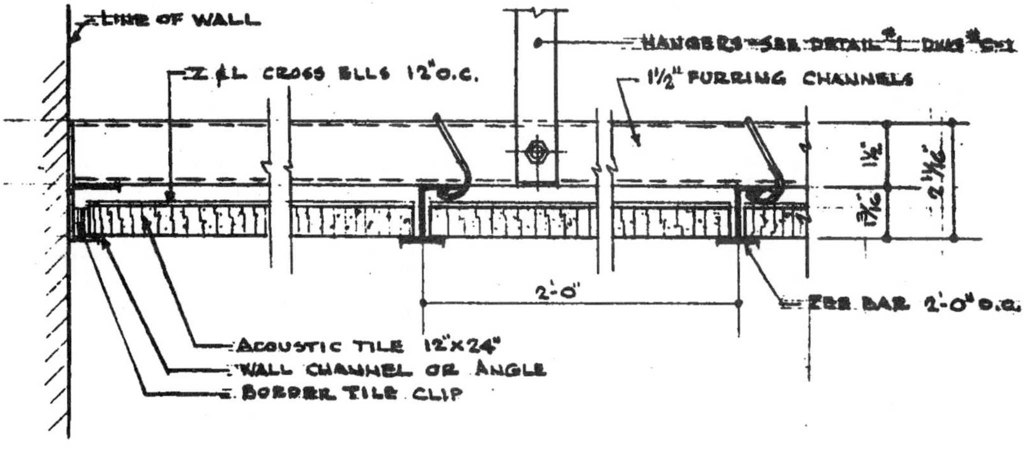

(6) ACOUSTIC TILE Z & L SUSPENSION SYSTEM

Nowhere is the personal safety and comfort of the user more important than in the design of stairs. This section, therefore, provides the planning data necessary to solve most problems of stair design. Various stair types are illustrated, including straight run, long L, wide L, double L, and narrow and wide U. Stair tables and related diagrams are provided that indicate vertical and horizontal areas, headroom clearances, and tread and riser dimensions for various stair systems. Information concerning nosings, landing widths, and so on, is also included. In addition to general planning data, this section includes barrier-free design data as well as actual construction details of wood, steel, and concrete stairs prepared by various design firms.

It should be noted that stair design must conform to local building codes. Most codes require that means-of-egress stairways not be less than 44 in (1118 mm) in width, that the least dimension of landings and platforms not be less than the required width of the stair, and that the minimum headroom in all parts of a stairway not be less than 6 ft 8 in (2032 mm) measured vertically from the tread nosing or from the floor surface of the landing or platform. In one- and two-family dwellings, most codes require that stairways not be less than 3 ft (915 mm) clear in width, and that hand rails not be less than 30 in (762 mm) nor more than 34 in (864 mm) measured vertically from the nosing of the treads and be provided on at least one side of stairways of four or more risers.

Critical Dimensions and Clearances

Dimensions indicated in Fig. 1 and listed in Table 1 determine the vertical and horizontal areas and headroom clearances for stair systems with tread and riser proportions shown. They can be used directly in developing sketches or working drawings and eliminate the need for experimental stair plans or sections. All dimensions refer to face of treads without nosing.

Tabular data refer only to minimum conditions for straight run stairs. All figures may be adjusted according to requirements of design or stair use. For similar dimensional information controlling other types of stairways, see the following pages.

Widths of stairways may vary with these requirements. For passage of furniture, minimum clear widths should be selected from Table 2.

Clearances for Furniture Passage

Width is not always a critical factor of stairway design but is important when the layout involves one or more turns with straight runs. Typical layouts for such stairways include the long L, double L, wide U, wide L, and narrow U. (See Fig. 3 for layouts and tabular data on these types.)

Stairways used solely as circulation from floor to floor can be 2 ft 0 in wide for comfortable passage of one individual or 3 ft 6 in for two, side-by-side. When furniture must be taken up and down, minimum clear widths of straight runs and landings must be carefully selected or corners will constitute obstructions in many instances.

Recommended minimum clear widths as shown in Table 2 are not necessarily the width of stairs, either rough or wall-to-wall. Projections of newels, handrails, or baseboards can obstruct passage of furniture and must be taken into account when determining actual stair widths.

Headroom is also a controlling factor of design. With minimum headroom conditions shown in Table 1, clear widths for furniture passage must be greater in most cases than may be necessary if headroom is unlimited or equal at least to the ceiling heights. This is particularly important at the first riser and at turns, where the under rake of the first stair limits the vertical clearance of the stairway below. Therefore, if stairs must be comparatively narrow and if furniture must be transported over them, headroom, or vertical clearance, must be increased accordingly.

Landing widths may be increased to provide greater turning space for maneuvering furniture. If this is done, minimum clear widths can be proportionately decreased. However, this expedient is not effective unless hallways at either end of the stairway are at least equal to the landing widths. Narrow hallways often offer as great an obstruction to furniture maneuvering as low headroom, narrow runs, or cramped turns.

Open-well stairways give more opportunity to maneuver furniture, since even very bulky but light pieces may often be lifted over rails or newels. In general, a closed-string stair should be wider than an open-string type for the same degree of convenience.

The data in Table 2 reflect safe *average* clearances for transportation of items listed. Dimensions of furniture are subject to wide variations. Consequently, the minimum clear widths recommended here are susceptible to adjustment in certain instances.

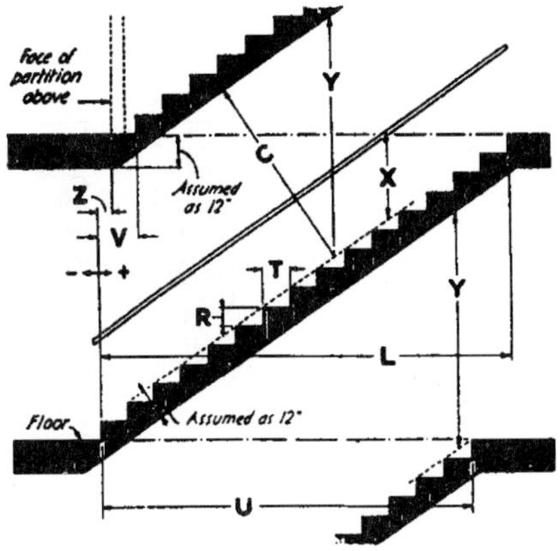

Fig. 1

Table 1 Stair table

(Dimensions in feet and inches)

Floor to Floor Height	No. of Risers	Riser R	Tread T	Total Run L	Min. Headroom Y	Handrail X	Clearance C	Partition Above Z*	First Riser Below - U	First Riser Above - V*
8'-0"	† 11	8.73"	8¼"	6'-10½"	8'-2"	2'-10"	5'-8"	-1'-10"	8'-6"	-1'-7"
	† 12	8.00	9	8-3	7-10	2-9½	5-10½	-1-8½	9-7½	-1-4
	13	**7.38**	**10½**	**10-3**	**7-7**	**2-9**	**6-2**	**-1-8½**	**11-6**	**-1-1½**
	14	**6.86**	**11½**	**12-5½**	**7-4**	**2-9**	**6-4**	**-1-7**	**13-5½**	**-9½**
	▲ 15	6.40	12½	14-7	7-3	2-9	6-7½	-1-6½	15-5½	-7½
	▲ 16	6.00	13½	16-10½	7-3	2-9	6-7½	-1-9	17-6	-8
8'-6"	† 12	8.50	8½	7-9½	8-1	2-9½	5-8½	-1-3½	8-10	-11
	† 13	7.85	9½	9-3	7-9	2-9½	5-10½	-1-1	9-10	-7½
	14	**7.29**	**10½**	**11-4½**	**7-6**	**2-9**	**6-2**	**-10½**	**12-9**	**-4**
	15	**6.80**	**11½**	**13-8½**	**7-4**	**2-9**	**6-4**	**-10½**	**13-10**	**-1½**
	▲ 16	6.38	12½	15-7½	7-3	2-9	6-5½	-7	15-5½	+3½
	▲ 17	6.00	13½	18-0	7-3	2-9	6-7	-7	17-8	+5
9'-0"	† 12	9.00	8	7-4	8-3	2-10	5-6	-11	8-1	-8
	† 13	8.31	8½	8-6	8-0	2-9½	5-9	-9	8-11½	-5
	14	**7.71**	**9½**	**10-3½**	**7-9**	**2-9½**	**6-0**	**-6**	**10-5**	**-½**
	15	**7.20**	**10½**	**12-3**	**7-6**	**2-9**	**6-2½**	**-3**	**11-10**	**+4½**
	16	**6.75**	**11½**	**14-8½**	**7-4**	**2-9**	**6-4**	**+2**	**13-11**	**+1-0**
	▲ 17	6.35	12½	16-8	7-3	2-9	6-5½	+5	15-5½	+1-4
	▲ 18	6.00	13½	19-1½	7-3	2-9	6-7½	+6	17-8	+1-6
9'-6"	† 13	8.77	8	8-0	8-2	2-10	5-5½	-3½	8-2	-½
	† 14	8.14	9	9-9	7-10	2-9½	5-9½	±0	9-5½	+5
	15	**7.60**	**9½**	**11-4½**	**7-7**	**2-9**	**5-11½**	**+4½**	**10-7**	**+10½**
	16	**7.13**	**10½**	**13-5½**	**7-5**	**2-9**	**6-2**	**+9½**	**12-2**	**+1-5½**
	17	**6.71**	**11½**	**15-8**	**7-4**	**2-9**	**6-4**	**+1-1½**	**13-11½**	**+1-11**
	▲ 18	6.33	12½	17-8½	7-3	2-9	6-5½	+1-5½	15-7	+2-4
	▲ 19	6.00	13½	20-3	7-3	2-9	6-8	+1-8	17-9	+2-7½
10'-0"	† 14	8.57	8½	9-2½	8-1	2-9½	5-8½	+2	8-8	+6
	† 15	8.00	9	10-6	7-10	2-9½	5-10½	+6½	9-7	+11
	16	**7.50**	**10**	**12-6**	**7-7**	**2-9**	**6-1**	**+1-1**	**10-11½**	**+1-6½**
	17	**7.06**	**11**	**14-8**	**7-5**	**2-9**	**6-2½**	**+1-7½**	**12-5½**	**+2-2½**
	18	**6.67**	**12**	**17-0**	**7-4**	**2-9**	**6-5**	**+2-0**	**14-3½**	**+2-9**
	▲ 19	6.32	12½	18-9	7-3	2-9	6-6	+2-5	15-8	+3-2½
	▲ 20	6.00	13½	21-4½	7-3	2-9	6-7½	+2-10	17-9	+3-8½
10'-6"	† 14	9.00	8	8-8	8-3	2-10	5-5½	+6	8-0	+9
	† 15	8.40	8½	9-11	8-1	2-9½	5-8½	+9½	8-10	+1-1
	16	7.88	9½	11-6½	7-9	2-9½	5-10½	+1-3½	9-10	+1-8½
	17	**7.41**	**10**	**13-4**	**7-7**	**2-9**	**6-1**	**+1-9½**	**11-0**	**+2-3½**
	18	**7.00**	**11**	**15-7**	**7-5**	**2-9**	**6-2½**	**+2-5**	**12-7½**	**+3-0½**
	19	**6.63**	**12**	**18-0**	**7-4**	**2-9**	**6-4½**	**+2-11**	**14-4**	**+3-6½**
	▲ 20	6.30	12½	19-9½	7-3	2-9	6-6	+3-5½	15-7	+4-3½
	▲ 21	6.00	13½	22-6	7-3	2-9	6-7½	+4-0	17-9	+5-0
11'-0"	† 15	8.80	8	9-4	8-2	2-10	5-6	+1-0½	8-1	+1-2½
	† 16	8.25	8½	10-11½	8-0	2-9½	5-10	+1-5	9-2½	+1-9
	17	**7.76**	**9½**	**12-8**	**7-9**	**2-9½**	**6-0**	**+2-0**	**10-3½**	**+2-4½**
	18	**7.33**	**10½**	**14-6½**	**7-6**	**2-9**	**6-1½**	**+2-7½**	**11-4½**	**+3-1½**
	19	**6.95**	**11**	**16-6**	**7-5**	**2-9**	**6-3**	**+3-3**	**12-8**	**+3-9**
	20	**6.60**	**12**	**19-0**	**7-4**	**2-9**	**6-5**	**+3-10½**	**14-5½**	**+4-7½**
	▲ 21	6.29	12½	20-10	7-3	2-9	6-6	+4-5	15-8	+5-3
	▲ 22	6.00	13½	23-7½	7-3	2-9	6-7½	+5-1	17-8	+6-0

*Dimensions given plus or minus, i.e., behind or in front of first riser (see Fig. 1).

Notes: Figures in boldface indicate stairs recommended for most interiors.
† indicates stairs allowable only for attics and cellars but not recommended.
▲ indicates stairs for exterior or monumental use.

STAIRS AND RAMPS
Planning Data

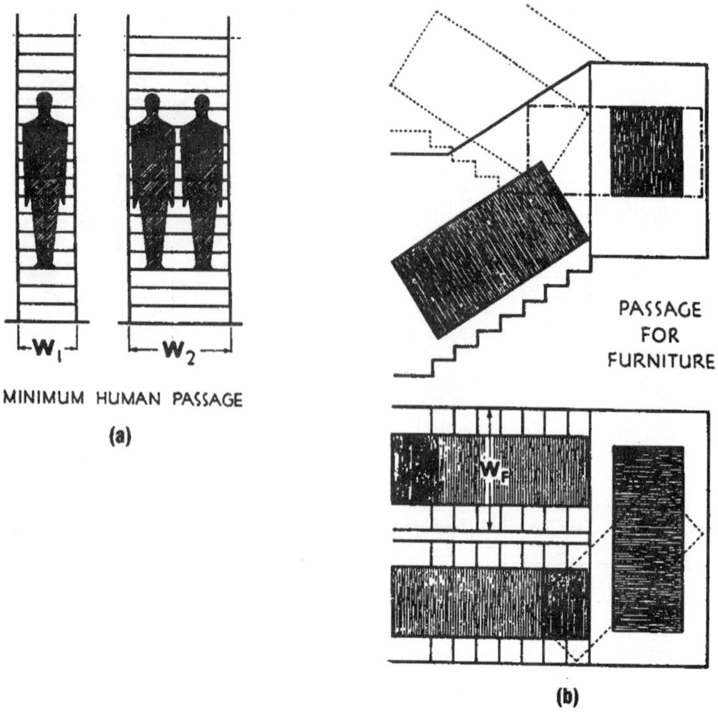

Fig. 2 Minimum stair widths. (*a*) Stairs designed for comfortable human passage only may be relatively narrow. W_1 may be 2 ft 0 in but 2 ft 6 in is better. W_2 should be at least 3 ft 6 in. (*b*) Furniture passage demands greater width. If stair landing is increased or headroom unlimited, W_F may be decreased. See Table 2

Table 2 Recommended minimum clear widths of stairs (W_F) for furniture movement*

Furniture		Min. Headroom ▲		Unlimited Headroom		
Article	Size	Wide U Type	Narrow U Type	Wide and Narrow U	Narrow U only● Stair	Narrow U only● Landing
Double Bed Box Spring	4'-6"x 6'-6"x 8"	3'- 2"	3'- 2"	2'- 3"		
Dressing Table	1'-10"x 4'-0"x 2'-6"	2'- 5"	2'- 5"	2'- 5"		
Bureau	2'-0"x 4'-0"x 3'-0"	2'- 8"	2'- 8"	2'- 8"		
Chiffonier	1'-8"x 3'-4"x 4'-8"	2'- 6"	2'- 6"	2'- 6"		
Chest of Drawers	1'-9"x 3'-4"x 4'-8"	2'- 7"	2'- 7"	2'- 7"		
Divan - Club	3'-6"x 7'-2"x 2'-9"	4'- 8"	4'- 8"	3'- 4"	3'-0"	3'-8"
Divan - Average	3'-0"x 6'-8"x 2'-6"	4'- 4"	4'- 4"	2'-11"		
Piano - Concert Grand	9'-0"x 5'-4"x 1'-8"	4'- 8"	4'- 8"	3'- 2" ■	3'-0" ■	3'-4" ■
Piano - Music Room Grand	7'-3"x 5'-2"x 1'-6"	3'-10"	3'-10"	3'- 0"		
Piano - Drawing Room Grand	6'-9"x 5'-0"x 1'-4"	3'- 6"	3'- 6"	2'-10"		
Piano - Baby Grand	5'-8"x 4'-10"x 1'-2"	3'- 0"	3'- 0"	2'- 8"		
Piano - Standard Upright	2'-2"x 5'-10"x 4'-6"	4'- 0"	3'- 9"	3'- 3"	3'-0"	3'-6"
Highboy - Large	2'-0"x 3'-6"x 7'-6"	4'- 4"	4'- 4"	2'-10"		
Highboy - Average	1'-8"x 3'-4"x 6'-0'	3'- 6"	3'- 6"	2'- 6"		
Secretary - Large	1'-10"x 3'-8"x 7'-2"	4'- 0"	4'- 0"	2'-10"		
Secretary - Average	1'-10"x 3'-0"x 6'-10"	3'-10"	3'-10"	2'- 6"		
Sideboard	1'-9"x 5'-0"x 3'-2"	2'- 6"	2'- 6"	2'- 6"		
Buffet	2'-1"x 3'-3"x 6'-6"	4'- 0"	4'- 0"	2'-10"		
Dresser	1'-9"x 6'-0"x 5'-6"	4'- 4"	3'- 6"	3'- 4"	3'-0"	3'-8"
Table (6 People)	3'-6"x 5'-0"x 2'-6"	3'- 2"	3'- 2"	3'- 2"	3'-0"	3'-4"
Table (8 People)	3'-6"x 7'-0"x 2'-6"	4'- 8"	4'- 4"	3'- 2"	3'-0"	3-4
Table (10 People) Rd.	6'-4" Diam.	4'- 8"	4'- 8"	3'- 0"		
Desk - Slope Top	2'-6"x 3'-8"x 3'-4"	3'- 3"	3'- 2"	3'- 2"	3'-0"	3'-4"
Desk - Flat Top	3'-0"x 5'-6"x 2'-6"	3'- 2"	3'- 0"	3'- 0"		
Desk - Executive's	3'-2"x 6'-0"x 2'-6"	4'- 2"	4'- 2"	3'- 1"	3'-0"	3'-2"
Trunk - Wardrobe	1'-11"x 2'-6"x 3'-7"	2'- 5"	2'- 5"	2'- 5"		

*Clear width between faces of rails, newels, etc., or between rail or newel and finish wall.
Notes: ▲ Headroom limited to minimum for comfortable human passage (see Table 1 and text).
● Narrow stairs and wide landings.
■ Absolute minimum not recommended (see text).

Purpose

The six diagrams in Fig. 3 represent unit plans for types of non-winder stairways which are most frequently encountered in the average residential planning problem. Tabular information with each was developed from data contained in Table 1.

Unit plans are drawn to ⅛-in scale and therefore can be supplied directly as a check of stair layouts to sketch plans and elevations. Each represents an average condition with a stair pitch well within the comfort zone. The basis is a 9 ft 6 in floor-to-floor height with 16 risers each 7.13-in in height. Width is 3 ft 0 in from wall to wall.

Tabular data with each unit plan indicate dimensional variations which occur when stairways of substantially similar pitches are planned for floor-to-floor heights from 8 to 11 ft.

Width is the only critical dimension missing from this unit plan information. This varies with requirements of design and stair use and should be selected from data in Table 2. Width is a dimension controlling critical clearances on all stairs that contain a turn.

Winders have not been included in these unit plans because they represent a stair condition generally regarded as undesirable. However, use of winders is sometimes necessary due to cramped space. In such instances, winders should be adjusted to replace landings so that the narrow portions of treads at the inside of the turn are at least equal to ¾ in T. When this is done, dimensions of L_1 and L_2 are decreased by approximately ½T, the exact figure depending on the width selected. The practice of adding a winder-riser to bisect the landing diagonally from the corner of a newel is to be avoided in all cases, for it produces a dangerously narrow step in a particularly undesirable place.

Application of Unit Plans

Diagrammatic data can be used on sketches as a graphic check as noted. Tabular data can be applied to either sketches or working drawings to eliminate the necessity of developing experimental stairway sections to determine run, proportional rise, horizontal and vertical areas, and location of under-rake minimum headroom.

Dimensional data have been confined to a single pitch for all floor-to-floor heights. The pitch indicated is that most generally desirable for human comfort. Data for other pitches listed as tread and riser proportions in Table 1 can be substituted for values of L_1, L_2, and M.

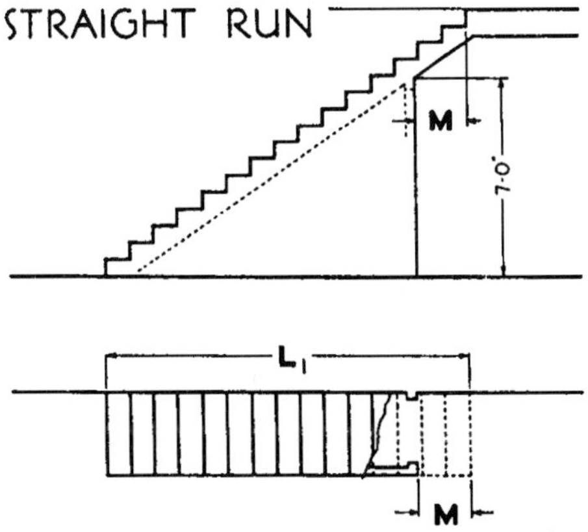

HEIGHT FLOOR TO FLOOR	NO OF RISERS	RISER	TREAD	L_1	M
8'-0"	13	7.38	10¼"	10'-3"	—
8'-6"	14	7.29	10½"	11'-4½"	4½"
9'-0"	15	7.20	10½"	12'-3"	1'-1½"
9'-6"	16	7.13	10¾"	13'-5¼"	1'-11¼"
10'-0"	17	7.06	11"	14'-8"	2'-9½"
10'-6"	18	7.00	11"	15'-7"	3'-7"
11'-0"	19	6.95	11"	16'-6"	4'-5"

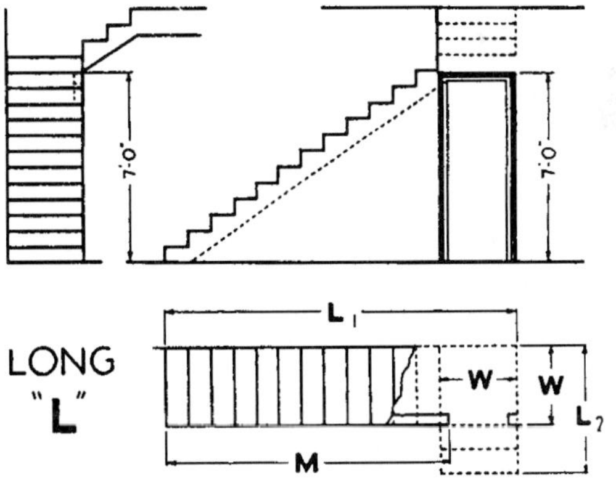

HEIGHT FLOOR TO FLOOR	Nº RISERS	RISER	TREAD	Nº RISERS	L_1	Nº RISERS	L_2	M
8'-0"	13	7.38	10¼"	13	10'-3" + W	0	W	10'-3"
8'-6"	14	7.29	10½"	13	10'-6" + W	1	W	10'-6"
9'-0"	15	7.20	10½"	13	10'-6" + W	2	10½" + W	10'-6"
9'-6"	16	7.13	10¾"	13	10'-9" + W	3	1'-9½" + W	11'-0"
10'-0"	17	7.06	11"	13	11'-0" + W	4	2'-9" + W	11'-4"
10'-6"	18	7.00	11"	13	11'-0" + W	5	3'-8" + W	11'-5"
11'-0"	19	6.95	11"	13	11'-0" + W	6	4'-7" + W	11'-6"

Fig. 3

STAIRS AND RAMPS
Planning Data

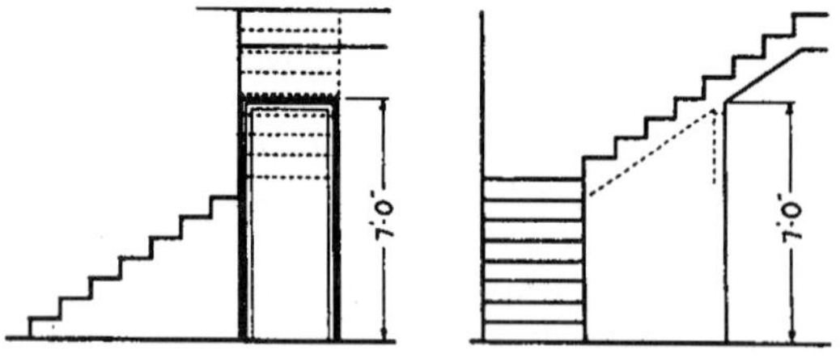

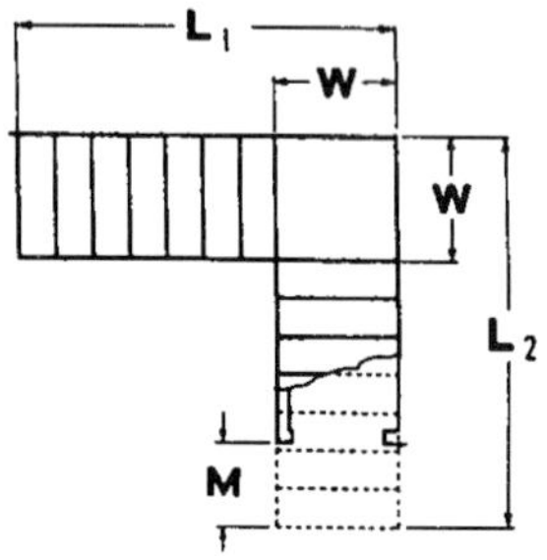

WIDE "L"

HEIGHT FLOOR TO FLOOR	Nº RISERS	RISER	TREAD	Nº RISERS	L_1	Nº RISERS	L_2	M
8'-0"	13	7.38	10¼"	7	5'-1½"+W	6	4'-3¼"+W	–
8'-6"	14	7.29	10½"	7	5'-3"+W	7	5'-3"+W	4½"
9'-0"	15	7.20	10½"	8	6'-1½"+W	7	5'-3"+W	1'-1½"
9'-6"	16	7.13	10¾"	8	6'-3¼"+W	8	6'-3¼"+W	1'-11¼"
10'-0"	17	7.06	11"	9	7'-4"+W	8	6'-5"+W	2'-9½"
10'-6"	18	7.00	11"	9	7'-4"+W	9	7'-4"+W	3'-7"
11'-0"	19	6.95	11"	10	8'-3"+W	9	7'-4"+W	4'-5"

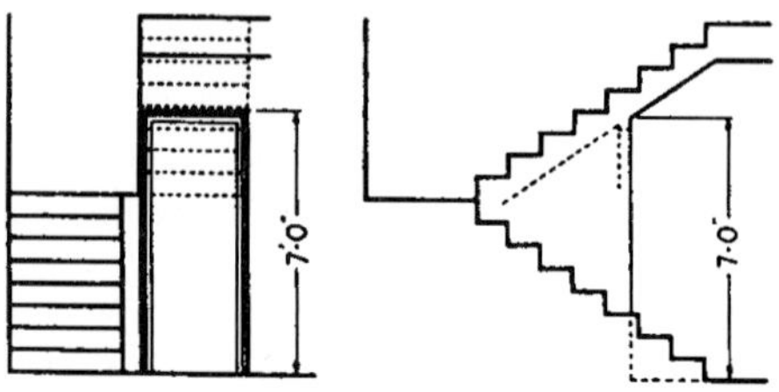

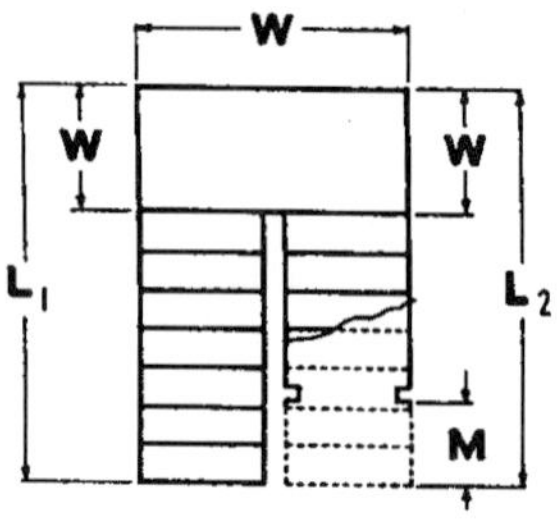

NARROW "U"

HEIGHT FLOOR TO FLOOR	Nº RISERS	RISER	TREAD	Nº RISERS	L_1	Nº RISERS	L_2	M
8'-0"	13	7.38	10¼"	7	5'-1½"+W	6	4'-3¼"+W	–
8'-6"	14	7.29	10½"	7	5'-3"+W	7	5'-3"+W	4½"
9'-0"	15	7.20	10½"	8	6'-1½"+W	7	5'-3"+W	1'-1½"
9'-6"	16	7.13	10¾"	8	6'-3¼"+W	8	6'-3¼"+W	1'-11¼"
10'-0"	17	7.06	11"	9	7'-4"+W	8	6'-5"+W	2'-9½"
10'-6"	18	7.00	11"	9	7'-4"+W	9	7'-4"+W	3'-7"
11'-0"	19	6.95	11"	10	8'-3"+W	9	7'-4"+W	4'-5"

DOUBLE "L"

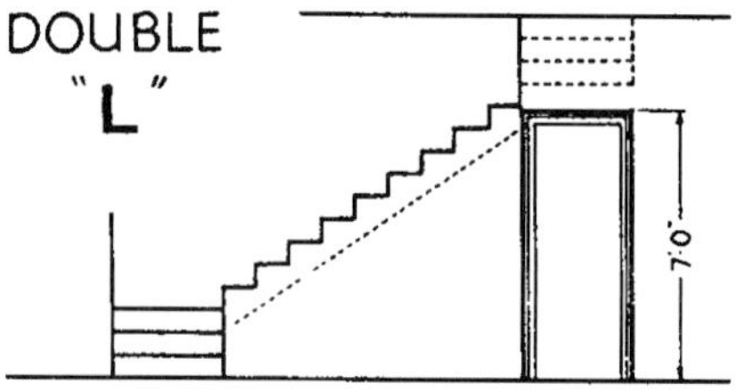

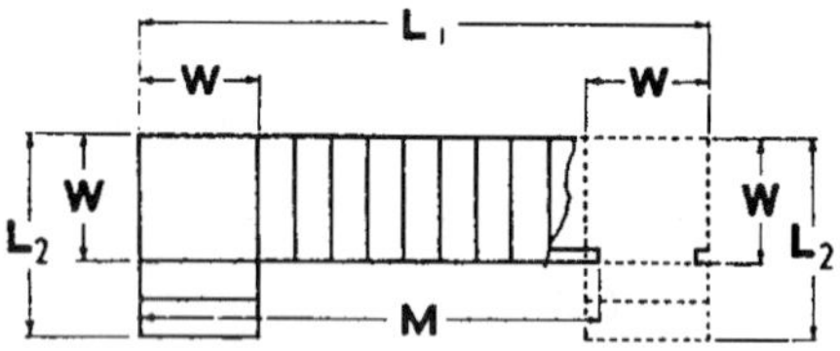

HEIGHT FLOOR TO FLOOR	Nº RISERS	RISER	TREAD	Nº RISERS	L_1	Nº RISERS	L_2	M
8'-0"	13	7.38	10¼"	13	10'-3"+2W	0	W	10'-3"+W
8'-6"	14	7.29	10½"	12	9'-7½"+2W	1	W	9'-7½"+W
9'-0"	15	7.20	10½"	11	8'-9"+2W	2	10½"+W	8'-9"+W
9'-6"	16	7.13	10¾"	10	8'-0¾"+2W	3	1'-9½"+W	8'-3¾"+W
10'-0"	17	7.06	11"	9	7'-4"+2W	4	2'-9"+W	7'-8"+W
10'-6"	18	7.00	11"	8	6'-5"+2W	5	3'-8"+W	6'-10"+W
11'-0"	19	6.95	11"	7	5'-6"+2W	6	4'-7"+W	6'-0"+W

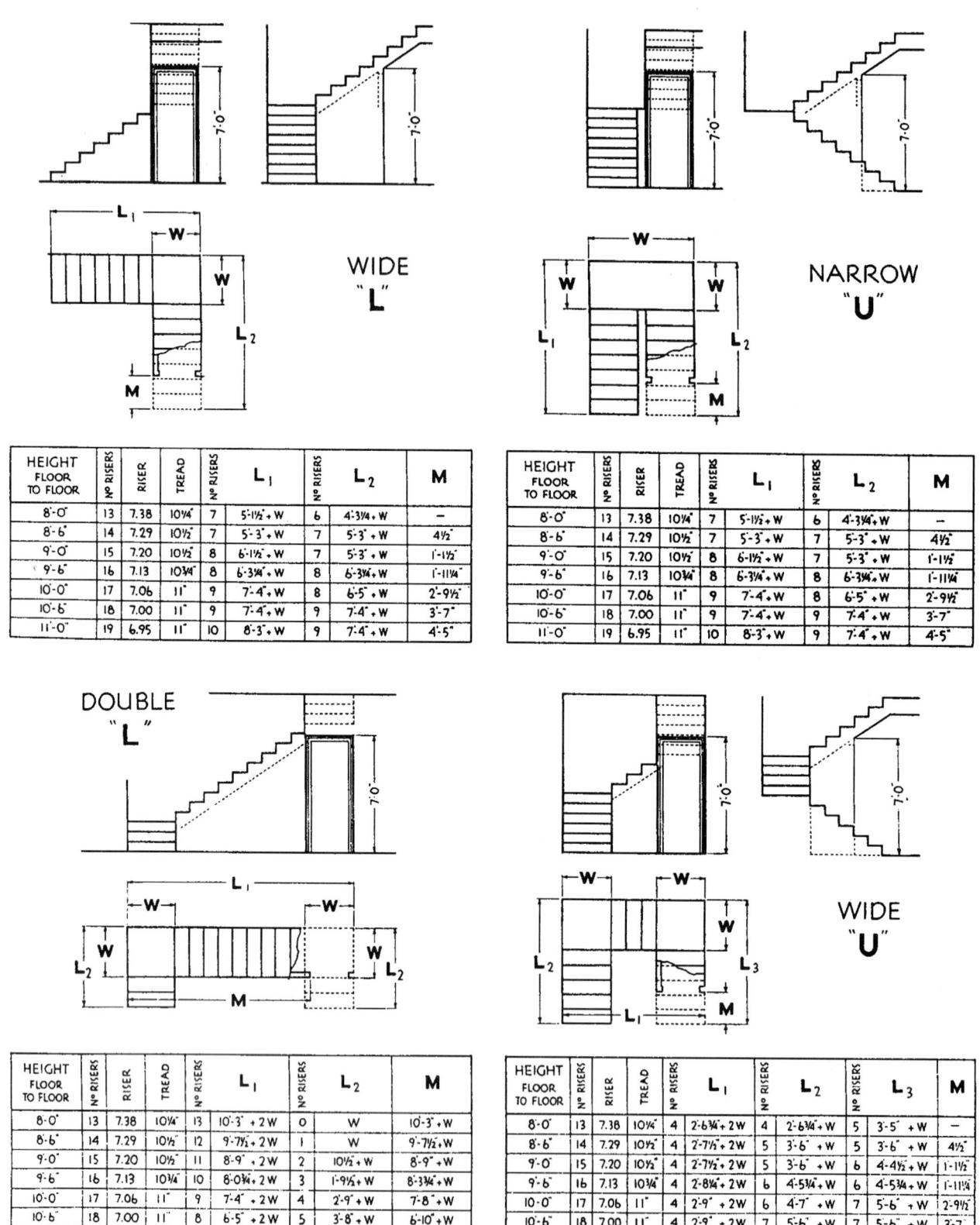

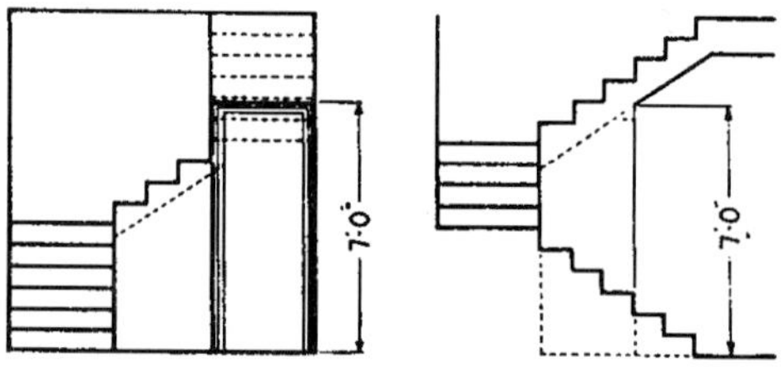

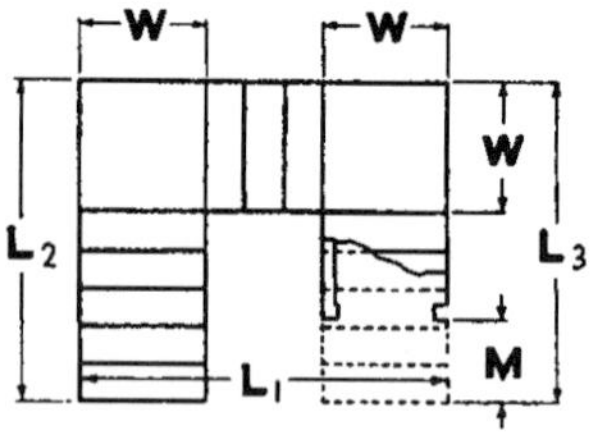

WIDE "U"

HEIGHT FLOOR TO FLOOR	Nº RISERS	RISER	TREAD	Nº RISERS	L_1	Nº RISERS	L_2	Nº RISERS	L_3	M
8'-0"	13	7.38	10¼"	4	2'-6¾"+2W	4	2'-6¾"+W	5	3'-5"+W	–
8'-6"	14	7.29	10½"	4	2'-7½"+2W	5	3'-6"+W	5	3'-6"+W	4½"
9'-0"	15	7.20	10½"	4	2'-7½"+2W	5	3'-6"+W	6	4'-4½"+W	1'-1½"
9'-6"	16	7.13	10¾"	4	2'-8¼"+2W	6	4'-5¾"+W	6	4'-5¾"+W	1'-11¼"
10'-0"	17	7.06	11"	4	2'-9"+2W	6	4'-7"+W	7	5'-6"+W	2'-9½"
10'-6"	18	7.00	11"	4	2'-9"+2W	7	5'-6"+W	7	5'-6"+W	3'-7"
11'-0"	19	6.95	11"	4	2'-9"+2W	7	5'-6"+W	8	6'-5"+W	4'-5"

Fig. 3 ***(Continued)***

Nosings

Nosings extending ¾ to 1½ in (usually 1¼ in) beyond the face of the riser are functionally necessary and are required by most building codes. Nosings may be provided by extending the treads or by sloping the risers. The latter method is customary in concrete stairs because of easier forming, and in any type of stair where carpet is to be installed. This type of nosing is also recommended for stairs to be used by people with disabilities.

Stairway Layouts

Comfortable stairways cannot be designed except in relation to dimensions of the average human figure. As applied to stairways, these dimensions and the equivalent of the average comfortable walking stride of about 24 in fix the gradient of stairways, the proportional relation of treads and risers, the height of the handrail, and the minimum necessary headroom.

Figure 4 indicates the influence of human figure dimensions and suggests the desirability of varying ceiling clearances and handrail heights according to variations in stair gradients. These variations are included in Table 3.

Treads and risers in curved stairs should be proportioned on an assumed *line of travel* 18 in from the inner (smaller radius) handrail.

All building codes have strict specifications for stairs which are required exits. The National Building Code of the American Insurance Association and the New York City code both require that treads and risers be proportioned by the formula T × R = 70 to 75, with risers not over 7¾ in high and treads not less than 9 in wide, exclusive of nosings. Minimum stair width for most uses is 44 in, based on two 22-in lanes of traffic. Handrails are required on both sides and may project a maximum of 3½ in into the required width. Winders and open risers are prohibited. The maximum vertical rise permitted between landings is 12 ft; in places of assembly it is 8 ft. Stairs must be designed for a live load of 100 lb/ft².

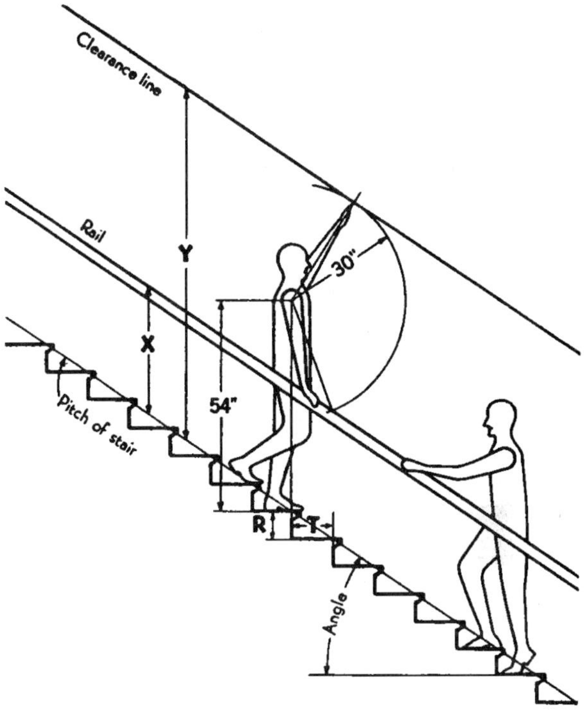

Fig. 4

Table 3 Dimensions for stairways

Step dimensions		Gradient designations		Headroom*	Handrail height
Riser **R** in inches	Tread **T** in inches	Per cent grade	Angle in degrees, minutes	**Y** in inches	**X** in inches
5	16	31.25	17 - 21	85	33½
5¼	15½	33.87	18 - 43	86	
5½	14¾	37.28	20 - 27		
5¾	14	41.07	22 - 20		
6	13½	44.44	23 - 58	87	33
6¼	13	48.07	25 - 40		
6½	12¼	53.06	27 - 57	88	
6¾	11¾	57.44	29 - 52		
7	11	63.63	32 - 28	89	
7¼	10½	69.04	34 - 37	90	
7½	10	75	36 - 52	91	
7¾	9½	81.57	39 - 12	93	33½
8	9	88.88	41 - 38	94	
8¼	8½	97.05	44 - 9	96	
8½	8¼	103.02	45 - 51	97	
8¾	8⅛	107.07	46 - 57	98	34
9	8	112.5	48 - 22	99	

NOTES

1. 7" by 11" is the proportion by which all steps are laid out
2. Risers from 5" to 6½" are suitable for exterior and "grand" interior stairs
3. Risers from 6¾" to 7¾" are most comfortable and most suitable for interior stairs
4. Risers for cellar and attic stairs may be up to 9" high
5. Width - minimum for single-file travel, 30"
6. Width - minimum for comfort, 36"
7. Width - desirable (for furniture passage etc.), 42"
8. Consult local building codes on all stair problems

Minimum for head clearance only can be safely taken as 84 in. for all gradients; HUD permits 80 in.

WOOD STAIRS

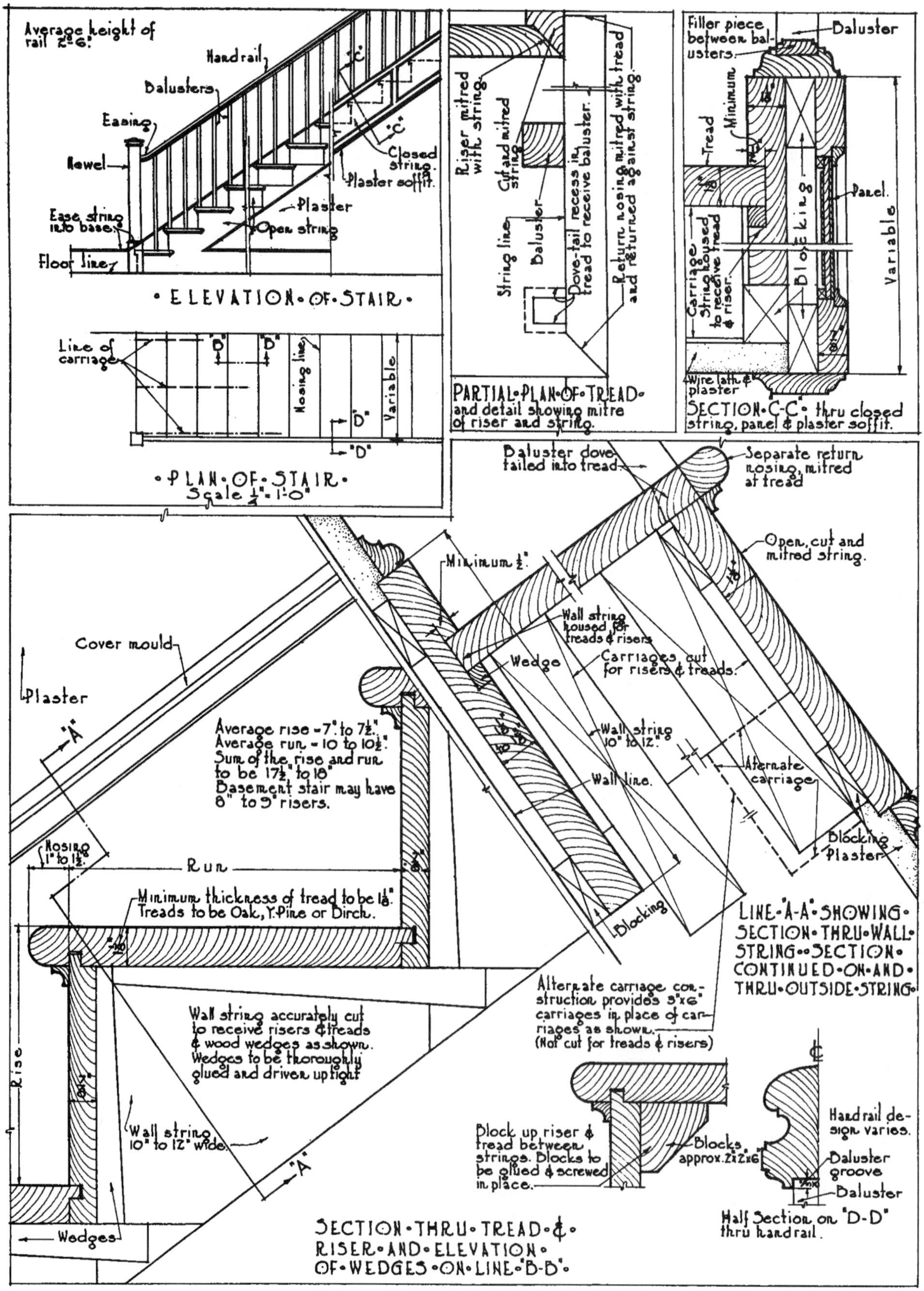
Average height of rail 2'-6".
Handrail
Balusters
Easing
Newel
Ease string into base.
Floor line
"C"
Closed string.
Plaster soffit.
Plaster
Open string
• ELEVATION • OF • STAIR •
Line of carriage
"D"
Nosing line
Variable
• PLAN • OF • STAIR •
Scale 1/4" = 1'-0"
Riser mitred with string.
Cut and mitred string
String line
Baluster
Dove-tail recess in tread to receive baluster.
Return nosing mitred with tread and returned against string.
PARTIAL • PLAN • OF • TREAD •
and detail showing mitre of riser and string.
Filler piece between balusters.
Baluster
Minimum
Tread
Panel.
Variable
Blocking
Carriage
String housed to receive tread & riser.
Wire lath & plaster
SECTION • C-C • thru closed string, panel & plaster soffit.
Baluster dove tailed into tread.
Separate return nosing, mitred at tread
Open, cut and mitred string.
Minimum 1/2".
Wall string housed for treads & risers
Wedge
Carriages cut for risers & treads.
Cover mould
Plaster
"A"
Average rise - 7" to 7 1/2".
Average run - 10 to 10 1/2".
Sum of the rise and run to be 17 1/2" to 18"
Basement stair may have 8" to 9" risers.
Wall string 10" to 12".
Wall line.
Alternate carriage
Blocking
Plaster
Nosing 1" to 1 1/8".
Run
Minimum thickness of tread to be 1 1/8".
Treads to be Oak, Y. Pine or Birch.
Blocking
LINE • A-A • SHOWING • SECTION • THRU • WALL • STRING • • SECTION • CONTINUED • ON • AND • THRU • OUTSIDE • STRING •
Rise
Wall string accurately cut to receive risers & treads & wood wedges as shown. Wedges to be thoroughly glued and driven up tight
Wall string 10" to 12" wide.
Alternate carriage construction provides 3"x6" carriages in place of carriages as shown. (Not cut for treads & risers)
Block up riser & tread between strings. Blocks to be glued & screwed in place.
Blocks approx. 2 1/2x2x6
Handrail design varies.
Baluster groove
Baluster
Half Section on "D-D" thru handrail.
Wedges
SECTION • THRU • TREAD • & • RISER • AND • ELEVATION • OF • WEDGES • ON • LINE • "B-B" •

NO. D-5.. DETAILS OF MAIN STAIRWAY.. TWO STORY COLONIAL HOUSE

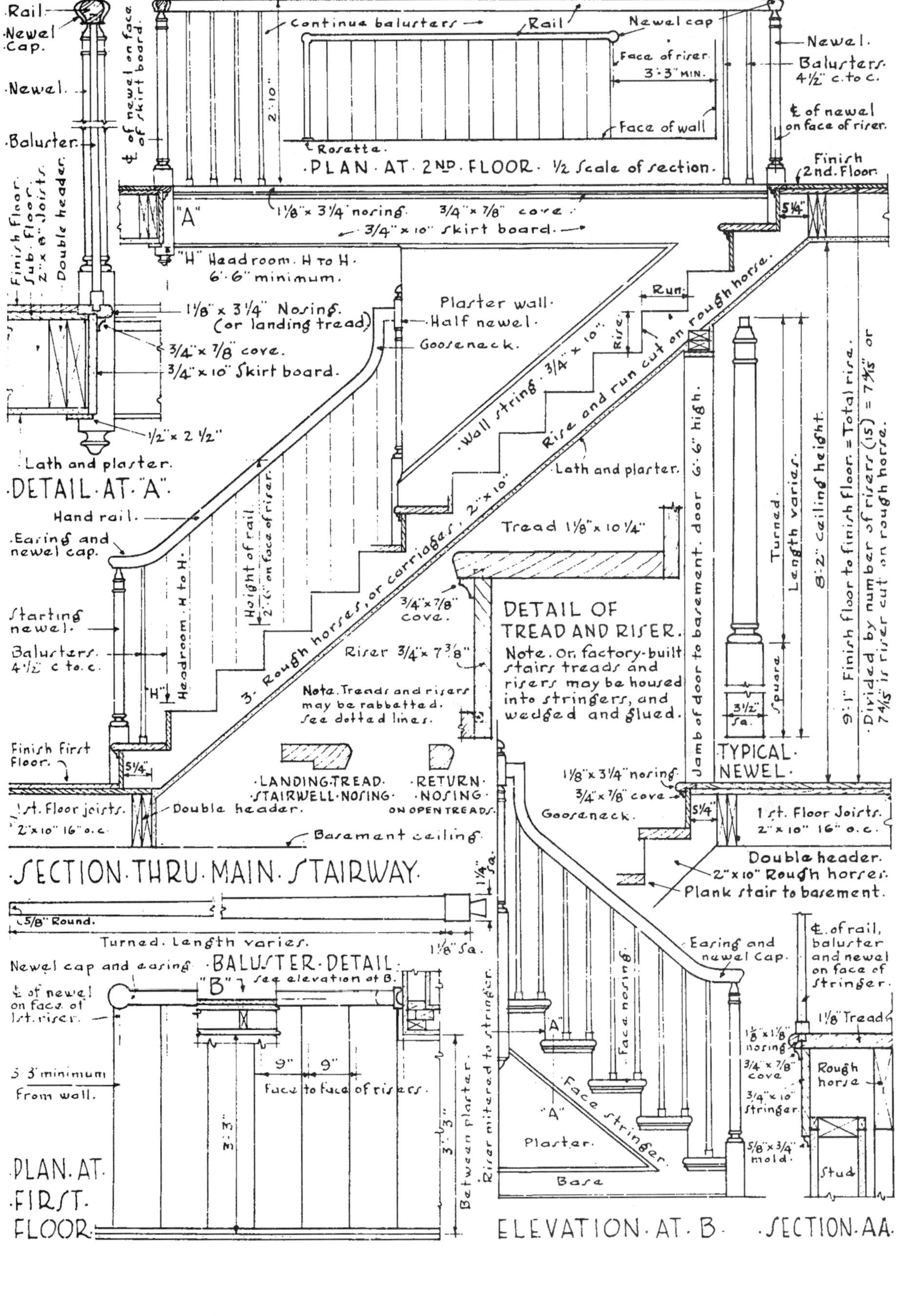

STAIRS AND RAMPS

Miscellaneous Stair Details

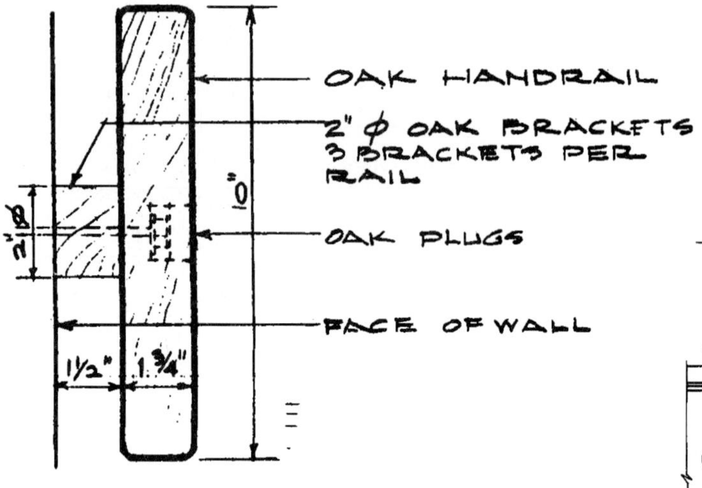

OAK HANDRAIL

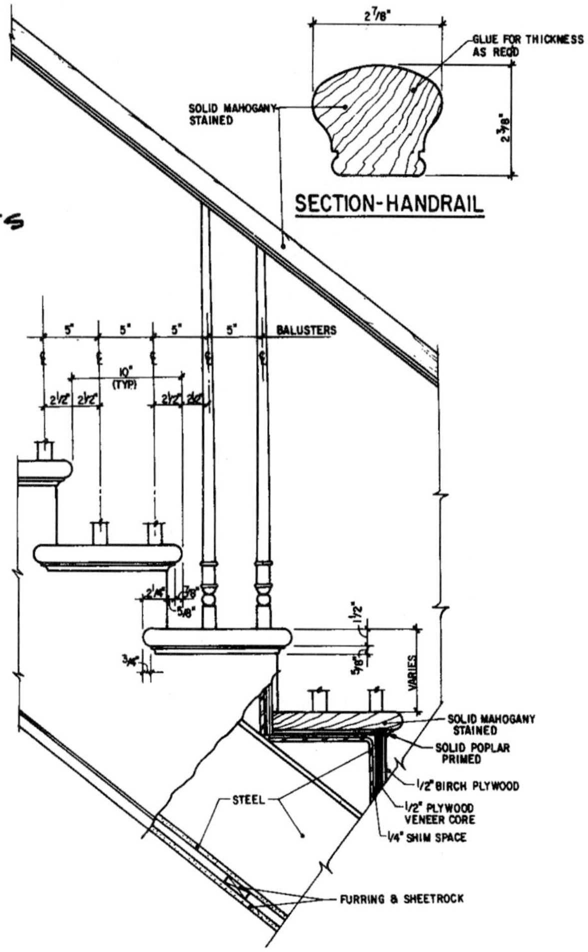

PARTIAL ELEVATION STAIR

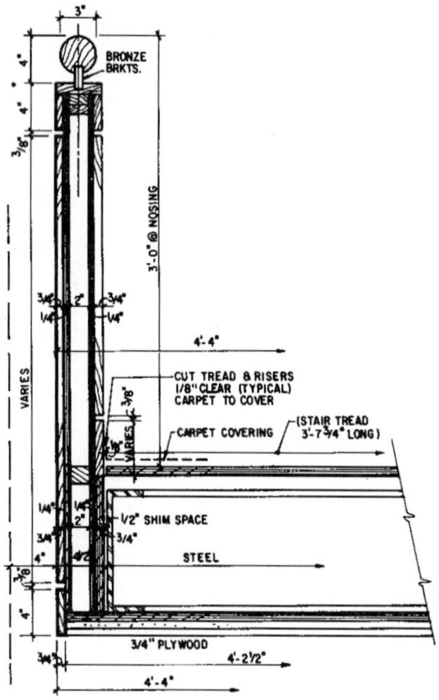

SECTION AT STAIRS

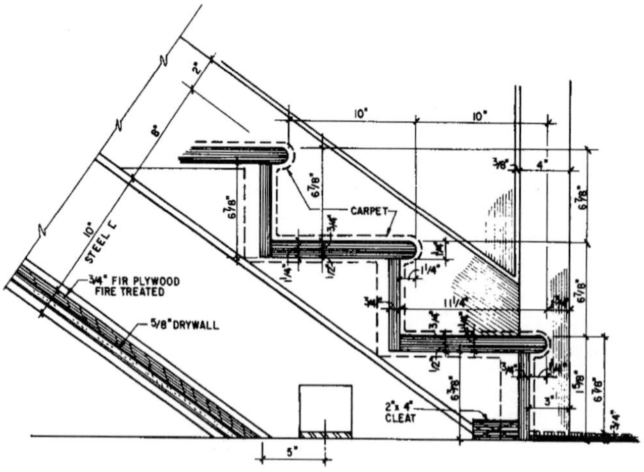

TYPICAL SECTION AT STAIRS

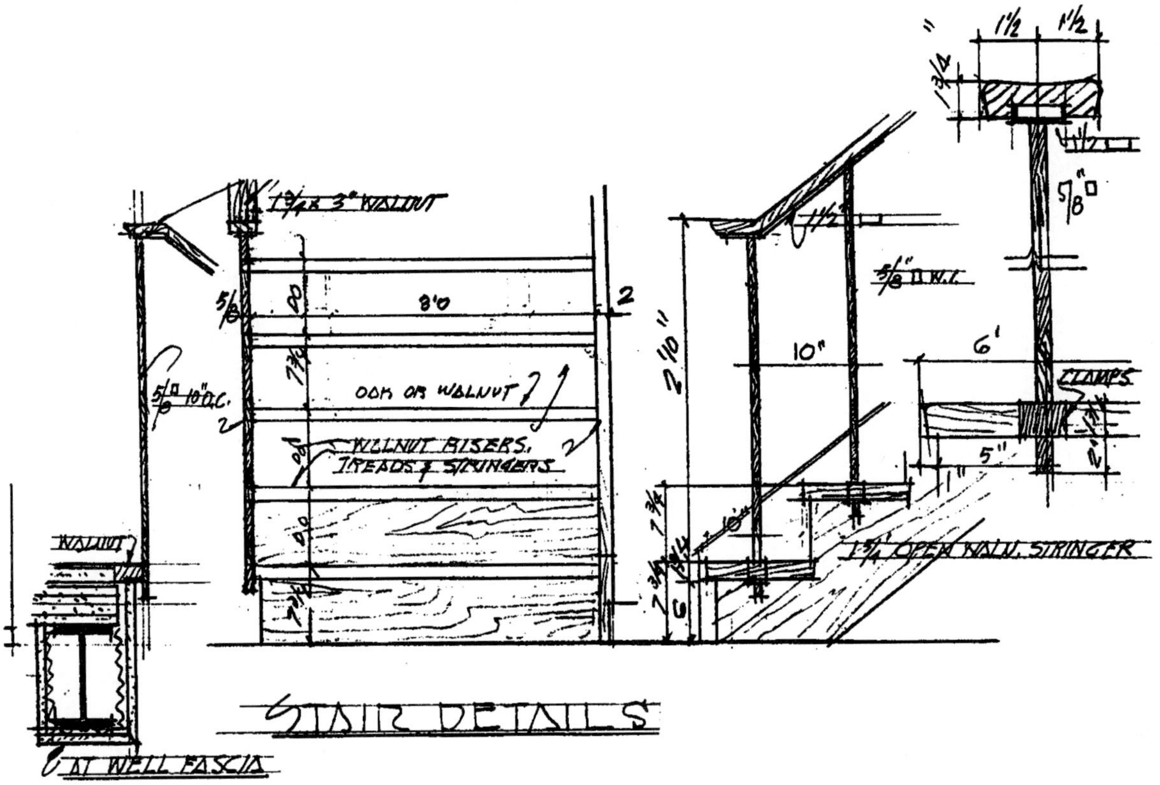

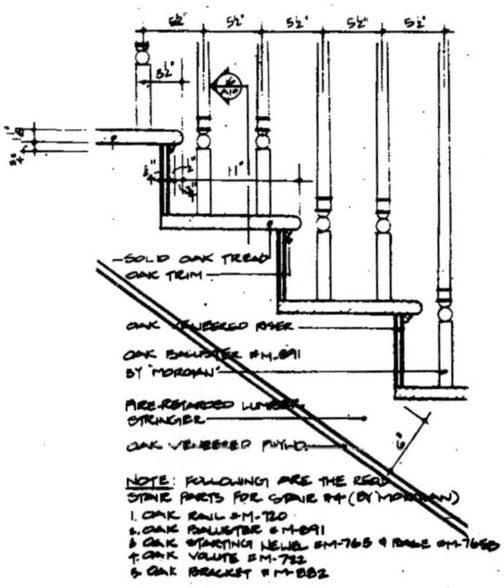

15/A10 DETAIL of TREAD & RISER at STAIR #4
SCALE: 3/4"=1'-0"

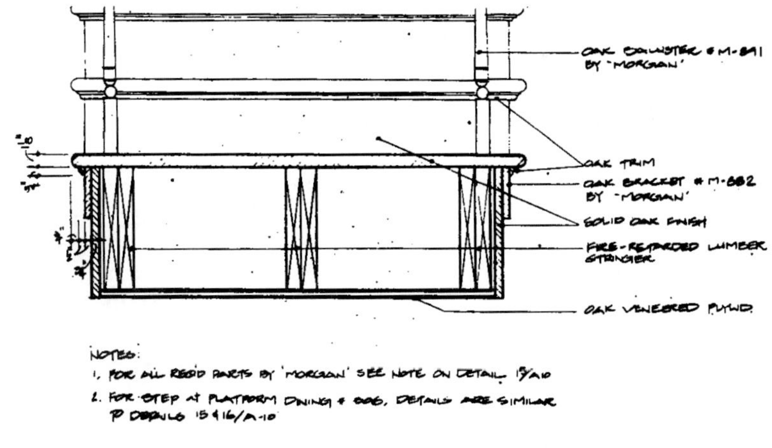

16/A10 DETAIL of STRINGER at STAIR #4
SCALE: 1½"=1'-0"

STAIRS AND RAMPS

Miscellaneous Stair Details

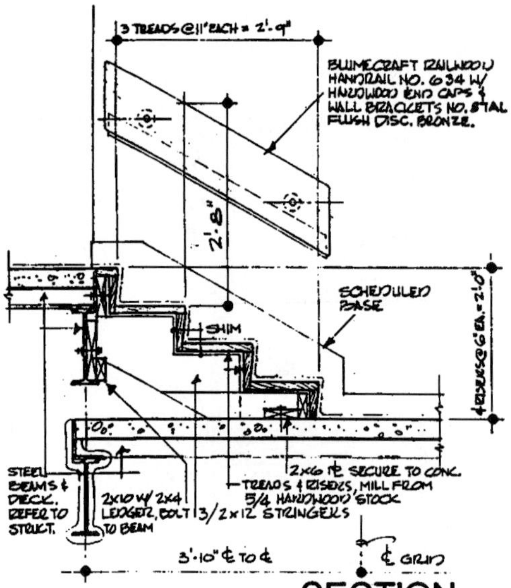

SECTION

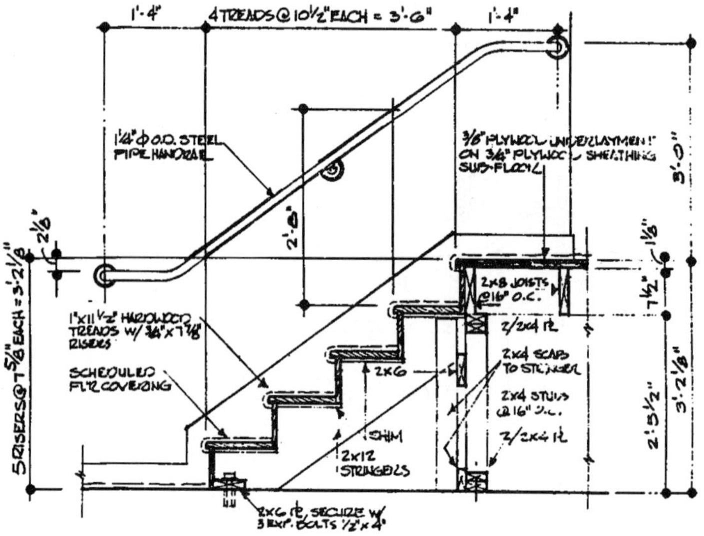

SECTION

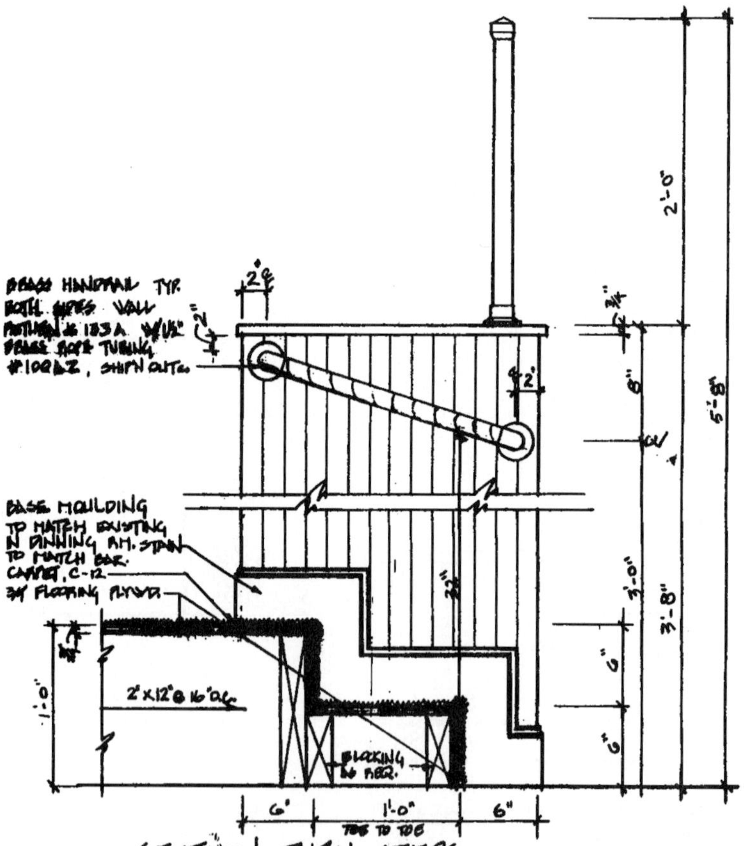

SECTION THRU STEPS

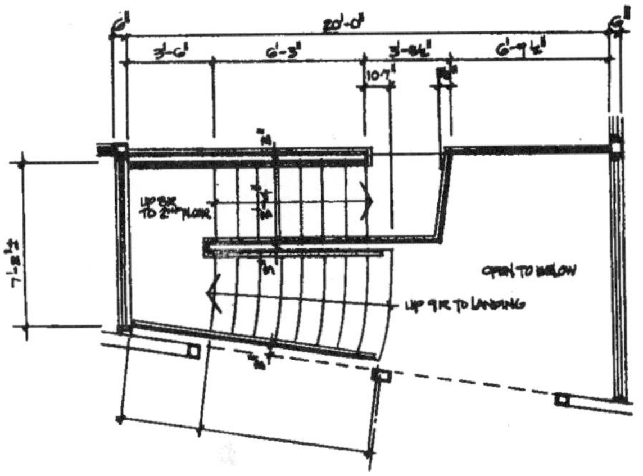

1 A16 PLAN ¼" = 1'-0"

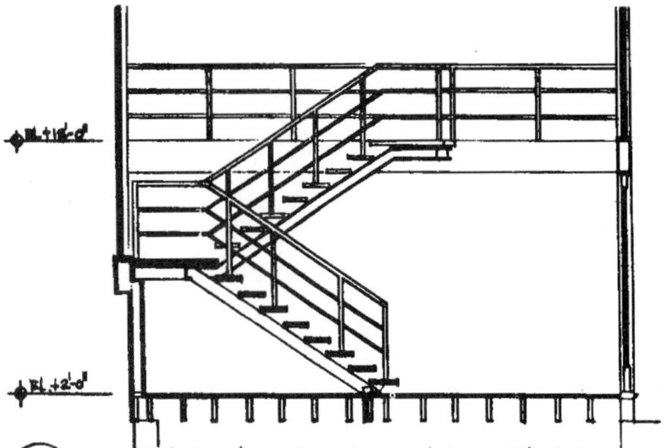

3 A16 SECTION THRU' LOWER FLIGHT LOOKING NORTH ¼" = 1'-0"

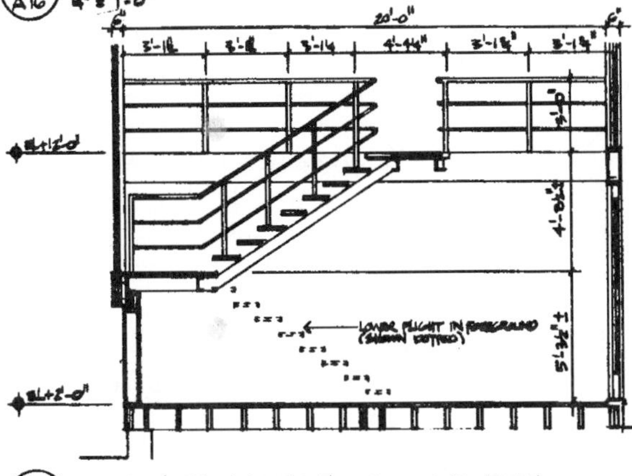

2 A16 SECTION THRU UPPER FLIGHT LOOKING NORTH ¼" = 1'-0"

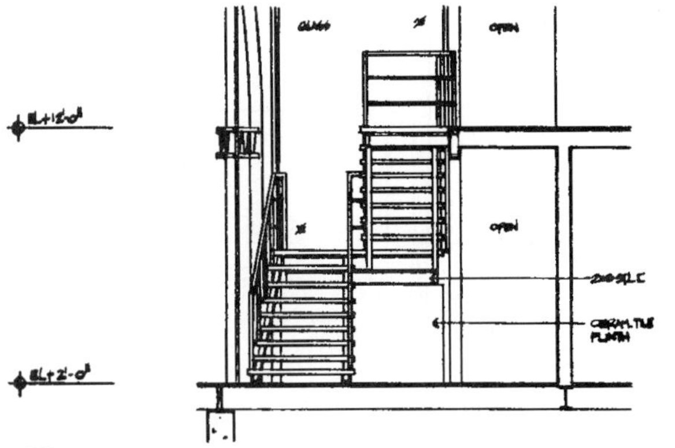

4 A16 WEST ELEVATION ¼" = 1'-0"

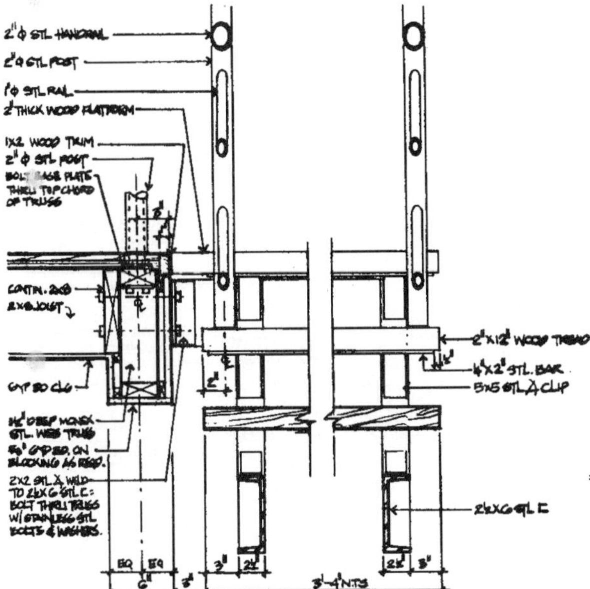

6 A16 CROSS SECTION THRU STAIR 1½" = 1'-0"

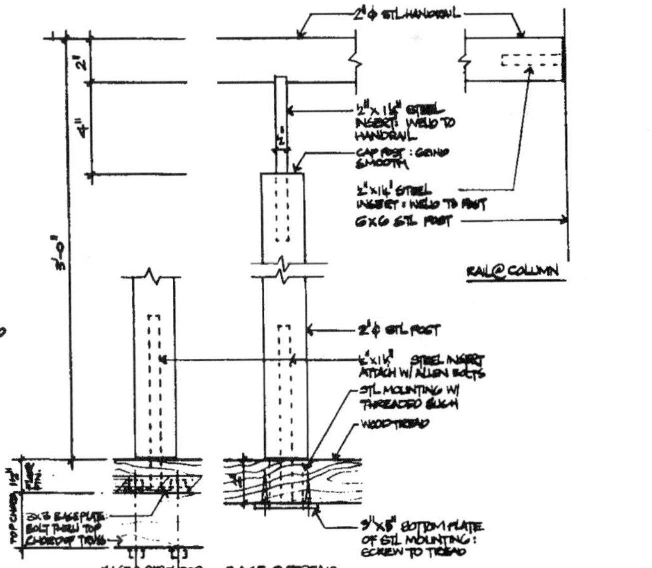

7 A16 HANDRAIL POST: DETAILS 3" = 1'-0"

STAIRS AND RAMPS

Wood and Steel Stairs

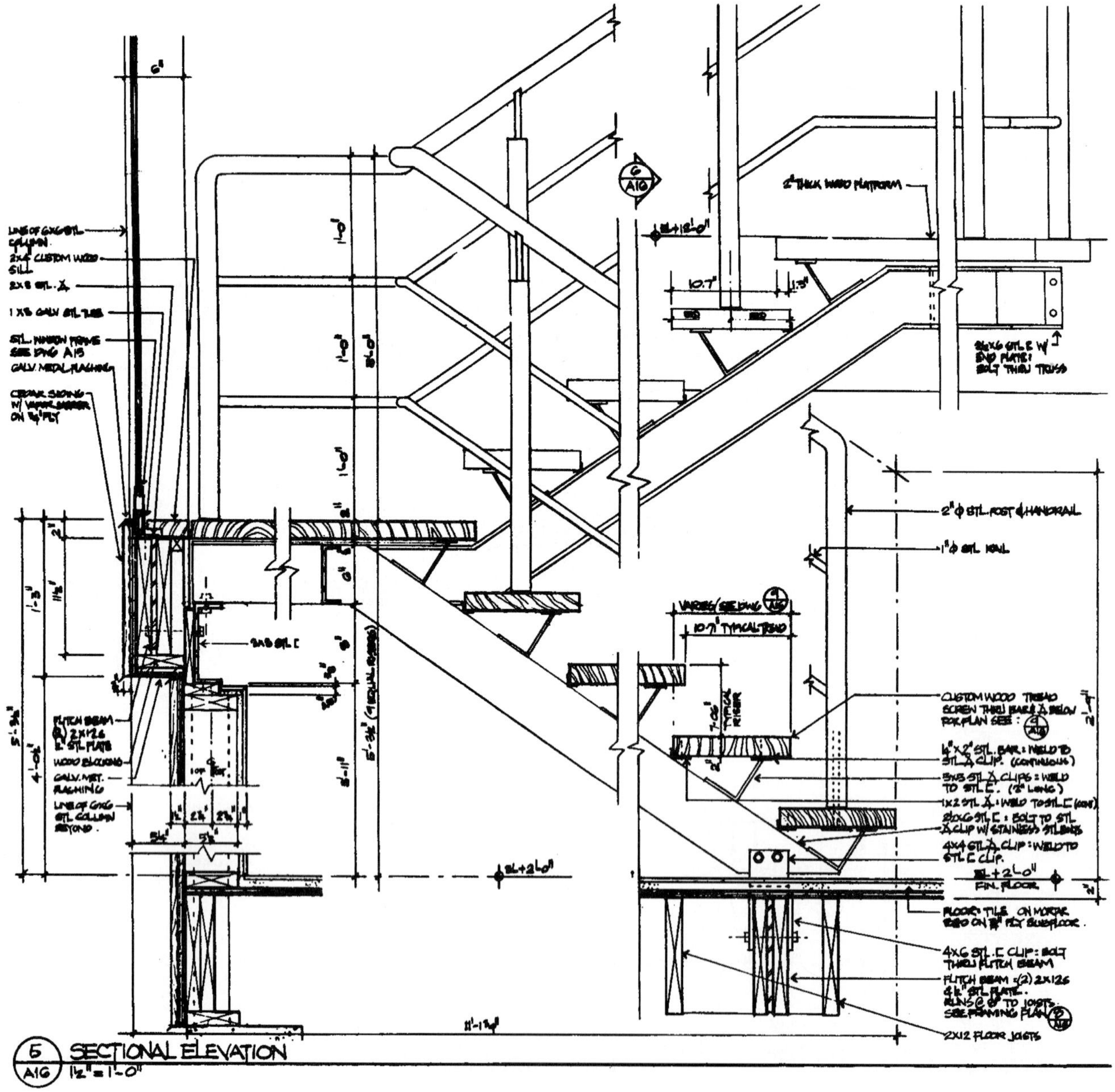

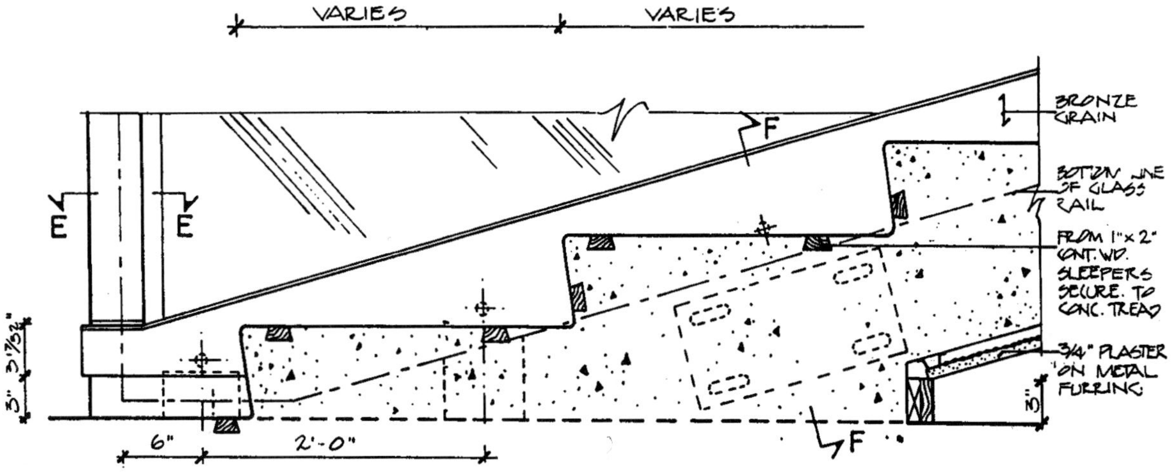
VARIES
VARIES
BRONZE GRAIN
F
BOTTOM LINE OF GLASS RAIL
E
E
FROM 1" x 2" CONT. WD. SLEEPERS SECURE. TO CONC. TREAD
3/4" PLASTER ON METAL FURRING
3"
3 7/32"
6"
2'-0"
F

DD Section

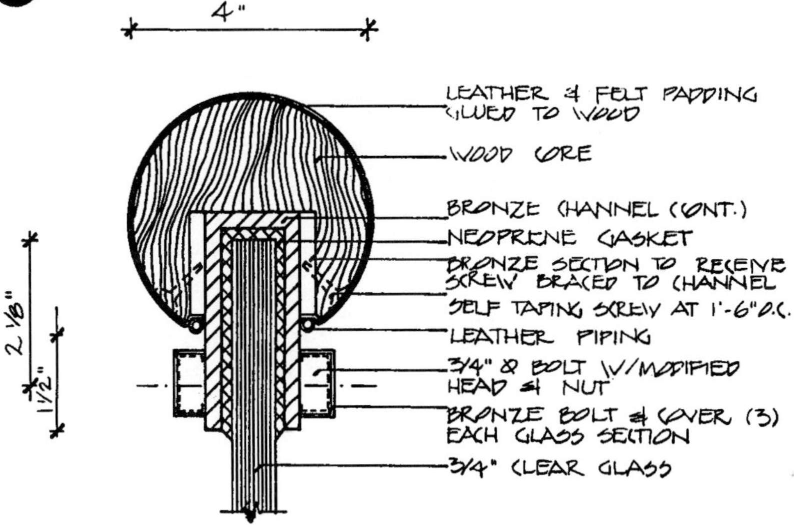
4"
LEATHER & FELT PADDING GLUED TO WOOD
WOOD CORE
BRONZE CHANNEL (CONT.)
NEOPRENE GASKET
BRONZE SECTION TO RECEIVE SCREW BRACED TO CHANNEL
SELF TAPING SCREW AT 1'-6" O.C.
LEATHER PIPING
3/4" ⌀ BOLT W/MODIFIED HEAD & NUT
BRONZE BOLT & COVER (3) EACH GLASS SECTION
3/4" CLEAR GLASS
2 1/8"
1 1/2"

EE Section

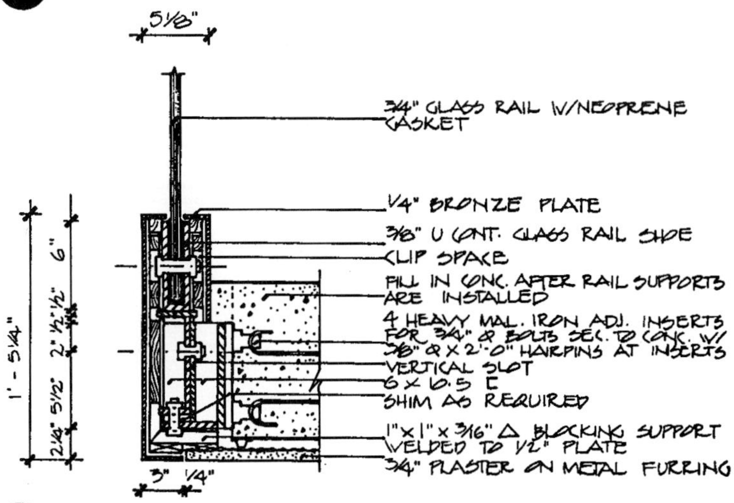
5 1/8"
3/4" GLASS RAIL W/NEOPRENE GASKET
1/4" BRONZE PLATE
3/8" U CONT. GLASS RAIL SHOE
CLIP SPACE
FILL IN CONC. AFTER RAIL SUPPORTS ARE INSTALLED
4 HEAVY MAL. IRON ADJ. INSERTS FOR 3/4" ⌀ BOLTS SEC. TO CONC. W/ 3/8" ⌀ X 2'-0" HAIRPINS AT INSERTS
VERTICAL SLOT
6 X 10.5 E
SHIM AS REQUIRED
1" x 1" x 3/16" △ BLOCKING SUPPORT WELDED TO 1/2" PLATE
3/4" PLASTER ON METAL FURRING
1'-5 1/4"
6"
3"
1/4"

FF Section

STAIRS AND RAMPS

Wood Handrail Components

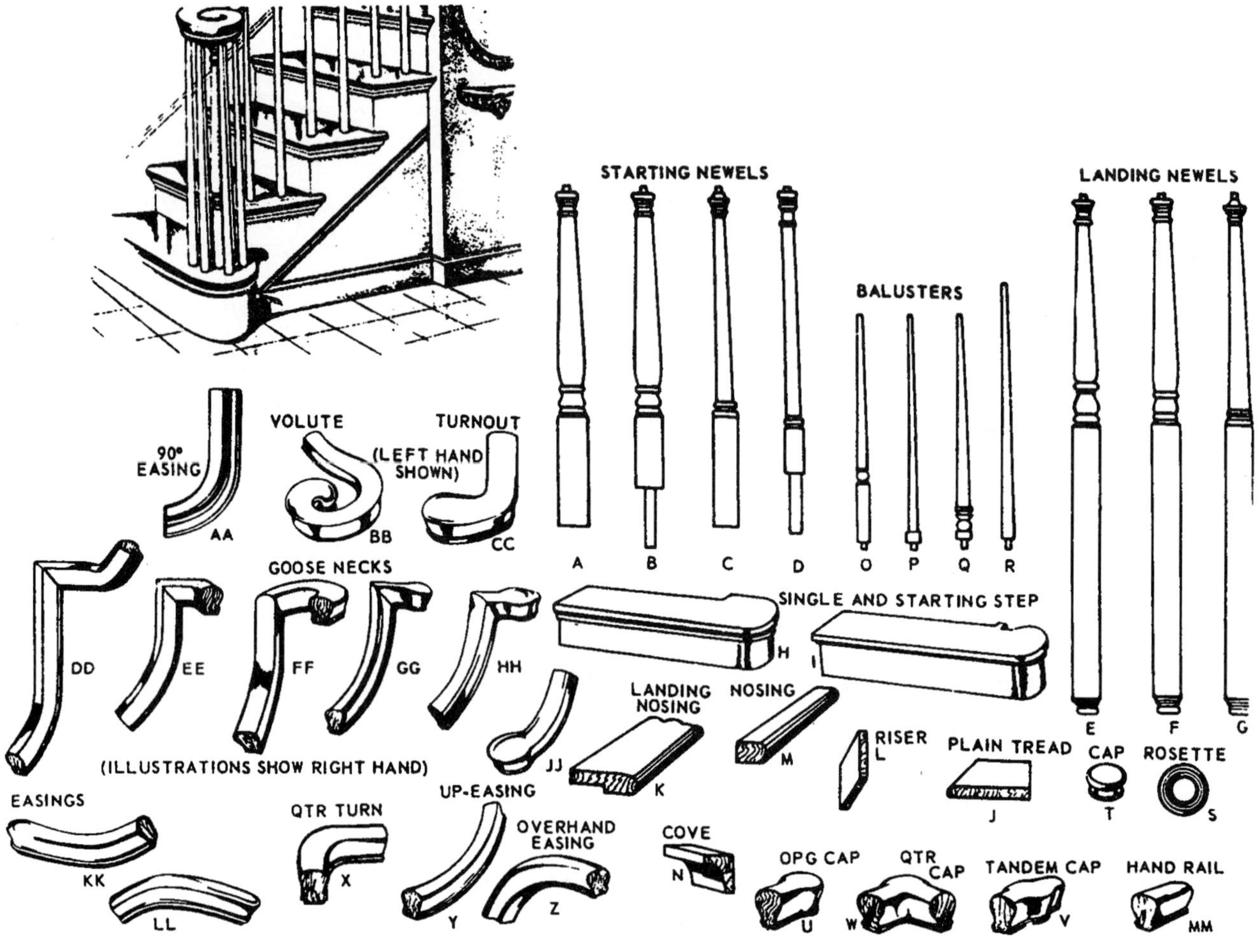

A-D Starting Newels
E-G Landing Newel
H-I Starting Step
J Stair Tread
K Landing Tread
L Risers
M Return Nosing
N Stair Cove
O-R Turned Balusters
S Wall Rosette
T Plain Cap
U One OPG Newel Cap
V Tandem Cap
W Quarter Turn Cap
X Quarter Turn
Y Up Easing

A Overhand Easing
AA 90 degree Up Easing
BB Volute
CC Turnout
DD Gooseneck 2 Riser
EE Gooseneck 1 Riser
FF Gooseneck 1 Riser Ledge Return
GG Gooseneck Riser with Cap
HH Gooseneck Riser Tandem Cap
JJ Starting Easing
KK Starting Easing with Return End
MM Hand Rail

SPIRAL STAIRS

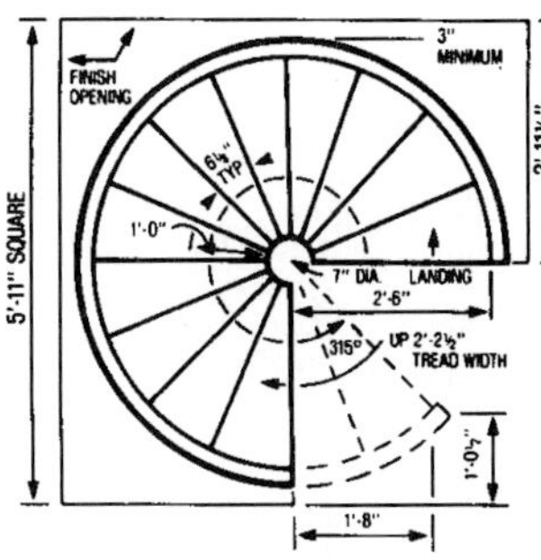

5′ diameter – spiral

5′ diameter – spiral

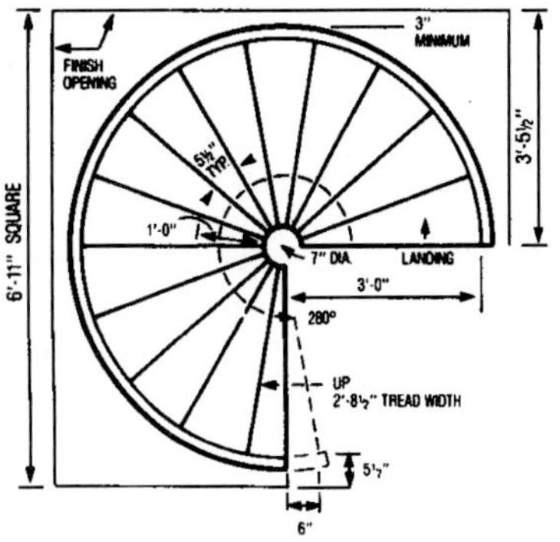

6′ diameter – spiral

CIRCULAR STAIRS

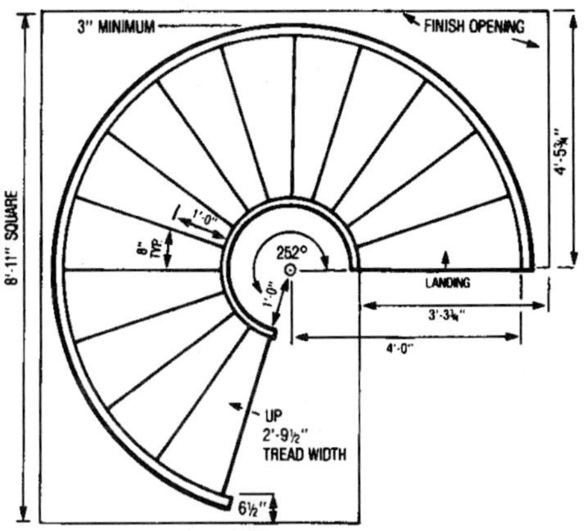

8′ diameter – circular

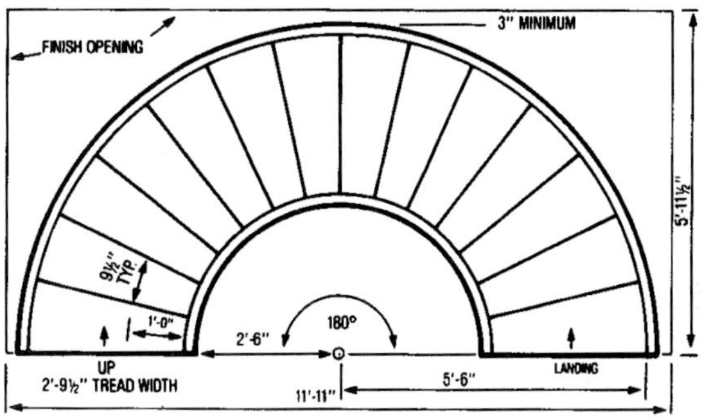

11′ diameter – circular

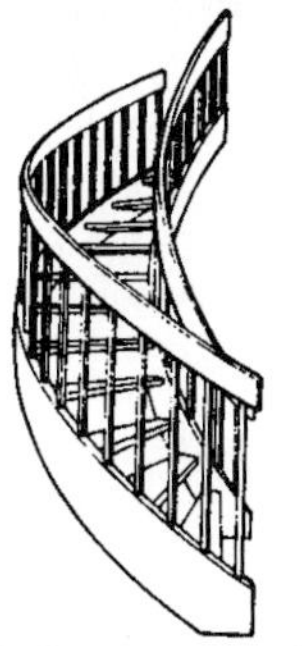

9′ diameter – circular

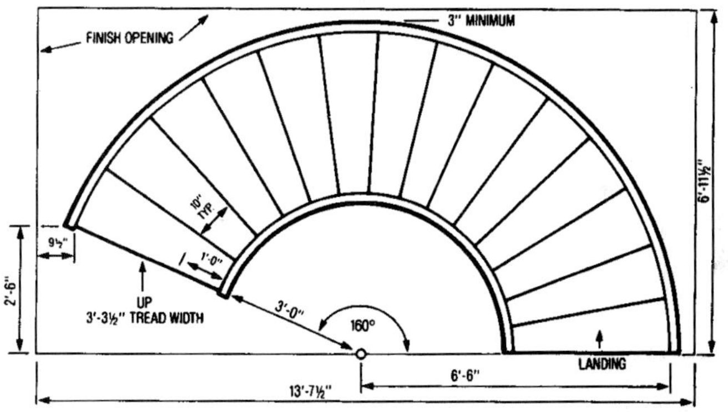

13′ diameter – circular

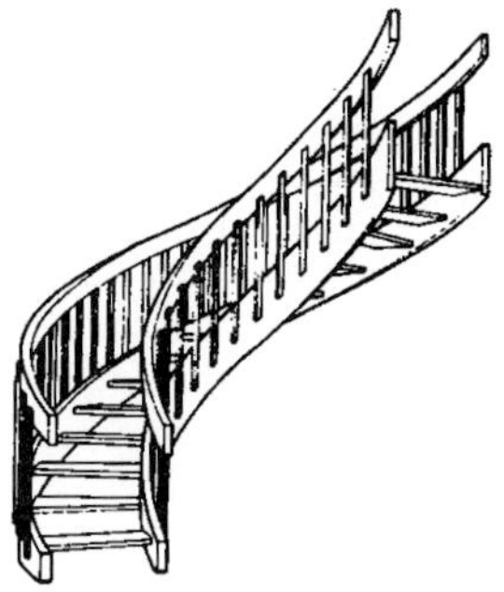

15′ diameter – circular

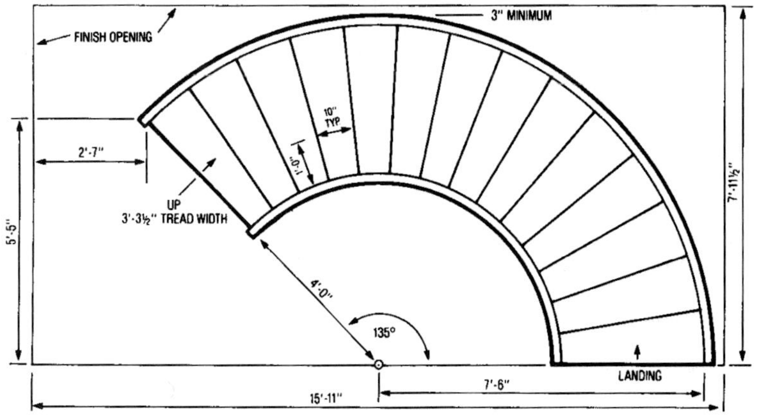

15′ diameter – circular

Note: All drawings left-hand turn (looking down).

STAIRS AND RAMPS
Spiral and Circular Stairs

Clockwise

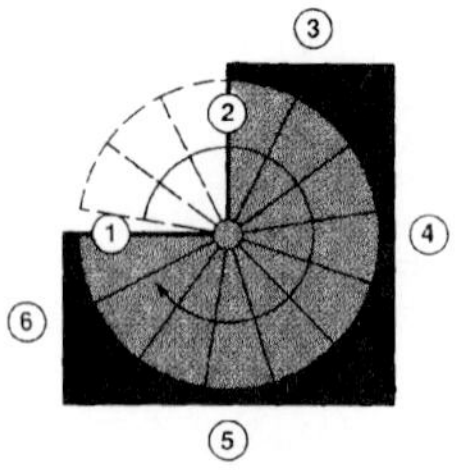

Left Hand Up
Standard 27°
13 1/2 Treads per circle
Riser height 7 1/2" to 8"

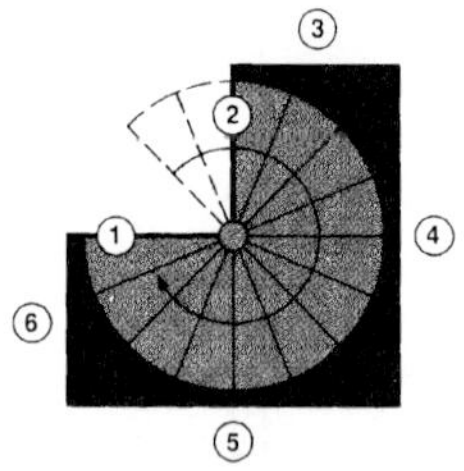

Left Hand Up
Standard 22 1/2°
16 Treads per circle
Riser height 6 1/2" to 7"

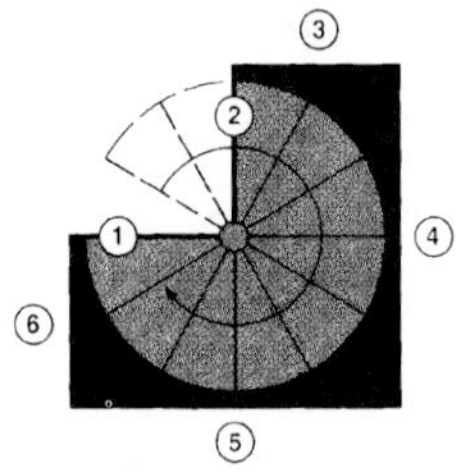

Left Hand Up
Standard 30°
12 Treads per circle
Riser height 8 1/2" to 9 1/2"

Layout

Locate the exact number of steps by using your elevation and refer to the Table of Riser's chart below. Standard degree is 27. If you have a code or special requirement, determine which chart will be used. Check the number of steps and degree of turn your stair will have. Rotate the diagram four different directions to determine which direction best meets your needs. You can have less of a turn by decreasing the number of steps.

Framing Dimensions

Model No.	1	2	3	4	5	6
40S	20"	20"	24"	44"	44"	24"
48S	24"	24"	28"	52"	52"	28"
52S	26"	26"	30"	56"	56"	30"
60S	30"	30"	34"	64"	64"	34"
64S	32"	32"	36"	68"	68"	36"
72S	36"	36"	40"	76"	76"	40"
76S	38"	38"	42"	80"	80"	42"
88S	44"	44"	48"	92"	92"	48"
96S	48"	48"	52"	100"	100"	52"

Framing Dimensions are used when stair passes through flooring. Notice the opening is an "L" shape, not square. For maximum head room taper 45" joist #2 (shaded area). If your joist is 10" or over, order with one less step and this will increase head room.

Counter Clockwise

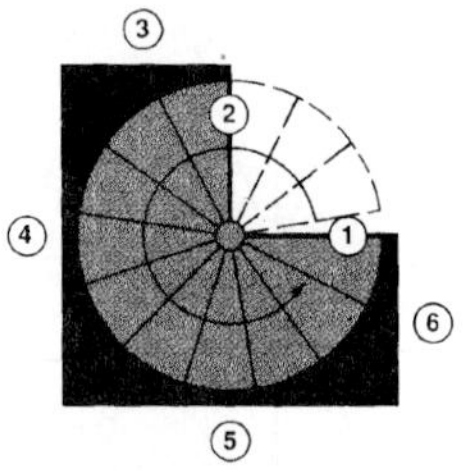

Right Hand Up
Standard 27°
13 1/2 Treads per circle
Riser height 7 1/2" to 8"

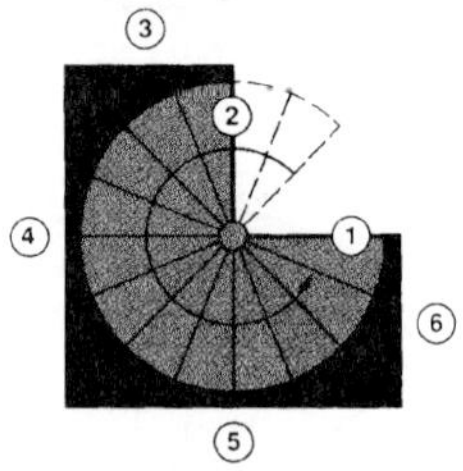

Right Hand Up
Optional 22 1/2°
16 Treads per circle
Riser height 6 1/2" to 7"

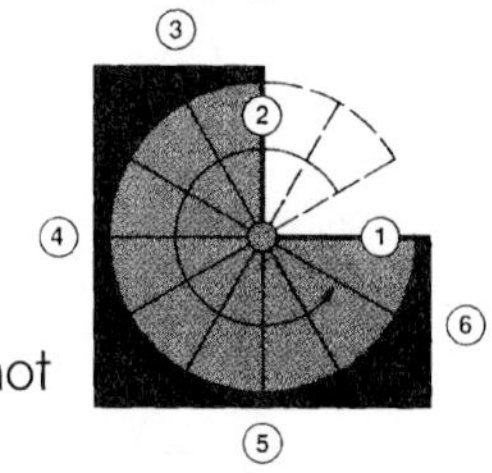

Right Hand Up
Optional 30°
12 Treads per circle
Riser height 8 1/2" to 9 1/2"

Table of Risers

27°			22 1/2°			30°		
Finish Floor Height	**Number of Steps 27°**	**Degree of Circle**	**Finish Floor Height**	**Number of Steps 22 1/2°**	**Degree of Circle**	**Finish Floor Height**	**Number of Steps 30°**	**Degree of Circle**
90" to 96"	11	297°	84" to 91"	12	270°	85" to 95"	9	270°
97" to 104"	12	324°	92" to 98"	13	292 1/2°	96" to 104"	10	300°
105" to 112"	13	351°	99" to 105"	14	315°	105" to 114"	11	330°
113" to 120"	14	378°	106" to 112"	15	337 1/2°	115" to 123"	12	360°
121" to 128"	15	405°	113" to 119"	16	360°	124" to 133"	13	390°
129" to 136"	16	432°	120" to 126"	17	382 1/2°	134" to 142"	14	420°
137" to 144"	17	459°	127" to 133"	18	405°	143" to 152"	15	450°
145" to 152"	18	486°	134" to 140"	19	427 1/2°	153" to 161"	16	480°
153" to 160"	19	513°	141" to 147"	20	450°	162" to 171"	17	510°
161" to 168"	20	540°	148" to 154"	21	472 1/2°	172" to 180"	18	540°

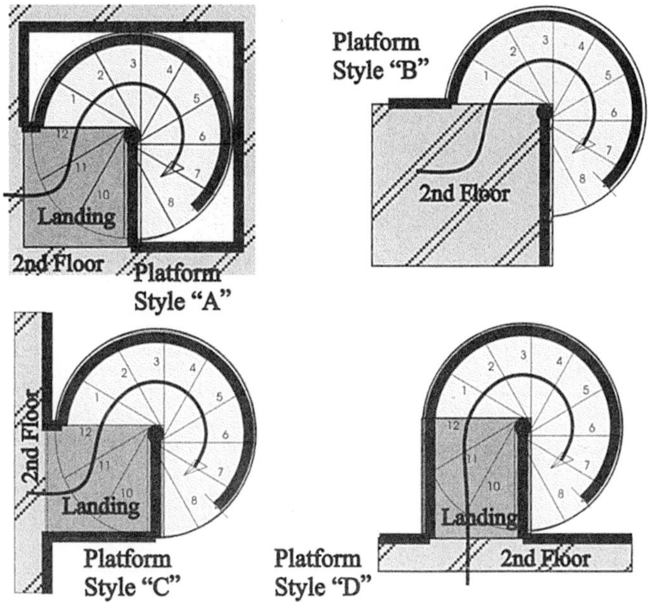

Stair Diameter	48"	54"	60"	72"	84"
Tread Angle	30°	27°	27°	25°	23.75°
- a 12 riser turn	330°	297°	297°	275°	261°
- a 13 riser turn	360°	324°	324°	300°	279°
- a 14 riser turn	390°	351°	351°	325°	303°
- a 15 riser turn	420°	378°	378°	350°	327°
- a 16 riser turn	450°	405°	405°	375°	350°
Maximum Rise	9"	8-3/4"	8-3/4"	8-1/2"	8-1/2"
Minimum Rise	8-1/4"	8"	8"	7-5/8"	7-5/8"
Center Column	6"	6"	6"	6"	6"
Floor opening needed					
- without stringer	53"	59"	65"	n/a	n/a
- with open stringer	53"	59"	65"	77"	89"
- with closed stringer	54"	60"	66"	78"	90"
Tread tickness	1-1/4"	1-1/4"	1-5/8"	1-5/8"	1-5/8"
Clear walkway	18"	21"	24"	30"	36"
Balusters spacing - 2 / tread	5-3/4"	6"	6-11/16"	n/a	n/a
Balusters spacing - 3 / tread	4"	4"	4-7/16"	5"	5-5/8"
Balusters spacing - 4 / tread	n/a	n/a	n/a	3-7/8"	4-1/4"

Floor to Floor Height	Qty of Treads	Degree
88-1/16" to 95"	9	270°
95-1/16" to 104-1/2"	10	300°
104-9/16" to 114"	11	330°
114-1/16" to 123-1/2"	12	360°
123-9/16" to 133"	13	390°
133-1/16" to 142-1/2"	14	420°
142-9/16" to 144"	15	450°

STAIRS AND RAMPS

Spiral and Circular Stairs

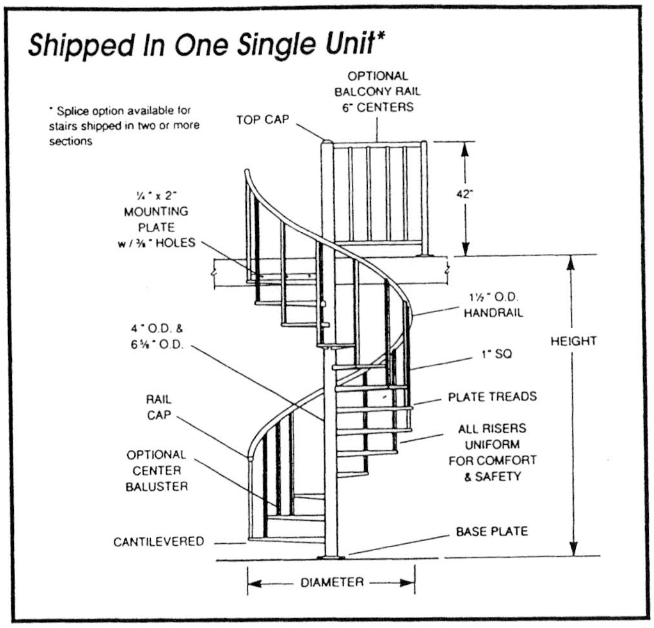

Dimension Chart

Model#	40S	48S	52S	60S	64S	72S	76S	88S	96S
Diameter	40"	48"	52"	60"	64"	72"	76"	88"	96"
Center Colum	4"	4"	4"	4"	4"	4"	6-5/8"	6-5/8"	6-5/8"
Lbs. per 9 ft.	205	220	235	250	365	310	322	435	485
Tread Detail A	3-1/2"	3-1/2"	3-1/2"	3-1/2"	3-1/2"	3-1/2"	5-5/8"	5-5/8"	5-5/8"
Tread Detail B	18"	22"	24"	28"	30"	34"	36"	42"	48"
22-1/2° Tread Detail C	7-13/16"	9-3/8"	10-1/8"	11-11/16"	12-1/2"	14-1/16"	14-13/16"	17-13/16"	18-3/4"
22-1/2° Tread Detail D	6-3/8"	6-3/4"	6-7/8"	7"	7-1/8"	7-1/4"	7-3/8"	8-7/8"	9"
27° Tread Detail C	9-5/16"	11-3/16"	12-1/8"	14"	14-15/16"	16-13/16"	17-3/4"	20-9/16"	22-7/16"
27° Tread Detail D	7-3/8"	7-3/4"	7-7/8"	8"	8-1/8"	8-1/4"	8-3/8"	9-3/4"	9-7/8"
30° Tread Detail C	10-3/8"	12-7/16"	13-7/16"	15-9/16"	16-9/16"	18-5/8"	19-11/16"	22-3/4"	24-7/8"
30° Tread Detail D	8-1/8"	8-3/8"	8-1/2"	8-3/4"	8-7/8"	9"	9-1/8"	10-3/8"	10-1/2"
Platform Size	22"	26"	28"	32"	34"	38"	42"	46"	50"

* Dimension D does not include the overlapping step above.

Tread Detail

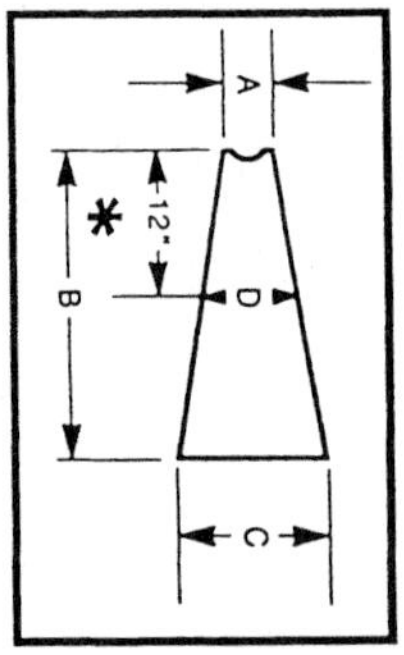

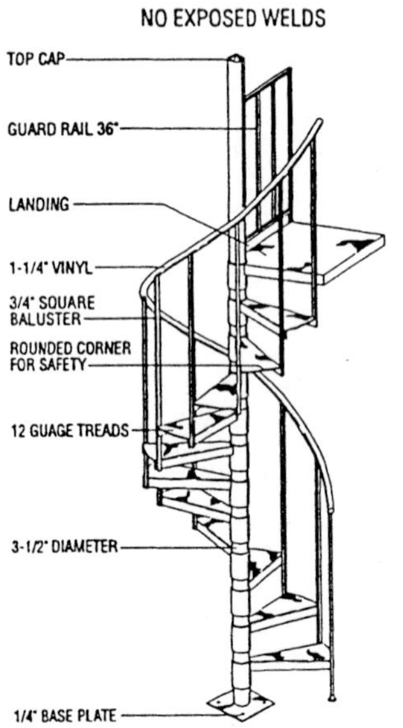

Standard Kit

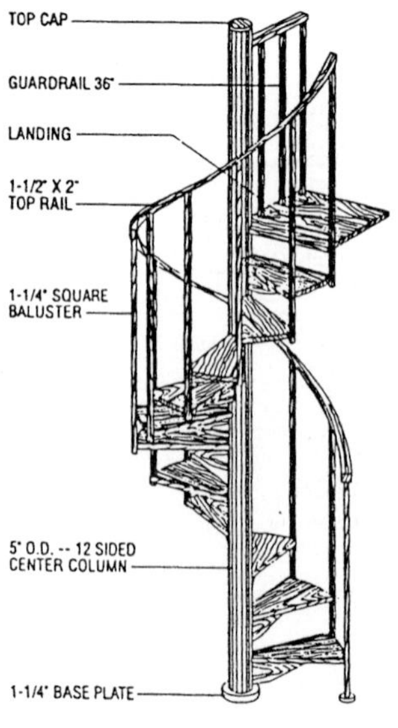

Wood Spiral Kit

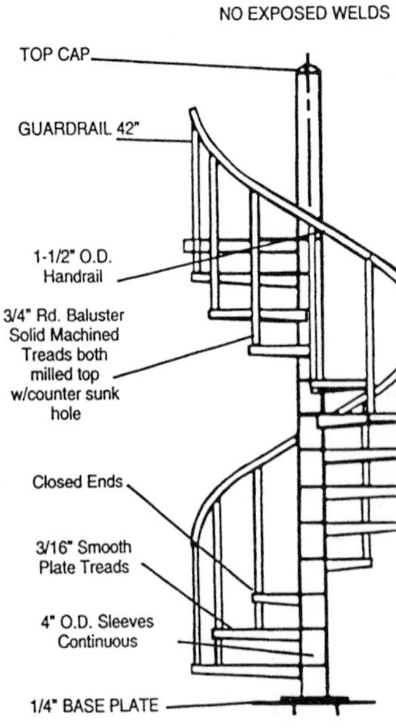

Heavy Duty Kit

Handrails

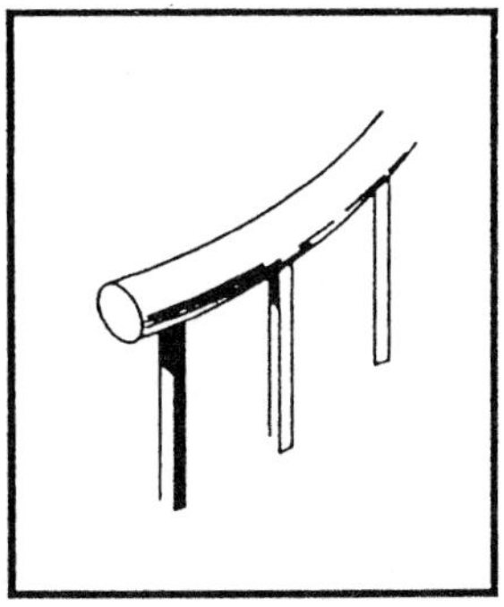

1-1/4″ Round
Steel
Aluminum
Brass

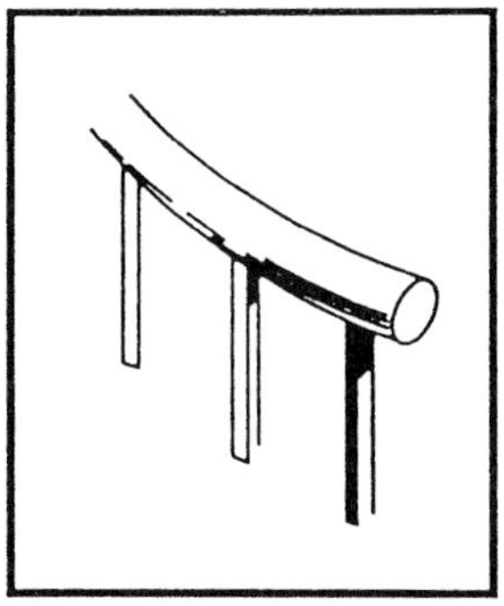

1-1/2″ Round
Steel
Aluminum
Brass

1-1/2″ x 2″ Square
Solid Wood
Oak
Specify

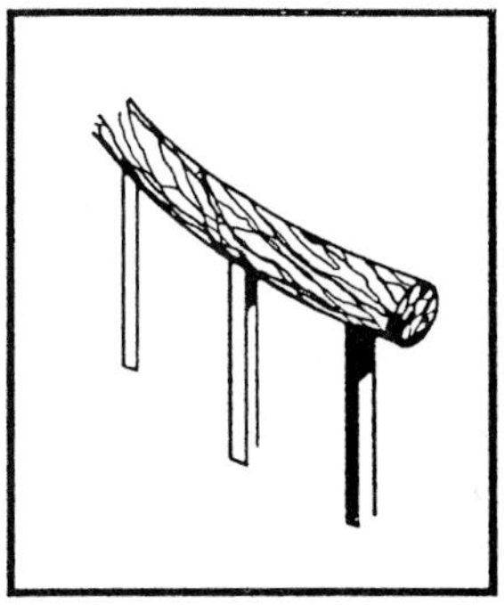

2″ Round
Solid Wood
Oak
Specify

Balusters

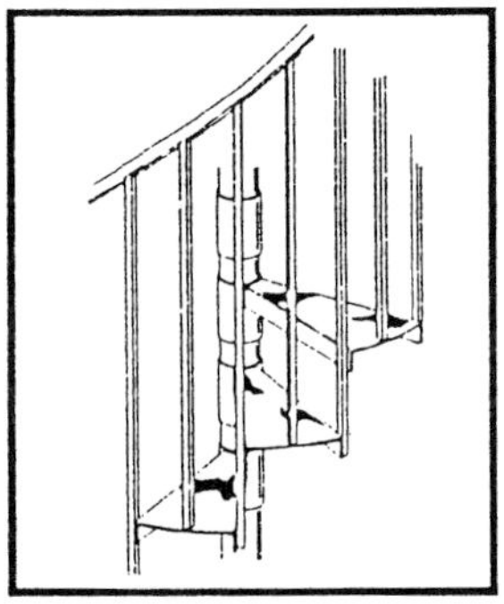

3/4″ Center
Square or Round
Steel
Aluminum
Brass

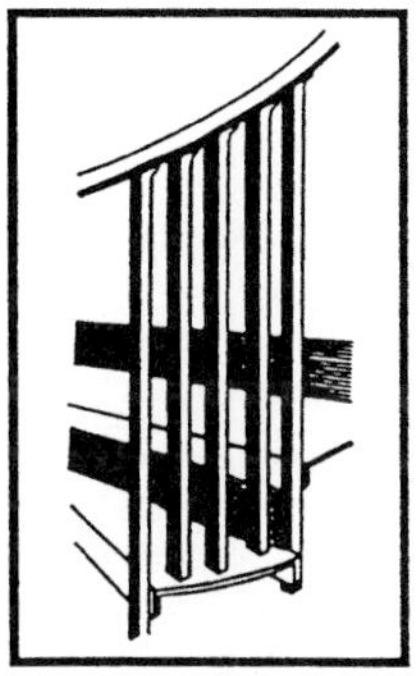

3/4″ Center
4″ Spacing
Steel
Aluminum
Brass

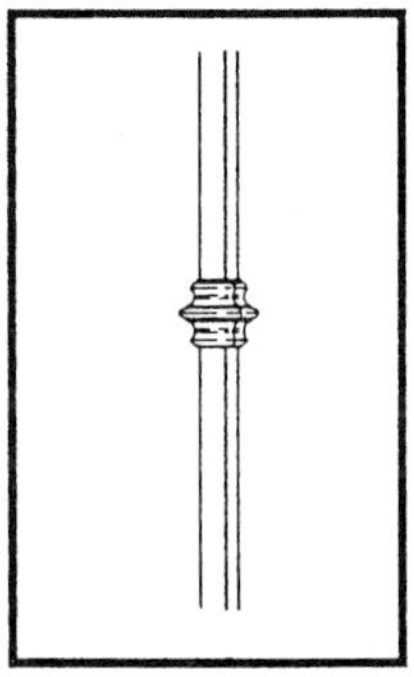

3/4″ Center
With Collar
Steel
Aluminum
Brass

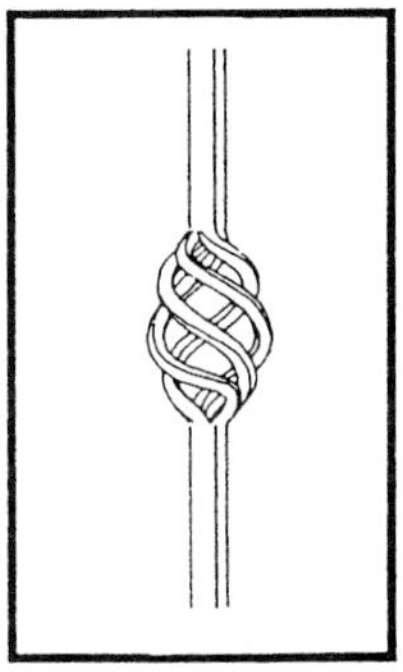

3/4″ Center
Spiral
Steel

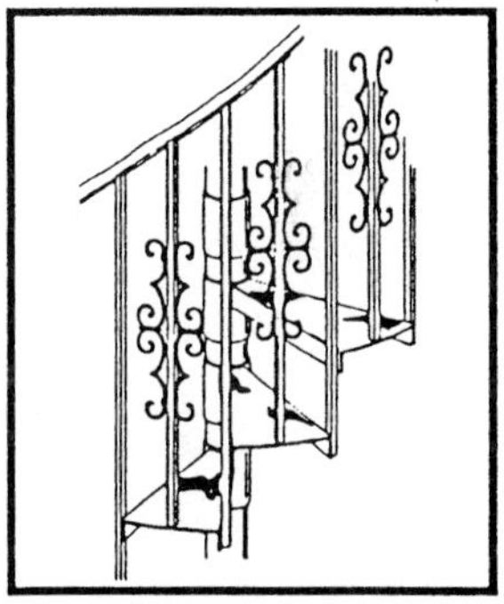

3/4″ Center
With Ornate Design
Steel
Aluminum
Brass

Treads

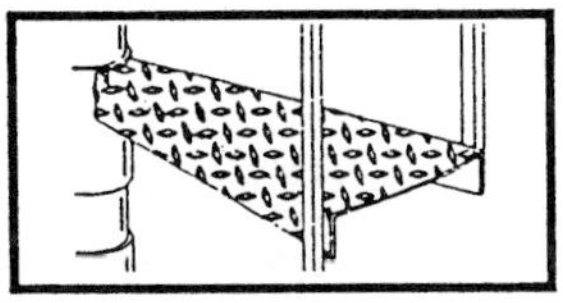

Checker Plate

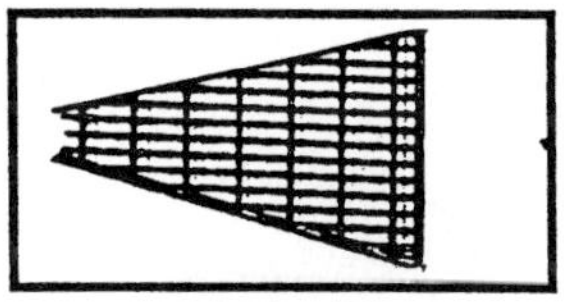

Bar Grating

Filigree Pattern

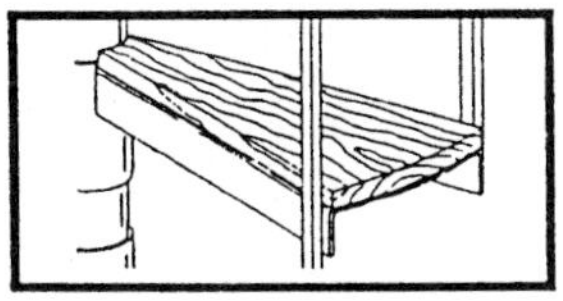

Oak

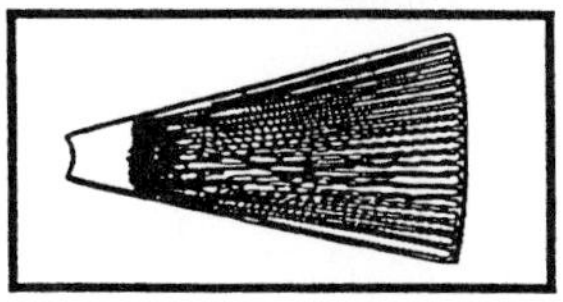

Radial Grating

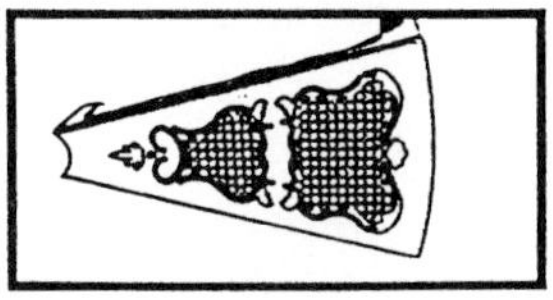

Traditional Pattern

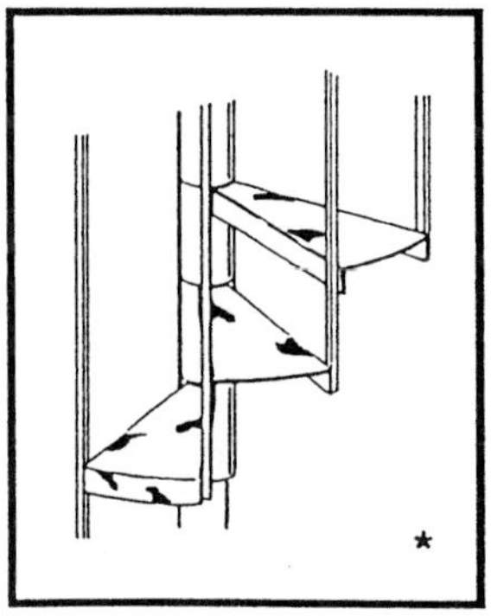

Continuous Sleeves
Each Tread Sleeve
Cut out to Exact Height
Metal Ends Closed

CURVED STAIRS

Standard Layouts – 14 Risers

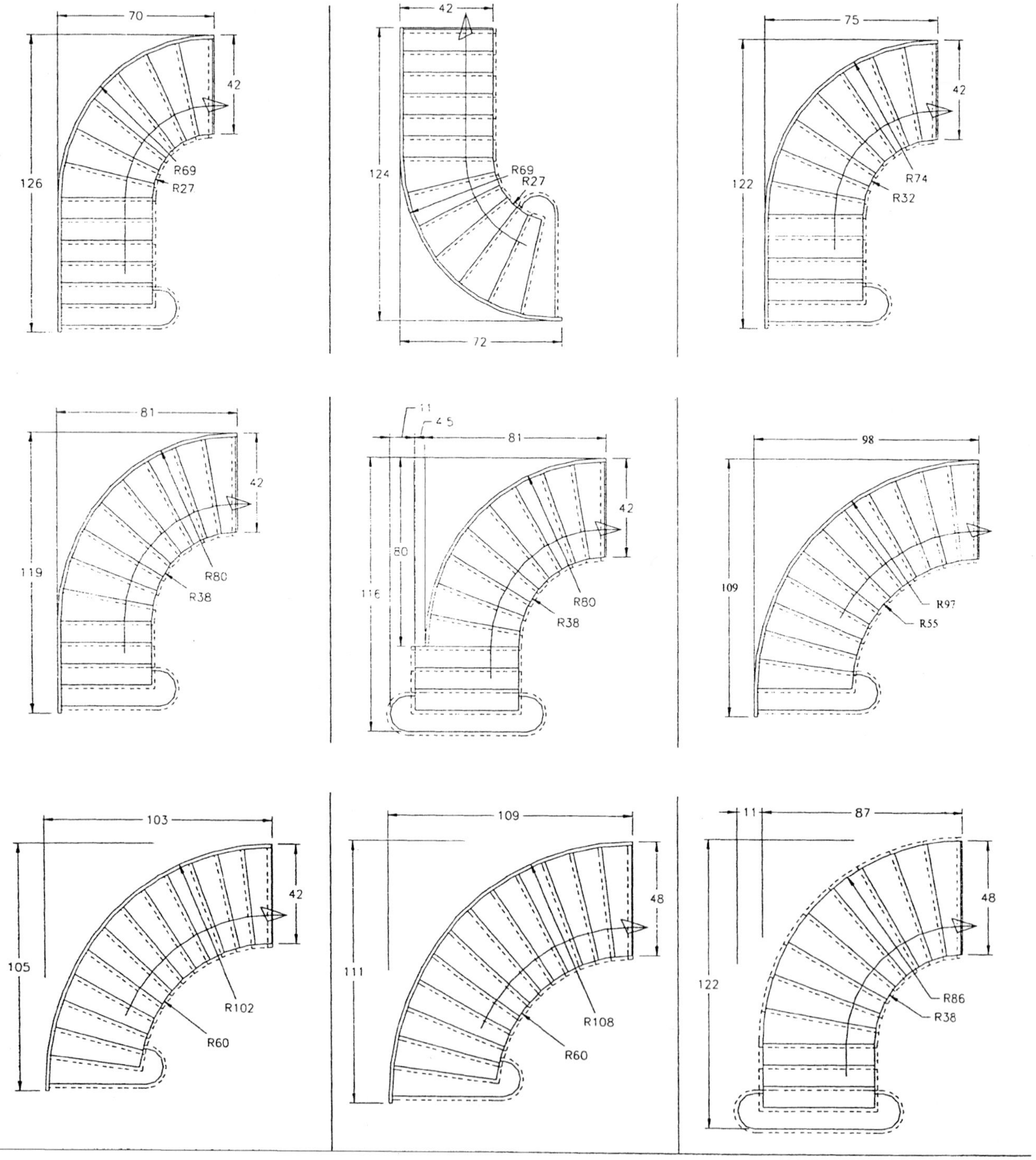

Standard Layouts – 14 Risers

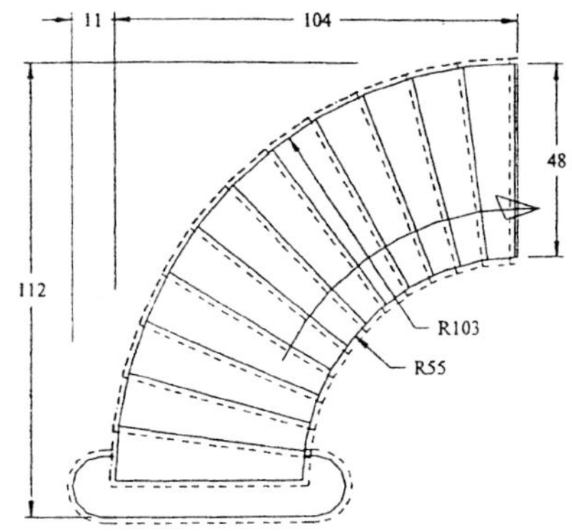

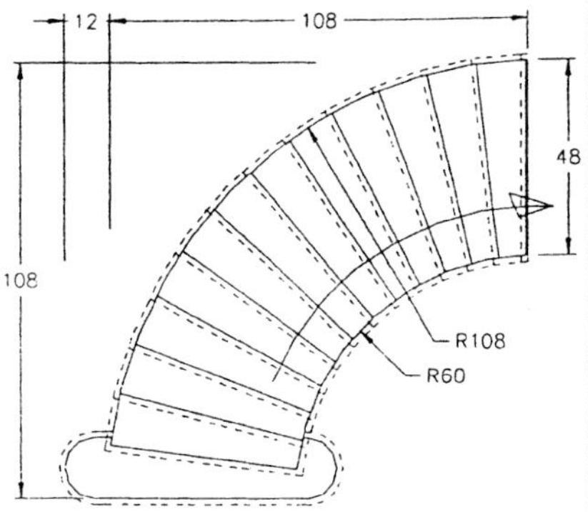

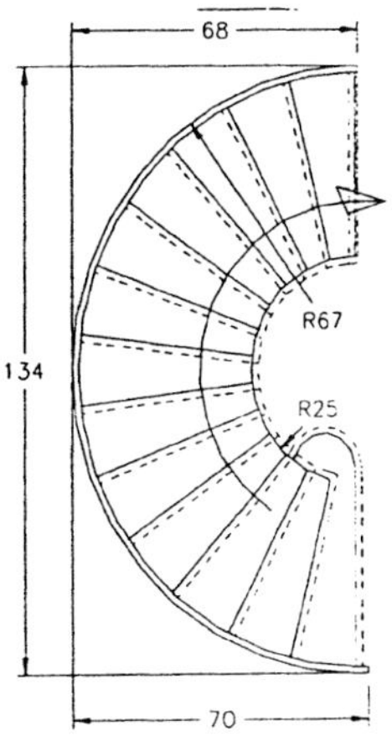

180° Turn

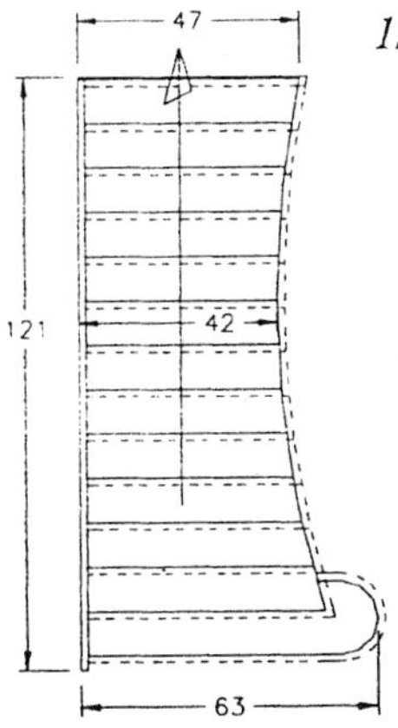

1/2 Hour Glass

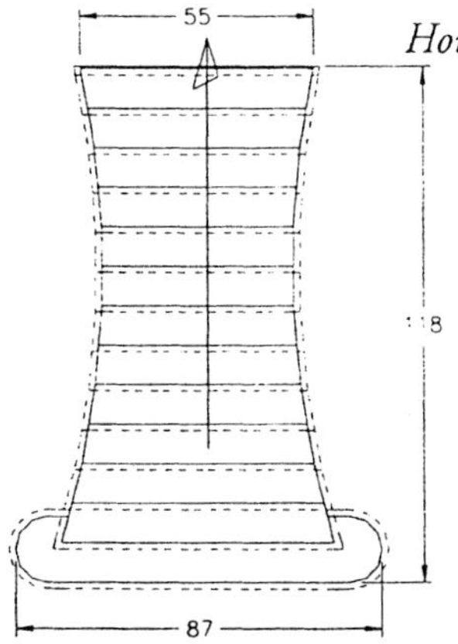

Hour Glass

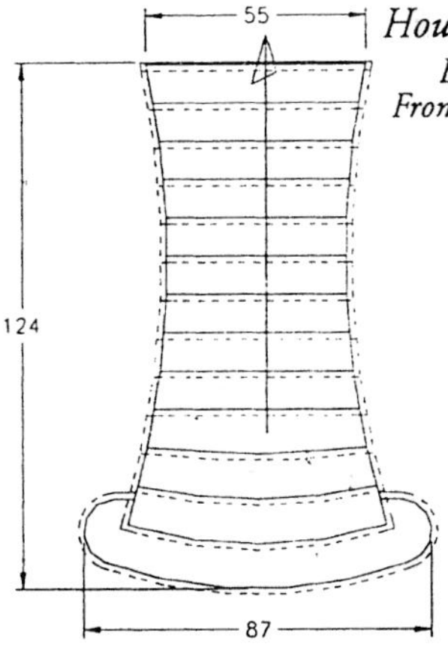

Hour Glass
Bowed Front Treads

"U" Shape Layout

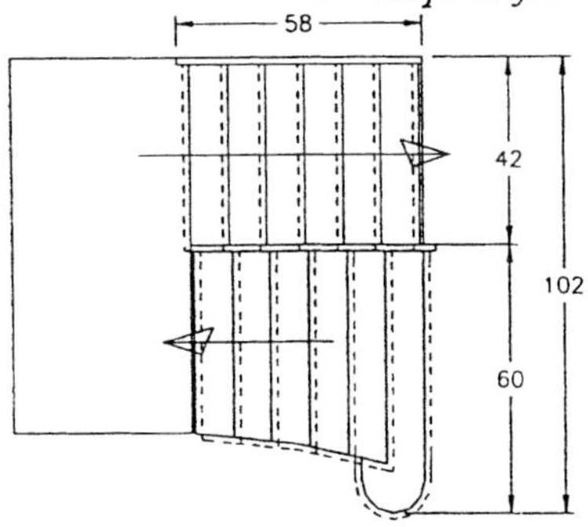

"L" Shape Layout

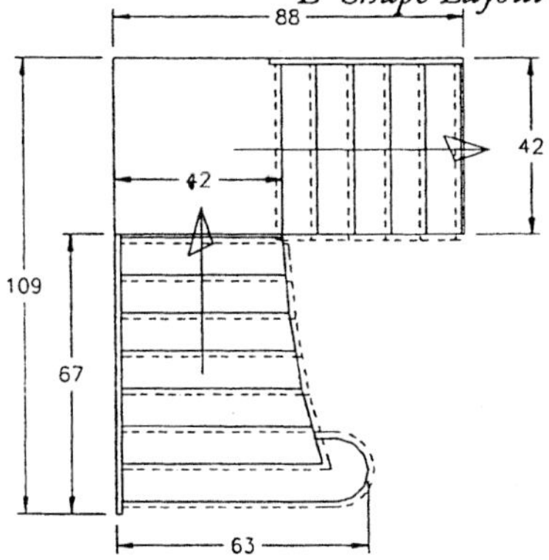

"T" Shape Layout

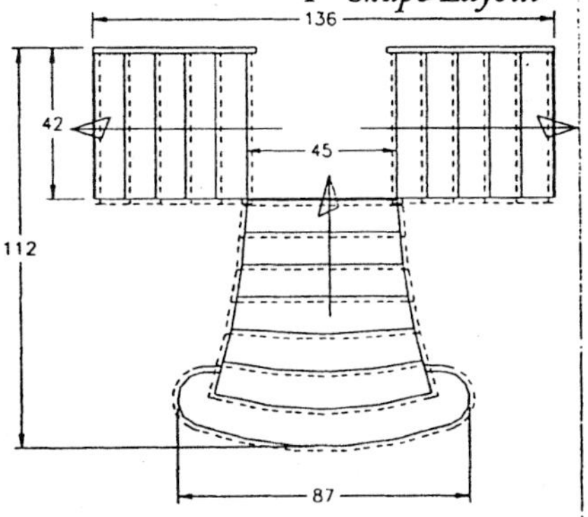

Standard Layouts – 15 Risers

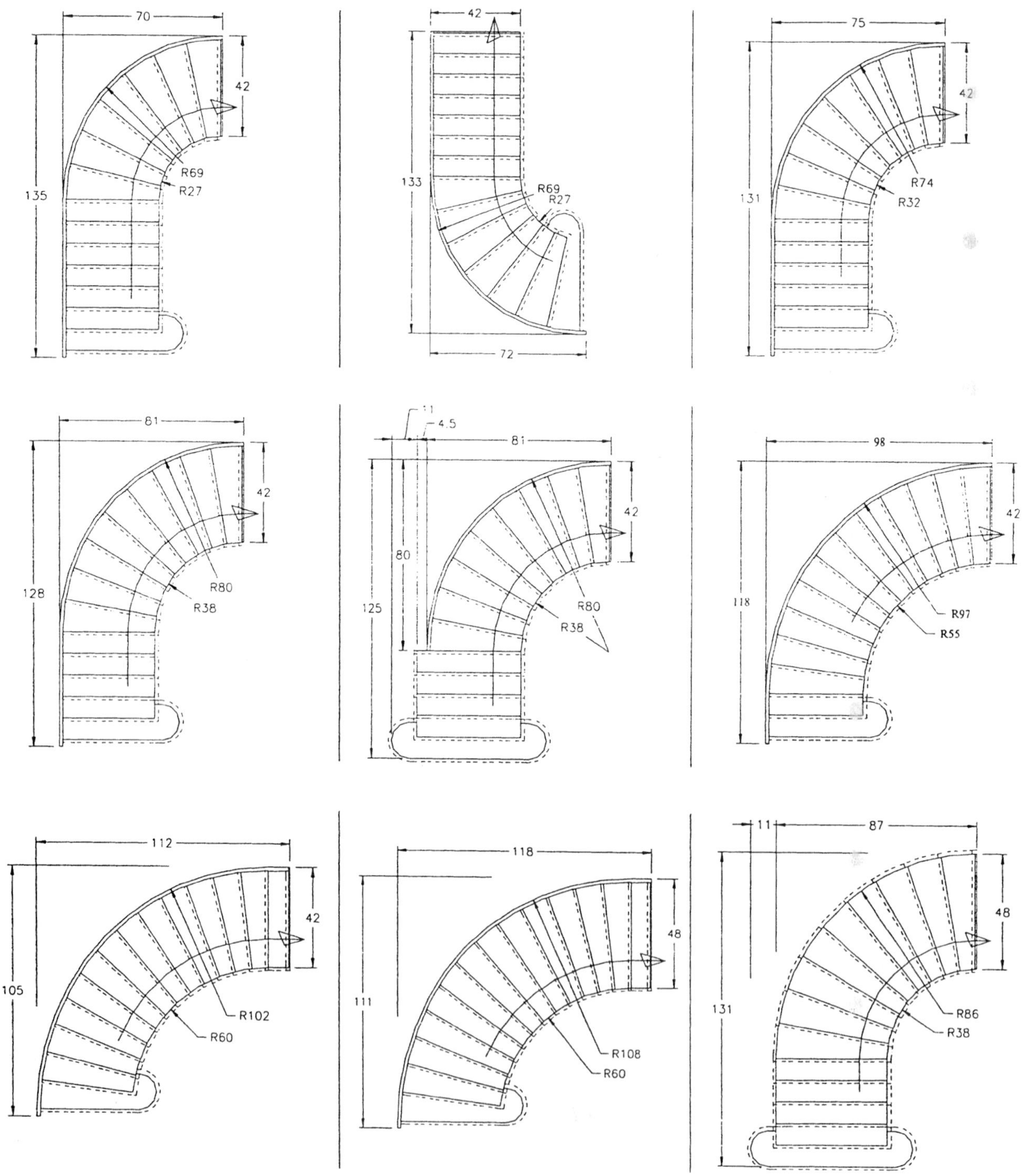

Standard Layouts – 15 Risers

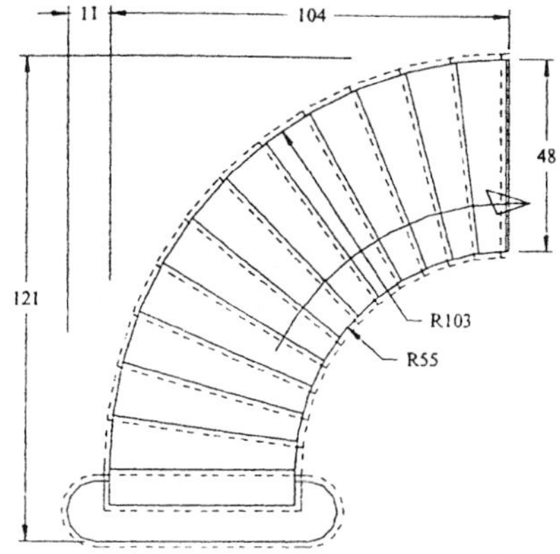

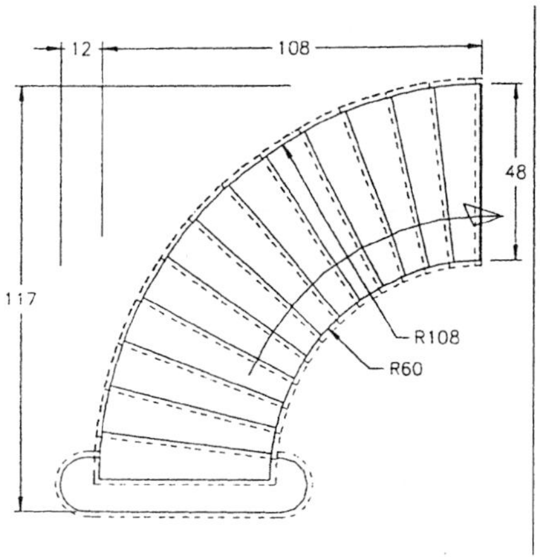

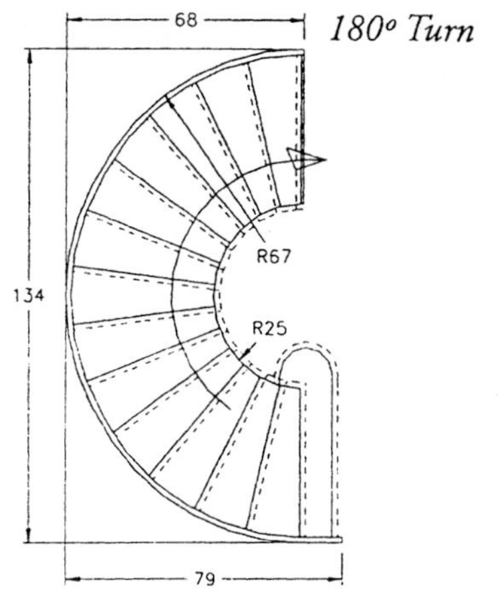

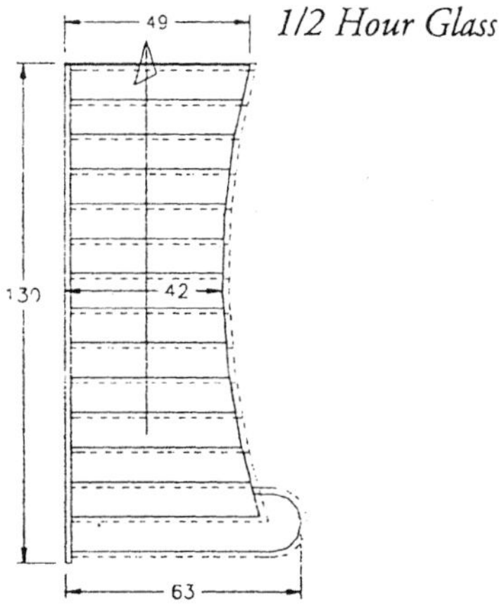

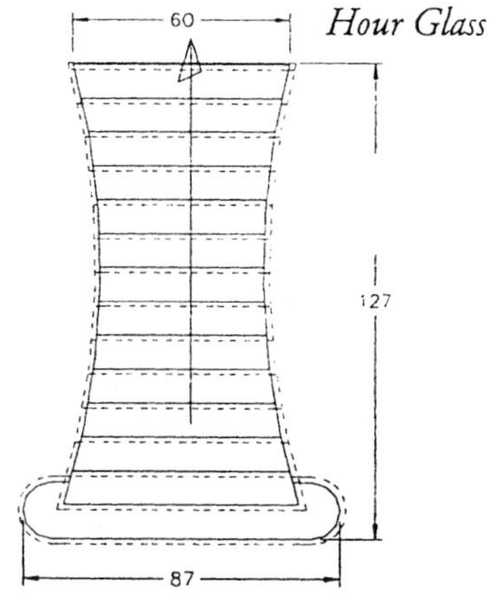

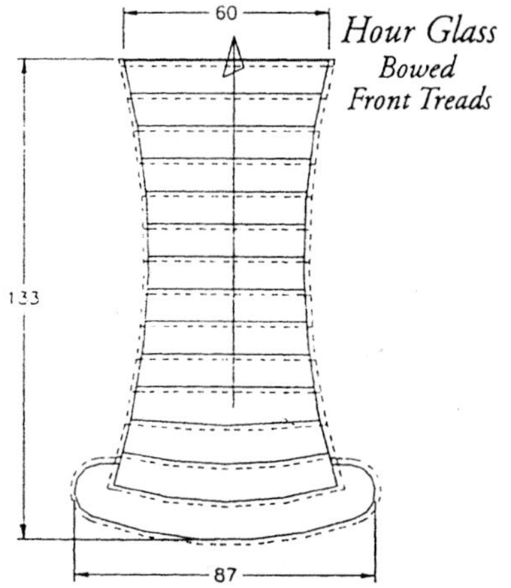

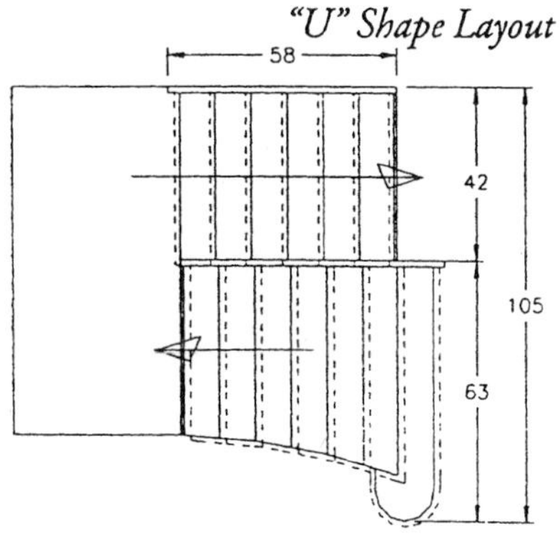

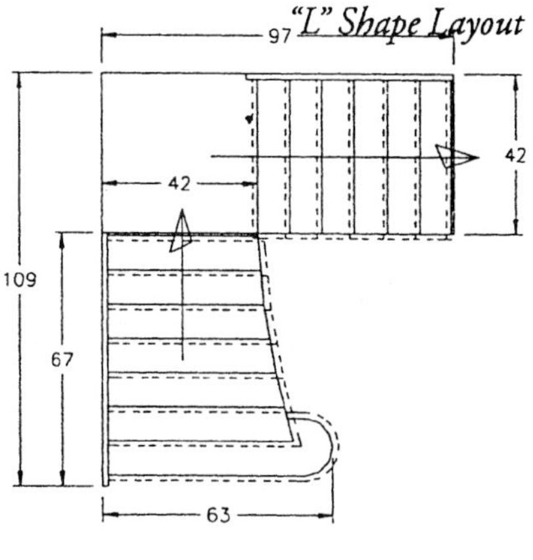

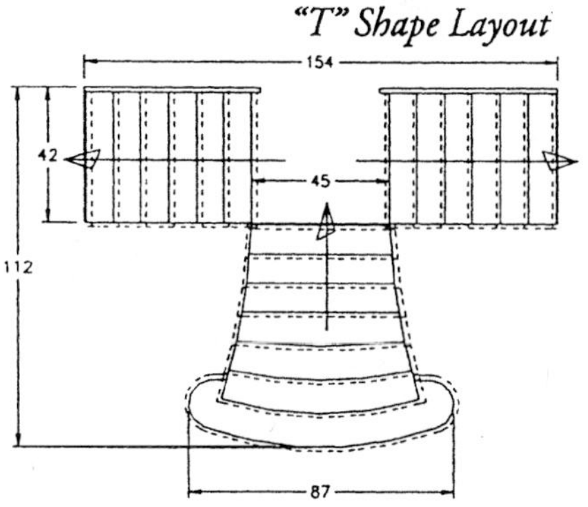

Standard Layouts – 16 Risers

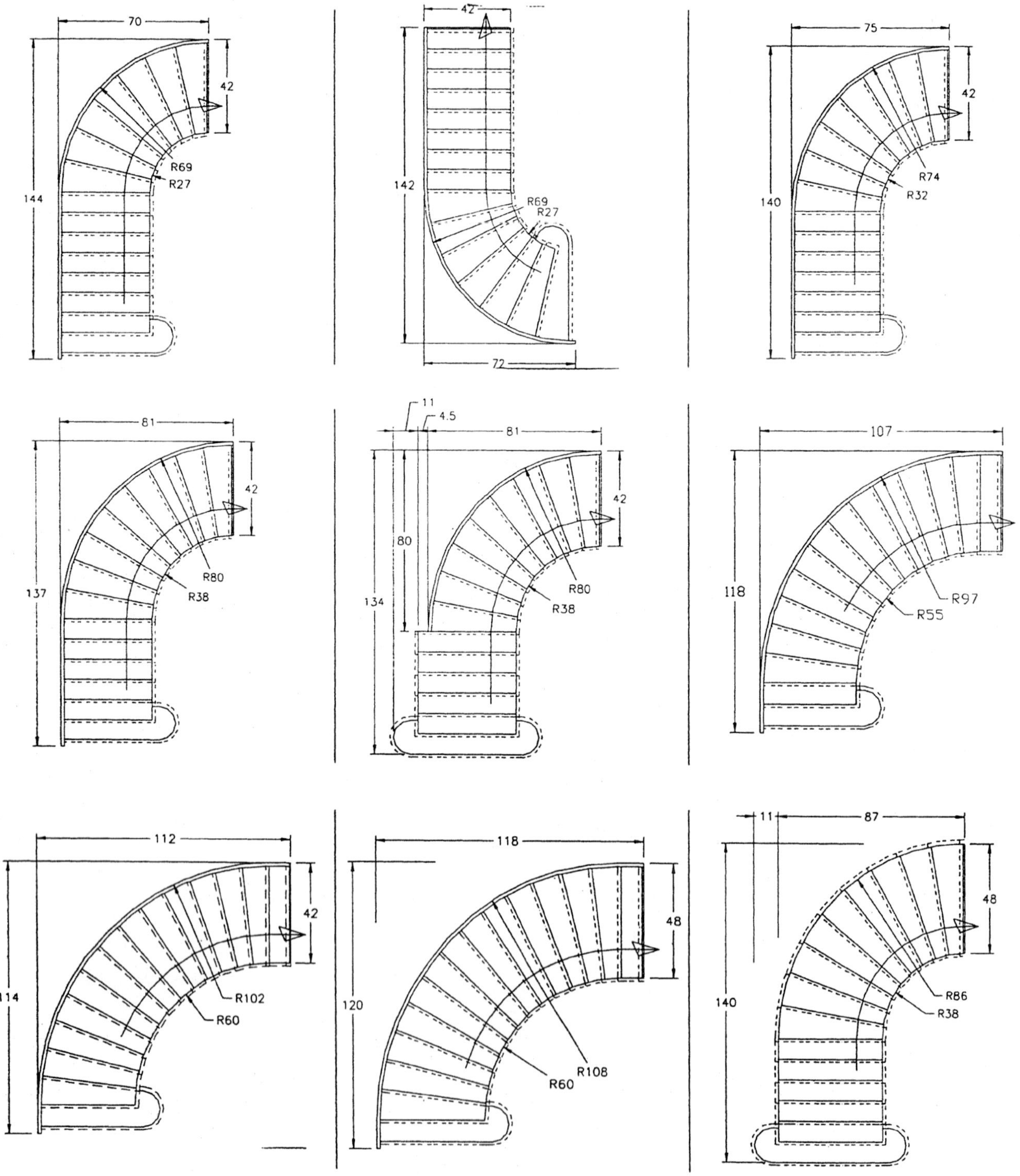

Standard Layouts – 16 Risers

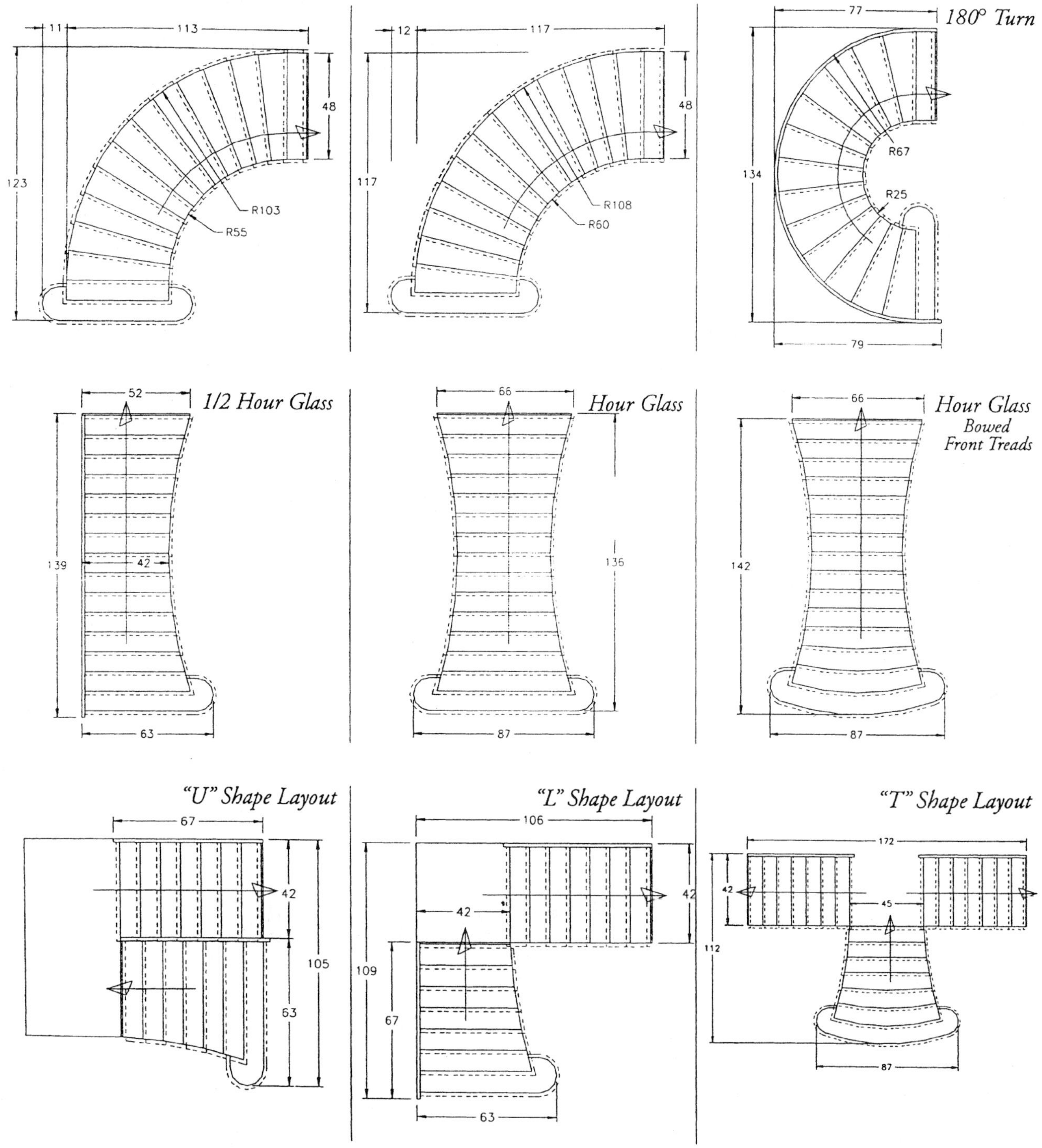

Rise Chart

Number of Risers	Minimum Rise (inches)	Ideal Rise (inches)	Maximum Rise (inches)
1	7	7 5/8	8 1/4
2	14	15 1/4	16 1/2
3	21	22 7/8	24 3/4
4	28	30 1/2	33
5	35	38 1/8	41 1/4
6	42	45 3/4	49 1/2
7	49	53 3/8	57 3/4
8	56	61	66
9	63	68 5/8	74 1/4
10	70	76 1/4	82 1/2
11	77	83 7/8	90 3/4
12	84	91 1/2	99
13	91	99 1/8	107 1/4
14	98	106 3/4	115 1/2
15	105	114 3/8	123 3/4
16	112	122	132
17	119	129 5/8	140 1/4
18	126	137 1/4	148 1/2

NOTE

These specifications and every stair layout should be compared with the building code requirement of the area where the stair is to be installed.

Building code adherence is the sole responsibility of the end user.

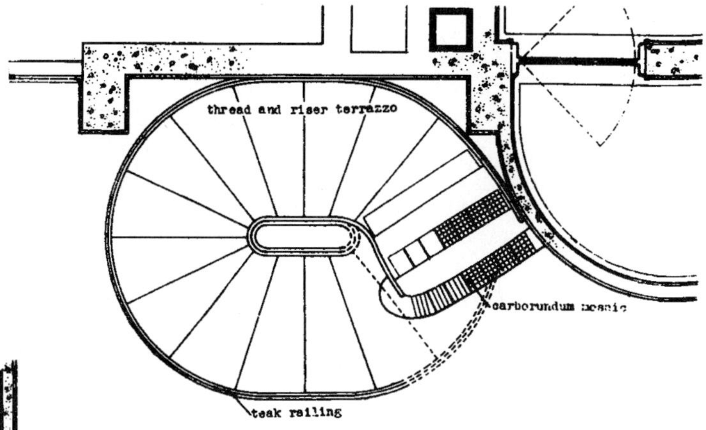

Plan

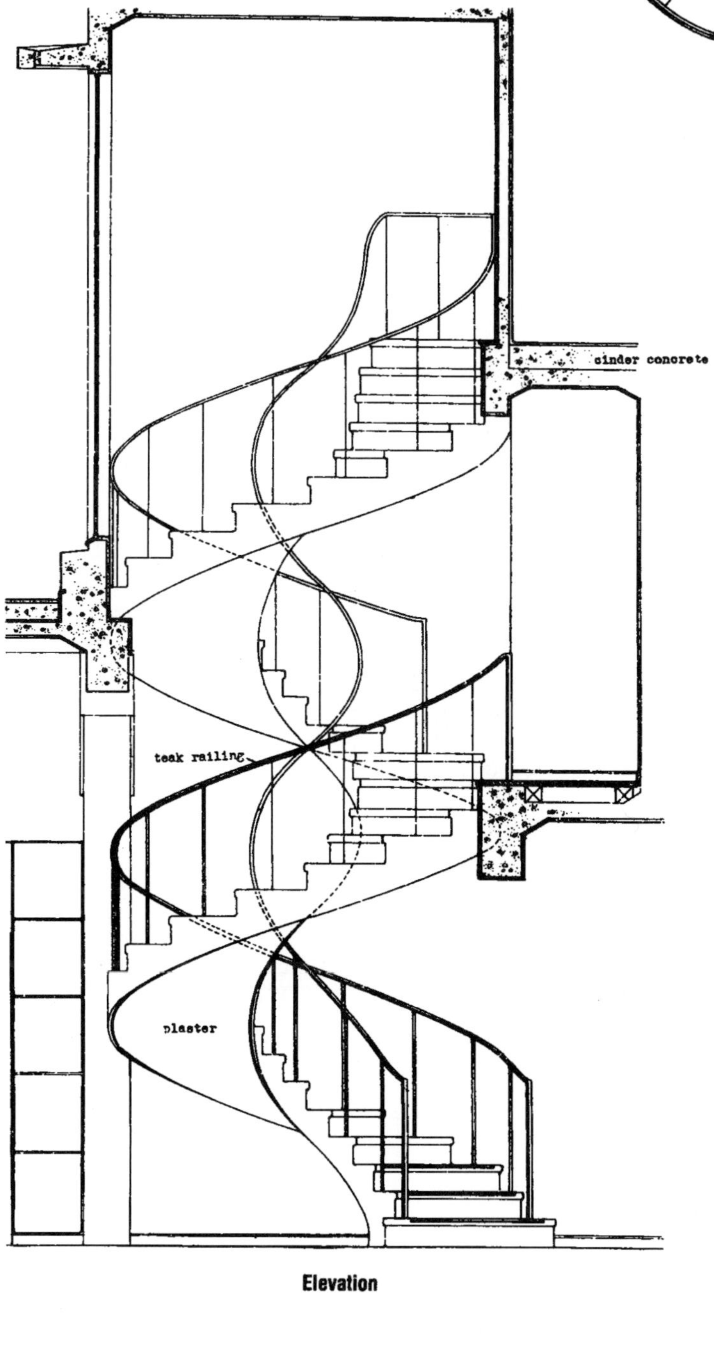

Elevation

STAIRS AND RAMPS

Spiral Stair Plan and Elevation

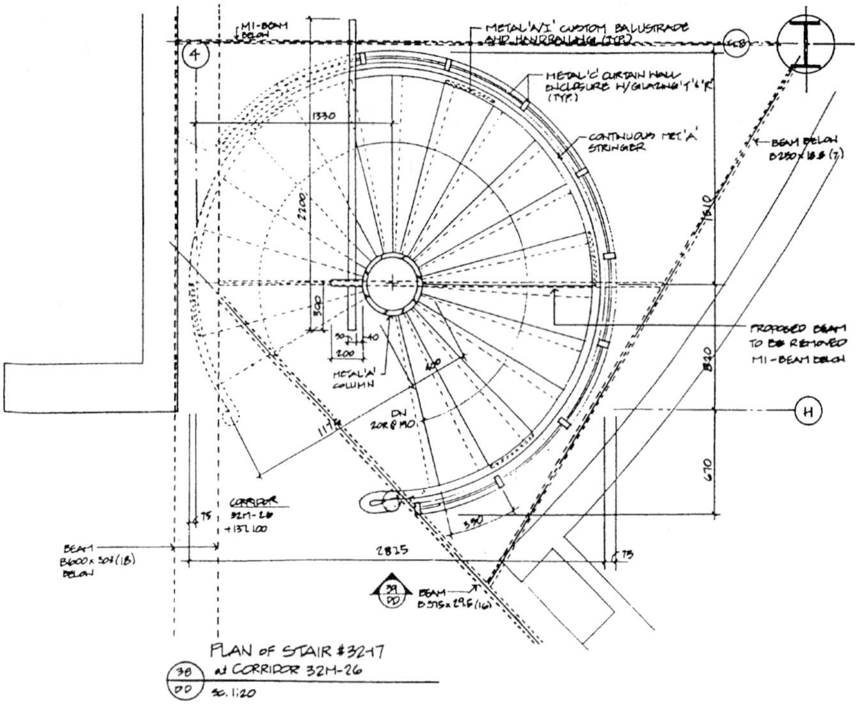

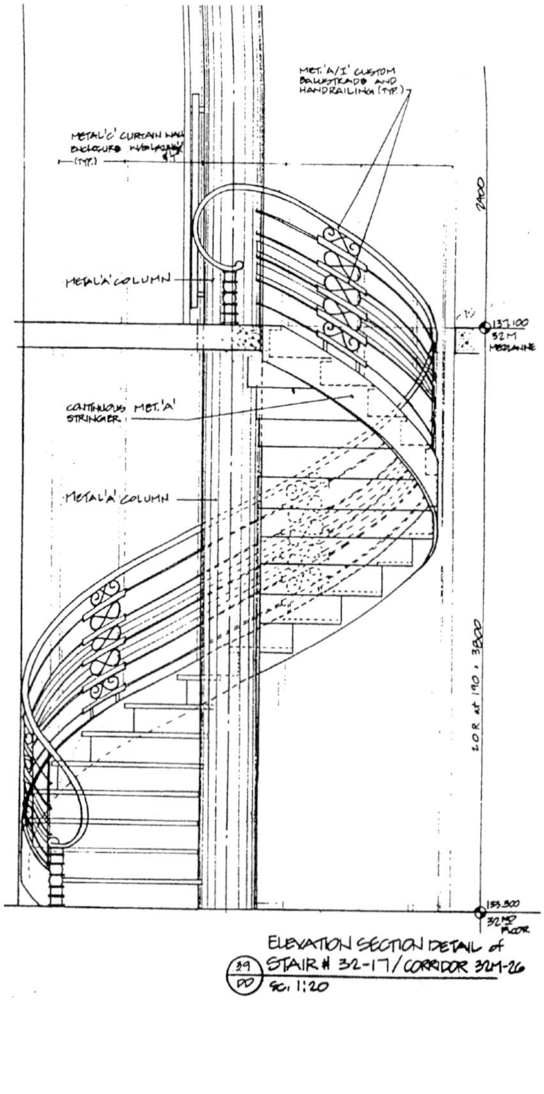

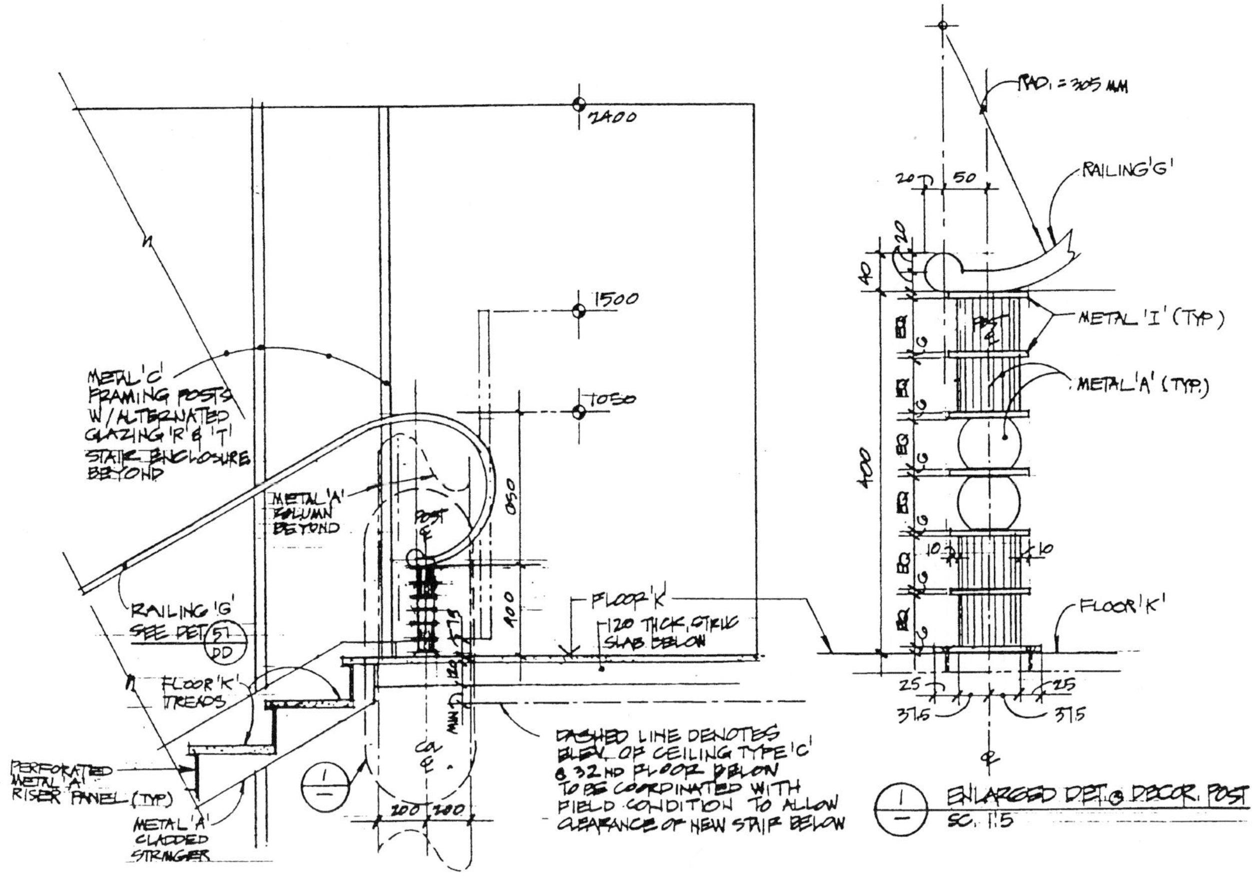

39A DD PARTIAL INTERIOR EAST ELEV. @ STAIR ENCLOSURE & RAIL'G.
SC. 1:20

39A DD RAILING DETAIL @ STAIR #32-17
SC. AS NOTED

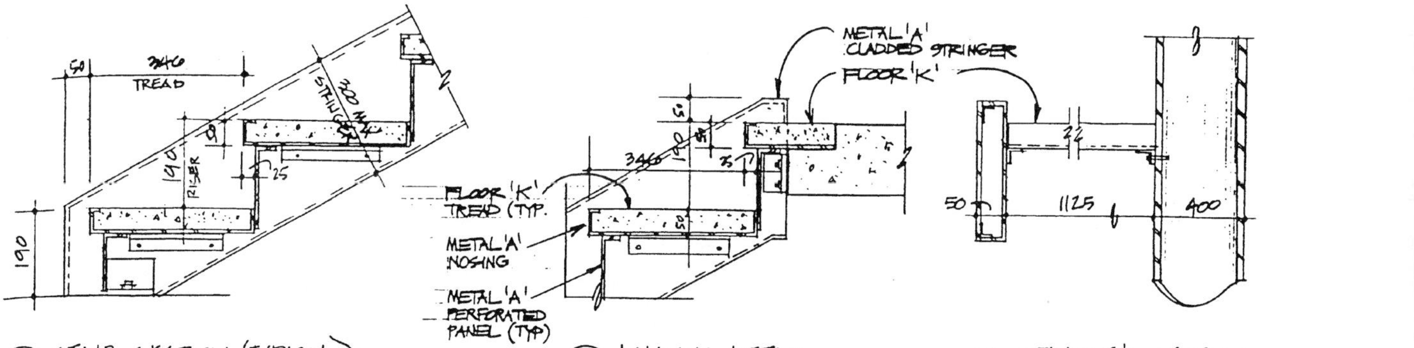

1 DD STAIR SECTION (TYPICAL)
SC. 1:10

2 DD LANDING DETAIL
1:10

3 DD STRINGER SECTION
1:10

39B DD STAIR DETAILS

STAIRS AND RAMPS
Spiral Stairs

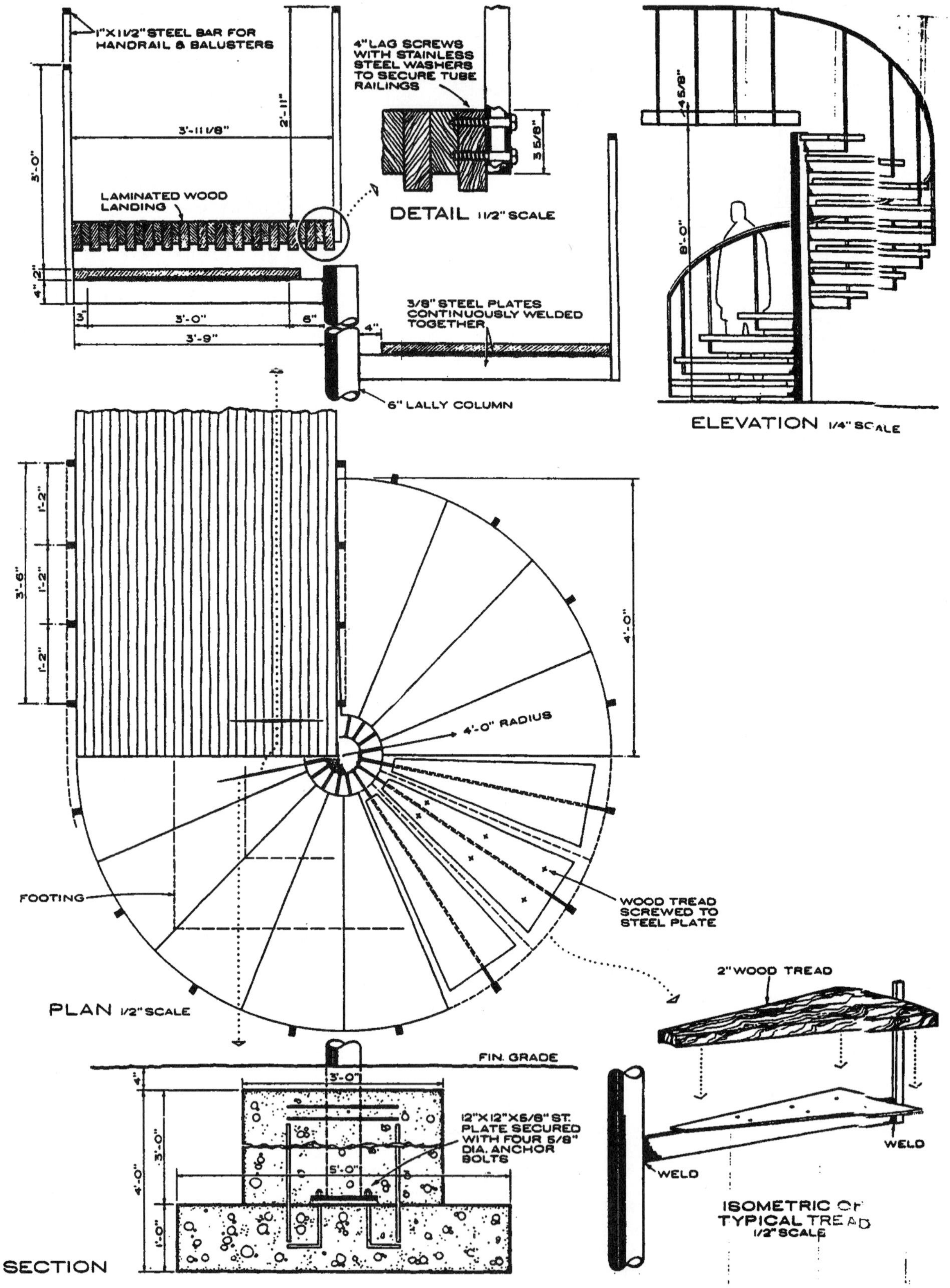

1"X1 1/2" STEEL BAR FOR HANDRAIL & BALUSTERS
4" LAG SCREWS WITH STAINLESS STEEL WASHERS TO SECURE TUBE RAILINGS
3'-11 1/8"
2'-11"
3'-0"
3 5/8"
LAMINATED WOOD LANDING
DETAIL 1 1/2" SCALE
3'-0"
6"
3'-9"
4"
3/8" STEEL PLATES CONTINUOUSLY WELDED TOGETHER
6" LALLY COLUMN
5/8"
8'-0"
ELEVATION 1/4" SCALE
1'-2"
1'-2"
1'-2"
3'-6"
4'-0"
4'-0" RADIUS
FOOTING
WOOD TREAD SCREWED TO STEEL PLATE
PLAN 1/2" SCALE
2" WOOD TREAD
WELD
WELD
ISOMETRIC OF TYPICAL TREAD 1/2" SCALE
FIN. GRADE
3'-0"
12"X12"X5/8" ST. PLATE SECURED WITH FOUR 5/8" DIA. ANCHOR BOLTS
5'-0"
3'-0"
4'-0"
1'-0"
SECTION

Types of Stairs

Four types of stairs are defined: straight stairs, circular stairs, curved stairs, and spiral stairs.

Straight stairs are by far the most common type, representing the bulk of the stair market. Though the term "straight" is self-explanatory, for purposes of classification a straight stair is defined as one in which the stringers are straight members. Straight stairs, unlike stairs of the other three types, may be arranged in several different ways:

Straight run: Either a single flight extending between floors, as shown in Fig. 5*A,* or a series of two or more flights in the same line, with intermediate platforms between them, as shown in Fig. 5*B.*

Parallel: Successive flights which parallel each other and are separated only by one or more intermediate platforms, as shown in Fig. 5*C.*

Angled: Successive flights placed at an angle of other than 180° to each other (often 90°), with an intermediate platform between them, as shown in Fig. 5*D* or *E.* The type shown in Fig. 5*D* is often referred to as a "trussed" stair.

Scissor: A pair of straight-run flights paralleling each other in plan and running in opposite directions on opposite sides of a dividing wall, as shown in Fig. 5*F.*

Circular stairs are stairs which, in plan view, have an open circular form, with a single center of curvature. They may or may not have intermediate platforms between floors.

Curved stairs are stairs which, in plan view, have two or more centers of curvature, being oval, elliptical, or some other compound curved form. They also may or may not have one or more intermediate platforms between floors.

Spiral stairs are stairs with a closed circular form, having uniform sector shaped treads and a supporting center column.

Classes of Stairs

The class designation of stairs, as already noted, is a key to the type of construction, the quality of materials, details and finish, and, in most cases, the relative cost. As stairs of all classes are built to meet the same standards of performance in respect to load-carrying capacity and safety, these class distinctions *do not represent differences in functional value, but in character and appearance.* It is important to recognize that where function is the prime concern, and esthetics are of minor importance, significant economics can be achieved by specifying one of the less expensive classes.

The following four classes of stairs are listed in order of increasing cost (as a general rule); the general construction characteristics of each class are described.

Industrial Class

Stairs of this class are purely functional in character and, consequently, they are generally the most economical. They are designed for either interior or exterior use, in industrial buildings such as factories and warehouses, or as fire escapes or emergency exitways. They do not include stairs which are integral parts of industrial equipment.

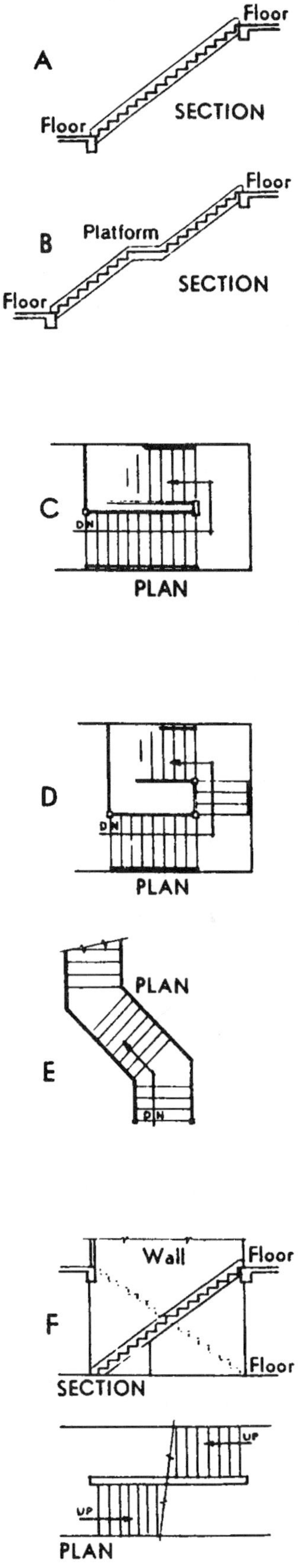

Fig. 5

STAIRS AND RAMPS
Classification of Steel Stairs

Industrial-class stairs are similar in nature to any light steel construction. Hex-head bolts are used for most connections, and welds, where used, are not ground. Stringers may be either flat plate or open channels; treads and platforms are usually made of grating or formed of floor plate, and risers are usually open, though in some cases filled pan type treads and steel risers may be used. Railings are usually of either pipe, tubing, or light steel angle construction.

Service Class

This class of stairs serves chiefly functional purposes, but is not unattractive in appearance. Service stairs are usually located in enclosed stairwells and provide a secondary or emergency means of travel between floors. In multistoried buildings they are commonly used as egress stairs. They may serve employees, tenants, or the public, and are generally used where economy is a consideration.

Stringers of service stairs are generally the same types as those used on stairs of the industrial class. Treads may be one of several standard types, either filled or formed of floor or tread plate, and risers are either exposed steel or open construction. Railings are typically of pipe construction or a simple bar type with tubular newels, and soffits are usually left exposed. Connections on the underside of the stairs are made with hex-head bolts, and only those welds in the travel area are smooth.

Commercial Class

Stairs of this class are usually for public use and are of more attractive design than those of the service class. They may be placed in open locations or may be located in closed stairwells or in public, institutional, or commercial buildings.

Stringers for this class of stairs are usually exposed open channel or plate sections. Treads may be any of a number of standard types, and risers are usually exposed steel. Railings vary from ornamental bar or tube construction with metal handrails to simple pipe construction, and soffits may or may not be covered. Exposed bolted connections in areas where appearance is critical are made with countersunk flat- or oval-head bolts; otherwise, hex-head bolts are used. Welds in conspicuous locations are smooth, and all joints are closely fitted.

Architectural Class

This classification applies to any of the more elaborate and usually more expensive stairs, those which are designed to be architectural features in a building. They may be wholly custom designed or may represent a combination of standard parts with specially designed elements such as stringers, railings, treads, or platforms. Usually this class of stair has a comparatively low pitch, with relatively low risers and correspondingly wider treads. Architectural metal stairs may be located either in the open or in enclosed stairwells in public, institutional, commercial, or monumental buildings.

The materials, fabrication details, and finishes used in architectural class stairs vary widely, as dictated by the architect's design and specifications. As a general rule, construction joints are made as inconspicuous as possible, exposed welds are smooth, and soffits are covered with some surfacing material. Stringers may be special sections exposed, or may be structural members enclosed in other materials. Railings are of an ornamental type and, like the treads and risers, may be of any construction desired.

General Requirements, All Classes of Stairs

All fixed metal stairs, regardless of class, are of fire-resistant construction and are designed and constructed to carry a minimum live load of 100 lb/ft^2 of projected plan area or an alternative concentrated load of 300 lb applied at the center of any tread span. Railings and handrails are designed and constructed to withstand a minimum force of 200 lb applied in any direction at any point on the rail.

STAIRS AND RAMPS
General-Purpose Steel Stairs

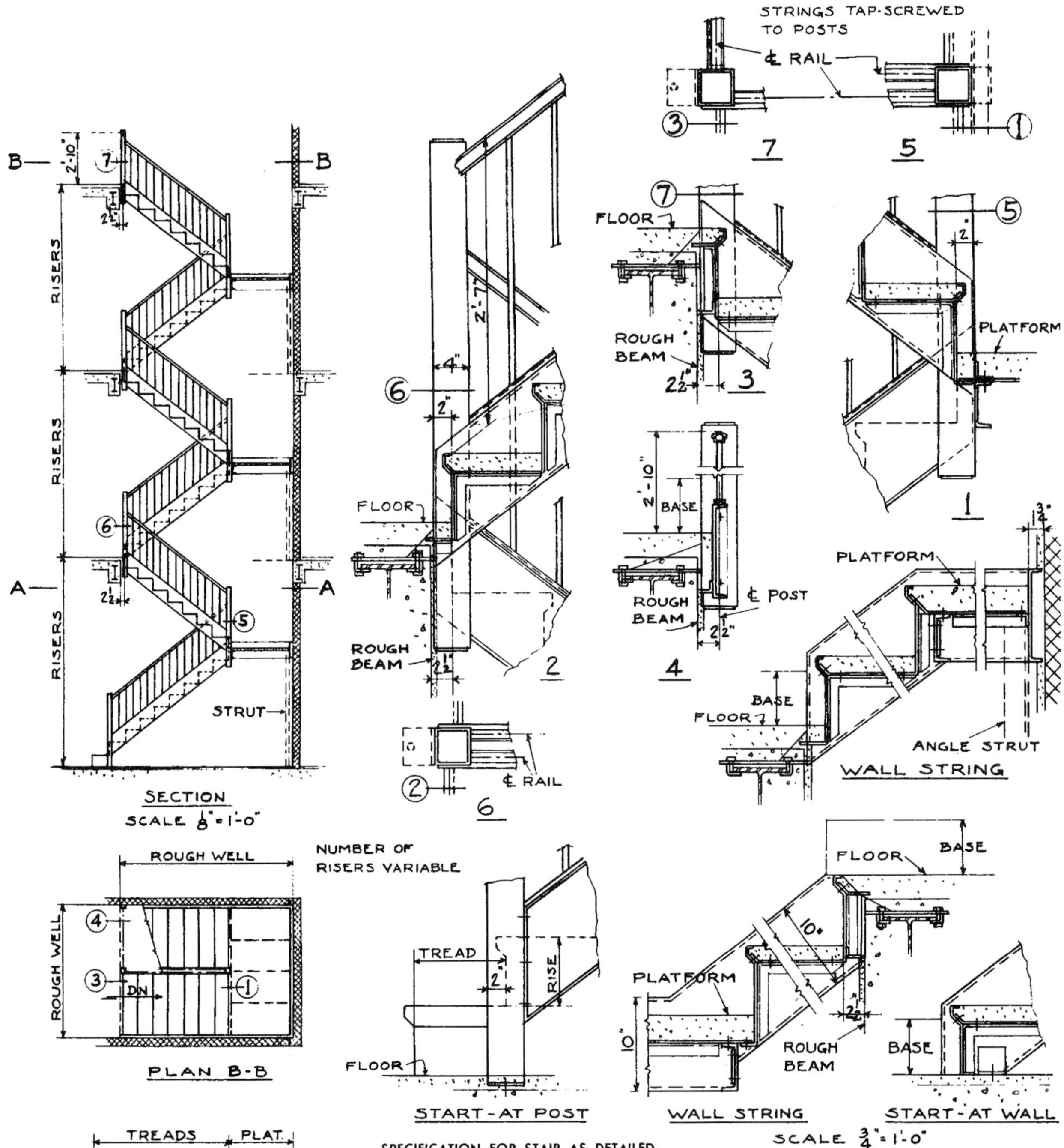

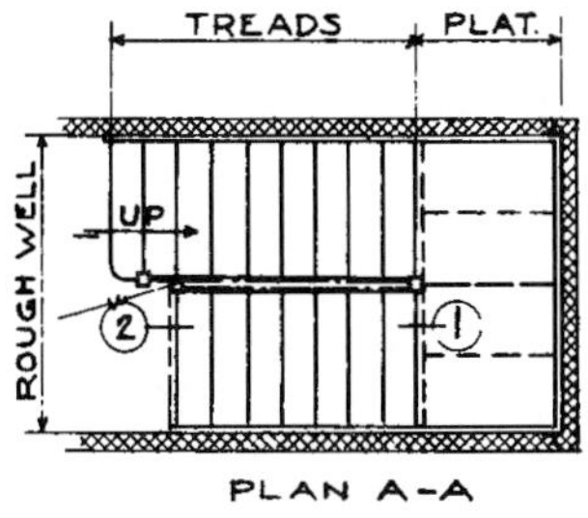

LAYOUT FOR:
MULTIPLE STORY
INTERMEDIATE PLATFORM
TWO RUNS PER STORY

SPECIFICATION FOR STAIR AS DETAILED:
Furnish and erect steel stairs and railings complete as detailed. Strings 10"x1 1/2"x8.4 lb. channels with 1 1/4"x1 1/4"x1/8" angle brackets, facias same section bolted to newels and floor construction. Headers of channels bolted or welded to newels and strings. Angle struts placed in wall, bolted to strings and to floor construction. Risers and sub-treads of 14 gauge steel, sub-platforms of 12 gauge steel reinforced with angle or tee stiffeners. Fill, 2" for treads, 3" for platforms, by others. Newels 4" square pipe, railing balusters 1/2" square spaced 4 1/2" and welded into 1"x1/2" channels top and bottom with handrail section as shown. All surfaces to be cleaned and painted one shop coat. Shop drawings, to show construction methods and fastenings, are to be approved before fabrication.

ALTERNATE SPECIFICATIONS:
Strings may be channels, flat plates, or formed plates.
Tread Brackets may be other size angles, or bars.
Riser Brackets may be omitted.
Hanger Rods may be used in place of struts.
Sub-Treads, Risers and **Sub-Platforms** may be heavier gauge.
Newels and **Railings** may be of other construction as designed by architect.
Wall Rails, where required, may have same handrail section as railing.
Prime Coat may be red lead, black graphite, zinc chromate, or other approved paint.

STAIRS AND RAMPS

Steel Stairs

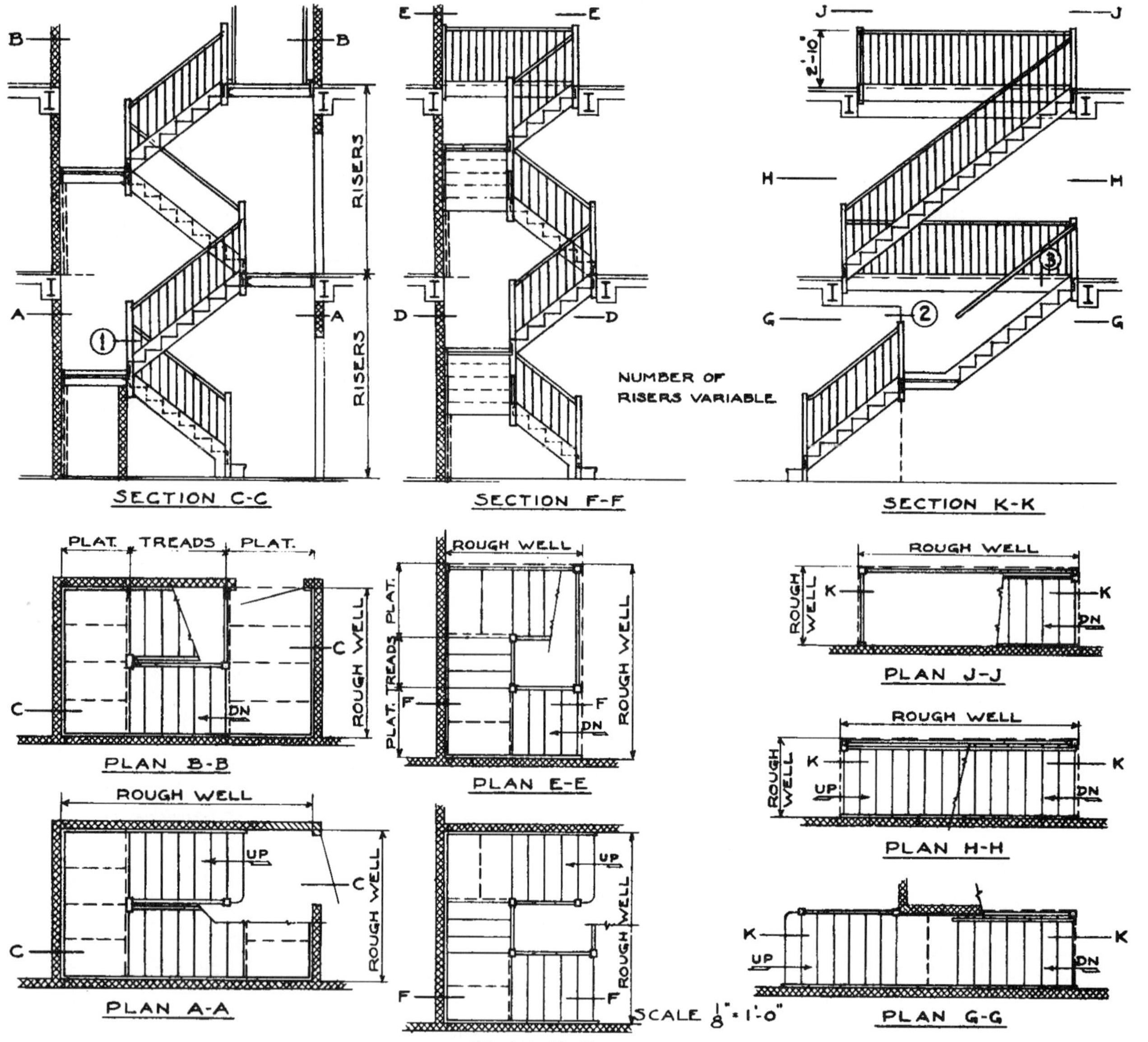

PLAN D-D

LAYOUT FOR:
MULTIPLE STORY
INTERMEDIATE PLATFORMS
PLATFORM AT FLOOR
TWO RUNS PER STORY

Strings and rails finishing against face of rectangular newels, allowing minimum hand clearance between strings and rails. For wider center well, two square newels replace one rectangular newel.

LAYOUT FOR:
MULTIPLE STORY
INTERMEDIATE PLATFORMS
THREE RUNS PER STORY

Open center well allowing intermediate stair runs at 90 degrees. One square newel at each platform.

LAYOUT FOR:
MULTIPLE STORY
INTERMEDIATE PLATFORMS
ONE AND TWO RUNS PER STORY

Arrangement for stairs in corridors, or other restricted spaces, either closed or open well.

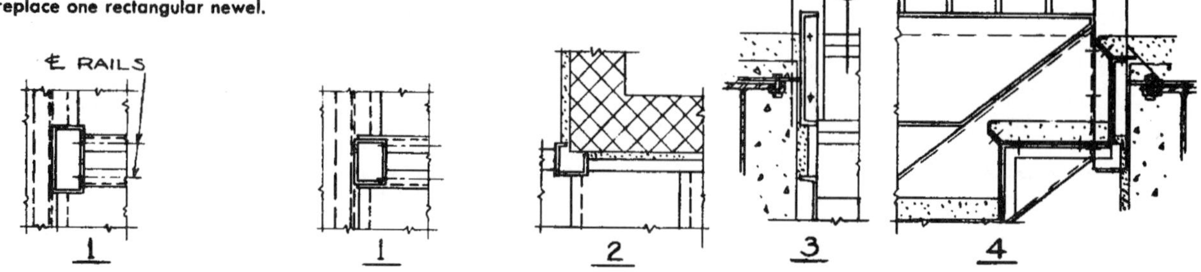

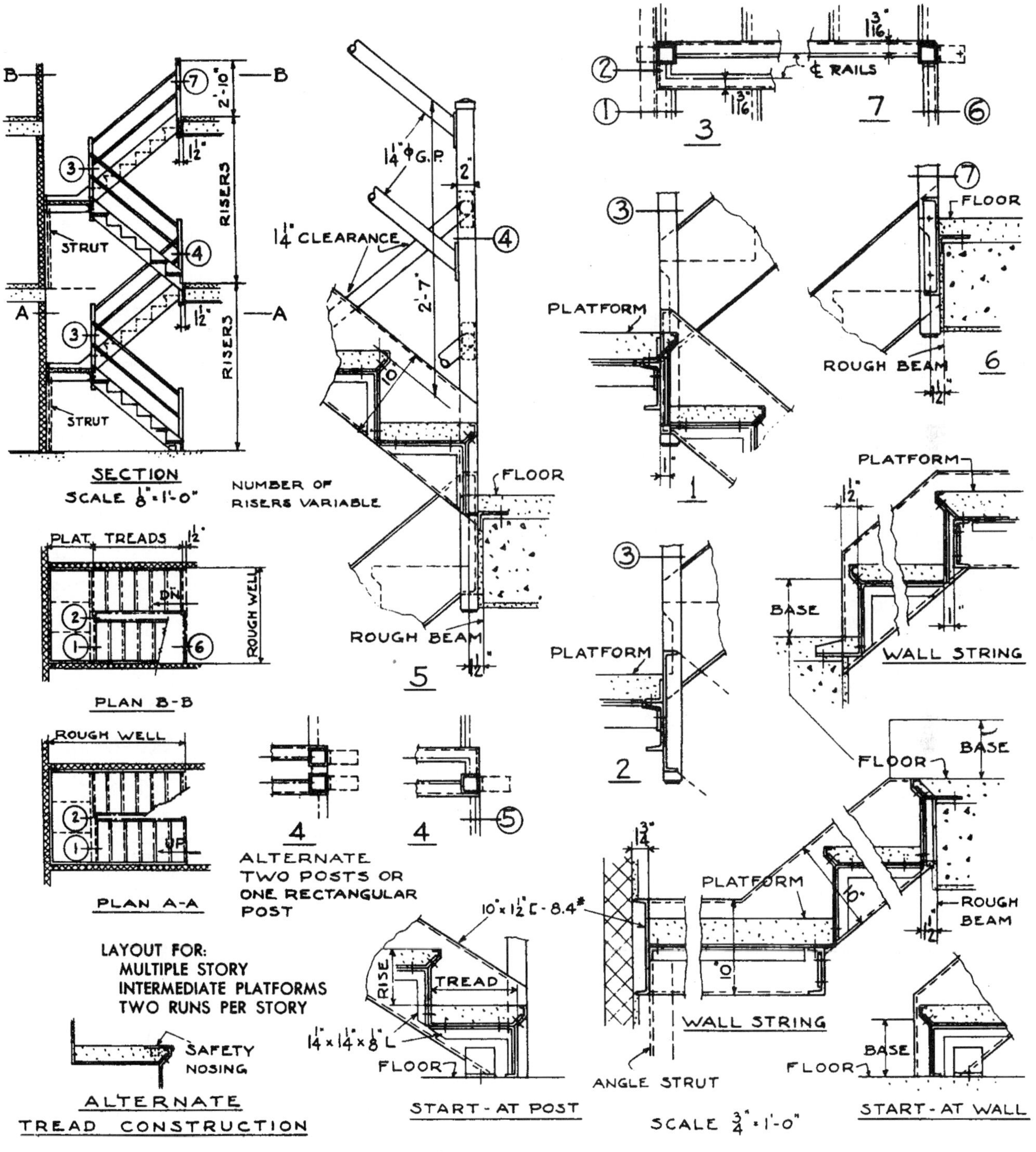
B
B
A
A
7
3
4
3
2'-10"
RISERS
RISERS
1½"
1½"
STRUT
STRUT
SECTION
SCALE ⅛"=1'-0"
NUMBER OF RISERS VARIABLE
PLAT. TREADS
ROUGH WELL
DN
PLAN B-B
ROUGH WELL
UP
PLAN A-A
1¼" ɸ G.P.
2"
1¼" CLEARANCE
2'-7"
10"
FLOOR
ROUGH BEAM
5
4
4
ALTERNATE TWO POSTS OR ONE RECTANGULAR POST
LAYOUT FOR:
MULTIPLE STORY
INTERMEDIATE PLATFORMS
TWO RUNS PER STORY
SAFETY NOSING
ALTERNATE TREAD CONSTRUCTION
3/16"
℄ RAILS
3
7
PLATFORM
1
FLOOR
ROUGH BEAM
6
PLATFORM
2
PLATFORM
BASE
WALL STRING
FLOOR
BASE
PLATFORM
ROUGH BEAM
10"x1½" [-8.4#
RISE
TREAD
1¼"x1¼"x⅛" L
FLOOR
START-AT POST
WALL STRING
ANGLE STRUT
SCALE ¾"=1'-0"
BASE
FLOOR
START-AT WALL

STAIRS AND RAMPS
Steel Stairs

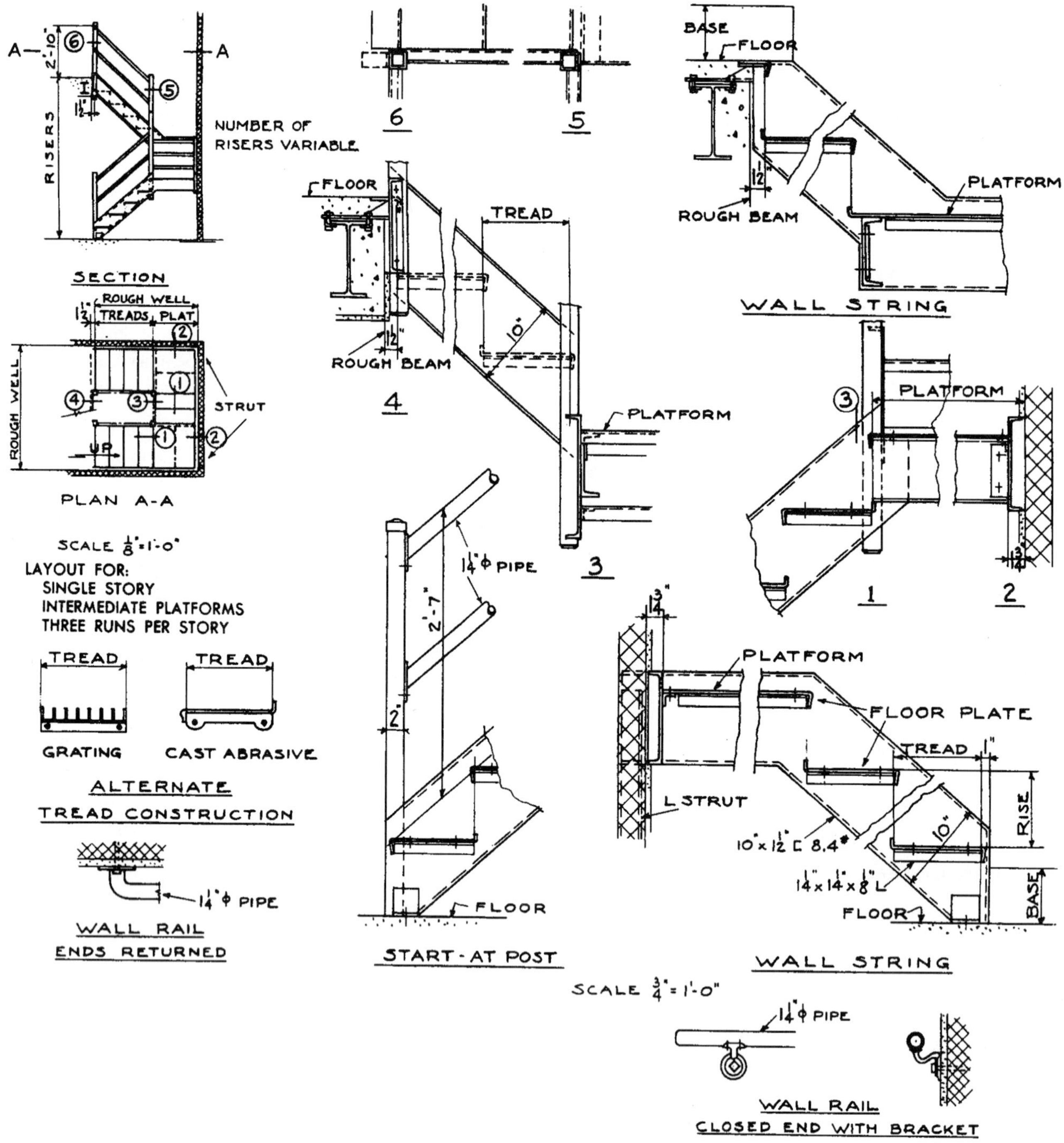

STAIRS AND RAMPS

Steel Stairs

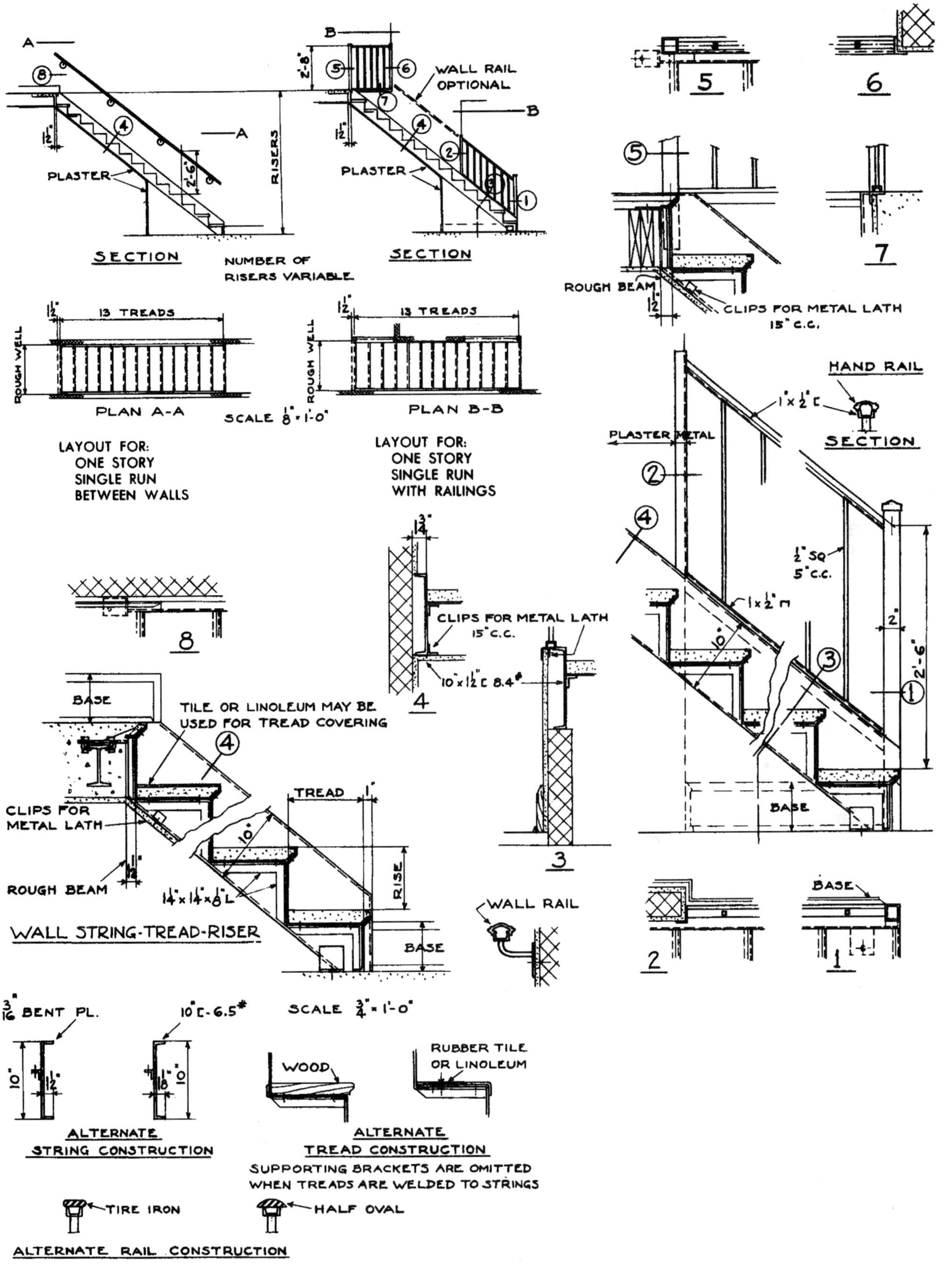
A
B
WALL RAIL OPTIONAL
2'-8"
2'-6"
1½"
PLASTER
RISERS
SECTION
NUMBER OF RISERS VARIABLE
SECTION
13 TREADS
ROUGH WELL
PLAN A-A
SCALE ⅛" = 1'-0"
PLAN B-B
LAYOUT FOR:
ONE STORY
SINGLE RUN
BETWEEN WALLS
LAYOUT FOR:
ONE STORY
SINGLE RUN
WITH RAILINGS
5
6
7
8
ROUGH BEAM
CLIPS FOR METAL LATH
15" C.C.
HAND RAIL
1"x½" C
SECTION
PLASTER METAL
½" SQ
5" C.C.
1x½" m
10"
2"
BASE
3
4
10"x1½" C 8.4#
¾"
TILE OR LINOLEUM MAY BE USED FOR TREAD COVERING
CLIPS FOR METAL LATH
TREAD
RISE
ROUGH BEAM
1¼"x1¼"x⅛" L
WALL STRING-TREAD-RISER
WALL RAIL
2
1
SCALE ¾" = 1'-0"
3/16" BENT PL.
10" C-6.5#
10"
1½"
WOOD
RUBBER TILE OR LINOLEUM
ALTERNATE STRING CONSTRUCTION
ALTERNATE TREAD CONSTRUCTION
SUPPORTING BRACKETS ARE OMITTED WHEN TREADS ARE WELDED TO STRINGS
TIRE IRON
HALF OVAL
ALTERNATE RAIL CONSTRUCTION

STAIRS AND RAMPS

Stair Platform Construction

The platform (Fig. 6) is shown constructed with a steel channel, A, of adequate strength to span the well on line X, through Secs. 1, 2, and 3, and supported at both ends by the wall strings. Newel posts rest on this channel through angle clips, around which the platform plate is cut (Sec. 3). Face strings have welded end plates with flathead screws tapped into the newels (Sec. 2).

The two platforms with two intermediate risers (Fig. 7) are shown constructed with the load carried on line Y by string B, post C, and channel D, which are shown bolted together (Secs. 8, 9, and 10) with through bolts. The load is also carried from post C on line Z in the same manner.

The members at post C may be brought together and welded and the post fitted over the connection, or the entire unit welded.

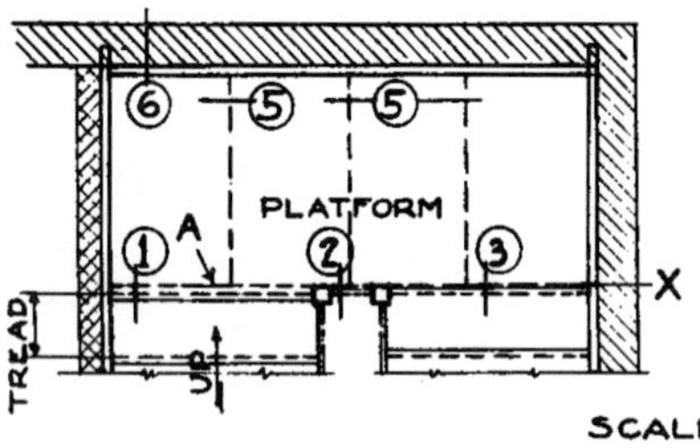

SCALE 1/4" = 1'-0"

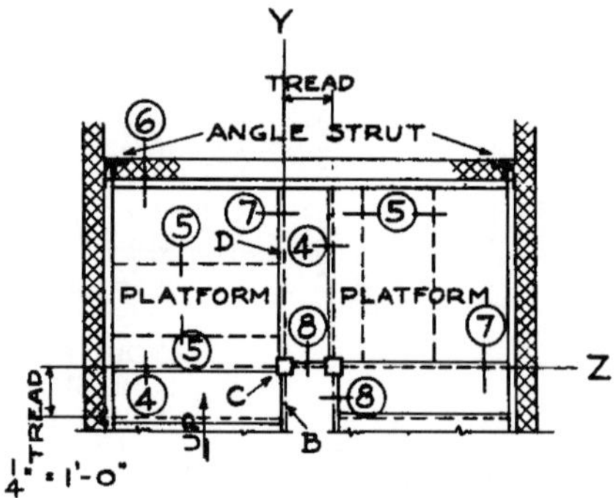

Fig. 6 Plan—one platform. Load carried on line X. Wall strings supported on masonry wall

Fig. 7 Plan—two platforms with two intermediate risers. Load carried on line Y and supplemented on line Z. Wall strings supported by struts

Stairs are supported by one or more of the following methods, (a) String at floor rests directly on floor construction; (b) String at landing or platform extends into adjacent load-bearing wall; or (c) String at landing or platform is supported by struts extending to the floor below, these being of angles, I-beams or pipes either set in the wall or exposed; or (d) String at landing or platform is supported by rods hung from the floor above, either set in walls or exposed; (e) String paralleling load-bearing wall may have shelf brackets on the back of the strings and set in wall; similar brackets may be used with struts or hanger rods.

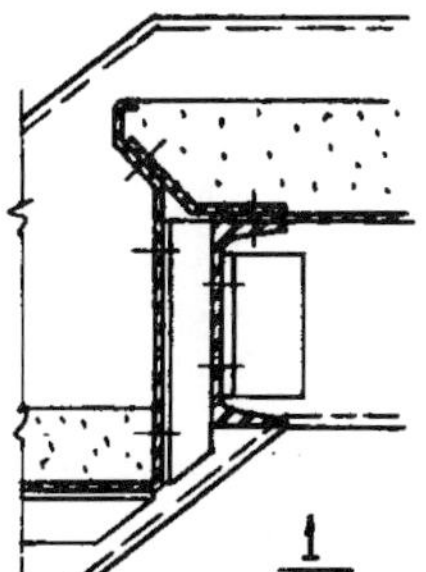

1

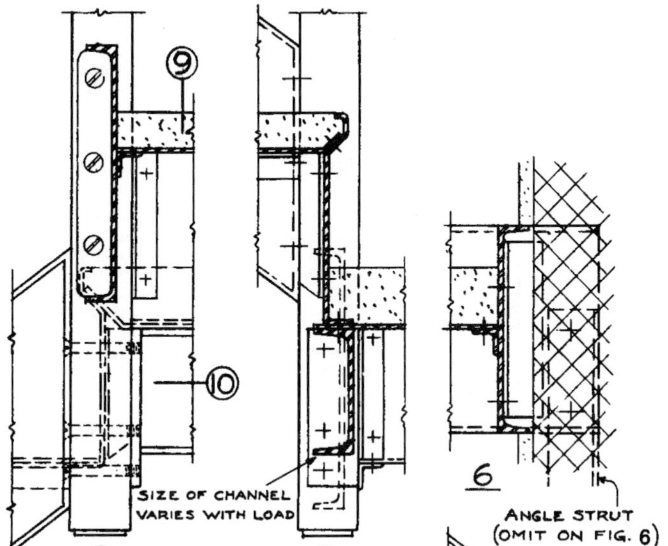

8 9 6

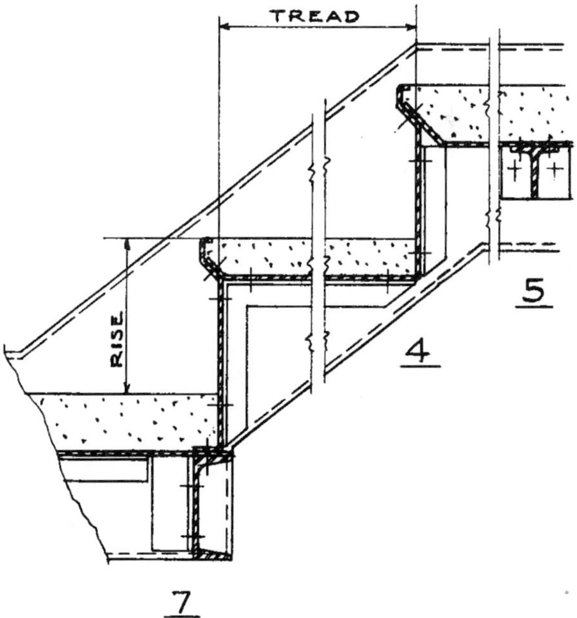

4 5 7

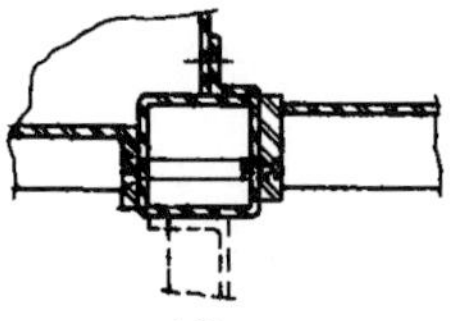

10

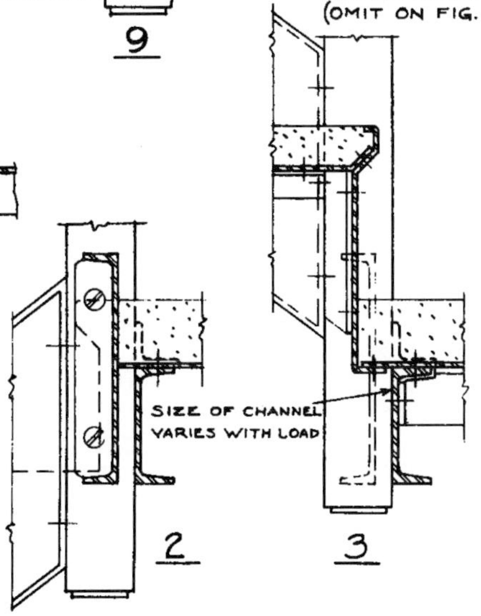

2 3

CONDITIONS ILLUSTRATED:
Concrete or terrazo fill.
Open unplastered soffit.
Square steel newel posts.
Steel Channel Strings.

STAIRS AND RAMPS
Stairwell

Width of stair is usually considered center line of rail to finished wall. When wall rail is required allowance should be made for clearance to comply with any legal requirements as to net width.

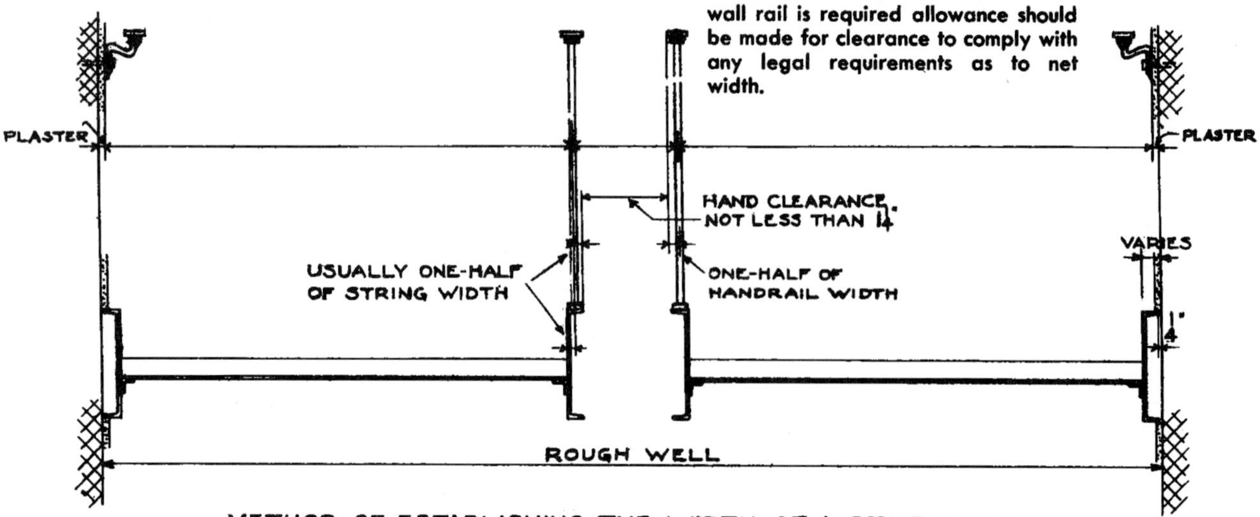

METHOD OF ESTABLISHING THE WIDTH OF A STAIR WELL

Height of riser and width of tread vary to fit the type of stair and its use. Legal requirements often limit the minimum tread and maximum rise. A tread of 10" and a rise of 7" to 7½" are considered average. Stairs of easy runs are often 10½" to 11" treads with risers under 7". Stairs used exclusively by maintenance and operating men are often constructed with a rise and tread to equal a pitch greater than 40°. Tread width is always face to face of riser.

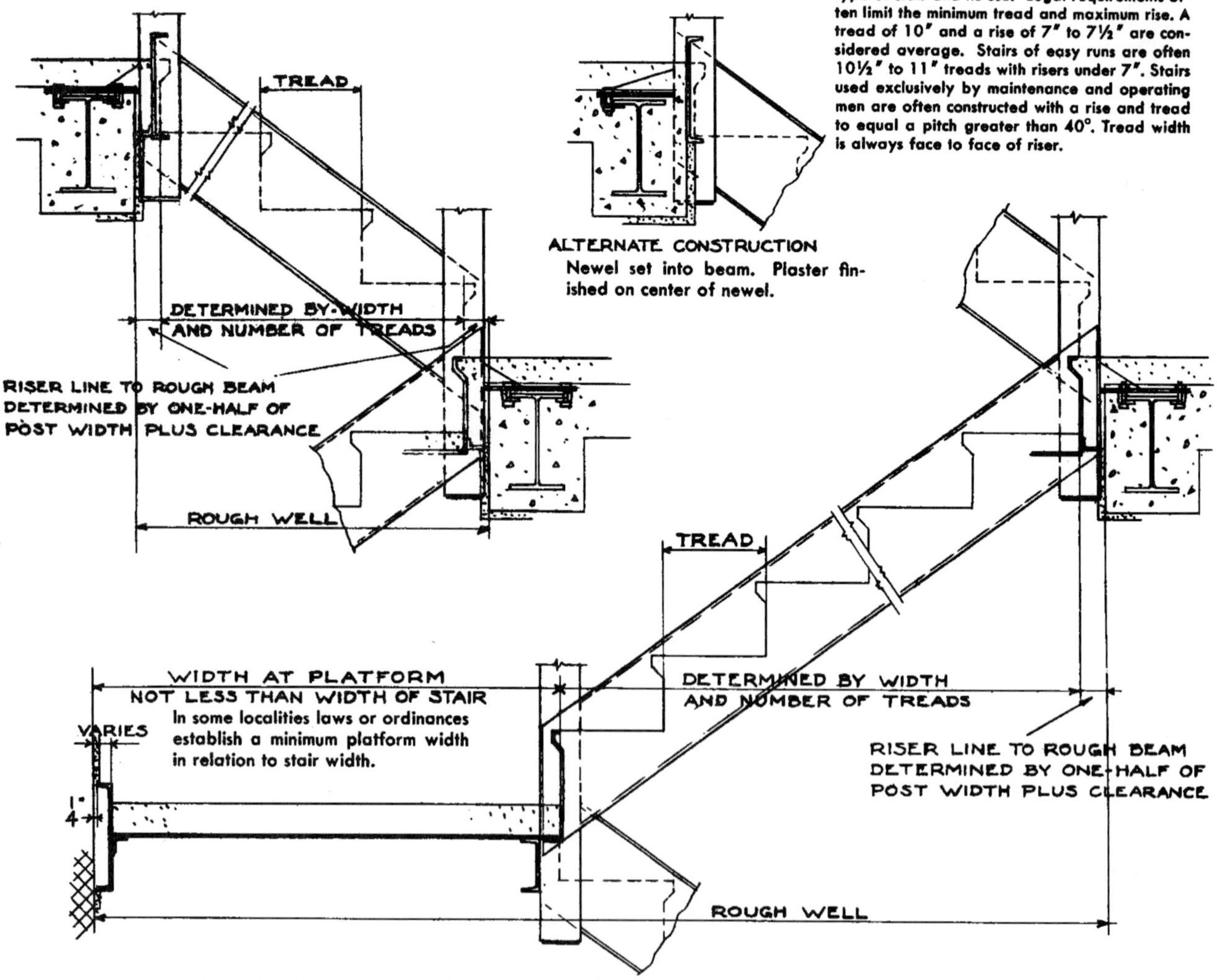

METHOD OF ESTABLISHING THE LENGTH OF A STAIR WELL

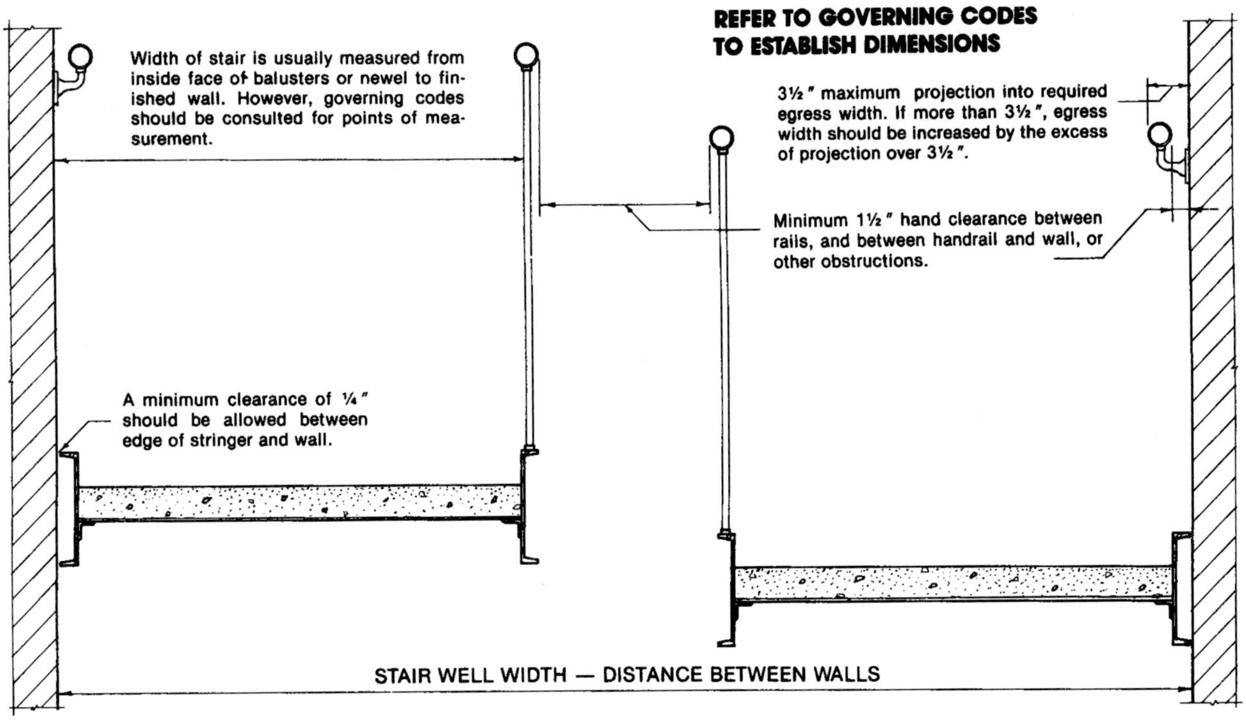
REFER TO GOVERNING CODES TO ESTABLISH DIMENSIONS
Width of stair is usually measured from inside face of balusters or newel to finished wall. However, governing codes should be consulted for points of measurement.
3½" maximum projection into required egress width. If more than 3½", egress width should be increased by the excess of projection over 3½".
Minimum 1½" hand clearance between rails, and between handrail and wall, or other obstructions.
A minimum clearance of ¼" should be allowed between edge of stringer and wall.
STAIR WELL WIDTH — DISTANCE BETWEEN WALLS

Minimum code requirements are usually measured from finished wall to finished wall. When establishing rough stair well dimensions, allowance should be made for thicknesses of any finish materials to be applied to the rough walls.

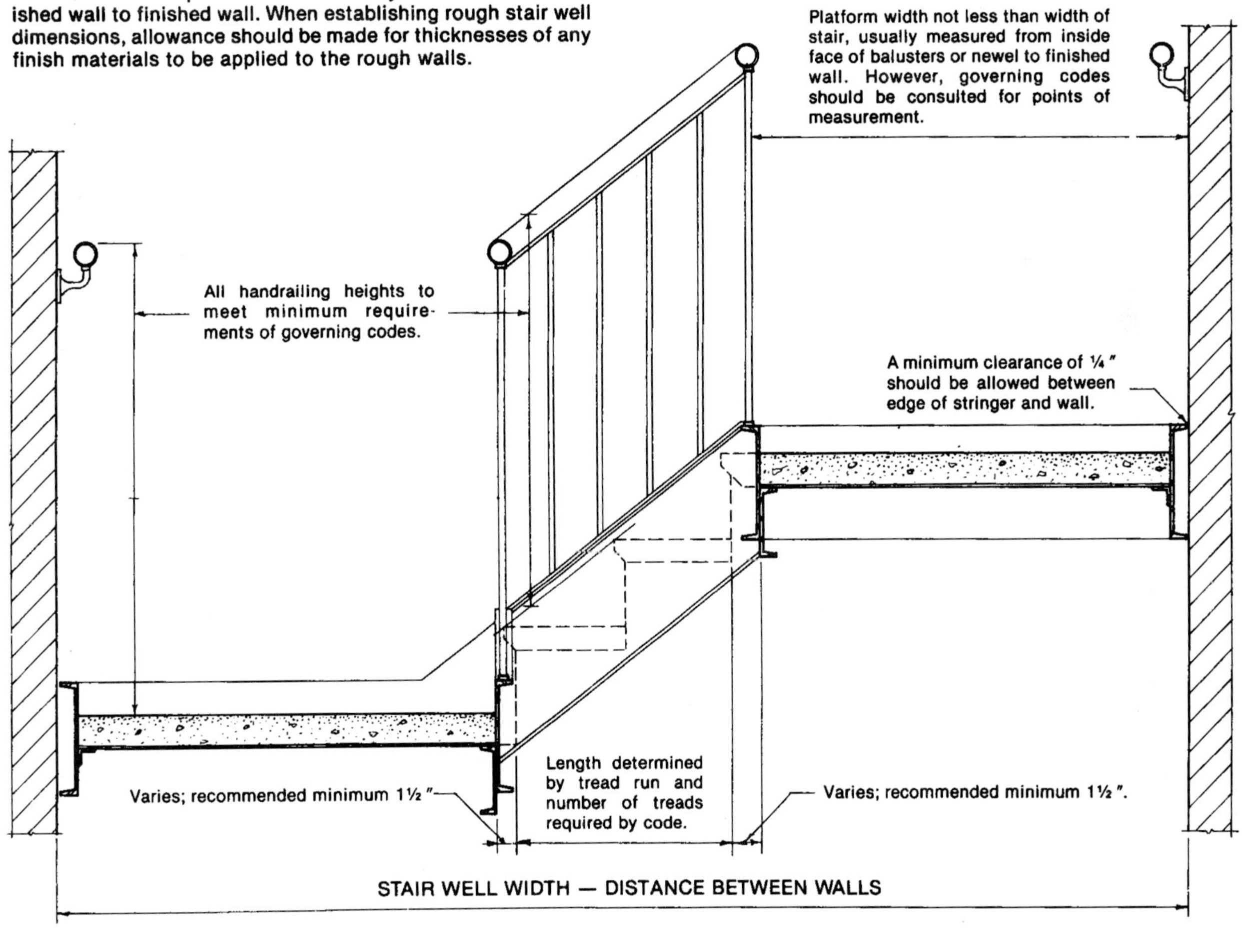
Platform width not less than width of stair, usually measured from inside face of balusters or newel to finished wall. However, governing codes should be consulted for points of measurement.
All handrailing heights to meet minimum requirements of governing codes.
A minimum clearance of ¼" should be allowed between edge of stringer and wall.
Varies; recommended minimum 1½"
Length determined by tread run and number of treads required by code.
Varies; recommended minimum 1½".
STAIR WELL WIDTH — DISTANCE BETWEEN WALLS

STAIRS AND RAMPS
Stair Length Dimensions

REFER TO GOVERNING CODES TO ESTABLISH DIMENSIONS

Height of riser and tread run vary according to governing codes. A tread of 10″ and a rise of 7″ to 7½″ are considered average. Stair treads for more comfortable runs are often 10½″ to 11″ with risers less than 7″. Treads and risers should be so proportioned that the sum of two risers and one tread run is not less than 24″ or more than 26″.

In establishing stair well dimensions, tread run is always face to face of riser.

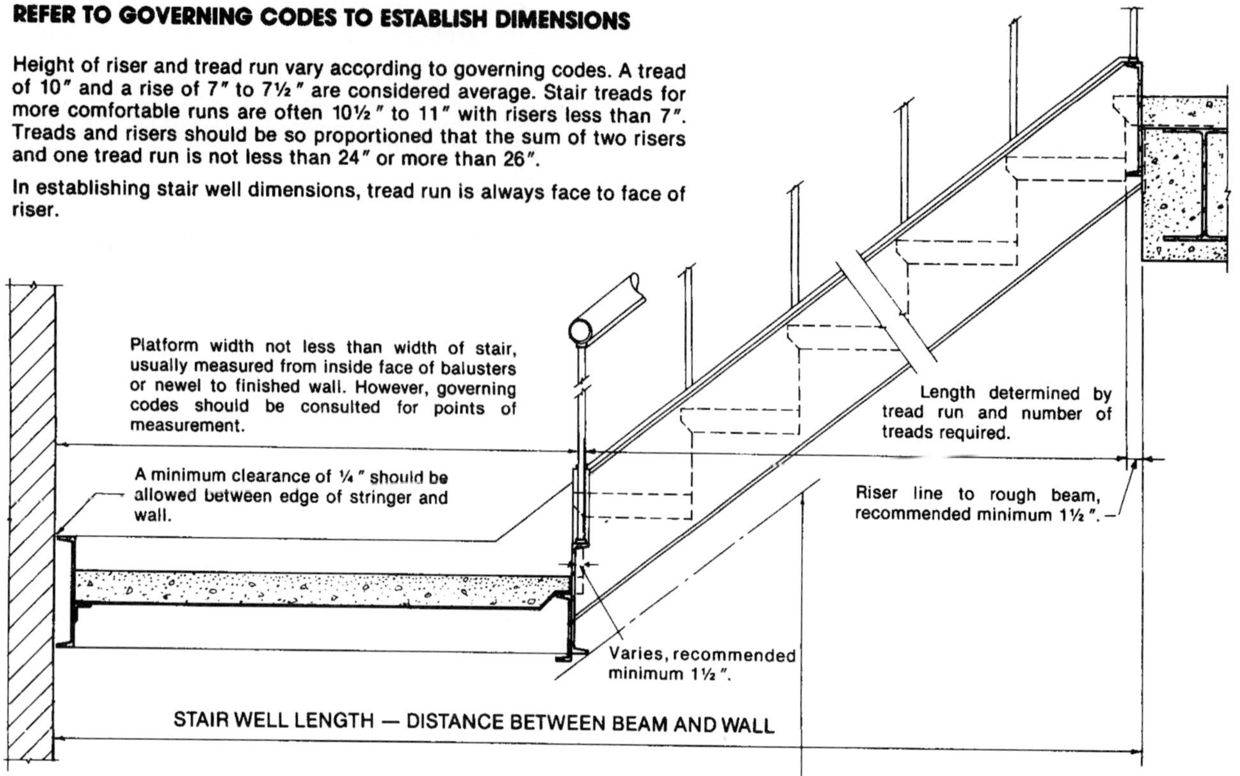

Platform width not less than width of stair, usually measured from inside face of balusters or newel to finished wall. However, governing codes should be consulted for points of measurement.
A minimum clearance of ¼″ should be allowed between edge of stringer and wall.
Length determined by tread run and number of treads required.
Riser line to rough beam, recommended minimum 1½″.
Varies, recommended minimum 1½″.
STAIR WELL LENGTH — DISTANCE BETWEEN BEAM AND WALL

Minimum code requirements are usually measured from finished wall to finished wall. When establishing rough stair well dimensions, allowance should be made for thickness of any finish materials to be applied to the rough walls.

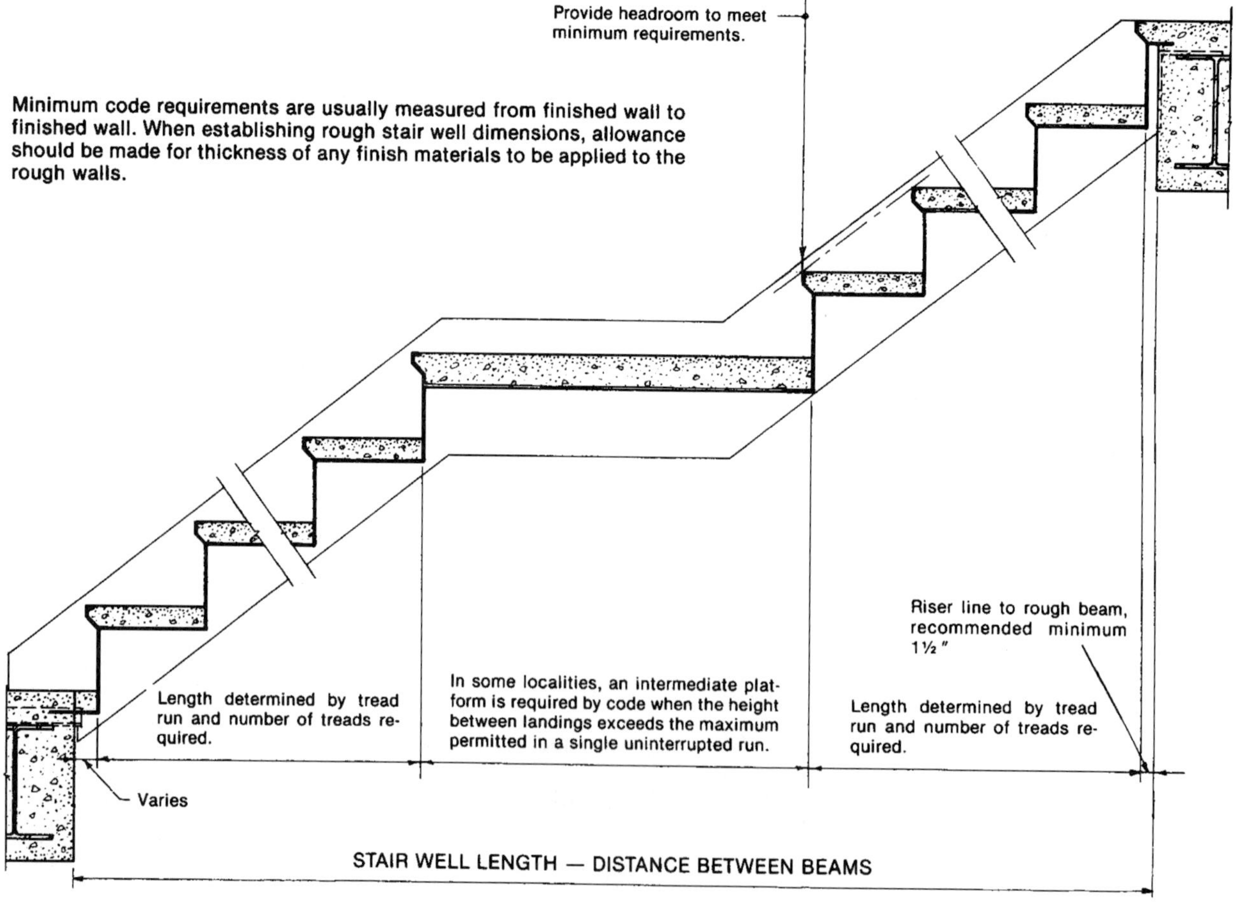

Provide headroom to meet minimum requirements.
Riser line to rough beam, recommended minimum 1½″
Length determined by tread run and number of treads required.
In some localities, an intermediate platform is required by code when the height between landings exceeds the maximum permitted in a single uninterrupted run.
Length determined by tread run and number of treads required.
Varies
STAIR WELL LENGTH — DISTANCE BETWEEN BEAMS

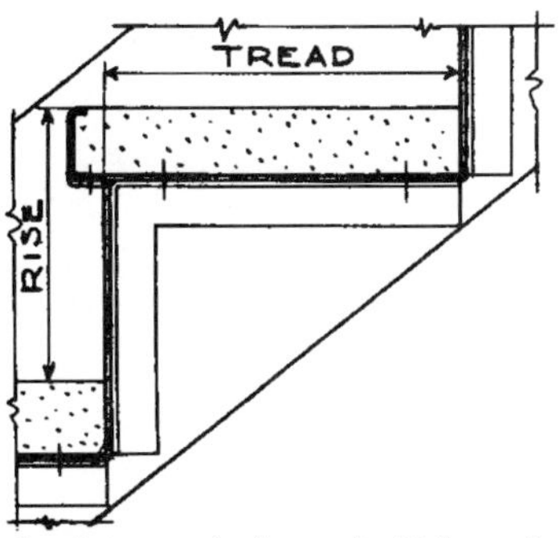

Steel riser and sub tread with formed nosing, angle supporting brackets.

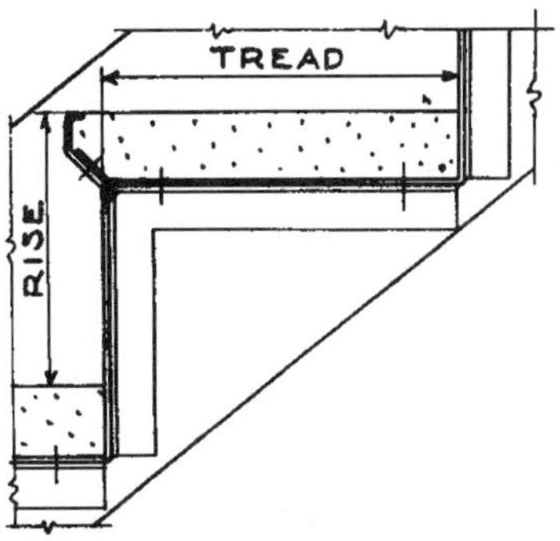

Steel riser and sub tread with formed nosing, angle supporting brackets.

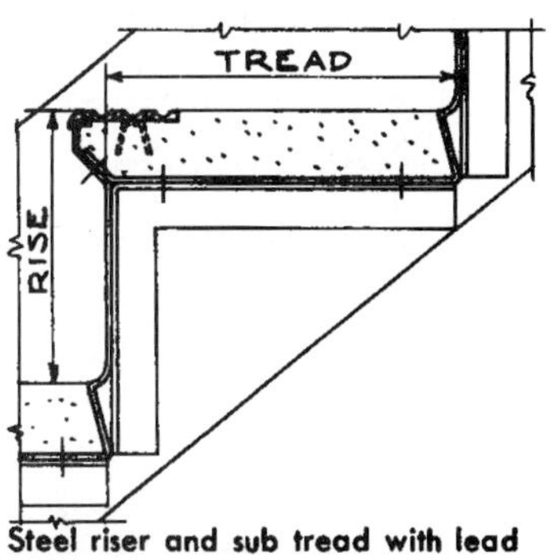

Steel riser and sub tread with lead filled safety nosing, sanitary cove, angle supporting brackets.

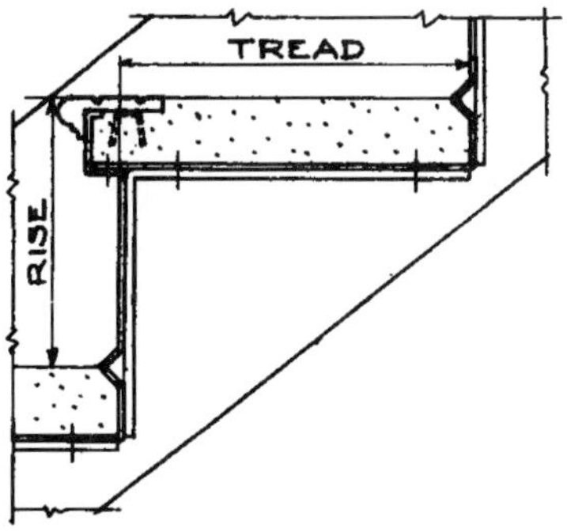

Steel riser and sub tread with abrasive safety nosing, sanitary cove, flat bar supporting brackets.

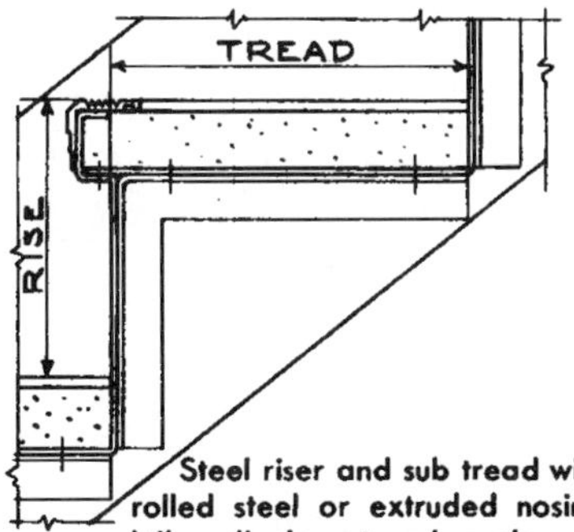

Steel riser and sub tread with rolled steel or extruded nosing and tile or linoleum tread, angle supporting brackets. Other types of safety nosing or tread covering may be used.

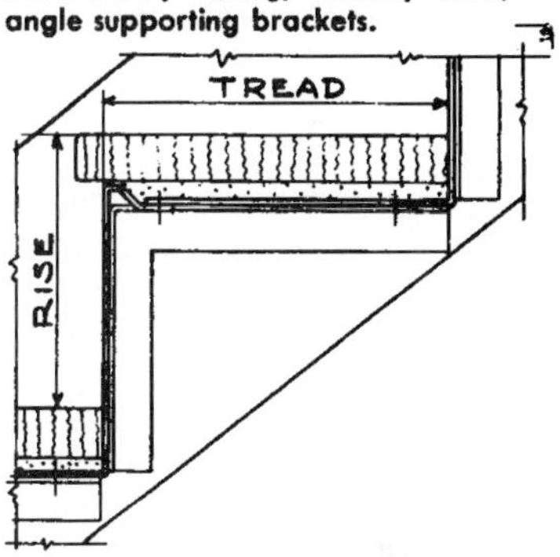

Steel riser and sub tread with marble, or pre-cast tread, angle supporting brackets.

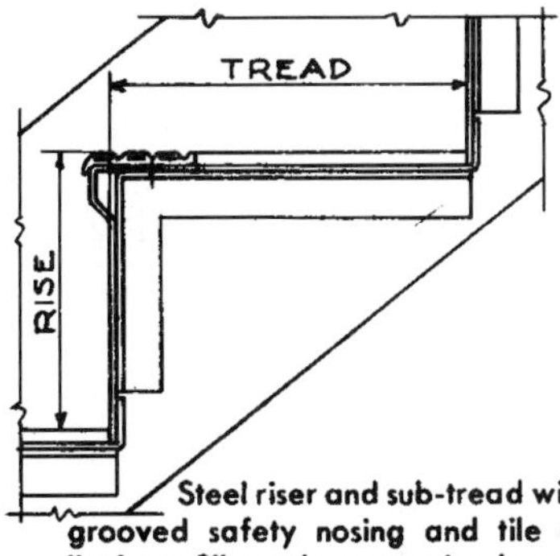

Steel riser and sub-tread with grooved safety nosing and tile or linoleum fill, angle supporting bracket. Other types of safety nosing or tread covering may be used.

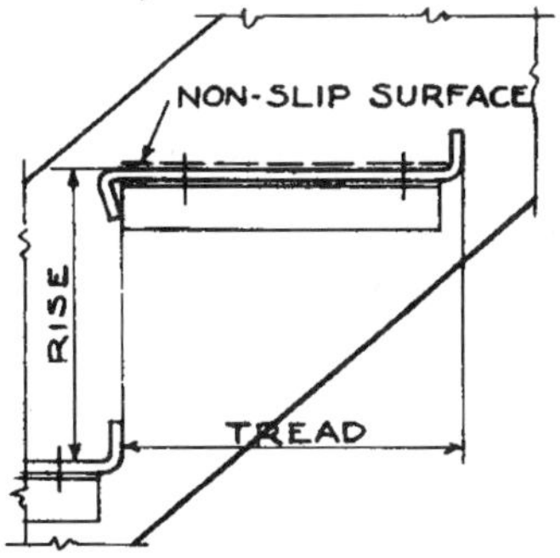

Steel floor plate tread, angle tread bracket, with or without steel riser.

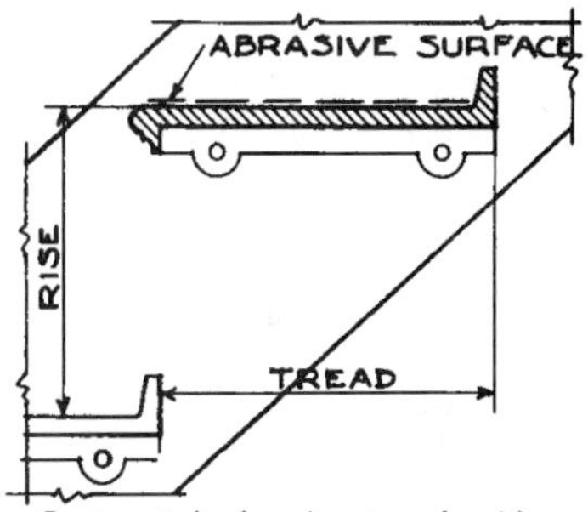

Cast metal abrasive tread, with or without steel riser.

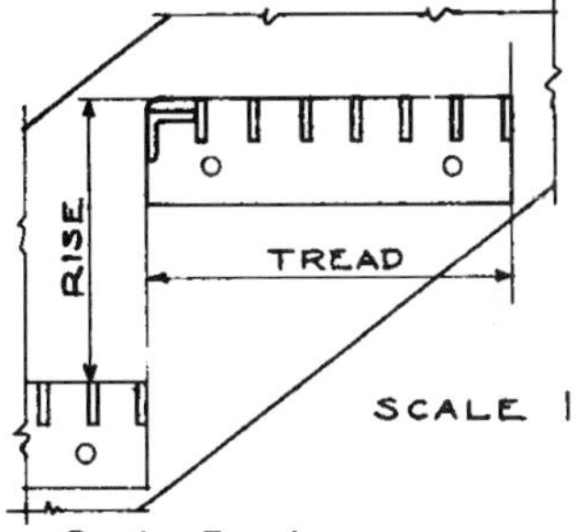

SCALE 1½" = 1'-0"

Grating Tread.

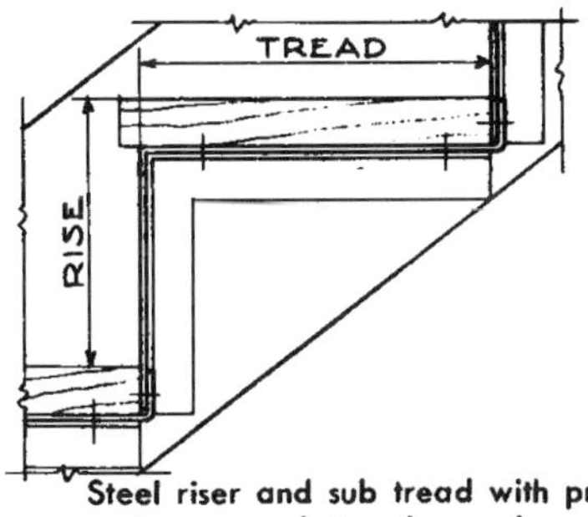

Steel riser and sub tread with pre-cast or wood treads, angle supporting brackets.

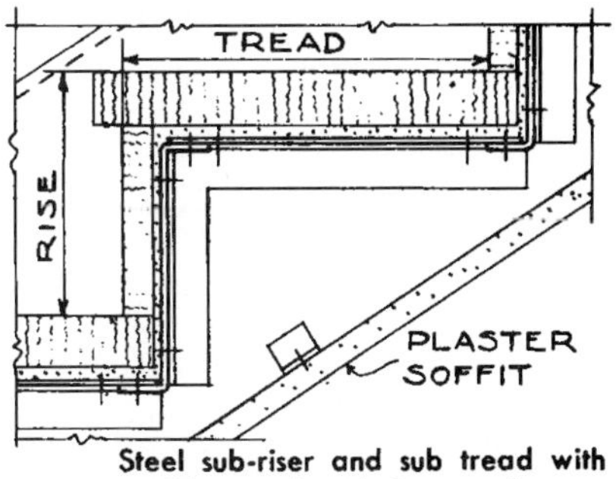

Steel sub-riser and sub tread with marble tread and riser, angle supporting brackets.

Stairs with concrete or terrazzo fill may be constructed with the top of supporting bracket 2" below the tread surface and 3" below the platform surface. These thicknesses may be less for narrow stairs or where use is limited.

Fill is always considered the distance from string bracket to finish tread.

Treads and riser brackets may be 1¼"x1¼"x3⁄16" or ⅛" angles, welded or riveted to string, or ¼"x1¼" bar welded. Treads and risers are usually bolted to brackets with round head bolts. Cast or grating treads are usually bolted to strings with two ⅜" bolts at each end. Brackets back of risers may be omitted when more economical construction is desired.

STAIRS AND RAMPS
Tread Sections

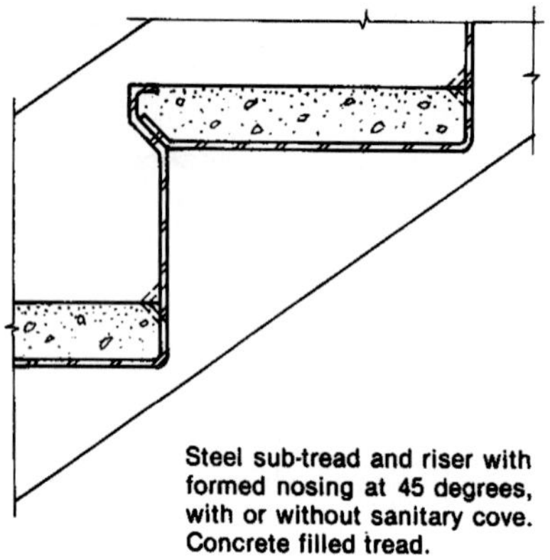

Steel sub-tread and riser with formed nosing at 45 degrees, with or without sanitary cove. Concrete filled tread.

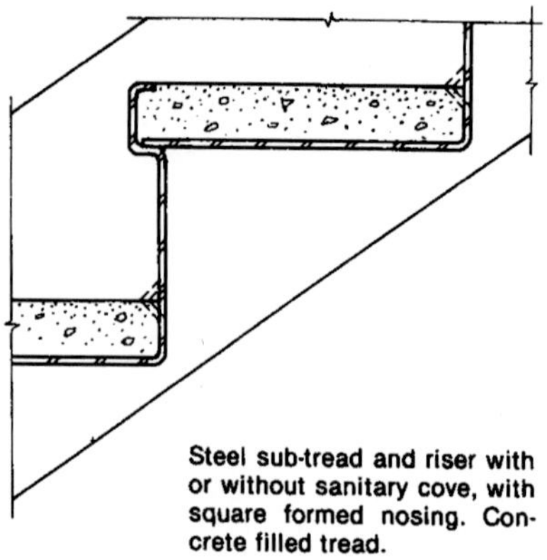

Steel sub-tread and riser with or without sanitary cove, with square formed nosing. Concrete filled tread.

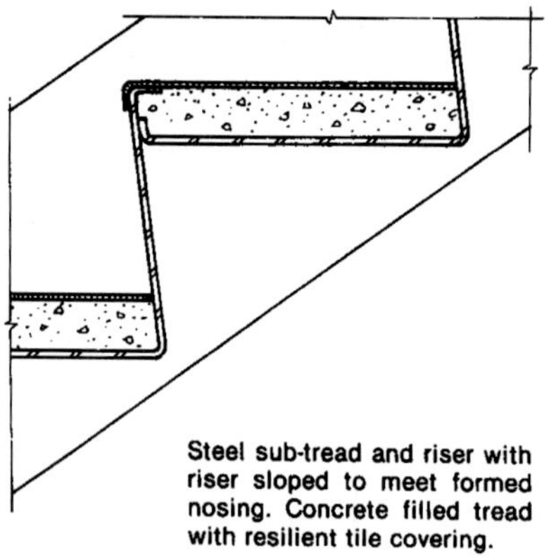

Steel sub-tread and riser with riser sloped to meet formed nosing. Concrete filled tread with resilient tile covering.

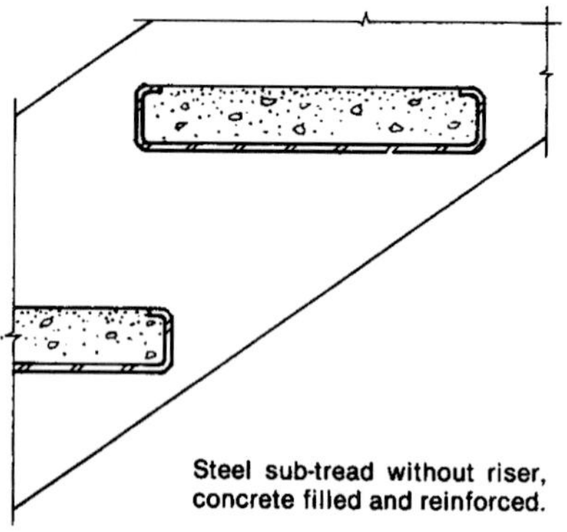

Steel sub-tread without riser, concrete filled and reinforced.

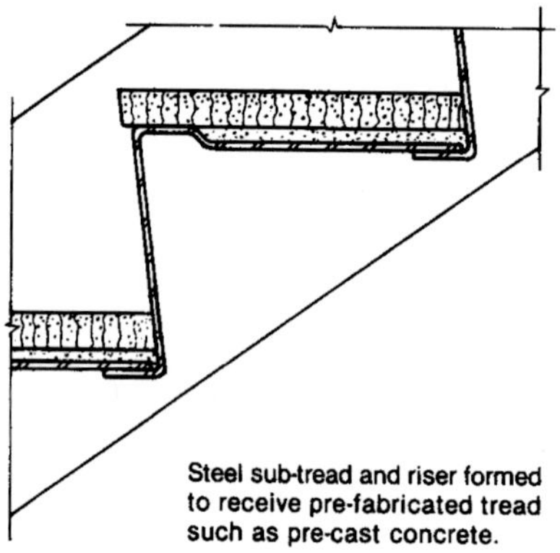

Steel sub-tread and riser formed to receive pre-fabricated tread such as pre-cast concrete.

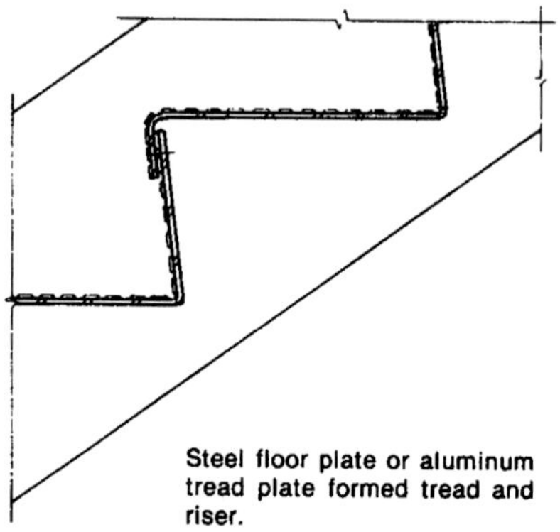

Steel floor plate or aluminum tread plate formed tread and riser.

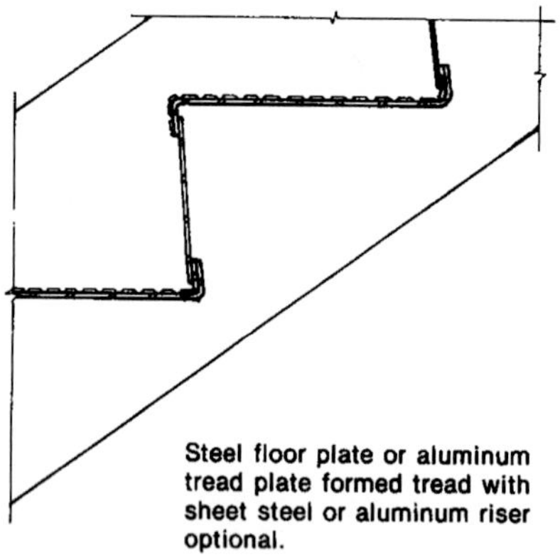

Steel floor plate or aluminum tread plate formed tread with sheet steel or aluminum riser optional.

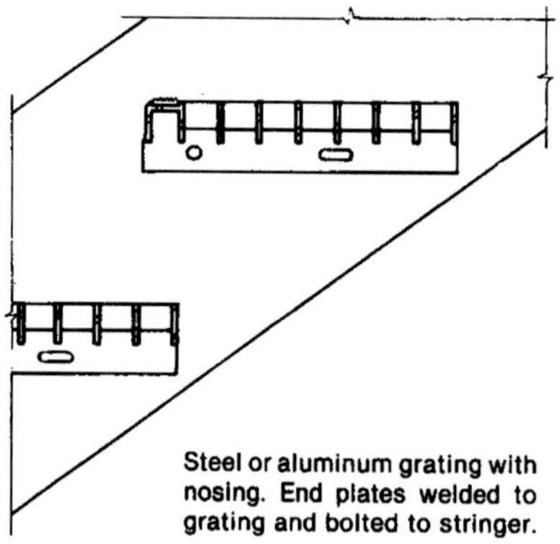

Steel or aluminum grating with nosing. End plates welded to grating and bolted to stringer.

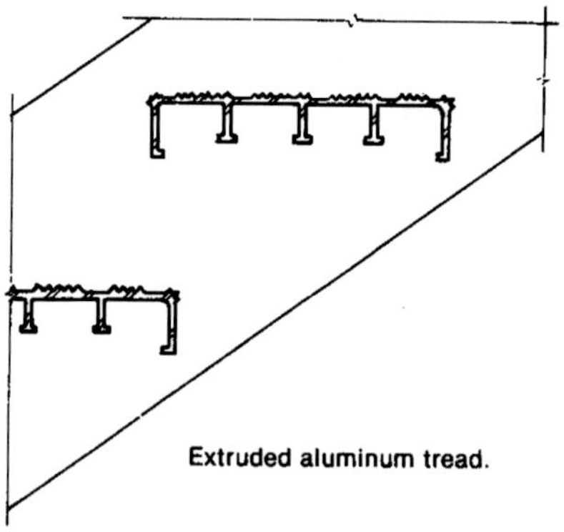

Extruded aluminum tread.

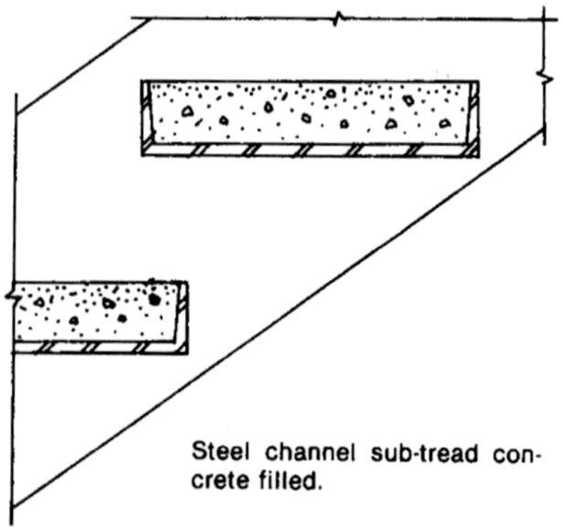

Steel channel sub-tread concrete filled.

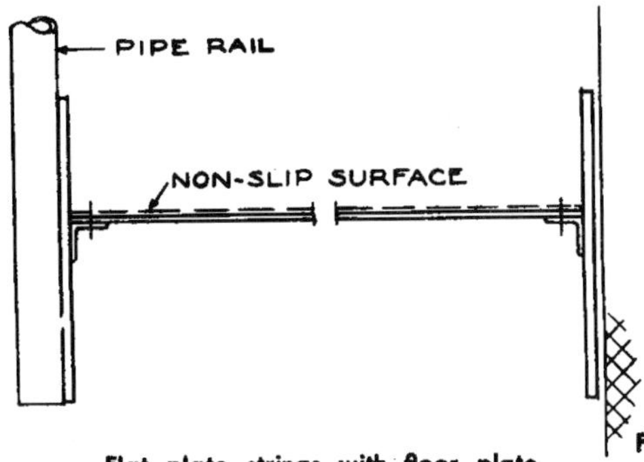

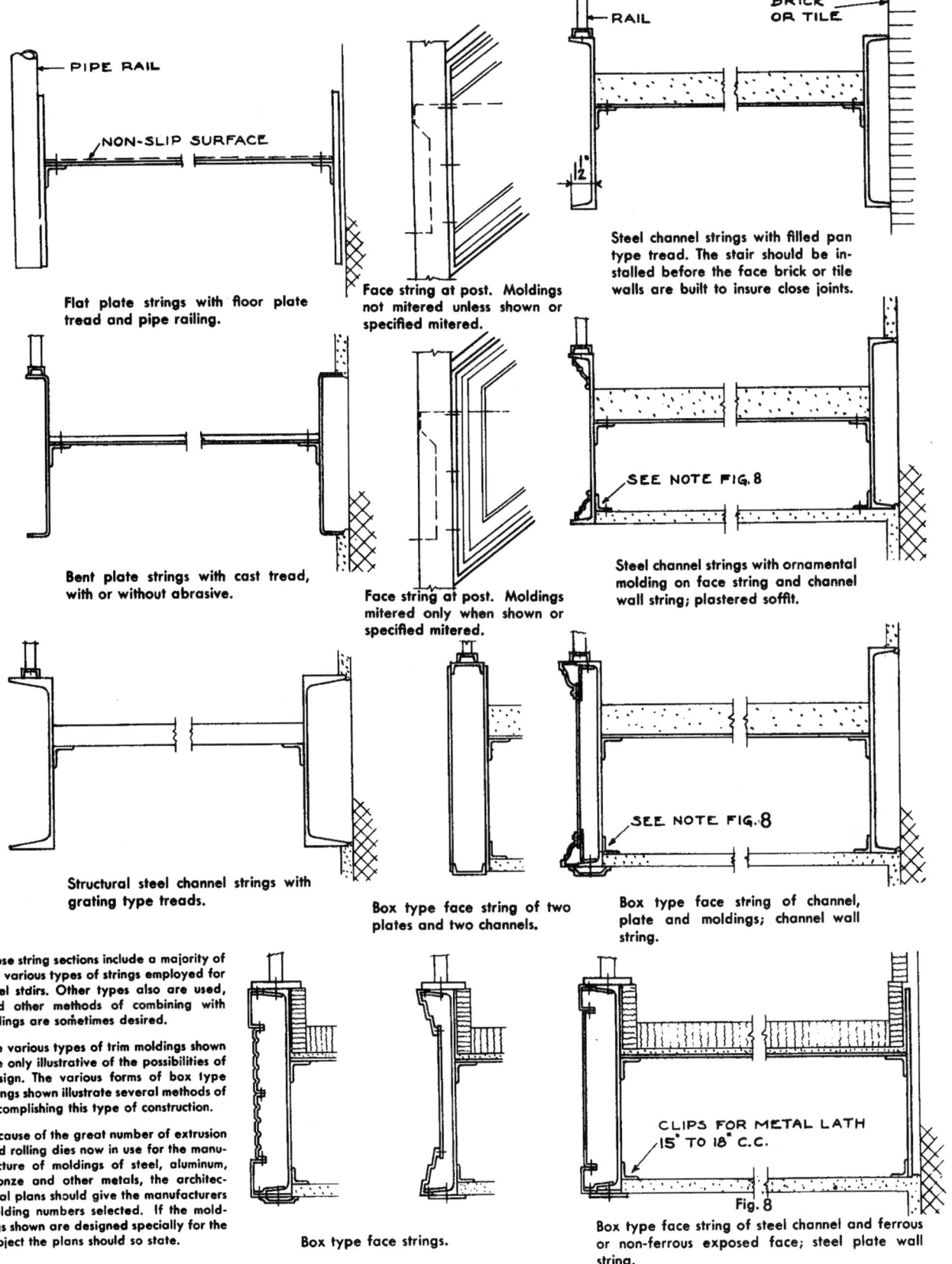

Flat plate strings with floor plate tread and pipe railing.

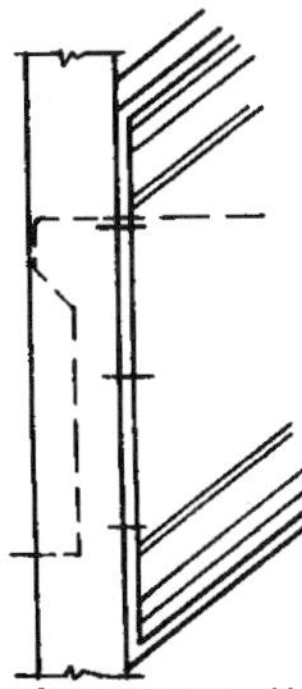

Face string at post. Moldings not mitered unless shown or specified mitered.

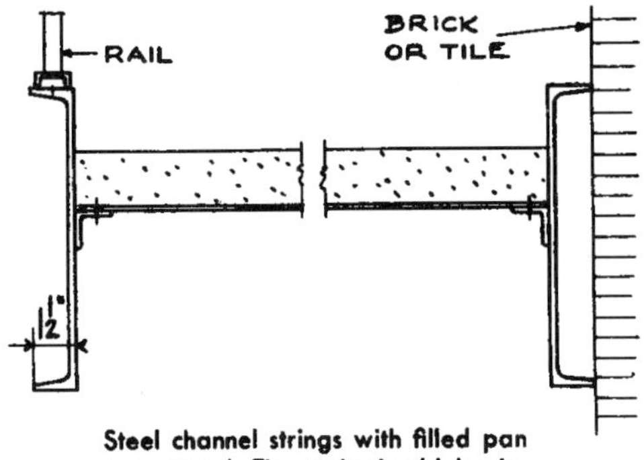

Steel channel strings with filled pan type tread. The stair should be installed before the face brick or tile walls are built to insure close joints.

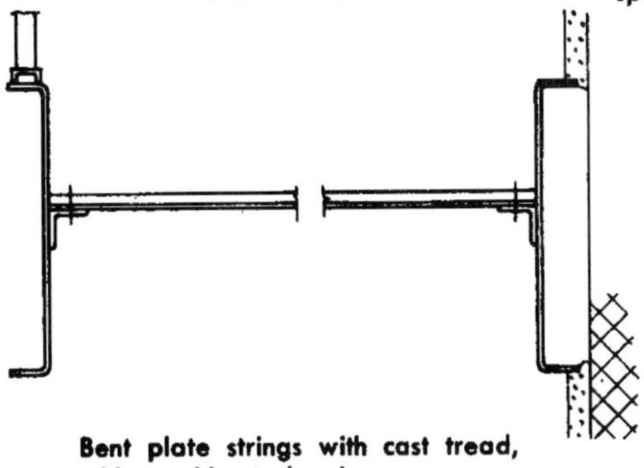

Bent plate strings with cast tread, with or without abrasive.

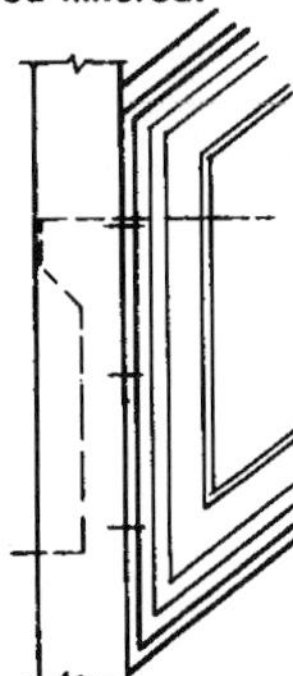

Face string at post. Moldings mitered only when shown or specified mitered.

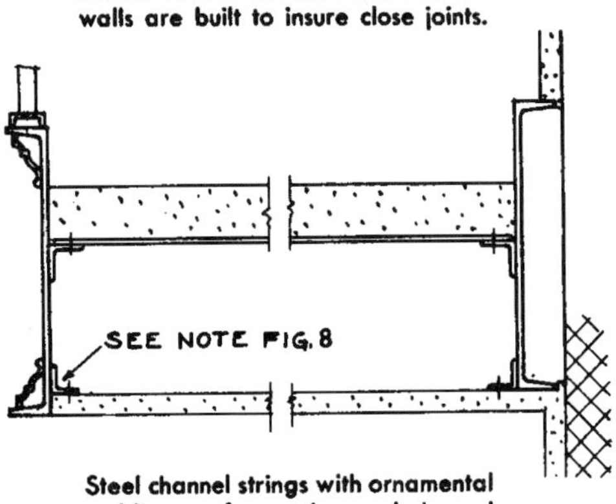

Steel channel strings with ornamental molding on face string and channel wall string; plastered soffit.

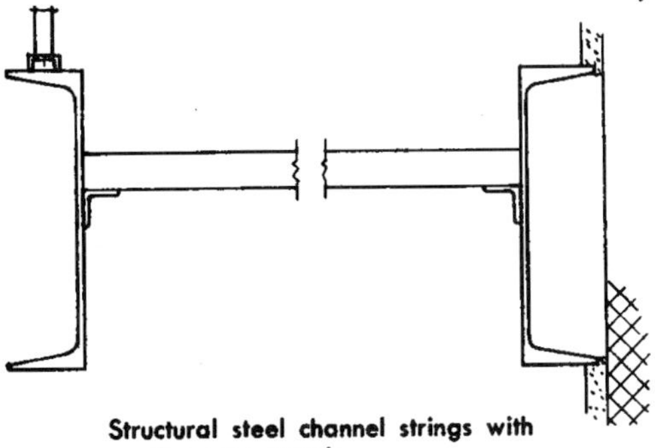

Structural steel channel strings with grating type treads.

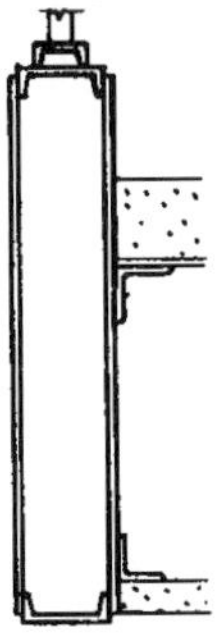

Box type face string of two plates and two channels.

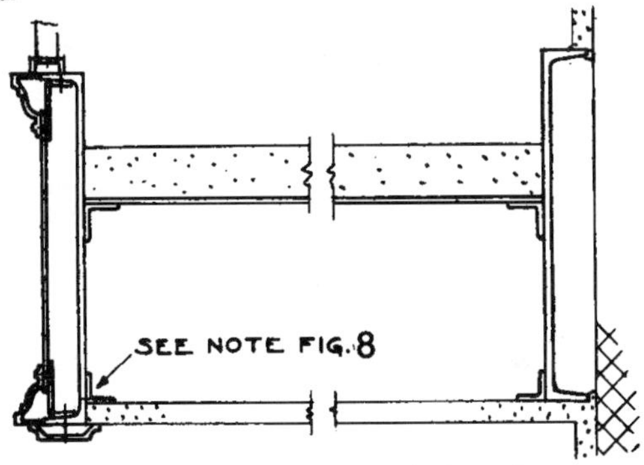

Box type face string of channel, plate and moldings; channel wall string.

These string sections include a majority of the various types of strings employed for steel stairs. Other types also are used, and other methods of combining with railings are sometimes desired.

The various types of trim moldings shown are only illustrative of the possibilities of design. The various forms of box type strings shown illustrate several methods of accomplishing this type of construction.

Because of the great number of extrusion and rolling dies now in use for the manufacture of moldings of steel, aluminum, bronze and other metals, the architectural plans should give the manufacturers molding numbers selected. If the moldings shown are designed specially for the project the plans should so state.

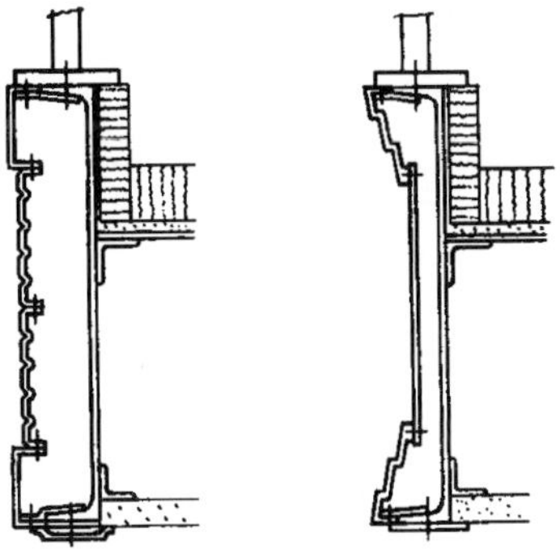

Box type face strings.

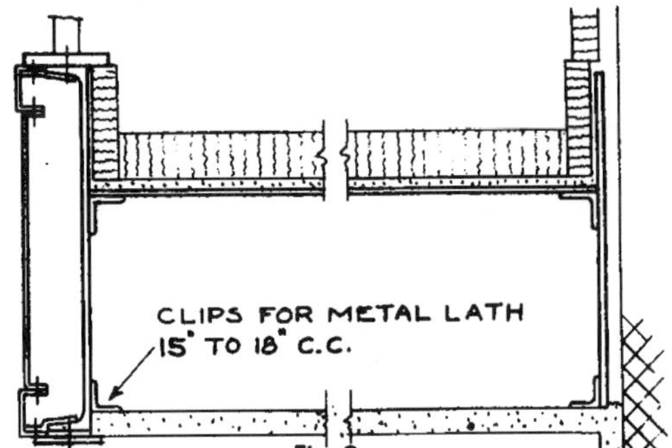

Fig. 8
Box type face string of steel channel and ferrous or non-ferrous exposed face; steel plate wall string.

STAIRS AND RAMPS
Stringer Sections

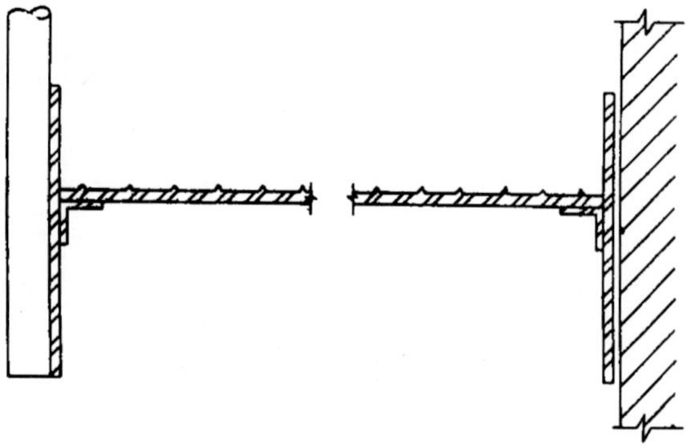

Steel plate stringers, carrier angles, floor plate treads, pipe railing on side of face stringer. Aluminum tread plate may be used when specified. Wall not plastered.

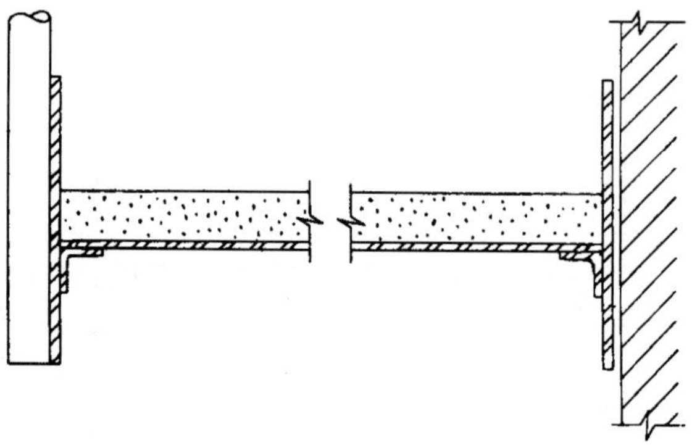

Steel plate stringers, carrier angles, steel sub-tread and riser, concrete filled tread. Pipe railing on side of face stringer, wall not plastered.

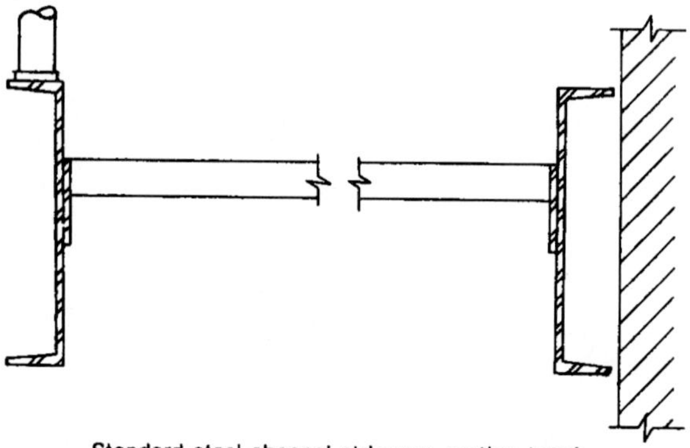

Standard steel channel stringers, grating tread bolted or welded to stringer, pipe railing bolted or welded to top flange of face stringer. Wall not plastered.

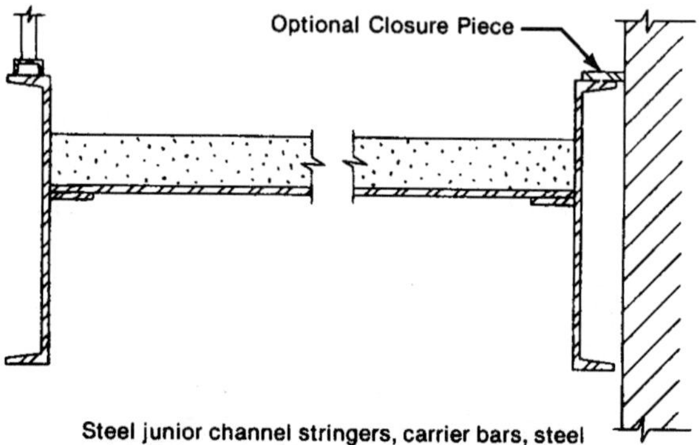

Steel junior channel stringers, carrier bars, steel sub-tread and riser. Concrete filled tread. Railing with bottom channel fastened to top flange of face stringer. Optional closure piece fastened to top flange of wall stringer in the field. Wall not plastered.

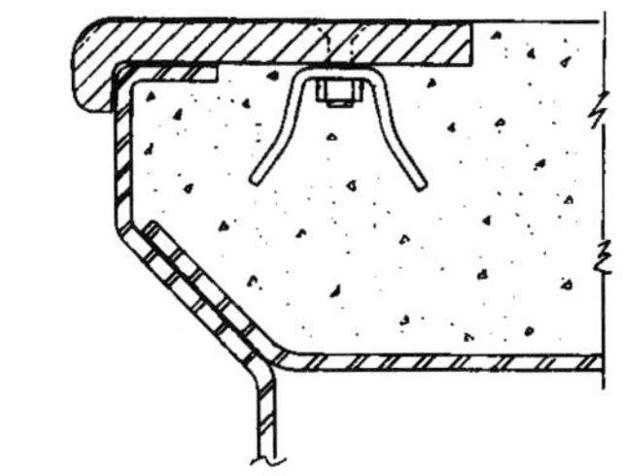

Cast abrasive nosing with short lip, available in iron, bronze or aluminum as specified. Standard drilling with wing anchors, bolts and nuts or drilled as required.

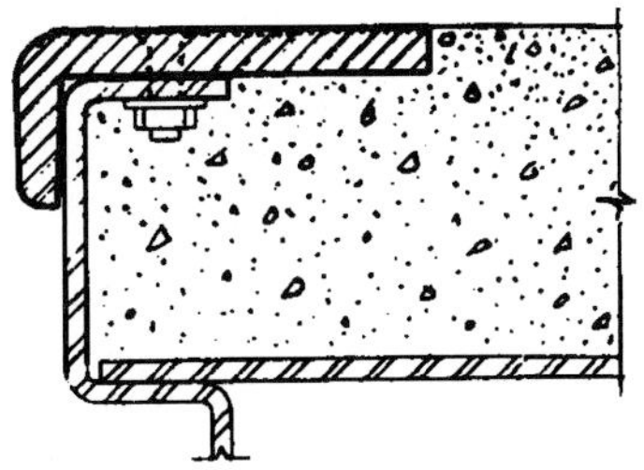

Cast abrasive nosing with deep lip, available in iron, bronze or aluminum as specified. Standard drilling with wing anchors, bolts and nuts or drilled as required.

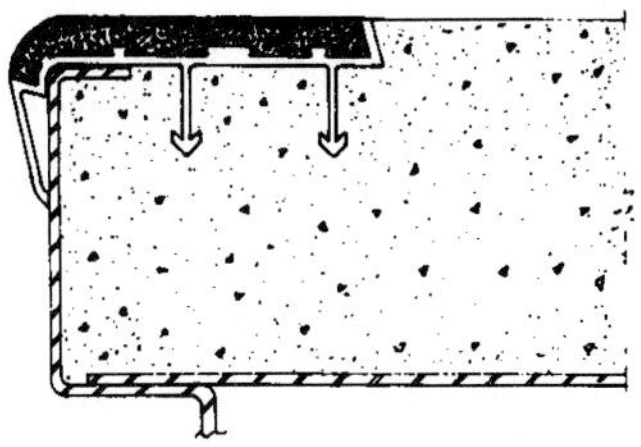

Extruded aluminum base with epoxy top, containing abrasive. Available in colors. Integral anchors for fresh concrete. Also available drilled to specifications without the anchors.

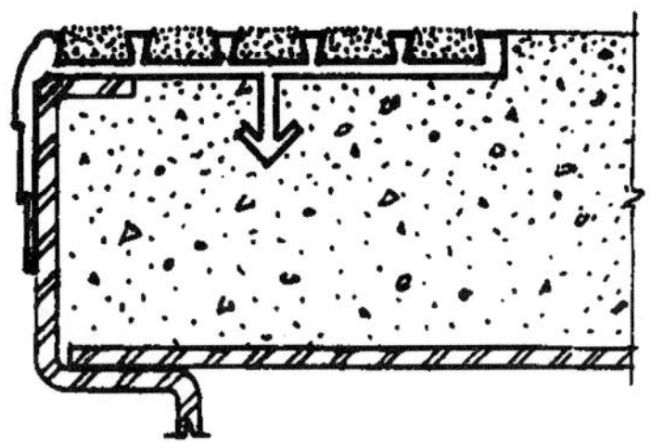

Extruded aluminum or brass with abrasive filled ribs. Concealed integral anchor runs full length of tread. Also available drilled to specifications, without the integral anchor.

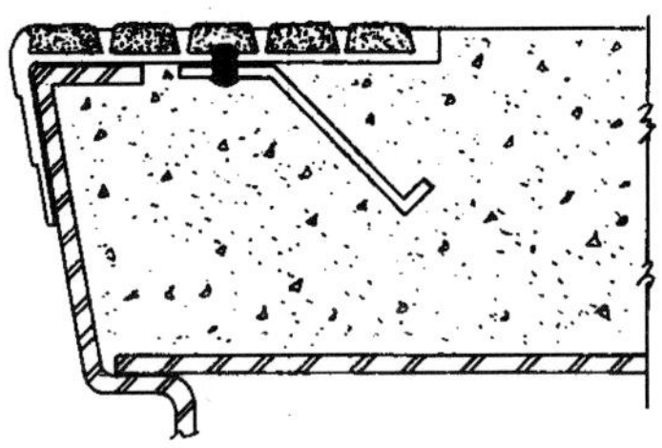

Extruded aluminum with abrasive ribs. Special design for pan stairs with sloped risers. Drilled to specification or furnished with strap anchors or wing anchors.

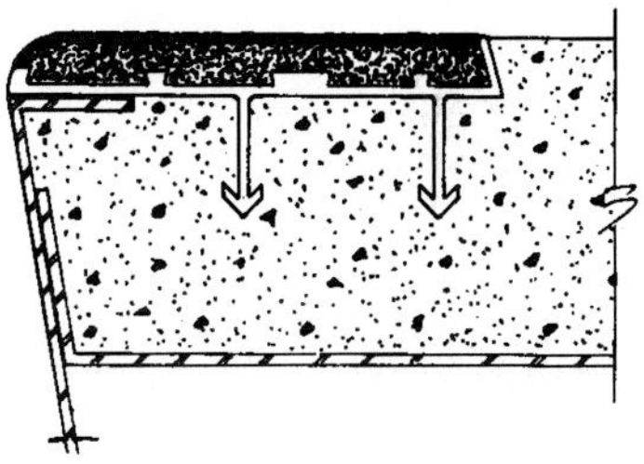

Barrier free design to meet standards for the physically handicapped. Aluminum base with epoxy containing abrasive top. Integral anchors for fresh concrete.

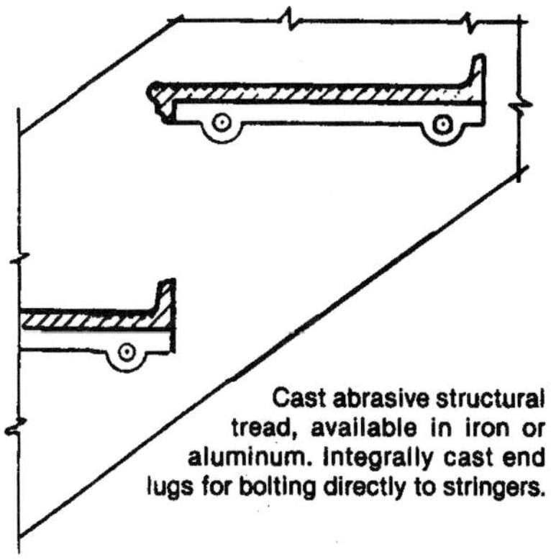

Cast abrasive structural tread, available in iron or aluminum. Integrally cast end lugs for bolting directly to stringers.

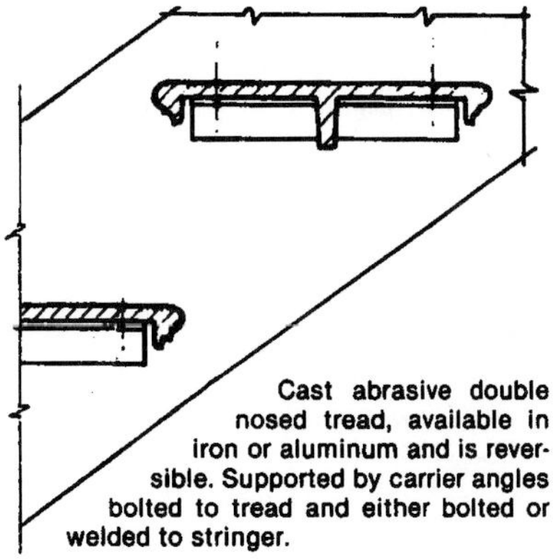

Cast abrasive double nosed tread, available in iron or aluminum and is reversible. Supported by carrier angles bolted to tread and either bolted or welded to stringer.

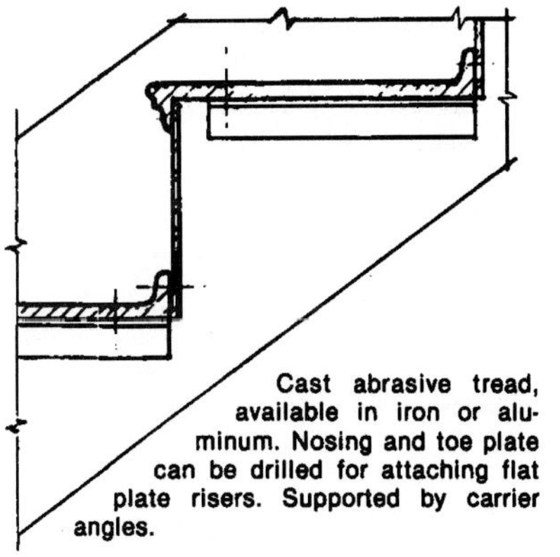

Cast abrasive tread, available in iron or aluminum. Nosing and toe plate can be drilled for attaching flat plate risers. Supported by carrier angles.

STAIRS AND RAMPS
Handrails

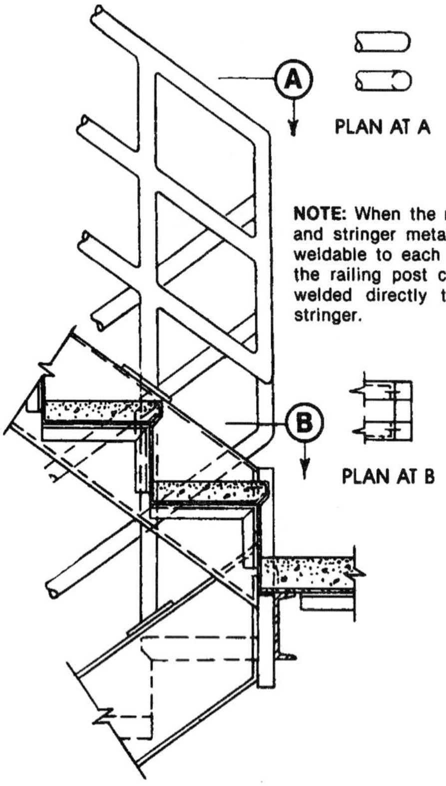

NOTE: When the railing and stringer metals are weldable to each other, the railing post can be welded directly to the stringer.

Stair platform or landing with pipe railings, railings not connected, for stairwell having minimum clearance. Short newels, supported on header.

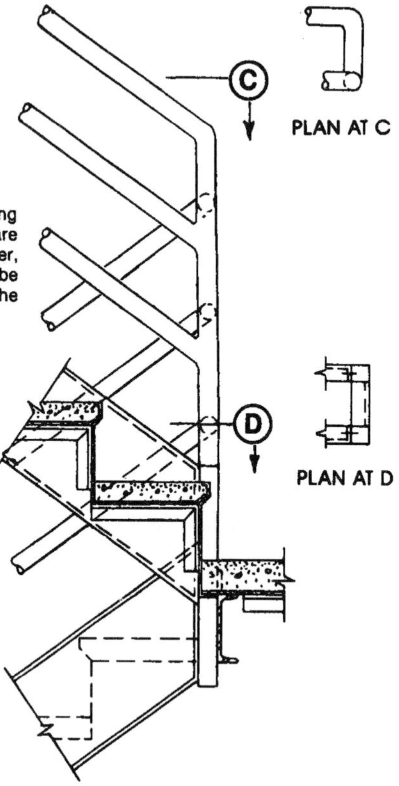

Stair platform or landing with pipe railing, one post at return. Lower rail returned into post, two or more posts used at wide wells. Short newels, supported on header.

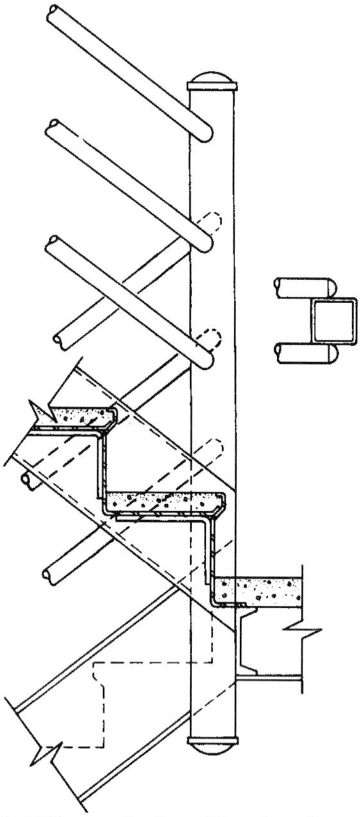

Stair platform or landing with rectangular or square newel, pipe railing members capped and welded to newel post.

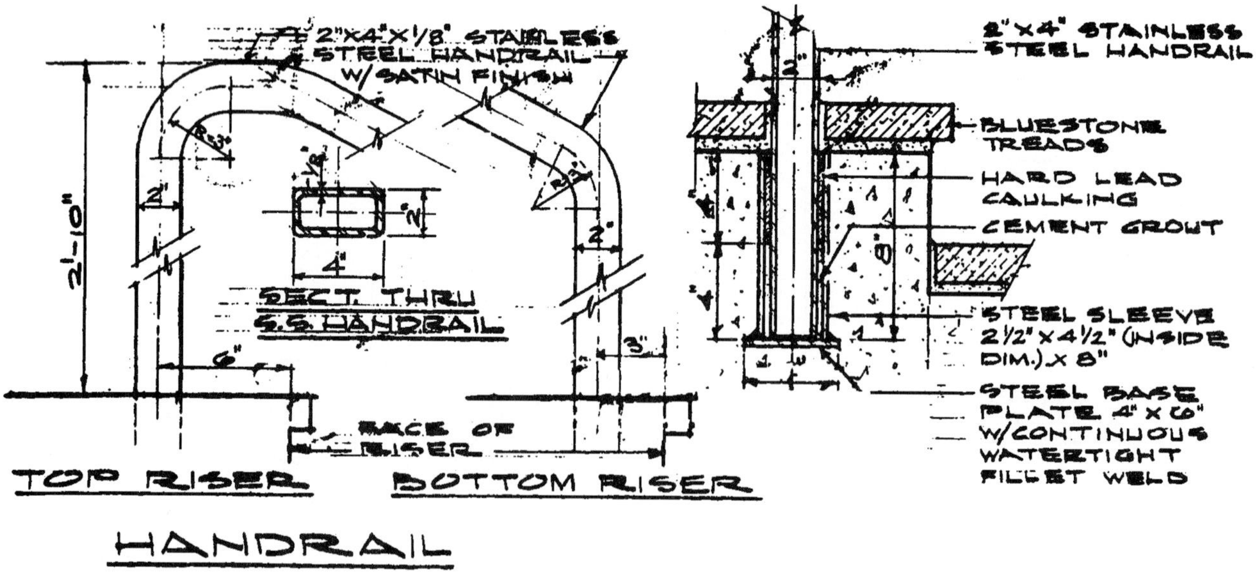

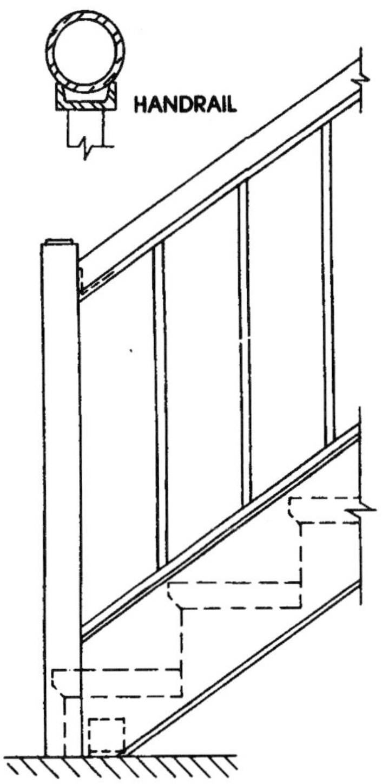

Stair start with square newel, baluster type railing with channel top and bottom, pipe handrail.

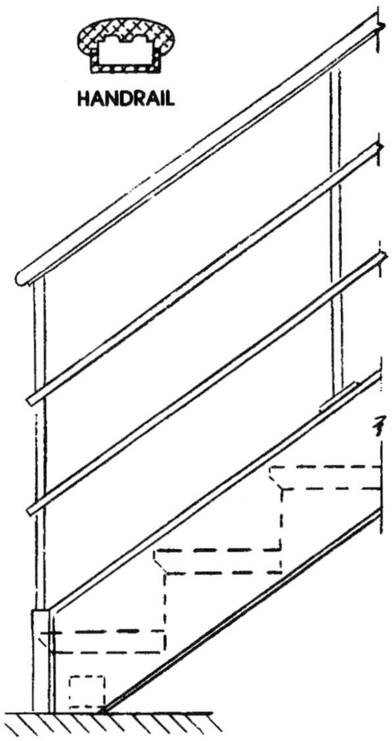

Stair start with short newel, parallel bar type railing with end and intermediate posts of square, rectangular or round section, extruded handrail with mitered, forged or cast terminal.

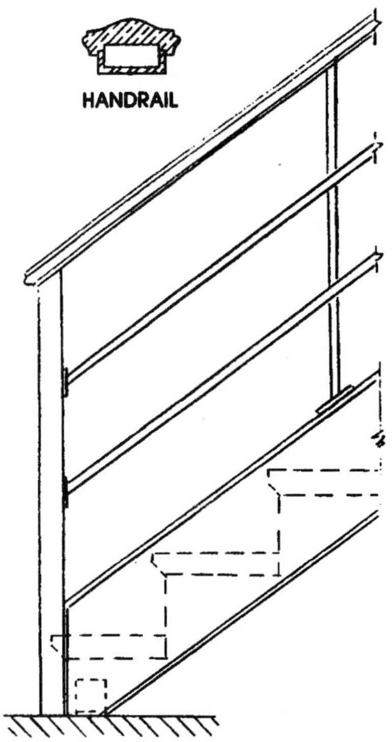

Stair start with square newel, parallel bar type railing with intermediate posts of square, rectangular or round section; extruded or rolled handrail section mitered to form cap over newel.

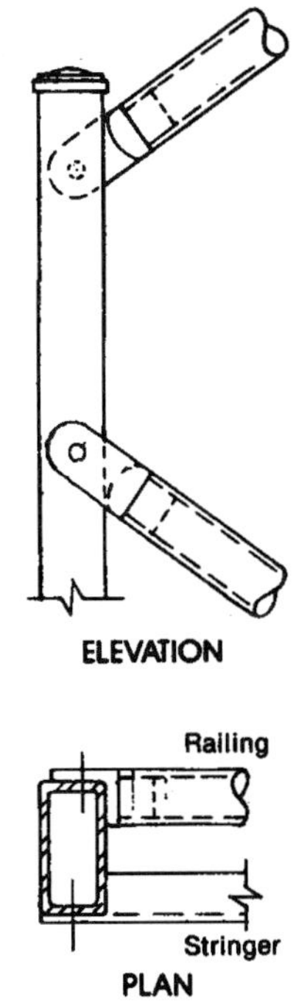

Square or rectangular newel, pipe rail fitted with offset lug to center on stringer.

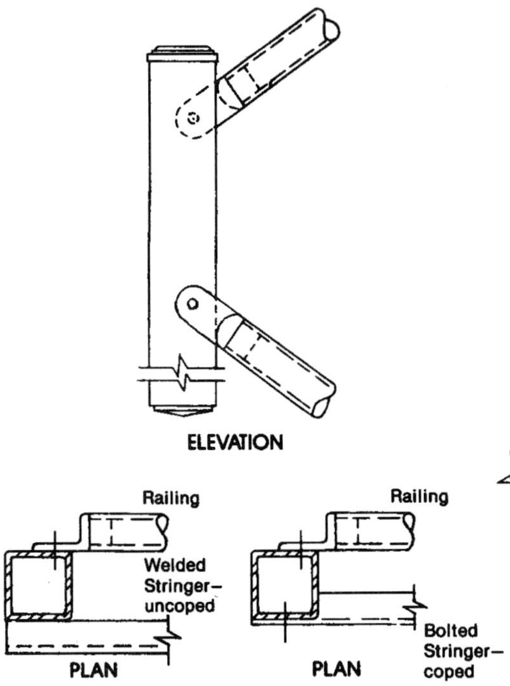

Square or rectangular newel, pipe rail fitted with offset lug for positioning inside of stringer.

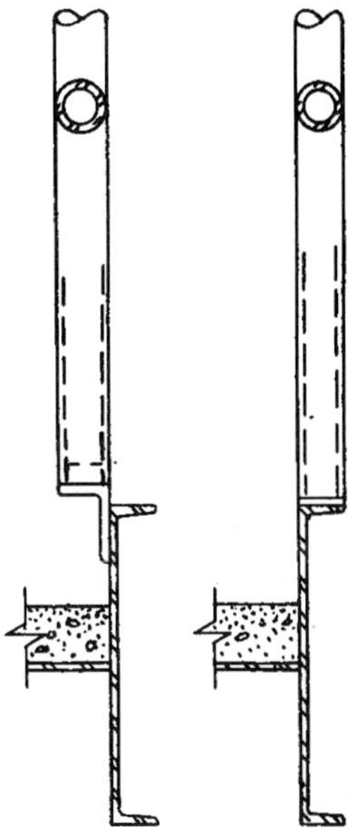

Section showing fastening for intermediate posts to stringers.

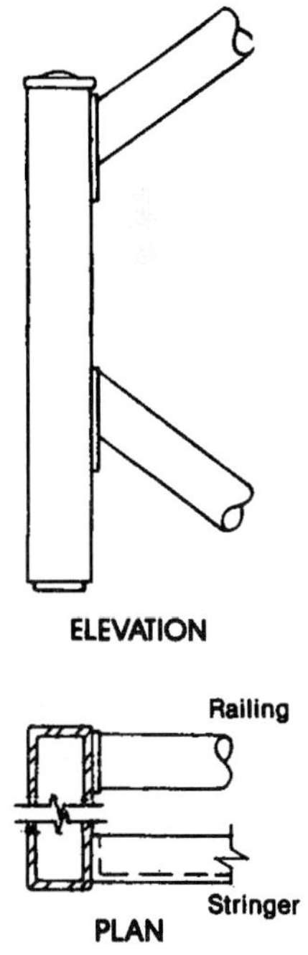

Rectangular newel, pipe rail and stringer welded or bolted to face.

STAIRS AND RAMPS

Newels and Railings

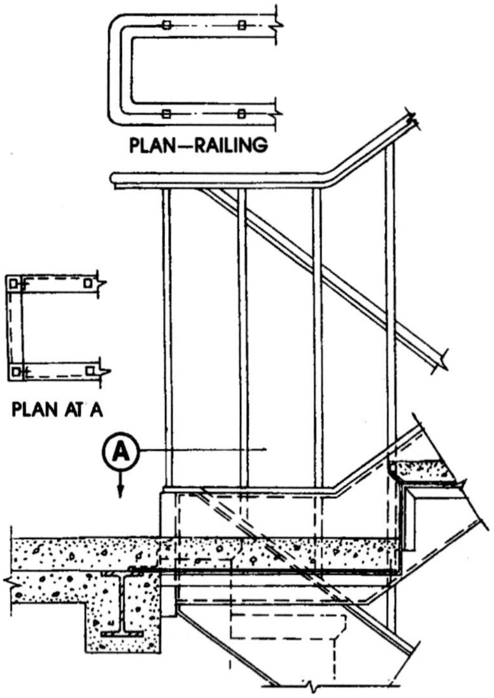

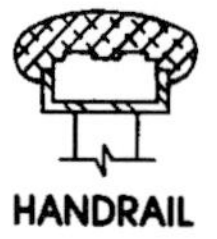

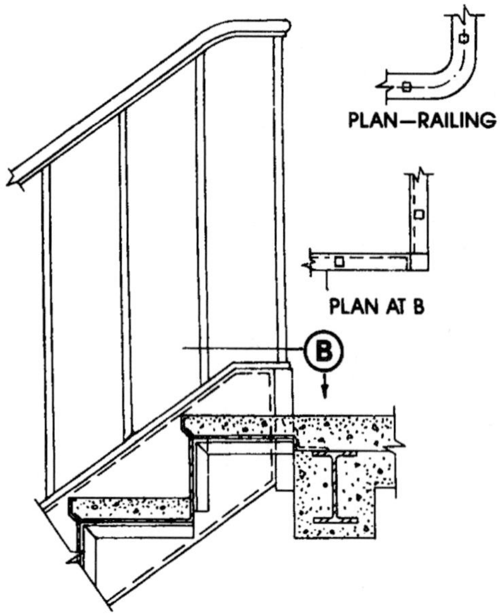

Stair landing with stringers and fascia framed square. Square railing return, end balusters centered on newels and landing extended on up flight to set-back riser.

Stair landing, with stringer and fascia at right angle. Landing extended on down flight to set-forward riser, producing easement in handrail.

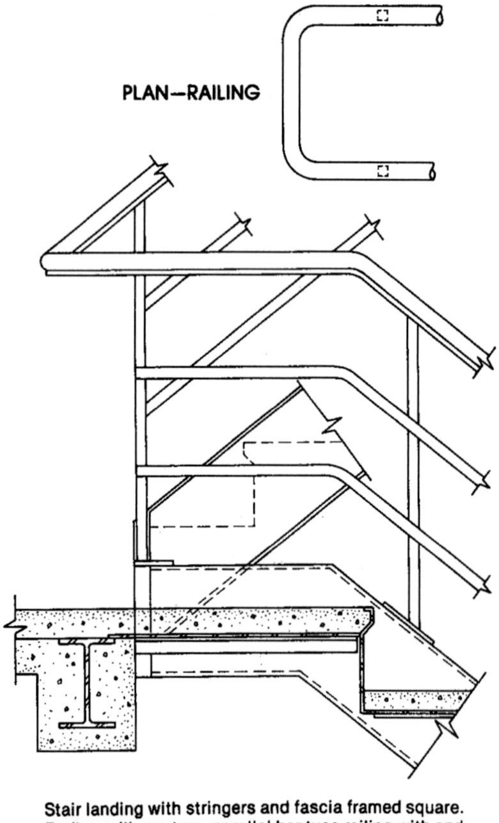

Stair landing with stringers and fascia framed square. Radius railing return, parallel bar type railing with end balusters centered on newels. Landing extended on down flight to set-forward riser.

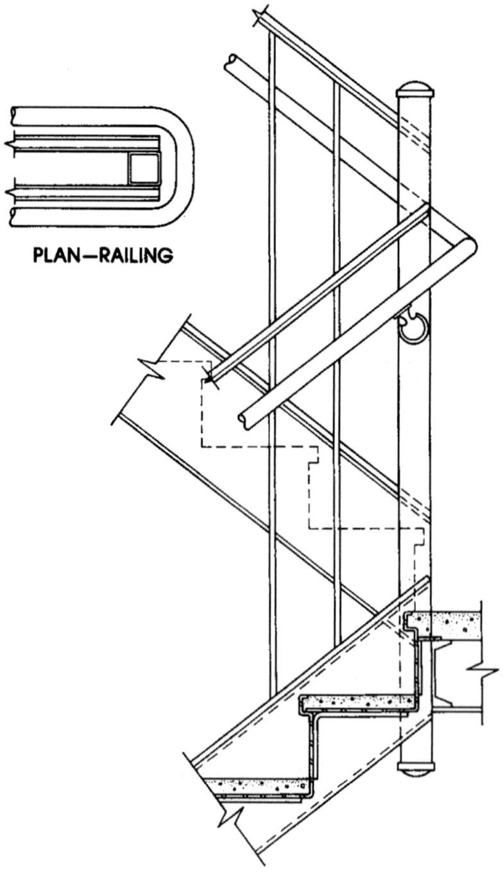

Stair landing with stringers and fascia framed into full height newel, baluster railing with channel top and bottom. Continuous pipe handrail offset from balusters and newels by brackets.

Figures 9 and 10 indicate typical railings for decks, platforms, balconies, roofs, and similar locations, adapted for residential, apartment, or hotel construction. These railings may be fastened with wood screws or lag bolts to wood, or with expansion bolts to masonry. On roofs or decks the setting of the post bases should be waterproofed.

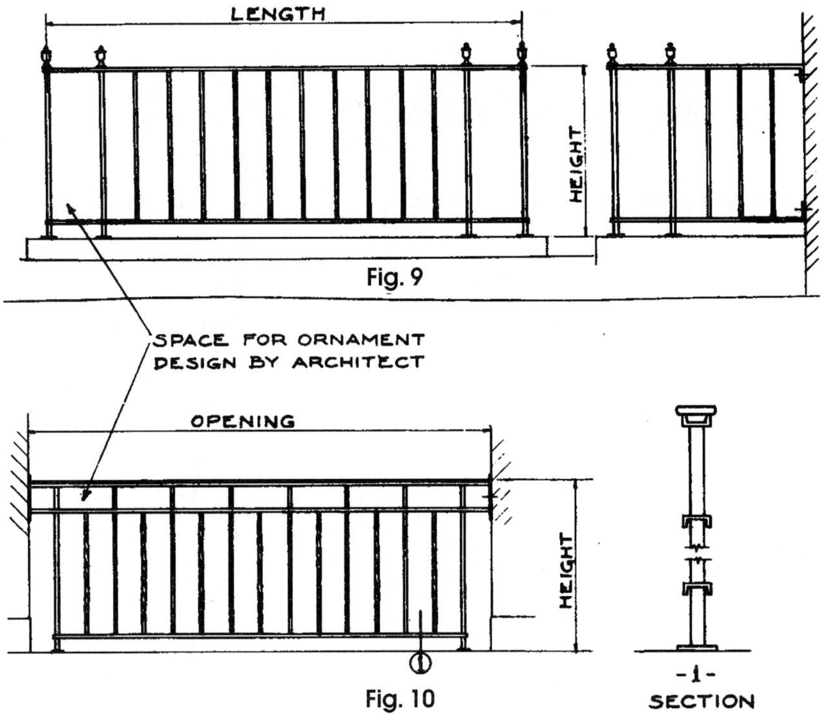

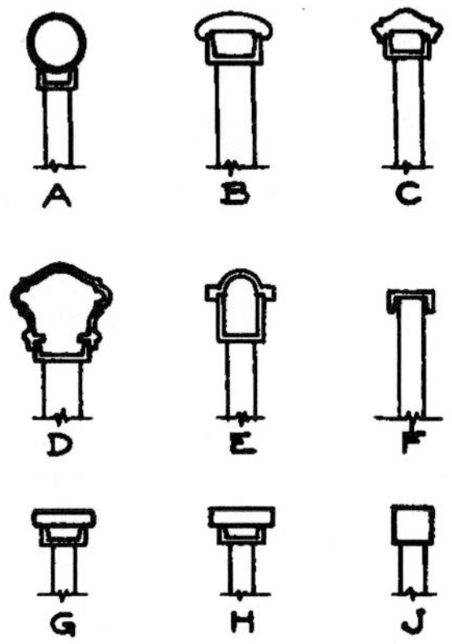

Methods of constructing railing top members.

SCALE 1½" = 1'-0"

TO SPECIFY:

Give locations.
Indicate kind of metal.
Specify finish.
Give sizes of members.
Give height.
Provide scale details of ornaments, finials and bases.

Specify method of fastening, or have fabricator provide fastenings best suited to each condition.

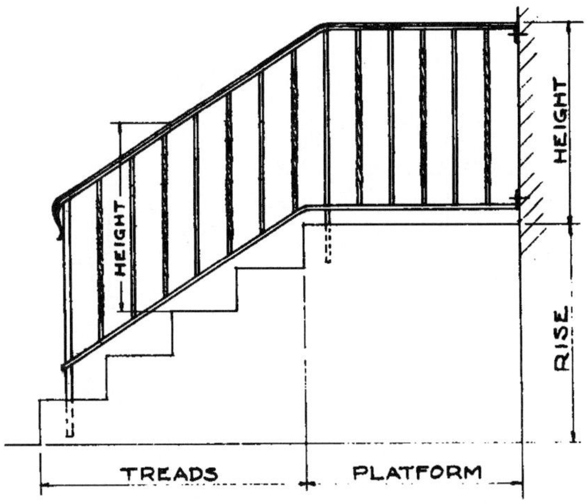

Railing with balusters and bottom longitudinal member supporting balusters. Posts extending into masonry.

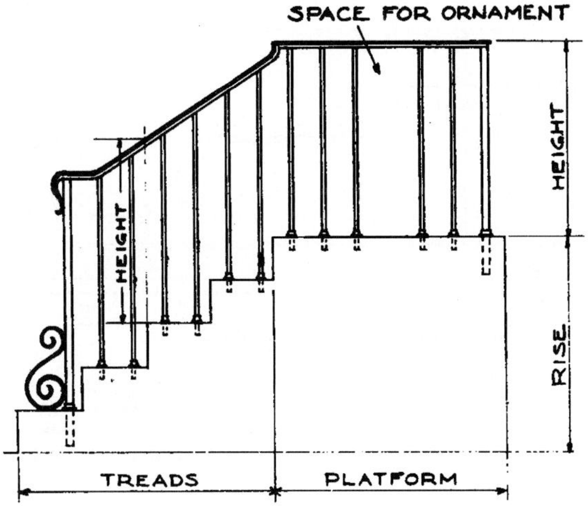

Railing without bottom longitudinal member, each baluster set in masonry and fitted with slip flange or base. Masonry specifications should specify holes.

STAIRS AND RAMPS

Ornamental Railings

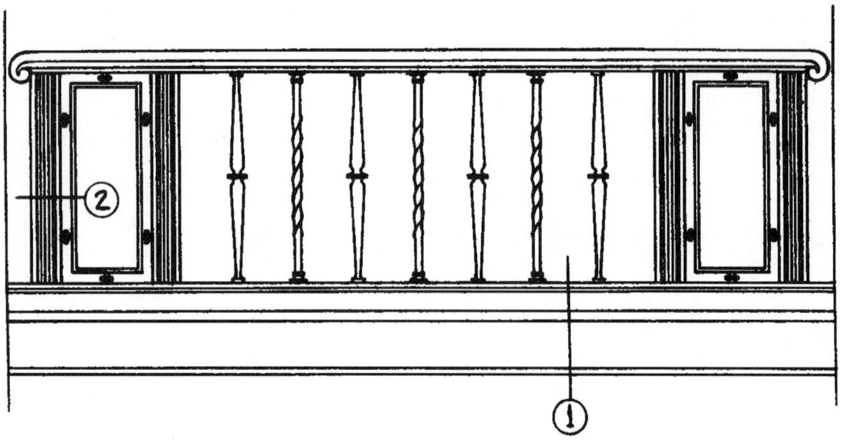

Railing panels set between columns or jambs. Posts extended to floor construction for support.

–2–

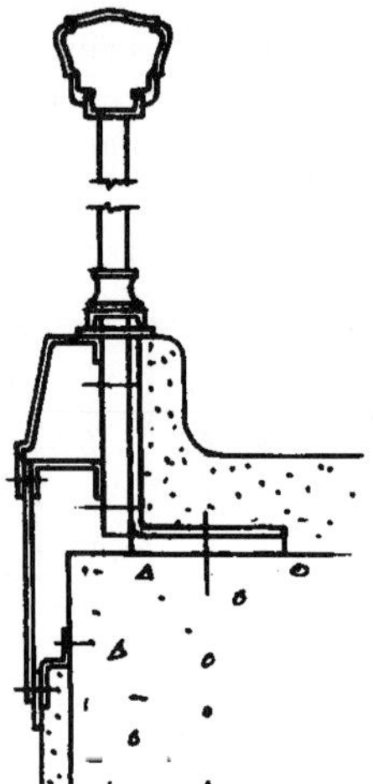

–1–

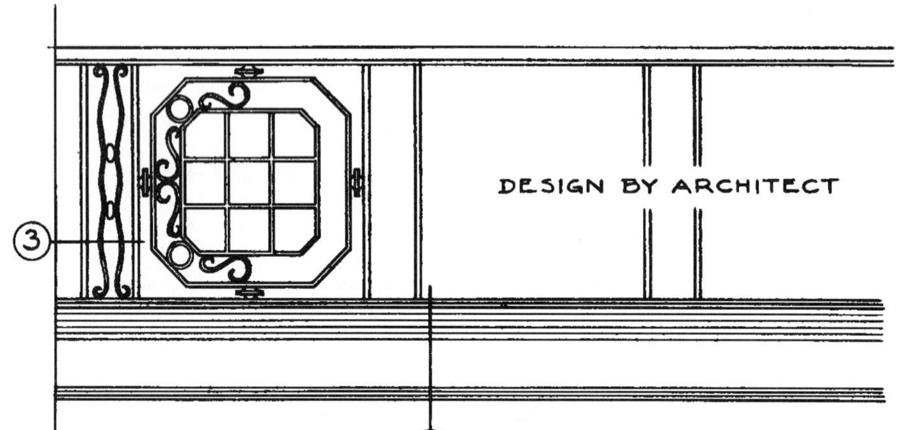

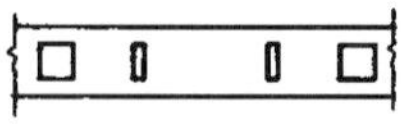

–3–

Railing for balcony or mezzanine with double posts and panels. Posts extended to support facia and fastened to floor construction.

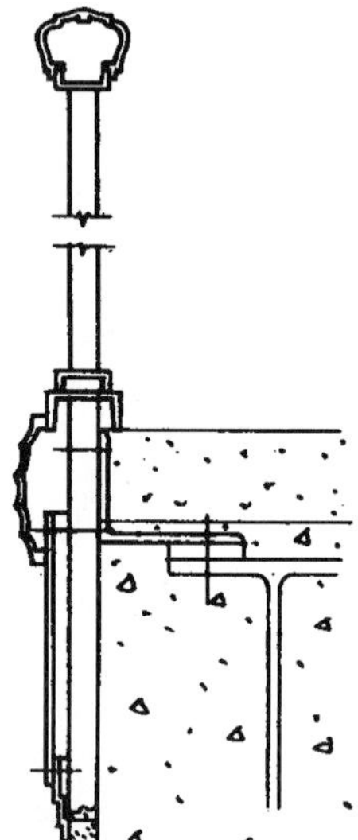

–4–

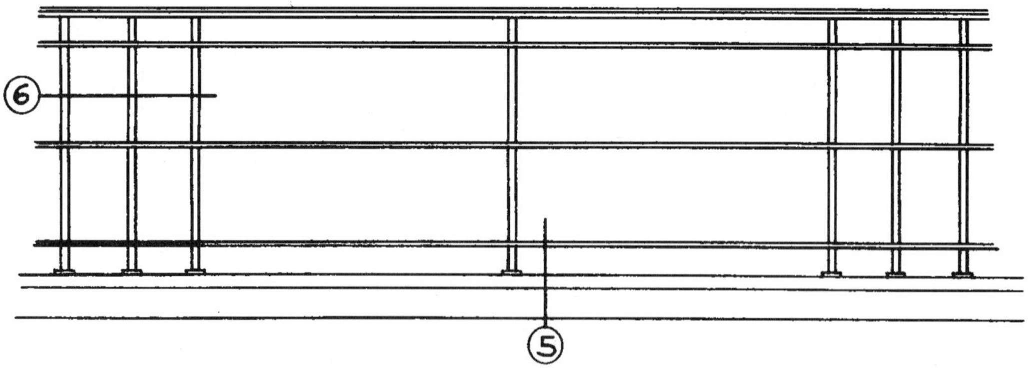

Railing for balcony or mezzanine with curved section. Facia fastened to floor construction. Railing fastened to facia.

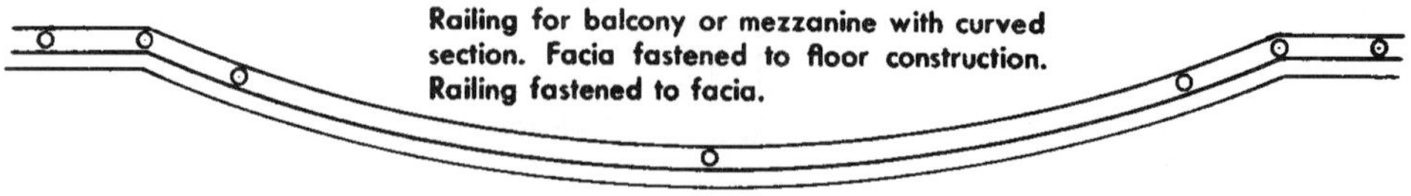

–6–

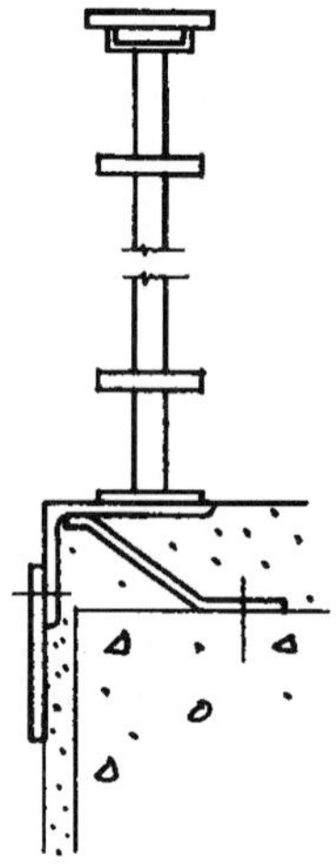

–5–

STAIRS AND RAMPS
Center Railings

Center railings are recommended for wide stairs. They may be a single pipe or tubing railing or they may be designed with double rails and panels of interesting design.

NOTE: A number of codes require that railings have a level extension beyond the nosings at the floors as indicated in Fig. 11 by dashed lines. This applies to both wall and center railings.

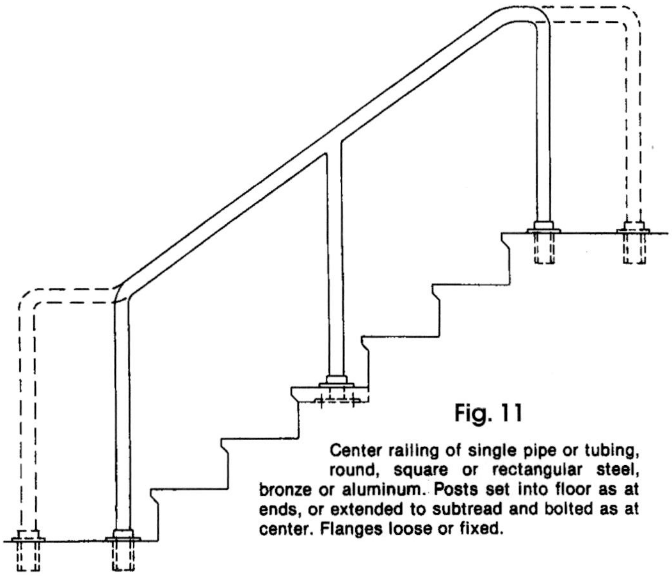

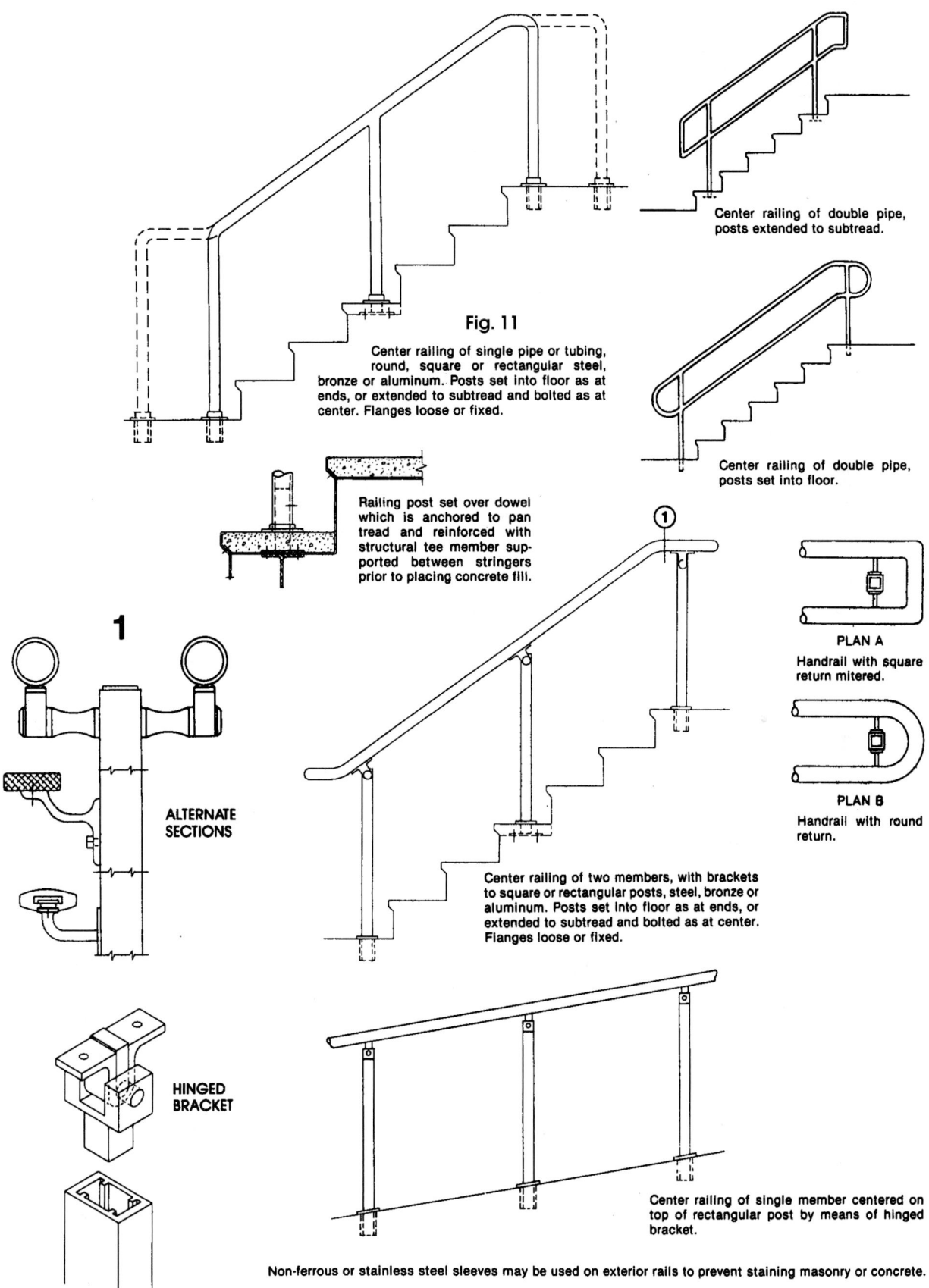

Fig. 11

Center railing of single pipe or tubing, round, square or rectangular steel, bronze or aluminum. Posts set into floor as at ends, or extended to subtread and bolted as at center. Flanges loose or fixed.

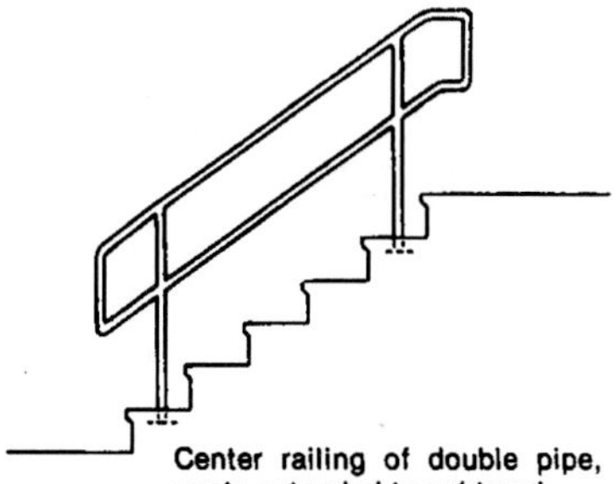

Center railing of double pipe, posts extended to subtread.

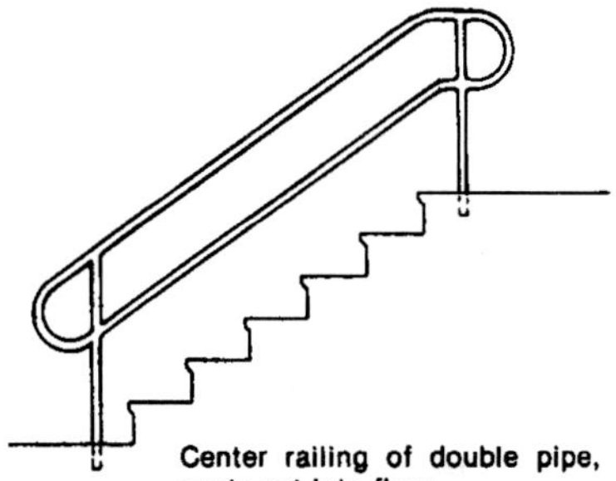

Center railing of double pipe, posts set into floor.

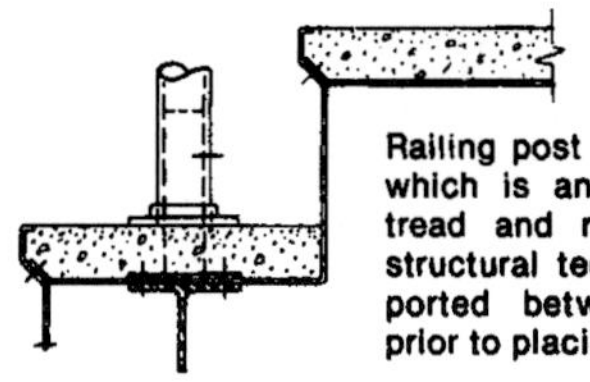

Railing post set over dowel which is anchored to pan tread and reinforced with structural tee member supported between stringers prior to placing concrete fill.

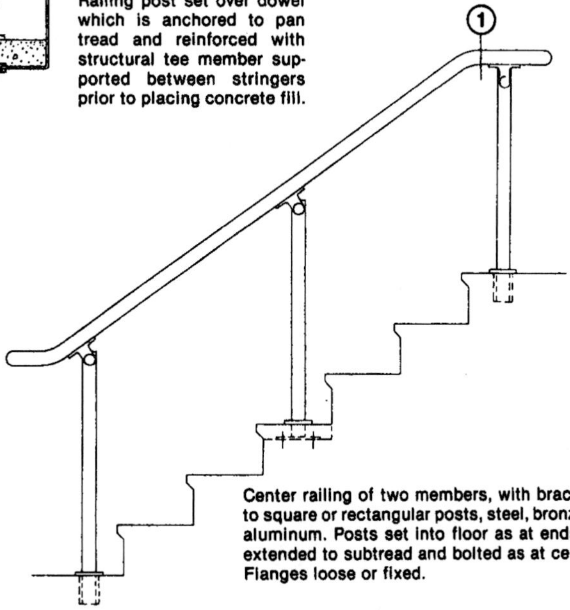

Center railing of two members, with brackets to square or rectangular posts, steel, bronze or aluminum. Posts set into floor as at ends, or extended to subtread and bolted as at center. Flanges loose or fixed.

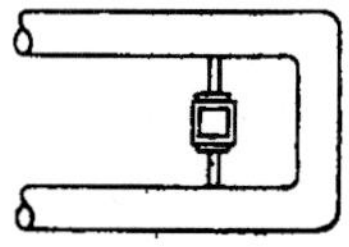

PLAN A

Handrail with square return mitered.

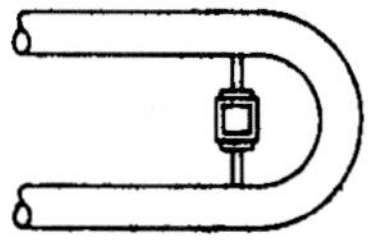

PLAN B

Handrail with round return.

1

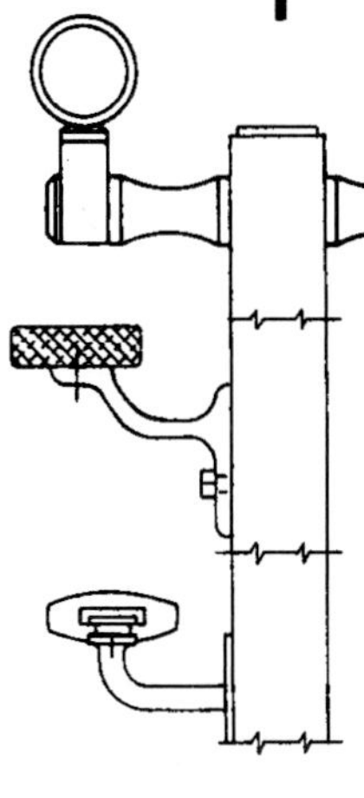

ALTERNATE SECTIONS

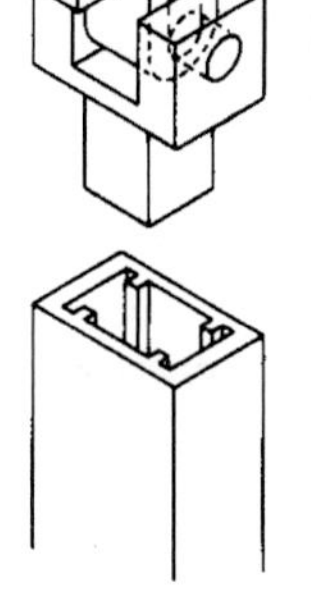

HINGED BRACKET

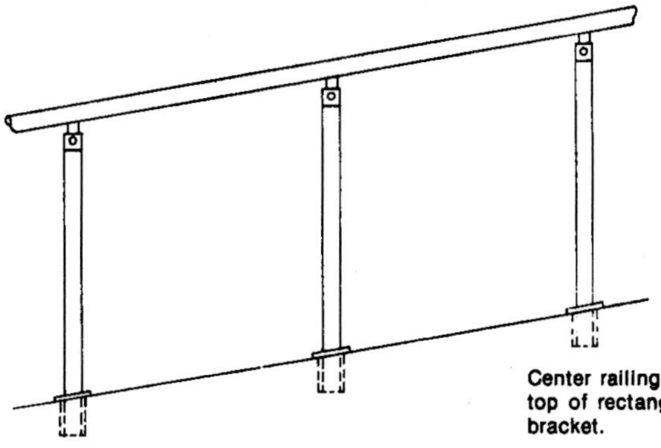

Center railing of single member centered on top of rectangular post by means of hinged bracket.

Non-ferrous or stainless steel sleeves may be used on exterior rails to prevent staining masonry or concrete.

STAIRS AND RAMPS

Railings

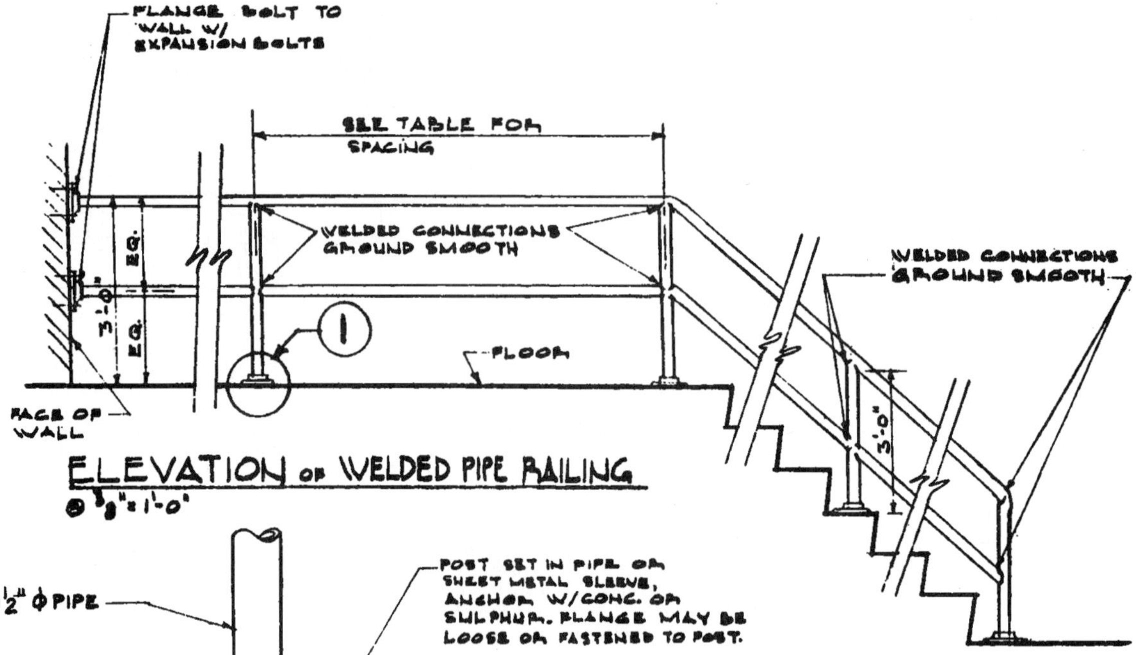

ELEVATION OF WELDED PIPE RAILING
@ 3/8" = 1'-0"

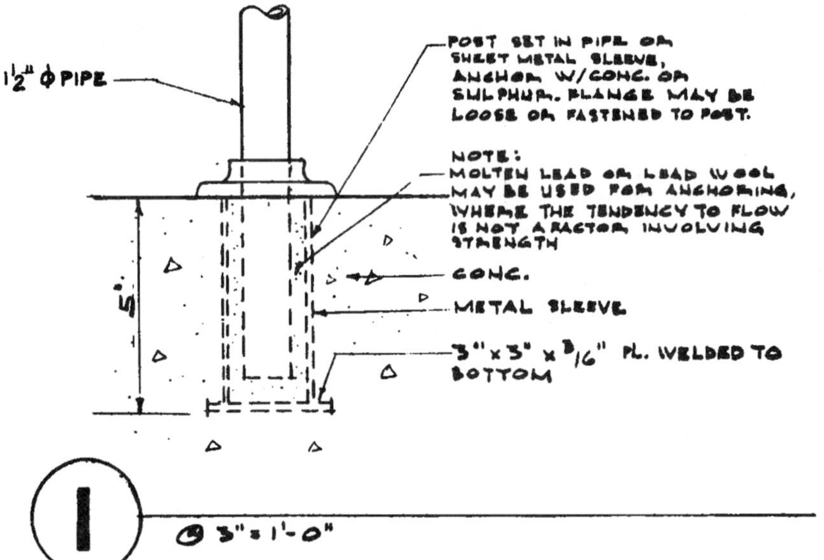

1 @ 3" = 1'-0"

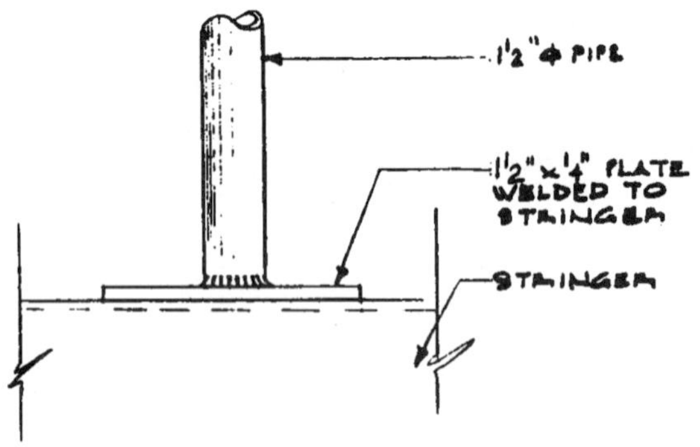

WELDED PIPE RAILING DETAIL FOR STEEL STAIRS
@ 3" = 1'-0"

RECOMMENDED POST SPACING FOR PIPE RAILING

SIZE OF PIPE	MAXIMUM SPACING
¾"	4'
1"	6'
1¼"	7'
1½"	8'
2"	9'
2½"	10'
3"	10'

TYPICAL EXTRUDED ALUMINUM AND BRONZE POST SECTIONS

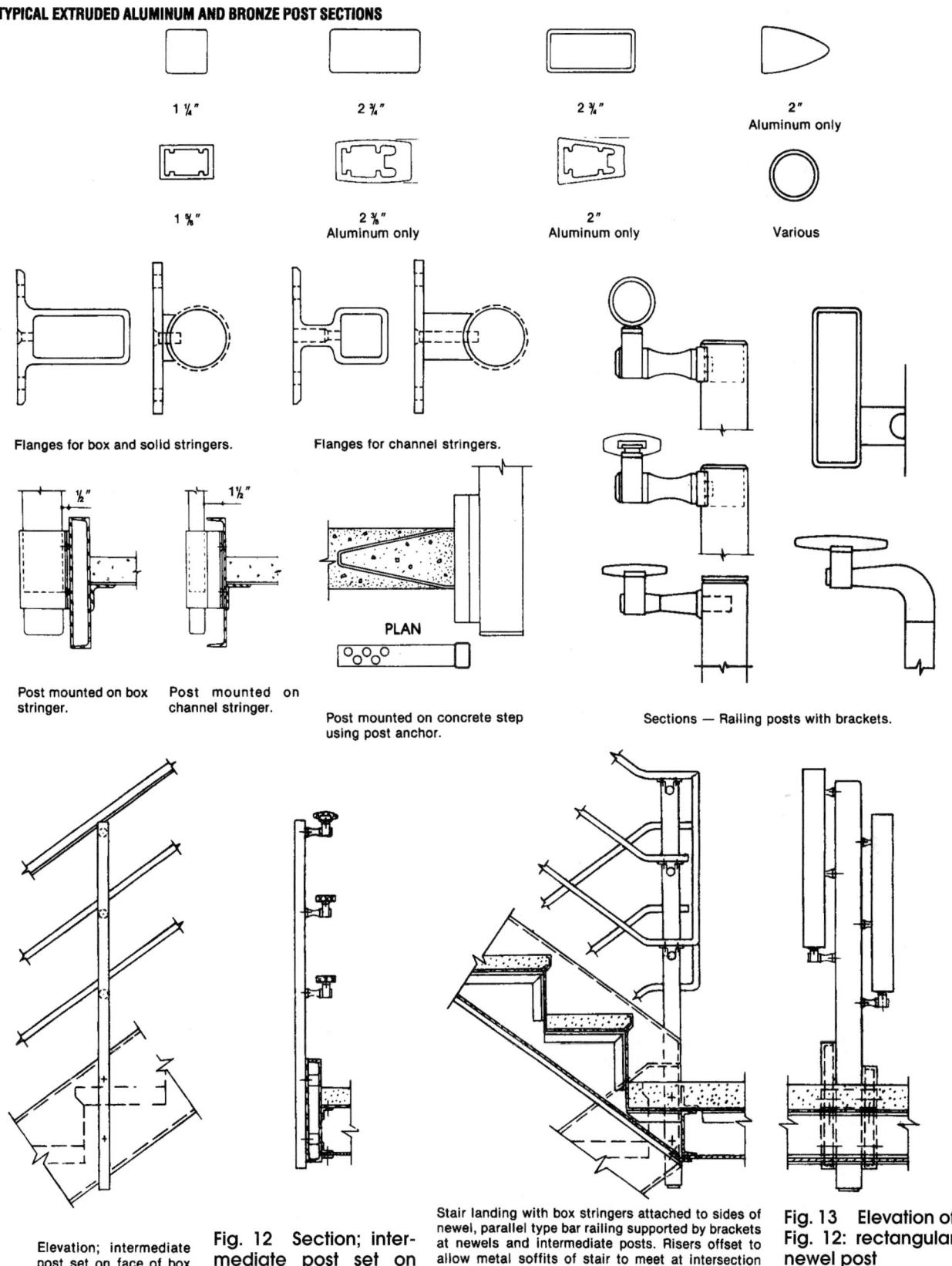

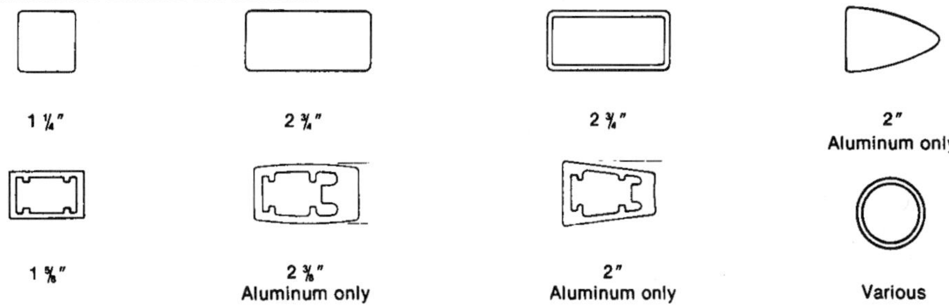

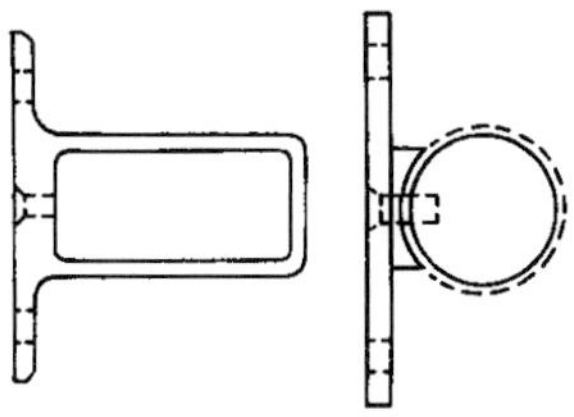

Flanges for box and solid stringers.

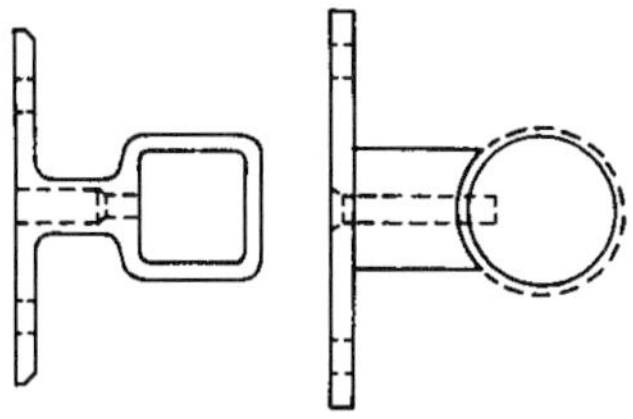

Flanges for channel stringers.

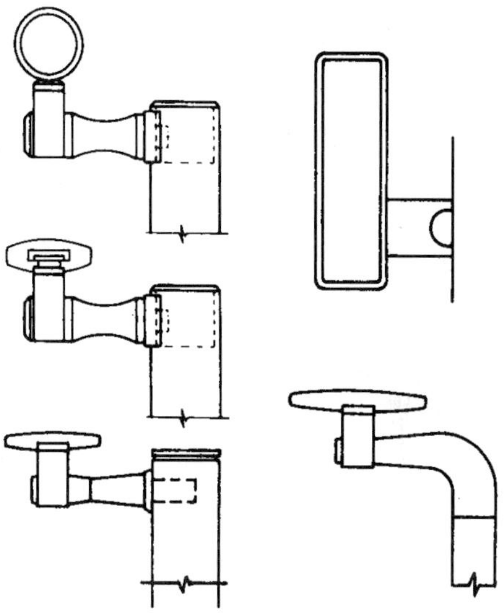

Sections — Railing posts with brackets.

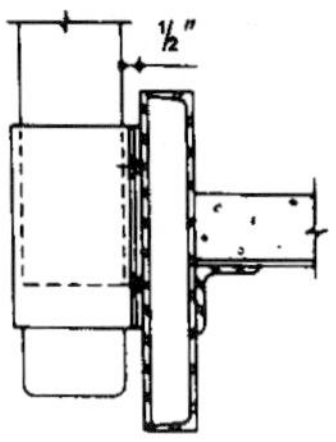

Post mounted on box stringer.

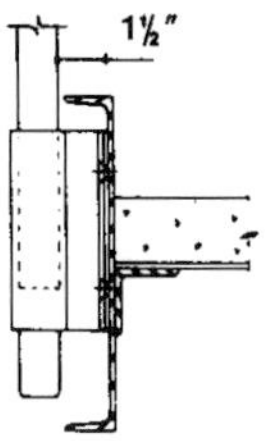

Post mounted on channel stringer.

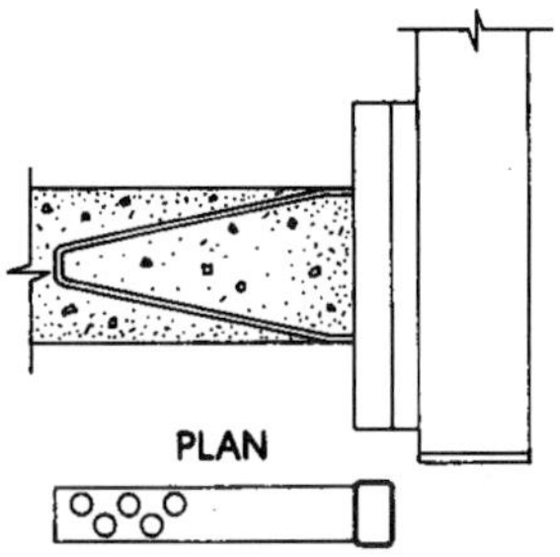

Post mounted on concrete step using post anchor.

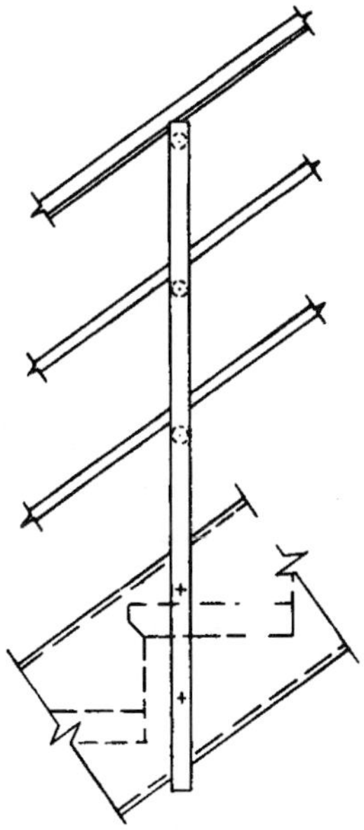

Elevation; intermediate post set on face of box stringer.

Fig. 12 Section; intermediate post set on face of box stringer

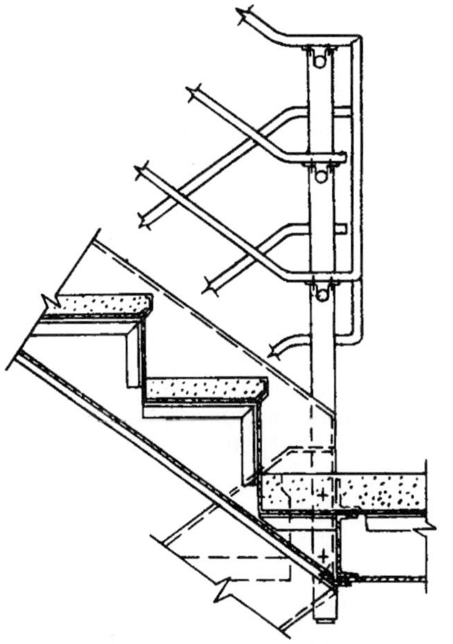

Stair landing with box stringers attached to sides of newel, parallel type bar railing supported by brackets at newels and intermediate posts. Risers offset to allow metal soffits of stair to meet at intersection with soffit of landing. Bottom and top rails must be the same and have symetrical cross section to obtain proper mitered connection.

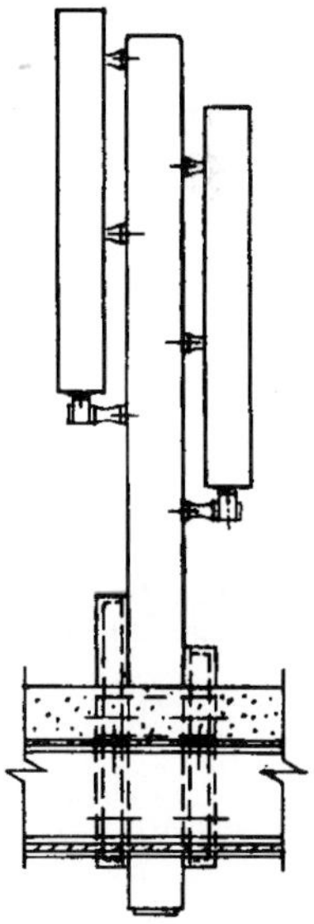

Fig. 13 Elevation of Fig. 12: rectangular newel post

STAIRS AND RAMPS

Handrail Sections

TYPICAL EXTRUDED ALUMINUM AND BRONZE HANDRAIL SECTIONS

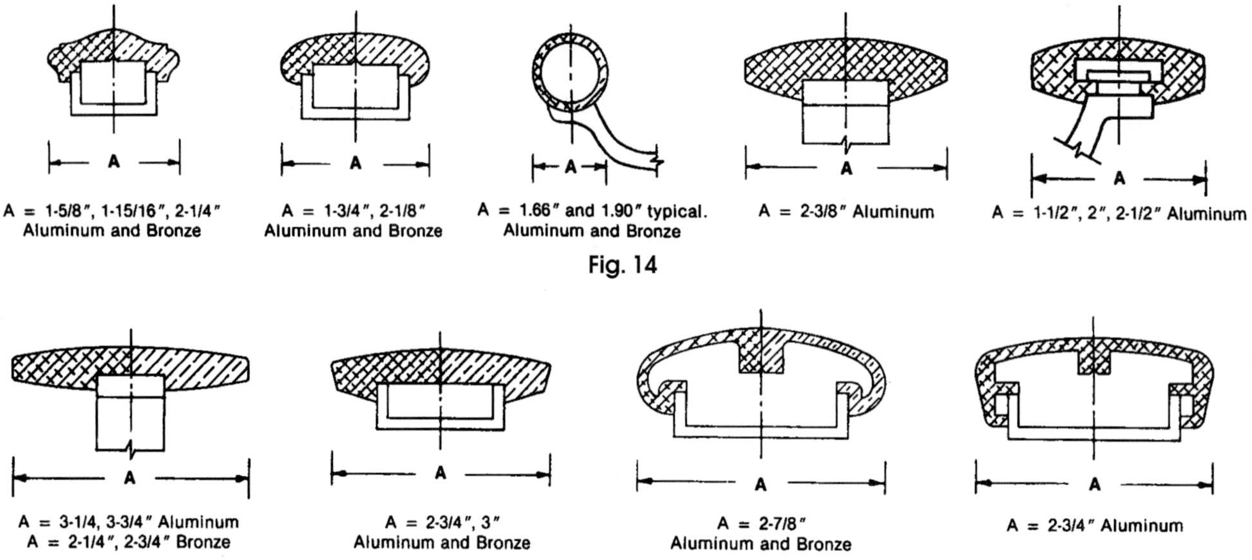

Fig. 14

Most of these sections can be mounted on channels or flats, secured by screws from below. Some are designed for mounting on handrail brackets. The use of channels instead of solid bars often simplifies the attachment of baluster and ornaments. The channels may be of the same or a different metal

TYPICAL ROLLED STEEL HANDRAIL SECTIONS

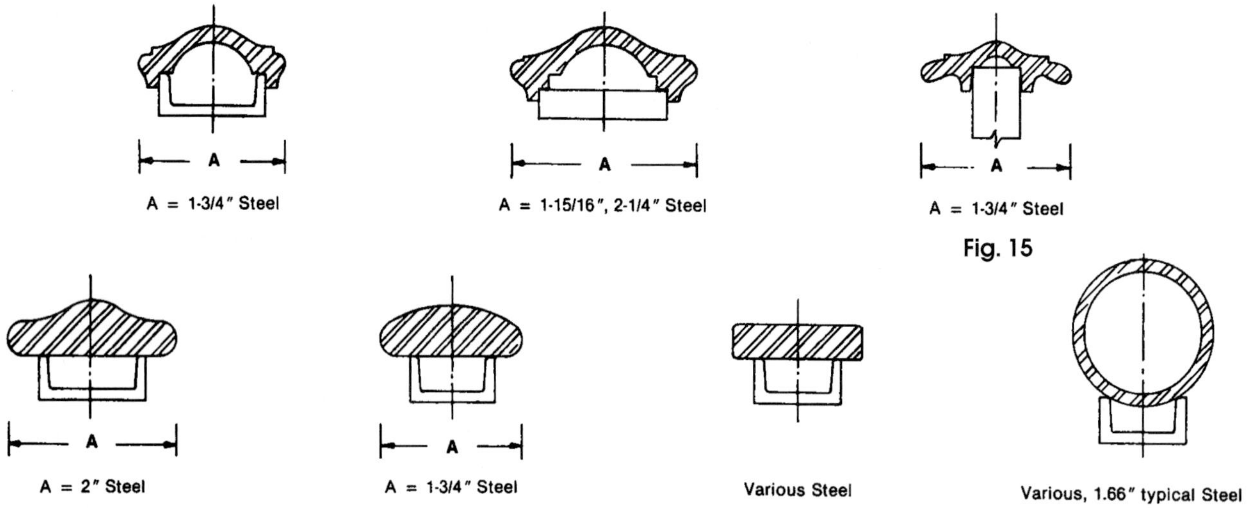

Fig. 15

Most of these sections can be mounted on channels or flats, secured by screws or welding from below. Sometimes they are welded directly to the baluster (see Fig. 15) or attached to handrail brackets (see Fig. 14). The use of channels often simplifies the attachment of balusters and ornaments

REPRESENTATIVE EXTRUDED AND TUBULAR STAINLESS STEEL HANDRAIL SECTIONS

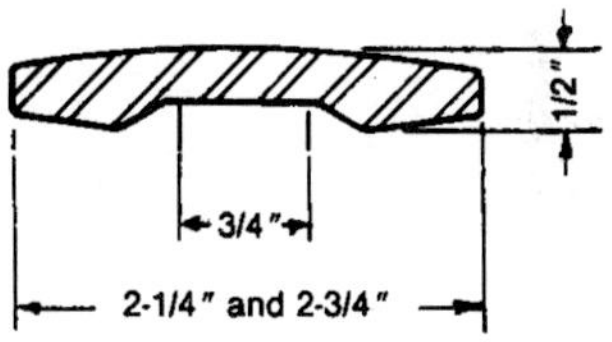

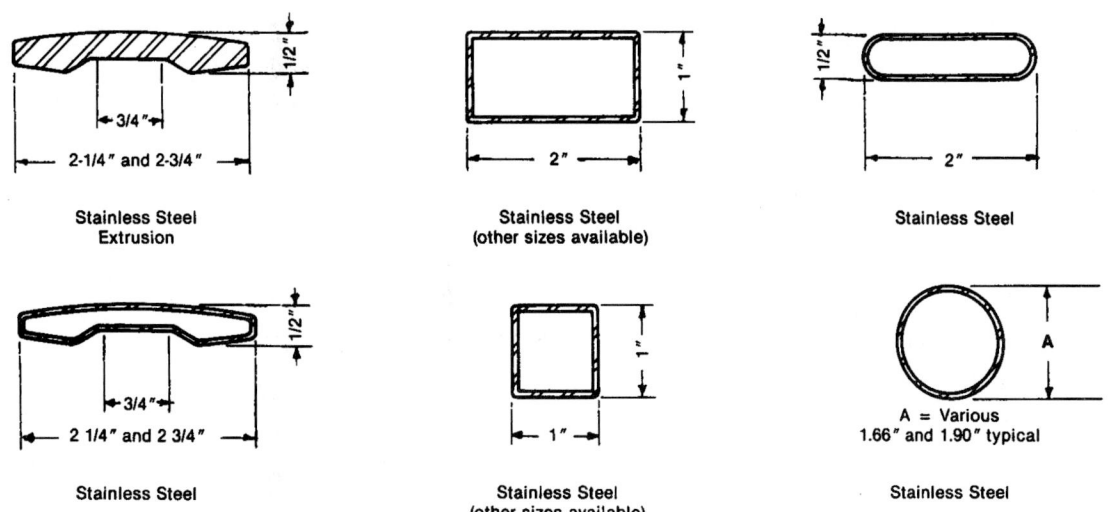

Stainless Steel
Extrusion

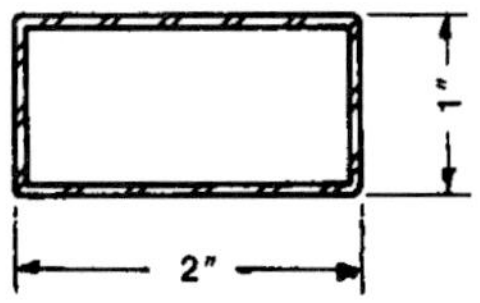

Stainless Steel
(other sizes available)

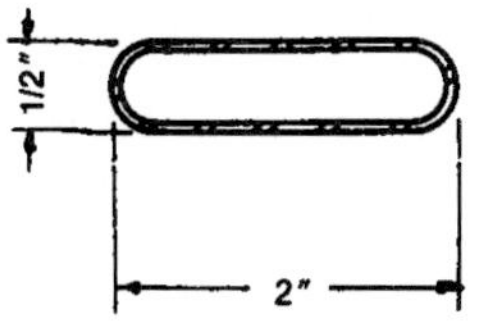

Stainless Steel

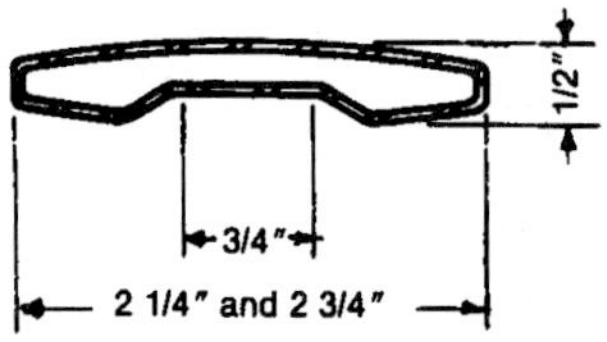

Stainless Steel

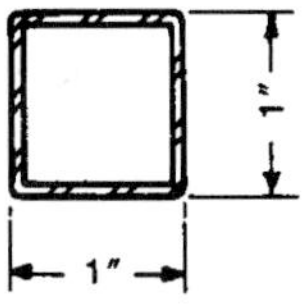

Stainless Steel
(other sizes available)

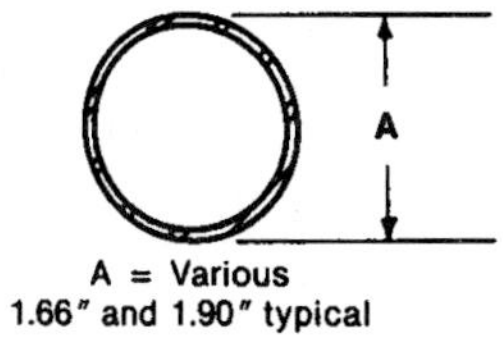

Stainless Steel

Stainless tubular handrail sections usually have a wall thickness of .065".

PLASTIC HANDRAIL COVERINGS

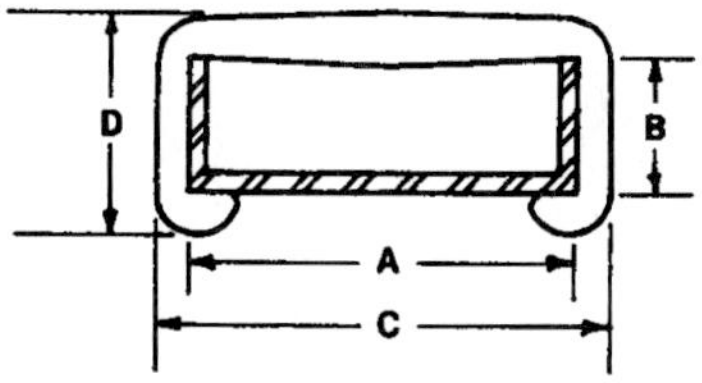

Fig. 16

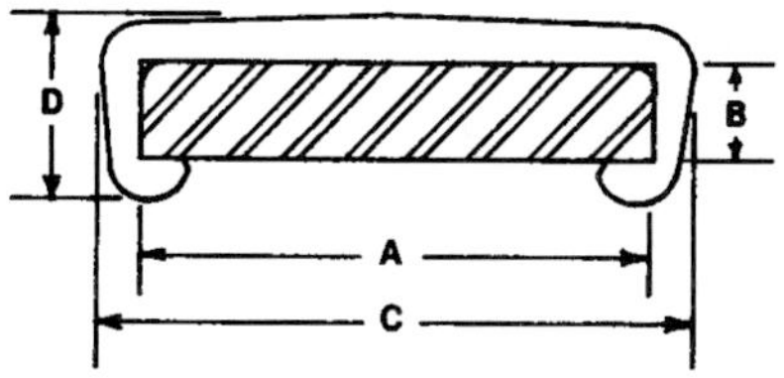

Fig. 17

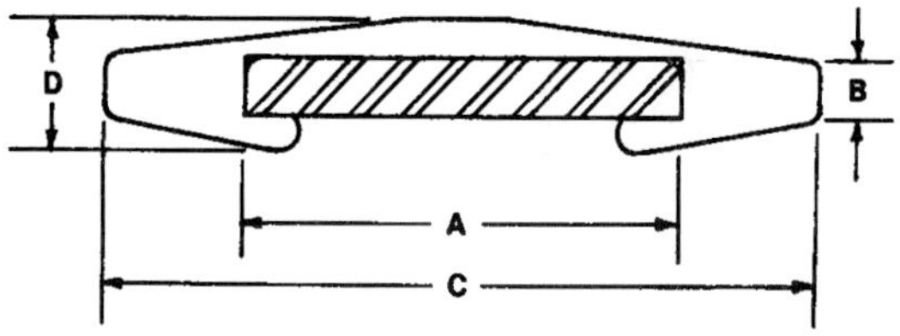

Fig. 18

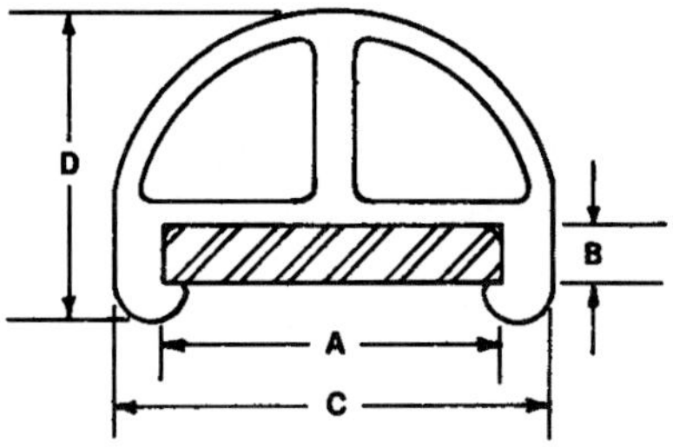

Fig. 19

Table 4 Table of dimensions for plastic handrail coverings

Fig.	A Inside width	B Inside height	C Outside width	D Outside height
16	1" 1 1/4" 1 1/2"	1/2"	1 5/16" 1 9/16" 1 13/16"	1 3/16"
17	1 1/4" 1 1/2" 2"	1/4" 1/4" 3/8"	1 9/16" 1 13/16" 2 5/16"	9/16" 9/16" 11/16"
18	1 1/2" 2"	1/4"	2 3/4" 3 1/4"	1/2" 9/16"
19	1 1/4" 1 1/2"	1/4"	1 5/8" 1 7/8"	1 3/16" 1 5/16"

Caution: Consult manufacturers for fabrication limitations.

General Information

Functional and decorative plastic handrail moldings of polyvinyl chloride plastics are available in a variety of sizes and profiles, several of which are illustrated in Figs. 16 to 19. Consult suppliers' current literature for variations in details and features.

Plastic handrail moldings are not structural and require bar, tube, or channel members to support vertical and horizontal loads.

Plastic handrail moldings are produced in a range of colors from subdued to bright, to suit either formal or informal design situations. The color is integral with the plastic, which is highly resistant to wear, weathering, and corrosion.

The thermoplastic material becomes pliable when heated (not over 165°F), at which time it can be fitted over the support member and conforms to vertical, horizontal, or combined vertical and horizontal curves within certain limitations.

Lateral bends should have a minimum centerline radius of not less than 2 times the width of the plastic section or 2½ to 3 times the width of the support section, whichever is greater. Mitered corners should be used if sharper turns are required.

Combined vertical and horizontal turns can be formed by twisting the molding.

The material can be joined by thermal welding, and end caps can be shaped using a knife, a file, or abrasives.

The use of a cleaning solution for removing grease and foreign material is recommended, after which a solvent is used for polishing or removing abrasive scratches. Normal cleaning requires only soap and water.

STAIRS AND RAMPS

Wall Handrail Brackets

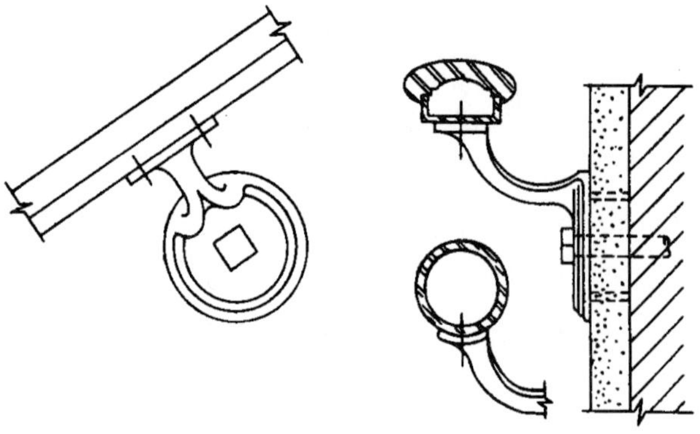

Wall rail bracket of conventional cast design, malleable iron, aluminum or bronze. 3/8″ bolt into wall.

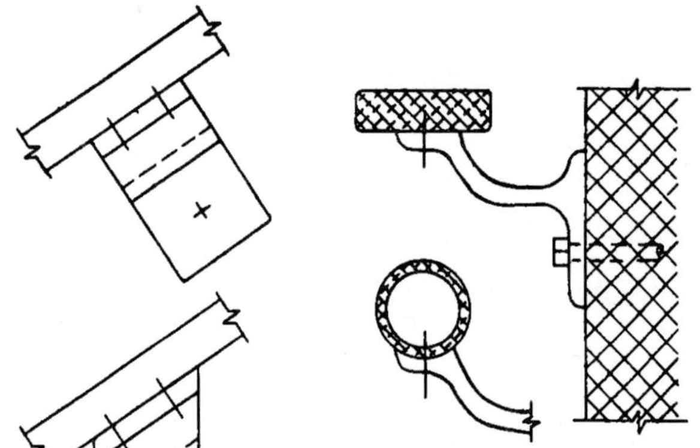

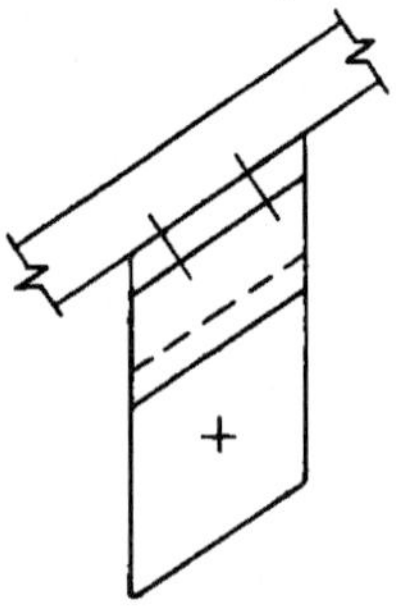

Wall rail bracket of extruded aluminum, made to set at right angle to wall rail or set vertically. 3/8″ bolt into wall.

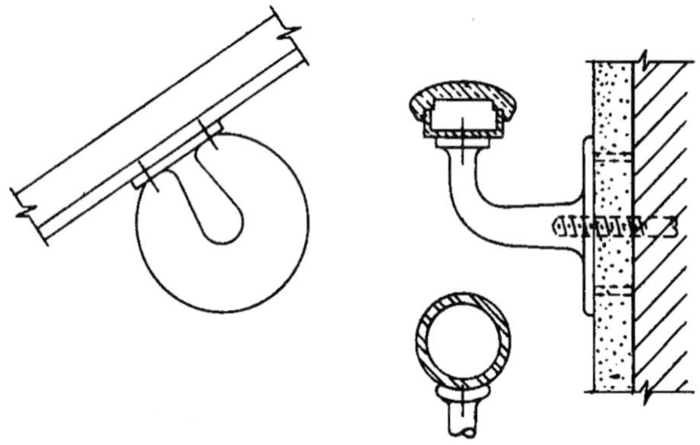

Wall rail bracket of conventional cast design, malleable iron, aluminum or bronze, 3/8″ stud into wall, tapped into arm of bracket.

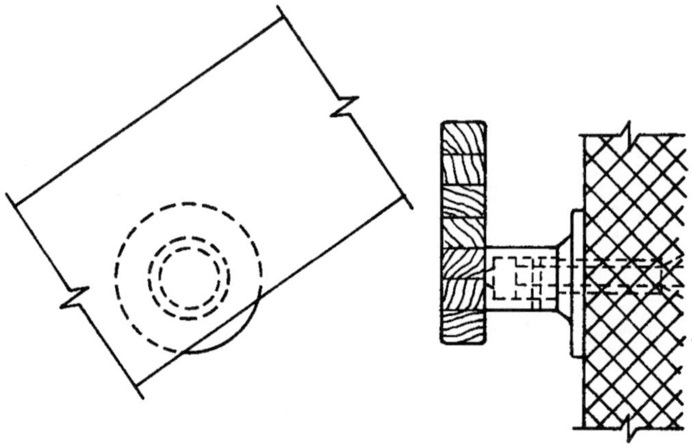

Two-piece wall rail bracket of aluminum. Wall plate bolted into wall through expansion type anchor. Outer sleeve screwed to rail. Outer sleeve fastened to wall plate by set screw.

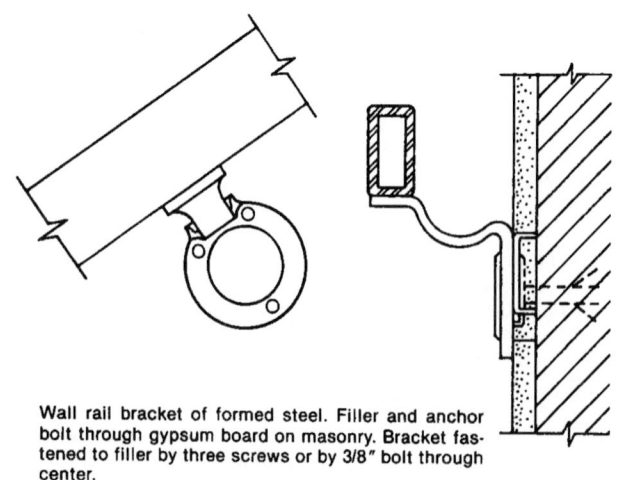

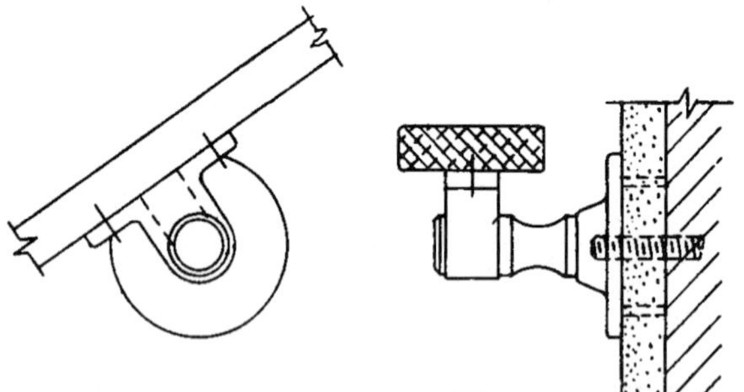

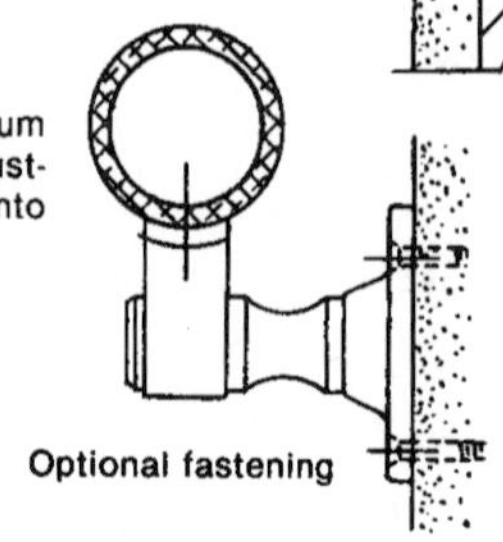

Wall rail bracket of aluminum with fittings to handrail adjustable to any pitch. 3/8″ stud into wall.

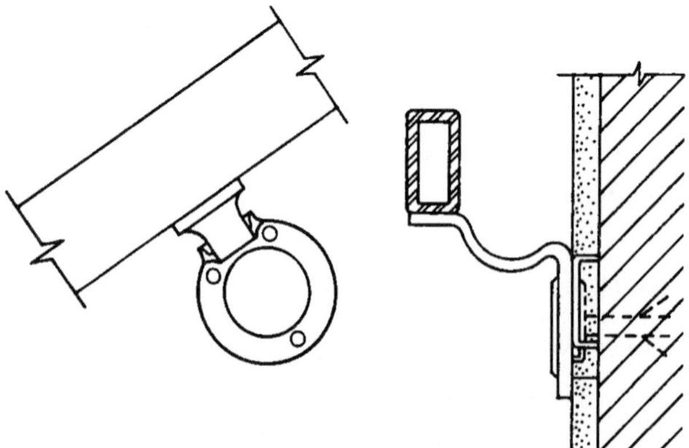

Wall rail bracket of formed steel. Filler and anchor bolt through gypsum board on masonry. Bracket fastened to filler by three screws or by 3/8″ bolt through center.

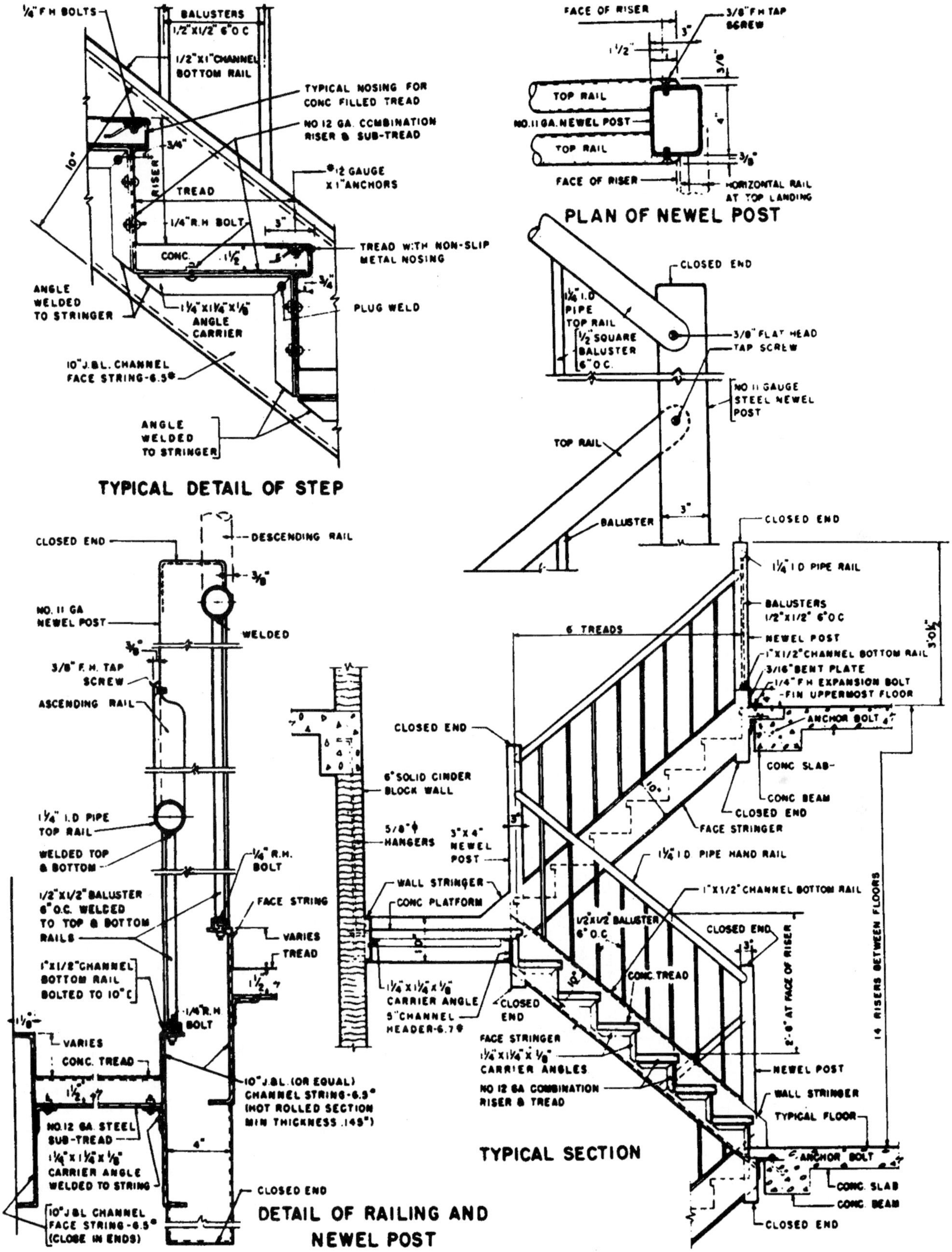

Typical steel stair construction

STAIRS AND RAMPS

Steel Stairs

PLAN·OF·FIRE-TOWER·SHOWING·STEEL·
STAIRS·(TYPICAL·FLOOR·) Scale ⅜"=1'-0"

DETAIL·FOR·MARBLE·OR·
SLATE·TREADS· 1½"=1'-0"

SIDE·VIEW·OF·PIPE·RAIL·
AT·NEWEL· Scale 1½"=1'-0"

SECTION·C-C·
THRU·WALL·
STRING·
Scale 1½"=1'-0"

SECTION·THRU·RISERS·
AND·TREADS·
Scale 1½"=1'-0"

SECTION·C-C·
THRU·FACE·
STRING· Scale 1½"=1'-0"

PLAN·OF·TRUSS·RISER·AT·NEWEL·X·INTER-
MEDIATE·LANDING· DETAIL·AT·NEWEL·Y·SIMILAR·
Scale ¾"=1'-0"·

ELEVATION·SHOWING·12"·TRUSS·RISER·
Scale ¾"=1'-0"

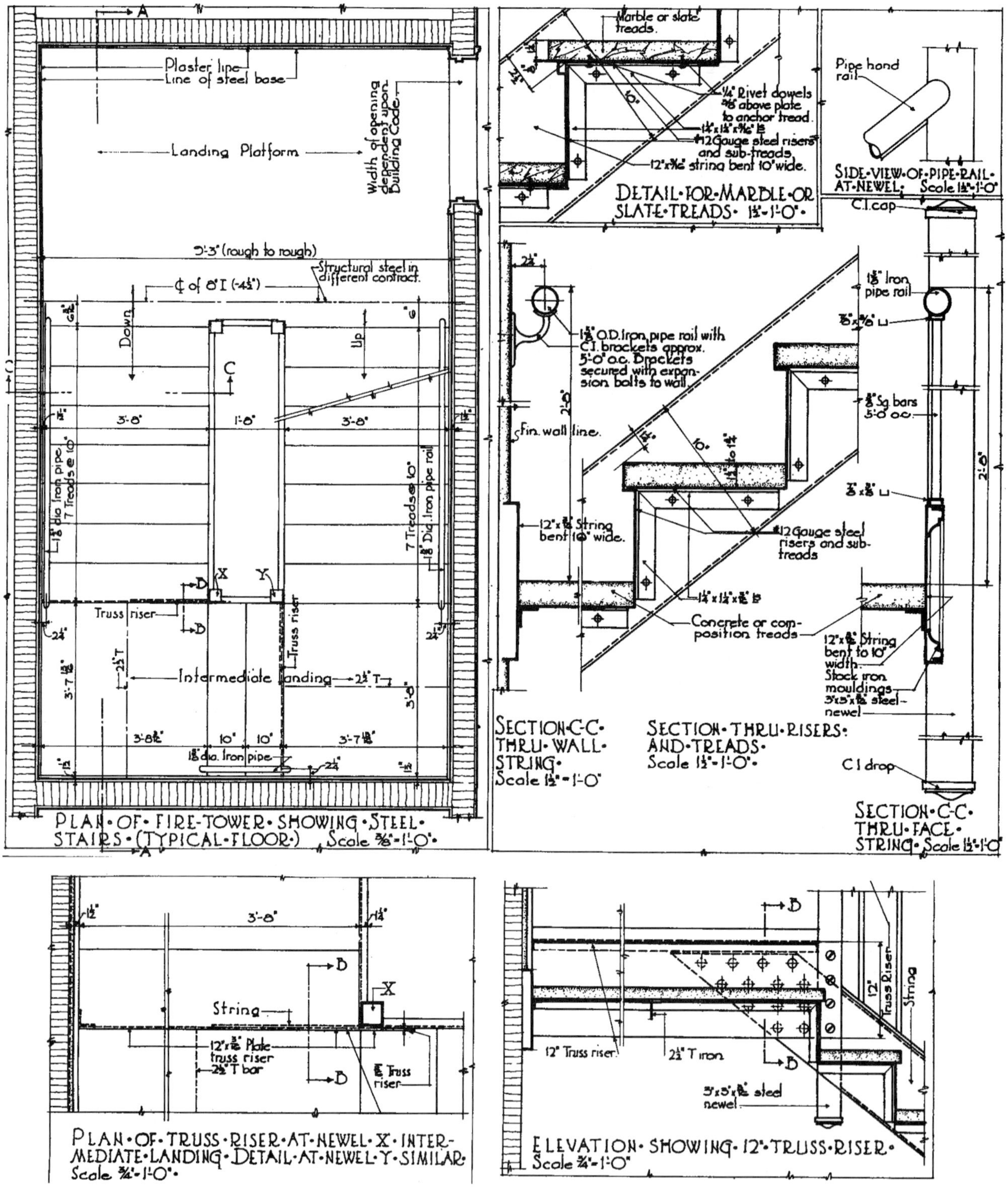

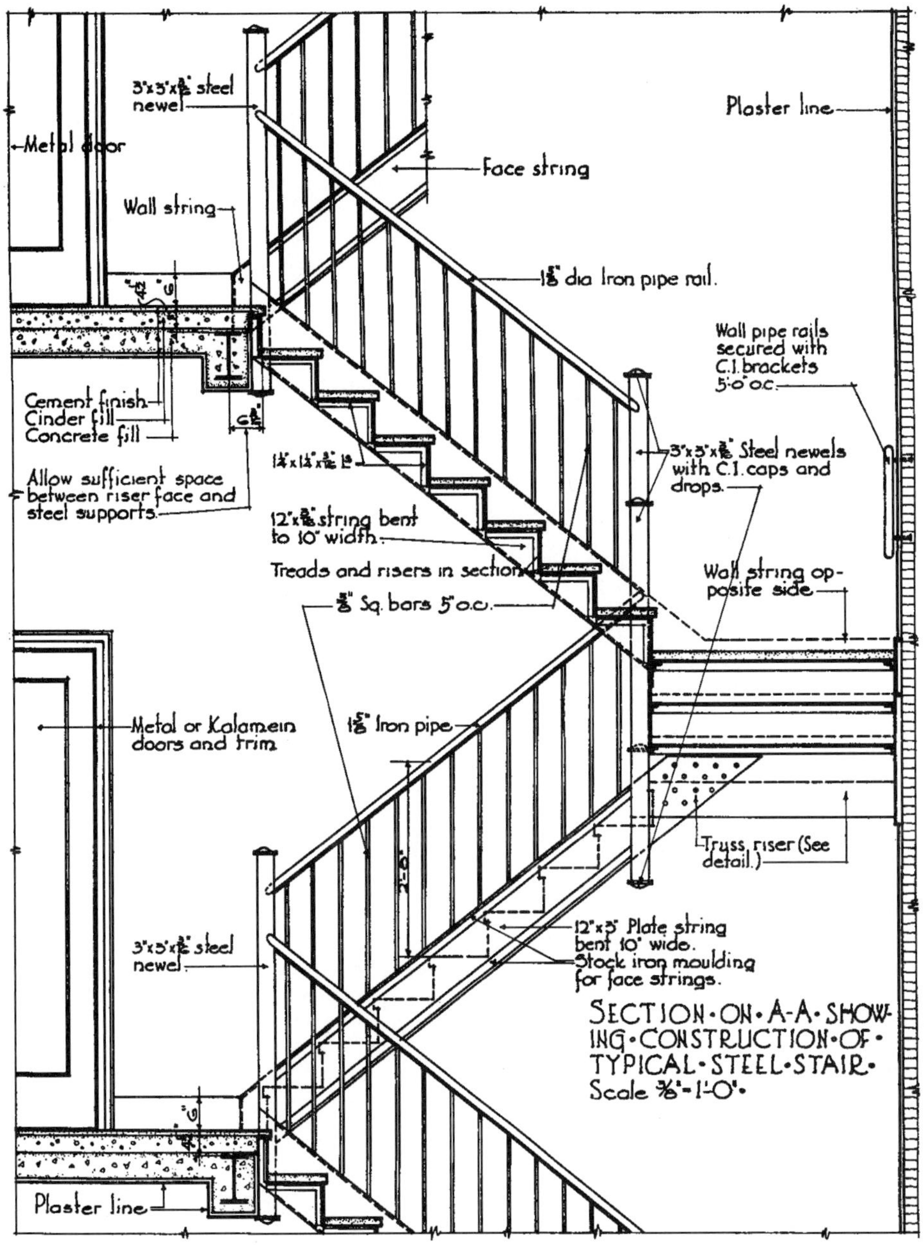

3"x3"x⅜" steel newel
Metal door
Wall string
Face string
Plaster line
1⅝" dia Iron pipe rail.
Wall pipe rails secured with C.I. brackets 5'0" o.c.
Cement finish
Cinder fill
Concrete fill
Allow sufficient space between riser face and steel supports.
3"x3"x⅜" Steel newels with C.I. caps and drops.
12"x⅜" string bent to 10" width.
Treads and risers in section
⅝" Sq. bars 5" o.c.
Wall string opposite side
Metal or Kalamein doors and trim
1⅝" Iron pipe
Truss riser (See detail.)
3"x3"x⅜" steel newel
12"x⅜" Plate string bent 10" wide.
Stock iron moulding for face strings.
SECTION·ON·A-A·SHOWING·CONSTRUCTION·OF·TYPICAL·STEEL·STAIR·
Scale ⅜"-1'-0"·
Plaster line
Pipe cap
1⅝" Pipe hand rail.
Wall bracket
ELEVATION·OF·BRACKET & HAND-(WALL) RAIL·
Truss Riser
String
SECTION·THRU·TRUSS·RISER·B-B ¾"-1'-0"·
·DETAIL·OF·SPLICE·FOR·STRING·
Non-slip nosing
Nosing anchor
DETAIL·OF·NON-SLIP·NOSING·FOR·TREAD· ·1½"-1'-0"·

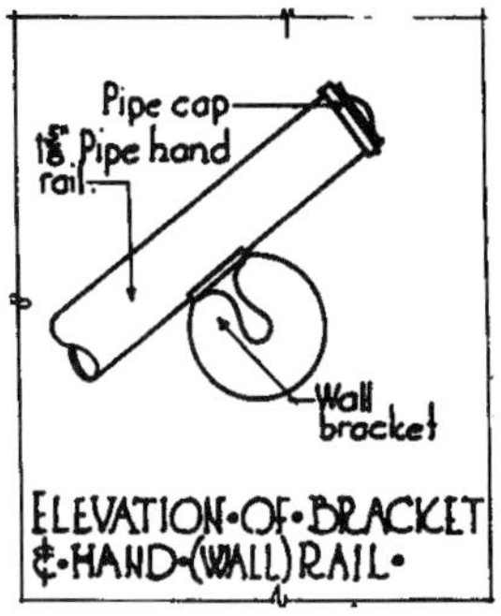

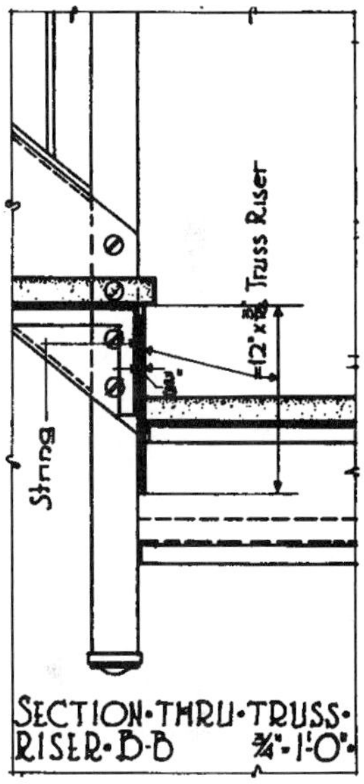

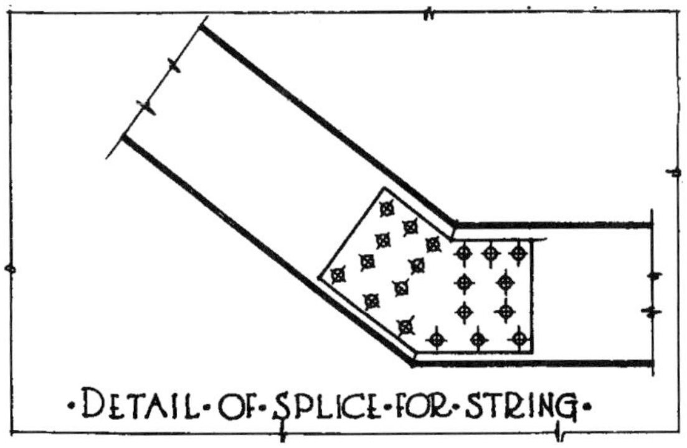

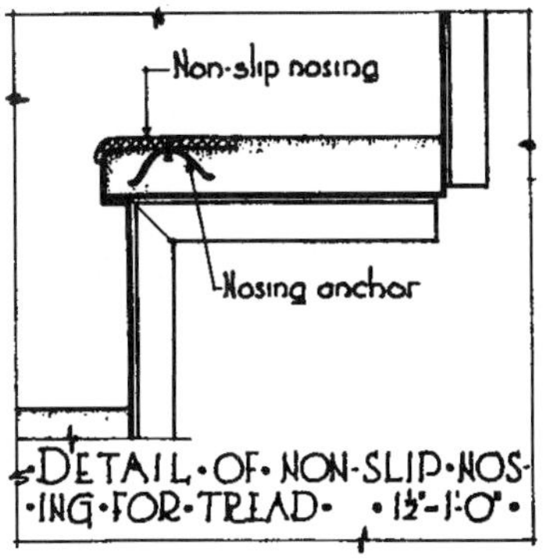

STAIRS AND RAMPS

Steel Stairs

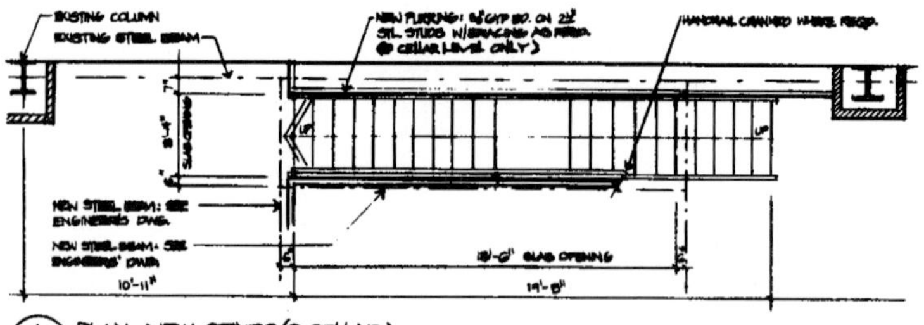

1 PLAN: NEW STAIRS(@ CELLAR)
A10 1/4" = 1'-0"

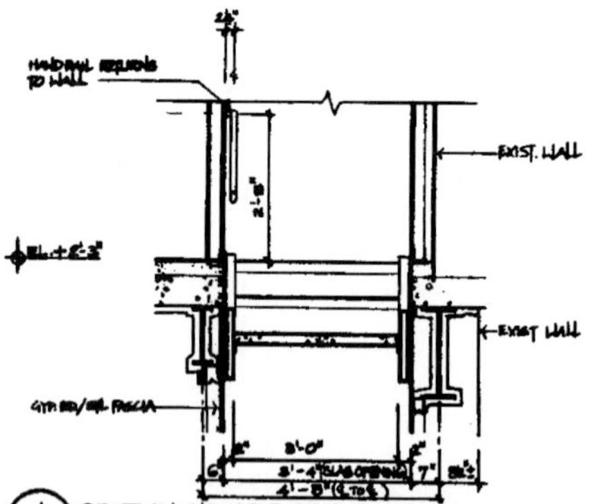

4 SECTION: NEW STAIRS @ FIRST FLOOR
A10 1" = 1'-0"

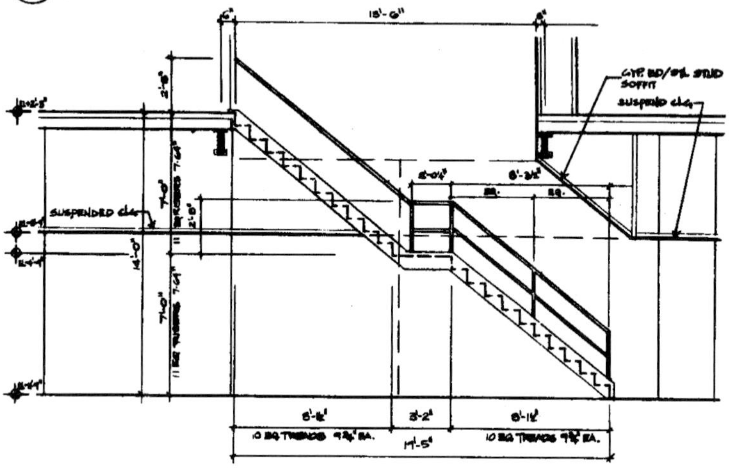

2 ELEVATION OF STAIRS
A10 1/4" = 1'-0"

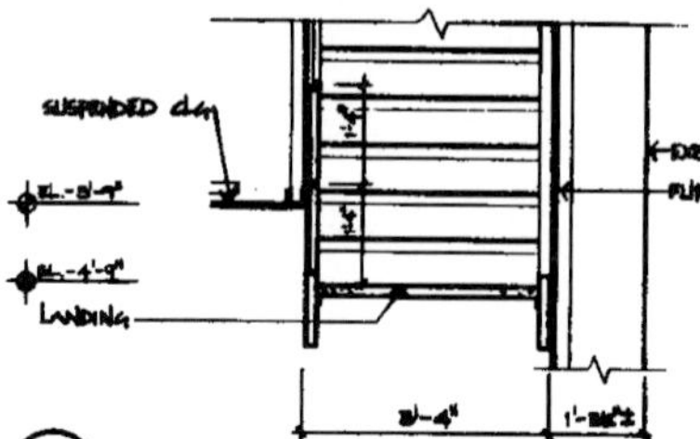

5 SECTION: NEW STAIRS @ LANDING
A10 1" = 1'-0"

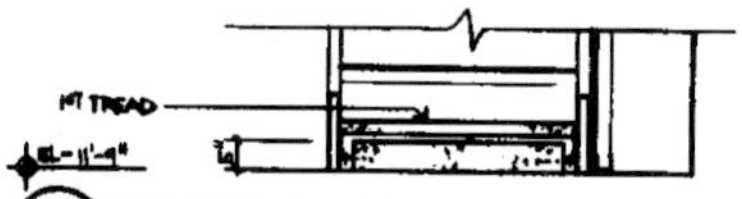

6 SECTION: NEW STAIRS @ CELLAR FLOOR
A10 1" = 1'-0"

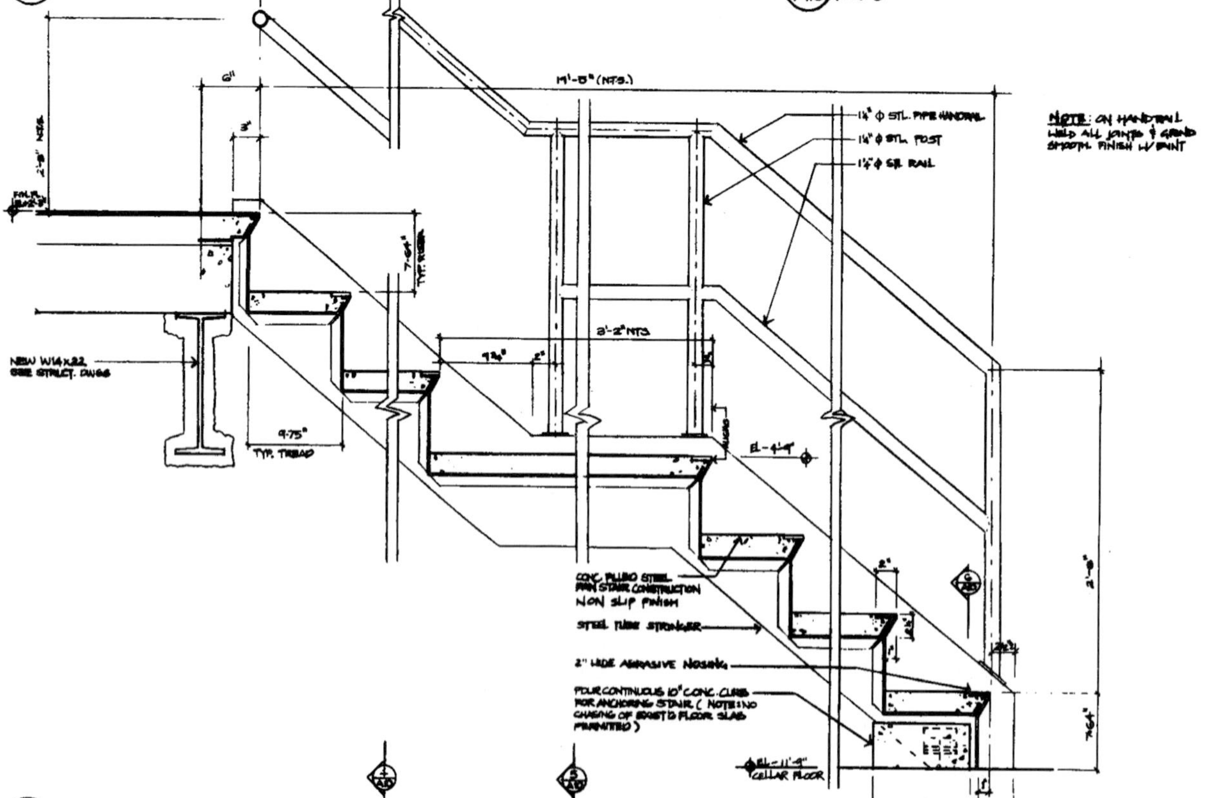

3 SECTION THRU STAIRS
A10 1 1/2" = 1'-0"

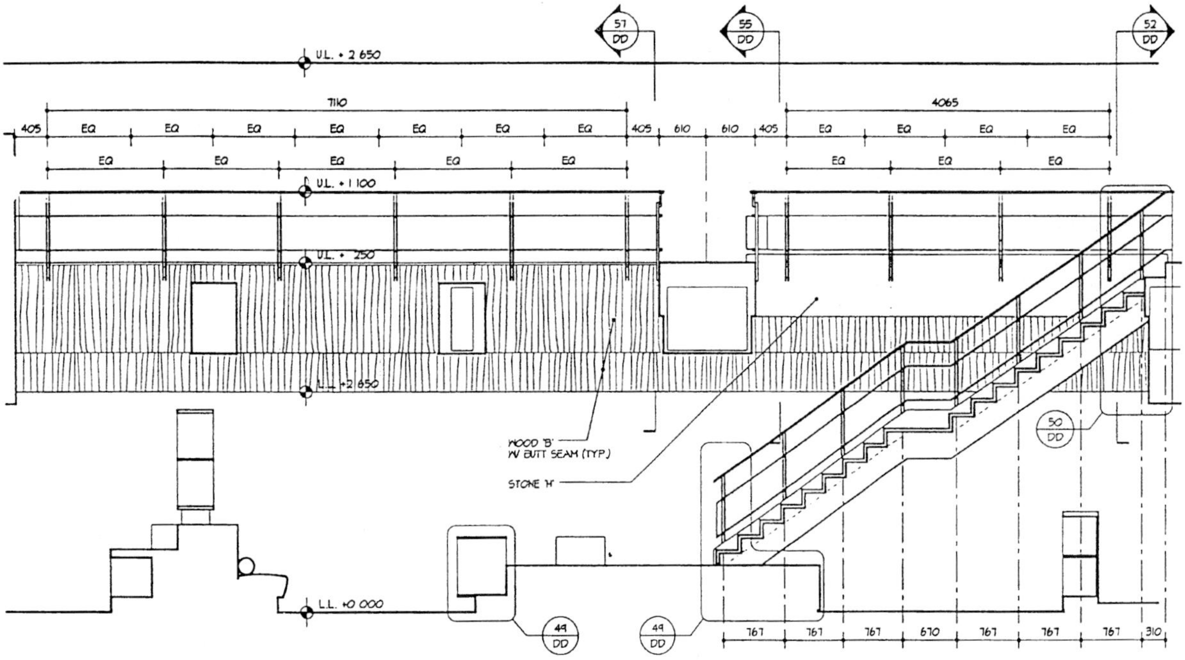

SECTION / ELEVATION THRU STAIRWELL TOWARDS MAIN DINING
JONES DETL 48 DD SC. 1:50 RM. 105/107

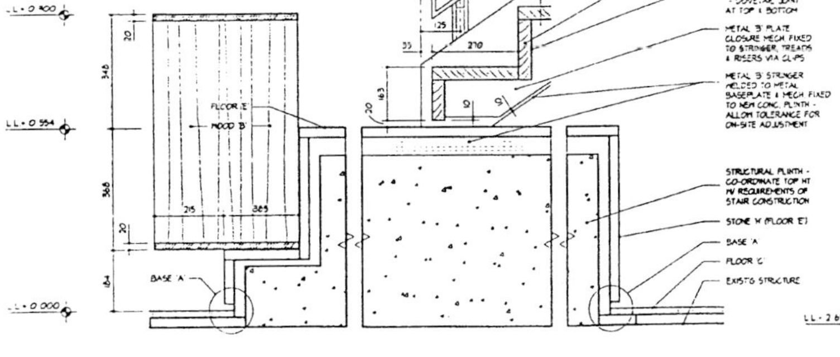

DETAIL SECTION OF STAIR @ LOWER LEVEL LANDING
JONES DETL 49 DD SC. 1:10 RM. 107

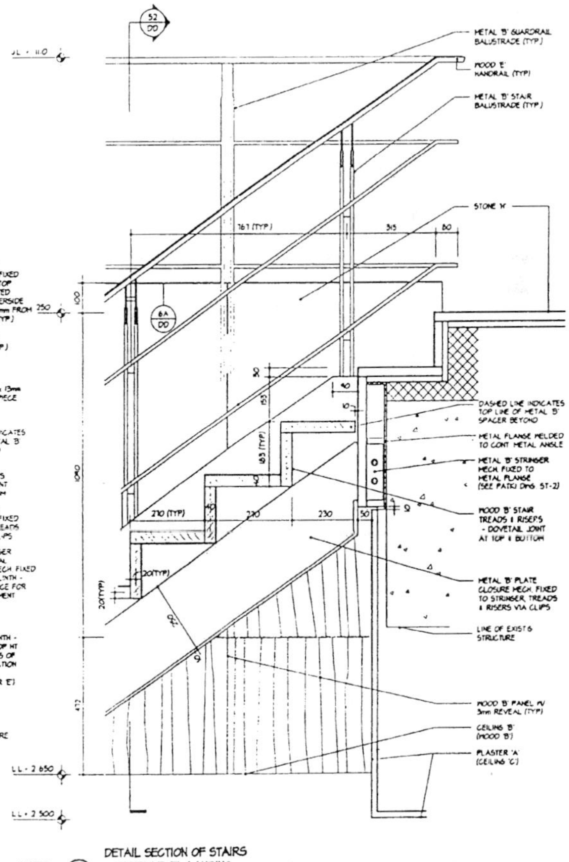

DETAIL SECTION OF STAIRS @ UPPER LEVEL LANDING
JONES DETL 50 DD SC. 1:10 RM. 202

STAIRS AND RAMPS

Steel Stair Railing Detail

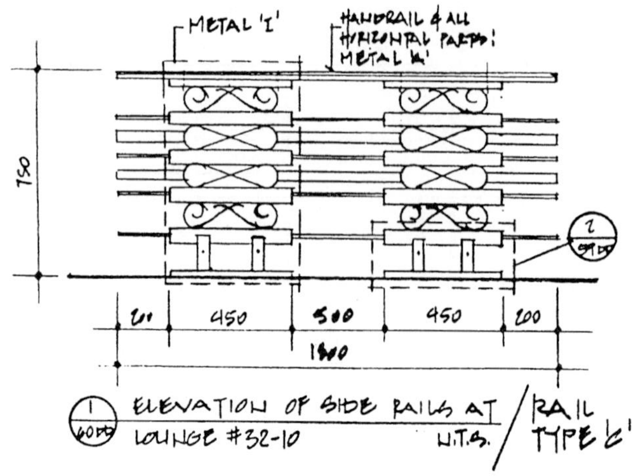

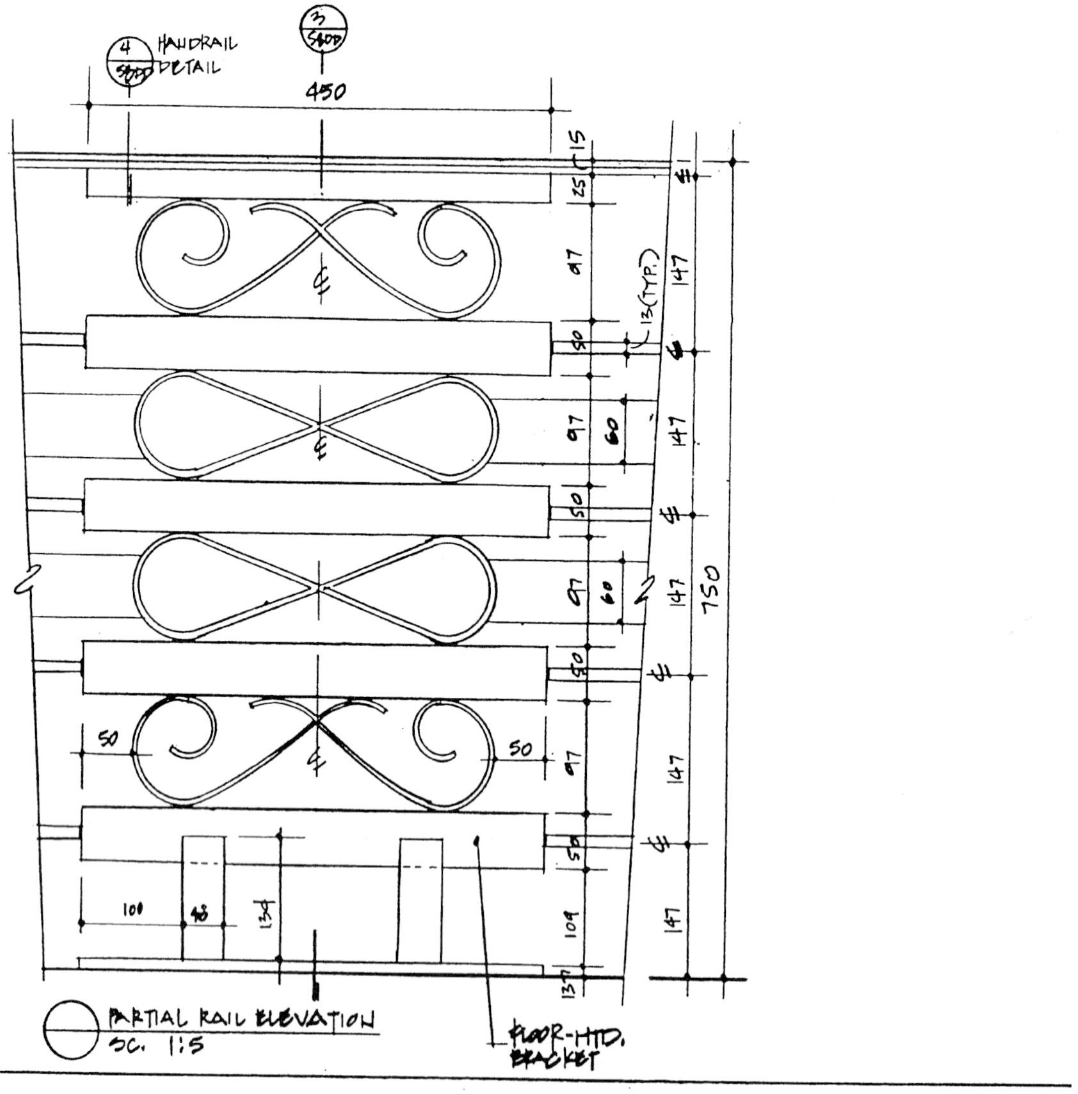

RAILS AT LOUNGE #32-10
SC.: AS SHOWN RAIL TYPE 'C'

STAIRS AND RAMPS

Steel Stair Railing Detail

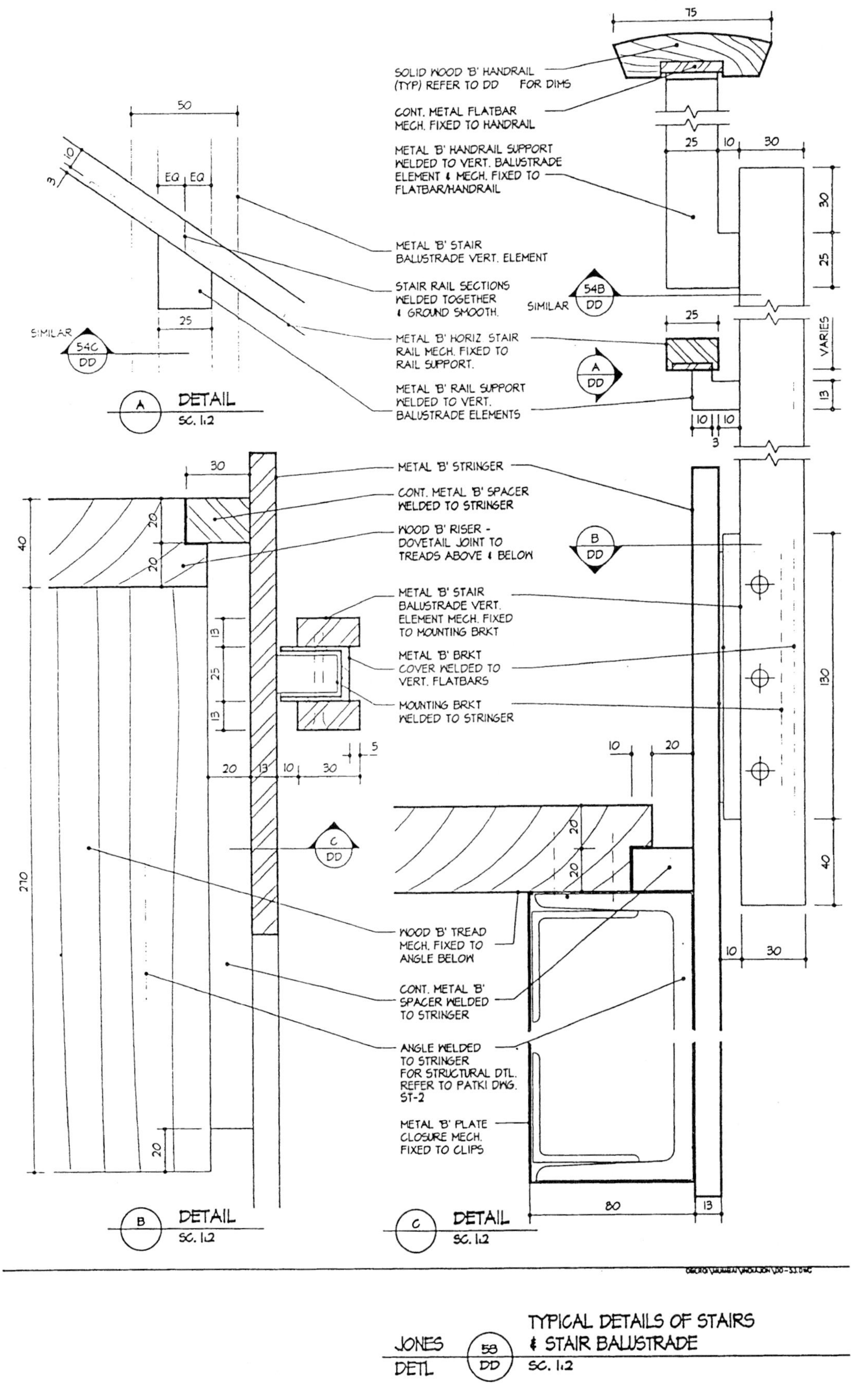
SOLID WOOD 'B' HANDRAIL (TYP) REFER TO DD FOR DIMS
CONT. METAL FLATBAR MECH. FIXED TO HANDRAIL
METAL 'B' HANDRAIL SUPPORT WELDED TO VERT. BALUSTRADE ELEMENT & MECH. FIXED TO FLATBAR/HANDRAIL
METAL 'B' STAIR BALUSTRADE VERT. ELEMENT
STAIR RAIL SECTIONS WELDED TOGETHER & GROUND SMOOTH.
SIMILAR
METAL 'B' HORIZ STAIR RAIL MECH. FIXED TO RAIL SUPPORT.
METAL 'B' RAIL SUPPORT WELDED TO VERT. BALUSTRADE ELEMENTS
DETAIL
SC. 1:2
METAL 'B' STRINGER
CONT. METAL 'B' SPACER WELDED TO STRINGER
WOOD 'B' RISER - DOVETAIL JOINT TO TREADS ABOVE & BELOW
METAL 'B' STAIR BALUSTRADE VERT. ELEMENT MECH. FIXED TO MOUNTING BRKT
METAL 'B' BRKT COVER WELDED TO VERT. FLATBARS
MOUNTING BRKT WELDED TO STRINGER
WOOD 'B' TREAD MECH. FIXED TO ANGLE BELOW
CONT. METAL 'B' SPACER WELDED TO STRINGER
ANGLE WELDED TO STRINGER FOR STRUCTURAL DTL. REFER TO PATKI DWG. ST-2
METAL 'B' PLATE CLOSURE MECH. FIXED TO CLIPS
DETAIL
SC. 1:2
DETAIL
SC. 1:2
TYPICAL DETAILS OF STAIRS & STAIR BALUSTRADE
JONES
DETL
58
DD
SC. 1:2

STAIRS AND RAMPS

Steel Stair Railing Detail

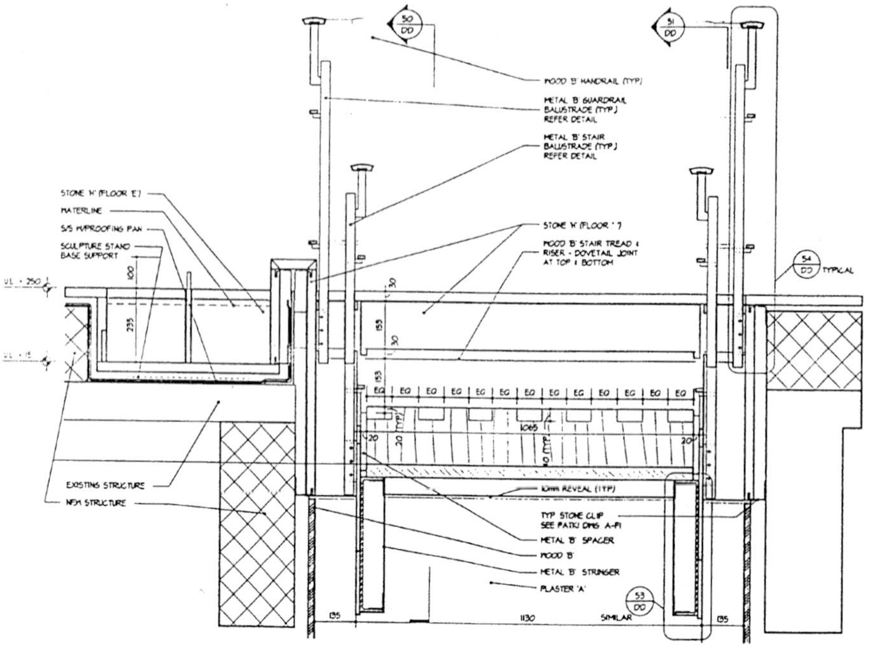

JONES DETL (52 DD) DETAIL SECTION THRU STAIRS AND SCULPTURE FOYER WATER FEATURE SC. 1:10 RM. 202

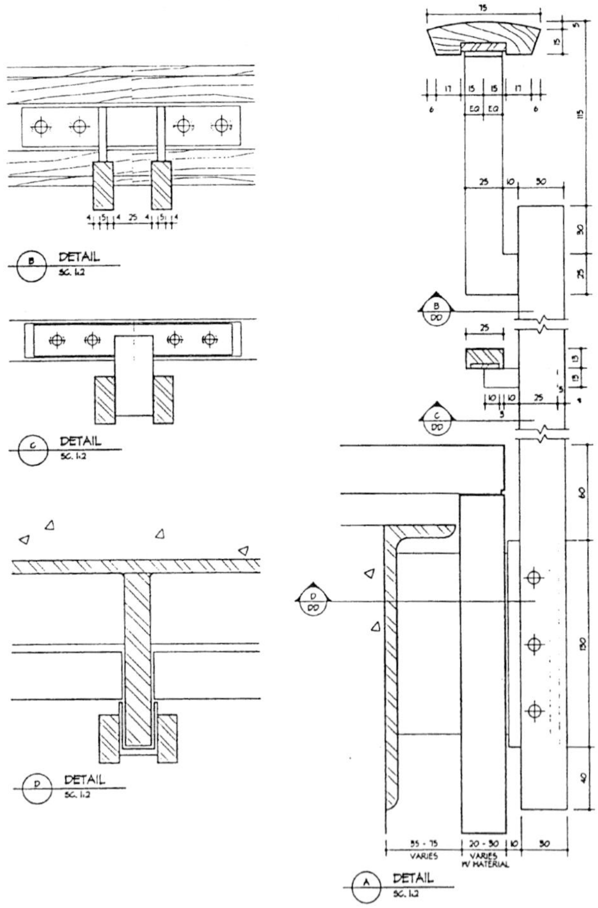

JONES DETL (54 DD) TYPICAL DETAILS OF GUARDRAIL BALUSTRADE SC. 1:2

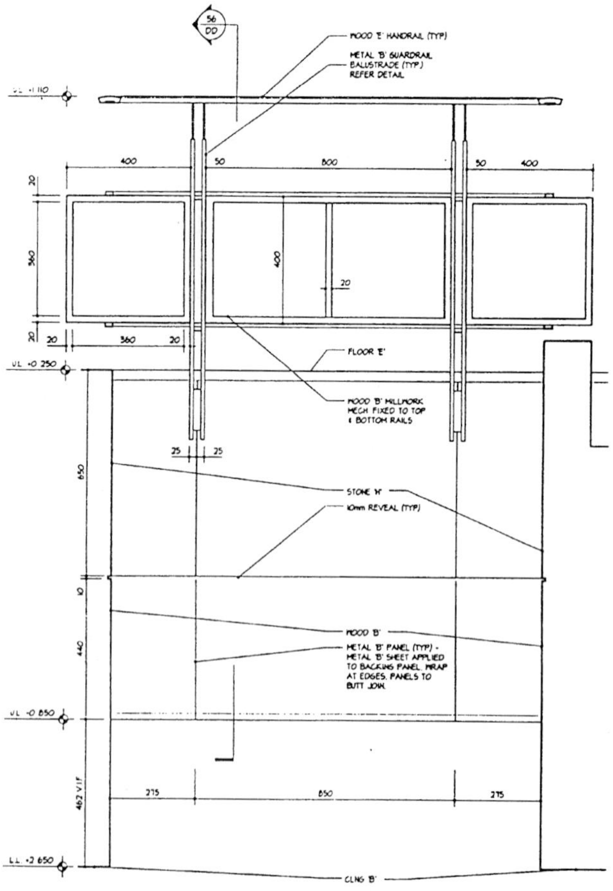

JONES DETL (55 DD) DETAIL ELEVATION OF BRIDGE SC. 1:10 RM. 202

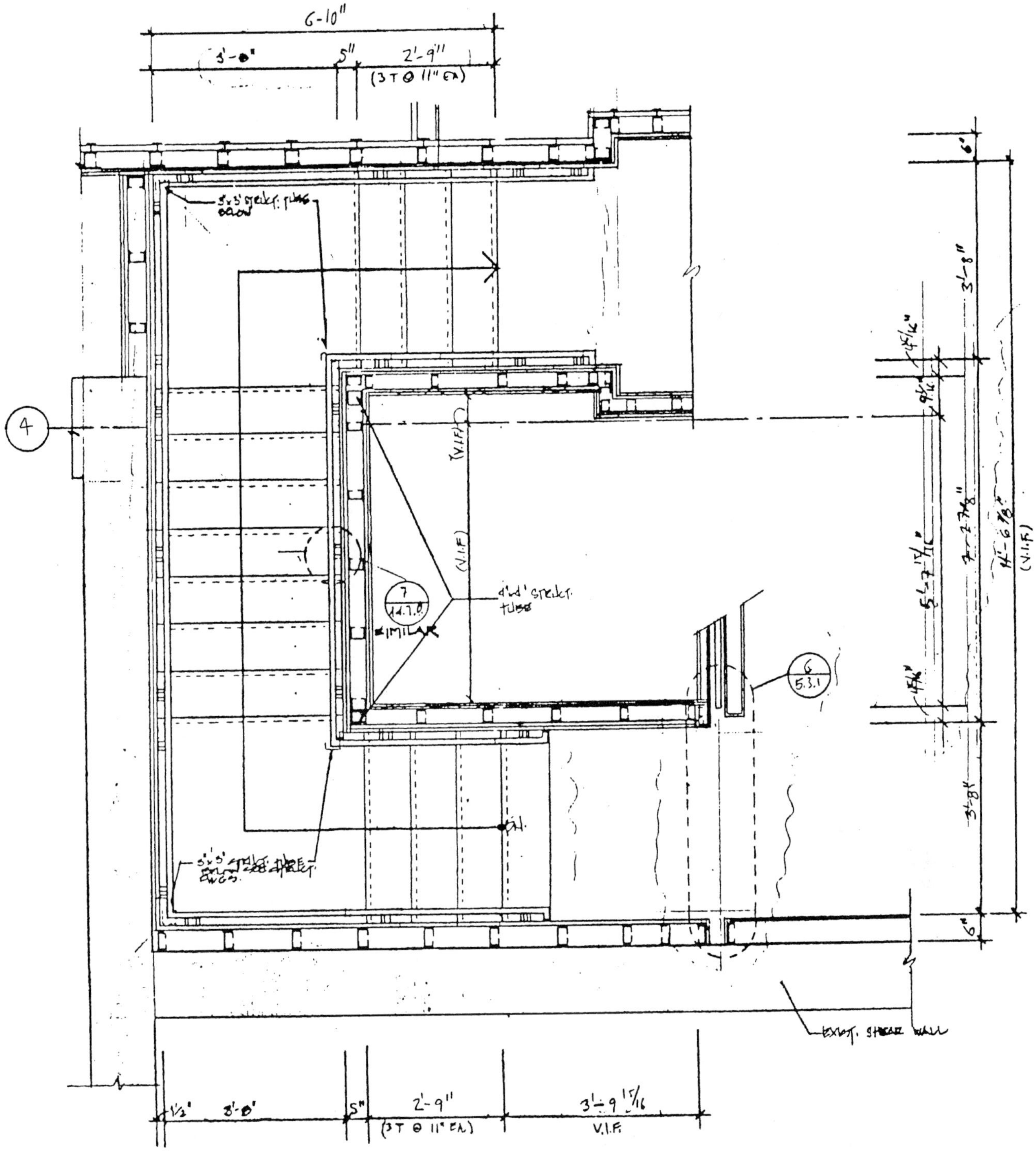

1 Plan: Basement & First Level Stair #2
1/2"=1'-0"

STAIRS AND RAMPS

U-Shape Steel Stair Elevations

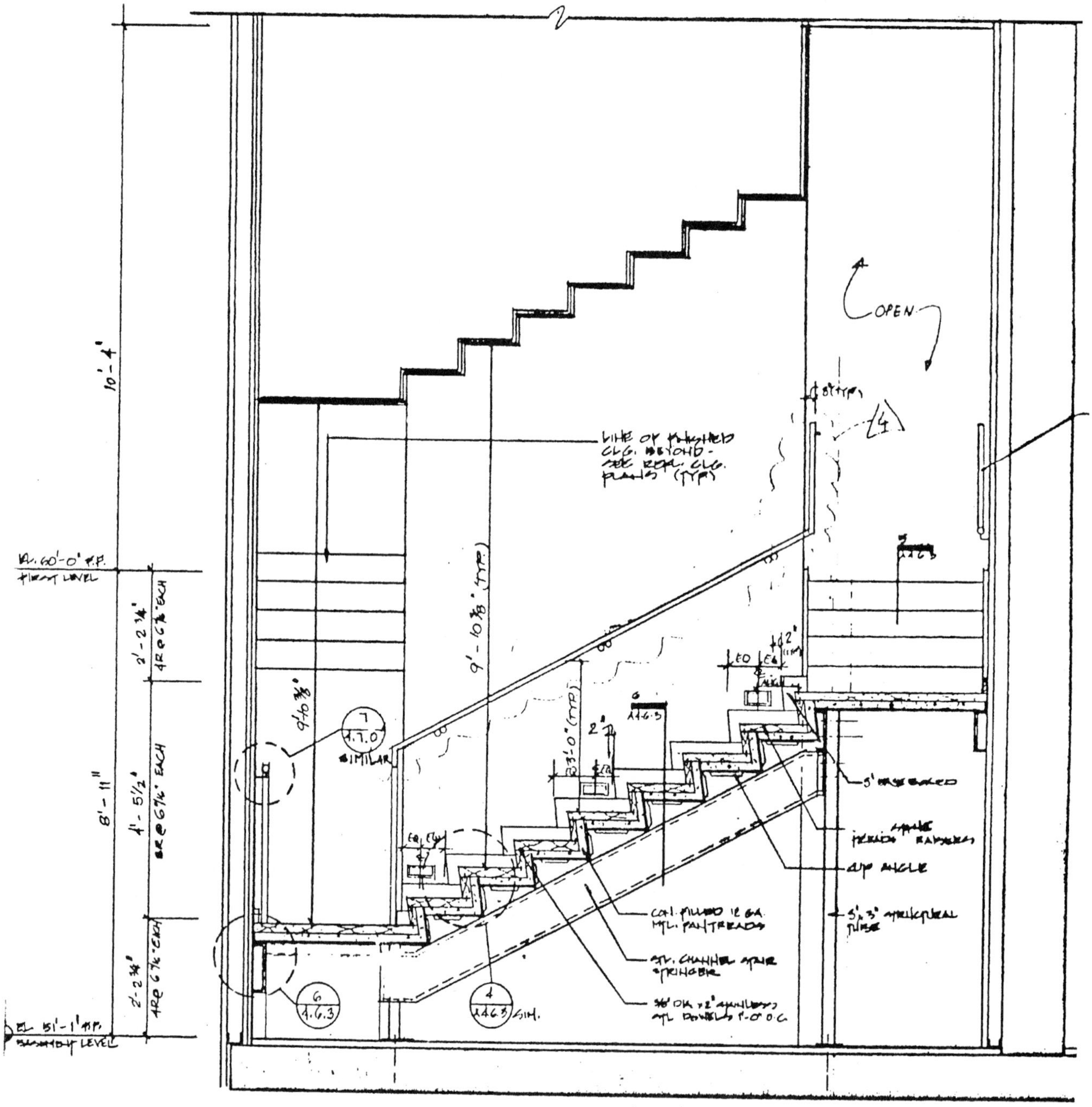

2 Section: East Stair #2
1/2"=1'0"

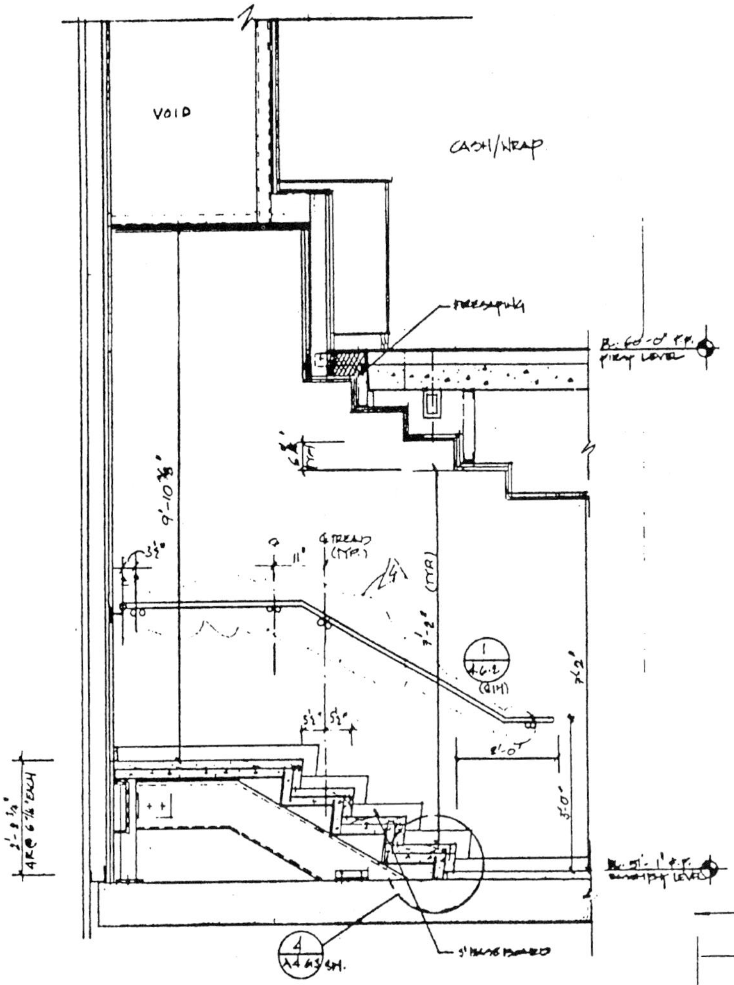

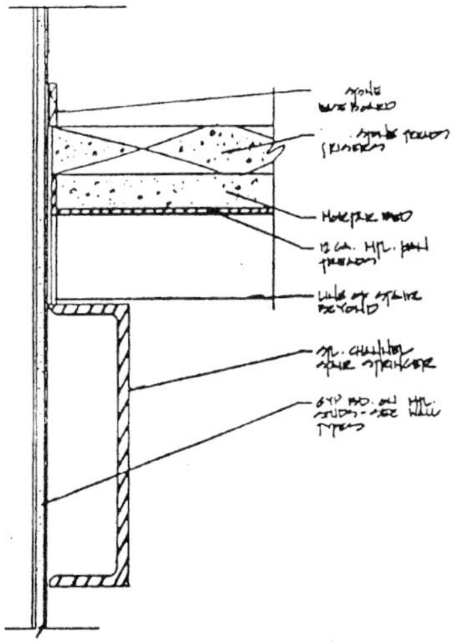

6 Detail
3"=1'-0"

3 Section: North St #2
1/2"=1'-0"

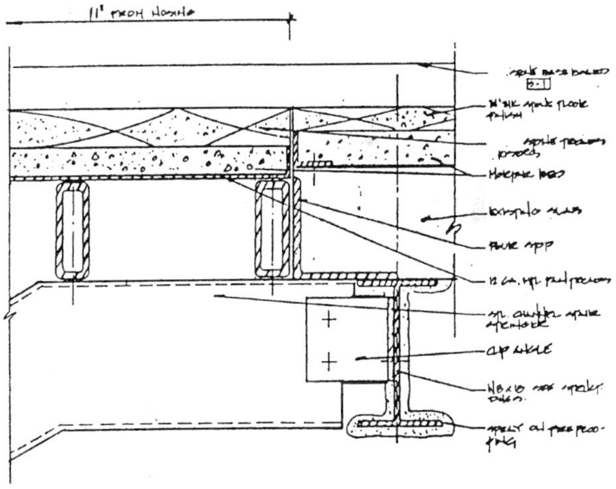

5 Detail
3"=1'-0"

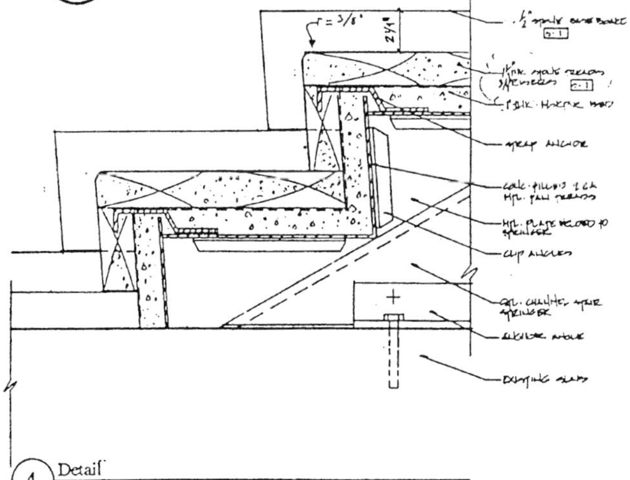

4 Detail
3"=1'-0"

STAIRS AND RAMPS

U-Shape Steel Stair Railing Details

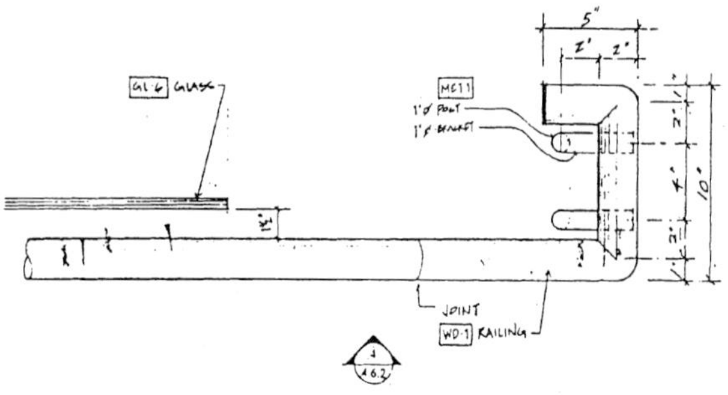

1 Detail

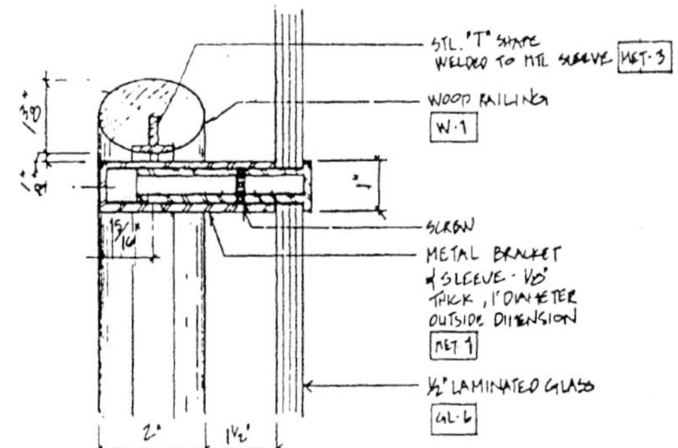

1 Detail

½ FULL SIZE

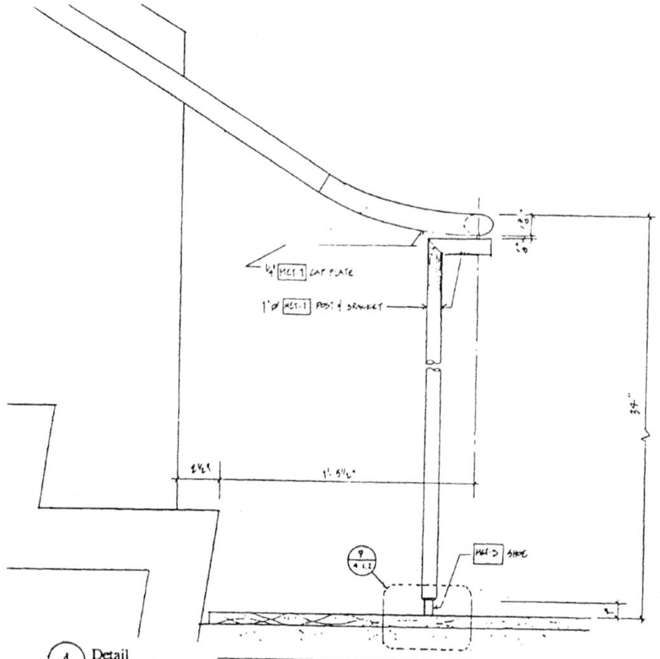

4 Detail

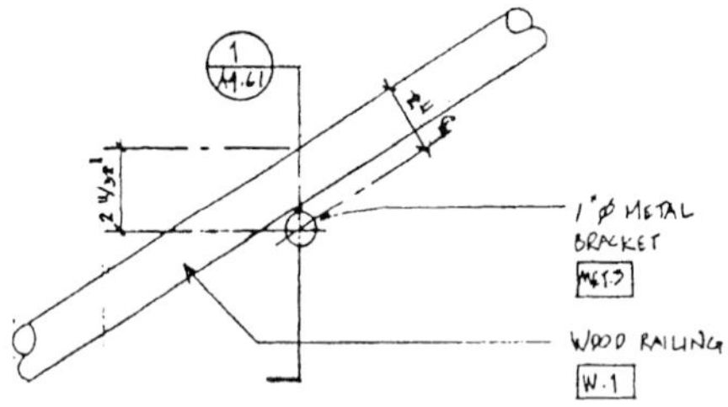

4 Detail

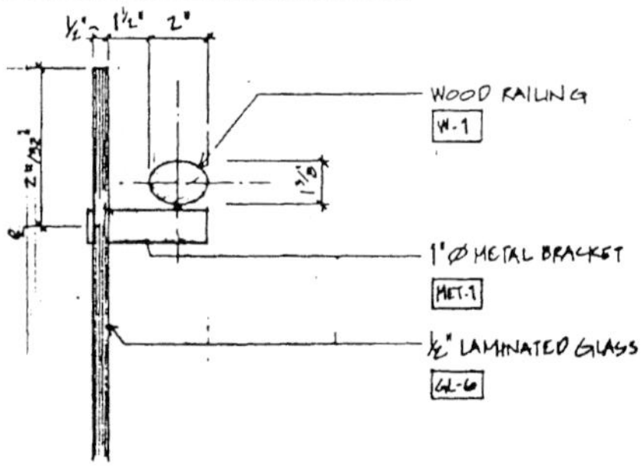

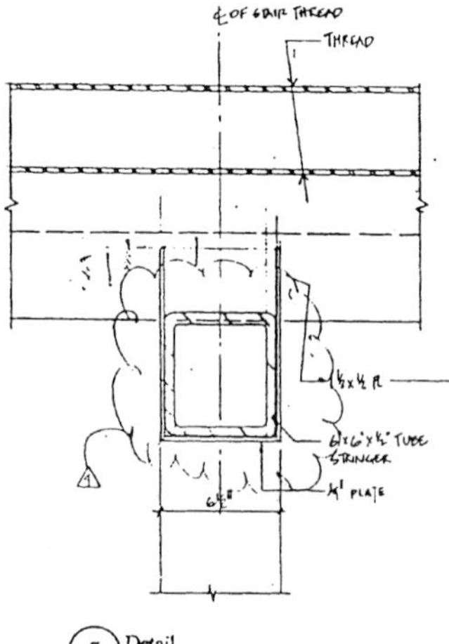

5 Detail

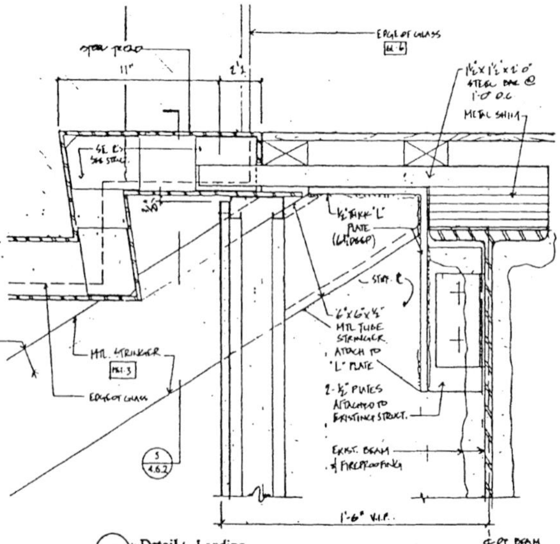

6 Detail @ Landing

STAIRS AND RAMPS

U-Shape Steel Stair Railing Details

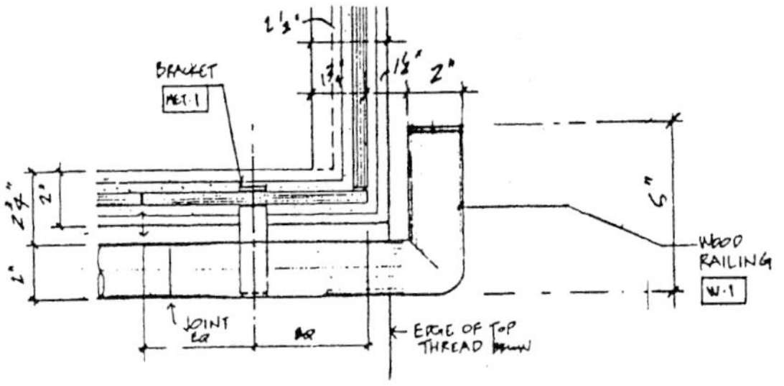

3 Detail

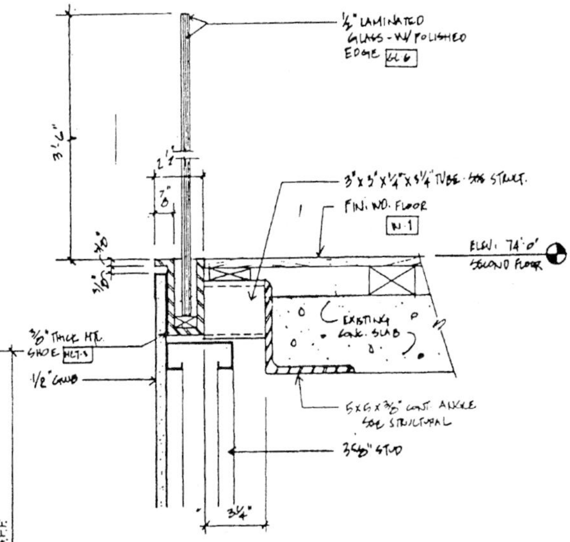

7 Detail - Guardrail @ 2nd. Level

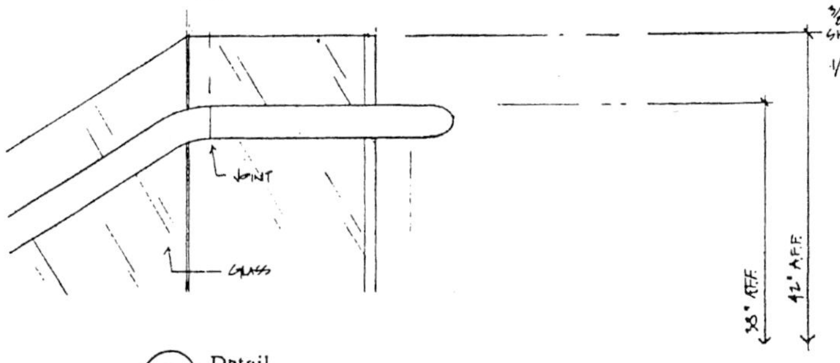

8 Detail

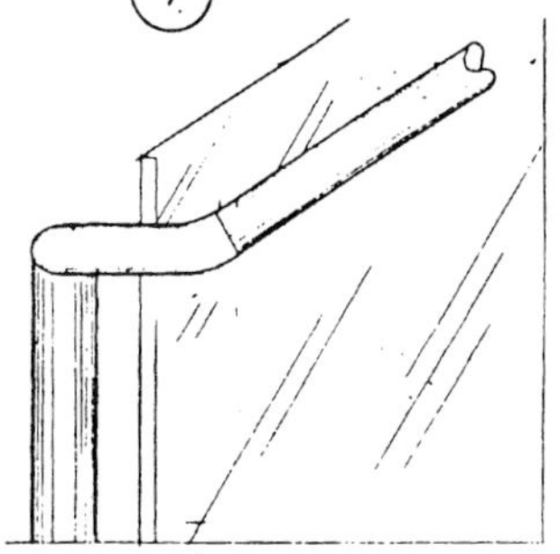

8 Detail

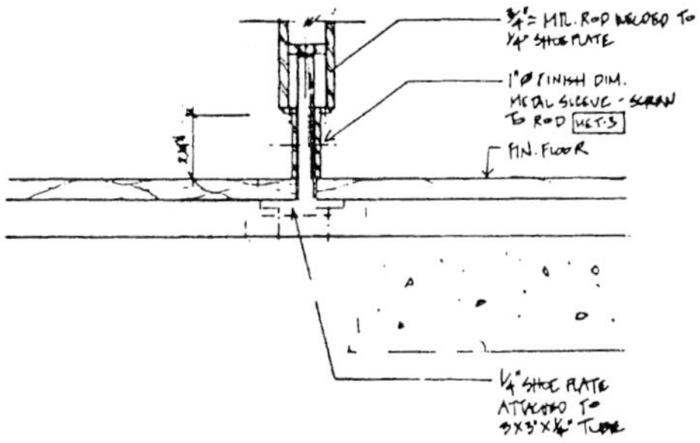

9 Detail

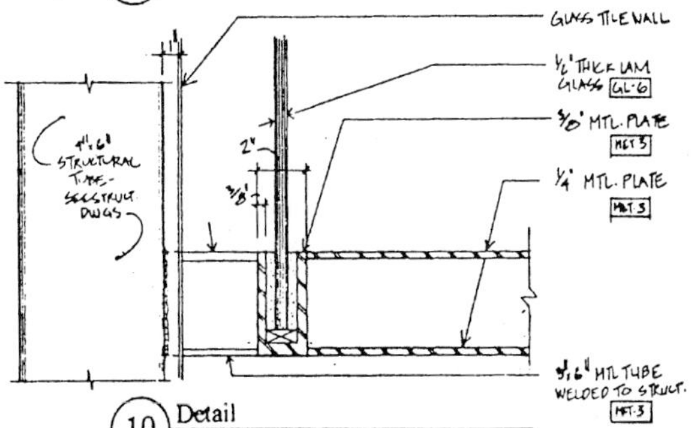

10 Detail

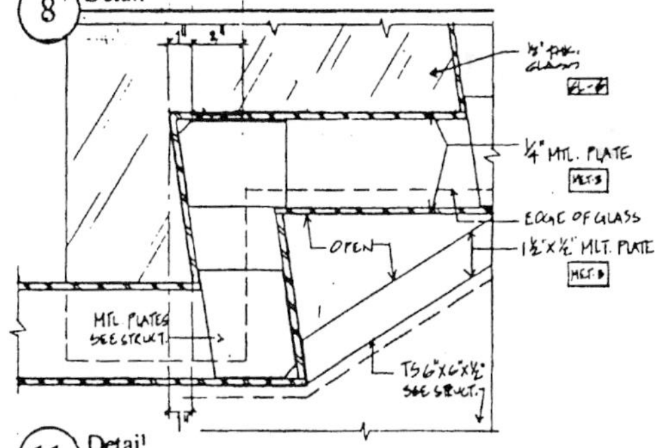

11 Detail

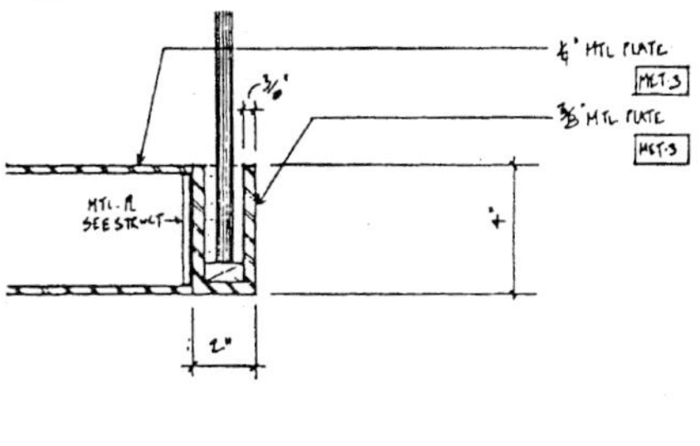

14 Detail

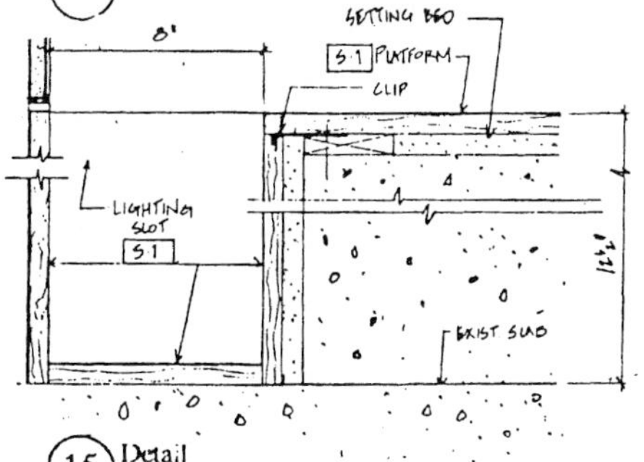

15 Detail

STAIRS AND RAMPS

U-Shape Steel Stair Railing Details

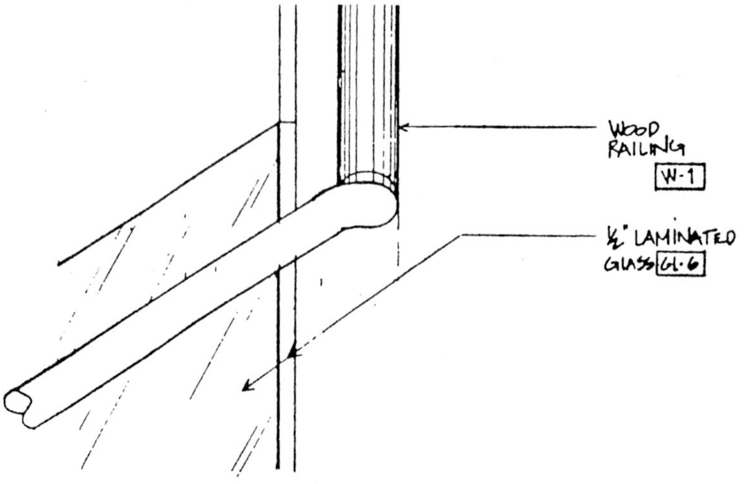

9 Detail

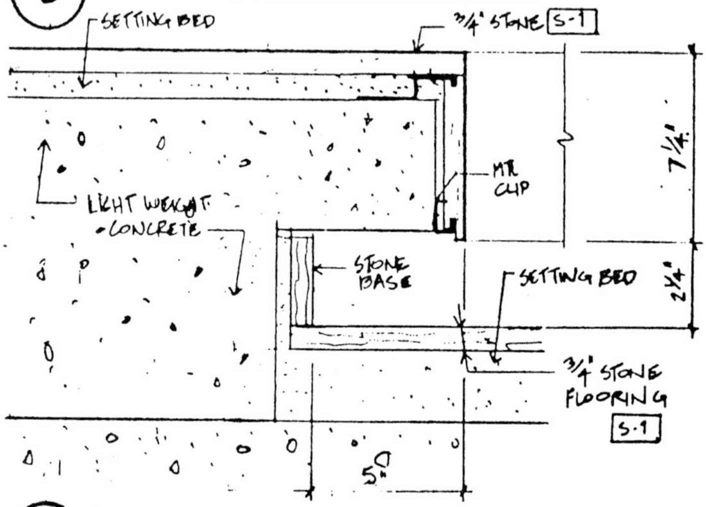

12 Detail

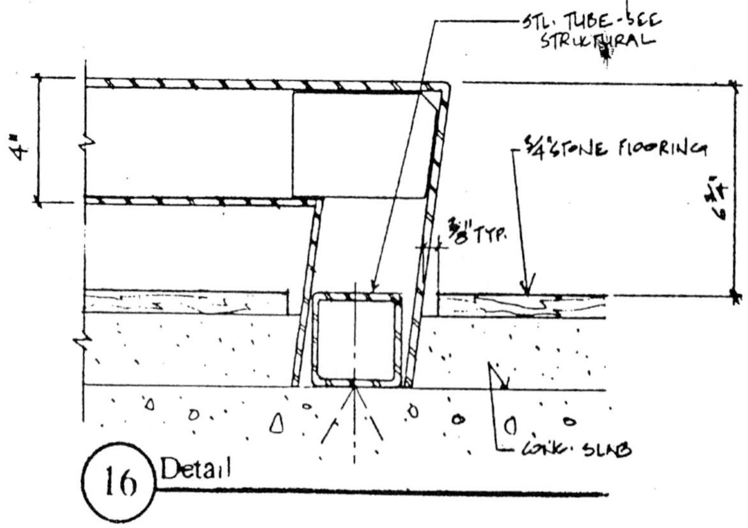

16 Detail

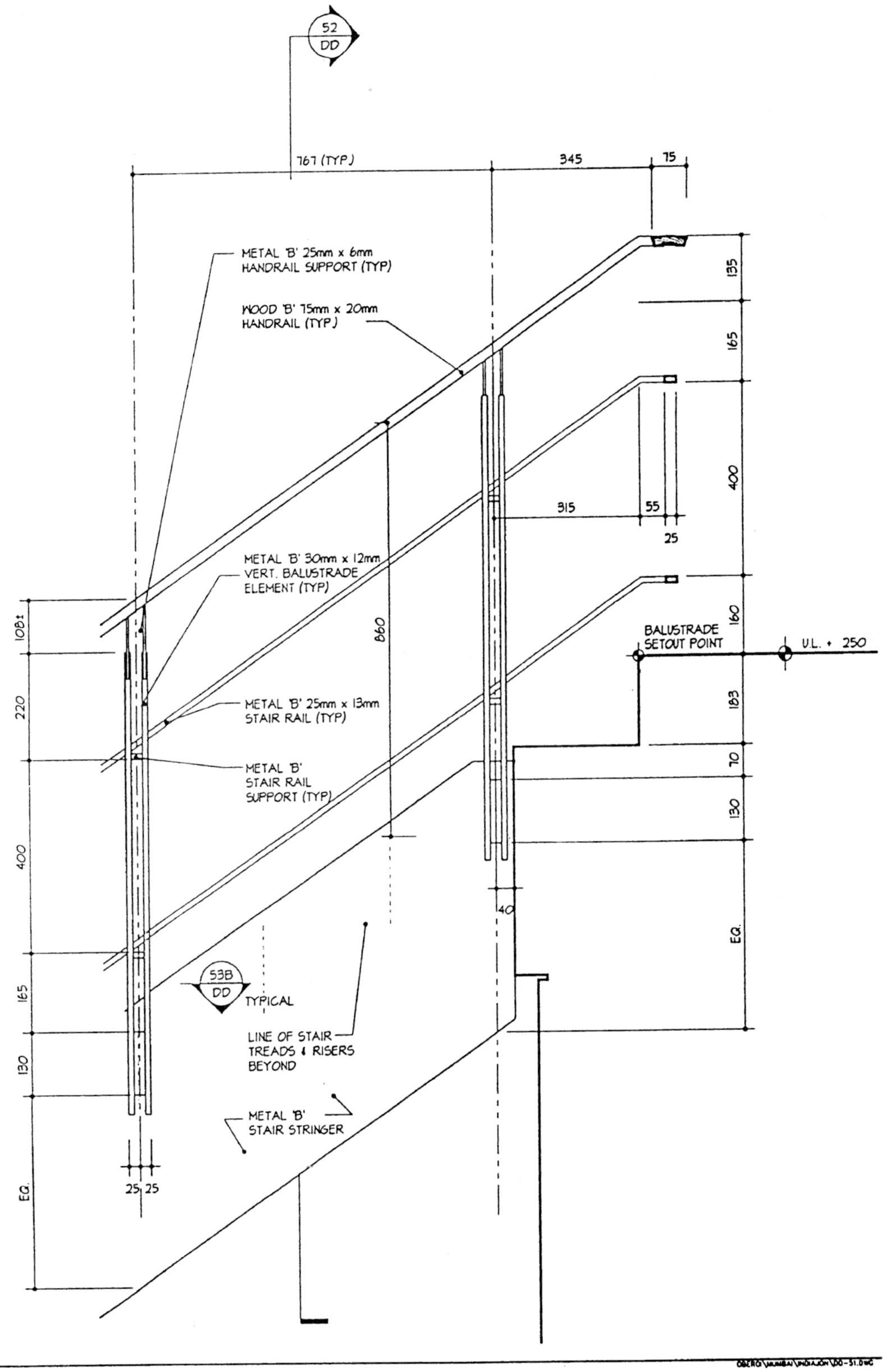

DETAIL SECTION OF STAIR
BALUSTRADE @ UPPER LEVEL LANDING

JONES DETL 51 DD SC. 1:10 RM. 202

STAIRS AND RAMPS

Steel Stair Details

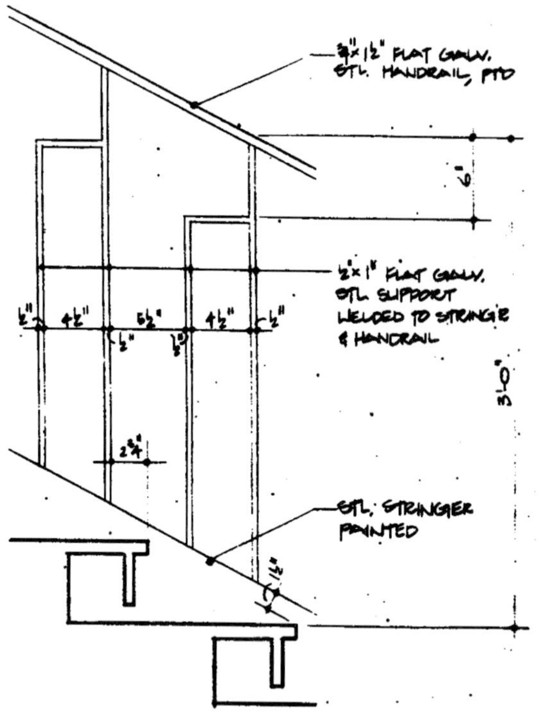

12 A10 DETAIL OF TYP. HANDRAIL at STAIR #1
SCALE: 1½"=1'-0"

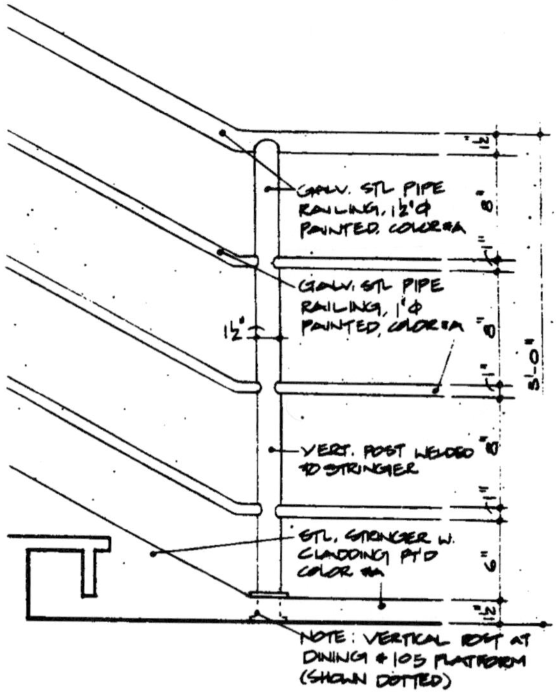

13 A10 DETAIL of HANDRAIL at STAIR #2
SCALE: 1½"=1'-0"

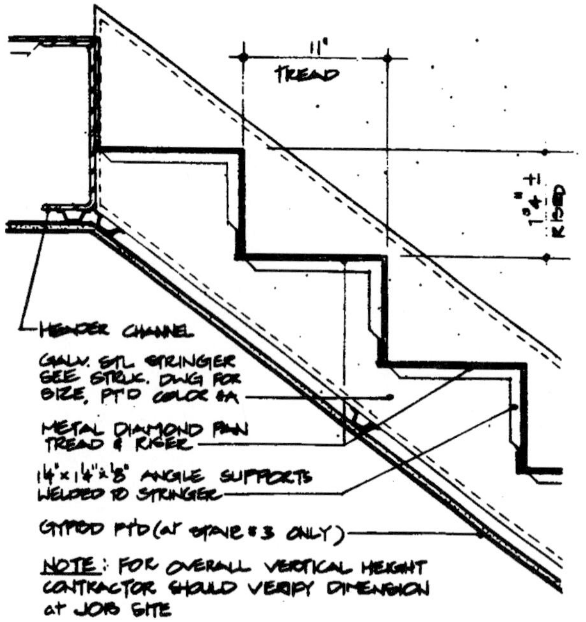

17 A10 DETAIL OF TREAD & RAISER at STAIRS #3 & #5
SCALE: 1½"=1'-0"

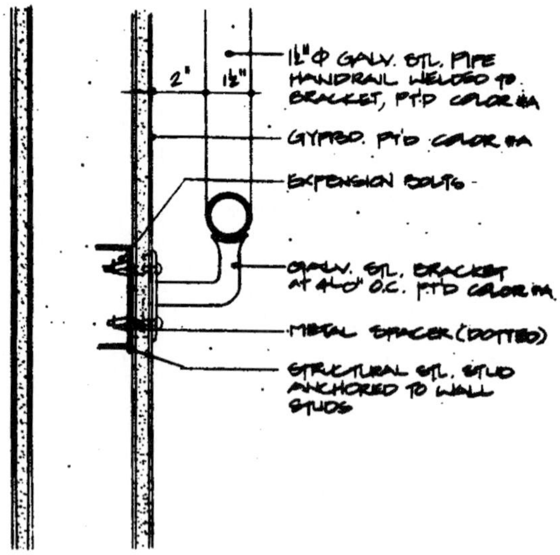

18 A10 DETAIL OF HANDRAIL at STAIRS #3 & #5
SCALE: 3"=1'-0"

STEEL STAIRS WITH TERRAZZO TREADS

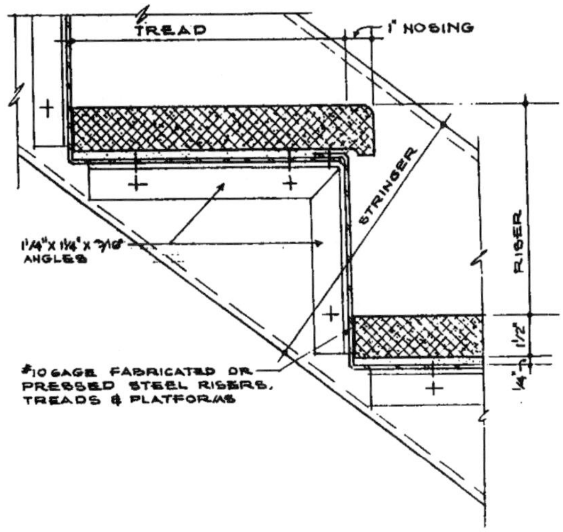

(1) STAIR DETAIL (TERRAZZO TREAD)
@ 3" = 1'-0"

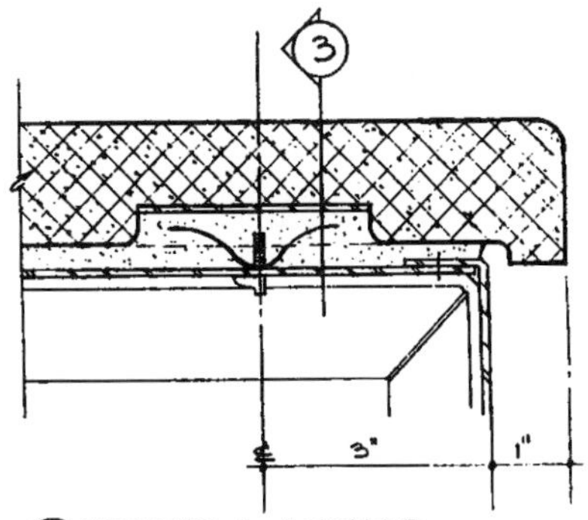

(2) DOVETAIL ANCHOR
@ 1/2 FULL SIZE

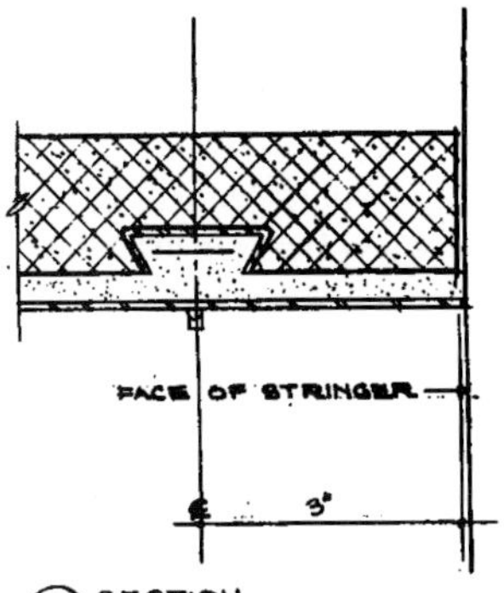

(3) SECTION
@ 1/2' FULL SIZE

LENGTH (FT.)	THICKNESS (MIN.) IN.
TO 4'-6"	1 1/2"
4'-6" TO 6'-6"	1 3/4"
6'-6" TO 8'-0"	2"
OVER 8'-0"	NOT RECOMMENDED

MINIMUM RECOMMENDED THICKNESS FOR TERRAZZO TREAD, RISERS, & STRINGERS

STEEL STAIRS WITH TERRAZZO TREADS AND RISERS

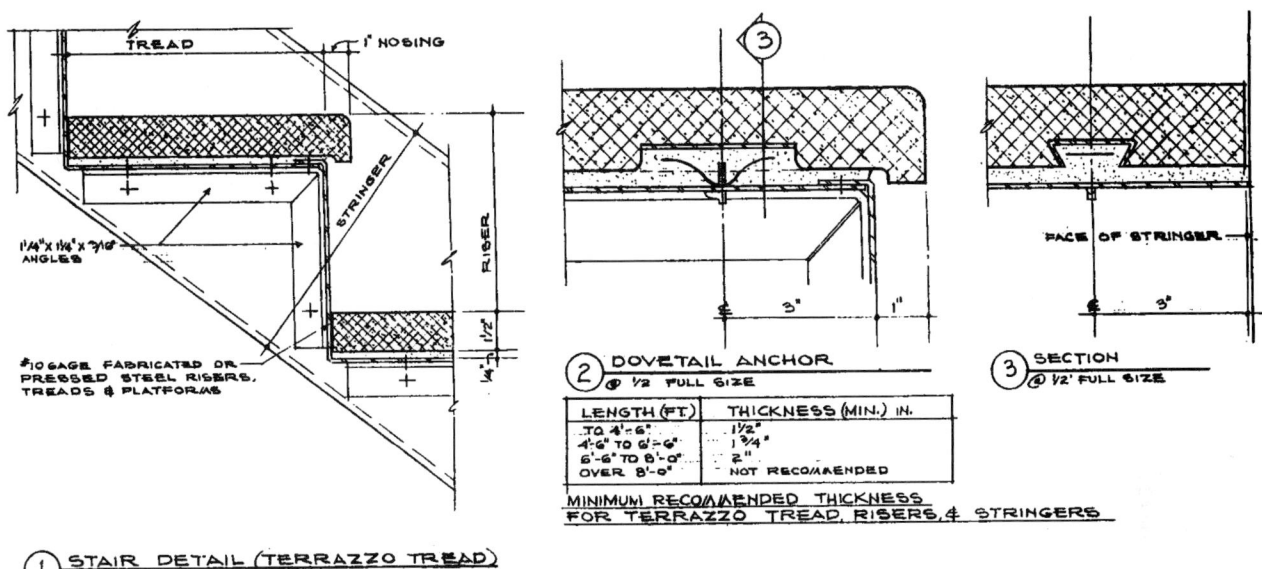

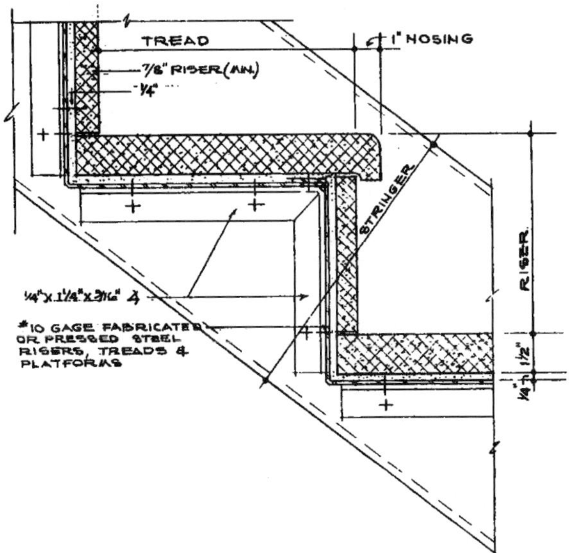

(1) STAIR DETAIL WITH TERRAZZO RISERS & TREADS

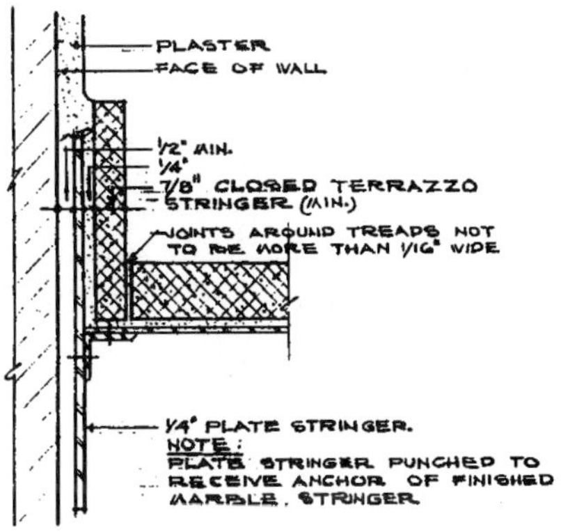

(2) STRINGER DETAIL

STAIRS AND RAMPS
Spiral Stairs

Construction

Material may be steel, stainless steel, cast iron, or aluminum. Treads are supported in cantilever fashion by the column, each consecutive tread being rotated at a predetermined angle. The platform attaches to the column and is fastened to the floor structure to hold the column secure. The spiral railing is supported by balusters attached to the outer ends of the treads.

Tread Designs

Fabricators provide several standard types and designs of treads and platforms. These include open riser, closed riser, and cantilever types, with surface of checkered plate, abrasive plate, steel grating, or plain surface to receive wood, resilient flooring, carpet, or other covering. Pan-type treads to receive concrete or terrazzo fill are also available.

Stair Height

Spiral stairs are adaptable to any height, the height being equal to the distance from finished floor to finished floor.

Stair Diameter

Spiral stairs are available in various diameters from 3 ft 6 in to 8 ft 0 in normally in 6-in increments. A 4 ft 0 in diameter is considered minimum for general access purposes; a 5 ft 0 in diameter provides a comfortable general-purpose stair. Larger diameters are used chiefly for architectural effect. Note that the diameter of the finished well opening should be at least 2 in greater than the stair diameter, to provide hand clearance.

Hand of Stairs

Left-hand stairs: User ascends in clockwise direction, with handrail at left.

Right-hand stairs: User ascends in counterclockwise direction, with handrail at right.

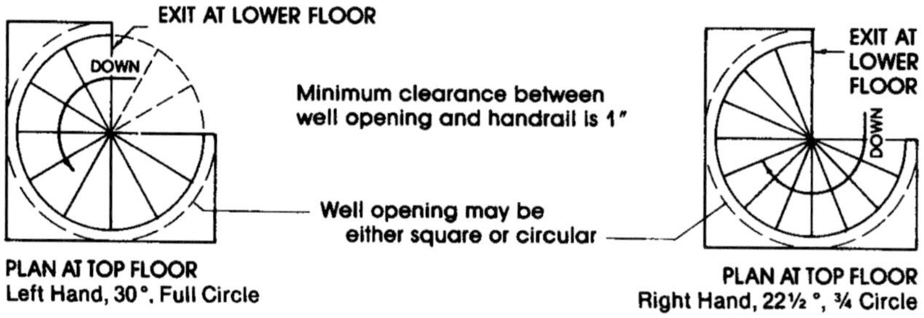

Fig. 20

Table 5 Riser heights for various tread angles

Tread angle	Min. height of riser*	Treads per ¾ circle	Treads per full circle
30°	8¹⁵⁄₁₆"	9	12
27°	8"	10	13=351°
24½°	7⁵⁄₁₆"	11	15=367½°
22½°	6¹¹⁄₁₆"	12	16

*Minimum height to attain 6'6" clear headroom using a 90° landing, 2" thick.

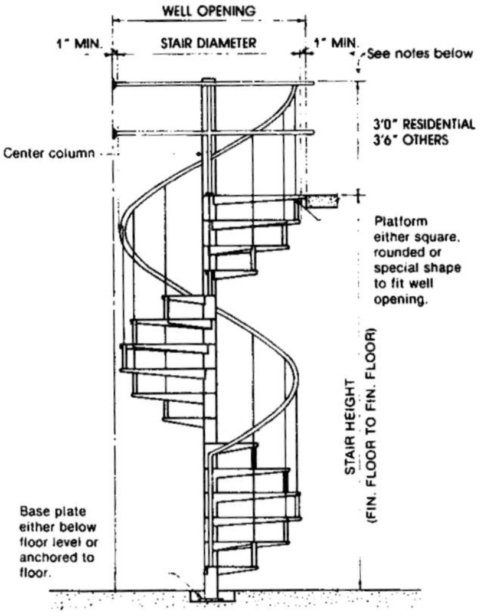

TYPICAL ELEVATION — RIGHT HAND OPEN RISER STAIR

Table 6 Chart for selection of number and height of risers

Floor to floor height	Number of risers and height of each in inches								
	10	11	12	13	14	15	16	17	18
7'0"	8.4	7.6	7.0						
7'4"	8.8	8.0	7.3	6.8					
7'8"	9.2	8.4	7.7	7.0					
8'0"	9.6	8.7	8.0	7.4	6.9				
8'2"	9.8	8.9	8.2	7.5	7.0				
8'4"		9.1	8.3	7.7	7.1	6.7			
8'6"		9.3	8.5	7.8	7.3	6.8			
8'8"		9.4	8.7	8.0	7.4	6.9			
8'10"			8.8	8.2	7.6	7.1	6.6		
9'0"			9.0	8.3	7.7	7.2	6.7		
9'2"			9.2	8.5	7.9	7.3	6.9		
9'4"			9.3	8.6	8.0	7.5	7.0		
9'6"				8.8	8.1	7.6	7.1	6.7	
9'8"				9.0	8.3	7.7	7.2	6.8	
9'10"				9.2	8.4	7.9	7.4	6.9	
10'0"				9.3	8.6	8.0	7.5	7.0	6.7
10'2"					8.7	8.1	7.6	7.2	6.8
10'4"					8.9	8.3	7.7	7.3	6.9
10'6"					9.0	8.4	7.9	7.4	7.0
10'8"					9.1	8.5	8.0	7.5	7.1
10'10"						8.6	8.1	7.6	7.2
11'0"						8.7	8.2	7.8	7.3
11'2"						8.9	8.4	7.9	7.4
11'4"						9.0	8.5	8.0	7.6
11'6"							8.6	8.1	7.7
11'8"							8.7	8.2	7.8
12'0"							9.0	8.5	8.0

STAIRS AND RAMPS
Spiral Stairs

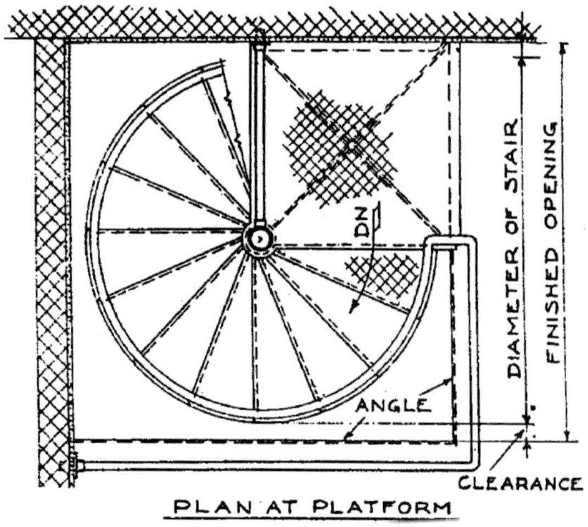

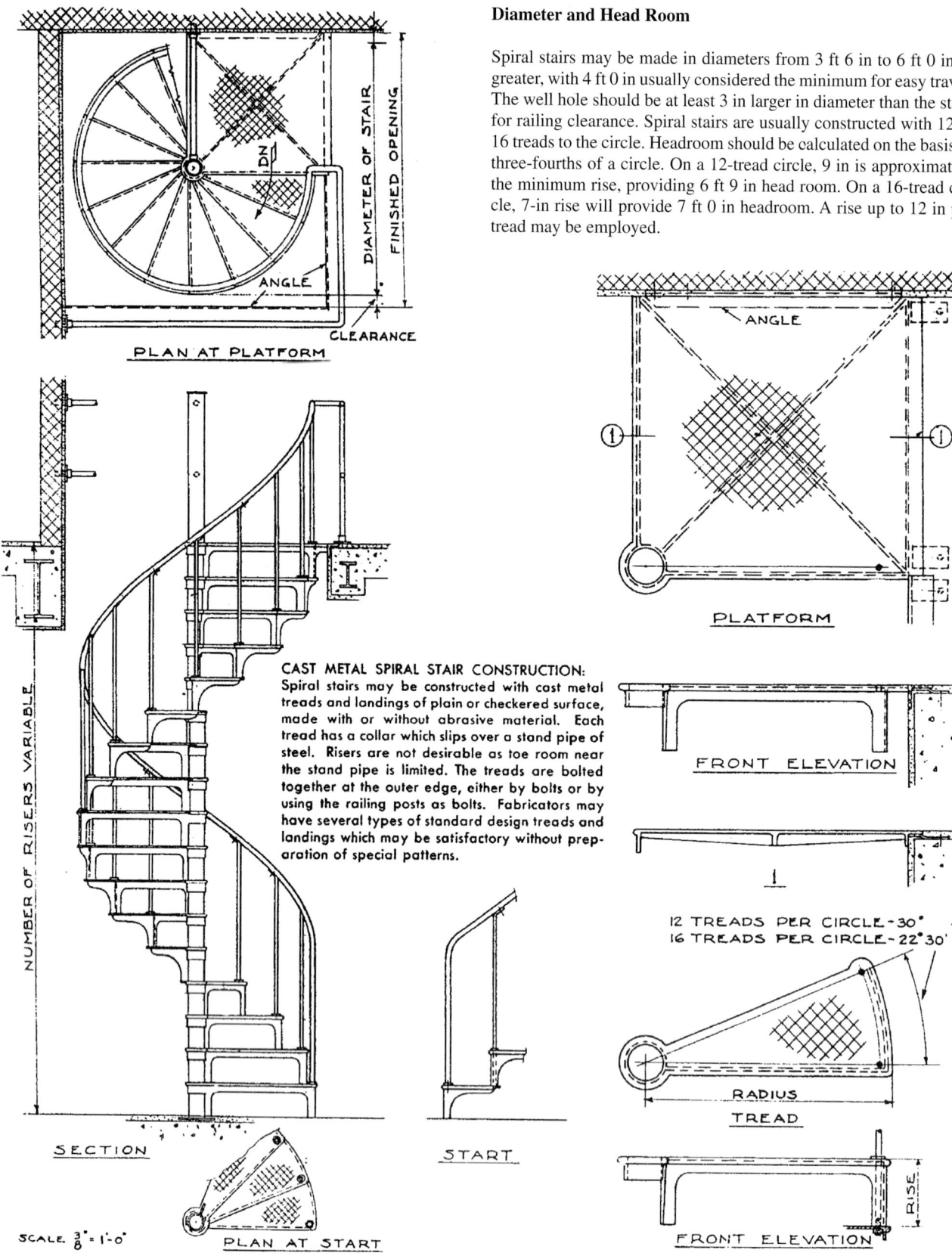

Diameter and Head Room

Spiral stairs may be made in diameters from 3 ft 6 in to 6 ft 0 in or greater, with 4 ft 0 in usually considered the minimum for easy travel. The well hole should be at least 3 in larger in diameter than the stair, for railing clearance. Spiral stairs are usually constructed with 12 or 16 treads to the circle. Headroom should be calculated on the basis of three-fourths of a circle. On a 12-tread circle, 9 in is approximately the minimum rise, providing 6 ft 9 in head room. On a 16-tread circle, 7-in rise will provide 7 ft 0 in headroom. A rise up to 12 in per tread may be employed.

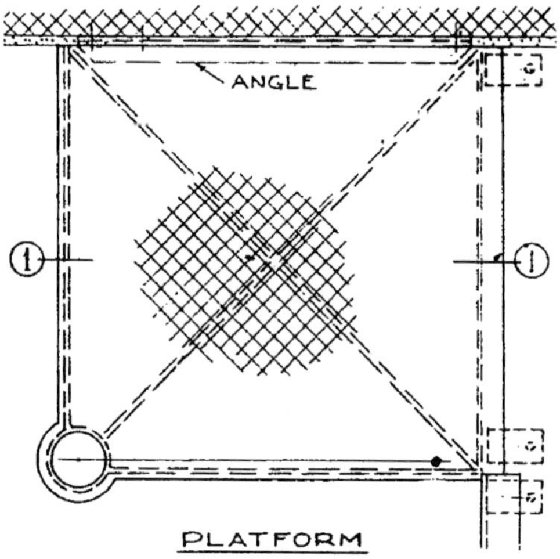

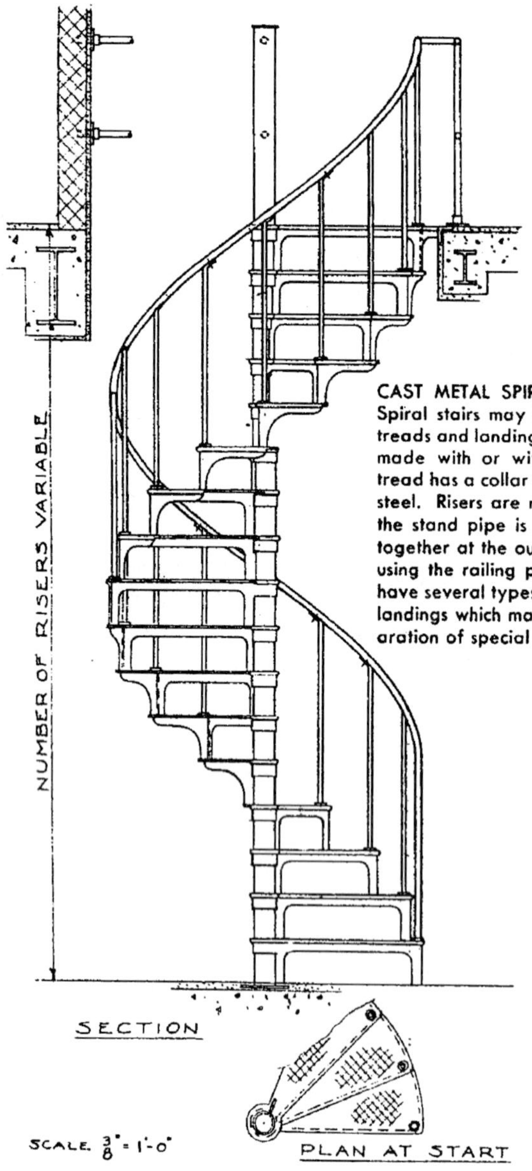

CAST METAL SPIRAL STAIR CONSTRUCTION: Spiral stairs may be constructed with cast metal treads and landings of plain or checkered surface, made with or without abrasive material. Each tread has a collar which slips over a stand pipe of steel. Risers are not desirable as toe room near the stand pipe is limited. The treads are bolted together at the outer edge, either by bolts or by using the railing posts as bolts. Fabricators may have several types of standard design treads and landings which may be satisfactory without preparation of special patterns.

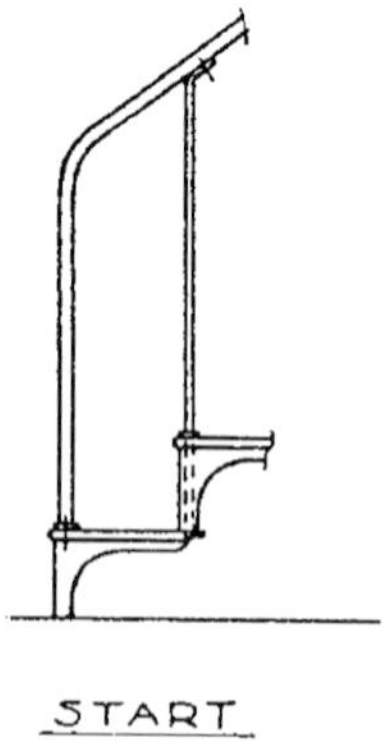

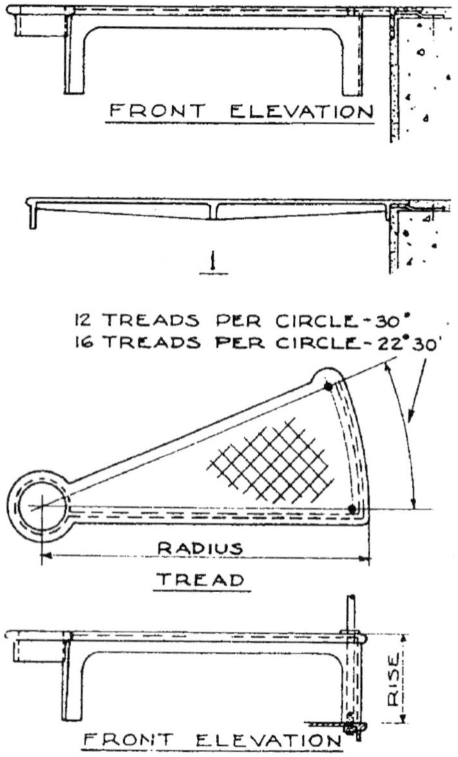

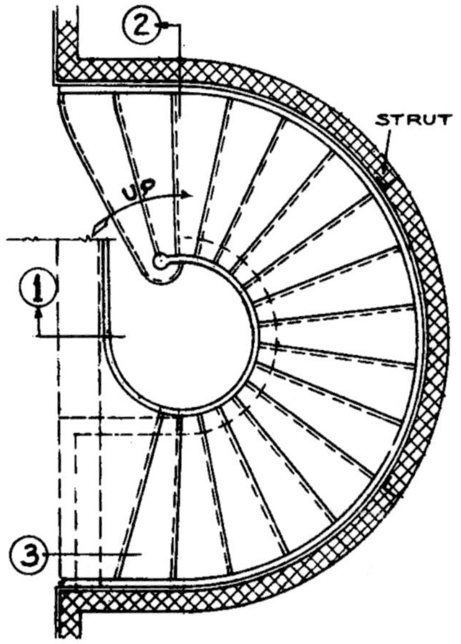

PLAN A-A

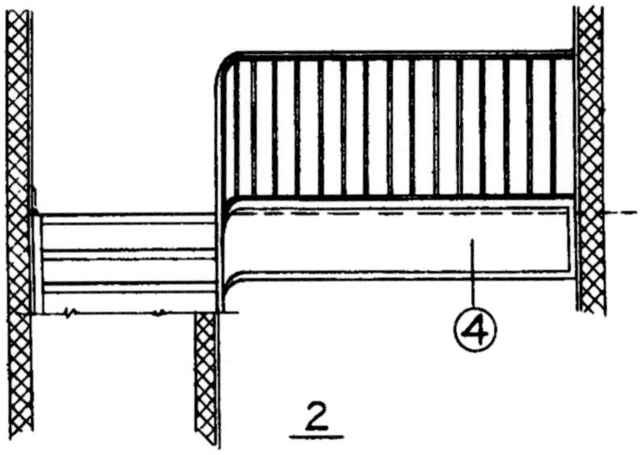

2

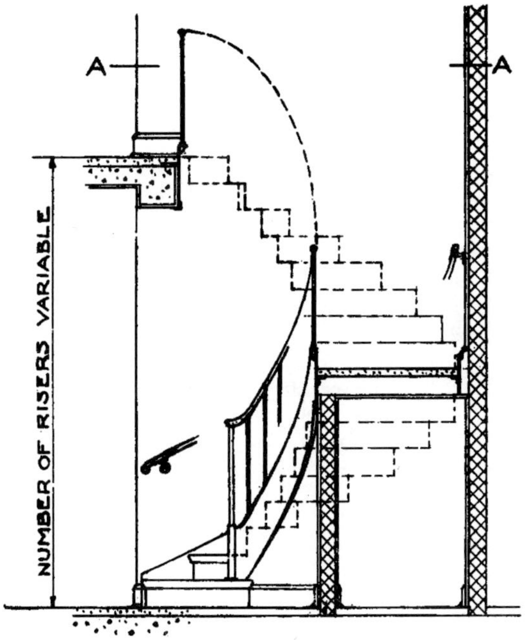

1

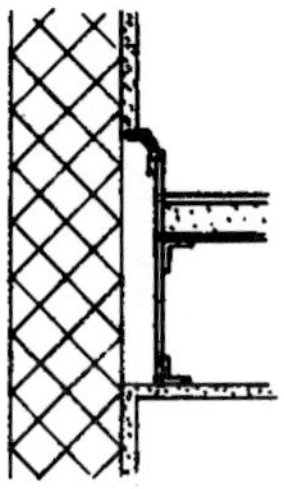

WALL STRING

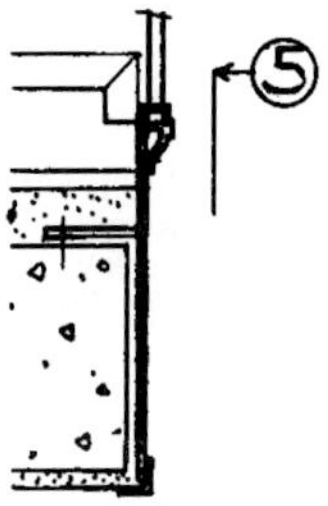

4

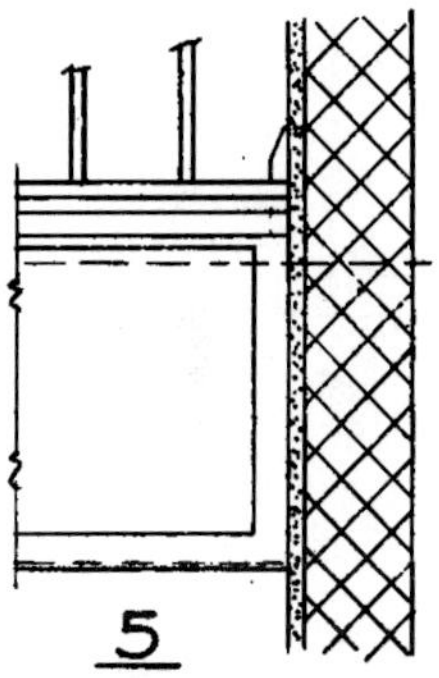

5

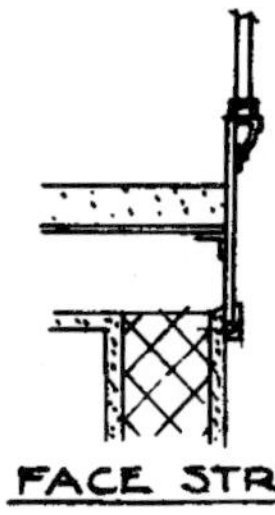

FACE STRING

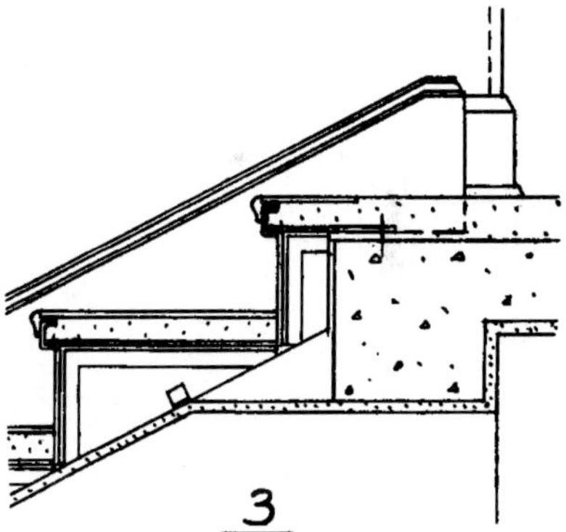

3

Circular stairs placed between walls may be built self-supporting at the inner string and be supported by concealed struts or hangers at the outer string. When completely exposed a circular stair may be designed to require few supports between floors.

In constructing a circular stair the overall size of the well and the tread length of the stairs may be adjusted to fit the particular conditions of the structure. Treads should be a minimum width of 8" at a distance 15" out from the inside railing. The treads may be of steel, abrasive cast iron, abrasive nonferrous metal, cement, tile, linoleum, wood, marble or other material.

Landings and platforms may be constructed as part of the stair, and may be supported by beam or cantilever construction. Wall rails and brackets may be constructed with handrail sections matching the railing.

Face strings and railings may be similar to those used on straight stairs but should be designed of shapes adaptable to abrupt curved construction. The small radius to which these are constructed offers possibilities of design that should not be overlooked. Combinations of contrasting metal colors can be effectively employed in such installations.

STAIRS AND RAMPS

Concrete Stairs

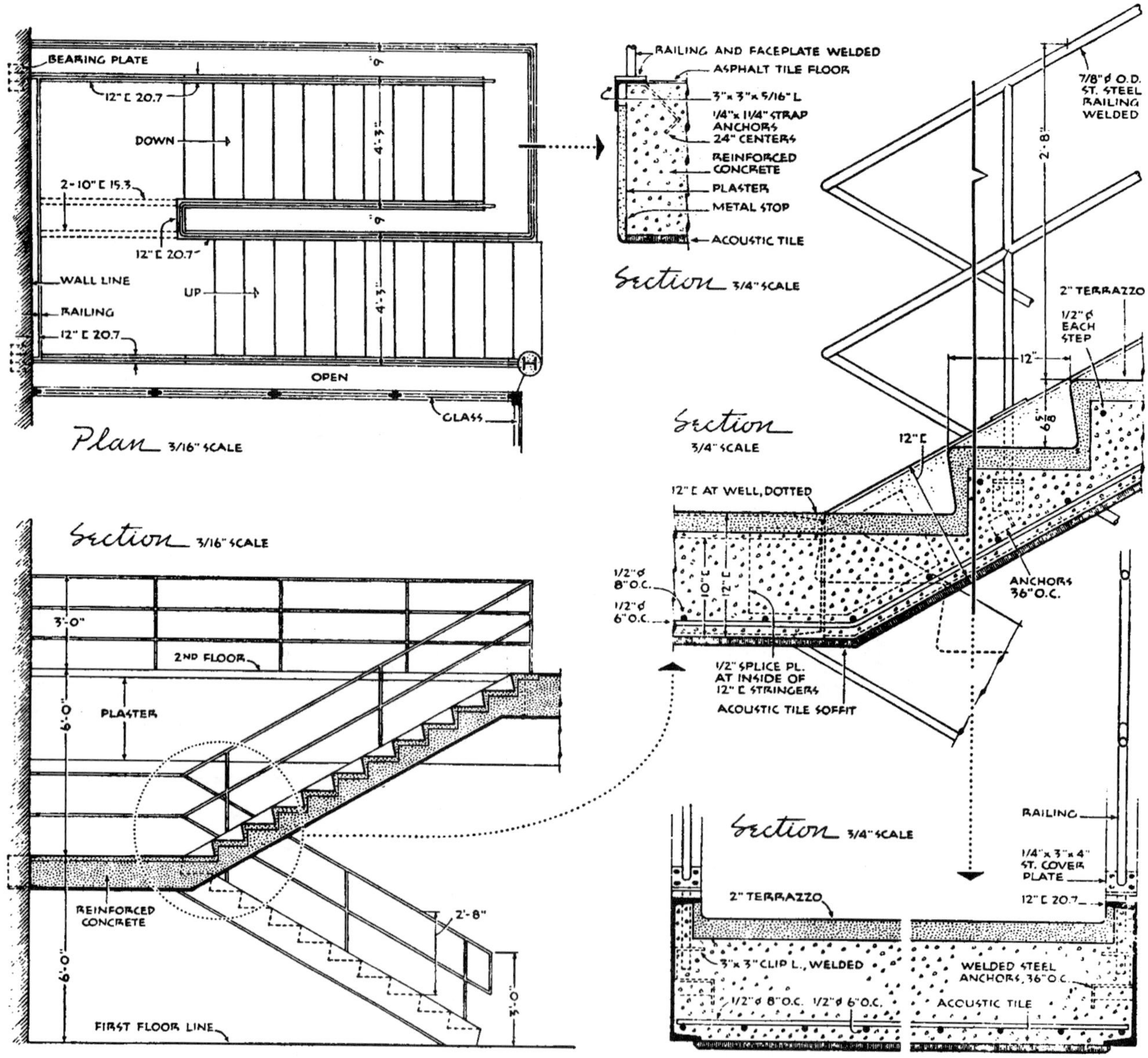

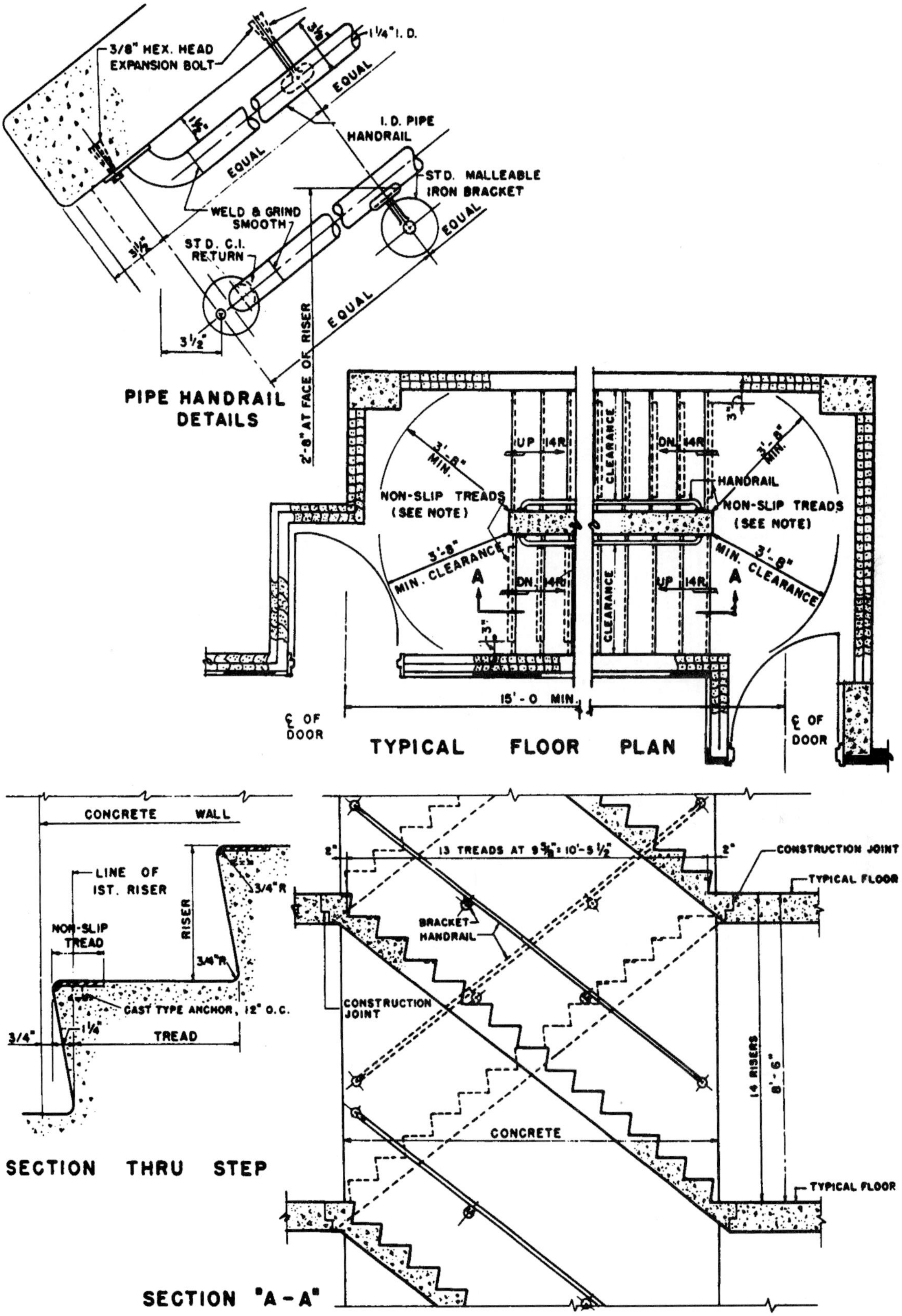

Typical reinforced concrete scissors stair

STAIRS AND RAMPS

Concrete, Steel, and Terrazzo Stairs

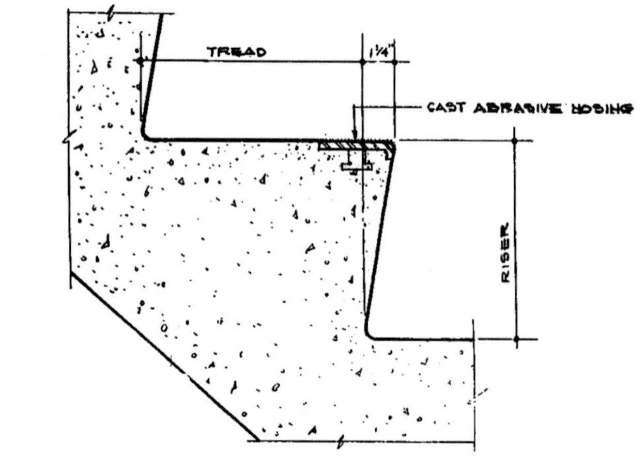

(1) STAIR DETAIL

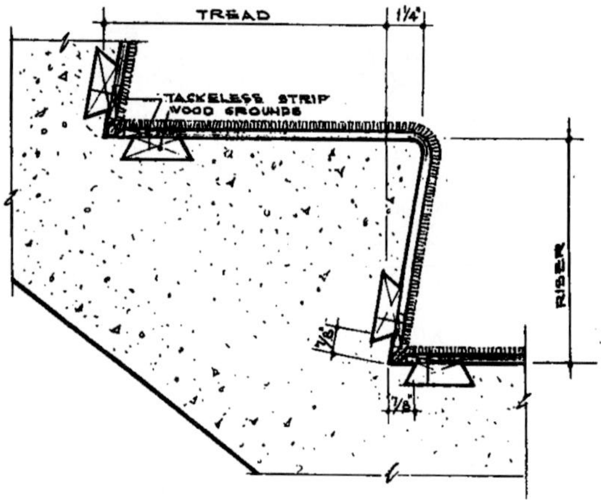

(1) STAIR DETAIL WITH CARPETING

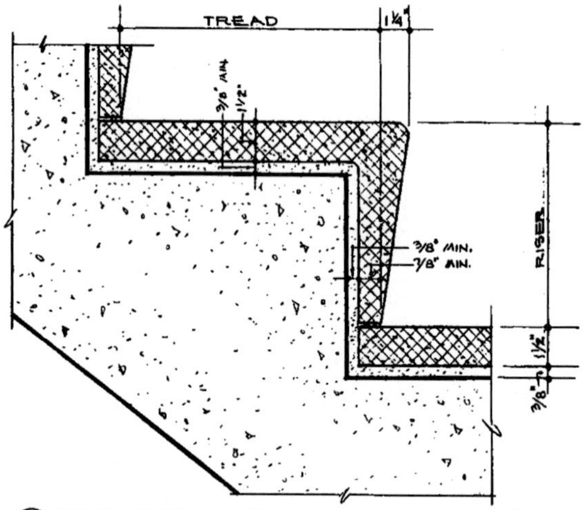

(2) STAIR DETAIL WITH TERRAZZO TREADS & RISERS

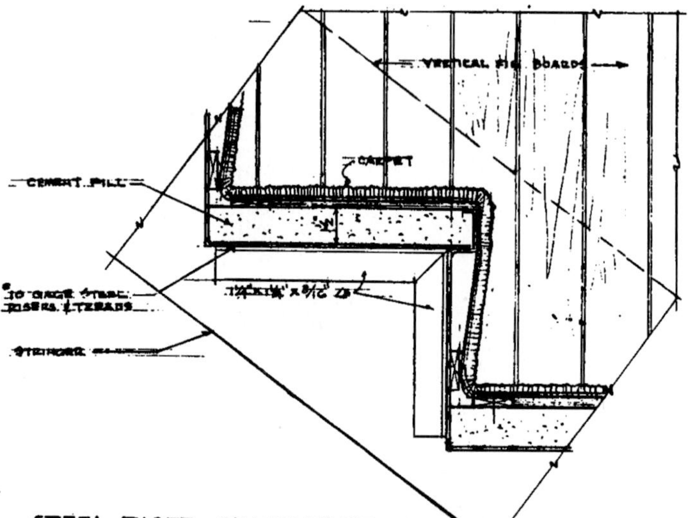

STEEL RISER CEMENT TREADS

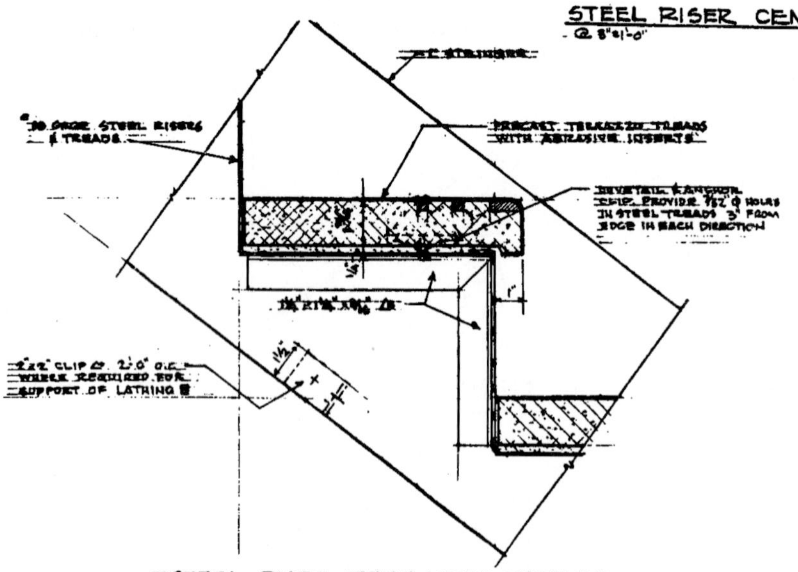

STEEL RISER TERRAZZO TREADS

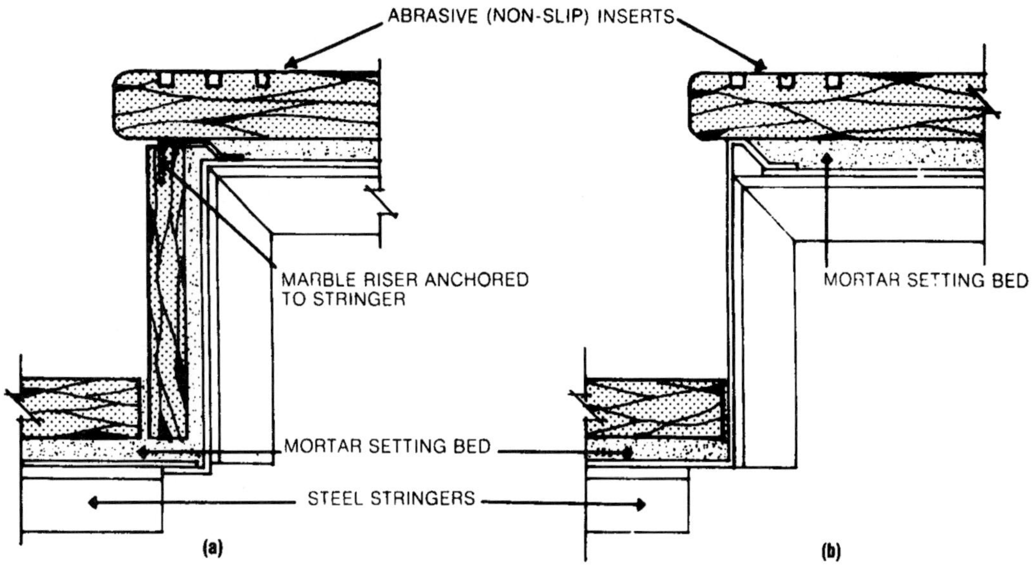

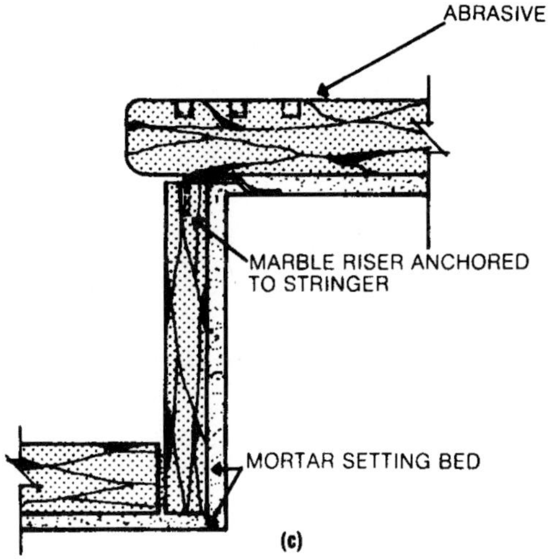

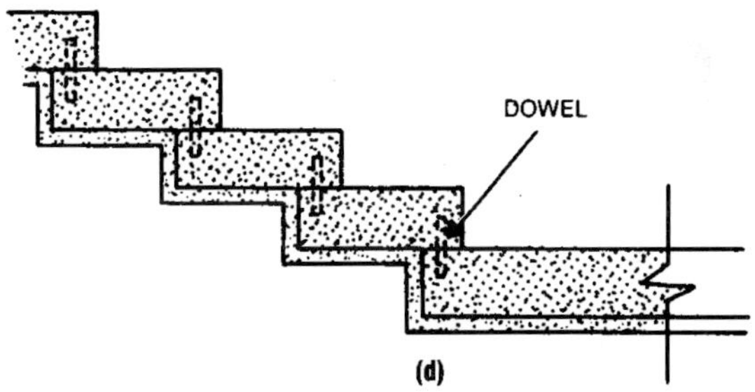

Fig. 21 Sections (*a*) and (*b*) are marble treads and risers supported by steel stringers; section (*c*), marble treads only; section (*d*), cubic marble treads supported by concrete or steel stringers

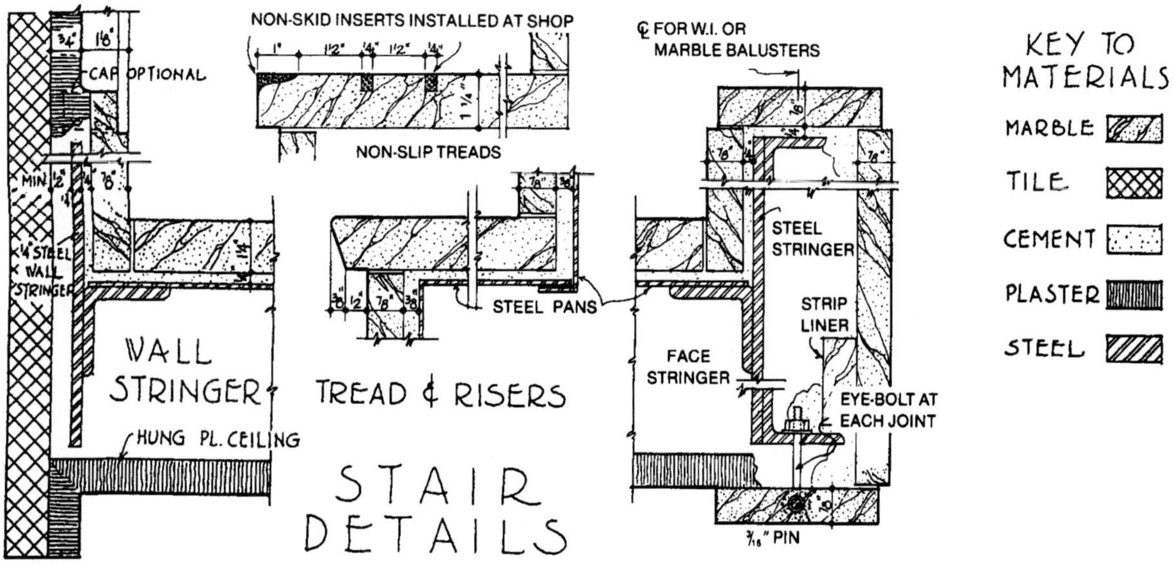

Fig. 22 Interior marble details

STAIRS AND RAMPS

Slate Treads

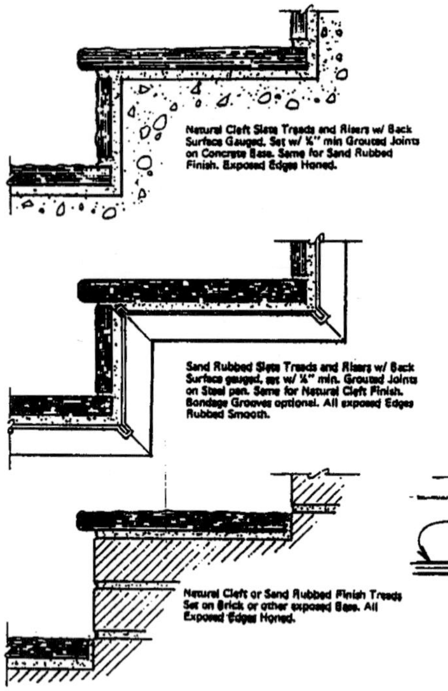

Suggested detail for slate treads and risers, exterior and/or interior

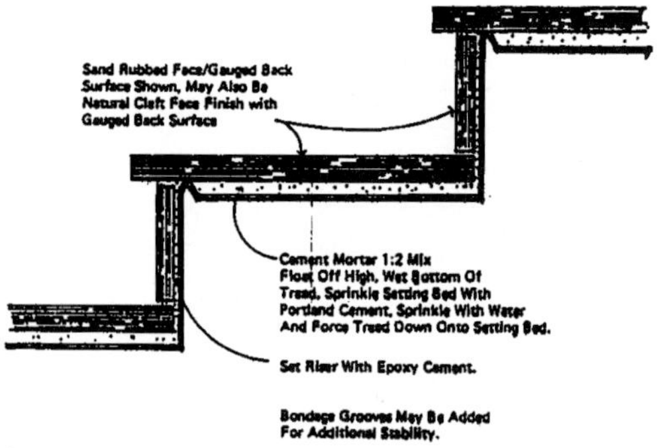

Slate treads and risers set on metal pan stair

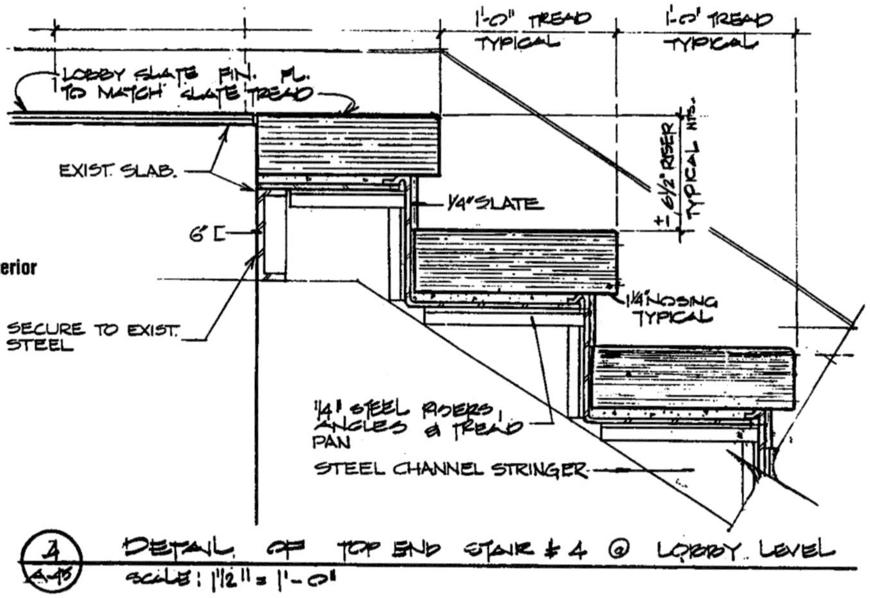

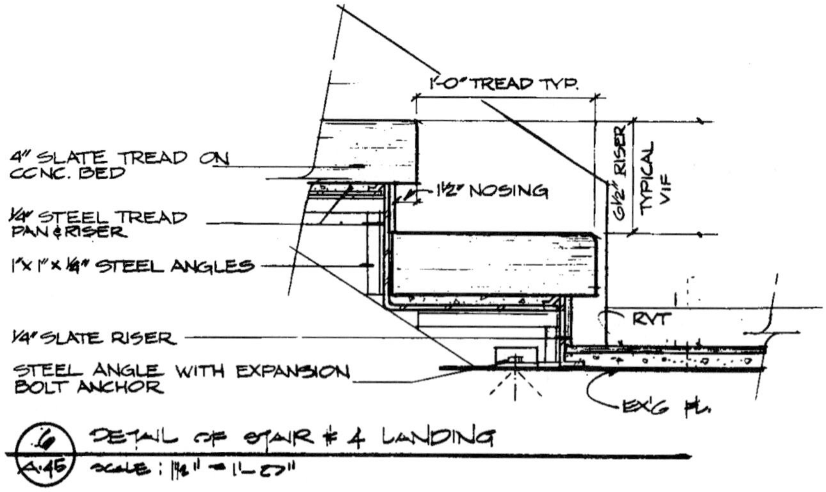

Any potential hazards must be eliminated. Stairs should be easy going; that is, there must be an appropriate relationship of riser to tread. Treads are of nonslip material, which is also extended onto platforms and landings for a distance equal to the width of the stair treads. Double handrails, one higher than the other, are provided on stairs for each line of short or tall pupils. The posts, which support the center handrails of double stairs, are extended high enough above the top handrail to prevent pupils from sliding down.

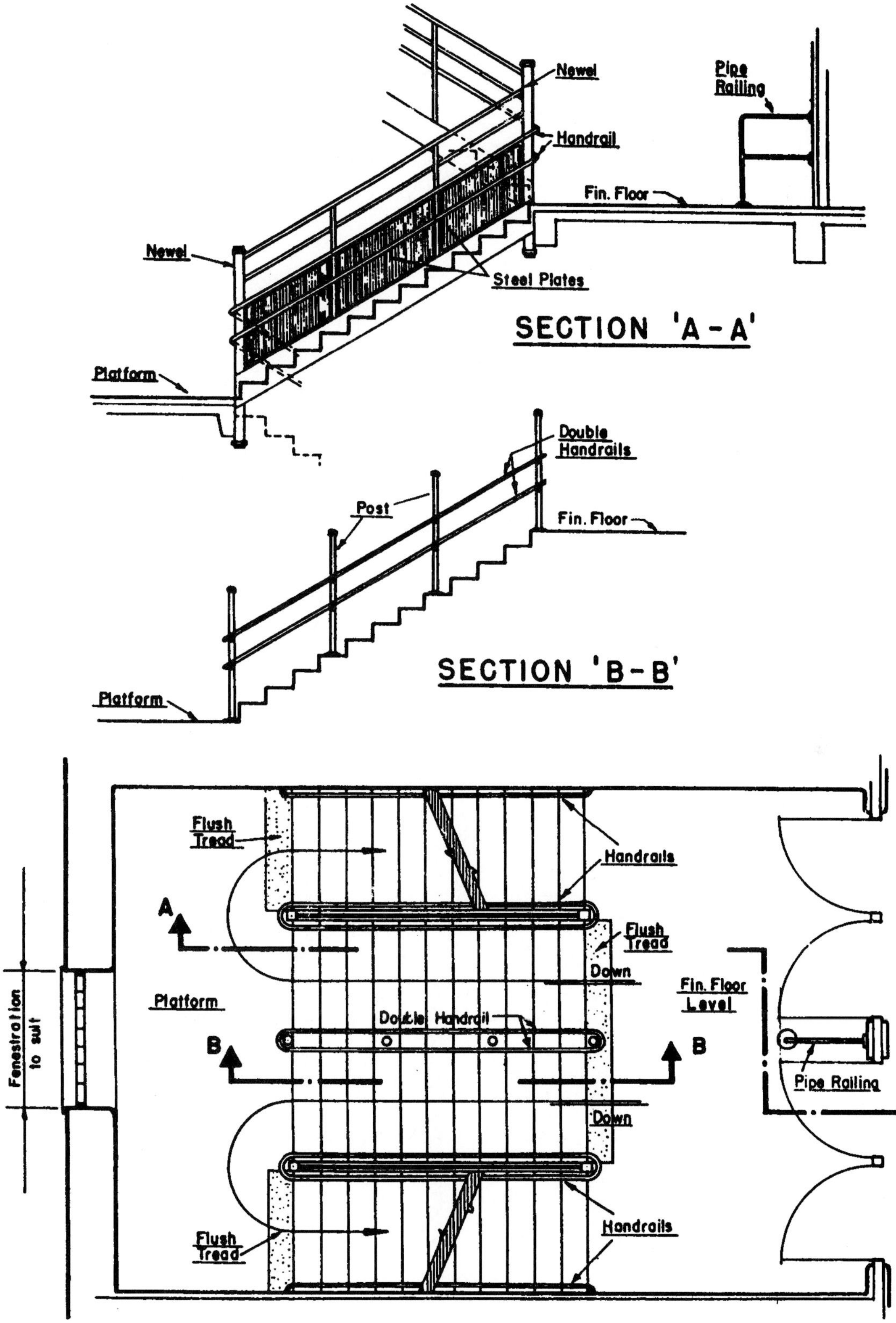

PLAN · VIEW ·

STAIRS AND RAMPS
Barrier-Free Design Data

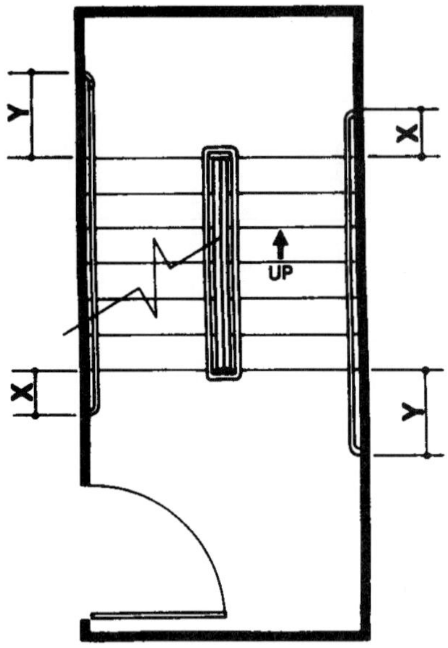

(a)
Plan

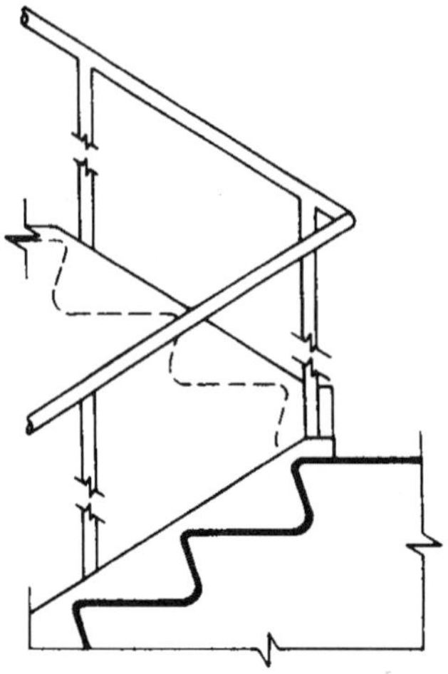

(b)
Elevation of Center Handrail

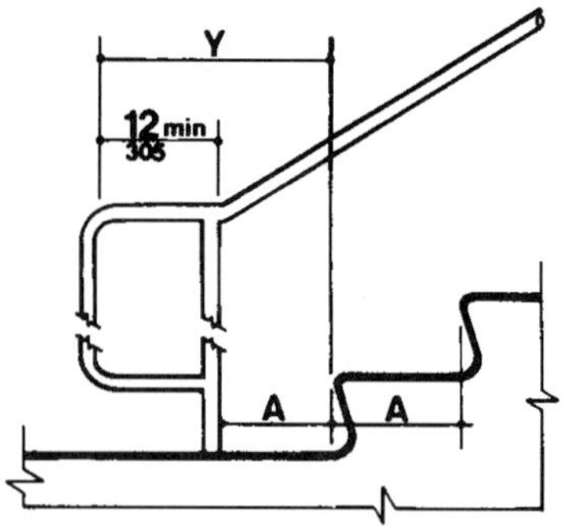

(c)
Extension at Bottom of Run

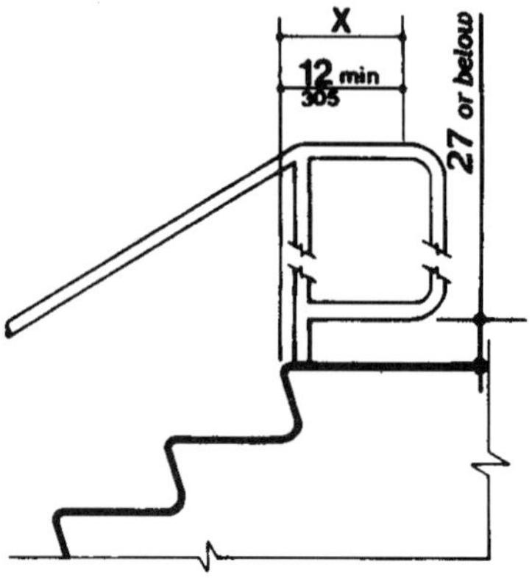

(d)
Extension at Top of Run

NOTE:

X is the 12 in minimum handrail extension required at each top riser.

Y is the minimum handrail extension of 12 in plus the width of one tread that is required at each bottom riser.

Fig. 23 Stair handrails

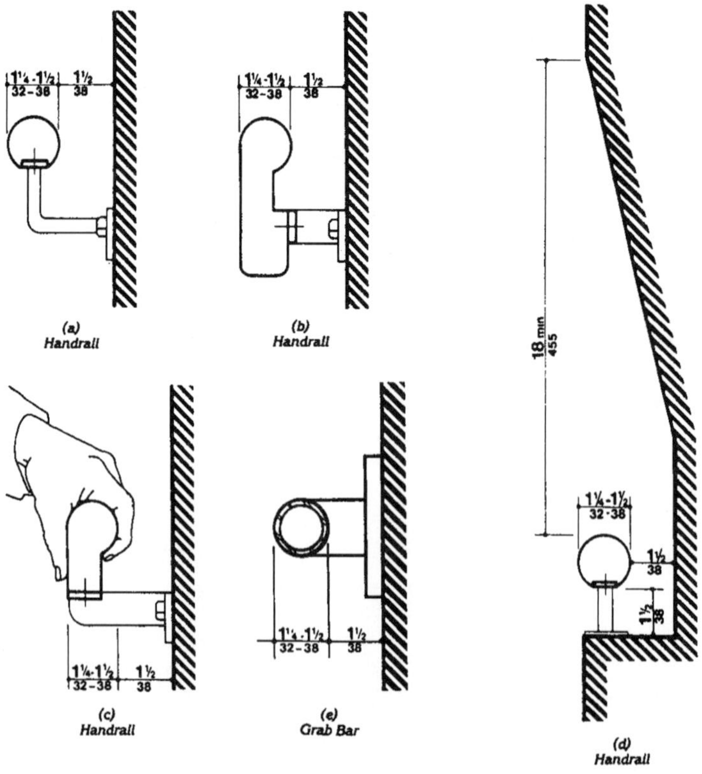

Fig. 24 Size and spacing of handrails and grab bars

Steps and Stairs

Steps and stairs should have nonprotruding nosings so that people with stiff joints, braces, artificial legs, or other leg or stability problems will not catch their toes as they climb.

Handrails should be oval or round with 1½-in/4-cm hand clearance between the rails and the wall: 1½-in/4-cm clearance will provide ease of grip but will prevent the hand or wrist from slipping between the handrail and the wall if the person loses balance. Handrails should be positioned on both sides of steps and stairs and should extend beyond the first and last steps on at least one side and preferably on both to allow people with long leg braces to pull themselves beyond these points. To guard against falls and to help children, some codes require another, lower, handrail.

Steps, stairs, and handrails should not be made of slippery material.

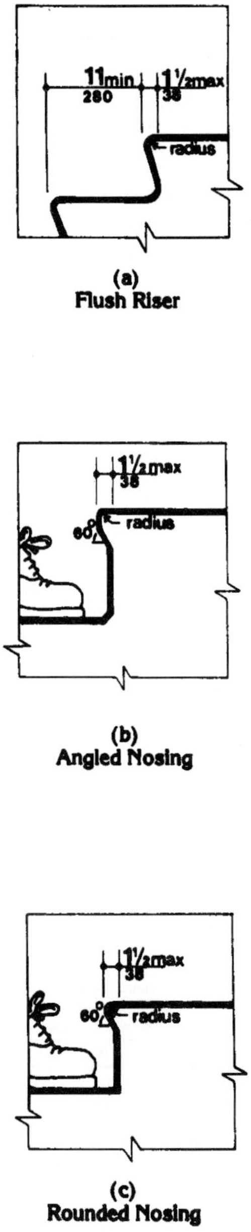

Fig. 25 Usable tread width and examples of acceptable nosings

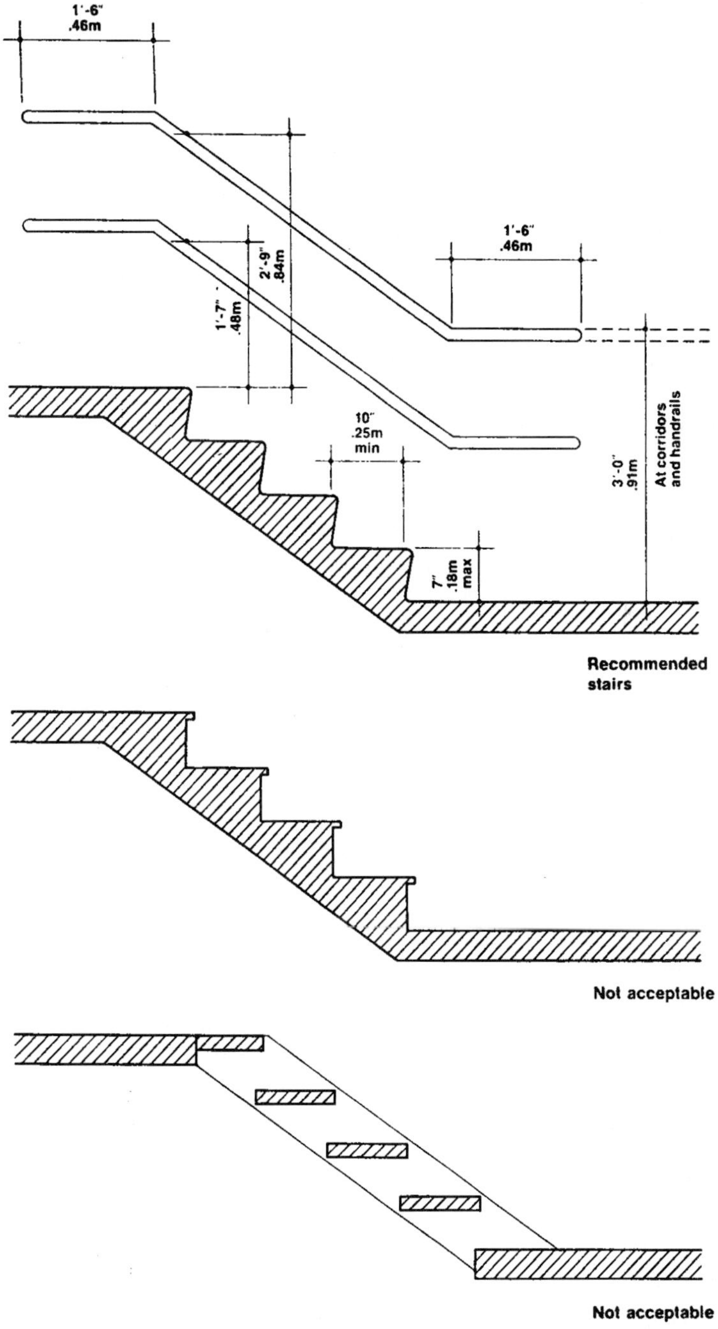

Fig. 26

STAIRS AND RAMPS
Ladders and Open Steel Stairs

LADDERS

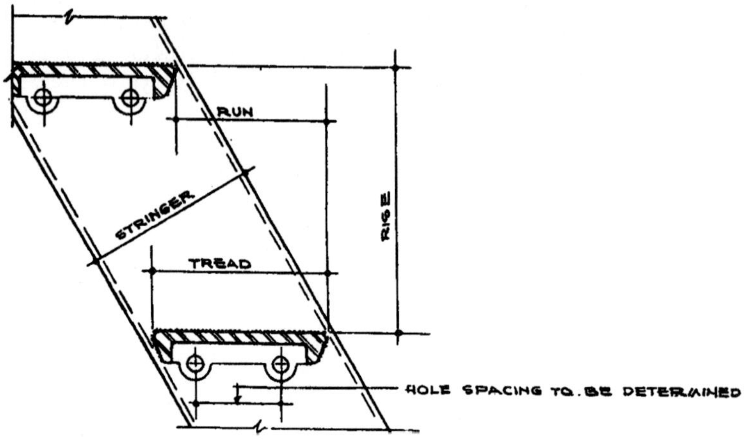

1 ENGINEERS LADDER WITH CAST ABRASIVE TREADS

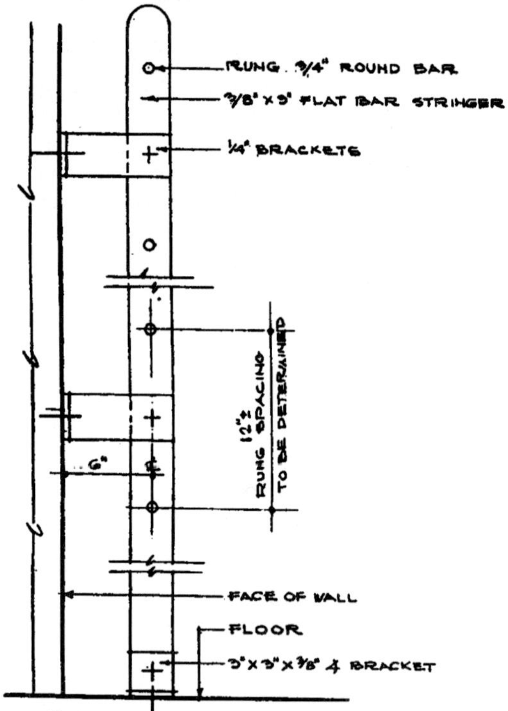

2 VERTICAL LADDER

OPEN STEEL STAIRS

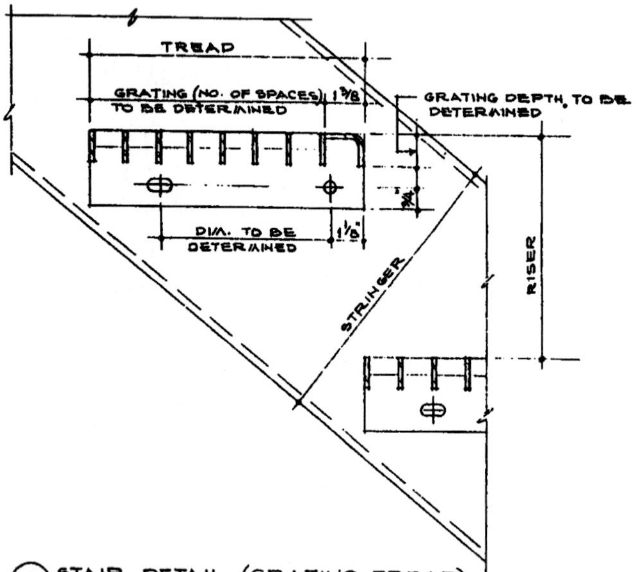

1 STAIR DETAIL (GRATING TREAD)

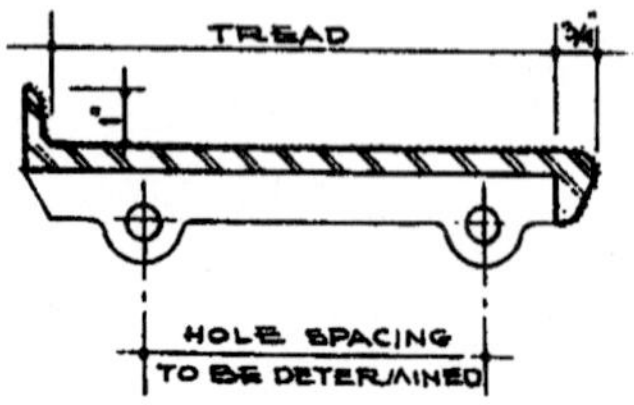

2 CAST ABRASIVE TREAD

WIDTH OVERALL	CENTER TO CENTER SPACING
5 INCHES	2 INCHES O.C.
6	3
7	3½
8	4
9	5
10	6

STANDARD HOLE SPACING FOR CAST ABRASIVE TREAD

THICKNESS IN INCHES	CAST IRON	CAST ALUMINUM	CAST BRONZE	CAST NICKEL-BRONZE
5/16"	UP TO 6" WIDE	UP TO 8" WIDE	UP TO 8" WIDE	UP TO 8" WIDE
3/8"	12"	18"	18"	18"
7/16"	24"	26"	24"	24"
1/2"	30"	36"	30"	30"
5/8"	42"	42"	36"	36"

THICKNESS LIMITATIONS FOR VARIOUS WIDTH CASTINGS

STAIRS AND RAMPS

Steel Pan Cement-Filled Stairs

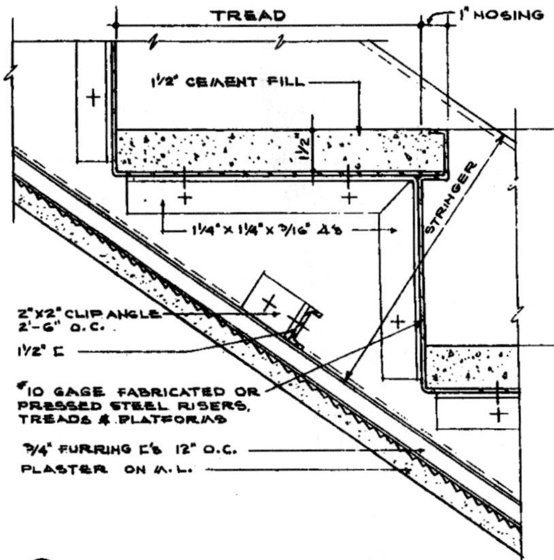

1 STAIR DETAIL

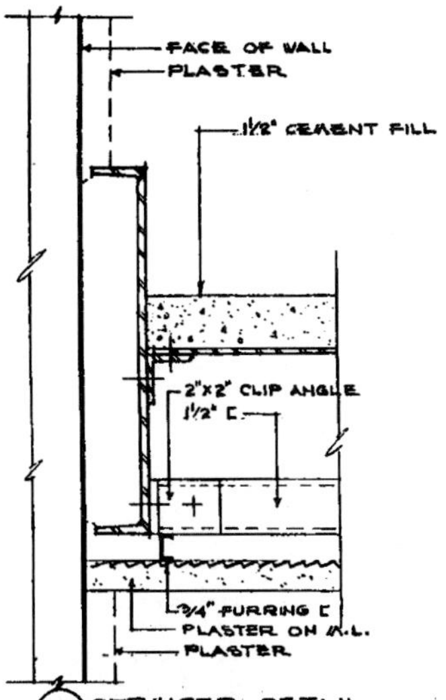

2 STRINGER DETAIL

NOTE:
STRINGER DETAIL SIMILAR FOR STAIRS WITH TERRAZZO OR MARBLE TREADS & RISERS

3 ABRASIVE SAFETY NOSING

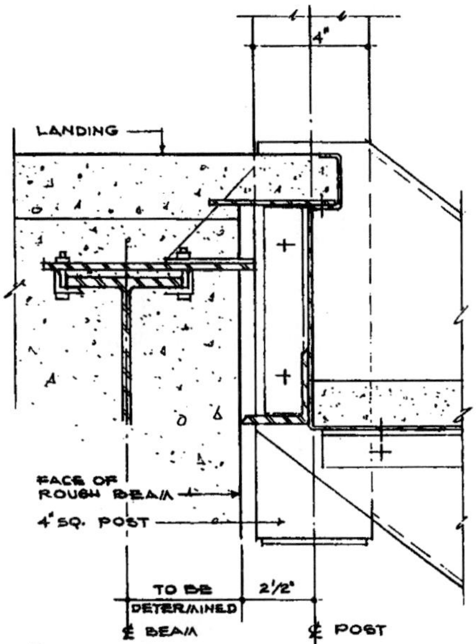

1 SECTION AT LANDING WITH POST

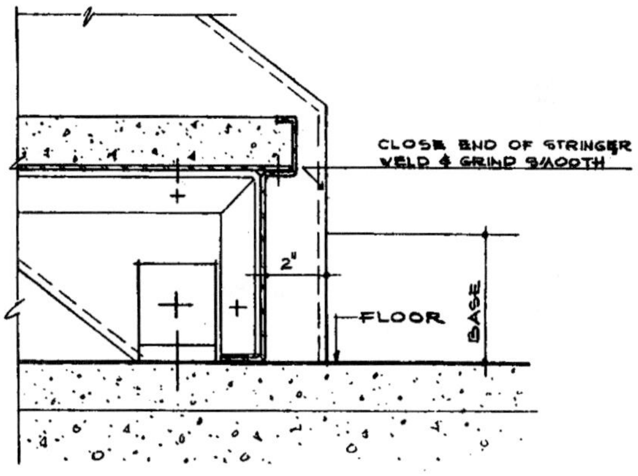

1 SECTION AT CONC. SLAB FLOOR

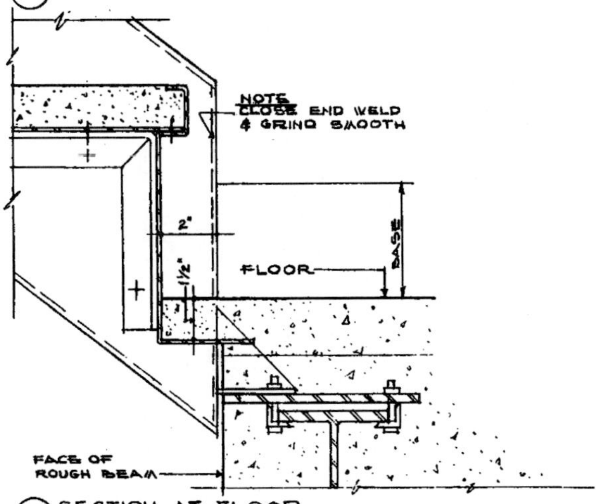

2 SECTION AT FLOOR

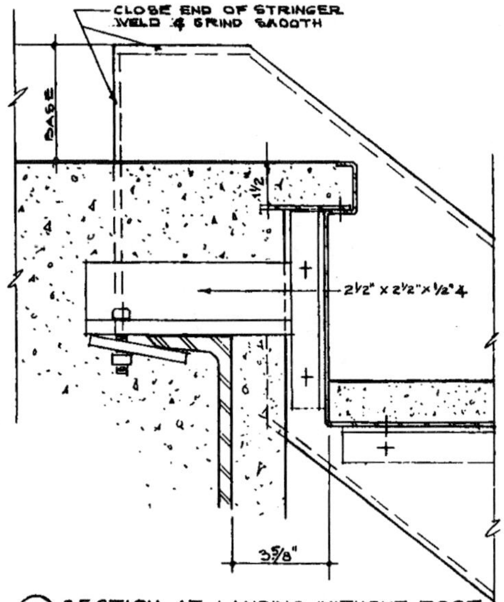

2 SECTION AT LANDING WITHOUT POST

STAIRS AND RAMPS
Barrier-Free Ramps

Slopes and Rise

Provide the least practical slope for any ramp or curb ramp, subject to the following new construction requirements:

1. Maximum running slope shall not exceed 1:12 (8.3 percent).
2. Maximum rise for any run shall not exceed 2 ft 6 in (760 mm).

Width

Ramps and curb ramps shall have a minimum clear width of 3 ft 0 in (915 mm) exclusive of edge protection or flared sides.

Cross-Slope and Surface

Cross-slope of ramp surfaces shall not exceed 1:48 (¼ in/ft).

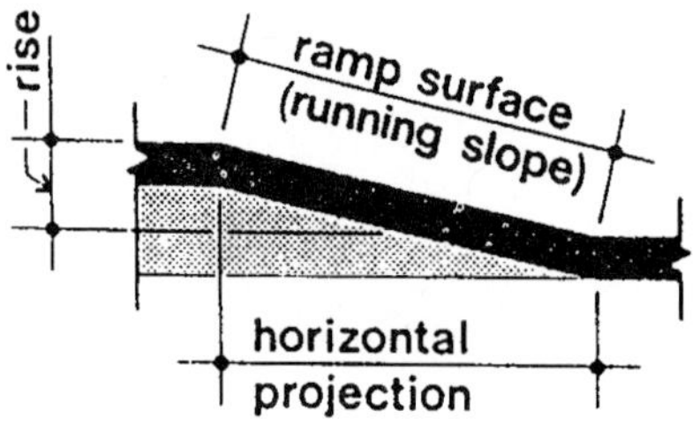

ramp slope

slope	maximum rise in	maximum rise mm	maximum projection ft	maximum projection m
1:12 to < 1:16	30	760	30	9
1:16 to < 1:20	30	760	40	12

maximum rise & projection
new construction

slope	maximum rise in	maximum rise mm	maximum projection ft	maximum projection m
1:10 to 1:8	3	75	2	0.6
1:12 to 1:10	6	150	5	1.5

maximum rise & projection
alterations to existing construction

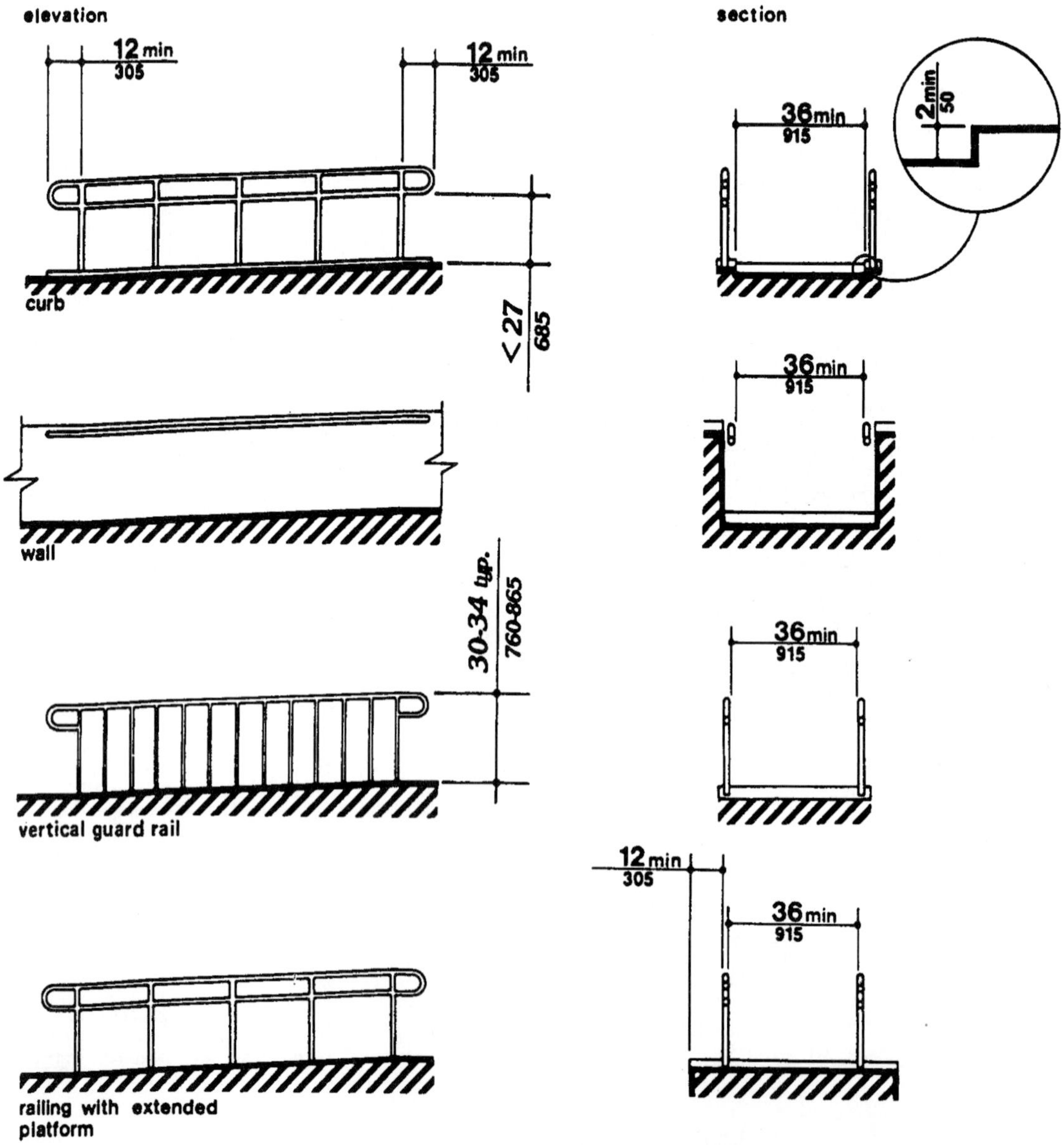

Fig. 27 Examples of edge protection and handrail extensions

STAIRS AND RAMPS

Barrier-Free Ramp Plan and Elevation

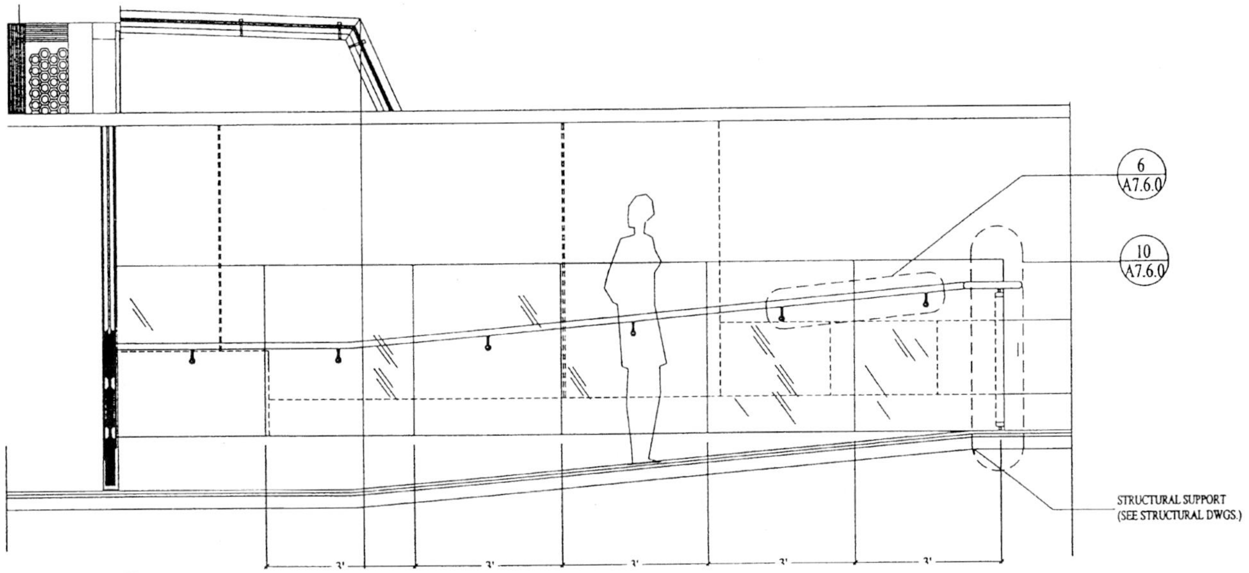

5 RAMP PLAN & ELEVATION
1/2" = 1'-0"

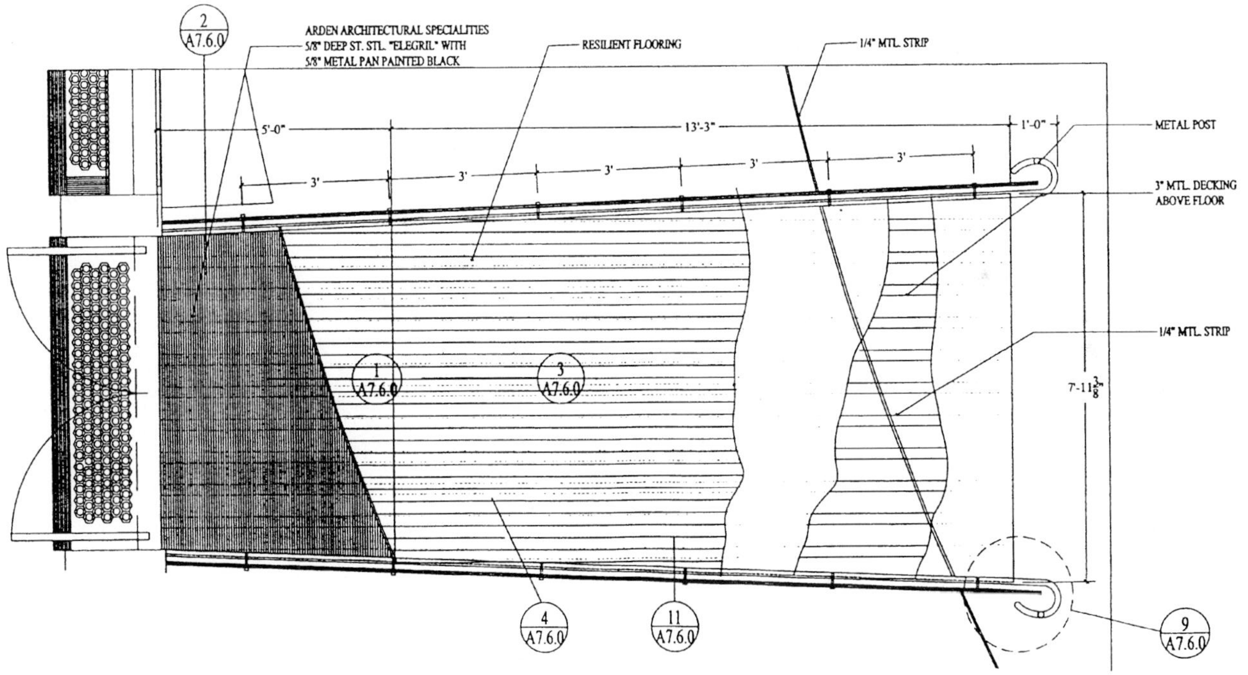

STAIRS AND RAMPS

Barrier-Free Ramp Details

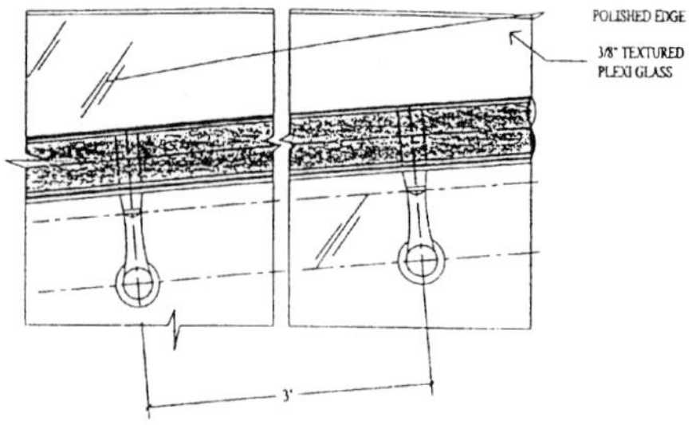

6 PARTIAL RAIL ELEVATION
3" = 1'-0"

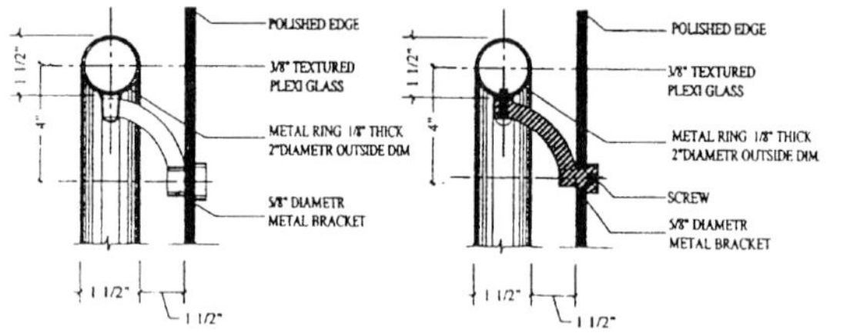

7 RAIL DETAIL AT RAMP
3" = 1'-0"

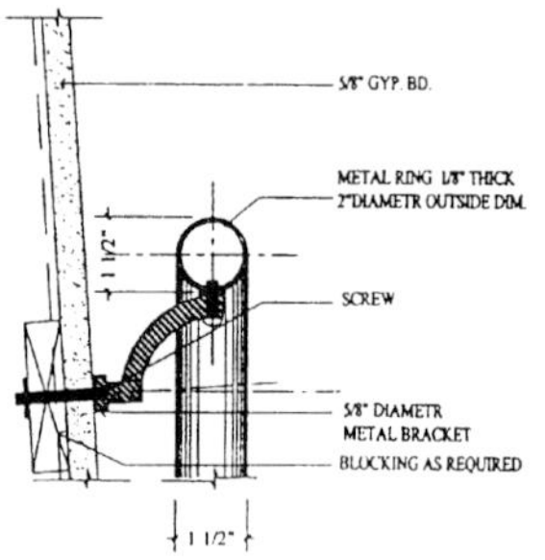

8 RAIL DETAIL AT STAIR
3" = 1'-0"

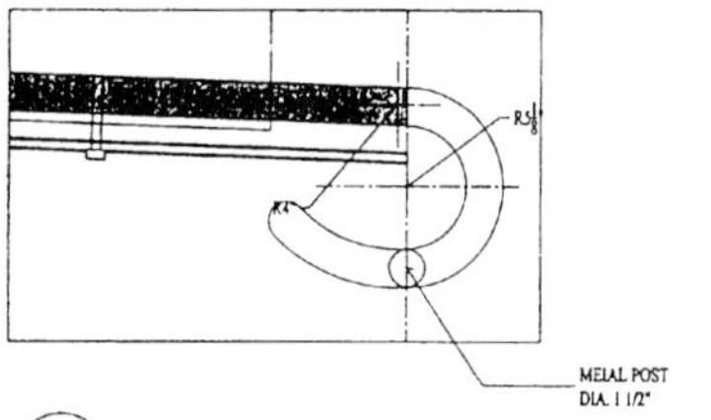

9 PARTIAL RAIL PLAN VIEW
1 1/2" = 1'-0"

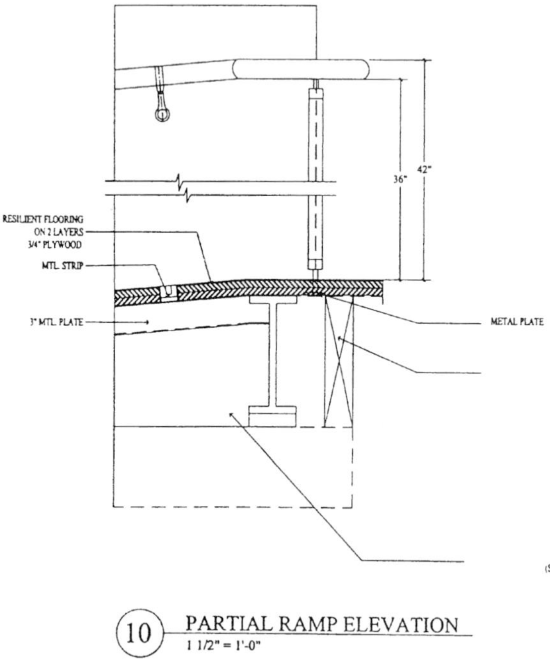

10 PARTIAL RAMP ELEVATION
1 1/2" = 1'-0"

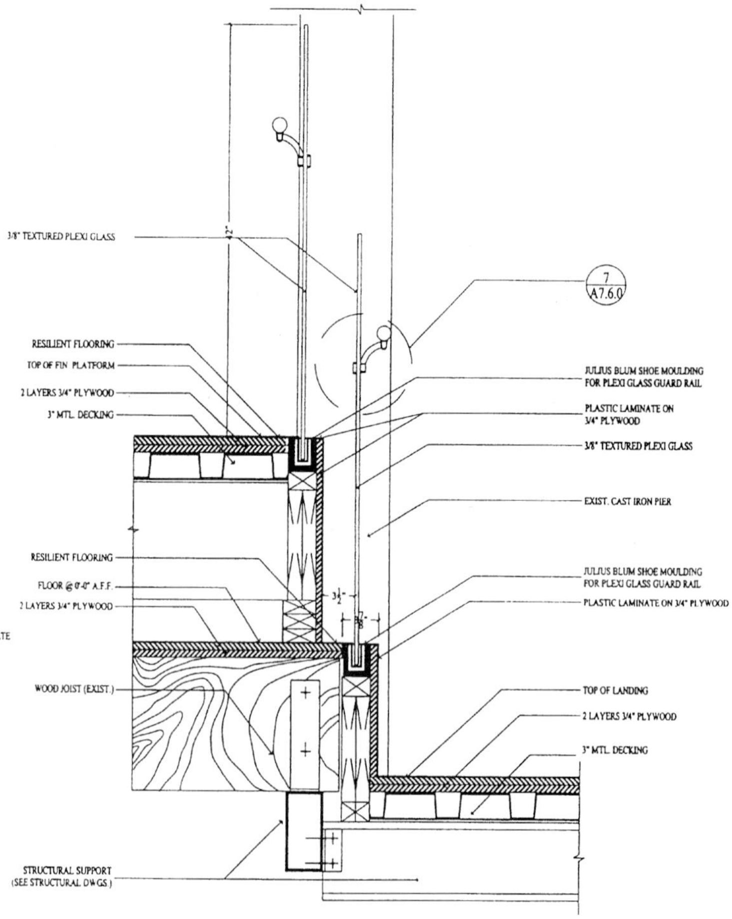

11 RAMP SECTION
1 1/2" = 1"-0"

FIREPLACES

The function of the fireplace today differs dramatically from its role of years ago. Whereas its original function was primarily to provide heat for warmth and/or cooking, today it serves more as a decorative asset and as the focal point of interior spaces and conversational groupings, providing the esthetic pleasure and comfort of firelight.

Of particular interest to the interior designer is the proportion and scale of the fireplace opening, the treatment of wall surfaces surrounding the fireplace, the design of mantel pieces and hearth extensions, and the array of fireplace accessories available. Accordingly, the information contained in this section addresses these considerations. Drawings include elevations, plans, and details of various fireplaces; elevations of a wide selection of prefabricated mantel types; and a sampling of fireplace accessories including andirons, wrought-iron fire sets, and log grates. It should be noted that, aside from their decorative aspects, the fireplace and chimney have important structural implications and require special foundations. Moreover, the fireplace must be designed to carry smoke away safely.

With respect to hearth extensions, most building codes require that for fireplaces having an opening of less than 6 ft^2 (0.56 m^2), the hearth must extend a minimum of 16 in (406 mm) beyond the face of the opening and a minimum of 8 in (203 mm) on each side. For fireplaces whose openings exceed 6 ft^2, the hearth must extend a minimum of 20 in (508 mm) beyond the face of the opening and 12 in (305 mm) on each side.

Most building codes also require that woodwork or other combustible materials not be placed within 6 in (153 mm) of a fireplace opening, and that combustible material within 12 in (305 mm) of a fireplace opening not project more than ⅛ in for each 1-in distance from such an opening.

Since building codes may vary, it is important that the designer have her or his plans checked for conformance with the applicable local or state codes. Any structural modifications to an existing fireplace and chimney or the design of a new fireplace and chimney should be reviewed by a professional engineer or registered architect.

A fireplace that draws properly can be ensured by applying proper principles of design. The size of flue should be adequate and should be based on the size of the fireplace opening. One rule commonly used is to take one-tenth of the area of the fireplace opening to find the minimum area of the flue. For example, if a fireplace had an opening 3 ft wide by 2 ft 6 in high, it would have an area of 1080 in^2. One-tenth of 1080 in^2 equals 108 in^2. The standard-size flue nearest to this requirement and readily available is a 13- by 13-in flue lining, which has an inside cross-sectional area of 126.56 in^2. One could also use a 13-in round flue that has a cross-sectional area of 113.0 in^2.

The front of the fireplace should be wider than the back and the upper part of the back should tilt forward to meet the throat in order to throw heat into the room instead of up the chimney. The arch over the top of the fireplace opening should be only 4 in thick, and the throat should project toward the front as much as possible to form the smoke shelf behind it. The area of the throat should be 1¼ times the area of the flue, with minimum and maximum width of 3 and 4½ in, respectively, so that the narrow throat will cause a quick suction into the flue. The sides of the fireplace above the throat are drawn together to form the flue, which always starts exactly over the center of the width of the fireplace. The smoke shelf is very necessary to stop back drafts. The depth of the fireplace should be one-half the height of the opening, with a maximum of 24 in. The back should rise one-half the height of the opening before sloping forward and should be two-thirds the opening in width.

The back, sides, and parts of the hearth that are under the fire must be built of heat-resistant materials. Firebrick laid in fire clay is the best combination.

The damper is a large valve that can be adjusted to regulate the draft. Many types of commercial damper units are manufactured. The position of a damper unit is important. The damper is generally set about 8 in above the top of the fireplace opening and is concealed by the brickwork. One advantage of these units is that they are correctly designed and have correctly proportioned throat damper and chamber to provide a form for the masonry and to reduce the risk of failure in the function of the completed fireplace.

The hearth consists of two parts, the front or finish hearth and the back hearth under the fire. The front hearth is simply a precaution against flying sparks and, while it must be noncombustible, it need not resist intense prolonged heat. Because the back hearth must withstand intense heat, it is built of heat-resistant materials. In buildings with wood floors, the hearth in front of the fireplace should be supported on masonry. The front hearth should project at least 16 in from the front of the fireplace.

At the back part of the hearth it is customary to have an ash dump for dropping the ashes into the ash pit, which is generally located in the basement, with a door for cleaning out ashes.

FIREPLACES
Components and Terminology

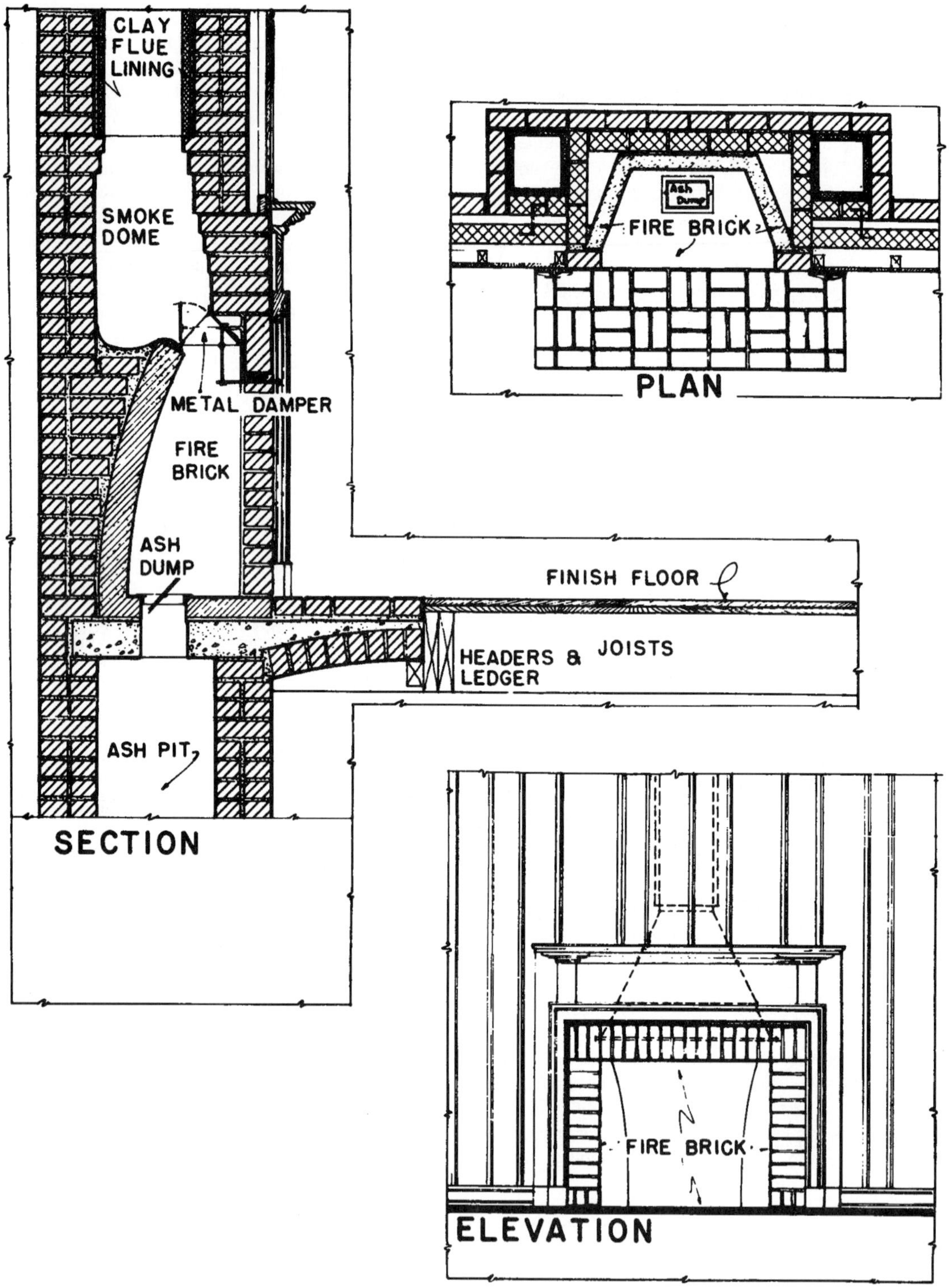

Fig. 1 Construction details of a typical fireplace

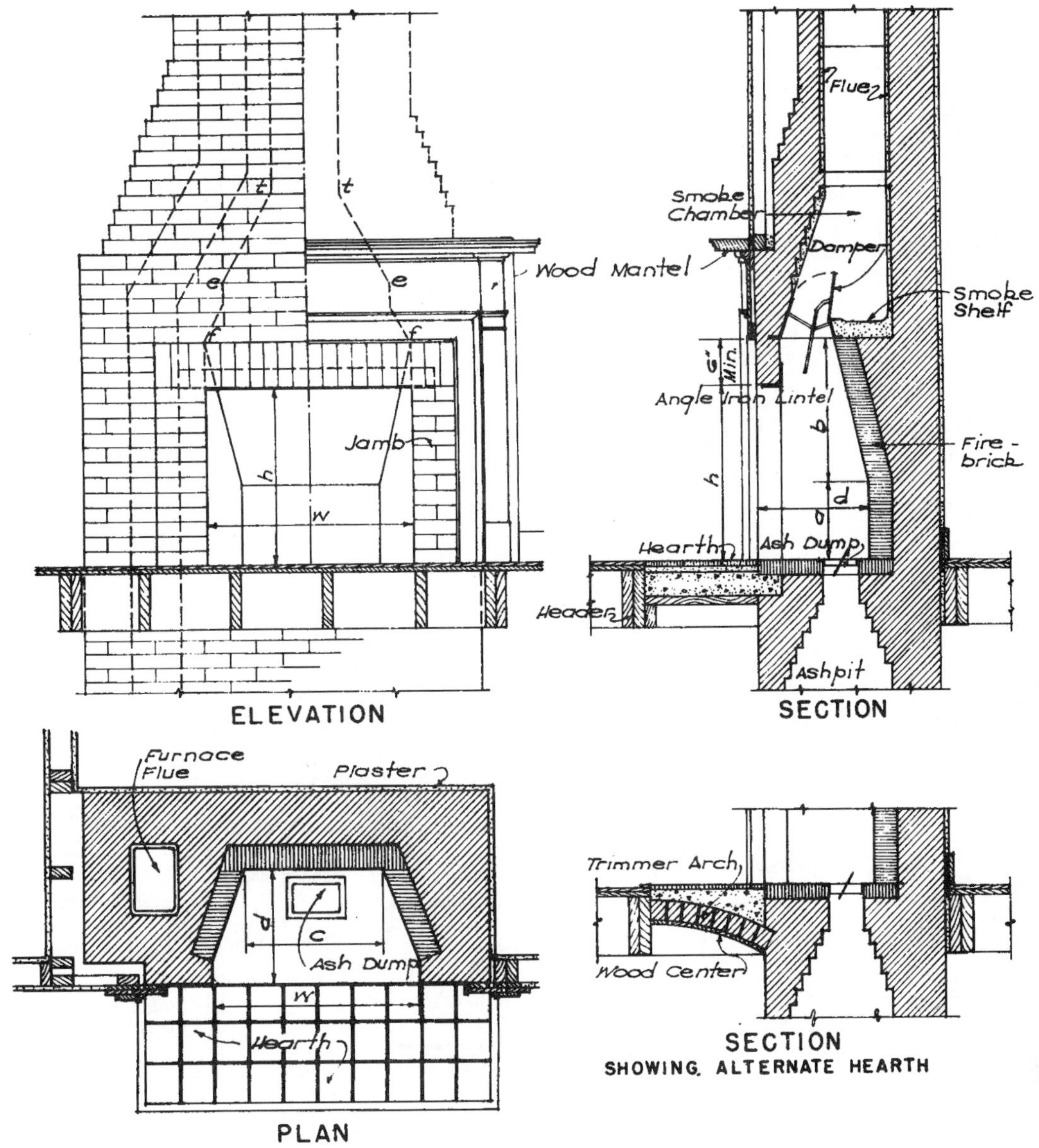

Fig. 2 Construction details of a typical fireplace

Table 1 Recommended dimensions for fireplaces and size of flue lining required

(Letters in column heads refer to Fig. 2; all dimensions in inches)

Size of fireplace opening						Size of flue lining required	
Width, *w*	Height, *h*	Depth, *d*	Minimum width of back wall, *c*	Height of vertical back wall, *a*	Height of inclined back wall, *b*	Standard rectangular (outside dimensions)	Standard round (inside diameter)
24	24	16–18	14	14	16	8½ × 13	10
28	24	16–18	14	14	16	8½ × 13	10
30	28–30	16–18	16	14	18	8½ × 13	10
36	28–30	16–18	22	14	18	8½ × 13	12
42	28–32	16–18	28	14	18	13 × 13	12
48	32	18–20	32	14	24	13 × 13	15
54	36	18–20	36	14	28	13 × 18	15
60	36	18–20	44	14	28	13 × 18	15
54	40	20–22	36	17	29	13 × 18	15
60	40	20–22	42	17	30	18 × 18	18
66	40	20–22	44	17	30	18 × 18	18
72	40	22–28	51	17	30	18 × 18	18

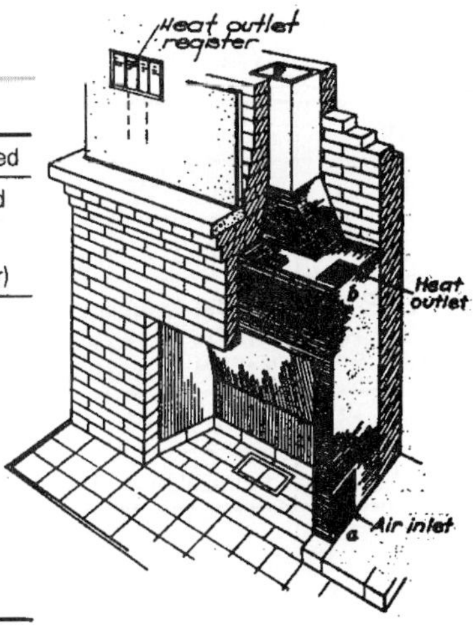

FIREPLACES
Design Data

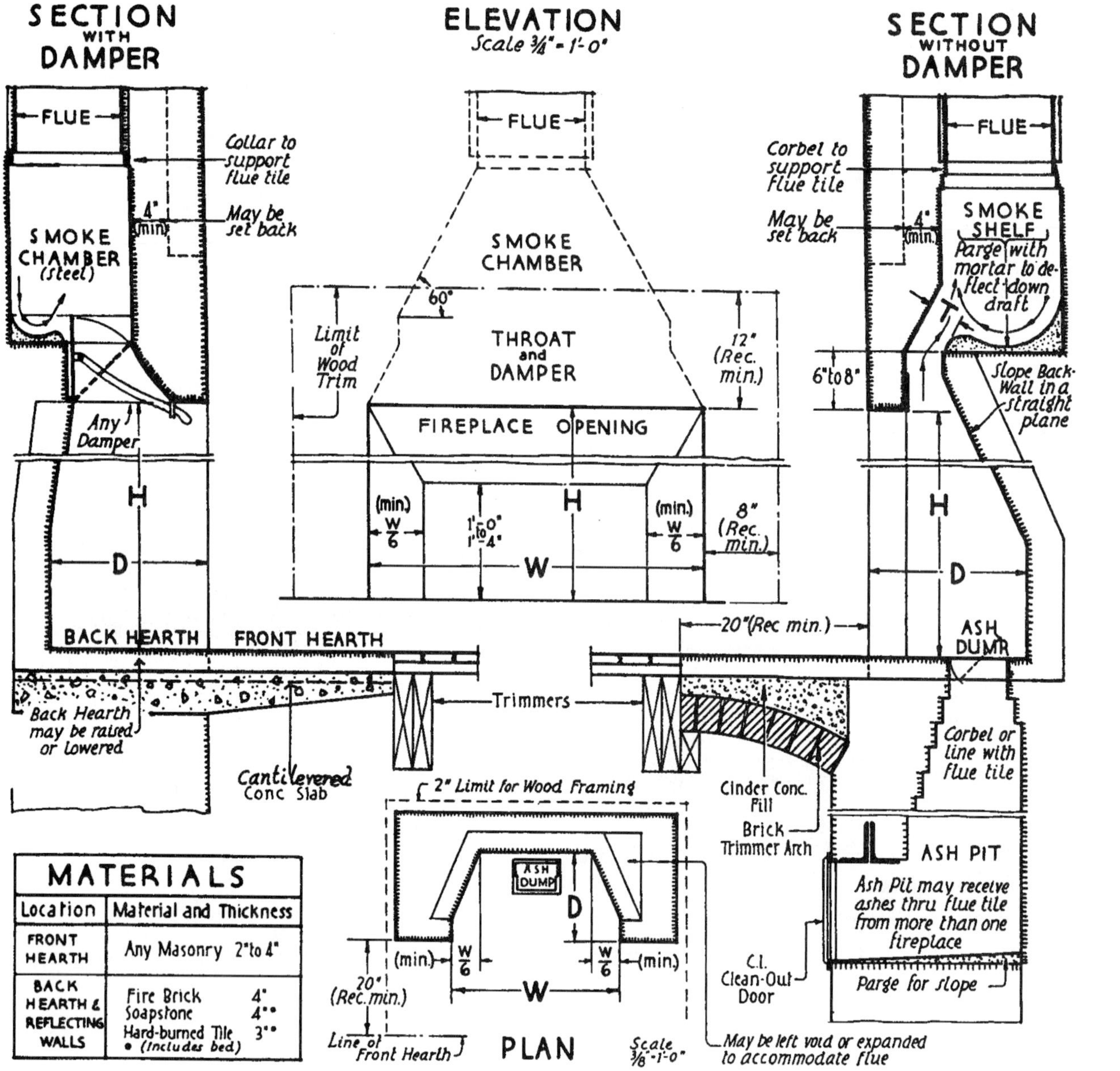

MATERIALS

Location	Material and Thickness
FRONT HEARTH	Any Masonry 2" to 4"
BACK HEARTH & REFLECTING WALLS	Fire Brick 4" Soapstone 4"* Hard-burned Tile 3"* * (Includes bed)

FIREPLACE DIMENSIONS *(In Inches)*

W	24 to 84
H	⅔ to ¾ W
D	½ to ⅔ H {16 to 24 (Rec) for Coal; 18 to 24 (Rec) for Wood}
FLUE *(Effective Area)*	⅛ WH for unlined flue ⅒ WH for rectangular lining 1/12 WH for circular lining
T *(Area)*	5/4 to 3/2 FLUE AREA
T *(Width)*	3" minimum to 4½" maximum

RECOMMENDED FLUE SIZES *(In Inches)*

FIREPLACE WIDTH W	RECTANGULAR FLUES: Nominal or Outside Dimension	Inside Dimension	Effective Area	EQUIVALENT ROUND: Inside Diameter	Effective Area
24	8½ X 8½	7¼ X 7¼	41**	8	50.3**
30 to 34	8½ X 13	7 X 11½	70**	10	78.54**
36 to 44	13 X 13	11¼ X 11¼	99**	12	113.0**
46 to 56	13 X 18	11¼ X 6¼	156**	15	176.7**
58 to 68	18 X 18	15¾ X 5¾	195**	18	254.4**
70 to 84	20 X 24	17 X 21	278**	22	380.13**

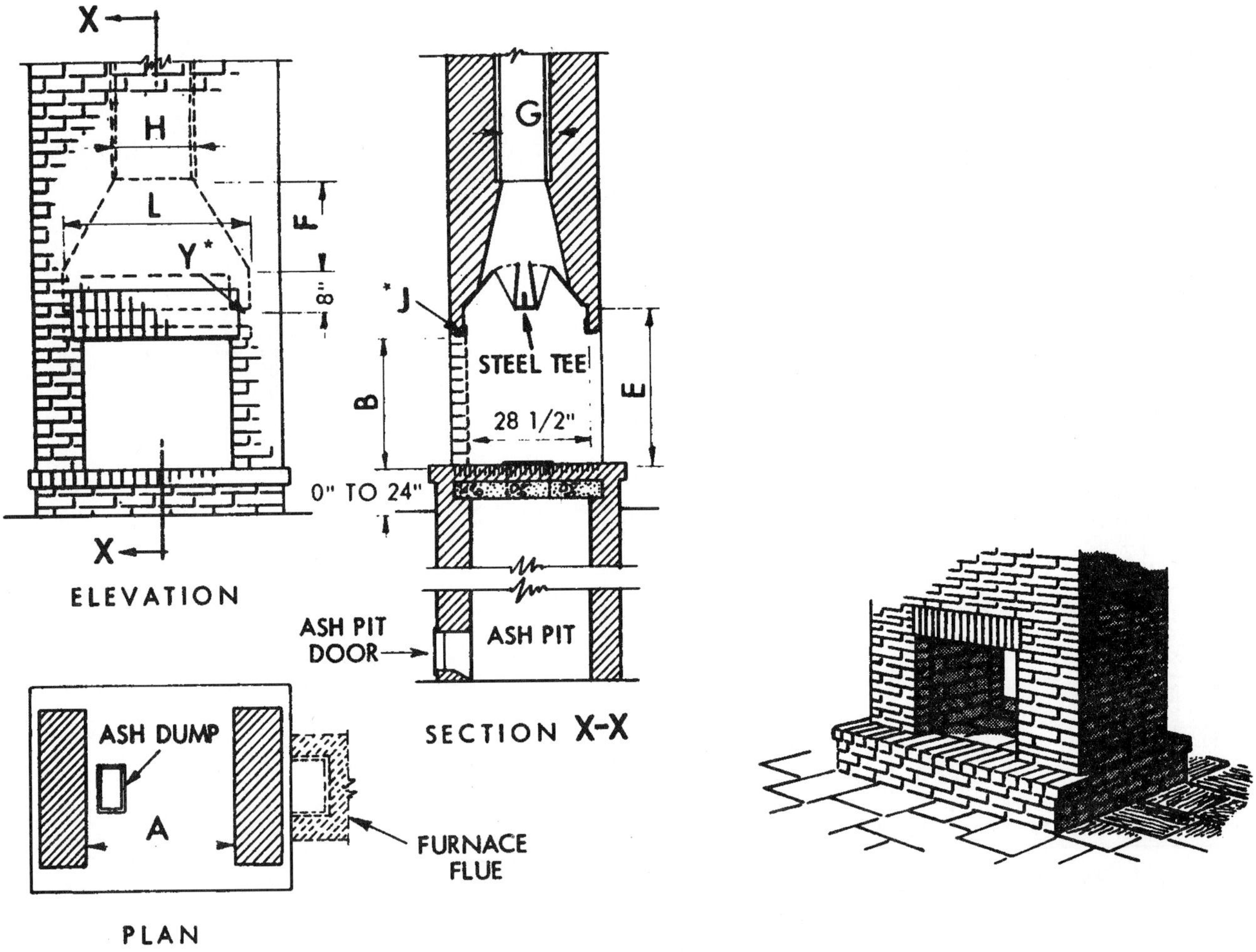

Fig. 3 Fireplace open on both sides

Table 2 Table of dimensions and equipment (in inches)

Width of opening, *A*	Height of opening, *B*	Damper height, *E*	Smoke chamber, *F*	Old flue size *G*	Old flue size *H*	New flue size *G*	New flue size *H*	Angle (2 req'd),* *J*	*L*	Tee	Ash dump	Ash-pit door
28	24	30	19	13	13	12	16	A-36	36	35	58	12 × 8
32	29	35	21	13	18	16	16	A-40	40	39	58	12 × 8
36	29	35	21	13	18	16	20	A-42	44	43	58	12 × 8
40	29	35	27	18	18	16	20	A-48	48	47	58	12 × 8
48	32	37	32	18	18	20	20	B-54	56	55	58	12 × 8

*Angle sizes: A—3 × 3 × 3⁄16; B—3½ × 3½ × ¼".

Note Y from Fig. 3: The damper and the steel T should not be built-in solid at the ends, but given freedom to expand with heat.

FIREPLACES
Corner Design

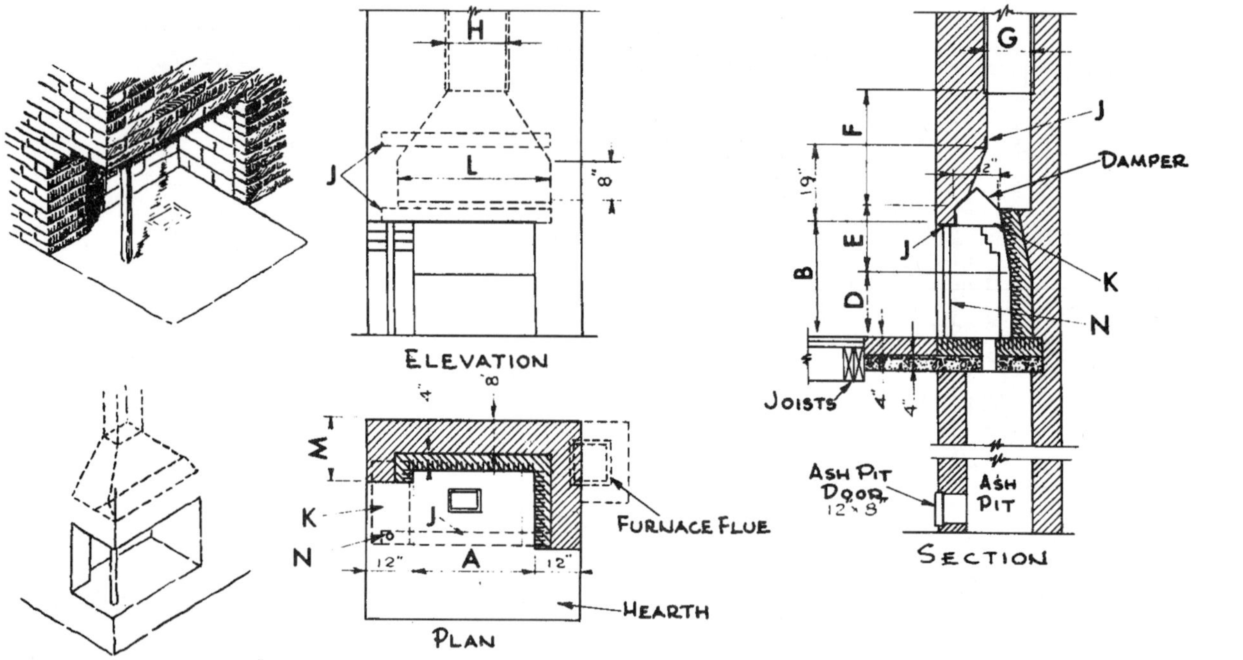

TABLE OF DIMENSIONS AND EQUIPMENT (IN INCHES)

A	B	C	D	E	F	OLD FLUE SIZES IN G	OUT	IN H	OUT	NEW FLUE SIZES IN G	OUT	IN H	OUT	L	M	STEEL ANGLE J*	PLATE LINTEL K	CORNER POST N
28	26½	20	14	20	29¼	11¼	13	11¼	13	10¼	12	10¼	12	36	16	*A-36	11x16	3ϕ x 26½
32	26½	20	14	20	32	11¼	13	11¼	13	10¼	12	13½	16	40	16	*A-42	11x16	3ϕ x 26½
36	26½	20	14	20	35	11¼	13	11¼	13	10¼	12	13½	16	44	16	*A-48	11x16	3ϕ x 26½
40	29	20	14	20	35	11¼	13	15¾	18	13½	16	13½	16	48	16	*B-54	11x16	3ϕ x 29
48	29	24	14	24	43	11¼	13	15¾	18	13½	16	13½	16	56	20	*B-60	11x16	3ϕ x 29

* ANGLE SIZES   *A 3 x 3 x 3/16   *B 3½ x 3½ x ¼

Fig. 4 Corner fireplace

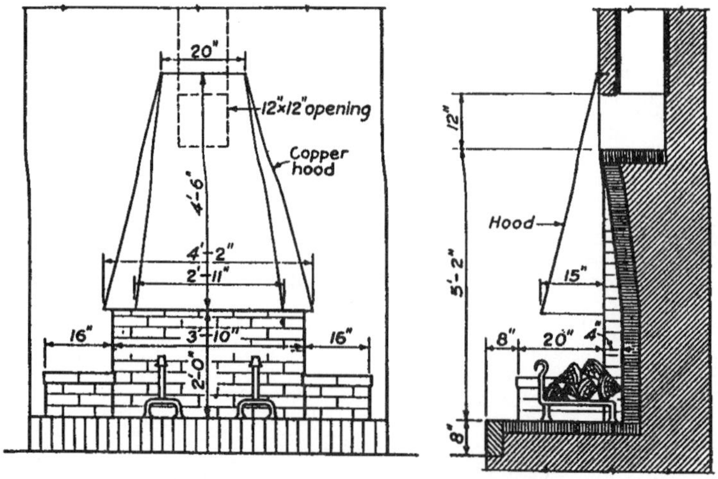

Fig. 5 A shallow fireplace with a copper hood, built as shown, throws out considerable heat after the hood gets hot. The wall should be of fire-resistant masonry

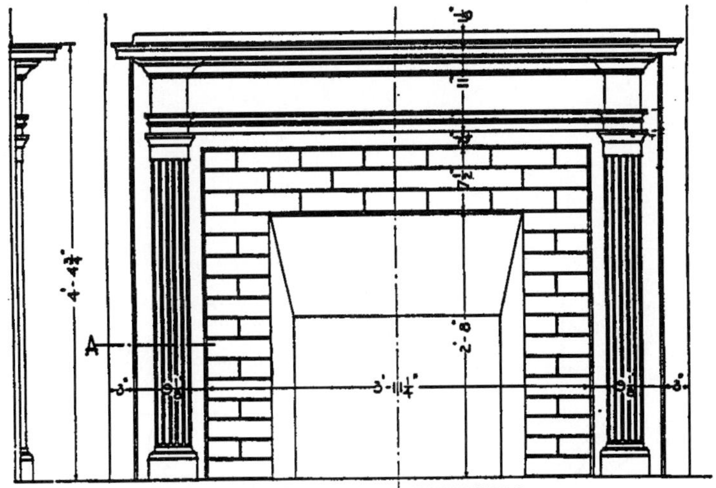

END FRONT ELEVATION

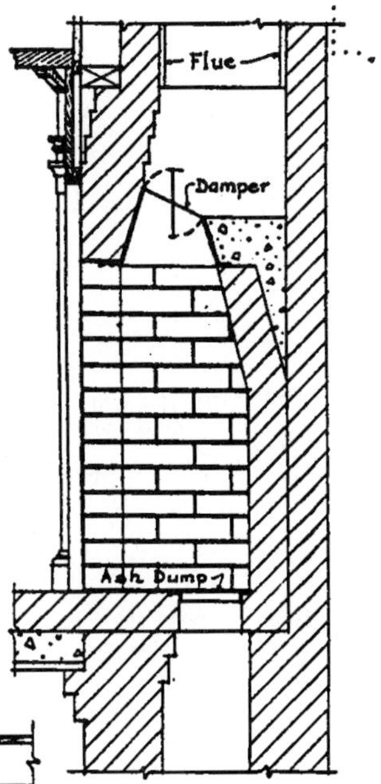

SECTION

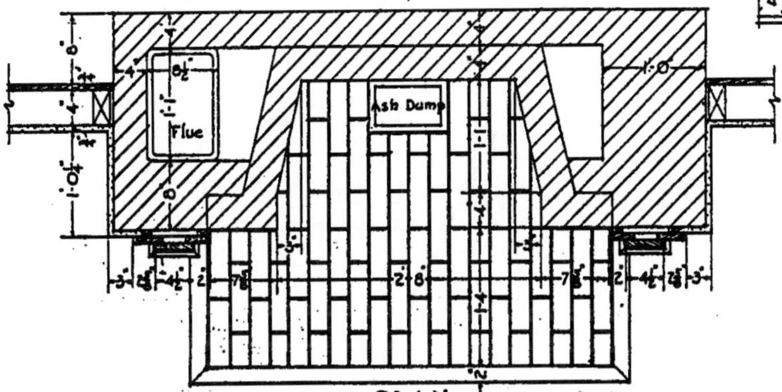

PLAN

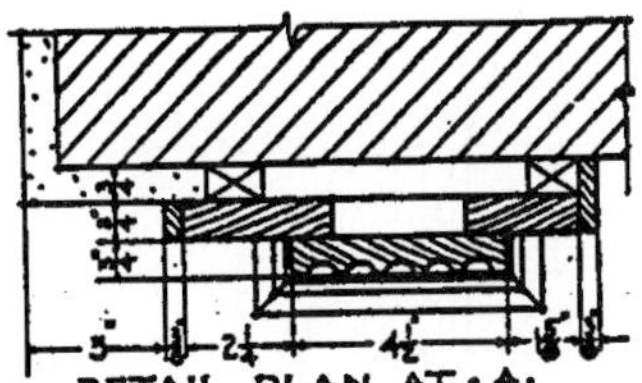

DETAIL PLAN AT · A ·

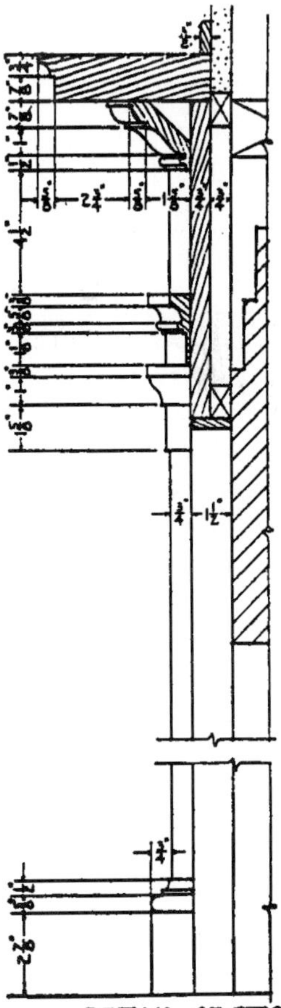

DETAIL SECTION
Scale 3" = 1 foot

FIREPLACES

Corner Design

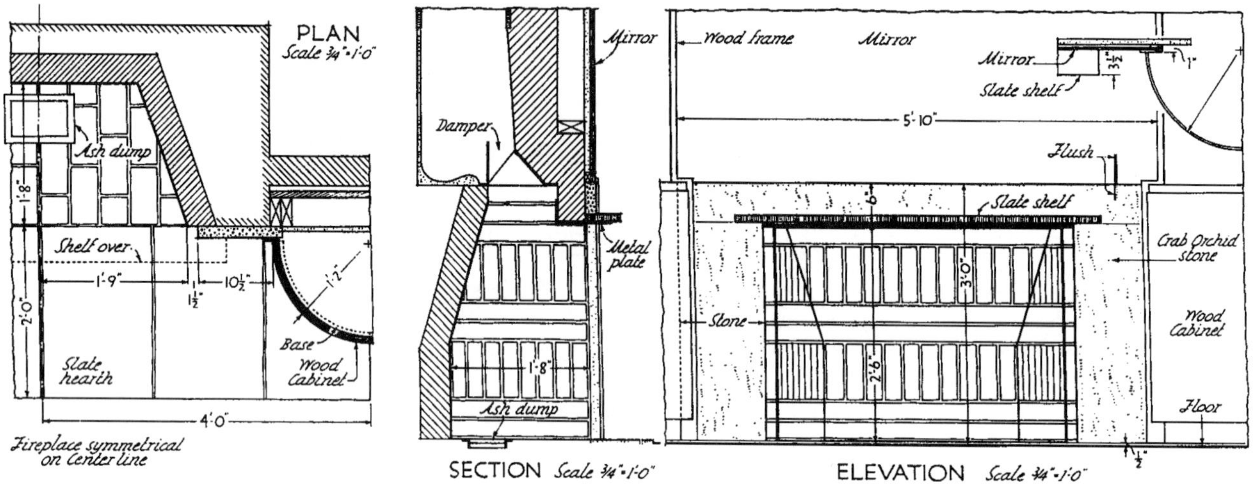

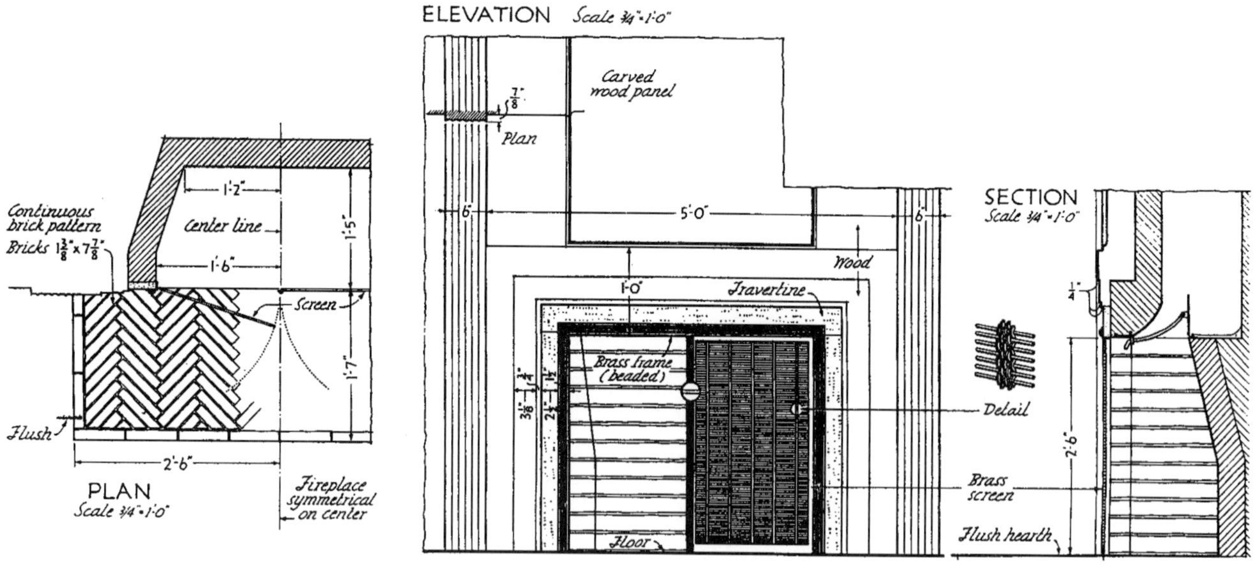

FIREPLACES
Corner Design

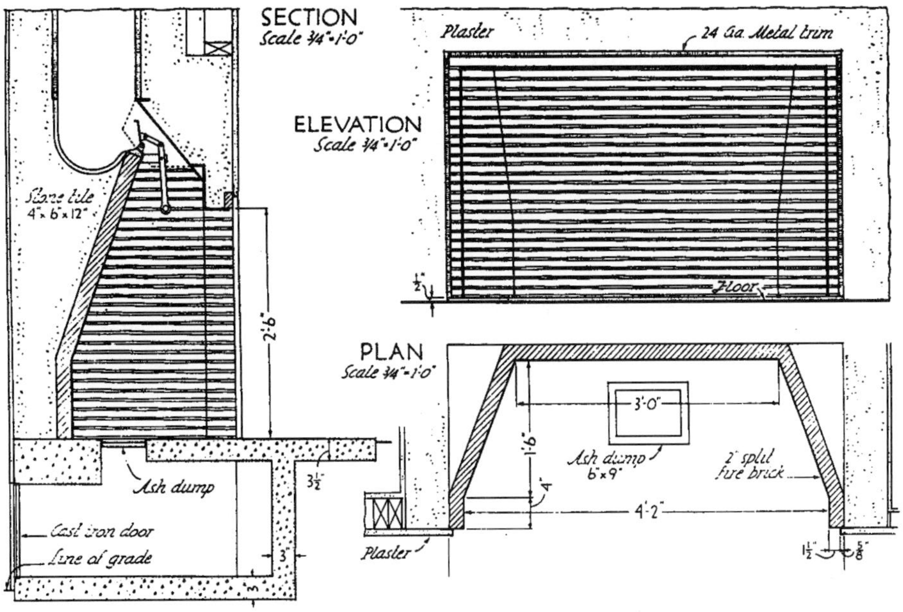

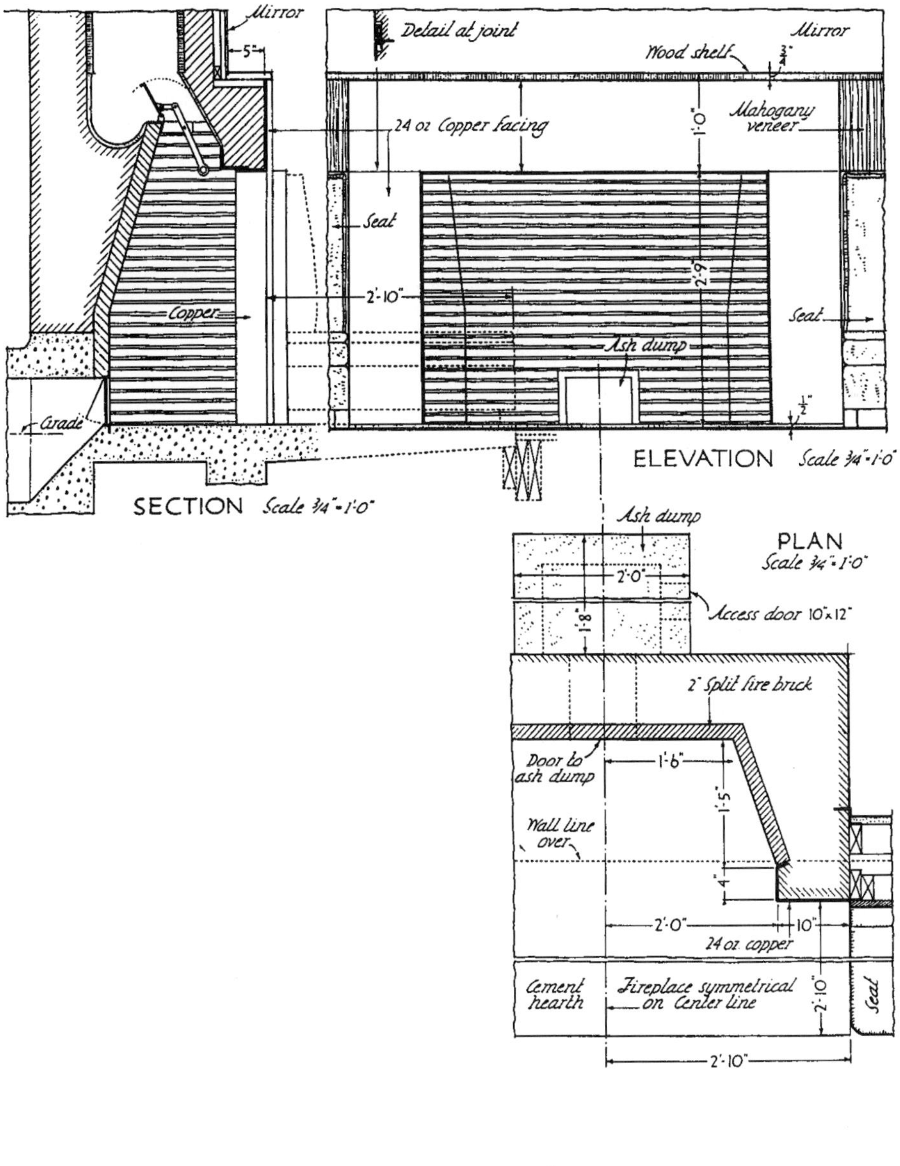

FIREPLACES

Direct Vent Installation Details and Data

DIRECT-VENT INSTALLATION
TOP VENT/REAR VENT

THROUGH THE ROOF INSTALLATIONS

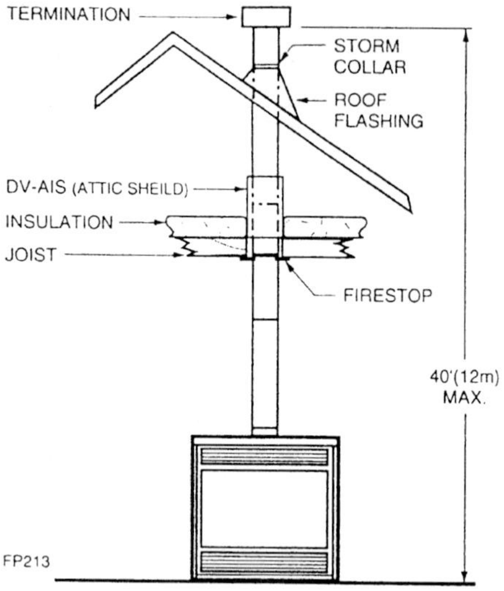

TYPICAL STRAIGHT-UP INSTALLATION

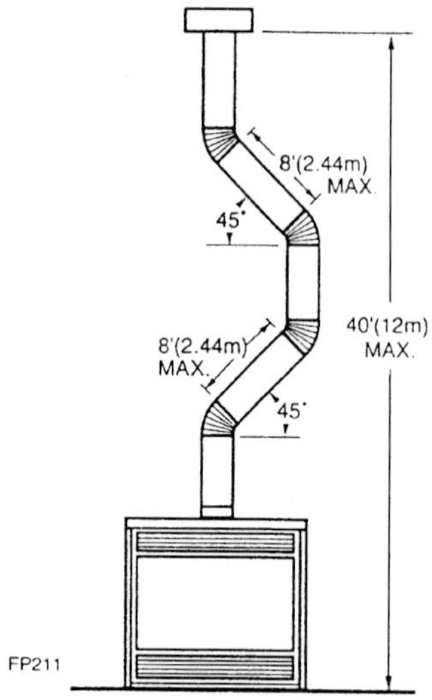

TYPICAL OFFSET INSTALLATION

DIRECT-VENT INSTALLATION
TOP VENT/REAR VENT

TOP VENT/REAR VENT: Venting applications are determined by a vent graph located in each installation manual. A maximum 20-ft. horizontal run may be used with a minimum 7.5-ft. vertical rise. Total number of elbows allowed is specified in each manual.

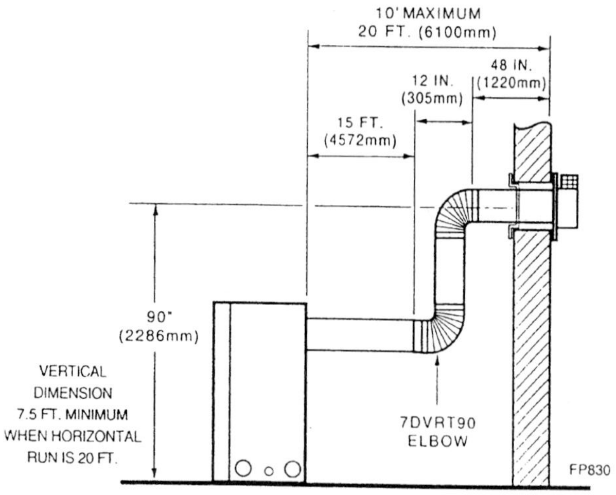

REAR VENT - SIDE VIEW

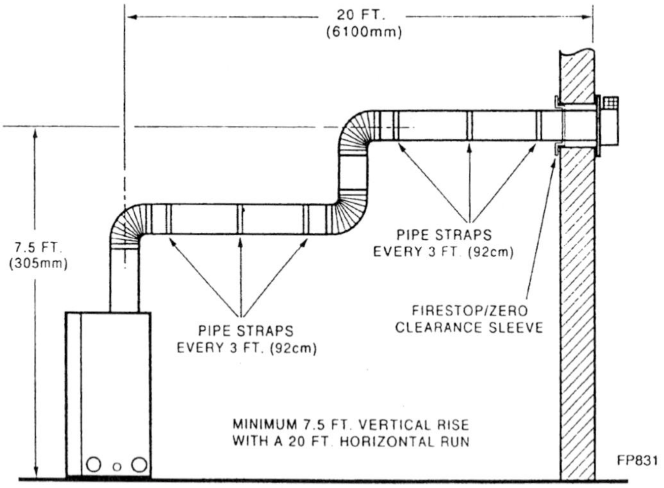

TOP VENT - SIDE VIEW

The information contained on this page demonstrates a typical venting method for a particular type fireplace. Safe installation of Majestic products must abide by the specific installation manual provided with each model.

DIRECT-VENT INSTALLATION
TOP VENT/REAR VENT

TYPICAL BASEMENT INSTALLATION

TOP VENT - SIDE VIEW

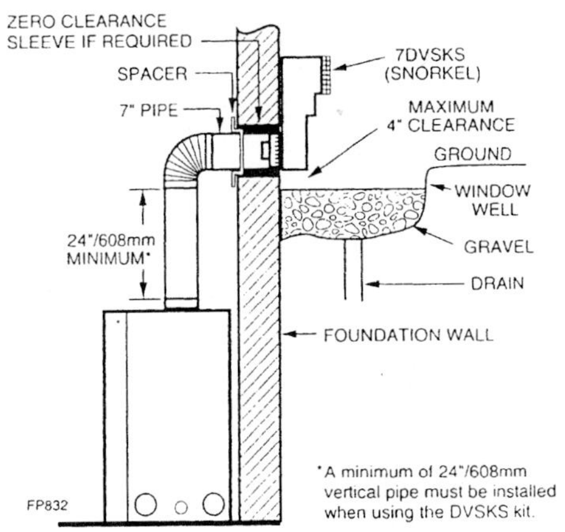

FP832

REAR VENT - SIDE VIEW

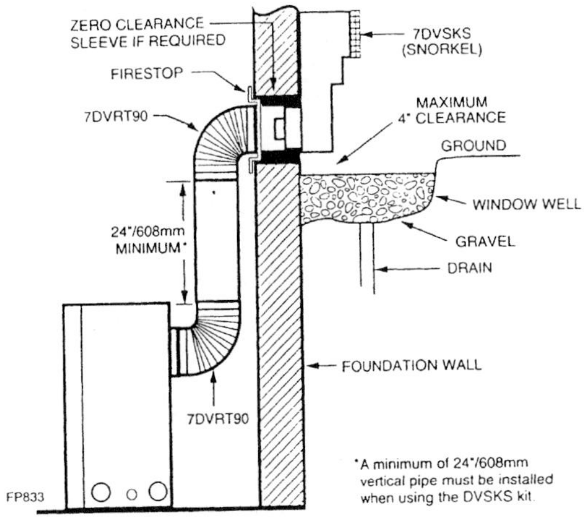

FP833

The information contained on this page demonstrates a typical venting method for a particular type fireplace. Safe installation of Majestic products must abide by the specific installation manual provided with each model.

DIRECT-VENT INSTALLATION
TOP VENT/REAR VENT

TYPICAL THROUGH THE WALL

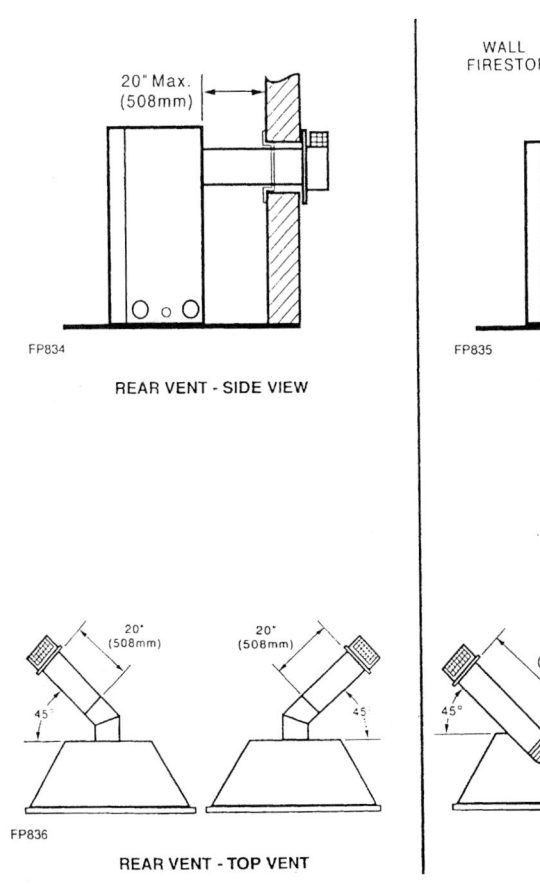

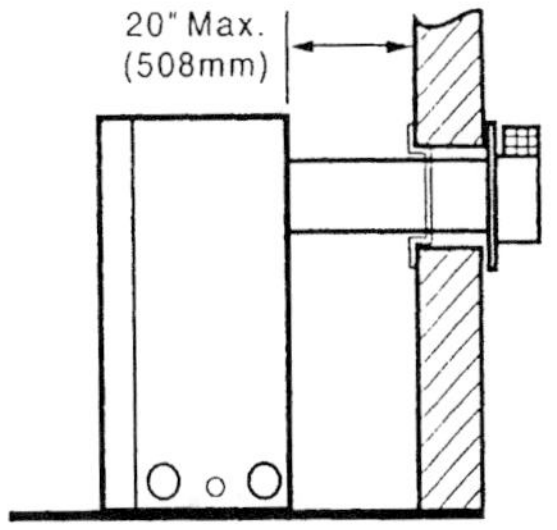

FP834

REAR VENT - SIDE VIEW

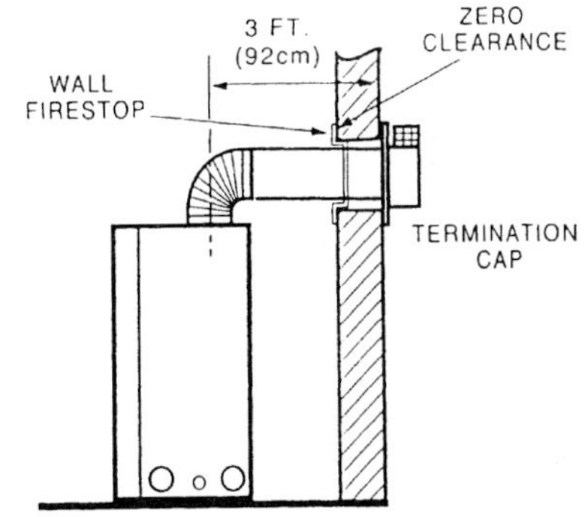

FP835

TOP VENT - SIDE VIEW

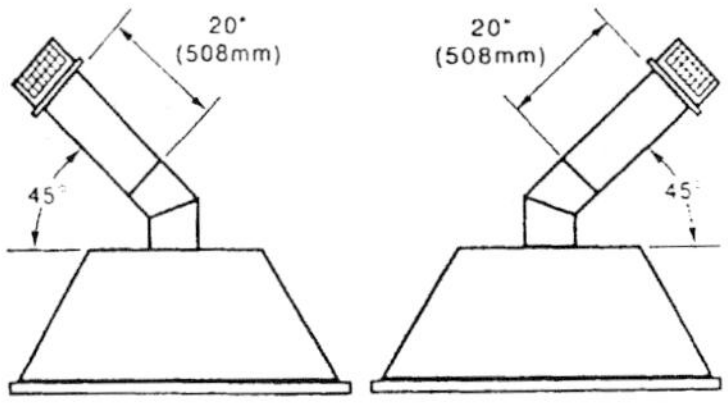

FP836

REAR VENT - TOP VENT

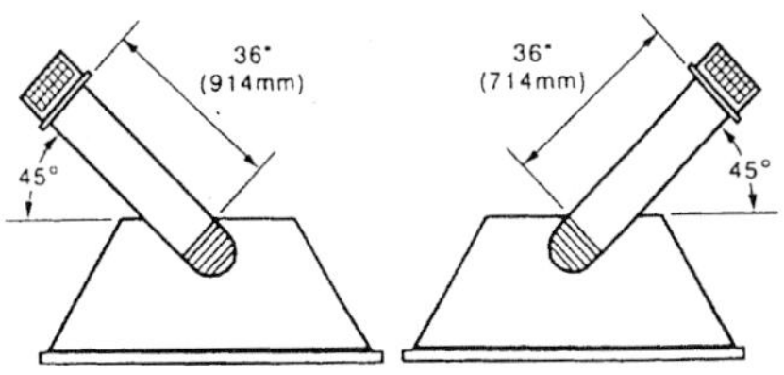

FP837

TOP VENT - TOP VIEW

FIREPLACES

Direct Vent Installation Details and Data

The information contained on this page demonstrates a typical venting method for a particular type fireplace. Safe installation of Majestic products must abide by the specific installation manual provided with each model.

MINIMUM-MAXIMUM HEIGHT INSTALLATION FOR WOOD-BURNING FIREPLACE

NOTE: *Firestops are required for safety and must be used for each ceiling the chimney system penetrates. If the area above the ceilings is not an attic, position the firestop on the ceiling side. If the area above the ceiling is an attic, position the firestop on the top side of the framed hole. A firestop is not required at the roof.

Maximum **TOTAL length of angled chimney system run **cannot exceed** 20 feet.

***If chimney is within 10' of roof peak, the top should extend a minimum of 24" above the roof peak, but never less than 3 feet in height above the highest point where it passes through the roof. When further than 10' from roof peak, the top of chimney should be positioned so that it is 10' or more from the closest point on roof in a horizontal direction, and a minimum of 24" above that point, but never less than 3 feet in height above the highest point where it passes through the roof. Minimum dimension for Major U.S. Building Codes. These minimum dimensions are recommended in the interest of safety, they do not assure a smoke-free operation.

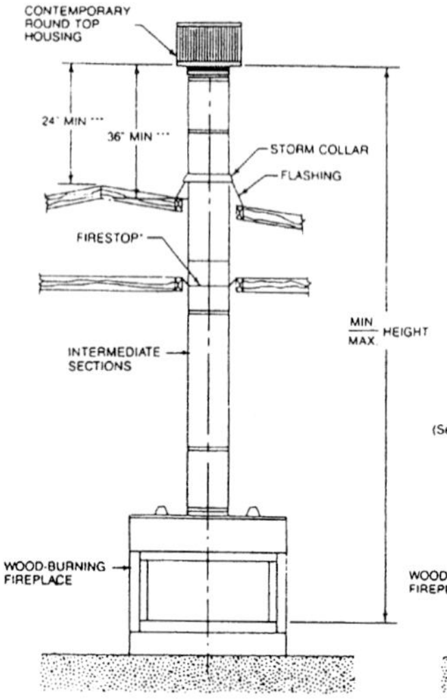

STRAIGHT-UP INSTALLATION

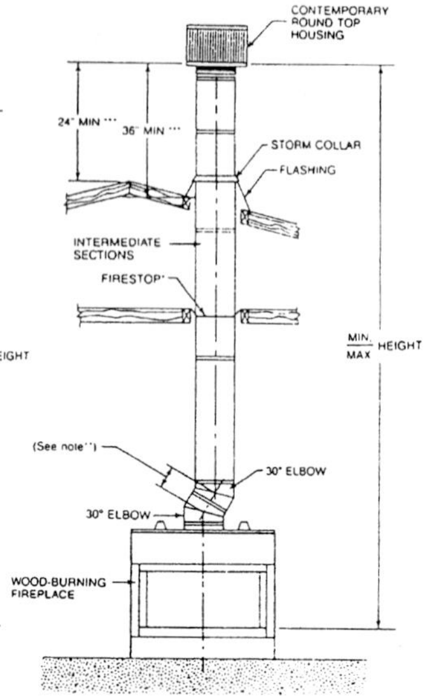

TWO-ELBOW INSTALLATION

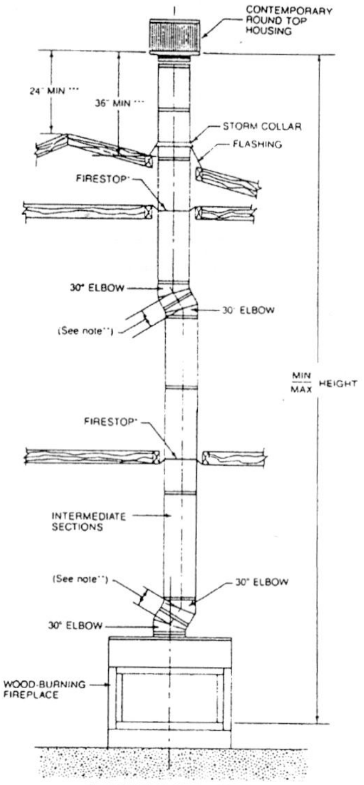

FOUR-ELBOW INSTALLATION

WOOD-BURNING FIREPLACES ON TWO FLOORS WITH FIREPLACE ON SAME CENTER LINE

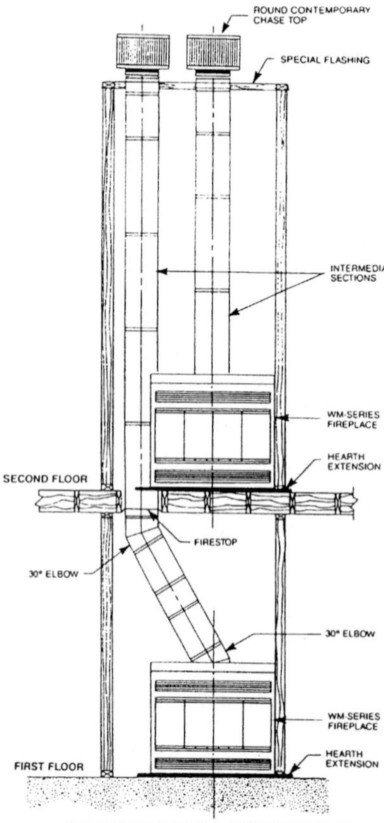

STRAIGHT UP AND 30° SINGLE OFFSET/TWO STORY CHASE INSTALLATION

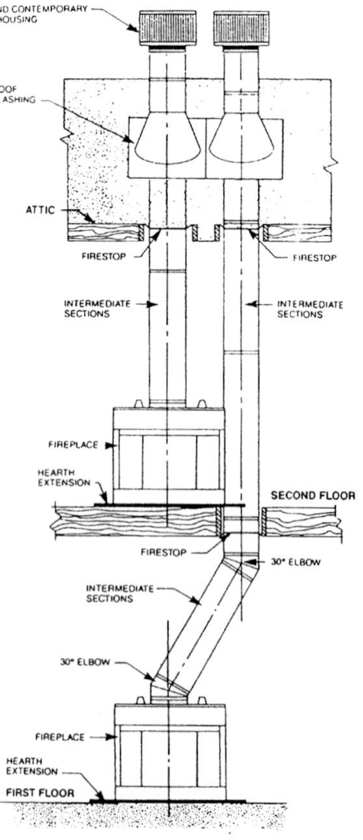

STRAIGHT UP AND 30° SINGLE OFFSET/TWO STORY SLOPED ROOF INSTALLATION

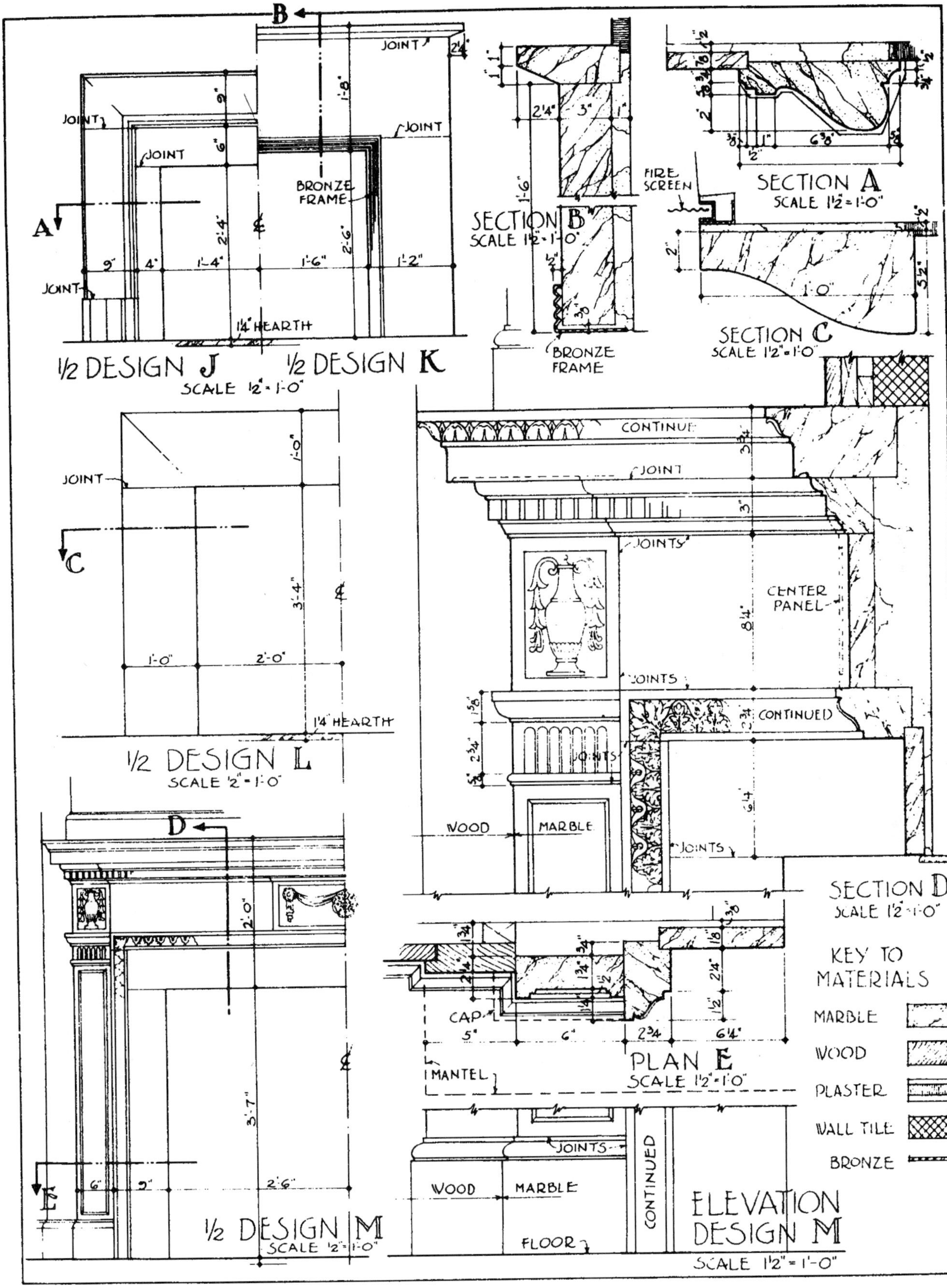
1/2 DESIGN J
1/2 DESIGN K
SCALE 1/2" = 1'-0"
JOINT
BRONZE FRAME
1/4" HEARTH
SECTION B
SCALE 1 1/2" = 1'-0"
BRONZE FRAME
FIRE SCREEN
SECTION A
SCALE 1 1/2" = 1'-0"
SECTION C
SCALE 1 1/2" = 1'-0"
1/2 DESIGN L
SCALE 1/2" = 1'-0"
CONTINUE
JOINTS
CENTER PANEL
CONTINUED
WOOD
MARBLE
SECTION D
SCALE 1 1/2" = 1'-0"
CAP
MANTEL
PLAN E
SCALE 1 1/2" = 1'-0"
KEY TO MATERIALS
MARBLE
WOOD
PLASTER
WALL TILE
BRONZE
1/2 DESIGN M
SCALE 1/2" = 1'-0"
FLOOR
ELEVATION DESIGN M
SCALE 1 1/2" = 1'-0"

FIREPLACES

Marble Mantels

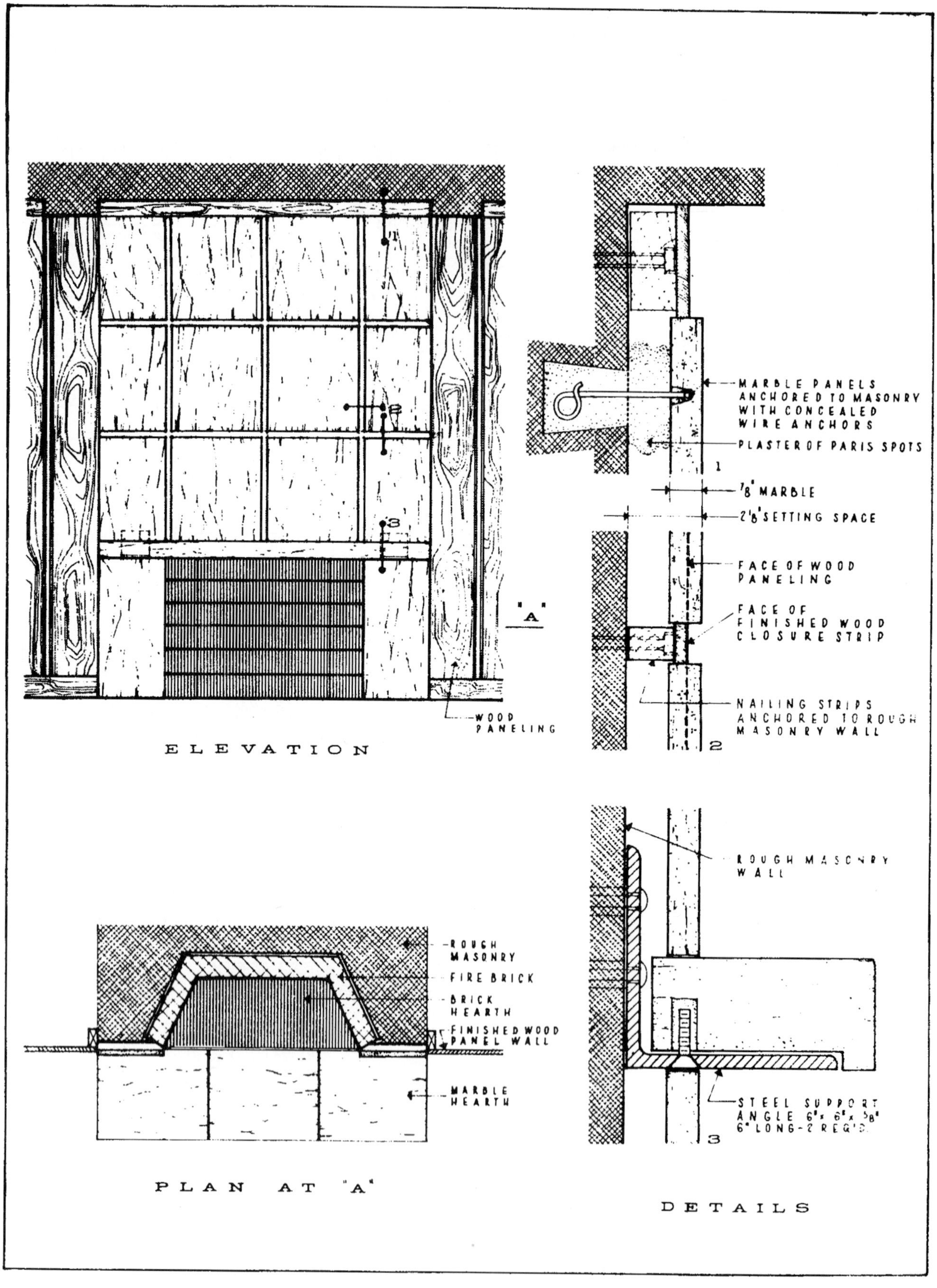
"A"
WOOD PANELING
ELEVATION
MARBLE PANELS ANCHORED TO MASONRY WITH CONCEALED WIRE ANCHORS
PLASTER OF PARIS SPOTS
1
7/8" MARBLE
2 1/8" SETTING SPACE
FACE OF WOOD PANELING
FACE OF FINISHED WOOD CLOSURE STRIP
NAILING STRIPS ANCHORED TO ROUGH MASONRY WALL
2
ROUGH MASONRY
FIRE BRICK
BRICK HEARTH
FINISHED WOOD PANEL WALL
MARBLE HEARTH
PLAN AT "A"
ROUGH MASONRY WALL
STEEL SUPPORT ANGLE 6"x 6"x 3/8" 6" LONG-2 REQ'D.
3
DETAILS

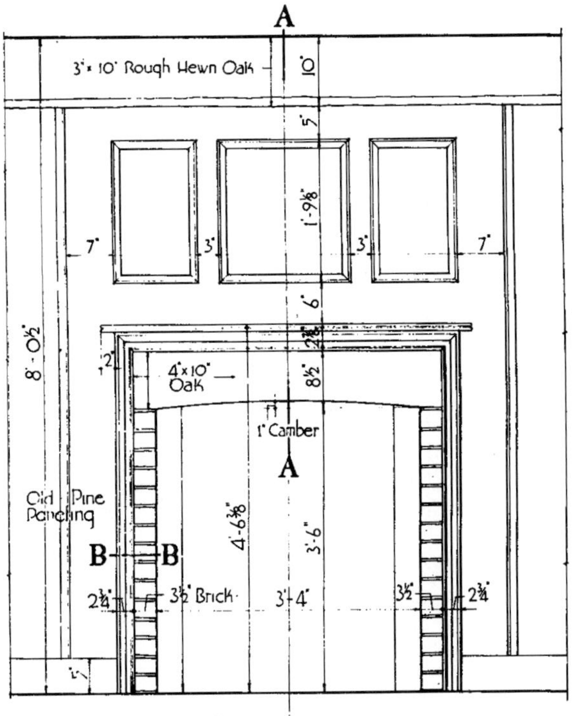

ELEVATION

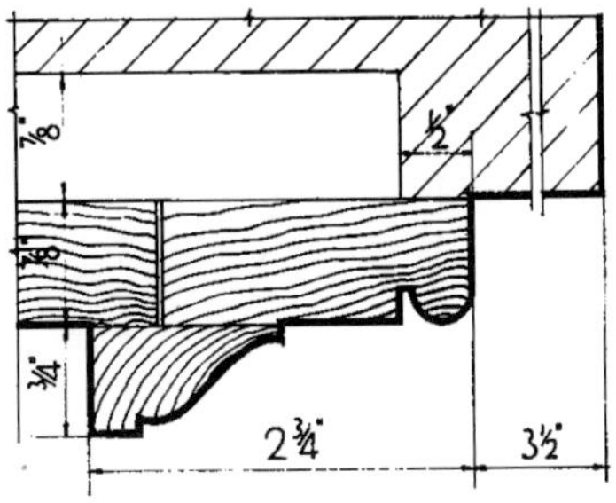

SECTION B—B

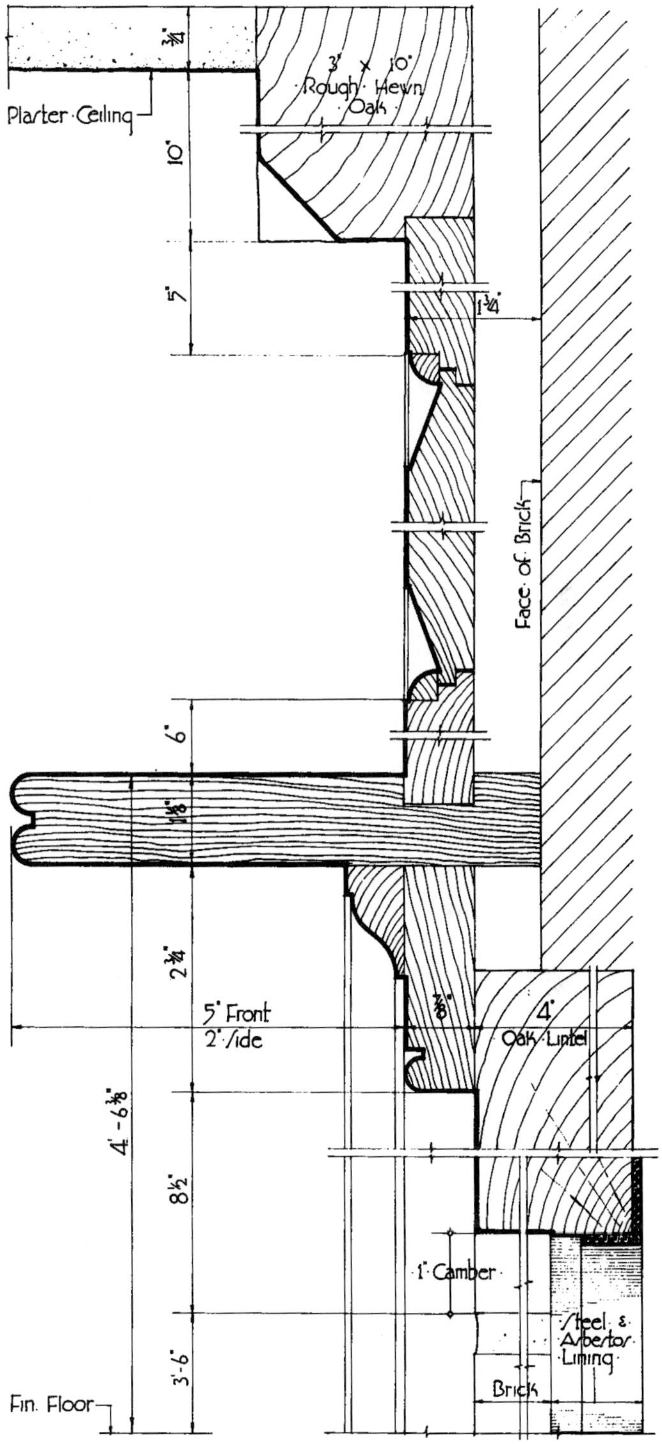

SECTION A—A

FIREPLACES

Wood Mantels

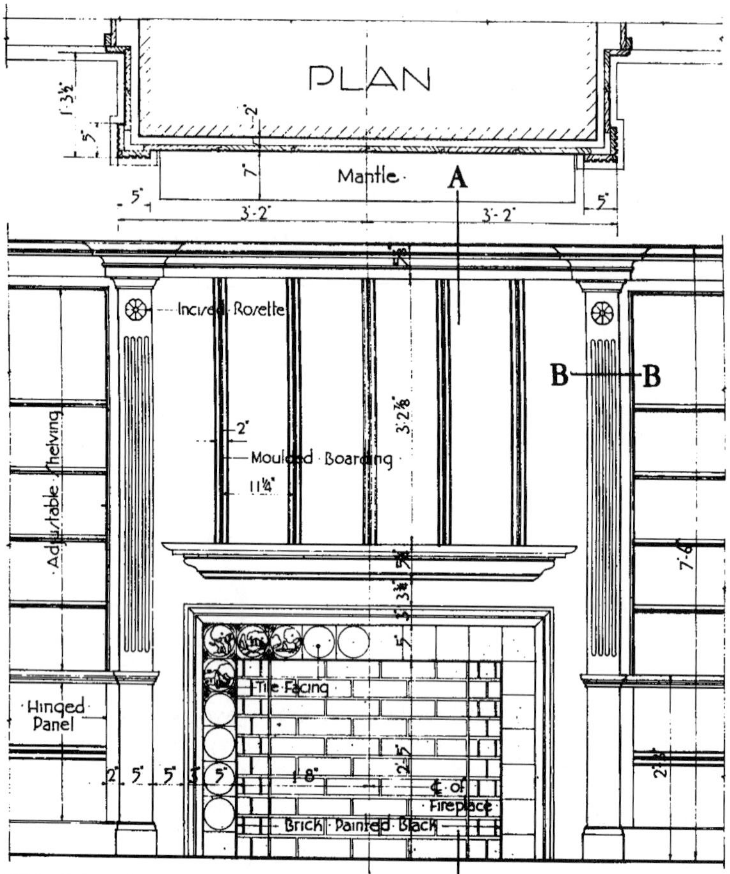

ELEVATION ·

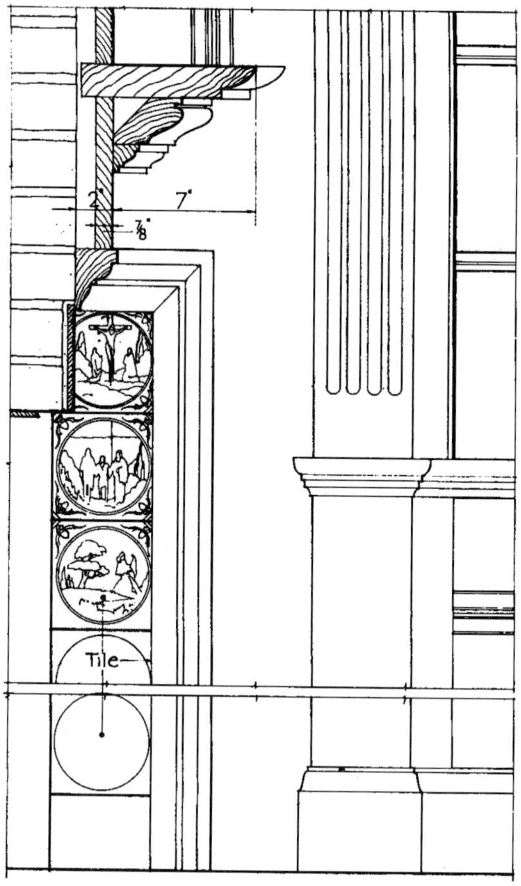

SECTION · A–A

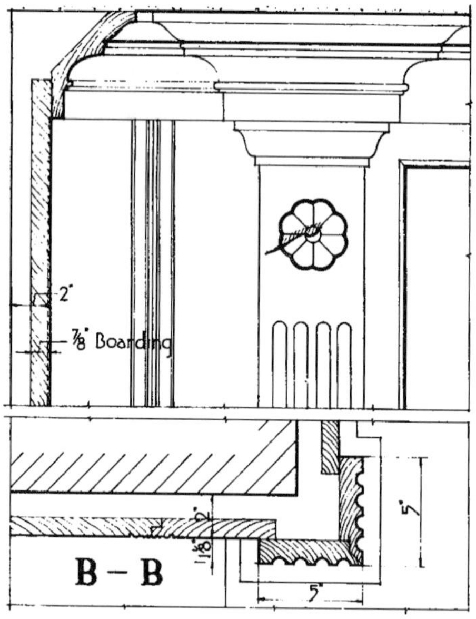

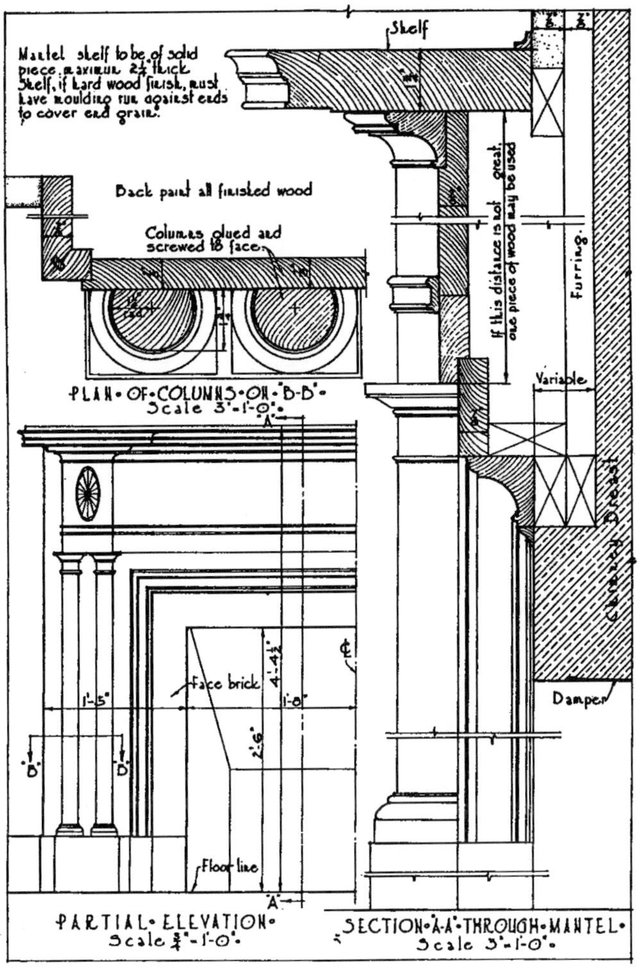
Shelf
Mantel shelf to be of solid piece, maximum 2¼ thick. Shelf, if hard wood finish, must have moulding run against ends to cover end grain.
Back paint all finished wood
Columns glued and screwed to face
PLAN OF COLUMNS ON B-B
Scale 3"-1'-0"
If this distance is not great, one piece of wood may be used
Furring
Variable
Chimney Breast
Face brick
Floor line
Damper
PARTIAL ELEVATION
Scale ¾"-1'-0"
SECTION A-A THROUGH MANTEL
Scale 3"-1'-0"

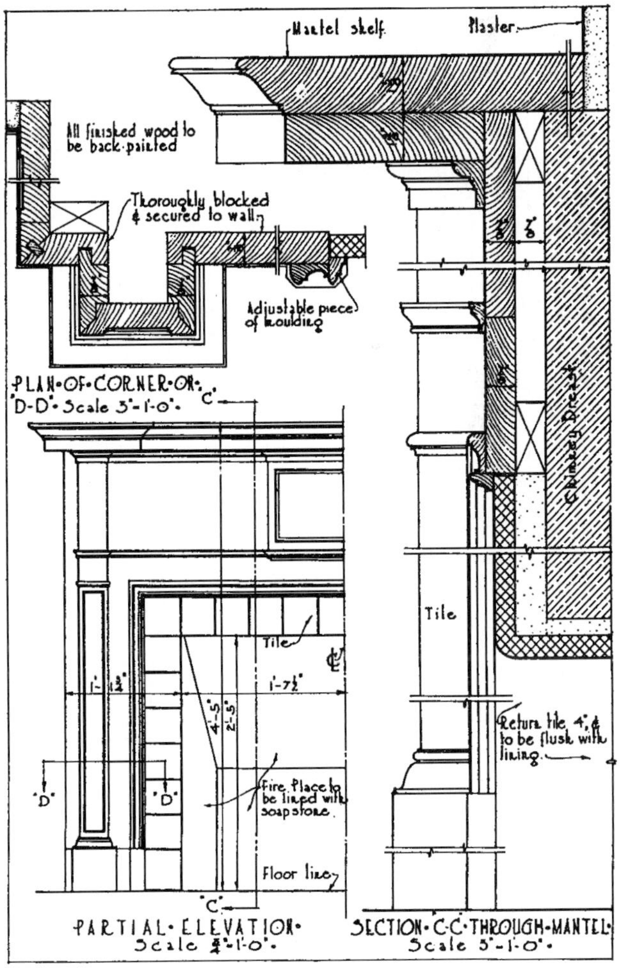
Mantel shelf
Plaster
All finished wood to be back-painted
Thoroughly blocked & secured to wall
Adjustable piece of moulding
PLAN OF CORNER ON D-D Scale 3"-1'-0"
Tile
Fire Place to be lined with soap stone
Return tile 4" & to be flush with lining
Floor line
Chimney Breast
PARTIAL ELEVATION
Scale ¾"-1'-0"
SECTION C-C THROUGH MANTEL
Scale 3"-1'-0"

FIREPLACES

Wood Mantels

Fig. 6 These wood mantels are readily available

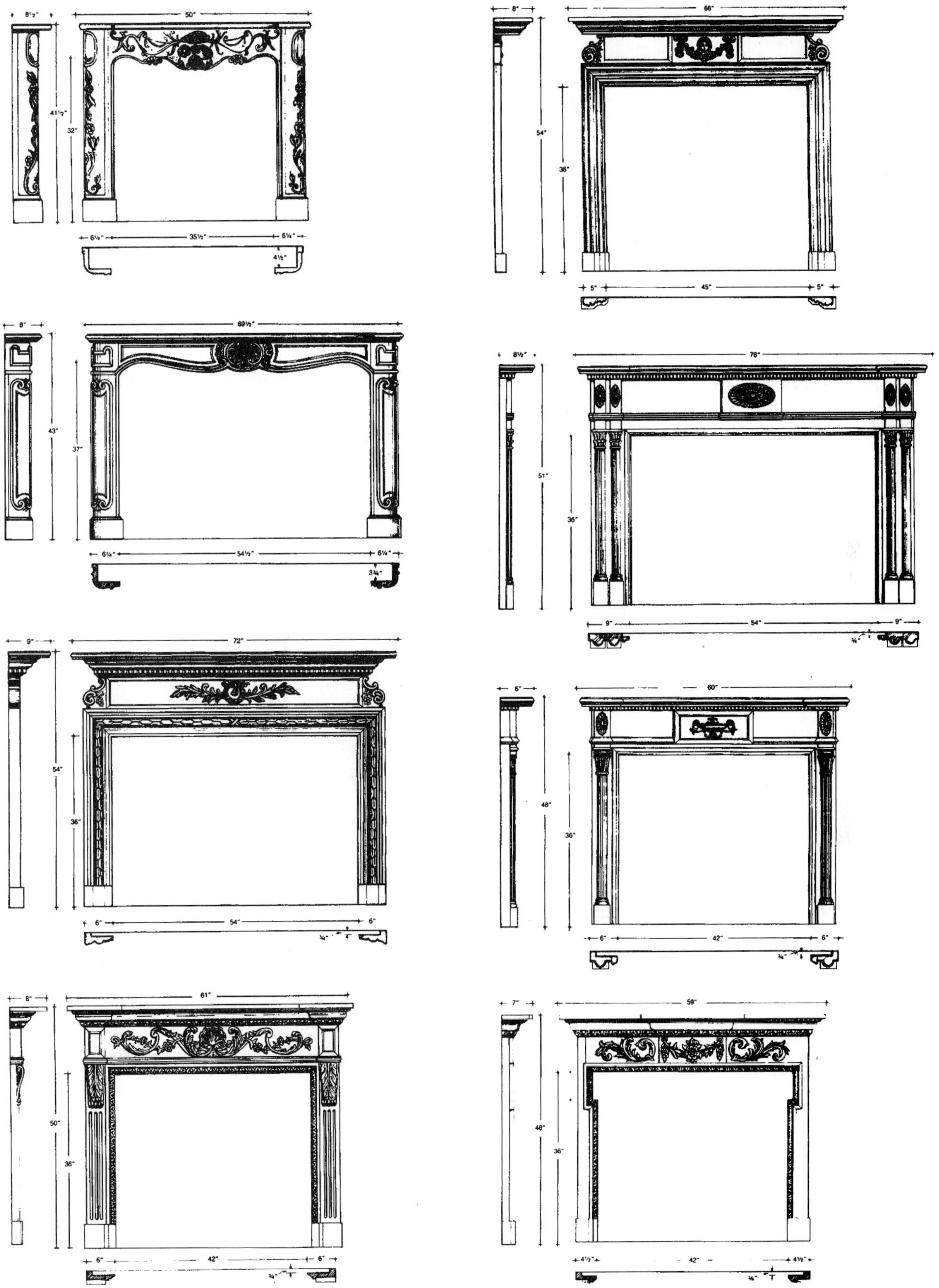

Fig. 6 *(Continued)*

FIREPLACES
Wood Mantels

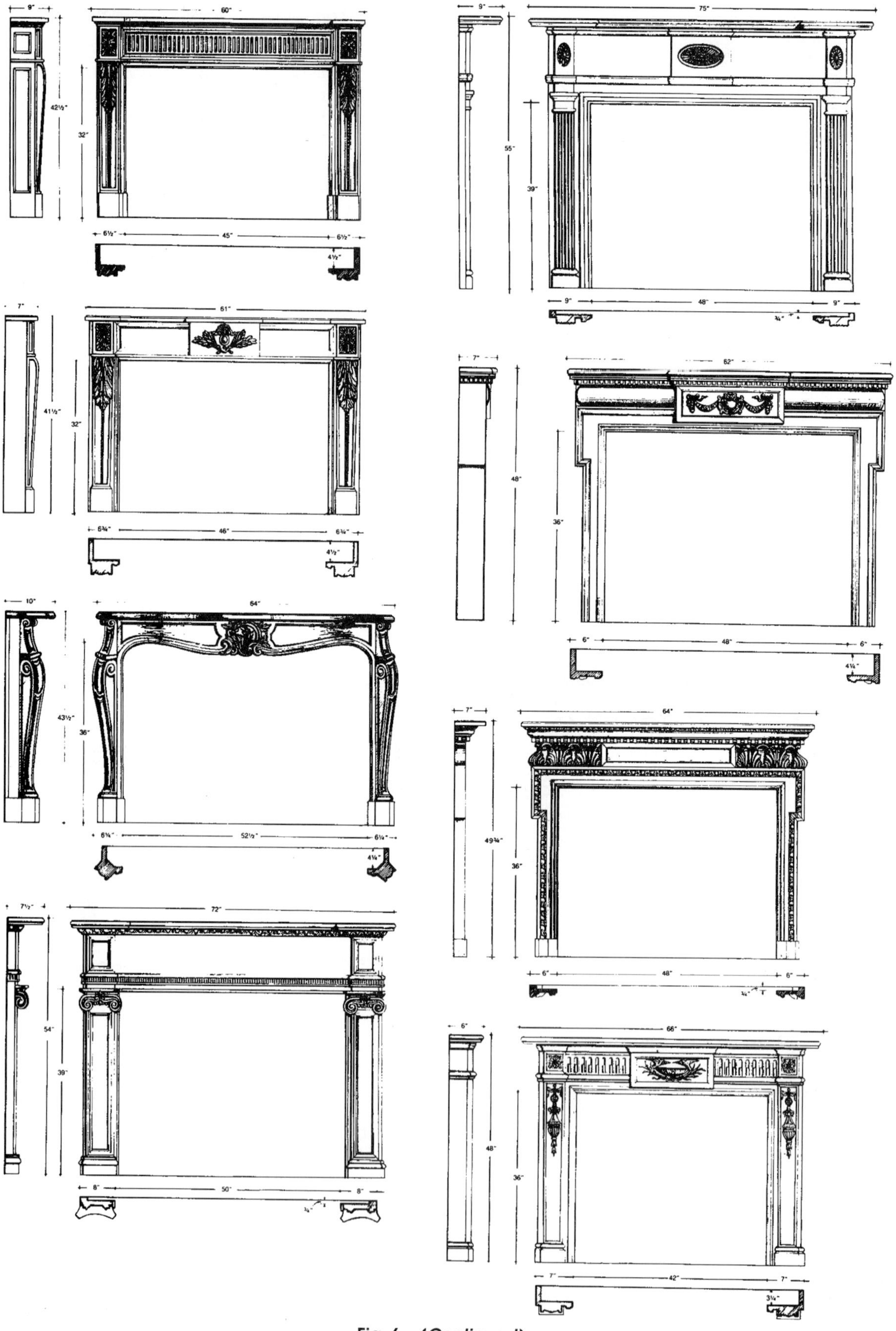

Fig. 6 ***(Continued)***

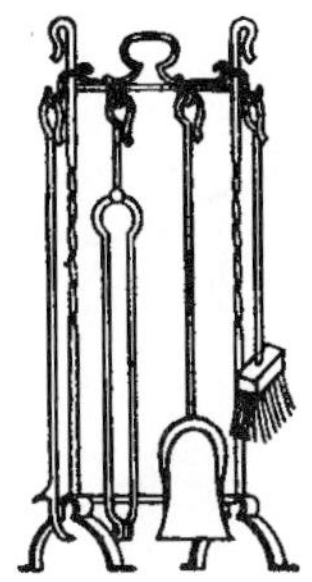

Fire set of wrought metal, stand and four tools.

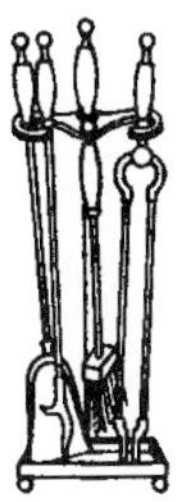

Fire set, polished brass, stand and four tools.

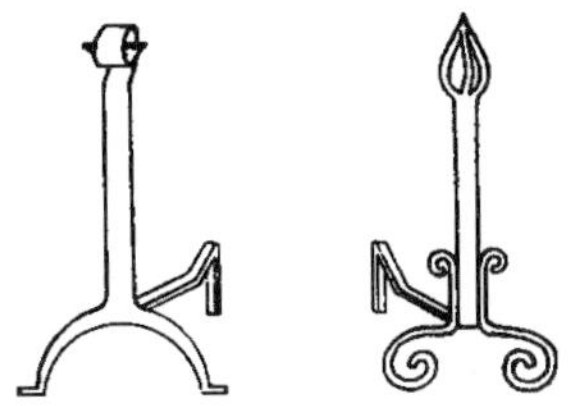

Andirons of wrought metal, smooth or hammered black finish.

Andirons of wrought and cast metal, smooth or hammered black, or polished brass finish.

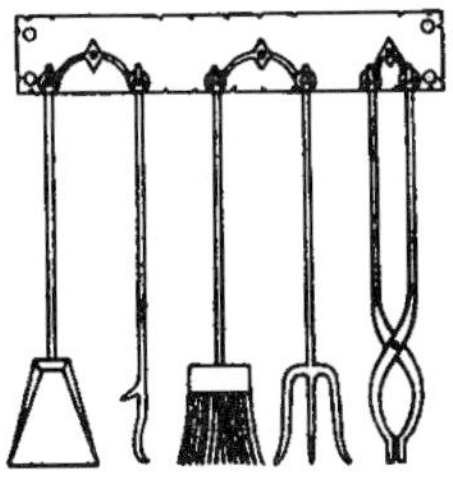

Fire set, wrought metal, back plate with jamb hooks, five tools.

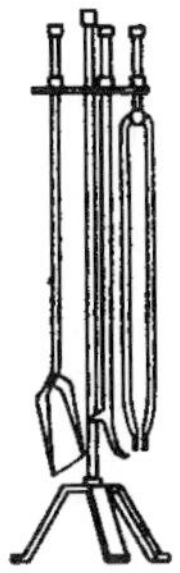

Fire set, wrought metal stand and three tools.

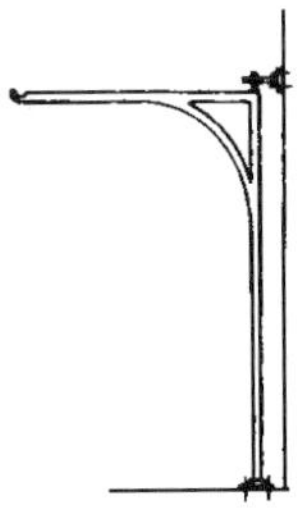

Crane, pivoted, of wrought metal.

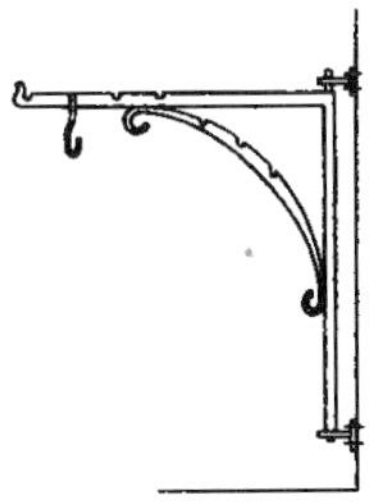

Crane, pivoted, of wrought metal, movable hook.

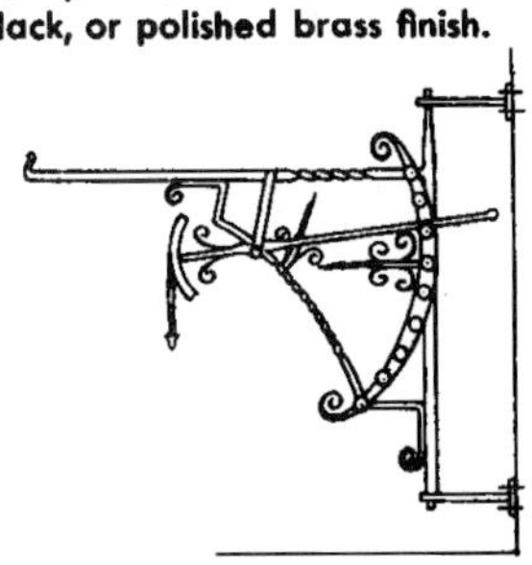

Crane, pivoted, of wrought metal, ornamental adjustable hook.

SCALE 1/2" = 1'-0"

Footman, wrought metal.

Trivet, wrought metal.

SCALE 3/4" = 1'-0"

Fire lighter, kerosene torch, can and drip pan, wrought metal.

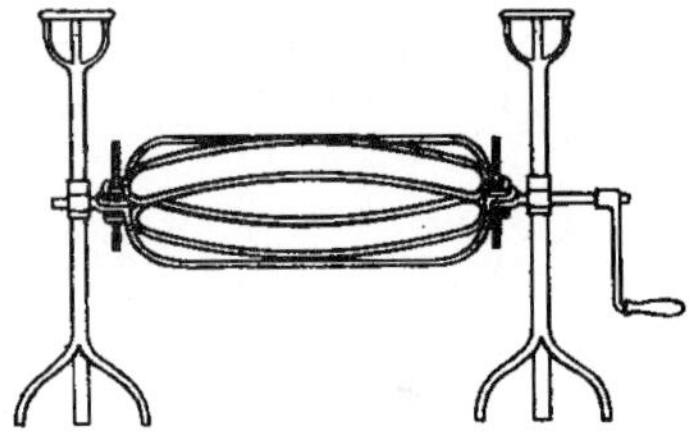

Spit with removable clamps. Hand turning crank may be replaced by pulley and operated by weight or spring clock mechanism.

SCALE 1/2" = 1'-0"

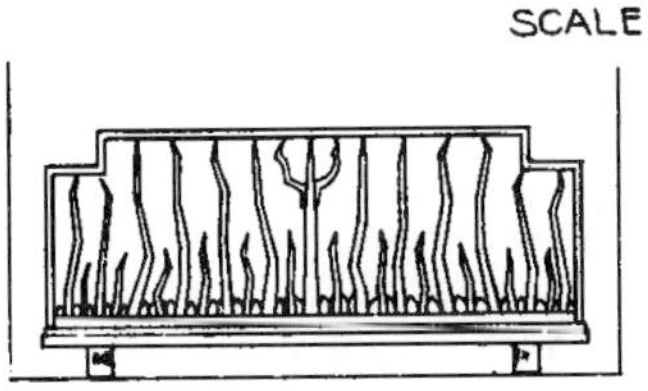

Log grate, wrought metal

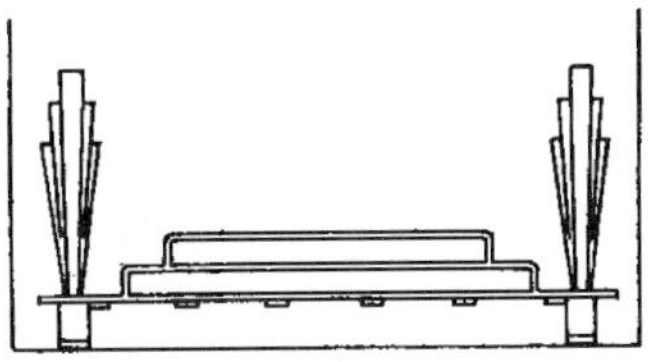

Log grate, wrought metal

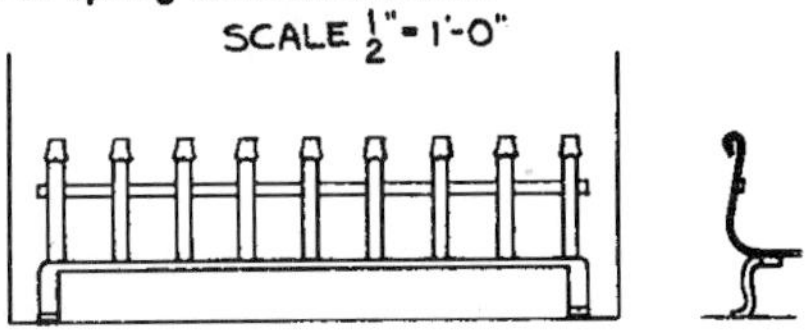

Log grate, wrought metal

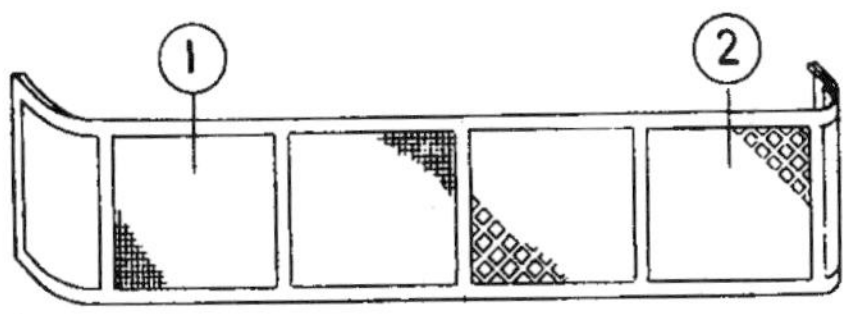

Fender with wire mesh screen. **Fender with stamped grille.**

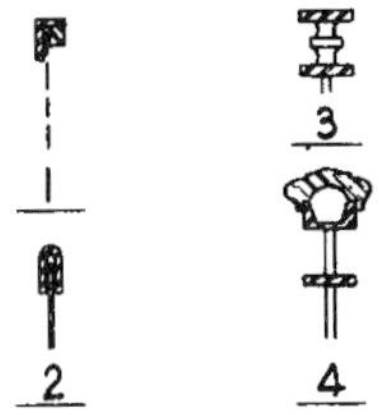

SCALE 1/2" = 1'-0"

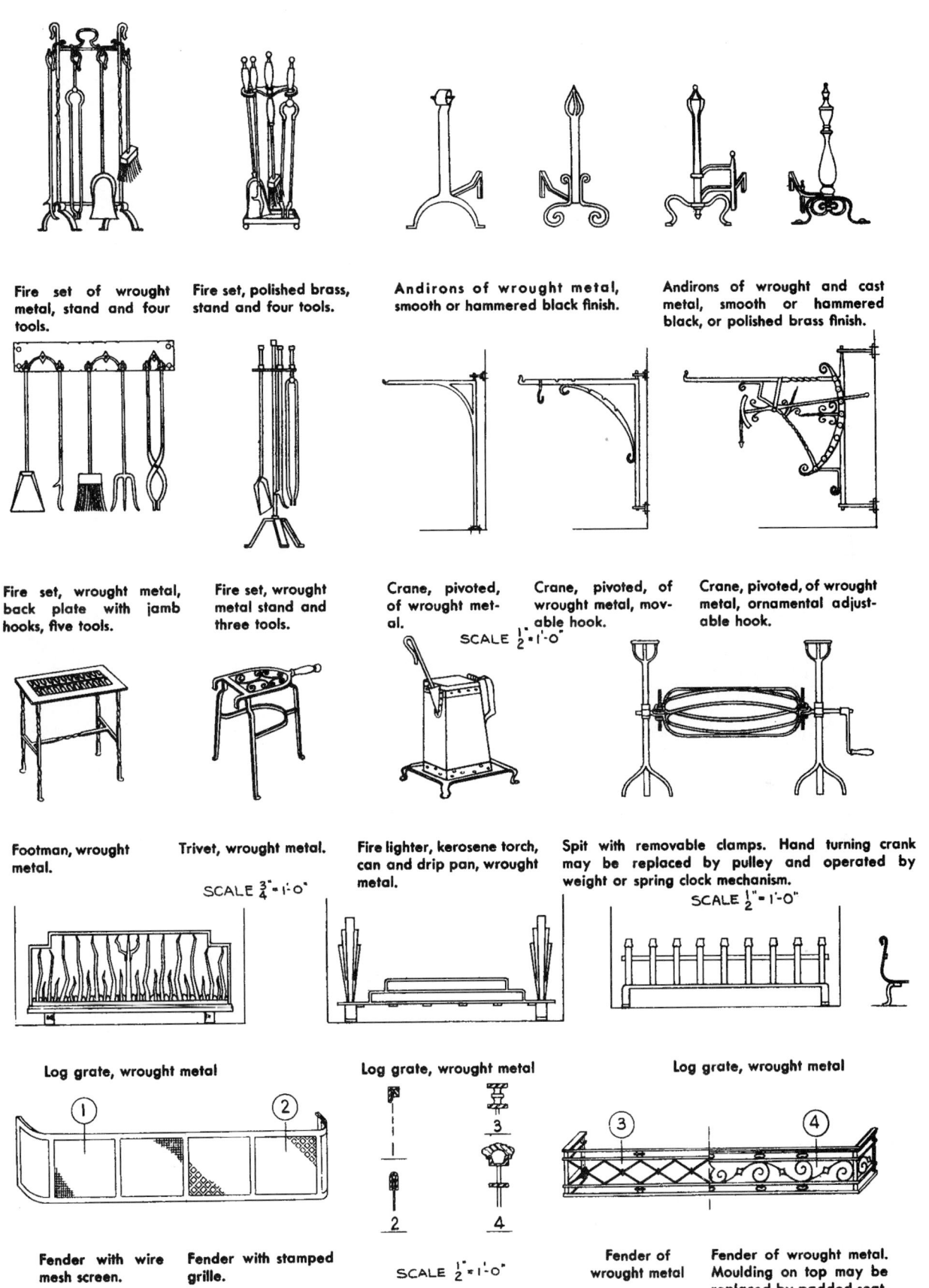

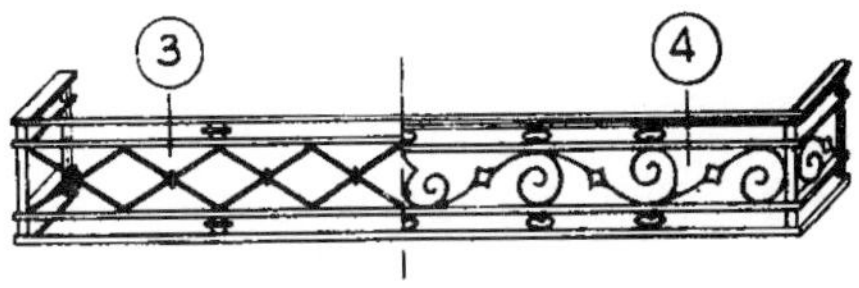

Fender of wrought metal

Fender of wrought metal. Moulding on top may be replaced by padded seat.

Fig. 7 Fireplaces offer opportunities for the use and display of a variety of metal items of decorative value. These may be selected or designed to match other material in the room. Metals used for wrought and cast fireplace products are usually cast iron, steel in a dark hammered finish, or polished brass.

LIGHTING

Planning Data: Minimum Shade Heights

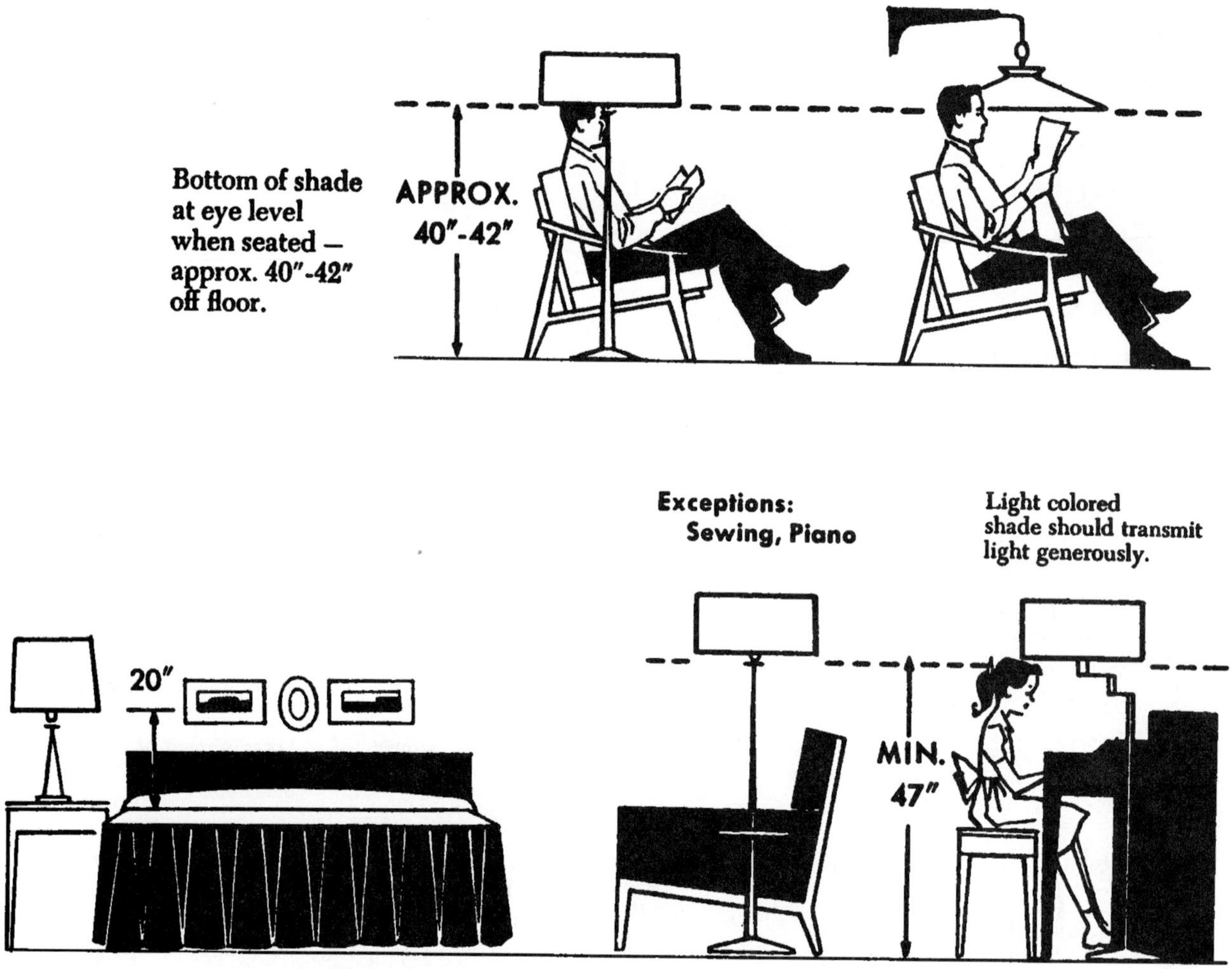
Bottom of shade at eye level when seated — approx. 40"-42" off floor.
APPROX. 40"-42"
Exceptions: Sewing, Piano
Light colored shade should transmit light generously.
20"
MIN. 47"

Fig. 1 Measuring when the lamp is at the side—when sitting, lying down, or playing the piano

When bottom of shade is above eye level, lamp stem should be about 10" behind shoulder — near rear corner of chair
MIN. 47"

Fig. 2 Measuring when the lamp is behind—when sitting

LIGHTING

Although lighting design is a discipline in and of itself, the interior designer and architect must be knowledgeable about the interface between lighting elements and the interior architecture. This section, therefore, focuses primarily on the detailing of this interface. Details from actual contract drawings, prepared by various interior design and architectural firms, are provided for the reader's reference. Among the details are those for valance and cove lighting and for the lighting of stairs, columns, and skylights. This section also provides some basic planning data including illuminance values for residences, offices, stores, and industrial spaces.

Recommended Minimum Shade Dimensions

LAMP TYPE	Top Dia. "	Depth "	Bottom Dia. "
Sr. Floor	10	10	18
Swing Type	10	10	16
Jr. Floor — Swing Type	10	9	16
Diffuser Type	14	6	16
Bridge	8	8	13
End Table	8	10	16
Diffuser Type	14	6	16
Sr. Table	14	13	16
Wall Lamp	8	8	13
Diffuser Type	4	6	14
Study Type — pair	6	7	10
Make-Up — pair	7	7	9-10
Double Dresser — pair	8	8	12-14

Base Height (measure from table to shade bottom)
+ Table Height
= Seated Eye Height (approx. 40"-42" off floor)

FLOOR LAMPS

Measure from floor to bottom of shade.

SHADES

Measure top and bottom diameters, and depth vertically through center.

Minimum 15" to shade bottom. Shade fairly dense, or opaque, in a light but not strong color

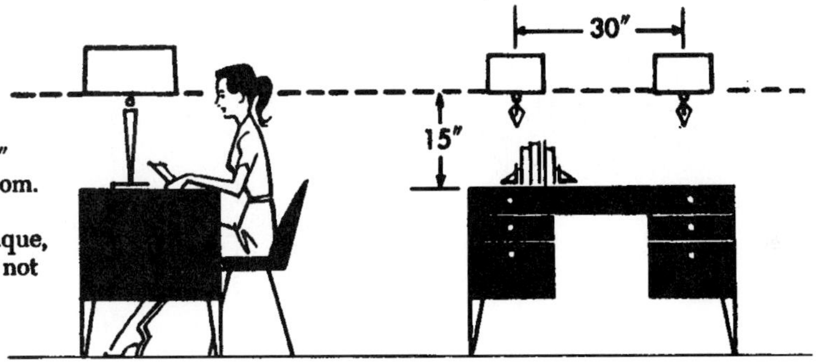

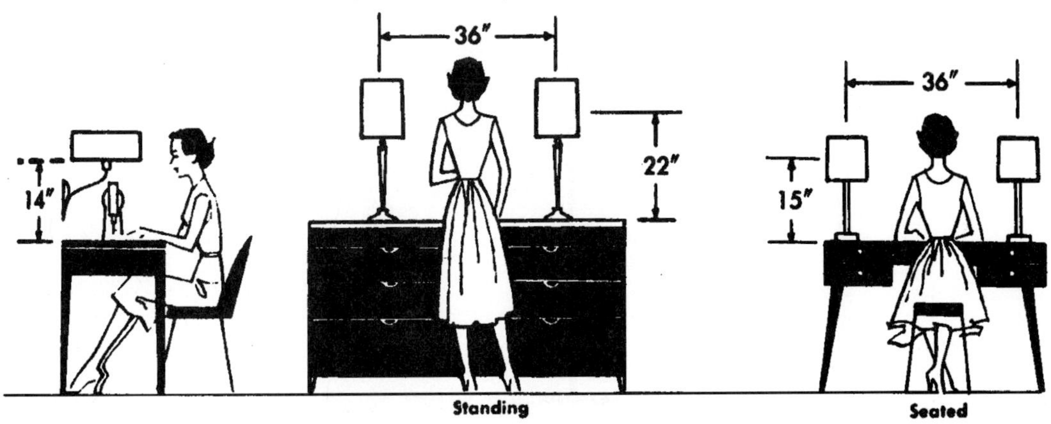

Fig. 3 Measuring when the lamp is in front—when studying, sewing, or grooming oneself

LIGHTING

Floor Lamps

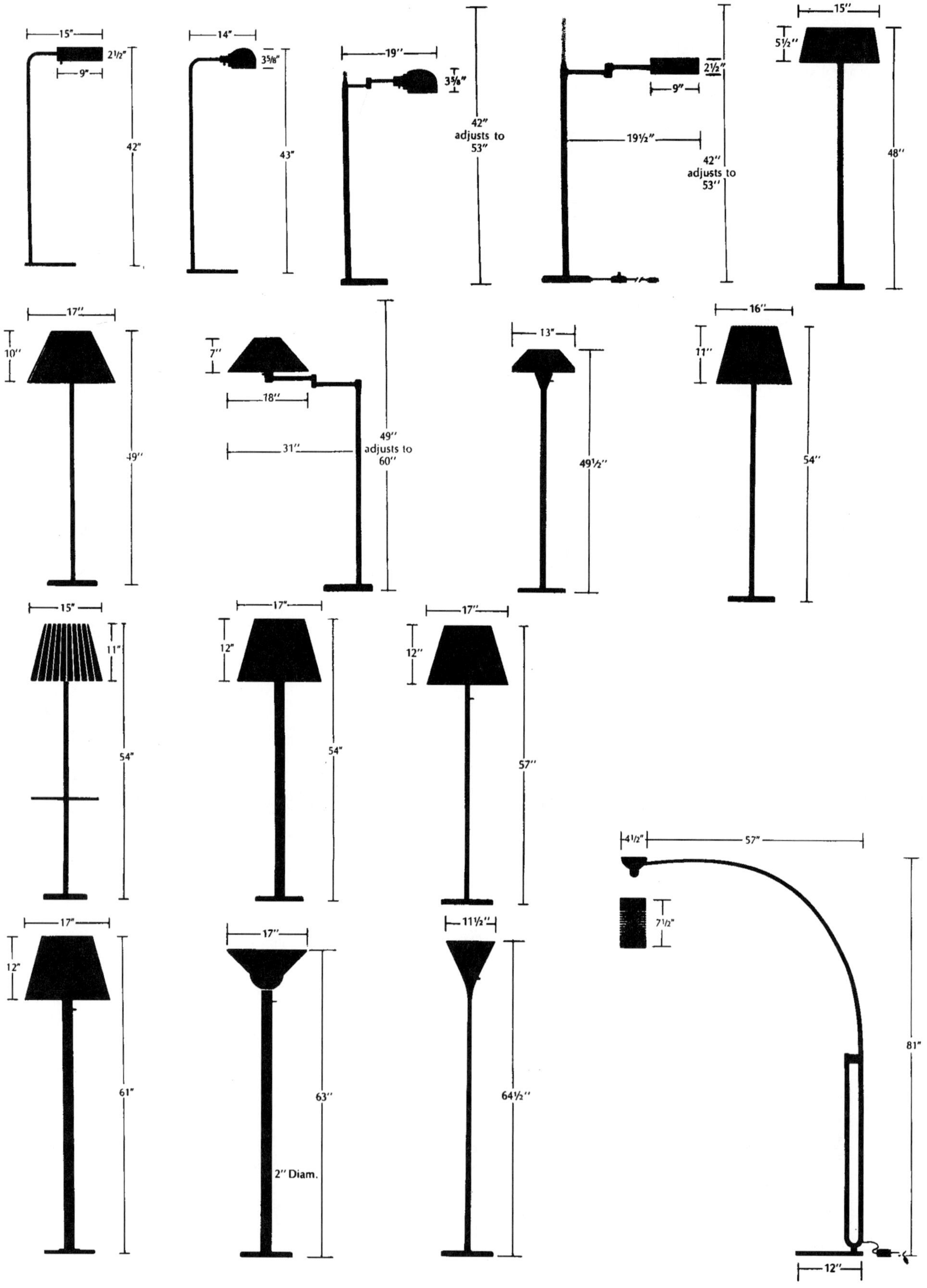

LIGHTING
Table Lamps

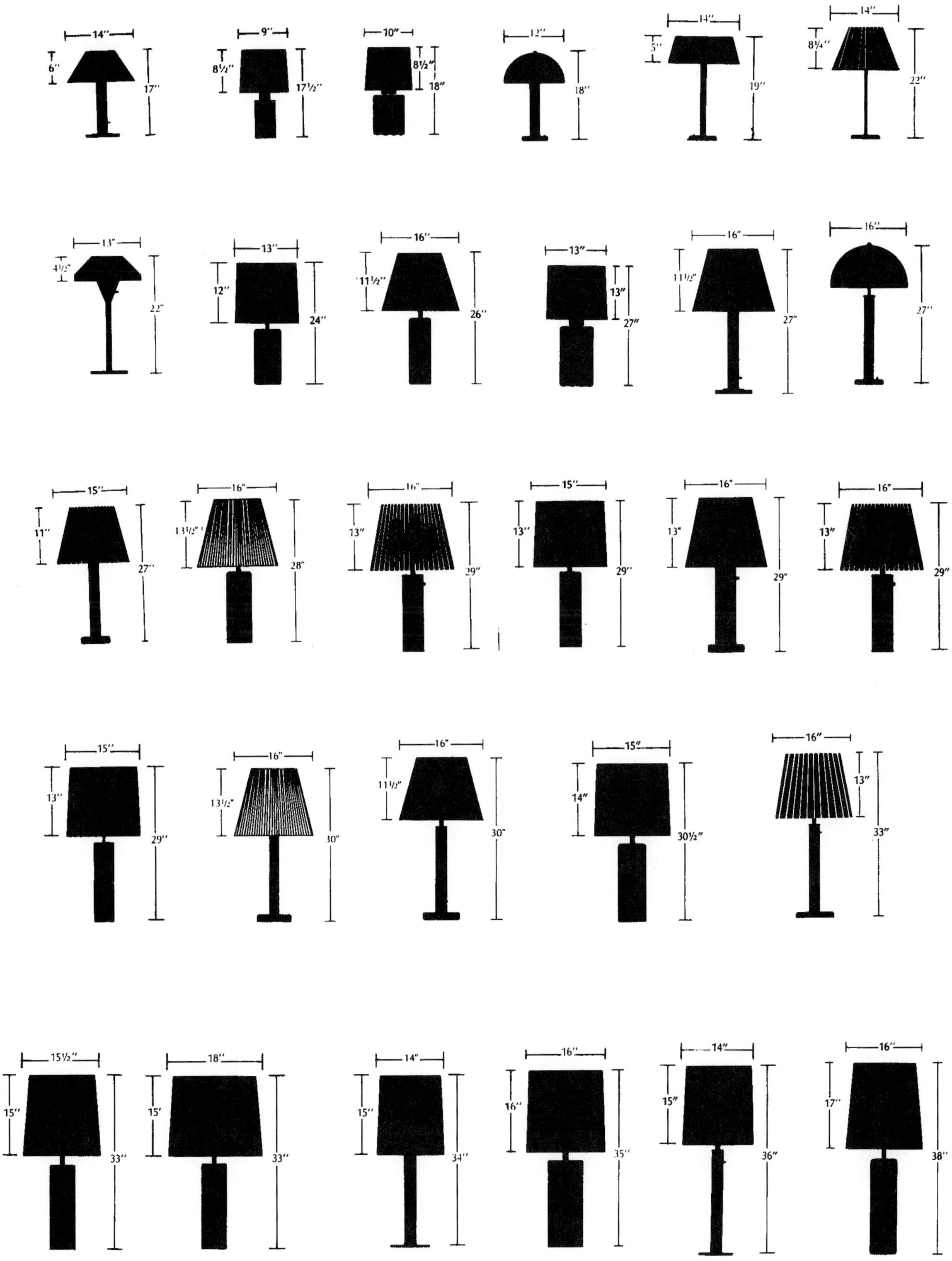

LIGHTING
Desk Lamps

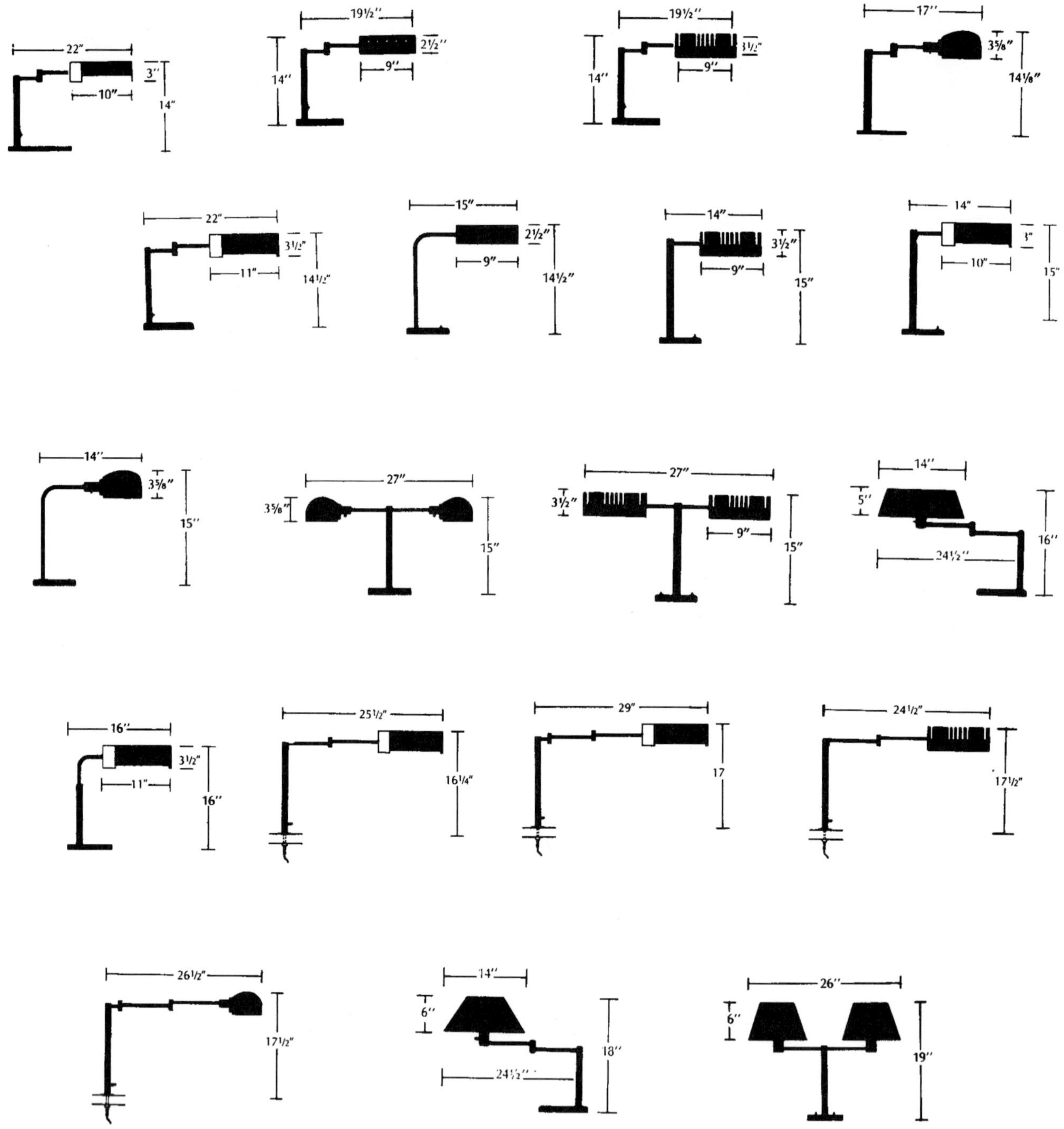

LIGHTING
Wall-Mounted Task Lamps

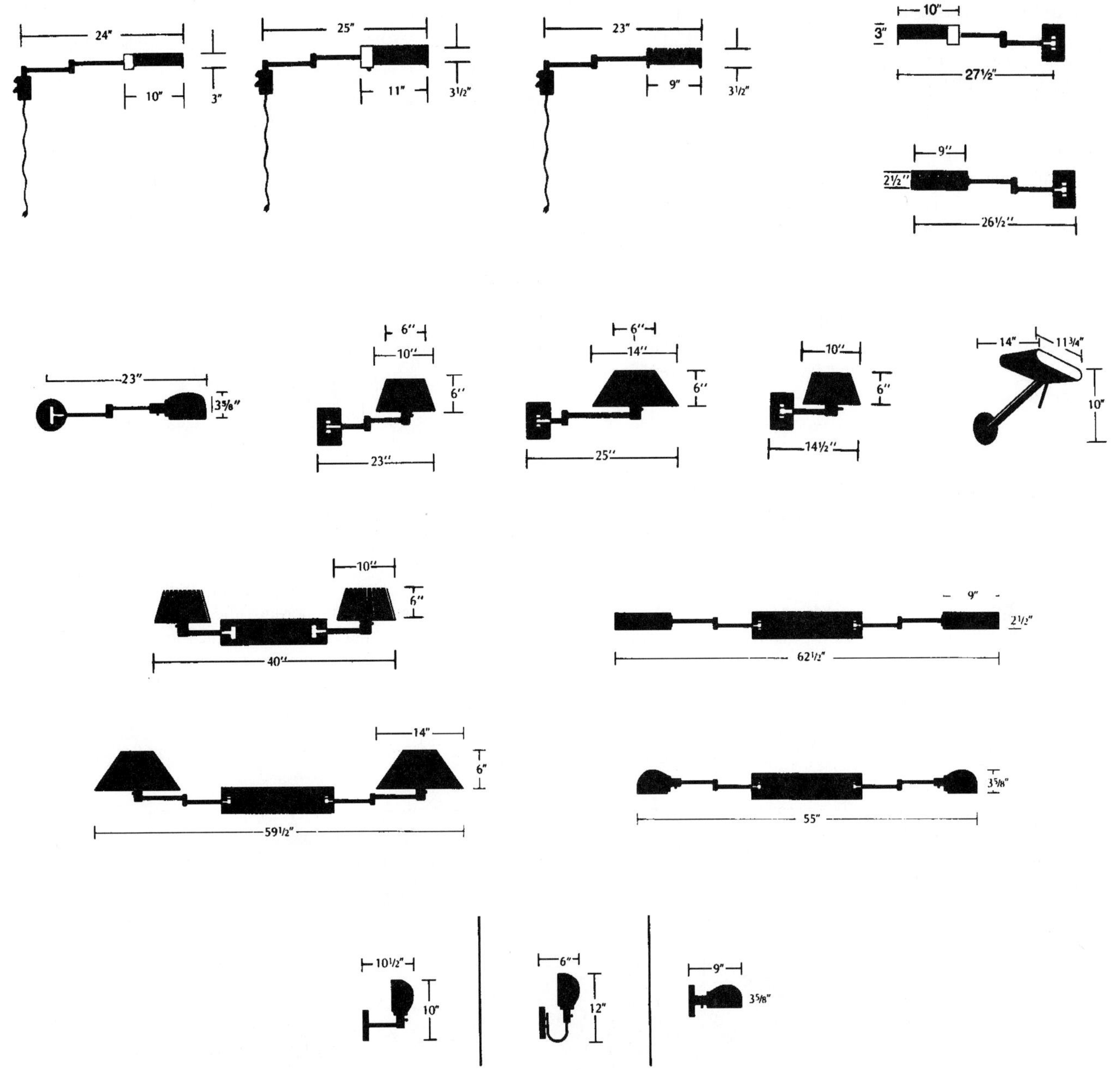

LIGHTING
Planning Data: Dining Spaces

What to Light and How to Light It

The lighting must make the dining room beautiful and functional for a variety of uses. It should make people, the table setting, food, and prized possessions look their best, as well as providing for other activities at the table or around the room. The plan, used to exemplify some typical lighting for dining, has a formal layout, with a table, sideboard, china cabinet, painting, and a pair of small tables on either side of a doorway leading to a patio. Two lighting schemes are shown to illustrate different approaches.

Focal Point

For the dining table, the main consideration is to enhance the color and texture of the food and the complexions and apparel of the diners, creating a festive mood by highlighting the table setting (*suggested illuminance 10–20 fc*).

General Lighting

This serves the need for flexible use of the room: buffet-dinner, cocktail party, cleanup (*suggested illuminance 5–10 fc*).

Accent Lighting

Accent lighting brings featured objects or special areas to light: the painting, the sideboard, the flower arrangements (*suggested illuminance on the table 25–50 fc*).

Controls

Use lighting controls to match the lighting to the activity: a dinner party, cleanup, breakfast the morning after. Use one dimmer for the overtable lighting and put other lights in the room on separate channels. A multiscene push-button control is particularly useful.

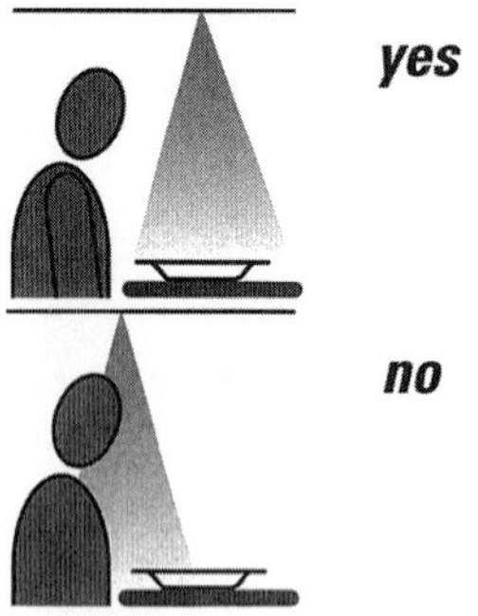

Accent lighting over the table must be kept well within the perimeter of the table. Do not place downlights over the chairs, as the beams from above will cast unpleasant shadows on people's faces and the heat can be uncomfortable

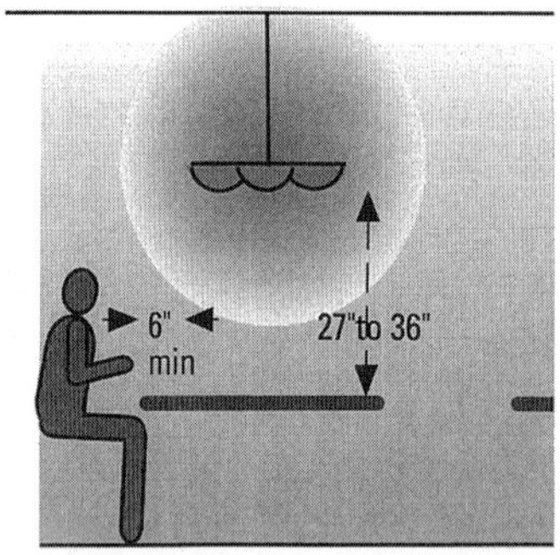

Chandeliers should be proportioned to both the table and the room; a diameter of 24 to 30 in will suit typical spaces. The diameter should not be larger than the width of the table, less 12 in or people may hit it when rising from the table

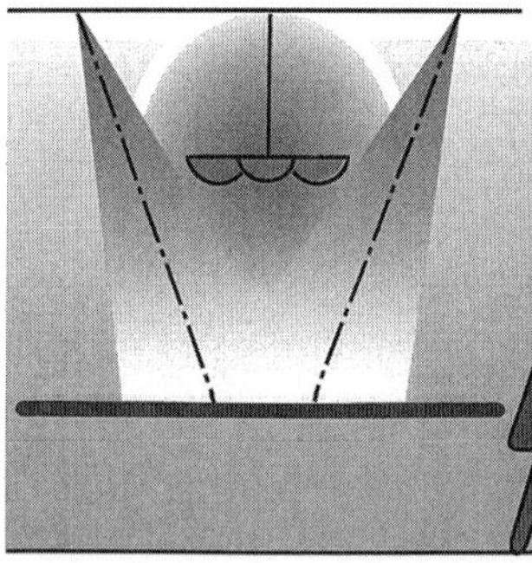

When the chandelier has no central downlight, the table setting and centerpiece can be enhanced by accent lighting using recessed adjustable fixtures with narrow- to medium-spread beams, spaced and angled to avoid casting shadows. Reflections from glass-top tables, however, must be considered when placing and adjusting the fixtures

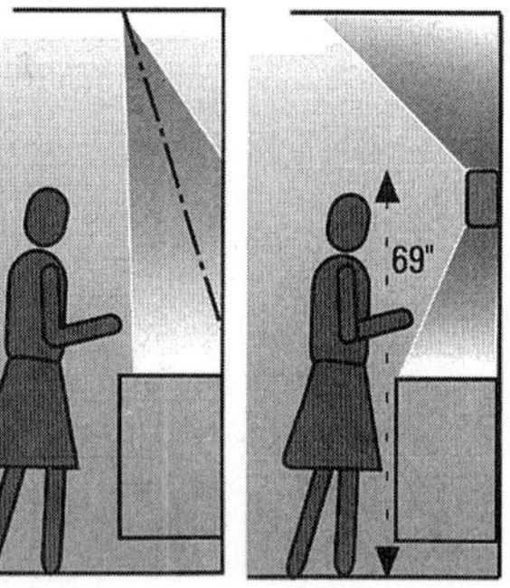

At the sideboard, carving and serving tasks should be provided with plentiful shadow-free lighting, from the ceiling or the wall (*suggested illuminance 30–50 f.c.*)

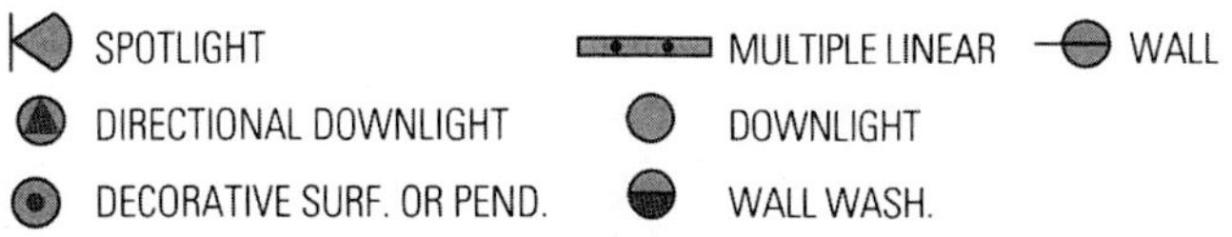

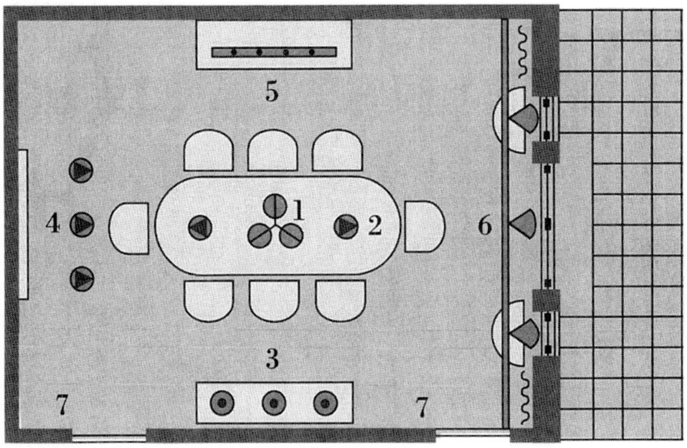

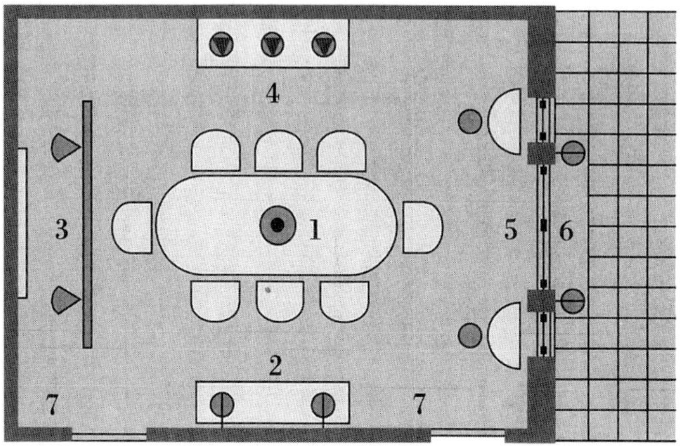

Lighting Scheme 1

1. Chandelier over the table provides general lighting and serves as a dramatic focal point of the room.
2. Recessed adjustable fixtures highlight the table setting.
3. Pendant low-voltage units provide decorative task lighting for carving or serving at the sideboard.
4. Recessed adjustable units bring light to the painting.
5. Undershelf track lighting shows off the china cabinet's contents.
6. Track-mounted units, aimed downward, wash the draperies and add soft ambient lighting to the room.
7. Lighting controls create the desired mood and atmosphere.

Location, Fixture, Lamp Characteristics

		Control channel
1. Granada chandelier	2-60W A19 and 3-60W Cand	1
2. Lytecaster® Adjust. Accent	20W MR16-EXZ 27°	2
3. Style Jacks® pendant	35W Bi-Pin 12V T4 Halogen	3
4. Lytecaster Mini-Swivel with Beam Elongator	35W MR16-FRA 20°	4
5. Lytetrim® with Basic Light	4-20W Krypton	4
6. Lytespan® Radius track with Par-Tech® aimed straight down	50W PAR20 WFL	5
7. MultiSet™ Control		

Lighting Scheme 2

1. Pendant indirect/direct lighting provides generous ambient lighting plus dramatic accent lighting of table.
2. Wall brackets highlight the sideboard and add visual intrigue.
3. Track lighting illuminates featured painting.
4. Recessed accent lighting adds appeal to display.
5. Recessed downlighting brings floral arrangements to life.
6. Wall brackets, mounted outside, fill the patio with light and carry the eye through the glass doors.
7. Lighting controls set the lighting for the scene.

Location, Fixture, Lamp Characteristics

		Control channel
1. Series 2000 chandelier	4-60W A19; 40W KX2000	1
	55W PAR16	2
2. Wall Sculpture	60W KX2000	3
3. Lytespan® Radius Track with Preview Flood	75W T4 Halogen	4
4. Lytecaster Mini-Swivel	20W MR16 BAB 40°	4
5. Lytecaster Aperture Cone	50W PAR20 NFL	4
6. Arco Oval Wall Bracket	75W A19	5
7. MultiSet™ Control		

LIGHTING

Planning Data: Living Rooms

What to Light and How to Light It

Most living rooms today serve many different functions. Whatever the activity, the room should be comfortable and beautiful, and the lighting should be flexible enough to provide for the range of tasks, situations, and desired aesthetic effects. The living room shown in the plan is intended to show some typical lighting applications. It has a window wall, a vaulted ceiling, a stone wall with fireplace and a niche for art objects (or TV), a wall of paintings, an audio/bookshelf section, and a bar. The piano, game table, and lounge seating complete the furnishings. Two lighting schemes are shown to illustrate possibilities.

Focal Point

The fireplace wall is the focal point. The main objectives are highlighting the texture and colors of the stonework and of the hood over the hearth and enhancing the beauty of the art objects—a small sculpture perhaps—in the niche (*suggested illuminance on wall 10–20 fc*).

General Lighting

This provides for ease of moving about in the room and serves to bring the various sections of the room together. General lighting is supplied in most positions of the room by reflections of light directed to the walls and furnishings (*suggested illuminance 5–10 fc*).

Task Lighting

This is needed to supply extra lighting for seeing small detail, such as music at the piano, the game table, and the titles of books and recordings, and for reading at the lounge chairs and sofa (*suggested illuminances 20–50 fc*).

Controls

Permit the lighting to be varied according to the occasion—quiet conversation, a party, reading, listening to recordings, singing around the piano, a game of cards.

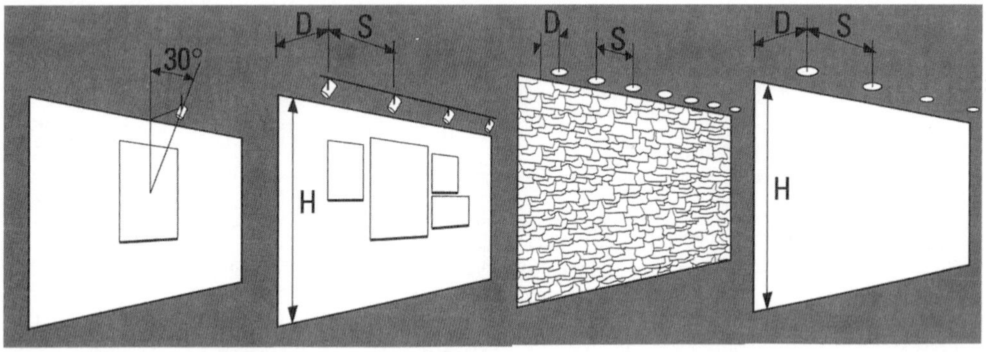

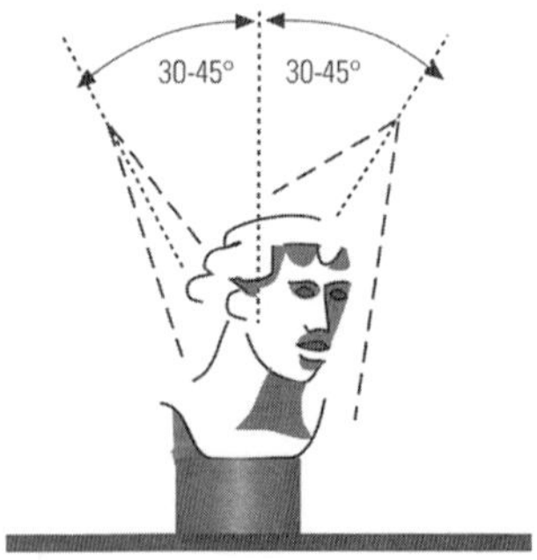

When lighting a small to medium-size picture, have the lighting reach the picture at an angle of about 30° from the vertical. See the table below for suggested spacing from the wall. Lighting placed much farther from the wall may cause disturbing reflections on the picture; lighting placed much closer may cause unwanted shadows cast by the frame

Ceiling height	*Distance from wall*
8 ft	2 ft
9 ft	3 ft
10 ft	4 ft

A group of pictures is best lighted by lighting the surface as a whole rather than by lighting the pictures individually. Use the same spacing from the wall as for a single picture and, for even illumination, make the space between units not more than twice that from the wall. Lighting from multiple units can be smoothed using a spread lens or beam elongator. These guidelines can also be used for lighting a very large picture

The texture of a surface can be raised by placing the fixtures close to the surface, so that the lighting strikes it at a grazing angle. If there are unwanted irregularities in the wall, place the fixtures well away from the wall

In wall washing the surface is illuminated smoothly and evenly from top to bottom. Wall washing makes spaces seem larger and is useful for achieving a comfortable level of balanced brightness

Three-dimensional objects, such as sculptures, often look best lighted from one side, in front and above, with a wide beam, and from the other side, in front and above, with a narrower beam. Glass objects, such as vases, however, often look best when seen resting on a translucent shelf or in front of a translucent wall

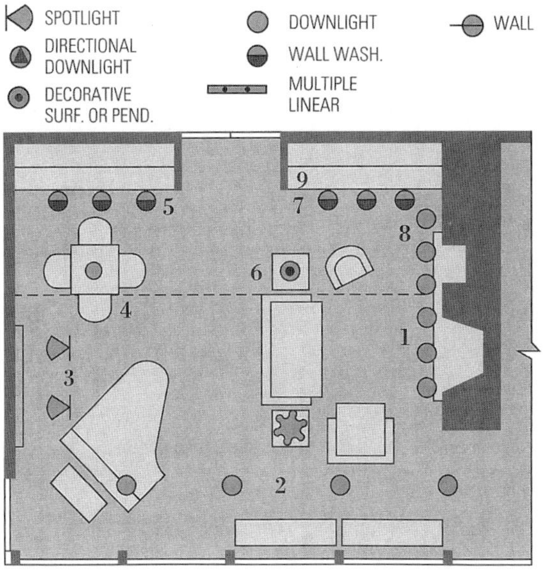

Lighting Scheme 1

1. Downlights, placed close to wall, enrich the texture of the stone.
2. Downlights provide general lighting and task lighting at the piano.
3. Spotlights, on individual outlets, illuminate the painting.
4. Concentrated beam from small aperture downlight illuminates game table.
5. The bar and cabinet above are illuminated by wall washers.
6. Reading light is provided by small pendant and table lamp.
7. Wall washers illuminate books, recordings, and audio equipment.
8. Matching downlights provide grazing light to stone wall and niche.
9. Lighting controls set the lighting for the activity.

Location, Fixture, Lamp Characteristics

		Control channel
1. Lytecaster Shallow Slope	50W PAR30 NSP	1
2. Same as above but with	75W PAR30 FL	2
3. Par-Tech Bezel on Monopoint	75W PAR30 NFL	3
4. Lytecaster Pinhole	35W MR16 FMW 40°	4
5. Lytecaster Step Baffle Wall Washer	60W A19	5
6. Style Jacks	35W Bi-Pin 12V T4 Halogen	4
7. Lytecaster Step Baffle Wall Washer	60W A19	5
8. Lytecaster Step Baffle	50W PAR30 FL	1
9. MultiSet Control		

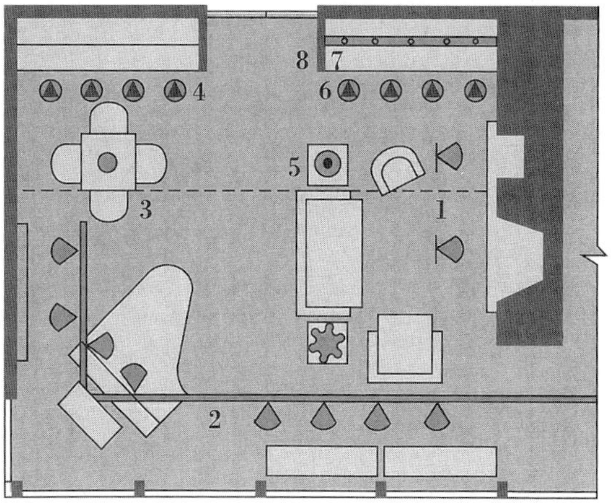

Lighting Scheme 2

1. Spotlights on individual outlets accent hood and objects in niche.
2. Track-mounted floods highlight the credenza; spots provide task light at piano, while floods illuminate large painting.
3. Decorative downlight illuminates the game table with style.
4. Recessed adjustable units illuminate the glass shelves above the bar.
5. A table lamp and a pendant provide task lighting for reading.
6. Recessed adjustable units light the bookshelves and audio equipment.
7. Undercabinet track lighting provides task lighting on the counter.
8. Lighting controls suit the lighting to the scene.

Location, Fixture, Lamp Characteristics

		Control channel
1. Focal Jack Geostar	50W MR16 EXZ 27°	1
2. Lytespan Advent 2-circuit track		
1st circuit: Par-Tech Bezel over piano	60W PAR16 NSP	2
2nd circuit: as above	60W PAR16 NFL	3
3. Lytegem® Pendant Disk	50W PAR30 FL	4
4. Lytecaster Mini Swivel	20W MR16 BAB 40°	4
5. Style Jacks	35W Bi-Pin 12V T4 Halogen	5
6. Lytecaster Mini Swivel	20W MR16 BAB 40°	4
7. Lytetrim with Basic Light	20W Krypton at 12-in centers	4
8. MultiSet Control		

LIGHTING
Planning Data: Kitchen Spaces

What to Light and How to Light It

The kitchen is fundamentally a work area for food preparation and cleanup, but it is often used for other activities: dining, homework, games, entertaining. It should be functional, comfortable, and beautiful; therefore, the lighting scheme should provide a combination of general, task, and accent lighting, controlled to suit the activity.

General Lighting

General lighting is needed to see into cabinets and drawers and for ease of moving about. It is best provided by surface-mounted fluorescent lighting or by an array of downlights. Fluorescent produces the most light for the lowest cost. Downlights are very flexible, as they can be arranged to provide even illumination throughout the kitchen, even if it has an irregular shape (*suggested illuminance 10–20 fc*).

Task Lighting

Task lighting is needed at the counter, the sink, and the stove. These areas are often in shadow, whether created by the person working or the cabinet above; therefore, the lighting should come from in front of the person. It must also be shielded from the view of others who may be seated nearby. Task lighting is also often required for reading at the kitchen table or dining counter; a pendant fixture not only can do the job, but adds visual appeal (*suggested illuminance 20–100 fc*).

Accent Lighting

Accent lighting of special objects, such as cookware, a noteboard, or a painting, contributes to making the kitchen the feature place it has become in so many homes (*suggested illuminance: 20–50 fc*).

Lighting Controls

Lighting controls allow one to set the lighting for the activity: food preparation, a late snack, or breakfast.

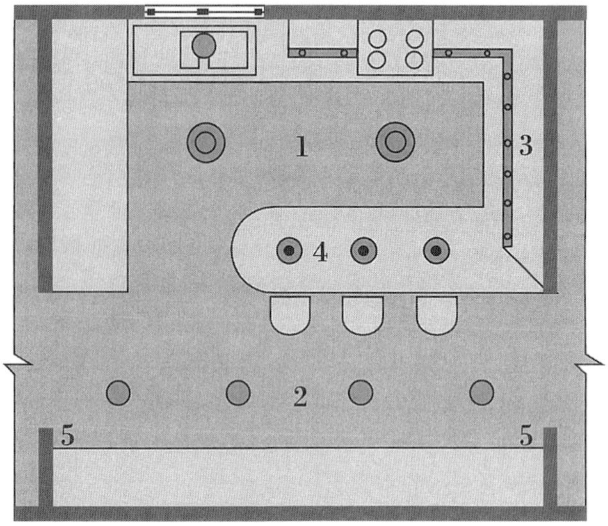

Kitchen 1

1. General lighting is from two decorative surface-mounted fluorescent and
2. an array of decorative recessed downlights, each providing generous lighting, as well as task lighting over the sink.
3. Shielded undercabinet track turns the corner to follow the countertop, providing the correct task lighting.
4. A group of small, glowing pendants over the dining counter provides light for reading and a visual focal point.
5. MultiSet controls, master and remote, enable one to set the lighting scene at either doorway.

Location, Fixture, Lamp Characteristics

		Control channel
1. Spill Ring	2-27W TT Compact Fluor	1
2. Lytecaster Glass Collar	75W MB19 Halogen	1
3. Lytetrim®/Basic Krypton	20W KX2000	2
4. Style Jack	35W Bi-Pin 12V T4 Halogen	
5. MultiSet Controls		

At the sink, use a concentrated beam from a downlight directly above

Relying on light from a ceiling fixture in the center of the room puts one's work in shadow

Task lighting is at the front edge of the cabinet. The lighting should be shielded from the view of those seated nearby

What to Light and How to Light It

Today, most homes contain two or more bathrooms: the master bath, children's bath, and guest bath or powder room. While the master bath may be larger and even include space for exercise, the children's bath simpler and more functional, and the guest bath something of a decorative statement, the lighting priority in each should be given to grooming at the mirror.

Lighting at the Mirror

Lighting at the mirror serves for cleaning, makeup, shaving, and dressing. It should be plentiful; evenly distributed over the face, hair, and neck; without shadows; and free from glare. Lighting placed in the center of the ceiling puts the face in shadow and, while useful for general lighting, cannot serve well for grooming (*suggested illuminance 20–50 fc*).

Fluorescent lighting of good color quality is now widely available and can provide high levels of illumination, with less heat and lower operating cost than incandescent. Incandescent and halogen offer greater decorative possibilities and, if well spaced and properly diffused, can be used very effectively.

Other Areas

Other areas in the bathroom that should be considered are the tub, where some people like to read; an enclosed toilet; and an exercise area, where general lighting from recessed or surface-mounted fixtures will serve to illuminate the space and closets (*suggested illuminance 5–10 fc*).

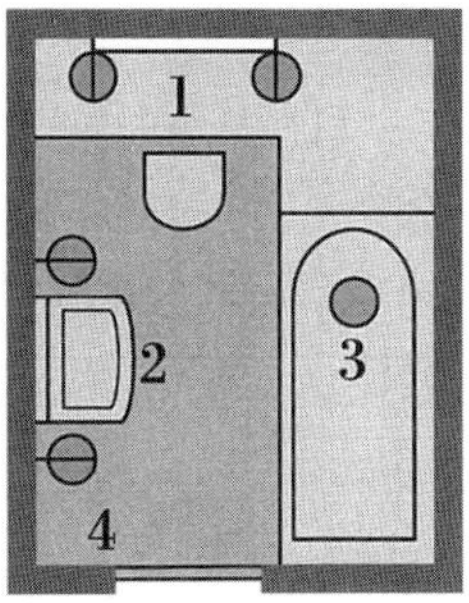

Small Bath

1. **Vanity dressing table has elongated fixtures with formed acrylic diffusers at either side of mirror.**
2. **Lighting at the lavatory mirror matches that of the vanity unit.**
3. **General lighting comes from recessed fixture over the tub, which is enclosed by a gasketed glass diffuser.**
4. **Dimmer control.**

Dimmer Controls

Dimmer controls are very helpful because they provide for attractive low-intensity night lighting, integrate with the decor, and permit persons to adapt the lighting to their individual liking.

Small bath: Location, Fixture, Lamp

		Controls
1. Capriccio	3-50W T4 Halogen Mini-Can	Sunrise 1
2. Capriccio	3-50W T4 Halogen Mini-Can	Switch 2
3. Lytecaster Opal Disk	100W A19	Sunrise 3
4. Sunrise slide dimmer		

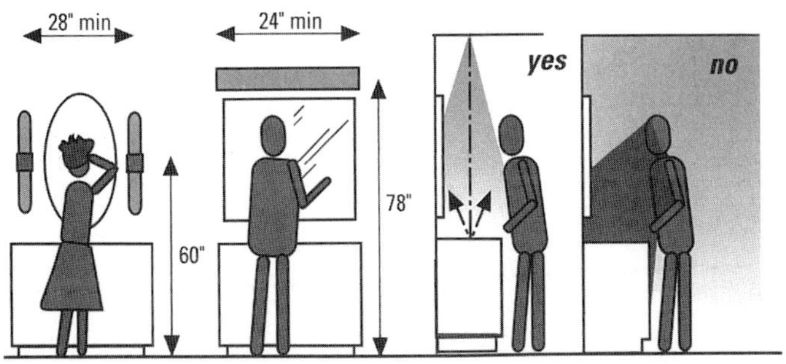

Elongated lighting at the side of the mirror works best. It should be at least 16 in long. Lighting above the mirror should be at least 24 in long to light both sides of the face and avoid shadows under the chin

Recessed downlights have the benefit of being unobtrusive, but will produce shadows under the eyelids, nose, and chin unless placed close to the mirror, spaced well apart and above a light-colored counter top, which can reflect the downlight upward to erase shadows

LIGHTING

Planning Data: Bathroom Spaces

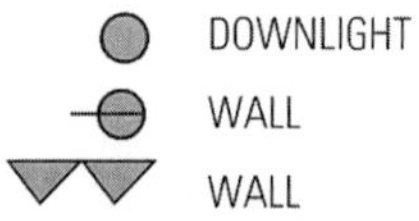

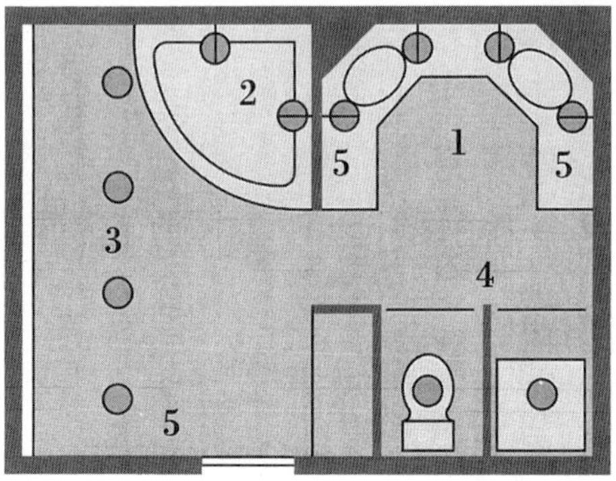

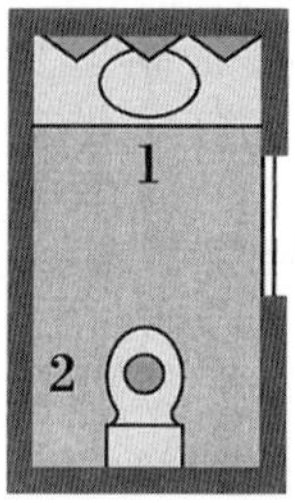

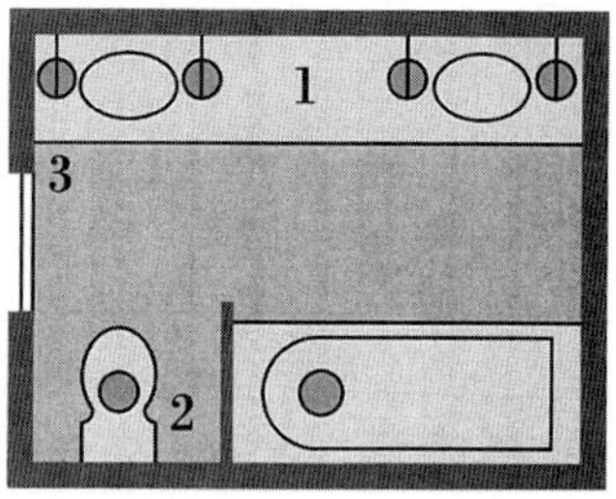

Powder Room

In a small powder room lighting is provided by:

1. A five-lamp fixture placed above the mirror, whose length serves to make the room seem larger. Lighting is softened by the glass diffusers.
2. Lighting of the toilet area from a decorative downlight having a luminous glass aperture.

Master Bath and Gym

1. Light at the mirrors is provided by long, decorative brackets, employing low-wattage lamps.
2. The tub area is brightened by waterproof wall-mounted units.
3. General lighting in the exercise area is from compact fluorescent downlights, shielded by white diffusers (minimal heat contribution, comfortable from all angles).
4. The enclosed toilet and shower each have dedicated lighting from a recessed fixture with gasketed diffusing enclosure.
5. Dimmers at the door and vanity control the lighting to suit individual needs at various times, day or night.

Location, Fixture, Lamp Characteristics

		Controls
1. Mini Bracelet	4-20W KX2000	Sunrise 1, 2
2. Arco, Oval	75W A19	Sunrise 3
3. Lytecaster Opal Dome	2-13W Quad Comp. Fluor.	Switch 3
4. Lytecaster Opal Dome	75W A19	Switch 4
5. Sunrise slide dimmer		

Children's Bath

In a large family home this bath has twin lavatories with:

1. Modular glass-enclosed wall brackets placed on either side of the mirrors.
2. General lighting provided by recessed fixtures shielded by gasketed diffusers.
3. Dimmer control.

Powder Room: Location, Fixture, Lamp

		Controls
1. Bracelet	5-40W A19	Switch 1
2. Lytecaster/Lytegem	60W A19	Switch 1

Children's Bath: Location, Fixture, Lamp

1. Rounder	3-60W A19	Sunrise 1
2. Lytecaster Basic Opalex	75W A19	Sunrise 2
3. Sunrise slide dimmer		

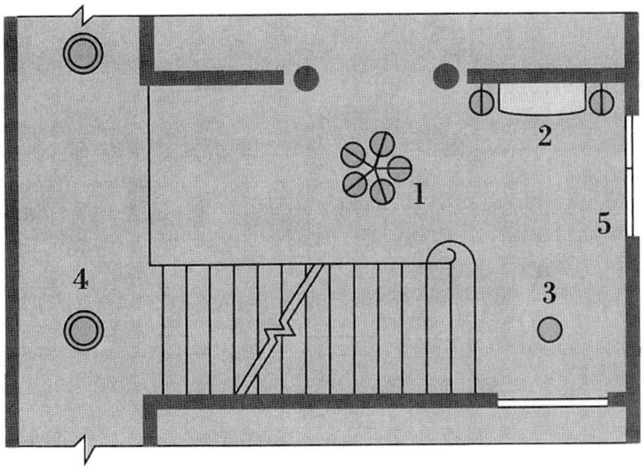

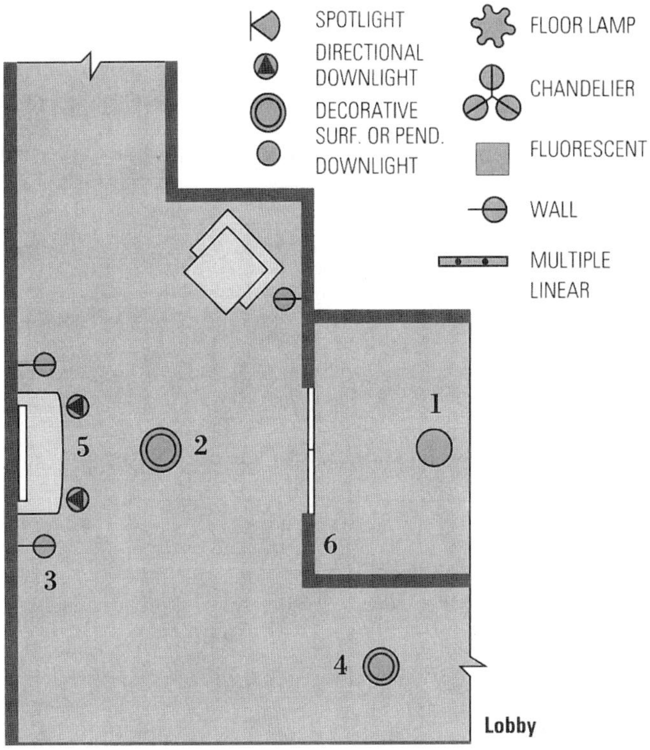

Where to Light and How to Light Them

The foyer and the lobby are places where first impressions are gained and where important transitions take place, between public and private space, and between outdoor and indoor lighting levels, whether by day or by night. The lighting of these areas is important not only because it gives a clue to the character of the interiors and of the inhabitants, but because it can assist in the comfortable adaptation from one level of lighting to a very different one.

Foyer/Stair Hall

1. In this entrance a chandelier establishes an elegant tone.
2. Sconces of coordinated style, at either side of the mirror, assist guests in adjusting their hair and attire.
3. A downlight with broad distribution safely lights the stairway and a doorway.
4. Close-to-ceiling decorative fixtures, comfortably shielded from below, light the upper stairway and hall.
5. Lighting controls set the scene for daily uses or festive occasions.

Location, Fixture, Lamps

		Control channel
1. Dauphine, alabaster	5-40W Candle	1
2. Dauphine, alabaster	40W Candle	1
3. Lytecaster Deep Alzak	100W A19	2
4. Alabaster	2-60W A19	2
5. MultiSet Controls		

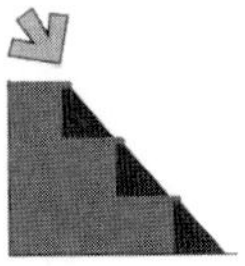

no

yes

LIGHTING
Planning Data: Foyers and Lobbies

Lobby

1. Lighting in the vestibule is from a decorative recessed downlight, providing a comfortable transition between outdoor and indoor light levels.

2, 3, 4. General lighting is from style-coordinated suspended and close-to-ceiling luminaries and sconces.

5. Flowers on the table are accented by beams from recessed adjustable downlights.
6. Controls facilitate change of lighting to suit daytime (bright-adapted) or nighttime (dark-adapted) conditions.

Location, Fixture, Lamps

		Control channel
1. Lytecaster/Lytegem	90W PAR38 FL	1
2. Alabaster	150W A21	2
3. Alabaster	60W A19	2
4. Alabaster	2-60W A19	3
5. Lytecaster PAR Recessed Adjust.	50W PAR20 SP	5
6. MultiSet Control		

Where to Light and How to Light Them

Work at home, whether the homework of a student, the after-hours efforts of an office worker, or the all-day work of a self-employed person, usually involves two kinds of tasks that pose different lighting problems: computer tasks and paper tasks.

Computer

The computer screen is self-illuminated, and if it receives much external light the contrast between the letters and the background is reduced and seeing becomes more difficult. Prolonged work under difficult visual conditions results in fatigue.

General Lighting

General lighting should be provided in order to balance the brightnesses in the field of view. This is often provided by a center-ceiling fixture, or a standing lamp (*suggested illuminance: 10–20 fc*).

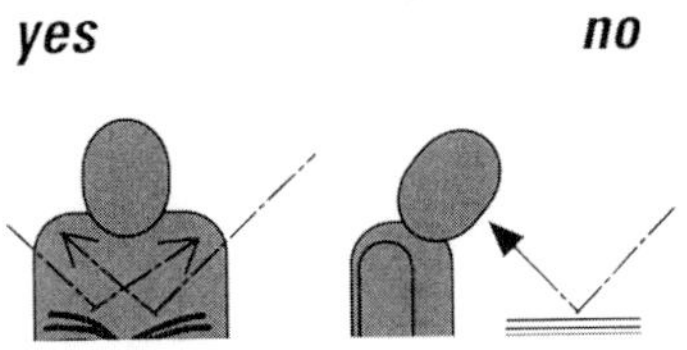

Task lighting for prolonged reading is often best provided by ceiling-mounted fluorescent, placed slightly behind or at either side of the desk

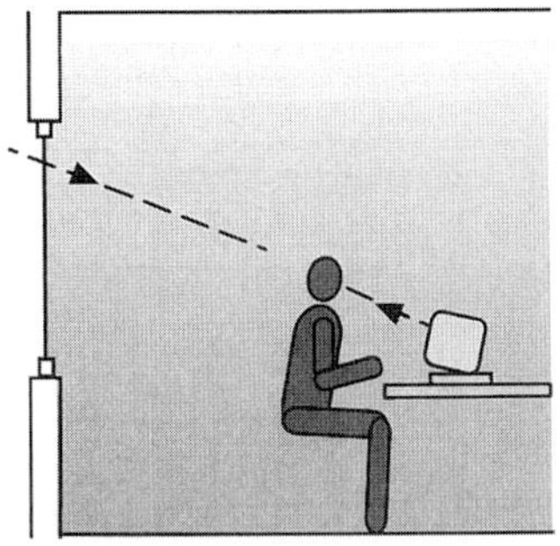

Avoid reflections of bright light sources on the screen, as those of a window, which should be shaded, or those of a ceiling fixture or a lampshade. Therefore, the screen should be oriented at right angles to a window and set so that no bright objects are reflected on it. *(The illuminance on the screen should be 10–20 fc)*

Alternatively, *local task lighting* can be used effectively. As noted above, this should be placed at the side, rather than in front of the task. The illuminance on the task should be 20–50 fc, and in the case of older eyes working with small detail, 100 fc

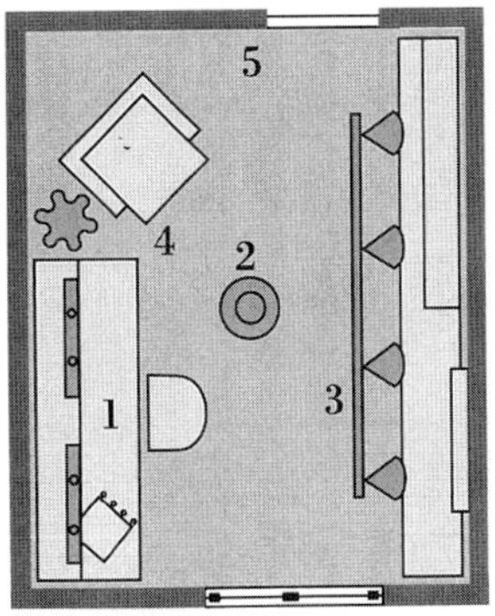

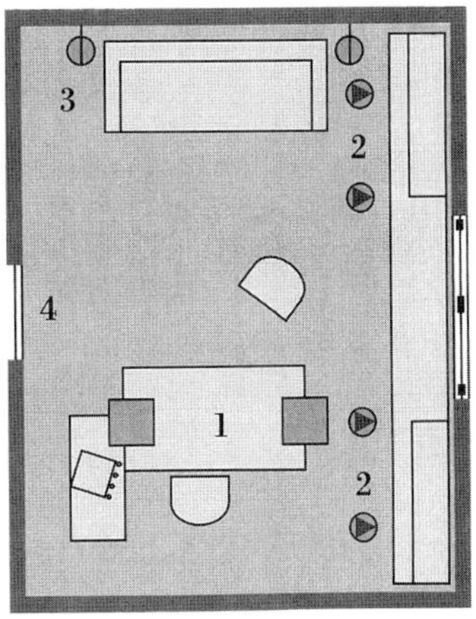

Study *above*
Office *right*

Paper Tasks

Paper tasks, especially those involving high-gloss paper, should be illuminated from either side rather than from in front, in order to avoid reflections of the light source in the surface of the task. These veiling reflections reduce the contrast between the print and the paper, imposing a veil over the task, which makes it hard to read.

Study

1. Shielded track mounted under shelf; miniature krypton lamps are positioned to the left and right of task for bilateral lighting.
2. Close-to-ceiling luminous indirect fixture provides general lighting.
3. Track lighting illuminates bookshelf.
4. Floor lamp.
5. Dimming controls, switch.

Location, Fixture, Lamp

		Controls
1. LyteTrim Basic	20W KX2000	Sunrise
2. Alabaster	2-13W TT Comp. Fluor.	Switch
3. Lytespan Radius with Sof-Tech spot	50W PAR30 FL	Sunrise
4. Sunrise Slide Dimmer		

LIGHTING

Planning Data: Offices and Studies

Office

1. Luminous square-surface fluorescent over desk, to left and right of task area.
2. Miniature recessed adjustable units, with spread lens, highlight bookshelves.
3. Wall brackets provide reading light at sofa, balance brightness.
4. Controls.

Location, Fixture, Lamp

		Controls
1. Copper Foil	2-27W TT Comp. Fluor.	Switch
2. Lytecaster Mini Swivel	50W MR16 FNV	Sunrise
3. Shoji	60W A19	Sunrise
4. Sunrise Slide Dimmer		

Accent lighting: Directional lighting used to emphasize a particular object or to draw attention to a part of the field view.

Adaptation: The process by which the visual system becomes accustomed to more or less light than it was exposed to during an immediately preceding period. It results in a change in the sensitivity of the eye to the light.

Ambient lighting: Lighting of a general, overall, uniform nature.

Ampere (amps or A): The unit of measurement of electric current flow.

Baffle: An opaque or translucent element that serves to shield a light source from direct view at certain angles, or serves to absorb unwanted light.

Ballast: An electrical device used in fluorescent fixtures to supply the necessary voltage and current to start and operate the lamp(s). Electronic ballasts are gradually replacing magnetic ballasts because they are more efficient, quieter, and lighter, and they facilitate dimming.

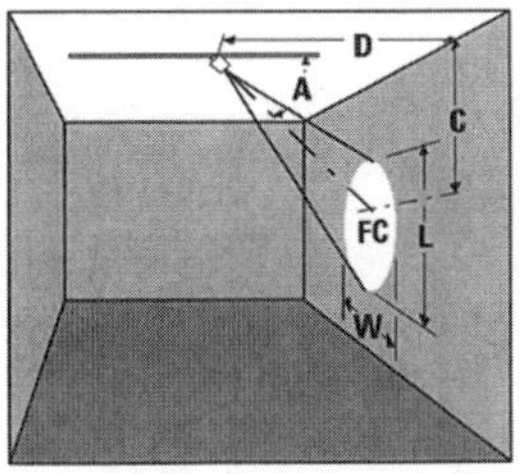

30°, 45° or 60° Vertical

Beam spread: The angle enclosed by two lines which intersect the candlepower distribution curve at the points where the candlepower is reduced to a stated percent of maximum (normally 50 percent of maximum).

Channel: A group of lights of the same type, or doing the same lighting task, that operate together. All the lights in a channel dim together, that is, they are all full-on, dimmed to 80 percent or 50 percent, and so on.

Circuit: The closed path over which an electric current flows. It includes the source of electric energy (usually the electric panel box or breaker, the wiring, and the electric load.

Color rendering index (CRI): Measure of the degree to which the perceived colors of objects illuminated by a source conform to those of the same objects illuminated by a reference source of comparable color temperature.

Color temperature (of a light source): The absolute temperature of a blackbody radiator having a chromaticity (apparent color) equal to that of the light source.

Contrast: The difference in the luminance of an object and its immediate background (e.g., between print and paper).

Current: The flow of electricity. Current is measured in amperes (amps or A).

Diffuser: A translucent glass or plastic that shields the light source and spreads the light evenly in all directions.

Diffusion: The scattering of light rays so that they are emitted or reflected in all directions.

Dimming ballast: Special fluorescent lamp ballast, which, when used with a dimmer control, permits varying the light output.

Efficacy: The ratio of output to input, measured in different units. The efficacy of a lamp is the ratio of its output (lumens) to the input power (watts).

Efficiency: The ratio of output to input, measured in the same units. The efficiency of a luminaire is the ratio of its output (in lumens) to the input (lumens from the lamps).

Energy: The power consumed over a period of time. Electrical energy is measured in kilowatt-hours (kWh).

Floodlighting: Lighting designed to light a scene or object to a luminance greater than that of its surroundings. It may be for utility, advertising, or decorative purposes.

Fluorescent lamp: A tubular electric lamp filled with mercury vapor and having a coating of fluorescent material on its inner surface. Light is emitted by the phosphors when excited by an arc discharge between cathodes at the ends of the lamp. The composition of the phosphors determines the color quality of the lamp.

Footcandle (fc): A unit of illuminance, the amount of light falling on a surface. 1 fc = 1 lumen/ft^2.

Footlambert (fl): A unit of luminance, the brightness of a surface. 1 fl = 1 lumen/ft^2.

Non-insulated ceiling (other than top floor).

Frame-in kit: The electrified mounting frame or housing which supports the optical assembly (reflector-trim) of a recessed fixture. Frame-in kits are of various types, according to the nature of the construction and the lamp.

Halogen: (tungsten halogen): A type of incandescent lamp filled with a halogen gas. The advantages over regular incandescent lamps include excellent lumen maintenance and compactness. They also provide whiter light and longer life at a given light output.

Illuminance: The density of luminous flux falling on a surface. The level of illumination. Measured in footcandles.

Incandescent (tungsten) lamp: A lamp in which light is produced by a tungsten filament heated to incandescence by an electric current.

Kilowatt-hour (kWh): A unit for measuring electrical energy consumption, kilowatt/hour = watts × hours/1000. Electric energy is sold by the kilowatt-hour (kWh).

Lamp: An artificial light source. (Portable luminaries, equipped with cord and plug, are more properly referred to as *portable lamps.*)

LIGHTING

Planning Data: Glossary

Lens: A glass or plastic element used in luminaries to change the direction of and control the distribution of light rays. Also called *prismatic lens.*

Light distribution, luminaires: Luminaires are classified according to the distribution of light up, down, or up/down: indirect, direct, or indirect/direct.

Louver: A shielding element used to intercept light traveling in undesirable directions. A louver is generally an assembly of baffle elements arranged in grid or concentric form.

Low-voltage lamps: Incandescent lamps that operate at low voltage, such as PAR 36 and MR-16 lamps that operate at 12 V.

Lumen: The unit of luminous flux. A measure of a lamp's or luminaire's light output.

Luminaire: A complete lighting unit consisting of a lamp or lamps, together with the parts designed to distribute the light, to position and protect the lamps, and to connect the lamps to the power supply.

Luminance: The luminous intensity of any light-emitting surface. Often referred to as *brightness.* Measured in footlamberts.

Matte surface: A dull surface, as opposed to a shiny (specular) surface. Light reflected from a matte surface is diffuse.

Parabolic reflector: A reflector shaped in cross-section like a parabola. A small light source at the focal point of the parabola produces an essentially parallel beam of light.

Power: The rate at which energy is developed or expended. Power is measured in watts.

Power factor: The ratio of watts to volt-amperes drawn by fluorescent ballasts. It is, in effect, a measure of ballast efficiency. Commercial jobs require high power factor (90 percent or higher) because, for a given load, they draw less current, permitting more fixtures on a circuit and lower wiring costs.

Reflection: The process by which incident light is returned by a surface. It can be classified as specular or diffuse. Specular reflectors are like mirrors, returning rays of light at the same angle as they arrive and preserving sharp images. Diffuse reflectors return light in many directions; images are blurred or absent altogether.

Refraction: The process by which the direction of a ray of light changes as it passes obliquely from one medium to another. Fresnel and prismatic lenses utilize refraction to control the distribution of light.

Shielding: An arrangement of light-controlling material to prevent direct view of the light source.

Shielding angle: The angle measured from the horizontal at which a light source in a luminaire first becomes visible. It is the complementary angle of the cutoff angle.

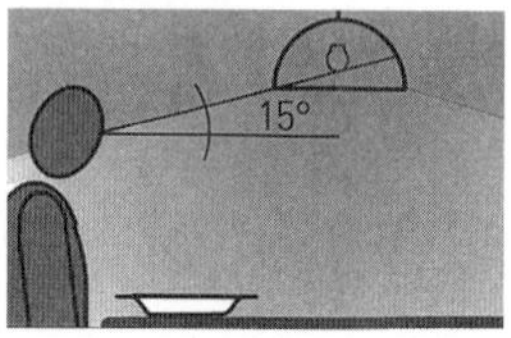

Spacing ratio: The spacing ratio for a particular luminaire is determined from its candlepower distribution curve and, when multiplied by the mounting height above the work plane, gives the maximum spacing of luminaires for even illumination.

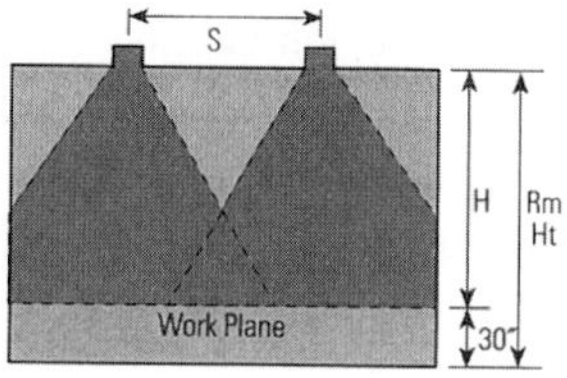

Specular reflector: A shiny, highly polished surface that acts like a mirror. It is used to control light precisely and looks dark except when viewed from the direction in which an image of the light source is projected.

Task (visual task): That which is to be seen. The visual function is performed.

Task lighting: Lighting directed to a specific surface or area to provide illumination for visual tasks.

Thermal protector: A device which disconnects power to a luminaire to protect against overheating due to abnormal conditions.

Transformer: A device used to raise (step up) or lower (step down) electrical voltage.

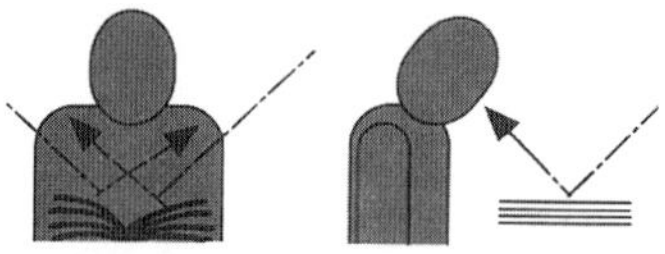

Veiling reflections: The reflections of light sources in a task which reduce the contrast between detail and background (e.g., between print and paper, or print and the computer screen), thus imposing a veil and decreasing task visibility.

Volt (V): The unit of measurement of voltage.

Voltage: Electromotive force. The force or pressure which causes electricity to flow. Voltage is measured in volts (V).

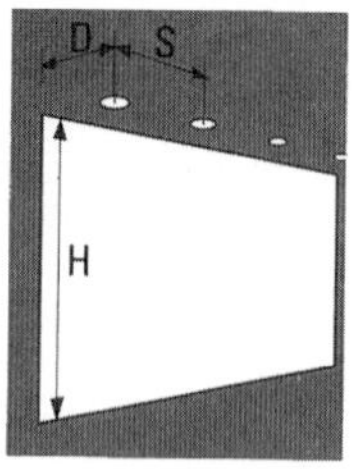

Wallwashing

Wall wash lighting: A lighting system that provides a smooth, even distribution of light over a vertical surface.

Watt: The unit of measurement of electrical power. When power is used over a period of time, energy is consumed, measured in watthours or kilowatthours.

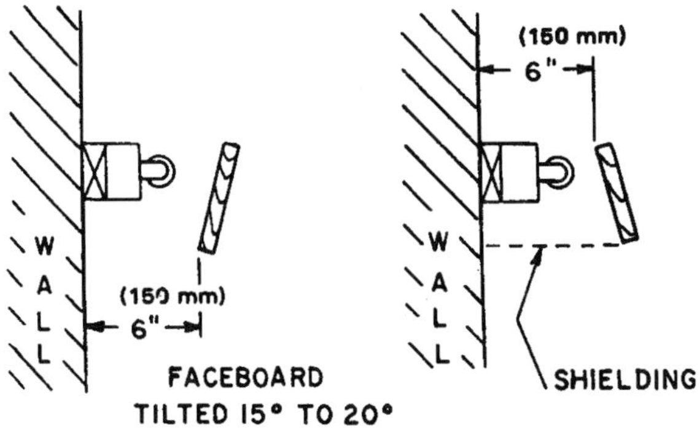

Fig. 4 Valance faceboard may be tilted

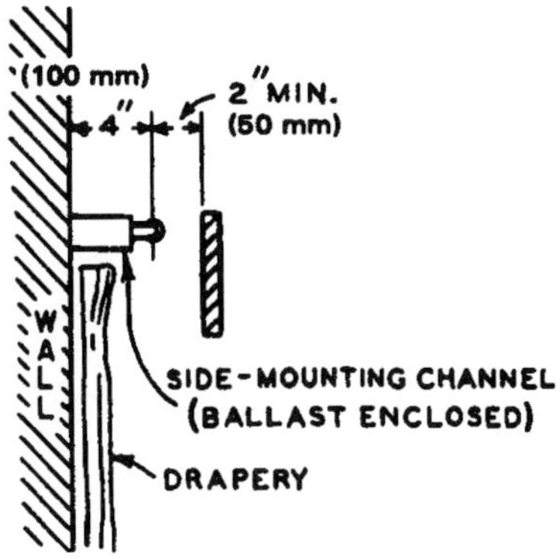

Fig. 5 With side-mounting channels, no extender is necessary

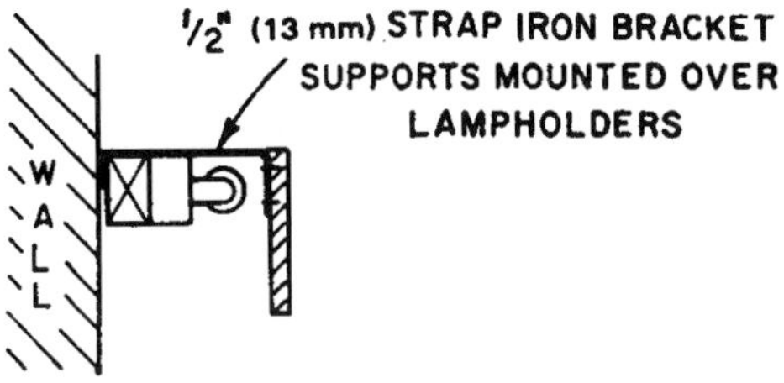

Fig. 6 Intermediate brackets are required to support long faceboards

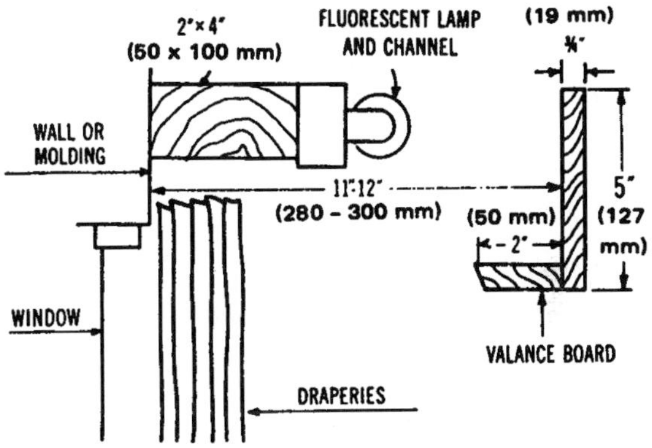

Fig. 7 Variation of valance lighting. (If distance between wall and lamp is increased, light will be distributed more evenly, but shielding may be required at the bottom of the faceboard.)

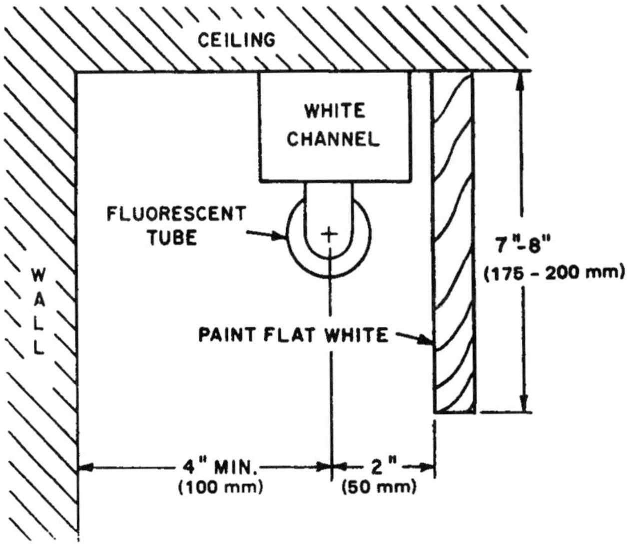

Fig. 8 Minimum dimensions for cornice lighting installation

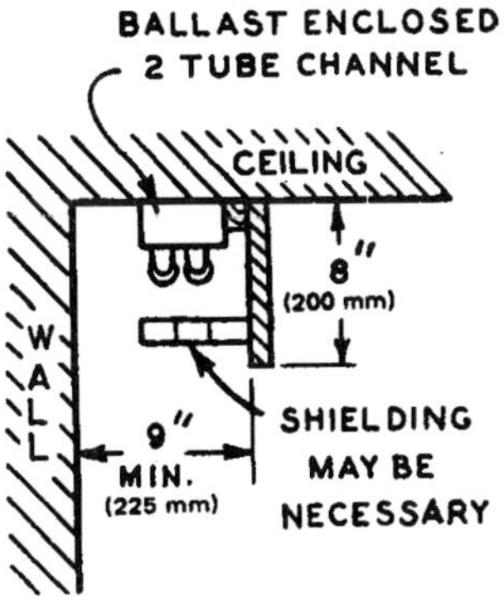

Fig. 9 Cornice lighting with two tubes may require shielding

LIGHTING

Planning Data: Residential Down Lighting

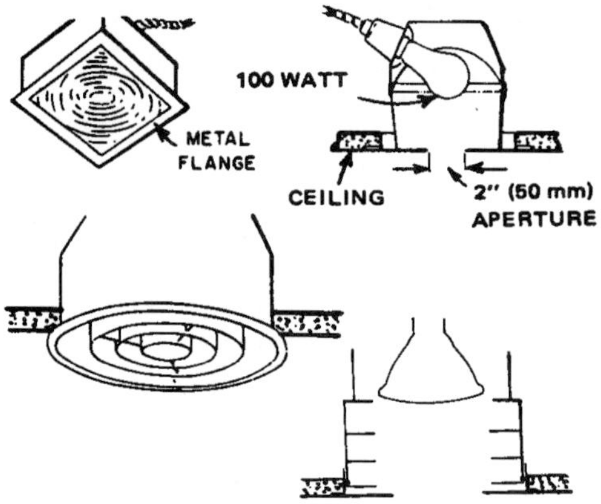

Fig. 10 Common types of downlights

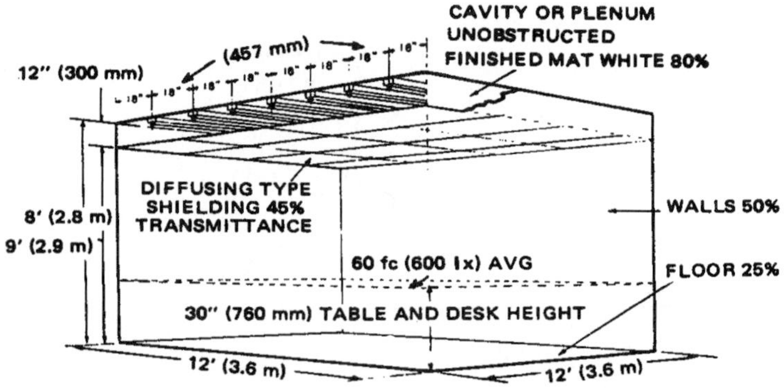

Fig. 15 Basic relation ship for the design of luminous panels. (A light level of 60 fc (600 lx) is produced by seven rows of three 40-W fluorescent tubes on 18-in (457 mm) centers. Light distribution and surface luminance are approximately uniform.)

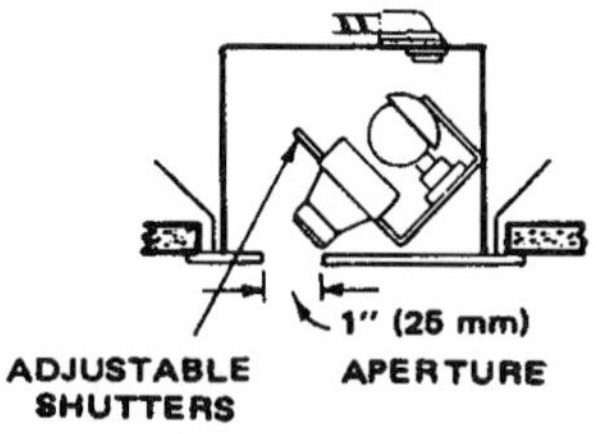

Fig. 11 Pinhole spot, a recessed downlight with adjustable shutters to shape beam pattern

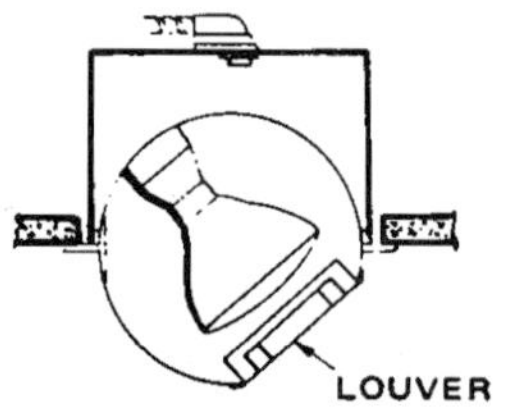

Fig. 12 "Eyeball" semirecessed fully adjustable downlight

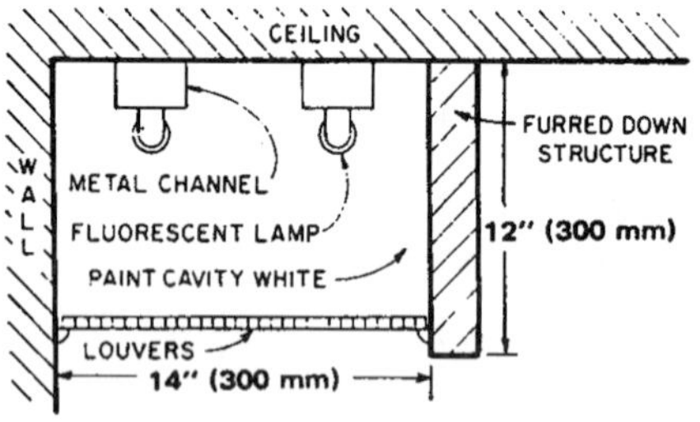

Fig. 13 Luminous panel or soffit lighting, used over a kitchen or bathroom counter

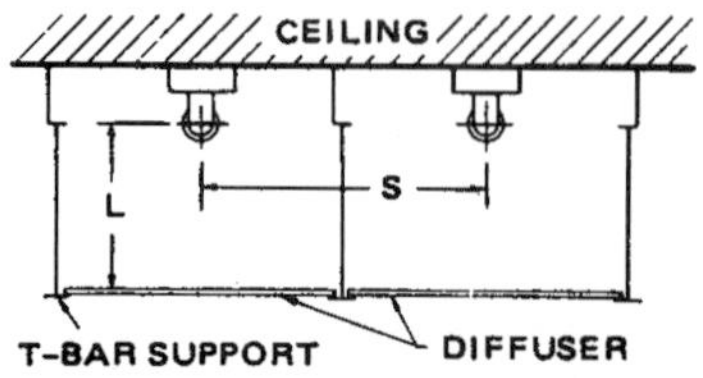

Fig. 14 Critical dimensions for luminous panel and luminous ceiling lighting. (S should not exceed 1½ to 2 times L.)

Table 1 Illuminance values for residences*

Specific visual tasks	Illuminance Foot-candles	Illuminance Lux†
Dining	15	150
Grooming, shaving, makeup	50	500
Handcraft		
Ordinary seeing tasks	70	700
Difficult seeing tasks	100	1000
Very difficult seeing tasks	150	1500
Critical seeing tasks	200	2000
Ironing (hand and machine)	50	500
Kitchen duties		
Food preparation and cleaning	150	1500
Serving and other noncritical tasks	50	500
Laundry		
Preparation, sorting, inspection	50	500
Tub area—soaking, tinting	50	500
Washer and dryer areas	30	300
Reading and writing		
Handwriting, reproductions, and poor copies	70	700
Books, magazines, newspapers	30	300
Reading piano or organ scores		
Advanced (substandard size)	150	1500
Advanced	70	700
Simple	30	300
Sewing (hand and machine)		
Dark fabrics	200	2000
Medium fabrics	100	1000
Light fabrics	50	500
Occasional—high contrast	30	300
Study	70	700
Table games	30	300
General lighting		
Conversation, relaxation, entertainment	10	100
Passage areas, for safety	10	100
Areas other than kitchen involving visual tasks	30	300
Kitchen	50	500

*Minimum on the task at all times.
†Lux is an SI unit equal to 0.0929 footcandle.

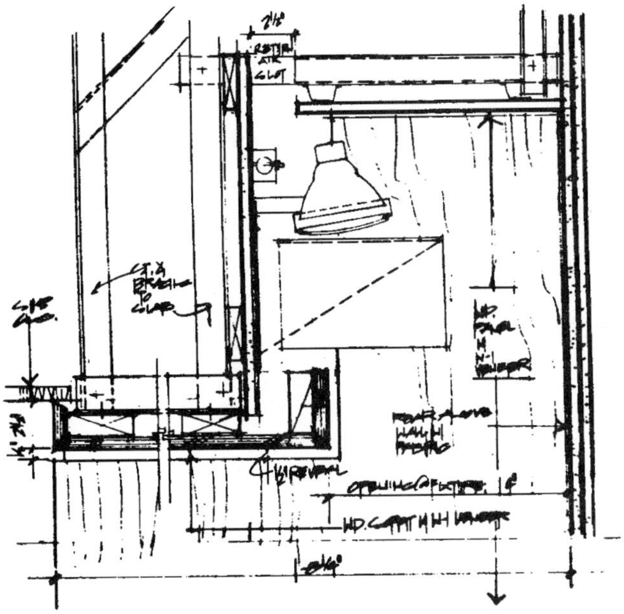

(17) WD SOFFIT SECTION @ ALCOVE

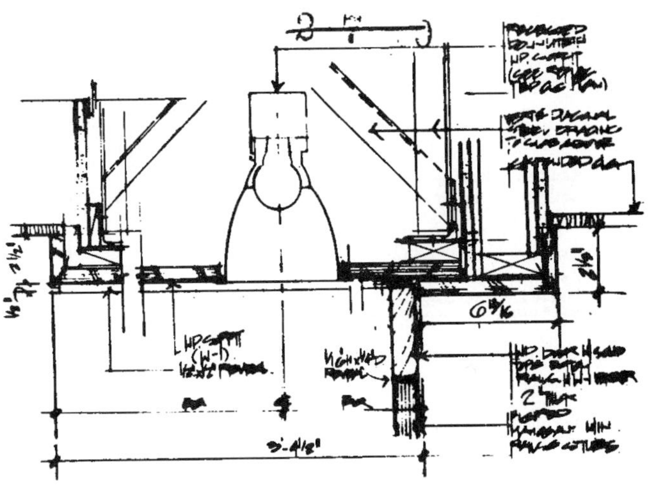

(18) WD. SOFFIT @ CONF. ROOMS

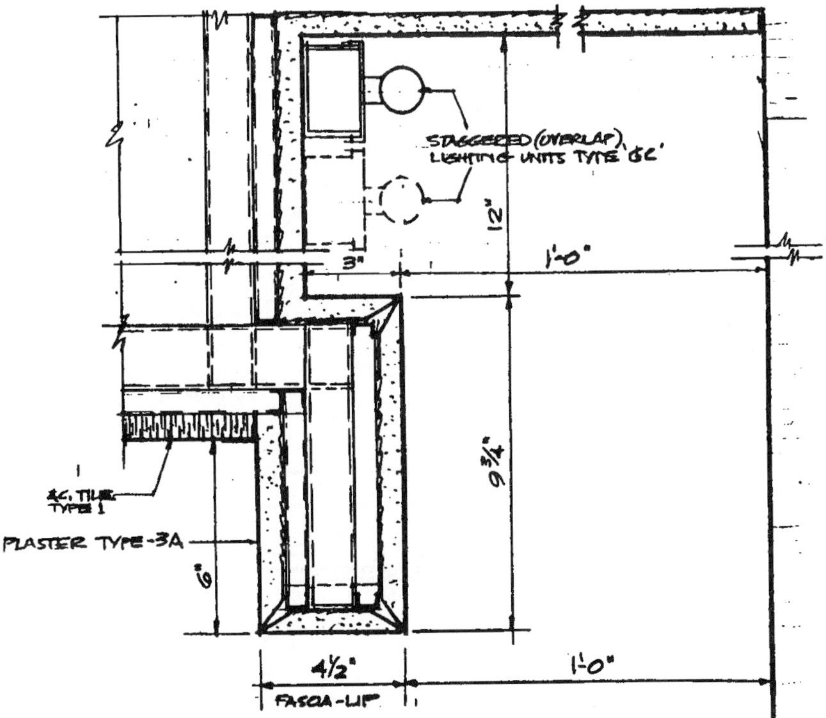

DETAIL OF LIGHT COVE RECESS
IN SANCTUARY @ 3"=1'-0"

LIGHTING

Cove Lighting Details

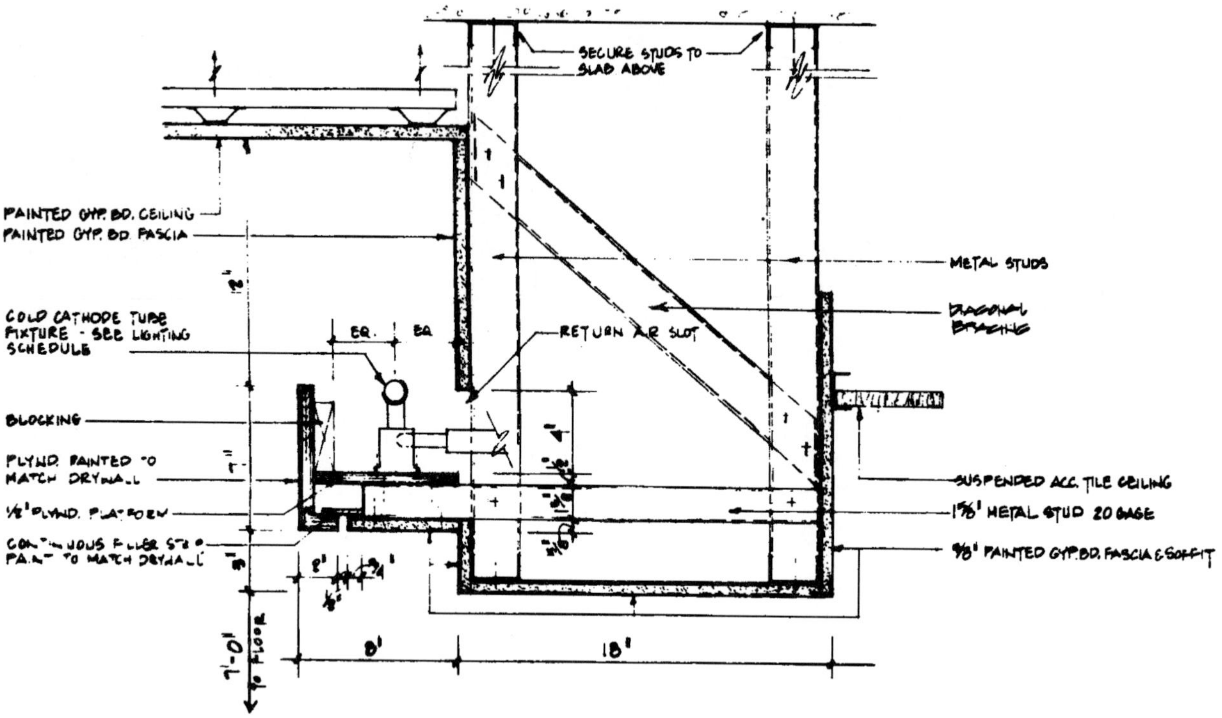

4 DETAIL - LIGHT COVE @ RECEPTION AREA

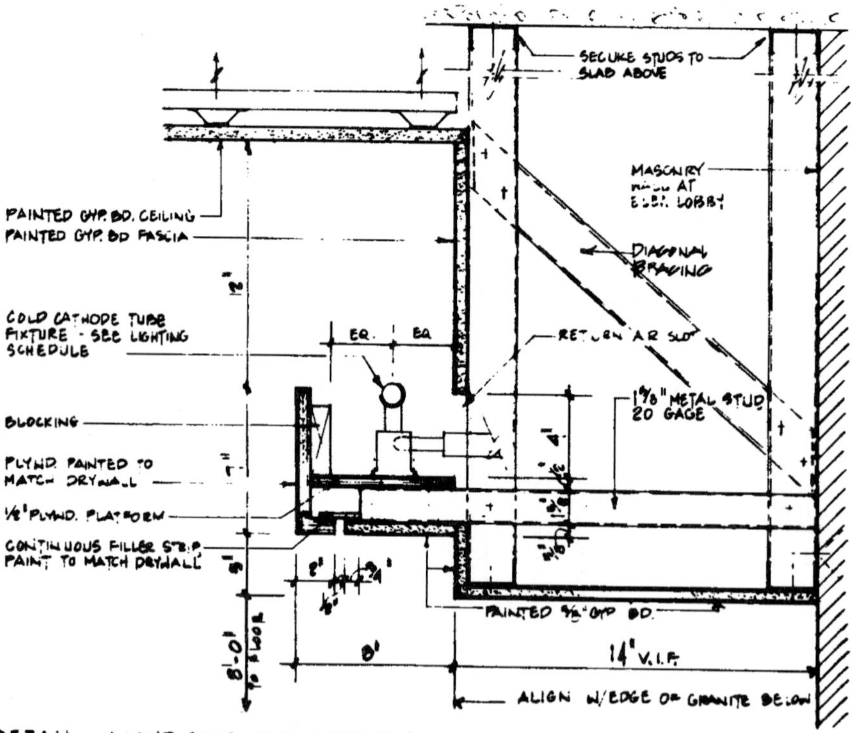

5 DETAIL - LIGHT COVE @ ELEVATOR LOBBY

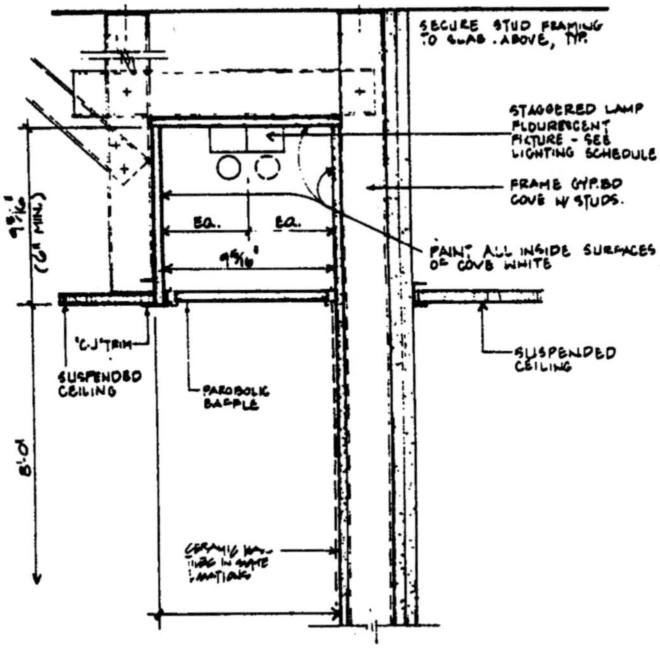

① DETAIL - LIGHT COVE @ TYPE "D" FIXTURE AT WALLS
3" = 1'-0"

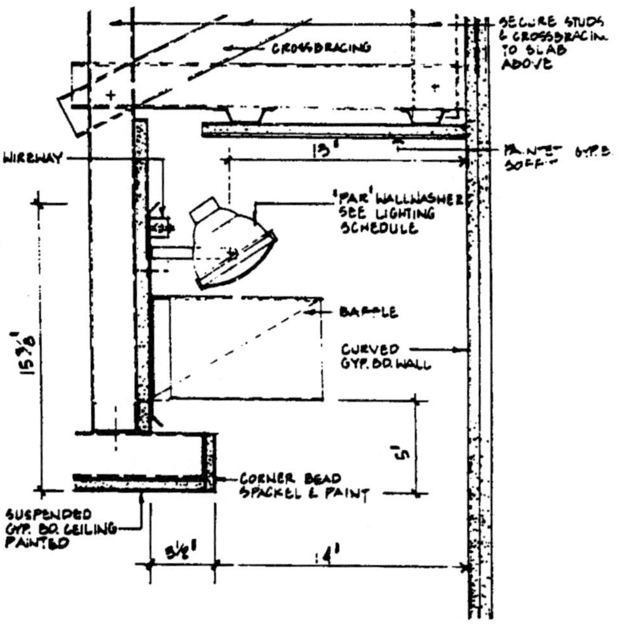

⑤ DETAIL - LIGHT COVE @ STAIR, TYPE 'K' FIXTURE
3" = 1'-0"

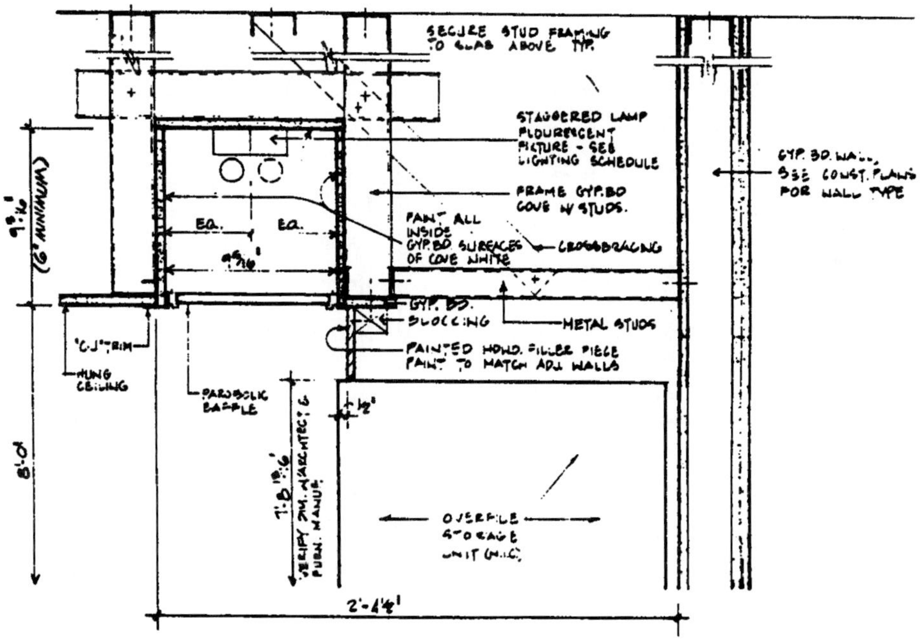

② DETAIL - LIGHT COVE @ TYPE "D" FIXTURE AT FILES
3" = 1'-0"

LIGHTING

Cove Lighting Details

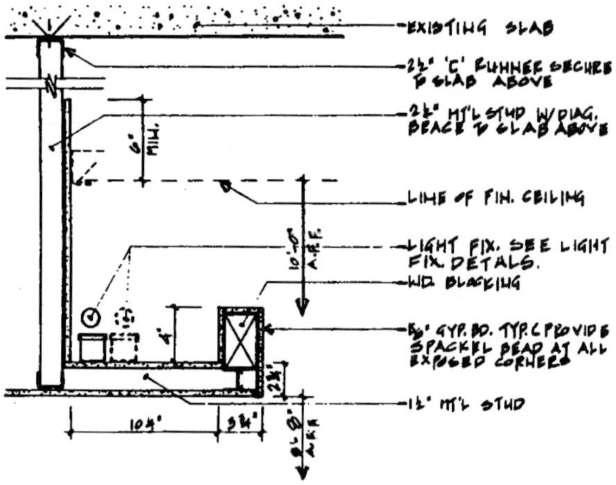

SECTION AT LIGHT COVE

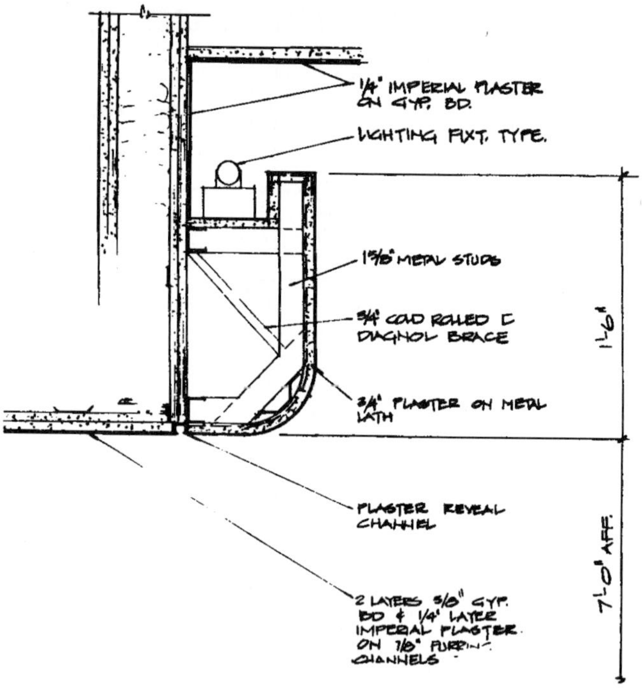

SECTION AT TROUGH AND SOFFIT
1½" = 1'-0"

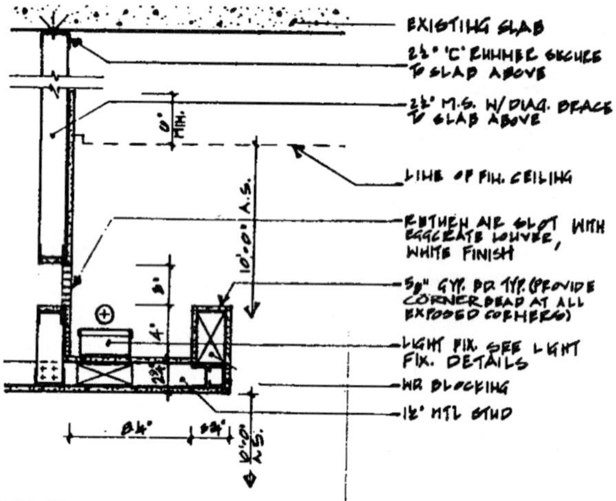

SECTION AT LIGHT COVE

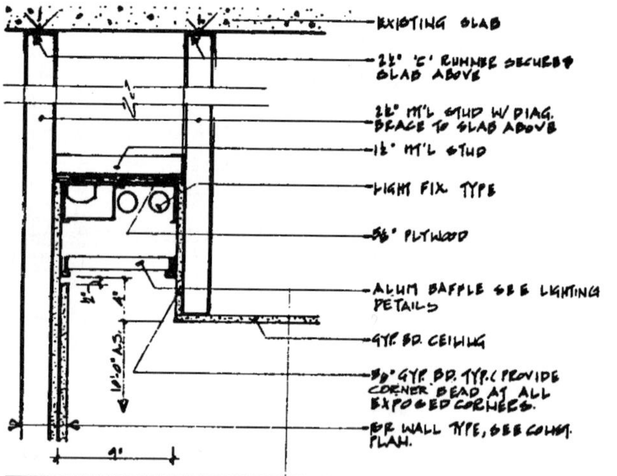

SECTION AT LIGHT COVE, DINING ROOM

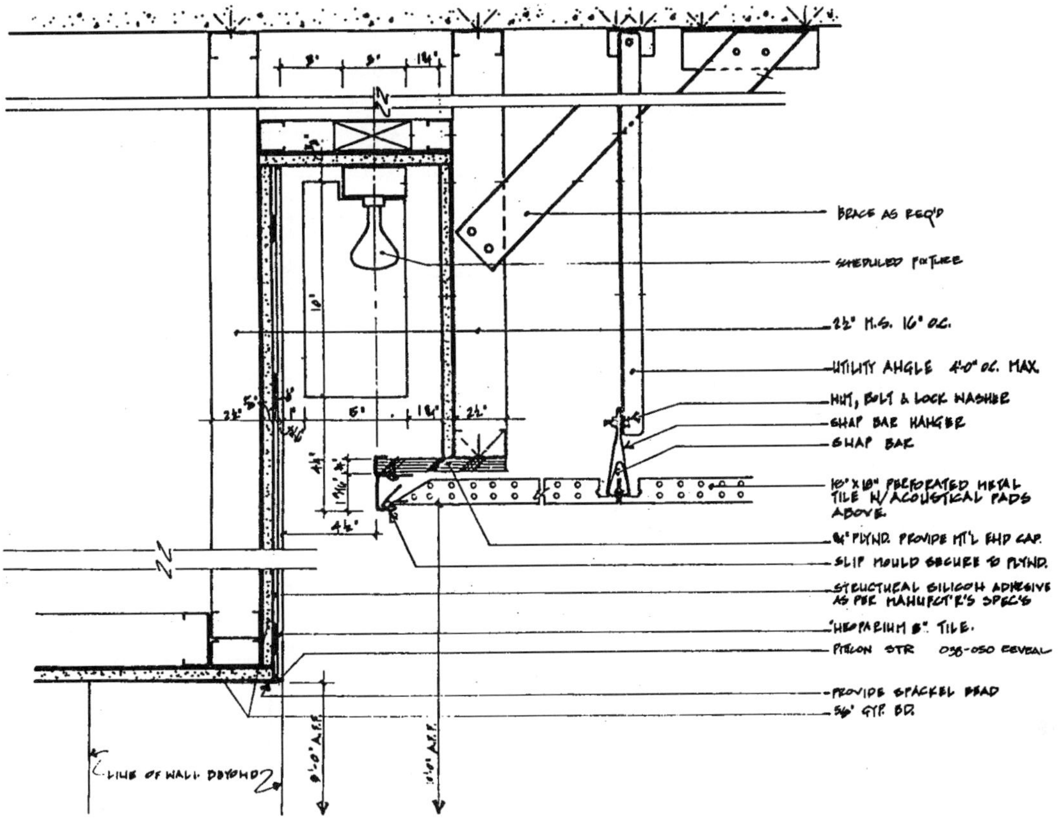
BRACE AS REQ'D
SCHEDULED FIXTURE
2½" M.S. 16" O.C.
UTILITY ANGLE 4'-0" O.C. MAX.
NUT, BOLT & LOCK WASHER
SNAP BAR HANGER
SNAP BAR
18" X 18" PERFORATED METAL TILE W/ACOUSTICAL PADS ABOVE.
¾" PLYWD. PROVIDE MT'L END CAP.
SLIP MOULD SECURE TO PLYWD.
STRUCTURAL SILICON ADHESIVE AS PER MANUFCT'R'S SPEC'S
"HEOPARIUM 8" TILE.
PITLON STR 038-050 REVEAL
PROVIDE SPACKEL BEAD
⅝" GYP. BD.
LINE OF WALL BEYOND

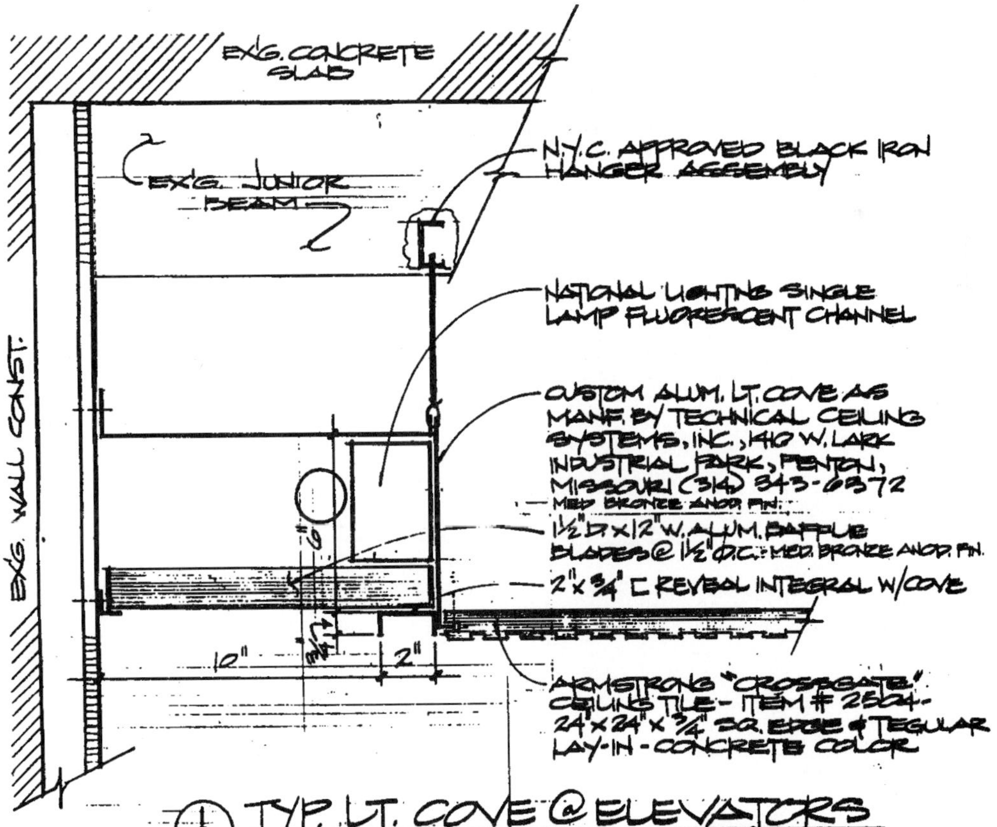
EX'G. CONCRETE SLAB
EX'G. JUNIOR BEAM
N.Y.C. APPROVED BLACK IRON HANGER ASSEMBLY
NATIONAL LIGHTING SINGLE LAMP FLUORESCENT CHANNEL
CUSTOM ALUM. LT. COVE AS MANF. BY TECHNICAL CEILING SYSTEMS, INC., 1410 W. LARK INDUSTRIAL PARK, FENTON, MISSOURI (314) 343-6372
MED BRONZE ANOD. FIN.
1½"D. x 12"W. ALUM. BAFFLE BLADES @ 1½" O.C. - MED. BRONZE ANOD. FIN.
2" x ¾" C REVEAL INTEGRAL W/COVE
ARMSTRONG "CROSSGATE" CEILING TILE - ITEM # 2524 - 24" x 24" x ¾" SQ. EDGE & TEGULAR LAY-IN - CONCRETE COLOR
EX'G. WALL CONST.
10"
2"

1/A57 TYP. LT. COVE @ ELEVATORS
Scale 3" = 1'-0"

LIGHTING

Fluorescent Cove Lighting Details

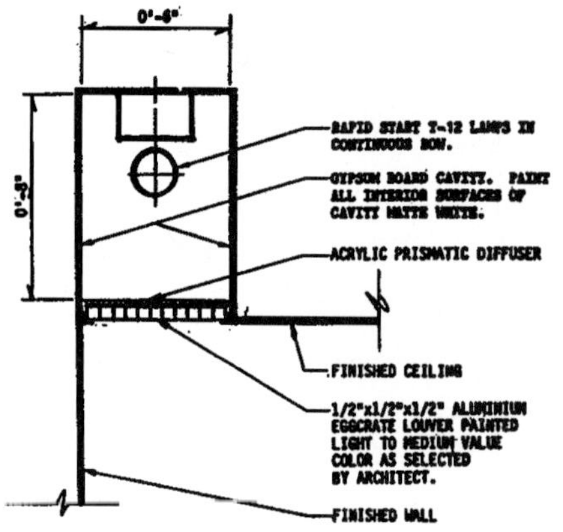

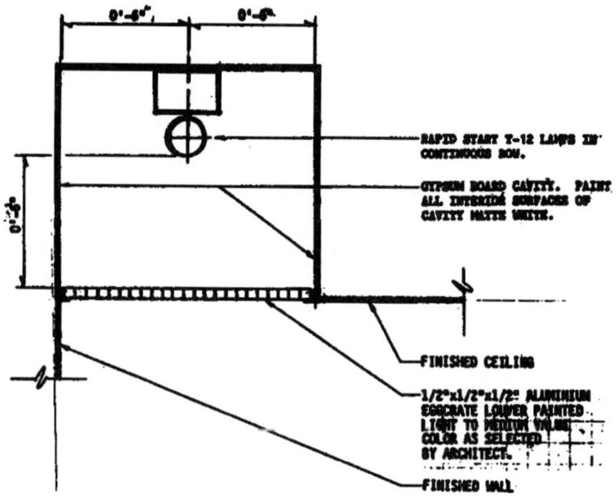

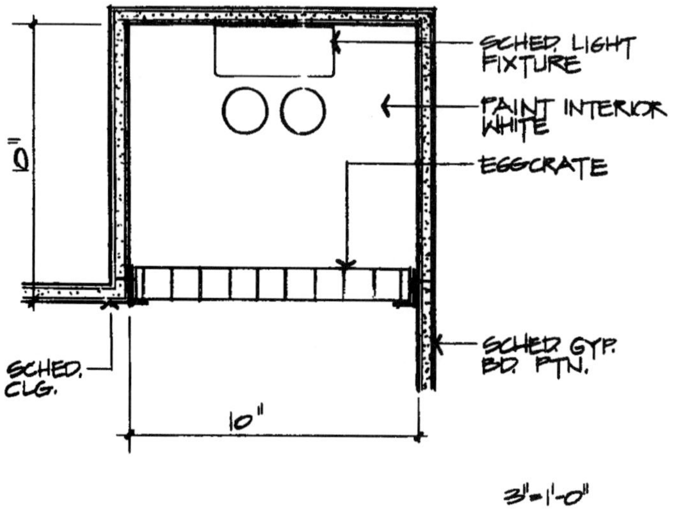

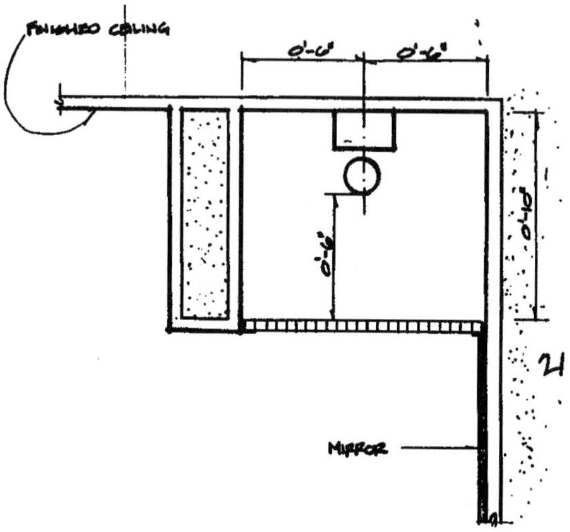

SECTION THRU CONTINUOUS COVE LIGHT

LIGHTING

Fluorescent Cove Lighting Details

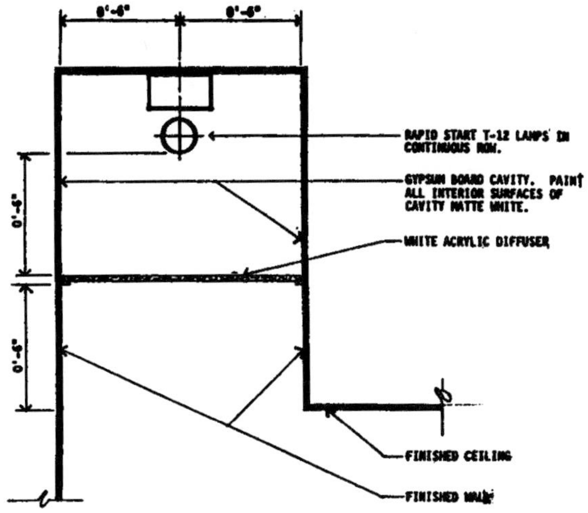

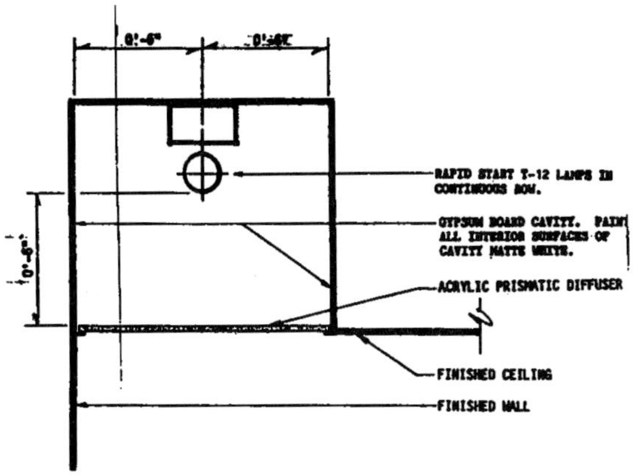

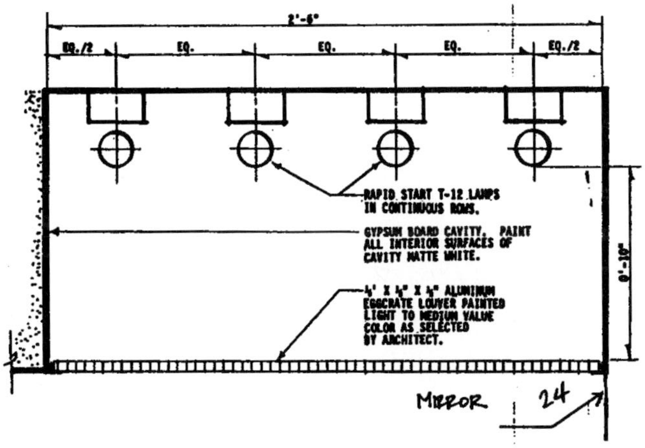

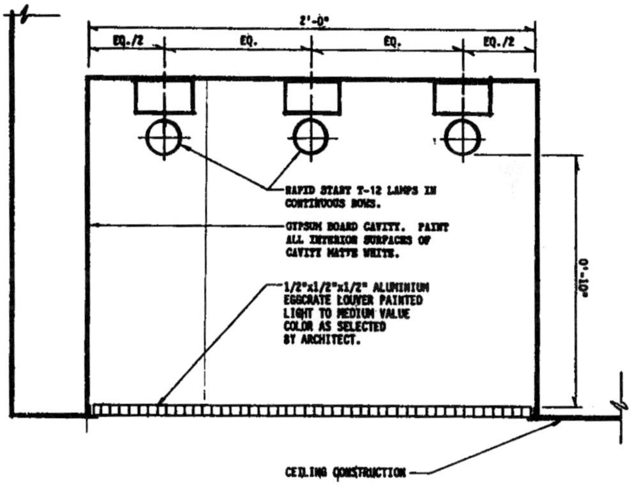

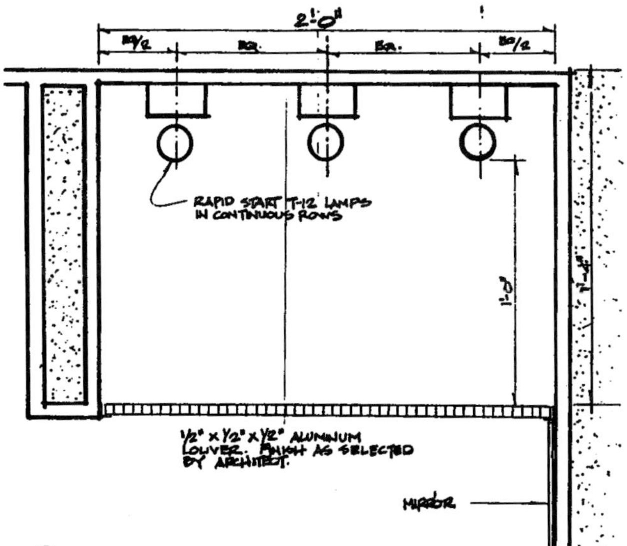

① VANITY LIGHTING SOFFIT DETAIL
3" = 1'-0"

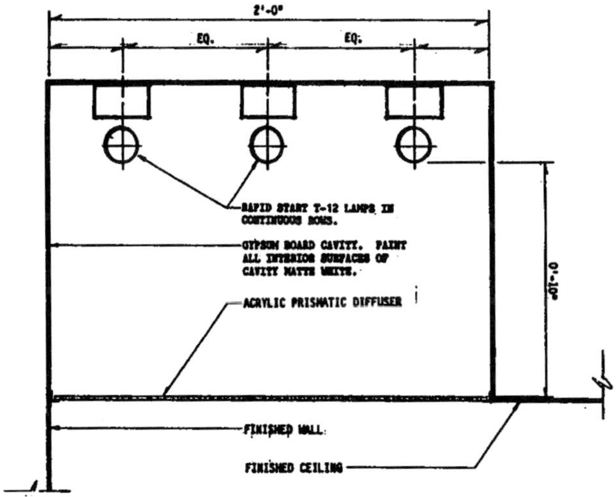

LIGHTING

Fluorescent Cove Lighting Details

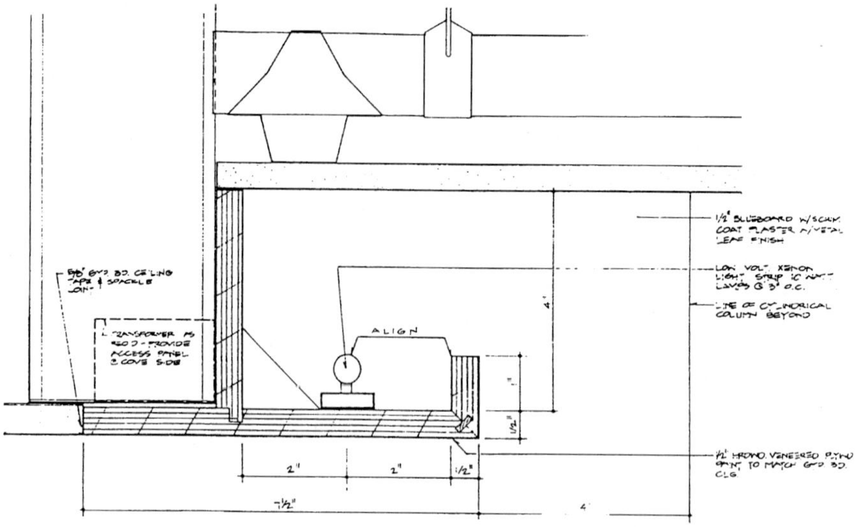

LIGHT COVE

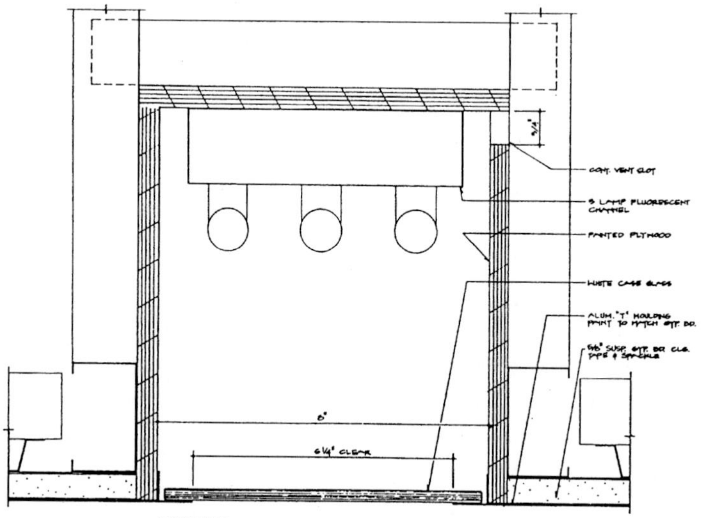

LIGHT COVE

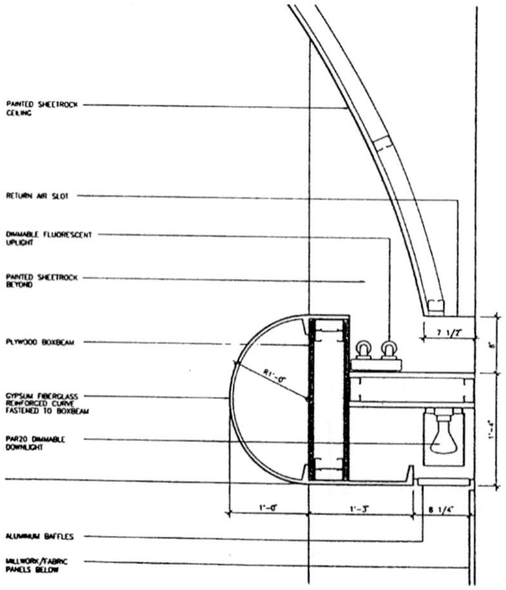

3-5/8" SW18 HANGER
@ 32" o.c
2-1/2" SW 20 BRACE MIN.2
PER EA. ROW IN BOTH
DIRECTIONS & 1st BAY
@EVERY HT. CHANGE
1-1/2" C.R.CHANNEL
5/8" GYPSUM BOARD
7/8" FURRING STRIP
5/8" GYP. BD.
7/8" FURRING STRIP
1-1/2" FURRING CHANNEL
MTL. TRIM PIECE
3/4" F.R. PLYWOOD
5/8" GYPSUM BOARD
LIGHTING FIX F-1 (TYP.)

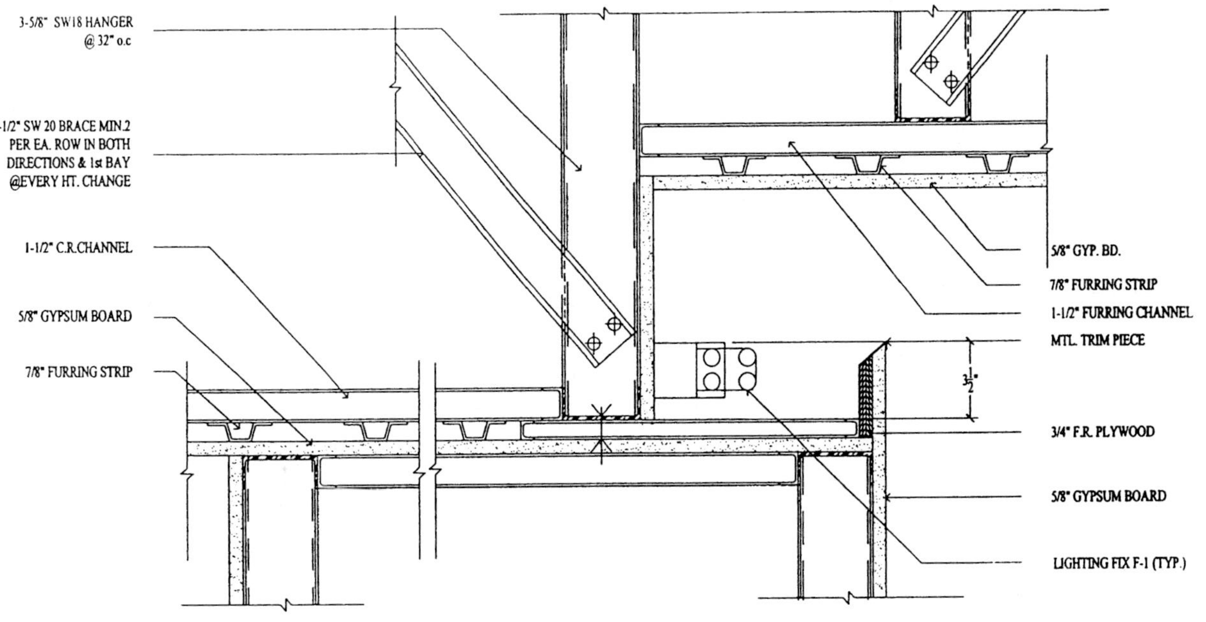

5
LIGHT COVE TYP.
VIDEO SCREEN
SCALE : 3" = 1' - 0"

3"

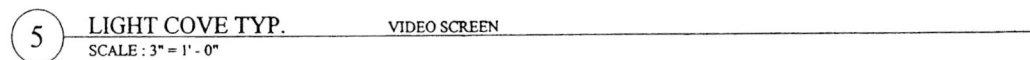

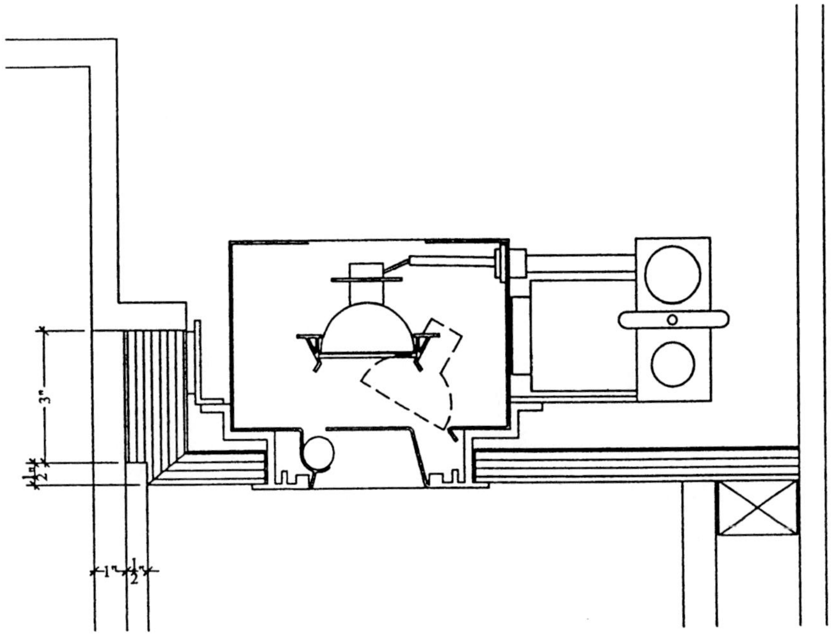

7
LIGHT FIXTURE DETAIL
SCALE 3" : 1'-0"

LIGHTING

Incandescent Cove Lighting Details

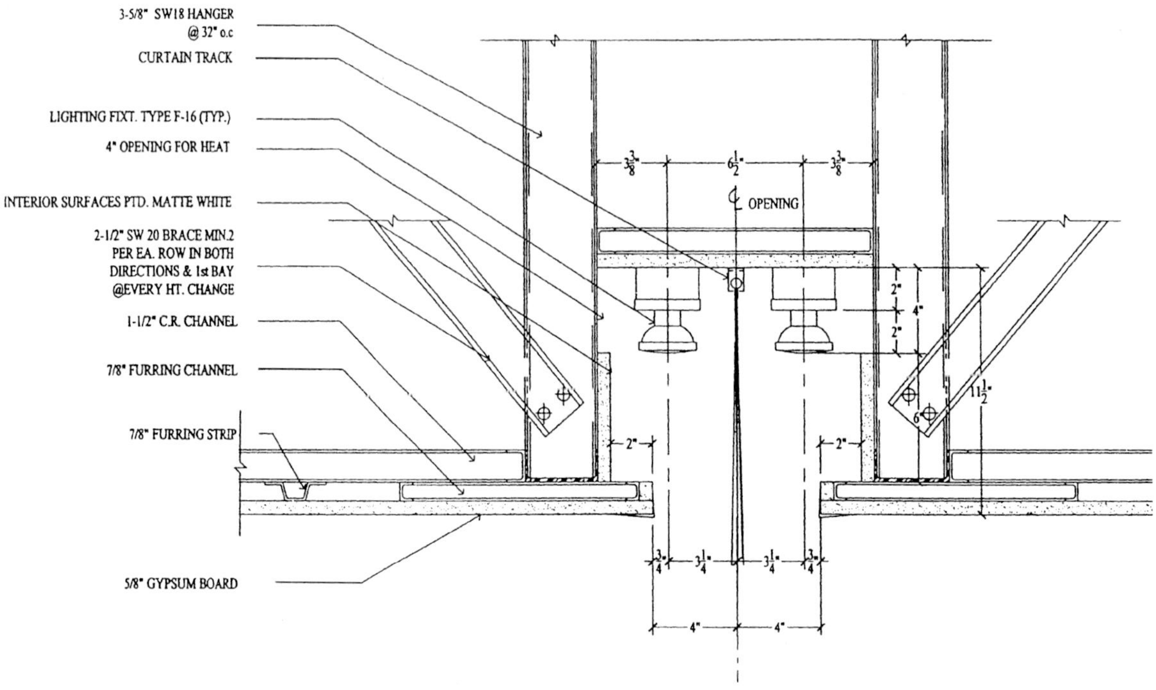

8 LIGHT COVE. HR EXPRESS, CURTAIN @ LIGHT
SCALE : 3" = 1' - 0"

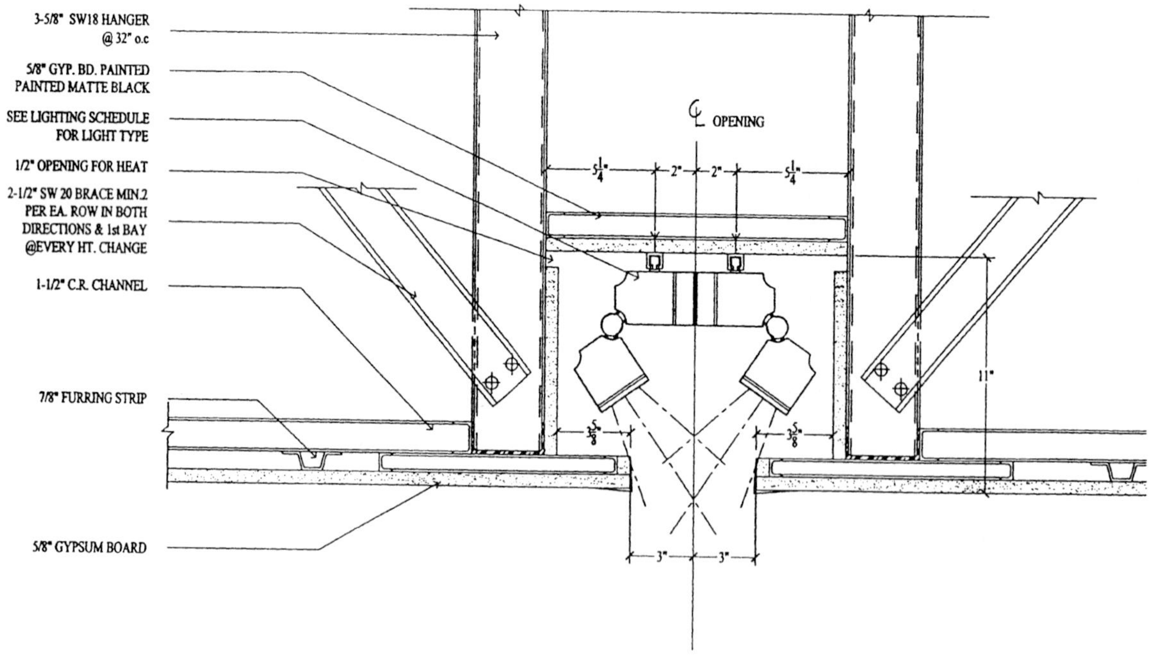

7 LIGHT COVE TYP. LIGHT POCKET
SCALE : 3" = 1' - 0"

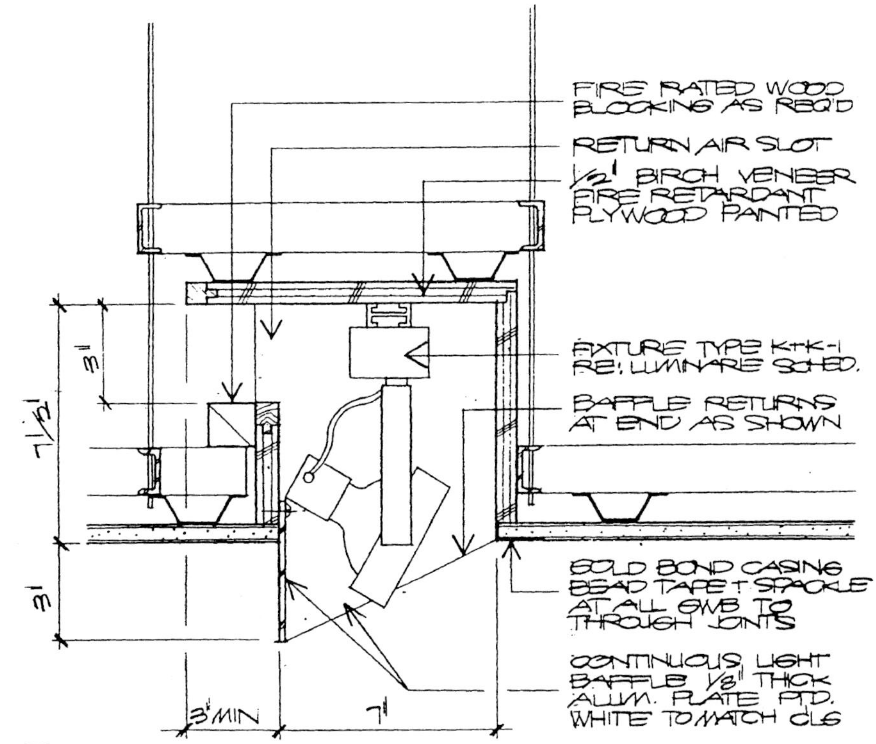

5 Section at Light Track Trough

Scale: 3" = 1'-0"

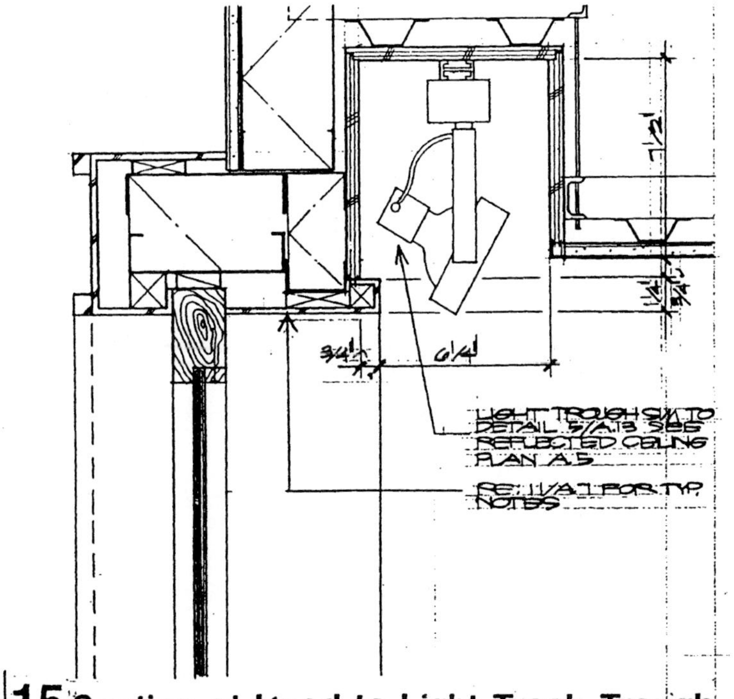

15 Section at Head to Light Track Trough

Scale: 3" = 1'-0"

LIGHTING

Fluorescent Cove Lighting Details

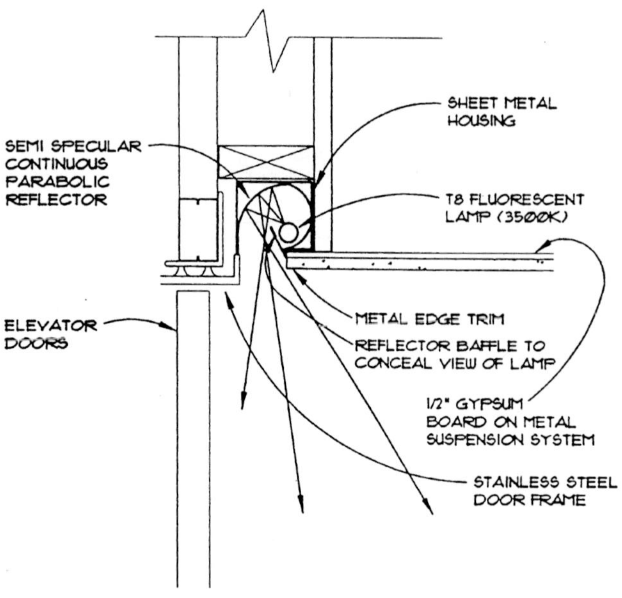
SHEET METAL HOUSING
SEMI SPECULAR CONTINUOUS PARABOLIC REFLECTOR
T8 FLUORESCENT LAMP (3500K)
ELEVATOR DOORS
METAL EDGE TRIM
REFLECTOR BAFFLE TO CONCEAL VIEW OF LAMP
1/2" GYPSUM BOARD ON METAL SUSPENSION SYSTEM
STAINLESS STEEL DOOR FRAME

SECTION "B-B"
COVE LIGHT DETAIL

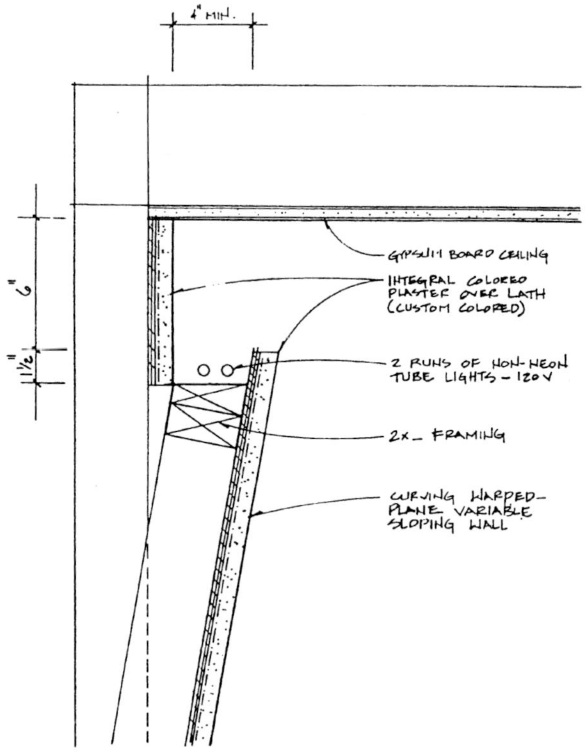
4" MIN.
GYPSUM BOARD CEILING
INTEGRAL COLORED PLASTER OVER LATH (CUSTOM COLORED)
2 RUNS OF NON-NEON TUBE LIGHTS – 120 V
2x_ FRAMING
CURVING WARPED-PLANE VARIABLE SLOPING WALL
6"
1 1/2"

1 SECTION @ LIGHT COVE
3" = 1'-0"

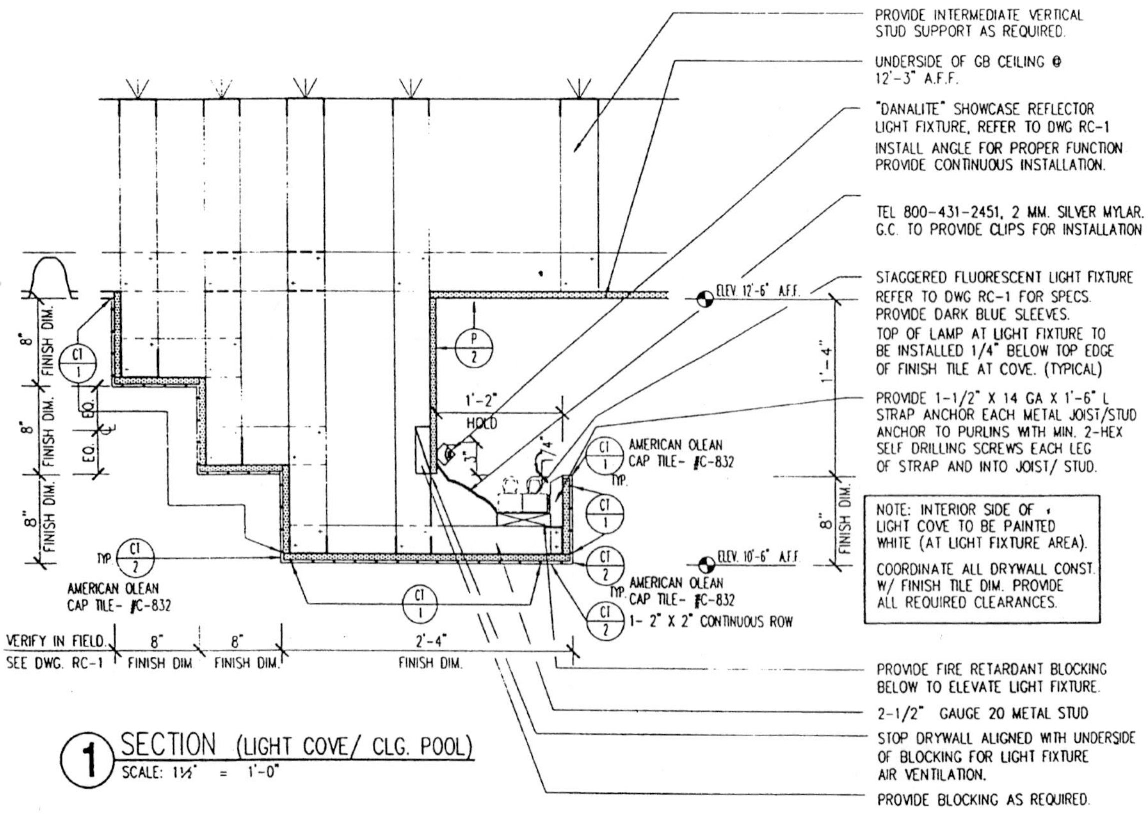
PROVIDE INTERMEDIATE VERTICAL STUD SUPPORT AS REQUIRED.
UNDERSIDE OF GB CEILING @ 12'-3" A.F.F.
"DANALITE" SHOWCASE REFLECTOR LIGHT FIXTURE, REFER TO DWG RC-1
INSTALL ANGLE FOR PROPER FUNCTION PROVIDE CONTINUOUS INSTALLATION.
TEL 800-431-2451, 2 MM. SILVER MYLAR. G.C. TO PROVIDE CLIPS FOR INSTALLATION
STAGGERED FLUORESCENT LIGHT FIXTURE REFER TO DWG RC-1 FOR SPECS. PROVIDE DARK BLUE SLEEVES. TOP OF LAMP AT LIGHT FIXTURE TO BE INSTALLED 1/4" BELOW TOP EDGE OF FINISH TILE AT COVE. (TYPICAL)
PROVIDE 1-1/2" X 14 GA X 1'-6" L STRAP ANCHOR EACH METAL JOIST/STUD ANCHOR TO PURLINS WITH MIN. 2-HEX SELF DRILLING SCREWS EACH LEG OF STRAP AND INTO JOIST/ STUD.
NOTE: INTERIOR SIDE OF LIGHT COVE TO BE PAINTED WHITE (AT LIGHT FIXTURE AREA).
COORDINATE ALL DRYWALL CONST. W/ FINISH TILE DIM. PROVIDE ALL REQUIRED CLEARANCES.
PROVIDE FIRE RETARDANT BLOCKING BELOW TO ELEVATE LIGHT FIXTURE.
2-1/2" GAUGE 20 METAL STUD
STOP DRYWALL ALIGNED WITH UNDERSIDE OF BLOCKING FOR LIGHT FIXTURE AIR VENTILATION.
PROVIDE BLOCKING AS REQUIRED.
ELEV. 12'-6" A.F.F.
ELEV. 10'-6" A.F.F.
1'-4"
1'-2" HOLD
AMERICAN OLEAN CAP TILE- #C-832
TYP.
1- 2" X 2" CONTINUOUS ROW
8" FINISH DIM.
EQ.
VERIFY IN FIELD. SEE DWG. RC-1
2'-4" FINISH DIM.

1 SECTION (LIGHT COVE/ CLG. POOL)
SCALE: 1½" = 1'-0"

LIGHTING

Fluorescent/Incandescent Cove Lighting Details

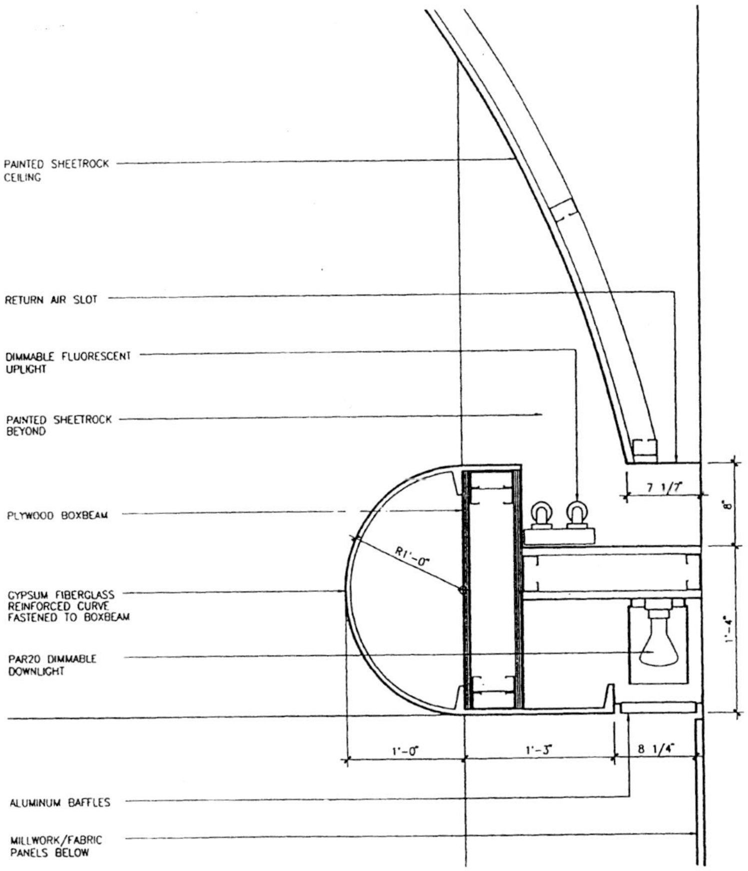
PAINTED SHEETROCK CEILING
RETURN AIR SLOT
DIMMABLE FLUORESCENT UPLIGHT
PAINTED SHEETROCK BEYOND
PLYWOOD BOXBEAM
GYPSUM FIBERGLASS REINFORCED CURVE FASTENED TO BOXBEAM
PAR20 DIMMABLE DOWNLIGHT
ALUMINUM BAFFLES
MILLWORK/FABRIC PANELS BELOW
R1'-0"
7 1/2"
8"
1'-4"
1'-0"
1'-3"
8 1/4"

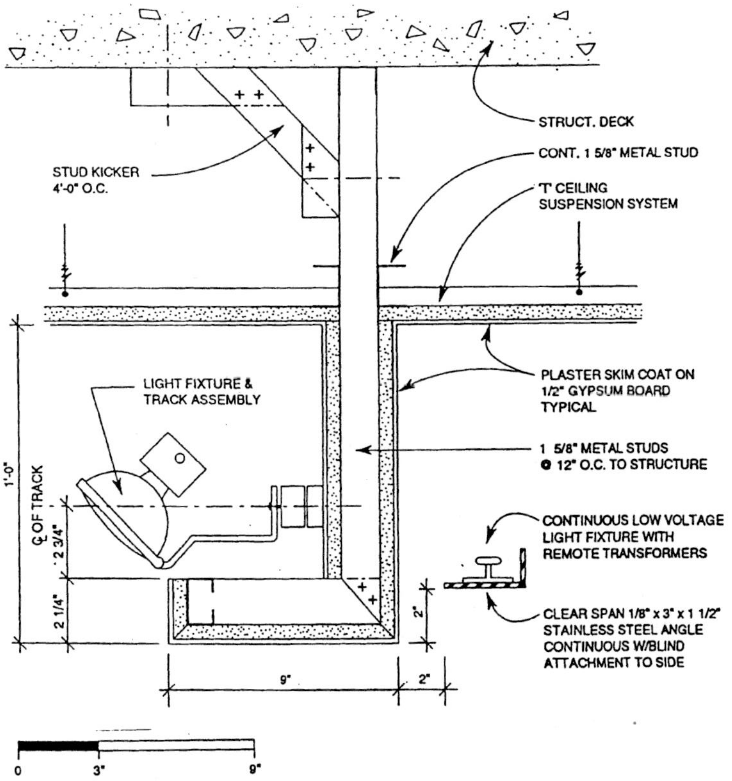
STRUCT. DECK
CONT. 1 5/8" METAL STUD
STUD KICKER 4'-0" O.C.
'T' CEILING SUSPENSION SYSTEM
PLASTER SKIM COAT ON 1/2" GYPSUM BOARD TYPICAL
LIGHT FIXTURE & TRACK ASSEMBLY
1 5/8" METAL STUDS @ 12" O.C. TO STRUCTURE
CONTINUOUS LOW VOLTAGE LIGHT FIXTURE WITH REMOTE TRANSFORMERS
CLEAR SPAN 1/8" x 3" x 1 1/2" STAINLESS STEEL ANGLE CONTINUOUS W/BLIND ATTACHMENT TO SIDE
1'-0"
℄ OF TRACK
2 3/4"
2 1/4"
2"
9"
2"
0
3"
9"

LIGHTING

Fluorescent Cove Lighting Details

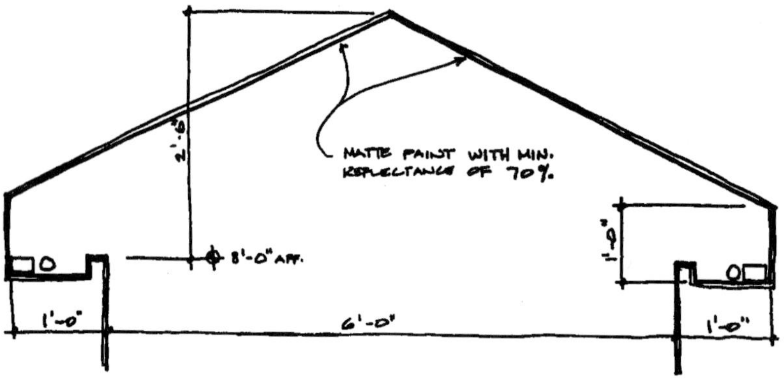

SECTION THRU COVE UPLIGHT

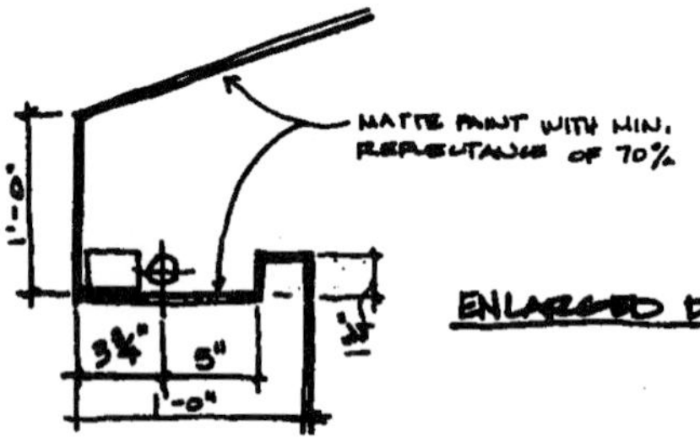

ENLARGED DETAIL

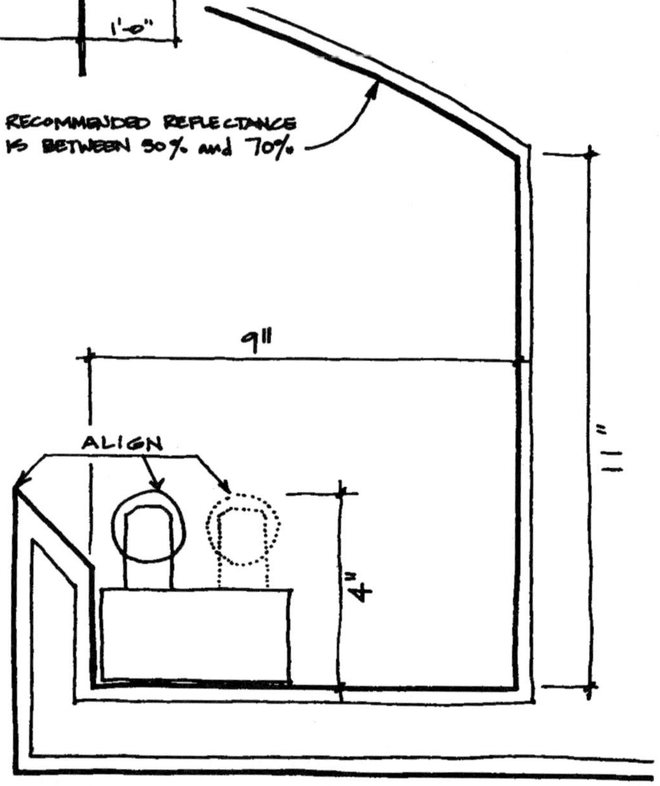

SECTION THRU COVE

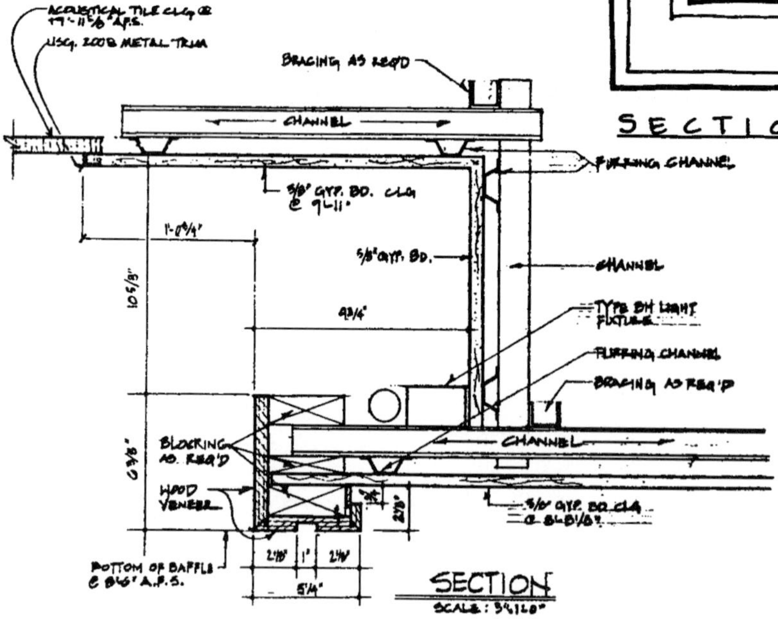

SECTION

SCALE: 3"=1'-0"

LIGHTING

Cove Lighting for Merchandise Displays

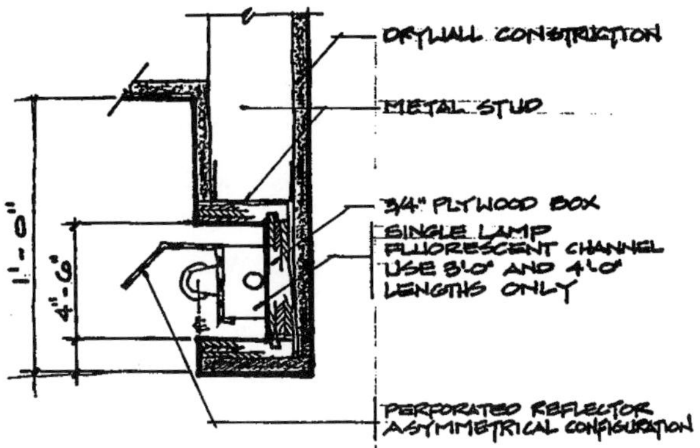

SHIELDED VALANCE WITH SINGLE LAMP FLUORESCENT CHANNEL "CURTAIN WALL" TYPE

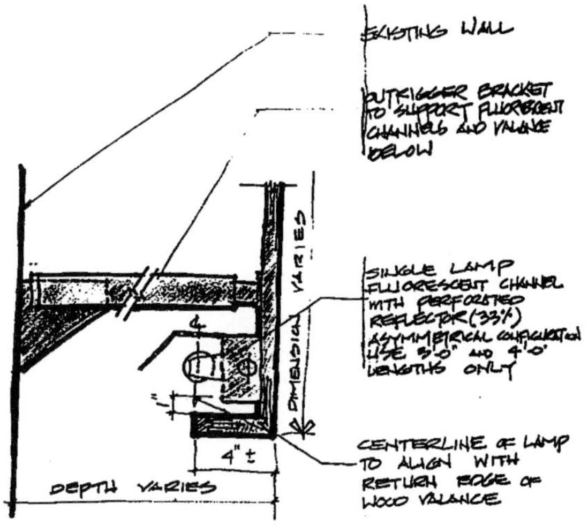

VALANCE WITH SINGLE LAMP FLUORESCENT CHANNEL

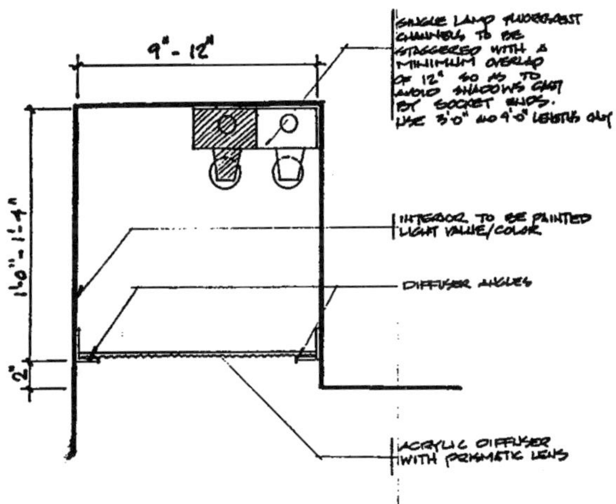

DIRECT COVE SINGLE/DOUBLE ROW STAGGERED FLUORESCENT

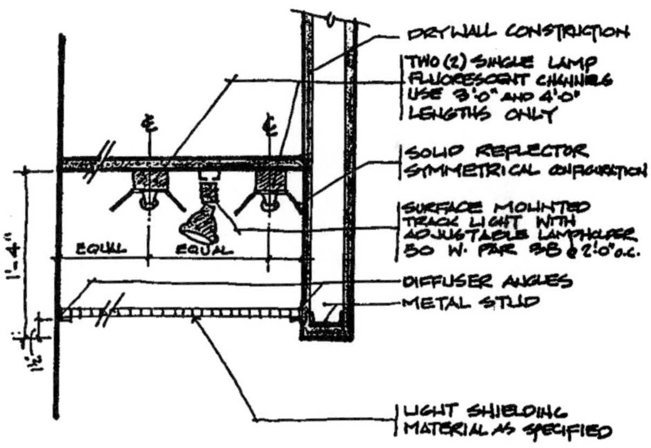

SHIELDED VALANCE WITH TWO (2) SINGLE LAMP FLUORESCENT CHANNELS AND TRACK LIGHT WITH INCANDESCENT "CURTAIN WALL" TYPE

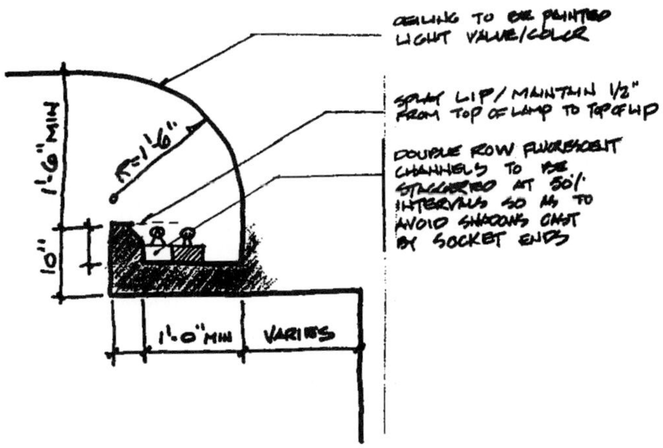

INDIRECT/CURVED COVE DOUBLE ROW FLUORESCENT

LIGHTING

Miscellaneous Lighting Details

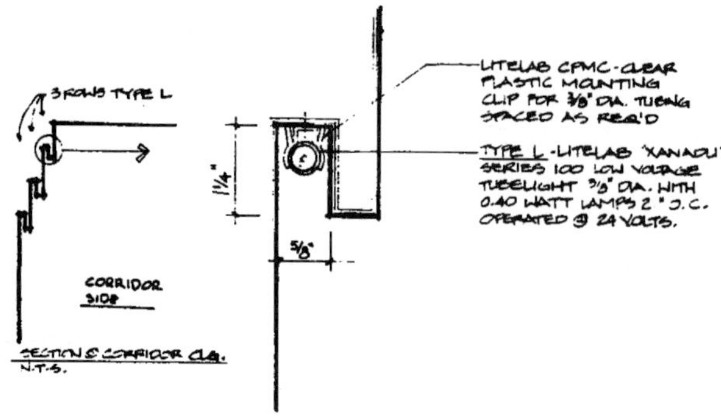

SECTION-TYPE L
SCALE: 3"=1'-0"

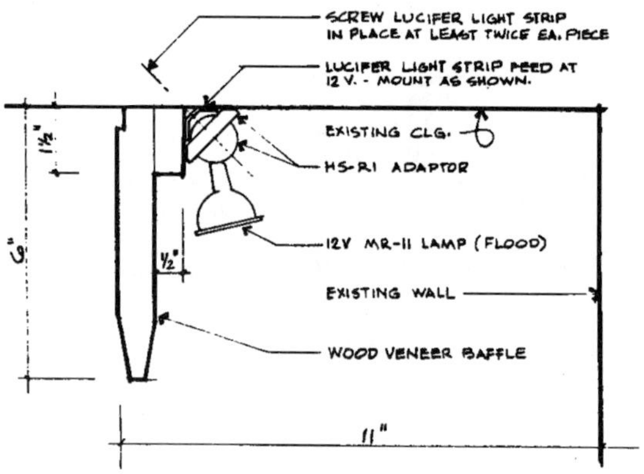

SECTION - TYPE M
SCALE: HALF SIZE

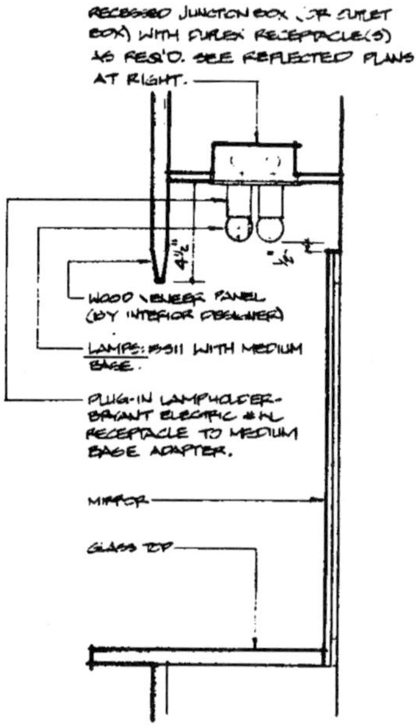

SECTION-TYPE G
SCALE: 3"=1'-0"

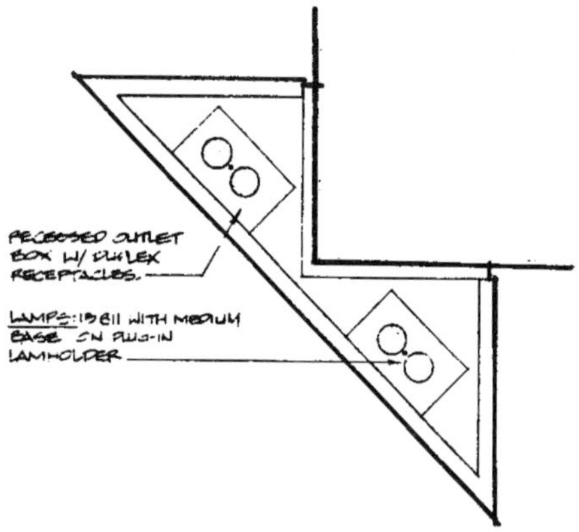

REFLECTED PLAN @ LIVING ROOM
SCALE: 3"=1'-0"

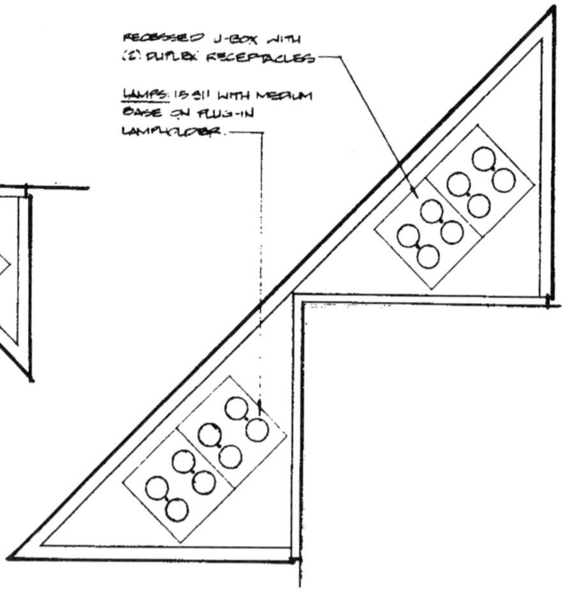

REFLECTED PLAN @ AUDIO VISUAL AREA
SCALE: 3"=1'-0"

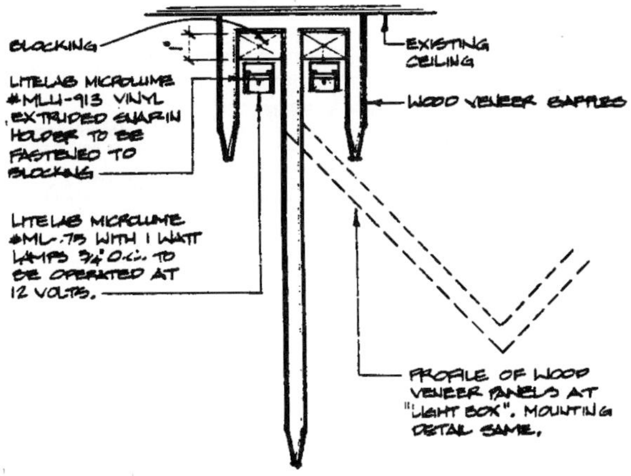
BLOCKING
EXISTING CEILING
LITELAB MICROLUME #MLU-913 VINYL EXTRUDED SNAP-IN HOLDER TO BE FASTENED TO BLOCKING
WOOD VENEER BAFFLES
LITELAB MICROLUME #ML-.75 WITH 1 WATT LAMPS 3/4" O.C. TO BE OPERATED AT 12 VOLTS.
PROFILE OF WOOD VENEER PANELS AT "LIGHT BOX". MOUNTING DETAIL SAME.

SECTION-TYPE A

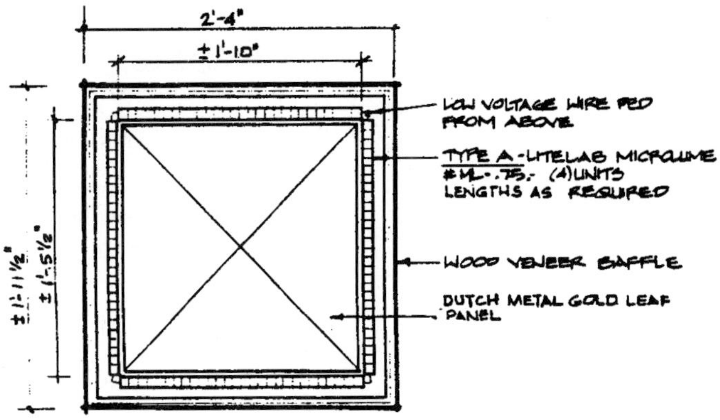
2'-4"
± 1'-10"
± 1'-11 1/2"
± 1'-5 1/8"
LOW VOLTAGE WIRE FED FROM ABOVE
TYPE A-LITELAB MICROLUME #ML-.75,- (4) UNITS LENGTHS AS REQUIRED
WOOD VENEER BAFFLE
DUTCH METAL GOLD LEAF PANEL

REFLECTED PLAN @ LIGHT BOX-

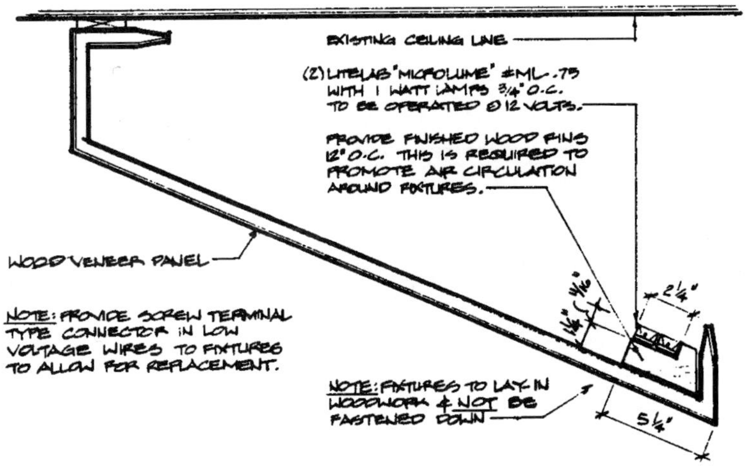
EXISTING CEILING LINE
(2) LITELAB 'MICROLUME' #ML-.75 WITH 1 WATT LAMPS 3/4" O.C. TO BE OPERATED @ 12 VOLTS.
PROVIDE FINISHED WOOD FINS 12" O.C. THIS IS REQUIRED TO PROMOTE AIR CIRCULATION AROUND FIXTURES.
WOOD VENEER PANEL
NOTE: PROVIDE SCREW TERMINAL TYPE CONNECTOR IN LOW VOLTAGE WIRES TO FIXTURES TO ALLOW FOR REPLACEMENT.
2 1/4"
NOTE: FIXTURES TO LAY IN WOODWORK & NOT BE FASTENED DOWN
5 1/4"

SECTION-TYPE B

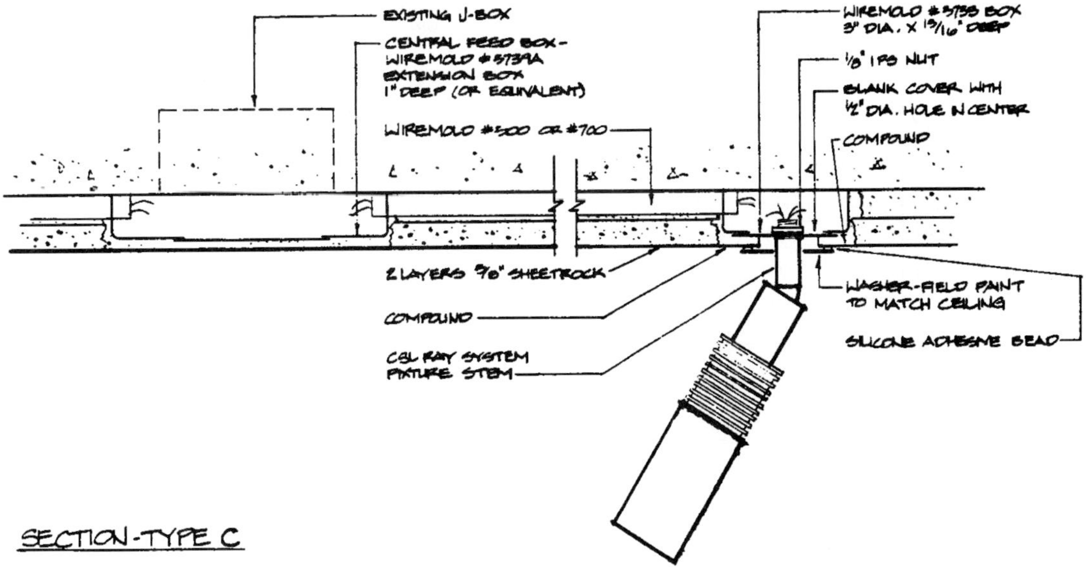
EXISTING J-BOX
CENTRAL FEED BOX- WIREMOLD #5739A EXTENSION BOX 1" DEEP (OR EQUIVALENT)
WIREMOLD #500 OR #700
WIREMOLD #5738 BOX 3" DIA. X 13/16" DEEP
1/8" IPS NUT
BLANK COVER WITH 1/2" DIA. HOLE IN CENTER
COMPOUND
2 LAYERS 5/8" SHEETROCK
COMPOUND
CBL RAY SYSTEM FIXTURE STEM
WASHER-FIELD PAINT TO MATCH CEILING
SILICONE ADHESIVE BEAD

SECTION-TYPE C

LIGHTING

Miscellaneous Lighting Details

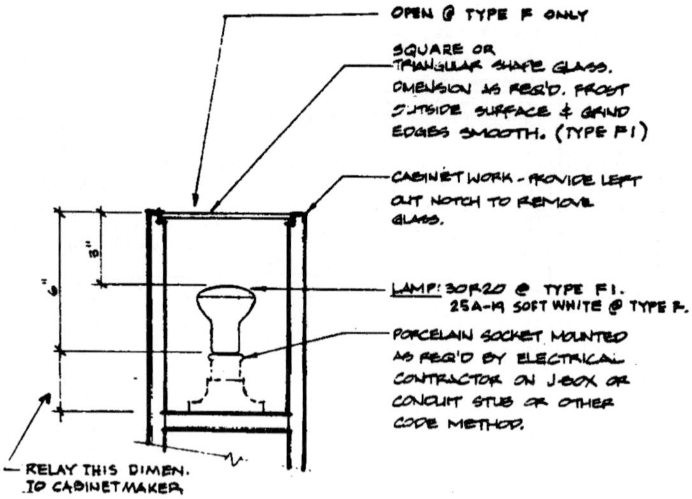
OPEN @ TYPE F ONLY
SQUARE OR TRIANGULAR SHAPE GLASS. DIMENSION AS REQ'D. FROST OUTSIDE SURFACE & GRIND EDGES SMOOTH. (TYPE F1)
CABINET WORK - PROVIDE LEFT OUT NOTCH TO REMOVE GLASS.
LAMP: 30R20 @ TYPE F1. 25A-19 SOFT WHITE @ TYPE F.
PORCELAIN SOCKET MOUNTED AS REQ'D BY ELECTRICAL CONTRACTOR ON J-BOX OR CONDUIT STUB OR OTHER CODE METHOD.
RELAY THIS DIMEN. TO CABINETMAKER

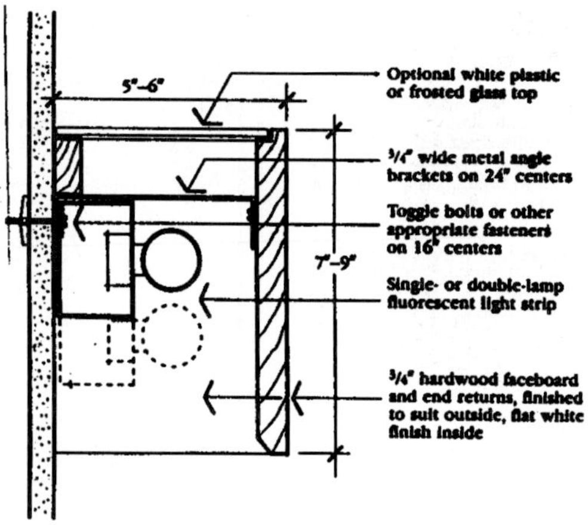
5"–6"
7"–9"
Optional white plastic or frosted glass top
3/4" wide metal angle brackets on 24" centers
Toggle bolts or other appropriate fasteners on 16" centers
Single- or double-lamp fluorescent light strip
3/4" hardwood faceboard and end returns, finished to suit outside, flat white finish inside

Wall bracket cross section

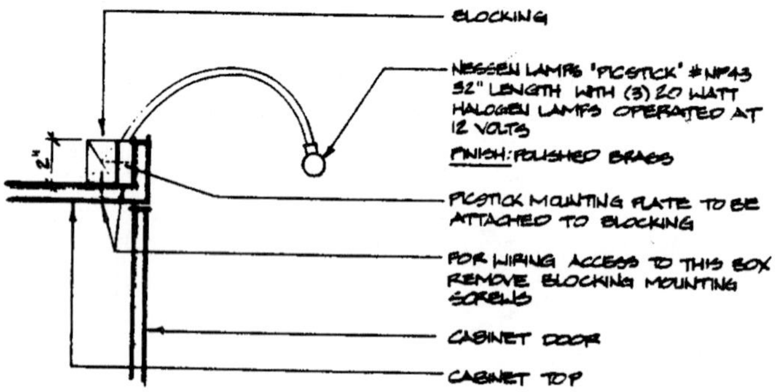
BLOCKING
NESSEN LAMPS 'PICSTICK' #NP43 32" LENGTH WITH (3) 20 WATT HALOGEN LAMPS OPERATED AT 12 VOLTS
FINISH: POLISHED BRASS
PICSTICK MOUNTING PLATE TO BE ATTACHED TO BLOCKING
FOR WIRING ACCESS TO THIS BOX REMOVE BLOCKING MOUNTING SCREWS
CABINET DOOR
CABINET TOP

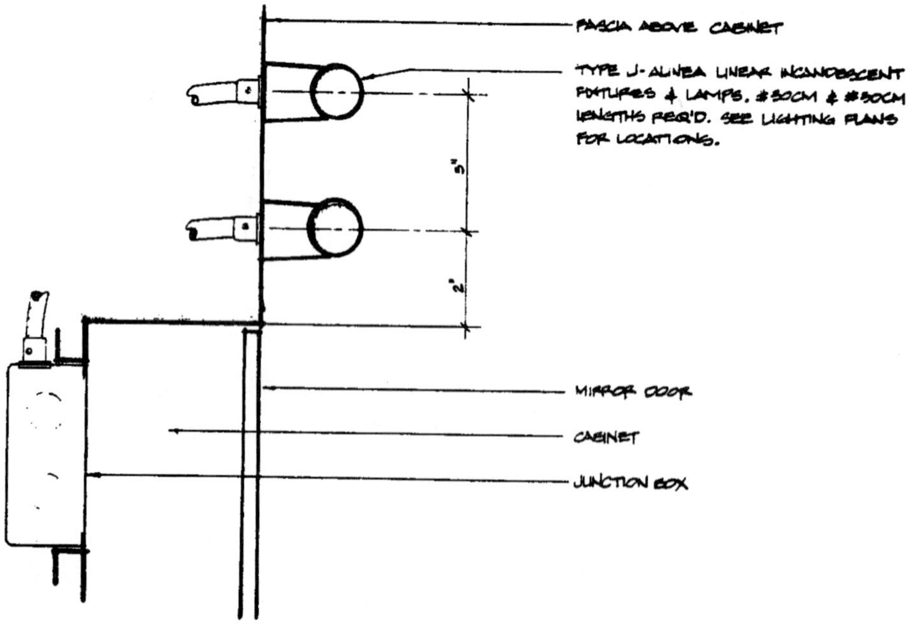
FASCIA ABOVE CABINET
TYPE J- ALINEA LINEAR INCANDESCENT FIXTURES & LAMPS. #30CM & #50CM LENGTHS REQ'D. SEE LIGHTING PLANS FOR LOCATIONS.
MIRROR DOOR
CABINET
JUNCTION BOX

LIGHTING

Miscellaneous Lighting Details

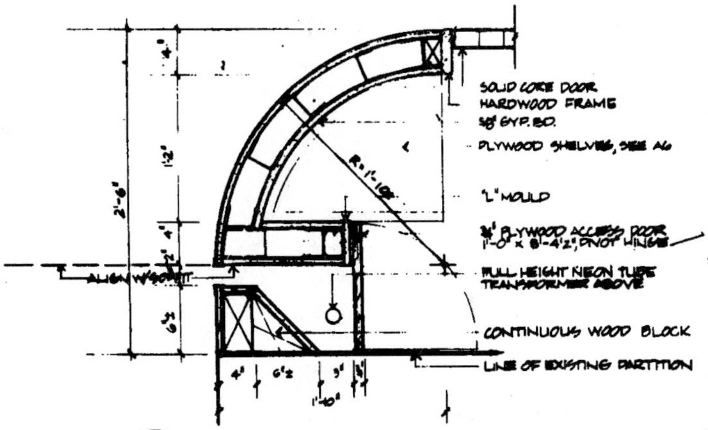

1 PLAN: NEON/NICHE: ENTRY
A4 1½" = 1'-0"

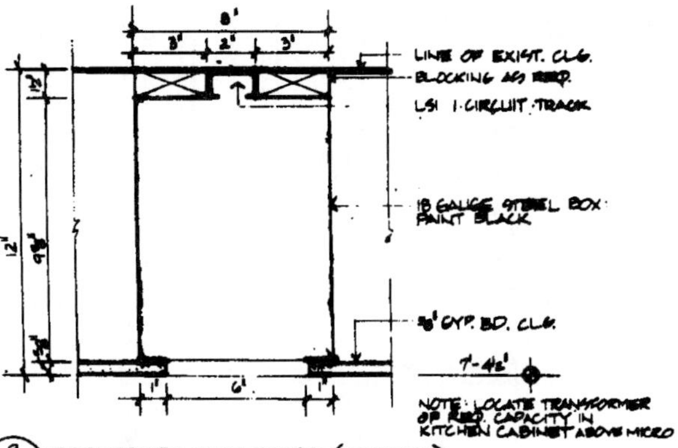

3 RECESSED LIGHT TROUGH (KITCHEN)
A4 3" = 1'-0"

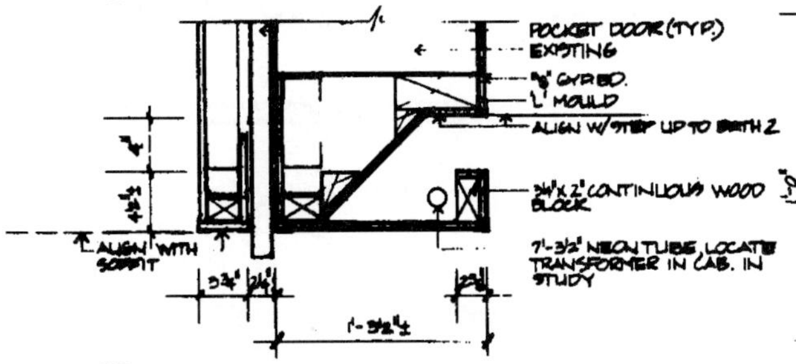

2 PLAN: NEON NICHE: STUDY
A4 1½" = 1'-0"

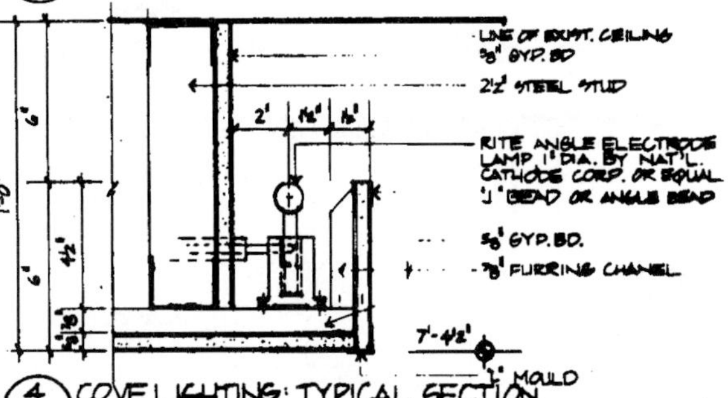

4 COVE LIGHTING: TYPICAL SECTION
A4 3" = 1'-0"

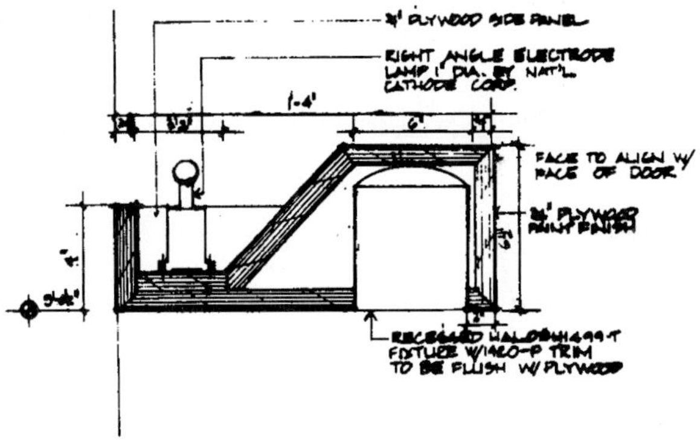

5 LIGHT FIXTURE OVER BED: BDRM 1
A4 3" = 1'-0"

LIGHTING

Miscellaneous Lighting Details

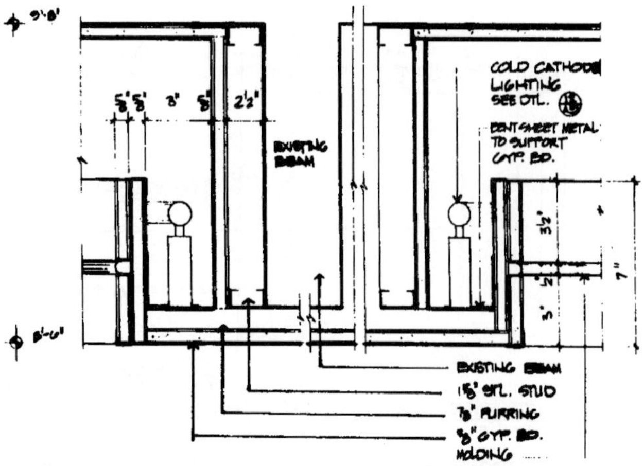

11/A9 DETAIL: COVE LIGHTING IN LIVING ROOM
3"=1'-0"

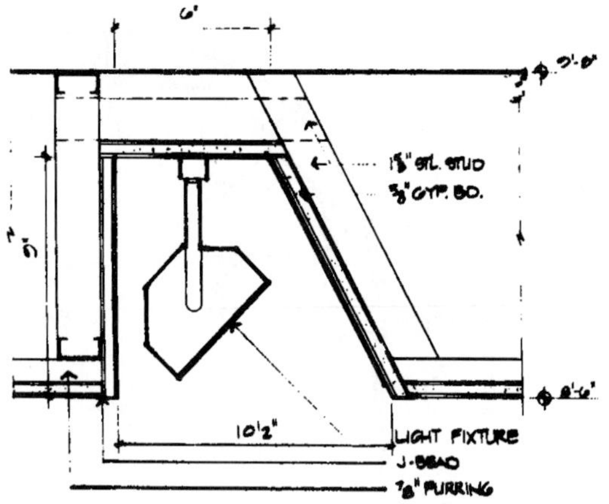

13/A9 DETAIL: COVE LIGHTING @ SLOPED WALL & HALL
3"=1'-0"

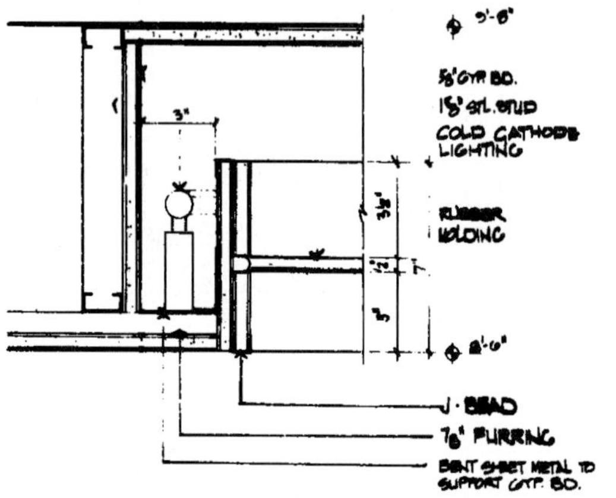

12/A9 DETAIL: COVE LIGHTING IN LIVING, DINING & FAM. RMS.
3"=1'-0"

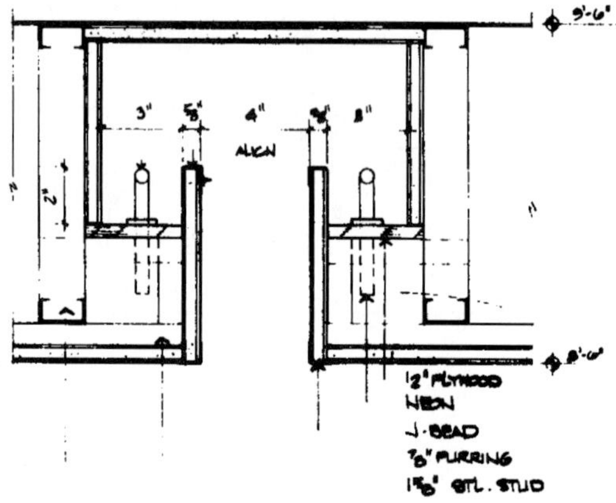

14/A9 DETAIL: NEON RECESS @ ENTRY
3"=1'-0"

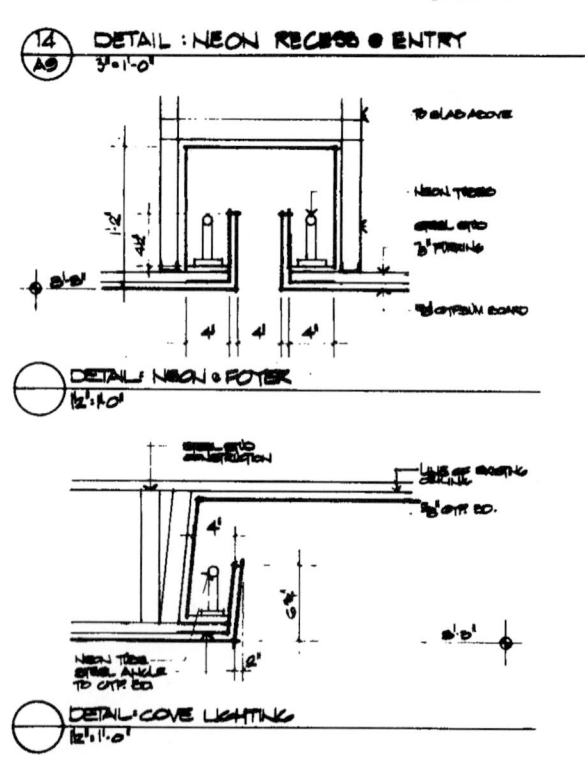

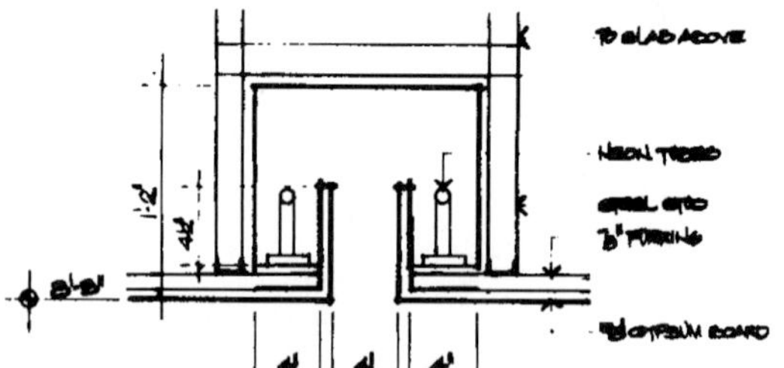

DETAIL: NEON @ FOYER
1½"=1'-0"

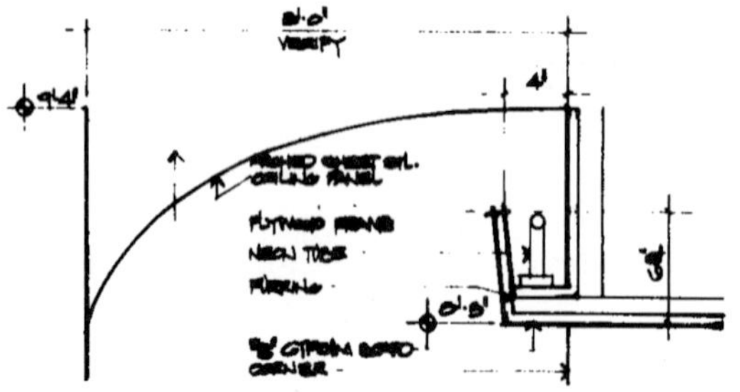

DETAIL: COVE LIGHT @ BAR
1½"=1'-0"

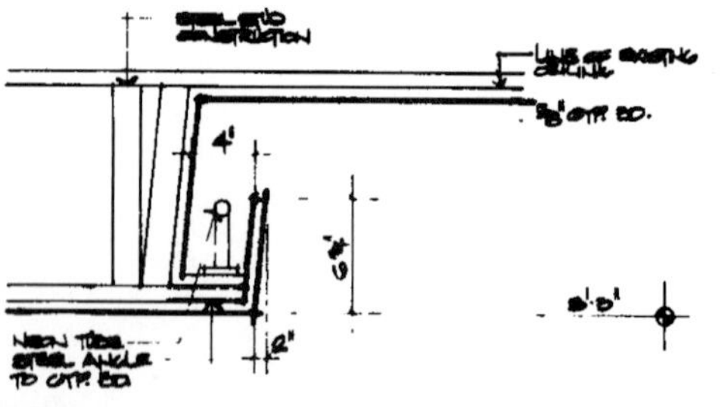

DETAIL: COVE LIGHTING
1½"=1'-0"

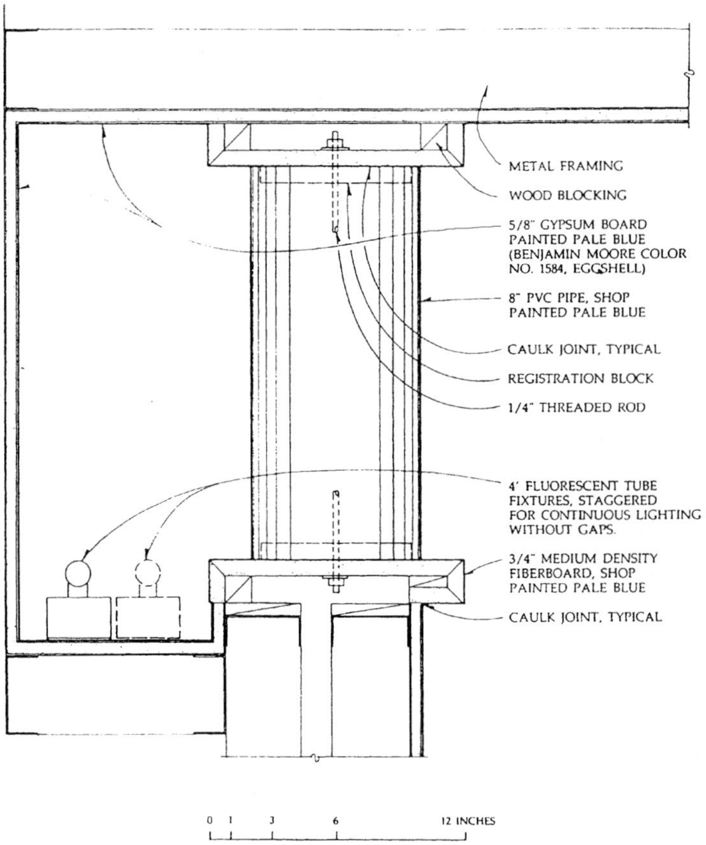
METAL FRAMING
WOOD BLOCKING
5/8" GYPSUM BOARD PAINTED PALE BLUE (BENJAMIN MOORE COLOR NO. 1584, EGGSHELL)
8" PVC PIPE, SHOP PAINTED PALE BLUE
CAULK JOINT, TYPICAL
REGISTRATION BLOCK
1/4" THREADED ROD
4' FLUORESCENT TUBE FIXTURES, STAGGERED FOR CONTINUOUS LIGHTING WITHOUT GAPS.
3/4" MEDIUM DENSITY FIBERBOARD, SHOP PAINTED PALE BLUE
CAULK JOINT, TYPICAL
0 1 3 6 12 INCHES

SECTION THROUGH LIGHT COVE

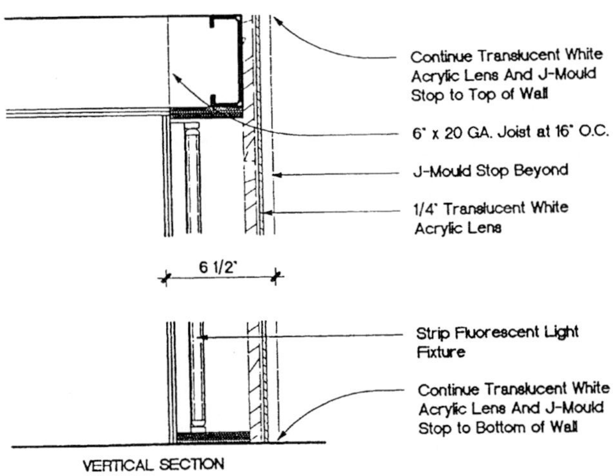
Continue Translucent White Acrylic Lens And J-Mould Stop to Top of Wall
6" x 20 GA. Joist at 16" O.C.
J-Mould Stop Beyond
1/4" Translucent White Acrylic Lens
6 1/2"
Strip Fluorescent Light Fixture
Continue Translucent White Acrylic Lens And J-Mould Stop to Bottom of Wall
VERTICAL SECTION

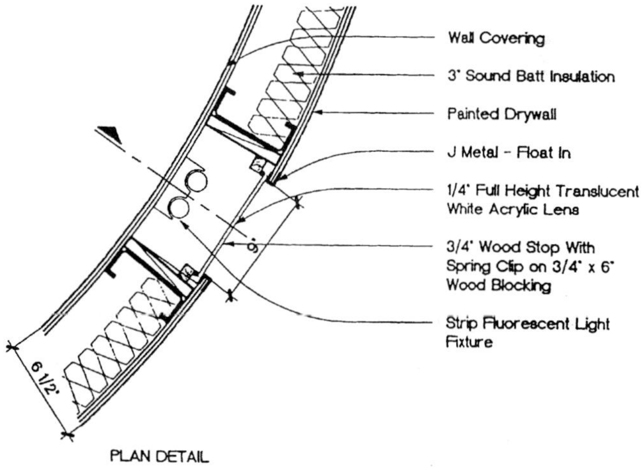
Wall Covering
3" Sound Batt Insulation
Painted Drywall
J Metal - Float In
1/4" Full Height Translucent White Acrylic Lens
3/4" Wood Stop With Spring Clip on 3/4" x 6" Wood Blocking
Strip Fluorescent Light Fixture
6 1/2"
PLAN DETAIL

VERTICAL LIGHT SHIFT

LIGHTING

Miscellaneous Lighting Details

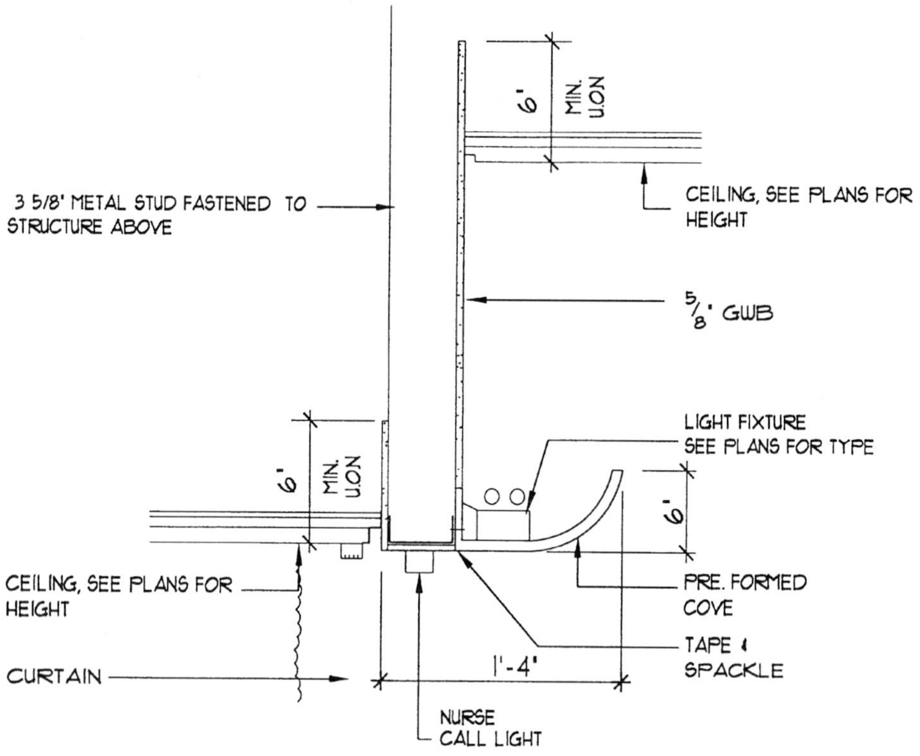

9 RECOVERY ROOM CEILING DETAIL

1½" = 1'-0"

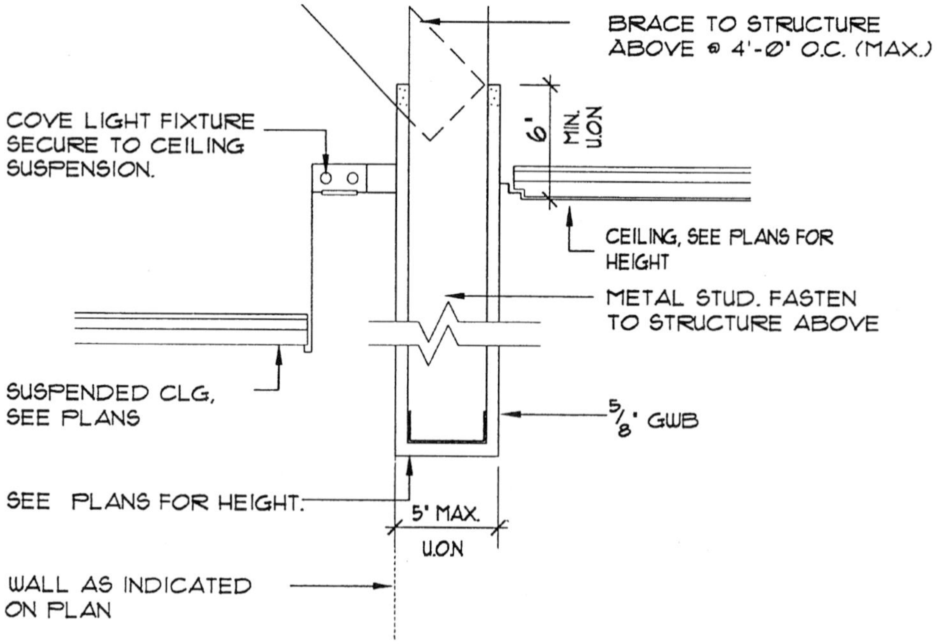

10 LIGHT SOFFIT DETAIL

1½" = 1'-0"

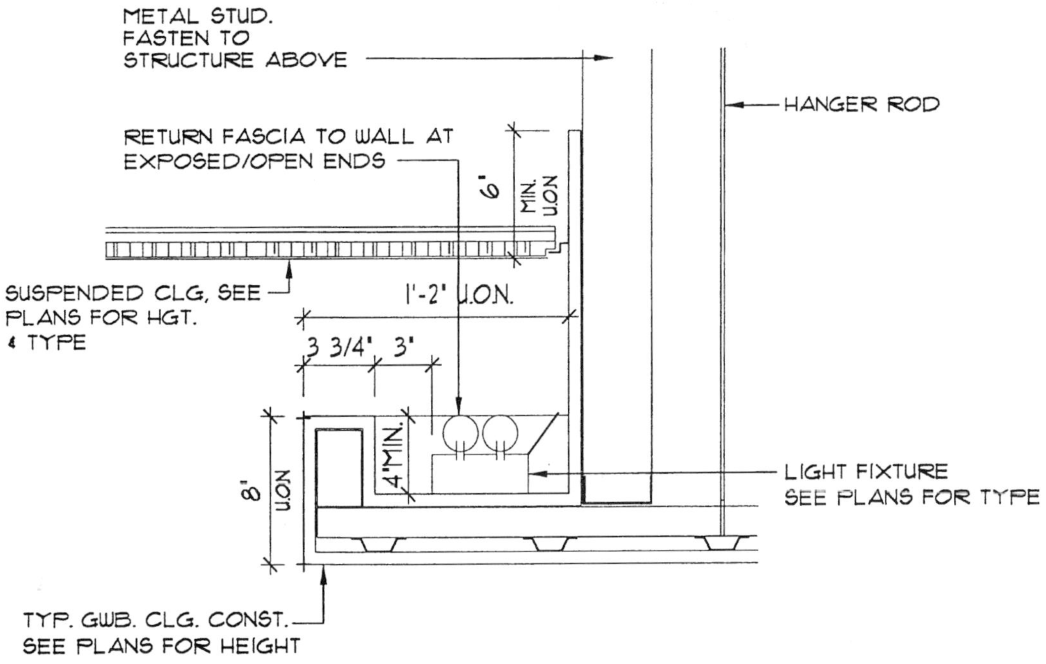

11 LIGHT COVE DETAIL
1½" = 1'-0"

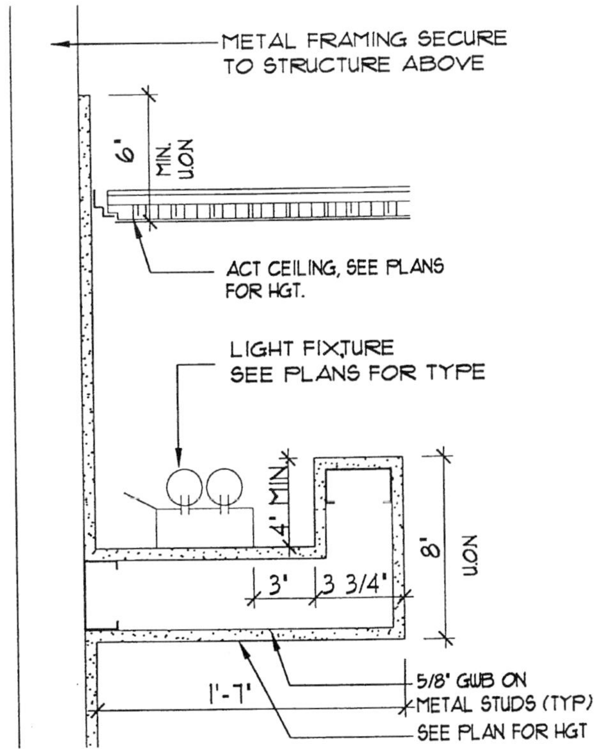

12 LIGHT COVE DETAIL
NOT TO SCALE

LIGHTING

Miscellaneous Lighting Details

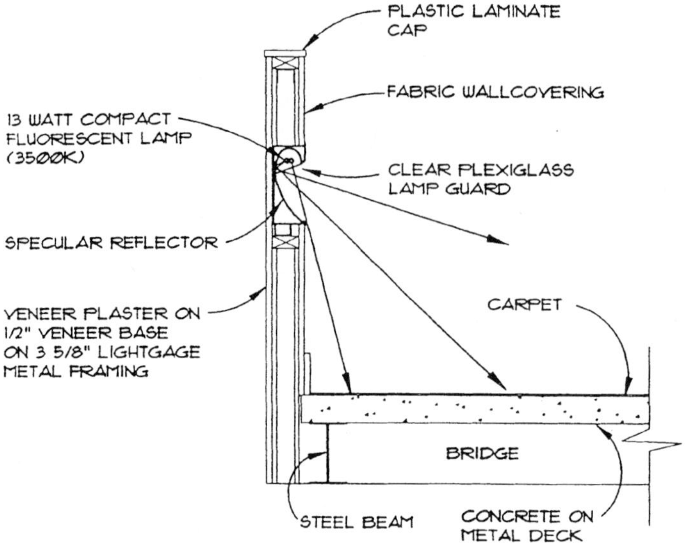

SECTION "A-A"

POCKETLIGHT DETAIL

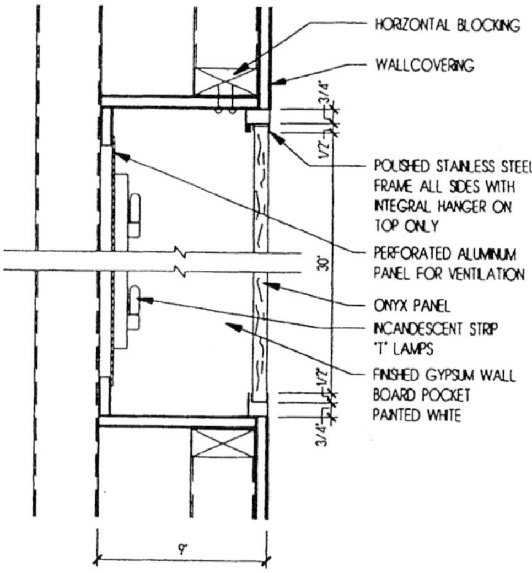

VERTICAL SECTION

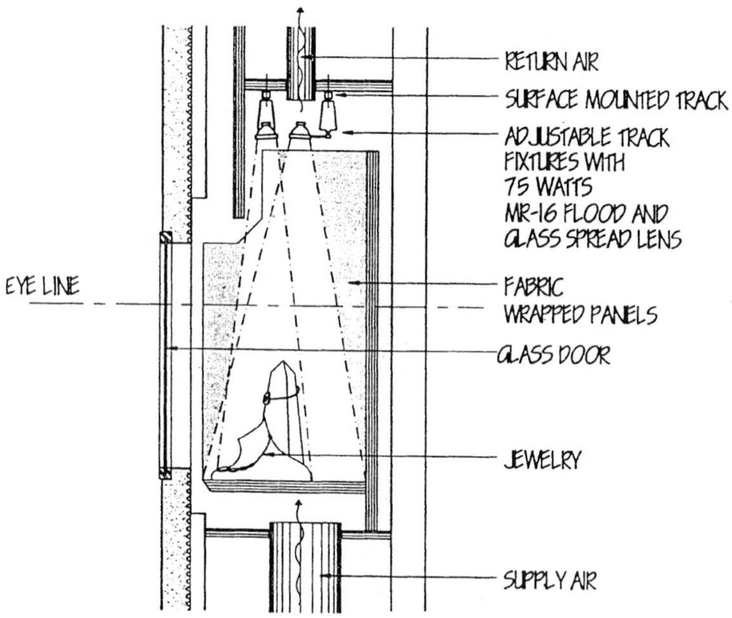

VITRINE LIGHTING

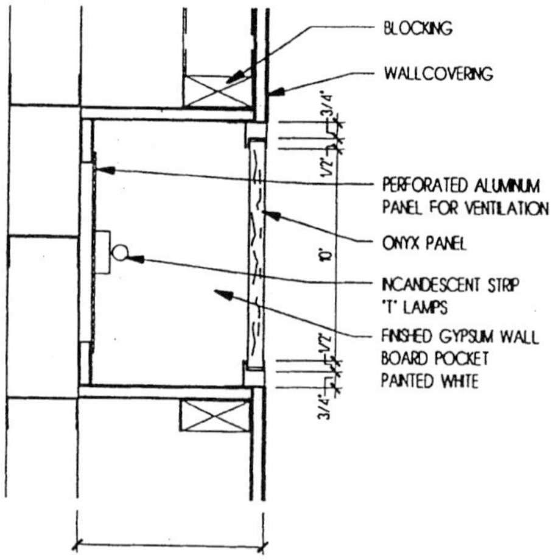

PLAN SECTION

WALL PANEL LIGHTS

LIGHTING

Miscellaneous Lighting Details

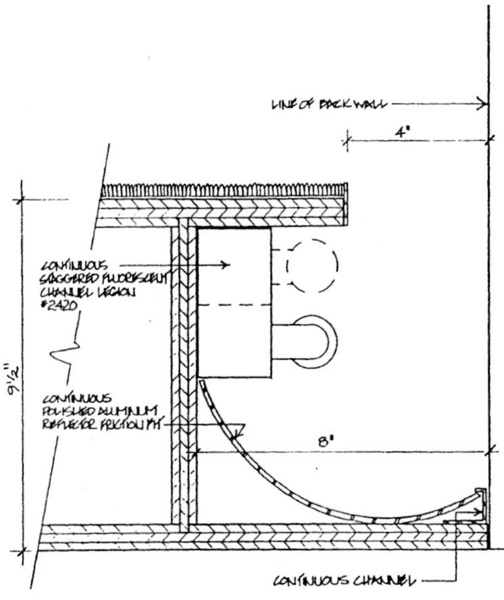

FLOOR COVE UPLIGHT

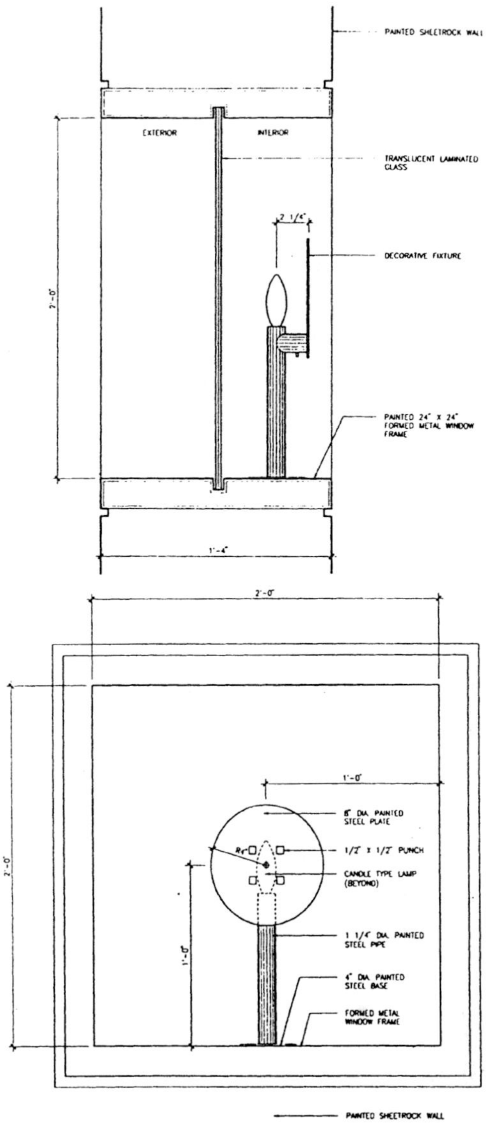

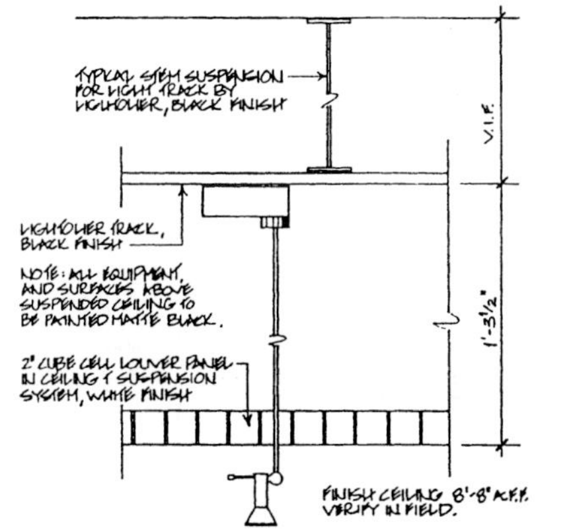

LOUVER CEILING
& ACCENT LIGHT

WINDOW "CUBE" LIGHTS

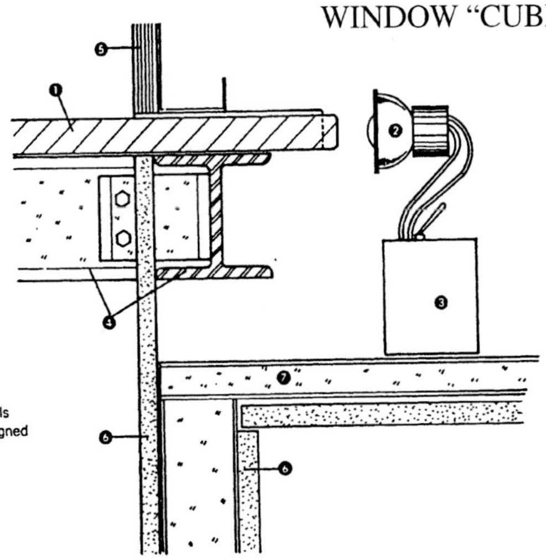

1. 1" Tempered laminated glass floor panels
2. MR 16 halogen lamp and lampholder aligned with exposed edge of glass, 1'0" o.c.
3. Transformer
4. Steel support structure
5. Plywood housing around HVAC unit
6. Drywall
7. Metal framing

LIGHTED GLASS FLOOR

LIGHTING
Miscellaneous Lighting Details

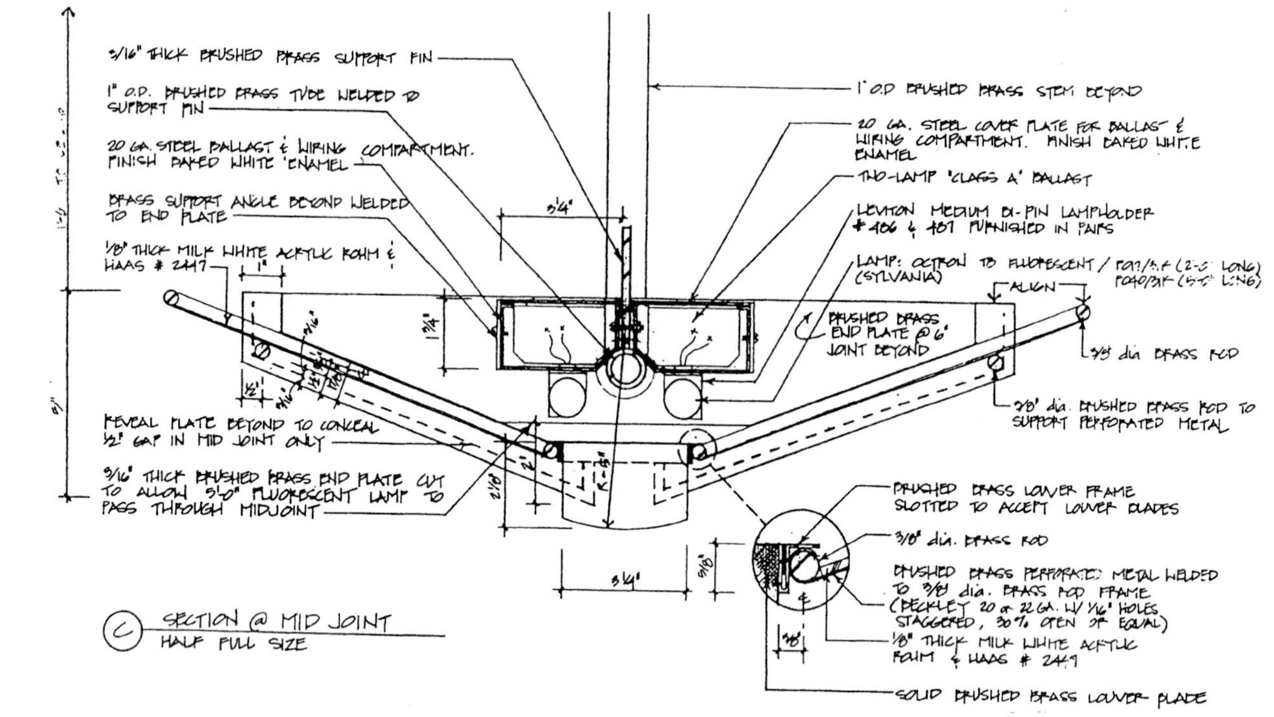

SUSPENDED BRASS & ACRYLIC LIGHT FIXTURE

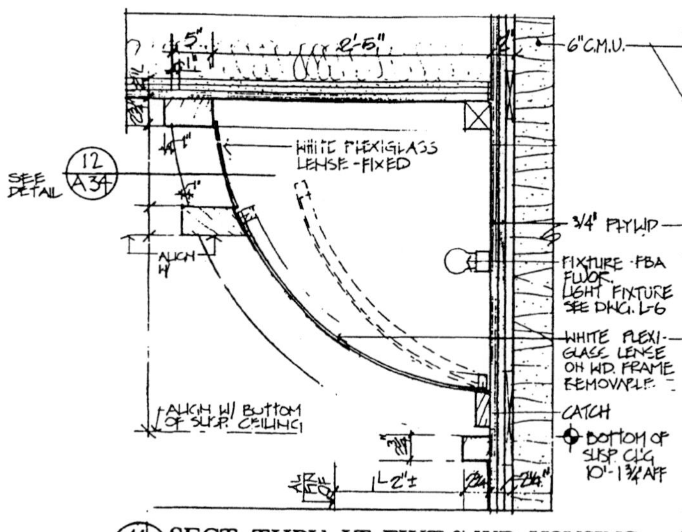

11 A34 SECT. THRU LT. FIXT.& WD. HOUSING

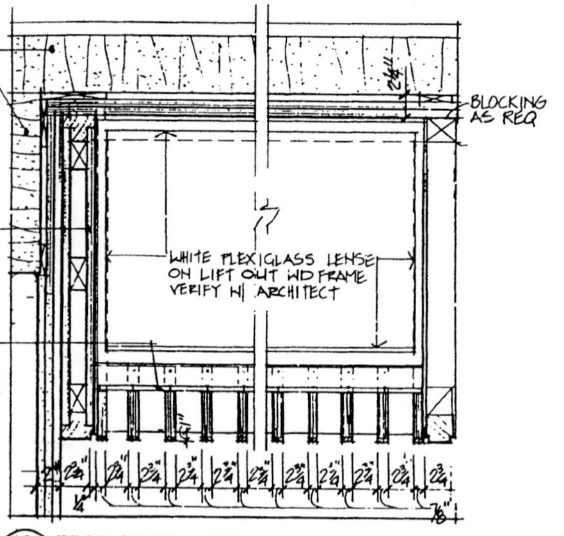

12 A34 PLN. SECT. THRU WD. LT. FIXT. HOUSING
SCALE: 3" = 1'-0"

"QUARTER TURN" WOOD & PLEXIGLASS LIGHT FIXTURE

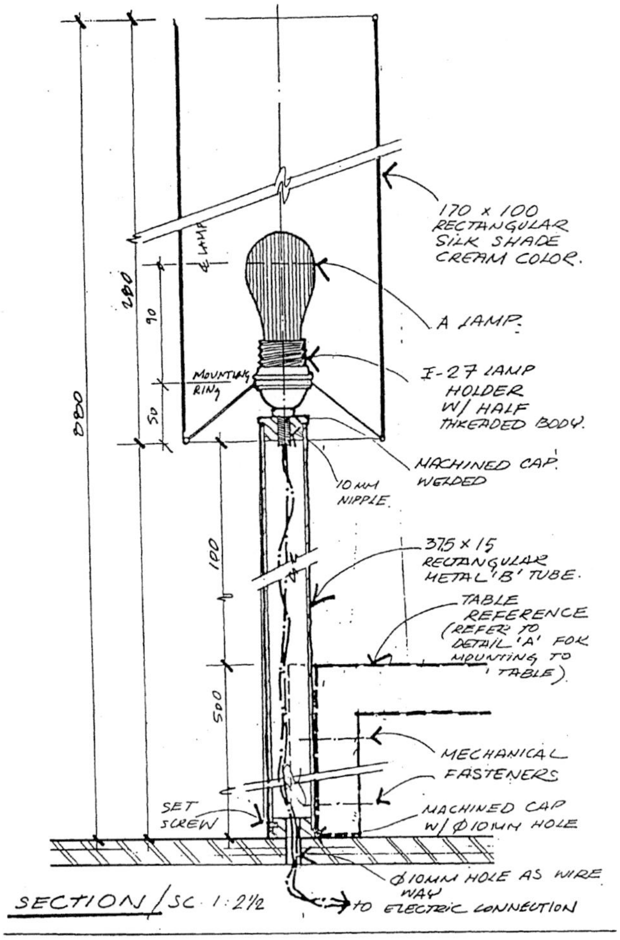
170 x 100 RECTANGULAR SILK SHADE CREAM COLOR.
A LAMP.
MOUNTING RING
E-27 LAMP HOLDER W/ HALF THREADED BODY.
MACHINED CAP. WELDED
10 MM NIPPLE.
37.5 x 15 RECTANGULAR METAL 'B' TUBE.
TABLE REFERENCE (REFER TO DETAIL 'A' FOR MOUNTING TO TABLE).
MECHANICAL FASTENERS
MACHINED CAP W/ Ø10MM HOLE
SET SCREW
Ø10MM HOLE AS WIRE WAY
TO ELECTRIC CONNECTION
SECTION / SC 1:2½
280
90
50
100
500
880

TABLE MOUNTED

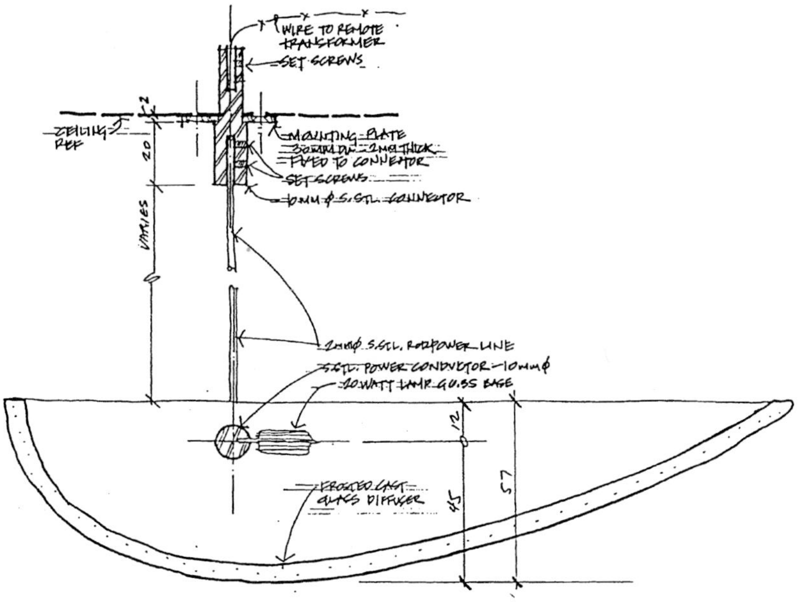
WIRE TO REMOTE TRANSFORMER
SET SCREWS
CEILING REF
MOUNTING PLATE
SET SCREWS
VARIES
FROSTED CAST GLASS DIFFUSER
20
12
45
57

PENDANT LIGHT

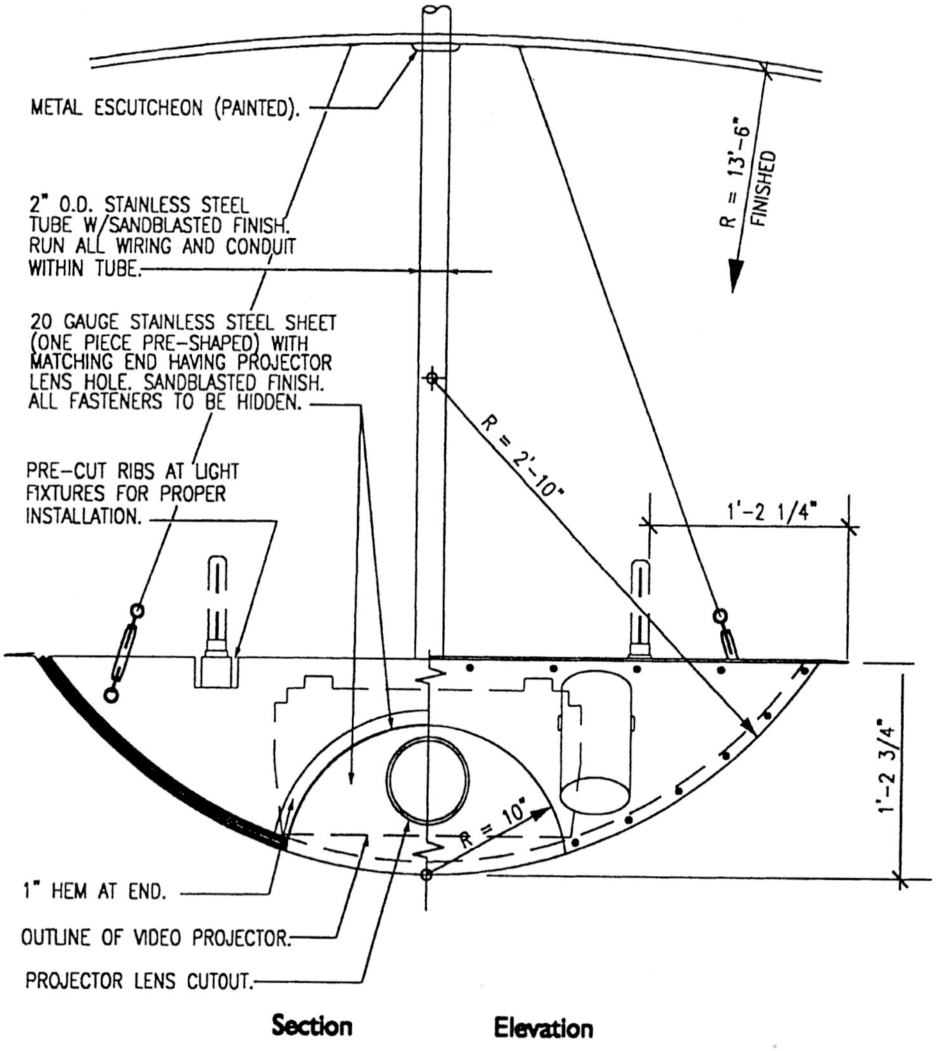

Lecture Hall Video Projector Enclosure

Detail

1" = 1'-0"

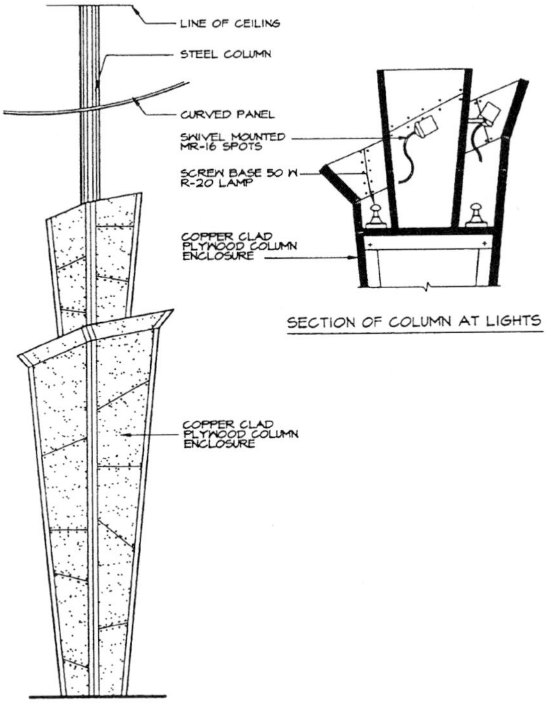
LINE OF CEILING
STEEL COLUMN
CURVED PANEL
SWIVEL MOUNTED MR-16 SPOTS
SCREW BASE 50 W R-20 LAMP
COPPER CLAD PLYWOOD COLUMN ENCLOSURE
SECTION OF COLUMN AT LIGHTS
COPPER CLAD PLYWOOD COLUMN ENCLOSURE

COLUMN ELEVATION

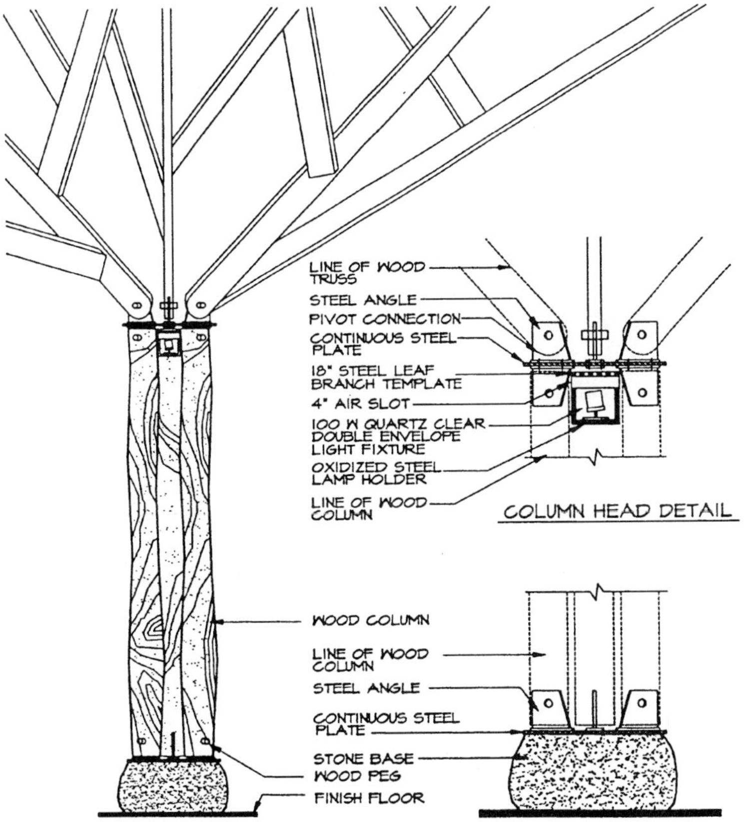
LINE OF WOOD TRUSS
STEEL ANGLE
PIVOT CONNECTION
CONTINUOUS STEEL PLATE
18" STEEL LEAF BRANCH TEMPLATE
4" AIR SLOT
100 W QUARTZ CLEAR DOUBLE ENVELOPE LIGHT FIXTURE
OXIDIZED STEEL LAMP HOLDER
LINE OF WOOD COLUMN
COLUMN HEAD DETAIL
WOOD COLUMN
LINE OF WOOD COLUMN
STEEL ANGLE
CONTINUOUS STEEL PLATE
STONE BASE
WOOD PEG
FINISH FLOOR

COLUMN ELEVATION

COLUMN BASE DETAIL

LIGHTING

Handrail Lighting Details

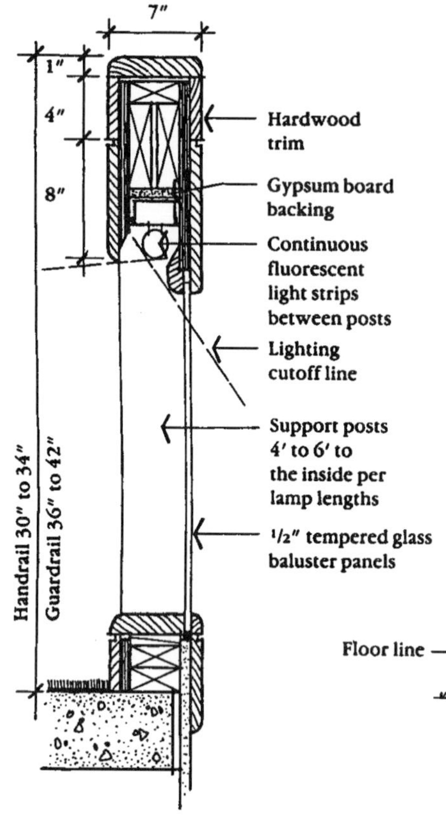

Lighted wood and glass guardrail

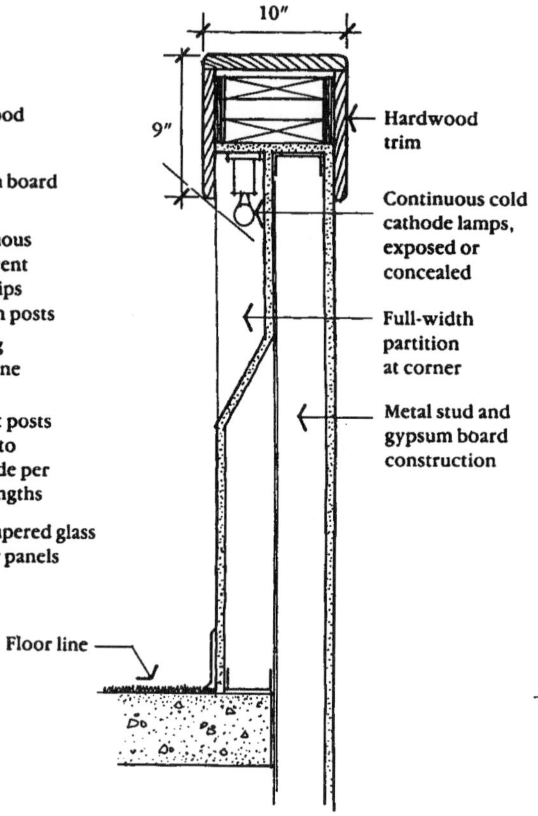

Lighted low-partition guardrail

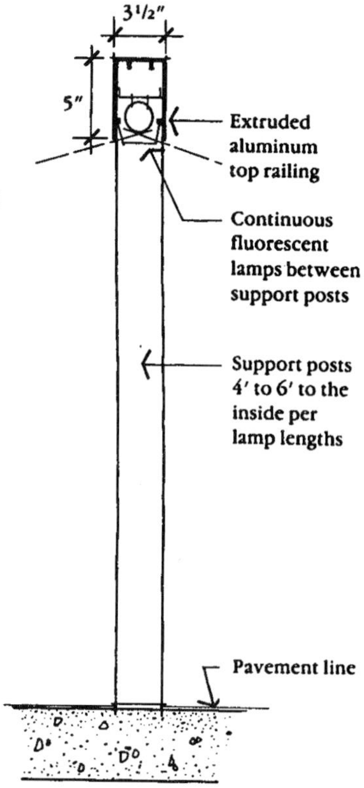

Extruded aluminum light rail

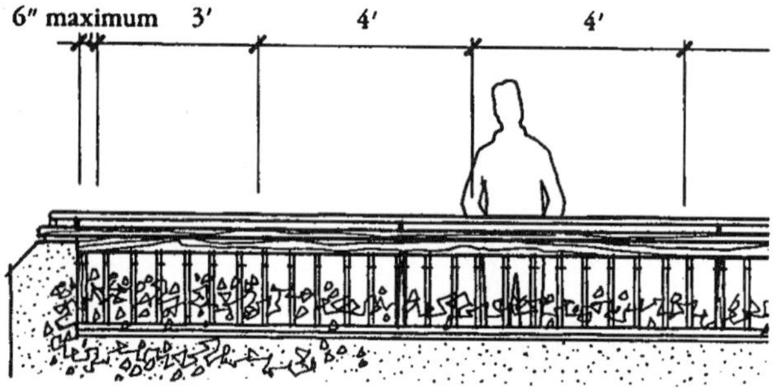

Elevation of lighted guardrail planter demonstrates the use of combined 3-foot and 4-foot fluorescent light strips to achieve overall lengths in 1-foot multiples. To minimize dark areas between lamps, use strips without end caps and install lamps back to back.

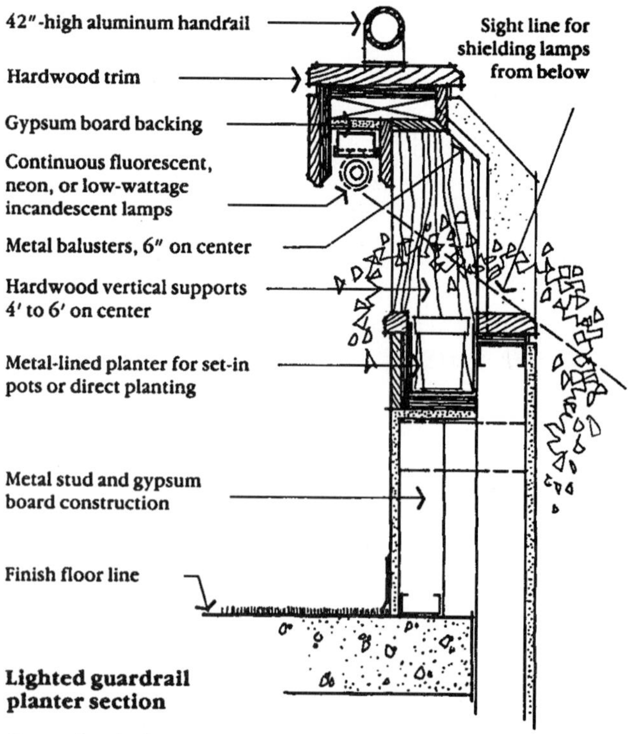

Lighted guardrail planter section

Open circulation areas can be illuminated with lighted railings, as shown in this section of a lighted guardrail planter.

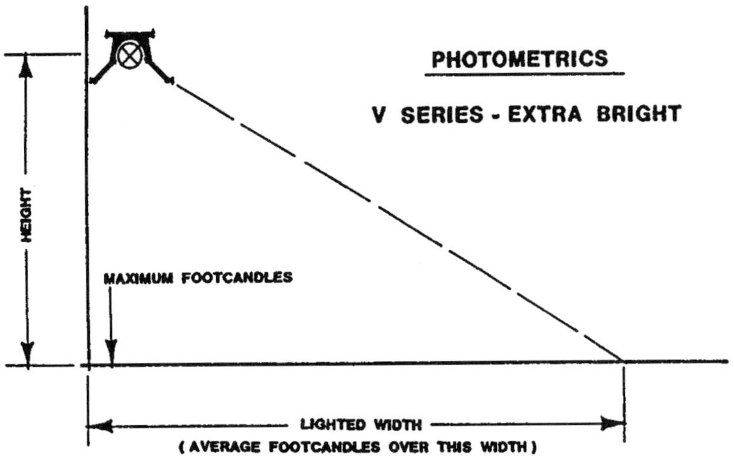

FOOTCANDLES

HT. ABOVE FLOOR IN.	LIGHTED WIDTH IN.(1)	AVERAGE(2)	MAXIMUM(3)
6	11	5.0	13.0
8	14	3.8	9.8
10	18	3.0	7.8
12	21	2.5	6.5
18	32	1.7	4.4
24	42	1.3	3.3
30	53	1.0	2.6
36	63	0.8	2.1

NOTES:

1. LIGHTED WIDTH TO POINT FOOTCANDLE LEVEL FALLS TO 10% OF MAXIMUM
2. AVERAGE FOOTCANDLES OVER LIGHTED WIDTH
3. FOOTCANDLES DIRECTLY BELOW LIGHT FIXTURE

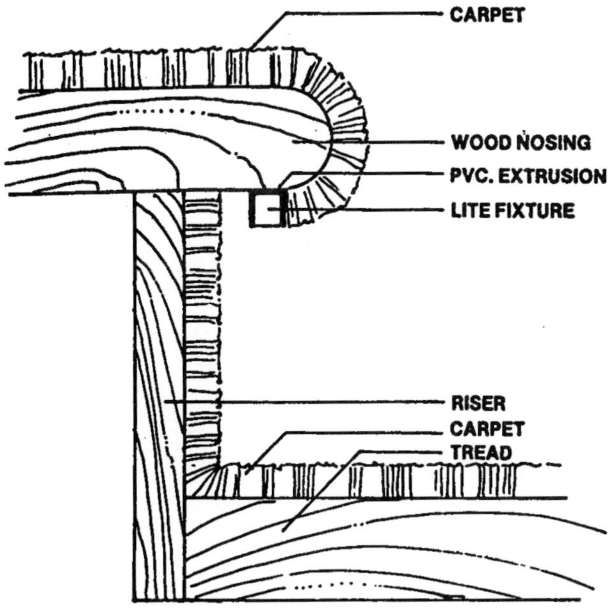

Fig. 16 Surface-mounted step light

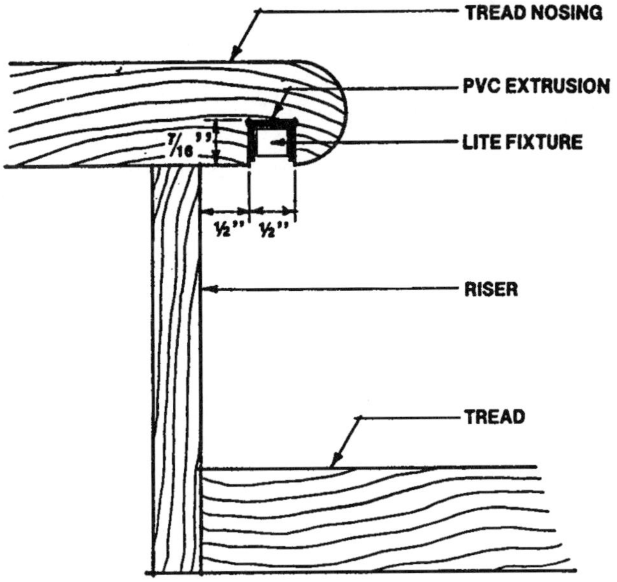

Fig. 17 Recessed step light

LIGHTING
Stair Lighting Details

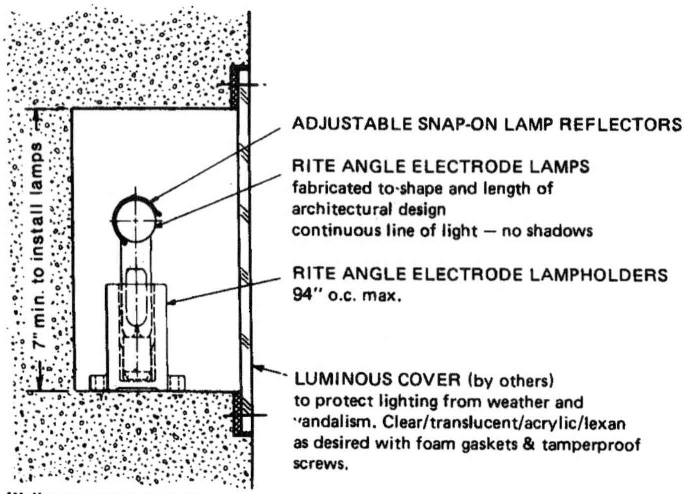

Wall recessed stair lighting

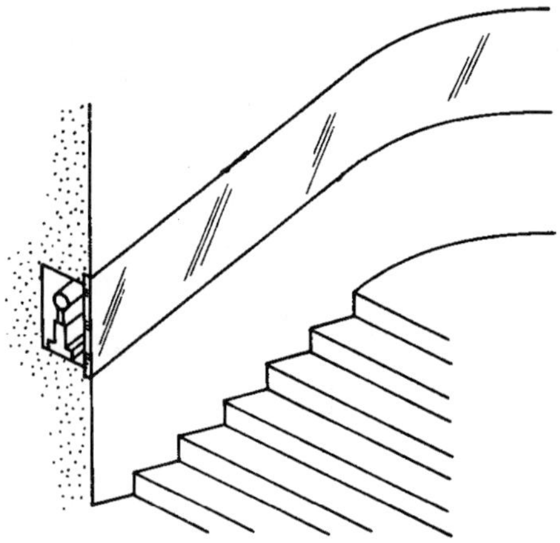

Schematic perspective

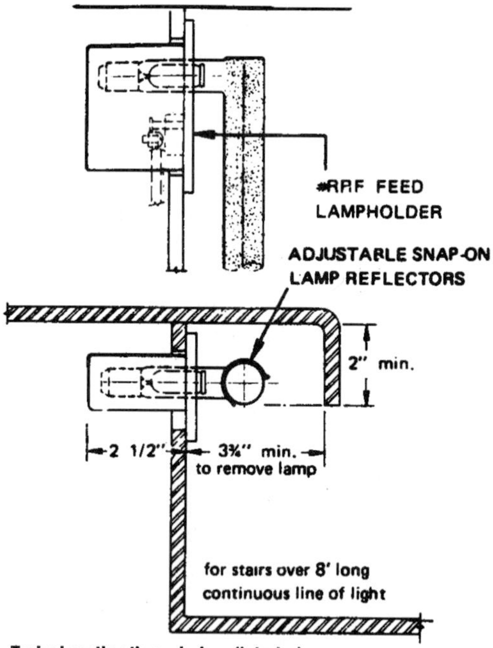

Typical section through riser (interior)

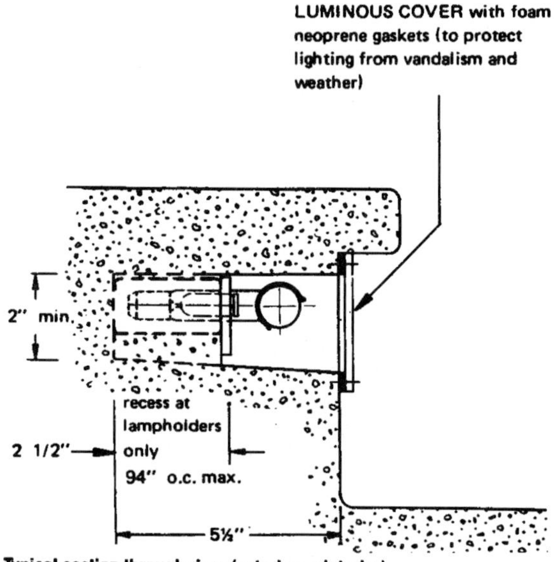

Typical section through riser (exterior or interior)

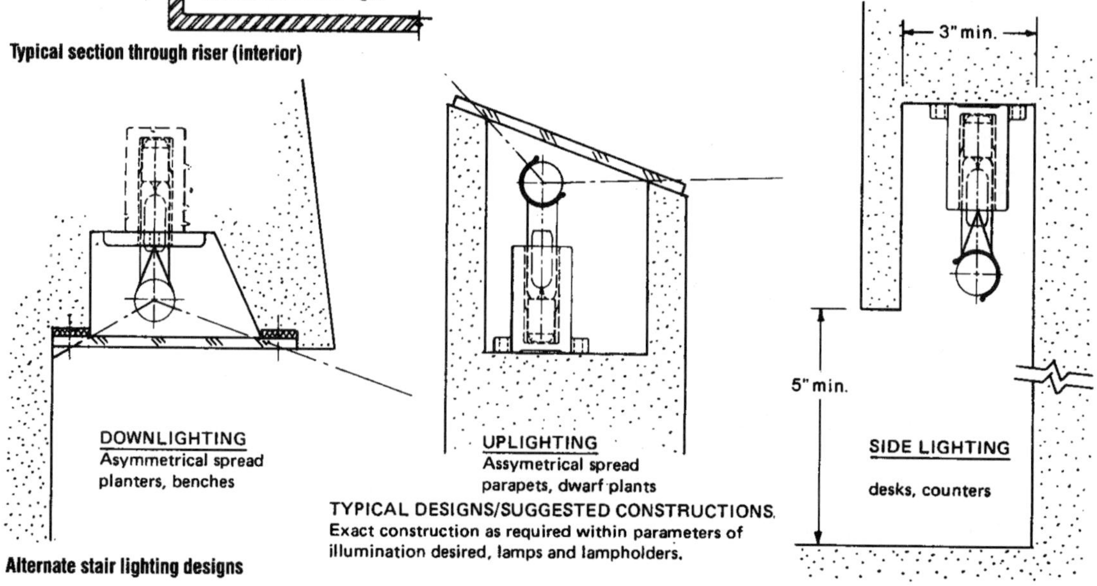

Alternate stair lighting designs

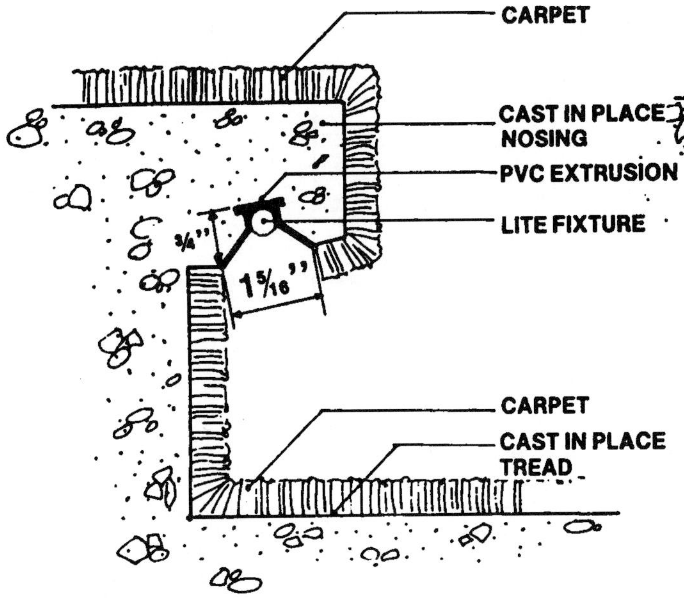

Carpeted cast-in-place step light

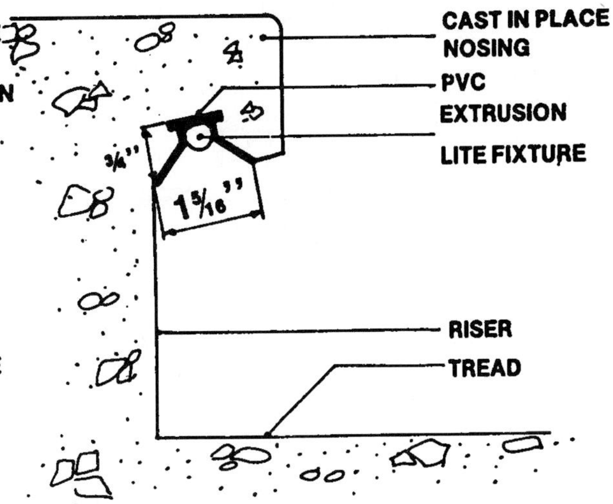

Exposed cast-in-place step light

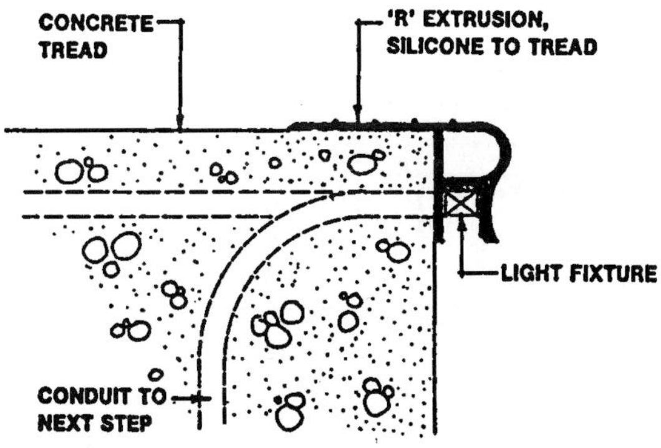

Concrete surface-applied bonded extrusion

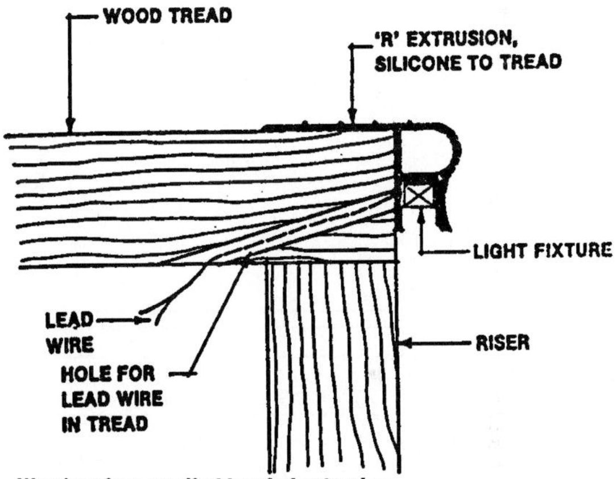

Wood surface-applied bonded extrusion

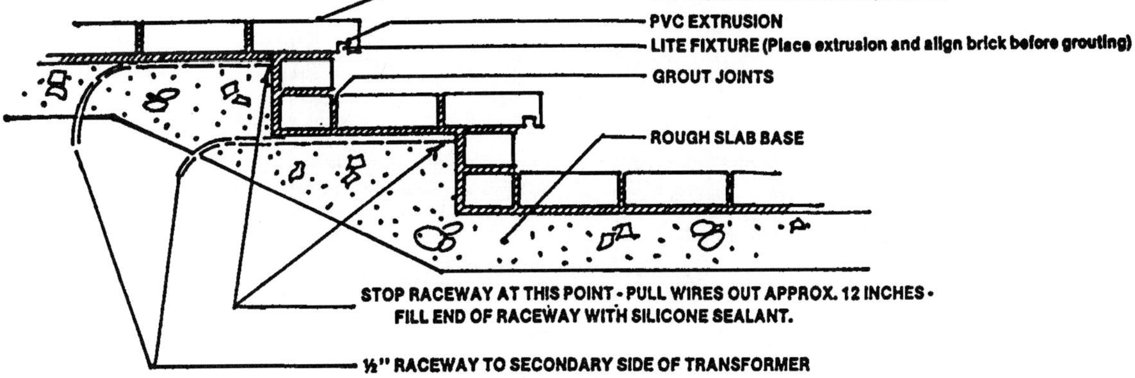

Brick steps with recessed light

LIGHTING

Stair Lighting Details

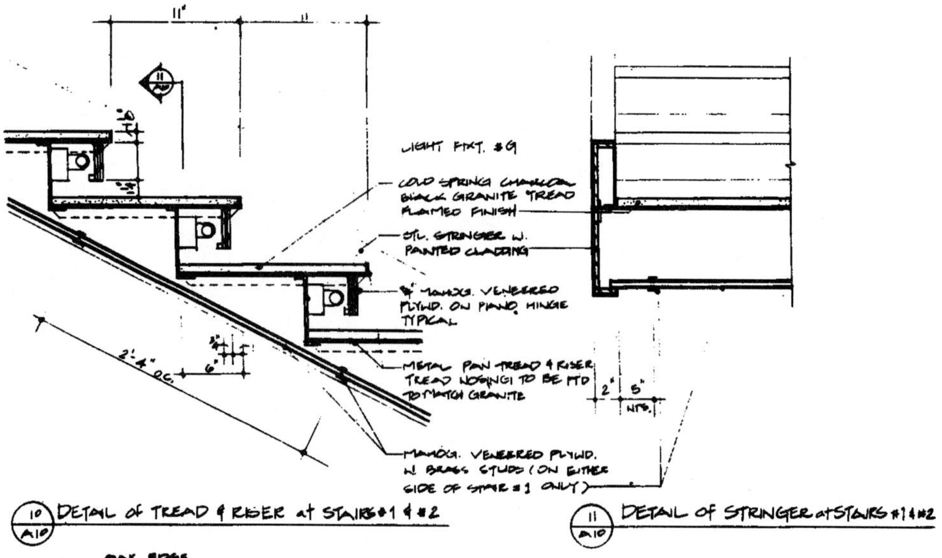

11"
11
LIGHT FIXT. #G
COLD SPRING CHARCOAL BLACK GRANITE TREAD FLAMED FINISH
STL. STRINGER W. PAINTED CLADDING
3/4" MAHOG. VENEERED PLYWD. ON PIANO HINGE TYPICAL
METAL PAN TREAD & RISER TREAD NOSINGS TO BE PTD TO MATCH GRANITE
MAHOG. VENEERED PLYWD. W/ BRASS STUDS (ON EITHER SIDE OF STAIR #1 ONLY)
2'-4" O.C.
6"
2"
5"
NTS.
DETAIL OF TREAD & RISER AT STAIRS #1 & #2
DETAIL OF STRINGER AT STAIRS #1 & #2

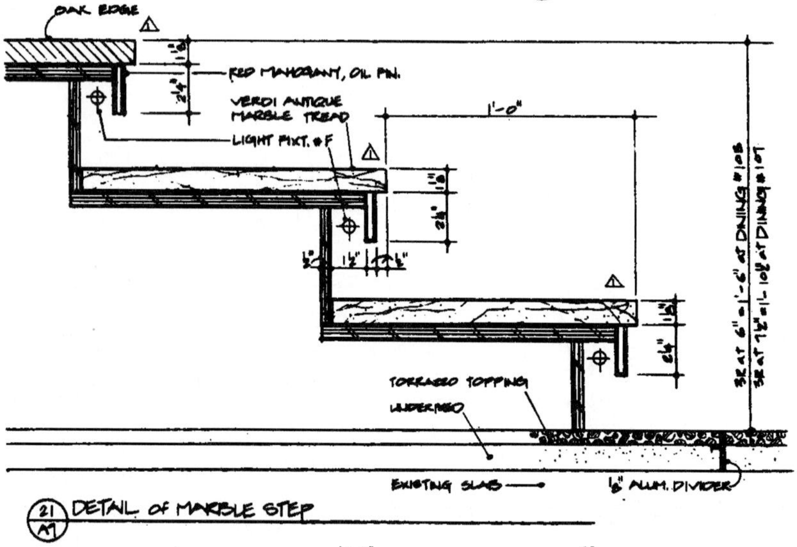

OAK EDGE
RED MAHOGANY, OIL FIN.
VERDI ANTIQUE MARBLE TREAD
LIGHT FIXT. #F
1'-0"
TERRAZZO TOPPING
UNDERBED
EXISTING SLAB
1/8" ALUM. DIVIDER
DETAIL OF MARBLE STEP

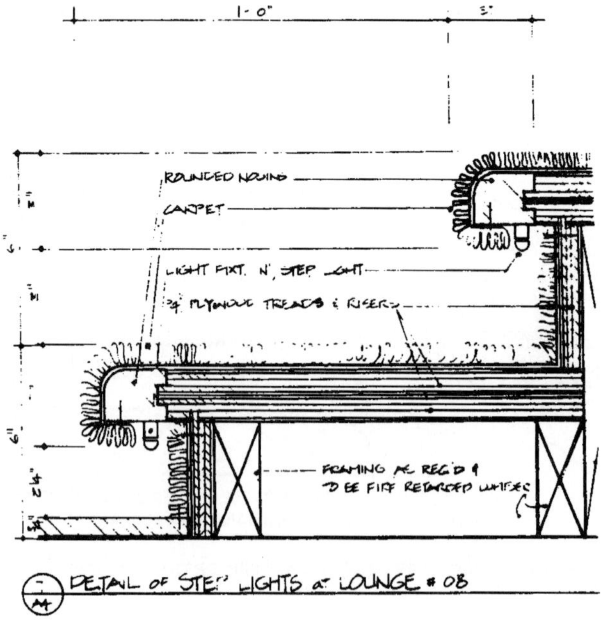

1'-0"
ROUNDED NOSING
CARPET
LIGHT FIXT. 'N', STEP LIGHT
3/4" PLYWOOD TREADS & RISERS
FRAMING AS REQ'D & TO BE FIRE RETARDED LUMBER
DETAIL OF STEP LIGHTS AT LOUNGE # 08

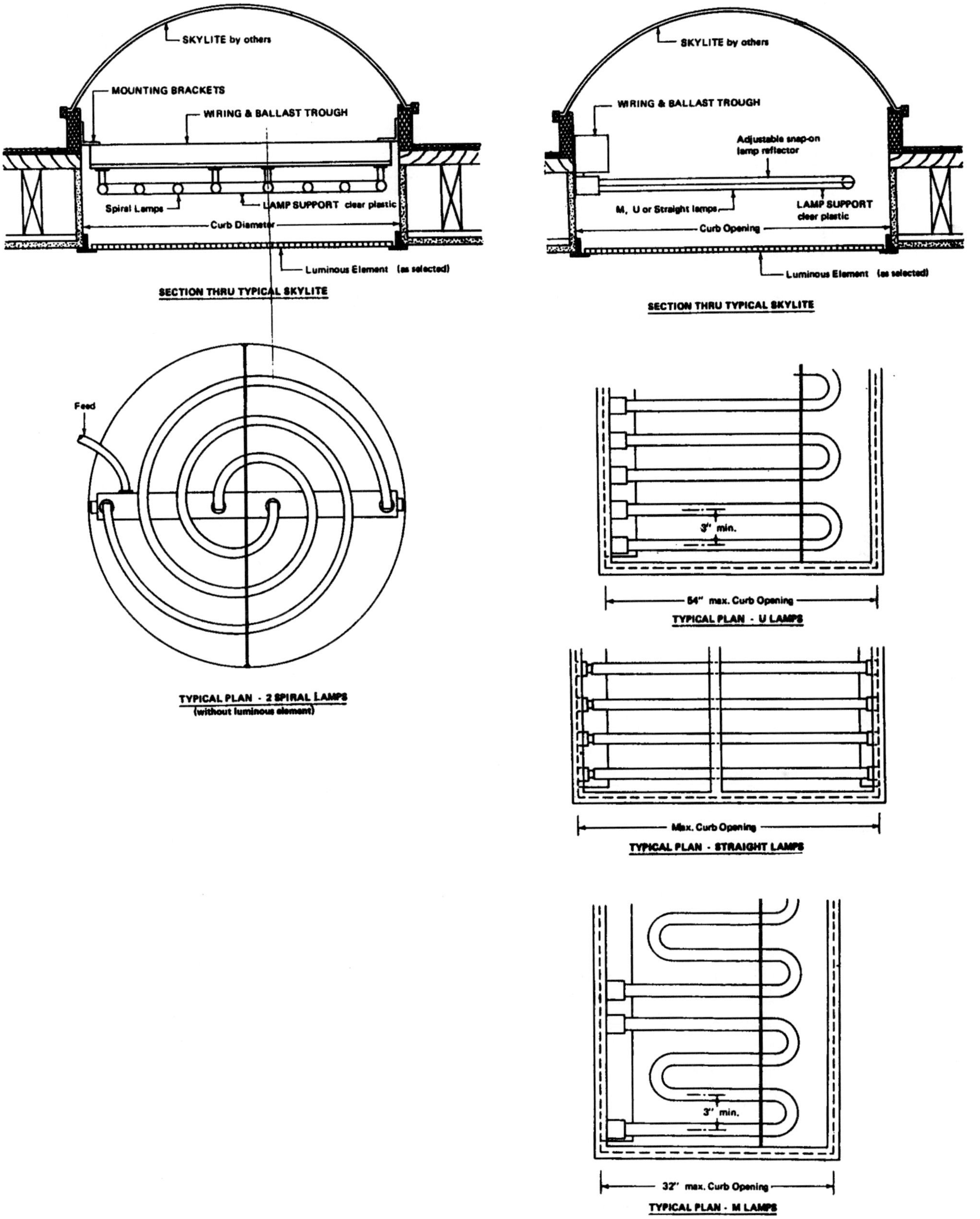

Fig. 18 Skylight lighting. Skylight serves as fixture—does not interfere with natural lighting, will not cast shadows on luminous element. Spiral, M, U, and straight lamps fabricated to fit curb opening

LIGHTING

Lighted Column Details

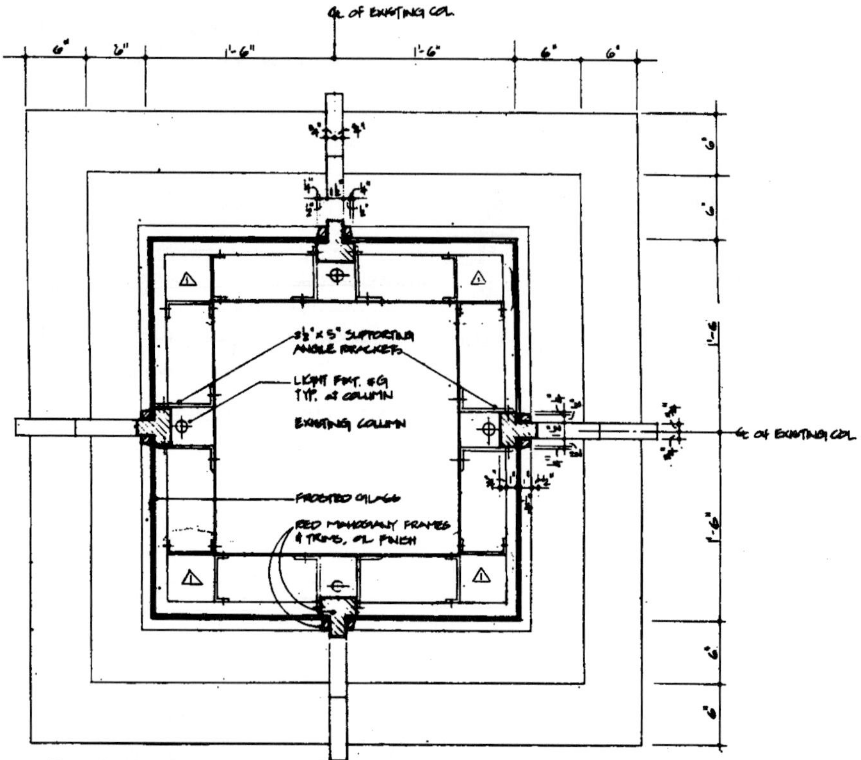

21 / A8 PLAN DETAIL of LIGHTED COLUMN
SCALE: 1½"=1'-0"

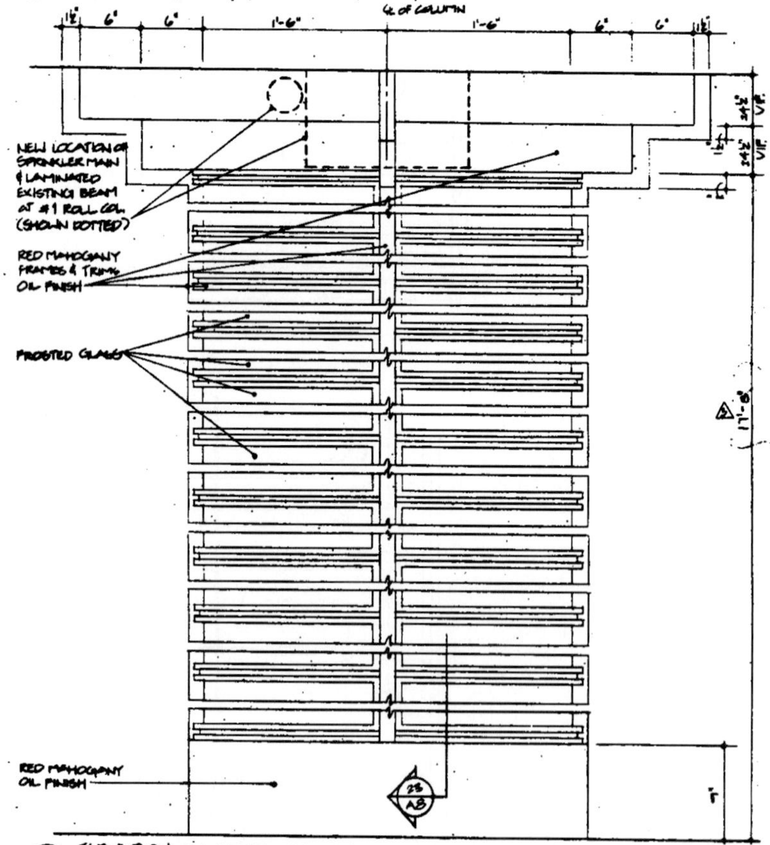

22 / A8 ELEVATION of LIGHTED COLUMN
SCALE: 1/2"=1'-0"

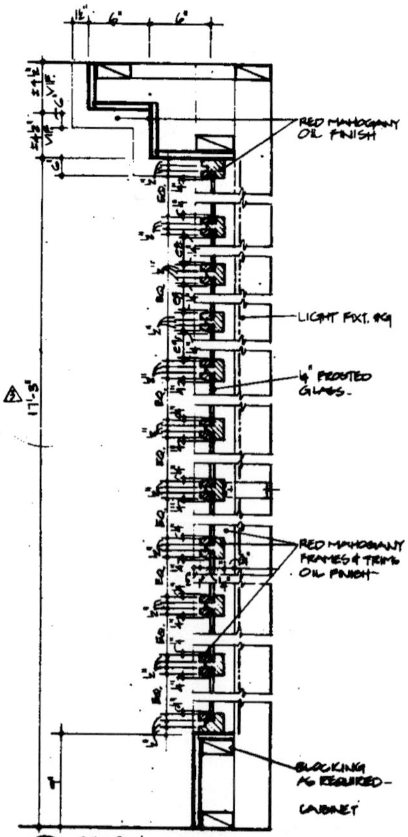

23 / A8 SECTION of LIGHTED COLUMN
SCALE: 1/2"=1'-0"

LIGHTING

Lighted Column Details

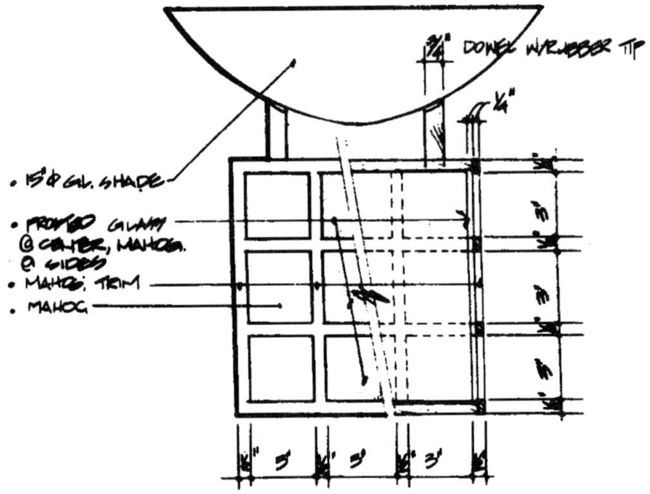

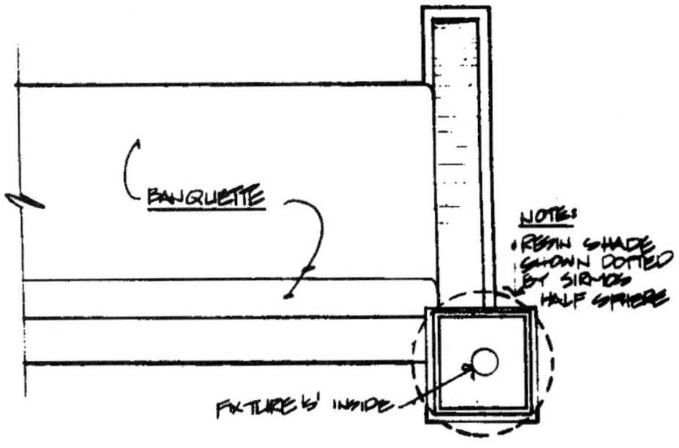

11/A5 BLOW-UP DETL. OF UPLIGHT • SEE DETL. 12/A5
SCALE: 3"=1'-0"

PLAN VIEW

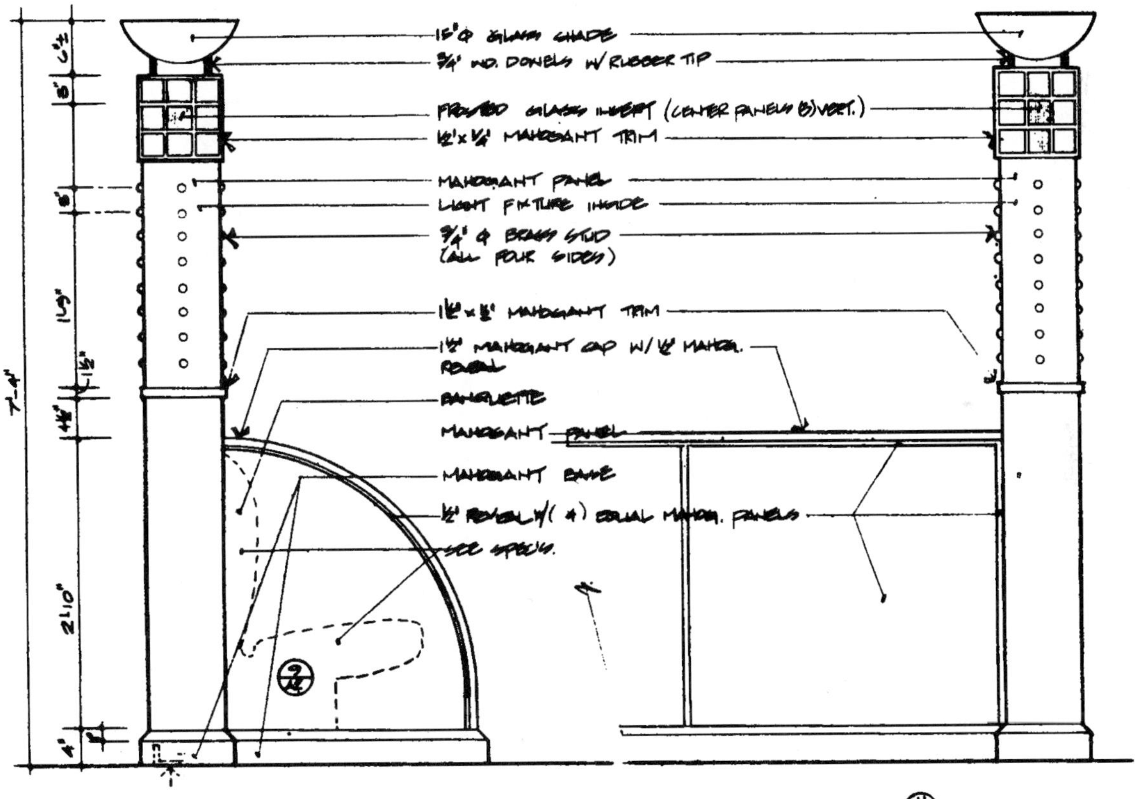

12/A5 CENTER BANQUETTE @ DINING 09 • SIDE/BACK & PLAN VIEW • SEE DETL. 11/A5
SCALE: 1"=1'-0"

LIGHTING
Lighted Column Details

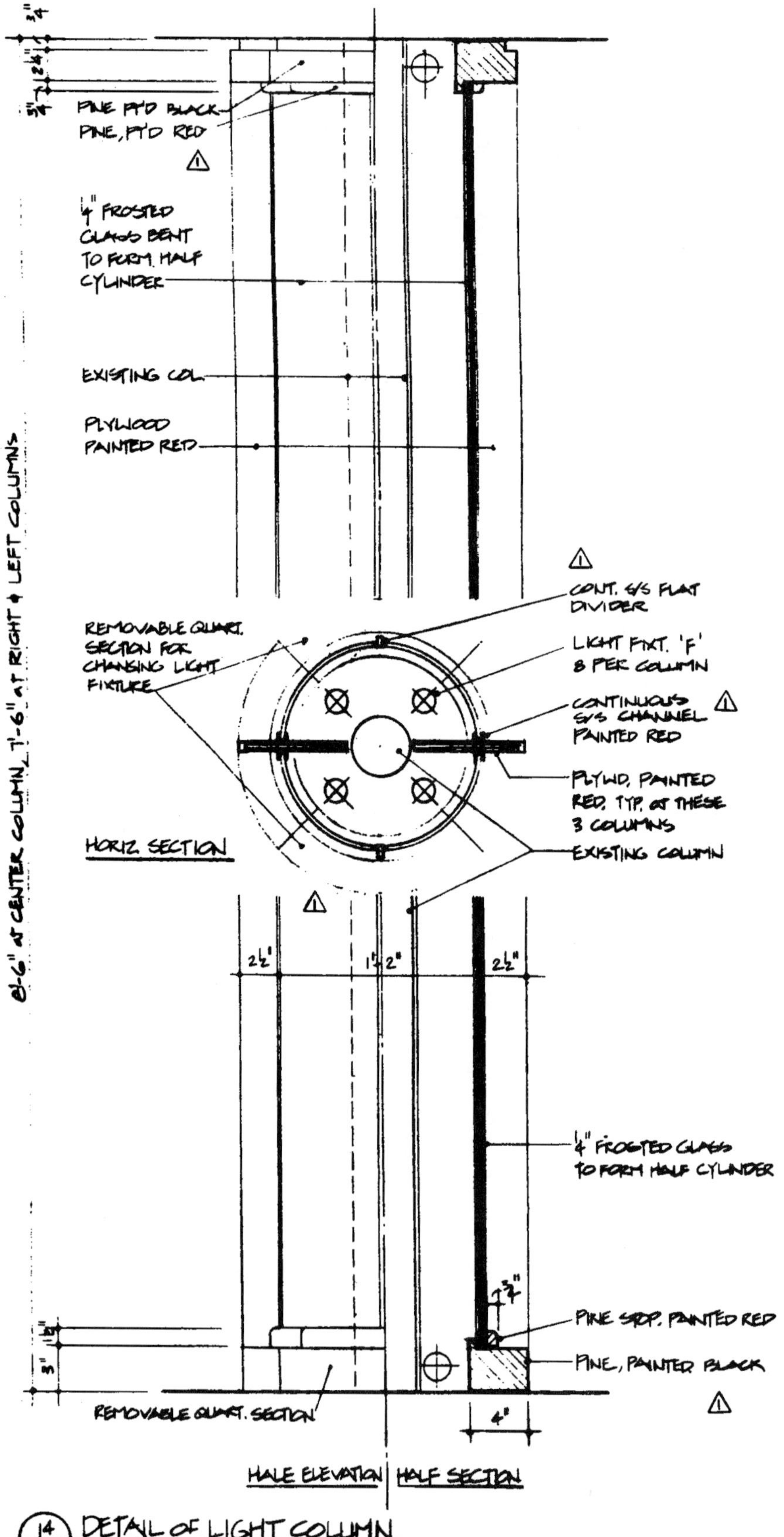

14/A4 DETAIL OF LIGHT COLUMN
SCALE: 1 1/2" = 1'-0"

Exposed/Sculpture Lamp Lighting

Cold cathode lighting is an architectural lighting tool with unusual flexibility:

- Lamps fabricated to the architectural design, continuous line of light—low brightness—no glare—high efficiency—long life—approaches a permanent light source.
- Remote transformers—no wiring troughs, ballasts, ballast failures, or hum. Only two leads for up to 120 ft of lamps.
- Excellent uniform dimming—no premature flickering of individual lamps as with hot cathode lighting.

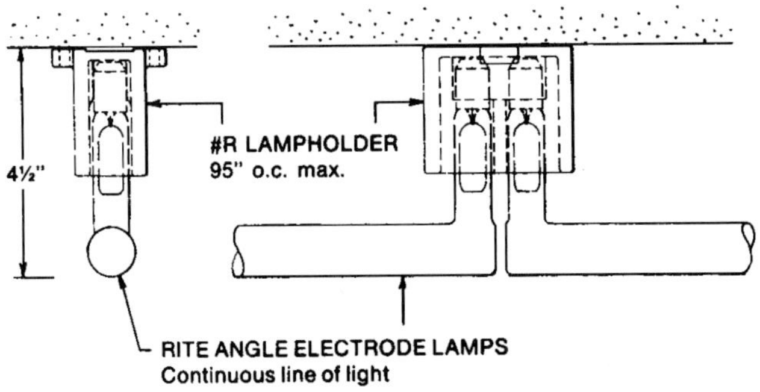

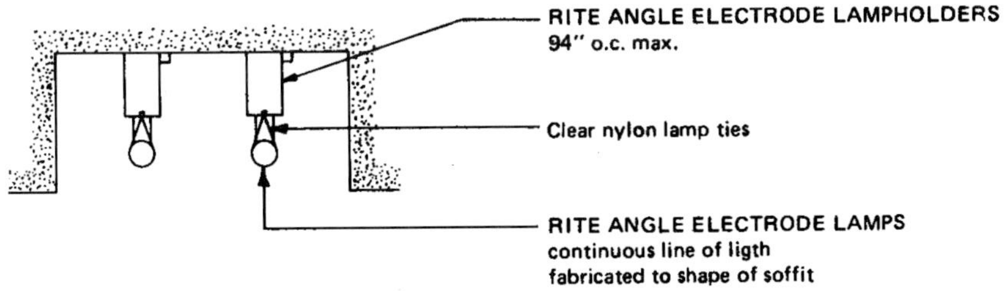

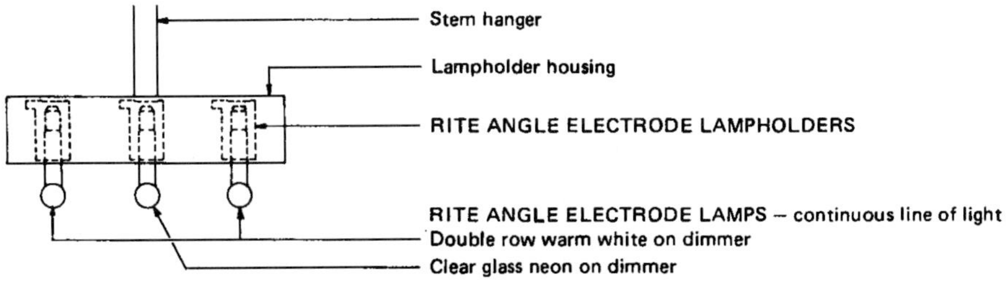

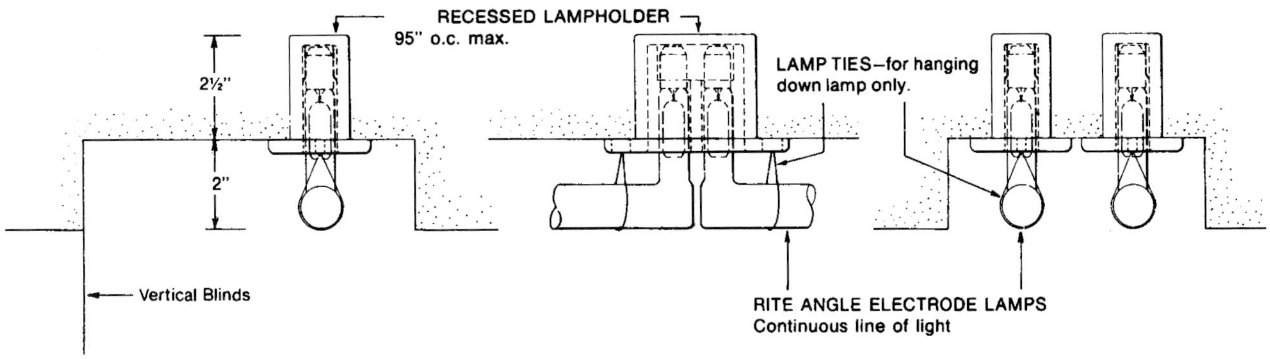

LIGHTING
Planning Data: Principal Lamp Types

Principal types of lamps for general lighting purposes

Category	Type	Maximum lamp efficacy lm/W	Average life hrs	Characteristic features	Typical application areas
Incandescent Lamps 	Normal incandescent lamps and reflector lamps	22	1,000	Easy to install, easy to use; many different versions; instant start; low cost price; reflector lamps allow concentrated light beams	General lighting in the home; decorative lighting; localized lighting; accent and decorative lighting (reflector lamps)
	Halogen	27	2,000	Compact; high light output; white light; easy to install; long life compared with normal incandescent lamps	Accent lighting; floodlighting
Fluorescent Lamps 	Tubular	104	20,000	Wide choice of light colors; high lighting levels possible; economical in use	All kinds of commercial and public buildings; streetlighting; home lighting
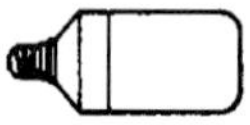	SL*	61	10,000	Energy-effective; direct replacement for incandescent lamps	Most applications where incandescent lamps were used before
	PL*	80	10,000	Compact; long life; energy-effective	To create a pleasant atmosphere in social areas, local lighting; signs, security, orientation lighting and general lighting
Gas-Discharge Lamps 	Self-ballasted	28	12,000/16,000	Long life; good color rendering; easy to install; better efficacy than incandescent lamps	Direct replacement for incandescent lamps; small industrial and public light projects; plant irradiation
	High pressure mercury	63	24,000 +	High efficacy; long life; reasonable color quality	Residential area lighting; sports grounds; factory lighting
	Metal halide	94	15,000	Very high efficacy combined with excellent color rendering; long life	Floodlighting, especially for color TV; industrial lighting; road lighting; plant irradiation
	High pressure sodium	125	24,000 +	Very high efficacy; extremely long life; good color rendering	Public lighting; floodlighting; industrial lighting; plant irradiation EL: direct replacement for mercury lamps
	Low pressure sodium	200	18,000	Extremely high efficacy; very long life; high visual acuity; poor color rendering: monochromatic light	Many different application areas: wherever energy/cost-effectiveness is important and color is not critical

INCANDESCENT BULBS

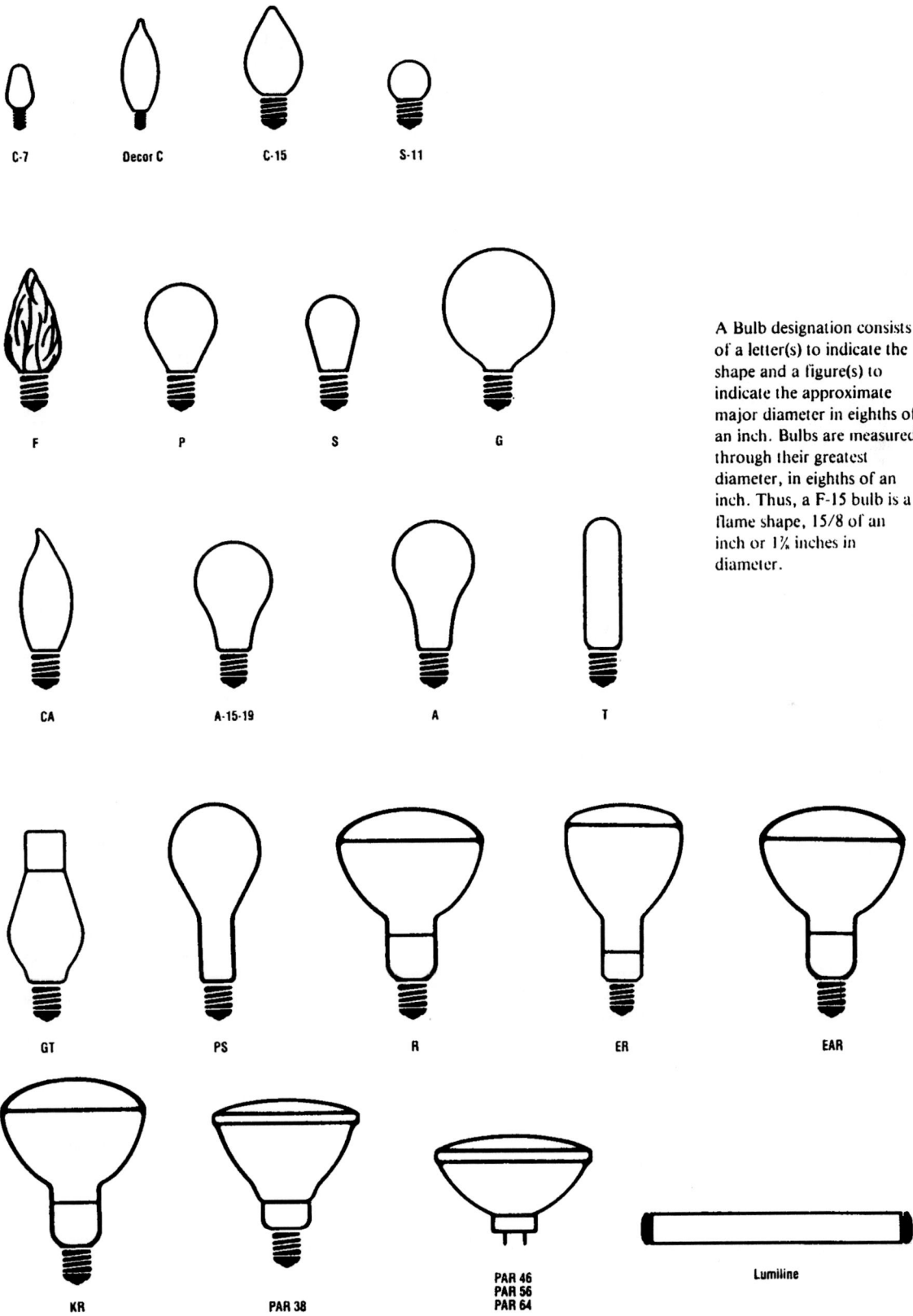

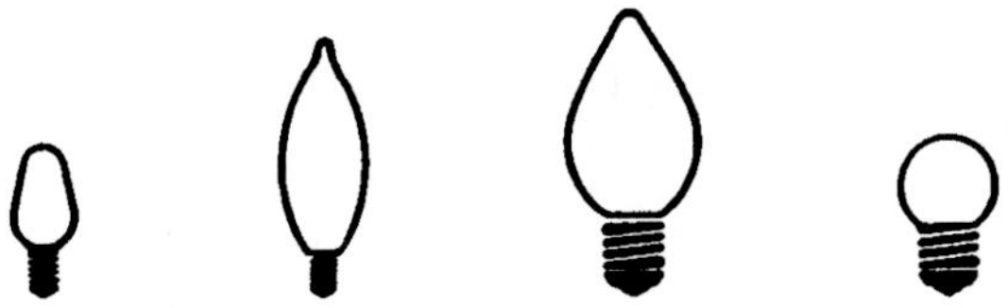

A Bulb designation consists of a letter(s) to indicate the shape and a figure(s) to indicate the approximate major diameter in eighths of an inch. Bulbs are measured through their greatest diameter, in eighths of an inch. Thus, a F-15 bulb is a flame shape, 15/8 of an inch or 1⅞ inches in diameter.

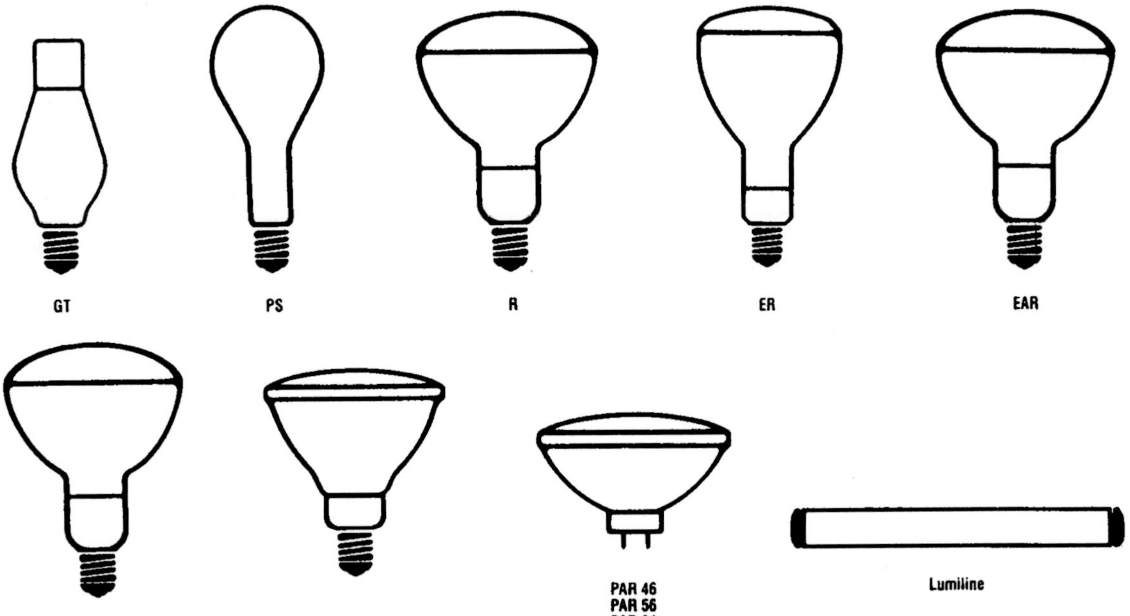

Light sources: selecting the right lamp

With so many lamps to choose from today, it is important to select the best ones for each job, while at the same time keeping the total number of different types to a minimum, to simplify maintenance. The criteria to be considered are:

Efficacy - a measure of efficiency, expressed in lumens per watt. This is a most important figure of merit wherever lamps are to be burned for long hours, because of energy conservation.

Color Rendering - a measure of the degree to which a light source shows the true colors of the objects it illuminates.

It is expressed in terms of a Color Rendering Index (CRI), on a scale of 0 to 100. The higher the CRI, the better people and objects look. On this scale, incandescent lamps rate 100, while fluorescent lamps, according to the quality of the phosphors used in their manufacture, are rated from the 70's to the 90's. This is a vast improvement over the fluorescent lamps commonly available a decade ago, many of which had a CRI in the 50's. Lamp catalogs now list the CRI of fluorescent sources, and the ordering code's first digit, a 7 or an 8, designates that the CRI is in the 70's or 80's.

Color Temperature - a measure of the apparent color of the light emitted from a light source, (sometimes referred to as the color appearance). It is expressed in degrees Kelvin; the lower the color temperature, the warmer the apparent color, and the higher the color temperature, the cooler the apparent color.

Most incandescent lamps have a color temperature of 2700 K, halogen lamps 2900 K, "warm" color fluorescent lamps, 2700 or 3000 K; "cool" fluorescent, 4100 K and a much specified fluorescent for many commercial uses, 3500 K.

The color temperature is indicated by the last two digits of the lamp ordering code, e.g., 835 signifies a color temperature of 3500K and a CRI in the 80s.

Lamp Life - the period of time until half the lamps in a typical installation fail. It is measured in hours, and typically runs for 750 hours for general service incandescent lamps, to 2000-4000 hours for halogen incandescent, to 10,000-20,000 hours for fluorescent. Fluorescent lamp life is measured on the basis of 3 hours per start. Frequent on-off switch of fluorescent results in diminished lamp life.

Incandescent

Incandescent lamps are the most familiar light source. They owe their popularity to their low cost, good color rendering, compact size, wide range of shapes and wattages and the fact that they are easily dimmed. Dimming causes incandescent lamps to run at lower temperatures, which results in longer lamp life, but also in a warmer color.

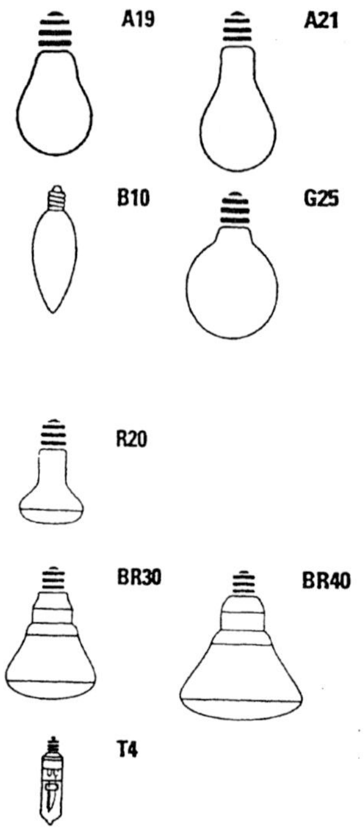

Annual Energy Cost Savings, Fluorescent vs. Incandescent
Approximate Dollars/Year @ $10/KWH

Equivalents in Light Output		24 hours/day 365 days/year Hallways	10 hours/day 260 days/year Offices	5 hours/day 365 days/year Kitchens
Fluorescent	Incandescent			
1-13 TT	60W A19	$40	$12	$8
2-13 TT	2-60W A19	$80	$24	$17
2-18 TT	2-75W A19	$100	$30	$21
2-26 TT	2-100W A19	$130	$39	$27

Output of typical lamps:*
Average Initial Lumens = lm

General Service Lamps A-line	lm
40 Watt A19	495
60 Watt A19	865
75 Watt A19	1190
100 Watt A19	1710
150 Watt A21	2850
Decorative Lamps	
Flame Shape, Candelabra Base	
25 Watts	220
40 Watts	400
Globe Shape, Candelabra Base	
25 G 16½ (white)	210
40 G 25 (Med.)	370

Halogen

Halogen lamps are a type of incandescent lamp that is filled with a halogen gas, allowing the lamp to burn more intensely, with a whiter light, and a slightly higher efficacy than ordinary incandescent. Moreover, the "halogen cycle" redeposits the evaporated tungsten filament, so that blackening is avoided and output is maintained throughout the life of the lamp.

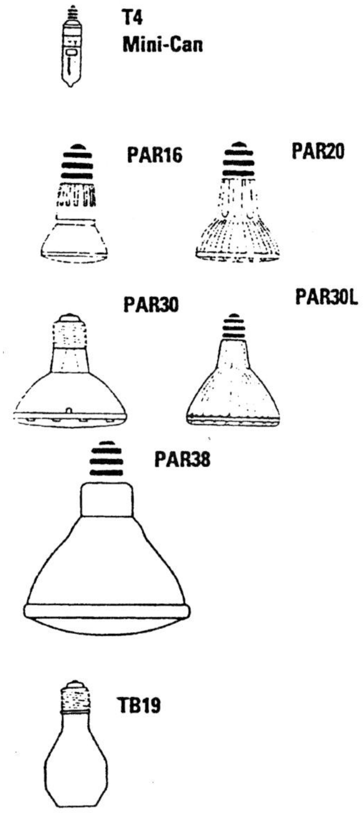

Low Voltage

Incandescent lamps designed to run at 12 volts are increasingly common, especially low voltage halogen lamps, because of their advantages: a smaller filament, permitting more precise beam control, smaller bulb size, smaller fixture size and whiter light.

Low voltage lamps require a transformer; this is normally part of the fixture, but sometimes it is remote, and because the life of low voltage lamps is dependent on the voltage with which they are operated, the transformer rating and the lamp wattage should be closely matched. Electronic transformers have advantages over magnetic types, especially when incorporated in the fixture: they are smaller, lighter and quieter.

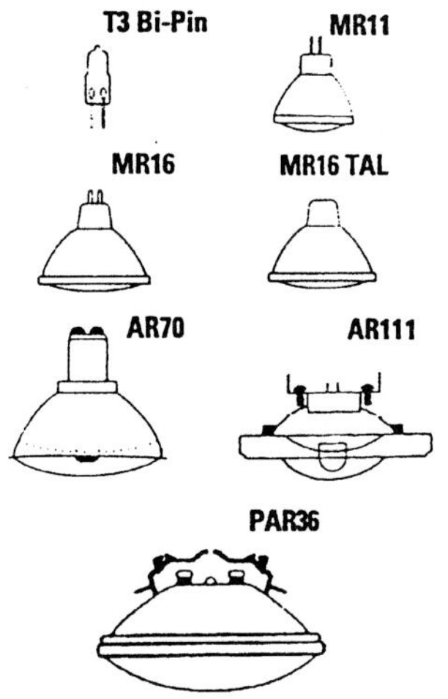

Fluorescent

Fluorescent lamps are much more efficient than incandescent, and therefore use much less energy for the same light output, as much as 80% less. They also last 10-20 times as long as incandescent.

With the advent of better color-rendering and new electronic technology, applications of fluorescent in the home, and other "people-oriented" spaces, are increasing rapidly.

Fluorescent lamps are essentially linear, and while they come in many lengths and several shapes, the light they produce is less readily controlled and is generally dispersed more evenly, resulting in uniform, largely shadowless illumination.

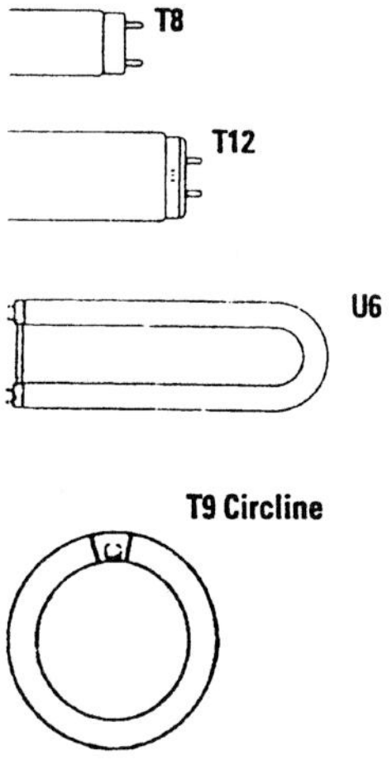

Compact fluorescent lamps, in Twin Tube and Quad Tube forms, can be more precisely controlled, however. They fit into smaller round and square fixtures, ceiling, wall and recessed types. The advantages they offer over the incandescent lamp versions of similar fixtures include a savings of up to 80% in energy costs, 10 times the lamp life, and a choice of color appearance, 2700, 3000, 3500, or 4100K, with excellent color rendition.

Fluorescent lamps require a ballast, whose function is to start the lamp and to control its operation. Electronic ballasts, which are replacing the older magnetic type, eliminate hum and flicker and are more efficient, smaller and lighter. They also make dimming more affordable.

Dimming of fluorescent has advanced greatly in recent years. For the latest information, contact a Lightolier representative.

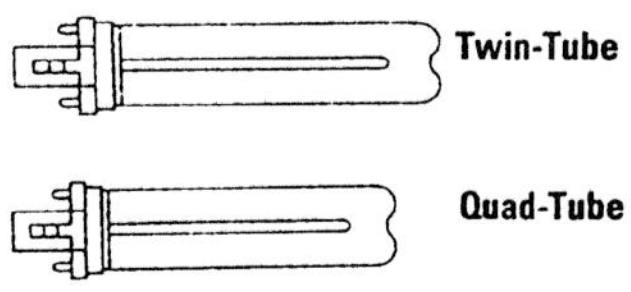

(Lamp families are not drawn to same scale.)

Output of typical lamps:*
Average Initial Lumens = lm

120 Volts, MiniCan Base	lm
75T3	1400
100 T4 (clear)	1800
150 T4 (clear)	2800

120 Volts, Medium Base	lm
50TB 19 Med.	710
90TB 19	1580

12 Volts, Bi-Pin Base:	lm
20 Watt T3	350
35 Watt T4	560
50 Watt T4	950

Large Fluorescent Lamps	lm
40 Watt T12	3250
40 Watt T12 U/6	3000
32 Watt T8	2950
32 Watt T8 U/6	2800
32 Watt T9, 12" Dia	2000
40 Watt T9, 16" Dia	2800

Compact Fluorescent (3000K)	lm
9 Watt T4 Twin Tube	600
13 Watt T4 Twin Tube	825
18 Watt T5 Twin Tube	1250
27 Watt T5 Twin Tube	1800
39 Watt T5 Twin Tube	2850
13 Watt T4 Quad Tube	900
18 Watt T4 Quad Tube	1200
26 Watt T4 Quad Tube	1800

LIGHTING
Planning Data: Beam Spreads

Accent lighting

Line Voltage Halogen and Incandescent Lamps

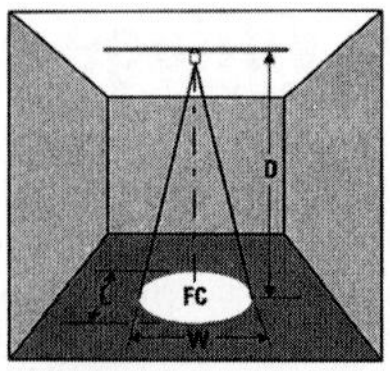

Head-on

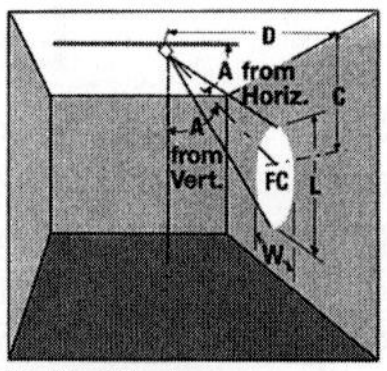

Vertical Surface

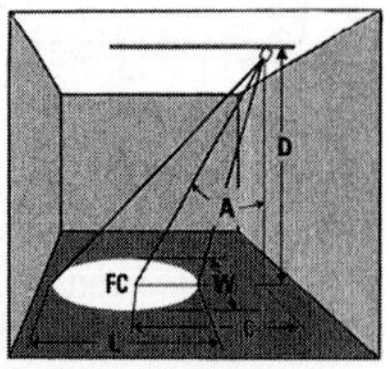

Horizontal Surface

FC is initial footcandles at center of beam. Beam length **(L)** and beam width **(W)** are to where the candlepower is reduced to 50% of center beam candlepower.

CBCP is center beam candlepower.
C is the distance to the center of beam.
A = AIMING ANGLE

dimensions shown are in feet

When Lighting Vertical Plane				0°				60° from V, 30° from H					45° from V or H					30° from V, 60° from H				
When Lighting Horizontal Plane				0°				30° from V, 60° from H					45° from V or H					60° from V, 30° from H				
Line Voltage Halogen and Incandescent Lamps				0° Aiming Angle				A = 30° Aiming Angle					A = 45° Aiming Angle					A = 60° Aiming Angle				
	Beam Spread (to 50% CBCP)	CBCP	Rated Life (hrs)	D	FC	L	W	D	C	FC	L	W	D	C	FC	L	W	D	C	FC	L	W
60W **PAR16** NFL	30°	1300	2000	3	144	1.6	1.6	3	1.7	94	2.2	1.9	2	2.0	115	2.3	1.5	1	1.7	163	2.7	1.1
				5	52	2.7	2.7	5	2.9	34	3.7	3.1	3	3.0	51	3.5	2.3	2	3.5	41	5.5	2.1
				7	27	3.8	3.8	7	4.0	17	5.1	4.3	4	4.0	29	4.6	3.0	3	5.2	18	8.2	3.2
				9	16	4.8	4.8	9	5.2	10	6.6	5.6	5	5.0	18	5.8	3.8	4	6.9	10	10.9	4.3
35W **PAR20** WFL	40°	600	2500	3	67	2.2	2.2	3	1.7	43	3.0	2.5	2	2.0	53	3.4	2.1	1	1.7	75	4.8	1.5
				5	24	3.6	3.6	5	2.9	16	5.1	4.2	3	3.0	24	5.0	3.1	2	3.5	19	9.7	2.9
				7	12	5.1	5.1	7	4.0	8	7.1	5.9	4	4.0	13	6.7	4.1	3	5.2	8	14.5	4.4
				9	7	6.6	6.6	9	5.2	5	9.1	7.6	5	5.0	8	8.4	5.1	4	6.9	5	19.3	5.8
50W PAR20 NSP	8°	6000	2000	6	167	0.8	0.8	5	2.9	156	0.9	0.8	3	3.0	236	0.8	0.6	2	3.5	188	1.1	0.6
				8	94	1.1	1.1	7	4.0	80	1.3	1.1	5	5.0	85	1.4	1.0	3	5.2	83	1.7	0.8
				10	60	1.4	1.4	9	5.2	48	1.7	1.5	7	7.0	43	2.0	1.4	4	6.9	47	2.3	1.1
				12	42	1.7	1.7	11	6.4	32	2.1	1.8	9	9.0	26	2.5	1.8	5	8.7	30	2.8	1.4
50W PAR20 SP	15°	3200	2000	6	89	1.6	1.6	5	2.9	83	1.8	1.5	3	3.0	126	1.6	1.1	2	3.5	100	2.2	1.1
				8	50	2.1	2.1	7	4.0	42	2.5	2.1	5	5.0	45	2.7	1.9	3	5.2	44	3.3	1.6
				10	32	2.6	2.6	9	5.2	26	3.2	2.7	7	7.0	23	3.8	2.6	4	6.9	25	4.4	2.1
				12	22	3.2	3.2	11	6.4	17	3.9	3.3	9	9.0	14	4.8	3.4	5	8.7	16	5.6	2.6
50W PAR20 NFL	27°	1850	2000	4	116	1.9	1.9	3	1.7	134	2.0	1.7	3	3.0	73	3.1	2.0	1	1.7	231	2.3	1.0
				6	51	2.9	2.9	5	2.9	48	3.3	2.8	4	4.0	41	4.1	2.7	2	3.5	58	4.6	1.9
				8	29	3.8	3.8	7	4.0	25	4.6	3.9	5	5.0	26	5.1	3.4	3	5.2	26	7.0	2.9
				10	19	4.8	4.8	9	5.2	15	5.9	5.0	6	6.0	18	6.1	4.1	4	6.9	14	9.3	3.8
50W **PAR30** NSP	8°	9200	2000	7	188	1.0	1.0	6	3.5	166	1.1	1.0	4	4.0	203	1.1	0.8	2	3.5	288	1.1	0.6
				10	92	1.4	1.4	9	5.2	74	1.7	1.5	6	6.0	90	1.7	1.2	3	5.2	128	1.7	0.8
				13	54	1.8	1.8	12	6.9	41	2.2	1.9	8	8.0	51	2.2	1.6	4	6.9	72	2.3	1.1
				16	36	2.2	2.2	15	8.7	27	2.8	2.4	10	10.0	33	2.8	2.0	5	8.7	46	2.6	1.4
50W PAR30 NFL	25°	2000	2000	4	125	1.8	1.8	3	1.7	144	1.8	1.5	3	3.0	79	2.8	1.9	1	1.7	250	2.1	0.9
				6	56	2.7	2.7	5	2.9	52	3.0	2.6	4	4.0	44	3.7	2.5	2	3.5	63	4.2	1.8
				8	31	3.5	3.5	7	4.0	27	4.2	3.6	5	5.0	28	4.7	3.1	3	5.2	28	6.2	2.7
				10	20	4.4	4.4	9	5.2	16	5.4	4.6	6	6.0	20	5.6	3.8	4	6.9	16	8.3	3.5
50W PAR30 FL	35°	1400	2500	3	156	1.9	1.9	3	1.7	101	2.6	2.2	2	2.0	124	2.8	1.8	1	1.7	175	3.6	1.3
				5	56	3.2	3.2	5	2.9	36	4.3	3.6	3	3.0	55	4.2	2.7	2	3.5	44	7.2	2.5
				7	29	4.4	4.4	7	4.0	19	6.1	5.1	4	40	31	5.6	3.6	3	5.2	19	10.8	3.6
				9	17	5.7	5.7	9	5.2	11	7.8	6.6	5	5.0	20	7.0	4.5	4	6.9	11	14.4	5.0
75W PAR30 NSP	9°	14000	2500	8	219	1.3	1.3	7	4.0	186	1.5	1.3	5	5.0	196	1.6	1.1	3	5.2	194	1.9	0.9
				12	97	1.9	1.9	10	5.8	91	2.1	1.8	7	7.0	101	2.2	1.6	4	6.9	109	2.6	1.3
				16	55	2.5	2.5	13	7.5	54	2.7	2.4	9	9.0	61	2.9	2.0	5	8.7	70	3.2	1.6
				20	35	3.1	3.1	16	9.2	36	3.4	2.9	11	11.0	41	3.5	2.4	6	10.4	49	3.6	1.9
75W PAR30 NFL	30°	3200	2500	6	89	3.2	3.2	5	2.9	83	3.7	3.1	3	3.0	126	3.5	2.3	2	3.5	100	5.5	2.1
				8	50	4.3	4.3	7	4.0	42	5.1	4.3	5	5.0	45	5.8	3.8	3	5.2	44	8.2	3.2
				10	32	5.4	5.4	9	5.2	26	6.6	5.6	7	7.0	23	8.1	5.3	4	6.9	25	10.9	4.3
				12	22	6.4	6.4	11	6.4	17	8.1	6.8	9	9.0	14	10.4	6.6	5	8.7	16	13.7	5.4
75W PAR30 FL	40°	2000	2500	4	125	2.9	2.9	3	1.7	144	3.0	2.5	3	3.0	79	5.0	3.1	1	1.7	250	4.8	1.5
				6	56	4.4	4.4	5	2.9	52	5.1	4.2	4	4.0	44	6.7	4.1	2	3.5	63	9.7	2.9
				8	31	5.8	5.8	7	4.0	27	7.1	5.9	5	5.0	28	8.4	5.1	3	5.2	28	14.5	4.4
				10	20	7.3	7.3	9	5.2	16	9.1	7.6	6	6.0	20	10.1	6.2	4	6.9	16	19.3	5.8
90W **PAR38** SP	12°	14500	2500	8	227	1.7	1.7	7	4.0	192	2.0	1.7	5	5.0	205	2.1	1.5	3	5.2	201	2.6	1.3
				12	101	2.5	2.5	10	5.8	94	2.8	2.4	7	7.0	105	3.0	2.1	4	6.9	113	3.5	1.7
				16	57	3.4	3.4	13	7.5	56	3.7	3.2	9	9.0	63	3.8	2.7	5	8.7	73	4.3	2.1
				20	36	4.2	4.2	16	9.2	37	4.5	3.9	11	11.0	42	4.7	3.3	6	10.4	50	5.2	2.5
90W PAR38 NFL	28°	4500	2500	6	125	3.0	3.0	5	2.9	117	3.4	2.9	3	3.0	177	3.2	2.1	2	3.5	141	4.9	2.0
				8	70	4.0	4.0	7	4.0	60	4.8	4.0	5	5.0	64	5.3	3.5	3	5.2	63	7.4	3.0
				10	45	5.0	5.0	9	5.2	36	6.1	5.2	7	7.0	32	7.4	4.9	4	6.9	35	9.8	4.0
				12	31	6.0	6.0	11	6.4	24	7.5	6.3	9	9.0	20	9.6	6.3	5	6.7	23	12.3	5.0
75W **R20**	46°	825	2000	2	206	1.7	1.7	2	1.2	134	2.4	2.0	2	2.0	73	4.1	2.4	1	1.7	103	7.4	1.7
				3	92	2.5	2.5	3	1.7	60	3.6	2.9	3	3.0	32	6.2	3.6	2	3.5	26	14.8	3.4
				4	52	3.4	3.4	4	2.3	33	4.8	3.9	4	4.0	18	8.3	4.8	3	5.2	11	22.2	5.1
				5	33	4.2	4.2	5	2.9	21	6.0	4.9	5	5.0	12	10.4	6.0	4	6.9	6	29.6	6.8

BASES

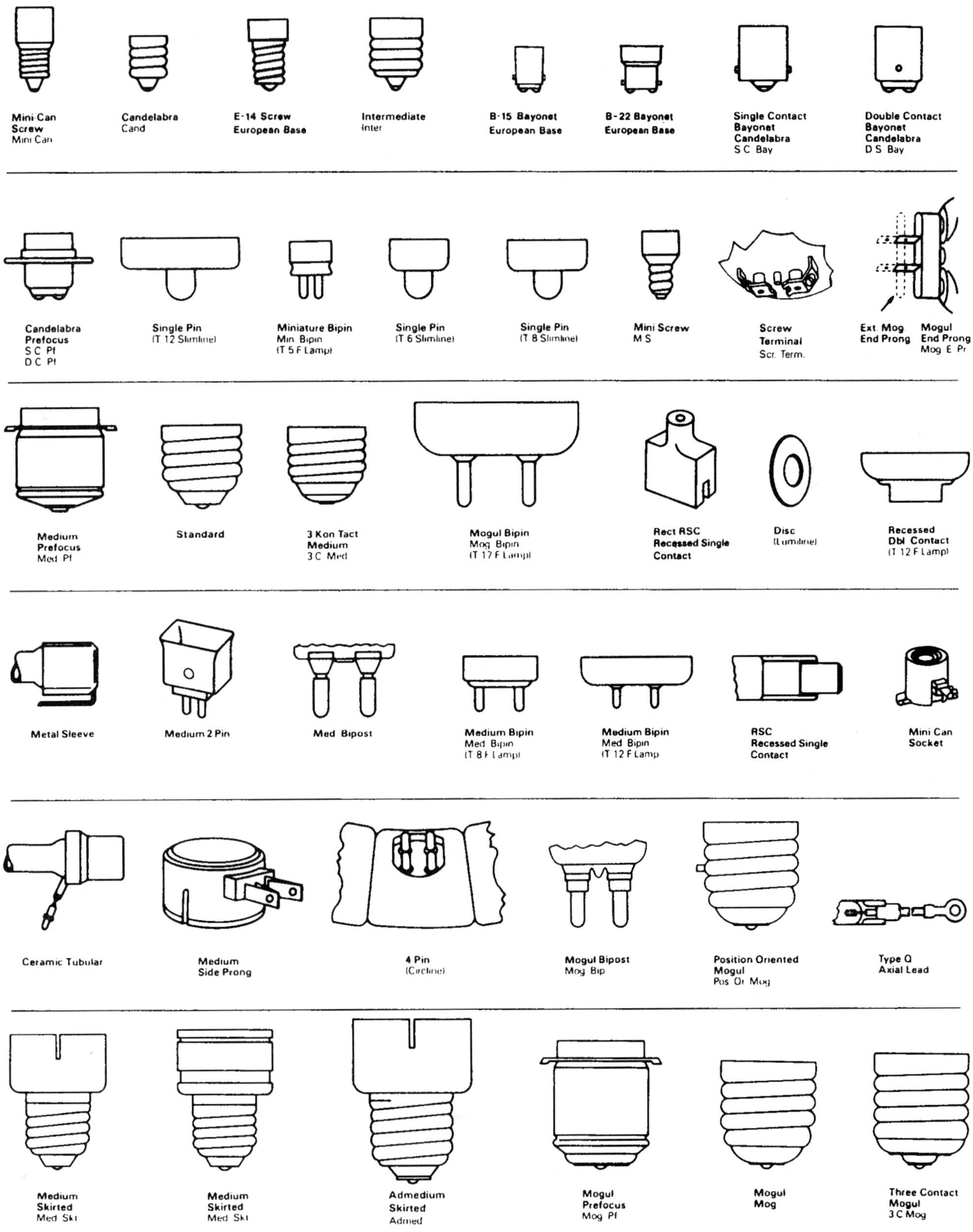
Mini-Can Screw
Mini Can
Candelabra
Cand
E-14 Screw
European Base
Intermediate
Inter
B-15 Bayonet
European Base
B-22 Bayonet
European Base
Single Contact Bayonet Candelabra
S C Bay
Double Contact Bayonet Candelabra
D S Bay
Candelabra Prefocus
S C Pf
D C Pf
Single Pin
(T 12 Slimline)
Miniature Bipin
Min Bipin
(T 5 F Lamp)
Single Pin
(T 6 Slimline)
Single Pin
(T 8 Slimline)
Mini Screw
M S
Screw Terminal
Scr. Term.
Ext. Mog End Prong
Mogul End Prong
Mog E Pr
Medium Prefocus
Med Pf
Standard
3 Kon Tact Medium
3 C Med
Mogul Bipin
Mog Bipin
(T 17 F Lamp)
Rect RSC
Recessed Single Contact
Disc
(Lumiline)
Recessed Dbl Contact
(T 12 F Lamp)
Metal Sleeve
Medium 2 Pin
Med Bipost
Medium Bipin
Med Bipin
(T 8 F Lamp)
Medium Bipin
Med Bipin
(T 12 F Lamp
RSC
Recessed Single Contact
Mini Can Socket
Ceramic Tubular
Medium Side Prong
4 Pin
(Circline)
Mogul Bipost
Mog Bip
Position Oriented Mogul
Pos Or Mog
Type Q
Axial Lead
Medium Skirted
Med Ski
Medium Skirted
Med Ski
Admedium Skirted
Admed
Mogul Prefocus
Mog Pf
Mogul
Mog
Three Contact Mogul
3 C Mog

BULB IDENTIFICATION

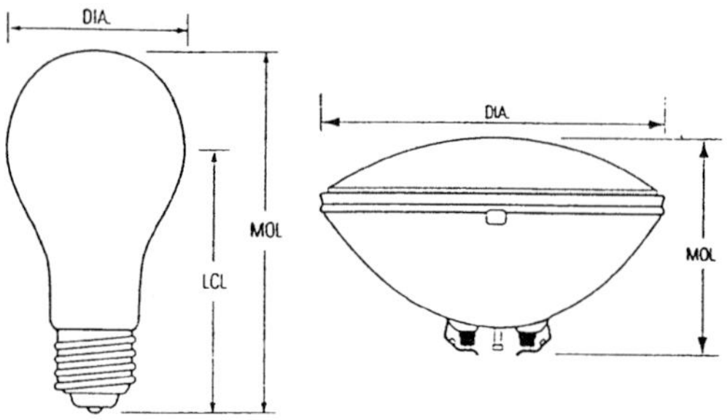

DIA: Diameter of bulb at widest point.

MOL: Maximum Overall Length including base or pins.

LCL: Distance between the center of the arc tube and the Light Center Length reference plane.

Note: Lamp drawings are not drawn to scale. Be sure to check size and dimension information when identifying each lamp.

To convert inches to millimeters, multiply the dimension (in inches) by 25.4 (i.e. 1.5" x 25.4 = 38.1 mm).

FILAMENT IDENTIFICATION

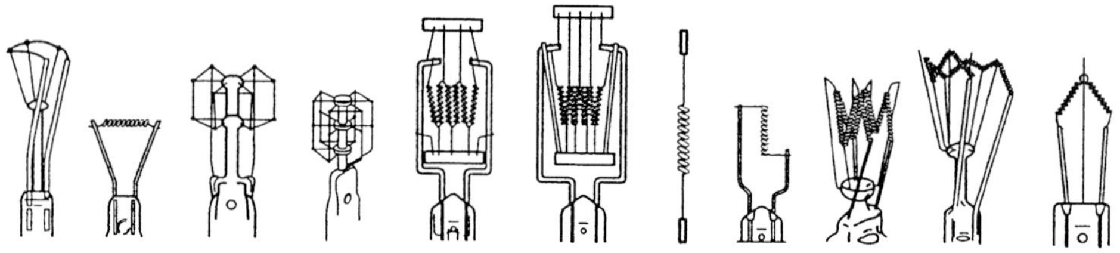

C-9 | *C-6 CC-6* | *C-17* | *C-22* | *C-13* | *C-13D* | *CC-8* | *C-8 CC-8* | *C-5* | *C-7A* | *C-2V CC-2V*

BASE IDENTIFICATION

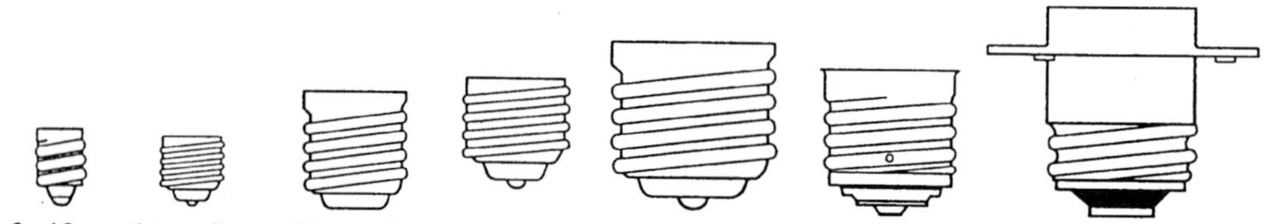

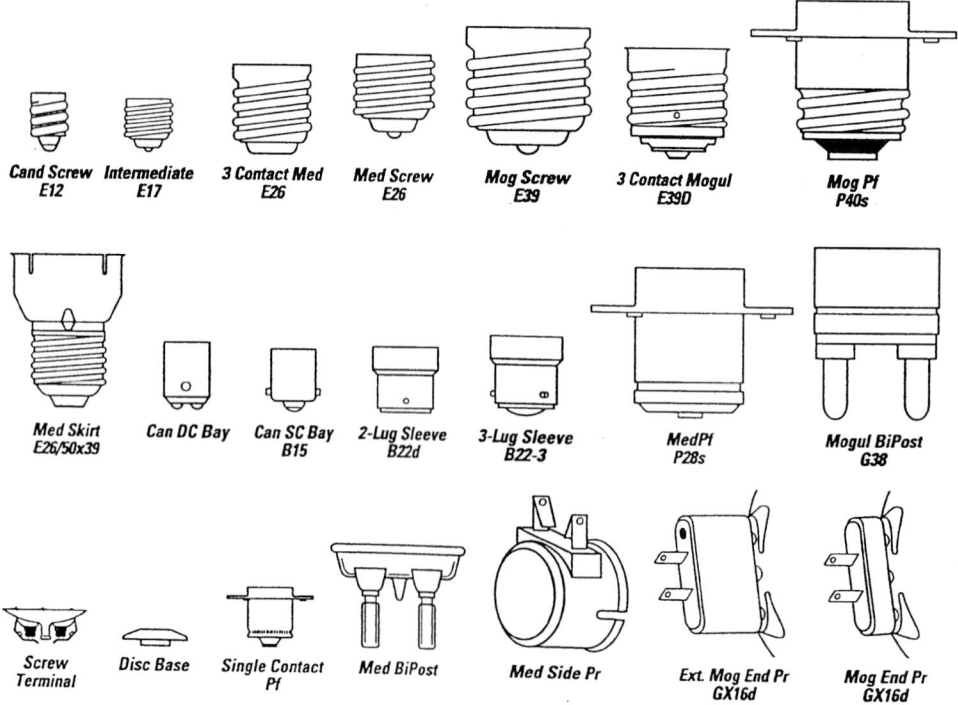

Cand Screw E12 | *Intermediate E17* | *3 Contact Med E26* | *Med Screw E26* | *Mog Screw E39* | *3 Contact Mogul E39D* | *Mog Pf P40s*

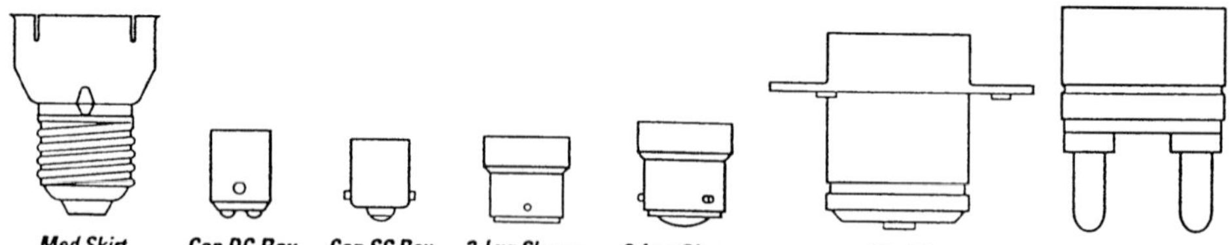

Med Skirt E26/50x39 | *Can DC Bay* | *Can SC Bay B15* | *2-Lug Sleeve B22d* | *3-Lug Sleeve B22-3* | *MedPf P28s* | *Mogul BiPost G38*

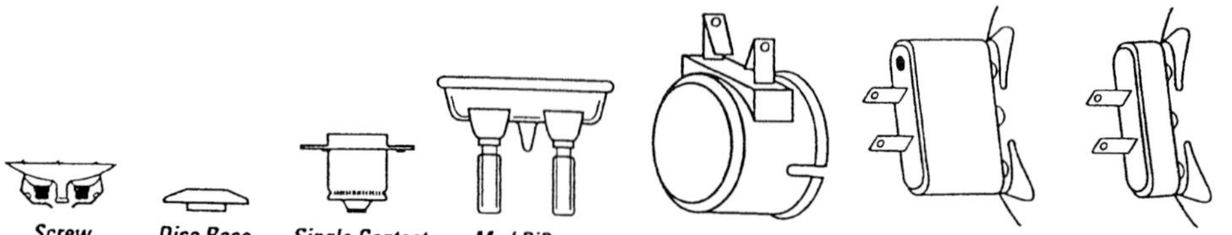

Screw Terminal | *Disc Base* | *Single Contact Pf* | *Med BiPost* | *Med Side Pr* | *Ext. Mog End Pr GX16d* | *Mog End Pr GX16d*

Incandescent Lamps

A Bulb designation consists of a letter(s) to indicate the shape and a figure(s) to indicate the approximate major diameter in eighths of an inch. Bulbs are measured through their greatest diameter in eighths of an inch. Thus, an F-15 bulb is a flame-shape, 15/8 of an inch or 1-7/8 inches in diameter.

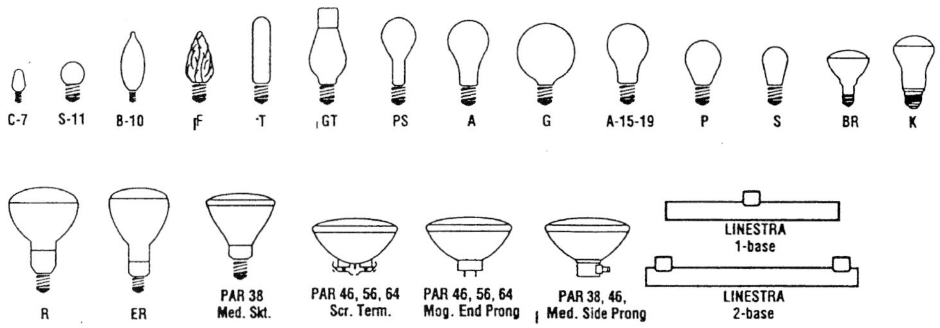

Incandescent Tungsten Halogen & Quartz Lamps

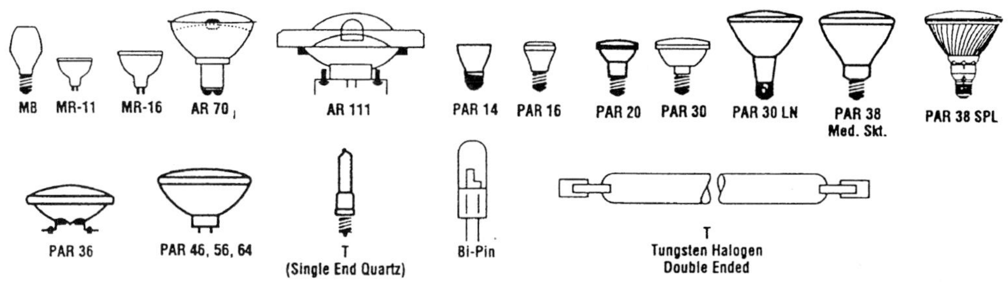

Filaments

A FILAMENT designation consists of a prefix letter to indicate whether the wire is straight or coiled, and a number to indicate the arrangement of the filament on the supports. Prefix letters include: C (coiled) — wire is wound into a helical coil or it may be deeply fluted; CC (coiled coil) — wire is wound into a helical coil and this coiled wire again wound into a helical coil.

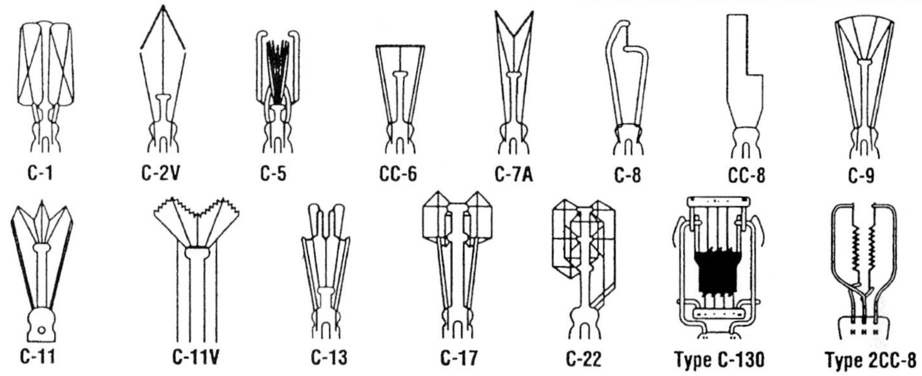

Bases

Typical screw base is shown. One lead-in wire is soldered to the center contact and the other soldered or welded to the upper rim of the base shell. Base shells are typically made of brass or aluminum. ANSI designations are in parentheses.

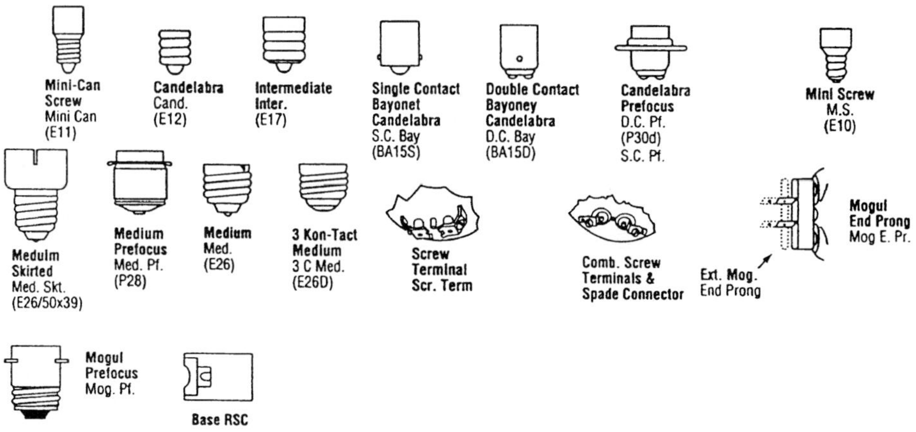

LIGHTING
Planning Data: Incandescent Bulb/Lamp Shapes

LAMP LOCATOR

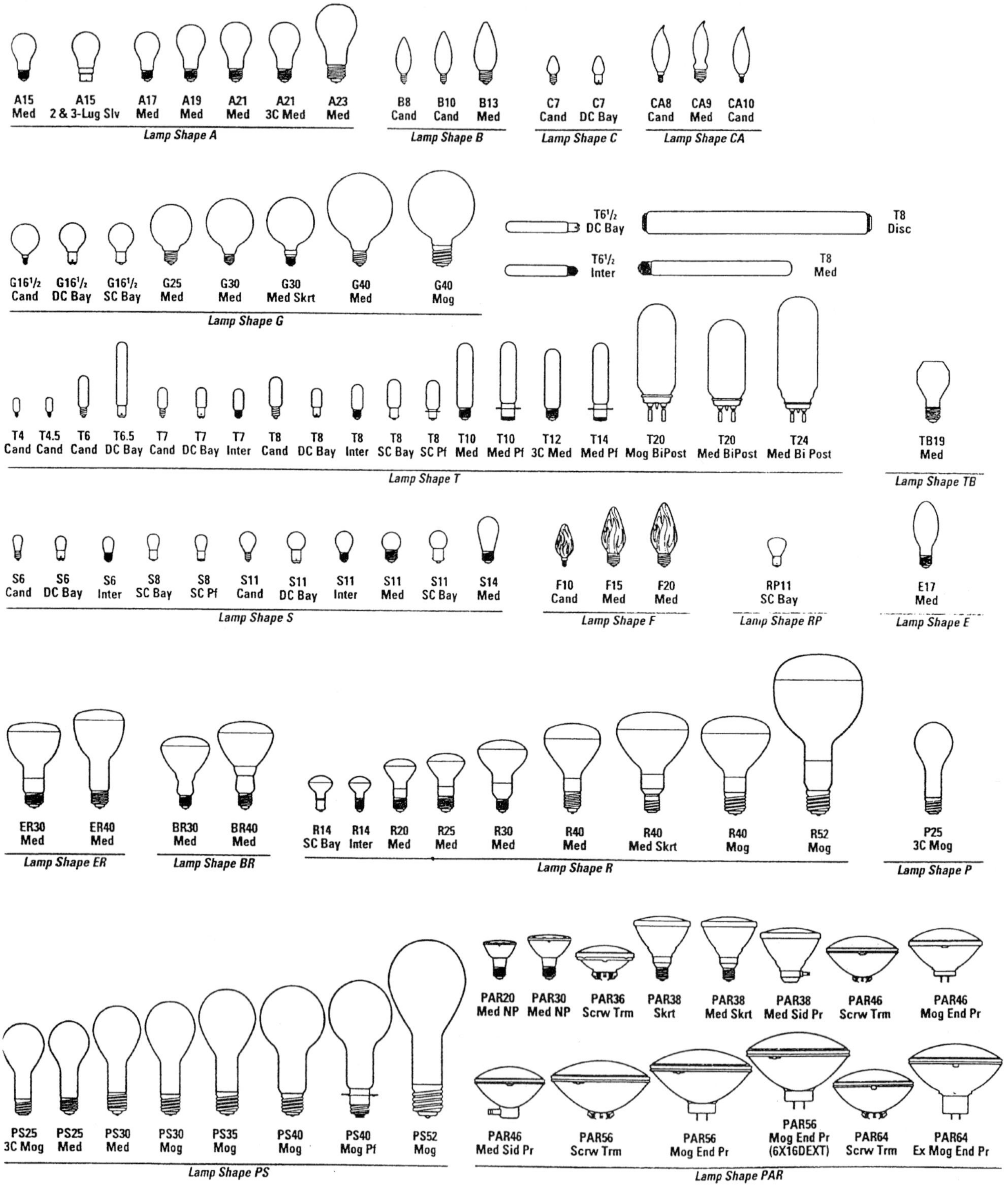
A15 Med
A15 2 & 3-Lug Slv
A17 Med
A19 Med
A21 Med
A21 3C Med
A23 Med
Lamp Shape A
B8 Cand
B10 Cand
B13 Med
Lamp Shape B
C7 Cand
C7 DC Bay
Lamp Shape C
CA8 Cand
CA9 Med
CA10 Cand
Lamp Shape CA
G16½ Cand
G16½ DC Bay
G16½ SC Bay
G25 Med
G30 Med
G30 Med Skrt
G40 Med
G40 Mog
Lamp Shape G
T6½ DC Bay
T6½ Inter
T8 Disc
T8 Med
T4 Cand
T4.5 Cand
T6 Cand
T6.5 DC Bay
T7 Cand
T7 DC Bay
T7 Inter
T8 Cand
T8 DC Bay
T8 Inter
T8 SC Bay
T8 SC Pf
T10 Med
T10 Med Pf
T12 3C Med
T14 Med Pf
T20 Mog BiPost
T20 Med BiPost
T24 Med Bi Post
Lamp Shape T
TB19 Med
Lamp Shape TB
S6 Cand
S6 DC Bay
S6 Inter
S8 SC Bay
S8 SC Pf
S11 Cand
S11 DC Bay
S11 Inter
S11 Med
S11 SC Bay
S14 Med
Lamp Shape S
F10 Cand
F15 Med
F20 Med
Lamp Shape F
RP11 SC Bay
Lamp Shape RP
E17 Med
Lamp Shape E
ER30 Med
ER40 Med
Lamp Shape ER
BR30 Med
BR40 Med
Lamp Shape BR
R14 SC Bay
R14 Inter
R20 Med
R25 Med
R30 Med
R40 Med
R40 Med Skrt
R40 Mog
R52 Mog
Lamp Shape R
P25 3C Mog
Lamp Shape P
PS25 3C Mog
PS25 Med
PS30 Med
PS30 Mog
PS35 Mog
PS40 Mog
PS40 Mog Pf
PS52 Mog
Lamp Shape PS
PAR20 Med NP
PAR30 Med NP
PAR36 Scrw Trm
PAR38 Skrt
PAR38 Med Skrt
PAR38 Med Sid Pr
PAR46 Scrw Trm
PAR46 Mog End Pr
PAR46 Med Sid Pr
PAR56 Scrw Trm
PAR56 Mog End Pr
PAR56 Mog End Pr (6X16DEXT)
PAR64 Scrw Trm
PAR64 Ex Mog End Pr
Lamp Shape PAR

BULB IDENTIFICATION

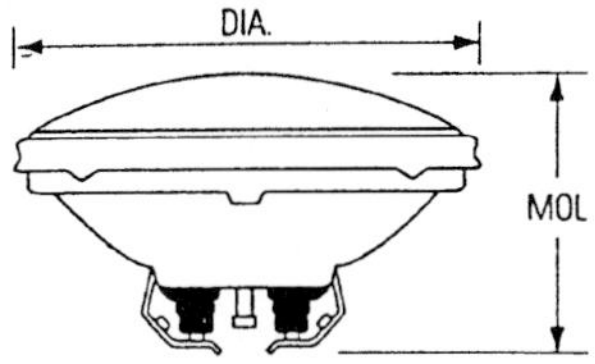

DIA. in.: Diameter of bulb at widest point.

MOL in.: Maximum Overall Length including base or pins.

LCL in.: Distance between the center of the filament and the Light Center Length reference plane.

Note: Lamp drawings are not drawn to scale. Be sure to check size and dimension information when identifying each lamp.

To convert inches to millimeters, multiply the dimension (in inches) by 25.4 (i.e. 1.5" x 25.4 = 38.1 mm).

FILAMENT IDENTIFICATION

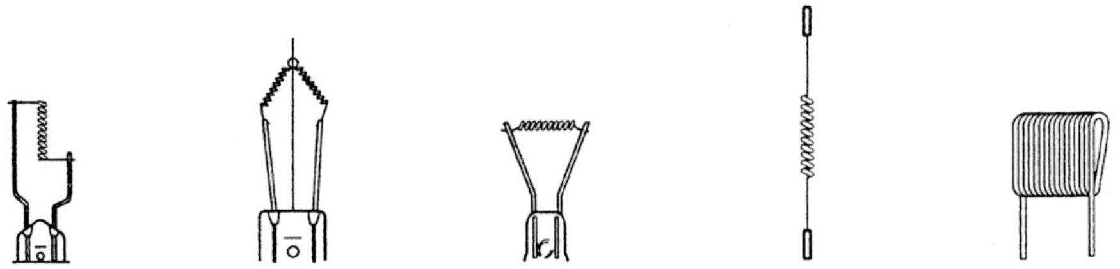

C-8 CC-8 | C-2V CC-2V | C-6 CC-6 | CC-8 | C-6 Oval

BASE IDENTIFICATION

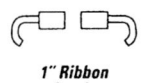

2-Pin (Round) GX5.3 | Can DC Bay | 2-Pin GY6.35 | Recessed Single Contact R7s | Screw Terminals | 4" Leads | 1" Ribbon Leads | 6" Flex Leads

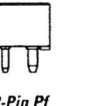

2-Pin GU-4 | 2-Pin GU-5.3 | 2-Pin G4 | Turn & Lock GU-7 | 2-Pin Pf | Min Screw E-10 | DC Bay BA15d | Min Cand E11

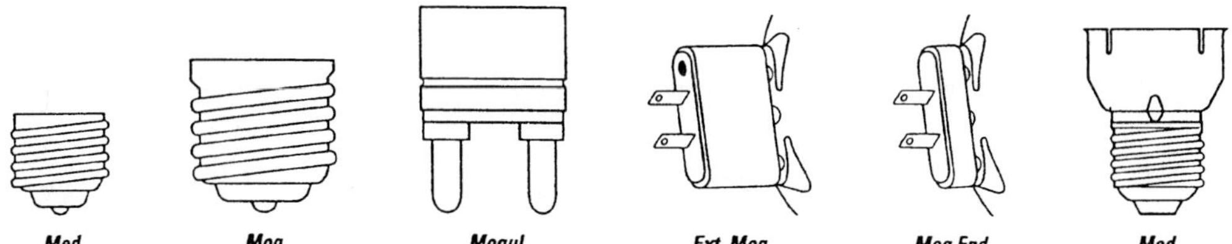

Med Screw E26 | Mog Screw E39 | Mogul BiPost G38 | Ext. Mog End Pr GX16d | Mog End PR GX16d | Med Skirted E26/50x39

BULB IDENTIFICATION

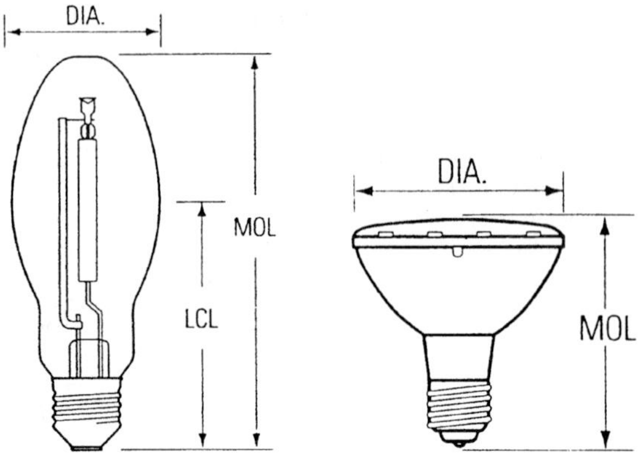

DIA: Diameter of bulb at widest point.

MOL: Maximum Overall Length including base or pins.

LCL: Distance between the center of the arc tube and the Light Center Length reference plane.

Note: Lamp drawings are not drawn to scale.
Be sure to check size and dimension information when identifying each lamp.

To convert inches to millimeters, multiply the dimension (in inches) by 25.4 (i.e. 1.5" x 25.4 = 38.1 mm).

LAMP LOCATOR

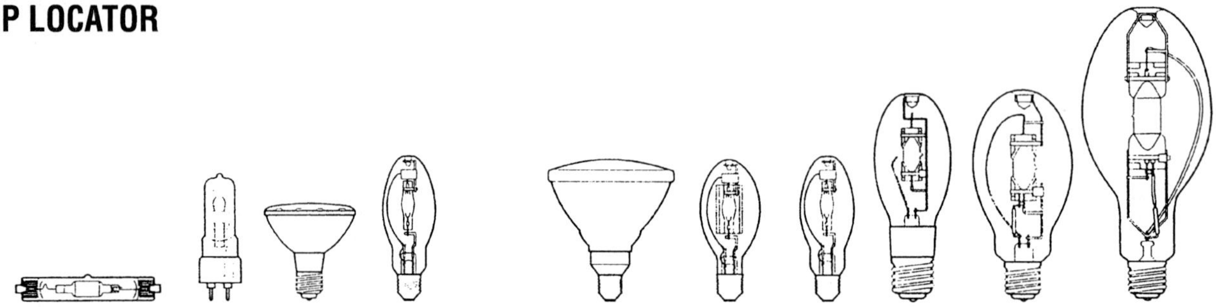

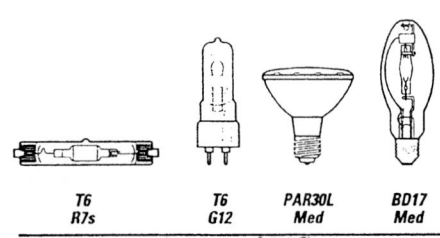

T6 R7s · *T6 G12* · *PAR30L Med* · *BD17 Med*
ConstantColor® CMH™

PAR38 Med · *ED17 Med* · *BD17 Med* · *ED23½ Mog* · *ED28 Mog* · *ED37 Mog*
PulseArc™ Metal Halide Lamps

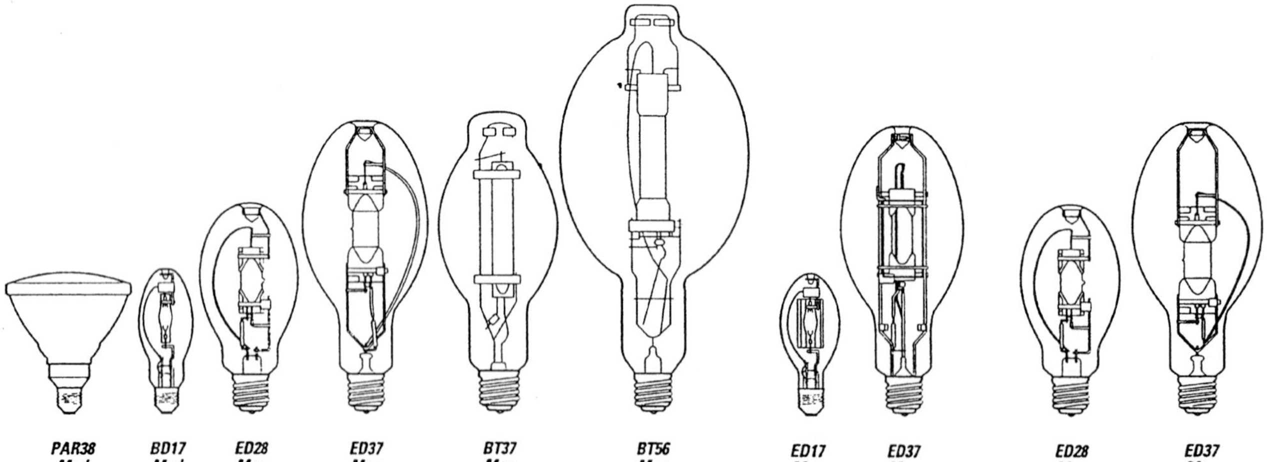

PAR38 Med · *BD17 Med* · *ED28 Mog* · *ED37 Mog* · *BT37 Mog* · *BT56 Mog*
Multi-Vapor® Metal Halide Lamps

ED17 Mog · *ED37 Mog*
Protected High Output Multi-Vapor® Lamps

ED28 Mog · *ED37 Mog*
ChromaFit™ Multi-Vapor® Lamps

LIGHTING

Planning Data: High-Intensity Discharge (HID) Bulb/Lamp Types

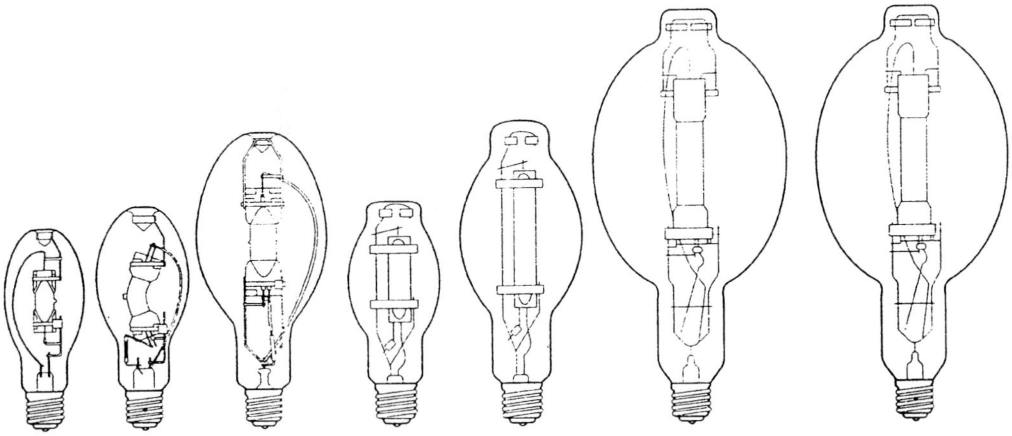

ED23½ Mog | ED28 PosMog | ED37 Mog | BT28 Mog | BT37 Mog | BT56 Mog | BT56 Pos Mog

High Output Multi-Vapor® Metal Halide Lamps

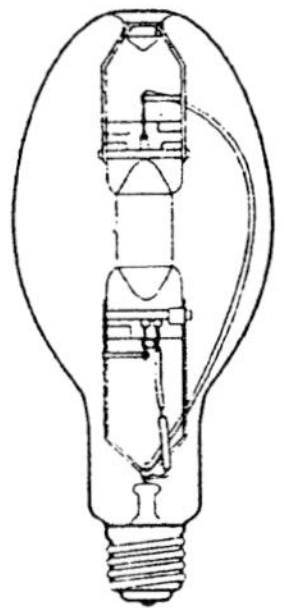

ED37 Mog

Saf-T-Gard® Self-Extinguishing Multi-Vapor Lamps

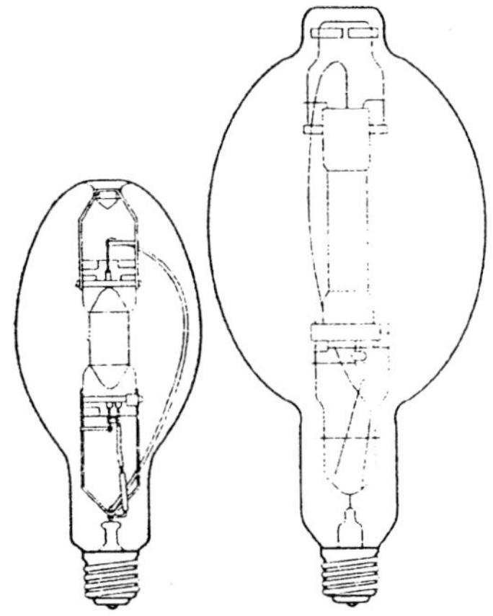

ED37 Mog | BT56 Mog

I-Line Multi-Vapor® Lamps

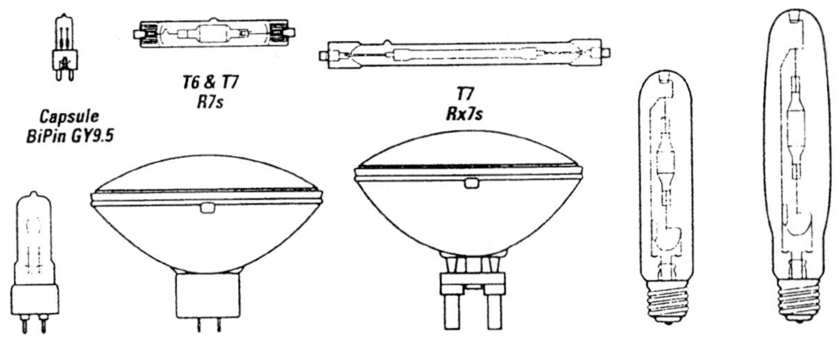

T6 BiPin G12 | PAR64 Ex Mog End Pr | PAR64 G38 | T15 Mog | ED18 Mog

Arcstream™ Metal Halide Lamps

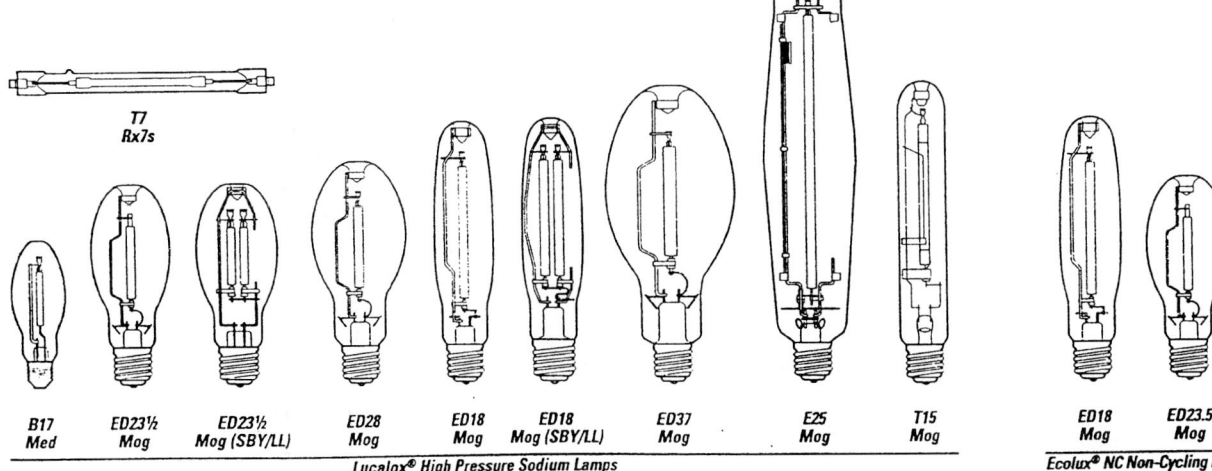

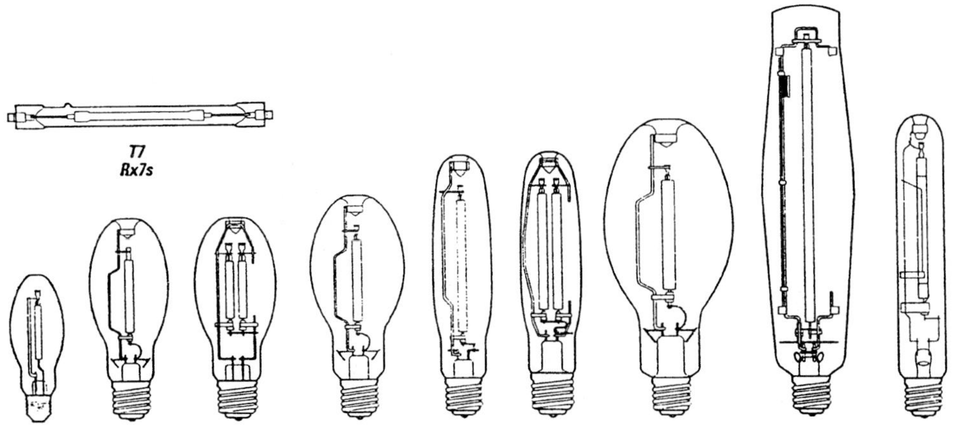

B17 Med | ED23½ Mog | ED23½ Mog (SBY/LL) | ED28 Mog | ED18 Mog | ED18 Mog (SBY/LL) | ED37 Mog | E25 Mog | T15 Mog

Lucalox® High Pressure Sodium Lamps

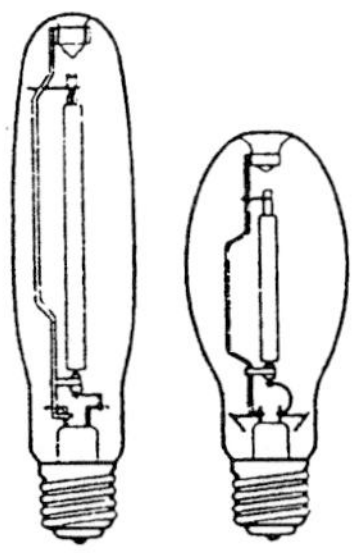

ED18 Mog | ED23.5 Mog

Ecolux® NC Non-Cycling High Pressure Sodium Lamps

LIGHTING

Planning Data: High-Intensity Discharge (HID) Bulb/Lamp Types

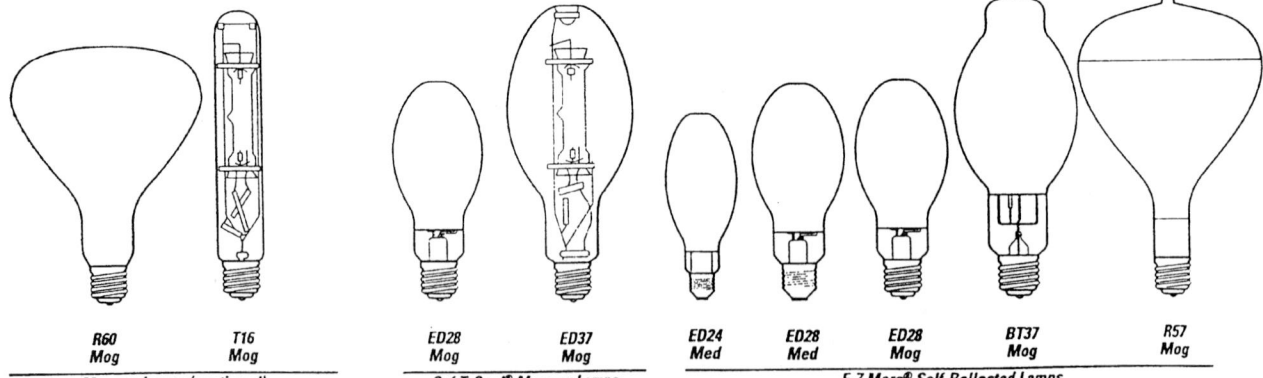

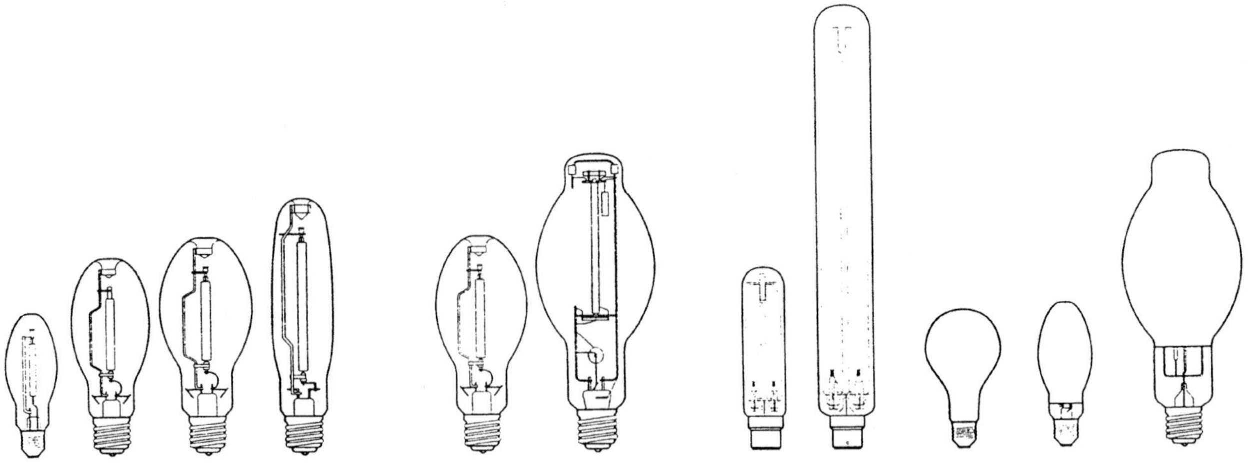

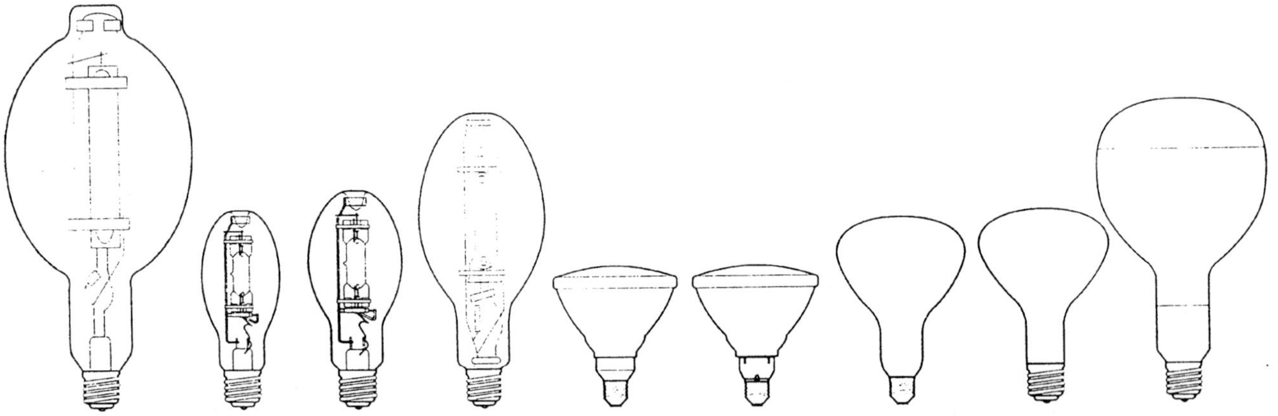

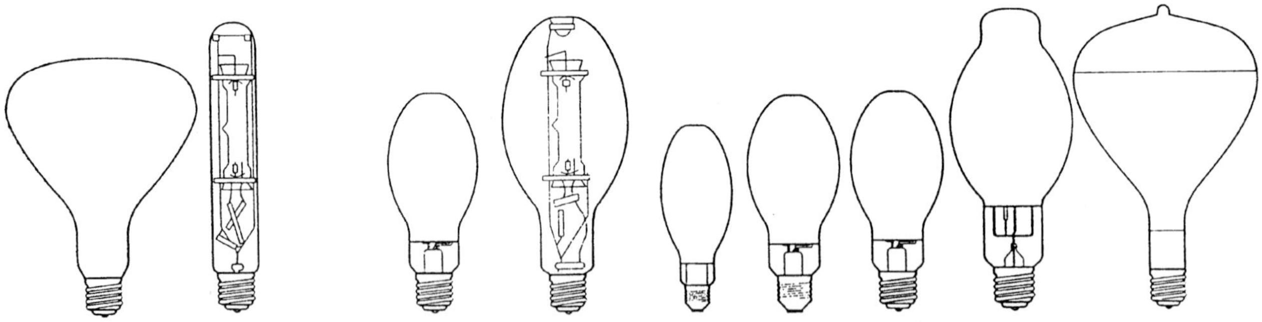

BASE IDENTIFICATION

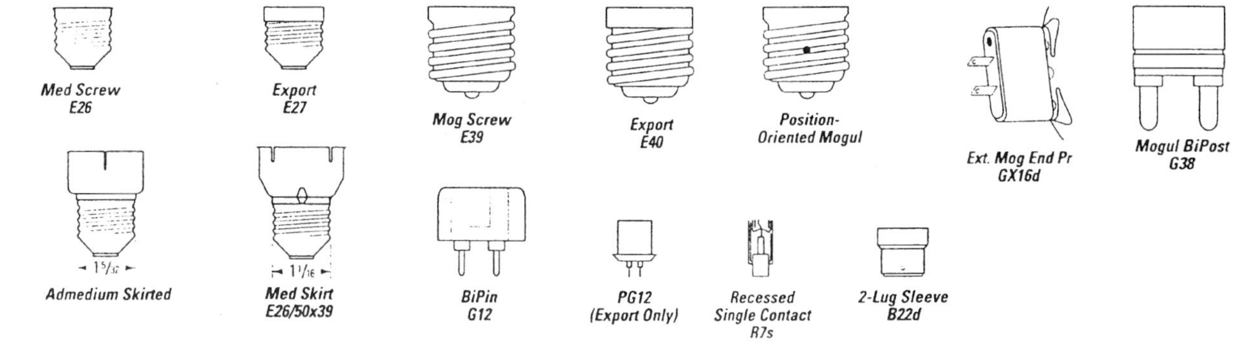

INTRODUCTION

GE HID lamps provide the following benefits:

High Efficacy/Low Operating Cost.
HID is generally the most efficient light source. Better efficiency almost always means lower operating cost.

Long Life.
Most HID lamps have life ratings that are better than incandescent lamps and similar to fluorescent lamps.

Compact Size.
An HID lamp produces high light output from a relatively compact source. Like incandescent, it is a "point" light source, which allows for good optical control.

The chart below shows how HID lamps compare to incandescent, halogen, and fluorescent in terms of efficiency and rated average life. Efficiency is measured in lumens per watt (LPW). Rated average life for most lamp types is the number of burning hours when 50% of the tested samples have failed and 50% are still operational. For both HID and fluorescent, lamp life depends on the number of hours per start.

The combination of high efficiency and long life makes HID an ideal light source for many commercial and industrial applications.

Typical Lamp Characteristics

Lamp Type	Typical LPW	Rated Avg. Life (in hours)
Incandescent	5 - 22	750 - 2000
Halogen	12 - 36	2000 - 6000
Compact Fluorescent	27 - 80	9000 - 20,000
Fluorescent	75 - 100	12,000 - 24,000 +
Mercury	50 - 60	12,000 - 24,000 +
ConstantColor® CMH™	80 - 90	6,000 - 10,000
Multi-Vapor® Metal Halide	80 - 115	10,000 - 20,000
Lucalox® High Pressure Sodium	90 - 140	10,000 - 40,000

SUGGESTED COLOR APPLICATIONS FOR HID LAMPS

CMH™: Stores, people places, display, accent.

MVR: Stores, public spaces, industrial, gymnasiums, floodlighting signs and buildings, parking areas, sports.

MVR/C: Same as MVR – warmer color – diffuse coating reduces glare.

MVR/SP30: Same as MVR – warmer than MVR or MVR/C – matches SP30 fluorescent.

MXR: Warm color (3200K) – good match for halogen.

LU: Street lighting, parking areas, industrial, floodlighting, security, CCTV.

LU/DX: Floodlighting, parking areas, indoor/outdoor pedestrian malls, industrial, security, roadway.

Deluxe (DX) Mercury: Stores, public spaces – Metal Halide lamps however, are preferred.

Clear Mercury: Landscape lighting, specialized floodlighting such as green copper roofs.

LAMP LOCATOR (Not Drawn to Scale)

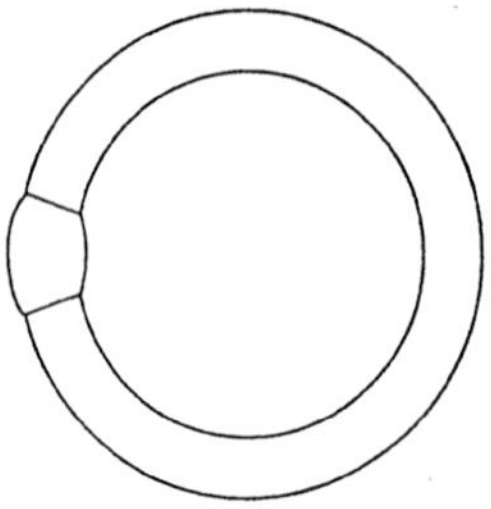

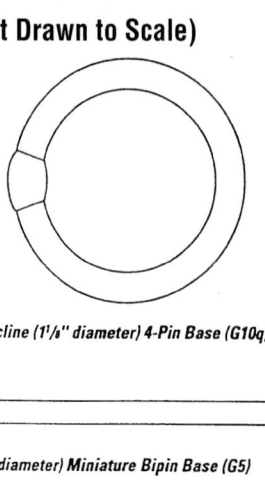

T9 Circline (1 1/8" diameter) 4-Pin Base (G10q)

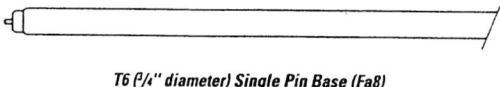

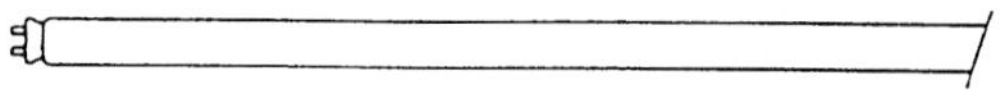

T5 (5/8" diameter) Miniature Bipin Base (G5)

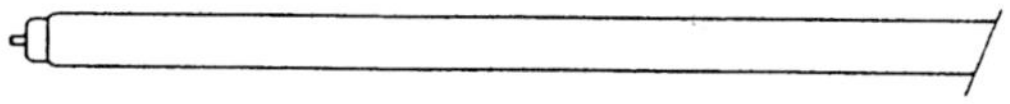

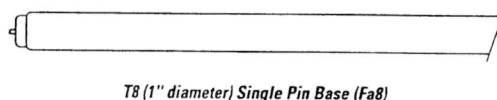

T6 (3/4" diameter) Single Pin Base (Fa8)

T8 (1" diameter) Single Pin Base (Fa8)

T8 (1" diameter) Medium Bipin Base (G13)

T8 (1" diameter) Recessed Double Contact Base (R17d)

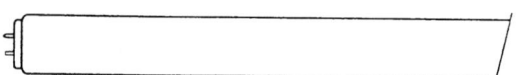

T10 (1 1/4" diameter) Recessed Double Contact Base (R17d)

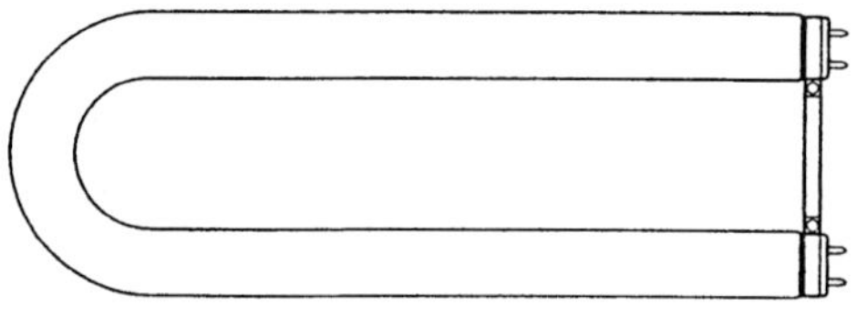

Mod-U-Line® T8/U6 (1" diameter) Medium Bipin Base (G13)

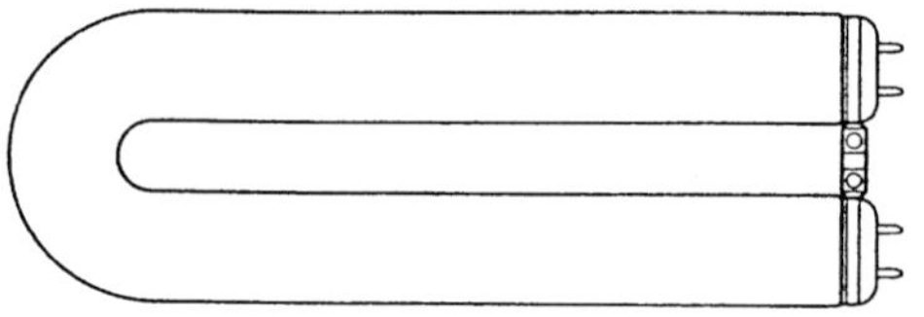

Mod-U-Line® T12/U3 (1 1/2" diameter) Medium Bipin Base (G13)

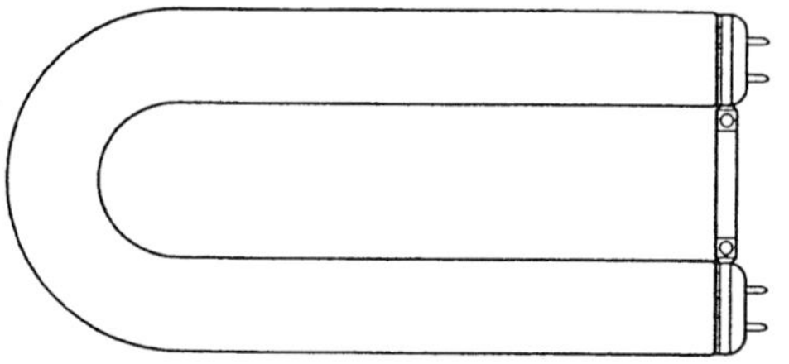

Mod-U-Line® T12/U6 (1 1/2" diameter) Medium Bipin Base (G13)

T12 (1 1/2" diameter) Single Pin Base (Fa8)

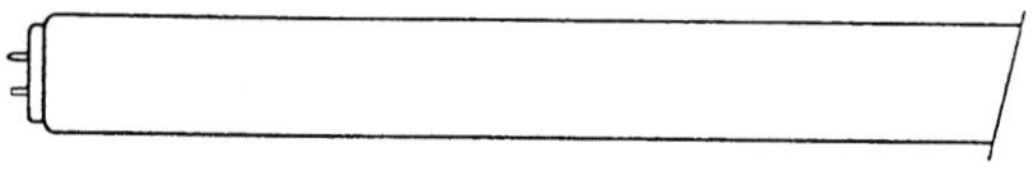

T12 (1 1/2" diameter) Medium Bipin Base (G13)

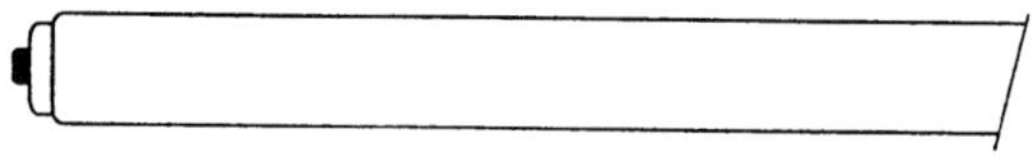

T12 (1 1/2" diameter) Recessed Double Contact Base (R17d)

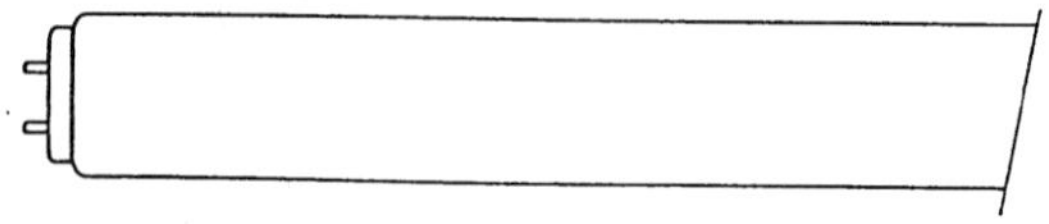

T17 (2 1/8" diameter) Mogul Bipin (G20)

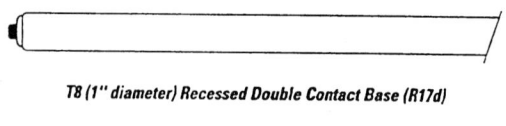

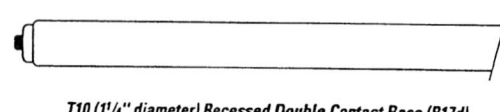

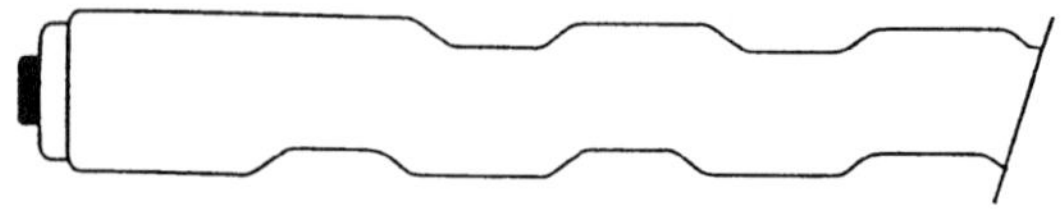

Power Groove® (2 1/8" diameter)
Recessed Double Contact Base (R17d)

FLUORESCENT LAMPS

The bulb shape and size of a fluorescent lamp are expressed by means of a code consisting of the letter "T" (which designates that the bulb is "tubular" in shape) followed by a number which expresses the diameter of the bulb in eighths of an inch. They vary in diameter from T-2 (¼ inch) to T-12 (1½ inches). In nominal overall length, fluorescent lamps range from 6 to 96 inches, which is always measured from back of lampholder to back of lampholder. For example, the actual overall length of the 40-watt rapid start T-12, 48 inch lamp is 47¾ inches. Circline lamps, which are circular, are available in four sizes: 6½ inches, 8 inches, 12 inches and 16 inches outside diameter. There are also U-shaped fluorescent types (Curvalume®) with T-8 and T-12 bulbs. The width of U shaped types are measured for the distance between the ends. The overall length is measured from the face of the bases to the outside of the glass bend.

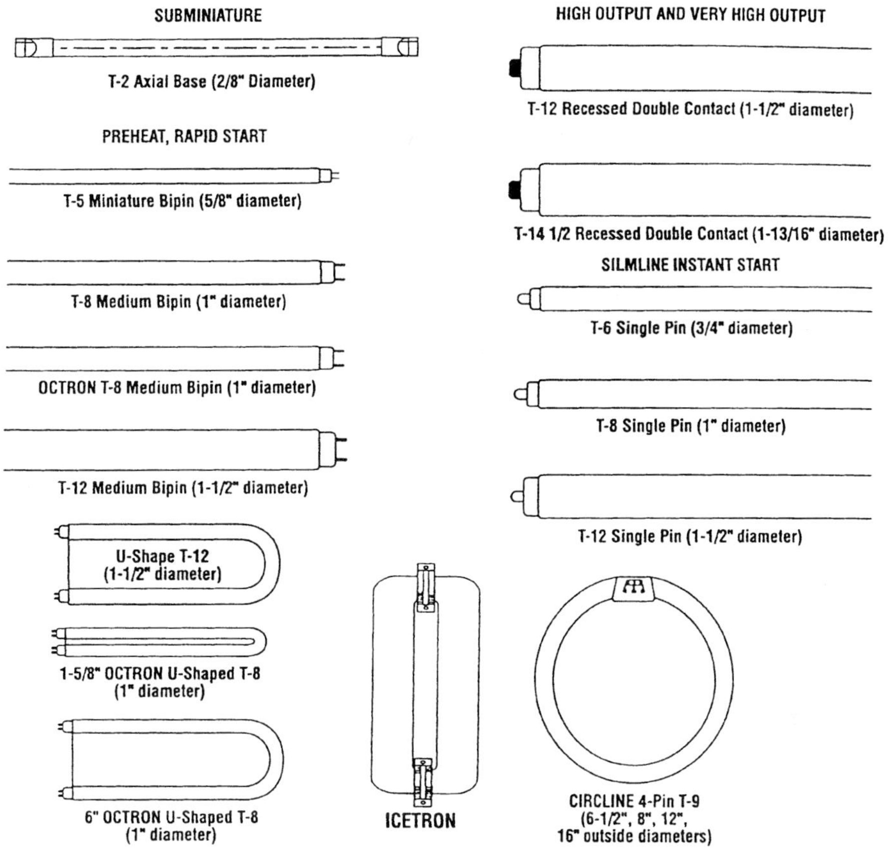

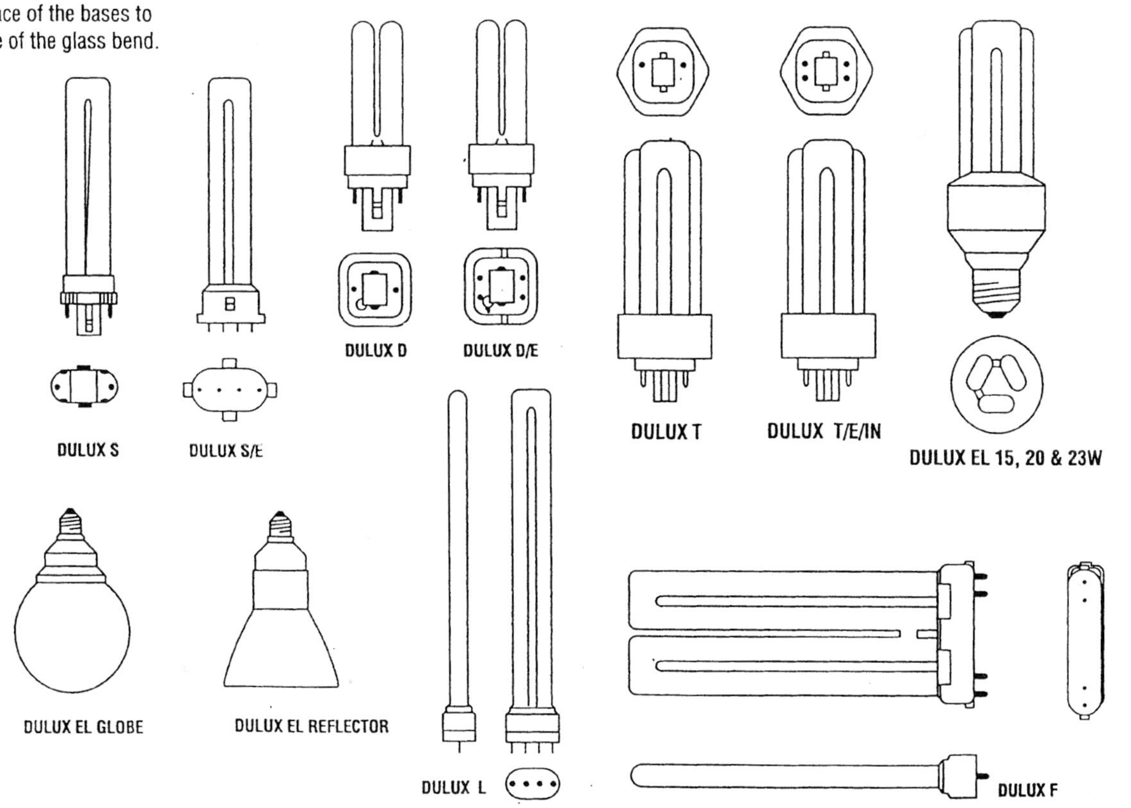

BASE IDENTIFICATION

Min Bipin
G5

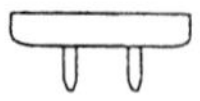

Med Bipin
G13

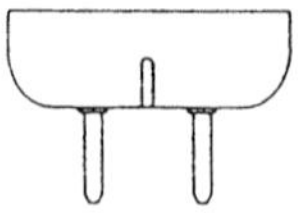

Mog Bipin
G20

Single Pin
Fa8

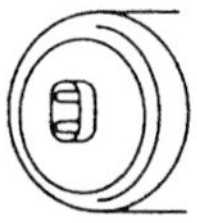

Recessed Double
Contact
R17d

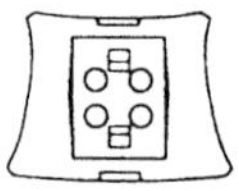

4-Pin
G10q
(Circline)

INTRODUCTION

GE introduced the first fluorescent lamp in 1939. Today, these lamps have become almost a universal standard in office and other lighting applications. The characteristics of fluorescent lamps vary widely according to the lamp type. In general, fluorescent lamps have the following advantages:

- **Low Operating Cost:**
  Efficient, fluorescent lamps can cost significantly less to operate over their lifetime than incandescent lamps.
- **Long Life:**
  Life ratings for fluorescent lamps range from 6000 to 24,000 hours based on the industry standard of 3 burning hours per start.
- **Light Quality:**
  GE Starcoat™ T8 lamps offer the best color rendering and highest lumen maintenance (95%) in the industry.
- **Flexibility:**
  Fluorescent lamps are available in a wide range of sizes, shapes, color performance, and wattage ratings.
- **Fast Starting:**
  Rapid-Start and Instant-Start lamps typically start within 1 second of being turned on.

FLUORESCENT BRAND NAME CROSS-REFERENCE

GE	OSRAM/SYLVANIA	PHILIPS
Aquarium/Terrarium	—	—
Chroma 50	Design 50®	Colortone 50
Cov-R-Guard™	—	—
Ecolux®	Ecologic	Alto
Ecolux® XL	—	—
Gro & Sho™/Plant & Aquarium	GRO-LUX®	Agro-Lite
Kitchen and Bath ULTRA™	Interior Design® (D30)	Softone Pastel FL (SPEC 30)
Mod-U-Line®	Curvalume®	U-Bent
Power Groove®	—	—
Specification Series (SP)®	Designer® Series (D)	SPEC Series
Specification Series (SPX)	Designer® "800" Series	Ultralume™
Starcoat™	—	—
T8	Octron®	TL70/TL80™
T10/1500MA	VHO/LT	—
/1500	VHO	VHO
Watt-Miser®	SuperSaver®	Econ-o-Watt
Watt-Miser® Plus	SuperSaver Plus®	—
XL	XP	Advantage

ATTENTION: This brand-name cross-reference chart is provided only as a quick reference. Other lamp company brand listings may only represent a near equivalent, versus an identical match to GE Lighting brands. Individual lamp manufacturer's performance specifications and product offerings should be consulted. Lamp performance may be affected by environmental conditions, ballast type and/or other auxiliary equipment.

OFFICE

LIGHT LEVEL RECOMMENDATIONS

Type of Work	Foot Candles*
Corridors, lobbies	10-15-20
Easy tasks (Typed originals, ball-point pen handwriting, large print)	20-30-50
Medium tasks (Poor copies, medium hard pencil, small print)	50-75-100
Difficult tasks (Very poor copies, hard pencil writing)	100-150-200

*Choose an illuminance value in the mid-range for your type of activity. Then decide upon a specific value (Same, lower, or higher) within that range by considering the age of the workers and the importance of the work.

SELECTING THE PROPER FIXTURE

- Light Output/Efficiency

  The more light, the fewer fixtures needed in new lighting systems and lower operating cost.

- Visual Comfort

  Fixtures should direct light to the task and away from the eyes. The fixture's VCP rating, available from the fixture manufacturer, should be 70 or above.

- Maintainability

  Check ease of lamp replacement, cleanability, and permanence of finishes.

- Fit In Application

  Should look right and cover the area to be lighted (consider smaller fixtures closer together, such as 2 × 2s instead of 2 × 4s, for lower ceilings, or lower light levels or high-panelled work stations).

- Shielding Materials

  Comparison of lighting characteristics for typical 2 × 4 troffer luminaries:

Shielding Material	Efficiency Range (%)	VCP Range
Clear Lens	50-70	55-85
Polarizer	55-60	60-70
Deep Cell Parabolic Louver	45-60	70-85
Diffuser	40-60	40-50
Plastic Louver Panel (45°)	45-55	50-70
White Metal Louver (45°)	35-45	65-85
Parabolic Louver Panel (45°)	40-50	99
Toned Lens	30-60	70-85
Dark Metal Louver	25-40	70-90

STORE

LIGHT LEVEL RECOMMENDATIONS	Circulation	Merchandising	Feature Displays
High Activity Area (Mass Merchandiser)	30	100	500
Medium (Family Dept. Store)	20	70	300
Low (Boutique, Specialty Stores)	10	30	150

INDUSTRIAL

LIGHT LEVEL RECOMMENDATIONS	Footcandles Maintained on the Task
GARAGES–SERVICE	
☐ repair	50-100fc
☐ active traffic areas	10-20fc
LOADING PLATFORM	20fc
MACHINE SHOPS AND ASSEMBLY AREAS	
☐ rough bench/machine work, simple assembly	20-50fc
☐ medium bench/machine work, moderately difficult assembly	50-100fc
☐ difficult machine work, assembly	100-200fc
☐ fine bench/machine work, assembly	200-500fc*
RECEIVING & SHIPPING	20-50fc
WAREHOUSES, STORAGE ROOMS	
☐ active-large items/small items, labels	15fc/30fc
☐ inactive	5fc

*Higher illuminance values may be achieved through a combination of supplementary and general lighting.

Material and color light reflectances

PLANNING DATA: ACCENT LIGHTING/BEAM SPREADS

Cloth	%
White linen (dull finish)	81%
White cotton	65
Red cotton (diamine fast red)	44
Black cotton (diamine)	33
Blue woolen	25
Blue flannel	17.5
Blue linen (navy blue)	17
Black woolen	12
Black velvet	1.8

Paper	%
Quality white	85%
White blotting	82
White drawing	70–80
Medium quality white	75
Light gray	73
Cheap white	70
Pink	60
Buff	60
Newsprint	55
Medium gray	45
Dark gray	20
Chocolate brown	20
Olive green	15
Matte black	5
Ultramarine blue	3.5
Hard pencil line	45
Soft pencil line	25
Printer's ink (good quality)	15
Black ink	4
Black velour	0.4

Accent Colors	%
White (diffuse)	80
Deep red	14–22
Red	21–31
Orange	38–48
Yellow	60–65
Yellow green	42–46
Saturated green	24–32
Blue	17–23
Violet purple	12–14
Red purple	16–23

Woods	%
Birch and beech	35–50%
Whitewood (plain)	45
Maple	42
Satinwood	34
Light oak	25–35
English oak	17
Walnut	16
Black Walnut	5–15
Dark oak and cherry	10–15
Mahogany	12

Glass and Plastic	%
Mirror glass	80–90%
Metabolized plastic	75–85
White structural glass	75–80
Reflective glass	20–30
Clear glass	7
Tinted glass	7
Black structural glass	5

Interior Surface Colors	%
Dull or flat white	75–90
Cream or eggshell	79
Pale pink, pale yellow	75–80
Ivory	75
Light green, blue, or orchid	70–75
Light beige and pale gray	70
Soft pink and light peach	69
Pink	64
Apricot	56–62
Tan or yellow gold	55
Light gray	35–50
Medium turquoise	44
Yellow green	45
Medium light blue	42
Old gold and pumpkin	34
Rose	29
Cocoa brown and mauve	24
Medium green and blue	21
Medium gray	20
Dark brown and dark gray	10–15
Olive green	12
Dark blue and blue green	5–10
Forest green	7

Recommended Levels of Artificial Illumination

The following is a guide for minimum levels of illumination for certain tasks. The values accommodate young adults with normal and better than 20/30 corrected vision. Values in one category can be used under other categories. The first value is for footcandles (fc) for the task, the second value is for lux (lx) for the task.

Office	*fc*	*lx*
Bookkeeping	150	1610
Typing	70	750
Filing	70	750
Conference rooms	30	320
Reception areas	20	220
Corridors	20	220
Drafting (low value is for rough work, high value is for fine work)	150–200	1610–2150

School	*fc*	*lx*
Chalkboards	150	1610
Desks (for study)	70	750
Drawing (art work)	70	750
Gymnasium	30	320
Auditorium	15	160

Theater	*fc*	*lx*
Lobby	20	220
During intermission	5	54
During movie	0.1	1

Industrial	*fc*	*lx*
Precision manual arc welding	1,000	10,750
Extra-fine machine work and inspection	1,000	10,750
Fine machine work	500	5,380
Medium machine work	100	1,080
Rough machine work	50	540
Sheet metal (scribing)	100	1,080
Steel and sheet metal fabrication	50	540
Paint mixing and matching	200	2,150
Receiving and shipping	10	110

Home	*fc*	*lx*
Reading, studying	30–70	320–750
Writing (with pencil)	70	570
Sewing, hand or machine (low value is for white cloth and high value is for black cloth)	50–200	540–2150
Kitchen sink and range	70	750
Kitchen counters	50–150	540–1600
Laundry work	50	540
Workbench hobbies	70–200*	750–2150
Washer, dryer, games	30	320

**Use if making jewelry.*

For instruments	*fc*	*lx*
Business machines, calculators, digital input, etc.	50–100	540–1080
Control panels, consoles	30–50	320–540
Dials	30	320
Meters	30–50	320–540
Gauges	50	540
Scales	30–50	320–540
Scales with 1/64-in divisions	180	1930

Medical	*fc*	*lx*
Operating table	2500	26,850
Emergency operating	2000	21,500
Dental work	1000	10,750
Examination room	50–100	540–1080

Train	*fc*	*lx*
Dining	50	540
Reading	30	320
Aisle, steps	10	110

Levels of Illumination in Daylight

Light condition	*fc*	*lx*
In direct sunshine (at noon)	6000–8000	64,500–87,000
In shade (outdoors at noon)	100–1000	1,080–10,750
Comfortable reading (in shade at noon)	200	2,150 minimum

ANSI (American National Standards Institute): The organization that develops voluntary guidelines and product performance standards for the electrical and other industries.

Ampere: A unit expressing the rate of flow of electric current.

Average rated life: An average rating, in hours, indicating when 50 percent of a large group of lamps have failed, when operated at nominal lamp voltage and current; manufacturers use 3 h per start for fluorescent lamps and 10 h per start for HID lamps when performing lamp life testing procedures; every lamp type has a unique mortality curve that depicts its average rated life.

Ballast: A device used with an electric-discharge lamp to obtain the necessary circuit conditions (voltage, current, and waveform) for starting and operating; all fluorescent and HID light sources require a ballast for proper operation.

Ballast factor (BF): The measured ability of a particular ballast to produce light from the lamp(s) it powers; ballast factor is derived by dividing the lumen output of a particular lamp/ballast combination by the lumen output of the same lamp(s) on a reference ballast.

Candela (cd): The unit of measure indicating the luminous intensity (candlepower) of a light source in a specific direction; any given light source will have many different intensities, depending on the direction considered.

Candlepower distribution: A curve that represents the variation in luminous intensity (expressed in candelas) in a plane through the light center of a lamp or luminaire; each lamp or lamp/luminaire combination has a unique set of candlepower distributions that indicate how light will be spread.

Center beam candlepower (CBCP): The intensity of light produced at the center of a reflector lamp, expressed in candelas.

Color rendering index (CRI): The measure of a light source is its ability to render the color of objects "correctly," as compared with a reference source with comparable color temperature.

Correlated color temperature (CCT): A specification of the color appearance of a lamp, relating its color to that of a reference source heated to a particular temperature, measured in degrees Kelvin (K); CCT generally measures the "warmth" or "coolness" of light source appearance.

Current (I): A measure of the flow of electricity, expressed in amperes (A).

Efficacy: Efficiency of a light source expressed in lumens per watt (LPW or Im/W).

Energy: A measure of work done by an electrical system over a given period of time, often expressed in kilowatthours (kWh).

Footcandle (fc): A unit of illuminance equal to 1 lumen per square foot.

Frequency: The number of times per second that an alternating current system reverses from positive to negative and back to positive, expressed in cycles per second or hertz (Hz).

Glare: Excessive brightness that may be caused by either direct or indirect viewing of a light source.

Harmonic: An electrical frequency that is an integer multiple of the fundamental frequency; for example, if 60 Hz is the fundamental frequency, then 120 Hz is the second harmonic and 180 Hz is the third harmonic; some electronic devices, such as ballasts or power supplies, can cause harmonic distortion, directly affecting power quality.

Illuminance: Light arriving at a surface, expressed in lumens per unit area; 1 lumen per square foot equals 1 footcandle, while 1 lumen per square meter equals 1 lux.

Lamp: Manufactured light source; the three broad categories of electric lamps are incandescent, fluorescent, and high intensity discharge (HID).

Light: Radiant energy that is capable of producing a visual sensation.

Light center length (LCL): The distance from a specified reference point on a lamp base to its light center, typically expressed in inches.

Lumen (lm): A unit of luminous flux; the overall light output of a luminous source is measured in lumens.

Lumen depreciation: The decrease in lumen output of a light source over time; every lamp type has a unique lumen depreciation curve (sometimes called lumen maintenance curve) depicting the pattern of decreasing light output.

Luminaire: A light fixture; the complete lighting unit, including lamp, reflector, ballast, socket, wiring, diffuser, and housing.

Luminance (L): Light reflected in a particular direction; the photometric quantity most closely associated with brightness perception, measured in units of luminous intensity (candelas) per unit area (square feet or square meters).

Lux (lx): A unit of illuminance equal to 1 lumen per square meter.

Maximum overall length (MOL): The total length of a lamp, from top of bulb to bottom of base, typically expressed in inches.

Power: The rate at which energy is taken from an electrical system or dissipated by a load, expressed in watts; power that is generated by a utility is typically expressed in volt-amperes.

Power factor: A measure of the effectiveness with which an electrical device converts volt-amperes to watts; devices with power factors (0.90) are high-power-factor devices.

Reflectance (ρ): The percentage of light reflected back from a surface, the difference having been absorbed or transmitted by the surface.

Resistance (R): A measure of resistance to flow of current, expressed in ohms (Ω).

Spectral power distribution (SPD): A curve illustrating the distribution of power produced by the lamp, at each wavelength across the spectrum.

Voltage (E): A measure of electrical potential, expressed in volts (V).

Wavelength (λ): Distance between two successive points of a periodic wave; the wavelengths of light are typically expressed in nanometers (nm), or billionths of a meter.

3
ARCHITECTURAL WOODWORK

Most residential and commercial projects require the design of a certain amount of architectural woodwork. Such woodwork may be in the form of built-in furniture, cabinets, display cases, reception desks, credenzas, work counters, kitchen cabinets, and so on. The extent of detail necessary to intelligently communicate and identify the scope and character of required woodwork is an important consideration in the preparation of contract drawings. It is necessary, therefore, that the designer have a knowledge of basic wood joinery and understand how to apply it in the preparation of construction details.

Accordingly, the information in this section can be used as a general guide in the detailing of most woodwork items and addresses four areas of concern. The first deals with basic joinery and typical casework details. This information is fundamental to an understanding of the detailing of woodwork. The typical joints illustrated vary in sophistication and structural integrity and represent the most common methods of joining any two wood members. The casework details are intended to illustrate the construction of routine casework and are divided into three categories: exposed face frame, flush overlay, and reveal overlay. The second area deals with custom woodwork and includes details of woodwork items selected directly from contract drawings contributed by various interior design and architectural firms. This information should prove helpful in providing the reader with a more global perspective of how different firms approach the detailing of some common types of woodwork items and the extent of that detailing. The third area of this section deals with standard cornices and moldings, and is intended to simply provide the designer with dimensional and design information relative to the many standard items available on the market. Since many woodwork items involve some movable elements, the fourth area of this section deals with furniture hardware.

STANDARD JOINERY AND CASEWORK DETAILS
Typical Joints

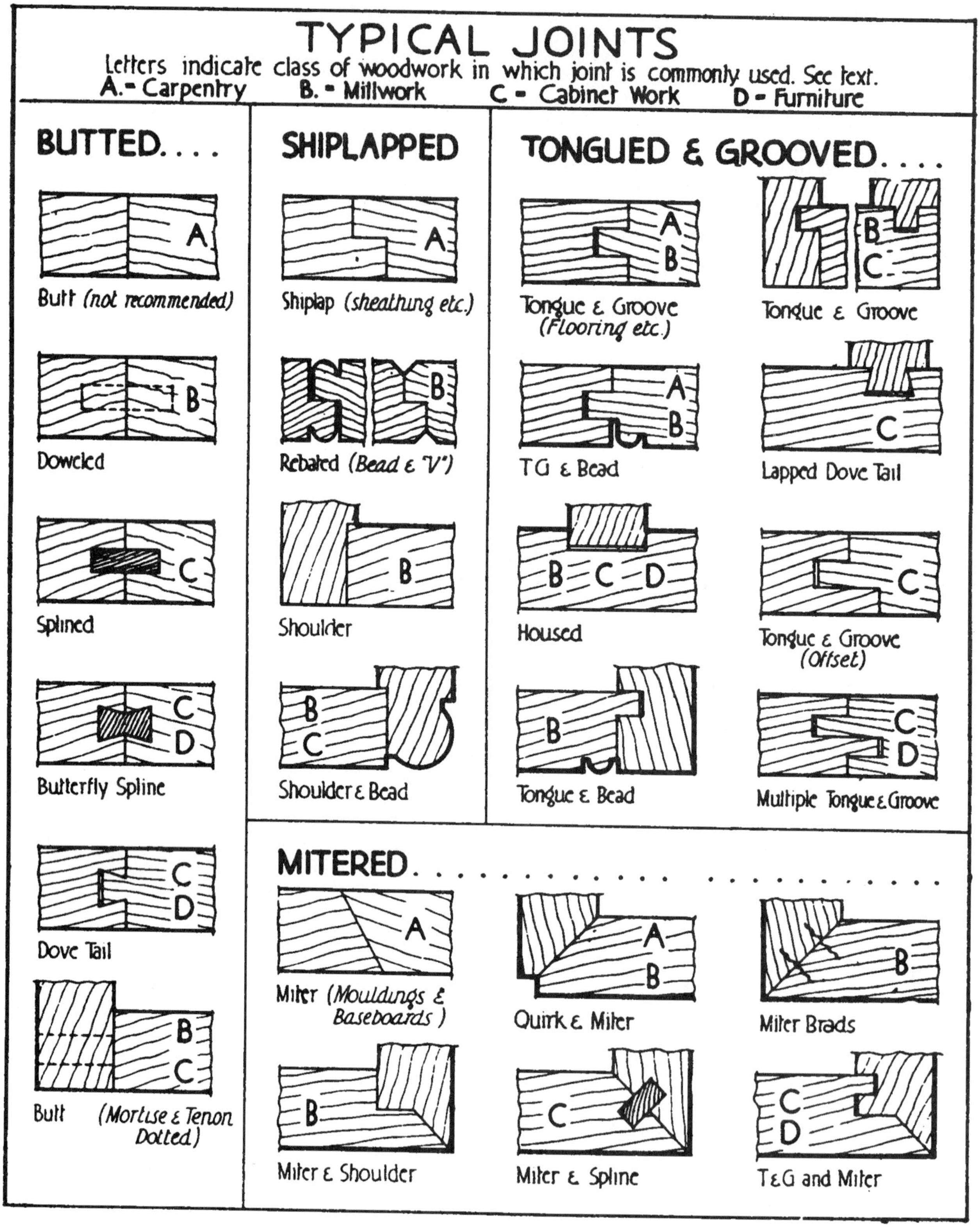
TYPICAL JOINTS
Letters indicate class of woodwork in which joint is commonly used. See text.
A.- Carpentry B.- Millwork C - Cabinet Work D - Furniture
BUTTED....
A
Butt (not recommended)
B
Doweled
C
Splined
C
D
Butterfly Spline
C
D
Dove Tail
B
C
Butt (Mortise & Tenon Dotted)
SHIPLAPPED
A
Shiplap (sheathing etc.)
B
Rebated (Bead & 'V')
B
Shoulder
B
C
Shoulder & Bead
TONGUED & GROOVED....
A
B
Tongue & Groove (Flooring etc.)
B
C
Tongue & Groove
A
B
TG & Bead
C
Lapped Dove Tail
B C D
Housed
C
Tongue & Groove (Offset)
B
Tongue & Bead
C
D
Multiple Tongue & Groove
MITERED....
A
Miter (Mouldings & Baseboards)
A
B
Quirk & Miter
B
Miter Brads
B
Miter & Shoulder
C
Miter & Spline
C
D
T&G and Miter

Characteristics of Joints

Joints may be divided into four general types: *butted, shiplapped, tongued-and-grooved,* and *mitered.* Used in their simple basic form, none is satisfactory for cabinet work except the tongued-and-grooved type in certain instances. However, when variously combined or when reinforced with gluing and dowels or splines, satisfactory joints can be developed.

Butt Joint

This is a simple but weak joint that opens easily and may show end wood when used at angles. Strength and range of use is greatly increased by use of the *mortise and tenon* and *dowels* and even more when a *straight spline* is included. Use of a glued *butterfly spline* with a butt joint produces an extremely strong joint. These variations are widely used to produce large flush surfaces of solid wood or backing for veneers.

Shiplap Joint

Stronger than a butt joint but subject to opening from shrinkage, shiplap joints are rarely used in a simple form in cabinet work except for door rebates. This joint is often molded to conceal shrinkage in quirks or combined as a *miter and shoulder* for corners. Another variation is the *shoulder joint.*

Tongue-and-Groove Joint

A strong joint, the tongue-and-groove joint is widely used for reentrant angles. The effect of wood shrinkage is concealed when the joint is beaded or otherwise molded. In expensive cabinet work, glued *dovetail* and *multiple tongue-and-groove* are used.

Miter Joints

Miter joints are weak and difficult to fit if used alone. Joints with *miter brads* are sufficiently strong for short lengths. Joints made in combination with other forms, as a *tongue-and-groove miter,* are tight and sturdy.

Use of Joints

Use of certain types of joints depends to a large degree on the type of work and skill involved. The following notes indicate use of joints in various categories, but cannot be regarded as an inclusive checklist.

For Panels and Shelving

For panels, shelving, or wherever the end of one piece butts against the face of another, use a *housed joint,* with or without cover mold, or some type of *tongue-and-groove* joint. Omit glue to avoid splitting due to swelling or shrinkage.

For Joining Stiles and Rails

Use *mortise and tenon,* glued in better work. Dowels may be used or hardwood wedges may be driven and glued into ends of tenons in high-grade work.

For Reentrant Corners

Use *shoulder joints* for inexpensive work. *Tongue-and-groove* is sturdier. Both should be glued, are often screwed together, and may be glued to a rough frame.

For External Corners

Simple *miter* and *quirk and miter* both lack strength. *Miter brads* are practical only for short lengths. *Miter and shoulder* glued and face-screwed or nailed is satisfactory (generally millwork). *Miter and spline* is preferable. In high-grade work exterior corners are reinforced by gluing to a corner post or short lengths of blocking.

Glued Joints

When screws, nails, and so on, can not be used, or when fine work is to be veneered, the strength of the joint depends on the accuracy of milling and total glue surface. Glue surface may be tremendously increased by using multiple or offset tongues and grooves, by forming miter cuts into waves, multiple shoulders, tongues and grooves, and so on. Such work is cabinet work. If done by a reliable cabinetmaker, a guarantee should be obtained and joint detail and composition of glue left to him or her.

Moldings

Moldings should be applied in continuous lengths if possible. Use simple miter for necessary joints, cope reentrant angles unless excessively undercut; miter external corners.

Terminology

Blind dado: Variation of conventional dado with applied edge "stopping" or concealing dado groove. Used when case body edge is exposed.

Conventional dovetail joint: Traditional method for joining drawer sides to fronts or backs. Usually limited to flush- or lipped-type drawers.

Conventional mortise and tenon joint: Joinery method for assembling square-edged surfaces such as case face frames.

Dowel joint: Alternative joinery method for serving same function as conventional mortise and tenon.

Drawer lock-joint: Another joinery method for joining drawer sides to fronts. Usually used for flush-type installation but can be adapted to lip- or overlay-type drawers.

Edge banding: Method of concealing plys or inner cores of plywood or particleboard when edges are exposed. Thickness or configuration will vary with manufacturers' practices.

Exposed end detail: Illustrates attachment of finished end of case body to front frame using butt joint.

Exposed end detail: Illustrates attachment of finished end of case body to front frame using mitered joint.

French dovetail joint: Method for joining drawer sides to fronts when fronts conceal metal extension slides or overlay the case faces.

Haunch mortise and tenon joint: Joinery method for assembling paneled doors or stile- and rail-type paneling.

Paneled door details: Joinery techniques when paneled effect is desired. Profiles are optional, as is the use of flat or raised panels. Solid lumber raised panels may be used when width does not exceed 10 in. Rim raised panels are recommended when widths exceed this dimension or when transparent finish is used.

STANDARD JOINERY AND CASEWORK DETAILS

Typical Joints

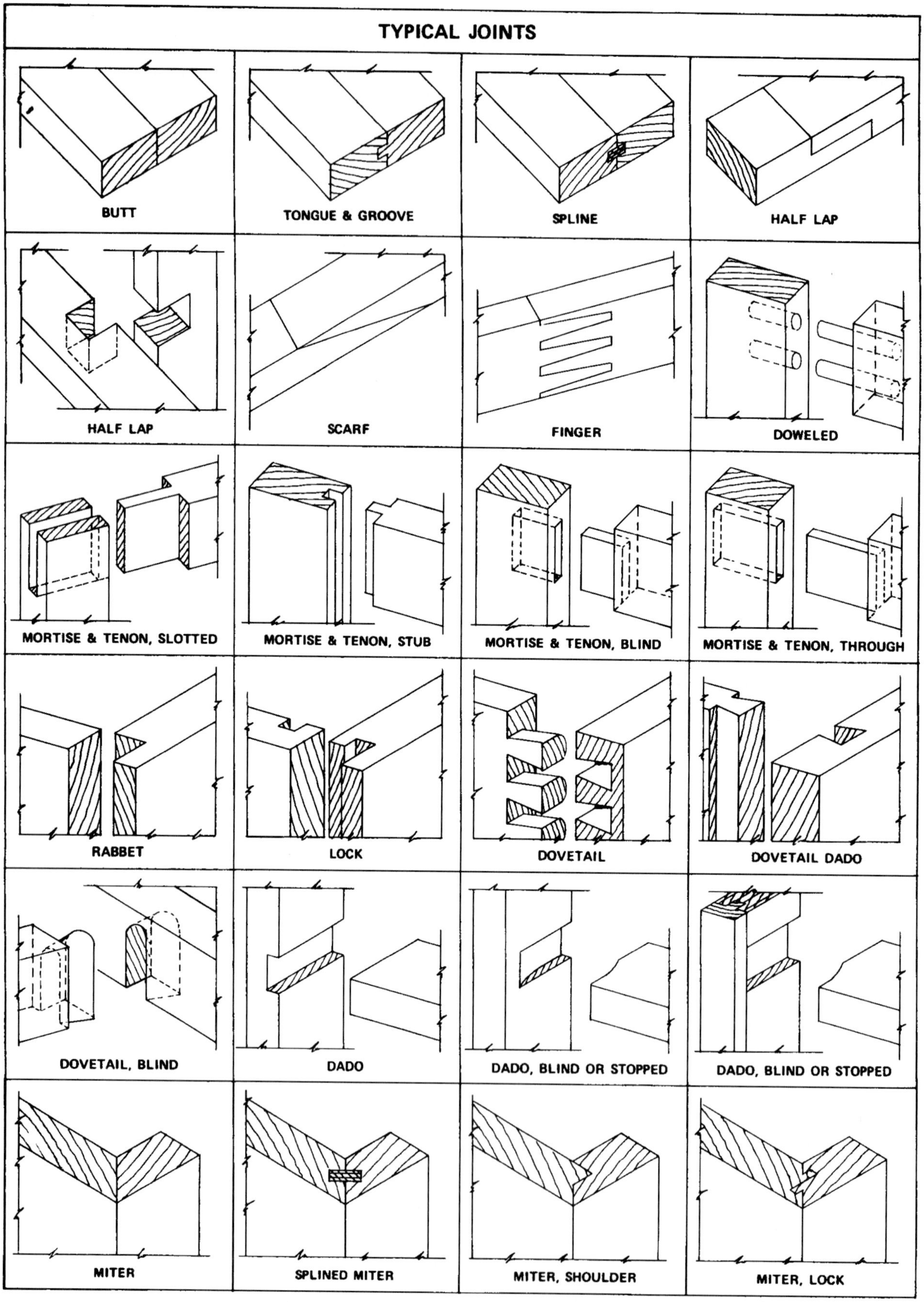

Spline joint: Used for gluing plywood in width or length. Since the spline serves to align faces, this joint is also used for items requiring site assembly.

Stop dado: Another method of concealing dado exposure. Applicable when veneer edging or solid lumber is used.

Stub tenon: Joinery method for assembling stile- and rail-type frames that are additionally supported, such as web or skeleton case frames.

Through dado: Conventional joint used for assembly of case body members—dado is usually concealed by application of case face frame.

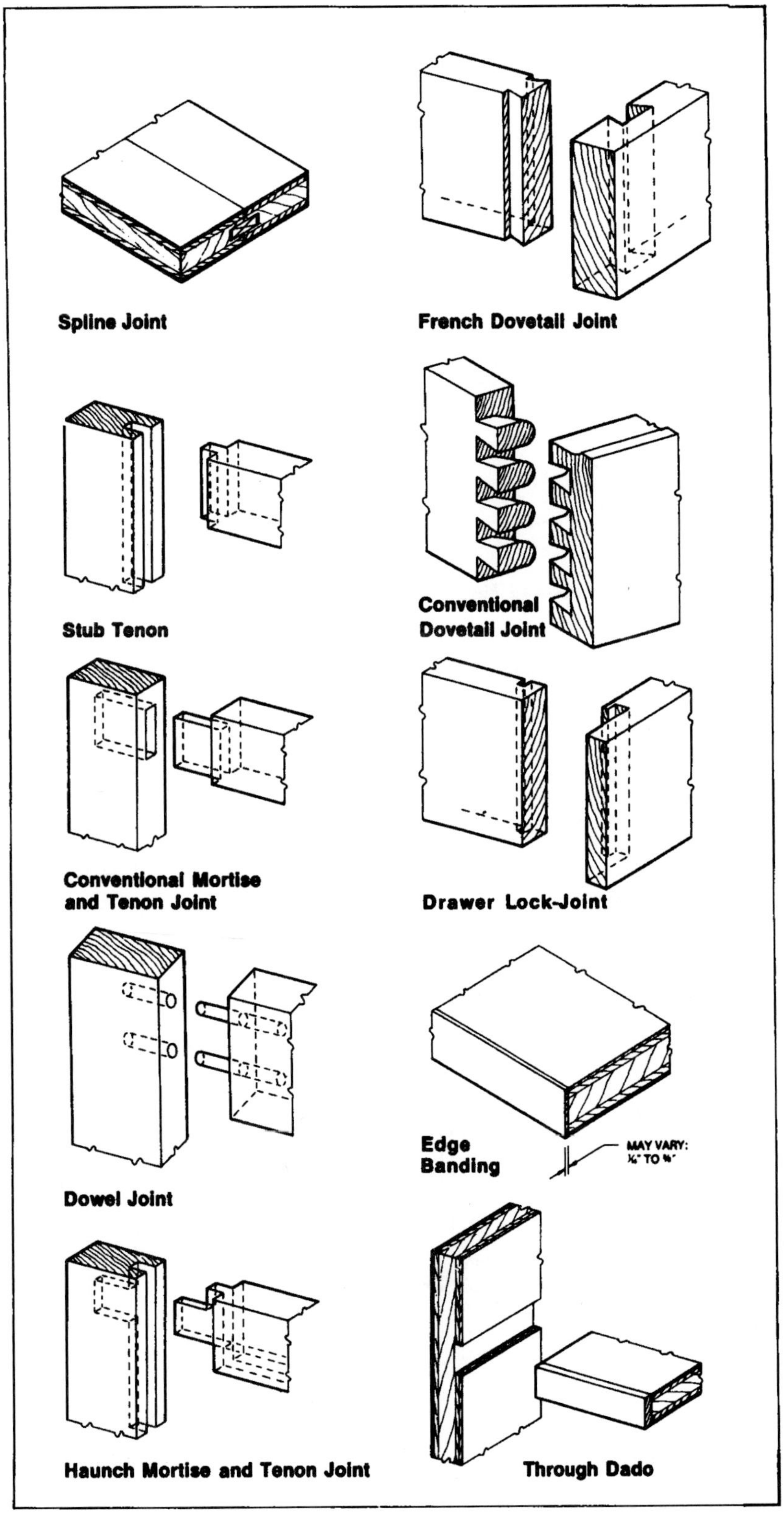

STANDARD JOINERY AND CASEWORK DETAILS
Typical Joints

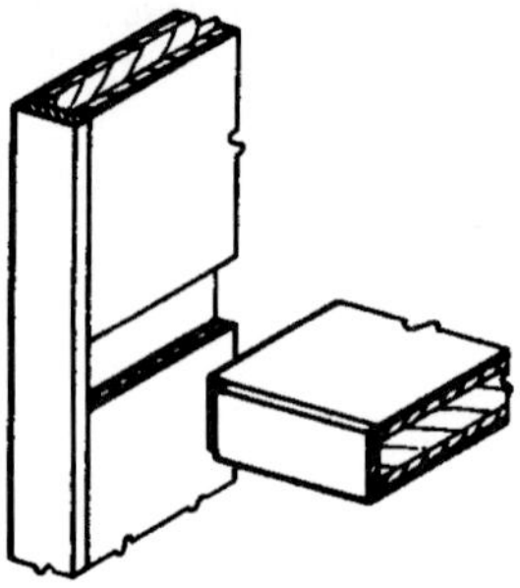

Blind Dado

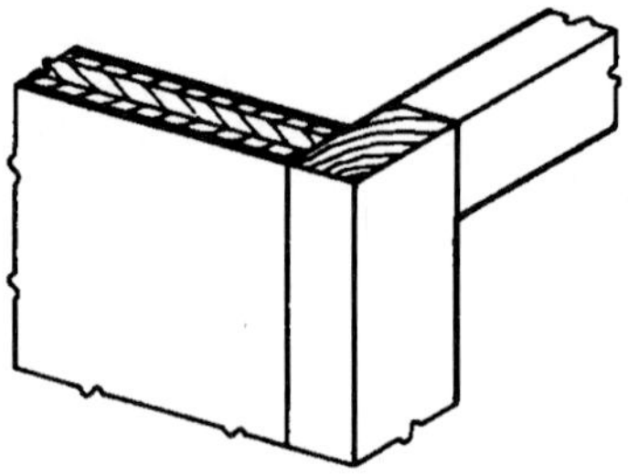

Exposed End Detail

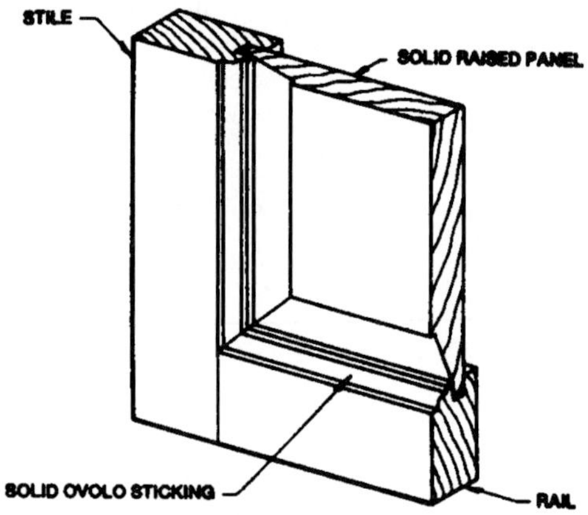

Paneled Door Detail

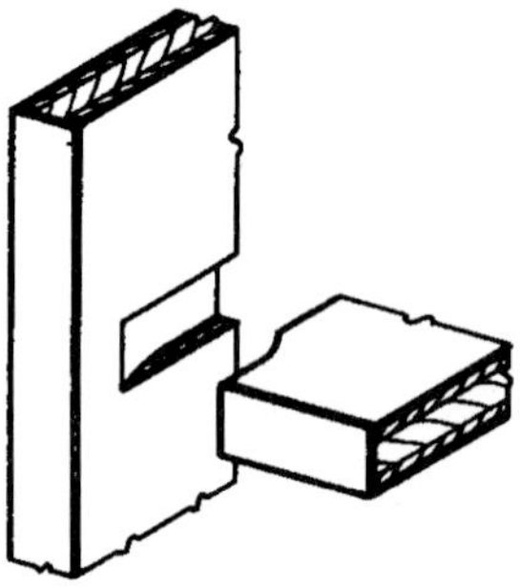

Stop Dado

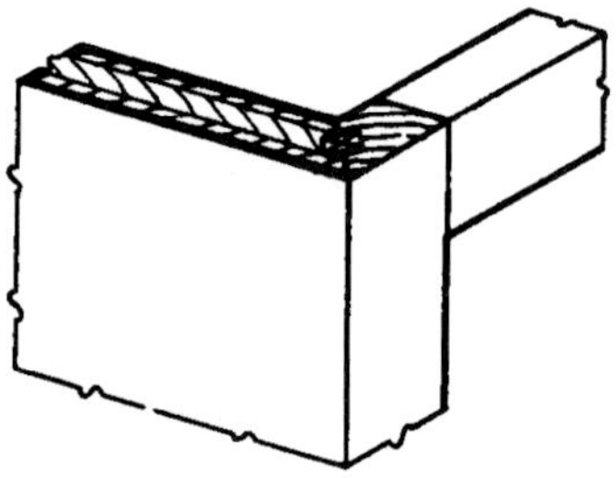

Exposed End Detail

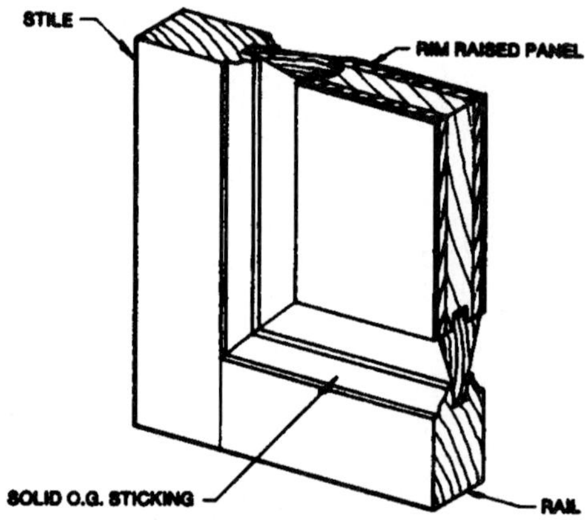

Paneled Door Detail

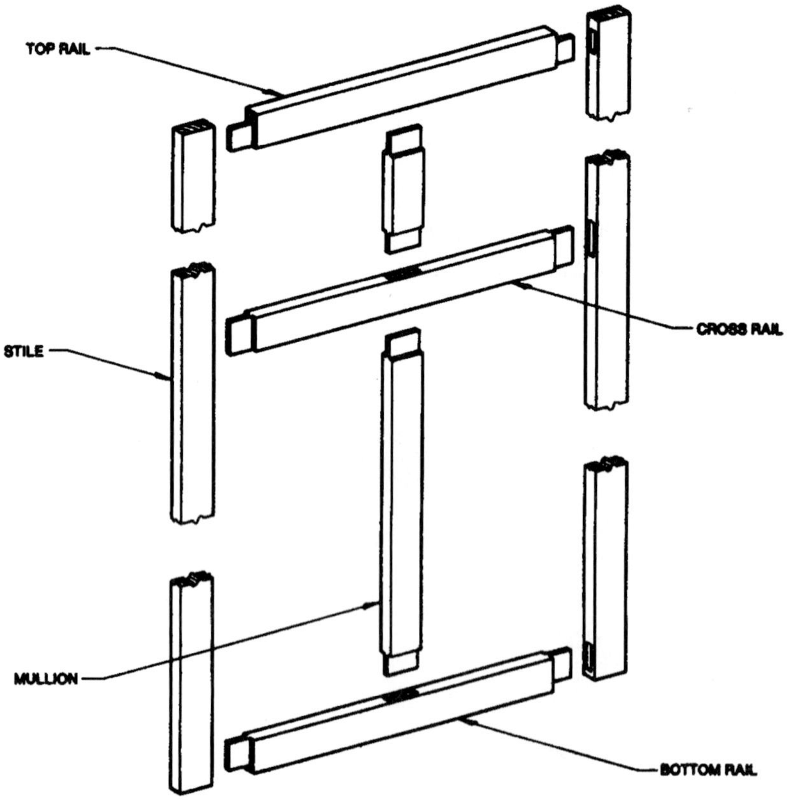

Typical Frame Parts

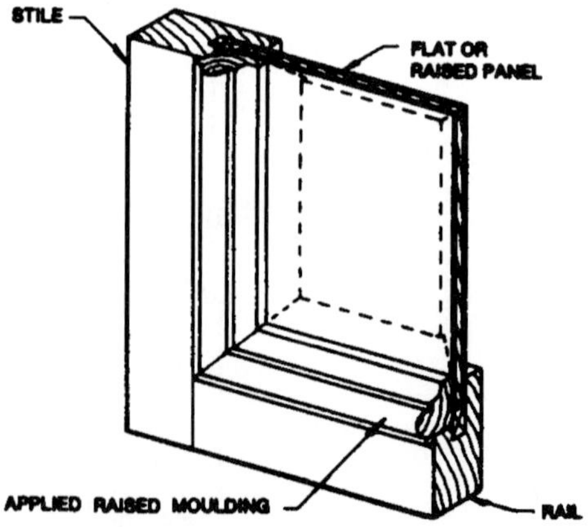

Paneled Door Detail

SEE ALSO

Man-made boards	34-38
Biscuit joints	136-137
Butt joints	216-217
Rabbet joints	218
Edge joints	222-223
Housing joints	224-225
Dowel joints	236-237
Dovetail joints	238-243

Plywood, blockboard, laminboard, chipboard and medium-density fiberboard (MDF) are all used for carcase construction. Man-made boards are more stable than panels of solid wood, but on the whole they do not have its long-grain strength. The means of joining these boards varies according to their composition. Most joints used for solid-wood carcase construction are suitable. Framing joints, such as mortise and tenon, lap and bridle joints, are unsuitable for joining man-made boards.

TYPICAL CARCASE JOINTS

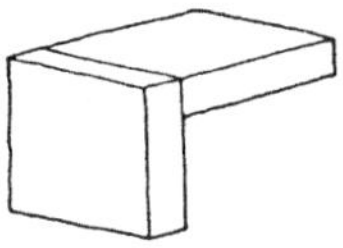

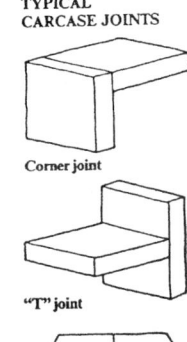

Corner joint

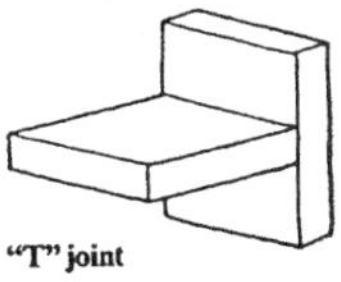

"T" joint

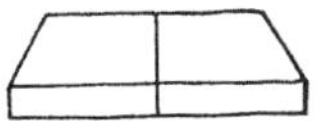

Edge-to-edge joint

JOINT GUIDE

The chart shows the typical range of man-made boards and the carcase joints suitable for a particular material. The first column indicates the strength of each joint in each material. The second column shows the best ways of making the joints. The third column indicates the relative difficulty in terms of hand-cutting and machine-cutting.

Treat solid-core laminated boards, such as blockboard and laminboard, like solid wood when selecting a joint for a particular application. A dovetail, for example, would be cut in the end grain only, not the side grain.

Dovetails are more difficult to cut in these materials because of the changing grain direction of the board's structure. Make coarse, even-sized tails and pins (machine-cut dovetails are preferable). For dovetail-joined cabinets that are to be veneered, use rabbet joints. The mitered variety is best, as it will not show the joint's construction through the veneer if the wood shrinks or swells.

Man-made boards that are ready-finished with a decorative veneer must be miter-joined if the core material is not to show on the face. The alternative is to use a corner lipping, which makes an attractive decorative feature.

CORNER-JOINT OPTIONS	SUITABILITY AND RELATIVE STRENGTH					SUITABLE METHOD OF MAKING				RELATIVE DIFFICULTY OF MAKING		COMMENTS
	PLYWOOD	BLOCKBOARD	LAMINBOARD	CHIPBOARD	MDF	HAND-CUT	HAND-CUT/JIG	MACHINE-CUT	MACHINE-CUT	HAND-CUT	MACHINE-CUT	
BUTT 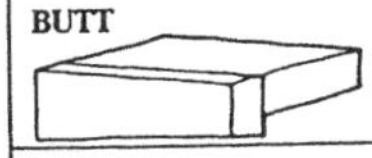	▮	▮	▮	▮	▮				▲	■	■	Has exposed core. Nail, screw or block reinforcement improves strength
MITERED BUTT 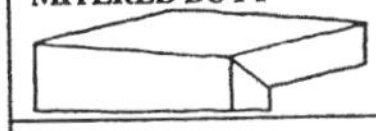	░	░	░	▮	░			△	▲	●	■	Core is hidden. Has similar strength to plain butt. Good for veneering.
SPLINED MITER 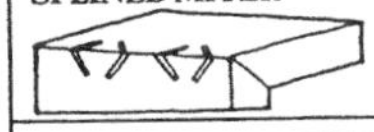	░	░	░	░	░			△		●	■	Stronger than plain miter. Can be used as decorative joint.
LOOSE-TONGUED MITER 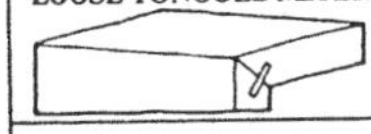	░	░	░	░	░				▲	●	■	A strong miter joint. Core is hidden. Good for veneering.
RABBET 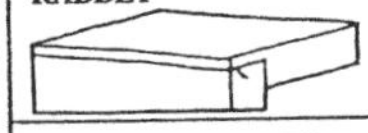	░	░	░	░	░			△	▲	■	■	Neater and stronger than a plain butt. Shows a little core at corner.
MITERED RABBET 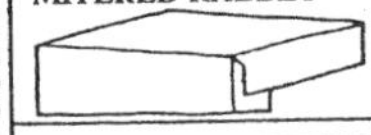	░	░	░	░	░				▲	●	■	Core is hidden. Better appearance than rabbet but more difficult to cut.
BAREFACED HOUSING 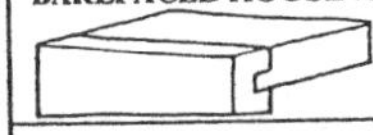	░	░	░	░	░			△	▲	■	■	Has exposed core. Has greater strength than plain butt.
DOWEL 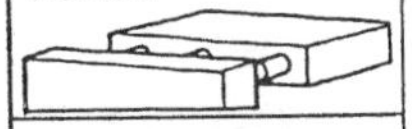	░	░	░	░	░		▲	△		■	■	Similar in appearance to plain butt joint but is much stronger.
MITERED DOWEL 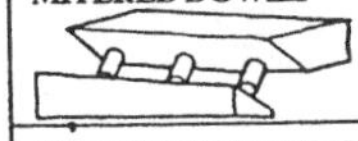	░	░	░	░	░		▲	△		●	■	Similar to loose-tongued miter in strength and appearance, cut with jig.
THROUGH DOVETAIL 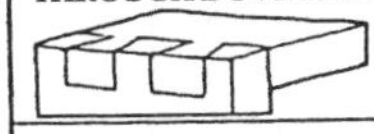	▮	▮	▮	▮	▮			△		●	■	A strong joint. May show through if covered with veneer.
HALF-BLIND DOVETAIL 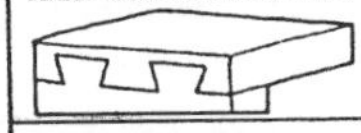	▮	▮	▮	▮	▮			△		●	■	Similar in strength to through dovetail with the joint hidden on one face.
BLIND DOVETAIL 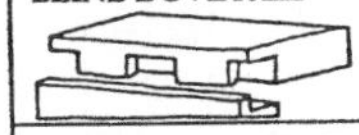	▮	▮	▮	▮	▮					●		Similar to the half-blind dovetail but only a thin edge of core exposed.
MITERED DOVETAIL 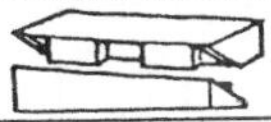	▮	▮	▮	▮	▮					●		Strong joint where core is hidden. Best version for veneering.
BISCUIT 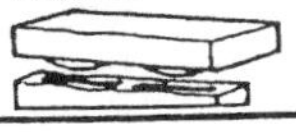	▮	▮	▮	▮	▮			△			■	A strong machine-made joint. Can be butted or mitered.

STANDARD JOINERY AND CASEWORK DETAILS
Board Joints

	Joint		Plywood	Blockboard	Laminboard	Chipboard	MDF	Hand-cut	Hand-cut/jig	Machine-cut	Machine-cut	Hand-cut	Machine-cut	Comments
			Suitability and relative strength					**Suitable method of making**				**Relative difficulty of making**		
T-JOINT OPTIONS	BUTT	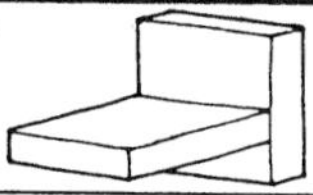	▮	▮	▮	▮	▮			▲	▲	■	■	Relatively weak. Nail or screw reinforcement improves strength.
T-JOINT OPTIONS	DADO	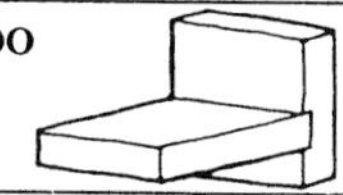	▮	▮	▮	▮	▮			▲	▲	■	■	Has greater strength than plain butt. Reinforcement not required.
T-JOINT OPTIONS	STOPPED DADO	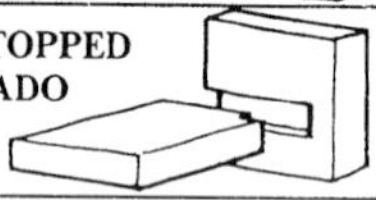	▮	▮	▮	▮	▮			▲		■	■	As above but neater at front edge.
T-JOINT OPTIONS	BAREFACED HOUSING		▮	▮	▮	▮	▮			▲	▲	■	■	Similar to plain dado.
T-JOINT OPTIONS	SLIDING DOVETAIL	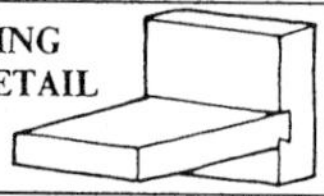	▮	▮	▮	▮	▮			▲		●	■	Greater strength than plain dado but more difficult to cut.
T-JOINT OPTIONS	DOWEL	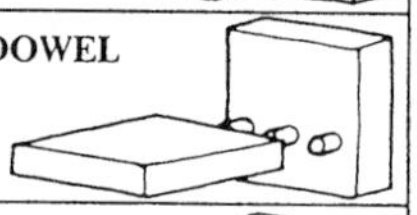	▮	▮	▮	▮	▮		▲	▲		■	■	Strong, simple to cut with aid of a dowel jig.
T-JOINT OPTIONS	BISCUIT	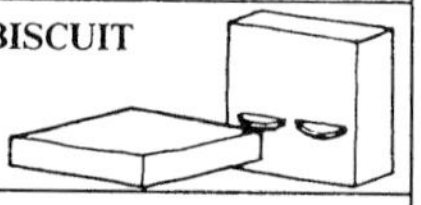	▮	▮	▮	▮	▮			▲			■	Strong machine-made joint.
EDGE-TO-EDGE JOINT OPTIONS	BUTT	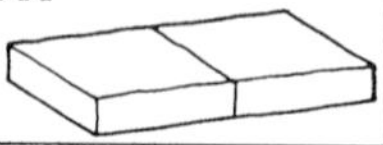	▮	▮	▮	▮	▮			▲	▲	■	■	Simple to cut. Use modern synthetic glues for improved strength.
EDGE-TO-EDGE JOINT OPTIONS	LOOSE TONGUE	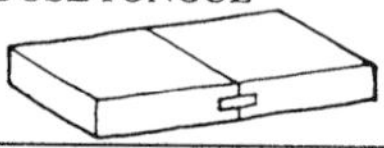	▮	▮	▮	▮	▮			▲	▲	■	■	Greater strength than plain butt. Tongue helps locate the edges.
EDGE-TO-EDGE JOINT OPTIONS	TONGUE & GROOVE	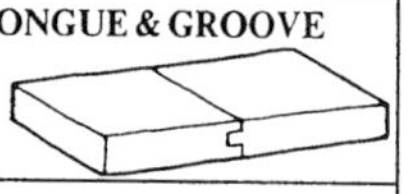	▮	▮	▮	▮	▮			▲	▲	■	■	As above.
EDGE-TO-EDGE JOINT OPTIONS	DOWEL	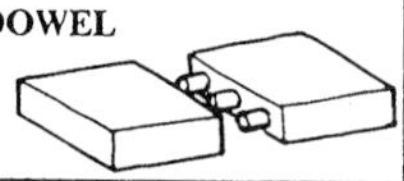	▮	▮	▮	▮	▮		▲	▲		■	■	As above.
EDGE-TO-EDGE JOINT OPTIONS	BISCUIT	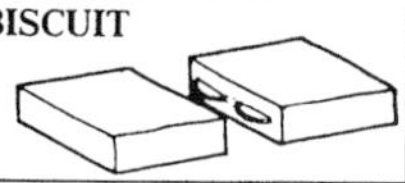	▮	▮	▮	▮	▮			▲			■	As above.

KEY TO CHART

Suitability and relative strength
- Excellent
- Good
- Fair
- Poor
- Unsuitable

Suitable method of making
- Hand-cut (Using hand tools)
- ▲ Hand-cut/jig (Using hand tools with jigs)
- ▲ Machine-cut (Using hand-held power tools)*
- ▲ Machine-cut (Using machine tools)*

**Jigs may also be used*

Relative difficulty of making
- ● Difficult
- ■ Simple

Using a Corner Lipping

For preveneered chipboard, a lipping can be used to make a corner joint that also masks the core. The grain of the lipping is set at right angles to the face veneer of the board and forms a feature. The lipping can be left square or you can shape it. You can also use contrasting wood.

Joints for Corner Lippings

Butt-join the lipping or, for improved strength, make a tongue-and-groove joint. Use a loose-tongued joint or cut the groove in the edge of the board and the tongue in the lipping. Whichever way you decide, stop the tongue and the groove so they do not show on the edge (**1**).

A stronger joint suitable for plinths or carcase construction can be made using a thicker lipping. Cut a barefaced tongue on the board and a matching goove in the lipping. The section can be shaped if required, as indicated by the broken line (**2**).

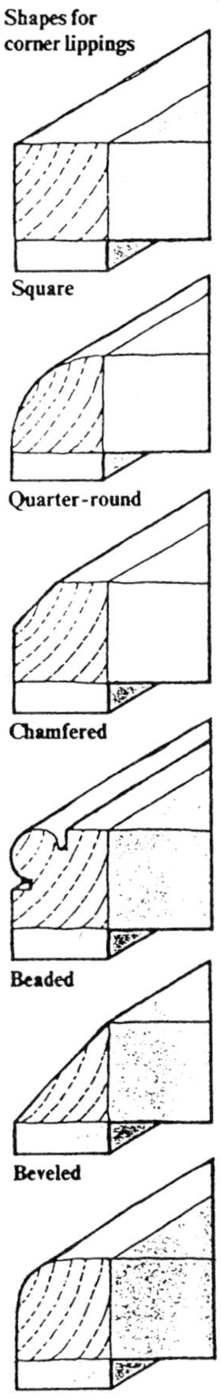

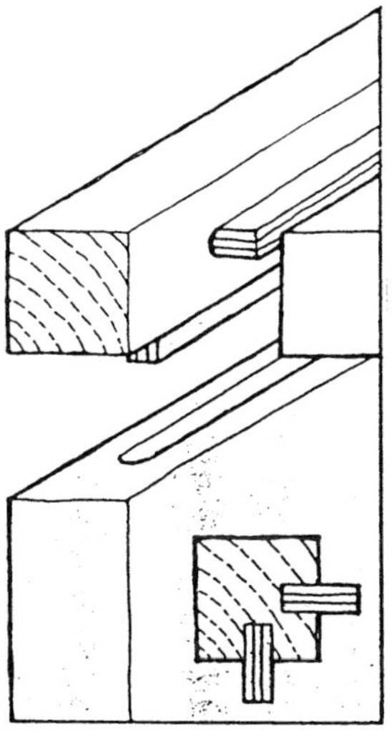

1 Loose tongue and groove joint

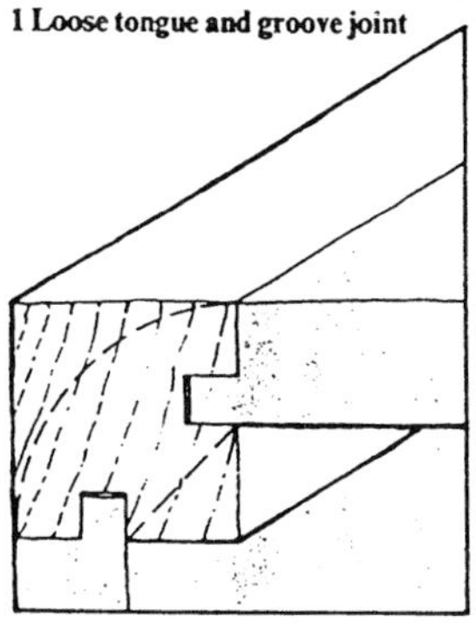

2 Shape the lipping if required

Types of Lipping

The edges of man-made boards must be finished with a lipping to cover the core material. You can use either long-grain or cross-grain veneer or a more substantial solid-wood lipping of matching or contrasting wood. Lippings can be applied before or after surface veneering. In the case of preveneered boards, you have no choice but to lip the edge last.

Applying Lippings

The simplest edging to apply is the preglued veneer type that is ironed onto the edge. These edge lippings are primarily sold for finishing veneered chipboard panels and are available in a limited range of matching veneer.

For a more substantial edging, and one that can be shaped, cut thick lippings from matching solid wood. Butt-join the lipping to the edge or tongue and groove it for greater strength.

Miter the corners of thick lippings to improve the finished appearance. This is particularly necessary if the edge is molded.

When gluing up a long lipping, use a stiff batten between the lipping and the clamp heads to help spread the clamping forces over the full length of the work.

When planing glued-on edge lippings to width, take care not to touch the surface veneer, particularly when working across the direction of the grain. Finish the edge with a sanding block.

Deep lippings will substantially stiffen the boards for use as shelves or worktops. Set the full thickness of the board into a rabbet cut in the lipping.

Working Man-Made Boards

Cutting by Machine

Man-made boards are best cut to finished dimensions with clean-cutting, high-speed machine tools. Use a circular saw blade with tungsten-carbide-tipped teeth if cutting a lot of board. The teeth of the saw blade should pierce the board from the face side. When using a hand-held power saw, have the panel face down, and for a table saw, face up. Run the board across the saw relatively quickly. If using a band saw, run the saw fast but feed the board slowly. You can also use a handheld router run against a long fence clamped to the work.

Cutting by Hand

For handsawing, use a 10- to 12-PPI panel saw. A tenon saw can also be used for smaller work. To prevent breakout of the surface, make all cutting lines with a knife to sever the fibers or laminate. Also, hold the saw at a shallow angle. Support the board close to the cutting line. Lay it face side up over the bench, or, if it is a particularly bulky piece, support it on sawhorses.

If cutting a large board, climb onto it so you can reach the cutting line comfortably. Have an assistant support the offcut if it is unmanageable. Otherwise, set up some means of support so it does not break away before you finish the cut.

Planing the Edges

Plane the edges as you would for solid wood, but treat each edge as though it were end grain. You should, therefore, plane from both ends toward the middle.

Wood Veneer Matching Patterns

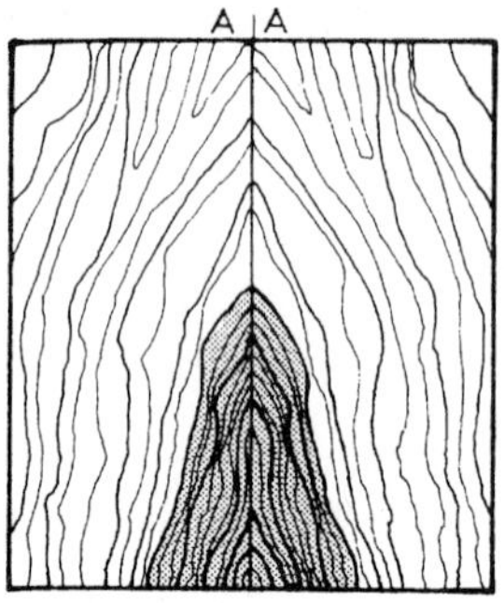

1 Book form (side matched)

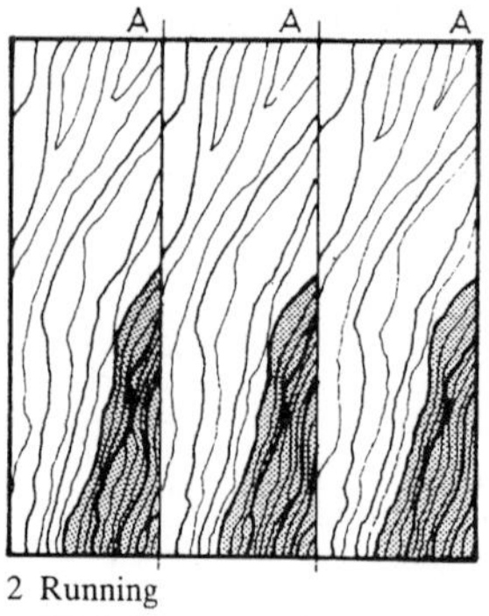

2 Running

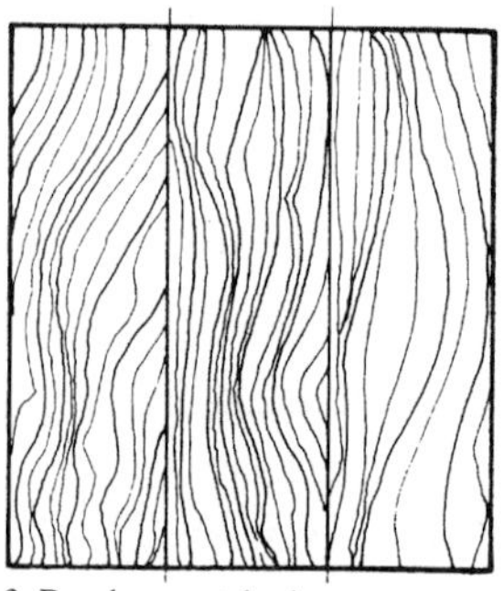

3 Random matched

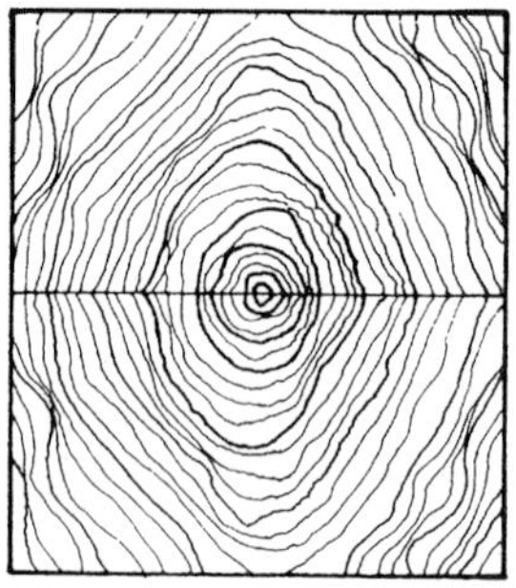

4 End or butt matched

5 Diamond quarter

6 Reverse diamond

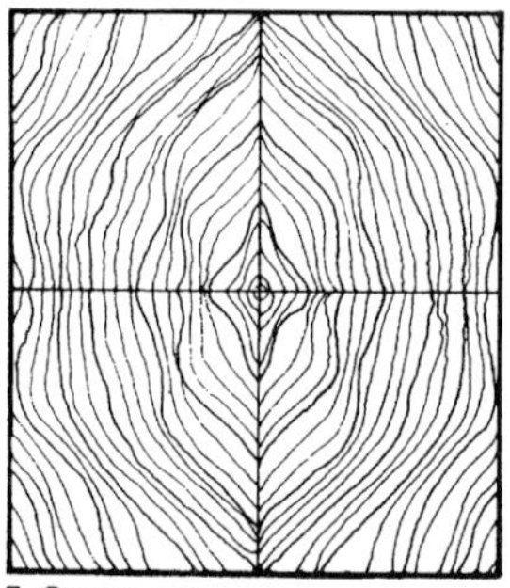

7 Quartered

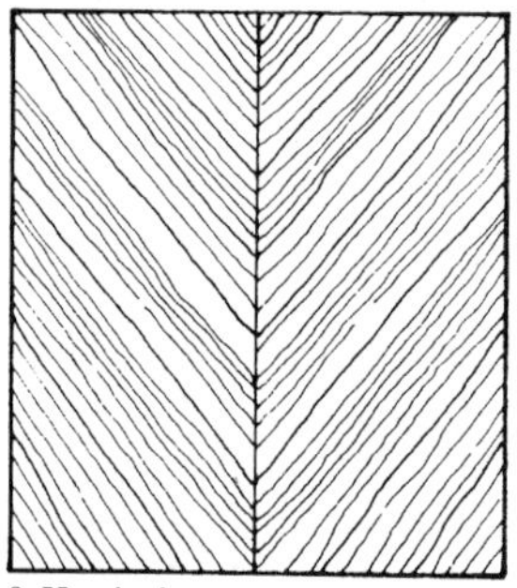

8 Herringbone

9 Inverted herringbone

1. **Book form or Side Matched:** The first leaf of the bundle is opened out as in the turning of the pages of a book, and matched at the sides with the next leaf.
2. **Running:** Consecutive veneer leaves are laid out side by side as they rise from the bundle.
3. **Random Matched:** Assorted veneer leaves not matched for grain and are not necessarily of the same width.
4. **End or Butt Matched:** The top leaf is folded down as in the book form matching.
5. **Diamond Quartered:** Four consecutive leaves are cut diagonally and then side and butt matched.
6. **Reverse Diamond:** Refer to diamond quartered.
7. **Quartered:** Four consecutive veneer leaves are side and butt matched.
8. **Herringbone:** Two consecutive veneer leaves are cut diagonally and side matched.
9. **Inverted Herringbone:** Refer to herringbone

Other Veneer Matching Terms: Slip, Reverse Slip, "V", Diamond, Box, Slip, Center, Balance, Vertical Butt/Horizontal Butt, Architectural End , Book and Butt , and Sunburst.

(For examples of actual wood veneers color plates, see color insert in Section 6)

TYPICAL CABINET CONSTRUCTION

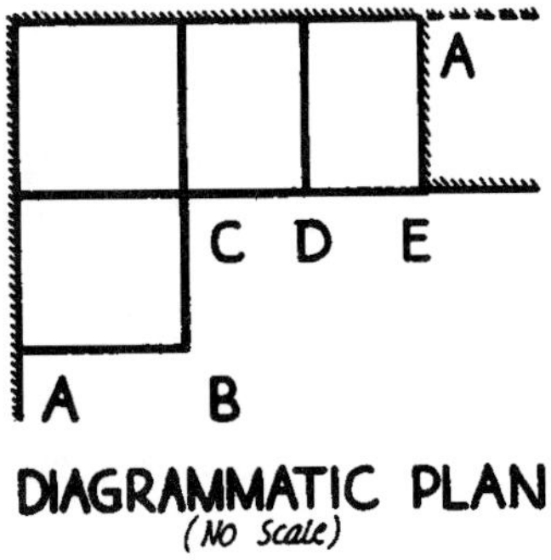
A
C D E
A B
DIAGRAMMATIC PLAN
(No Scale)

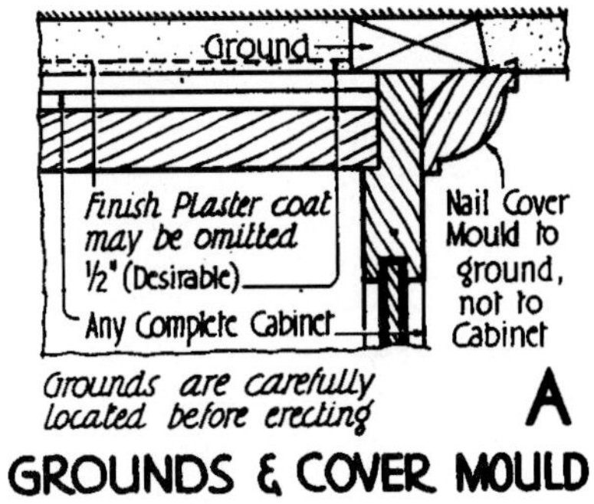
Ground
Finish Plaster coat may be omitted
½" (Desirable)
Any Complete Cabinet
Nail Cover Mould to ground, not to Cabinet
Grounds are carefully located before erecting
A
GROUNDS & COVER MOULD

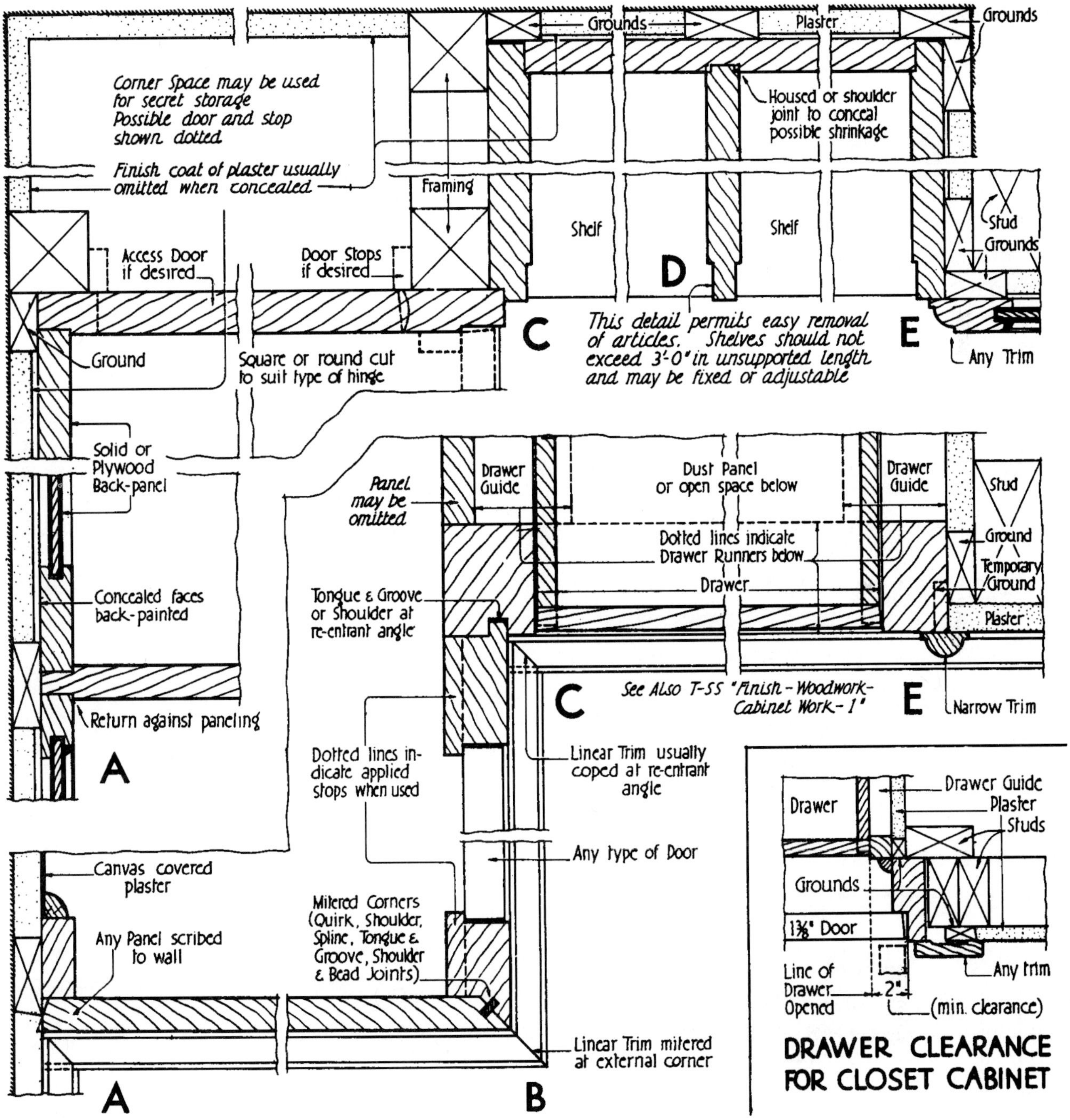
Grounds
Plaster
Grounds
Corner Space may be used for secret storage Possible door and stop shown dotted
Finish coat of plaster usually omitted when concealed
Framing
Housed or shoulder joint to conceal possible shrinkage
Shelf
Shelf
Stud
Grounds
Access Door if desired
Door Stops if desired
D
C
E
Ground
Square or round cut to suit type of hinge
This detail permits easy removal of articles. Shelves should not exceed 3'-0" in unsupported length and may be fixed or adjustable
Any Trim
Solid or Plywood Back-panel
Concealed faces back-painted
Return against paneling
A
Panel may be omitted
Drawer Guide
Dust Panel or open space below
Drawer Guide
Stud
Dotted lines indicate Drawer Runners below
Drawer
Ground
Temporary Ground
Plaster
Tongue & Groove or Shoulder at re-entrant angle
C
See Also T-SS "Finish - Woodwork - Cabinet Work - 1"
E
Narrow Trim
Dotted lines indicate applied stops when used
Linear Trim usually coped at re-entrant angle
Any type of Door
Canvas covered plaster
Any Panel scribed to wall
Mitered Corners (Quirk, Shoulder, Spline, Tongue & Groove, Shoulder & Bead Joints)
Linear Trim mitered at external corner
A
B
Drawer
Drawer Guide
Plaster
Studs
Grounds
1⅜" Door
Any trim
Line of Drawer Opened
2"
(min. clearance)
DRAWER CLEARANCE FOR CLOSET CABINET

STANDARD JOINERY AND CASEWORK DETAILS
Cabinet Work

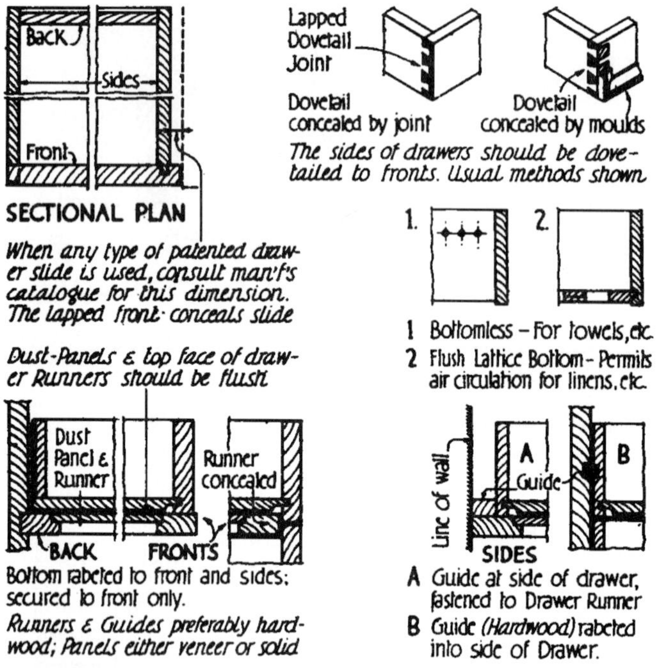
Back
Sides
Front
SECTIONAL PLAN
When any type of patented drawer slide is used, consult man'f's catalogue for this dimension. The lapped front conceals slide
Lapped Dovetail Joint
Dovetail concealed by joint
Dovetail concealed by moulds
The sides of drawers should be dovetailed to fronts. Usual methods shown.
1.
2.
1 Bottomless – For towels, etc.
2 Flush Lattice Bottom – Permits air circulation for linens, etc.
Dust-Panels & top face of drawer Runners should be flush
Dust Panel & Runner
Runner concealed
BACK
FRONTS
Bottom rabeted to front and sides; secured to front only.
Runners & Guides preferably hardwood; Panels either veneer or solid
Line of wall
A
Guide
B
SIDES
A Guide at side of drawer, fastened to Drawer Runner
B Guide (Hardwood) rabeted into side of Drawer.

DRAWERS

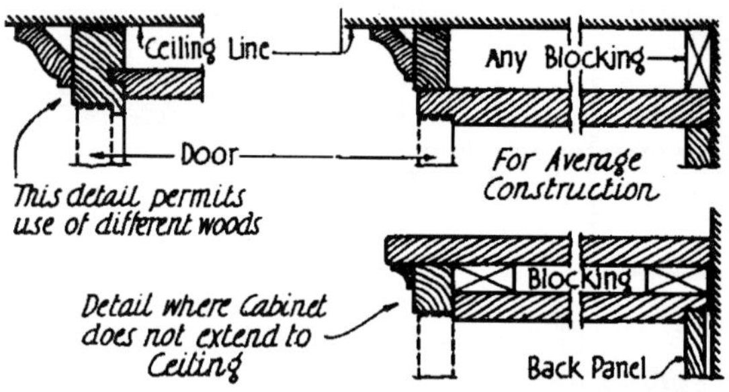
Ceiling Line
Door
This detail permits use of different woods
Any Blocking
For Average Construction
Detail where Cabinet does not extend to Ceiling
Blocking
Back Panel

CORNICE

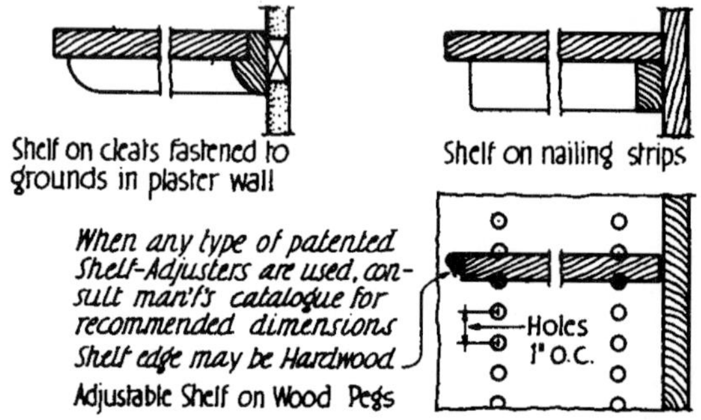
Shelf on cleats fastened to grounds in plaster wall
Shelf on nailing strips
When any type of patented Shelf-Adjusters are used, consult man'f's catalogue for recommended dimensions
Shelf edge may be Hardwood
Adjustable Shelf on Wood Pegs
Holes 1" O.C.

SHELVES

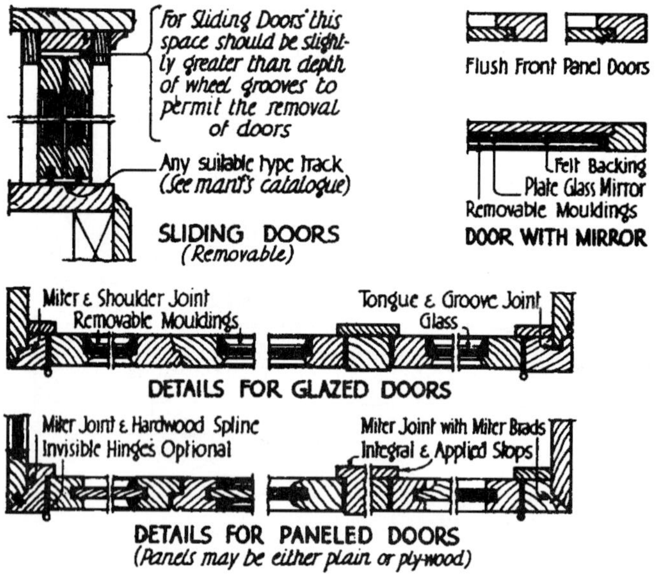
For Sliding Doors this space should be slightly greater than depth of wheel grooves to permit the removal of doors
Any suitable type track (See man'f's catalogue)
SLIDING DOORS (Removable)
Flush Front Panel Doors
Felt Backing
Plate Glass Mirror
Removable Mouldings
DOOR WITH MIRROR
Miter & Shoulder Joint
Removable Mouldings
Tongue & Groove Joint
Glass
DETAILS FOR GLAZED DOORS
Miter Joint & Hardwood Spline
Invisible Hinges Optional
Miter Joint with Miter Brads
Integral & Applied Stops
DETAILS FOR PANELED DOORS (Panels may be either plain or ply-wood)

DOORS

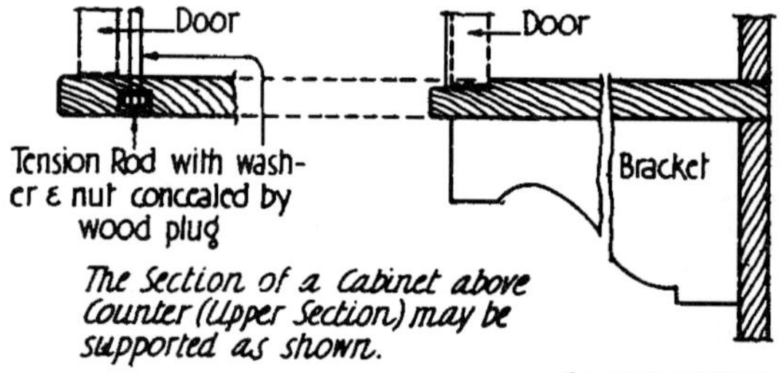
Door
Door
Tension Rod with washer & nut concealed by wood plug
Bracket
The Section of a Cabinet above Counter (Upper Section) may be supported as shown.

SUPPORTS

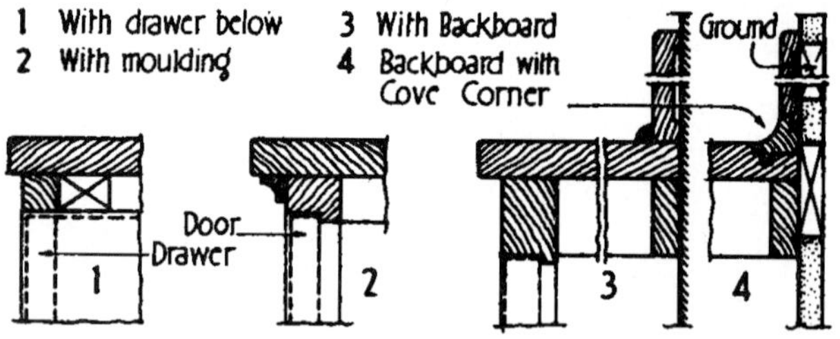
1 With drawer below
2 With moulding
3 With Backboard
4 Backboard with Cove Corner
Ground
Door
Drawer
1
2
3
4

COUNTERS

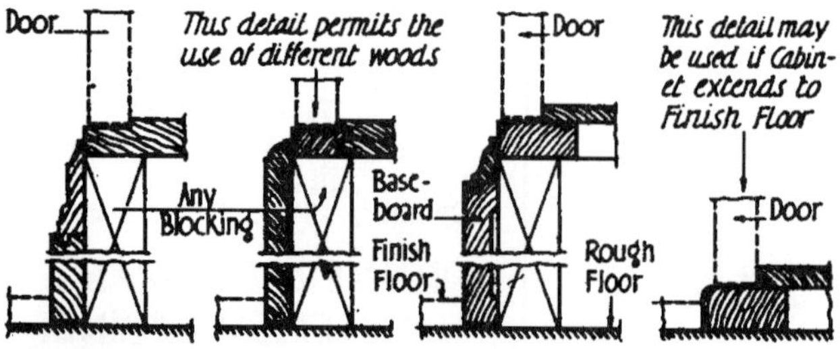
Door
This detail permits the use of different woods
Door
This detail may be used if Cabinet extends to Finish Floor
Any Blocking
Baseboard
Finish Floor
Rough Floor
Door

BASES

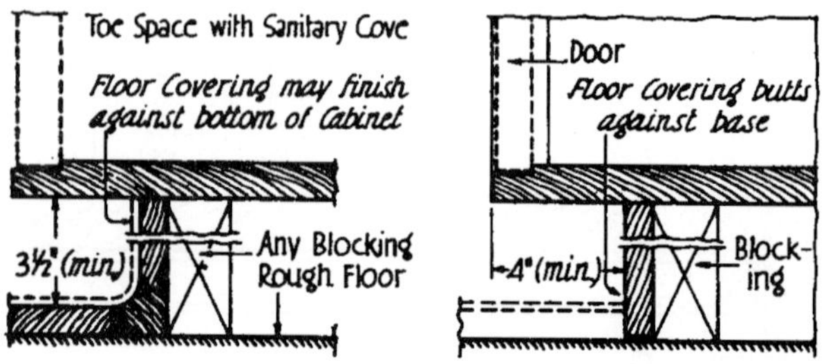
Toe Space with Sanitary Cove
Floor Covering may finish against bottom of Cabinet
3½" (min)
Any Blocking
Rough Floor
Door
Floor Covering butts against base
4" (min)
Blocking

TOE SPACE

Purpose

The following information outlines methods of assembly and installation of common cabinet work. Solutions of typical problems are presented without attempting to detail specific cabinets.

Assembly

High-grade cabinet and veneered work is assembled as far as possible at the shop. Joints are glued and blocked, and sometimes secured with finishing nails or screws. Carpentry and millwork are generally put together with finishing nails if of soft wood, or with screws if of hardwood. Hardwood should be drilled to prevent splitting before using nails or screws, and heads should be countersunk and concealed by cover molds, molding quirks, or putty, plastic wood, or other filler, colored to match the finish. No nails, screws, or joints should be visible unless they are intentionally incorporated in design.

Shrinkage and Warping

Such effects can be largely eliminated by proper detailing and construction. *Wide flat surfaces* (solid or veneered) should be made up of several narrow strips glued and doweled, splined, or dovetailed together. Cleats may also be screwed or keyed to backs of wide surfaces. *Joints in corners, sheathing, and so on,* should be concealed within quirks of molds (as in molded tongue and groove) or return faces (shoulder joints). *Panels* should be rigidly secured on one side only, and are often left entirely loose. Housed joints, not glued, permit panels to expand and contract without splitting.

Large Molded Surfaces

These surfaces (such as cornices or mantels) should always be shop-assembled and delivered with scribe-molds (see "Scribing") loosely tacked to assembled units.

Installation

All grades of woodwork should be preservative treated or back painted before erection, preferably before delivery to the job. Satisfactory priming coats are aluminum paint or white lead in linseed oil, thinned with turpentine or mineral spirits.

Preparation

On frame walls plaster may be limited to one or two coats, recessed between studs, or omitted. In the latter case, building paper should be used between woodwork and studs. On masonry, plaster may consist of one or two coats or may be omitted. Masonry surfaces, particularly exterior walls, should be waterproofed or woodwork should be protected by a layer of waterproof paper and should always be furred out. When finish of the interior of cabinets is plaster, either plain or canvas covered, the final coat of plaster is applied after erection of cabinet.

Grounds

Grounds of soft wood for attaching cabinet work must be accurately located, are secured directly to framing members or furring, and must be concealed.

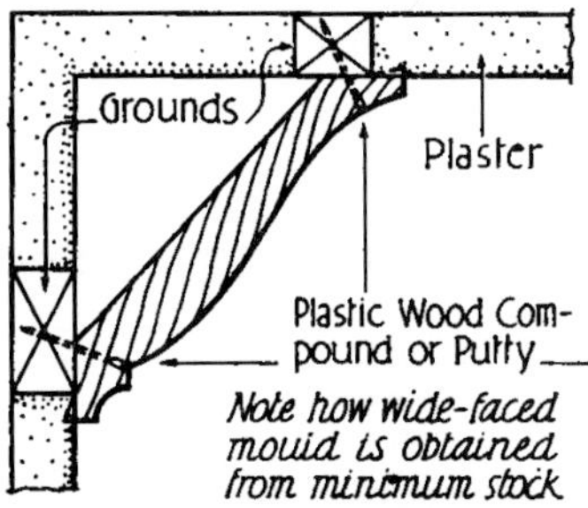
Grounds
Plaster
Plastic Wood Compound or Putty
Note how wide-faced mould is obtained from minimum stock

NAILING TO GROUNDS

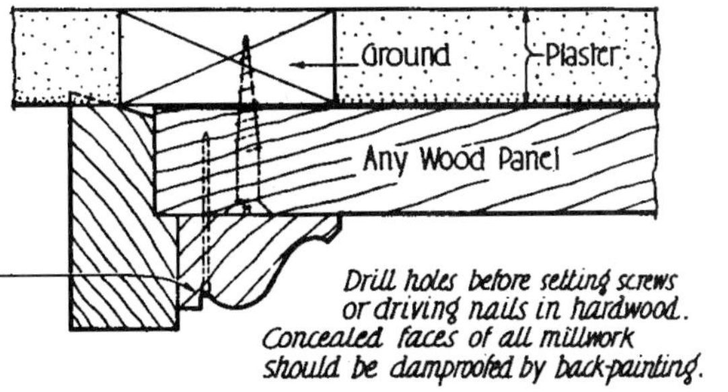
Ground
Plaster
Any Wood Panel
Drill holes before setting screws or driving nails in hardwood.
Concealed faces of all millwork should be damproofed by back-painting.

CONCEALING ATTACHMENT OF HARDWOODS

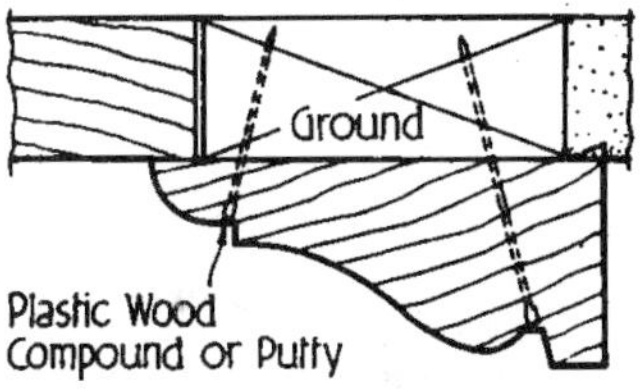
Ground
Plastic Wood Compound or Putty

NAILING IN QUIRKS

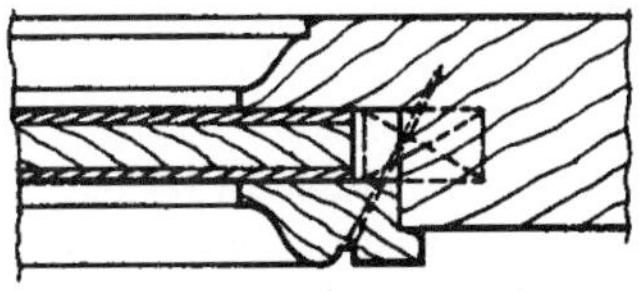

Nail to stiles or rails; avoiding panel

NAILING PANEL MOULD

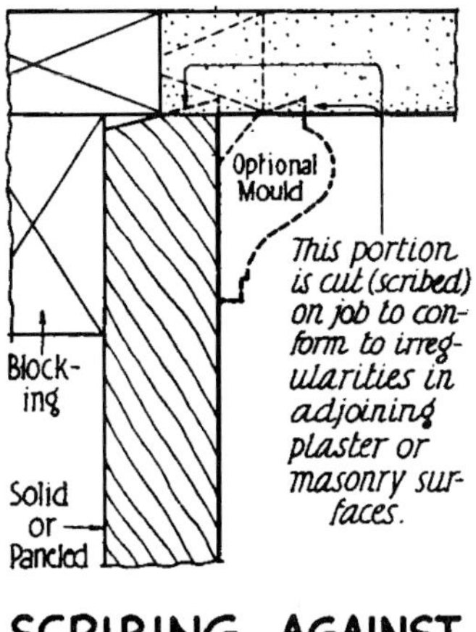
Optional Mould
This portion is cut (scribed) on job to conform to irregularities in adjoining plaster or masonry surfaces.
Blocking
Solid or Paneled

SCRIBING AGAINST PLASTER OR MASONRY

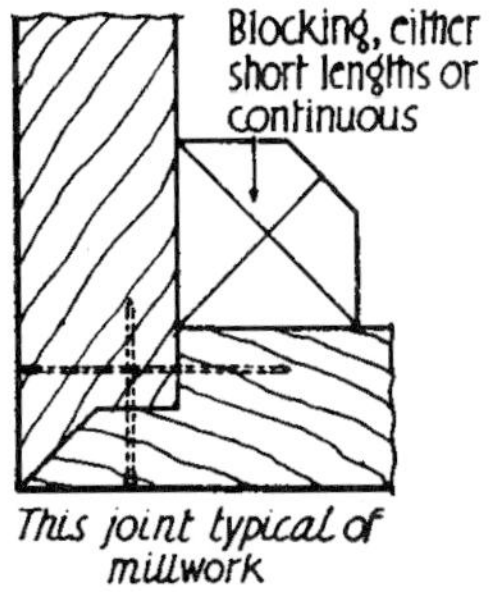
Blocking, either short lengths or continuous
This joint typical of millwork

Nailing & gluing a mortise and shoulder provides a strong, reasonably permanent joint

GLUING AND BLOCKING

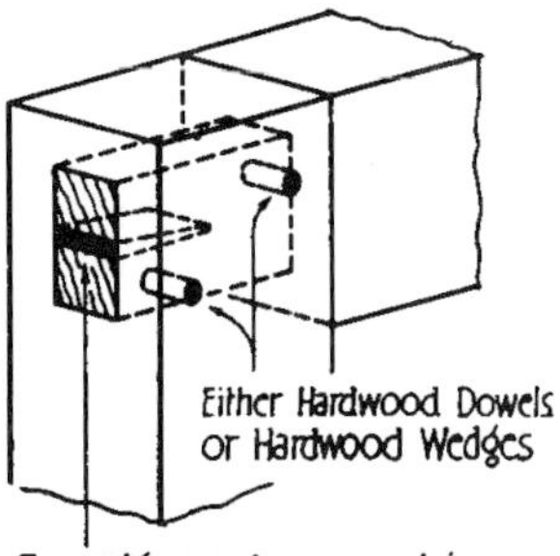
Either Hardwood Dowels or Hardwood Wedges

For wedges, make saw-cut in tenon before assembling. Holes for dowels may be offset to draw joint tight.

SECURING MORTISE & TENON

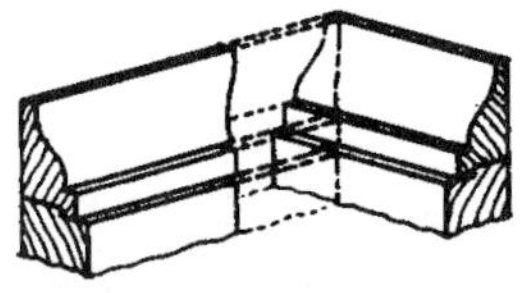

Cope by hand on job unless excessively undercut; if so, use miter. Flat members may be butted or Tongued-and-Grooved

COPING MOULDINGS RE-ENTRANT ANGLE

Blocking

Blocking of rough lumber should be erected for supporting raised floors and large or heavy cabinet work, if it can be concealed. Blocking must be accurately placed and secured with nails.

Shimming

Minor irregularities in blocking, furring, or placement of studs may be corrected by using shims (wedge-shaped pieces of wood, often shingles) to bring completed work to plumb and level lines. Shimming should be concealed.

Scribing

Scribing is the practice of fitting edges of cabinet work accurately to all irregularities of finish plaster, masonry, or other abutting surfaces. Wood moldings, panel frames, or cabinet returns to be scribed should be provided with a beveled edge.

Prefabricated Woodwork

Prefabricated woodwork is generally delivered knocked down for assembly on the job and is erected similarly to custom-made work. Consult manufacturers' data.

PLASTIC-COVERED CASEWORK

Casework Definitions

A. Exposed portions
  1. All surfaces visible when doors and drawers are closed.
  2. Underside of bottoms of cabinets over 4 ft 0 in above finished floor.
  3. Cabinet tops under 6 ft 0 in above finished floor or if over 6 ft 0 in and visible from an upper building level or floor.
  4. Visible front edges of web frames, ends, divisions, tops, shelves, and hanging stiles.
  5. Sloping tops of cabinets that are visible.
  6. Visible surfaces in open cabinets or behind glass for premium grade only.
  7. Interior faces of hinged doors for premium grade only.
  8. Visible portions of bottoms, tops, and ends in front of sliding doors in custom and premium grades only.

B. Semiexposed portions
  1. Shelves.
  2. Divisions.
  3. Interior face of ends, backs, and bottoms.
  4. Drawer sides, subfronts, backs, and bottoms.
  5. The underside of bottoms of cabinets between 2 ft 6 in and 4 ft 0 in above the finished floor.
  6. Interior faces of hinged doors, except premium grade.
  7. Visible surfaces in open cabinets or behind glass for economy and custom grades and all rooms designated as storage, janitor, closet, or utility.
  8. Visible portion of bottoms, tops, and ends in front of sliding doors in economy grade only.

C. Concealed portions
  1. Toe space unless otherwise specified.
  2. Sleepers.
  3. Web frames, stretchers, and solid subtops.
  4. Security panels.
  5. Underside of bottoms of cabinets less than 2 ft 6 in above the finished floor.
  6. Flat tops of cabinets 6 ft 0 in or more above the finished floor, except if visible from an upper building level.
  7. The three nonvisible edges of adjustable shelves.
  8. The underside of countertops, knee spaces, and drawer aprons.
  9. The faces of cabinet ends of adjoining units that butt together.

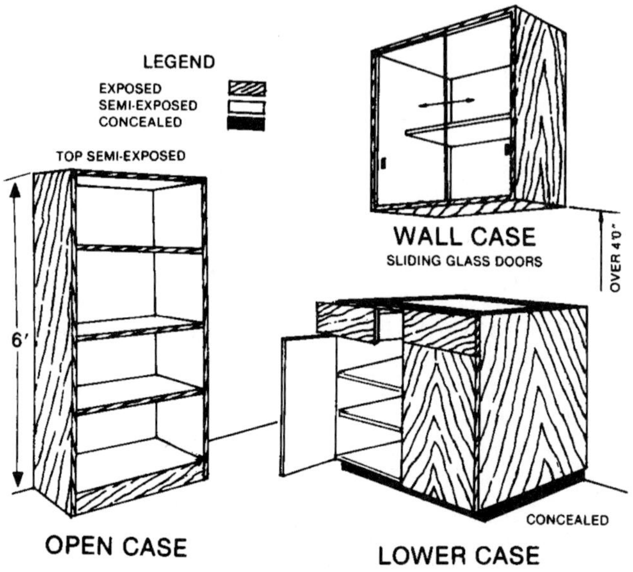

Fig. 1 Inside surfaces of open shelf cabinets and behind glass are considered exposed for premium grade, and tops of tall cabinets and upper cabinets 6 ft above the floor that are exposed from upper levels are considered exposed

STANDARD JOINERY AND CASEWORK DETAILS
Typical Base Cabinet Details

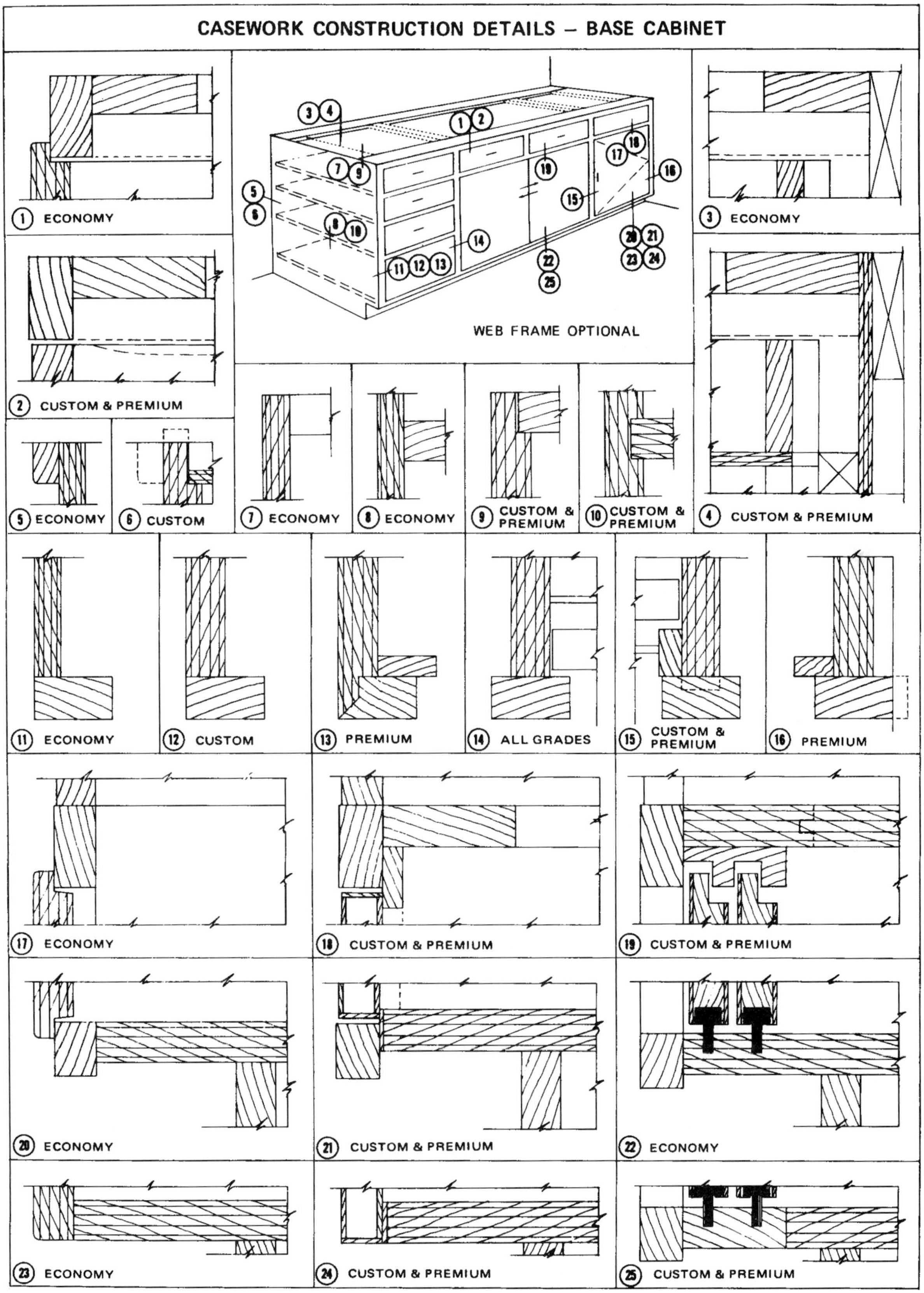

Fig. 2 Casework construction details—base cabinet

STANDARD JOINERY AND CASEWORK DETAILS

Typical Upper Cabinet Details

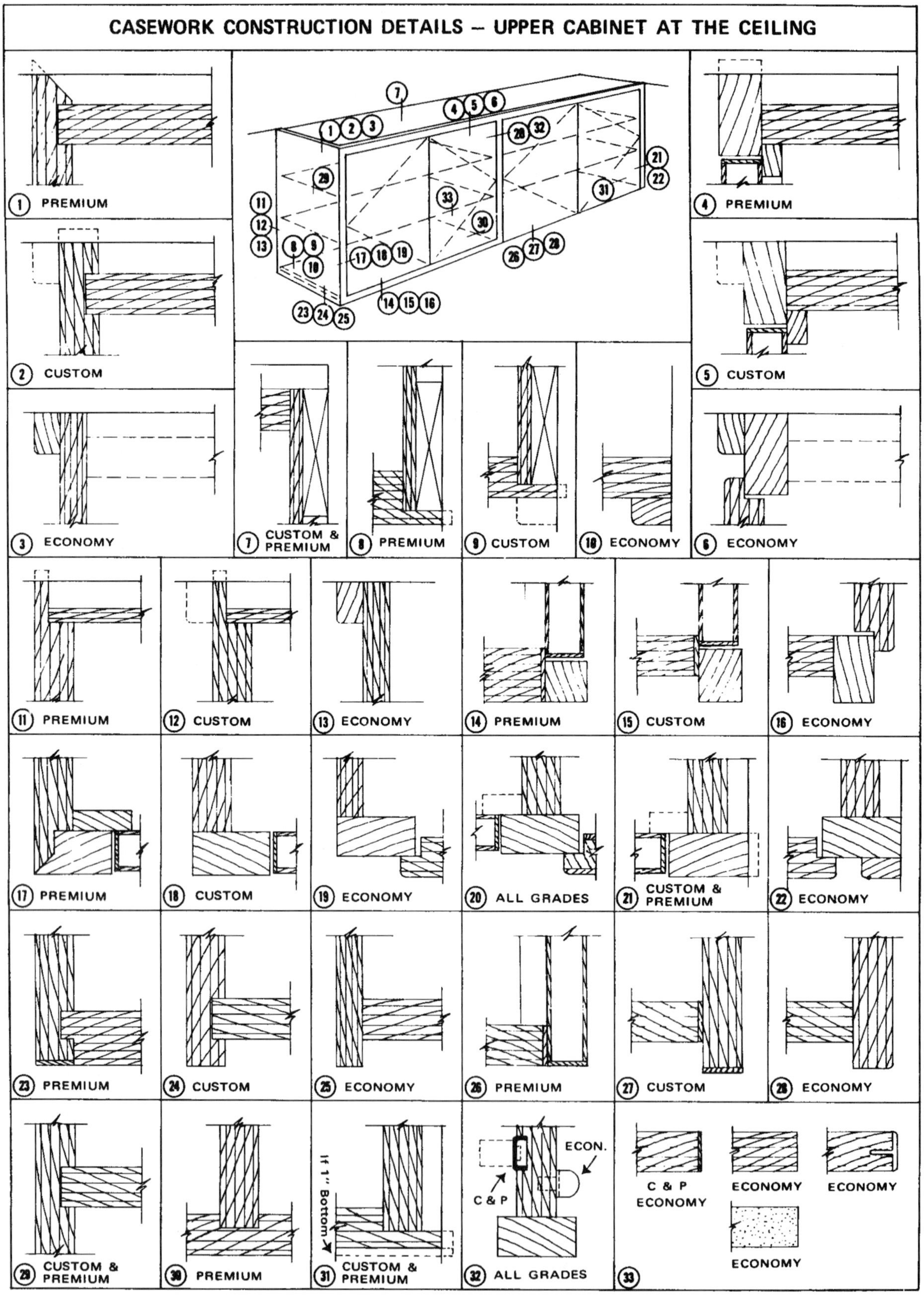

Fig. 3 Casework construction details—upper cabinets at the ceiling

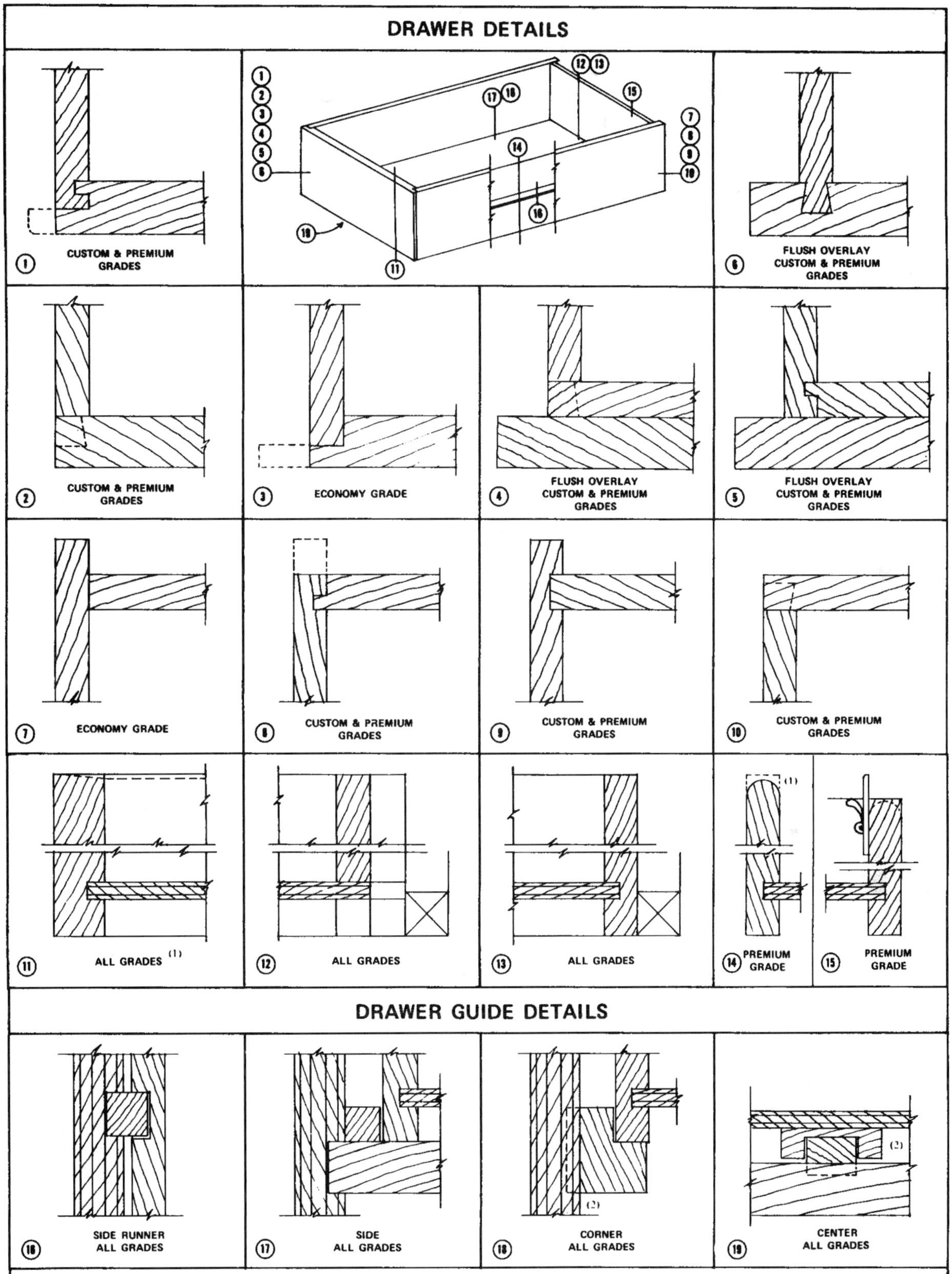

(1) Premium Grade requires top edge of sides to be shaped or stop shaped.
(2) Dado not required. Must be securely attached.

Fig. 4 Drawer details

STANDARD JOINERY AND CASEWORK DETAILS
Typical Flush Overlay Casework Construction

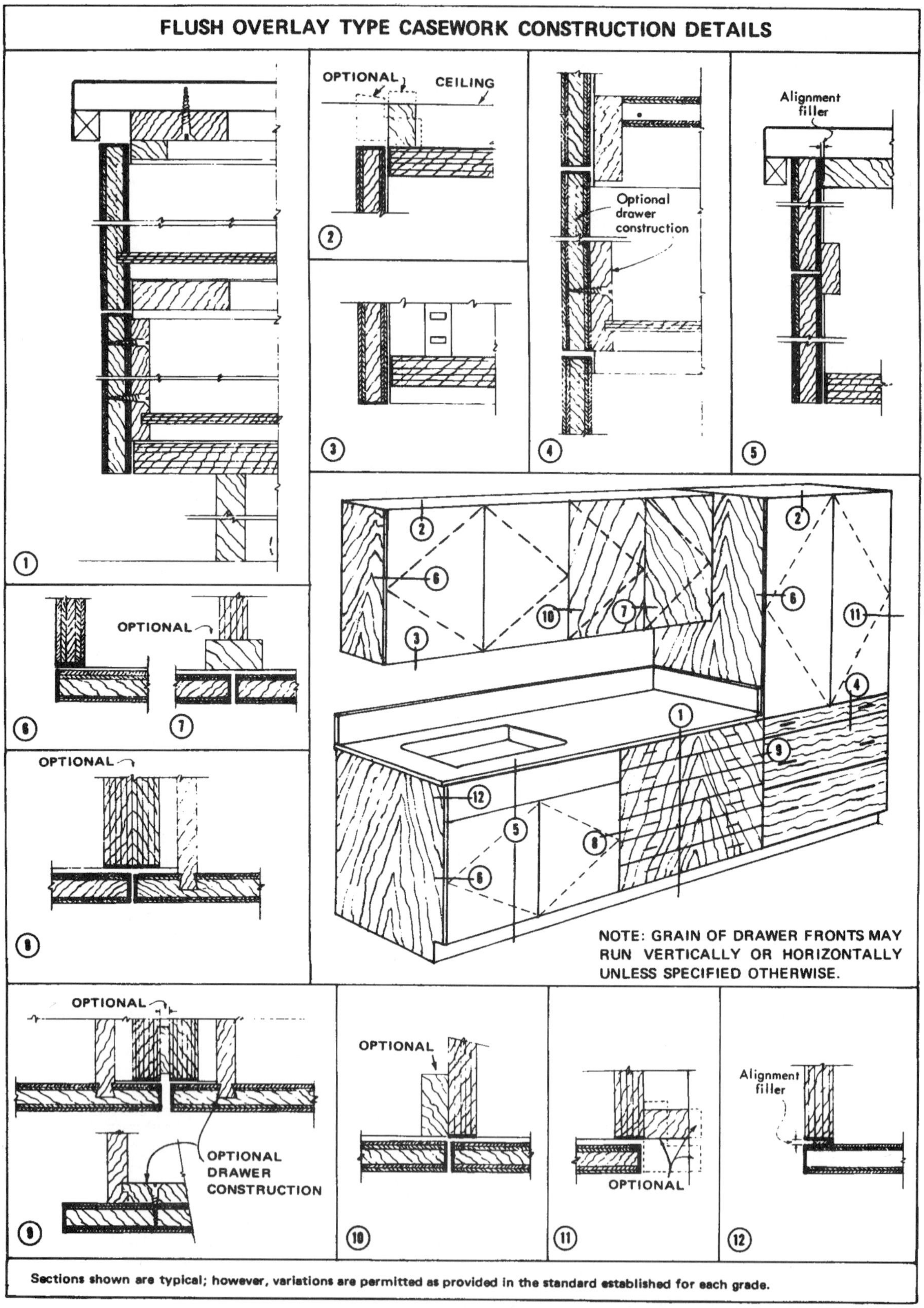

Fig. 5 Flush overlay-type casework construction details

STANDARD JOINERY AND CASEWORK DETAILS
Typical Flush Overlay Casework Construction

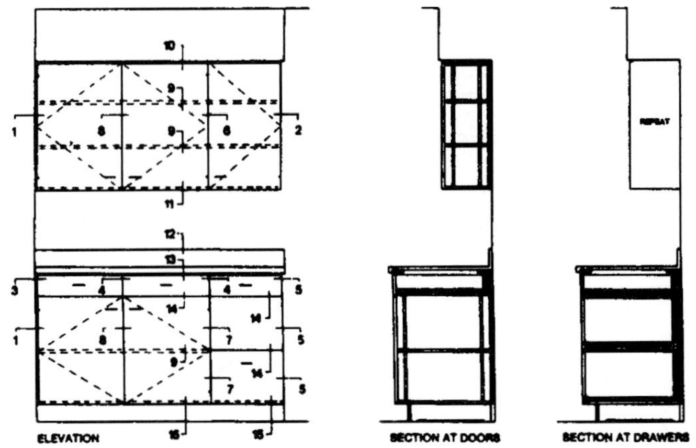

ELEVATION SECTION AT DOORS SECTION AT DRAWERS

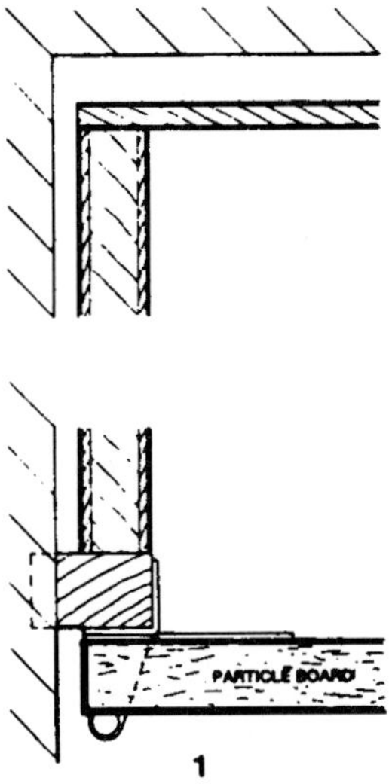

1

6

8

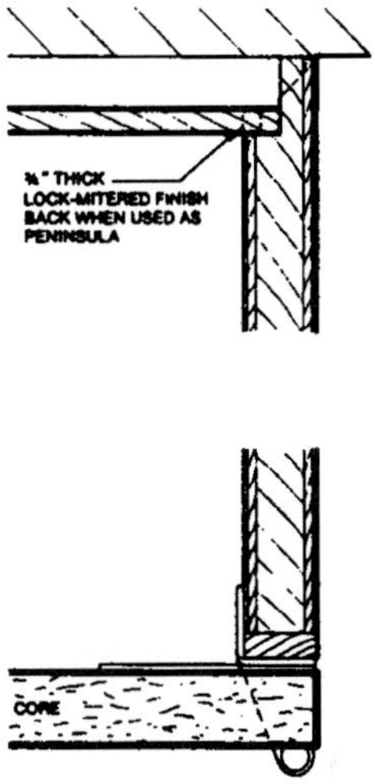

2

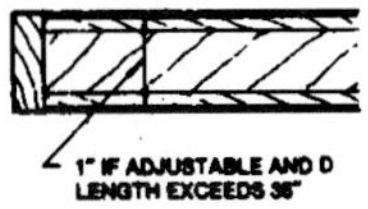

9

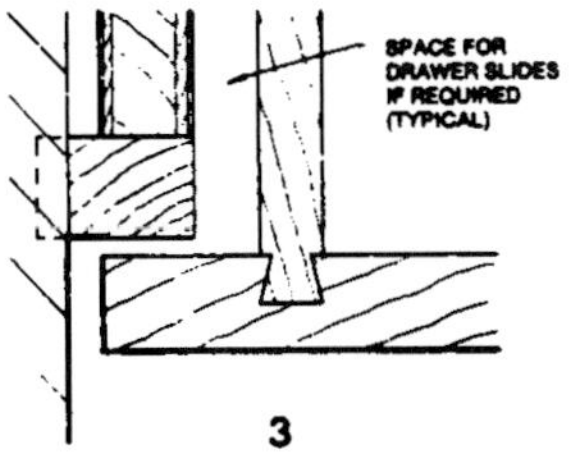

3

4

5

7

STANDARD JOINERY AND CASEWORK DETAILS
Typical Flush Overlay Casework Construction

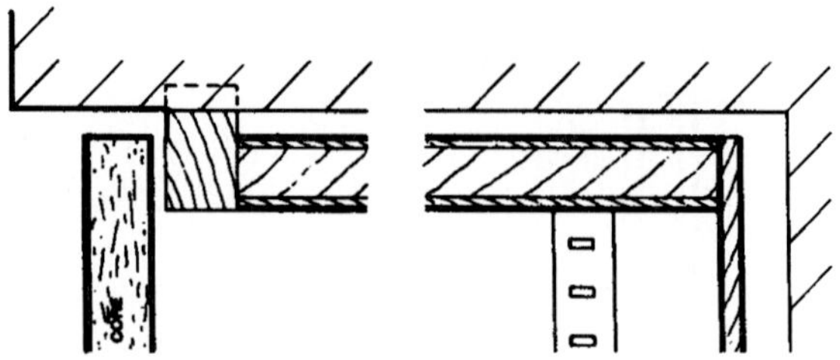

10

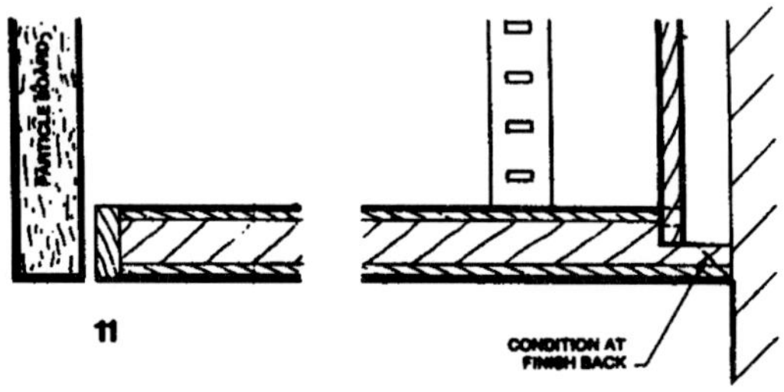

11

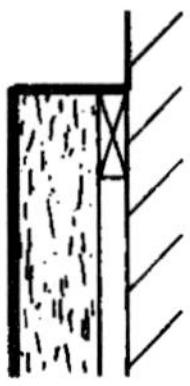

12

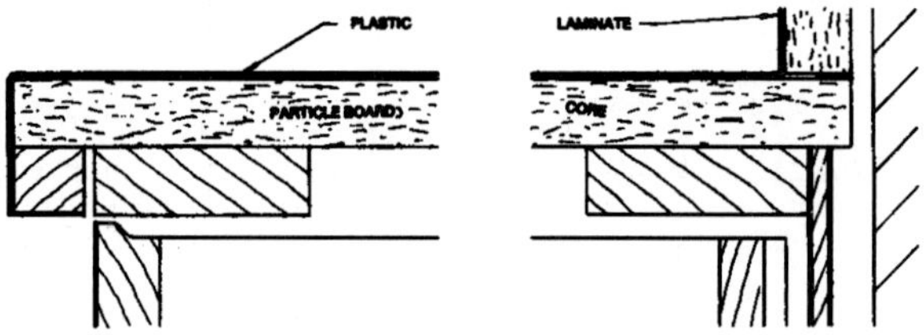

13

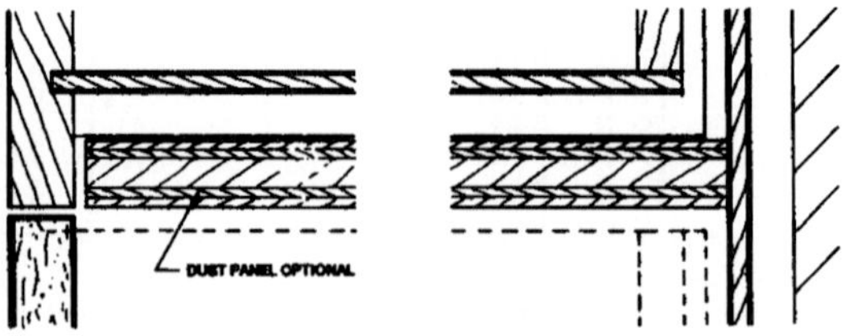

14

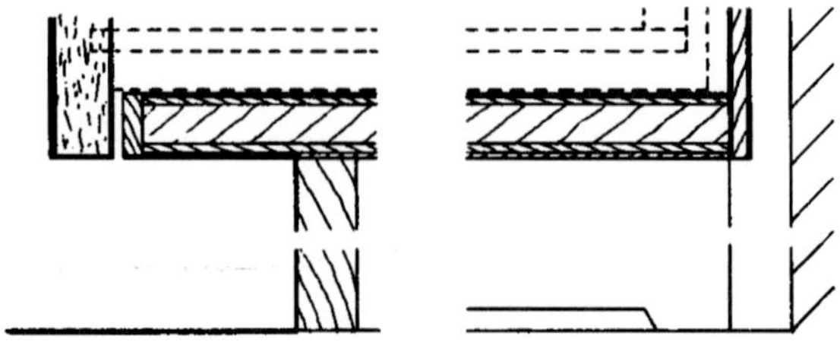

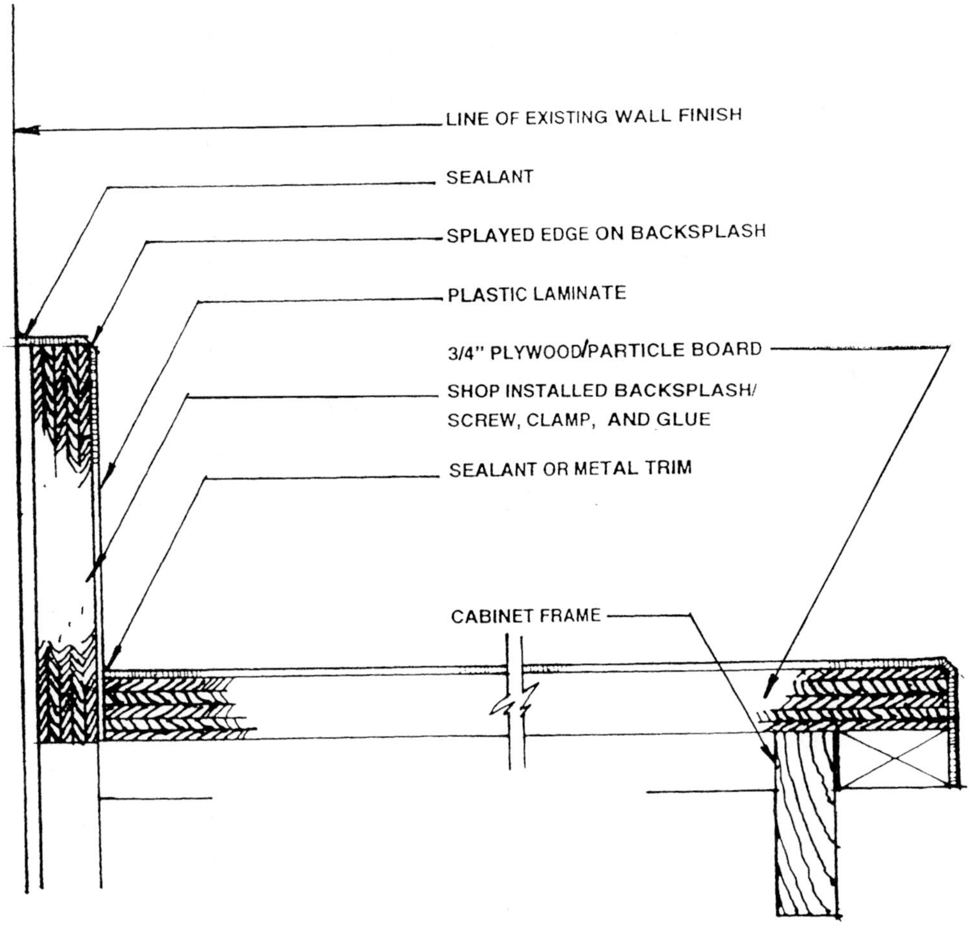

TYPICAL SECTION THRU PLASTIC LAMINATE COUNTER TOP

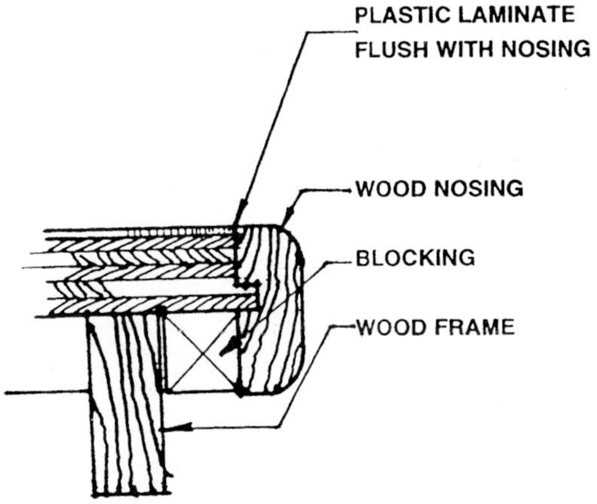

PLASTIC LAMINATE / WOOD NOSING

Backsplash components can be installed in the field or in a woodworking shop.
A field installed backsplash can be secured to the wall with construction adhesive or can be installed to the counter top by means of a metal or plastic clip that is fastened securely to the plastic laminate counter top. The plastic laminate backsplash has a kerfed bottom with screws that slide into clip. This latter form of installation is not typical, and in general, may lack structural integrity.

Careful attention should be given to the horizontal joint at the top of the back splash. While typically removed from exposure to objects that may damage the edge, a splayed or beveled edge will tend minimize chipping of the laminate.

STANDARD JOINERY AND CASEWORK DETAILS
Countertops/Edge Details

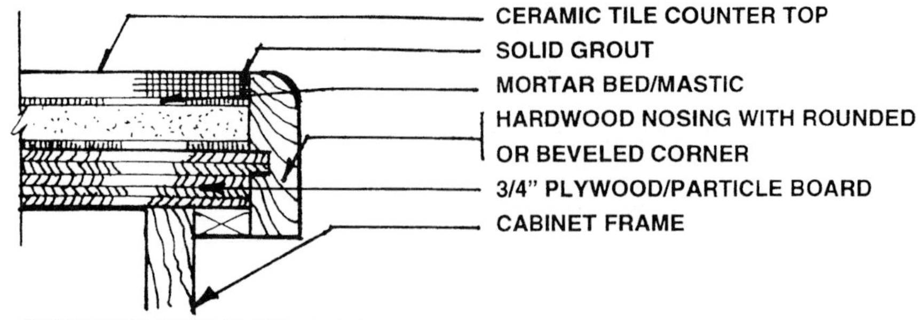

SECTION THRU TILE COUNTER TOP/SOLID WOOD NOSING

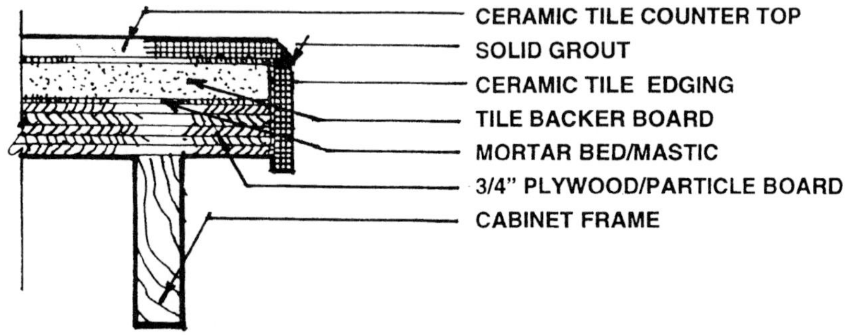

SECTION THRU TILE COUNTER TOP/TILE EDGING

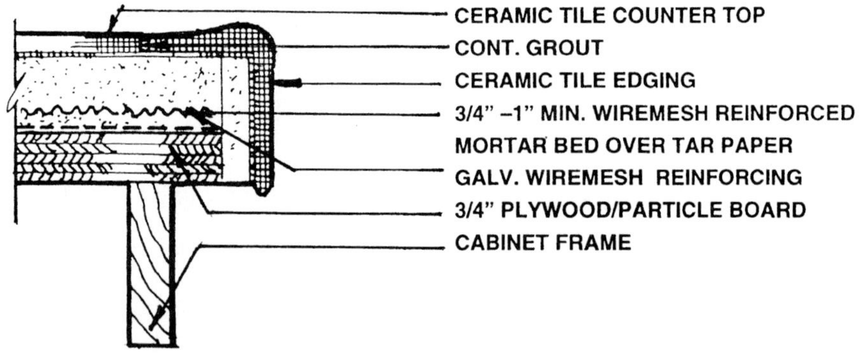

SECTION THRU TILE COUNTER TOP/ONE PIECE CERAMIC TILE EDGING

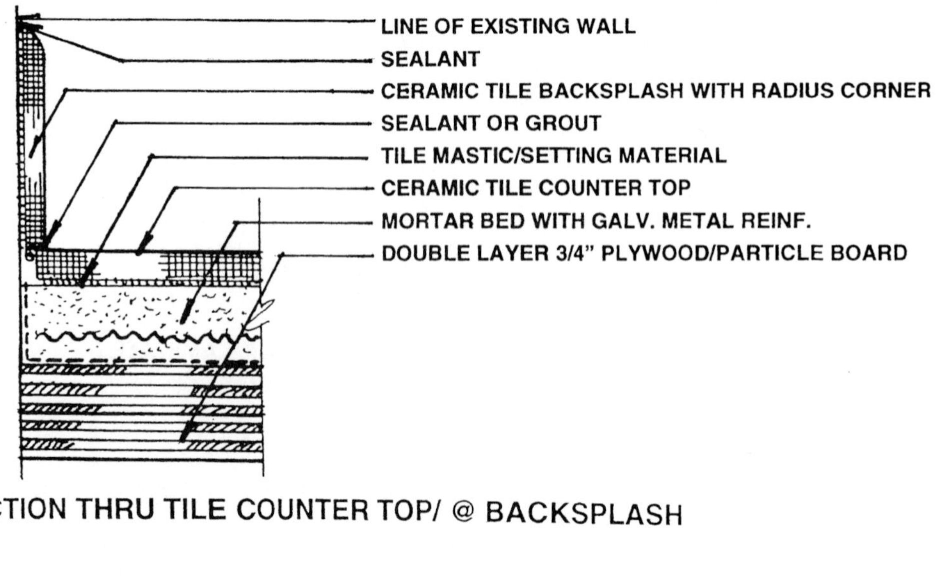

SECTION THRU TILE COUNTER TOP/ @ BACKSPLASH

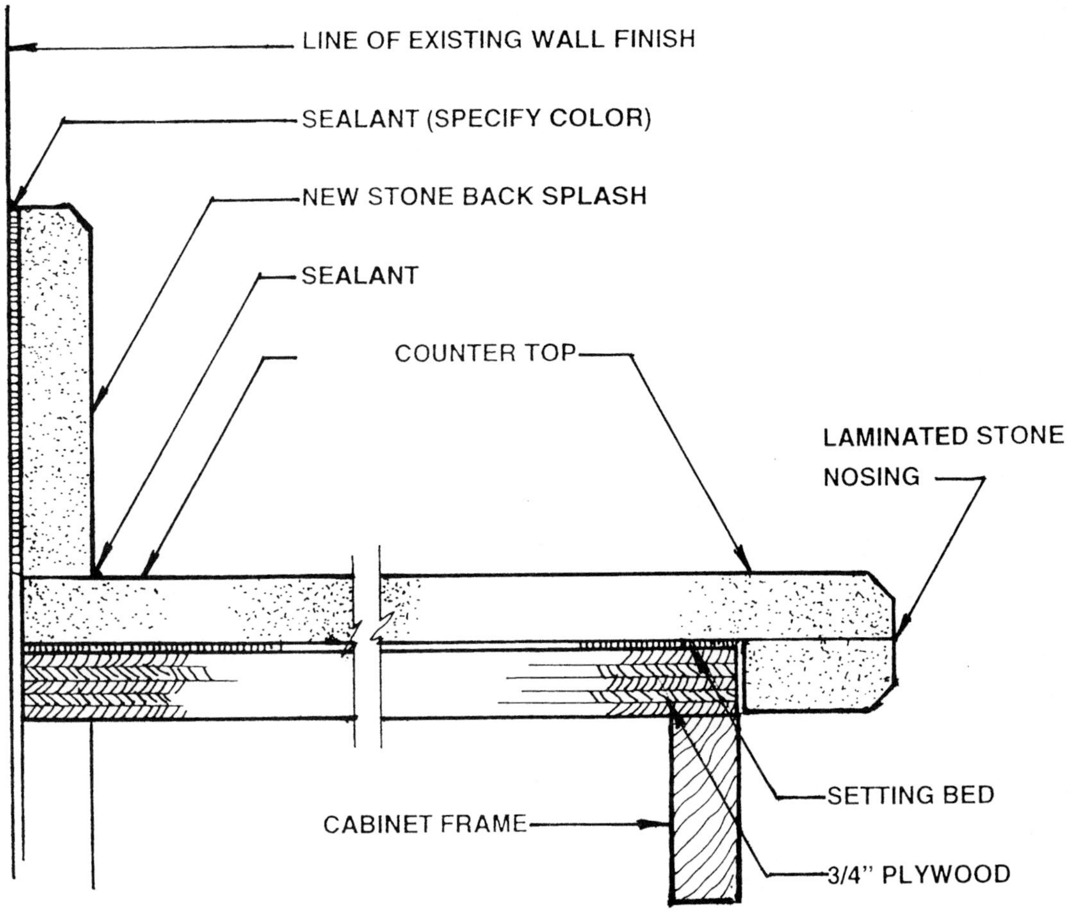

TYPICAL SECTION THRU STONE COUNTER TOP

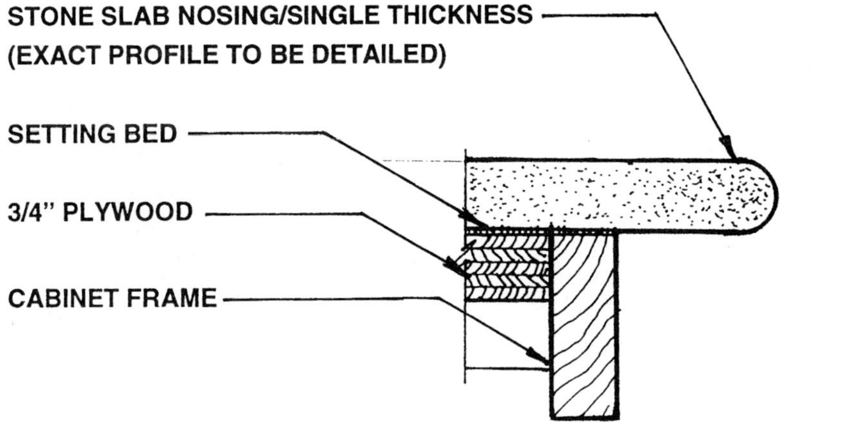

SINGLE THICKNESS NOSING

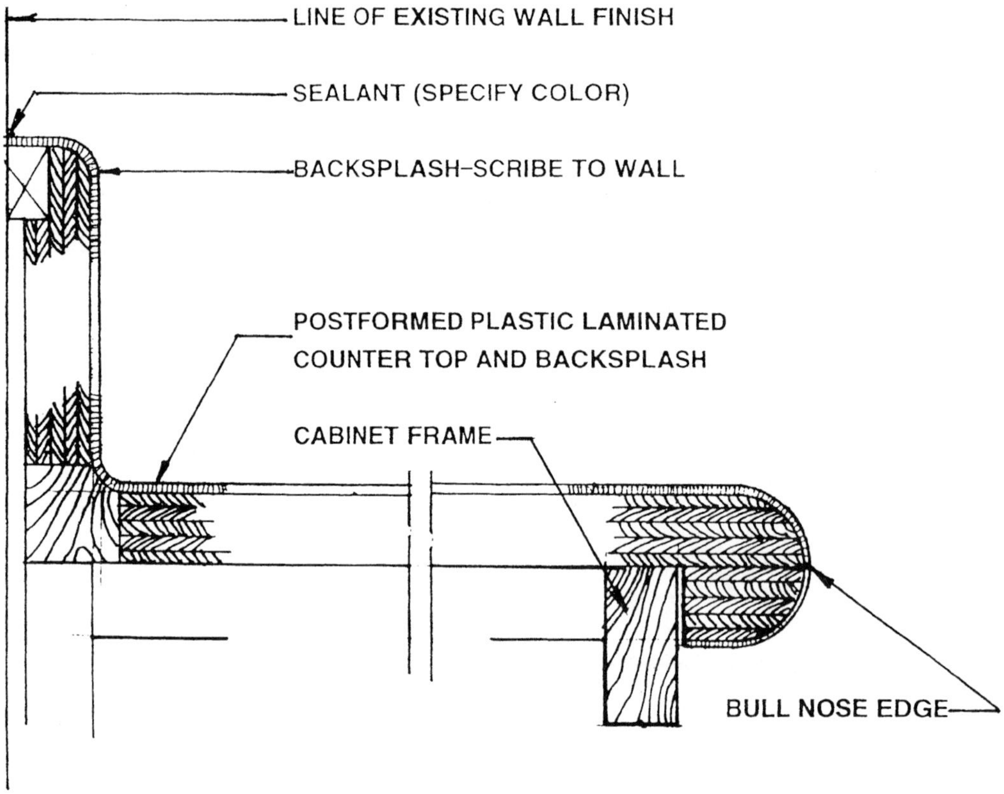

TYPICAL SECTION THRU POSTFORMED
PLASTIC LAMINATE COUNTER TOP

Typically there are two edge details possible when designing a postformed counter top. One is a curved or "bull nose" edge detail as shown in the typical detail above.

The other is a "no-drip" edge detail as shown in the detail to the right. This edge detail will contain spills more efficiently than the bull nose. The no-drip is more functional while the bull nose will provide simple sleek lines at the sacrifice of surface area.

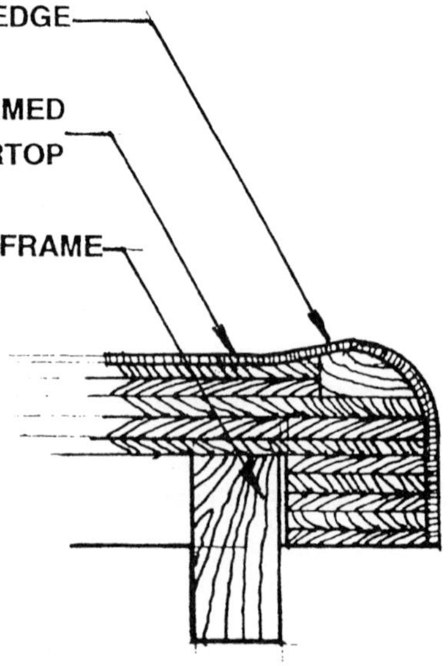

ALTERNATE NO-DRIP EDGE

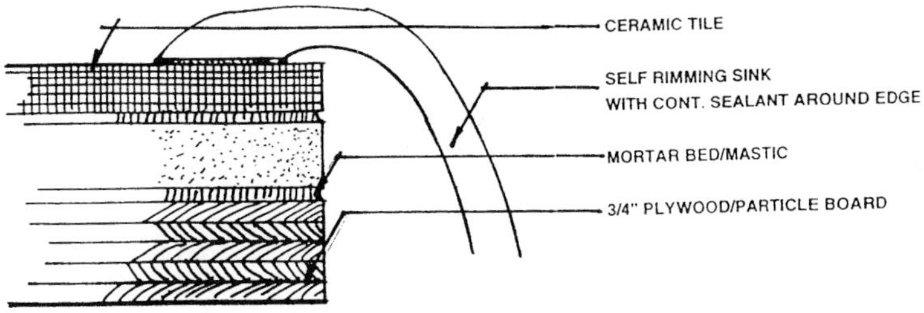

SECTION THRU TILE COUNTER TOP/
SELF RIMMING SINK

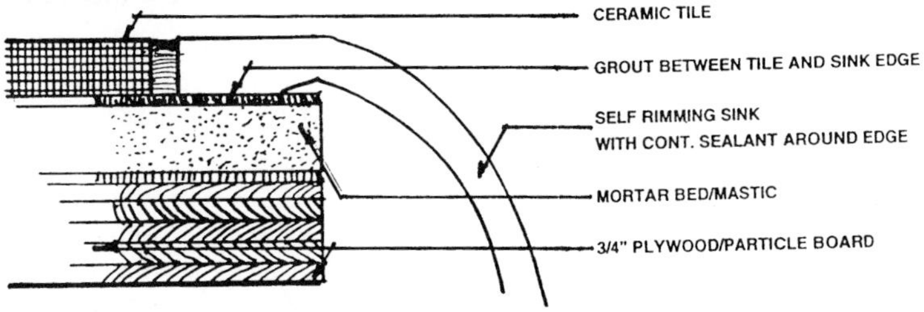

SECTION THRU TILE COUNTER TOP/
FLUSH MOUNTED SINK

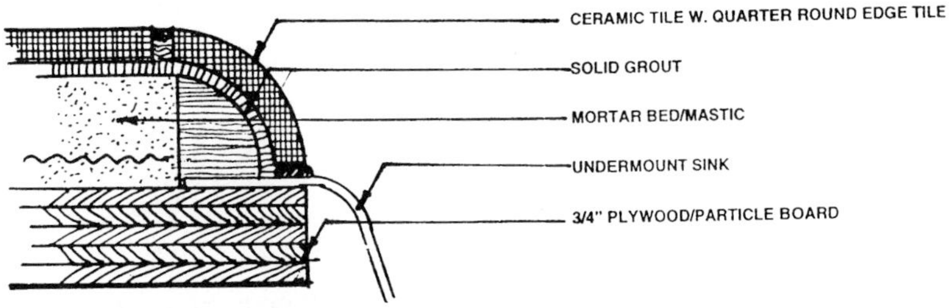

SECTION THRU TILE COUNTER TOP/
UNDERMOUNT SINK

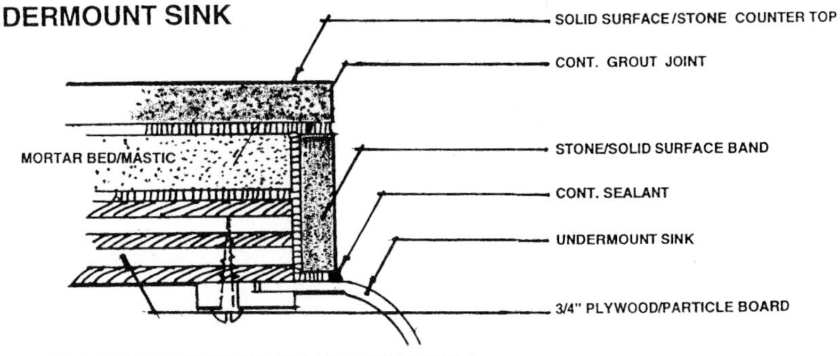

SECTION THRU STONE COUNTER TOP/
FLUSH MOUNTED SINK

In the case of tile counter tops and the use of self rimming sinks, the designer is cautioned that the more irregular the tile, the greater the difficulty in achieving a neat and fitted seal between the sink and the tile. For economy, however, the self rimming sink is most cost effective.

Undermount sinks will provide a more aesthetically pleasing installation when installed within a ceramic tile or stone counter top, albeit at greater expense due to cost of installation and finishing the exposed edges. The finish of inside corner details is to be carefully considered.

STANDARD JOINERY AND CASEWORK DETAILS
Countertops/Solid Surface

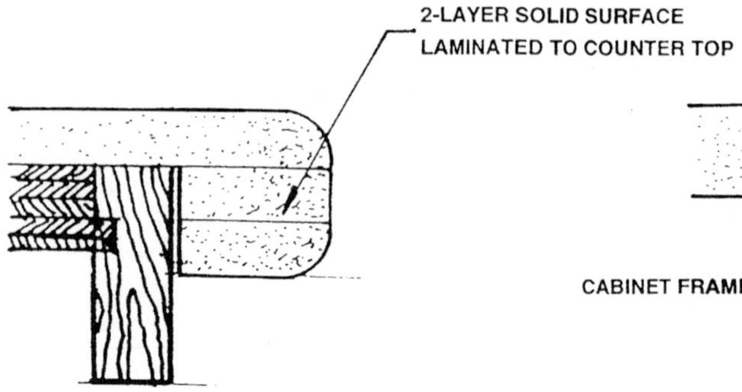

SOLID SURFACE NOSING/LAMINATED

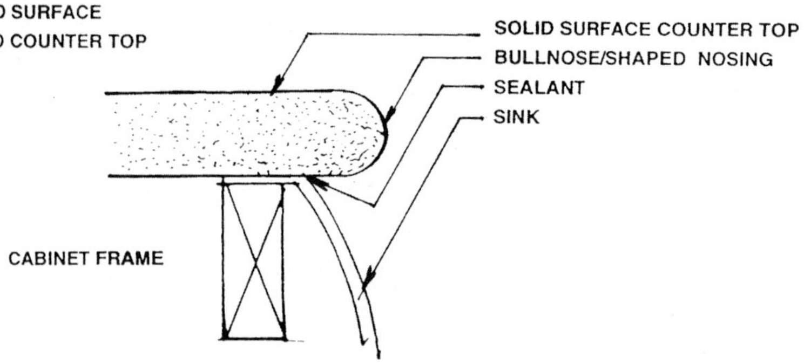

SOLID SURFACE COUNTER TOP/ UNDERMOUNT SINK

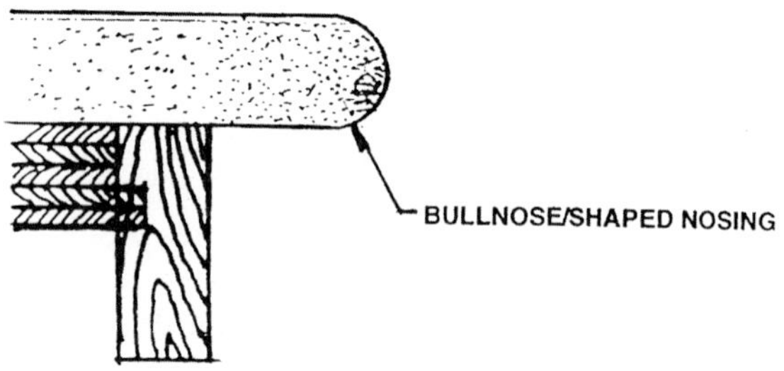

SOLID SURFACE NOSING/ONE PIECE

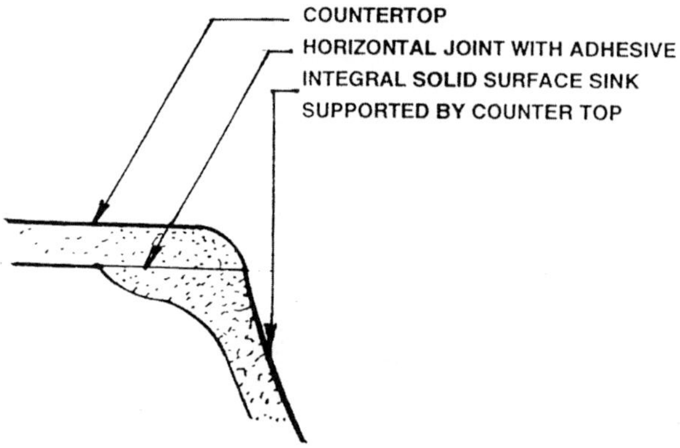

SOLID SURFACE COUNTER TOP/ SOLID SURFACE SINK

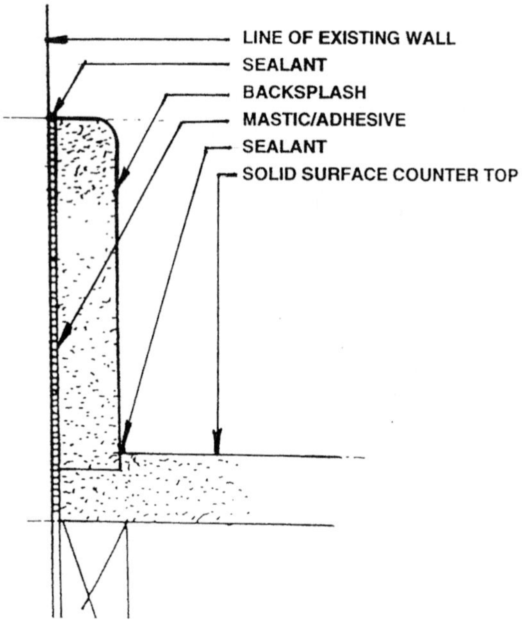

SOLID SURFACE BACK SPLASH

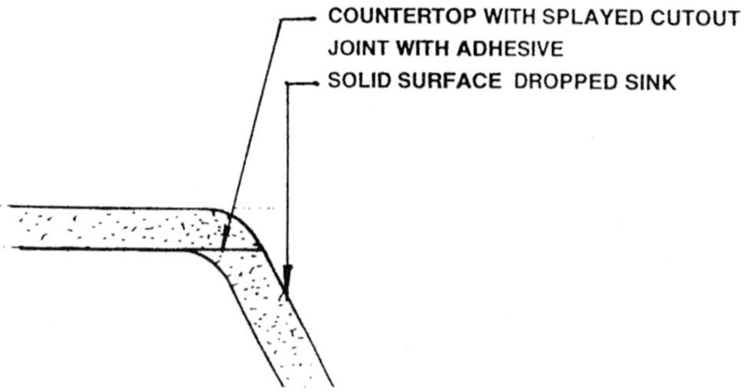

SOLID SURFACE COUNTER TOP/ FLUSH SOLID SURFACE SINK

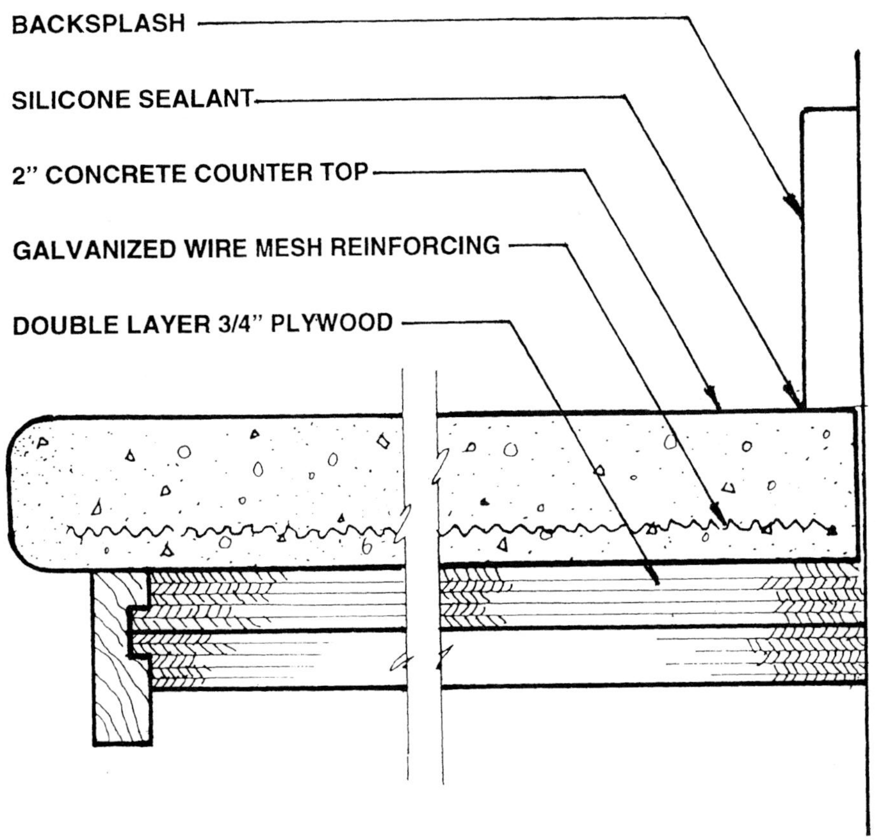

TYPICAL SECTION THRU PRECAST CONCRETE COUNTER TOP

It should be noted that the designer has a number of options to control both the texture and the color of the concrete counter top, whether precast or cast in place. Although a smooth finish is recommended, a variety of surface textures are possible, depending on the type and design of the float employed in the finishing of the concrete, or the grinding after the concrete has cured.

With regard to color, white or black cement can be used. In addition, colored aggregates can also be used to produce interesting and, in some cases, dramatic effects.

It is important that a sealant be applied at such time that the finishing operation has been completed. In kitchens or other food preparation areas, it is important that nontoxic sealers be used.

It is highly recommended that sample panels be made up ahead of time, showing the intended color, texture, and finish of the counter top.

STANDARD JOINERY AND CASEWORK DETAILS
Countertops/Edge Details

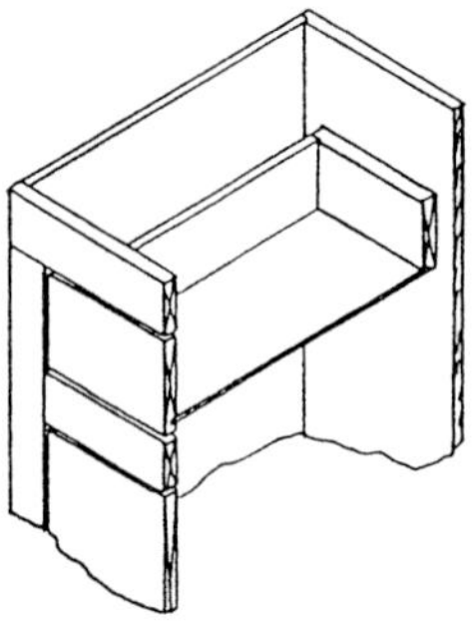

Doors flush with cabinets

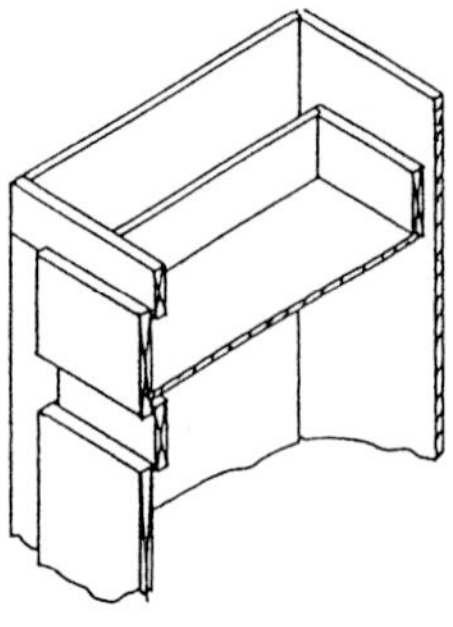

Doors extend past cabinets

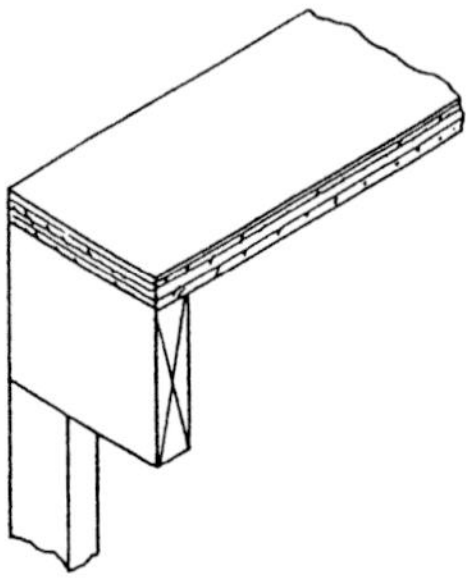

Subtop flush with cabinet face

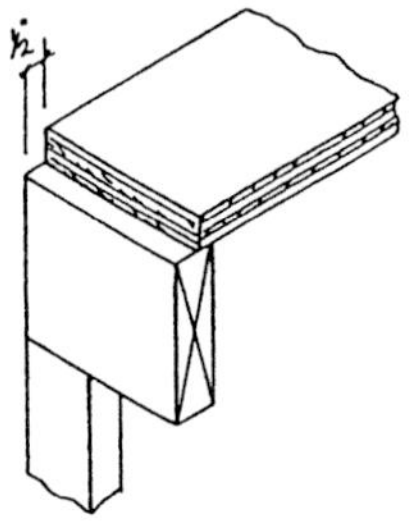

Subtop set back from cabinet face

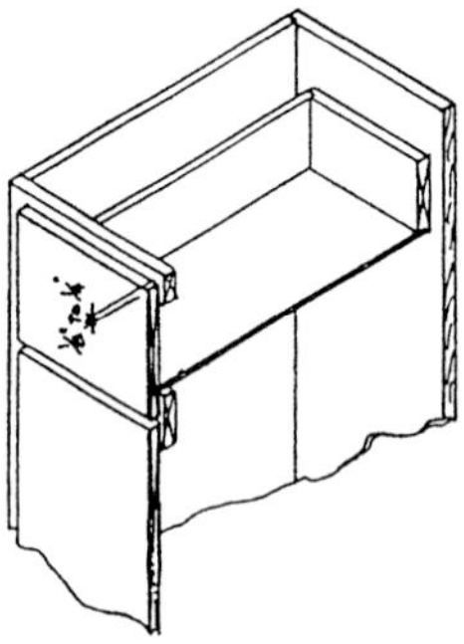

Doors cover cabinets

CONSIDERATIONS:

1. Are cabinets set firmly in place?
2. Are cabinet fronts set in a straight line or do they follow the profile of the wall?
3. Are the tops of the cabinets set level and flush or do they have lips where they meet?

CABINET TYPES

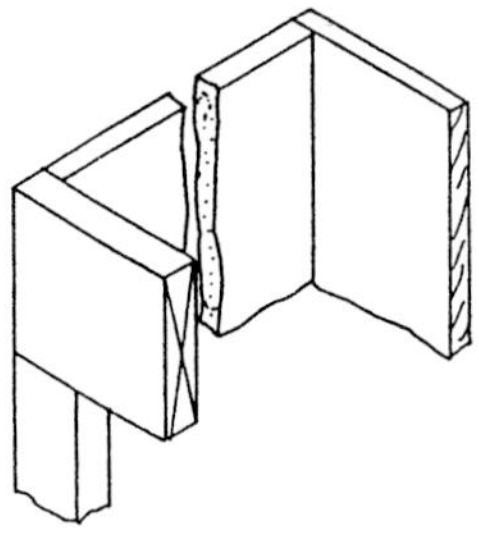

No subtops

CONSIDERATIONS:

1. Allowance should be made for the actual stone thickness in the thickness of the subtops. 3/4" stone is a nominal 2 cm and usually measures from 5/8" to 7/8".
2. Joints should be located at the cabinet joints or centered over the center of the cabinets or the doors.
3. Holes for the sinks, faucets and ranges should be located and sized as well as the method of supporting.
4. The dishwasher should be located and the method of stabilizing should be considered.

SUBSTRUCTURES

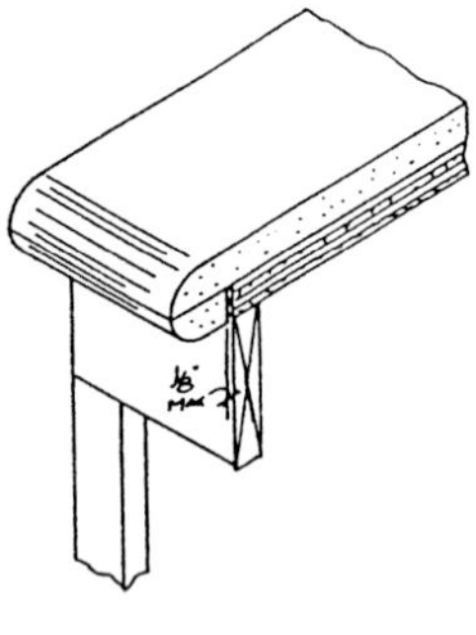

Typical at flush subtops

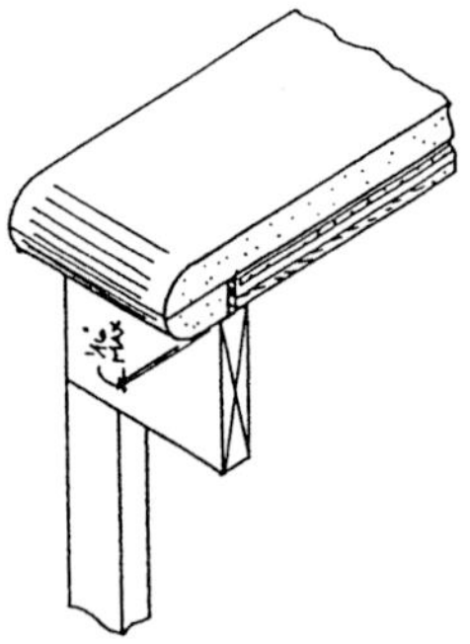

Typical at set back subtops

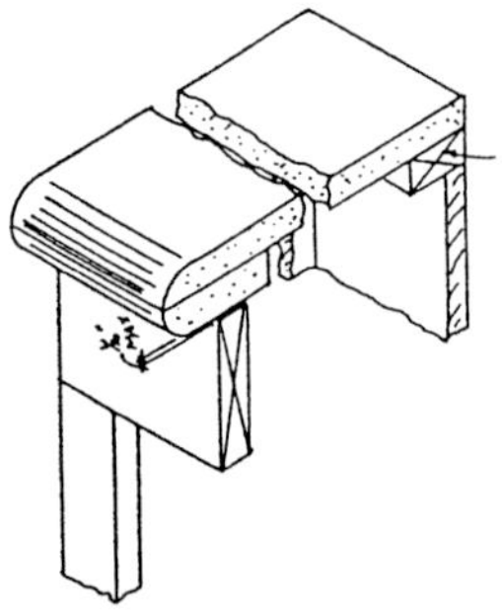

Typical when no subtops

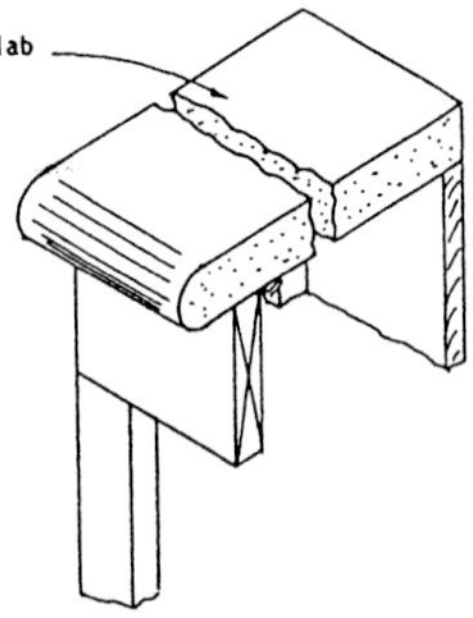

Typical at thicker slabs (note: slabs may have to be gauged to maintain a consistent thickness throughout)

COUNTERTOP PLACEMENT

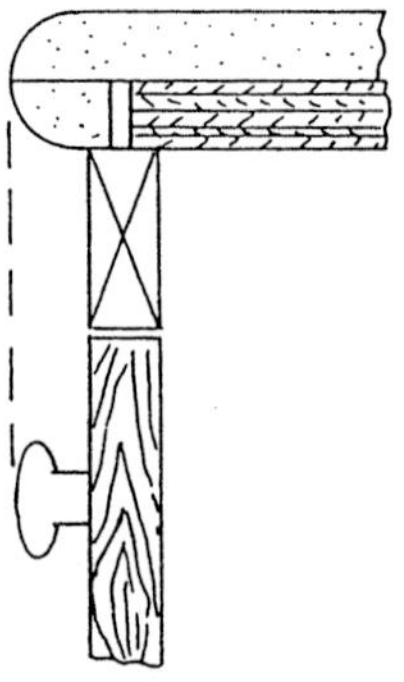

Doors flush with cabinets

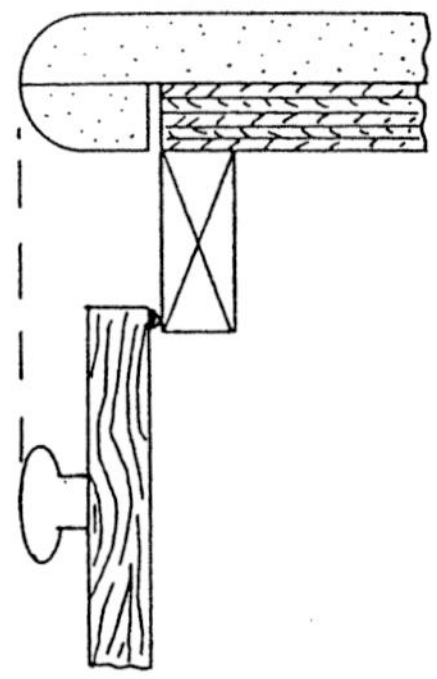

Doors overlapping cabinets

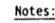

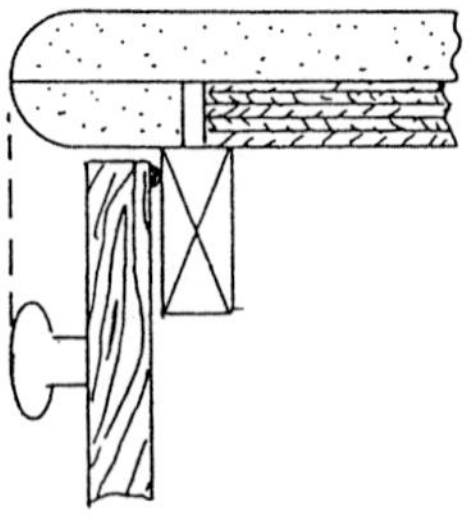

Doors covering cabinets

Notes:

1. Countertops should extend to or beyond handles on doors.
2. Consideration should be given to sides of cabinets to maintain the same basic look as the fronts.
3. Sides may not have the same nose profile or overhang as the front of the cabinet due to obstructions, appliances or other factors.

COUNTERTOP CLEARANCE

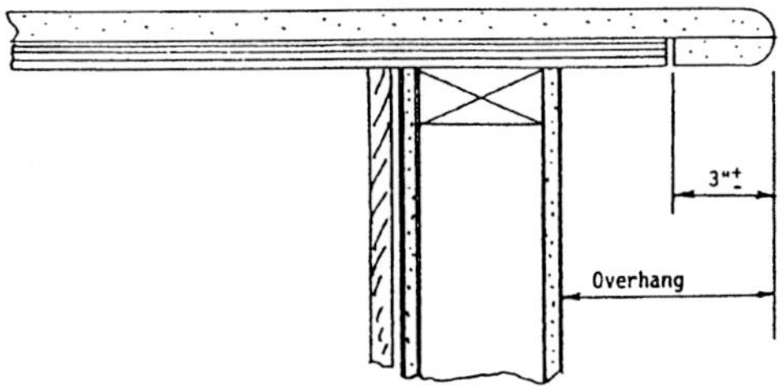

Cabinet backed by stud wall

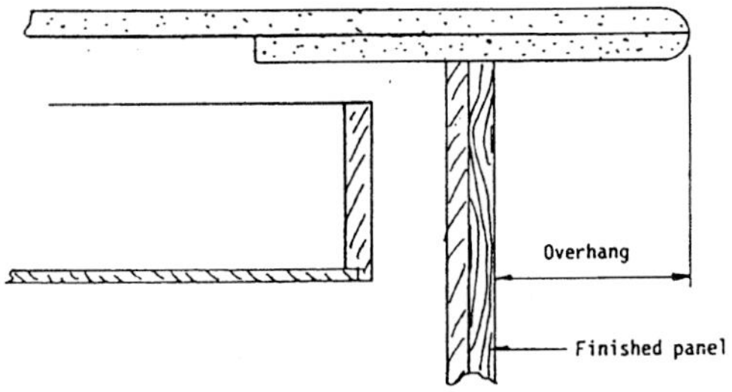

Cabinet back covered by paneling

COUNTERTOP EXTENSION

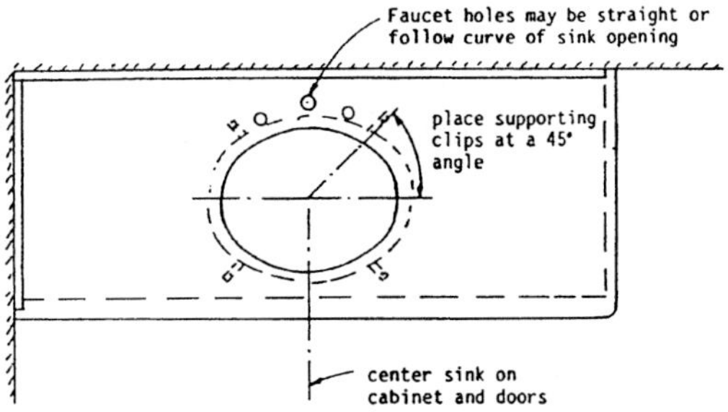

Typical vanity plan

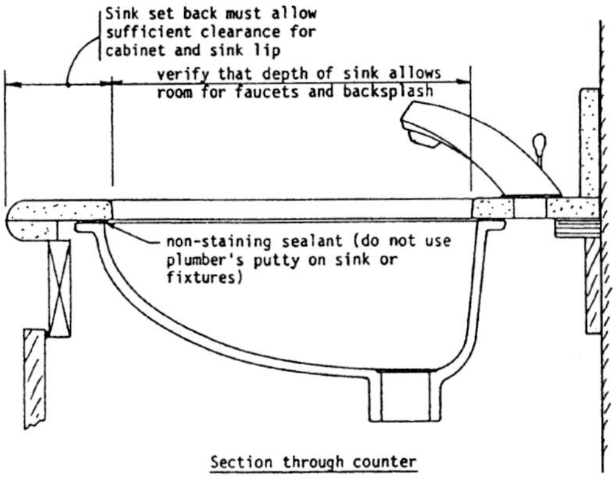

Section through counter

VANITIES

	ADVANTAGES	DISADVANTAGES
EPOXY	Achieve better color match Leaves joint most flush	Harder than stone material so settling can crack the stone Does not allow for any movement
GROUT	Easiest to use Simple to install Relatively easy to color match	Color not consistent May crack Does not have a shiny finish Contrast with the surface of a polished stone
CAULK	Allows for most flexibility Leaves a slick joint that will match the surface of a polished stone Latex version is easier to use than the silicone version	Not as many colors available May stain the surface of some types of stone

ADVANTAGES AND DISADVANTAGES OF JOINT FILLERS
INTERIOR APPLICATIONS

STANDARD JOINERY AND CASEWORK DETAILS
Countertops/Backsplash Details

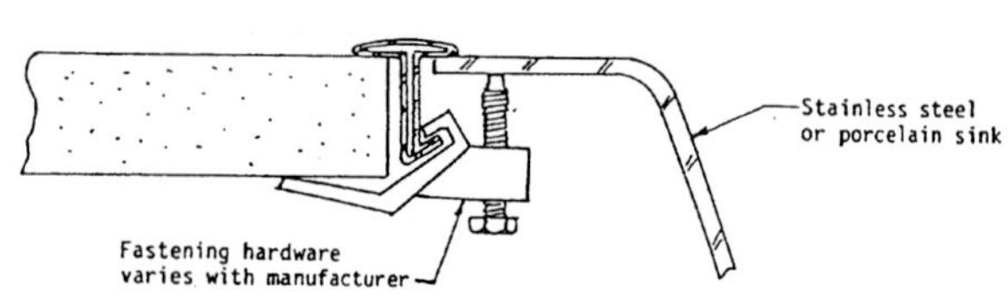

Supported by metal frame

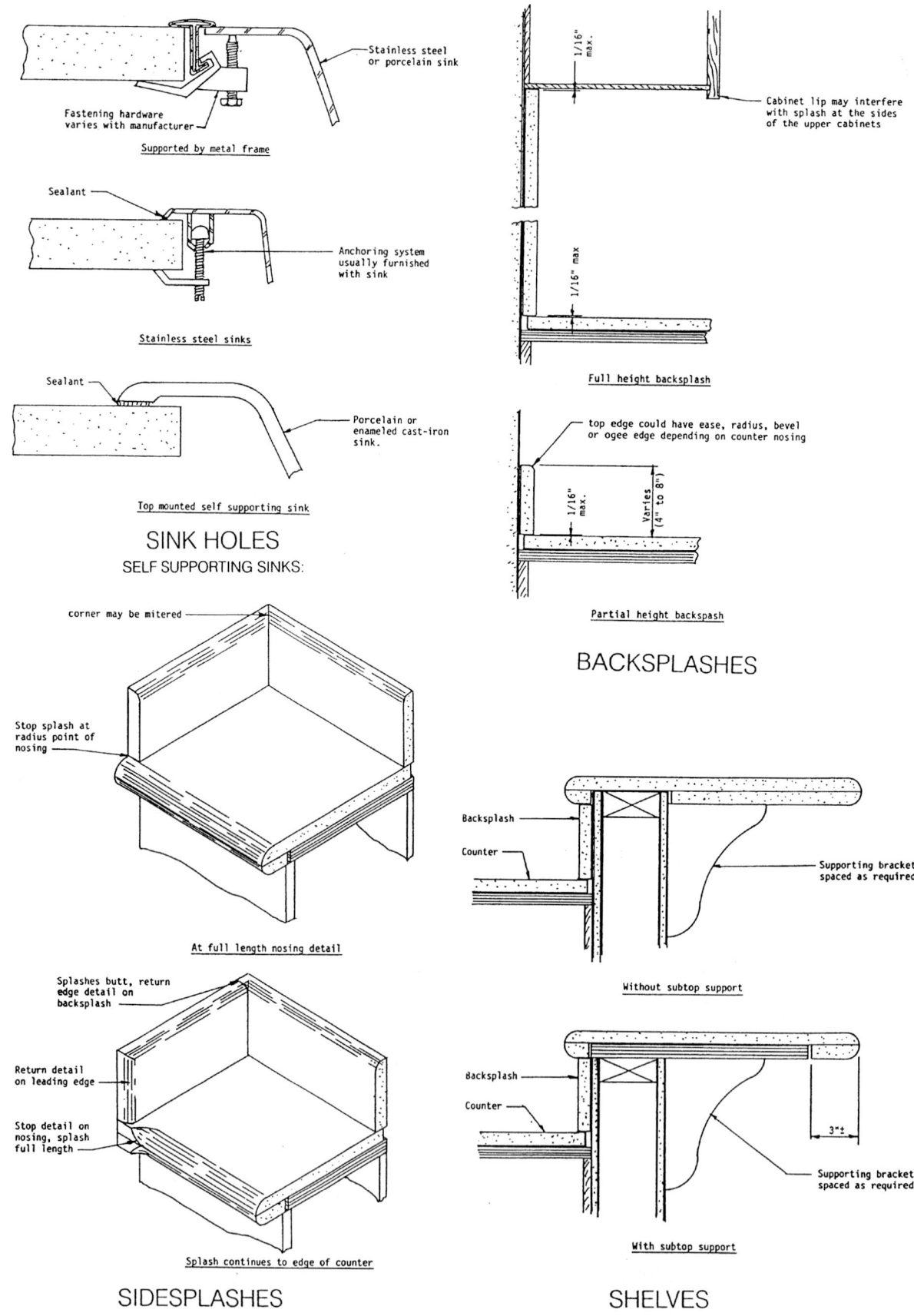

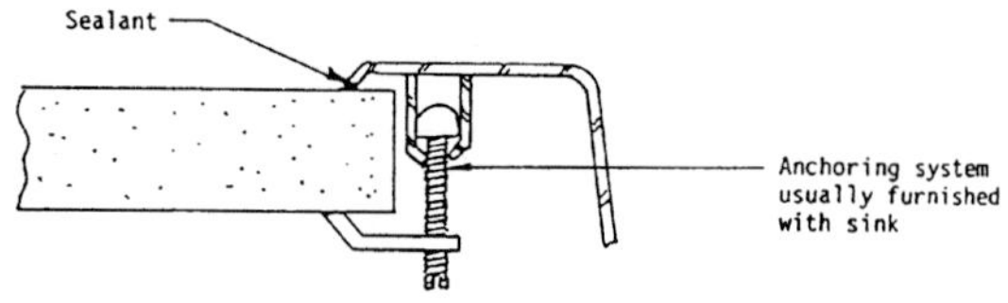

Stainless steel sinks

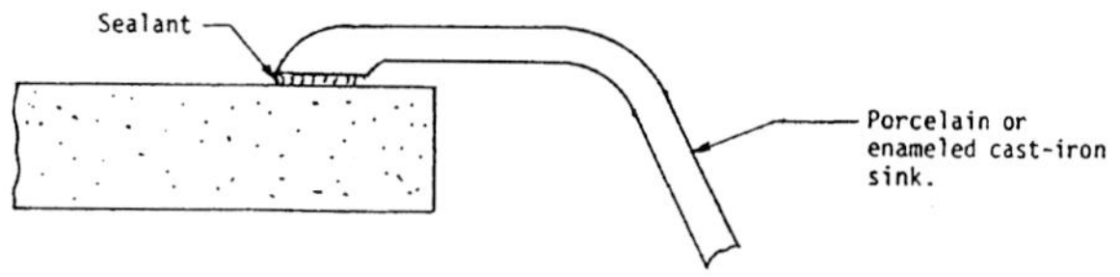

Top mounted self supporting sink

SINK HOLES
SELF SUPPORTING SINKS:

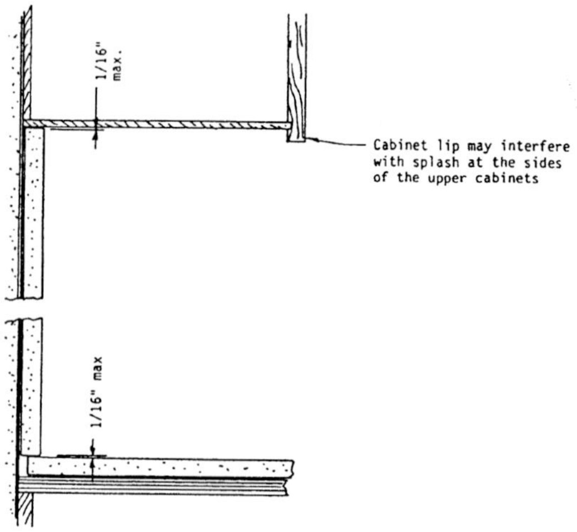

Full height backsplash

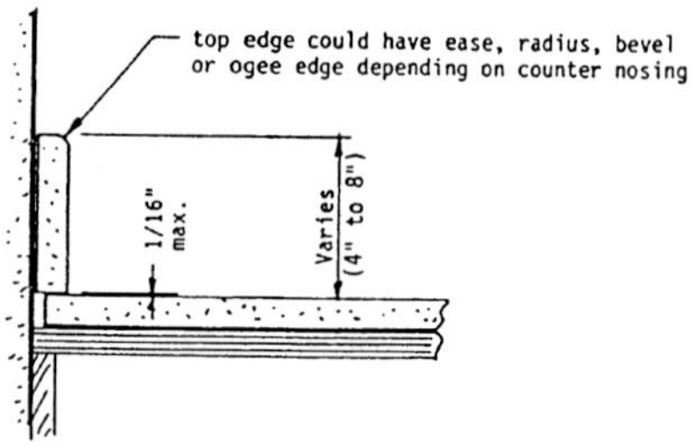

Partial height backspash

BACKSPLASHES

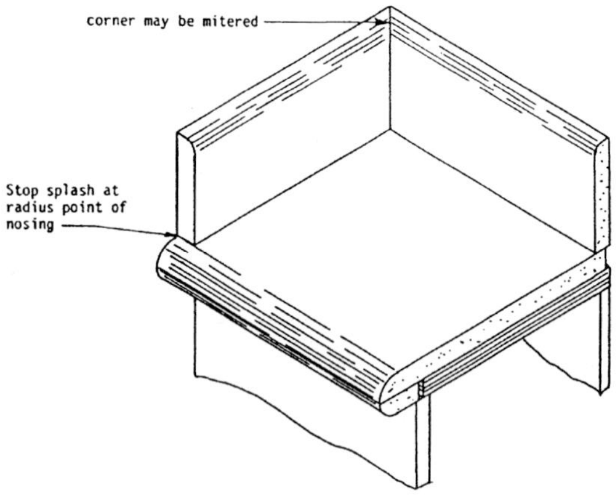

At full length nosing detail

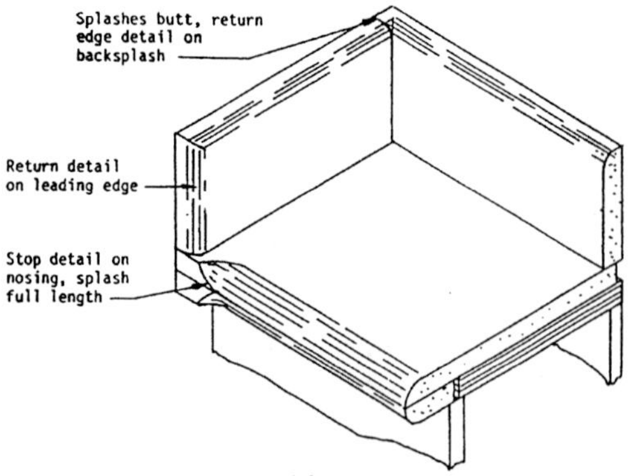

Splash continues to edge of counter

SIDESPLASHES

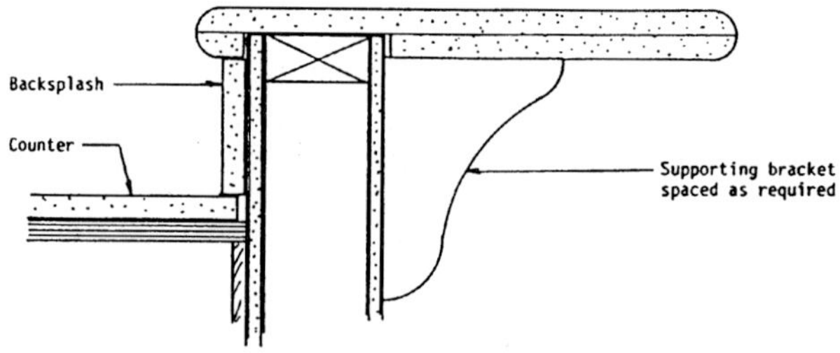

Without subtop support

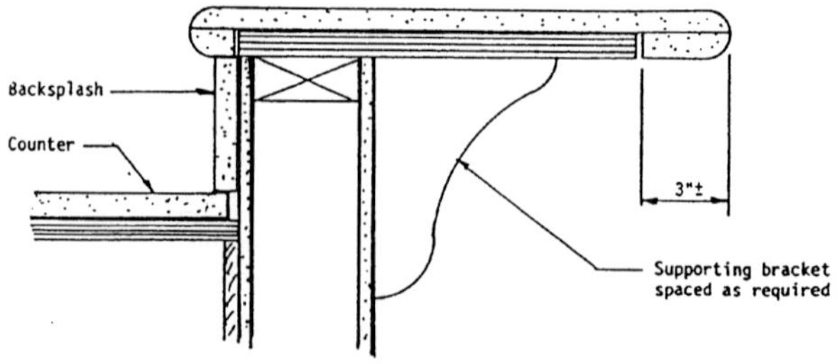

With subtop support

SHELVES

STANDARD JOINERY AND CASEWORK DETAILS
Countertop/Sink Details

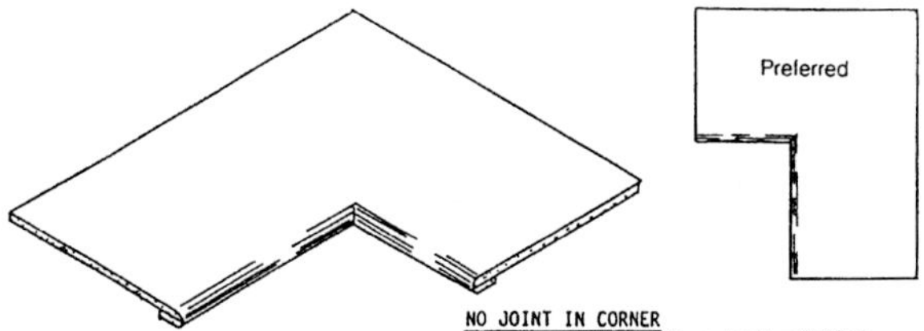

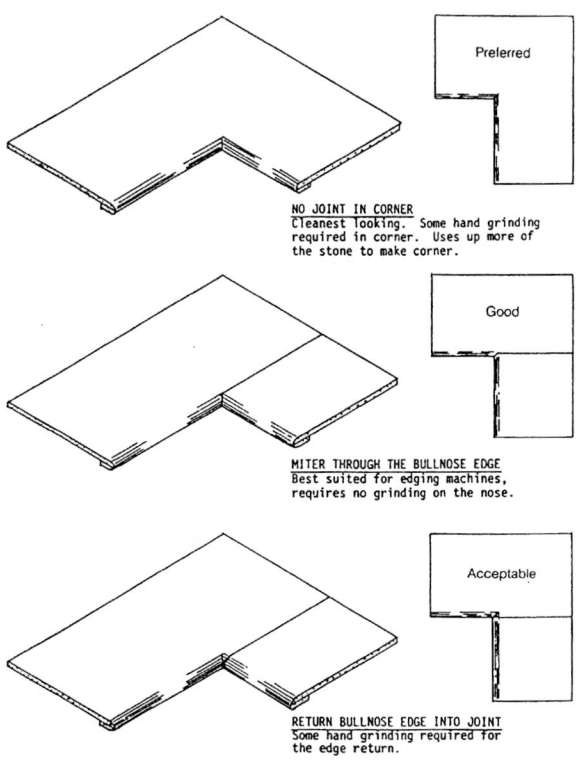

NO JOINT IN CORNER
Cleanest looking. Some hand grinding required in corner. Uses up more of the stone to make corner.

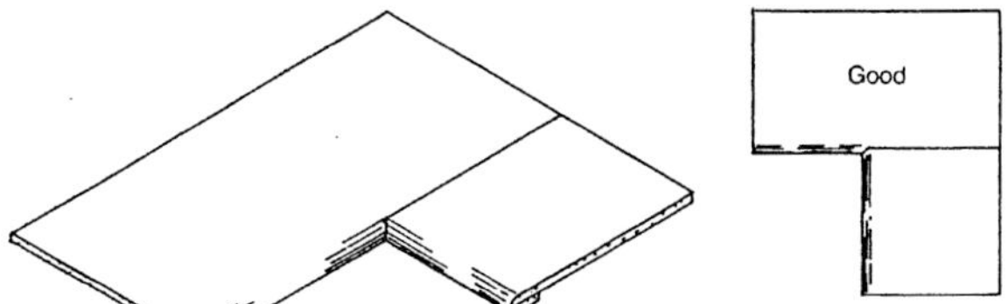

MITER THROUGH THE BULLNOSE EDGE
Best suited for edging machines, requires no grinding on the nose.

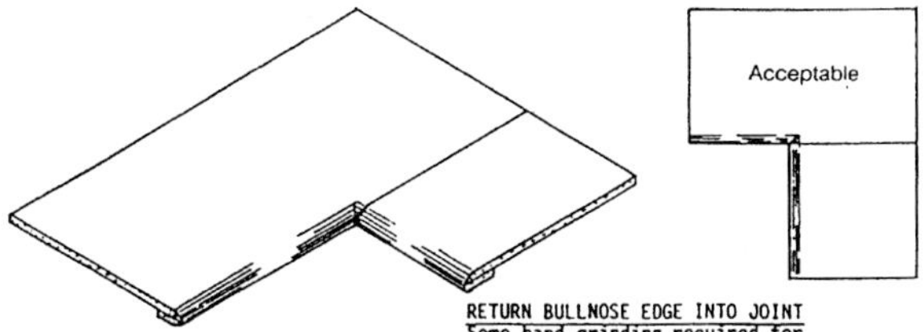

RETURN BULLNOSE EDGE INTO JOINT
Some hand grinding required for the edge return.

CORNER CONDITIONS

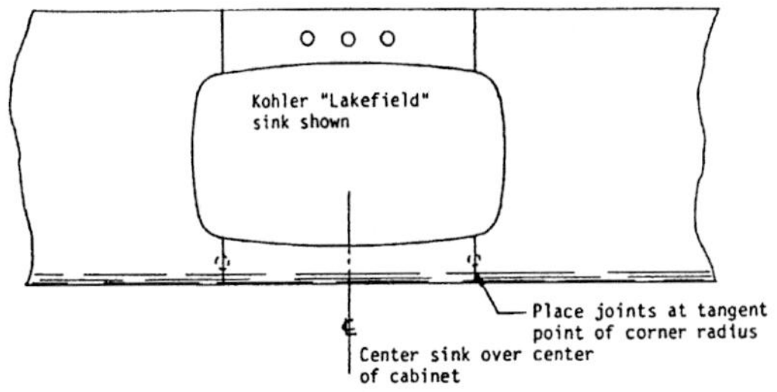

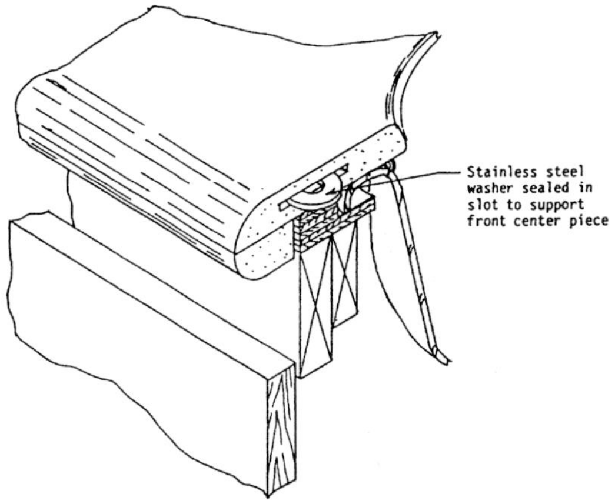

POLISHED SINK HOLES
JOINTS LOCATED AT SINK:

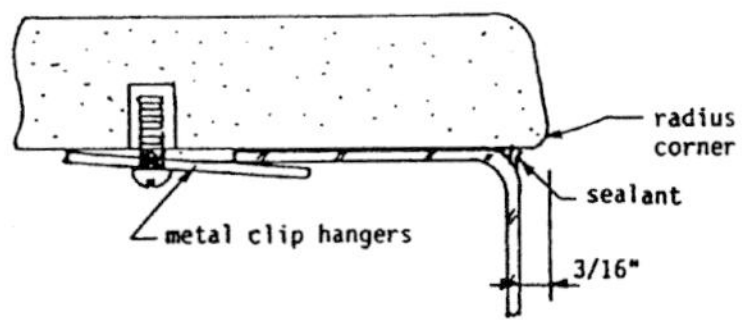

Top overhangs edge of sink

1. Silicone sealer color should blend with the stone and/or the sink.
2. Metal clip hangers should be placed with 2 minimun per side or 4 minimum on oval sinks.

Note: Sometimes mounting screws may be hard to reach.

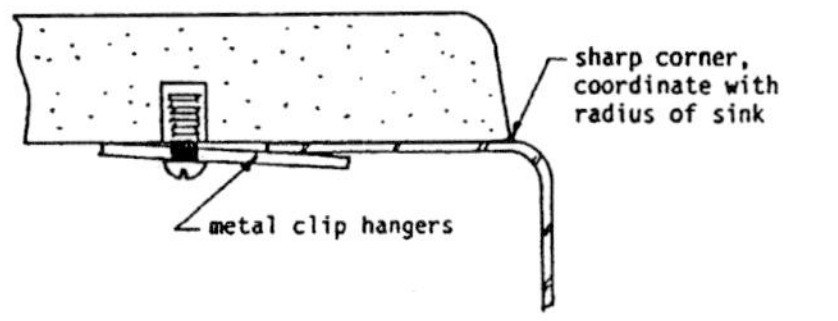

Top set back from edge of sink

1. This design allows for a larger opening which makes it less likely to be hit by pots, pans or glasses.
2. Gives a cleaner looking opening at some double sink designs.

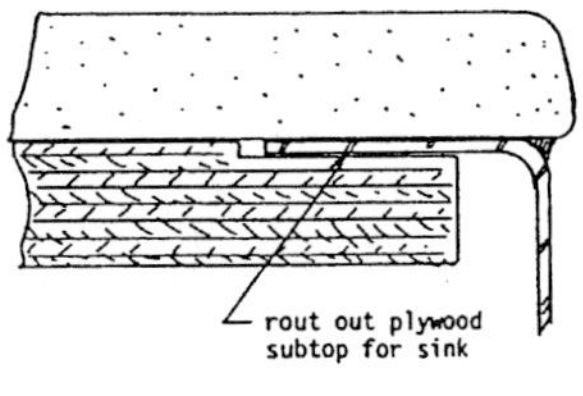

Sink set into plywood subtop for support

1. Allows for consistent support around sink perimeter.
2. Impossible to remove in the future.

POLISHED SINK HOLES
STAINLESS STEEL SINKS

NOTE: This type of sink is generally quite heavy and should be supported by the cabinet, substrate or other system (metal or wood frame). Stone tops are not to be relied upon for support of large cast iron sinks.

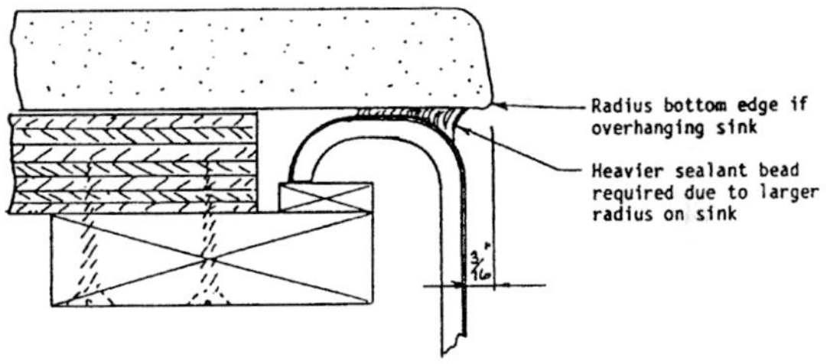

Top overhangs the edge of the sink

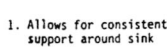

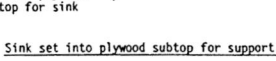

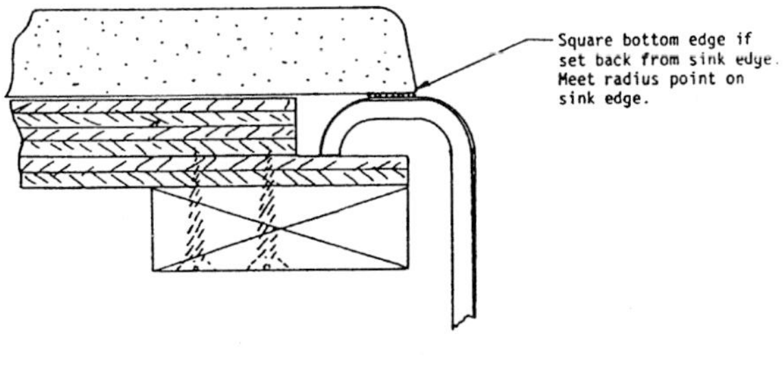

Sink extends past edge of sink hole on counter

POLISHED SINK HOLES
ENAMELED CAST IRON SINKS

STANDARD JOINERY AND CASEWORK DETAILS

Solid Core Wood Flush Doors

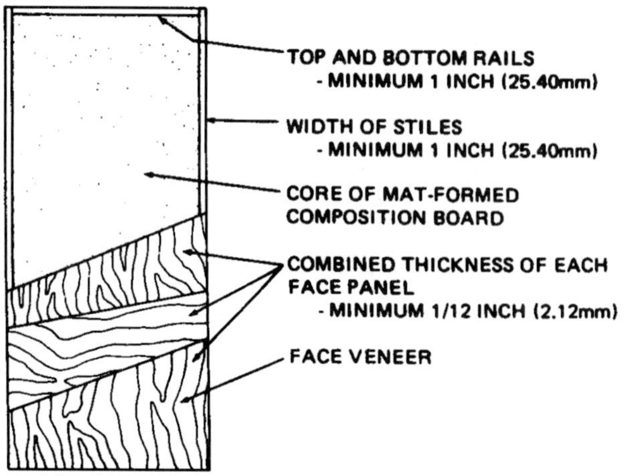

Fig. 6 Mat-formed wood particleboard core (seven-ply construction illustrated)

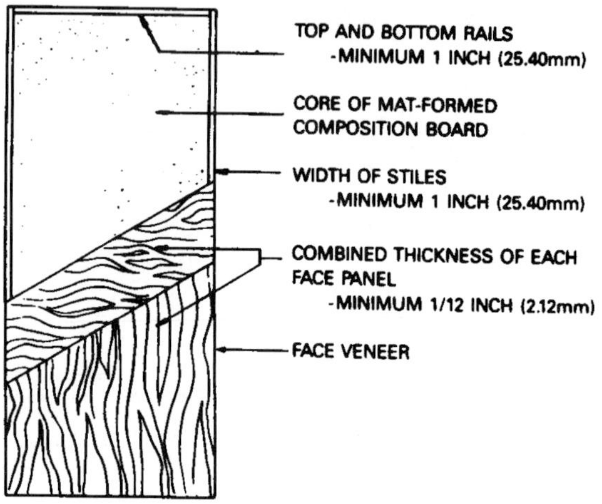

Fig. 7 Mat-formed wood particleboard core (five-ply construction illustrated)

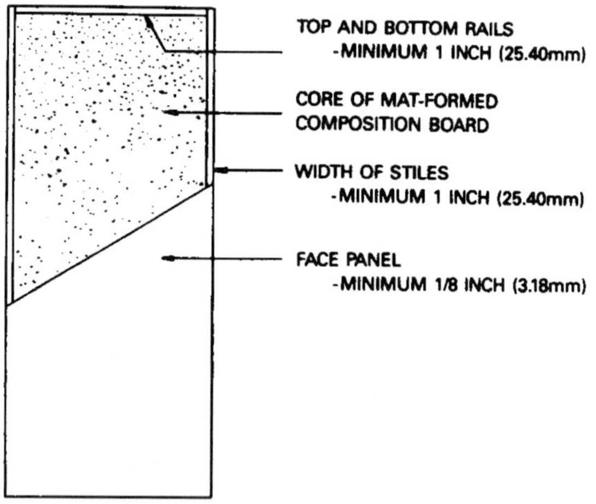

Fig. 8 Mat-formed wood particleboard core (three-ply construction illustrated)

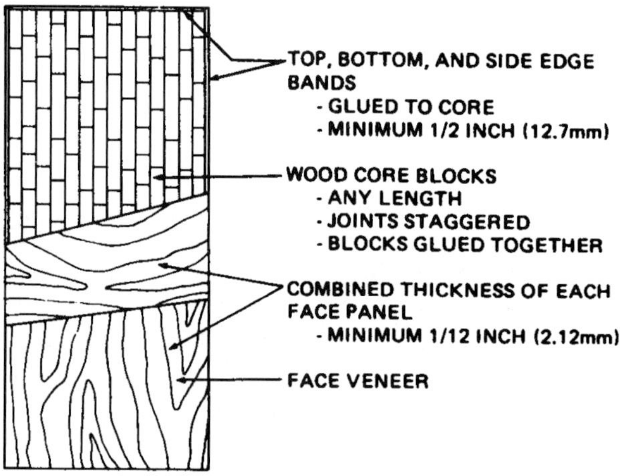

Fig. 9 Glued block core (five-ply construction illustrated)

SOLID CORE WOOD FLUSH DOORS

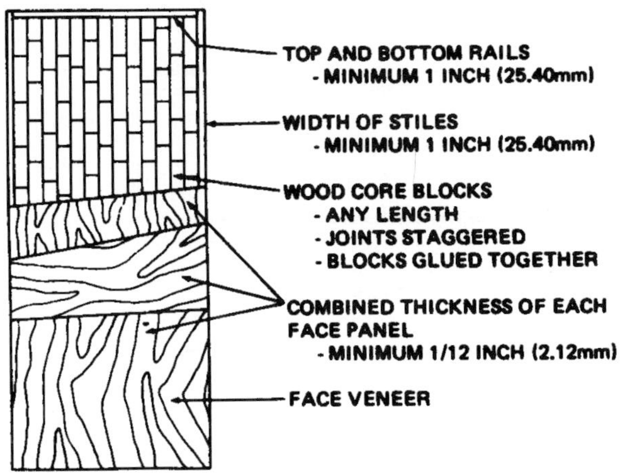

Fig. 10 Framed block glued core (seven-ply construction illustrated)

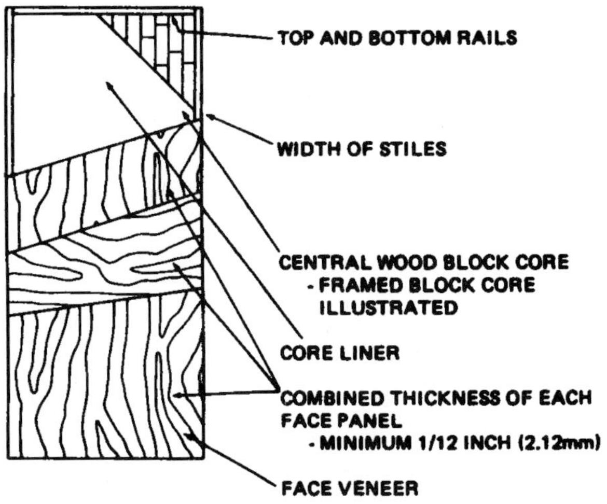

Fig. 11 Wood block lined core (seven-ply construction illustrated)

HOLLOW CORE WOOD FLUSH DOORS

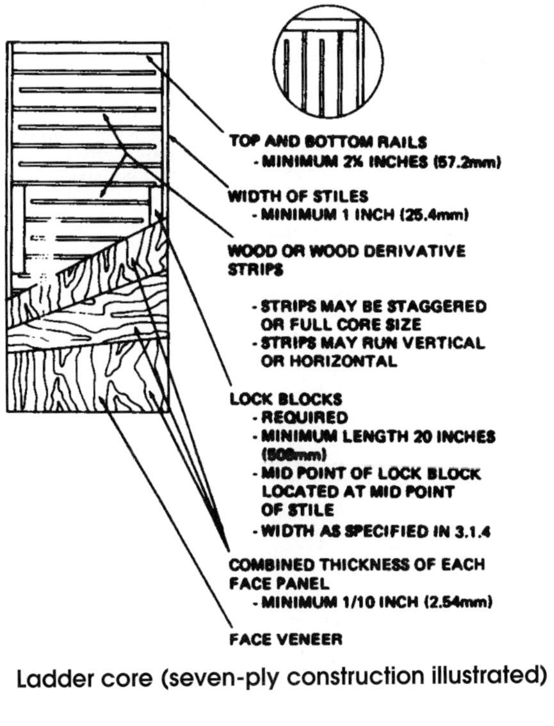

Fig. 12 Ladder core (seven-ply construction illustrated)

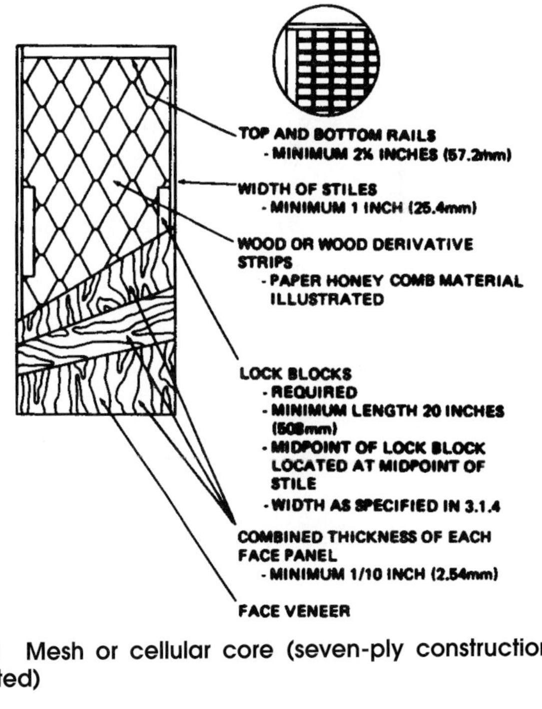

Fig. 13 Mesh or cellular core (seven-ply construction illustrated)

STANDARD JOINERY AND CASEWORK DETAILS
Cabinet Door and Banding Types

a. **FLUSH CABINET DOORS. All WIC Grades.**

TYPE "1"
Veneer/tape banding, 1/16″ maximum.

TYPE "2"
Solid banding.

TYPE "3" — Medium Density Fiberboard.
Banding not required for **Economy and Custom Grades.**
Band required for Premium Grade.

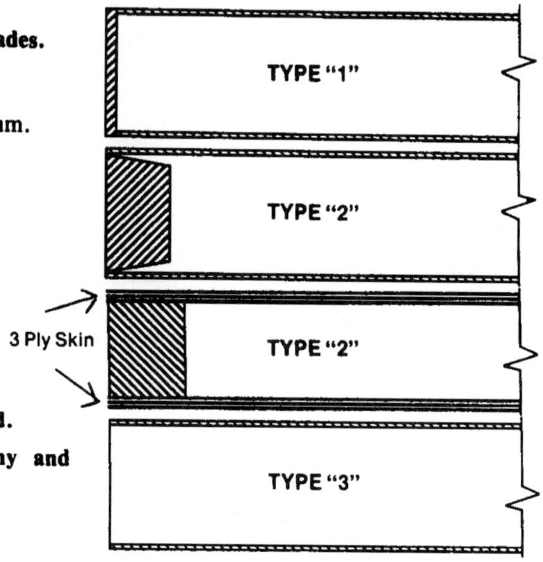

b. **LIPPED CABINET DOORS.**

TYPE "4"
Veneer/tape banding, 1/16″ maximum, required.

TYPE "5"
Solid banding.

TYPE "6" — Medium Density Fiberboard.
Banding not required for **Economy and Custom Grades.**
Band required for Premium Grade.

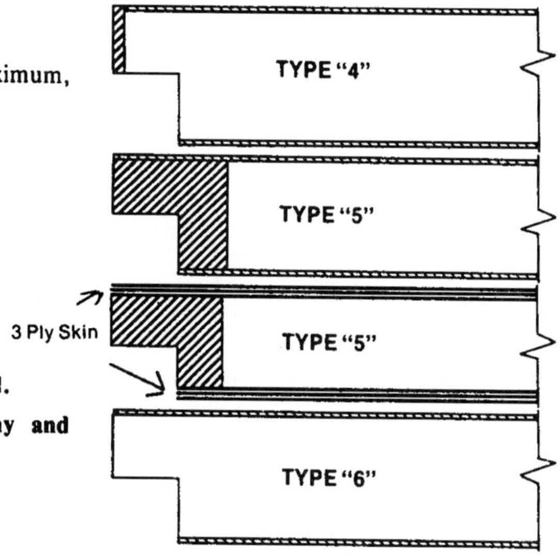

c. **STILE AND RAIL CABINET DOORS. All WIC Grades.**

TYPE "7", S4S Stop.

TYPE "8", Solid Stuck.

TYPE "9", Moulded Stop.

d. **The top and bottom edges of sliding doors do not require an edge band.**

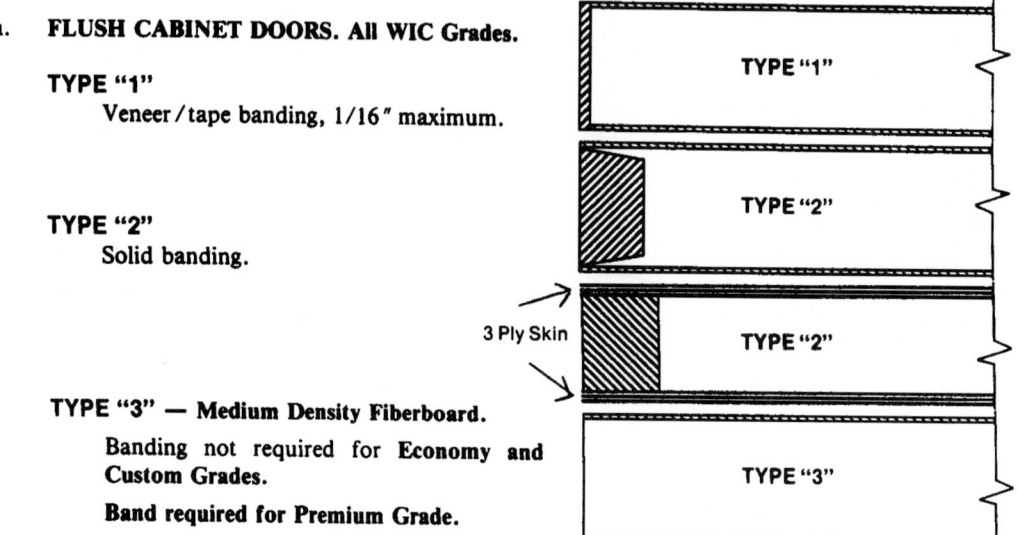

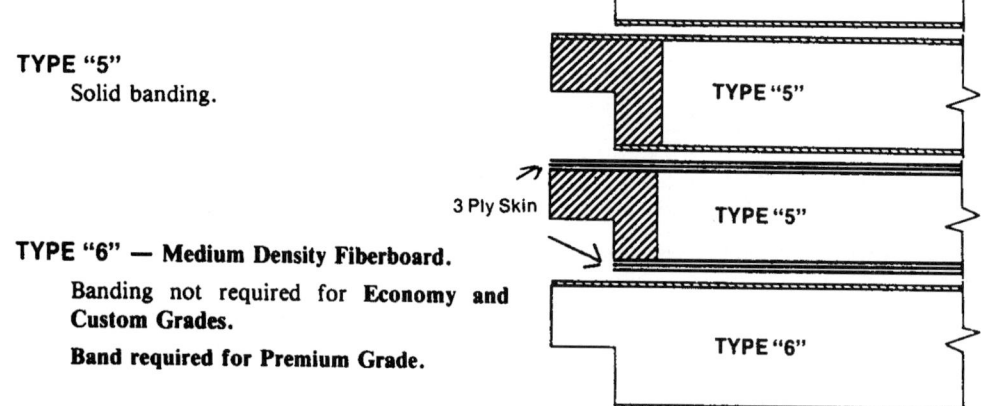

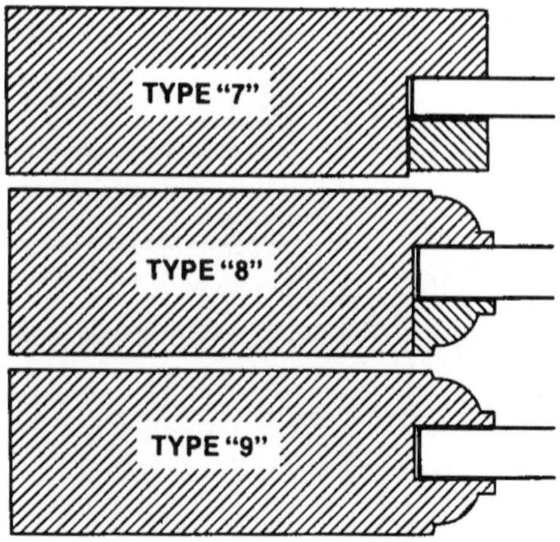

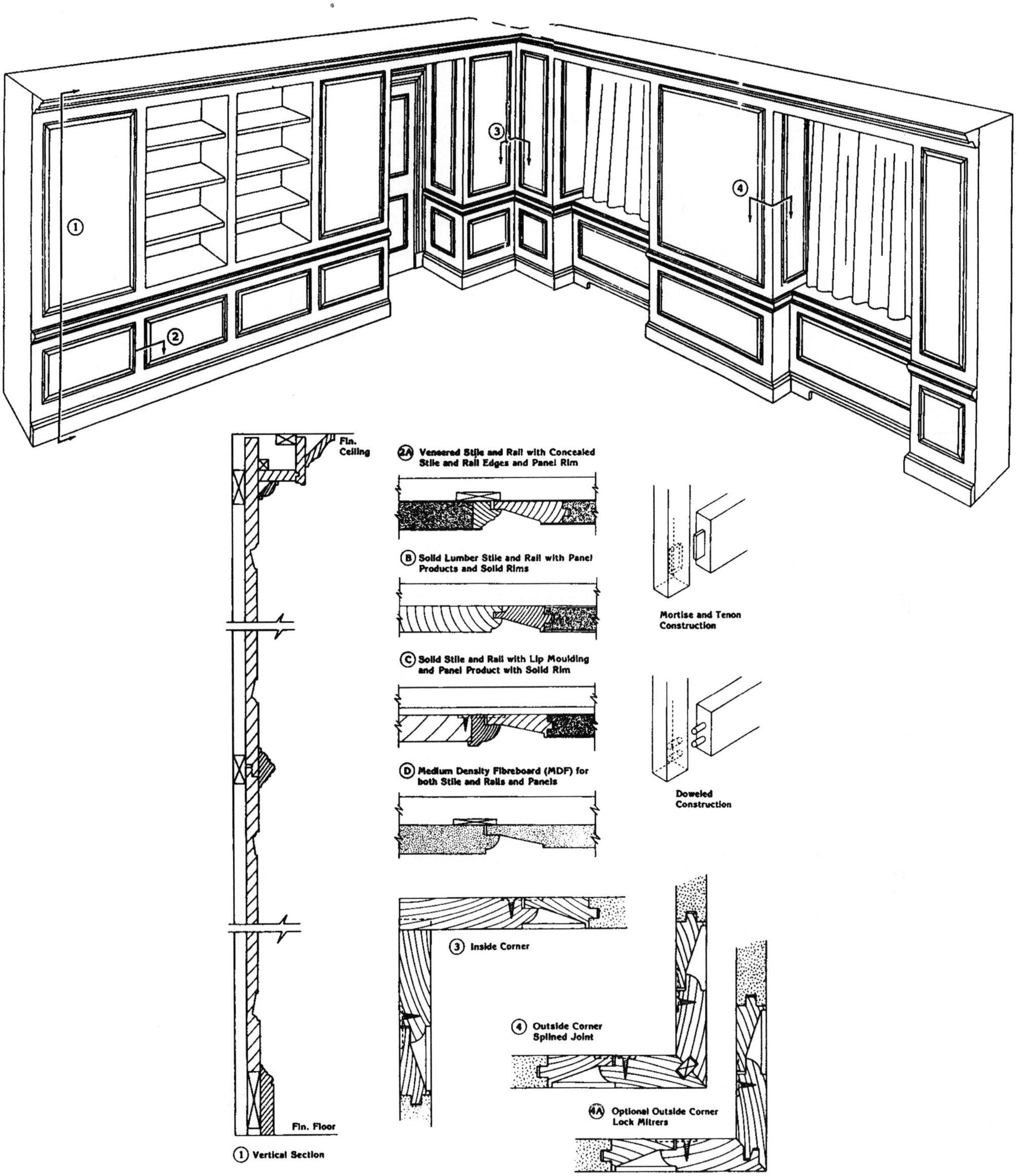

Fig. 14 Full-height stile-and-rail raised paneling. Stile-and-rail wall paneling accented by raised panels creates a beautiful effect of traditional architectural woodwork. Framed within the stiles and rails and accented by the shadow lines, this construction offers limitless opportunities for various effects through the use of different wood species and veneer cuts. Each design creates a unique atmosphere, complemented by the finely proportioned paneling

STANDARD JOINERY AND CASEWORK DETAILS

Paneled Wainscot and Doors

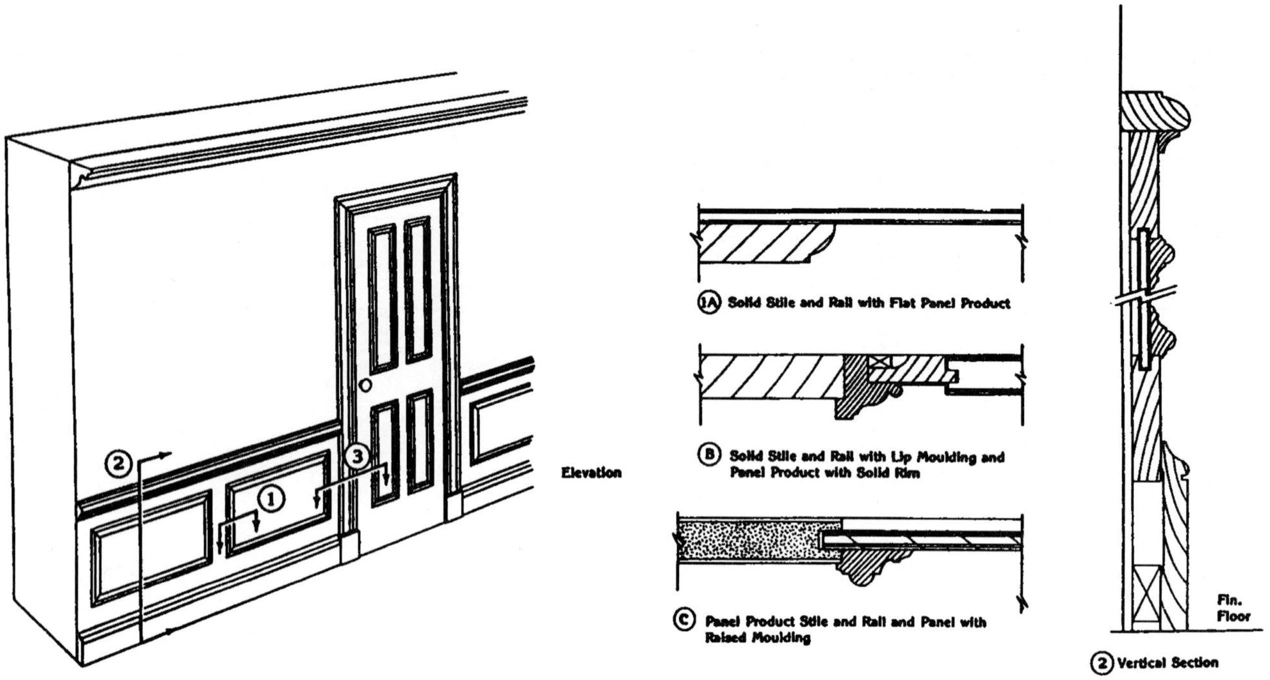

Fig. 15 Flat paneled wainscot. Flat panels set within the frame of the stile and rail create a rich effect of traditional architectural woodwork. Different results can be produced through the use of veneer selections with transparent finish or painted finishes chosen by the architect or designer

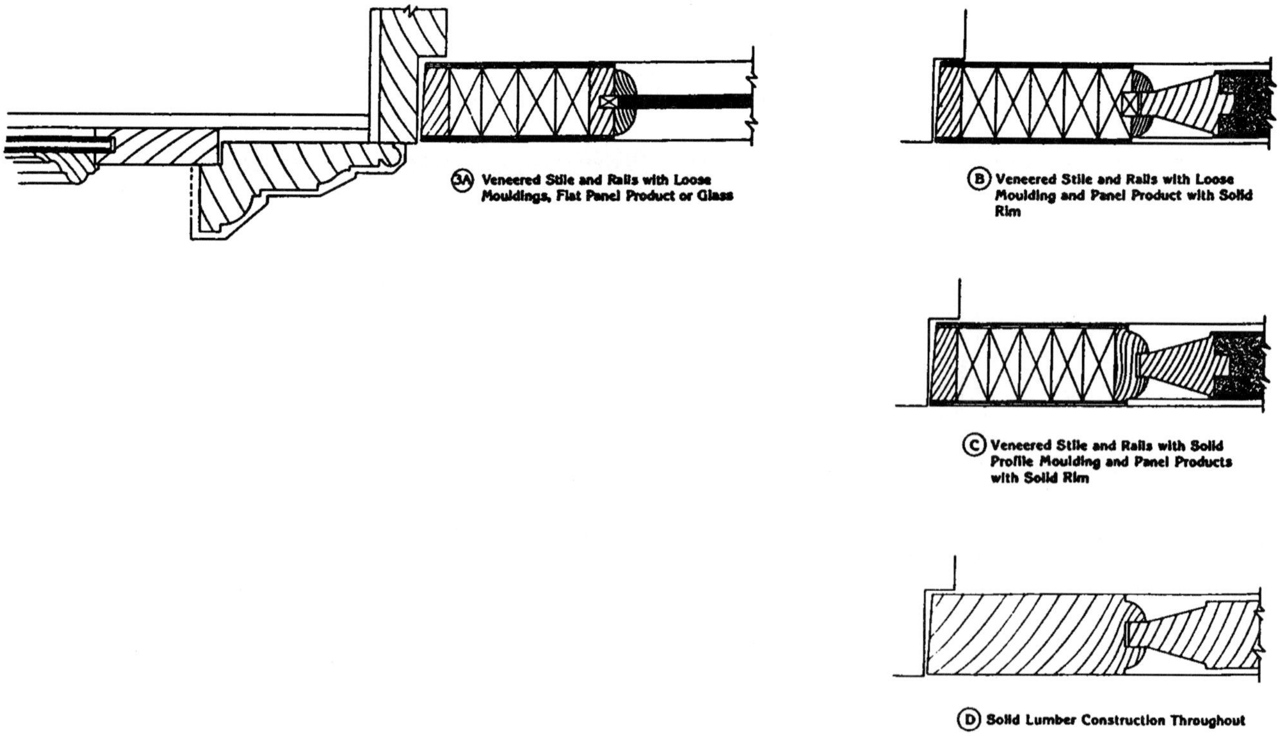

Fig. 16 Paneled doors. Stile-and-rail doors designed to accent the adjacent wall paneling, whether traditional or contemporary or used alone, beautify an entryway or area

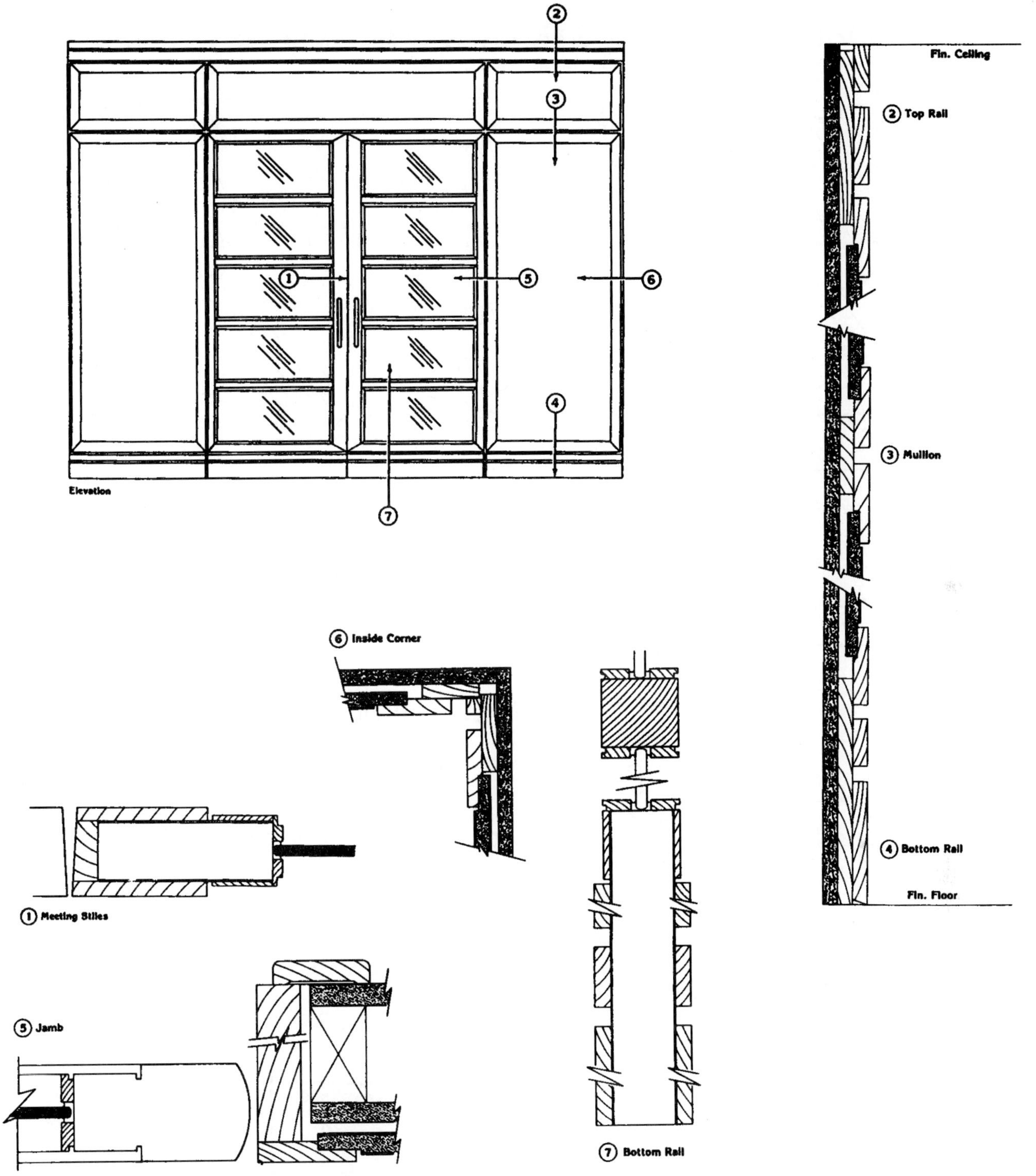

Fig. 17 Full-height contemporary raised paneling. This design, distinguished by its simplicity, is a contemporary expression of the stile-and-rail construction

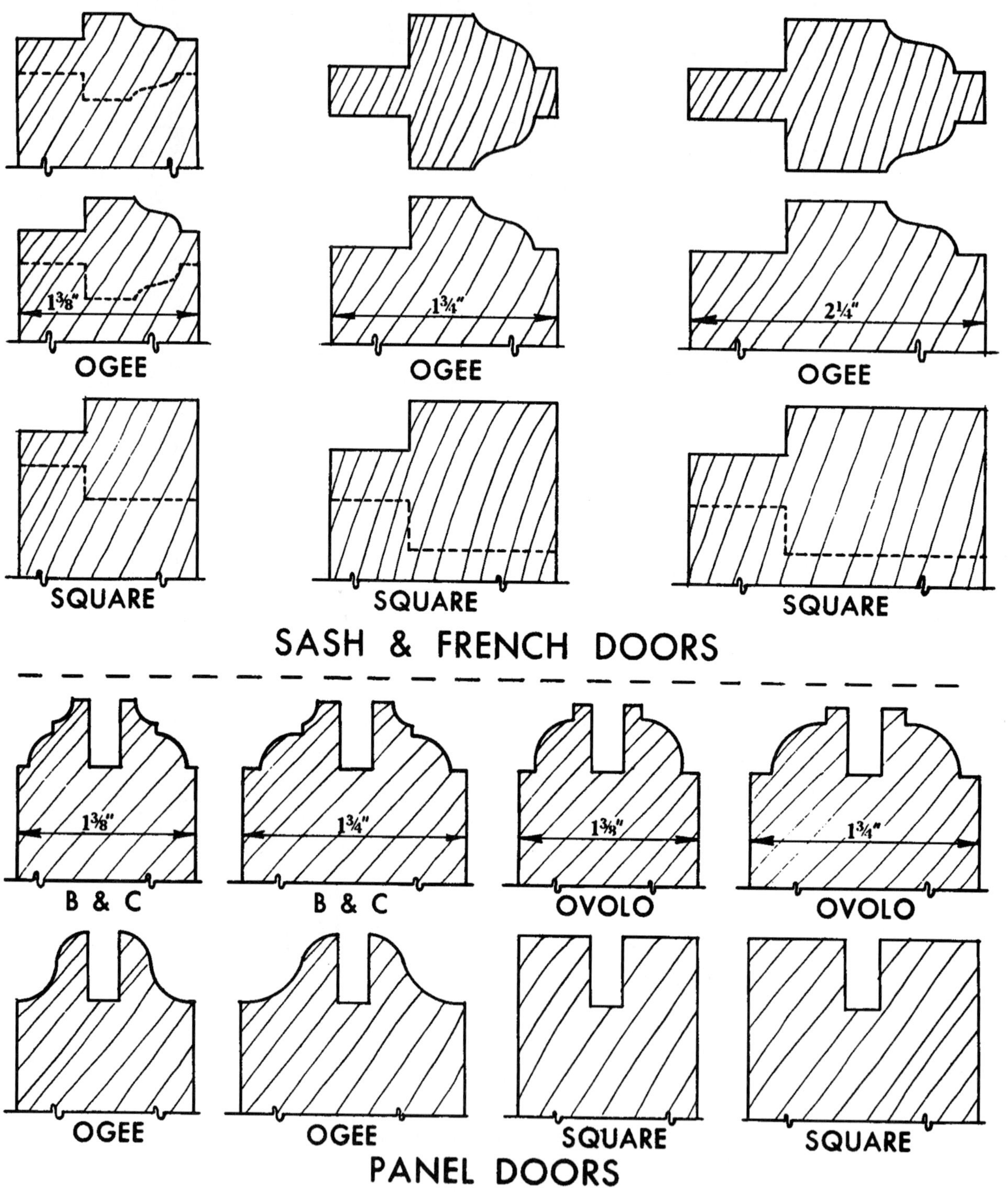
PROFILES OF STOCK STICKING FOR SASH & DOORS
1⅜"
OGEE
1¾"
OGEE
2¼"
OGEE
SQUARE
SQUARE
SQUARE
SASH & FRENCH DOORS
1⅜"
B & C
1¾"
B & C
1⅜"
OVOLO
1¾"
OVOLO
OGEE
OGEE
SQUARE
SQUARE
PANEL DOORS

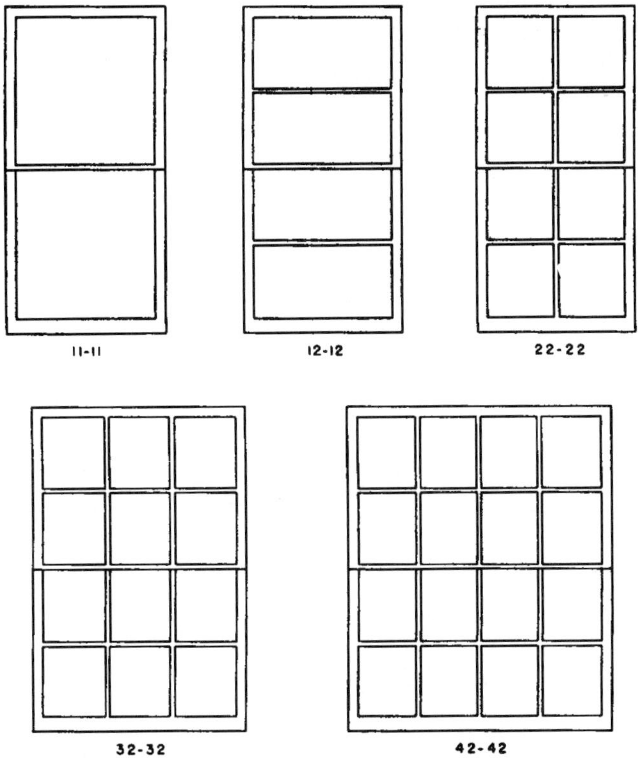

Fig. 18 Double-hung windows: stock designs. Standard widths are 1 ft 6 in, 2 ft 0 in, 2 ft 6 in, 3 ft 0 in, 3 ft 6 in, 4 ft 0 in, 4 ft 6 in, and 5 ft 0 in. Standard heights are 2 ft 0 in, 2 ft 6 in, 3 ft 0 in, 3 ft 6 in, 4 ft 0 in, 4 ft 6 in, 5 ft 1 in, 5 ft 6 in, and 6 ft 0 in. Standard thicknesses are 1⅜ and 1¾ in. Stock thickness is 1⅜ in. Standard glazing is s.s.b. glass—not bedded

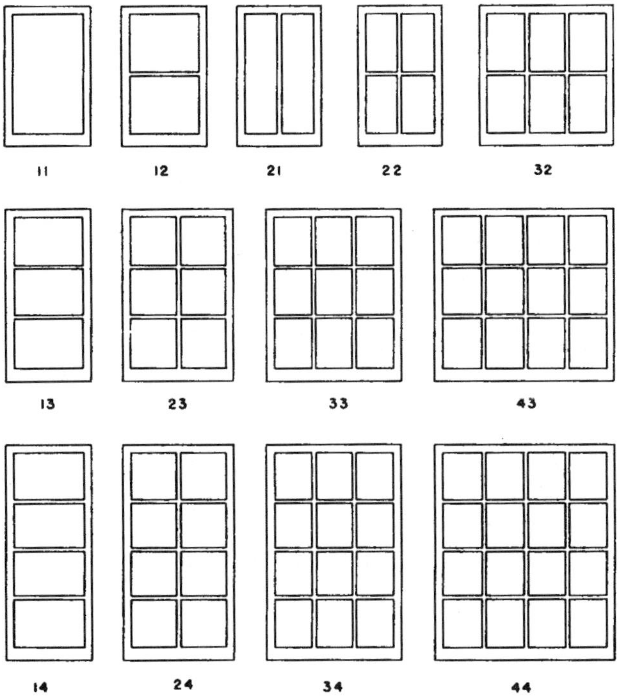

Fig. 19 Single sash: stock designs. Standard widths are 2 ft 0 in, 2 ft 6 in, 3 ft 0 in, 3 ft 6 in, 4 ft 0 in, 4 ft 6 in, 5 ft 0 in, 5 ft 6 in and 6 ft 0 in. Standard heights are 2 ft 0 in, 2 ft 6 in, 3 ft 0 in, 3 ft 6 in, 4 ft 0 in, 4 ft 6 in, 5 ft 1 in, 5 ft 6 in, 6 ft 0 in, 6 ft 6 in, and 7 ft 0 in. Standard thicknesses are 1⅜ and 1¾ in. Stock thickness is 1⅜ in. Standard glazing is s.s.b. glass—not bedded

STANDARD JOINERY AND CASEWORK DETAILS

Casement Windows

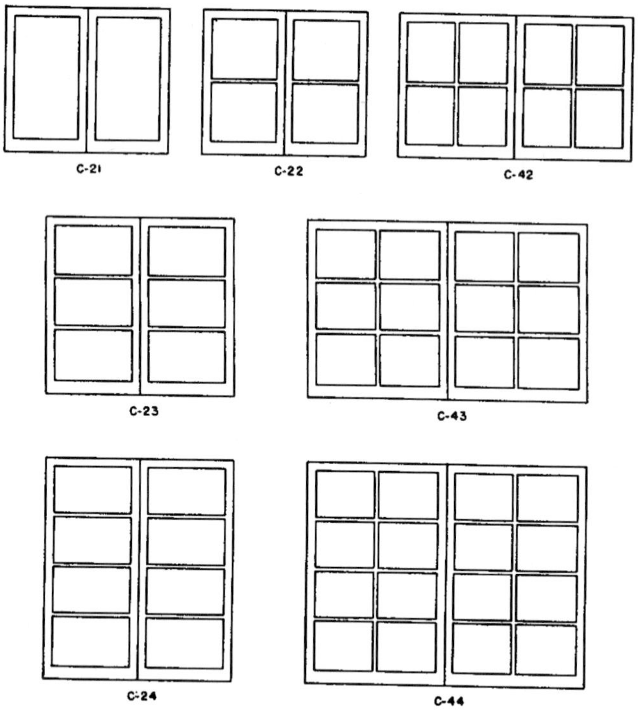

Fig. 20 Casements in pairs: stock designs. Standard widths are 2 ft 6 in, 3 ft 0 in, 3 ft 6 in, 4 ft 0 in, 4 ft 6 in, and 5 ft 0 in. Standard heights are 2 ft 0 in, 2 ft 6 in, 3 ft 0 in, 3 ft 6 in, 4 ft 0 in, 4 ft 6 in, 5 ft 1 in, 5 ft 6 in, and 6 ft 0 in. Standard thicknesses are 1⅜ and 1¾ in. Stock thickness is 1⅜ in. Standard glazing is s.s.b. glass—not bedded

Fig. 21 Windows and sash: typical diamond light cutups

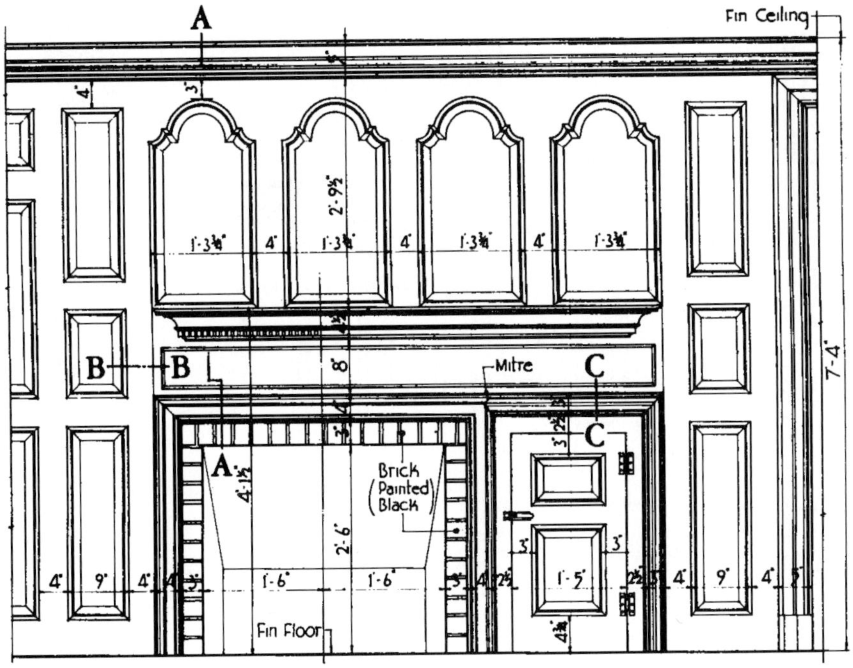

A
Fin Ceiling
B
B
Mitre
C
C
A
Brick (Painted) Black
Fin Floor
ELEVATION ·
Scale: ½" = 1' - 0"
B — B
3" = 1' - 0"
C — C
3" = 1' - 0"
Cornice
· Wall · Board
· Blocking
TYPICAL PANEL HEAD
℄ · of Panel
· Dotted Lines Indicate ⅜" Face of Rails at Side of Fireplace ·
· Face · of Brick
DETAIL · ON · LINE · A – A

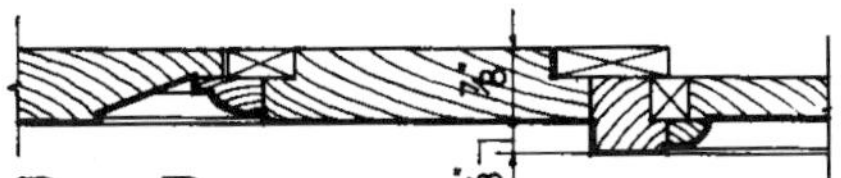

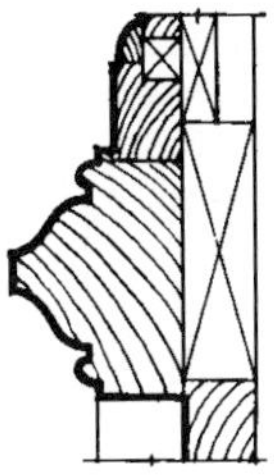

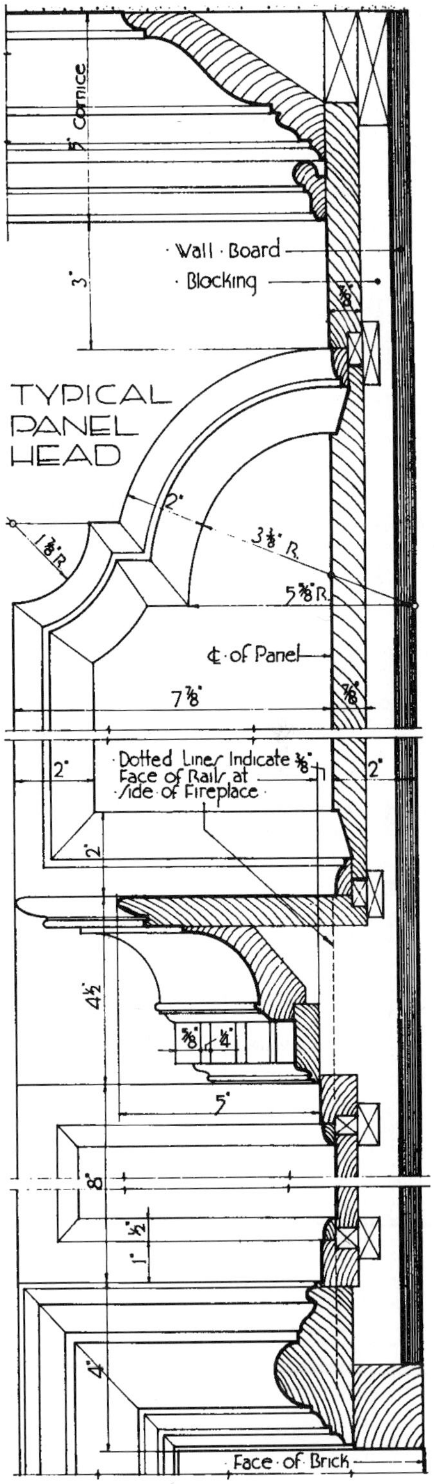

WOODWORK DETAILS

Wood Paneling

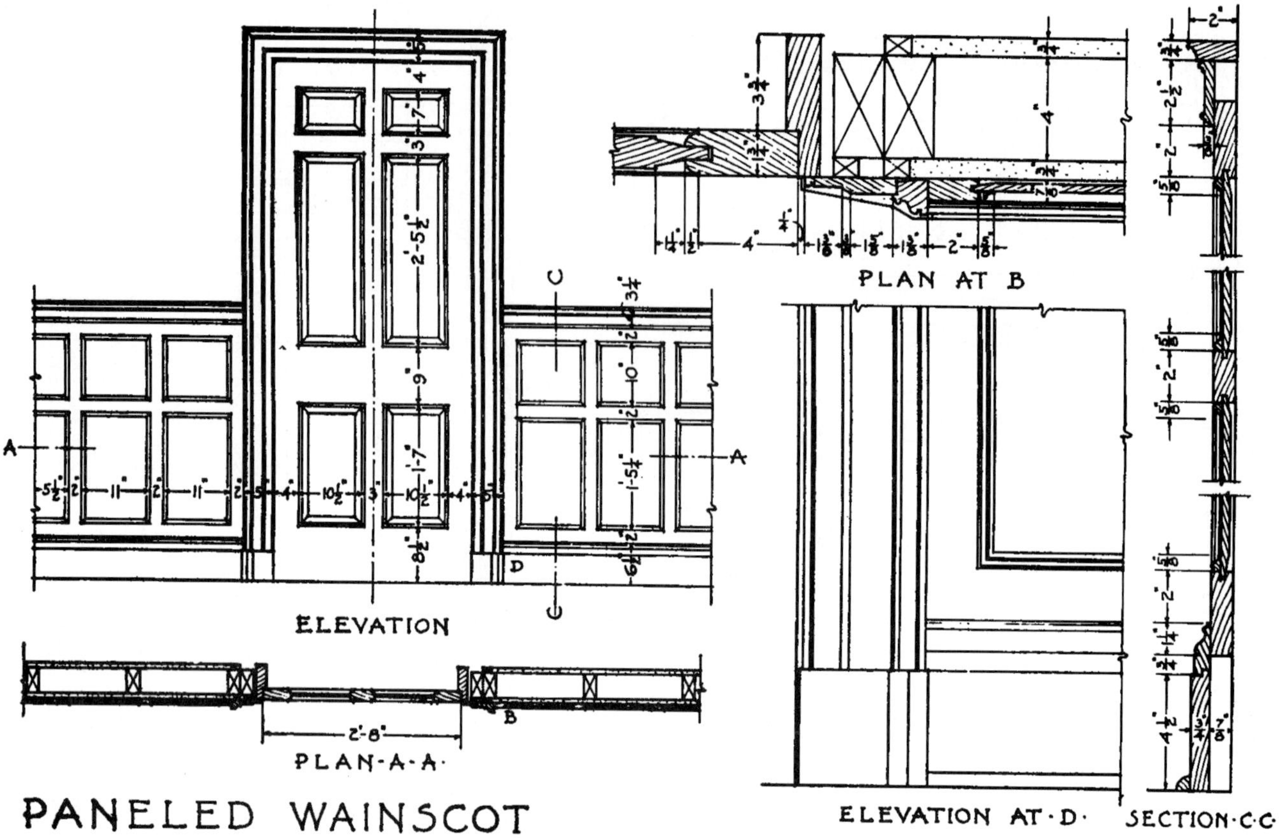

PANELED WAINSCOT

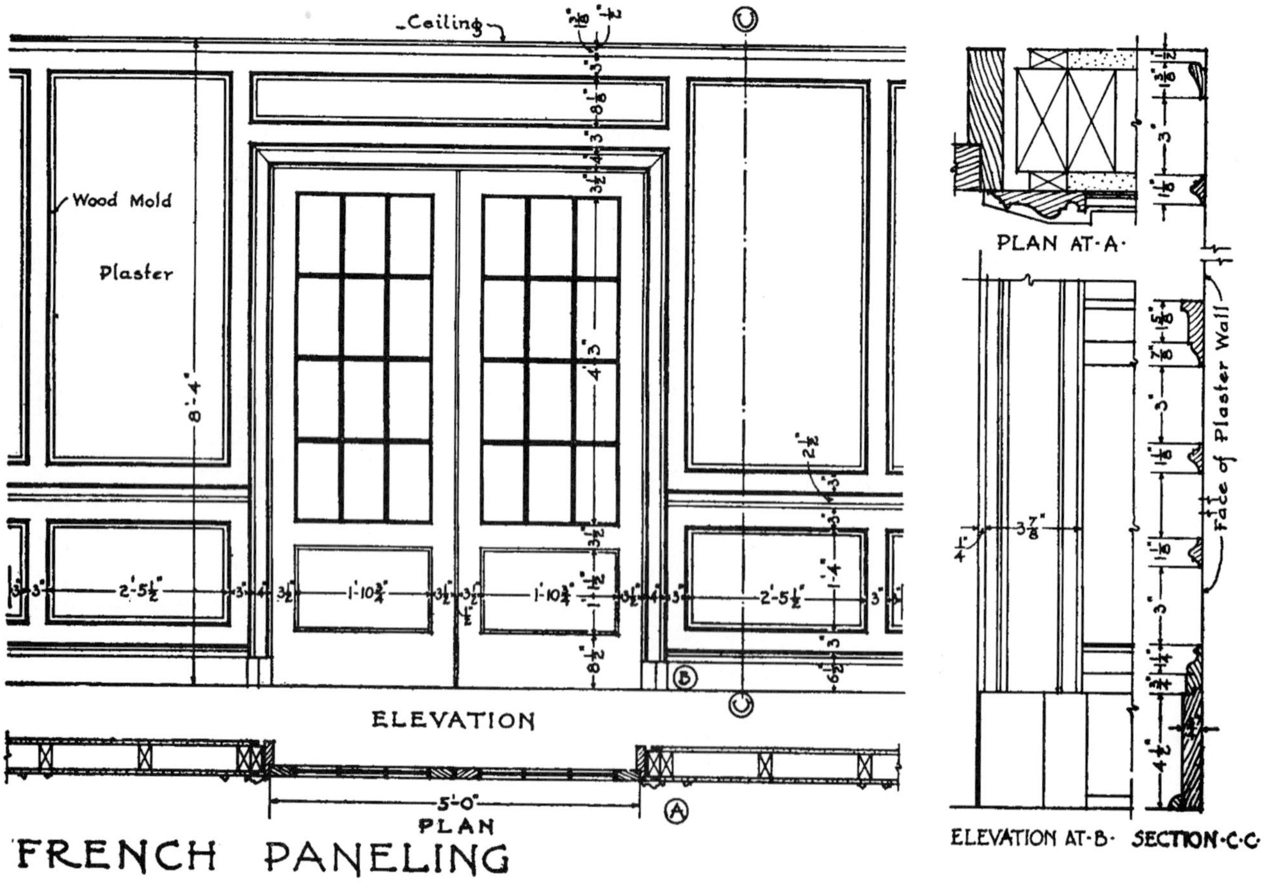

FRENCH PANELING

fin ceiling
"A"
Notch Carving
"A"
8'-0½"
1'-0¼"
1'-1¼"
1'-2¼"
"B"
"C" "C"
W I Hinges
6"
6"
2'-3"
⅞" shelf
fin floor
"B"
ELEVATION
Scale : ¾" = 1'—0"
2'-9"
2'-9"
equal
equal
equal
2'-2⅜"
3'-10⅝"
PLAN
¾" = 1'-0"

SECTION
"A-A"
Carving
SECT
"C - C"
top of cut-out
SECTION
"B-B"
Note:
Scale of Sections is half full Size

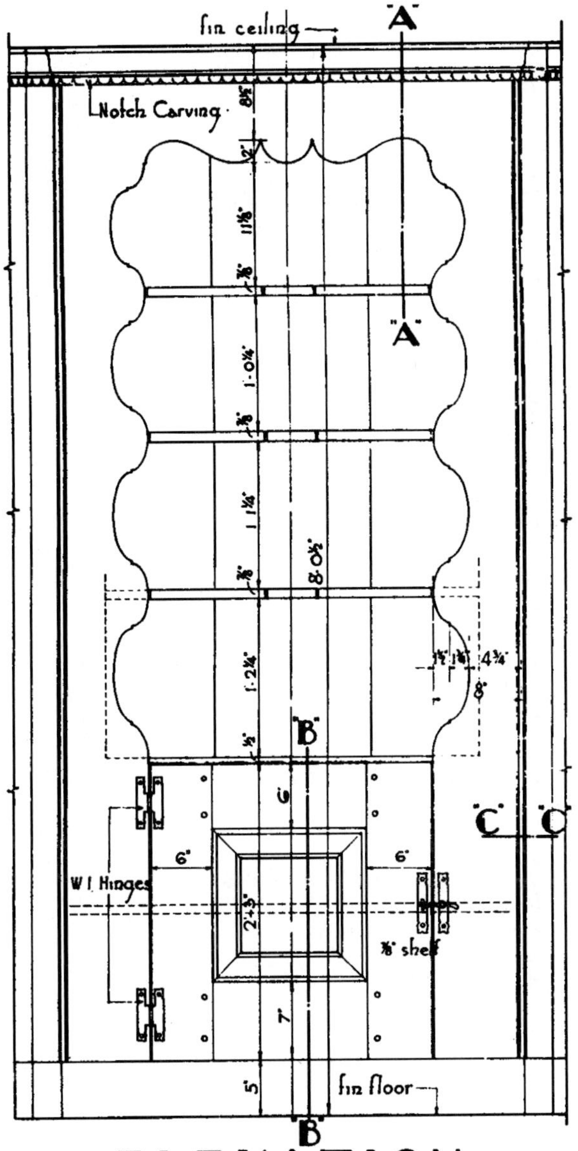

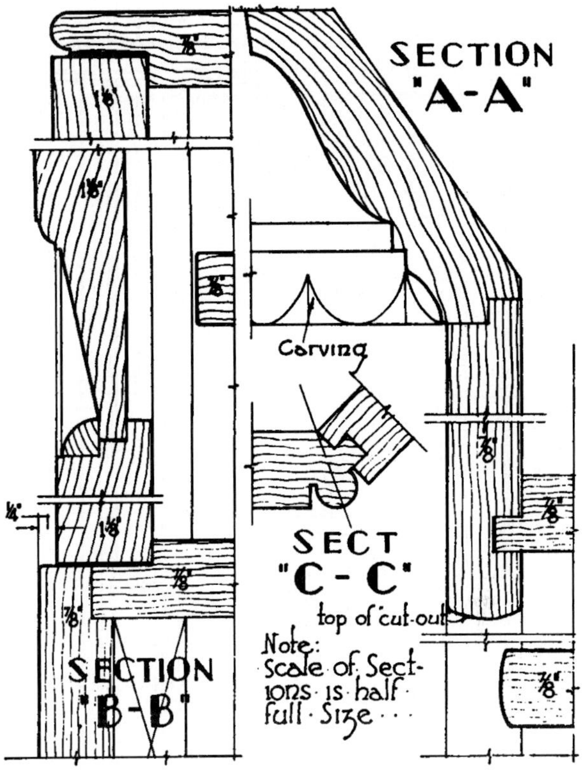

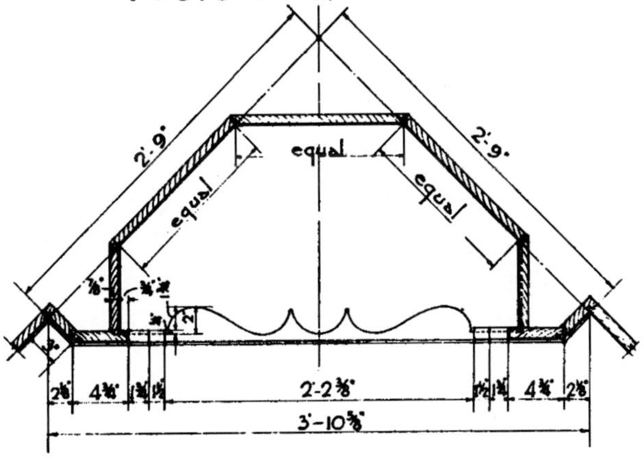

WOODWORK DETAILS
Corner Cupboard

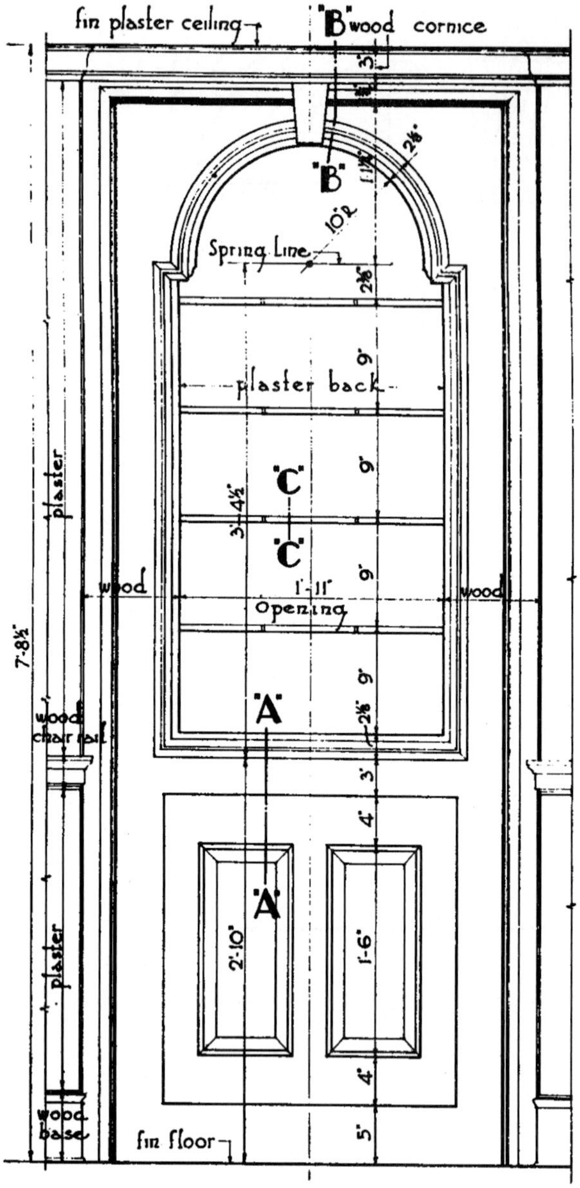

ELEVATION
Scale 3/4" - 1'—0"

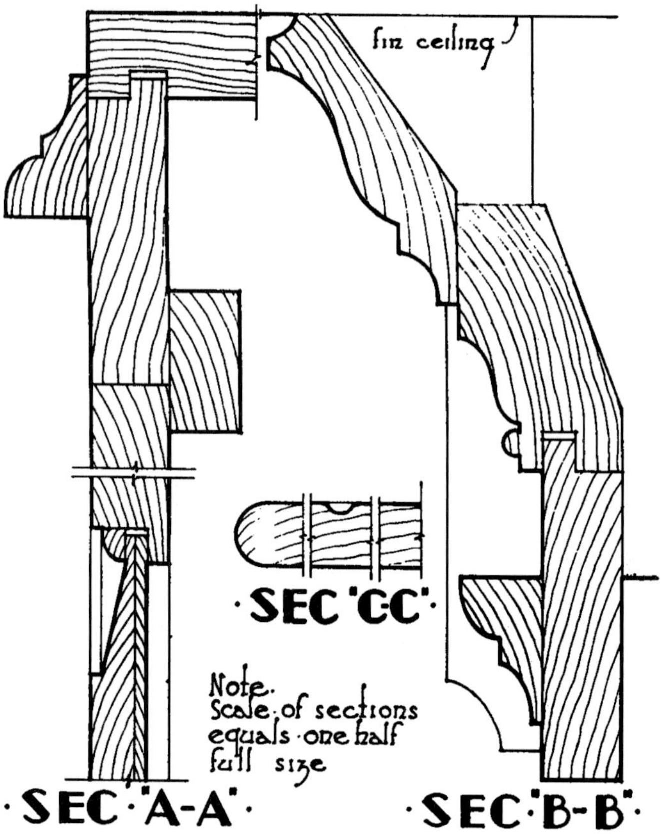

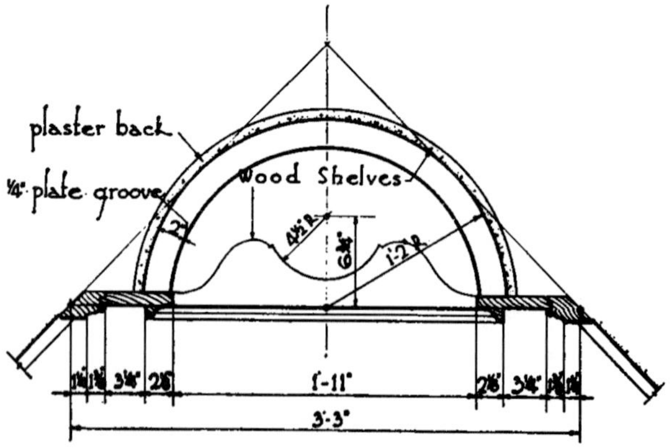

PLAN
3/4" - 1'-0"

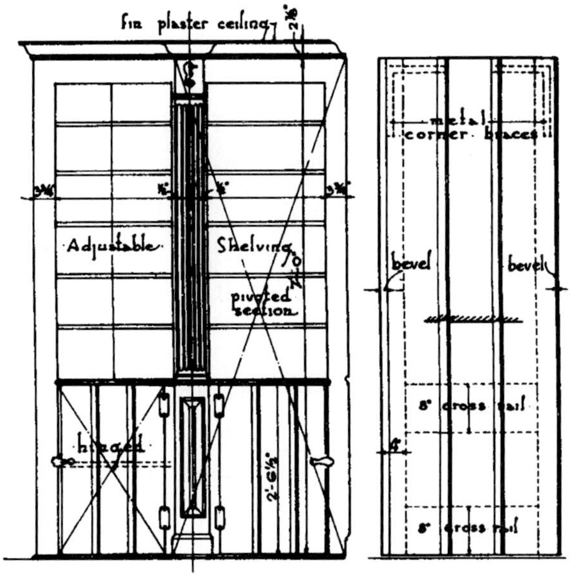

·3/8" SCALE·ELEVATION· ·DOOR·BACK·
Showing book shelving and secret Door to a silver closet · · ·

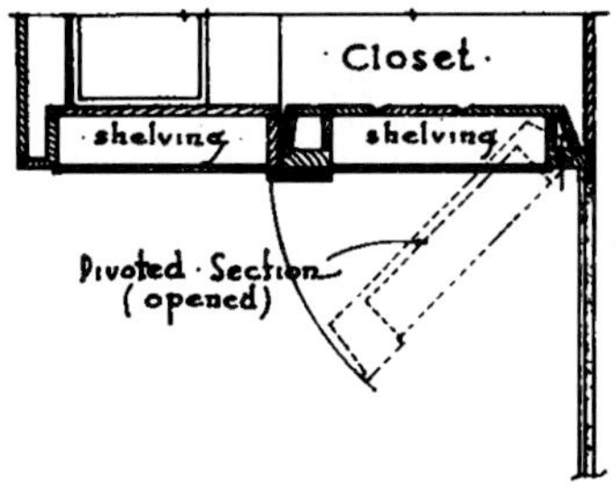

·3/8" SCALE PLAN· of ·BOOK·SHELVES· ·&·SECRET·DOOR·

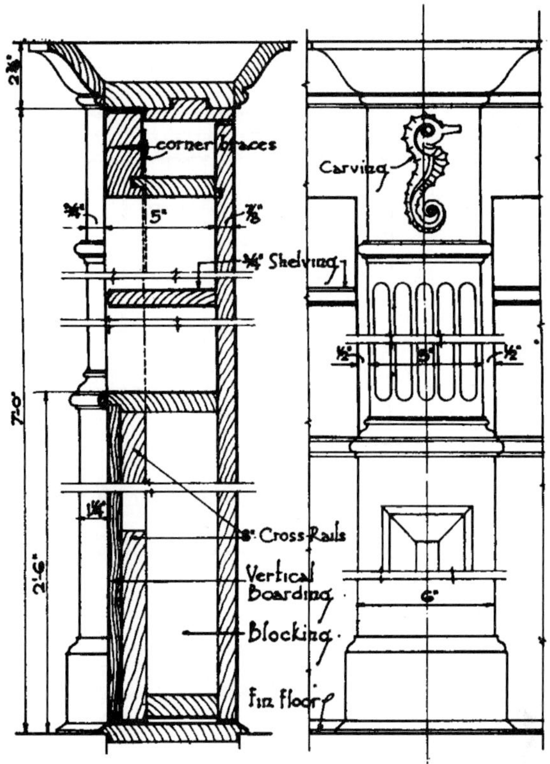

·VERTICAL·SECTION· ·THROUGH·DOOR· ·ELEVATION· OF PILASTER
·Scale: 1½" = 1'-0"

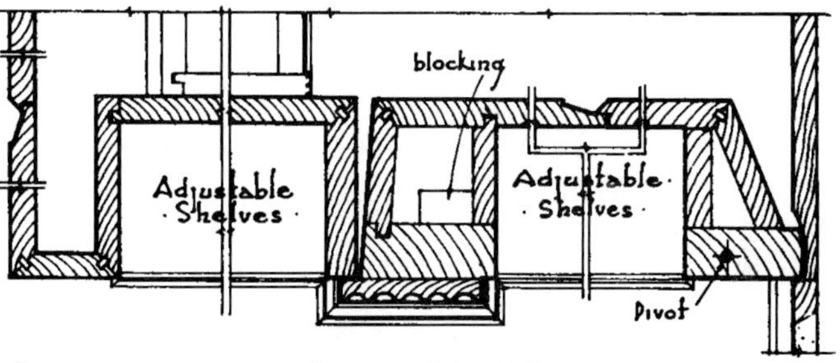

·SECTION ON·LINE·"A-A"·THRU·SHELVING·
Scale : 1½" = 1'—0"

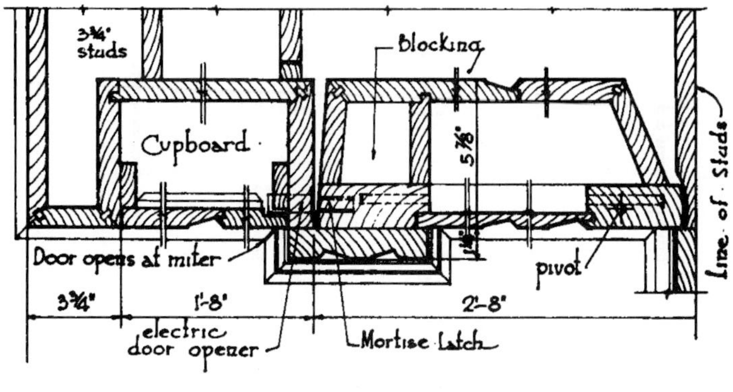

·SECTION·ON·LINE·"B-B"·THRU·CUPBOARD·
Scale: 1½" — 1'—0"

WOODWORK DETAILS

Bookcases

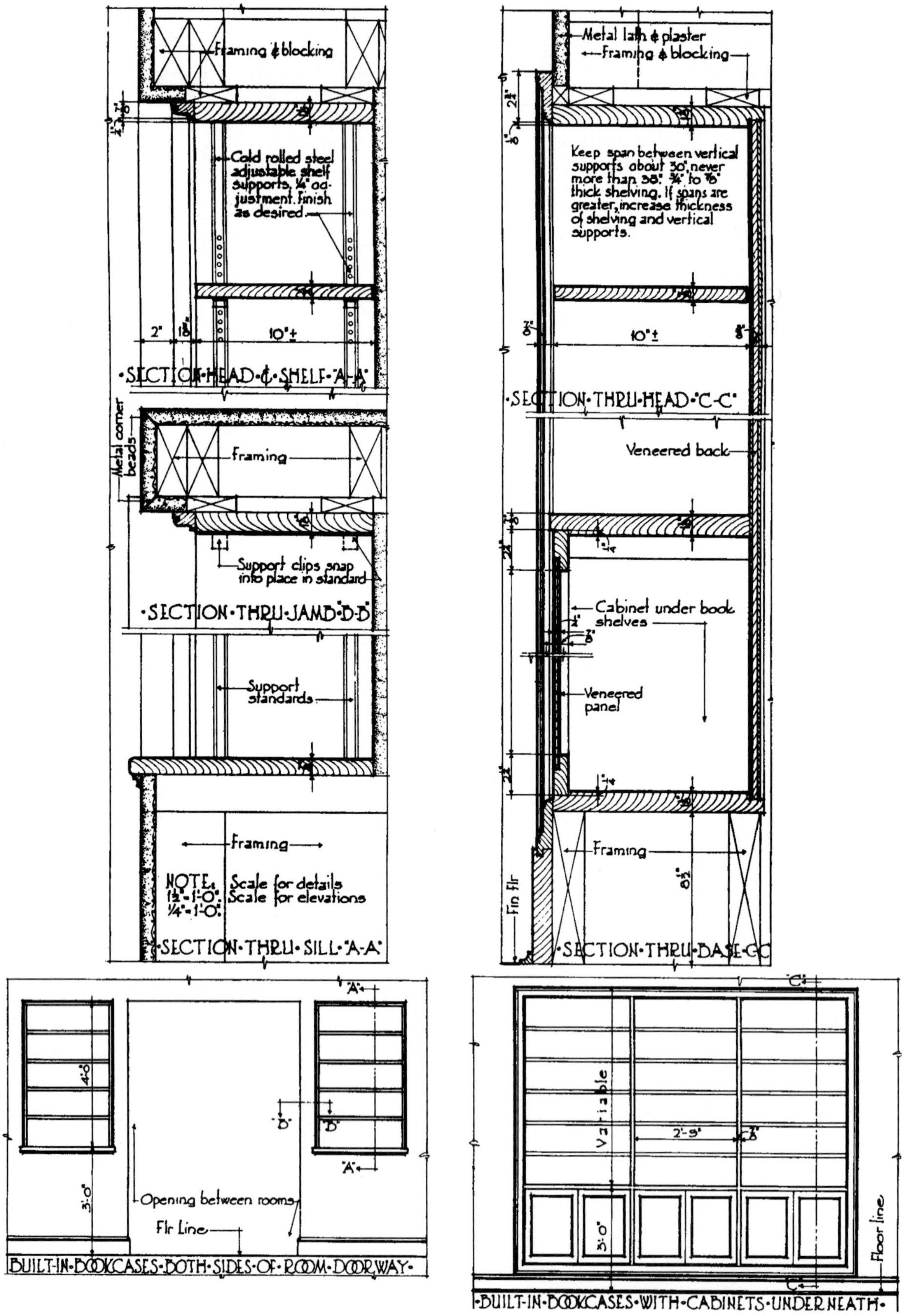
Framing & blocking
Cold rolled steel adjustable shelf supports, ¼" adjustment. Finish as desired
2"
10"±
·SECTION·HEAD·&·SHELF·"A-A"·
Metal corner beads
Framing
Support clips snap into place in standard
·SECTION·THRU·JAMB·"D-D"·
Support standards
Framing
NOTE: 1½"=1'-0". Scale for details
¼"=1'-0". Scale for elevations
·SECTION·THRU·SILL·"A-A"·
Metal lath & plaster
Framing & blocking
Keep span between vertical supports about 30", never more than 38". ¾" to ⅞" thick shelving. If spans are greater, increase thickness of shelving and vertical supports.
10"±
·SECTION·THRU·HEAD·"C-C"·
Veneered back
Cabinet under book shelves
Veneered panel
Framing
Fin Flr
·SECTION·THRU·BASE·C-C·
4'-0"
3'-0"
Opening between rooms
Flr Line
BUILT-IN·BOOKCASES·BOTH·SIDES·OF·ROOM·DOORWAY·
Variable
2'-9"
3'-0"
Floor line
·BUILT-IN·BOOKCASES·WITH·CABINETS·UNDERNEATH·

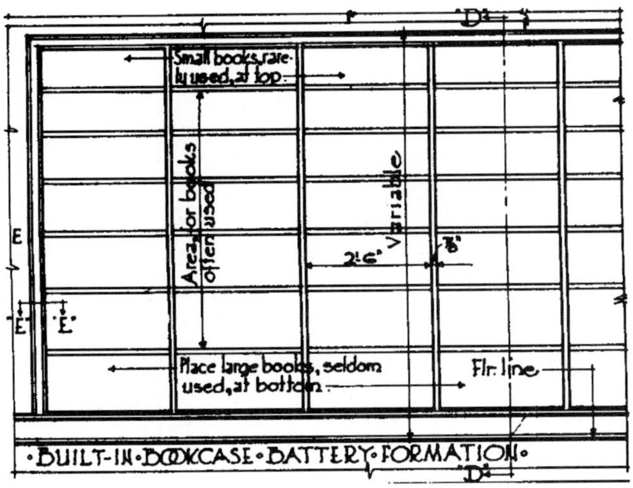
Small books,rarely used,at top
Area for books often used
Variable
2'-6"
Place large books, seldom used,at bottom
Flr. line
•BUILT-IN•BOOKCASE•BATTERY•FORMATION•
"D"
"E"

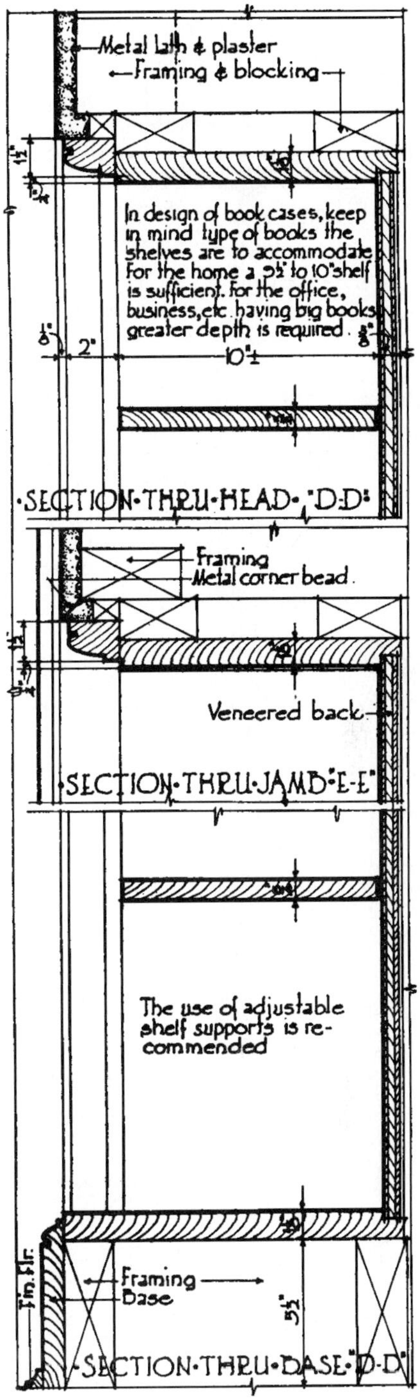
Metal lath & plaster
Framing & blocking
In design of book cases, keep in mind type of books the shelves are to accommodate. For the home a 9½" to 10" shelf is sufficient. For the office, business,etc. having big books greater depth is required.
2"
10"±
•SECTION•THRU•HEAD• "D-D"
Framing
Metal corner bead.
Veneered back
•SECTION•THRU•JAMB•"E-E"
The use of adjustable shelf supports is recommended
Fin. flr.
Framing
Base
•SECTION•THRU•BASE•"D-D"

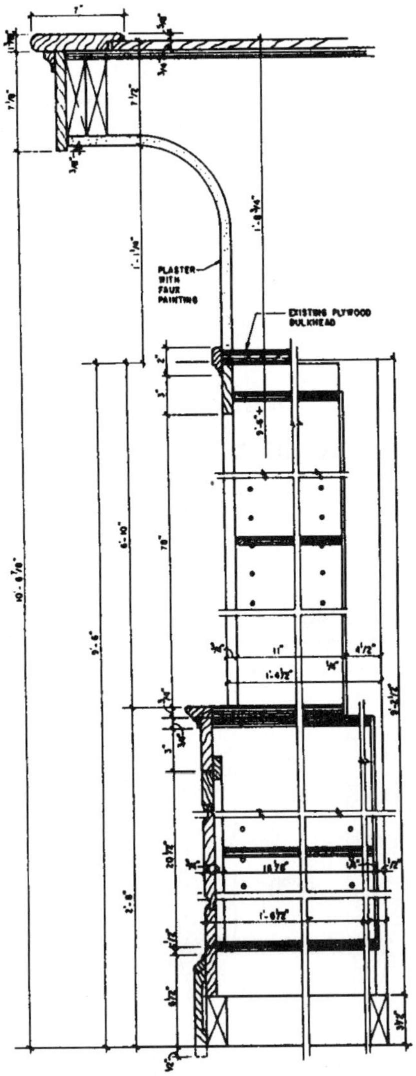
PLASTER WITH FAUX PAINTING
EXISTING PLYWOOD BULKHEAD

SECTION - BOOKCASE UNIT

WOODWORK DETAILS

Wall Cabinet and Paneling Details

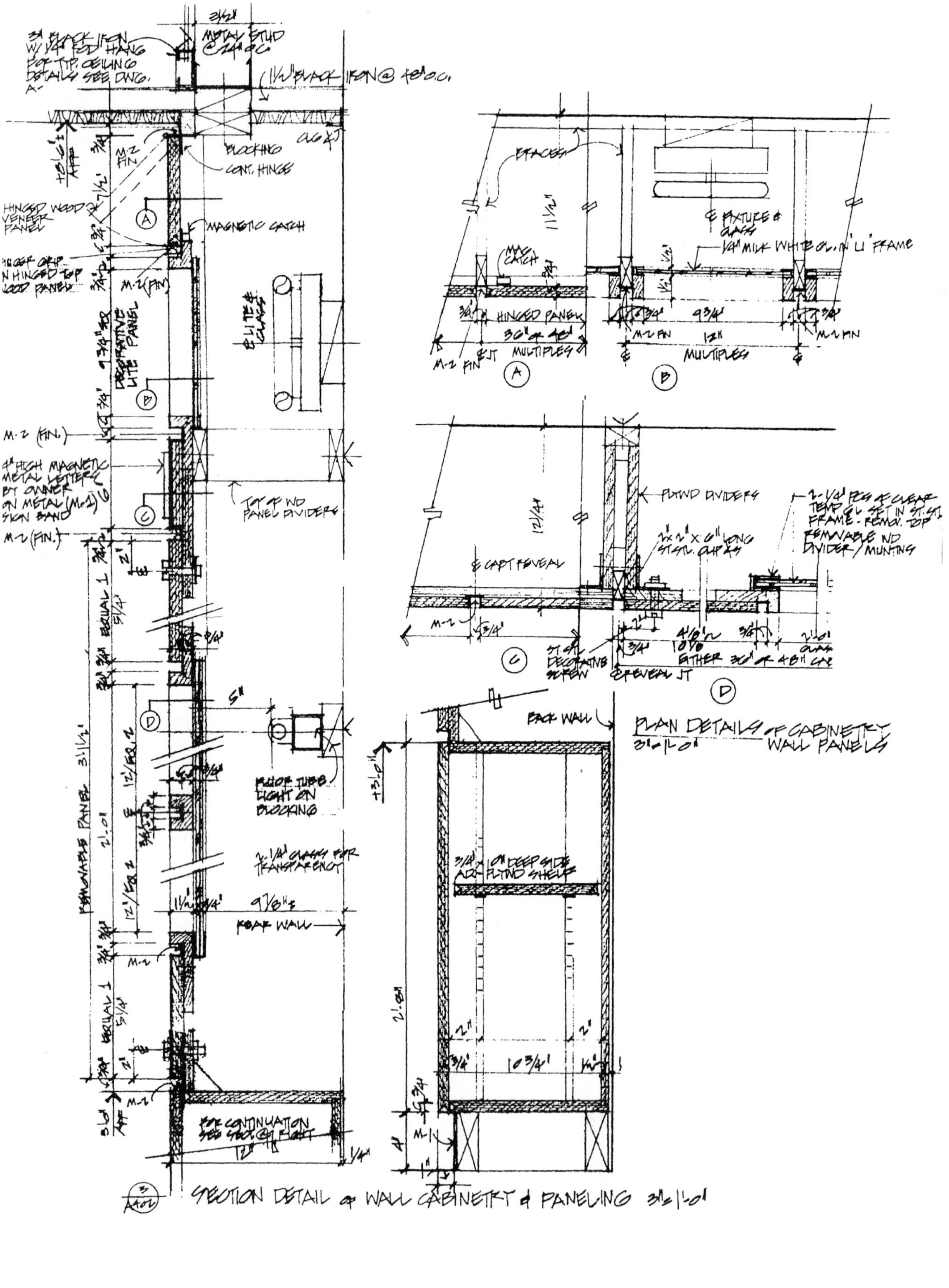

WOODWORK DETAILS

Coat Closet with Base Cabinet

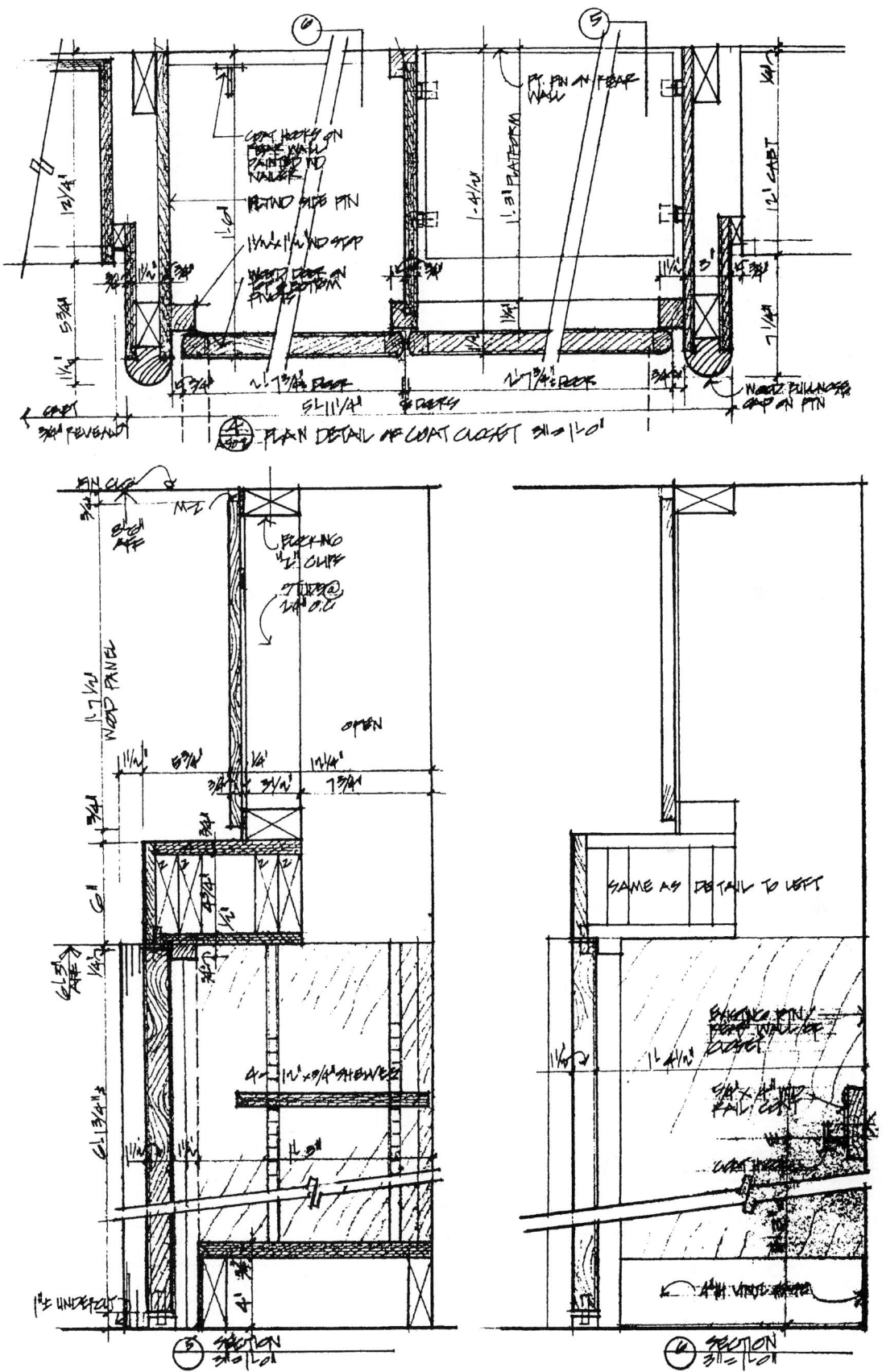

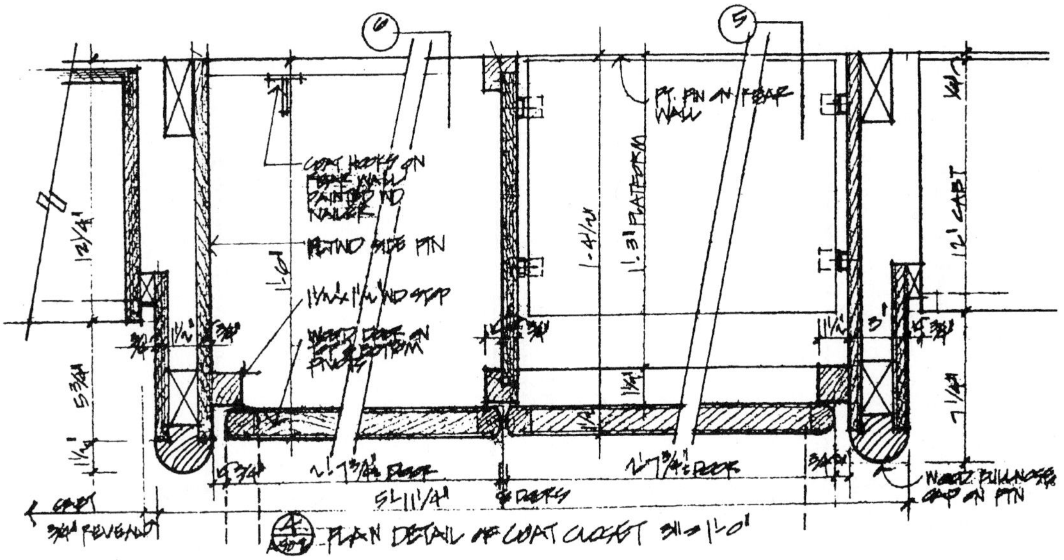

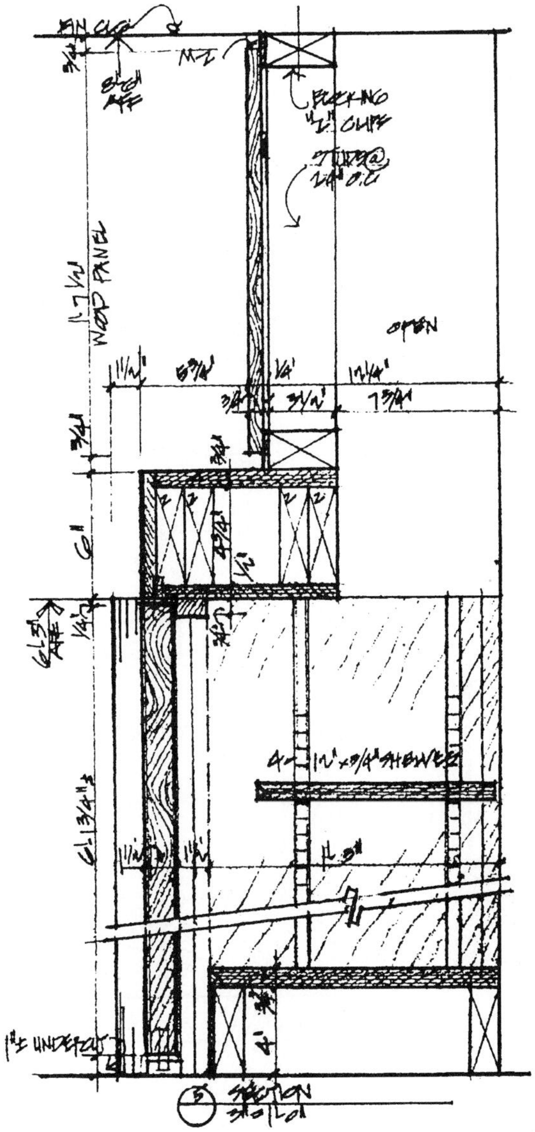

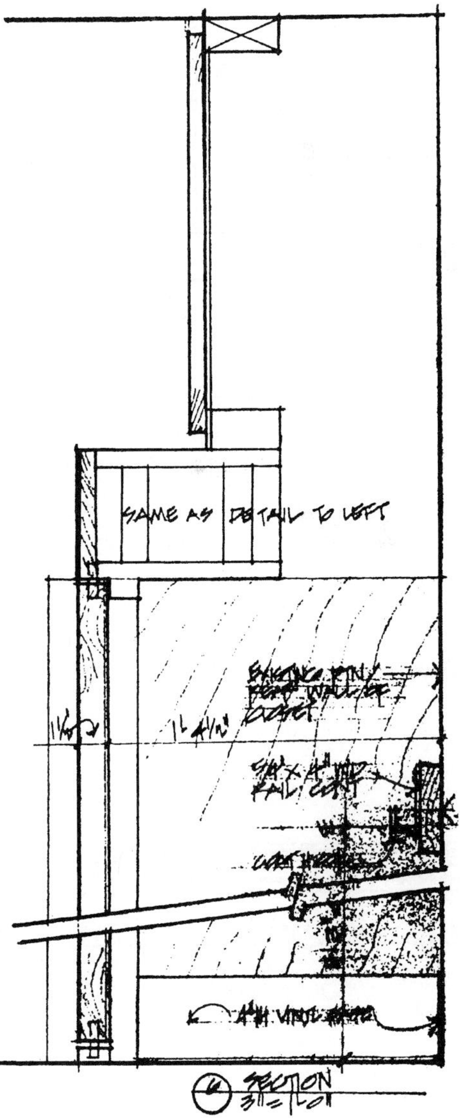

WOODWORK DETAILS
Bookcases

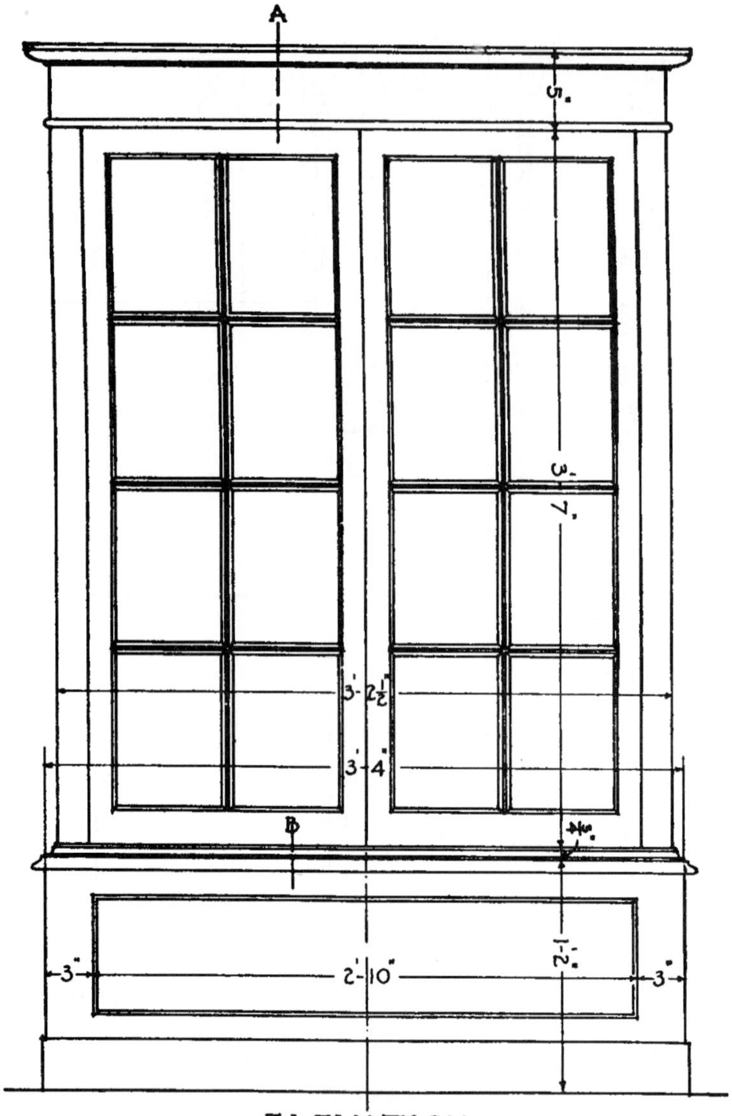

ELEVATION

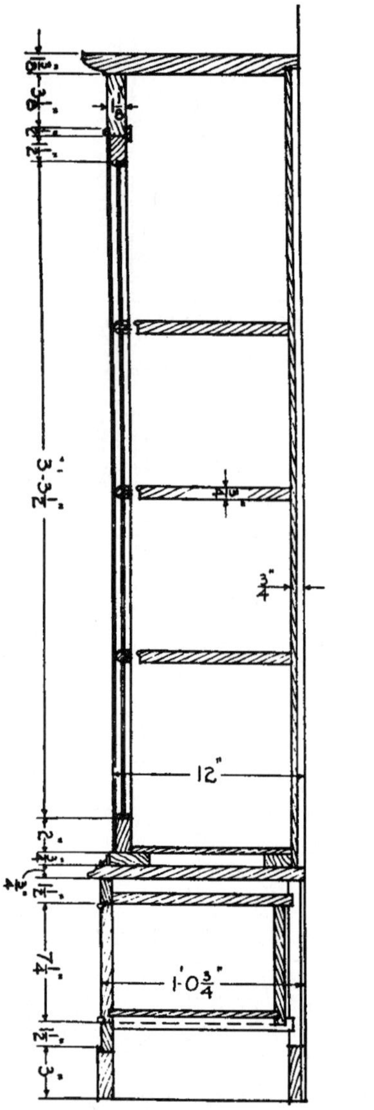

SECTION

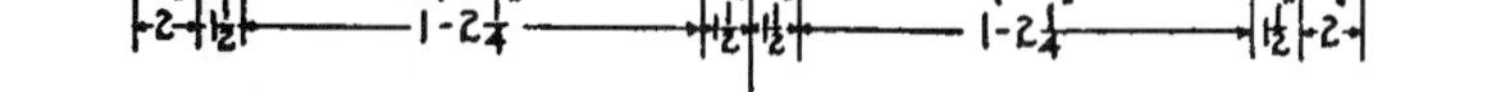

PLAN

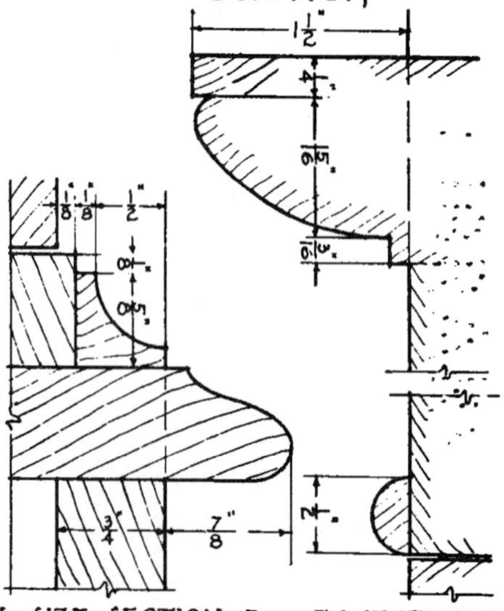

FULL SIZE SECTION · B · F.S. SECTION A

WOODWORK DETAILS
Library Cabinets and Bookcases

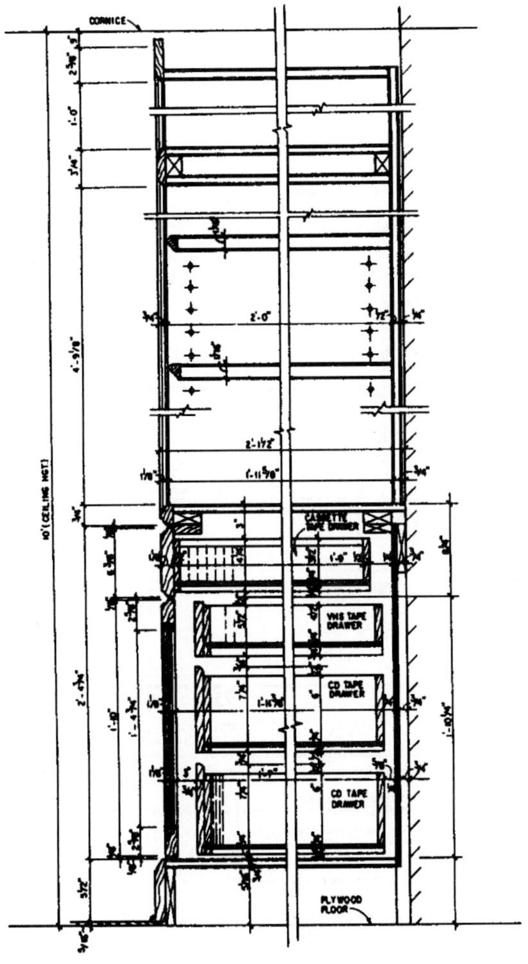

VERTICAL SECTION
LIBRARY CABINETS

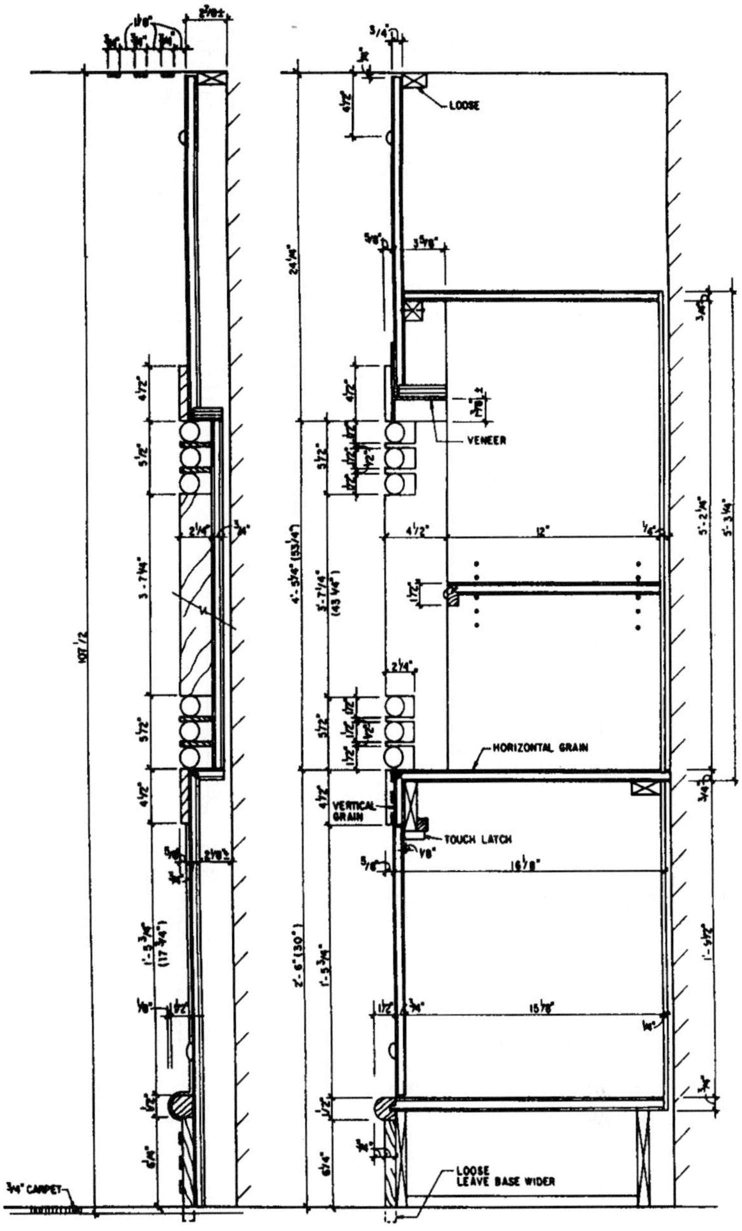

VERTICAL SECTION - LIBRARY BOOKCASE

WOODWORK DETAILS

Trader's Wall

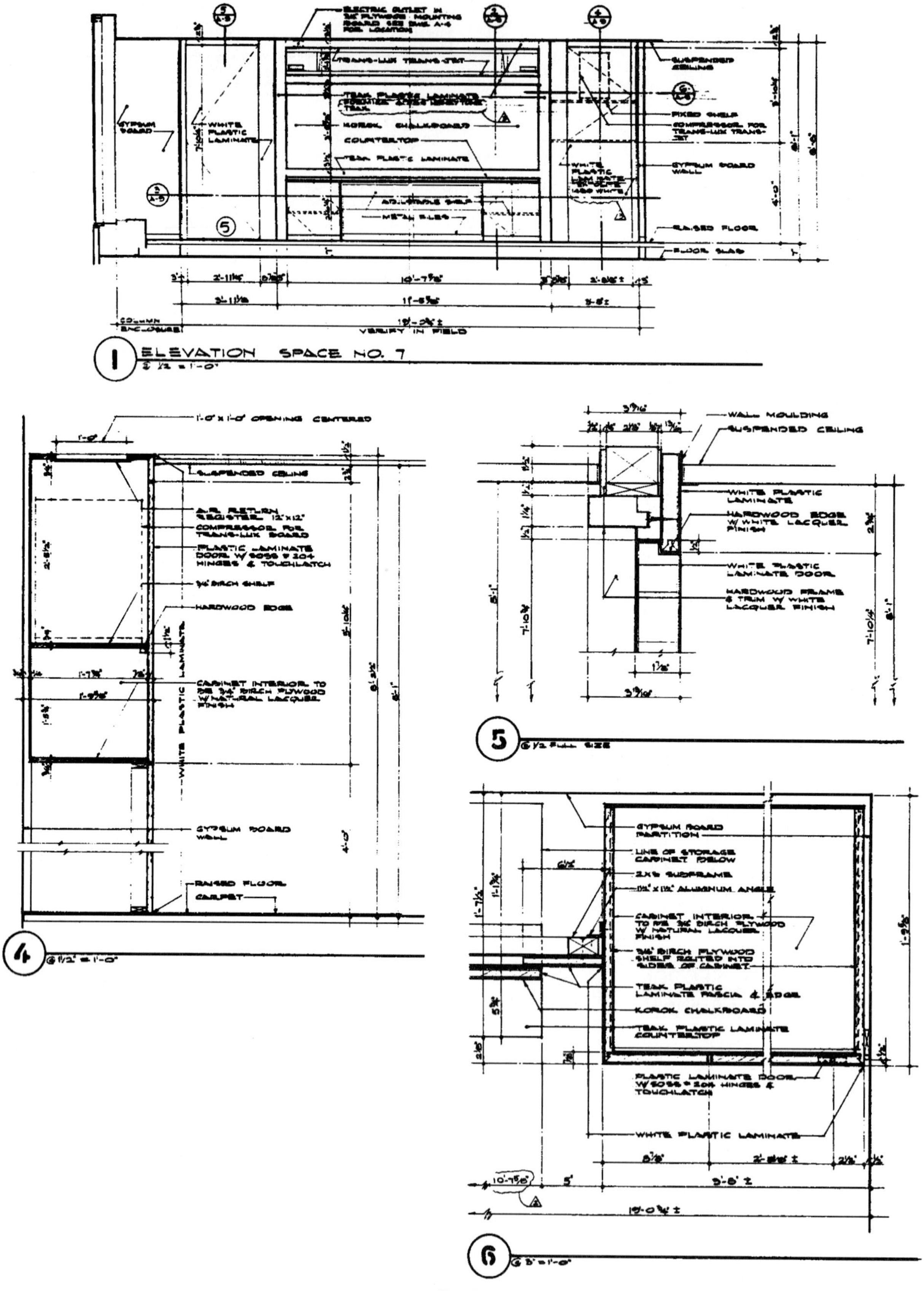

Fig. 1

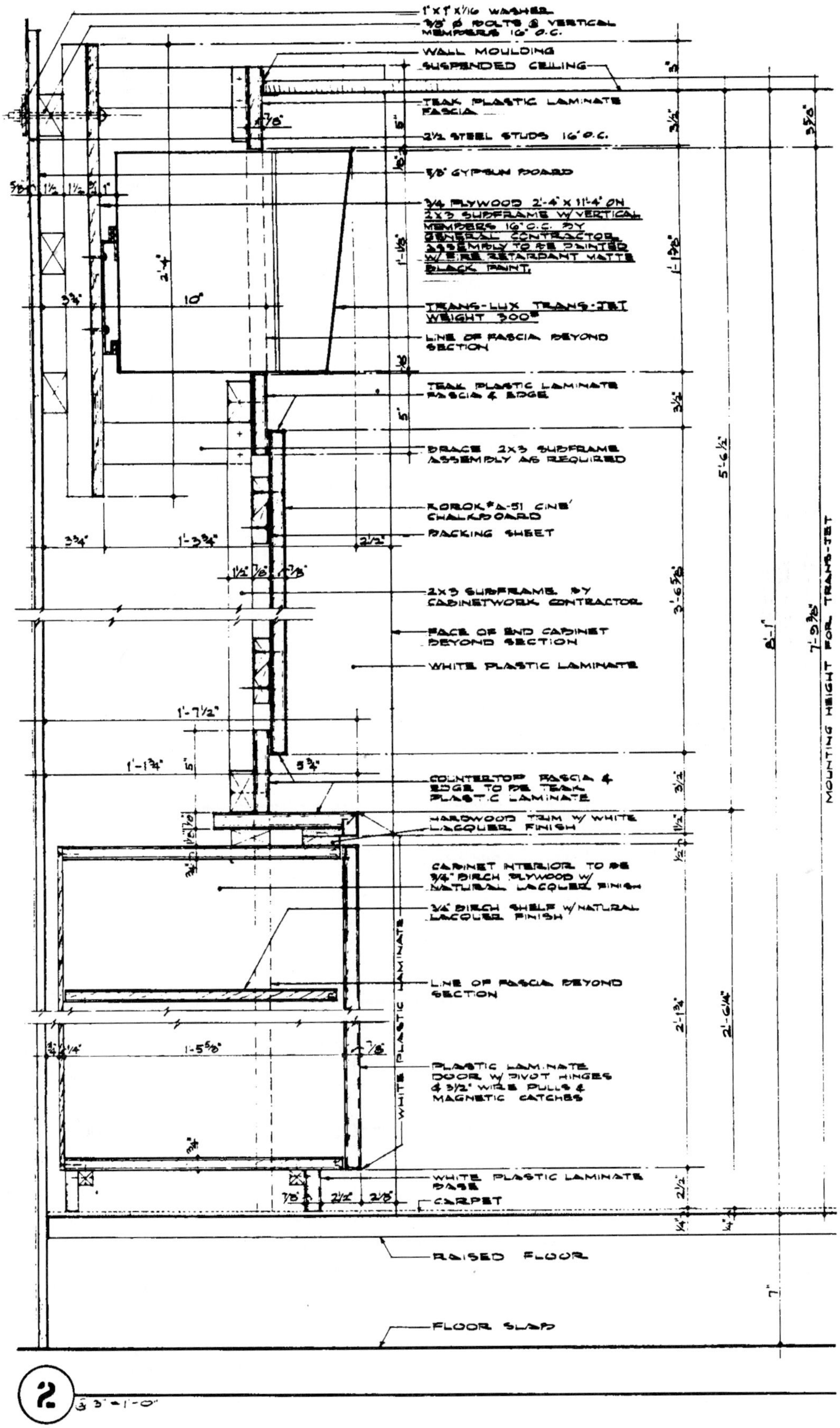

Fig. 1 *(Continued)*

WOODWORK DETAILS
Storage Cabinets

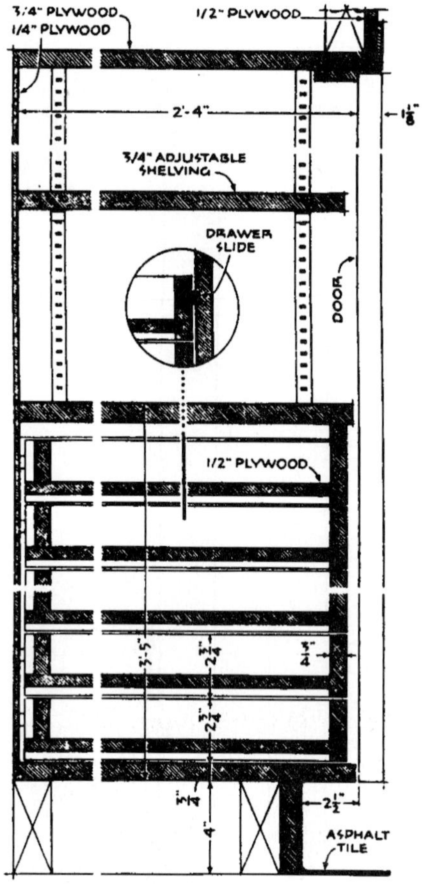

Section A 1 1/2" SCALE

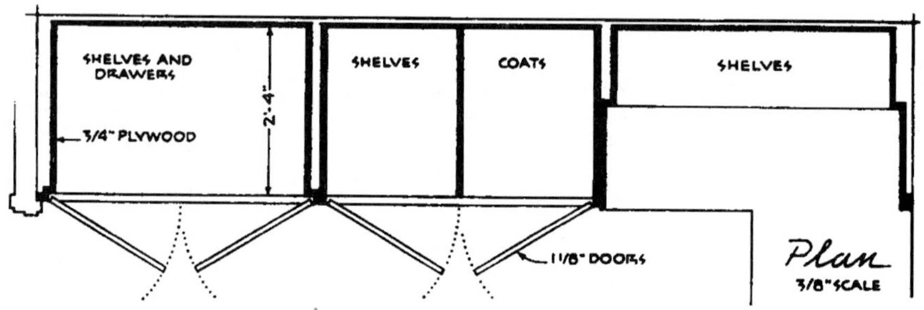

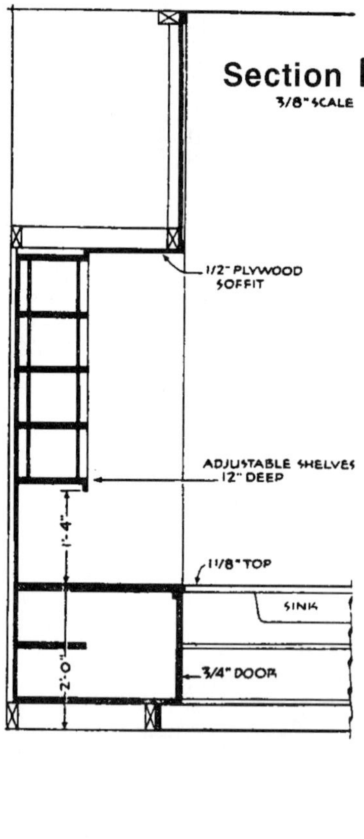

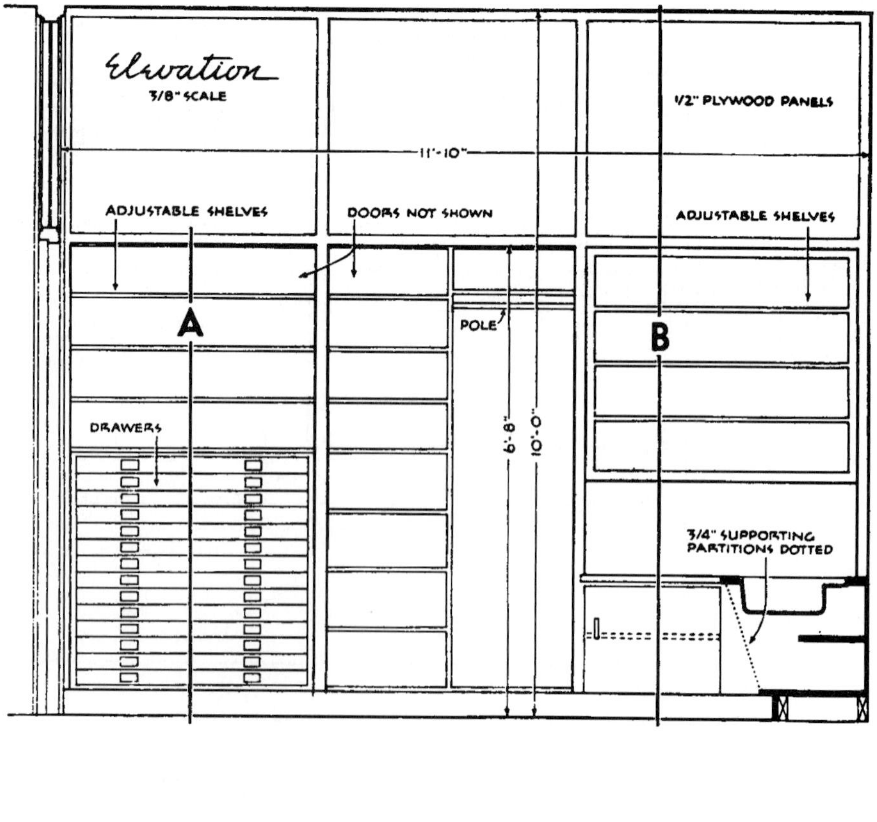

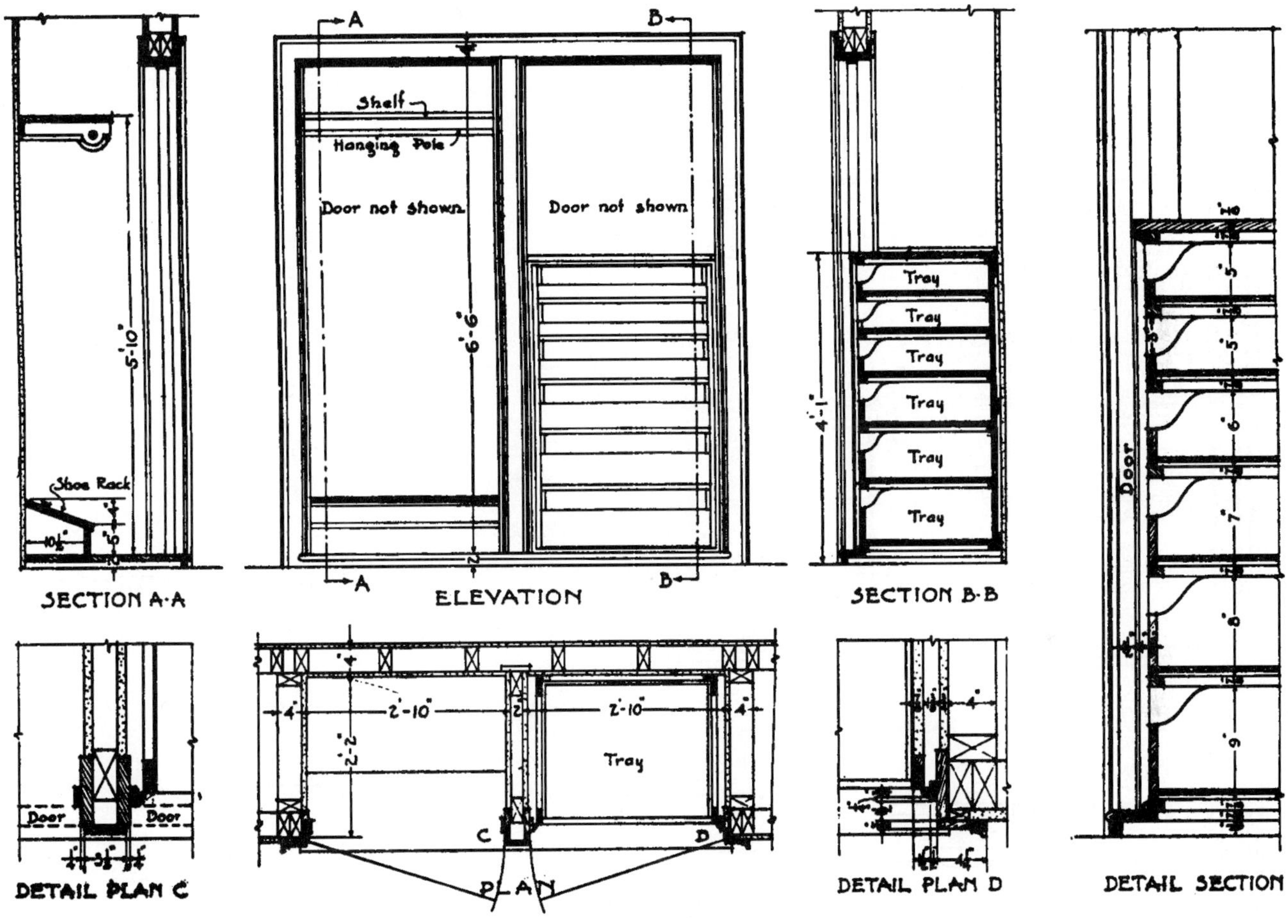
Shelf
Hanging Pole
Door not shown
Door not shown
6'-6"
5'-10"
Shoe Rack
10½"
4'-1"
Tray
Tray
Tray
Tray
Tray
Tray
Door
SECTION A-A
ELEVATION
SECTION B-B
2'-10"
2'-10"
2'-2"
Tray
Door
Door
DETAIL PLAN C
PLAN
DETAIL PLAN D
DETAIL SECTION

WOODWORK DETAILS

Bar Sink

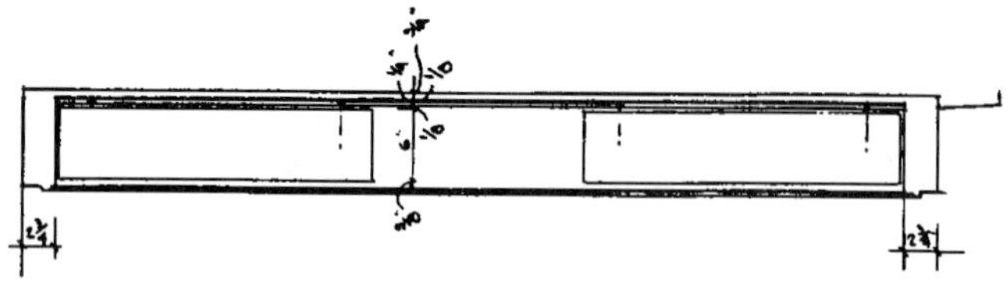

UPPER PLAN

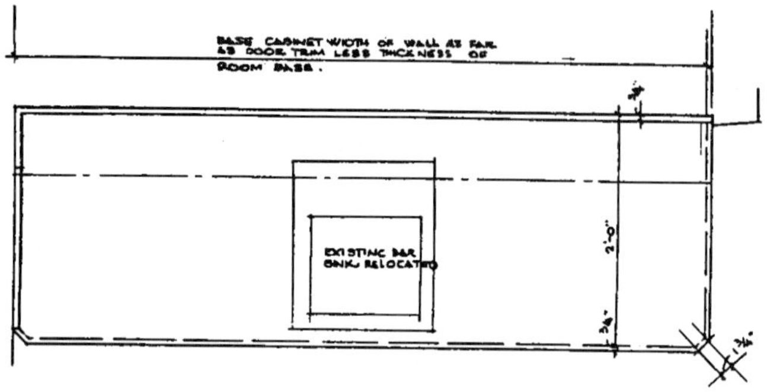
BASE CABINET WIDTH OF WALL AS FAR AS DOOR TRIM LESS THICKNESS OF ROOM BASE.
EXISTING BAR SINK, RELOCATED
2'-0"

LOWER PLAN

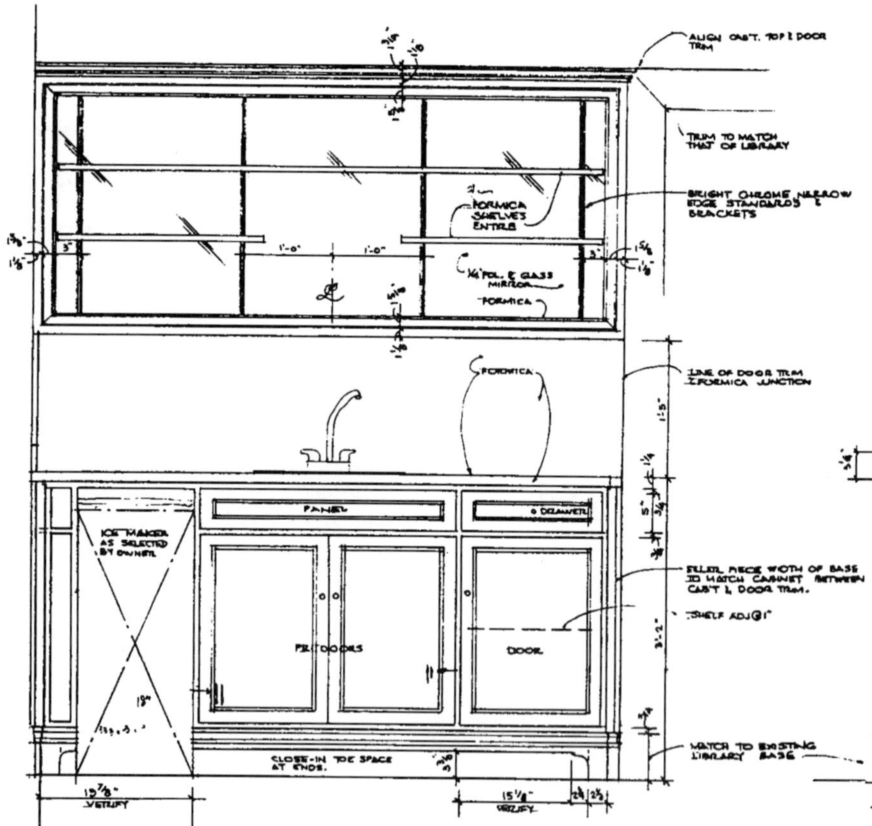
ALIGN CAB'T. TOP & DOOR TRIM
TRIM TO MATCH THAT OF LIBRARY
BRIGHT CHROME NARROW EDGE STANDARDS & BRACKETS
FORMICA SHELVES ENTIRE
1/4" POL. & GLASS MIRROR
FORMICA
1'-0"
1'-0"
LINE OF DOOR TRIM & FORMICA JUNCTION
FORMICA
1'-5"
PANEL
DRAWER
ICE MAKER AS SELECTED BY OWNER
PR. DOORS
DOOR
FILLER PIECE WIDTH OF BASE TO MATCH CABINET BETWEEN CAB'T & DOOR TRIM.
SHELF ADJ @ 1"
3'-2"
MATCH TO EXISTING LIBRARY BASE
CLOSE-IN TOE SPACE AT ENDS.
VERIFY
VERIFY

ELEVATION

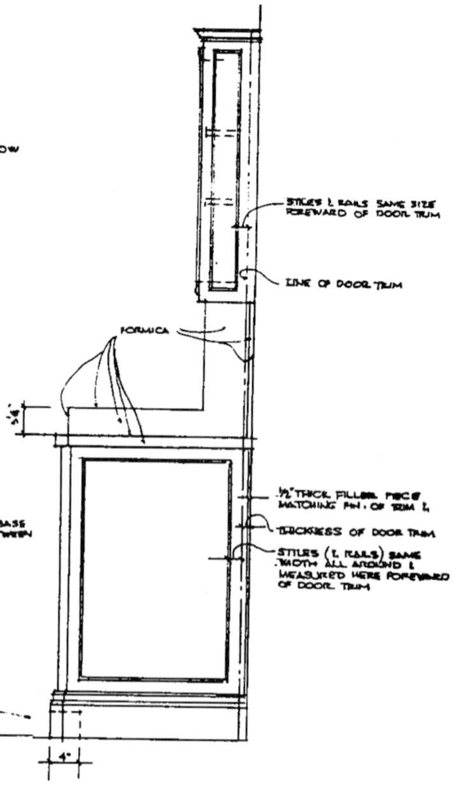
STILES & RAILS SAME SIZE FOREWARD OF DOOR TRIM
LINE OF DOOR TRIM
FORMICA
1/2" THICK FILLER PIECE MATCHING FIN. OF TRIM &
THICKNESS OF DOOR TRIM
STILES (& RAILS) SAME WIDTH ALL AROUND & MEASURED HERE FOREWARD OF DOOR TRIM
4"

SIDE ELEVATION

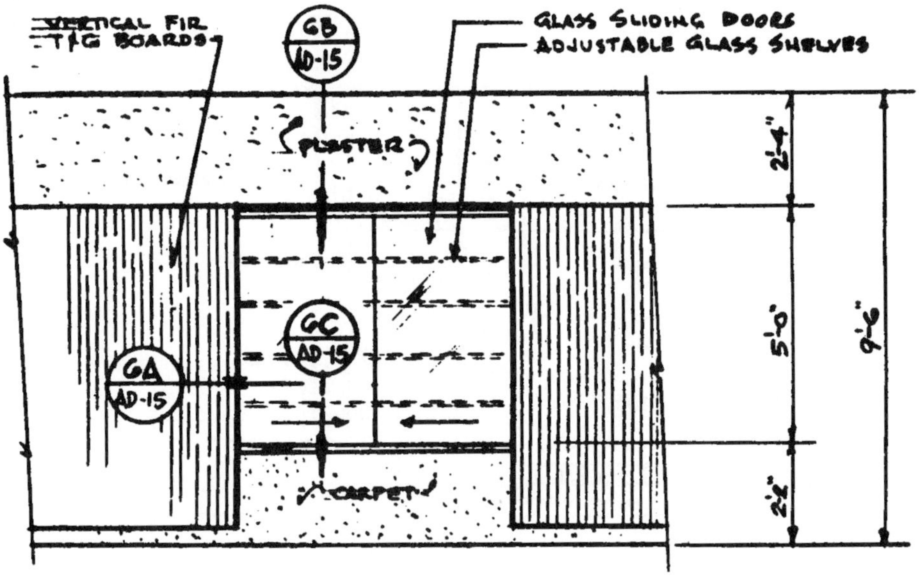

ELEVATION OF GIFT DISPLAY CASE

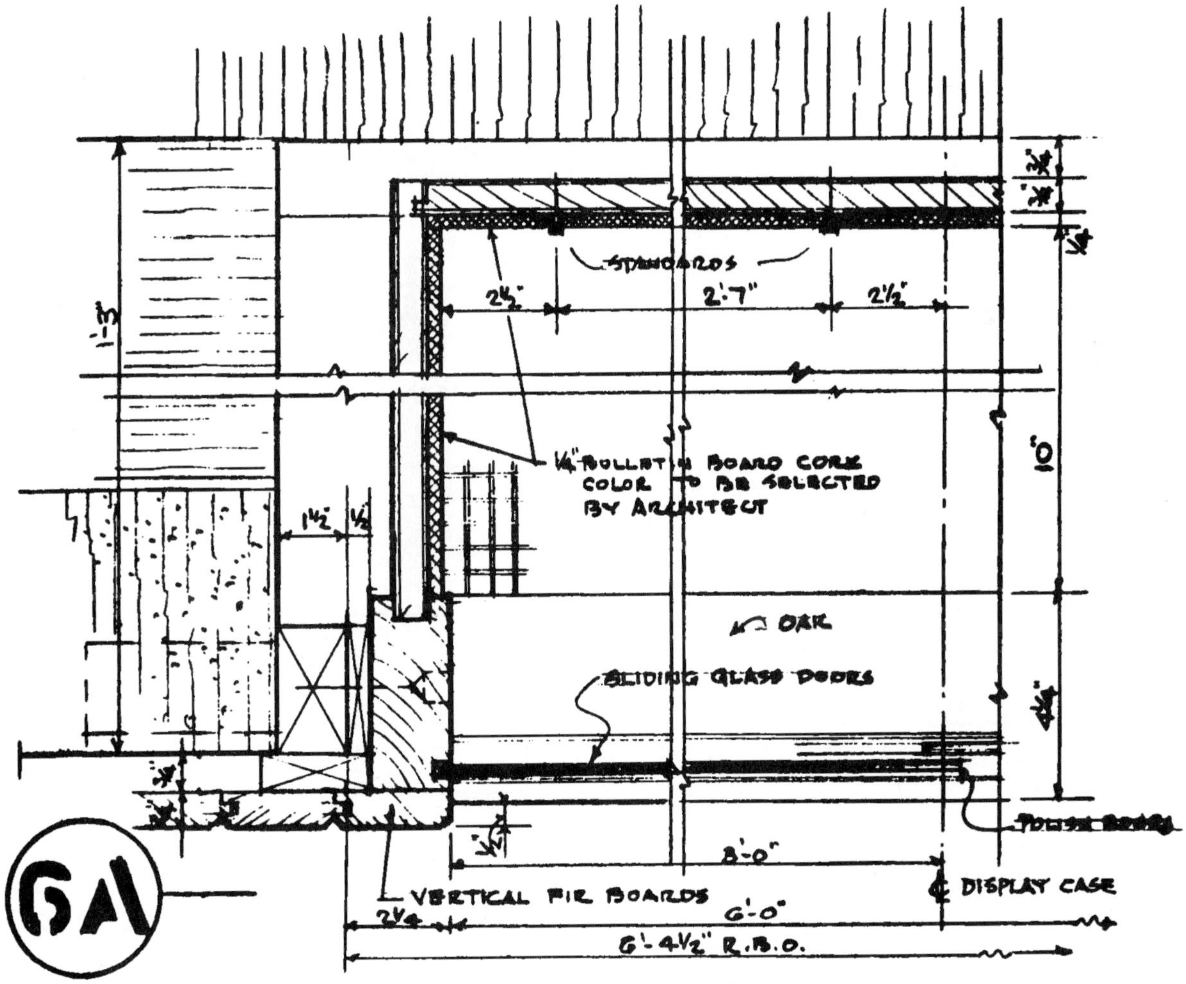

WOODWORK DETAILS

Display Case

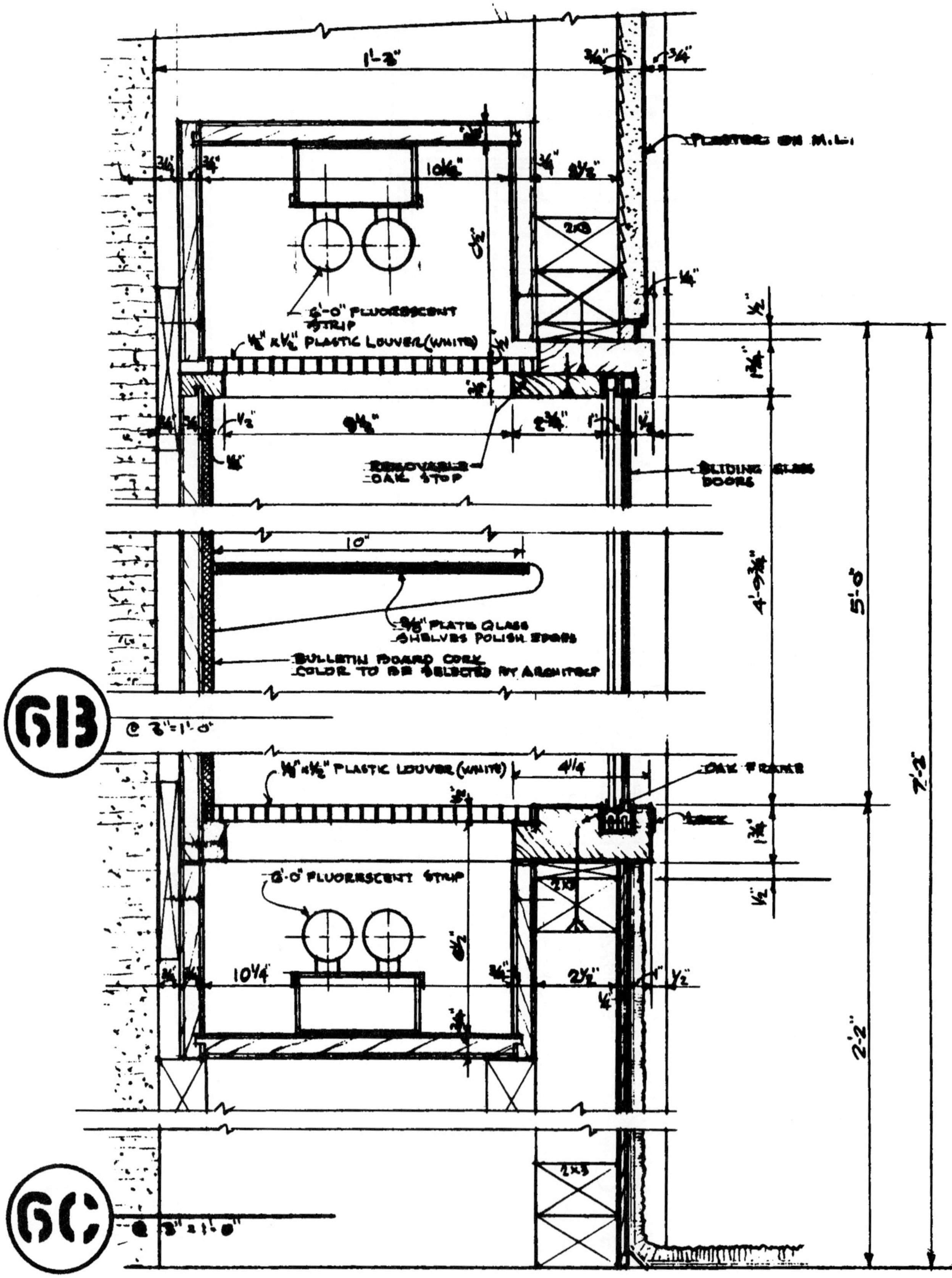

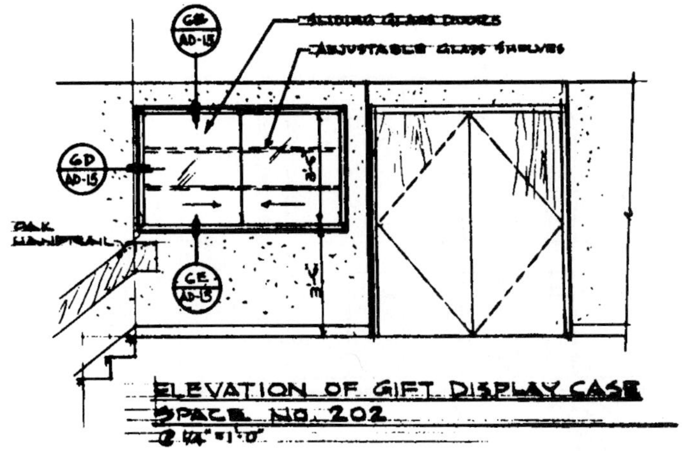
SLIDING GLASS DOORS
ADJUSTABLE GLASS SHELVES
6E
AD-15
6D
AD-15
ELEVATION OF GIFT DISPLAY CASE
SPACE NO. 202

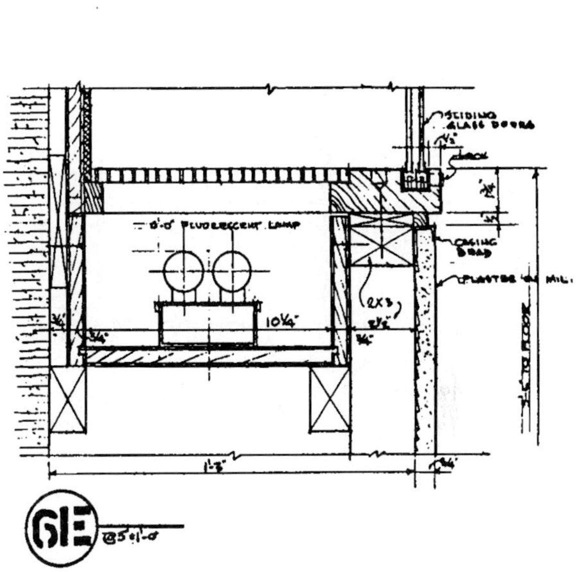
SLIDING GLASS DOORS
PLASTER ON MIL.
1'-3"
6E

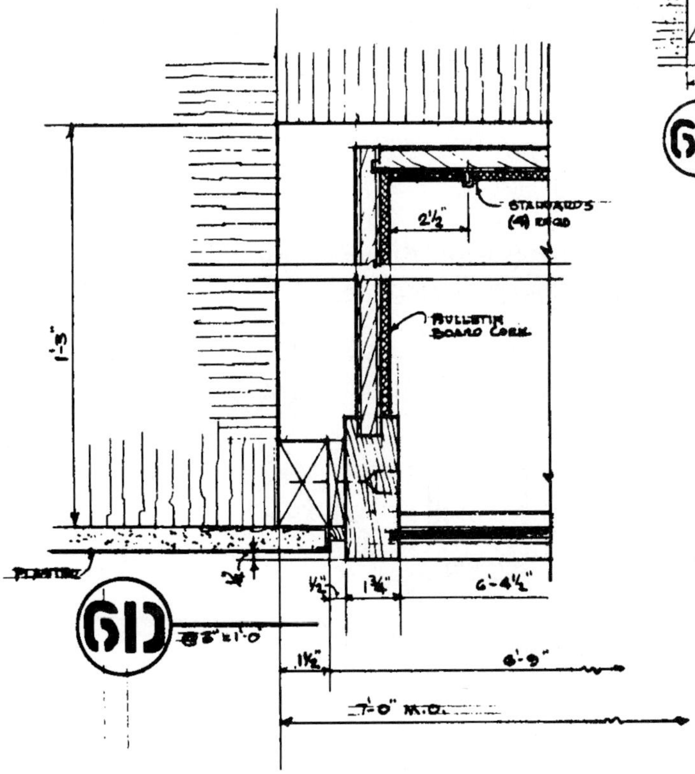
2½"
BULLETIN BOARD CORK
1¾"
6'-4½"
1½"
6'-9"
7'-0" M.O.
6D

WOODWORK DETAILS
Display Case

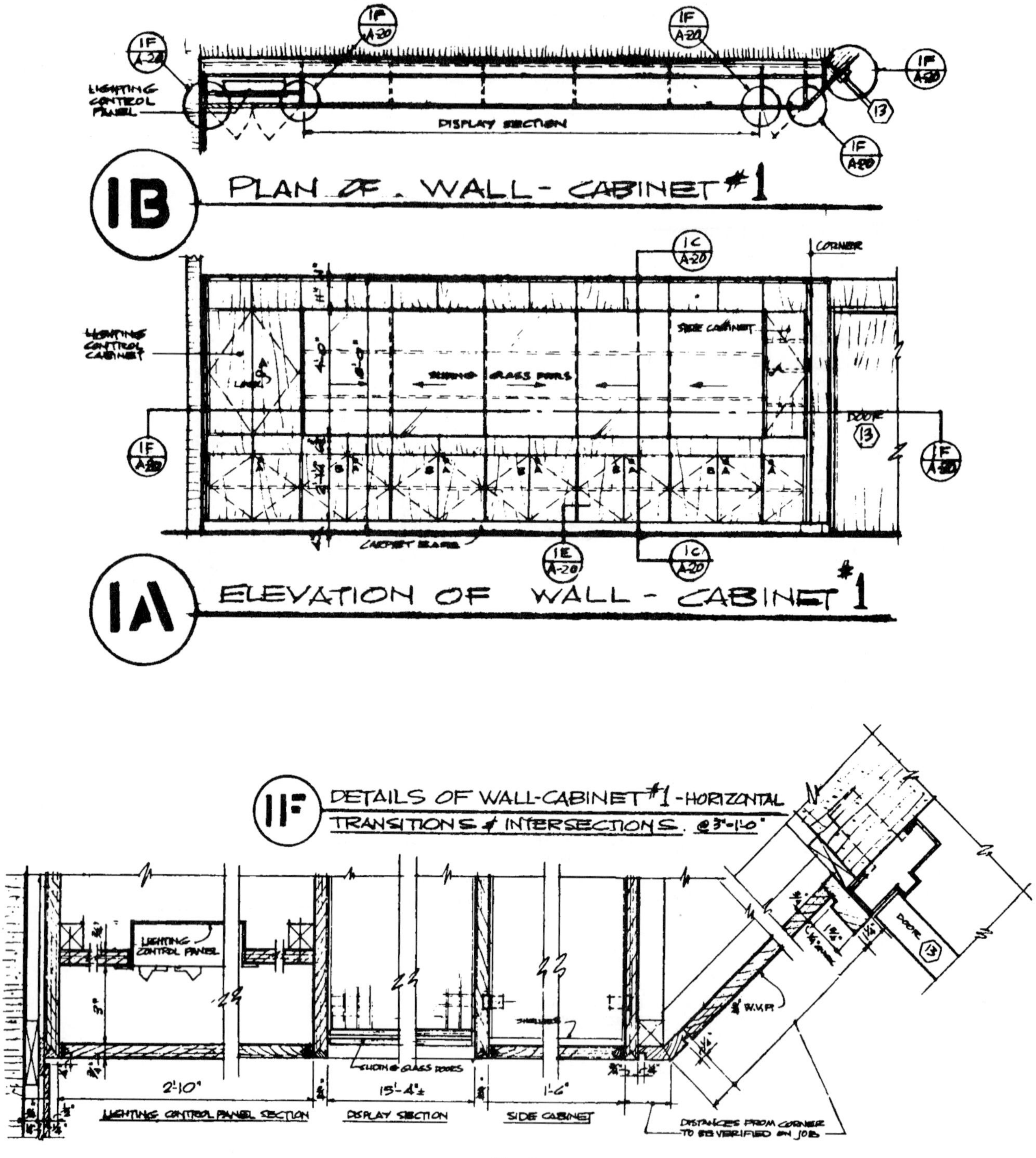

Fig. 2

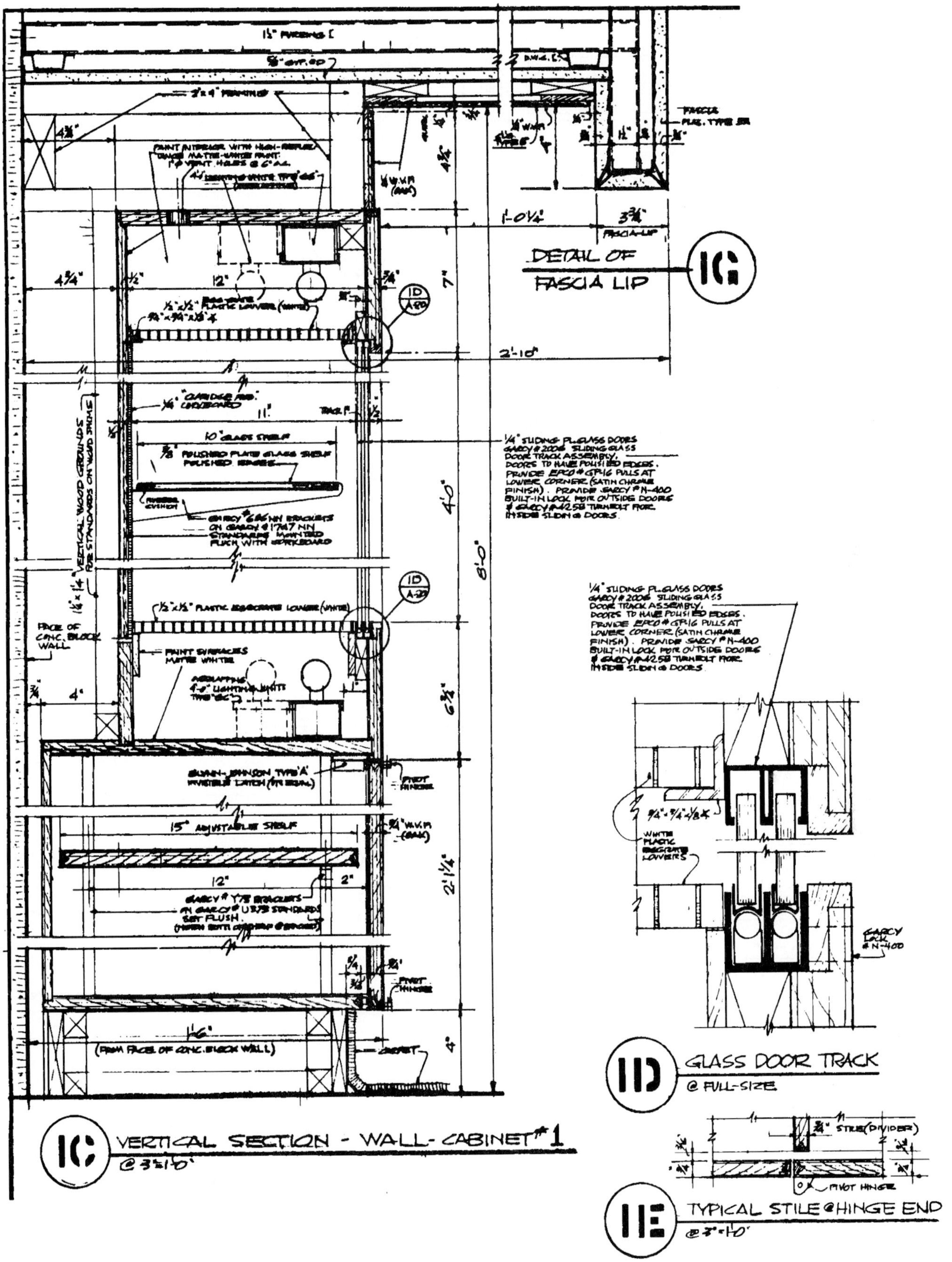

Fig. 2 *(Continued)*

WOODWORK DETAILS
Work Counter

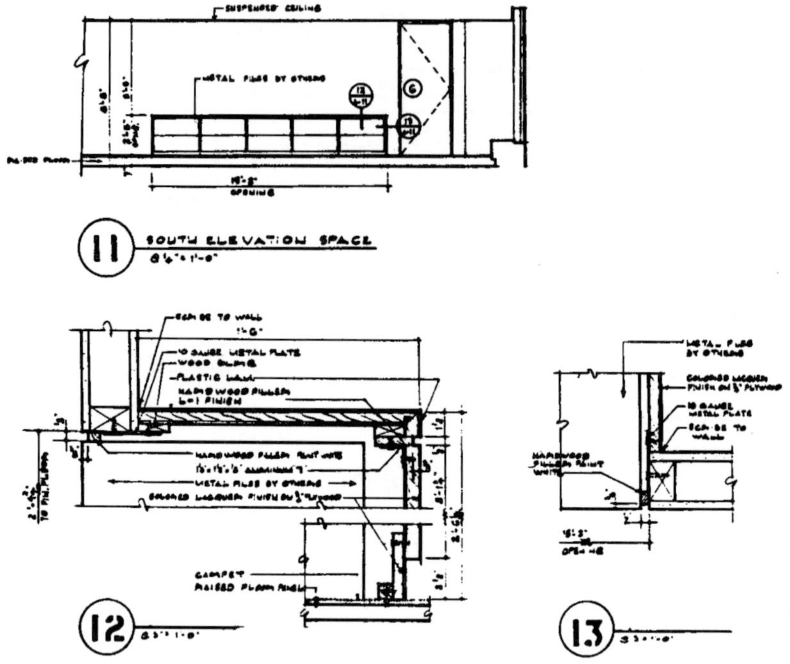

Fig. 3 Countertop

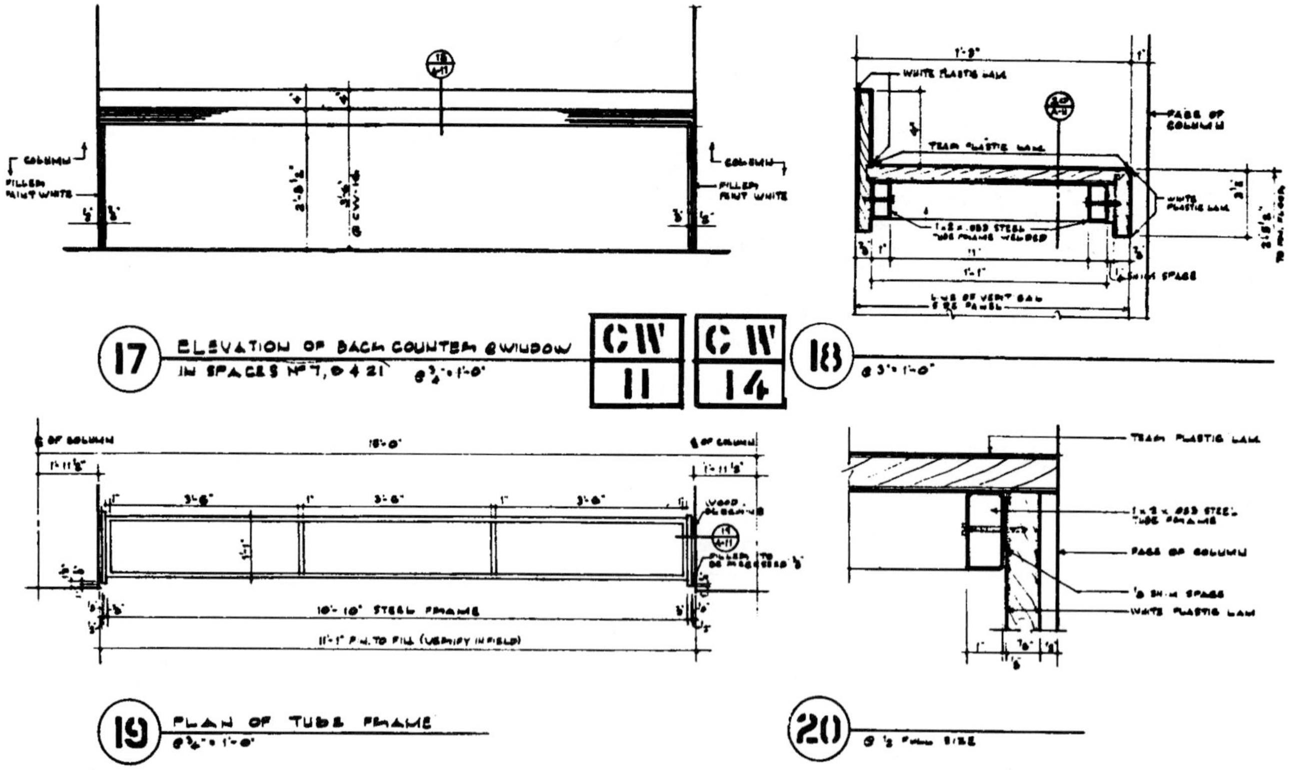

Fig. 4 Back counter

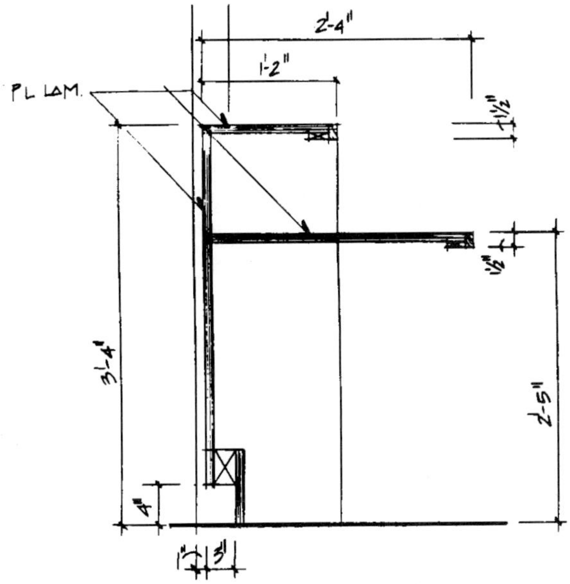

Fig. 5 Word processing counter

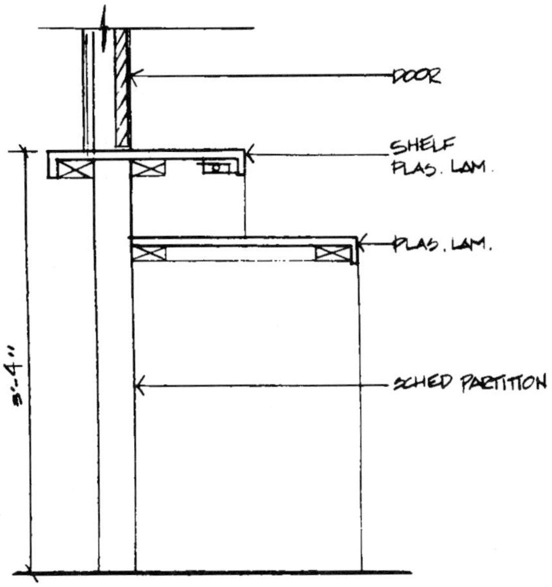

Fig. 6 Cashier counter

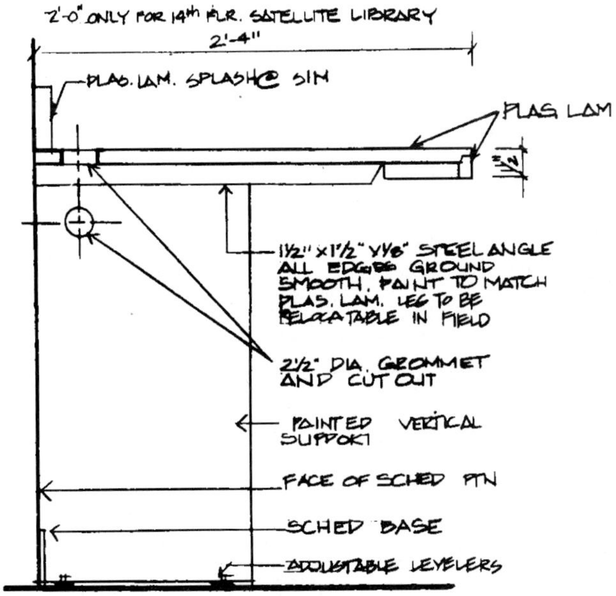

Fig. 7 Base and work counter

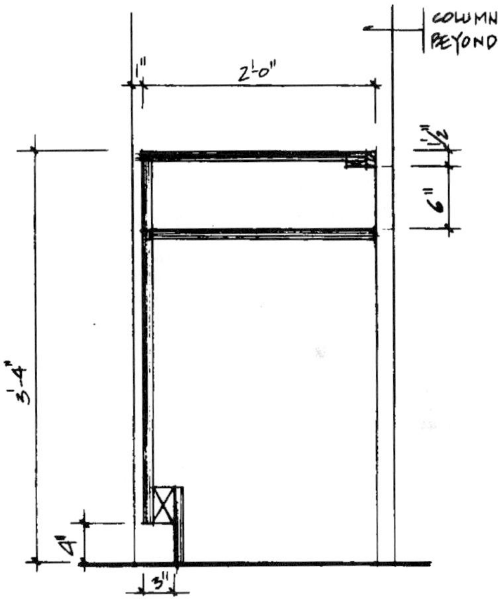

Fig. 8 Walk-up counter

WOODWORK DETAILS
Work Counter

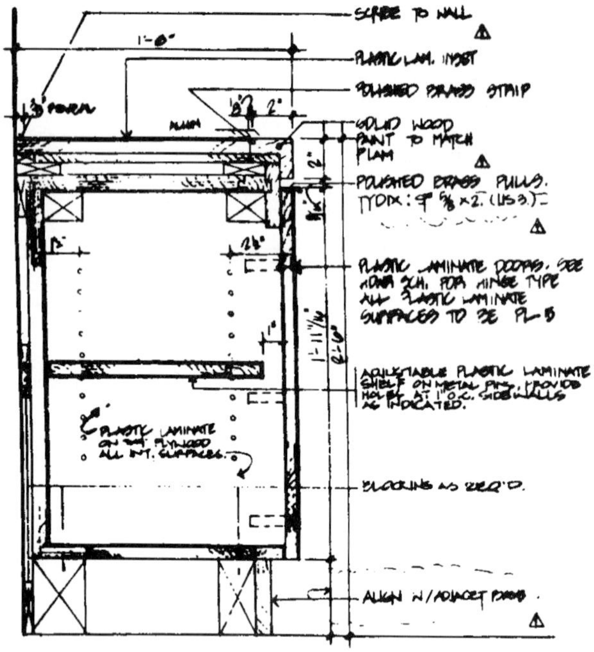

(3) CONF RM. CREDENZA @ RM. 45:08
NTS

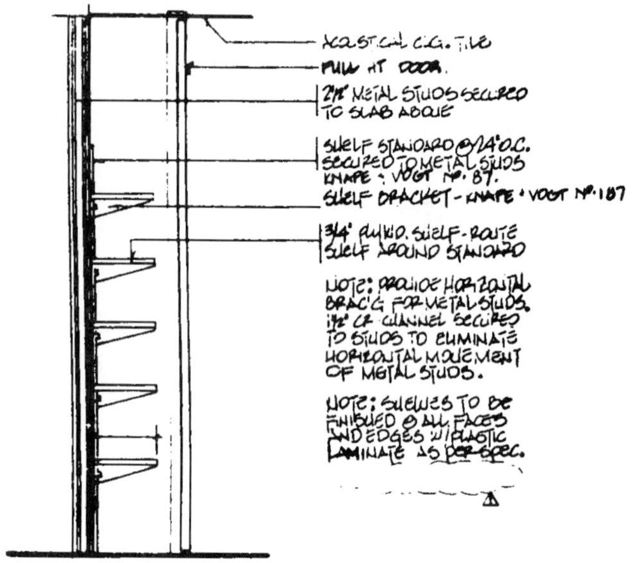

(5) SHELF UNIT
¾" = 1'-0"

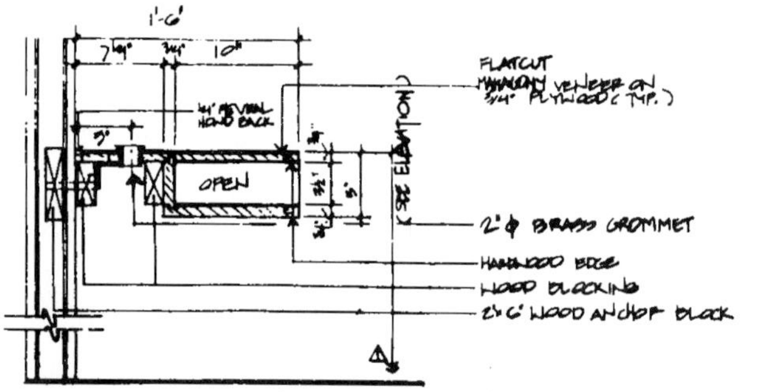

(4) DET SECTION THRU TELEPHONE COUNTER
1½" = 1'-0"

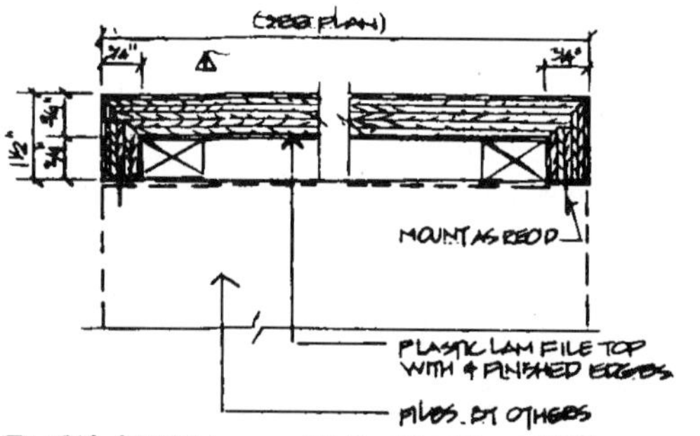

(6) TYP. SECTION thru FILE COUNTER TOP
HALF SCALE

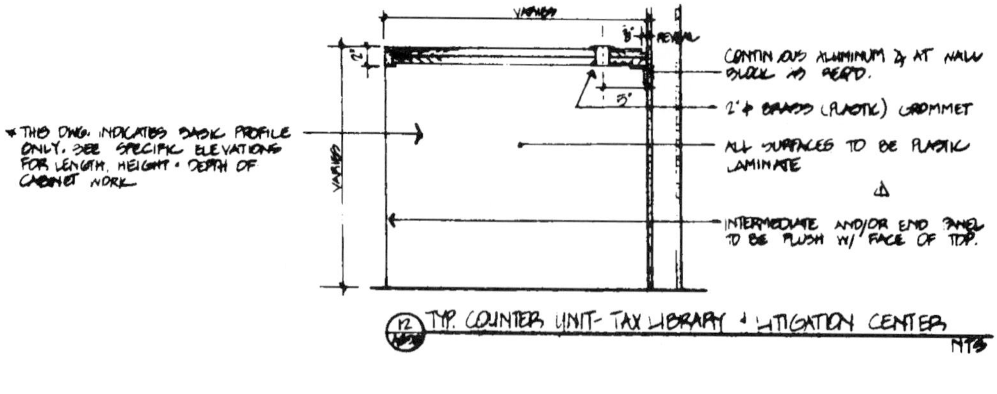

(12) TYP. COUNTER UNIT- TAX LIBRARY & LITIGATION CENTER
NTS

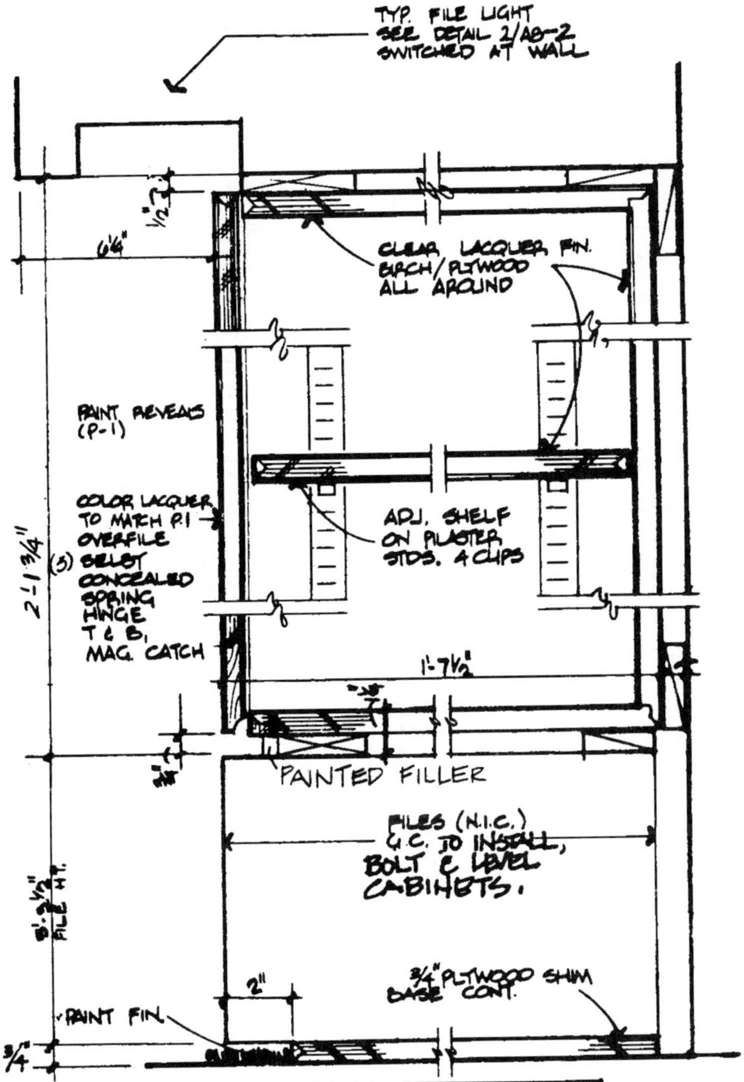
TYP. FILE LIGHT
SEE DETAIL 2/A8-2
SWITCHED AT WALL
CLEAR LACQUER FIN.
BIRCH/PLYWOOD
ALL AROUND
PAINT REVEALS
(P-1)
COLOR LACQUER
TO MATCH P.1
OVERFILE
(3) SELECT
CONCEALED
SPRING
HINGE
T & B,
MAG. CATCH
ADJ. SHELF
ON PILASTER
STDS. 4 CLIPS
1'-7½"
2'-1 3/4"
PAINTED FILLER
FILES (N.I.C.)
G.C. TO INSTALL,
BOLT & LEVEL
CABINETS.
3/4" PLYWOOD SHIM
BASE CONT.
2"
PAINT FIN.
3/4"

OVERFILE

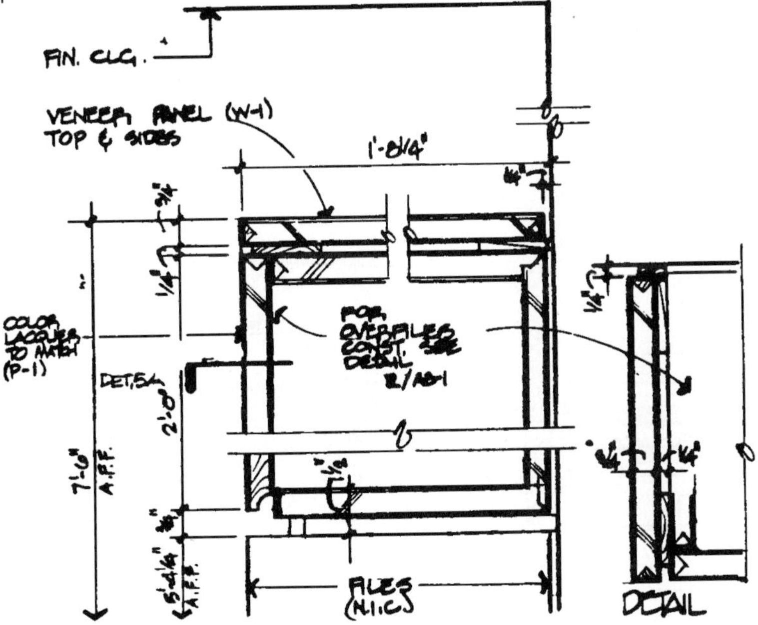
FIN. CLG.
VENEER PANEL (W-1)
TOP & SIDES
1'-8¼"
COLOR LACQUER
TO MATCH
(P-1)
DET. 5/-
FOR OVERFILES
CONST. SEE
DETAIL
2/A8-1
2'-0"
7'-0"
A.F.F.
FILES
(N.I.C.)
DETAIL

FILE END

PNL

WOODWORK DETAILS
Overfile Cabinet

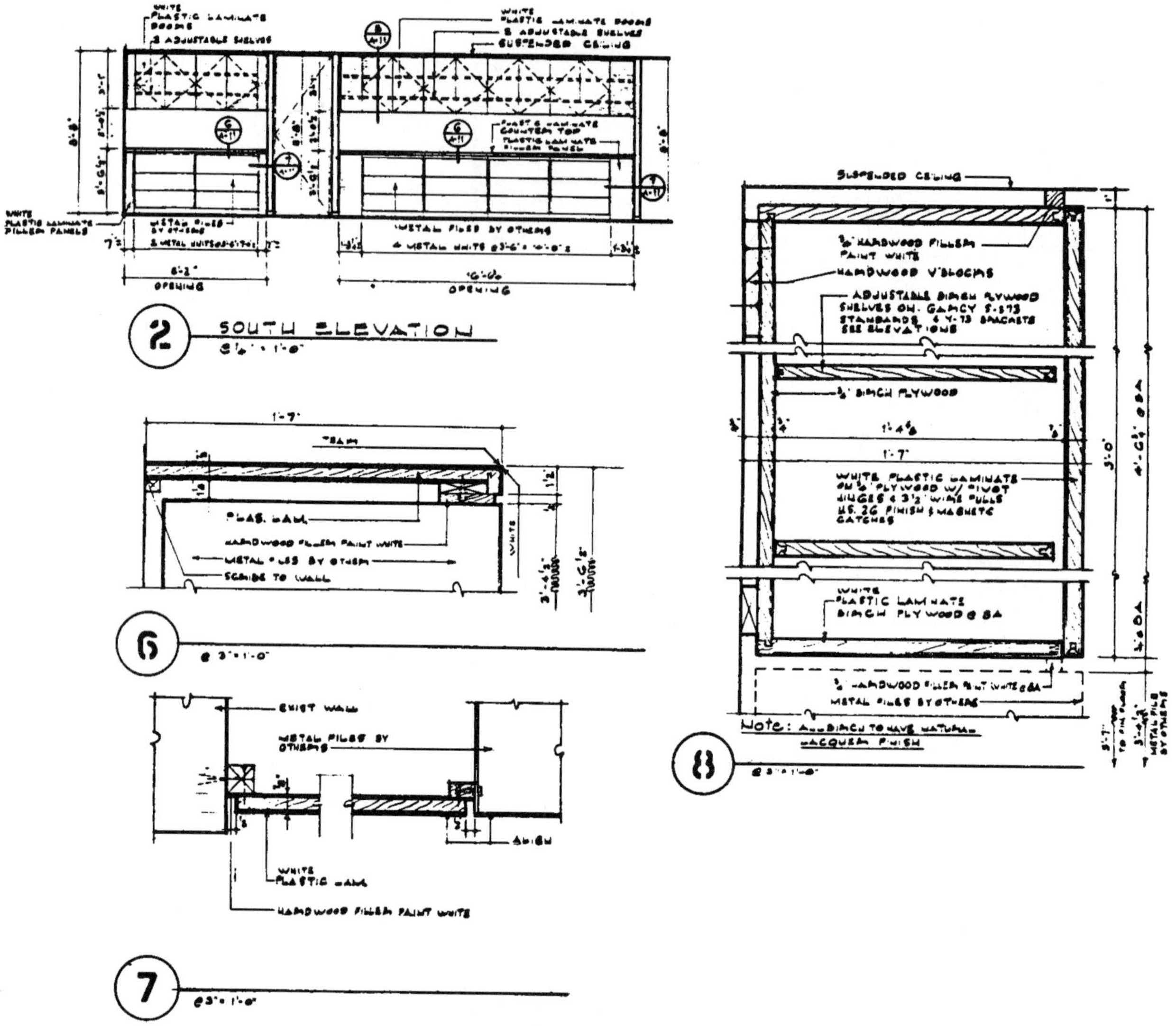

Fig. 9 Wall unit with overhead cabinets

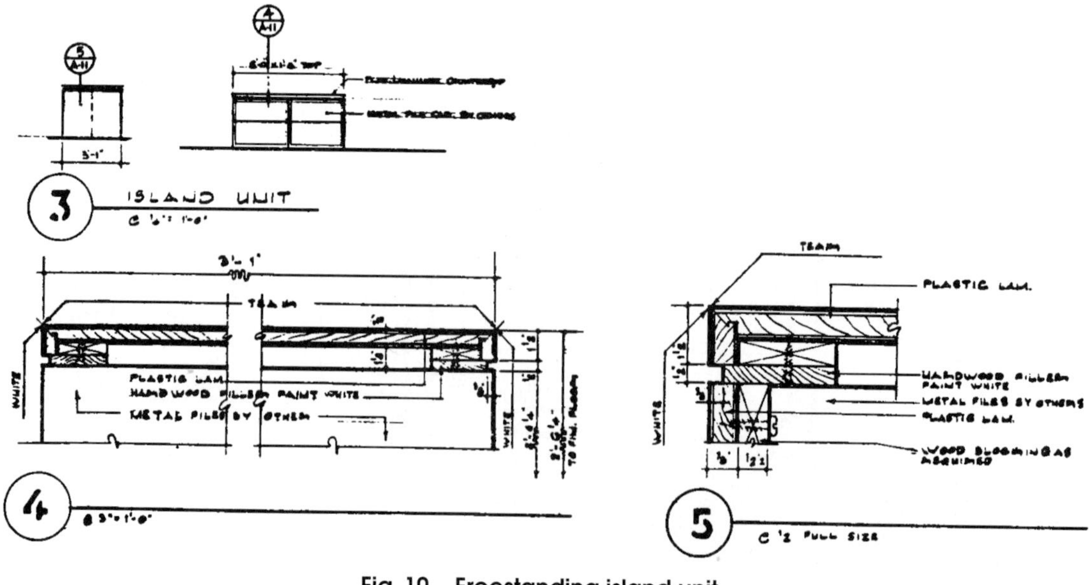

Fig. 10 Freestanding island unit

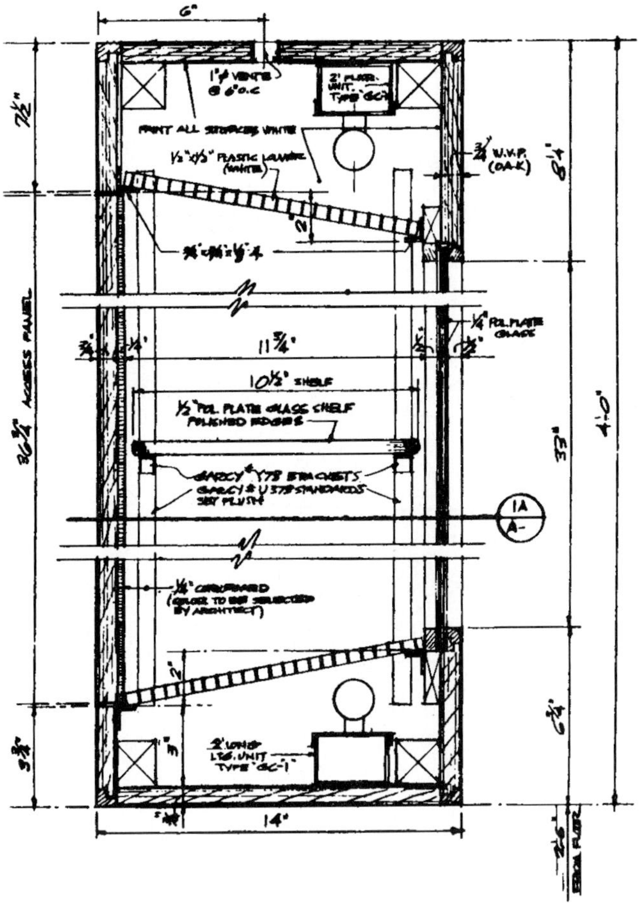

1 LOBBY DISPLAY CABINET #1
VERTICAL SECTION @ 3"=1'-0"

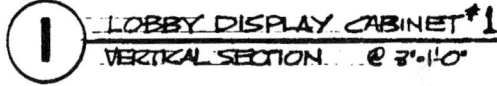

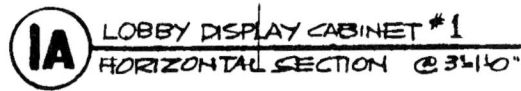

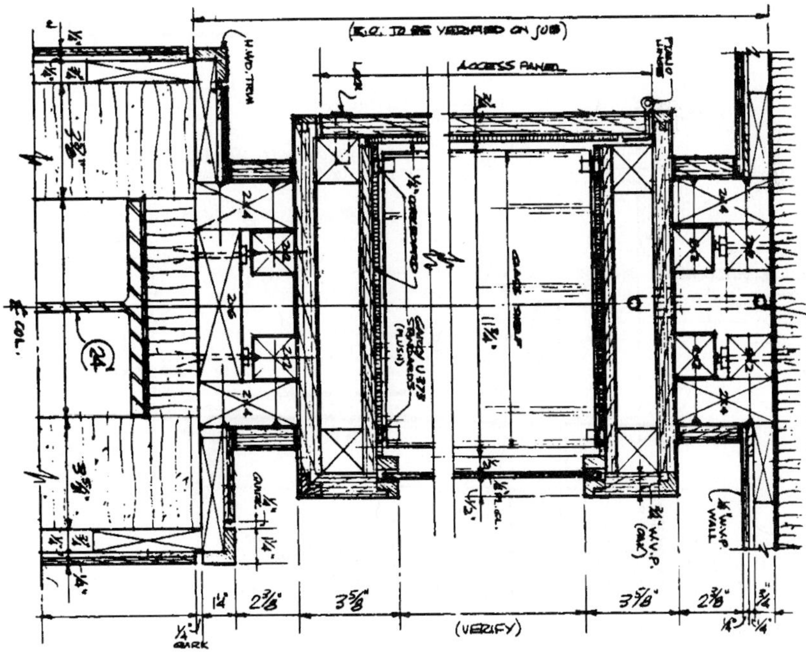

1A LOBBY DISPLAY CABINET #1
HORIZONTAL SECTION @ 3"=1'-0"

WOODWORK DETAILS

Credenza

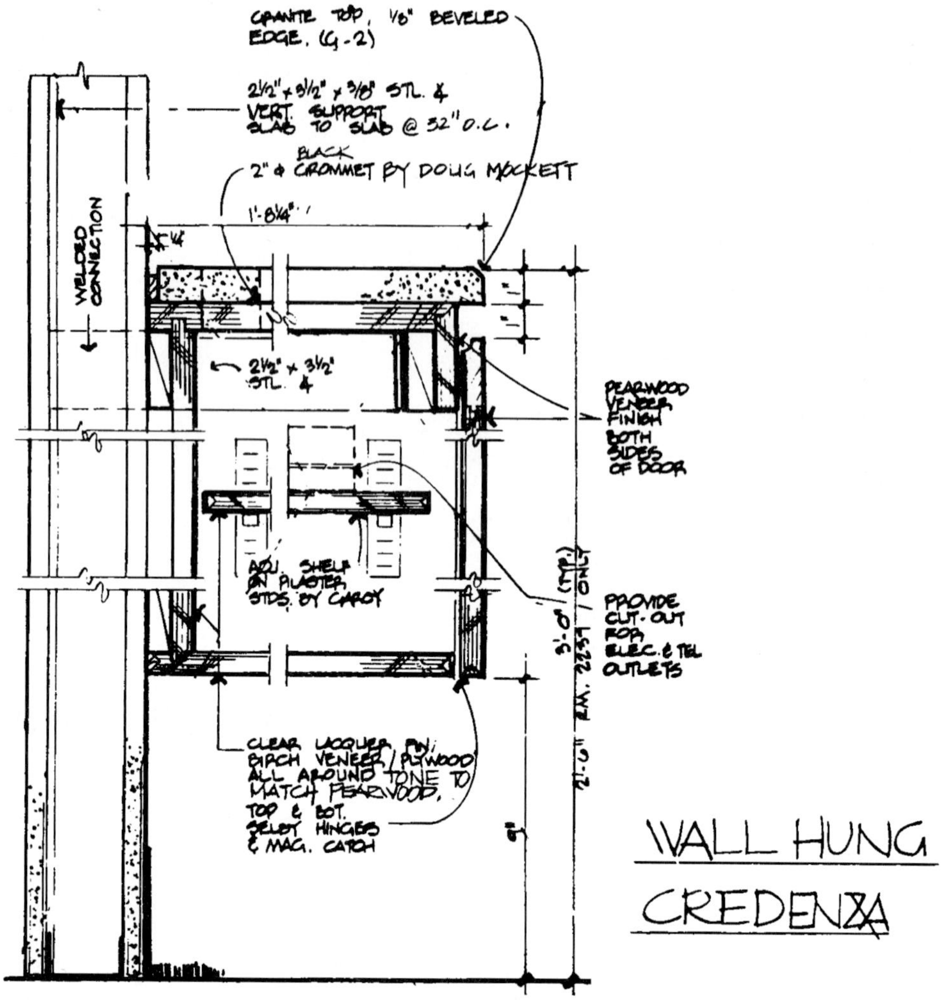
GRANITE TOP, 1/8" BEVELED EDGE. (G-2)
2½" x 3½" x 3/8" STL. ∠ VERT. SUPPORT SLAB TO SLAB @ 32" O.C.
2" ⌀ BLACK GROMMET BY DOUG MOCKETT
1'-8¼"
WELDED CONNECTION
2½" x 3½" STL. ∠
PEARWOOD VENEER FINISH BOTH SIDES OF DOOR
ADJ. SHELF ON PILASTER STDS. BY GAROY
PROVIDE CUT-OUT FOR ELEC. & TEL OUTLETS
CLEAR LACQUER FIN; BIRCH VENEER/PLYWOOD ALL AROUND TONE TO MATCH PEARWOOD. TOP & BOT.
SELECT HINGES & MAG. CATCH
WALL HUNG CREDENZA

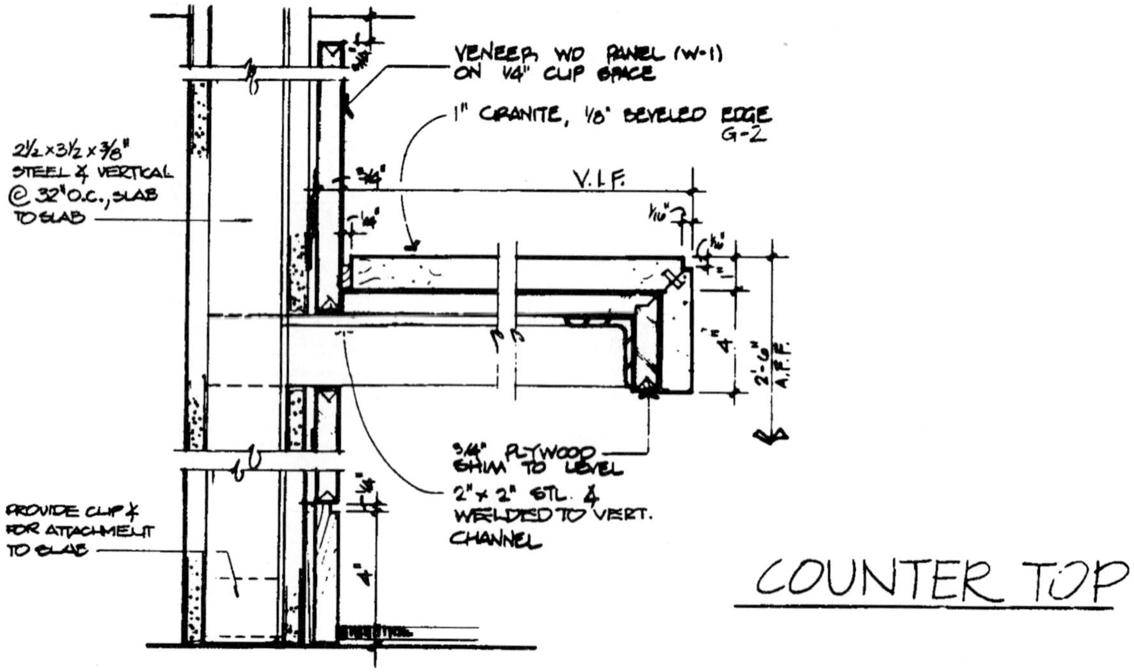
VENEER WD PANEL (W-1) ON ¼" CLIP SPACE
1" GRANITE, 1/8" BEVELED EDGE G-2
2½ x 3½ x 3/8" STEEL ∠ VERTICAL @ 32" O.C., SLAB TO SLAB
V.I.F.
3/4" PLYWOOD SHIM TO LEVEL
2" x 2" STL. ∠ WELDED TO VERT. CHANNEL
PROVIDE CLIP ∠ FOR ATTACHMENT TO SLAB
2'-6" A.F.F.
COUNTER TOP

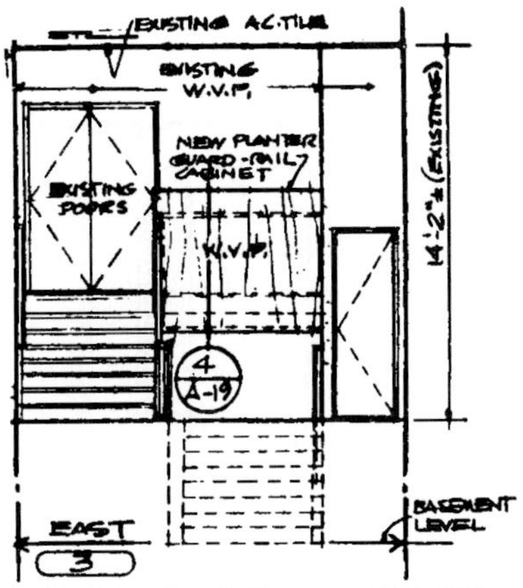
EXISTING AC.TILE
EXISTING W.V.P.
NEW PLANTER GUARD-RAIL CABINET
EXISTING DOORS
W.V.P.
14'-2"± (EXISTING)
4
A-19
BASEMENT LEVEL
EAST
3

ENTRY FOYER

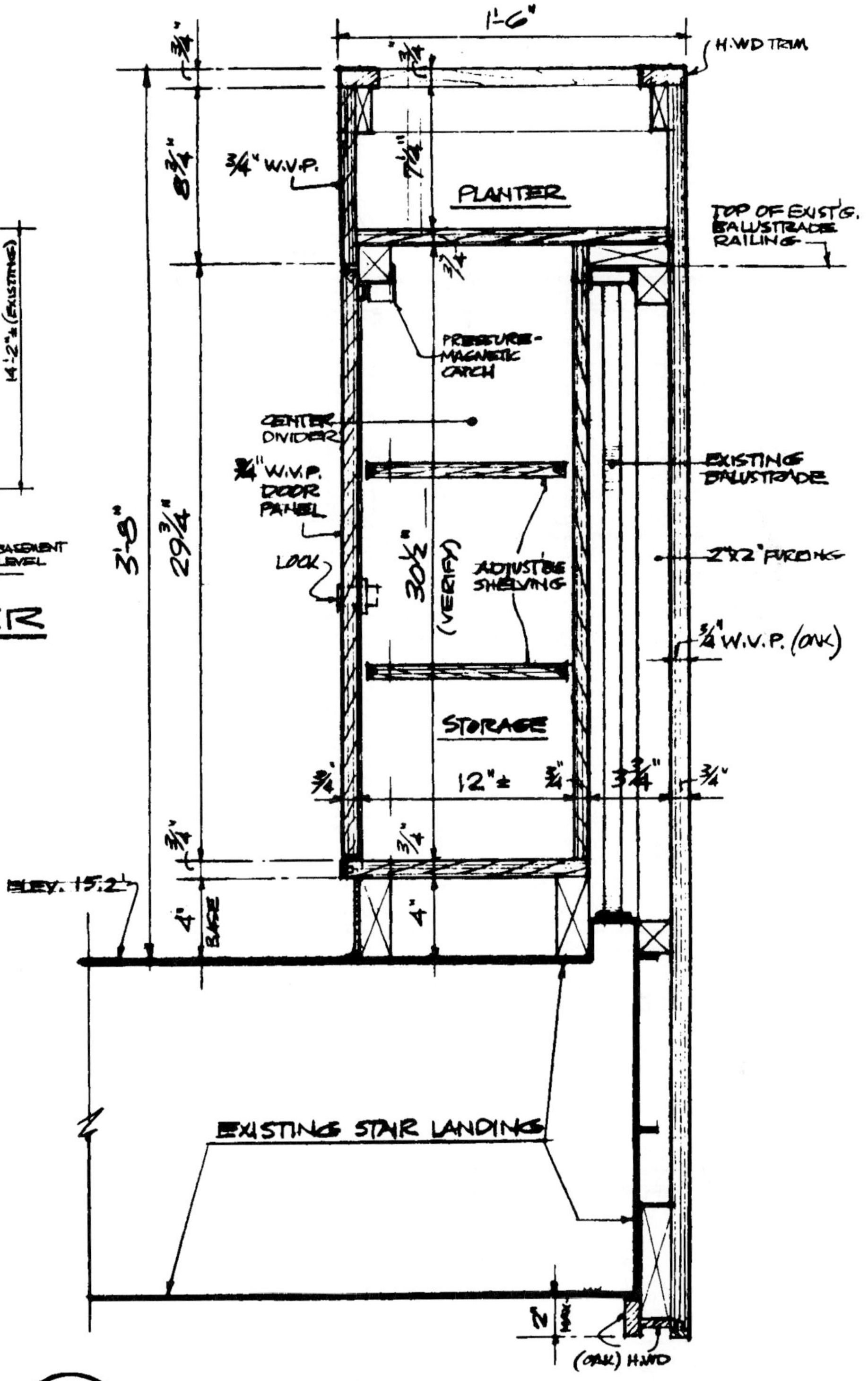
1'-6"
H.WD TRIM
3/4"
3/4"
8 3/4"
7 1/4"
3/4" W.V.P.
PLANTER
TOP OF EXIST'G. BALUSTRADE RAILING
3/4"
PRESSURE-MAGNETIC CATCH
CENTER DIVIDER
EXISTING BALUSTRADE
3/4" W.V.P. DOOR PANEL
3'-8"
29 3/4"
30 1/2" (VERIFY)
ADJUSTBLE SHELVING
LOCK
2"x2" FURRING
3/4" W.V.P. (OAK)
STORAGE
3/4
12"±
3/4"
3 1/4"
3/4"
3/4"
3/4"
ELEV. 15.2'
4"
BASE
4"
EXISTING STAIR LANDING
(OAK) H.WD

4 SECTION THRU PLANTER-CABINET

WOODWORK DETAILS

Book and Shawl Cabinet

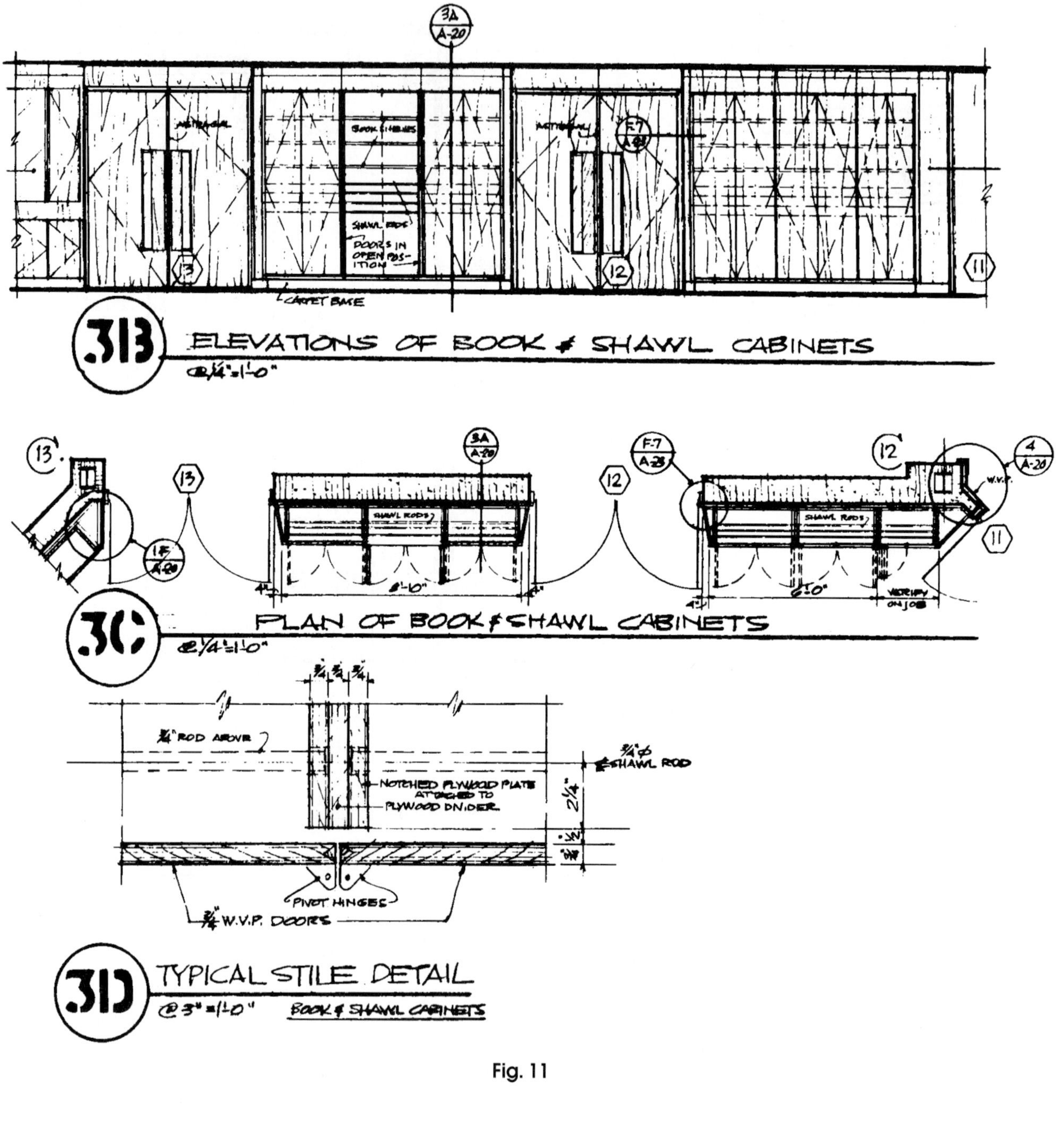

Fig. 11

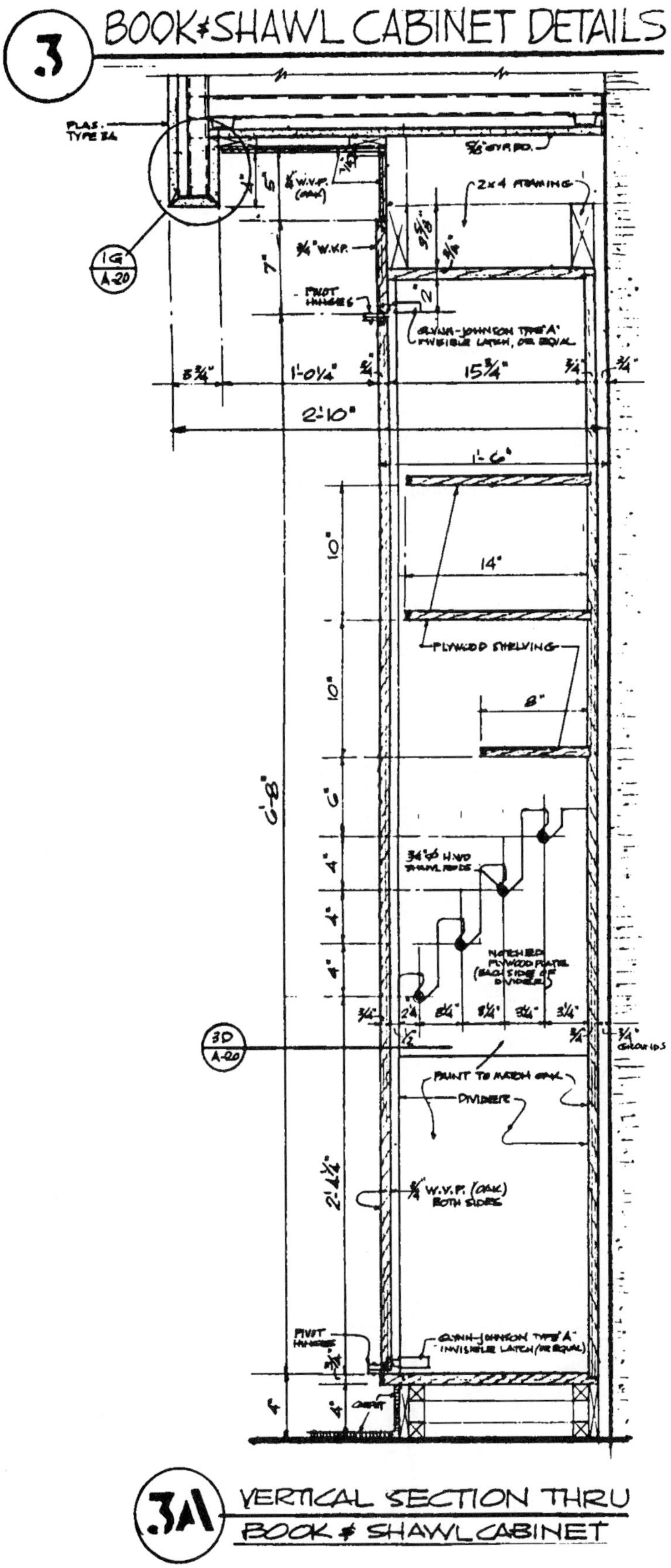

Fig. 11 *(Continued)*

WOODWORK DETAILS
Storage Shelves

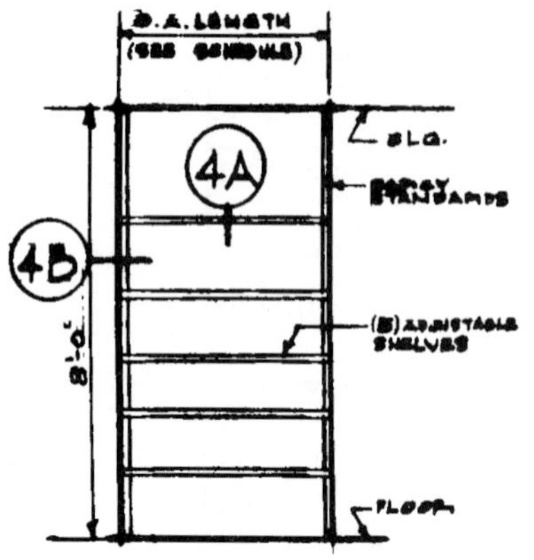

ELEVATION OF STORAGE CLOSETS 4'-0" OR LESS IN LENGTH
@ ¼" = 1'-0"

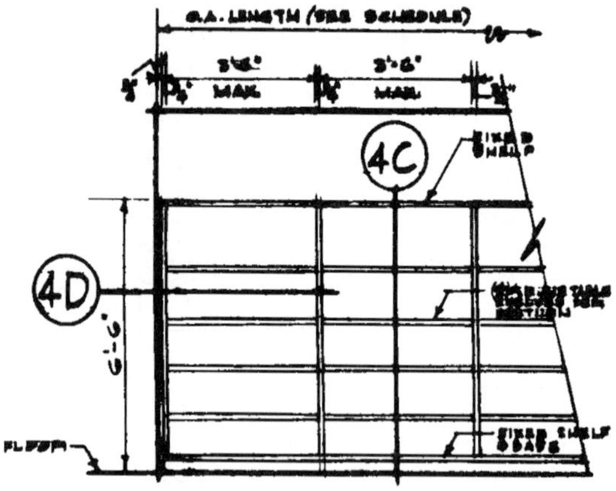

ELEVATION OF STORAGE CLOSETS OVER 4'-0" IN LENGTH
@ ¼" = 1'-0"

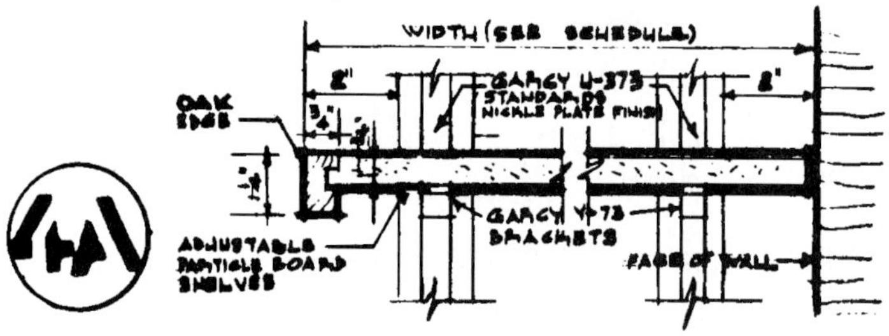

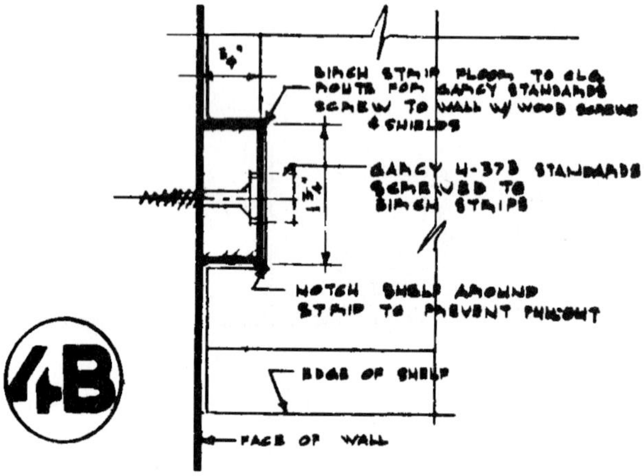

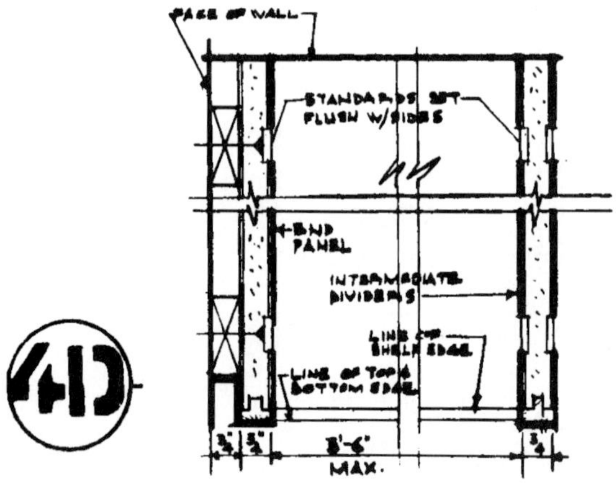

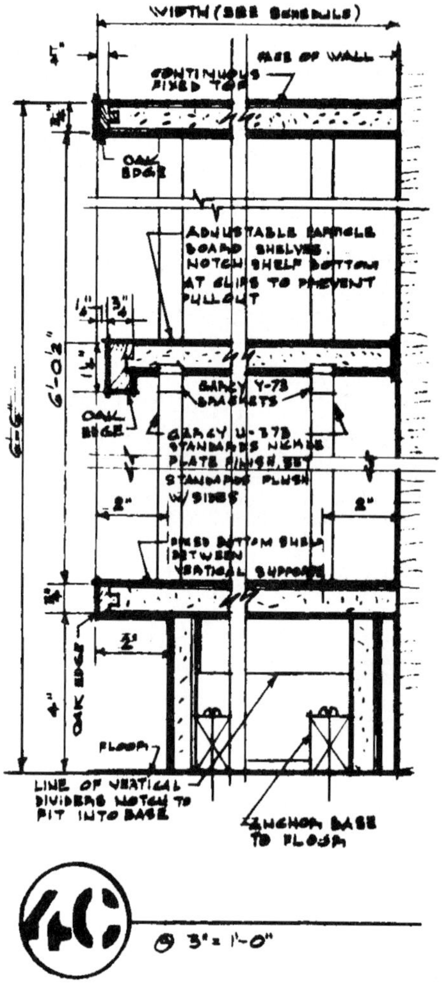

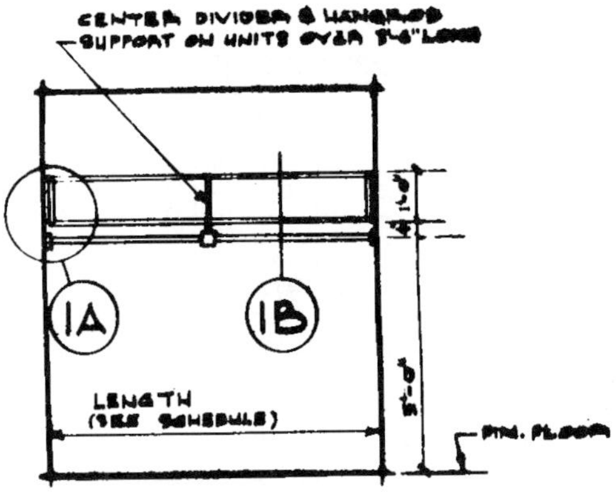

ELEVATION OF UNIT
@ 1/4" = 1'-0"

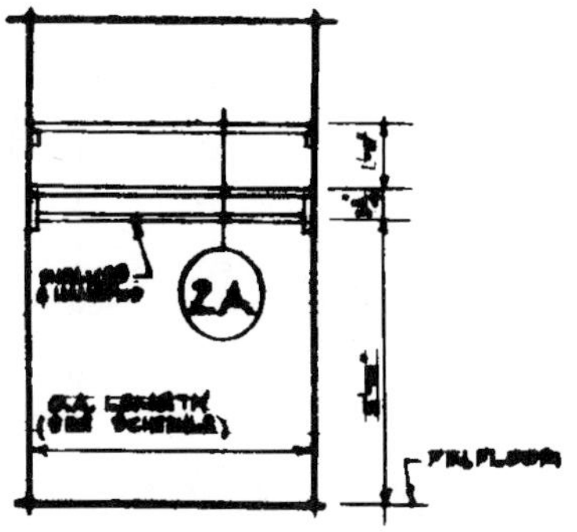

ELEVATION OF UNIT
@ 1/4" = 1'-0"

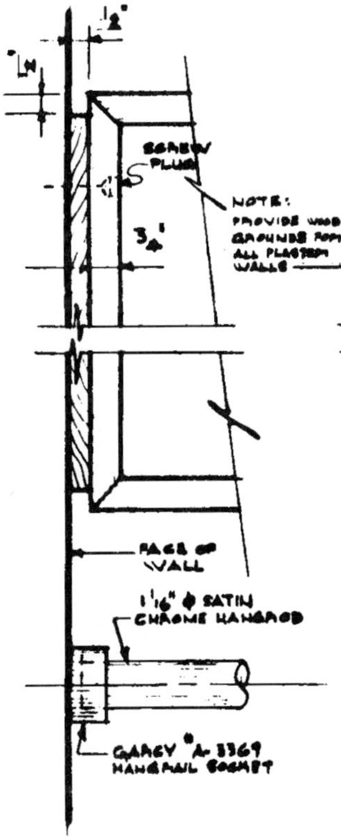

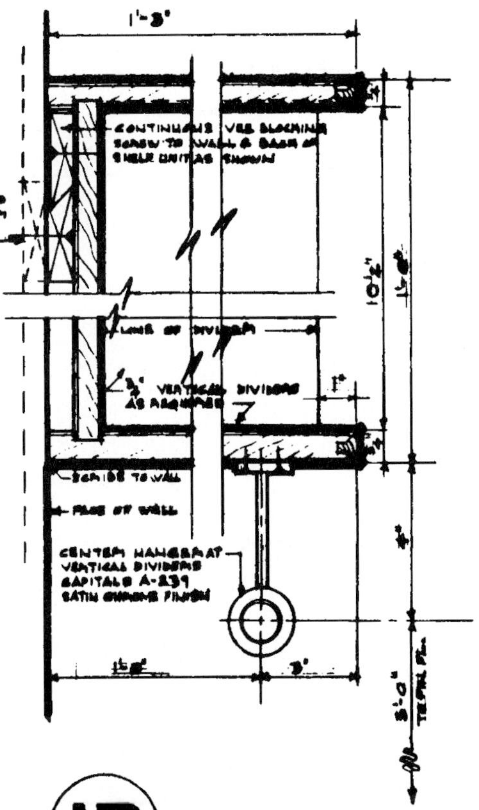

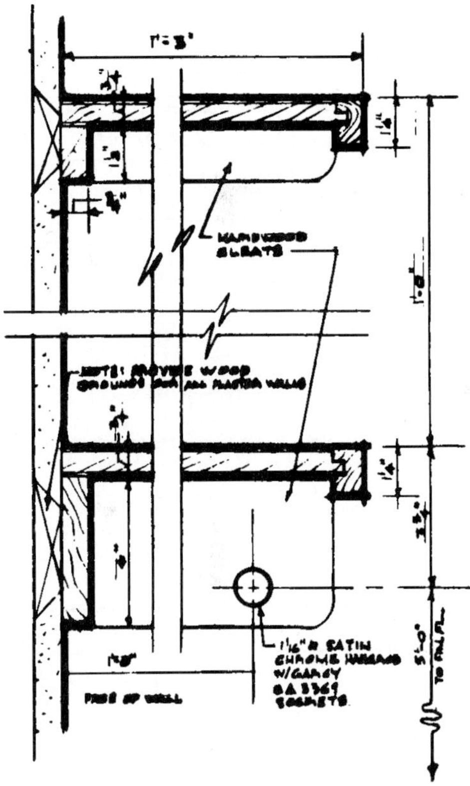

1A @ 3" = 1'-0"

1B @ 3" = 1'-0"

2A @ 3" = 1'-0"

WOODWORK DETAILS
Credenza and File Storage

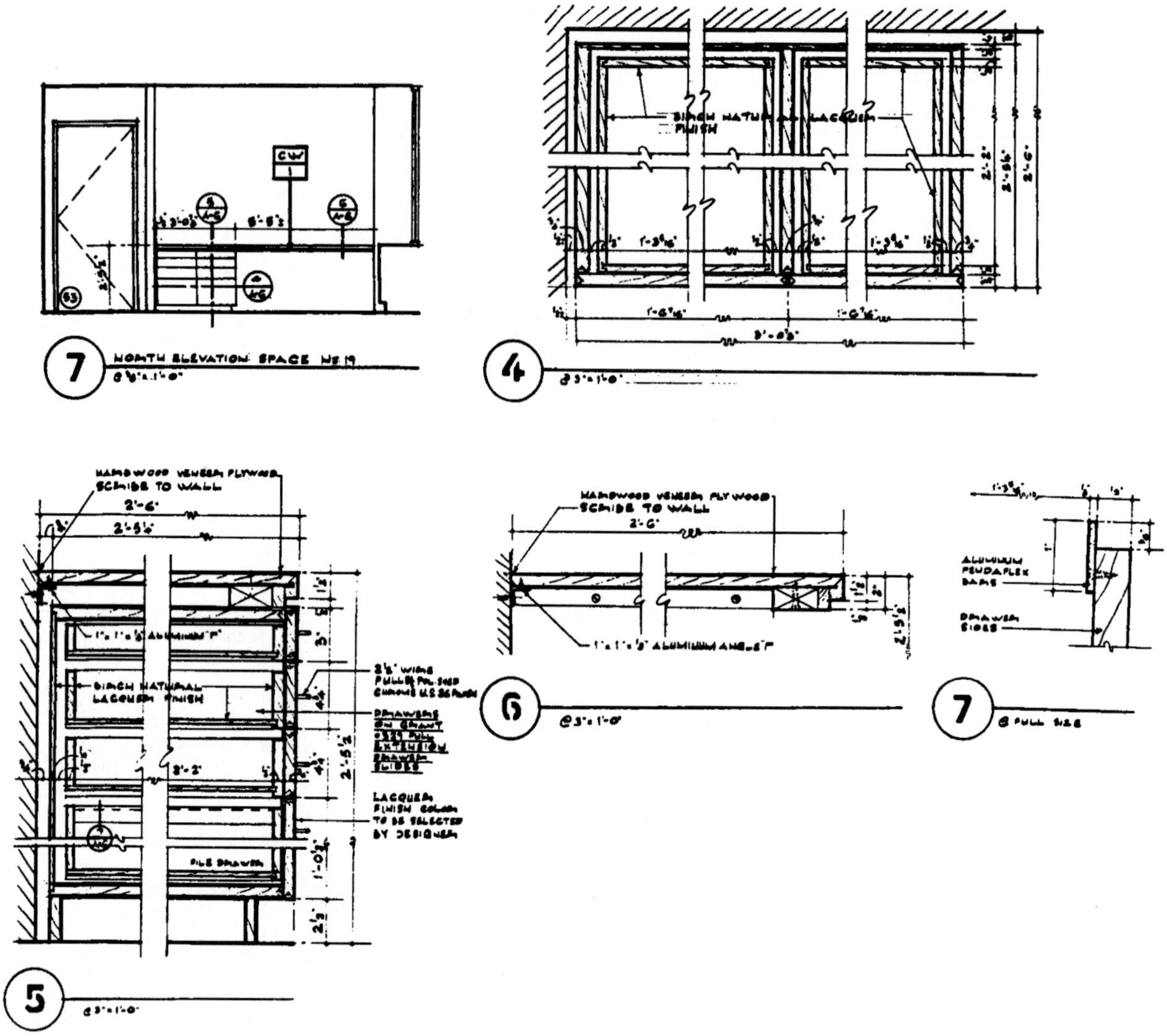

Fig. 12 Credenza

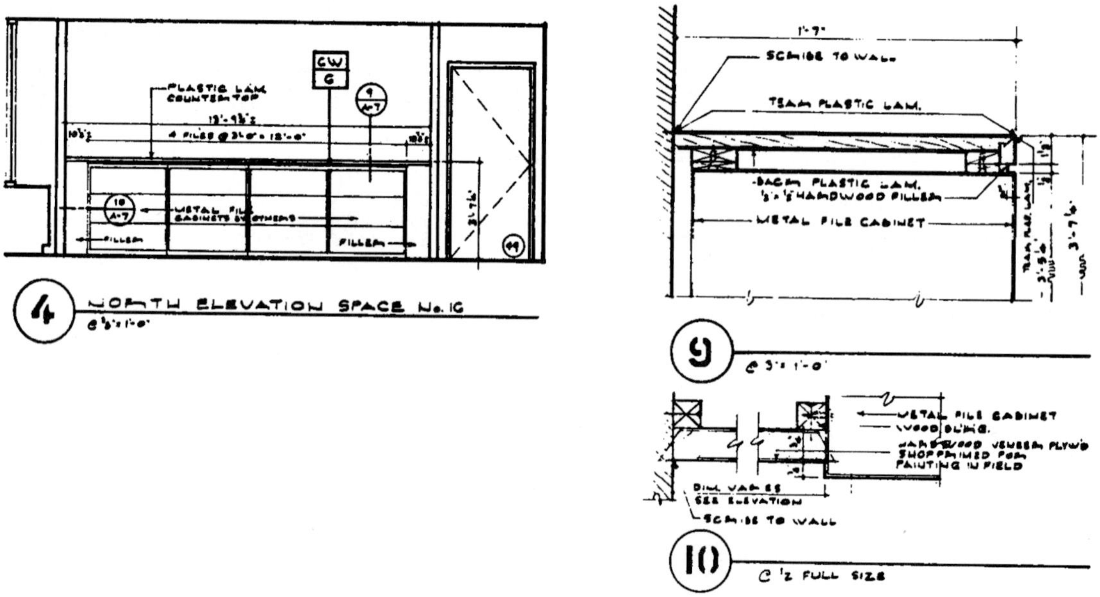

Fig. 13 File countertop

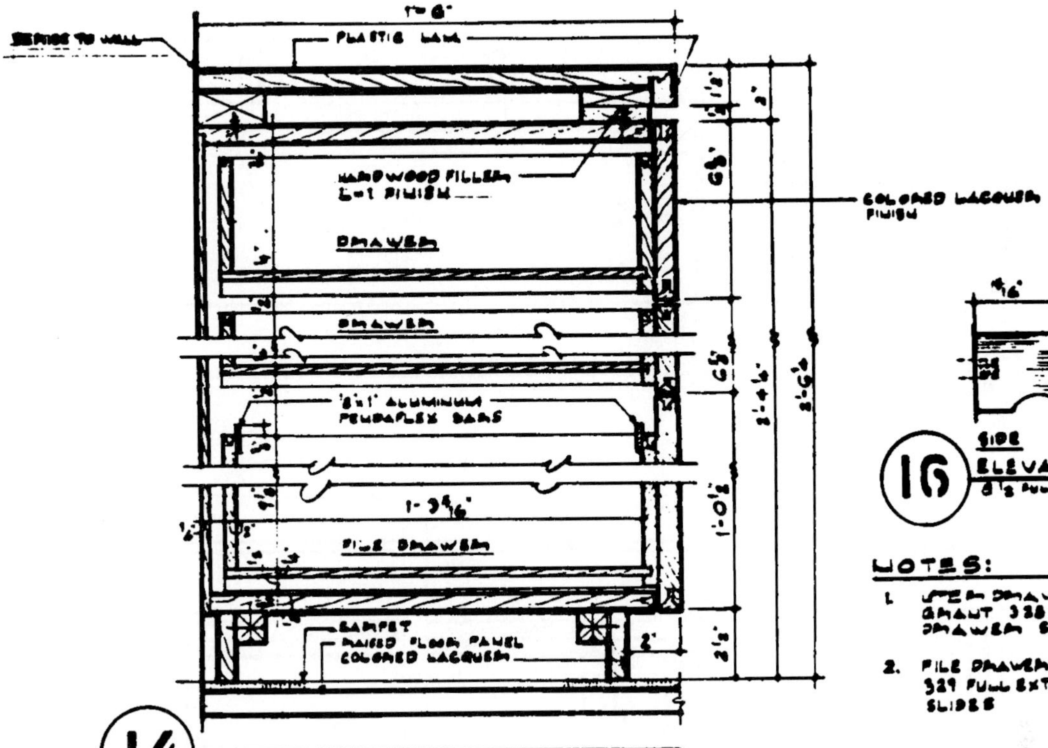

14 @ 3" = 1'-0"

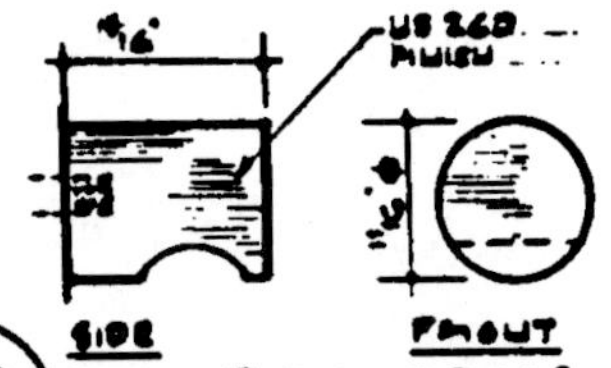

16 ELEVATION OF PULLS
@ ½ FULL SIZE

NOTES:

1. UPPER DRAWERS SHALL HAVE GRANT 328 FULL EXTENSION DRAWER SLIDES
2. FILE DRAWER SHALL HAVE GRANT 329 FULL EXTENSION DRAWER SLIDES

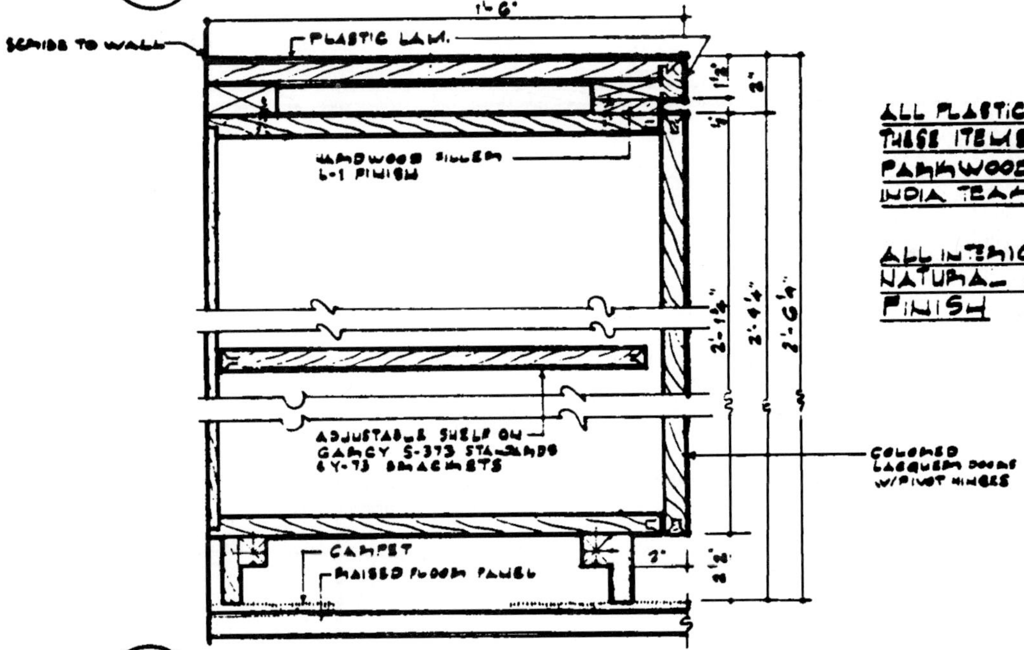

ALL PLASTIC LAMINATE FOR THESE ITEMS TO BE: PARKWOOD # 51202E INDIA TEAK

ALL INTERIORS TO HAVE NATURAL LACQUER FINISH

15 @ 3" = 1'-0"

WOODWORK DETAILS
Base Cabinets

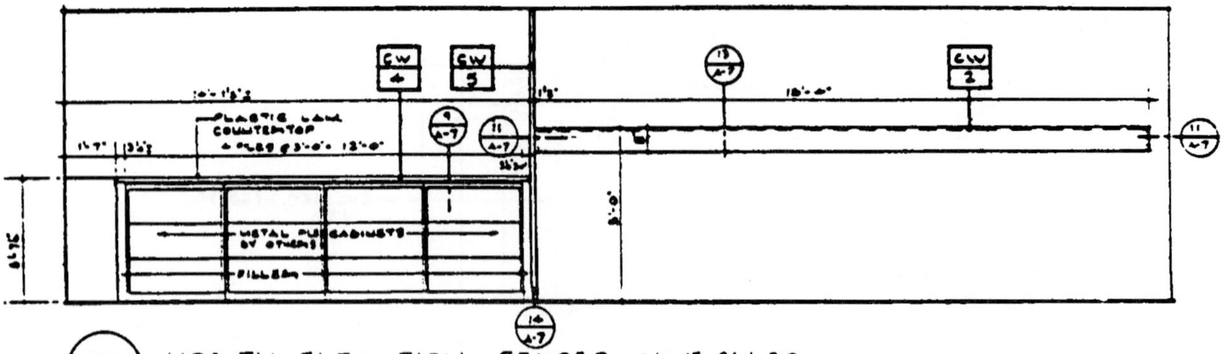

3 NORTH ELEVATION SPACES №s 15, 21 & 20
@ 3/8" = 1'-0"

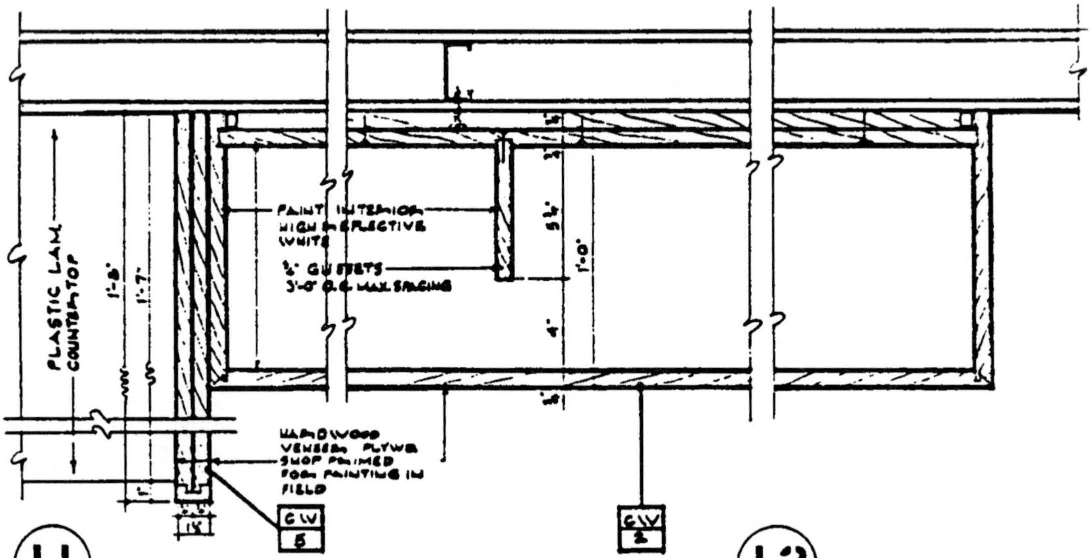

11 @ 3" = 1'-0"

12 @ 3" = 1'-0"

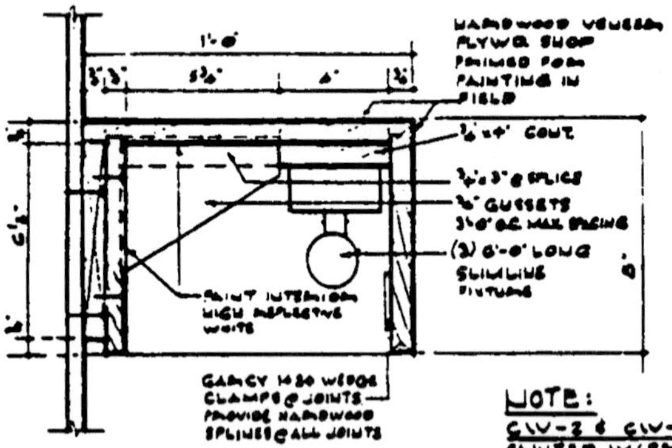

NOTE:
CW-2 & CW-5 SHALL BE PAINTED W/PRATT & LAMBERT #C124 TIGER LILY SEMI-GLOSS

13 @ 3" = 1'-0"

CW
2

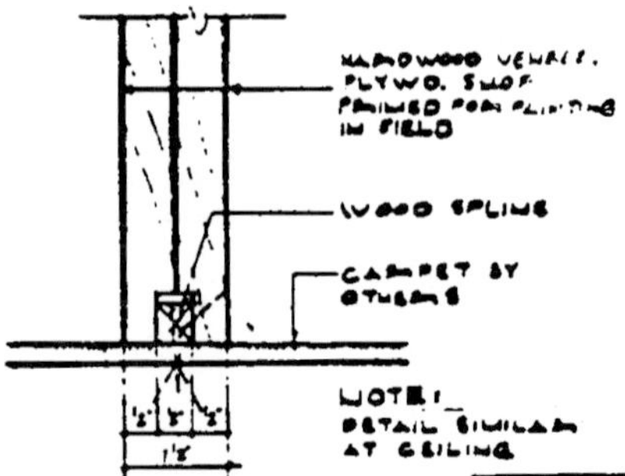

14 @ 1/2 FULL SIZE

CW
5

WOODWORK DETAILS
Pantry Cabinets

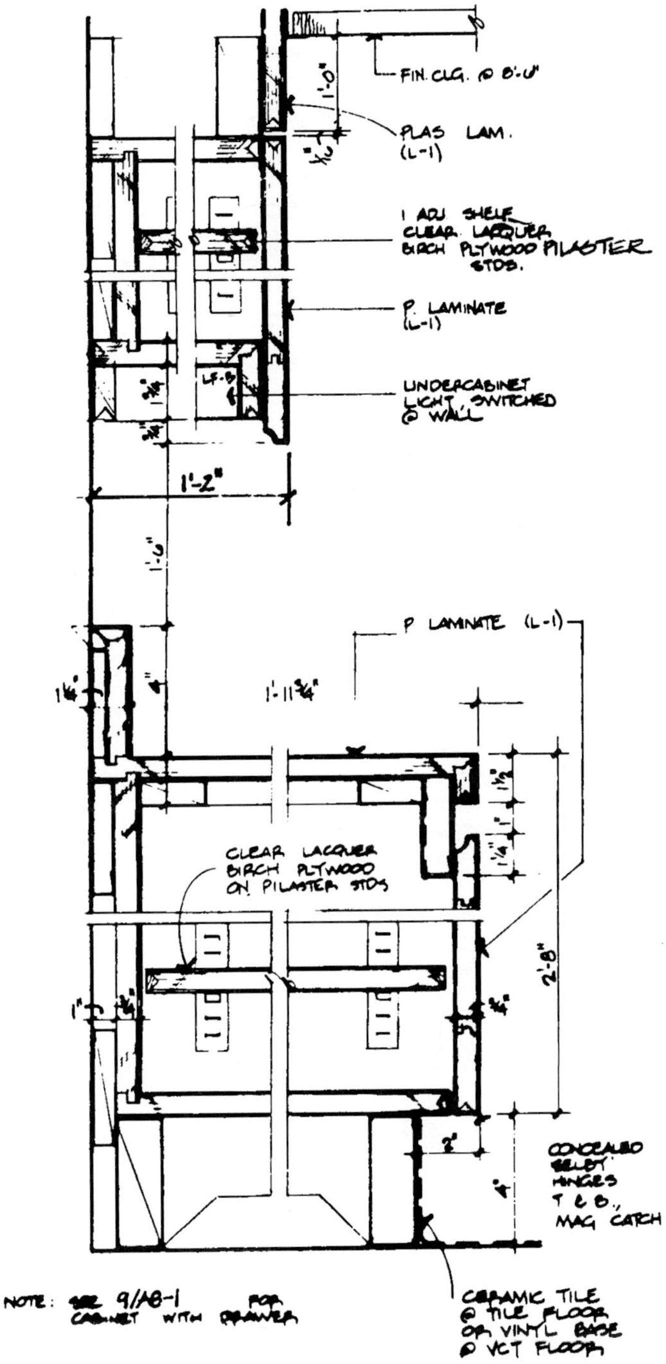

PANTRY CABINETS

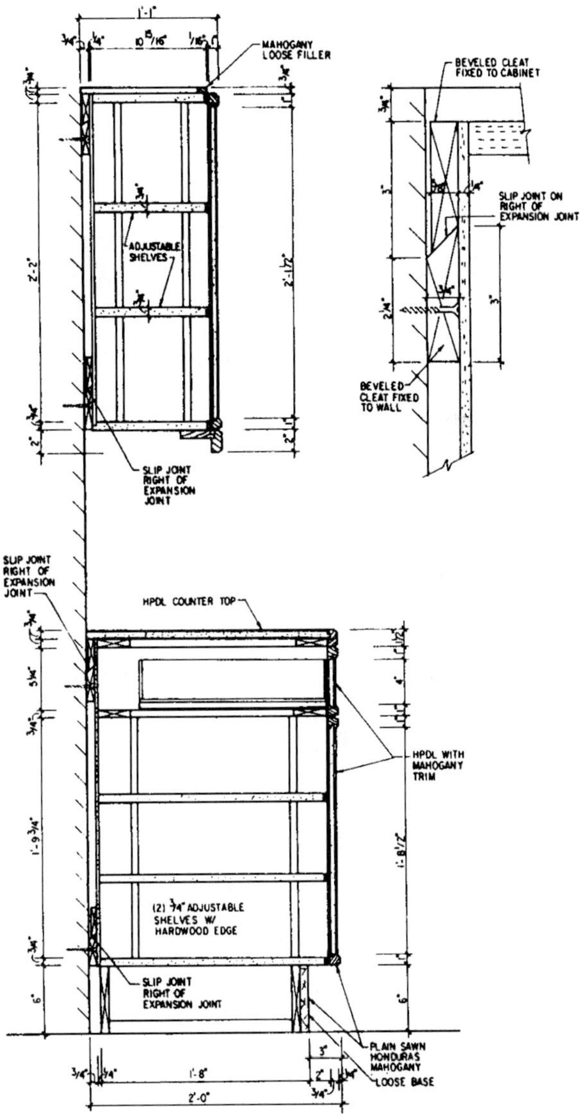

VERTICAL SECTION-PANTRY CABINETS

WOODWORK DETAILS
Altars

Pulpit
3′9″ High x 3′6″ Wide x 1′8½″ D
Table
2′7″ High x 5′0″ Long x 2′ D
Center Pulpit Chair
4′ High x 2′2½″ Wide x 1′10″ D
Side Pulpit Chair
3′9″ High x 2′2½″ Wide x 1′10″ D
Communion Chair
3′4″ High x 1′8½″ Wide x 1′7½″ D
Flower Stand
2′6″ High x 1′3″ Square

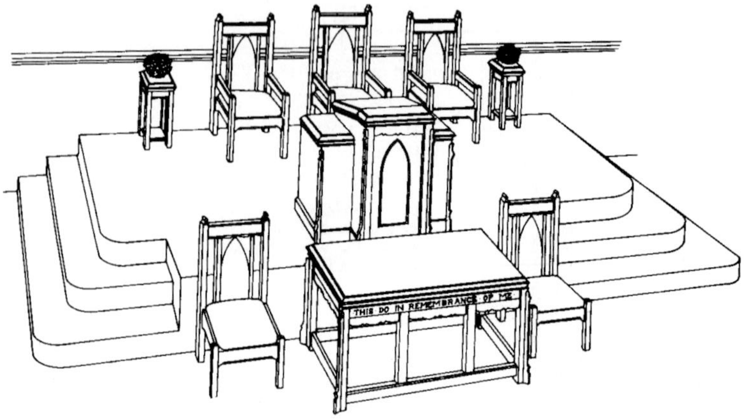

Pulpit
4′0″ High x 3′6″ Wide x 1′8″ D
Table
2′9″ High x 6′0″ Long x 2′0″ D
Flower Stand
2′0″ High x 1′2″ Square

Pulpit
3′9″ High x 3′4″ Wide x 1′8″ D
Table
2′9″ High x 6′0″ Long x 2′0″ D
Flower Stand
2′0″ High x 1′2″ Square
Clergy Pew End

Pulpit
4′0″ High x 3′8″ Wide x 1′9″ D
Table
2′9″ High x 4′6″ Long x 2′0″ D
Flower Stand
2′0″ High x 1′2″ Square
Clergy Pew End

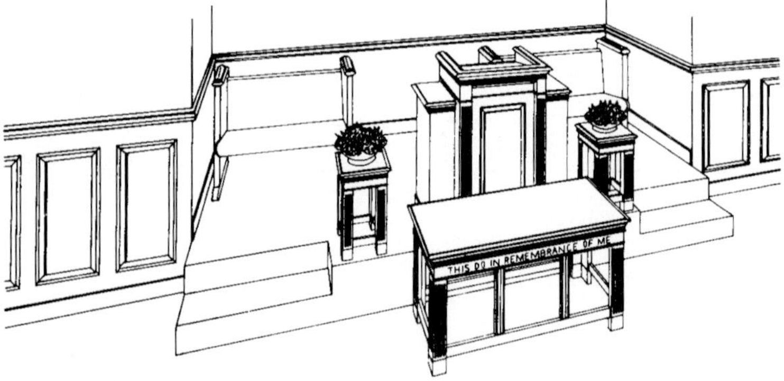

Fig. 14

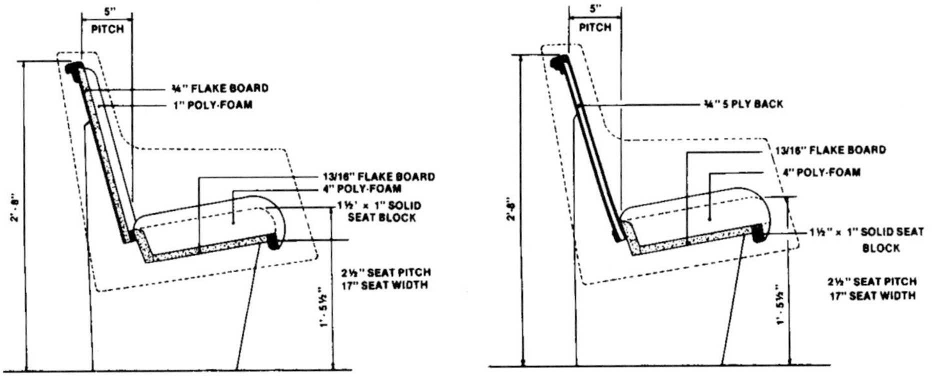

Fig. 15 Fully upholstered seat. All exposed surfaces of the seat and back are fully upholstered

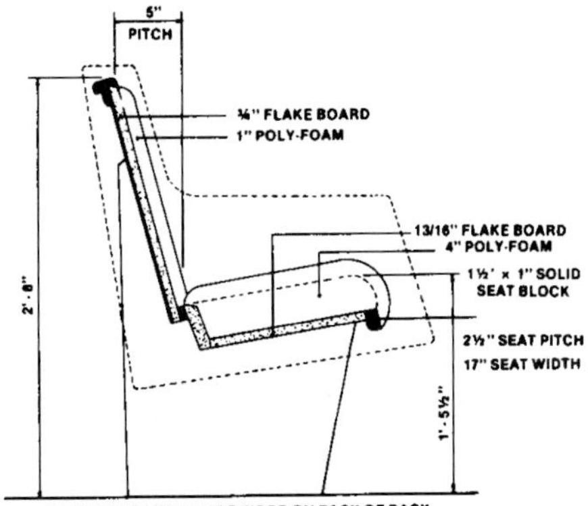

* #46 BODY SAME EXCEPT WOOD ON BACK OF BACK.

Fig. 16 Combination upholstered/wood seat. An upholstered seat with a wooden back (either solid or veneer laminate)

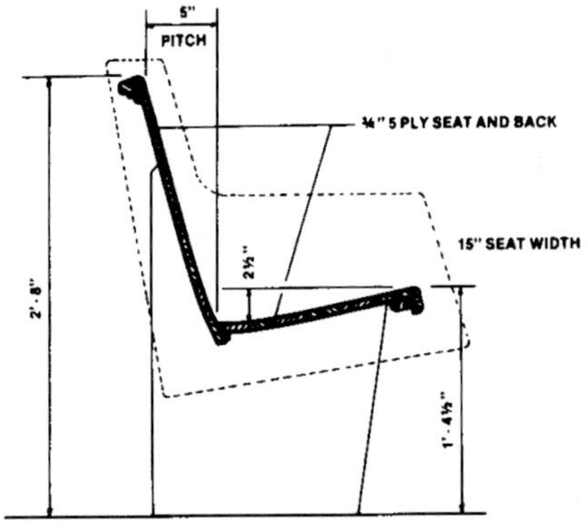

Fig. 17 All wood seat. Either solid wood or veneered seat and back. Generally the most expensive option. Wood seats and back can be contoured for increased comfort

WOODWORK DETAILS

Sanctuary Doors and Miscellaneous Details

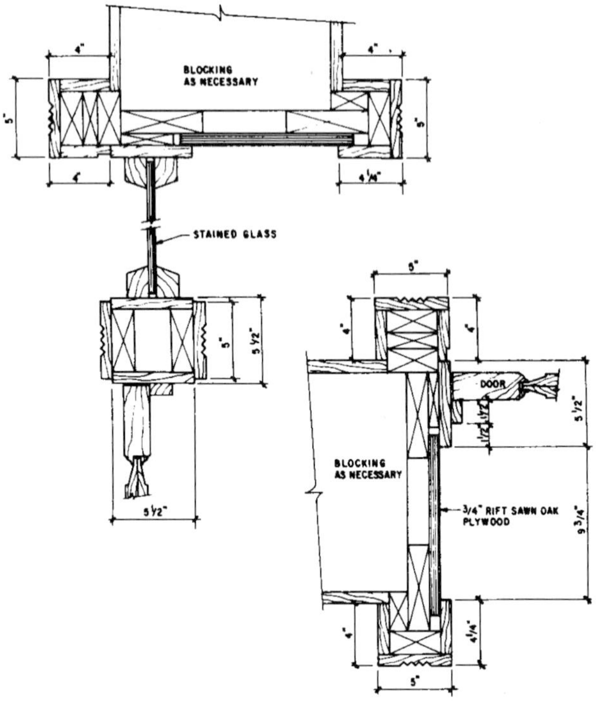

SECTIONS-SANCTUARY DOORS

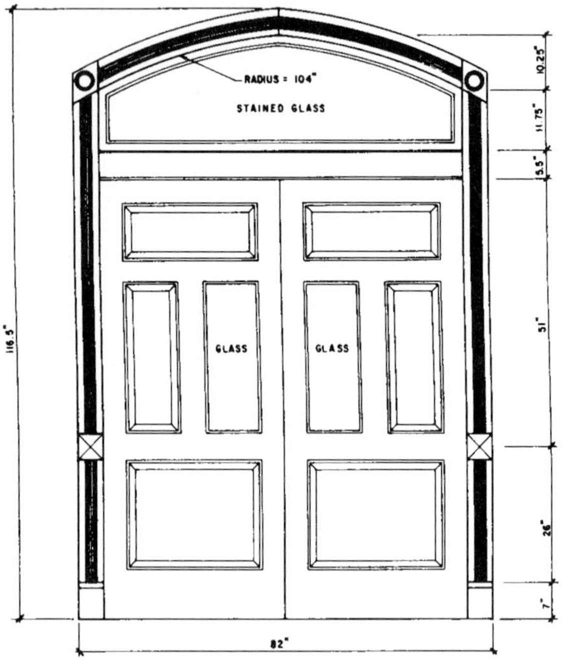

ELEVATION - SANCTUARY DOORS

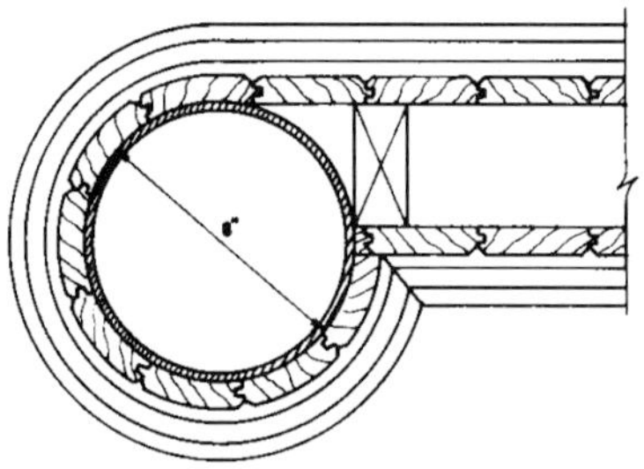

PLAN AT INTERSECTION
OF CHANCEL RAIL AND COLUMN

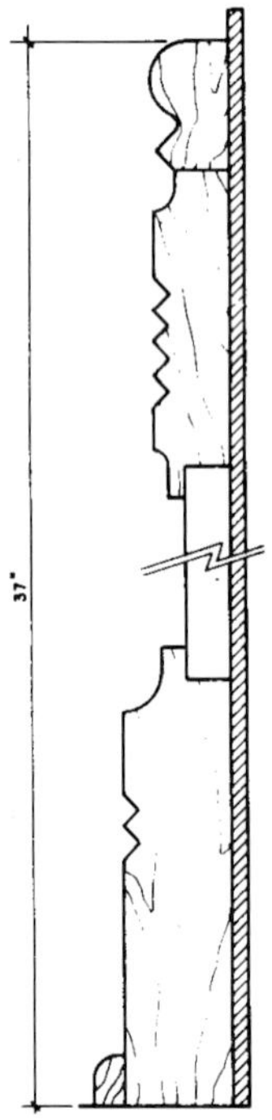

SECTION
AT SANCTUARY COLUMN

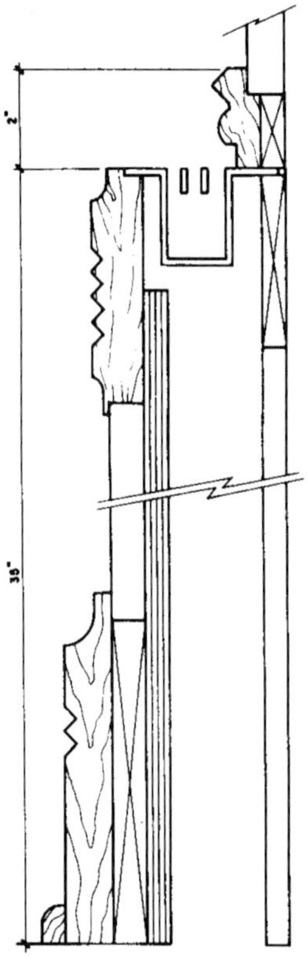

SECTION
AT WAINSCOAT

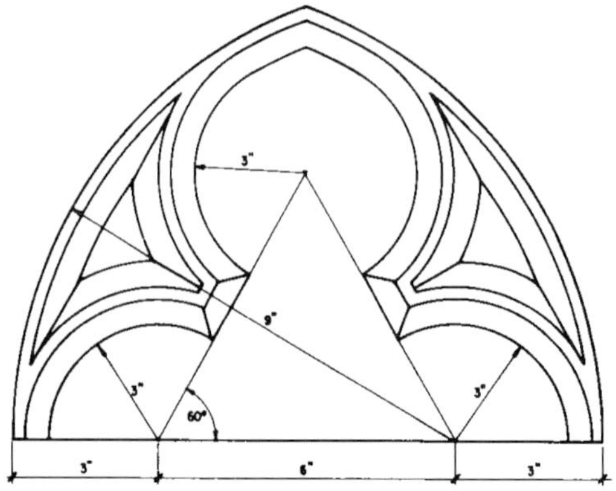

TREFOIL LAYOUT

WOODWORK DETAILS
Lectern

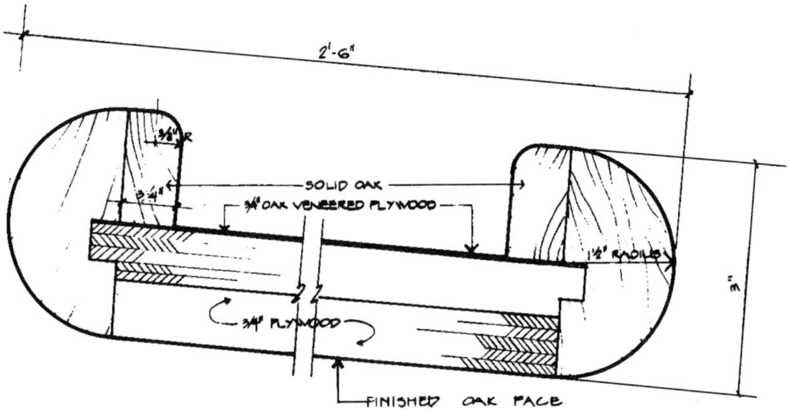

2 FULL SIZE SECTION THRU BIMAH TOP

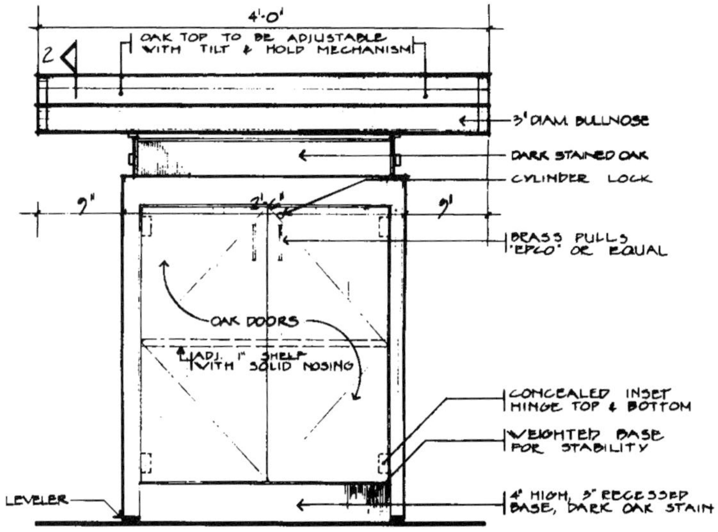

4 FRONT ELEVATION (EAST SIDE)
SCALE: 1 1/2" = 1'-0"

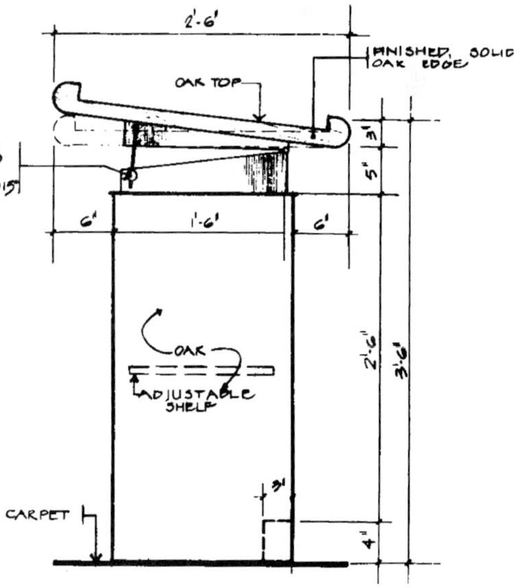

3 SIDE ELEVATION (SOUTH SIDE)
SCALE: 1 1/2" = 1'-0"

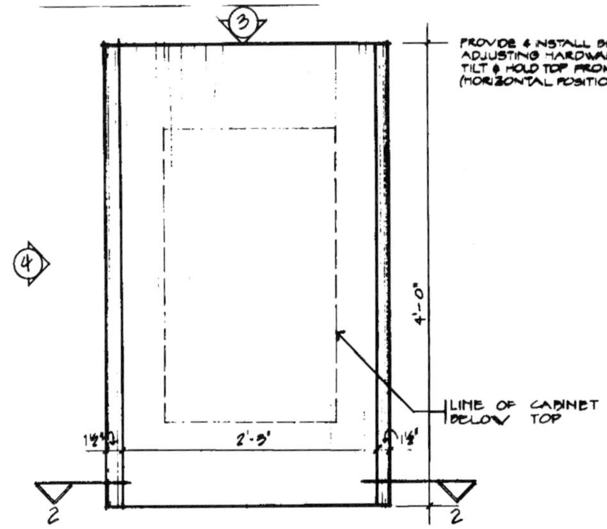

1 PLAN OF BIMAH TOP
SCALE: 1 1/2" = 1'-0"

WOODWORK DETAILS
Lectern

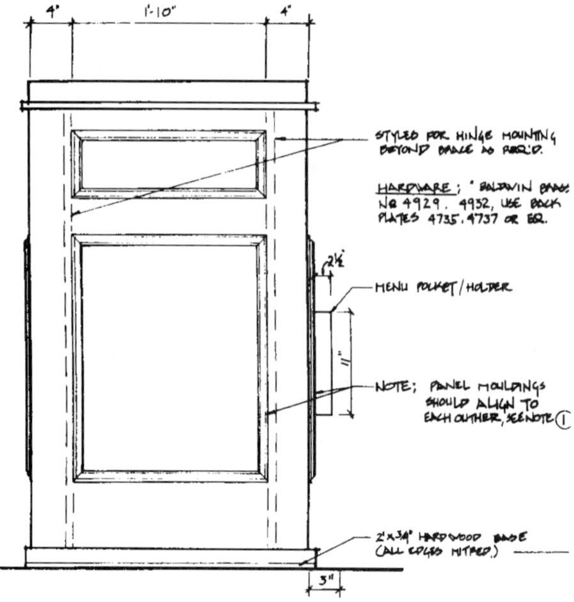

STYLED FOR HINGE MOUNTING BEYOND BRACE AS REQ'D.
HARDWARE; "BALDWIN BRASS Nº 4929, 4932, USE BACK PLATES 4735, 4737 OR EQ.
MENU POCKET/HOLDER
NOTE; PANEL MOULDINGS SHOULD ALIGN TO EACH OTHER, SEE NOTE 1
2"x3/4" HARDWOOD BASE (ALL EDGES MITRED)

ELEVATION FRONT VIEW 5

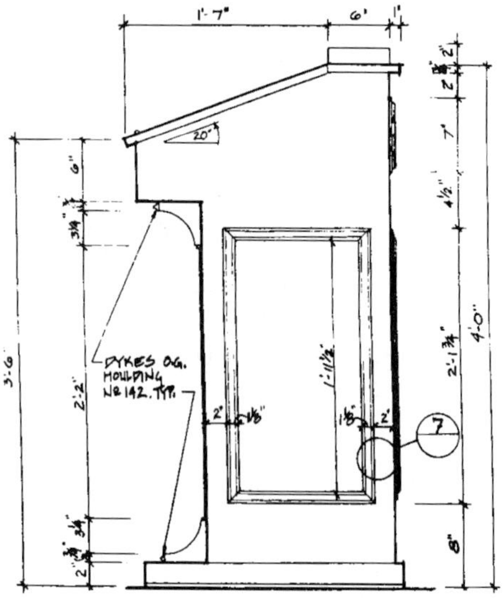

DYKES OG. MOULDING Nº 142. TYP.

ELEVATION SIDE 2

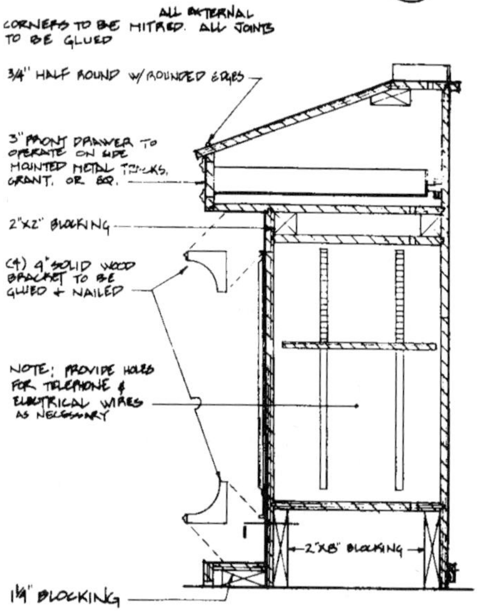

ALL EXTERNAL CORNERS TO BE MITRED. ALL JOINTS TO BE GLUED
3/4" HALF ROUND W/ROUNDED EDGES
3" FRONT DRAWER TO OPERATE ON SIDE MOUNTED METAL TRACKS, GRANT, OR EQ.
2"x2" BLOCKING
(4) 4" SOLID WOOD BRACKET TO BE GLUED + NAILED
NOTE; PROVIDE HOLES FOR TELEPHONE & ELECTRICAL WIRES AS NECESSARY
2"x8" BLOCKING
1 1/4" BLOCKING

SECTION 3

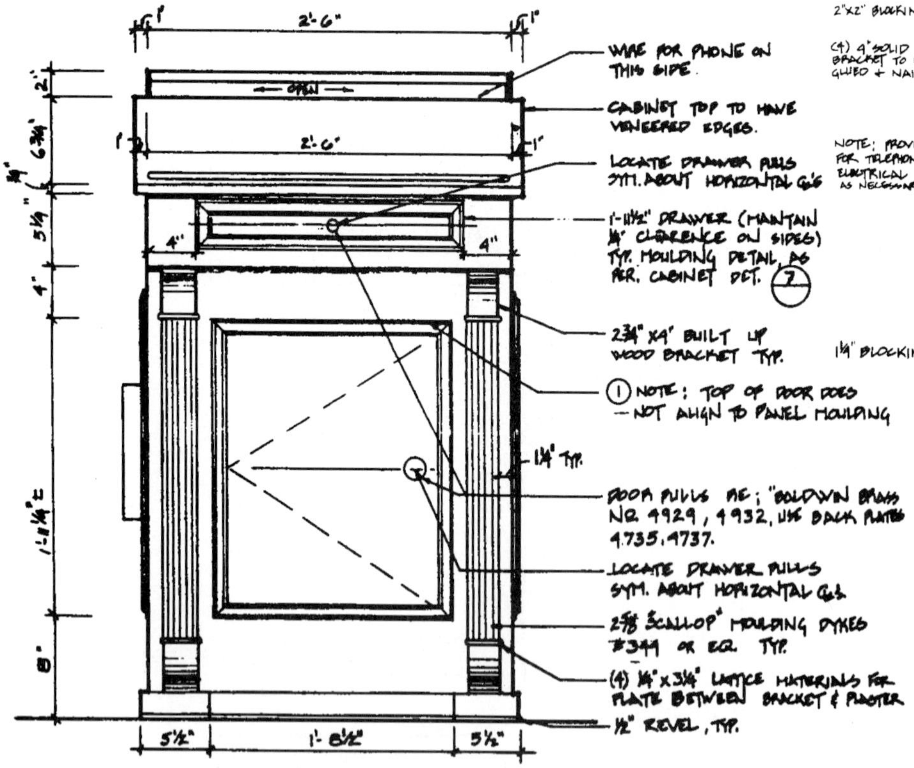

WIRE FOR PHONE ON THIS SIDE.
CABINET TOP TO HAVE VENEERED EDGES.
LOCATE DRAWER PULLS SYM. ABOUT HORIZONTAL C's
1'-1 1/2" DRAWER (MAINTAIN 1/4" CLEARENCE ON SIDES) TYP. MOULDING DETAIL AS PER. CABINET DET. 7
2 3/4" X4" BUILT UP WOOD BRACKET TYP.
1 NOTE: TOP OF DOOR DOES NOT ALIGN TO PANEL MOULDING
DOOR PULLS ARE; "BALDWIN BRASS Nº 4929, 4932, USE BACK PLATES 4735, 4737.
LOCATE DRAWER PULLS SYM. ABOUT HORIZONTAL C's.
2 3/8" SCALLOP" MOULDING DYKES #344 OR EQ. TYP.
(4) 1/4"x3/4" LATTICE MATERIALS FOR PLATE BETWEEN BRACKET & PLASTER
1/2" REVEL, TYP.

ELEVATION BACK VIEW 1

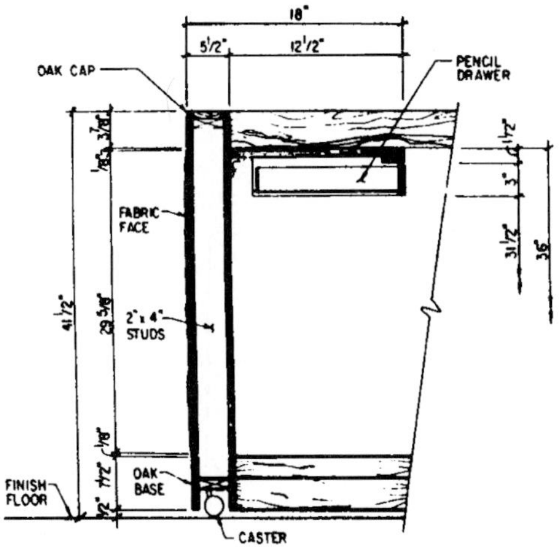

SECTION VIEW THRU LECTERN STANDS

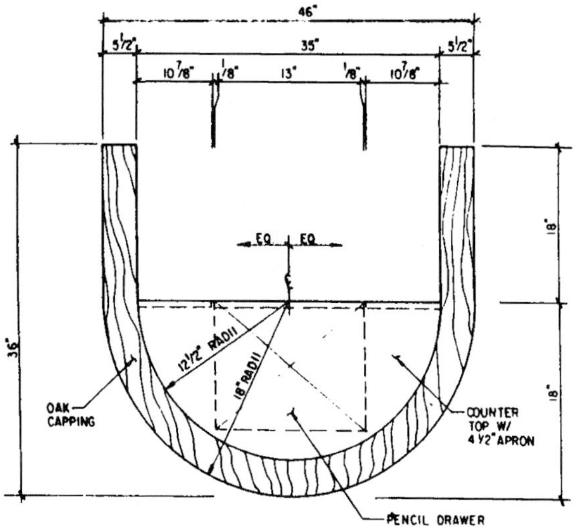

PLAN VIEW OF LECTERN STANDS

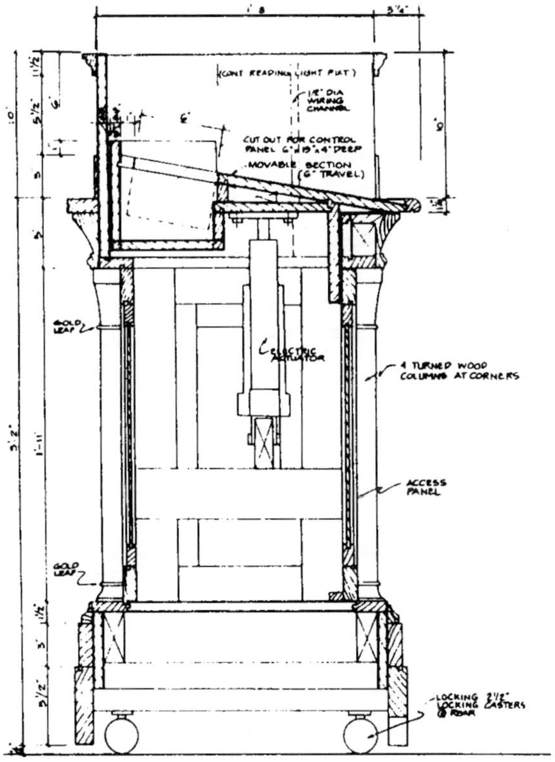

CROSS SECTION @ PODIUM

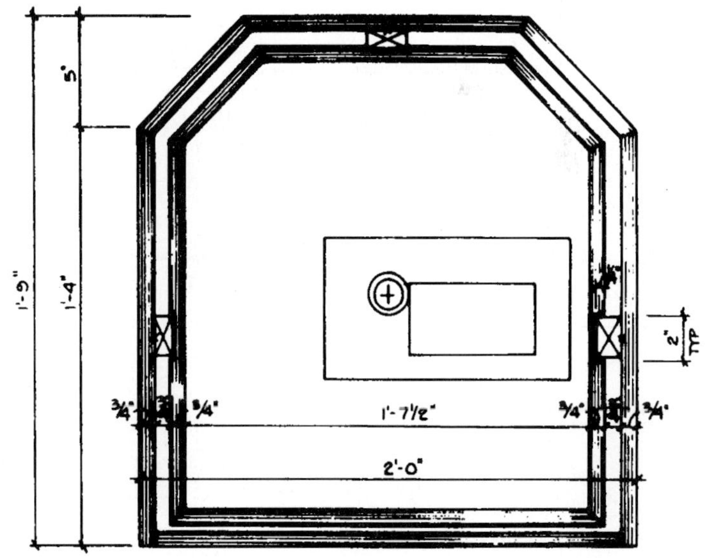

PLAN SECTION

WOODWORK DETAILS
Lectern

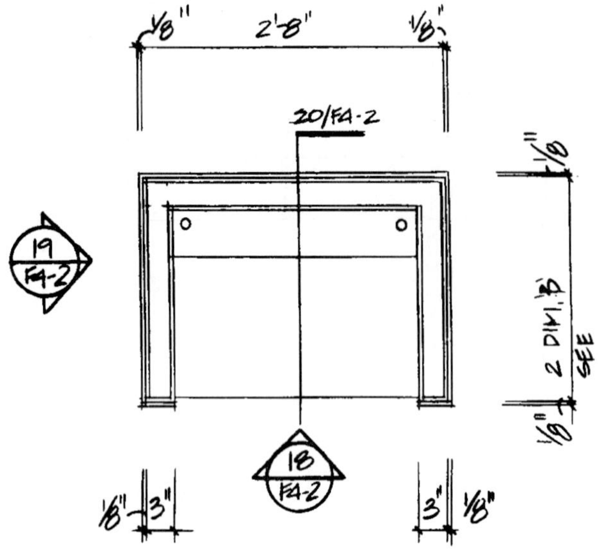

17 F4-2 LECTURN PLAN

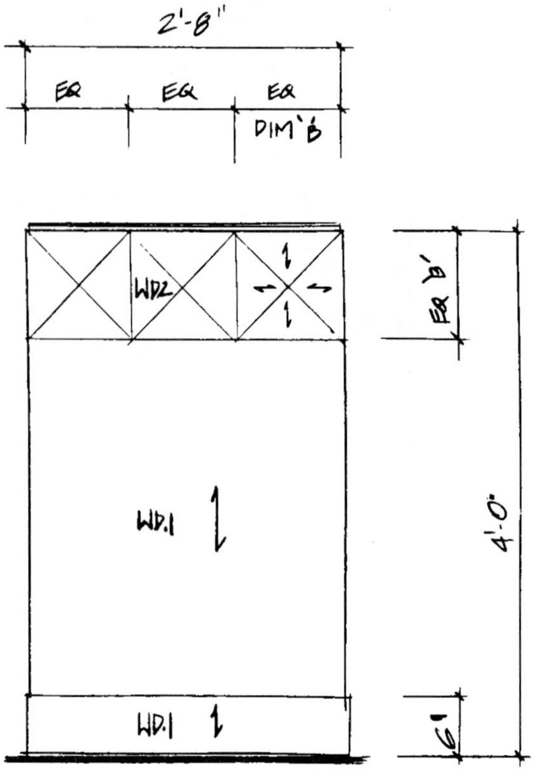

18 F4-2 FRONT VIEW

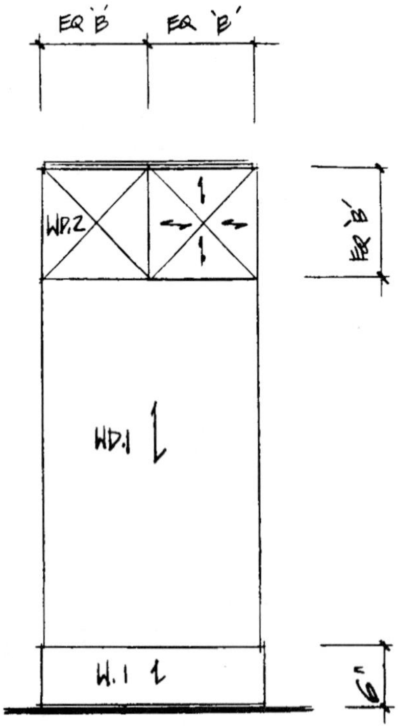

19 F4-2 M.317 SIDE VIEW

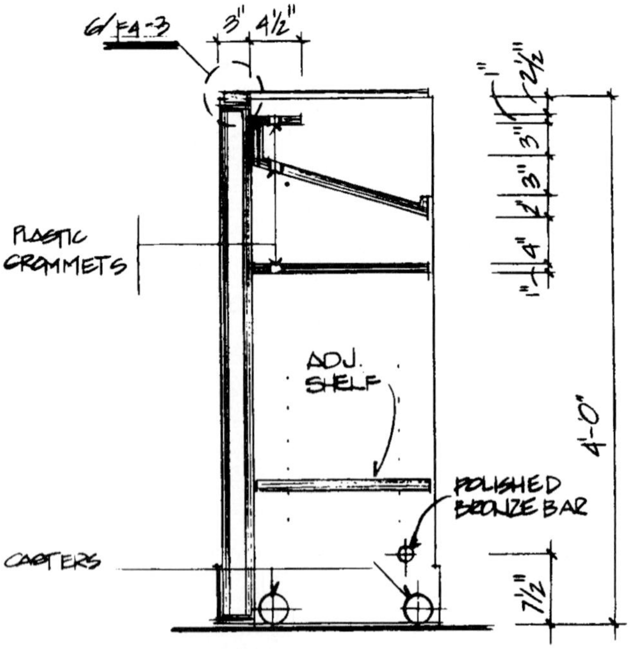

20 F4-2 M.317 SECTION

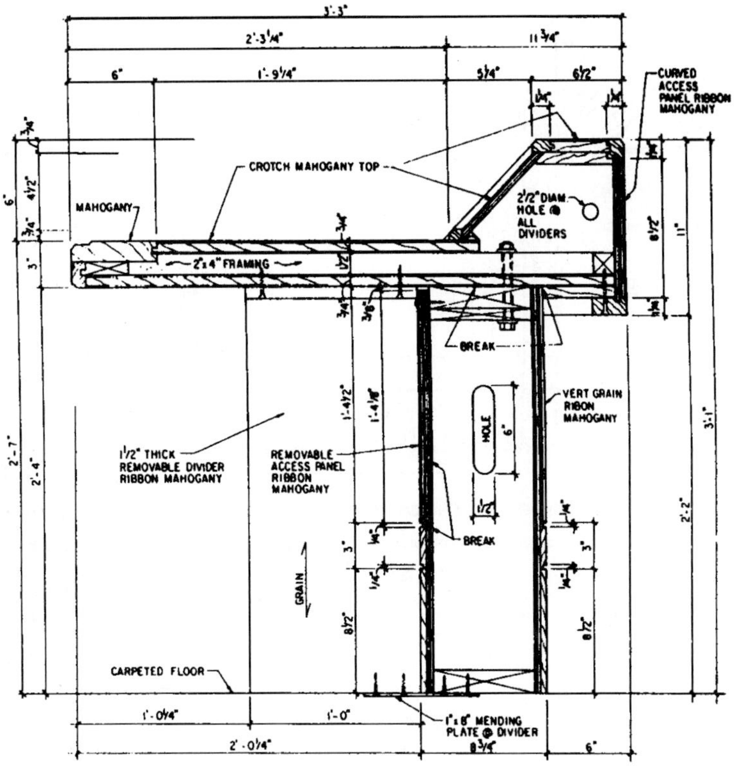

VERTICAL SECTION- BOARDROOM TABLE

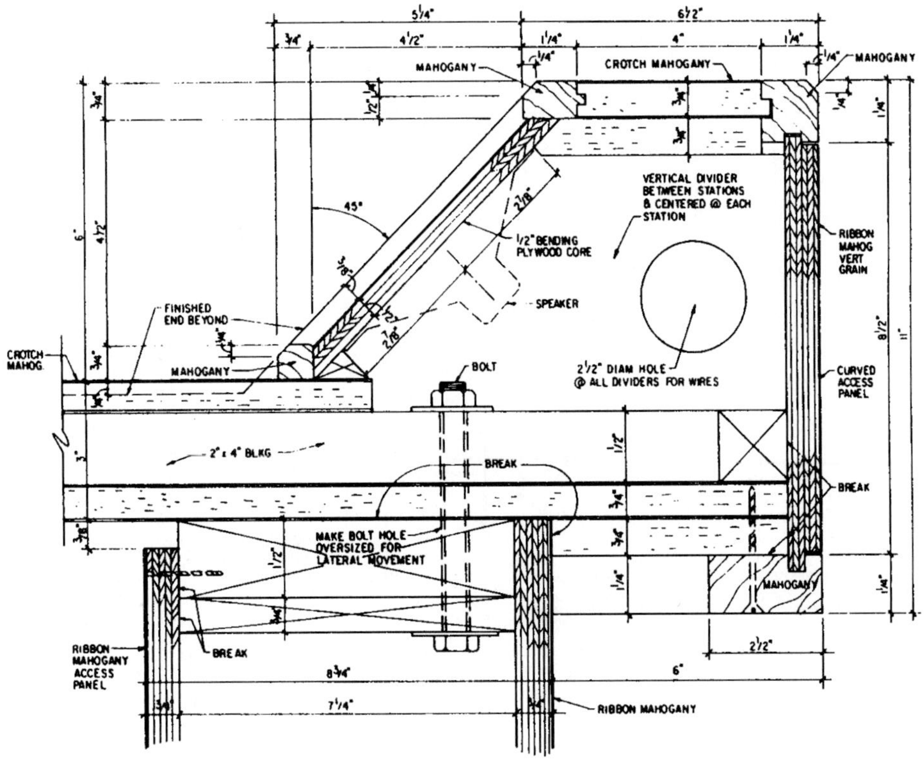

SECTION

WOODWORK DETAILS
Boardroom Table

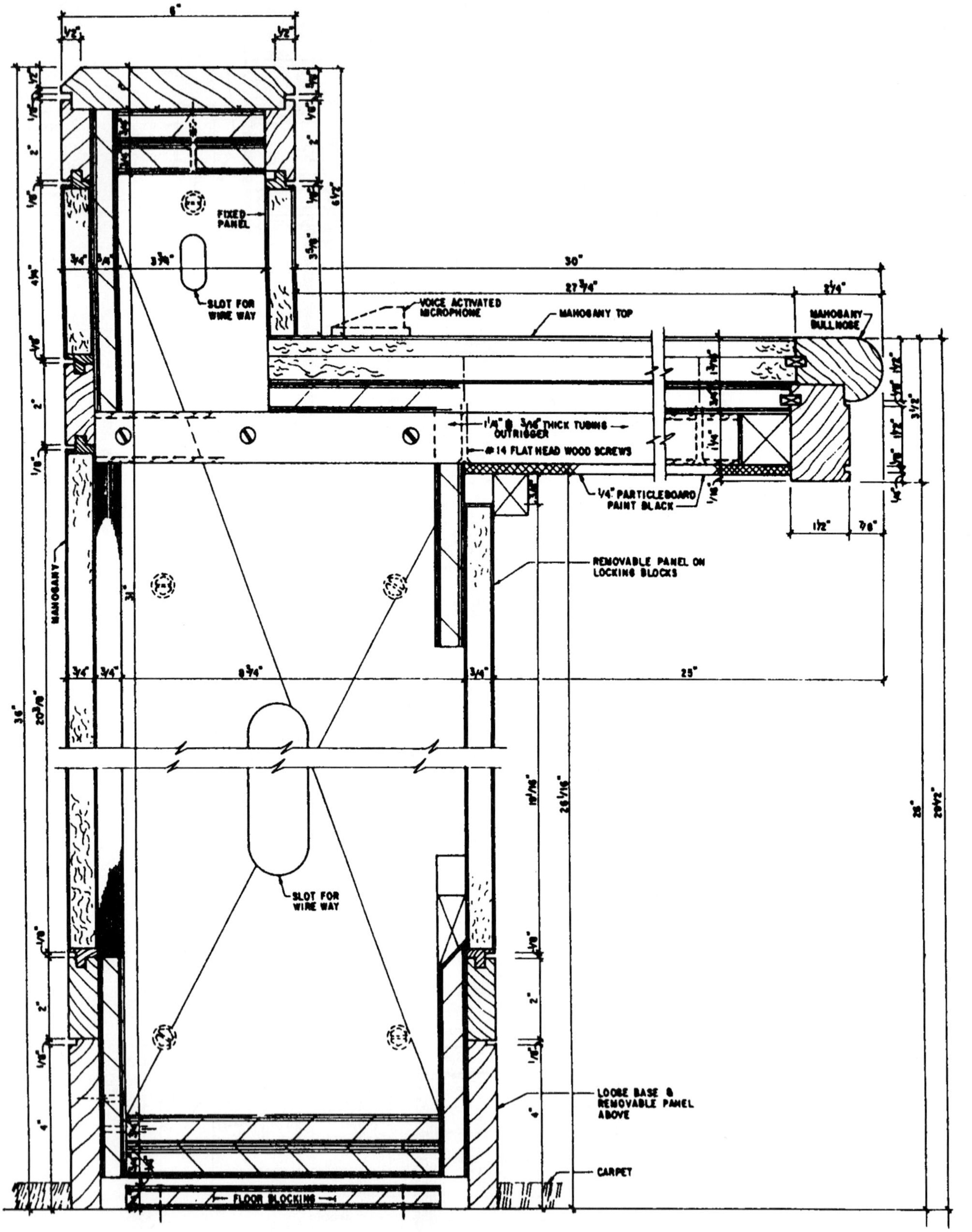

CROSS SECTION AT BOARDROOM TABLE

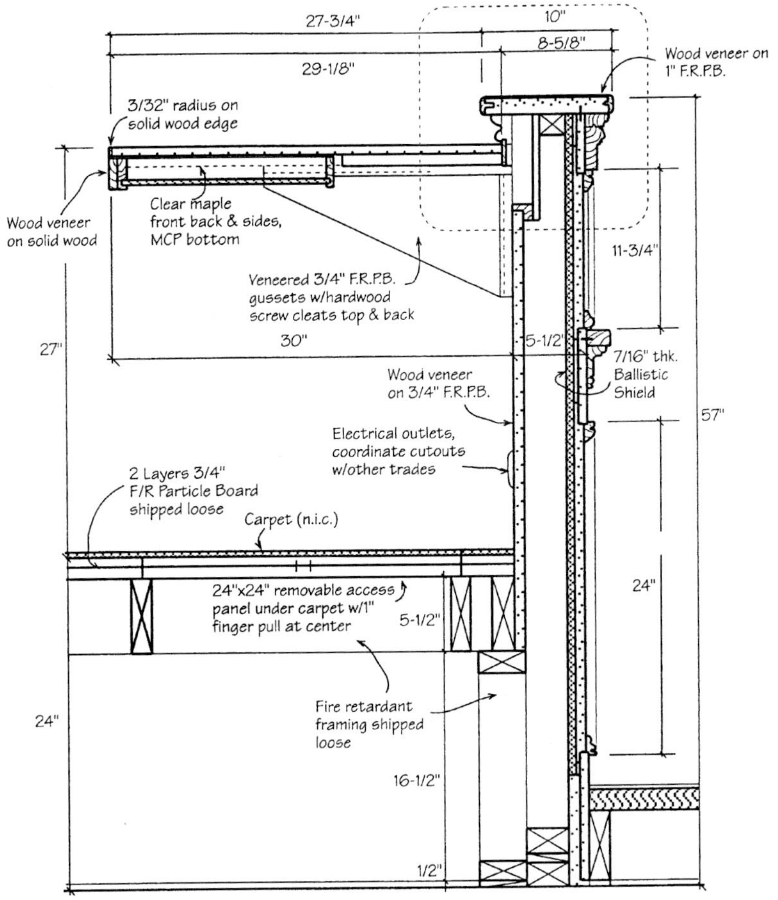
27-3/4"
10"
8-5/8"
29-1/8"
Wood veneer on 1" F.R.P.B.
3/32" radius on solid wood edge
Wood veneer on solid wood
Clear maple front back & sides, MCP bottom
Veneered 3/4" F.R.P.B. gussets w/hardwood screw cleats top & back
11-3/4"
30"
5-1/2"
27"
7/16" thk. Ballistic Shield
Wood veneer on 3/4" F.R.P.B.
57"
Electrical outlets, coordinate cutouts w/other trades
2 Layers 3/4" F/R Particle Board shipped loose
Carpet (n.i.c.)
24"x24" removable access panel under carpet w/1" finger pull at center
5-1/2"
24"
Fire retardant framing shipped loose
24"
16-1/2"
1/2"

Judges' Bench Vertical Section

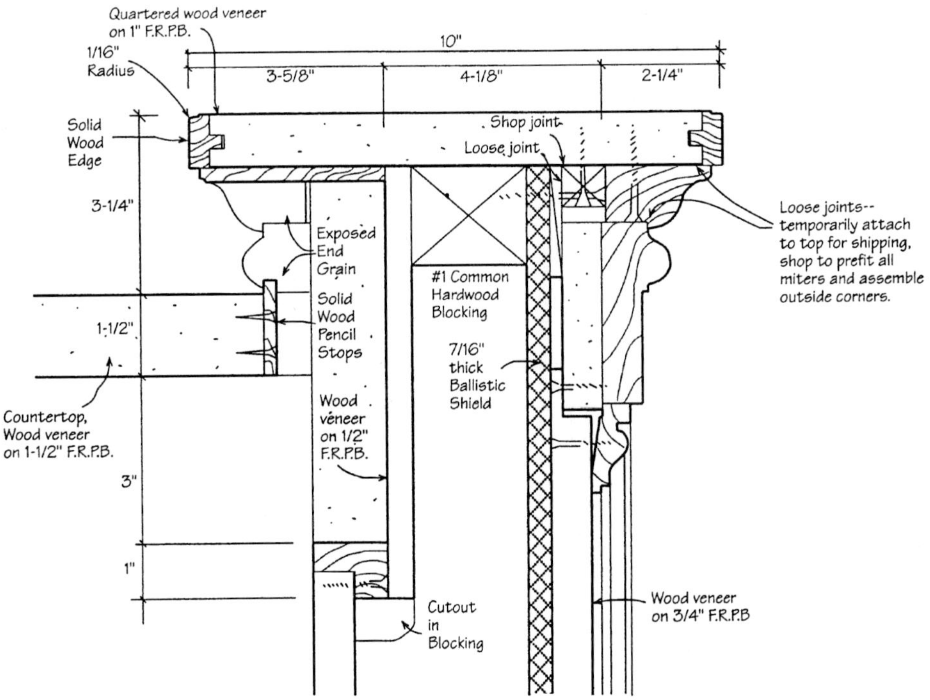
Quartered wood veneer on 1" F.R.P.B.
1/16" Radius
10"
3-5/8"
4-1/8"
2-1/4"
Solid Wood Edge
Shop joint
Loose joint
3-1/4"
Exposed End Grain
Loose joints-- temporarily attach to top for shipping, shop to prefit all miters and assemble outside corners.
#1 Common Hardwood Blocking
1-1/2"
Solid Wood Pencil Stops
7/16" thick Ballistic Shield
Wood vêneer on 1/2" F.R.P.B.
Countertop, Wood veneer on 1-1/2" F.R.P.B.
3"
1"
Cutout in Blocking
Wood veneer on 3/4" F.R.P.B

Bench Detail

WOODWORK DETAILS

Courtroom Seating and Judge's Bench

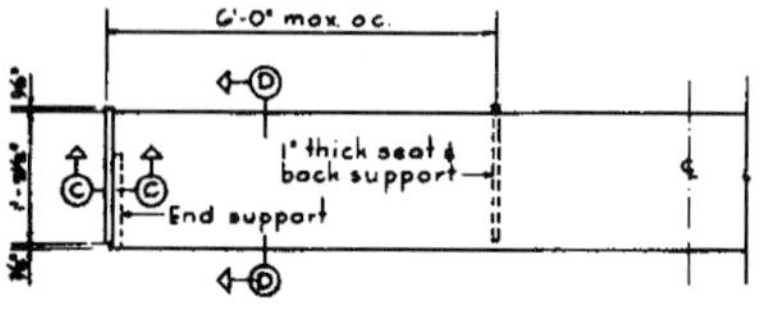

PARTIAL PLAN OF BENCH

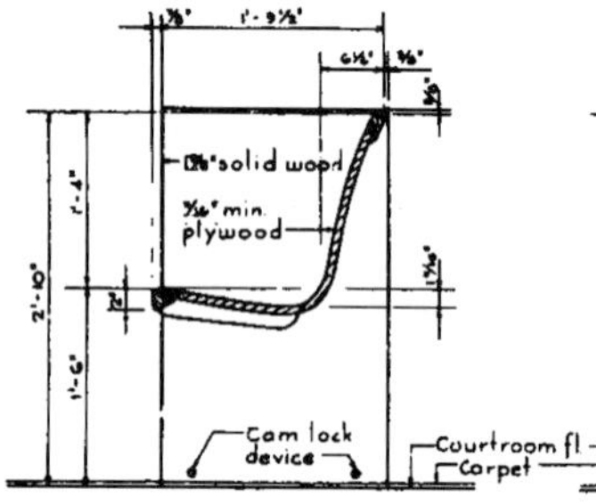

SECTION D-D

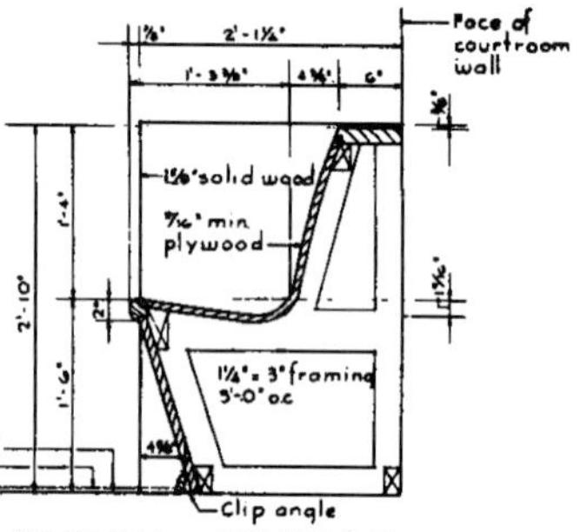

TYPICAL SECTION THRU REAR BENCH

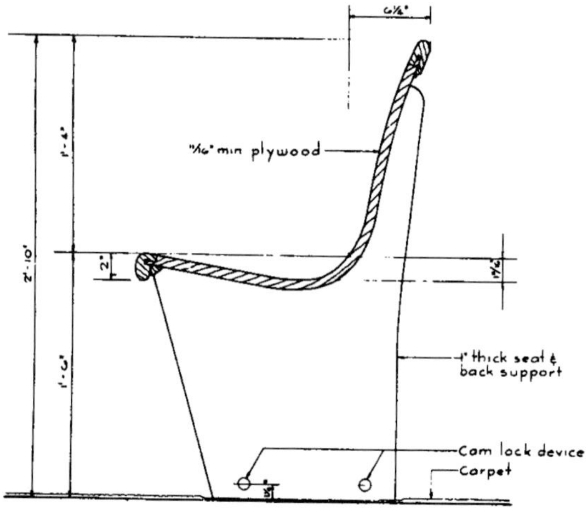

SEAT AND BACK SUPPORT

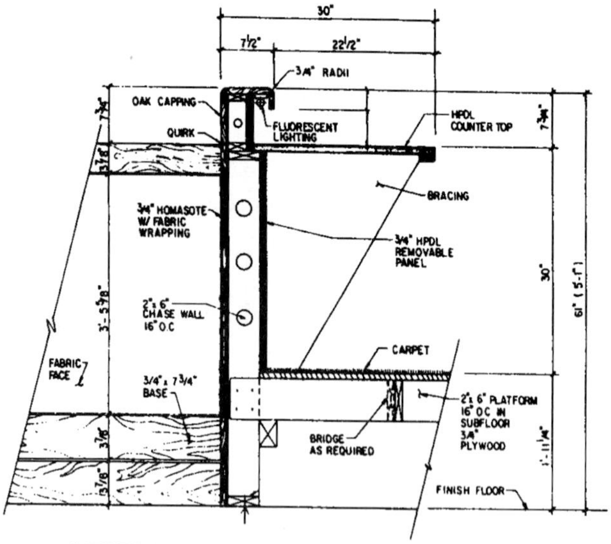

SECTION THRU JUDGES BENCH

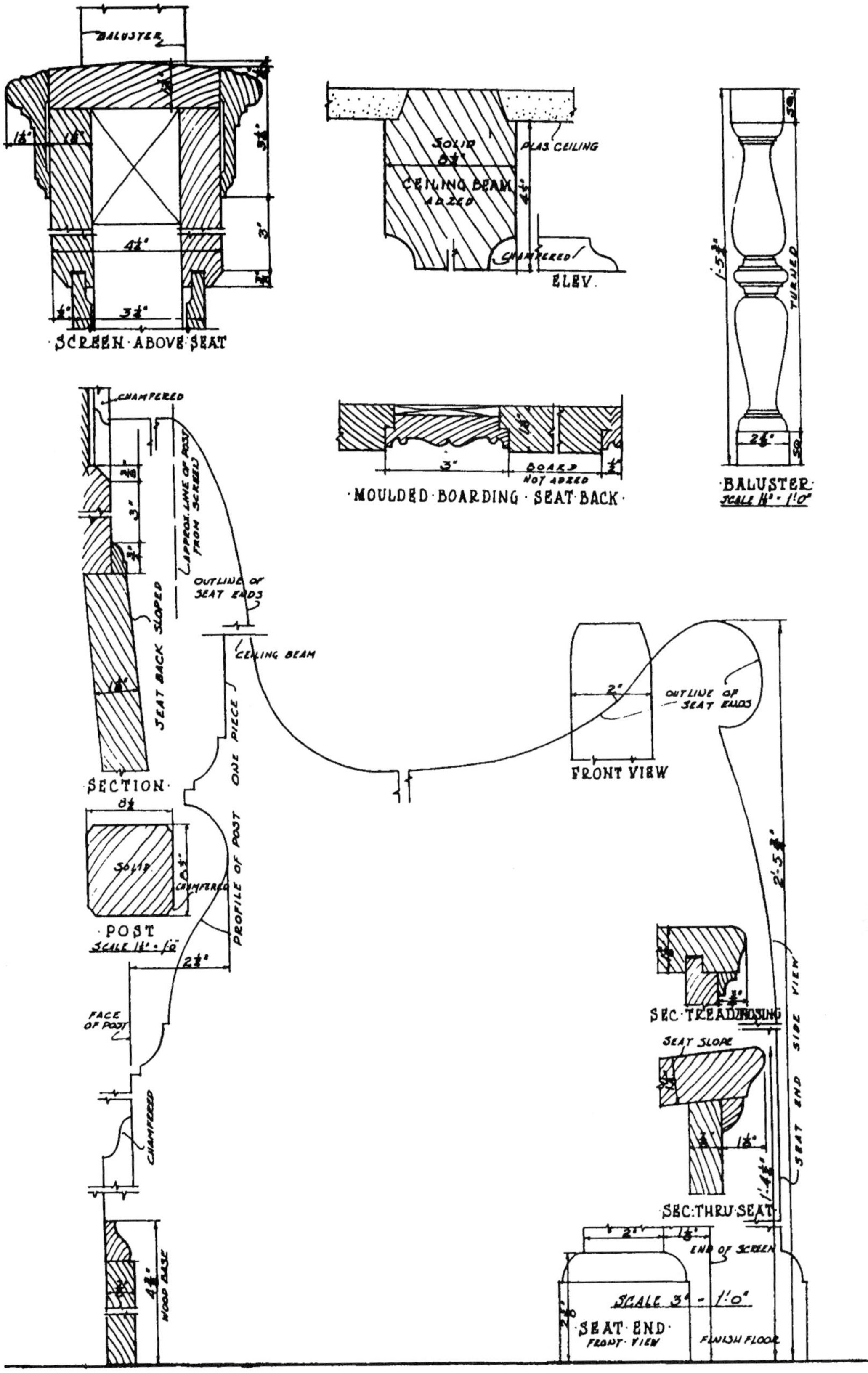

DETAIL · OF · STAIR · SCREEN · & · SEAT · MAIN · HALL ·

WOODWORK DETAILS
Window Seat

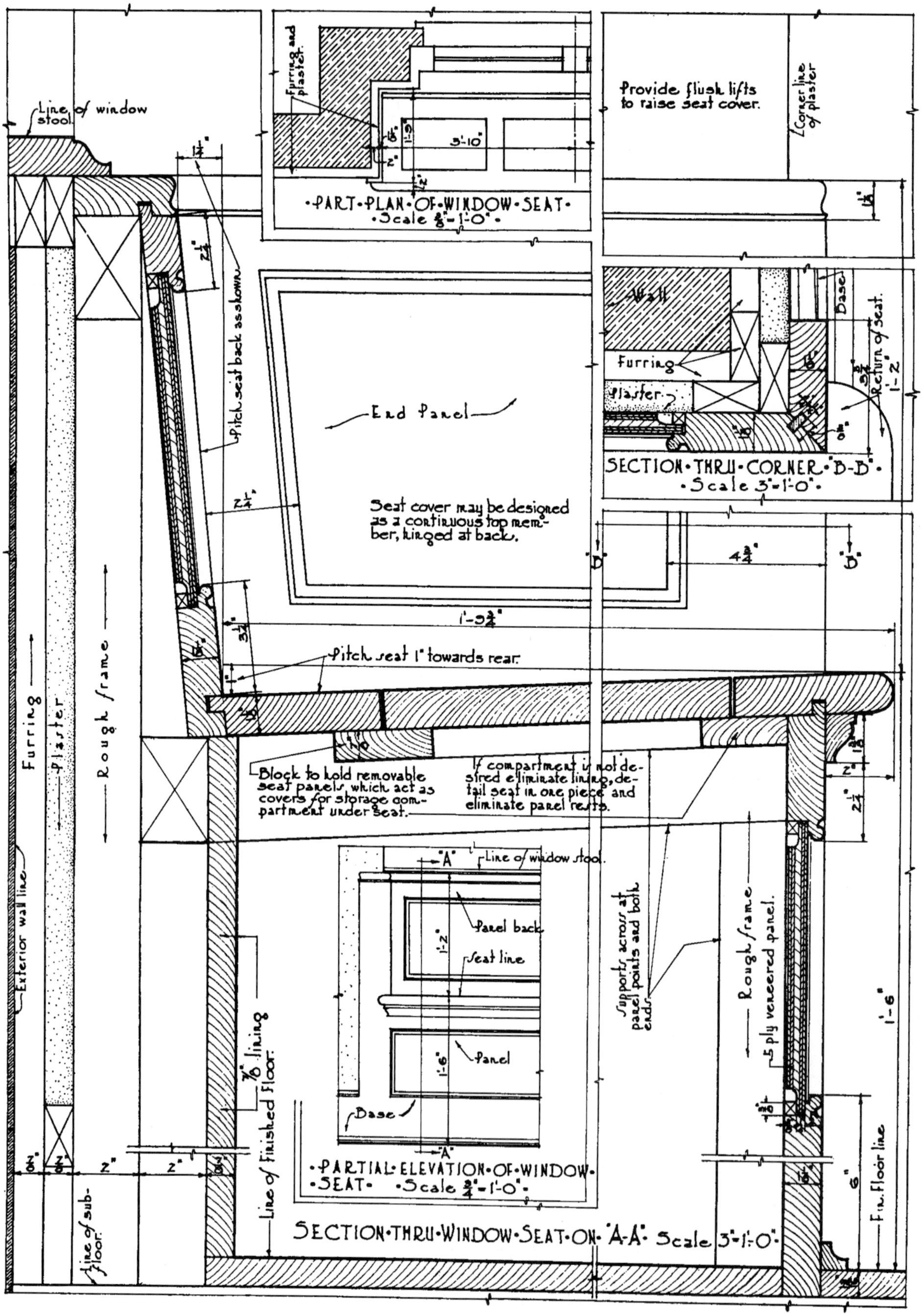
Line of window stool.
Provide flush lifts to raise seat cover.
Corner line of plaster
Furring and plaster.
•PART•PLAN•OF•WINDOW•SEAT•
•Scale ⅜"=1'-0"•
Wall
Furring
Plaster
Base
Return of seat.
SECTION•THRU•CORNER•"B-B"•
•Scale 3"=1'-0"•
Pitch seat back as shown
End Panel
Seat cover may be designed as a continuous top member, hinged at back.
Pitch seat 1" towards rear.
Exterior wall line
Furring
Plaster
Rough frame
Block to hold removable seat panels which act as covers for storage compartment under seat.
If compartment is not desired eliminate lining, detail seat in one piece and eliminate panel rests.
Line of window stool.
Panel back
Seat line
Panel
Base
Supports across at panel points and both ends.
Rough frame
5 ply veneered panel.
⅞" lining
Line of finished floor.
Line of sub-floor.
Fin. Floor line
•PARTIAL•ELEVATION•OF•WINDOW•
•SEAT• •Scale ¾"=1'-0"•
SECTION•THRU•WINDOW•SEAT•ON•"A-A"• Scale 3"=1'-0"•

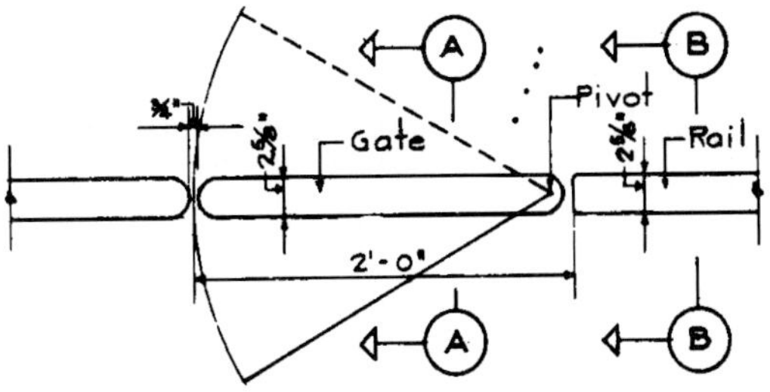

PLAN OF RAIL AND GATE

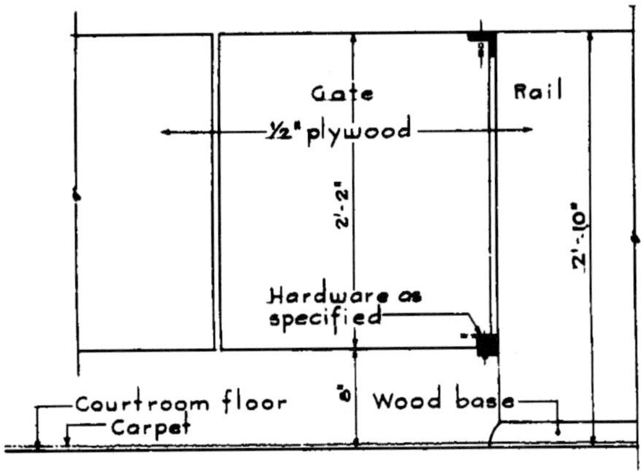

ELEVATION OF RAIL AND GATE

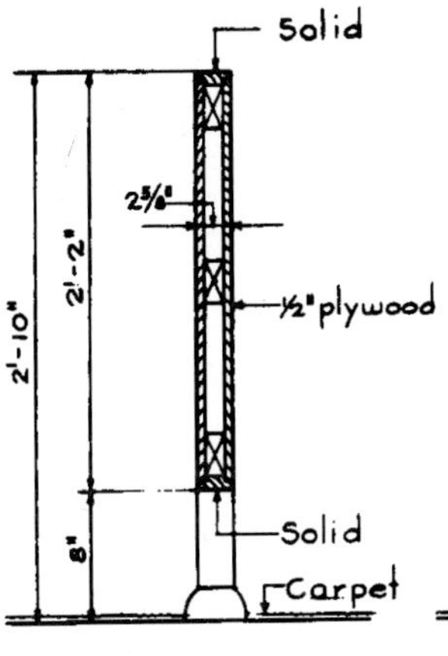

SECTION A-A

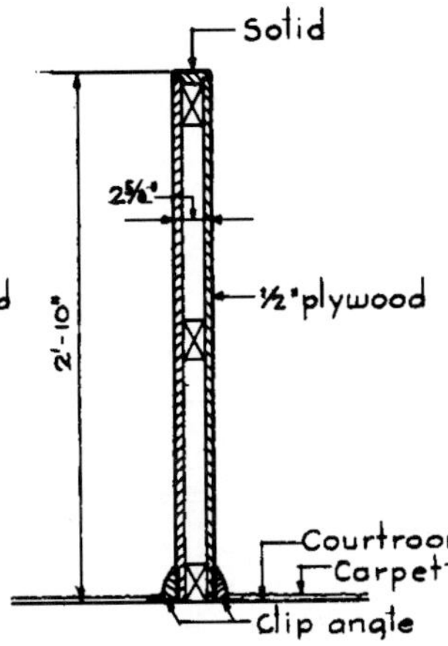

SECTION B-B

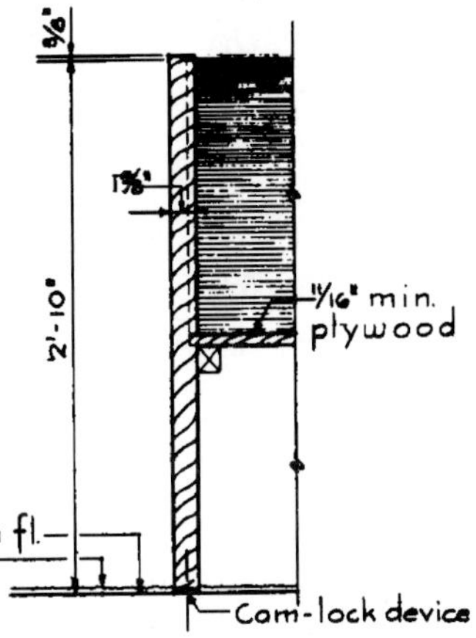

SECTION C-C

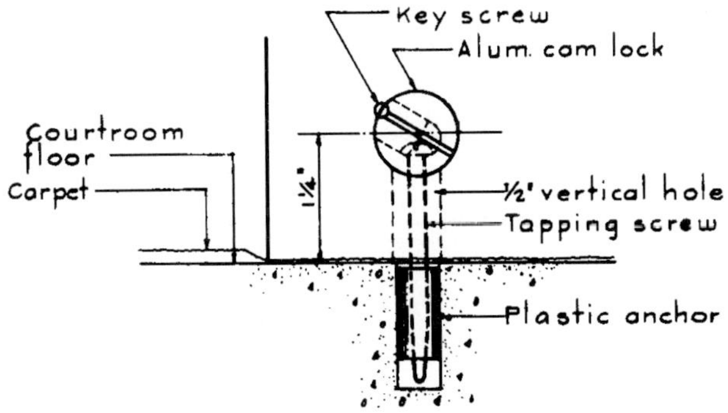

ELEVATION

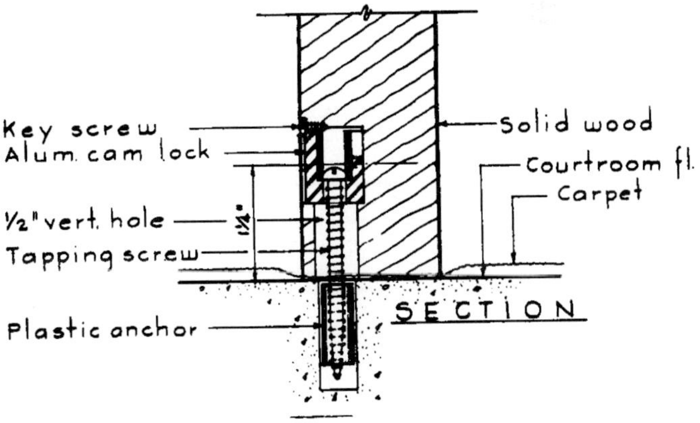

CAM LOCK ASSEMBLY

WOODWORK DETAILS
Hidden Wood Door

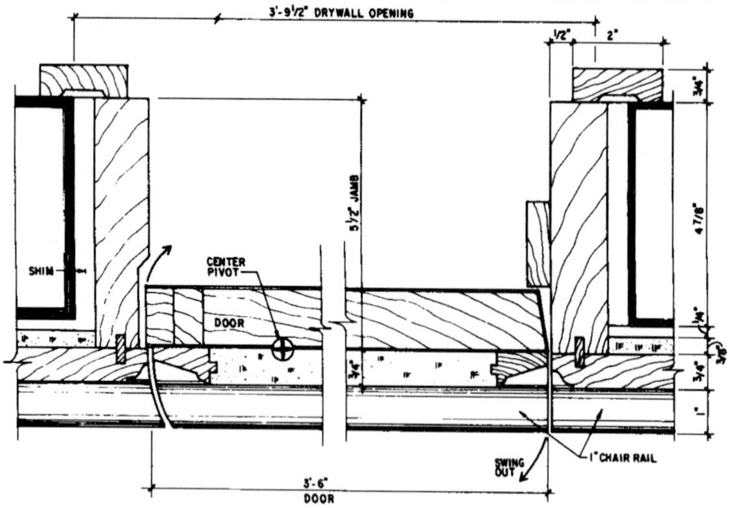

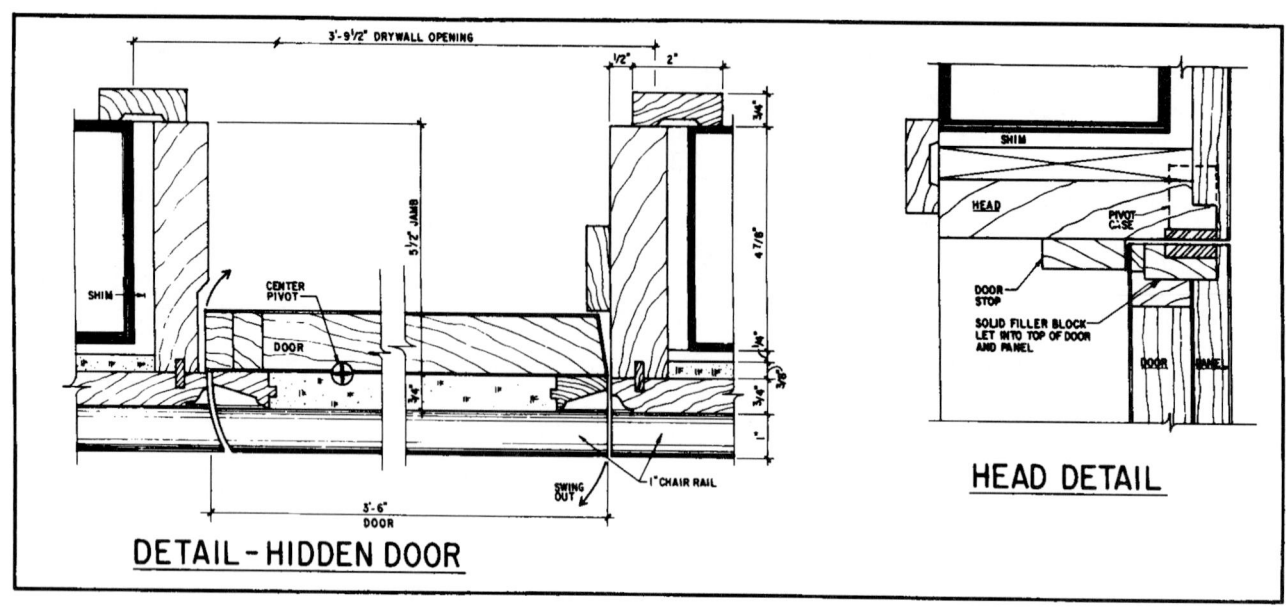

DETAIL - HIDDEN DOOR

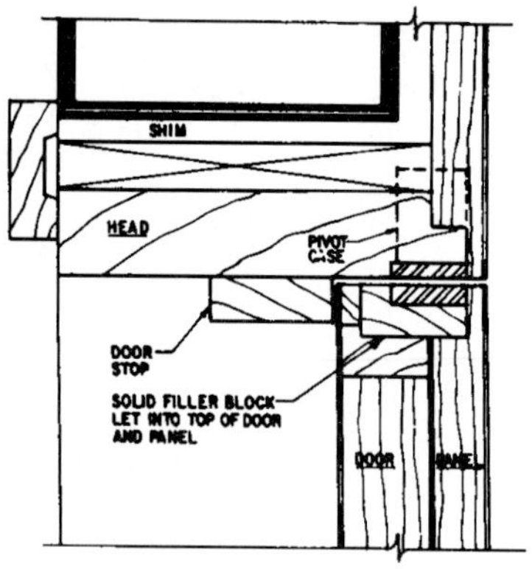

HEAD DETAIL

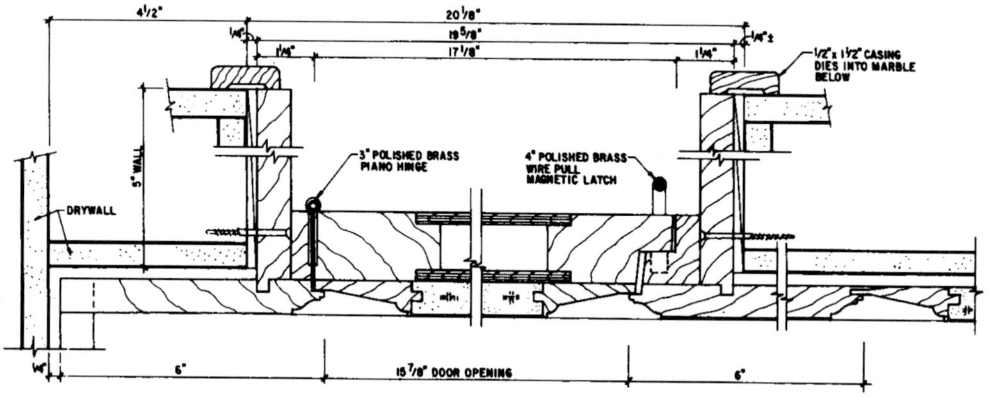

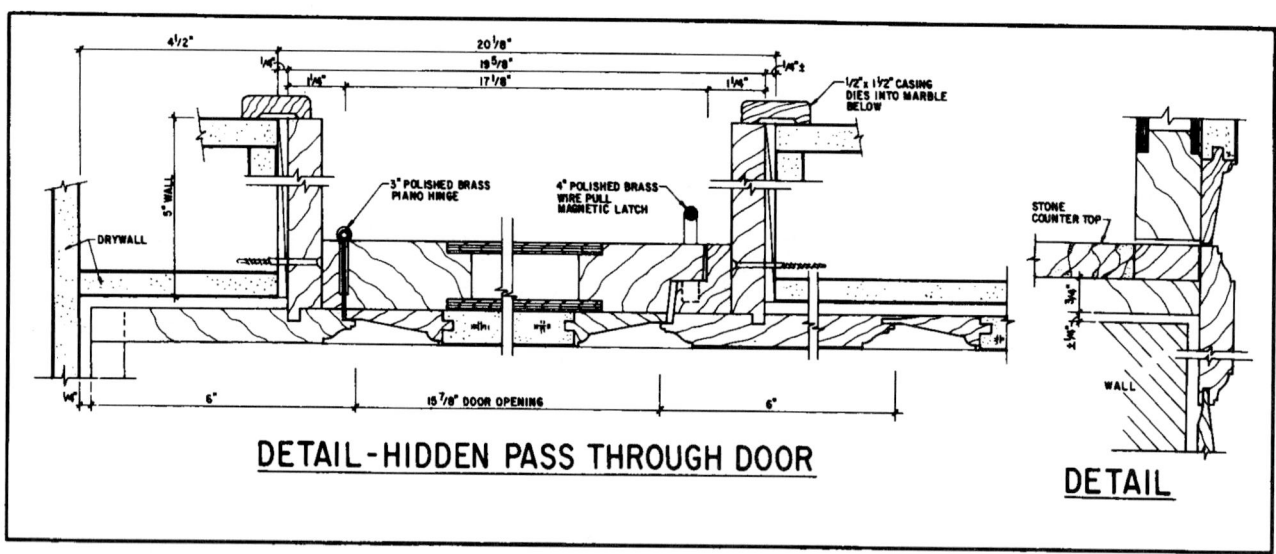

DETAIL - HIDDEN PASS THROUGH DOOR

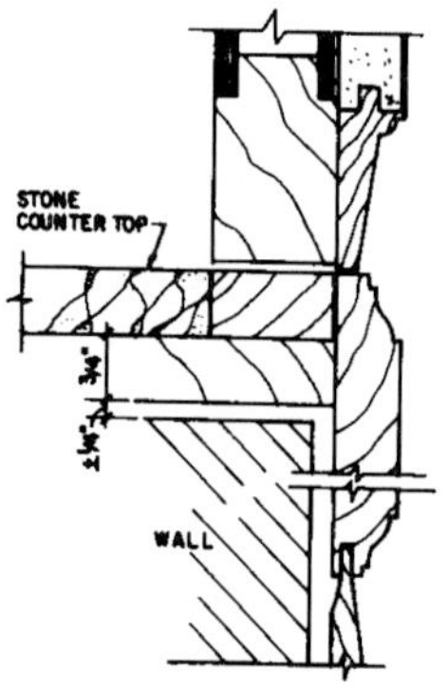

DETAIL

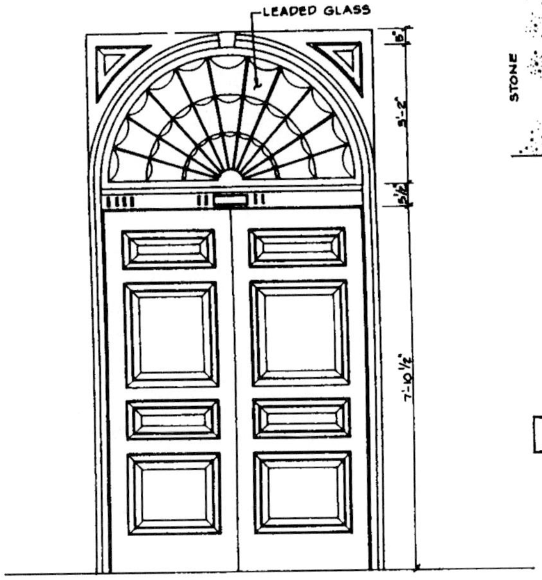

ELEVATION-FRONT ENTRY

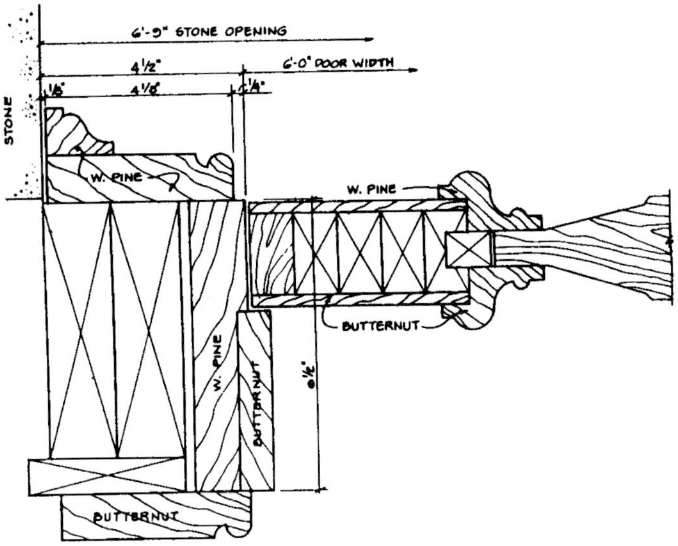

JAMB DETAIL AT ENTRY

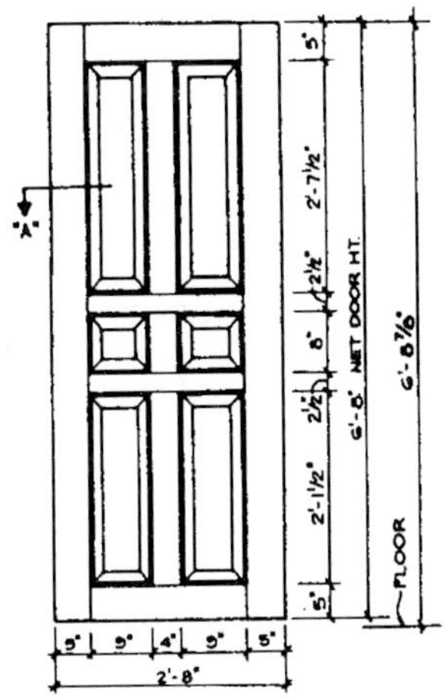

ELEVATION OF SPECIAL DOOR

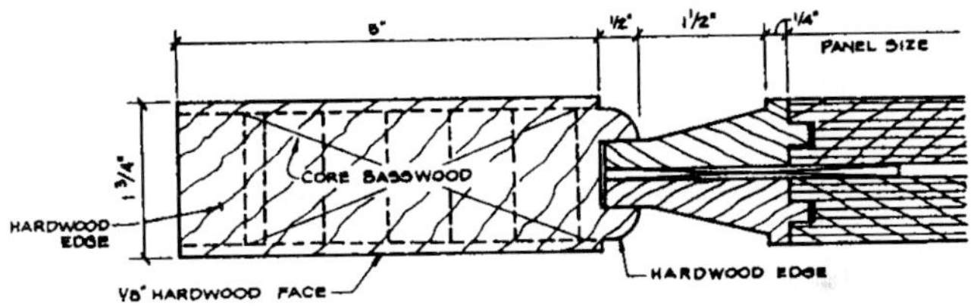

SECTION "A" TYPICAL DOORS

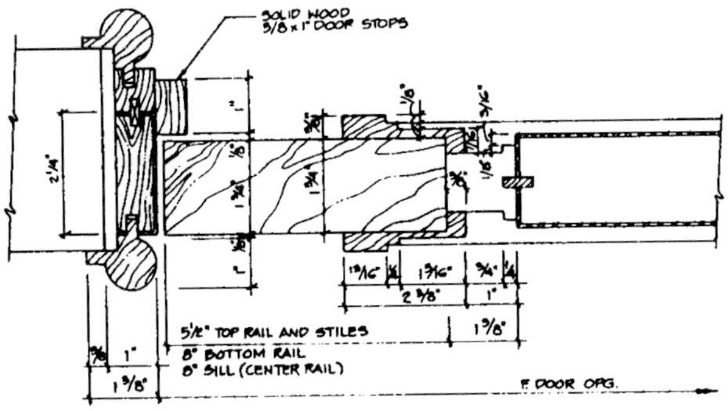

JAMB DETAIL AND DOOR DETAIL

WOODWORK DETAILS

Miscellaneous Details

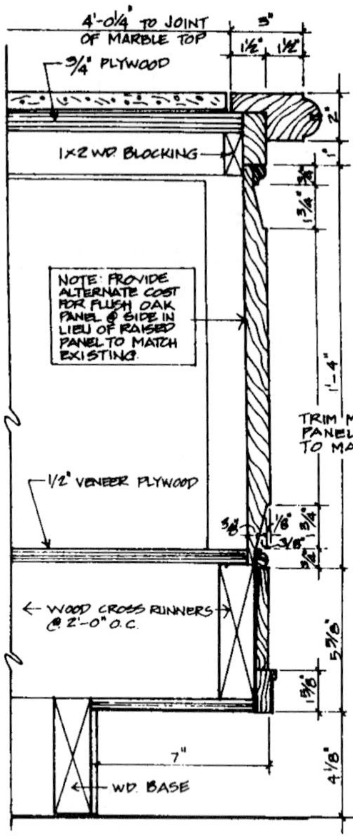

SECTION

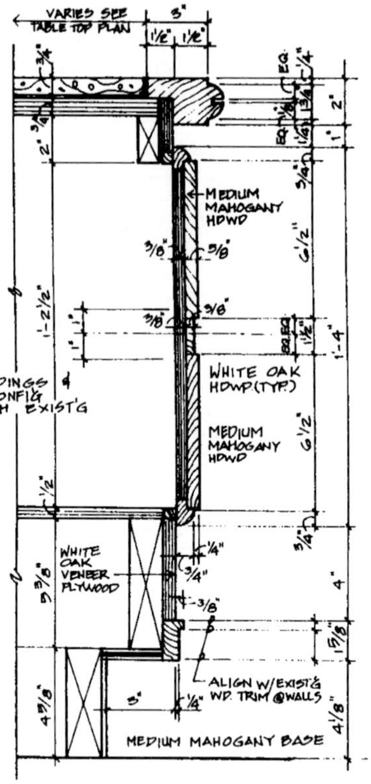

SECTION

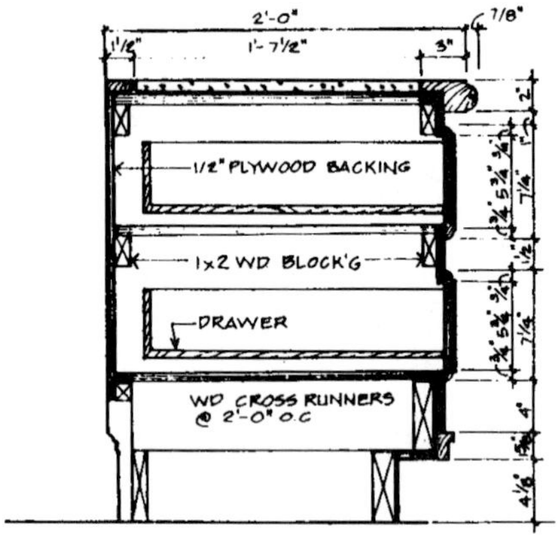

SECTION

CREDENZA

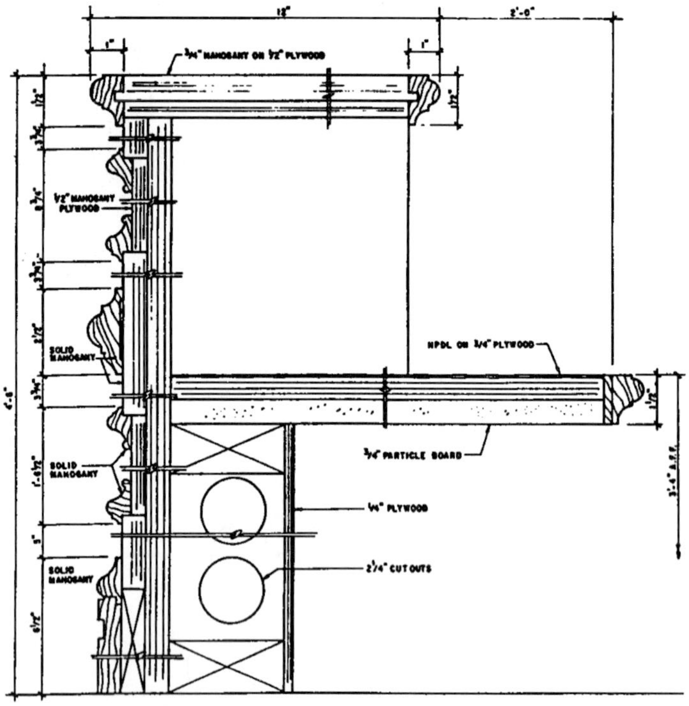

VERTICAL SECTION AT TELLERS COUNTER

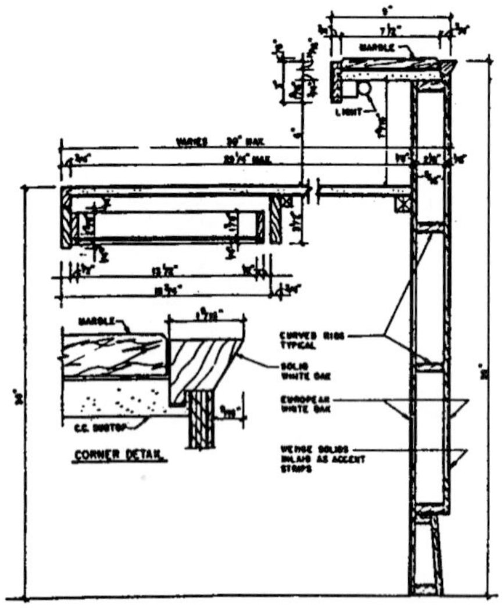

VERTICAL SECTION-RECEPTION DESK

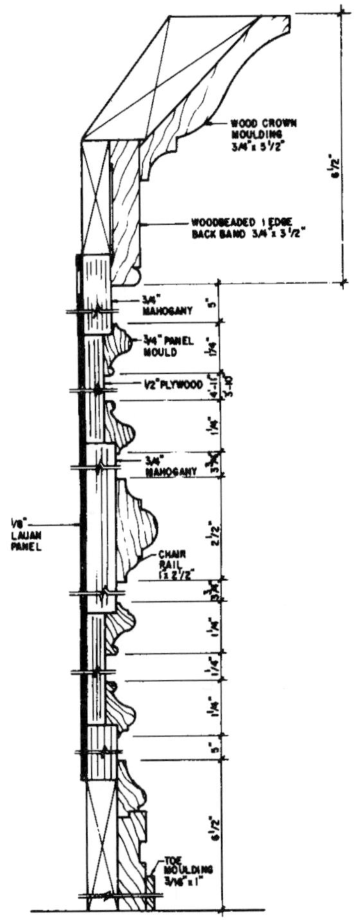

TYPICAL TRIM AND CORNICE

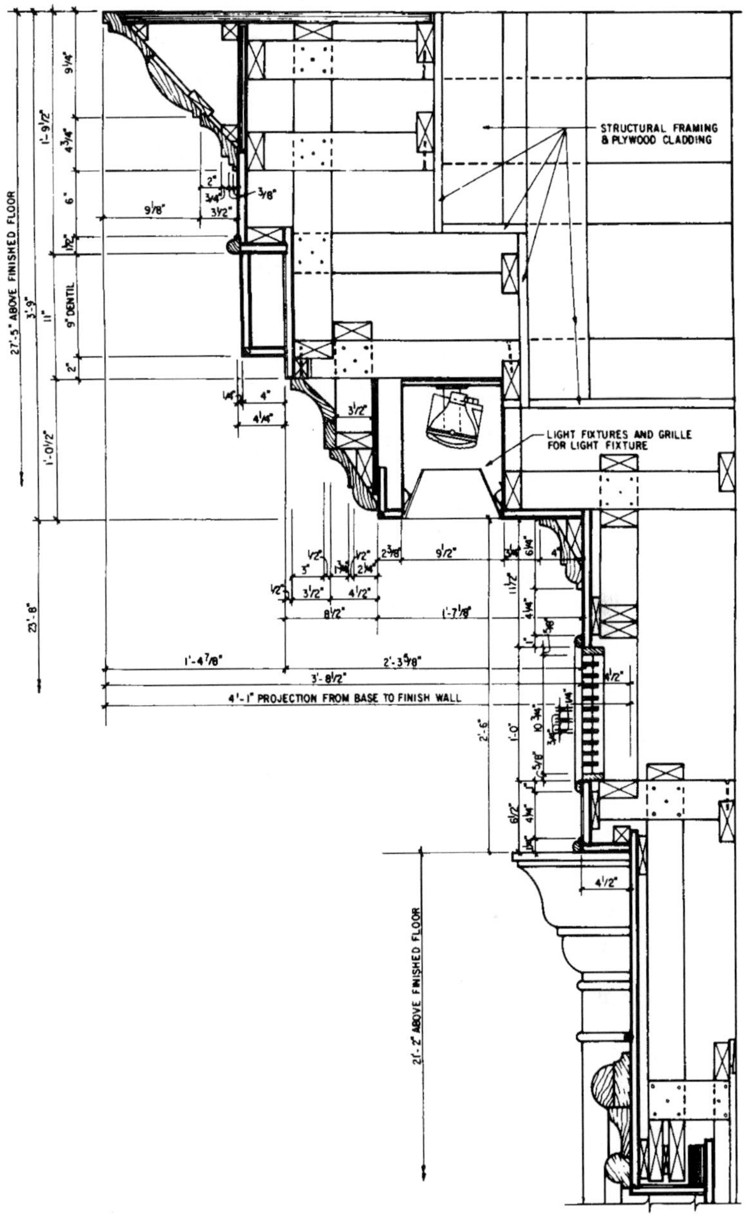

SECTION AT ENTABLATURE

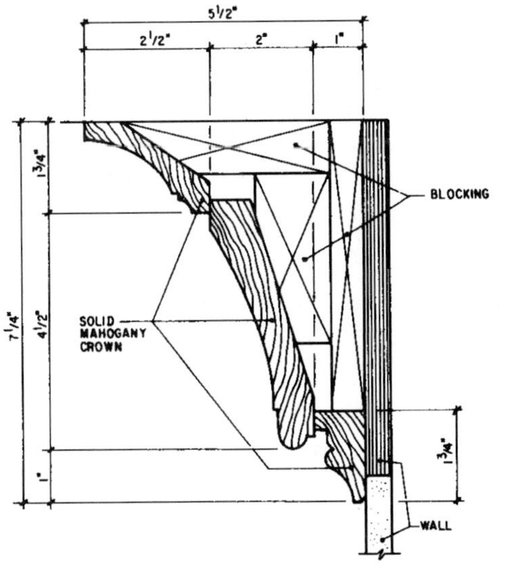

SECTION-TYPICAL CEILING MOULDINGS

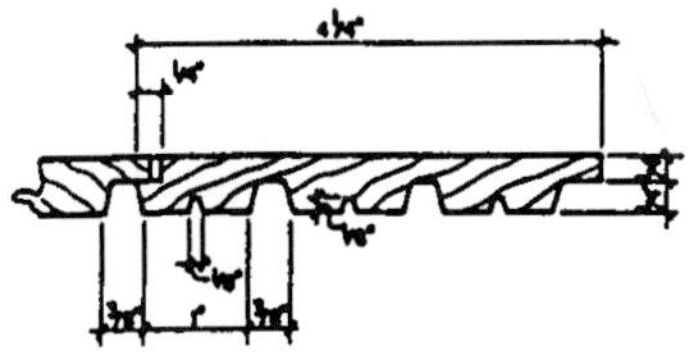

PANELING

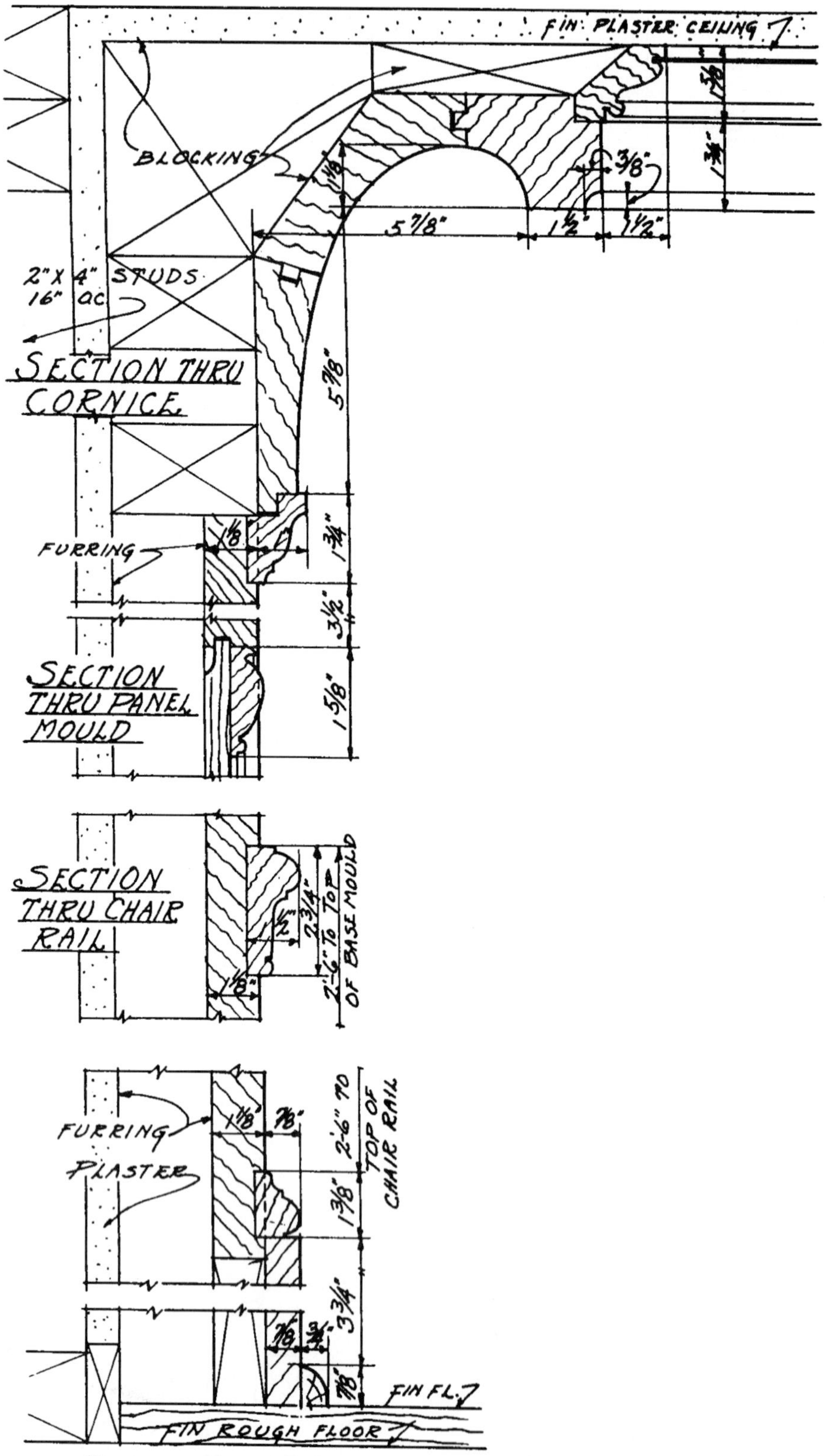

Section Thru Base

DETAIL OF WOOD CORNICE AND PANELING

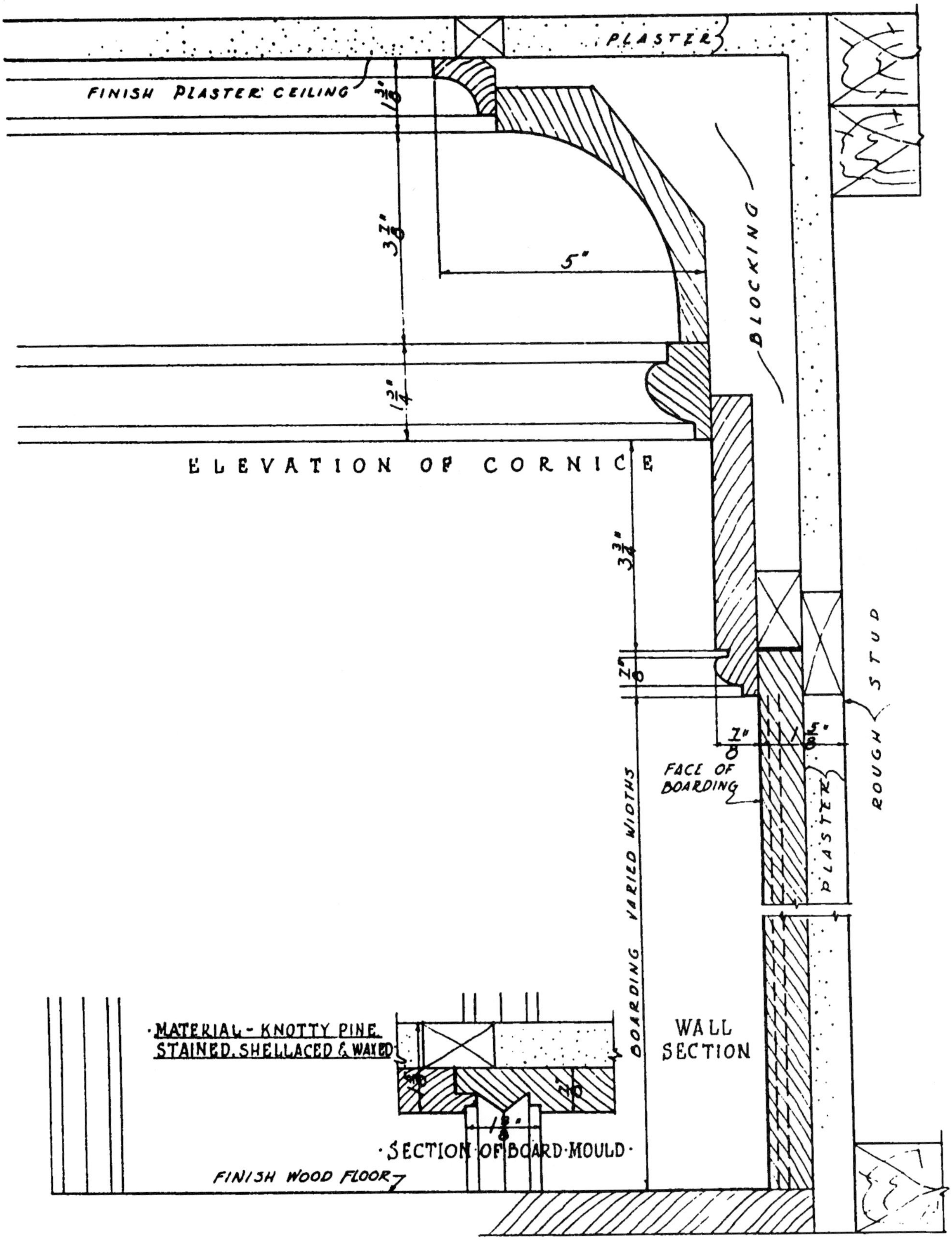

• DETAIL•OF•WOOD•WALL•&•CORNICE•LIBRARY •

WOODWORK DETAILS

Cornice Details

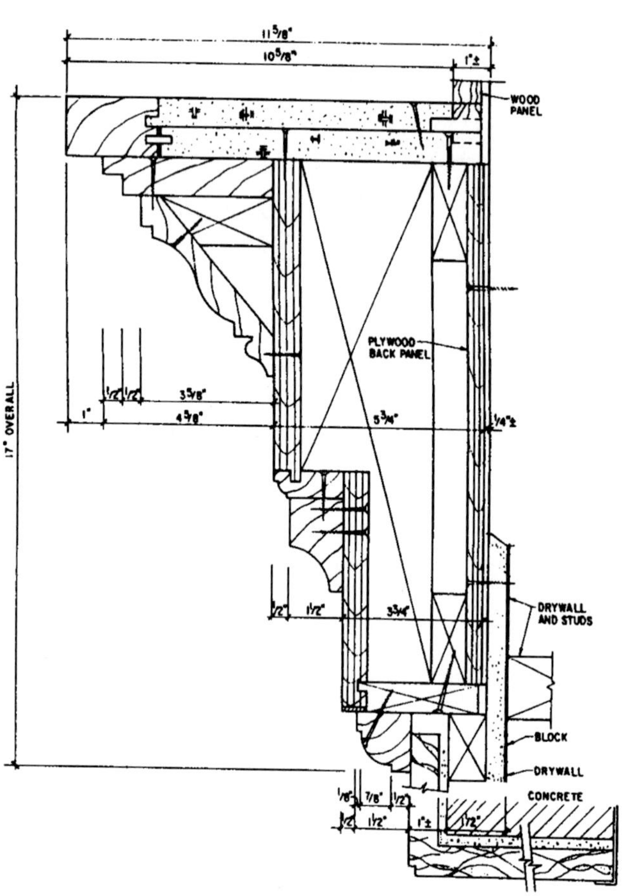

DETAIL-FIREPLACE MANTEL

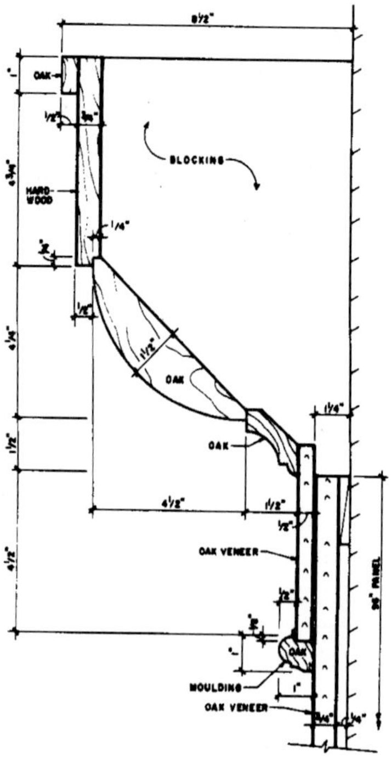

DETAIL AT COLUMN CAPITAL

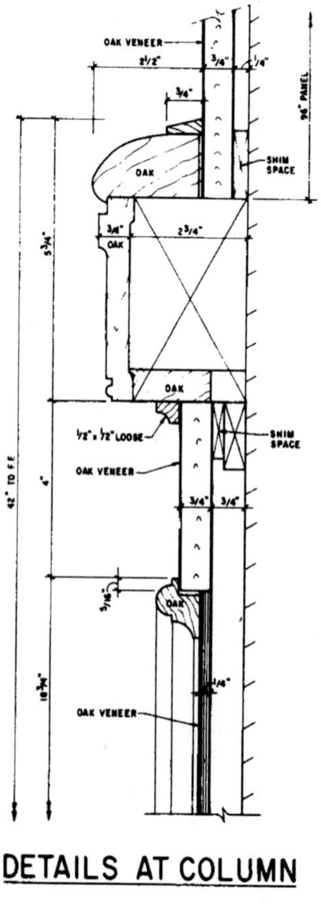

DETAILS AT COLUMN

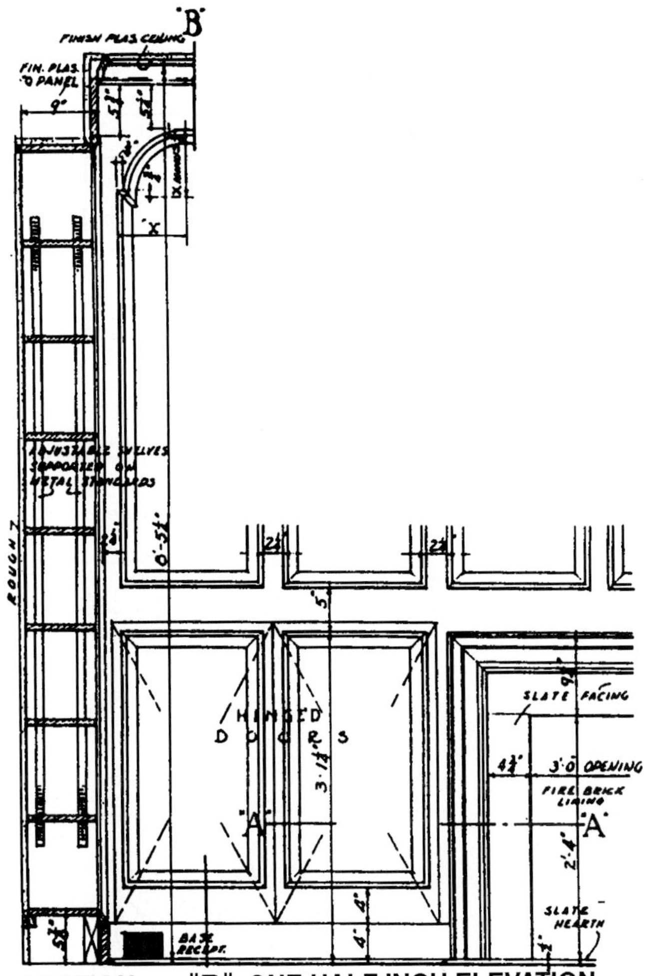

•SECTION• "B" •ONE HALF INCH ELEVATION

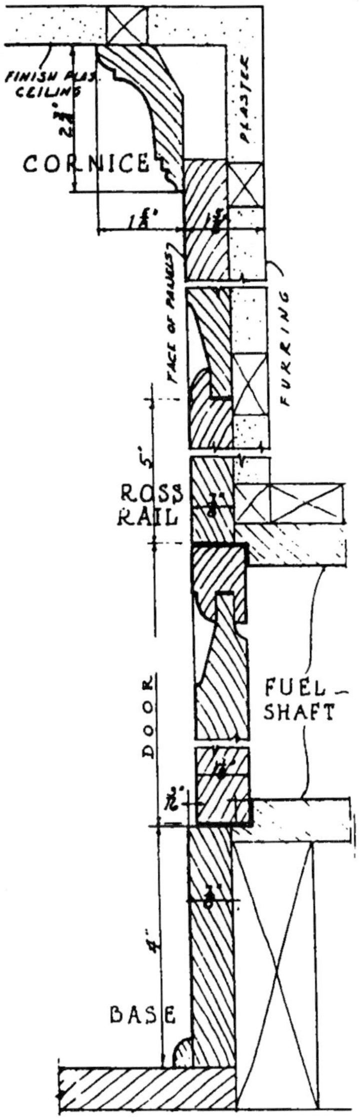

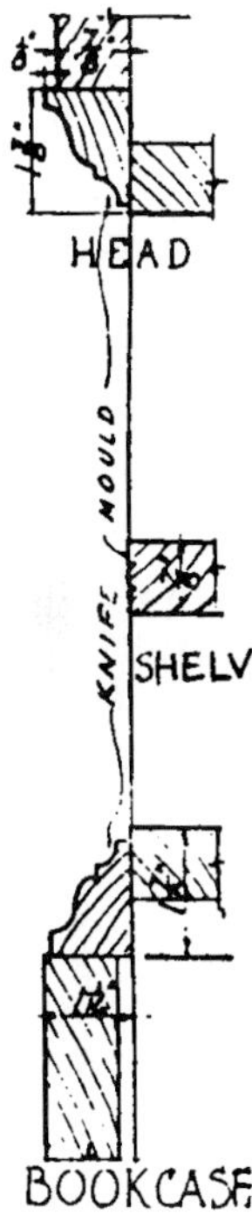

•SECTION• "B"
• $\frac{1}{4}$ FULL-SIZE•
MATERIAL - KNOTTY PINE
STAINED AND WAXED

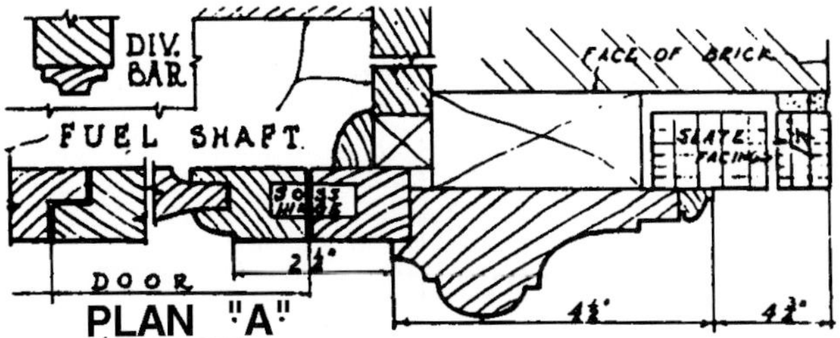

PLAN "A"
$\frac{1}{4}$ FULL SIZE

WOODWORK DETAILS
Cornice and Baluster Details

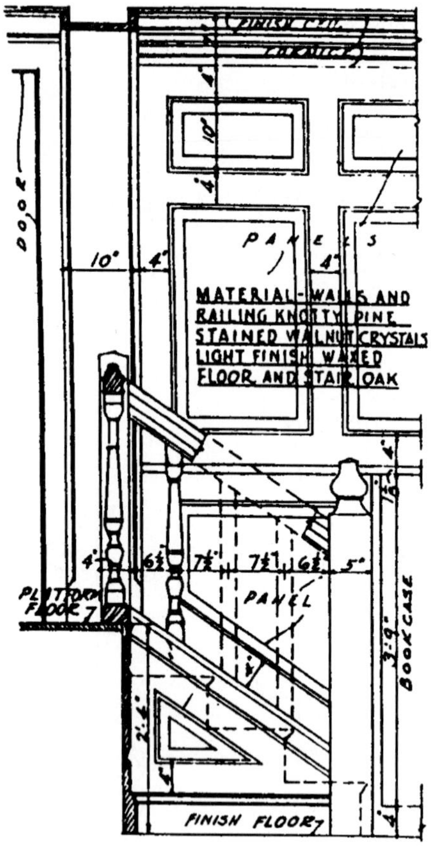

•3/8" SCALE ELEVATION•

MOULD
POST & BEAM

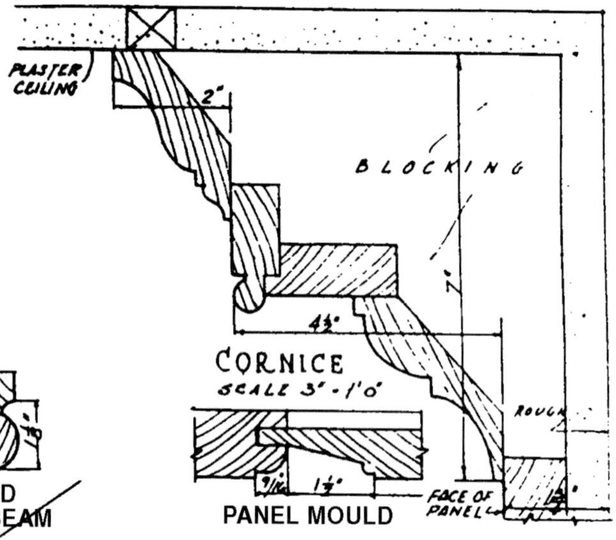

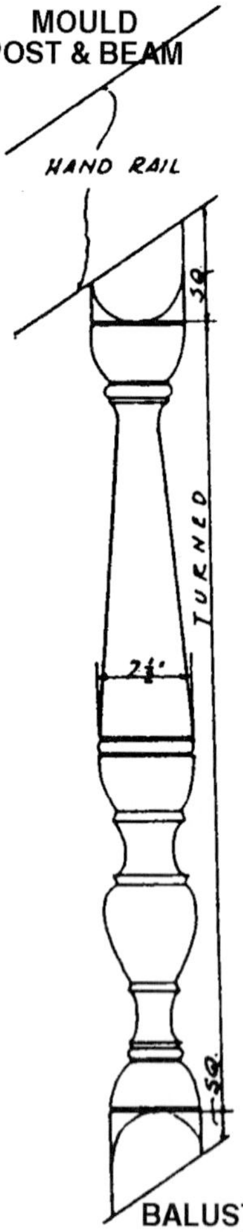

BALUSTER
SCALE 1½"-1'0"

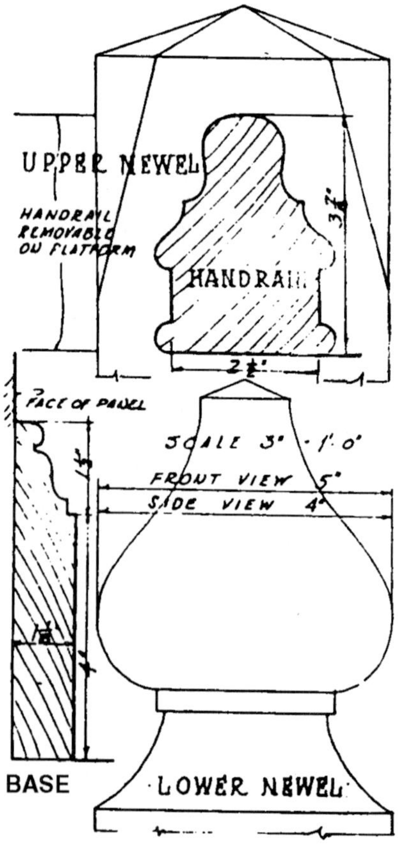

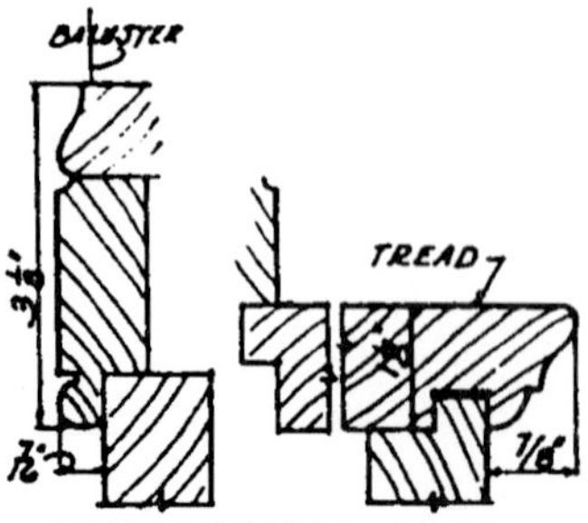

OUTER•STRING• •STAIR•

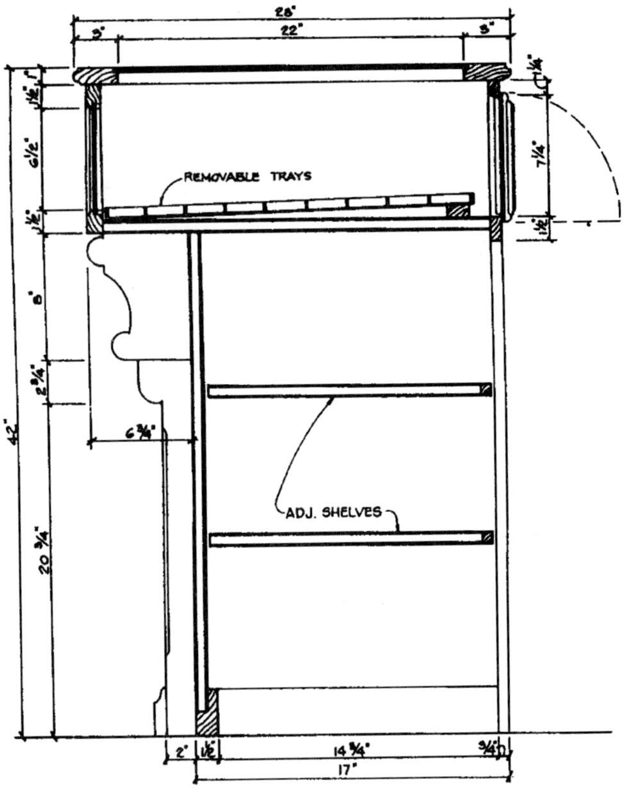

SHOWCASE SECTION

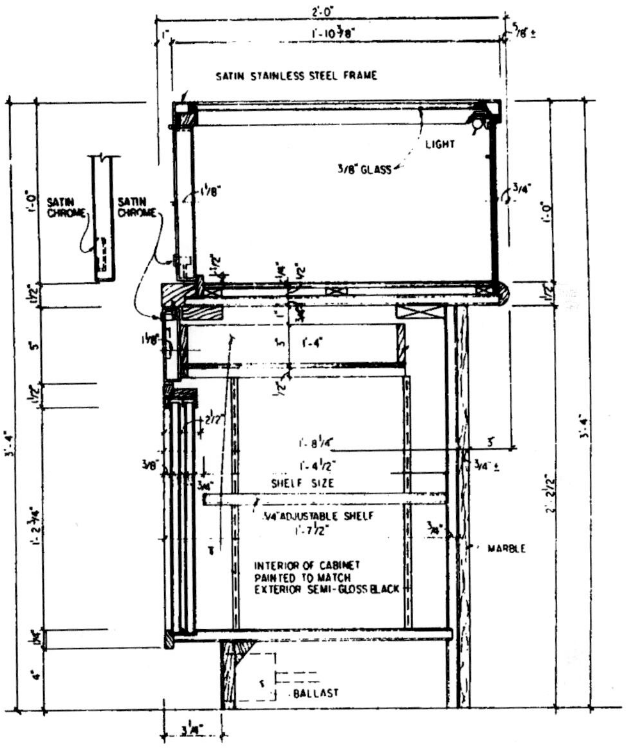

VERTICAL SECTION-DISPLAY CASE

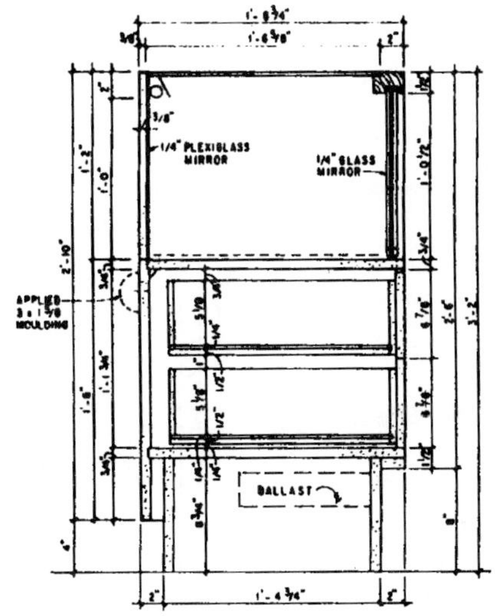

VERTICAL SECTION
JEWELRY CASE

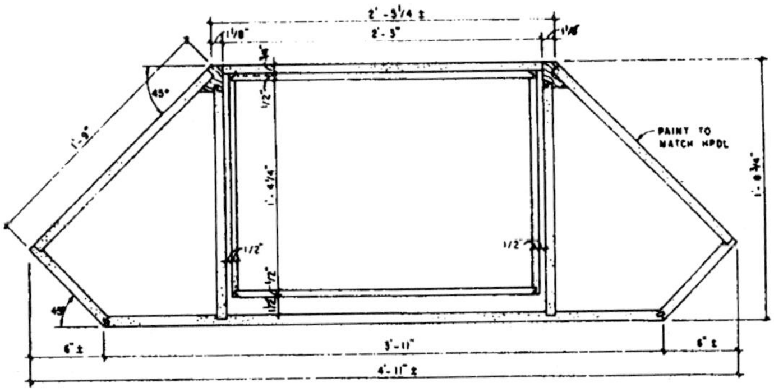

PLAN SECTION JEWELRY CASE

WOODWORK DETAILS
Display Cases

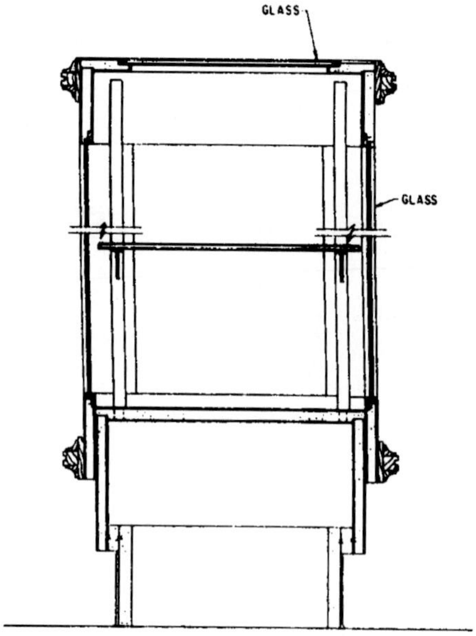

VERTICAL SECTION
AT DISPLAY CASE

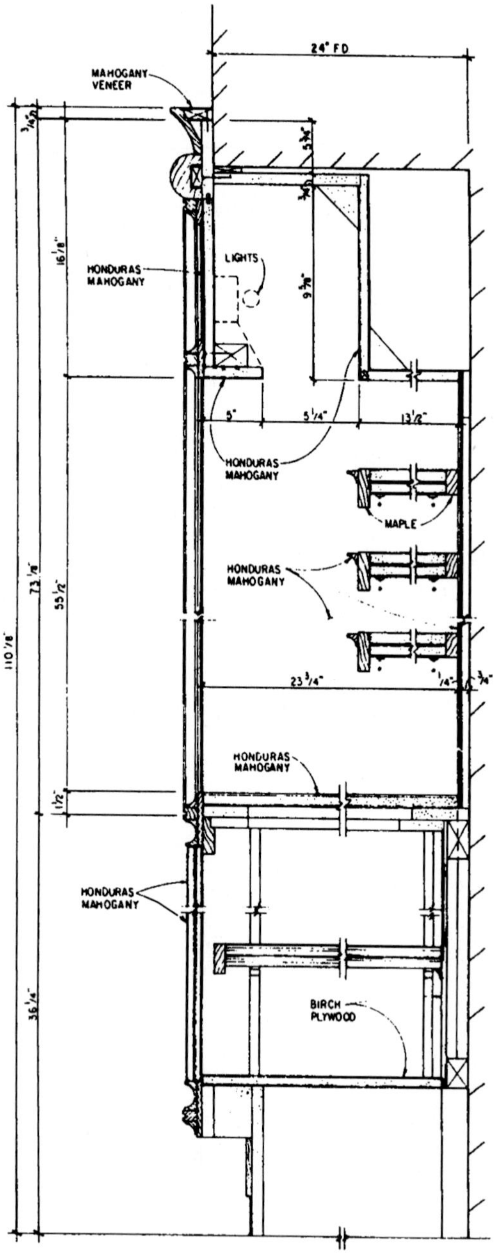

TYPICAL VERTICAL SECTION
AT WALL UNIT

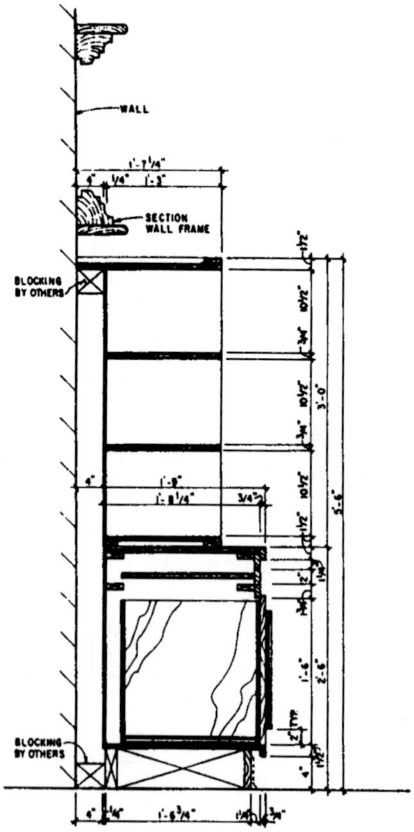

VERTICAL SECTION
SHIRT DISPLAY

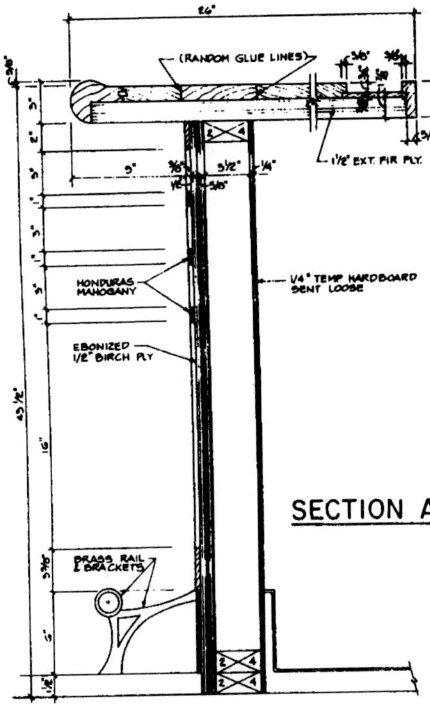

SECTION AT BAR

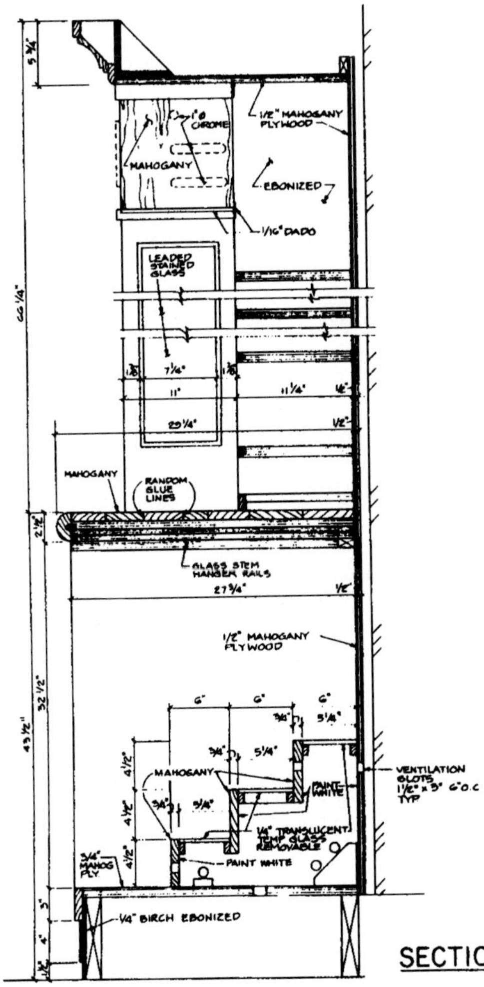

SECTION AT BACK BAR

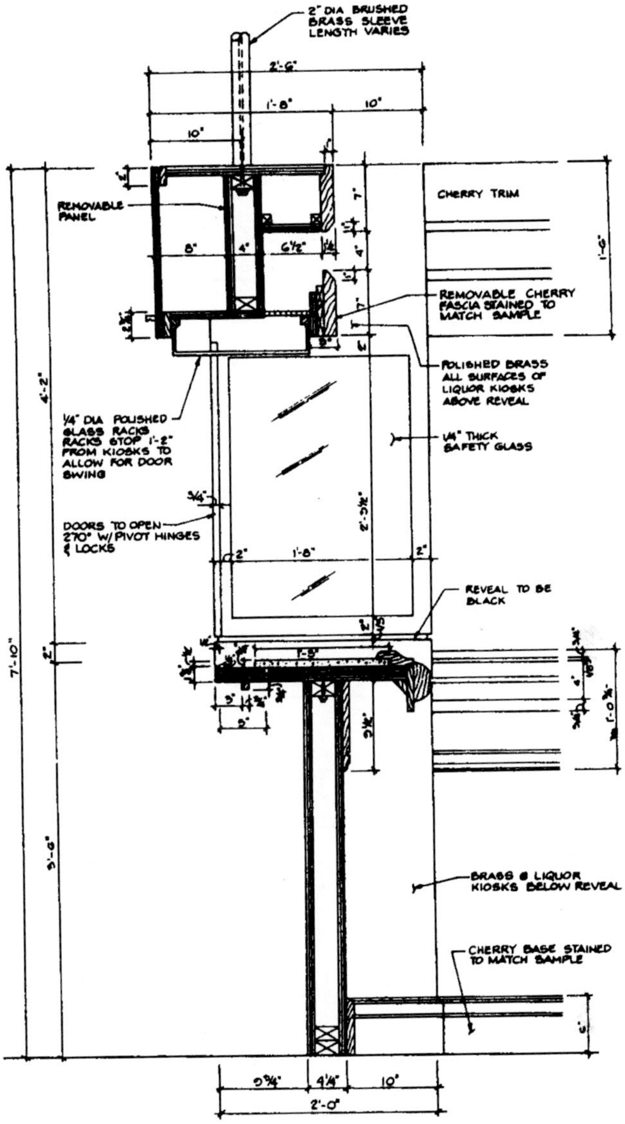

VERT. SECTION AT BAR & OVERHEAD CABINETS

WOODWORK DETAILS
Wood Column

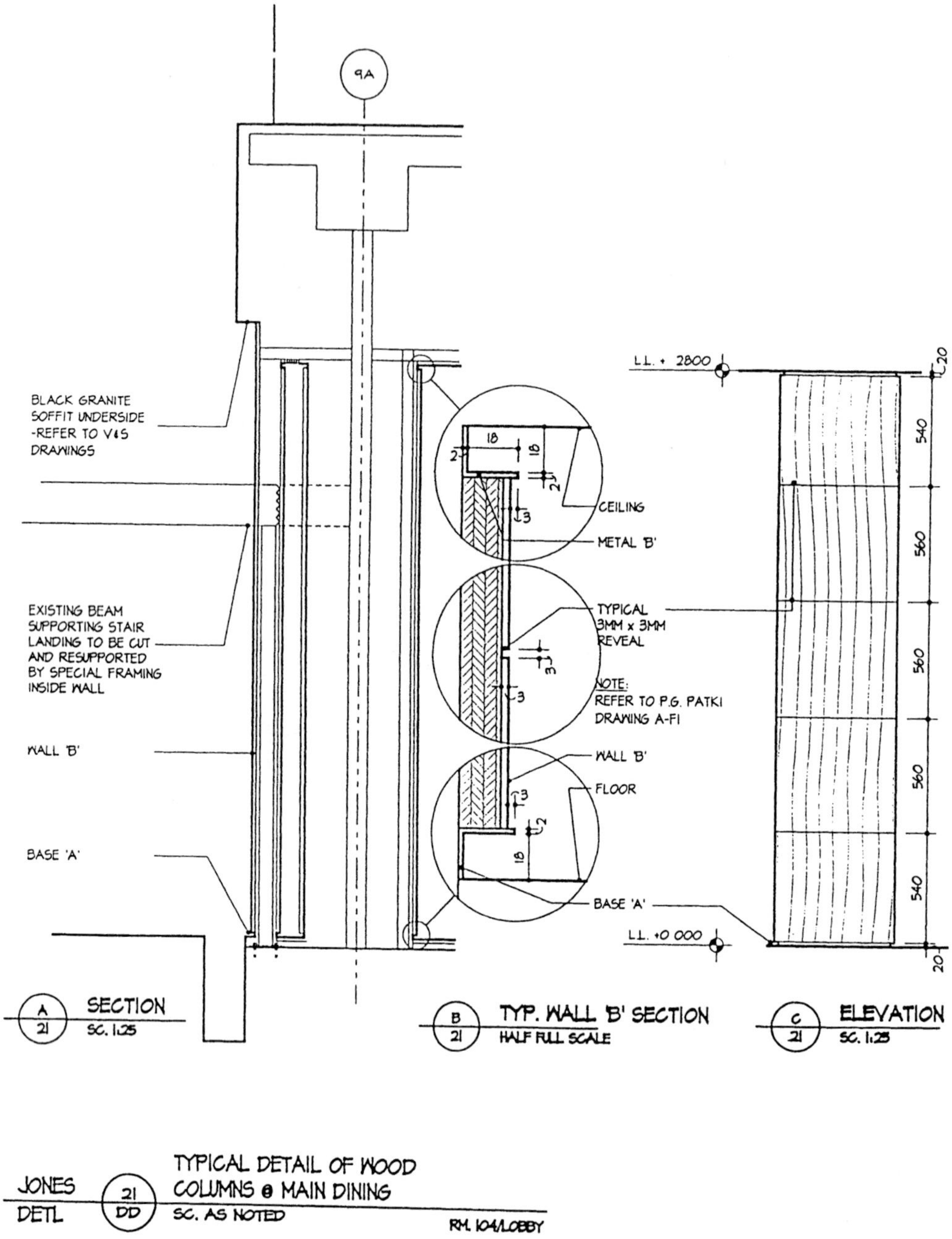
9A
BLACK GRANITE SOFFIT UNDERSIDE -REFER TO V&S DRAWINGS
EXISTING BEAM SUPPORTING STAIR LANDING TO BE CUT AND RESUPPORTED BY SPECIAL FRAMING INSIDE WALL
WALL 'B'
BASE 'A'
CEILING
METAL 'B'
TYPICAL 3MM x 3MM REVEAL
NOTE: REFER TO P.G. PATKI DRAWING A-F1
WALL 'B'
FLOOR
BASE 'A'
L.L. + 2800
L.L. +0 000
540
560
560
560
540
20
20
A 21 SECTION SC. 1:25
B 21 TYP. WALL 'B' SECTION HALF FULL SCALE
C 21 ELEVATION SC. 1:25
JONES DETL
21 DD
TYPICAL DETAIL OF WOOD COLUMNS @ MAIN DINING
SC. AS NOTED
RM. 104/LOBBY

Generic type	Recommended usage	Characteristics
System #1		
Lacquers	For all wood surfaces except medium to heavy acid areas; interior use.	Good coverage; easy to apply; sands easily; poor water resistance.
Catalyzed lacquers	For wood surfaces requiring medium acid resistance; interior use.	Tough-wearing surface; good water resistance; can be repaired.
System #2		
Varnishes	For all wood surfaces; interior use; exterior use—spar varnishes.	Good build; tends to amber with age; slow drying.
Conversion varnishes	For all wood surfaces; some acid resistance; interior use.	Good build and solids; can be repaired.
System #3		
Polyurethane	For all wood surfaces; interior use.	Tough surface; excellent wear and abrasion resistance; can be repaired.
Catalyzed polyurethane	For all wood surfaces; high acid resistance; interior use.	Tough surface; excellent wear and abrasion resistance; can be repaired.
System #4		
Epoxy	For all wood surfaces; high acid resistance; interior use.	Very hard surface; excellent wear and abrasion resistance; limited pot life; high water resistance.
System #5		
Penetrating oils	For all wood surfaces; performs well on oak, teak, walnut, etc.	Easy to apply; makes touch-up easy; average wear and abrasion qualities; easy to repair.
System #6		
Synthetic enamels	Most wood and wood product surfaces; interior use; most colors available.	Good coverage; tough wearing; can be recoated or repaired; easy to apply.
System #7		
Vinyl lacquer	For all wood products; interior use; light acid resistance.	Tough surface; good wearing; resists light chemicals.
Catalyzed vinyl	For all wood products; interior use; excellent for residential kitchens, etc.; better acid resistance.	Tough surface; good wearing; repairs not easy.
System #8		
Fire-retardant coatings (intumescent)	For surfaces of wood products requiring flame spread protection (See WIC Technical Bulletin No. 423—Section 19.) Interior use only. UL Rated-UL-723; NFPA-255, and ASTM E-84; Tested for flame spread, fuel contributed, and smoke developed.	Leaching will result if exposed directly to high humidity or direct water. Can be coated with compatible overcoat system or waterproofing materials. Available for transparent and opaque finishes.

CORNICES AND MOLDINGS
Deep Sculpt and Crown Moldings

Deep Sculpt Moldings

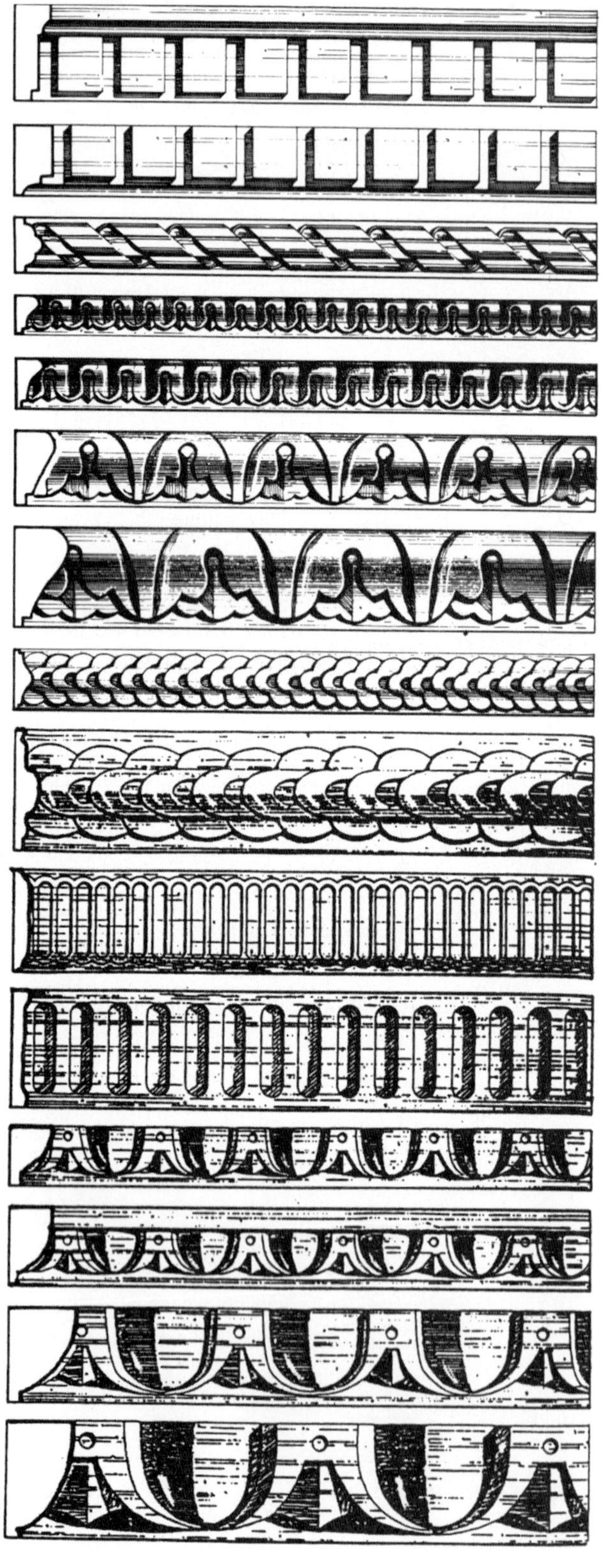

Crown Moldings

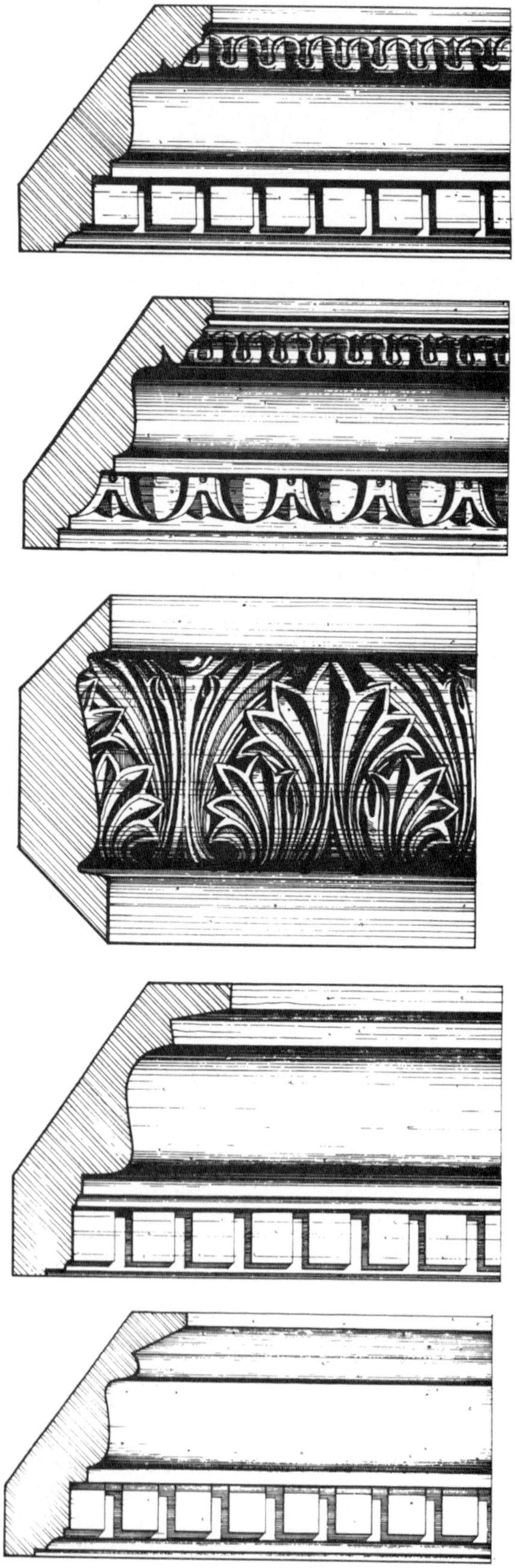

CORNICES AND MOLDINGS
Crown Moldings

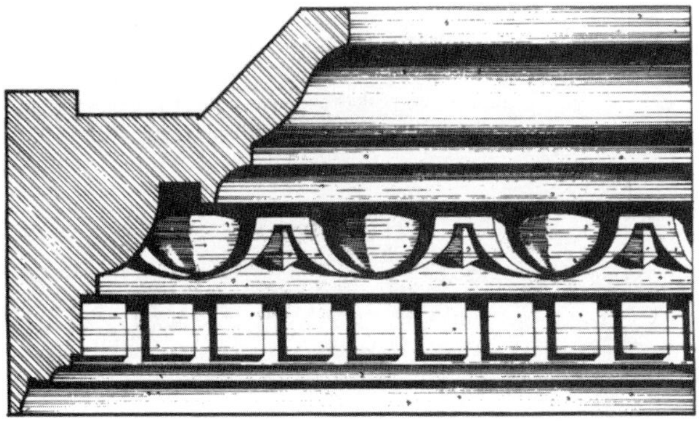

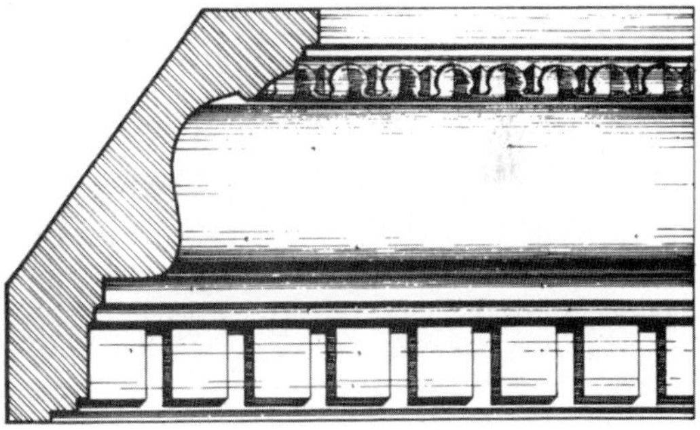

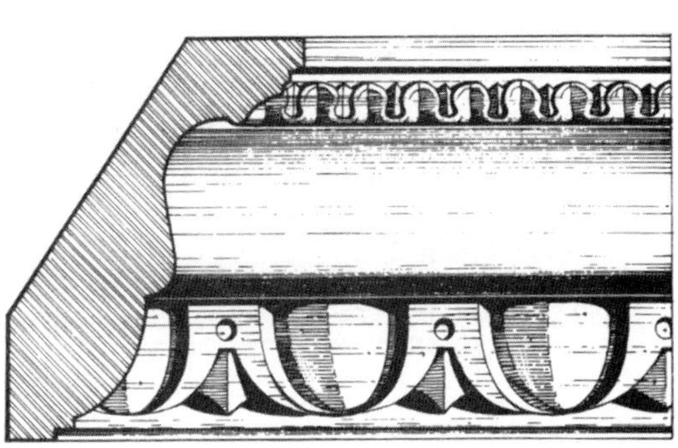

CORNICES AND MOLDINGS
Crown Moldings

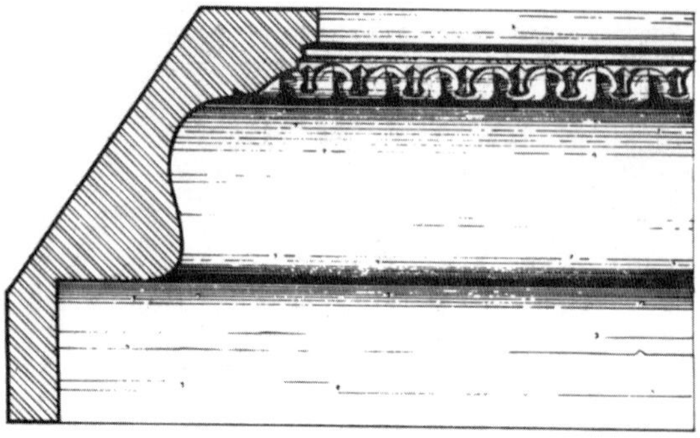

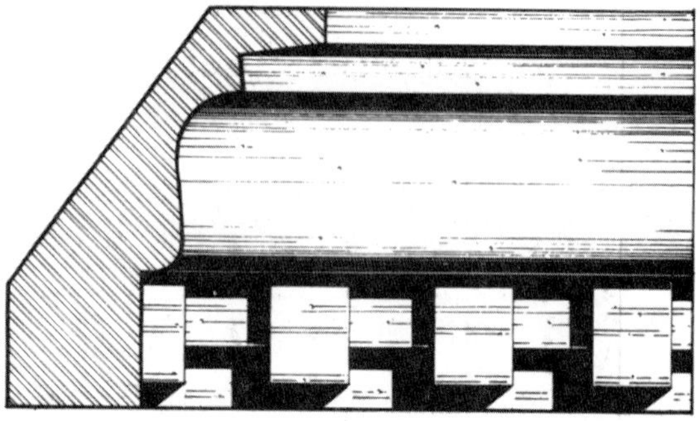

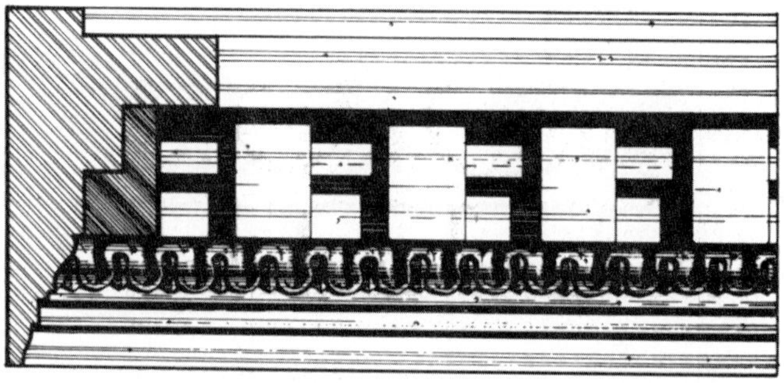

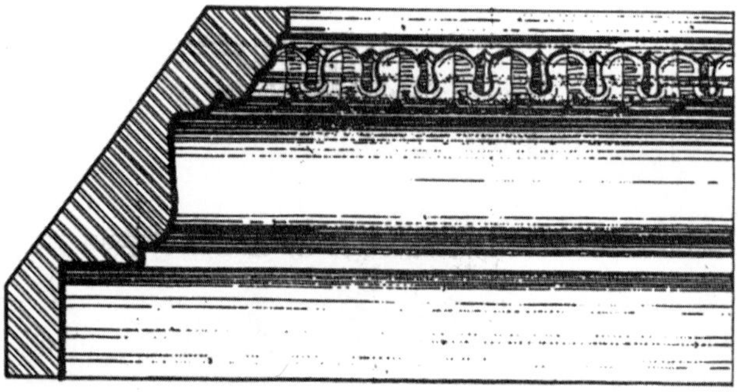

CORNICES AND MOLDINGS

Door Trim Moldings

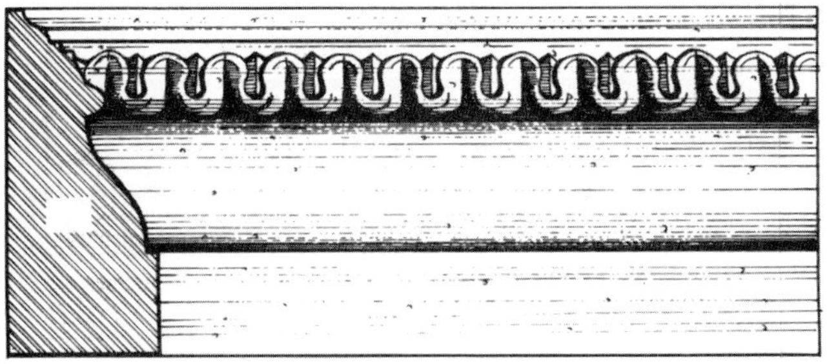

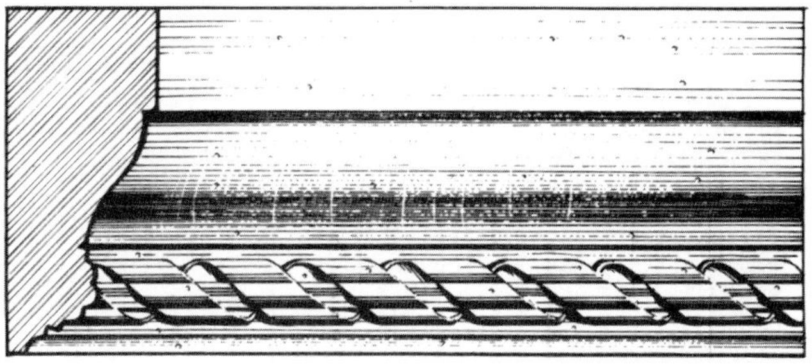

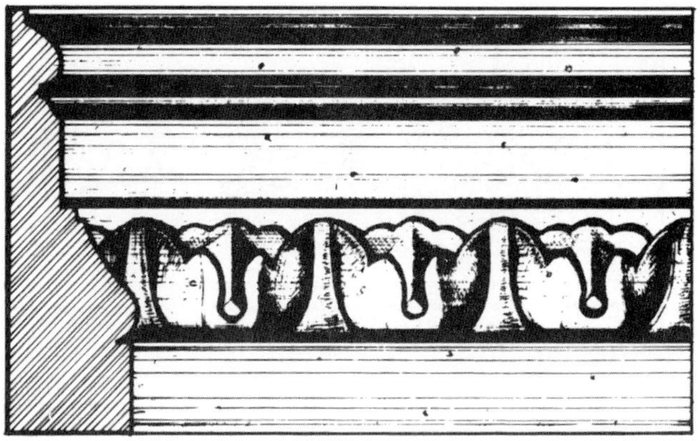

CORNICES AND MOLDINGS
Miscellaneous Moldings

Chair Rail Moldings

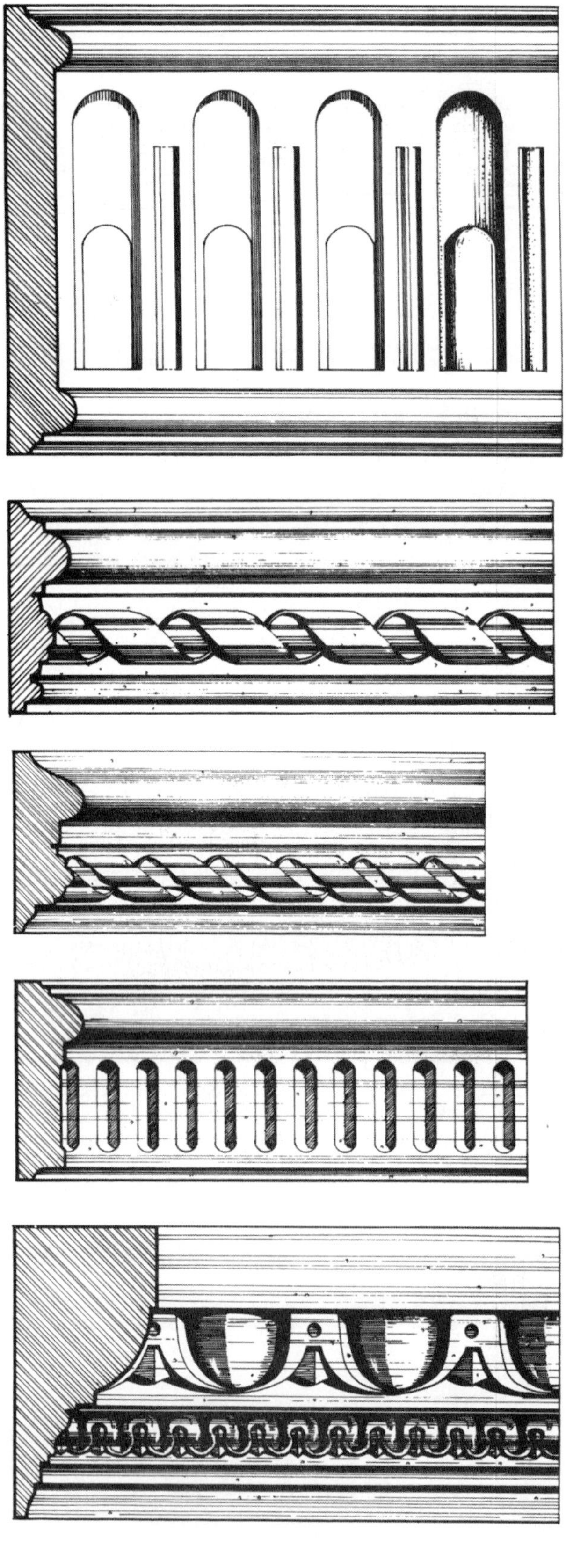

Picture/Mirror Hanging Moldings

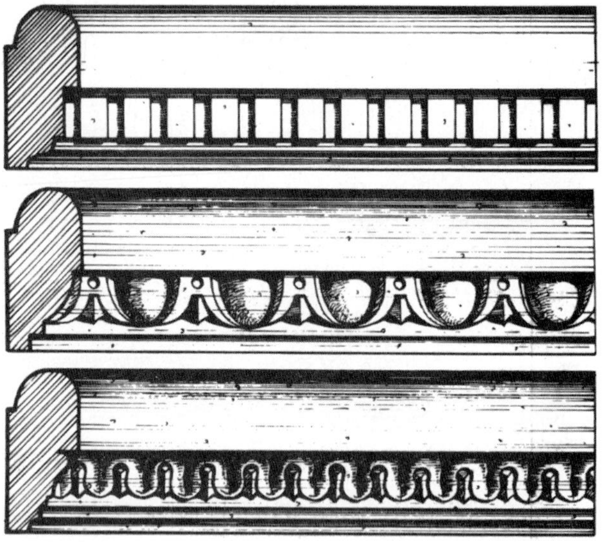

Door Trim Moulding

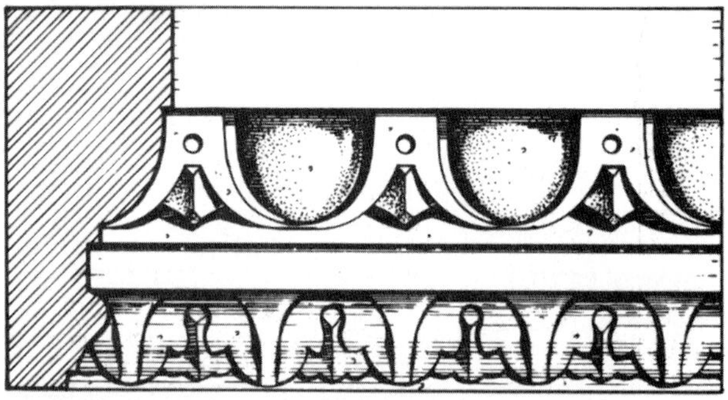

Panel and Trim Mouldings

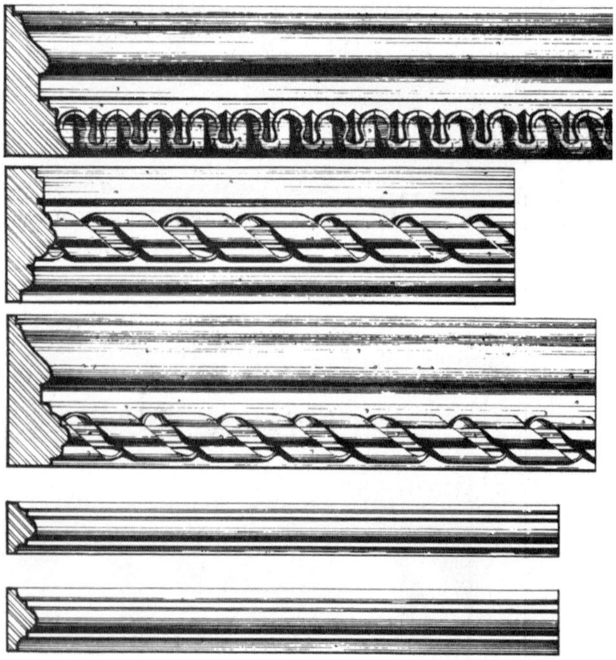

CORNICES AND MOLDINGS
Crown Moldings

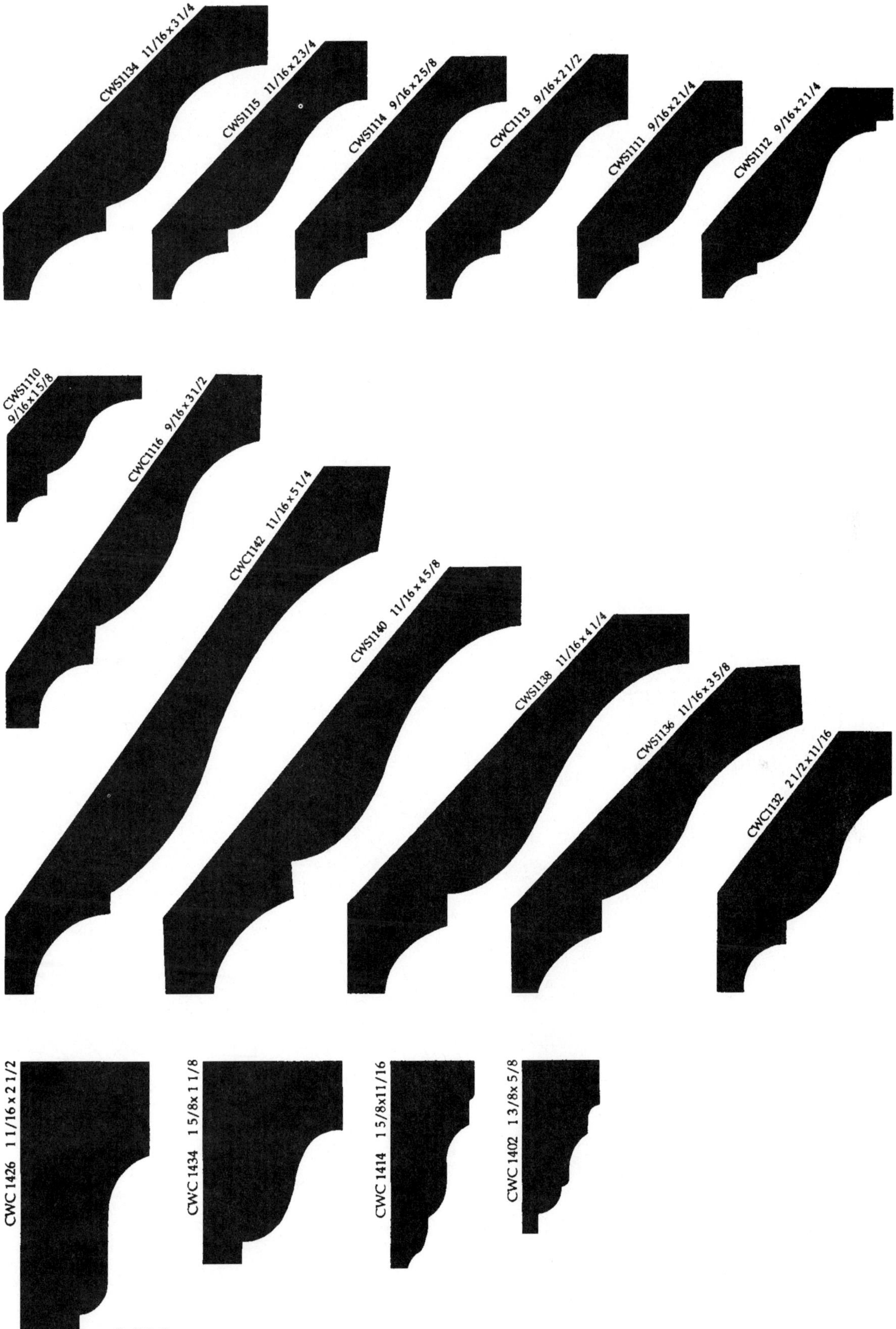

Solid Crowns

CORNICES AND MOLDINGS

Crown Moldings

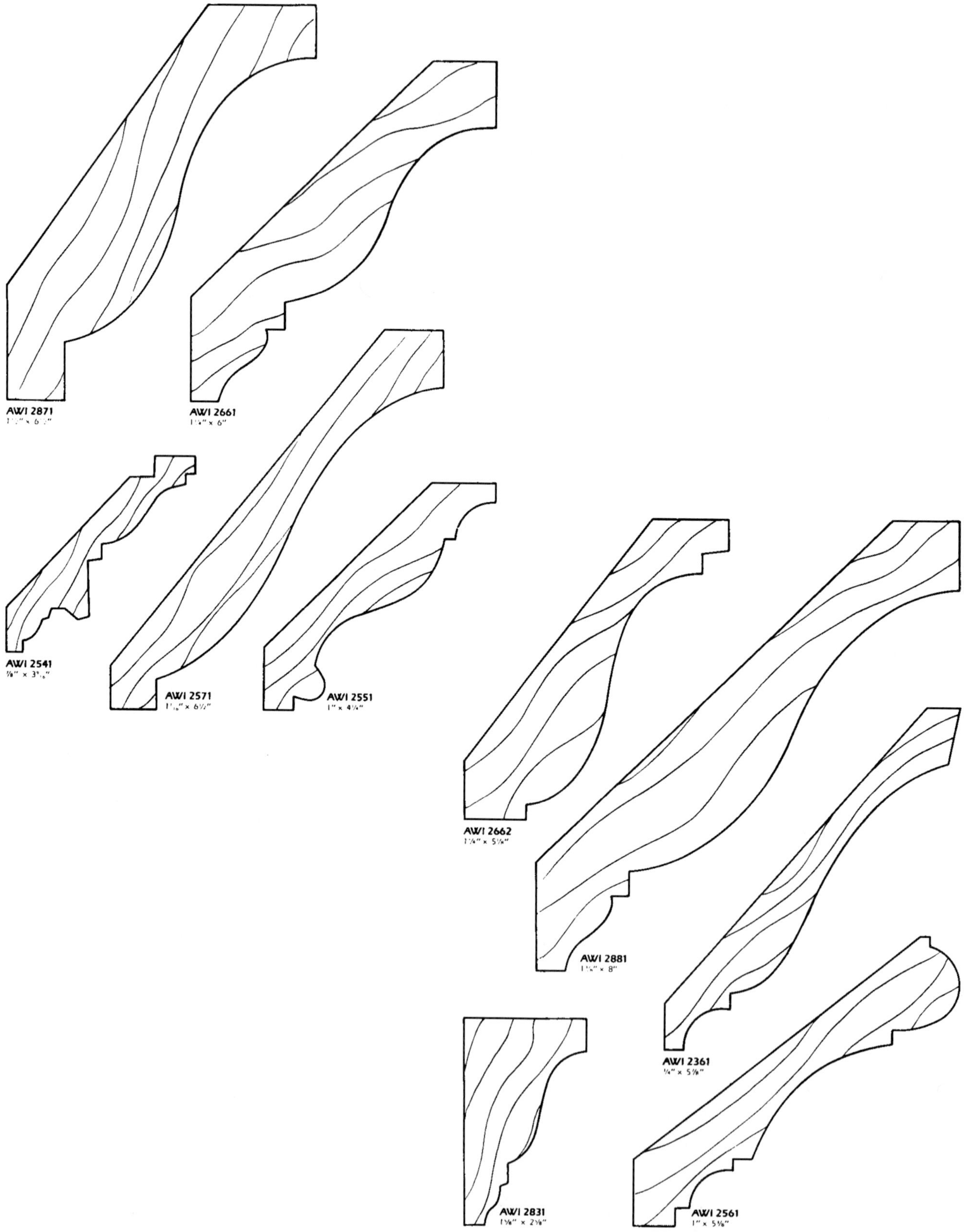

CORNICES AND MOLDINGS
Classic Molding Shapes

The next two pages illustrate the classic moulding shapes. Used alone and in combination, they form the basis for the classic proportions and arrangement of elements which appear in each order.

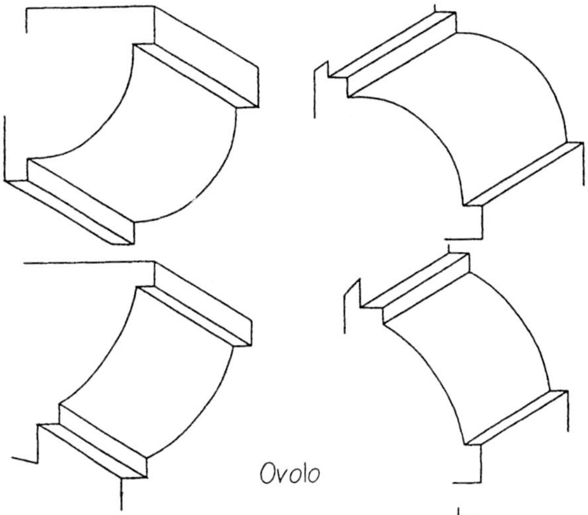

Ovolo

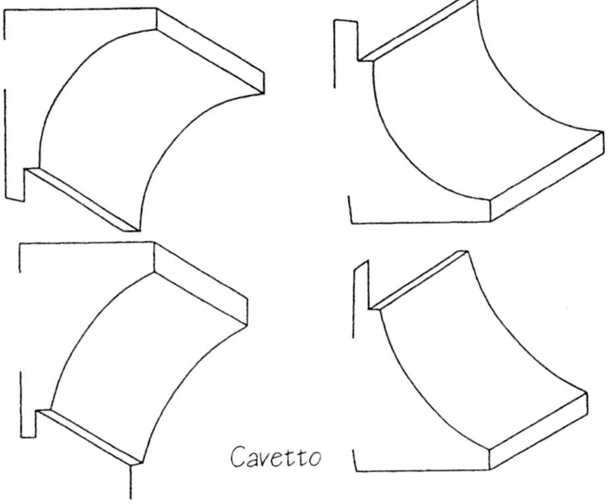

Cavetto

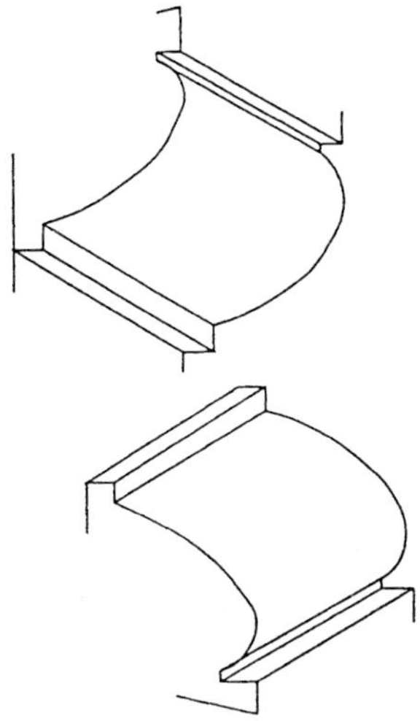

Thumb Moldings

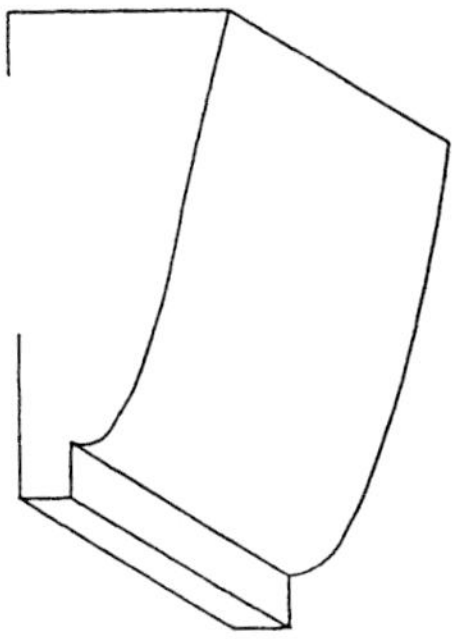

Venetian Molding

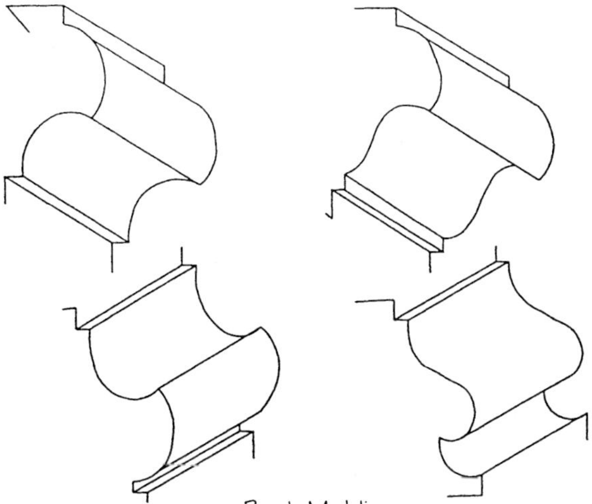

Beak Moldings

Scotia

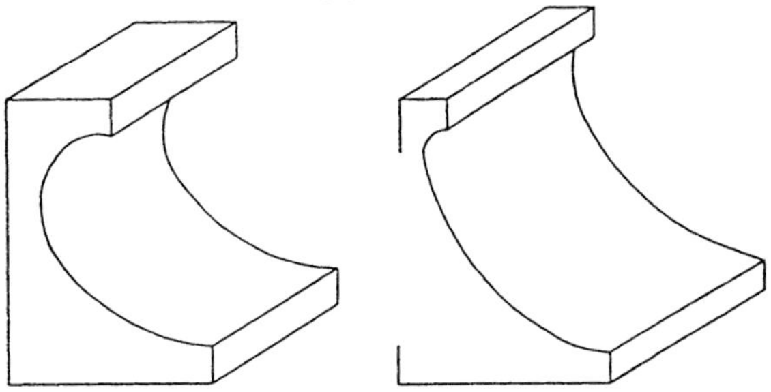

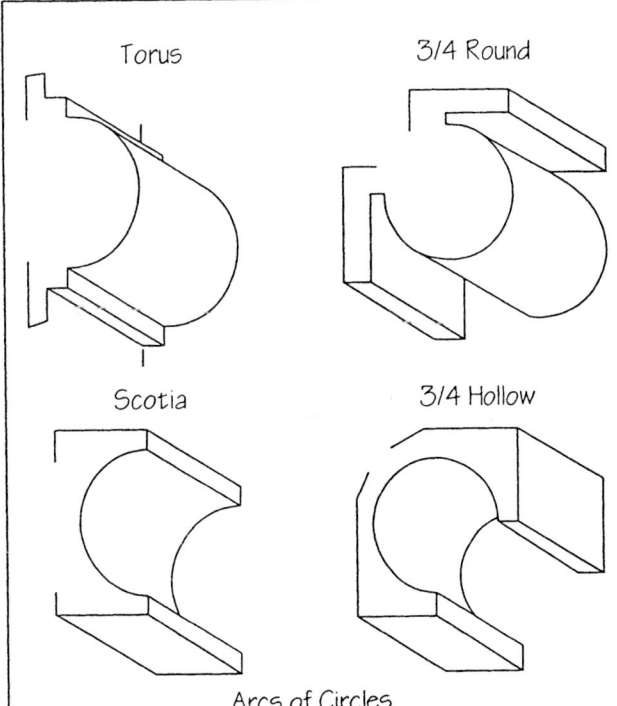

Torus

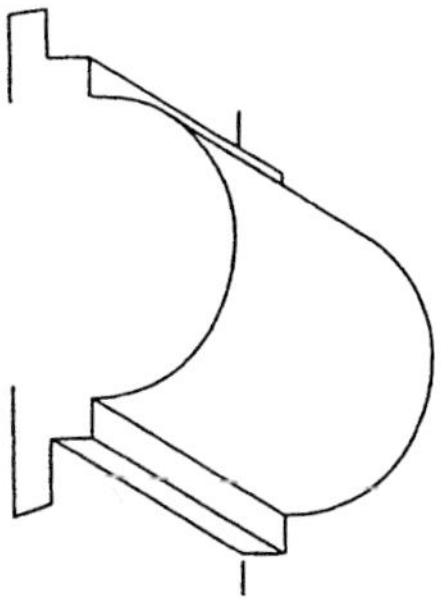

3/4 Round

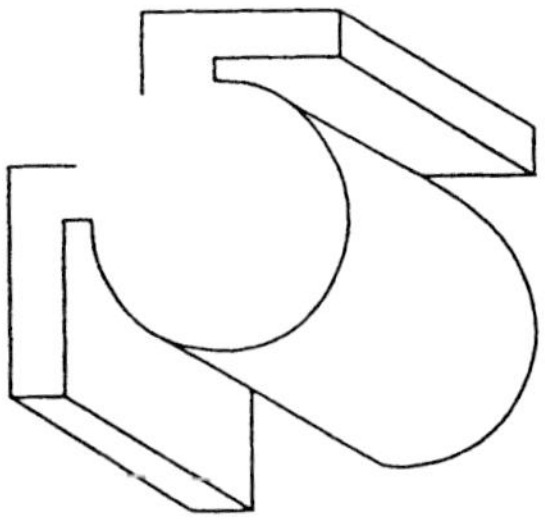

Scotia

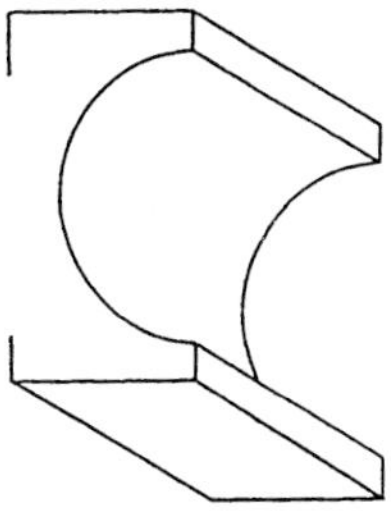

3/4 Hollow

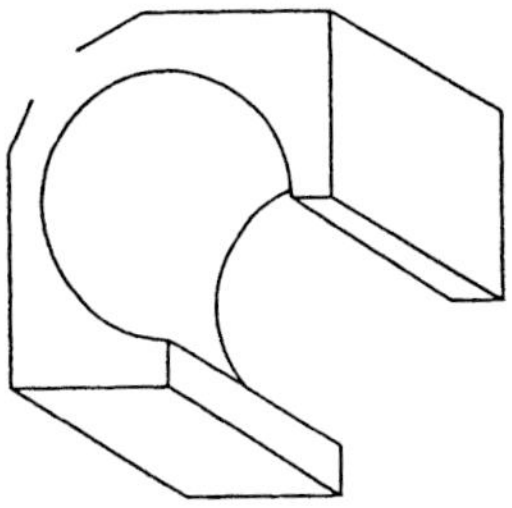

Arcs of Circles

CORNICES AND MOLDINGS

Classic Molding Shapes

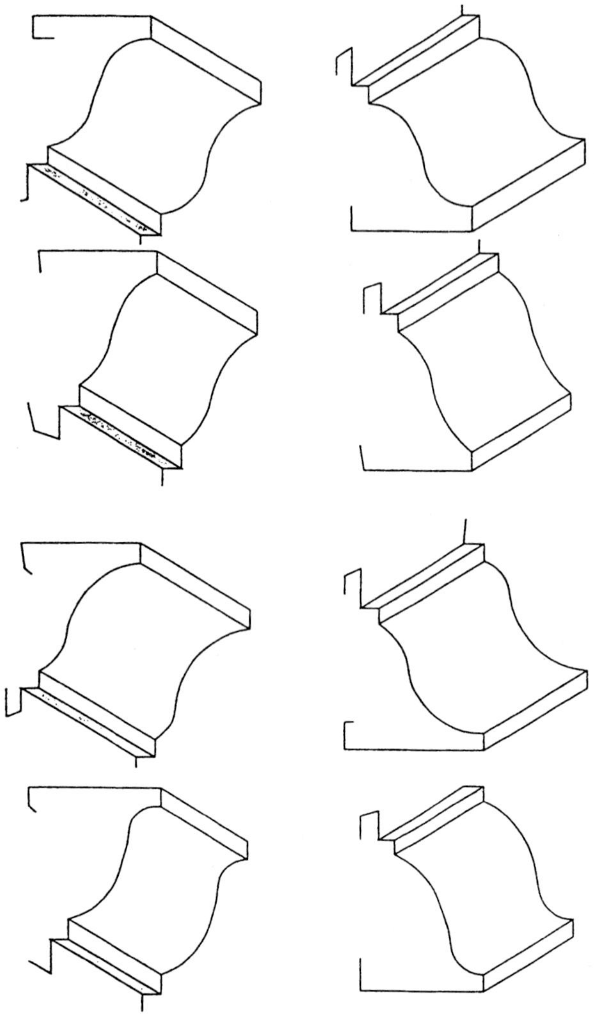

Cyma Recta

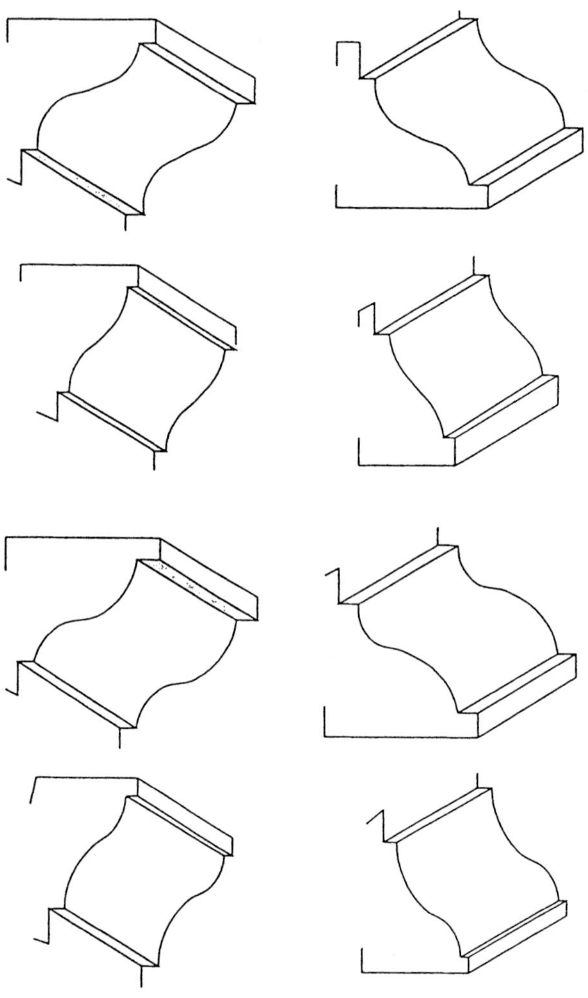

Cyma Reversa

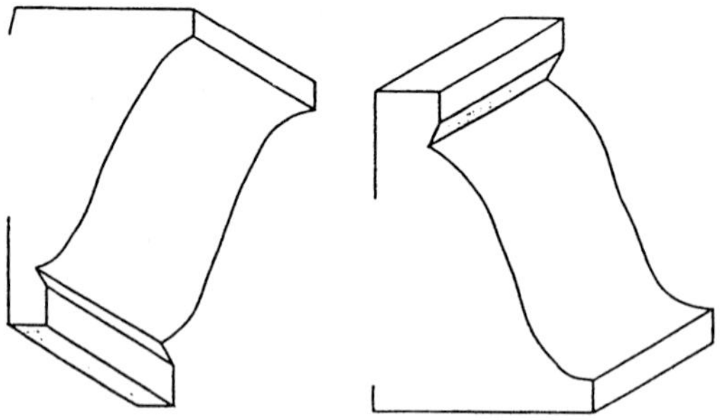

Quirked Cyma Recta

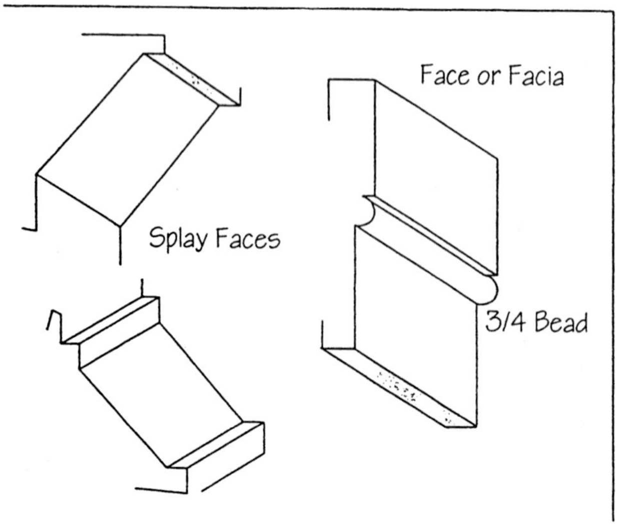

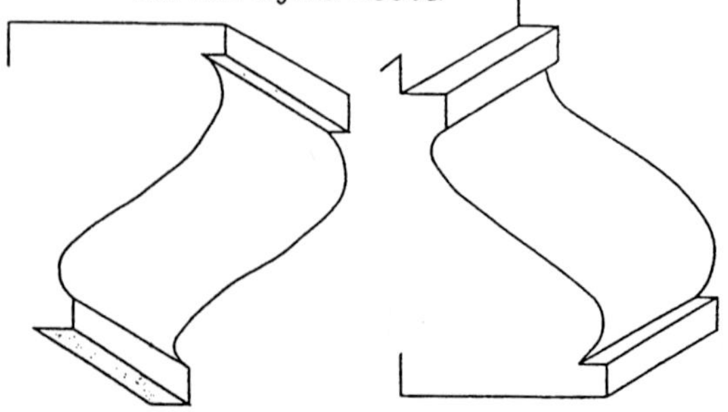

Quirked Cyma Reversa

CORNICES AND MOLDINGS

Crown Molding Details

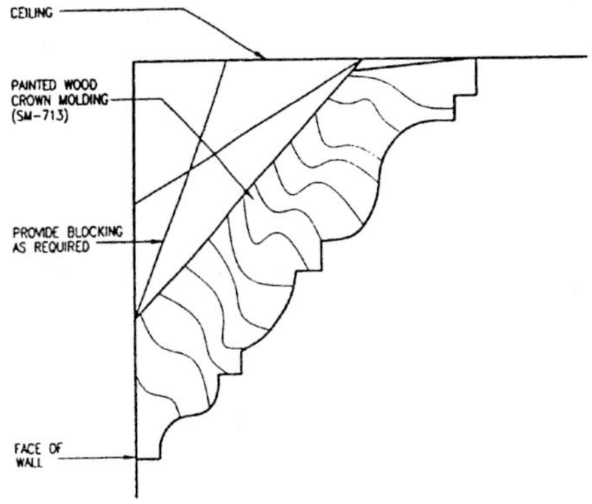

1 CROWN MOLDING DETAIL @ 1,2,3 BAYS
SCALE: FULL SIZE

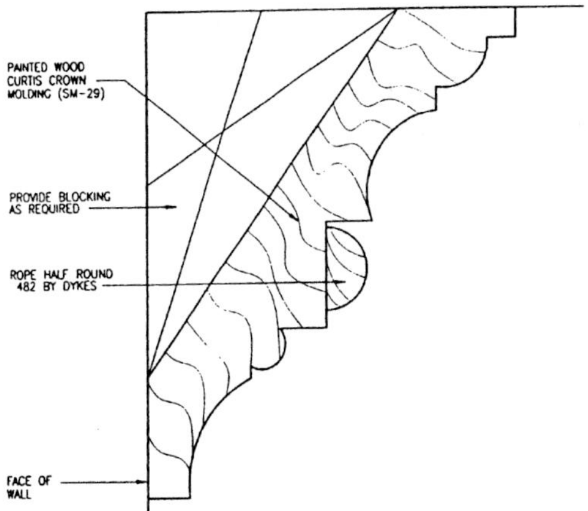

2 CROWN MOLDING DETAIL @ 4,5,7 BAYS
SCALE: FULL SIZE

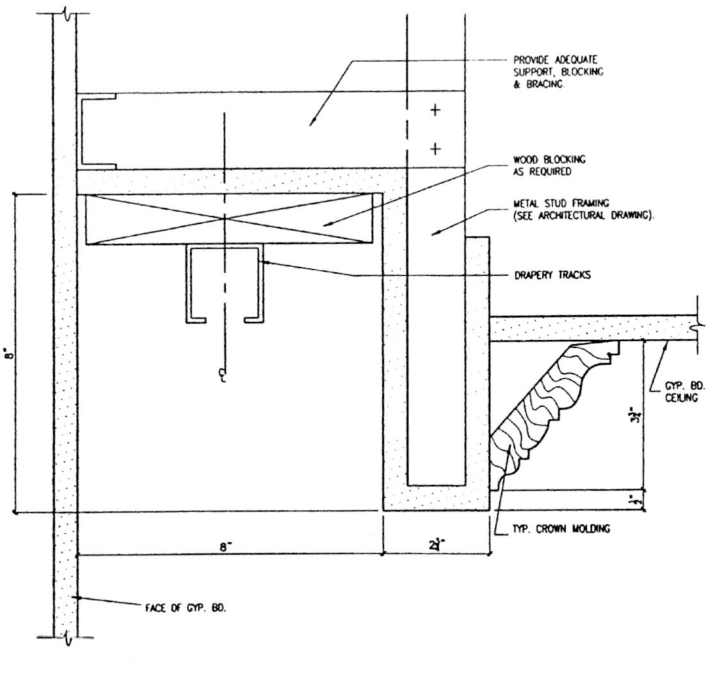

3 DRAPERY POCKET DETAIL
SCALE: HALF FULL SCALE

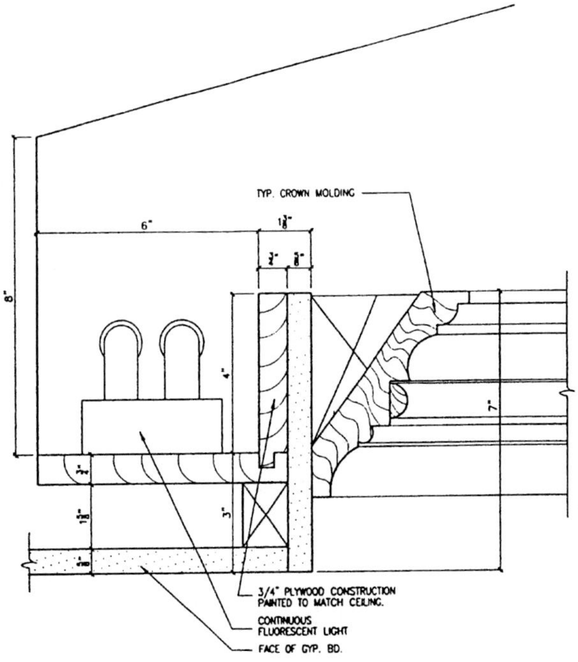

4 TYP. LIGHT COVE DETAIL
SCALE: HALF FULL SCALE

CORNICES AND MOLDINGS
Miscellaneous Moldings

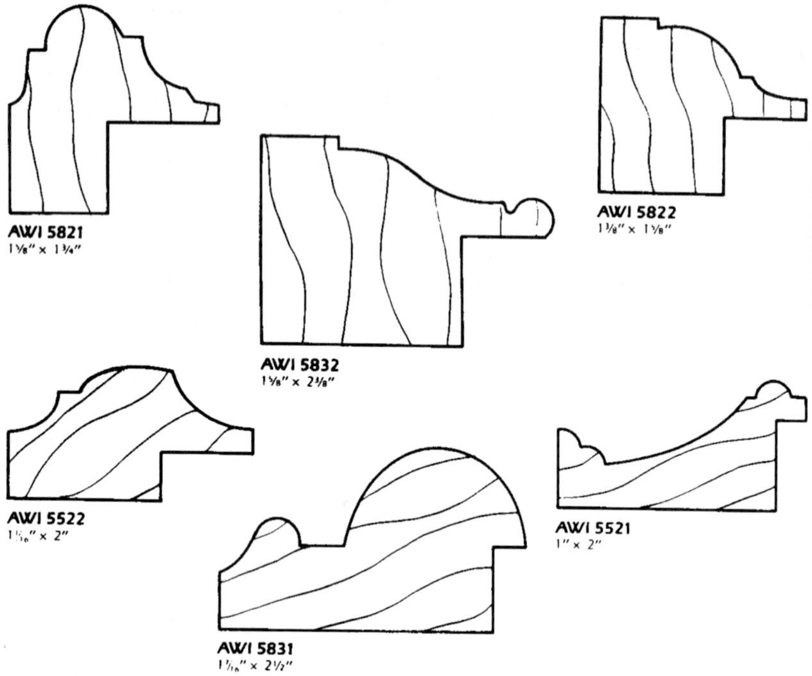

Picture Moldings

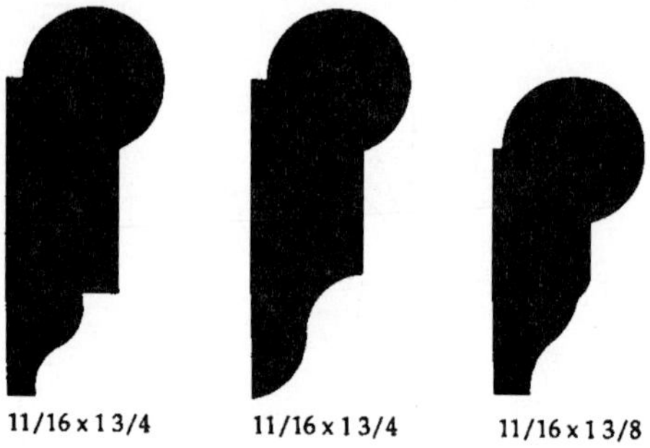

Picture Molds

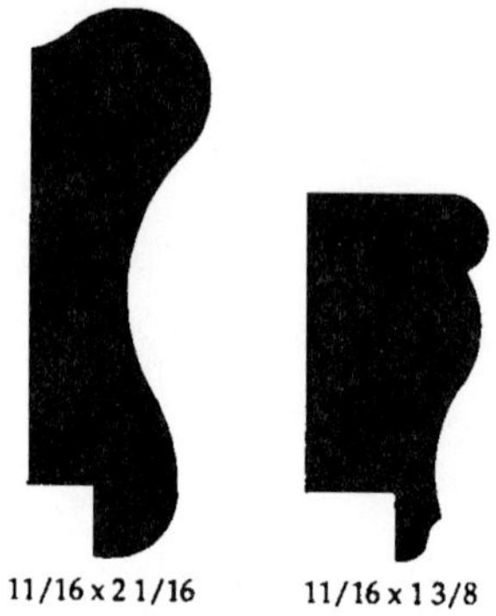

Picture Frame

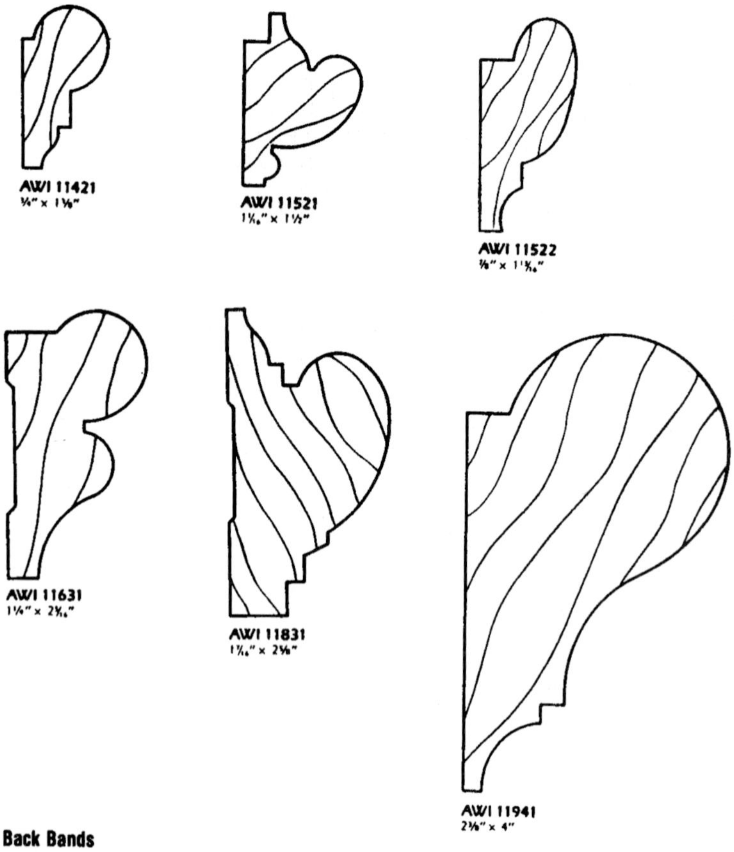

Back Bands

Step Molds

1 1/8 x 5 1/2 & 1 1/8 x 7 1/2

Pilaster

3/16 x 1 3/4

Tongue and Groove Siding

11/16 x 1 3/4

Fluted Pilaster

1 5/16 x 2

1 5/8 x 1 1/2

1 1/8 x 1 1/4

1 1/4 x 2

1 1/2 x 2

1 11/16 x 1 7/8

1 1/16 x 2

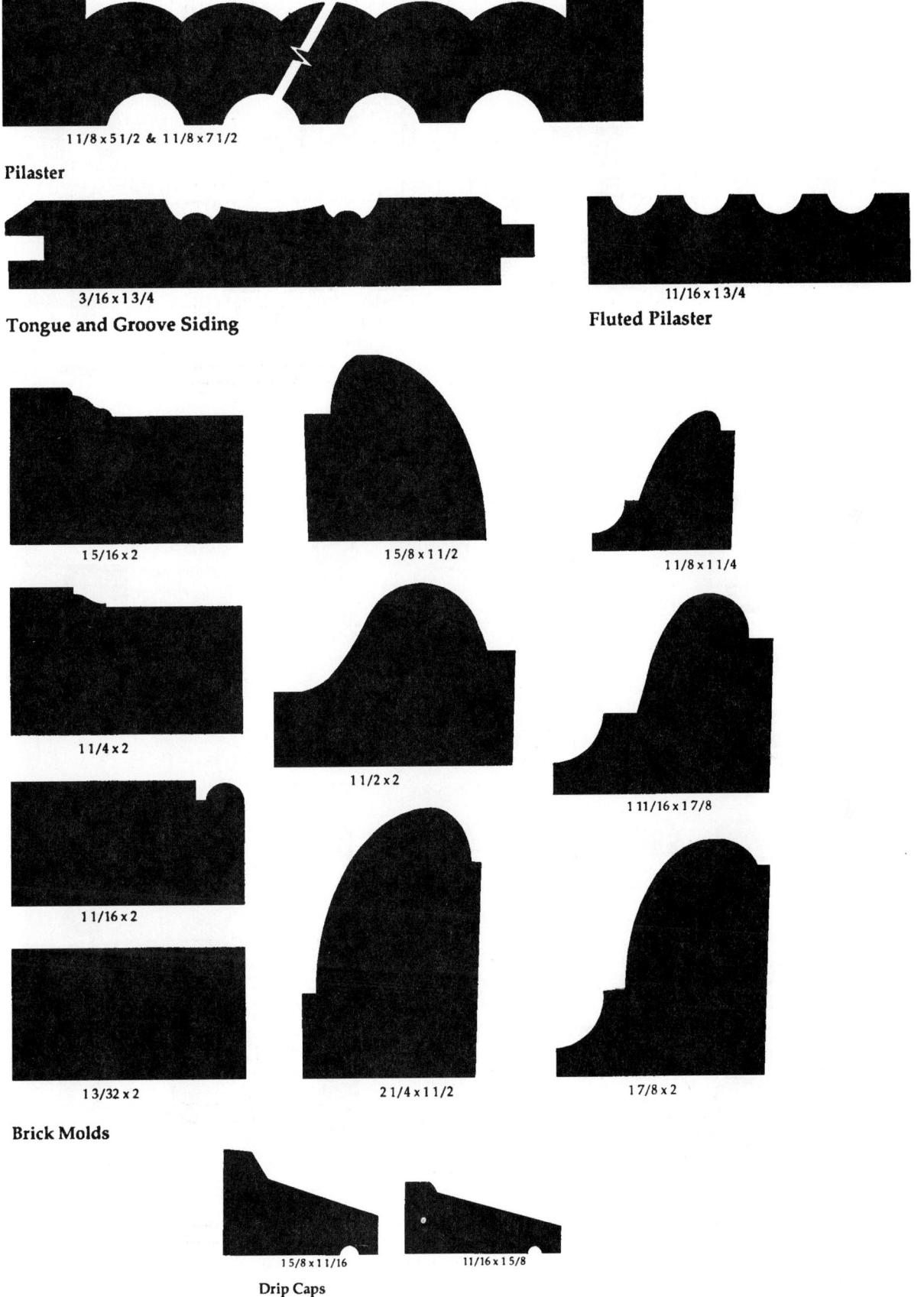

2 1/4 x 1 1/2

1 7/8 x 2

1 3/32 x 2

Brick Molds

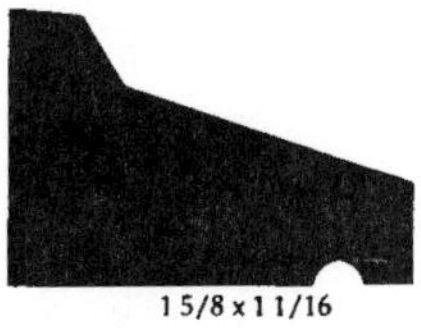

1 5/8 x 1 1/16

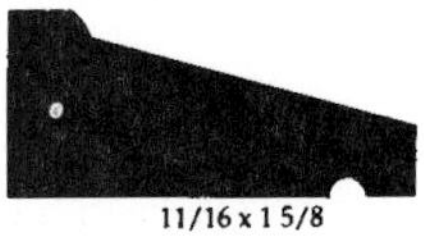

11/16 x 1 5/8

Drip Caps

CORNICES AND MOLDINGS
Miscellaneous Moldings

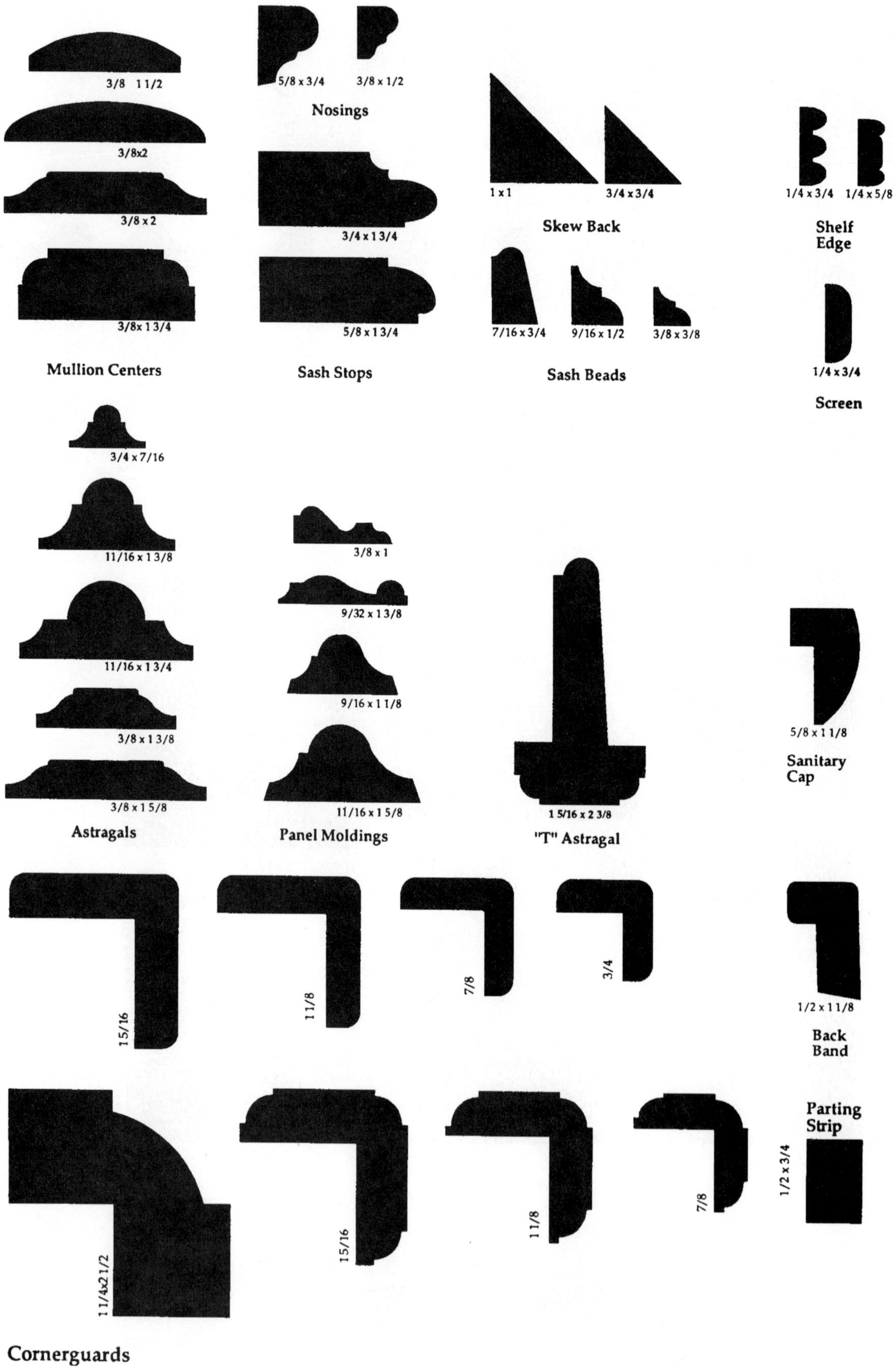

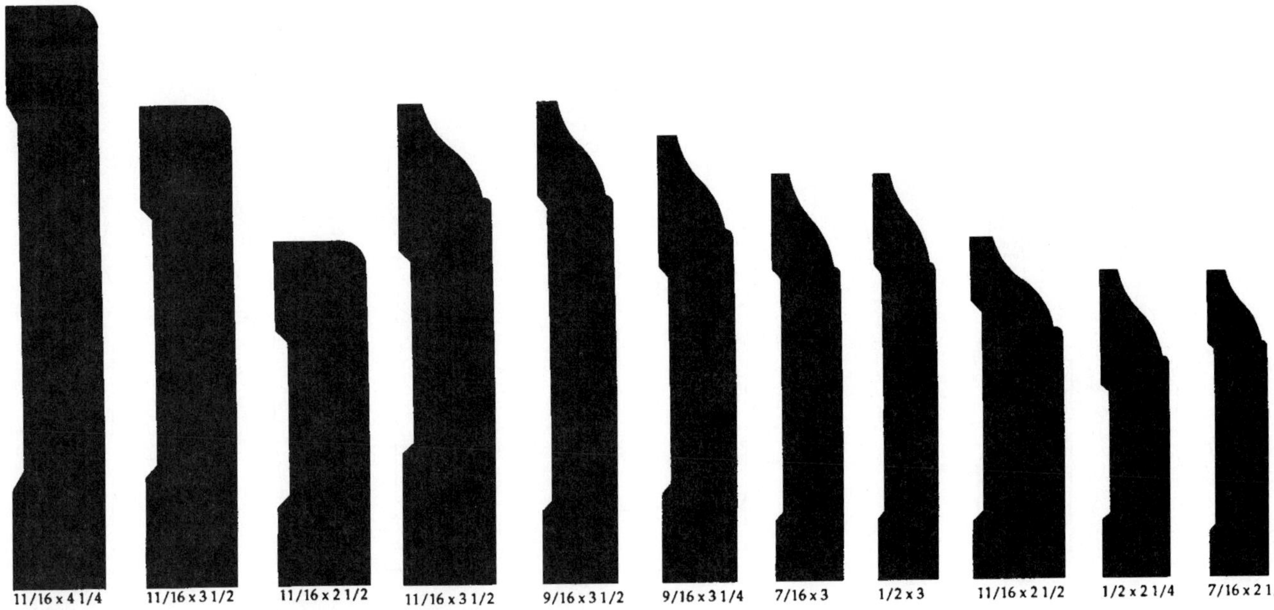

11/16 x 4 1/4 — 11/16 x 3 1/2 — 11/16 x 2 1/2 — 11/16 x 3 1/2 — 9/16 x 3 1/2 — 9/16 x 3 1/4 — 7/16 x 3 — 1/2 x 3 — 11/16 x 2 1/2 — 1/2 x 2 1/4 — 7/16 x 2 1/4

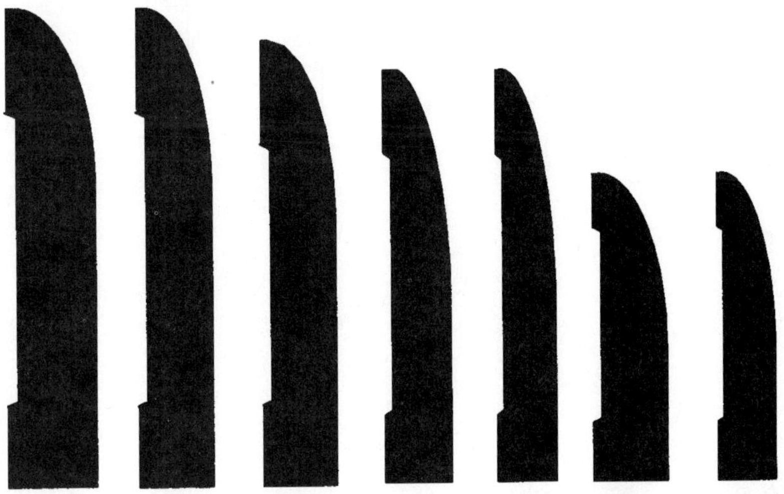

9/16 x 3 1/2 — 11/16 x 3 1/2 — 9/16 x 3 1/4 — 1/2 x 3 — 7/16 x 3 — 9/16 x 2 1/4 — 7/16 x 2 1/4

9/16 x 5 1/4 — 9/16 x 4 1/4

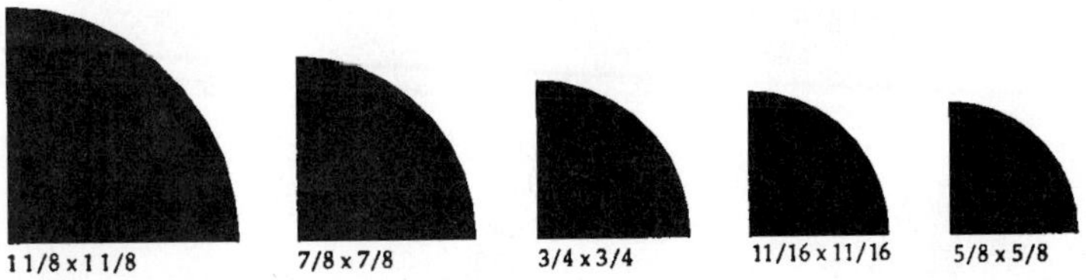

1 1/8 x 1 1/8 — 7/8 x 7/8 — 3/4 x 3/4 — 11/16 x 11/16 — 5/8 x 5/8

Quarter Round Molds

1/2 x 3/4 — 7/16 x 3/4 — 7/16 x 11/16 — 1/2 x 3/4 — 1/2 x 1/2 — 3/8 x 3/8 — 1/4 x 1/4

Base Shoe & Floor Molds

CORNICES AND MOLDINGS

Base Moldings

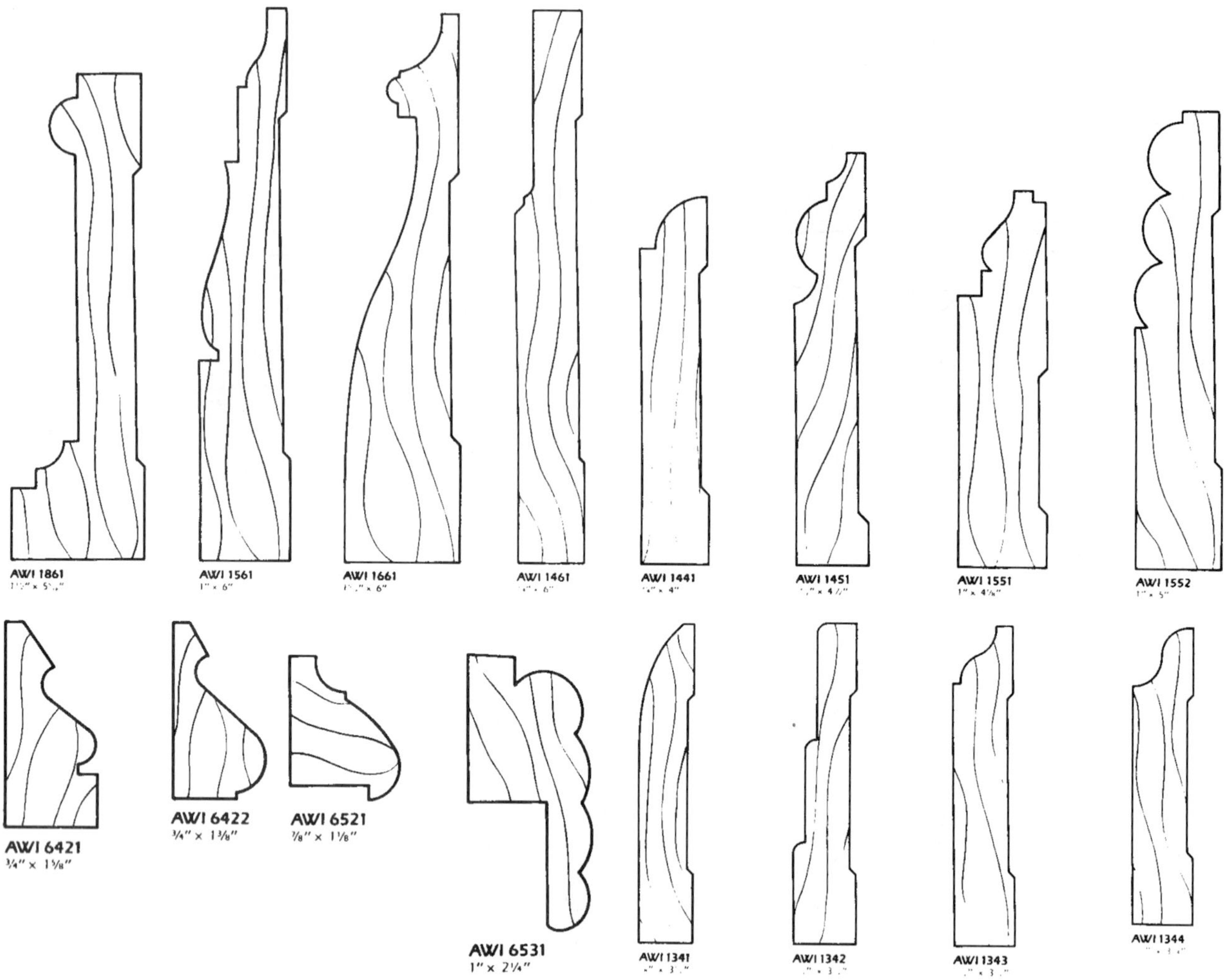

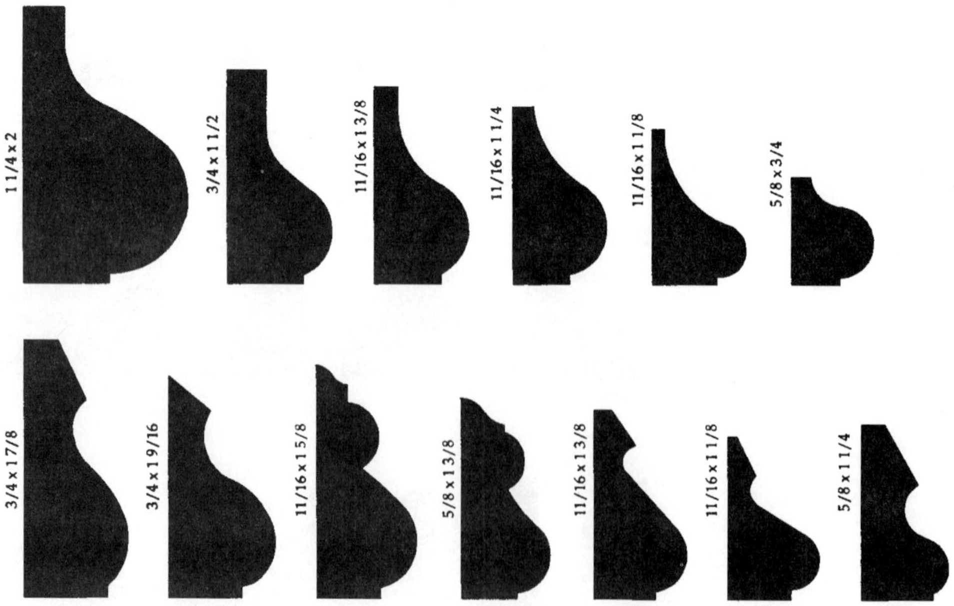

Base Cap Molds

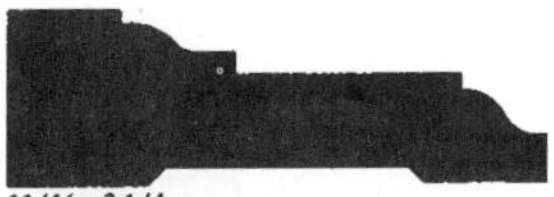
11/16 x 2 1/4

11/16 x 2 1/4

11/16 x 2 1/2

3/4 x 2 1/2

11/16 x 2 1/2

11/16 x 2 5/8

11/16 x 3 1/2

11/16 x 3 1/2

5/8 x 2 1/4

5/8 x 2 3/8

9/16 x 2 1/4

5/8 x 2 1/4

11/16 x 2 1/4

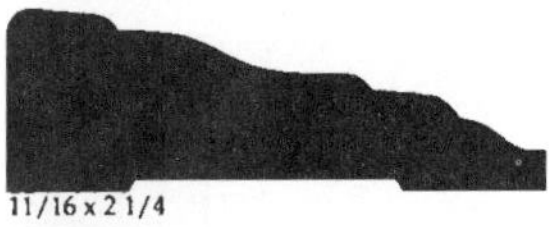
11/16 x 2 1/4

11/16 x 2 1/2

11/16 x 2 1/2

5/8 x 3 1/4

1/2 x 3 1/4

9/16 x 3 1/4

9/16 x 3 1/4

11/16 x 3 1/2

11/16 x 2 1/4

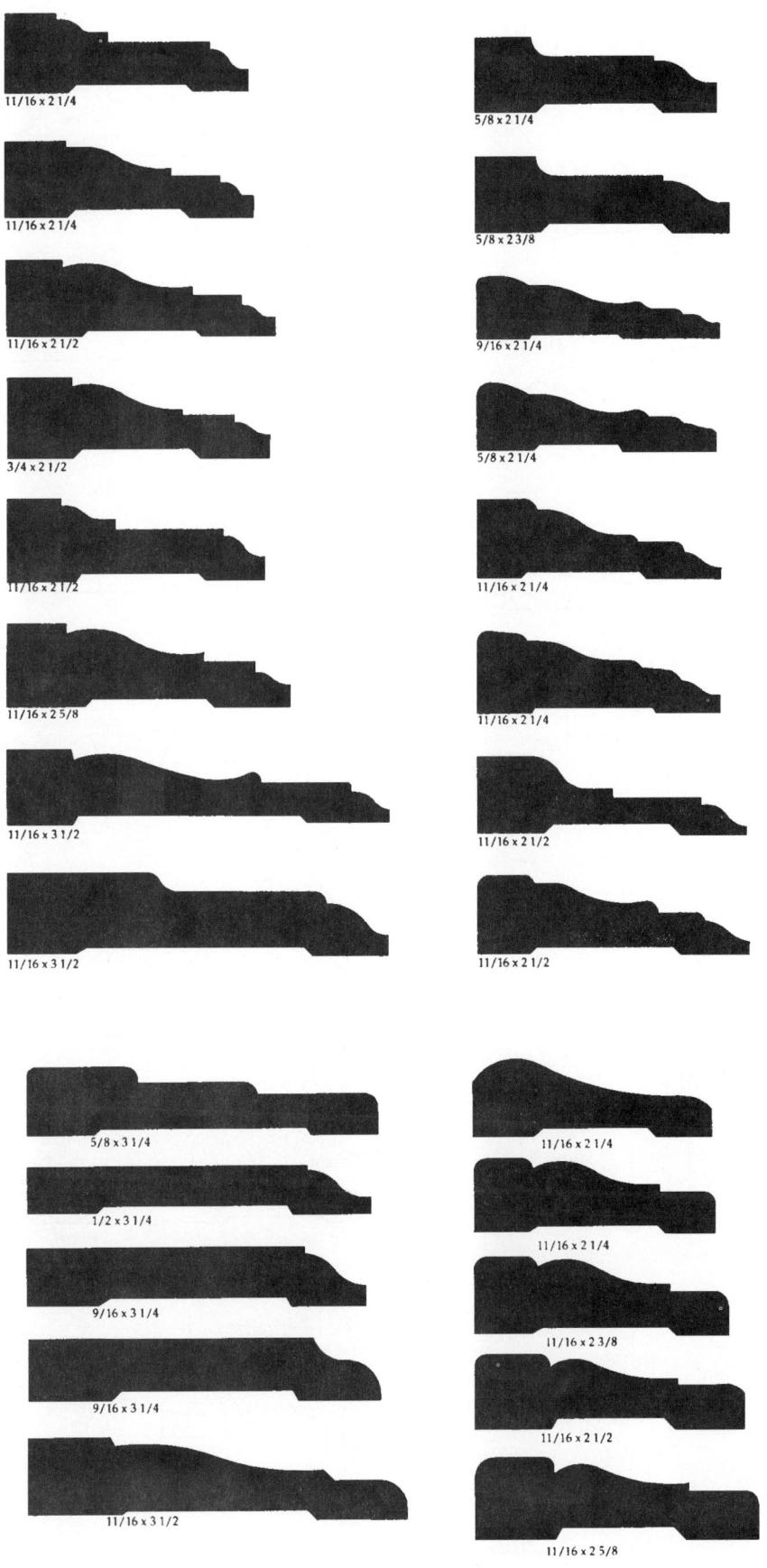

11/16 x 2 1/4

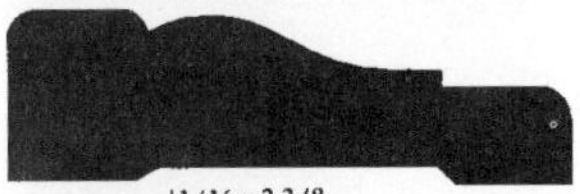
11/16 x 2 3/8

11/16 x 2 1/2

11/16 x 2 5/8

CORNICES AND MOLDINGS
Casings

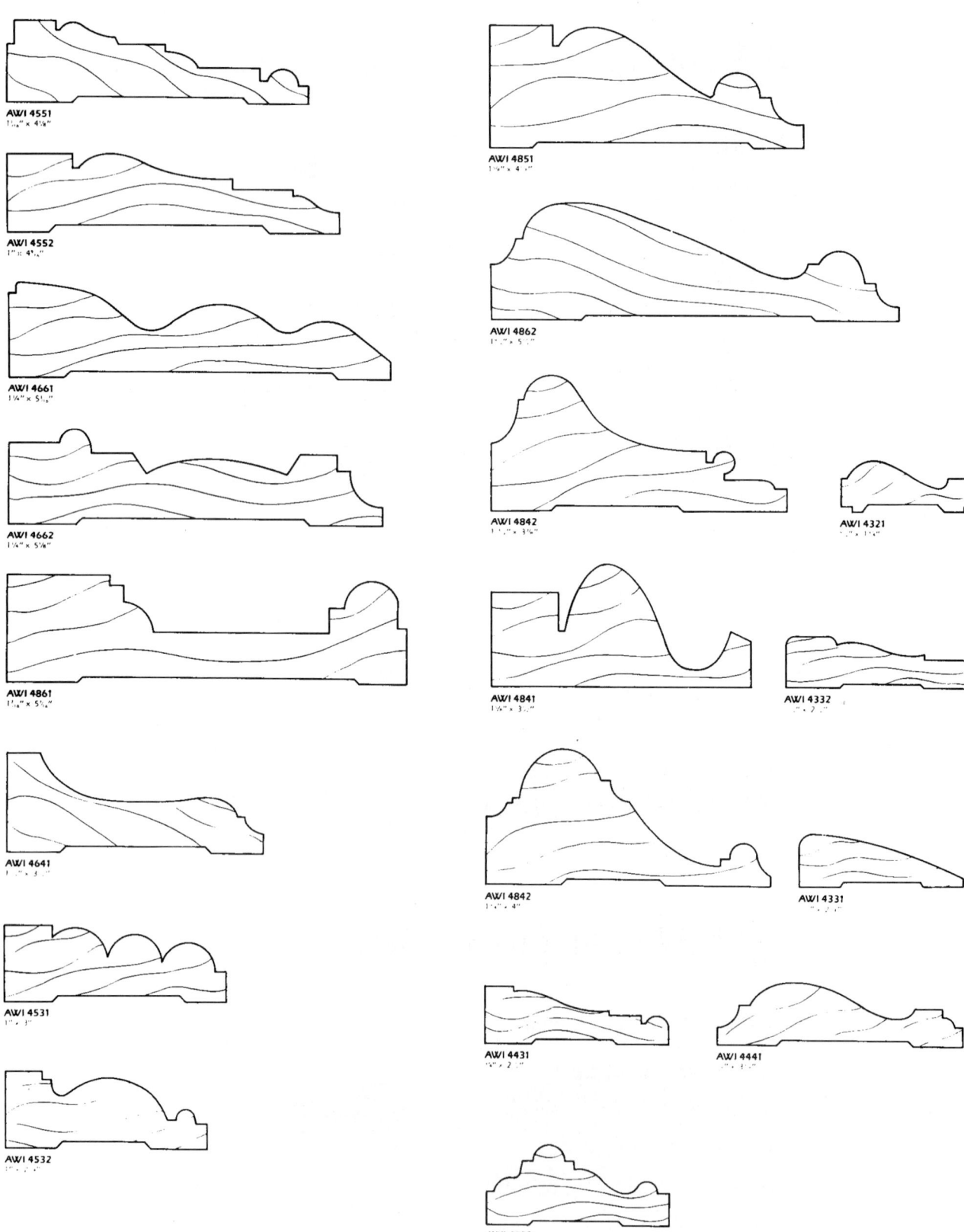

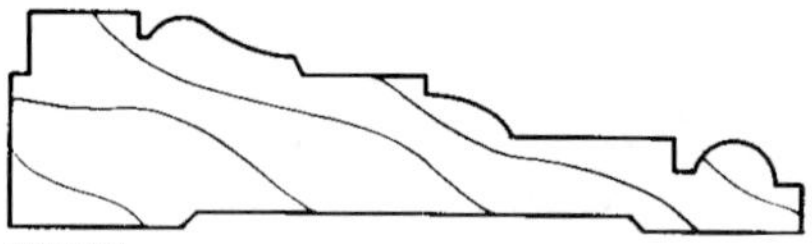
AWI 4551

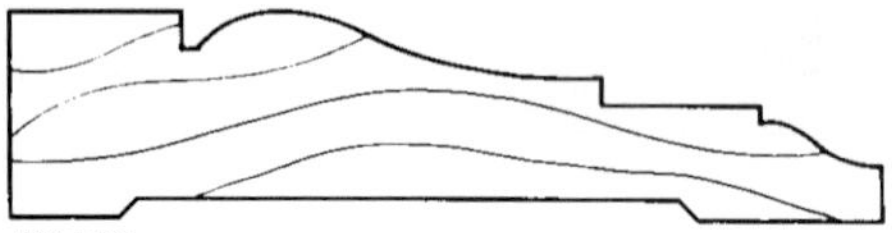
AWI 4552

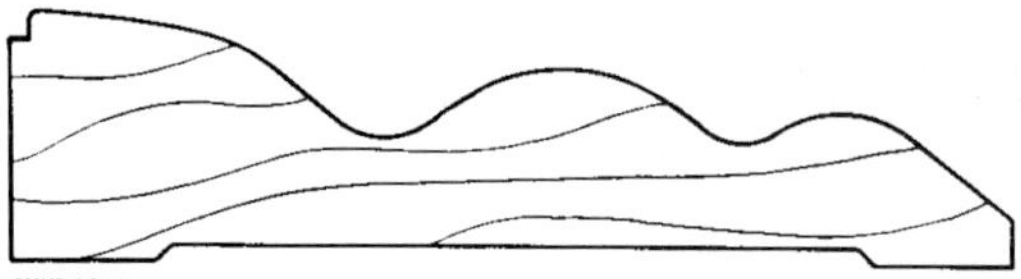
AWI 4661
1¼" × 5¹⁄₁₆"

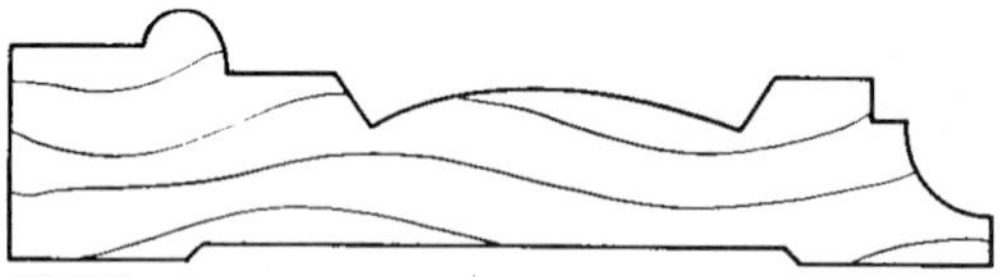
AWI 4662
1¼" × 5⅛"

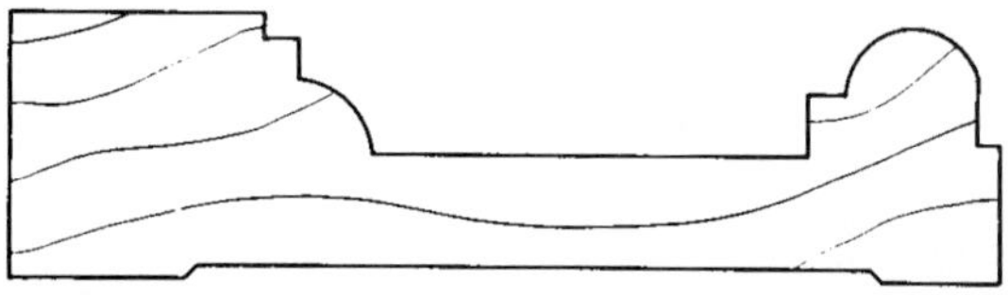
AWI 4861

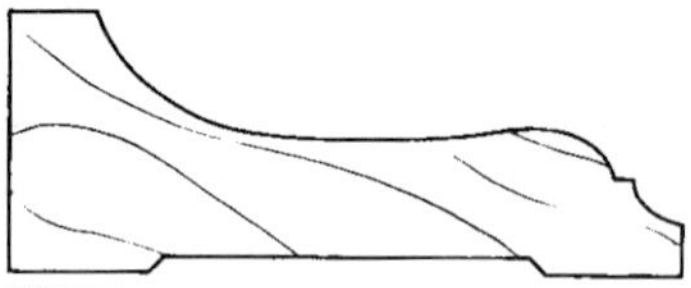
AWI 4641

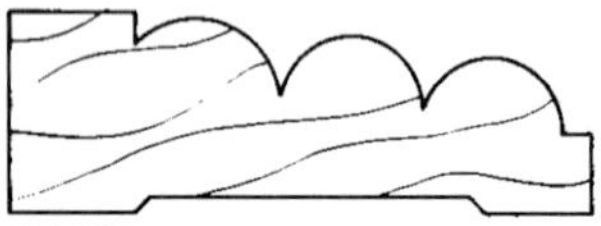
AWI 4531

AWI 4532

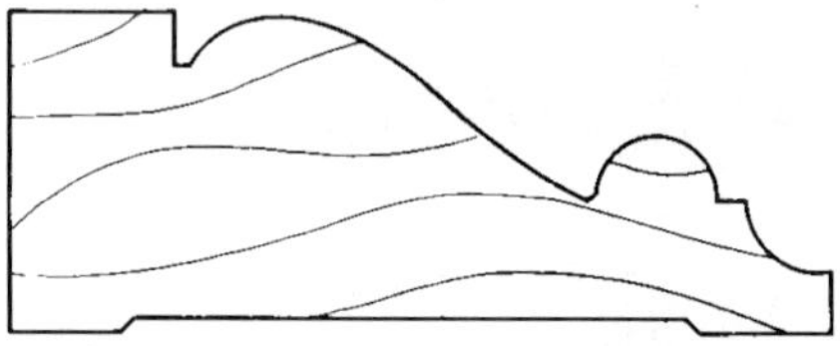
AWI 4851

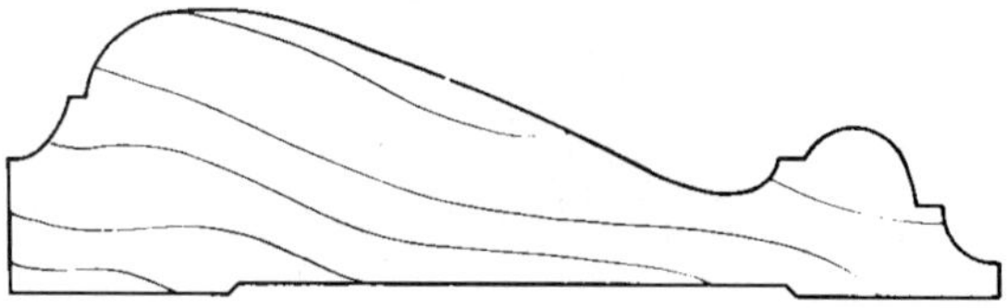
AWI 4862

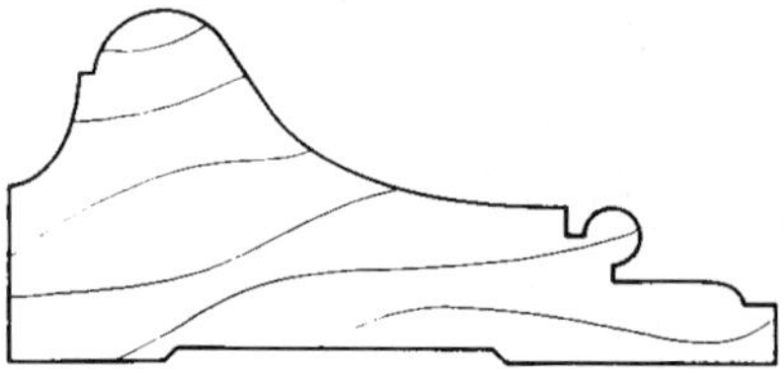
AWI 4842

AWI 4321

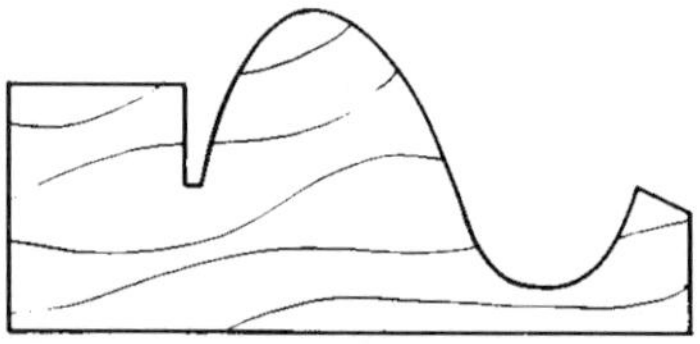
AWI 4841

AWI 4332

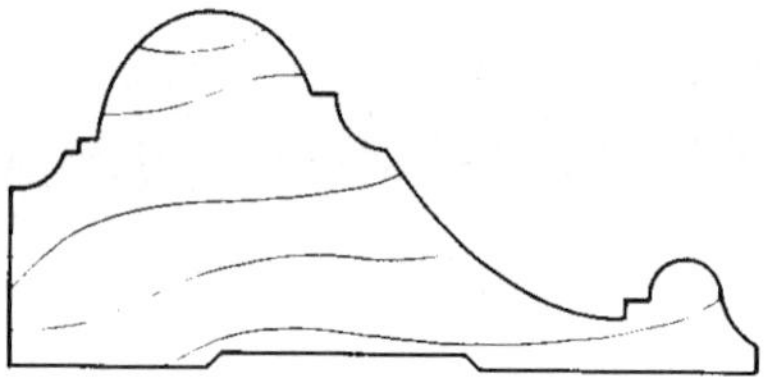
AWI 4842

AWI 4331

AWI 4431

AWI 4441

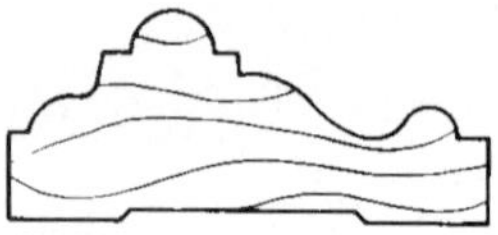
AWI 4533

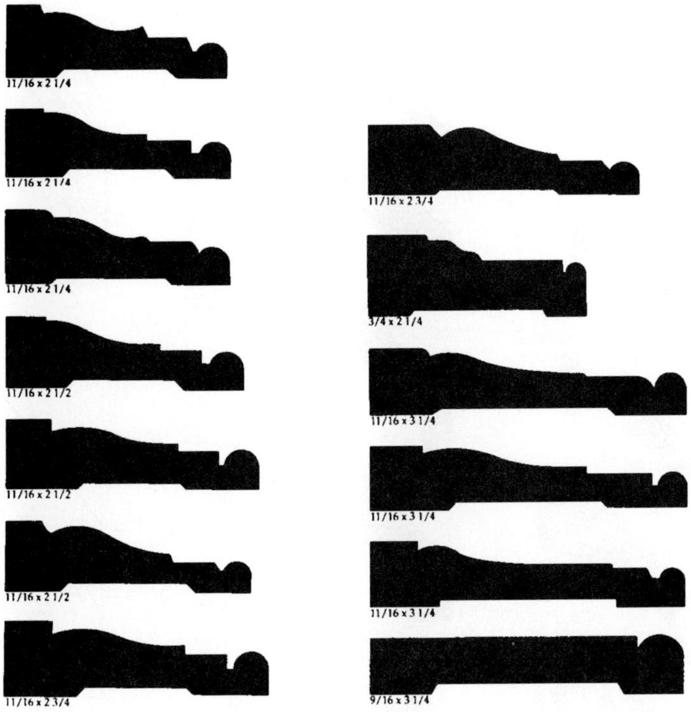

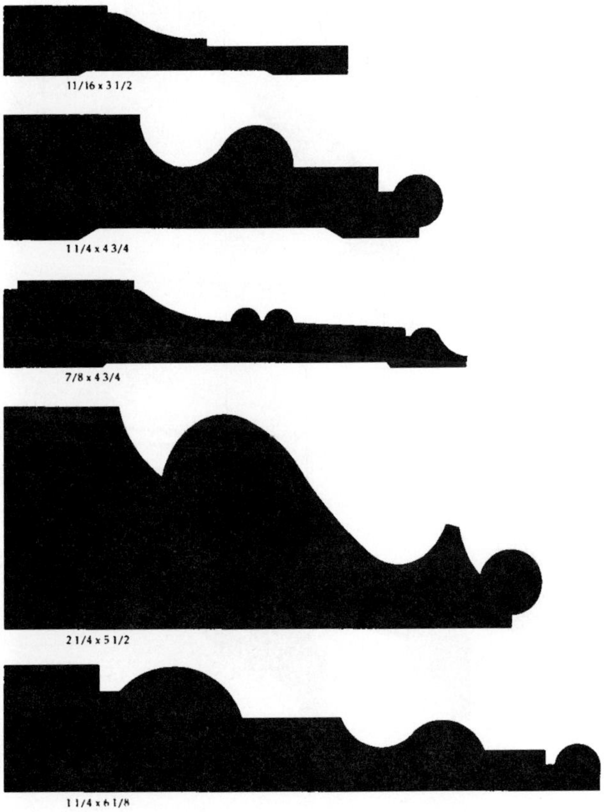

Specialty casings

CORNICES AND MOLDINGS
Cove Moldings

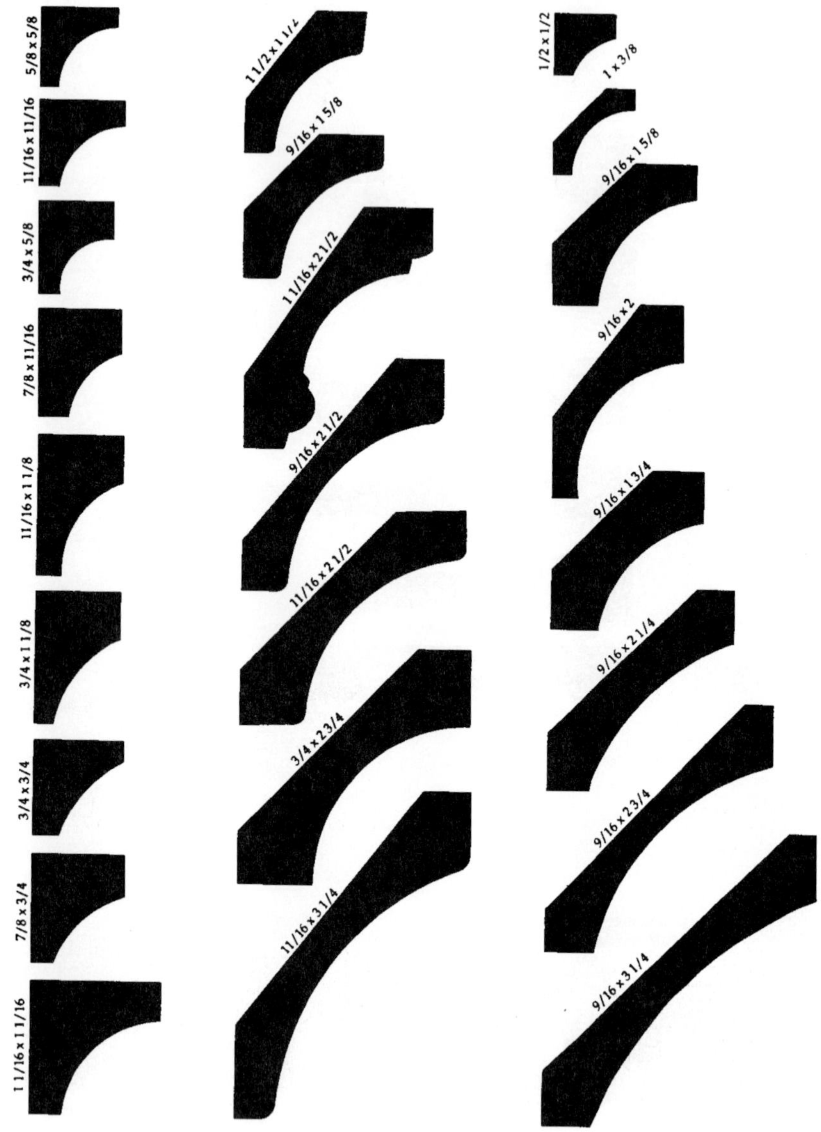

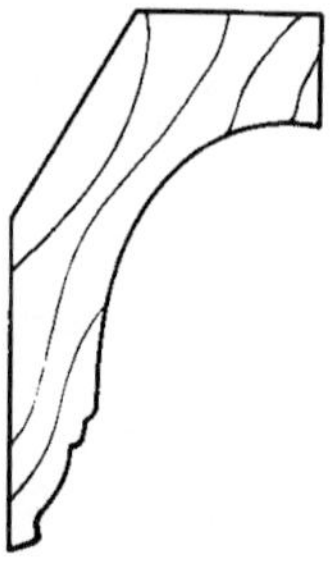
AWI 3531
1 1/16″ × 3″

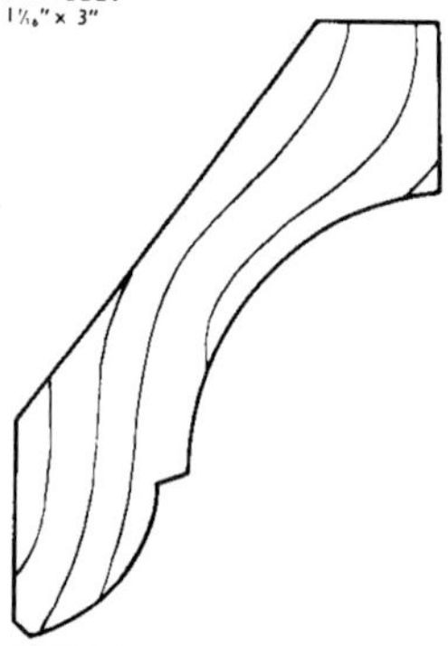
AWI 3542
1 1/16″ × 3 11/16″

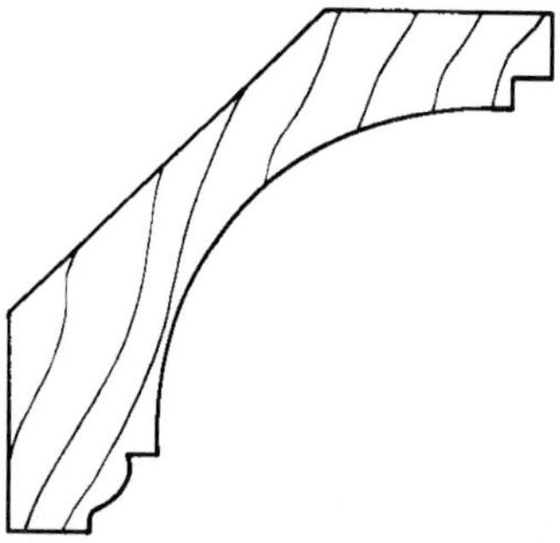
AWI 3651
1 1/8″ × 4 1/4″

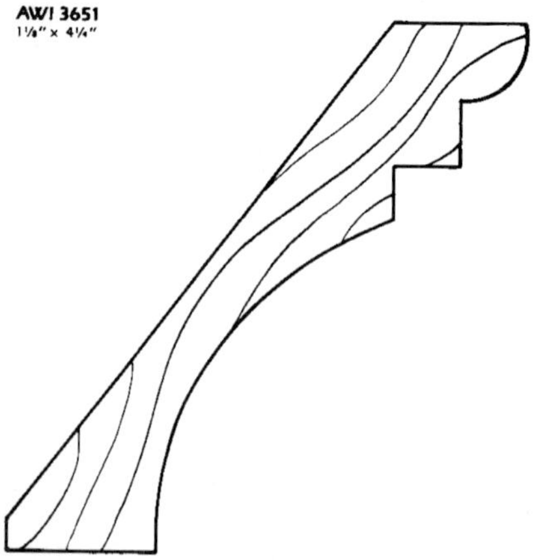
AWI 3561
1 1/16″ × 5 1/2″

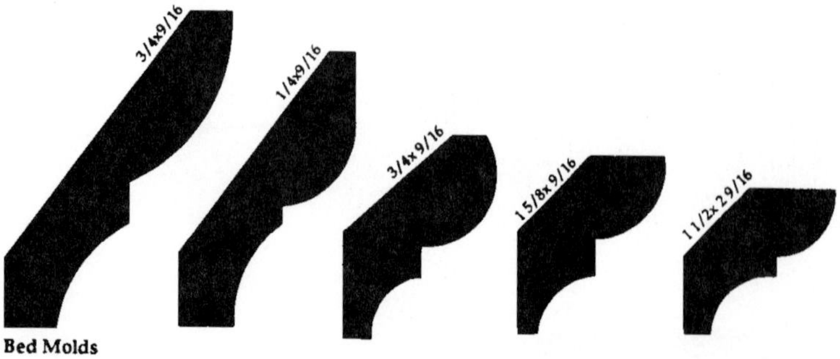

Bed Molds

CORNICES AND MOLDINGS

Panel Moldings

AWI 12631
1 1/4" × 3"

AWI 12531
1" × 2 1/2"

AWI 12522
1" × 2"

AWI 12523
1" × 1 1/2"

AWI 12321
11/16" × 1 15/16"

AWI 12322
11/16" × 1 1/2"

AWI 12521
7/8" × 2"

AWI 12421
13/16" × 1 1/2"

AWI 12422
13/16" × 1 5/16"

AWI 12423
3/4" × 1 1/4"

AWI 12424
11/16" × 1 5/16"

AWI 12323
11/16" × 1 3/8"

AWI 12221
9/16" × 1 3/8"

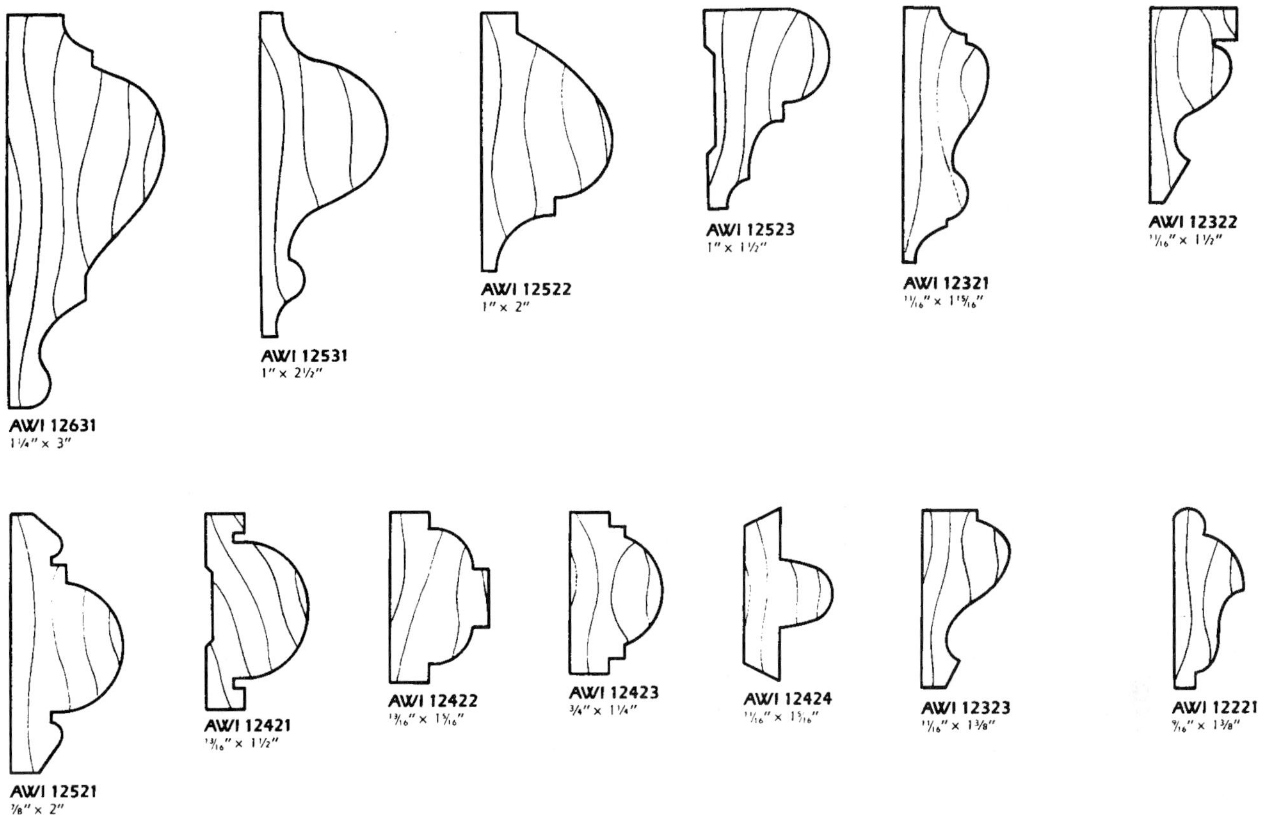

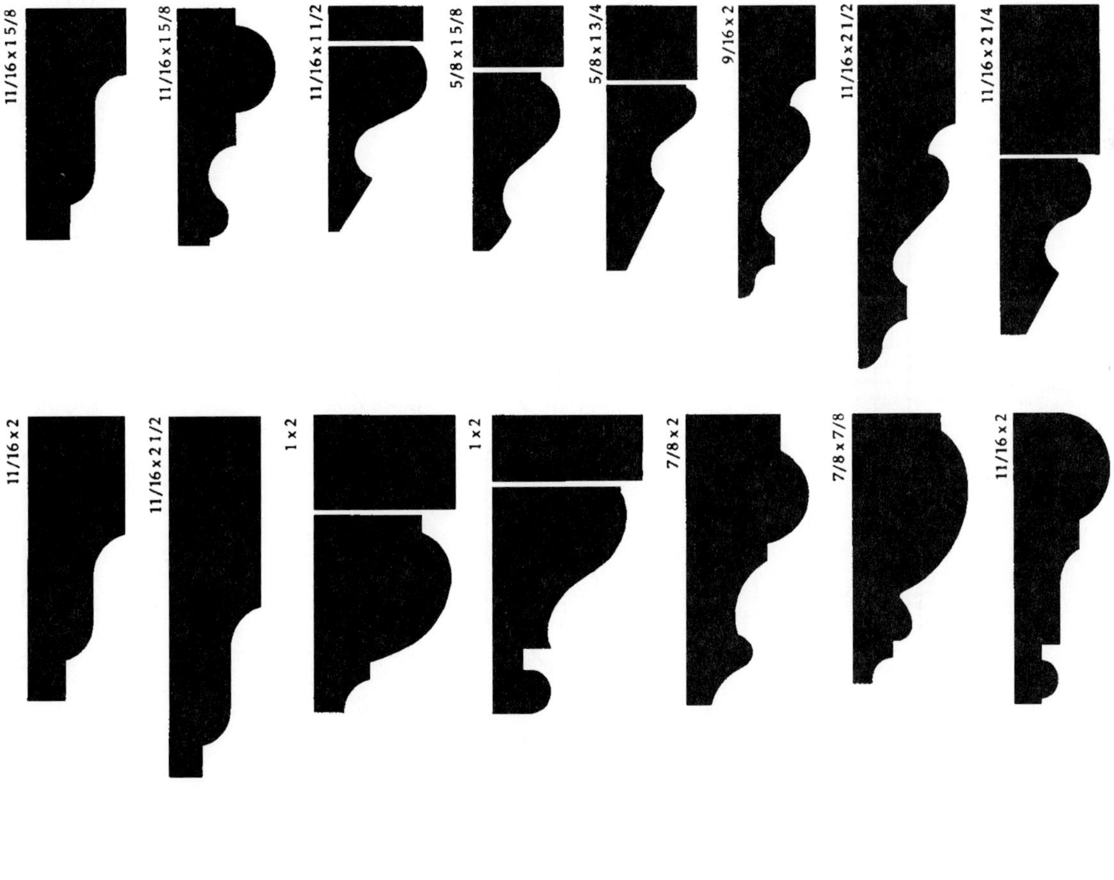

CORNICES AND MOLDINGS
Chair Rail Moldings

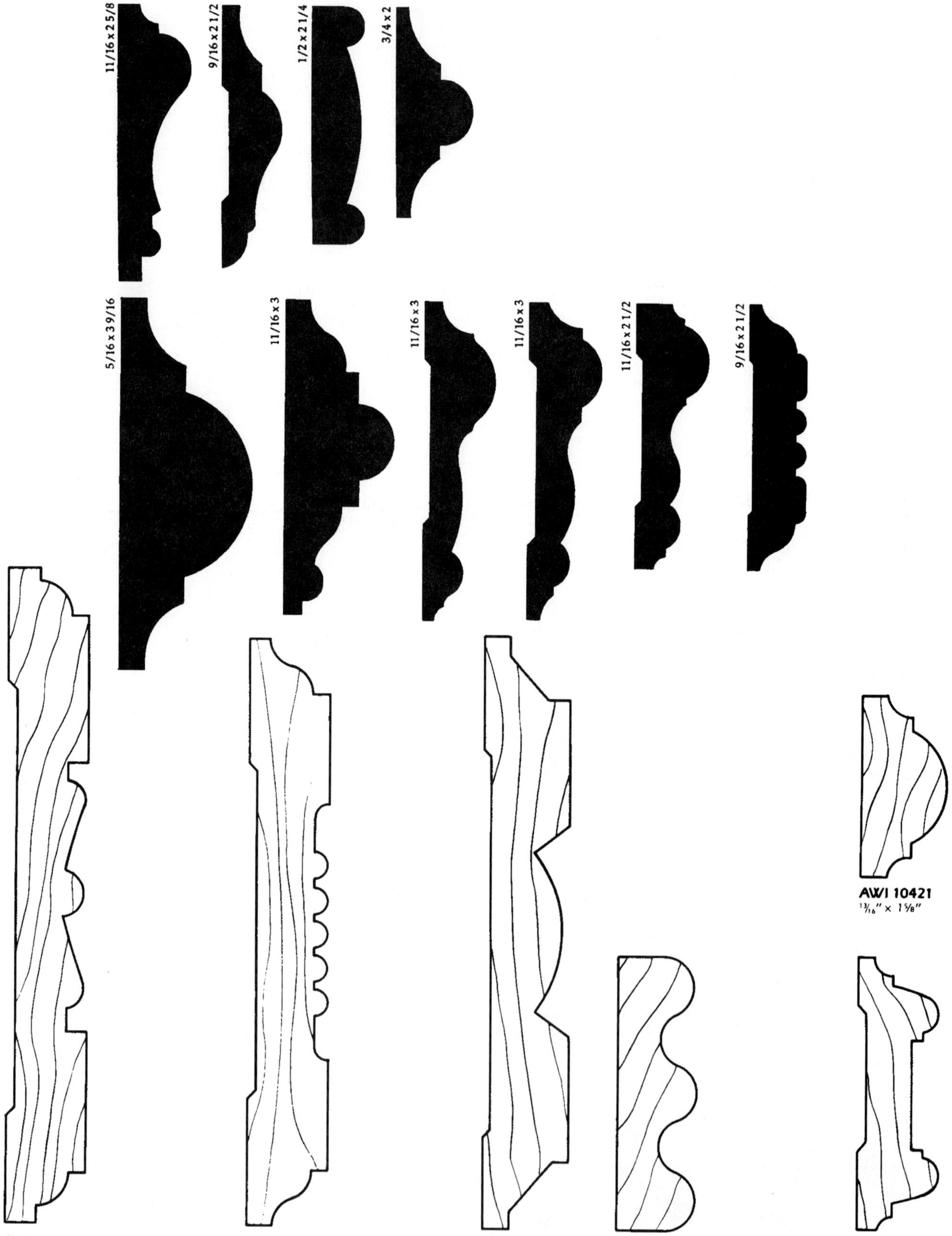

AWI 10461 3/4" × 6"

AWI 10462 3/4" × 5 3/8"

AWI 10463 13/16" × 5 7/16"

AWI 10431 3/4" × 2 1/2"

AWI 10421 13/16" × 1 5/8"

AWI 10432 3/4" × 2 1/2"

Handrails

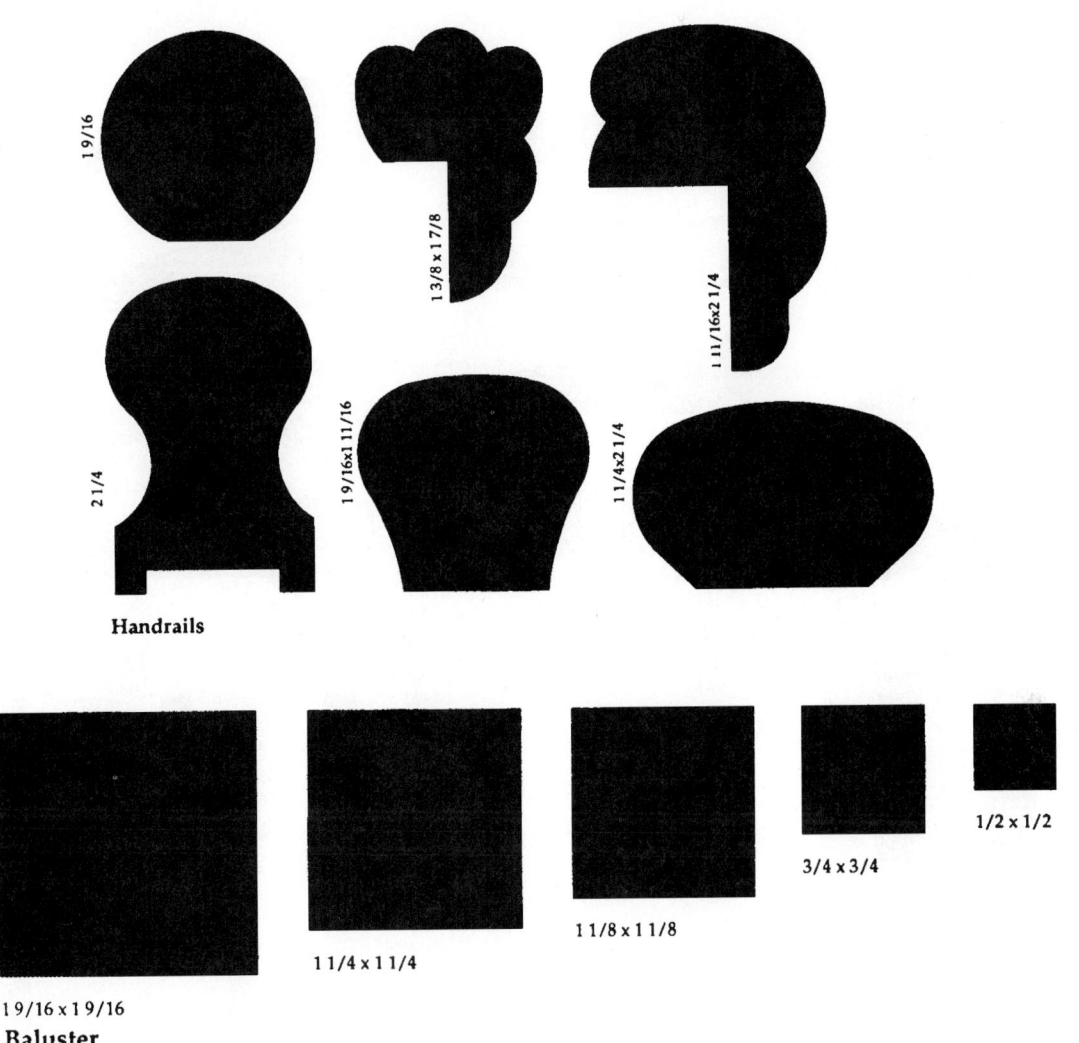

Baluster

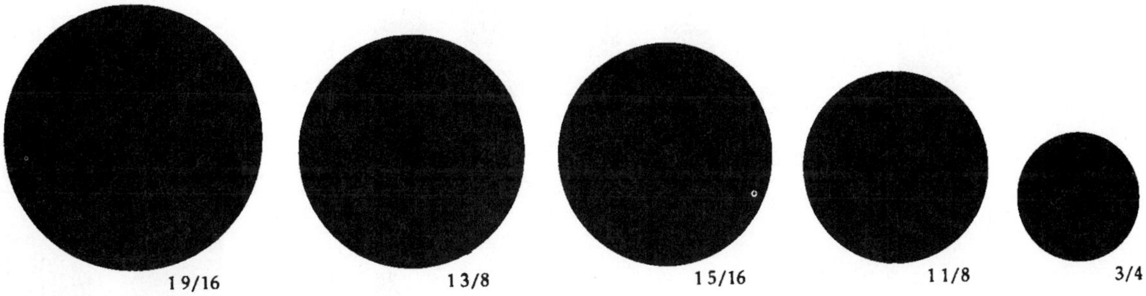

Round Molds

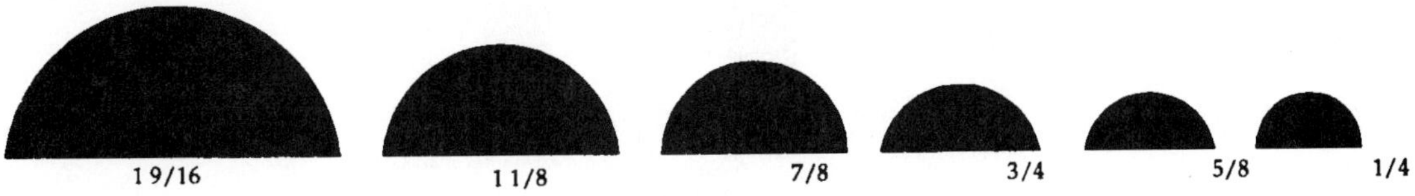

Half Rounds

CORNICES AND MOLDINGS
Clamshell and Stop Moldings

CLAMSHELL MOLDINGS

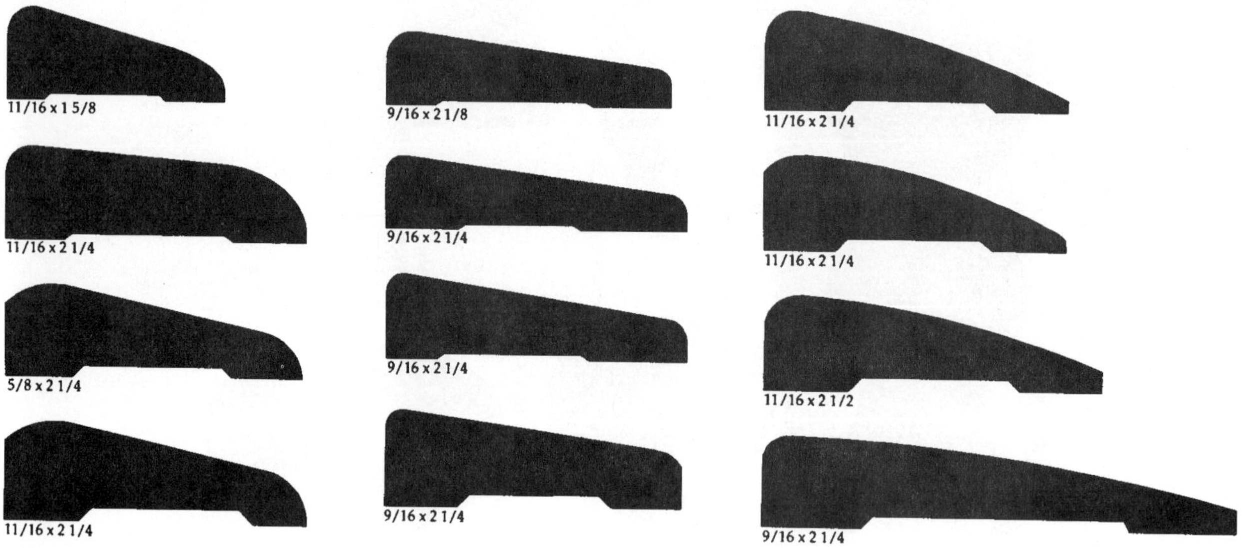

STOP MOLDINGS

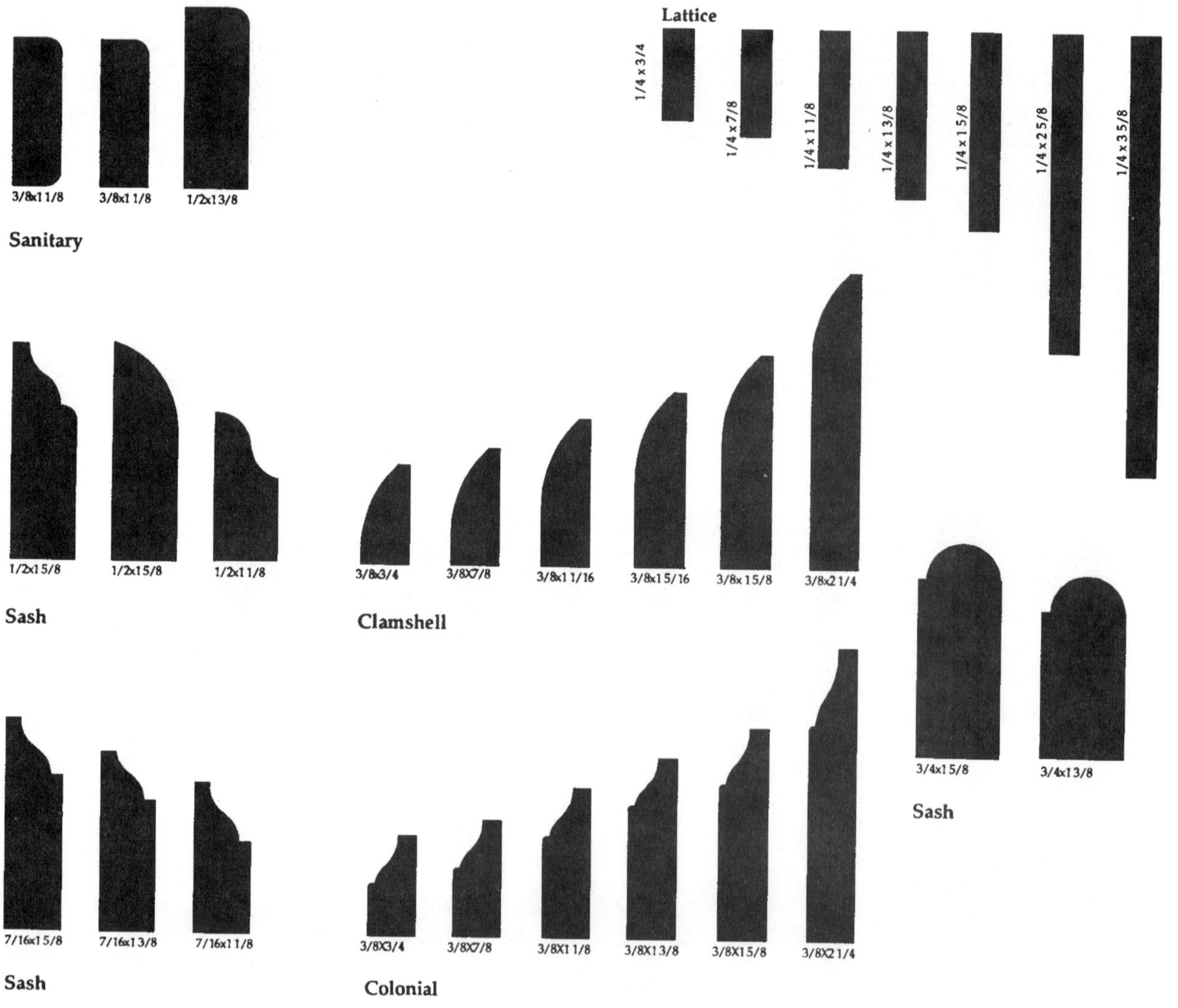

CORNICES AND MOLDINGS

Hand-Carved Brackets

Flute & Lyre
10½"W x 11"H

Bracket
6½"W x 12½"H x 5¼"D.

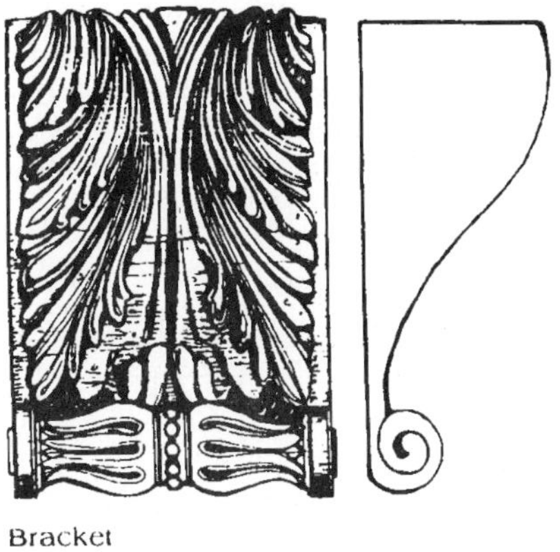

Bracket
8"W x 12"H x 4"D.

Left & Right Scroll
8¼"W x 11½"H

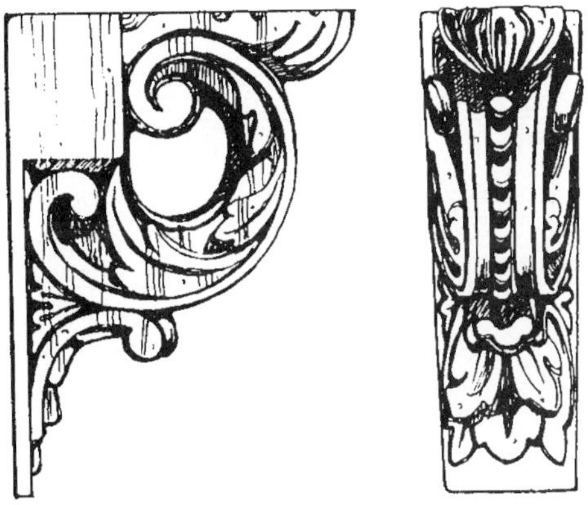

Bracket
4½"W x 13"H x 9½"D.

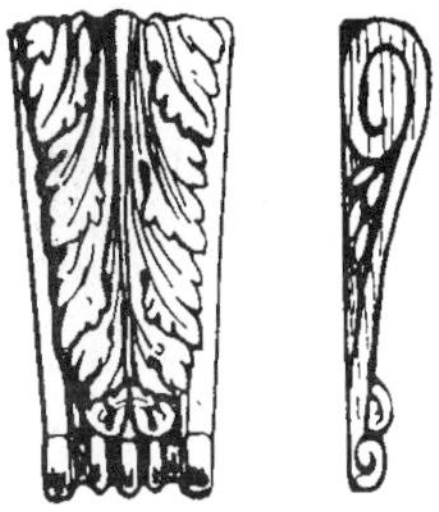

Bracket
4"W x 8½"H x 1¾"D.

Bracket
2¾"W x 12"H x 7"D

Bracket
7½"W x 14"H x 7½"D

CORNICES AND MOLDINGS
Classical Composite Column

The columns of the classical orders of Greek and Roman architecture are often adapted for modern construction. These orders are Tuscan, Doric, Ionic, Corinthian, and Composite. The Composite figure (below) names the basic features of a classical order and gives some of the proportions of the column in relation to the shaft diameter as a basic unit of measurement.

Pilasters are rectangular in plan, without taper from top to bottom. If used structurally they are usually referred to as *piers,* but are treated architecturally as columns. The typical pilaster extends a third or less of its width from the wall surface behind it.

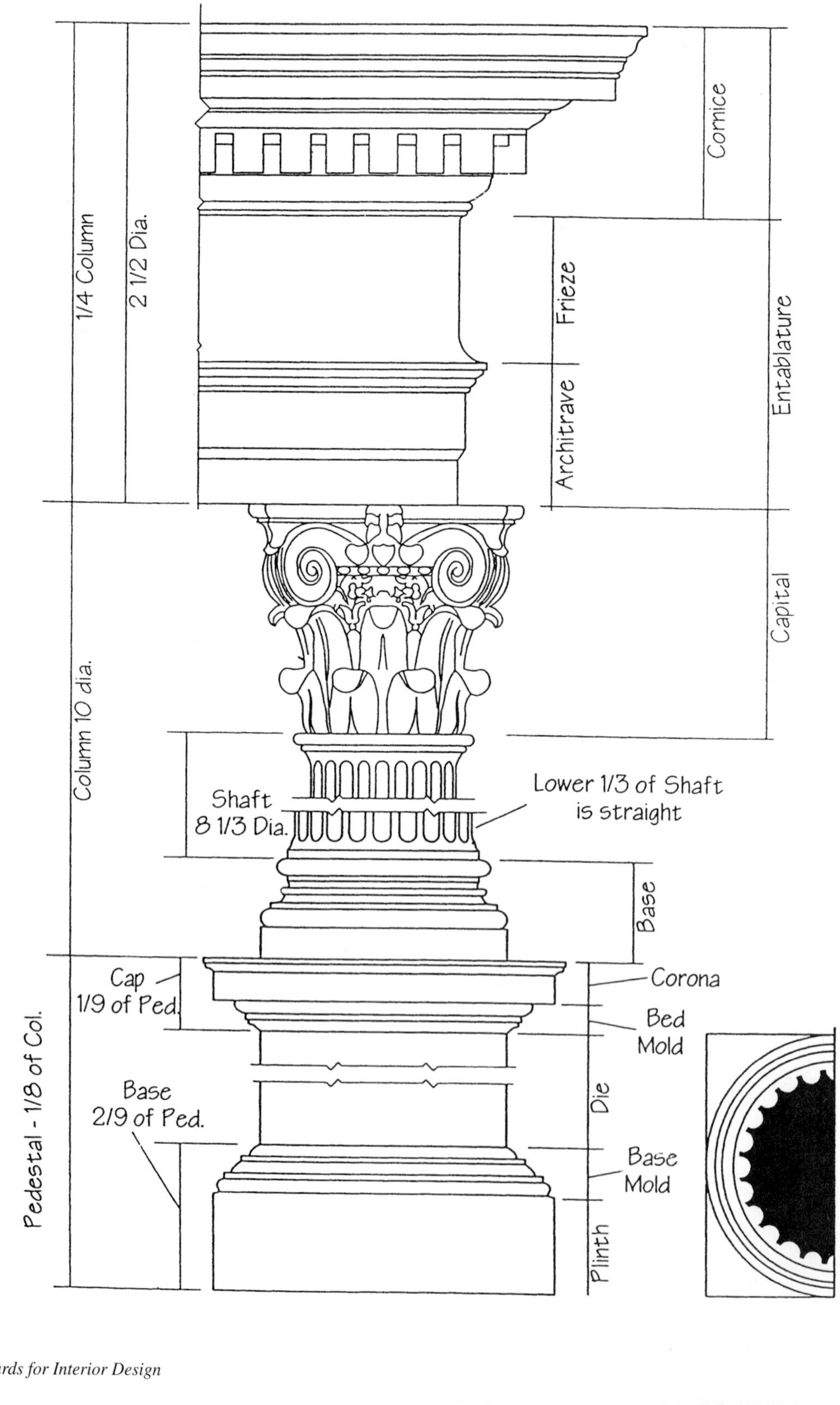

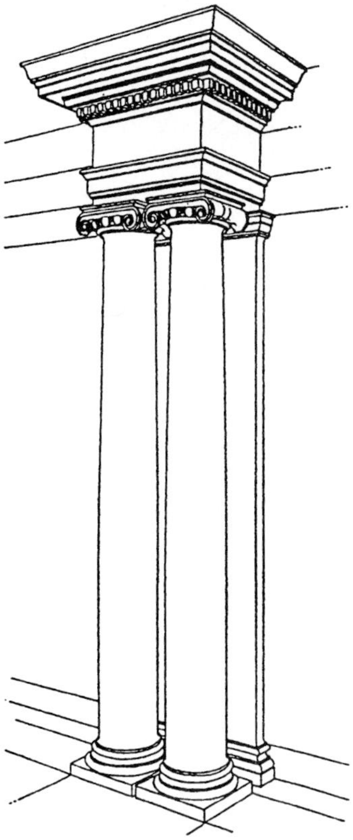

IIONIC ORDER

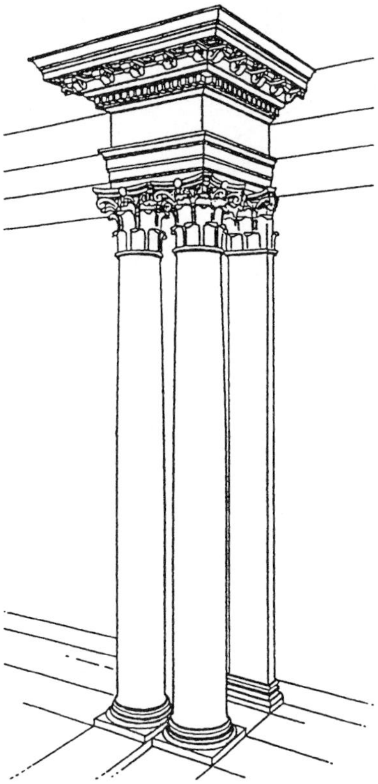

CORINTHIAN ORDER

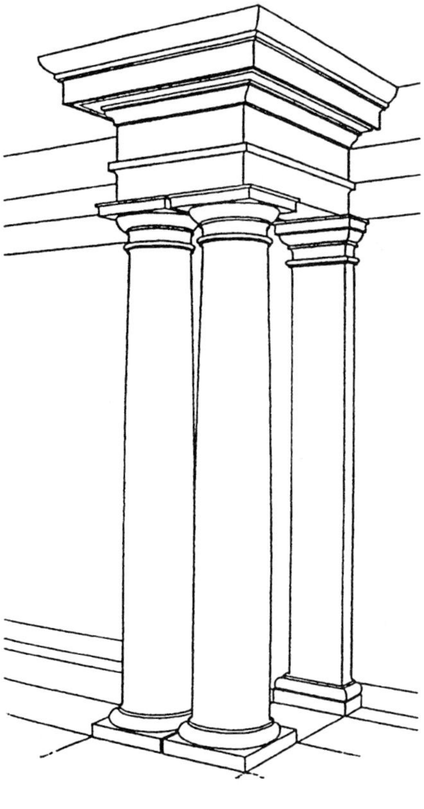

TUSCAN ORDER

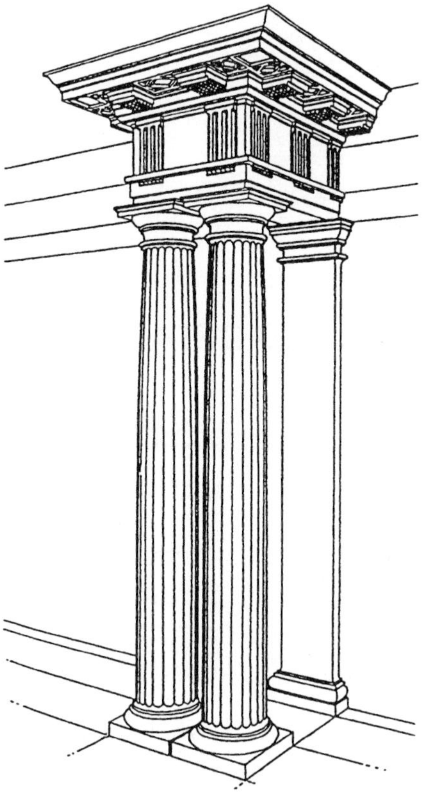

DORIC ORDER

PEDIMENTS

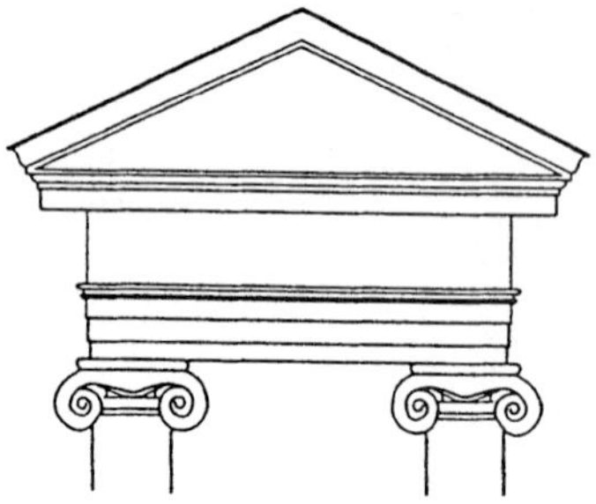

Greek Ionic

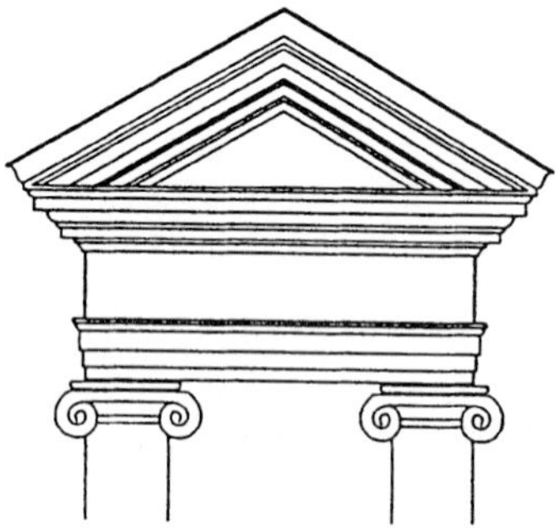

Roman Ionic

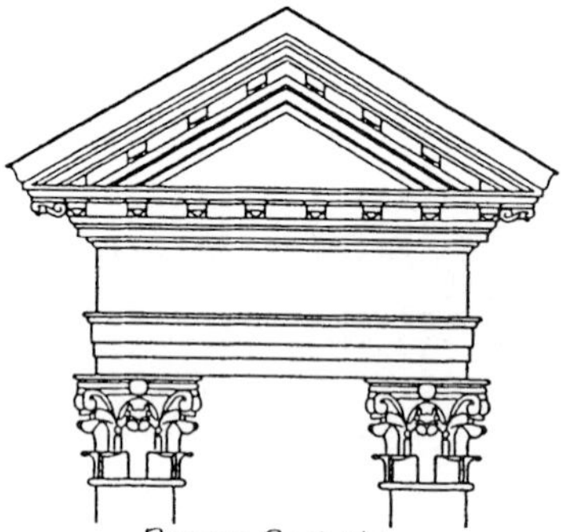

Roman Corinthian

ENTRANCE AND DETAILS

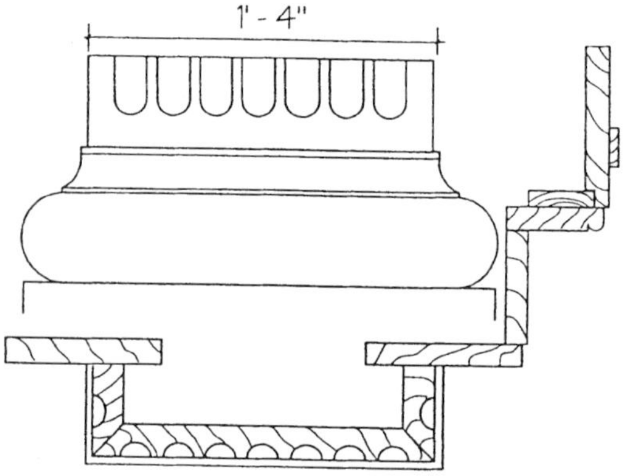

MANTEL AND DETAILS

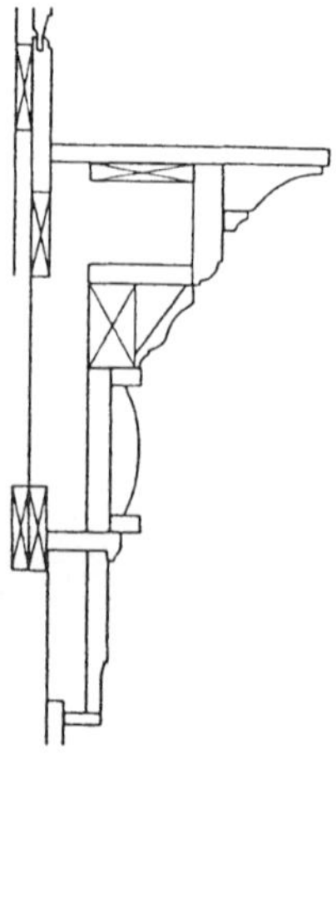

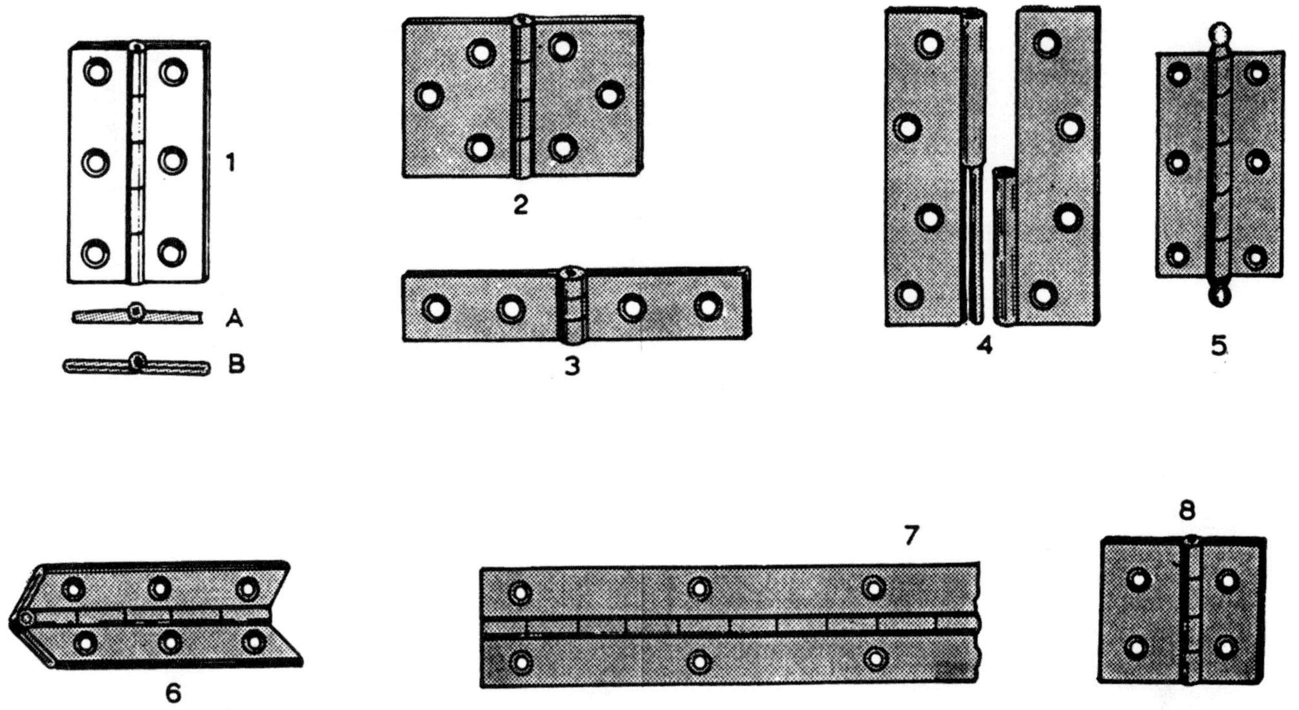

FURNITURE HARDWARE

BUTT HINGES

Table 1 Butt Hinges

No.	Type	Comments
1	Standard brass butt: A, solid drawn type; B, pressed pattern	General usage
2	Back flap hinge	With wide plates for table leaves and rebated or rabbeted fallflaps
3	Strap hinge	For narrow sections
4	Lift-off butt	For doors which have to be removed from time to time without disturbing setting
5	Loose pin hinge; ball-tipped hinge	Where it is necessary to throw door clear of carcase frame with the whole or the hinge knuckle protruding
6	Stopped hinge	Opens through 90° only for box lids, etc.
7	Piano hinge	Continuous strip form for supporting long lengths; supplied in drilled and countersink or undrilled blanks
8	Clock case hinge	One plate is wider to allow for a projecting door

FURNITURE HARDWARE
Hinges

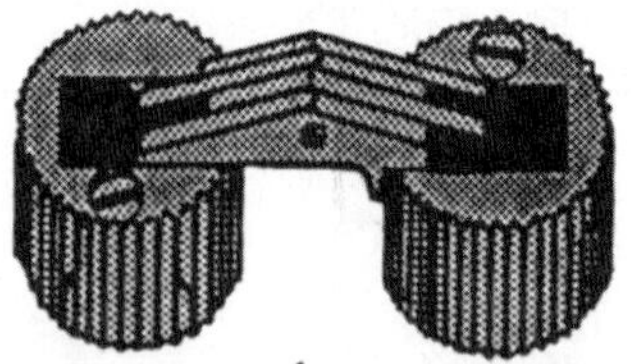

1
CYLINDRICAL DOORHINGE
CONCEALED/180° OPENING

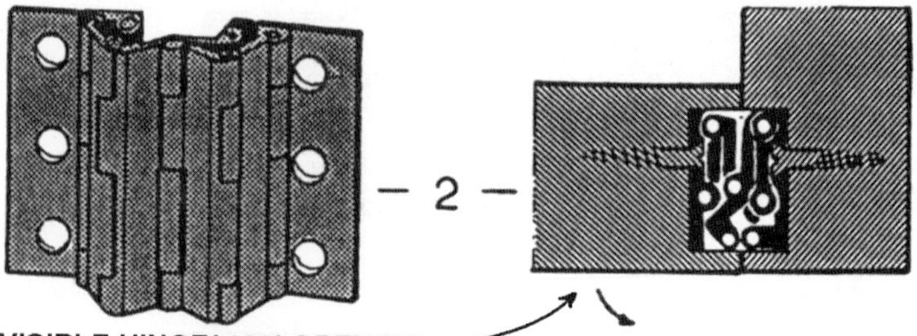

INVISIBLE HINGE/ 180° OPENING

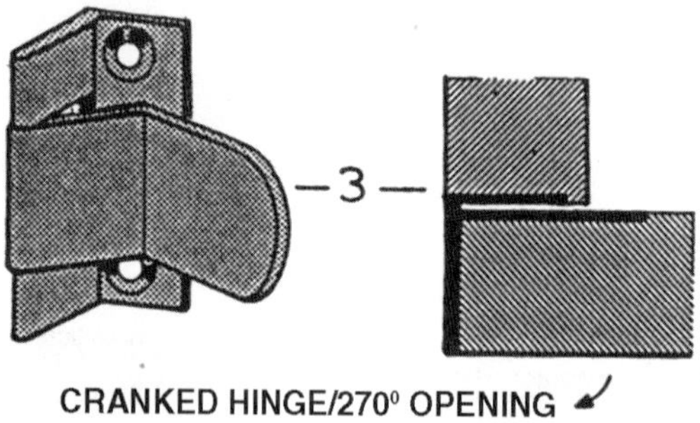

CRANKED HINGE/270° OPENING

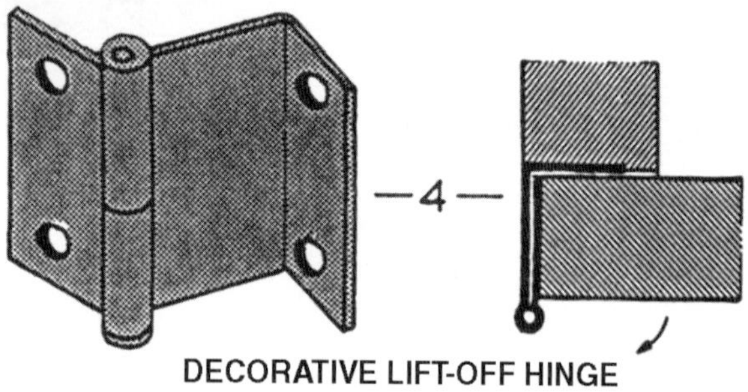

DECORATIVE LIFT-OFF HINGE

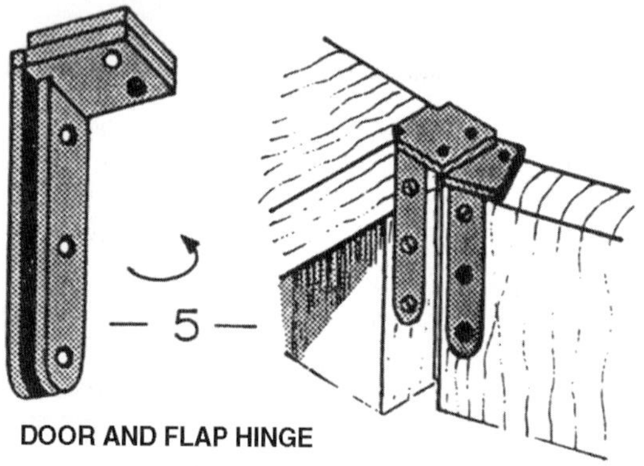

DOOR AND FLAP HINGE

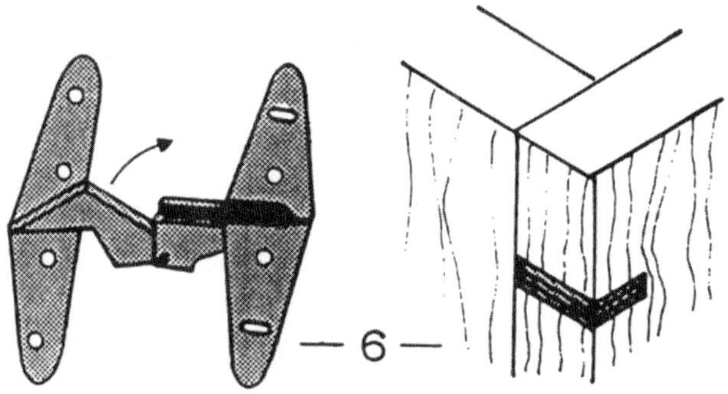

PIVOT HINGE FOR OVERLAYED
(ONSET) DOORS

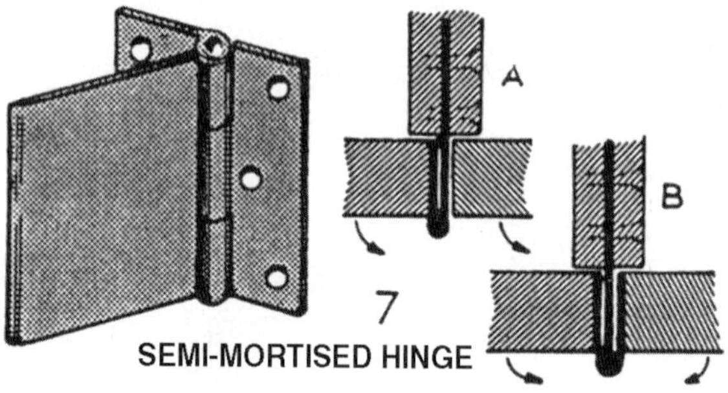

7
SEMI-MORTISED HINGE

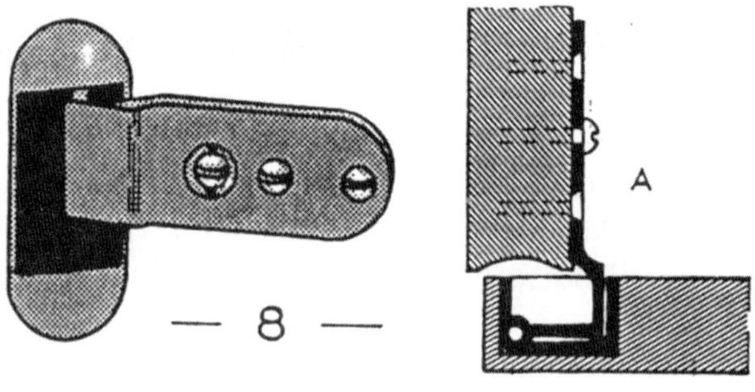

CONCEALED HINGE

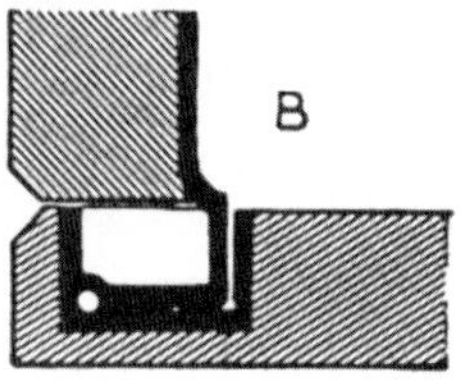

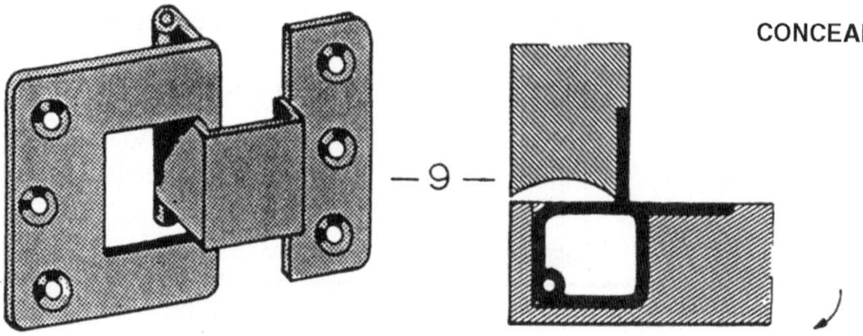

SEMI-INVISIBLE HINGE WITH CONCEALED
PIVOT POINT

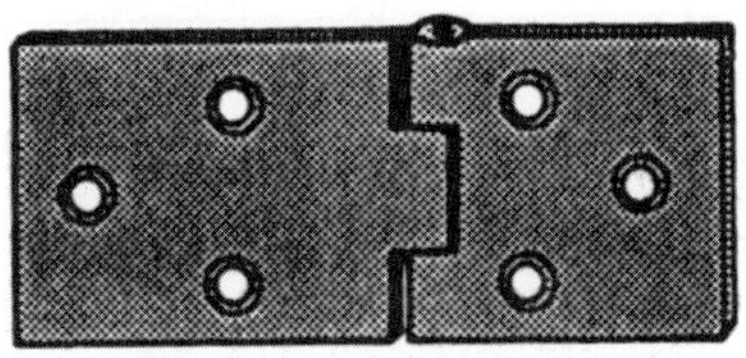

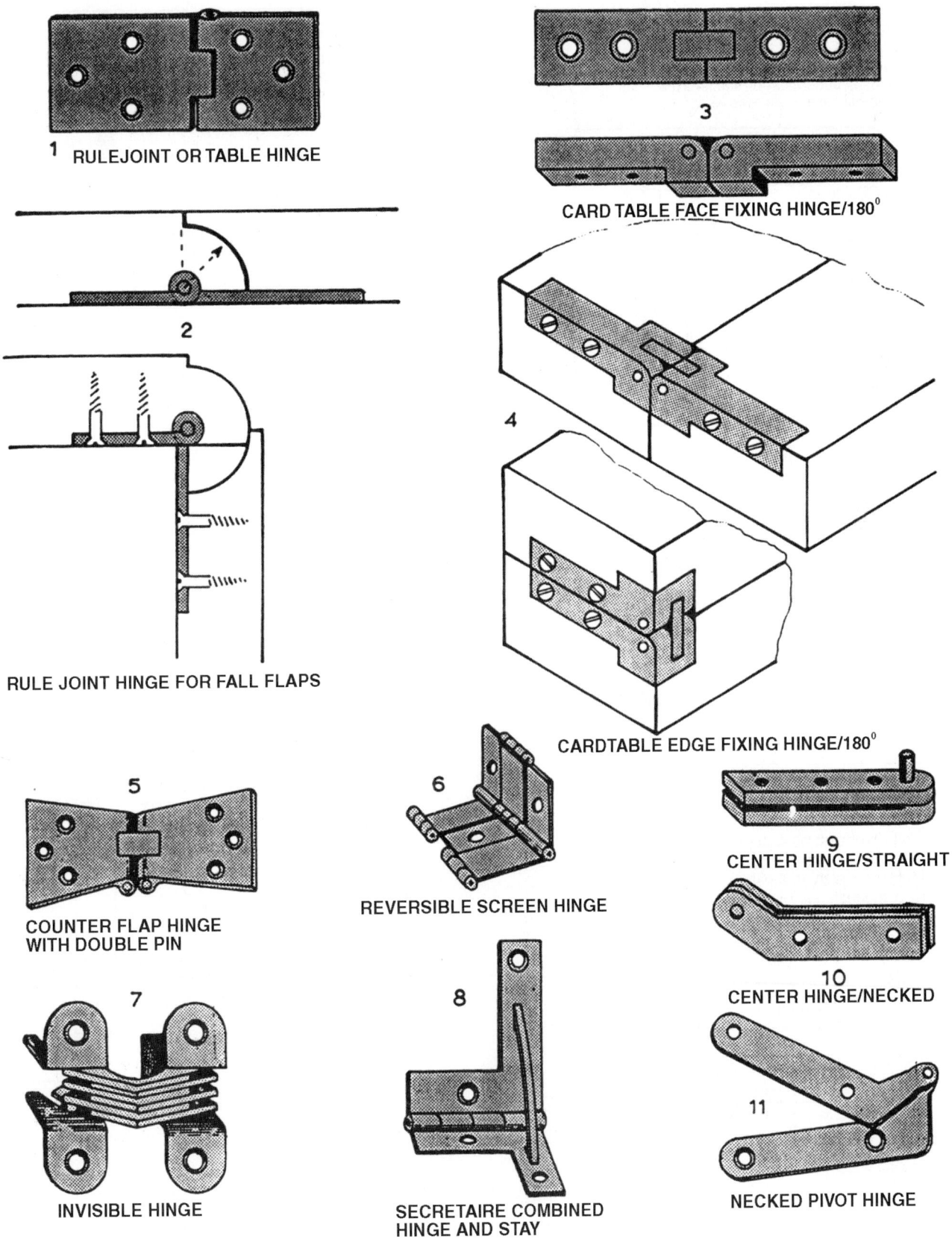

1 RULEJOINT OR TABLE HINGE

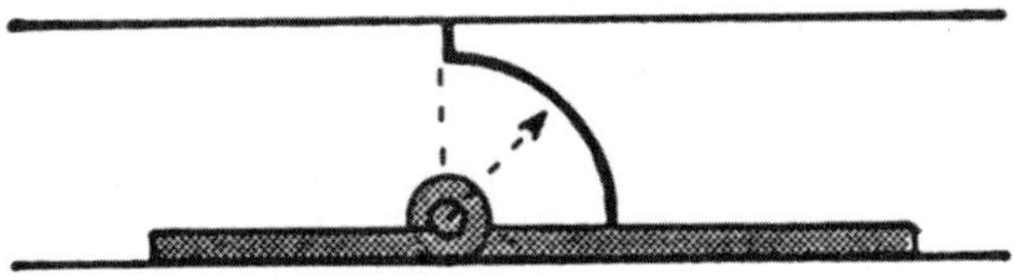

2

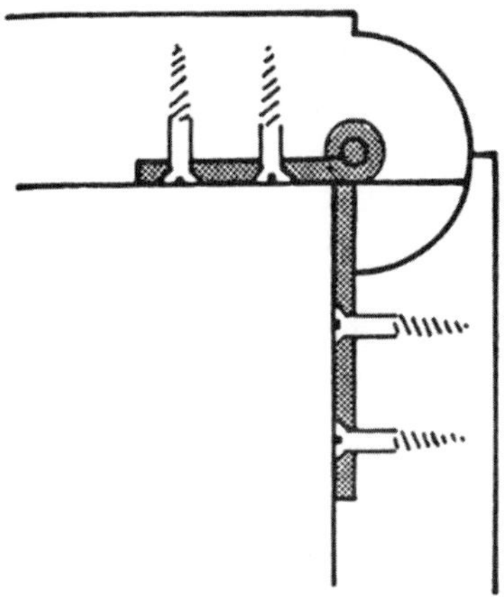

RULE JOINT HINGE FOR FALL FLAPS

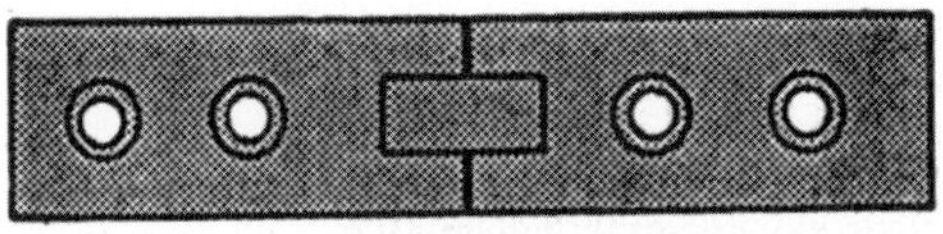

3

CARD TABLE FACE FIXING HINGE/180°

4

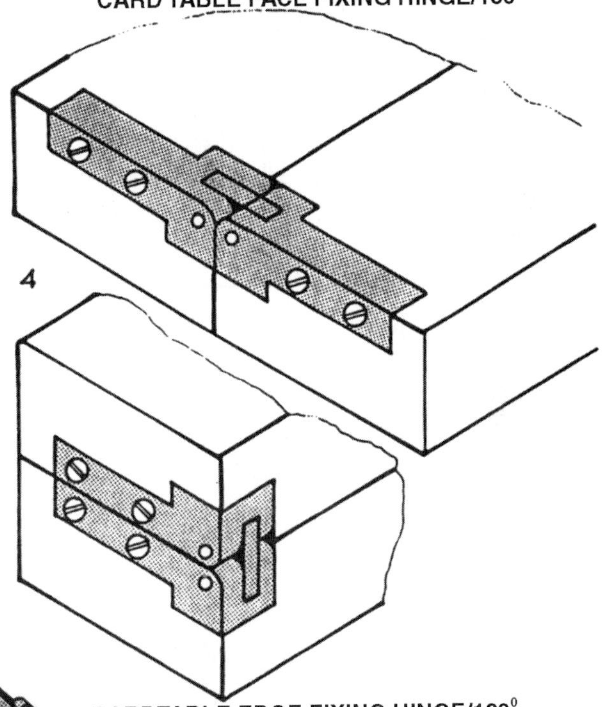

CARDTABLE EDGE FIXING HINGE/180°

5

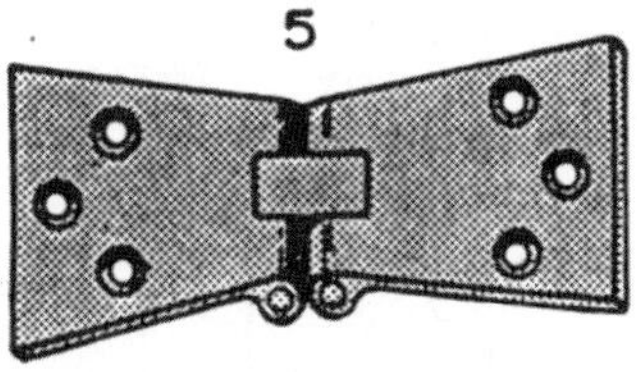

COUNTER FLAP HINGE
WITH DOUBLE PIN

6

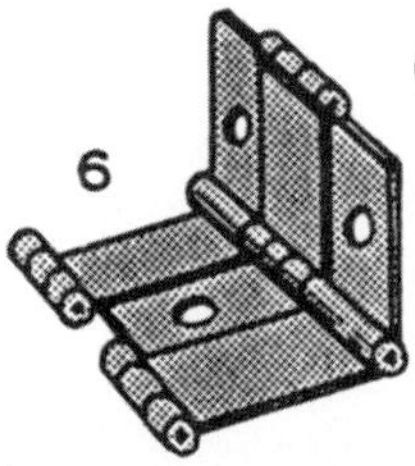

REVERSIBLE SCREEN HINGE

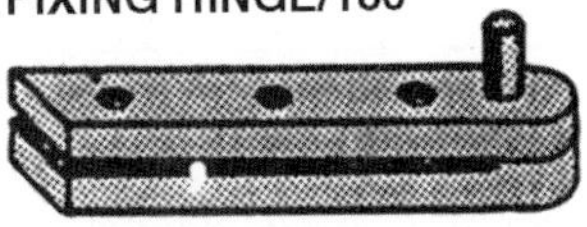

9
CENTER HINGE/STRAIGHT

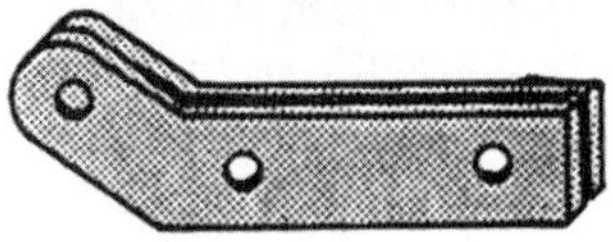

10
CENTER HINGE/NECKED

7

INVISIBLE HINGE

8

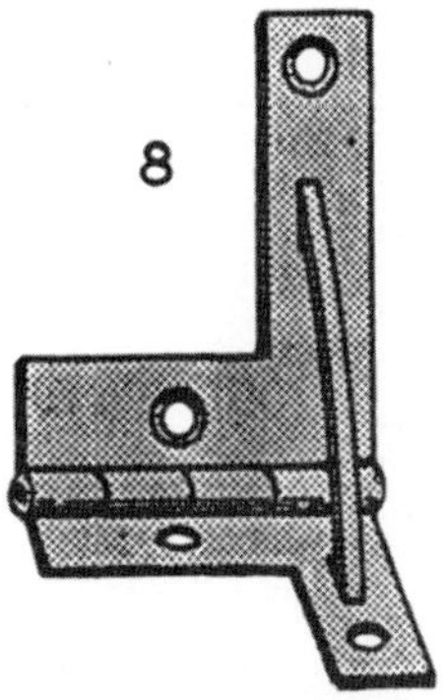

SECRETAIRE COMBINED
HINGE AND STAY

11

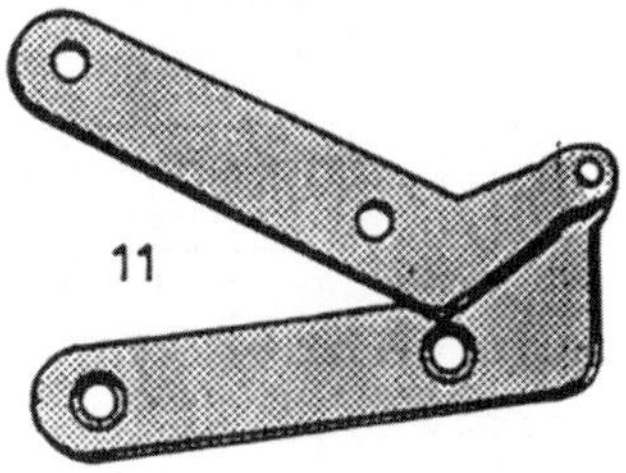

NECKED PIVOT HINGE

FURNITURE HARDWARE
Hinges

Left- and Right-Hand Hinges

Hinges with screw-mounted flanges should be viewed as if in mounted condition with the countersunk screw holes facing you. If the female flange is uppermost on the left, the hinge is a left-hand hinge and vice versa.

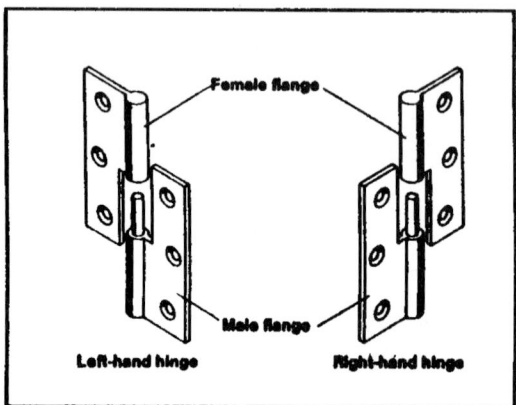

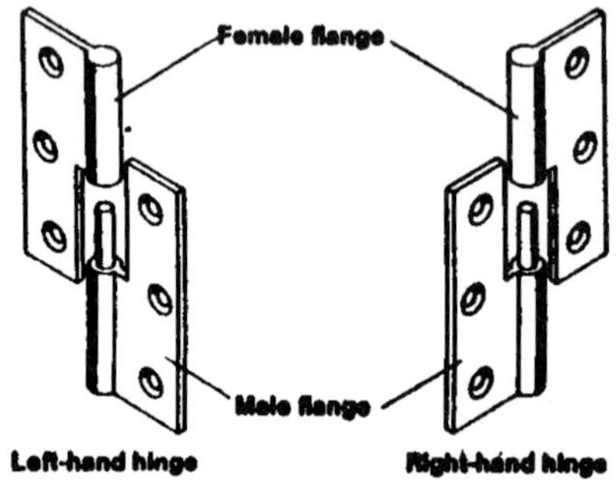

Cranked Hinges and Their Uses

The position of the door relative to the side panel can vary considerably, being decided at the design stage in accordance with the final effect required. A wide variety of hinge types has developed from variations in door mounting methods, which must be coordinated at the design stage.

Straight hinge
For butting, flush or front-hung doors. The barrel is positioned centrally between the two flanges.

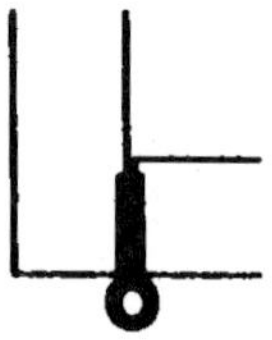

Crank B
Mounting with set-back doors. One flange is cranked by an amount equivalent to the thickness of the material.

Crank C
Similar to crank B but for forward-set doors.

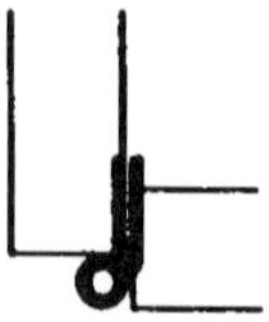

Crank D
Mounting with rebated doors with flanges of non-uniform width (reduced female flanges).

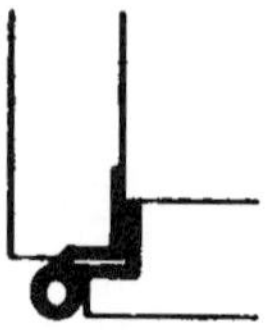

Crank L1
Mounting with butting front-hung doors
Door opening range 270°.
Crank features internal roll.

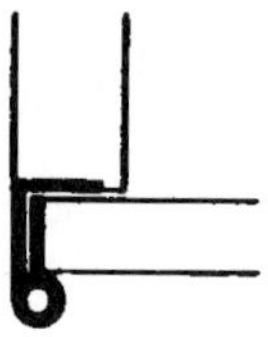

Butt Hinge Designations

Butt hinges for cupboards, windows, and doors, and hinges with mortise-type flanges should be viewed with the barrel facing you. If the female flange is positioned on the left of the barrel, it is a left-hand hinge and vice versa.

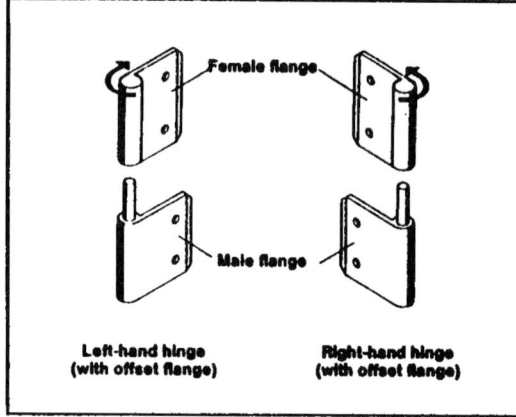

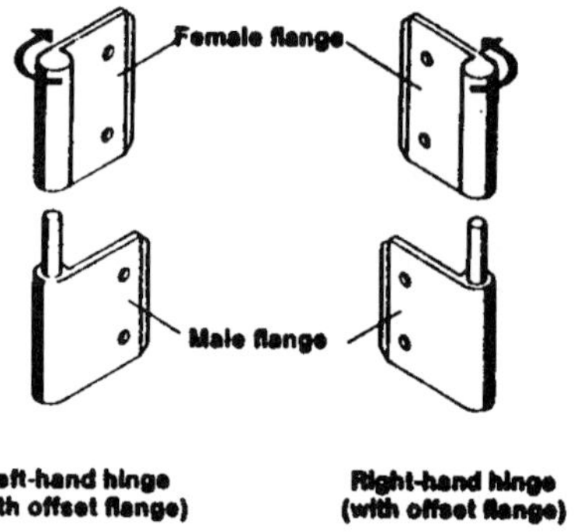

The same rule applies to hinges with symmetrical flanges.

Butt hinge
The hinge is made with offset flanges for mortised mounting. The door-mounted flange is secured with screws or pins from the rear or front (giving exposed heads).

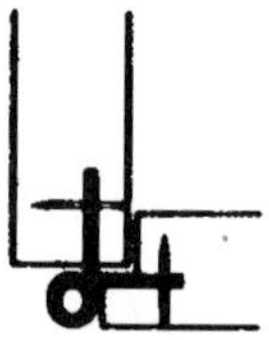

Double butt hinge
Suitable for mounting two doors to a single center panel. The door opening range is 180° each (center flange only mortised).

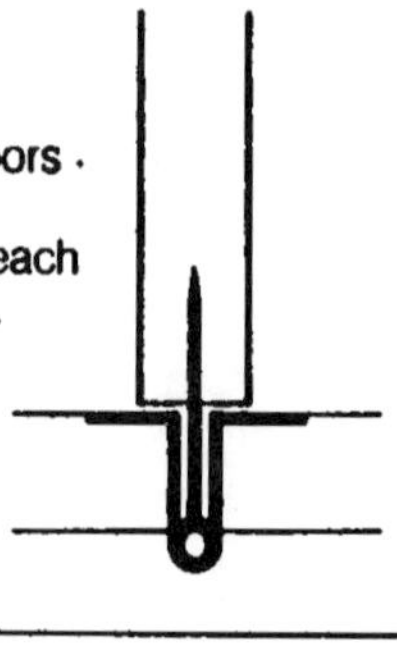

FOLDING TABLE HINGE

Functional diagram

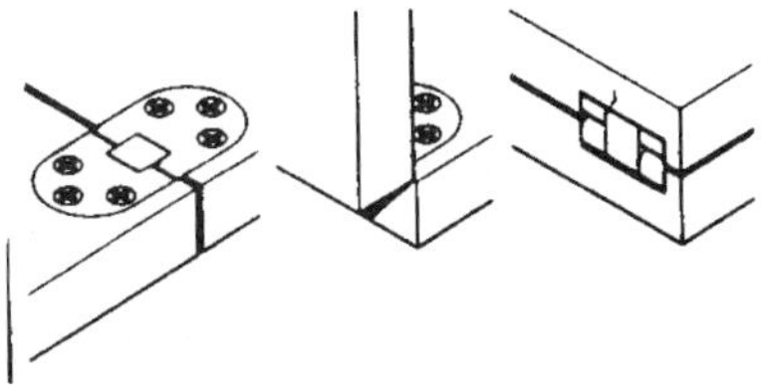

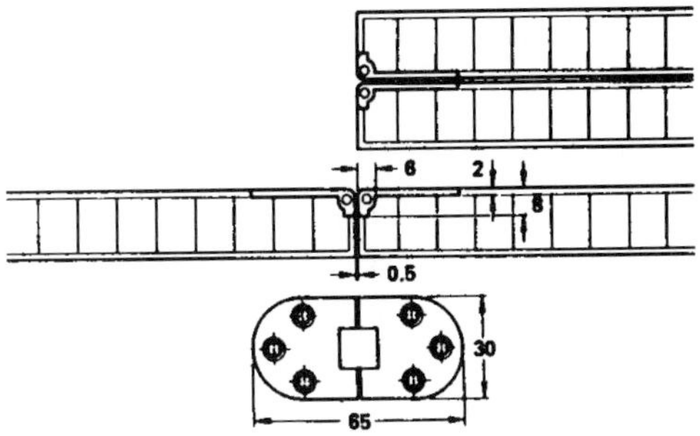

Self-supporting hinge,
for folding and sewing machine tables,
flush-mounted

Functional diagram
(seen from below)

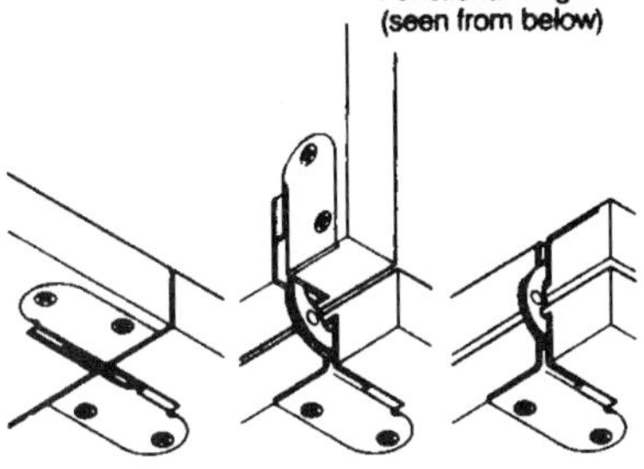

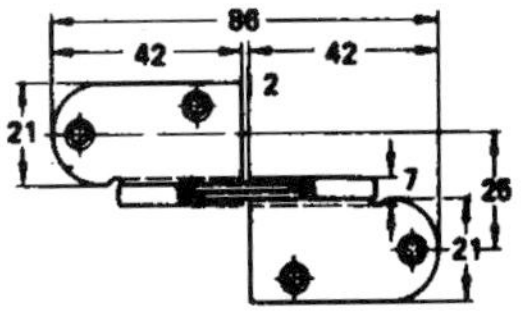

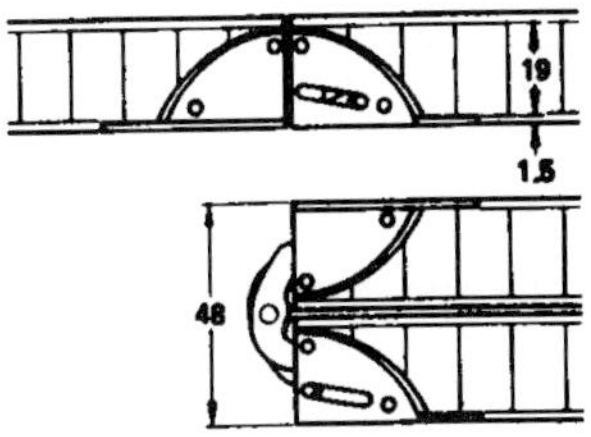

Folding table hinge,
flush-mounted

Functional diagram

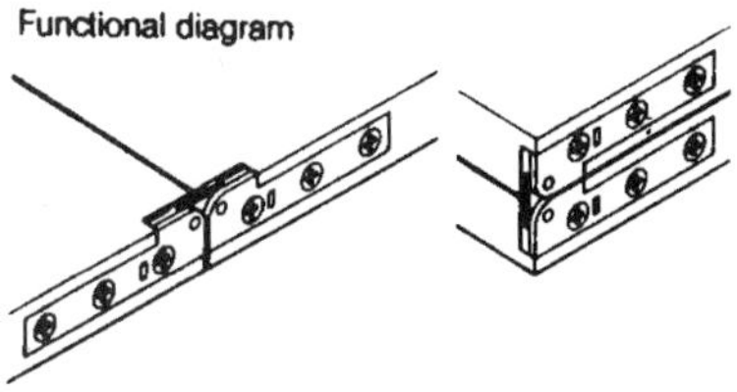

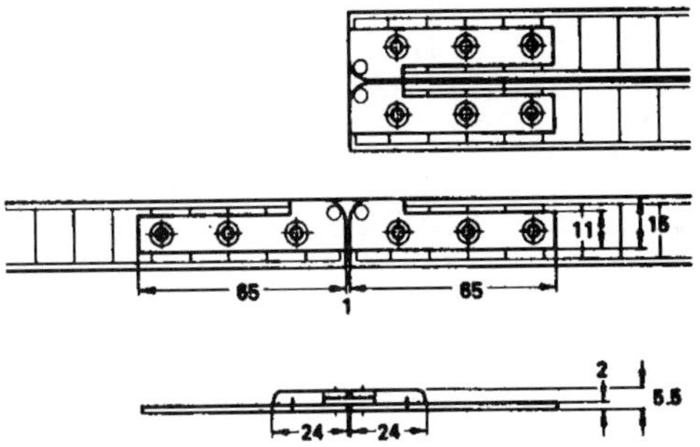

Card table hinge
Two-way table-leaf hinge,
flush-mounted

FLAP HINGES

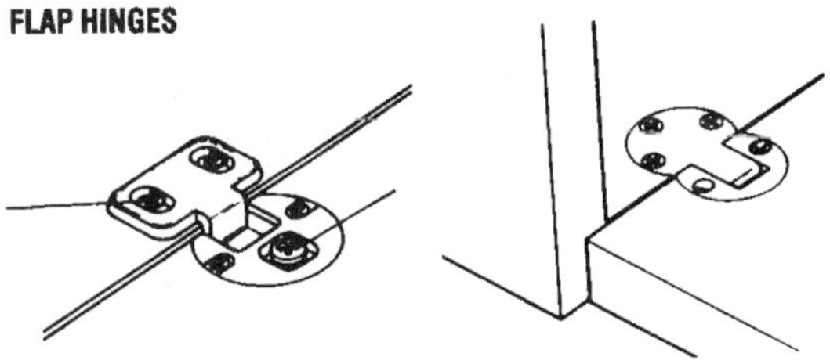

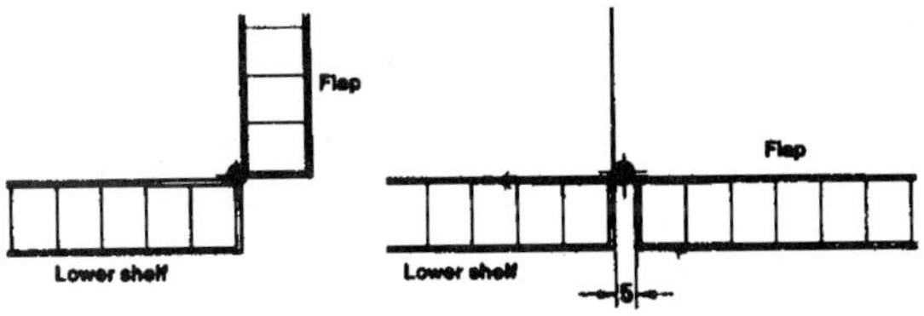

Flap closed Flap open

Specimen mounting

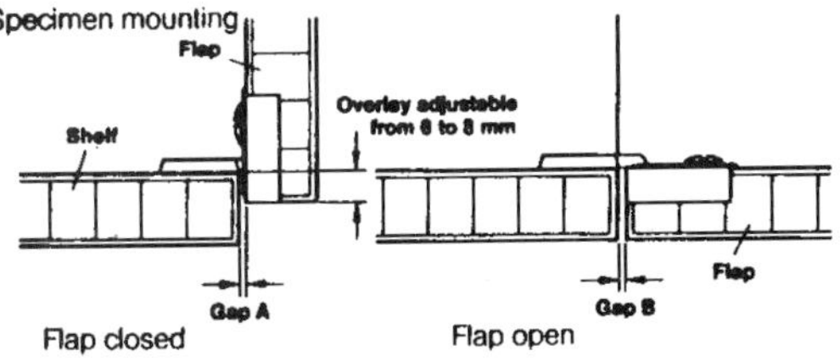

Flap closed Flap open

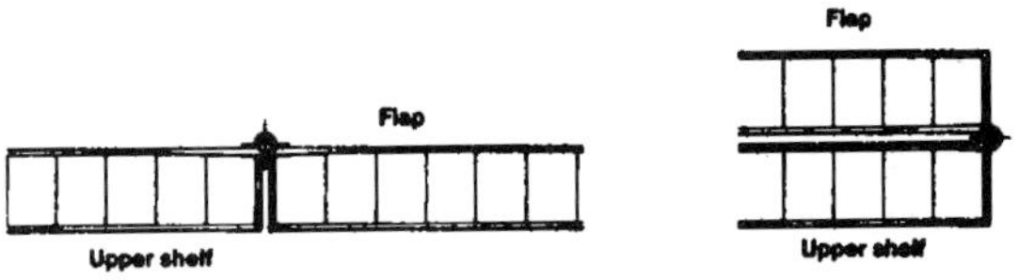

Flap closed Flap open

Dimensions in mm.

FURNITURE HARDWARE
Mitered and Concealed Hinges

MITERED HINGE

The hinges are suitable for wooden doors and side panels from 16 mm to 22 mm in thickness, chamfered at an angle of 45°.

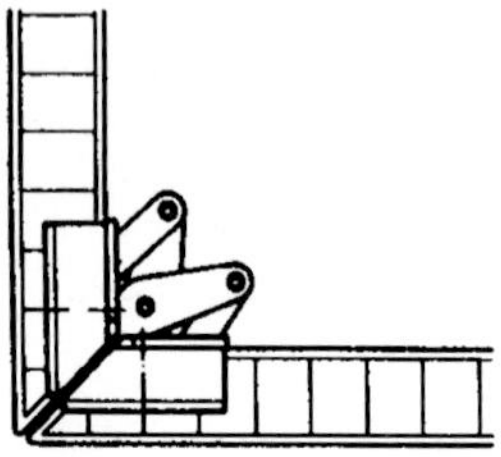

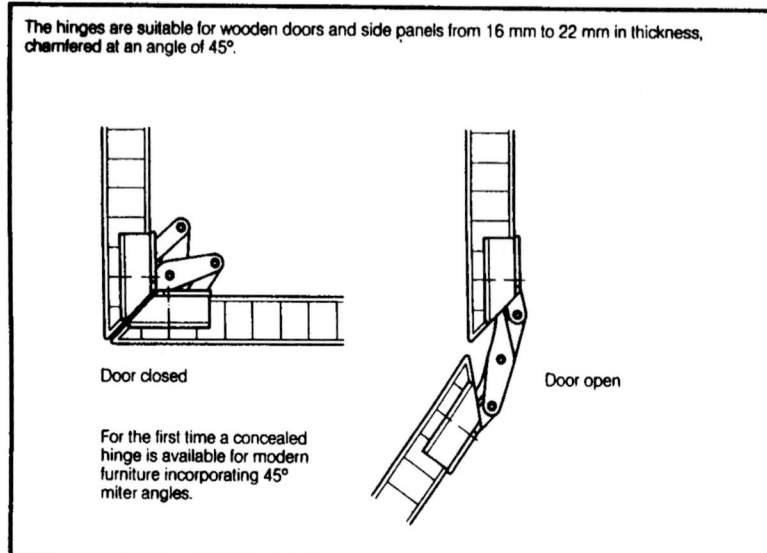

Door closed

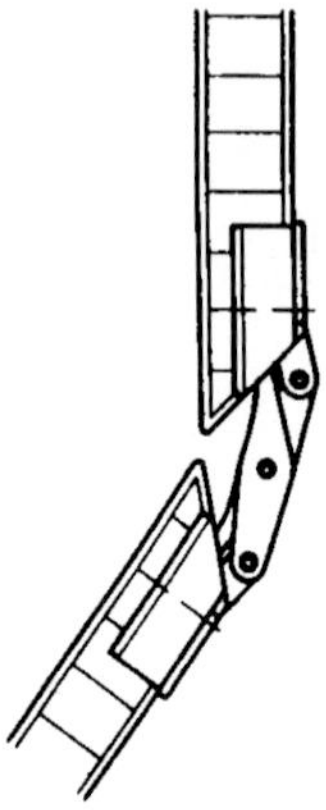

Door open

For the first time a concealed hinge is available for modern furniture incorporating 45° miter angles.

An all-metal mitered hinge, specially designed to enable door and carcase edges to meet at an angle of 45°.

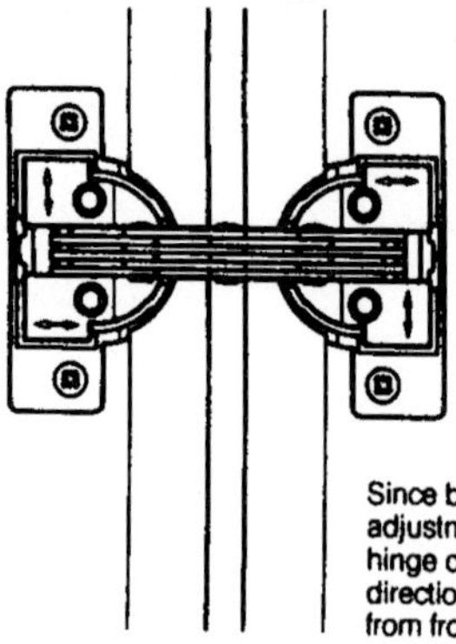

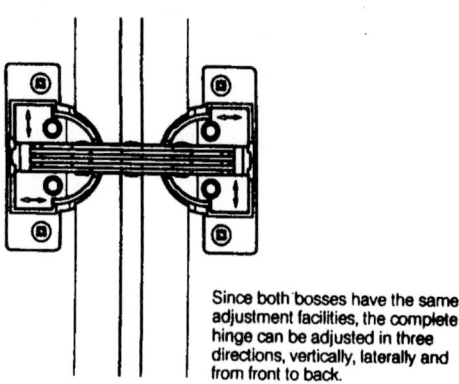

Since both bosses have the same adjustment facilities, the complete hinge can be adjusted in three directions, vertically, laterally and from front to back.

CONCEALED HINGES

Specimen installation of a butting, flush-fitting cupboard door. Doors may, however, be set back or forward if preferred, provided the housing recesses are appropriately offset. If doors are set back, care must be taken to ensure that the opening angle is restricted as little as possible.

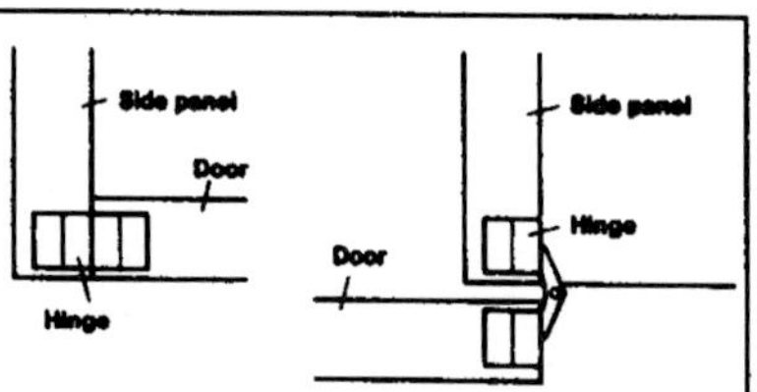

Door closed   Door open

Specimen installation of a butting, front-hung door, fitting flush with the cupboard side in the conventional manner. Doors may, however, be hung with inset edge if preferred, provided the housing recesses are offset accordingly. It is important in such cases to ensure that center doors are not mounted with groove gap clearance.

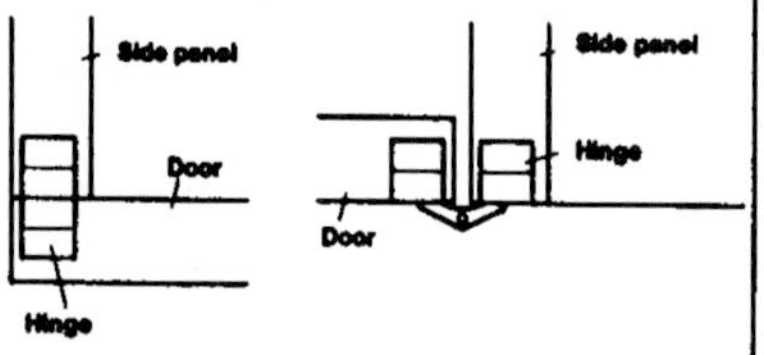

Door closed   Door open

Specimen installation of a butting, front-hung, flap-type door. On opening, the flap projects downwards by its own thickness. Thus, if doors or other panels are situated below the flap, a degree of clearance exceeding the flap thickness will be necessary.

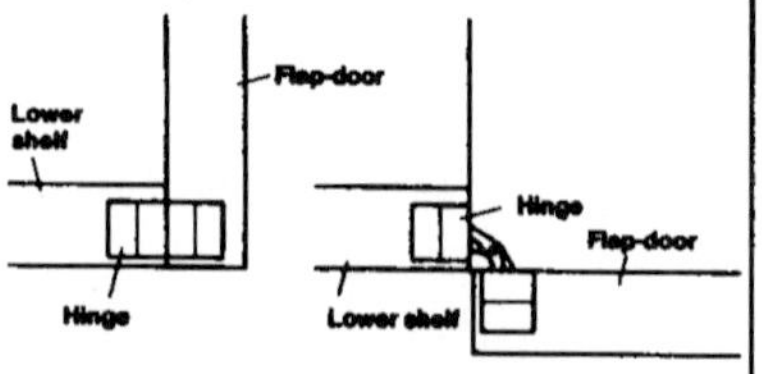

Flap closed   Flap open

Specimen installation joining two panels. In this way folding doors can be constructed for furniture or room dividers:

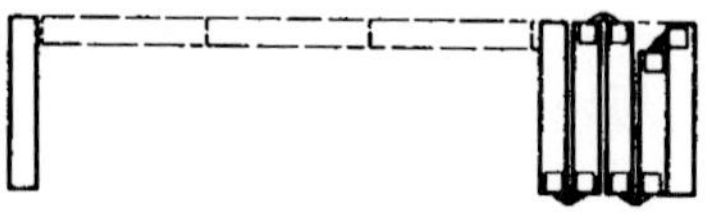

Typical folding door

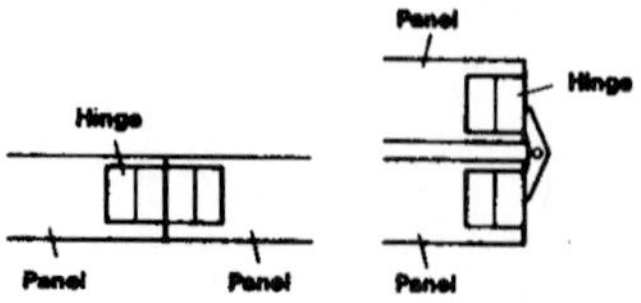

Door closed   Door open

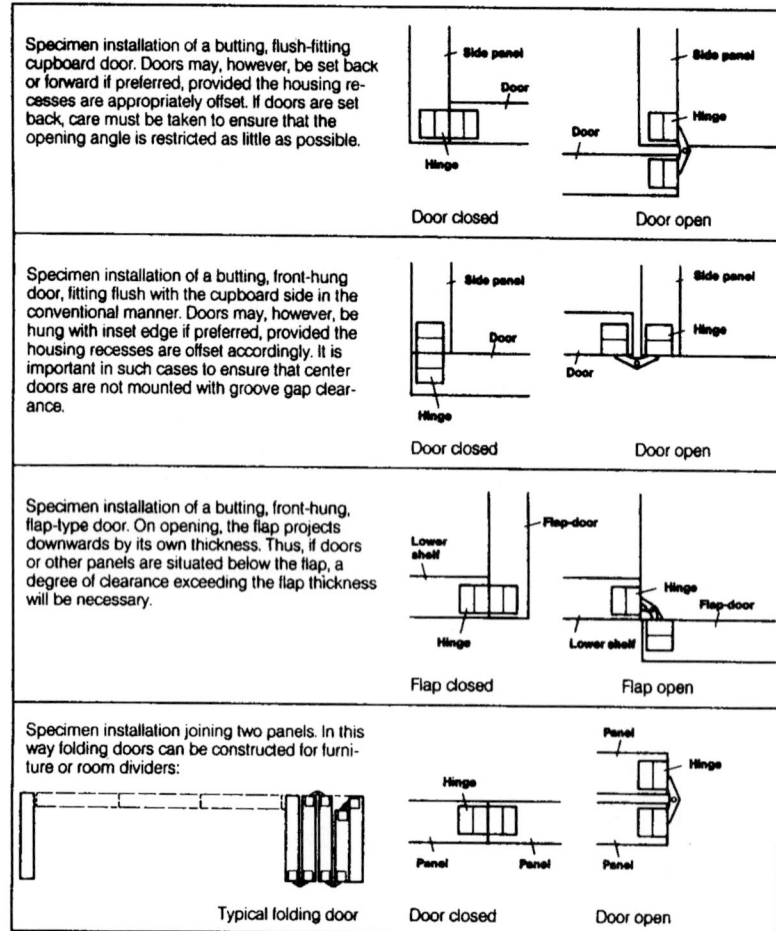

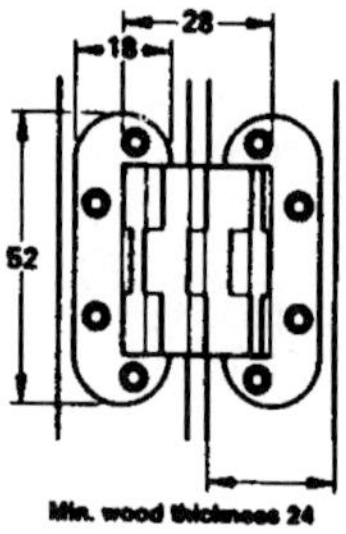

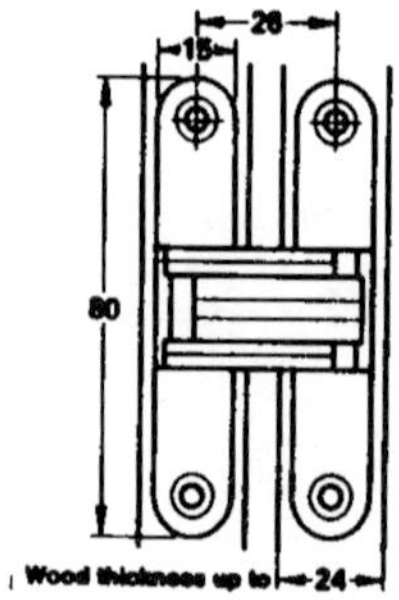

Dimensions in mm.

FURNITURE HARDWARE
Pivot Hinges

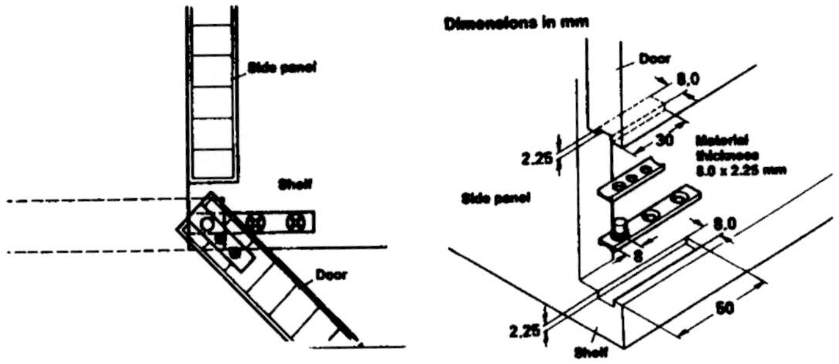

Pivot hinge, without stop
Hollow drawn, with one short flange

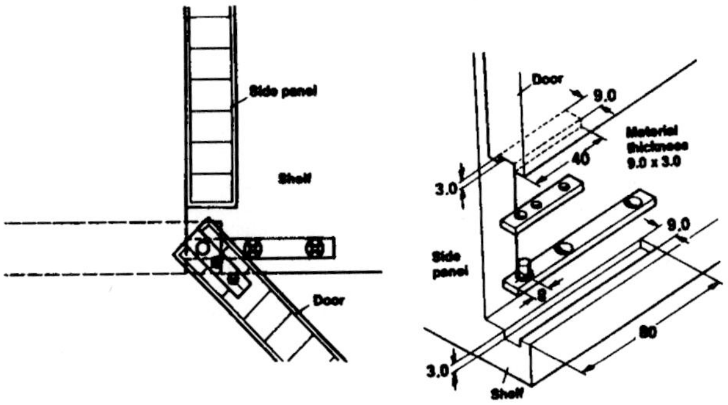

Pivot hinge, without stop
Smooth drawn, with one short flange

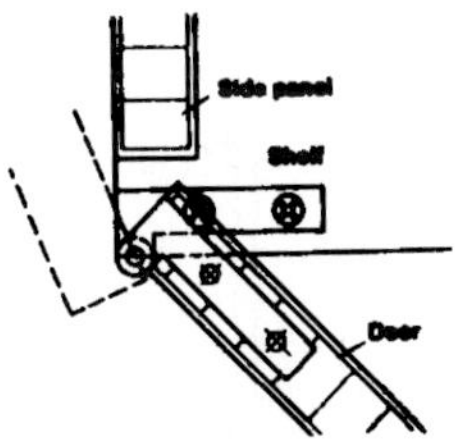

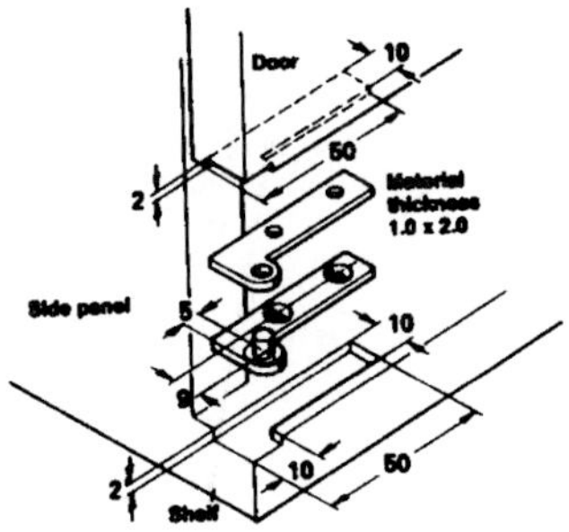

Corner pivot hinge, without stop
With outer knuckle, **straight**

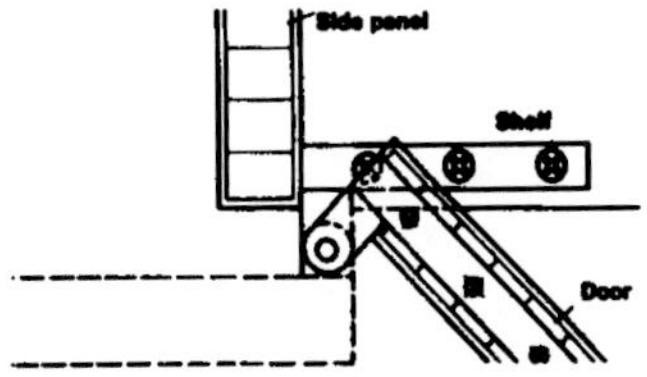

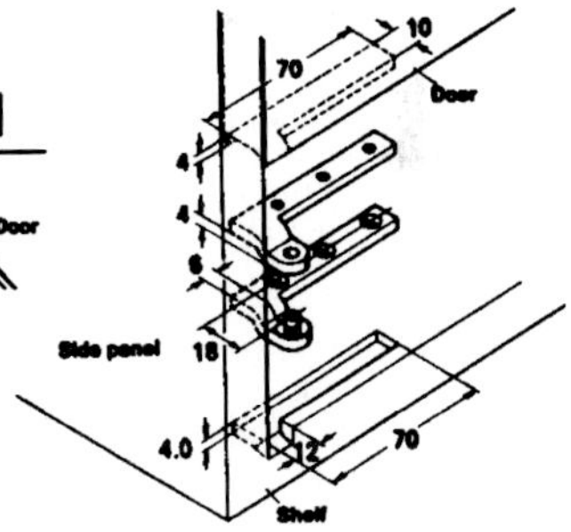

Corner pivot hinge, without stop
With outer knuckle, **cranked**

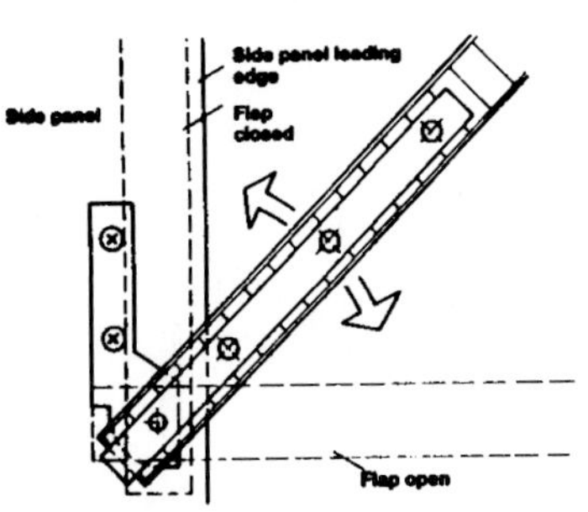

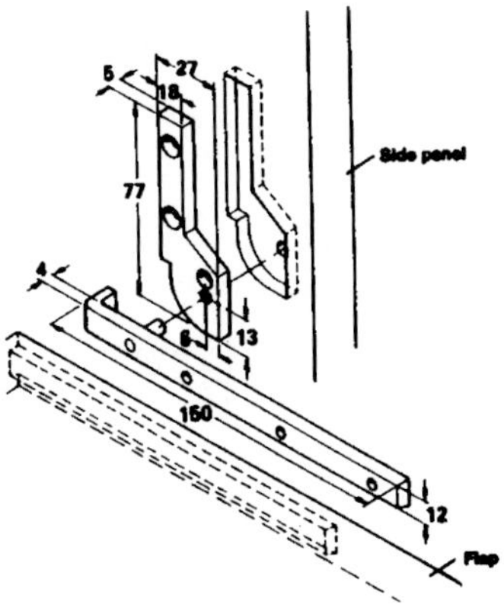

Pivot hinges for writing bureau drop leaf mounting, smooth drawn.

Dimensions in mm.

FURNITURE HARDWARE

Glass Door Hinges

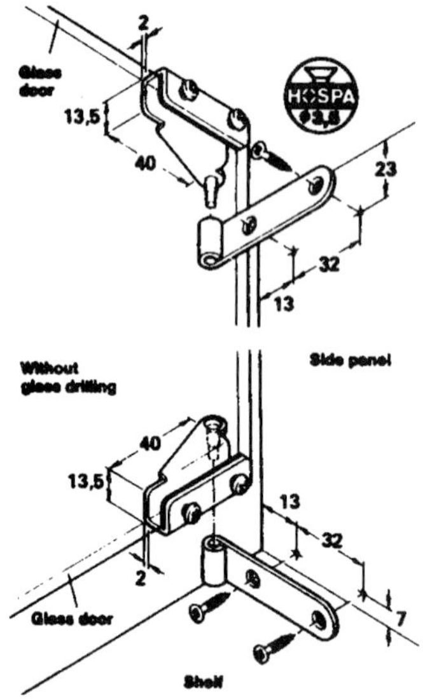

For flush-fitted doors

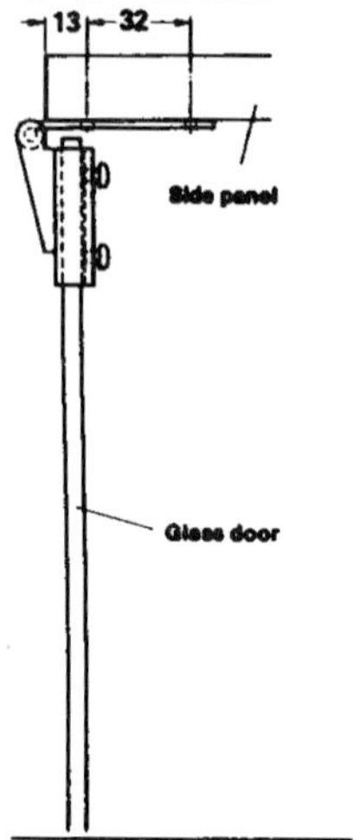

One upper and one lower hinge per mounting

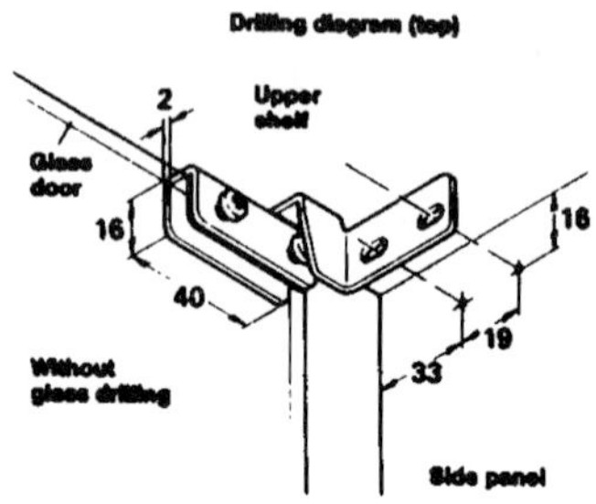

For flush-fitted doors

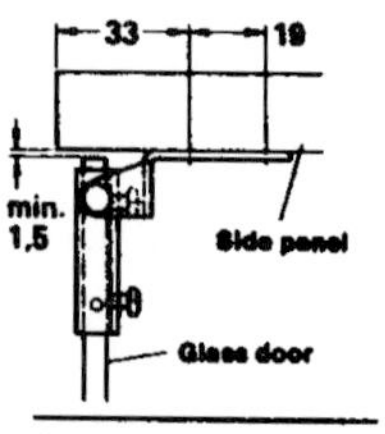

One left and one right hinge per mounting

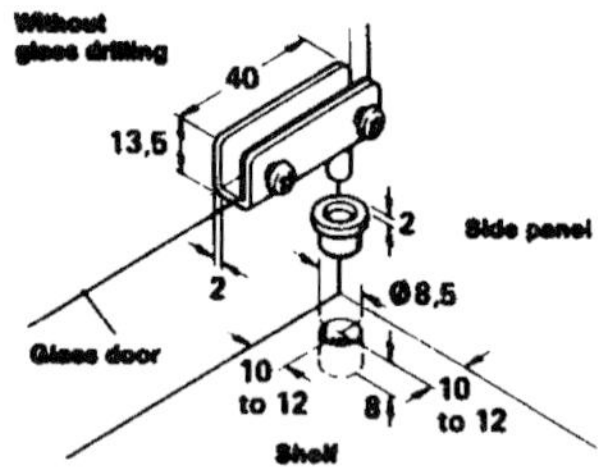

For flush-fitted doors

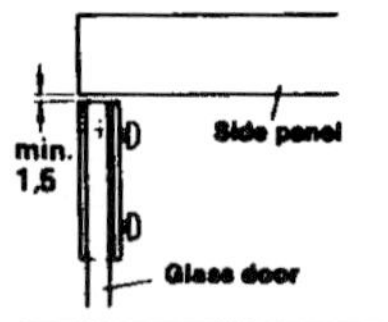

One left and one right hinge per mounting

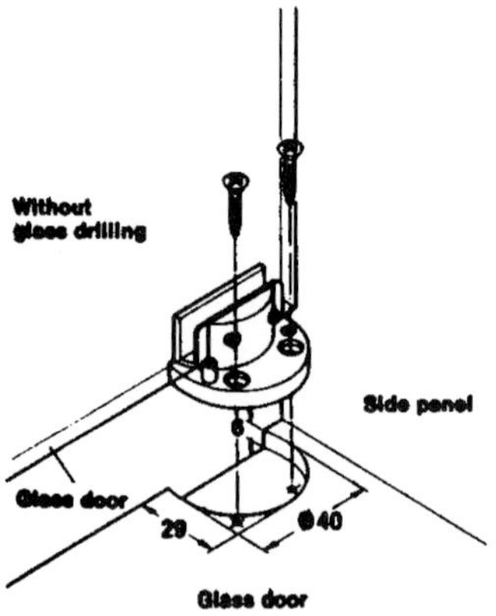

For flush-fitting doors

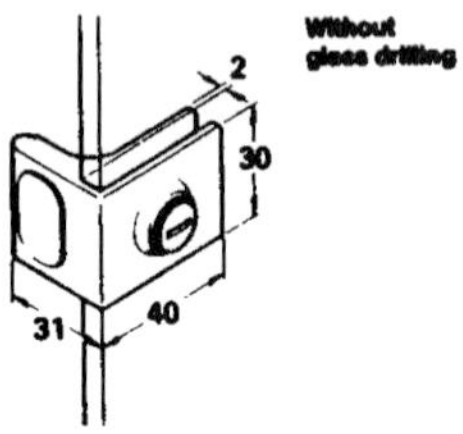

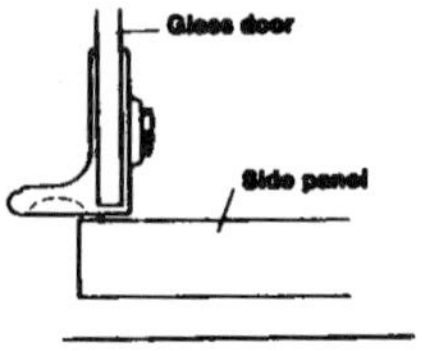

One pull per mounting

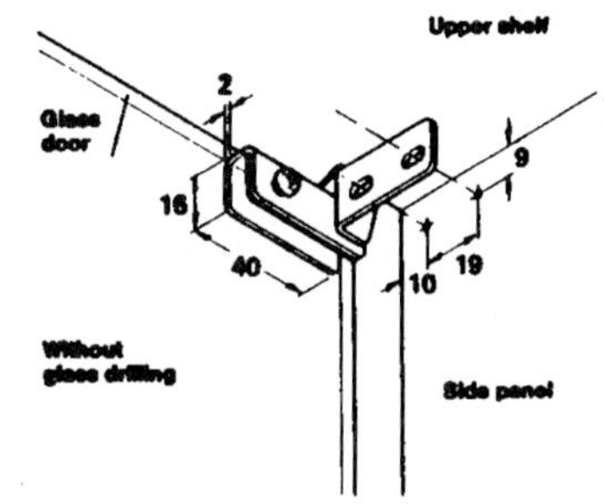

For front-hung doors

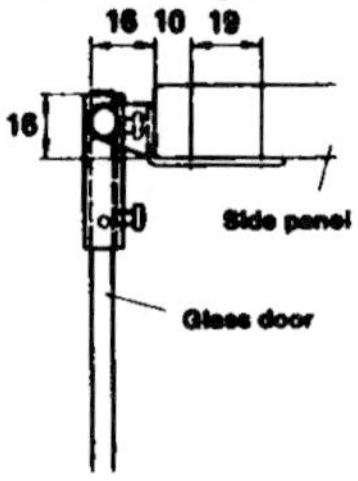

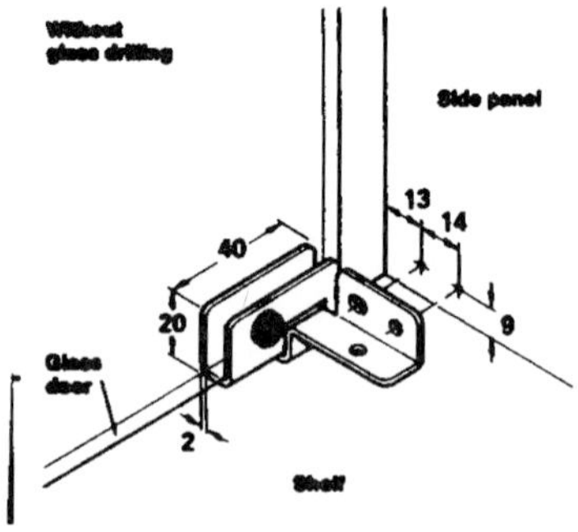

For front-hung doors

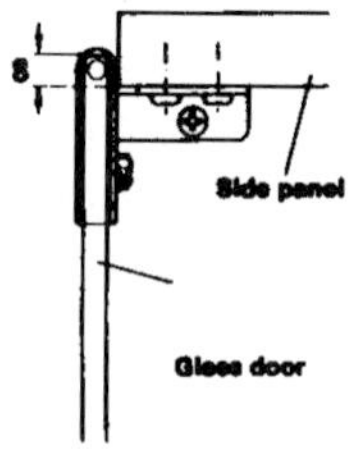

One left and one right hinge per mounting

Magnetic Pressure Catches

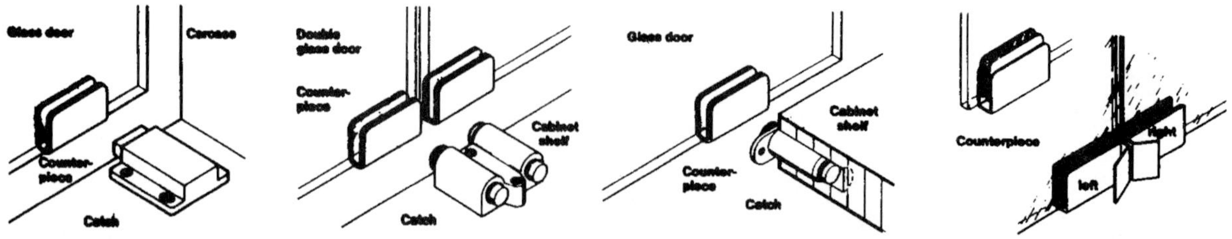

Dimensions in mm.

FURNITURE HARDWARE
Flap Stays with Brake

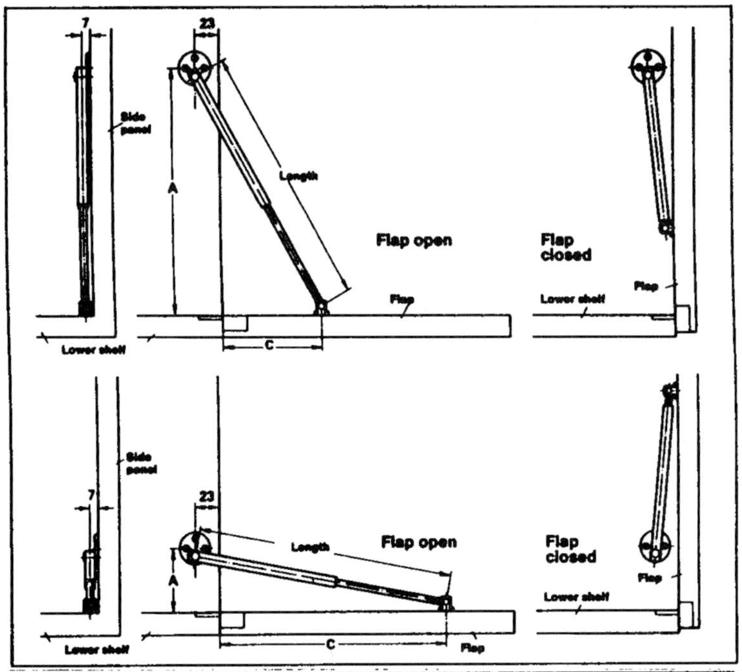

Vertical mounting

Length (mm)	Internal carcase height (mm)	Distance A (mm)	Distance C (mm)
250	300 to 400	240	Determine by trial mounting
325	350 to 450	308	
450	400 to 500	430	

Horizontal mounting

Length (mm)	Internal carcase height (mm)	Distance A (mm)	Distance C (mm)
250	300 to 400	65	Determine by trial mounting
325	350 to 450	100	
450	400 to 500	150	

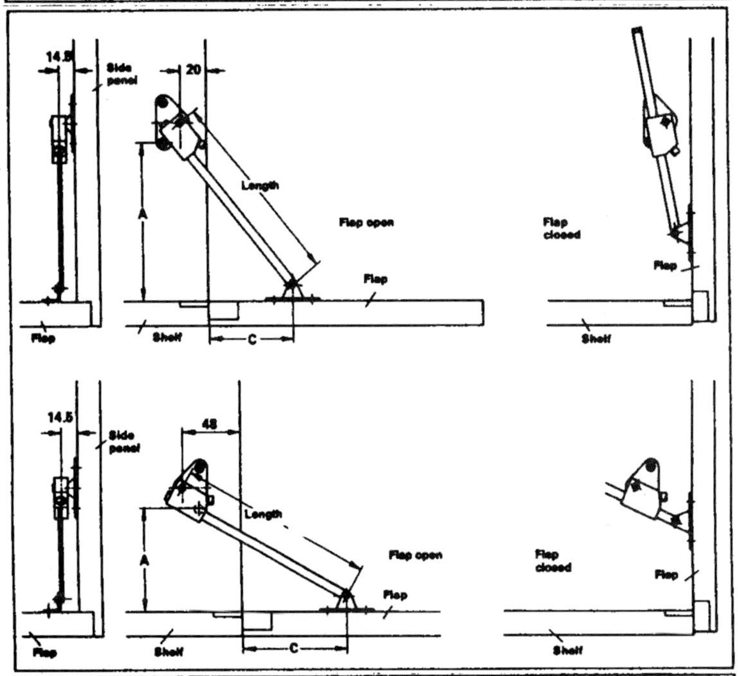

Vertical mounting

Length (mm)	Internal carcase height (mm)	Distance A (mm)	Distance C (mm)
160	250 to 350	127	Determine by trial mounting
190	300 to 400	151	
220	350 to 450	175	
250	400 to 500	198	
280	450 to 550	222	

Horizontal mounting

Length (mm)	Internal carcase height (mm)	Distance A (mm)	Distance C (mm)
160	200 to 300	82	Determine by trial mounting
190	230 to 330	105	
220	260 to 360	127	
250	290 to 430	148	
280	320 to 460	171	

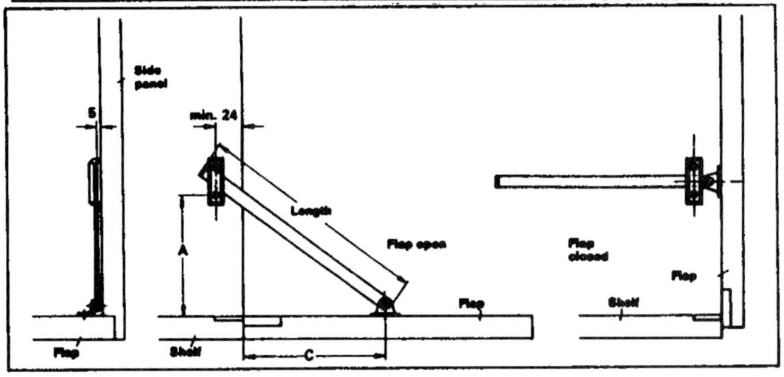

Length (mm)	Internal carcase height (mm)	Distance A (mm)	Distance C (mm)
150	min. 130	70	Determine by trial mounting
200	min. 170	105	
250	min. 210	140	

Dimensions in mm.

FURNITURE HARDWARE

Lid Stays

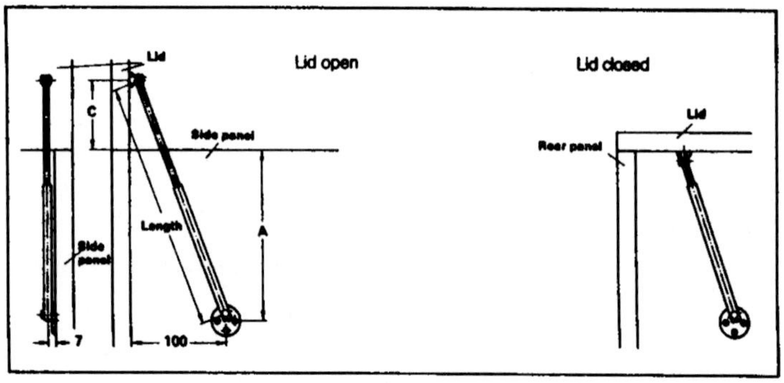

Length (mm)	Lid height (mm)	Distance A (mm)	Distance C (mm)
250	up to 300	170	Determine by trial mounting
325	up to 450	205	
450	over 450	275	

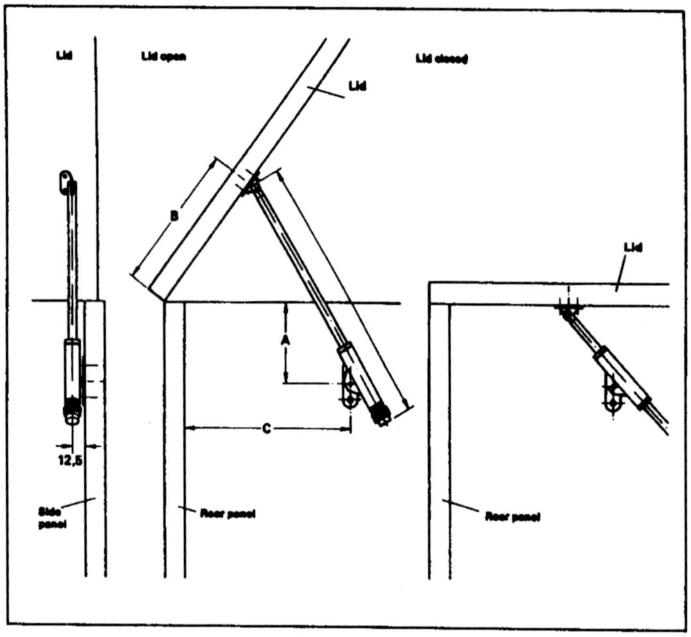

Length (mm)	Distance A (mm)	Distance B (mm)	Distance C (mm)
145	Determine by trial mounting depending on opening angle of lid.		
260			
330			

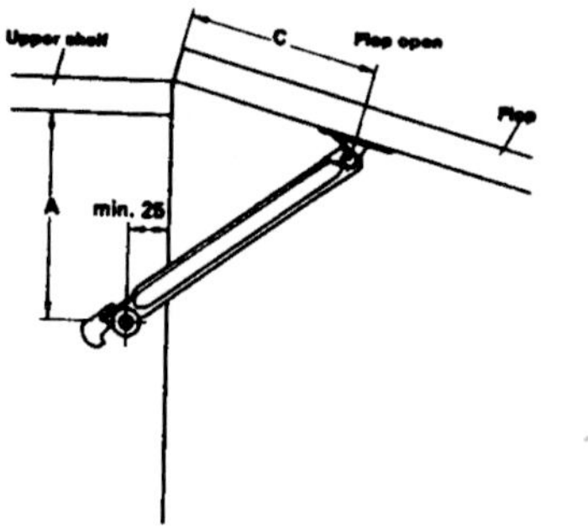

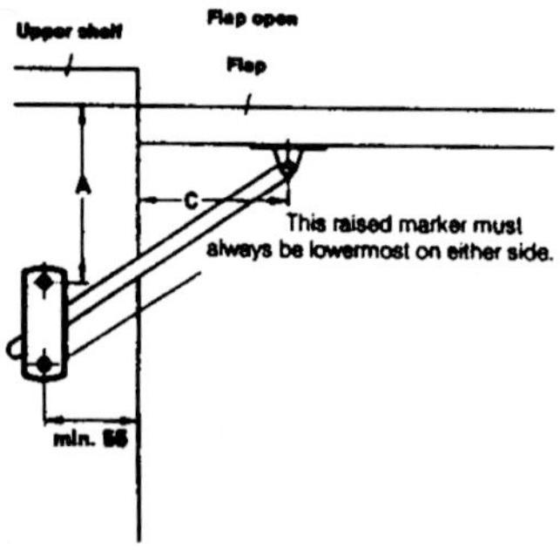

Length (mm)	Carcass depth (mm)	Distance A (mm)	Distance C (mm)
200	210	150	Determine by trial mounting
250	260	180	
300	310	230	

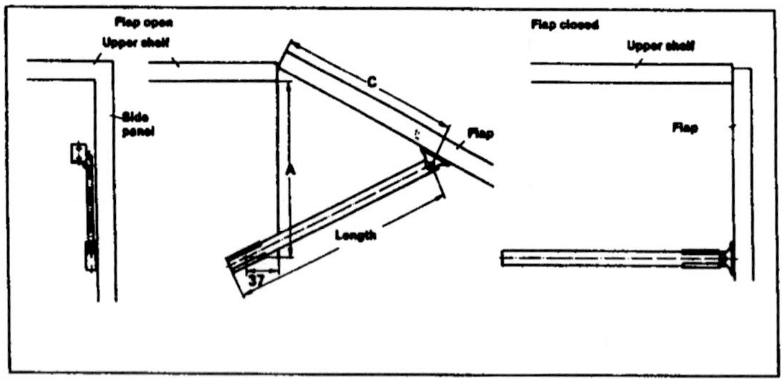

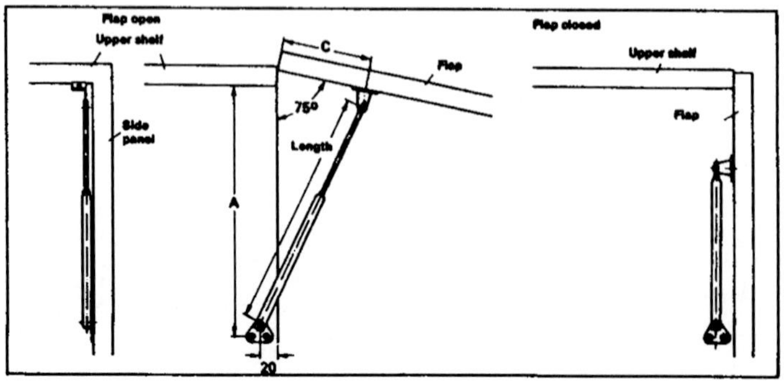

Length (mm)	Distance A (mm)	Distance C (mm)
130	150	Determine by trial mounting
250	260	

Dimensions in mm.

Extension type

Soft-Roller systems are capable of varying degrees of extension, depending on design. Basically, three types are employed:

E = Single extension

The withdrawal distance offered by single extensions is designed to be less than the installation length. Drawers cannot be opened clear of the carcase.

V = Full extension

The full extension model incorporates a pull-out distance as great as, or greater than, the installation length.
Drawers can be opened completely clear of the carcase.

T = Telescopic extension

Telescopic extensions are fully extending systems. Their particular design is such that all the elements travel on a central axis resulting in a particularly neat, space-saving, compact assembly.

Mounting method

An indication as to how the rails are secured to the drawer or pull-out element.

A = Base mounted

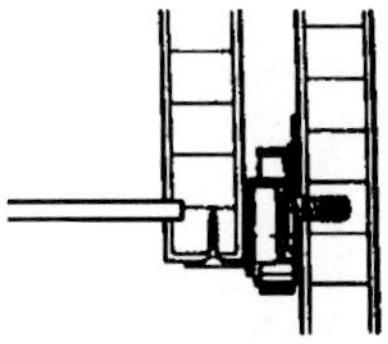

S = Side mounted

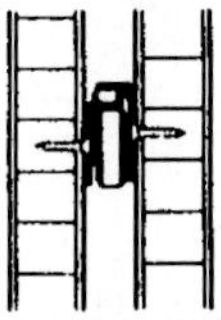

N = Groove mounted

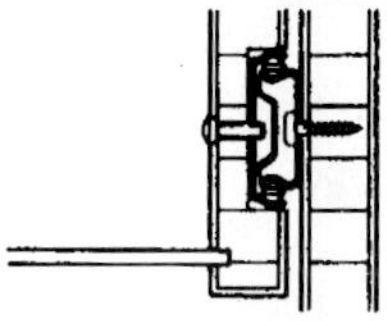

T = Shelf mounted

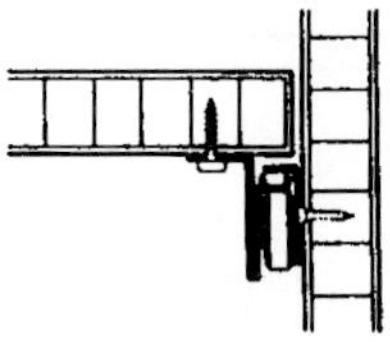

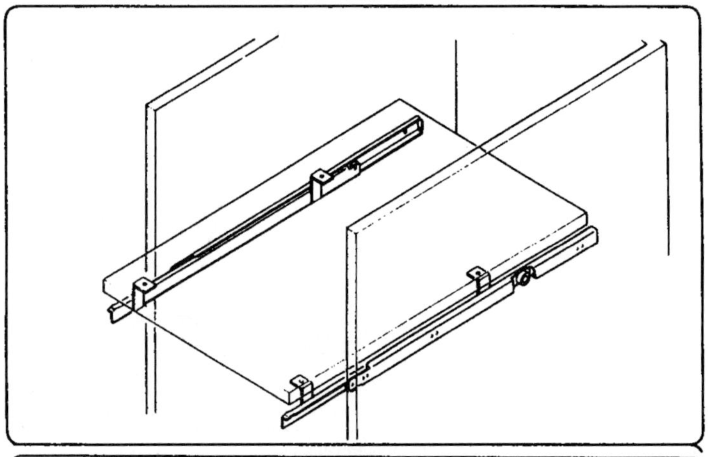

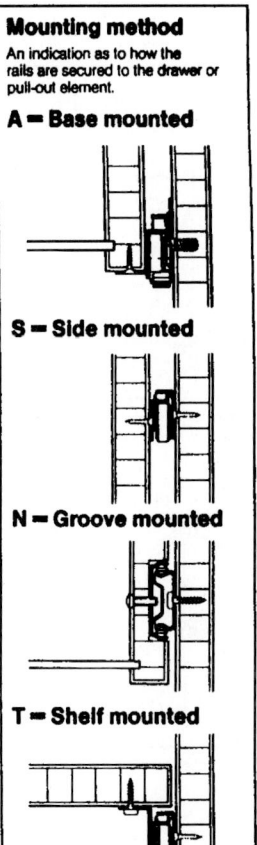

Single extensions with friction bearing mounted nylon rollers

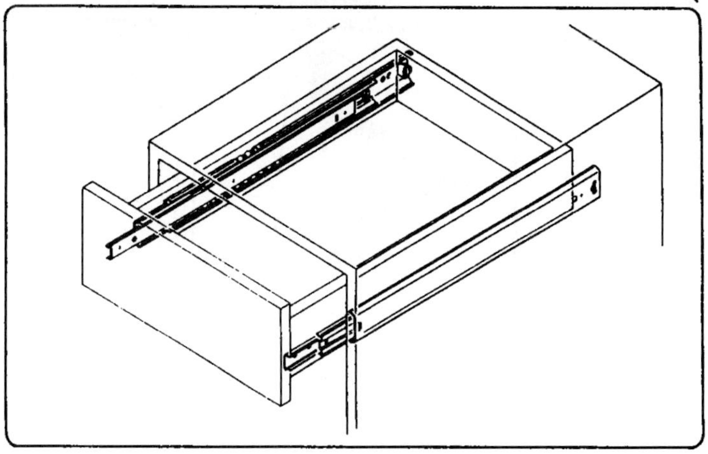

Telescopic extensions guided by means of ball cages

FURNITURE HARDWARE
Magnetic and Spring Catches, and Bolts

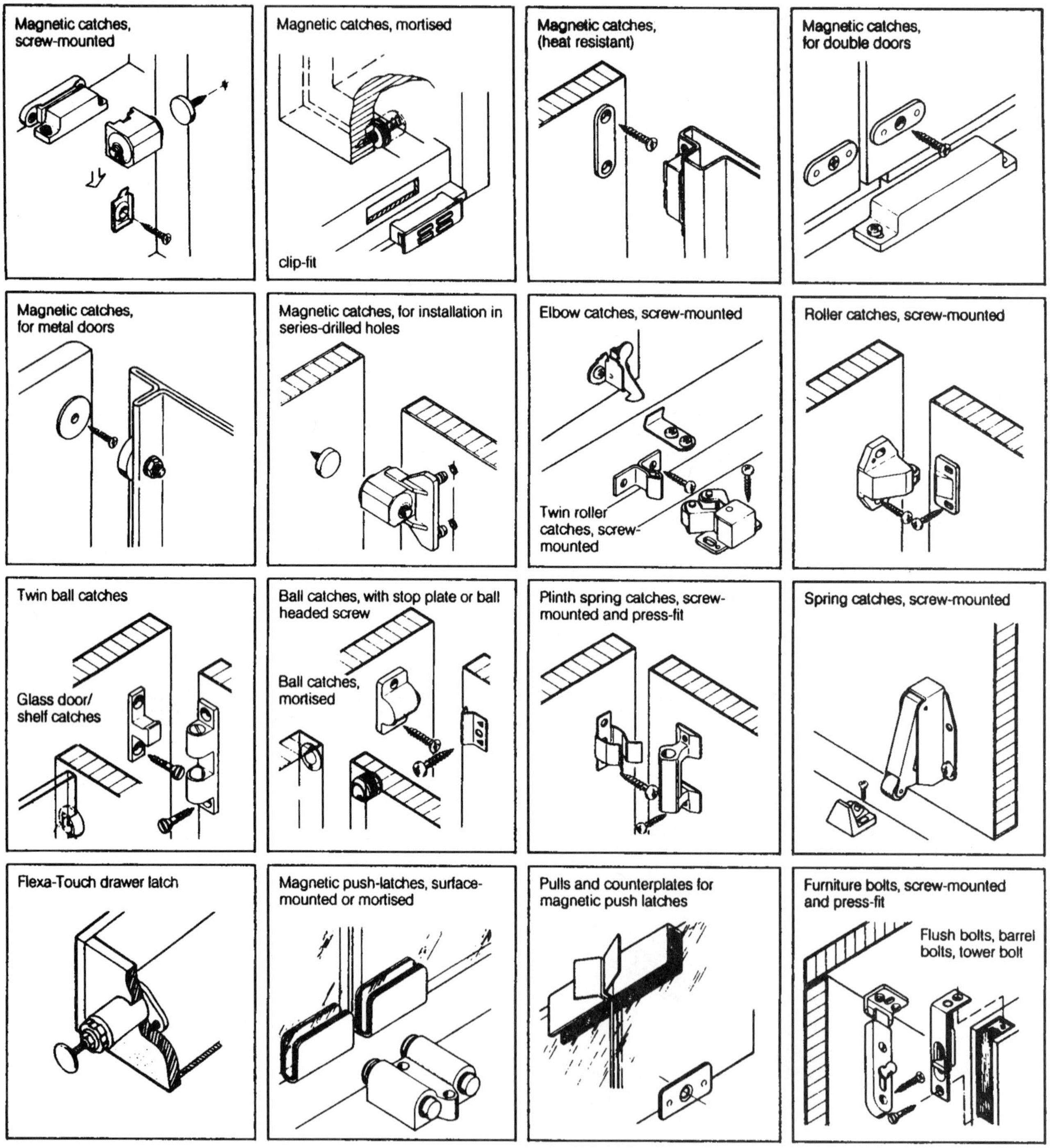
Magnetic catches, screw-mounted
Magnetic catches, mortised
clip-fit
Magnetic catches, (heat resistant)
Magnetic catches, for double doors
Magnetic catches, for metal doors
Magnetic catches, for installation in series-drilled holes
Elbow catches, screw-mounted
Twin roller catches, screw-mounted
Roller catches, screw-mounted
Twin ball catches
Glass door/ shelf catches
Ball catches, with stop plate or ball headed screw
Ball catches, mortised
Plinth spring catches, screw-mounted and press-fit
Spring catches, screw-mounted
Flexa-Touch drawer latch
Magnetic push-latches, surface-mounted or mortised
Pulls and counterplates for magnetic push latches
Furniture bolts, screw-mounted and press-fit
Flush bolts, barrel bolts, tower bolt

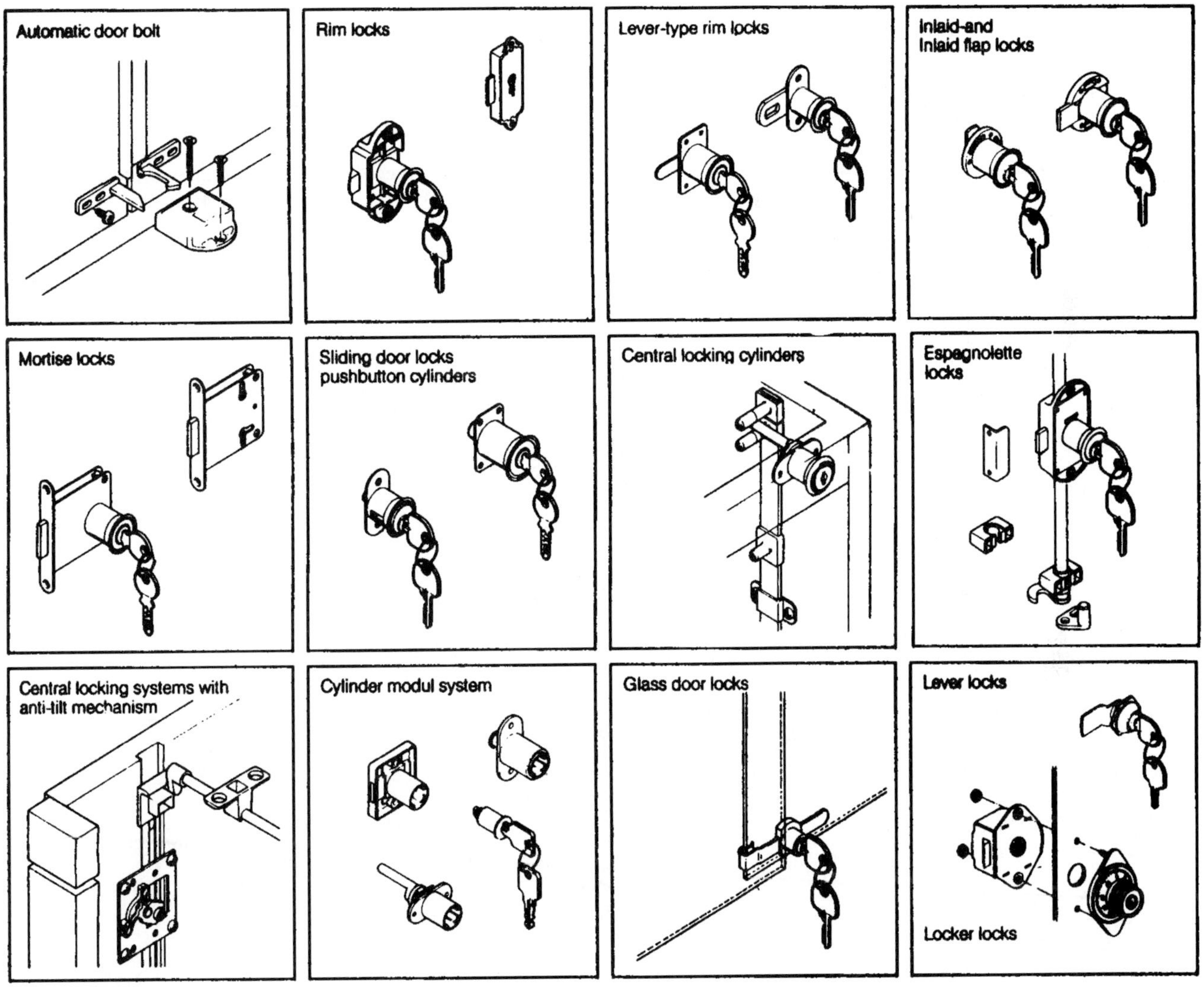
Automatic door bolt
Rim locks
Lever-type rim locks
Inlaid-and
Inlaid flap locks
Mortise locks
Sliding door locks
pushbutton cylinders
Central locking cylinders
Espagnolette
locks
Central locking systems with
anti-tilt mechanism
Cylinder modul system
Glass door locks
Lever locks
Locker locks

FURNITURE HARDWARE

Shelf Supports

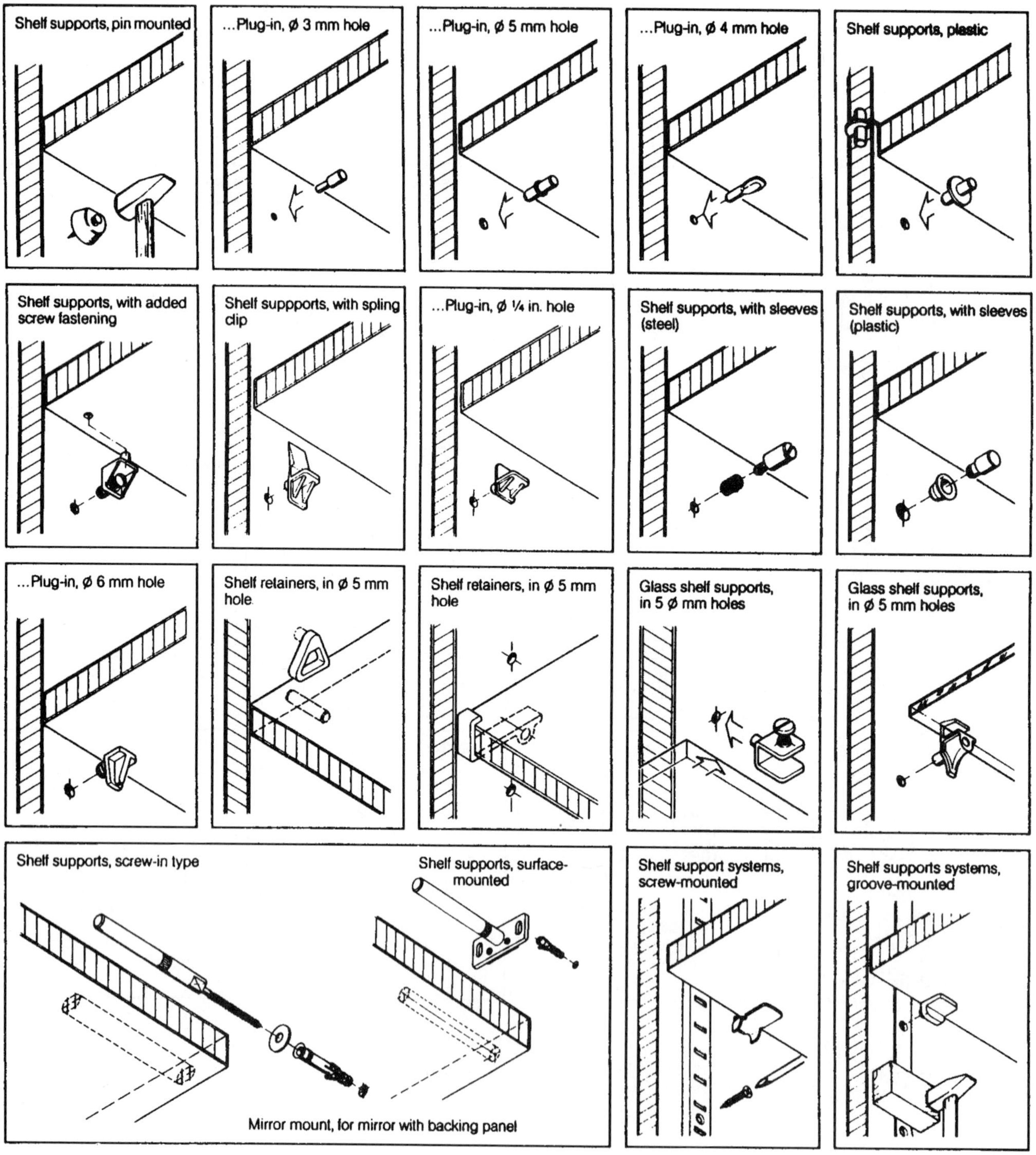
Shelf supports, pin mounted
...Plug-in, ø 3 mm hole
...Plug-in, ø 5 mm hole
...Plug-in, ø 4 mm hole
Shelf supports, plastic
Shelf supports, with added screw fastening
Shelf suppports, with spling clip
...Plug-in, ø ¼ in. hole
Shelf supports, with sleeves (steel)
Shelf supports, with sleeves (plastic)
...Plug-in, ø 6 mm hole
Shelf retainers, in ø 5 mm hole
Shelf retainers, in ø 5 mm hole
Glass shelf supports, in 5 ø mm holes
Glass shelf supports, in ø 5 mm holes
Shelf supports, screw-in type
Shelf supports, surface-mounted
Mirror mount, for mirror with backing panel
Shelf support systems, screw-mounted
Shelf supports systems, groove-mounted

WARDROBE RAILS AND SUPPORTS

OVA wardrobe rails
and supports

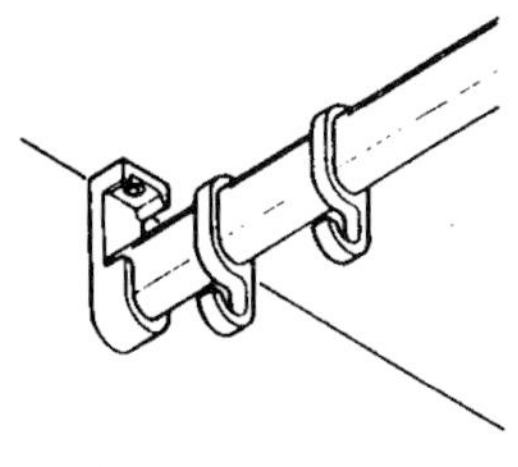

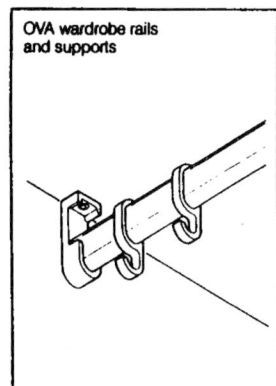

Shoe racks

Universal storage rack
Pull-relief plug

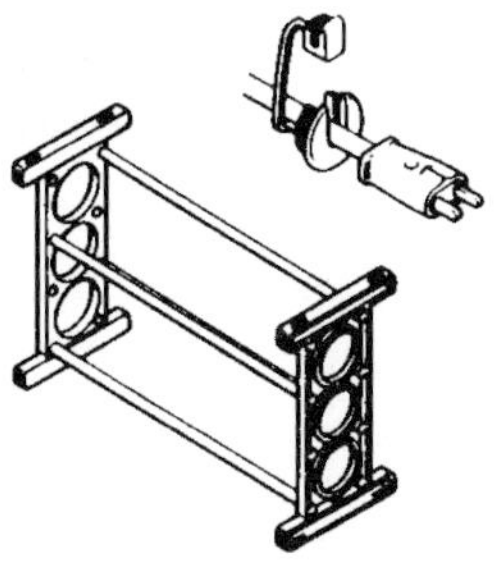

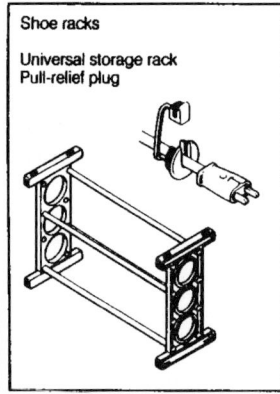

Single and double hooks,
pew hooks

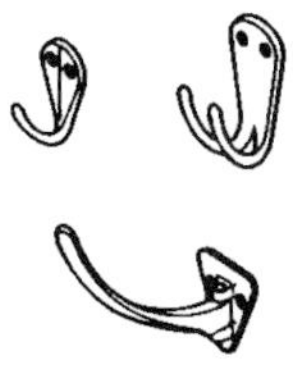

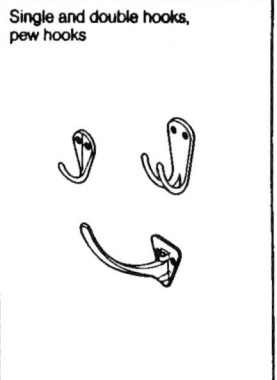

ø 18 mm, ø 20 mm,
ø 25 mm wardrobe rails
and supports

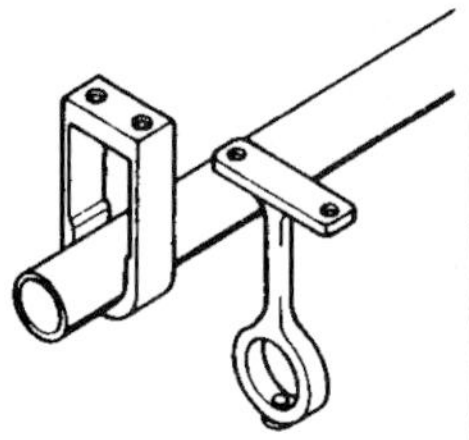

Wardrobe lifts,
hanging rails

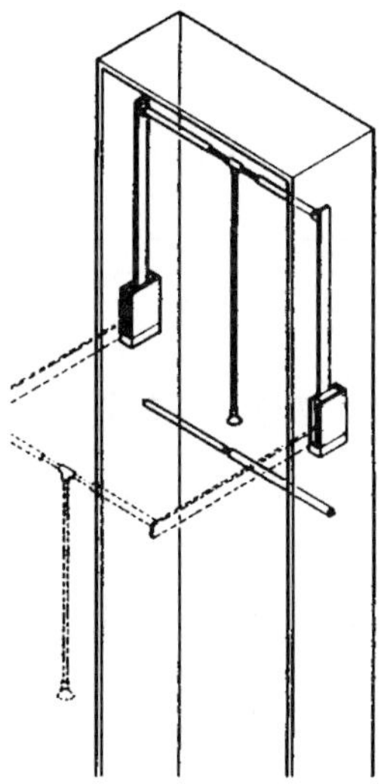

Cloakroom, wall and
ceiling hooks, nylon

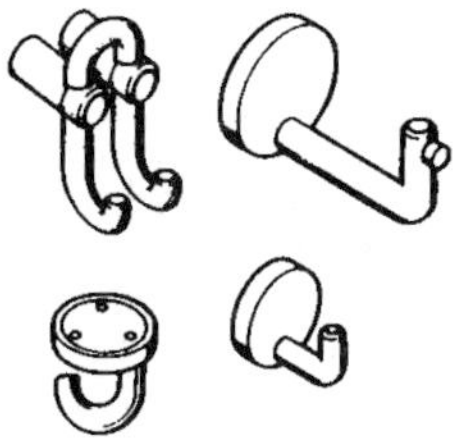

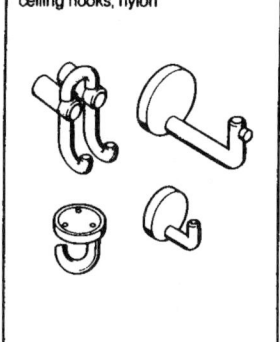

Cloakroom fittings
Thiefproof cloakroom fittings

Nylon tubular rails and coat
hangers

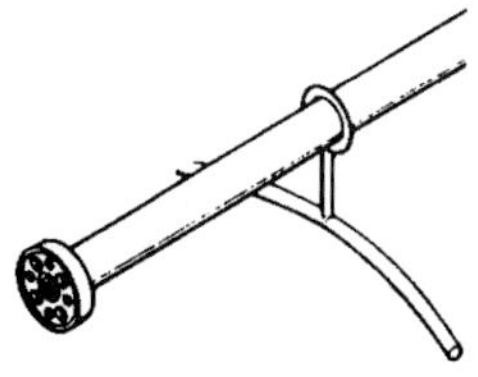

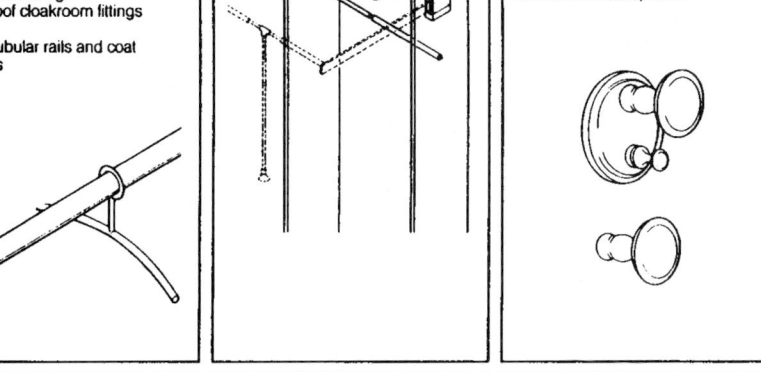

Cloakroom hooks, wood

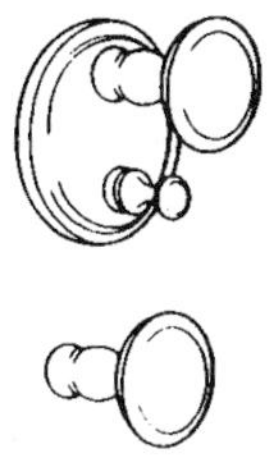

Wardrobe rails

Tie rails and hat racks

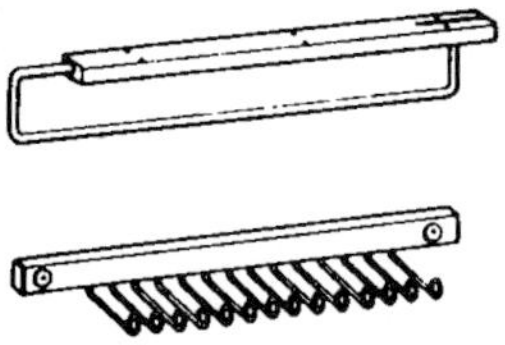

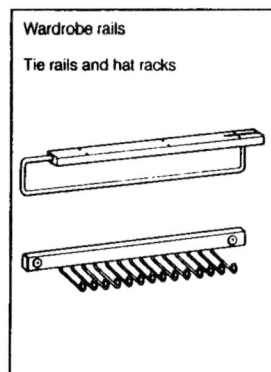

Hat and coat hooks

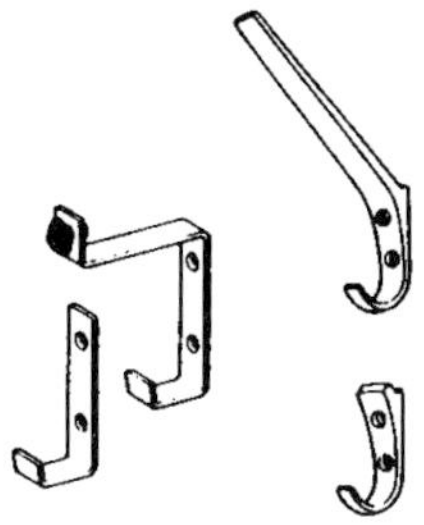

Wardrobe hanging bars
and rails

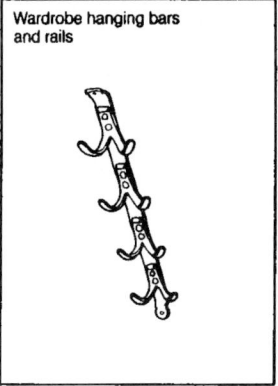

CASTORS AND GLIDES

Twin-Wheel Castors
Audio and
Audio-Stop

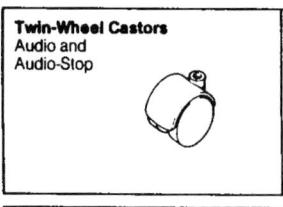

Enclosed Castors

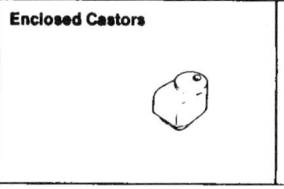

Furniture Glides

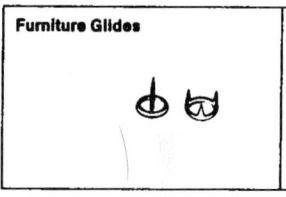

Furniture Glides
Cylindrical

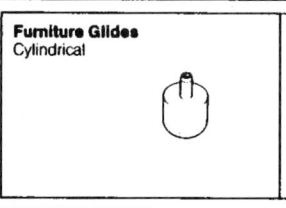

Furniture Legs
Furniture Glides

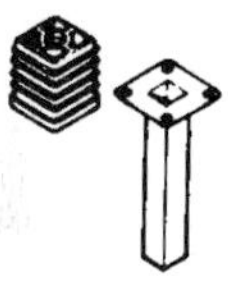

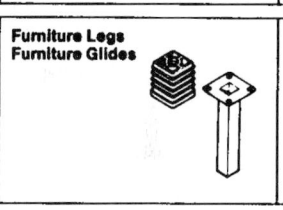

Bed Box Castors
Ball Castors

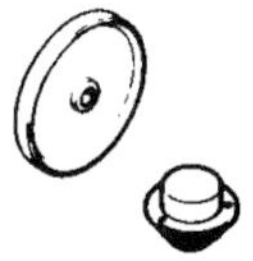

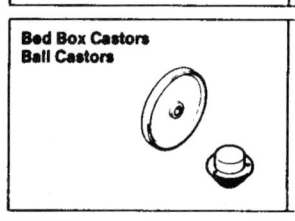

Coal Box Castors
Light Duty
Swivel Castors

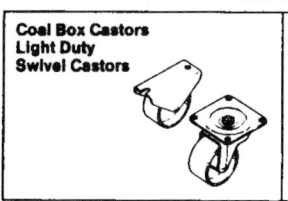

FURNITURE HARDWARE
Furniture Glides

knock-in furniture glides

Furniture glide
With two pins
Finish: white plastic

Size	45 × 20 × 5 mm

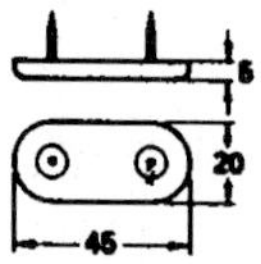

Dimensions in mm

Chairleg glide (pin type)
Finish: nickel-plated steel

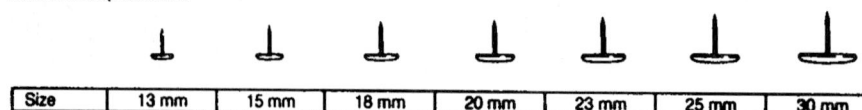

Size	13 mm	15 mm	18 mm	20 mm	23 mm	25 mm	30 mm

Chairleg cups with three lugs
Finish: nickel-plated steel

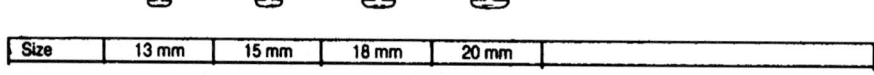

Size	13 mm	15 mm	18 mm	20 mm			

Glide (pin type)
With rubber washer
Finish: nickel-plated steel; black rubber

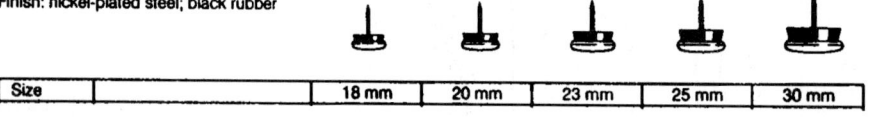

Size			18 mm	20 mm	23 mm	25 mm	30 mm

Felt glide
Finish: felt, in plastic case, grey

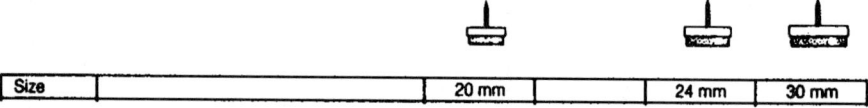

Size				20 mm		24 mm	30 mm

Plastic glide
Finish: white plastic

Size	10 mm	13 mm	16 mm	19 mm	22 mm		

Plastic glide (pin type)
With rubber washer
Finish: white plastic; black rubber

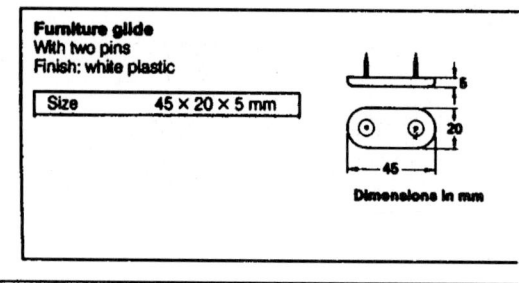

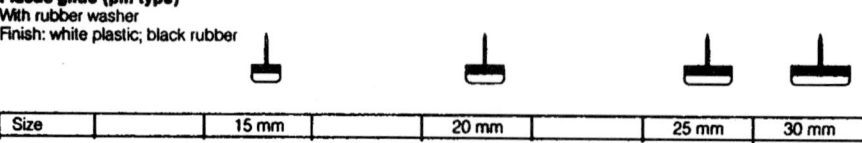

Size		15 mm		20 mm		25 mm	30 mm

4
SPECIALTIES

INTRODUCTION

In most instances, the design process requires a knowledge of, or at the very least an awareness of, certain specialized elements that can contribute heavily to the success or failure of a project in terms of aesthetics or function, or both. These elements may take the form of manufactured off-the-shelf products or consist of design theories, standards, and guidelines for certain areas of expertise. Accordingly, this section deals with 10 such elements, ranging from plantscaping to accessories.

Information can be found concerning the height, spacing, and diameter of indoor trees and floor plants. Also included are planting standards, details, and maintenance information. The section dealing with signage and graphics provides information on signage systems, symbols, mounting heights, and locations. Other sections provide data on audiovisual systems, including projection room layouts and details, and auditorium seating arrangements and sightlines. The section dealing with security includes information on door and window hardware, mailbox rooms, lighting, and security systems. Still other sections provide information on color theory and window treatments, including draperies and curtains, shutters and shades, and rods, holdbacks, and ties.

PLANTSCAPING

DESIGN GUIDELINES

Designing with Plants

Any successful design uses plants that are compatible not only in an aesthetic design sense, but also in their growing requirements. No matter how beautiful the design, if neighboring plants are not matched to the correct growing conditions, parts of the design will either deteriorate or require elaborate maintenance. The aesthetic design considerations involve choosing the proper variety of plant textures, heights, and spacing to give the desired effect. The growing considerations involve the proper matching of light intensity, soil, and water, as well as proper container size, to the plant environmental requirements.

Of all the growing conditions, the most important is the light intensity. It is easy to underestimate the amount of available light, since the human eye can easily see in 20 footcandles of light, while even the plant needing the lowest light requires 50 to 75 footcandles to remain healthy. If the light intensity is to be below 100 footcandles, even these low-light plants must be slowly acclimatized prior to installation.

No matter if the space to be planted is a small office, a large interior garden, or a cafeteria, the first step is to ascertain the actual level of the existing or planned lighting. To allow maximum creativity in the planting design, the light intensity should be considered in the initial planning stages, especially in large areas such as those in shopping malls or corporate interior gardens. Adding the needed lighting fixtures after the initial electrical installation is often expensive or impossible. In smaller-scale situations, such as offices or homes, extra light fixtures should be added or the plants should be chosen according to the available light. If the plants do not have the proper light intensity, they will die. The lower the light intensity below the minimum needed by the species, the faster they will do so.

Since the light source (incandescent, fluorescent, sun, or other) is not important, but the light intensity is, accurate intensity measurements are essential. For these measurements we recommend the General Electric Model 213 or 214 light meter or its equivalent. The measurements must be made at the level of the plant foliage; they must be made several times a day on several days typical of the location if sunlight is used; and they must take curtains, tinted glass, and other light-shielding devices into account. Only light hitting the top of the leaves is effective. While underlighting with spotlights can create dramatic effects, it does very little to help the plant.

After the light intensity is determined, the plants should be selected from the appropriate light-level group (see Fig. 7), consistent with the design aims. Plants that will be growing near one another should also have similar water requirements (also given in Fig. 7). If plants with different watering requirements must be close, they should be kept in their own growing containers so they can be watered separately.

An interior planting designer creates the mood through the interplay of plant texture and plant height, working only with those plants that will live under the predetermined light intensity. Color cannot really be used as a design element, since the average interior light intensity is seldom more than 100 footcandles and brightly colored plants or blooming flowers need up to 1000 footcandles. If flowering plants are used where the lighting conditions are normal, they will generally have to be replaced every few days.

Plant Texture

The good designer will provide for design variety through the clever use of plant texture. The term is used here to describe the general structure, shape, and appearance of the plant, regardless of height. It includes the size, shape, edging, and thickness of the plant's leaves, as well as its overall shape and the arrangement and number of leaves on the plant.

Five general rules concerning texture should be kept in mind.

1. Juxtapose fragmented foliage (such as that of a palm) with solid foliage (say, that of a dracaena).
2. Avoid too much of the same type of foliage (e.g., large flat leaves) in one area, unless a border or hedge effect is desired.
3. An exception to these previous rules on groupings is the palm. Although all palms have similar foliage, they vary slightly in color and interest, so that different types of palms may be planted together.
4. To create interest, mix small-leaved with large-leaved plants, and narrow-leaved with broad-leaved plants.
5. When using plants as specimens, especially as interior design elements in offices or homes, pick the plant with the background fabric, carpet, or wallpaper in mind. For example, a busy foliage plant will fight with a busy fabric.

Plant Height

Plant height not only determines the scale of the design, but adds variety to the plant groupings. There are six general rules regarding plant height selection to keep in mind.

1. In the plant grouping, build up with the low plants in front. If the grouping can be seen from all sides, the grouping must be well balanced throughout and built up to the center height.
2. If a plant has canes with no lower foliage, try to place the lower plants in front to conceal the absence of foliage of the taller plants in the rear.
3. Uneven sizes throughout a grouping add more interest than consistent levels of foliage.
4. If a single plant is desired to hide a column or some other object, be sure that the plant height, including its container, is about three-fourths the height of the object to be concealed.
5. Keep the scale of the surroundings in mind when choosing the plant height. A 3-ft plant is fine next to a desk, but a plant of at least 6 ft should be selected if it is to be viewed when entering a room.
6. By convention, interior plant heights are measured from the bottom of the root ball or planter, while exterior plant heights are measured from the top of the root ball. The reason is that interior plants are usually placed in a container or raised planter, and the total available height from floor to ceiling is fixed.

Plant Spacing

Under certain conditions, the plants of an interior landscaping design will grow. Therefore, any possible change in the plant size must be considered by the designer. If the lighting intensity is at or below the recommended level, there will be little or no plant growth and the plant size and relationships will change little over time. If the lighting intensity is well above the required level, there will be plant growth, with different plant species growing at different rates.

Unlike outdoor plants, indoor tropical plants seldom grow outward; most of their growth occurs upward. The main exceptions are the *Ficus* family, the schefflera, and the *Philodendron Selloum,* which will spread somewhat outward. If a full plant design is desired, the required number of plants should be placed close together at the time of installation since future growth will seldom fill in the bare spots.

Even if the light intensity is high enough, before the plant can grow significantly, its root system must be able to expand. Thus, the best way to ensure that the size relationships of the plants do not change is to keep them in their original growing containers and not to replant them into a growing medium. If they are kept in the original containers, they will become pot-bound and future growth will be automatically limited.

Plant material is sold on the basis of height or growing-container size, and one must be familiar with the particular species to know what the spread will be. For each plant species considered here, Fig. 1 lists the height range for each plant in each standard growing-container size and gives a recommended minimum center-to-center plant spacing. This recommended spacing is based on experience with the plant's branching habits and growth patterns and will give a full plant design. If an open or a less full design is called for, the spacing should be increased.

When the plants are to be displayed in individual planters or decorative containers, each plant, still in its growing can, is placed directly into the planter or container, on top of a layer of drainage material of the appropriate depth. However, many standard planters have lips that reduce the interior diameter to less than the overall diameter. This inner diameter should be larger than the growing can's diameter so that the plant can be placed directly into it without being repotted and risking the attendant danger of root damage. To emphasize this requirement, Fig. 2 gives the standard planter diameter needed for each standard size of growing container. The size of the lip changes when a nonstandard type is used. If space is limited, this measurement should be carefully checked.

PLANTSCAPING
Plant Height, Spacing, and Diameter

Species	*Height Range*	*Recommended Center-to-Center Plant Spacing*	*Growing Can Diameter*
INDOOR TREES			
Fiddle-leaf fig *(Ficus lyrata)*	3- 4 ft	24-36 in	10 in
	4- 6 ft	30-42 in	14 in
	6-11 ft	42 in & up	17 in
Indian laurel *(Ficus retusa)*	5- 7 ft	42-54 in	14 in
	7- 9 ft	48-60 in	17 in
	9-12 ft	60 in & up	22 in
Rubber plant (*Ficus elastica* cv. 'Decora'), tree standard	4-5 ft	48-60 in	10 in
	5-6 ft	54-66 in	12 in
	6-7 ft	60-72 in	14 in
Rubber plant (*Ficus elastica* cv. 'Decora'), bush type	1½-2 ft	12-18 in	6 in
	2 -2½ ft	12-24 in	8 in
	3 -4 ft	24-36 in	10 in
	4 -5 ft	36-48 in	12 in
	4 -5 ft	48-60 in	14 in
Weeping fig *(Ficus benjamina)*	3- 4 ft	24-36 in	10 in
	4- 5 ft	30-42 in	12 in
	5- 7 ft	36-48 in	14 in
	6- 8 ft	48-60 in	17 in
	9-10 ft	60 in & up	22 in
	9-12 ft	60 in & up	28 in
	10-12 ft	72 in & up	36 in
Norfolk Island pine *(Araucaria heterophylla)*	1½-2 ft	18-30 in	6 in
	2 -3 ft	24-36 in	8 in
	3 -5 ft	30-42 in	10 in
	4 -5 ft	36-48 in	12 in
	4 -6 ft	42-54 in	14 in
	6 -7 ft	54-66 in	17 in
Schefflera *(Brassaia actinophylla)*	3- 4 ft	36-48 in	10 in
	4- 5 ft	36-48 in	10 in
	5- 7 ft	55-66 in	14 in
	7- 8 ft	60-72 in	17 in
	8- 9 ft	60 in & up	22 in
	9-12 ft	72 in & up	Metal tubs
FLOOR PLANTS			
Bamboo palm *(Chamaedorea erumpens)*	3-4 ft	30-42 in	10 in
	4-6 ft	36-48 in	12 in
	5-7 ft	42-54 in	14 in
	7-9 ft	48-60 in	17 in
Corn plant (*Dracaena fragrans* cv. 'Massangeana')	1½-2 ft	24-30 in	6 in
	3½-4 ft	24-36 in	10 in
	4½-6 ft	30-42 in	12 in
	5 -7 ft	36-48 in	14 in
Corn plant bush (*Dracaena fragrans* cv. 'Massangeana')	1 -1½ ft	18-24 in	6 in
	1½-2½ ft	18-30 in	8 in
	3 -4 ft	24-36 in	10 in
	4 -5 ft	30-42 in	14 in
	5 -7 ft	36-48 in	17 in
Dwarf date palm *(Phoenix Roebelenii)*	2-3 ft	30-42 in	10 in
	3-4 ft	36-48 in	12 in
	4-5 ft	42-54 in	14 in
	5-6 ft	48-60 in	17 in
	5-6 ft	54-66 in	22 in

Fig. 1 Spacing recommendations

Species	Height Range	Recommended Center-to-Center Plant Spacing	Growing Can Diameter
Dwarf dragon tree (*Dracaena marginata)*	3-4 ft	24-36 in	10 in
	4-5 ft	30-42 in	12 in
	5-7 ft	36-48 in	14 in
	7-9 ft	48 in & up	17 in
Dwarf schefflera *(Brassaia arboricola)*	1 -1½ ft	18-24 in	6 in
	1½-2½ ft	30-42 in	8 in
	3 -4 ft	36-48 in	10 in
	4 -5 ft	42-54 in	14 in
False aralia *(Dizygotheca elegantissima)*	1½-2 ft	18-30 in	6 in
	3 -4 ft	30-42 in	10 in
	5 -7 ft	36-48 in	14 in
	7 -8 ft	42-54 in	17 in
Green dracaena (*Dracaena deremensis* cv. 'Janet Craig')	1 -1½ ft	18-24 in	6 in
	1½-2½ ft	18-30 in	8 in
	3 -4 ft	24-36 in	10 in
	4 -5 ft	30-42 in	14 in
	5 -7 ft	36-48 in	17 in
Green pleomele *(Dracaena reflexa)*	1½-2 ft	12-18 in	6 in
	3 -4 ft	18-30 in	10 in
	4 -5 ft	30-45 in	14 in
	5 -6 ft	36-48 in	17 in
Kentia palm *(Howea Forsterana)*	3-4 ft	36-48 in	10 in
	4-5 ft	42-54 in	12 in
	5-8 ft	48-60 in	14 in
Lady palm *(Rhapis excelsa)*	3-4 ft	36-48 in	10 in
	4-5 ft	42-54 in	12 in
	5-7 ft	48-60 in	14 in
Mock orange *(Pittosporum Tobira)*	1¼-1½ ft	24-36 in	10 in
	1½-2½ ft	30-42 in	12 in
	2 -3 ft	36-48 in	14 in
Narrow-leaved pleomele *(Dracaena angustifolia honoraii)*	3-4 ft	24-36 in	12 in
	5-6 ft	30-42 in	14 in
	6-7 ft	36-48 in	17 in
Neantha bella palm *(Chamaedorea elegans)*	1 -1½ ft	18-30 in	6 in
	1½-2½ ft	24-36 in	8 in
	2½-3½ ft	30-42 in	10 in
	4 -5 ft	36-48 in	14 in
Ponytail *(Beaucarnea recurvata)*	1½-2 ft	24-36 in	10 in
	2 -3 ft	30-42 in	12 in
	3 -4 ft	36-48 in	14 in
	4 -5 ft	42-54 in	17 in
Reed palm *(Chamaedorea Seifrizii)*	4-6 ft	36-48 in	12 in
	6-7 ft	42-54 in	14 in
	7-9 ft	48-60 in	17 in
Self-heading philodendron *(Philodendron Selloum)*	3 ft	30-42 in	10 in
	4 ft	42-54 in	14 in
	5 ft	54-66 in	17 in
Southern yew (*Podocarpus macrophyllus* var. Maki)	4-5 ft	36-48 in	10 in
	5-6 ft	42-54 in	12 in
	5-6 ft	48-60 in	14 in
	6-7 ft	54-66 in	17 in

Fig. 1 *(Continued)*

PLANTSCAPING

Plant Height, Spacing, and Diameter

Species	Height Range	Recommended Center-to-Center Plant Spacing	Growing Can Diameter
TABLE OR DESK PLANTS—GROUND COVER			
Boston fern (*Nephrolepis exaltata* cv.	1 ft	24-30 in	6 in
'Bostoniensis')	1 -1½ ft	30-36 in	8 in
	1½-2 ft	36-42 in	10 in
Common philodendron (*Philodendron*	1 ft	18-24 in	8 in
scandens oxycardium)	1¼-1½ ft	24-30 in	10 in
	1¼-1½ ft	24-36 in	12 in
Chinese evergreen (*Aglaonema*	1¼-1½ ft	18-24 in	6 in
commutatum var. maculatum)	1½-2 ft	24-30 in	8 in
	2 -2½ ft	30-36 in	10 in
Dumb cane (*Dieffenbachia maculata* cv.	1 ft	18-24 in	6 in
'Rudolph Roehrs')	2 ft	24-30 in	8 in
	3 ft	30-36 in	10 in
	3 -3½ ft	36-42 in	12 in
	3½-4 ft	42-48 in	14 in
Golden pothos *(Epipremnum aureum* or	1 ft	12-18 in	6 in
Scindapsus aureus)	1 ft	18-24 in	8 in
	1¼-1½ ft	24-30 in	10 in
	1¼-1½ ft	30-36 in	12 in
Grape ivy *(Cissus rhombifolia)*	1 ft	18-24 in	6 in
	1 -1¼ ft	18-30 in	8 in
	1¼-1½ ft	24-36 in	10 in
	1¼-1½	24-36 in	12 in
Jade plant *(Crassula argentea)*	1 ft	18-24 in	8 in
	2 ft	24-36 in	10 in
	2 -2½ ft	30-42 in	12 in
	2½-3½ ft	36-48 in	14 in
Prayer plant *(Maranta leuconeura)*	1 ft	18-24 in	8 in
	1 ft	24-30 in	10 in
	1-1½ ft	24-30 in	12 in
Swedish ivy *(Plectranthus australis)*	1 ft	18-24 in	6 in
	1 -1¼ ft	18-30 in	8 in
	1¼-1½ ft	24-36 in	10 in
	1¼-1½ ft	24-36 in	12 in
Wax plant *(Hoya carnosa)*	1 ft	12-18 in	6 in
	1 ft	18-24 in	8 in
	1 ft	24-30 in	10 in
White flag (*Spathiphyllum* cv. 'Clevelandii')	1¼-1½ ft	24-36 in	6 in
	2 -3 ft	30-42 in	8 in
	2½-3½ ft	36-48 in	10 in
	3 -4 ft	48-54 in	14 in
White-striped Dracaena (*Dracaena*	1¼-1½ ft	18-24 in	6 in
deremensis cv. 'Warneckii')	2 ft	24-30 in	8 in
	3 -4 ft	24-36 in	10 in
	4 -5 ft	30-42 in	12 in
	4 -7 ft	36-48 in	14 in
Green dracaena (*Dracaena deremensis* cv.	1 -1½ ft	18-24 in	6 in
'Janet Craig')	1½-2½ ft	24-30 in	8 in
	3 -4 ft	30-42 in	10 in
Neantha bella palm *(Chamaedorea elegans)*	1 -1½ ft	18-30 in	6 in
	1½-2½ ft	24-36 in	8 in
	2½-3½ ft	30-42 in	10 in
Self-heading philodendron *(Philodendron*	1 ft	18-24 in	6 in
Selloum)	2 ft	24-36 in	8 in
	3 ft	30-42 in	10 in

Fig. 1 *(Continued)*

Plant Growing Container Diameter	Recommended Planter Exterior Diameter
4 in	6 in
6 in	8 in
8 in	10 in
10 in	12 in
11 in	14 in
12 in	14 in
13 in	16 in
14 in	16 in
17 in	18-22 in
22 in	24 in

Fig. 2 Planter selection. These recommendations are based on the fact that most standard planters have either a 1-in lip or no lip at all. Because the growing cans sometimes have ridges or become deformed, it is always best to allow for a little extra leeway, even for planters with no lip. Some manufacturers, however, put 2-in lips on their planters, a possibility that should be checked. If the planter is an automatic watering type, the inside and outside diameters will be quite different, depending on the manufacturer.

DESIGN GUIDELINES

Writing Specifications

The interior landscaping business is very competitive, and a common practice is for the architect or designer to send out the landscaping specifications for bids. Unless the specifications for the job are well written, however, there are many ways for the contractor to cut corners and still be within the specifications. Consequently, the final installation may not be what the designer had in mind. The lowest bid is not necessarily the best bargain, unless the specifications are very tightly written or unless the architect is dealing with a well-established landscape contractor with a reputation for high-quality work.

The following are some suggested guidelines to use in writing specifications. If they are observed, the bids received will accurately reflect the design requirements of the job.

1. Specify the plant heights within a 6-in bracket. For example, designate 5 to 5½ ft or 5½ to 6 ft. If the specification were simply "5 to 6 ft," the supplier could use all 5-ft plants, which are considerably less expensive than 6-ft plants.
2. For corn plants, dwarf dragon trees, and the like, specify the number of canes and approximate number of foliage heads, as well as the height. The difference in cost between a two-cane and a three-cane corn plant of the same height is not minor.
3. For reed palms, bamboo palms, and the like, specify the number of stems desired, five to six being medium full.
4. For the green dracaena and white-striped dracaena, list the number of main foliage stems desired. They range from one to three stems.
5. For ficus trees, it should be specified whether the bush style or standard tree style is desired. In the bush style, the plant has multiple stems (ranging from two to five in number) branching out from the base of the plants. The standard tree or "lollipop" style has one main 5- to 6-ft stem with a sheared, ball-shaped foliage head.
6. Small plants should be specified as to single plants or combinations or several plants. Examples are dumb cane, Chinese evergreen, and white flag.
7. If ivy trailers are desired, their length should be specified. The trailers take up to eight months to grow, depending on the length, so the designer must plan for these up to a year before installation. Examples are grape ivy, swedish ivy, golden pothos, common philodendron, and wax plant.
8. Specifications should call for plant cleaning and spraying before installation.
9. Perlite should be specified as the drainage material for both planters and decorative containers. Styrofoam, which is much cheaper, is often used but has little long-term value.
10. The amount of ingredients in large planters (soil mixture, drainage material, soil separator) should be specified, as should the composition of each of the ingredients.
11. If bark chips, moss cover, or other soil coverings are desired, they should be specified.
12. Special attention should be given to the description of specimen plants, including the number of heads, stems, or canes, and any unusual stem structure that is desired. If canes with character (such as angle and peculiarity of growth), tufts of foliage at various heights, or other unusual features are wanted, they should be specifically mentioned.
13. If the landscape contractor will not maintain the plants after installation, provision should be made for a training program for the maintenance crew. Also, the contractor should provide for two weeks' initial maintenance of the plants and replacement of any that fall below specifications during the period.
14. If the landscape contractor is to maintain the plants after the installation (usually the best all-around solution), such an agreement should be reached before the plants are installed and a maintenance contract should be signed. This contract should include a provision for the replacement of any plant that falls below specifications because of faulty maintenance. This stipulation gives the contractor incentive for professional-quality maintenance.
15. If a large garden is planned and the landscape contractor is given design responsibility for it, the contractor should provide a floor plan of the garden for the designer's approval, before the installation.
16. If the architect or designer provides the landscape contractor with a detailed planting floor plan and the contractor finds it impossible to meet all the specifications (because of unavailability of certain species, etc.), the contractor and the designer or architect should agree in writing on any changes.

PLANT USE AND PROCEDURES

Use of Interior Plants and Procedures

The general rule of interior planting design is to vary the plant heights, shapes, and textures to give the desired design feeling consistent with the available light level and planting space. The best way to learn to apply this rule to specific situations is to study successful designs.

Interior planting designs have usually been found to fall into one of two categories: (1) interior gardens, both large and small, such as those seen in residential and hotel lobbies, corporate headquarters reception areas, and enclosed shopping mall public spaces; and (2) open plan or specimen design, like office landscaping designs and designs that use individual plants as living sculptures. In both categories of design, the main requirements to be considered are the available light intensity, the scale of the design, and the client's wishes and budget. After these basic requirements are determined, however, the design considerations are somewhat different for the two types of design.

Interior Gardens

Interior gardens are planting areas, sometimes contained in built-in planters, that have a variety of plants and that convey their design feeling through plant arrangements rather than through individual plant specimens. Small gardens generally contain only a single grouping of plants, act as a single design element, and have uniform lighting and watering requirements throughout. Large gardens have a variety of plant groupings and varying design feelings among the groupings, and they can encompass areas of different lighting and watering requirements. Since any garden conveys its effects through the juxtaposition of different plants, a single dominant plant cannot be considered a garden from the design point of view, even if it is in a built-in planter with ground-cover plants.

In designing any built-in planter, enough planter depth must be provided to allow the root ball or the planting can be covered with soil and to rest on 4 to 8 in of drainage material. Since soil and gravel are expensive, it is best not to overdesign the planter by making it larger than necessary and not to buy too much soil to fill in between the plants. (For example, a depth of 1½ to 2 ft is usually enough for most small gardens.) Figure 1 lists the size of the growing can for different sizes of plants of each species. The depth of the largest growing can, plus the depth of the drainage material, yields the minimum planter depth for the garden. The volume of the planter minus the total volume of all the growing cans indicates the amount of additional soil and drainage material to be provided.

If the planter is already in place, its depth may limit the size of the plants that may be used. Since soil must reach to the top of the root ball or can, the only way to utilize too shallow a planter is to put the large plant in the center and to build up from the edge inward. The planter must be wide enough to slant the soil gradually so that the slope is not too great.

Small gardens While a garden may be large enough to have only a single design function, that function can be quite varied, provided that the lighting intensity is appropriate. It can serve as a small glen or a space separator, or it can be simply a large decorative planter. The garden can be airy and open or it can be dense and closed. Planter depth of 1½ to 2 ft is usually sufficient.

Also, some small gardens can be designed to be changed with the seasons. Often, flowering plants, such as chrysanthemums or azaleas, are used, but the plants must then be replaced every two weeks. If the seasonal or flowering plant changes are desired, the plants should be left in their containers so that they may be easily moved. Some care should be given to the planter design so that the growing cans are not obvious and do not detract from the arrangement.

Creative additions of volcanic rocks, small ponds, or fountains can be quite attractive and set off and enhance the plants. However, with the usually limited space in the small garden, these additions can produce a crowded or overdone appearance. Overcrowding will give a jungle effect that is rarely desired.

Just as in other design fields, good proportion and good sense will create a pleasing design that is neither overlooked or overbearing.

Large gardens Large gardens are simply larger versions of small gardens, but their very size opens up more design possibilities, since they may be subdivided into related sections. The shape, height, and texture of the planters may be varied from section to section. The plants may be chosen to reflect varying design moods and functions. The lighting and watering requirements may differ between sections. In fact, variety is often necessary for good large-garden design, since a large mass of similar plants or plant groupings will create the impression of a monotonous forest or field.

Because large indoor gardens usually are in areas of high ceilings, the light level must be very carefully considered. Just the presence of windows or skylights does not guarantee enough light. In addition, if the light sources are distant from the plants, the taller plants may effectively block some of the light from reaching the lower plants and foliage.

When large areas are to be planted, there is a tendency to use rocks, pools, gravel, or fountains to cut down the plant costs and simplify the maintenance. Care is essential when using these elements to prevent the plant arrangement from looking bare and sterile.

Large gardens are most commonly used in shopping malls. The skilled designer will take this illumination into account, as well as design the garden to enhance the shopper's view of the stores.

The designer will always remember that large gardens achieve their effectiveness by both the proper variation of plant groupings and the proper variation of plants within the groupings.

Procedures for planting gardens As pointed out earlier, a successful garden needs proper planting, since improper procedures can inflict severe damage. Correct planting involves not only correct technique and design but also correct organization.

The techniques of proper drainage, spacing, and handling will ensure that the plants remain healthy once they are installed. Experienced supervision of the installation staff will be important in this regard, since a large installation of expensive plants is no place for the on-the-job training of the supervisor.

Proper planning and organization will ensure that the plants remain healthy between unloading and planting. If the plants are left on an unheated loading dock or stored in an unlighted or unheated room until they are installed, irreversible damage may occur.

Drainage Overwatering of plants leads to root rot and is often more harmful than underwatering. To minimize this danger, the planter or container should be installed with proper drainage. The simplest technique is to provide a porous reservoir below the planting soil; any excess water will then drain into it from the root ball and be slowly fed back to the soil as the soil dries out.

To prepare the planter or decorative container, the drainage material is poured into the bottom and leveled. The plant growing can is placed on top of the drainage layer and surrounded with more of the drainage material. For the smaller plants (in pots 6 in or less in diameter), a 1-in depth of drainage material is usually enough. For the larger plants, a layer of 3 to 4 in is suggested. For very large gardens, about one-third of the planter depth should be the drainage layer, provided it leaves enough room for the root ball or planting can.

The drainage material can be perlite (a readily available synthetic material) alone or mixed with small pebbles or gravel. The perlite is suggested since it is porous enough to feed back the excess water to the soil as the soil dries out. If only gravel or pebbles are used, the excess water will sit and stagnate in the reservoir and will not be fed back to the plants.

Even with the proper drainage layer, overwatering is possible if so much excess water is used that it fills up the reservoir. The water level in a small container can be determined by tapping the container at various intervals and listening for the change in sound. In large planted areas, it is wise to provide for dipstick readings of the water level. To take such a reading, rigid hollow plastic tubes, with a cloth over their lower ends, are planted at intervals along with the plants. The hollow tubes reach from the top of the container to just above the drainage layer and the cloth on the bottom prevents soil or drainage material from entering the tube. A dipstick is lowered into the tube until it touches the cloth. If the stick, upon removal, shows more than ½ in of water, there is too much water in the bottom of the planter.

If gravel is used as part of the drainage material, it should be ⅜ to ½ in in diameter. Under no circumstances should limestone be used, since it is alkaline and will raise the pH of the water to a level that is too high for most tropical plants.

Soil separator If the plants are removed from their growing cans and replanted in growing soil, it is usually best to use a soil separator

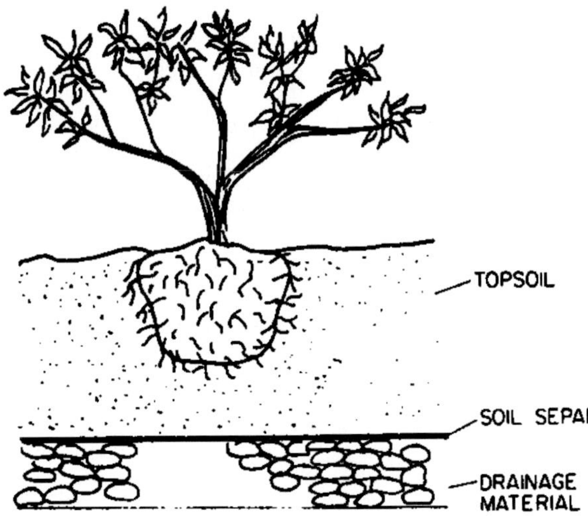

Fig. 3 Soil separation

between the drainage layer and the planting soil. The separator is a semiporous sheet, often composed of fiberglass wool, which serves to keep the soil from falling into the drainage material. If the separator is not used, soil will clog the drainage material. Fiberglass wool of building material grade should not be used, as it contains chemicals that will damage the plant (Fig. 3).

Planting medium Because the root systems of tropical plants are much finer than those of outdoor plants, pure topsoil is too heavy and too easily compacted to be used as a planting medium. It will constrict the plant roots and will retain too much water.

For the common tropical plants discussed here, we recommend the use of the foliage plant mix developed by Cornell University. Because it is easiest to calculate the quantity of needed soil in terms of the volume of the planter to be filled, the formula given here is for 1 yd^3 of soil. For conversion purposes, 1 yd^3 equals 21.7 bushels, 765 L, or 27 ft^3.

Sphagnum peat moss: ½ yd^3 = 383 L
Vermiculite #2: ¼ yd^3 = 191 L
Perlite, medium fine: ¼ yd^3 = 191 L
Ground limestone, dolomitic: 0.85 gal = 13.5 cup = 3.2 L
Superphosphate 20% solution: 0.21 gal = 3.4 cup = 0.79 L
10-10-10 fertilizer: 0.32 gal = 5.1 cup = 1.2 L
Iron sulphate: 0.11 gal = 1.7 cup = 0.41 L
Potassium nitrate: 0.11 gal = 1.7 cup = 0.41 L

While this Cornell foliage plant mix gives the best all-around results, a simpler mix that gives good results in most cases is as follows:

⅓ by volume sterilized commercial mix of peat moss and vermiculite
⅓ by volume sterilized topsoil
⅓ by volume perlite

This mix is particularly effective for container planting. If it is to be used in a larger garden planting, such as a shopping mall garden, more perlite should be added for improved drainage.

The peat and topsoil mix is considerably heavier than the Cornell mix and both are heavier wet than dry. If the garden is not situated at grade level, this weight can be an important consideration. Figure 4 gives guidelines to be used in estimating the weight of the planting medium.

Planting organization The basic ingredients for a large planting installation are drainage material, planting medium, soil separator, plant material, material-handling equipment, light, water, and labor. Organization of all these ingredients is important since every one must be ready and available for a successful installation. Arrangements for all these factors should be made ahead of time, and they should be ready and waiting when the plants are delivered.

The amount of interior volume in the planters and containers determines the amount of needed drainage material, soil separator, and planting medium. If detailed blueprints are not available, actually measuring the planters is generally a good way to obtain this volume. The relationship between planting medium, drainage material, and soil separator can be determined using the guidelines of the previous subsection. If the plants are to be left in their cans (as generally recommended), the space between the plants is filled with drainage material. If they are removed from their cans, the space between plants is filled with planting medium. In either case, the volume displaced by the plants is simply the sum of the volume contained in the growing cans. Information for each standard size of growing container is given in Fig. 5.

The installation should not be started unless all lights and water connections are operating, as the plants will need both light and water during the installation—especially the light. If the plants are delivered dry, they should be watered in their cans unless they are to be planted at once and watered immediately after planting. If the plants are removed from their cans and placed into dry planting medium, they and the planting medium should be thoroughly watered immediately afterward.

Fewer design mistakes will be made if the plants are installed one section at a time, under the direction of a supervisor familiar with the design of the section. If the installation is in an office building, it may be necessary to arrange for a workroom and a freight elevator with access both to the loading dock and to the workroom. Depending on the exact arrangements, a crew of four to six workers per supervisor is generally optimum.

It is recommended that each section be planted in the following order. First, leftover building material and other debris are removed from the planting areas. Second, drainage material is added to the proper depth and leveled. Third, the plants, either in or out of their growing containers, are placed on top of the drainage material and the soil separator if present, and arranged according to the design. The spaces between the plants are then filled in with drainage material or planting medium, depending on whether the plants are in or out of their growing containers. If planting medium is used, it should be lightly compacted to prevent its settling later. (If the light intensity is below specifications and periodic replacement of the plants is expected, the plants should be left in their cans.)

After the spaces between the large plants have been filled in, the ground cover, if any, is planted. The use of decorative bark or marble chips on top of the soil is not recommended, as they easily mix with the soil and are hard to remove if the plants are replaced.

After all the spaces have been filled, the plants should be thoroughly watered and the maintenance schedule begun. If dry planting medium

PLANTSCAPING
Plant Use and Procedures

Planting Bed Material	Dry Weight	Wet Weight
Cornell foliage mix	12-18 lb/cu ft	25-35 lb/cu ft
Peat/topsoil mix	38-42 lb/cu ft	70-90 lb/cu ft
Topsoil (loam)	80-100 lb/cu ft	100-120 lb/cu ft
Gravel	120-135 lb/cu ft	120-135 lb/cu ft
Sand	95-110 lb/cu ft	120-130 lb/cu ft

Note: For conversion to metric system: 1 lb = 0.454 kg; 1 cu ft = 0.028 cu m.

Fig. 4 Planting material weight. These figures are the normal weight for each of the materials in both the dry and the wet state. The exact weight depends on the degree of compaction of the material

is used, it should be watered thoroughly several times during the first week to ensure that it is completely wet.

Removing plants from cans or burlap A healthy root system is necessary for the maintenance of a healthy plant. It is the new, very fine, feathery roots that are the most important and also the most easily damaged. This damage is very likely if the soil between the fine roots is dislodged in the course of repotting. Whether the tropical plants are delivered in growing cans or with their roots wrapped in burlap, the root system must be handled with care.

The best procedure for removing a plant from its container is to lean the pot on its side, tap on the container sides and bottom, and carefully slide out the plant. In large container-grown plants (in 17-in or larger cans), the root system may be held very tightly in the can. In this case, a can cutter, which works on either metal or rubber cans, may be the most gentle way of removing the can. Once the can is removed, the root ball of soil and roots should be scored by making ¼-in deep vertical cuts at 3-in intervals around the root ball from top to bottom. If the can removal and ball scoring are done near the planting site, the exposed root system is subjected to minimum handling.

Very large plants and trees are frequently field-grown rather than container-grown. The root balls of such plants will come wrapped in burlap. When planting them, only the upper half of the burlap should be removed. The lower portion will disintegrate in the soil after the plant is installed.

Rock formations and decorative pools Natural elements, such as rock formations, decorative pools, water fountains, and waterfalls, can add an artistic touch and turn an unimaginative large planting arrangement into a full garden. Unfortunately the overuse of such design elements is tempting, since they are usually inexpensive compared with the cost of filling the same area with plants. Provided they are not overused, they can serve as natural sculpture or as the answer for areas with too little light to support plants or where conditions limit the variety of plants that can be used.

In rock formations, volcanic rock is the most commonly used type because it is much lighter than ordinary rock. This weight factor can be of considerable importance when the weight of the garden must be limited. This type of rock is also easy to shape with a hammer and chisel.

Pot Size	Soil Volume	Pot Diameter x Height
6 in	1 gal	6½ in x 6 in
8 in	2 gal	8 in x 7 in
10 in	3 gal	10 in x 9½ in
12 in	4 gal	11 in x 10½ in
14 in	7 gal	13½ in x 12 in
17 in	10 gal	17 in x 16 in
22 in	20 gal	21 in x 17 in
30 in	35 gal	29 in x 17 in
32 in	65 gal	32 in x 22 in
36 in	95 gal	36 in x 24 in

Note: For conversion to different units, use the following factors. 1 gal = .00495 cu yd = .0038 cu m = .134 cu ft = 3.79 lit; 1 in = 2.54 cm.

Fig. 5 Pot-size and volume proportions

Although a large decorative pool or fountain must be custom designed, there are small fiberglass pools that can be purchased in a variety of sizes and are available in kidney, free-form, or rectangular shapes. They are usually no longer than 6 ft, but they are of a standard 16-in depth, which is deep enough to accommodate any water plants, recirculating pump, and a filter tray with mat and gravel. Their high-capacity, low-pressure pumps are usually adequate for small fountains and waterfalls.

If decorative pools are used, some thought might be given to using water plants in them. These plants are very attractive and can be easily grown indoors. As with all plants, different species have different growing and flowering habits. A reputable dealer should be consulted for information.

The use of fish in pools should be carefully studied in light of the plant maintenance requirements. Fertilizer, plant chemicals, and limestone runoff from the planting area may enter the circulating water system and kill the fish. Fish can be an attractive design element, but their maintenance requirements must be considered along with the maintenance requirements of the plants.

Open Plan and Specimen Design

Modern offices are sometimes sterile places in which to work. The introduction of live plants into such an environment is one way of making the space seem less austere and more comfortable without disrupting the integrity of the original design. For windowless offices, plants provide an attractive natural setting appreciated by the occupants. For offices and other windowed areas, the plants provide a transition which makes indoors and outdoors seem to flow together.

In all locations, however, the light intensity must be at the proper level before the plants are introduced. The intensity cannot be taken for granted, since artificial lighting designed for office vision is seldom enough for any but the lowest-light plant species. Even a large window will not provide enough light if it has an overhang or a northern exposure. If the light intensity cannot be directly measured or calculated from detailed ceiling plans, one must assume the worst and use only low-light material. There is sometimes a tendency to use plants to fill in otherwise forgotten spots, such as corners, stairwells, and hallways. Such areas are often poorly lit and no plant will survive there unless additional lighting is installed.

In large areas with barely enough light, the usual design problem is how to arrange the limited number of low-light species so that different areas stand out from one another. Design interest can be accomplished by using different types of foliage (for example, fragmented and solid) in the different areas, varying the plant sizes among the areas or using specimen plants selectively.

Specimen plants usually have fuller foliage or an unusual stem structure and hence appear to be different from other plants of that species. The true specimen plants are more expensive than ordinary plants of the same species, but can solve many a design problem. However, a plant with fuller foliage than most will also require more light than most to maintain the foliage.

If the office has floor-to-ceiling walls, the best design procedure is to select specimen plants that act as living sculptures. Since these plants are used for visual emphasis, the plant height and container size should conform to the scale of the rest of the interior design. The plant texture and container finish should blend with each other and with the wall and floor treatments. The particular plant specimen chosen should have an inherently interesting shape and texture.

If the office area is very large or is designed along an "office landscaping" plan with movable partitions, the plants can become an integral part of the design. They can be used with the partitions as space dividers and are excellent for indicating the importance of the space. They also may be effective in relating widely separated areas with one another. They break the monotony of the partitions with both color and texture. They act as sound absorbers. Also, specimen plants can be used in the office landscaping scheme for visual emphasis.

Planting into individual planters Individual decorative containers are used for individual plants or small plant groupings. The plants are left in their growing containers and placed directly into the decorative planter on top of 4 to 6 in of perlite as the drainage material. The decorative planter or container must be tall enough to accommodate the growing can and the perlite, and wide enough to accommodate the width of the growing can. The space between the growing can and the inner wall of the planter can be filled with additional perlite. (See Fig. 2 for size-selection guidance.) As a decorative finishing, bark chips or sheet moss may be placed on the surface of the soil in the growing can. This decorative cover can be easily removed if the plant is replaced and it does not mix with the soil, as sometimes happens in large gardens.

Removing the plant from the growing can and repotting it directly into the planter is not generally recommended. Replacing the plant, if necessary, is a messy job unless drainage material and soil separator are added to the bottom of the container. Also, once removed from its growing container, the plant may take up to four weeks to adjust fully to its new environment.

Plant Containers

Decorative Containers: Different Types

A plant container should be more than decorative. Its proper selection is the first element of proper maintenance, since the container must provide the plant roots with sufficient growing room and with adequate drainage.

All small to medium-size plants are received from the grower in growing containers, usually metal cans or rubber tubs. Large plants are either in large growing containers or their root balls are wrapped in burlap. As a rule, these growing cans provide the proper volume of soil for the size of the plant and have a hole in the bottom for drainage. There is seldom any need to remove the plant from its growing container, especially since rough handling of the root system can shock the plant. Only the smaller plants, such as ivy, can be repotted without much disturbance of the root system. If it is absolutely necessary to repot a larger plant, it should be done carefully, as outlined earlier, and it should be always into a larger volume of soil, never into a smaller volume.

The decorative container should be chosen so that its inside dimensions are large enough that the plant-growing container can be dropped directly into it. In addition, it should be deep enough for the growing container to rest on at least 2 in of perlite or other drainage material, and leave about 1 in between the top of the growing can and the top of the decorative container. Some care must be taken in the choice since the interior dimensions of the decorative container are often not uniformly related to the exterior dimensions. For example, some fiberglass containers have a large lip which limits the size of the growing can that can be dropped directly into them. Also some containers have a large false bottom, which makes the interior depth much less than the outside height.

With these simple size-selection rules in mind, the proper decorative container can be selected using Fig. 6 as a guide. Figure 6 lists the decorative pros and cons of the most common types of containers.

Excess Water in Container

Overwatering of plants is more harmful than underwatering. This problem is most likely to occur when the plants are in individual decorative containers that do not allow the excess water to flow off. To minimize this danger, we have recommended that a plant in a decorative container be double-potted. In the bottom of the decorative container, below the plant growing can, there should be at least 2 in of perlite or other drainage material to act as a reservoir for excess water. Nevertheless, if the plant is continually overwatered, this reservoir will fill up and lead to root rot because the roots are in a pool of water.

Container Type	*Pros*	*Cons*
Fiberglass	Large selection of sizes, shapes, and colors. Light weight, easy to move. Some types have casters. Reasonable prices. Many manufacturers.	Easily scratched. Some types have large lips.
Ceramic	Large selection of sizes, shapes, colors, and textures. Rich appearance. Can be put on casters.	Expensive. Easily broken in shipping and handling.
Metal	Large selection of sizes and styles. Rich appearance. Polished or brushed finish.	Expensive.
Baskets, traditional	Good range of styles and textures. Combines well with all furniture styles. Reasonable prices.	Limited sizes. Tend to sag. Need saucer under plant can to prevent water spillage.
Baskets woven around metal	Good texture range. Reasonable prices. Do not sag. Need no saucers. Combine well with all furniture styles.	Sizes limited.
Plastic	Least expensive. Good for table plants. Versatile.	Available mostly in green or white. Sizes largely limited to standard pot sizes. Need saucers underneath. Cheap appearance.
Hanging planters (Heavy; must be used with a rotating hook which can support the weight and allow for easy plant access.)	Available in ceramic, fiberglass, plastic, and metal. Ceramic in various shapes and textures, metal in various finishes. Plastic and fiberglass are inexpensive. All are versatile.	Makes plants susceptible to drafts from heating and air conditioning. Difficult to water without spilling on floor. Metal very expensive. All need inner pot to allow for drainage. Ceramic is porous and presents condensation problem.

Fig. 6 Comparison of container types

If the plant soil is continually wet to the touch, excess water may be the problem. The water level in the container may be determined by tapping the sides of the container. If the water level indicates excess water, the container is tilted on its side, the plant gently pulled from the container, and the excess water drained from the perlite. If the perlite is completely saturated or appears old, it must be discarded and replaced with new drainage material. If the plant has been sitting in a pool of water for some time, the root ball should be allowed to dry before repotting.

If a very large container or garden has been overwatered and there is no way to drain out the excess water, not really much can be done short of using a small electric pump. One must simply avoid watering the plant or garden at all until the soil has begun to dry out and feels dry to the touch.

Automatic Watering Devices

In areas where regular maintenance would be difficult, the use of automatic watering devices can be of considerable help. Even when they are used, however, the plant must be checked periodically to see that the device is working properly, that its water reservoir is full, and that no other maintenance problems have developed.

Automatic watering devices are either external to the container or are built into the planter. The external devices tend to work well only with small plants, and also, they are likely to detract from the design. For these reasons, the built-in type of device is preferred. The planters with this type come in both cylindrical and rectangular shapes and in several colors. The planter has a hollow space within its double-wall sides, which serves to hold a three- to four-week water supply, feeding the water to the plant soil by a wick mechanism, sensor, or capillary action. Most types have a float to indicate the amount of water remaining in the reservoir.

Since the soil must be in contact with the wick or capillary tubes for the device to work, the plant must be removed from its original growing can and repotted directly in the planter. As the soil never dries out, the plant must be watched for symptoms of overwatering. Because different plants use water at different rates under different humidity and temperature conditions, a timetable should be kept for each container so the maintenance staff will know when to refill each reservoir.

The use of automatic watering devices will not eliminate maintenance personnel, but it will reduce the number of workers needed. One person can handle many more plants, devoting more time to cleaning and trimming, since the reservoir has to be refilled only every month or so. Occasionally, however, one will find a client who will resist the use of the automatic devices because he or she likes the assurance of seeing a person with a watering can once a week.

The use of the automatic watering devices is expected to increase in the future as more architects and designers become aware of them and convince their clients of their usefulness, and as the manufacturers produce more colors and styles and improve the efficiency of the devices.

Design Type	Plant Name	Watering Requirements
HIGH-LIGHT PLANTS—150 FOOTCANDLES AND UP		
T	Fiddle-leaf fig *(Ficus lyrata)*	W
T	Indian laurel *(Ficus retusa)*	W
T	Rubber plant (*Ficus elastica cv.* 'Decora')	W
T	Weeping fig *(Ficus benjamina)*	W
T	Norfolk Island pine *(Araucaria heterophylla)*	LF
T	Schefflera *(Brassaia actinophylla)*	W
FP	Dwarf date palm *(Phoenix Roebelenii)*	LF
FP	Dwarf schefflera *(Brassaia arboricola)*	W
FP	False aralia *(Dizygotheca elegantissima)*	W
FP	Lady palm *(Rhapis excelsa)*	W
FP	Mock orange *(Pittosporum Tobira)*	W
FP	Ponytail *(Beaucarnea recurvata)*	LF
FP	Southern yew (*Podocarpus macrophyllus* var. Maki)	LF
DTP	Jade plant *(Crassula argentea)*	LF
DTP	Swedish ivy *(Plectranthus australis)*	MF
DTP	Wax plant *(Hoya carnosa)*	MF
MEDIUM-LIGHT PLANTS—100 TO 150 FOOTCANDLES		
T	Indian laurel *(Ficus retusa)*	W
T	Schefflera *(Brassaia actinophylla)*	W
T	Weeping fig *(Ficus benjamina)*	W
FP	Bamboo palm *(Chamaedorea erumpens)*	MF
FP	Corn plant (*Dracaena fragrans* cv. 'Massangeana')	W
FP	Dwarf date palm *(Phoenix Roebelenii)*	LF
FP	Dwarf dragon tree *(Dracaena marginata)*	LF
FP	Dwarf schefflera *(Brassaia arboricola)*	W
FP	Green dracaena (*Dracaena deremensis* cv. 'Janet Craig')	W
FP	Green pleomele *(Dracaena reflexa)*	W
FP	Kentia palm *(Howea Forsterana)*	W
FP	Narrow-leaved pleomele *(Dracaena angustifolia honoraii)*	W
FP	Neantha bella palm *(Chamaedorea elegans)*	W
FP	Reed palm *(Chamaedorea Seifrizii)*	MF
FP	Self-heading philodendron *(Philodendron Selloum)*	LF
DTP	Boston fern (*Nephrolepis exaltata* cv. 'Bostoniensis')	W
DTP	Chinese evergreen (*Aglaonema commutatum* var. maculatum)	LF
DTP	Common philodendron *(Philodendron scandens oxycardium)*	W
DTP	Dumb cane (*Dieffenbachia maculata* cv. 'Rudolph Roehrs')	LF
DTP	Golden pothos *(Epipremnum aureum)*	LF
DTP	Grape ivy *(Cissus rhombifolia)*	W
DTP	Prayer plant *(Maranta leuconeura)*	W
DTP	Swedish ivy *(Plectranthus australis)*	W
DTP	White flag (*Spathiphyllum* cv. 'Clevelandii')	W
DTP	White-striped dracaena (*Dracaena deremensis* cv. 'Warneckii')	W
LOW-LIGHT PLANTS—50 TO 100 FOOTCANDLES		
FP	Corn plant (*Dracaena fragrans* cv. 'Massangeana')	W
FP	Dwarf dragon tree *(Dracaena marginata)*	LF
FP	Green dracaena (*Dracaena deremensis* cv. 'Janet Craig')	W
FP	Green pleomele *(Dracaena reflexa)*	W
FP	Kentia palm *(Howea Forsterana)*	W
FP	Neantha bella palm *(Chamaedorea elegans)*	W
FP	Reed palm *(Chamaedorea Seifrizii)*	W
FP	Self-heading philodendron *(Philodendron Selloum)*	W
DTP	Chinese evergreen (*Aglaonema commutatum* var. maculatum)	LF
DTP	Common philodendron *(Philodendron scandens oxycardium)*	W
DTP	White Flag (*Spathiphyllum* cv. 'Clevelandii')	W

A Final Word about Lighting Intensity The preceding lighting-intensity recommendations are based on experience and the assumption that these levels will be provided eight hours a day, five days a week, and that the plants have been fully acclimatized. If light can be provided for more hours each day or more days each week, the plant material will look its best for longer periods. On the other hand, often the energy costs of the longer lighting exposure are more than the costs of plant replacement. However, if the plants are not to be maintained by the landscape contractor with a plant replacement guarantee, provision should be made for giving the plants light exposure seven days a week.

Fig. 7 Growing requirements. Design type: T = tree; FP = floor plant; DTP = desk or table plant or ground cover. Watering requirements: W = water weekly; MF = water more frequently, as required; LF = water less frequently, as required

PLANTSCAPING
Typical Plants

(False) Aralia

The aralia is a plant of grace and elegance with narrow, ribbonlike, notched leaves of dark green, usually borne on slender, single stems. The aralia is attractive if two or three plants are planted together in one pot. It grows very quickly, so prune the stem tips from time to time to prevent the foliage from thinning at the bottom.

Temperature

The aralia is tolerant of warm temperatures if there is plenty of humidity.

Light/Sun

The plant likes a semisunny to semishady window; an east or west window is ideal.

Water/Humidity

Keep the soil damp but not soggy. The false aralia likes a humid atmosphere. Place your plant on a pebble tray and mist the foliage daily.

Soil

The soil should be equal parts loam, sand, and peat moss.

Special care

You can rejuvenate leggy plants by drastically cutting the stems back to four to six in from the pot. Do this in the spring and leave the plant in a sheltered location, being sure to fertilize and water frequently.

African Violet

The African violet, a longtime favorite houseplant, does insist on more care and attention, but its beautiful blossoms make the effort worthwhile.

Temperature

African violets are more contented and grow best within a temperature range of 65 to 80 degrees. Be careful that your plants are not in an open window or a draft.

Light/Sun

The African violet enjoys a place in an east or west window. Direct sun is too strong, unless filtered through a curtain. Excess sun will cause spotting and loss of color, and too little light causes elongated stems and no blooms.

Water/Humidity

African violets should be watered from the saucer underneath in the morning with *lukewarm* water. Water when the soil begins to dry out. Do not keep it soggy. If the air is dry in your home, place the potted plant in a tray of moistened pebbles.

Soil

The soil should be porous for good drainage and should contain ample organic matter such as compost or peat moss. Commercial African violet soil mixture is specially prepared for these plants; however, add sand or perlite to ensure adequate drainage. A plastic pot is less likely to cause the lower leaves to rot where they touch the pot.

Asparagus Fern—Emerald Feather

The bright feathery green of this delightful plant is best displayed in a hanging container. The long branches drape gracefully and are studded with tiny white flowers that ripen into red-orange berries.

Temperature

Asparagus fern is not fussy about temperatures, but prefers a range of 60 to 68 degrees.

Light/Sun

The bright filtered sun of an east or west window is a good location for this plant.

Water/Humidity

Soak the soil in the pot thoroughly and allow it to become dry to the touch before rewatering.

Soil

Use a well-drained potting soil or a mixture of equal parts of loam, peat moss, and sand or perlite.

How to Start New Plants

Allow the berries to ripen and when dry sow the seeds they contain. Asparagus fern can usually be grown from seed quite well.

Avocado

The avocado comes easily from seed and is grown for its ornamental foliage. It makes a nice tree for your indoor garden. Allow the plant to reach the desired height and then begin regular pinching to force branching and encourage bushy growth.

Temperature

Temperatures between 60 and 70 degrees suit the avocado well.

Light/Sun

Keep your avocado in bright light but protected from direct sun. Avocados are easily sunburned, especially when they are first moved outside.

Water/Humidity

Use tepid water and keep the soil moist. Place the plant on a pebble tray to raise the humidity level around it. This plant likes a fair amount of humidity and benefits from regular misting. Any sign of

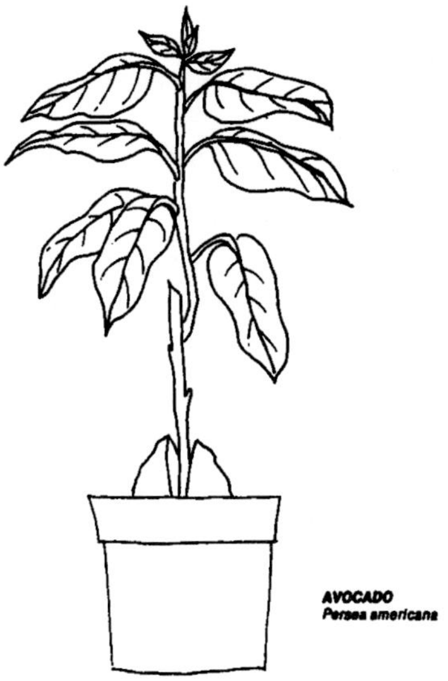

browning or crispness at the tips and along the edges of the leaves means the plant needs more humidity.

Soil

Use a mixture consisting of equal parts of sand, loam, and peat moss.

Boston Fern

Exultant is a good adjective for this family of ferns that can fill a corner with rich green foliage. These ferns are excellent for hanging baskets. Initially the ferns may need a lot of attention until the right combination of environmental factors is achieved, but the effort is well worth it. The leaflets grow on a midrib that is covered with fine brown hairs and vary from smooth-edged to feathery and even ruffled. A mature fern can have fronds ranging in length from 2 to 3 ft and 2 to 3 in across.

Temperature

With lots and lots of humidity, ferns will do well in house temperatures in the 60- to 70-degree range.

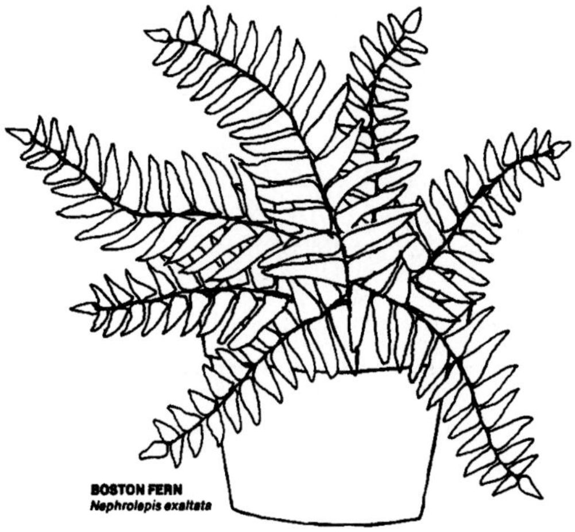

PLANTSCAPING
Typical Plants

Light/Sun

Ferns need a location with good, bright light, but this means filtered sunlight. *Avoid direct sunlight.*

Water/Humidity

It is essential that the roots of the ferns never dry out at any time. Soak the soil regularly. Clay pots and hanging baskets can be soaked in a bucket or the sink for half an hour and then drained. The soil should be checked daily to make sure that it is not drying out. Humidity is the most important ingredient to successful fern growing. Place pots of ferns on a pebble tray. Mist the foliage daily with room temperature water.

Soil

Ferns need a soil that is loose and easily penetrated by their dense root system. The soil mixture should be rich in peat moss and organic matter with a liberal amount of sand for drainage. A sprinkling of charcoal mixed in the soil helps to keep the soil from becoming sour from the frequent waterings. When potting ferns, place a layer of bits of broken pots or gravel in the bottom of the pot. Ferns do not take kindly to having their roots tampered with, so be careful not to damage them when repotting.

Chinese Evergreen

This beautiful foliage plant has waxy dark green leaves. The leaves grow on a canelike stem and are oblong, tapering to a thin tip. Some of the varieties are variegated with splashes of creamy white or yellow. Under optimal conditions, it will produce a flower spike surrounded by a white spathe. The flower is similar to a calla lily. The great thing about this plant is that it will adapt to a variety of environments, which makes it a good plant for a beginner or a difficult location.

Temperature

A range of 60 to 70 degrees suits this plant well.

Light/Sun

A shady spot, an artificial light, or any other location will suit this plant. The Chinese evergreen is an excellent plant for a north window.

Water/Humidity

Keep the soil moist but not soggy. To avoid waterlogged soil, allow the surface soil to become dry to the touch before rewatering. The Chinese evergreen can be grown in water. The roots are attractive, so a clear glass container shows them off to best advantage. It is important to wash the leaves regularly to keep them dust free.

Soil

The soil should be equal parts of garden loam, peat moss, and sand.

Dracaenas

There are several varieties of dracaenas, which vary in foliage color, variegation, and size. Here are three that are commonly available.

Dracaena deremensis "Warneckei" is a good choice for a location without much light. The gray-green foliage is striped with white and gray.

Dracaena marginata has clusters of narrow deep green leaves edged with red, and gray stems strongly marked with leaf scars. This variety will reach a height of 5 or 6 ft.

Dracaena sanderiana resembles a corn plant in the brightness of the green and the size and shape of the leaves, with the difference that the leaves are striped with white.

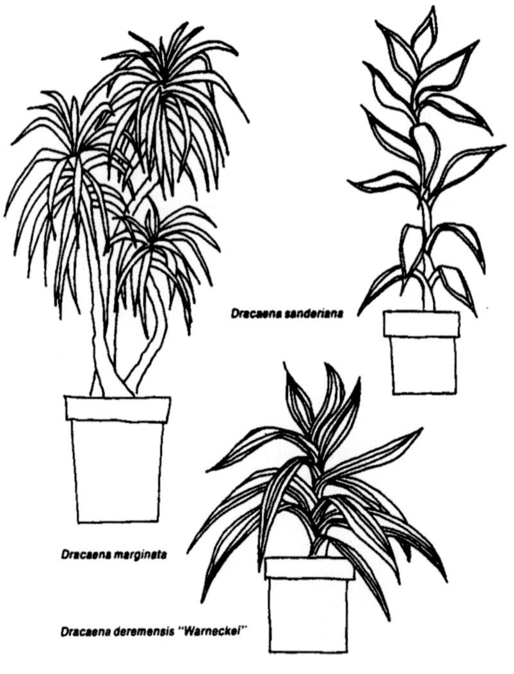

Temperature

Moderate household temperatures in the 60- to 70-degree range suit these plants best. It is important to keep plants away from heating vents.

Light/Sun

The marginata and sanderiana should get only filtered sun or bright light. The Warneckei will fare well in a spot with very little light; it will flourish when more light is available.

Water/Humidity

These plants all like soil that is kept evenly moist but not soggy. Soak the soil in the pot thoroughly and then rewater when the soil surface feels dry to the touch. Humidity is a must. Brown, crispy leaf tips and margins mean too little moisture in the air. It is a good idea to place the dracaenas in pebble trays and mist the foliage daily.

Soil

Commercial potting soil is adequate, but added drainage material such as sand or perlite is advisable.

Dumb Cane

The cool-looking foliage of this plant is yellow-green, mottled with white. The leaves are pointed ovals that become quite large as the plant matures. The dieffenbachia is known as the mother-in-law plant or dumb cane because when a piece of the stem is placed on the tongue it causes temporary numbness and loss of speech. All joking aside, *this plant is poisonous.*

Temperature

The dieffenbachia prefers warm temperatures and will tolerate hot, dry places with added humidity.

Light/Sun

This plant does well in an east or west window where it can bask in the sun for a few hours.

Water/Humidity

The soil should be allowed to dry out for a few days before rewatering. The plants indicate a need for water when the leaves show signs of dropping. Regular misting keeps the foliage dust free and luxuriant.

Soil

A porous soil of equal parts loam, peat moss, and sand is fine.

Gardenia

The gardenia is a handsome foliage plant with intensely fragrant blooms, but it has an extremely temperamental nature. It is a challenging plant to grow successfully indoors. The most frequently available varieties are *Gardenia radicans floraplena,* a low spreading plant with small double flowers, and *Gardenia florida,* which blooms in summer.

Temperature

The temperature must be kept above 65 degrees to maintain healthy foliage and flower buds. These plants hate drafts. Loss of flower buds is often due to sudden changes in temperature.

Light/Sun

The gardenia needs lots of light, but avoid strong sun that might burn the leaves.

Water/Humidity

The soil must be kept constantly moist without becoming soggy. Submerge the pot in a bucket of lukewarm water and allow it to soak for half an hour or until the soil is moist on the surface. Do not allow the pot to sit in water, as that will cause the roots to rot. Gardenias need very high humidity at all times. Place the pot in a tray of moistened pebbles. Mist the foliage daily with tepid water. Leaf or bud drops indicate the air is too dry.

Soil

Potting soil should be a mixture of equal parts peat moss, loam, and well-decayed manure, with sand or perlite added for drainage.

DUMB CANE
Dieffenbachia maculata

GARDENIA
Gardenia radicans floraplena

PLANTSCAPING
Typical Plants

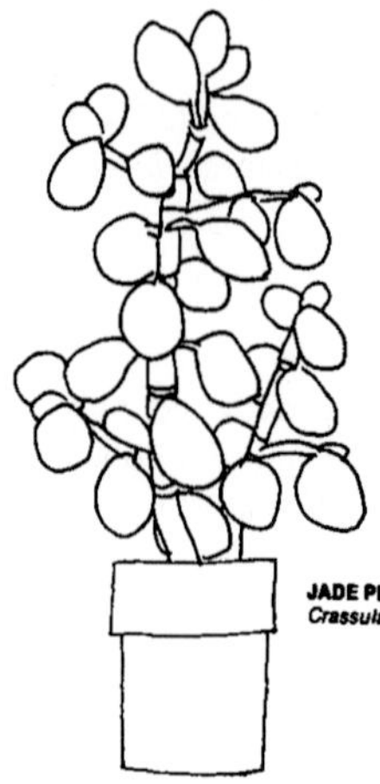

Grape Ivy

Grape ivy is a climber or trailer. The olive-colored green leaves look a bit like those of holly without the stiffness of the sharp tips. The leaves form attractive groups of three and are accompanied by furry tendrils.

Temperature

The plant is fairly tolerant of a wide temperature range. Increase the amount of humidity as the temperature goes up.

Light/Sun

Grape ivy will do all right in low light and is often used in low-light areas. But it flourishes with bright light or filtered sunlight.

Water/Humidity

Soak the pot and soil thoroughly and then allow the soil to become dry to the touch before rewatering. Mist frequently and wash the foliage regularly to remove dust and restore the luster of the leaves.

Soil

A potting soil that is rich in organic matter is the best. Be sure to add plenty of drainage material to the soil mixture.

Jade Plant

The jade plant is a tough plant well-suited to the hot, dry conditions so prevalent in office and apartment buildings. The rounded leaves are in pairs on the branched, treelike stem. A plant that is six to eight years old will produce clusters of lacy-looking, star-shaped flowers.

Temperature

Temperatures ranging from 65 to 75 degrees are fine. Lower and higher temperature will be tolerated.

Light/Sun

The jade plant will require full sunlight, with shade at midday if possible. A west or south window would be a good location. If you put the plant outside in the summer, place it in a lightly shaded spot.

Water/Humidity

The soil should remain dry for several days between waterings. The fleshy leaves soak up the soil water and store it for future use. Too much water will cause stem and root rot and certain death.

Soil

The jade plant will do well in rich garden soil that has coarse sand or fine bits of broken pots added to it for drainage. Each year give the pot a top dressing of humus. A new pot will be necessary only after about three or four years.

Norfolk Island Pine

The delightful symmetry of this evergreen makes it a desirable houseplant. The branches grow in tiers of six, each tier representing a year's growth. The bright green needles are soft and pleasant to touch.

Temperature

The ideal temperature is between 50 and 60 degrees. High temperatures are tolerated when sufficient humidity is available.

Light/Sun

The filtered sun of an east or west window is best. Yellowing of the needles might mean too much sun.

Water/Humidity

Provide the plant with a well-drained soil and pot. Water thoroughly and allow the soil surface to become dry before rewatering. Daily misting is necessary for the warmer temperatures of most houses and offices. A pebble tray will help to add more moisture to the air around the plant.

Soil

Garden loam mixed with equal parts of sand and peat moss makes a suitable potting mixture. Repot the Norfolk Island pine only when it has become pot-bound (the pot is crammed with roots). This would be about every two or three years.

Parlor Palm

The palm trees are not the easiest plants to grow. However, once you have discovered their basic needs, they are a delightful addition to your indoor garden. This palm grows to about 4 ft tall. It is most attractive when two or three plants are grouped together in a pot. The long feathery fronds grow out of a single stem. Other varieties to try are *C. seifrizii, C. erumpens,* and *C. costarincana.*

Temperature

The best growing temperatures for palms range between 60 and 75 degrees.

Light/Sun

Palms are good plants for locations without much light. They do not like direct sunlight.

Water/Humidity

During the active growing season, between March and October, the palm needs moist soil, but it will not tolerate soggy soil. In the winter months, allow the soil to dry on the surface before rewatering. If the foliage shows signs of browning and drying on the tips, it needs more humidity. Misting regularly is recommended to keep the foliage healthy.

Soil

The palm needs well-drained soil of equal parts rich garden loam, peat moss, and sand. It will need repotting only every two or three years. It prefers being a bit pot-bound.

Philodendron

By nature, the philodendron is a climbing plant, but it also trails. It looks best on a bracket beside the window frame, and for good effect must be kept strongly pinched back so that the plant is full of bushy young growth and does not deteriorate into two or three stringlike stems.

Temperature

Normal house or office temperatures are fine.

Light/Sun

The philodendron is quite hardy and robust and will grow almost anywhere. However, it will fare better in a well-lighted area.

Water/Humidity

The plant should be kept evenly moist and never allowed to dry out. Be certain water does not remain in the saucer after watering. The foliage should be misted daily and the leaves cleaned of accumulated dust.

Soil

Potting soil mixed with perlite, vermiculite, or sand and peat moss is recommended.

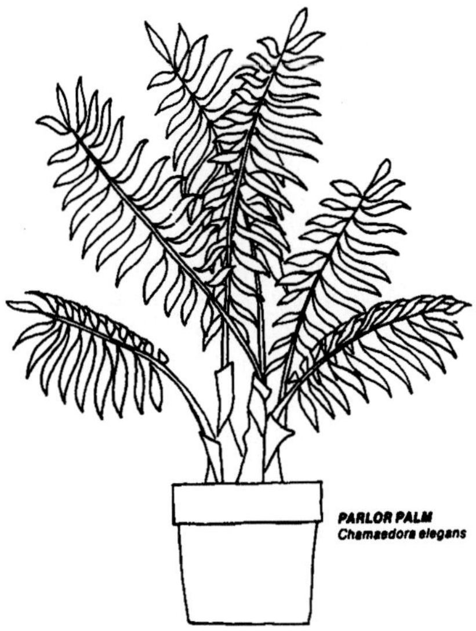

PARLOR PALM
Chamaedora elegans

COMMON PHILODENDRON
Philodendron oxycardium

PLANTSCAPING
Typical Plants

Windowleaf Philodendron

This philodendron has large, heart-shaped leaves that are slashed irregularly. It is an enthusiastic climber and needs a piece of bark or totem for support. The aerial roots can be inserted in the soil or encouraged to attach to the totem. Keep the growing tips pinched back so that the plant doesn't get leggy.

Temperature

The windowleaf prefers temperatures between 65 and 70 degrees.

Light/Sun

Bright light is best for this plant. However, avoid putting the plant in a location where the plant would get direct sun.

Water/Humidity

Soak the plant thoroughly and allow the soil surface to remain dry for a day or two before rewatering. Mist the foliage daily and wash the leaves weekly to remove dust.

Soil

A soil mixture of equal parts garden loam, peat moss, and sand is fine.

Purple Passion Plant—Velvet Plant

The strikingly rich royal purple coloring and velvety texture of the foliage and stems attract many growers. The green leaves and stems are covered with tiny purple hairs. The straggly growth habit is best kept in check by frequent prunning.

Temperature

The purple passion plant likes temperatures in the 65- to 70-degree range.

Light/Sun

Direct or partial sun will promote the color.

Water/Humidity

It is important that the velvet plant not dry out. Keep the soil evenly moist at all times. A humid atmosphere is important to keep the brilliant color. Mist the foliage frequently and place the pot in a tray of moistened pebbles to raise the humidity.

Soil

Use potting soil of equal parts garden loam, peat moss, and sand. This plant will also grow in water.

Rubber Tree Plant

This houseplant with dark green glossy leaves can grow to be 4 ft high with a little care and not too much water.

Temperature

Due to its hardy nature, the plant does well in any normal household temperature.

Light/Sun

The plant will do well in almost any light, but a well-lighted area is best for the rich green foliage characteristic of the rubber tree plant.

Water/Humidity

Water only when the soil is completely dry all through the pot. You should set the entire pot in a bucket when watering, so that moisture can penetrate the deepest roots. Clean the leaves every two weeks or so with a damp cloth. Do not artificially shine the leaves, as this clogs the plant's pores and does not allow it to breathe!

Soil

Soil should be a well-drained mixture of equal parts of sand, peat moss, and garden loam. If pot is plastic or rubber, be sure to provide plenty of drainage material in the bottom of the pot.

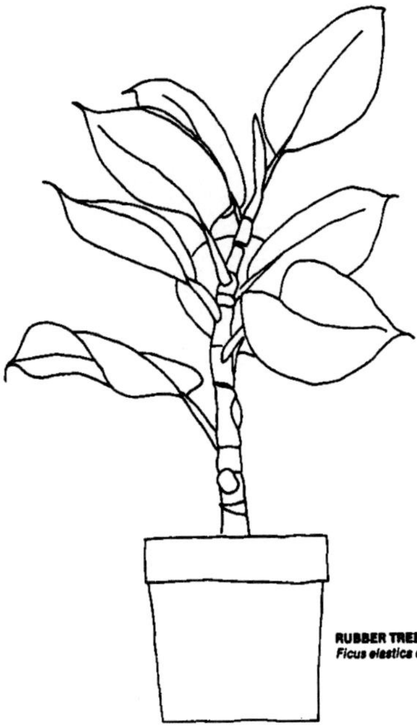

RUBBER TREE PLANT
Ficus elastica decora

Wandering Jew

This is a particularly attractive hanging plant. It is hardy and easy to grow, with only one special requirement, which is regular pinching to keep it full and bushy. There are several plants called Wandering Jew, distinguished from each other by their different colorings and markings. The illustration shows a *Zebrina pendula.* The leaf is a pointed oval with a deep purple underside, and the upperside is dark green striped with pale silvery green. *Tradescantia fluminensis* has small oval green leaves marked with white, silver and white, or yellow.

Temperature

These plants prefer warm temperatures.

Light/Sun

Bright indirect sunlight keeps the foliage brilliant. Avoid direct sunlight, as they are susceptible to sunburn.

WANDERING JEW
Zebrina pendula

Water/Humidity

Water generously, keeping the soil moist at all times. During the winter months, it will not need quite as much water.

Soil

This plant grows in a well-drained potting soil or water.

Schefflera—Umbrella Tree

If you are looking for a tree for your indoor garden, a schefflera is a good choice. It has handsome deep green leaves that radiate out from a long, slender stalk rather like the ribs of an umbrella.

Temperature

The umbrella tree does well in a room where the temperature ranges from 55 to 75 degrees.

Light/Sun

The schefflera does not like direct sunlight. It grows best in good light from a shaded window.

Water/Humidity

When watering your schefflera, soak the pot thoroughly and then allow the soil to dry before rewatering. The plant likes a humid atmosphere and responds well to daily misting with warm water. This is essential if the plant is in a room with forced hot air heat. This plant needs a pebble tray.

Soil

The soil mixture for the umbrella tree should be equal parts of peat moss, garden soil, and sand. The pot should have a layer of gravel or bits of broken pots underneath the soil to ensure good drainage.

SCHEFFLERA - UMBRELLA TREE
Schefflera venulosa

PLANTSCAPING
Typical Plants

Snake Plant

Seen in many homes and offices, this spikey, banded plant will take almost any abuse.

Temperature

Normal household temperatures are best, *but* do not allow the plant to become suddenly chilled!

Light/Sun

The snake plant is a good low-light plant but needs sun in order to bloom.

Water

The plant likes the dryness of the home and should never be overwatered. The leaves should be cleaned with clear water every two weeks.

Soil

Garden loam, peat moss, and sand mixed together provide the best soil for the snake plant.

Spider Plant

With its green and white foliage, the spider plant makes one of the best hanging plants. The graceful trailing runners have plantlets and white, star-shaped flowers. There are all-green varieties, but the more commonly seen one has a green leaf striped with white.

Temperature

The plant lives best in a warm location.

Light/Sun

This lovely plant does very well hanging in indirect sun or a moderately lighted area.

Water/Humidity

The spider plant should be allowed to dry out before rewatering. Drying leaf tips usually indicate lack of humidity. To tidy up the plant, just snip these off.

Soil

The plant grows contentedly in a rich soil composed of garden loam, sand, and peat moss.

Zebra Plant

The zebra plant is one of the showiest houseplants one can grow. Its spike of waxy yellow flowers and deep shiny green leaves veined in white makes it a striking specimen.

Temperature

The zebra plant needs warm temperatures free from drafts.

Light/Sun

The plant wants bright light but not direct sunlight.

Water/Humidity

It is important never to allow the soil to dry out. Set the pot in a pebble tray and mist the foliage daily.

Soil

The zebra plant likes loose soil consisting of one part garden loam, one part sand or perlite, and two parts peat moss.

PLANTING DETAIL

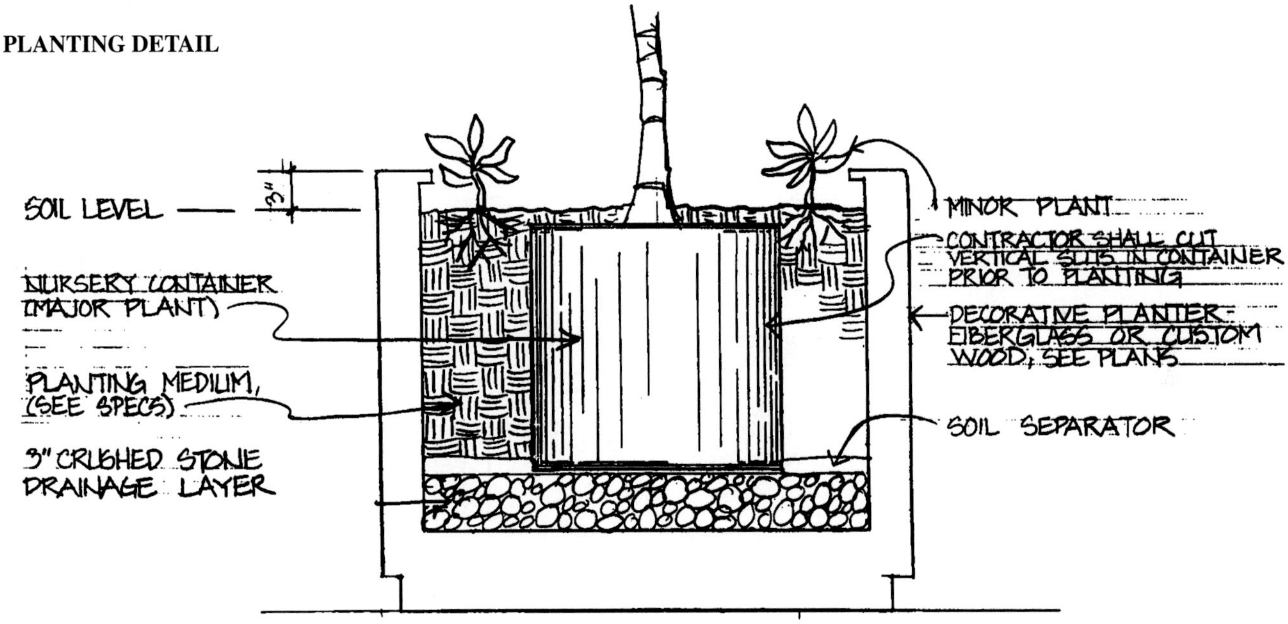

PLANTSCAPING

Planting Standards and Details

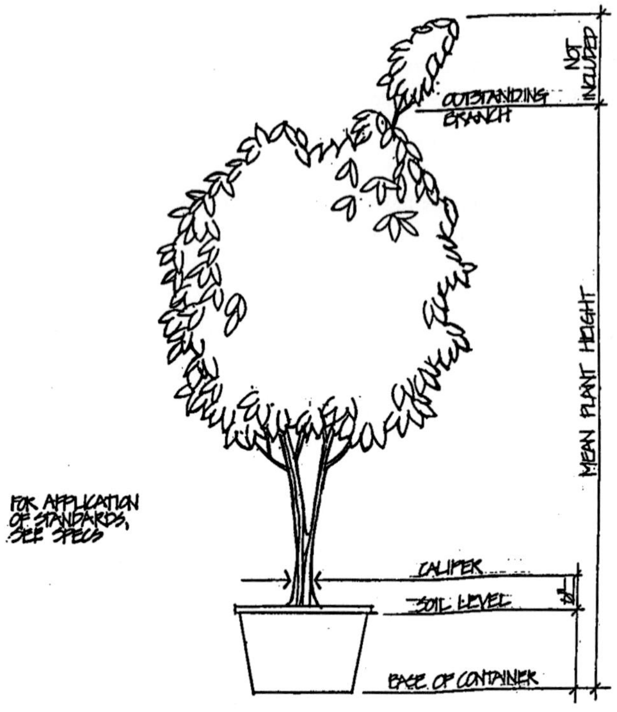

(1) PLANT STANDARDS: OVERALL PLANT HEIGHT
NOT TO SCALE

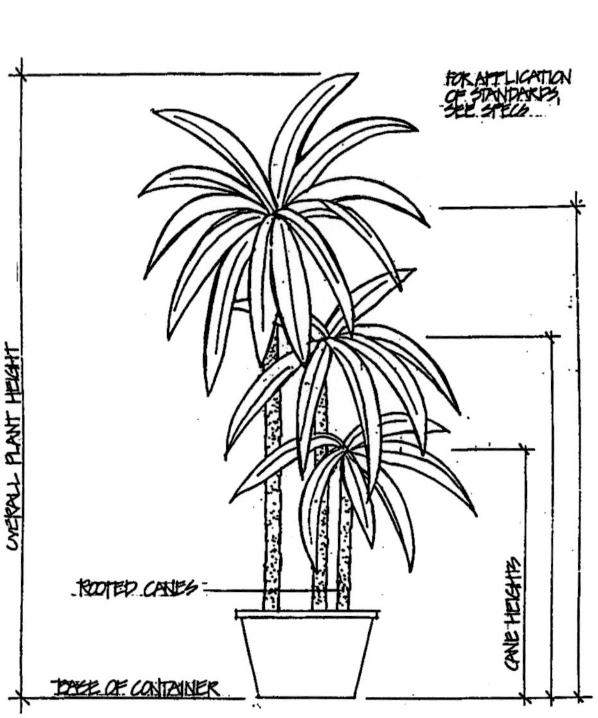

(2) PLANT STANDARDS: CANE HEIGHT
NOT TO SCALE

THIS DETAIL APPLIES TO ALL SHRUBS OVER 5' HIGH

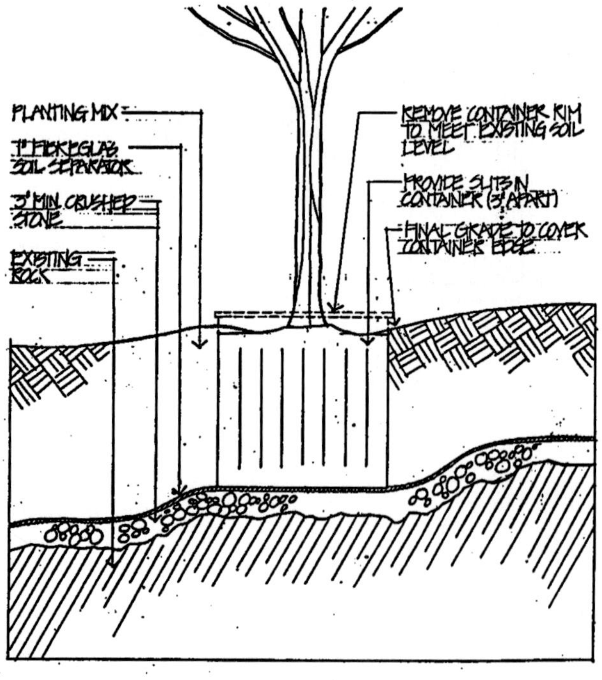

(3) TREE PLANTING DETAIL
NOT TO SCALE

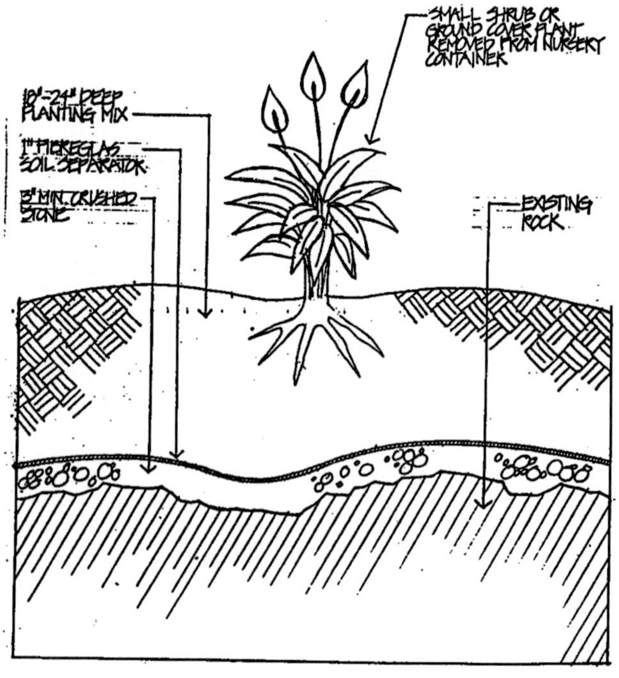

(4) SHRUB PLANTING DETAIL
NOT TO SCALE

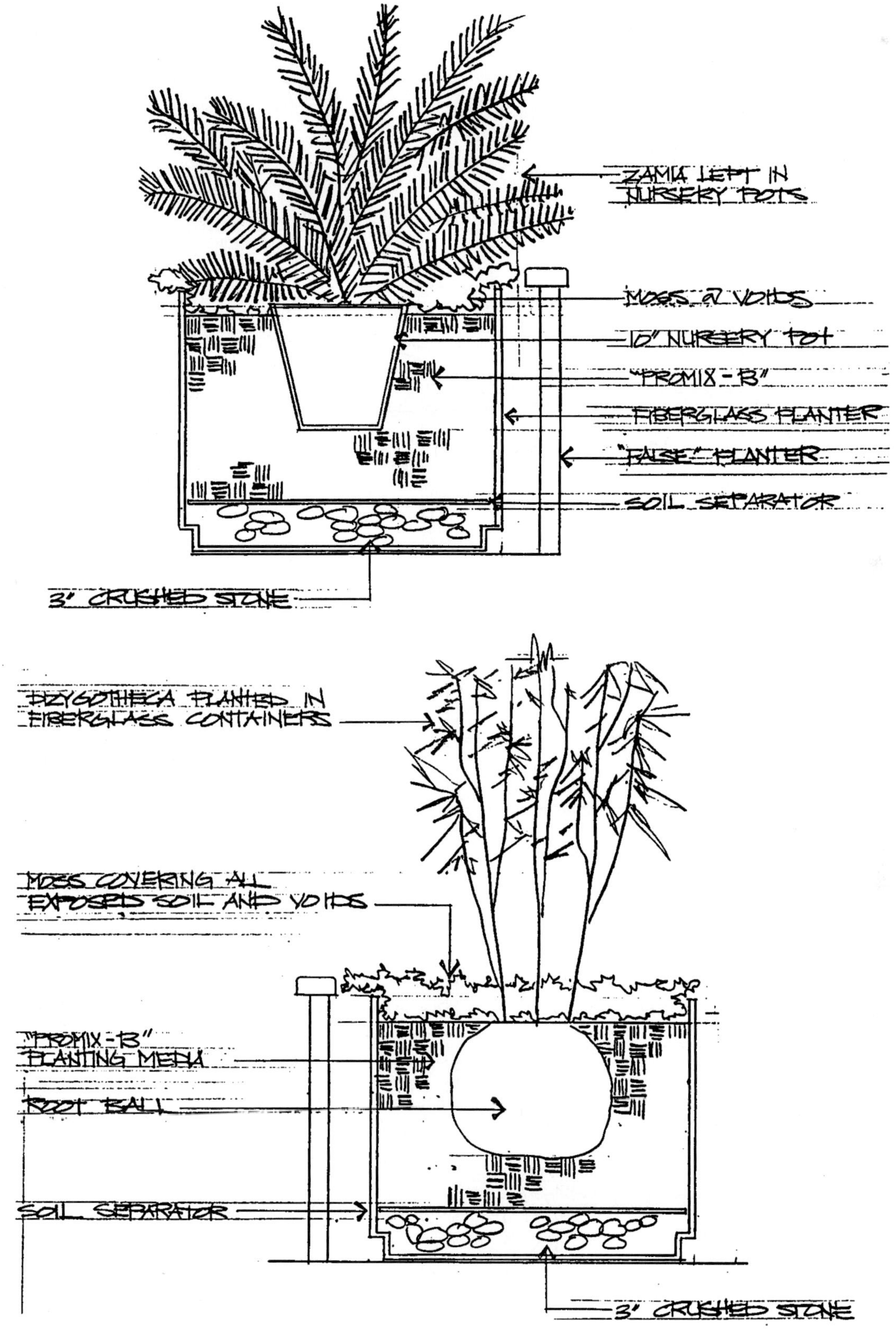

PLANTING DETAIL IN "FALSE" PLANTER

PLANTSCAPING

Plant Containers

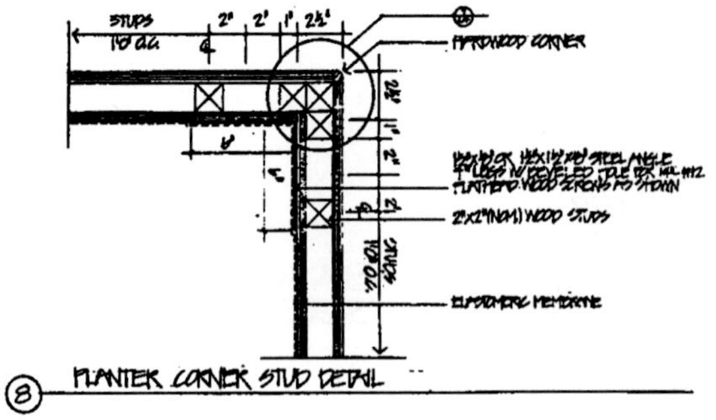

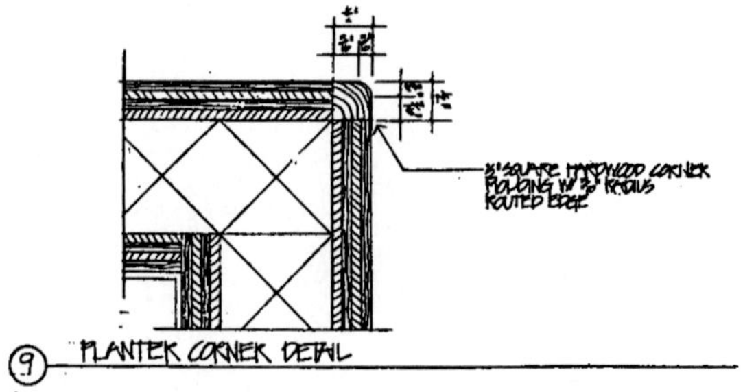

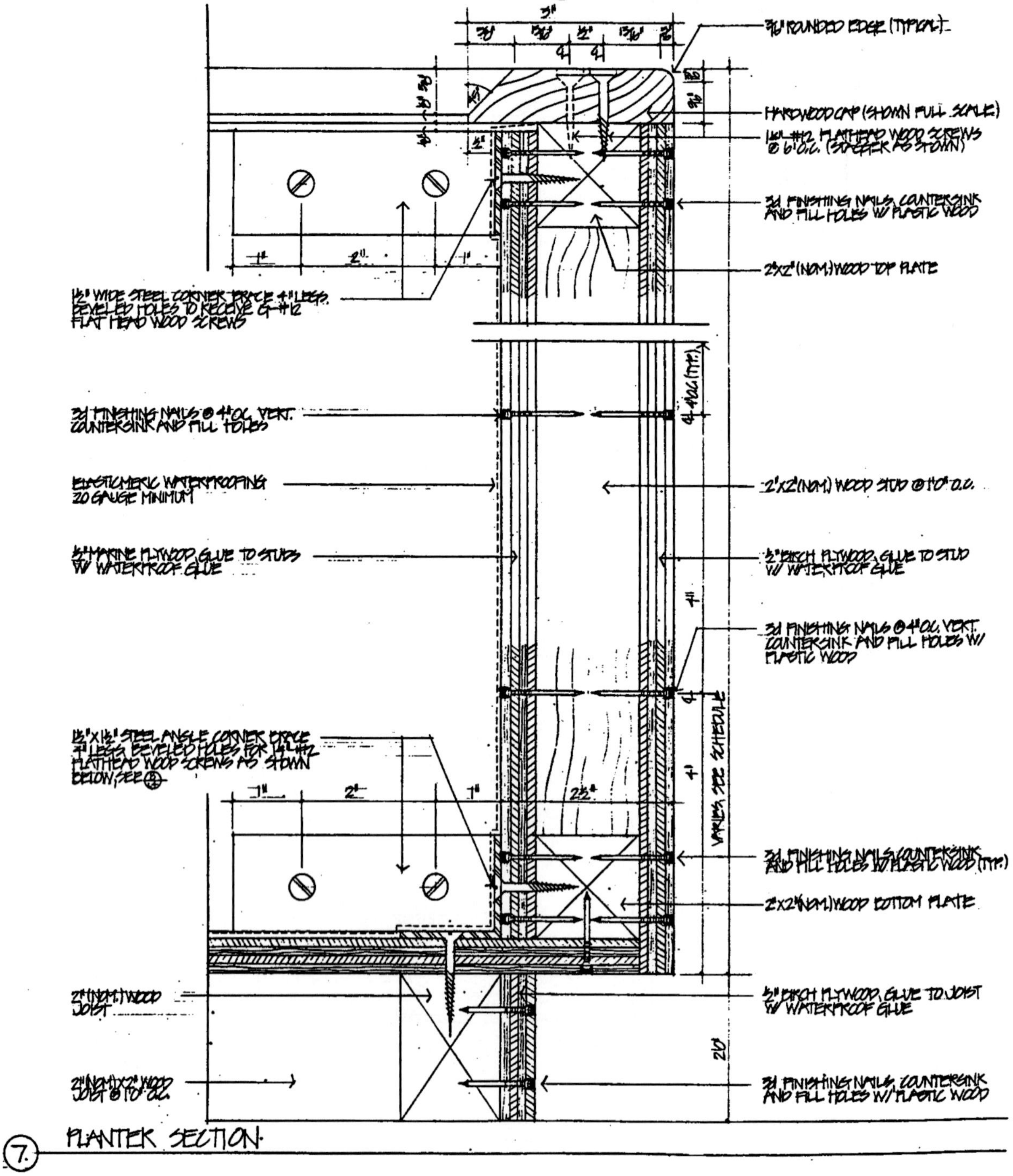

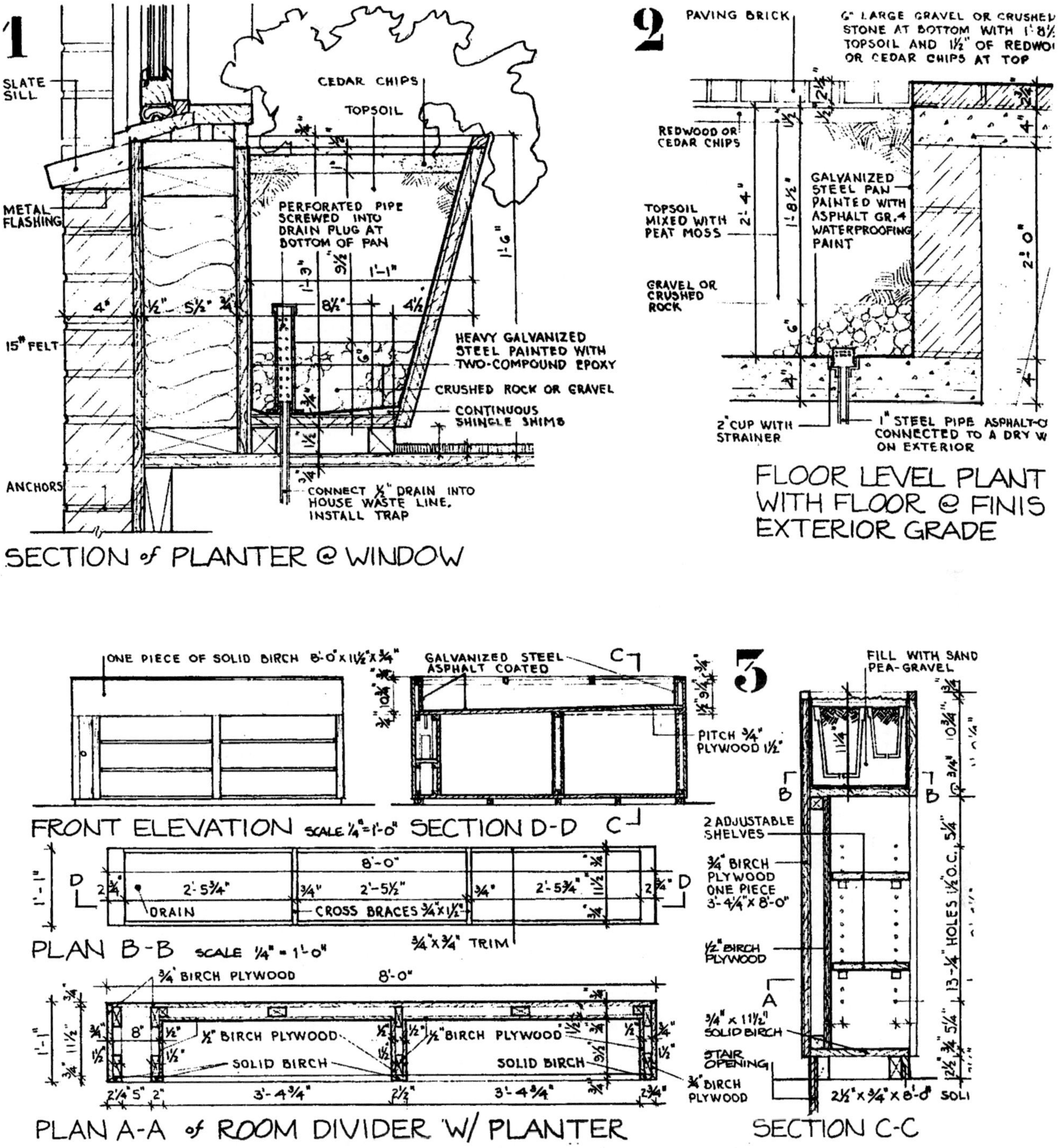

Fig. 8 Detail 1: In this window planter, the plants are placed directly in the earth or growing medium filling the planter and continue to grow and blossom there. The entire planter is contained within a galvanized steel pan with drain. The 6-in-high perforated pipe allows for drainage of excess water over a long period of time before the entire planter has to be cleaned out and started anew. Detail 2: This is a simple floor-level planter where the drainage can easily be connected to the building's drainage system. Here also, plants are installed and grow naturally until a complete planting change is required. Detail 3: A room divider planter for the Ackermann residence, Southampton, New York, consists of a planter-bookcase combination. Here the plants remain in their clay pots and are inserted in the planter with or without gravel or some other type of filler. The entire planter is pitched toward one end, where the drain empties into a small container, which catches any extra water

PLANTSCAPING

Planters

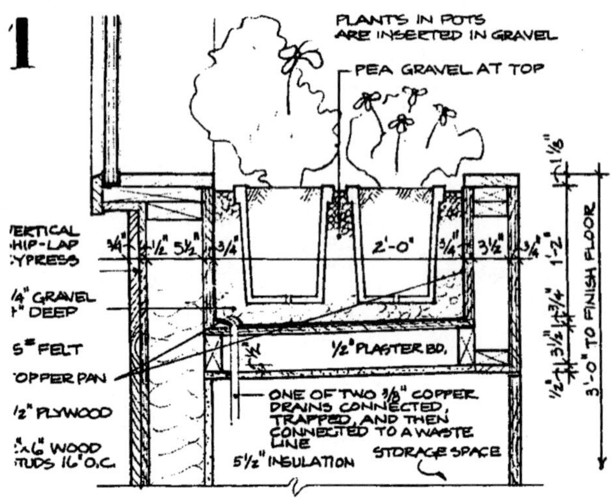

Section of window planter in a south wall

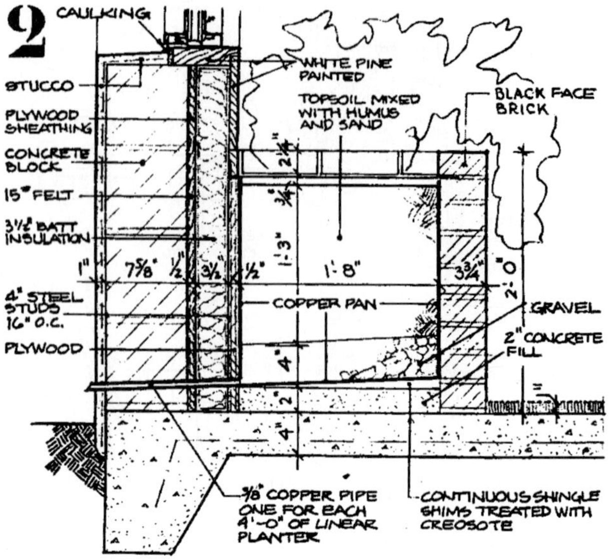

Planter for a warm climate

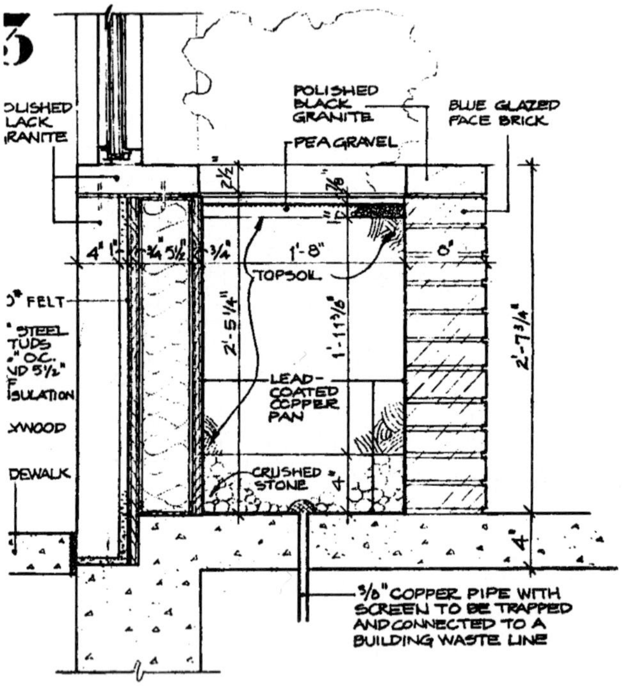

Planter for a restaurant or store

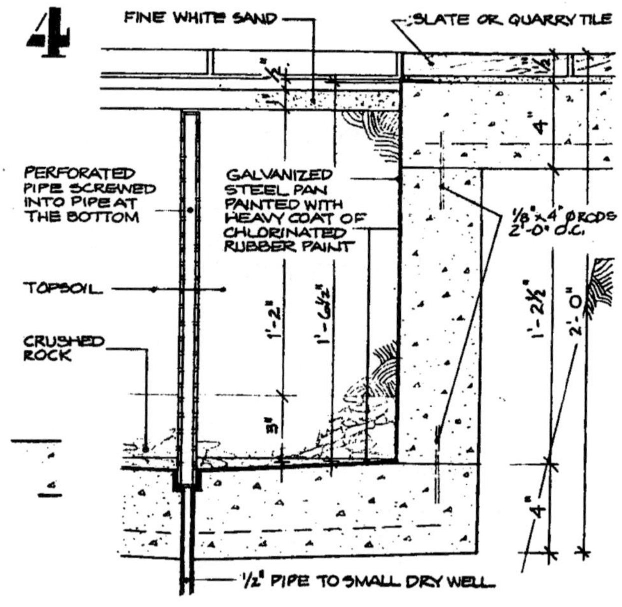

Floor planter

Fig. 9 Detail 1: The plants remain in their own clay pots. The use of pea gravel at top and only 4 in of ¾-in gravel at bottom permits easy changes of the plants. To take care of watering and drainage, the copper pan is simply sloped to one side and two screened drains are connected, trapped, and joined to a waste line. This takes care of any excess water, as it is eliminated by gravity drainage. Detail 2: This planter is for areas where freezing does not occur, and the drainage of excess water can be taken care of by simply extending small pipes directly to the exterior. Detail 3: In this planter the plants remain within the planter and excess water is carried off by a screened pipe at the bottom. Pea gravel is used as a 1-in topping so that odds and ends dropped into the planter can easily be removed. Detail 4: A planter in a commercial lobby or entrance is shown in this detail. The plants are permanently installed and the tall drainage pipe takes care of any top-applied water. The white sand at the top is to bring contrast to the colors of the plants

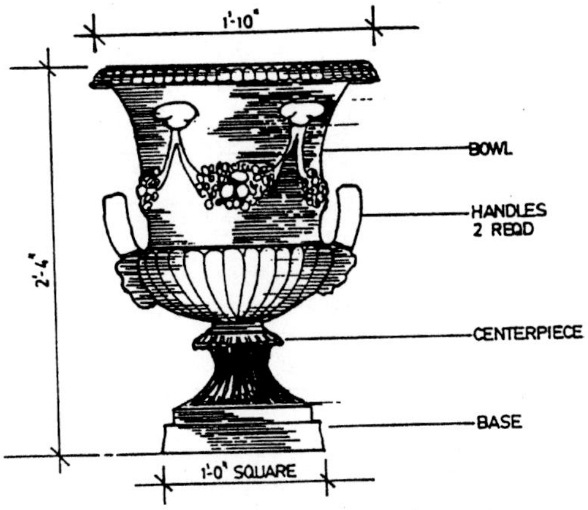
1'-10"
BOWL
HANDLES
2 REQD
2'-4"
CENTERPIECE
BASE
1'-0" SQUARE

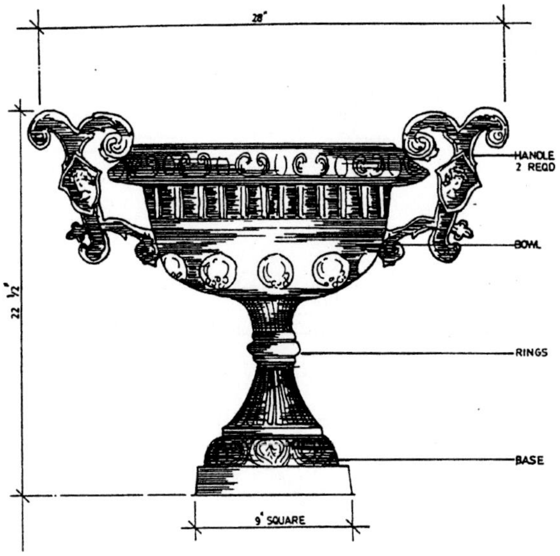
28"
HANDLE
2 REQD
BOWL
22 1/2"
RINGS
BASE
9" SQUARE

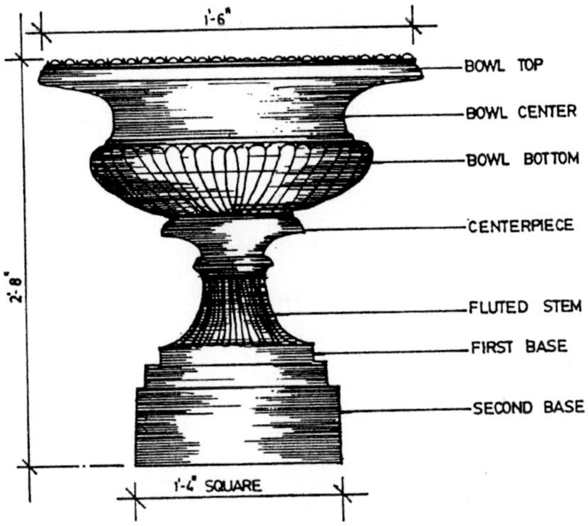
1'-6"
BOWL TOP
BOWL CENTER
BOWL BOTTOM
CENTERPIECE
2'-8"
FLUTED STEM
FIRST BASE
SECOND BASE
1'-4" SQUARE

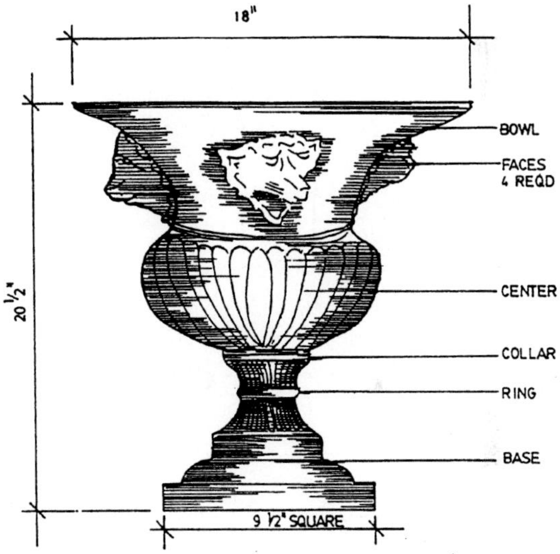
18"
BOWL
FACES
4 REQD
20 1/2"
CENTER
COLLAR
RING
BASE
9 1/2" SQUARE

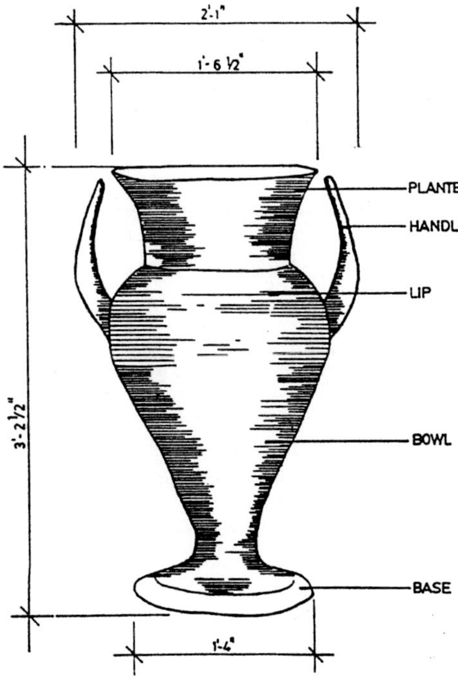
2'-1"
1'-6 1/2"
PLANTER
HANDLE
LIP
3'-2 1/2"
BOWL
BASE
1'-4"

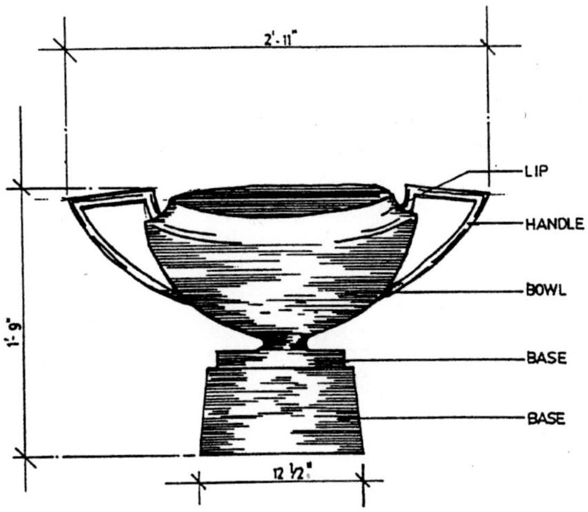
2'-11"
LIP
HANDLE
BOWL
1'-9"
BASE
BASE
12 1/2"

PLANTSCAPING

Urns and Fountains

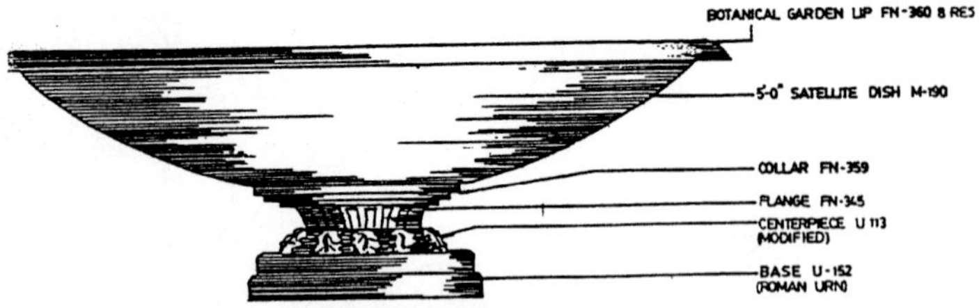

ELEVATION

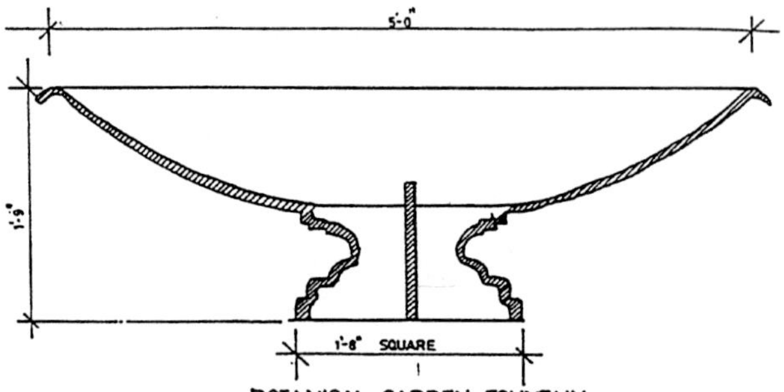

BOTANICAL GARDEN FOUNTAIN

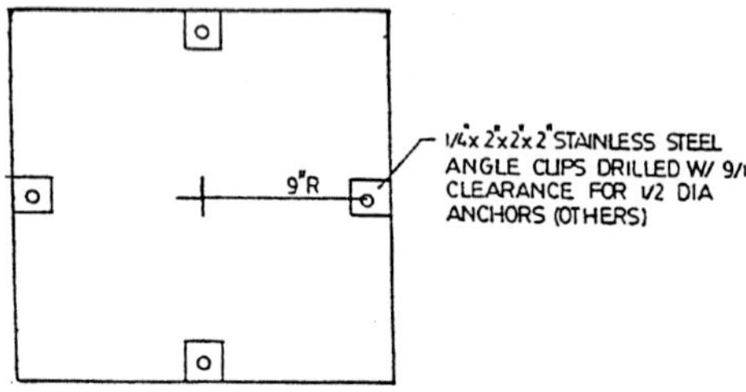

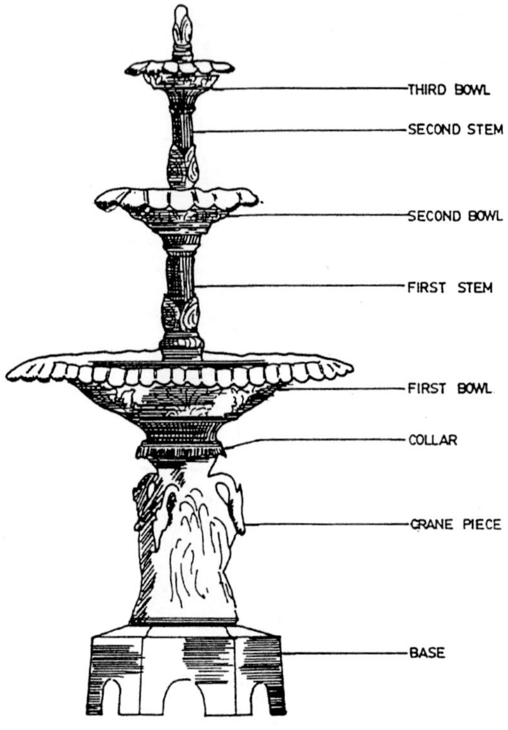

ELEVATION

ELEVATION

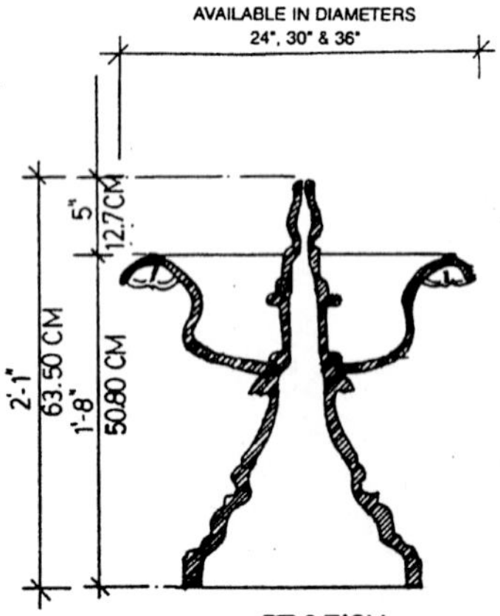

SECTION

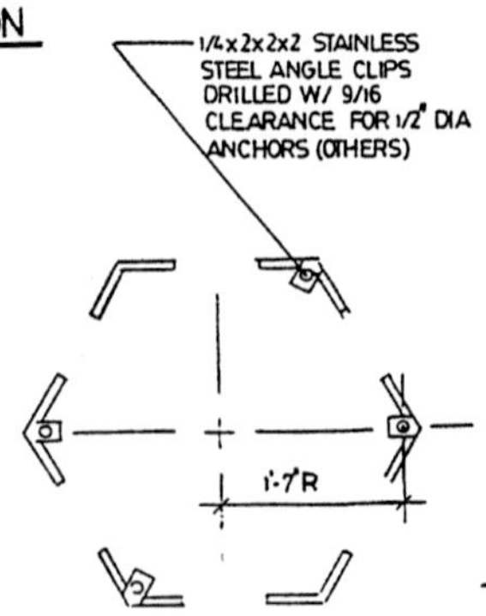

BASE DIAGRAM

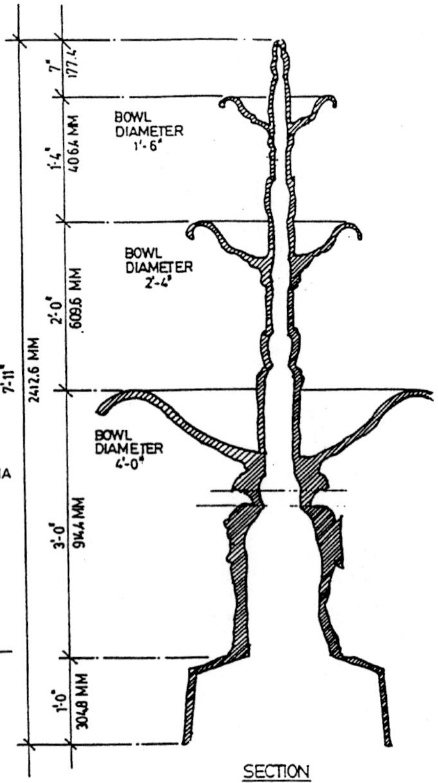

SECTION

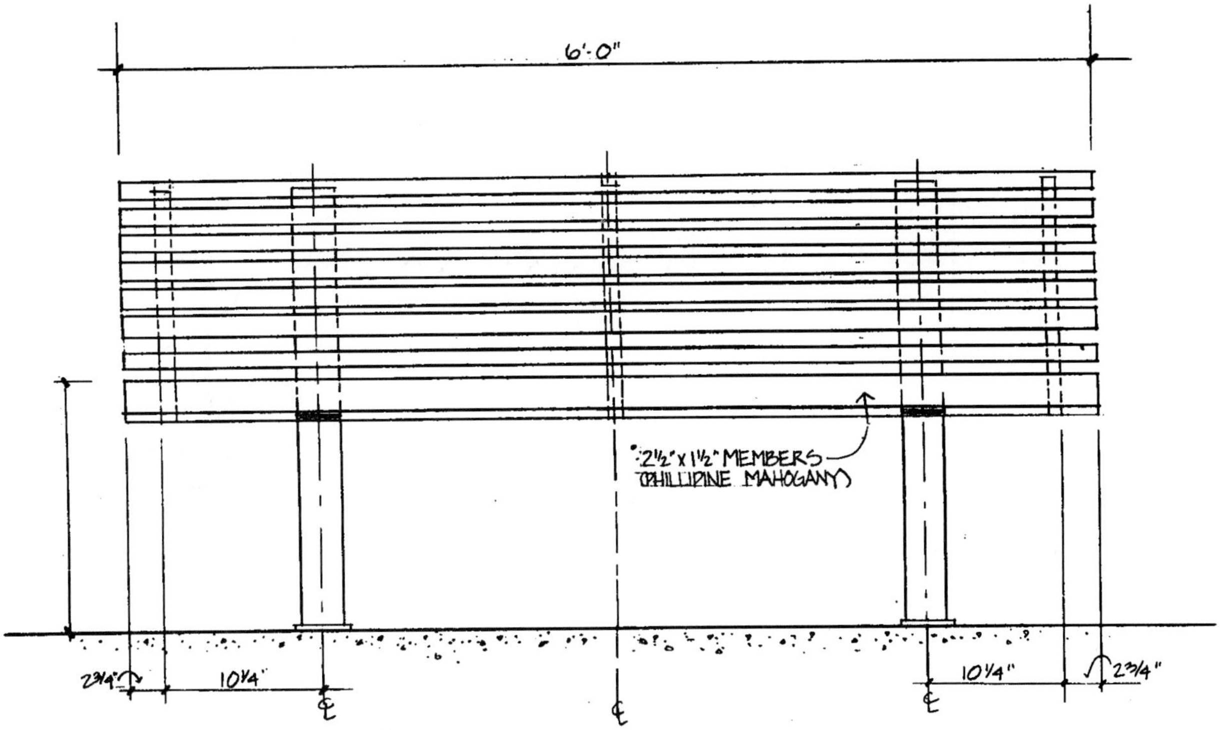
6'-0"
2½" x 1½" MEMBERS (PHILLIPINE MAHOGANY)
2¾"
10¼"
10¼"
2¾"

FRONT ELEVATION

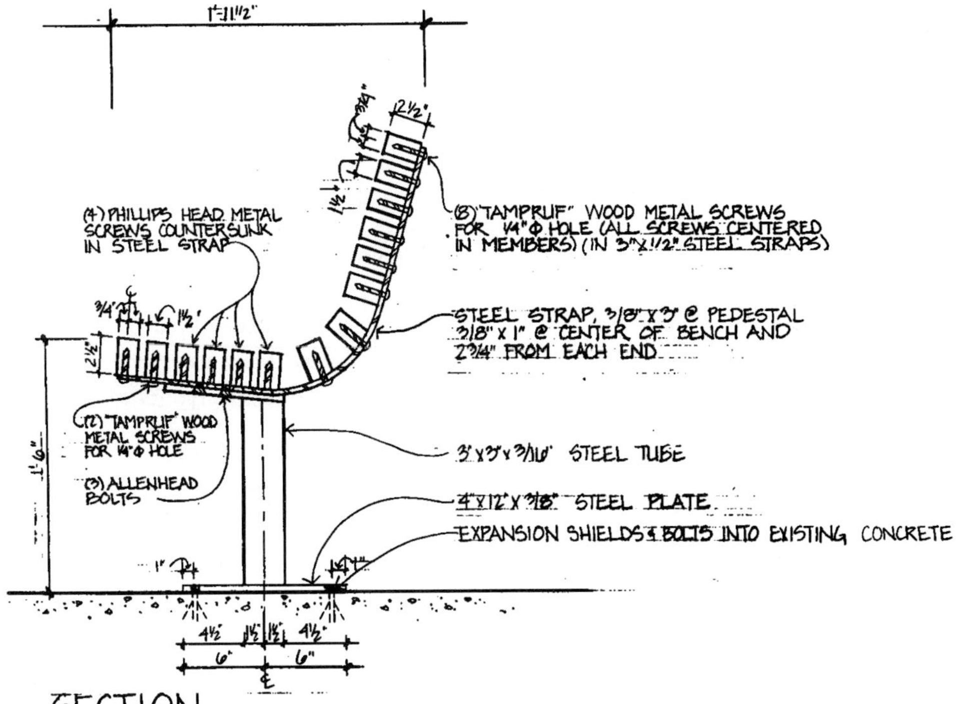
1'-11½"
2½"
1½"
(4) PHILLIPS HEAD METAL SCREWS COUNTERSUNK IN STEEL STRAP
(8) "TAMPRUF" WOOD METAL SCREWS FOR ¼"Φ HOLE (ALL SCREWS CENTERED IN MEMBERS) (IN 3"x½" STEEL STRAPS)
STEEL STRAP, 3/8"x3" @ PEDESTAL 3/8" x 1" @ CENTER OF BENCH AND 2¾" FROM EACH END
(2) "TAMPRUF" WOOD METAL SCREWS FOR ¼"Φ HOLE
(3) ALLENHEAD BOLTS
3"x3"x3/16" STEEL TUBE
4"x12"x3/8" STEEL PLATE
EXPANSION SHIELDS & BOLTS INTO EXISTING CONCRETE
1'-6"
1"
4½"
1½"
1½"
4½"
6"
6"

SECTION

PLANTSCAPING

Benches

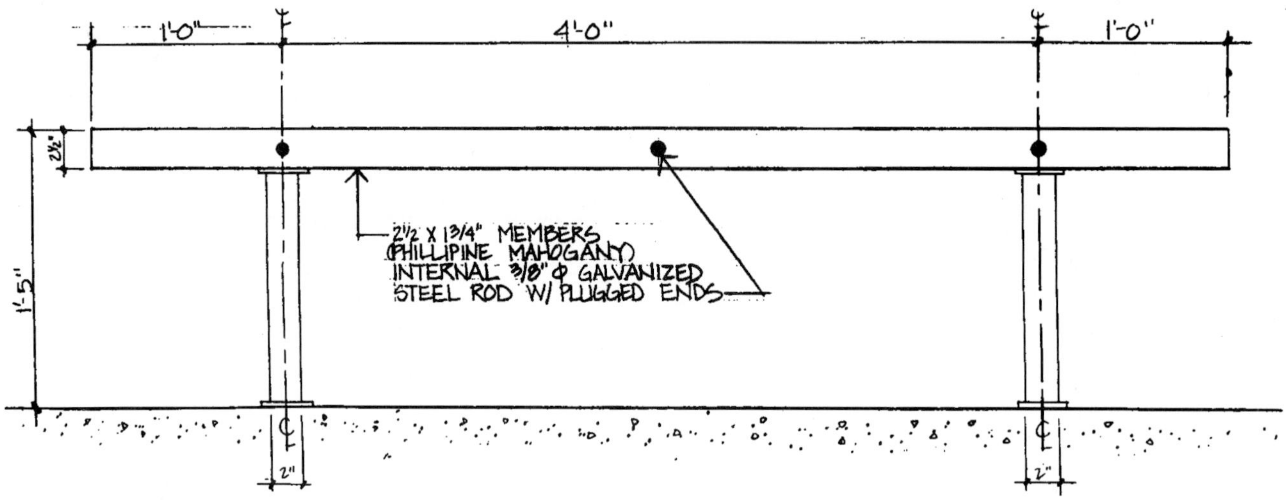

FRONT ELEVATION

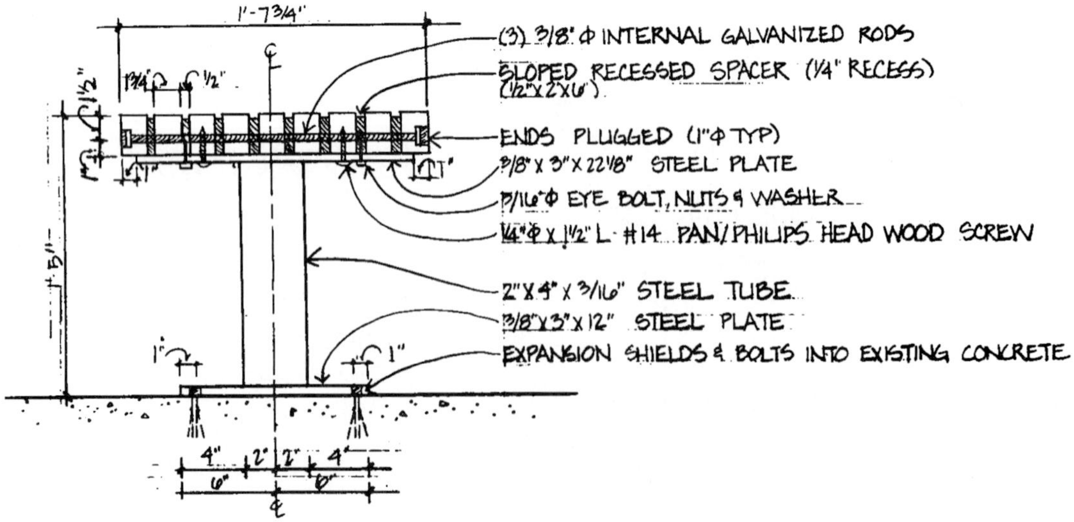

SECTION

Initial consideration should be directed toward determining the basic parameters required in developing the sign system. Each of them merits discussion here.

Performance Requirements

Signs usually must be designed to meet specific performance requirements. The good designer will determine how a system is to perform within given space relationships. The sign system may function entirely on its own merit, or it may be supplemented by staff personnel at major decision-making locations, such as the main lobby and reception areas. Sign devices may become decorative amenities to be featured within the environment, or they may be subtle and low-key elements of minor importance. Supergraphics may be considered in certain areas simply as an art form, or as a functional graphic device presented in large scale for emphasis of context. Certainly, a combination of the two is feasible. These are only several performance considerations that should be addressed prior to the development of the signage system. The designer must evaluate the needs of the client, the unique traffic flow requirements and mounting restrictions dictated by the structure, and the basic performance requirements desired of the signing devices to be utilized.

Usage Considerations

The general nature of the building complex often defines how signs are to be used. They may be given an appearance of being fixed and an integral part of the architecture by the appropriate selection of materials, colors, and mountings, or they may appear changeable and temporary should need so dictate. Some signage requires constant change to properly relate information to people or people to facility, while most sign devices are considered permanent fixtures within a given space. The designer is responsible for determining how signs are to be used most effectively and, at the same time, for enhancing the environment.

Durability Requirements

Prior to the selection of materials for a signing system, durability requirements must be considered. The vast assortment of materials available for signs covers a wide spectrum of durability, from soft plastics to metals. The sign copy and background material should be evaluated both individually and jointly when considering durability requirements.

Vandalism Considerations

Signs located in controlled spaces are often free from destructive vandalism; however, in many instances vandalism becomes rampant and uncontrolled. There are no materials that may accurately be labeled "vandal-proof." However, some materials are more vandal-resistant than others. Where vandalism is of prime importance, only materials and graphic techniques engineered to resist destruction should be considered.

Flexibility to Accommodate Changes and Additions

Modern architectural structures are designed to accommodate inner spacial changes to meet tenant needs. Partition systems, prehung door units, room dividers, and modular furniture have ensured ease of change in officescapes. The sign system may also require alterations to preserve continuity. Changes and additions to a sign system should be considered by the designer prior to the selection of materials, graphic techniques, and mounting methods to be used.

Readability Factors

Sign readability is determined by the letter style selected, size of copy, interletter spacing, copy position relative to background, colors, and angle of observance.

Letter Style

Letter styles are classified as sans serif and serif. Sans serif letters, such as Helvetica, are more contemporary than serif letters, such as Clarendon (Fig. 1). Each letter style has its own unique personality and flavor. Printers carry alphabets in most letter styles, including lowercase letters as well as uppercase (Fig. 2). Test results indicate that messages starting with an initial uppercase letter and followed by lowercase characters are more recognizable than messages formed with uppercase characters only. Lowercase letters have more personality because their shape is varied by ascenders and descenders, resulting in characteristic word forms that are much easier to recognize than all-uppercase word forms. Also, people are more accustomed to reading text in upper- and lowercase than in all uppercase. The proper selection of a particular alphabet should be carefully considered, not only from a legibility point of view, but also from a personality standpoint. The letter style should make a concise and meaningful impression in the environment it serves.

Readability

Readability is directly related to the size of copy. Visibility studies indicate that 1-in-high Helvetica Medium, for example, is readable

Helvetica Medium
Clarendon

Fig. 1

HELVETICA MEDIUM
CLARENDON

Fig. 2

Architectural Signage Systems
Architectural Signage Systems
Architectural Signage Systems

Fig. 3

from a distance of 40 ft. Using this as a measure for comparison, 1-in-high Clarendon style would be readable from a somewhat lesser distance, approximately 25 ft. The distance visibility per 1-in height may be used as a guideline to determine distance readability for larger letters; that is, 2-in-high Helvetica Medium will be readable at 80 ft, and 3-in-high at 120 ft. This direct proportion may be helpful for determining copy (text) sizes for signs used in pedestrian situations. However, the direct proportion may not hold true for vehicular traffic applications, where many other factors are involved. The designer must exercise caution after selecting the alphabet and copy size to make certain the lettering will fit properly on the sign background. The sign size should be determined using the longest line of copy and the maximum number of copy lines that may be required.

Letters and Line Spacing

Interletter spacing and interline spacing of copy greatly affect the overall readability of a sign. Message legibility and ease of recognition are increased when proper visual relationships are established between individual characters, words, and lines of copy. Copy with spacing too tight becomes very difficult to read; copy with too open spacing tends to break the message down into fragments (Fig. 3). Proper spacing depends largely on the distance from which the message is to be read. Messages to be read at close distances should employ tighter spacing than messages that will be read at greater distances. Spacing is also affected by the angle at which the message is to be viewed: greater angles of observance require wider interletter spacing to prevent the characters of the message from appearing to run together.

Copy Position

The position of copy on the sign background influences the overall readability. Signs on which copy occupies most of the background are not as readable as signs that have sufficient background material surrounding the copy to form a visual barrier separating the message from the environment (Figs. 4 and 5).

Emphasis should be placed on selecting an appropriate sign size to best accommodate the sign message. There are nine basic copy placement positions to be considered in determining the important relationship of copy to sign background. They are: upper left, upper centered, upper right, centered left, centered, centered right, lower left, lower centered, and lower right. Traditionally, the most popular placement selections have been the centered and upper left positions.

Color

Color of copy and sign background greatly affect readability. Strong contrasting colors are more readable than less dramatic color combinations. White copy on a black background offers the greatest contrast and readability. Color also influences the apparent relationship between the copy size and the background. For example, white copy on a black field appears larger than black copy on a white field, although letter height, size, and copy position remain the same in both examples (Fig. 6).

Colors in a signage system should also relate harmoniously with the pallette of colors selected for the building and its environment. The designer may choose to select colors that blend with the environment or vibrant primary colors that accent the sign system and perhaps contrast with the architectural color scheme.

The Viewing Angle

The angle of observance is influential in the design of a signage system, since it affects interletter spacing and overall readability. Normally, interior signs are viewed chiefly from a straight-on position; however, exterior signs are frequently seen from more than one angle. Signs to be read from vehicles moving at varying speeds with different angles of observance may require a compromise in letter spacing to best communicate the message.

Multilingual Needs

The jet age is a contributing factor in bringing people together from all over the world to visit and transact business. Transportation terminals and public facilities that may be used by visitors unaccustomed to reading English should employ sign systems that bridge any visual communication gap. Multilingual messages in English and the dominant foreign languages used by visitors may be combined and presented on one sign background. However, sign design and graphic formats become very critical to prevent confusion. A more popular solution involves the use of pictorial symbols as word substitutes. Pictographic signs are bold, recognizable images not bound by language barriers.

Regulatory Considerations

The designer should become aware of regulations governing signs. Federal regulations concerning safety signs are enumerated in Occupational Safety and Health Administration (OSHA) publications. The American National Standards Institute (ANSI) publishes standards

Fig. 4

Fig. 5

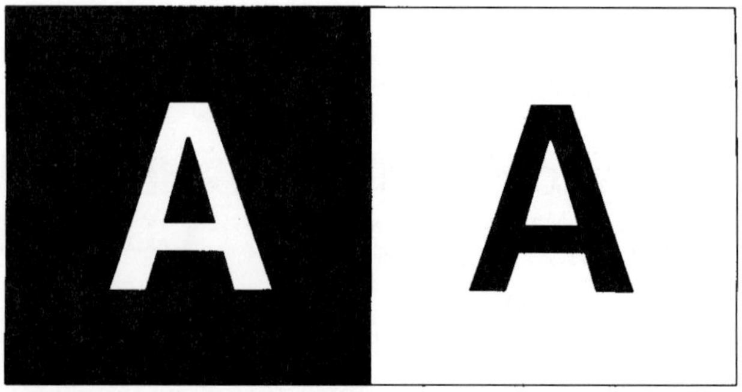

Fig. 6

concerning signage for the physically handicapped. Underwriters' Laboratory (UL) issues standards applicable to illuminated signs. State and local codes contain regulatory information concerning sign sizes, mounting locations and heights, quantities of signs allowable in various zoning areas, and other restrictions relating to exterior signs. These rules, and those of other regulatory bodies, should be taken under advisement prior to completing a comprehensive signage program.

Need for Illumination

Many signs are required to relate their messages after dark as well as during natural daylight. The careful designer will determine which signs require artificial illumination and decide on the method of illumination. Signs can be externally illuminated by readily available stock fixtures produced by many manufacturers, or they can be internally illuminated. Fluorescent lighting is the most common source of internal illumination, although metal arc lamps, incandescent lamps, and neon are frequently employed.

Need for a Graphics Manual

Many signage programs are developed for institutions that have a continuing need not only to maintain, but also to augment or change, their signage systems. The preparation of a signage manual containing all the information required to create additional signs or components would benefit the client and ensure continuity in the system as changes and additions are made. The designer should determine this potential need and include the manual with other documents developed for the signage program.

SIGN TYPES CATEGORIZED BY FUNCTION

Signage systems should be logically broken down into various types of signs to be utilized on a particular project. Many categories of sign types may be developed, but one of the most conclusive listings is based on function. The following discussion of signage system components, including sign requirements for specific applications, covers these functions.

Exterior Signs

Exterior sign system components are normally viewed from vehicles or by pedestrians who have parked their vehicles and are walking toward their destination.

Primary Identification

All architectural projects require some form of identification that is both easily readable and recognizable. A person's first association with a building is the identifying device selected to label the structure. The importance of the first impression created by this device should be recognized. A sign that produces an image in keeping with the environment it serves reflects the quality of the people associated with that environment. Major corporations spend large sums of money on corporate identity programs to ensure that the visual image presented to the public best reflects corporate philosophy and product desirability. Equal emphasis should be placed on the image presented by the device employed to identify an architectural structure.

Secondary Identification

Many complexes containing more than one basic structure require secondary identification signs to properly identify the various elements within the complex. A systems approach to design will provide continuity in the relationship of primary to secondary identification signs.

Vehicular Advance Notice

A system of road signs suitably located in advance of decision-making points will allow vehicular traffic to execute the proper decisions smoothly and safely at the appropriate times.

Vehicular Directional

Intersections and parking facility entrances are major decision-making locations requiring directional devices to guide drivers toward their destination.

Traffic Regulatory and Control

Vehicular traffic can be systematically controlled by employing signing devices. Traffic codes are usually clear as to what signs are required, where they are to be located, and the height at which they are to be mounted. Usually, colors, sizes, and shapes are standardized by the traffic authorities. Stop, yield, and speed limit signs are representative of this classification of signs.

Instructional

Frequently, signs are required to instruct vehicular and pedestrian traffic. These notices must be properly installed in carefully selected locations to be effective. Examples include parking procedures, delivery and service directions, and the like.

Informational

Signs are required to present information that is both relevant to the location and important to the viewer. This information may pertain to parking rates, hours of operation, and security, or it may relate to items of interest within the environment.

Decorative

Decorative graphics may be employed to enhance the beauty or decor of a particular area; form, color, and design may be utilized to create interest and to become features of the exterior landscape.

Interior Signs

Interior sign system components should assist visitors to travel from the building entrances throughout the complex until they reach their desired destination.

Identification

Multiple-occupancy buildings require tenant identification; frequently, buildings with only one tenant will also utilize identification in the main lobby or reception areas to reinforce the corporate signature. Criteria for multiple-tenant signage are very important and should be included in lease documents to provide for visual continuity and architectural harmony. When individuals are allowed to implement their own desires concerning signage, each will attempt to outdo the other, resulting in clutter, confusion, and visual pollution. Signs that are too big, too gaudy, too competitive, and poorly conceived and executed will become commonplace unless controls on tenant identification are established and enforced.

SIGNAGE AND GRAPHICS
Sign Types Categorized by Function

Primary Directory

Information relevant to one's location within a complex should be clearly enumerated on the primary directory, usually located in a very visible area of the main lobby. Alphabetized listings of tenants, departments, and individuals should be concise and should designate the floor and room numbers. Such directories may be flush or recessed wall mounts, horizontal projected wall mounts, or pedestal or kiosk mounts, and internally illuminated or not, depending on the ambient lighting conditions.

Elevator Lobby Floor Directory

High-rise structures require well-positioned signage that not only identifies each individual floor, but also serves as a secondary directory system for that floor. Frequently, the floor identification, directory, and corridor directional signage may be included in one device. When a visitor exits from an elevator on a chosen floor, a sign showing the floor number and also the direction of the office or room number sought is both helpful and reassuring.

Pictorial "You Are Here" Indicators

Pictorial schematic maps may become an integral part of directory systems, or they may be utilized separately as visual aids in depicting one's intended passage through a complex. Hospitals, sports complexes, and transportation centers are good examples of structures that may require pictorial maps to supplement word messages. Caution will be exercised by the expert designer to keep the pictorial map simple and correctly oriented in the building, according to where the viewer is standing, and to evaluate the need of color coding as part of the visual aid. Too frequently, designers employ a complicated color-coded system that becomes very confusing to the viewer and, in fact, compromises the effectiveness of the system.

Primary Directional

The maze that often results from interior corridor layouts creates many decision-making points for a visitor. Primary directional signs may be ceiling-mounted, wall-mounted, or floor-mounted as kiosk-type units in open areas. Areas with heavy pedestian traffic should have directional signs located so that people do not obstruct the line of sight to the sign device. Normally, ceiling-suspended or kiosk-type units are the best choice to enhance visibility.

Secondary Directional

Directional signs should be considered in locations where traffic flow and corridor layouts do not demand primary directional devices but do require some guidance for direction control. Corridors within suites of offices and corridors that change direction should be considered as decision-making points that may require a secondary directional signage device.

Area Identification

Specific areas within a complex should be properly identified. These areas may be tenant spaces, divisions, or departments. When occurring along main corridors, they are usually designated by wall-, door-, or transom-mounted devices. Ceiling-suspended signs are a good solution in open office spaces.

Room Identification

Wall- or door-mounted room identification signs are required to label the function of a particular room. Work functions are properly identified within tenant areas, while service and maintenance functions should be suitably designated in most situations.

Desk Identification

Reception areas may require a sign device located on a desk or counter to identify a particular service or individual rendering assistance to visitors. Such signs may be permanently affixed or removable, and may provide for changeable name inserts.

Personnel Identification

Persons rendering a service to the public, such as nurses, maintenance personnel, and food service personnel, generally are identified by name badges or pins.

Regulatory and Control Signs

Signs that authorize or prohibit certain functions are required, frequently by law or code, to inform people using the facility. Examples include signs for the handicapped and signs relevant to no-smoking areas, elevator capacities, "no entry" areas, fire control, and "authorized personnel only" areas. These signs are usually mounted on doors or their adjacent walls; they may employ colors which deviate from the standard colors used in the comprehensive signage system to emphasize a dangerous situation or the need for caution.

Exits

Exit signs are required by codes to designate exits effectively in times of emergency. Supplemental devices are used to give additional information pertaining to a particular exit, such as "Emergency Exit Only" and "Alarm Sounds When Door Is Opened." OSHA-approved exit signs are standard items manufactured by many lighting companies and are generally provided by the electrical contractor.

Information Exhibit Cases

Notices, posters, attractions, and promotional pieces should be contained within an appropriately designed case to control the display of this type of information. Standard units featuring vinyl-covered cork panels housed within extruded aluminum frames with lockable doors are available from many directory manufacturers.

Decorative Features

Decorative designs may be reproduced on walls as interior features. Reproduction processes include appliqués, painting, and screen printing on location; or mural processes, which are applied much like wall-coverings, may be considered. Doors may also receive supergraphic treatments in which copy may become an integral part of the design.

Dedicatory Plaques

Building dedication plaques should be carefully conceived and implemented, using materials that reflect favorably on the talents involved in the realization of the project. Historically, these plaques have been bronze or aluminum castings. However, modern technology has provided photographic methods and photochemical processes which offer the designer a freedom of size, format, letter form, and color not available in the casting operation.

Donor Recognition

Buildings constructed in part by contributions from donors require special recognition for the donors. Hospitals, performing arts centers, and service institutions rely on gifts to assist in financing buildings, additions, and furnishings, and usually stipulate that donors be remembered and recognized in some prestigious location in the building. The designer is responsible for establishing controls and developing a system that fulfills promises made by those soliciting funds, while allowing flexibility to expand the system as future needs may dictate. Location selection is very important in the overall effectiveness of the donor recognition signage.

Mechanical, Instrumentation, and Control System Markings

Many industrial and mechanical installations require equipment, control, and pipe markings to meet codes, assist maintenance and service personnel, and ensure safety. Often, these locations are not public spaces and require an industrial, rather than an architectural, approach to signage. Elevator floor-indicator panels, however, should receive special attention and be considered in a comprehensive signage program.

CONCEPTUAL DESIGN OF THE SIGN FACE

Emphasis will not be placed on the graphic design of each sign required in a comprehensive signage program. However, the following considerations will help to ensure continuity, correctness, and aesthetic acceptability.

Alphabet Selection

An alphabet must be carefully chosen that best exemplifies the graphic image to be portrayed to the public without compromising legibility and performance requirements. More than one alphabet may be selected, should need dictate. However, good design practices should be maintained in choosing the family of alphabets to be employed.

Interletter, Word, and Line Spacing

Each alphabet has its own personality and visual impact; therefore, spacing between characters, words, and lines of copy must be carefully developed to give the best legibility and visual harmony possible (Fig. 8).

Arrow Selection

Directional arrows should be designed to reflect the personality of the letter form selected. Stroke width and size relationships are important considerations (Fig. 9).

Copy Determination

The message for each sign must be accurately determined and the copy condensed to the fewest words that will still relay the desired message. Wordy signs are frequently misread or not read at all. The message must be concise, clear, and informative (Fig. 10 and 11).

Copy Placement Format

The placement of copy on a sign face may take one of the nine basic positions or a custom format for special situations (Fig. 12).

Size Determination of the Sign Face

After the copy for each sign is in final form, the sign with the greatest amount of copy is selected from each of the sign types utilized and the desired copy height is determined for each type. This height should be based on the distance from which the sign will be read and the graphic design portrayed. Using this letter height, the message should be laid out with photographic type or transfer lettering to scale, incorporating the copy placement and spacing requirements. The most pleasing shape and size for the message to be contained are then determined, realizing that this particular layout is for the maximum copy required for that particular sign type. A shape and size format should be chosen that works well as a module which can be proportioned and become applicable to the entire family of sign types. While this may be ideal, frequently the proportional system is not applicable. An example of each sign type should be drawn to scale and fully dimensioned to serve as a production guide for signs within that type (Fig. 13).

Color Selections

Selection is then made of the copy and background colors that offer good contrast and harmoniously blend with the prominent colors in the environment. It is also wise to consider any corporate colors required by the client.

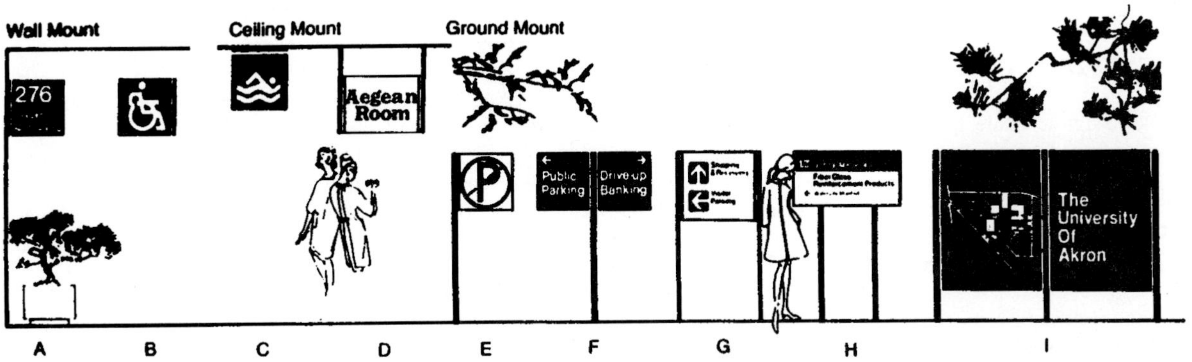

Fig. 7

Architectural Signage Systems
Planning · Design · Implementation

Fig. 8

Fig. 9

These Doors Should
Not Be Opened
Except During
An Emergency

Fig. 10

Emergency
Exit Only

Fig. 11

SIGNAGE SYSTEM DEVELOPMENT CHECKLIST

The completed sign schedule, location plans, scaled drawings of typical examples from each sign type, construction or assembly details or both, mounting details, and specifications form the documents required to bid competitively or to negotiate signage projects. Well-prepared documents prevent individual interpretation by vendors and result in comparable competitive bids.

The following systematic approach to the design and development of a comprehensive signage program will serve as a guideline to problem solving, employing the concepts contained in this chapter. This checklist may be expanded or condensed to meet individual project parameters. The basic systematic thought process, however, is applicable to all projects.

1. Develop the signage system design criteria based on:
   a. Performance requirements
   b. Usage considerations
   c. Durability requirements
   d. Vandalism considerations
   e. Flexibility to accommodate changes and additions
   f. Readability factors
   g. Multilingual needs
   h. Regulatory considerations
   i. Need for illumination
   j. Need for graphics manual for ongoing implementation and system maintenance
2. Study the traffic flow patterns, determine all sign locations, and draw the location symbols on the site and floor plans.
3. Evaluate and select the sign types required from the following list, categorized by function, that meet the design criteria:
   a. Exterior sign types:
      Type A—Primary identification
      Type B—Secondary identification
      Type C—Vehicular advance notice
      Type D—Vehicular directional
      Type E—Traffic regulatory and control
      Type F—Instructional
      Type G—Informational
      Type H—Decorative
   b. Interior sign types:
      Type I—Primary identification
      Type J—Primary directory
      Type K—Elevator lobby floor directories
      Type L—Pictorial "You Are Here" indicators
      Type M—Primary directional
      Type N—Secondary directional
      Type O—Area identification
      Type P—Room identification
      Type Q—Desk identification
      Type R—Personnel identification
      Type S—Regulatory and control
      Type T—Exit
      Type U—Information exhibit cases
      Type W—Dedicatory
      Type X—Donor recognition
      Type Y—Mechanical, instrumentation, and control system markings
      Type Z—Other (to be specified by designer)
4. Select the best signing devices for each sign type designated above from the following lexicon of signage system components that most effectively satisfy the design criteria established:
   a. Elevated pylons
   b. Monolithic sign structures
   c. Panel and post assemblies
   d. Illuminated sign cabinets
   e. Directory and informational systems

   f. Die-cut pressure-sensitive lettering
   g. Dimensional graphics
   h. Plaque signage
   i. Environmental graphics
   j. Other (to be defined by the designer)
5. Conceptually design the sign face for each sign type selected, indicating:
   a. Alphabet selection
   b. Interletter, word, and line spacing
   c. Arrow selection
   d. Copy determination
   e. Copy placement format
   f. Size determination of copy and sign face
   g. Color selections
6. Complete the location plans by filling in the symbol indicating sign number and type.
7. Prepare scaled drawings of typical examples from each sign type.
8. Prepare the detailed sign schedule.
9. Prepare typical construction and assembly details, mounting details, and engineering drawings for wind loading, foundations, and illumination.
10. Prepare detailed specifications for all materials, techniques, and components required in the system.

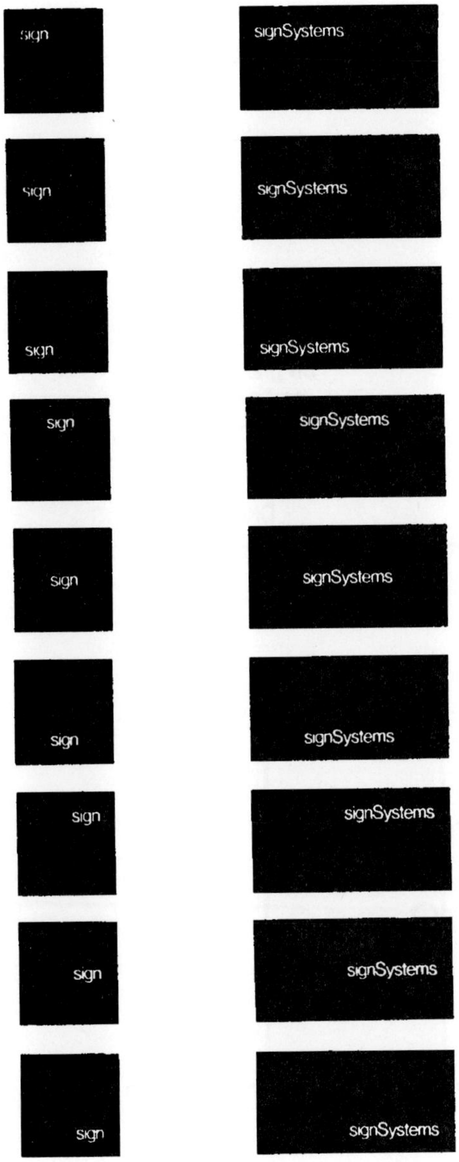

Fig. 12

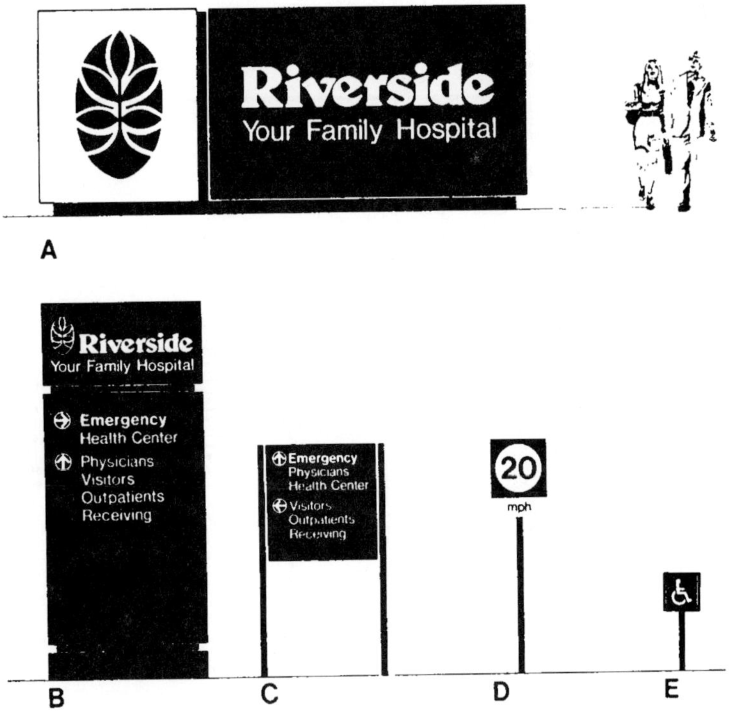

Fig. 13

STANDARD SIGN SYSTEM

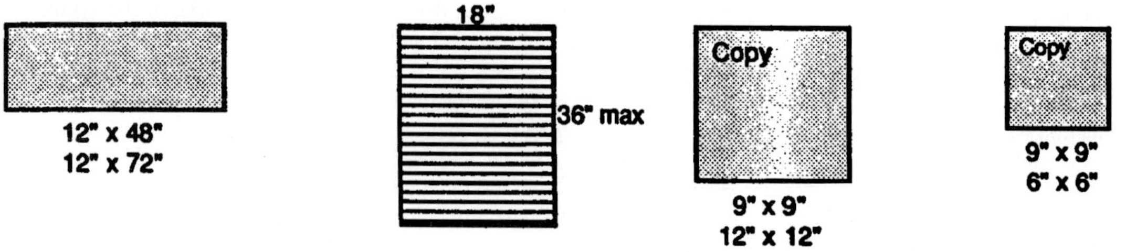

Overhead · Directional · Area · Room

CODE SIGNS

Elevator · Stair · Distraction strips

STANDARD MOUNTING HEIGHTS AND LOCATIONS

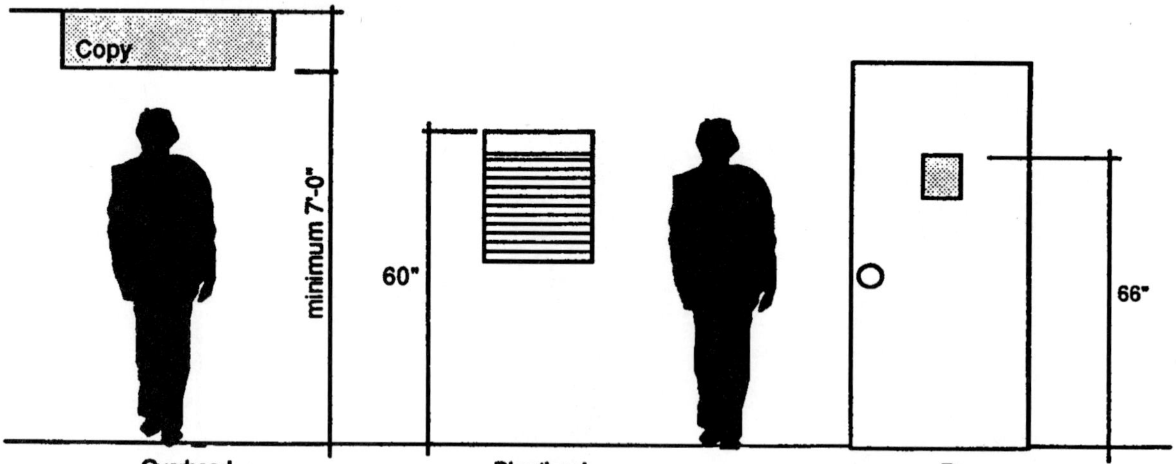

Overhead · Directional · Door

SIGNAGE AND GRAPHICS
Standard Sign Type and Mounting Heights

Sign Type

DIRECTIONAL (CEILING-HUNG)

Material Choices

MDO board, acrylic

Finishes

Painted, plastic laminate, metal laminate

Graphics

Vinyl die cuts, silkscreen, dimensional applied letters

Standard Mounting Detail

1. Threaded rod: pendant, flush
2. Scissor clip

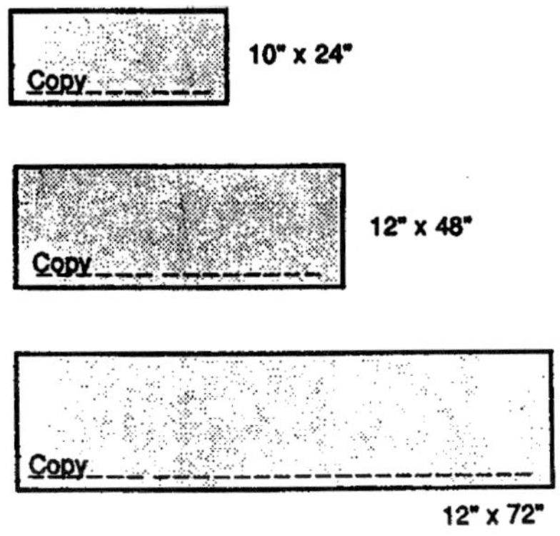

Standard sizes

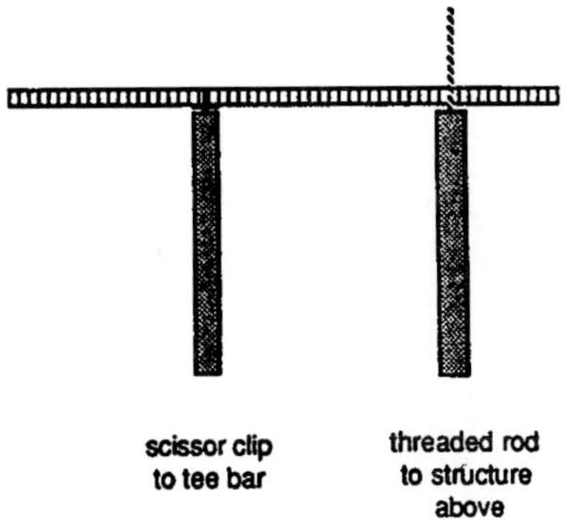

Section

Sign Type

DIRECTIONAL (WALL-MOUNTED)

Material Choices

Acrylic, aluminum, acrylic with metal laminate face

Finishes

Painted acrylic or aluminum, natural aluminum or brass (satin or polished), laminates available in standard laminate finishes

Graphics

Silkscreen, front surface or reverse

Standard Mounting Materials

1. Backpanel: backplate with countersunk screws with shields; magnetic, form, or vinyl tape with adhesive
2. Strips: vinyl tape

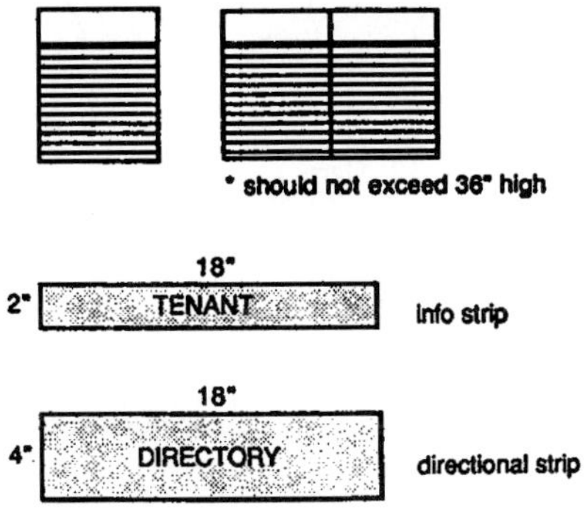

Standard sizes

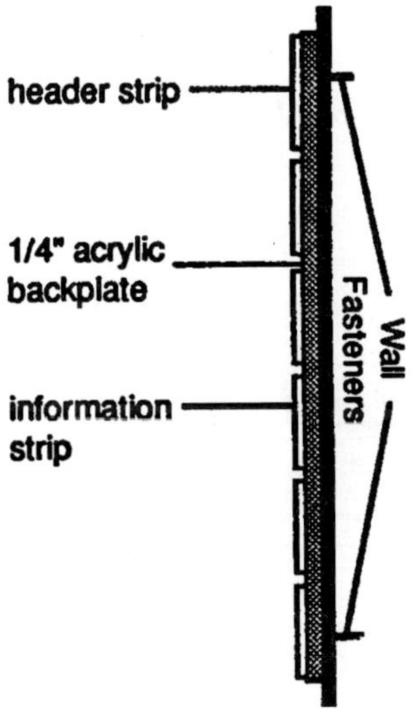

Section

Sign Type

AREA DESIGNATION (WALL-MOUNTED)

Material Choices

Acrylic, aluminum, acrylic with metal laminate face

Finishes

Painted acrylic or aluminum, natural aluminum or brass (satin or polished), laminates available in standard laminate finishes

Graphics

Silkscreen, front surface or reverse; vinyl die cuts

Standard Mounting Materials

Vinyl or magnetic tape, foam tape, silastic adhesive

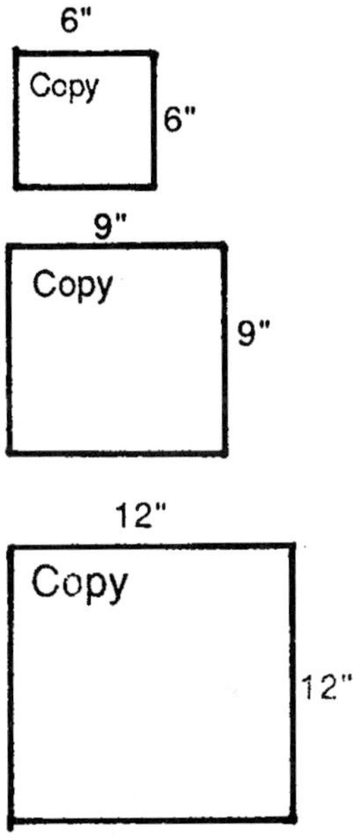

Standard sizes

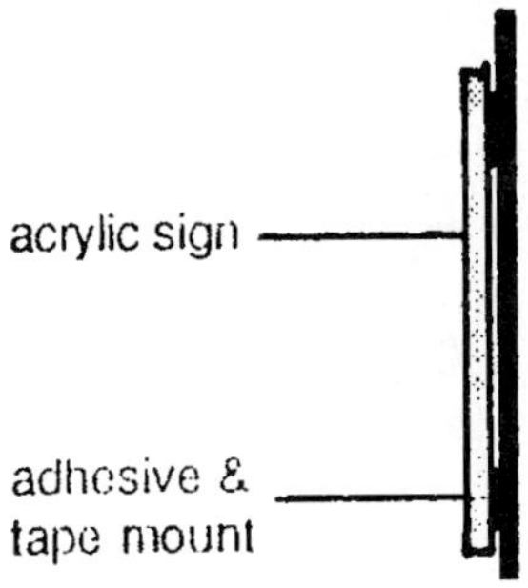

Section

SIGNAGE AND GRAPHICS

ADA Signage Mounting Heights and Details

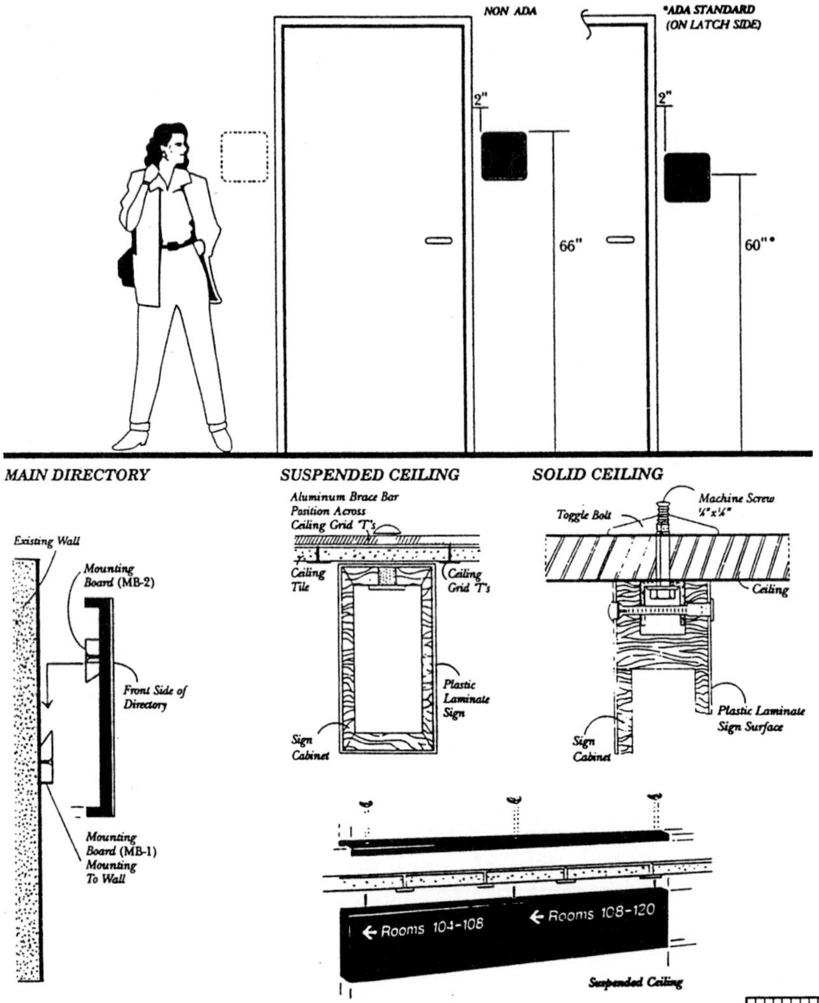

TYPICAL MOUNTING LOCATION AND METHODS

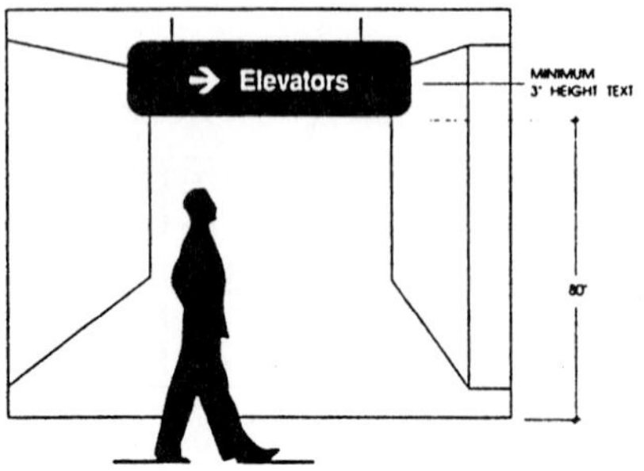

D. Overhead Signage (Typical)

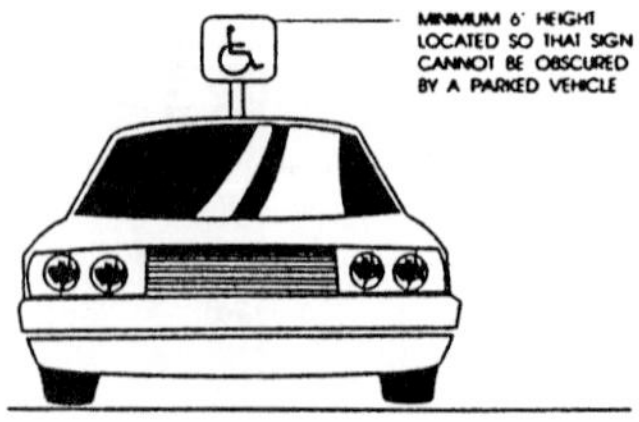

E. Accessible Parking

PROPORTIONS FOR INTERNATIONAL SYMBOL OF ACCESSIBILITY

DISPLAY CONDITIONS FOR INTERNATIONAL SYMBOL OF ACCESSIBILITY

INTERNATIONAL SYMBOL OF TELECOMMUNICATIONS DEVICE FOR THE DEAF (TDD)

INTERNATIONAL SYMBOL OF ACCESS FOR HEARING LOSS

SYMBOLS OF ACCESSIBILITY

SYMBOLS OF ACCESSIBILITY

F. International Symbol of Accessibility
G. International Symbol of Access for Hearing Loss
H. International TDD Symbol

F. G. H.

Sign Type

ROOM IDENTIFIER (WALL-MOUNTED)

Material Choices

Acrylic, aluminum, acrylic with metal laminate face

Finishes

Painted acrylic or aluminum, natural aluminum or brass (satin or polished), laminates available in standard laminate finishes

Graphics

Silkscreen, front surface or reverse

Standard Mounting Materials

Vinyl tape, foam tape, magnetic tape, silastic adhesive

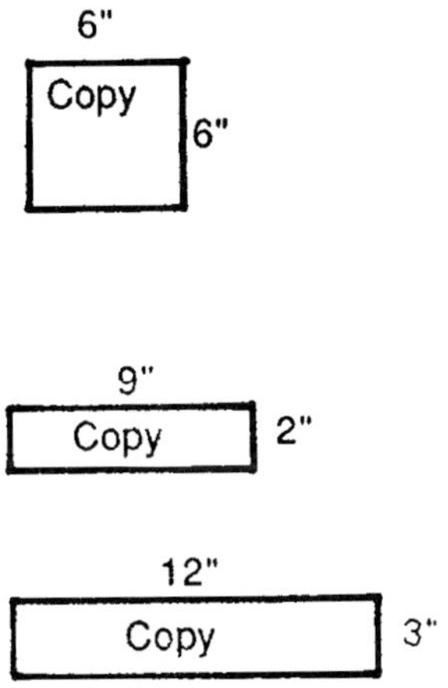

Standard sizes

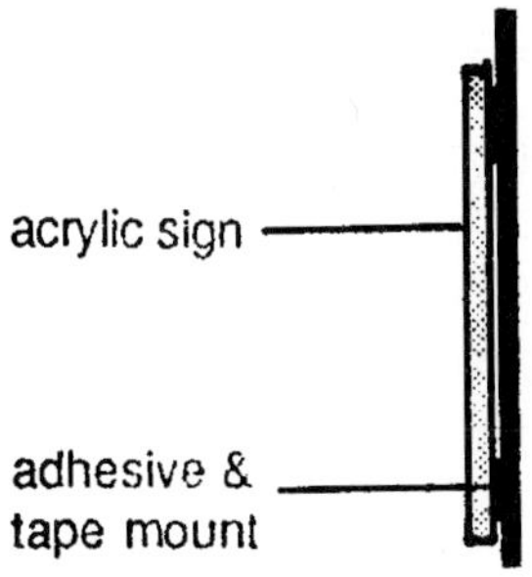

Section

Sign Type

ROOM IDENTIFIER, CHANGEABLE MESSAGE (WALL-MOUNTED)

Material Choices

Holder, acrylic; insert, vinyl

Finishes

Painted (surface or subsurface)

Graphics

Silkscreen or vinyl die cuts

Standard Mounting Materials

Vinyl tape, foam tape, silastic adhesive

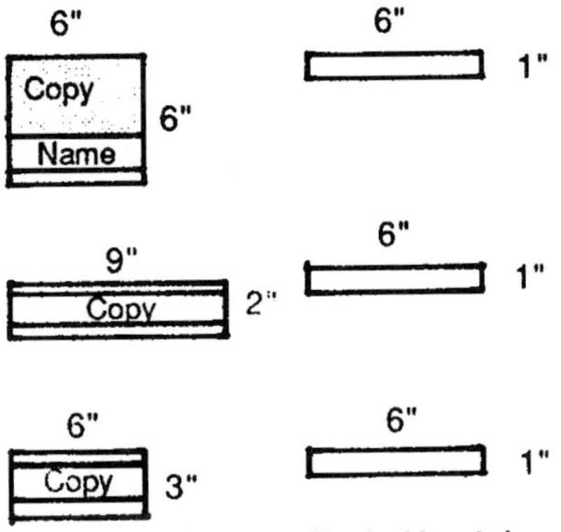

Standard sign sizes **Standard insert sizes**

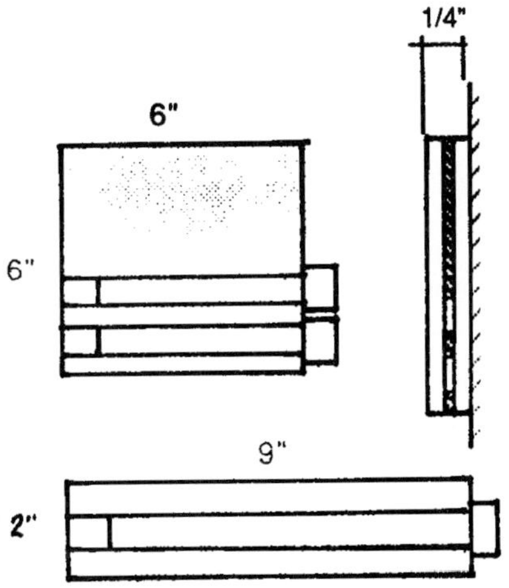

Elevation and section

Sign Type

FRAMED PLAQUE SIGNS, WALL-MOUNTED (previous plaque types are insertable into standard frame signs)

Material Choices

Molded acrylic, aluminum, brass

Finishes

Painted, satin, polished

Standard Frame Mounting Materials

1. Frame: screw mount, tape and adhesive
2. Insert: adhesive or magnetic tape, Velcro, magnet

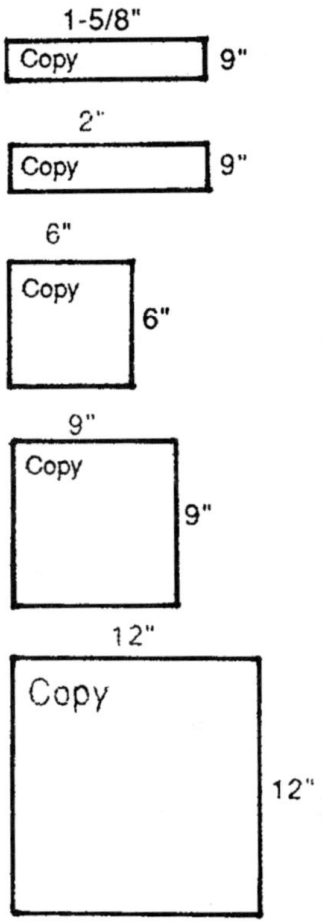

Standard insert sizes

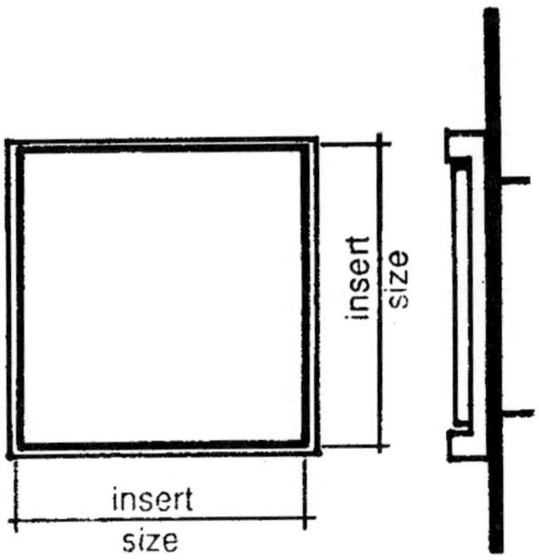

Elevation and section

SIGNAGE AND GRAPHICS

ADA Signage Mounting Heights and Details

Sign Type

COUNTERTOP/FLAG MOUNT

Extrusion Material

Aluminum

Insert Material

Acrylic, aluminum, acrylic with metal laminate

Graphics

See area and room plaques

Standard Mounting Details

1. Counter: free-standing with extruded aluminum base
2. Flag mount: countersunk screws and shields

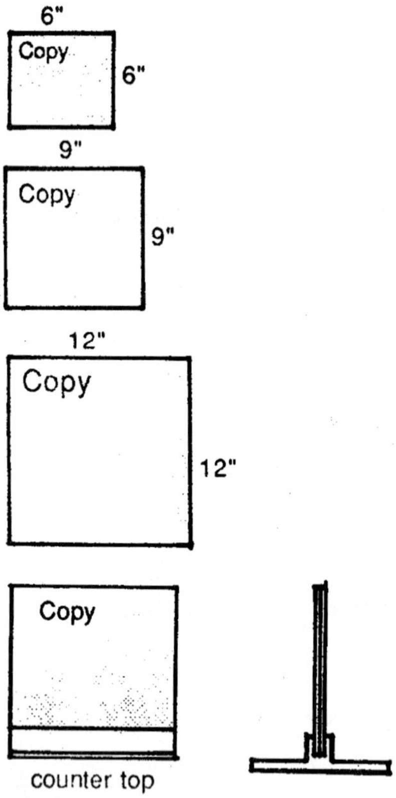

Standard sizes

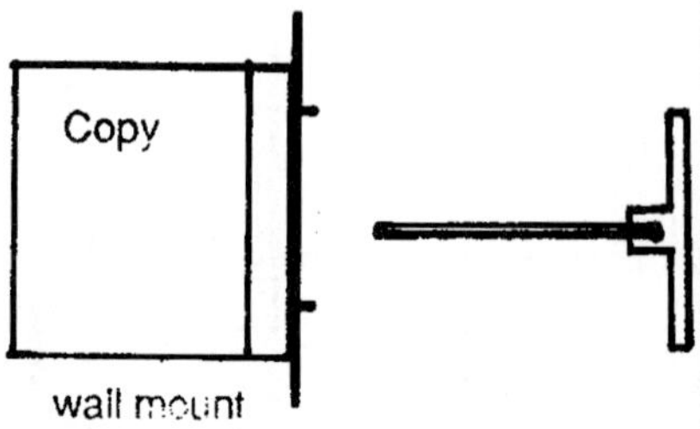

Elevation and section

Sign Type

DESKBAR (DESK TOP)

Material Choices

Aluminum, molded acrylic

Finishes

Painted, satin, polished

Graphics

Vinyl die cuts; silkscreen on acrylic plaque, front surface or reverse

Standard Mounting Detail

Free-standing on desks or countertops

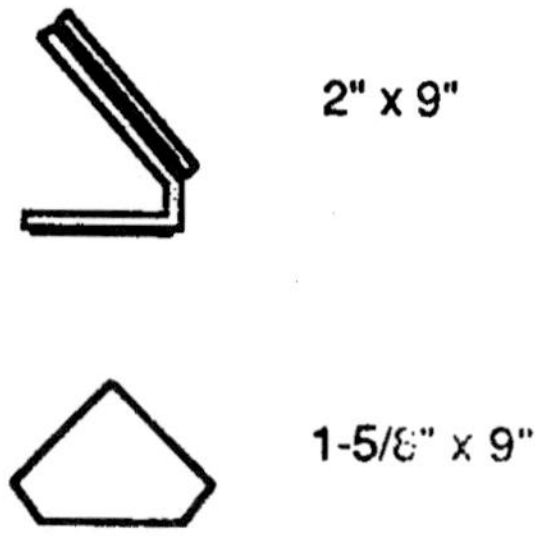

Standard sizes

Note: Changeable face available by using acrylic sign plaque.

Sign Type

CUT LETTERS: FLUSH, PROJECTED

Material Choices

Acrylic, acrylic with metal laminate face, brass, aluminum

Finishes

Polished, painted, brushed, sand blasted

Standard Mounting Details

Adhesive mount, flush pin mount, standoff mount

Standard Letter Sizes

Varies from 2" to 18"

Front View

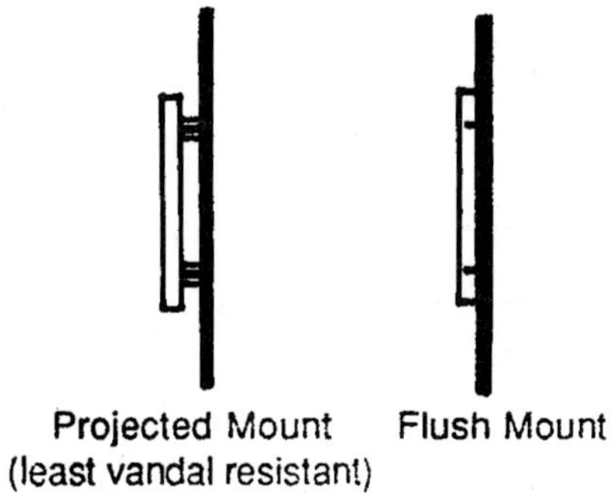

Sections

Medical

Nursing Homes
Medical Complexes
First-Aid Centers

Picto grafics not shown:

1.516	Parking	1.413	Health
1.372	Playroom	2.531	Warning
1.150	Library or Reading	1.147	Chest

Hospital
Pharmacy
Dental Care
Wheelchair

1.508

1.518
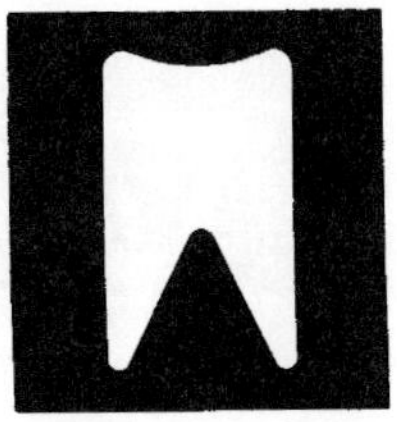
1.184

1.188

X-Ray
Physiotherapy
General Medicine, Female
General Medicine, Male

1.146

1.148

1.440

1.450

Coronary Care
Hematology
Urology
Eye

1.446
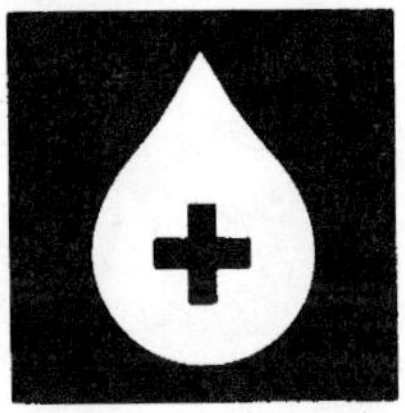
1.417
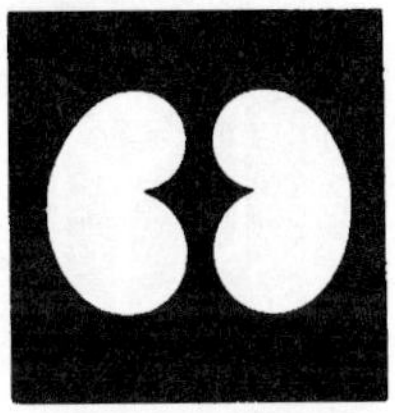
1.448
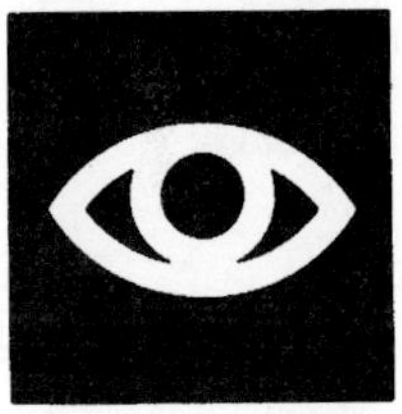
1.123

Podiatry
Mental Health
Ear, Nose & Throat
Oxygen

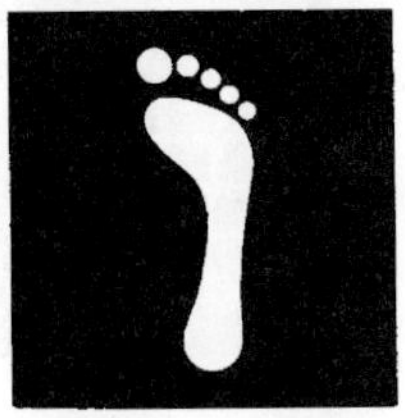
1.129

1.473

1.137

1.368

Shower
Isolation
Nursery
Laboratory

1.376

1.411

1.302

1.359

Conference
Occupational Therapy
Rehabilitation
Ambulatory Patients

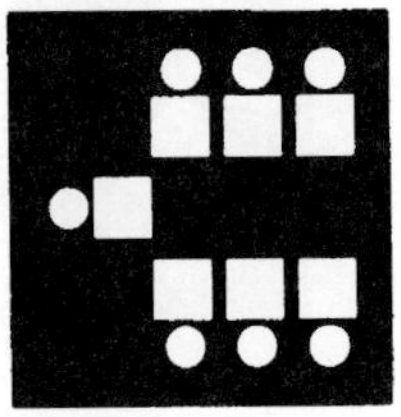
1.406

1.347

1.483

1.152

SIGNAGE AND GRAPHICS
Commercial Symbols

Commercial

Shopping Centers
Stores & Shops
Eating Facilities
Community Services

Picto'grafics not shown:
1.218 Concrete Mixer
1.219 Cushman Vehicle
1.222 Dump Truck
1.226 Flatbed Truck
1.250 Pickup Truck
1.304 Basket
1.314 Vegetable Produce
1.363 Newspaper Vendor
1.370 Record Store
1.394 Cooking

Cocktail Lounge
Pub
Coffee Shop
Liquor Store

1.344

1.361

1.360

1.307

Mens' Furnishings
Furniture
Cinema
Camera Store

1.352

1.315

1.126

1.338

Gift Shop
Florist
Dress Shop
Shoe Store

1.339

1.393

1.321

1.375

Restaurant
Soda Fountain
Grocery Store
Tobacco Shop

1.354

1.341

1.337

1.316

Bookstore
Record Shop
Fuel
Toy Shop

1.305

1.455

1.336

1.372

Theater
Van
Beauty Salon
Barber Shop

1.449

1.290

1.192

1.149

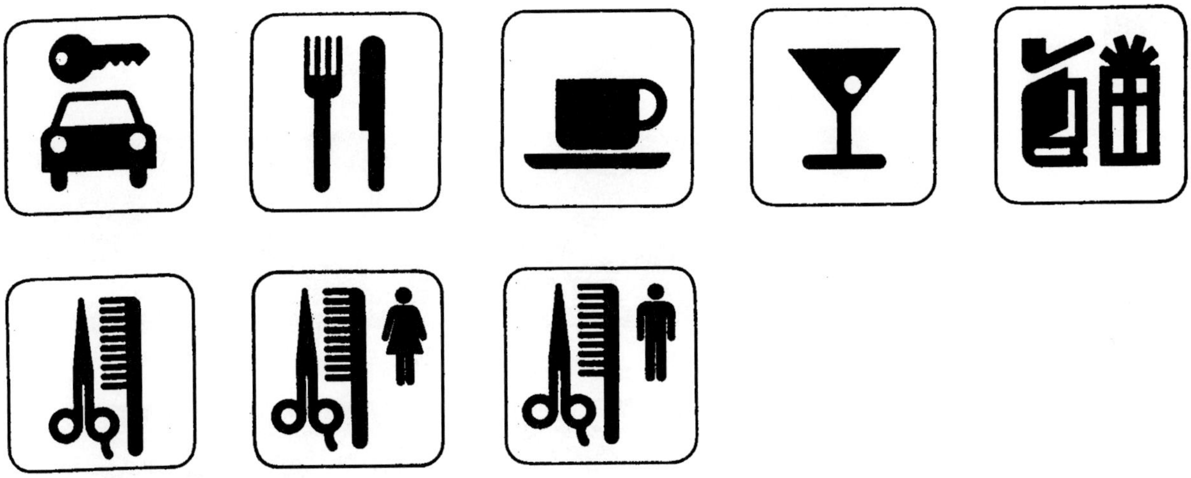

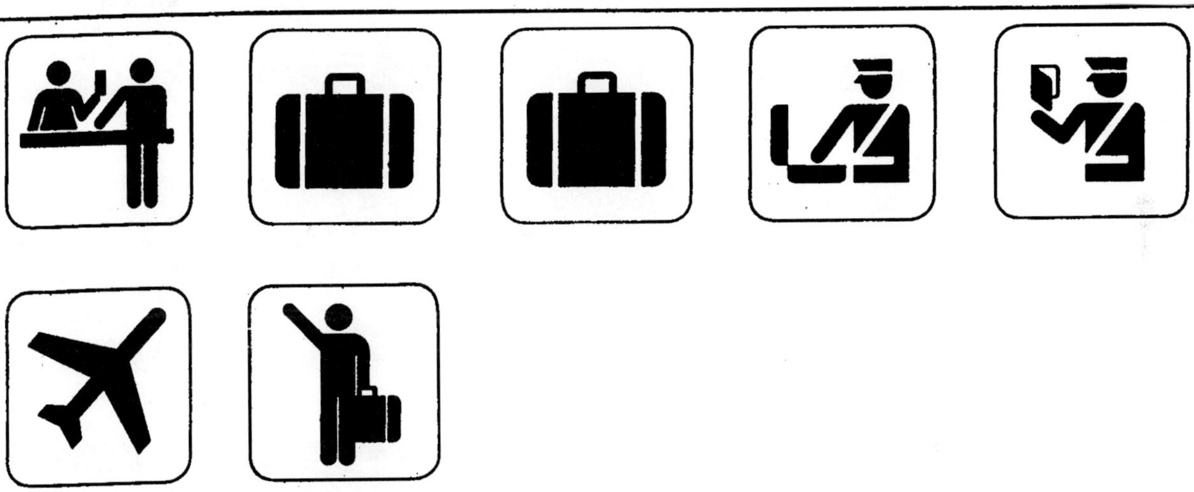

SIGNAGE AND GRAPHICS
Travel Symbols

Travel

Picto'grafics not shown:

1.350 Motel
1.266 Seaplane Base

Airport
Departures
Arrivals
Car Rentals

1.253

1.255

1.254

1.202

Bus
Subway
Train
Taxi

1.208

1.268

1.278

1.203

Monorail
Ferry
Cable Car
Automobile

1.239

1.225

1.215

1.201

Lost & Found
Porter
Locker
Fuel

1.310

1.319

1.308

1.336

Baggage Claim
Customs
Immigration
Money Exchange

1.303

1.125

1.464

1.532

Motorcycle
Moving Sidewalk
Lodging
Ice Cubes

1.241

1.145

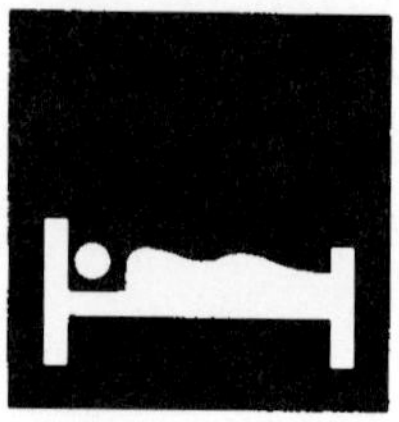
1.173

1.353

Recreation and Sports

Sports Arenas
Parks
Recreation Facilities
Amusement Parks

Picto'grafics not shown:
1.112 Curling
1.115 Dancing
1.140 LaCrosse
1.138 Hockey
1.183 Tobogganing
1.471 Wintersports
1.387 Outdoor Recreation

Campers
Picnic Area
Midway
Trailer Train

1.276

1.366

1.313

1.185

Water
Swimming
Canoeing
Sailing

1.492

1.177

1.217

1.265

Marina, Boating
Life Preserver
Snowmobiling
Camping

1.401

1.357

1.267

1.385

Judging
Bicycling
Women's/Girl's Toilet
Fishing

1.370

1.211

1.910

1.334

Skiing
Soccer
Ice Skating
Football

1 172

1.176

1.181

1.130

Hunting, Shooting
Golf
Baseball
Tennis, Badminton

1 170

1.133

1 105

1.182

Universal

Applicable to any building or facility

Picto'grafics not shown:

1.110 Children
1.144 Man with boy
1.340 Fragile
1.372 Playroom
1.410 Church
1.472 Synagogue
1.469 Police
1.493 Smoke
1.516 Parking
1.488 Keep Dry
1.155 Janitor

Entry
Exit
Ramp up
Ramp down

1.403

1.404

1.461

1.462

Emergency
Women's Toilet
Men's Toilet
Stairs

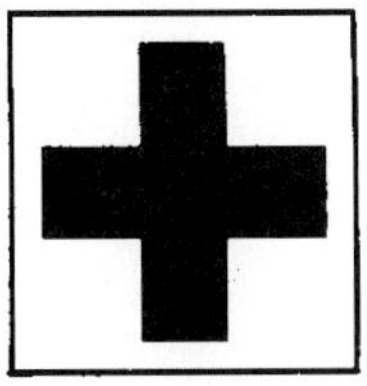
4.412

1.189

1.143

1.377

Handicapped
No Smoking
Telephone
Escalator

1.188

3.316

1.365

1.328

Elevator
Down
No Parking
Drinking fountain

1.311

1.402B

3.516

1.139

Mail Box
Check Room
Up
No Entry

1.326

1.317

1 402A

3 463

Shower
Waiting Room
Telegraph Office
Information

1 376

1 151

1 327

1 530

International symbol of accessibility

SIGNAGE AND GRAPHICS
General Type Styles

Alternate GOTHIC NO. 3
Americana
Americana ITALIC
Aster
Avant Garde GOTHIC MEDIUM
Baker Danmark 2
Baker Sans MONO REGULAR
Baskerville BOLD ITALIC
Bodoni
Bookman
Caledonia BOLD ITALIC
Caslon BOLD
Century SCHOOLBOOK
Century SCHOOLBOOK BOLD
Cheltenham MEDIUM
Columbus
COPPERPLATE GOTHIC LIGHT
Craw Clarendon BOOK
Craw Clarendon
Craw Modern
Delta MEDIUM
Eastern Souvenir MEDIUM
Eurostile
Eurostile BOLD
Eurostile EXTENDED
Eurostile BOLD EXTENDED
Firmin Didot
Folio MEDIUM
Folio MEDIUM EXTENDED
Fortuna LIGHT
Franklin Gothic

Futura MEDIUM
Futura DEMIBOLD
Garamond BOLD
Gerstner Program MEDIUM
Gill Sans
Harry FAT
Hellenic WIDE
Helvetica LIGHT
Helvetica
Helvetica MEDIUM
Helvetica MEDIUM OUTLINE
Horizon MEDIUM
Karen BOLD
Korinna
Korinna BOLD
Lydian
Melior
Melior SEMIBOLD
MICROGRAMMA NORMAL
MICROGRAMMA BOLD
MICROGRAMMA BOLD EXTENDED
Modula MEDIUM
News Gothic BOLD
Olive ANTIQUE
Optima
Optima SEMIBOLD
Palatino
Palatino SEMIBOLD
Permanent MEDIUM
Perpetua ROMAN
Plantin

Quorum MEDIUM
Romana NORMAL
Schadow ANTIQUA SEMIBOLD
Serif Gothic REGULAR
Serif Gothic BOLD
Solitaire BOLD
Souvenir LIGHT
Souvenir MEDIUM ITALIC
Standard MEDIUM
Stymie BOLD
Times ROMAN
Times ROMAN BOLD
Trooper ROMAN LIGHT
Trooper ROMAN
Univers 55
Univers 56
Univers 65
Univers 67
Univers 53
Univers 63
Univers 55 OUTLINE
Univers 65 OUTLINE
Univers 83 OUTLINE
Venus MEDIUM
Venus EXTRABOLD
Venus EXTRABOLD CONDENSED
Venus BOLD EXTENDED
Walbaum MEDIUM
Weiss ROMAN EXTRABOLD
Windsor
Windsor OUTLINE

Clarendon Medium

abcdefghijklmnopqrstuvwxyz
ABCDEFGHIJKLM
NOPQRSTUVWXYZ
0123456789 !"#$%&'*()"+¢£:?-=;/,.

Optima Regular

abcdefghijklmnopqrstuvwxyz
ABCDEFGHIJKLM
NOPQRSTUVWXYZ
0123456789 !"$%&'()"¢£:?-;/,.

Helvetica Medium

abcdefghijklmnopqrstuvwxyz
ABCDEFGHIJKLM
NOPQRSTUVWXYZ
0123456789 ®!"#$%&'°()"+¢£:?-=;/,.

Times New Roman

abcdefghijklmnopqrstuvwxyz
ABCDEFGHIJKLM
NOPQRSTUVWXYZ
0123456789 !"#$%&'()+¢£:?-=;,.

General Symbols Extended

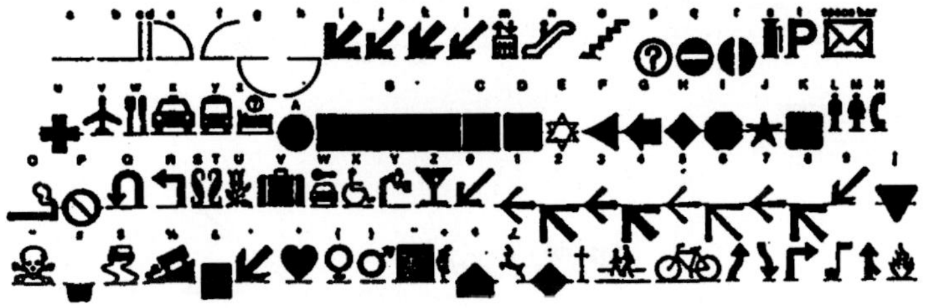

Fig. 14 General type styles with maximum readability. ½-in cap height is legible up to 25 ft, ¾-in to 1-in cap height is legible up to 50 ft, 1- to 2-in cap height is legible up to 100 ft

AUDIOVISUAL SYSTEMS
Planning Guideline Summary

Designing the System

The formulation of a communications program is based on the functional requirements delineated in the feasibility study. The presentation modes to be utilized are a part of such a program. They might include slides, films, videotape, and a sound-recording and playback system. The detailed design of the facility includes the selection of basic equipment, possible modification of that equipment, and provision for additional optical elements, as well as the engineering of the electrical control circuitry and the design of the electromechanical devices that may be needed.

The implementation of a proposed audiovisual (AV) system is not merely an exercise in mechanical assembly. It is a highly complex process of logistics that involves providing specific functional requirements within architectural and economic constraints. Careful engineering and balancing of the alternatives available will generally achieve optimum results.

A large number of variables is encountered in every AV design problem. As an example, the dimensions of the presentation room have a significant effect on the audience size, the acoustic characteristics, the size of the projected image, the choice of equipment, and the location and the interrelationship of the components.

The AV consultant who is responsible for the program planning, the design, and the engineering of this complex, multifaceted discipline should be intimately familiar with the problems of fabrication, installation, and operation of such systems. This knowledge will enable the consultant to plan a facility whose execution will not create difficulties and whose construction and operation can be effected without costly changes. However, even when the consul-

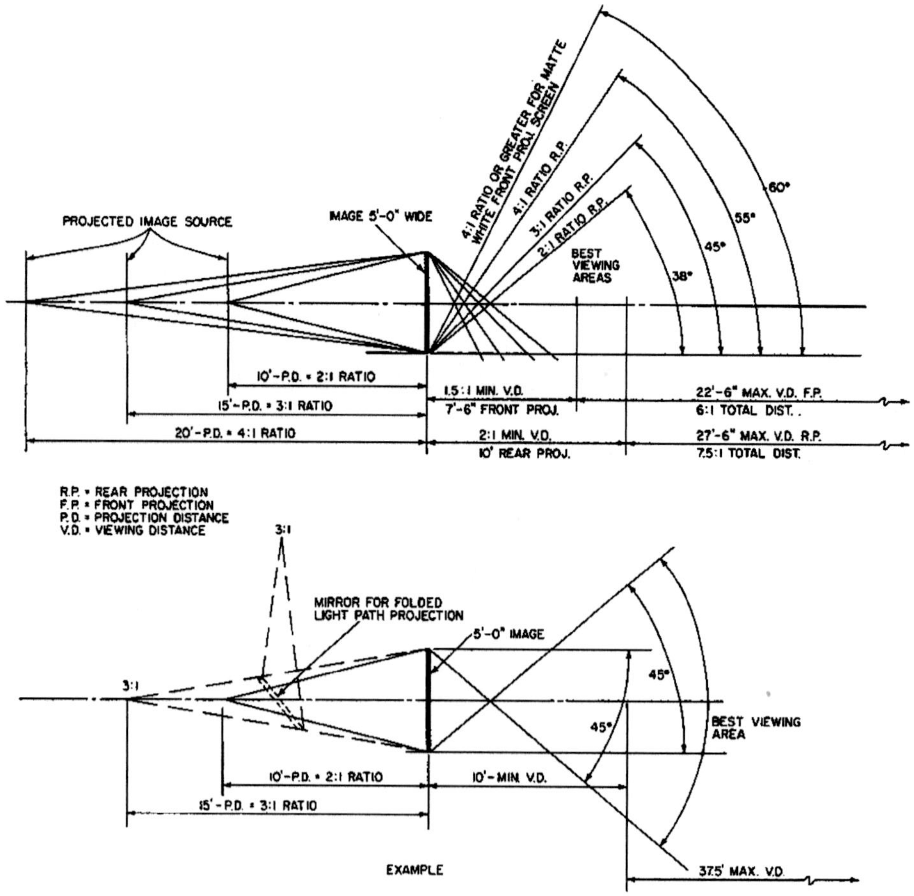

Fig. 1 The interrelationship of projection distance, image size, and viewing area

tant has experience as an adviser to members of the architectural and engineering professions, the creation of a well-integrated facility is not necessarily assured. His or her work and the completed facilities should be viewed and evaluated.

Optical Aspects

It is of critical importance for an AV system to have the ability to display bright, sharp images to all viewers and to maintain the stability and consistency of those images in a simple and straightforward manner. The picture quality is a function of a number of factors requiring careful attention during all phases of the project. These include:

- The quality of the original photography or artwork
- The density, contrast, and sharpness of the actual material being projected
- The output intensity of the projector light source
- The optical characteristics of each projection unit
- The optical characteristics of the integrated system
- The ratio of the projection distance to the image size
- The centering integrity of the light path from the material being projected to its image on the screen
- The characteristics of the projection screen or other viewing surface

Projection Engineering

Room size Ideally, the dimensions of the viewing room should be an outgrowth of the estimate of the audience size that was established in the original AV study. In many cases, however, the AV design engineer must utilize a predetermined space. Given the characteristics of that space, the designer can determine the ideal audience size for each type of seating arrangement, and also ascertain whether a front or rear projection mode is feasible and what the image size should be.

The type of relationship that is desired between the person making the presentation and the audience will determine the seating configuration: theater, lecture, or conference format. That configuration will in turn dictate the number of viewers that can be comfortably seated for optimum viewing (Fig. 1).

As an illustration, a room 20 ft by 32 ft can accommodate about 49 people in a theatre configuration (Fig. 2); in a lecture arrangement, the audience size would be 24 (Fig. 3); a U-shaped table would seat 18 (Fig. 4); and 15 people could fit comfortably at a conference table (Fig. 5). Circular and multiuse arrangements (Figs. 6 and 7) are additional examples of the relationship of seating configuration and audience size.

Other seating configurations have been devised for other types of communication program modes, each with a direct relationship between room size and audience size. The audience size is also affected by the angle of view between each member of the audience and the screen (Fig. 1).

Whenever the AV design engineer has the opportunity of establishing the dimensions of the presentation room, he or she should be aware of the important fact that a longer projection throw for a particular

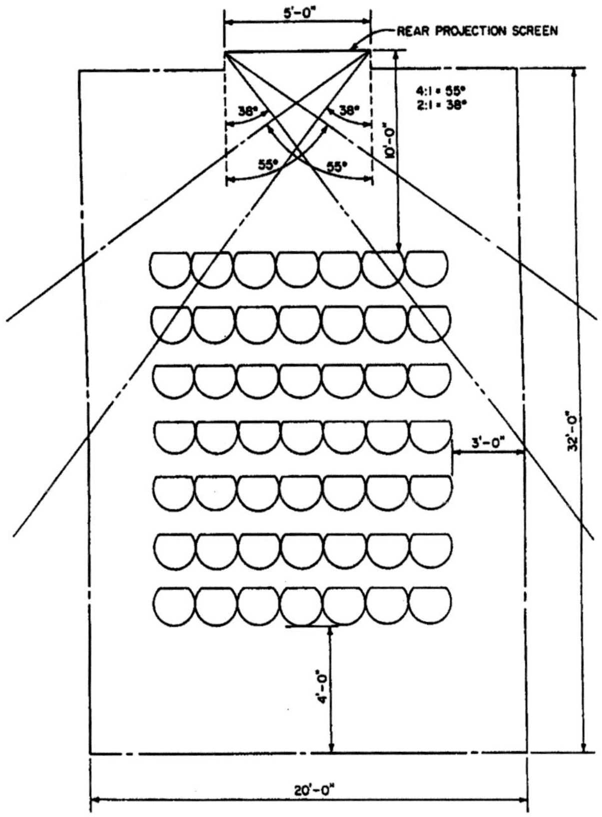

Fig. 2 A room 20 ft by 32 ft, seating 49 people in theater style

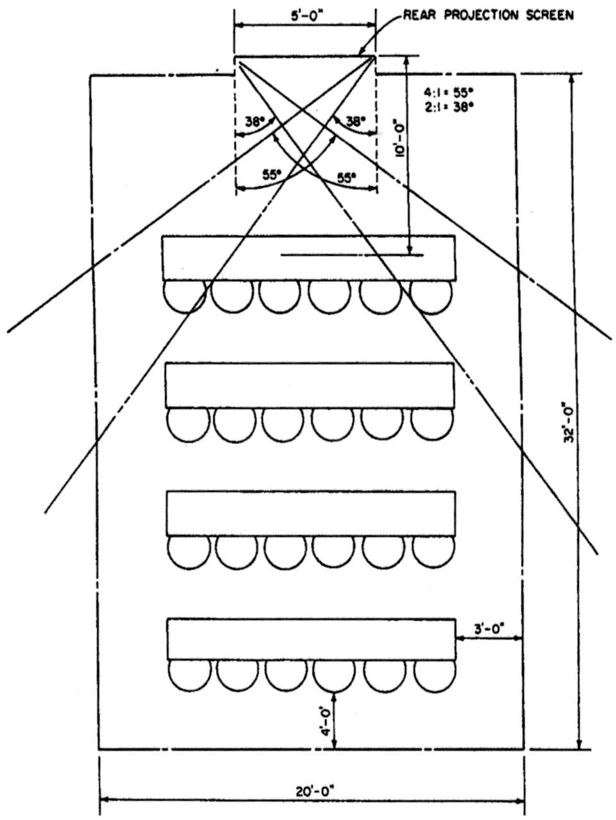

Fig. 3 A room 20 ft by 32 ft, seating 24 people in lecture style

AUDIOVISUAL SYSTEMS

Typical Projection Room Layout and Sightlines

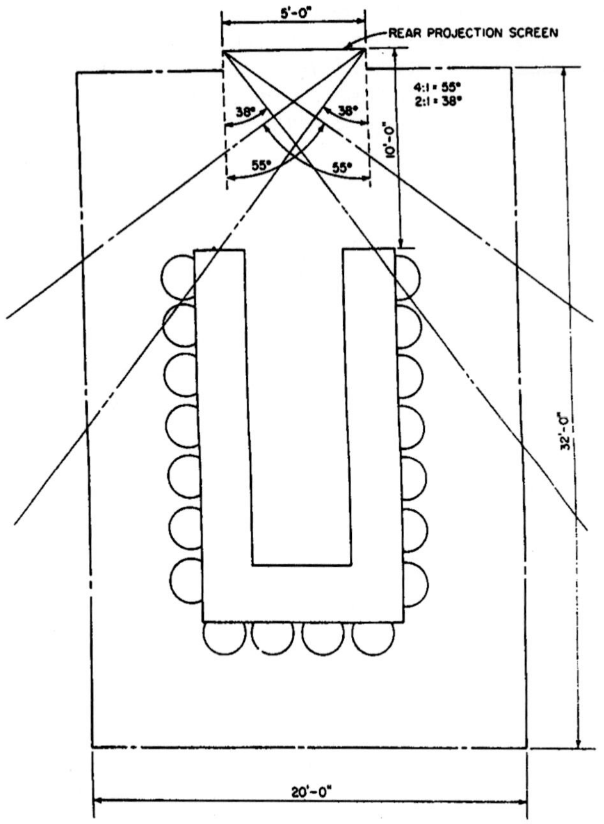

Fig. 4 A room 20 ft by 32 ft, seating 18 people at a U-shaped table

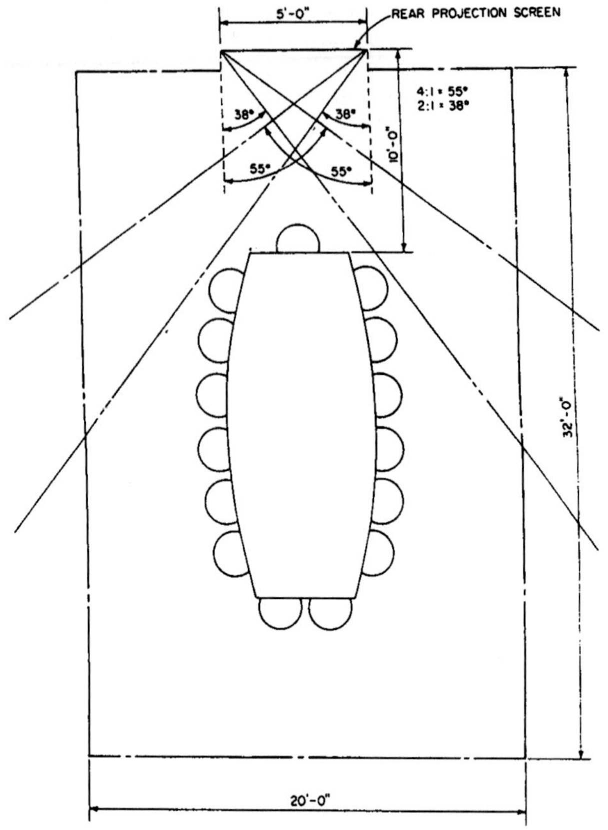

Fig. 5 A room 20 ft by 32 ft, seating 15 people at a boat-shaped conference table

image size results in more even light distribution and sharpness as well as a better angle of view. Consequently, a larger audience can be accommodated than would be possible using a system with a short projection distance and a narrower angle of view. This question of projection distance applies to both front and rear projection systems. However, as the throw is normally quite short when a rear projection screen is used, this factor of design in rear projection facilities is an extremely critical planning element.

Distortion, sometimes called "keystoning," will result if the viewing surface is not precisely parallel to the plane of the image being projected. Therefore, the light path, which is usually perpendicular to the projected material, must be carefully controlled in relation to the projector and the screen. The size of the audience and the room, as well as the mode of projection, will determine whether the screen will be vertical or at an angle (Fig. 8). Normally, a rear projection screen will permit a vertical viewing surface.

AUDIOVISUAL SYSTEMS

Typical Projection Room Layout and Sightlines

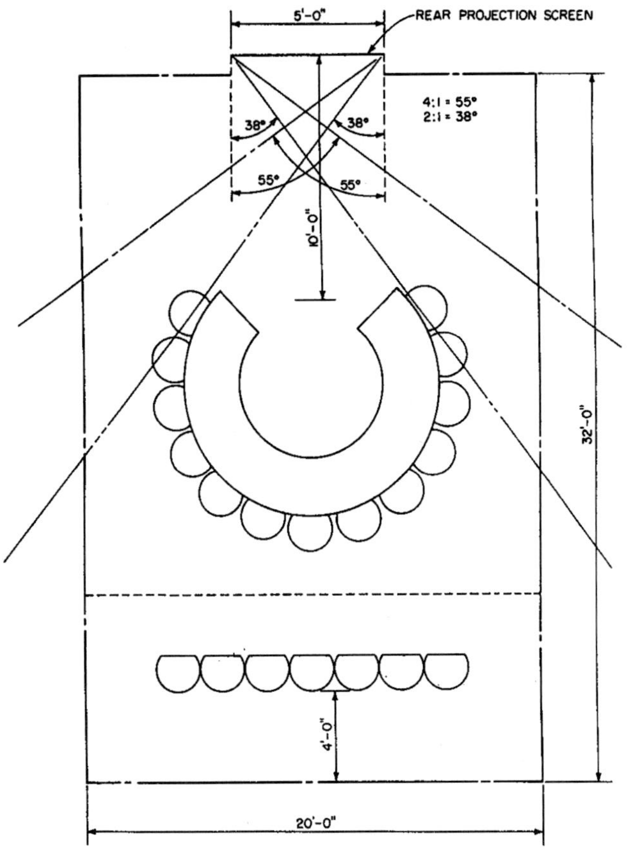

Fig. 6 A room 20 ft by 24 ft, seating 13 people at a circular table. With the depth increased to 32 ft, from 7 to 14 observers can also be accommodated

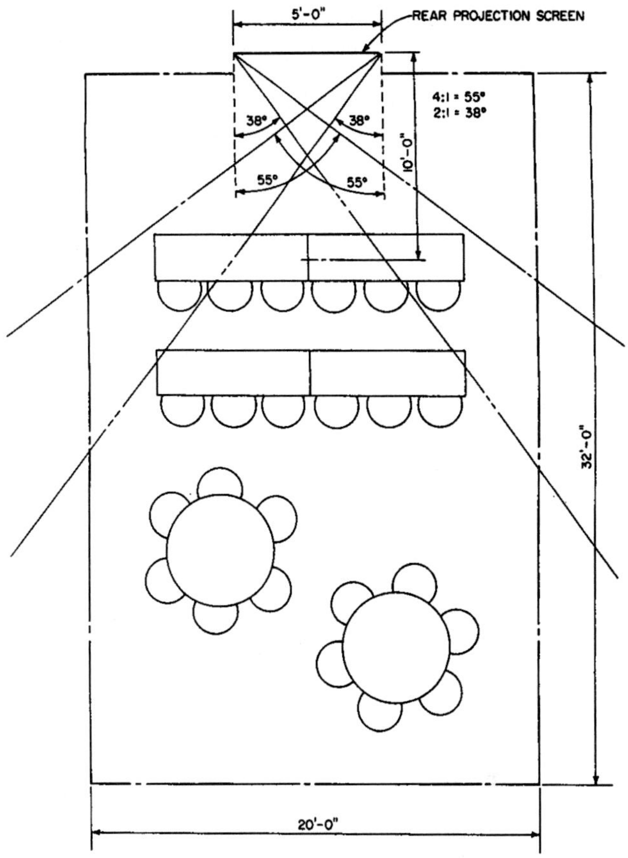

Fig. 7 A modified classroom arrangement including both lecture and separate tables

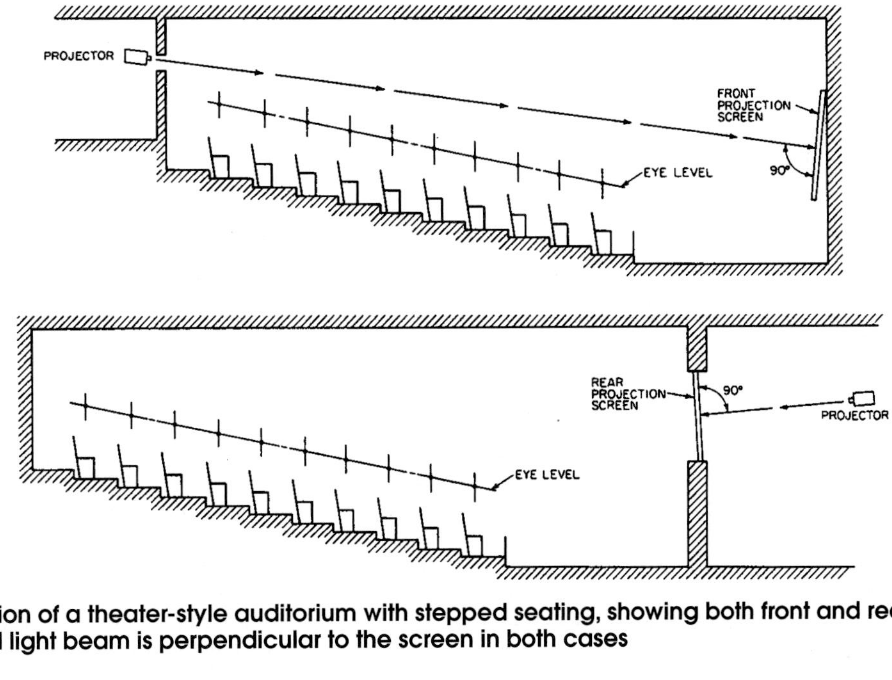

Fig. 8 Cross section of a theater-style auditorium with stepped seating, showing both front and rear projection. Note that the projected light beam is perpendicular to the screen in both cases

AUDIOVISUAL SYSTEMS
Planning Guidelines Summary

Screen image area The most useful screen is one that is square, as it will permit both vertical and horizontal images, as well as square ones, of course (Fig. 9). A single image format will need one such screen, while a dual format will have a viewing surface that is the width of two images placed side by side (Figs. 9 and 10).

It is an easy matter to determine the minimum image size necessary for a room of a given size. For a front projection screen, the minimum size is the distance between it and the farthest viewer divided by 6. For a rear projection screen, the division factor is 7.5. As an illustration, when the distance between the front projection screen and the last row of viewers is 45 ft, the minimum image size would be 7.5 ft; with a rear projection screen, the minimum image should be 6 ft. These calculations assume that the original artwork from which the projection materials are made meets the generally accepted basic minimum standards.

Front projection The projector in a front projection system transmits the image in the form of a light beam to an opaque screen, where it is reflected back to the viewers, creating the image. As the screen reflects any light falling on its surface, the general light level in the room during a presentation must be extremely low. If the full color and contrast of the projected image are to be retained, the ambient light should be no greater than 0.3 percent of the average screen brightness.

Projectors are generally noisy and should be separated from the audience to avoid distractions. If the space is available, a separate projection booth can be built behind the room's rear wall. Besides insulating the viewers from unwanted sound and light spill, this arrangement provides the opportunity for equipment to remain in place, ready for use. There are other possible arrangements when space is constricted (Figs. 11, 12, and 13).

Creating an AV front projection system that is both aesthetically pleasing and functionally efficient requires a high level of technical expertise and design skill. The results of such a combination can be effective yet unobtrusive. Fig. 16 provides an example of a multimedia front projection system that is compatible with the decor of the room and its formalized seating arrangement.

Rear projection The image in a rear projection system is focused on the back of a translucent screen and is visible to the audience on the other side. Since the light passes through the screen rather than being reflected off its front surface, there can be a reasonable light level in the viewing room during the presentation without affecting the quality of the image. It is only in the immediate vicinity of the screen that the room lights need be dimmed.

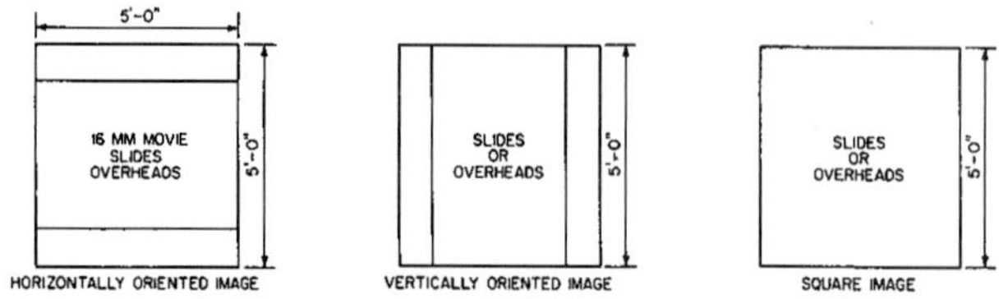

Fig. 9 A square screen will permit horizontal, vertical, and square images to be shown

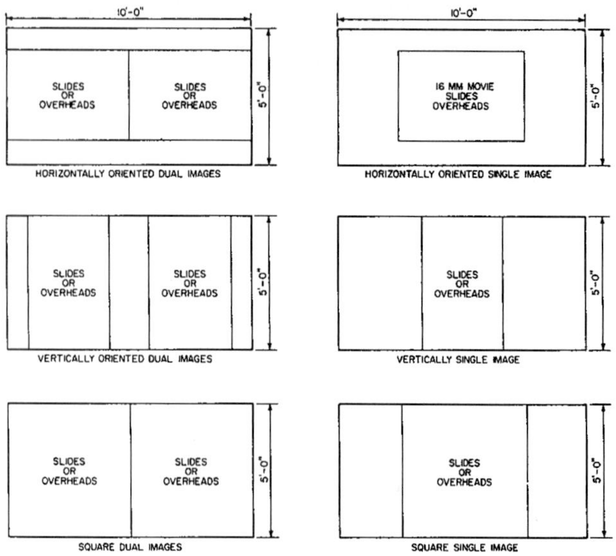

Fig. 10 A dual-image format uses a screen that is a double square—giving the same flexibility of image shape for each of the two images or for a single central image

As is the case with all projection systems, for minimum distractions the equipment should be separated from the audience. This can be effected by means of a separate projection booth or by an enclosed cabinet within the viewing room. A separate room usually requires more space, but it may be the best solution for a particular situation. A cabinet within the viewing room permits front access to the projectors, enabling the presenter to load the equipment without assistance.

While technical expertise and design skill are needed for the creation of a front projection AV system, they are even more important for a system intended for rear projection, as a rear-mode arrangement has more inherent problems to overcome.

A rear projection system utilizing the indirect deep method in a separate projection booth requires a considerable amount of space. In addition, if more than one projector is used in such a system, either the projectors must be optically aligned each time a change is made (as there is only one true screen axis), or they are permanently positioned a little off axis, resulting in a slight keystone or distortion effect in the projected image (Fig. 17).

For good image clarity, the distance between the image source and the screen must be at least twice the picture size. To achieve this clarity within a limited amount of space, the folded light-path method can be used (Figs. 18 and 19). As the name implies, the light path from the projector is "folded" by means of a large mirror, usually placed some distance away. This arrangement has the advantage of reducing the depth required behind the screen while retaining an adequate projection distance. As a further advantage, several projectors can be aligned in optically true positions by the use of a movable mirror with preset position stops.

The use of the folded light-path method of projection and a movable mirror can also be engineered in a cabinet that is directly accessible from the presentation room for hands-on operation by the person making the presentation. Both single-image and side-by-side dual-image systems can be designed in this manner (Figs. 20 and 21).

A great number of variations are possible using the same basic engineering concepts. These variations can accommodate different functional requirements, spatial limitations, and image-quality parameters. Figures 14, 15, 22, and 23 illustrate some of the possible arrangements. User requirements and job conditions will guide the AV engineer in the design of a specific system.

The Optical Design Factor

A projection system—of whatever nature—is only as good as the quality of the image on the screen. The clarity, sharpness, resolution, and angle of view that can be expected are a direct result of the thought and care that go into the optical design of the system. The more complex the system becomes, the more critical is the system optics. The need for larger images, sharper images, multiple images, and multiple image sources, and the existence of physically constraining parameters all add to the conflicting requirements that must be satisfied. And they must be satisfied if an acceptable image quality is to be achieved.

The Sound System

The quality and the functional characteristics of the sound system that is part of an audiovisual facility are as important as the quality and functional characteristics of the optical system. The two aspects of a facility are complementary and the one should not be neglected in relation to the other if the goal of an effective and useful facility is to be attained.

The quality of the sound, as perceived by the listener, will be influenced by such factors as:

- Sensitivity of controls
- Quality of the amplifiers
- Quality of the speakers

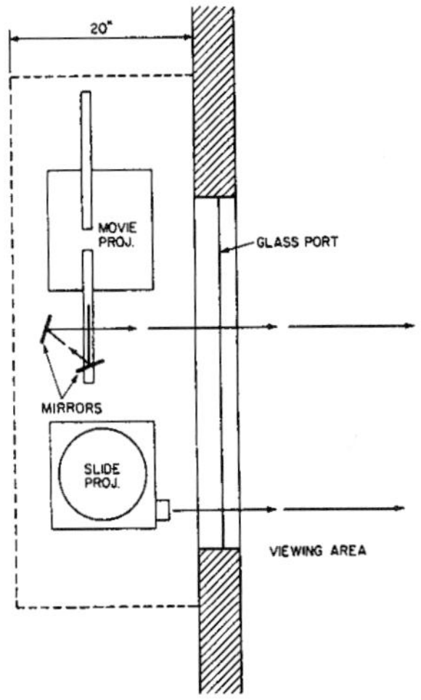

Fig. 12 A rear-access reduced-depth arrangement of equipment for front projection

- Location of the speakers
- Elimination of extraneous sounds
- Overall acoustical characteristics of the space

The design factors that govern the functional characteristics of the sound system might include the following:

Sound sources: Voice, movie soundtrack, videotape, audiotape
Telecommunication facilities for outside program sources
Mixing and control requirements
Quantity and placement of speakers
Room size and function: Conference room, classroom, auditorium
Provision for flexibility and future expansion

The Remote-Control System

Most people who make informational presentations are not audiovisual specialists. Their primary concern is with the material they are

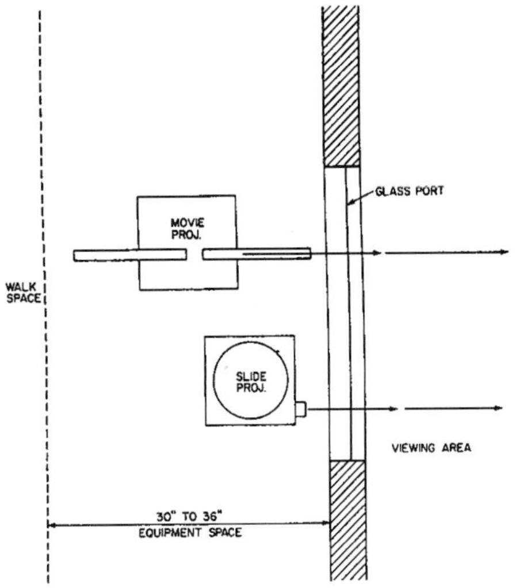

Fig. 11 A typical rear-access equipment arrangement for front projection

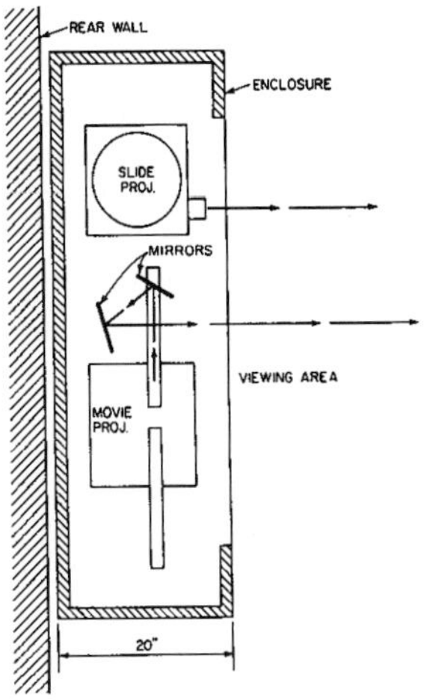

Fig. 13 A front-access equipment cabinet for front projection

presenting and not with the mechanics of how it is to be presented. As a result, any control devices they may be required to operate should be simple and logical. The presenter should be asked to make only a minimum of effort to determine how to manipulate the controls in order to achieve a desired result. The fewer the operations necessary to reach a particular goal, the better. For example, in order for a change to be made from one presentation mode to another, it may be necessary to alter the ambient room lighting, reposition a mirror, turn one machine off and then another on. If all these things can be accomplished merely by flipping one clearly marked switch, the presenter is freed from mechanical distractions and can concentrate full attention on the message being delivered. The location and spacing of the various switches on the panel, as well as the use of nomenclature unmistakable to a nontechnical person, are important parts of the design of a remote-control system that will aid the presenter in the use of the audiovisual facility.

Other considerations that may affect the design of a remote-control system include:

- Seating configuration
- Room lighting
- Number of control points required
- Use of a lectern incorporating a control module
- Number and type of functions to be controlled
- Degree of automation required to meet system objectives

SUMMARY

An audiovisual presentation facility is made up of many components and subsystems which are interdependent and must perform as an integrated unit. Regardless of its size or scope, the AV system must be conceived, designed, and installed to function as a totality—as a single entity that works with optimum efficiency and effectiveness in an unobtrusive manner.

In order to achieve this goal—that of developing a logical and workable solution to any particular communication problem—careful and detailed preliminary investigations must be made. These will determine the functional requirements that make up the design program. From this program, the space needs for the equipment and for the audience can be established early enough in the development of the project to avoid undesirable procrustean solutions later. The selection, adaptation, manufacture, assembly, and installation of equipment and components should be carefully coordinated to ensure their functional integrity and performance.

Ultimately, a successful audiovisual system is one that serves as a logical and natural extension of the human capabilities of the person using it. It should respond easily and unobtrusively to the communicator's needs, and it should reproduce the material being communicated with the highest possible degree of fidelity.

RECAP

Front Projection

1. Viewing distance factor is 6. (For example, if image size is 5 ft, the alphanumerics would be clear at a maximum distance of 30 ft to a viewer with 20/40 vision if characters are 3⁄16 in on 6- by 9-in original copy area.)
2. Advantages
   a. Good angle of view
   b. Good for checking laboratory quality of all projectuals
   c. Virtually no apparent falloff to the sides
3. Disadvantages
   a. High ceilings are required to utilize a square screen to accommodate vertical as well as horizontal images.
   b. Distraction occurs when the presenter or viewers interrupt the light beam.
   c. Any ambient light adversely affects image quality. The room must be relatively dark to achieve the desired picture contrast.
   d. An overhead projector cannot be used most effectively.

Rear Projection (Rigid or Flexible Material)

1. Viewing distance factor is 7.5. (For example, if image size is 5 ft, the maximum viewing distance would be 37.5 ft.)
2. Advantages
   a. A 20 percent smaller image than is required by front projection permits minimum standards to be met in low-ceilinged rooms.
   b. Can be used in higher ambient light conditions.
   c. No distracting light beam. (Presenter can more comfortably point at details).
   d. In a brighter room, the presenter easily maintains eye contact.
   e. An overhead projector can be used, so that neither it nor the presenter blocks the image from the viewers.
3. Disadvantages
   a. The inherent grain and directional quality of the rear screen eliminate it as a viewing medium to determine laboratory quality of projectuals.
   b. The projection system must be designed to overcome apparent illumination falloff at the sides and improve the angle of view.
   c. Mirrored image is required for proper use.
   d. More space is required than with front projection.
   e. Usually costs more.

Seating

(Plan should permit several arrangements.)

1. A U- or V-table layout provides for best viewing and viewer/presenter interaction (lowest audience capacity).
2. Conference table (boat shape or oval) provides good interaction for conferences but not so good as the U- or V-table layout for audiovisual communication.
3. Random seating style (usually with writing tablets) is frequently selected for high-level visitor presentations. It permits larger capacity and creates a more luxurious atmosphere than the two arrangements previously mentioned.
4. Classroom style (shallow tables parallel to front wall with chairs behind) is the next best method, but is less conducive to student interraction.
   a. Stepped, curved seating (lecture hall) provides unobstructed viewing.
   b. When classroom style is contemplated, study and programmed-learning carrels should be considered.
5. Auditorium style provides the largest seating capacity and is generally used for large group-orientation and overview types of presentation.

Rear Projection System Factors

1. The physical center of all projector lenses must be in perfect alignment with the physical center of the screen to eliminate any keystone effect. (For dissolve mode, 2° off center vertically is permitted.)

2. A front-surface mirror should be used to reverse the image so the equipment can be loaded much as it is for front projection; slides in magazines need not be reversed, and special reversed prints are not needed for motion pictures. The use of a mirror can also extend the projection distance appreciably by folding the light path. Remember, the longer the projection distance, the better the viewing angle. Minimum projection distance should be at least two times the image size.
3. The screen-image area should be considered to be square to accommodate vertical and horizontal images unless the system is to be used for a special, limited requirement.
4. Apparent light falloff at the sides can be diminished or eliminated by increasing the projection distance and projector illumination. Another minor contributor is slide density. A dense or underexposed slide reduces the amount of light transmission. This condition increases apparent light falloff.

EQUIPMENT ARRANGEMENT

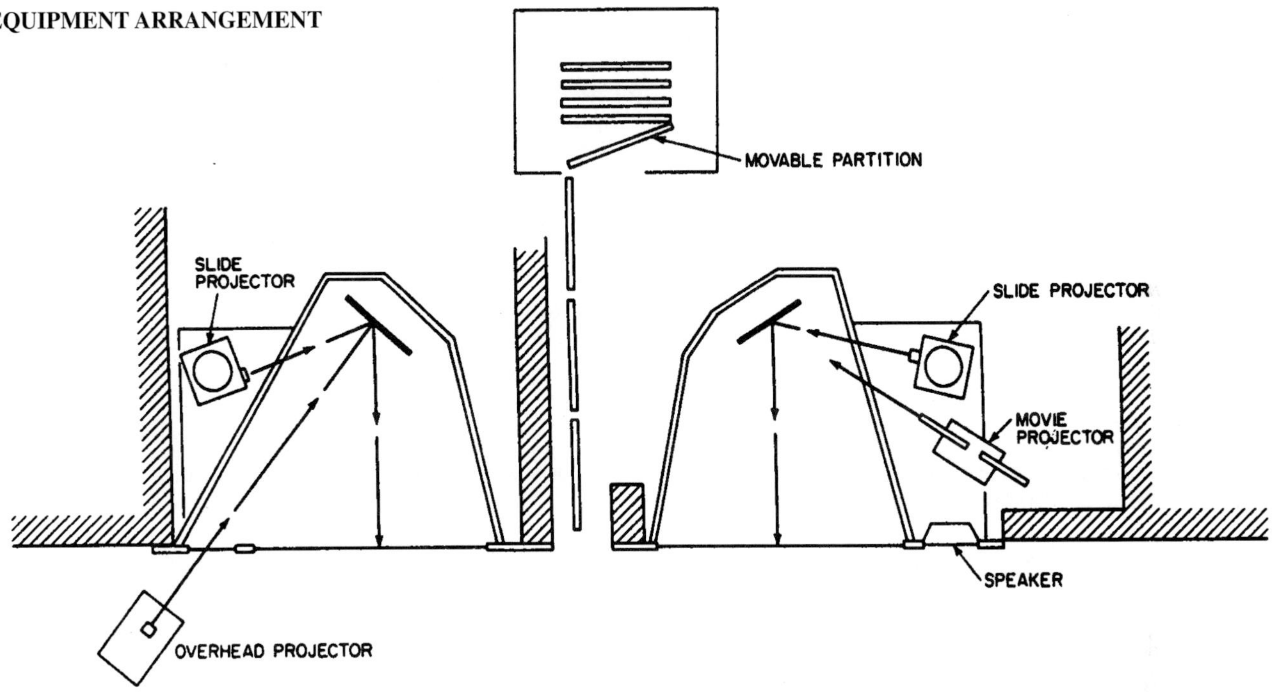

Fig. 14 An arrangement of two enclosed rear projection systems serving a single large room

AUDIOVISUAL SYSTEMS
Equipment Arrangement

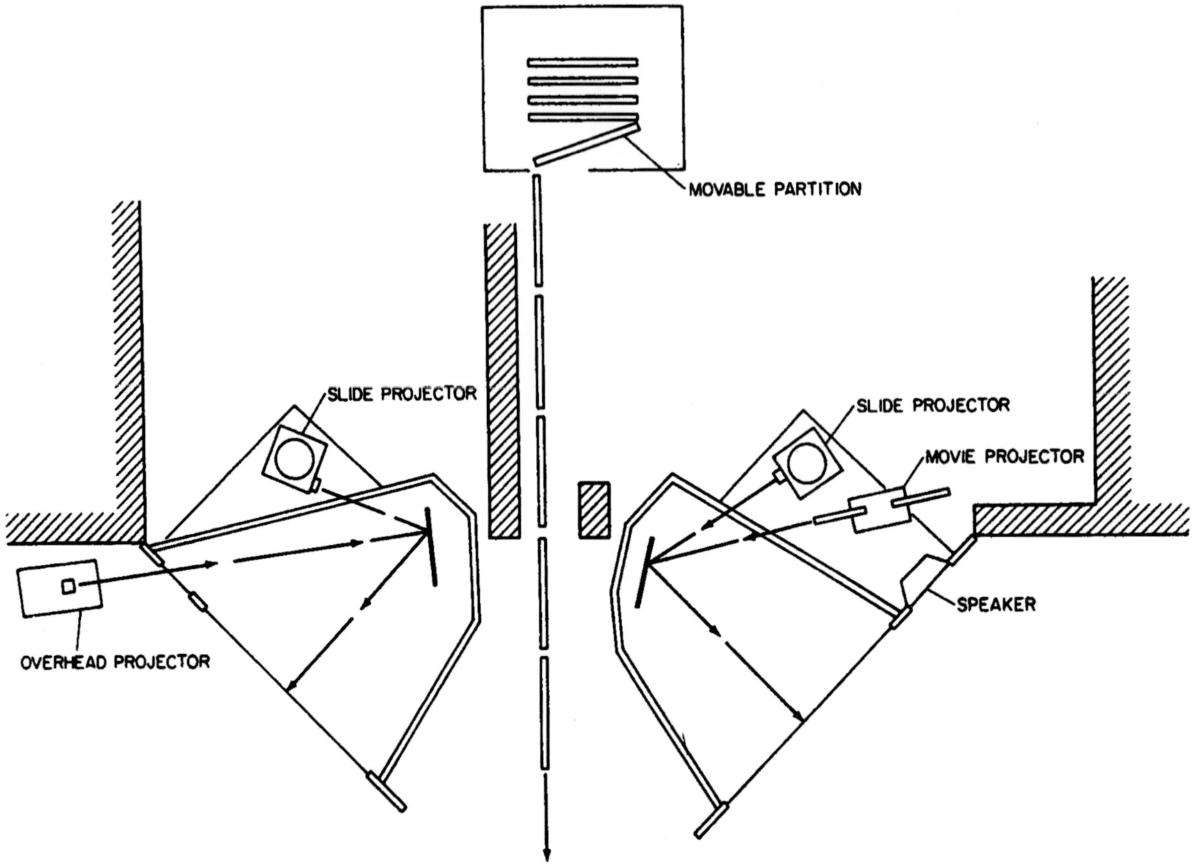

Fig. 15 The two enclosed and pivoted rear projection systems positioned to serve the two separate rooms that are created when a hidden dividing partition is extended

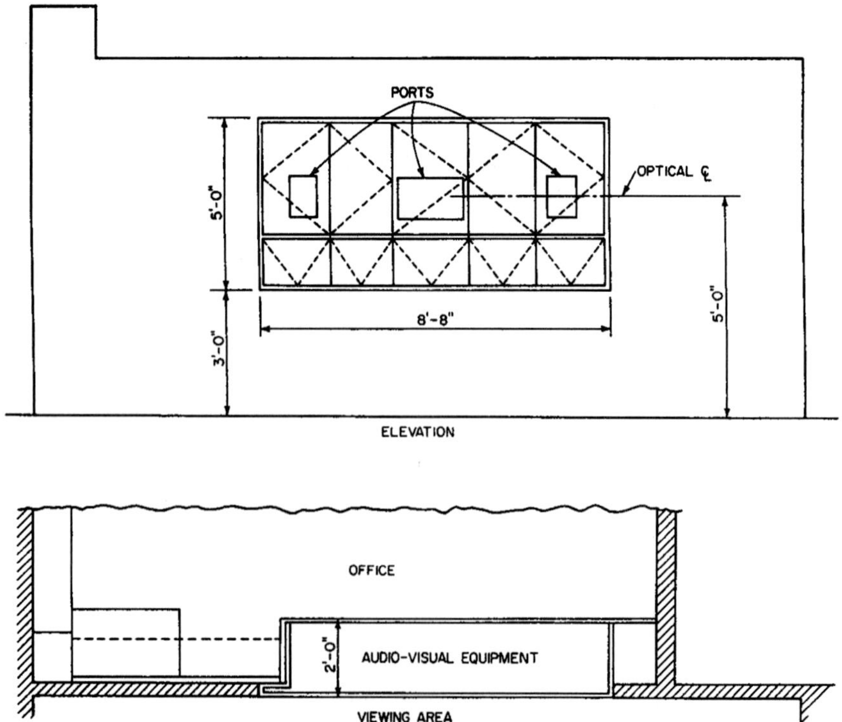

Fig. 16 A custom-designed recessed front-access equipment cabinet for a multi-image front projection system

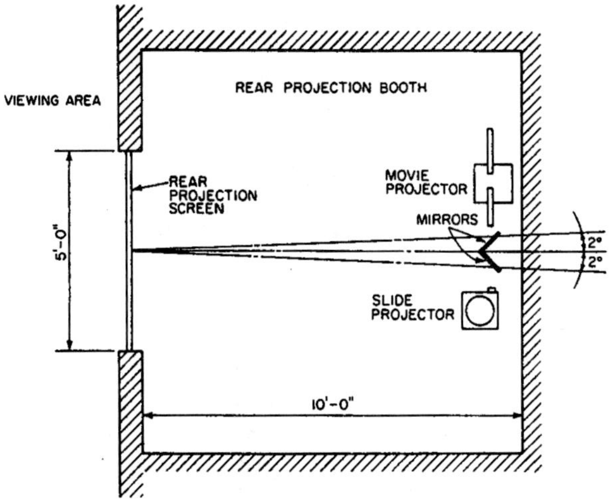

Fig. 17 A deep, indirect-method, rear projection arrangement using the minimum recommended ratio of 2 to 1 between projection distance and image size

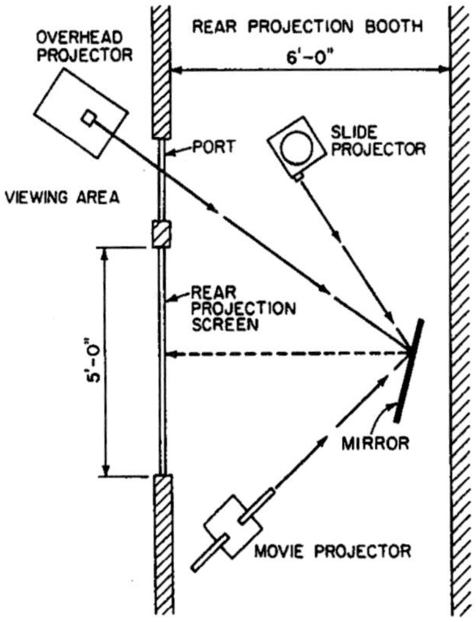

Fig. 19 An indirect rear projection arrangement using the folded light-path method and the minimum recommended 2-to-1 ratio of projection distance to image size. This permits a flexible equipment arrangement within tight space limitations

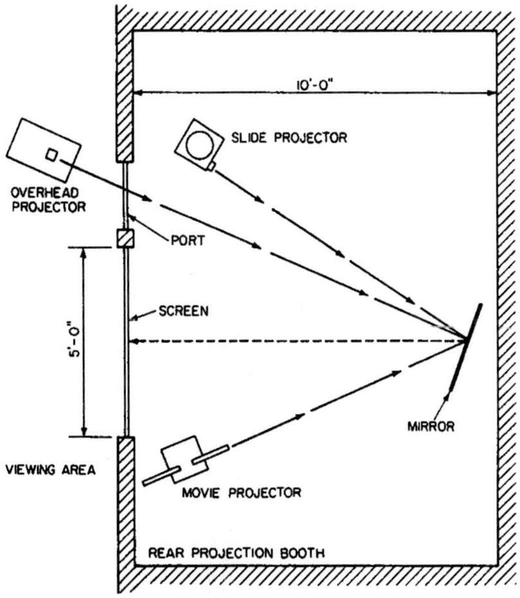

Fig. 18 An indirect rear projection arrangement using the folded light-path method, resulting in a ratio of 3.5 to 1 within the same depth. This improves the image quality and increases the possible viewing angle as well as allowing rear projection of overhead transparencies with the overhead projector in the presentation room

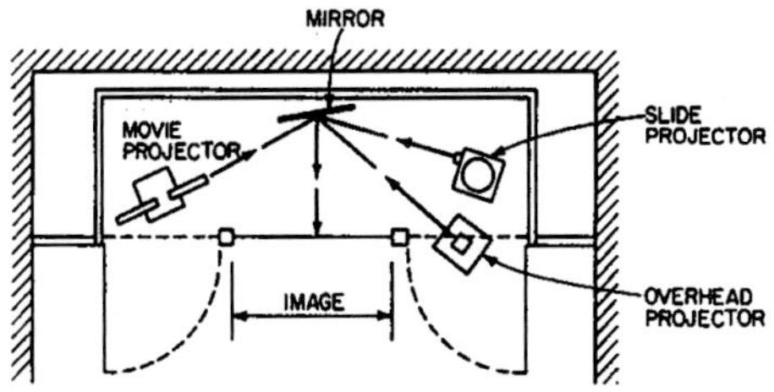

Fig. 20 A front-access rear projection arrangement using the folded light-path method for single-image presentations

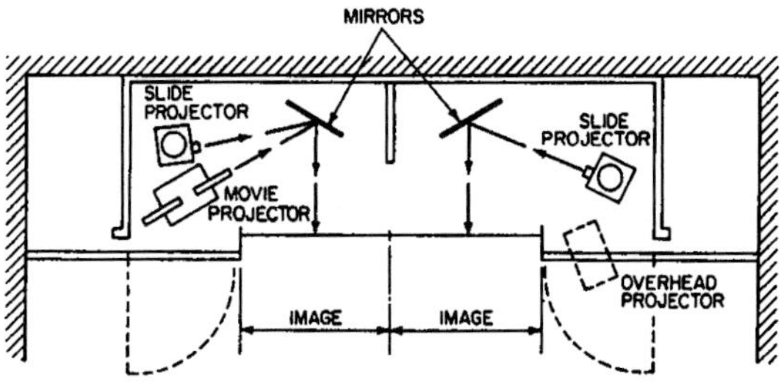

Fig. 21 A front-access rear projection arrangement using the folded light-path method for dual-image presentations

AUDIOVISUAL SYSTEMS
Equipment Arrangement

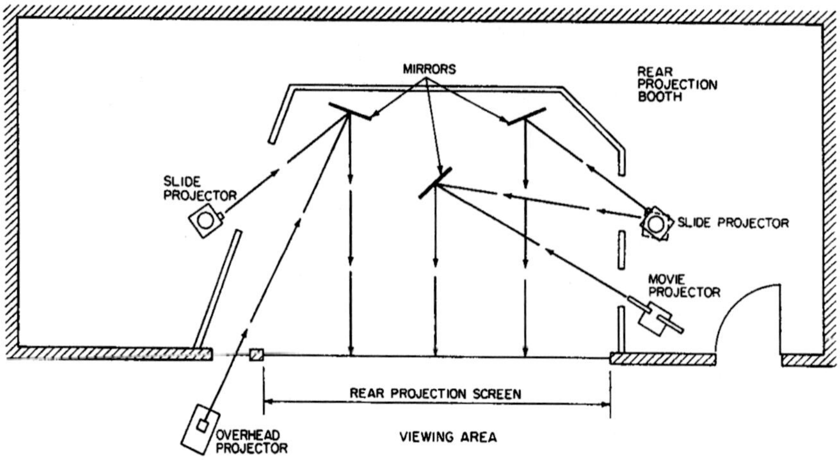

Fig. 22 A rear-access rear projection arrangement using the folded light-path method for dual-image or single-central-image presentations

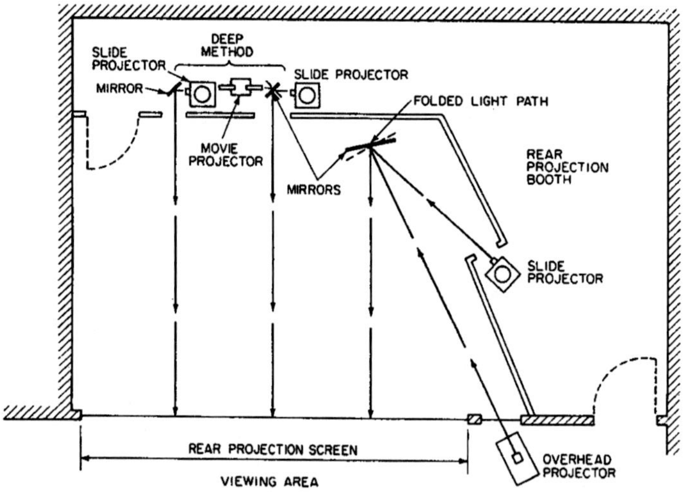

Fig. 23 A rear projection arrangement for dual-image and single-central-image presentations utilizing both deep indirect projection and the folded light-path method

AUDIOVISUAL SYSTEMS
Typical Projection Room Layout

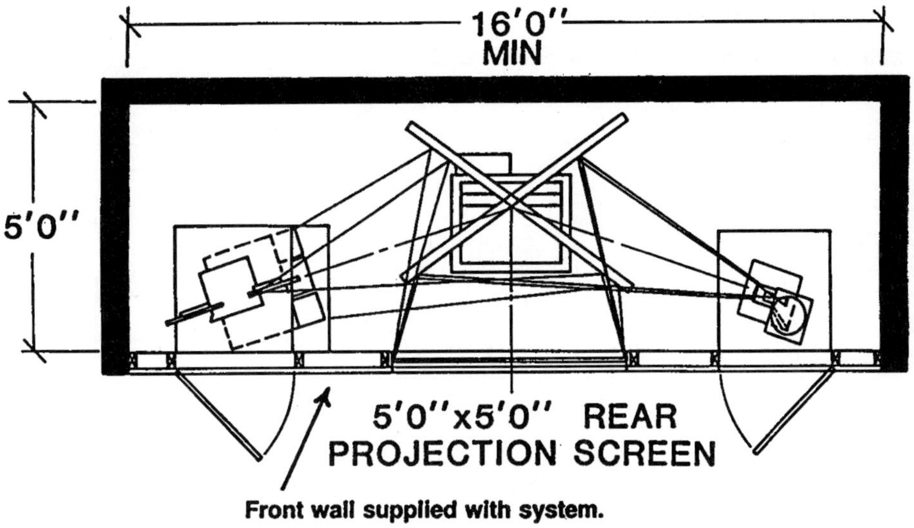

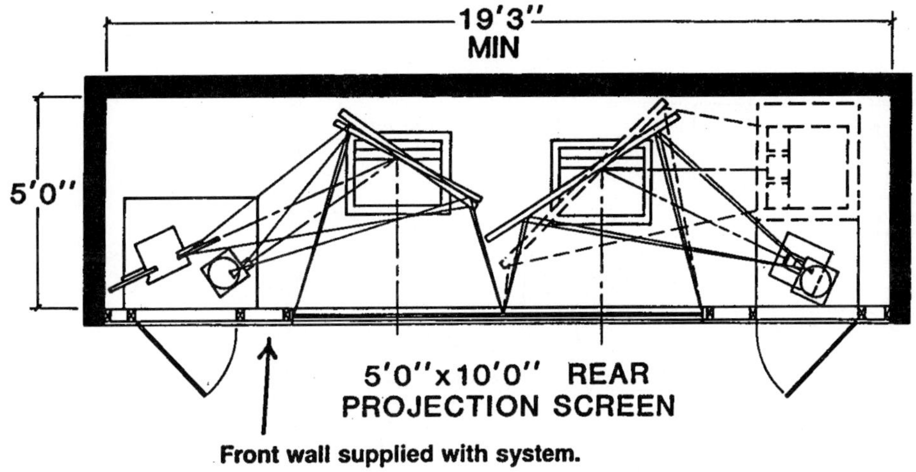

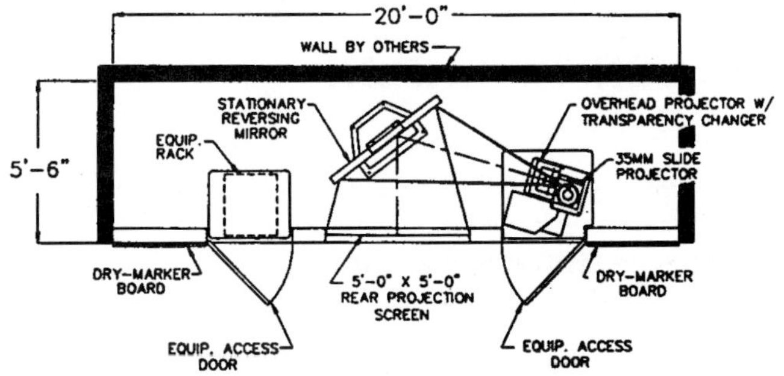

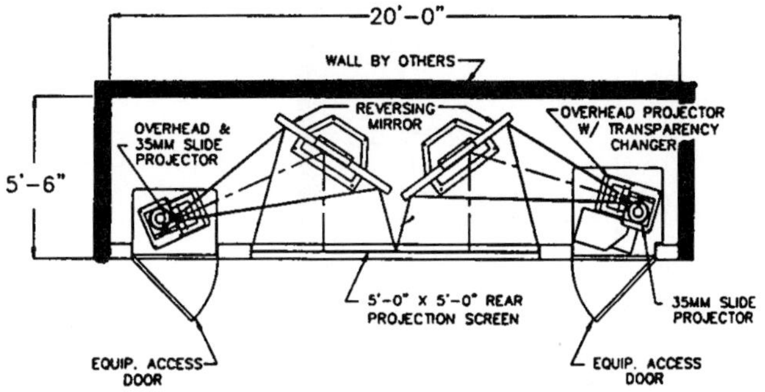

AUDIOVISUAL SYSTEMS
Typical Projection Room Layout

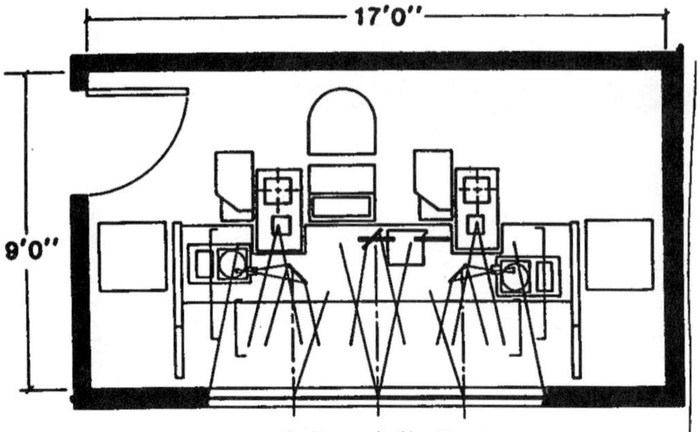

5'0"x10'0" REAR

PROJECTION SCREEN

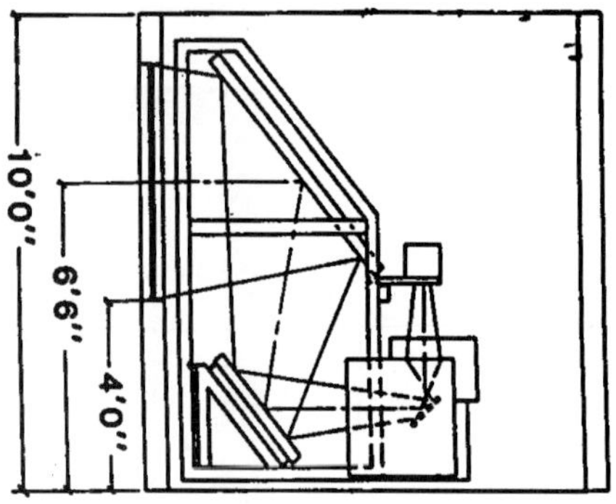

SECTION

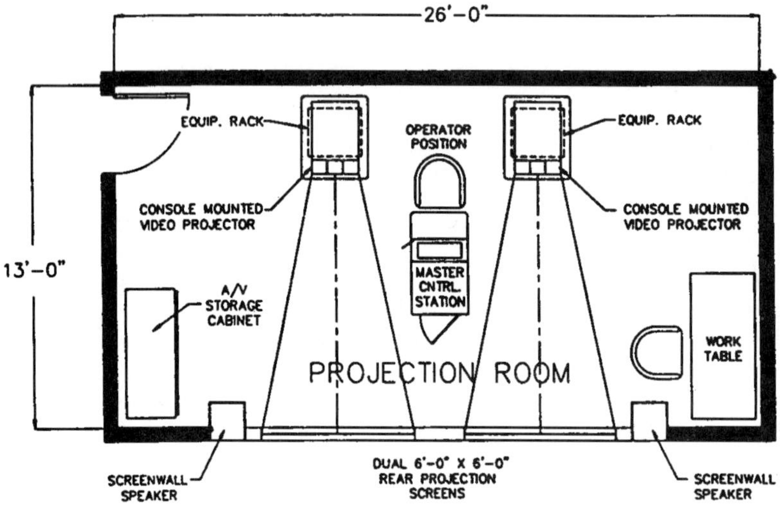

TYPICAL CONFIGURATION

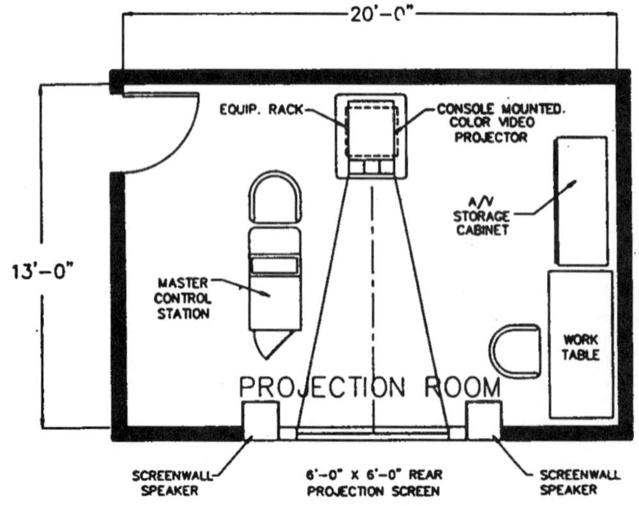

TYPICAL CONFIGURATION

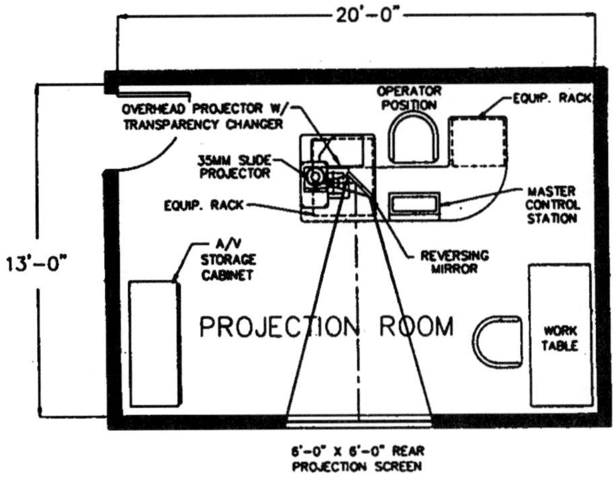

TYPICAL CONFIGURATION

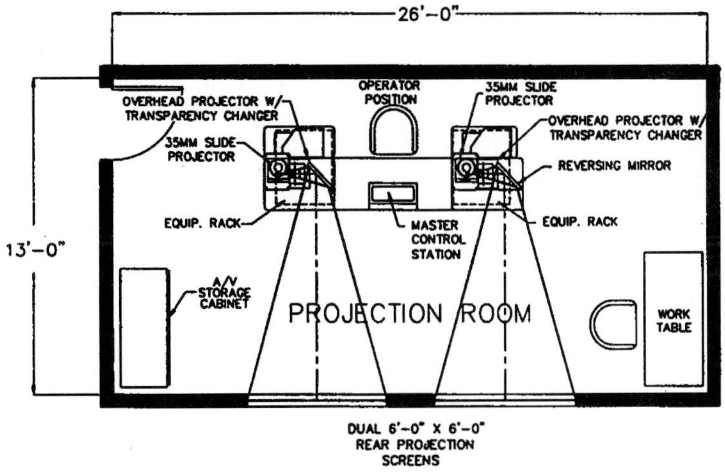

TYPICAL CONFIGURATION

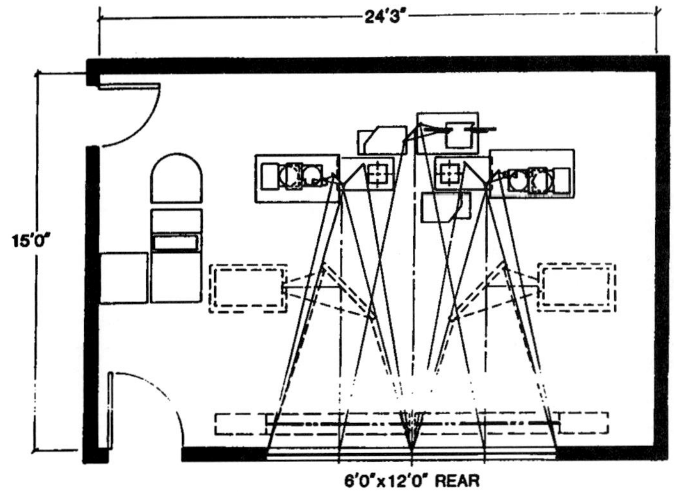

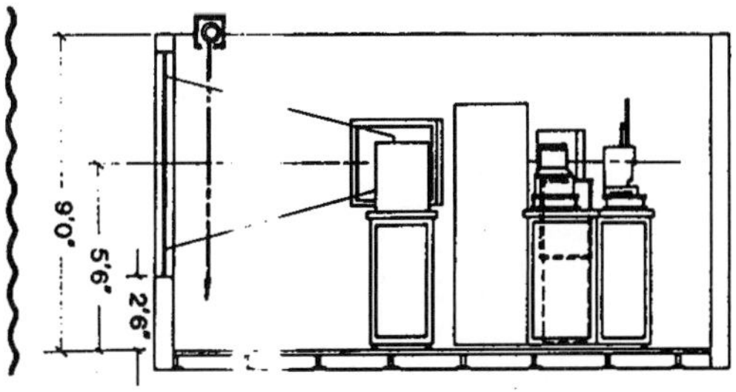

SECTION

PROJECTION SCREEN

(AUDIENCE AREA)

AUDITORIUM SEATING
Sightlines and Building Codes

Sightline studies vary depending on the particular event and seating configuration. The following are some basic design elements.

NOTE: Remember to review and verify slope, riser heights, tread depths, etc., with pertinent national and local code requirements.

Refer to the visibility profile shown in Fig. 1:

Angle A: Shifting position to look between heads in row immediately in front of spectator and over all other heads.
Angle B: Shifting position to look between heads of two rows immediately in front of spectators and over all other heads.

Generally, the variables considered in determining these angles are:

- 3 ft 8 in eye level in the seated position
- 5-in minimum eye clearance
- Row spacing and row rise

Angle A is commonly used in determining floor slope for auditorium, performing arts, or theater-type seating configurations. When the angle A profile is used in conjunction with a staggered seating arrangement (chairs staggered or alternated in arrangement of sizes opposite every other row), it allows spectators an unobstructed view to a determined focal point at the screen on stage. The final analysis is to have all sightlines intersect the desired focal point (usually 5 ft 6 in elevation either at the screen or 12 ft 0 in back from the front of the stage).

Angle B is most commonly used in determining riser or stepped applications for gymnasium, arena, or stadium-type seating configurations. When the angle B profile is used (generally associated with an aligned seating arrangement), it allows spectators an unobstructed view to a determined focal point at the court line or line of play. The final analysis is to have all the critical sightlines intersect the focal point or line of play at generally a 3 ft 0 in elevation.

Legal responsibility lies with the owners and users of equipment in acquiring acceptance with local officials. The following are some basic guidelines.

Standard Seating

1. Row spacing shall provide a clear space of not less than 12 in (30.5 cm) from the back of one chair to the front of the most forward projection of the chair directly behind it when measured with the self-rising seat in the up position.
2. Rows of chairs shall not exceed 14 chairs between aisles and exceed seven chairs from an aisle to a row end.
3. Aisles serving 60 seats or less shall be a minimum of 30 in (76 cm) wide. Aisles serving more than 60 seats shall be at least 3 ft (91 cm) wide when serving seats on one side and at least 3 ft 6 in (107 cm) wide when serving seats on both sides. These minimum widths, measured at the point farthest from an exit, cross aisles, or foyer shall be increased 1½ in (3.8 cm) for each 5 ft (152 cm) in length toward the exit, cross aisle, or foyer. Where egress is possible in either direction, aisles shall be uniform in width. Dead-end aisles are not allowed over 20 ft 0 in (61.0 m) in length.
4. Cross aisles, foyer, or exit widths shall be not less than the sum of the required width of the widest aisle plus 50 percent of the total required width of the remaining aisles that it serves.

Continental Seating

1. Row spacing shall provide a clear space of not less than: 18 in (45.7 cm) between rows of 18 chairs or less; 20 in (50.8 cm) between rows of 35 chairs or less; 21 in (53.3 cm) between rows of 45 chairs or less; 22 in (55.9 cm) between rows of 45 chairs or more to a maximum of 100 chairs per row, measured from the back of one chair to the front of the most forward projection of the chair directly behind it with the self-rising seat in the up position.
2. There shall be exits of 66 in (168 cm) minimum clear width along each side aisle of the chair rows for each five rows of chairs.
3. Aisles shall not be less than 44 in (112 cm) in clear width.

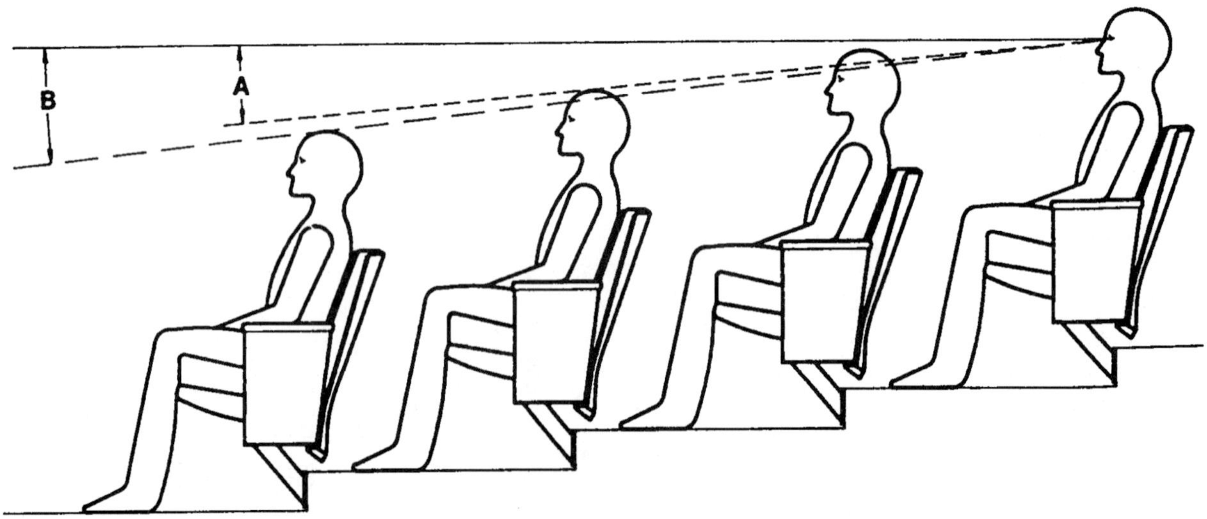

Fig. 1

Row length = ℄ to ℄ + (2A) measured at the Chair Size Line

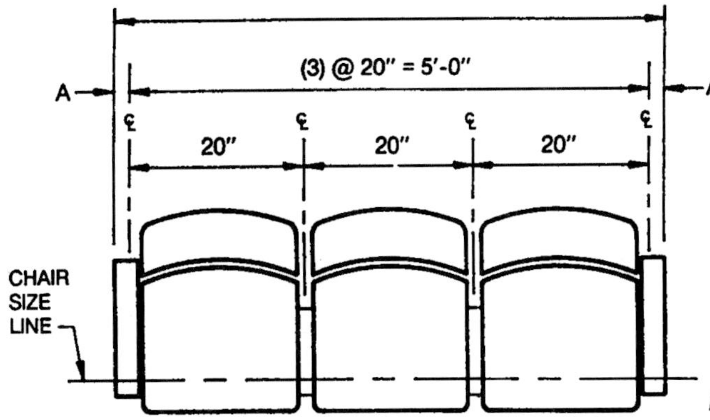

Note: End dim. A varies 2" to 3" for end tablet arm applications.

EXAMPLE:
(3) 20" chairs = 5'-4" row length.

DIMENSIONS: Center line to center line (℄ to ℄)											
QTY	SIZE					QTY	SIZE				
	18"	19"	20"	21"	22"		18"	19"	20"	21"	22"
2	3'-0"	3'-2"	3'-4"	3'-6"	3'-8"	32	48'-0"	50'-8"	53'-4"	56'-0"	58'-8"
3	4'-6"	4'-9"	5'-0"	5'-3"	5'-6"	33	49'-6"	52'-3"	55'-0"	57'-9"	60'-6"
4	6'-0"	6'-4"	6'-8"	7'-0"	7'-4"	34	51'-0"	53'-10"	56'-8"	59'-6"	62'-4"
5	7'-6"	7'-11"	8'-4"	8'-9"	9'-2"	35	52'-6"	55'-5"	58'-4"	61'-3"	64'-2"
6	9"-0"	9'-6"	10'-0"	10'-6"	11'-0"	36	54'-0"	57'-0"	60'-0"	63'-0"	66'-0"
7	10'-6"	11'-1"	11'-8"	12'-3"	12'-10"	37	55'-6"	58'-7"	61'-8"	64'-9"	67'-10"
8	12'-0"	12'-8"	13'-4"	14'-0"	14'-8"	38	57'-0"	60'-2"	63'-4"	66'-6"	69'-8"
9	13'-6"	14'-3"	15'-0"	15'-9"	16'-6"	39	58'-6"	61'-9"	65'-0"	68'-3"	71'-6"
10	15'-0"	15'-10"	16'-8"	17'-6"	18'-4"	40	60'-0"	63'-4"	66'-8"	70'-0"	73'-4"
11	16'-6"	17'-5"	18'-4"	19'-3"	20'-2"	41	61'-6"	64'-11"	68'-4"	71'-9"	75'-2"
12	18'-0"	19'-0"	20'-0"	21'-0"	22'-0"	42	63'-0"	66'-6"	70'-0"	73'-6"	77'-0"
13	19'-6"	20'-7"	21'-8"	22'-9"	23'-10"	43	64'-6"	68'-1"	71'-8"	75'-3"	78'-10"
14	21'-0"	22'-2"	23'-4"	24'-6"	25'-8"	44	66'-0"	69'-8"	73'-4"	77'-0"	80'-8"
15	22'-6"	23'-9"	25'-0"	26'-3"	27'-6"	45	67'-6"	71'-3"	75'-0"	78'-9"	82'-6"
16	24'-0"	25'-4"	26'-8"	28'-0"	29'-4"	46	69'-0"	72'-10"	76'-8"	80'-6"	84'-4"
17	25'-6"	26'-11"	28'-4"	29'-9"	31'-2"	47	70'-6"	74'-5"	78'-4"	82'-3"	86'-2"
18	27'-0"	28'-6"	30'-0"	31'-6"	33'-0"	48	72'-0"	76'-0"	80'-0"	84'-0"	88'-0"
19	28'-6"	30'-1"	31'-8"	33'-3"	34'-10"	49	73'-6"	77'-7"	81'-8"	85'-9"	89'-10"
20	30'-0"	31'-8"	33'-4"	35'-0"	36'-8"	50	75'-0"	79'-2"	83'-4"	87'-6"	91'-8"
21	31'-6"	33'-3"	35'-0"	36'-9"	38'-6"	51	76'-6"	80'-9"	85'-0"	89'-3"	93'-6"
22	33'-0"	34'-10"	36'-8"	38'-6"	40'-4"	52	78'-0"	82'-4"	86'-8"	91'-0"	95'-4"
23	34'-6"	36'-5"	38'-4"	40'-3"	42'-2"	53	79'-6"	83'-11"	88'-4"	92'-9"	97'-2"
24	36'-0"	38'-0"	40'-0"	42'-0"	44'-0"	54	81'-0"	85'-6"	90'-0"	94'-6"	99'-0"
25	37'-6"	39'-7"	41'-8"	43'-9"	45'-10"	55	82'-6"	87'-1"	91'-8"	96'-3"	100'-10"
26	39'-0"	41'-2"	43'-4"	45'-6"	47'-8"	56	84'-0"	88'-8"	93'-4"	98'-0"	102'-8"
27	40'-6"	42'-9"	45'-0"	47'-3"	48'-6"	57	85'-6"	90'-3"	95'-0"	99'-9"	104'-6"
28	42'-0"	44'-4"	46'-8"	49'-0"	51'-4"	58	87'-0"	91'-10"	96'-8"	101'-6"	106'-4"
29	43'-6"	45'-11"	48'-4"	50'-9"	53'-2"	59	88'-6"	93'-5"	98'-4"	103'-3"	108'-2"
30	45'-0"	47'-6"	50'-0"	52'-6"	55'-0"	60	90'-0"	95'-0"	100'-0"	105'-0"	110'-0"
31	46'-6"	49'-1"	51'-8"	54'-3"	56'-10"	—	—	—	—	—	—

AUDITORIUM SEATING
Row Spacing

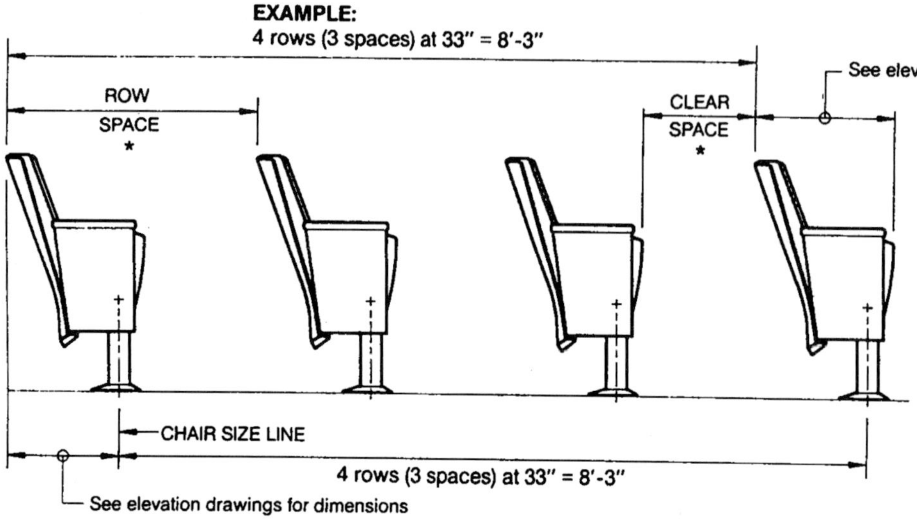

***Notes:**
1. Refer to applicable building codes.
2. Spacing varies with tablet arm applications.
3. Row space dimension will be the sum of "clear space" (see building codes) plus "chair envelope" (see chair dimensions) plus any additional space as desired for convenience to permit patron easy access to concessions, restrooms, etc.

Number of seating rows (spaces + 1)	OVERALL SPACING OF CHAIRS (back to back) — ROW SPACE DIMENSIONS										
	32"	33"	34"	35"	36"	37"	38"	39"	40"	41"	42"
2	2'-8"	2'-9"	2'-10"	2'-11"	3'-0"	3"-1"	3'-2"	3'-3"	3'-4"	3'-5"	3'-6"
3	5'-4"	5'-6"	5'-8"	5'-10"	6'-0"	6'-2"	6'-4"	6'-6"	6'-8"	6'-10"	7'-0"
4	8'-0"	8'-3"	8'-6"	8'-9"	9'-0"	9'-3"	9'-6"	9'-9"	10'-0"	10'-3"	10'-6"
5	10'-8"	11'-0"	11'-4"	11'-8"	12'-0"	12'-4"	12'-8"	13'-0"	13'-4"	13'-8"	14'-0"
6	13'-4"	13'-9"	14'-2"	14'-7"	15'-0"	15'-5"	15'-10"	16'-3"	16'-8"	17'-1"	17'-6"
7	16'-0"	16'-6"	17'-0"	17'-6"	18'-0"	18'-6"	19'-0"	19'-6"	20'-0"	20'-6"	21'-0"
8	18'-8"	19'-3"	19'-10"	20'-5"	21'-0"	21'-7"	22'-2"	22'-9"	23'-4"	23'-11"	24'-6"
9	21'-4"	22'-0"	22'-8"	23'-4"	24'-0"	24'-8"	25'-4"	26'-0"	26'-8"	27'-4"	28'-0"
10	24'-0"	24'-9"	25'-6"	26'-3"	27'-0"	27'-9"	28'-6"	29'-3"	30'-0"	30'-9"	31'-6"
11	26'-8"	27'-6"	28'-4"	29'-2"	30'-0"	30'-10"	31'-8"	32'-6"	33'-4"	34'-2"	35'-0"
12	29'-4"	30'-3"	31'-2"	32'-1"	33'-0"	33'-11"	34'-10"	35'-9"	36'-8"	37'-7"	38'-6"
13	32'-0"	33'-0"	34'-0"	35'-0"	36'-0"	37'-0"	38'-0"	39'-0"	40'-0"	41'-0"	42'-0"
14	34'-8"	35'-9"	36'-10"	37'-11"	39'-0"	40'-1"	41'-2"	42'-3"	43'-4"	44'-5"	45'-6"
15	37'-4"	38'-6"	39'-8"	40'-10"	42'-0"	43'-2"	44'-4"	45'-6"	46'-8"	47'-10"	49'-0"
16	40'-0"	41'-3"	42'-6"	43'-9"	45'-0"	46'-3"	47'-6"	48'-9"	50'-0"	51'-3"	52'-6"
17	42'-8"	44'-0"	45'-4"	46'-8"	48'-0"	49'-4"	50'-8"	52'-0"	53'-4"	54'-8"	56'-0"
18	45'-4"	46'-9"	48'-2"	49'-7"	51'-0"	52'-5"	53'-10"	55'-3"	56'-8"	58'-1"	59'-6"
19	48'-0"	49'-6"	51'-0"	52'-6"	54'-0"	55'-6"	57'-0"	58'-6"	60'-0"	61'-6"	63'-0"
20	50'-8"	52'-3"	53'-10"	55'-5"	57'-0"	58'-7"	60'-2"	61'-9"	63'-4"	64'-11"	66'-6"
21	53'-4"	55'-0"	56'-8"	58'-4"	60'-0"	61'-8"	63'-4"	65'-0"	66'-8"	68'-4"	70'-0"
22	56'-0"	57'-9"	59'-6"	61'-3"	63'-0"	64'-9"	66'-6"	68'-3"	70'-0"	71'-9"	73'-6"
23	68'-8"	60'-6"	62'-4"	64'-2"	66'-0"	67'-10"	69'-8"	71'-6"	73'-4"	75'-2"	77'-0"
24	61'-4"	63'-3"	65'-2"	67'-1"	69'-0"	70'-11"	72'-10"	74'-9"	76'-8"	78'-7"	80'-6"
25	64'-0"	66'-0"	68'-0"	70'-0"	72'-0"	74'-0"	76'-0"	78'-0"	80'-0"	82'-0"	84'-0"
26	66'-8"	68'-9"	70'-10"	72'-11"	75'-0"	77'-1"	79'-2"	81'-3"	83'-4"	85'-5"	87'-6"
27	69'-4"	71'-6"	73'-8"	75'-10"	78'-0"	80'-2"	82'-4"	84'-6"	86'-8"	88'-10"	91'-0"
28	72'-0"	74'-3"	76'-6"	78'-9"	81'-0"	83'-3"	85'-6"	87'-9"	90'-0"	92'-3"	94'-6"
29	74'-8"	77'-0"	79'-4"	81'-8"	84'-0"	86'-4"	88'-8"	91'-0"	93'-4"	95'-8"	98'-0"
30	77'-4"	79'-9"	82'-2"	84'-7"	87'-0"	89'-5"	91'-10"	94'-3"	96'-8"	99'-1"	101'-6"
31	80'-0"	82'-6"	85'-0"	87'-6"	90'-0"	92'-6"	95'-0"	97'-6"	100'-0"	102'-6"	105'-0"

AUDITORIUM SEATING
Chair Dimensions

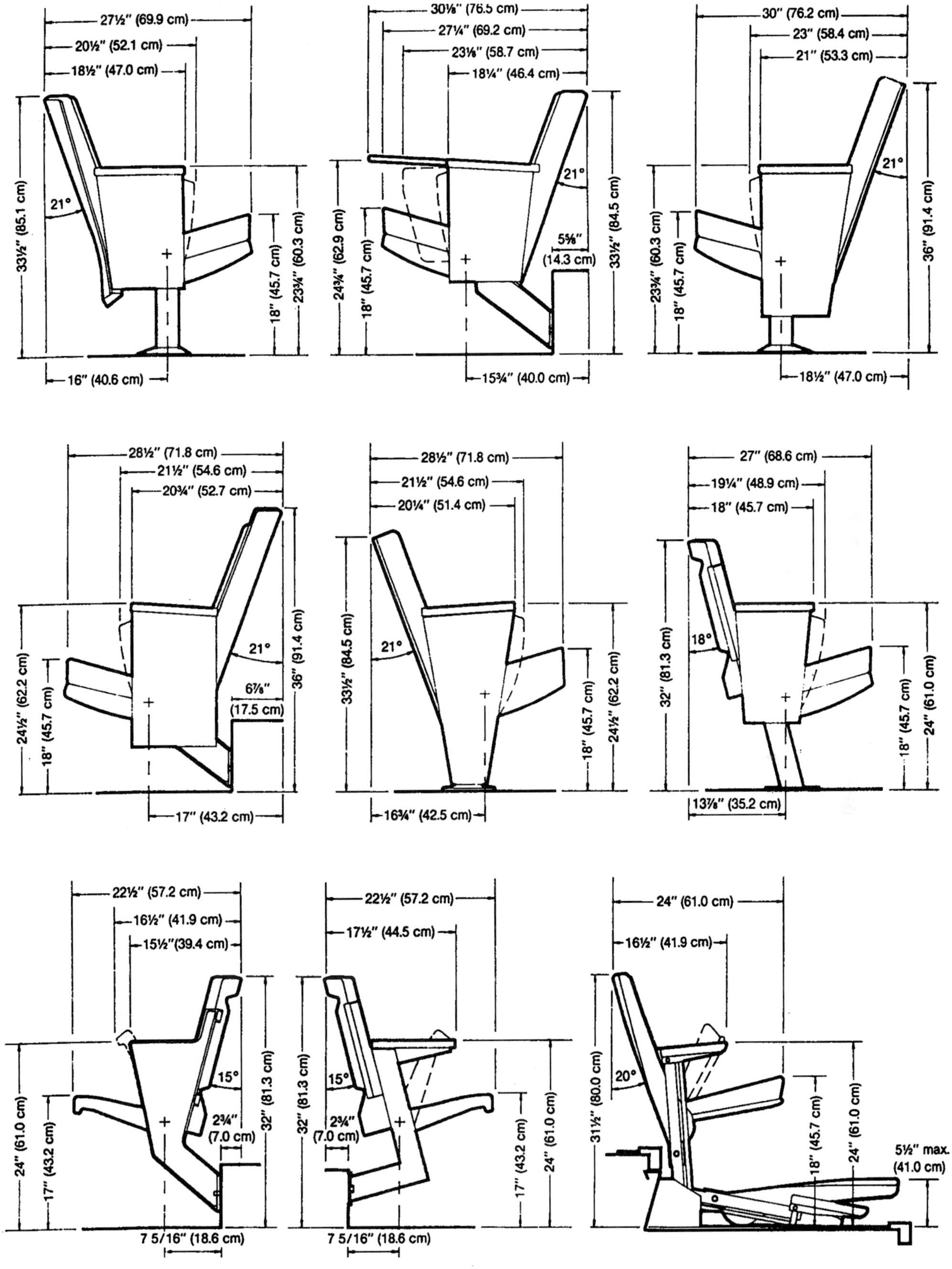

AUDITORIUM SEATING
Chair Dimensions and Row Seating

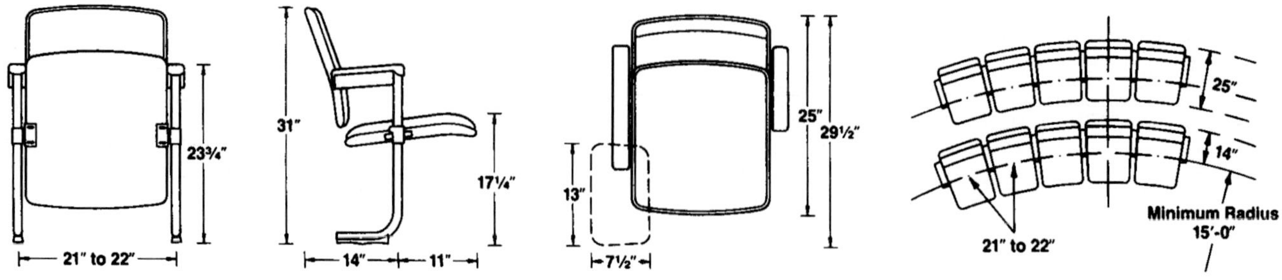

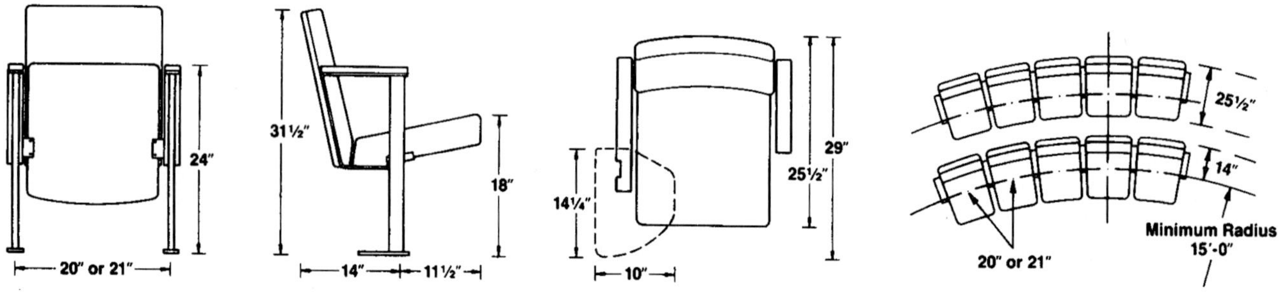

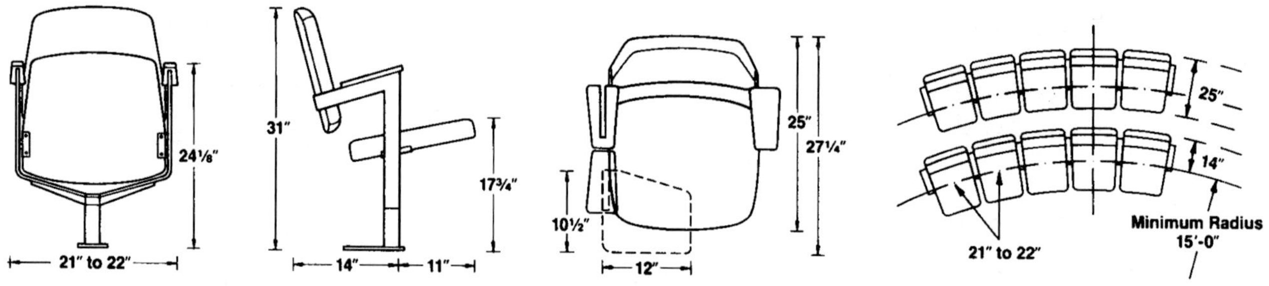

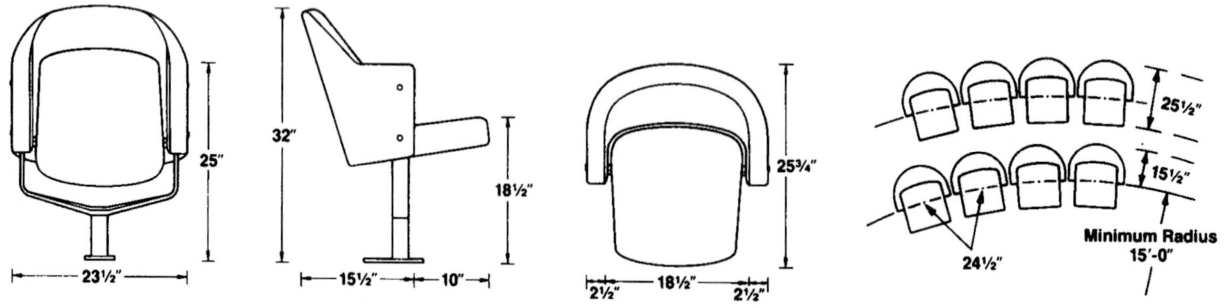

GENERAL SEATING ARRANGEMENT

Seating arrangements in an assembly space will be identified as either *multiple-aisle* or *continental*. These terms are commonly found in design standards manuals, building codes, and similar architectural reference documents. Each is unique, with specific guidelines governing row size, row spacing, and exitways.

Basically, a multiple-aisle arrangement (Fig. 2) will have a maximum of 14 to 16 chairs per row with access to an aisleway at both ends. If an aisle can be reached from one end of a row only, the seat count may then be limited to 7 or 8. It should be noted here that the maximum quantities will always be established by the governing building code.

In a continental arrangement (Fig. 3) all seats are located in a central section. Here the maximum quantity of chairs per row can greatly exceed the limits established in a multiple-aisle arrangement. In order to compensate for the greater length of rows allowed, building codes will require wider row spacing, wider aisles, and strategically located exit doors.

Although more space would appear to be called for, a continental seating plan is often not any less efficient than a multiple-aisle arrangement. In fact, carefully planned, a continental arrangement can frequently accommodate more seating within the same space. For early planning an average 7.5 ft^2 per person may be used. This will include both the seating area and space necessary for aisleways.

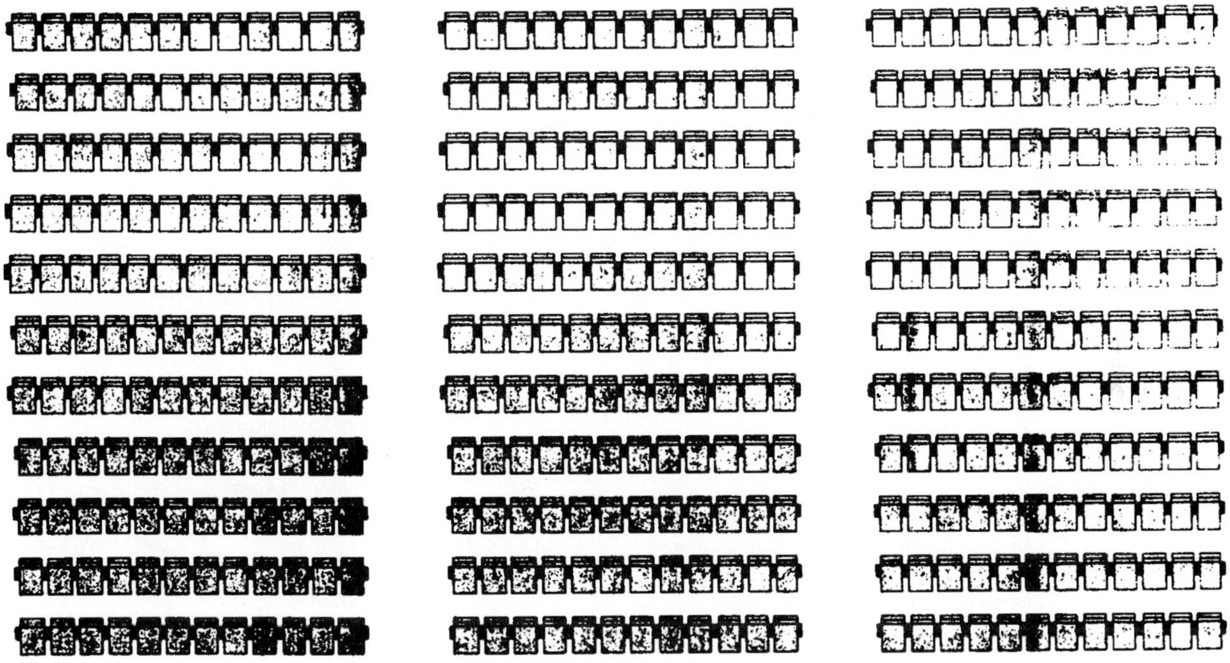

Fig. 2 Multiple-aisle arrangement

AUDITORIUM SEATING
Row Seating

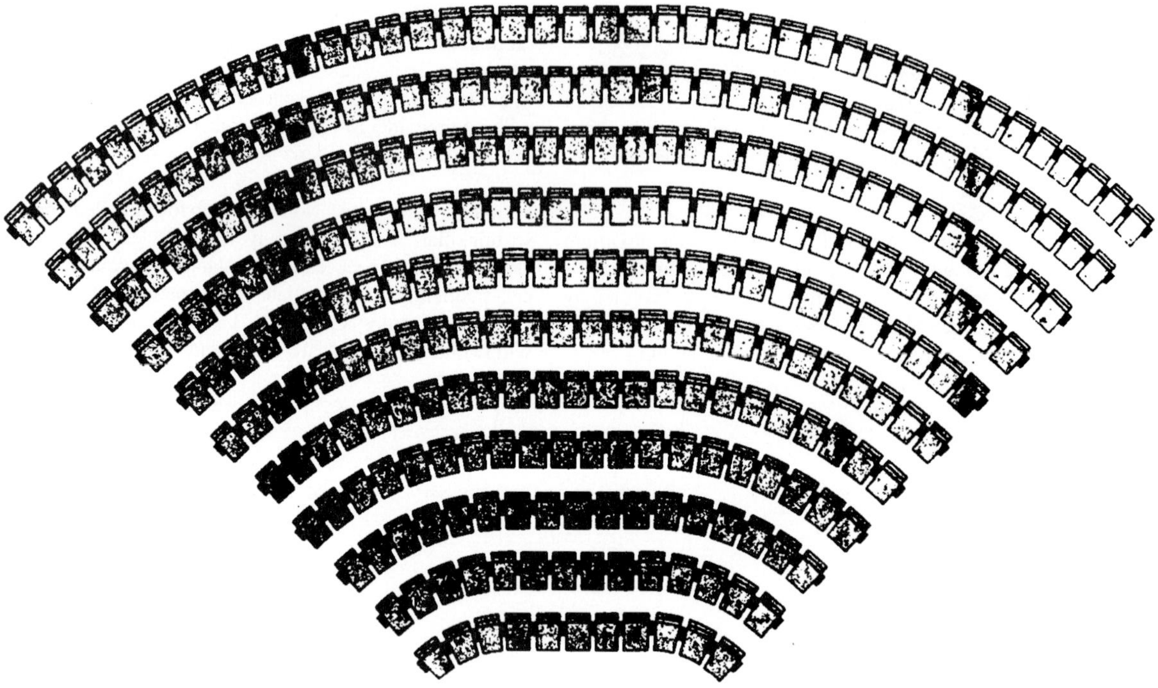

Fig. 3 Continental arrangement

LAYOUT INFORMATION

Design Considerations

1. Lay out per applicable building and life safety codes, regulations, and ordinances.
2. Allow sufficient distance between aisles for desired quantity and size of chairs plus end space.
3. Space rows to allow for proper seat to back clear space.
4. Determine radius or straight rows and locate by the chair size line.
5. Allow 1 in minimum clearance from either side or rear of chair to any adjacent side wall, end walls, and so on.
6. Provide adequate sightlines for either sloping or stepped (riser) floor configurations.
7. Seating area should be free of obstructions.
8. To allow for sufficient aisle illumination, aisle lights are generally located in the end panel standards at least every other row. Locate aisle light junction box 6 in from the standard.
9. Provide adequate floor or riser materials for sound anchorage.

ROW SEATING

Seat widths Seating comfort is initially established by individual chair widths. Available sizes range from 18 to 24 in; however, all may not be produced by a single manufacturer. The most commonly used chair widths are 20, 21, and 22 in. It should be noted that these dimensions are nominal, being measured from center to center of the support legs. If seating comfort is a high priority, thought must be given to a particular width and the space taken up by chair arms to determine an actual size. Usually, smaller sizes of 18 and 19 in have limited application due to the minimum clear width provided. Typically, all manufacturers size their chairs along an imaginary line, which may be referred to as a *datum line, chair radius line,* or a *similar name.* For accurate planning in an assembly area, this line must be identified so as not to over- or underestimate the potential of a row of chairs.

Row spacing Row spacing or back-to-back spacing of seats is also very important in developing a comfortable assembly area. A minimum dimension occasionally used is 2 ft 8 in (32 in). This spacing provides marginal clearance between a seated person's knees and the back of the chair in the next forward row. At the same time, however,

TYPICAL PLAN OF SEATING AND TERMINOLOGY

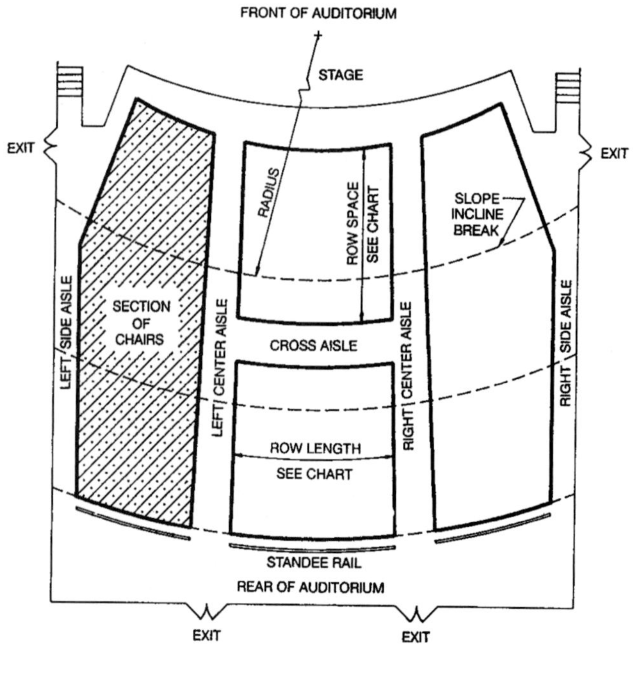

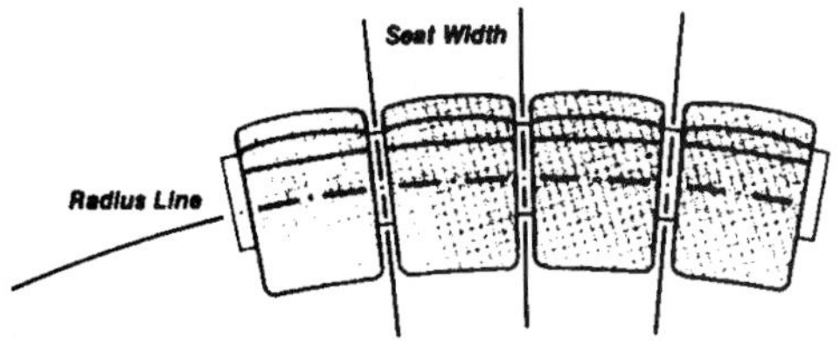

it will require that a seated person stand to permit the passage of another individual. As the row spacing is increased to 3 ft 0 in (36 in), seating comfort is dramatically improved and passage along a row of seated persons is accomplished with less disruption.

Floor design Seating comfort will also be affected by the design of the assembly space floor. Flat or less steeply sloped floors will usually allow a person to extend their knees and legs even under minimum row spacing dimensions. Here an individual can take advantage of the open area under a seat and the free space created by the pitched back of a chair. As the floor slope is increased, this free space diminishes. The extreme condition exists where a large elevation change between rows is combined with a minimum row spacing. An example would be a 12-in-high riser and a 32-in-wide row spacing. At this point, it becomes necessary to consider increasing the back-to-back dimension to provide more leg room.

The free space under a chair is also lost when a row of seats is located directly behind a low wall. In this case a recommended minimum clearance would be 11 in, measured from seat edge in the lowered position to face of wall. The back-to-back dimension of a row of seats abutting a rear wall should also be carefully studied. Normally, the pitched back of a chair will overlap a riser face, automatically reducing the width of that row unless succeeding rows are similarly positioned. Where a rear wall exists, the recommended procedure is to increase the dimension of the last row sufficiently to accommodate any overlap plus a minimal space between the wall and top edge of the chair back.

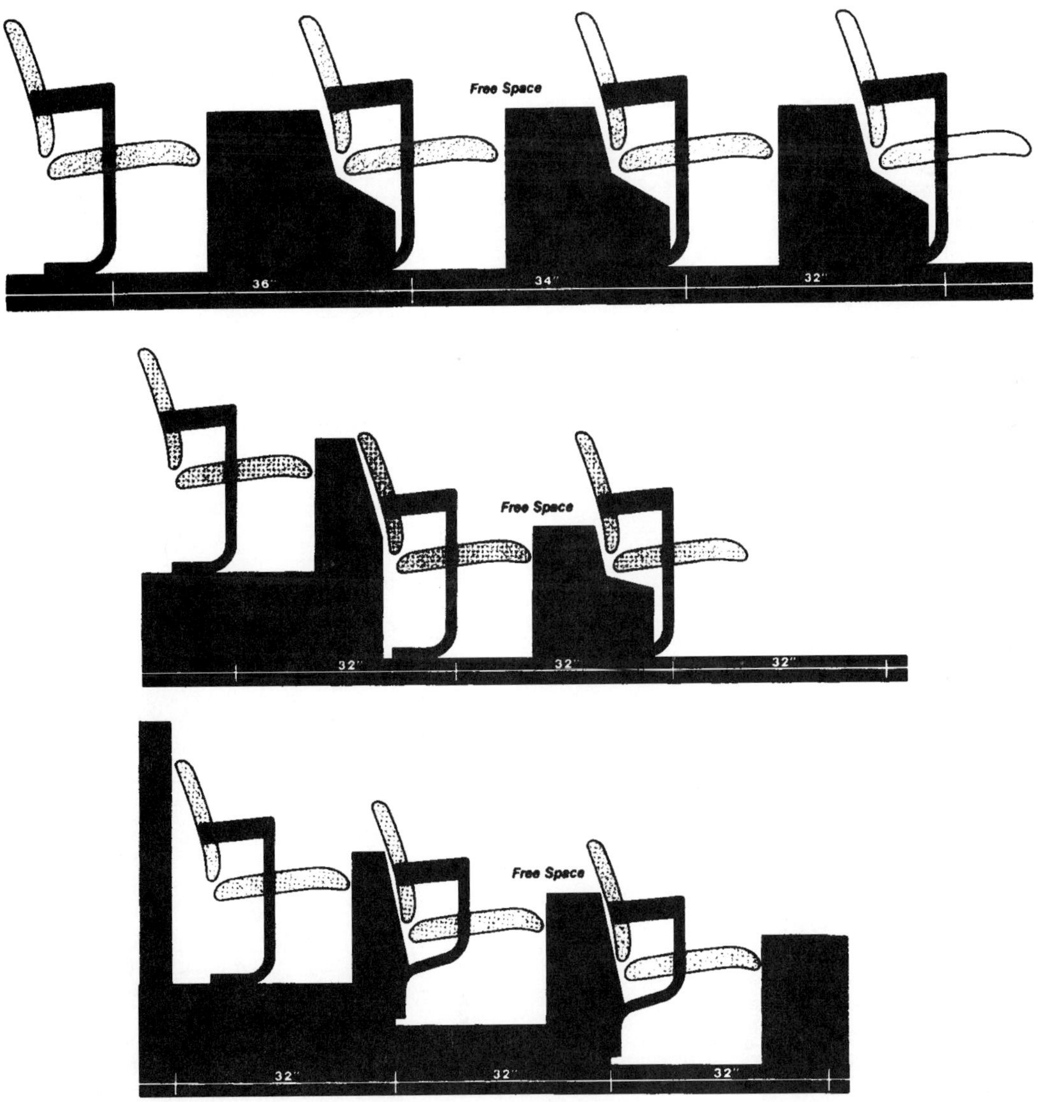

AUDITORIUM SEATING
Visibility

Visibility in an assembly space is a function of seat location. As stated earlier, building codes, comfort guidelines, floor design, and the overall form of an assembly space will play a part in seating arrangements. This information, combined with a basic understanding of sightline analysis and related planning guidelines, can result in achieving an acceptable, if not optimum, level of viewing for spectators.

Perhaps film projection requires the most critical sightline analysis, since poor seat location will result in distorted images. For this activity, the seating parameters are established by the screen or image size. An angle of 30° up to 45°, measured perpendicular to the far and near edges of the screen, can establish a side-to-side seating limit, while the screen or image height may determine the maximum distance. The minimum dimension or closest recommended seat will also be set by the screen height. (It should be noted that these figures are approximate and apply principally to flat screen projection.)

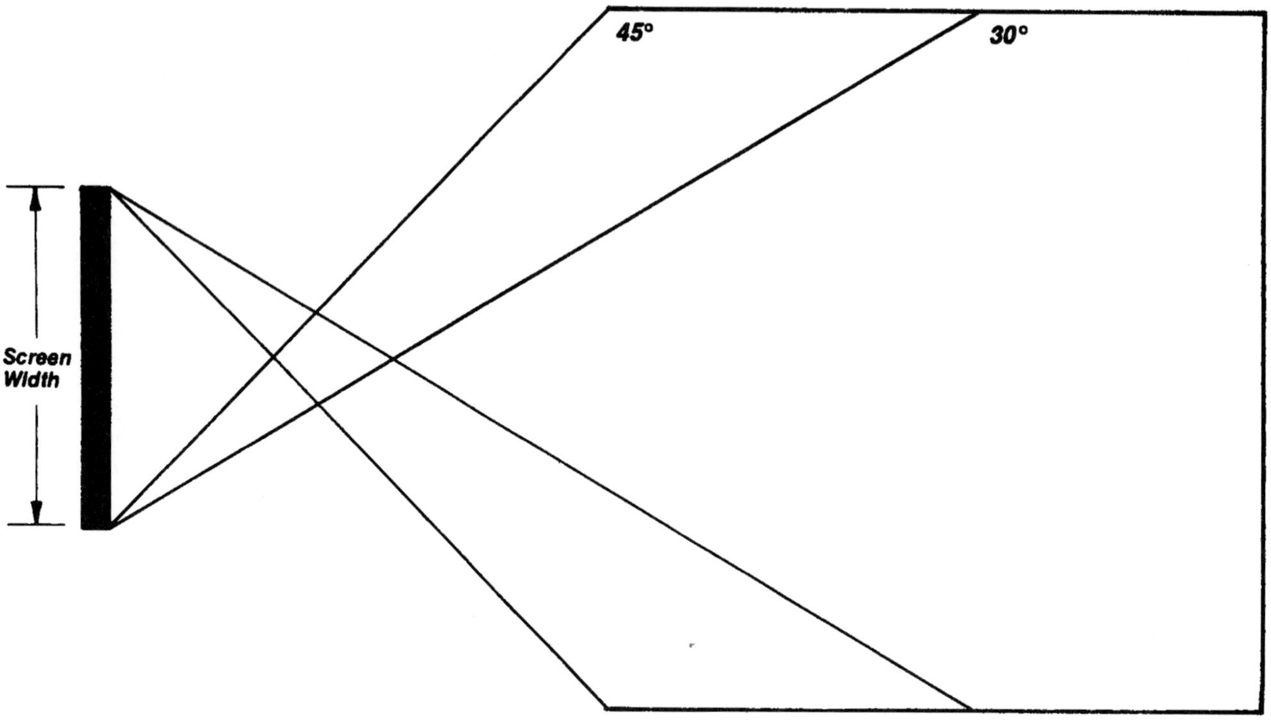

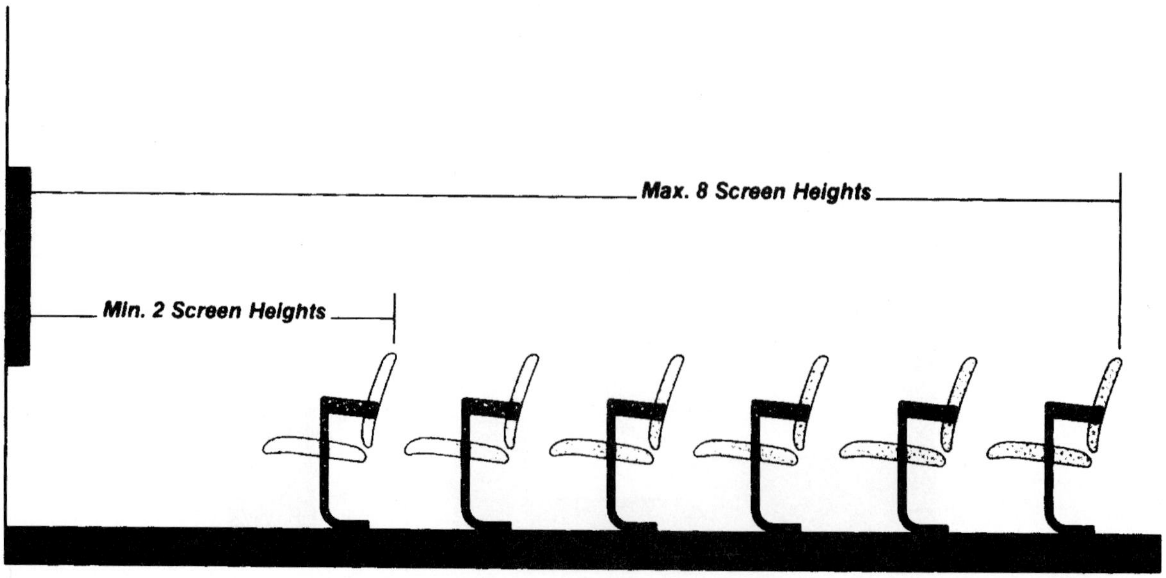

AUDITORIUM SEATING
End Stage and ¾ Arena

Basic Theater Form	End Stage
Quantity of Seats	55
Seating Area	450 Sq. Ft.
Space per Seat	8.23 Sq. Ft.
Row Spacing	2'-9"
Most Distant Seat	22'-0"
Stage Elevation	None
Floor Design	Flat/One Riser 8"

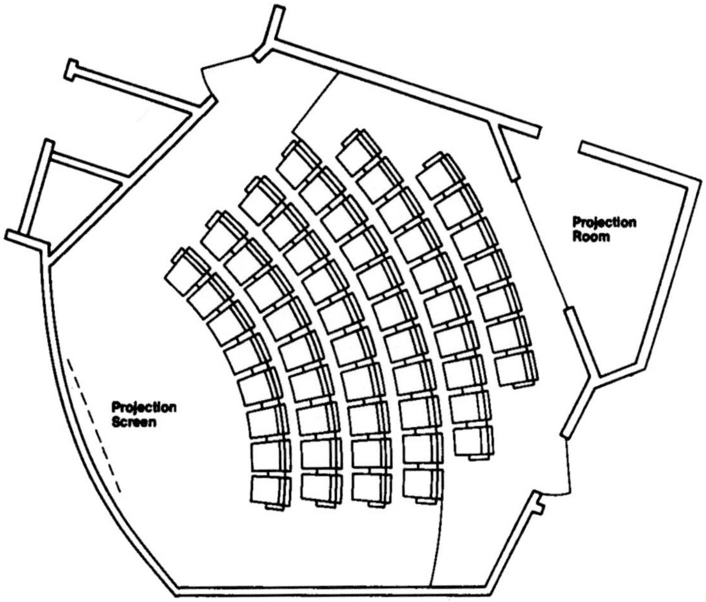

Basic Theater Form	¾ Arena
Quantity of Seats	56
Seating Area	622 Sq. Ft.
Space per Seat	11.1 Sq. Ft.
Row Spacing	3'-3"
Most Distant Seat	32'-0"
Stage Elevation	None
Floor Design	Risers 4"

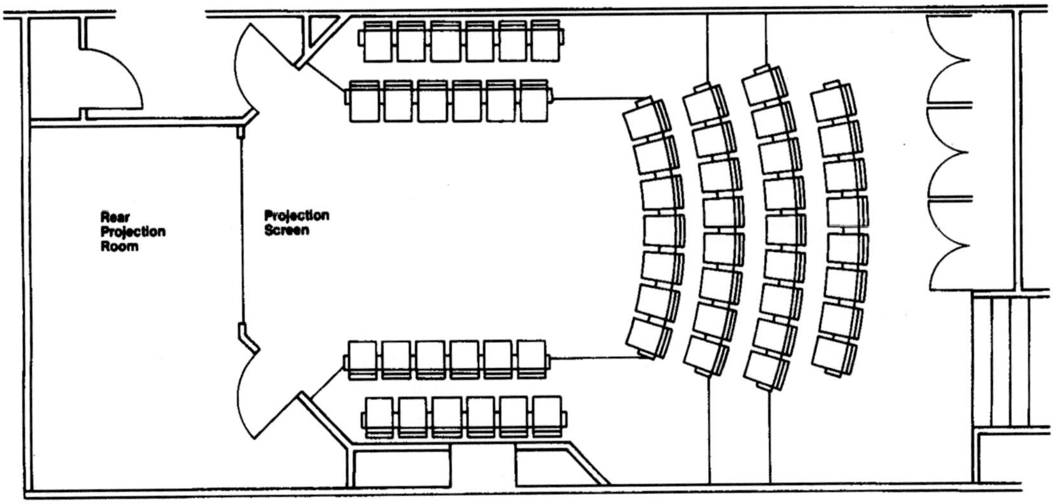

AUDITORIUM SEATING
End Stage

Basic Theater Form	End Stage
Quantity of Seats	80
Seating Area	700 Sq. Ft.
Space per Seat	8.75 Sq. Ft.
Row Spacing	3'-6"
Most Distant Seat	25'-0"
Stage Elevation	3'-6"
Floor Design	Risers 6"

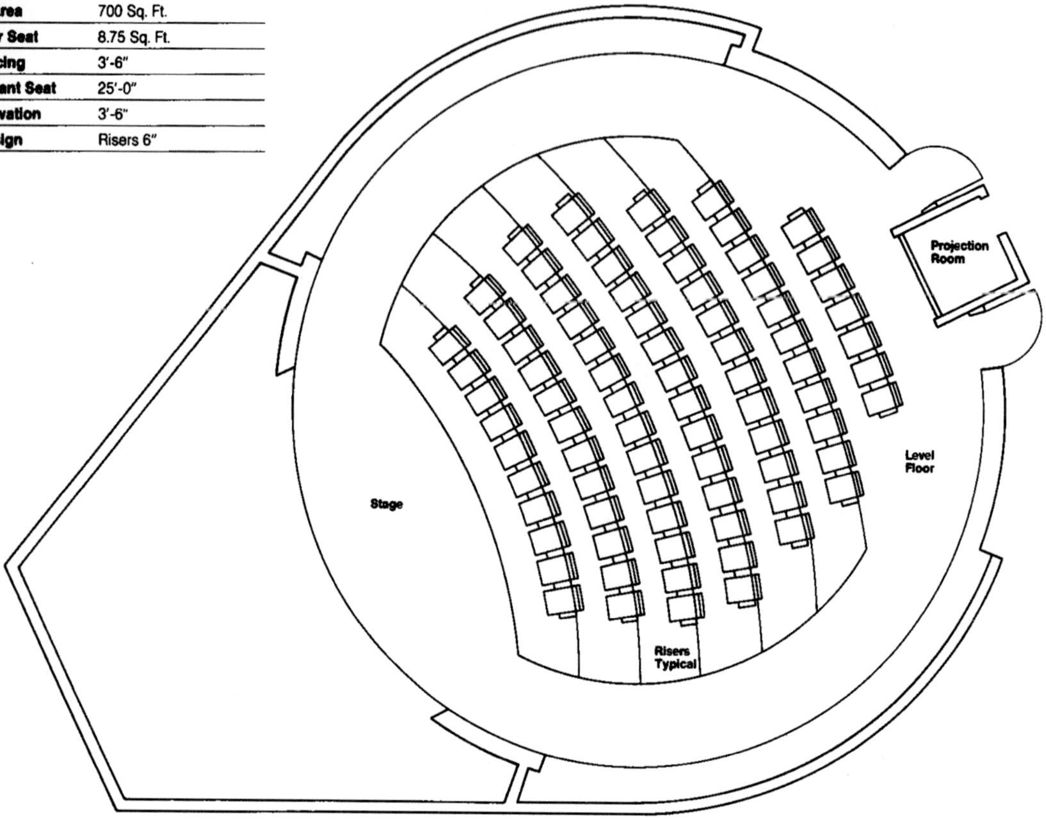

Basic Theater Form	End Stage
Quantity of Seats	92
Seating Area	956 Sq. Ft.
Space per Seat	10.4 Sq. Ft.
Row Spacing	3'-0"
Most Distant Seat	37'-0"
Stage Elevation	12"
Floor Design	Flat

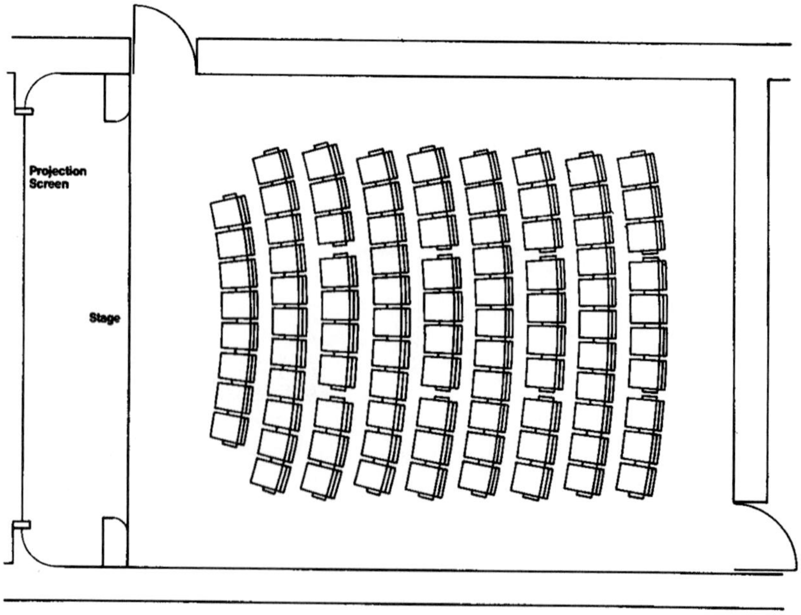

Basic Theater Form	End Stage
Quantity of Seats	99
Seating Area	953 Sq. Ft.
Space per Seat	9.62 Sq. Ft.
Row Spacing	3'-5"
Most Distant Seat	32'-0"
Stage Elevation	12"
Floor Design	Risers 12"

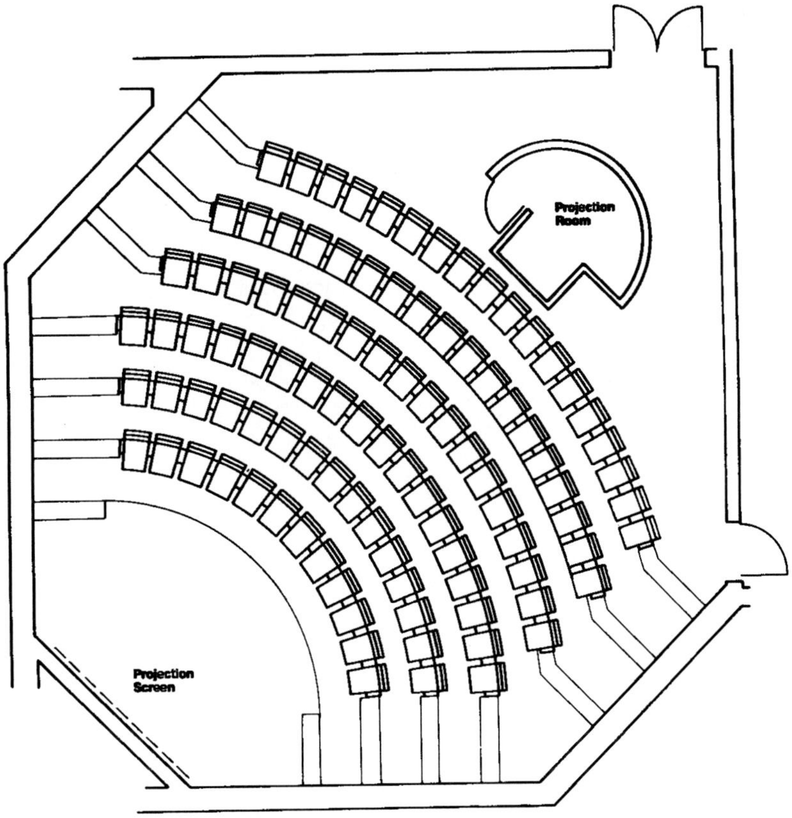

Basic Theater Form	End Stage
Quantity of Seats	105
Seating Area	903 Sq. Ft.
Space per Seat	8.6 Sq. Ft.
Row Spacing	3'-0"
Most Distant Seat	35'-0"
Stage Elevation	5"
Floor Design	Risers 12"

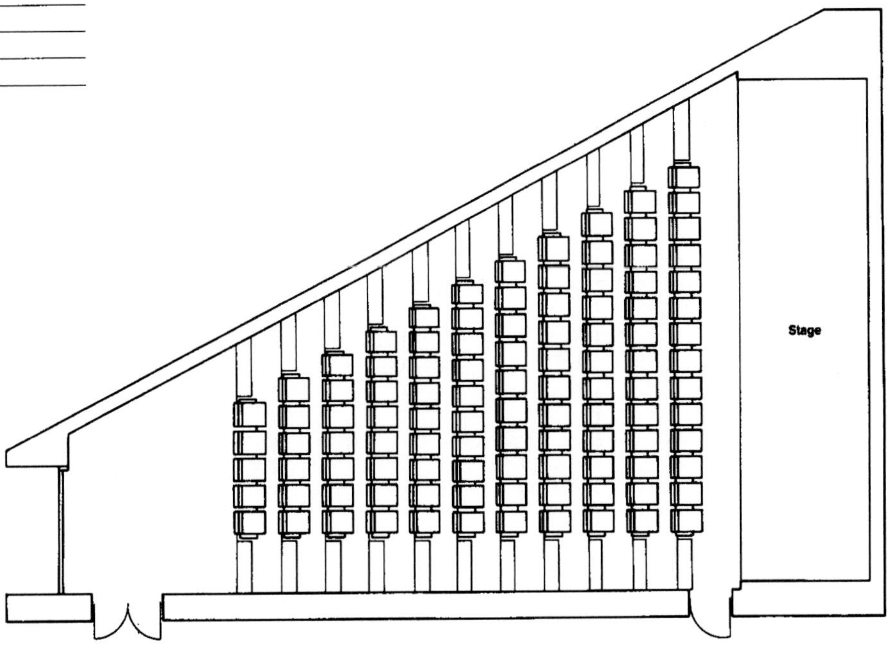

AUDITORIUM SEATING
¾ Arena and End Stage

Basic Theater Form	¾ Arena
Quantity of Seats	108
Seating Area	1200 Sq. Ft.
Space per Seat	11.1 Sq. Ft.
Row Spacing	3'-0"
Most Distant Seat	45'-0"
Stage Elevation	Varies
Floor Design	Risers 12"

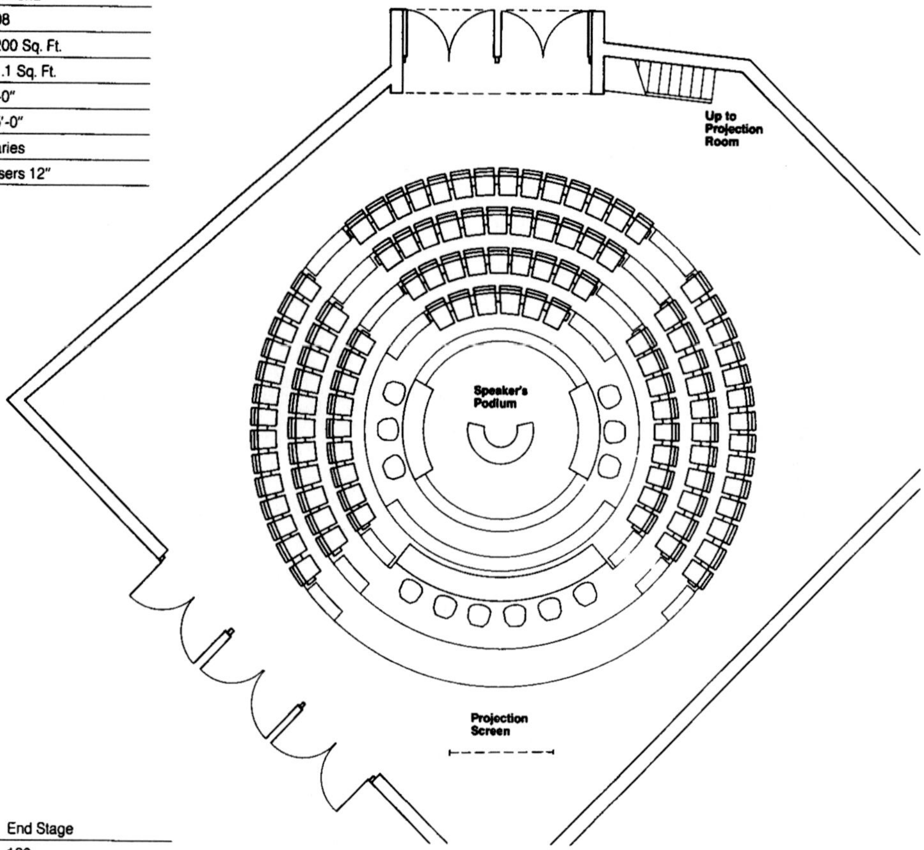

Basic Theater Form	End Stage
Quantity of Seats	120
Seating Area	1088 Sq. Ft.
Space per Seat	9.1 Sq. Ft.
Row Spacing	3'-3"
Most Distant Seat	41'-0"
Stage Elevation	1'-6"
Floor Design	Iscidomal Slope 2.4°, 4.7°, 7.1°

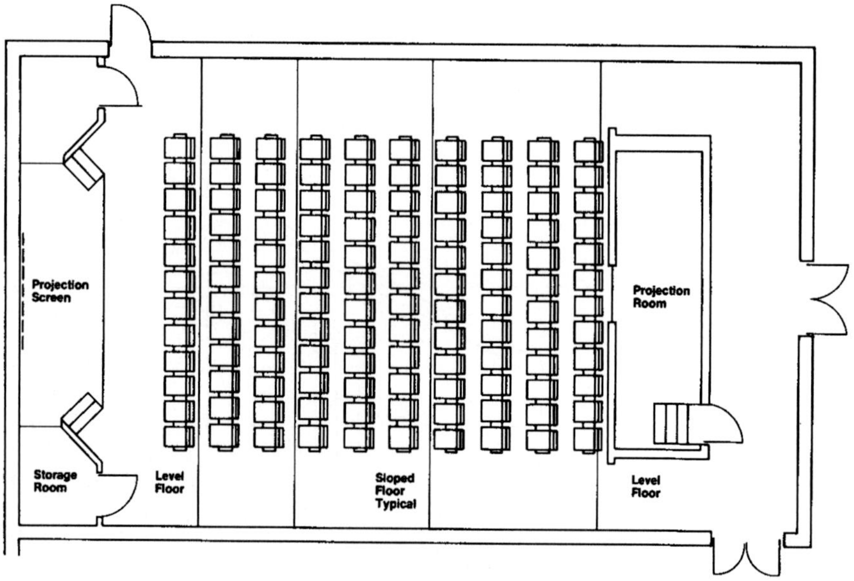

AUDITORIUM SEATING
End Stage and Wide Fan

Basic Theater Form	End Stage
Quantity of Seats	180
Seating Area	1218 Sq. Ft.
Space per Seat	6.8 Sq. Ft.
Row Spacing	2'-8"
Most Distant Seat	50'-0"
Stage Elevation	1'-6"
Floor Design	Iscidomal Slope -1° to 10°

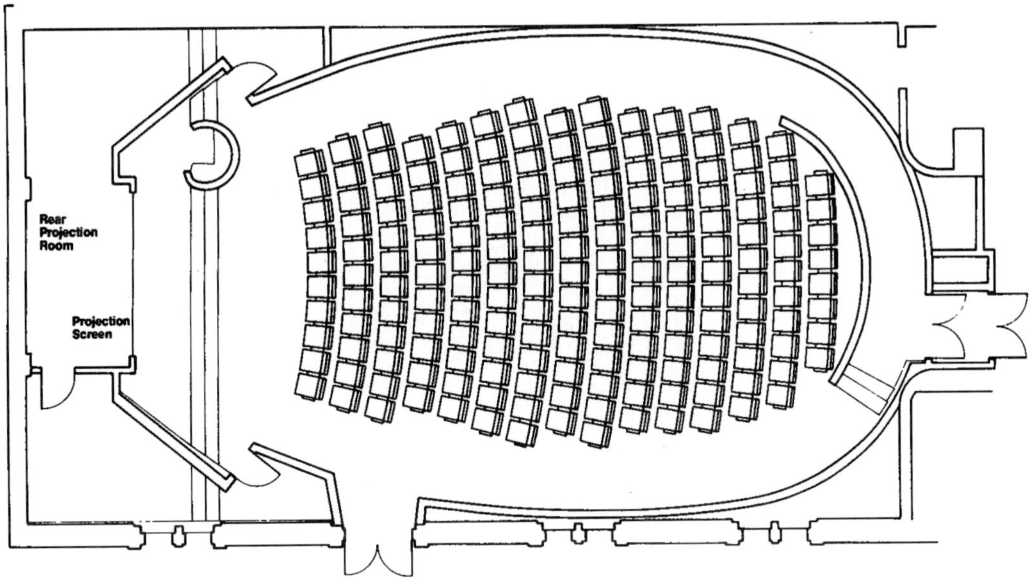

Basic Theater Form	Wide Fan
Quantity of Seats	253
Seating Area	1790 Sq. Ft.
Space per Seat	7.1 Sq. Ft.
Row Spacing	3'-0"
Most Distant Seat	48'-0"
Stage Elevation	None
Floor Design	Risers—Varying Height 10½" to 16"

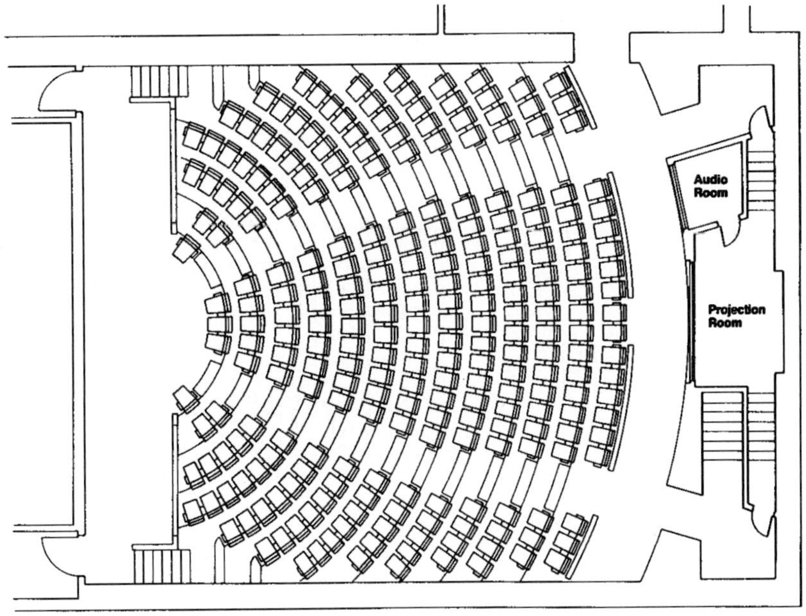

AUDITORIUM SEATING
End Stage

Basic Theater Form	End Stage
Quantity of Seats	430
Seating Area	2586 Sq. Ft.
Space per Seat	6.0 Sq. Ft.
Row Spacing	2'-8¾"
Most Distant Seat	58'-0"
Stage Elevation	2'-6"
Floor Design	Sloped 7.1°

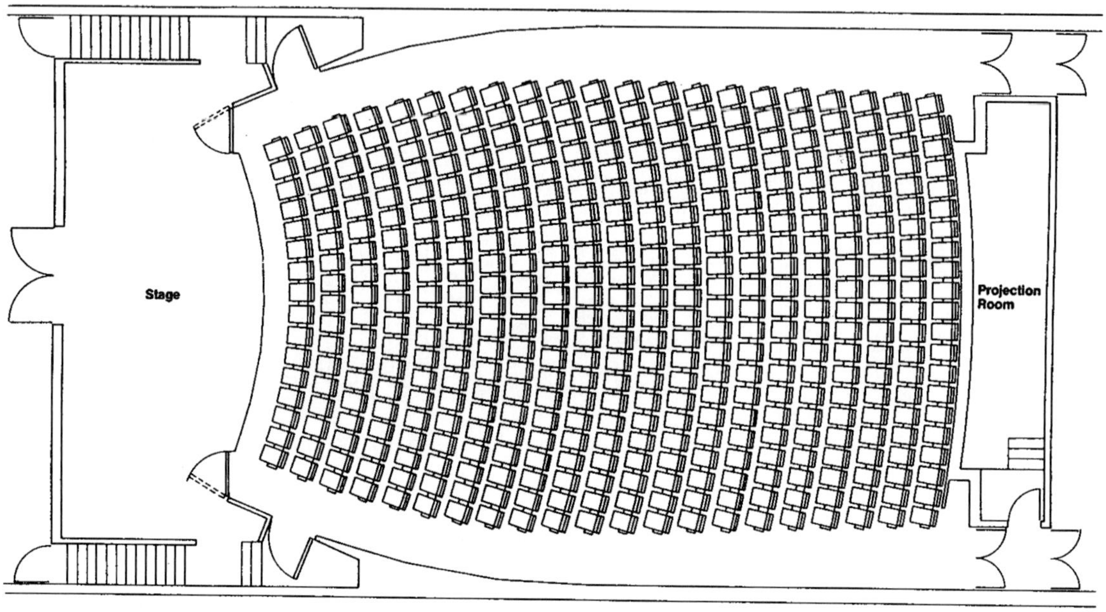

Basic Theater Form	End Stage
Quantity of Seats	224
Seating Area	1660 Sq. Ft.
Space per Seat	7.4 Sq. Ft.
Row Spacing	2'-9"
Most Distant Seat	60'-0"
Stage Elevation	None
Floor Design	Sloped 7.1°/Risers 13¾"

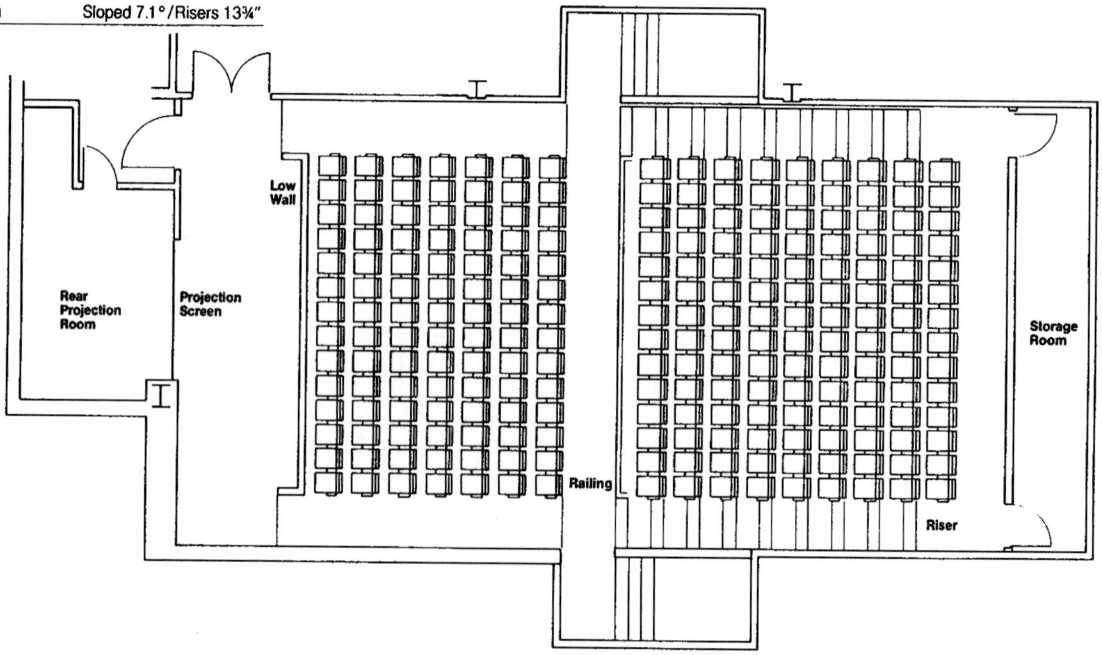

Plan shows the main (Lloyd Rigler) theater and small (Steven Spielberg) theater and lobby contained within the shell of the Egyptian Theatre.

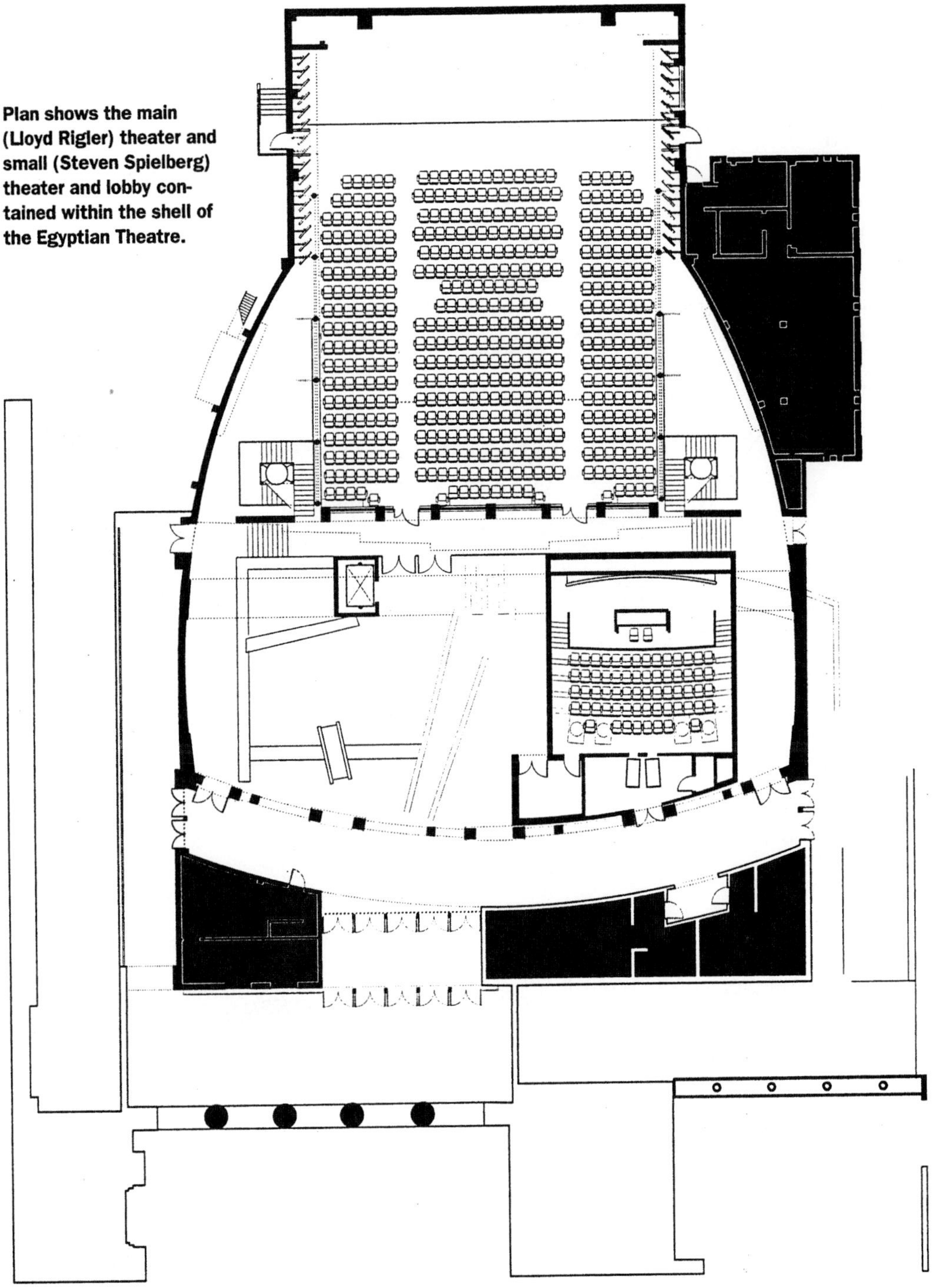

Basic theater form—end stage (large auditorium). Quantity of seats—478.

AUDITORIUM SEATING
Wide Fan

Basic Theater Form	Wide Fan
Quantity of Seats	208
Seating Area	1557 Sq. Ft.
Space per Seat	7.5 Sq. Ft.
Row Spacing	2'-8"
Most Distant Seat	48'-0"
Stage Elevation	5"
Floor Design	Risers 14"

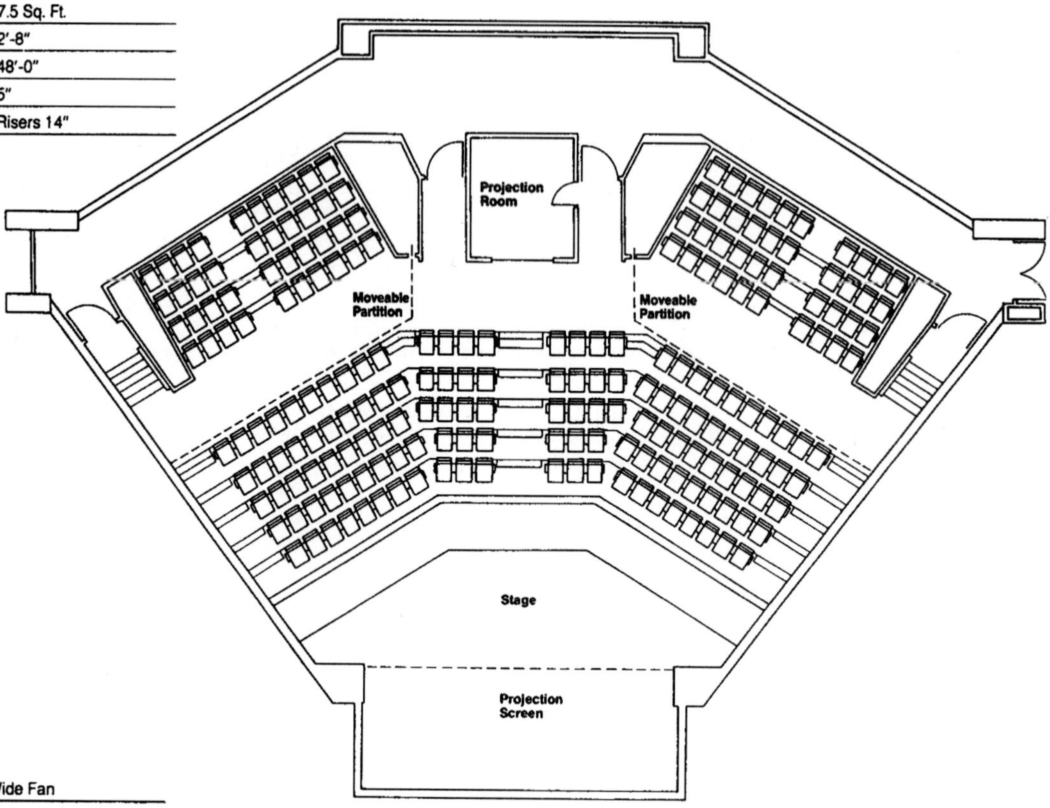

Basic Theater Form	Wide Fan
Quantity of Seats	207
Seating Area	1428 Sq. Ft.
Space per Seat	6.9 Sq. Ft.
Row Spacing	3'-4"
Most Distant Seat	40'-0"
Stage Elevation	2'-3"
Floor Design	Sloped 6.6°

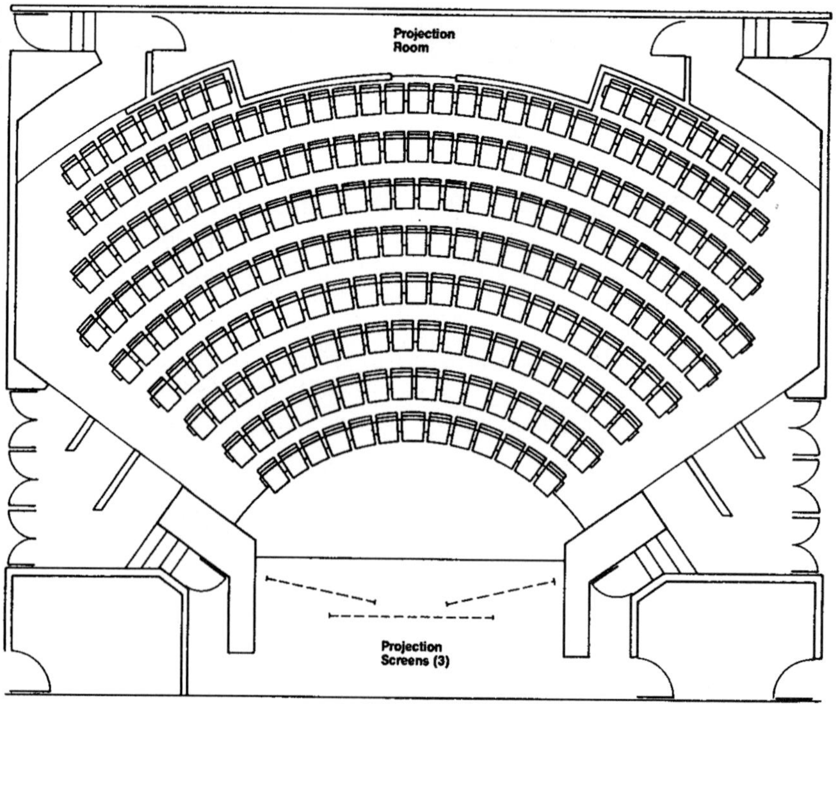

SECURITY

GENERAL CONTROL GUIDELINES

Control of Grounds

Fencing can be a very effective means of limiting access to secondary exits and to vulnerable ground-level dwellings. Fencing functions as a control by requiring entry through a single, limited, highly visible area. The fencing surrounding most single-family homes does not have locked gates. It is intended primarily to protect children, pets, and gardens, and to define the area immediately around the home as the private outdoor space of that household. Any intrusion into the area within the fence is therefore noticeable. As a security measure, such fencing, used symbolically, is of minimal value against premeditated crime, but it does make criminal intent visible and so is an important deterrent.

A conventional use of fencing in multifamily complexes is to limit access to backyards and windows of a housing cluster. On conventional city blocks, backyards of row housing are accessible only through one of the houses. However, in many superblock designs, such backyards are left open to public access. In this situation, addition of a limited amount of fencing can protect a large group of homes (see Fig. 1). This approach can also subdivide the superblock and so create small, natural clusters.

The Lobby

Improving visibility is the most important ingredient in providing a naturally secure lobby. It is crucial that a tenant entering a building be able to see what is going on in the lobby from the outside. Hidden nooks and blind curves provide perfect hiding places. Where such features cannot be removed structurally, the use of mirrors, windows, and improved lighting may ease the situation.

Ideally, a person walking down a path to enter a building should be able to see anyone standing in the lobby and elevator waiting area. In fact, it is often advantageous if the arriving person can see into the elevator from across the lobby.

Control of Interior Public Spaces of Multifamily Dwellings

The most vulnerable locations in multifamily buildings are the interior public spaces: lobbies, elevators, stairwells, and corridors. These are areas open to the public but without the attending surveillance given a public street by passersby and police. The crimes that occur in these interior public spaces are the most fearful types of crimes, involving acts of personal confrontation such as robbery, assault, and rape. Limiting access to these spaces through the use of a doorman or intercom/door lock system can be of substantial benefit.

Lobby visibility discourages a number of different kinds of crime. Crimes of personal confrontation may be deterred primarily because the potential victim can readily perceive and avoid a suspicious person in the lobby. The potential criminal must also fear the possibility that another tenant or the police may be viewing the crime in the well-lit open area.

Mailbox crime—generally the theft of checks—can be deterred when mailboxes are located in a highly protected area of the lobby. This protection can consist of placing the mailboxes behind an intercom or in a locked mailroom. It is essential that the mailboxes be visible from as many different viewpoints as possible. Improved visibility in this context can be a significant deterrent to crime.

Some managers designate an area of the lobby as a legitimate resting place, where chairs and other lounging items are provided. Lounging may aid security, particularly if the building includes a high proportion of elderly. The best locations for such seating are areas with high visibility. Often tenant patrols use this space as a station and provide still another dimension of security.

A bulletin board is an inexpensive device that can improve lobby security by providing a diversion. If, for example, a tenant enters the lobby and sees someone he or she doesn't recognize waiting for an

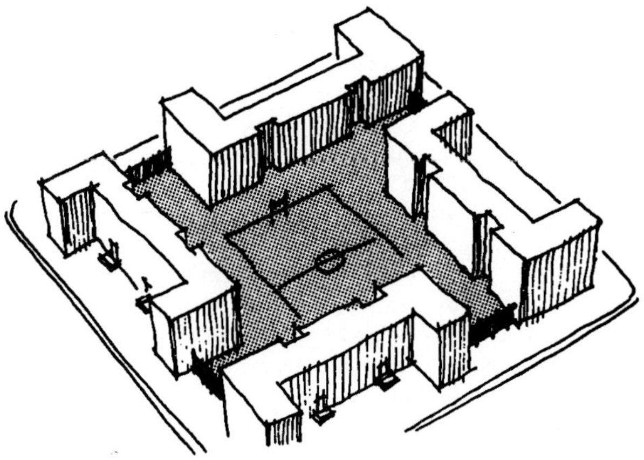

Fig. 1 Use of fencing to define and secure large semiprivate areas

elevator, the bulletin board provides the tenant with a natural excuse to pause and survey the situation.

The area around the main entry to a multifamily building should be clearly distinguished from the public walkway which leads to it. A person entering through the main door should feel distinctly that he or she is entering a space controlled by the residents of the building. The main entry should be well lit and clearly visible from outside.

Entry doors should be constructed of a transparent material covering as large an area as possible. In vandalism-prone areas, the main entry doors should be made of unbreakable glass or other, similar, very sturdy transparent material. Because of the need for good visibility, replacing glass panels with metal or other material should be avoided. For window walls and doors where the incidence of vandalism is extreme, glass panels less than 2 ft from the ground and higher than 7 ft from the ground may be replaced by solid materials.

Fire Doors and Fire Stairs

Secondary exit doors are the weakest link in security of buildings. An ideal secondary exit door would be one that allows exit but not entrance. Unfortunately, there is no acceptable emergency exit system that allows egress only.

In the design of any security system there is a continuing clash between the need for security against crime and the need for safety in case of fire. Fire doors are frequently used for entry and exit by criminals. Installation of panic hardware and the absence of exterior hardware sometimes prevent criminal use. These measures will not suffice, however, where tenants do not cooperate in avoiding use of secondary exits and ensuring that they are kept closed.

To a large extent, the design and location of secondary fire exits determine tenant attitudes about the exits. For example, a building's main entry may face the street, but the parking lot may be to the rear of the building. If the secondary exit is also at the rear and close to this destination, the temptation to use the fire door as an entry or exit will be difficult to resist. Similarly, security is decreased in buildings where the main entries face the interior of the project while the fire doors face the surrounding streets with their parking and shopping facilities. Where the fire exit does not represent any shortcut or improved convenience to the tenant, it is far more likely to remain closed. A securely designed building is one in which the fire door exits to an area that is less convenient or desirable than the area outside the main door.

In cases of persistent breaks in security of secondary exits, it is possible to modify the building plan at the ground level and open a new doorway in a better location. However, this improvement is costly and can only be done where architecturally possible.

Another architectural modification to improve security involves making a fire exit into a legitimate secondary entry and developing a security system that protects both the main and secondary entries. If a fire door exits to a parking area, for example, this modification may be more successful than efforts to prevent tenants from using that exit. If the main entry is equipped with an intercom system, the secondary entry should be similarly equipped and made easily surveillable through the use of lighting and windows.

Other mechanisms can be used to limit access to and prevent circulation through the emergency exit system. A fire exit passageway, for example, can be modified by installing a second door inside the building a short distance from the existing exterior door. Both doors should be equipped with hardware so that they can be opened only from the inside. The point of this system is that it is unlikely that both doors will be propped or jammed open at the same time. A tenant entering an open exterior fire door which leads only to the locked second door will have to exit and use another door. A few experiences of this kind will convince most tenants that it is probably more convenient to go directly through the main entrance. This double-door system generally does not conflict with fire codes.

An extension of this concept is to have the fire door on each floor above ground level openable from the corridor only. Thus, once someone has gone into a stairwell he can exit only at the ground level. This system may be somewhat inconvenient to tenants accustomed to moving easily between floors, but it does create roadblocks for anyone attempting to enter the building from the ground-level exit door.

The improvements outlined here are generally applicable to all dwellings. In buildings which have such security personnel, additional measures are possible.

A doorman or security guard can only be effective if he controls all access to the building, including access through fire doors. In a well-designed building, the doorman can see the fire doors from his position at the main entry. Where this is not possible, an inexpensive and effective solution is to install panic hardware with an alarm, and make sure the doorman can hear and respond to the alarm. Where the doorman or guard has access to closed-circuit TV, this may be used to monitor the fire doors. If the doorman can also be given a device for controlling the secondary door, it becomes very difficult for a criminal to use the fire entry.

Elevators

There are virtually no structural modifications that can improve security within elevators. The only possible improvements are use of mirrors, communication devices, emergency buttons, or an electronic surveillance system.

Security modifications to other areas of a building improve security within the elevator. If the elevator waiting area and the elevator cab are a visible extension of the lobby, the residents are afforded some protection. Similarly, if the fire door and fire stairs are secure, there is less chance of a criminal entering the elevator on an upper floor. In this sense, the safety of the elevator is dependent on the general security of the building.

Securing the Dwelling

Illegal entry into dwelling units is traditionally prevented by use of hardware. However, there are building design features which in themselves limit access, improve surveillance, and promote neighbor recognition.

Windows

Ground-level windows are generally most vulnerable to illegal entry and breakage. (All windows whose lower ledges are less than 7 ft off the ground should be considered ground level.) There are three ways to discourage criminal entry through ground-floor windows: design ground-floor areas which need few windows, house activities on the ground floor which hold no interest to the burglar, and assign the grounds immediately adjacent to the building for the use of the neighboring resident and fence off the grounds for his protection.

Elaborate architectural details—protruding ledges, for example—often increase the vulnerability of lower windows. Fences, garbage containers, and parked cars, when located near windows, are used as stepping stones to an otherwise inaccessible window. Care should be taken to prevent this type of situation.

Most windows above the ground floor are relatively inaccessible, with very important exceptions. Fire escapes make windows accessible. Little can be done to modify fire escapes, except in terms of hardware, because of fire safety and fire codes. One solution is to ensure that the ladder from the lowest fire escape is at least 12 ft above the ground. The ground area under the fire escape should be highly visible.

Another point of entry to the fire escape is the roof, which can be secured with panic hardware and possibly patrolled. The roof also provides possible entry to windows or balconies on the top floor. Therefore, security of the roof is quite essential, particularly to top-floor residents. Other accessible windows are those located diagonally across from a stairwell window. The criminal can open a stairwell window and cross from the stairwell into the units. It is not advisable to board up stairwell windows, as they provide the security of visibility to the stairwell and may have a fire safety function.

Accessible windows are also those located above or near door canopies. Criminals can reach the canopy by climbing onto it from the ground or from a stair or hall window.

Doors

Security of doors, beyond the hardware aspect, depends on surveillance and neighbor recognition. An experienced burglar needs just a few seconds to enter a locked apartment door equipped with minimal hardware. Within this interval, the crucial factors are: will the intruder be seen or heard by tenants, will the viewer perceive that the potential criminal is in fact an intruder, and will the viewer respond by calling authorities or in some way challenge the criminal?

Physical design can directly influence the opportunity for surveillance of doors. Corridors that are open to view, either single loaded or with windows, are more easily surveillable by residents and police. Thus the opportunity for the criminal to attempt entry undetected is reduced.

In most single-family homes (detached or row) where the entrance door is on the street, the only means of improving surveillance is to avoid placing trees and shrubs where they hide the doors and windows, and to locate lighting to improve visibility around these openings.

In multiple-family dwellings, the apartment doors, located on interior corridors, are generally difficult to keep under surveillance. Any windows, mirrors, or lighting that allow someone inside an apartment or outside the building to view the hallway and doors can be helpful.

DOORS AND HARDWARE

Hardware

This section describes hardware devices that secure the individual residential dwelling and the multifamily dwelling. Much of this material is intended to prevent burglary. However, some of the measures, particularly those directed at multifamily dwellings, will also deter forcible entry, robbery, and vandalism.

The Residential Dwelling

Door Materials

The major security tests of door material are its ability to withstand efforts to force entry by brute strength and its ability to retain securely the locking devices attached. Materials most commonly used for doors are wood, aluminum, steel, and glass, often in combination with hardboard, fiberboard, asbestos, and plastic. The two most common door designs are panel and flush. Panel doors consist of vertical and horizontal members framing rectangular areas in which opaque panels, panes of glass, or louvers are located. Flush doors consist of flat panels running the full height and width of the door. (See Fig. 2.)

Solid-steel flush doors, although most secure, are rarely used except in very high security areas such as banks and prisons. Steel-clad doors, which are flush doors constructed of 24-gauge sheet metal facing bonded to a nonresinous, kiln-dried wood interior, provide an optimum weight-strength situation for ordinary residential use. Hollow steel doors (1¾-in flush-type) are satisfactory in multiple-dwelling buildings. Aluminum doors can provide sufficient protection but may be comparatively expensive.

While less strong than steel-clad doors, wood doors can be secure. All exterior wooden doors should be of solid-core construction with a minimum thickness of 1¾ in. Although flush doors provide better security, if panel doors are desired for aesthetic reasons, the panels should have a minimum ½-in thickness (see Fig. 3). Both hollow-core wood doors and thin-wood panel doors are unacceptable where security is a factor.

Door Frames

The sides and top of a doorway are provided with a door frame which holds the door in position. The side members of the door frame are called *jambs;* the top member is called the *head* (see Fig. 4). The *strike* is the portion of the jamb which is cut out or drilled out to allow installation of a metal plate, which accepts the latch or bolt from the door lock (see Fig. 5).

Wooden frames provide an unacceptable level of security unless they are at least 2 in thick. Metal-covered wood frames provide an optimum cost-security investment when used in combination with metal-covered wood doors. If a hollow steel frame is used, the residual air space behind the frame should be filled with a crush-resistant material such as cement grout, especially in the area of the strike (see Fig. 6). This will prevent an intruder from wedging a crowbar between the door and frame and crushing the frame to free the lock.

For doors swinging in, rabbeted jambs should be used. These are jambs containing a metal extension that protrudes beyond the edges of the closed door, thus preventing tampering in the area of the strike (see Fig. 7).

For doors without rabbeted jambs, an L-shaped piece of angle-iron at least 2 ft long, mounted in the area of the strike, gives extra protection (see Fig. 8). The iron acts as a lip which protects the strike from attack.

SECURITY
Doors and Hardware

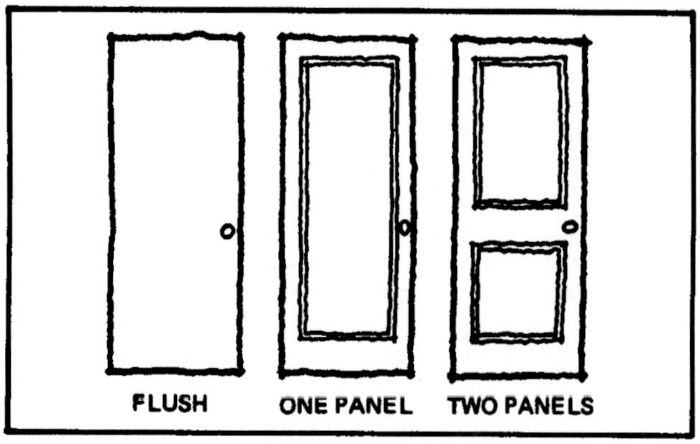

Fig. 2 Door types

Fig. 5 Door strike

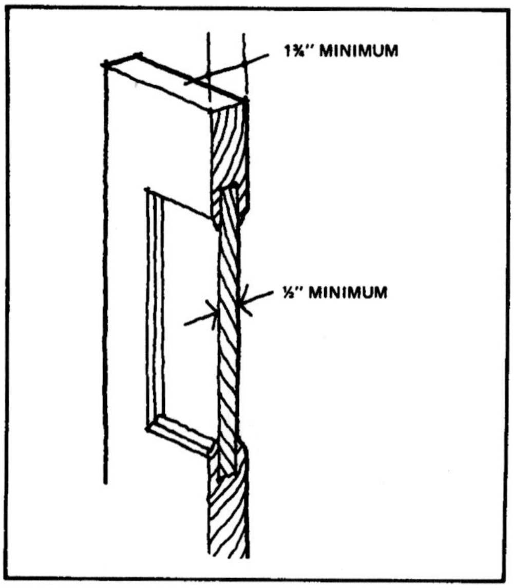

Fig. 3 Panel door

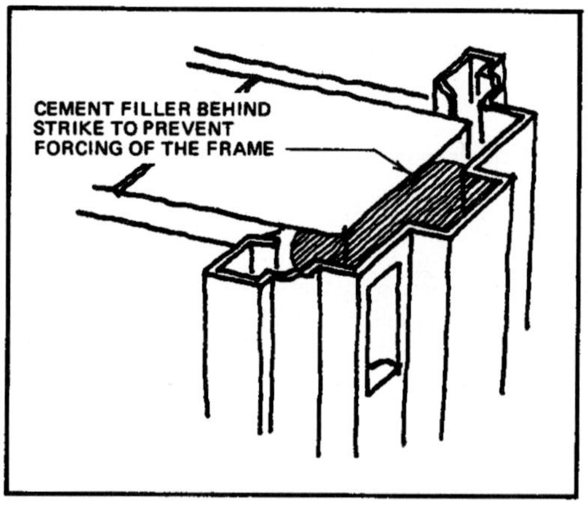

Fig. 6 Hollow metal door frame

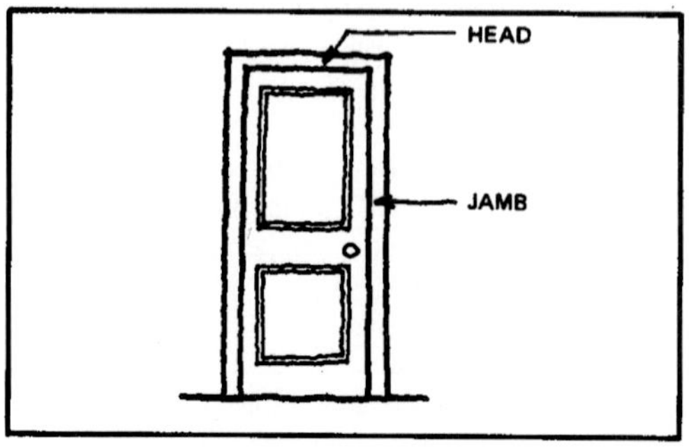

Fig. 4 Door frame

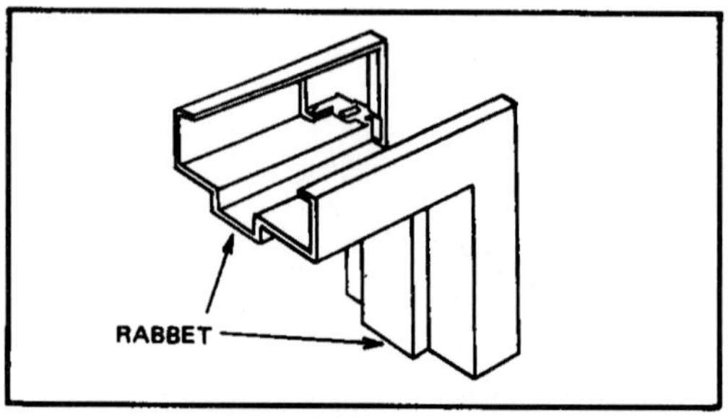

Fig. 7 Rabbeted jamb

For doors opening out, a flat metal plate, called an *escutcheon plate,* can be mounted to the face of the door in the area of the lock. This plate, which extends beyond the edge of the door and fits flush with the jamb when the door is closed, will protect the lock from attack in the area of the strike (see Fig. 9).

All plates located on the outsides of doors should be attached with tamper-resistant connectors such as round-headed carriage bolts or one-way screws.

Door Hinges and Closers

Spring hinges close the door automatically by using spring force. A spring hinge prevents a criminal from slipping in behind a resident who has neglected to close the door immediately upon entering. Also, spring hinges prevent the resident from leaving the door open when he or she exits. Door closers (see Fig. 10) serve the same purpose. These are for more heavy duty and are commonly used in lobbies and commercial facilities.

Hinges should be mounted on the inside of the door so that burglars cannot remove the door from the hinges to enter. If hinges must be placed on the outside, they should have nonremovable pins. Pins can be made nonremovable by peening the straight end or by drilling and tapping a machine screw into the middle portion of each pin from the inside of the open hinge (see Fig. 11). Doors with outside hinge pins can also be protected by screwing two screws halfway into the jamb edge of the door. One screw is placed near each hinge, and a receiving hole is drilled into the jamb for each screw. These protruding screws hold the door when it is closed, even if the hinge pins are removed.

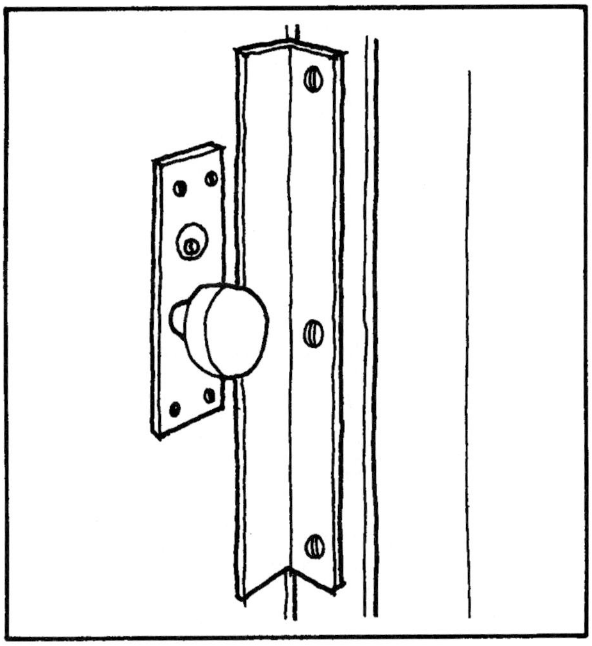

Fig. 8 Protective angle-iron for doors opening in

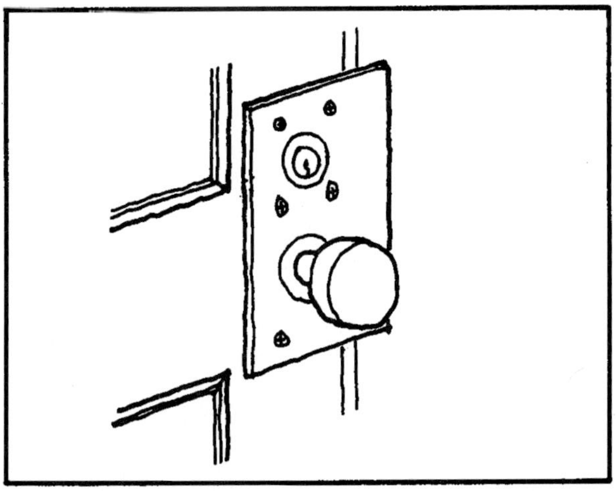

Fig. 9 Escutcheon plate for doors opening out

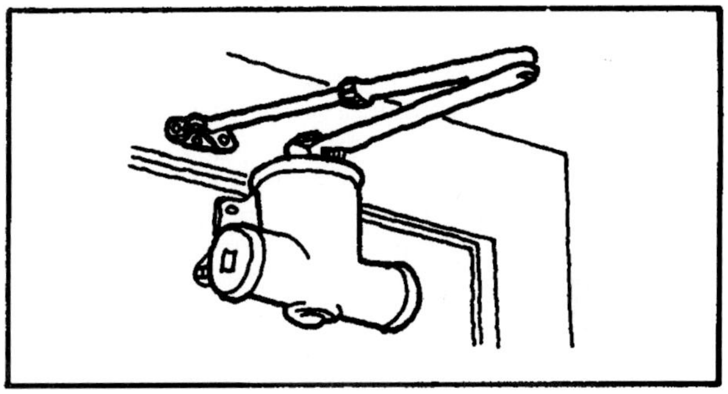

Fig. 10 Door closer

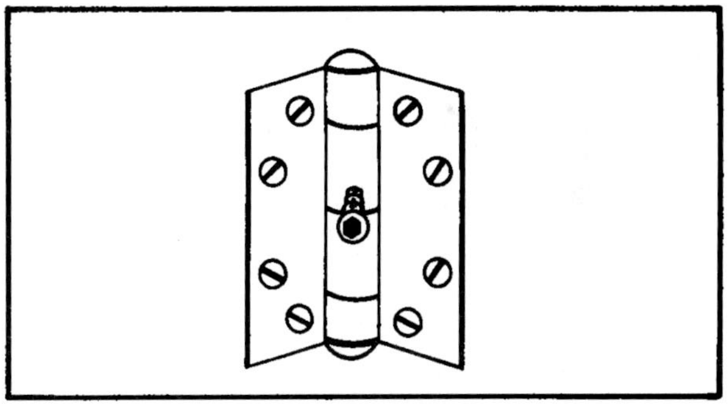

Fig. 11 Nonremovable hinge pin

Door Locks

Locks must withstand or seriously delay not only a simple forced entry but also sophisticated criminal attack. Locks may also guard against window entry-door exit crimes.

Parts of the a lock are defined as follows:

Cylinder: A cylinder is that part of the lock into which the key is inserted. If the proper key is used, the cylinder will allow the key to turn, thus moving a bolt or latch.
Deadbolt: A deadbolt (or bolt lock) is a heavy metal bar which moves horizontally into the strike of the door jamb, thus locking the two together. It is called a deadbolt because it cannot be pushed back unless the knob is turned by the correct key.
Latch: A latch (or spring lock) is the part of the lock that keeps the door in a closed position by extending into the strike automatically when the door is closed. The latch is most often operated by the doorknob. Most latches can be pushed back by external pressure without having to turn the doorknob.
Deadlatch: In a deadlatch, the latch is positively held in the projected position by an automatic mechanism which is depressed against the strike plate (see Fig. 12).
Strike: The strike is the portion of the jamb where a metal plate has been placed to receive the deadbolt and/or the latch (see Fig. 5).
Stopworks: Stopworks consist of two buttons located under the latch. Pressing the top button in allows the doorknob to turn freely and operate the latch, from both inside and out. Pressing the lower button in allows the inside doorknob to operate the latch, but freezes the outside doorknob.
Throw: The throw of a lock is the length (in inches) that the deadbolt extends beyond the face of the lock.

Primary locks Primary locks operate in conjunction with the latch. There are two major types: mortise locks and cylindrical or bore-in tubular locks (commonly called key-in-the-knob locks).

Mortise locks (see Fig. 13) are more common than key-in-the-knob locks and will provide good security. All mortise locks with latches should contain a deadbolt with at least a 1-in throw constructed of case-hardened steel, brass or zinc alloy, or bronze. Federal FF-H 106a heavy-duty series 86 mortise locks or 185 latch and 190K modified deadbolts are recommended. The deadbolt and latch should be key-operated from the exterior and operated from the inside by a device not requiring a key.

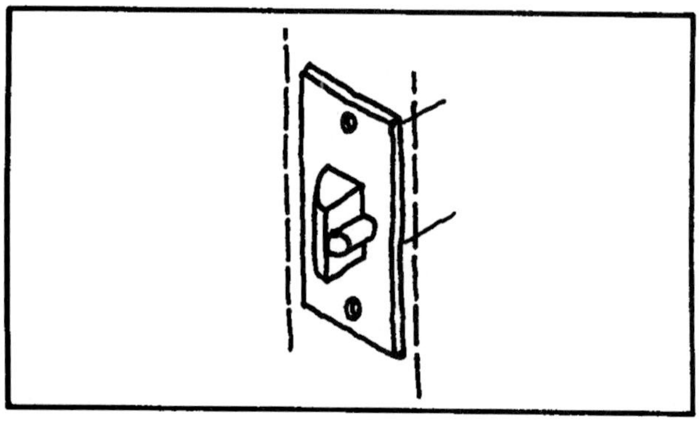

Fig. 12 Deadlatch

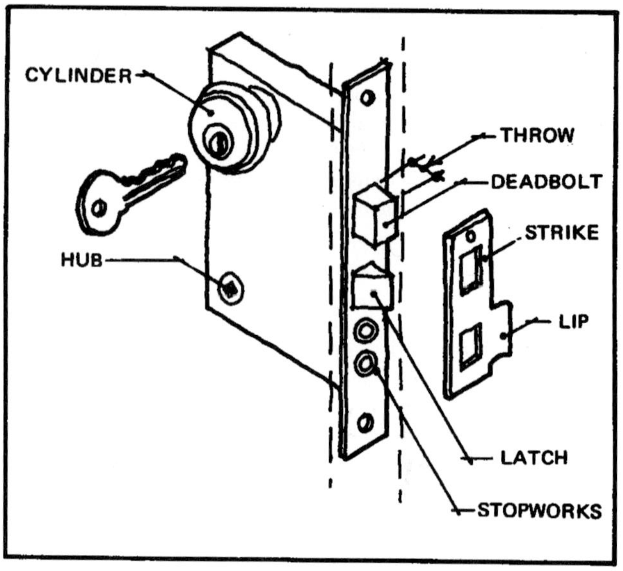

Fig. 13 Mortise lock

Mortise locks with latches used in residences should not contain an automatic spring latch with stopworks. Although stopworks prevent the outside knob from being turned, they leave the premises open to easy entry because they do not prevent the latch from being pushed back. An intruder need only insert a credit card into the strike area, push back the spring latch, and open the door (called "loiding" or "shimming" the lock). In locks without stopworks, the deadbolt (which cannot be loided) must be thrown by the key of the resident. Eliminating the stopworks prevents the resident from relying on the stopwork and latch mechanism alone.

Key-in-the-knob locks (see Fig. 14) are less secure than mortise locks. Although inexpensive due to easy installation, key-in-the-knob locks can be easily gripped by a tool and twisted until they break. A key-in-the-knob lock can include a deadbolt, at a comparable to slightly higher price than a mortise lock.

Secondary locks A secondary lock (rim lock) operates independently of the latch. "Secondary" is perhaps a poor name, since this type of lock is essential for good security. Secondary locks are usually mounted above the primary lock at shoulder level. They are operated by a key from the outside, and by a turnbolt from the inside. Both mortise and secondary locks may require keys to open them from inside and outside—useful where access to premises may be gained through a small opening other than the door (window transom), since this will prevent the thief from using the door to remove large objects or to escape.

There are three major types of secondary locks: spring bolt, horizontal deadbolt, and vertical deadbolt. The spring bolt lock operates much the same as the primary door latch. Because the bolt must be spring loaded and bevelled to allow automatic latching, the bolt can be easily opened. A button (slide stop) may be set to deadlock the bolt. However, the button must be set from the inside and can only be used when another means of egress is available. The spring bolt is not recommended as a secondary lock (see Fig. 15).

Horizontal bolt rim locks operate much the same as deadbolts on primary locks. While horizontal deadbolts afford much better protection than spring bolts, they still can be easily overcome. By inserting a crowbar between the door and the jamb, the intruder can pry them apart to release the bolt from the strike. For this reason, the longer the throw of the deadbolt, the greater the protection it affords. However, throws of over 1½ in may have excessive cantilever. The recommended minimum throw is 1 in (see Fig. 16).

Vertical bolt deadlocks should be used as secondary locks wherever possible. These utilize two deadbolts that fit vertically into eyeholes or sockets attached to the jamb. This creates a firm bond between the door and the jamb. The vertical bolt deadlock made by Segal is highly recommended, both for its pressed-steel construction and for its ability to hold up under heavy use (see Fig. 17). For additional security, a pick-resistant cylinder should be installed in a good vertical deadbolt body. This combination provides excellent security.

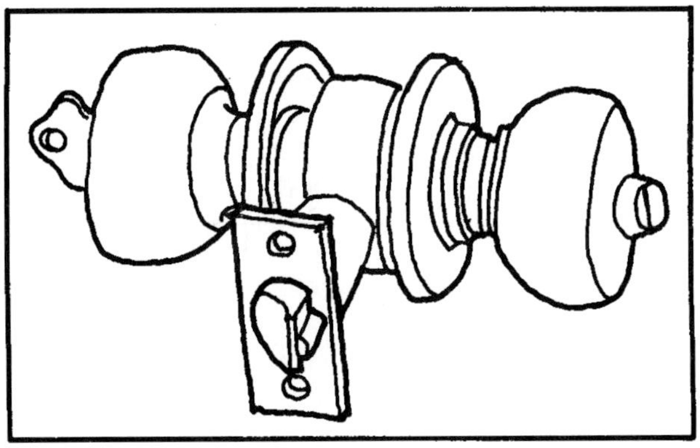

Fig. 14 Key-in-knob lock

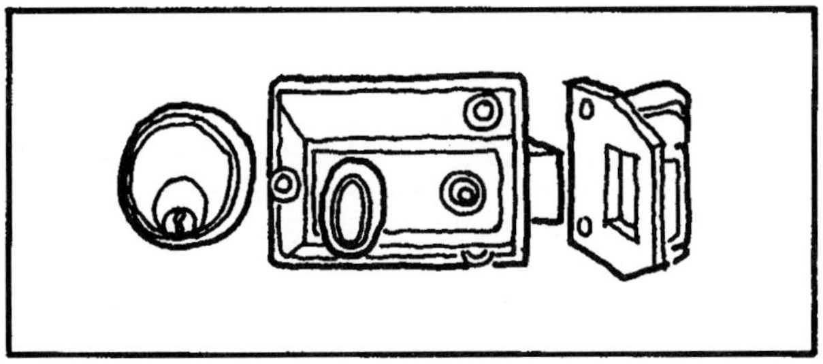

Fig. 15 Spring bolt

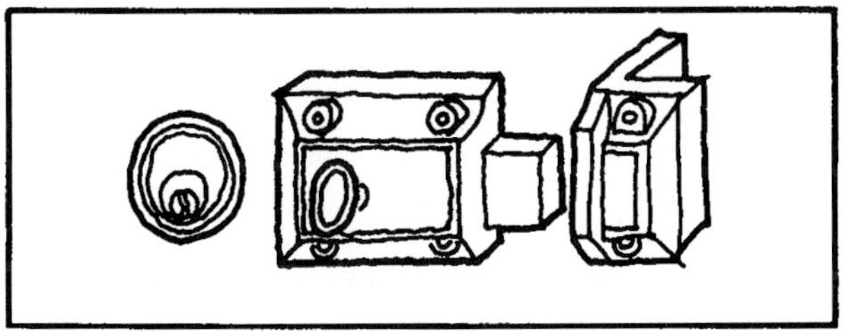

Fig. 16 Horizontal bolt

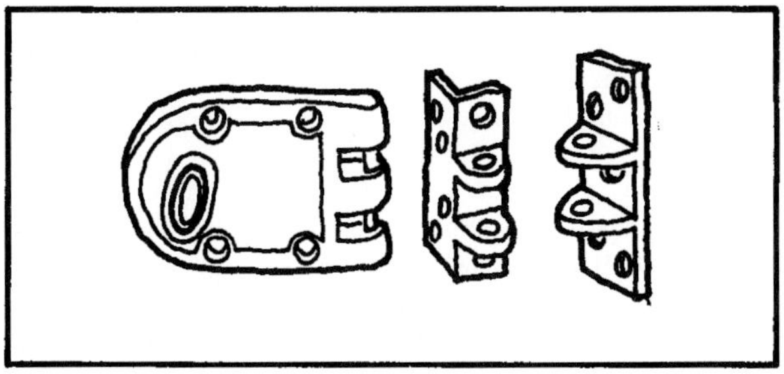

Fig. 17 Vertical bolt

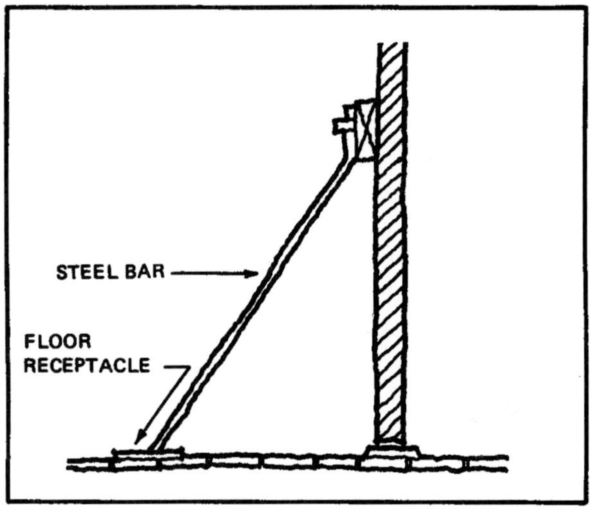

Fig. 18 Buttress door lock

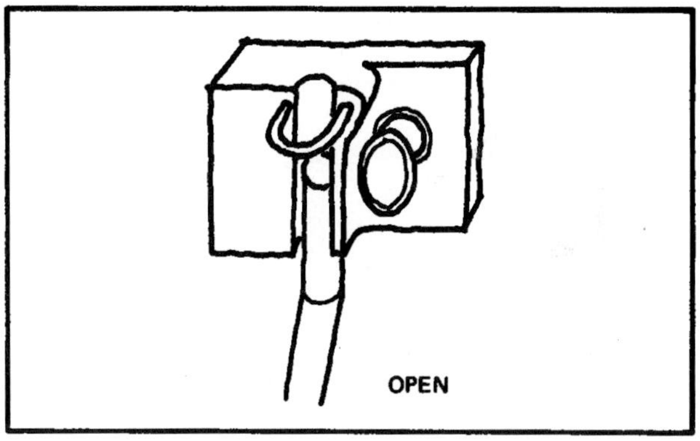

Fig. 19 Magic Eye lock with thumb turn

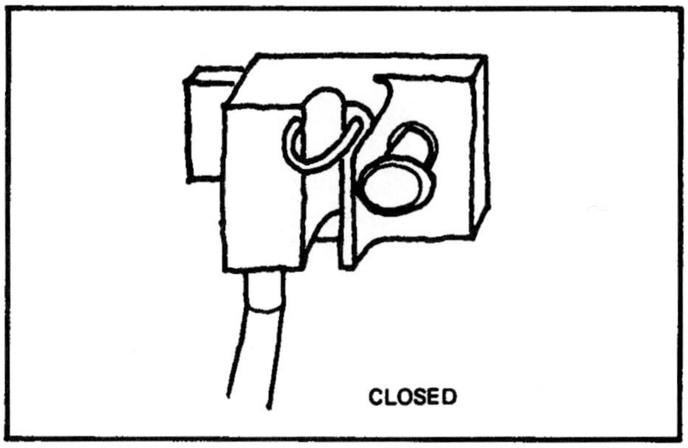

Fig. 20 Buttress door lock with deadbolt

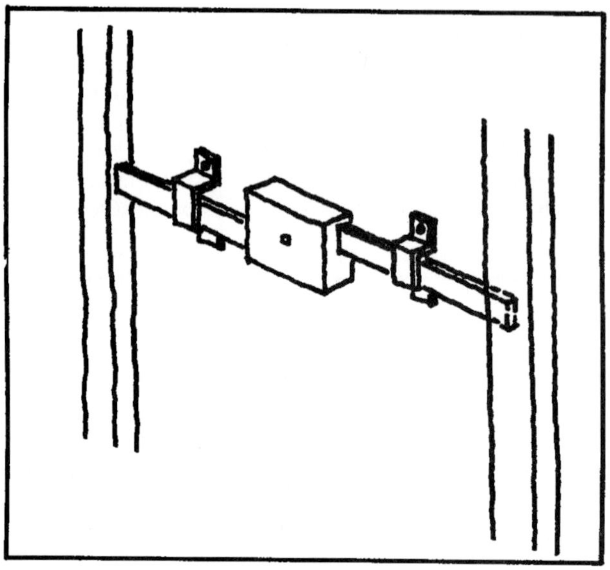

Fig. 21 Double-bar lock

The locks discussed so far rely on the rigidity of an existing door frame to resist attacks on the lock. Since older buildings may contain weak door frames, a buttress-type door lock is advisable. Locks of this type include a bar set against a plate on the door and into a receptacle in the floor, thus forming a triangular buttress (see Fig. 18). Most of these locks can be operated only by a key from the outside. The Magic Eye Company buttress lock can be operated from the outside by a key and from the inside by a turnbolt to prevent accidental locking (see Fig. 19). One model contains a heavy-duty deadbolt as well as the buttress bar, and affords still further protection (see Fig. 20).

The double-bar lock may also be used to increase the strength of a door, by means of two steel bars that extend up to 2½ in into each side of the jamb (see Fig. 21). The cylinder is protected on the outside by an escutcheon plate to prevent forcible removal. A pick-resistant cylinder can be installed for added protection. The Fox Police Lock and the Fichet Locking Bar are examples of high-quality double-bar locks.

Cylinders Regardless of the type of lock purchased, the cylinder is critical in providing protection. It must withstand efforts by sophisticated criminals such as lock pick experts.

The cylinder is the part of the lock into which the key is inserted. The most common type of cylinder is the pin tumbler, which operates as follows: As the key is inserted, spring-loaded pins are raised to the proper position to allow the barrel and the key to turn; the turning causes the bolt or latch (or both) to move. If the wrong key is used, the pins will line up incorrectly and prevent the barrel from turning (see Fig. 22).

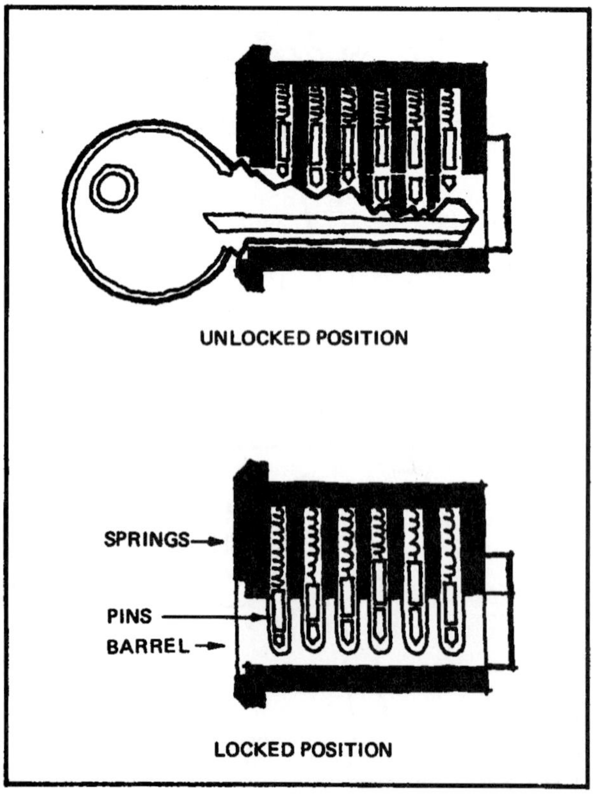

Fig. 22 Cylinders

Recently, cylinders have become available which utilize special keyways and keys to make the cylinder pick proof or pick resistant (see Fig. 23). Medeco, Illinois Duo, Sargent, Keso, Eagle Three Star, Mela, Fitchet, and Miracle Magnetic are highly pick resistant. Such cylinders provide improved security, but may require registered keys that can be duplicated only at the factory upon receipt of a signed request. A compromise is the use of a key type whose blank is not available normally, but for which spare blanks are kept for replacements.

Of all cylinders on the market, Medeco has proven most difficult to overcome. Medeco utilizes twisting tumblers operated by a key with angular or criss-cross cuts. Only if the proper key is inserted will the pins twist the exact amount needed to allow the barrel to turn.

If special keyway cylinders are deemed unnecessarily secure or costly (Medeco cylinders cost about two times the next adequate), the cylinder used should be of solid-bar-stock bronze and machined for a tight fit.

The cylinders of a master-key system of locks are constructed so that individual keys fit only one lock, but a single master key can open all locks in the system. Use of a master-key system makes maintenance and other authorized access simpler, but the dangers of improper use of a lost or stolen master key far outweigh the benefits.

From a security standpoint, a cylinder should have at least six pins. This often results in the cylinder being longer than the thickness of the door. In mortise locks (which are recessed into doors), a six-pin cylinder often extends slightly beyond the surface of the door, thus making it susceptible to forcible removal by use of a gripping tool. To prevent use of such a tool, protruding cylinders should be protected by one of the following:

Door Interviewers

Interviewers are devices installed on opaque doors to allow residents to see and hear who is outside the door without opening it.

An optical interviewer (peephole) should be installed on each door that provides entry into private dwellings. Many types of interviewers are available, ranging in diameter from 2/10 to 3 in. Optics of the interviewer include one-way glass, plastic, and wide-angle glass.

Interviewers with openings of over 1/4 in are not recommended. Larger interviewers can easily be punched out to allow insertion of tools to open the door from the inside. Someone also may stick a knife, wire, or gun through the hole while the person is looking through it. Interviewers are located approximately 4 ft 9 in from the floor (see Fig. 31). The best interviewers contain a double glass for safety. Wide-angle glass allows maximum visibility. Although a wide-angle lens does produce a curved, fisheye image, clarity of the image is not impaired. If wide-angle glass is not used, the person outside cannot be seen unless he or she is standing in a direct line with the interviewer (see Fig. 32).

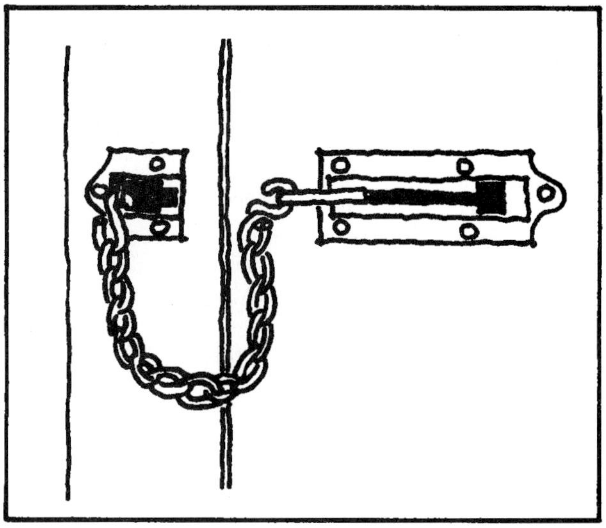

Fig. 33 Chain lock

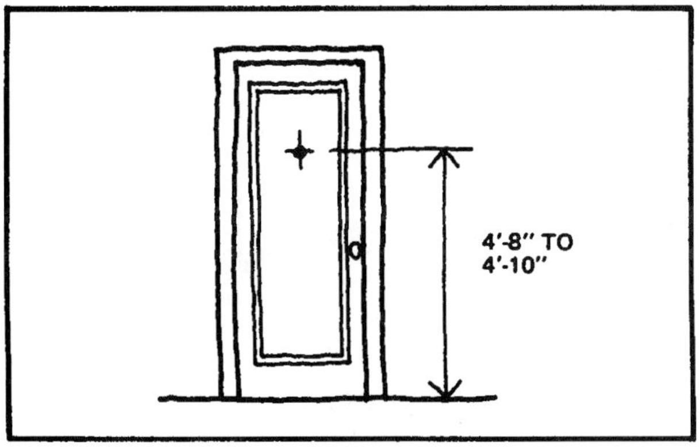

Fig. 31 Interviewer location

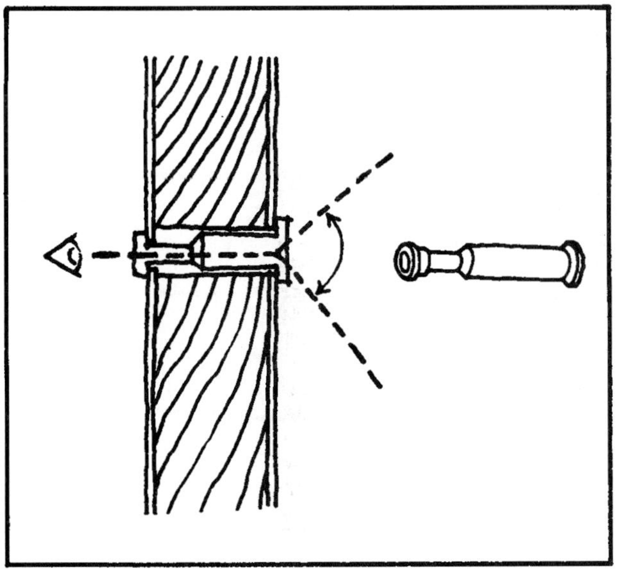

Fig. 32 Interviewer angles

Instead of an optical interviewer, a case-hardened steel chain which fits into a horizontally mounted slide track on one end of the door jamb may be installed (see Fig. 33). The chain allows the door to open slightly (preferably not more than 2 in) to permit easy conversation without fully unlocking the door. These chains should be used for interviewing only, not to protect a locked door. The swing of the door, even if only 2 in, allows the criminal to exert strong force with momentum, which breaks most chain devices. The interviewing space also allows insertion and use of tools. Some slide chains have a locking mechanism which prevents use of a thumb tack (or piece of tape) and rubber band to pull back the slide mechanism and remove the chain from the track. Even when equipped with a locking mechanism, steel chains and slides are readily overcome by simple tools and brute force.

Windows and Hardware

Window Materials

Because windows contain large sections of glass, they naturally impose a security problem. Windows most vulnerable are those on the first floor (or otherwise accessible from the ground) and those leading to fire escapes. Less vulnerable, but still easily reached, are windows over a canopy (as above a main entrance), windows adjacent to stairwell windows, and windows on the top floor.

Window Locks

Among the common window locks are the crescent sash lock, often standard on residential windows; various friction or pressure devices, such as the thumb-screw latch; pin-type latches, such as the simple steel pin-in-the-hole device; and the slide-bolt latch. All of these devices can easily be overcome, especially if an intruder is willing to risk the noise of breaking a small section of the glass. (See Figs. 34–37.)

SECURITY
Doors and Hardware

Normal windowpane glass is approximately ⅛ in thick and extremely brittle, and it breaks easily. Plate glass is usually ¼ in thick and is tempered to withstand an accidental knock. Plate glass is used for larger areas because of its greater strength and because the initial cost is worth the extra protection. Tempered glass has a thin, hardening coating and, while no stronger than plate glass, will not cut someone who breaks it.

Several companies have developed unbreakable, transparent polycarbonate materials which look like glass but are very difficult to break. GE's Lexan, for example, is guaranteed unbreakable. It costs two to three times as much as glass and has low resistance to scratching. An improved material, Lexan MR-4000, is slightly more expensive but is much less easily scratched. These polycarbonate materials have not yet been extensively used for private dwellings.

Another type of durable "glass" is fabricated much like the safety glass used in automobiles: two layers of high-quality glass are bonded together with a layer of tough vinyl between. This is sold by one company as Secur-lite. While Secur-lite can eventually be broken, the noise and trouble required to do so are considerable deterrents.

Oversized glazed areas should be avoided. Anything beyond standard size (6 ft by 8 ft for glass, for example) is expensive and may be difficult to obtain.

The only reliable devices are those with a key-operated locking mechanism. Yale and Ideal Security manufacture a window lock which is a modification of the pin-type lock. It can be locked in either of two positions, one of which allows the window to be open slightly at the bottom for ventilation (see Fig. 38). Fox makes a window lock combining a pin-type lock and a hasp and padlock. Although somewhat unsightly, it provides excellent protection. Ideal Security manufactures a modification of the crescent sash lock, which requires a key to operate.

All of these devices provide adequate security for normal residential use. A set of keys should be convenient to the window for use in emergencies but far enough away so that a burglar cannot reach them.

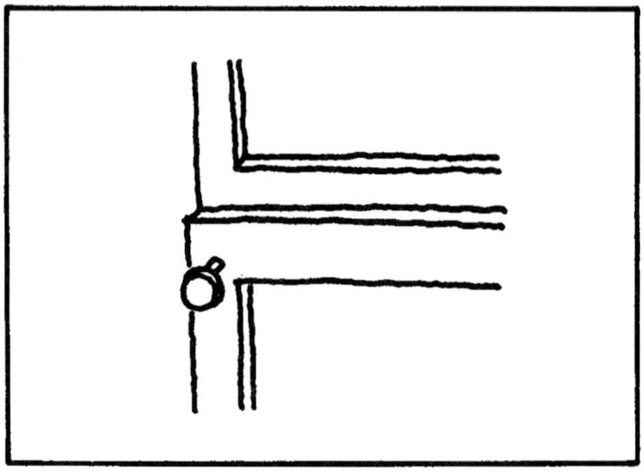

Fig. 35 Thumb screw lock

Fig. 36 Pin latch

Fig. 34 Crescent sash lock

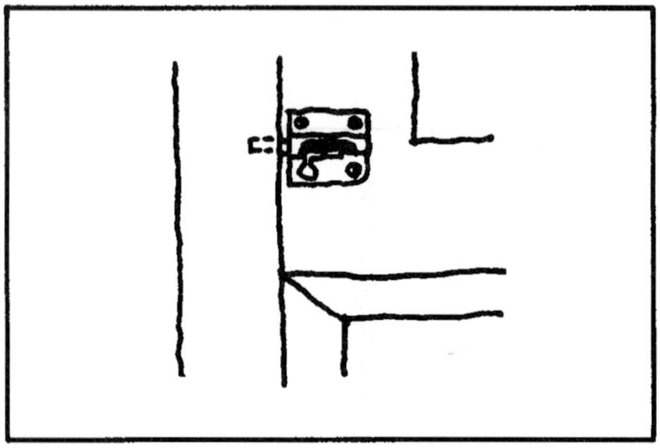

Fig. 37 Slide bolt

Window Bars, Grilles, and Gates

Where tighter security is desired, metal bars, grilles, and gates have proven most reliable. If a wire mesh grille is used, the metal should be at least ⅛ in in diameter and the openings should not exceed 2 in (see Figs. 39 and 40). The grille should be attached to the window frame with machine or roundhead bolts which cannot be removed from the outside.

If bars are used, they should be placed not more than 5 in apart. The bars should have a diameter of at least ¾ in and be set at least 3 in into the masonry.

Sliding gates afford excellent protection and can be pushed aside or opened for emergency exit. The gates should be set in tracks on the top and bottom to prevent them from being pulled or pried away from the window (see Fig. 41). Protect-A-Guard gates are highly recommended for residential and commercial use.

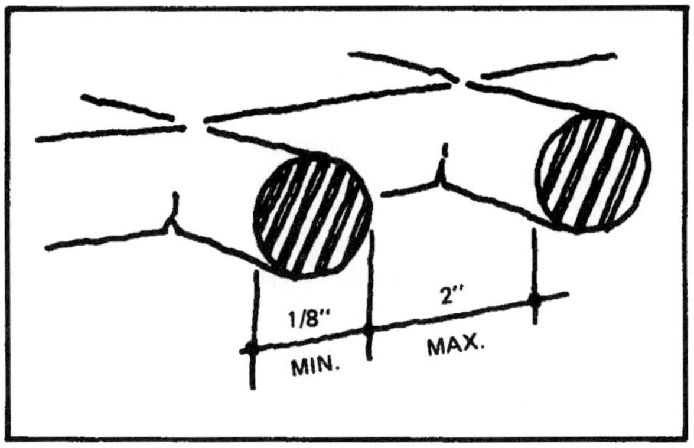

Fig. 40 Wire mesh dimensions

Fig. 38 Keyed window lock

Fig. 41 Window guard

Fig. 39 Mesh window grille

All of these devices should be installed inside the window for maximum security.

Skylights

The best protection for skylights is installation of metal bars, grilles, or mesh. Bars should be made of steel not less than ¾ in in diameter and should be placed not more than 5 in apart (see Fig. 42). If mesh is used, it should be at least ⅛ in thick and the spaces should not be greater than 2 in. Mesh should be secured firmly by machine or roundhead bolts that cannot be removed from the outside.

If metal is undesirable, a securely fastened hasp and padlock will discourage entry and exit through the roof, if the glass is not removed.

Both hook-in-eye and sliding-bolt devices are unacceptable security measures for skylights.

SECURITY
Doors and Hardware

Multifamily Dwellings

Lobby Doors and Walls

All lobby entrance doors should provide maximum visibility of the lobby. This often requires large glass areas in the lobby doors. Where there is a high degree of vandalism and crime, use of Lexan is recommended. In all cases, oversized glass sheet should be avoided. Glazed areas should be divided so that sheets larger than 6 by 8 ft are not needed. The door frame should be constructed of rugged, heavy-duty metal. The vertical jamb incorporating the lock should withstand a concentrated load of 500 lb and be a minimum of 5 in thick so that it can receive heavy-duty mortise lock sets.

The main outer lobby door should have a key-operated lock with a pin-tumbler cylinder containing at least six pins. The key for this lock should not open any other door (such as an apartment door), as this makes the lobby-door cylinder susceptible to picking. An antifriction latch (see Fig. 43) and a sturdy door closer should be used in conjunction with the lock.

Lobby doors, especially if locked or equipped with intercoms, should open out for fire safety and to reduce vandalism (tenants who have misplaced their keys can kick an in-swinging door hard enough to break the locking mechanism).

Secondary Exits

In multifamily dwellings, exit doors leading to fire stairwells on each landing should have self-locking deadlatches to allow free egress while prohibiting entry. The stairside surface of the door should be free of hardware to prevent access to one floor from another via the stairwell. Hardware should limit access to the roof or ground-floor exits via the stairwell.

Panic hardware, if required, should be in the form of vertical-bolt latches on the top and bottom of the door. This hardware makes the door more sturdy and makes entry from the outside difficult (see Fig. 44).

Doors leading into the buildings from garage areas should have self-locking deadlatches with a minimum throw of ½ inch, which allow free egress but require a key for entry into the building. The door should be protected in the area of the strike. All exit doors should be equipped with a self-closing apparatus that can be adjusted to the desired tension.

Since fire doors are required by law to be operable from the inside, they are often a means of escape. Exit alarms (see Fig. 45) bring immediate attention to fire doors that are opened when there is no apparent fire. A panic bar or other device simultaneously opens the door and sounds a local alarm. However, effectiveness of the alarm as a security measure depends on the speed and consistence of response to the signal.

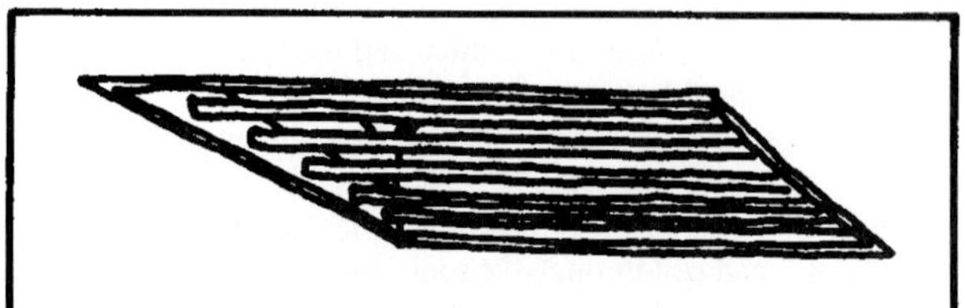

Fig. 42 Skylight protection

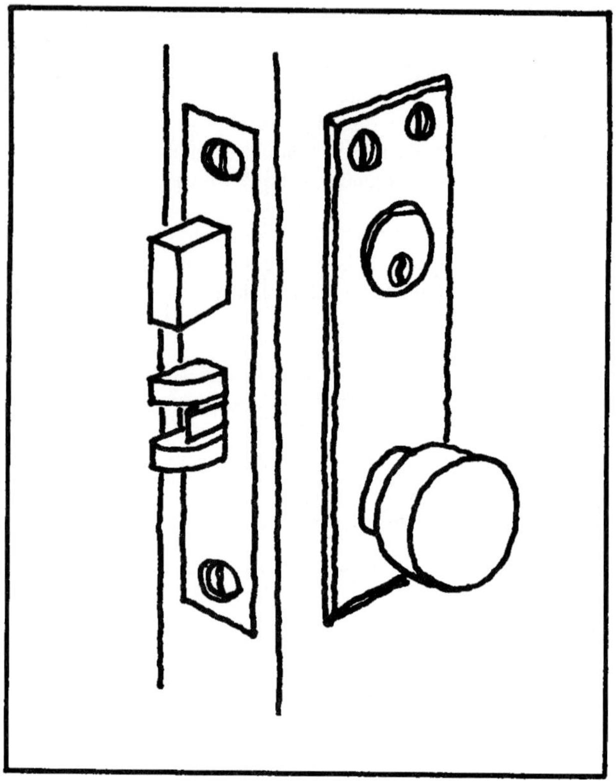

Fig. 43 Antifriction latch bolt

Exit alarms on fire exits leading to roofs keep burglars from using the roof for escape or for access to top-floor apartments. However, the alarm may prove more a nuisance than a good security measure if teenage vandalism is prevalent. Teenagers often set off the alarm to harass the local official, who must respond to the signal and reset the alarm.

Elevators

In most middle-income multifamily dwellings, vandalism of elevators is relatively rare. However, in many high-crime areas and low-income housing developments, this vandalism is reaching a critical level. In New York City Housing Authority projects, vandalism to elevators and elevator equipment is responsible for almost 60 percent of elevator outages. Parts of the elevator most commonly vandalized are the hall buttons, indicator lights, hatch door glass, hatch door interlock, and buttons located inside the cab, especially the emergency and light switches.

Hall buttons are most commonly vandalized because of their accessibility. Impatient tenants push the buttons excessively and often kick or smash them in frustration. To prevent damage to the button and the electrical contacts inside, a stainless steel mushroom-type button should be used (see Fig. 46). The shape of the button prevents the contacts from being damaged by the button's being pushed too heavily against them. Another stainless steel button has been developed on the

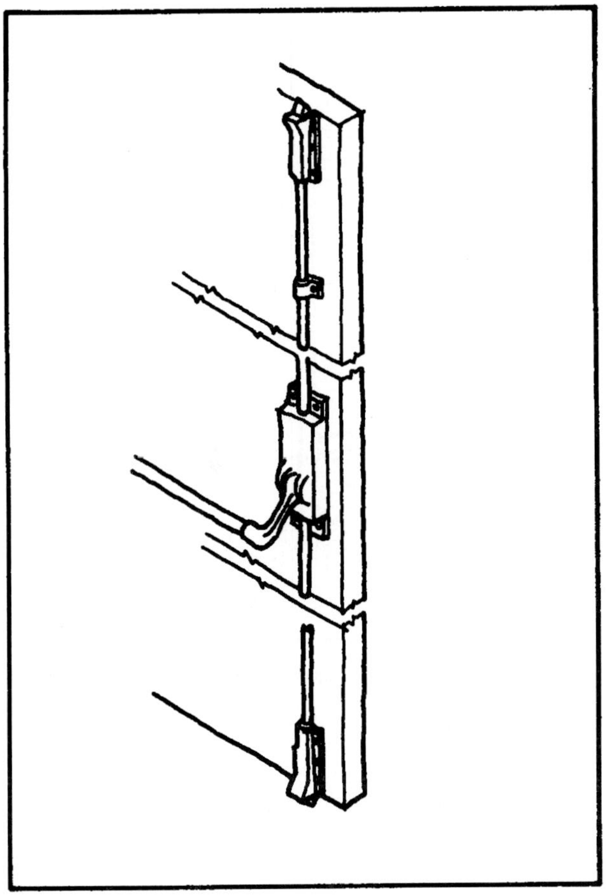

Fig. 44 Vertical bolt on exit door

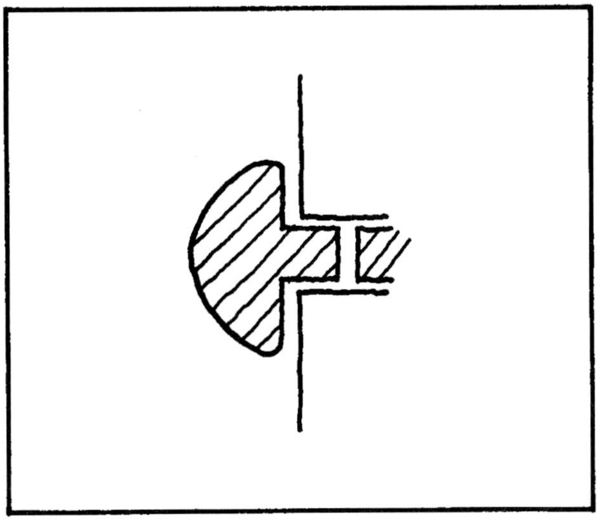

Fig. 46 Mushroom button

same principle, except that the stopper is inside the mechanism so that the button has the more familiar stunted-cone appearance.

Use of indicator lights for the lobby, the cab, and the other floors should be decided by the management. In some projects, indicator lights are so vandalized that it is easier to eliminate them. In other developments, indicator lights dampen user impatience and the result is less wear and tear on the buttons. If indicator lights are used, they should be protected by a heavy-duty plastic shield.

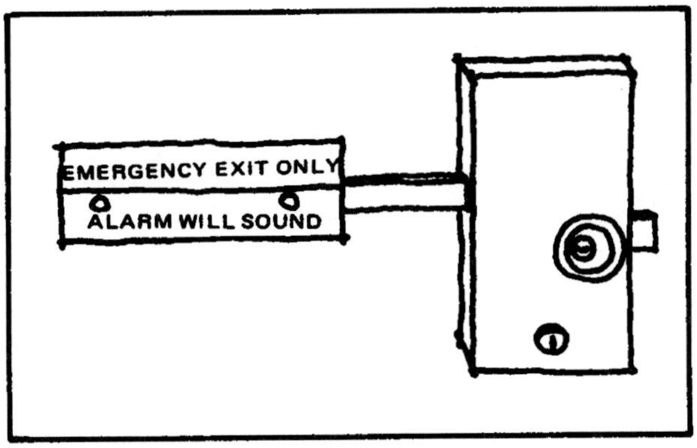

Fig. 45 Exit alarm

There are two types of elevator doors: swing and slide. This nomenclature refers to the doors on each floor; the cab door is always a slide door. Slide doors, which are automatic, are becoming increasingly popular despite higher initial cost, because they increase protection against vandalism. Swing doors are inconvenient and more subject to vandalism (short-circuiting of door interlocks, jamming of closing mechanisms, and joyriding on top of cabs).

In many older elevators (especially the swing-door type), the hatch and cab door contain small glass windows, which allow people to see inside before entering and allow passengers to see what floor they're passing. In high-crime areas, this glass has proven more dangerous than helpful. Vandals smash the glass readily, even if wire glass is used. The opening left when the glass is broken presents a very dangerous situation. Hatch door glass should be eliminated by welding or bolting a piece of metal over the opening. Where this is prohibited by a strict building code, a variance is often granted in a high-crime area. A less desirable modification is to install a heavy steel grille over the opening and replace the glass with Lexan.

Interlocks are more commonly vandalized on swing-door elevators. Causes of damage are excessive pulling on the elevator door while the cab is at another floor and short-circuiting due to water or urine damage. The latter problem can be solved by installing interlocks with hydrophilic (non-water-absorbing) contacts. When damaged, this type of interlock requires replacement of only the contact plates rather than the entire mechanism. Damage caused by excessive pulling may be alleviated by signs cautioning tenants against such pulling. Closing mechanisms (keepers) can be made to fit more securely when the bolt is in place to prevent too much play in the door.

The emergency stop button presents a problem because it is often misused. The button may be activated to stop the elevator between floors to commit crimes such as mugging, rape, and drug abuse. Because every elevator has several automatic safety mechanisms that prevent it from falling freely down the shaft, the stop button is primarily a psychological comfort to passengers. Wherever possible, the stop button should be eliminated. The building code requirement for stop buttons is being challenged in New York and several other cities. If code change is unlikely, a variance should be applied for where elevator crime is common. A constant-pressure alarm switch is also somewhat better than the conventional toggle switch.

Secer Light and Kendall are among the manufacturers of elevator dome lights that are highly vandal resistant (see Fig. 47). They are constructed of durable steel and contain a shatterproof plastic plate to protect the bulb. Where use of these lights is economically prohibitive, Lexan or an equivalent should be used to protect the light bulb.

Aside from vandalism, joyriding on top of elevator cabs is becoming prevalent in high-crime areas. Injury occurs most often when children are struck by the counterweight when the cab and counterweight pass each other. In other cases, children are crushed between cabs, struck by dividing beams, or squashed under a cab in the pit.

There are numerous means of access to elevator roofs and shafts: door interlocks are jammed by using simple household tools, emergency stop switches are abused, and roof escape hatch doors are forced. Once on top, children often abuse passengers inside the cabs and interfere with normal elevator operation.

It is difficult to prevent crime by modifying elevator equipment. Restricted access to the building through the use of a buzzer-reply system, tenant patrol groups, or doormen is more likely to be effective. Closed-circuit television and audio-intercom systems mounted on elevators are other possible crime control devices.

A common device used to increase visibility in an elevator is a convex mirror placed in the upper back corner of the elevator. This allows a person to see if anyone is waiting inside the elevator *before* he or she walks into a possible assault situation (see Fig. 48).

An elevator modification that may deter crime is the up-discharge, down-collect system. When controlled in this way, an elevator will stop only for a person who has selected "up" (discharge) at the ground-floor level. Passengers on the upper floor can enter the elevator only on its way down (collect). The advantage is that a person entering the elevator on the first floor can be assured that the elevator will not stop at another floor to allow a suspicious person to enter. Such a system may be inconvenient for residents—a person wishing to go from the fifth to the seventh floor would have to travel down to the ground floor and then up again. The system is far from foolproof, as criminals can operate in other ways, but the modification is inexpensive and may deter crime in buildings without security personnel.

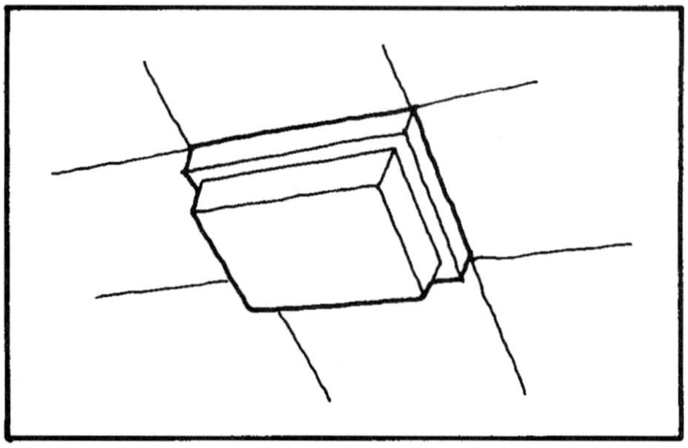

Fig. 47 Unbreakable light fixture

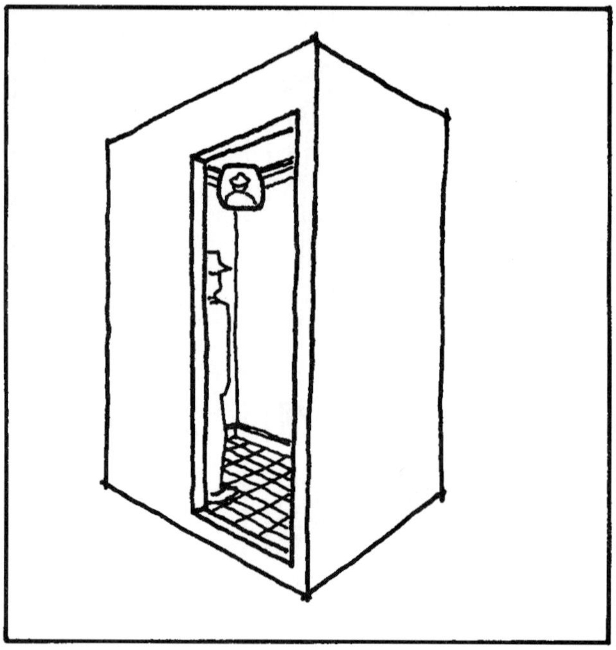

Fig. 48 Elevator mirror

Garage Doors and Secondary Entries

Doors to interior garages provide a means of entry that circumvents many security precautions. If access to the building is to be limited, entry through the garage door must be carefully controlled.

The most practical solution is to have a locked door which tenants can open but which automatically closes behind them, usually within 15 seconds. A large number of manufacturers provide such self-closing doors. The major variation is the means for opening the garage door. Radio-controlled devices, requiring each auto to have a transistor, are expensive and far from foolproof. If a device is stolen from one car, all the devices should be replaced (an expensive procedure). A convenient and less elaborate system has a key-operated switch mounted on the driver's side of the garage, allowing the driver to use a key without leaving his car.

Despite these controls, the garage door should be monitored by tenants, security personnel, or electronic equipment if a building is to retain a high level of security.

A door leading directly from a parking area to the building interior must be treated the same as a main entry. Such a door will be used continually and requires equivalent security measures.

The secondary lock recommended for storage rooms containing valuables is the Fox double-bar lock.

Mailboxes and Mailbox Rooms

Mailboxes are a major target for criminals within multifamily dwellings, particularly in low-income communities. The mail includes welfare, social security, and veterans' checks as well as others. These checks are particularly vulnerable because they arrive on set days of the month.

The bank of mailboxes should be located in the most secure and easily surveyed space available. Some brands of mailboxes do provide security, but any mailbox can be opened in the 10 minutes required to force open the door. If there is any control of access to the building (intercom or doorman), mailboxes should be located inside the protected area.

Mailboxes may be located in a locked room. Such a room must contain a large window to make it visible from the lobby, and be lighted 24 hours a day to reduce its potential as a location for muggings and other crimes. The door to a mailbox room should have sturdy self-locking hardware. Where back-loading mailboxes (generally secure) are used, a separate mail-loading room is often provided (see Fig. 49).

The better mailboxes are constructed of 16-gauge metal. The doors are tightly fitted and are without holes, to prevent prying them open and to prevent matches from being dropped in. The metal may be corrugated for additional strength. Cylinder locks with at least five pins should be used. Door size should be kept to a minimum to further limit the possibility of prying doors open (see Fig. 50). American and Gorth manufacture such mailboxes.

LIGHTING

Good lighting in a residential development permits adequate visibility and surveillance. Generally, the higher the lighting level, the better the security. An appropriate level of lighting should be provided in each area, the light should be without excessive glare and generate no heavy shadows, and lighting should be resistant to vandalism and easy to maintain.

Fluorescent lamps are tubular glass lights that require special current-control devices called *ballasts.* Operating costs of fluorescent lamps are significantly lower than for incandescent bulbs: fluorescent tubes typically produce 3 to 4 times as much light per watt and operate 7 to 10 times longer than incandescent bulbs (due in part to lower operating temperatures).

Interior Lighting

Lobbies, elevators, stairwells, and corridors must be well lit. Interior lighting normally requires only conventional incandescent bulbs, but low-glare or frosted incandescent or fluorescent luminaries are preferable. Low wattages of 25 to 200 W generally suffice. It is usually desirable to install low-wattage fixtures at close intervals to minimize shadows and glare.

The most common problem of interior lighting is vandalism. Naked bulbs provide maximum illumination at minimal installation cost, but they are so often and so easily broken that maintenance costs are very high, and crime is encouraged by lack of lights. Recessed lighting suffers less from accidental breakage and vandalism. Transparent bulb protectors allow nearly total passage of light, but since the bulb can be seen, a vandal will likely try to break it. Translucent bulb covers are therefore preferable, even though some of the light is blocked by the cover.

Secer and Kendall have developed fixtures that are vandal resistant. They are made of plastic and come in a variety of shapes and sizes.

Exterior Lighting

All heavily used spaces such as paths, entries, and parking areas should be lit by 5 to 10 foot candles. Higher fixture locations have a variety of advantages. As a general rule, the useful ground coverage of an elevated light fixture is roughly twice the height of the fixture. Thus, a 150-W incandescent lamp mounted 8 ft above the ground can provide adequate light for 16 ft along a walk. Higher luminaries are safer from vandalism. However, lighting fixtures mounted higher than the second floor may create a feeling of being in a compound.

A variety of specialized, high-intensity light sources can illuminate large outdoor areas such as recreation facilities and parking lots. Mercury-vapor and sodium-vapor lamps are available in sizes up to 1500 W; the eerie bluish light of early mercury-vapor lamps may be avoided by selecting one of the newer, color-corrected models. Once again, the point is to provide an appropriate level of light without creating glare or shadows.

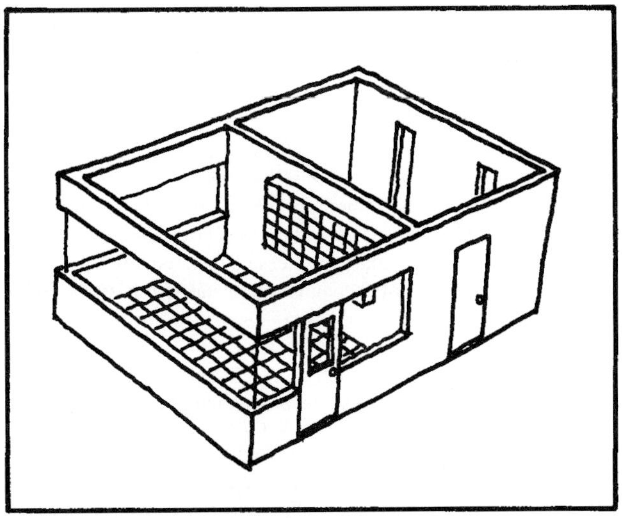

Fig. 49 Mailroom and loading room

Fig. 50 Mailboxes

Lamp and fixture breakage can be controlled in part by installing fixtures of tough, break-resistant plastic. The spherical, white glass fixtures so common today are less vulnerable, though not as tough as the more expensive plastic models.

A final comment on lighting is specifically relevant to a building or residential development inhabited primarily by the elderly. The pupil in the human eye gradually decreases in size due to advancing age. As a result, about twice as much actual brightness is required to create the same degree of brightness on the retina of a 60-year-old as on the retina of a 20-year-old (the ratio reaches 3 by age 75). Therefore, lighting levels in residences for the elderly should be well in excess of conventional standards and much higher than what seems adequate to a (younger) management staff.

ELECTRONIC SYSTEMS

Electronic security equipment includes alarms designed to detect unauthorized entrance; closed-circuit television systems, apartment-to-lobby intercom locks, and various audio equipment. While the initial cost of many of these systems is high, each could reasonably be installed in moderate-income residential complexes and could prevent future need for more costly measures.

Alarms

An alarm performs two functions: it detects the presence of an intruder, and it reports the intrusion. The quality of an alarm mechanism is measured by its ability to perform these two functions.

A wide range of devices detect intrusion of a criminal into a building. These fall roughly into two categories: contact devices and motion-detection devices.

Contact Devices

Contact devices are mechanical switches that detect movement or perhaps the breakage of glass. A common type consists of a contact on the door (or window) and a contact on the frame. When the door is closed, the two contacts form part of an electrical circuit. When the door is opened, the contact is broken, the circuit is opened, and the alarm circuit is activated (see Fig. 51). A similar device, called a *string-pull alarm,* employs a slight variation in that the opening of the door pulls a string, which closes a switch that trips the alarm. Many contact devices are purely mechanical (as just described), while others include magnetic and mercury switches.

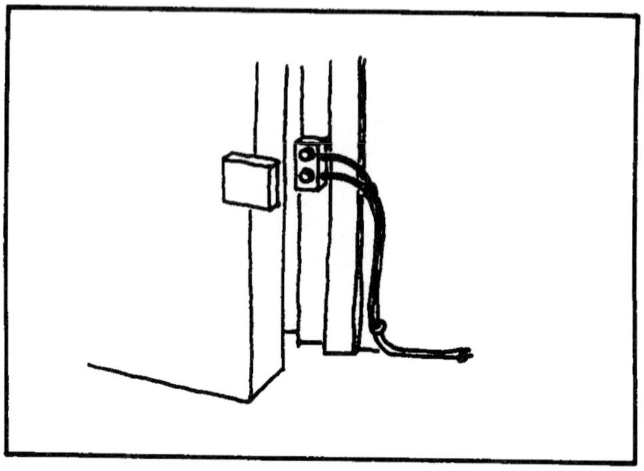

Fig. 51 Contact switch on door

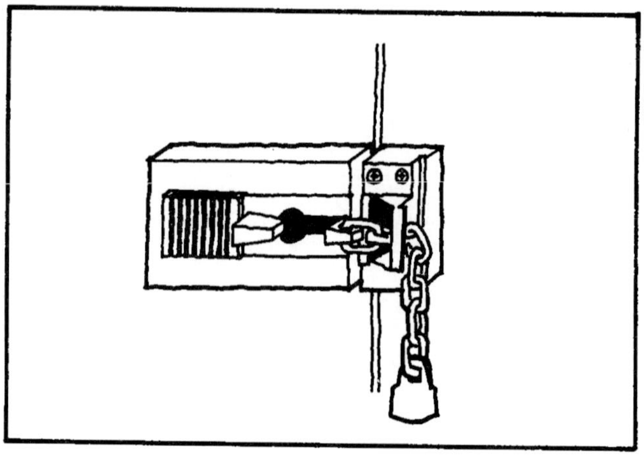

Fig. 52 Lock alarm.

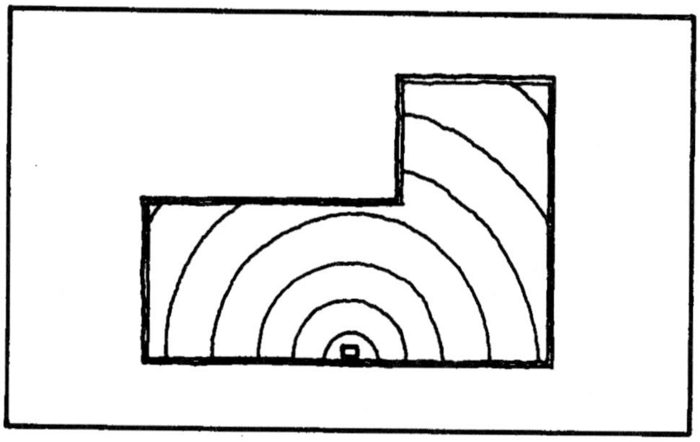

Fig. 53 Ultrasonic detector

Usefulness of a contact depends on its sensitivity (how much the device can be jarred without being activated) and its reliability. Most situations call for a device sufficiently sensitive that a skilled burglar cannot enter without setting off the alarm, but not so delicate that innocent jostling will disturb it.

Foil strips are a related mechanism used primarily to detect breakage of glass in windows and doors. A delicate strip of metal foil is glued or taped to the glass. The foil strip acts as one long, continuous electrical circuit. If the glass is broken, the foil is broken, which interrupts the circuit and activates the alarm. Foil can be circumvented if it is possible to break the glass or release a lock without breaking the foil. Primarily because of their unattractiveness, foil strips are seldom installed in residences.

Contact devices can be made part of a lock mechanism (see Fig. 52). This type of alarm is set off whenever an attempt is made to force or pick the lock.

Contact devices themselves are very inexpensive; a simple magnetic contact pair costs about $2. But each contact device can protect only one opening; therefore, even a single-family house requires several devices to protect all points of entry. In addition, it is often expensive to install the alarms and connect them to an alarm-reporting device.

Contacts may be hidden so criminals cannot locate and dismantle them easily. Hiding an alarm system lessens its value as a deterrent, but increases the criminal's chances of being apprehended while committing a crime. Since deterrence is the primary goal of residential security efforts, it is quite common to advertise the existence of an alarm without revealing the location of the mechanisms. This advertising is sometimes done where no alarm system exists. Considering the minimal expense involved in such a ruse, it may be worth the cost, but even very unsophisticated criminals can pick out such fake systems.

Heat-sensitive devices are sometimes combined with contact switches to provide an inexpensive fire-security alarm system.

Motion-Detection Devices

These devices detect the motion of an intruder as he or she moves about the protected space. This detection can be accomplished in a variety of ways. Seismographic devices are turned on by vibrations or weight on the floor (these devices have been perfected so they are not triggered by a passing truck). Photoelectric cells ("seeing-eye" mechanisms) use a beam of light to detect any motion across a protected span. Ultrasonic devices send inaudible sound waves through a room (see Fig. 53). Movement by an intruder changes the pattern of reflected sound waves and thus triggers an alarm. Increased sensitivity improves the effectiveness of each of these systems, but also raises their costs.

Motion detectors are far more expensive than contact devices, but one motion device can protect an entire area, regardless of the number of points of entry. Installation costs are often minimal, as the detection device need not be connected to any part of the structure. Motion detectors are most useful in spaces not used during scheduled periods of time, such as in commercial establishments which are totally empty at night and in homes left empty during vacation. More expensive motion-detection devices can protect limited areas, such as a single door or window.

Alarm-Reporting Systems

The term "alarm-reporting system" describes the mechanism that receives the message of an intrusion and reacts. Essentially, there are only two kinds of alarm-reporting systems. Intrusion is reported either by a loud alarm on the premises (called a *local alarm*) or via wires to a security force, which is prepared to react when notified (called a *central alarm* or *silent alarm*).

A local alarm has a bell or buzzer connected to the intrusion device, which produces a loud audio signal on the premises when the alarm is activated. This is the simplest type of alarm and can be installed readily. The deterrent effect is dependent on the burglar's being intimidated and driven off immediately by the noise. Noise of the local alarm can also stop a crime in progress and aid in apprehension if someone responds to the alarm. Local alarms are often operated by batteries (see Fig. 54). Instead of an alarm being sounded, lights in the building can be turned on by an alarm system, or both lights and alarm can be activated.

This local system also protects people sleeping in a house by alerting them that a break-in is being attempted. Generally, keys are required to shut off local alarms.

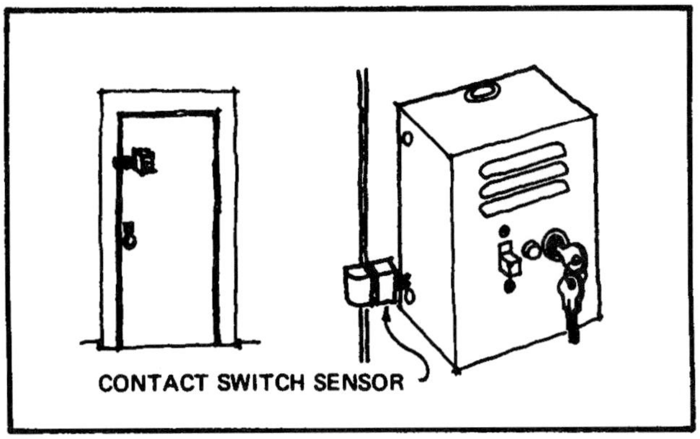

Fig. 54 Local alarm

A central alarm-reporting system sounds an alarm at a remote point usually connected to the detection device by wires (telephone lines are used in many cases). The remote point is sometimes the residence of the owner of a protected business establishment and sometimes the local police station, but generally it is the headquarters of a private protective agency. These agencies have guards stationed at this headquarters who will respond to the alarm signal. Usefulness of the alarm system is dependent on the speed and reliability of the response.

A local alarm signal is often activated at the same time as a central alarm, thus simultaneously frightening the criminal and alerting the authorities. If only a central alarm-reporting system is activated, the criminal is not warned that an alarm has been sent. This system (called a *silent alarm*) increases the possibility of apprehension while eliminating the possibility of driving the intruder off with noise.

A variation on this central-alarm arrangement is to utilize regular city police to respond to the central alarm. In high-income, low-density, high-burglary-risk communities, the city police allow alarms to be hooked up to the police headquarters, where the dispatcher serves as monitor. Another arrangement is for the detection device to trigger a tape-recorded message that is automatically telephoned to the police, telling them the location of a burglary in progress.

The single major problem of all alarm systems is the possibility of false alarms. They can be caused by defects in the intrusion-detection device or the reporting system. False alarms diminish the credibility of the entire system.

If neighbors experience repeated false alarms, if security guards are called out unnecessarily, or if police are accidentally telephoned a tape-recorded message, response by all of these persons slows dramatically and will eventually cease. Thus, the intrusion device must be designed so that it is not accidentally activated by noncriminal occurrences.

Related to the false alarm issue is the question of how the alarm is turned off. The most common method is for the alarm to operate after a 20-second delay; that is, the alarm will not sound for 20 seconds after a contact is broken or motion detected, allowing the resident a brief period in which to switch off the entire system. The switch can be simply a button located in a hidden place. A key-operated switch is more secure, but the possibility of false alarms increases because residents often forget or cannot locate their keys. However, the turnoff mechanism should not be so simple or accessible that the criminal can activate it.

Selecting Alarm Systems

The security alarm business is large and complex. It is therefore impossible to specify manufacturers or even types of alarm systems for general use. The quality of installation and the maintenance program that backs up the system are crucial elements that should outweigh initial price in the selection of equipment. The best advice is to deal with firms that have a verifiable history of quality installation, a reliable guarantee/warranty record, and an established repair and maintenance program.

The concept of a consistent level of security avoids excessive expenditures for one piece of equipment while other means of entry are unprotected. Equipment characteristics should fit specific installation situations. It is often difficult to install contact switches in older houses because window frames often have warped or buckled. String-pull devices have to be set from the inside and therefore cannot be used for a normal exit door.

Selection of alarm equipment should be based on specific system characteristics desired: Is deterrence of crime or apprehension of criminals the primary goal? Should the system be visible to deter attempted burglary, or should it be hidden to increase the likelihood of apprehending a burglar?

Closed-Circuit Television

When used in residential settings, closed-circuit television (CCTV) is intended to provide "electronic windows"—that is, a visual surveillance where physical design has obviated unaided surveillance. The purpose is to create an environment in which residents know that normal restraints of surveillance by citizens and their authorized agents exist, albeit aided by electronics. While initially costly, CCTV often reduces security personnel requirements or obviates the need for expensive redesign of existing structures.

Electronically aided surveillance is not equal to personal surveillance. A corrective response to a detected crime is obviously a step further away if the viewer sees the crime on a TV receiver rather than on the spot. The deterrent of having police or another person on hand is lost. There is also the possibility of equipment malfunction. But CCTV has a quality of its own: being watched while unable to ascertain who, if anyone, is doing the watching is somehow unnerving, and definitely is a deterrent. A remotely controlled surveillance camera can be fitted with an automatic panning device so that the camera swings from side to side continuously, even when no one is monitoring the system.

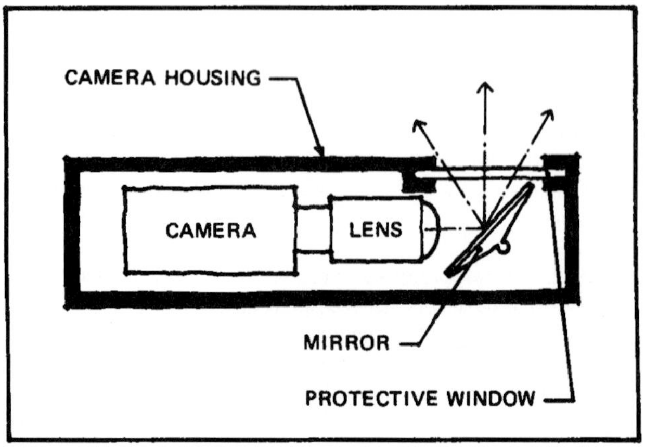

Fig. 55 Recessed camera

CCTV System Requirements

In general, a CCTV system should perform at approximately the same level as commercial broadcast receivers. Specific equipment and the quality of image needed are determined by characteristics of the area under surveillance, schedules of operation, makeup of the monitoring staff and their expected responses to emergencies, and use of special equipment.

American and foreign manufacturers have TV cameras suitable for security work. All equipment should meet the standards of the Electronic Industries Association for CCTV. Service and maintenance are generally more difficult and expensive than installation; therefore, the capability and reputation of a local supplier is crucial. City police or traffic departments often have had experience with manufacturers, suppliers, and maintenance operations. To encourage reliance on the system by users and to prevent criminals from taking advantage of a lapse, the CCTV system should break down as infrequently as possible and be repaired quickly in the event of a breakdown.

Picture resolution depends primarily on camera quality and lighting levels; higher lighting levels permit the use of less sensitive, less expensive cameras.

The entire system should operate unattended. This requires electronically stable equipment—meaning, for example, that no one should be required to constantly adjust the lens of the camera.

It is difficult to project costs of CCTV systems because of the variety of system sizes and configurations and the range of equipment costs. Camera prices start as low as $200, but more sophisticated models, such as those sensitive to very low light levels, cost up to $10,000 each. Complicated accessories, including zoom lenses, remote pan (side-to-side movement) and tilt (up-and-down movement) mechanisms, and low-light equipment, can increase installation and maintenance costs tremendously. The cost of monitoring equipment can be as low as the cost of a conventional television receiver, but more specialized and sensitive equipment is far more expensive.

Camera Locations

The location of a CCTV camera and the light level at that point are key cost-effectiveness factors. A camera's location defines the area to be observed by the camera, and the nature of the location greatly influences the camera's vulnerability to theft and vandalism. Available lighting dictates the type of camera needed to produce a final image of adequate quality. Of course, supplemental lighting may be provided at additional cost.

The camera must be able to view an area that is significant in terms of crime control. Wide-angle or other special lenses should be avoided by choosing a different camera location. Most important, the camera itself must be protected from theft and vandalism. This means that the body and lens of the camera should be in an inaccessible place. A mirror is often used to reflect the image into the lens, so that the expensive lens will not be broken by pointed instruments, thrown objects, or bullets (see Fig. 55). All interior cameras should be placed inside sturdy housings which are installed with tamper-proof connectors. Cameras must be accessible for maintenance and repair, however.

A number of locations meet all of these requirements. An elevator in a high-rise building is often protected by CCTV. The camera is generally mounted on the outside of the elevator cab wall so that the image passes via a mirror in a corner of the elevator to the protected lens. In case of camera failure, the elevator must be stopped so that the camera maintenance person can step onto the top of the cab and reach over the side to repair the units. This is not overly inconvenient for repairpersons, but it does make access to the camera more difficult for a potential thief.

Building lobbies are another common location of interior cameras. Lobby cameras are commonly hung from the ceiling or recessed into the ceiling. The elevated locations require that repair personnel use a ladder. Use of a ladder, however, would make a thief very conspicuous.

Outdoor locations usually depend on inaccessibility to protect equipment from theft and vandalism. Cameras are located atop steel poles or on poles extending from roofs or walls. An alternative is to place the camera in a wall or window of an accessible apartment.

Lighting for CCTV Systems

Lighting plays a key role in the cost and effectiveness of a CCTV system. For camera locations inside buildings, it is almost always less expensive to raise the light level than to use low-light-level equipment. The required lighting level is only slightly higher than normal for building interiors, can be achieved without glare, and has an intrinsic value as a crime deterrent.

Exterior lighting can be very expensive. Cameras used outdoors are almost always more flexible and sensitive, being capable of adapting to full sun, cloudiness, and dusk. But as indicated earlier, camera costs rise dramatically for low-light-level equipment. While increasing of lighting levels is also expensive, well-designed extra lighting again has an intrinsic value as a crime deterrent.

Monitoring of CCTV Systems

The effectiveness of CCTV depends on the nature and quality of monitoring. Many people may be used as monitors: city police, project security personnel, members of organized tenant patrols, tenants acting as individuals, and various combinations of these groups. The choice depends principally on availability of personnel and their monitoring costs.

City police will monitor CCTV systems only if they believe it is the most efficient use of personnel. Thus an area being surveyed must suffer large numbers of crimes to warrant hiring police or civilians whose function is simply sitting, watching, and adjusting. Crime reduction or criminal apprehension through CCTV monitoring would have to be substantial to justify continued use of such personnel. Police use of CCTV systems is generally limited to shopping districts and city-center areas. Police normally monitor large systems that include several cameras (each equipped with pan, tilt, and zoom capability) and a monitoring console, so that the viewer can watch activity in several places at once and adjust the equipment to concentrate on a particular place, incident, or individual.

Commercial and industrial facilities often hire private security personnel to monitor CCTV systems. Guards are used less frequently in residential complexes. The major advantage of using guards is that a single guard can control several entrances to a building or complex of buildings. Usually the guard can see all entrance doors, the lobby, and the elevator interiors on the monitor screens. The guard can be given audio contact with the lobby area. With the use of an intercom system, the guard can also control garage and front door entrances, and can also be given the ability to stop the elevator in midflight. Thus the security guard can see and hear every person entering the premises, prevent them from entering, and even exert some control after they enter.

It is also possible to staff a monitoring panel with members of tenant patrols. Use of volunteer personnel eliminates payment of guard salaries. Because they are personally acquainted with the project residents, tenant monitors can easily pick out strangers and perhaps distinguish a minor argument among friends from an impending fight.

But, there are serious drawbacks in using tenant monitors. It is difficult to guarantee the performance of unpaid people. The novelty of working with TV monitors will wear off quickly, and declining interest increases the likelihood of patrol members simply not showing up. Additionally, tenant patrol members are not equipped or empowered to take much action. The tenant monitoring the CCTV has no real authority over police or security personnel. Finally, there is the problem of tenant patrol members using their position to harass or intimidate other tenants.

An alternative is in-apartment tenant monitoring. Tenants of a building or housing project can monitor CCTV on their home TV screens. By connecting CCTV equipment to a master antenna within a building, tenants can have the option of tuning in to unused TV channels to monitor lobby, elevator, playground, or parking lot activity. Tenants may watch CCTV when they are expecting someone to arrive, or when a child is playing within viewing range of a camera in a playground area. Older people may watch for less specific reasons. Obviously, this does not ensure continuous monitoring, but if one or more of 200 tenants is watching, it would be risky for intruders to take chances.

An in-apartment tenant monitoring system requires that a cable TV or master antenna system be in operation in the building. CCTV is clearly most suited to large high-rise dwellings. Picture quality of the CCTV systems should be comparable to that of commercial broadcasting to promote tenant usage. While some picture disintegration may be acceptable in a conventionally monitored CCTV system, there should be no distortion in a system designed for in-apartment monitoring. It is desirable (and generally not expensive) to install a microphone system so that sound accompanies the TV picture, which makes the system more interesting and enjoyable.

It is possible to organize a voluntary in-apartment monitoring program to improve coverage. A tenant organization could arrange for persons to watch CCTV in their homes during specified hours. Such a scheduled system would promote better coverage and facilitate participation because there would be no requirement that residents leave their apartments.

Also, CCTV monitors should be placed where responsible individuals, such as management staff and patrolling guards, are at work or pass by continually.

Intercom Systems

Most urban multifamily dwellings are equipped with buzzer-reply systems to limit access to the building to tenants and to people who have been interviewed by tenants on an intercom system. A typical buzzer-reply intercom system in an apartment building functions as follows. A panel located outside the lobby entrance door lists the names and apartment numbers of all tenants in the building. Next to each tenant's name is a call button that, when pressed, rings a bell or buzzer within that tenant's apartment. The tenant responds to the call by walking to a panel mounted on the wall of his apartment and speaking via an intercom system to the person outside the door. When identification is satisfactorily established, the tenant pushes a button on the panel, which momentarily allows the entrance door to be opened without a key. Because the costs involved in installing wiring for such a system in an existing building are very high, buzzer-reply systems should be installed in all new buildings during the construction phase.

A modified version of the traditional buzzer-reply system has recently come into use. Local telephone companies install and service front-door intercom systems that use existing telephone wires instead of a separately wired system. The panel mounted outside the lobby door differs from a conventional panel in that it is supplied with a telephone receiver, and the list of residents has a three-digit number next to each name. A person wishing to enter the building dials the appropriate three-digit number, which makes the phone of the tenant buzz (not ring). The tenant then speaks with the person over the phone. If recognition is established, the tenant dials "4" to open the front door. If a tenant is speaking on the phone when the buzzer sounds, he or she can depress the receiver once, speak to the person in the lobby, buzz the visitor in by dialing "4," and then depress the receiver again to return to the initial telephone conversation. For tenants without telephones, a special unit that can be used only for the intercom can be installed. Fees for installation and service are billed by the phone company and added to the tenants' monthly rent.

Elevator Audio Systems

Use of audio systems in elevators is rapidly increasing. An elevator audio system is an uncomplicated sound transmission installation consisting of a microphone and speaker located in the elevator cab and connected to similar devices near the elevator doors on each floor. The system allows someone inside the elevator to speak to anyone standing in the elevator waiting area, and vice versa. In office buildings or high-income residential buildings, an additional connection is made so that a doorman, guard, or maintenance person can respond to persons inside the elevator. In low-income housing, the equipment in the cab is simply connected to the elevator on each floor.

Some systems are designed to remain on at all times, but most require the person in the cab to push a button before being able to talk to the outside location. A continuous voice relay system reassures the elevator rider that he or she can communicate with the outside if any trouble arises, whereas the need to push a button limits the usefulness of a noncontinuous audio system in crime situations. Any elevator audio device is useful when breakdowns occur and someone is trapped inside the cab.

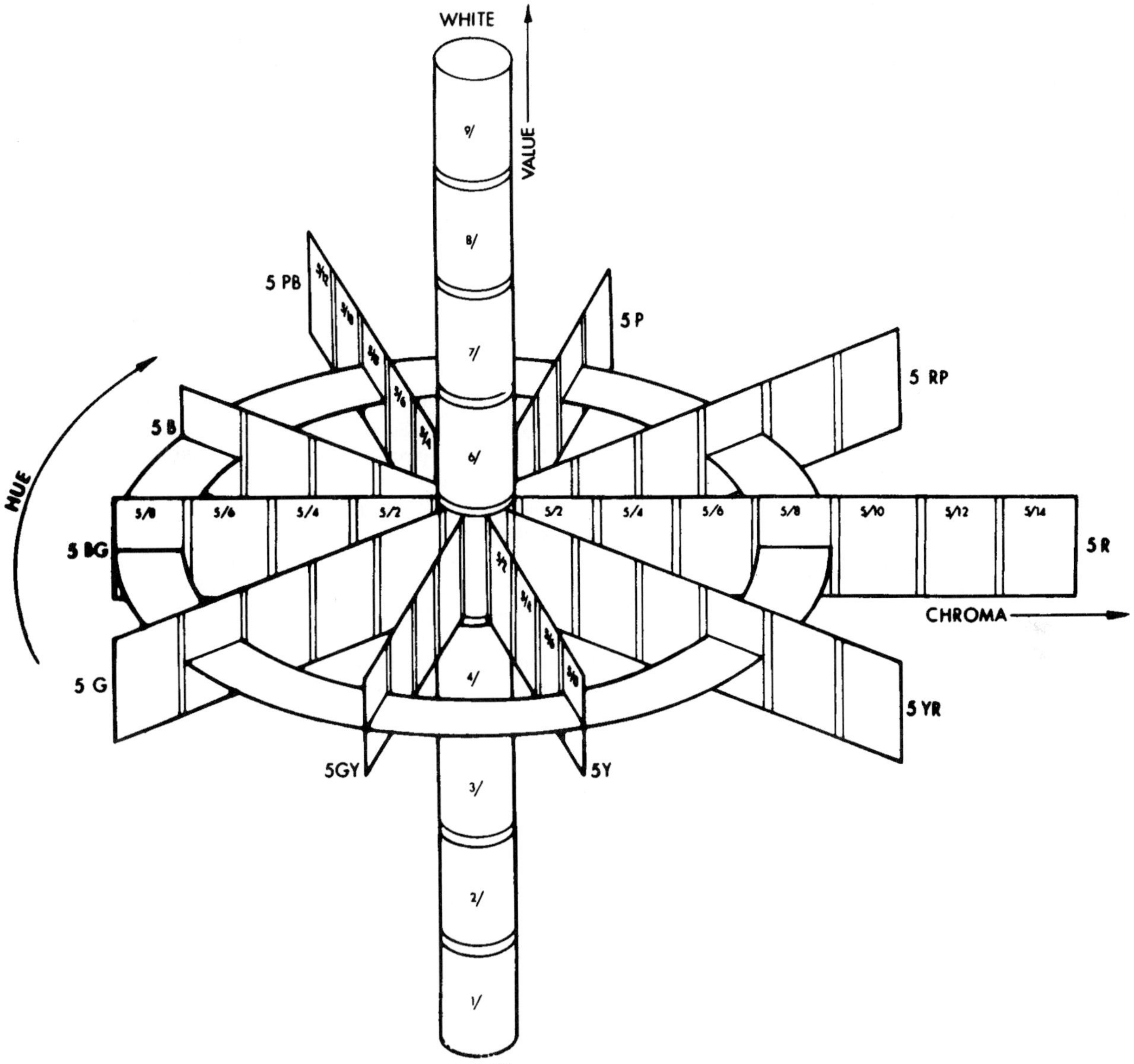

Fig. 1 The basic wheel with a three-dimensional projection of the attributes of color—hue, value, and intensity—as shown in their relation to one another. The circular band represents the hues: G, green; B, blue; P, purple; R, red; and Y, yellow. The upright center axis is the scale of value. Paths leading from the center indicate color intensity

COLOR THEORY

Primary colors The longest extended slices on the color wheel (Fig. 1) show the three primary colors: red, yellow, and blue. They're called *primary* because all the other colors come from combinations of these three colors.

Secondary colors Mix any two primary colors and you get the *secondary* colors: orange (red and yellow), violet (red and blue), and green (blue and yellow).

Tertiary colors All of the other six colors on the wheel are called *tertiary,* or intermediate, colors. They are a mixture of the primary colors plus an adjacent secondary color. Thus:

Yellow orange (yellow and orange)
Yellow green (yellow and green)
Blue green (blue and green)
Blue violet (blue and violet)
Red violet (red and violet)
Red orange (red and orange)

COLOR THEORY
Basic Color-Scheme Planning

Color has three dimensions: the *hue,* distinguishing one color from another—such as red, green, blue, and so on; the *value,* denoting lightness or darkness; and the *tone* or *intensity,* which is the brightness or dullness.

These hues, values, and intensities can appear to change when different ones are used together. Two or more light values combined afford little contrast, nor will darker values in combination provide much interest. But when a light value is used with a dark, the light appears lighter while the dark appears darker. White is the lightest of all colors, and values range from it through varying gradations of gray to black. Colors that are nearer white in value are called *tints* and colors that are closer to black in value are called *shades.*

Intensities or tones also have similar effects. A brightly upholstered chair will appear brighter and will stand out when used with a carpet of dull color, as it will produce a spot of interest. In contrast, a few dull-colored pieces of furniture will sink into the background if the room contains brighter-colored rugs, draperies, and other furnishings.

Contrasting or opposite hues will emphasize one another. Red with green will make the red look redder and the green appear more orange, while the red-purple will take on a bluish tone.

There are many ways of combining colors for interest. Related color schemes such as reds, purples, and blues together can produce very pleasing effects. Contrasting hues, such as blues with oranges, can also be combined to give more vibrant results.

Some people enjoy excitement. Warm colors such as yellow, orange, and red are exciting because they are associated with things like sunshine, fire, heat, and even blood. Warm colors tend to advance, and a predominantly warm-colored wall will seem to come forward. They are especially effective in rooms that are on the east or north side of a house, because light entering from those directions seems to be cool light. The warm colors and cool light complement each other and make the room seem cozier and warmer.

Cool colors are those associated with water, verdure, and the sky—blues, greens, and violets. These tend to recede, and under most conditions, light, cool-colored walls will create an illusion of greater space. They are good choices for rooms on the south and west sides of the house, since these areas receive a lot of sunlight all year around. Theirs is a cooling effect in the warm-light areas, another complementary association.

Black, white, gray, and brown—and the tones of the latter two, known as griege and beige—are not considered to be colors so much as *neutrals.* In practice, they are the "no-color" colors, which are used with other colors to modify them or to contrast with them. But they are far from being negative. As you work with color, you will find that all colors are influenced by the company they keep. This is particularly true of the tints, shades, and so-called neutral colors. A juxtaposition of two muted colors, such as a gray and a tan, will bring out latent greens, lavenders, and pinks you did not see before. Colors also have visual weights. Dark and bright appear heavy, while light or dull seem to weigh less. Remember that a dominant color is the one that controls a room, while the others are accents.

BASIC COLOR-SCHEME PLANNING

Successful decorating often depends on how well the total effect is anticipated. Here are four types of schemes that professional decorators have in mind when they start to plan a job. They are no guarantee of perfect results, but they do make an unwieldy subject easier to handle.

Monochromatic This scheme is built around one color, using it somewhere in its full intensity, and then varying it with a number of shades and tints of the same color. For example, in a monochromatic scheme of yellow, the range could be from dark shades of gold, through clear yellow, to light, pale-yellow tints. A monochromatic color scheme can be restful, can create a feeling of spaciousness, and provides a good background for art objects, collections, or similar decorations. But, generally, when employing a monochromatic color scheme, the interest of the room comes through by using a variety of textures and patterns.

Analogous or related Because it's the easiest color scheme to work with, an analogous scheme is the one that enjoys the greatest popularity at the present time. It is based on two or three colors, such as yellow, yellow orange, and red orange, that lie close to each other on the color wheel, with relief provided by tints and shades of the same that have been tinged with adjacent greens or vermilion. The analogous color scheme is restful and refreshing also, and the colors are more interesting because of their variations in intensity and value. It is the kind of color scheme that is easily changed; a slight shift of emphasis here and there is all that is necessary to completely change the character of the room.

Complementary or contrasting This scheme, which is rapidly coming into favor, uses colors that are opposite each other on the color wheel—blue and orange, red and green, yellow and violet. One color is usually a primary color and the other a secondary color. Using such contrasting colors will give a lively and vibrant room, but it is a color scheme that must be used with caution. One color should always dominate, with the others being primarily dramatic accents. The shock impact of a complementary color scheme can be softened by selecting unexpected shades and tints of the two colors. That is, a vivid color and its complement can be quieted, if you prefer, by graying them, or reducing their values. Employing a pair of opposites in this manner means that there will be both cool and warm colors in a room, which makes a complementary association. A complementary color scheme tends to make a room seem smaller.

Accented This is a combination of adjacent, related, or analogous colors—call them what you will—accented by a bold touch of color from the opposite side of the wheel. An example would be a scheme ranging through a number of strong, soft, and grayed yellows, spiked with purple or violet.

There are also other color schemes, such as *triad* and *split-complementary,* that you can adapt from the color wheel, but the four suggested here are the easiest to visualize and to carry out.

In whatever basic scheme you use, do not forget the neutrals: black, white, the grays, and browns—to which you might add metallic gold and silver. Since they will appear, of themselves, in the wood and metal of your furnishings, they must at all times be considered for the part they play in the total effect. If you wish, the neutrals can constitute a fifth, and very sophisticated, color scheme of their own. But usually they must be more or less just accepted and played up or played down by the colors you combine them with. Incidentally, some black and white is an asset to almost any color scheme, but too many and indefinite neutrals, used with stronger colors, tend to compromise a color scheme and make it look confused or merely drab. It is best to think of any neutral as a distinctive note of color, whether it is the fieldstone of a fireplace or a hardwood floor.

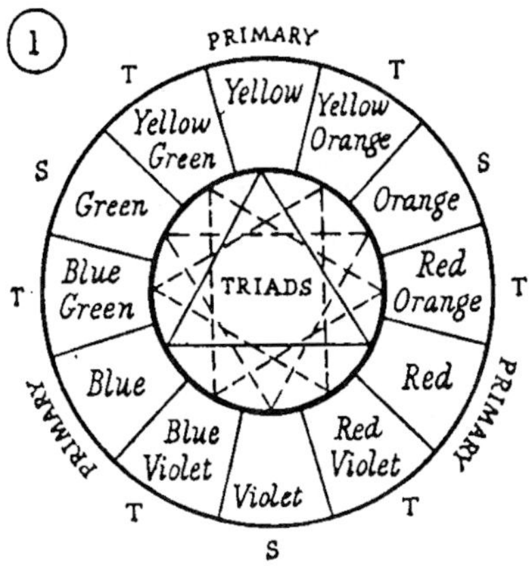

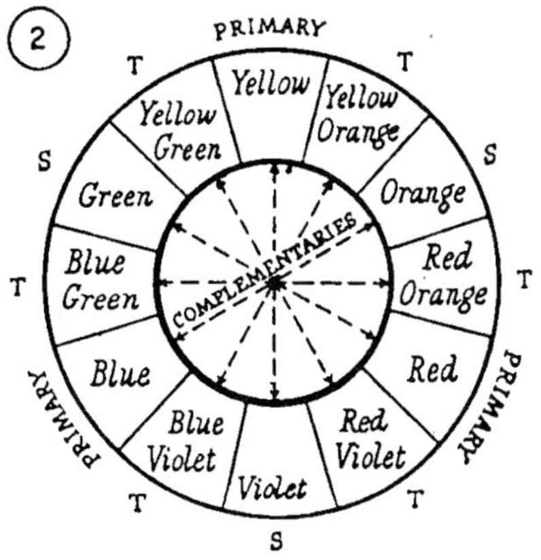

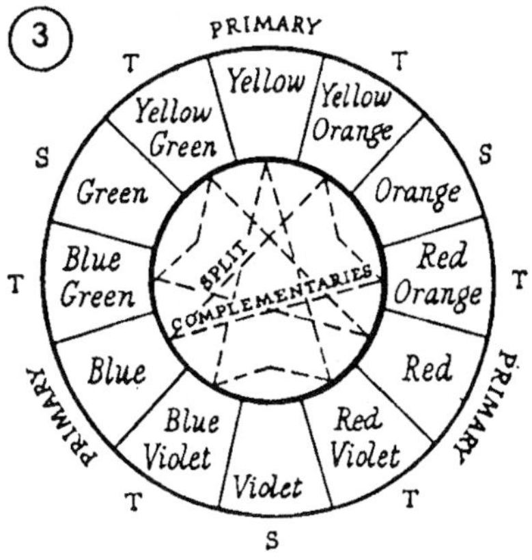

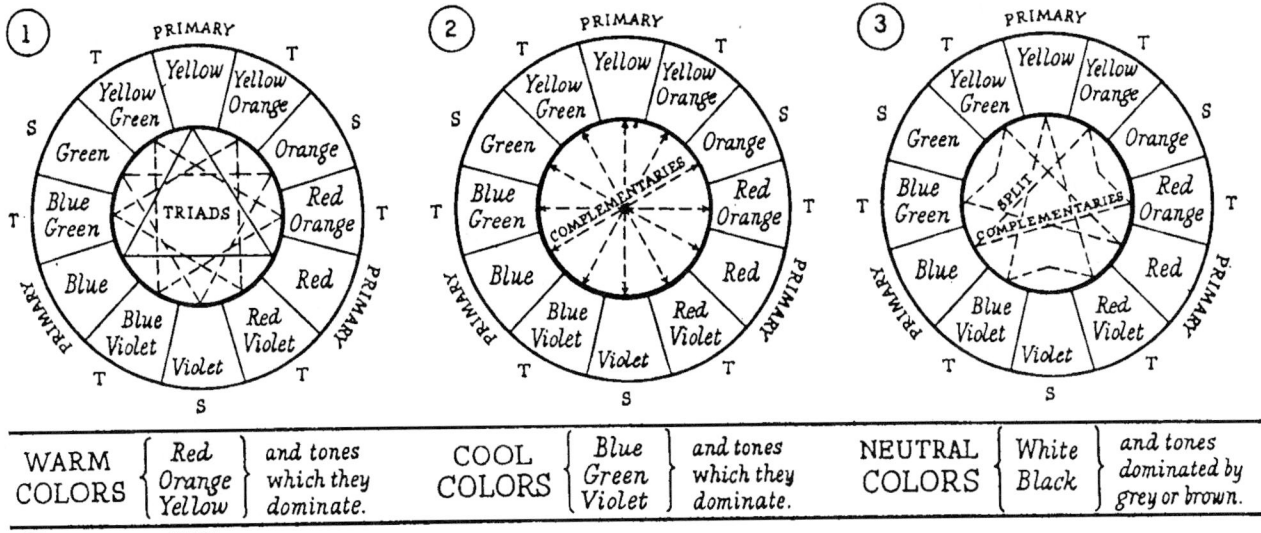

WARM COLORS	Red Orange Yellow	and tones which they dominate.	COOL COLORS	Blue Green Violet	and tones which they dominate.	NEUTRAL COLORS	White Black	and tones dominated by grey or brown.

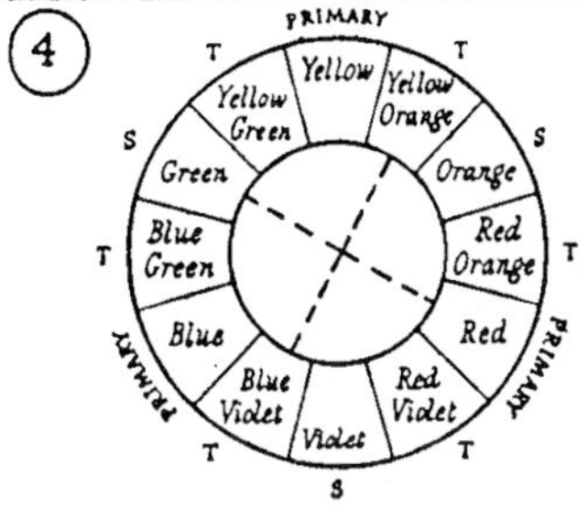

EXAMPLES OF ANALOGOUS (RELATED) COLOR SCHEMES

DIRECTIONS FOR USING COLOR COMBINATION CHARTS

COLOR WHEEL NUMBER 1 illustrates color combinations in which the three primaries are used together, or the three secondary colors, or three tertiary colors. The three points of each triangle link the colors used in this TRIAD COLOR SCHEME. The rule for success is to use only one of them in a strong, bright tone, in small areas, with the other two in softened (or grayed) tones.

COLOR WHEEL NUMBER 2 illustrates the color pairs which are effective together through contrast. This is called the COMPLEMENTARY COLOR SCHEME. As the arrows indicate, the pairs are exactly opposite each other on the wheel. One should be used in a bright tone for smaller areas, the other in grayed tones and larger areas.

COLOR WHEEL NUMBER 3 illustrates the use of a color with the two which are next to its opposite on the wheel, one on each side. This SPLIT COMPLEMENTARY COLOR SCHEME follows the rule for complementaries, and may include the direct contrast color also, if desired. For example, yellow may be used with blue-violet, and red-violet, with or without the true violet shade which comes between them.

To avoid confusion, not all of the triangles are indicated. Cut a piece of paper the size of the triangle and lay it with the top point at any color you choose. The other points will rest on the correct colors.

COLOR WHEEL NUMBER 4 illustrates how an ANALOGOUS COLOR SCHEME is developed by using colors which are related because they are side by side on the wheel. Any group can be used, all around the wheel, as indicated by the dotted lines. For an accent color you can use a contrast color opposite any one of your group. For instance, in the yellow-orange to red group, complementary blue could be used for accent (shown on color wheel 2).

Black, white, gray and other definitely neutral tones can be used with any combination of colors.

BASIC PRINCIPLES FOR WORKING OUT A COLOR SCHEME

1. DOMINANT OR CONTROLLING COLOR

Decide on your dominant or controlling color, which may dominate by covering a large area or by strength of color in a smaller area. Decide whether your foundation or background color is to be the dominant or a secondary color. Plan to use a large amount of quiet background color, a small amount of bold, strong color. All large foundation areas should be in light or grayed tones.

2. GRAYING

Clear colors are gayer, more cheerful, but grayed tones are more restful, their harmonies more subtle. Mixing gray with bright colors brings them into relation with other colors in the room. As . . . red and yellow in bright tones seem to clash. Mixed with gray, they become rose and tan and go very well together. Use this principle also in buying materials. Avoid too much graying. It gives muddy tones, dirty grays, flat greens. A little gray goes far.

3. RELIEF AND CONTRAST COLORS

Decide on relief and contrast colors and bring them into all parts of the room composition. Remember the order in the amount of space allowed each one—foundation, then relief, then contrast. All colors—including background colors—should be keyed to the dominant color. Soften strong contrast colors with white. Contrast is less in lighter tints. Soften darker contrasts with gray.

4. ACCENT COLORS

Use pure bright intense colors only in accessories, etc. Distribute them so they will not be spotty. The smaller the area the brighter the color may be. The larger the area the softer the tone should be. Don't use large amounts of pure bright color.

5. KEYING

This is another means of creating harmony. A key color is the one about which the color scheme is built—the dominant, or controlling color. All other colors in the room must be "keyed" with it—harmonized. Two colors in which any part of a third color is present will be linked together. Example: To key red and yellow to each other, mix them both with a little of the third primary hue—blue. Violet and green will result, and these are harmonious to use with your strong tones. Remember this principle in buying as well as mixing colors. A lovely print or art object will have these tones keyed for you, and you can use them for your own composition. The safe rule is to avoid too many colors and too strong tones except in accents, etc. Most colors will "go together" if you soften them.

COLOR THEORY
Terminology and Combinations

WHAT DECORATORS MEAN WHEN THEY USE THESE COLOR TERMS

HUE: Each section in the color wheel is called a hue. To change a hue, another color (not black, white or pure gray) must be added to it. Every hue has a different wave length from every other hue. Mixed with its complement equally it produces gray.

PRIMARY COLORS: Also called "normal," also "fundamental." Primaries are the three pigment colors which cannot be produced by any mixture of other pigments. These are red like that of a geranium flower, yellow like that of ripe lemons, blue like the deep clear hue of a sunny southern sky.

SECONDARY COLORS: Secondaries are the three colors which are produced by mixing two of the three primaries in equal amounts. Red + yellow = orange; red + blue = purple (or violet); yellow + blue = green.

TERTIARY COLORS: Tertiaries are the colors produced by mixing a primary with a secondary, the exact shade depending upon the proportion. Red + orange produces shades such as russet, burnt orange, coral, etc. Red + purple—mulberry, amethyst, orchid, etc. Blue + purple—heliotrope, periwinkle, lavender, etc. Blue + green—turquoise, aquamarine, bottle green, etc. Yellow + orange—maize, primrose, flame, etc. Yellow + green—jade, Nile, olive, chartreuse, etc. Mixtures of complementaries not included because these produce shades of gray—a neutral. Some authorities consider, also, the shades produced by mixing two secondaries as tertiaries, such as slate, citron, buff, sage, etc.

COMPLEX COLORS: All colors which are made up of more complicated mixtures than those producing secondary and tertiary colors are called complex.

NEUTRAL COLORS: Black and white are considered neutral. Also all those tints and shades in which tones of gray or brown predominate.

TINTS: The light tones resulting when white is mixed with a color. Much white makes a color cold.

SHADES: The dark tones resulting when black is mixed with a color. Much black deadens the color.

TONE: Each hue has many tones. By tone—or tonal value—we mean the relative strength of the hue as it approaches black or white at the opposite ends of the value scale. Mixed with white, a color is "pale" in tone; mixed with black, it is "dark" in tone. The upper and lower extremes of any color would be white (or very pale gray), and black.

CHROMA: This term is used interchangeably with value, tonal value, and intensity. The chroma of a color such as yellow is "light"; the chroma of a color such as Navy blue is "dark." When a color fades, it loses chroma.

LUMINOSITY: This term is used to describe a quality of warm clear colors in light-reflecting tones and finishes, such as light golden-yellow. Clear white is also luminous. Literally "luminous" are only metals in gold, silver, platinum, or clear plastics.

COLOR	SUGGESTED COLOR GROUPS TO USE WITH IT
RED	Green, gray, blue (for accent)
SCARLET	Light blue, ecru (or Navy and taupe)
CRIMSON	Pearl gray, mauve
GARNET	Sapphire blue, mauve, pearl gray
CARDINAL	Marine blue, turquoise, gray
WINE	Black, old blue, beige
ROSE	Flesh, light blue, green
OLD ROSE	Blue in various shades
CEDAR ROSE	Blue, cream
PINK	Green, orchid, blue for accent
ORANGE	Violet, light blue, indigo for accent
BURNT ORANGE	Electric blue, light brown
SALMON	Turquoise, lavender
HENNA	Peacock green, royal blue, gray
PEACH	Rust, blue, tan
MAIZE	Powder blue, pink
YELLOW	Violet, blue, green
PRIMROSE	Lavender, dusty rose, soft green
SOFT YELLOW	Brown, French blue
GOLD	Soft gray-green, deep red
DARK GREEN	Brown, beige (or sage green and gold)
MYRTLE	Heliotrope, yellow
SOFT GREEN	Rosewood, deep violet
TARRAGON	Heliotrope, pearl gray
CHINESE JADE	Rose, ivory
NILE	Cornflower, orange
LIGHT GREEN	Rose, dark green, mauve
BLUE	Yellow, sand, orange for accent
COPENHAGEN BLUE	Burgundy, gray
FLEMISH BLUE	Olive-green, cardinal
LIGHT BLUE	Orchid, champagne
DEEP PURPLE	Orange, gray
VIOLET	Green, light and dark shades
LAVENDER	Green, mauve, gray
HELIOTROPE	Light blue, cream
HYDRANGEA	Old rose, primrose yellow
MAUVE	Emerald green, dark red, brown
BROWN	Orange, tan, cardinal for accent
GRAY	Violet, crimson, lavender.

COLOR AREAS AND SAMPLES

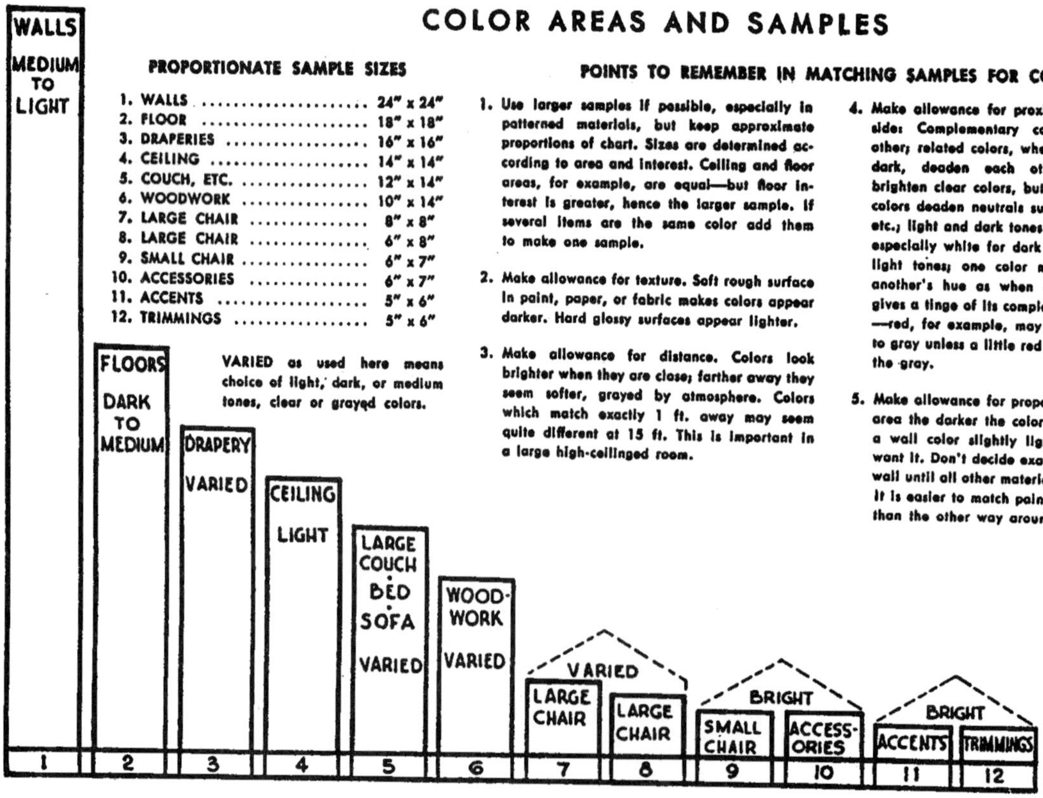

PROPORTIONATE SAMPLE SIZES

1.	WALLS	24" x 24"
2.	FLOOR	18" x 18"
3.	DRAPERIES	16" x 16"
4.	CEILING	14" x 14"
5.	COUCH, ETC.	12" x 14"
6.	WOODWORK	10" x 14"
7.	LARGE CHAIR	8" x 8"
8.	LARGE CHAIR	6" x 8"
9.	SMALL CHAIR	6" x 7"
10.	ACCESSORIES	6" x 7"
11.	ACCENTS	5" x 6"
12.	TRIMMINGS	5" x 6"

VARIED as used here means choice of light, dark, or medium tones, clear or grayed colors.

POINTS TO REMEMBER IN MATCHING SAMPLES FOR COLOR

1. Use larger samples if possible, especially in patterned materials, but keep approximate proportions of chart. Sizes are determined according to area and interest. Ceiling and floor areas, for example, are equal—but floor interest is greater, hence the larger sample. If several items are the same color add them to make one sample.

2. Make allowance for texture. Soft rough surface in paint, paper, or fabric makes colors appear darker. Hard glossy surfaces appear lighter.

3. Make allowance for distance. Colors look brighter when they are close; farther away they seem softer, grayed by atmosphere. Colors which match exactly 1 ft. away may seem quite different at 15 ft. This is important in a large high-ceilinged room.

4. Make allowance for proximity. When side by side: Complementary colors brighten each other; related colors, when both light or both dark, deaden each other; neutral colors brighten clear colors, but pure strong primary colors deaden neutrals such as grays, browns, etc.; light and dark tones brighten each other, especially white for dark colors and black for light tones; one color may seem to change another's hue as when a strong clear color gives a tinge of its complementary to a neutral—red, for example, may give a greenish cast to gray unless a little red has been mixed with the gray.

5. Make allowance for proportion. The larger the area the darker the color will appear. Choose a wall color slightly lighter than you really want it. Don't decide exact shade of a painted wall until all other materials have been chosen. It is easier to match paint to fabric and paper than the other way around.

COLOR COMBINATION CHARTS

S = SECONDARY . . . . . T = TERTIARY

MUNSELL SYSTEM OF COLOR

One of the best-known and widely respected systems of color standardization used in the United States today is that developed by Albert H. Munsell. He became greatly interested in the practical application of color and was disturbed by the fact that the popular names for colors did not describe them adequately for professional purposes. They are named after flowers or plants, such as violet, indigo, old rose, primrose; after fruits, such as peach, pomegranate, grape, avocado, plum; after places, such as french blue, naples yellow, or prussian blue; or after persons, such as Davy's gray or Hooker's green.

Essentially the system consists of an orderly arrangement of colors in the shape of a three-dimensional color solid. The system is based on a color circle of 10 major hues made up of 5 principal hues (red, yellow, green, blue, and purple) and 5 intermediate hues (yellow-red, green-yellow, blue-green, purple-blue, and red-purple). Each hue is indicated by a symbol as follows:

Red: R
Yellow: Y
Green: G
Blue: B
Purple: P
Yellow-red: YR
Green-yellow: GY
Blue-green: BG
Purple-blue: PB
Red-purple: RP

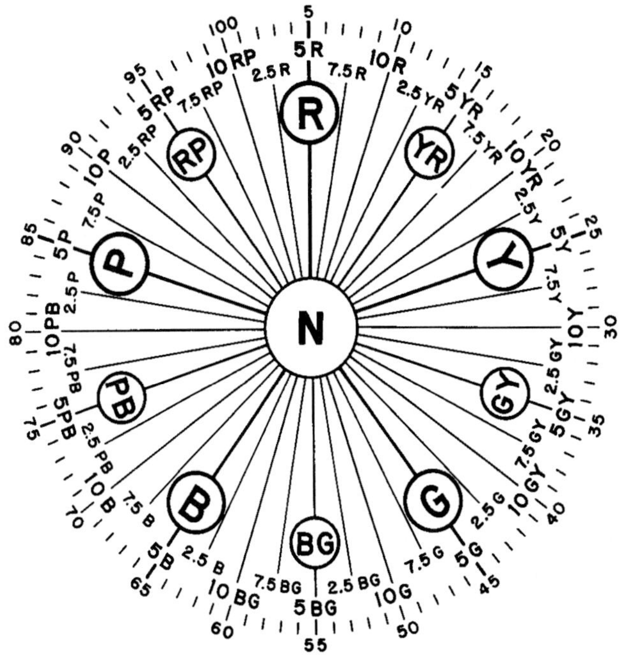

Fig. 2 Munsell hue symbols and their relation to one another

Each of the major hues has been given a value of 5 in the inner scale around the hue circle (see Fig. 2, hue symbols): 5 R, 5 YR, 5 Y, 5 GY, 5 G, 5 BG, 5 B, 5 PB, 5 P, and 5 RP. Between each of the major hues are values of 2.5, 10, and 7.5 for rough indication of hue. The outer scale of the hue circuit is divided into 100 segments to provide greater accuracy for indicating hue where needed.

In the Munsell color tree each hue (H) is allotted 10 segments of the hue circle, making 100 hues, and these hues form the horizontal center, or equator, of the color solid. The center segment of each color is considered the true color, and the remaining segments in each hue section vary according to their proximity to adjoining colors; for example, as red gets closer to yellow it contains more yellow, and this is indicated by the numerical designation.

The value (V) notation denotes the lightness or darkness of a hue, which is determined by a neutral core at the center of the hue circle. The core contains 10 gradations from a supposedly perfect white (one having 100 percent reflectance) at the top to 0, a perfect black (having 0 percent reflectance) at the bottom.

The chroma (C) notation indicates the saturation of the hue, or the strength of the color. The chroma scale extends outward from the central core or axis, and the increments vary from 0 at a neutral gray to as high as 16, according to the amount of saturation produced by a given hue at a given value level. Since colors vary in chroma, or saturation, some colors extend farther from the neutral axis than others, and the solid is therefore not symmetrical, Pure red, with a chroma of 14, for instance, extends farther than blue-green, with a chroma of only 6 (see Fig. 1).

A Munsell notation indicating hue, value, and chroma (H V/C) might be given as follows:

Vermilion: 5R 5/14
Rose: 5R 5/4

With this information it is possible to describe exactly any given hue and to locate its place in the color solid. Furthermore, as Munsell stated, one can "select one familiar color, and study what others will combine with it to please the eye," by the use of three typical paths: one vertical, with rapid change of value; another lateral, with rapid change of hue; and a third, inward, through the neutral center, to seek out the opposite color field. All other paths are combined by two or three of these typical directions in the color solid.

COLOR THEORY

Color Families: Red

THE RED FAMILY

REPRESENTATIVE MEMBERS OF THE RED FAMILY . . . FLESH . . . DUSTY-PINK . . . SHELL-PINK . . . ROSE . . . DUSTY ROSE . . . OLD ROSE . . . CARDINAL OR CRIMSON . . . RASPBERRY . . . RED-BURGUNDY OR WINE RED . . . MAROON . . . ETC.

CHARACTERISTICS . . . Warm, advancing . . . Cheerful, hospitable, active . . . In strong tones, stimulating, bold, vital, dramatic, exciting.

WHAT THEY CAN DO . . . Make objects seem closer, larger . . . Make room seem smaller by bringing background closer . . . Focus attention on wall or object . . . Bring life, brightness, warmth, to drab, dark or too-cool rooms.

CORRECT USES . . . In light tints, charming backgtound for fairly light, large rooms . . . In bright tones, highly decorative when used for comparatively small areas, as in accessories, accents, etc. . . . In darker shades, rich and warm for draperies, carpets, upholstery, especially in large rooms with heavy furniture.

CAUTION . . . Do not use too much red—especially in clear, bright tones, and in light rooms . . . Safer to soften a little by "graying," except when used for accent . . . Do not use the Red Family for background of a room that is small or crowded . . . Do not use bright red for large objects, unless you want to call attention to them . . . Do not forget when using the Red Family to include cool colors in your color schemes . . . It takes two cool colors, or a large area of one cool color, to balance red.

SUGGESTED COLOR SCHEMES IN WHICH MEMBERS OF RED FAMILY PLAY A DOMINANT ROLE

DOMINANT COLOR	MAJOR WALL COLOR	MAJOR FLOOR COLOR	DRAPERIES AND UPHOLSTERY	ACCENT COLORS	REMARKS
SHELL-PINK	Shell-pink	Light Blue	Off-white background, powder-blue and shell-pink in pattern	Italian Red	Charming for bedroom. In slightly darker tones of same colors, could be adapted to living rooms. Feminine feeling
MELON PINK (like Pompeiian terra cotta)	Melon Pink	Brown	Light tan background, melon-pink with green olive in design	Green Olive	Good for living or dining room with mahogany or walnut furniture
VENETIAN PINK	Venetian Pink	Patterned rug, soft tones, green, mauve, red	Draperies, yellow and white stripes Upholstery, green and dull pink stripes	Red	Good for living room with 18th Century furniture
DUSTY PINK	Dusty Pink Woodwork, cocoa brown	Deep Brown	Draperies, pale aquamarine (dusty pink curtains) Chair and bed covers, cocoa and pink stripes with cocoa brown trimming	White	Interesting for modern bedroom with furniture in cocoa tones
BOIS DE ROSE	Bois de Rose	Sage Green	Draperies, pearl gray, trimmed with bois de rose Upholstery, pale gray with sulphur yellow	Green and Sulphur yellow	Living room color scheme with feminine feeling
DAWN ROSE	Dawn Rose	Dark Green	Neutral background, dawn rose and leaf-green in pattern	Wet Leaf-green	Attractive for bedroom
LIGHT ROSE	Light Rose	Deep Blue-green	Draperies, dusty rose background, blue-green and foliage tones in design Upholstery, blue, blue-green and green, plain, pattern and stripes	Blue	Suitable for fairly large room with average light
ROSE (1)	Warm Gray	Rose Taupe	Draperies, rose Upholstery, rose and cream stripes	Blue or Green	Appropriate for almost any living or bedroom
ROSE (2)	Oyster White	Rose Red	Draperies, oyster white Upholstery, oyster white with reds, blues and soft green	Red	Charming for bedroom or woman's living room
ASHES OF ROSES	Ashes of Roses	Cafe au lait	White	Strong Blue	Adaptable to bedroom or living room
DUSTY ROSE (1)	Deep dusty Rose	Brown	Lighter dusty rose, white and brown	Silver	Good color scheme for living room or dining room
DUSTY ROSE (2)	Pickled wood	Pinkish Beige	Draperies, dusty rose Upholstery, foam green and natural	Pale Green	Adaptable to living room, traditional or modern
OLD ROSE (1)	Old Rose	Warm Gray	Blue dnd pale yellow, with touch of old rose	Jade Green	This color scheme is charming and delicate, suitable for bedrooms and dressing rooms
OLD ROSE (2)	Paper, Old Rose, cream and gray	Mulberry	Old rose and gray	Blue and Silver	With woodwork painted warm gray, this scheme would be attractive for bedroom or dressing room
OLD ROSE (3)	Paper, Blue and rose pattern	Ivory	Draperies, ivory background, rose, blue and green in pattern Upholstery, old rose, and drapery fabric	Green	Attractive for formal living room
RED (1)	Soft grayed Green	Patterned rug with red background	Draperies, pale gray background, red in pattern Upholstery, plain green, red and green stripes	Blue and Orange	Suitable living room or dining room

RED (2)	Paper, granite flecked with red	Patterned rug, red predominating	Chintz, red predominating in pattern	Green and Pewter	Good for Early American room, with pine or maple
RED (3)	Paper, red toile design; woodwork, white	Hooked rugs Floors, painted blue	Draperies, textured beige Upholstery, textured beige trimmed with red	Blue (chairs painted blue)	Colonial type living room or library
RED (4)	Old white Woodwork, dark green	Red rug	Red and white brocade	Green	Living room in period feeling with walnut furniture
RED (5)	Paper, light background, red with green and brown in pattern	Dark blue	Red	Blue	Early American dining room, with pine and maple
SOFT RED (1)	Neutral	Soft Red	Draperies, blue-green background, deep red in design Upholstery, blue-green	Yellow	Nice for living room
SOFT RED (2)	White	Rug, blue, red and white pattern	Draperies, linen color with red in pattern Upholstery, chair seats, blue	Silver	18th Century dining room
CRIMSON (1)	Bone white	Crimson	White background, floral design in red and soft green	White	Mahogany furniture of very nice design would be lovely with white walls
CRIMSON (2)	Soft Gray	Crimson	Draperies, white, gray and crimson Upholstery, white, trimmed with crimson	Black	A smart sophisticated color scheme
CRIMSON (3)	Slate Gray	Soft Crimson	Draperies, bluish white, trimmed with soft crimson Upholstery, bluish white	Gold	Adaptable to modern styles
CHINESE RED	Grayed soft Green	Chinese Red	Draperies, grayed soft green Upholstery, deep beige	Light Beige	Good for living room or dining room
LACQUER RED (1)	Gray	Brown	Gray and lacquer red	Green	Colorful living room with some red lacquer furniture
LACQUER RED (2)	Paneling, Red Lacquer, silver trim	Black	Silver gray, with red and black in design	Silver	Modern library
ITALIAN RED	Yellow	Floor, stained dark Patterned rug in old reds and dark blues, red predominating	Draperies, Italian red damask. Upholstery, red damask, yellow, glazed chintz with white ground and red in design	Gold	Living room English in feeling; also good for Federal American
CRANBERRY RED	Paper with light ground and cranberry pattern Paneled fireplace and painted blue	Deep soft red	Draperies, rose Upholstery, blue, and chintz-like wallpaper pattern	Green	Cheerful living room color scheme
WINE RED (1)	Green	Wine Red	Draperies, wine red Upholstery, grayed green and off white	Crystal	Attractive for living room with cool North or East light
WINE RED (2)	Soft grayed Blue	Deep Gray	Draperies, wine red Upholstery, wine red, grayed white and blue	Silver	For fairly formal living room, average size
WINE RED (3)	Paper in yellow, pale gray and white	Dark Wine Red	Draperies, Ruby taffeta Upholstery, glazed maroon chintz with yellow flowers Chair seats, bright yellow leather	Gold	Specially appropriate for Victorian dining room
AMERICAN BEAUTY	Linen color	Fawn	Draperies, fawn and American beauty Upholstery, American beauty, fawn, blue and gray	Blue	Dramatic color scheme for fairly large living room
RED DAHLIA	Gray	Red Dahlia	Draperies, light neutral background with dahlia and melon green in pattern Upholstery, melon green	Larkspur Blue	Adaptable to various types of living rooms
OLD RED	Soft light shade Old Red	Deep Old Red	Draperies, old red, beige and white stripes Upholstery, light tan	Copper	Warm, colorful plan for a room inclined to be cold
BURGUNDY (1)	Pale clear yellow	Burgundy	Draperies, white, valance and trimming Upholstery, burgundy and white	Gold	Rich color scheme for formal room
BURGUNDY (2)	Burgundy	Darker Burgundy	Burgundy and natural	Chartreuse	For large room, living room or library
BURGUNDY (3)	Warm Gray with pinkish cast	Burgundy	Draperies, primrose yellow Upholstery, pale grayed blue and white	White	Good for any room not too small or too sunny
BURGUNDY (4)	Beige with pinkish cast	Burgundy	Draperies, beige background, shell pink and burgundy in pattern Upholstery, shell pink	Grayed White	Same as above

COLOR THEORY
Color Families: Orange

THE ORANGE FAMILY

REPRESENTATIVE MEMBERS OF THE ORANGE FAMILY . . . IVORY . . . PEACH . . . CORAL . . . BEIGE . . . RUST . . . TERRA COTTA . . . WARM BROWN.

CHARACTERISTICS . . . Always warm, advancing . . . Cheerful, welcoming, gay, vibrant, glowing . . . In strong tones, akin to red . . . In softer tones, a good mixer.

WHAT THEY CAN DO . . . In slightly less degree, Orange repeats the activities of the Red Family . . . Effective for "toning" up a room in too dull or quiet colors, or warming a cold room.

CORRECT USES . . . Best in off shades, except for accent . . . In softened tones, excellent background color for dark or cold rooms . . . Wonderful accent color in proper combinations.

CAUTION . . . Do not use too much of the clear color . . . In large areas it has the disturbing quality of red . . . Do not use for background of small room unless you want it to be very "cozy."

SUGGESTED COLOR SCHEMES IN WHICH MEMBERS OF ORANGE FAMILY PLAY A DOMINANT ROLE

DOMINANT COLOR	MAJOR WALL COLOR	MAJOR FLOOR COLOR	DRAPERIES AND UPHOLSTERY	ACCENT COLORS	REMARKS
IVORY	Ivory Woodwork, Ivory	Floor, painted ivory Rug, Jade Green	Ivory background, rose and blue green in pattern	Rose and Jade Green	Charming for bedroom or lady's sitting room with ivory painted furniture
PEACH (1)	Peach	Peach	Apple green	Bittergreen	Attractive for bedroom, modern or traditional
PEACH (2)	Peach	Old Green	Draperies and upholstery, peach, with old blue	Old Blue	For a room that needs warming up, with cool touches
PEACH (3)	Peach	Warm Brown	Draperies, brown and coral stripes Upholstery, brown background, with coral, beige and tan	Copper	Modern color scheme appropriate for living room or library
PEACH (4)	Paper, shades of yellow, through peach to brown	Brown	Draperies, brown Upholstery, light and dark peach	Yellow	Good modern living room color scheme
PEACH (5)	Floral pattern paper, white ground, peach and green	Rust	Draperies, peach Upholstery (chair seats), green	Green	Very good for late Colonial dining room with Duncan Phyfe style furniture
PEACH (6)	Yellowish Pink	Eggplant	Draperies, peach background, blue in design Upholstery, peach and blue	Coral and yellow	Good color scheme to lighten dark bedroom
APRICOT	Apricot	Rose and Cream	Draperies, old rose Bed and furniture covering, apricot, trimmed with black	Orchid	Charming for young girl's room
CORAL (1)	Paper, silver ground, coral-rose design; Woodwork, coral	Aquamarine	Aquamarine	Aquamarine and Silver	Charming for woman's bedroom
CORAL (2)	Coral Woodwork, soft Blue	Gray Blue	Draperies, off-white background rose and green in design, Coral valance; Bed and furniture covering, copper rose and same chintz used for hangings	Off-white	Attractive for bedroom with furniture painted blue
WARM BEIGE (1)	Warm Beige	Warm Beige	Brown and Copper	Bright Green	Modern living room or library
WARM BEIGE (2)	Pink and Beige wallpaper	Warm Beige	Draperies, old white and beige Upholstery, dusty pink and pale olive green	Terra Cotta	Restful living room color scheme
WARM BEIGE (3)	Warm Beige	Warm Beige	Draperies, burgundy background, white and beige in design; Upholstery, burgundy and natural	White	Good for living room, library, or man's bedroom
WARM BEIGE (4)	Warm Beige	Dark Taupe	Draperies, russet (beige glass curtains) Upholstery, brown with tan cushions	Tan	Restful, chromatic color scheme
WARM BEIGE (5)	Beige with pink cast	Light warm beige	Brown, beige and white stripes or checks	Sky Blue	Appropriate for informal living room or boy's room
HENNA (1)	Grass cloth, tan and gold	Henna and black	Henna, green and gray	Gold	Living room or man's bedroom
HENNA (2)	Mint Green Woodwork, Cream	Henna	Draperies, henna with valance of bedspread material Bedspread, henna, light and dark green and tan stripes Upholstery, same combination in patterned material	White	Man's bedroom
TERRA COTTA	Pink Terra Cotta	Eggplant	Draperies, pinkish yellow, trimmed with terra cotta Upholstery, bois de rose	Pale Green	Charming for dining room in Directoire feeling with furniture painted yellow and gold
COPPER (1)	Pine paneled	Floor, Pine Rugs (hooked) in tones of orange, yellow, green	Draperies, copper toned background with orange, yellow and green in pattern	Blue and copper	Appropriate for living room in Early American feeling with Early American style furniture
COPPER (2)	Rough plaster with oak paneling	Oak plank floor Patterned rug, tones of brown, green, copper	Draperies, copper colored, coarsely woven material Upholstery, neutral green, trimmed with brown and copper	Green	Good color scheme for large, formal, English-style living room, with furniture in natural oak and walnut
BURNT ORANGE	Neutral Woodwork, walnut	Rug, greenish background, with burnt orange and henna	Burnt orange and henna	Blue	Good for dining room with walnut furniture
WARM BROWN (1)	Tobacco Brown	Warm Beige	Chintz in clear yellow, beige and warm brown in design	White	Modern living room or library
WARM BROWN (2)	Tan	Warm Brown	Draperies, copper and topaz; Upholstery, warm browns	Orange, French Blue	Appropriate for boy's room
WARM BROWN (3)	Yellow Brown	Orange Brown	Burnt orange and apple green	Greenish Blue	Restful, cheerful color scheme for library
WARM BROWN (4)	Pale Yellow	Orange Brown	Shades of warm browns and orange	Silver	Attractive for modern living room or dining room

THE YELLOW FAMILY

REPRESENTATIVE MEMBERS OF THE YELLOW FAMILY . . . CREAM . . . BUFF . . . STRAW . . . CANARY . . . GOLD . . . TAN . . . BROWN.

CHARACTERISTICS . . . Warm, somewhat advancing . . . The sunlight color—gay, happy, bright, cheerful . . . In light tones, luminous, radiant.

WHAT THEY CAN DO . . . Diffuse and increase light by reflection, making dark rooms seem lighter and brighter . . . In pale tints, yellow lights up a small room without making it seem smaller because reflective radiance of yellow balances its advancing quality as a warm color.

CORRECT USES . . . Excellent background for all average rooms . . . In light tints, best wall-background for poorly lighted rooms . . . In clear, bright tones, safe accent color almost everywhere.

CAUTION . . . Do not use yellow without testing under artificial light, and providing lamp shades to offset color changes . . . Don't use in wide expanses in a very sunny room . . . Don't use bright tones without restful combination color.

SUGGESTED COLOR SCHEMES IN WHICH MEMBERS OF YELLOW FAMILY PLAY A DOMINANT ROLE

DOMINANT COLOR	MAJOR WALL COLOR	MAJOR FLOOR COLOR	DRAPERIES AND UPHOLSTERY	ACCENT COLORS	REMARKS
CREAM	Cream Woodwork, cream	Patterned rug, mulberry, green and cream	Draperies, green, cream trimming Upholstery, green and green yellow	Mulberry	Appropriate for bedroom, especially in Directoire feeling with cream and gold furniture
BUFF	Buff	Buff	Copenhagen blue and burgundy	Orange, Tete de Negre	Glowing color scheme for living room or man's bedroom
PALE YELLOW (1)	Pale Yellow	Soft Beige	Draperies, light yellow background, soft reds, greens and blue in pattern Upholstery, soft blue, chintz of draperies	Green and Red	Good color scheme for medium-sized dark room
PALE YELLOW (2)	Pale Yellow	Pale Yellow	Turquoise	Coral	Colorful for bedroom or small sitting room
BRIGHT LEMON (1)	Bright Lemon	Beige	Draperies, beige background, yellow green and lavender Seat covers, wet leaf green	Wet Leaf Green	This color scheme will brighten up a dark dining room
PALE LEMON (2)	Pale Lemon Yellow Woodwork, white	Tobacco Brown	Draperies, white with yellow trimming Upholstery, emerald green; some pieces white, yellow, dull orange	Orange	Suitable for living room with north light
JONQUIL YELLOW (1)	Jonquil Yellow	Gray	Draperies, white, trimmed with Chinese red Upholstery, warm gray and white	Chinese Red	Charming for living room, modern or traditional
JONQUIL YELLOW (2)	Jonquil Yellow	Soft Blue-Green	Draperies, white and yellow Upholstery, soft blue, green and white	White	Good for any room without too much light
YELLOW (1)	Yellow	Brown	Blue and apple green	Black	Good for room with cold light
YELLOW (2)	Yellow	Brown	Dutch blue and white	Bright Red	Attractive for informal living room
YELLOW (3)	Marbleized yellow paper Woodwork, deep green	Deep Green	Draperies, green, yellow trimming Chair seat upholstery, yellow	Blue	Charming for dining room, especially in Directoire feeling
YELLOW (4)	Paper in Yellow and ivory stripes, divided by narrow plum lines	Yellow Tan	Draperies, gray background, yellow, plum and rose in pattern Upholstery, blue and light tan	Old Gold	Good combination for dark maple woodwork
GRAYED YELLOW	Grayed Yellow	Brown	Draperies, brown and beige stripes Upholstery, yellow, beige, moss green	White	Pleasant for living room or man's bedroom
SOFT YELLOW	Soft Yellow	Deep Brown	Draperies, yellow Upholstery, cinnamon brown	Chartreuse	Attractive and restful for library or living room
EMPIRE YELLOW	Slate Gray	Lime Green	Draperies, Empire yellow Upholstery, Strong clear yellow	Silver	Suitable for living room or dining room
CITRON YELLOW	Citron Yellow	Citron Yellow	Coral	Silver	Modern or traditional living room
LEMON YELLOW	Lemon Yellow	Tete de Negre	Brown and henna	Orange	Distinctive for modern living room
SULPHUR YELLOW	Sulphur Yellow	Olive Green	Shades of green and sulphur	Coral	Colorful modern living room

COLOR THEORY
Color Families: Yellow

DEEP YELLOW	Deep Yellow	Red	Draperies, gold damask Upholstery, plum, wine red, gold with red, blue, lavender in pattern	Gold	Suitable for period room with Queen Anne, Sheraton, and other Georgian style furniture
MUTED GOLD	Caramel	Bleached wood, rubbed with gold and waxed	Draperies, soft caramel taffeta, trimmed with brown Upholstery, brown and yellow	Ebony	Unusual modern living room scheme where there is plenty of light
GOLD (1)	Yellow, flat finish Woodwork, Olive Green	Old gold carpet	Draperies, old gold, trimmed with green Upholstery, olive green and paprika	Light Green	Charming for modern living room with blond wood
GOLD (2)	Gray and pale Yellow paper	Harvest Gold and Gray	Draperies, oyster white, trimmed with multi-color fringe Upholstery, rust-shot silk	Brass	Traditional or modern dining room
TAN (1)	Neutral Tan	Dark Tan	Draperies, burnt orange Upholstery, brown and burnt orange	Rich Chocolate	Good with natural wood tones
TAN (2)	Tan linen color	Light and dark Tan	Draperies, tan and rose stripes Upholstery, linen color with rose, tan, gray and blue in pattern	Rose	Attractive for living room or library with walnut woodwork and furniture
TAN (3)	Tan	Brown Taupe	Dark green and vermilion	Brown	Rich, warm color scheme for living room or library, especially with walnut furniture and paintings
TAN (4)	Brownish Tan	Floor, Oak Multi-colored scatter rugs	Draperies, brown with red, yellow and blue pattern Upholstery, old red and yellow chintz	Blue	Suitable for bedroom with oak furniture in Early English feeling
BROWN (1)	Brown paneled	Deep Brown	Beige background with brilliant gold, scarlet and orange tones of fall foliage	Blue	Attractive for living room with plenty of light
BROWN (2)	Pine paneled	Pine	Old chintz in blue and brown	Silver and Pewter	Dining room in French Provincial style
BROWN (3)	Warm Beige with brown cast	Brown	Draperies, brown, beige and dusty pink Upholstery, brown and off-white	White	Appropriate for modern living room
BROWN (4)	Pine paneled	Hooked Rugs	Yellow, copper and blue chintz	Green	Suitable Early American living room with maple furniture
BROWN (5)	Chalk White	Brown	Turquoise	Peach	Charming bedroom color scheme
SABLE BROWN (1)	Sable Brown	Off-white	Draperies, off-white with turquoise Upholstery, shell pink and off-white	Turquoise	Distinctive modern living room
SABLE BROWN (2)	Sable Brown	Deep warm Beige	Draperies, bright yellow Upholstery, plain chartreuse with white pattern	Earth Brown	Same as above
CHESTNUT BROWN	Fawn	Chestnut Brown	Champagne background, beaver, turquoise and apricot in pattern and trimming	Turquoise	Appropriate for living or dining room
TAWNY BROWN	Tawny Brown Pine	Light beige and taupe	Blue on light ground	Yellow	Good for dining room in French period feeling
GOLDEN BROWN	Knotty Pine	Golden Brown Navajo rug	Draperies, colorful hunting print Upholstery, red leather	Blue and Green	Library or Den
NUT BROWN	Nut Brown Pine	Moss Green	Draperies, dark linen Upholstery, green, brown and white	Yellow	Restful living room color scheme
TOBACCO BROWN	Tobacco Brown	Beige	Clear yellow chintz with beige and dark brown in design	White	Suitable modern dining room with much sunlight
CHOCOLATE BROWN	Chocolate Brown	Eggshell	Draperies, white Upholstery, chartreuse, brown and eggshell	Chartreuse	Interesting modern color scheme for living room or dining room
DARK BROWN (1)	Deep Beige	Dark Brown	Draperies, pale, clear blue Upholstery, cinnamon brown	Pale Clear Blue	Good for dining room or living room
DARK BROWN (2)	Light Chartreuse	Dark Brown	Light tan and brown	White	Good for modern living room
BROWNS	Light Brown	Deep Brown	Draperies, off-white Upholstery, Wedgwood green and off-white	Gold	Suitable for living or dining room

THE GREEN FAMILY

REPRESENTATIVE MEMBERS OF THE GREEN FAMILY . . . NILE . . . LETTUCE . . . PEA . . . GRASS . . . SEA . . . OLIVE . . . BOTTLE . . . ETC.

CHARACTERISTICS . . . Cool, receding—except when mixed with a warm color . . . Most restful color . . . Friendly with all other colors, refreshing, versatile . . . Endless variety of tones and combinations.

WHAT THEY CAN DO . . . In light, soft tints, makes rooms seem larger because the wall seems farther away . . . Makes objects seem farther away, therefore smaller . . . Brings atmosphere of rest and relaxation to room.

CORRECT USES . . . One of best background colors for average rooms, especially where restfulness is important . . . Great corrective value for rooms too small or too warm . . . Suitable in proper tones for background in any part of room—floor, walls, ceiling.

CAUTION . . . Do not use in quantity in cold, dark or overlarge rooms—choose warm, advancing colors for backgrounds, keeping green for smaller areas.

SUGGESTED COLOR SCHEMES IN WHICH MEMBERS OF GREEN FAMILY PLAY A DOMINANT ROLE

DOMINANT COLOR	MAJOR WALL COLOR	MAJOR FLOOR COLOR	DRAPERIES AND UPHOLSTERY	ACCENT COLORS	REMARKS
PALE GREEN (1)	Pale Green	Dark Green	Draperies, off-white background, with pale blues, greens, and mauve in pattern Upholstery, darker blue	Mauve and Violet	Appropriate for average living room and bedroom
PALE GREEN (2)	Pale Green	Plum	Draperies, natural linen color, with flowered plum and green in design Upholstery, plum, gold, green	Gold	Especially good for traditional living room
LIGHT GREEN (1)	White	Light Green	Draperies, white with dark green pattern Upholstery, dark green and white	Yellow	Pleasant color scheme for modern room
LIGHT GREEN (2)	Pickled Pine	Light Green	Draperies, off-white and light green Upholstery, light green	Brown	Attractive for living room or library
LIGHT GREEN (3)	Off-white	Soft Light Green	Shell-pink, green and off-white	Crystal	Charming and cool for small living room or sitting room
APPLE GREEN (1)	Apple Green	Plum	Draperies, apple green Upholstery, gold, yellow and ivory	Gold	Good for small living room
APPLE GREEN (2)	Apple Green	Yellow Green	Gray, blue, and touches of light yellow	Light Yellow	This combination makes cool room
APPLE GREEN (3)	Pale Apple Green	Floor, brown walnut Rug, blue and tan	Draperies, royal blue background, with rose and green leaves in pattern Upholstery, same drapery chintz, also rose, antique salmon, apple green and cream stripes	Black, gold, white and ruby	Early American living room with maple or cherry furniture
SOFT GREEN (1)	Soft Green	Deeper Green	Draperies, plum background with beige and green in pattern Upholstery, plum, beige and green	Orange	Restful Color Scheme
SOFT GREEN (2)	Soft Grayed Green	Deeper Green	Draperies, corn yellow Upholstery, grayed green and off-white	Pine Green	Adaptable to living room, dining room or bedroom
SOFT GREEN (3)	Pale Soft Grayed Green	Ivy Green	Draperies, soft grayed green Upholstery, golden yellow and white	Lacquer Red	Excellent to add feeling of space to small room
FOAM GREEN	Slate Gray	Foam Green	Draperies, lemon yellow and white Upholstery, lemon yellow and gray	Gold	Good modern color scheme
IVY GREEN	Clear Beige	Ivy Green	Draperies, beige with light and dark green floral design Upholstery, same chintz and some clear beige	Black	Appropriate for living room
DEEP LIME	Deep Lime	Deep Lime	White, green and melon pink	White	Dramatic modern scheme, especially good with blond wood

COLOR THEORY
Color Families: Green

NILE GREEN	Nile Green	Green	Glazed chintz with green background and white in design, red lining and trimming	Crystal	Cool, airy bedroom
MINT GREEN	Pure White Woodwork, white	Painted Mint Green, spatter-dashed with turquoise and yellow	Turquoise, yellow and mint green	White	Adaptable for informal living room, dining room or bedroom
JADE GREEN	Pale Jade	Dark Blue	Draperies, blue Upholstery, blue and jade green	Silver	Attractive for modern living room
SAGE	Slate Gray	Soft Deep Sage	Gray and blue with green touches	Silver	Excellent color to make small sunny room seem larger and cooler
BOTTLE GREEN	Pale Apricot	Bottle Green	Green, apricot and topaz	Topaz	Good for living room or dining room
CHARTREUSE GREEN	Chartreuse Green	Shades of Tete de Negre	Draperies, chartreuse green Upholstery, shades of heliotrope	Silver	Modern bedroom. Good with furniture painted chartreuse
CHARTREUSE GREEN	Gray	Chartreuse	Chartreuse and bright blue	Silver	Adaptable to any modern room
TURQUOISE	Light Turquoise	Patterned rug, Green with Moss Rose	Draperies, turquoise, green and rose stripes Upholstery, turquoise	Rose	Attractive for bedroom with mahogany furniture
BLUE GREEN (1)	Deep Cream	Blue Green	Apple green, greenish blue, touch of burnt orange	Burnt Orange	Versatile color scheme for average room
BLUE GREEN (2)	Blue Green	Blue Green	Draperies, light grayish tan background, turquoise, rose and green in pattern Upholstery, same print and some soft rose	Green	Very restful for living room or bedroom
BLUE GREEN (3)	Dull Blue Green	Rug, light field, red violet and green leaves in pattern	Draperies, white Upholstery, red violet	Dark Green	Dining room in period feeling with walnut furniture
WET LEAF GREEN	Deep Lime	Bronze	White background, wet leaf green, dawn rose and bright lemon in pattern	Rose	Sophisticated modern color scheme
DEEP GREEN (1)	Deep Green	Gray	Draperies, sky blue chintz with rose and green pattern Upholstery, emerald green and gray	Gold and Rose	Suitable for living room or man's bedroom
DEEP GREEN (2)	Gray and White paper, Block pattern	Deep Green	Draperies, yellow Upholstery, yellow flowers and pale green leaves on gray background	White and Green	Modern living room or dining room
DEEP GREEN (3)	Green, lighter than carpet	Deep Soft Green	Draperies, off-white Upholstery, off-white and Wedgwood green	Yellow	Very cool and fresh
DEEP GREEN (4)	Greenish Gray	Deep Green	Draperies, apple green Upholstery, grayed greens and white	Salmon	Good combination to make small room seem larger
DEEP GREEN (5)	Deep Soft Green	Light Brown	Golden yellow and white	White	Modern or traditional setting
GEORGIAN GREEN	Deep Georgian Green	Deep Green	Draperies, soft golden yellow Upholstery, golden yellow and deep green	Gold	Very cool and restful for period living room or library
DARK GREEN (1)	Ivory Green	Dark Green	Draperies, white with dark green pattern Upholstery, off-red, off-white and dark green	Black	Subtle color combination. Good for living room or dining room
DARK GREEN (2)	Warm Gray	Dark Green	Draperies, dark green or gray background Upholstery, light green	Yellow	Cool and restful for living room
DARK GREEN (3)	Dark Green	Tan	Draperies, chintz in blue-green and soft red Upholstery, same chintz, also some soft red	Copper	Charming for sunny living room
GREEN OLIVE	Green Olive	Red-Coral	Lime green, red-coral, antique white	Coral and White	Daring modern color scheme. Good with traditional or modern furniture in light finish

THE BLUE FAMILY

REPRESENTATIVE MEMBERS OF THE BLUE FAMILY . . . PALE . . . BABY . . . SKY . . . POWDER . . . NAVY . . . MIDNIGHT . . . ETC.

CHARACTERISTICS . . . Coldest, most receding, unless mixed with warm colors . . . Serene, quiet, "spacious" . . . Much-loved hue . . . Too much of it in dull tones may be depressing.

WHAT THEY CAN DO . . . Make room seem larger, cooler, more airy and spacious . . . Make objects look smaller because they seem more distant . . . In dark tones, make lighter contrast colors more luminous.

CORRECT USES . . . In light tones, excellent background for small, dark, warm rooms . . . Good combining color, especially in soft tones . . . Effective background for many other colors.

CAUTION . . . Do not use in quantity in cold or dark or over-large rooms . . . Do not use too much in dull shades . . . Do not use without some warm bright accent color.

SUGGESTED COLOR SCHEMES IN WHICH MEMBERS OF BLUE FAMILY PLAY A DOMINANT ROLE

DOMINANT COLOR	MAJOR WALL COLOR	MAJOR FLOOR COLOR	DRAPERIES AND UPHOLSTERY	ACCENT COLORS	REMARKS
PALE BLUE (1)	Pale Blue	Dark Blue	Tan draperies and upholstery	Silver	Modern color scheme for bedroom with furniture in lemon color
SKY BLUE	Garden Sky Blue	Champagne	Champagne, sky blue and orchid	Orchid	Modern color scheme, good with light natural finish woods
POWDER BLUE (1)	Powder Blue	Delft Blue	Draperies, canary yellow Upholstery, yellow and powder blue	Off-white	Cool and fresh for bedroom
POWDER BLUE (2)	Powder Blue	Powder Blue	White draperies and upholstery	Peach	Dainty feminine bedroom
LARKSPUR BLUE (1)	Larkspur Blue	Pale Gray	Draperies, wine, trimmed with white Upholstery, deep blue and white	Deep Blue and Wine	Good modern living room combination
LARKSPUR BLUE (2)	Larkspur Blue	Blue	Neutral background, blue and pink in pattern	Red Dahlia	Any period room with enough light
BLUE (1)	Pale Blue, deep Rose and Ivory paper	Blue	Blue, gold and rose with touches of black—in stripes or plain	Black	Attractive for traditional living room
BLUE (2)	Faded Blue (middle value)	Floor, dark Brown Carpet, Gray and Yellow	Draperies, old yellow Upholstery, yellow, old yellow, and touch of Venetian red, also some blue	Blue	Bedroom with Directoire feeling and walnut furniture
BLUE (3)	Striped wallpaper in tones of light and medium blue and White	Dark Blue	Draperies, blue with white in pattern and trimming Upholstery, lemon yellow	Dark Blue	Good for small, low-ceilinged but light room
HYDRANGEA BLUE (1)	Pale Hydrangea Blue	Eggplant	Draperies, peach background with white, copper, gold and hydrangea blue in design Upholstery, same chintz, also old blue	Old Blue	Good for room with strong light, especially with 18th Century furniture
HYDRANGEA BLUE (2)	Hydrangea Blue	Deeper Blue	Draperies, salmon pink Chair seats, black and gold	Gold	Dining room with Directoire feeling
COPENHAGEN BLUE	Copenhagen Blue	Burgundy	Gray with blue and burgundy	Rose and Silver	Attractive for traditional living room
PENCIL BLUE	Lemon Yellow	Pencil Blue	Blue background with yellow in pattern and trim	Silver	Setting for dining room with modern furniture

COLOR THEORY
Color Families: Blue

MEDIUM BLUE (1)	Blue	Mulberry ground	Draperies, cherry red Upholstery, chintz in blue, rose and mauve, some pieces in cherry red and gold	Gold	Good for living room, especially in 18th Century French feeling
MEDIUM BLUE (2)	Blue	Mole	Lavender, gray, and some rose	Rose	Adaptable for lady's bedroom in lighter blues, also to living room in darker shades of duller blues
MEDIUM BLUE (3)	Cream	Blue	French Blue	Jade Green	Good for south living room or bedroom
DUSTY BLUE	Dusty Blue	Dark Burgundy	Draperies, gray, trimmed with soft blue Upholstery, soft blue and gray	Crystal	Restful for living room or dining room
SOFT DULL BLUE	Ivory	Soft Dull Blue	Ivory background with blue, rose and green in design, some pieces in old rose	Green	Bedroom or informal living room
OLD BLUE	Old Blue	Deeper Blue	Faded Pink, or chintz with blue, green and pink	Green	Charming for living room or bedroom
GRAYED BLUE	Gray Blue	Deeper grayed Blue	Yellow, white, and gold	Red	Dining room in Directoire feeling with mahogany
TURQUOISE BLUE	Pale Turquoise Blue	Turquoise	Draperies, golden yellow Upholstery, golden yellow and white	White	Any room not too large or too dark
TURQUOISE BLUE	Grayed Turquoise	Grayed Turquoise	Wine and Ivory	Polished Brass	Dignified but friendly living room
GREEN BLUE	Green Blue	Plum rug; flowered pattern	Draperies, peach Upholstery, green-blue with some plum	Peach	Simple living room in French Provincial feeling
ROYAL BLUE (1)	Walls, Silver Woodwork, Royal Blue	Floor, painted Gray Rug, Blue	Draperies, blue, trimmed with silver Upholstery (chairs), silver and blue leather	Silver and Black	Distinctive modern dining room
ROYAL BLUE (2)	Old White	Royal Blue	Clear yellow	Silver	Modern living or dining room
ROYAL BLUE (3)	Dull White	Rug, Deep Blue ground with honey-yellow in pattern	Draperies, royal blue Chair Seats, royal blue Morocco	Silver	Attractive for modern dining room, especially with lemon wood furniture
DEEP BLUE (1)	Pale Amethyst	Deep Blue	Deep blue, trimmed with gold	Amethyst and Gold	Cool and charming for living room not too dark
DEEP BLUE (2)	Deep Blue Woodwork, Ivory	Dark Blue rug with Tan and Rose in pattern	Draperies, dull ivory Upholstery (chairs), ivory or rosy red leather	Red	Colorful for dining room with plenty of light
DEEP BLUE (3)	Deep Blue	Deep Blue	Draperies, deep sea blue Upholstery, canary yellow	White	Modern living room or dining room
DEEP BLUE (4)	Pale Yellow	Natural	Draperies, deep sea blue (gold gauze glass curtains) Upholstery, deep blue	White	Good when blue is dominant color in a dark room
DEEP BLUE (5)	Creamy White	Blue	Draperies, deep blue Upholstery, yellow with dash of white	Gold, Rose-Pink and Blue	Good for bedroom, furniture painted blue with flower decorations, and some smaller oyster white pieces
GARDEN POOL BLUE	Ivory	Garden Pool Blue	Draperies, garden pool blue Chair Seats, red leather	White and Silver	Dramatic modern living room with furniture in rich mahogany or walnut tones
DARK BLUE	Cream and beige paper	Dark Blue rug with rose and tan in pattern	Draperies, linen color with blues, greens and rosy reds in pattern Chair Seats, dark blue	Blue and Silver	Good for dining room where light is needed

THE VIOLET (OR PURPLE) FAMILY

REPRESENTATIVE MEMBERS OF THE VIOLET FAMILY . . . ORCHID . . . LAVENDER . . . MAUVE . . . VIOLET . . . PLUM . . . PURPLE.

CHARACTERISTICS . . . Cool when mixed with blue, warm when mixed with red . . . In pure form, cold and formal . . . In purple tones, rich and dignified but not friendly . . . May be depressing.

WHAT THEY CAN DO . . . Add to impression of room size and coolness, especially when mixed with blue . . . Create restful, quiet atmosphere when used in soft tones.

CORRECT USES . . . In light, soft tints, excellent wall and ceiling background for an average room . . . Strong shades good for accent . . . In deep, soft tones, attractive for carpets, upholstery, draperies.

CAUTION . . . Do not use blue tones of violet in cold, dark, over-large rooms . . . Be careful when using strong shades for dominant color . . . Do not use without some warm contrast.

SUGGESTED COLOR SCHEMES IN WHICH MEMBERS OF VIOLET FAMILY PLAY A DOMINANT ROLE

DOMINANT COLOR	MAJOR WALL COLOR	MAJOR FLOOR COLOR	DRAPERIES AND UPHOLSTERY	ACCENT COLORS	REMARKS
ORCHID (1)	Orchid	Blue	Champagne, orchid and blue	Black and Silver	Attractive for living room
ORCHID (2)	Paneled paper in Orchid and Pale Yellow	Mulberry	Green, yellow and orchid chintz	Green	Cool, airy bedroom
LAVENDER (1)	Lavender	Lavender with mauve border	Gray, light blue and touches of jade green	Jade Green	Good for sunny room
LAVENDER (2)	Lavender, Blue and White paper	Plum	Lavender	Rose	Feminine bedroom
LAVENDER (3)	Pale Lavender	Rose	Pink, lavender and white	Lavender	Bedroom with warm light
HELIOTROPE (1)	Gray	Beige	Heliotrope draperies and upholstery	Violet and Silver	Lovely color scheme for woman with gray hair
MAUVE (1)	Gray	Mauve	Light blue, Nile green, some rose	Rose	Good for sunny bedroom
MAUVE (2)	Paneled wall painted Pale Mauve	Deep Violet	Mauve and yellow	Crystal and Sepia	Especially attractive for Louis XVI style bedroom with walnut furniture
HELIOTROPE (2)	Pearl Gray	Heliotrope	Draperies, heliotrope trimmed with silver Upholstery, Tarragon green, gray and heliotrope	Green	Cool and restful living room
VIOLET	Dove Gray	Black and White	Draperies, violet Upholstery, coral and old gold	Silver and Black	Attractive with silver gray painted woodwork and violet lines, also white and gold furniture
MULBERRY (1)	Dusty Mulberry	Mahogany	Draperies, clear blue chintz with mulberry and brown in pattern Upholstery, clear blue	White	Very good for traditional living room or dining room
MULBERRY (2)	Dusty Mulberry	Ebony	Draperies, creamy peach chintz with gray, old rose and ebony design Upholstery, creamy peach	Black	Good for sunny living room or dining room
MULBERRY (3)	Scenic paper Woodwork, walnut	Deep Mulberry	Mulberry	Orange	Traditional dining room
PURPLE	Paper in Gray and soft Purple stripes	Gray	Purple, with blue, green and gray	Burnt Orange	Hall or living room

COLOR THEORY
Reflective Values/Safety Color Guides

Table 1 Reflective values

Color	Approx. percent of reflection
White, dull or flat	75–85
White, gloss	85–90
Light tints	
Cream or eggshell	79
Ivory	75
Pale pink and pale yellow	75–80
Light green, light blue, light orchid	70–75
Soft pink, light peach	69
Light beige, pale gray	70
Medium tones	
Apricot	56–62
Pink	64
Tan, yellow gold	55
Light grays	35–50
Medium turquoise	44
Medium light blue	42
Yellow green	45
Old gold, pumpkin	34
Rose	29
Deep tones	
Cocoa brown, mauve	24
Medium green, medium blue	21
	20
Unsuitable dark colors	
Dark brown, dark gray	10–15
Olive green	12
Dark blue, blue green	5–10
Forest green	7
Natural wood tones	
Birch and beech	35–50
Light maple	25–35
Light oak	25–35
Dark oak, cherry	10–15
Redwood	10–15
Black walnut, mahogany	5–15

Recommended ceiling values should be in the range of 60–90%. Floor reflection values should be in the range of 15–35%. Overall reflection values of a room should be in the 35–60% range.

SAFETY COLOR GUIDES

Physical hazards:

Red: Fire protection equipment and apparatus; danger; stop
Orange: Dangerous parts of moving machinery
Yellow: Physical hazards that might cause stumbling, falling, etc.
Green; Safety—first aid dispensary or kits, stretchers, safety deluge showers, etc.
Blue: Caution against movement or use of equipment being worked on such as elevators, scaffolding, etc.
Black and white: Traffic direction; sanitation

Equipment in industrial plants:

Red: Fire protection systems and equipment
Orange: Dangerous materials, nonflammable, such as acids, alkalis, toxic materials, gases, oxygen
Yellow: Dangerous materials, flammable, such as fuel oil, gasoline, kerosene, alcohol, propane, butane, acetylene, hydrogen, and solvent
Green: Safe materials, such as drinking water, service water, brine
Blue: Protective materials
Violet: Valuable materials
Black: Electrical conduit

Table 2

Color Effects of White Fluorescent Lamps

	Cool* White	Deluxe* Cool White	Warm† White	Deluxe† Warm White	Daylight	White	Soft White—Natural
Lamp appearance; effect on neutral surfaces	White	White	Yellowish white	Yellowish white	Bluish white	Pale yellowish white	Pinkish white
Effect on "atmosphere"	Neutral to moderately cool	Neutral to moderately cool	Warm	Warm	Very cool	Moderately warm	Warm, pinkish
Colors strengthened	Orange, yellow, blue	All nearly equal	Orange, yellow	Red, orange, yellow, green	Green, blue	Orange, yellow	Red, orange
Colors grayed	Red	None appreciably	Red, green, blue	Blue	Red, orange	Red, green, blue	Green, blue
Remarks	Blends with natural daylight	Best overall color rendition; simulates natural daylight	Blends with incandescent light	Excellent color rendition; simulates incandescent light	Usually replaceable with CW	Usually replaceable with CW or WW	Usually replaceable with CWX or WWX

Color Effects of Mercury and Filament Lamps

	Mercury	White Mercury	Color-Improved Mercury	Deluxe White Mercury	Filament
Lamp appearance; effect on neutral surfaces	Greenish blue white	Greenish white	Yellowish white	White	Yellowish white
Effect on "atmosphere"	Very cool, greenish	Moderately cool, greenish	Warm, yellowish	Moderately cool	Warm
Colors strengthened	Yellow, green, blue	Yellow, green, blue	Yellow, green	Orange, yellow, blue	Red, orange, yellow
Colors grayed	Red, orange	Red, orange	Blue	Green	Blue
Remarks	Poor overall color rendering		Color rendering often acceptable, but not equal to any white fluorescent	Color rendering good; compares favorably with CWX fluorescent	Excellent color rendering

* Greater preference at higher levels.

† Greater preference at lower levels.

WINDOW TREATMENTS

Window Types

OPERATION		VENTILATION	REMARKS
Double-hung window: upper and lower sections slide vertically to open; spring balance; lock at meeting rail	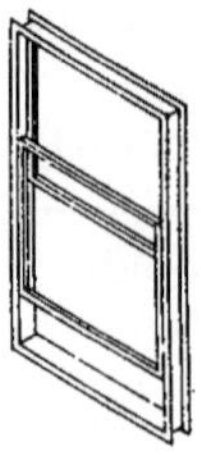	Substantial airflow, but not directed well; drafty without a shield	No parts project even when open; sometimes difficult to open if schoolroom has usual shelving at sill level; usually a glass deflector is installed to prevent drafts
Casement window: with fixed glass section at bottom, two swing-out sections at top; crank-operated	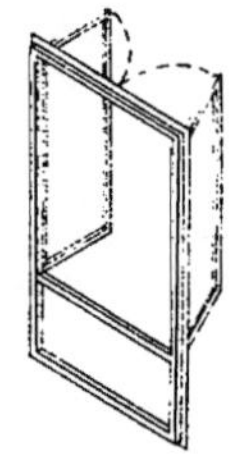	Substantial airflow, but not directed well; drafts are difficult to avoid	Easily operated; shades can be drawn without obstruction when window is open (but they will billow in breeze); these windows must be placed carefully—there is danger of children running into them outdoors if open; rarely used in schools
Projected window: with fixed upper section of glass, vent (hopper type) at bottom opening in; crank-operated	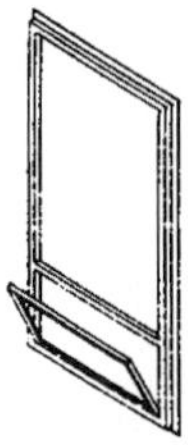	Adequate airflow in most climates; well directed, not drafty	Easily operated, can be used with shades or blinds closed over most of its area; view is unobstructed, even when window is closed
Projected window: with sections opening out at top, in at bottom; crank-operated	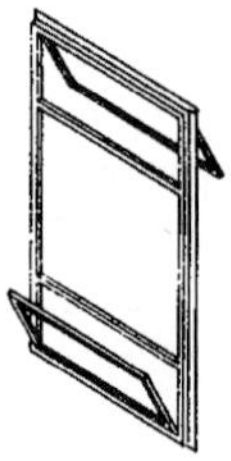	Very good airflow, both in quantity and quality (not drafty)	Easily operated; does provide some ventilation even when partially shaded; view through this type is almost unhindered with few obstructions at eye level
Awning window: four horizontal sections project out; crank-operated	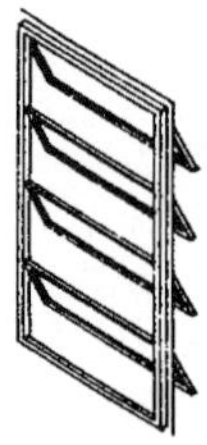	Large quantities of airflow are easily controlled, with fairly good draft control	Can be opened quite wide even during rainstorms; is easily operated; shades can be drawn without obstruction; framing does obstruct outdoor view somewhat whether window is open or closed
Sliding window with lower fixed section	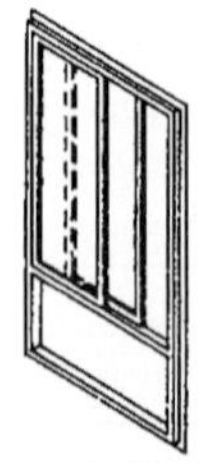	Substantial airflow, but hard to control, drafty	No parts project either inward or outward when open, but window is sometimes difficult to slide with the usual schoolroom shelf at sill level
Combination window: upper section is of glass block, supported on angle and channel girts attached to columns; lower section is half fixed glass, and half hopper (crank-operated)	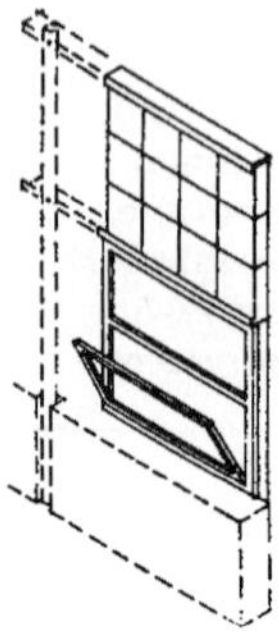	Adequate, well directed air flow for most climates	Some types of glass block refract light to ceiling, providing good light distribution across classroom and eliminating need for shades or blinds; however, designer must take care to use properly; this type does not always meet brightness tests for good schoolroom lighting

Windows are available in many types, each having advantages. The principal types are double-hung, casement, stationary, awning, and horizontal sliding. They may be made of wood or metal. Heat loss through metal frames and sash is much greater than through similar wood units. Glass blocks are sometimes used for admitting light in places where transparency or ventilation is not re-quired.

Insulated glass, used both for stationary and movable sash, consists of two or more sheets of spaced glass with hermetically sealed edges. This type has more resistance to heat loss than a single thickness and is often used without a storm sash.

TYPE | **DESCRIPTION**

SIDE HINGED

CASEMENT

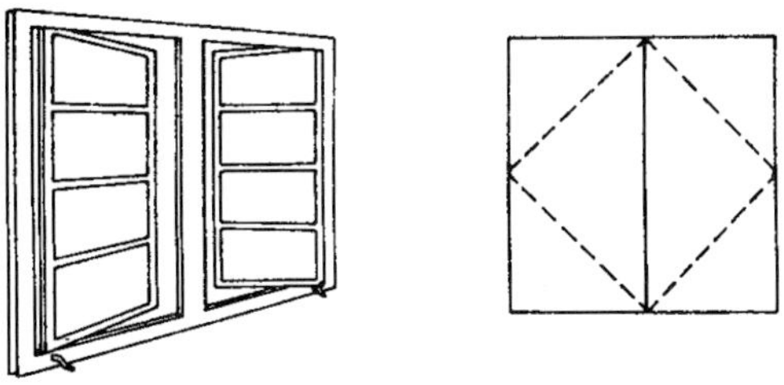

materials • wood, steel, aluminum
use • common in residences and apartments
operation • rotary crank or lever operators hold the vent open to desired position, up to 180°, but usually 90°
note • available also as a single vent
• generally allow exterior of glazing to be cleaned from inside when outswinging.
• provide 100 percent opening in the ventilation area
• will be subject to wind pressures when opened.

CASEMENT-HOPPER

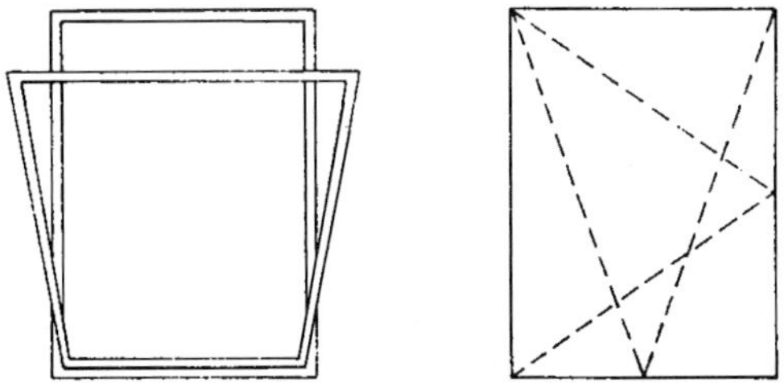

materials • wood, aluminum
use • especially appropriate for high-rise, life safety installations
operation • sophisticated hardware
note • no protection from rain when open
• available to limited extent as "tilt and turn" type which acts as a bottom hung window in normal use, but which can be converted by use of secondary hinges into a side-hung, inswinging type, allowing for easy cleaning.

CASEMENT-COMBINATION

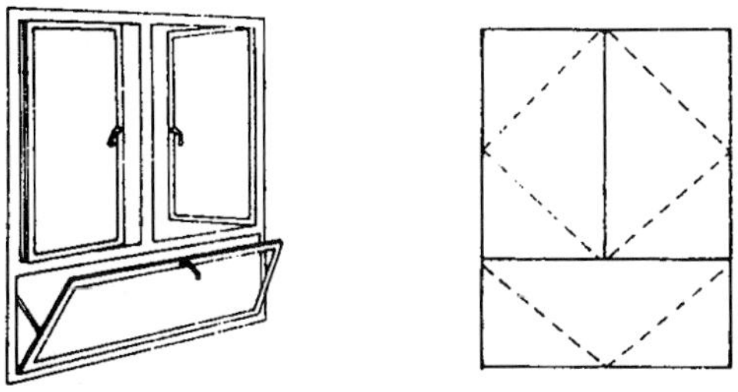

materials • wood, aluminum, steel in varied quality grades
use • commonly known as the "classroom window"
operation • combination of in-swinging hopper and out-swinging casement vents offer flexibility for ventilation control

BOTTOM HINGED

HOPPER

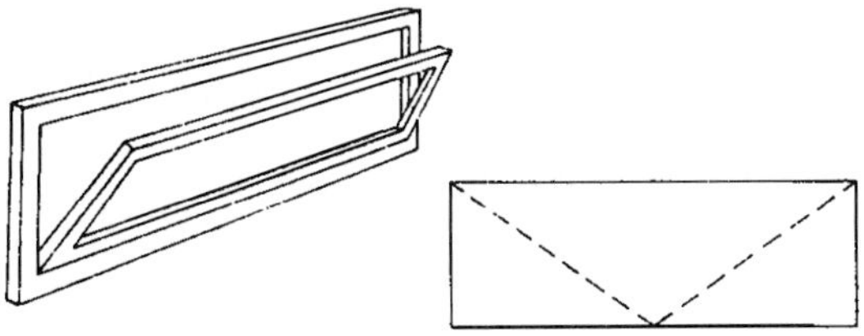

materials • wood, aluminum and steel
use • where vent will not interfere with interior conditions
• lower cost utility quality is commonly used for residential basements
note • no protection from rain when open

WINDOW TREATMENTS
Window Types

TYPE | **DESCRIPTION**

BOTTOM HINGED, continued

HOPPER-SPECIAL

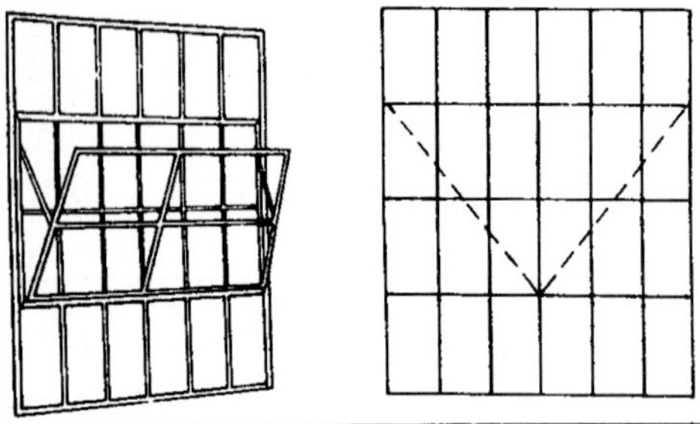

materials
- steel, stainless steel

use
- in commercial and industrial buildings where appearance is not of major importance and resistance to forced entry is
- to prevent forcible exit; sometimes called "guard" windows

operation
- combined with fixed lights or with projecting vents above, which offer high and low openings that are best for natural-air circulation (due to principles of stratification)
- separate vent frames usually swing in as hoppers
- jalousie-like vents also available
- frames often reinforced with steel rods

notes
- vents limited in size
- muntins usually separate openings of 88 inches square

HOPPER-MULTIPLE

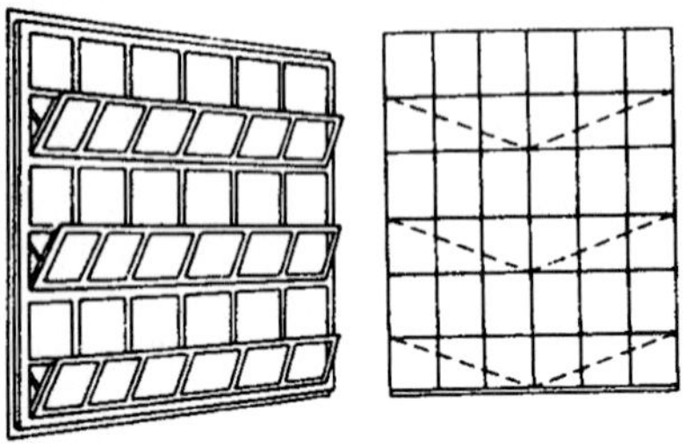

materials
- steel

use
- in housing for mental patients, to provide protection against exit while minimizing appearance of restraint

note
- vents have a maximum clear opening of about 6 inches

TOP HINGED

AWNING

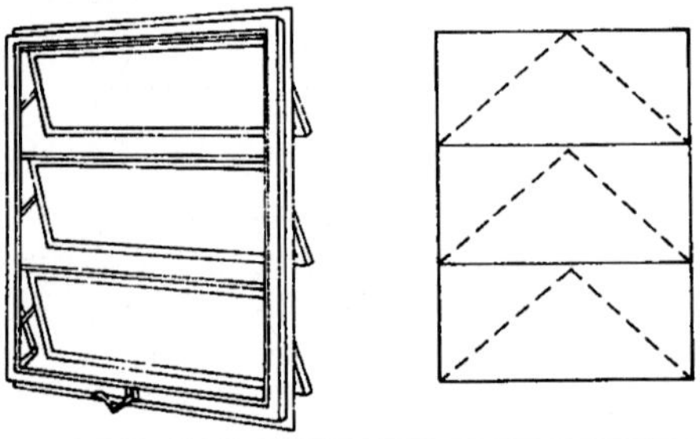

materials
- wood, steel, aluminum

use
- multiple assemblies are used mostly in steel for industrial buildings
- separate units are commonly combined with fixed lights, or with hoppers for maximum stratification ventilation (These are available also in wood and aluminum.)

operation
- are out-swinging projected windows that create a "canopy" against rain penetration
- when in multiple, vertical stacks, the mechanical operation will allow for the bottom vent to open before the other vents, which will then open in unison

PROJECTED

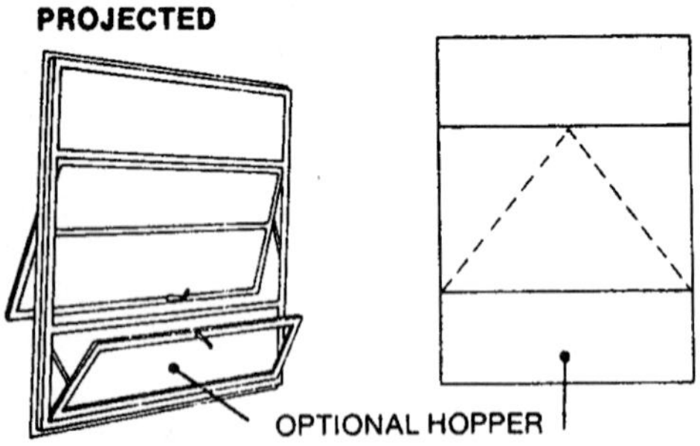

materials
- steel or aluminum

use
- medium quality grade is called "intermediate" and is commonly used in commercial, institutional and industrial type buildings
- architectural windows are frequently used for schools, hospitals, office buildings, etc.

operation
- similar to awning windows but with optional fixed glass lights and/or hoppers.

JALOUSIE

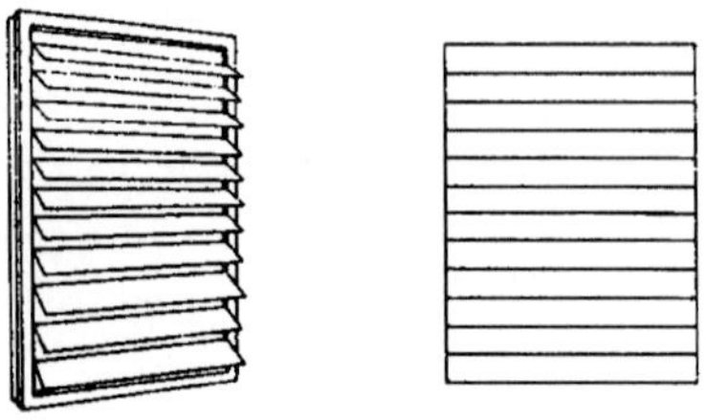

materials
- wood, steel, aluminum

use
- primarily for sunrooms, porches, and the like where protection from the weather is desired with maximum fresh air

operation
- multiple vents combine unobstructed vision with controlled ventilation
- the louvers are fully adjustable and can be set in any position

note
- can be fitted with storm sash on the inside to provide more weather tightness
- screens, interchangeable with storm sash, are furnished
- various types of glass, including obscure and colored, often are used for privacy or decoration

TYPES — **DESCRIPTION**

GLIDING

DOUBLE-HUNG

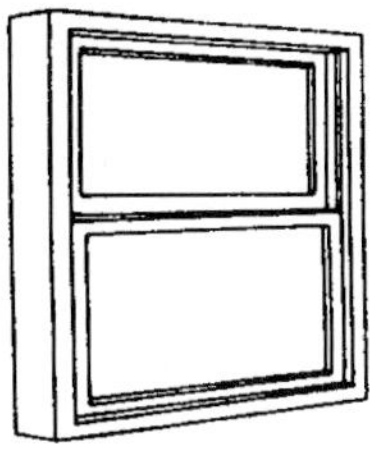
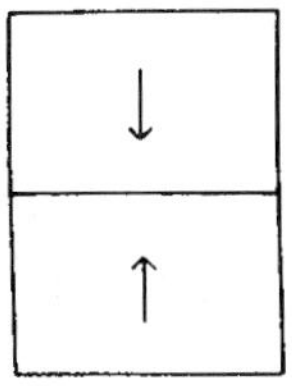

materials • wood, aluminum, steel in different designs and weights to meet various service requirements for all types of buildings

use • with combination of fixed windows for maximum window openings
• use in buildings other than residential and light commercial has been declining

operation • top and bottom openings optimize natural stratification ventilation

note • also available in single-hung (only one sash operating) and triple hung (three operable sash)

SLIDING

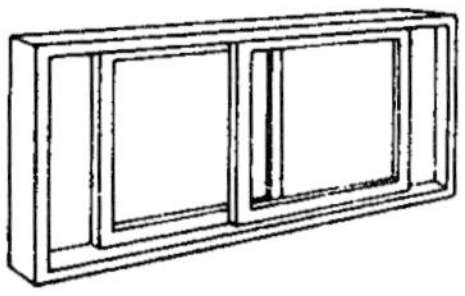
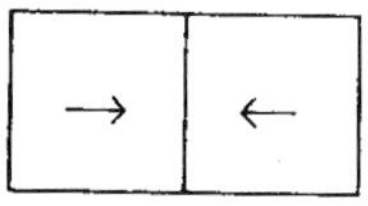

materials • wood, aluminum (with various coatings and claddings)

use • mostly in residential buildings

operation • provide only one half of opening for ventilation;
• sash height to width ratio should not exceed 1 to 2 for good operation

note • sash usually removable for cleaning and may be very large

DUAL-VENT

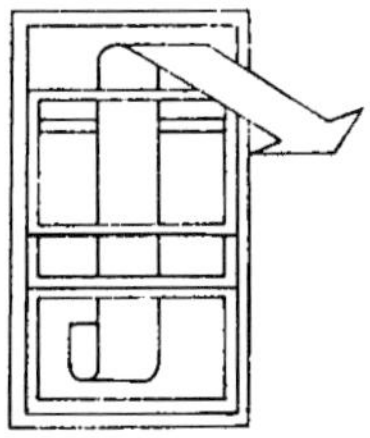
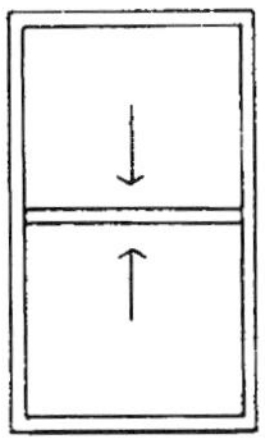

materials • aluminum

use • mostly in hospitals

operation • essentially two sets of double-hung sash—air circulates through the bottom outer sash and then through the top inner sash

note • provides ventilation while protecting from rain and drafts
• check cost

PIVOT

VERTICAL PIVOT

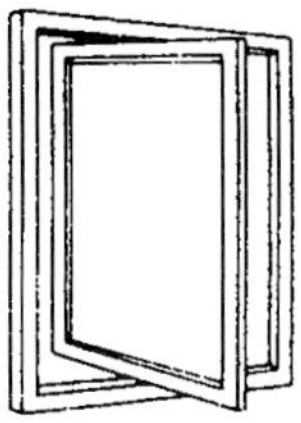
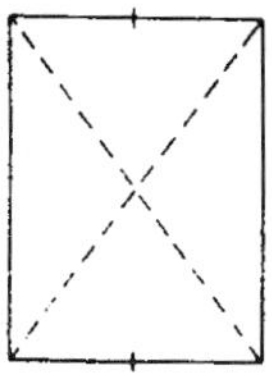

materials • wood, aluminum and steel

use • mostly in air conditioned buildings

operation • consists of large vent, usually pivoted in the center of the head and sill of the main frame, which rotates 180° or 360° around its vertical axis for cleaning

note • not primarily designed for ventilation, although may be held open up to 4'' with special hardware (unless unlocked by maintenance personnel)

WINDOW TREATMENTS
Window Types

TYPES | **DESCRIPTION**

PIVOT, continued

HORIZONTAL PIVOT

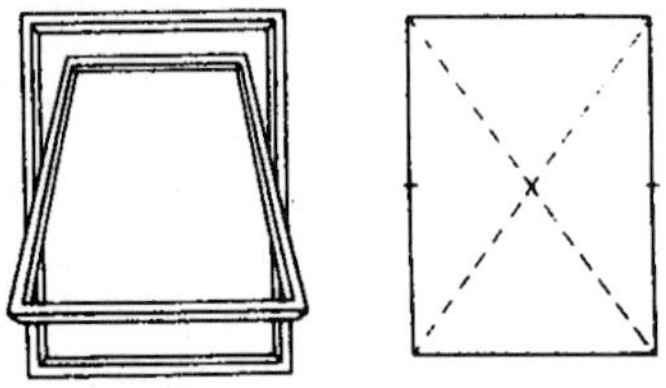

operation • similar to vertically pivoted but rotates around a horizontal axis

INDUSTRIAL PIVOT

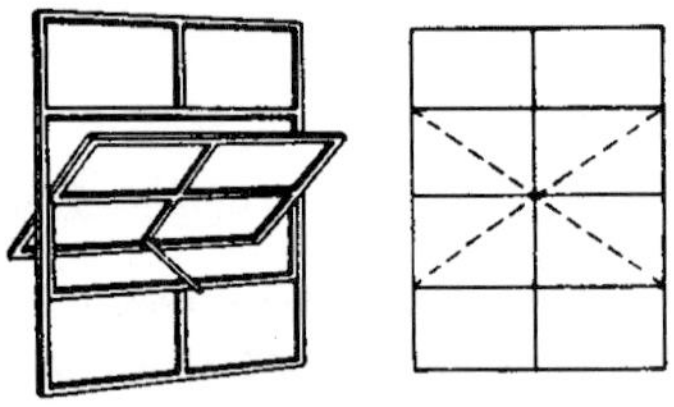

materials • steel, aluminum
use • often used horizontally and vertically to form entire walls
• lower cost for use in industrial and utilitarian buildings
note • mechanical operators are available

SPECIAL

CONTINUOUS

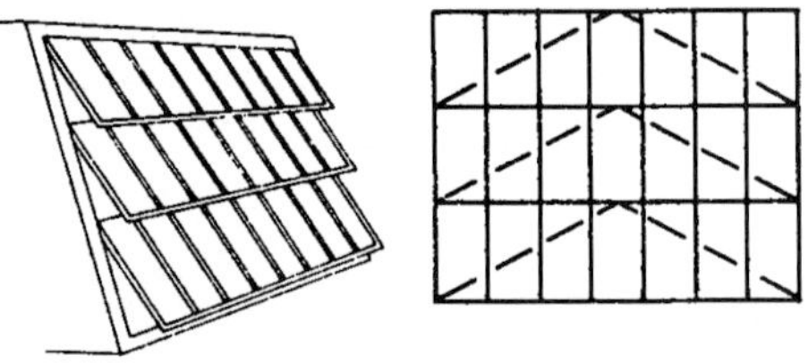

materials • steel
use • for top lighting and ventilation in monitor and sawtooth roof construction
operation • hinged at the top to the structural-steel framing members of the building and swing outward at the bottom
• two-floor lengths are connected end to end on the job
note • mechanical operators may be either manual or motor-powered

AUSTRAL

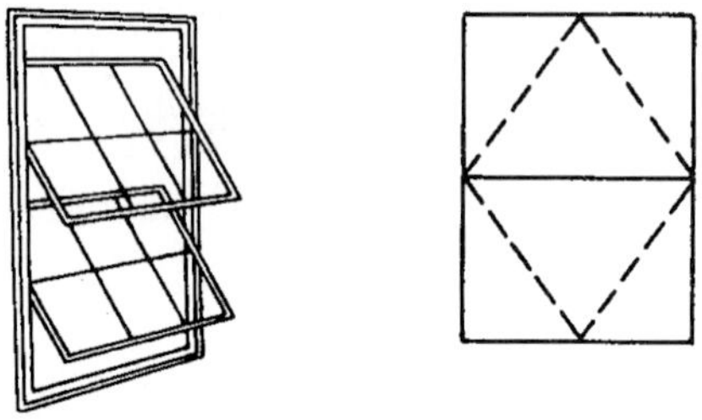

materials • wood and steel
use • schools, hospitals and other institutional buildings
• upper and lower sash counterbalanced on arms pivoted to frame
• upper and lower sash operate simultaneously
note • difficult to screen, shade or curtain

REVERSIBLE

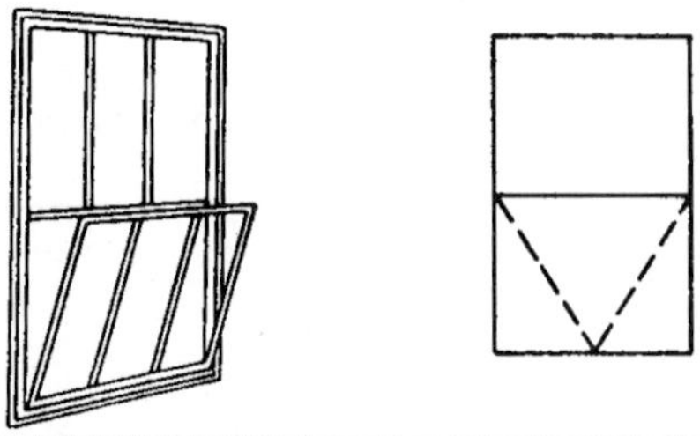

materials • wood and steel
use • residential and industrial buildings
operation • similar to double-hung in appearance, but may be tilted for better control of ventilation, or reversed for cleaning
note • not universally available

CUSTOM TYPES VARIOUS CONFIGURATIONS

materials • aluminum, steel, stainless steel
use • special types for windows in houses of worship, mausoleums, and memorial buildings
operation • various arrangements available

1. Round Top over casements

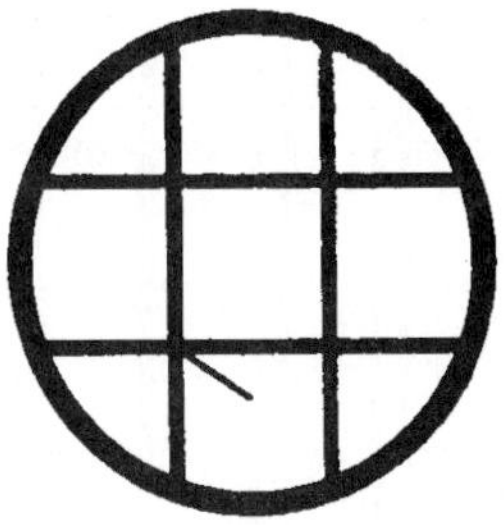

2. Full Round with operating center

3. Round Top with authentic divided lites

4. Separated Round Top

5. Eyebrow with Gothic divided lites

6. Round Top over double-hung

7. Simulated Round Top

8. Round Top with quarter panes

9. Transom Round Top

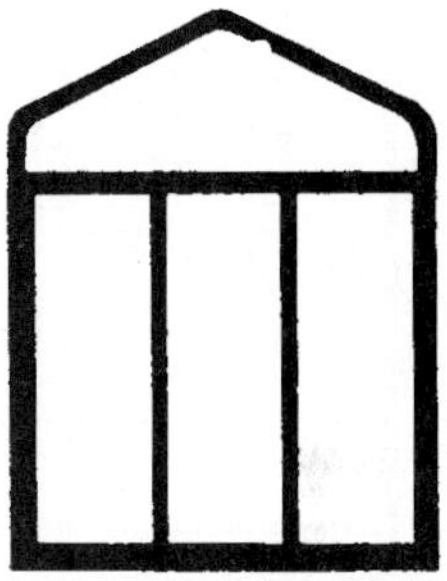

10. 3 point Round Top

11. Quarter Rounds

12. Round Top over picture window

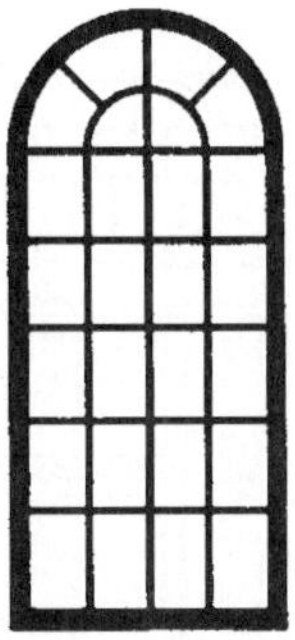

13. 12 foot Round Top with decorative divided lites

14. Inverted corners

15. 12 foot wide Round Top with operating center

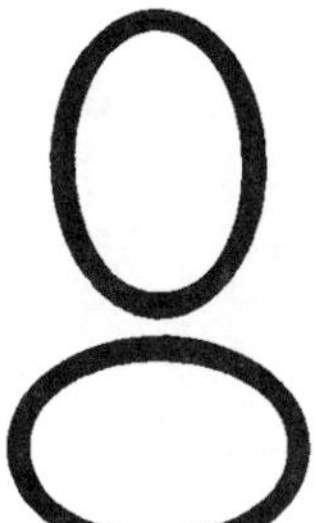

16. Ovals

17. Spider Web

18. Gothic head

19. Rounded casements

20. Rounded double hung with Gothic lite pattern.

WINDOW TREATMENTS

Window Types

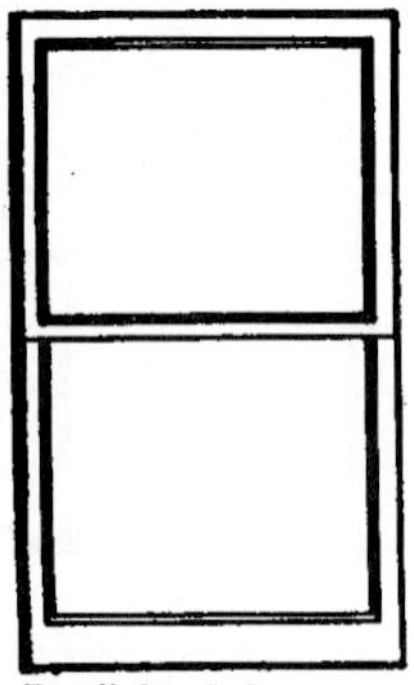

Two-light window, the all-purpose window

Two-light window, three lights over one light

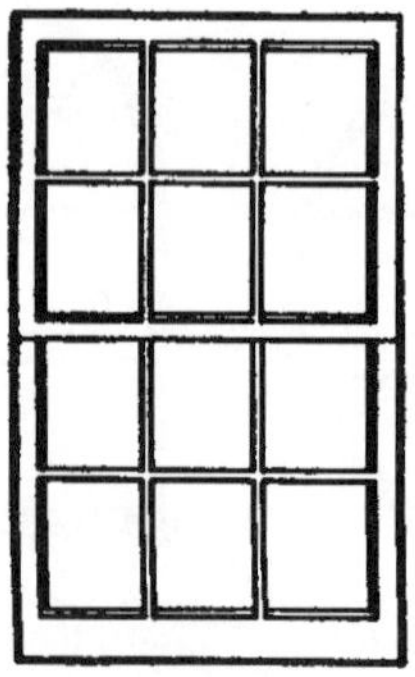

Two-light window, divided twelve lights

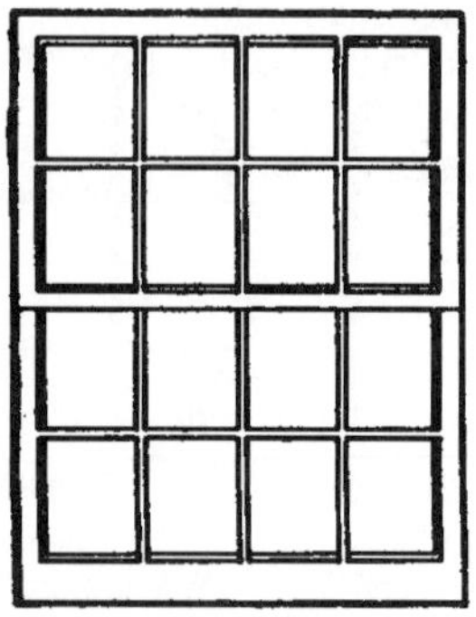

Two-light window, divided sixteen lights

Two-light window, six lights over one light

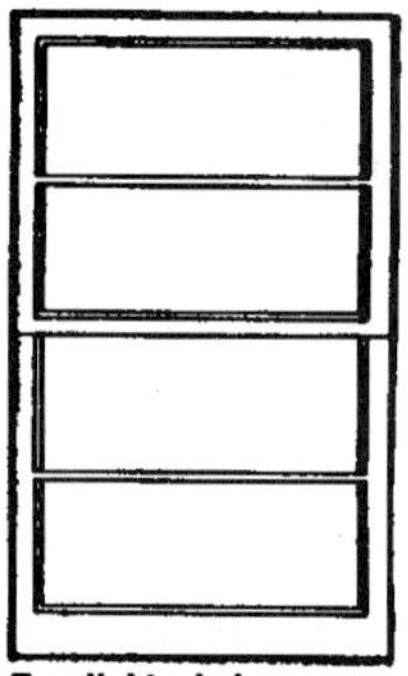

Two-light window, four horizontal lights high

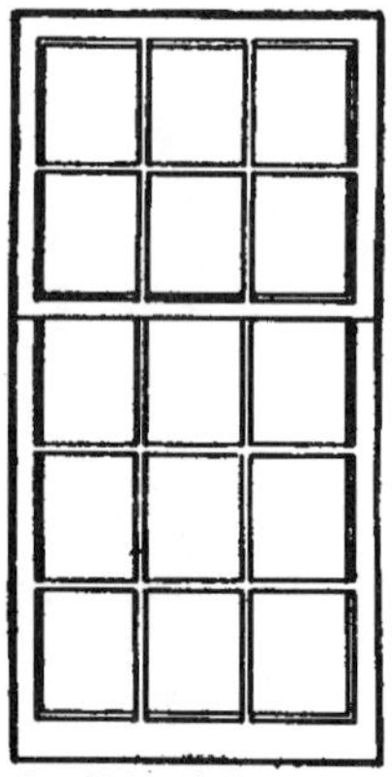

Two-light window, six lights over nine

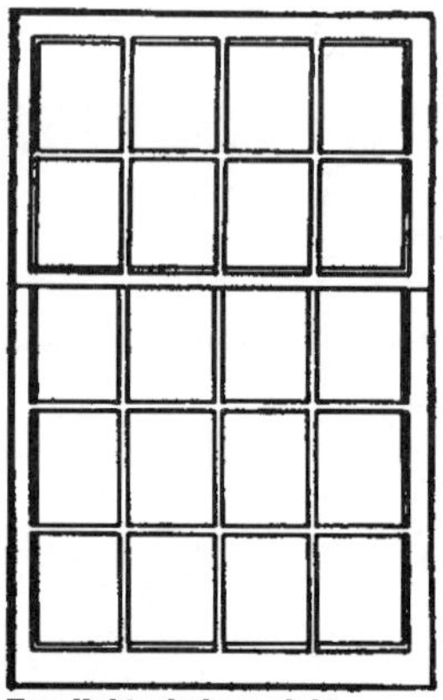

Two-light window, eight lights over twelve

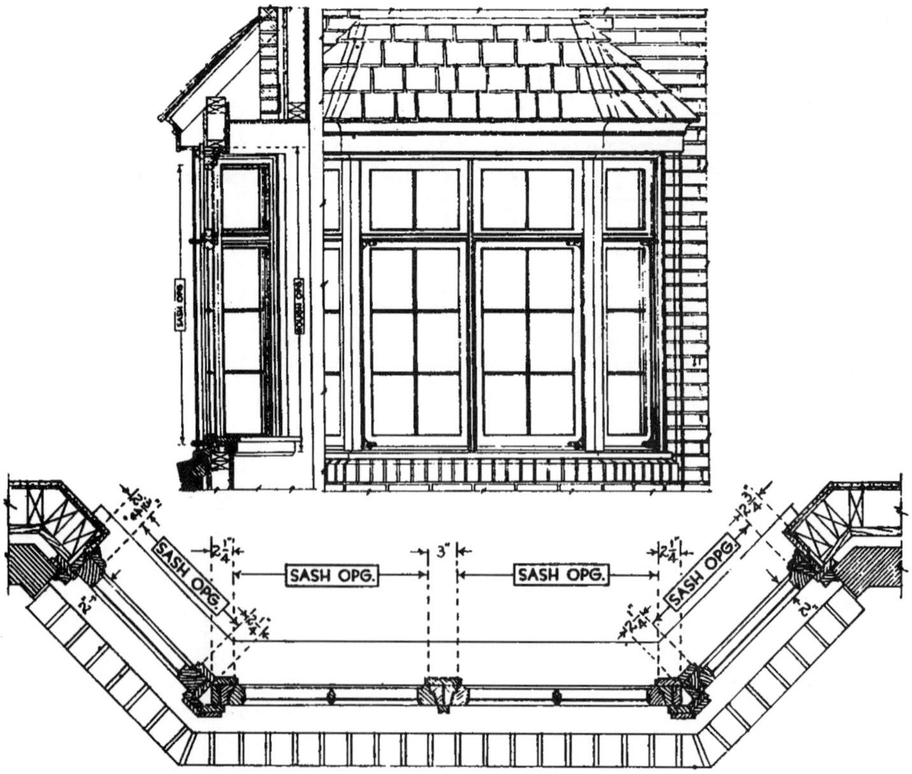

Typical styles of windows

Wood sash and door and window frames should be made from a clear grade of all-heartwood stock of a decay-resistant wood species or from wood which is given a preservative treatment. Species commonly used include ponderosa and other pines, the cedars, cypress, redwood, and the spruces.

Double-Hung Windows

The double-hung window is perhaps the most familiar window type. It consists of an upper and lower sash that slide vertically in separate grooves in the side jambs or in full-width metal weatherstripping. This type of window provides a maximum face opening for ventilation of one-half the total window area. Each sash is provided with springs, balances, or *compression weatherstripping* to hold it in place in any location. Compression weatherstripping, for example, prevents air infiltration, provides tension, and acts as a counterbalance; several types allow the sash to be removed for easy painting or repair.

The *jambs* (sides and top of the frames) are made of nominal 1-in lumber; the width provides for use with drywall or plastered interior finish. Sills are made from nominal 2-in lumber and sloped at about 3 in 12 for good drainage. Sash is normally 1⅜ in thick and wood combination storm and screen windows are usually 1⅛ in thick.

Sash may be divided into a number of lights by small wood members called *muntins*. A ranch-type house may provide the best appearance, with top and bottom sash divided into two horizontal lights. A colonial or Cape Cod house usually has each sash divided into six or eight lights. Some manufacturers provided preassembled dividers which snap in place over a single light, dividing it into six or eight lights. This simplifies painting and other maintenance.

Assembled frames are placed in the rough opening over strips of building paper put around the perimeter to minimize air infiltration. The frame is plumbed and nailed to side studs and header through the casings or the blind at the sides. Where nails are exposed, such as on the casing, use the corrosion-resistant type.

Hardware for double-hung windows includes the sash lifts that are fastened to the bottom rail, although they are sometimes eliminated by providing a finger groove in the rail. Other hardware consists of sash locks or fasteners located at the meeting rail. They not only lock the window, but draw the sash together to provide a windtight fit.

Double-hung windows can be arranged in a number of ways—as a single unit, doubled (or mullion) type, or in groups of three or more. One or two double-hung windows on each side of a large, stationary, insulated window are often used to effect a window wall. Such large openings must be framed with headers large enough to carry roofloads.

Casement Windows

Casement windows consist of side-hinged sash, usually designed to swing outward because this type can be made more weathertight than the inswinging style. Screens are located inside these outswinging windows, and winter protection is obtained with a storm sash or by using insulated glass in the sash. One advantage of the casement window over the double-hung type is that the entire window area can be opened for ventilation.

Weatherstripping is also provided for this type of window, and units are usually received from the factory entirely assembled with hardware in place. Closing hardware consists of a rotary operator and sash lock. As in the double-hung units, casement sash can be used in a number of ways—as a pair or in combinations of two or more pairs. Style variations are achieved by divided lights. Snap-in muntins provided a small, multiple-pane appearance for traditional styling.

Metal sash is sometimes used but, because of low insulating value, should be installed carefully to prevent condensation and frosting on the interior surfaces during cold weather. A full storm-window unit is sometimes necessary to eliminate this problem in cold climates.

Stationary Windows

Stationary windows used alone or in combination with double-hung or casement windows usually consist of a wood sash with a large single light of insulated glass. They are designed to provide light, as well as for attractive appearance, and are fastened permanently into the frame. Because of their size (sometimes 6 to 8 ft wide), 1¾-in-thick sash is used to provide strength. The thickness is usually required because of the thickness of the insulating glass.

Double-Hung and Casement

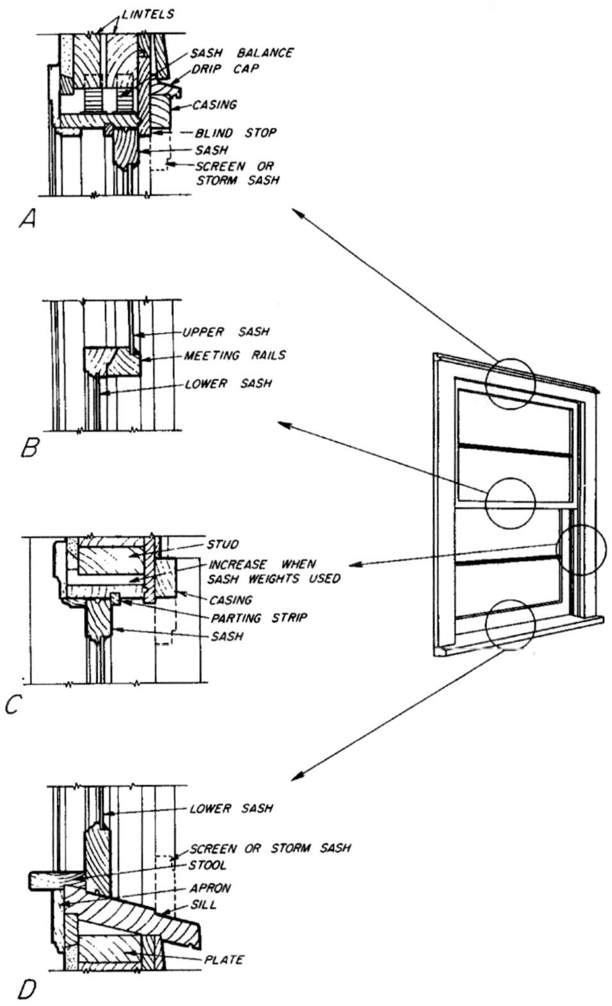

Fig. 3 Double-hung windows. Cross sections: *A*, head jamb; *B*, meeting rails; *C*, side jamb; *D*, sill

WINDOW TREATMENTS
Curtains/Draperies

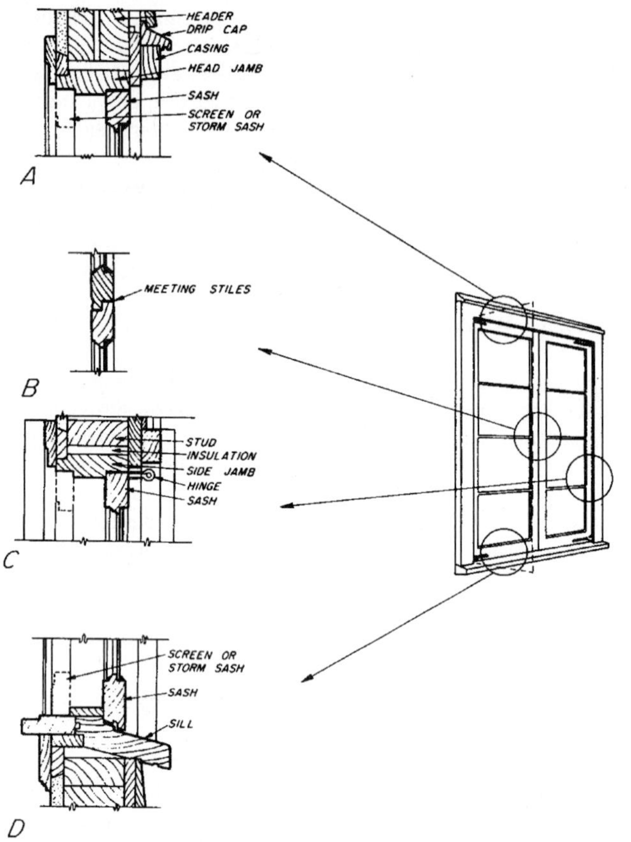

Fig. 4 Outswinging casement sash. Cross sections: *A*, head jamb; *B*, meeting stiles; *C*, side jambs; *D*, sill

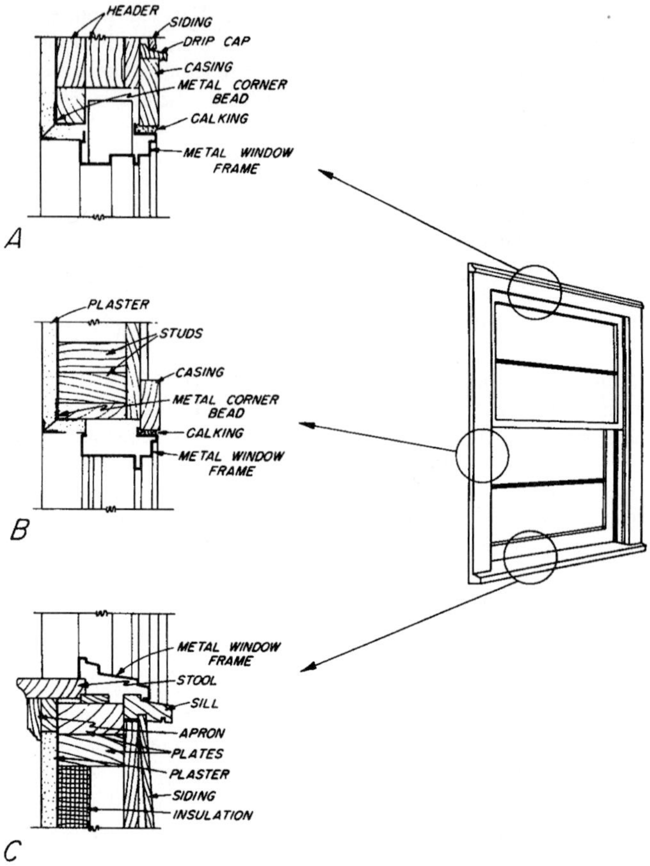

Fig. 5 Double-hung metal windows. Cross sections: *A*, head; *B*, side jamb; *C*, sill

Wood Trim

The casing around the window frames on the interior of the house should be the same pattern as that used around the interior door frames. Other trim which is used for a double-hung window frame includes the sash stops, stool, and apron (Fig. 7A). Another method of using trim around windows has the entire opening enclosed with casing (Fig. 7B). The stool is then a filler member between the bottom sash rail and the bottom casing.

The *stool* is the horizontal trim member that laps the window sill and extends beyond the casing at the sides, with each end notched against the plastered wall. The *apron* serves as a finish member below the stool. The window stool is the first piece of window trim to be installed and is notched and fitted against the edge of the jamb and the plaster line, with the outside edge being flush against the bottom rail of the window sash (Fig. 7A). The stool is blind-nailed at the ends so that the casing and the stop will cover the nailheads. Predrilling is usually necessary to prevent splitting. The stool should also be nailed at midpoint to the sill and to the apron with finishing nails. Face-nailing to the sill is sometimes substituted or supplemented with toe-nailing of the outer edge to the sill (Fig. 7A).

The casing is applied and nailed as described for door frames, except that the inner edge is flush with the inner face of the jambs so that the stop will cover the joint between the jamb and casing. The window stops are then nailed to the jambs so that the window sash slides smoothly. Channel-type weatherstripping often includes full-width metal subjambs into which the upper and lower sash slide, replacing the parting strip. Stops are located against these instead of the sash, to provide a small amount of pressure. The apron is cut to a length equal to the outer width of the casing line (Fig. 7A). It is nailed to the window sill and to the 2- by 4-in framing sill below.

When casing is used to finish the bottom of the window frame as well as the sides and top, the narrow stool butts against the side window jamb. Casing is then mitered at the bottom corners (Fig. 7B) and nailed as previously described.

CURTAINS/DRAPERIES

Curtains

Curtains are soft window coverings that generally are shirred (gathered onto a rod) or have headings attached to solid-wood rods, round or oval metal rods, or café rods rather than cord-operated traverse rods. Curtains may be either stationary fabric panels or slid open and closed by hand. They are flexible in that they can be short or long, layered or tiered, or used alone or in combination with other soft or

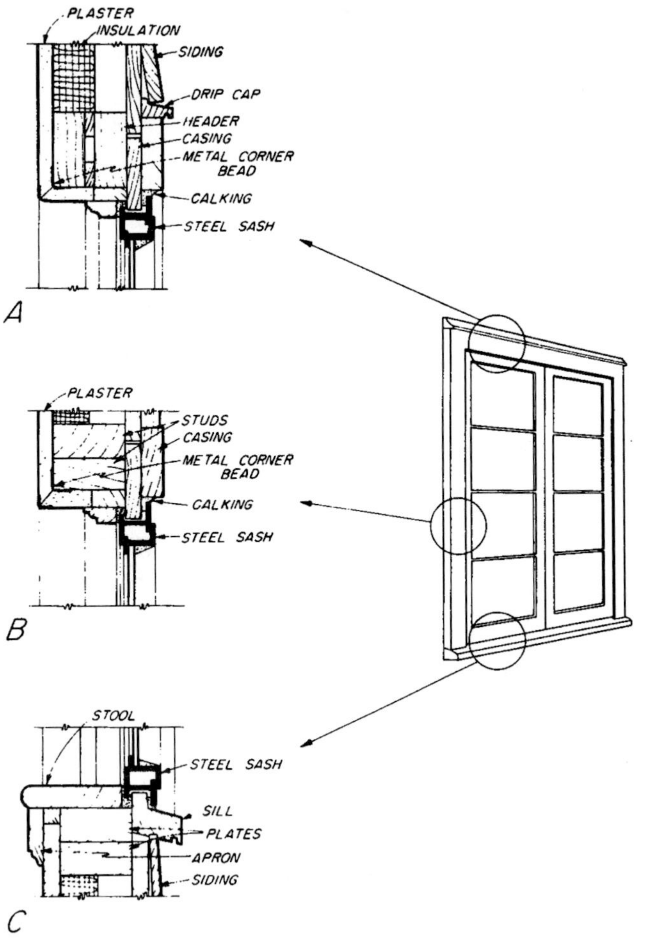

Fig. 6 Solid-section steel outswinging casement sash. Cross sections: *A*, head jamb; *B*, side jamb; *C*, sill

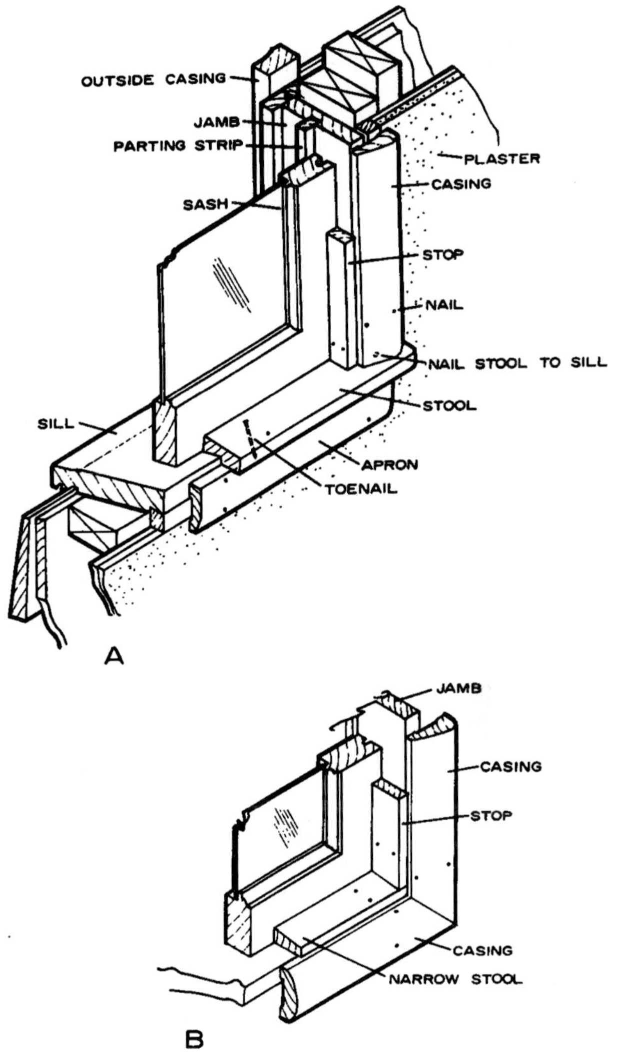

Fig. 7 Installation of window trim: *A*, with stool and apron; *B*, enclosed with casing

with hard treatments. *Curtain* is traditionally a term for informal treatments, such as café curtains. However, curtains also may be quite formal, as are shirred and elegant tied-back fabric treatments.

Even though curtains are generally thought to be shirred treatments, other headings might be included in this category. Indeed, there is a crossover of terminology between draperies and curtains. Generally draperies are installed on cord-operated traverse rods, although they may be stationary pleated panels. Curtains may be installed on traverse rods (as in a pleated café curtain, for example), and headings such as the pencil pleat, drawstring pencil pleat, shirred spaced pencil pleat, alternate pencil pleat, ruffled shirring tape heading, and smocked heading may be called either curtain or drapery treatments.

Draperies

Draperies are made with pleats. They are hung with drapery hoods onto carriers of conventional, architectural, or decorative traverse rods or into the rings of wood rods or café curtain rods, or they may thread onto spring-system traverse rods. Generally draperies are either hung straight to the floor or tied back. Thus they operate, or *draw,* by opening and closing with a cord or a wand or by hand. The

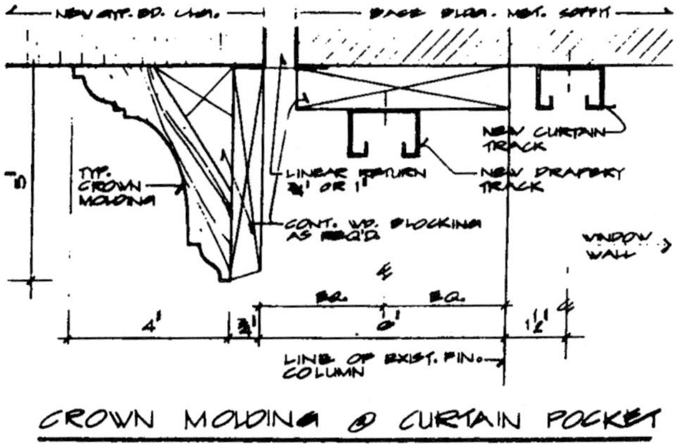

exception is tied-back draperies, which sometimes are let down at night. However, tied-back draperies are trained to tie back at an angle and therefore should not be handled to any extent. Draperies draw in a pair and meet in the center (center-meet) or draw one way from left to right or from right to left. One-way draw draperies require one-way traverse rods.

Draperies that hang at a doorway rather than at a window are called *portières*. They may be pleated in any fashion or shirred. They may be placed on a traverse rod, but historically (and they were used extensively in the Victorian era), they were tied-back stationary panels made of a heavy fabric that were let down when privacy or insulation was needed.

Draperies can be made of any fabric. The selection will depend on the style, use, and needs. Sheer fabrics do best as diffusers of glare and as providers of daytime privacy. Medium- to heavyweight fabrics are excellent choices for overdraperies and plain tieback draperies. Lining fabrics are the right weight for privacy liners or underdraperies. If a drapery is given a ruffled edge or a banding, that trim should be a lightweight, semicrisp, flexible fabric, not a heavy, stiff fabric or a sheer, slippery fabric.

Table 1 Draperies

Period style	Fabric	Colors	Design	Upholstery fabrics
Early English Tudor Jacobean Charles II	Crewel, embroideries, hand-blocked linen, silk and worsted damask, velvet, brocade	Full-bodied crimson, green, and yellow	Large bold patterns: tree branch, fruits, flowers, oak leaf, animals, heraldic designs	Tapestry, leather, needlework, velvet, brocade
Anglo-Dutch William & Mary Queen Anne	Crewel, embroideries, hand-blocked linen, silk and worsted damask, velvet, brocade, India print	Full-bodied crimson, green, and yellow	Large bold patterns: tree branch, fruits, flowers, oak leaf, animals, heraldic designs	Tapestry, leather, needlework, velvet, brocade
Early Georgian Chippendale	Crewel, embroideries, hand-blocked linen, silk and worsted damask, velvet, brocade, Indian print	Full-bodied crimson, green, and yellow	Jacobean motifs, classic medallions and garlands	Tapestry, leather, needlepoint, velvet, brocade
Late Georgian Adam Hepplewhite Sheraton Empire Federal	Brocade, damask, chintz, taffeta, satin, toile de jouy	Delicate subdued hues of rose, yellow, mauve, green, and gray	Classic designs, small in scale: garlands, urns, floral, animals, etc.	Damask, brocade, velour, satin, petit point, leather in libraries
Louis XIV Louis XV Louis XVI	Silk, satin, damask, taffeta, muslin, brocade, toile de jouy	Delicate powder blue, oyster white, pearl, rose, pale greens, mauve, yellow	Stripes sprinkled with ribbons, flowers, medallions, lyres, and other classic motifs	Petit point, satin, moire, velour, chintz, damask, brocade, tapestry
Spanish renaissance	Velvet, damask, crewel, India print, printed and embroidered linen	Rich vigorous colors, red, green, and gold	Bold patterns in classic and heraldic designs; also arabesques	Leather, tapestry, velvet, linen, brocatelle
Early colonial	Crewel, embroideries, hand-blocked linen, silk and worsted damask, velvet, brocade	Full-bodied crimson, green, and yellow	Large bold patterns: tree branch, fruits, flowers, oak leaf, animals, heraldic designs	Tapestry, leather, needlepoint, velvet, brocade
Early American	Toile de jouy, damask, chintz, organdy, cretonne	All colors, but more subdued than in early period	Scenic, birds, animals, floral	Haircloth, mohair, linen, chintz, velours
Modern	Textured and novelty weaves, all fabrics	All colors, bright to pastel	Solid colors, modern designs, stripes	All fabrics, novelty weaves, plastics
French provincial	Chintz, cretonne, hand-blocked linen, velvet	Subdued colors, pastel shades	Screen prints, block prints	Solid colors, textured weaves, tapestry
Victorian	Velvet, brocade, damask	Turkey red, other rich colors	Solid colors, formal patterns	Haircloth, needlework

Decorative Rods

Measuring for Most Windows

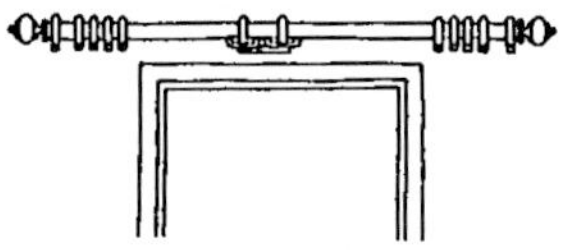

Outside mount Decorative rods should be mounted on the wall. Measure width of glass; if total glass exposure is desired, add for stackback (see Table 4). Rods should be hung so that drapery headings (pleated tops of panels) are at least 4 in above the glass, so they can't be seen from the outside.

Figuring Stackback

Stackback is the amount of wall space needed if open panels are to clear the glass completely. This dimension, added to the window opening, gives you the proper rod length.

Begin by measuring the window opening, then consult Table 4. Find your opening measurement and read across for the right rod length.

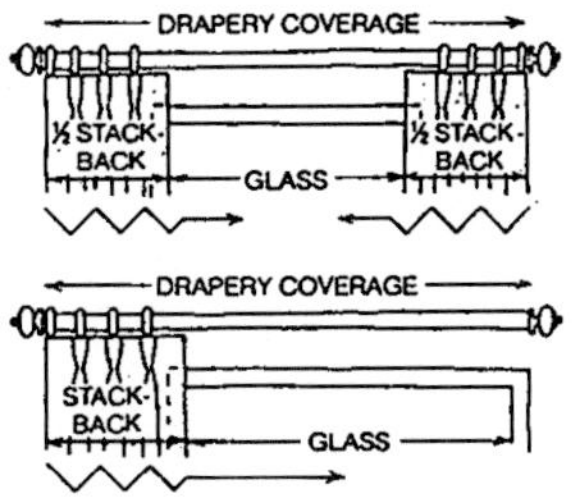

Table 4 Stackback: average pleating and medium weight fabric

Window opening	Stackback*	Rod length
24″	21″	45″
30″	23″	53″
36″	25″	61″
42″	26″	68″
48″	29″	77″
54″	30″	84″
60″	31″	91″
66″	32″	98″
72″	34″	106″
78″	36″	114″
84″	37″	121″
90″	38″	128″
96″	39″	135″
102″	42″	144″
108″	44″	152″
114″	45″	159″
120″	48″	168″

*Deduct 7″ for one-way draw.

Measuring for Special Windows

Sliding doors Measure as for outside mounted rod. Convert rod from two- to one-way draw.

Corner and bay windows Decorative rods may be used at these windows. However, it is best to consult your dealer or designer about the measuring.

Layered Treatments

Decorative traverse rods are often used for overtreatments. If the undertreatment is inside mounted or is an outside-mounted miniblind, pleated shade, Romanette woven wood, or a café curtain, set the brackets for maximum clearance. Drapery returns will be 4½ in.

If you are using an undercurtain, you will want a utility curtain rod. It comes with its own bracket supports.

If you are using underdraperies, double brackets are available. They hold both rods and automatically align the headings. Overdrapery returns will be 6 to 7 in.

If using a decorative rod over an outside mounted vertical blind or a woven wood shade other than Romanette, special brackets are available. Overdrapery returns will be 6 to 7 in.

Pleated Shades

Measuring for Most Windows

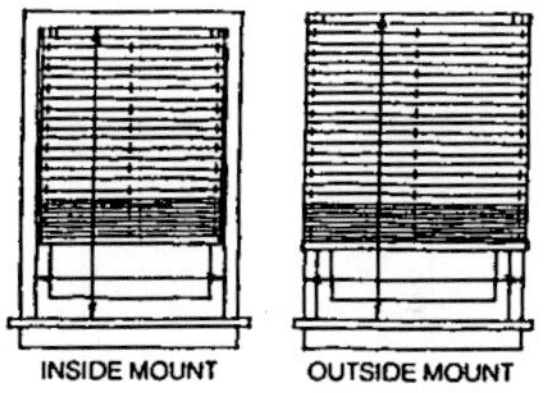

Inside mount Measure width at top, center, and bottom. Use narrowest measurement. Shades will be made narrower to slip inside easily. Measure length from inside top of opening to sill. A 1⅝-in-deep recess is needed for flush mounting; 2¼ in for Duette in ¾.

Outside mount Measure width of opening. Add at least 1½ in on each side for overlap. Measure from top of frame to sill or 1½ in below opening if there is no sill. (If brackets are to go above window frame, add an extra 1½ in for bracket bases.)

Ceiling mount Measure desired width and length of blind. Overlap window openings by at least 1½ in on each side.

Measuring for Special Windows

Multiple shades At very wide or sectioned windows and at sliding doors, it's wise to use two shades hung from one headrail. Make a drawing of the window; include measurements of glass, woodwork, and overall size. Your dealer will do the rest.

Corner windows Inside-mounted shades need no special measuring instructions. If outside- or ceiling-mounted shades are used, they can be overlapped. Make a drawing of the windows; include measurements of glass, woodwork, and overall size. Your dealer will do the rest.

WINDOW TREATMENTS
Guidelines

Other special windows Bays and other unusual windows can frequently be fitted for pleated shades. Make a drawing of the window; include measurements of glass, woodwork, and overall size, or ask your dealer to do the measuring for you.

Layered Treatments

Pleated shades are most often used with an undertreatment. If inside mounted, no extra projection is needed for the overtreatment. If outside mounted, the overtreatment must have a clearance of 2½ in to clear the headrail. A cornice used over pleated shades should have a 4½-in return.

Table 5 Stack chart

Shade length	Stack
24″	1¾″
36″	1⅞″
48″	2″
60″	2⅛″
72″	2¼″
84″	2⅜″
96″	2½″

Measurements are from top of headrail to bottom of bottom rail.

Conventional Traverse Rods

Measuring for Most Windows

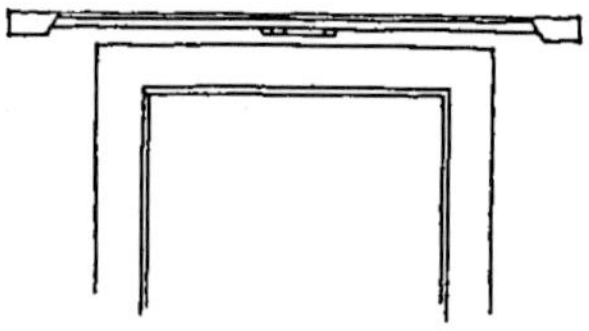

Outside or ceiling mount Conventional rods may be mounted on the wall or ceiling. Measure the width of glass; if total glass exposure is desired, add for stackback (see Table 4). Rods should be hung so that drapery headings (pleated tops of panels) are at least 4 in above the glass, so they can't be seen from the outside.

Figuring Stackback

Stackback is the amount of wall space needed if open panels are to clear the glass completely. This dimension, added to the window opening, gives you the proper rod length.

Begin by measuring the window opening, then consult Table 4. Find your opening measurement and read across the right rod length.

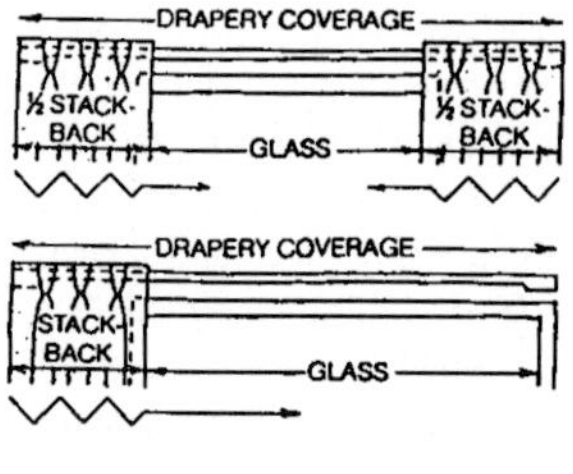

Measuring for Special Windows

Sliding doors Measure as for outside mounted rod. Use a one-way draw rod.

Corner and bay windows Measure each window as if it were set flat into the wall. At corners, run one rod into the corner and butt the other into it. At bays, butt all rods. Use either one- or two-way draw rods for corners. For bays, use 3 two-way rods or 2 one-ways with a two-way in the center.

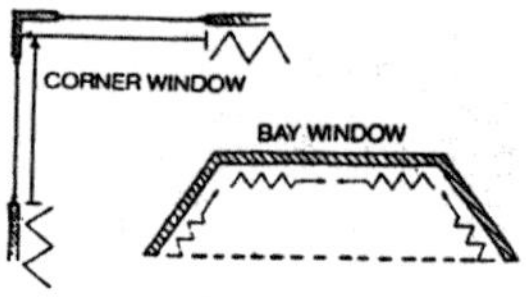

Layered Treatments

Conventional traverse rods come in sets specifically for layered treatments. If you are using an undercurtain, you will want a traverse and plain rod set; both rods are on one set of brackets. Overdrapery returns will be 4½ to 5½ in.

If you are using underdraperies, use a double traverse rod set. Again, one set of brackets holds both rods. Overdrapery returns will be 5½ to 6½ in.

If the undertreatment is inside mounted or is an outside-mounted miniblind, pleated shade. Romanette woven wood, or a café curtain, use a single rod and set the brackets for maximum clearance. Drapery returns will be 4½ in.

If the undertreatment is an outside-mounted vertical blind or a woven wood shade other than Romanette, special extender plates for brackets and supports are available. Overdrapery returns will be 5½ to 6½ in.

Remember, whenever you change the clearance of the brackets, you also change the drapery return.

Vertical Blinds

Measuring for Most Windows

Inside mount Measure width at top, center, and bottom. Use narrowest measurement. Verticals will be made slightly narrower to slip inside easily. Measure length from inside top of opening to sill. A minimum 3¼-in recess is required for track; 4½-in if open vanes are to be flush with front of opening.

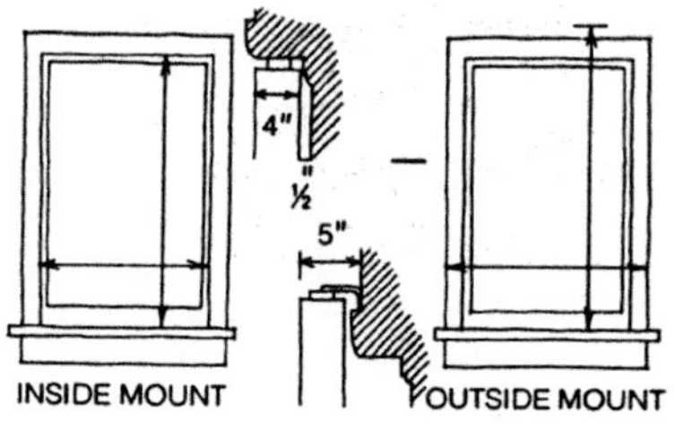

Outside mount Measure width of opening. Add for stackback (see Tables 6 and 7). Measure from a point 2½ in above top of frame to sill or floor; deduct ¾ in for clearance.

Minimum projection of front of vane from wall is 5 in; maximum is 6½ in. Minimum clearance of back of vane from wall is 1 in; maximum is 2½ in.

Ceiling mount Measure desired width and length of verticals; deduct at least ¾ in for floor clearance.

Cirmosa 2000 Ask your designer, decorator, or store to measure for you.

Measuring for Special Windows

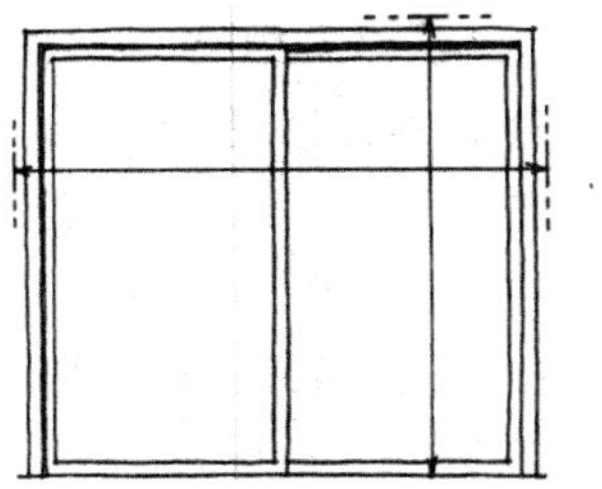

Sliding doors Use a one-way draw. Measure width from trim to trim. Add to this measurement desired extra width for overlap beyond door. If total glass exposure is desired, also add for stackback (see Tables 6 and 7). Measure from a point 2½ in above door trim to floor; deduct ¾ in for clearance.

Layered Treatments

When layered, verticals are most often used as an undertreatment. If inside mounted, no extra clearance is needed for the overtreatment. If outside mounted, the overtreatment must have a clearance of 6 in to clear the open vanes. A cornice used over verticals should have a 6-in return.

Table 6 Two-way draw stackback

Window opening	Stackback	Track
24"	9"	33"
30"	10"	40"
36"	11"	47"
42"	12"	54"
48"	14"	62"
54"	15"	69"
60"	16"	76"
66"	17"	83"
72"	19"	91"
78"	20"	98"
84"	21"	105"
90"	22"	112"
96"	23"	119"
102"	25"	127"
108"	26"	134"
114"	27"	141"
120"	29"	149"

Table 7 One-way draw stackback

Window opening	Stackback	Track
24"	7"	31"
30"	8"	38"
36"	9"	45"
42"	11"	53"
48"	12"	60"
54"	13"	67"
60"	14"	74"
66"	15"	81"
72"	17"	89"
78"	18"	96"
84"	19"	103"
90"	20"	110"
96"	21"	117"
102"	22"	124"
108"	23"	131"
114"	25"	139"
120"	26"	146"

Figuring Stackback

Stackback is the amount of wall space needed if open verticals are to clear the glass completely. This dimension, added to the window opening, gives you the proper track length.

Begin by measuring the window opening, then consult Table 6 or 7 for the type of treatment you desire—one- or two-way draw. Find your opening measurement and read across for the right track. (NOTE: Stackback figure for two-way draw is total stack; one-half of this is on each side of the window.)

If your window opening is somewhere in between the measurements in the tables, go to the next smallest opening. Add the stackback listed there to your opening dimension.

Miniblinds

Measuring for Most Windows

Inside mount Measure width at top, center, and bottom. Use narrowest measurement. Blinds will be made slightly narrower to slip inside easily. Measure length from inside top of open to sill. A 1⅜-in-deep recess is needed for flush mounting of Mono-Rail minis; however, a difference of ¼-in is not objectionable.

Outside mount Measure height and width of area to be covered. It is recommended that blinds overlap window opening by at least 1½-in on each side. Measure from top of frame to sill or 1½ in below opening if there is no sill.

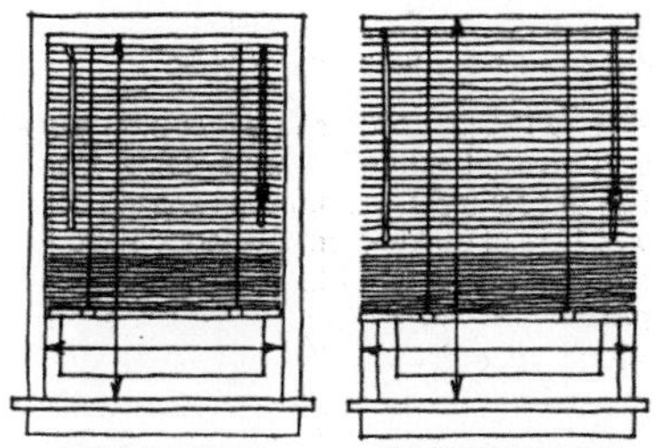

WINDOW TREATMENTS
Guidelines

Ceiling mount Measure desired width and length of blind. Overlap window openings by at least 1½-in on each side.

Table 8 Stack chart

Window opening	Stackback	Track
24″	7″	31″
30″	8″	38″
36″	9″	45″
42″	11″	53″
48″	12″	60″
54″	13″	67″
60″	14″	74″
66″	15″	81″
72″	17″	89″
78″	18″	96″
84″	19″	103″
90″	20″	110″
96″	21″	117″
102″	22″	124″
108″	23″	131″
114″	25″	139″
120″	26″	146″

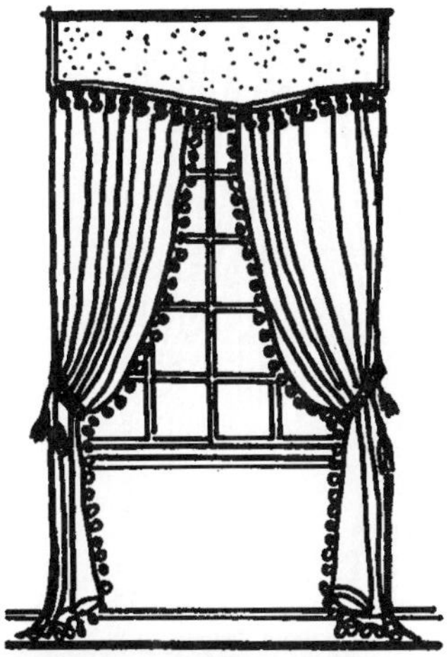

18th-century colonial: tieback damask drapery with balled fringe

18th-century colonial: staggered tieback with plain edge asymmetric panels

18th-century colonial: swagged valance over bishop sleeve draperies over holdback

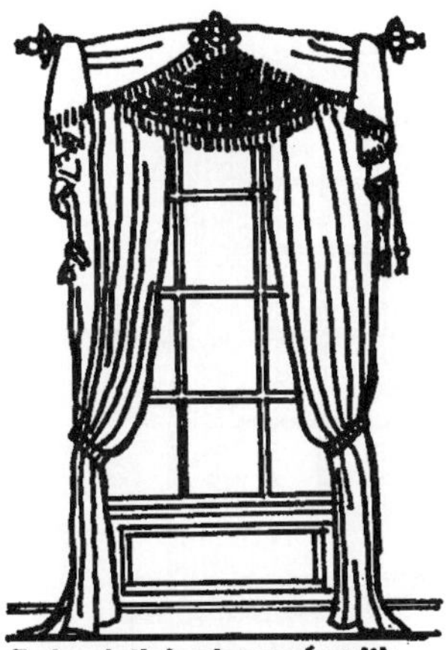

Federal: tieback panels with fringed raised valance of contrasting color

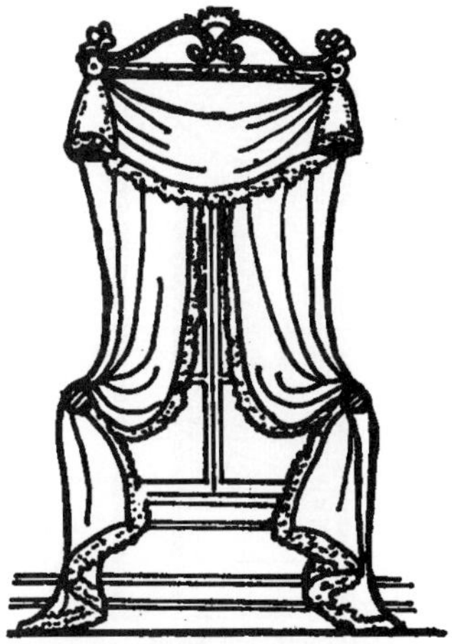

Federal: waterfall over holdback with draped valance

Federal: asymmetric tieback with fringed valance

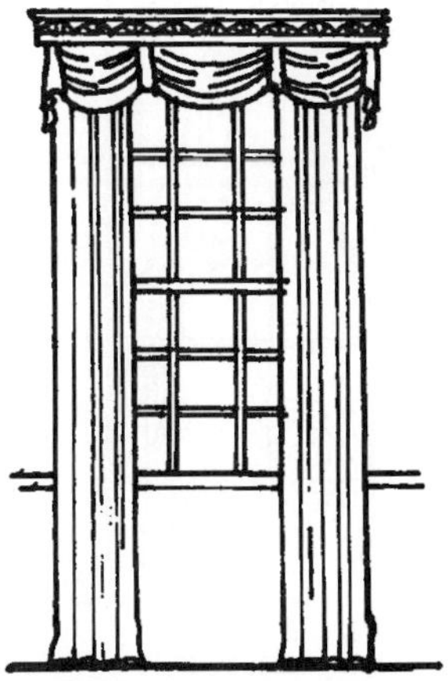

Federal: heavy valance over straight draperies

WINDOW TREATMENTS

Curtains/Draperies of Georgian and Directoire Periods

Georgian: tieback drapery with Austrian valance with fringes

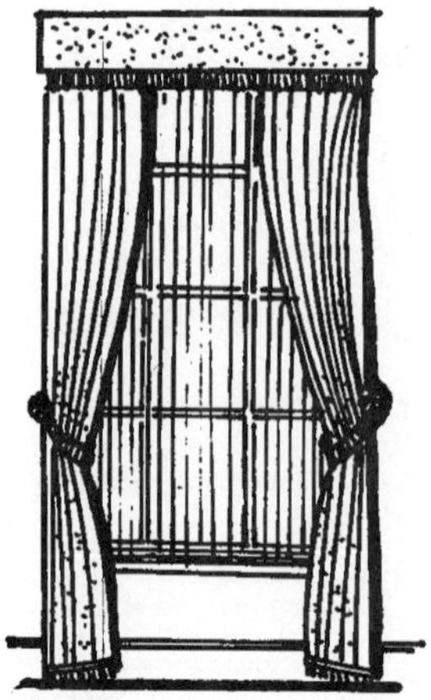

Georgian: tieback heavy woven drapery with fabric-covered heading – sheer curtains behind

Georgian: tieback drapery with tapered French pleat heading

Late Georgian: curved fabric cartridge valance over holdback draperies

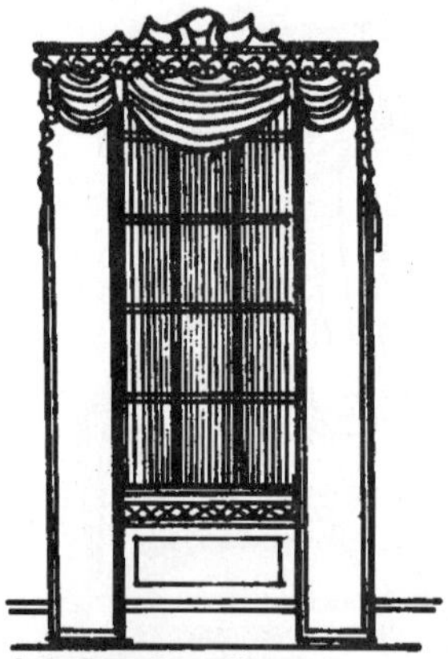

Late Georgian: gilt wood cornice over fixed lambrequins and sheer curtains

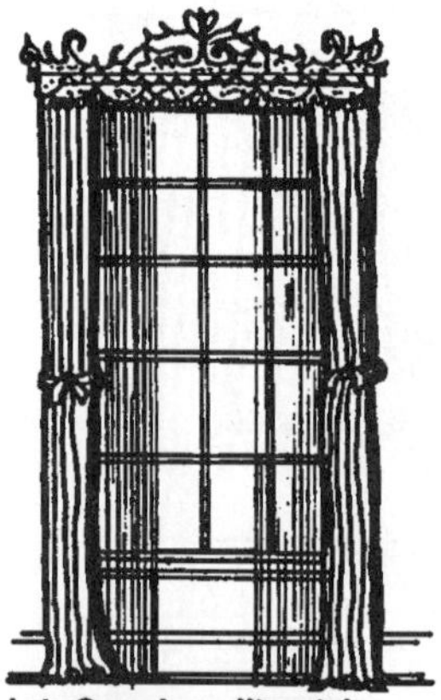

Late Georgian: gilt metal cornice over fixed tieback draperies and sheer curtains

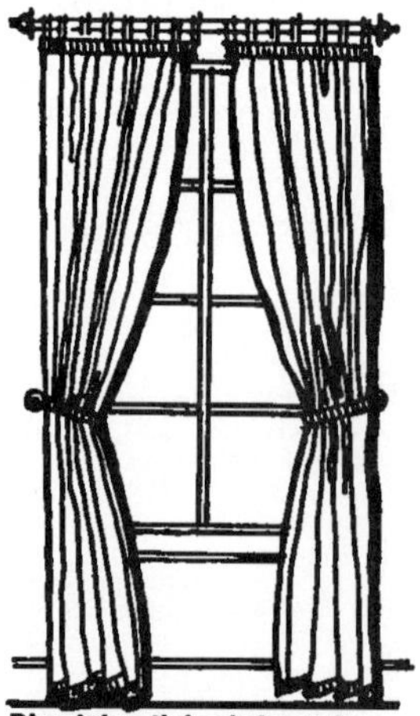

Directoire: tieback draperies with contrasting edging on decorative brass rod

Directoire: fringed overdrapery valance on fringed sleeved tiebacks and fringed drapery

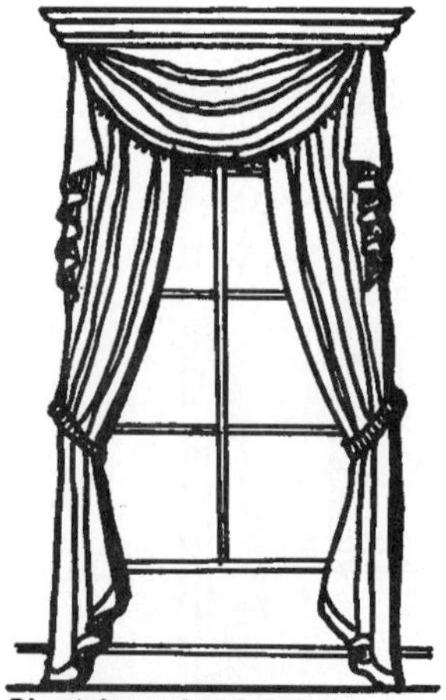

Directoire: painted stepped wood cornice over swag with twin cascades and tieback draperies

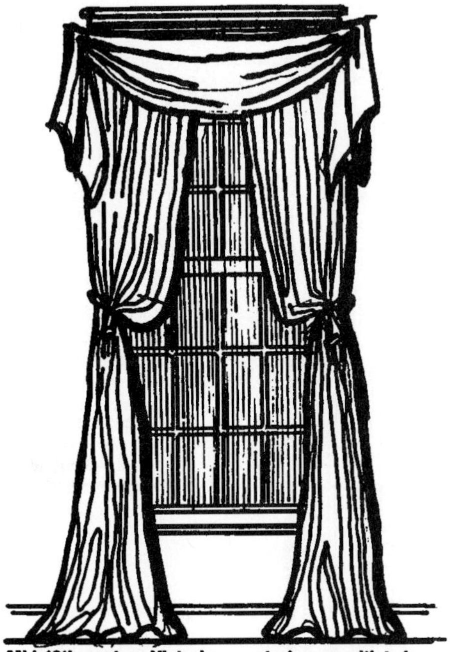

Mid-19th-century Victorian: central swag with twin cascades over heavy draperies with braided tieback over sheer undercurtain

Late-19th-century Victorian: looped festoon over decorative brass rod

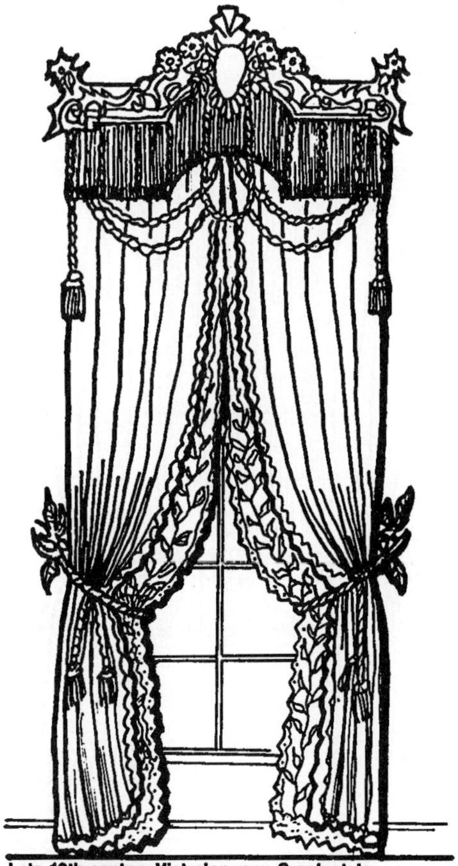

Late-19th-century Victorian: neo-Greek-style cornice with fringed valance over tieback fringed fabric with lace undercurtains

WINDOW TREATMENTS
Curtains/Draperies of 1940s

Fringed finger festoon over brackets over straight line draperies with sheer undercurtains

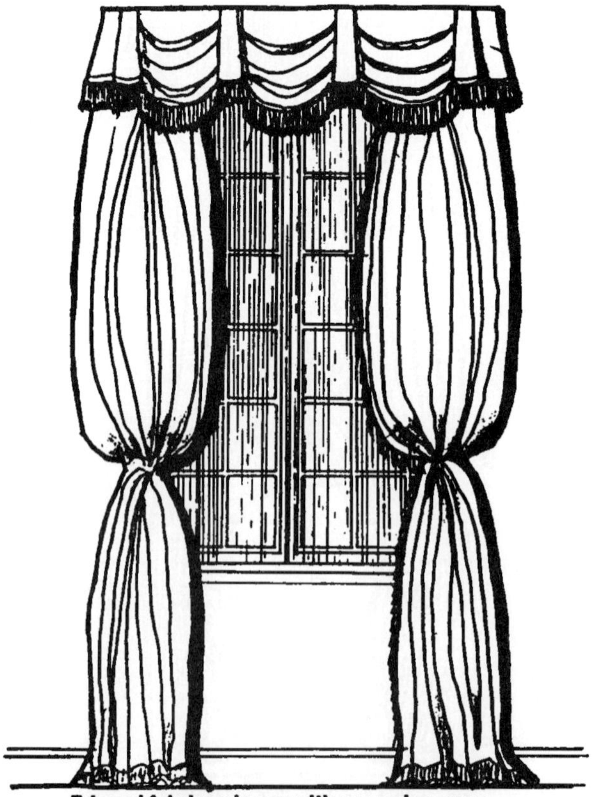

Fringed fabric valance with cascades over bishop sleeve draperies

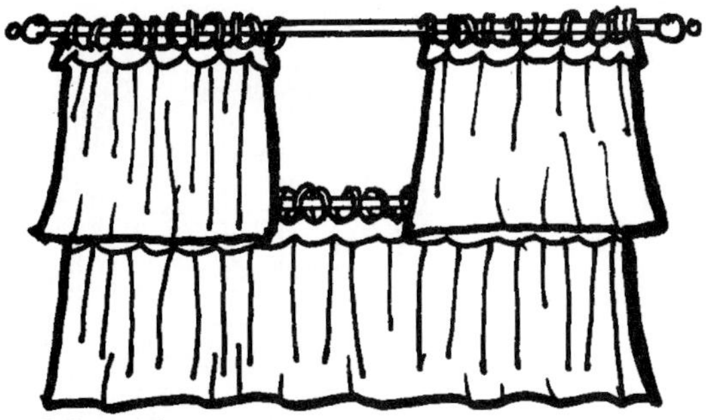

Cafe curtains

Ruffled tieback curtains

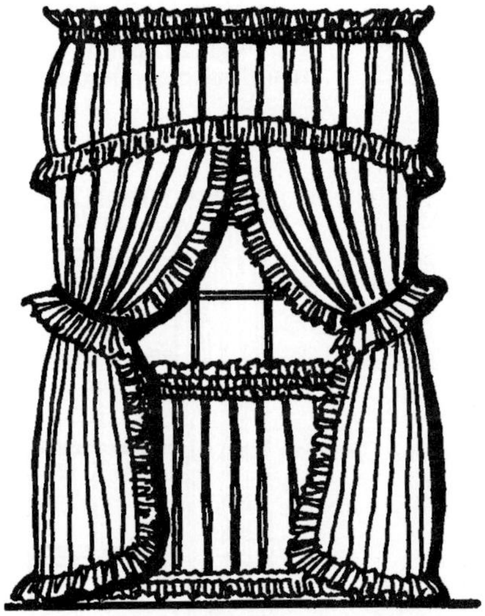

Fringed segmented valance with ruffled trim – tieback draperies over café curtains

Fabric-wrapped-pole draped valance

Café curtains with gathered valance and ball fringe trim

WINDOW TREATMENTS
Curtains/Draperies

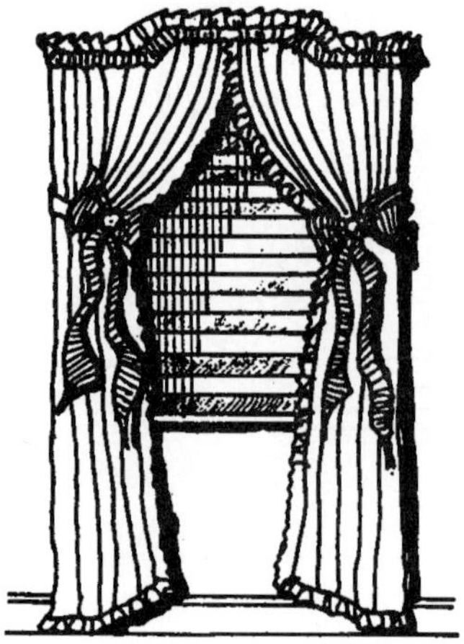

Tieback draperies with ruffles on center arch rod — pleated shade beneath

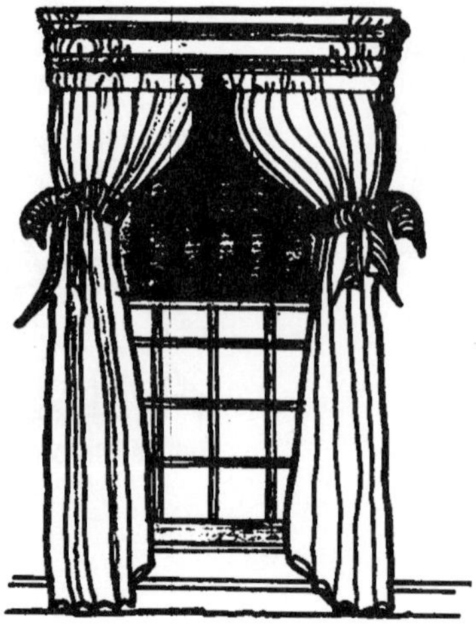

High tieback draperies with ruffled multirow valance — woven shade beneath

Full-length straight draperies with ruffled valance — decorative bows

Shirred, ruffled balloon valance over ruffled, shirred heading on narrow rod

Shirred heading on brass pole — fixed draperies with rosette tieback

Shirred heading on brass pole — fixed panel draperies

Shirred balance with shirred tieback draperies over blinds

Penta balloon valance over ribbon tieback draperies

Shirred valance with horizontal accent banding — tieback draperies with matching edge banding

Bishop sleeve fringed-tip valance with ribbon tieback draperies

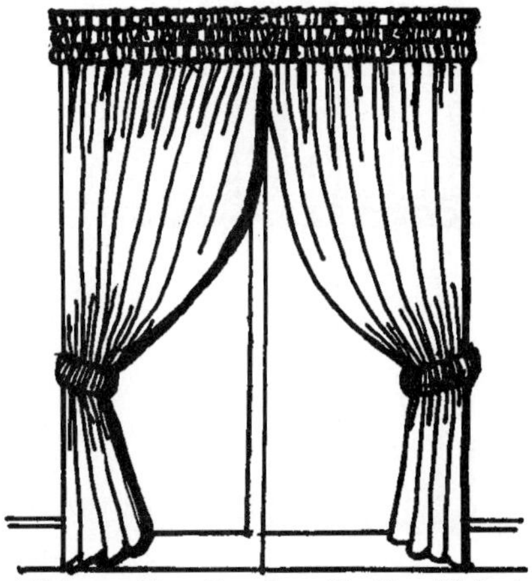

Triple-row fringed heading with shirred tieback draperies

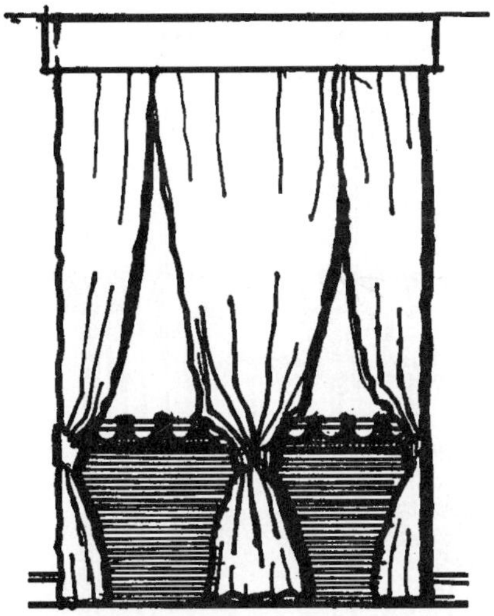

Fabric-covered straight cornice over paired tieback draperies and scalloped curtain on brass rod

Pinch pleated draperies with horizontal tiebacks over standard roller shades

WINDOW TREATMENTS
Curtains/Draperies

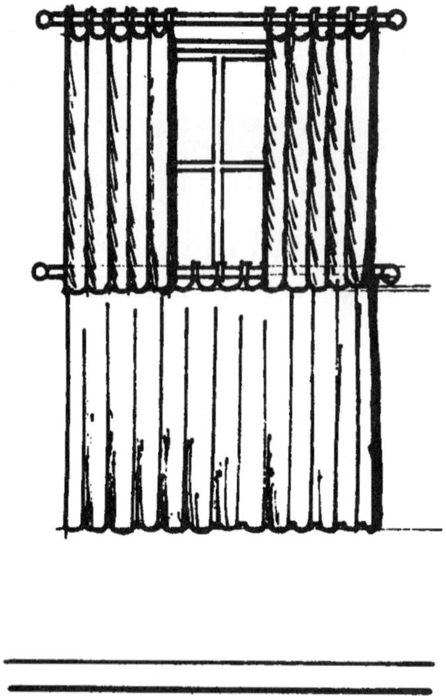

Café curtains with scalloped edges on brass rods

Single pleated draperies over paired double hung windows with tab headed café curtains on rod

Fabric-covered cornice board valance – ribbon tiebacks on drapery

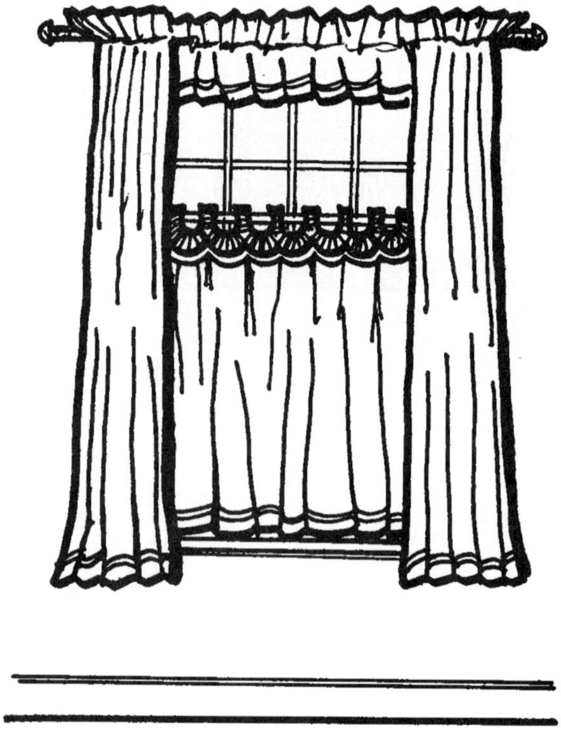

Ruffled valance heading over brass rod with straight draperies over scalloped café curtain

Simple traditional swag with cascade draperies

Rosette tieback priscilla curtains with continental heading

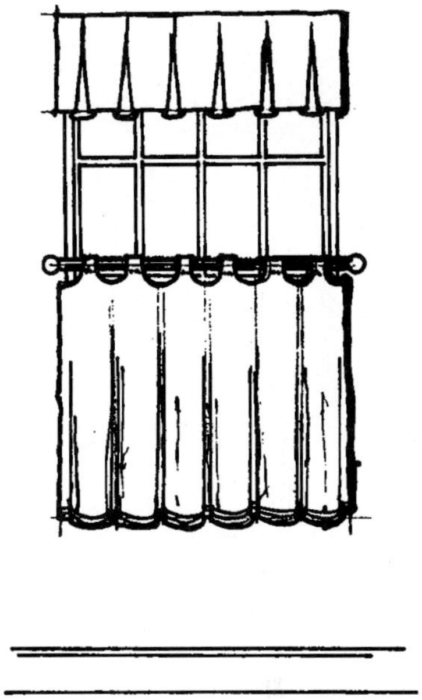

Scalloped café curtains on brass rod with pleated valance

Bow tieback curtains with fringed trim and gathered valance

Bow tieback gathered curtains on brass rod

WINDOW TREATMENTS
Curtains/Draperies

Overlapping swag on rod with ball-fringed cascades

Swag with bow and asymmetric cascades

Symmetrical swags and cascades with center rosette

Symmetrical draped swag over brass rod

Asymmetrical swag drapery over brass rod with sheer curtain

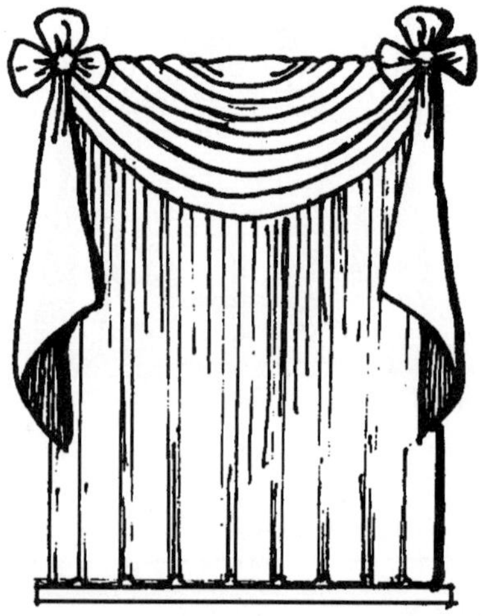

Symmetrical draped swag on rod with ties at end over sheer or solid curtain

Triple-tail cascades with dual swags and rosette holds

Swag over rod with rosette holds

Swag, draped valance, cascading ends

WINDOW TREATMENTS
Curtains/Draperies

Asymmetrical double-rod-supported swags and draperies – contemporary

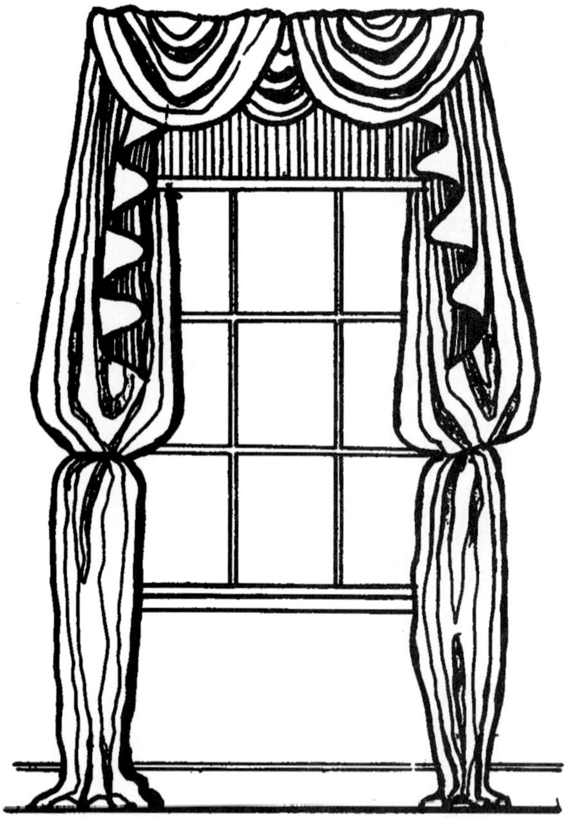

Symmetrical long cascades and swags with center swag and bishop sleeve draperies

Overlapped double swag thrown over door-high holdbacks, with draperies billowed at floor

Flared cornice box with geometric trimmed scallops over reverse swags and asymmetric floor-tip cascades

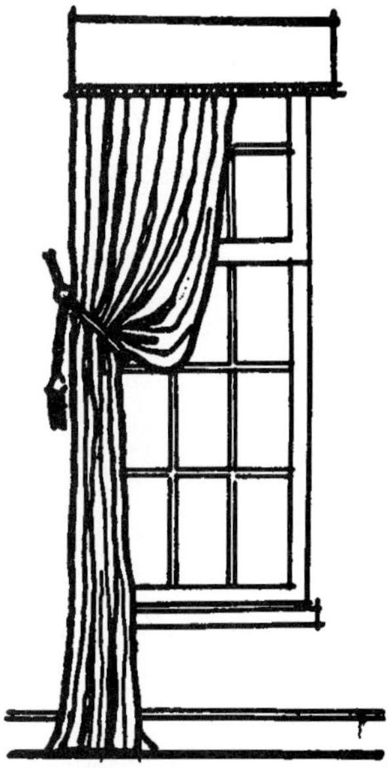

Trimmed cornice box over asymmetric tieback drapery

Symmetrical box-pleated draperies on brass rod with double-tiered rosette holdbacks

WINDOW TREATMENTS
Curtains/Draperies

Pleated shade

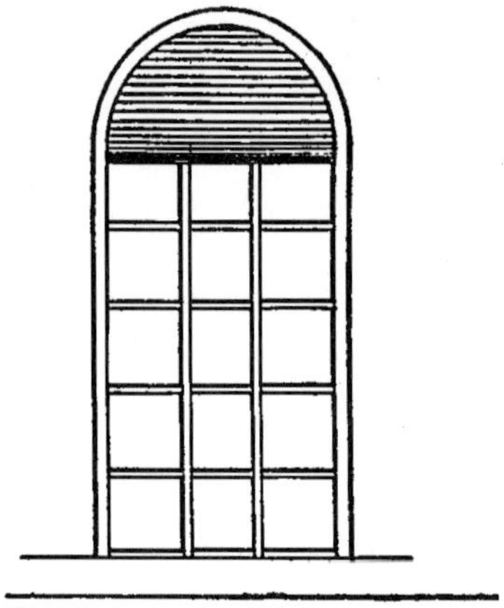

Miniblind – custom fitted

Wooden shutters

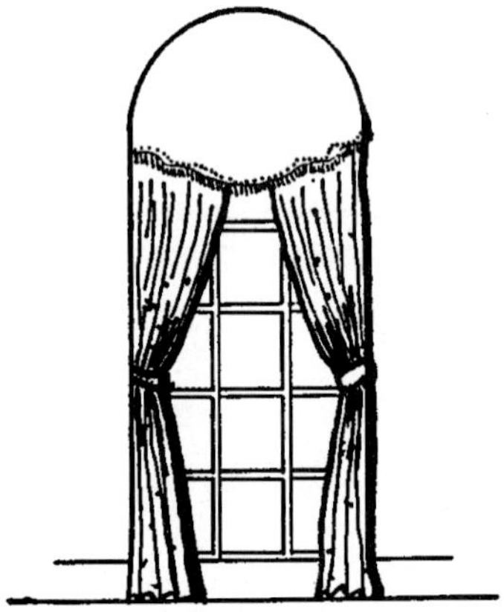

Rounded valance with drapery

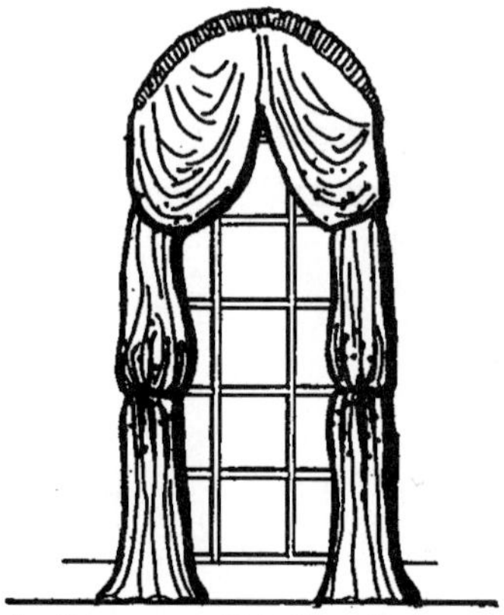

Double swags with balloon drapery

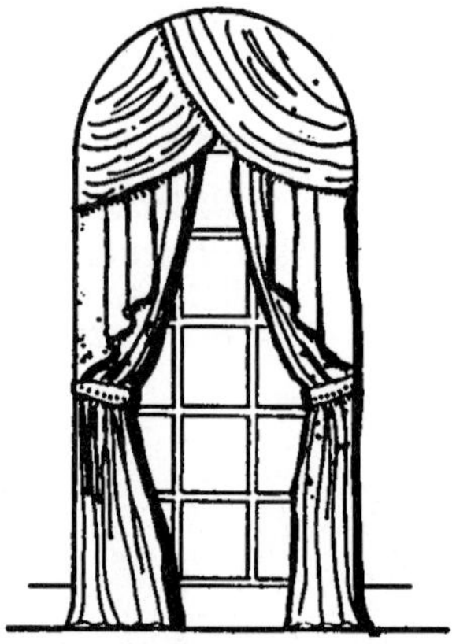

Double swags with cascades and drapery

Shirred curtain with sunburst

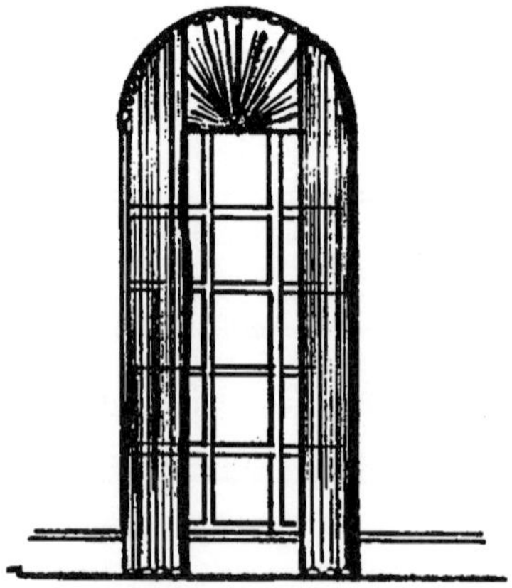

Pleated shade with shirred curtain

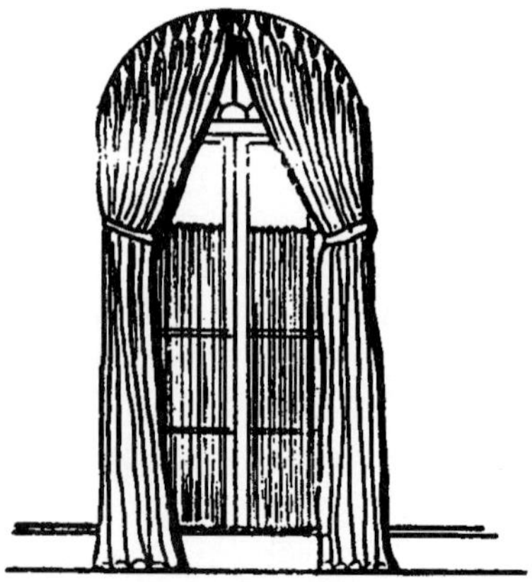

French pleats with shaped top under curtain

Semiformal box pleats, evenly spaced

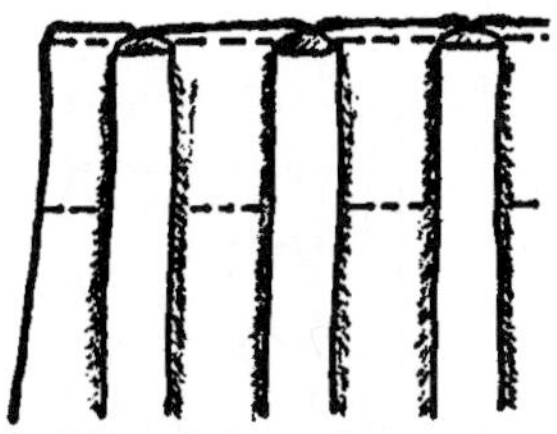
Cartridge pleat, evenly spaced

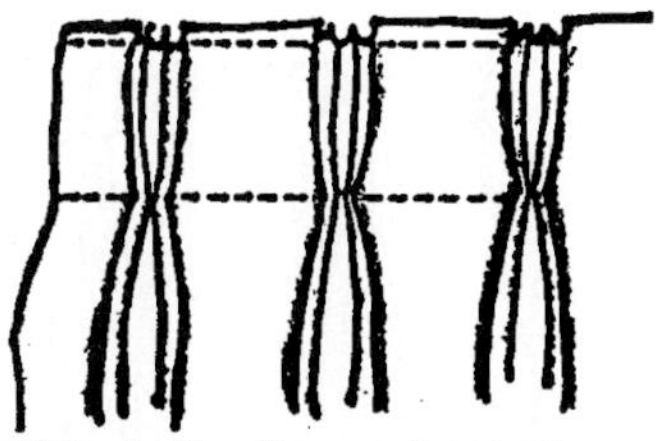
Triple pleat heading, evenly spaced

Shirred heading on a narrow rod

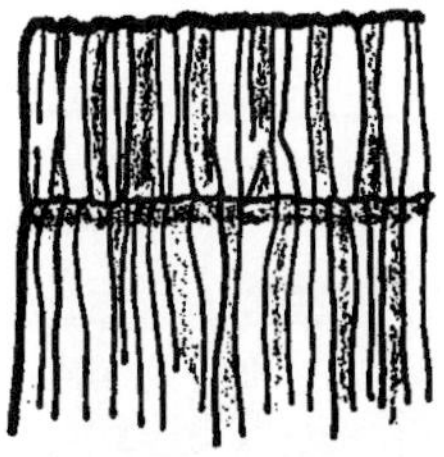
Shirred heading gathering on a wide rod

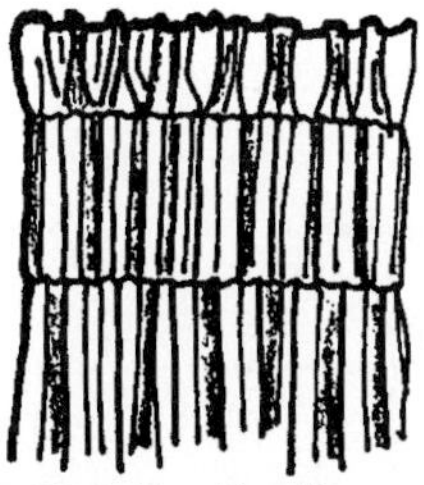
Ruffled shirred heading on an extra- wide rod

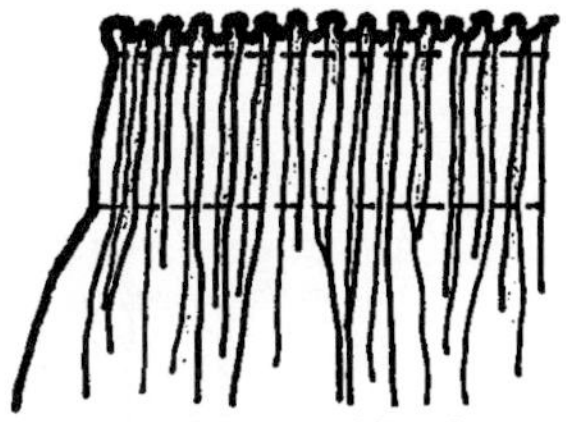
Pencil heading on a wide rod

Shirred heading gathered on an extra-wide rod

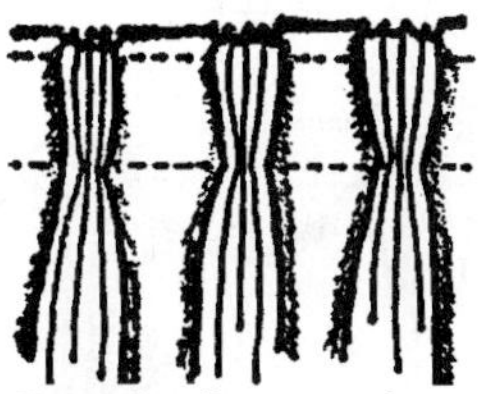
Cluster heading, spaced evenly

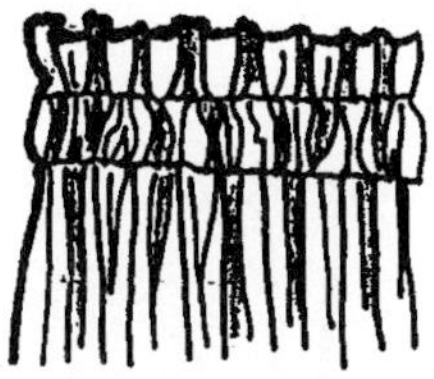
Ruffled shirred heading on a narrow rod

Standard heading on a narrow rod

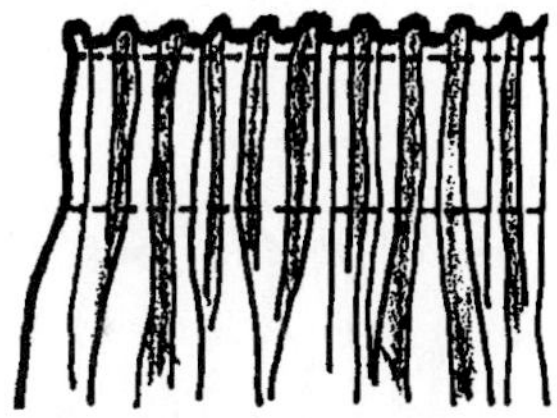
Spaced pencil pleats heading on a wide rod

WINDOW TREATMENTS
Headings

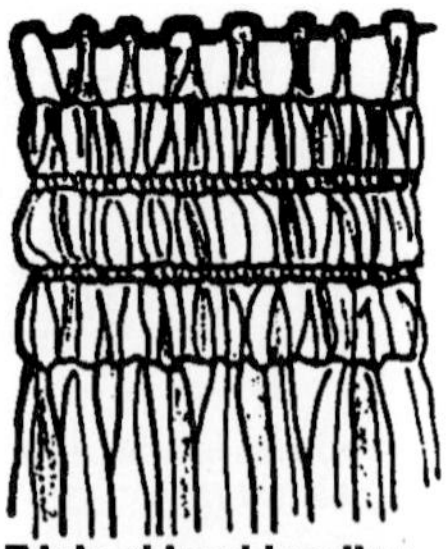

Triple shirred heading with ruffle gathered on 3 narrow rods

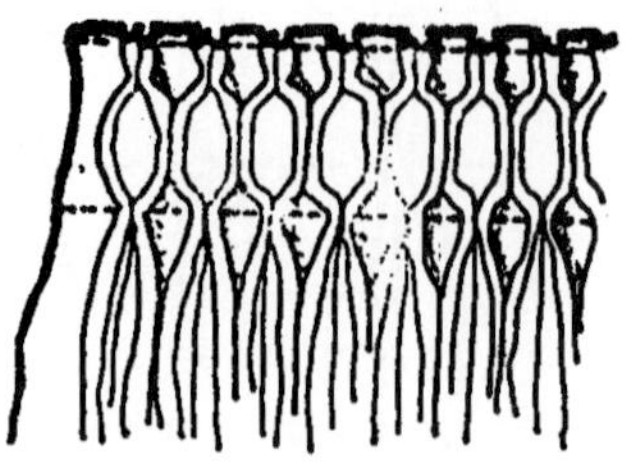

Decorative heading on a wide rod

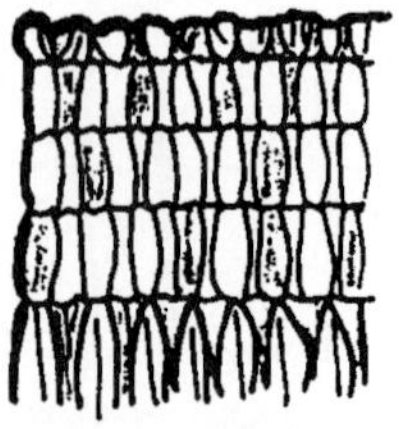

Triple shirred heading gathered on 3 narrow rods

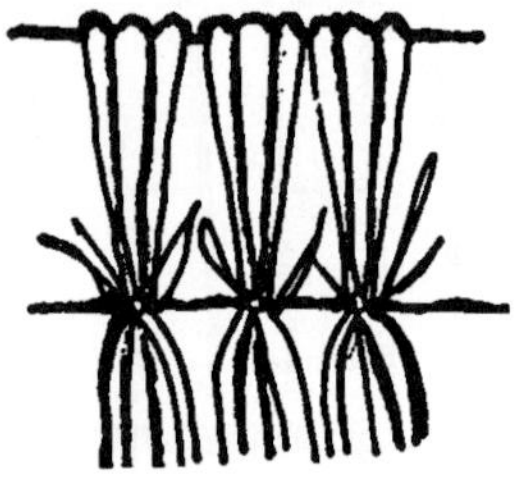

Grouped French pleats

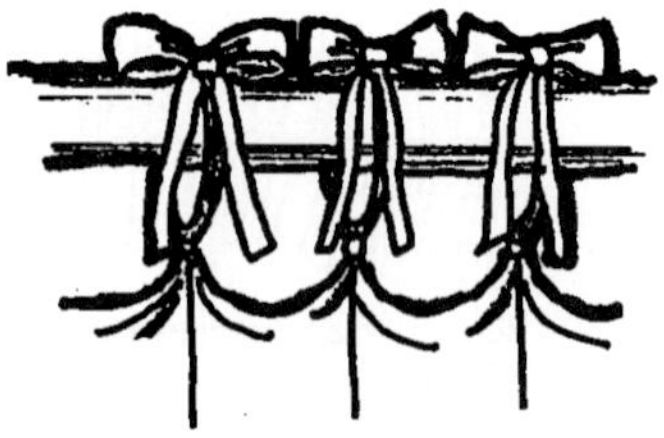

Scalloped heading with rings and bows

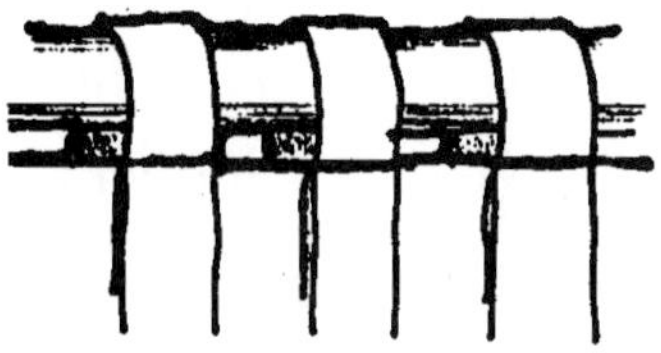

Tab heading spaced evenly on rod

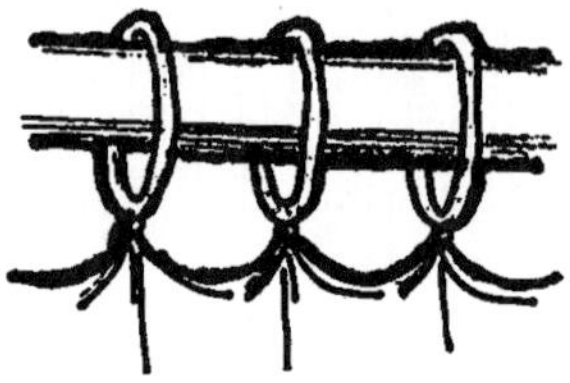

Scalloped heading with rings

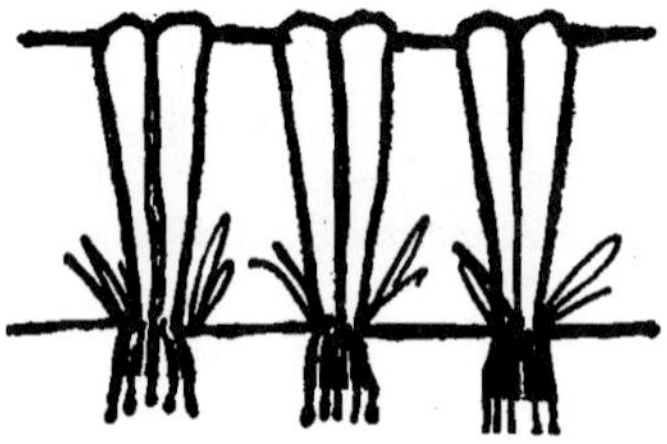

Double butterfly pleat heading

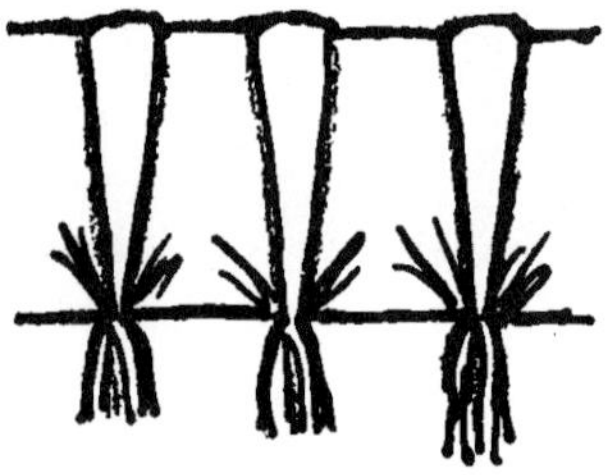

Single butterfly pleat heading

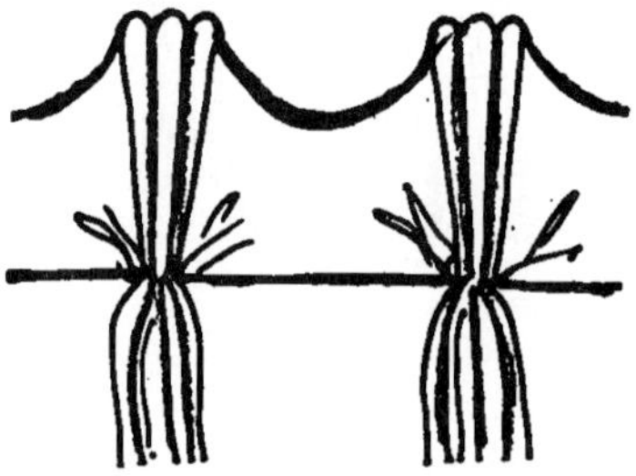

French pleats with scalloped heading

WINDOW TREATMENTS
Tiebacks and Holdbacks

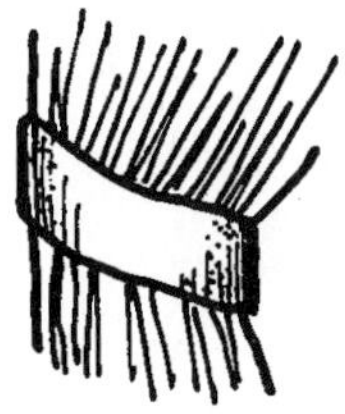
Straight

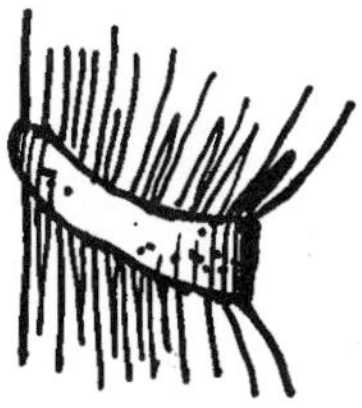
Tapered

Banded

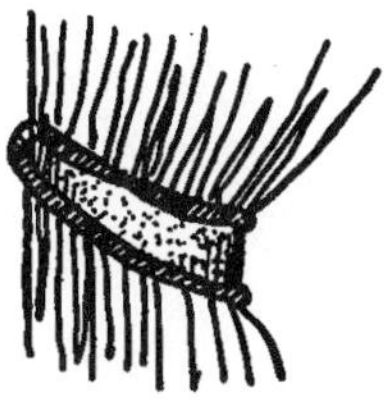
Tapered with welting

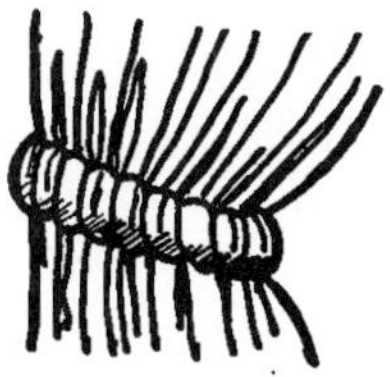
Oversized welting

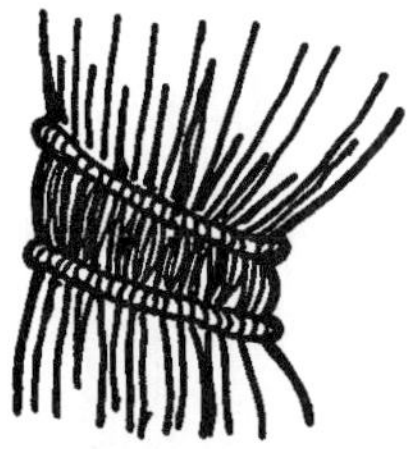
Shirred with welting

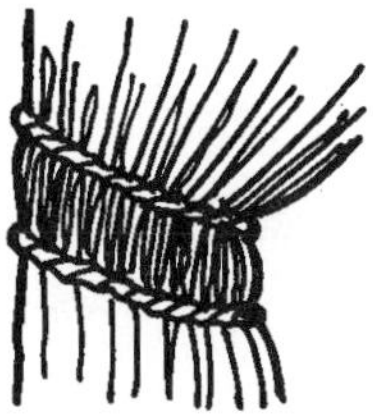
Shirred with braided trim

Braided

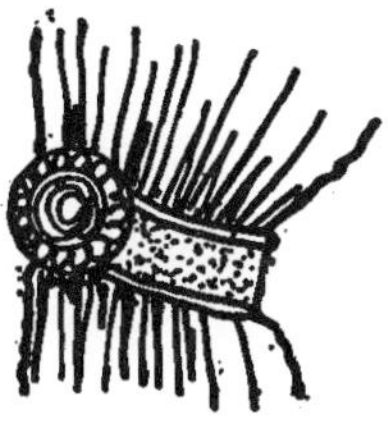
Rosette

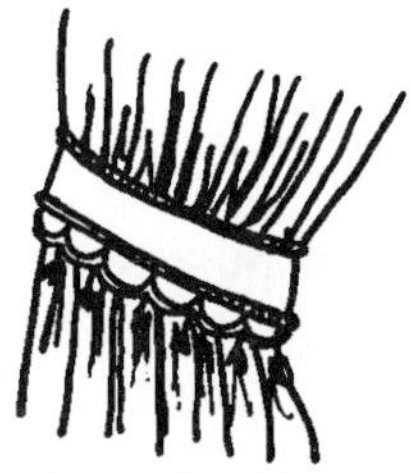
Fringed with welting

Scalloped

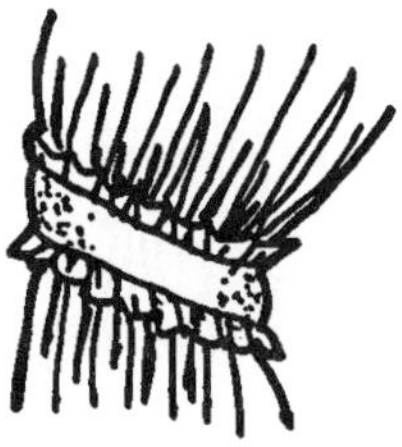
Frilled

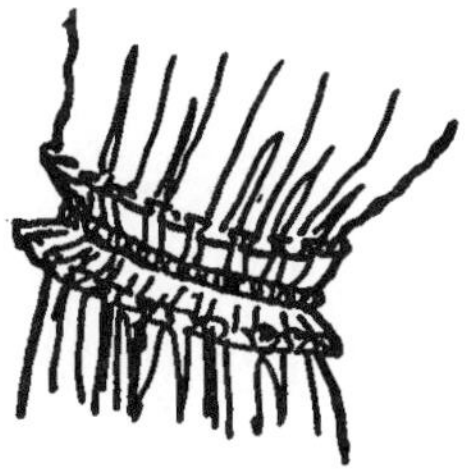
Twin ruffles

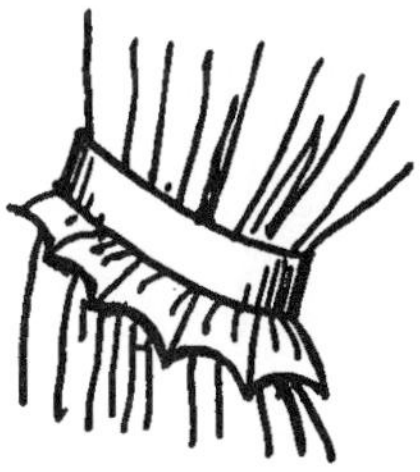
Straight with scallops

Twin welting with box pleating

Rosette with cascade

Ruffles

Bow/ribbon

Bow with welting and tassel

Tapered with welting, rosette, and tassels

WINDOW TREATMENTS
Tiebacks and Holdbacks

Leaf motif

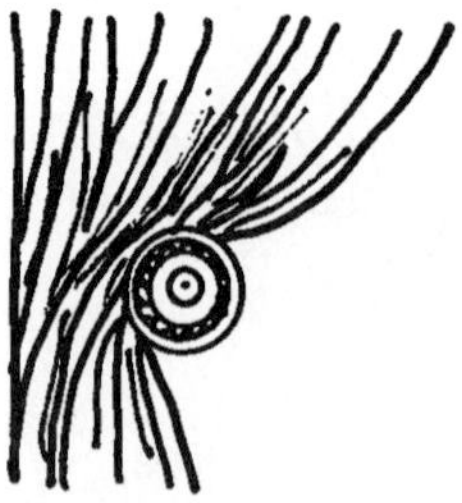

Decorative holdback

Scalloped with welting

Layered with pleats

Decorative with tassel

Decorative bow and ribbon

Square holdback with insert

Decorative knob with 2 inserts

Decorative knob holdback with tassel

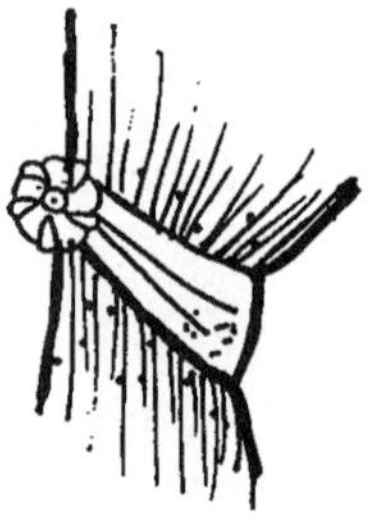

Stylized rosette

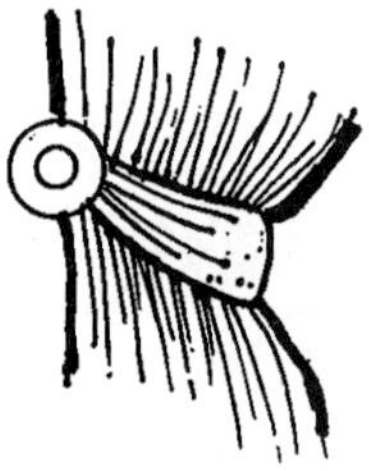

Decorative knob with inserts

Decorative knob holdback with two tassels

Decorative bow holdback

Standard knob with cascade

Decorative knob with circular insert and cascade

MOUNTS

Flush mount — closed top

Outside mount — open top

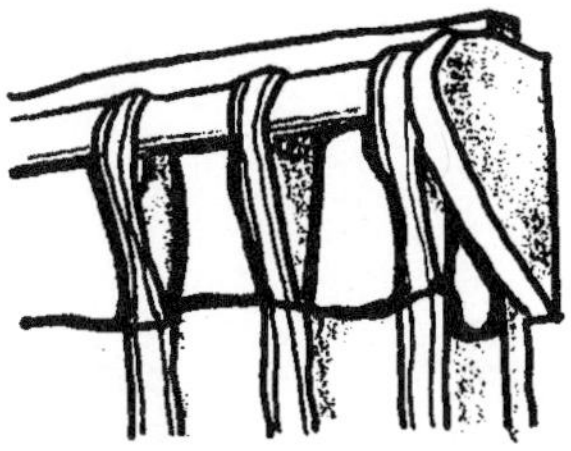
Outside mount — closed side

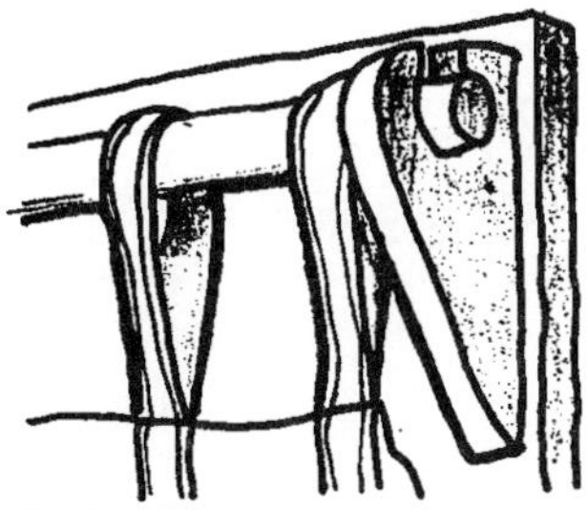
Flush mount — open top

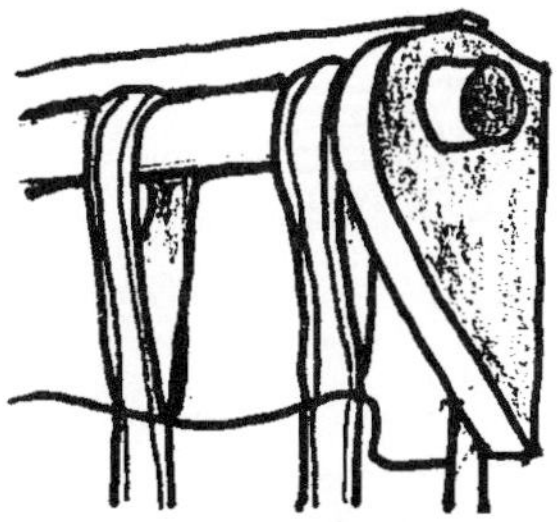
Outside mount — closed top

Inside mount bracket

BRACKETS

Flush extra-projection bracket

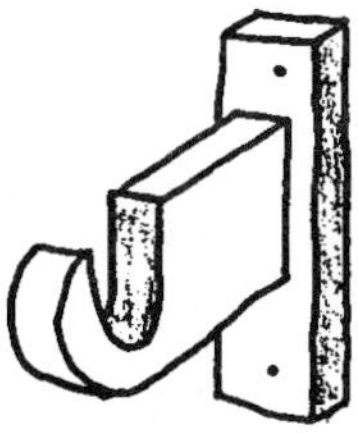
Base-mounted extra-projection bracket

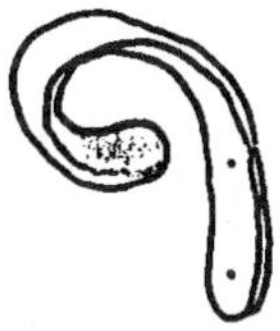
Curved bracket

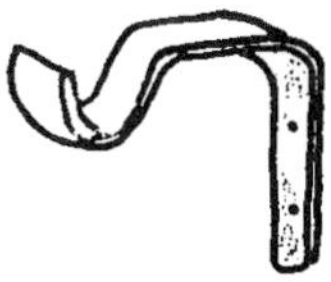
Support bracket

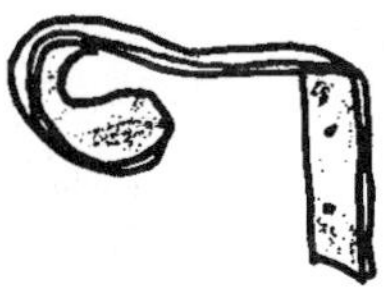
Curved support bracket

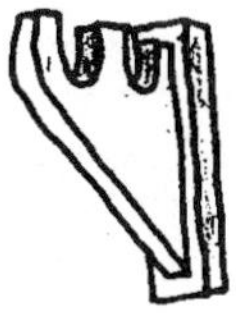
Double rod bracket

COUPLERS

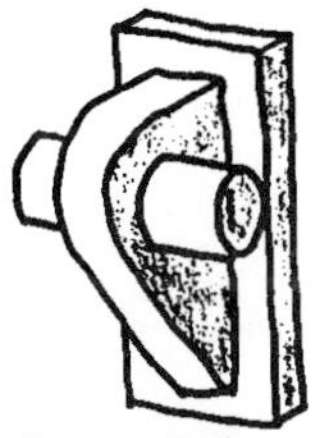
Extra-projection base-mounted coupler

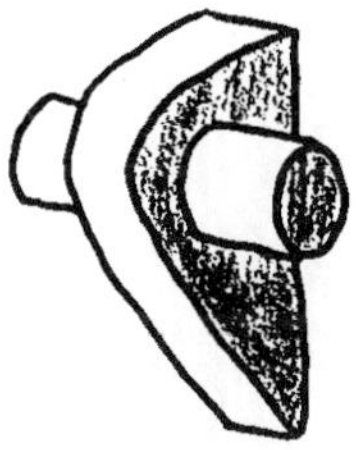
Base-mounted coupler

WINDOW TREATMENTS
Finials, Rings, and Hooks

FINIALS

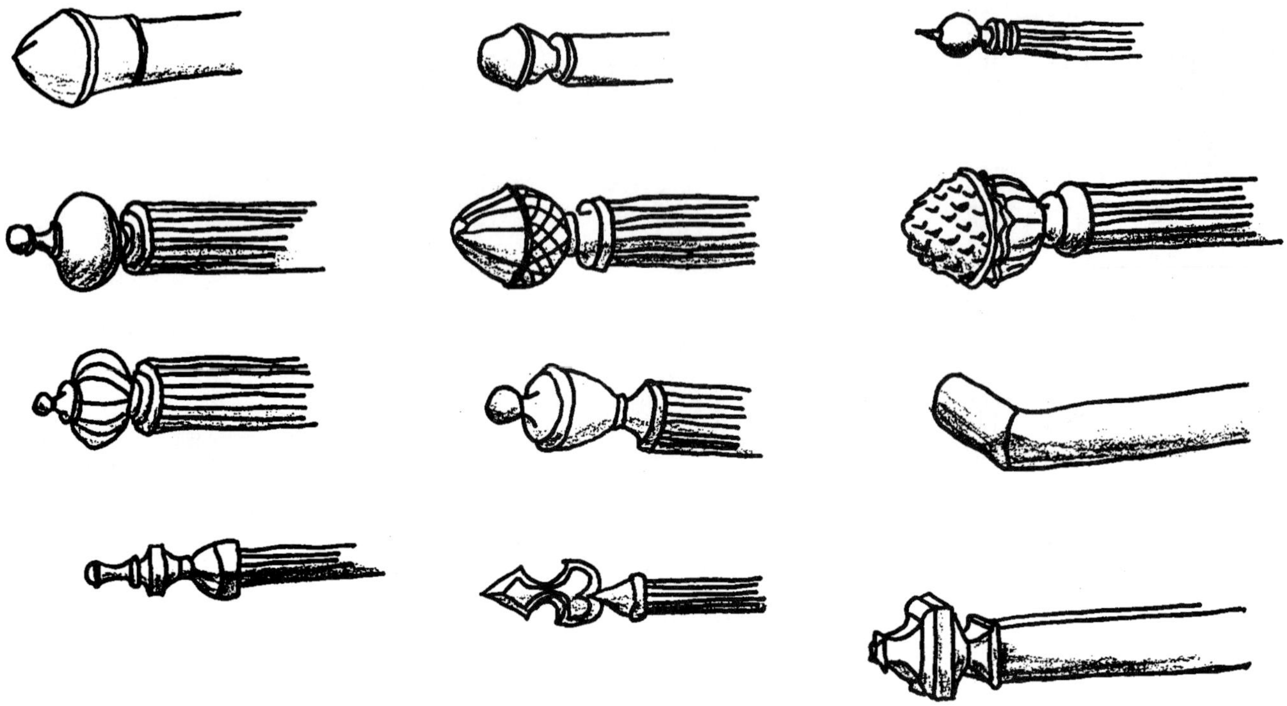

RINGS

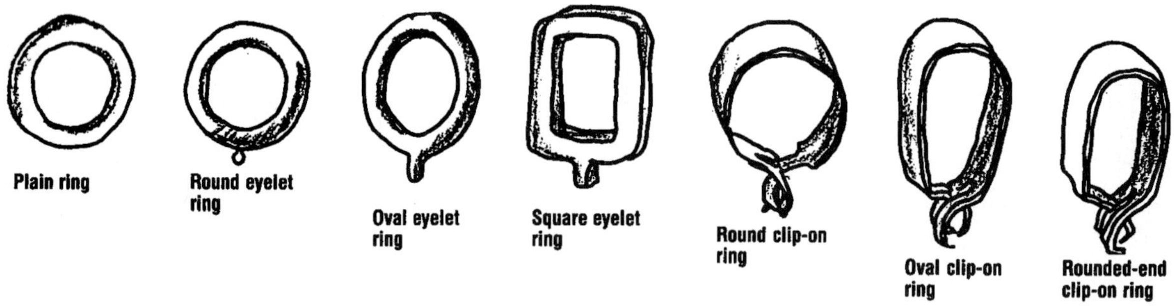

HOOKS

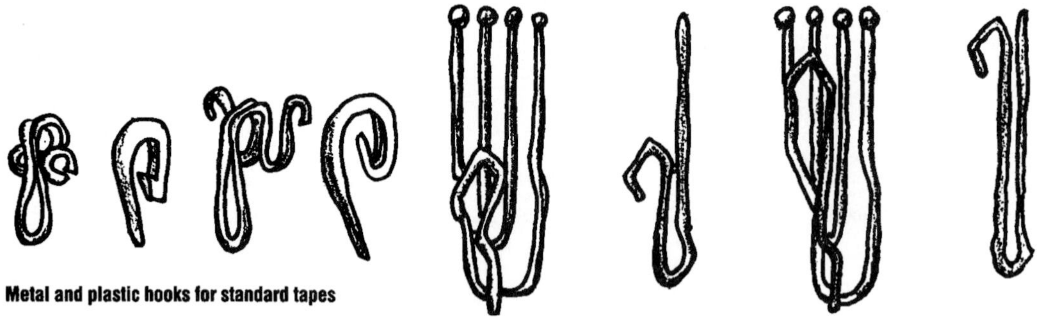

Metal and plastic hooks for standard tapes

Metal hooks for decorative tapes

Flat curtain rod

Double flat curtain rod

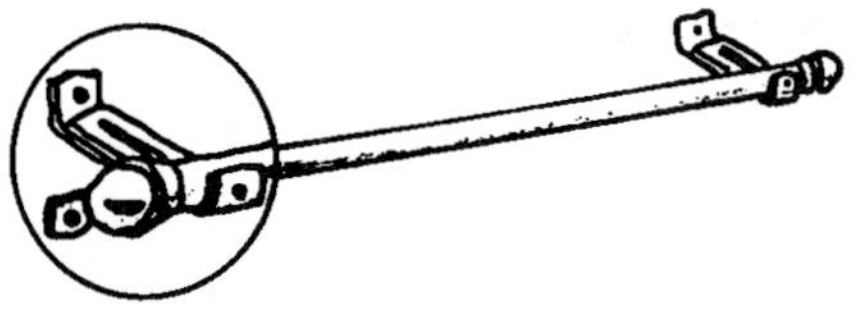

Cafe curtain rod

Fluted wood rod

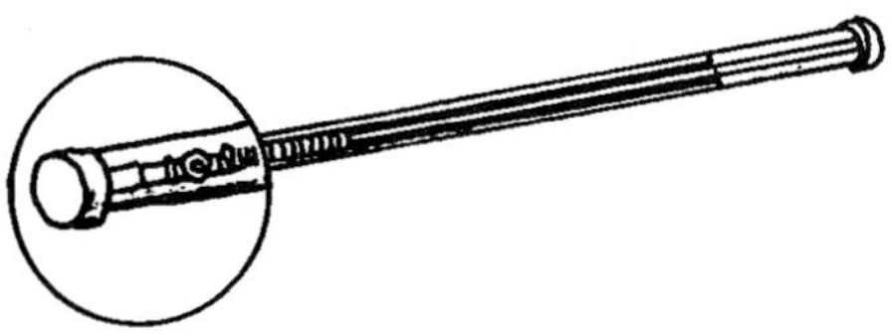

Tension rod with adjustable screw

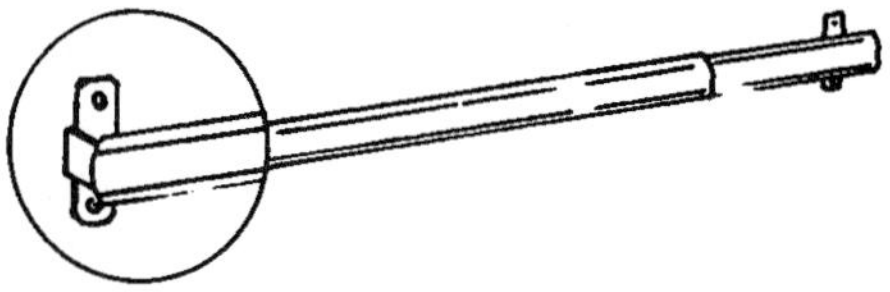

Sash rods

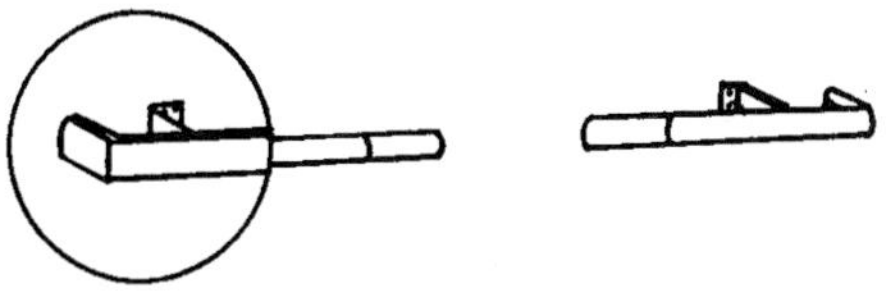

Separated curtain rod

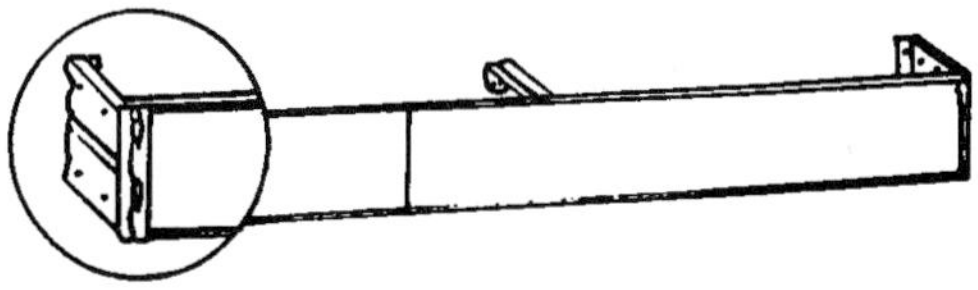

Extra wide telescoping projection rod

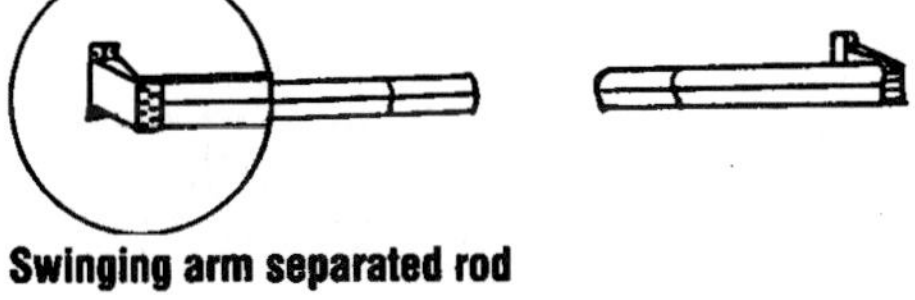

Swinging arm separated rod

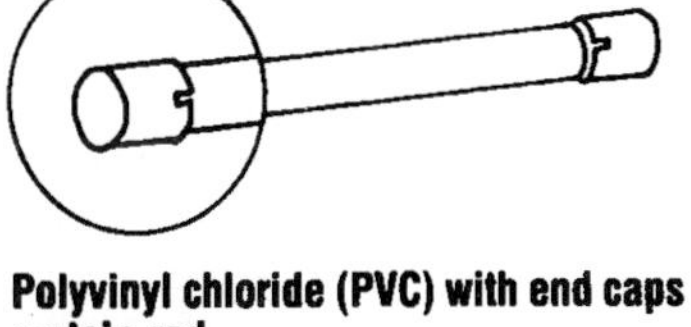

Polyvinyl chloride (PVC) with end caps curtain rod

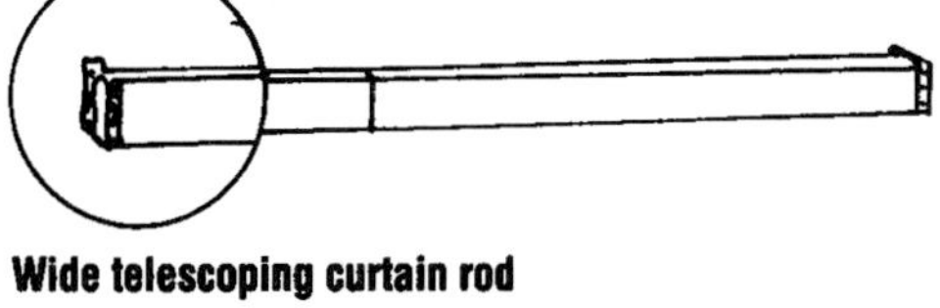

Wide telescoping curtain rod

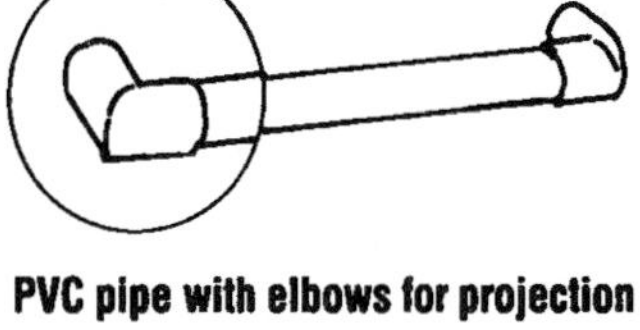

PVC pipe with elbows for projection

WINDOW TREATMENTS
Traverse Rods

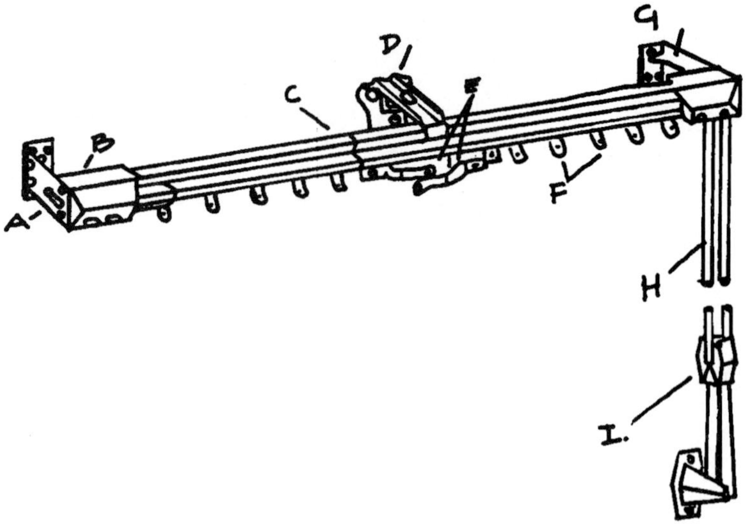

Conventional single hung traverse rod – A, projecting end brackets; B, end housing; C, telescoping rod; D, center support; E, master carriers; F, carriers; G, end bracket; H, cord; I, tension pulley

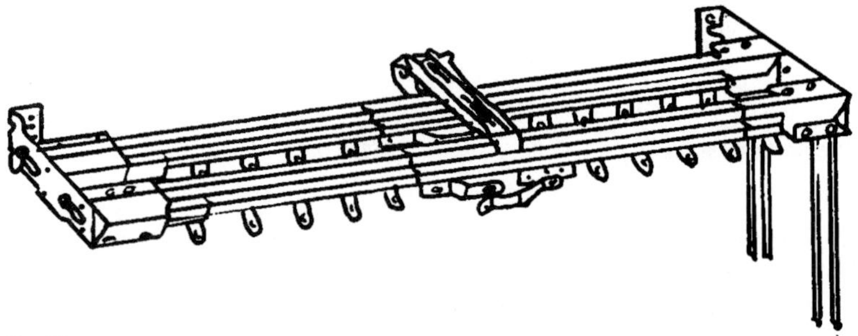

Double traverse rod

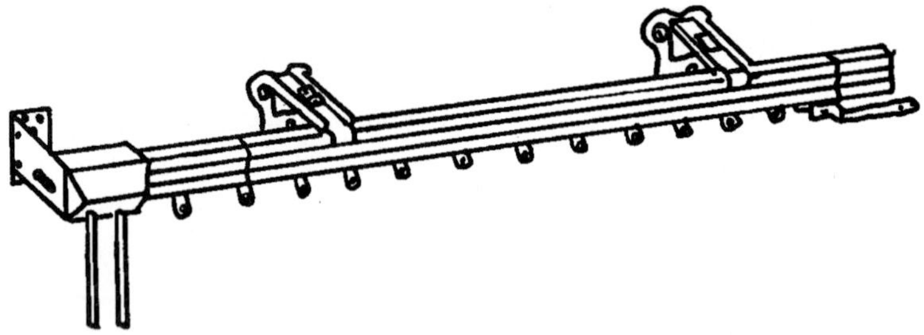

One-way traverse rod with two center supports

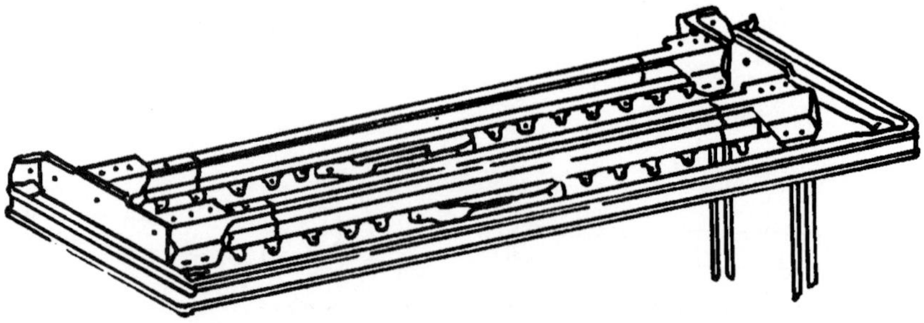

Double traverse rod with valence

Table 2 Fabric panel widths and pleating guidelines

Desired pleated panel coverage	Flat fabric without hems	Hemmed flat fabric	Number of 4″ flat spaces between pleats	Number of pleats	Width of fabric in each pleat
16″	43″	39″	4	5	3⅛″
20″	51″	47″	5	6	3¼″
24″	59″	55″	6	7	3⅜″
28″	67″	63″	7	8	3½″
32″	75″	71″	8	9	3½″
36″	83″	79″	9	10	3⁹⁄₁₆″
40″	91″	87″	10	11	3⅝″
44″	99″	95″	11	12	3⅝″
48″	107″	103″	12	13	3⅝″
52″	115″	111″	13	14	3⅝″
56″	123″	119″	14	15	3¾″
60″	131″	127″	15	16	3¾″
64″	139″	135″	16	17	3¾″
68″	147″	143″	17	18	3¾″
72″	155″	151″	18	19	3¾″
76″	163″	159″	19	20	3¾″
80″	171″	167″	20	21	3¾″
84″	179″	175″	21	22	3¾″
88″	187″	183″	22	23	3¾″
92″	195″	191″	23	24	3¾″
96″	203″	199″	24	25	3¾″
100″	211″	207″	25	26	3¾″
104″	219″	215″	26	27	3¾″
108″	227″	223″	27	28	3¾″
112″	235″	231″	28	29	3¾″
116″	243″	239″	29	30	3¾″
120″	251″	247″	30	31	3⅞″
124″	259″	254″	31	32	3⅞″
128″	267″	263″	32	33	3⅞″

Table 3 Rod lengths needed for various widths of windows and stackback spaces

If the glass is	The stackback* should be	Your rod length and drapery coverage should be (add for overlaps and returns)
38″	26″	64″
44″	28″	72″
50″	30″	80″
56″	32″	88″
62″	34″	96″
68″	36″	104″
75″	37″	112″
81″	39″	120″
87″	41″	128″
94″	42″	136″
100″	44″	144″
106″	46″	152″
112″	48″	160″
119″	49″	168″
125″	51″	176″
131″	53″	184″
137″	55″	192″
144″	56″	200″
150″	58″	208″
156″	60″	216″
162″	62″	224″
169″	63″	232″
175″	65″	240″
181″	67″	248″
187″	69″	256″

*For one-way draws, deduct 7″ from stackback.

Note: Figures are based on average pleating and medium-weight fabric. For extra bulky fabrics, add to stackback to compensate for the additional space they require.

WINDOW TREATMENTS
Shades

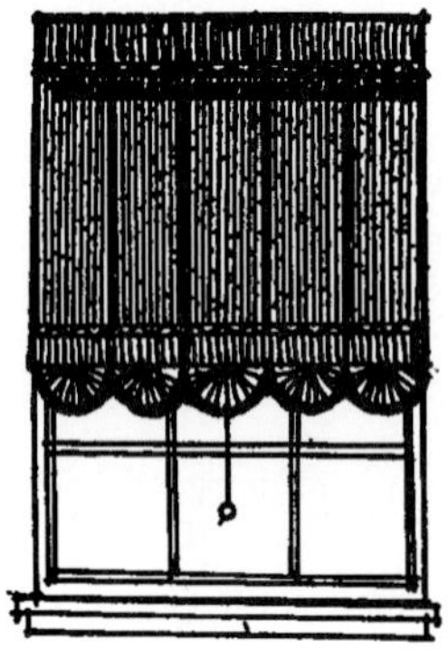

Overlapping trimmed valance over scalloped shade

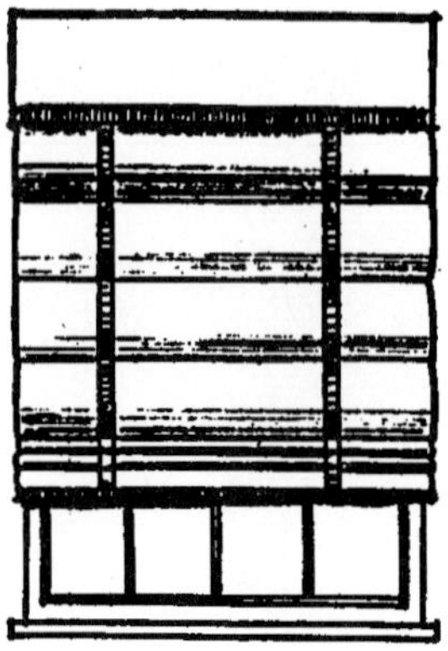

Banded valance over Roman shade

Shirred cornice box over tri-part balloon shade

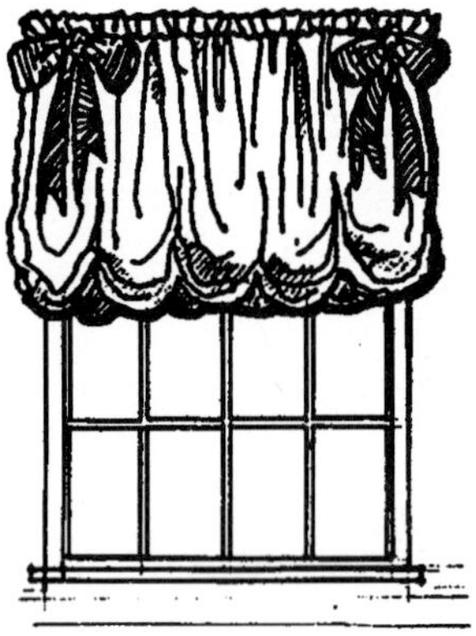

Twin bow cloud shade with gathered heading

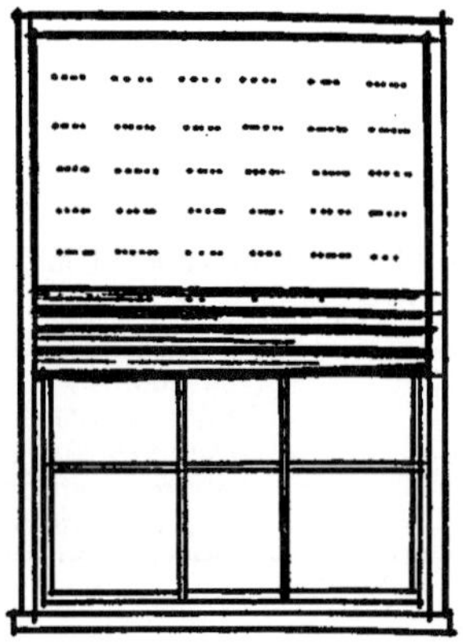

Inset flush Roman shade with horizontal folds

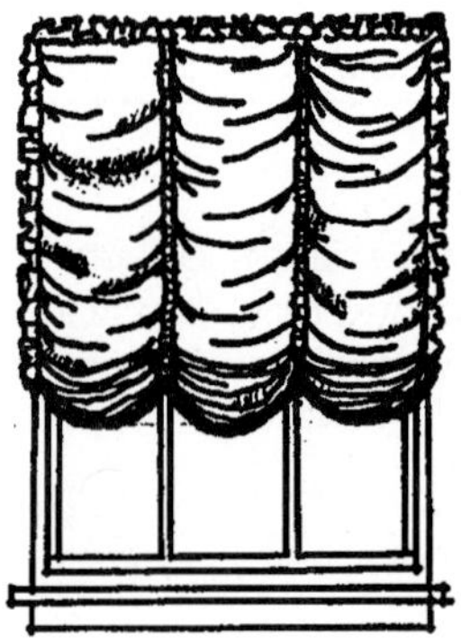

Tri-part Austrian shade with ruffled trim

Inset flush bottom pull Roman shade with horizontal folds

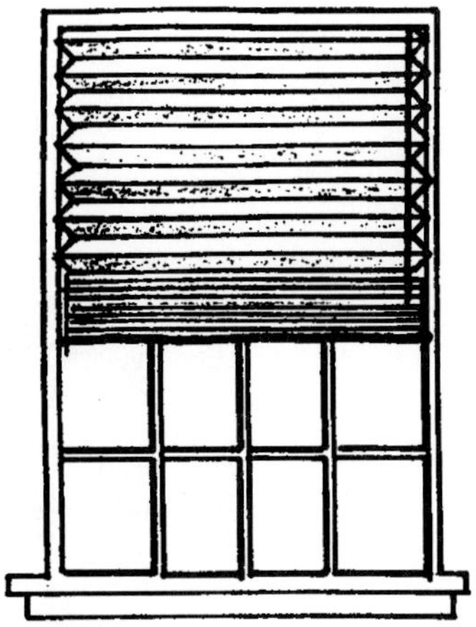
Pleated shade

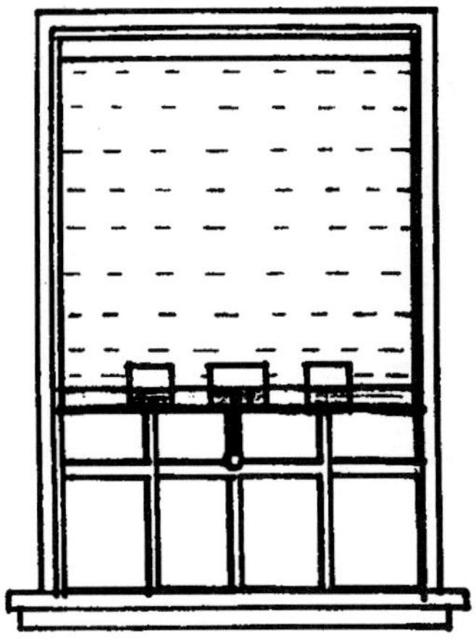
Crenellated edge

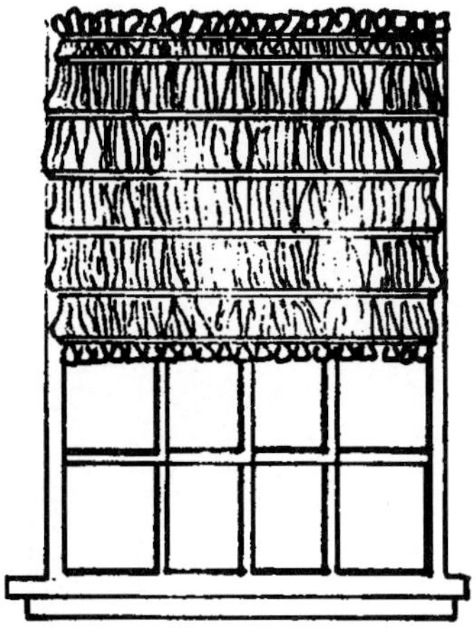
Shirred shade

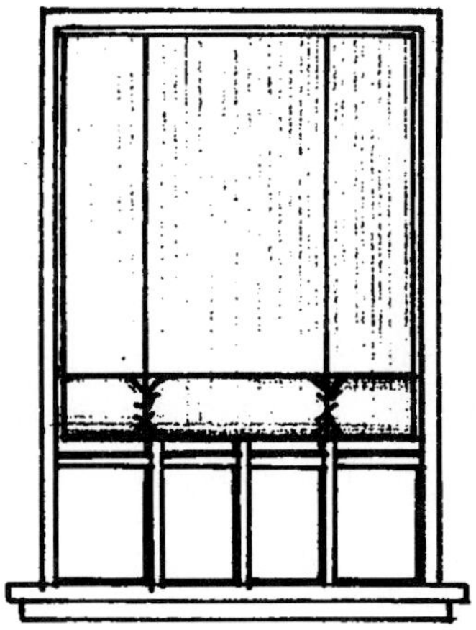
Rolldown shade

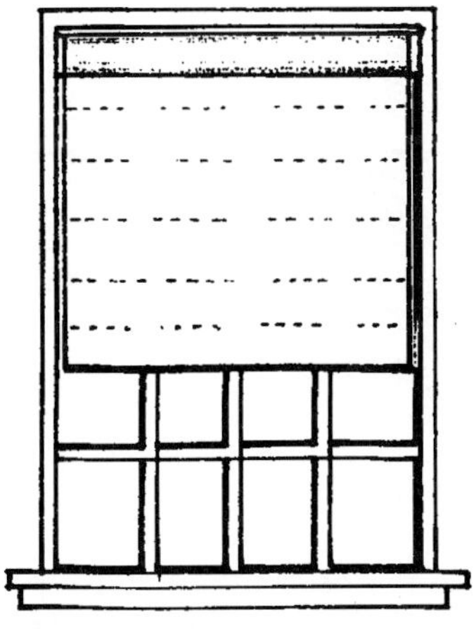
Rolldown shade

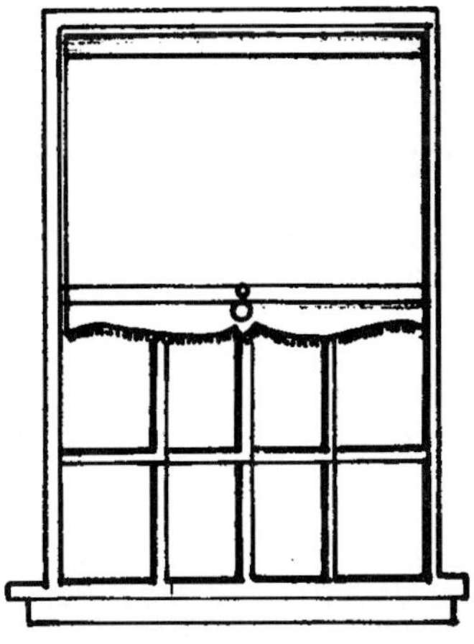
Pulldown shade

WINDOW TREATMENTS
Shades

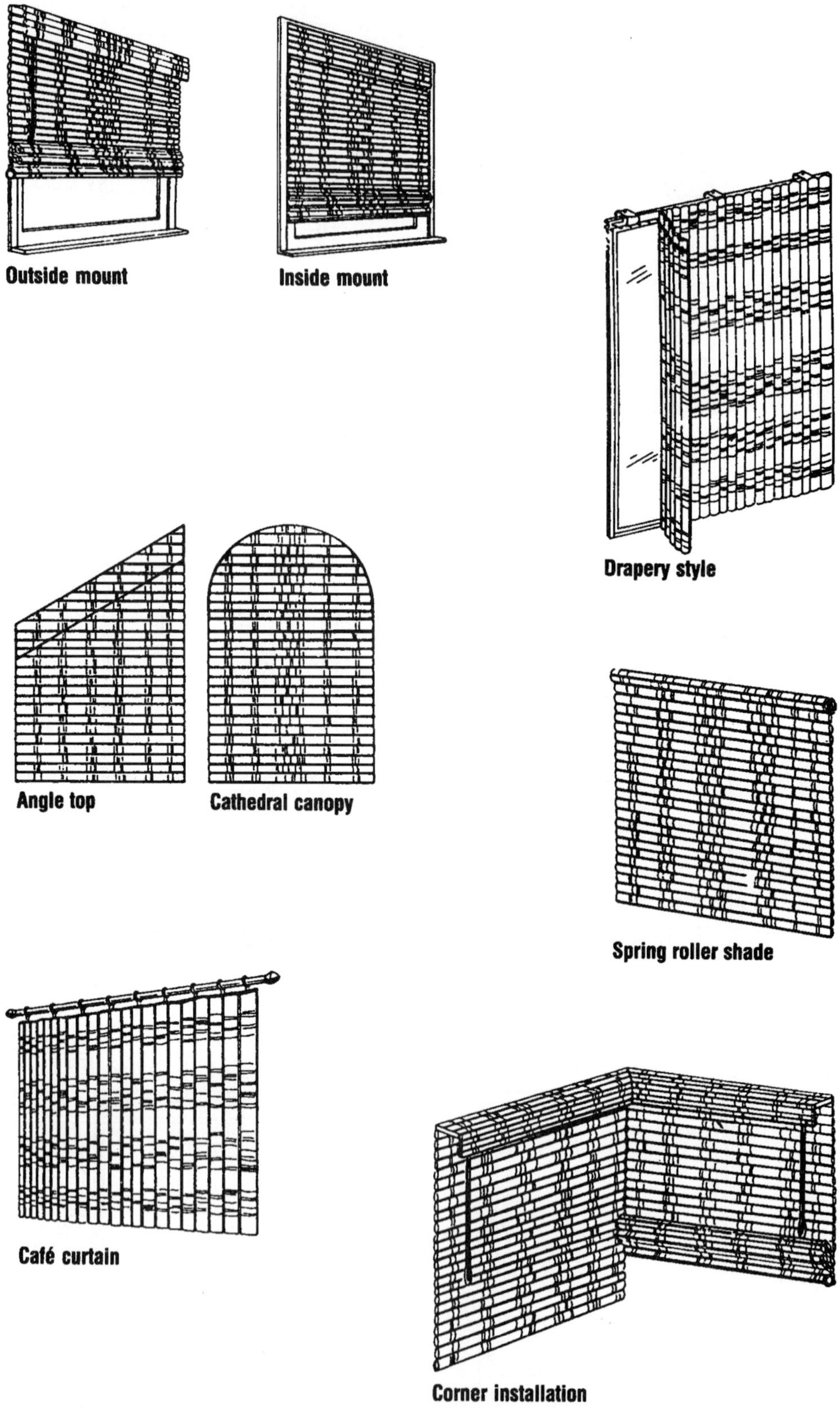

Fig. 8 Woven wood blinds. These blinds have horizontal or vertical reeds—long slats of wood from ¼ to 1 in width—that are held together by decorative vertical yarns. They range in designs from those that are made mostly from exposed wood to those that are mainly yarns of several colors, creating various interesting effects. Woven wood blinds can be used with many window treatments including draperies and café curtains, and such shade types as Roman-fold, spring-rolls, cord and pulley, and duofold. Top treatments include canopies, valances, and arches, while scallops, fringes, and trims are suitable for the bottom. Because woven wood blinds add color and texture to a window, they are particularly adaptable to the natural look in decorating

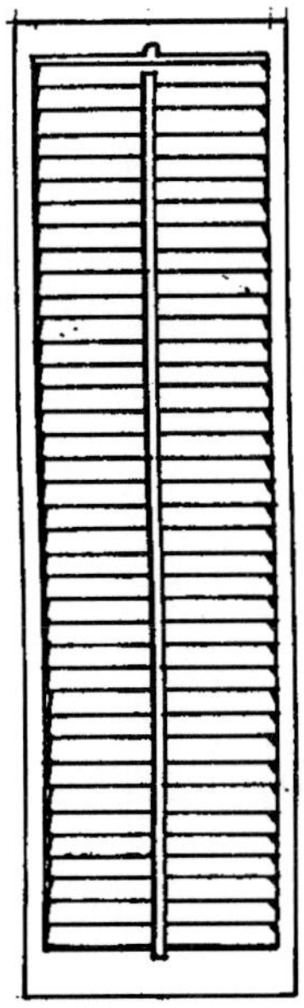

Louvers: 1⅞", 2½", 3½", 4½"; thickness: 1¼"; width of stile: 2"; width: 8" to 36" in ¼" increments

Louvers: 1⅞", 2½", 3½", 4½"; thickness: 1¼"; width of stile: 2"; width: 8" to 36" in ¼" increments.

Louvers: 2½".

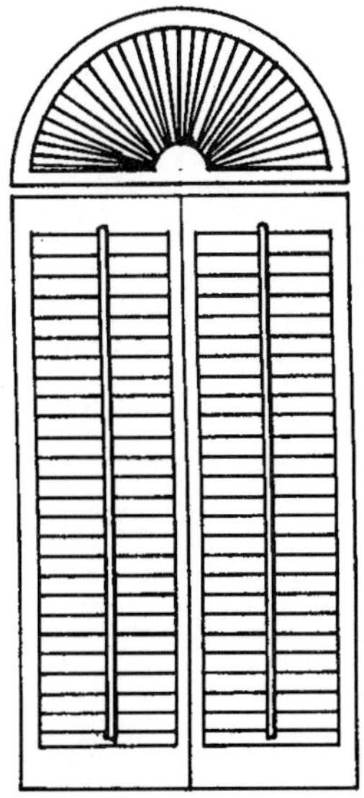

Fan top (nonadjustable louvers); louvers: 2½"; thickness: 1¼".

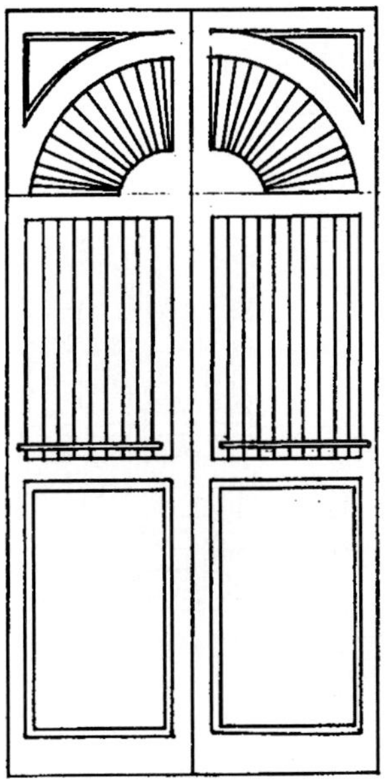

Louvers: 2½"; thickness: 1¼".

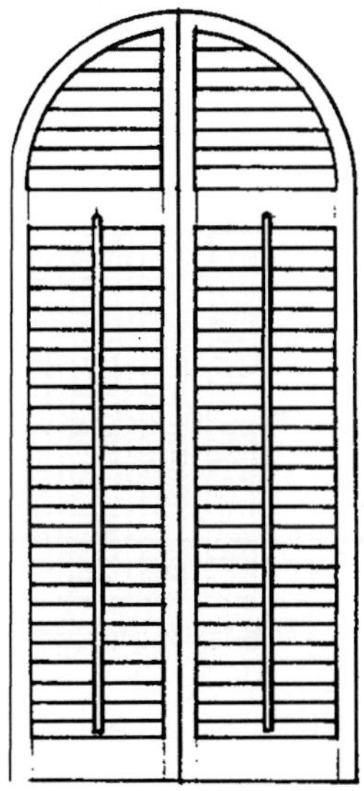

Louvers: 2½"; thickness: 1¼".

Louver grid. Standard: 4' x 8" unframed; standard framing: 1 1/16" wide x 2¼" thick.

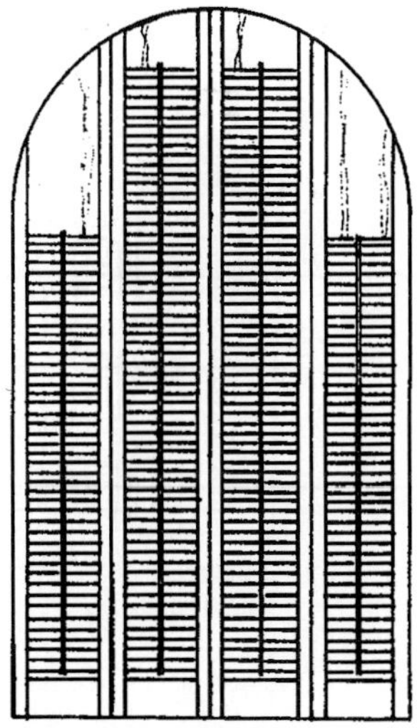

Traditional/Dixie panel; louvers: 1¼"; thickness: 1⅛".

Fig. 9 Inside shutters can be used next to windows in place of curtains. Some are put under curtains or draperies; others are used café style, either above or beneath café curtains. Shutters may be made from wood or metal. Natural wood tones are often used to enhance the beauty of the shutters. The inside section may be made from any of the following materials: fabric mesh, cane, grille cloth, or screening

WINDOW TREATMENTS
Shutters

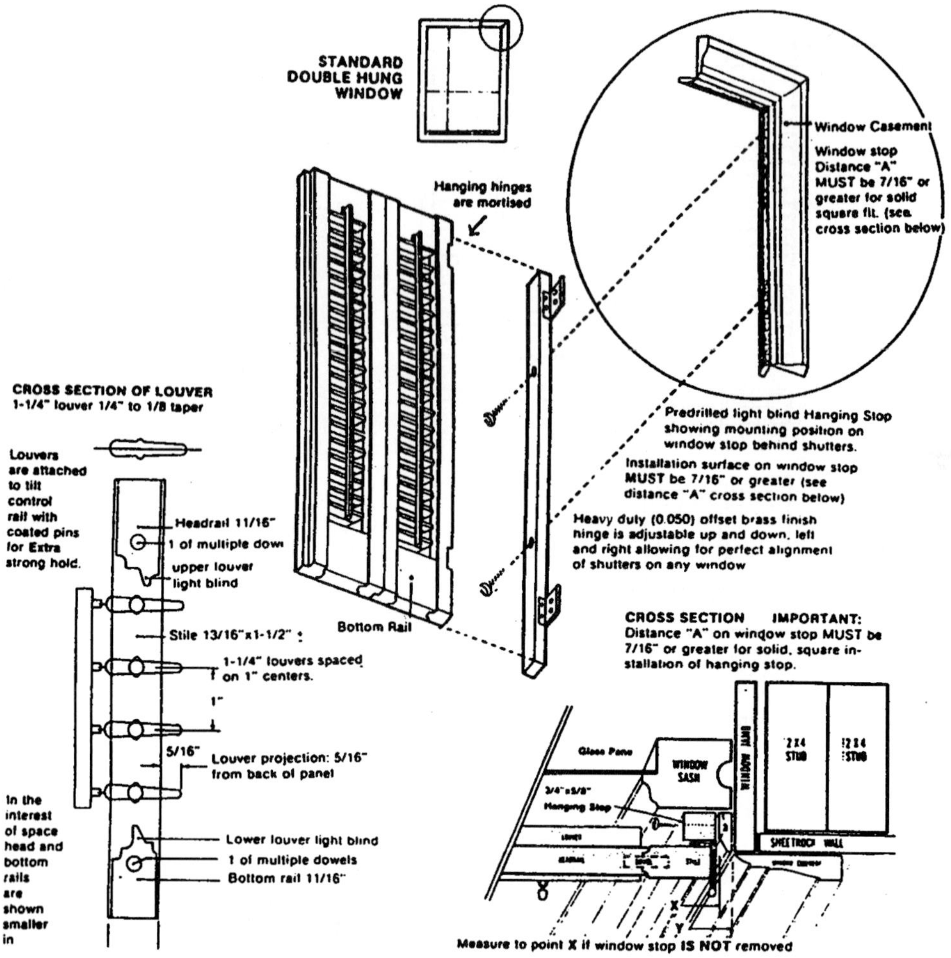
STANDARD DOUBLE HUNG WINDOW
Hanging hinges are mortised
Window Casement
Window stop Distance "A" MUST be 7/16" or greater for solid square fit. (see cross section below)
CROSS SECTION OF LOUVER
1-1/4" louver 1/4" to 1/8 taper
Louvers are attached to tilt control rail with coated pins for Extra strong hold.
Headrail 11/16"
1 of multiple dow
upper louver light blind
Stile 13/16"x1-1/2"
Bottom Rail
1-1/4" louvers spaced on 1" centers.
1"
5/16"
Louver projection: 5/16" from back of panel
In the interest of space head and bottom rails are shown smaller in
Lower louver light blind
1 of multiple dowels
Bottom rail 11/16"
Predrilled light blind Hanging Stop showing mounting position on window stop behind shutters.
Installation surface on window stop MUST be 7/16" or greater (see distance "A" cross section below)
Heavy duty (0.050) offset brass finish hinge is adjustable up and down, left and right allowing for perfect alignment of shutters on any window
CROSS SECTION IMPORTANT: Distance "A" on window stop MUST be 7/16" or greater for solid, square installation of hanging stop.
Glass Pane
WINDOW SASH
3/4"x5/8" Hanging Stop
SHEETROCK WALL
X
Y
Measure to point X if window stop IS NOT removed

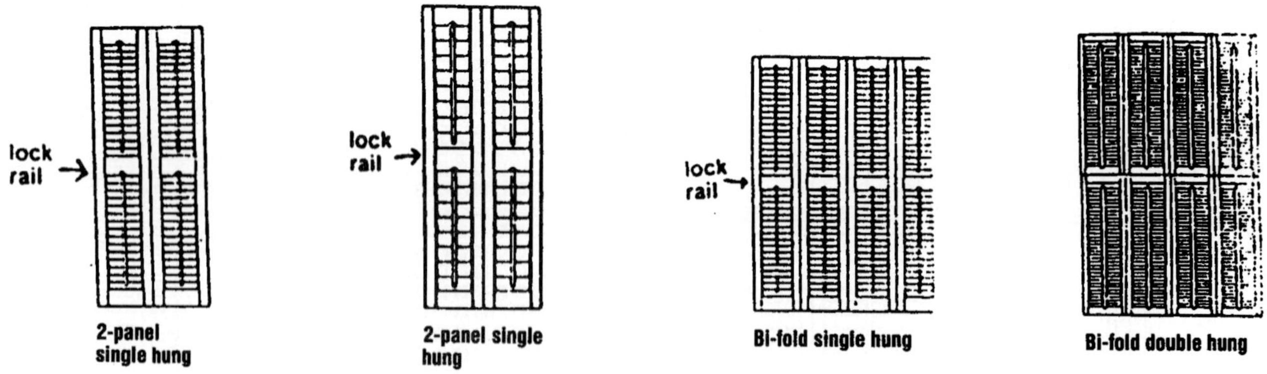
lock rail
2-panel single hung
lock rail
2-panel single hung
lock rail
Bi-fold single hung
Bi-fold double hung

WINDOW TREATMENTS
Shutters and Venetian Blinds

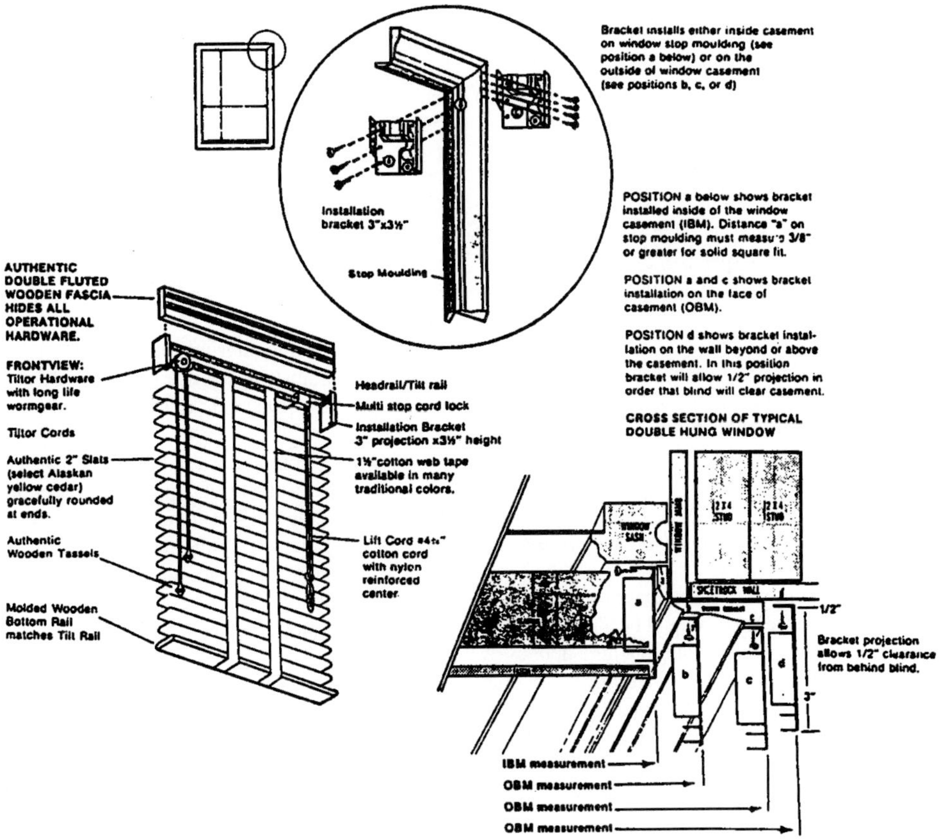
Bracket installs either inside casement on window stop moulding (see position a below) or on the outside of window casement (see positions b, c, or d)
Installation bracket 3"x3½"
Stop Moulding
POSITION a below shows bracket installed inside of the window casement (IBM). Distance "a" on stop moulding must measure 3/8" or greater for solid square fit.
POSITION a and c shows bracket installation on the face of casement (OBM).
POSITION d shows bracket installation on the wall beyond or above the casement. In this position bracket will allow 1/2" projection in order that blind will clear casement.
CROSS SECTION OF TYPICAL DOUBLE HUNG WINDOW
AUTHENTIC DOUBLE FLUTED WOODEN FASCIA HIDES ALL OPERATIONAL HARDWARE.
FRONTVIEW: Tiltor Hardware with long life wormgear.
Tiltor Cords
Authentic 2" Slats (select Alaskan yellow cedar) gracefully rounded at ends.
Authentic Wooden Tassels
Molded Wooden Bottom Rail matches Tilt Rail
Headrail/Tilt rail
Multi stop cord lock
Installation Bracket 3" projection x3½" height
1½"cotton web tape available in many traditional colors.
Lift Cord cotton cord with nylon reinforced center.
WINDOW SASH
2X4 STUD
SHEETROCK WALL
1/2"
Bracket projection allows 1/2" clearance from behind blind.
3"
IBM measurement
OBM measurement
OBM measurement
OBM measurement

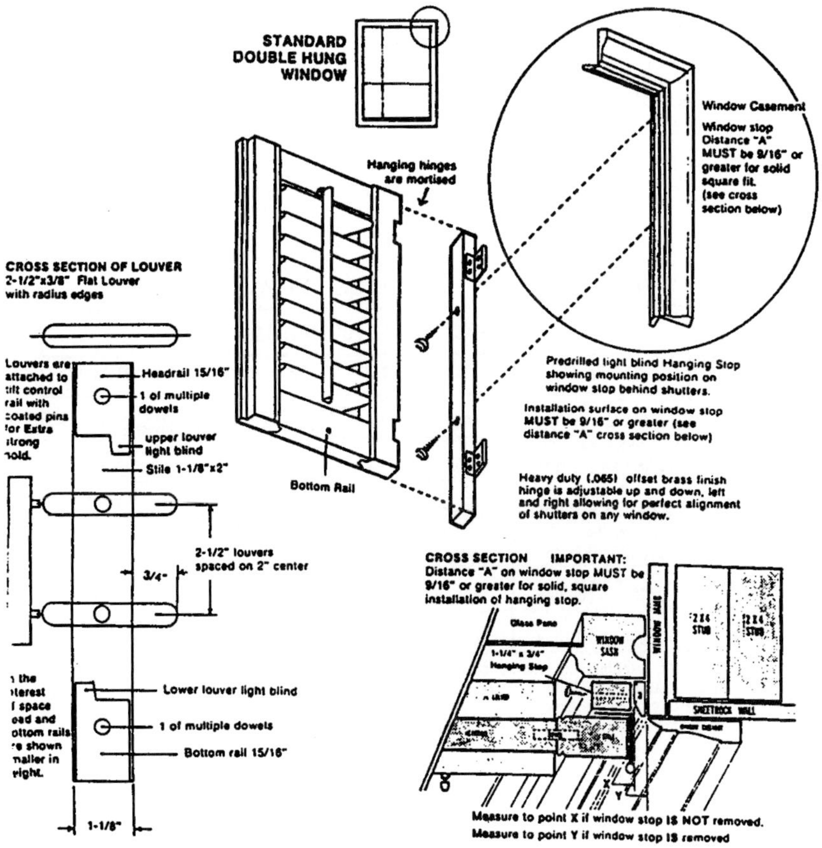
STANDARD DOUBLE HUNG WINDOW
Window Casement
Window stop Distance "A" MUST be 9/16" or greater for solid square fit. (see cross section below)
Hanging hinges are mortised
CROSS SECTION OF LOUVER 2-1/2"x3/8" Flat Louver with radius edges
Louvers are attached to tilt control rail with coated pins for Extra strong hold.
Headrail 15/16"
1 of multiple dowels
upper louver light blind
Stile 1-1/8"x2"
Bottom Rail
2-1/2" louvers spaced on 2" center
3/4"
Lower louver light blind
1 of multiple dowels
Bottom rail 15/16"
1-1/8"
Predrilled light blind Hanging Stop showing mounting position on window stop behind shutters.
Installation surface on window stop MUST be 9/16" or greater (see distance "A" cross section below)
Heavy duty (.065) offset brass finish hinge is adjustable up and down, left and right allowing for perfect alignment of shutters on any window.
CROSS SECTION IMPORTANT: Distance "A" on window stop MUST be 9/16" or greater for solid, square installation of hanging stop.
Glass Pane
1-1/4" x 3/4" Hanging Stop
WINDOW SASH
2X4 STUD
SHEETROCK WALL
Measure to point X if window stop IS NOT removed.
Measure to point Y if window stop IS removed

ELEVATORS AND WHEELCHAIR LIFTS
Elevator Types and Planning

Elevator Types

Hydraulic: For low-rise buildings—speeds up to 200 ft/min. Ideal where design limitations preclude overhead supports and machine rooms. Economical to install and maintain; no penthouse or load-bearing walls required.

Geared traction: For low- to medium-rise buildings—speeds up to 400 ft/min. Recommended for all types of buildings where higher speeds are not essential.

Gearless traction: Recommended for high-rise applications requiring the ultimate in service—speeds of 500 ft/min and up.

Elevator Planning

Starting Point Recommendations for All Types of Buildings

When preparing schematics for a particular type of building, select the quantity, capacity, and speed from one of Tables 1 to 4 and keep in mind that generally:

- Passenger elevators should be wide and shallow with center-opening or single slide doors.
- Service elevators should be narrow and deep with two-speed doors.
- Combination passenger/service elevators should be almost square with either center-opening or two-speed center-opening doors.
- Freight elevator size and shape should be determined by the dimensions of goods to be carried and by the loading/unloading methods used. Doors should be of the vertical biparting type.

The data contained in Tables 1 to 4 are based on the following criteria.

Office buildings 100 ft^2 per person; an interval of 30 sec.; net rentable area = 80 percent of gross area; 5-min carrying capacity of 12 percent of building population; typical floor heights were estimated at 12 ft and the main floor at 18 ft. When the building exceeds 250,000 ft^2 total, it is suggested that consideration be given to the use of separate freight elevators which are not included in Table 1.

Hospitals Five-minute vehicular demand = .04 × the number of beds; interval of 35 to 50 seconds for vehicular traffic; visitor and staff population = 3 × number of beds; 5-min carrying capacity equal to 12 percent of building population.

Hotels Registration during conventions = 1.5 × the total number of rooms; maximum 1-h peak is 1.15 × total registrations; 5-minute carrying capacity = 10 percent of total 1-h peak load.

Apartments Population established at two persons per bedroom; 5-min carrying capacity of 7 percent; maximum waiting interval of 60–90 sec; average of 9 ft 0 in floor height. Further, Table 4 applies only for average or middle-income apartments. For applications beyond the scope of Table 4, such as local-express arrangements, luxury apartment buildings, and other considerations, please consult your local elevator company representative.

NOTE: If a restaurant or general assembly area is located in your building (on any but the main floor) and is not served by a separate elevator, the information contained in Tables 1 to 4 may not apply.

Table 1 Office buildings—passenger elevators only

Number of Floors, Including Main	GROSS SQUARE FOOTAGE/FLOOR			
	5000 Sq. Ft.	8000 Sq. Ft.	12000 Sq. Ft.	16000 Sq. Ft.
5 floors	2 Elev. 2500# @ 250 fpm	2 Elev. 2500# @ 250 fpm	3 Elev. 2500# @ 250 fpm	3 Elev. 2500# @ 300 fpm
6 to 8 floors	3 Elev. 2500# @ 350 fpm	3 Elev. 2500# @ 350 fpm	3 Elev. 2500# @ 400 fpm	4 Elev. 2500# @ 400 fpm
9 to 12 floors	4 Elev. 2500# @ 400-500 fpm	4 Elev. 2500# @ 400-500 fpm	4 Elev. 3000# @ 500 fpm	5 Elev. 3500# @ 600 fpm
13 to 15 floors	4 Elev. 2500# @ 600 fpm	4 Elev. 2500# @ 600 fpm	5 Elev. 3000# @ 700 fpm	6 Elev. 3500# @ 700 fpm
16 to 19 floors	5 Elev. 2500# @ 700 fpm	6 Elev. 2500# @ 700 fpm	*	*
20 to 22 floors	5 Elev. 2500# @ 800 fpm	6 Elev. 3000# @ 800 fpm	*	*

* Because of the complexities such as local and express arrangements and service requirements inherent in taller and larger buildings, we suggest you contact your Armor representative when the limitations of this chart are exceeded.

Table 2 Hospitals

Number of Floors	BEDS/FLOOR			
	Up to 20 Beds	21 to 30 Beds	31 to 40 Beds	41 to 50 Beds
Up to 6 Floors	3 Elev. 4500# @ 200 fpm	4 Elev. 2-3000# @ 300 fpm 2-4500# @ 300 fpm	5 Elev. 2-3000# @ 350 fpm 3-4500# @ 350 fpm	5 Elev. 2-3000# @ 350 fpm 3-4500# @ 350 fpm
7 to 9 floors	6 Elev. 3-3000# @ 500 fpm 3-4500# @ 500 fpm	7 Elev. 3-3000# @ 500 fpm 4-4500# @ 500 fpm	8 Elev. 4-3000# @ 500 fpm 4-4500# @ 500 fpm	9 Elev. 4-3000# @ 500 fpm 5-4500# @ 500 fpm
10 to 12 floors	7 Elev. 3-3000# @ 500 fpm 4-4500# @ 500 fpm	8 Elev. 4-3000# @ 500 fpm 4-4500# @ 500 fpm	9 Elev. 4-3000# @ 500 fpm 5-4500# @ 500 fpm	10 Elev. 4-3000# @ 500 fpm 6-4500# @ 500 fpm

NOTE: The number of elevators listed above will most likely be reduced if automatic cart and/or container handling equipment for food. laundry, surgical instrument and central supply distribution is used.

Table 3 Hotel buildings—passenger elevators only

Number of Floors	UNITS/FLOOR			
	Up to 14 Units	15 to 20 Units	21 to 28 Units	29 to 32 Units
4 to 5 floors	2 Elev. 3000# @ 150 fpm	2 Elev. 3000# @ 175 fpm	2 Elev. 3000# @ 200 fpm	2 Elev. 3000# @ 200 fpm
6 to 9 floors	2 Elev. 3000# @ 300 fpm	2 Elev. 3000# @ 350 fpm	2 Elev. 3000# @ 400 fpm	3 Elev. 3000# @ 300 fpm
10 to 12 floors	3 Elev. 3000# @ 300 fpm	3 Elev. 3000# @ 350 fpm	4 Elev. 3000# @ 350 fpm	4 Elev. 3000# @ 350 fpm
13 to 15 floors	4 Elev. 3000# @ 350 fpm	4 Elev. 3000# @ 350 fpm	4 Elev. 3000# @ 350 fpm	4 Elev. 3000# @ 350 fpm
16 to 20 floors	4 Elev. 3000# @ 350 fpm	4 Elev. 3000# @ 400 fpm	4 Elev. 3000# @ 400 fpm +1 Service 3500# @ 400 fpm	4 Elev. 3000# @ 400 fpm +2 Service 3500# @ 400 fpm

NOTE: Because of the complexities such as local and express and service requirements inherent in taller and larger hotels, we suggest that you contact your Armor representatives when the limitations of this chart are exceeded.

Table 4 Apartment buildings—passenger elevators only

Number of Floors Including Main	BEDROOMS/FLOOR			
	10 Bedrooms	16 Bedrooms	22 Bedrooms	30 Bedrooms
6 floors	1 Elev. 2000# @ 150 fpm	1 Elev. 2000# @ 150 fpm	2 Elev. 2000# @ 150 fpm	2 Elev. 2000# @ 150 fpm
12 floors	2 Elev. 2000# @ 200 fpm	2 Elev. 2000# @ 200 fpm	2 Elev. 2500# @ 250 fpm	3 Elev. 2500# @ 250 fpm
18 floors	3 Elev. 2000# @ 350 fpm	3 Elev. 2000# @ 350 fpm	3 Elev. 2500# @ 350 fpm	4 Elev. 2500# @ 350 fpm
25 floors	3 Elev. 2500# @ 400 fpm	3 Elev. 2500# @ 400 fpm	4 Elev. 2500# @ 400 fpm	*
32 floors	3 Elev. 2500# @ 500 fpm	4 Elev. 2500# @ 500 fpm	*	*
40 floors	4 Elev. 2500# @ 700 fpm	*	*	*

LOW- AND MID-RISE ELEVATORS

Hydraulic Elevators

Ideal for use in buildings up to six floors. Supported and raised by a powerful hydraulic plunger, the Oildraulic is renowned for smooth performance, quiet operation, and accurate floor leveling. And since it's supported from below, no vertical load is placed on the building. That means hoistways can be of lighter construction and no penthouse is needed. The machine room can be located nearly anywhere to let you maintain a flat roof line *and* save money on construction.

ELEVATORS AND WHEELCHAIR LIFTS
Low- and Mid-Rise Elevators

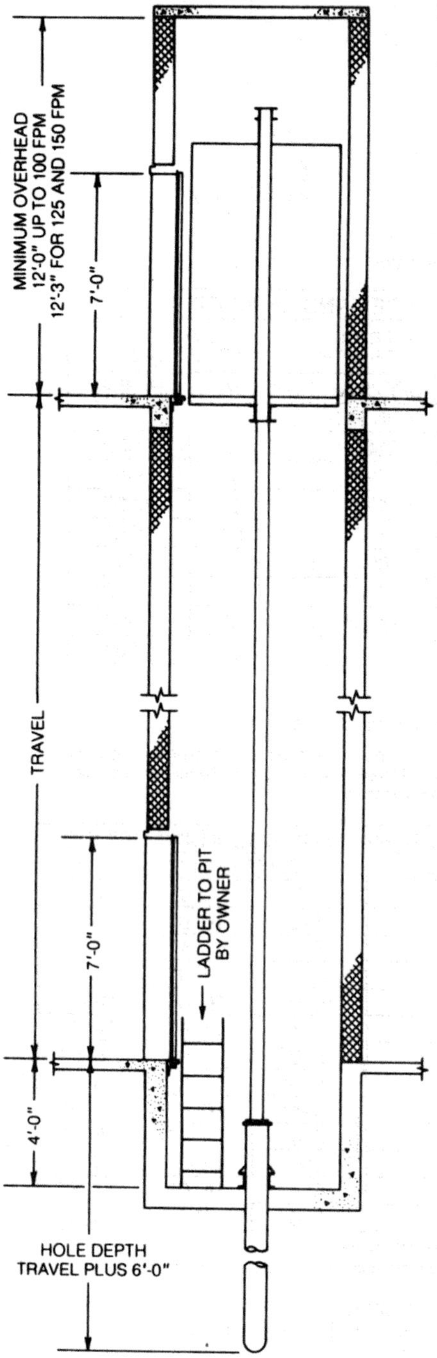

HOISTWAY PLAN

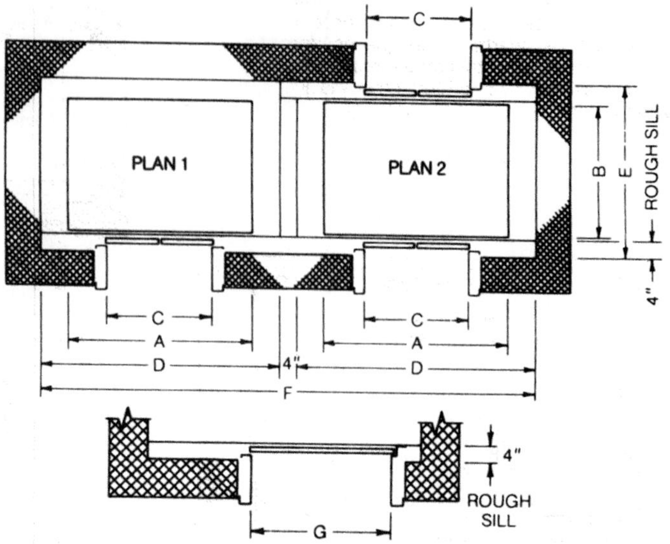

RIGHT HAND DOOR SHOWN: LEFT HAND AVAILABLE

RECOMMENDED SIZES AND CAPACITIES					
TYPE BUILDING	APART-MENT	AVERAGE OFFICE/HOTEL		LARGE OFFICE/STORE	
MODEL	FLEET-WOOD 21-H	PLAN 1 MARQUIS-25	PLAN 2 MARQUIS-25	SEVILLE-30	SEVILLE-35
CAPACITY (IN POUNDS)					
DIMENSIONS	2100 ♿	2500 ♿	2500 ♿	3000 ♿	3500 ♿
A[1]	5'-8"	6'-8"	6'-8"	6'-8"	6'-8"
B[1]	4'-3"	4'-3"	4'-3½"	4'-9"	5'-5"
C	–	3'-6"	3'-6"	3'-6"	3'-6"
D[2]	7'-4"	8'-4"	8'-4"	8'-4"	8'-4"
E	5'-9"	5'-9"	6'-8¾"	6'-3"	6'-11"
F	15'-0"	17'-0"	17'-0"	17'-0"	17'-0"
G	3'-0"	3'-6"	3'-6"	3'-6"	3'-6"

[1] Inside dimensions.
[2] Single car dimensions.
♿ These models meet minimum size for handicapped use.
Hoistway dimensions are based on no provisions for seismic conditions and 8'-0" O.A. nominal cab height.
Standard speeds available: 75, 100, 125 150 FPM.

POWER UNIT (MACHINE) LOCATION

The most desirable machine room location is on the lowest floor, adjacent to the elevator hoistway. It may, however, be located remote from hoistway if necessary. Typical size for one-car installation: 7 ft 10 in × 5 ft 6 in × 8 ft 0 in high; for two cars: 10 ft 9 in × 6 ft 6 in × 8 ft 0 in high. Enclosure to meet local code requirements must be provided. A sound-isolated machine room is recommended for quietest operation. Adequate heating and ventilation of machine spaces must be provided.

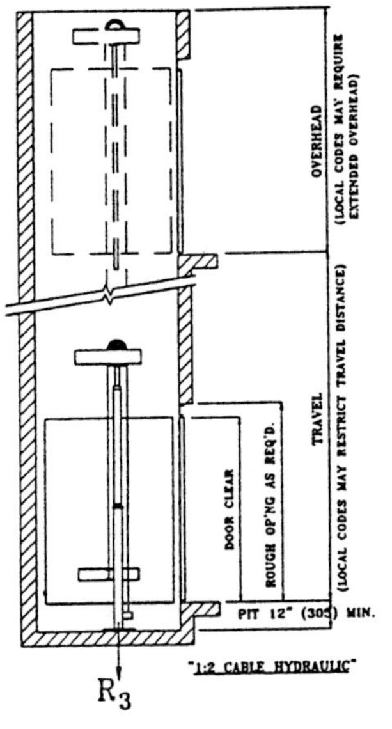

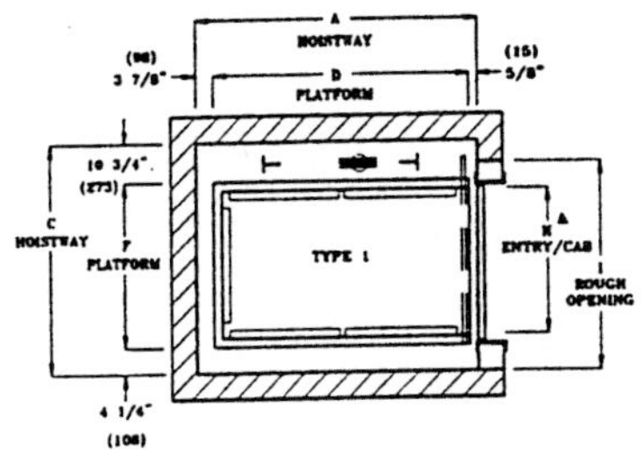

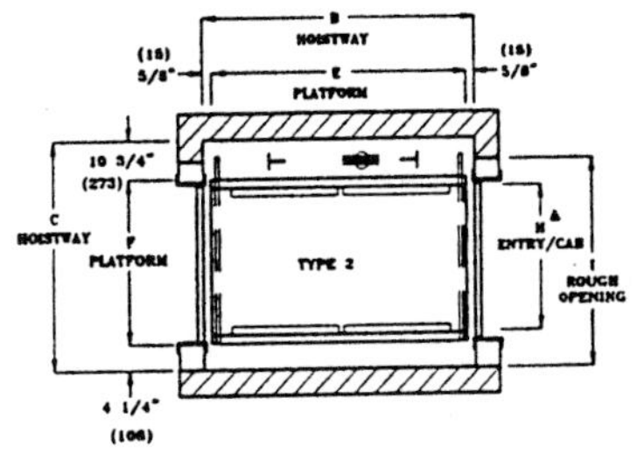

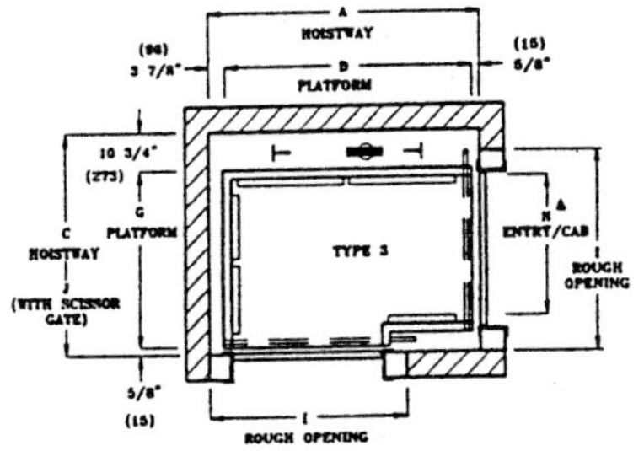

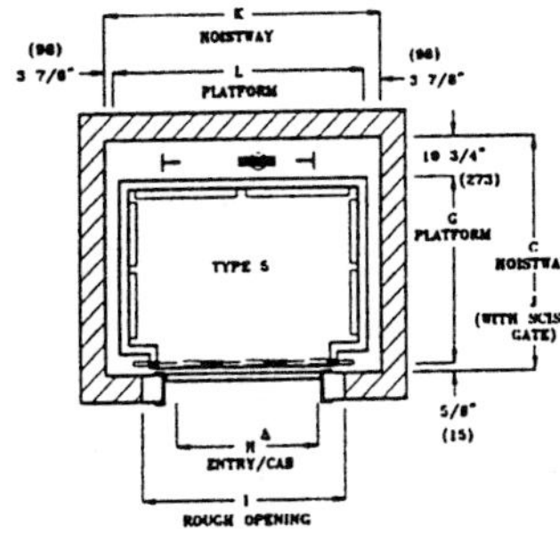

CAB HEIGHT	OVERHEAD (MIN)
80" (2032)	98" (2490)
84" (2134)	104" (2642)
90" (2286)	110" (2794)

NOTE:
HOISTWAY MUST BE PLUMB AND SQUARE AND TO SIZES SHOWN.... ALL DIMENSIONS INDICATED ARE FINISHED DIMENSIONS.

* LAYOUTS FOR "RIGHT HAND" MODELS SHOWN. "LEFT HAND" MODELS ARE OPPOSITE AND DIMENSIONS ARE IDENTICAL AND ARE CALLED TYPE 4

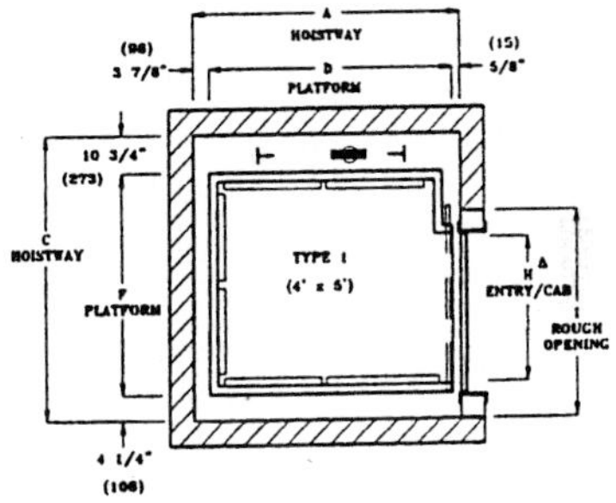

LAYOUTS FOR STANDARD SIZES SHOWN

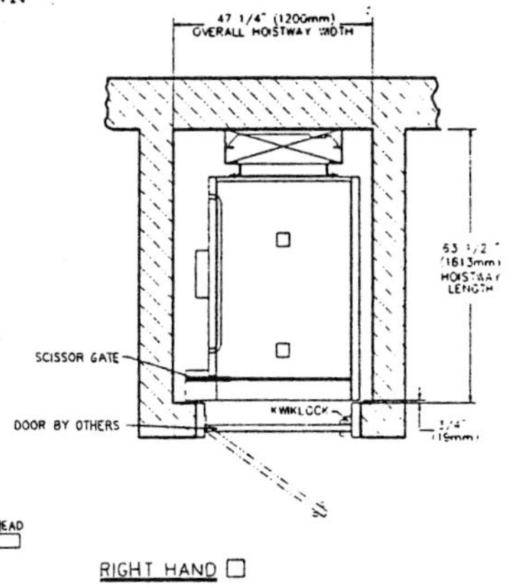

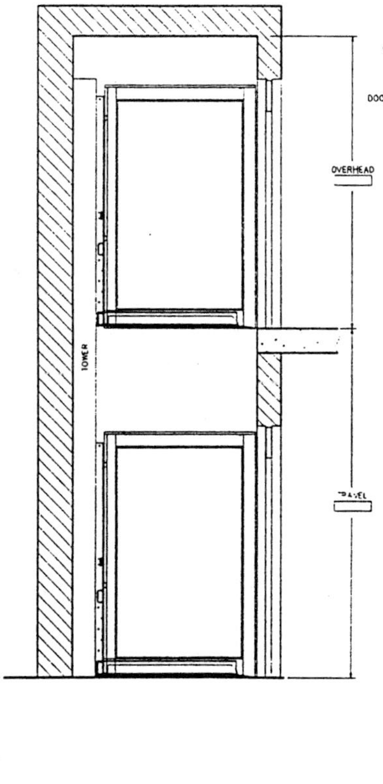

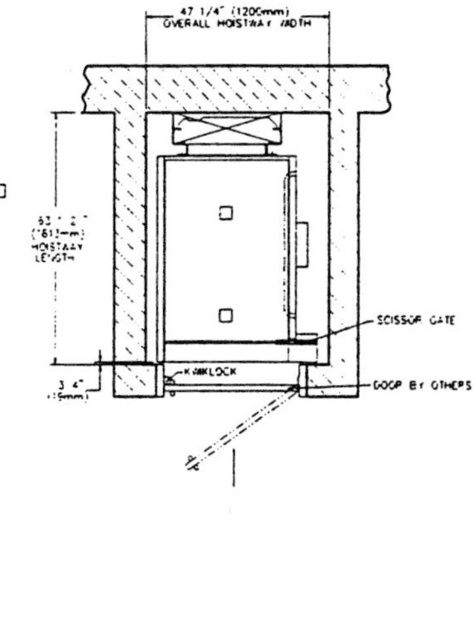

ELEVATORS AND WHEELCHAIR LIFTS
Residential Installations

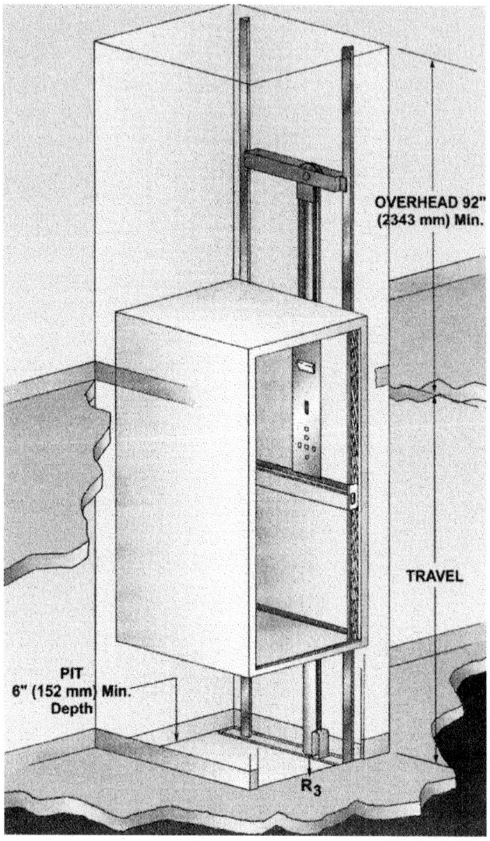

HOISTWAY PLANS LAYOUTS FOR STANDARD SIZES SHOWN

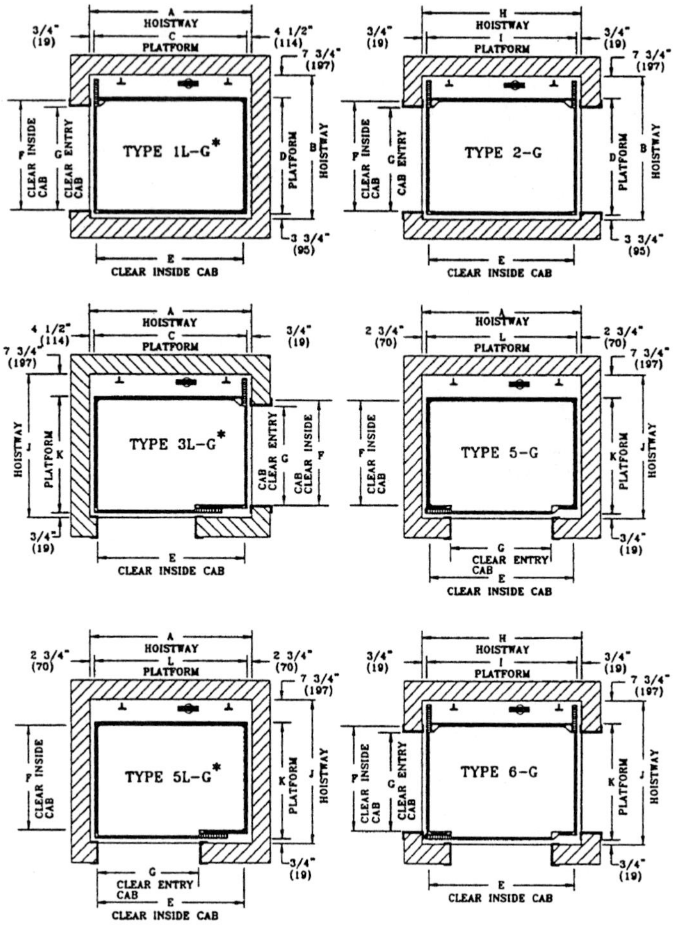

Δ NOMINAL SIZE

PLATFORM SIZES	A	B	C	D	Δ E	Δ F	G	H	I	J	K	L
3' x 4' (914 x 1220)	56" (1420)	50" (1270)	50 3/4" (1289)	38 1/2" (978)	48" (1220)	36" (915)	SEE BELOW	52 1/2" (1335)	51" (1295)	48 1/4" (1225)	39 3/4" (1010)	50 1/2" (1280)
3' x 5' (914 x 1525)	68" (1730)	50" (1270)	62 3/4" (1594)	38 1/2" (978)	60" (1525)	36" (915)	SEE BELOW	64 1/2" (1640)	63" (1600)	48 1/4" (1225)	39 3/4" (1010)	62 1/2" (1585)

HIGH-RISE ELEVATORS

Traction Elevators

Traction elevators are for use in buildings over six floors. They can serve up to 27 landings and can be used in office buildings, apartment complexes, dormitories, hotels, and other structures. These elevators can travel up to 1000 ft/min and are ideal for high-rise buildings of all kinds.

HOISTWAY PLAN

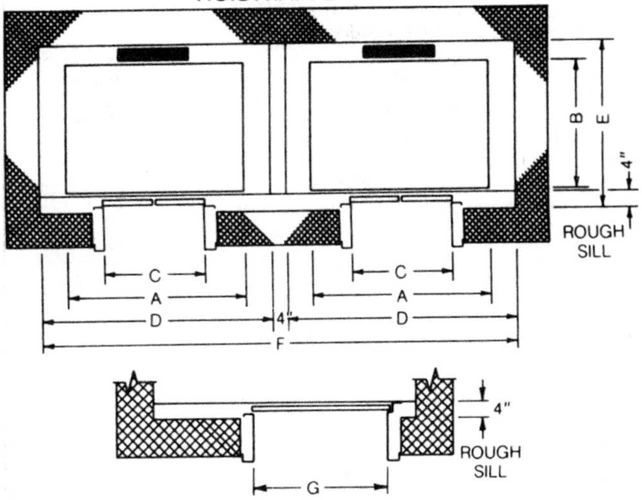

RIGHT HAND DOOR SHOWN: LEFT HAND AVAILABLE

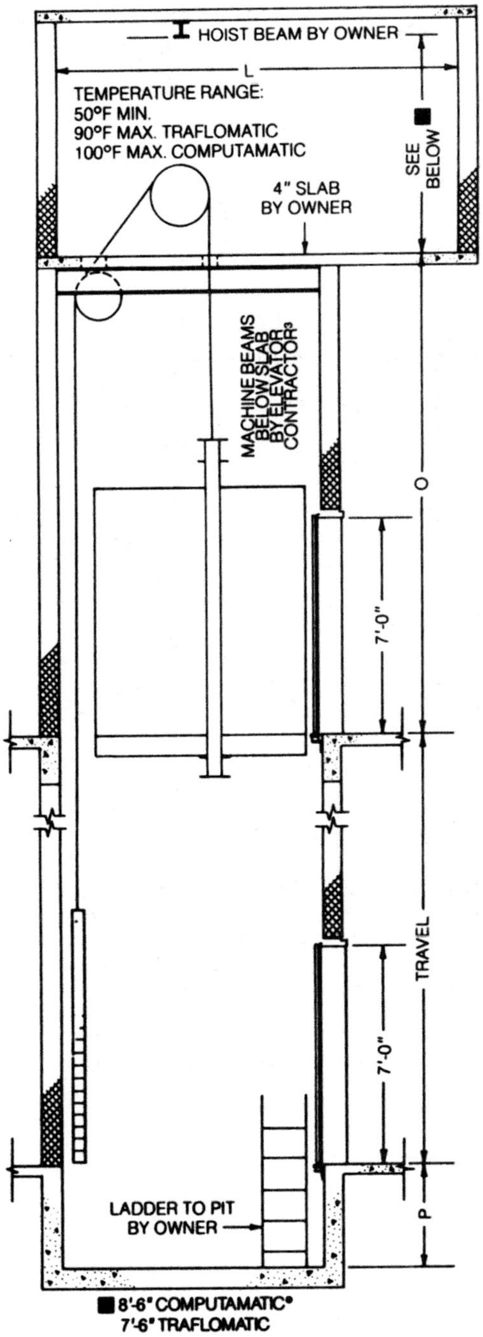

RECOMMENDED SIZES AND CAPACITIES				
TYPE BUILDING	SMALL OFFICE/ APARTMENT	AVERAGE OFFICE/HOTEL	LARGE OFFICE/STORE	
MODEL	SPF21-H♿	SPF25♿	SPF30♿	SPF35♿
	CAPACITY (IN POUNDS)			
DIMENSIONS	2100	2500	3000	3500
A[1]	5'-8"	6'-8"	6'-8"	6'-8"
B[1]	4'-3"	4'-3"	4'-9"	5'-5"
C	—	3'-6"	3'-6"	3'-6"
D[2]	7'-4"	8'-4"	8'-4"	8'-4"
E	6'-8"	6'-8"	7'-2"	7'-10"
F	15'-0"	17'-0"	17'-0"	17'-0"
G	3'-0"	3'-6"	3'-6"	3'-6"

[1] Inside dimensions
[2] Single car dimensions
♿ These models meet minimum size for handicapped use.

Hoistway dimensions are based on 1" out of plumb, no provisions for seismic conditions, and no occupied space below hoistway. If these conditions cannot be met, then consideration must be given for additional required space.

MINIMUM PIT, OVERHEAD, MACHINE ROOM DIMENSIONS				
CAPACITY (IN LBS.)	DIMENSIONS	SPEED (FEET PER MINUTE)		
		200	350	450
2100	L	16'-0"	16'-0"	—
	O	15'-4"	15'-4"	—
	P[4]	5'-0"	5'-0"	—
2500	L	16'-0"	16'-0"	16'-0"
	O	15'-4"	15'-4"	16'-4"
	P[4]	5'-0"	5'-0"	6'-6"
3000	L	16'-0"	16'-0"	16'-0"
	O	15'-4"	16'-0"	16'-4"
	P[4]	5'-0"	5'-0"	6'-6"
3500	L	16'-0"	16'-0"	16'-0"
	O	15'-4"	16'-0"	17'-6"
	P[4]	5'-0"	5'-0"	6'-6"

Overhead "O" based on 8'-0" O.A. nominal cab height.
[3] Machine beams designed per ANSI/ASME code A17.1 and does not include floor weight and loads on floor.
[4] 6'-0" min. "P" travel above 250'-0" SPF21 SPF25; travel above 225'-0" SPF30; travel above 200'-0" SPF35 } for speeds up to 350 F/M

ELEVATORS AND WHEELCHAIR LIFTS

High-Rise Elevators

HOISTWAY PLAN

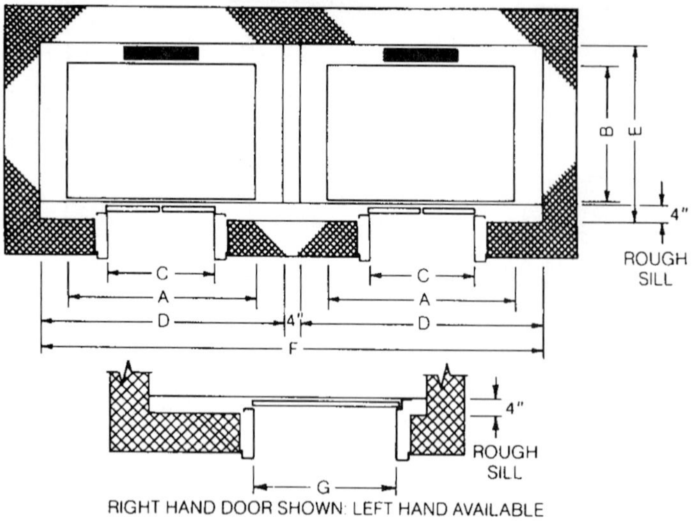

RIGHT HAND DOOR SHOWN: LEFT HAND AVAILABLE

RECOMMENDED SIZES AND CAPACITIES						
TYPE BUILDING	SMALL OFFICE/APARTMENT		AVERAGE OFFICE/HOTEL		LARGE OFFICE/STORE	
	CAPACITY (IN POUNDS)					
DIMENSIONS	2000♿	2100♿	2500♿	3000♿	3500♿	4000♿
A[1]	6'-0"	5'-8"	6'-8"	6'-8"	6'-8"	7'-8"
B[1]	3'-7"	4'-3"	4'-3"	4'-9"	5'-5"	5'-5"
C	3'-0"	—	3'-6"	3'-6"	3'-6"	4'-0"
D[2]	7'-8"	7'-4"	8'-4"	8'-4"▲	8'-4"▲	9'-4"▲
E[3]	6'-0"	6'-8"	6'-8"	7'-2"	7'-10"	7'-10"
F	15'-8"	15'-0"	17'-0"	17'-0"●	17'-0"●	19'-0"●
G	—	3'-0"	3'-6"	3'-6"	3'-6"	4'-0"

[1] Inside dimensions [2] Single car dimensions [3] Add 3" when speed = 500 FPM or above
▲ Add 2" when speed = 1000 FPM ● Add 4" when speed = 1000 FPM

Hoistway dimensions are based on 1" out of plumb, no provisions for seismic conditions, and no occupied space below hoistway. If these conditions cannot be met then consideration must be given for additional required space.

MINIMUM PIT, OVERHEAD, MACHINE ROOM DIMENSIONS								
		SPEED (FEET PER MINUTE)						
CAPACITY (IN LBS.)	DIMENSIONS	200	350	450	500	700	800	1000
2000	L O P[5]	16'-0" 15'-4" 5'-0"	16'-0" 15'-4" 5'-0"	16'-0" 16'-4" 6'-6"				
2100	O O P[5]	16'-0" 15'-4" 5'-0"	16'-0" 15'-4" 5'-0"	16'-0" 16'-4" 6'-6"				
2500	L O P[5]	16'-0" 15'-4" 5'-0"	16'-0" 15'-4" 5'-0"	16'-0" 16'-4" 6'-6"	16'-6" 18'-6" 10'-1"	16'-6" 20'-6" 11'-5"		
3000	L O P[5]	16'-0" 15'-4" 5'-0"	16'-0" 16'-0" 5'-0"	16'-0" 16'-4" 6'-6"	17'-0" 18'-6" 10'-1"	17'-0" 20'-6" 11'-5"	18'-0" 20'-0" 11'-6"	18'-0" 20'-0" 11'-6"
3500 4000	L O P[5]	16'-0" 15'-4" 5'-0"	16'-0" 16'-0" 5'-0"	16'-0" 17'-6" 6'-6"	17'-0" 18'-6" 10'-1"	17'-0" 20'-6" 11'-5"	18'-0" 20'-6" 11'-6"	18'-0" 20'-6" 11'-6"

NOTE: These dimensions are for general application to custom designed elevators.
Overhead "O" based on 8'-0" O.A. nominal cab height.

[4] Machine beams designed per ANSI/ASME code A17.1 and does not include floor weight and loads on floor.

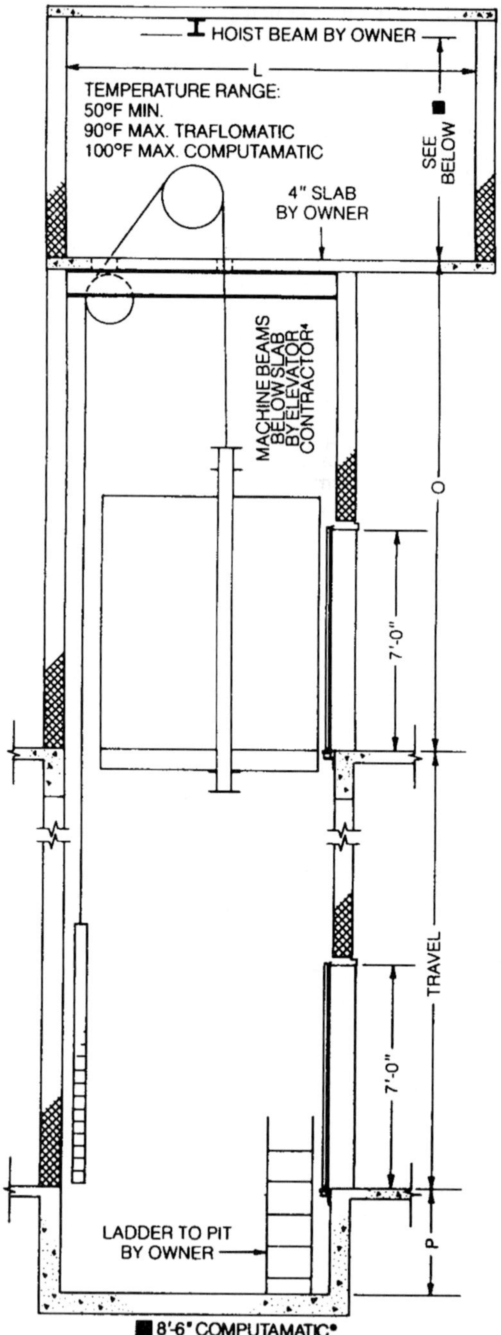

■ 8'-6" COMPUTAMATIC®
7'-6" TRAFLOMATIC

CENTER-OPENING DOORS

These permit quickest entry and exit, thus speeding elevator service, and provide an attractive balanced appearance both in the hallway and inside the elevator car. They should always be used in high-speed applications.

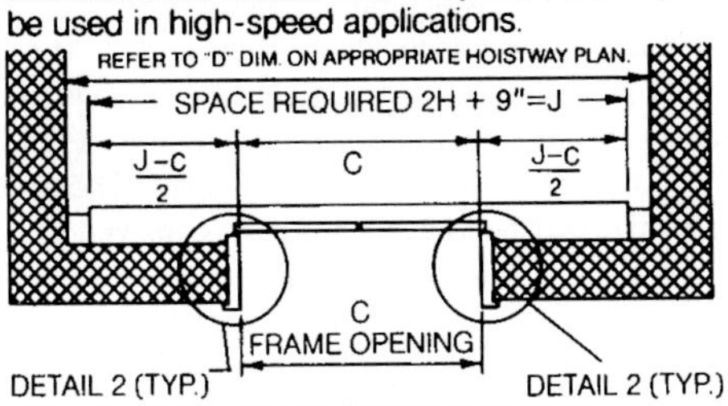

NOTE: H=opening in 2" increments only (use next higher even dimension for odd size door).
C=actual frame opening

TWO-SPEED SLIDING DOORS

Doors of this type provide the widest possible opening width for small cars but do not afford the entry and exit speed of center-opening doors. The two doors move in the same direction, one sliding behind the other.

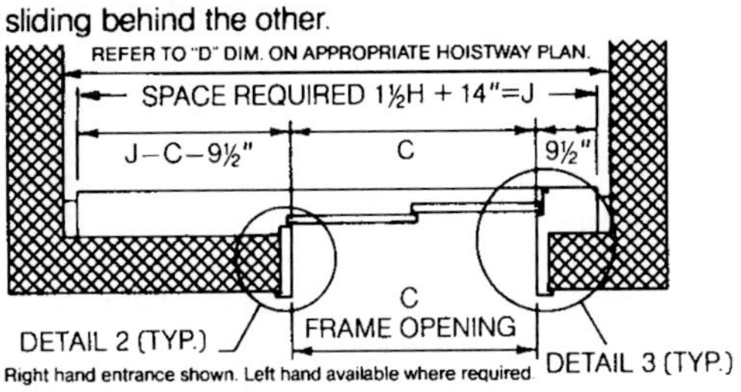

Right hand entrance shown. Left hand available where required.

NOTE: H=opening in 2" increments only (use next higher even dimension for odd size door).
C=actual frame opening

SINGLE SLIDING DOORS

This is the most economical type of elevator door, and also the slowest. The single door moves either to right or left from one side of the elevator car, the opening being limited by the width of the door and car.

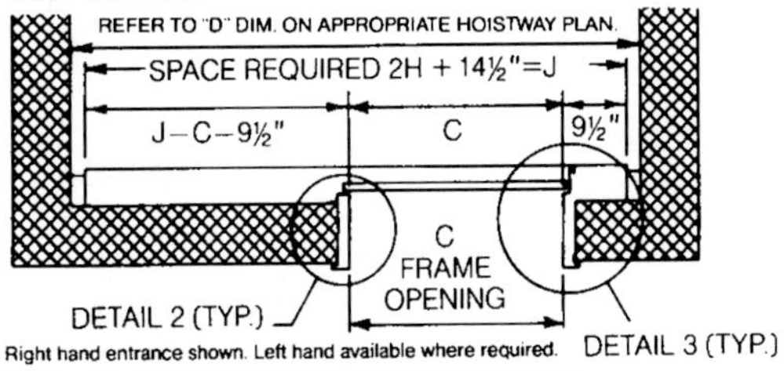

Right hand entrance shown. Left hand available where required.

NOTE: H=opening in 2" increments only (use next higher even dimension for odd size door).
C=actual frame opening

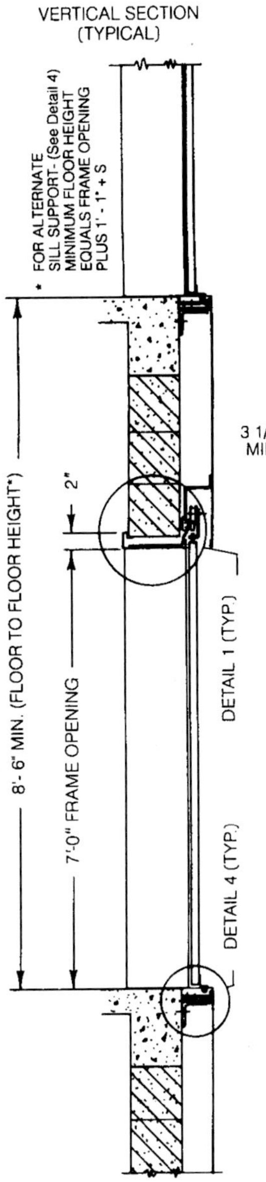

DRYWALL CONSTRUCTION

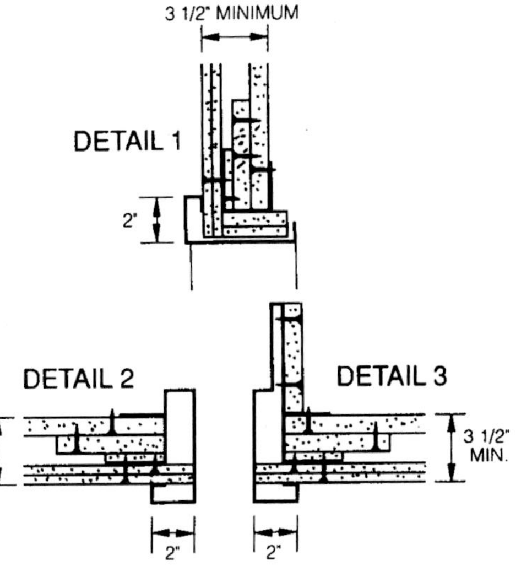

NOTE: These diagrams show minimum wall thickness and construction detail required in order to supply UL Label on entrances with no cutouts.

MASONRY CONSTRUCTION

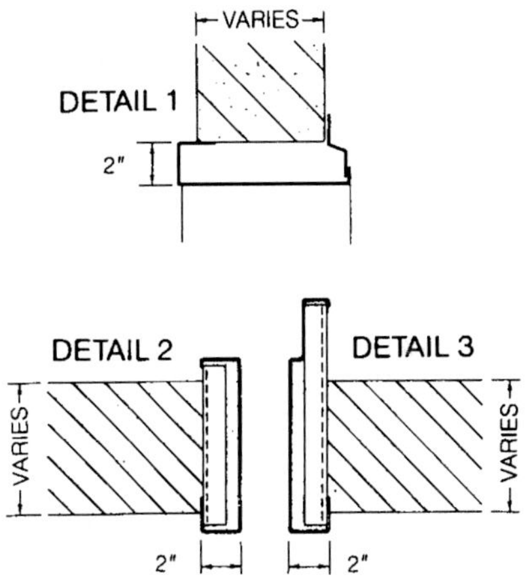

DETAIL 4 — SILL SUPPORTS

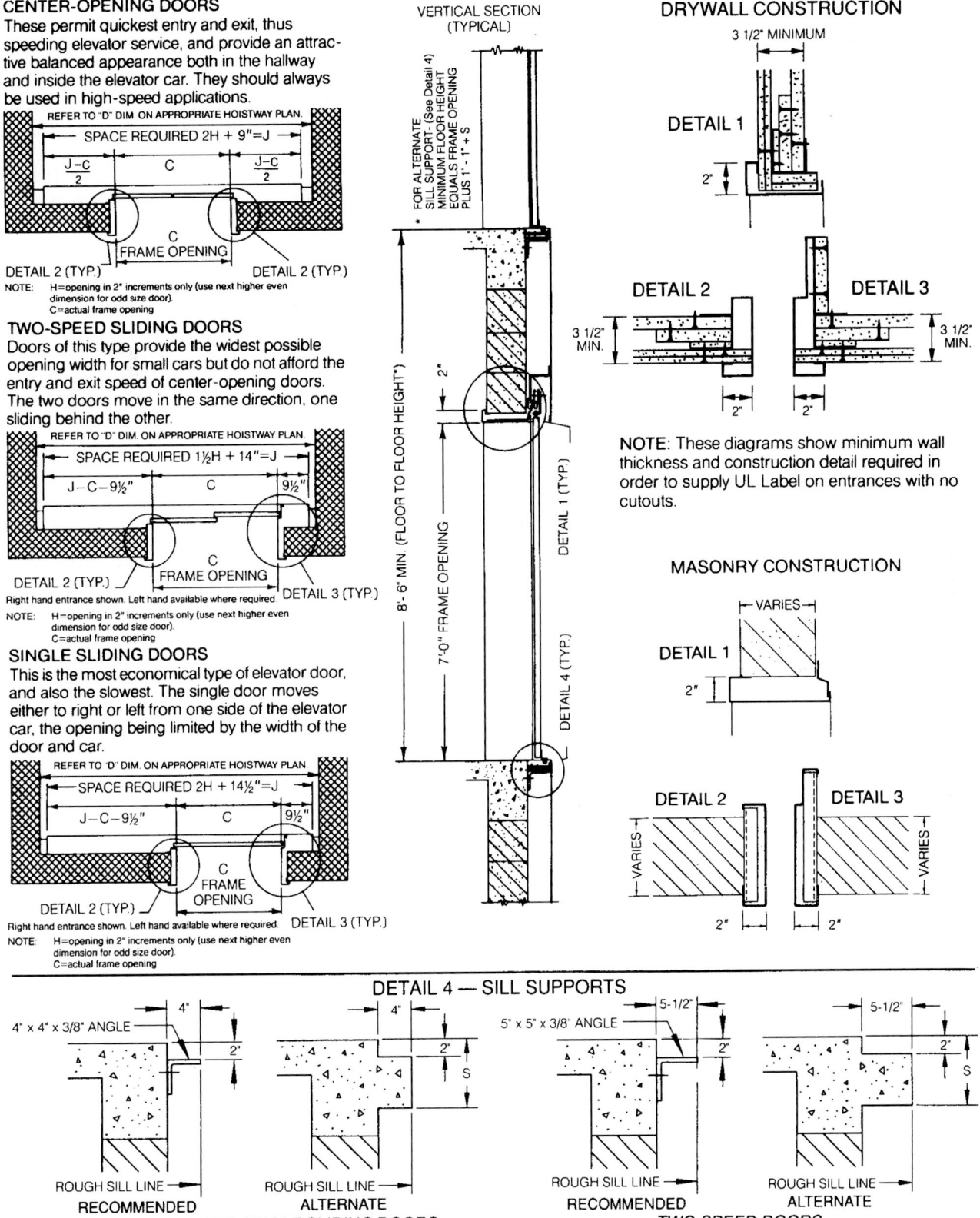

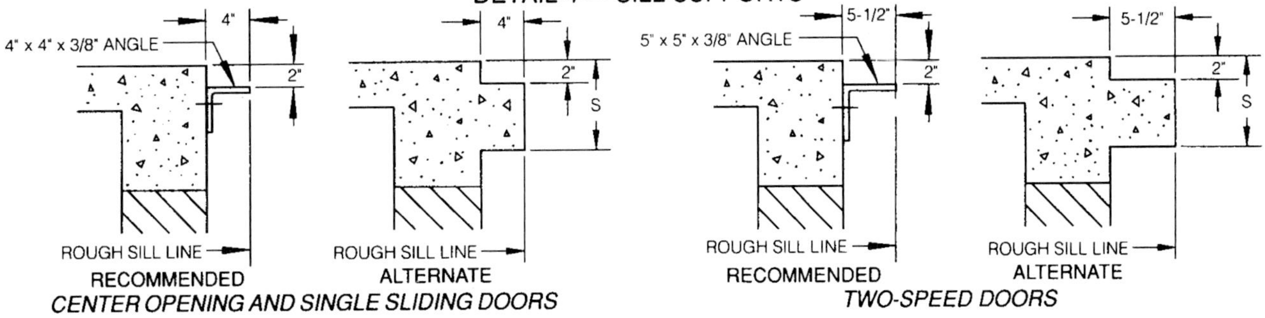

ELEVATORS AND WHEELCHAIR LIFTS
Barrier-Free Considerations

Floor Plan of Elevator Cars

The floor area of elevator cars shall provide space for wheelchair users to enter the car, maneuver within reach of controls, and exit from the car. Acceptable door opening and inside dimensions shall be as shown in Fig. 1. The clearance between the car platform sill and the edge of any hoistway landing shall be no greater than 1¼ in (32 mm).

Illumination Levels

The level of illumination at the car controls, platform, and car threshold and landing sill shall be at least 5 footcandles (53.8 lux).

Car Controls

Elevator control panels shall have the following features:

1. *Buttons.* All control buttons shall be at least ¾ in (19 mm) in their smallest dimension. They may be *raised* or flush.
2. *Tactile and visual control indicators.* All control buttons shall be designated by *raised* standard alphabet characters for letters, Arabic characters for numerals, or standard symbols as shown in Fig. 3*a*, and as required in ANSI A17.1-1978 and A17.1a-1979. The call button for the main entry floor shall be designated by a *raised* star at the left of the floor designation (see Fig. 3*a* and *b*). All *raised* designations for control buttons shall be placed immediately to the left of the button to which they apply. Applied plates, permanently attached, are an acceptable means to provide *raised* control designations. Floor buttons shall be provided with visual indicators to show when each call is registered. The visual indicators shall be extinguished when each call is answered.
3. *Height.* All floor buttons shall be no higher than *48 in (1220 mm), unless there is a substantial increase in cost, in which case the maximum mounting height may be increased to 54 in (1370 mm),* above the floor. Emergency controls, including the emergency alarm and emergency stop, shall be grouped at the bottom of the panel and shall have their centerlines no less than 35 in (890 mm) above the floor (see Fig. 3*a* and *b*).
4. *Location.* Controls shall be located on a front wall if cars have center opening doors, and at the side wall or at the front wall next to the door if cars have side opening doors (see Fig. 3*c* and *d*):

Car Position Indicators

In elevator cars, a visual car position indicator shall be provided above the car control panel or over the door to show the position of the elevator in the hoistway. As the car passes or stops at a floor served by the elevators, the corresponding numerals shall illuminate and an audible signal shall sound. Numerals shall be a minimum of ½ in (13 mm) high. The audible signal shall be no less than 20 dB with

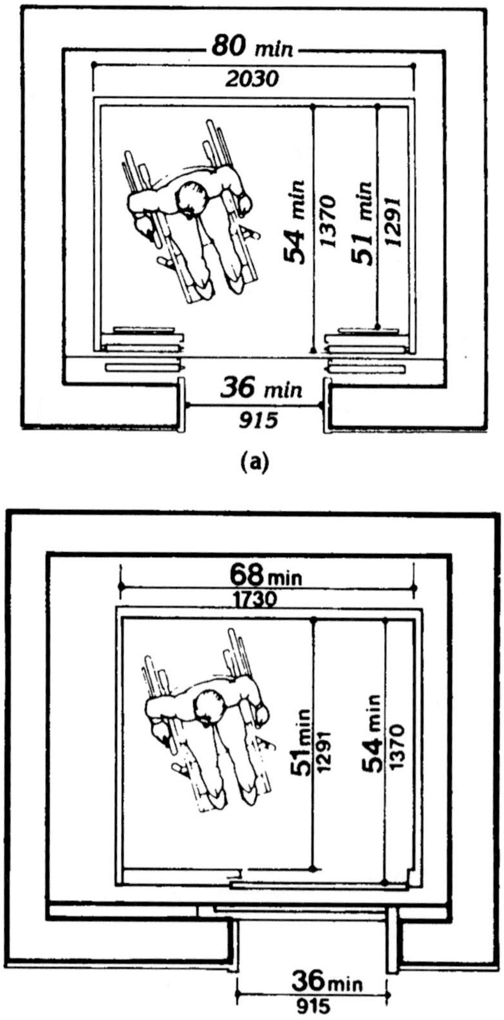

Fig. 1 Minimum dimensions of elevator cars

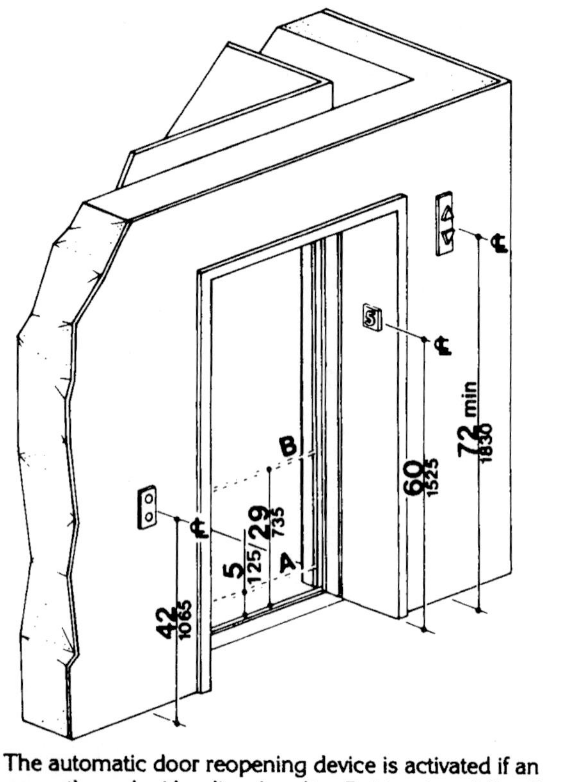

NOTE: The automatic door reopening device is activated if an object passes through either line A or line B. Line A and line B represent the vertical locations of the door reopening device not requiring contact.

Fig. 2 Hoistway and elevator entrances

a frequency no higher than 1500 Hz. An automatic verbal announcement of the floor number at which a car stops or which a car passes may be substituted for the audible signal.

Emergency Communications

If provided, emergency two-way communication systems between the elevator and a point outside the hoistway shall comply with ANSI A17.1-1978 and A17.1a-1979. The highest operable part of a two-way communication system shall be a maximum of 48 in (1220 mm) from the floor of the car. It shall be identified by a raised or recessed symbol and located adjacent to the device. If the system uses a handset, then the length of the cord from the panel to the handset shall be at least 29 in (735 mm). The emergency intercommunication system shall not require voice communication.

AMERICANS WITH DISABILITIES ACT REQUIREMENTS

ADA Checklist for Elevators

Automatic operations: Elevator operation shall be automatic and include two-way self-leveling.

Hall call buttons: Call Buttons to be ¾-in in the smallest dimension (minimum). Button arrangement must be vertical (not horizontal). Buttons to be either flush or raised (projected). Buttons must be of the illuminating type to indicate the registration of a hall call.

Hall lanterns: The visual element must be a minimum of 2½-in in the smallest dimension. Lantern(s) must be visible from the proximity of the hall call button. In addition to visual signal, the hall lantern is to have an audible signal sounding once for up and twice for down or shall have verbal annunciator. Note that in-car lanterns shall satisfy this requirement if they are as stipulated in the foregoing.

Raised and Braille characters (hoistway entrance jambs): Floor designation characters to be a minimum of 2 in high, raised 1/32 in, uppercase, and accompanied by corresponding Braille indications.

Door protective/reopening device: Doors shall stop and reopen automatically when the door becomes obstructed by an object or person. This device must function without requiring contact and may be of the photocell design or may be of another type of photoelectric registration.

Door and signal timing for hall calls: The minimum acceptable time between notification that a car is answering a call until the doors of that car begin to close shall be 5 seconds.

Door closing time delay for car calls: The minimum time for elevator doors to remain fully open in response to a car call shall be 3 seconds.

Elevator floor plan: Car door size, type, and clear inside car dimensions shall be in accordance with details provided elsewhere. Maximum elevator running clearance shall not exceed 1¼ in.

Inside car illumination: The level of illumination at the car controls, platform, car threshold, and landing sill shall be at least 5 footcandles (53.8 lux).

Car controls: All floor buttons shall illuminate when pressed to indicate registration of a car call. Buttons shall be flush or raised (projected). Tactile markings are required and are to include raised characters, numerals, and/or symbols along with corresponding Braille designations. Main entry floor to also be designated by a star. These tactile markings shall be placed immediately to the left of the button to which they apply. Characters and symbols shall contrast with their background.

Car position indicator: Floor indications shall illuminate and be a minimum of ½-in high, located for ease of visibility by riding passengers. This device shall also include an audible signal to record floors served by the elevator in either the up or down direction.

Emergency communications: A means of emergency two-way communication shall be provided in accordance with ASME A17:1-1990. The emergency communications system shall not rely solely on voice communication. The highest operable part of this device shall be no more than 48 in from the floor of the car and shall be identified by a raised symbol adjacent to the device.

ELEVATORS AND WHEELCHAIR LIFTS

ADA Requirements

Door Jamb Designation Height (Both Jambs)

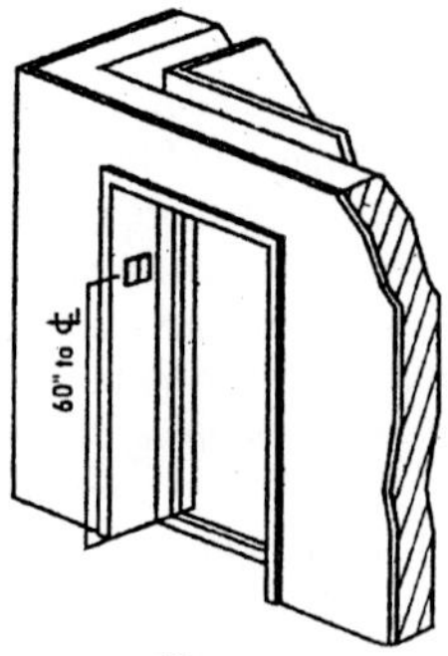

Hall/Car Lantern-Minimum Height

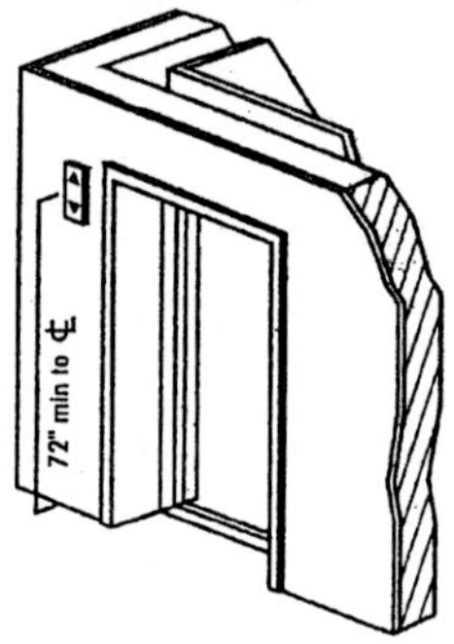

Automatic Door Reopening Device Locations

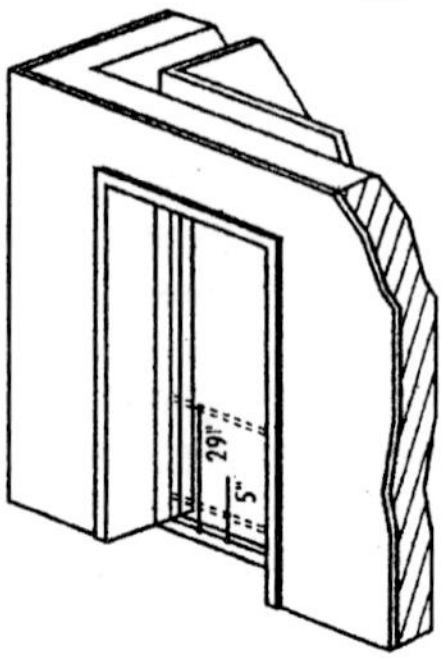

Hall Call Button Height

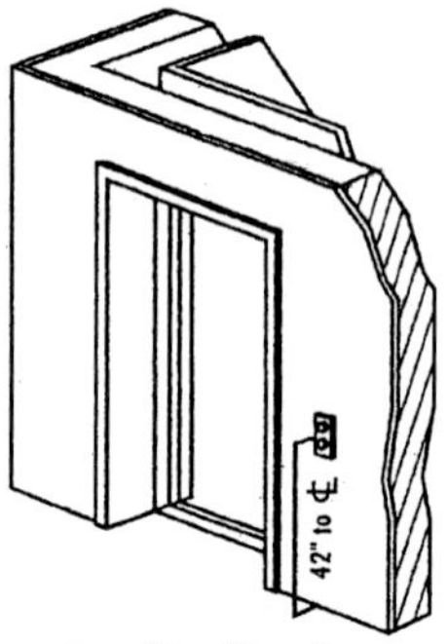

Side Opening Door Floor Plan

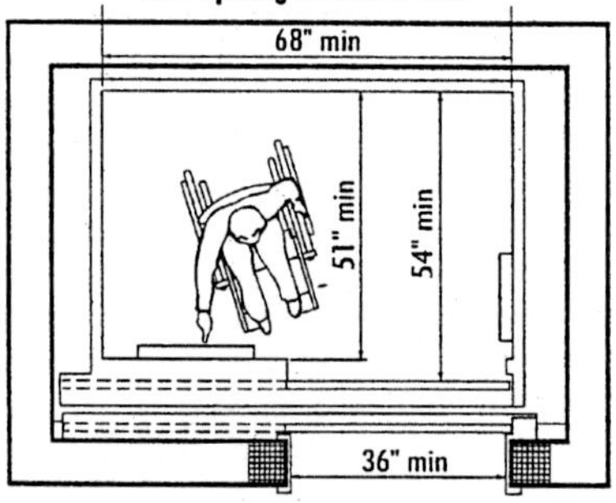

Alternate Control Panel Locations – Side Opening Door

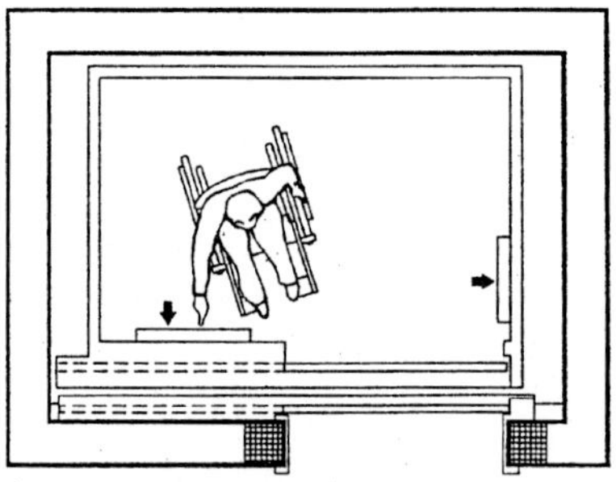

Center Opening Door Floor Plan

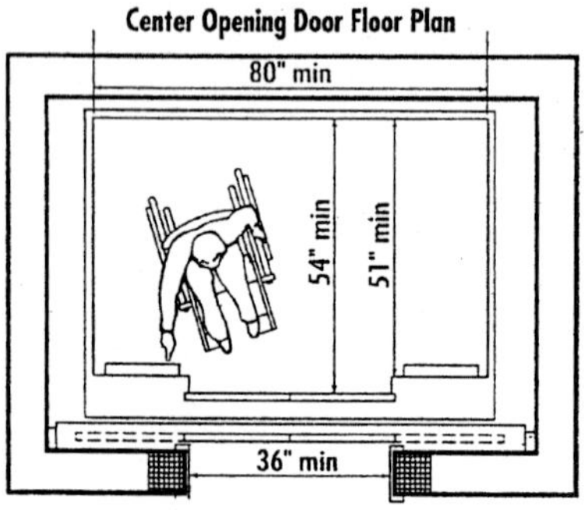

Alternate Control Panel Locations – Center Opening Door

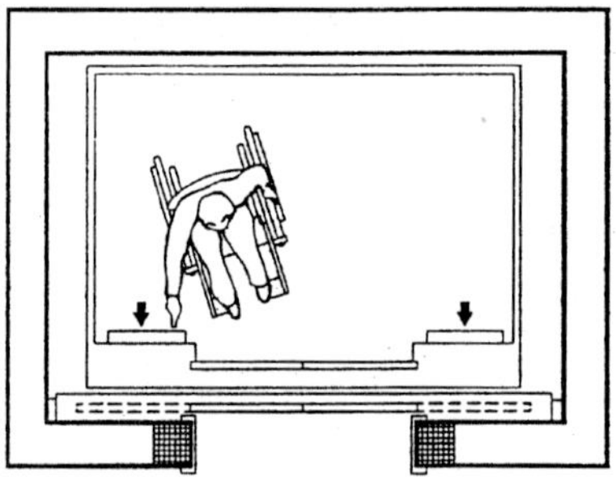

Control Panel Height

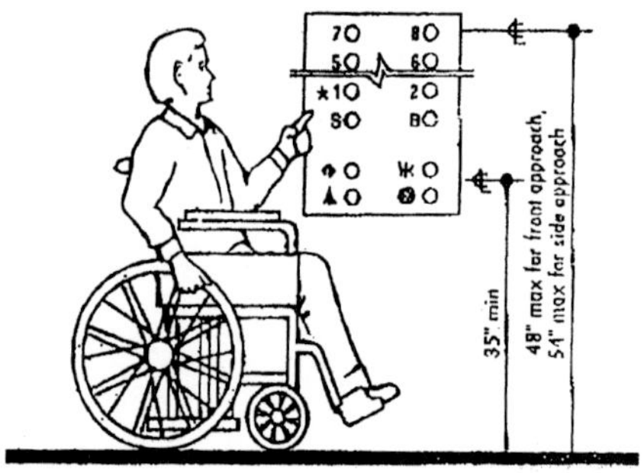

Control Panel Detail

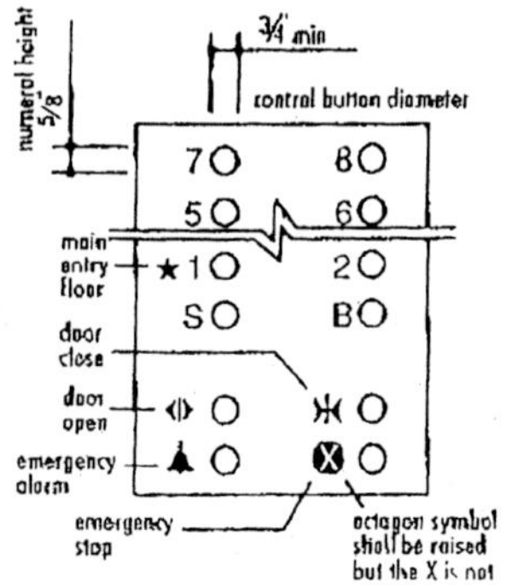

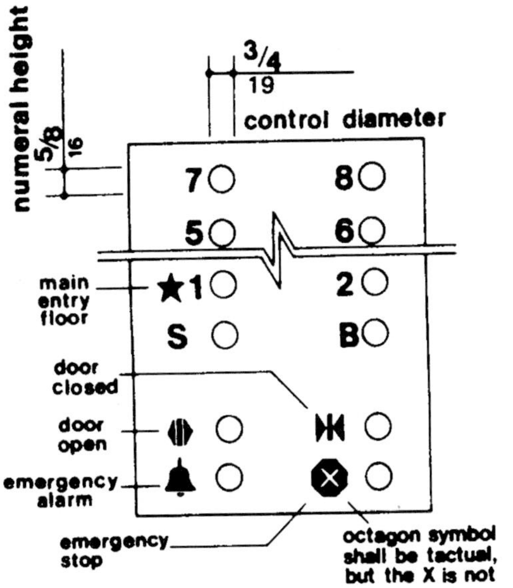

(a)
Panel Detail

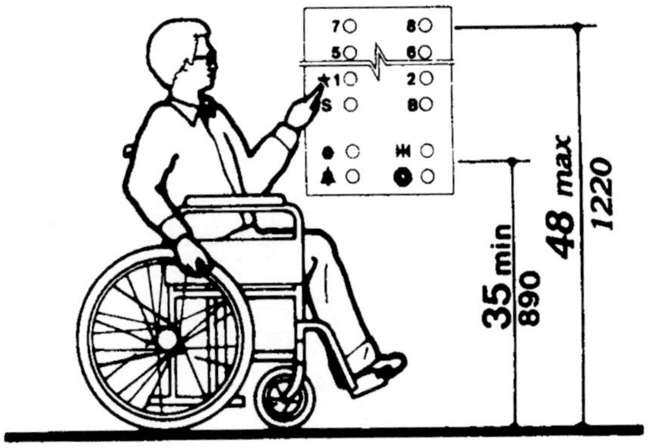

(b)
Control Height

(c)
Alternate Locations of Panel with Center Opening Door

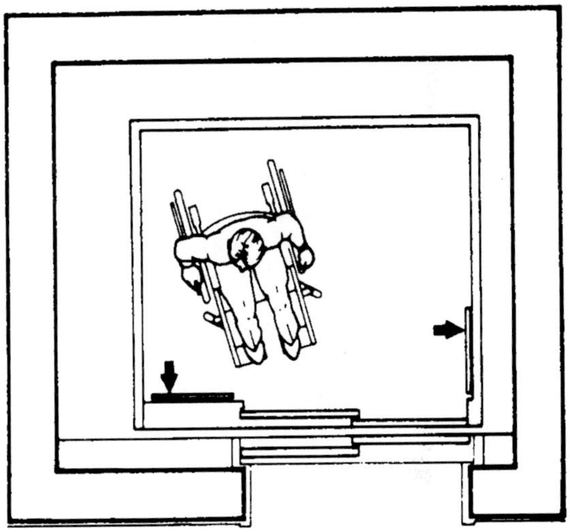

(d)
Alternate Locations of Panel with Side Opening Door

Fig. 3 Car controls

ELEVATORS AND WHEELCHAIR LIFTS
Typical Section of Escalator

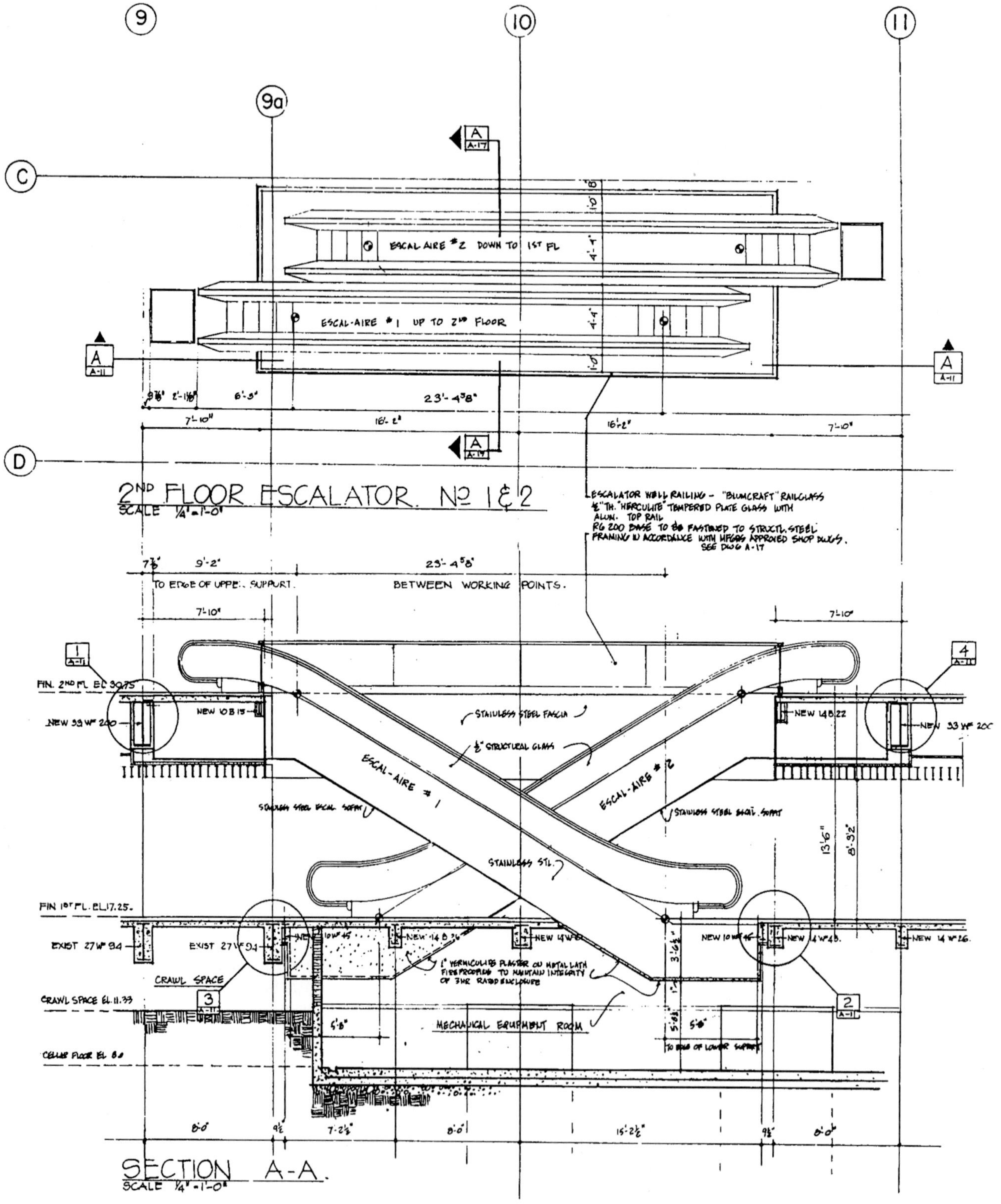

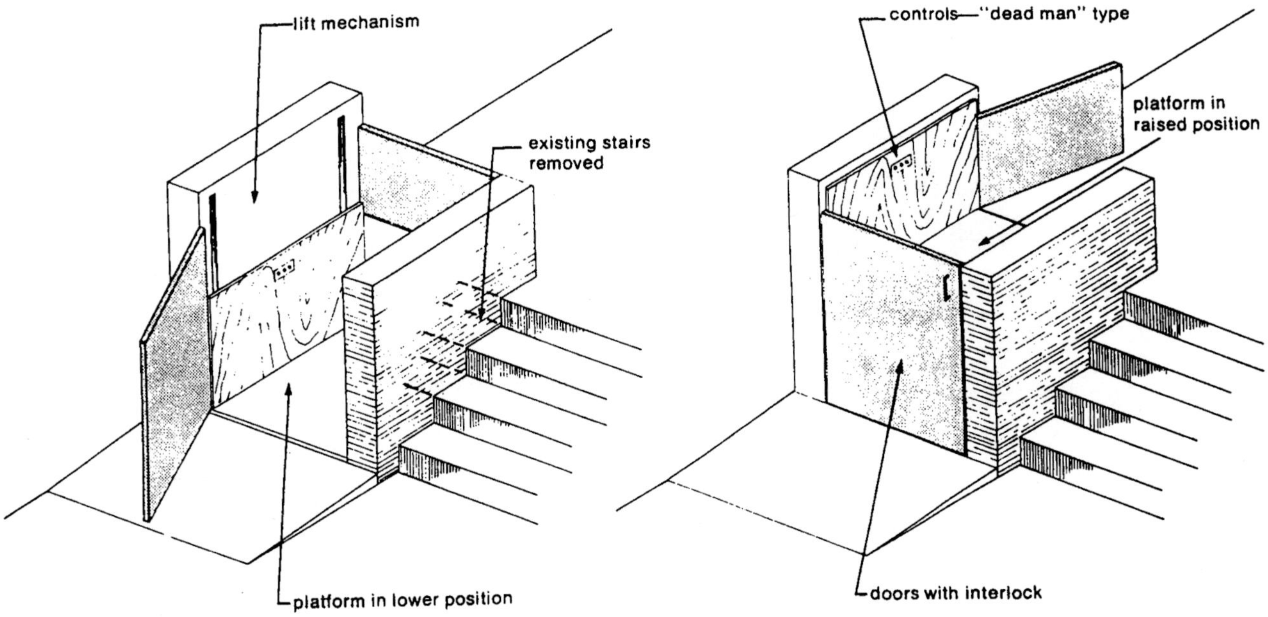

Fig. 4 Wheelchair lift. In certain installations where ramps may be impossible due to space limitations, small mechanical wheelchair lifts can be installed to overcome level changes. Manufactured lifts have a lift range from 2 to several feet and are either electromechanical, hydraulic, or pneumatically operated. Lifts can be semienclosed and equipped with entrance interlocks for safety, and either key operated for limited use or button type. "Dead-man" controls are recommended for safety

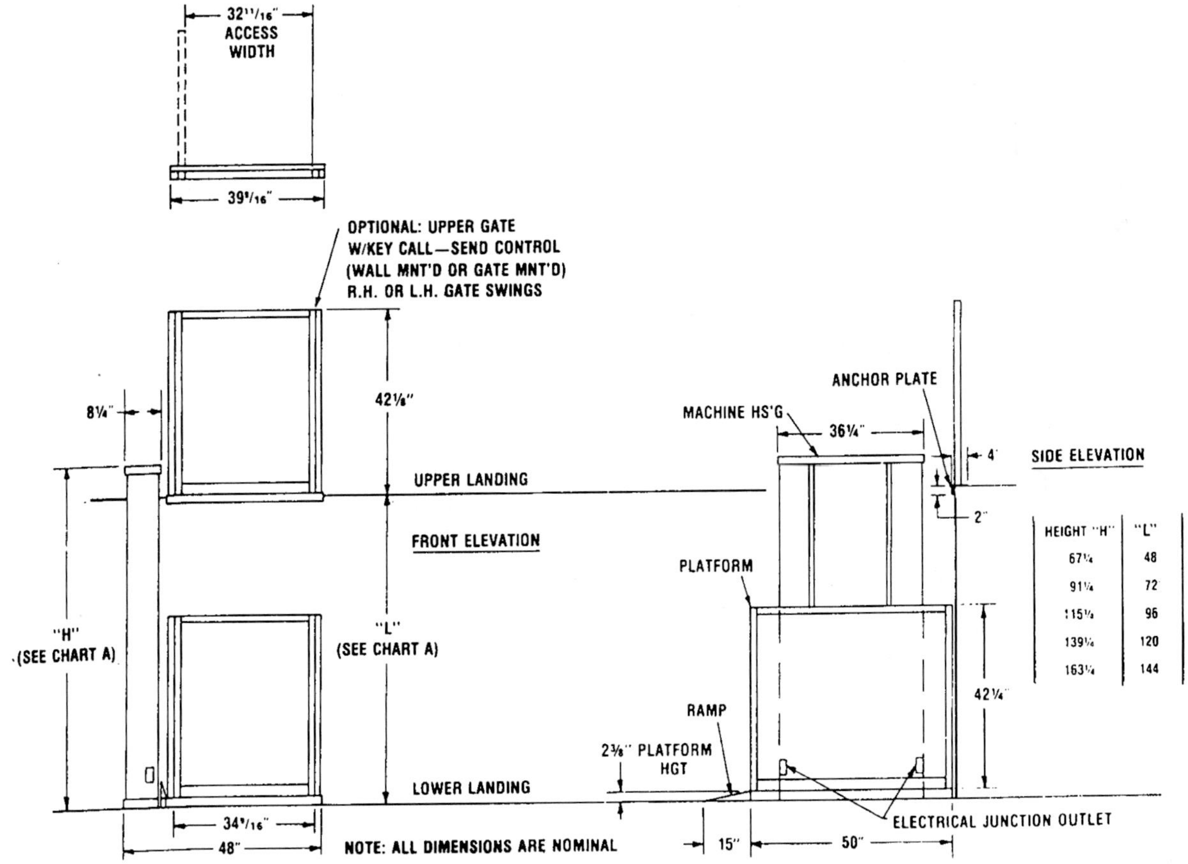

HEIGHT "H"	"L"
67¼	48
91¼	72
115¼	96
139¼	120
163¼	144

ELEVATORS AND WHEELCHAIR LIFTS
Wheelchair/Platform Lifts

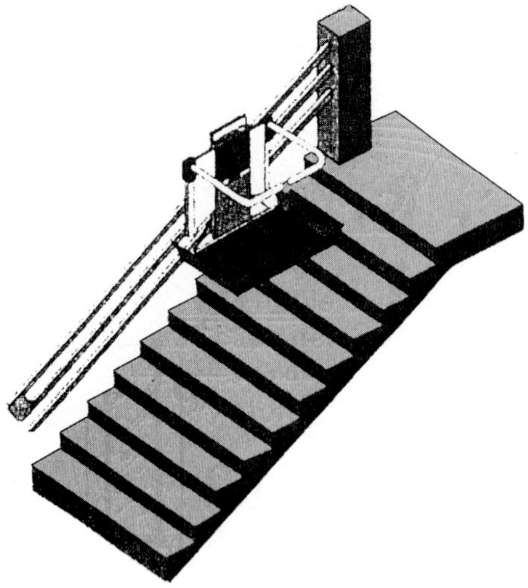

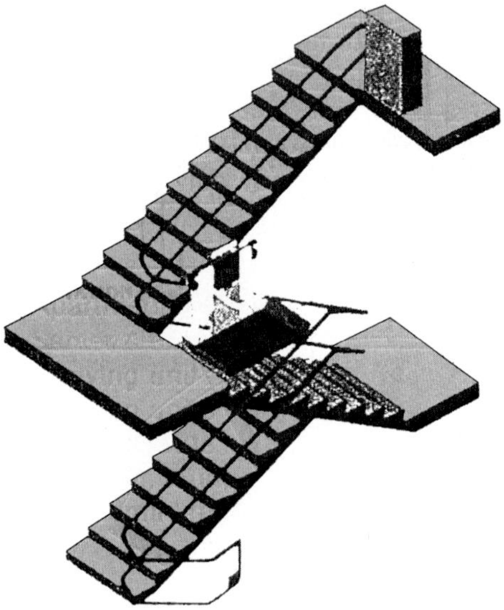

WHEELCHAIR/PLATFORM LIFTS

4.1.3(5) Exception 4: In new construction, platform lifts may be used in lieu of an elevator only under the following conditions and where state and local codes permit.

- To provide an accessible route to a performing area in an assembly occupancy.
- To comply with the wheelchair viewing position, line-of-sight, and dispersion requirements in assembly areas with fixed seating.
- To provide access to incidental occupiable rooms and spaces that are not open to the general public and that house no more than five persons. (This includes, but is not limited to, equipment control rooms and projection booths.)
- To provide access where existing site constraints or other constraints make use of a ramp or an elevator infeasible.

4.1.6(3)(g): In alterations, the use of platform lifts is not limited to the above conditions. Platform lifts may be used as part of an accessible route in alterations.

Section	*Item*	*Technical requirements*
4.1.3(5) Exception 4	Lifts	In new construction, if a lift is installed in lieu of an elevator or ramp, was it installed consistent with 4.1.3(5) Exception 4 (above) and in compliance with applicable state and local codes?
4.11.3	Independent use	Can the lift be entered, operated, and exited without assistance?
4.11.2 4.2.4	Platform size	Is the lift platform at least 30 by 48 in?
4.11.2 4.2.4	Clear space outside lift	Is there at least a 30- by 48-in clear space outside the lift positioned for a wheelchair user to reach the controls from a parallel or forward approach and to enter the lift?
4.11.2 4.27.3 4.2.5	Controls—forward reach	Where a forward reach is provided, is the height of the lift control no more than 48 in?
4.11.2 4.27.3 4.2.6	Side reach	Where a side reach is provided is the height of the lift control no more than 54 in?
4.11.2 4.27.4	Operation	Are the controls operable with one hand and without tight grasping, pinching, or twisting of the wrist? Is the force required to operate the controls no greater than 5 lbf?
4.1.2(1) 4.3.2	Accessible route	Is the lift on an accessible route?
4.11.2 4.3.6 4.5.1	Surface	Is the surface of the lift, as well as the accessible route to which it connects, stable, firm, and slip resistant?
4.11.2 4.5.2	Edge bevel	If there is a change in level of between ¼ and ½ in, is the edge beveled with a slope of 1:2 or less?
4.11.2	Safety code	Does the lift meet the ASME A17.1 Safety code for Elevators and Escalators, Section XX, 1990?

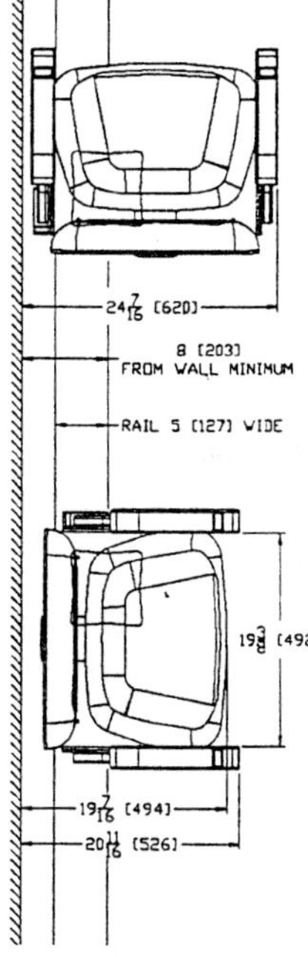

TOP VIEW - WITH 90° SWIVEL

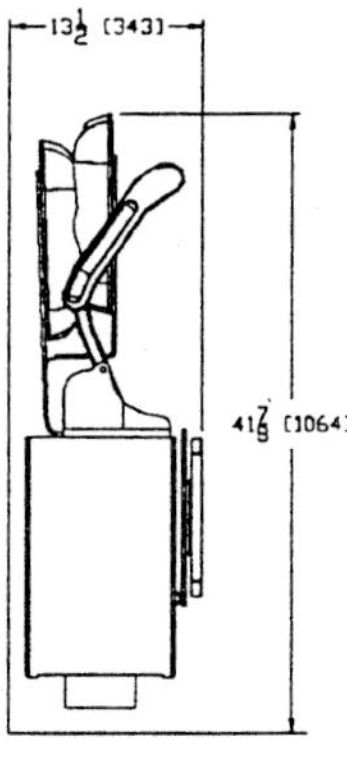

SIDE VIEW - FOLDED

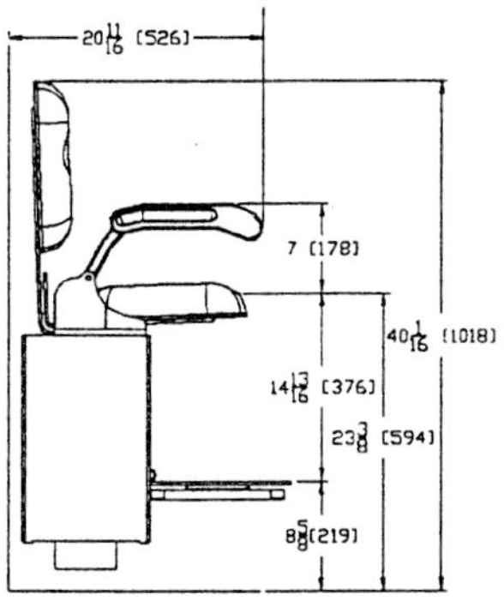

SIDE VIEW - UNFOLDED

Liberty RE-S Model

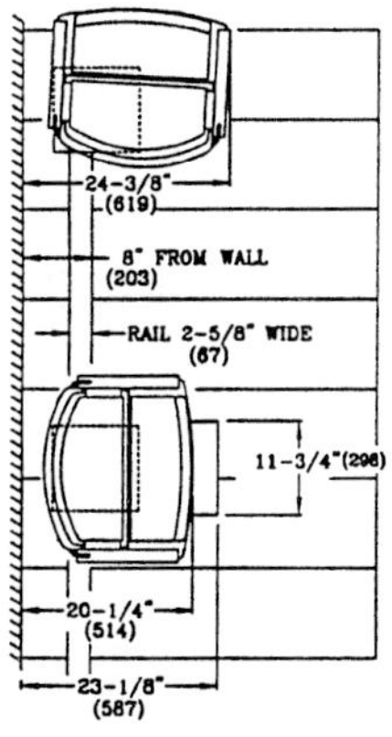

Top View - with 90° swivel

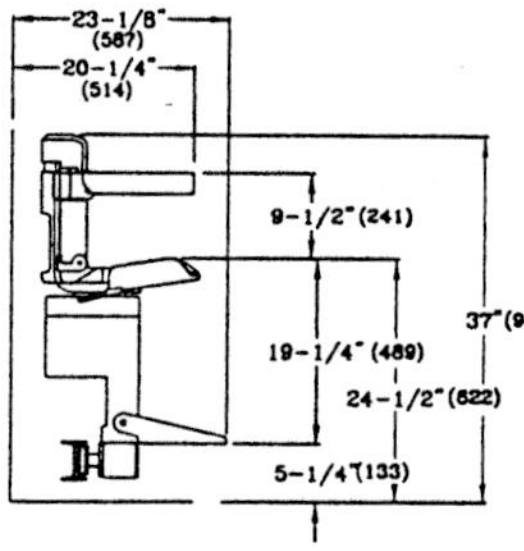

Side View - Unfolded

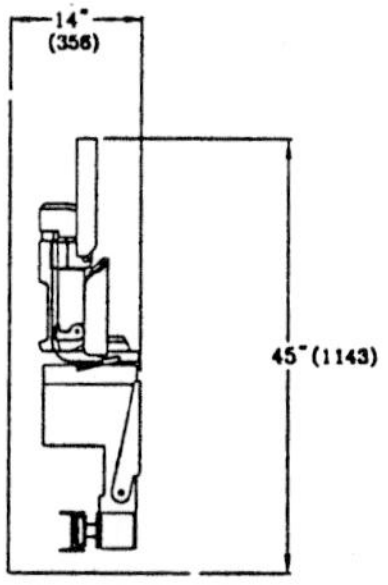

Side View - Folded

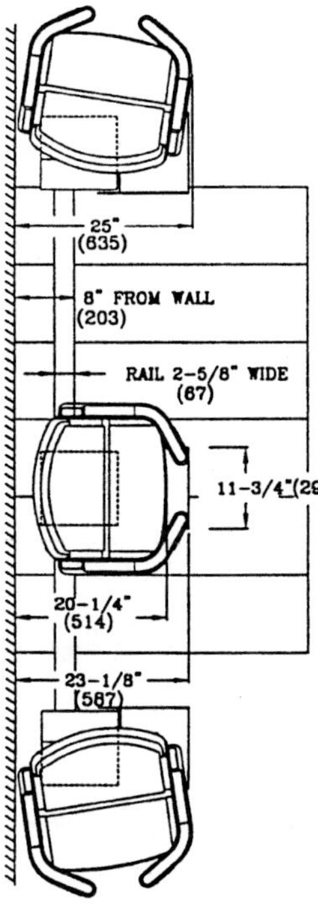

Top View - with 180° swivel

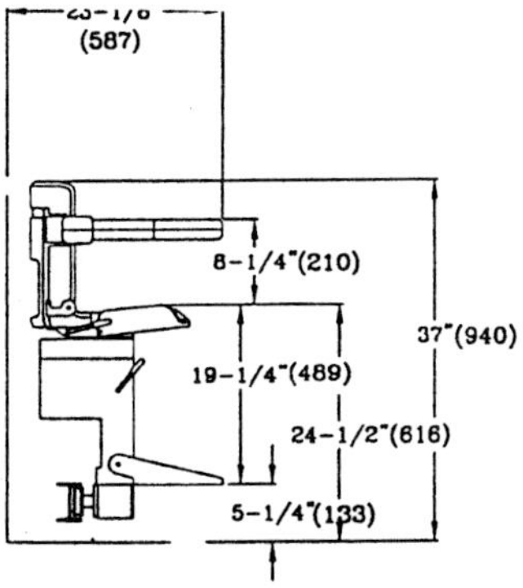

Side View - Unfolded

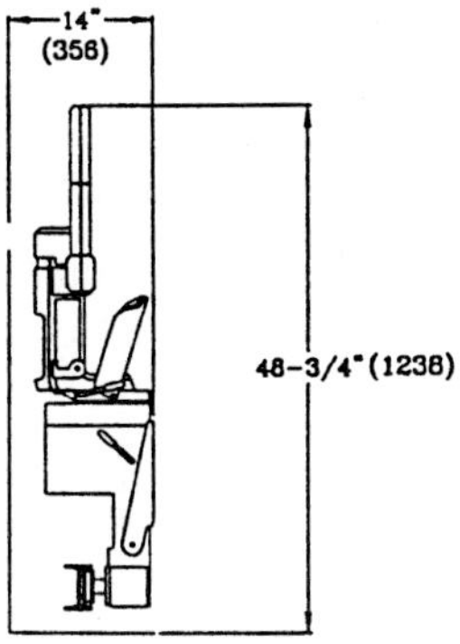

Side View - Folded

Liberty LX Model

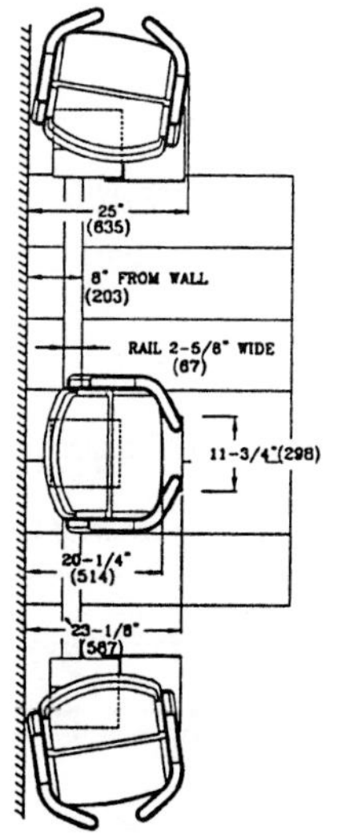

Top View - with 180° swivel

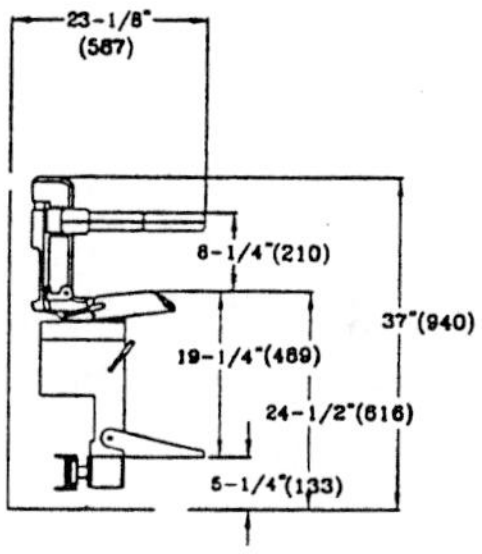

Side View - Unfolded

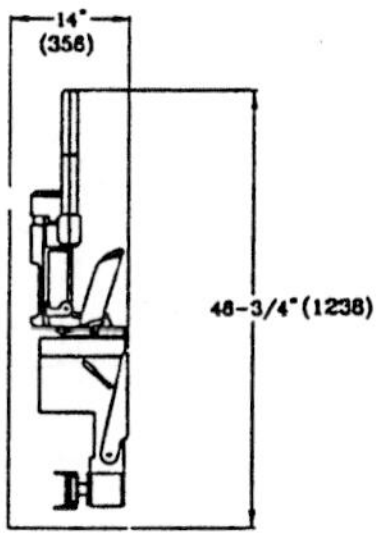

Side View - Folded

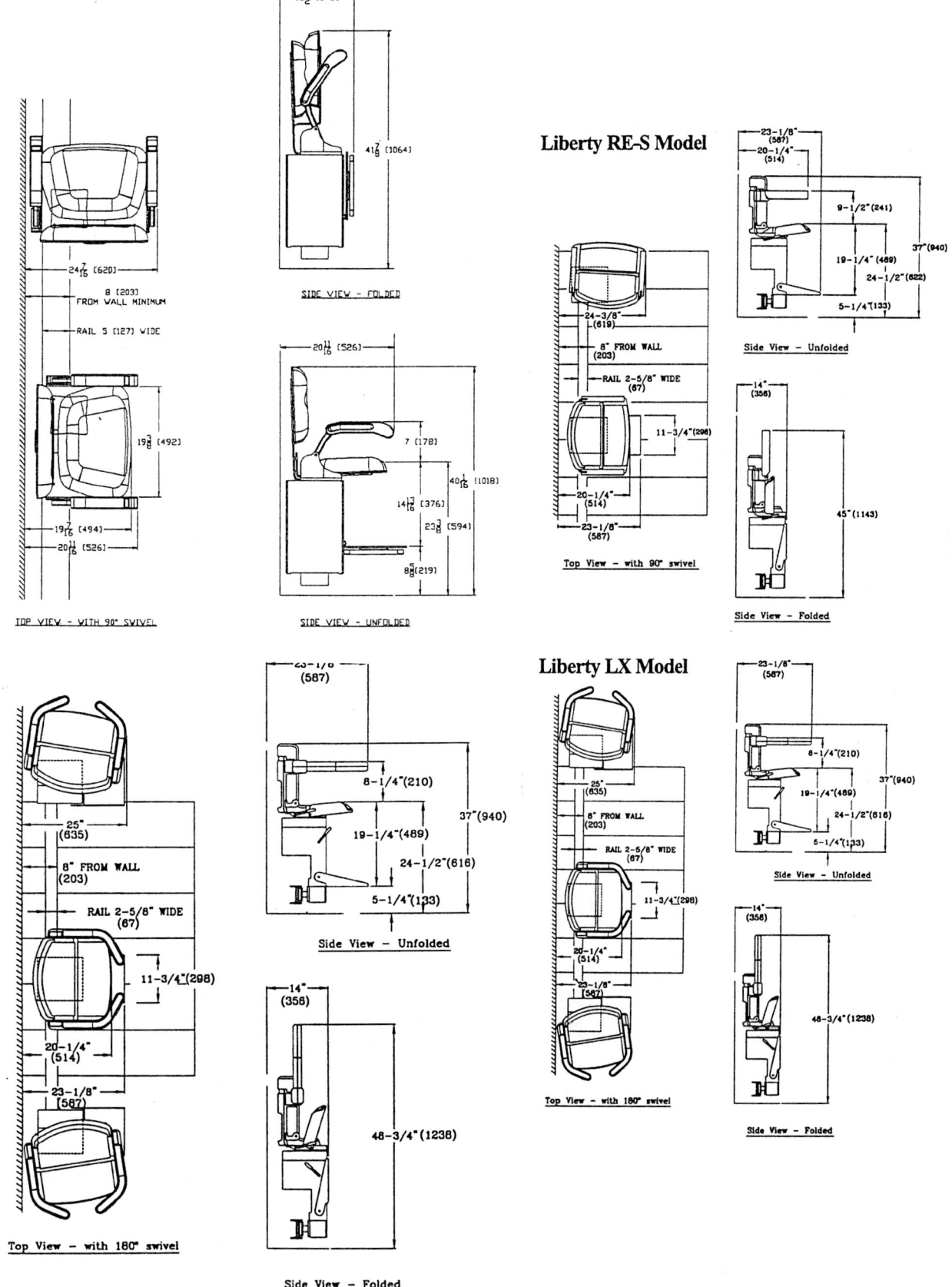

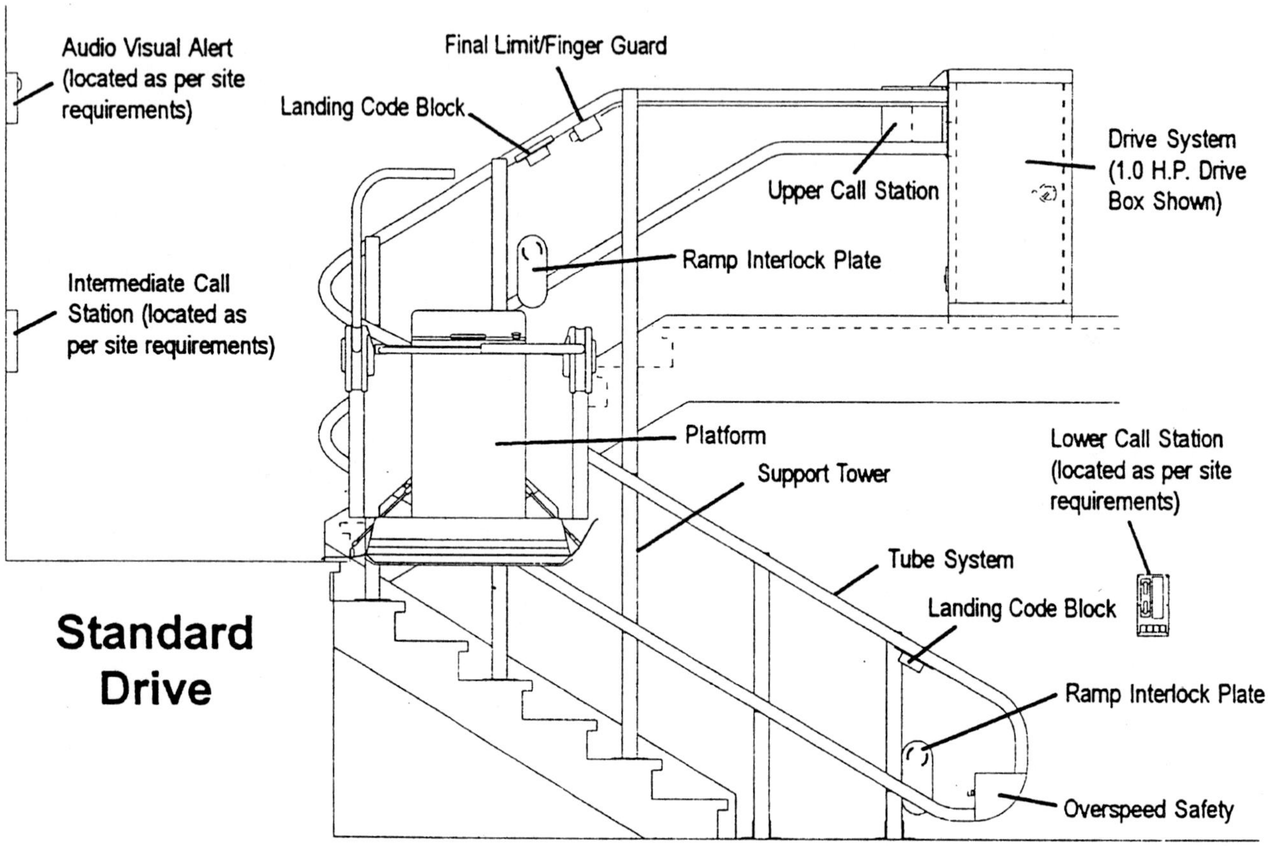

The Garaventa Stair-Lift is a versatile, aesthetically pleasing and cost-effective accessibility solution. It can be used on turning or straight stairways, with or without landings.

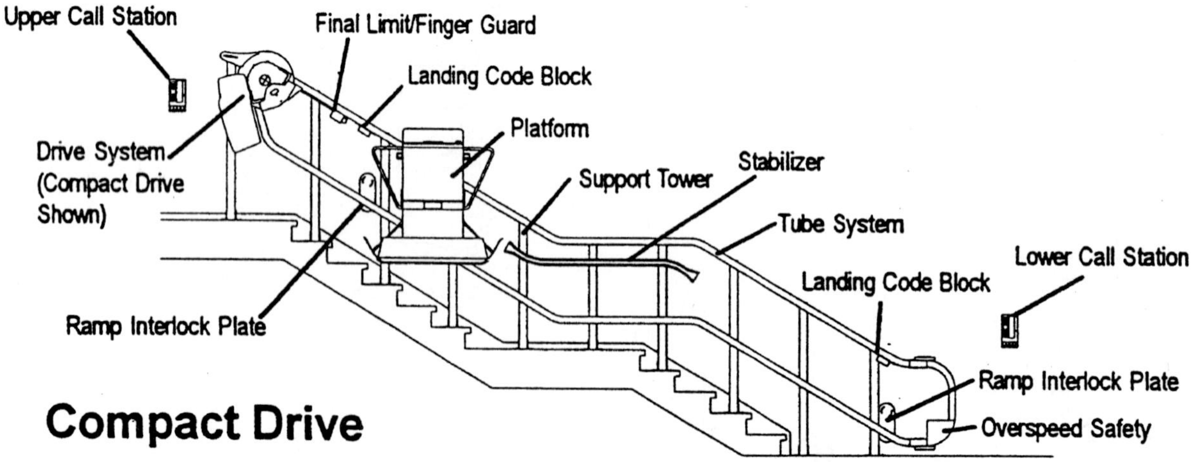

Attachment Methods

There are a multitude of attachment methods for the Garaventa Stair-Lift. Below are some of the most common mounting arrangements. Consult Garaventa for more details.

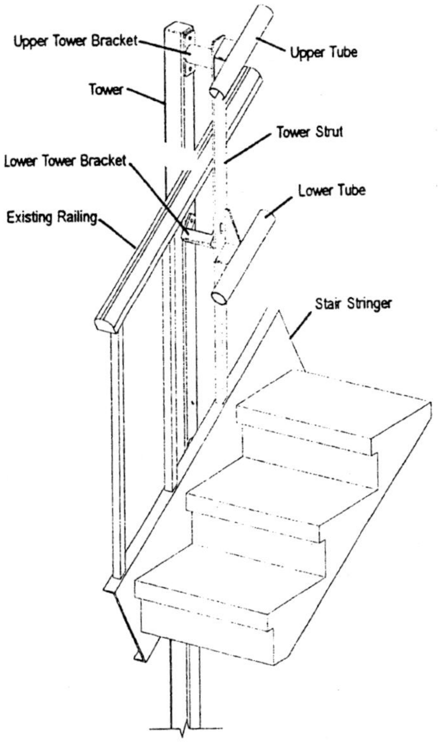

Tower Mount in Open Balustrade

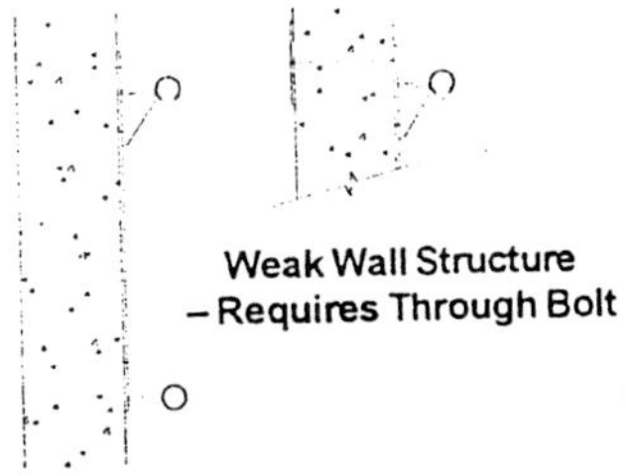

Direct Mount to Wall

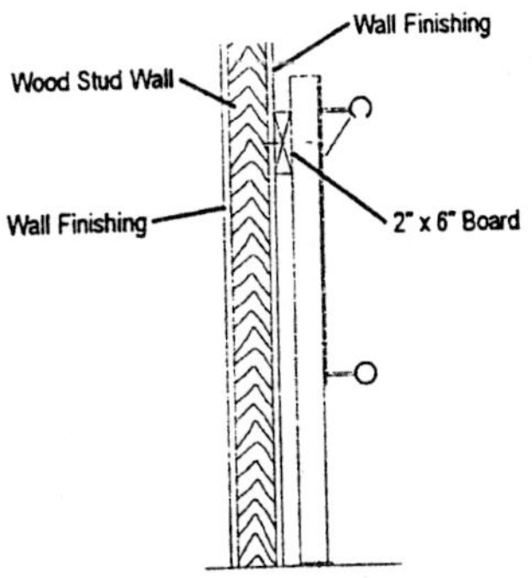

Tower Mount to 2" x 6" Board on Wall

System Operation

Two parallel steel tubes, custom built for the **stairway, support** the platform. These tubes contain a continuous loop of wire haul rope that attaches through a slot in the upper tube. An electrical motor at the top of the system turns a drive cog, which moves the haul rope carrying the wheelchair platform up and down the stairway. (Note: affixed to the rope are Delrin spheres and knuckles, which keep the rope in the center of the tube)

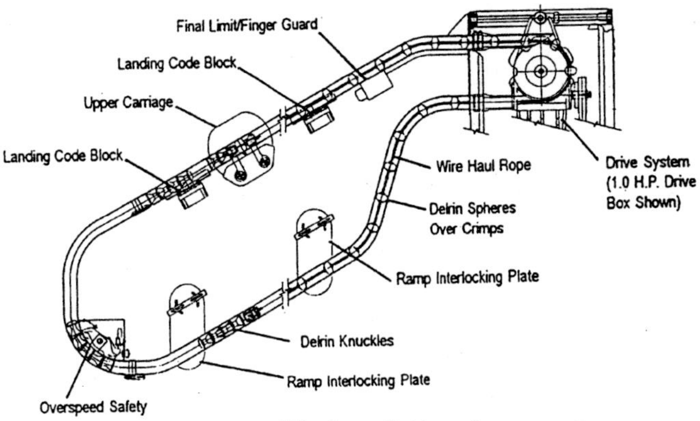

Tube Attachment

The wheelchair platform travels on two steel tubes 51mm (2 in) in diameter that are affixed 600mm (23.6 in) apart vertically. To maintain the vertical separation, the tubes are welded to distance struts with gussets. The struts are attached either directly to the wall or to square/rectangular support towers.

Note: A variety of tower bases are available, based on stairway construction.

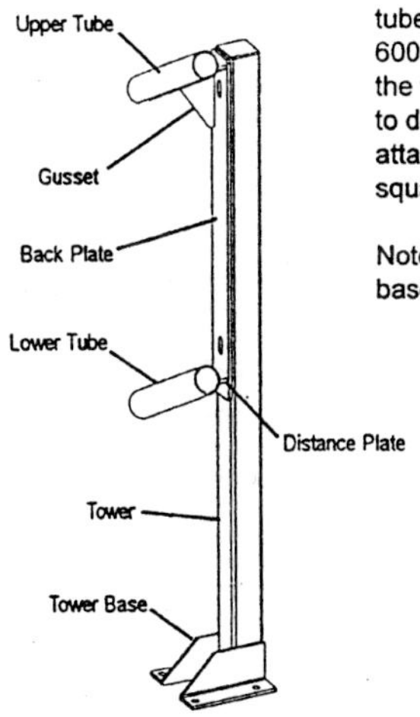

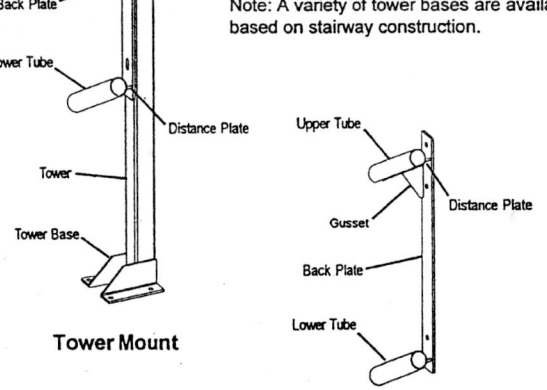

Tower Mount

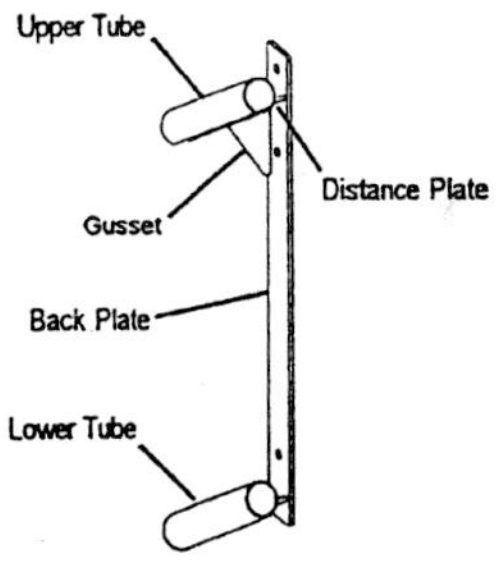

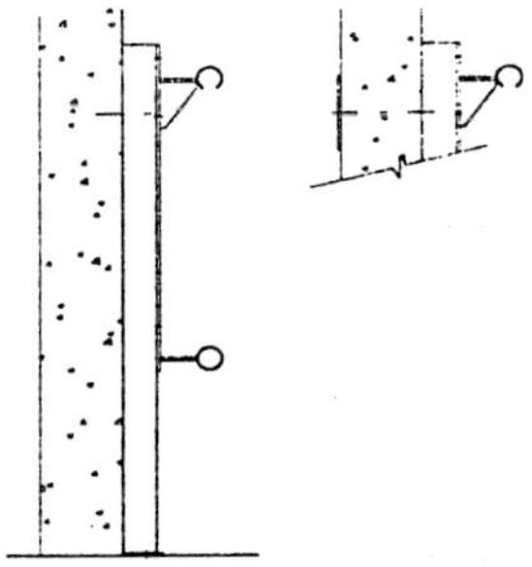

Tower Mount to Wall

ELEVATORS AND WHEELCHAIR LIFTS
Straight Stairways

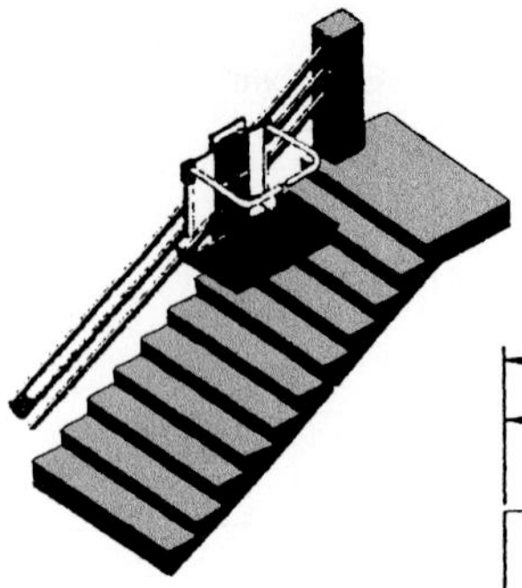

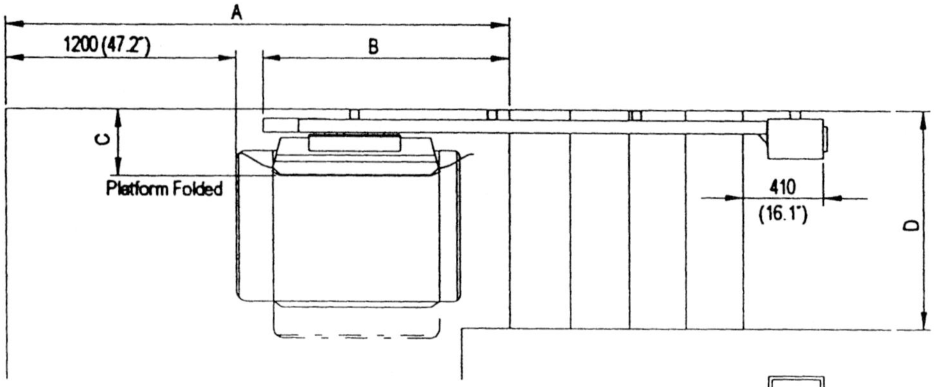

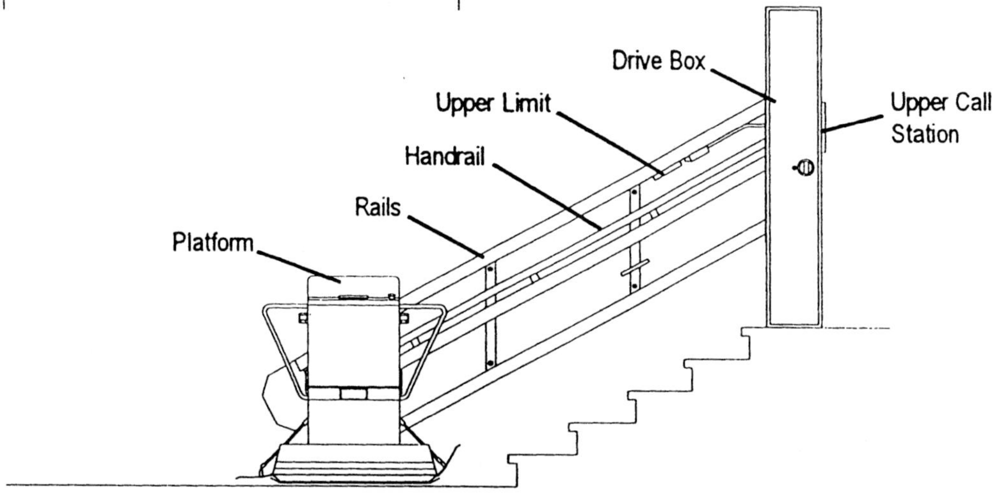

GSL-2 Clearances

			Minimum clearance dimensions					
			900 × 760 platform		*1050 × 760 platform*		*1220 × 760 platform*	
Dim.	*Clearance required for:*	*Stair angle (X°)*	*mm*	*in*	*mm*	*in*	*mm*	*in*
A	Loading:	25	2777	109.3	2927	115.2	3097	121.9
	end load	30	2705	106.5	2855	112.4	3025	119.1
		35	2652	104.4	2802	110.3	2972	117.0
		40	2611	102.8	2761	108.7	2931	115.4
	Loading:	25	1610	63.4	1760	69.3	1930	76.0
	side load	30	1538	60.6	1688	66.5	1858	73.2
		35	1485	58.5	1635	64.4	1805	71.1
		40	1444	56.8	1594	62.7	1764	69.4
B	Rail extension	25	1452	57.2	1527	60.1	1612	63.4
	(straight loading)*	30	1352	53.2	1427	56.2	1512	59.5
		35	1268	49.9	1343	52.9	1428	56.2
		40	1193	47.0	1268	49.9	1353	53.3

			Minimum clearance dimensions					
			900 × 760 platform		*1050 × 760 platform*		*1220 × 760 platform*	
Dim.	*Drive configuration*	*Attachment method*	*mm*	*in*	*mm*	*in*	*mm*	*in*
C	Standard drive and	Direct mount	325	12.8	325	12.8	325	12.8
	flush drive at 90°	Towers to wall	330	13.0	330	13.0	330	13.0
		Towers w/2 in × 6 in	368	14.5	368	14.5	368	14.5
		Freestanding	343	13.5	343	13.5	343	13.5
	Flush drive (straight wall)		400	15.8	400	15.8	400	15.8
D	Standard drive and	Direct mount	1007	39.6	1007	39.6	1007	39.6
	flush drive at 90°	Towers to wall	1012	39.8	1012	39.8	1012	39.8
		Towers w/2 in × 6 in	1050	41.3	1050	41.3	1050	41.3
		Freestanding	1025	40.4	1025	40.4	1025	40.4
	Flush drive (straight wall)		1082	42.6	1082	42.6	1082	42.6

ELEVATORS AND WHEELCHAIR LIFTS

Turning Stairways

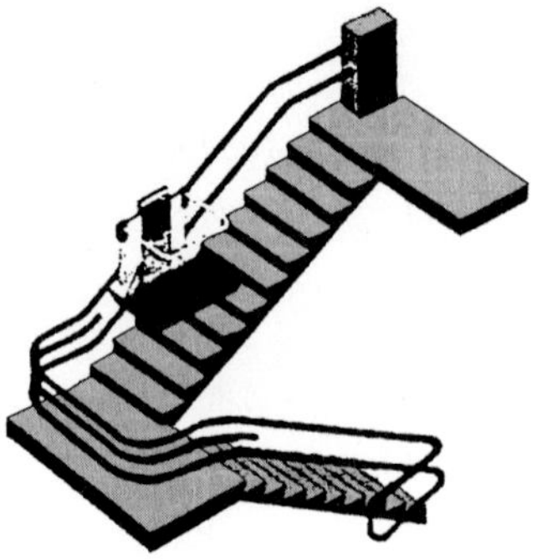

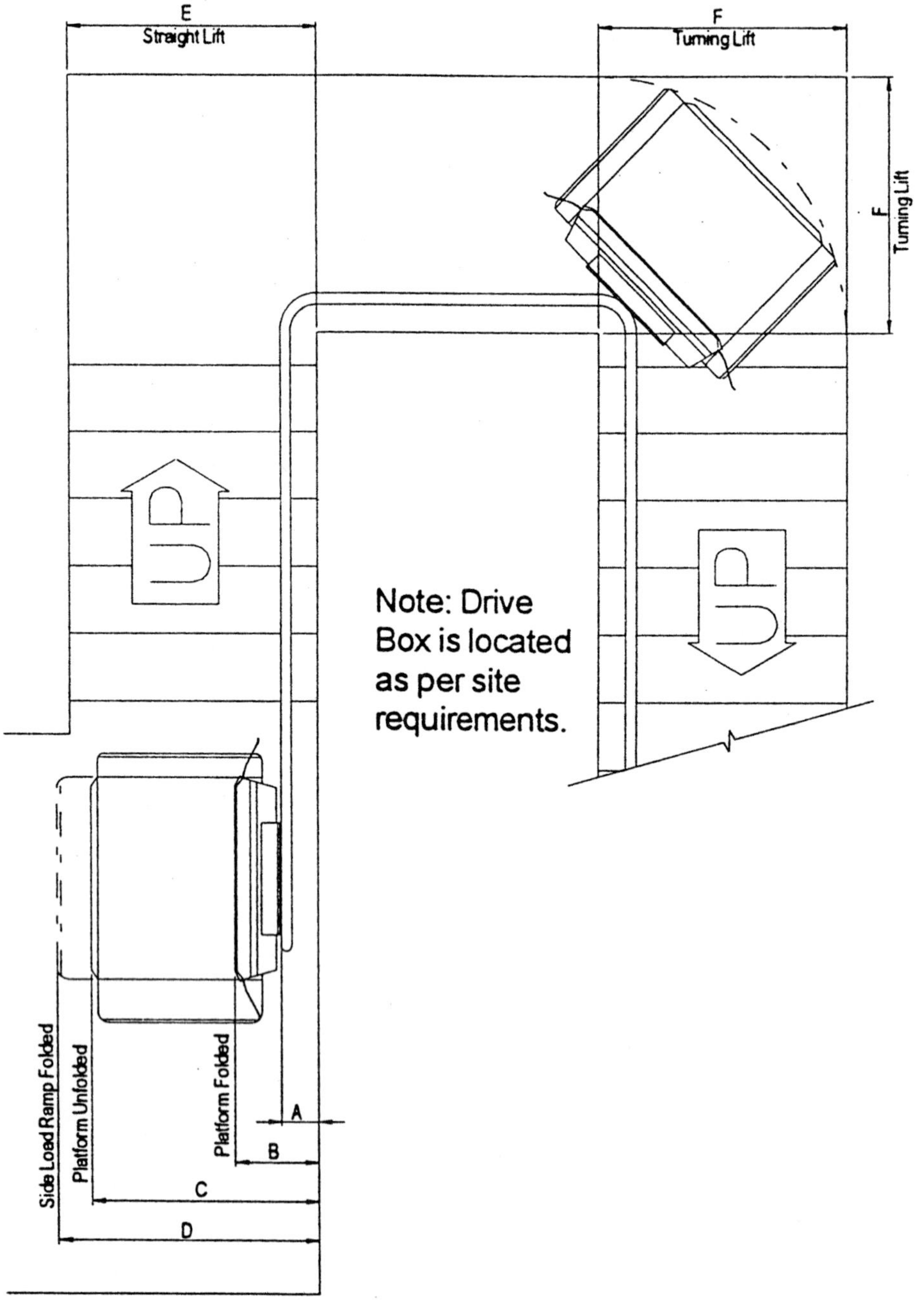

GSL-1 Turning Clearances

		Minimum clearance dimensions					
		900 × 760 platform		*1050 × 760 platform*		*1220 × 760 platform*	
Dim.	*Attachment method*	*mm*	*in*	*mm*	*in*	*mm*	*in*
A	Direct mount	130	5.1	130	5.1	130	5.1
	Towers	175	6.9	175	6.9	175	6.9
	Towers w/2 in × 6 in	213	8.4	213	8.4	213	8.4
B	Direct mount	349	13.7	349	13.7	349	13.7
	Towers	394	15.5	394	15.5	394	15.5
	Towers w/2 in × 6 in	432	17.0	432	17.0	432	17.0
C	Direct mount	1010	39.8	1010	39.8	1010	39.8
	Towers	1055	41.5	1055	41.5	1055	41.5
	Towers w/2 in × 6 in	1093	43.0	1093	43.0	1093	43.0
D	Direct mount	1164	45.8	1164	45.8	1164	45.8
	Towers	1209	47.6	1209	47.6	1209	47.6
	Towers w/2 in × 6 in	1247	49.1	1247	49.1	1247	49.1
E	Direct mount	1030	40.6	1030	40.6	1030	40.6
	Towers	1075	42.3	1075	42.3	1075	42.3
	Towers w/2 in × 6 in	1113	43.8	1113	43.8	1113	43.8
F	Direct mount	1155	45.5	1196	47.1	1247	49.1
	Towers	1180	46.5	1221	48.1	1272	50.1
	Towers w/2 in × 6 in	1218	48.0	1259	49.6	1310	51.6

ELEVATORS AND WHEELCHAIR LIFTS
Turning Stairways

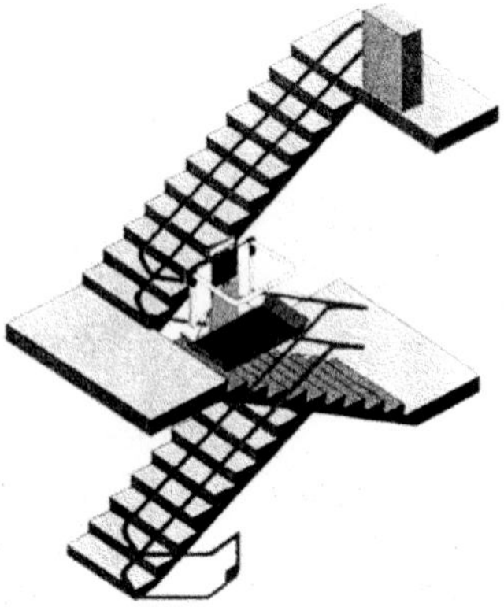

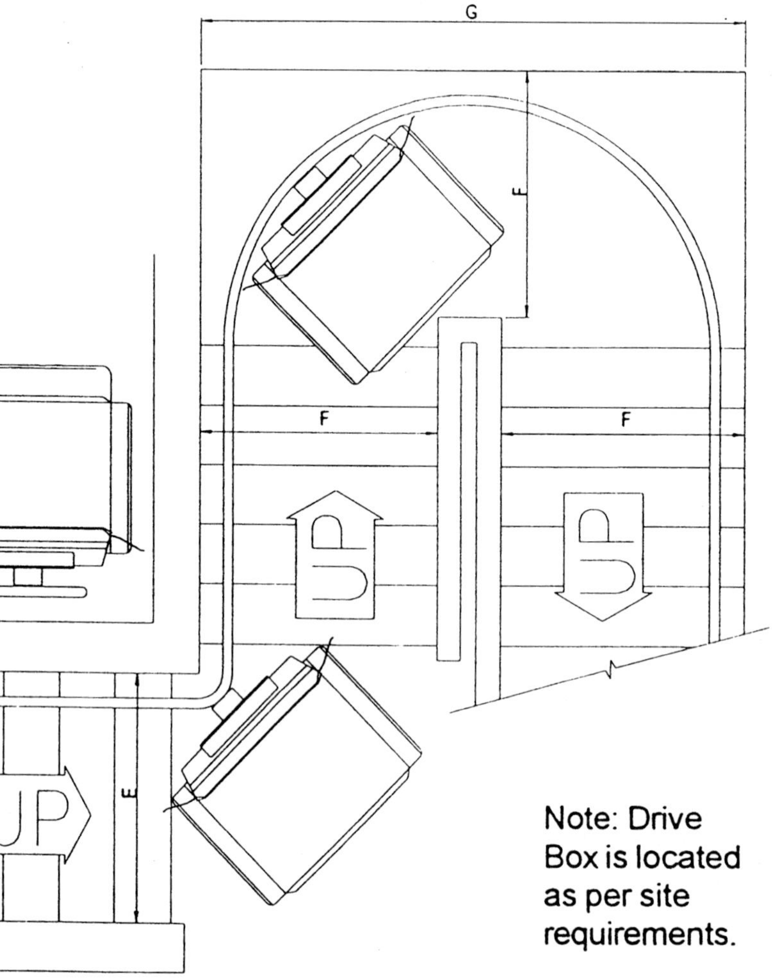

GSL-3 Turning Clearances

		Minimum clearance dimensions					
		900 × 760 platform		*1050 × 760 platform*		*1220 × 760 platform*	
Dim.	*Attachment method*	*mm*	*in*	*mm*	*in*	*mm*	*in*
A	Direct mount	130	5.1	130	5.1	130	5.1
	Towers	175	6.9	175	6.9	175	6.9
	Towers w/2 in × 6 in	213	8.4	213	8.4	213	8.4
B	Direct mount	434	17.1	434	17.1	374	14.7
	Towers	479	18.9	479	18.9	419	16.5
	Towers w/2 in × 6 in	517	20.4	517	20.4	457	18.0
C	Direct mount	1095	43.1	1095	43.1	1035	40.7
	Towers	1140	44.9	1140	44.9	1080	42.5
	Towers w/2 in × 6 in	1178	46.4	1178	46.4	1118	44.0
D	Direct mount	1249	49.2	1249	49.2	1189	46.8
	Towers	1294	50.9	1294	50.9	1234	48.6
	Towers w/2 in × 6 in	1332	52.4	1332	52.4	1272	50.1
E	Direct mount	1189	46.8	1227	48.3	1226	48.3
	Towers	1234	48.6	1272	50.1	1271	50.0
	Towers w/2 in × 6 in	1272	50.1	1310	51.6	1309	51.5
F	Direct mount	1186	46.7	1259	49.6	1612	63.5
	Towers	1231	48.5	1304	51.3	1657	65.2
	Towers w/2 in × 6 in	1269	50.0	1342	52.8	1695	66.7

ELEVATORS AND WHEELCHAIR LIFTS

Commercial Inclined Wheelchair Platform Lift

Dimension Drawings

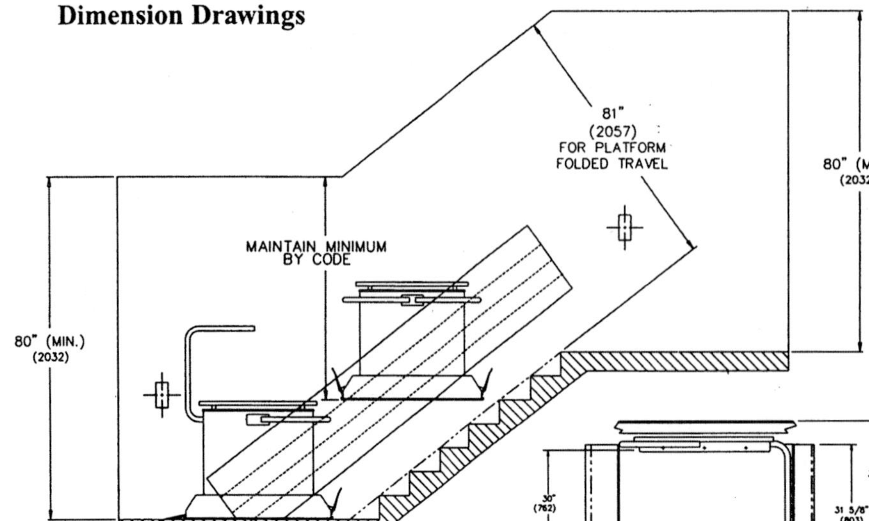

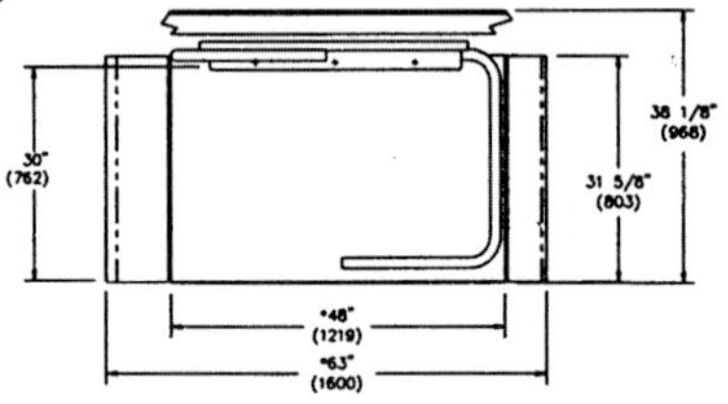

Top View (platform at landing)

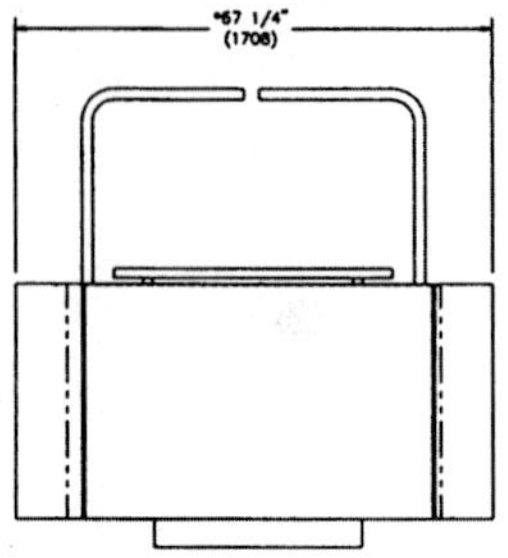

Front View (platform up)

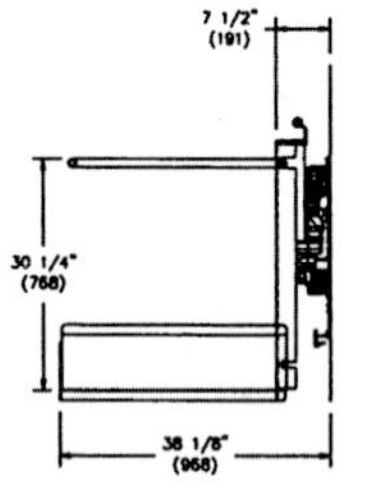

Side View
(platform in motion)

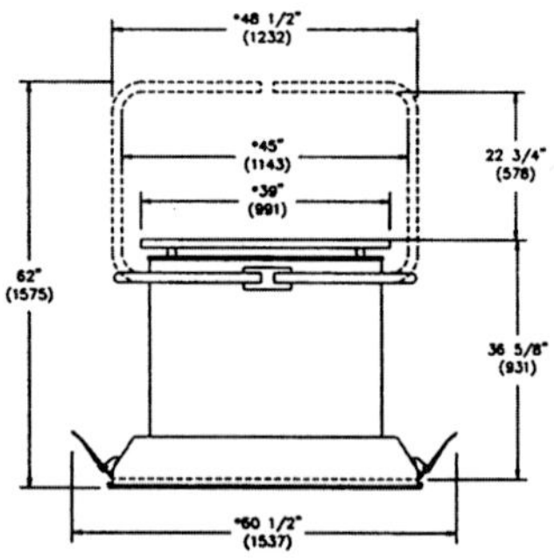

Front View
(platform in motion)

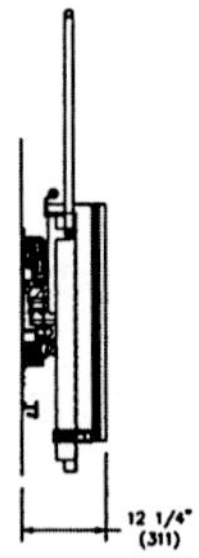

Side View
(platform up)

Dimension Drawings

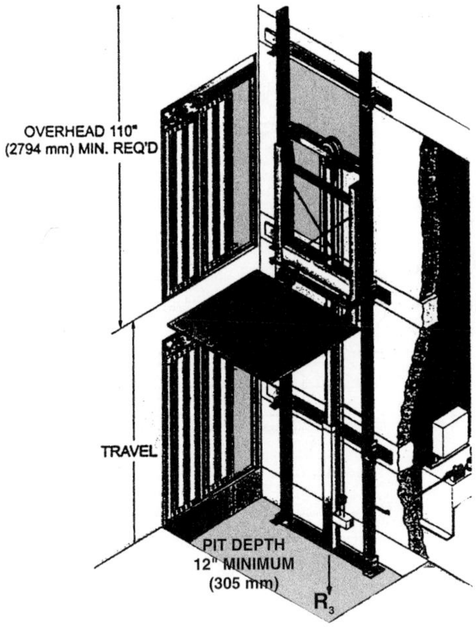

HOISTWAY PLANS

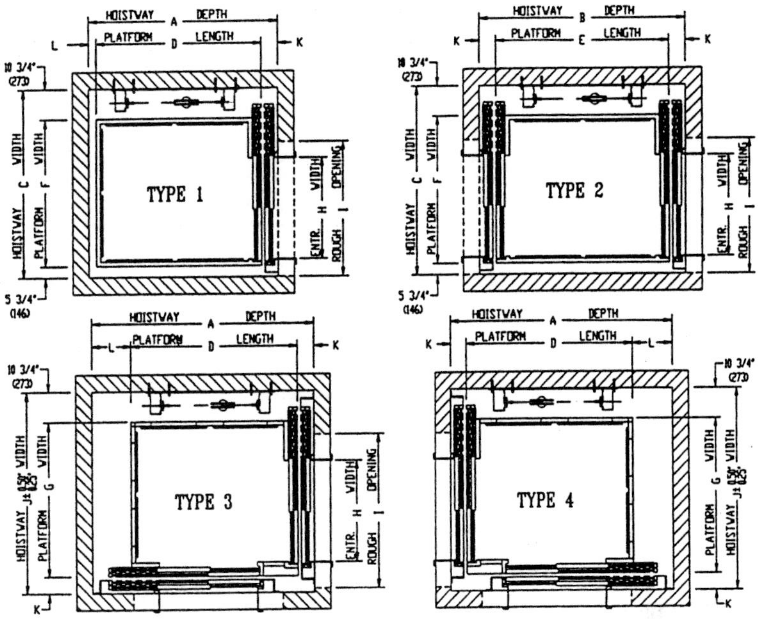

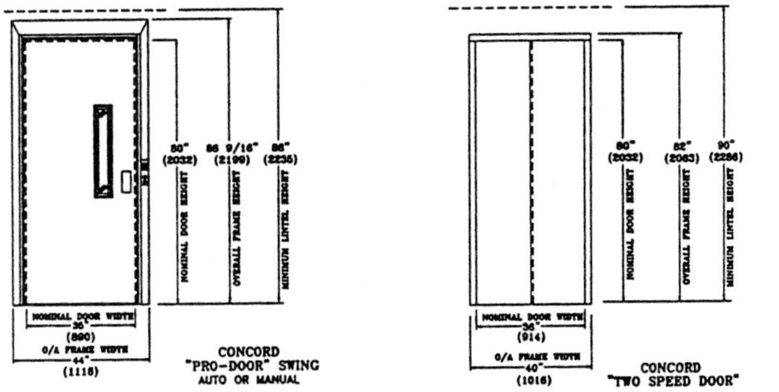

COMMERCIAL WITH TWO SPEED HORIZONTAL SLIDING DOOR (TYPE 1 AND 2 ONLY) Δ NOMINAL SIZE

PLATFORM SIZES	A	B	C	D	E	F	ΔH	I	K	L
48" x 54" (1220 x 1372)	73" (1854)	82" (2083)	69" (1753)	62 3/4" (1594)	67" (1702)	52 1/2" (1334)	36" (914)	55" (1397)	7 1/2" (191)	2 3/4" (70)
54" x 48" (1372 x 1220)	67" (1702)	76" (1930)	75" (1905)	56 3/4" (1441)	61" (1550)	58 1/2" (1486)	36" (914)	55" (1397)	7 1/2" (191)	2 3/4" (70)
54" x 54" (1372 x 1372)	73" (1854)	82" (2083)	75" (1905)	62 3/4" (1594)	67" (1702)	58 1/2" (1486)	36" (914)	55" (1397)	7 1/2" (191)	2 3/4" (70)

COMMERCIAL WITH TWO SPEED HORIZONTAL SLIDING DOOR (TYPE 3 AND 4 ONLY) Δ NOMINAL SIZE

PLATFORM SIZES	A	D	G	ΔH	I	J	K	L
48" x 54" (1220 x 1372)	85" (2159)	62 3/4" (1594)	56 3/4" (1441)	36" (914)	55" (1397)	75" (1905)	7 1/2" (191)	14 3/4" (375)
54" x 48" (1372 x 1220)	85" (2159)	56 3/4" (1441)	62 3/4" (1594)	36" (914)	55" (1397)	81" (2057)	7 1/2" (191)	20 3/4" (527)
54" x 54" (1372 x 1372)	85" (2159)	62 3/4" (1594)	62 3/4" (1594)	36" (914)	55" (1397)	81" (2057)	7 1/2" (191)	14 3/4" (375)

ELEVATORS AND WHEELCHAIR LIFTS

Hoistway Plans

Dimension Drawings

LAYOUTS FOR STANDARD SIZES SHOWN "VARIOUS MODELS AND SIZES AVAILABLE"

HOISTWAY PLANS

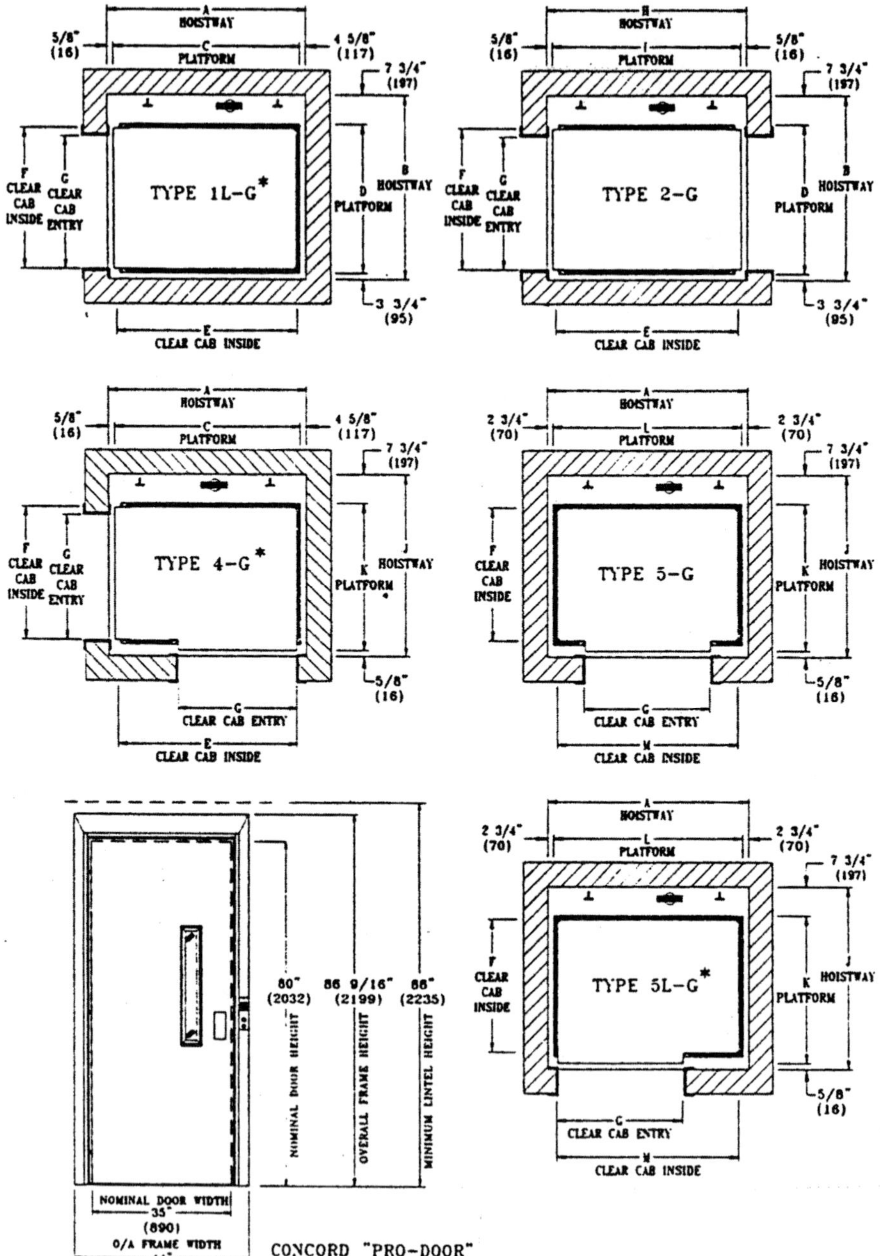

CONCORD "PRO-DOOR" (MANUAL)

Approximate reactions					
R1		*R2*		*R3*	
KIPS	kN	KIPS	kN	KIPS	kN
0.25	1.13	0.17	0.76	4.00	17.8

Rail reactions are based on 750 lb (340 kg) capacity and a STD. 3′ × 4′ cab.

Clear cab entry "Δ G"	
Panelfold/visifold gate	*No gate*
34″	36″
(864)	(914)

Δ Nominal size

Platform sizes	*A*	*B*	*C*	*D*	*ΔE*	*ΔF*	*ΔG*	*H*	*I*	*J*	*K*	*L*	*M*
36″ × 48″	56″	50″	50¾″	38½″	49½″	36″	SEE	52¼″	51″	48⅛″	39¾″	50½″	48″
(914 × 1220)	(1422)	(1270)	(1289)	(978)	(1257)	(915)	ABOVE	(1327)	(1295)	(1223)	(1010)	(1282)	(1220)
36″ × 54″	62″	50″	56¾″	38½″	55½″	36″	SEE	58¼″	57″	48⅛″	39¾″	56½″	54″
(914 × 1372)	(1574)	(1270)	(1441)	(978)	(1410)	(915)	ABOVE	(1480)	(1448)	(1223)	(1010)	(1434)	(1372)
36″ × 60″	68″	50″	62¾″	38½″	61½″	36″	SEE	64¼″	63″	48⅛″	39¾″	62½″	60″
(914 × 1525)	(1727)	(1270)	(1594)	(978)	(1562)	(915)	ABOVE	(1632)	(1600)	(1223)	(1010)	(1587)	(1525)

ELEVATORS AND WHEELCHAIR LIFTS
Through the Floor

Side View Cab Interior

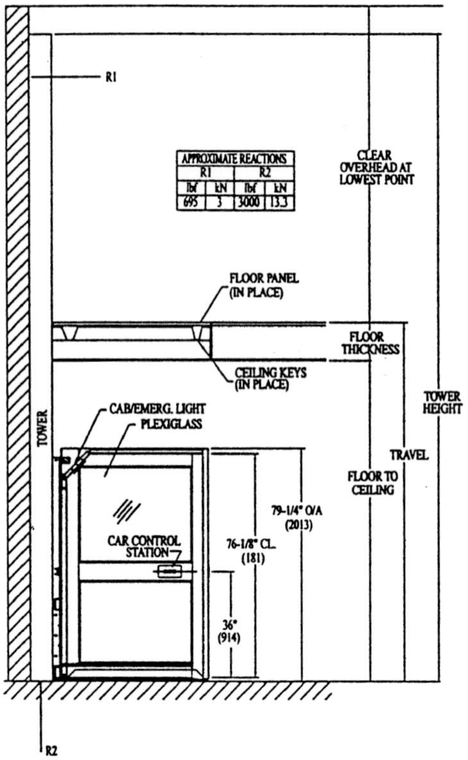

Plan View

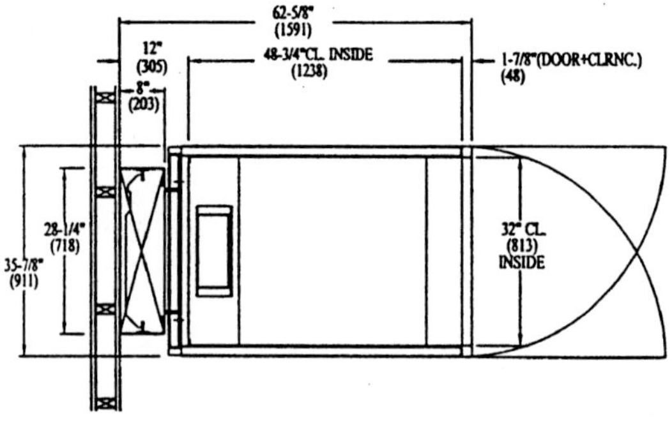

Floor Cutout

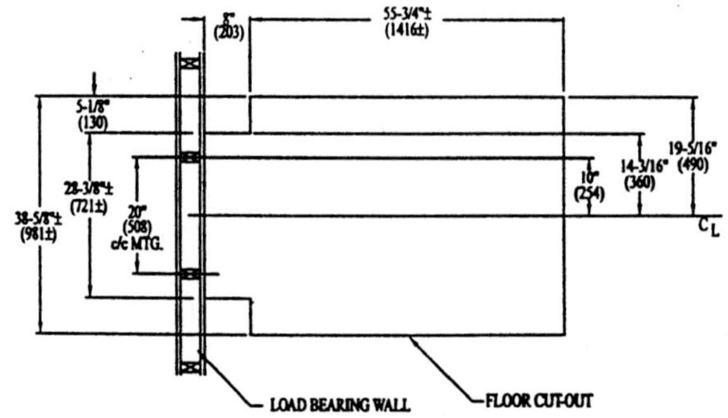

Dimensional Drawings: **Handilift Standard Model Shown**

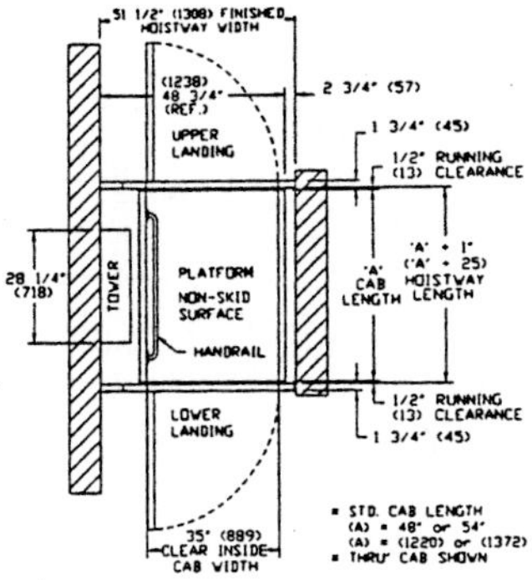

Handilift Standard Model

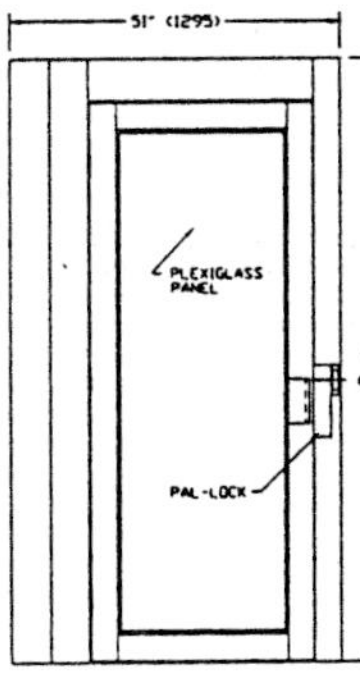

Lower Door

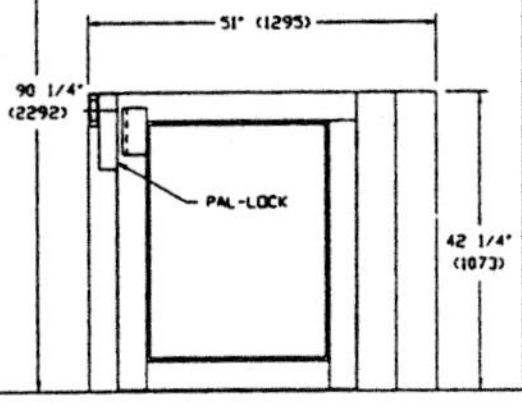

Upper Gate

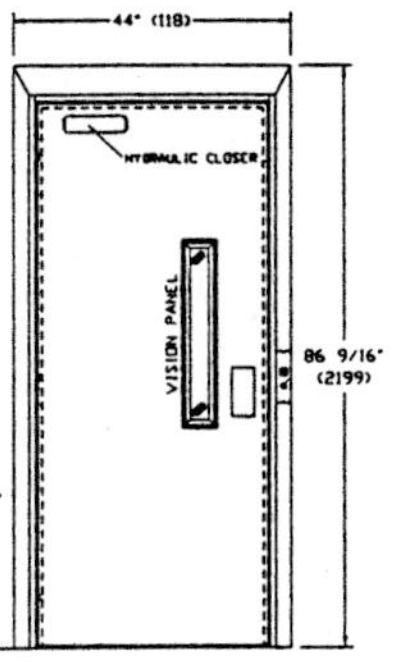

Fire Rated Door

Dimensional Drawings: **Handilift-EN Model Shown**

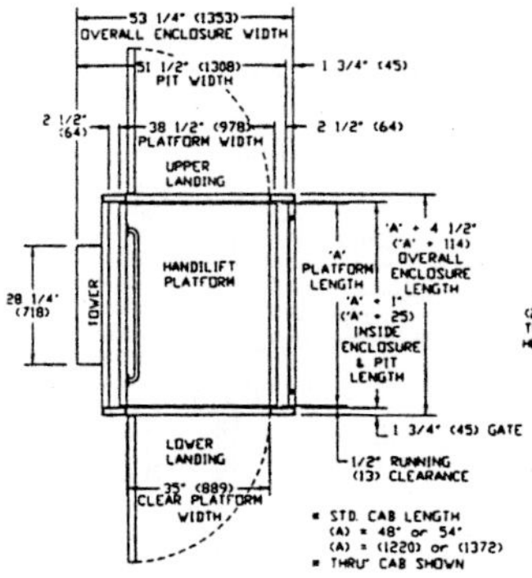

Handilift-EN Model

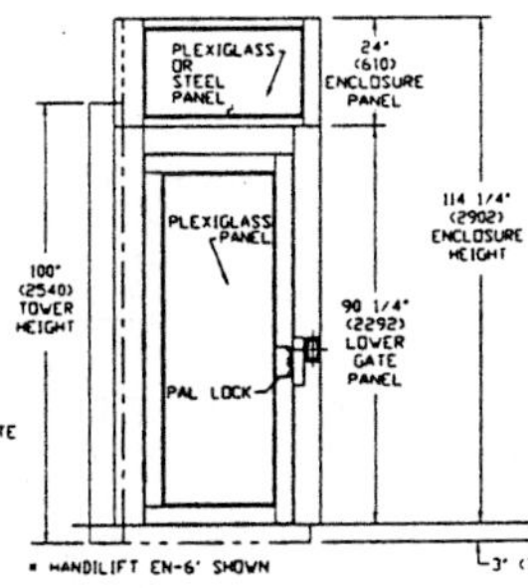

Lower Door

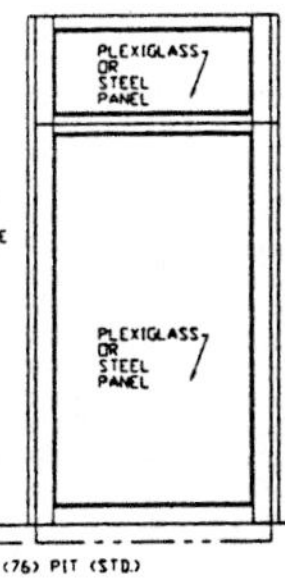

Side Wall

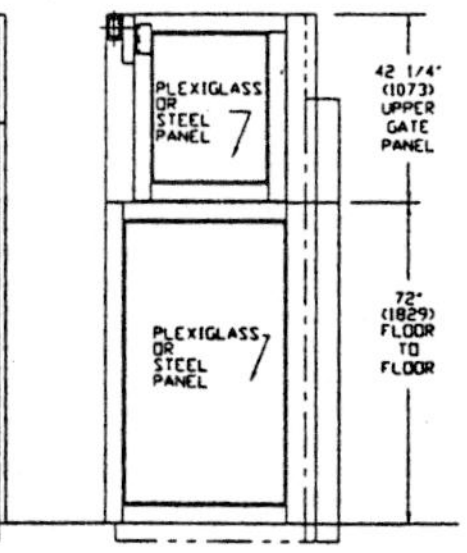

Upper Gate

Dimensional Drawings: **Handilift-SE Model Shown**

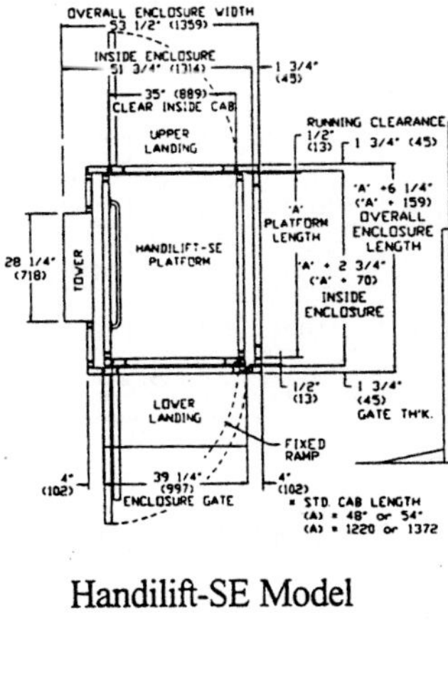

Handilift-SE Model

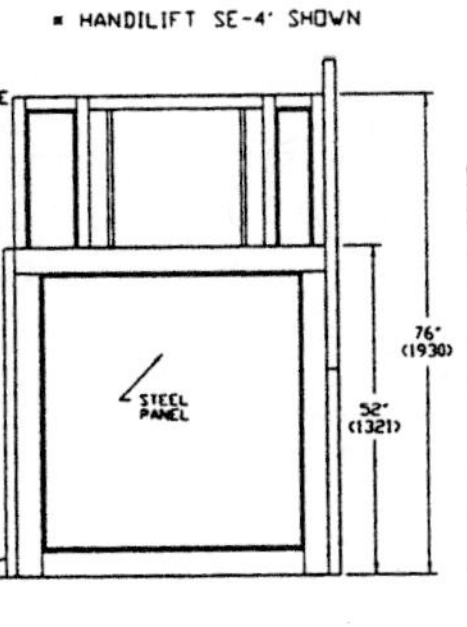

Lower Door

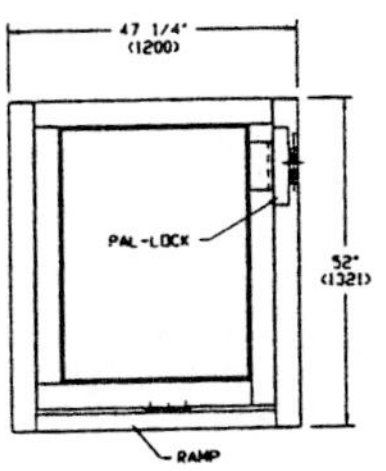

Upper Gate

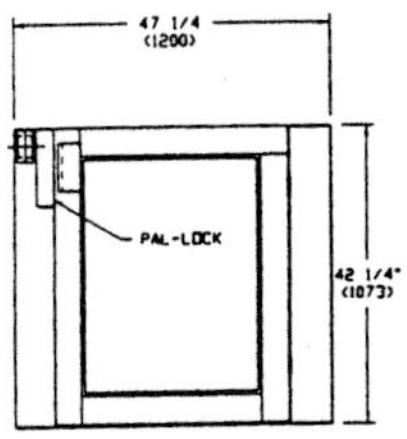

Fire Rated Door

ELEVATORS AND WHEELCHAIR LIFTS
Enclosed Lifts

HOISTWAY PLANS LAYOUTS FOR STANDARD SIZES

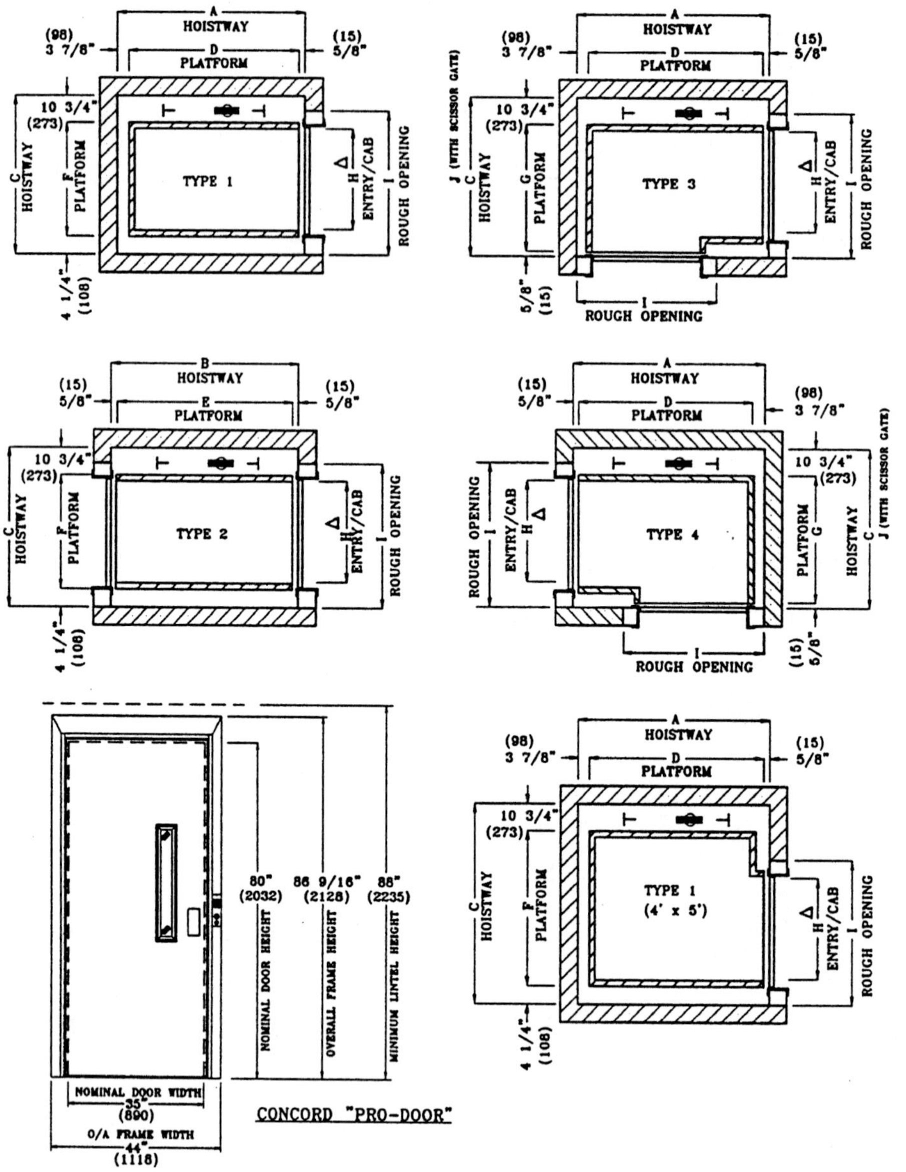

NOTE: HOISTWAY MUST BE PLUMB AND SQUARE AND TO SIZES SHOWN.... ALL DIMENSIONS INDICATED ARE FINISHED DIMENSIONS.

COMMERCIAL LIFT

Δ NOMINAL SIZE

PLATFORM SIZES	A	B	C	D	E	F	G	Δ H	I
35" x 48" (890 x 1220)	54" (1372)	49 1/4" (1251)	53" (1345)	49 1/2" (1257)	48" (1220)	38" (965)	41 1/8" (1045)	35" (890)	48" (1220)
35" x 60" (890 x 1525)	66" (1675)	61 1/4" (1555)	53" (1345)	61 1/2" (1560)	60" (1525)	38" (965)	41 1/8" (1045)	35" (890)	48" (1220)
48" x 60" (1220 x 1525)	66" (1675)	61 1/4" (1555)	66" (1675)	61 1/2" (1560)	60" (1525)	51" (1295)	54 1/8" (1375)	35" (890)	48" (1220)

RESIDENTIAL LIFT (WITH SCISSOR GATE)

N.B. WHEN A LIFT HAS A SCISSOR GATE DIMENSIONS A, B, D, E & G CHANGE. DIMENSION J IS THE HOISTWAY WIDTH FOR A TYPE 3, 4 UNIT WITH SCISSOR GATES.

PLATFORM SIZES	A	B	C	D	E	F	G	Δ H	I	J
35" x 48" (890 x 1220)	55 5/8" (1413)	52 1/2" (1334)	53" (1345)	51 1/8" (1299)	51 1/4" (1302)	38" (965)	42 3/4" (1086)	35" (890)	48" (1220)	54 5/8" (1388)
35" x 60" (890 x 1525)	67 5/8" (1718)	64 1/2" (1638)	53" (1345)	63 1/8" (1603)	63 1/4" (1606)	38" (965)	42 3/4" (1086)	35" (890)	48" (1220)	54 5/8" (1388)

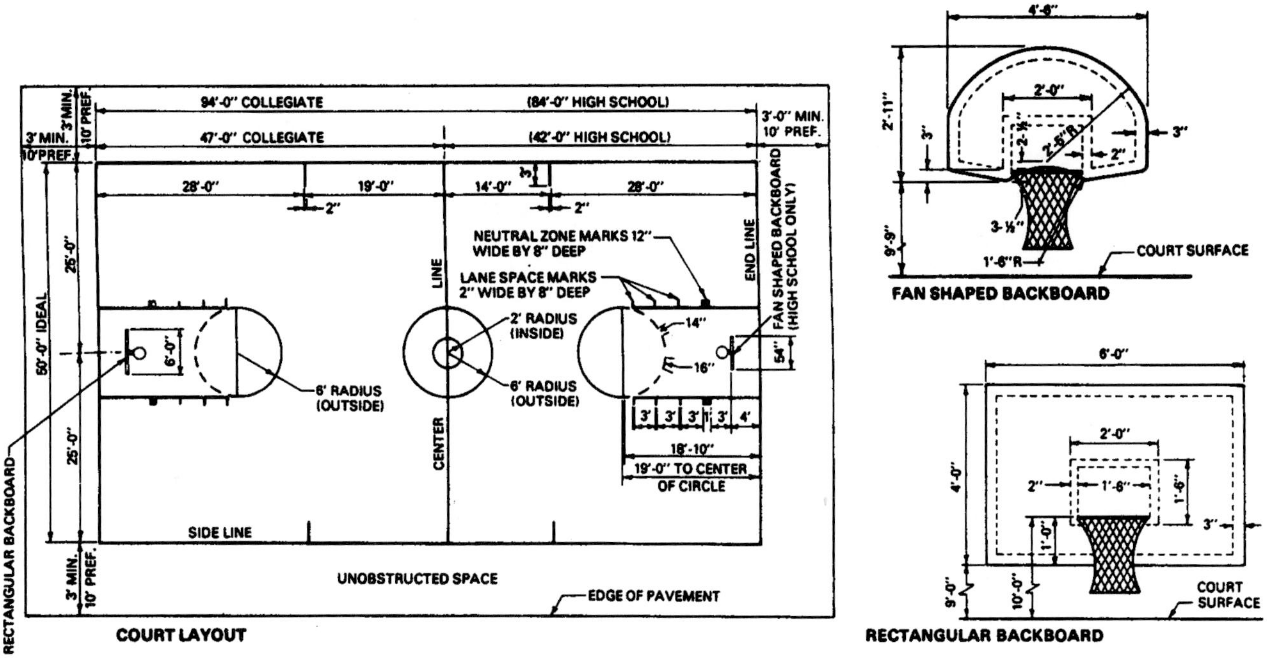

Fig. 1 NCAA basketball. The color of the lane space marks and neutral zone marks shall contrast with the color of the bounding lines. The midcourt marks shall be the same color as the bounding lines. All lines shall be 2 in wide (neutral zone excluded). All dimensions are to inside edge of lines except as noted. Backboard shall be of any rigid weather-resistant material. The front surface shall be flat and painted white unless it is transparent. If the backboard is transparent, it shall be marked with a 3-in-wide white line around the border and an 18- × 24-in target area bounded with a 2-in-wide white line. (High school recommended court is 84 × 50 ft with a 10-ft unobstructed space on all sides (3 ft minimum). Collegiate recommended court is 94 × 50 ft with a 10-ft unobstructed space on all sides (3 ft minimum))

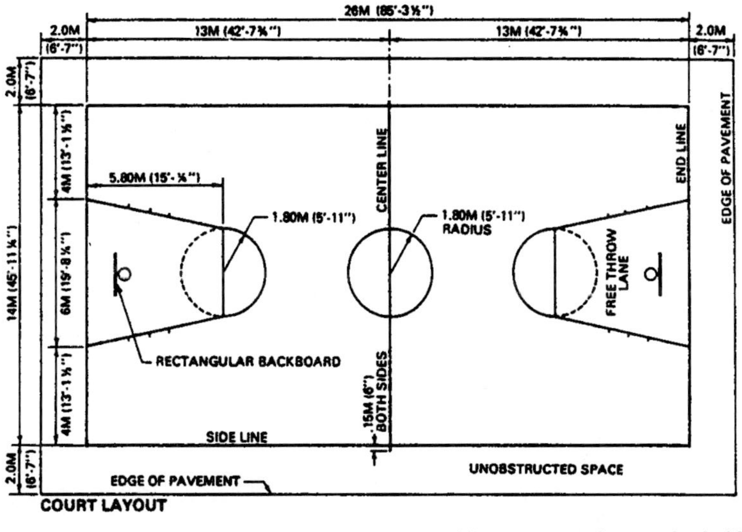

Fig. 2 AAU basketball court. All dimensions are to inside edge of lines except as noted. All lines to be 0.05 m (2 in) wide. Backboard shall be of any rigid weather-resistant material. The front shall be flat and painted white unless it is transparent. If the backboard is transparent, it shall be marked with a 0.05-m-wide white line around the border and a 0.45 × 0.59-m target area bounded with a 0.05-m-wide white line

INDOOR RECREATION

Basketball: College (NCAA), High School, and National Basketball Association (NBA)

HIGH SCHOOL AND N.C.A.A. COLLEGE BASKETBALL COURTS

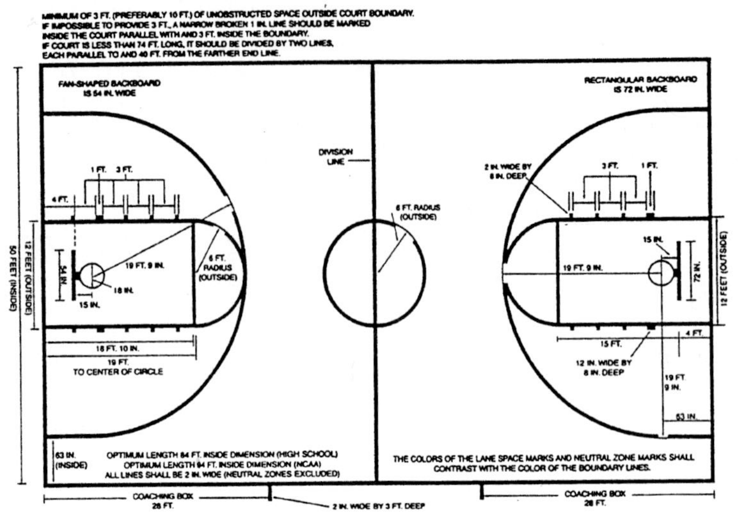

LEFT SIDE SHOWS HIGH SCHOOL COURT MARKINGS AND BACKBOARD DIMENSIONS.

OPTIMUM LENGTH 84' OR 94' (INSIDE DIMENSION). ALL LINES SHALL BE 2" (5.1 CM) WIDE (NEUTRAL ZONES EXCLUDED).

THE COLOR OF THE LANE SPACE MARKS AND NEUTRAL ZONE MARKS SHALL CONTRAST WITH THE COLOR OF THE BOUNDING LINES. THE MIDCOURT MARKS SHALL BE THE SAME COLOR AS THE BOUNDING LINES.

RIGHT SIDE SHOWS COLLEGE COURT MARKINGS AND BACKBOARD DIMENSIONS.

High School —
The 3 point line is the same color as the free throw lane line and semicircle. Division line must be visible through any logos.

High School Court Marking reprinted with permission of :
National Federation of State High School Associations
11724 NW Plaza Circle
P.O. Box 20626
Kansas City, MO 64195 – 0626
(816) 464-5400

NCAA & High School —
Minimum of 3' (91.4 cm) preferably 10' (304.8 cm) of unobstructed space outside.

High School —
If impossible to provide 3' (91.4 cm) unobstructed space outside the court boundary, a narrow broken 1" (2.5 cm) line should be marked inside the court parallel with and 3' (91.4 cm) inside the boundary.

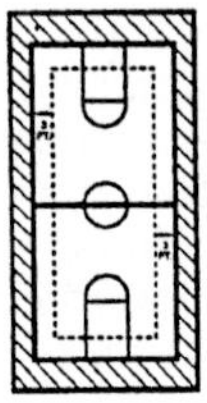

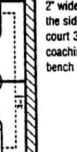

Slash Hash Mark NCAA —
2" wide lines extend from the sideline away from the court 3' to frame the coaching boxes on the bench side

NCAA Court Making reprinted with permission of:
National Collegiate Athletic Association*
6201 College Boulevard
Overland Park, KS 66211 – 2422
(913) 339-1906
*This diagram is subject to annual review and change.

NBA COURT

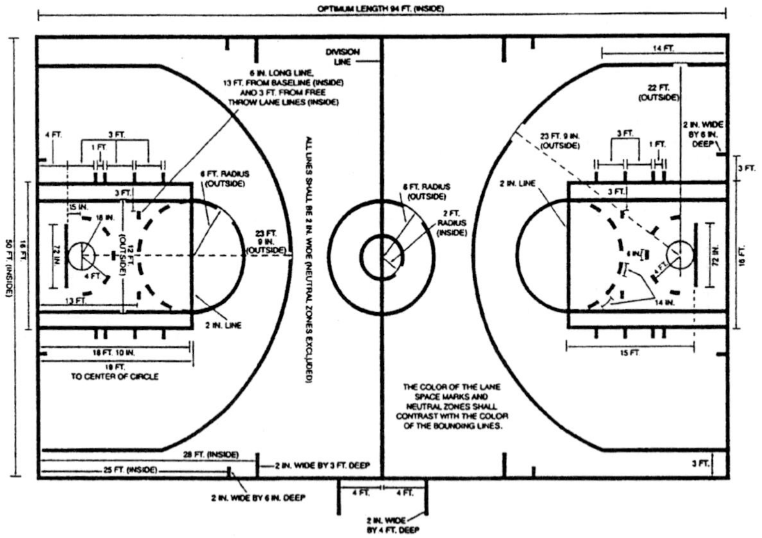

Section 1 — Court and Dimensions

a. The playing court shall be measured and marked as shown in court diagram.

b. A free throw lane shall be marked at each end of the court with dimensions and markings as shown on court diagram. All boundary lines are part of the lane; lane space marks and neutral zone marks are not. The color of the lane space marks and neutral zones shall contrast with the color of the boundary lines and college lanes, if applicable. The areas identified by the lane space markings are two inches by eight inches and the neutral zone marks are twelve inches by eight inches.

c. A free throw line, 2" wide, shall be drawn across each of the circles indicated in the court diagram. It shall be parallel to the end line and shall be 15' from the plane of the face of the backboard.

d. Three-point field goal area which has parallel lines 3' from the sidelines, extending 14' from the baseline, and an arc of 23'9" from the middle of the basket which intersects the parallel lines.

NBA Court Marking reprinted with permission of:
National Basketball Association
Olympic Tower, 645 Fifth Avenue, New York, NY 10022 • (212) 826-7000

4

e. Four hash marks shall be drawn (2" wide) perpendicular to the sideline on each side of the court and 28' from the baseline. These hashmarks shall extend 3' onto the court.

f. Four hashmarks shall be drawn (2" wide) perpendicular to the sideline on each side of the court and 25' from the baseline. These hashmarks shall extend 6" onto the court.

g. Four hashmarks shall be drawn (2" wide) perpendicular to the baseline on each side of the free throw lane line. These hashmarks shall be 3' from the free throw lane line and extend 6" onto the court.

h. Four hashmarks shall be drawn (2" wide) parallel to the baseline on each side of the free throw circle. These hashmarks shall be 13' from baseline and 3' from the free throw lane lines and shall be 6" in length.

i. Two hashmarks shall be drawn (2" wide) perpendicular to the sideline, in front of the scorer's table, and 4' on each side of the mid-court line. This will designate the Substitute Box area.

j. A half-circle shall be created 4' from the center of the basket. Five hash marks (2" x 6") shall be placed on the floor. Two shall be at the bottom of the half circle. One at a 90 degree angle from the baseline and the other two at a 45 degree angle from the center of the basket.

INTERNATIONAL OLYMPIC BASKETBALL COURT

FULL SIZE REGULATION COURT

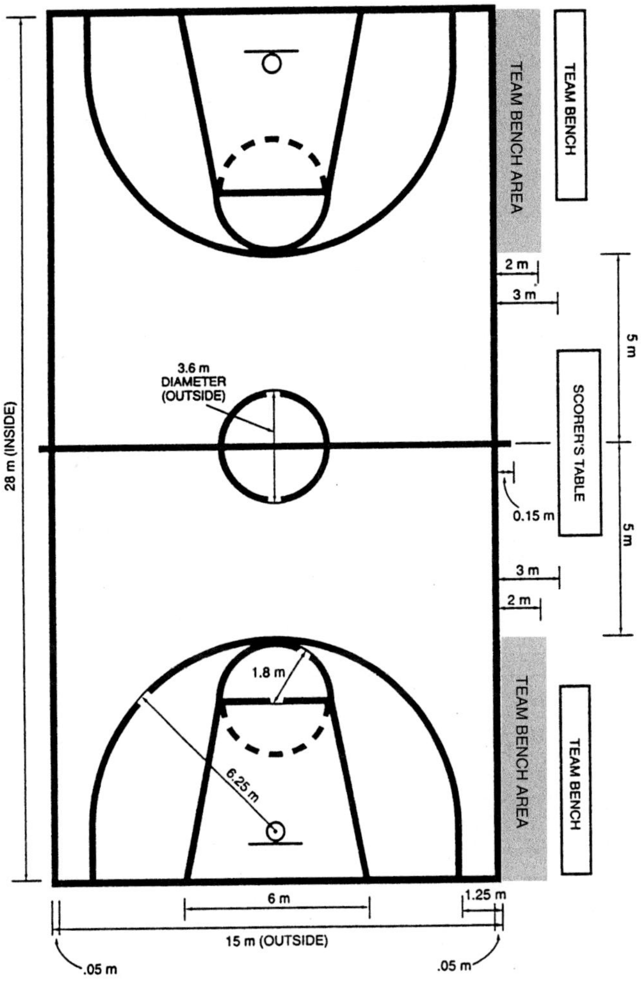

REGULATION FREE THROW LANE

ALL LINES ARE 5 cm WIDE

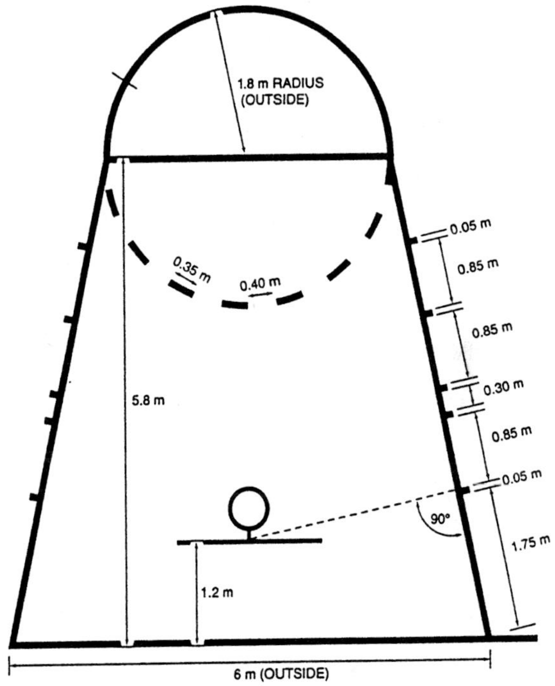

ALL LINES ARE 5 cm. WIDE.
Reprinted with permission of:
USA Basketball
1750 East Boulder St.
Colorado Springs, CO 80909-5777
(719) 590-4800

INDOOR RECREATION
One-, Three-, and Four-Wall Handball

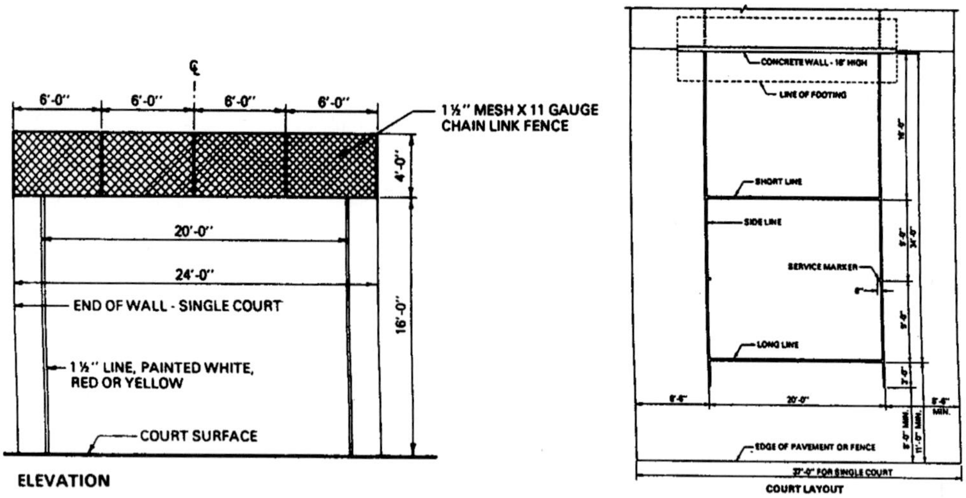

Fig. 3 One-wall handball. Playing court is 20 ft 0 in wide by 34 ft 0 in long plus a required 11 ft 0 in minimum width of surfaced area to the rear and a recommended 8 ft 6 in minimum width on each side. Courts in battery are to be a minimum of 6 ft 0 in between courts. Court markings: 1½-in-wide lines painted white, red, or yellow

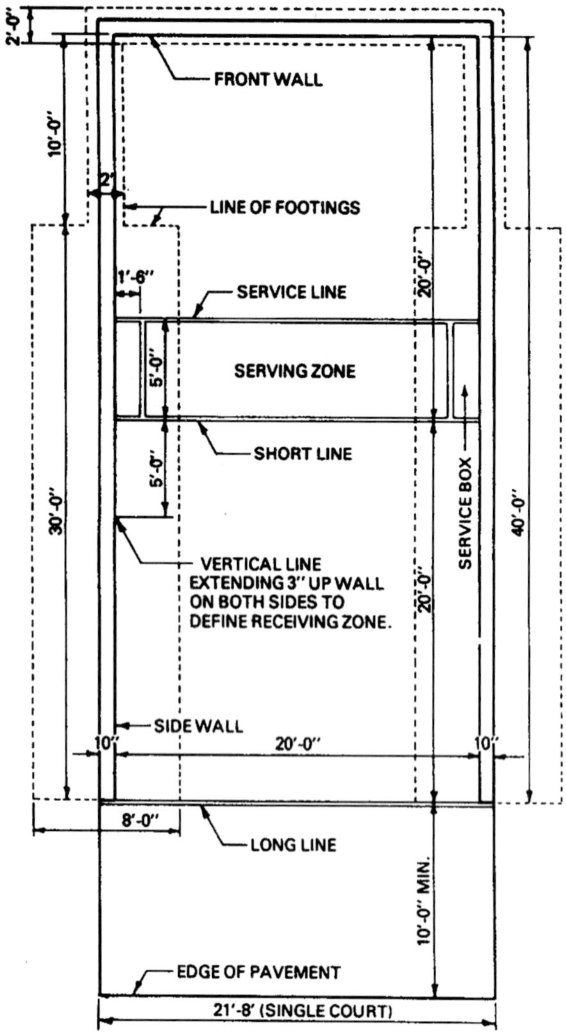

Fig. 4 Handball court layout—four-wall. All court markings to be 1½ in wide and painted white, red, or yellow.

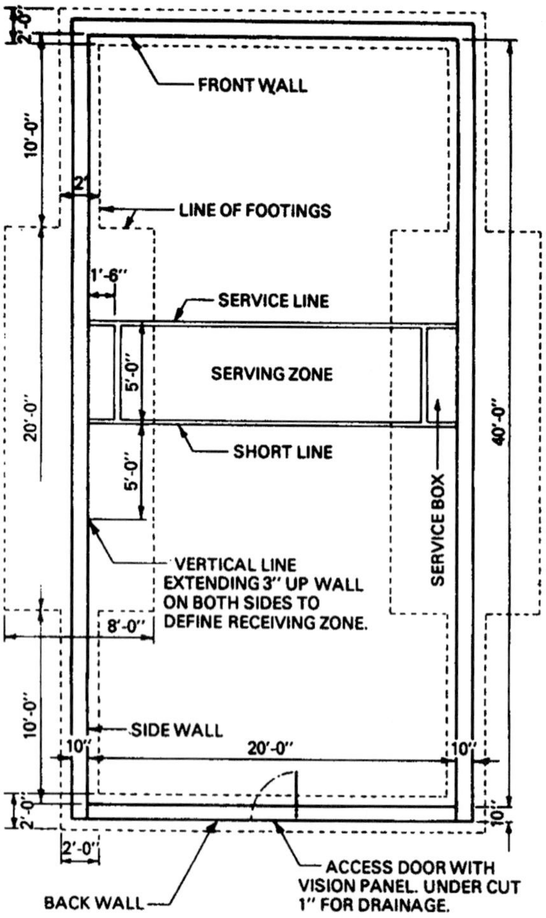

Fig. 5 Handball court layout—three-wall. All court markings to be 1½ in wide and painted white, red, or yellow. Playing court is 20 ft 0 in wide by 40 ft 0 in long plus a minimum 10 ft 0 in to the rear of the three-wall court. Overhead clearance required is 20 ft 0 in minimum

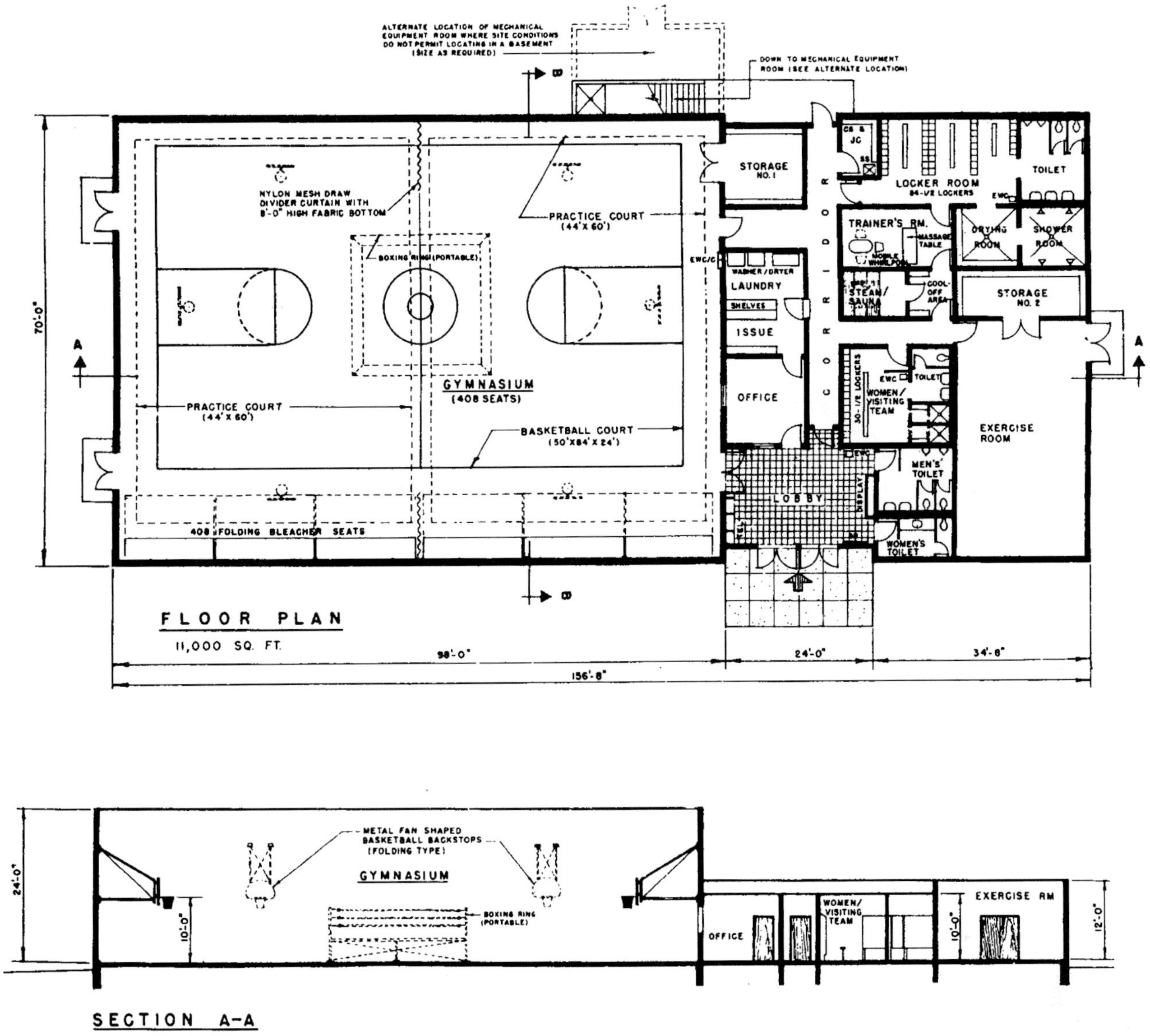

Fig. 6 Gymnasium plan and section

INDOOR RECREATION
Tennis and Paddle Tennis

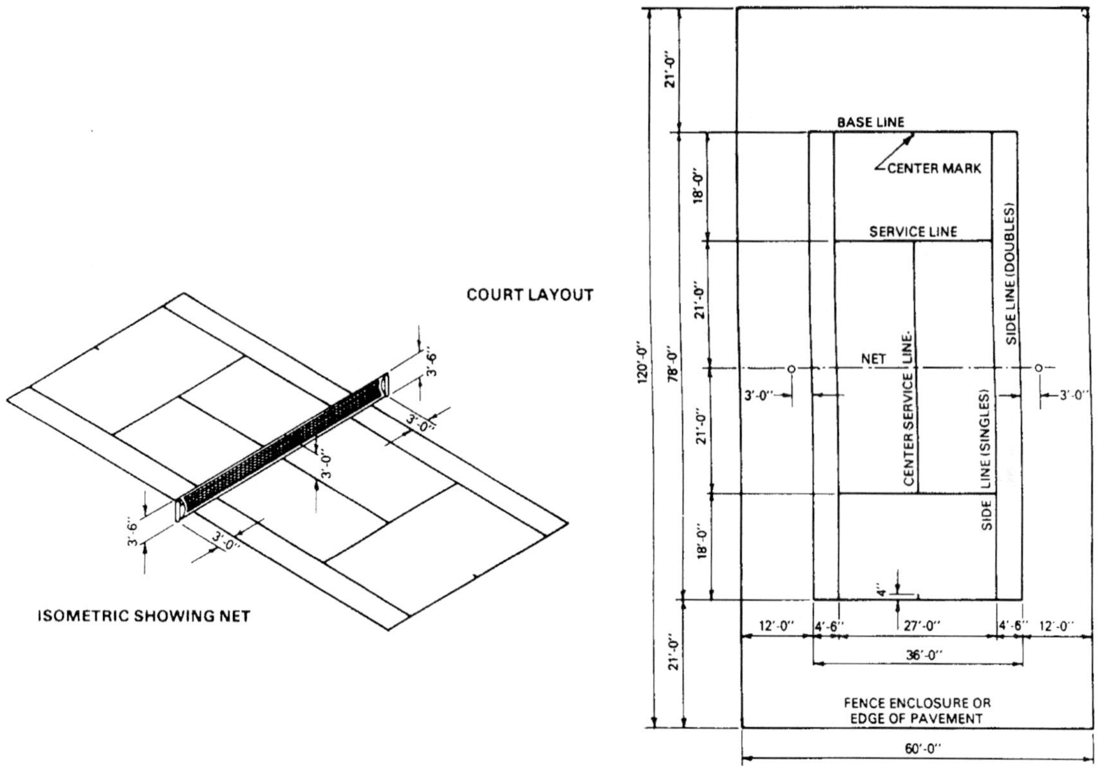

Fig. 7 Tennis court. All measurements for court markings are to the outside of lines except for those involving the center service line, which is equally divided between the right and left service courts. All court markings to be 2 in wide

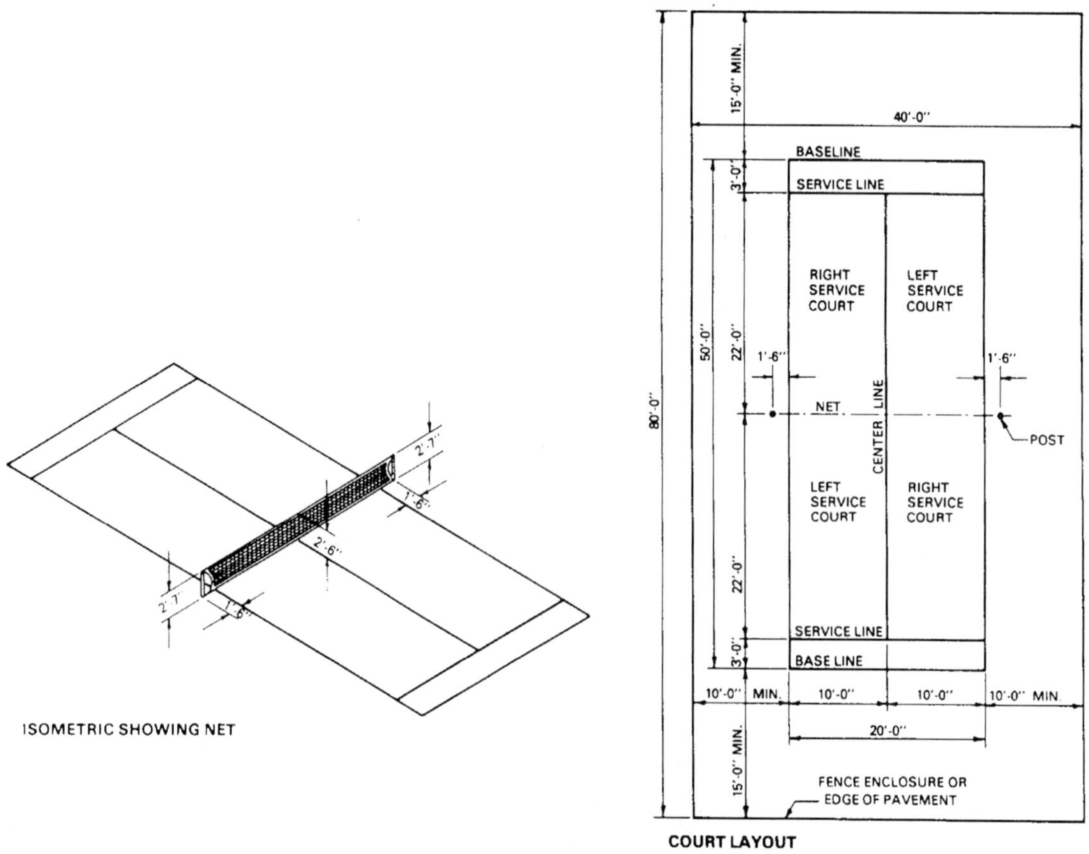

Fig. 8 Paddle tennis court. All measurements for court markings are to the outside of lines except for those involving the center service line, which is equally divided between right and left service court. All court markings to be 1½ in wide

STANDARD SQUASH COURT

SINGLES

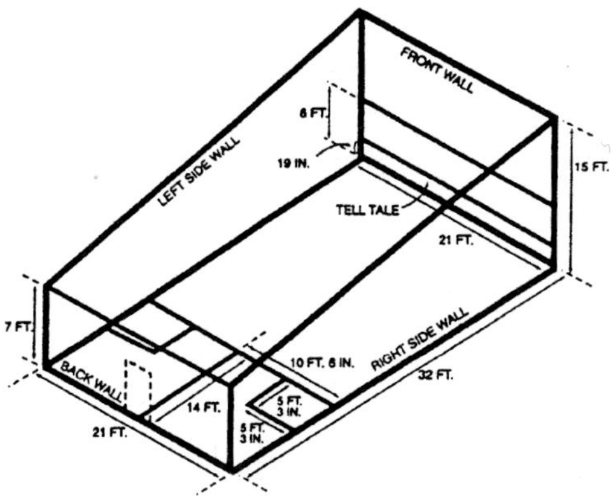

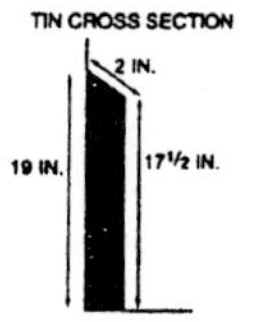

DOUBLES

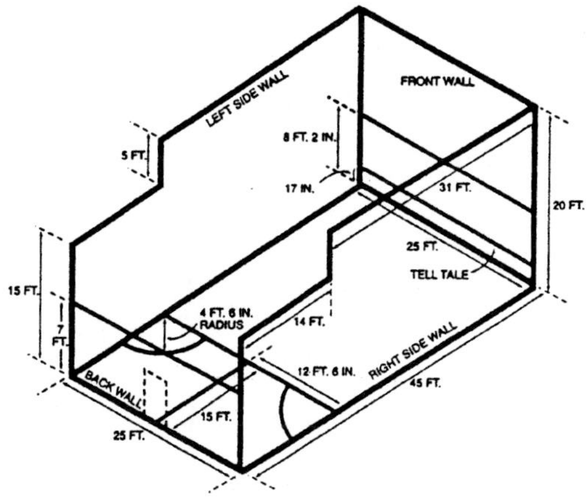

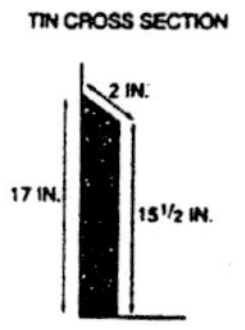

Dimensions are measured to the center of all lines. All boundary lines shall be 1" (2.5 cm) wide, and shall be colored red.

NOTE: One side wall must be moved 1' 6" in from the racquetball dimension (if possible) in order to form a regulation size squash court.

SQUASH "CONVERSION" COURT

Reprinted with permission of:
United States Squash Racquets Association Inc.
P.O. Box 1216, 23 Cynwyd Road, Bala Cynwyd, PA 19004
(610) 667-4006

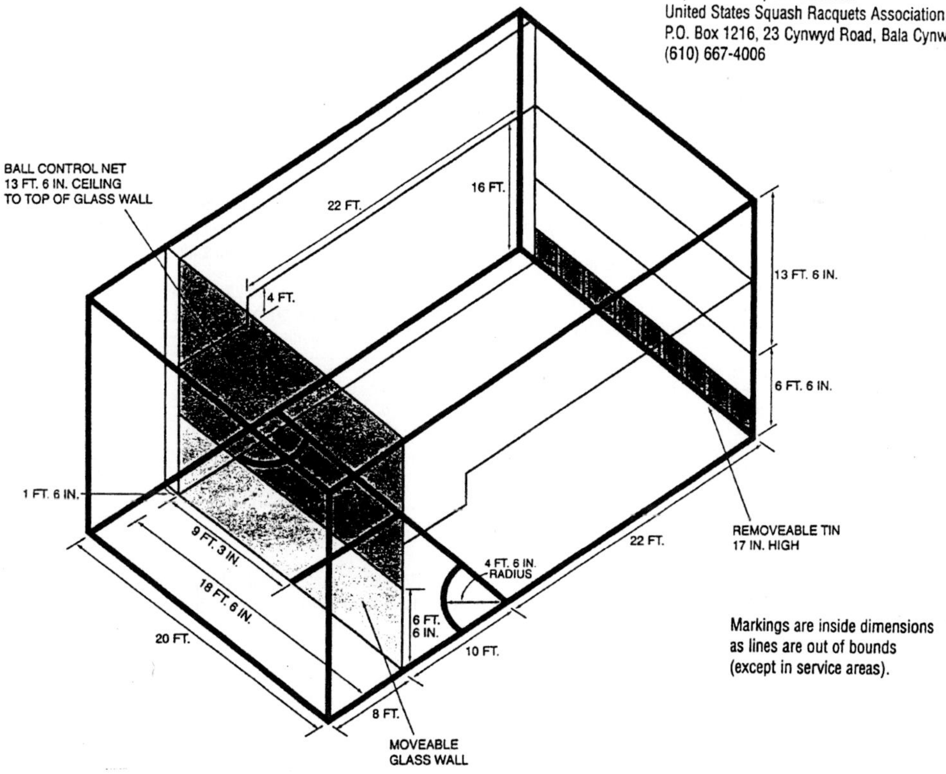

Markings are inside dimensions as lines are out of bounds (except in service areas).

Dimensions shown above are preceded by "S" for singles court; by "D" for doubles court.

The top of the front wall service line is 6' 6" from the floor. The bottom of the back wall service line is 6' 6" from the floor.

Dimensions are measured to the center of all lines. All boundary lines shall be 1" (2.5 cm) wide, and shall be colored red.

INDOOR RECREATION

Four-Wall Handball and Racquetball Courts

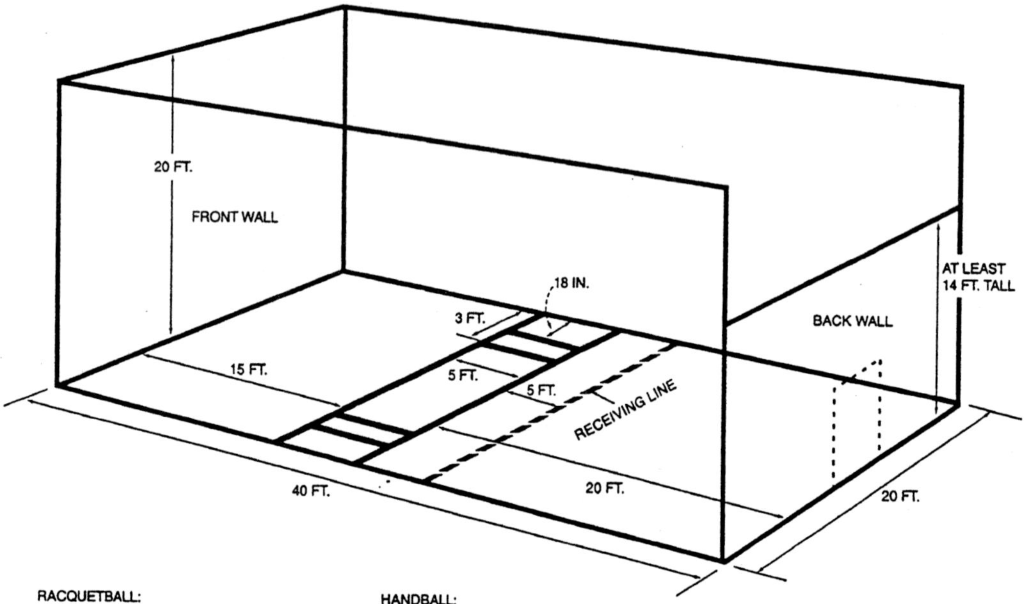

RACQUETBALL:
1 1/2 IN. PAINTED LINES
(BRIGHT RED, WHITE OR BLACK)

HANDBALL:
2 IN. PAINTED LINES
(WHITE OR RED)

Racquetball Four-Wall Rules

Rule 2.1 — Court. The specifications for a standard four-wall racquetball court are:

(a) Dimensions. The dimensions shall be 20 feet high and 40 feet long with each back wall at least 14 feet high.

(b) Lines and Zones. Racquetball courts shall be divided and marked on the floors with 1-1/2 inch wide lines as follows:

(1) Short Line. The back edge of the short line is midway between, and is parallel with, the front and back walls.

(2) Service Line. The front edge of the service line is parallel with, and five feet in front of, the back edge of the short line.

(3) Service Boxes. The service boxes are located at each end of the service zone and are designated by lines parallel with the side walls. The inside edges of the lines are 18 inches from the side walls.

(4) Drive Serve Lines. The drive serve lines, which form the drive serve zone, are parallel with the side wall and are within the service zone. The outside edge of the line is three feet from the side wall.

(5) Receiving Line. A broken line parallel to the short line. The back edge of the receiving line will be five feet from the back edge of the short line. The receiving line will begin with a line 21 inches long that extends from each side wall: the two lines will be connected by an alternate series of six-inch spaces and six-inch lines (17 six-inch spaces and 16 six-inch lines).

Reprinted with the permission of:
United States Handball Association
930 N. Benton Ave., Tucson, AZ 85711 • (520) 795-0434

American Amateur Racquetball Association
1685 West Uintah, Colorado Springs, CO 80904-2921 • (719) 635-5396

High School Volleyball Court

The Court and Markings

(1) The court shall be 60 feet (18 m) long and 30 feet (9 m) wide, including the outer edges of the boundary lines. An area above the court which shall be clear of any obstruction and at least 27 feet high is recommended.

(2) It is recommended all boundary lines shall be of one clearly visible color.

(3) Boundary lines shall be 2 inches wide and at least 6 feet from walls or obstacles. The end lines are the boundary lines on the short sides of the court. The sidelines are the boundary lines on the long sides of the court.

(4) A centerline, 2 inches wide, parallel to and equidistant from the end lines, shall separate the court into two playing areas.

(5) An attack line, 2 inches wide, shall be drawn across each playing area from sideline to sideline, the midpoint of which shall be 10 feet from the midpoint of the center line and parallel to it.

(6) A serving area which is 30 feet wide shall be provided behind and excluding the end line. It shall be laterally limited by 2 short lines each 6 inches long by 2 inches wide, drawn 8 inches behind and perpendicular to the end line as extensions of the sidelines. Both lines are included in the width of the serving area. Each serving area shall be a minimum of 6' in depth. In the event that such a space is not available, the serving area shall extend into the court to whatever distance necessary to provide the minimum depth and be so marked.

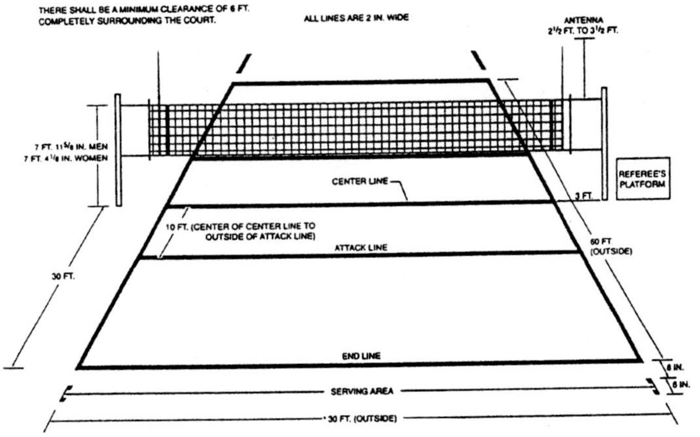

NOTE:
ALL LINES ARE ARE 2" (5.1 cm) WIDE

*7' 4-1/8" FOR WOMEN
7' 11-5/8" FOR MEN

Reprinted with permission of:
National Federation of State
High School Associations
11724 NW Plaza Circle
P.O. Box 20626
Kansas City, MO 64195-0626
(816) 464-5400

All Volleyball Courts Including International (Olympic) Except High School

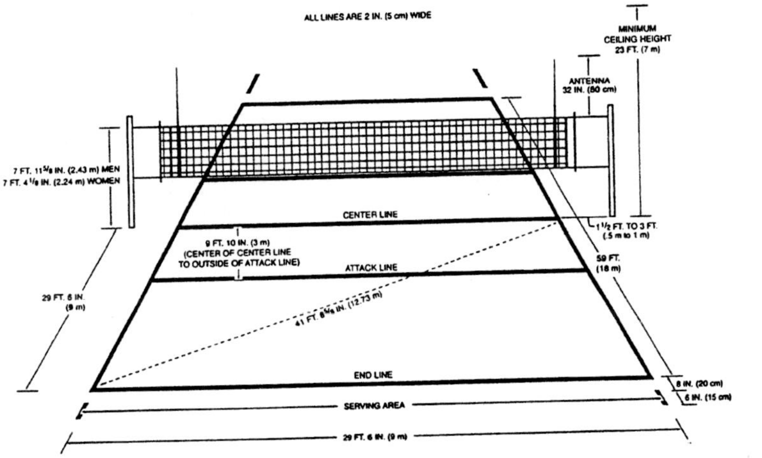

Dimensions are measured to the outside edges of all lines, except attack line, which is measured from middle of center line to rearmost edge of attack line.

Reprinted with permission of:
National Association for
Girls and Women in Sport
1900 Association Drive
Reston, VA 22090
(703) 476-3450

Reprinted with permission of:
USA Volleyball
3595 E. Fountain Blvd., Suite I-2
Colorado Springs, CO 80910-1740
(719) 637-8300

INDOOR RECREATION
Badminton and Volleyball

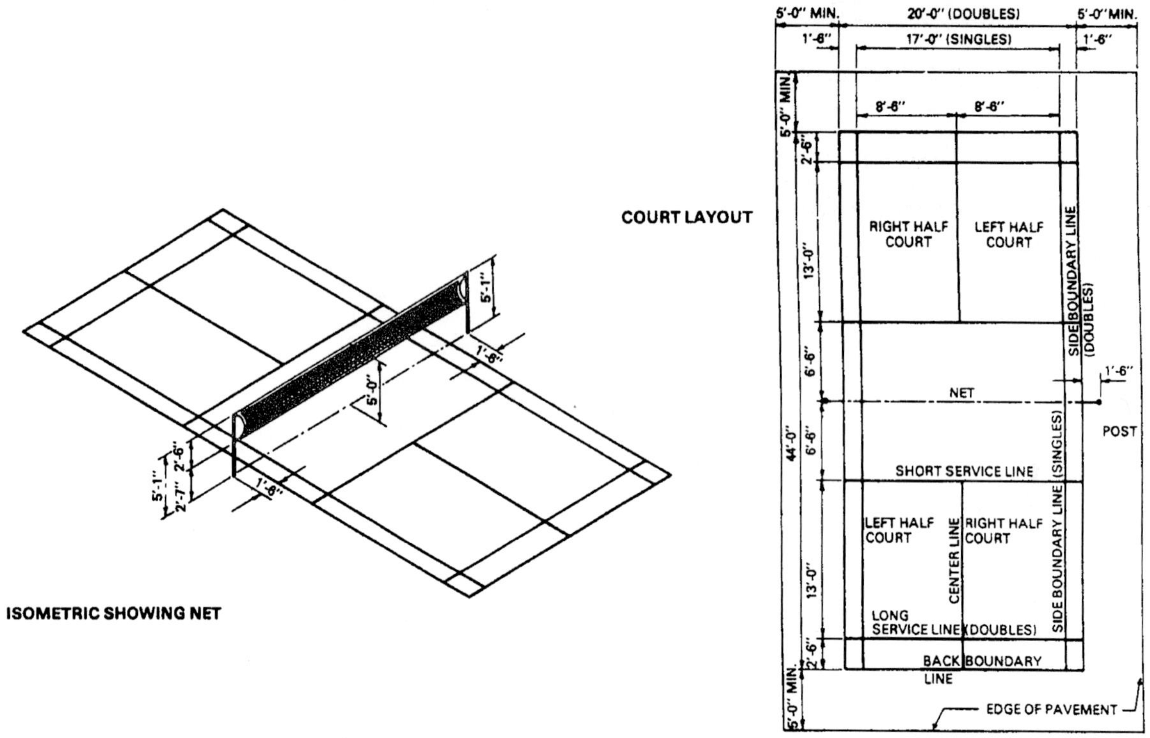

Fig. 9 Badminton court. All measurements for court markings are to the outside of lines except for those involving the center service line, which is equally divided between right and left service courts. All court markings to be 1½ in wide and preferably white or in color. Minimum distance between sides of parallel courts to be 5 ft 0 in

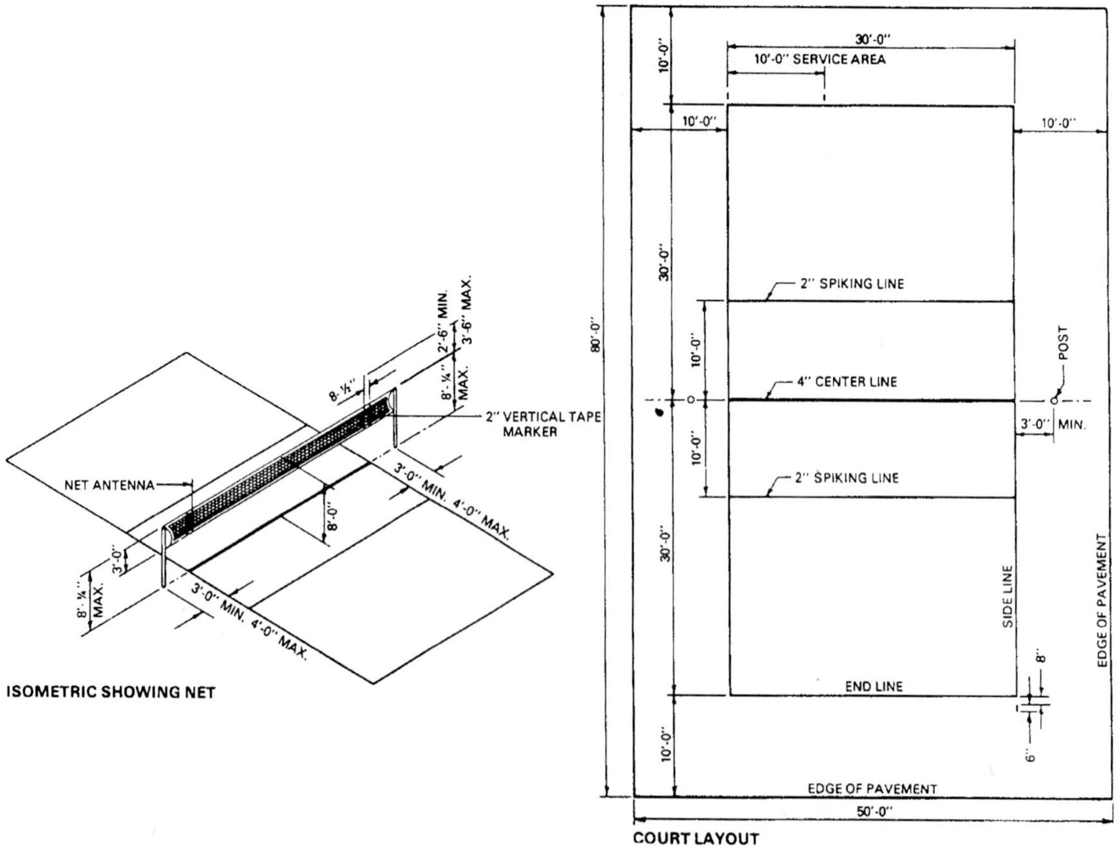

Fig. 10 Volleyball court. All measurements for court markings are to the outside of lines except for the centerline. All court markings to be 2 in wide except as noted

BADMINTON COURT

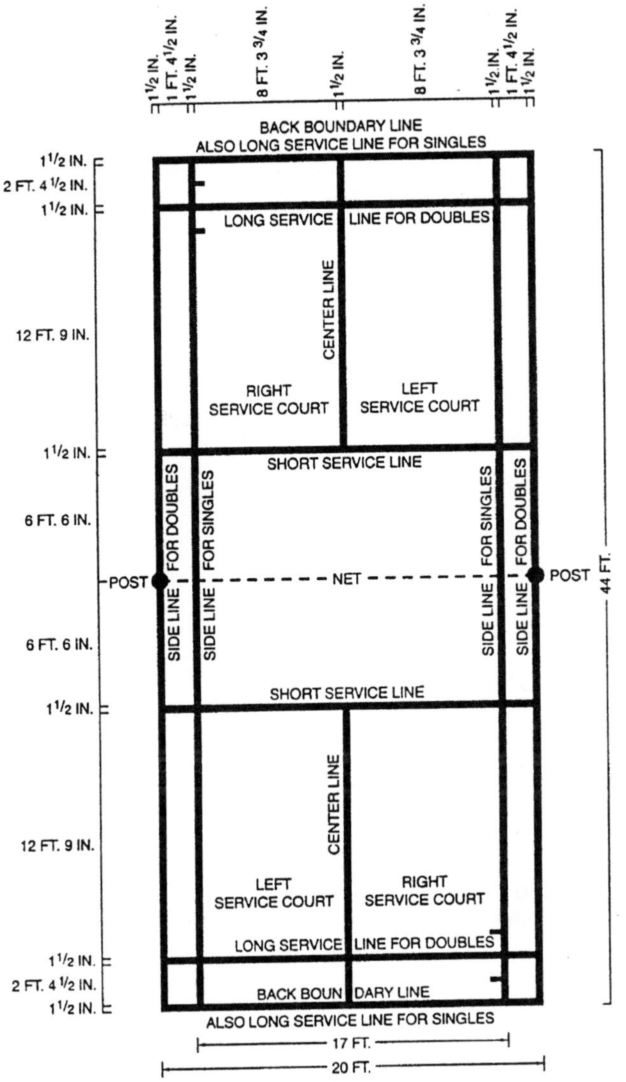

Dimensions are measured to the outside edges of all lines. All boundary lines shall be 1-1/2" wide, and shall be easily distinguishable and preferably colored white or yellow.

NOTE: The above court may be used for singles or doubles play. For singles play only, remove zones created by Singles Long Service Line and Doubles Side Line.

Reprinted with permission of:
U.S. Badminton Association (USBA)
One Olympic Plaza
Colorado Springs, CO 80909
(719) 578-4808

STANDARD SHUFFLEBOARD COURT

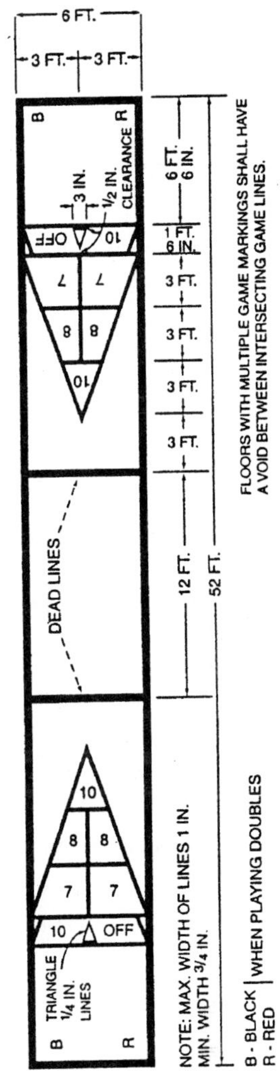

NOTE: Number markings are optional. All line dimensions must be measured from line centers.

Reprinted with permission of:
National Shuffleboard Association, Inc.
c/o Howard J. Rayle
2508 Westmoor Road
Findlay, OH 45840
(419) 422-7263

INDOOR RECREATION
Shuffleboard

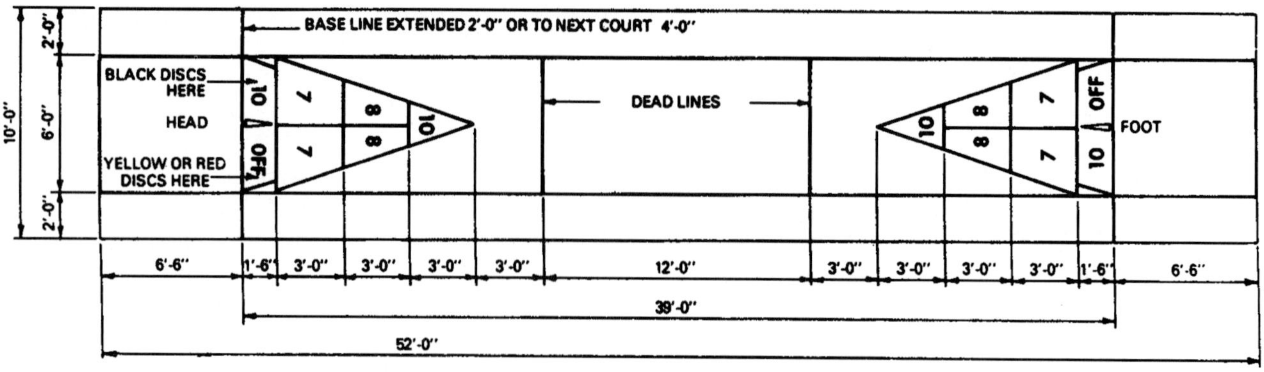

COURT LAYOUT

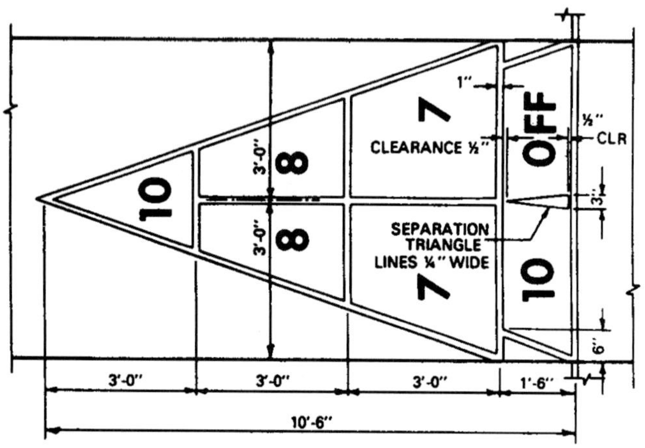

COURT MARKING DETAIL

Fig. 11 Shuffleboard court. All dimensions are to centers of lines and to edge of court. Maximum line width 1½ in, minimum ¾ in. Playing court is 6 ft 0 in × 52 ft 0 in plus a recommended minimum of 2 ft 0 in on each side or 4 ft 0 in between courts in battery

LETTER BOXES
Wall Recessed

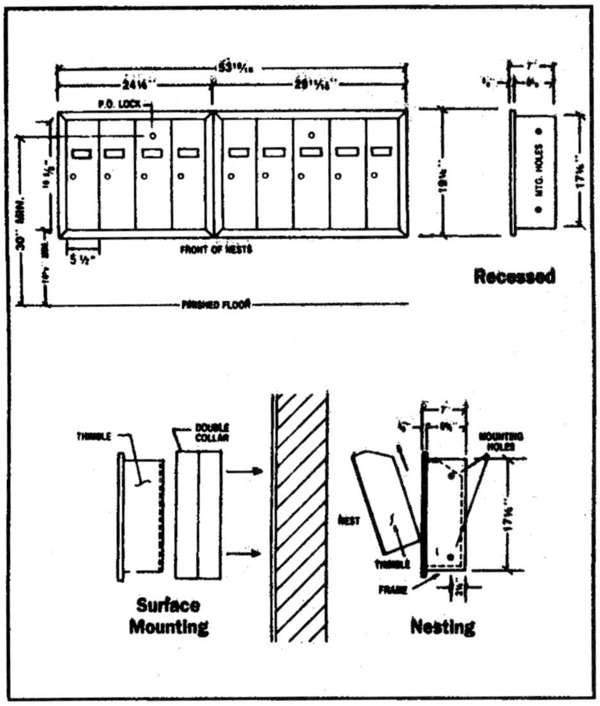

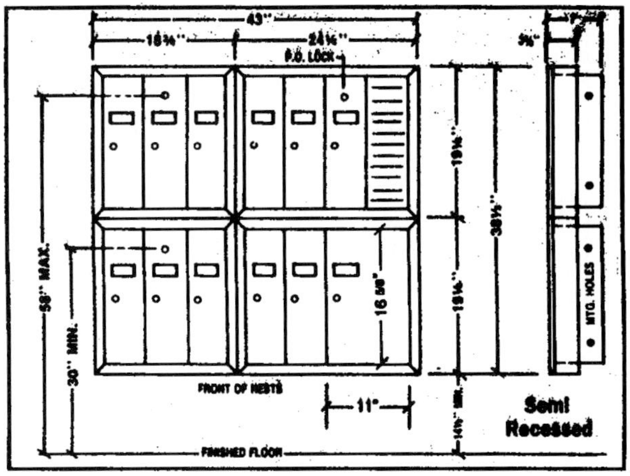

NO. OF OPENINGS		FOR 3-4 & 5 WIDE NESTS			All dimensions in inches.
SINGLE	DOUBLE	SUGGESTED ARRANGEMENT	ROUGH OPENING	CABINET	NET OVERALL WIDTH
3	6	3	17 3/4	16 3/4	18 3/4
4	8	4	23 1/4	22 1/4	24 1/4
5	10	5	28 11/16	27 11/16	29 11/16
6	12	3-3	36 1/2	35 1/2	37 1/2
7	14	3-4	42	41	43
8	16	4-4	47 1/2	46 1/2	48 1/2
9	18	4-5	52 15/16	51 15/16	53 15/16
10	20	5-5	58 3/8	57 3/8	59 3/8
11	22	4-3-4	66 1/4	65 1/4	67 1/4
12	24	4-4-4	71 3/4	70 3/4	72 3/4
13	26	4-5-4	77 3/16	76 3/16	78 3/16
14	28	5-4-5	82 5/8	81 5/8	83 5/8
15	30	5-5-5	88 1/16	87 1/16	89 1/16
16	32	4-4-4-4	96	95	97
17	34	5-4-4-4	101 7/16	100 7/16	102 7/16
18	36	5-4-4-5	106 7/8	105 7/8	107 7/8
19	38	5-4-5-5	112 5/16	111 5/16	113 5/16
20	40	5-5-5-5	117 3/4	116 3/4	118 3/4
21	42	4-4-5-4-4	125 11/16	124 11/16	126 11/16
22	44	5-4-4-4-5	131 1/8	130 1/8	132 1/8
23	46	5-5-3-5-5	136 1/2	135 1/2	137 1/2
24	48	5-5-4-5-5	142	141	143
25	50	5-5-5-5-5	147 7/16	146 7/16	148 7/16
26	52	5-4-4-4-4-5	155 3/8	154 3/8	156 3/8
27	54	5-4-5-4-5-4	160 13/16	159 13/16	161 13/16
28	56	5-5-4-4-5-5	166 1/4	165 1/4	167 1/4
29	58	5-5-4-5-5-5	171 11/16	170 11/16	172 11/16
30	60	5-5-5-5-5-5	177 1/8	176 1/8	178 1/8
31	62	5-4-4-5-4-4-5	185 1/16	184 1/16	186 1/16
32	64	5-5-4-4-4-5-5	190 1/2	189 1/2	191 1/2
33	66	5-5-4-5-4-5-5	195 15/16	194 15/16	196 15/16
34	68	5-5-5-4-5-5-5	201 3/8	200 3/8	202 3/8
35	70	5-5-5-5-5-5-5	206 13/16	205 13/16	207 13/16
36	72	5-5-4-4-4-4-5-5	214 3/4	213 3/4	215 3/4
37	74	5-5-5-4-4-4-5-5	220 3/16	219 3/16	221 3/16
38	76	5-5-5-4-4-5-5-5	225 5/8	224 5/8	226 5/8
39	78	5-5-5-5-4-5-5-5	231 1/16	230 1/16	232 1/16
40	80	5-5-5-5-5-5-5-5	236 1/2	235 1/2	237 1/2
41	82	4-4-5-5-5-5-5-4-4	244 7/16	243 7/16	245 7/16
42	84	5-5-5-4-4-4-5-5-5	249 7/8	248 7/8	250 7/8
43	86	5-5-5-5-3-5-5-5-5	255 1/4	254 1/4	256 1/4
44	88	5-5-5-5-4-5-5-5-5	260 3/4	259 3/4	261 3/4
45	90	5-5-5-5-5-5-5-5-5	266 3/16	265 3/16	267 3/16

LETTER BOXES
Mail Collection Boxes

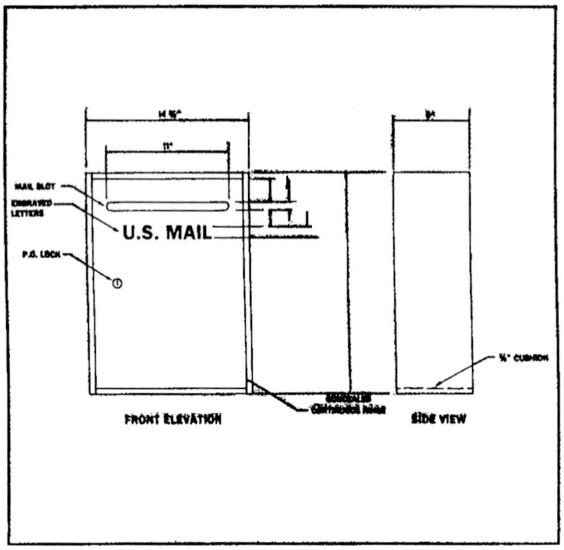

19 1/4" H x 14 3/8" W x 6" D

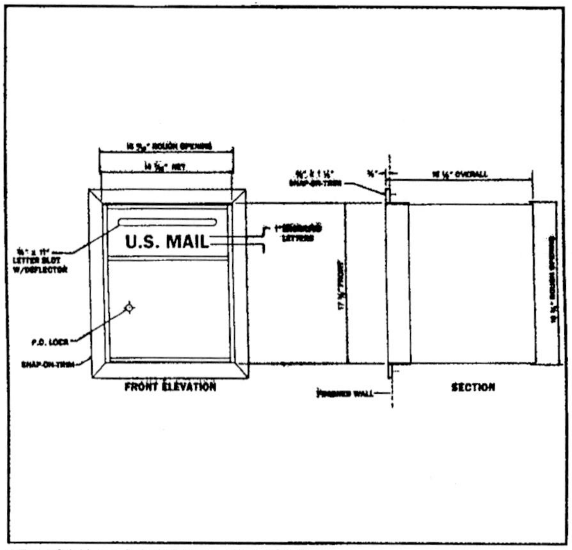

17 1/8" H x 14 1/16" W x 16 1/8" D

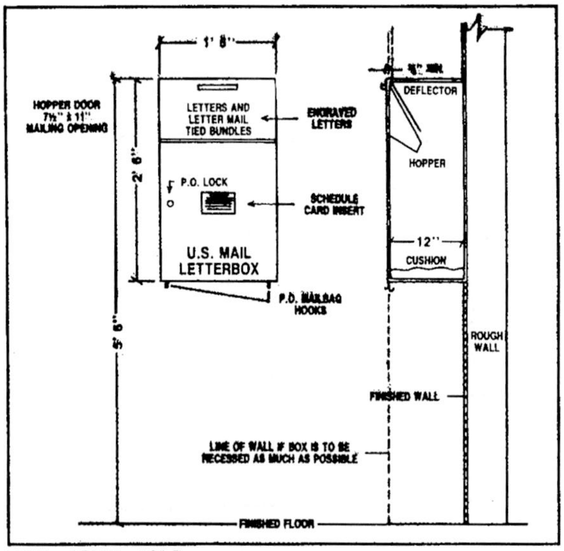

30" H x 18" W x 12" D

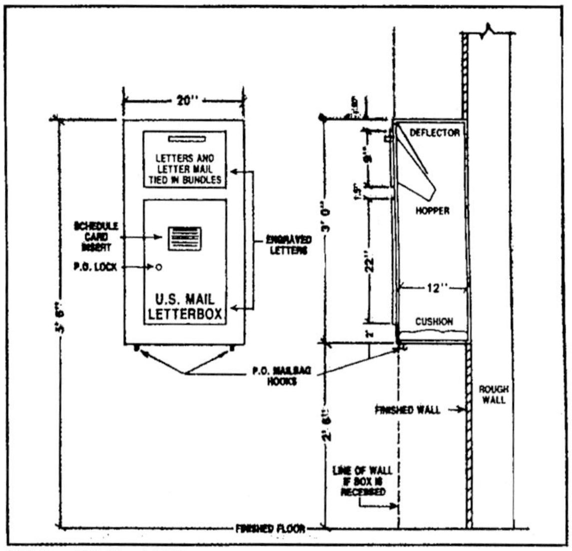

36" H x 20" W x 12" D

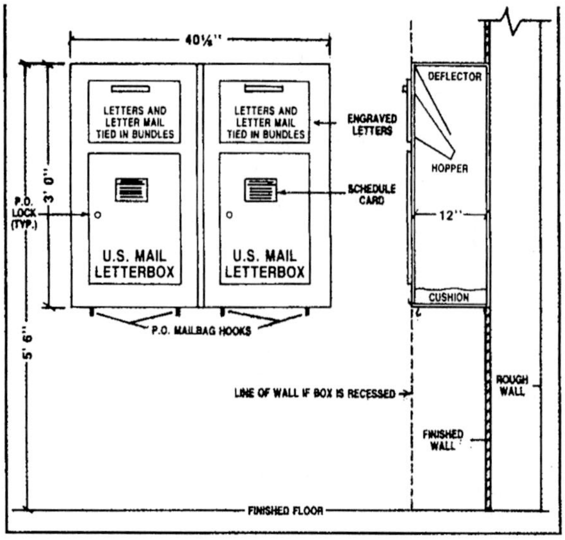

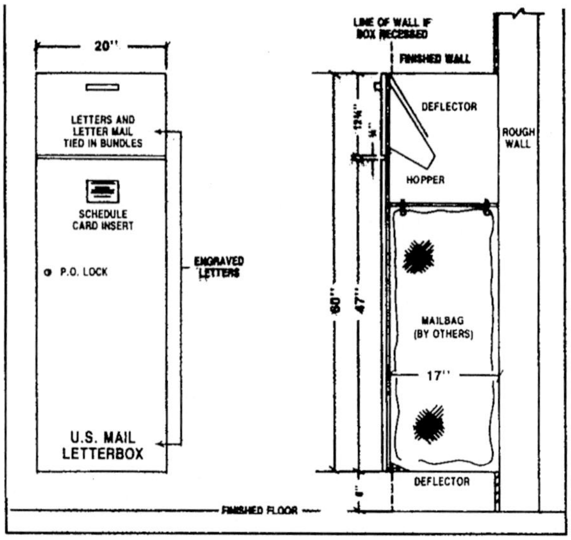

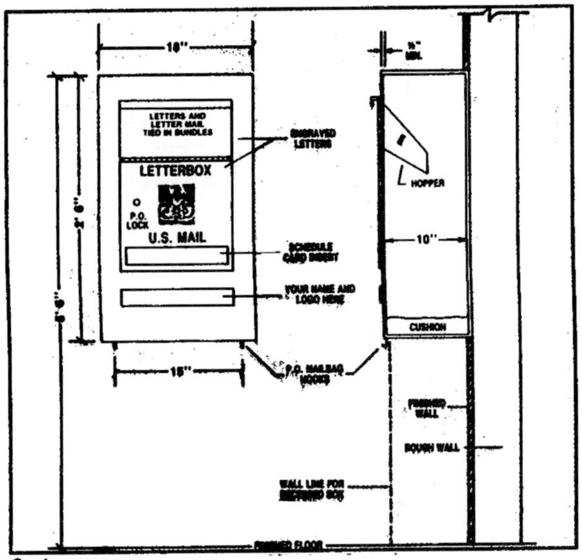

Contemporary
30" H x 18" W x 10" D

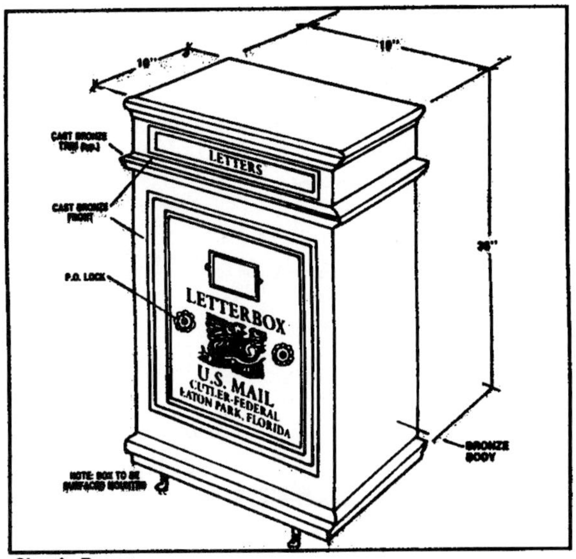

Classic Bronze
36" H x 19" W x 10" D

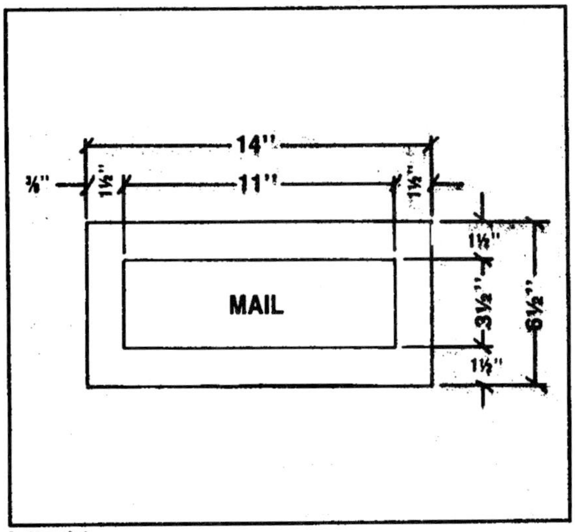

Letterslot
6 1/2" H x 14" W

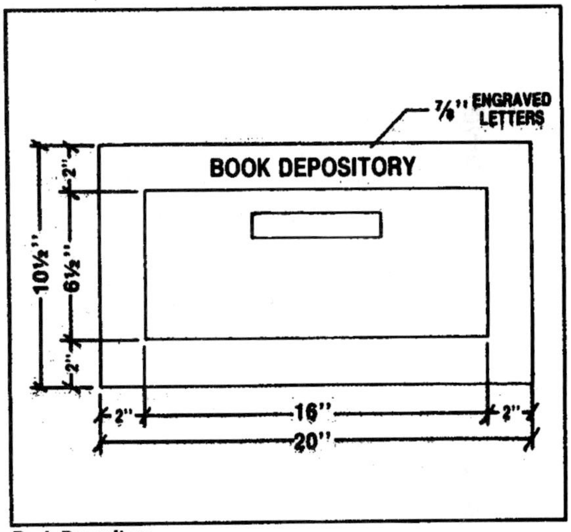

Book Depository
10 1/2" H x 20" W

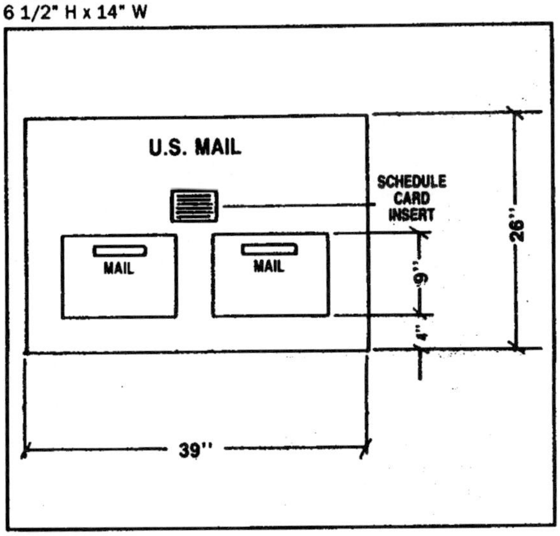

Plate Front
26"H x 39"W

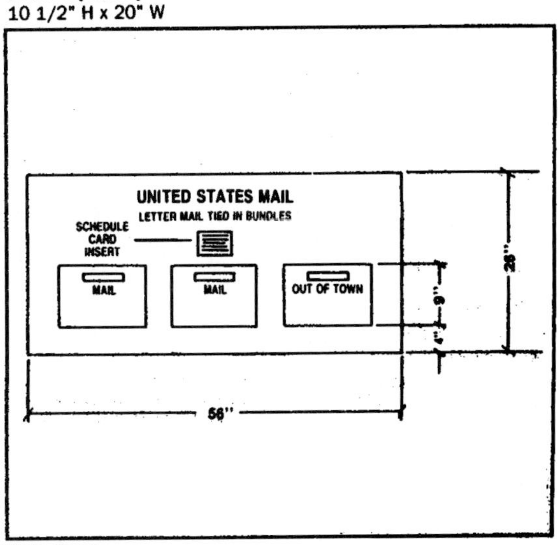

Plate Front
26" H x 56" W

LETTER BOXES
Mail Chutes, Parcel Lockers, and Key Cabinets

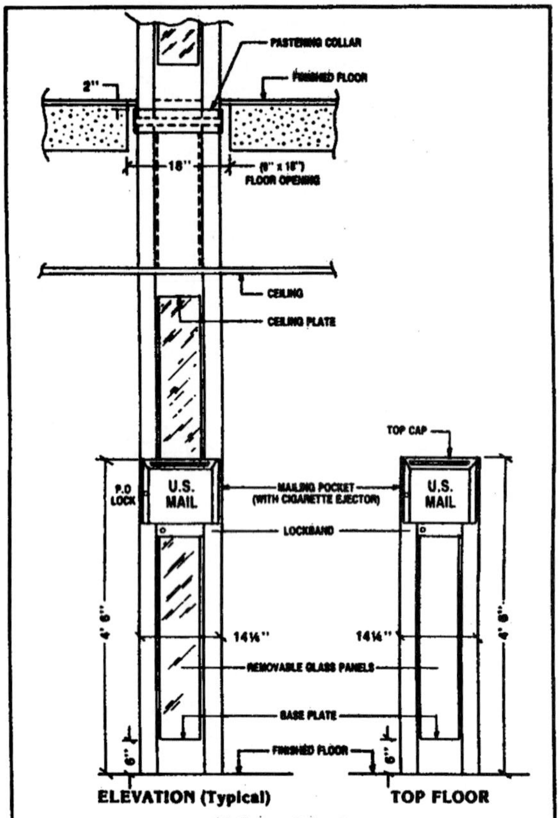

Wide Chute

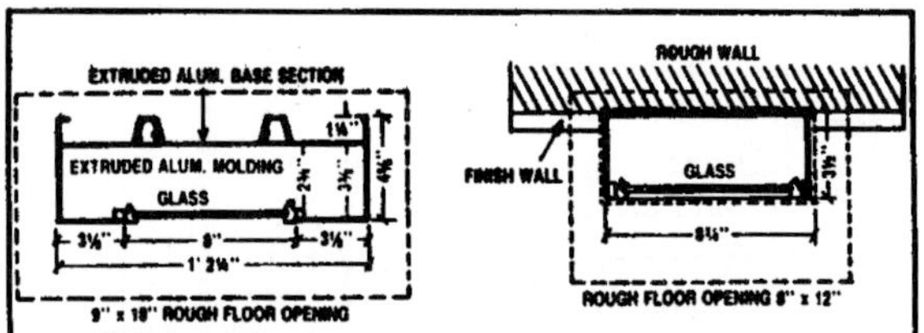

Wide Chute

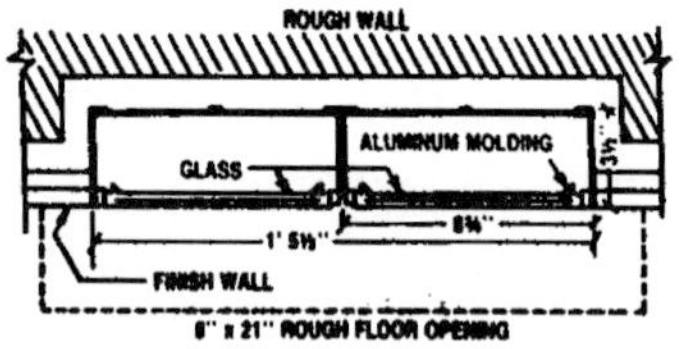

Twin

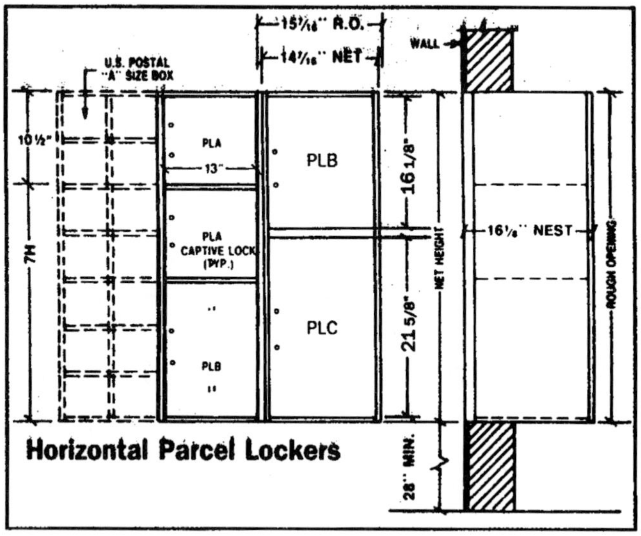

Horizontal Parcel Lockers

Key Storage Cabinet

The safest way to keep keys stored in one central secure location. Available in four different sizes, holding from 32 to 128 keys.

Holds 32 Keys
9 1/4" H x 13 5/8" W

Holds 64 Keys
16 5/16" H x 13 5/8" W

Holds 96 Keys
23 1/4" H x 13 5/8" W

Holds 128 Keys
30 1/4" H x 13 5/8" W

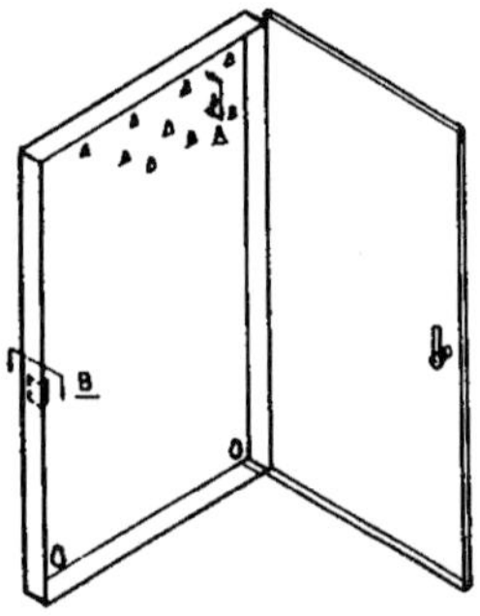

Key Keeper

For use in a mail room (rear loading) installation. The arrow lock is accessed by the postman to retrieve the mail room door key, and stored safely when not in use.

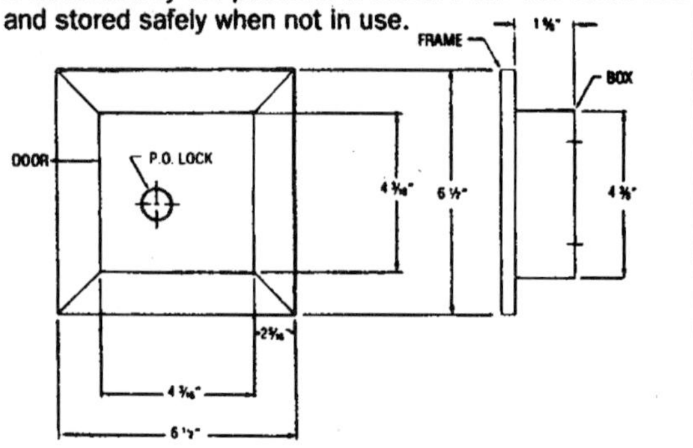

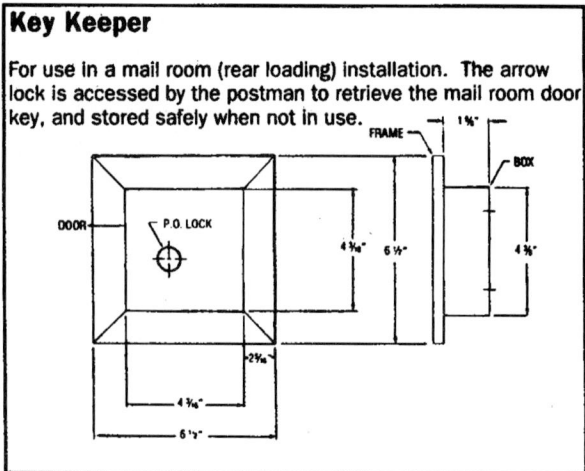

TELEPHONE BOOTHS

Freestanding and Wall-Mounted

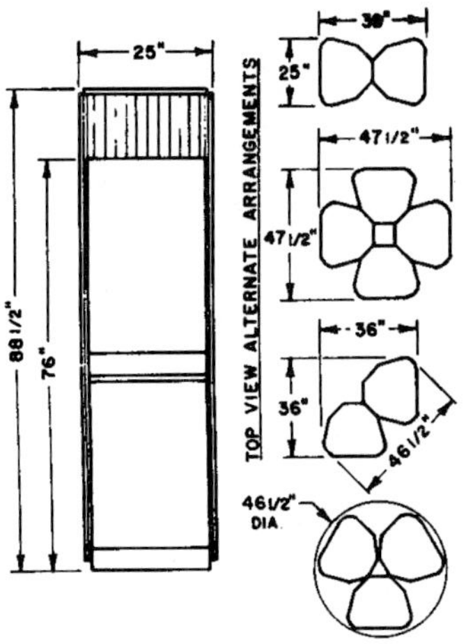

Cluster

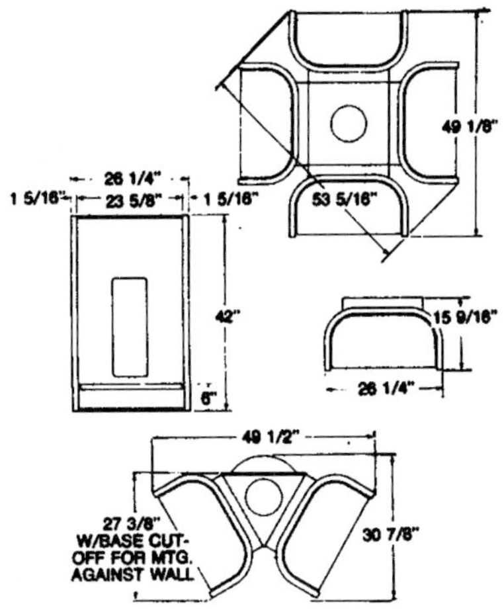

Cluster

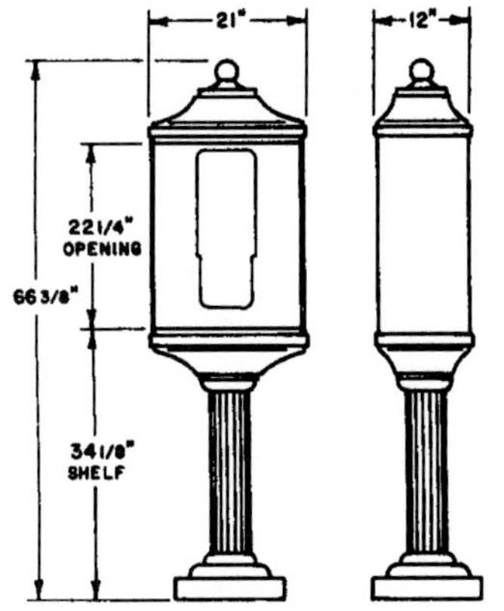

Free-standing

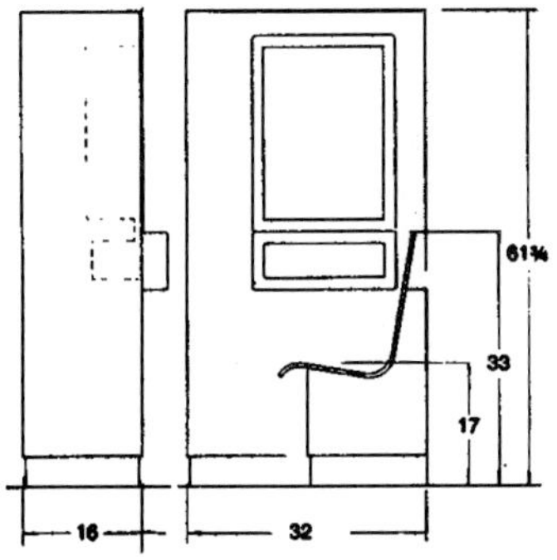

Freestanding

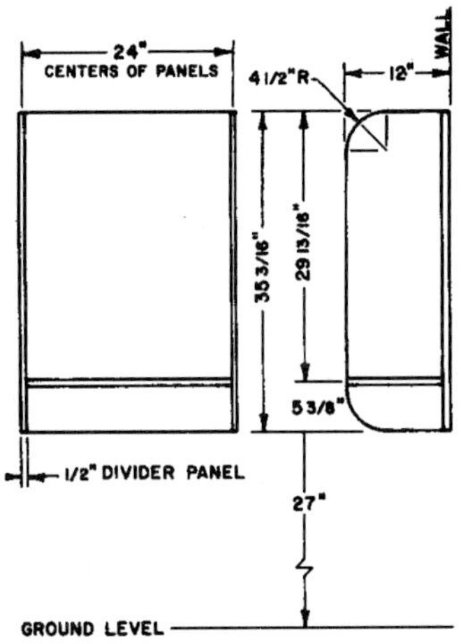

Wall-mounted

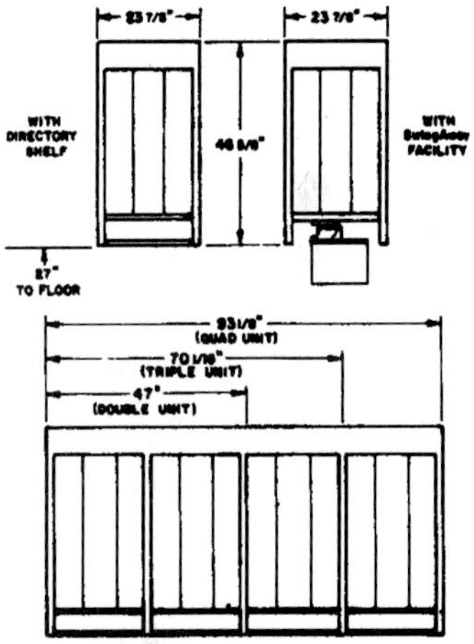

Wall-mounted

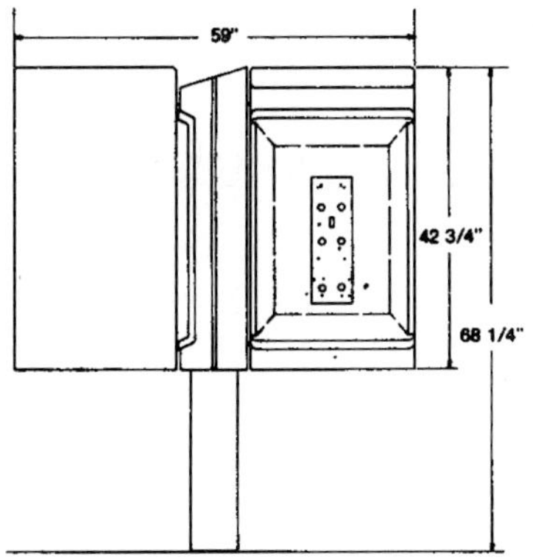

Freestanding

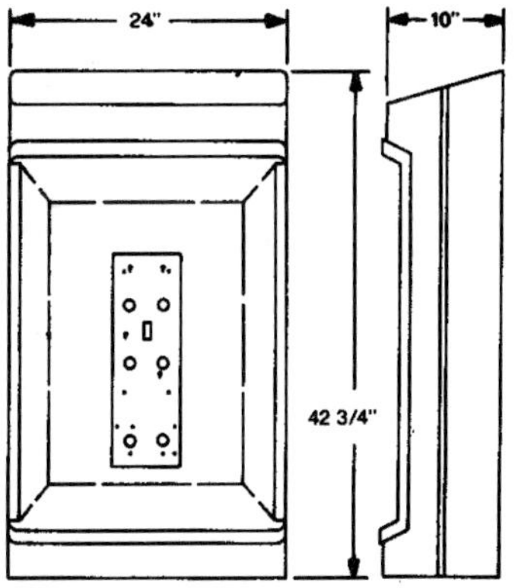

Wall-mounted

GRILLES
Cast Metal

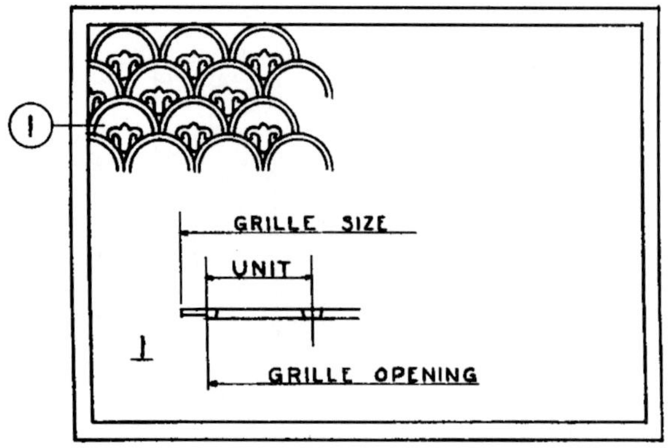

Cast metal grille of unit design, cast in one piece. Grille size is governed by unit sizes plus width of border.

Cast metal grille of Renaissance design, ferrous or non-ferrous metal.

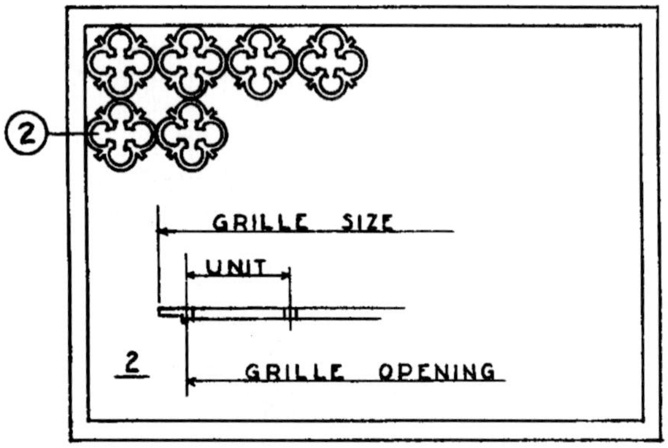

Cast metal grille of unit design, units cast separately and built into frame. Grille size is governed by unit sizes plus width of border.

Cast metal grille panels of various sizes cast in units and fitted into cast or wrought metal frame.

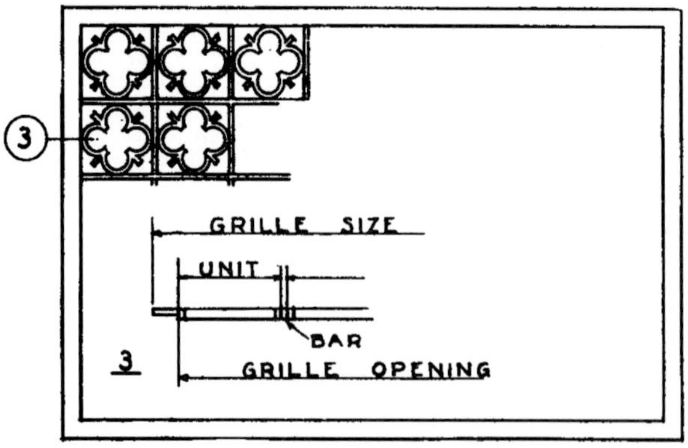

Cast metal grille of unit design. Units cast separately and built into grille spaces. Grille size must conform to unit sizes plus widths of bars and borders.

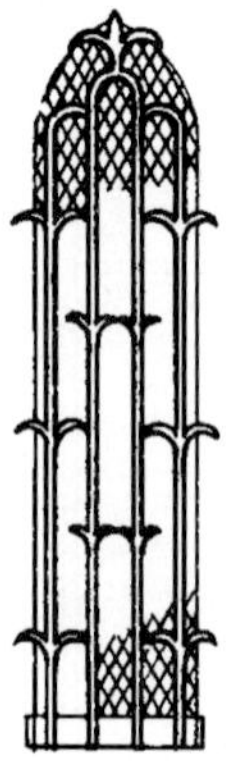

Cast metal grille for ventilator opening; may be fitted with metal screen and may be formed to curved wall or cove.

Cast metal grille for ventilator opening of special architectural form.

Fig. 1 Cast metal grilles may be designed and built in various combinations. They may be made in small units cast separately or as one complete piece

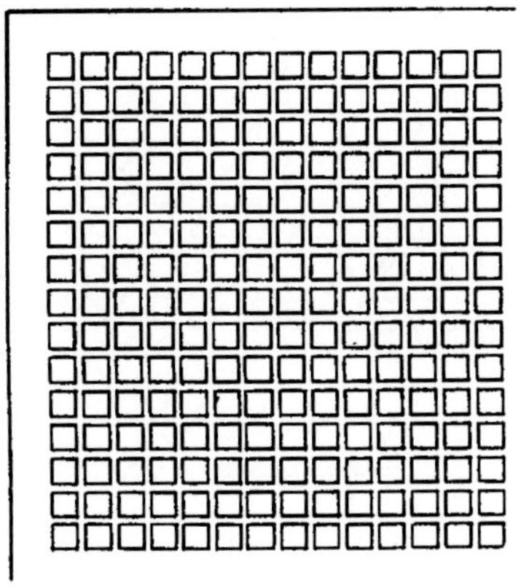

Stamped metal grille, square holes. Holes may be from ¼" to 1½" or larger, in ⅛" steps, with bars or frets from ⅛" to ⅜" or greater.

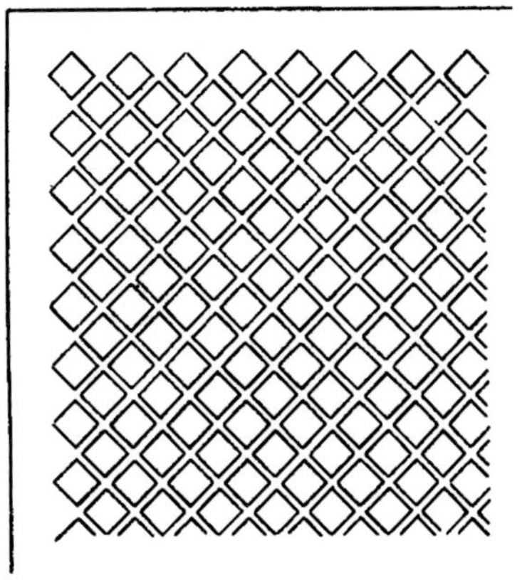

Stamped metal grille, square holes diagonally arranged.

Stamped metal grille, Grecian or Union Jack design, made in a number of unit sizes and variations.

Stamped metal grille, shell or fish scale design, made in several unit sizes and variations.

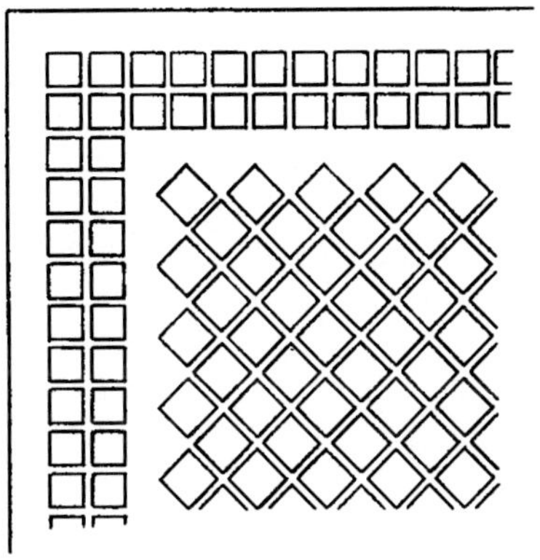

Stamped metal grille, square holes arranged to form plain border with diagonal center.

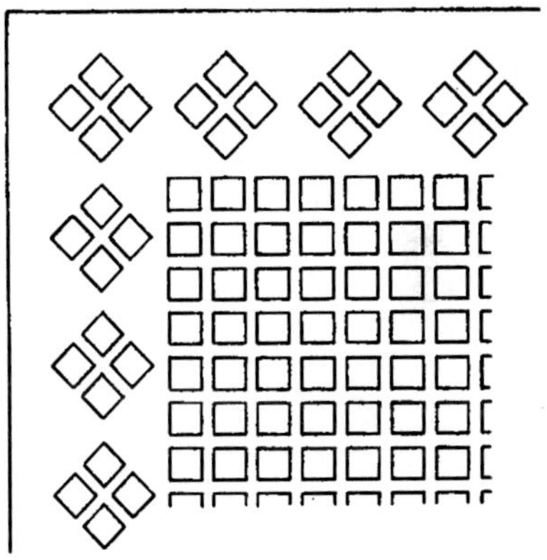

Stamped metal grille, square holes arranged to form diagonal border, with plain center.

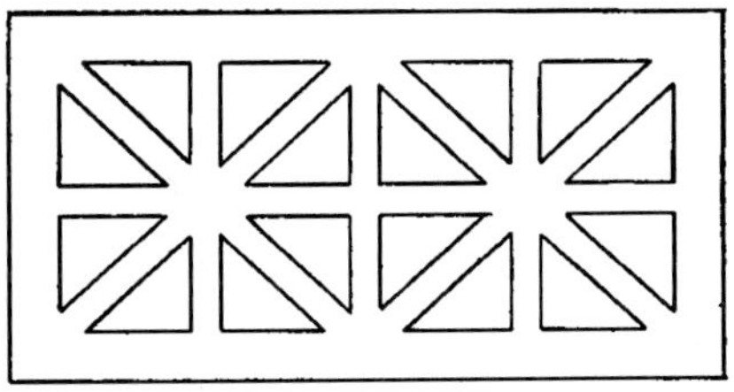

Foundation or Bulkhead Grille

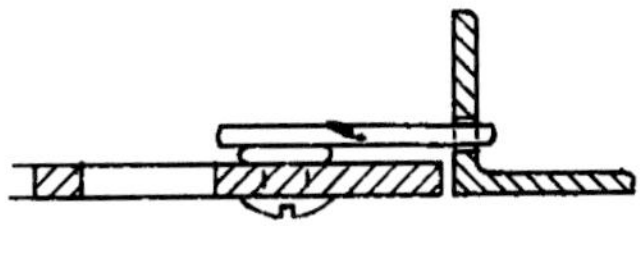

Screwdriver Operated Catch

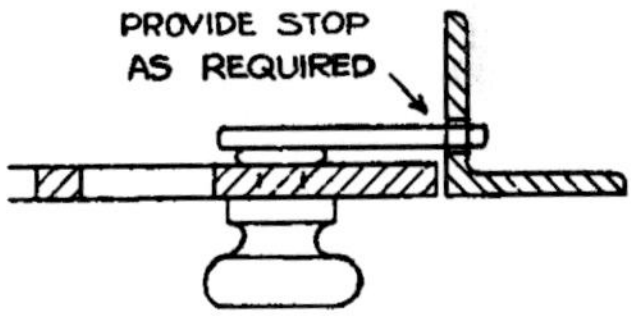

Thumb Latch

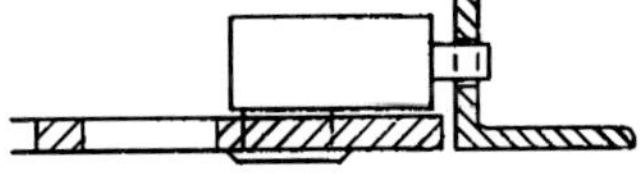

Lock and Dead Bolt

SCALE 1½" = 1'-0" AND ½" = 1"

SPECIFY:
- **Sizes of holes or unit stampings**
- **Thickness**
- **Metal and finish**
- **Approximate width of margins**
- **Method of fastening**
- **Hinges and locks where required**
- **Invisible hand hole doors.**

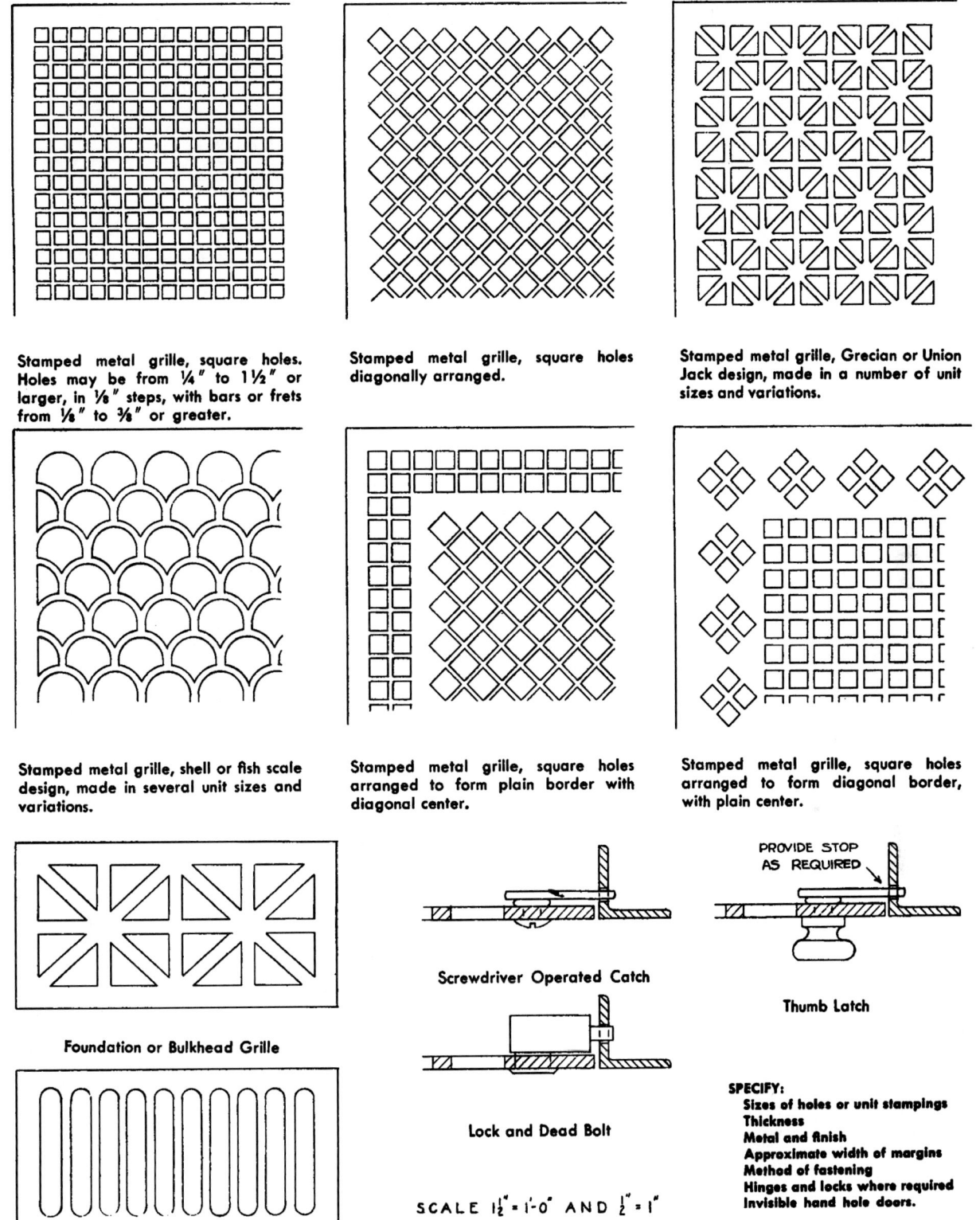

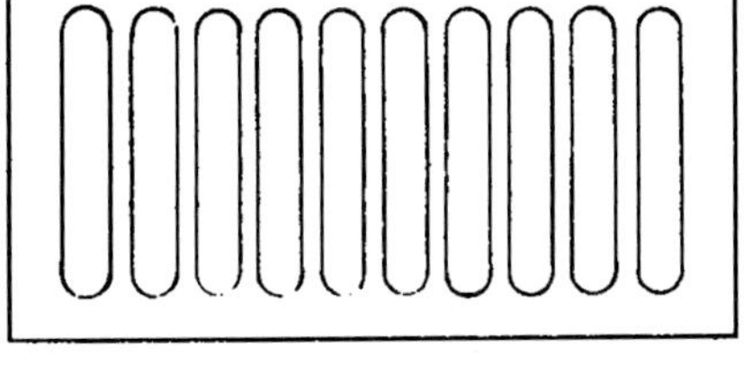

Foundation or Bulkhead Grille

Fig. 2 Stamped metal grilles are produced in a great variety of designs, metals, thicknesses, and sizes. Percentage of free area of stamped grilles may vary from about 25 percent to over 70 percent, with a great many designs in the 55 to 65 percent range. Margin widths can be made to accord with requirements of particular installations, consideration being given to duct openings and overall dimensions. Metal may be steel, painted or otherwise finished, bronze, aluminum, monel metal, or other nonferrous metals, in thicknesses from 16 gauge to ¼ in

GRILLES

Types of Grilles

Perforated Metal Grilles

Perforated Metal Grilles

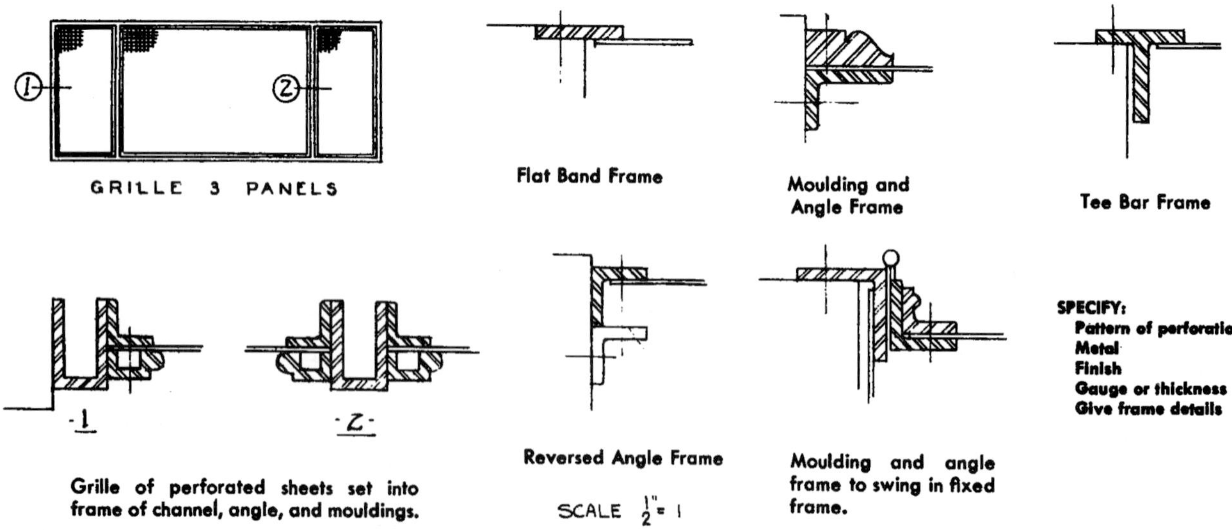

Flat Band Frame

Moulding and Angle Frame

Tee Bar Frame

Grille of perforated sheets set into frame of channel, angle, and mouldings.

Reversed Angle Frame

Moulding and angle frame to swing in fixed frame.

SPECIFY:
- **Pattern of perforations**
- **Metal**
- **Finish**
- **Gauge or thickness**
- **Give frame details**

Fig. 3 Perforated metal grilles may be obtained in several designs and are produced of 19-gauge steel in sheets of standard sizes. Sheets may be cut to any size and placed in frames of metal or other material. Perforated metal grilles are used for vent openings, panels, covers, shelves, partitions, cabinets, metal furniture, boxes, machinery guards, enclosures, and many other purposes. They are also available in many other patterns in any ferrous or nonferrous metal that can be perforated, and in thicknesses from about 24 gauge in the smaller perforations to ¼ or ⅜ in in the larger perforations

Wrought metal grille of heavy close construction, for radiator or ventilator openings.

Wrought metal grille for glass door.

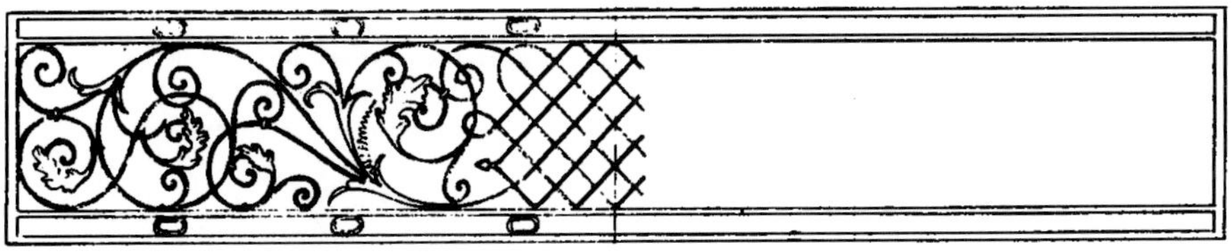

Wrought metal grille for railing or ornamental construction.

Wrought metal grille of light construction, with silhouette work, leaves, flowers, and husks, for arch decoration.

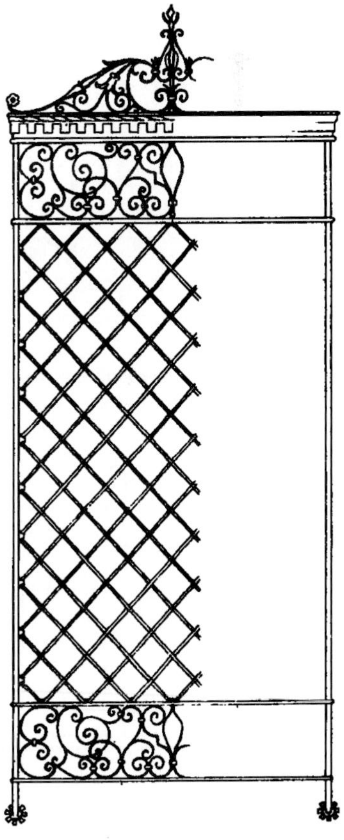

Wrought metal grille for large window or opening.

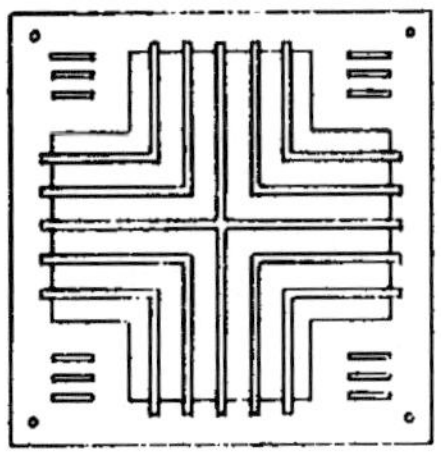

Wrought metal grille of sheet and flat bars, for ventilating opening.

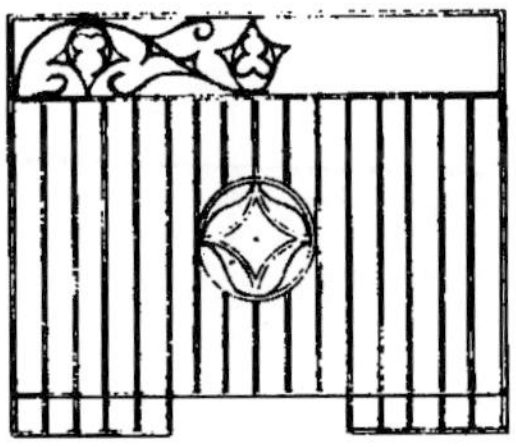

Wrought metal grille for counter.

Fig. 4 Design of wrought metal grilles includes the use of other metal forms, such as sheets, extruded moldings, castings, and stampings. Thus, in addition to plain bar sections and forged items, use is made of the unlimited number of extruded moldings in nonferrous metals; stamped leaves, rosettes, and ornaments of many kinds; cast iron, bronze, nickel silver, and aluminum items of every character; and rolled or drawn sections of many shapes

GRILLES

Window Guards

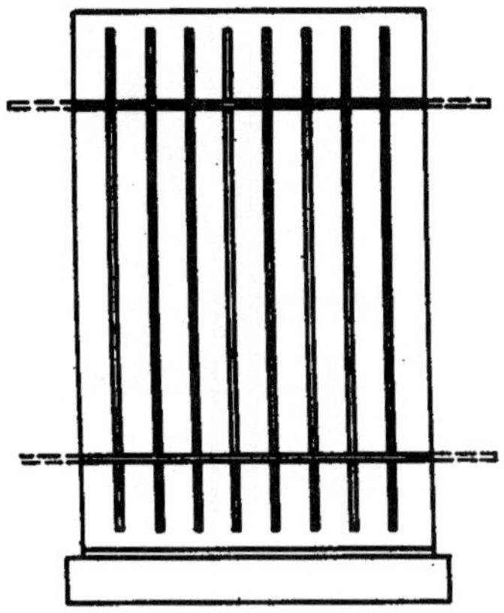

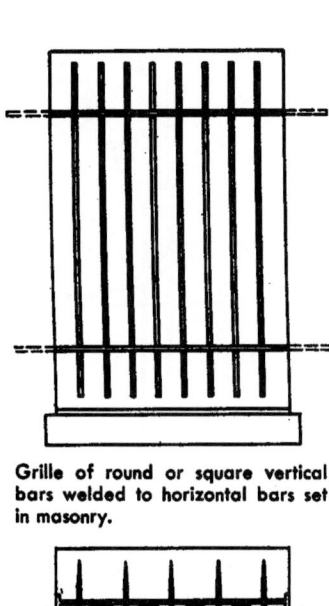

Grille of round or square vertical bars welded to horizontal bars set in masonry.

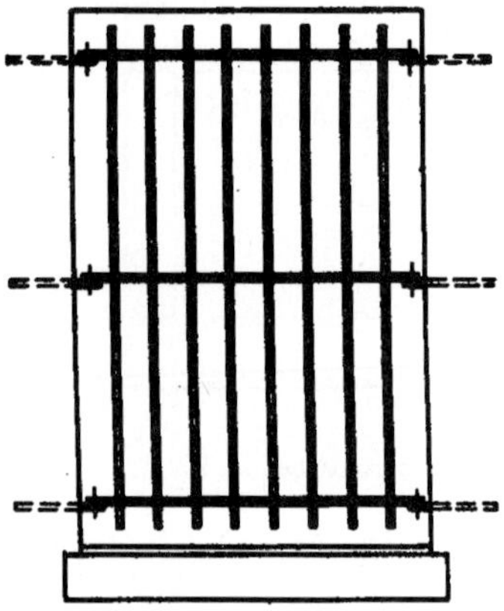

Grille with anchors set in masonry and grille bolted or riveted to anchors.

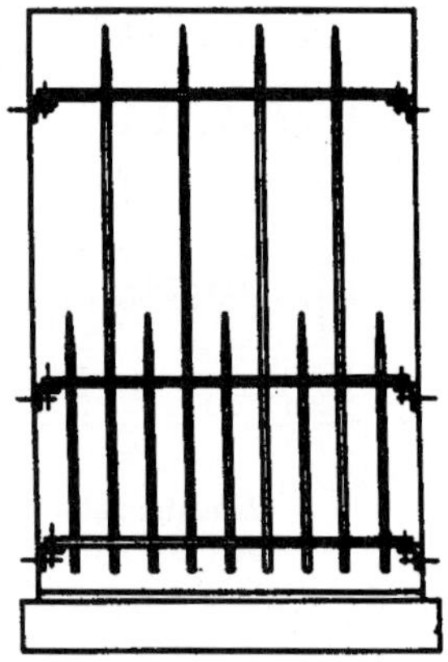

Grille with short alternate vertical bars, angle clips fastened to opening jambs.

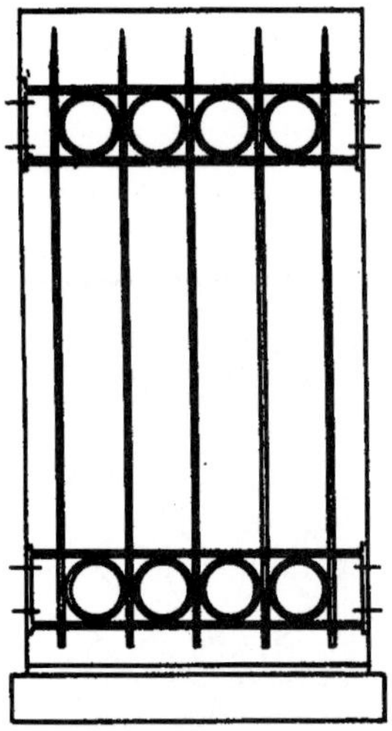

Grille, with ornament between bars, set in masonry opening.

Grille of welded construction set on face of wall.

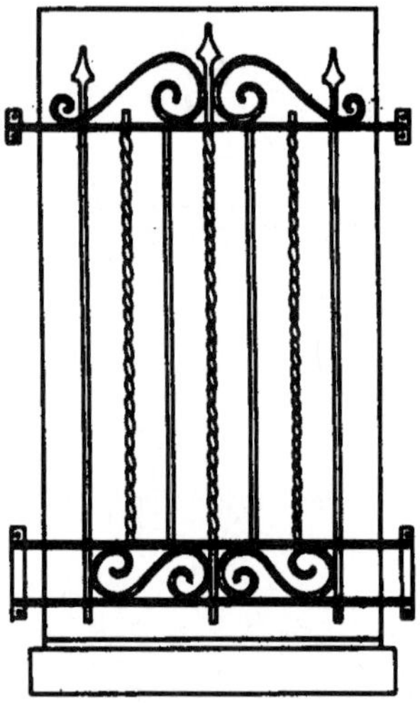

Grille of welded construction set on face of wall.

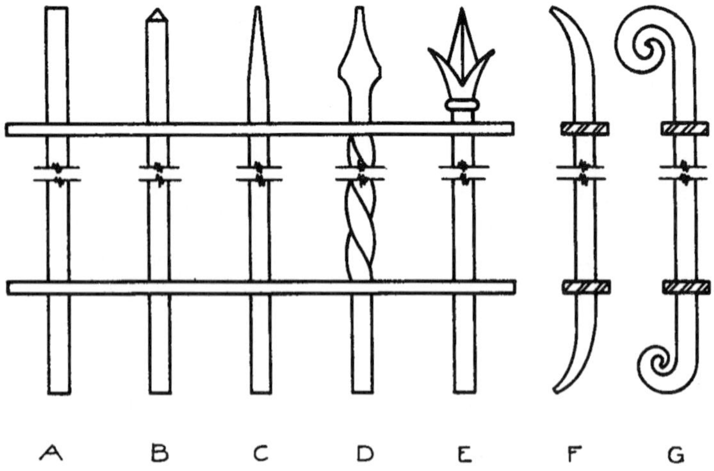

Methods of forming vertical bars.

Fig. 5 Window grilles are of plain construction when used for protection only, and when used for ornamental effect, may be designed with many unique and interesting ideas. Window grilles may be set in the masonry openings or on the face of the wall, with either plain or ornamental brackets or supports. They may also be attached to window frames, or may be arranged to swing, with hinges and locks. Material sizes in window grilles may vary according to the degree of protection required and in proportion to the size of the grille

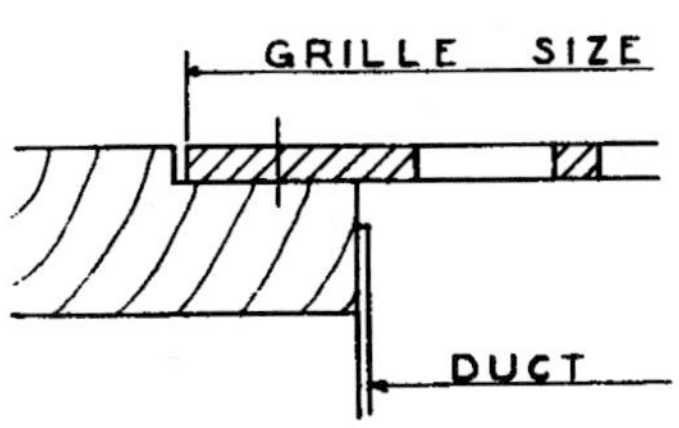

Set in Rabbet

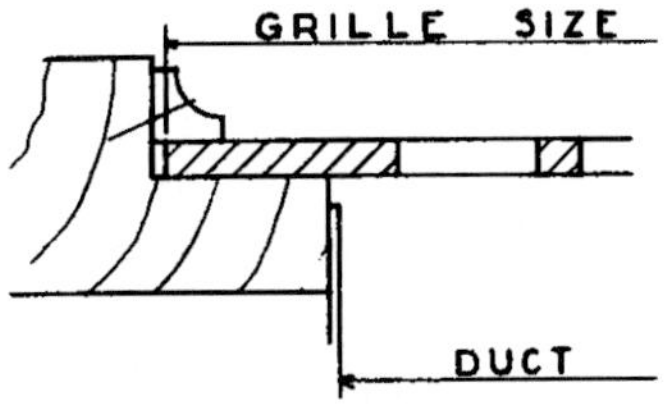

Secured by Moulding

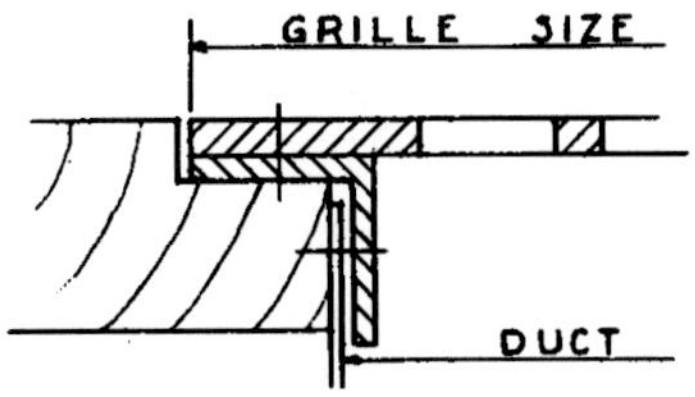

Angle Frame on Back

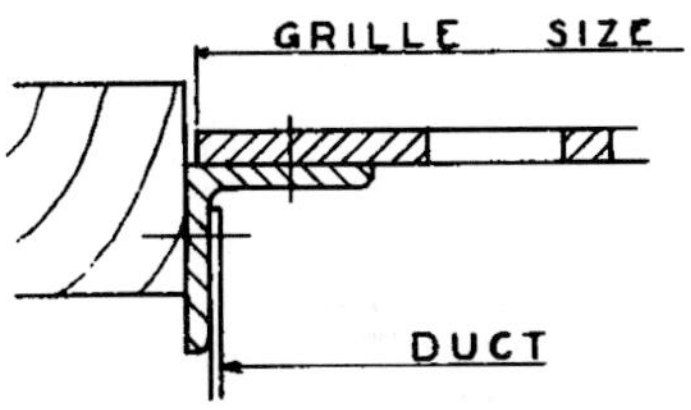

Reversed Angle Frame on Back

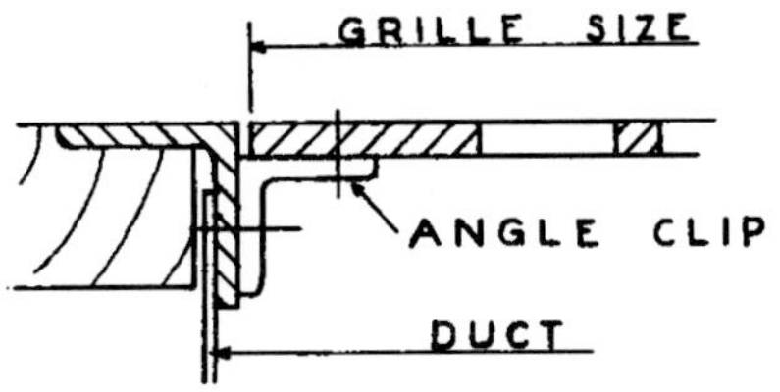

Angle Frame Exposed

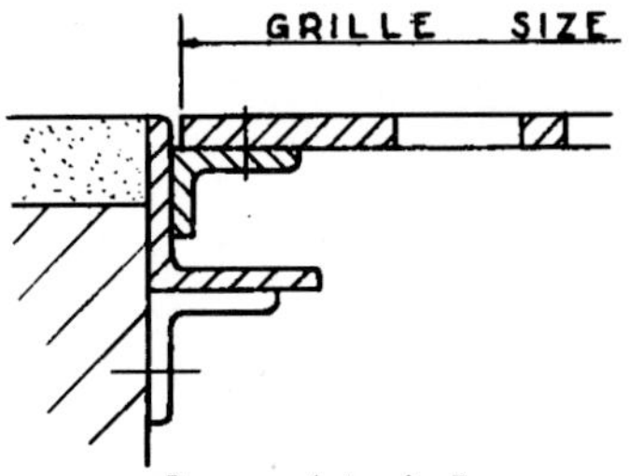

Reversed Angle Frame Exposed

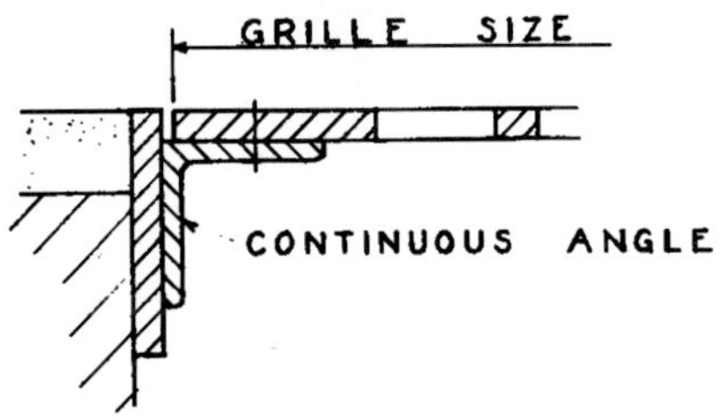

Band and Angle Frame

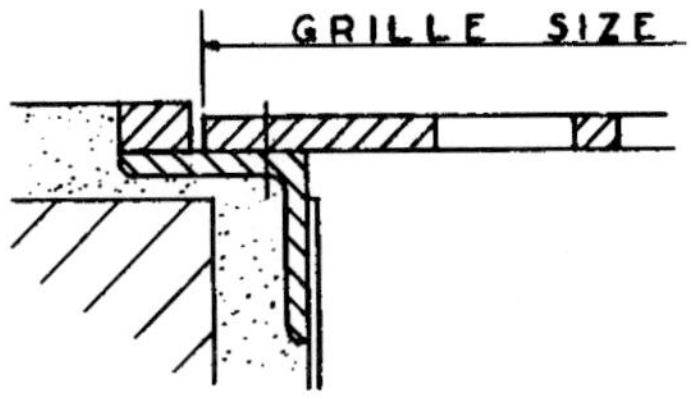

Angle and Plaster Ground

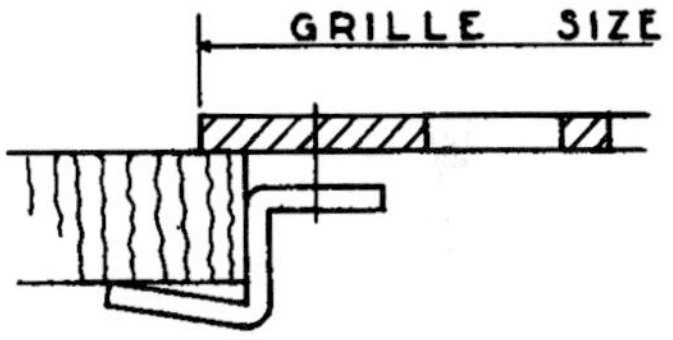

Lugs for Marble

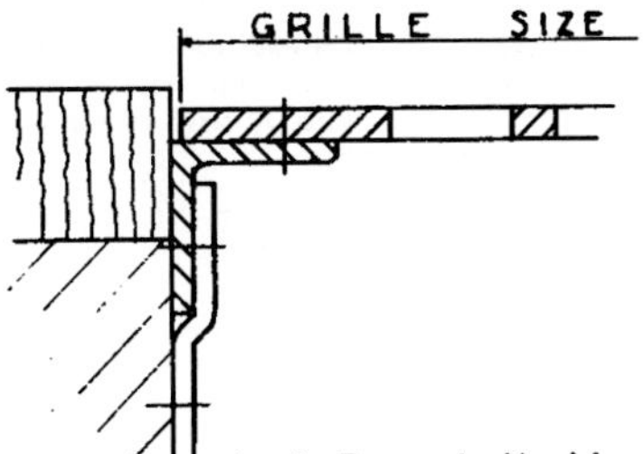

Angle Frame in Marble

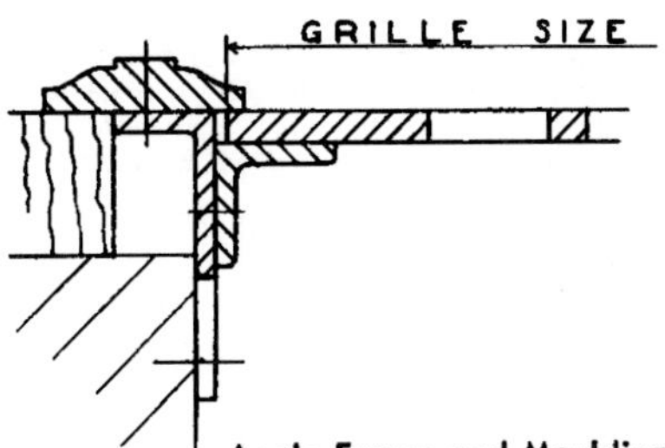

Angle Frame and Moulding

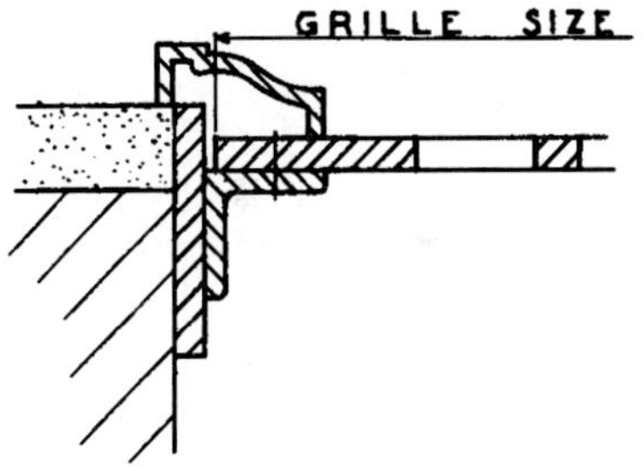

Band Frame and Moulding

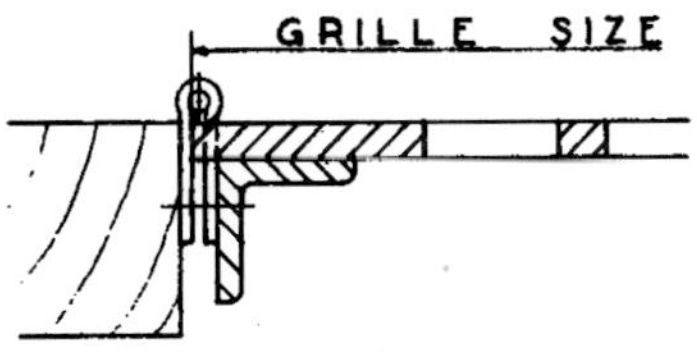

Hinged to Woodwork

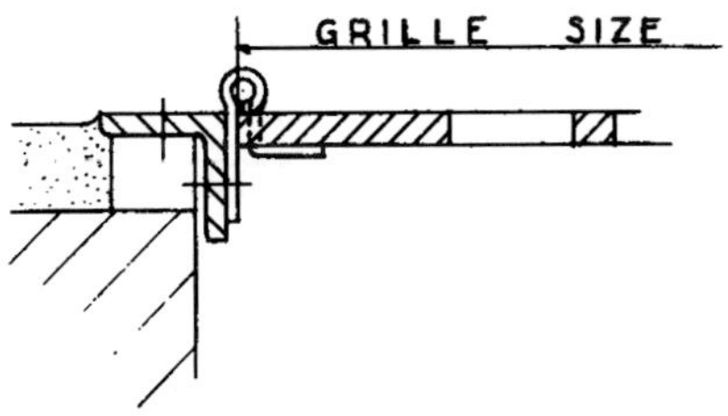

Hinged to Angle Frame

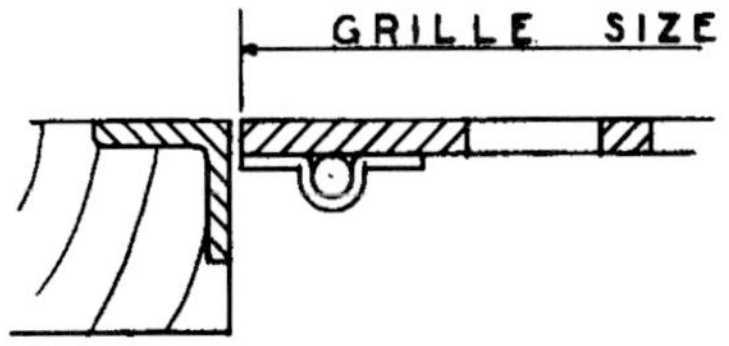

Round Rod Hinge

SCALE $\frac{1}{2}'' = 1''$

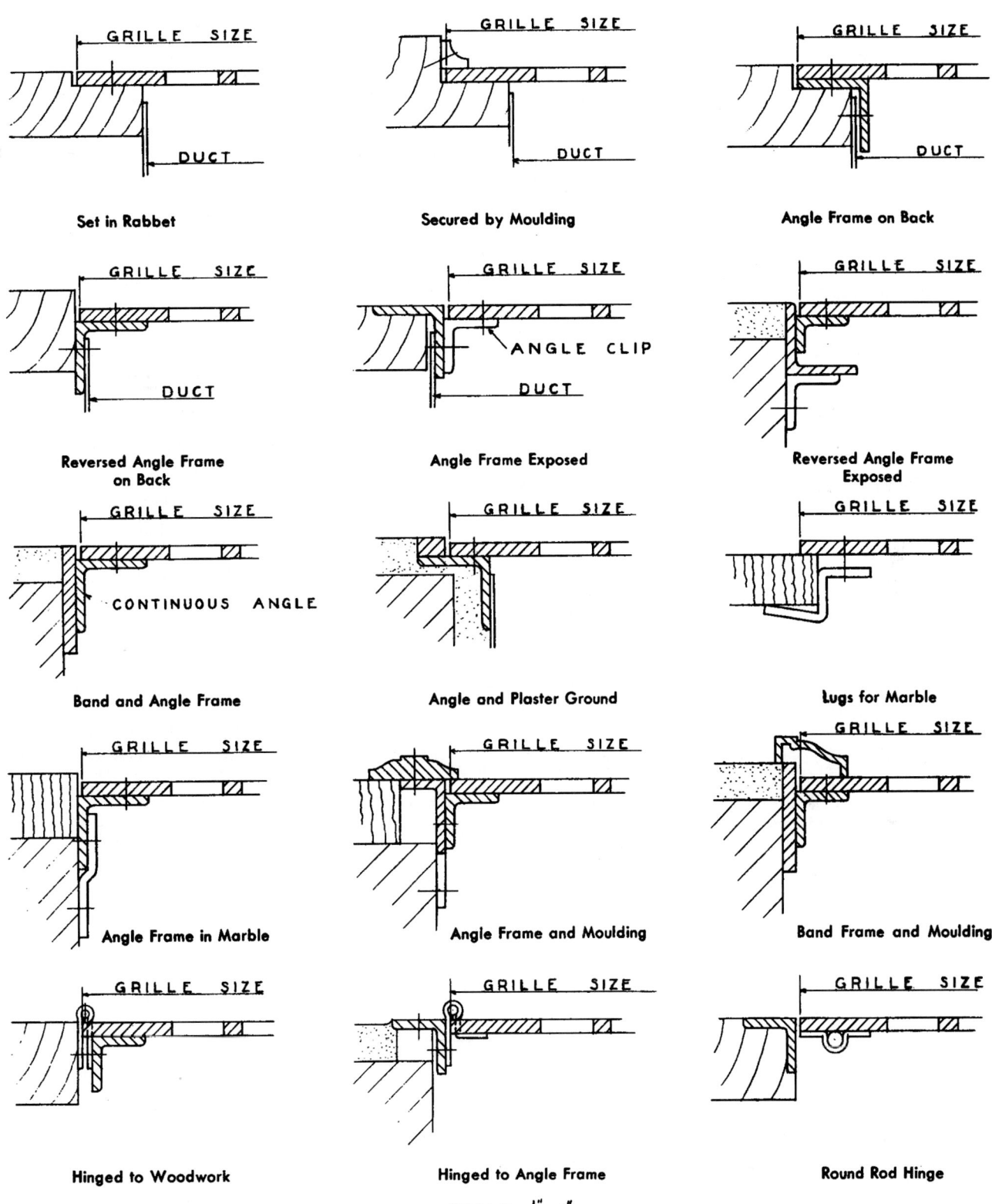

Fig. 6 Methods of fastening grilles. Cast and stamped metal grilles may be fastened by screws or hinges and locks to walls of wood, plaster, marble, or other material in a variety of ways, depending on the type of the grille, the type of framing to be used around the grille, and the appearance or effect desired. These methods show a number of ways in which cast and stamped grilles may be fastened. In selecting the method desired, consideration should be given to whether the grille will require frequent removal. The size and weight of the grille will have a bearing on the size of frames, screws, and hinges

GRILLES
Fastening Methods

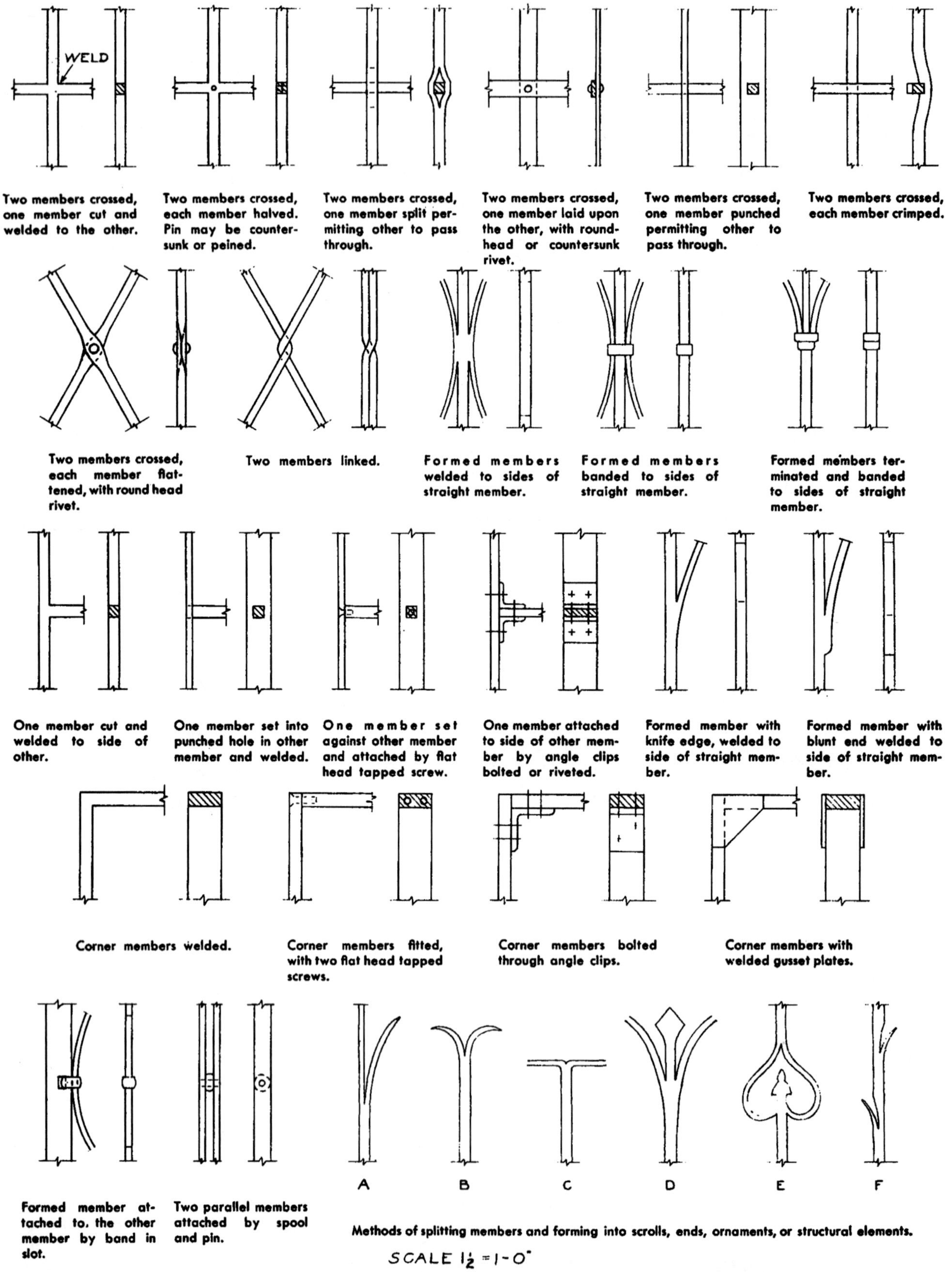
WELD
Two members crossed, one member cut and welded to the other.
Two members crossed, each member halved. Pin may be countersunk or peined.
Two members crossed, one member split permitting other to pass through.
Two members crossed, one member laid upon the other, with roundhead or countersunk rivet.
Two members crossed, one member punched permitting other to pass through.
Two members crossed, each member crimped.
Two members crossed, each member flattened, with round head rivet.
Two members linked.
Formed members welded to sides of straight member.
Formed members banded to sides of straight member.
Formed members terminated and banded to sides of straight member.
One member cut and welded to side of other.
One member set into punched hole in other member and welded.
One member set against other member and attached by flat head tapped screw.
One member attached to side of other member by angle clips bolted or riveted.
Formed member with knife edge, welded to side of straight member.
Formed member with blunt end welded to side of straight member.
Corner members welded.
Corner members fitted, with two flat head tapped screws.
Corner members bolted through angle clips.
Corner members with welded gusset plates.
Formed member attached to the other member by band in slot.
Two parallel members attached by spool and pin.
A
B
C
D
E
F
Methods of splitting members and forming into scrolls, ends, ornaments, or structural elements.
SCALE 1½ = 1-0"

Fig. 7 Wrought metal grilles are fabricated by the use of a great many different methods of crossing and joining members. Some of the more widely employed of these methods are shown here

VINYL WALL PROTECTION GUARDS

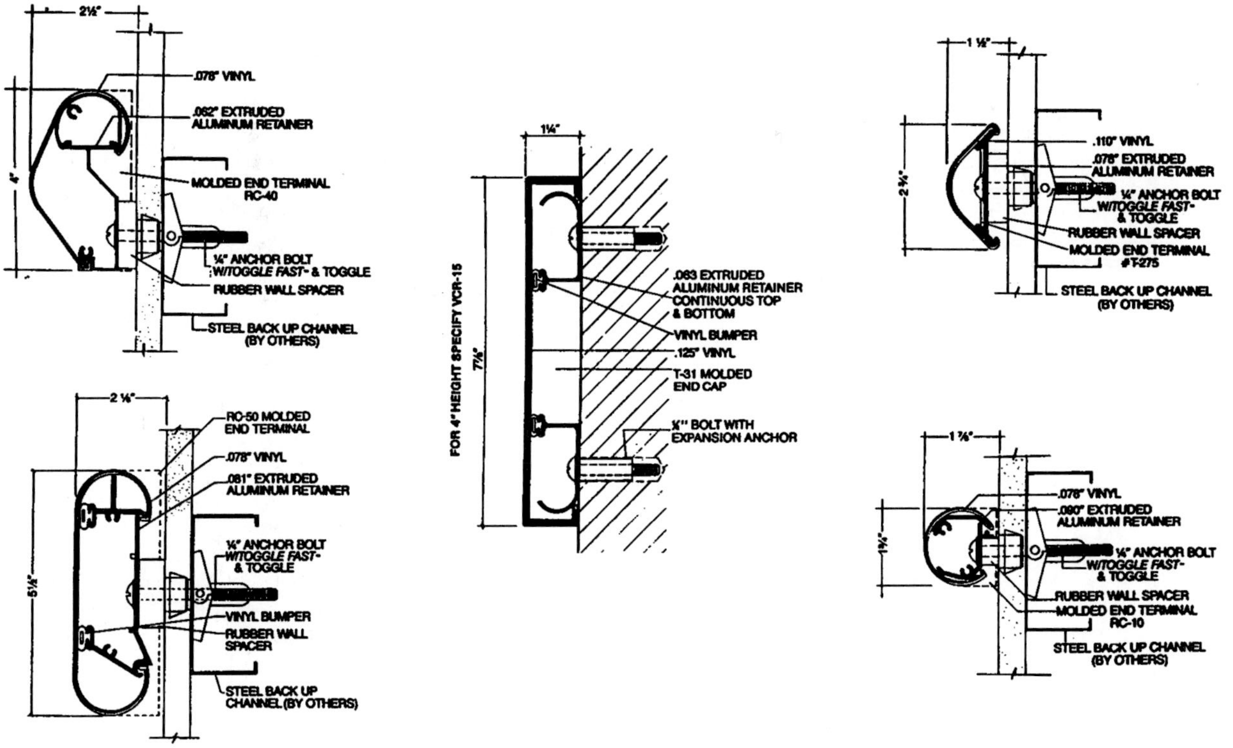

ALUMINUM WALL PROTECTION GUARDS

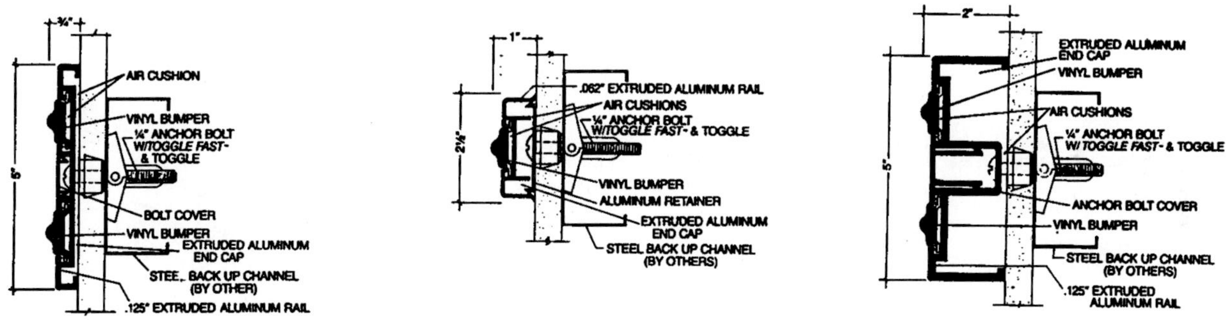

FLUSH-MOUNTED CORNER PROTECTION GUARDS

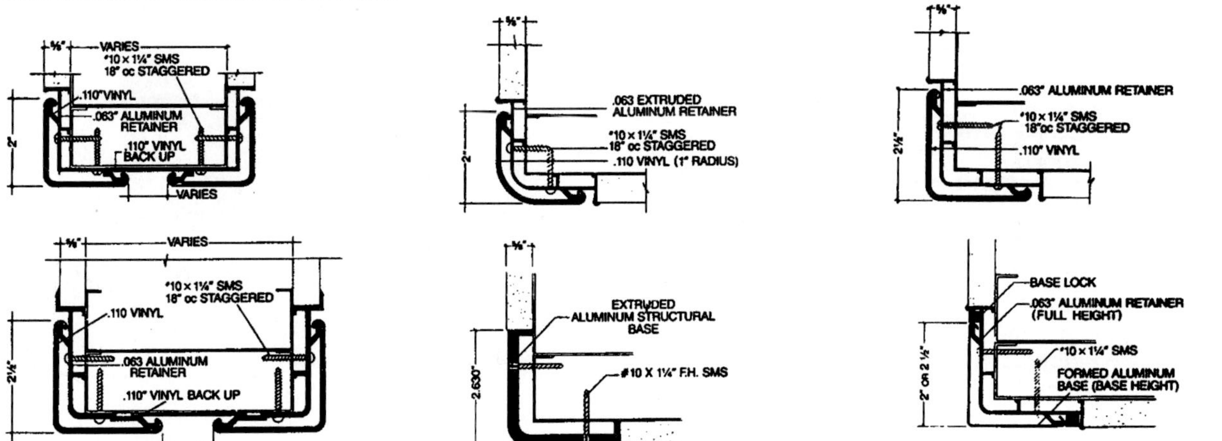

HANDRAILS AND PROTECTION GUARDS

Vinyl Wall Protection Guards

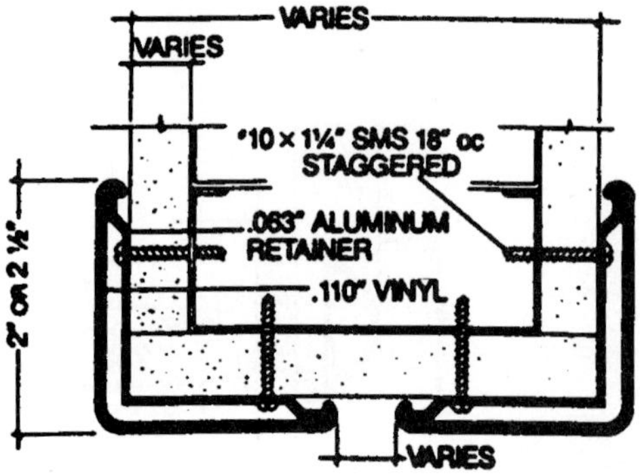

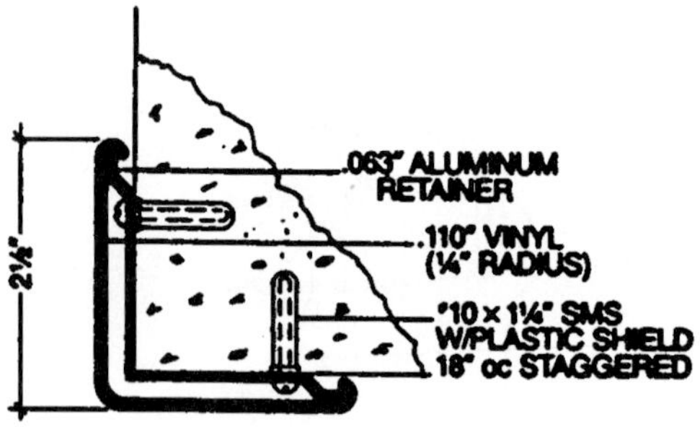

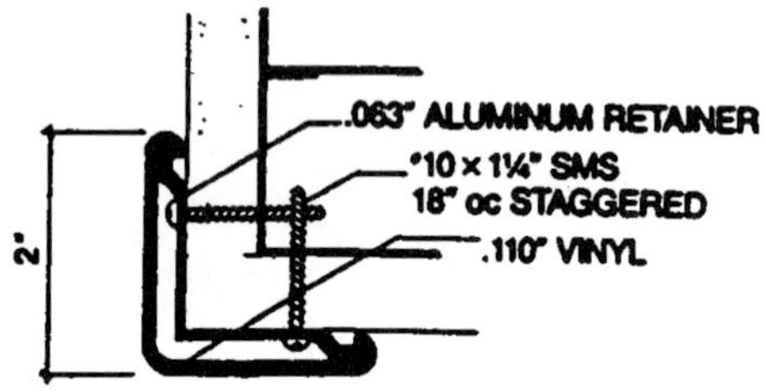

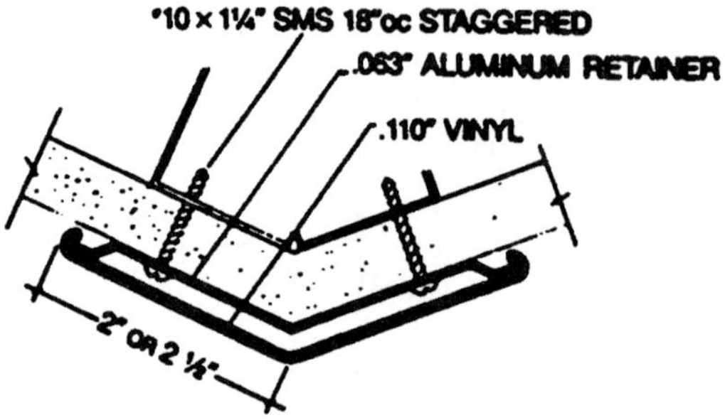

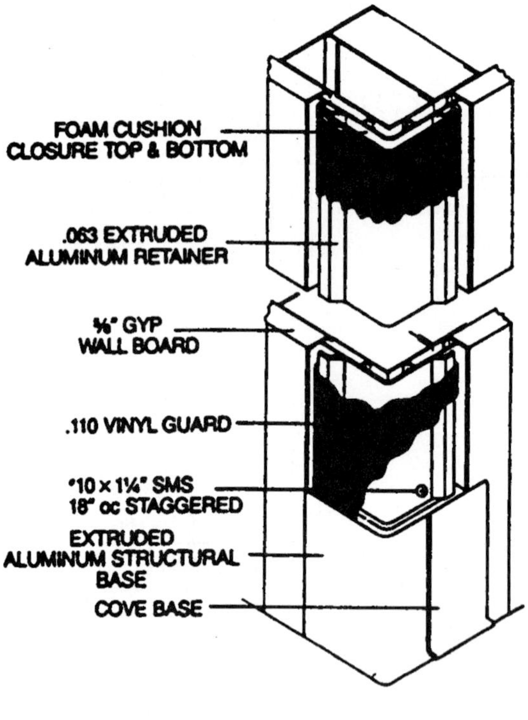

Ceiling height – flush mount

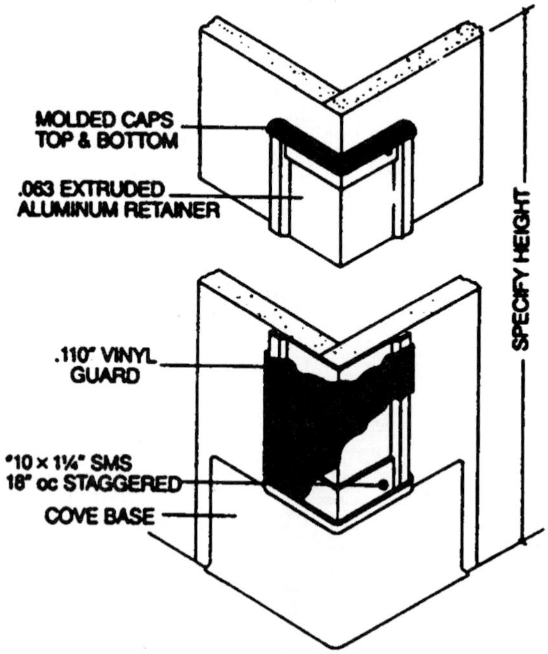

Wainscot installation – surface mount

VINYL HANDRAILS

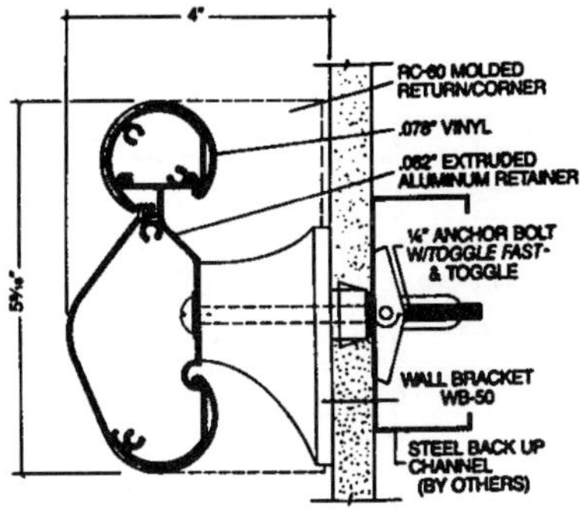

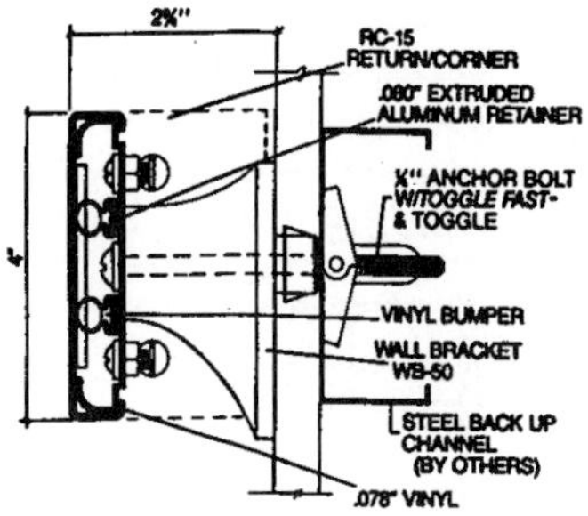

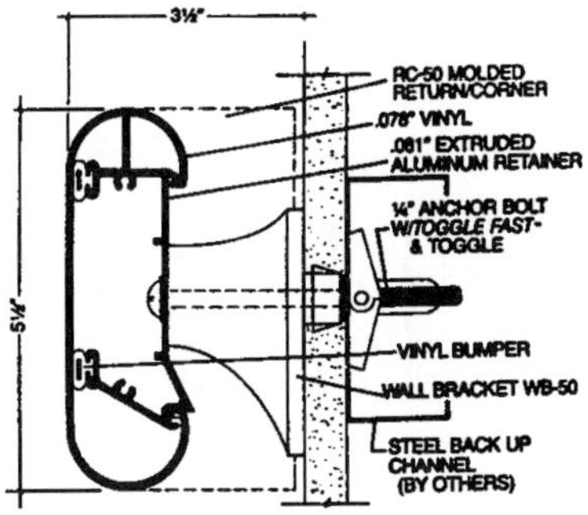

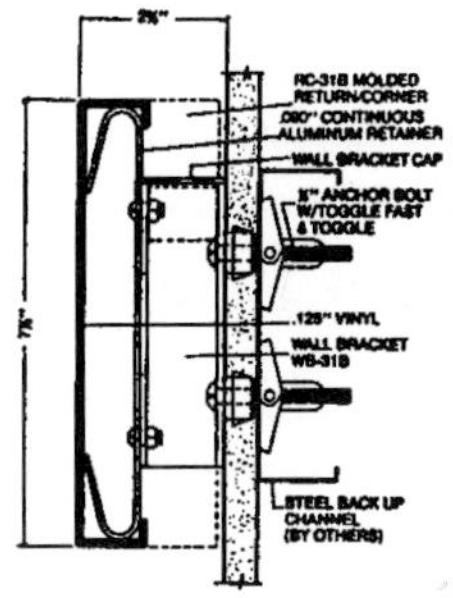

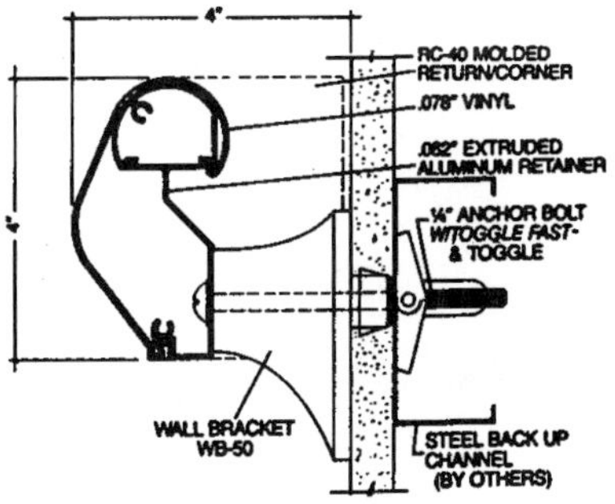

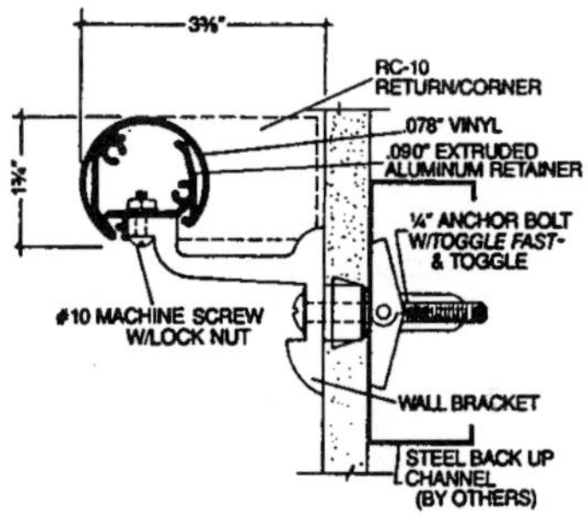

ALUMINUM HANDRAILS

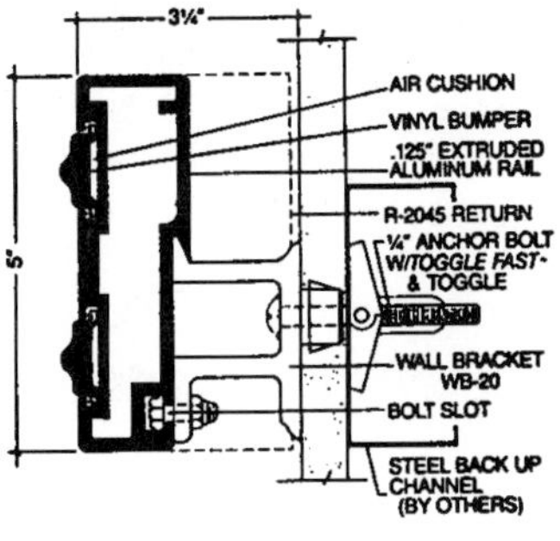

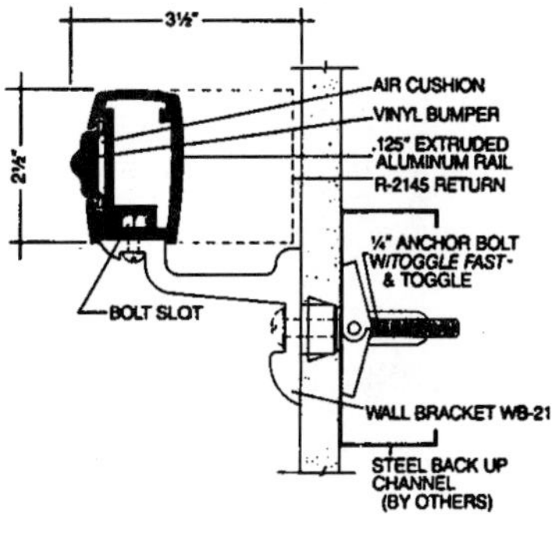

CHALKBOARDS
Elevations and Details

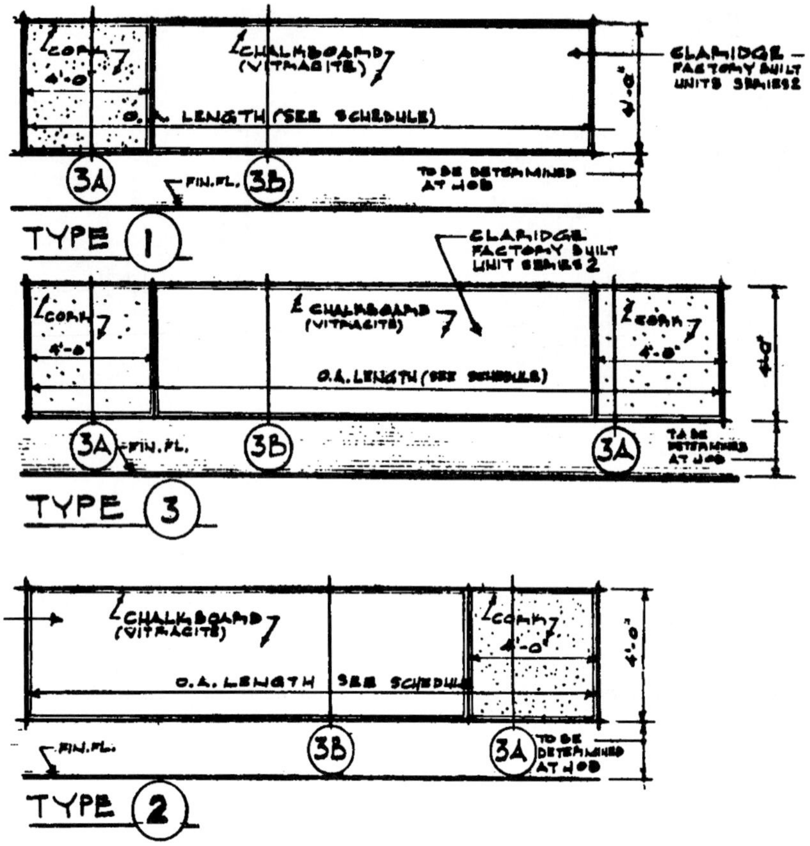

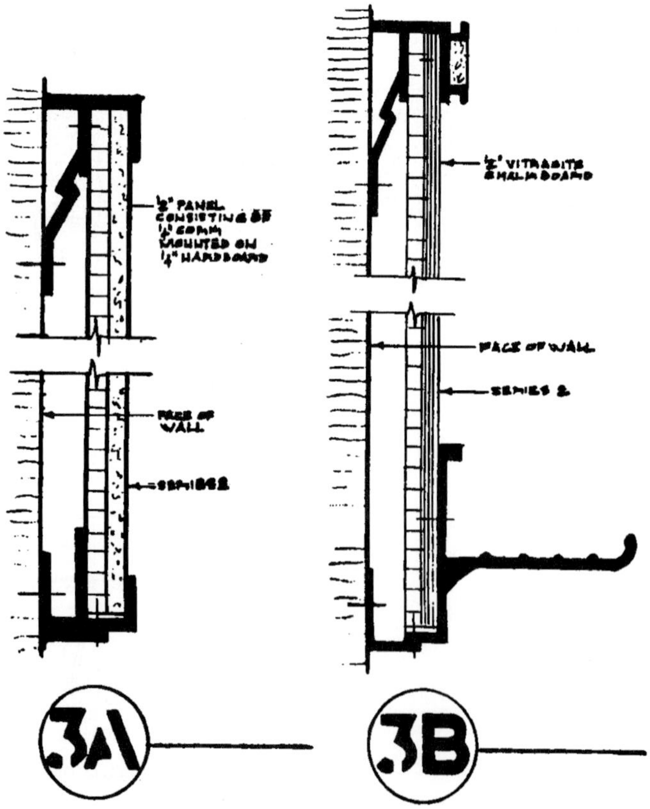

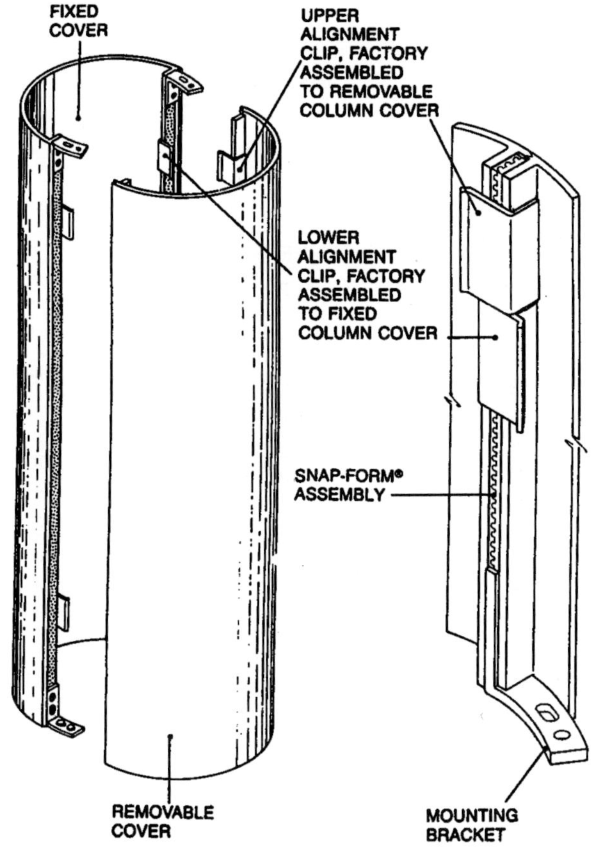

COLUMN ASSEMBLY
PERSPECTIVE

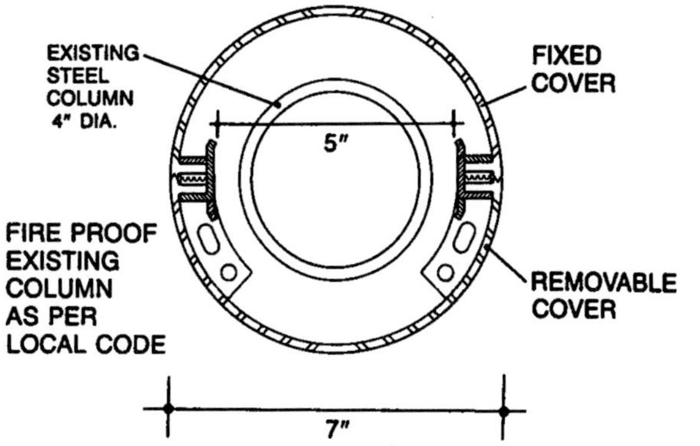

COLUMN COVER
7" DIAMETER

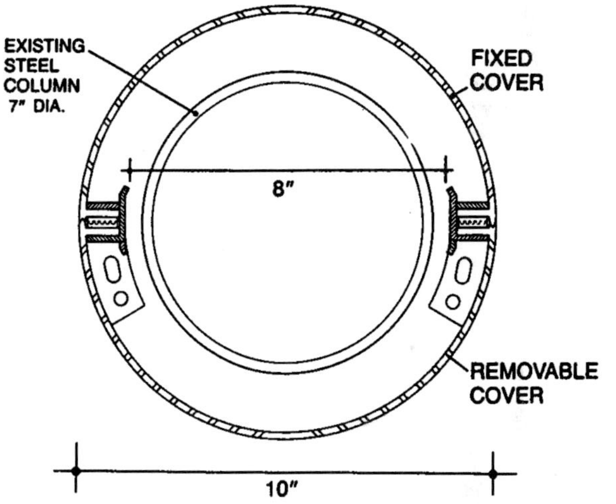

COLUMN COVER
10" DIAMETER

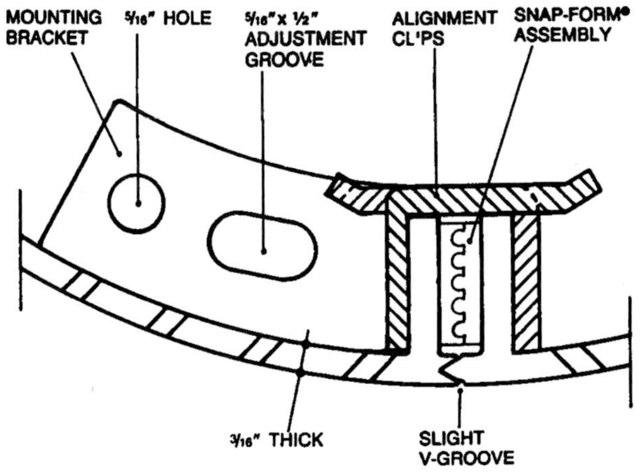

JOINT DETAIL
PLAN

COLUMN COVERS
Details

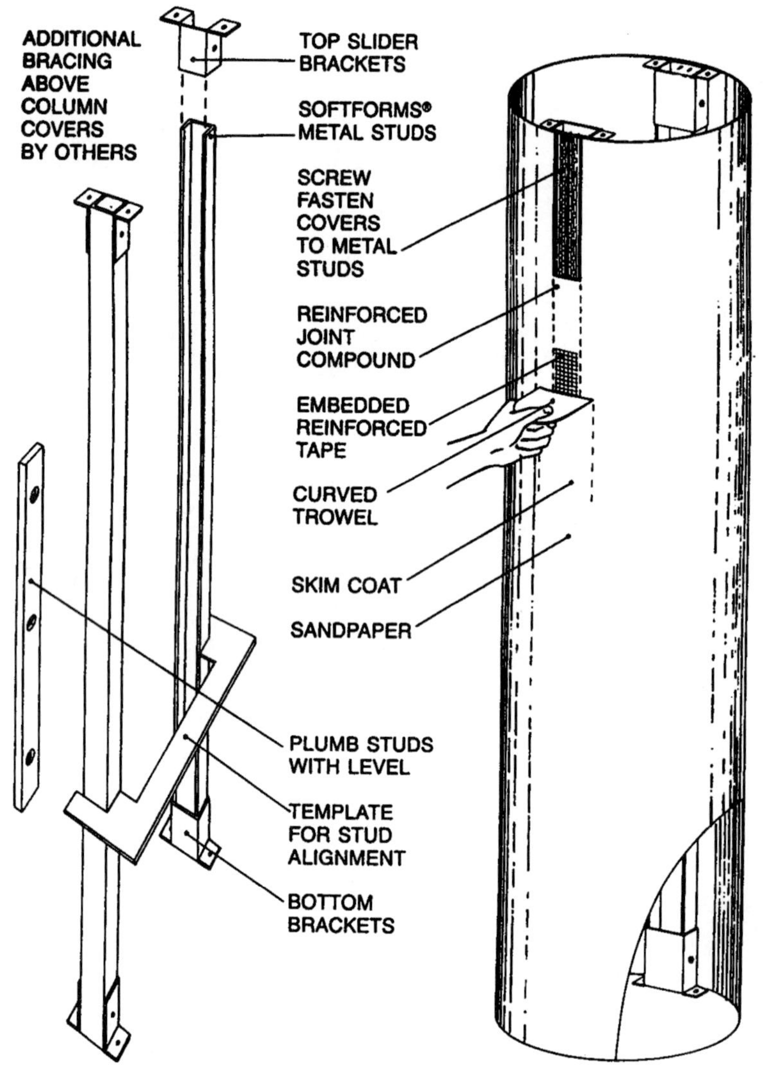

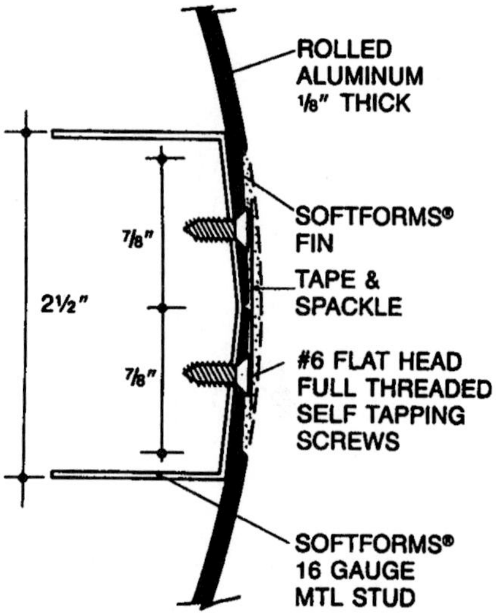

SERIES 100K TYPICAL JOINT DETAIL

NO SCALE SECTION

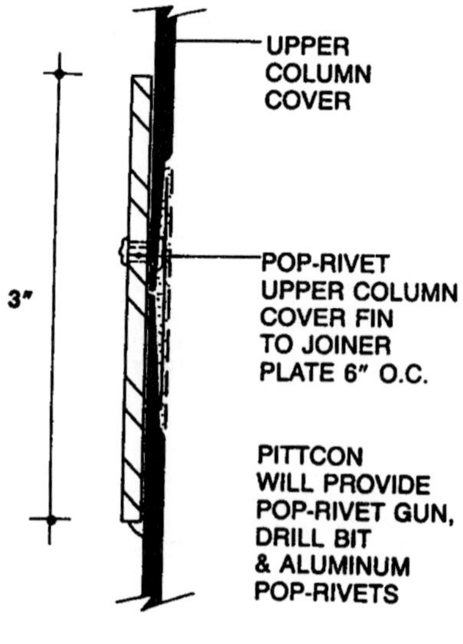

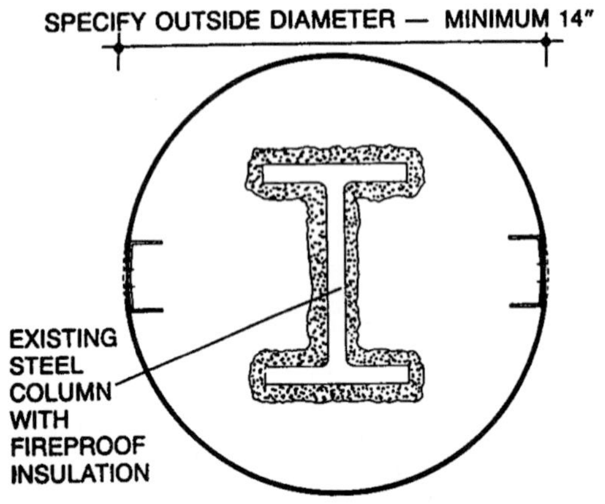

SOFTFORMS® COLUMN COVERS

SECTION

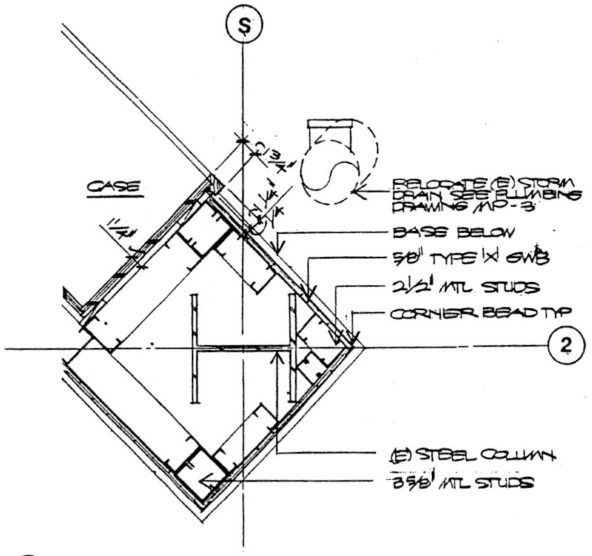

2 Plan Section
Scale: 1 1/2" = 1'-0"

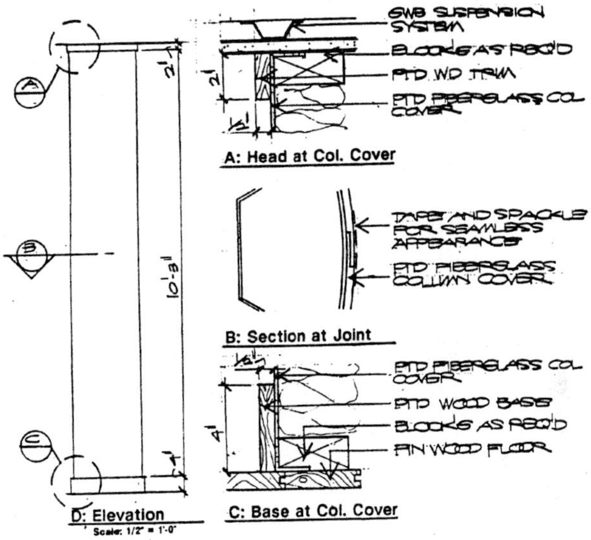

4 Details at Col. Cover
Scale: 3" = 1'-0" UON

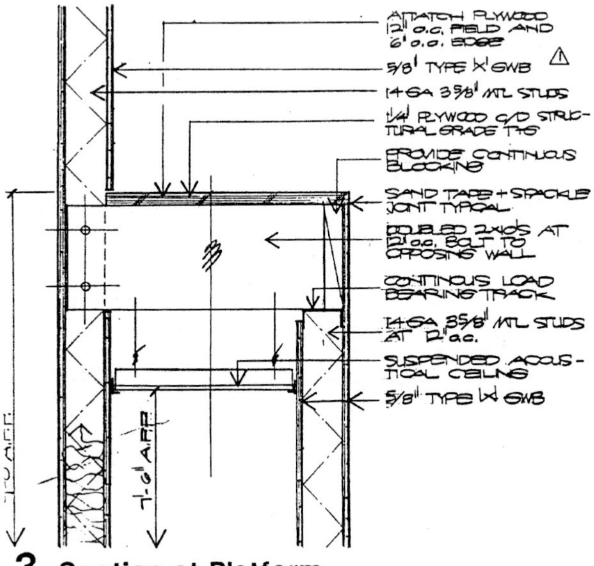

3 Section at Platform
Scale: 1 1/2" = 1'-0"

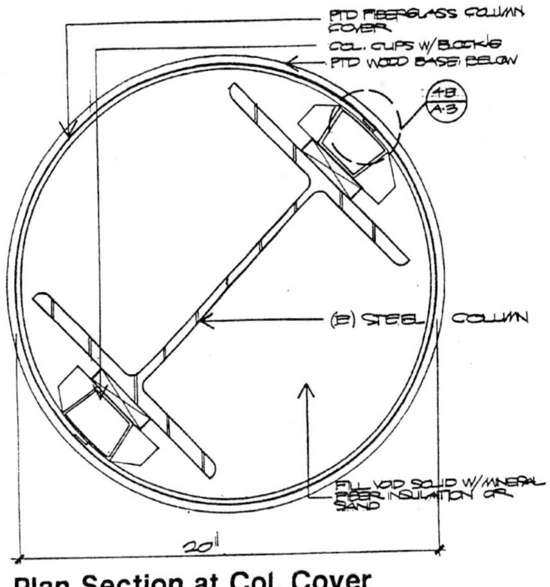

5 Plan Section at Col. Cover
Scale: 3" = 1'-0"

COLUMN COVERS
Section and Elevation

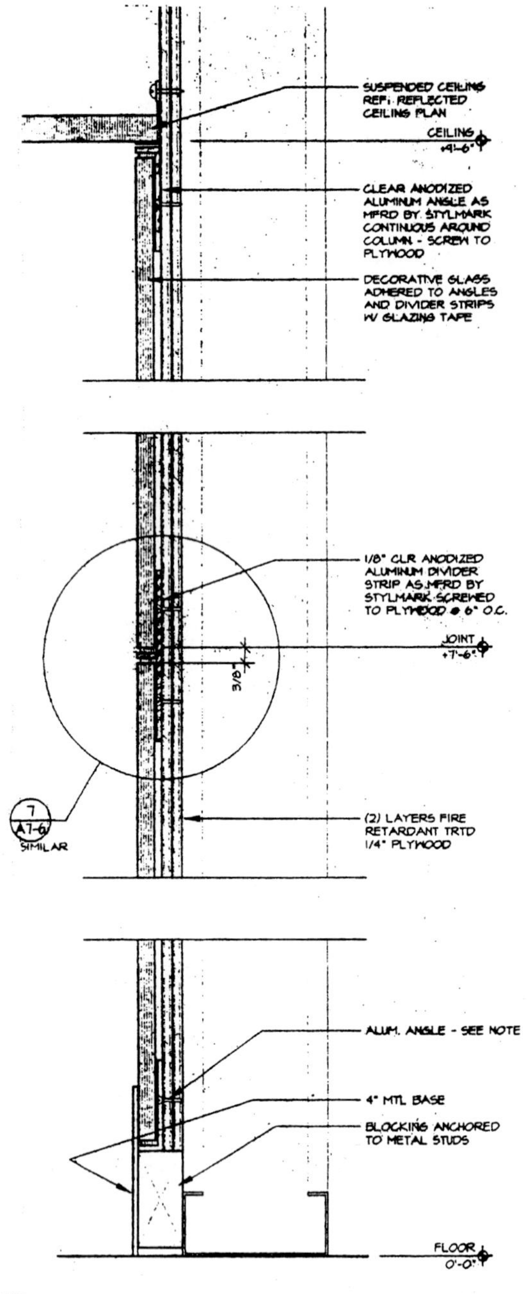

9 A7-6 COLUMN SECTION
SCALE: 3" = 1'-0"

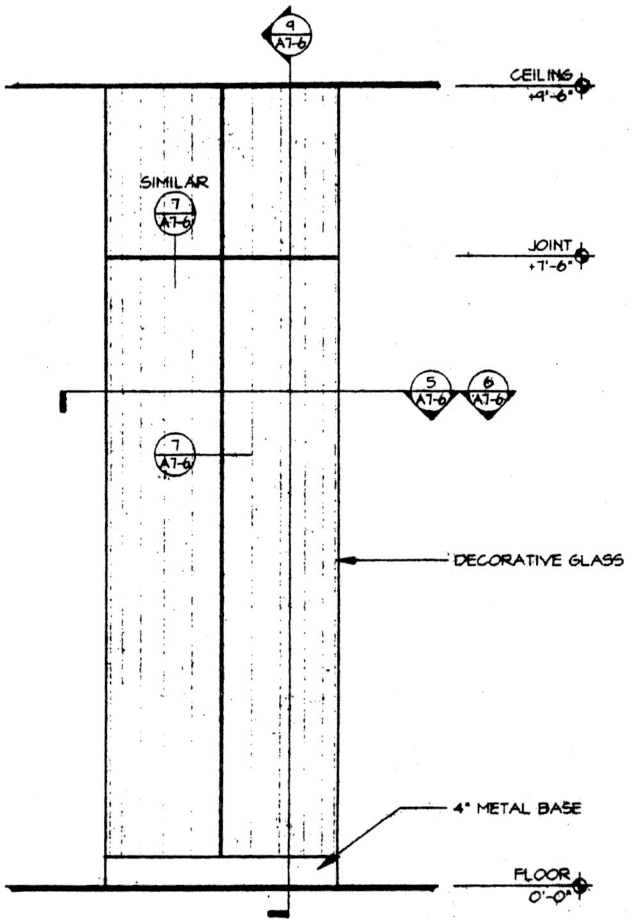

8 A7-6 COLUMN ELEVATION
SCALE: 3/4" = 1'-0"

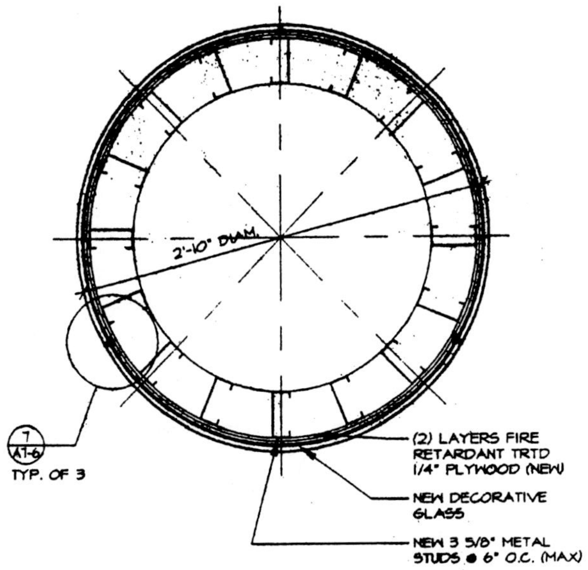

2'-10" DIAM.
7
A7-6
TYP. OF 3
(2) LAYERS FIRE RETARDANT TRTD 1/4" PLYWOOD (NEW)
NEW DECORATIVE GLASS
NEW 3 5/8" METAL STUDS @ 6" O.C. (MAX)
5 COLUMN SECTION
A7-6 SCALE: 1 1/2" = 1'-0"
1/8" CLR ANODIZED ALUMINUM DIVIDER STRIP AS MFRD BY STYLMARK SCREWED TO PLYWOOD @ 6" O.C.
(2) LAYERS FIRE RETARDANT TRTD 1/4" PLYWOOD
DECORATIVE GLASS ADHERED TO DIVIDER STRIPS W/ GLAZING TAPE
7 JOINT DETAIL
(3) JOINTS SPACED EQUALLY AROUND COLUMN
A7-6 HALF FULL SCALE
EXPANSION JOINT IN FLOOR
TYP. OF 3
EXIST. STEEL COLUMN W/ BRICK SURROUND
2'-10" DIAM.
COLUMN WRAP AT EXPANSION JOINT FURRING CHANNELS TO BE ANCHORED TO MASONRY - NOT TO FLOOR
(2) LAYERS FIRE RETARDANT TRTD 1/4" PLYWOOD (NEW)
NEW DECORATIVE GLASS
NEW MTL FURRING CHANNELS @ 6" O.C. (MAX) ANCHORED TO EXISTING MASONRY
6 COLUMN SECTION
A7-6 SCALE: 1 1/2" = 1'-0"
POLISHED STAINLESS STEEL ANGLE ATTACHMENT W/ SET SCREW ANCHOR (TYPICAL OF 2)- SEE DETAIL 12/A7-6
SET SCREW
ANCHOR ANGLE ATTACHMENT TO WALL, AND TO MIRROR
3"
2 1/2"
FACE OF WALL (FINISH VWC-1)
FACE OF TRIM BEYOND
1/4" CLEAR PLATE MIRROR W/ CONTINUOUS BEVELED EDGE- ADHERE TO PLYWOOD
3/4" BIRCH VENEER PLYWOOD- BIRCH VENEER TO BE EXPOSED AND PAINTED FINISH PT-2 (MATTE), OTHER SIDE TO FACE BACK OF MIRROR & BE PRIMED
1 1/4" X 1 1/4" X 1/4" METAL TRIM- FINISH TO BE M-3
11 MIRROR EDGE DETAIL
A7-6 SCALE: 3" = 1'-0"

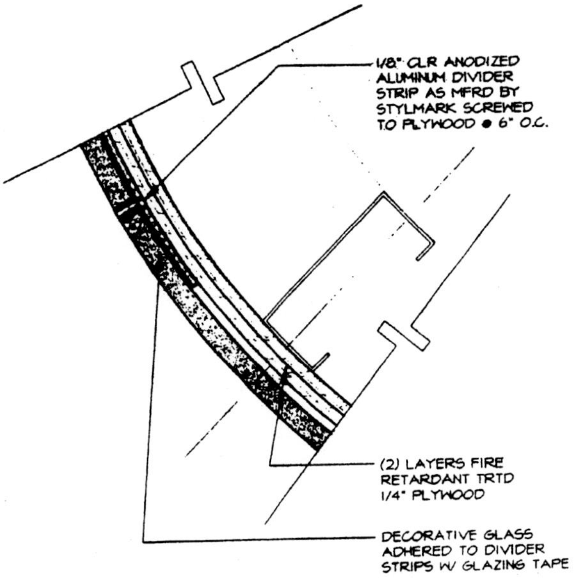

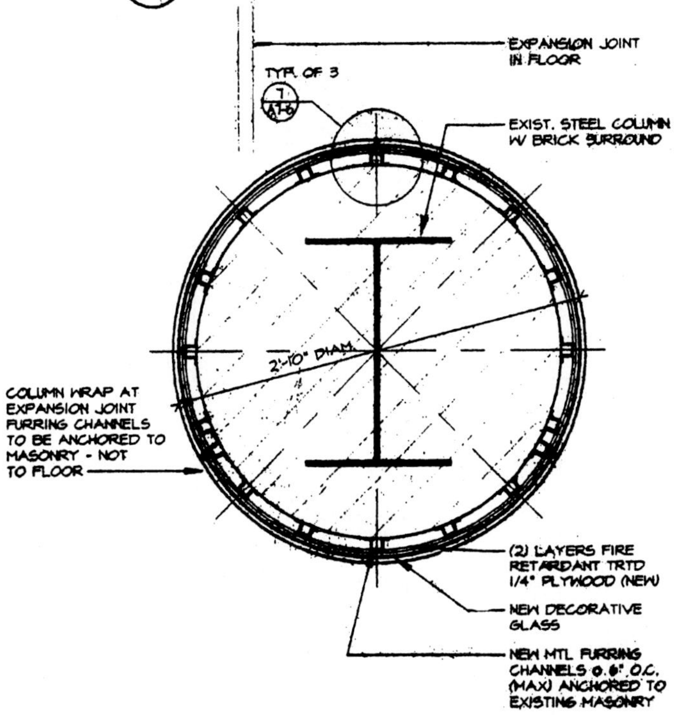

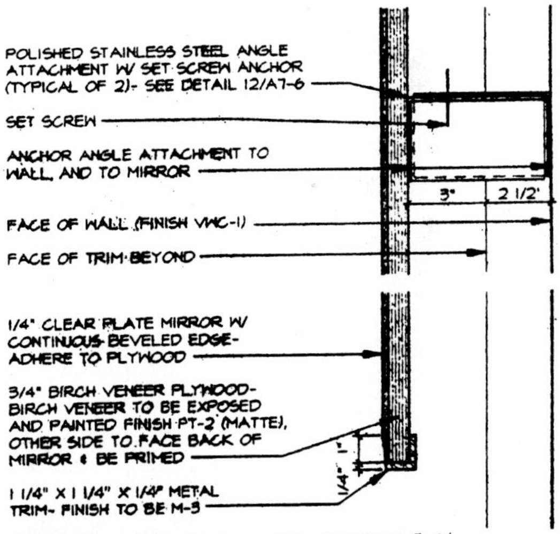

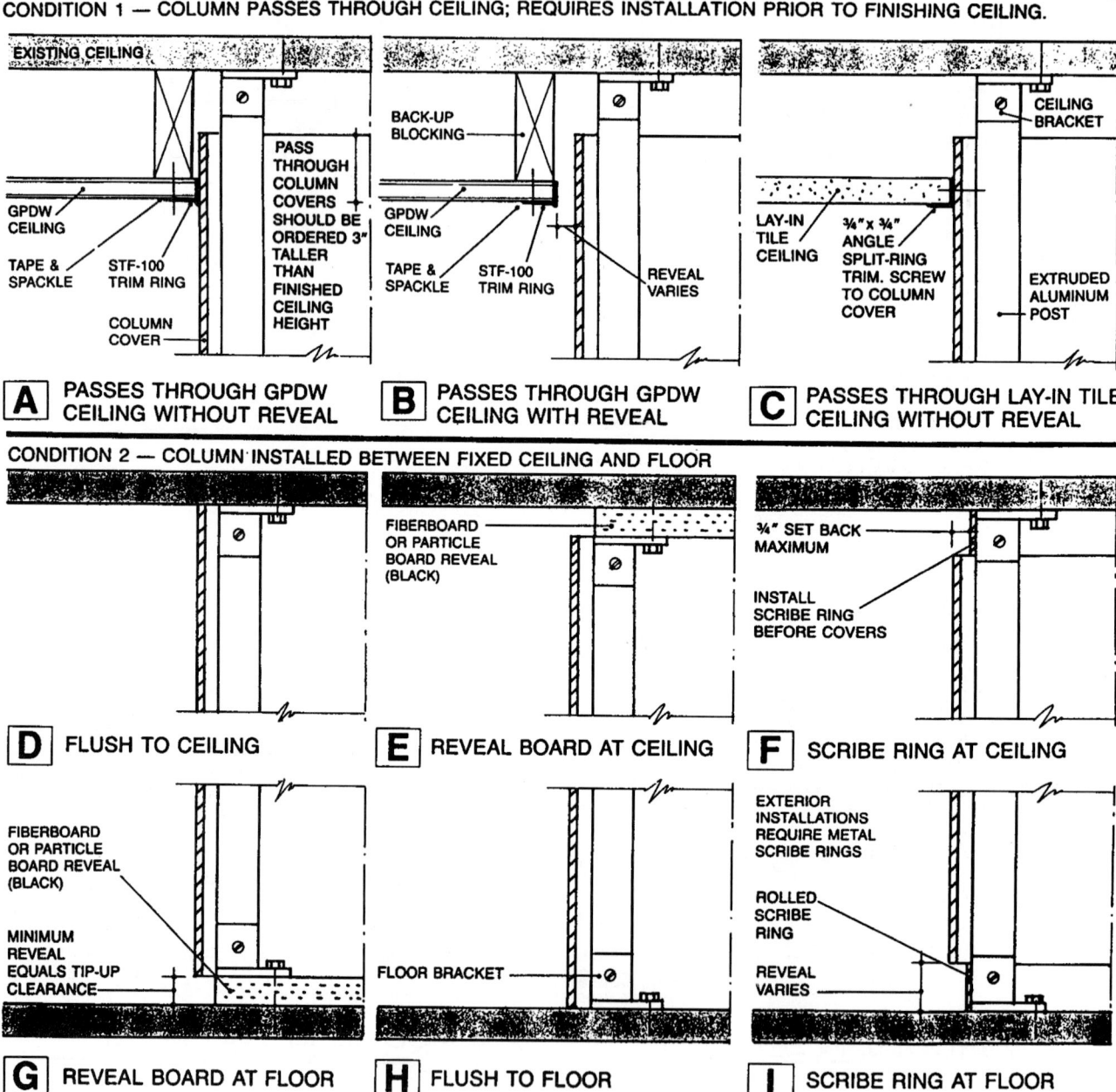

COLUMN COVERS
Details

CONDITION 1 — COLUMN PASSES THROUGH CEILING; REQUIRES INSTALLATION PRIOR TO FINISHING CEILING.

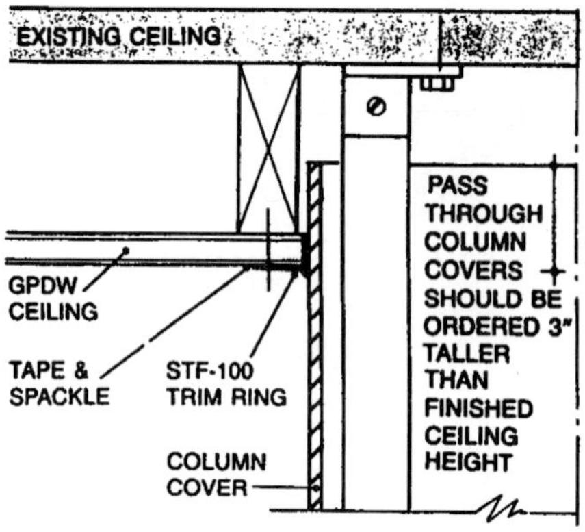

A PASSES THROUGH GPDW CEILING WITHOUT REVEAL

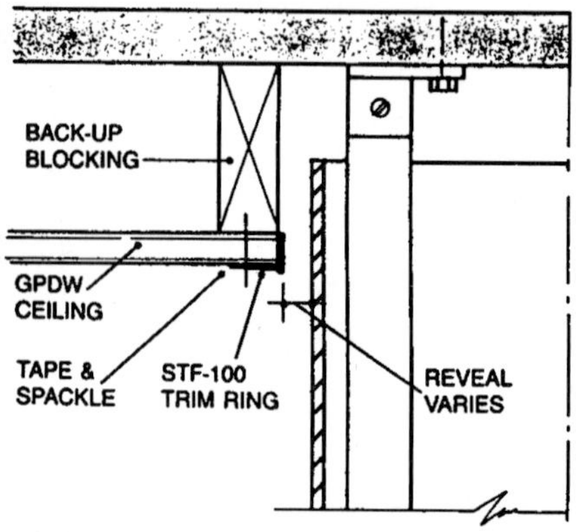

B PASSES THROUGH GPDW CEILING WITH REVEAL

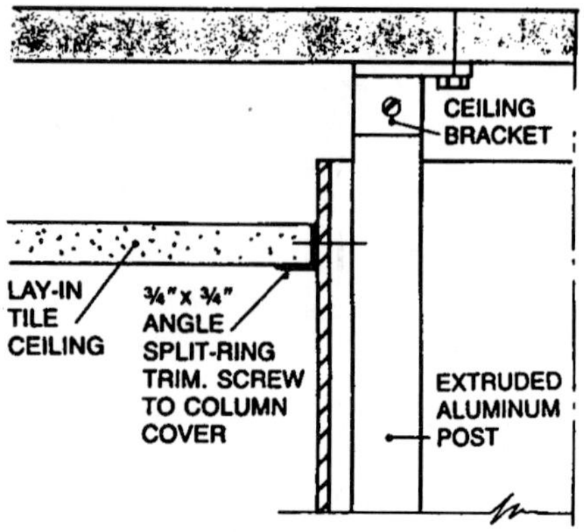

C PASSES THROUGH LAY-IN TILE CEILING WITHOUT REVEAL

CONDITION 2 — COLUMN INSTALLED BETWEEN FIXED CEILING AND FLOOR

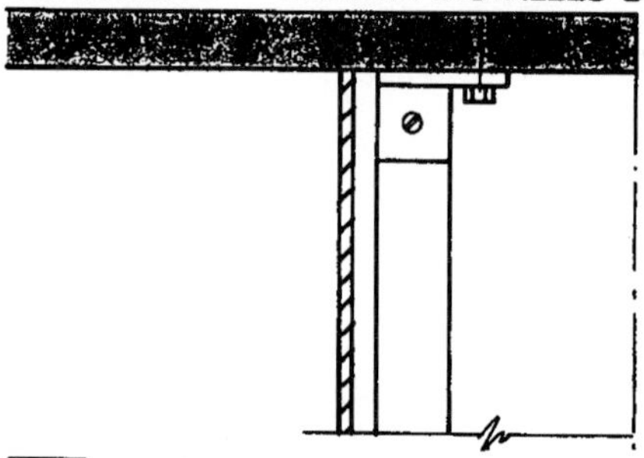

D FLUSH TO CEILING

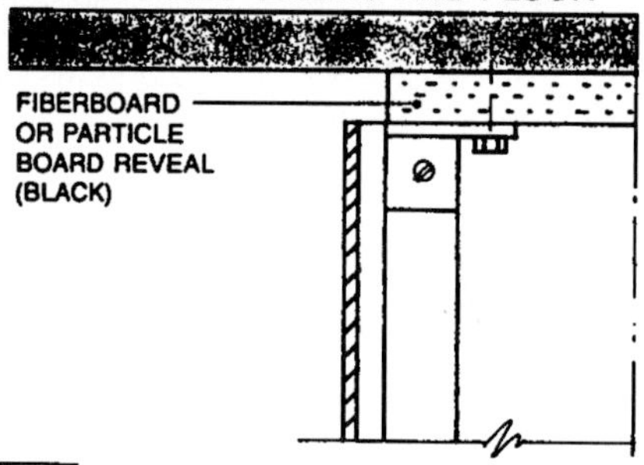

E REVEAL BOARD AT CEILING

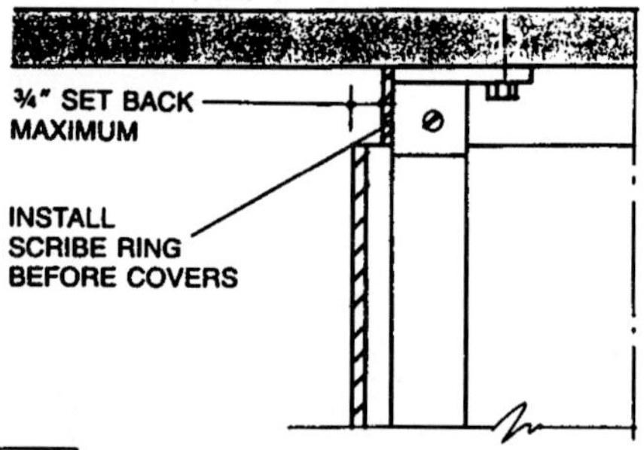

F SCRIBE RING AT CEILING

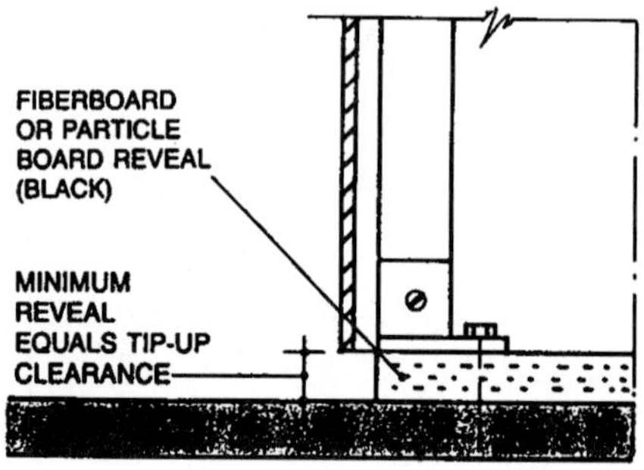

G REVEAL BOARD AT FLOOR

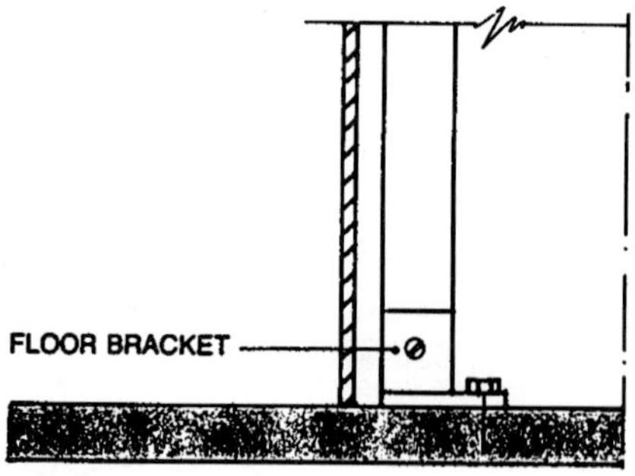

H FLUSH TO FLOOR

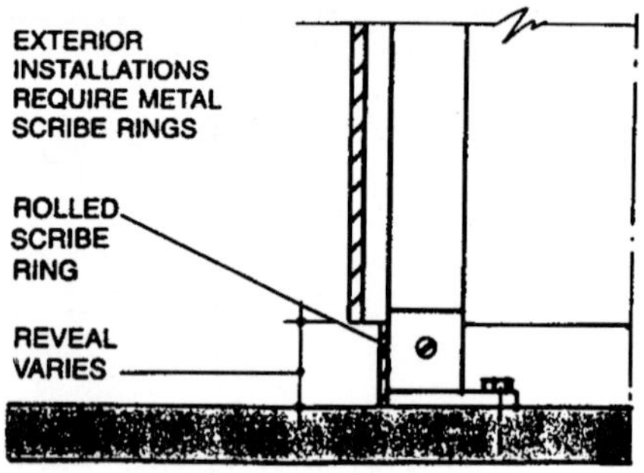

I SCRIBE RING AT FLOOR

COLUMN COVERS
Plan and Corner Details

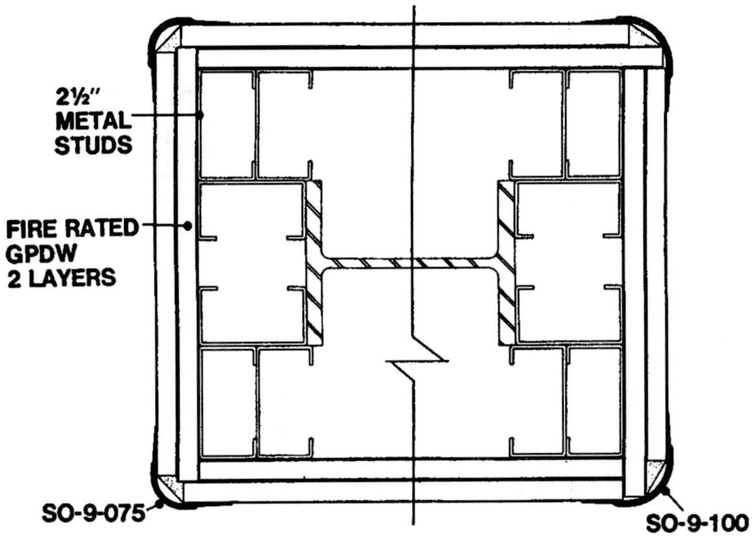

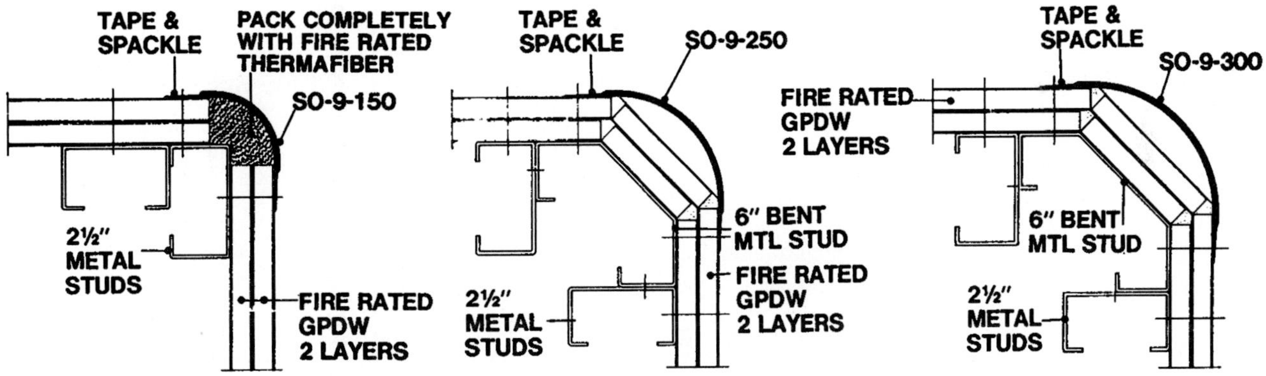

COLUMN COVERS
Details

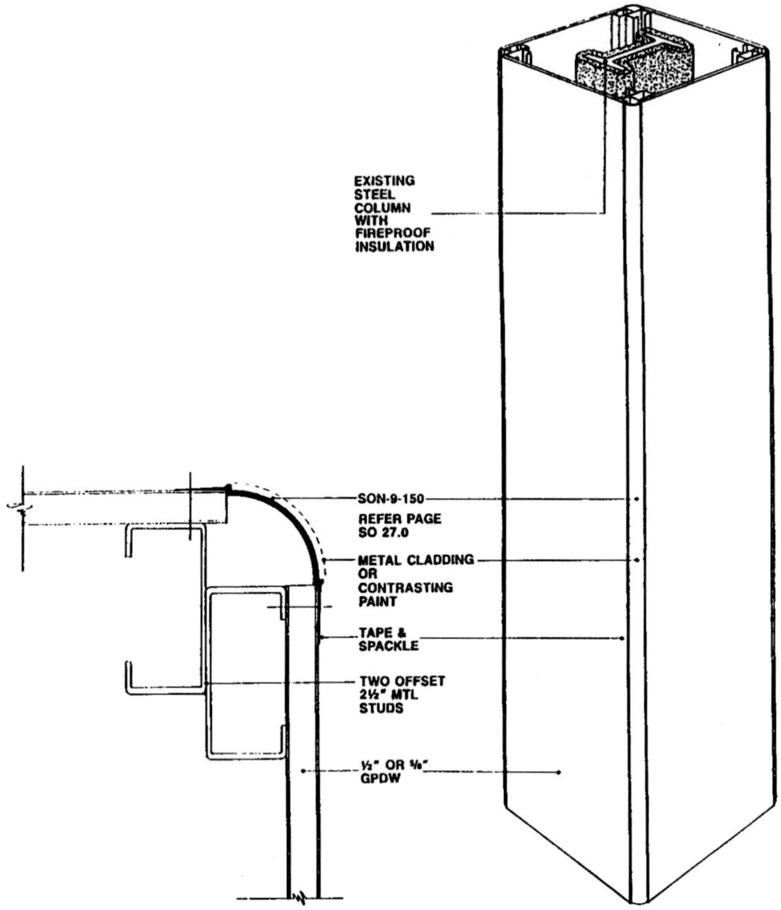

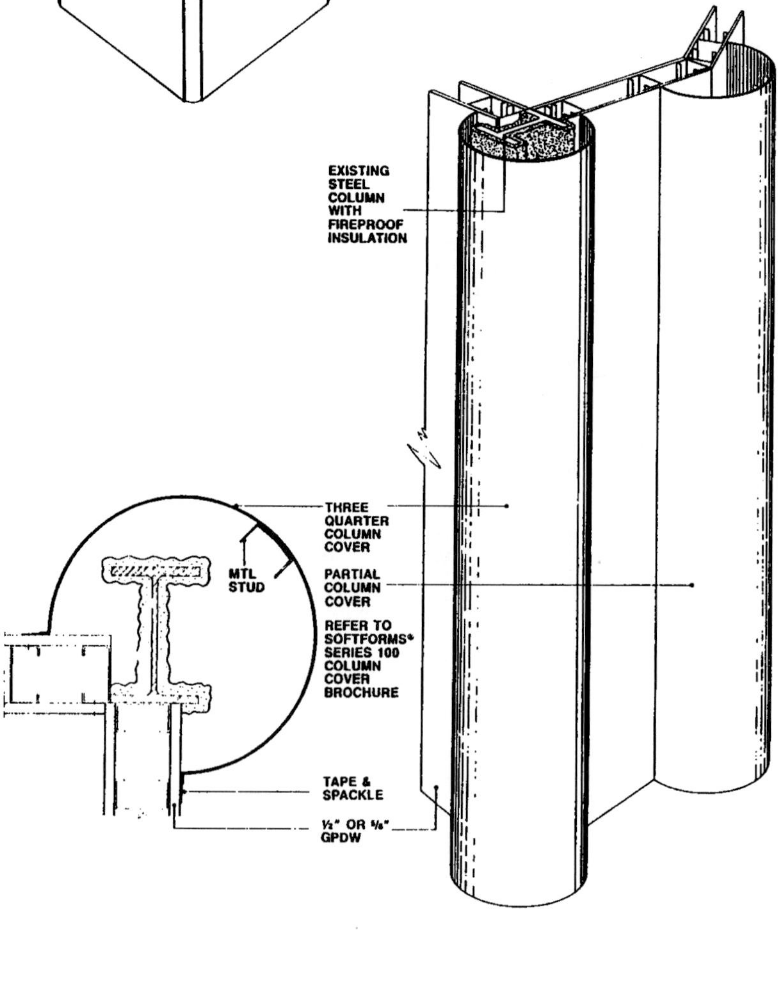

3-ARM HIGH-TRAFFIC MANUAL AND ELECTRIC TURNSTILES
1.18
1.19
3.87
2" DIA. SHOWN CONDUIT
WIRE HOLES - 2 TYP.
24.63
Plan
A
A
FINISHED FLOOR
SEE DETAIL "B"
Side elevation
Front elevation
DETAIL "B"
CUP
ANCHOR BOLT
FINISHED FLOOR
CONCRETE
HALF SCALE
ANCHOR
Vertical section
25"
15½"
Plan
27"
39¾"
Side elevation
55°
90°
34"
Front elevation
3.5"
1.5"
Socket Plug
Socket Plug
3.5"
1.365"
Square Socket for Yokes & Turnstiles
Round Socket for Posts
1.75" O.D.
1.5" O.D.
Anchor details

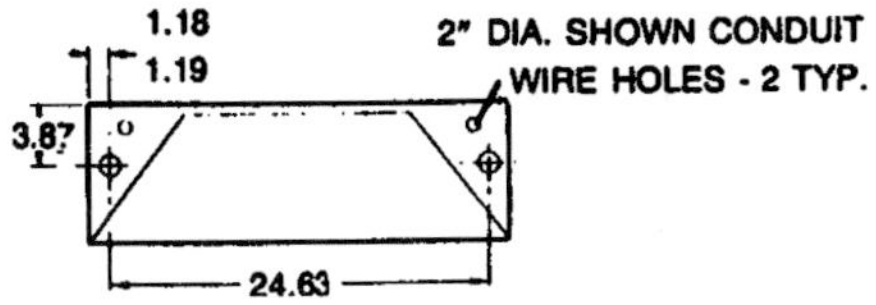

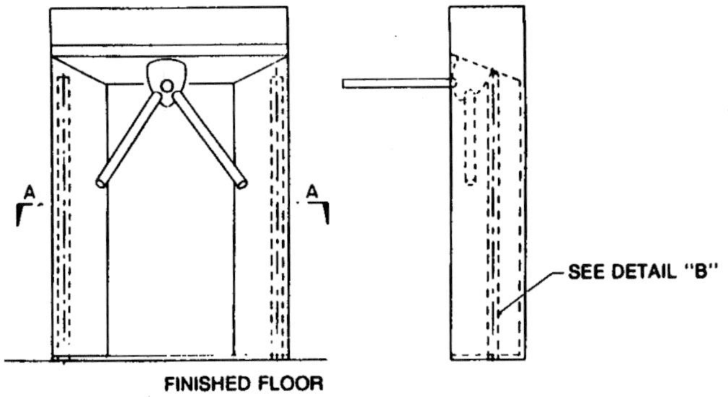

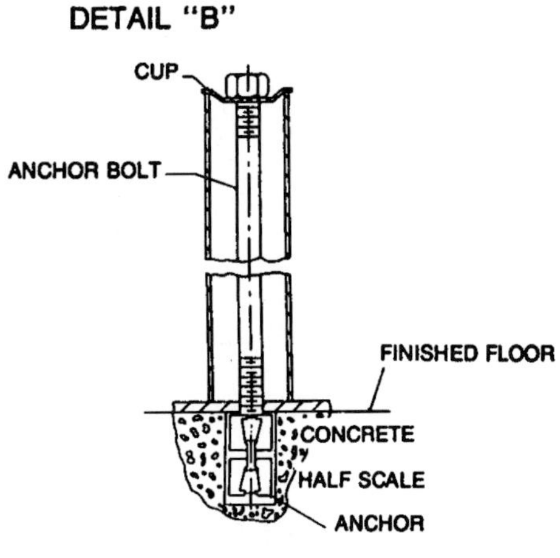

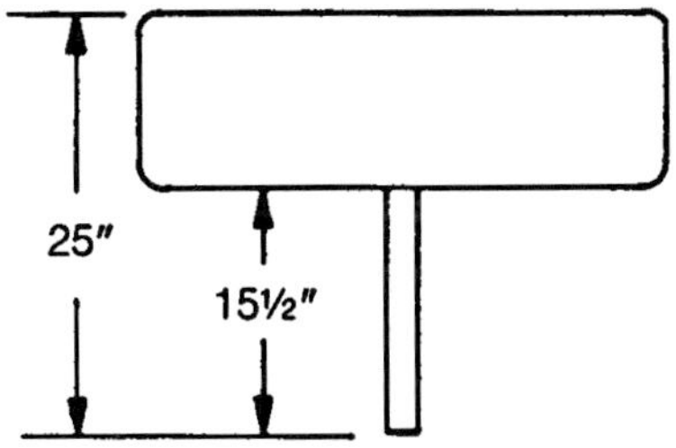

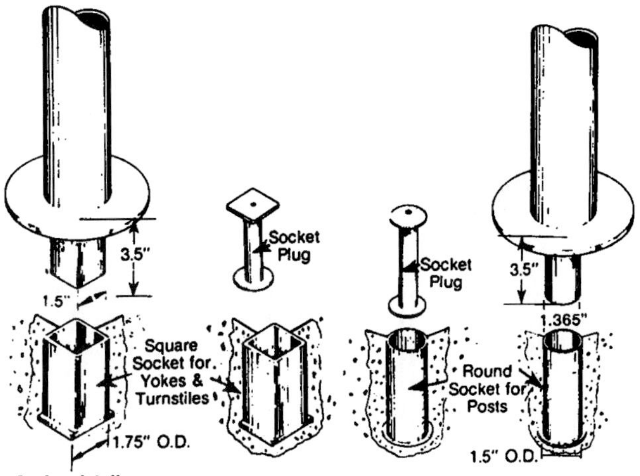

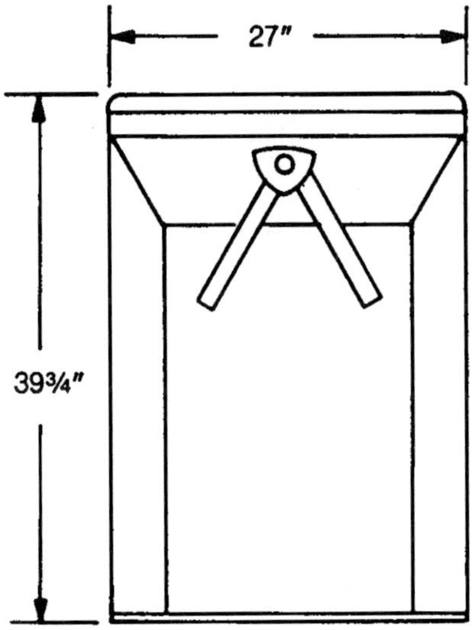

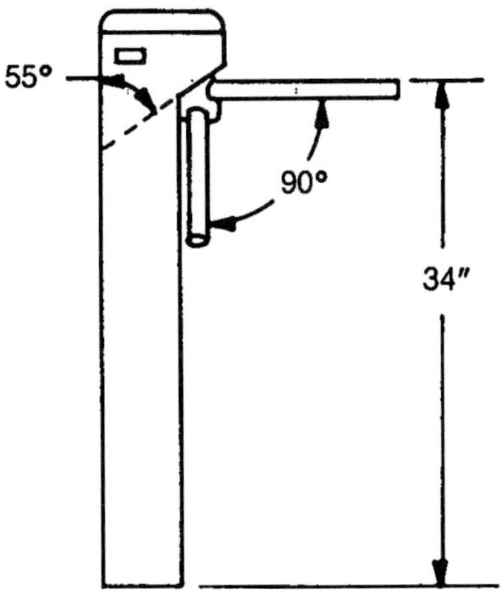

TURNSTILES

Arm High and Full Height

4-ARM MANUAL AND ELECTRIC TURNSTILES

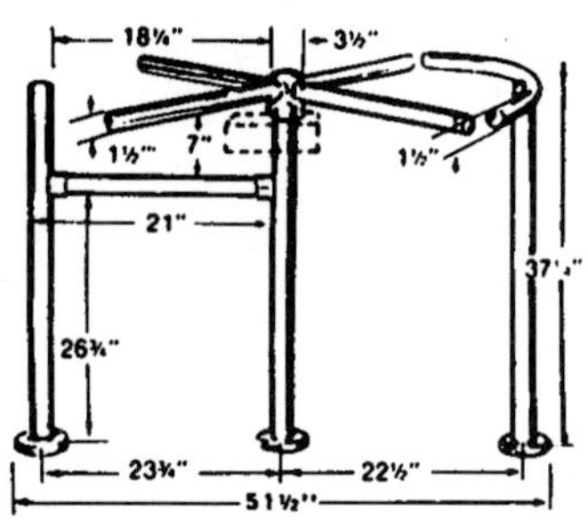

Basic customer security

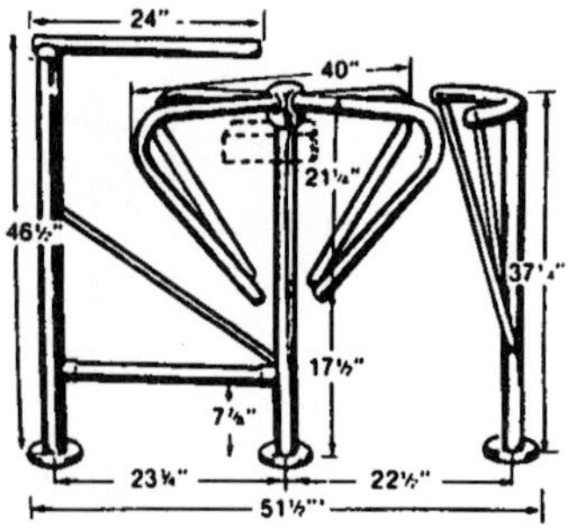

Enhanced security

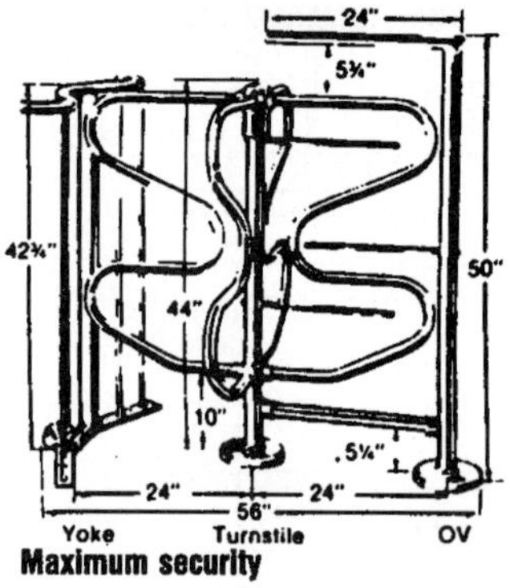

Maximum security

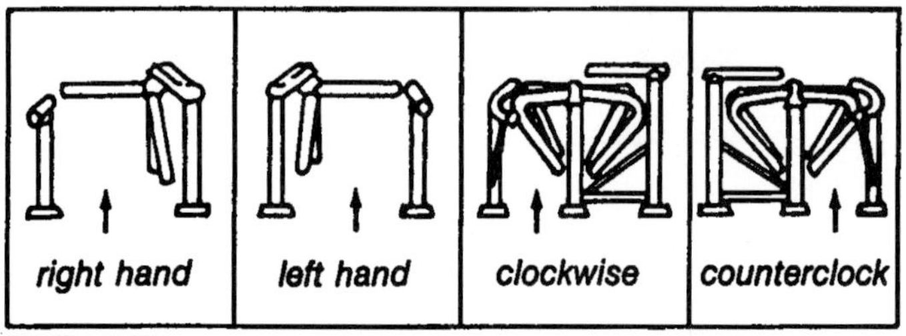

Rotation guide

HIGH-SECURITY TURNSTILES

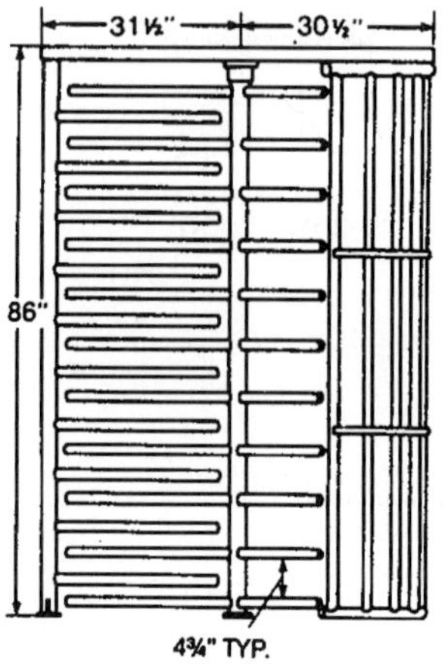

Manual

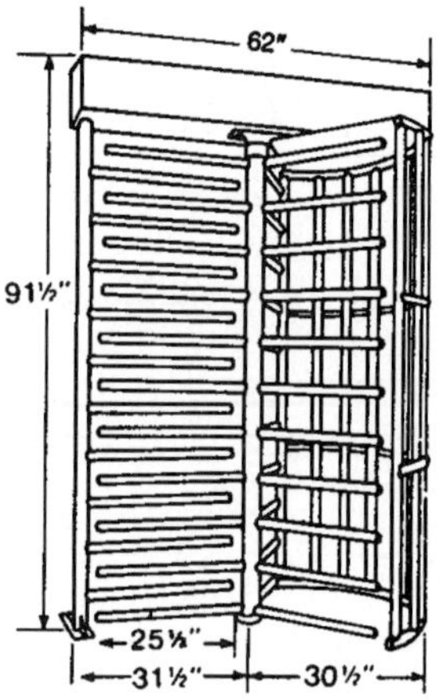

Electric

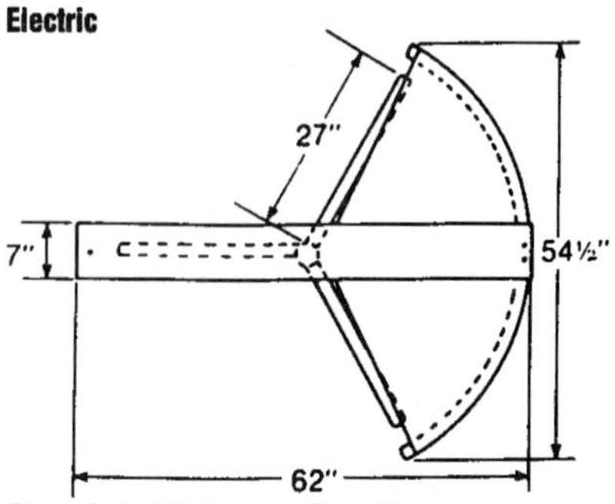

Plan of electric type configuration

3-ARM MANUAL AND ELECTRIC TURNSTILES

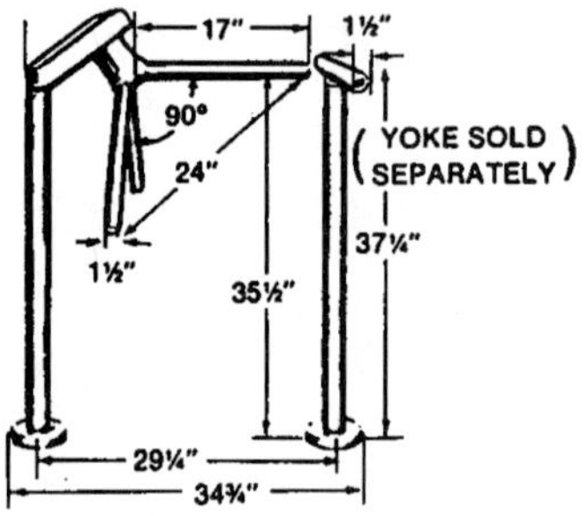

Post-mounted

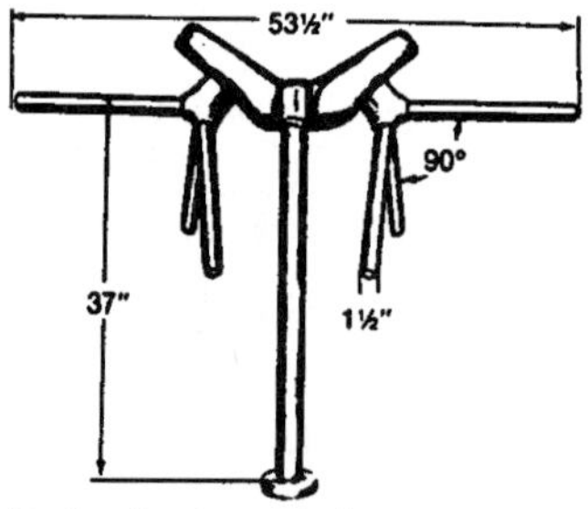

Tandem (post-mounted)

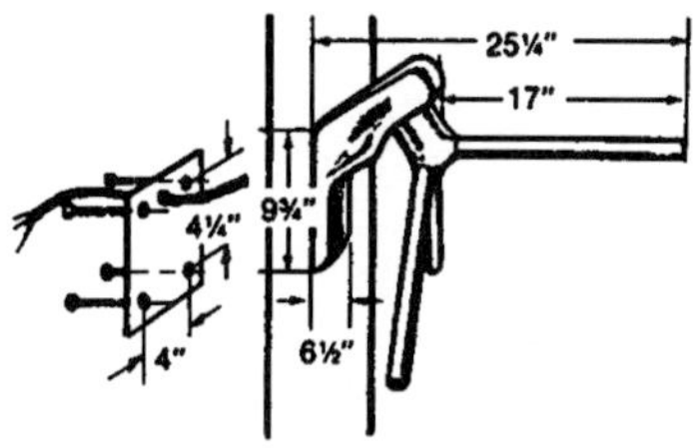

Wall-mounted

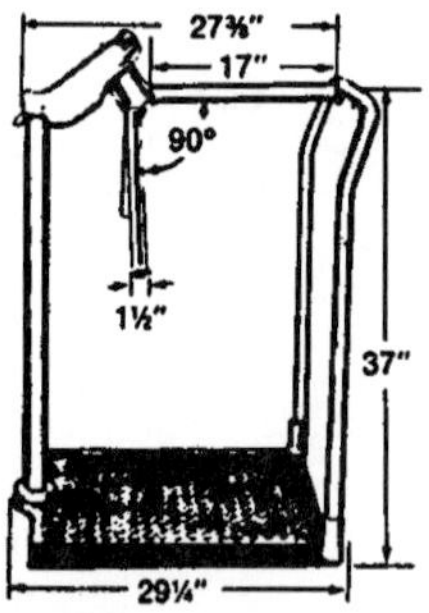

Portable

TURNSTILES
Arm High

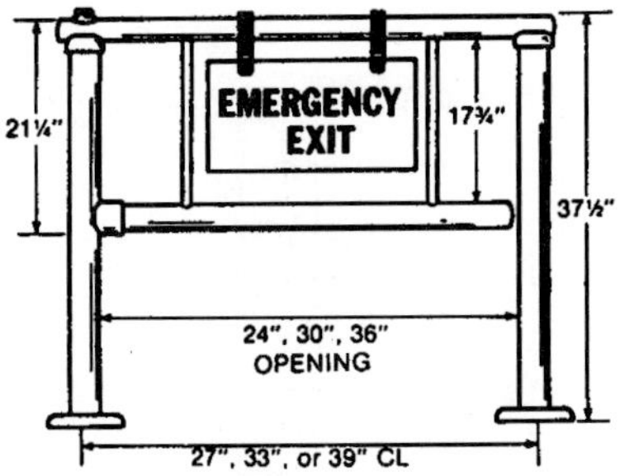

Emergency – quick release

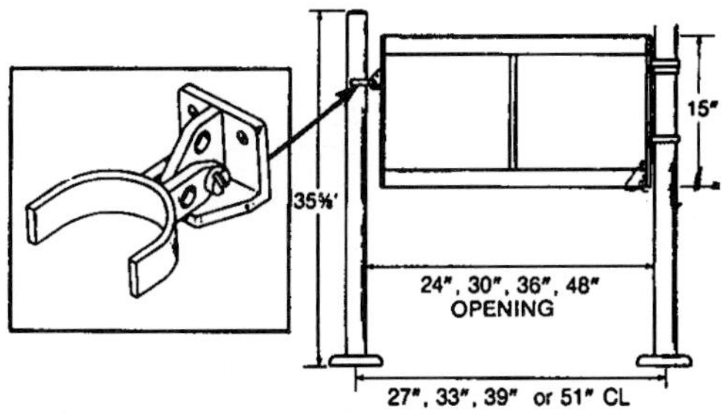

Double rail – flip sleeve latch

MODEL BA-1
Break-away finger latch
features an adjustable
tension setting. SAME
mounting as Gate

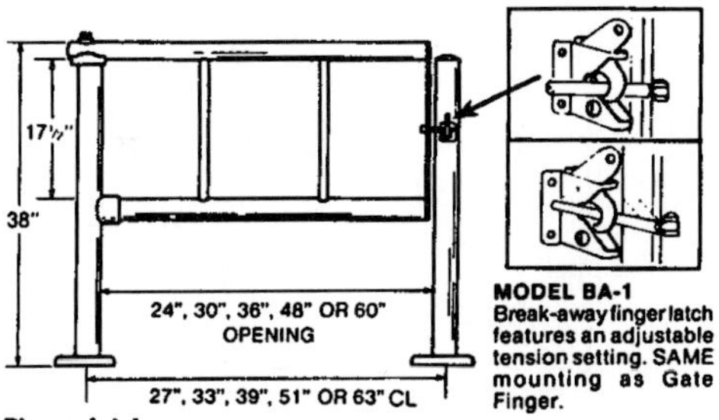

Finger latch

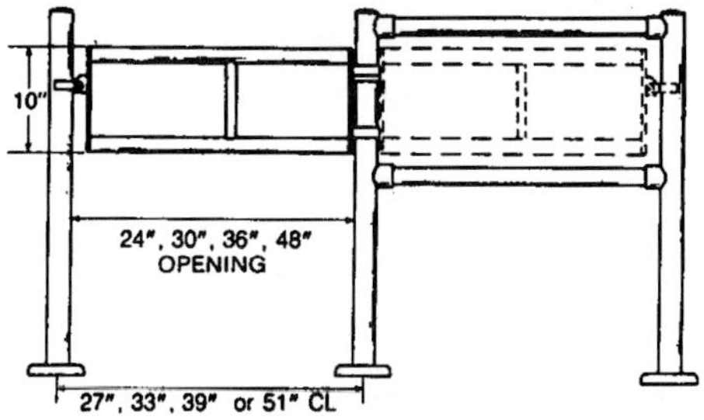

Double rail – aisle closure with flip sleeve latch

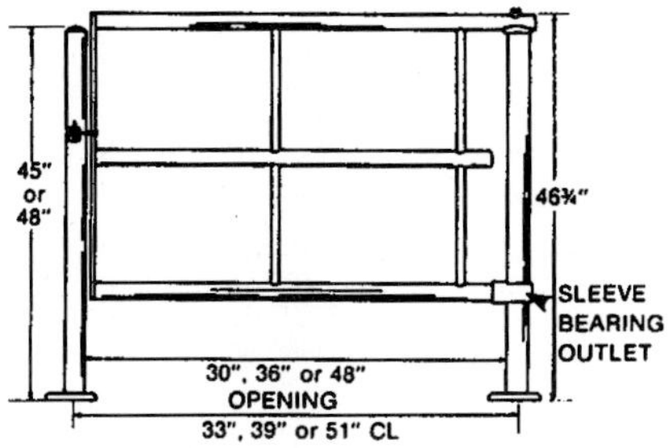

Triple rail – finger latch

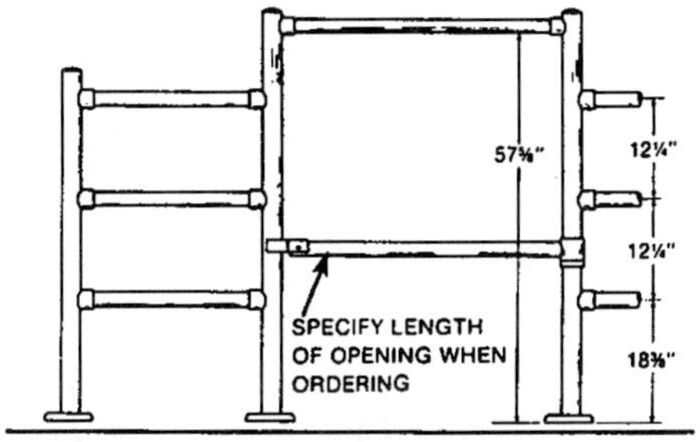

Single rail – cart security with flip sleeve latch

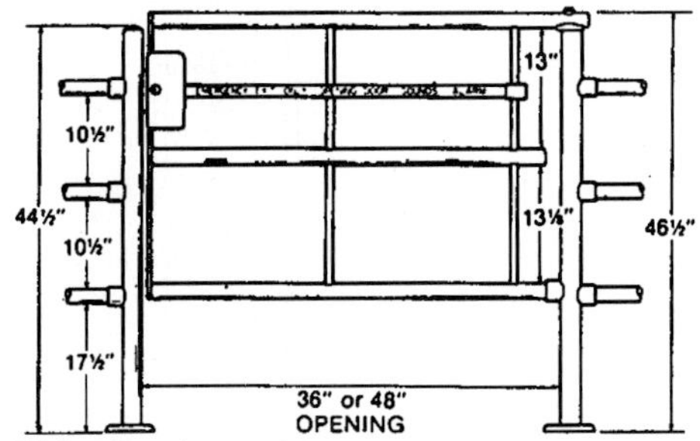

Triple rail – alarm system

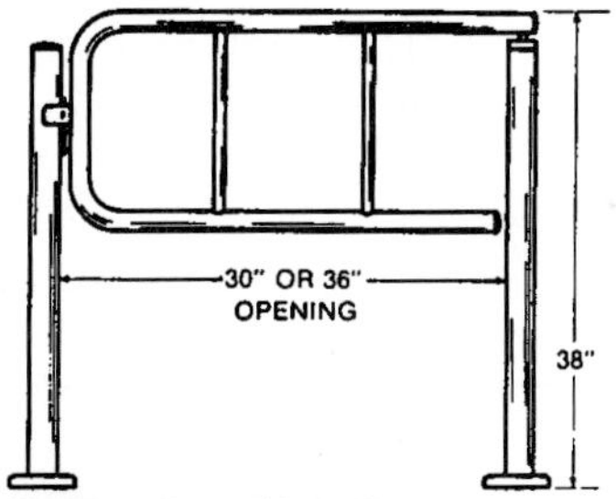

Single section welded rail – electrically controlled gate latch, wheelchair access

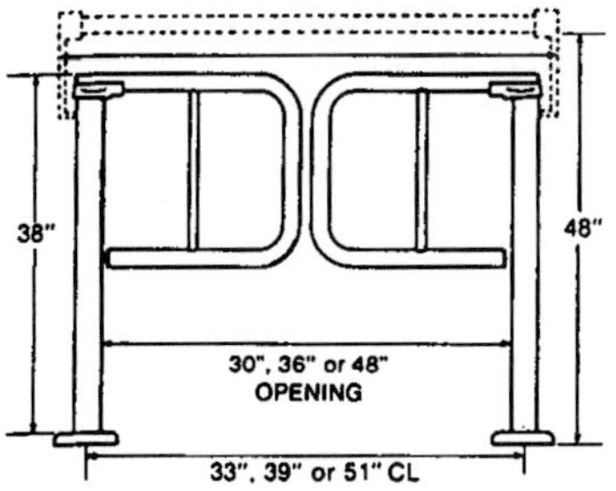

Double rail

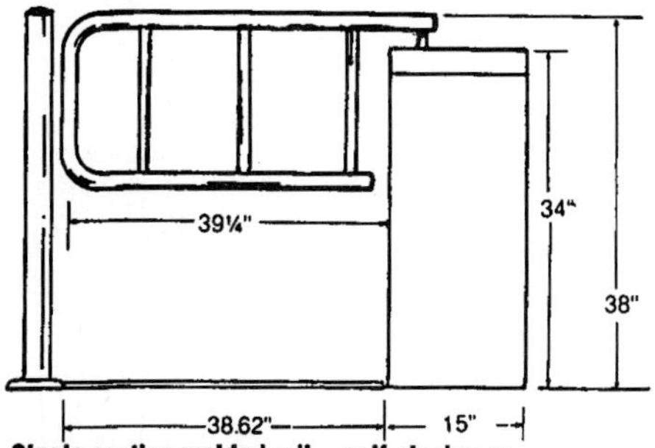

Single section welded rail – self-closing or self-opening

DRINKING FOUNTAINS

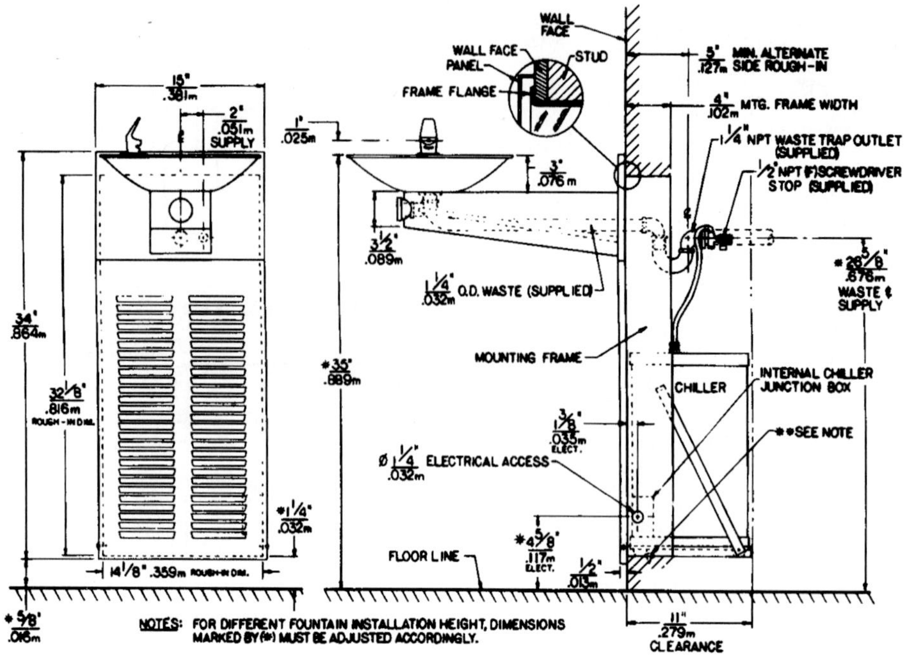

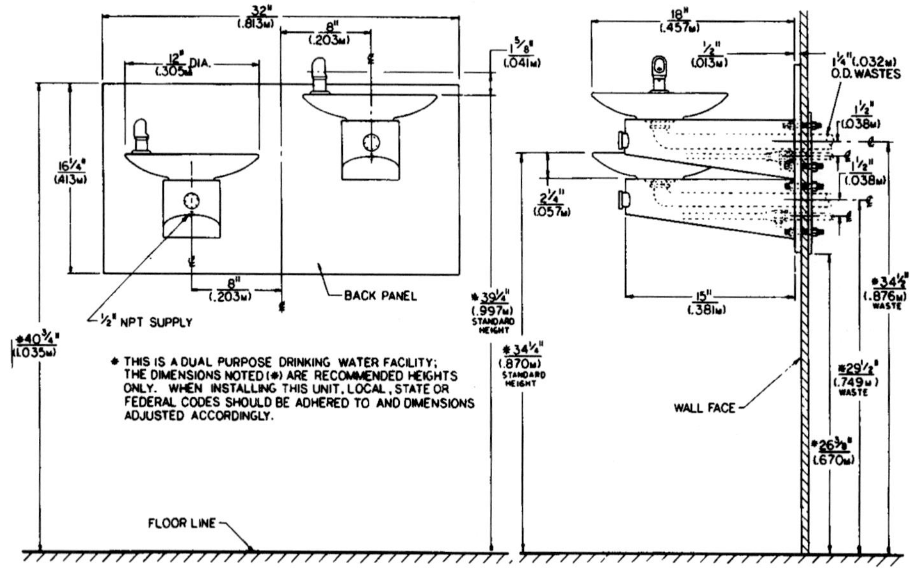

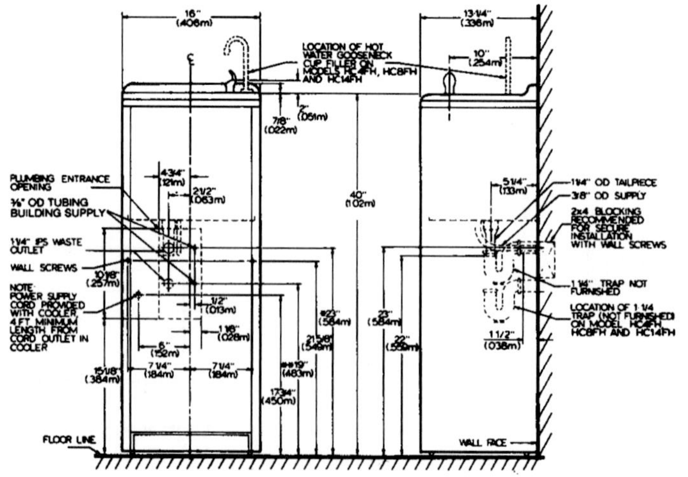

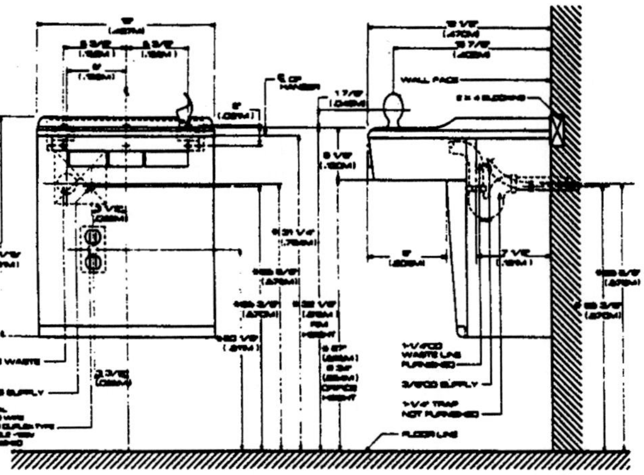

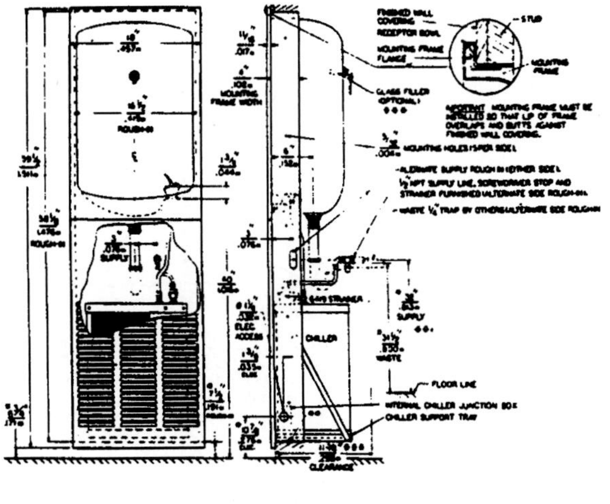

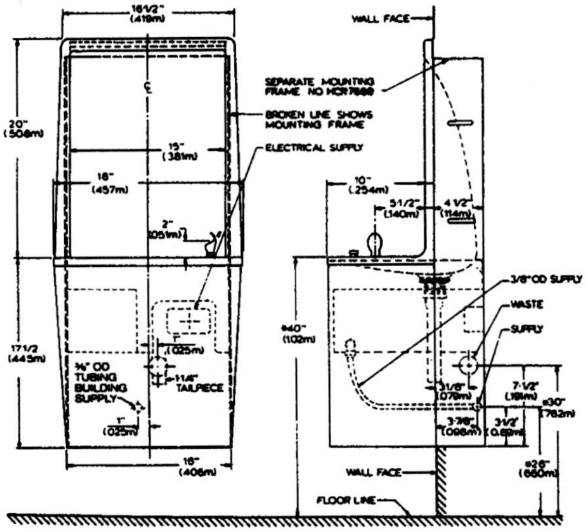
WALL FACE
SEPARATE MOUNTING FRAME NO HCR7689
BROKEN LINE SHOWS MOUNTING FRAME
ELECTRICAL SUPPLY
3/8" OD SUPPLY
WASTE
SUPPLY
1/4" OD TUBING BUILDING SUPPLY
1 1/4" TAILPIECE
WALL FACE
FLOOR LINE

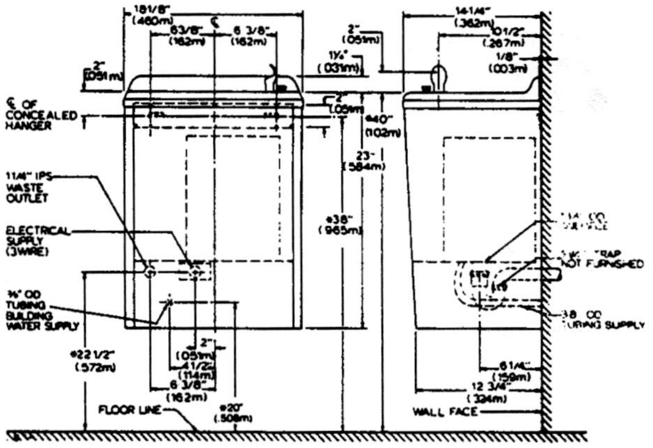
℄ OF CONCEALED HANGER
1 1/4" IPS WASTE OUTLET
ELECTRICAL SUPPLY (3 WIRE)
3/8" OD TUBING BUILDING WATER SUPPLY
FLOOR LINE
WALL FACE

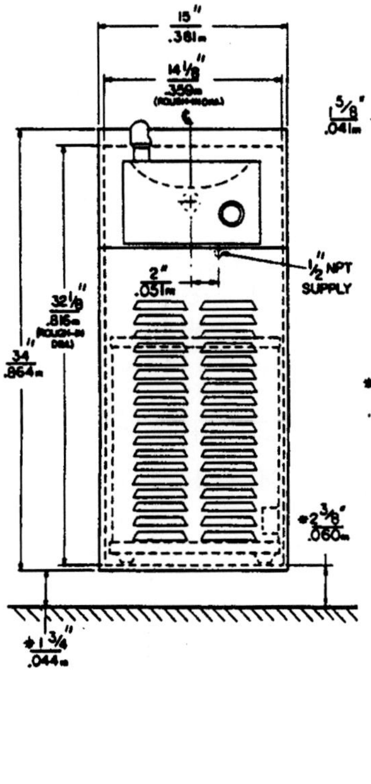
15"
.381m
14 1/8"
.359m
1/2" NPT SUPPLY
32 1/8"
.816m
34"
.864m
2"
.051m
2 3/8"
.060m
1 3/4"
.044m

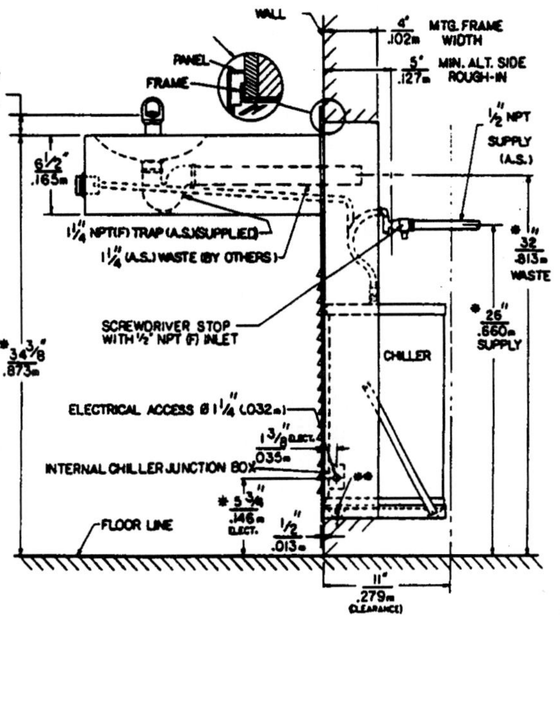
WALL
4" .102m MTG. FRAME WIDTH
5" .127m MIN. ALT. SIDE ROUGH-IN
PANEL
FRAME
1 5/8"
.041m
6 1/2"
.165m
1/2 NPT SUPPLY (A.S.)
1 1/4 NPT(F) TRAP (A.S.)(SUPPLIED)
1 1/4 (A.S.) WASTE (BY OTHERS)
32
.813m
WASTE
SCREWDRIVER STOP WITH 1/2" NPT (F) INLET
26
.660m
SUPPLY
34 3/8
.873m
CHILLER
ELECTRICAL ACCESS Ø 1 1/4 (.032m)
1 3/8" ELECT.
.035m
INTERNAL CHILLER JUNCTION BOX
5 3/4
.146m
ELECT.
FLOOR LINE
1/2"
.013m
11"
.279m
(CLEARANCE)

DRINKING FOUNTAINS
Accessible

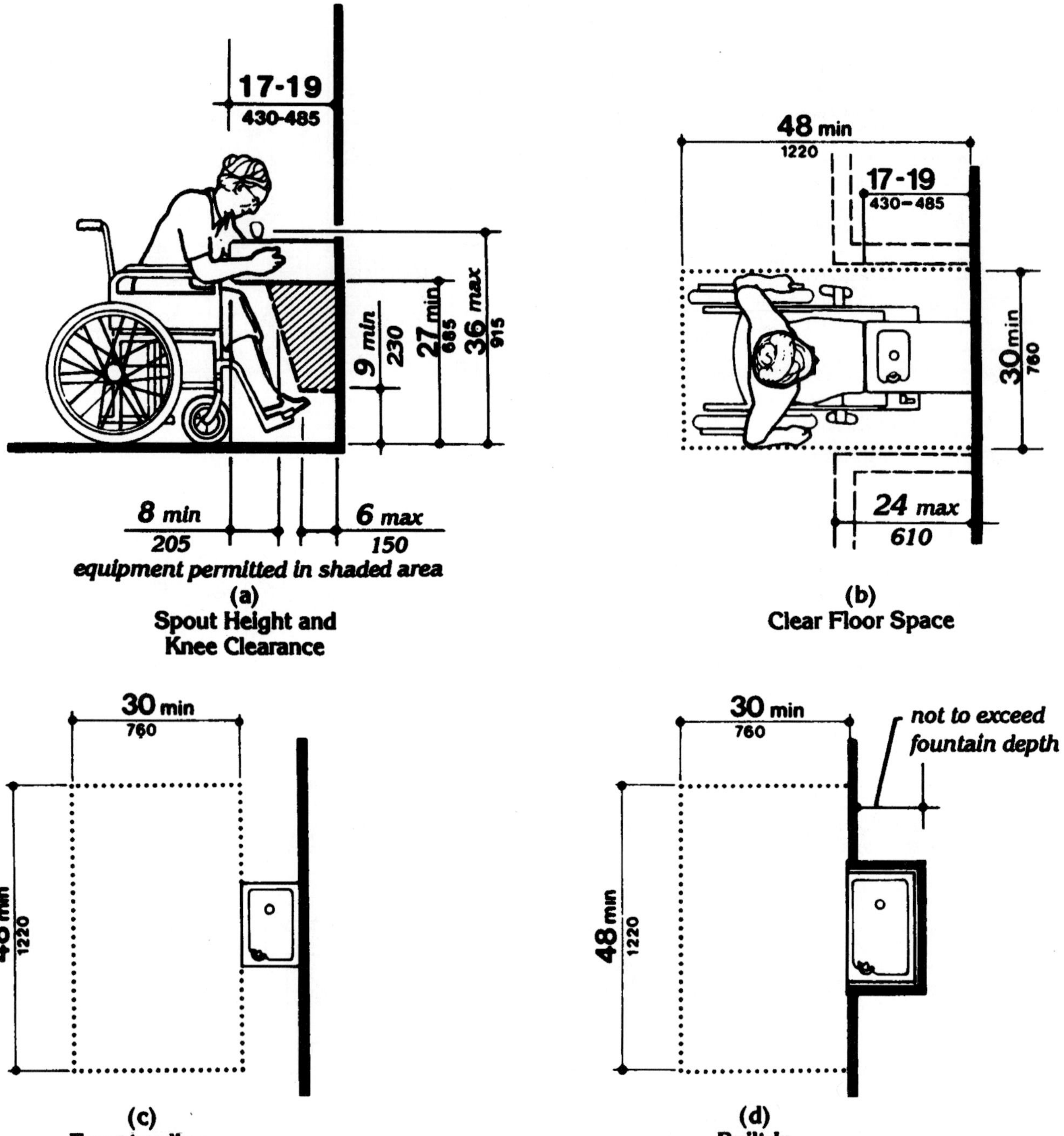

(a) Spout Height and Knee Clearance

(b) Clear Floor Space

(c) Freestanding Fountain or Cooler

(d) Built-In Fountain or Cooler

Drinking Fountains and Water Coolers

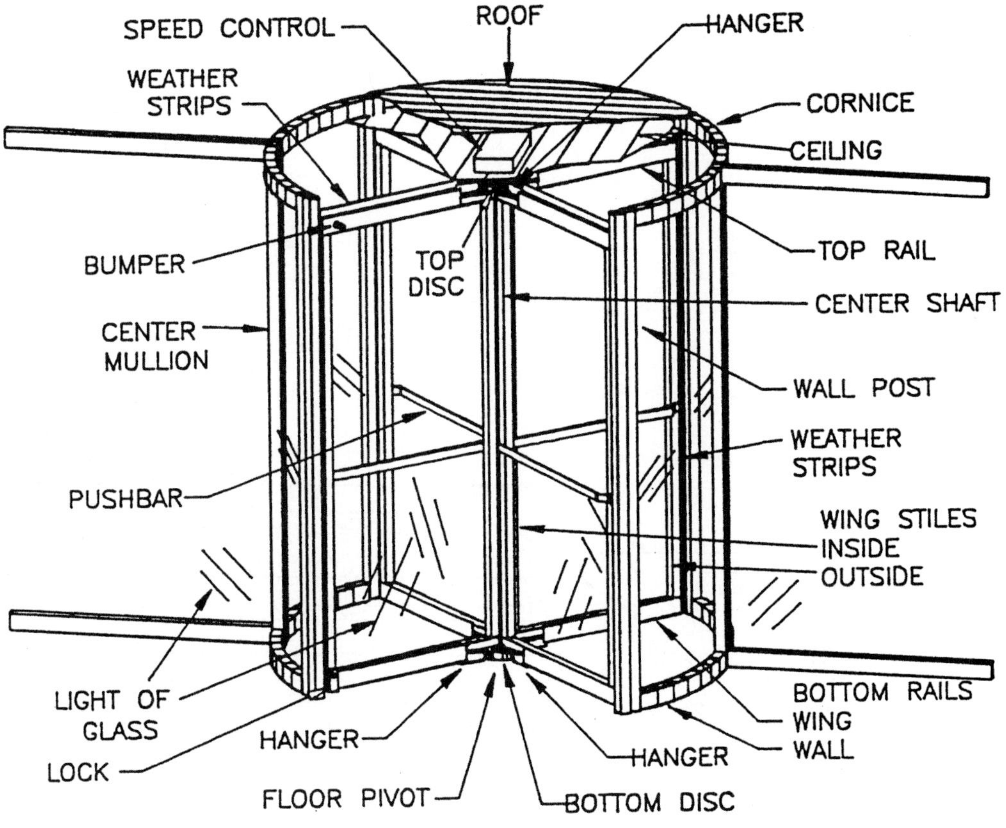

Common Entry Plans
(Any Model)

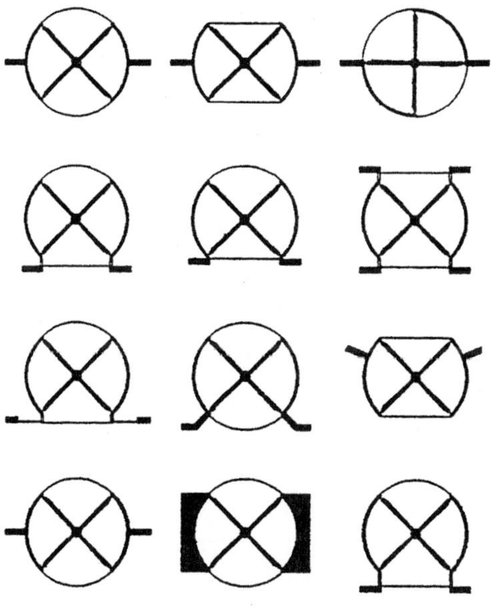

Common Entry Plans
(Any Model)

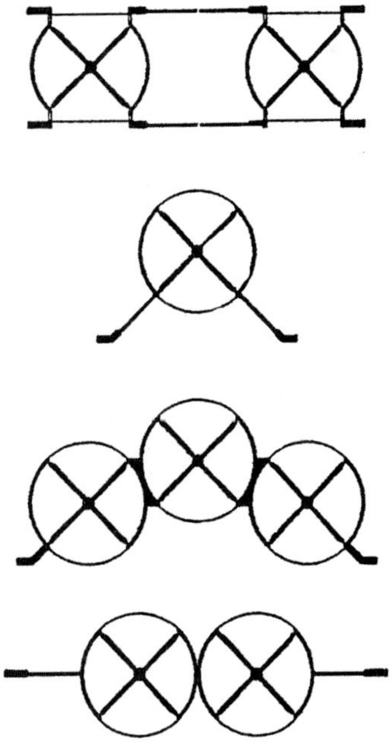

REVOLVING DOORS
Three-Wing and Four-Wing Types

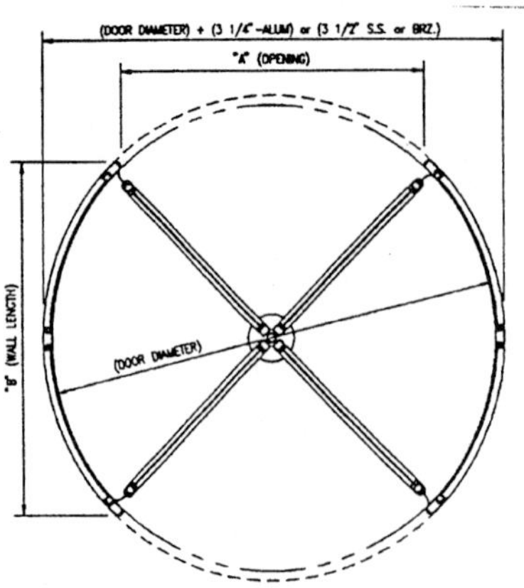

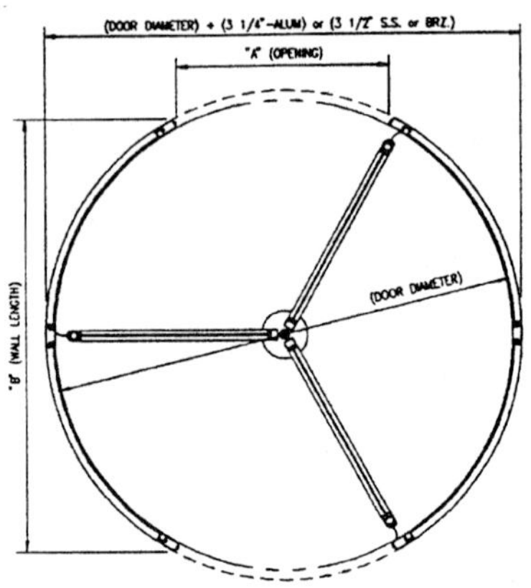

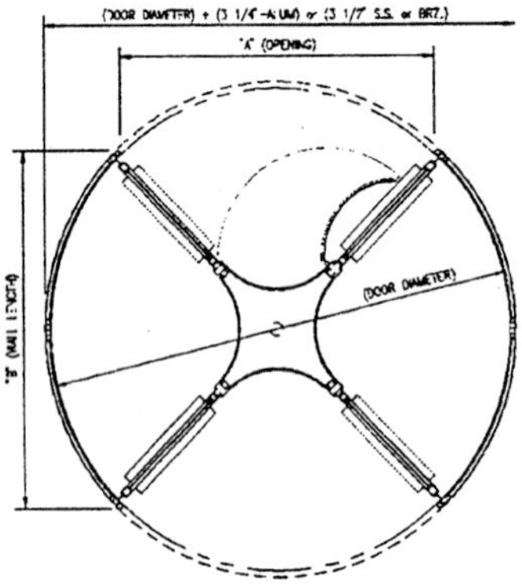

SATURN-ALUMINUM 4-WING			SATURN-ALUMINUM 3-WING		
DIAMETER	"A" OPENING	"B" WALL LENGTH	DIAMETER	"A" OPENING	"B" WALL LENGTH
6'-6"	4'-5 1/4"	4'-11 5/16"	7'-6"	3'-6 1/2"	6'-9 15/16"
7'-0"	4'-9 1/2"	5'-3 9/16"	8'-0"	3'-9 1/2"	7'-3 1/16"
7'-6"	5'-1 3/4"	5'-7 13/16"	8'-6"	4'-0 1/2"	7'-8 5/16"
8'-0"	5'-6"	6'-0"	9'-0"	4'-3 1/2"	8'-1 1/2"
9'-0"	6'-2 1/2"	6'-6 1/2"	9'-6"	4'-6 1/2"	8'-6 3/4"
10'-0"	6'-11"	7'-5"	10'-0"	4'-9 1/2"	8'-11 15/16"

SATURN-STAINLESS STEEL & BRONZE 4-WING			SATURN-STAINLESS STEEL & BRONZE 3-WING		
DIAMETER	"A" OPENING	"B" WALL LENGTH	DIAMETER	"A" OPENING	"B" WALL LENGTH
6'-6"	4'-5 1/4"	4'-11 1/2"	7'-6"	3'-6 1/2"	6'-10 1/8"
7'-0"	4'-9 1/2"	5'-3 3/4"	8'-0"	3'-9 1/2"	7'-3 5/16"
7'-6"	5'-1 3/4"	5'-8"	8'-6"	4'-0 1/2"	7'-8 1/2"
8'-0"	5'-6"	6'-0 3/16"	9'-0"	4'-3 1/2"	8'-1 11/16"
9'-0"	6'-2 1/2"	6'-8 3/4"	9'-6"	4'-6 1/2"	8'-6 15/16"
10'-0"	6'-11"	7'-5 3/16"	10'-0"	4'-9 1/2"	9'-0 1/8"

JUPITER-STAINLESS STEEL & BRONZE 4-WING			JUPITER-STAINLESS STEEL & BRONZE 3-WING		
DIAMETER	"A" OPENING	"B" WALL LENGTH	DIAMETER	"A" OPENING	"B" WALL LENGTH
12'-0"	8'-2 9/16"	8'-11 9/16"	12'-0"	5'-8 3/4"	10'-10 7/16"
14'-0"	9'-7 9/16"	10'-4 9/16"	14'-0"	6'-8 3/4"	12'-7 1/4"
16'-0"	11'-0 1/2"	11'-9 1/2"	16'-0"	7'-8 3/4"	14'-4"

WHY A THREE-WING DESIGN? Revolving doors with a three-wing design create an intriguing focal point for an entrance and they are more functional than a four-wing design in some applications.

- Each compartment in a three-wing door is 33% larger. An excellent choice for more comfortable passage where baggage handling or wheelchairs will be common.
- Three-wing doors are aesthetically unusual. Use one when you would like to draw special attention to an entrance.

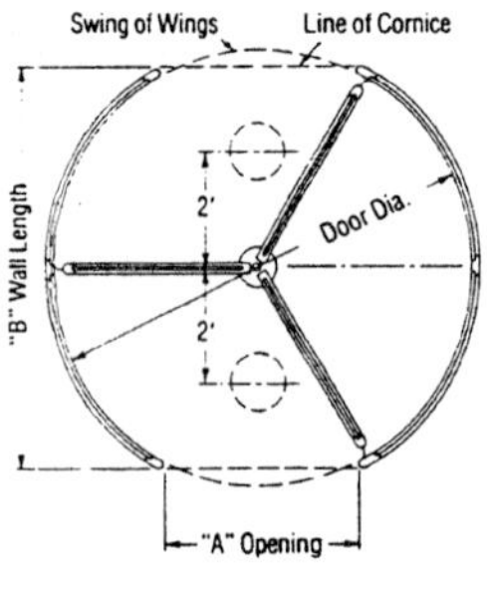

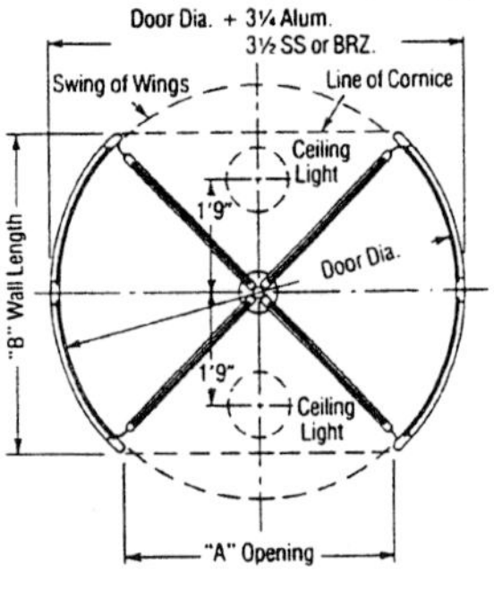

THE FOUR-WING DESIGN has a proven tradition of practicality and economy.

- The "A" opening dimension is larger than the three-wing design, permitting quicker access and egress for high volume passage.
- There is better air seal performance. Less air is transferred with the use of each quadrant of the door. When locked, the weatherstrip is in continuous contact at all four wings.

Dia.	"A" (Opening)	"B" (Wall Length) Alum.	"B" (Wall Length) S/Stl. Bronze
7'-6"	3'-6½"	6'-9 15/16"	6'-10⅛"
8'-0"	3'-9½"	7'-3⅛"	7'-3 5/16"
9'-0"	4'-3½"	8'-1½"	8'-1 11/16"
10'-0"	4'-9½"	8'-11 15/16"	9'-0⅛"
11'-0"	5'-3½"	9'-10 5/16"	9'-10½"
12'-0"	5'-9½"	10'-8 11/16"	10'-8⅞"

Dia.	"A" (Opening)	"B" (Wall Length) Alum.	"B" (Wall Length) S/Stl. Bronze
6'-6"	4'-5¼"	4'-11 5/16"	4'-11½"
6'-10"	4'-8⅛"	5'-2 3/16"	5'-2⅜"
7'-0"	4'-9½"	5'-3 9/16"	5'-3¾"
7'-6"	5'-1¾"	5'-7 13/16"	5'-8"
8'-0"	5'-6"	6'-0"	6'-0 3/16"
9'-0"	6'-2½"	6'-6½"	6'-8¾"
10'-0"	6'-11"	7'-5"	7'-5 3/16"
11'-0"	7'-7 7/16"	8'-1½"	8'-1 11/16"
12'-0"	8'-3 15/16"	8'-10"	8'-10 3/16"

Door Diameters and Related Dimensions

REVOLVING DOORS
Plans and Elevations

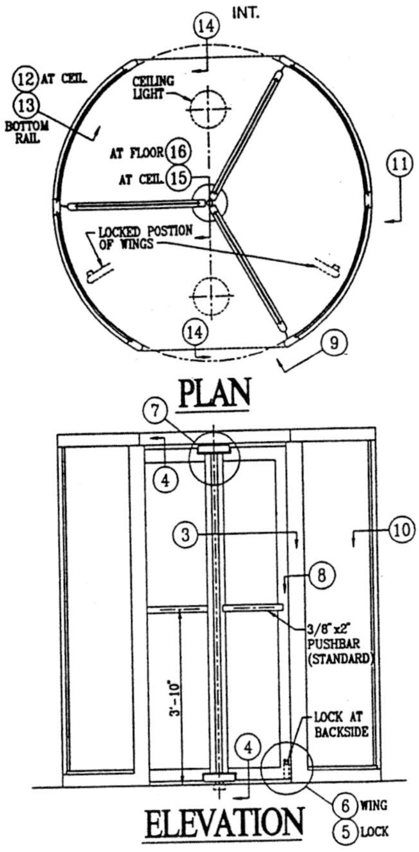

ALUMINUM
KEY PLAN & ELEVATION
3 - WING DOOR

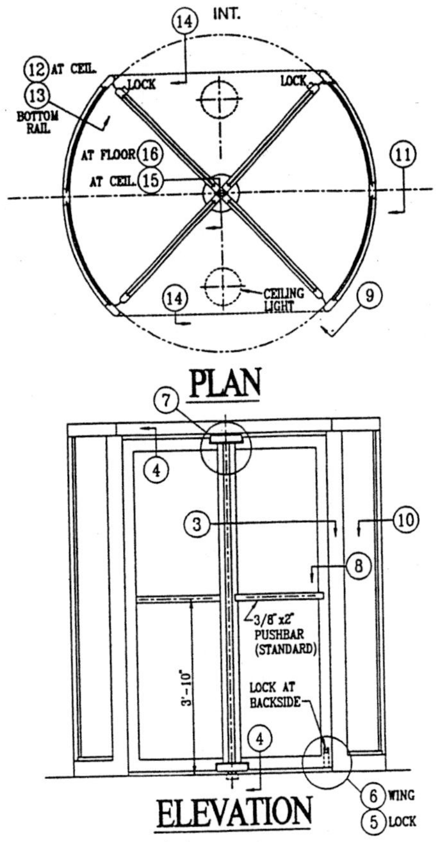

ALUMINUM
KEY PLAN & ELEVATION
4 - WING DOOR

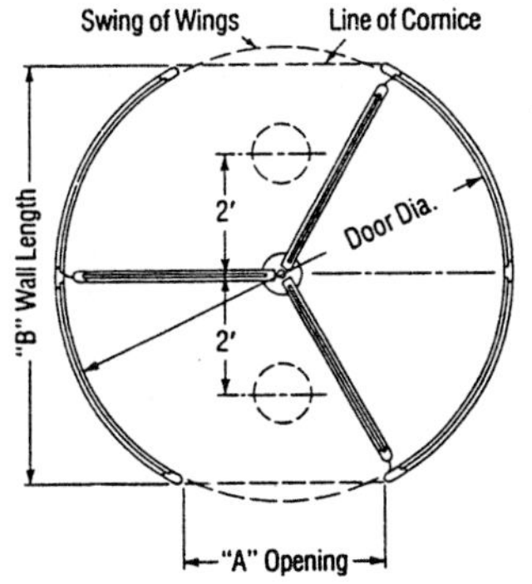

Dia.	"A" (Opening)	"B" (Wall Length) Alum.	S/Stl. Bronze
7'-6"	3'-6½"	6'-915⁄16"	6'-10⅛"
8'-0"	3'-9½"	7'-3⅛"	7'-3⁵⁄16"
9'-0"	4'-3½"	8'-1½"	8'-1¹¹⁄16"

Door Diameters and Related Dimensions

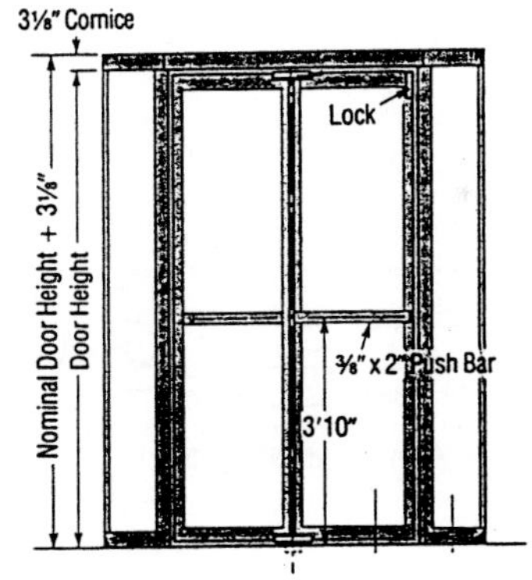

Diameter	Height
6'-6"	10'-0"
7'-0"	9'-0"
7'-6"	8'-6"
8'-0"	8'-0"
9'-0"	7'-0"

Other sizes manufactured on request

Door Heights

REVOLVING DOORS
Sections and Details

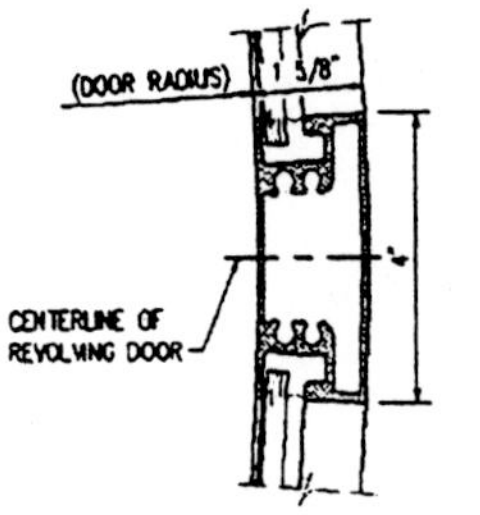

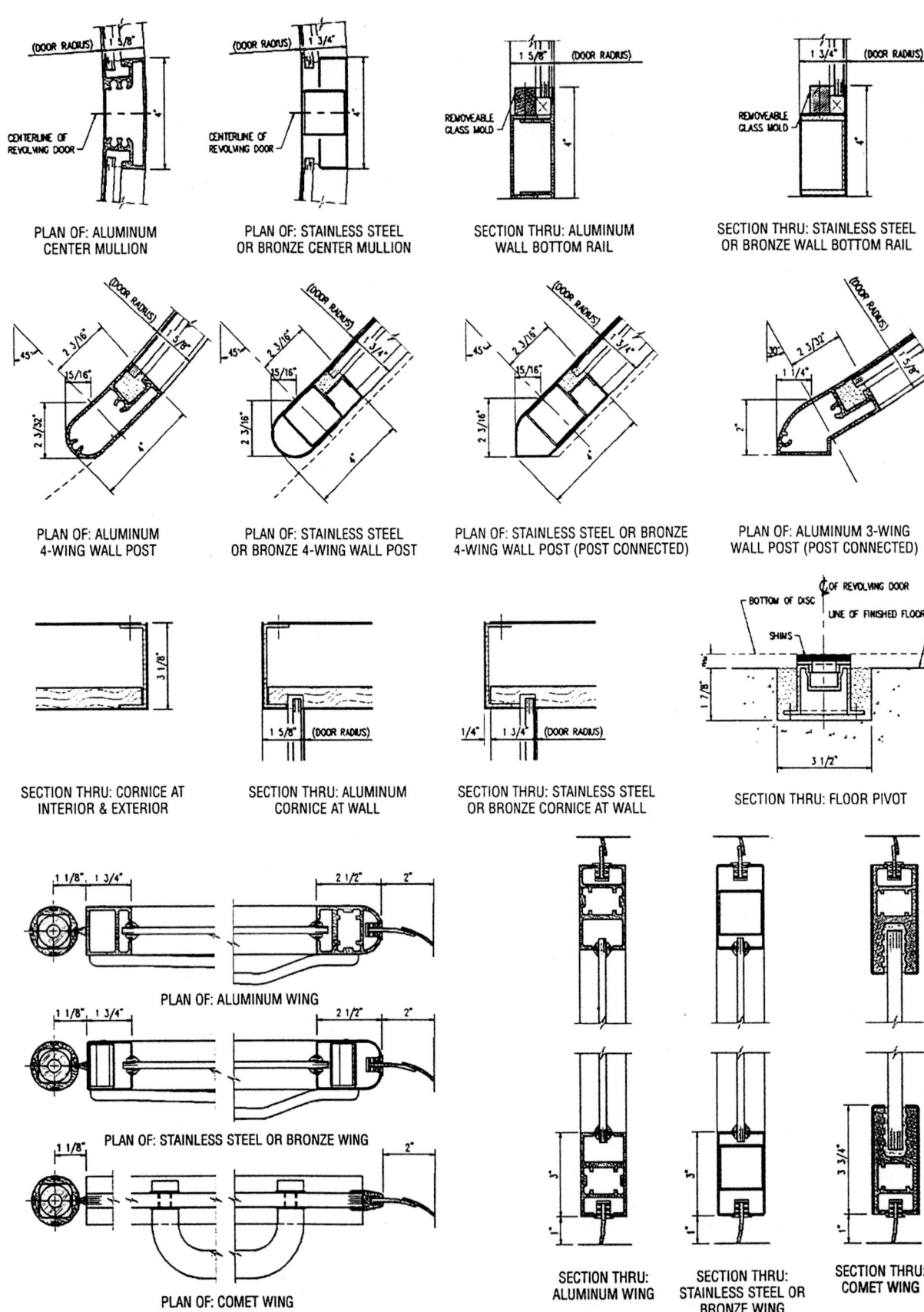

PLAN OF: ALUMINUM CENTER MULLION

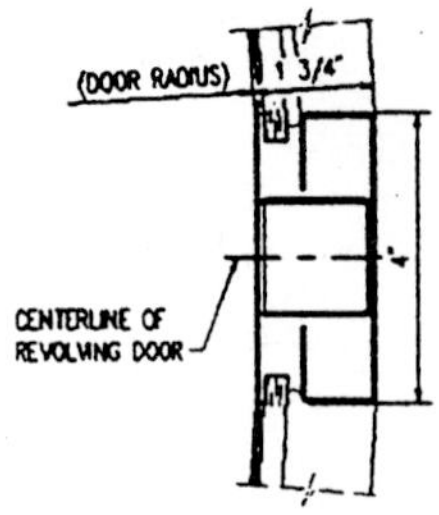

PLAN OF: STAINLESS STEEL OR BRONZE CENTER MULLION

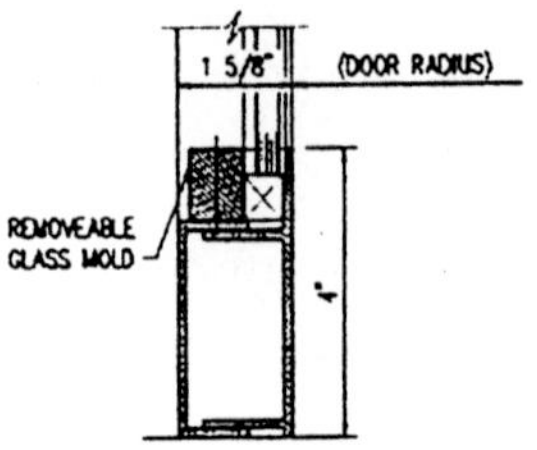

SECTION THRU: ALUMINUM WALL BOTTOM RAIL

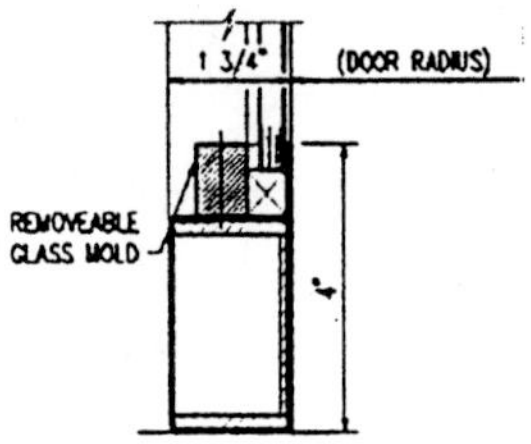

SECTION THRU: STAINLESS STEEL OR BRONZE WALL BOTTOM RAIL

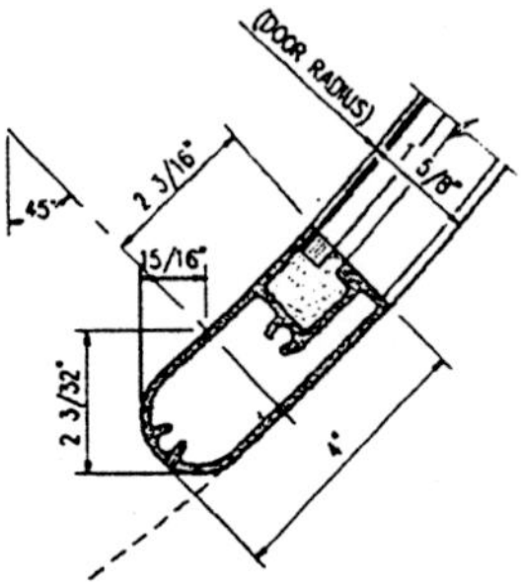

PLAN OF: ALUMINUM 4-WING WALL POST

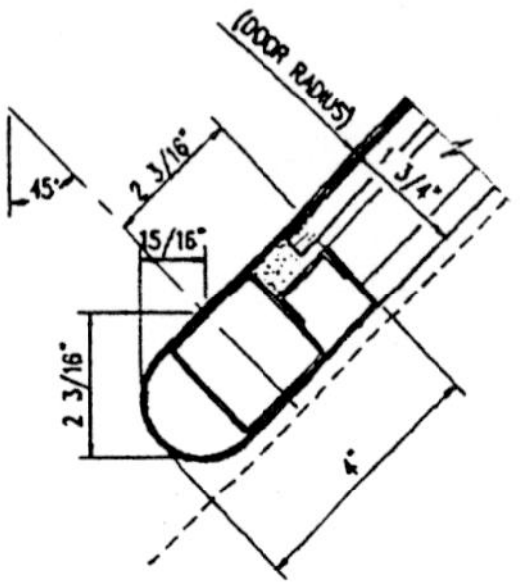

PLAN OF: STAINLESS STEEL OR BRONZE 4-WING WALL POST

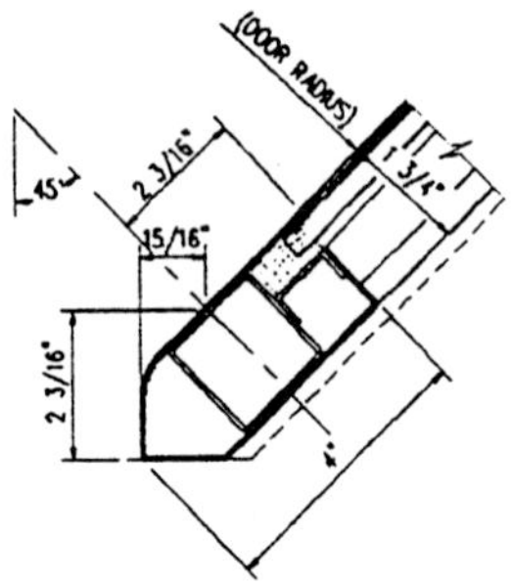

PLAN OF: STAINLESS STEEL OR BRONZE 4-WING WALL POST (POST CONNECTED)

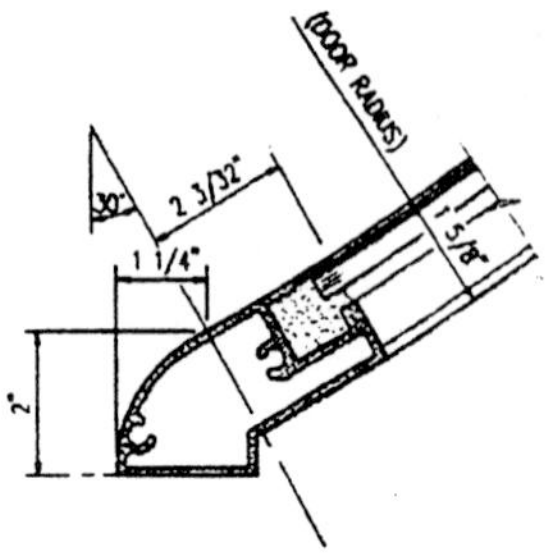

PLAN OF: ALUMINUM 3-WING WALL POST (POST CONNECTED)

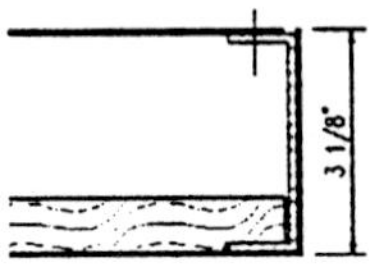

SECTION THRU: CORNICE AT INTERIOR & EXTERIOR

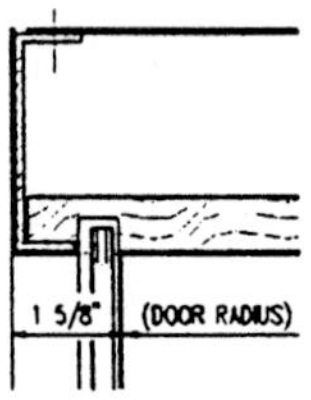

SECTION THRU: ALUMINUM CORNICE AT WALL

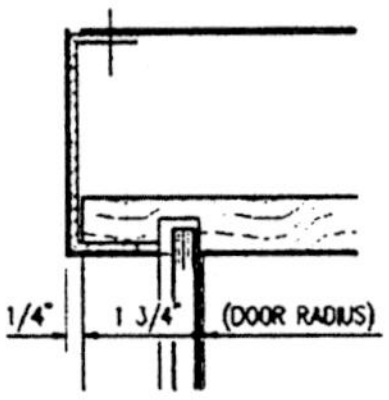

SECTION THRU: STAINLESS STEEL OR BRONZE CORNICE AT WALL

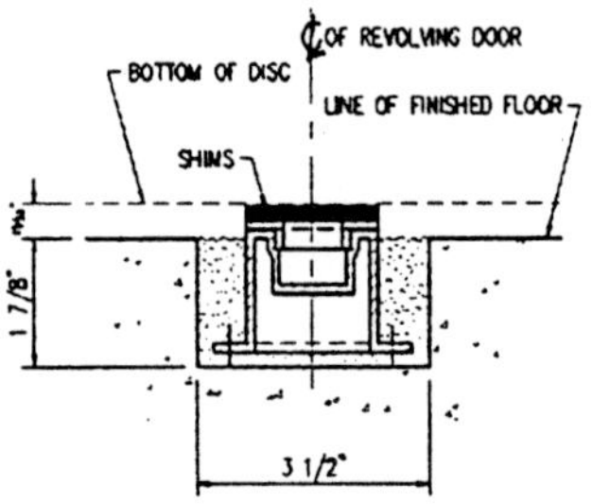

SECTION THRU: FLOOR PIVOT

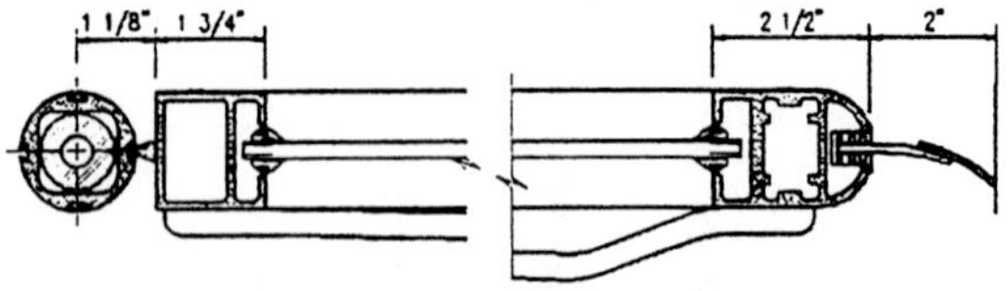

PLAN OF: ALUMINUM WING

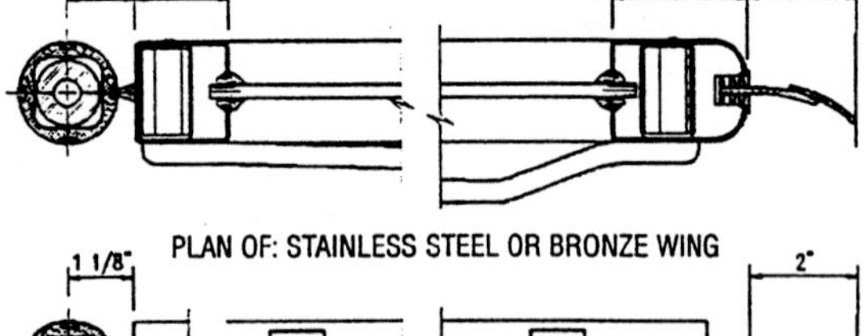

PLAN OF: STAINLESS STEEL OR BRONZE WING

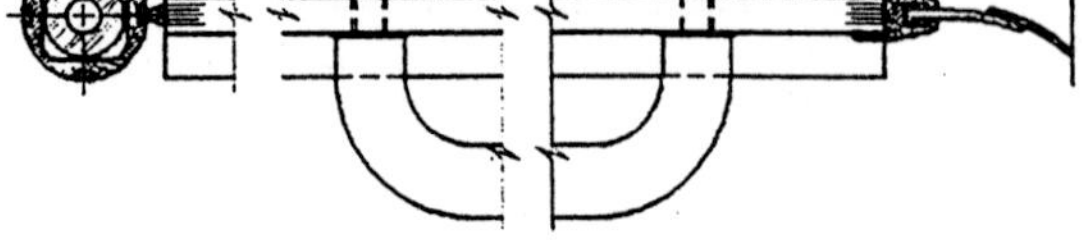

PLAN OF: COMET WING

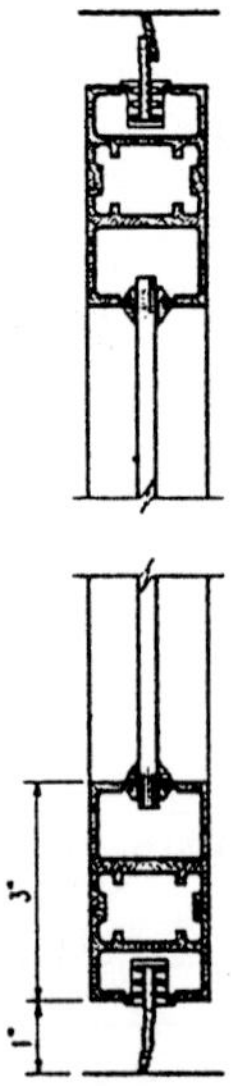

SECTION THRU: ALUMINUM WING

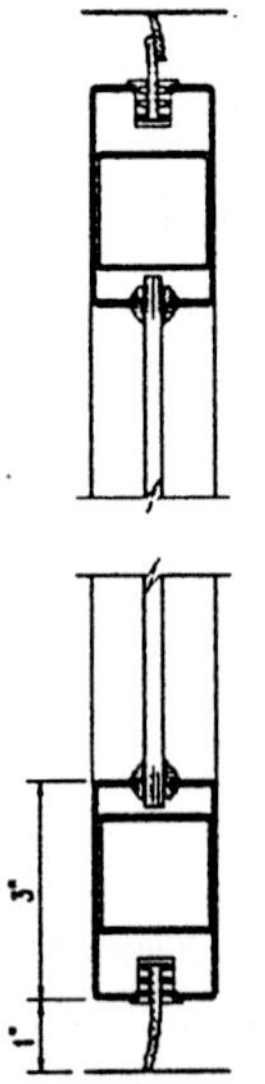

SECTION THRU: STAINLESS STEEL OR BRONZE WING

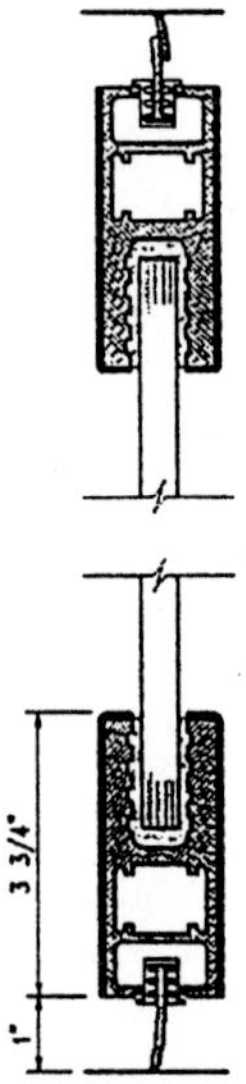

SECTION THRU: COMET WING

CLOCK FACES
Types

Face AI - Hands WS

Face B - Hands HS

Face C - Hands VS

Face T - Hands WS

Face I - Hands LS

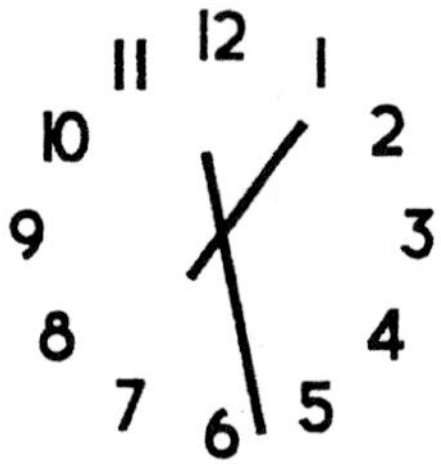

Face J - Hands LS

Face L - Hands LS

Face N - Hands AS

Face O - Hands MS-A

Face P - Hands LS

Face Z - Hands CS

Face Y - Hands DS

Face NI - Hands WS

Face Q - Hands IS

Face R - Hands AS

Face U - Hands IS

Face V - Hands WS

Face X - w/Pointer
*Available in Degrees Centigrade

CLOCK FACES
Clock Elevation and Section

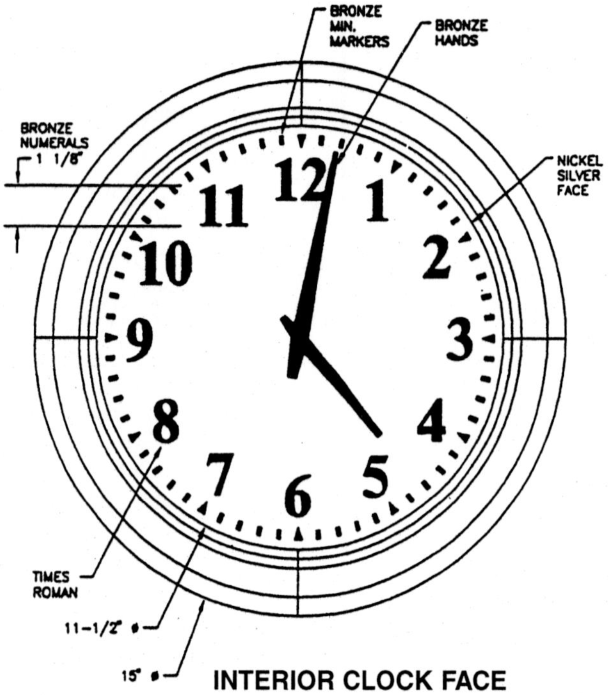

INTERIOR CLOCK FACE

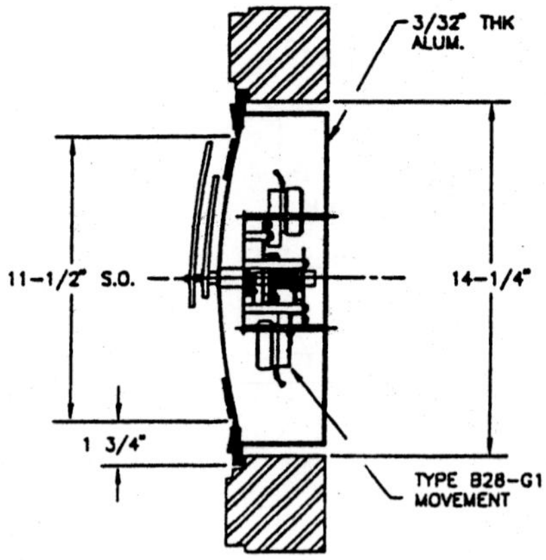

SIDE VIEW

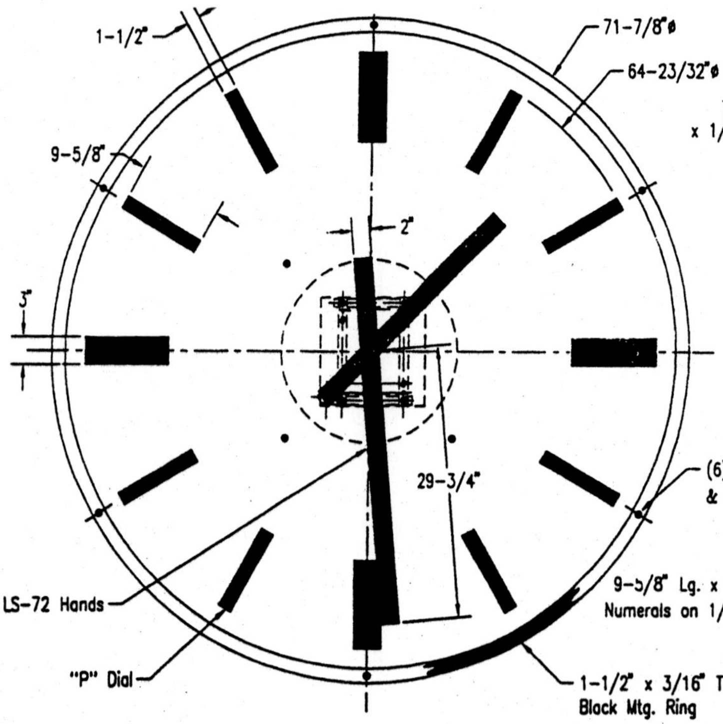

FRONT VIEW

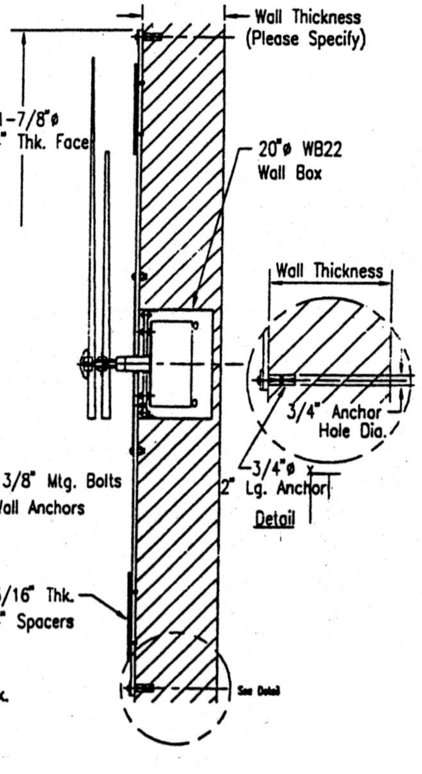

SECTION

CLOCK FACES
Details

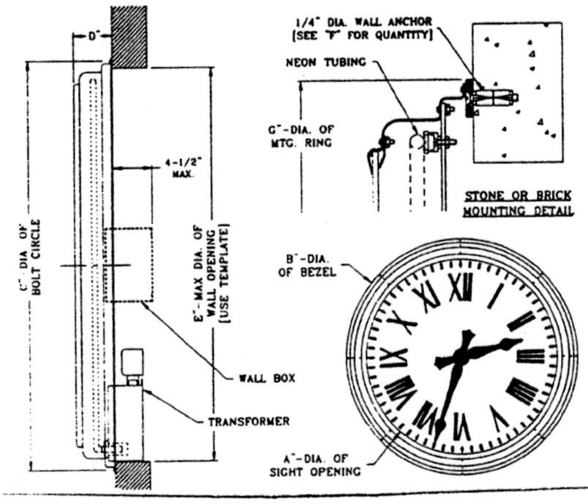

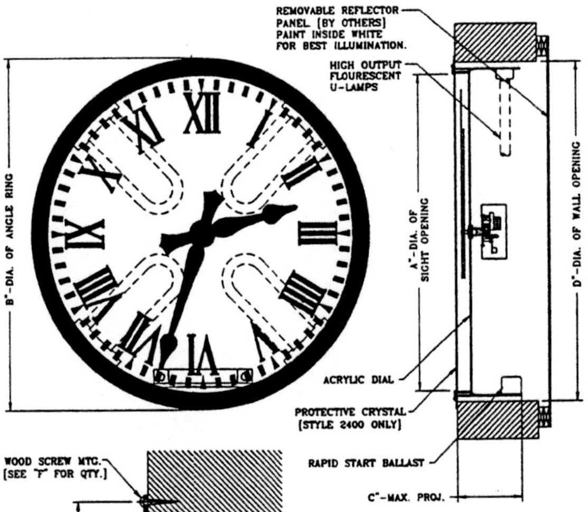

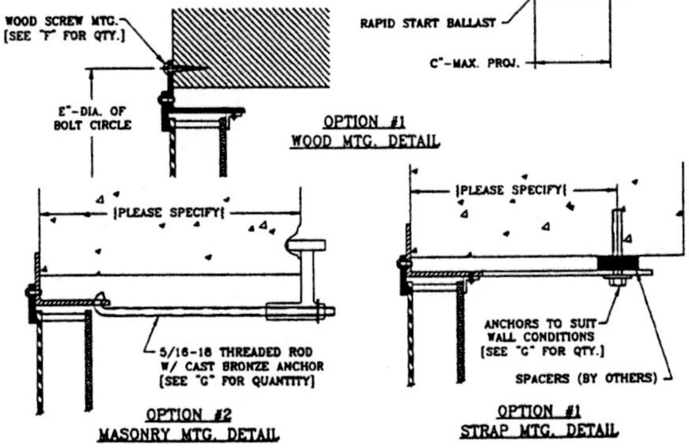

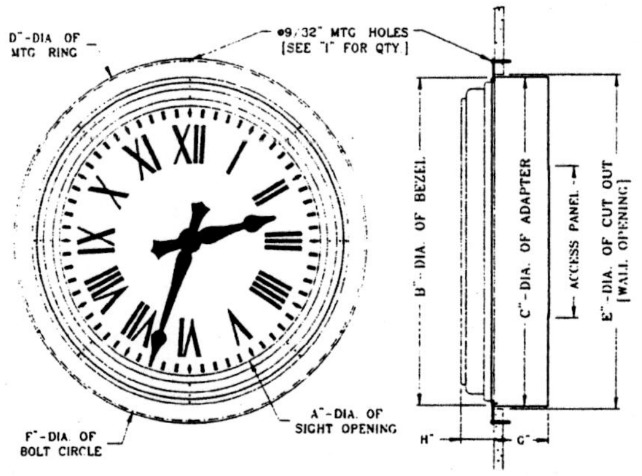

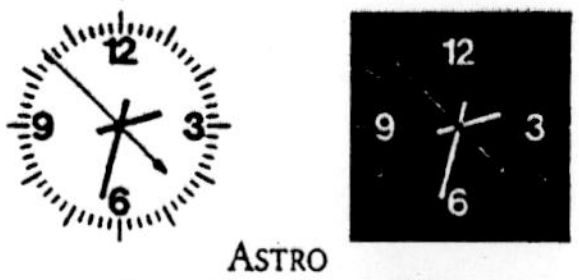
ASTRO
STYLE E STYLE ER

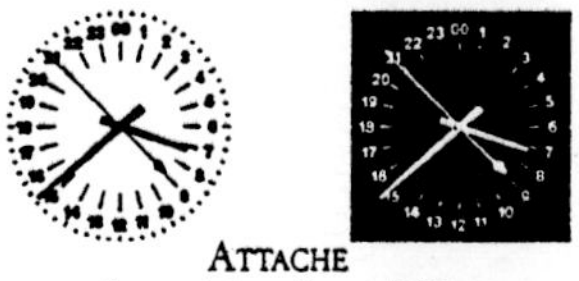
ATTACHE
STYLE M STYLE MR

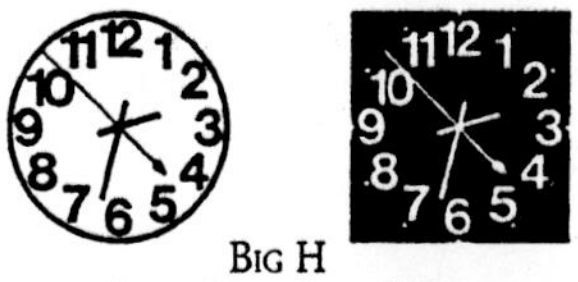
BIG H
STYLE H STYLE HR

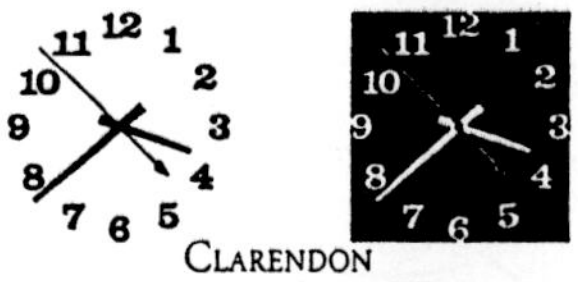
CLARENDON
STYLE T STYLE TR

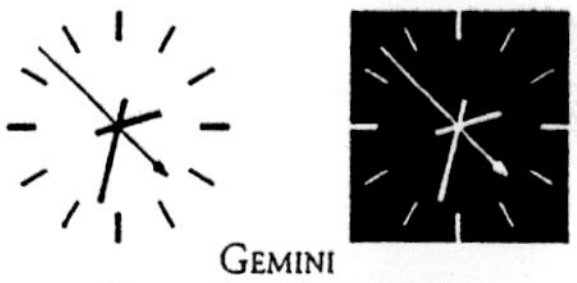
GEMINI
STYLE D STYLE DR

MONITOR
STYLE G STYLE GR

PATRIOT
STYLE F STYLE FR

URBANITE
STYLE K STYLE KR

SOLARIS
STYLE S

WIRE MANAGEMENT

Grommets: Types and Sizes

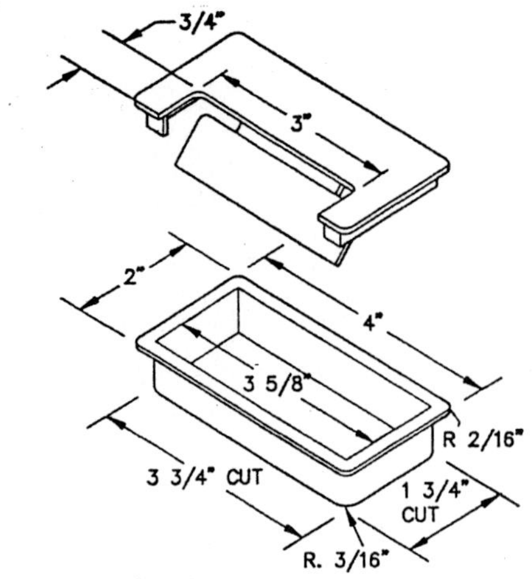

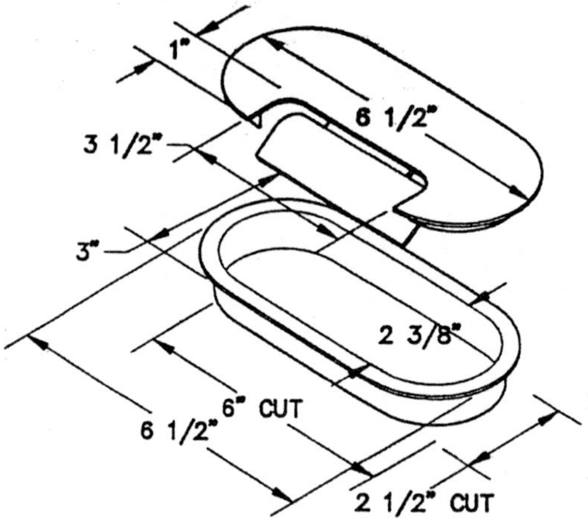

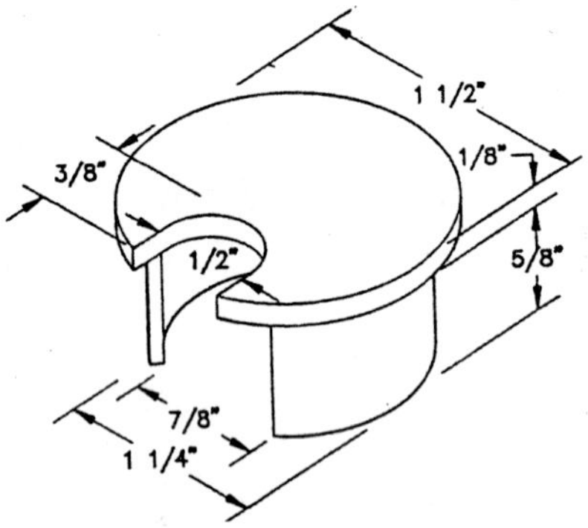

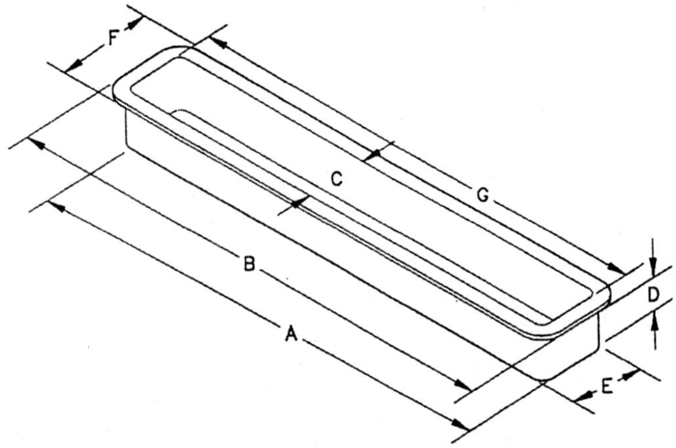

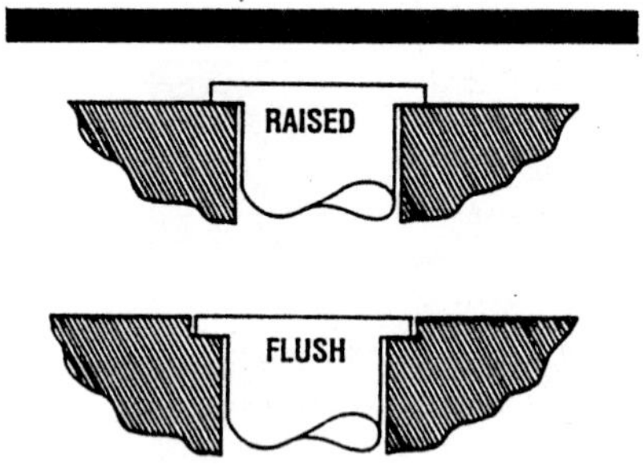

	A	B	C	D	E	F	G
CP-1	17" 432mm	17-1/2" 445mm	1-9/16" 40mm	1-1/8" 29mm	1-3/4" 45mm	2-1/4" 57mm	16-3/4" 426mm
CP-2	12" 305mm	12-1/2" 318mm	1-9/16" 40mm	1-1/8" 29mm	1-3/4" 45mm	2-1/4" 57mm	11-3/4" 299mm

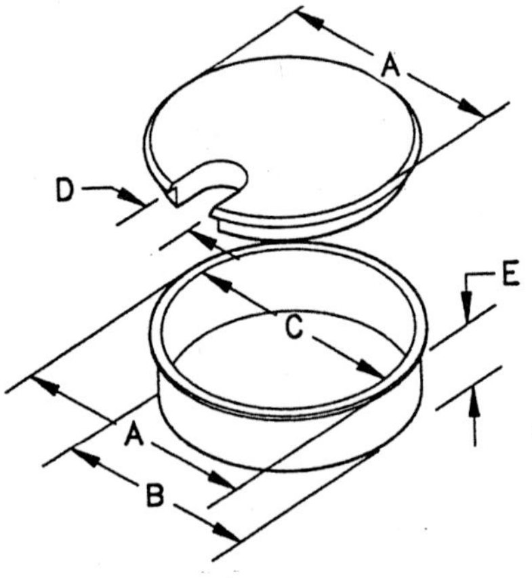

GROMMET CAP	A OVERALL DIAMETER OR SIZE	B HOLE SIZE TO CUT	C INSIDE DIAMETER OR SIZE	D CORD SLOT SIZE	E DEPTH
MM-3	2" 51mm	1-3/4" 43.5mm	N/A	5/8" 16mm	N/A
MM-4	2-1/2" 63.5mm	2-3/16" 55.5mm	N/A	5/8" 16mm	N/A
MM-5	3" 76mm	2-3/4" 70mm	N/A	3/4" 19mm	N/A
LINER					
MM-3A	2" 51mm	1-7/8" 48mm	1-3/4" 43.5mm	N/A	3/4" 19mm
MM-4A	2-1/2" 63.5mm	2-3/8" 60mm	2-3/16" 55.5mm	N/A	5/8" 16mm
MM-5A	3" 76mm	2-7/8" 73mm	2-3/4" 70mm	N/A	11/16" 17.5mm

Large P&C Grommet with four 110v outlets and up to 6 data ports | ***Small P&C Grommet with one electrical outlet and two data ports***

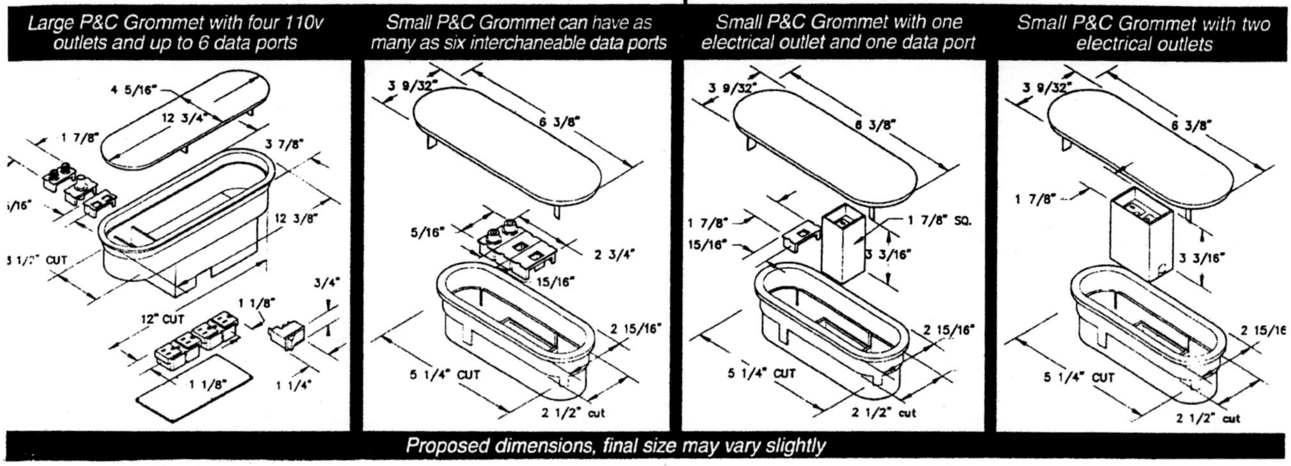

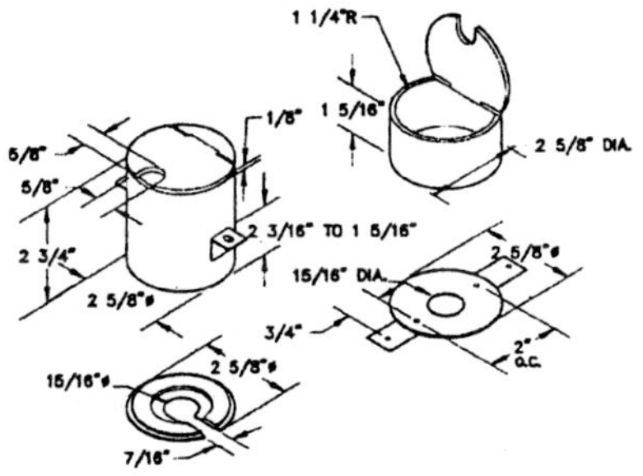

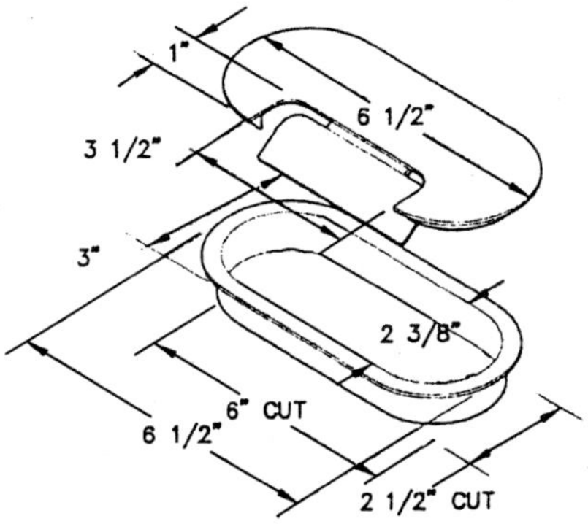

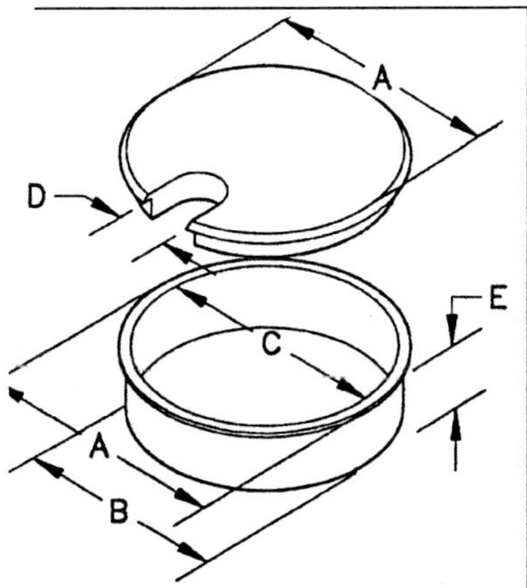

GROMMET CAP	A OVERALL DIAMETER OR SIZE	B HOLE SIZE TO CUT	C INSIDE DIAMETER OR SIZE	D CORD SLOT SIZE	E DEPTH
MM-3	2" 51mm	1-3/4" 43.5mm	N/A	5/8" 16mm	N/A
MM-4	2-1/2" 63.5mm	2-3/16" 55.5mm	N/A	5/8" 16mm	N/A
MM-5	3" 76mm	2-3/4" 70mm	N/A	3/4" 19mm	N/A
LINER					
MM-3A	2" 51mm	1-7/8" 48mm	1-3/4" 43.5mm	N/A	3/4" 19mm
MM-4A	2-1/2" 63.5mm	2-3/8" 60mm	2-3/16" 55.5mm	N/A	5/8" 16mm
MM-5A	3" 76mm	2-7/8" 73mm	2-3/4" 70mm	N/A	11/16" 17.5mm

WIRE MANAGEMENT
Grommets: Types and Sizes

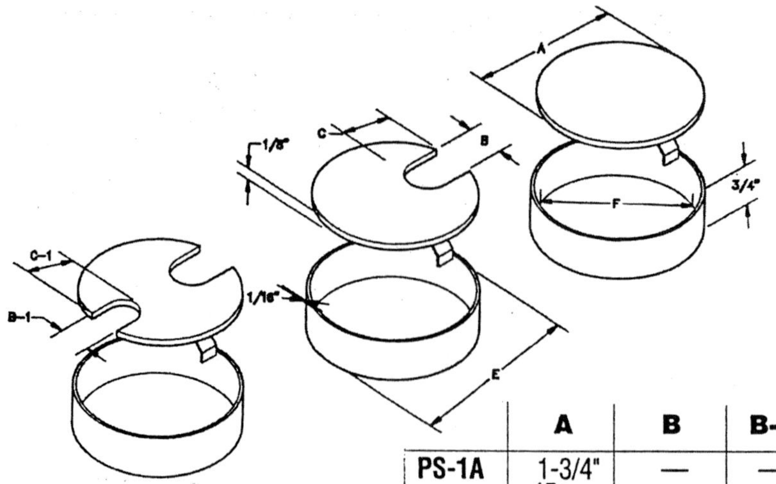

	A	B	B-1	C	C-1	D	E
PS-1A	1-3/4" 45 mm	— —	— —	— —	— —	1-3/4" 45mm	1-5/8" 41mm
PS-1B	1-3/4" 45mm	9/16" 14mm	— —	5/8" 16mm	— —	1-3/4" 45mm	1-5/8" 41mm
PS-1C	1-3/4" 45 mm	9/16" 14mm	3/8" 9.5mm	5/8" 16mm	3/8" 14mm	1-3/4" 45mm	1-5/8" 41mm
PS-2A	2-1/2" 64mm	— —	— —	— —	— —	2-1/2" 64mm	2-3/8" 60mm
PS-2B	2-1/2" 64mm	7/8" 22mm	— —	3/4" 19mm	— —	2-1/2" 64mm	2-3/8" 60mm
PS-2C	2-1/2" 64mm	7/8" 22mm	5/8" 16mm	3/4" 19mm	9/16" 14mm	2-1/2" 64mm	2-3/8" 60mm
PS-3A	3" 76mm	— —	— —	— —	— —	3" 76mm	2-7/8" 73mm
PS-3B	3" 76mm	1" 25mm	— —	7/8" 22mm	— —	3" 76mm	2-7/8" 73mm
PS-3C	3" 76mm	1" 25mm	7/8" 22mm	7/8" 22mm	13/16" 21mm	3" 76mm	2-7/8" 73mm

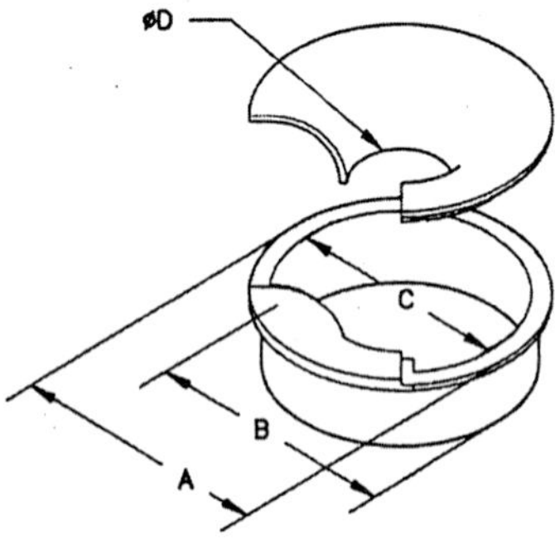

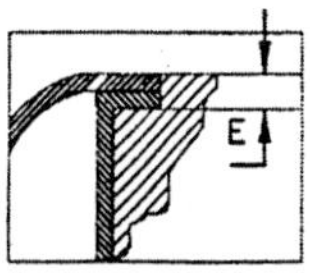

	A	B	C	D	E	F
WG-2	1-3/4" 45mm	2-1/4" 57mm	5/8" 16mm	1/4" 6mm	7/8" 22mm	9/16" 14mm
WG-3	2-1/2" 64mm	3" 76mm	7/8" 22mm	1/4" 6mm	1-3/16" 30mm	15/16" 24mm

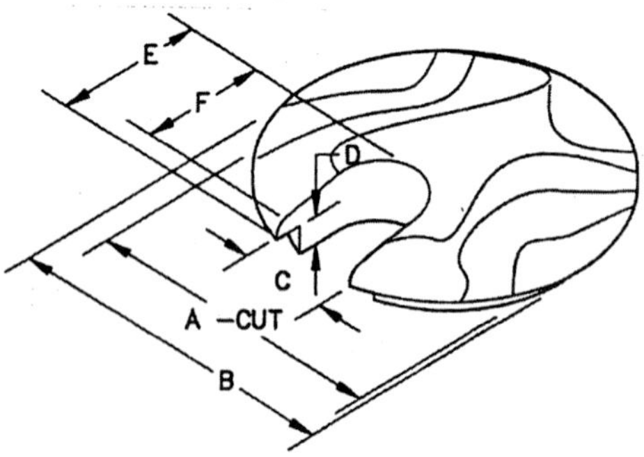

	A	B	C	D	E
SS-3	2" 51mm	1-3/4" 45mm	1-5/8" 41mm	5/8" 16mm	5/32" 4mm
SS-3A	3" 76mm	2-3/4" 70mm	2-5/8" 67mm	1" 25mm	5/32" 4mm

5 ACCESSIBLE DESIGN/ADA

INTRODUCTION/OVERVIEW

Although the Americans with Disabilities Act (ADA) was signed by President Bush on July 26, 1990, the notion of making buildings and products usable and accessible to those with disabilities has been with us for at least four decades. At various times and in various venues, terms such as "inclusive design," "barrier-free design," "humane design," "design for all," "accessible design," and, more recently, "universal design" have been employed to identify and describe this concept. In most instances the differences in terms have been essentially a question of semantics. In other instances the terms represent a strong, disciplined, and well-structured philosophical design approach, while in still other instances the terms have been used to identify a body of design standards that have been codified and made part of local and state legislation.

It is the intent of this section, however, to deal exclusively with specific federal legislation, including the ADA and its related design guidelines, directed to making buildings and products usable and accessible to the disabled.

Accordingly, and in a more national context, the issue of accessible design had it origins as far back as 1961, at which time the American National Standards Institute (ANSI), formerly known as the American Standards Association (ASI), issued A117.1, "Specifications for Making Buildings and Facilities Accessible and Usable by the Physically Handicapped." However, the first federal law to require so-called barrier-free design was the Architectural Barriers Act of 1968, which still requires that buildings and facilities be accessible if they are designed, built, or altered with certain federal funds, or leased for occupancy by federal agencies

The Rehabilitation Act of 1973, the precursor to the ADA, followed and became one of the most significant pieces of federal legislation requiring access to programs and facilities that are designed and built by recipients of federal funds. This act also created the Architectural and Transportation Barriers Compliance Board (ATBCB). The board, also known as the "Access Board," is the federal agency that develops guidelines issued under the ADA, the Architectural Barriers Act of 1968, the Telecommunications Act of 1996, and Section 508 of the Rehabilitation Act of 1973, as amended in 1998.

While the Access Board has enforcement authority for the Architectural Barriers Act, four other federal agencies actually develop the enforceable standards, based on the Access Board's Minimum Guidelines and requirements for Accessible Design. These agencies are the General Services Administration, the Department of Defense, the Department of Housing and Urban Development, and the U.S. Postal Service. The currently enforceable standards are the Uniform Federal Accessibility Standards (UFAS). These four federal standards-setting agencies may, on a case-by-case basis, waive or modify the standards.

The two most recent pieces of legislation dealing with accessible design are the Fair Housing Amendments Act of 1988 and the ADA. The former requires that all newly constructed multifamily housing be adaptable—not fully accessible but modifiable—by a tenant with a disability, to suit his or her individual accessibility requirements. The latter is the most current legislation, the purpose of which is to prohibit discrimination against individuals with disabilities. Prohibited actions include, but are not limited to, failure to design and construct in compliance with federal standards for accessible design.

The ADA is the most recent law affecting people with disabilities and is the most far-reaching. Of particular importance to designers are Titles II and III of the ADA. The Department of Justice (DOJ) and the Department of Transportation (DOT) have responsibility for enforcing Titles II and III. As part of that responsibility they must establish design standards with which covered entities must comply. The process by which the DOJ, DOT, and ADA standards for accessible design are developed involves two steps.

First, the Access Board publishes the ADA Accessibility Guidelines (ADAAG) as a final rule. Then, the DOJ and the DOT independently adopt standards. Both the DOJ and the DOT are required under the statute to establish standards that are "consistent with" the ADAAG. Although both the DOJ and the DOT have adopted the ADAAG as their design standards, the standards must be read in the context of the applicable rule or title. While the Access Board from time to time supplements, refines, and otherwise modifies its original guidelines, they do not have the force of law until Titles II or III are modified to incorporate the changes in their standards.

A designer wanting to plan ahead is cautioned that provisions may be modified in the ADAAG that have the effect of establishing a lesser or differing standard from the currently enforceable standard. Where ADAAG is changed, or proposed by the Access Board to be changed, designers should make certain that the guidelines used are the most current recognized by the enforcing authorities. If the Access Board's changes go beyond the current requirements, it is prudent to consider using the more stringent standard, but no one is bound to use standards not yet recognized by the DOJ or the DOT

The Eastern Paralyzed Veterans Association (EPVA) offers the following overviews of the four key pieces of federal accessibility legislation, while the chart on page 1581 provides comparative descriptions of the various federal accessibility legislation. Also included in this section are the complete Americans with Disabilities Act Accessibility Guidelines (ADAAG).

OVERVIEW OF THE ARCHITECTURAL BARRIERS ACT OF 1968

The Architectural Barriers Act of 1968 was the first federal law to require barrier-free design. More than 30 years old, the law still applies where buildings are constructed, altered, leased, or financed in whole or part with federal funds.

OVERVIEW OF THE REHABILITATION ACT OF 1973

The Rehabilitation Act of 1973, and particularly Section 504 and its prohibition against discrimination against persons with disabilities, is the precursor of the Americans with Disabilities Act (ADA) of 1990. It still applies to public and private entities that receive federal funds and may impose on them barrier-free design requirements that are far stricter than the ADA's mandates. For example, a two-story private school building is not required by the ADA to have an elevator, but would be required to have an elevator if the school received federal funding. Religious colleges are exempt from all ADA accessibility requirements, but most are covered by the Rehabilitation Act mandates for barrier-free design. Also, federal departments and agencies are not covered by the ADA, but must provide access under the requirements of Section 504 of the Rehabilitation Act.

OVERVIEW OF THE FAIR HOUSING AMENDMENTS ACT OF 1988 (42 USC 3600 *ET SEQ.*)

The Fair Housing Amendments Act of 1988 extends the nondiscrimination protections of the Fair Housing Act to persons with disabilities and persons with families.

It should be noted that the Fair Housing Accessibility Guidelines are in fact *guidelines* only and have no force of law. The actual guidelines are reprinted in Section 3 of the guideline material, and those alone are enforced by the Department of Housing and Urban Development (HUD) and the federal courts.

Finally, though the guidelines are for "accessible/adaptable dwellings," the level of accessibility afforded by the HUD criteria is significantly lower than that provided by either the Uniform Federal Accessibility Standards (UFAS) or CABO/ANSI A117, 1-1992 standard. As of this writing, the latest edition of the accessibility standard, Icc/ANSI A117.1-1998 has technical requirements for "Type B dwelling units, meant to reflect the Fair Housing requirement, though the A117 Accredited Standard Committee makes clear that these dwelling units are not "accessible" in the traditional sense.

OVERVIEW OF THE AMERICANS WITH DISABILITIES ACT OF 1990 (42 USC 12101 *ET SEQ.*)

The Americans with Disabilities Act (ADA) of 1990 is the most comprehensive law ever passed to protect the civil rights of individuals with disabilities. Its protections far exceed its requirements for barrier-free design, though its access requirements are all that are addressed in this publication. Please refer to EPVA's publication, *Understanding the ADA,* for a general overview of the act.

The ADA comprises five titles: Title I—Employment, Title II—Public Services, Title III—Public Accommodations and Services by Private Entities, Title IV—Telecomunication Relay Services, Title V—Miscellaneous. While the requirements in Title I, to accommodate a qualified employee with a disability, may involve structural alterations to the workplace, it is Title II and III that contain the major barrier-free requirements of the act. It is important to remember that the accessibility requirements of the ADA apply *in addition to,* and not *instead of,* the accessibility requirements of state and local building codes. Where the latter are more restrictive than the ADA, they take precedence over the federal regulations

As mentioned previously, Title II and Title III of the ADA deal with the major barrier-free issues. The applicability and design guidelines related to each are as follows.

TITLE II

Applicability

Title II regulations apply to public services provided by state and local governments, including public school districts, throughway and port authorities, and other governmental units, whether or not they receive federal funds. In order to make the services offered accessible to people with disabilities, new construction and alterations are required to incorporate barrier-free design. Moreover, program accessibility in existing buildings may necessitate alterations in order to enhance the present degree of accessibility.

Design Guidelines

At present, Title II regulations allow the use of either the 1984 Uniform Federal Accessibility Standards (UFAS) or the ADA Accessibility Guide lines (ADAAG). However, the designer is cautioned of the following:

FEDERAL ACCESSIBILITY LEGISLATION

Legislation	*Applies to*	*Jurisdiction*	*Design guidelines*	*Comments*
ADA/Americans with Disabilities Act of 1990 Title I	Employment practices	Equal Employment Opportunities Commission	Not applicable	
Title II	Programs and services of state and local governments	Dept. of Justice (**DOJ**)	**ADAAG** **UFAS**	Extends to *all* activities of state and local governments, whether or not they receive federal funds
Title III	Commercial facilities, public accommodations, private entities (offering exams and courses related to educational and occupational certification)	Dept. of Justice (**DOJ**)	**ADAAG** certified equivalent	
Title IV	Requires relay operators for telephone systems	Federal Communications Commission (**FCC**)	Not applicable	
Architectural Barriers Act of 1968	**Facilities** designed, constructed, altered, and leased with federal funds	**ATBCB (Access Board)**	**UFAS** guidelines	**UFAS** issued by GSA, U.S. Postal Service, Dept. of Defense, Dept. of Housing and Urban Development
Rehabilitation Act of 1973 / Section 504	Programs that receive federal financial assistance	**ATCB (Access Board)**	ANSI 117.1	Precursor of ADA of 1990 (can at times be stricter than **ADA**)
Fair Housing Amendment Act of 1988	Multifamily dwellings	HUD DOJ	**FHAG (Fair Housing Accessibility Guidelines)**	Compliance with guidelines does not provide relief from other requirements such as Rehab Act of 1973 and Architectural Barriers Act of 1968

- Indications are that the UFAS may be phased out as a design criteria option and that a number of federal agencies have already revised their regulations to require compliance with the ADAAG but without the elevator exception.
- If ADAAG design criteria are used, it should be noted that the elevator exception does not apply.
- The ADAAG do not address residential construction or construction of jails and correctional facilities. Under Title II, these types of facilities must be subject to UFAS guidelines.

TITLE III

Applicability

Title III regulations apply primarily to commercial facilities. All newly constructed and altered commercial facilities are subject to the accessibility requirements of Title III. Existing public accommodations may also be subject to additional access requirements through the barrier removal provisions of the law. In order to be considered a "public accommodation" covered under Title III, an entity must be private and must own, lease, lease to, or operate a place of public accommodation. Moreover, places of public accommodation must fall within at least one of the following 12 categories:

1. *Places of lodging:* An inn, hotel, motel, or other place of lodging, except for an establishment located within a building that contains no more than five rooms for rent or hire and that is actually occupied by the proprieter of the establishment as the residence of the proprieter.
2. *Establishments serving food or drink:* A restaurant, bar, or other establishment serving food or drink.
3. *Places of exhibition or entertainment*
4. *Places of public gathering:* An auditorium, convention center, lecture hall, or other place of public gathering.
5. *Sales or rental establishments:* A bakery, grocery store, clothing store, hardware store, shopping center, or other sales or rental establishment.
6. *Service establishments:* A laundromat, dry cleaner, bank, barber shop, travel service, shoe repair service, funeral parlor, gas station, office of an accountant or lawyer, pharmacy, insurance office, professional office of a health care provider, hospital, or other service establishment.
7. *Stations used for specified public transportation:* A terminal, depot, or other station used for specified public transportation.
8. *Places of public display or collection:* A museum, library, gallery, or other place of public display or collection.
9. *Places of recreation:* A restaurant, bar, or other establishment serving food or drink.
10. *Places of education*
11. *Social service center establishments:* A day care center, senior citizen center, homeless shelter, food bank, adoption agency, or other social service center establishment.
12. *Places of exercise or recreation:* A gymnasium, health spa, bowling alley, golf course, or other place of exercise or recreation.

NOTE: The 12 categories above constitute an exhaustive list. The examples given, however, are not, and are intended to apply as illustrations. Accordingly, many of the categories listed could include many facilities other than those listed. For additional and more detailed information, the reader is referred to the Access Board web site (www.access-board.gov), from which ADAAG and other invaluable information may be downloaded. The Access Board can also be contacted by e-mail (info@access-board.gov) or by fax (202-272-5447).

Design Guidelines

The Americans with Disabilities Act Accessibility Guidelines (ADAAG) set the guidelines for accessibility to places of public accommodation and commercial facilities by individuals with disabilities. It should be noted that departures from these guidelines are permitted where the alternative designs will provide equivalent or greater access to the facility. The ADAAG also provide procedures for departure from the guidelines in the case of historic buildings when compliance with said guidelines would destroy or threaten the historic significance of the building.

It is not possible to include in this publication the entire ADAAG text. The ADAAG graphics, however, are included on the following pages. The reader is cautioned that these graphics are frequently increased in quantity and subject matter. It is essential, therefore, that the designer ensure that he or she is working with the most current graphics available at the time.

National and State Building Codes

Article 2.2 of the ADAAG allows for departures from particular scoping and technical requirements by use of other designs and technologies "where the alternative designs and technologies used will provide substantially equivalent or greater access to and usability of the facility." Accordingly, if the accessibility requirements of certain national and state building codes do, in fact, provide such equivalent or greater access, they may be employed where required.

Local and state governmental agencies having jurisdiction must submit their building codes to the DOJ for review, to determine if they meet the same or comparable accessibility standards. Once the DOJ so certifies, a project that complies with that state or local code will be considered to comply with the ADA.

Where the ADA (or Fair Housing) requirements are more restrictive, they take precedence over state or local codes. The reader is cautioned, however, that in many instances it may be difficult to determine which requirements are more restrictive.

While state or local authorities having jurisdiction may submit their codes to the DOJ for review, these jurisdictions are not mandated to have any accessibility requirements, much less requirements that meet or exceed the federal regulations. Far too many designers still assume that compliance with a local code constitutes compliance with federal law.

In addition, HUD has no similar certification process for state and local codes vis-à-vis the Fair Housing requirements. However, HUD has indicated that compliance with ICC International Building Code 2000 with the 2001 supplement is substantially equivalent to compliance with the Federal Housing regulations.

ADAAG
Wheelchair Clearances/Circulation Spaces

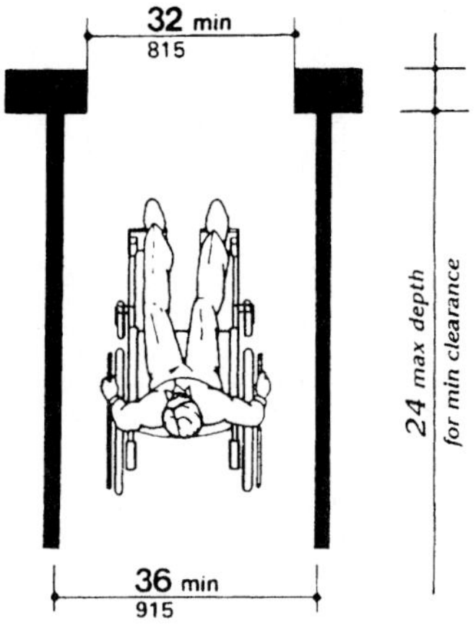

Fig. 1 Minimum clear width for single wheelchair

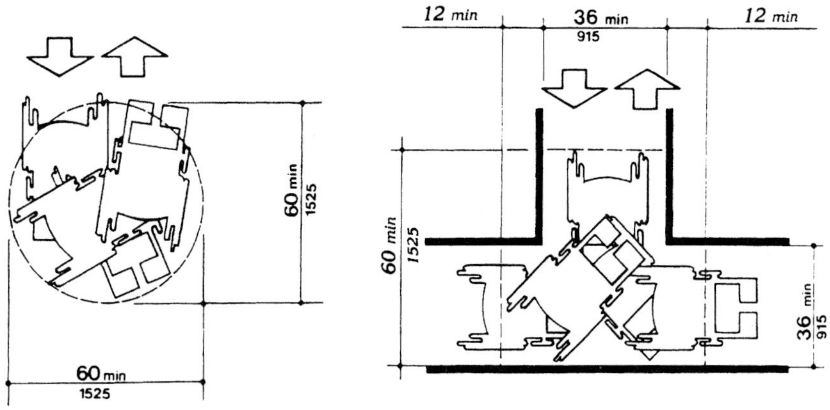

(a)
60-in (1525-mm)-Diameter Space

(b)
T-Shaped Space for 180° Turns

Fig. 3 Wheelchair turning space

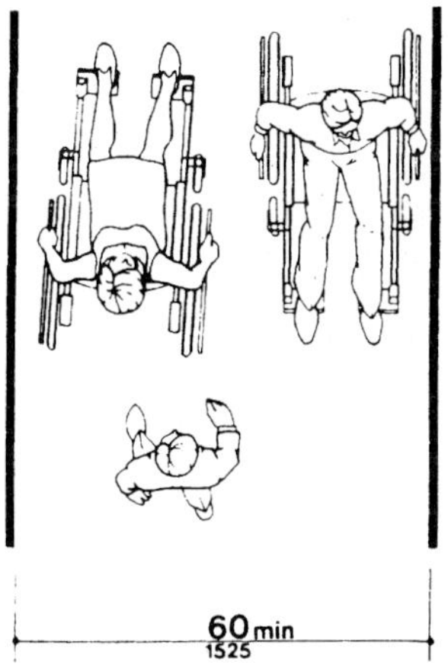

Fig. 2 Minimum clear width for two wheelchairs

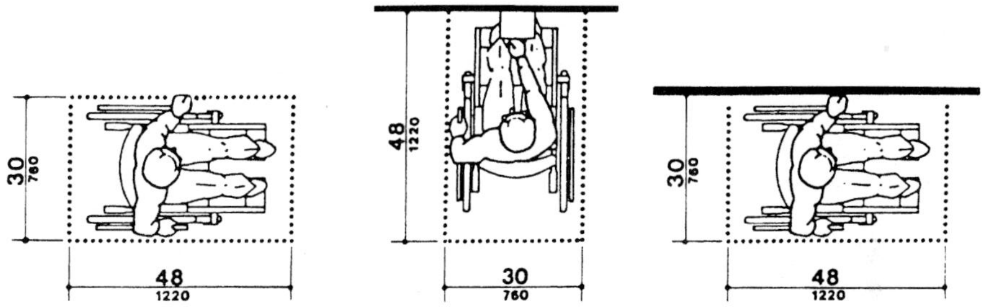

(a)
Clear Floor Space

(b)
Forward Approach

(c)
Parallel Approach

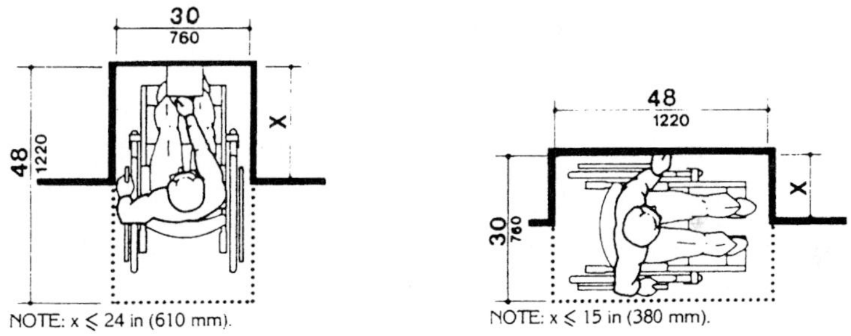

NOTE: x ≤ 24 in (610 mm).

NOTE: x ≤ 15 in (380 mm).

(d)
Clear Floor Space in Alcoves

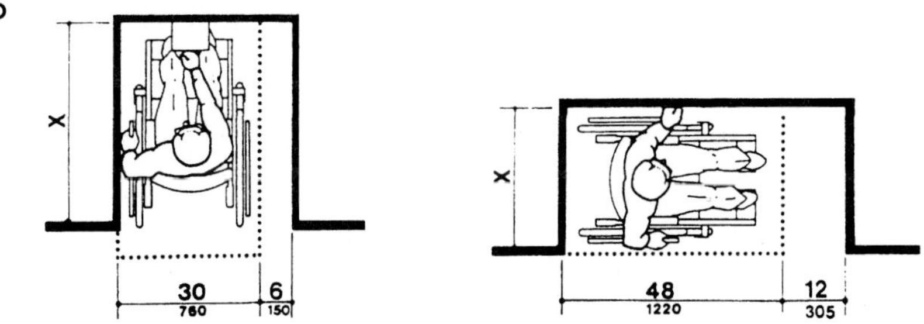

NOTE: If x > 24 in (610 mm), then an additional maneuvering clearance of 6 in (150 mm) shall be provided as shown.

NOTE: If x > 15 in (380 mm), then an additional maneuvering clearance of 12 in (305 mm) shall be provided as shown.

(e)
Additional Maneuvering Clearances for Alcoves

Fig. 4 Minimum clear floor space for wheelchairs

ADAAG
Wheelchair Clearances/Forward and Side Arm Reach

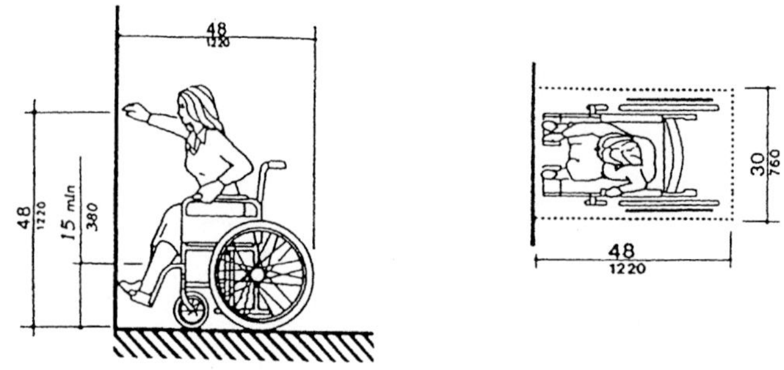

(a)
High Forward Reach Limit

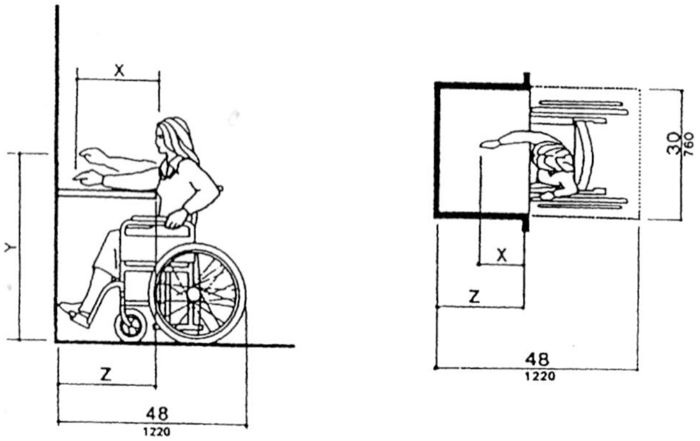

NOTE: x shall be ≤ 25 in (635 mm); z shall be ≥ x. When x < 20 in (510 mm), then y shall be 48 in (1220 mm) maximum. When x is 20 to 25 in (510 to 635 mm), then y shall be 44 in (1120 mm) maximum.

(b)
Maximum Forward Reach over an Obstruction

Fig. 5 Forward reach

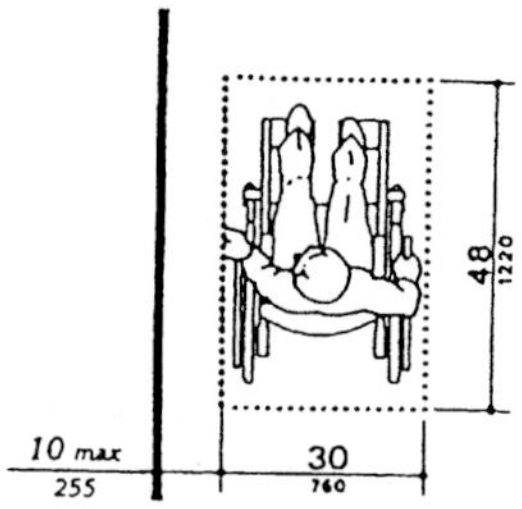

(a)
Clear Floor Space Parallel Approach

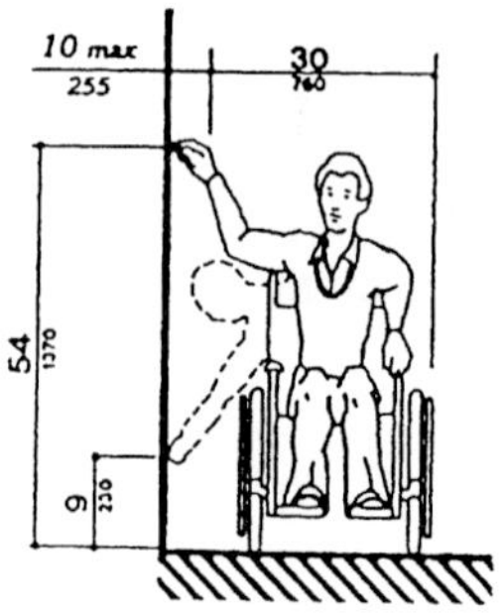

(b)
High and Low Side Reach Limits

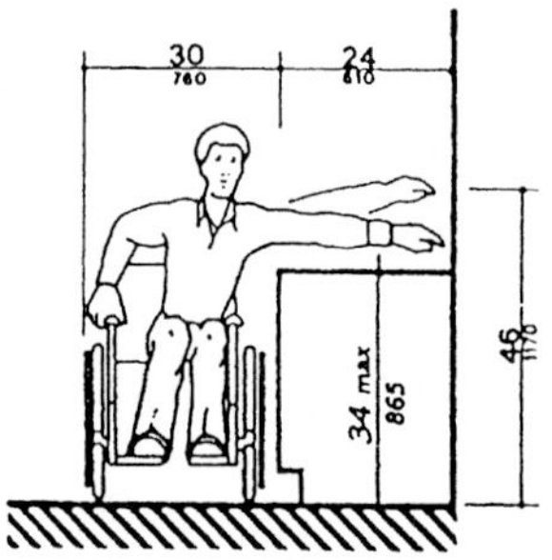

(c)
Maximum Side Reach over an Obstruction

Fig. 6 Side reach

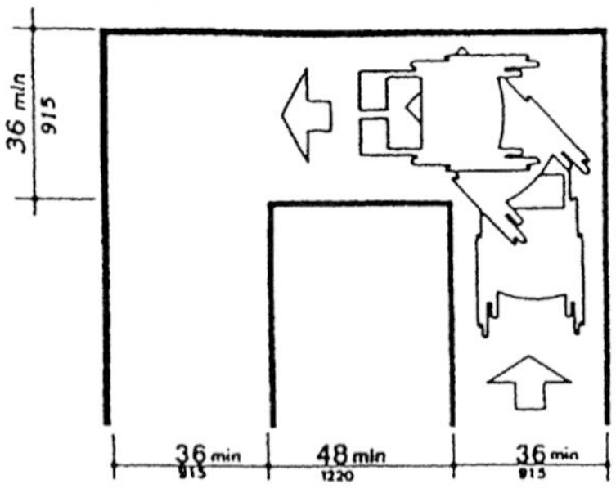

(a)
90° Turn

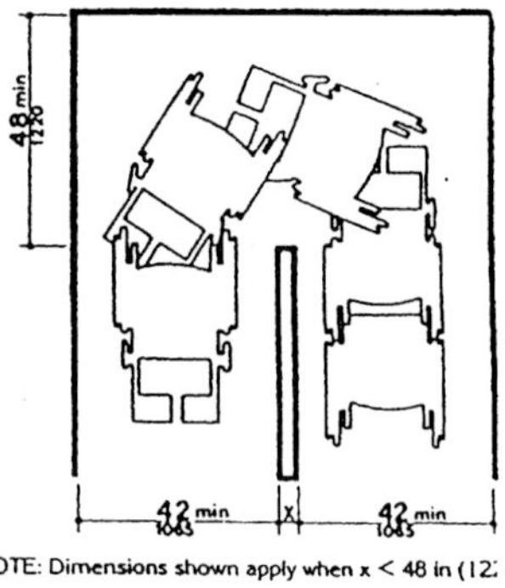

NOTE: Dimensions shown apply when x < 48 in (12:

(b)
Turns around an Obstruction

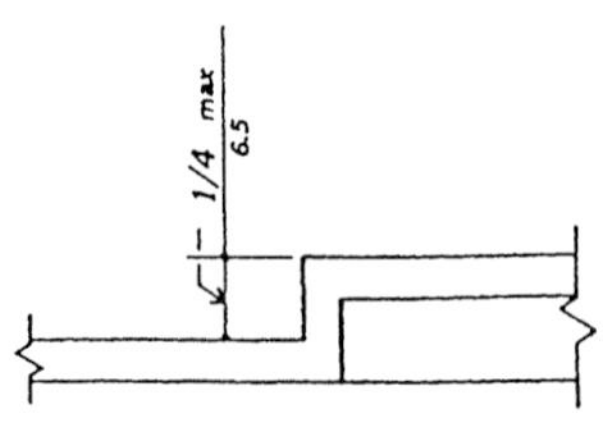

(c)
Changes in level

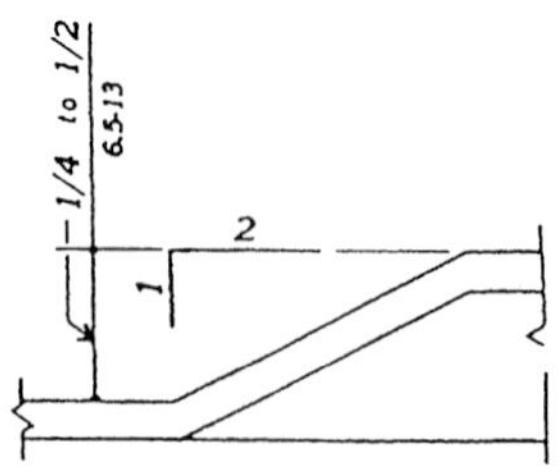

(d)
Changes in level

Figure 7

(a)
Walking Parallel to a Wall

(b)
Walking Perpendicular to a Wall

(c)
Free-Standing Overhanging Objects

(c-1)
Overhead Hazards

(d)
Objects Mounted on Posts or Pylons

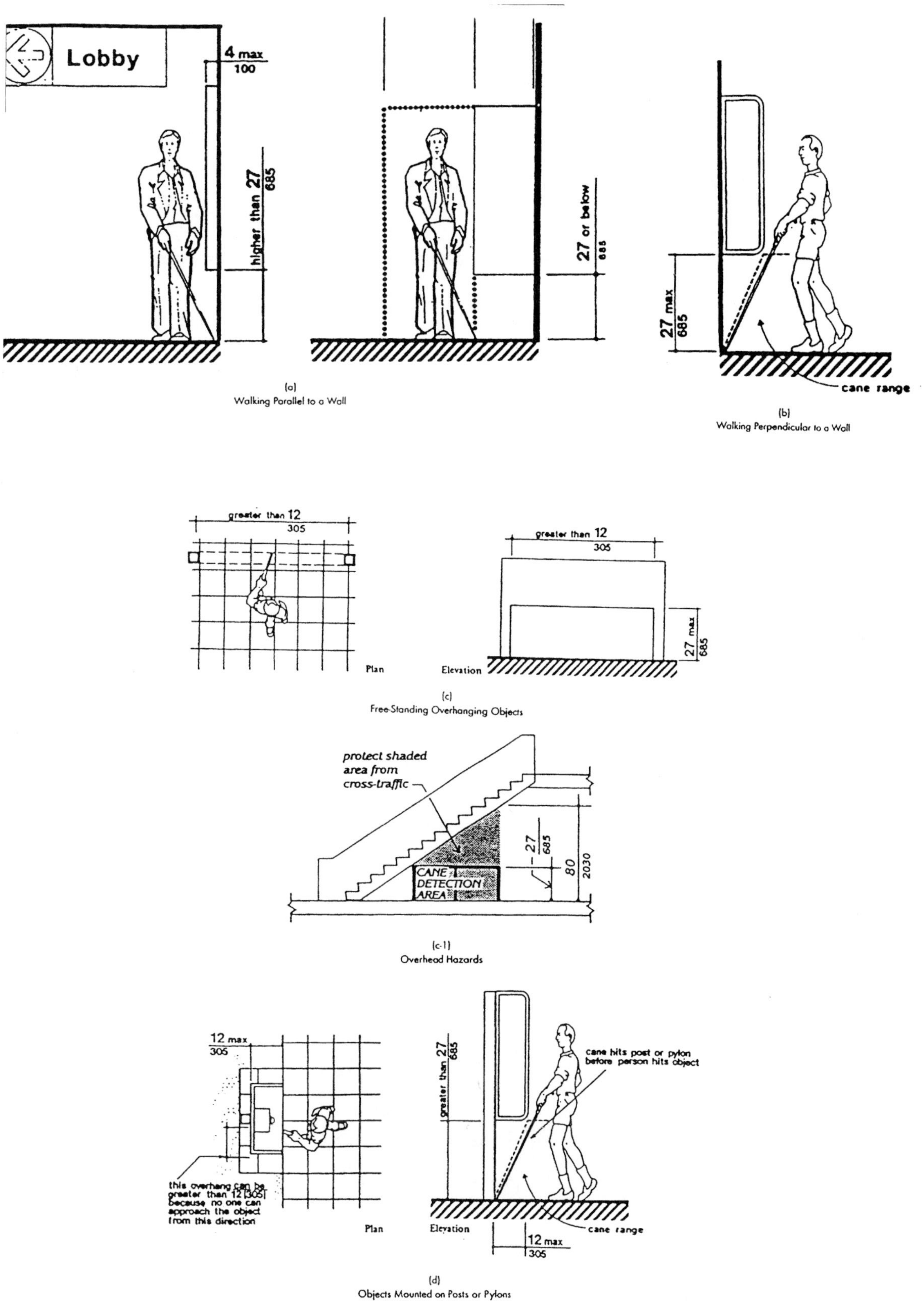

Fig. 8 Protruding objects

ADAAG
Wall-Mounted Object Protection/Carpets/Gratings

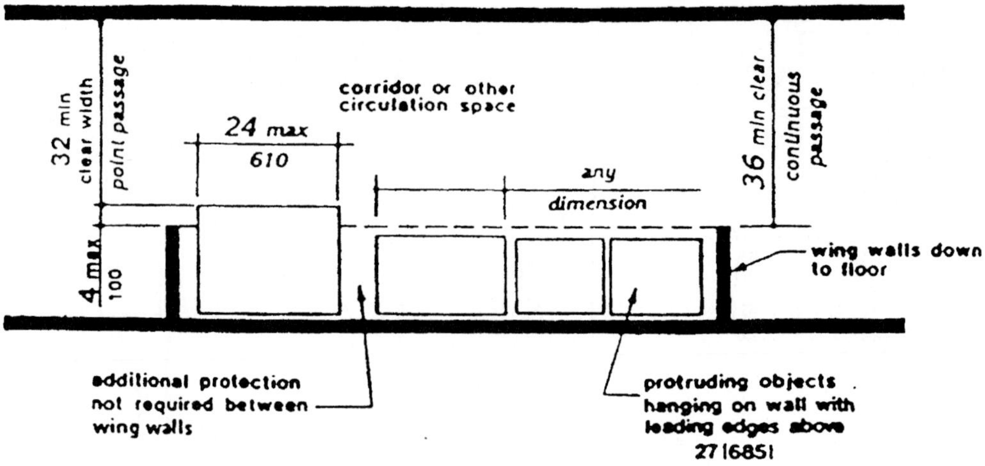

(e)
Example of Protection around Wall-Mounted Objects and Measurements of Clear Widths

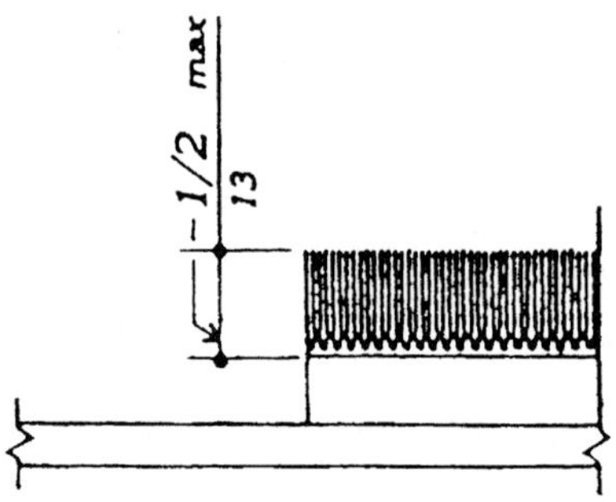

(f)
Carpet Pile Thickness

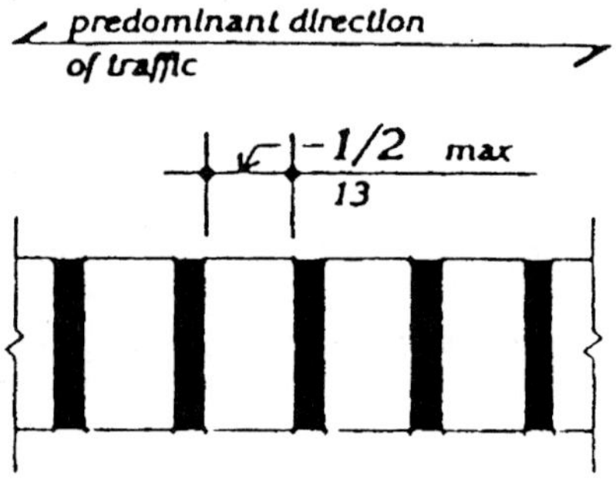

(h)
Gratings

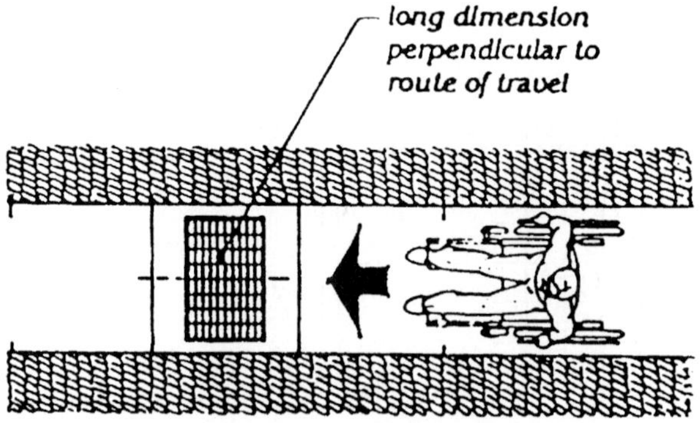

(h)
Grating Orientation

Fig. 8 Protruding objects (*cont.*)

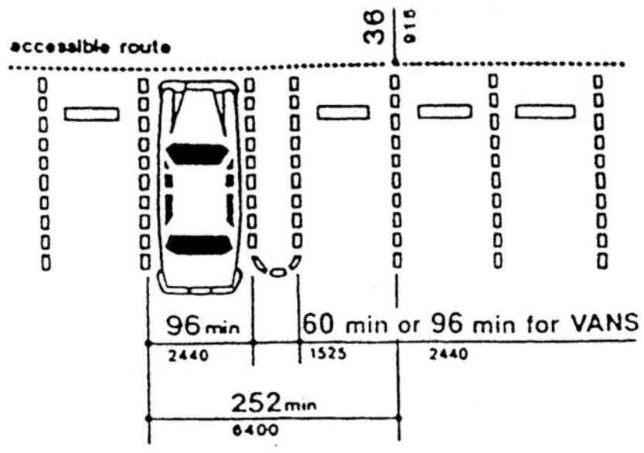

Fig. 9 Dimensions of parking spaces

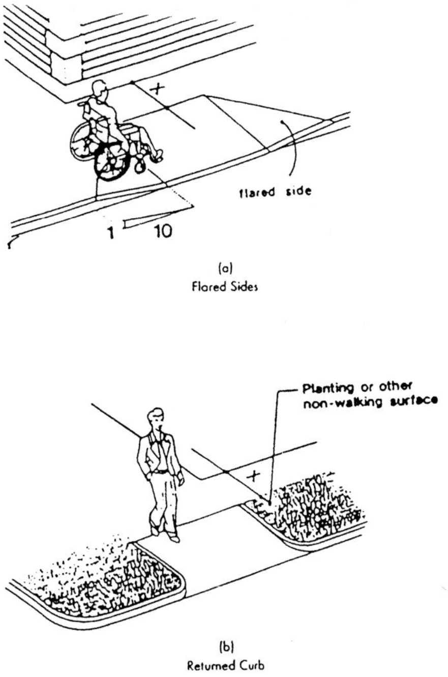

Fig. 12 Sides of curb ramps

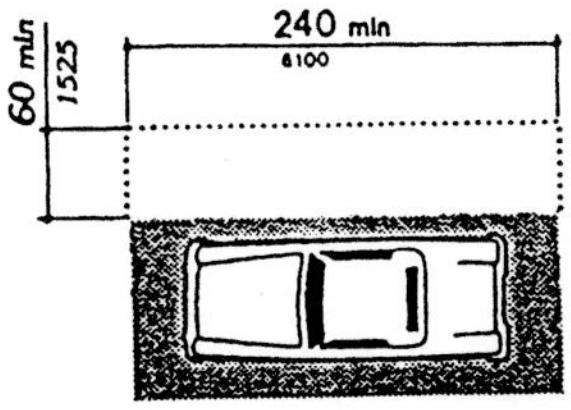

Fig. 10 Access aisle at passenger loading zones

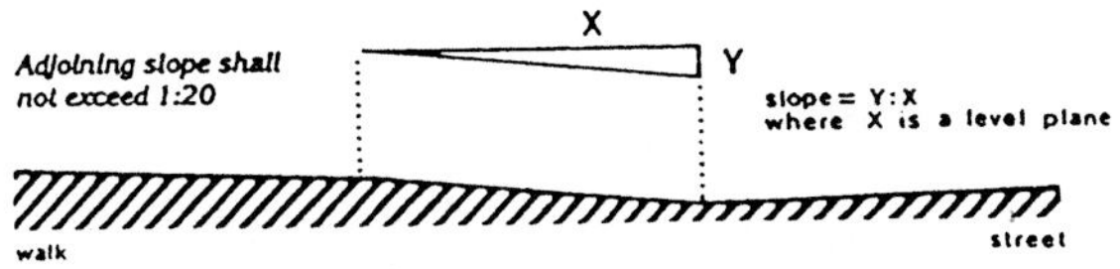

Fig. 11 Measurement of curb ramp slopes

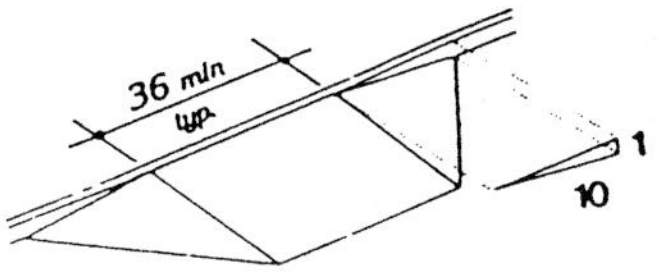

Fig. 13 Built-up curb ramp

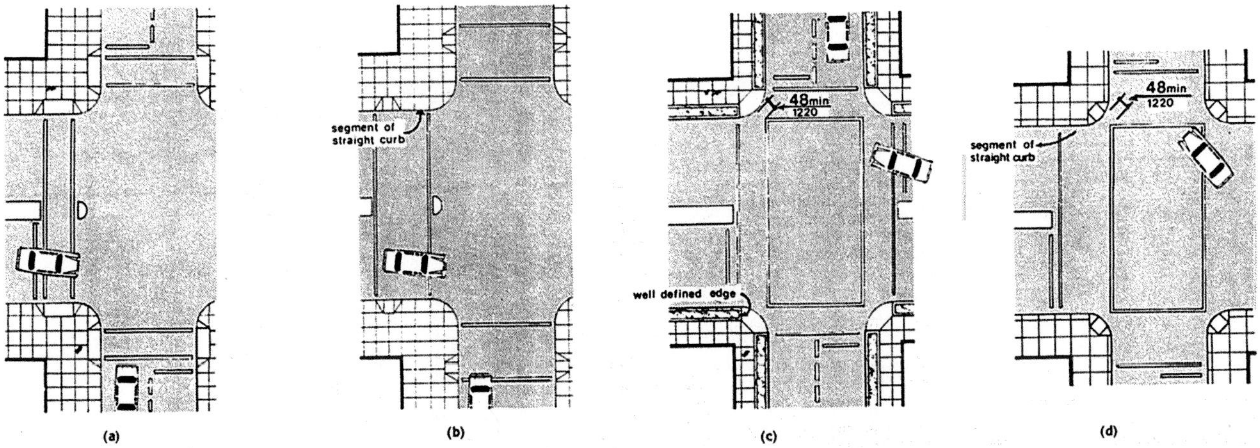

Fig. 15 Curb ramps at marked crossings

ADAAG
Ramp/Railing/Step Details

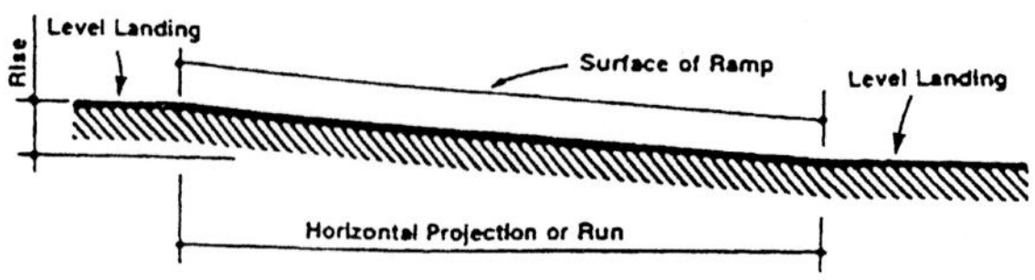

Slope	Maximum Rise in	Maximum Rise mm	Maximum Horizontal Projection ft	Maximum Horizontal Projection m
1:12 to < 1:16	30	760	30	9
1:16 to < 1:20	30	760	40	12

Fig. 16 Components of a single ramp run and sample ramp dimensions

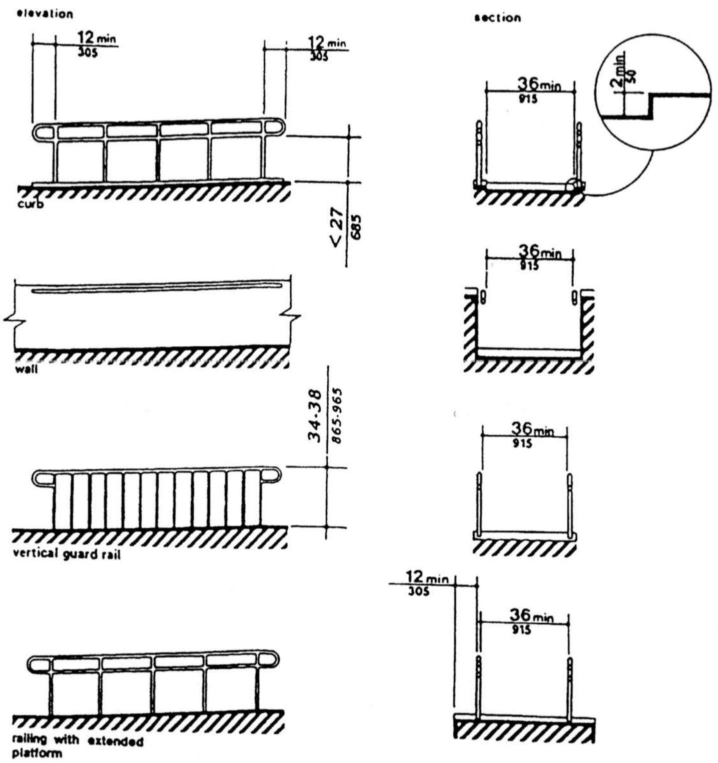

Fig. 17 Examples of edge protection and handrail extensions

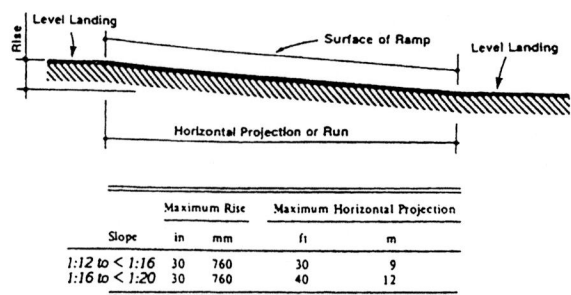

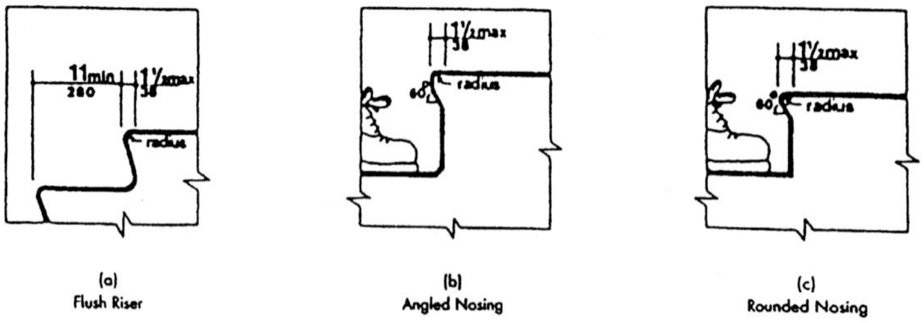

Fig. 18 Usable tread width and examples of acceptable nosings

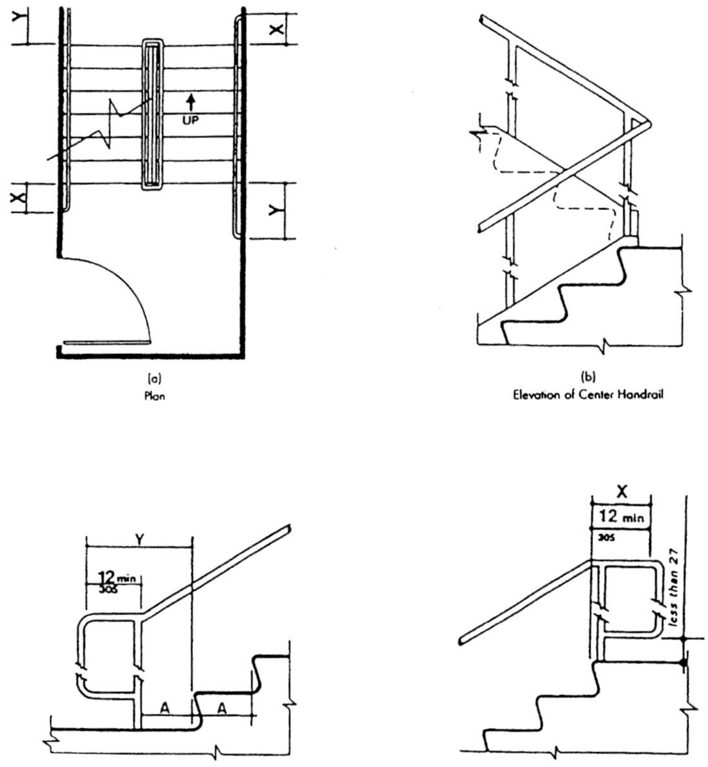

(a)
Plan

(b)
Elevation of Center Handrail

(c)
Extension at Bottom of Run

(d)
Extension at Top of Run

NOTE.
X is the 12 in minimum handrail extension required at each top riser.
Y is the minimum handrail extension of 12 in plus the width of one tread that is required at each bottom riser.

Fig. 19 Stair handrails

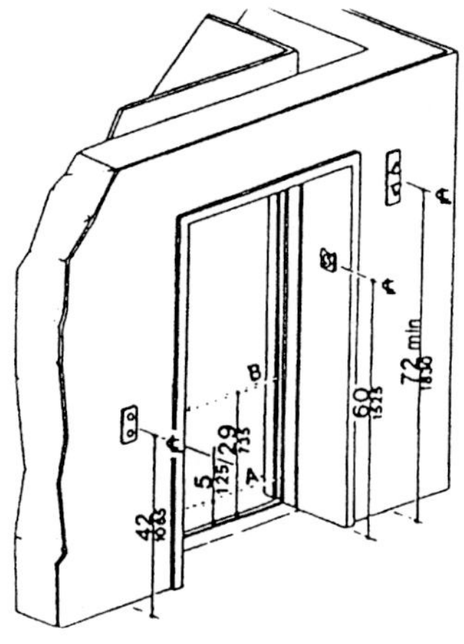

Fig. 20 Hoistway and elevator entrances

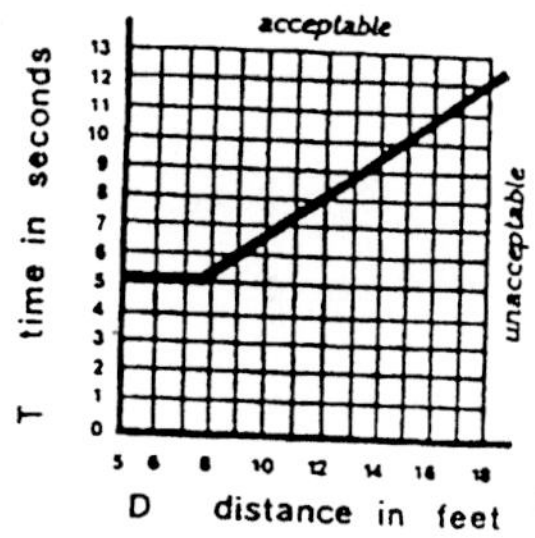

Fig. 21 Graph of timing equation

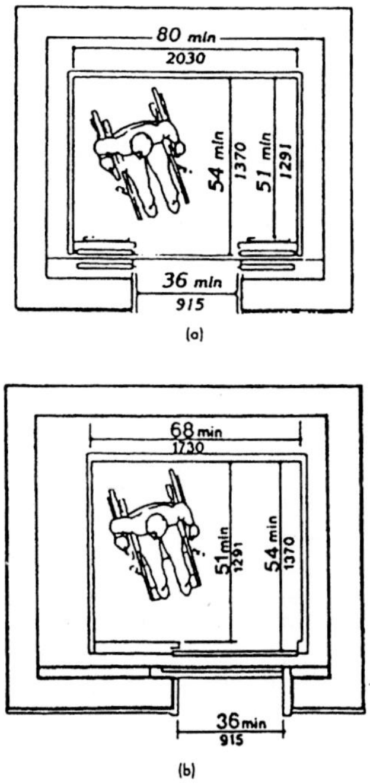

(a)

(b)

Fig. 22 Minimum dimensions of elevator cars

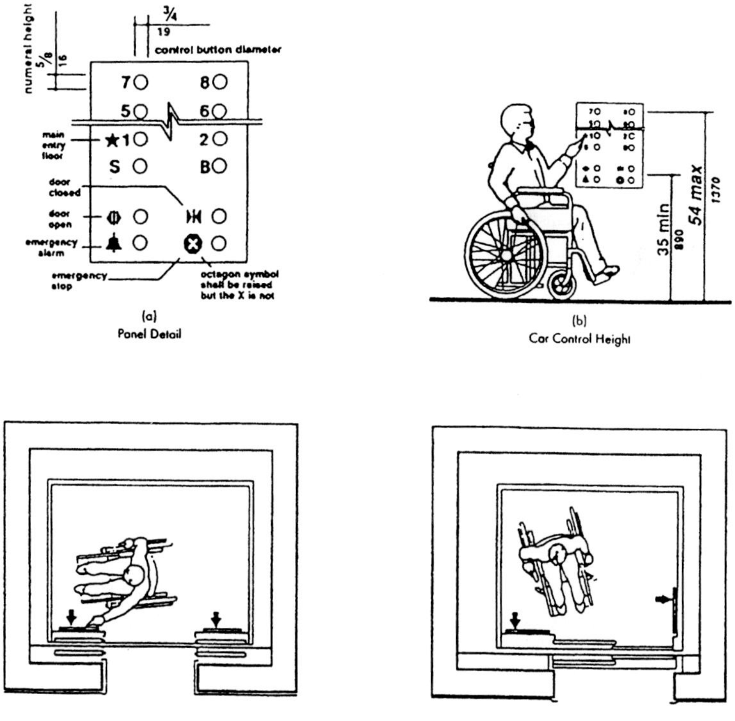

(a)
Panel Detail

(b)
Car Control Height

(c)
Alternate Locations of Panel with Center Opening Door

(d)
Alternate Locations of Panel with Side Opening Door

Fig. 23 Car controls

ADAAG
Wheelchair Clearances/Door Openings

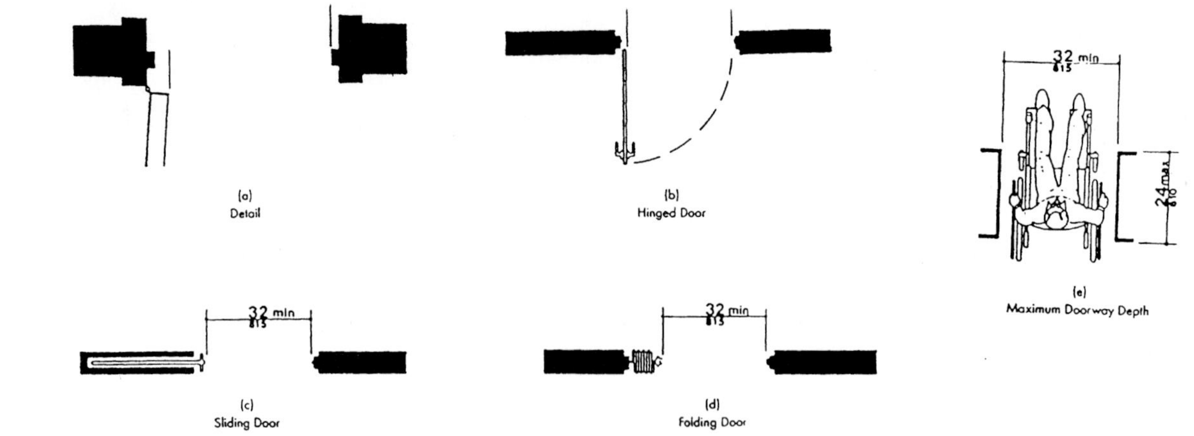

Fig. 24 Clear doorway width and depth

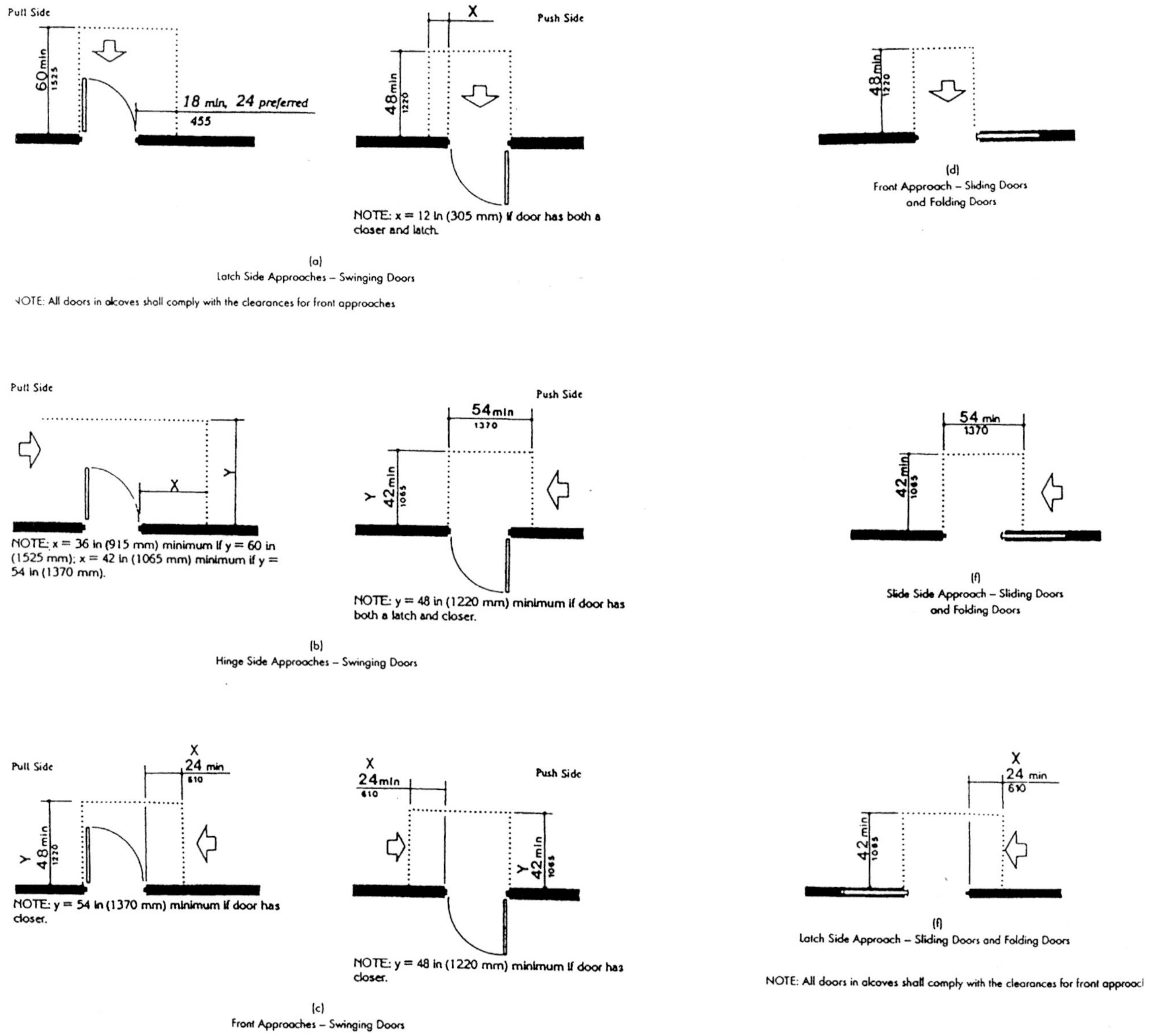

Fig. 25 Maneuvering clearances of doors

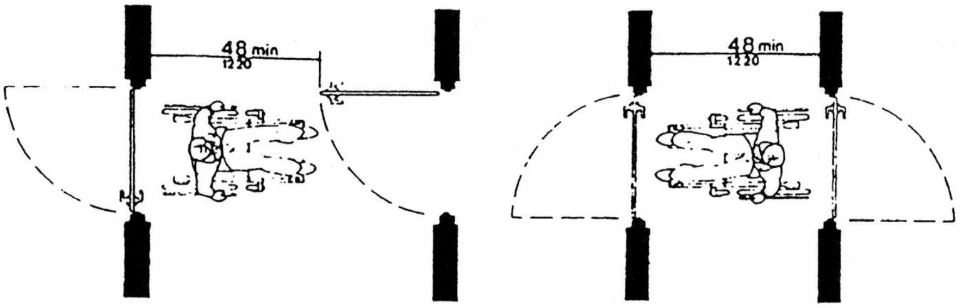

Fig. 26 Two hinged doors in series

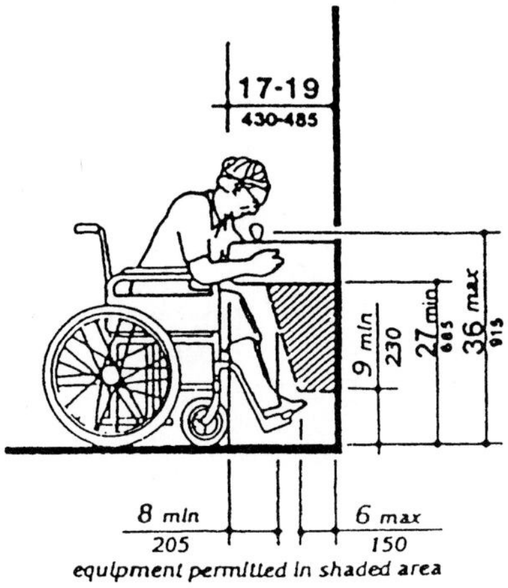

(a)
Spout Height and
Knee Clearance

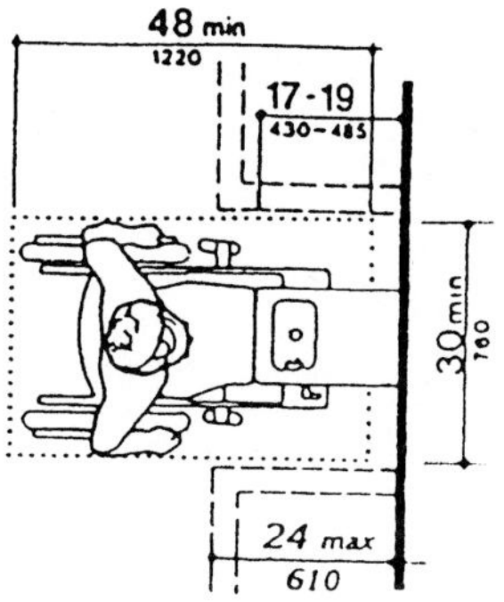

(b)
Clear Floor Space

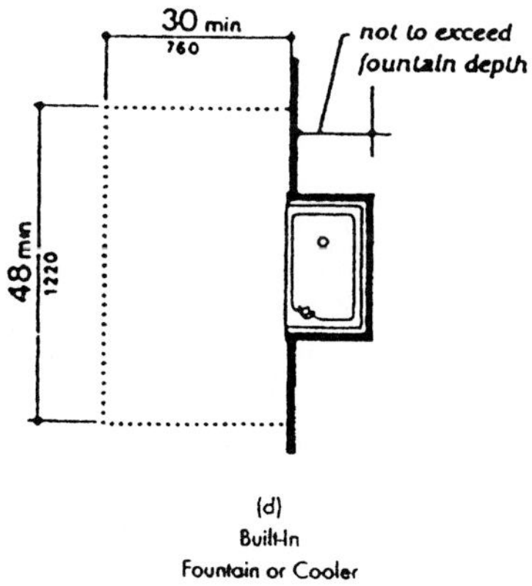

(d)
Built-In
Fountain or Cooler

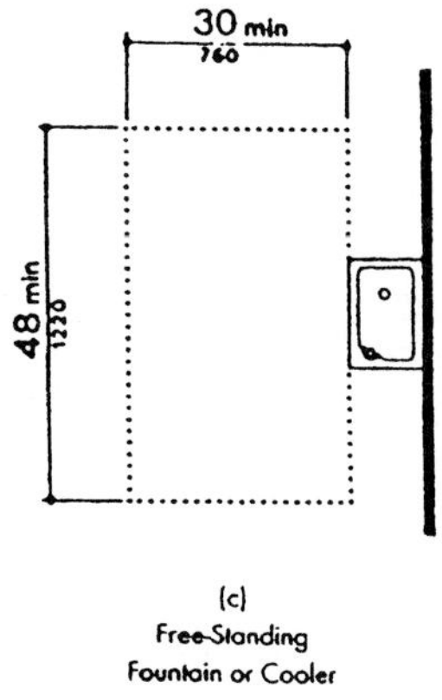

(c)
Free-Standing
Fountain or Cooler

Fig. 27 Drinking fountains and water coolers

ADAAG

Wheelchair Clearances/Water Closets/Lavs

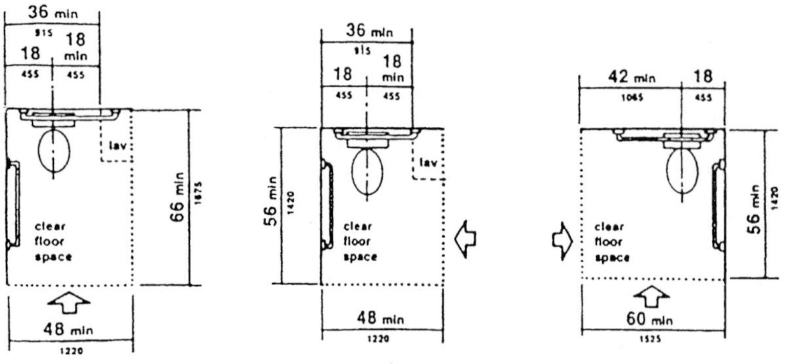

Fig. 28 Clear floor space at water closets

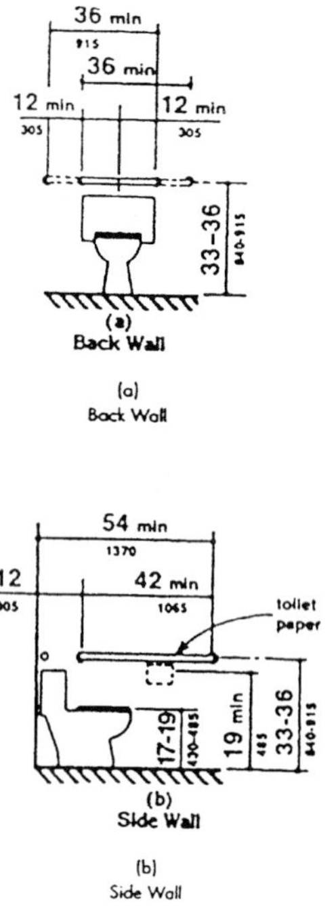

Fig. 29 Grab bars at water closets

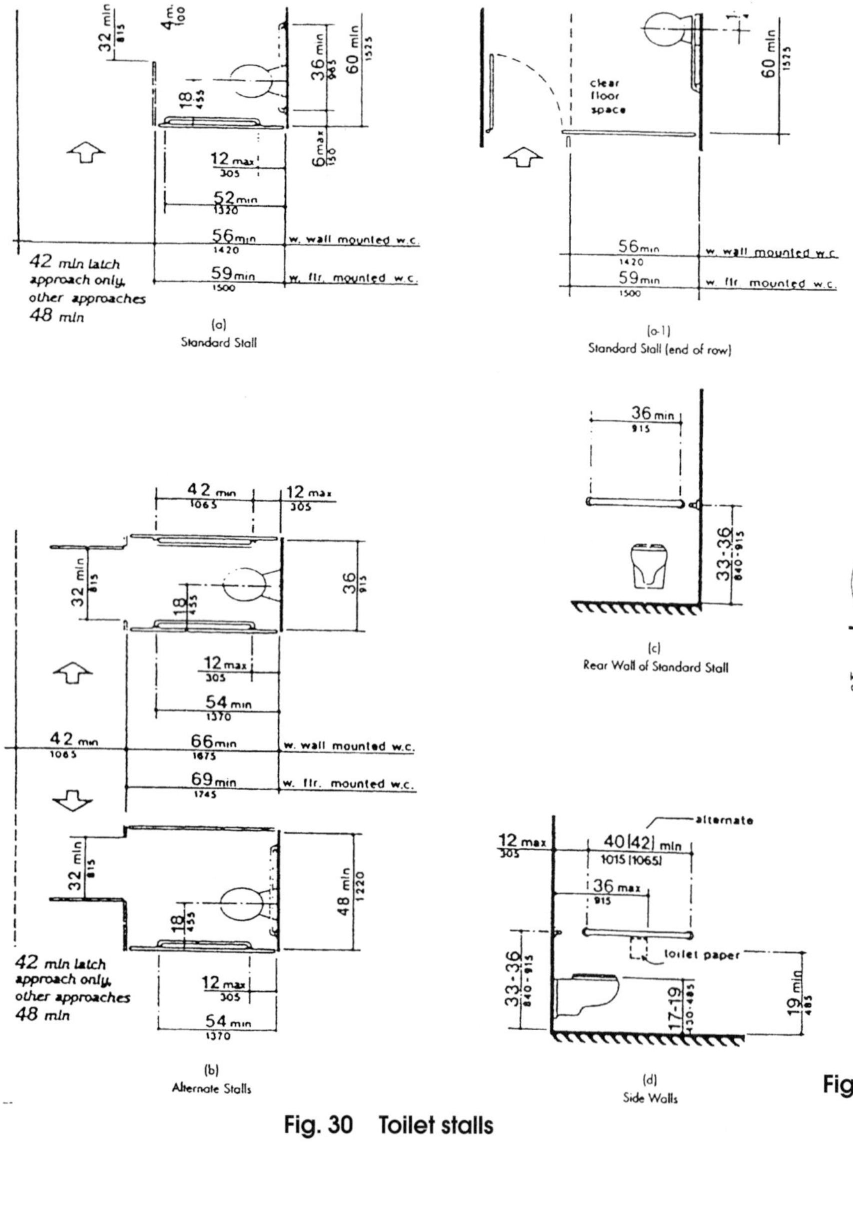

Fig. 30 Toilet stalls

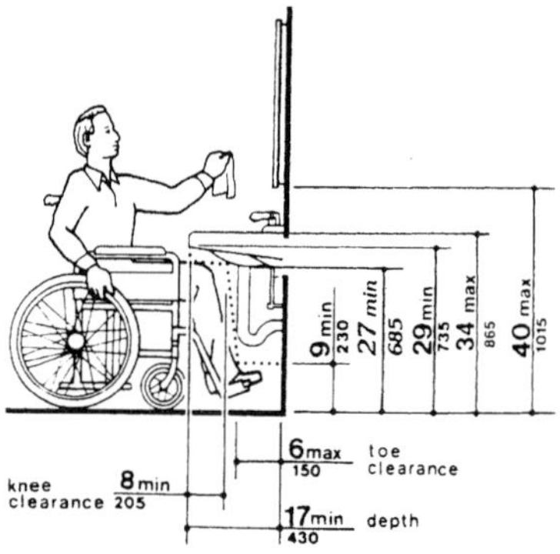

Fig. 31 Lavatory clearances

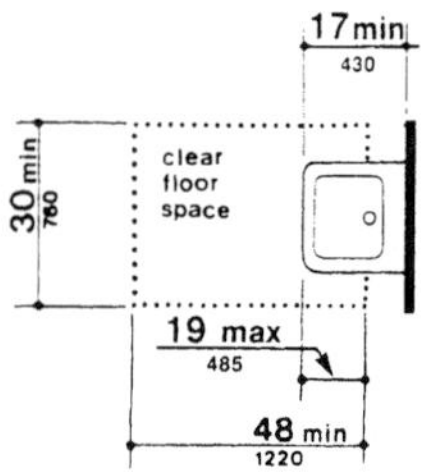

Fig. 32 Clear floor space at lavatories

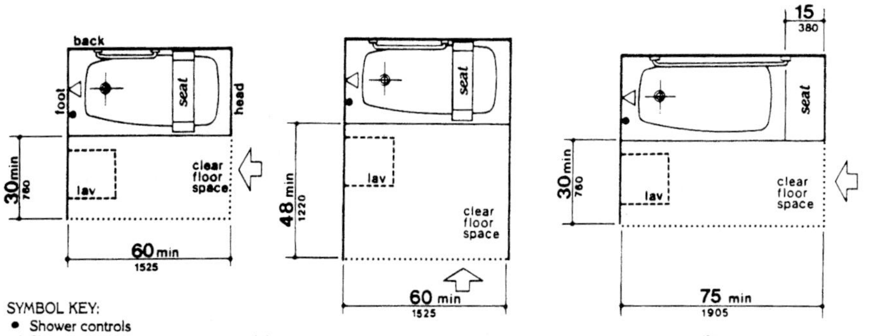

SYMBOL KEY:
• Shower controls
◁ Shower head
Drain

(a)
With Seat in Tub

(b)
With Seat at Head of Tub

Fig. 33 Clear floor space at bathtubs

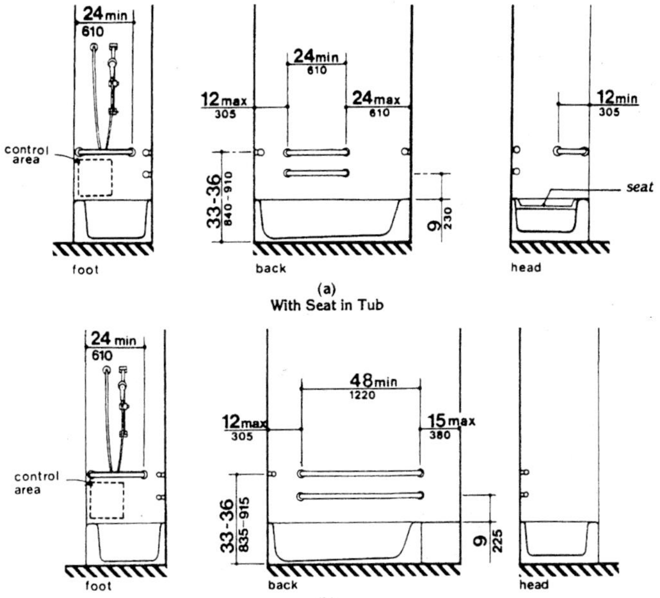

(a)
With Seat in Tub

(b)
With Seat at Head of Tub

Fig. 34 Grab bars at bathtubs

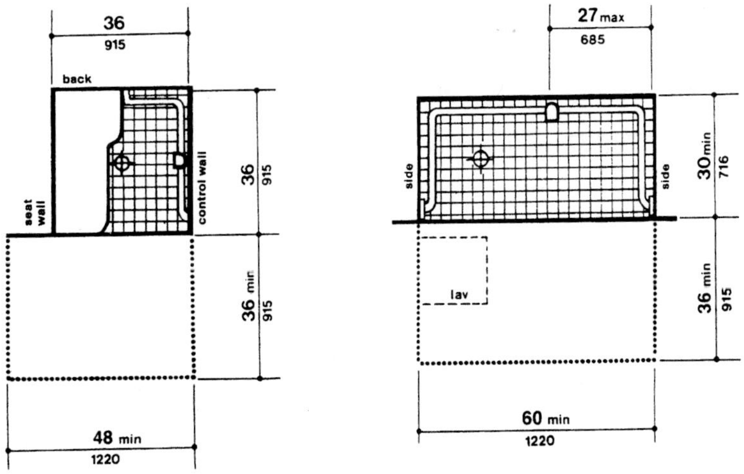

(a)
36-in by 36-in
(915-mm by 915-mm) Stall

(b)
30-in by 60-in
(760-mm by 1525-mm) Stall

Fig. 35 Shower size and clearances

ADAAG
Shower Seats/Grab Bars/Shelving

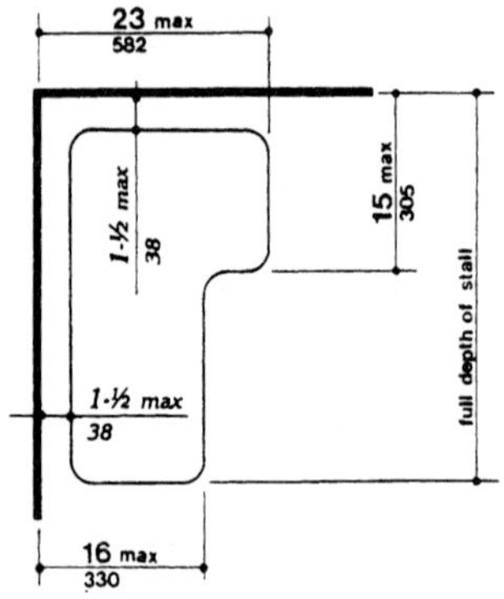

Fig. 36 Shower seat design

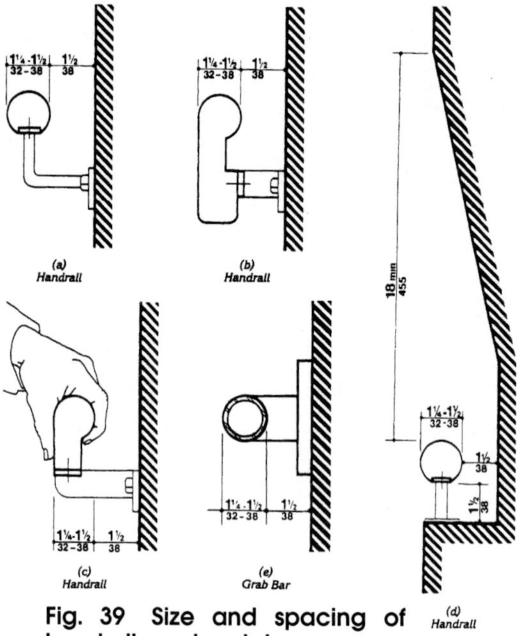

Fig. 39 Size and spacing of handrails and grab bars

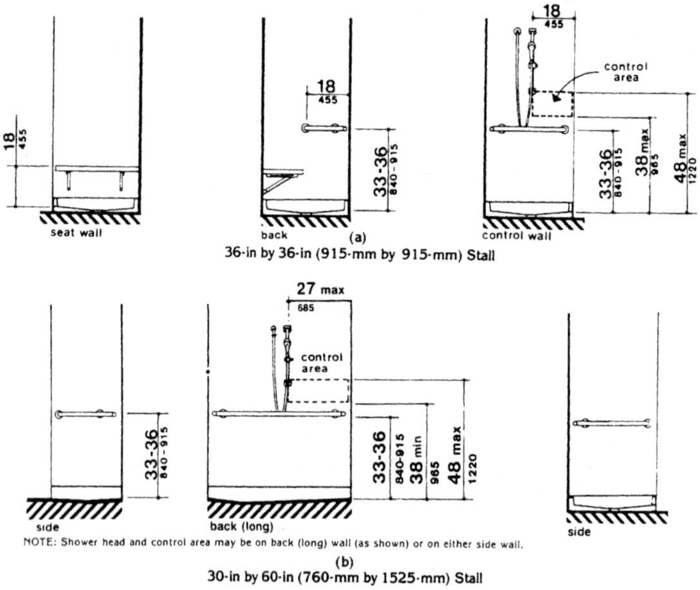

Fig. 37 Grab bars at shower stalls

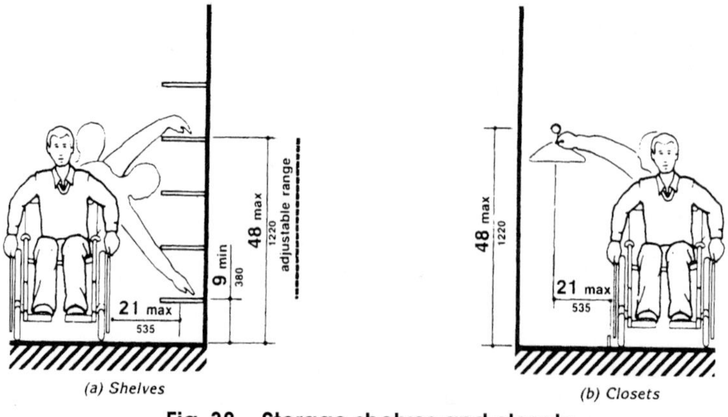

Fig. 38 Storage shelves and closets

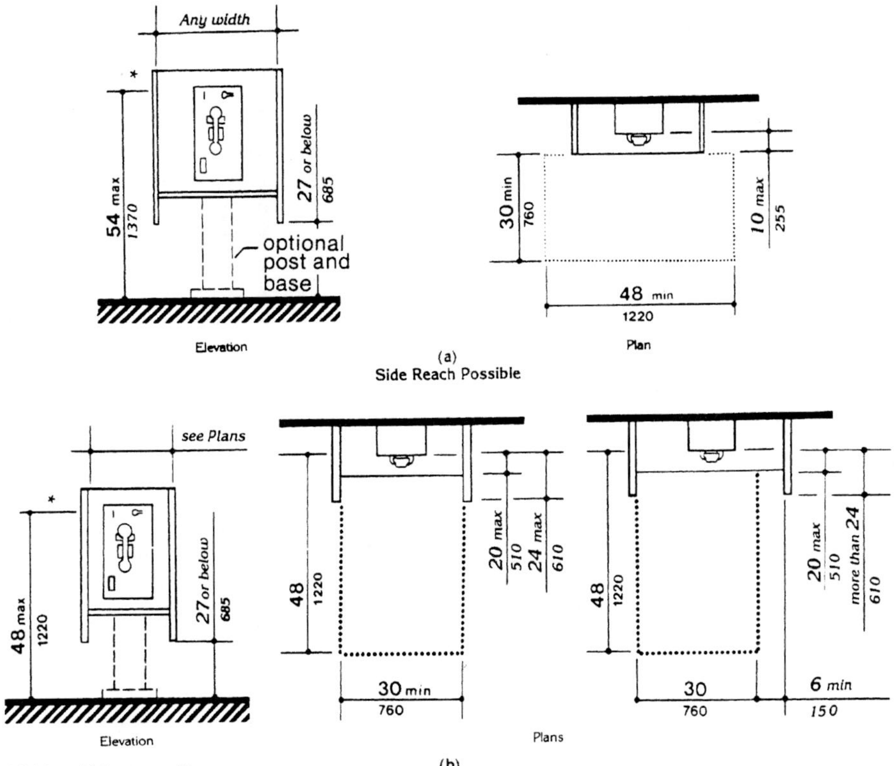

*Height to highest operable parts which are essential to basic operation of telephone.

Fig. 44 Mounting heights and clearances for telephones

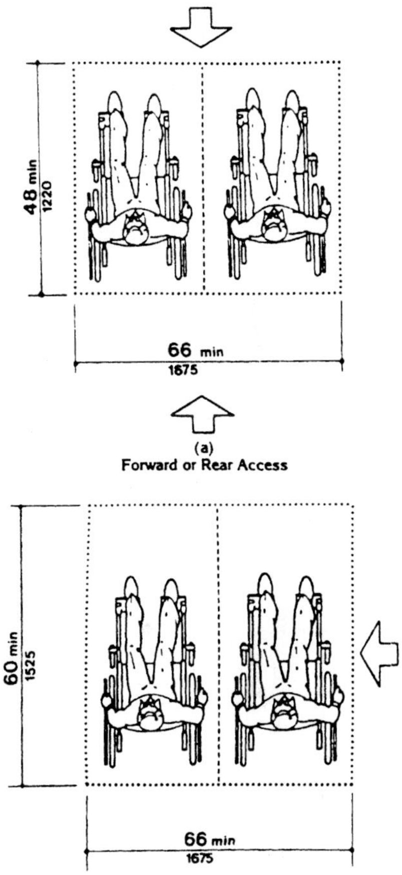

Fig. 46 Space requirements for wheelchair seating spaces in series

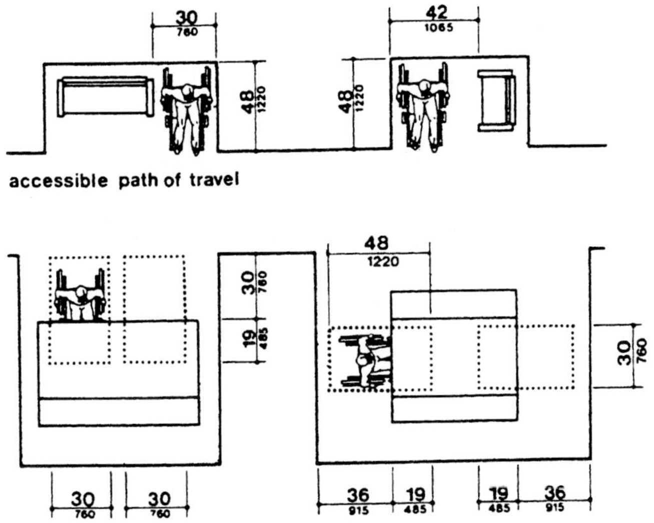

Fig. 45 Minimum clearances for seating and tables

ADAAG

Wheelchair Clearance/Food Service/Roll-in Shower

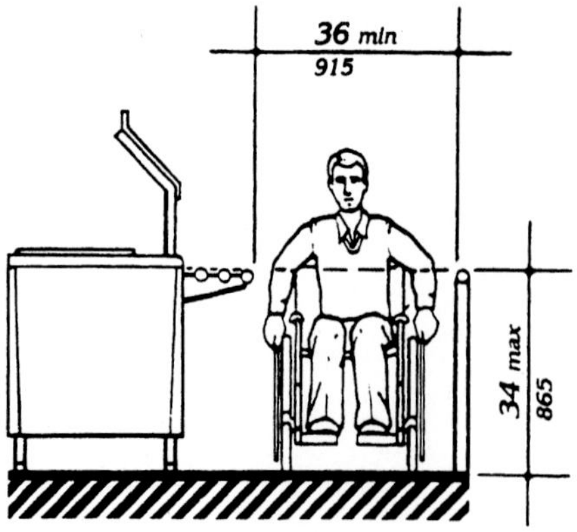

Fig. 53 Food service lines

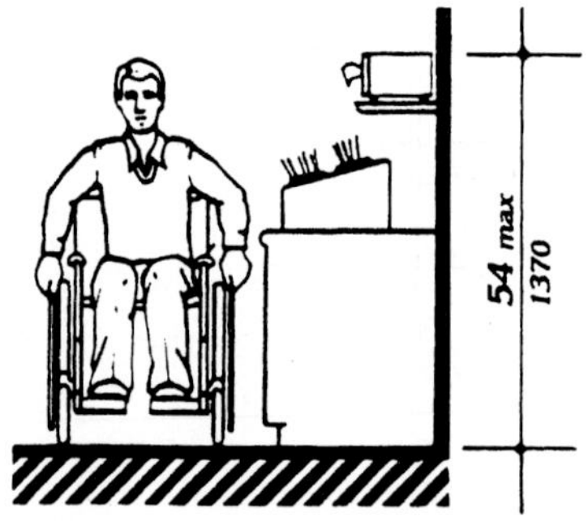

Fig. 54 Tableware areas

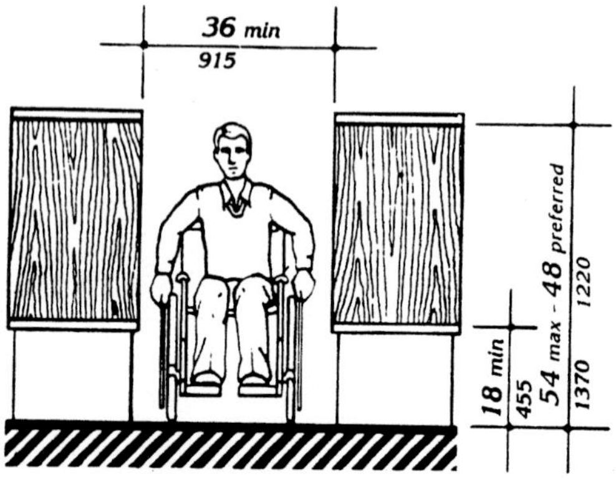

Fig. 55 Card catalog

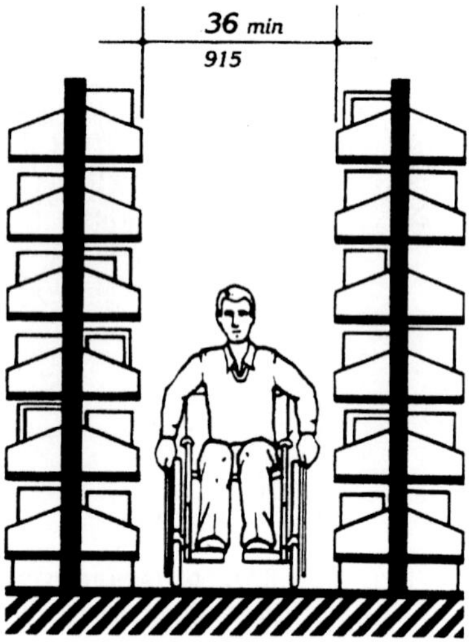

Fig. 56 Stacks

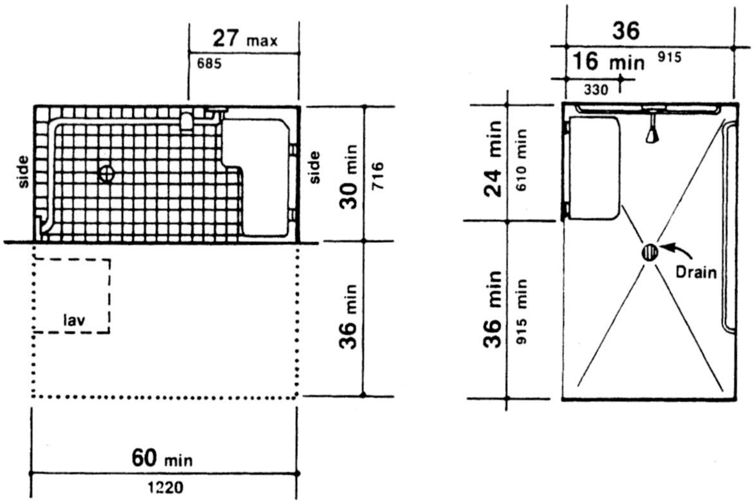

(a) (b)

Fig. 57 Roll-in shower with folding seat

ADAAG
Wheelchair Dimensions/Clearances/Parking Space Design

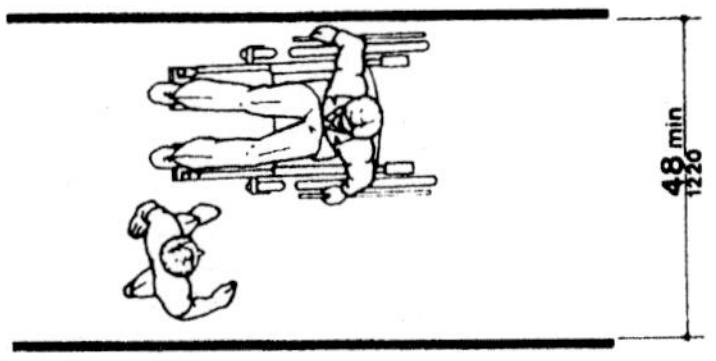

Fig. A1
Minimum Passage Width for One Wheelchair and One Ambulatory Person

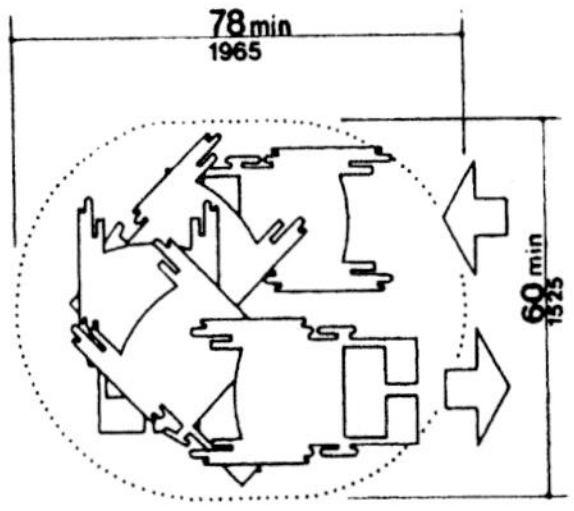

Fig. A2
Space Needed for Smooth U-Turn in a Wheelchair

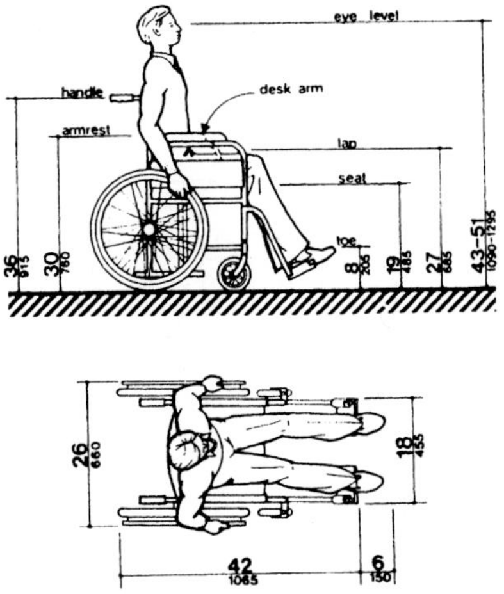

NOTE: Footrests may extend further for tall people

Fig. A3
Dimensions of Adult-Sized Wheelchairs

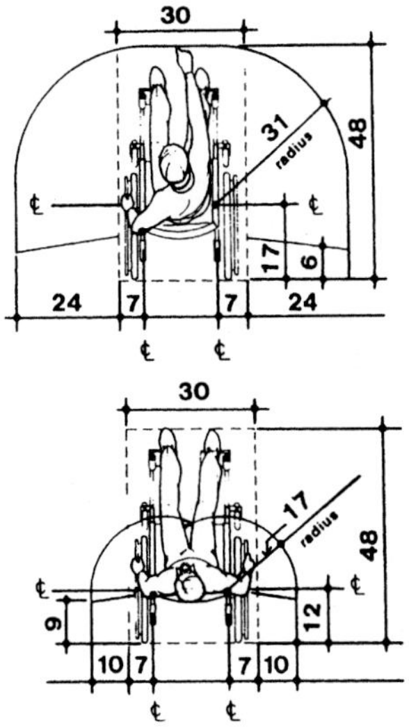

Fig. A3 (a)

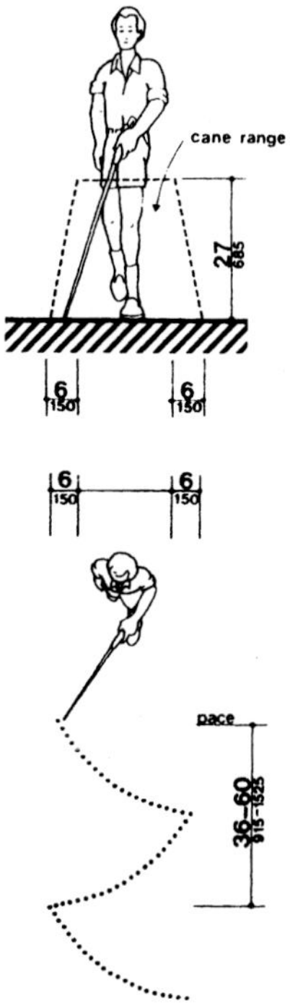

Fig. A4
Cane Technique

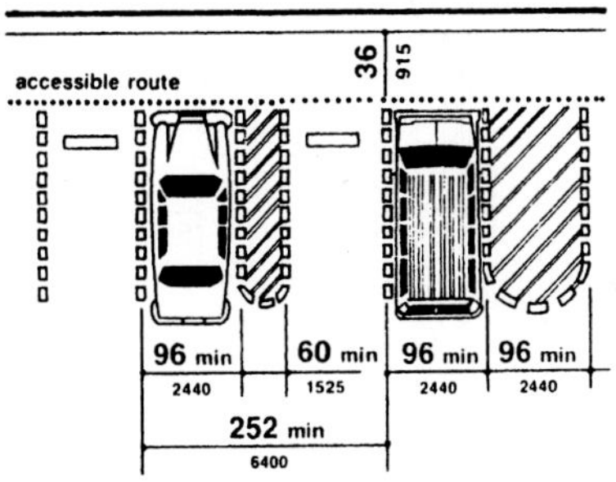

(a)
Van Accessible Space at End Row

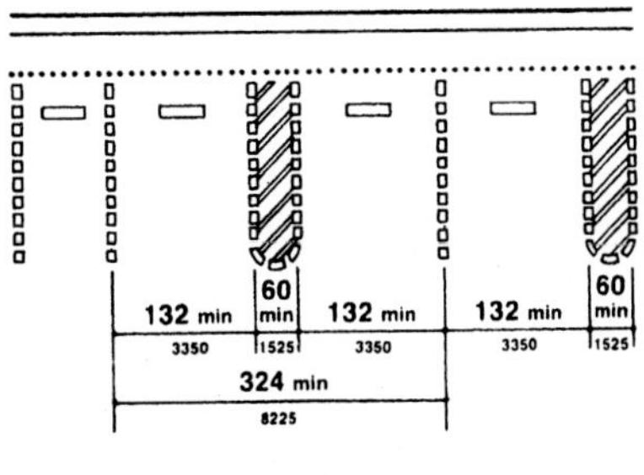

(b)
Universal Parking Space Design

Fig. A5
Parking Space Alternatives

ADAAG
Wheelchair Transfer Details/Bathroom Dimensions

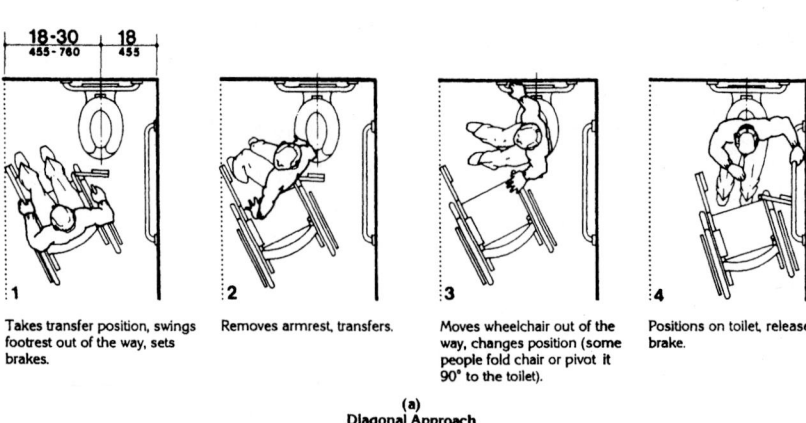

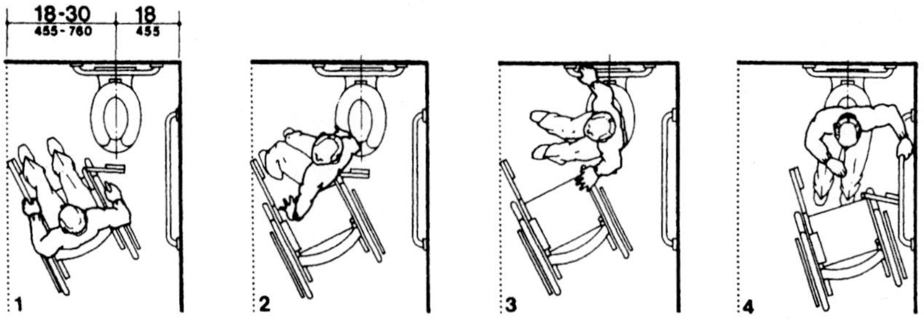

Takes transfer position, swings footrest out of the way, sets brakes.

Removes armrest, transfers.

Moves wheelchair out of the way, changes position (some people fold chair or pivot it 90° to the toilet).

Positions on toilet, releases brake.

(a)
Diagonal Approach

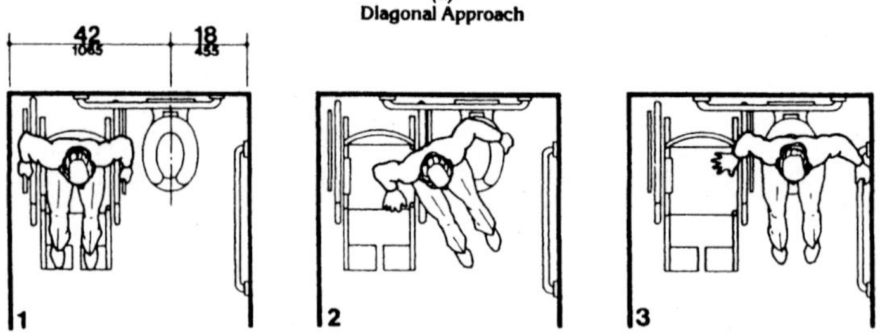

Takes transfer position, removes armrest, sets brakes.

Transfers.

Positions on toilet.

(b)
Side Approach

Fig. A6
Wheelchair Transfers

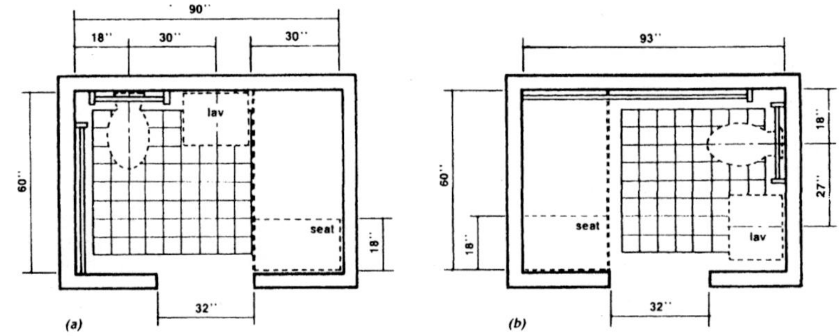

Fig. A7

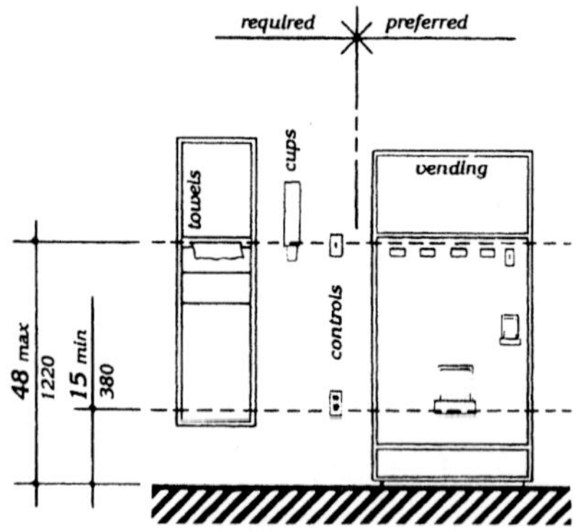

(a)
Forward Reach Possible

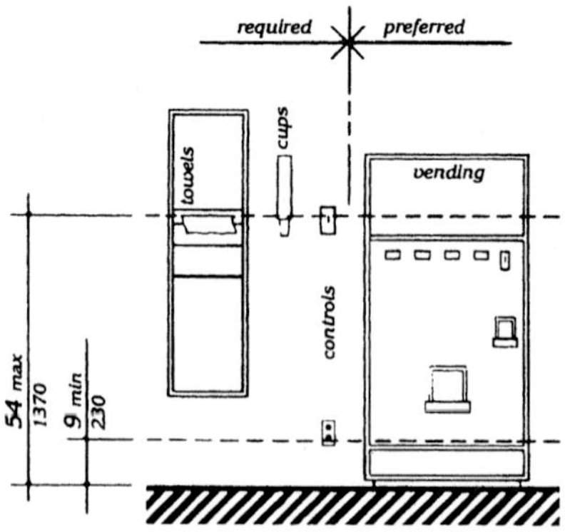

(b)
Side Reach Possible

Fig. A8
Control Reach Limitations

6
GENERAL REFERENCE DATA

INTRODUCTION

This section provides a variety of time-saving reference material in the form of tables, charts, formulas, and planning guidelines. Included are area requirements for the preliminary space planning of various building types and human factors data related to anthropometrics, space, and acoustics. Also included are a number of tables for determining carpet and wall covering yardage quantities. In addition, a series of tables dealing with electrical data provides typical amperage ratings for office and electronic equipment and for residential appliances. Still other tables and charts contain mathematical data relative to functions of numbers, metric system conversions, and areas of plane figures.

SPACE PLANNING
Area Requirements by Use

The first portion of Table 1 shows some of the planning guidelines for several types of office use. Of course, usable areas per employee vary greatly depending on the type of work performed and types of support space and common areas required, such as file rooms, data processing, and conference rooms.

Rules of Thumb

Office use: 125 to 150 net ft^2 area per person
Retail space: 30 net ft^2 per person on ground floor; 50 net ft^2 per person on upper floors
Classrooms: 20 net ft^2 per pupil

Table 1 Space planning by building type

Building/Use Type	Sq. Ft. per Unit		Area Basis
Office buildings, all types	100-250	net	usable
Work station, minimum clerical	40	person	usable
Work station, clerical with VDT	55	person	usable
Work station, with visitor space	65	person	usable
Work station, supervisor	100	person	usable
Manager, private office	150-225	person	usable
Law firm	450	attorney	total usable
Law firm library	25-30	attorney	usable
Law firm conference	25-30	attorney	usable
Insurance company, branch	100 average	work station	usable
Insurance company, branch Total, includes common areas and circulation	155-165	employee	total usable
Energy company	255	employee	total usable
Conference and dining rooms	15	person	net
Restaurants			
Dining areas (includes dining room but not waiting, coat room, etc.)			
Banquet	10-15	seat	net
Cafeteria, college	12-15	seat	net
Cafeteria, commercial	16-18	seat	net
Counter service	18-20	seat	net
Table service, hotel or restaurant	15-18	seat	net
Table service, minimum	11-14	seat	net

Kitchens

Type	Meals per Hour: < 200	200-400	400-800	800-1300
Cafeterias	7.5-5.0	5.0-4.0	4.0-3.5	3.5-3.0
Hotels	18.0-4.0	7.5-3.0	6.0-3.0	4.0-3.0
Restaurants	7.0-4.0	5.0-3.6	5.0-3.6	5.0-3.0

Serving and service areas			
Cafeterias	6	person	net
Restaurants	5	person	net

Add to totals space for food storage, administration, waiting.

Table 1 Space planning by building type (*Continued*)

Building/Use Type	Sq. Ft. per Unit		Area Basis
Night clubs	25	person	net
Bars	18	person	net
Hotel			
1.5 persons per room without extensive conferencing facilities	550-600	room	gross
	Retail		
Large stores	30-50	person	net
	Cultural		
Public library			
Stack space	0.08	bound vols.	net
Reading rooms	20-35	user	net
Staff space	100	staff person	net
Overall	50	person	net
Museums, exhibition areas	15	person	net
Theater and assembly areas			
Seating area, fixed seats	7.5	seat	net
Seating, movable seating	15	seat	net
Theaters, fixed seating (Does not include stage, lobby, etc.)	8-12	seat	net
Stage/backstage Performing arts theater	100%	seating area	
Lobbies	3	person	net
Lobbies	30%	seating area	
	Educational		
Elementary			
The following figures are based on the number of students in the particular space listed.			
Small classrooms	20-30	student	net
Library	40	student	net
Art room	40	student	net
Secondary			
The following figures are based on the number of students in the particular space listed.			
Cafeteria	12-15	student	1/3 of total
Small classrooms	20-25	student	net
Large classrooms	15	student	net
Art classrooms	50-60	student	net
Home economics	50-60	student	net
Laboratory classrooms	55-70	student	net
Library	40	student	20% of total
Music rooms	30-35	student	net
Physical education	125	student	net
Shops/vocational rooms small	50	student	net
Shops/vocational rooms wood, metal, etc.	120-140	student	net
University			
Classrooms, small	20	student	net
Classrooms, large	12-15	student	net

SPACE PLANNING
Area Requirements by Use

Table 1 Space planning by building type (*Continued*)

Building/Use Type	Sq. Ft. per Unit		Area Basis
Lecture halls	9–12	seat	net
Dormitory, no dining	160	student	net
Dormitory, no dining	210–240	student	gross
Dormitory, dining	235–260	student	gross
Food service, table service	18–26	seat	net, all areas
Food service, cafeteria	14–19	seat	net, all areas
Laboratories	34–45	student	net
Laboratory storage	6–10	student	net
Library			
Book stacks, less than 300,000 volumes	0.10	volume	net
Book stacks, 300,000–1,000,000 volumes	0.7–0.8	volume	net
Book stacks, over 1,000,000 volumes	0.5	volume	net
Reading, study	25–35	station	net
(provide stations equal to 25% to 40% of student population):	6.25–10	student	net
Total service space	25%	of reading	net
Residential			
Apartments	250	Occupant	net
Senior citizen housing			
Living units	300–380	1-person unit	net
Living units	350–425	2-person unit	net
Living units	400–600	unit	gross
Dining, lounge, lobby, administration, etc.	33%–45% of living unit space, gross area		
Health Care Facilities			
General hospital	1000	bed	gross
Medical center	1100	bed	gross

The above figures are based on *usable* square footage, which in the language of leasing includes the area within the boundaries of the leased space. Most building owners lease space based on the *rentable* area, which includes a tenant's prorated share of common areas such as toilet rooms, elevator lobby, public corridors, and so on. The multiplying figure can be obtained from the building owner, or a figure of 1.1 to 1.15 can be used as an estimated multiplying factor.

Table 2 Gross to net ratios for common building types

Building Type	Multiplying Factor	Building Type	Multiplying Factor
Office	1.25–1.35	Library reading space	1.5
Retail	1.35	Museum	1.2
Bank	1.4	Theater	1.3–1.7
Restaurant, table service	1.4–1.5	School, classroom	1.5–1.65
Restaurant, cafeteria	1.5	School, dormitory	1.5–1.8
Bars, nightclubs	1.3–1.4	School, laboratory	1.7
Hotel	1.4–1.6	School, gymnasium	1.4–1.45
Public library	1.25–1.3	Apartment	1.25–1.5
Library stack space	1.1–1.3	Hospital	1.5–1.85

Libraries represent a unique building type in that a majority of space is devoted to housing books and not people. The number of volumes to be housed, rather than numbers of people, becomes the primary planning parameter. For a detailed layout of book stacks, you can use the figures given in Table 3. For preliminary planning, the following general guidelines are useful.

Rules of Thumb

Public library: 12 to 18½ volumes per ft^2
Law library: 5 to 7 volumes per ft^2

To stack space, add a configuration loss of from 6 to 20 percent, to account for inefficiencies in stack layout.

Minimum aisle between open stacks: 3 ft 0 in
Staff spaces: 100 net ft^2 per person
Reading room seating: 15 to 35 ft^2 per person plus 6 percent configuration loss
Net/gross multiplier: 1.25
Maximum of 15,000 to 20,000 ft^2 per floor

Example A 100,000-volume public library is planned. How much space should be devoted to open stacks?

Plan about 15 volumes per square foot (100,000 ÷ 15 = 6667 ft^2). Add a configuration loss of 10 percent, to give a total area of 6667 + 667, or 7333 ft^2 of stack space.

Table 3 Library shelving—volumes per linear foot of shelf based on subject

(Standard stack section 3 ft wide x 7½ ft high with 7 shelves)

Subject	Volumes per foot of shelf	Volumes per single face section
Art (excluding oversize)	7	147
Circulating, nonfiction	8	168
Economics	8	168
Fiction	8	168
General literature	7	147
History	7	147
Law	4	84
Medical	5	105
Periodicals, bound	5	105
Public documents	5	105
Technical and scientific	6	126
Average for overall estimating		125

These figures should be reduced by at least 10% to avoid overcrowding and to allow for expansion.

Appropriateness

It is essential, because of the many variables involved, that the data selected be appropriate to the user of the space or furniture to be designed. It becomes necessary, therefore, for the intended user population to be properly defined in terms of such factors as age, sex, occupation, and ethnicity. If the user is an individual or constitutes a very small group, it may, in certain situations, be feasible to develop your own primary anthropometric data by actually having individual body measurements taken. Surely, if one is prepared to take the time to be fitted for a dress or a suit, one should be willing to spend the time to be fitted for an interior environment or components of that

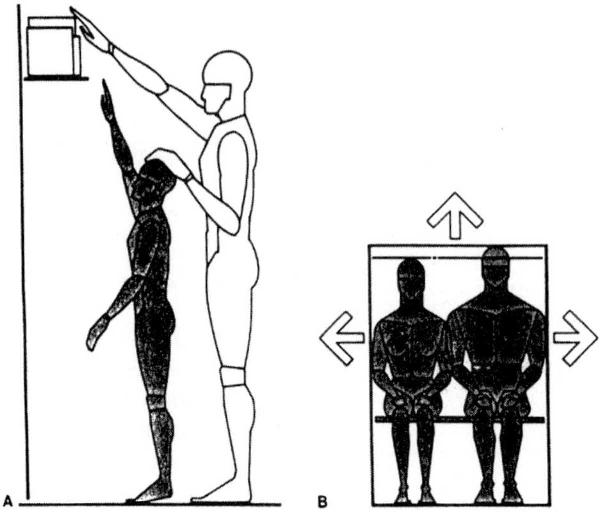

Fig. 1 (*a*) People of smaller body dimensions and, correspondingly, the lower-range percentile data should be used to establish dimensions where reach is the determining factor. (*b*) Larger-size people and, correspondingly, the high percentile range data should be used in establishing clearance dimensions

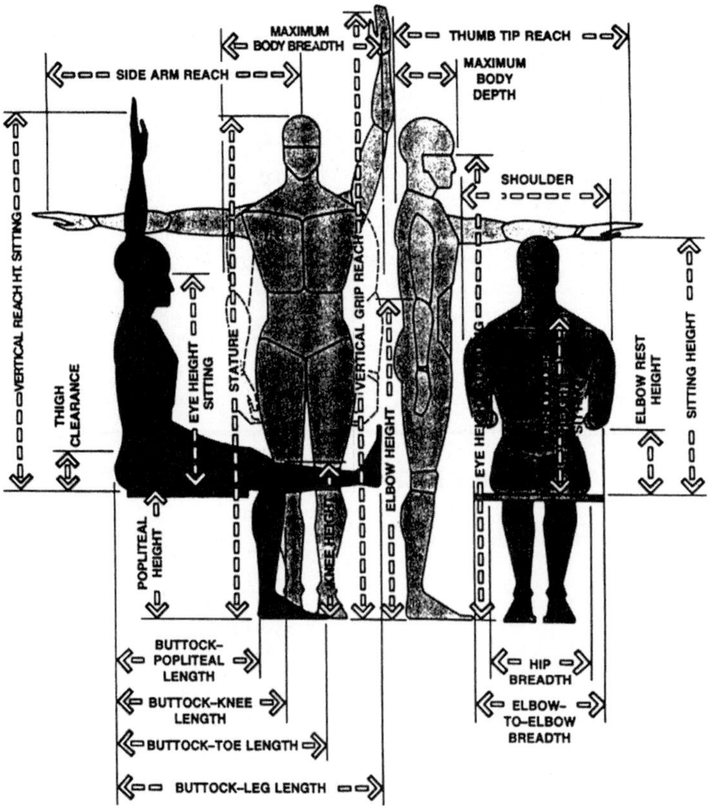

Fig. 2 Body measurements of most use to the designer of interior spaces

environment, particularly since, in most cases, the latter will reflect a far greater financial investment. The measurements, in the event that individual data are generated, should, however, be taken with proper instruments by a trained observer. In situations where specific body dimensions or other data for a particular user population are unavailable, and both time and funds prevent undertaking sophisticated studies, an engineering anthropometrist can be consulted to discuss the statistical methods of obtaining the necessary information.

"Average Man" Fallacy

As suggested previously, a very serious error in the application of data is to assume that the 50th-percentile dimensions represent the measurements of an average man and to create a design to accommodate 50th-percentile data. The fallacy in such an assumption is that, by prior definition, 50 percent of the group may suffer. There simply is no average man. Depending on the nature of the design problem, the design should usually be conceived to accommodate the 5th or the 95th percentile, so that the greatest portion of the population is served.

Dr. H.T.E. Hertzberg, one of the country's most distinguished research physical anthropologists, in discussing the so-called average man, indicated, "there is really no such thing as an 'average' man or woman. There are men who are average in weight, or in stature, or in sitting height, but the men who are average in two dimensions constitute only about 7 percent of the population; those in three, only about 3 percent; those in four, less than 2 percent. There are no men average in as few as 10 dimensions. Therefore, the concept of the 'average' man is fundamentally incorrect, because no such creature exists. Work places to be efficient should be designed according to the measured range of body size."

Reach, Clearance, and Adjustability

The selection of appropriate anthropometric data is based on the nature of the particular design problem under consideration. If the design requires the user to reach from a seated or standing position, the 5th-percentile data should be utilized. Such data for arm reach indicate that 5 percent of the population would have an arm reach of short (or shorter) dimension, while 95 percent of the population—the overwhelming majority—would have longer arm reaches. If the design in a reach situation can accommodate the user with the shortest arm reach, obviously it will function for the users with longer reaches as well; it is equally obvious that the opposite is not true, as shown in Fig. 1*a*.

In designs where clearance is the primary consideration, the larger or 95th-percentile data should be used. The logic is simple. If the design will allow adequate clearance for the users with the largest body size, it would also allow clearance for those users with smaller body size. Here, too, it can be seen from Fig. 1*b* that the opposite is not true.

In other situations it may be desirable to provide the design with a built-in adjustment capability. Certain chair types, adjustable shelves, and so on, are examples of such. The range of adjustment should be based on the anthropometrics of the user, the nature of the task, and the physical or mechanical limitations involved. The range should allow the design to accommodate at least 90 percent of the user population involved.

It should be noted that the foregoing examples were used primarily to illustrate the basic logic underlying the selection of the body dimensions involved and the particular percentiles to be accommodated. Wherever possible, however, it is naturally more desirable to accommodate the greatest percentage of the user population. In this regard, there is no substitute for common sense. If a shelf can just as easily be placed an inch or two lower, without significantly impacting on other design or cost factors, thereby accommodating 98 or 99 percent of the user population, obviously that is the correct design decision.

The clearances shown in Fig. 3 are intended to introduce general guidelines for barrier-free design. While we have utilized the wheelchair as our design subject, it does not represent the largest number of people with disabilities. However, it is usually the most demanding for which to design. To provide practical limits for this design, we have chosen to plot the range of reach for the short female to the tall male. The overlapping areas of ability for those with and without disabilities demonstrate the field of good design practice common to both.

When planning for accessibility, it is important to consider the attitude at which the wheelchair approaches the object desired. Reach limits differ for frontal and side reach. Because of this, range of reach is plotted for each. The elevation targets represent the maximum height at which controls requiring manual dexterity should be located.

Wheelchairs vary in size. They are fitted to their users in much the same manner as clothing is. A range of sizes is given, with the dimensions for the typical collapsible, manual chair indicated. Electrically powered wheelchairs require more space. Further, the wheelchair must be considered in its occupied state, as the user imparts additional space requirements with arms and feet as well as basic maneuvering space.

We consider the basic space requirement for an occupied wheelchair to function to be 3 ft wide by 4 ft deep. This same space will accommodate most people who use canes, crutches, and walkers. Blind people using the cane technique for perceiving obstacles can also be accommodated in this space. For a person in a wheelchair to make a complete turn, an area of approximately 5 ft by 5 ft is required. As the elevations of surrounding surfaces change, so do the space requirements. The length of time that one is confronted by close quarters also affects the required clearance. An opening through a wall may be 2 ft 8 in clear, as it represents only a short time involvement. As travel distance and traffic increase, passage width must also.

The complexity of space also affects minimum clearance. To make a simple 90° turn, adjoining passages 3 ft wide are required (and 3 ft 6 in preferred if a normal walking is to be maintained). A 180° turn around a fixed partition requires more space.

As clearances relate to general circulation requirements, space needs again increase with traffic speed and volume. Narrow corridors (4 ft) should be restricted to basically short, one-directional traffic patterns. Generally, maintain at least 5-ft clearances or more, as determined by code.

HUMAN FACTORS
Anthropometrics

Adult Male and Female Miscellaneous Structural Body Dimensions in Inches and Centimeters by Age and Selected Percentiles

Percentile		A in	A cm	B in	B cm	C in	C cm	D in	D cm	E in	E cm	F in	F cm	G in	G cm
95	MEN	36.2	91.9	47.3	120.1	68.6	174.2	20.7	52.6	27.3	69.3	37.0	94.0	33.9	86.1
	WOMEN	32.0	81.3	43.6	110.7	64.1	162.8	17.0	43.2	24.6	62.5	37.0	94.0	31.7	80.5
5	MEN	30.8	78.2	41.3	104.9	60.8	154.4	17.4	44.2	23.7	60.2	32.0	81.3	30.0	76.2
	WOMEN	26.8	68.1	38.6	98.0	56.3	143.0	14.9	37.8	21.2	53.8	27.0	68.6	28.1	71.4

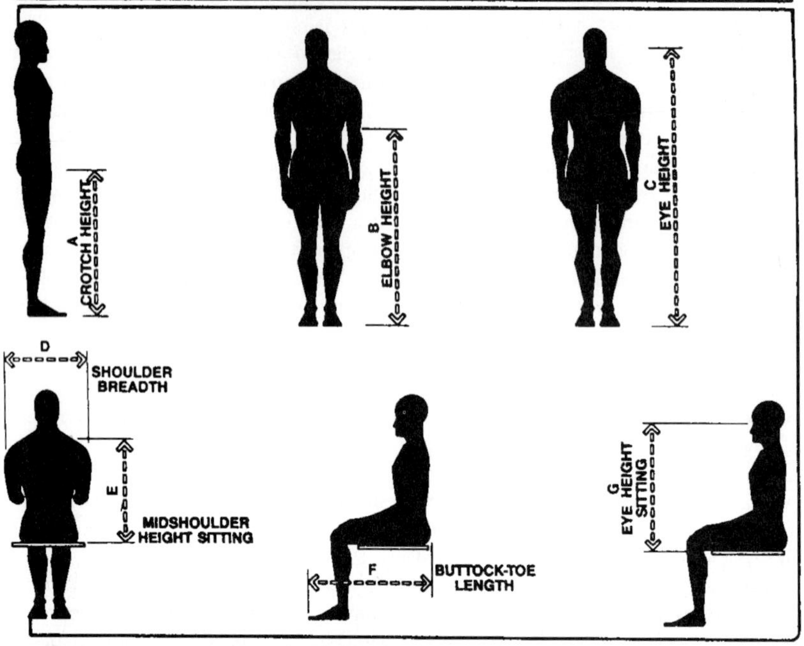

Adult Male and Female Functional Body Dimensions in Inches and Centimeters by Age, Sex, and Selected Percentiles

Percentile		A in	A cm	B in	B cm	C in	C cm	D in	D cm	E in	E cm	F in	F cm
95	MEN	38.3	97.3	46.1	117.1	51.6	131.1	35.0	88.9	39.0	86.4	88.5	224.8
	WOMEN	36.3	92.2	49.0	124.5	49.1	124.7	31.7	80.5	38.0	96.5	84.0	213.4
5	MEN	32.4	82.3	39.4	100.1	59.0	149.9	29.7	75.4	29.0	73.7	76.8	195.1
	WOMEN	29.9	75.9	34.0	86.4	55.2	140.2	26.6	67.6	27.0	68.6	72.9	185.2

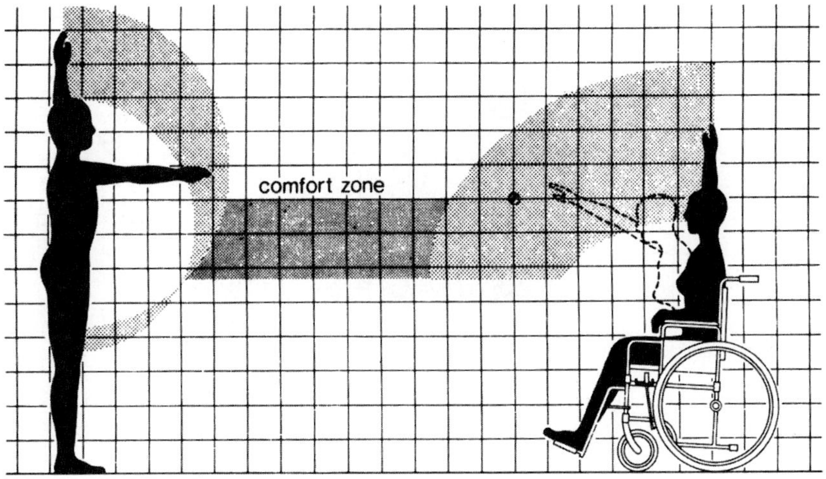

range of reach (a/1)
scale: 3/8"= 1'-0"

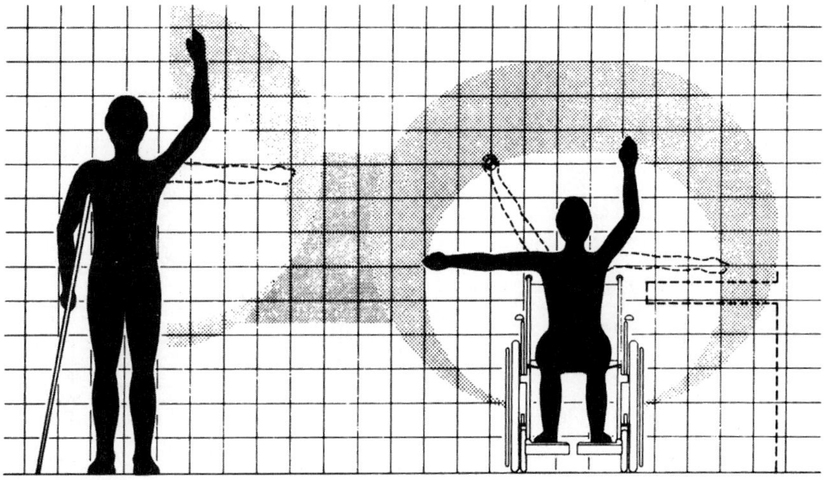

range of reach (b/1)
scale: 3/8"= 1'-0"

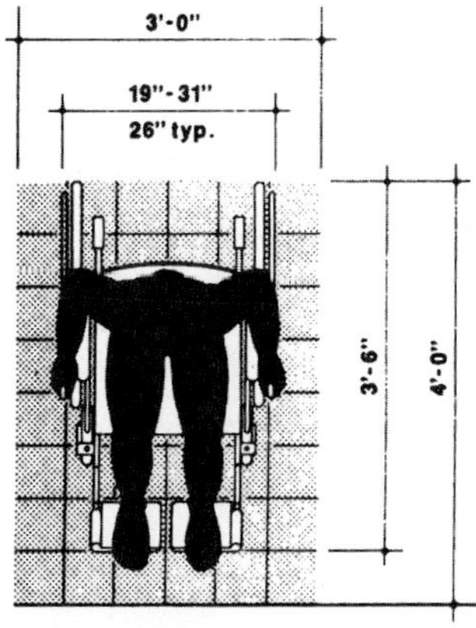

wheelchair (c/1)
scale: 3/8"= 1'-0"

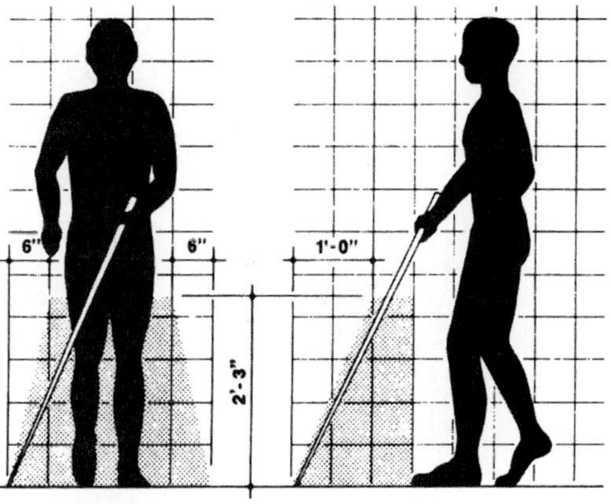

cane technique (d/1)
scale: 3/8"= 1'-0"

Fig. 3

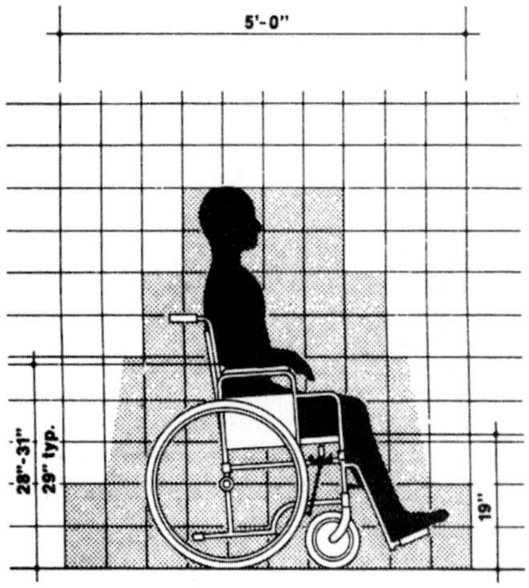

clearance (e/1)

scale: 3/8" = 1'-0"

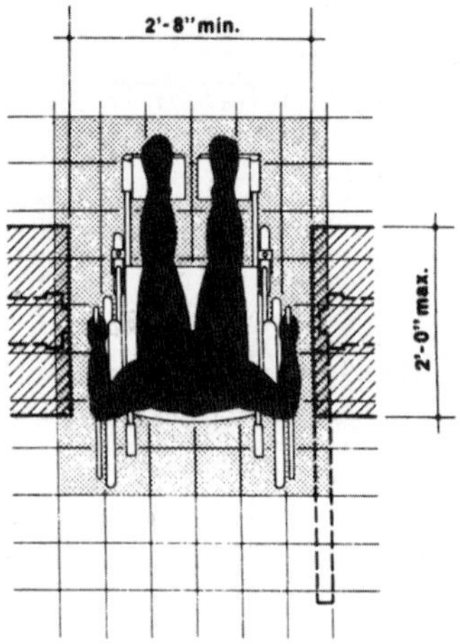

openings (f/1)

scale: 3/8" = 1'-0"

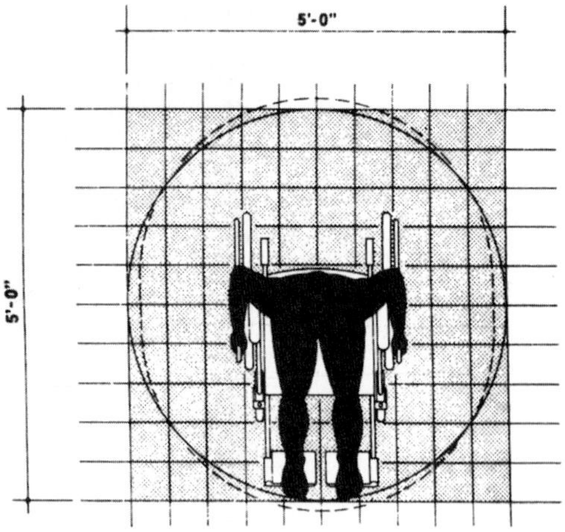

360° turn (g/1)

scale: 3/8" = 1'-0"

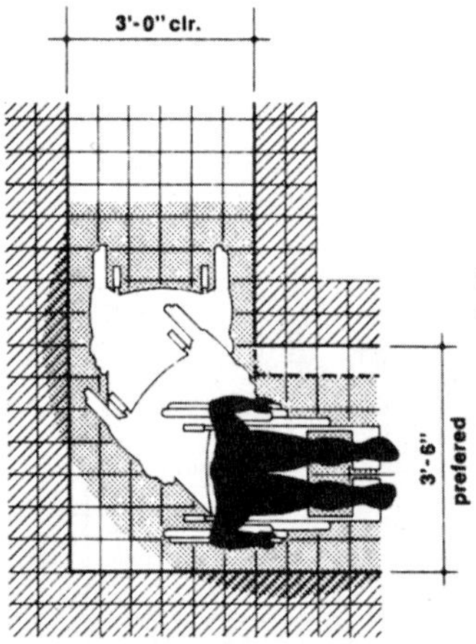

90° turn (h/1)

scale: 1/4" = 1'-0"

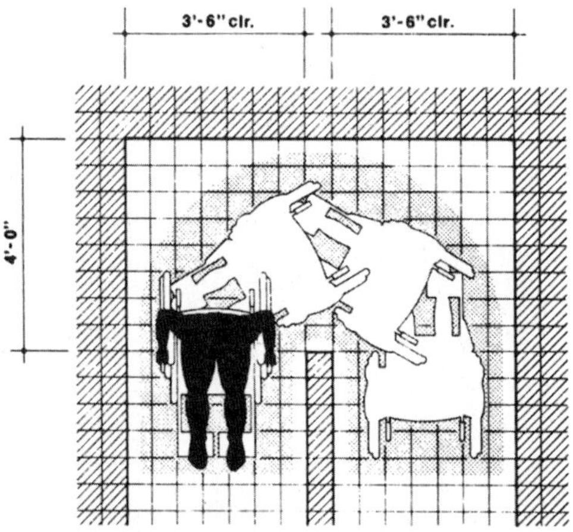

180° turn (j/1)

scale: 1/4" = 1'-0"

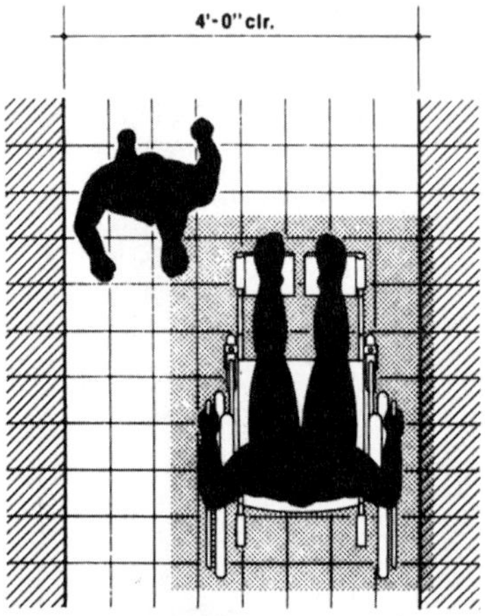

one-way (k/1)

scale: 3/8" = 1'-0"

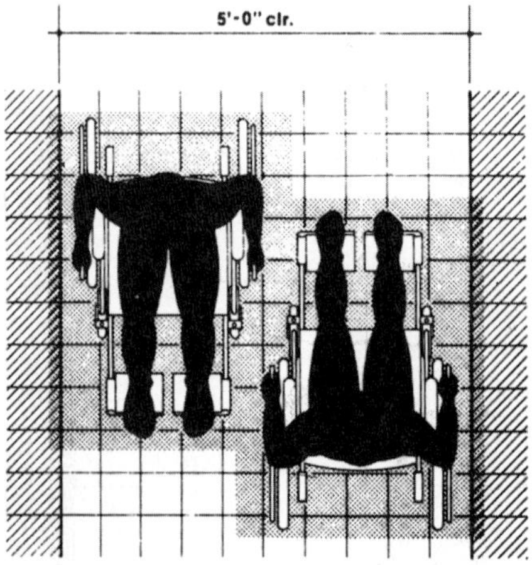

two-way (m/1)

scale: 3/8" = 1'-0"

Fig. 3 *(Continued)*

Clothing Increases for Men and Women

Clothing must be taken into consideration when designing compartments and seating arrangements. If a condition exists that must accommodate the 99th-percentile man and the 1st-percentile woman, add the heaviest clothing required to the large man and add the lightest clothing to the small woman. Hats are important; include a 2-in clearance between the highest hat and the ceiling to allow for rising and falling during walking. Shoe heights are important to determine ceiling clearance and seat heights. Spacing between arm rests will depend on the sitting buttock width, with the bulkiest clothing anticipated.

Gloves affect space requirements. A bare hand opening of 1.5 × 3.8 in (38 × 97 mm) has to be increased, for heavy gloves, to 2 × 4.5 in (51 × 114 mm). Gloved hands are not as sensitive. A push-button travel of 0.1 in (3 mm) must be increased to 0.3 in (8 mm) for heavy gloves.

Table 1 shows the increase required on each side for various types of clothing, is both for civilian increases for men and women, and for military men. Values are approximate, for styles of clothing change. Military and safety helmets are about 12 × 10.25 in (305 × 260 mm).

Table 1 Clothing increases for men and women (approximate, in inches and millimeters)

	Men		*Women*		*Military men*		*Arctic*	
	Street clothes	*Winter clothes*	*Street clothes*	*Winter clothes*	*Army light*	*Army heavy*	*Flying heavy*	*Parka and boots*
Stature	1.2 (30)	3.2 (80)	1.2 (30)	4 (100)	2.65 (67)	2.65 (67)	3 (75)	4.3 (110)
Sitting hgt	0.1 (2.5)	2.3 (60)	0.1 (2.5)	2.7 (70)	1.39 (35)	1.61 (41)	1.61 (41)	NA
Head hgt	Bare	2 (50)	Bare	3 (75)	1.4 (36)	1.4 (36)	1.35 (35)	NA
Head w	Bare	2 (50)	Bare	3 (75)	2.8 (71)	2.8 (71)	2.8 (71)	NA
Head lg	Bare	2 (50)	Bare	3 (75)	3.5 (89)	3.5 (89)	3.5 (89)	NA
Shoulder w	0.5 (13)	2 (50)	0.25 (6.4)	1 (25)	0.24 (61)	1.52 (39)	1.52 (39)	4.7 (120)
Shoulder hgt	0.6 (15)	2 (50)	0.35 (9)	1.25 (32)	0.24 (61)	1.52 (39)	0.92 (23)	NA
Hip w sit	0.5 (13)	2 (50)	0.25 (6.4)	1 (25)	0.56 (14.2)	1.4 (36)	1.44 (37)	5.2 (132)
Abdomen	0.9 (23)	1.7 (43)	0.3 (7.6)	1 (25)	1.2 (30)	2.5 (65)	1.4 (36)	NA
2 elbow w	0.8 (20.3)	4 (100)	0.4 (10)	2 (50)	1 (25)	2.1 (55)	1.84 (47)	5.9 (150)
Elbow lg	0.4 (10)	2 (50)	0.2 (5)	1 (25)	0.56 (14.2)	1.84 (48)	0.94 (25)	NA
Hand w	Bare	0.4 (10)	Bare	0.4 (10)	Bare	0.3 (7.6)	0.4 (10)	1.2 (30)
Hand lg	Bare	0.2 (5)	Bare	0.2 (5)	Bare	0.2 (5)	0.3 (7.6)	0.6 (16)
Hand thk	Bare	0.5 (12.7)	Bare	0.5 (12.7)	Bare	0.4 (10)	0.4 (10)	0.6 (16)
Thigh clear	0.5 (12.7)	1 (25)	0.3 (7.6)	0.8 (20.3)	0.3 (7.6)	0.4 (10)	2 (50)	NA
2 knee w	0.3 (7.6)	0.4 (10)	0.1 (2.5)	0.1 (2.5)	0.5 (12.7)	1.7 (43)	0.72 (18)	NA
Knee to fl	1.5 (38)	1.6 (40)	1.3 (33)	1.3 (33)	1.32 (35)	1.44 (37)	1.44 (37)	NA
Knee to back	0.8 (20)	3 (75)	0.6 (15)	1.8 (45)	0.2 (5)	0.7 (18)	0.54 (14)	1 (25)
Foot w	0.5 (12.7)	1 (25)	0.3 (7.6)	0.5 (12.7)	0.2 (5)	0.2 (5)	0.2 (5)	NA
Foot lg	1.3 (33)	1.5 (38)	0.5 (12.7)	1.5 (38)	1.6 (40)	1.6 (40)	1.6 (40)	NA
Heel hgt	1.2 (30)	1.5 (38)	1.2 (30)	1.5 (38)	1.3 (33)	1.3 (33)	1.3 (33)	1.3 (33)
Wt lb (kg)	5 (2.3)	10.0 (4.5)	3.5 (1.6)	7 (3.2)	9.4 (4.3)	11.8 (5.4)	20. (9)	NA

(*Source:* Humanscale 1/2/3, 1974.)

Children Ages 3 to 18

Table 2 Work and play stations for combined 50th-percentile male and female children (in inches and millimeters)

	Sitting				*Standing*			
Age	*Chair height*	*Elbow height*	*Desk height*	*Desktop reach*	*Chair height*	*Elbow height*	*Desk height*	*Desktop reach*
3	8 (205)	13.7 (350)	15 (380)	12 (305)	37 (940)	21 (535)	20 (510)	14 (355)
4	9 (230)	14.6 (370)	16 (405)	14 (355)	40 (1020)	23 (585)	22 (560)	15 (380)
5	10 (255)	15.7 (400)	17 (430)	15 (380)	43 (1095)	24.5 (622)	23 (585)	17 (430)
6	11 (280)	17.2 (440)	18 (460)	16 (405)	45 (1145)	26 (660)	24 (610)	18 (460)
7	11.5 (290)	18.1 (460)	19 (480)	18 (460)	48 (1220)	28.5 (725)	26 (660)	20 (510)
8	12 (305)	18.8 (480)	20 (510)	19 (480)	50 (1270)	30 (760)	27 (685)	21 (535)
9	13 (330)	19.7 (500)	21 (535)	20 (510)	52.5 (1330)	31 (790)	28 (710)	22 (560)
10	13.5 (345)	20.2 (515)	22 (560)	21 (535)	54 (1375)	32.5 (825)	29 (740)	23 (585)
11	14 (355)	20.8 (530)	23 (585)	22 (560)	56.5 (1435)	34 (865)	30 (760)	24 (610)
12	15 (380)	21.4 (545)	24 (610)	23 (585)	59 (1495)	35 (890)	31 (790)	25 (635)
13	15 (380)	22.1 (560)	25 (635)	24 (610)	61 (1550)	36.5 (925)	32 (815)	26 (660)
14	16 (405)	23 (585)	26 (660)	24 (610)	63 (1600)	37.5 (950)	33 (840)	27 (685
15	16 (405)	23.6 (600)	26.5 (675)	24 (610)	65 (1650)	38.5 (980)	34 (865)	28 (710)
16	16.5 (420)	24.4 (620)	27.5 (700)	24 (610)	66.5 (1690)	40 (1015)	35 (890)	29 (735)
17	16.5 (420)	24.9 (630)	28 (710)	24 (610)	66.5 (1690)	40 (1015)	35 (890)	29 (735)
18	16.5 (420)	24.9 (630)	28 (710)	24 (610)	68 (1725)	41 (1040)	36 (915)	30 (760)

(*Source:* SAE, 1977.)

Standing height includes shoes and a slight slump in posture.

Maximum elbow rise at table is 3 in (76 mm).

Maximum distance from chair to desktop is 12 in (305 mm).

It is difficult to accommodate all children in one age bracket; the 5th-percentile might prefer a chair 1 in (25.4 mm) lower and the 95th-percentile might prefer a chair 1 in higher.

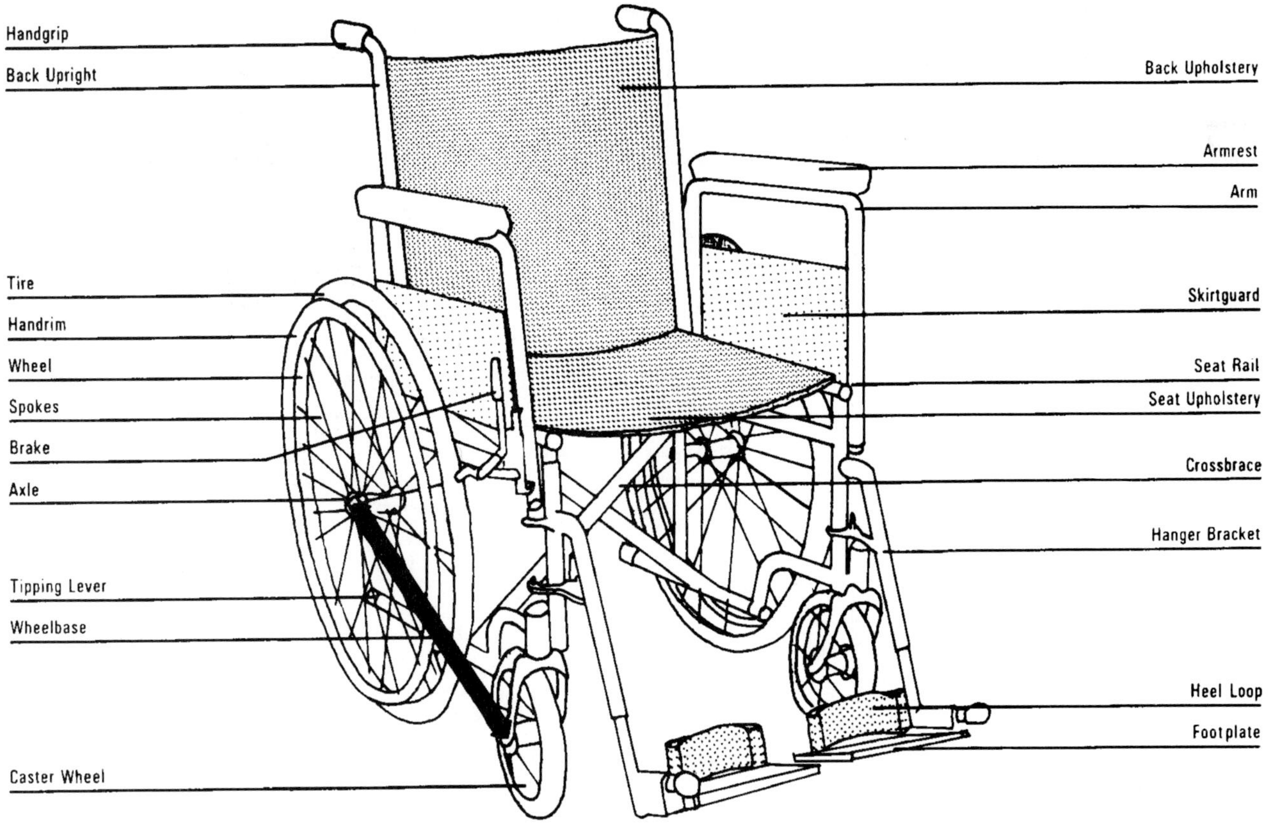

Handgrip

Back Upright

Tire

Handrim

Wheel

Spokes

Brake

Axle

Tipping Lever

Wheelbase

Caster Wheel

Back Upholstery

Armrest

Arm

Skirtguard

Seat Rail

Seat Upholstery

Crossbrace

Hanger Bracket

Heel Loop

Footplate

Fig. 4

eye level

handle

desk arm

armrest

lap

seat

toe

Overall length: 40" to 50"

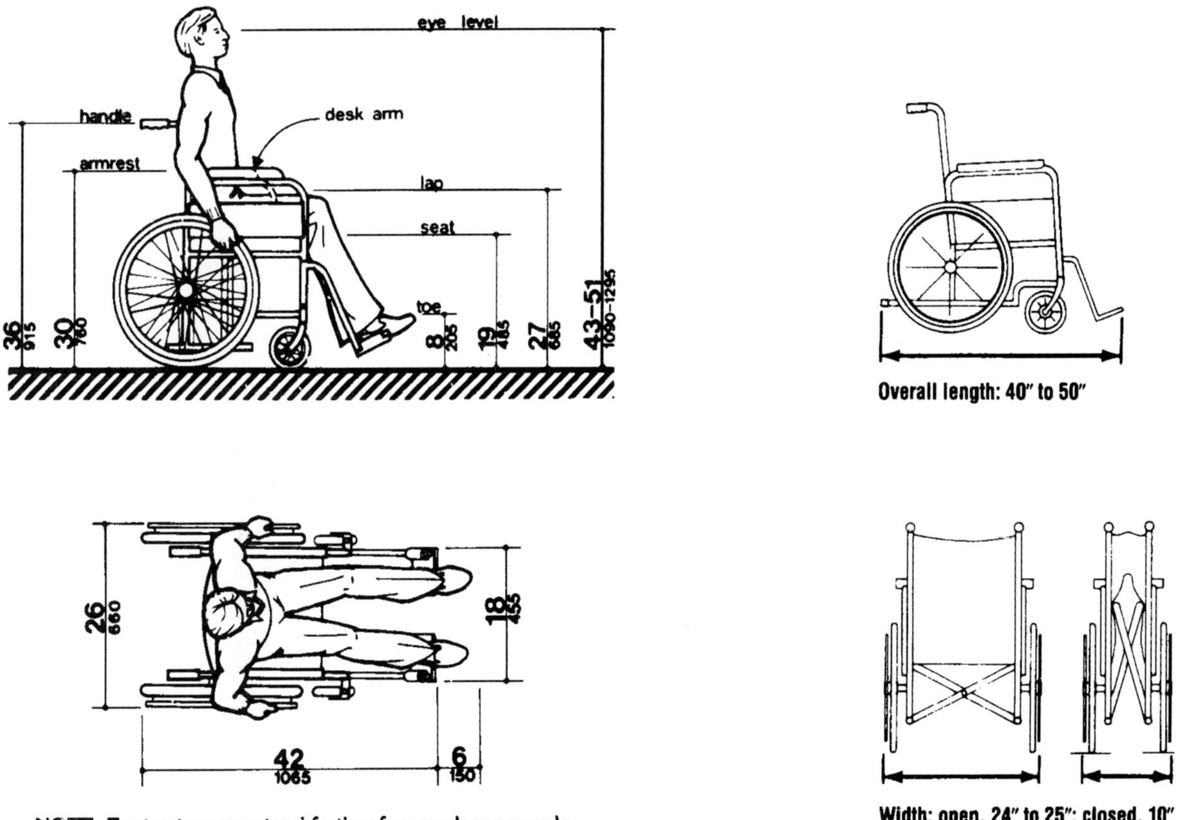

NOTE: Footrests may extend further for very large people.

Width: open, 24" to 25"; closed, 10"

Fig. 5   Dimensions of adult-sized wheelchairs

HUMAN FACTORS
Floor Space for Wheelchairs

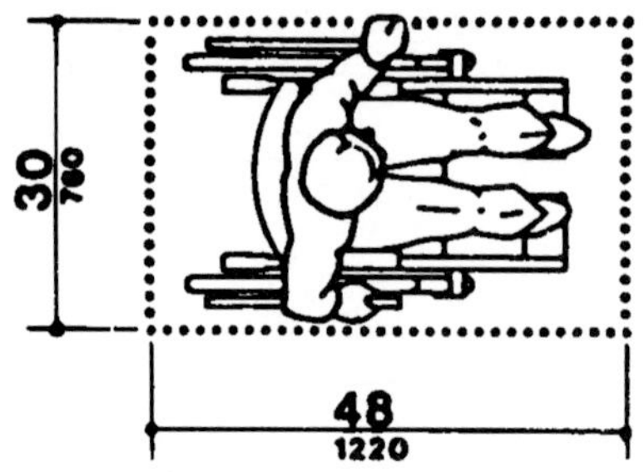

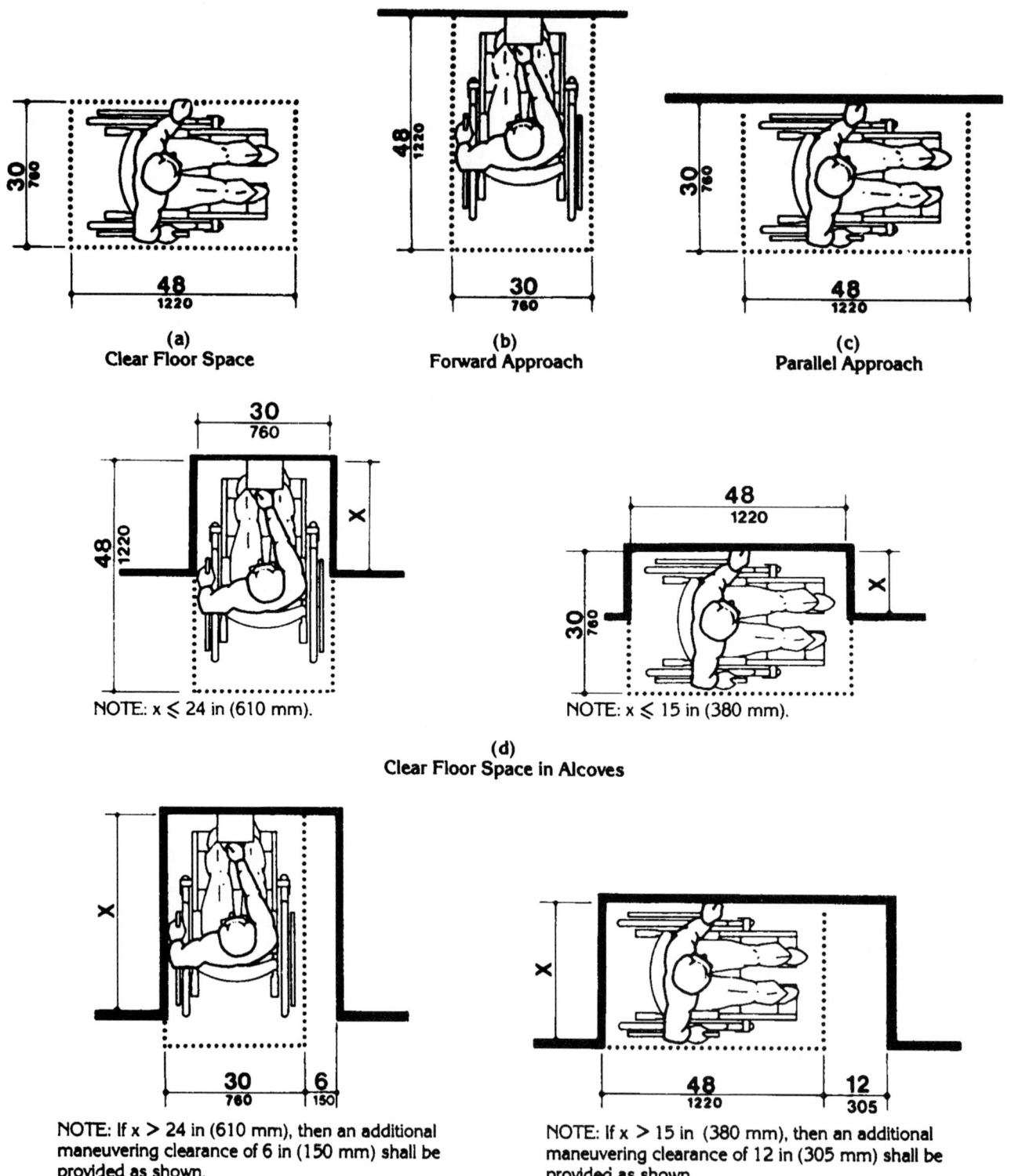

(a)
Clear Floor Space

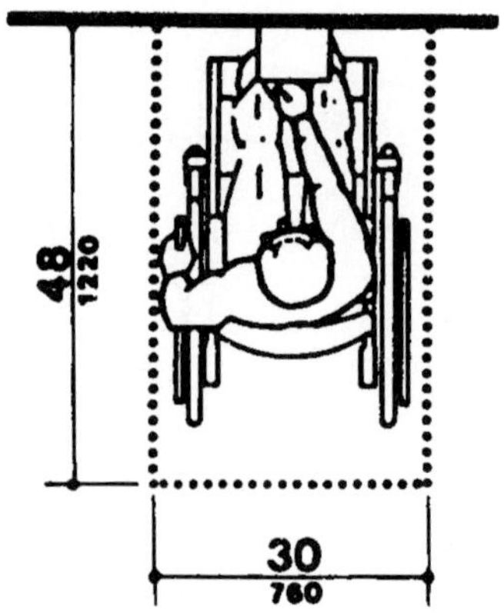

(b)
Forward Approach

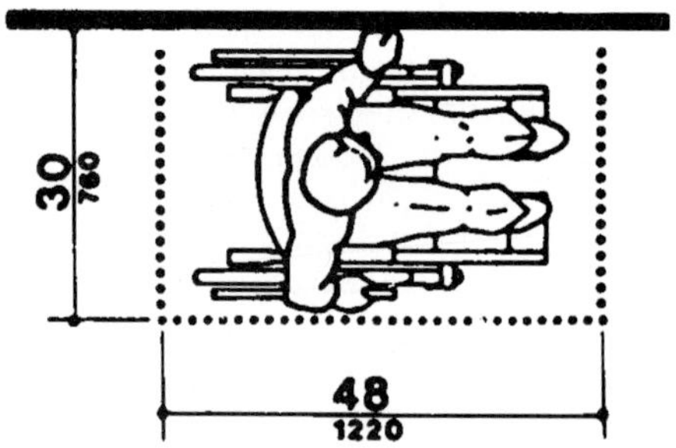

(c)
Parallel Approach

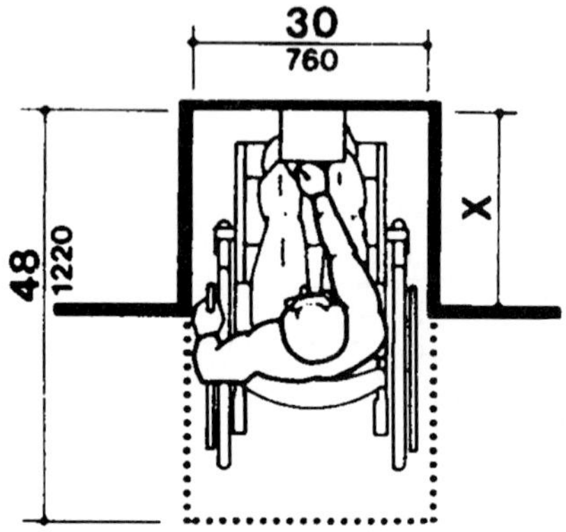

NOTE: x ≤ 24 in (610 mm).

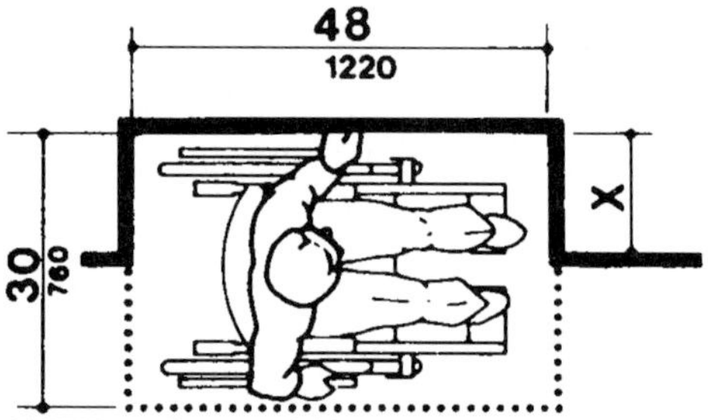

NOTE: x ≤ 15 in (380 mm).

(d)
Clear Floor Space in Alcoves

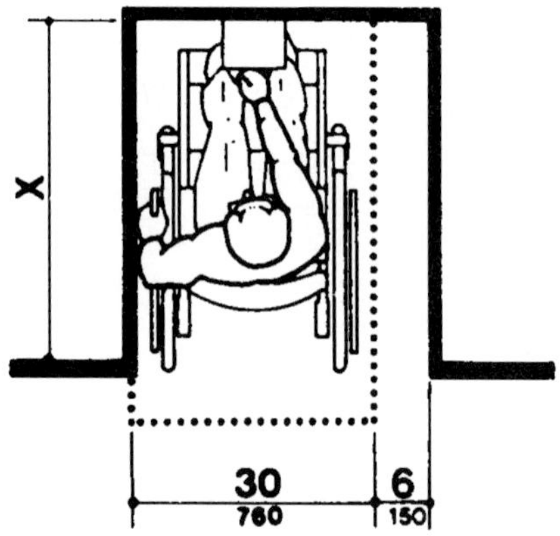

NOTE: If x > 24 in (610 mm), then an additional maneuvering clearance of 6 in (150 mm) shall be provided as shown.

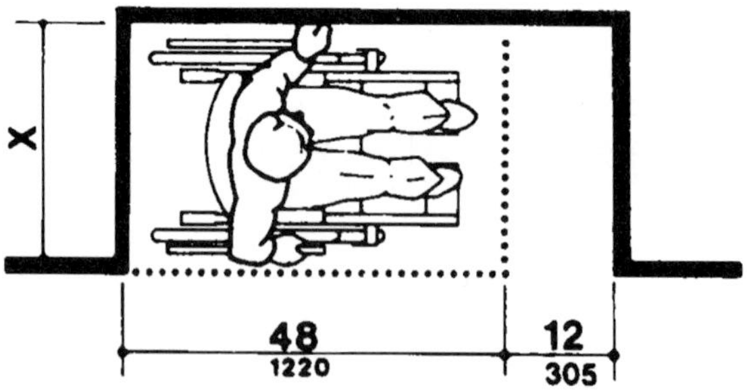

NOTE: If x > 15 in (380 mm), then an additional maneuvering clearance of 12 in (305 mm) shall be provided as shown.

(e)
Additional Maneuvering Clearances for Alcoves

Fig. 6 Minimum clear floor space for wheelchairs

Types of Space

Besides needing enough space in order to move about and perform various tasks, people react to space in a variety of ways. Several researchers have defined the space surrounding the individual in terms of the limits within which people categorically respond (see Figs. 7 and 8). *Intimate space* is that area in which a person tends not to allow anyone to intrude unless intimate relationships are expected. *Personal space* is that area within which a person allows only selected friends or fellow workers with whom personal discussion is mandatory. *Social space* is that area within which the individual expects to make purely social contacts on a temporary basis. And, finally, *public space* is that area within which the individual does not expect to have direct contact with others. Obviously, the more intimate the spatial relationship becomes, the more people resist intrusion by others. Personal space factors are important in establishing the privacy requirements for architectural design.

Distance Relationships Among People
(Hall)

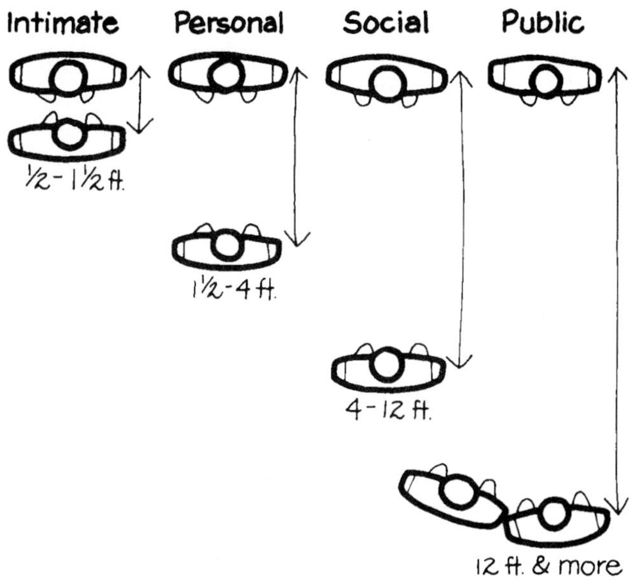

Fig. 7

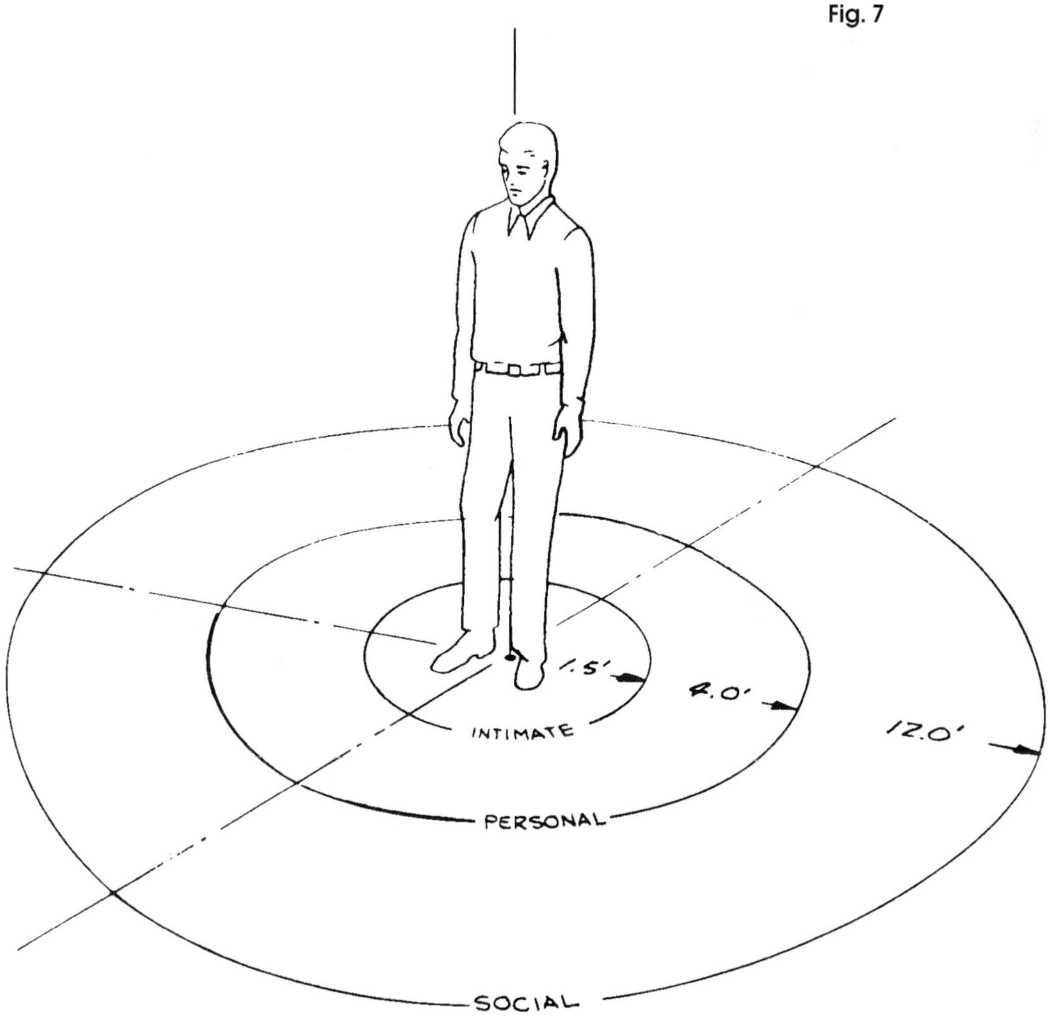

Fig. 8

Typical Subjective Responses to Selected Spatial Features

Although few research data have been generated with regard to how people respond to specific spatial factors (at least in terms of being able to prescribe precise, quantitative guidelines), it is important for the designer to reflect on potentially negative reactions that often result when a given space is not made compatible with what the user expects in terms of the size, shape, organization, color, and illumination of a particular space. The considerations listed in Table 3 are suggested as a checklist for the designer.

Table 3

Space characteristic	*Probable response*
Size (generally, volume)	If the space is too small for the number of people, furnishings, equipment, or other objects that occupy it, people will consider it to be crowded. Although they may accept a crowded condition on a temporary basis, they will object to living or working in such a space for extended periods of time. If the space is too large for the people, furnishings, equipment, or other objects that occupy it, people will consider it unfriendly, inconvenient, and/or overly demanding in terms of communicating, travel distance, maintenance, etc. Although they may accept the "barnlike" atmosphere for temporary periods, they will object to living or working in such a space for extended periods of time.
Shape (generally, proportion)	If the space is out of proportion (too narrow, wide, long, high, etc.) for the intended use, people will consider it awkward and often distracting or oppressive. Although they may accept proportional distortion on a short-term basis (i.e., as they pass through briefly), they will object to living or working in such a space for extended periods of time. If the space contains such distortions as all curved surfaces, acute wall junctures, and too many projections or surface changes, people will consider it confusing and difficult to maneuver in and/or furnish. Although they may accept such distortions (or even consider them interesting) on a temporary or one-time basis, they will object to living or working in such a space for extended periods of time. It should also be noted that blind people depend on the constant proportions of right-angle corners to aid them in negotiating a space; such individuals are easily confused by curved surfaces, walls that are not at right angles, and periodic projections that imply they may have reached a turning point. When a ceiling is extremely high relative to the lateral dimension of a space, people feel as though they are working in a pit and that the walls are closing in on them. When a ceiling is extremely low and the space in front of the observer is very long, people feel as though the room is "endless" or as if they will hit their heads unless they duck.
Color and illumination	If a space is dark (unless this is required for a particular operation, such as a motion picture presentation), people tend to become lethargic and less active, or they may feel anxious. As a rule, the less bright a room is, the less cheerful it seems. A small space will seem even smaller. If a space is too bright, people will feel overly exposed, or they will complain of glare or thermal discomfort (even though actual glare in terms of accepted light levels or inappropriate thermal conditions for comfort are not present). If there are too many different colors, too large expanses of very saturated color, or too many and too "busy" patterns of color within a space, most people become irritated after more than a brief exposure to the space. If there is too little color, no visual pattern, or no other decorative break in the visual environment, people will find the space monotonous, boring, and eventually irritating to the point of wanting to escape. Although isolated points of highly reflective surface provide interest, all-metallic and highly reflective surface treatments create both subjective and directly objective interference for most people who have to work in the space.
Windows	Generally, most people do not like to live and work in a space that is devoid of windows. First and foremost, people seem to need visual contact with the outside world. Too many windows, on the other hand, can cause the following possible negative reactions: too much glare, too much exposure (fishbowl effect), lack of protection from outside elements, true anxiety (caused by floor-to-ceiling glass at high elevations).
Space organization	The internal components within a space and the traffic corridors and entrance and exit locations will seem either well organized or badly organized. The furnishings, partitions, decorative objects, etc., will appear as being either organized or disorganized, depending on the observer's ability to comprehend what things are and where they are with respect to his or her vantage point. Key behavioral response issues include apparent capability to find one's way to specific locations, apparent ease for interacting and communicating with others with whom the individual must associate, and apparent privacy provisions necessary to perform individual tasks. Although these are sometimes conflicting needs, the people who use a space will perform on the basis of how well each of these factors has been executed for *them,* not for the designer or the boss. The organization of internal space components obviously interacts with all the other space characteristics; i.e., the individual perceives and reacts to the combined effects of size, shape, color and illumination, windows, and organization simultaneously. A significant behavioral response will be an individual's interpretation of whether sufficient options are available for local modification of his or her own portion of the space. Even though people may never require a modification, they react to their own space in terms of permanently established restrictions that eventually elicit the feeling that the space is too small, the wrong shape, too dark, or isolated from the rest of the world, for example.
Furnishings	As a general rule, people are sensitive to improperly proportioned furniture, i.e., furniture that is too large, too small, or the wrong shape for the space in which it is placed. Although the designer normally tries to select furnishings that are properly proportioned for the space he or she has created, this may ultimately restrict the efficiency of the individual (e.g., a desk or storage cabinet may be too small). Thus, although the general visual proportions of furniture in relation to space must be taken into account to avoid negative observational responses, shortchanging the individual in terms of specific furniture and use requirements soon stimulates an even stronger negative response.

Table 4 Comparison of sound pressure levels and loudness sensations

Sound Pressure Level (decibels—A scale)	Source	Sensation
130	Jet Aircraft at 100′ Bass Drum at 3′ Auto Horn at 3′	Physical Pain
120		
110	Thunder, Artillery, Nearby Riveter Elevated Train Discotheque	Deafening
100		
90	Loud Street Noise Noisy Factory Truck Unmuffled Police Whistle	Very Loud
80		
70	Cocktail Party Noisy Office Average Street Noise Average Radio Average Factory	Loud
60		
50	Noisy Home Inside General Office Face to Face Conversation Quiet Radio	Moderate
40		
30	Quiet Home Private Office Empty Auditorium Quiet Conversation	Faint
20		
10	Rustle of Leaves Whisper Soundproof Room	Very Faint
0	Threshold of Audibility	

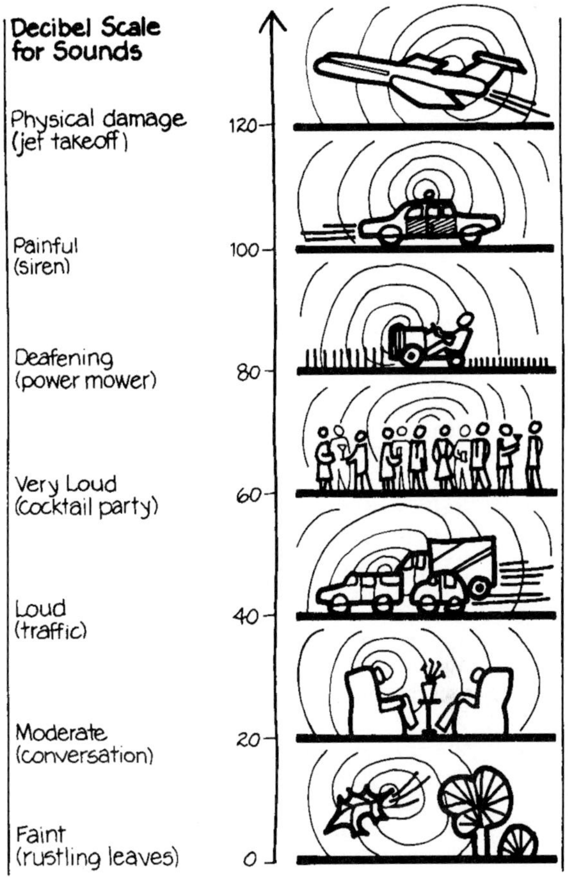

Fig. 9

Table 5 Speech-interference levels that barely permit reliable conversation

Distance between talker and listener, ft	Speech-interference level, dB			
	Normal	Raised	Very loud	Shouting
0.5	71	77	83	89
1.0	65	71	77	83
2.0	59	65	71	77
3.0	55	61	67	73
4.0	53	59	65	71
5.0	51	57	63	69
6.0	49	55	61	67
12.0	43	49	55	61

Table 6 Speech interference levels (SIL) and noise criteria (NC) recommended for rooms

Type of room	Maximum permissible level (measured in vacant rooms)	
	SIL	NC
Secretarial offices, typing	60	50–55
Coliseum for sports only (amplification)	55	50
Small private office	45	30–35
Conference room for 20	35	30
Movie theater	35	30
Conference room for 50	30	20–30
Theaters for drama, 500 seats (no amplification)	30	20–25
Homes, sleeping areas	30	20–25
Assembly halls (no amplification)	30	
Schoolrooms	30	25
Concert halls (no amplification)	25	15–20

FLOOR AND WALL COVERING
Length and Width of Carpet Roll Converted to Area

Table 1 Length and width of carpet roll converted to area

	Width of carpet roll										Width of carpet roll								
	9 ft			12 ft			15 ft				9 ft			12 ft			15 ft		
Length, ft	ft²	yd²	m²	ft²	yd²	m²	ft²	yd²	m²	Length, ft	ft²	yd²	m²	ft²	yd²	m²	ft²	yd²	m²
2	18	2	1.67	24	2.67	2.23	30	3.33	2.79	51	459	51	42.64	612	68	56.86	765	85	71.07
3	27	3	2.51	36	4	3.34	45	5	4.18	52	468	52	43.48	624	69.33	57.97	780	86.67	72.46
4	36	4	3.34	48	5.33	4.46	60	6.67	5.57	53	477	53	44.31	636	70.67	59.09	795	88.33	73.86
5	45	5	4.18	60	6.67	5.57	75	8.33	6.97	54	486	54	45.15	648	72	60.20	810	90	75.25
6	54	6	5.02	72	8	6.69	90	10	8.36	55	495	55	45.99	660	73.33	61.32	825	91.67	76.64
7	63	7	5.85	84	9.33	7.80	105	11.67	9.76	56	504	56	46.82	672	74.67	62.43	840	93.33	78.04
8	72	8	6.69	96	10.67	8.92	120	13.33	11.15	57	513	57	47.66	684	76	63.55	855	95	79.43
9	81	9	7.52	108	12	10.03	135	15	12.54	58	522	58	48.49	696	77.33	64.66	870	96.67	80.83
10	90	10	8.36	120	13.33	11.15	150	16.67	13.94	59	531	59	49.33	708	78.67	65.77	885	98.33	82.22
11	99	11	9.20	132	14.67	12.26	165	18.33	15.33	60	540	60	50.17	720	80	66.89	900	100	83.61
12	108	12	10.03	144	16	13.38	180	20	16.72	61	549	61	51	732	81.33	68	915	101.67	85.01
13	117	13	10.87	156	17.33	14.47	195	21.67	18.12	62	558	62	51.84	744	82.67	69.12	930	103.33	86.40
14	126	14	11.71	168	18.67	15.61	210	23.33	19.51	63	567	63	52.68	756	84	70.23	945	105	87.79
15	135	15	12.54	180	20	16.72	225	25	20.90	64	576	64	53.51	768	85.33	71.35	960	106.67	89.19
16	144	16	13.38	192	21.33	17.84	240	26.67	22.30	65	585	65	54.35	780	86.67	72.46	975	108.33	90.58
17	153	17	14.21	204	22.67	18.95	255	28.33	23.69	66	594	66	55.18	792	88	73.58	990	110	91.97
18	162	18	15.05	216	24	20.07	270	30	25.08	67	603	67	56.02	804	89.33	74.69	1005	111.67	93.37
19	171	19	15.89	228	25.33	21.18	285	31.67	26.48	68	612	68	56.86	816	90.67	75.81	1020	113.33	94.76
20	180	20	16.72	240	26.67	22.30	300	33.33	27.87	69	621	69	57.69	828	92	76.92	1035	115	96.15
21	189	21	17.55	252	28	23.41	315	35	29.26	70	630	70	58.53	840	93.33	78.04	1050	116.67	97.55
22	198	22	18.39	264	29.33	24.53	330	36.67	30.66	71	639	71	59.36	852	94.67	79.15	1065	118.33	98.94
23	207	23	19.23	276	30.67	25.64	345	38.33	32.05	72	648	72	60.20	864	96	80.27	1080	120	100.33
24	216	24	20.07	288	32	26.76	360	40	33.44	73	657	73	61.04	876	97.33	81.38	1095	121.67	101.73
25	225	25	20.90	300	33.33	27.87	375	41.67	34.84	74	666	74	61.87	888	98.67	82.50	1110	123.33	103.12
26	234	26	21.74	312	34.67	28.99	390	43.33	36.23	75	675	75	62.71	900	100	83.61	1125	125	104.52
27	243	27	22.57	324	36	30.10	405	45	37.63	76	684	76	63.55	912	101.33	84.73	1140	126.67	105.91
28	252	28	23.41	336	37.33	31.21	420	46.67	39.02	77	693	77	64.30	924	102.67	85.84	1155	128.33	107.30
29	261	29	24.25	348	38.67	32.33	435	48.33	40.41	78	702	78	65.22	936	104	86.96	1170	130	108.70
30	270	30	25.08	360	40	33.44	450	50	41.81	79	711	79	66.05	948	105.33	88.07	1185	131.67	110.09
31	279	31	25.92	372	41.33	34.56	465	51.67	43.20	80	720	80	66.89	960	106.67	89.19	1200	133.33	111.48
32	288	32	26.76	384	42.67	35.68	480	53.33	44.59	81	729	81	67.73	972	108	90.30	1215	135	112.88
33	297	33	27.59	396	44	36.79	495	55	45.99	82	738	82	68.56	984	109.33	91.42	1230	136.67	114.27
34	306	34	28.43	408	45.33	37.90	510	56.67	47.38	83	747	83	69.40	996	110.67	92.53	1245	138.33	115.66
35	315	35	29.26	420	46.67	39.02	525	58.33	48.77	84	756	84	70.23	1008	112	93.65	1260	140	117.06
36	324	36	30.10	432	48	40.13	540	60	50.17	85	765	85	71.07	1020	113.33	94.76	1275	141.67	118.45
37	333	37	30.94	444	49.33	41.25	555	61.67	51.56	86	774	86	71.91	1032	114.67	95.88	1290	143.33	119.84
38	342	38	31.77	456	50.67	42.36	570	63.33	52.95	87	783	87	72.74	1044	116	96.99	1305	145	121.24
39	351	39	32.61	468	52	43.48	585	65	54.35	88	792	88	73.58	1056	117.33	98.11	1320	146.67	122.63
40	360	40	33.44	480	53.33	44.59	600	66.67	55.74	89	801	89	74.41	1068	118.67	99.22	1335	148.33	124.03
41	369	41	34.28	492	54.67	45.71	615	68.33	57.13	90	810	90	75.25	1080	120	100.33	1350	150	125.42
42	378	42	35.12	504	56	46.82	630	70	58.53	91	819	91	76.09	1092	121.33	101.45	1365	151.67	126.81
43	387	43	35.95	516	57.33	47.94	645	71.67	59.92	92	828	92	76.92	1104	122.67	102.56	1380	153.33	128.21
44	396	44	36.79	528	58.67	49.05	660	73.33	61.32	93	837	93	77.76	1116	124	103.68	1395	155	129.60
45	405	45	37.63	540	60	50.17	675	75	62.71	94	846	94	78.6	1128	125.33	104.79	1410	156.67	130.99
46	414	46	38.46	552	61.33	51.28	690	76.67	64.10	95	855	95	79.43	1140	126.67	105.91	1425	158.33	132.39
47	423	47	39.30	564	62.67	52.40	705	78.33	65.50	96	864	96	80.27	1152	128	107.02	1440	160	133.78
48	432	48	40.13	576	64	53.51	720	80	66.89	97	873	97	81.10	1164	129.33	108.14	1455	161.67	135.17
49	441	49	40.97	588	65.33	54.63	735	81.67	68.28	98	882	98	81.94	1176	130.67	109.25	1470	163.33	136.57
50	450	50	41.81	600	66.67	55.74	750	83.33	69.68	99	891	99	82.78	1188	132	110.37	1485	165	137.96
										100	900	100	83.61	1200	133.33	111.48	1500	166.67	139.36

Table 2 Paperhanging walls and ceilings

Size of room, ft	Height of ceiling 8 ft	9 ft	10 ft	Yards of border	Rolls of ceiling
	Single rolls for walls				
4 × 8	6	7	8	9	2
4 × 10	7	8	9	11	2
4 × 12	8	9	10	12	2
6 × 10	8	9	10	12	2
6 × 12	9	10	11	13	3
8 × 12	10	11	13	15	4
8 × 14	11	12	14	16	4
10 × 14	12	14	15	18	5
10 × 16	13	15	16	19	6
12 × 16	14	16	17	20	7
12 × 18	15	17	19	22	8
14 × 18	16	18	20	23	8
14 × 22	18	20	22	26	10
15 × 16	15	17	19	23	8
15 × 18	16	18	20	24	9
15 × 20	17	20	22	25	10
15 × 23	19	21	23	28	11
16 × 18	17	19	21	25	10
16 × 20	18	20	22	26	10
16 × 22	19	21	23	28	11
16 × 24	20	22	25	29	12
16 × 26	21	23	26	31	13
17 × 22	19	22	24	28	12
17 × 25	21	23	26	31	13
17 × 28	22	25	28	32	15
17 × 32	24	27	30	35	17
17 × 35	26	29	32	37	18
18 × 22	20	22	25	29	12
18 × 25	21	24	27	31	14
18 × 28	23	26	28	33	16
20 × 26	23	28	28	33	17
20 × 28	24	27	30	34	18
30 × 34	27	30	33	39	21

Allowance for waste is included in all figures.
Deduct one roll for every 36 sq ft of openings.
Deduct one roll for every 2 doors.
Deduct for windows as area of each opening.
One roll of wallpaper equals 36 sq ft (24 ft by 18 in.).

Table 3 Covering capacity

Material	Surface or use	Coverage per gallon, sq ft
Exterior Painting		
Priming paint	Wood	450
	Metal	500
Flat house paint	Over primer	500
	Repainting 1 coat	400
Oil paint	Masonry	300
	Concrete	250
	Stucco (smooth)	200
	Stucco (rough)	150
Stain	Wood shingle siding, first coat	150
	Wood shingle siding, second coat	200
Interior Painting		
Priming paint	Wood	500
Metal primer	Metal	600
Undercoat (enamel)	Over primer	400
Flat	Finish coat	500
Semigloss enamel	Finish coat	450
Satin-gloss enamel	Finish coat	450
Gloss enamel	Finish coat	400
Floor enamel	Floors	500
Aluminum paint	Aluminum, first coat	600
	Aluminum, second coat	700
Spar varnish	Finishing woodwork	600
Clear gloss varnish	Finishing woodwork	600
Lacquer	Over stain	450
Interior stain	Woodwork, first coat	500
	Woodwork, second coat	600
	Woodwork, third coat	700
Miscellaneous		
Barn red oil paint	Repaint barn	450
Rust inhibitor (zinc paint)	Metal	650
Furniture sealer and stain	Unpainted furniture	600

Table 4 Flooring tile

(Net covering capacity per 100 sq ft)

Tile size, in.	No. of pieces per 100 sq ft	No. of pieces per sq ft
6 × 6	400	4.00
6 × 12	200	2.00
9 × 9	178	1.78
12 × 12	100	1.00
12 × 24	50	0.50
18 × 18	45	0.45
18 × 24	34	0.33
18 × 36	23	0.23
36 × 36	11	0.11

FLOOR AND WALL COVERING

Wall Areas of Rooms

Table 5 Wall area of rooms (8-ft ceiling), ft²

	Feet								
Feet	3	4	5	6	7	8	9	10	11
3	96	112	128	144	160	176	192	208	224
4	112	128	144	160	176	192	208	224	240
5	128	144	160	176	192	208	224	240	256
6	144	160	176	192	208	224	240	256	272
7	160	176	192	208	224	240	256	272	288
8	176	192	208	224	240	256	272	288	304
9	192	208	224	240	256	272	288	304	320
10	208	224	240	256	272	288	304	320	336
11	224	240	256	272	288	304	320	336	352
12	240	256	272	288	304	320	336	352	368
13	256	272	288	304	320	336	352	368	384
14	272	288	304	320	336	352	368	384	400
15	288	304	320	336	352	368	384	400	416
16	304	320	336	352	368	384	400	416	432
17	320	336	352	368	384	400	416	432	448
18	336	352	368	384	400	416	432	448	464
19	352	368	384	400	416	432	448	464	480
20	368	384	400	416	432	448	464	480	496
21	384	400	416	432	448	464	480	496	512
22	400	416	432	448	464	480	496	512	528
23	416	432	448	464	480	496	512	528	544
24	432	448	464	480	496	512	528	544	560
25	448	464	480	496	512	528	544	560	576

	Feet								
Feet	12	13	14	15	16	17	18	19	20
3	240	256	272	288	304	320	336	352	368
4	256	272	288	304	320	336	352	368	384
5	272	288	304	320	336	352	368	384	400
6	288	304	320	336	352	368	384	400	416
7	304	320	336	352	368	384	400	416	432
8	320	336	352	368	384	400	416	432	448
9	336	352	368	384	400	416	432	448	464
10	352	368	384	400	416	432	448	464	480
11	368	384	400	416	432	448	464	480	496
12	384	400	416	432	448	464	480	496	512
13	400	416	432	448	464	480	496	512	528
14	416	432	448	464	480	496	512	528	544
15	432	448	464	480	496	512	528	544	560
16	448	464	480	496	512	528	544	560	576
17	464	480	496	512	528	544	560	576	592
18	480	496	512	528	544	560	576	592	608
19	496	512	528	544	560	576	592	608	624
20	512	528	544	560	576	592	608	624	640
21	528	544	560	576	592	608	624	640	656
22	544	560	576	592	608	624	640	656	672
23	560	576	592	608	624	640	656	672	688
24	576	592	608	624	640	656	672	688	704
25	592	608	624	640	656	672	688	704	720

Table 6 Wall area of rooms (9-ft ceiling), ft²

	Feet								
Feet	3	4	5	6	7	8	9	10	11
3	108	126	144	162	180	198	216	234	252
4	126	144	162	180	198	216	234	252	270
5	144	162	180	198	216	234	252	270	288
6	162	180	198	216	234	252	270	288	306
7	180	198	216	234	252	270	288	306	324
8	198	216	234	252	270	288	306	324	342
9	216	234	252	270	288	306	324	342	360
10	234	252	270	288	306	324	342	360	378
11	252	270	288	306	324	342	360	378	396
12	270	288	306	324	342	360	378	396	414
13	288	306	324	342	360	378	396	414	432
14	306	324	342	360	378	396	414	432	450
15	324	342	360	378	396	414	432	450	468
16	342	360	378	396	414	432	450	468	486
17	360	378	396	414	432	450	468	486	504
18	378	396	414	432	450	468	486	504	522
19	396	414	432	450	468	486	504	522	540
20	414	432	450	468	486	504	522	540	558
21	432	450	468	486	504	522	540	558	576
22	450	468	486	504	522	540	558	576	594
23	468	486	504	522	540	558	576	594	612
24	486	504	522	540	558	576	594	612	630
25	504	522	540	558	576	594	612	630	648

	Feet								
Feet	12	13	14	15	16	17	18	19	20
3	270	288	306	324	342	360	378	396	414
4	288	306	324	342	360	378	396	414	432
5	306	324	342	360	378	396	414	432	450
6	324	342	360	378	396	414	432	450	468
7	342	360	378	396	414	432	450	468	486
8	360	378	396	414	432	450	468	486	504
9	378	396	414	432	450	468	486	504	522
10	396	414	432	450	468	486	504	522	540
11	414	432	450	468	486	504	522	540	558
12	432	450	468	486	504	522	540	558	576
13	450	468	486	504	522	540	558	576	594
14	468	486	504	522	540	558	576	594	612
15	486	504	522	540	558	576	594	612	630
16	504	522	540	558	576	594	612	630	648
17	522	540	558	576	594	612	630	648	666
18	540	558	576	594	612	630	648	666	684
19	558	576	594	612	630	648	666	684	702
20	576	594	612	630	648	666	684	702	720
21	594	612	630	648	666	684	702	720	738
22	612	630	648	666	684	702	720	738	756
23	630	648	666	684	702	720	738	756	774
24	648	666	684	702	720	738	756	774	792
25	666	684	702	720	738	756	774	792	810

Table 7 Wall area of rooms (10-ft ceiling), ft^2

	Feet								
Feet	3	4	5	6	7	8	9	10	11
3	120	140	160	180	200	220	240	260	280
4	140	160	180	200	220	240	260	280	300
5	160	180	200	220	240	260	280	300	320
6	180	200	220	240	260	280	300	320	340
7	200	220	240	260	280	300	320	340	360
8	220	240	260	280	300	320	340	360	380
9	240	260	280	300	320	340	360	380	400
10	260	280	300	320	340	360	380	400	420
11	280	300	320	340	360	380	400	420	440
12	300	320	340	360	380	400	420	440	460
13	320	340	360	380	400	420	440	460	480
14	340	360	380	400	420	440	460	480	500
15	360	380	400	420	440	460	480	500	520
16	380	400	420	440	460	480	500	520	540
17	400	420	440	460	480	500	520	540	560
18	420	440	460	480	500	520	540	560	580
19	440	460	480	500	520	540	560	580	600
20	460	480	500	520	540	560	580	600	620
21	480	500	520	540	560	580	600	620	640
22	500	520	540	560	580	600	620	640	660
23	520	540	560	580	600	620	640	660	680
24	540	560	580	600	620	640	660	680	700
25	560	580	600	620	640	660	680	700	720

	Feet								
Feet	12	13	14	15	16	17	18	19	20
3	300	320	340	360	380	400	420	440	460
4	320	340	360	380	400	420	440	460	480
5	340	360	380	400	420	440	460	480	500
6	360	380	400	420	440	460	480	500	520
7	380	400	420	440	460	480	500	520	540
8	400	420	440	460	480	500	520	540	560
9	420	440	460	480	500	520	540	560	580
10	440	460	480	500	520	540	560	580	600
11	460	480	500	520	540	560	580	600	620
12	480	500	520	540	560	580	600	620	640
13	500	520	540	560	580	600	620	640	660
14	520	540	560	580	600	620	640	660	680
15	540	560	580	600	620	640	660	680	700
16	560	580	600	620	640	660	680	700	720
17	580	600	620	640	660	680	700	720	740
18	600	620	640	660	680	700	720	740	760
19	620	640	660	680	700	720	740	760	780
20	640	660	680	700	720	740	760	780	800
21	660	680	700	720	740	760	780	800	820
22	680	700	720	740	760	780	800	820	840
23	700	720	740	760	780	800	820	840	860
24	720	740	760	780	800	820	840	860	880
25	740	760	780	800	820	840	860	880	900

FLOOR AND WALL COVERING
Panel Conversion Chart

Table 8 Standard modular panel conversion chart

(For plywood, architectural woodwork, sheathing, plastic laminate, gypsum board, and other modular wall components)

No. of units	Size (areas in square feet)				No. of units	Size (areas in square feet)			
	4′ x 8′	4′ x 10′	4′ x 12′	4′ x 14′		4′ x 8′	4′ x 10′	4′ x 12′	4′ x 14′
10	320	400	480	560					
11	352	440	528	616	36	1152	1440	1728	2016
12	384	480	576	672	37	1184	1480	1776	2072
13	416	520	624	728	38	1216	1520	1824	2128
14	448	560	672	784	39	1248	1560	1872	2184
15	480	600	720	840	40	1280	1600	1920	2240
16	512	640	768	896	41	1312	1640	1968	2296
17	544	680	816	952	42	1344	1680	2016	2352
18	576	720	864	1008	43	1376	1720	2064	2408
19	608	760	912	1064	44	1408	1760	2112	2464
20	640	800	960	1120	45	1440	1800	2160	2520
21	672	840	1008	1176	46	1472	1840	2208	2576
22	704	880	1056	1232	47	1504	1880	2256	2632
23	736	920	1104	1288	48	1536	1920	2304	2688
24	768	960	1152	1344	49	1568	1960	2352	2744
25	800	1000	1200	1400	50	1600	2000	2400	2800
26	832	1040	1248	1456	51	1632	2040	2448	2856
27	864	1080	1296	1512	52	1664	2080	2496	2912
28	896	1120	1344	1568	53	1696	2120	2544	2968
29	928	1160	1392	1624	54	1728	2160	2592	3024
30	960	1200	1440	1680	55	1760	2200	2640	3080
31	992	1240	1488	1736	56	1792	2240	2688	3136
32	1024	1280	1536	1792	57	1824	2280	2736	3192
33	1056	1320	1584	1848	58	1856	2320	2784	3248
34	1088	1360	1632	1904	59	1888	2360	2832	3304
35	1120	1400	1680	1960	60	1920	2400	2880	3360

Table 9 Drywall conversion chart

	Size (areas in square feet)					*Size (areas in square feet)*			
No. of pieces	*4″ × 8″*	*4″ × 10″*	*4″ × 12″*	*4″ × 14″*	*No. of pieces*	*4″ × 8″*	*4″ × 10″*	*4″ × 12″*	*4″ × 14″*
10	320	400	480	560					
11	352	440	528	616	36	1152	1440	1728	2016
12	384	480	576	672	37	1184	1480	1776	2072
13	416	520	624	728	38	1216	1520	1824	2128
14	448	560	672	784	39	1248	1560	1872	2184
15	480	600	720	840	40	1280	1600	1920	2240
16	512	640	768	896	41	1312	1640	1968	2296
17	544	680	816	952	42	1344	1680	2016	2352
18	576	720	864	1008	43	1376	1720	2064	2408
19	608	760	912	1064	44	1408	1760	2112	2464
20	640	800	960	1120	45	1440	1800	2160	2520
21	672	840	1008	1176	46	1472	1840	2208	2576
22	704	880	1056	1232	47	1504	1880	2256	2632
23	736	920	1104	1288	48	1536	1920	2304	2688
24	768	960	1152	1344	49	1568	1960	2352	2744
25	800	1000	1200	1400	50	1600	2000	2400	2800
26	832	1040	1248	1456	51	1632	2040	2448	2856
27	864	1080	1296	1512	52	1664	2080	2496	2912
28	896	1120	1344	1568	53	1696	2120	2544	2968
29	928	1160	1392	1624	54	1728	2160	2592	3024
30	960	1200	1440	1680	55	1760	2200	2640	3080
31	992	1240	1488	1736	56	1792	2240	2688	3136
32	1024	1280	1536	1792	57	1824	2280	2736	3192
33	1056	1320	1584	1848	58	1856	2320	2784	3248
34	1088	1360	1632	1904	59	1888	2360	2832	3304
35	1120	1400	1680	1960	60	1920	2400	2880	3360

FLOOR AND WALL COVERING
Gypsum Board Framing Standards

Gypsum board framing standards for wood or steel framed construction (maximum frame spacing and fastener spacing)

Ceilings (wood- or steel-framed)

Thickness	*Application*	*Frame spacing*	*Fastener spacing*	
			Nails	*Screws*
½ in	Parallel	16 in o.c.	7 in o.c.	12 in o.c.
	Perpendicular	16 in o.c.	7 in o.c.	12 in o.c.
⅝ in	Parallel	16 in o.c.	7 in o.c.	12 in o.c.
	Perpendicular	24 in o.c.	7 in o.c.	12 in o.c.

Walls

Thickness	*Frame spacing**	*Fastener spacing*
½ in	24 in o.c.	12 in o.c.
	16 in o.c.	16 in o.c.
⅝ in	24 in o.c.	12 in o.c.
	16 in o.c.	16 in o.c.

*16 in o.c. recommended for abuse-resistant applications.

Basic Single-Layer System, Treated Joints

1. Position all ends and edges of all gypsum fiber panels over framing members, except when joints are at right angles to framing members, as in perpendicular application or when end joints are back-blocked.
2. Apply gypsum fiber panels first to the ceiling, then to the walls. Extend ceiling board into corners and make firm contact with top plate. To minimize end joints, use panels of maximum practical lengths. Fit ends and edges closely, but not forced together. Stagger end joints in successive courses with joints on opposite sides of a partition placed on different studs.
3. Attach panels to framing supports by standard single nailing method, double nailing method, or power-driven screws. Space fasteners not less than ⅜ in from edges and ends of panels and drive as recommended for specified fastening method. Drive fasteners in field of panels first, working toward ends and edges. Hold panel in firm contact with framing while driving fasteners. Drive fastener heads slightly below surface of gypsum fiber panels in a uniform dimple.
4. For UL fire-rated partition designs, refer to the specific UL design for proper fastener spacing.
5. Install trim at all internal and external angles formed by the intersection of either panel surfaces or other surfaces. Apply metal or paper-faced corner bead to all vertical or horizontal external corners in accordance with manufacturer's directions.

Estimating the Amount of Hardwood Strip Flooring Required

An allowance for side matching, plus 5 percent for end matching and normal waste are incorporated into these percentages.

Take the square footage and add the percentage below opposite the size of strip flooring to be used.

When using	¾ × 1½ in strip	*add*	55%
	¾ × 2 in		42½%
	¾ × 2¼ in		38⅓%
	¾ × 3¼ in		29%
	⅜ × 1½ in		38⅓%
	⅜ × 2 in		30%
	½ × 2½ in		38⅓%
	½ × 2 in		30%

The above percentages are for laying flooring straight across the room. Additional flooring should be estimated for diagonal applications and bay windows or other projections.

Converting Square Feet of Floor Space to Board-Feet of Strip Flooring Required

Floor space	*Board-feet required (5% cutting waste included)*				
Square feet	*¾ × 2¼ in*	*¾ × 1½ in*	*¾ × 3¼ in*	*½ × 2 in*	*⅜ × 1½ in*
5	7	8	6	7	7
10	14	16	13	13	14
20	28	31	26	26	28
30	42	47	39	39	42
40	55	62	52	52	55
50	69	78	65	65	69
60	83	93	77	78	83
70	97	109	90	91	97
80	111	124	103	104	111
90	125	140	116	117	125
100	138	155	129	130	138
200	277	310	258	260	277
300	415	465	387	390	415
400	553	620	516	520	553
500	692	775	645	650	692
600	830	930	774	780	830
700	968	1085	903	910	968
800	1107	1240	1032	1040	1107
900	1245	1395	1161	1170	1245
1000	1383	1550	1290	1300	1383

FLOOR AND WALL COVERING
Carpet Construction

Carpets are manufactured in three different ways: woven, knitted, or tufted.

Woven Carpet

The surface pile and backing of woven carpet are interwoven at the same time, creating a single fabric. Due to the interweaving, which locks all of the yarns together in the single woven fabric, the pile yarns cannot be pulled out. Some carpet weaves presently available are velvet, wilton, and axminster. Velvet is best suited for solid-color carpet; however, tweeds, stripes, and salt-and-pepper effects can be produced on velvet looms. The usual velvet is a solid-color carpet with smooth surface and even pile. Sometimes the pile is cut to produce a plushlike surface (see Fig. 1*a*). It may also be had in loop pile, or twist.

Wilton weave comes in almost unlimited numbers of textures and sculptured effects, as well as patterns. The pile is sometimes cut, sometimes left uncut; a combination of cut and uncut may also be obtained. In multicolor wiltons, one color may be seen on the surface pile, while other colors are hidden in the body of the carpet. Embossed and sculptured effects are also made by the wilton looms, and cut and uncut pile can be combined with cut pile for the top level, with loops at other levels. Another variation is to have some pile yarn straight and others twisted (see Fig. 1*b*).

In the axminster weave, which is similar in appearance to handweaving, we find a complete flexibility in the use of color. In this method, each tuft is inserted separately and, while solid-color carpets can be made by this method, it is nearly always used for multicolored pattern carpet such as orientals, or modern and geometric designs (see Fig. 1*c*).

Tufted Carpet

In the tufted process, which was only recently perfected, the tufts are attached to a previously made backing, as compared with the methods previously described, in which the backing and pile are integral. The tufts are held in place by a heavy coating of latex applied to the backing, which is usually cotton, jute, or kraft cord. By the use of this method, a wide variety of textures is possible. For example, the tufted pile can be made in several levels, it can be cut or uncut, and carved or striated effects can be obtained. The pile can be looped or plush. Tufted carpets are made in multicolor patterns with an increasing number of textural effects and refinements (see Fig. 1*d*).

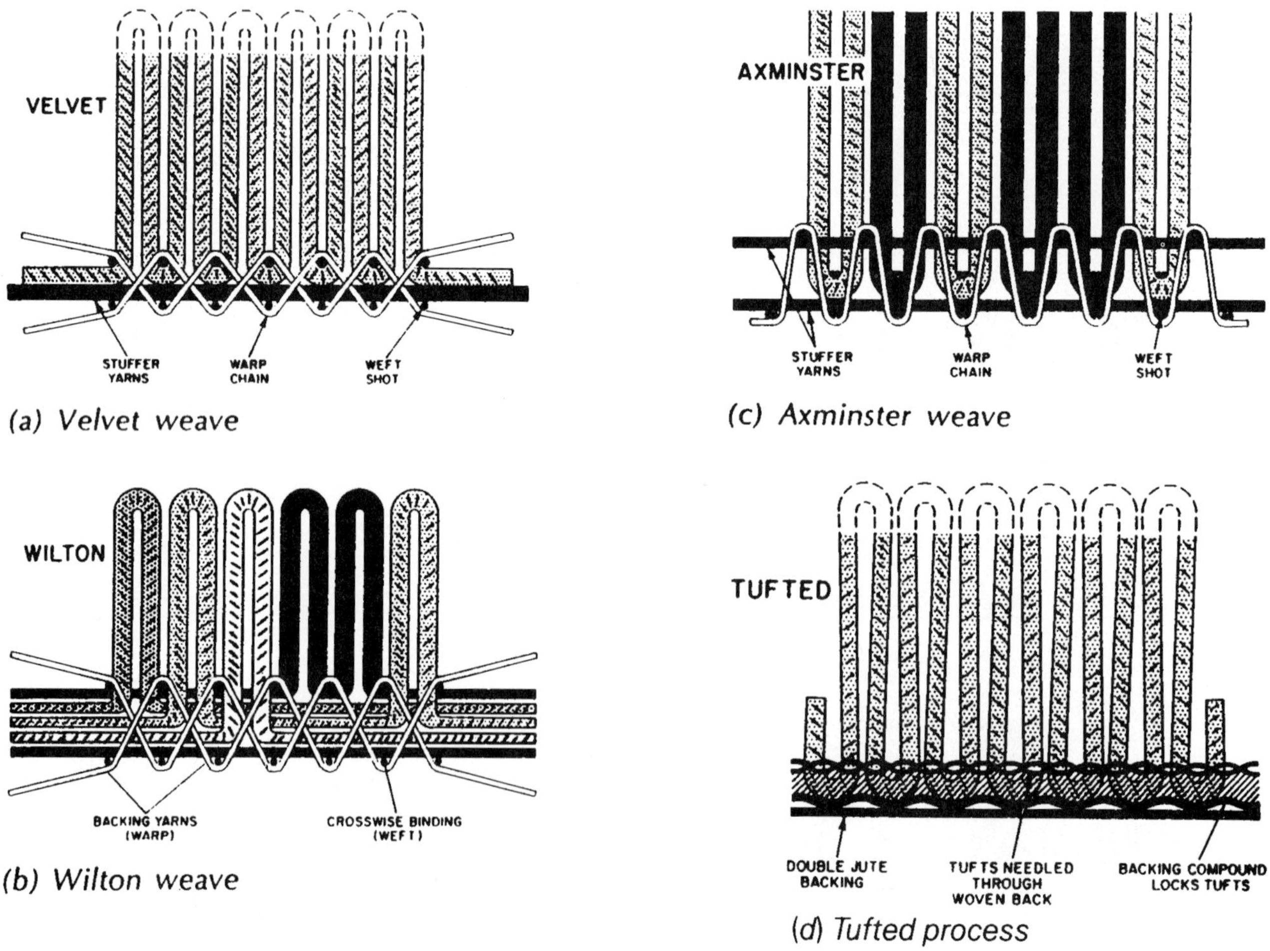

(*a*) *Velvet weave*

(*b*) *Wilton weave*

(*c*) *Axminster weave*

(*d*) *Tufted process*

Fig. 1

Carpet Types

Type of Weave — Characteristics and Best Uses

LEVEL LOOP: EVEN HEIGHT, TIGHTLY SPACED UNCUT LOOPS. TEXTURE IS HARD AND PEBBLY. HARD WEARING AND EASY TO CLEAN. IDEAL FOR OFFICES AND HIGH-TRAFFIC AREAS.

MULTILEVEL LOOP: UNEVEN HEIGHT IN PATTERNS. TIGHTLY SPACED UNCUT LOOPS. TEXTURE IS HARD AND PEBBLY. HARD WEARING AND EASY TO CLEAN. IDEAL FOR OFFICES AND HIGH-TRAFFIC AREAS.

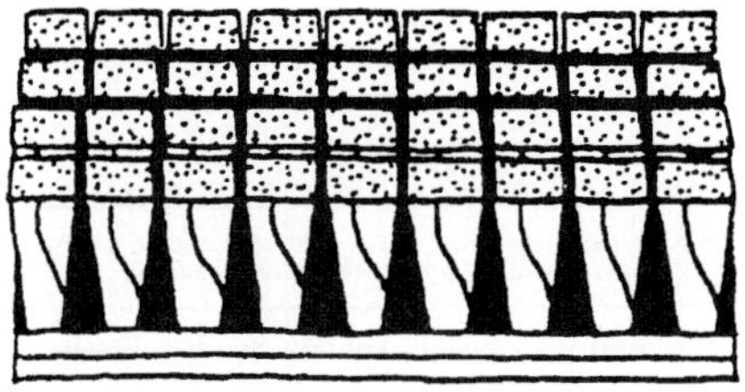

PLUSH CUT PILE: EVENLY CUT YARNS WITH MINIMAL TWIST. EXTREMELY SOFT, VELVETY TEXTURE. VACUUMING AND FOOTPRINTS APPEAR AS DIFFERENT COLORS, DEPENDING ON LIGHT CONDITIONS. IDEAL FOR FORMAL ROOMS WITH LIGHT TRAFFIC.

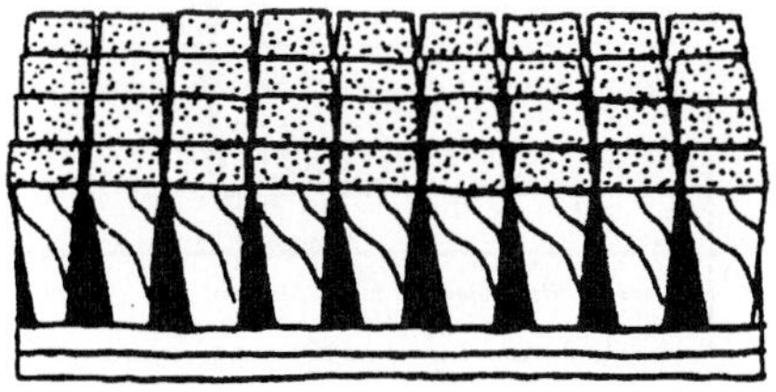

FRIEZE CUT PILE: EVENLY CUT YARNS WITH TIGHT TWIST. EXTREMELY SOFT, VELVETY TEXTURE. VACUUMING AND FOOTPRINTS APPEAR AS DIFFERENT COLORS, DEPENDING ON LIGHT CONDITIONS. IDEAL FOR FORMAL ROOMS WITH LIGHT TRAFFIC.

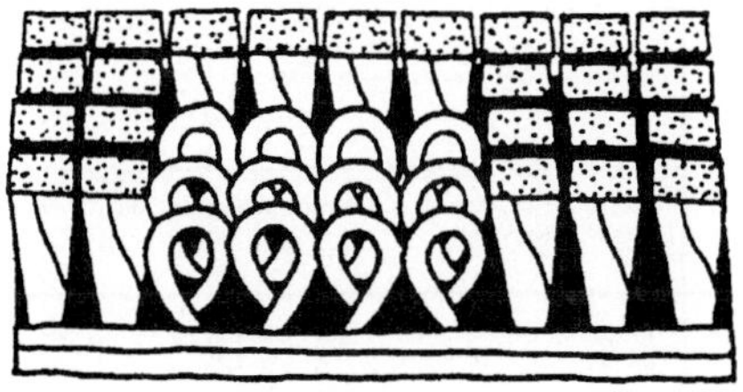

CUT AND LOOP: COMBINATION OF BOTH PLUSH AND LEVEL LOOP. HIDES DIRT FAIRLY WELL. IDEAL FOR RESIDENTIAL APPLICATIONS.

INDOOR-OUTDOOR: CUT, TIGHTLY TWISTED YARNS THAT TWIST UPON THEMSELVES. TEXTURE IS ROUGH. HIDES DIRT EXTREMELY WELL AND IS NEARLY AS TOUGH AS LEVEL LOOP. IDEAL FOR RESIDENTIAL APPLICATIONS.

HOME-DECORATING FABRIC CHART

In the chart below are listed the fabrics usually classified as primarily decorating materials. In addition to these, practically all dress materials may be used, and are often woven in extra widths for this purpose. Among these are: light weight cottons such as cambric, challis, chambray, gingham, muslin, percale, poplin, seersucker, silkaline all used for informal draperies, bed coverings, dressing tables, etc.; stiff fabrics such as buckram and crinoline for interlining curtain tops, valances, etc.; cottons such as Canton flannel used for interlinings, and sateen for linings; heavy utility cottons such as crash, denim, drill, gabardine, pique, all suited to certain types of draperies, couch covers, etc.; sheer cottons such as cheesecloth, dimity, plain and dotted Swiss, lace, lawn, organdy, voile, all used for glass curtains, bed coverings, etc.; pile fabrics such as corduroy, panne velet, velour, velvet, velveteen, all excellent for upholstery, draperies, etc.; silk fabrics such as faille, moire (watered silk), pongee and shantung, satin, taffeta, all used for draperies, bed coverings, slipcovers, sometimes upholstery; sheer silks such as chiffon for glass curtains, lamp shades, etc.

FABRIC	DESCRIPTION	SUITABLE FOR
ARMURE	Ribbed silk, cotton, rayon (sometimes wool), fabric with small design on the surface.	Draperies. Medium-weight upholstery.
ARTIFICIAL LEATHER	Available under many trade names. A woven cotton fabric, coated with nitrocellulose preparation and stamped surface to simulate different kinds of leather.	Medium-weight upholstery. Panels. Other decorative uses.
BATIK	Javanese process of coloring fabrics by blocking out various parts of the pattern with wax before dyeing.	Curtains and panels. Other decorative effects.
BOBBINET	Net with hexagonal openings. Originally handmade with a bobbin.	Glass curtains. Dressing table skirts, etc.
BROCADE	Rich, colorful fabric with embroidery effects on taffeta, twill, satin or damask weave background. Gold or silver metal threads sometimes introduced in the figures. Brocade is also the name designating a certain type of Jacquard weave.	Draperies. Medium-weight upholstery. Especially good for rooms of Queen Anne, Chippendale, Hepplewhite or Sheraton furnishings of 18th Century.
BROCATELLE	A heavy fabric with general characteristics of damask, but figures more raised and velvety in quality giving embossed effect.	Draperies on very large studio-size windows. Heavy-weight upholstery.
BROCHE	Brocade with small floral pattern.	Lined or unlined draperies. Medium-weight upholstery.
BURLAP	Coarse, plain-weave fabric made of jute or hemp. Comes in variety of colors and widths. Inexpensive.	Drapery or upholstery purposes.
CALICO	Light-weight cotton fabric in plain weave. May be printed, plain or patterned, in deep colors. Designs usually small. (Also for dresses.)	Curtains, draperies, bedspreads, comfortables. Excellent with Early American or French Provincial furnishings.
CANDLEWICK	Cotton yarn used for hand tufting on muslin sheeting. Yarn may be white or in color and design simple or elaborate.	Bedspreads, draperies, and other decorative purposes.
CANVAS	A coarse, firm cotton or linen material, rough finish, plain weave. May be bleached, unbleached, starched, dyed, or printed.	Awnings, couch covers, etc.; also used for stiff interlining as at top of draperies.
CASEMENT CLOTH	Light, plain, and usually neutral in color. Made in cotton, linen, mohair, silk, wool or rayon. Sometimes comes in small figures.	Fine for draw-curtains; also glass curtains in sheer textures.
CELLOPHANE	Glossy, transparent synthetic product woven on warp threads of cotton. Often woven in with other materials and used for many novelty effects.	Draperies in modern interiors. Trimmings, etc.
CHENILLE	Various types of fabrics woven with chenille yarn of silk, wool, mercerized cotton, or rayon.	Draperies. Yarn used for tufting, fringes, etc.
CHEVRON CLOTH	Fabric with broken twill weave forming chevron pattern.	Draperies, etc.
CHINTZ	A firm plain weave cotton fabric usually printed in gay pattern, but may be had in plain colors. May be semi-glazed or fully glazed. Some chintz has special finish so that it will retain glaze after washing. Glazed chintz is more resistant to dirt, while its shiny surface and stiff texture adds to its charm. There are many grades of chintz, and many have soil-resistant special finish.	May be formal or informal in pattern. Suitable to any room according to pattern, quality and treatment. Used for draperies, upholstery, slip covers, lamp shades, etc.
CRETONNE	Cotton or linen fabric named for French town of Creton, with plain, rep or damask weave background printed in large designs. Does not muss easily and can be washed often.	Draperies, upholstery, slip covers, bed covers, etc. Often more formal than chintz.
CREWEL EMBROIDERY	A type of wool embroidery worked on unbleached cotton or linen ground in large floral, bird, or tree designs.	Draperies and upholstery. Used extensively during Jacobean period.
DAMASK	The name originated with the beautiful silks woven in Damascus during the 12th Century. Damasks are now made of linen, cotton, wool, or any of the synthetic fibers, or combinations of the two. In taffeta weave on satin ground, this fabric in flat woven pattern is usually reversible. Damask is also the name given to a kind of Jacquard weave.	In silk or cotton it is used for draperies and upholstery. Appropriate for Queen Anne, Chippendale, Hepplewhite or Sheraton furnishings of 18th Century.
DRUID'S CLOTH	A fabric of loosely twisted cotton yarn, or cotton mixed with jute, in basket weave. Something like monk's cloth but not as rough in texture.	Draperies. Couch covers.
DUCK	Heavy plain weave cotton fabric.	Outdoor cushions, etc.
FELT	A material made by matting together, under heat or pressure, woolen fibers, mohair, cowhair, or mixed fibers.	Upholstery and couch covers. Rugs.

HOME-DECORATING FABRIC CHART CONTINUED

FABRIC	DESCRIPTION	SUITABLE FOR
FILET NET	Cotton or linen net with square mesh. Hand netted filet has a knot at each corner of square mesh.	Curtains, tablecloths, scarves, etc.
FORTUNY PRINTS	Fabrics produced in Venice by a secret printing process which gives cotton cloth the effect of antique brocades and damasks. Comes in beautiful color combinations.	Draperies. Wall hangings, screens, etc.
FRIAR'S CLOTH	Like druid's cloth but with finer basket weave.	Same as druid's cloth.
FRISE	Uncut pile fabric of wool, mohair, cotton or linen. Patterns may be printed or produced by using yarns of different colors, or by cutting some of the loops to give sculptured effect. Very durable.	Upholstery.
GAUZE	Thin, sheer transparent fabric of plain weave, sometimes printed. May be all silk, or cotton, linen, wool, mohair, synthetic fibers, or combinations.	Glass curtains.
HAIR CLOTH	A fabric with warp of cotton, worsted, or linen, and horsehair weft, woven plain, striped or patterned. May now be obtained in colors and variety of woven designs.	Upholstery. Used extensively in England and America during middle of 19th Century.
HOMESPUN	Coarse hand-woven woolen, cotton or linen fabrics. Also trade name given to imitations made on power looms.	Curtains and upholstery in informal rooms. Bedspreads in cotton.
INDIA PRINTS	Printed cotton cloth with clear colors and characteristic designs of India or Persia. Handprinted with many colors on white or natural background.	Draperies. Wall hangings. Bed coverings, etc.
JASPE	Fabrics having warp threads of different colors giving material streaked or mottled effect, resembling jasper.	Draperies and other decorative effects.
LAME	A fabric with silk and metal threads in plain weave or with a woven pattern.	Drapery. Panels.
LAMPAS	A fabric similar to damask in appearance and brocatelle in weave. Generally all silk with multi-colored pattern on plain background, often classic in design.	Used as damask is used.
MARQUISETTE	Sheer cloth in gauze weave of cotton, silk, rayon, often with woven figure. It comes in wide range of colors, and may be dyed or printed.	Excellent for glass curtains. Fluffy, dainty, tailored spreads.
METALASSE	Fabric with brocaded pattern in raised, padded or blistered effect.	Draperies.
MOHAIR	Various types of fabrics made from the fleece of the Angora goat. Most durable of all textiles. Now woven in combination with cotton, linen, silk or wool into many types of plain, twill or pile fabrics.	Very durable and widely used for upholstery.
MONK'S CLOTH	Heavy cotton fabric of coarse basket weave.	Drapery material.
MOQUETTE	Pile fabric resembling frise, woven on Jacquard loom with small set pattern in different colors.	Used for upholstery in mohair, wool, or heavy cotton.
NINON	A semi-transparent fabric of silk or rayon.	Glass curtains.
PLUSH	High pile fabric resembling fur, made of silk, wool, cotton or any synthetic fiber. Pile may be cut or uncut.	Upholstery.
REP	Plain weave fabric of heavy rib made of silk, cotton or wool, or synthetic fibers. Unpatterned and reversible.	Draperies. Upholstery.
SAIL CLOTH	Stout, firm, plain weave cotton material similar to canvas in construction but lighter. Has a stiff, hard texture and is printed in gay, bright colors.	Draperies. Slip covers. Bedspreads, etc.
SLIPPER SATIN	Sleek, smooth very heavy satin in rayon or silk; may be slightly stiff because of thickness.	Drapery and upholstery, bed coverings, etc. Suitable in formal and period rooms for draperies.
SCRIM	Fabric of coarse two-ply yarns in plain, open weave. Often mercerized.	Curtains, bedspreads, etc.
STRIE	Term used to designate fabric with uneven streaked effect. This process gives two-toned appearance to taffeta, satin, etc.	According to fabric.
TERRY CLOTH	Light cotton fabric similar to bath toweling. Woven with uncut loops. May be dyed or printed, in designs of one or two colors. Rich texture and reversible.	Draperies. Draw-curtains.
THEATRICAL GAUZE	Loosely woven, transparent plain-weave fabric of cotton or linen. Obtainable in brilliant as well as soft colors. Inexpensive.	Glass curtains.
TOILES DE JOUY	Printed cotton material with repeat designs showing landscapes, or historical scenes. Reproductions of famous printed fabric woven at Jouy, near Paris, France. Designs and figure groups usually in colors on white or cream background.	Draperies, wall hangings, upholstery, bed coverings. Excellent for French, English and American period rooms of late 18th Century and early 19th Century; also French Provincial.
TWEED WEAVES	Term applied to a large group of woolen goods made from worsted yarns, woven in plain, twill, or herringbone twill weaves in homespun type.	Draperies and upholstery. Very good for modern or masculine rooms.
VELOUR	Really a French word for velvet. Through common usage, a short-pile velvet.	Same as velvet.

FABRIC AND FURNITURE

Fabric Patterns and Measurements

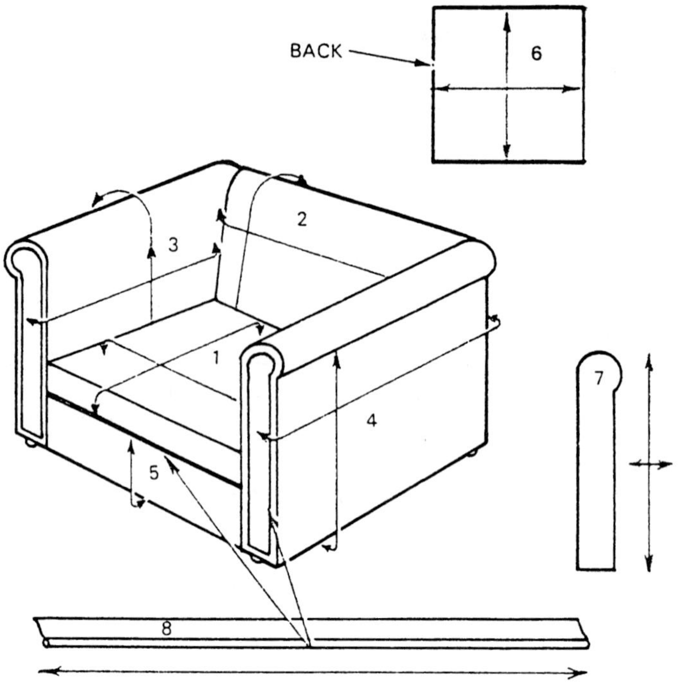

Fig. 1

Making Fabric Patterns from Existing Upholstered Furniture

When existing patterns or old covers do not exist, use the diagram in Fig. 1 as an example of where to take measurements. The lines, numbers, and arrows indicate measurement locations.

Part no.	*Part name*	*Pieces req.*	*Width*	*Length*
1	Seat (S)	1	38 in	25 in
2	Inside back (1B)	1	38 in	26½ in
3	Inside arm (1A)	2	26½ in	26½ in
4	Outside arm	2	26½ in	23 in
5	Bottom band (or seat boxing)	1	37 in	8 in
6	Outside back (OB)	1	36 in	25 in
7	Front panel (FP)	2	8 in	26 in
8	Welting (W)	6	54 in	1½ in

This chart provides an example of how to record the sizes of panels. Width measurements should always be indicated first. Abbreviations are noted in parentheses.

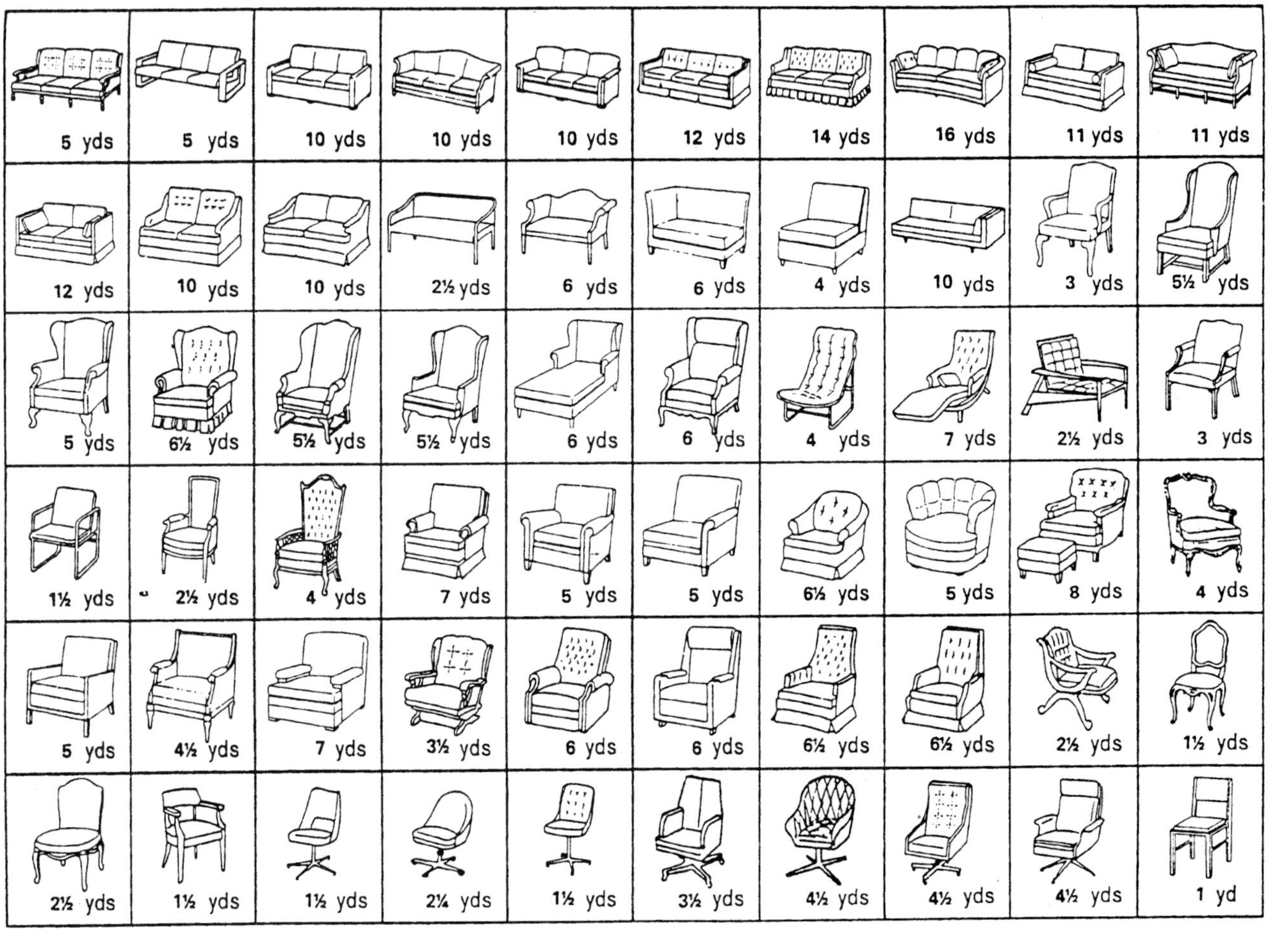

NOTE: This chart provides an approximate amount of fabric or leather yardage that might be needed for generic furniture types similar to those illustrated. If possible, always check with the manufacturer or take precise measurements of the piece.

FABRIC AND FURNITURE

Comparison of Fibers Suitable for Upholstery Fabrics

Fiber	*Cost comparison*	*Strength*	*Abrasion resistance*	*Feel*	*Main advantage*	*Main disadvantage*
Cotton	Low cost	Strong	Good	Soft, cool	Can be used for many applications	Burns and wrinkles easily
Linen	Expensive	Very strong	Very good	Much like cotton	Durable, has natural luster	Wrinkles easily, needs special care
Wool	Moderately expensive	Moderate	Moderate	Warm, soft, resilient	Easy to sew and shape	Needs careful handling, cleaning
Silk	Very expensive	Strong	Good	Very soft, warm	Beautiful luster, easy to work	High cost, needs careful treatment
Mohair	Expensive	Moderate	Moderate	Quite soft, warm, very resilient	Lustrous and resilient	Difficult to spin evenly
Viscose rayon	Low	Fairly strong	Moderate	Soft, limp fiber, cool	Has many uses	Weak if wet, wrinkles easily
Modified rayon	Low	Fairly strong	Moderate	Warmer than ordinary rayon	Warmer, deeper texture	Weak when wet, wrinkles easily
Acetate	Moderately low	Moderate	Fair	Soft, not very resilient	Easily worked	Heat sensitive, moderately durable
Triacetate	Moderate	Moderate	Fair	Like acetate	Like acetate but can be heat set and is drip dry	Only moderately durable
Polyamides (nylon)	Moderately expensive	Very strong	Excellent	Glassy or slippery	Strong and tough, can be heat set, drip dry	Nonabsorbent, uncomfortable feel in tight weaves
Acrylics (Orlon, Acrilan, Creslan, and Zefran)	Moderately expensive	Fairly strong	Fairly good	Soft, warm, resilient	Like wool in texture	Sensitive to heat and moisture
Olefin polyethylene	Relatively low	Moderately strong	Good	Like wool	Dense fiber, easy to clean with detergents	Does not accept dyes easily
Polypropylene	Relatively low	Strong	Good	Like wool	Dense fiber, easy to clean with detergents	Does not accept dyes readily
Saran	Very expensive	Strong	Good	Silky	Dense fiber, easy to clean	High cost

Mattress types and sizes (juvenile, youth, and adult)

	Width (in/cm)		*Length (in/cm)*	
Mattress type	*Minimum*	*Maximum*	*Minimum*	*Maximum*
Bassinet	17/43	23/81	36/91	40/90
Portable crib	22/56	26/66	45/114	52/132
Junior crib	24/61	31.5/80	46/116	58/147
Youth bed	33/84	36/91	66/168	76/193
Bunk bed	30/76	33/84	75/191	76/193
Dorm bed	32/81	36/91	75/191	80/203
Hospital bed	36/91	36/91	74/188	80/203
Narrow twin	36/91	36/91	74/188	75/191
Twin bed	39/99	39/99	75/191	81/206
Super twin	45/114	45/114	75/191	80/203
Full-size	54/137	54/137	74/188	75/191
Double bed	54/137	54/137	74/188	75/191
Extra long double	54/137	54/137	80/203	80/203
Queen-size	60/152	60/152	80/203	84/213
King-size	76/193	78/198	80/203	84/213

Pillow types and sizes

	Width (in/cm)		*Length (in/cm)*	
Pillow type	*Minimum*	*Maximum*	*Minimum*	*Maximum*
Standard	18/46	20/51	26/66	27/69
Queen	19/48	21/53	29/74	30/76
King	20/51	22/56	35/89	36/91

Note: Many manufacturers also make and merchandise undersized pillows for cribs and youth beds as well as oversized pillows for larger beds.

ELECTRICAL
Office and Electronic Equipment

Table 1 Typical amperage ratings

Equipment	Amperage
Electronic Equipment	
Video Display Terminals (Detached Keyboards)	
Normal maximum	2.50
Burroughs/MT 983 TP110	.08
Digital/VT 278 Decmate	1.25
Form-Phase Systems/8115-2	.48
Harris/8680A	1.00
Hewlett-Packard/2382A	.75
IBM/3101	1.20
IBM/3278 or 3276	1.33
IBM/3279	2.50
IBM/5251 Model 11	2.10
IBM/6580	4.80
ITT Courier/2790-2A	1.50
Perkin/Elmer/1251	1.30
Prime/PT-45	1.00
Raytheon/PTS100	.80
Sperry-Univac/UTS20 (313)	.50
Texas Instruments/940/200	2.00
Texas Instruments/DS990	2.20
Wang/5503	3.00
Xerox/8000 Series	.50
Video Display Terminals (Integrated Keyboard)	
Normal maximum	3.00
Hewlett-Packard/HP-9845A	4.50
Lear Siegler/ADM31	.50
NCR/7900-01	.60
Perkin-Elmer/550B	.80
Tektronics/4112	3.00
Wang/5536	2.00
Printers (Stand Alone)	
Digital Equipment/LA-120AA	3.00
Wang/5503	4.00
Xerox/8000 Print Server	11.00
Printers (Desk Top)	
Normal maximum	3.50
Centronics/7030	1.50
Digital Equipment/Decwriter IV	1.30
Form-Phase Systems/8125	1.60
Hewlett-Packard/7221B	1.00
Hewlett-Packard/HP7240A	2.50
IBM/3287	2.36
IBM/5256	4.70
Epson/FX 185	.70
NEC/3510	2.50
ITT Courier/8700	1.60
Lear Siegler/300 Series	1.60
Perkin-Elmer/650	1.50
Raytheon/PTS 1200 3472	1.50
Sperry-Univac/0786	4.00
Tektronix/4612	3.30
Texas Instruments/Omni-800 810R0	5.00
Wang/5531-2 w/floor mount	1.70
Wang/5577 (DW-20 Series)	1.20

Equipment	Amperage
Electronic Equipment	
Memory Storage Devices (Desk Top)	
Wang/5503 Disk	4.00
Xerox/8000 NS	12.00
Digital Equipment/RX02	3.00
Hewlett-Packard/8290 ZM	1.00
Hewlett-Packard/9895A	1.60
Sperry-Univac/8406	1.50
Texas Instruments/WD-500	3.00
Bell/Western Electric/Dataphone 300/1200	.08
Office Equipment*	
General	
Typewriter	1.50
Transcriber	.15
Microfiche	.85
Manuscript holder	.75
Calculator	.25
A.C. adapter	.05
Electric eraser	.25
Pencil sharpener	.25
Fan	1.00
Space heater (1,000 watts)	8.50
Space heater (1,250 watts)	10.50
Space heater (1,500 watts)	12.50
Coffee pots	10.00
Copy machine	15.00
Clock	.03
CRT (average)	1.50
Printer (average)	3.50
Lighting	
Adjustable task light	.80
2" task light (20 watt)	.27
2" task light (30 watt)	.40
2" task light (40 watt)	.48
2" task light (35 watt, energy-saving ballast)	.38
Indirect ambient light	
(30 watt/2 lamp)	.68
(30 watt/3 lamp)	1.08
(40 watt/2 lamp)	.80
(40 watt/3 lamp)	1.28
(35 watt/2 lamp)	.63
(35 watt/3 lamp with energy-saving ballast)	1.01
HID light (400 watt)	4.00
(250 watt)	2.50
(175 watt)	1.80
PLP light (20 watt)	.65
(40 watt)	.80

Note: These figures are for quick reference only. For specific information consult the manufacturer.

*Some appliances – such as large copiers, coffee makers, or space heaters – require most of the current available on a 20-amp circuit. It is recommended that such devices be supplied with their own receptacle, directly from the building. This leaves the capacity of Series 9000 circuits available for the more dynamic requirements of the office occupants.

Table 1 Residential appliance, load, and circuit chart*

Appliance	Typical wattage	Voltage needed	Amps load	Wires and size†	Size fuse or breaker‡	Type of circuit and comments
Range	12,000	115/230	52	3#6	50A	Separate circuit—grounded
Countertop range	6,000	115/230	26	3#10	30A	Separate circuit—grounded
Oven built-in	5,000	115/230	22	3#10	30A	Separate circuit—grounded
Dishwasher	1,200	115	10	2#12 w/grd§	20A	These two can be connected on one circuit; must be grounded.
Waste disposal	500	115	5	2#12 w/grd	20A	
Broiler	1,500	115	13	2#12	20A	Two or more 20-amp circuits needed for these appliances depending on number used at once. A 115/230 V "splitwired" circuit provides capacity of two ordinary circuits at any outlet. Ask your wiring inspector about this.
Fryer	1,300	115	11	2#12	20A	
Coffeemaker	800	115	7	2#12	20A	
Refrigerator	400	115	4	2#12	20A	
Toaster	1,100	115	10	2#12	20A	
Frypan	1,200	115	10	2#12	20A	
Roaster	1,500	115	13	2#12	20A	
Clothes dryer	5,000 to 9,000	115/230	25	3#10 to 3#6	30A to 45A	Separate circuit—grounded.
Washer	500	115	9	2#12 w/grd	20A	Grounded—advise fused outlet for motor protection.
Hand iron	1,000	115	9	2#12 w/grd	20A	A 20-A circuit will carry only one of these in addition to washer.
Hot plate	1,500	115	13	2#12 w/grd	20A	
Ironer	1,650	115	15	2#12 w/grd	20A	
Workshop	——	115	—	2#12	20A	Separate circuit grounded.
Portable heater	1,500	115	13	2#12	20A	Use on general-use circuits.
Television	300	115	3	2#14	15A	
Portable lights—(up to)	300	115	3	2#14	15A	
Lighting, general (each)	100	115	1¼	2#14	15A	(Not over 9 per circuit, including convenience outlets.)
Air conditioner (window unit)	1,500	115 or 230	13 or 7	2#12 w/grd	20A	Requires separate circuit; 230 volt operation preferred.
Air conditioner (central unit)	3,400	115/230	20	3#10	—	Check manufacturer's recommendations; should be grounded.
Water system	500	115	5	2#12 w/grd	20A	Separate circuit—grounded. Provide motor protection (230V. for ½ hp. or larger).
Heating plant	600	115	6	2#12 w/grd	20A	Separate circuit—grounded. Provide motor protection.
Electric heaters (built-in)	750 to 4,500	230	—	—	—	Wiring should be planned with heating. Provide separate circuits for heating.
Water heater	1,500 to 4,500	230	7 to 20	2#12 w/grd / 2#10 w/grd	20A to 30A	Separate circuit—grounded.

† Wire sizes are for copper wire. For aluminum, use next larger size.
‡ Fustats advised in place of ordinary fuses up to 30 amp as they do not blow on harmless short-time overloads and cannot be replaced by a larger size.
§ W/grd means with groundwire. This is usually a bare wire run inside the same cable but can be installed separately. Portable equipment is grounded through the third prong on the plug. Permanent equipment is grounded by direct connection of the third wire to the frame of the appliance.
* Courtesy Agricultural Extension Service, South Dakota State University.

Table 2 Typical office amperage loads

CAD station*	10.00–20.00
Calculator	.25
Coffee pot*	8.50–15.00
Clock	.03
Radio	.03
Stereo	.33
Tape recorder	.07
Laser printer*	6.00–10.00
Desktop copier*	10.00–15.00
Electric eraser	.25
Fan	1.10
Freestanding copier*	15.00–20.00
Pencil sharpener	1.00
Task light (4′)	.67
Adding machine	.35
Letter opener	1.90
Dictaphone	.25
Telecopier	.50
Word processor	1.50– 3.00
Postage meter	2.80
Tape dispenser	1.80
Personal computer	3.50– 8.00
Desktop printer	1.50– 5.00
CRT	1.00– 3.00
Space heater*	12.50
Typewriter	1.50
Microfiche reader	.85
Transcriber	.15
A.C. adapter	.05
100-W lamp	.80

*Some appliances such as coffee pots, copiers, printers, and heaters consume most of the amperage available on a circuit. It is recommended that these devices be connected directly to the building power supply, leaving flexibility for other circuit planning.

Table 3 Common house circuits

Type	Wire size	Ampere rating of fuse or circuit breaker	Volts	Load capacity in watts	Use of circuit	Types of outlets
General purpose	minimum #14 recommended #12	15 20	115-120	1725-1800	Installed lighting, outlets for lamps and low wattage appliances all over the house	Those for attached light fixtures; ordinary convenience outlets
Appliance	minimum #12 recommended #10	20 25	115-120	2300-2400 2875-3000	Portable appliances in kitchen, dining room, work room, laundry	Ordinary or grounded convenience outlets
Individual appliance	#12	20	115-120	2300-2400	Automatic washer, refrigerator, freezer	Ordinary or grounded convenience outlets
Individual power	#6 or #8	30-60	220-240	6600-14400	Range, water heater, clothes dryer	Receptacle for plug with 3 heavy prongs or appliances may be attached

COLOR AND LIGHT

Material and Color Light Reflectances

Cloth	%
White linen (dull finish)	81
White cotton	65
Red cotton (diamine fast red)	44
Black cotton (diamine)	33
Blue woolen	25
Blue flannel	17.5
Blue linen (navy blue)	17
Black woolen	12
Black velvet	1.8

Paper	%
Quality white	85
White blotting	82
White drawing	70–80
Medium-quality white	75
Light gray	73
Cheap white	70
Pink	60
Buff	60
Newsprint	55
Medium gray	45
Dark gray	20
Chocolate brown	20
Olive green	15
Matte black	5
Ultramarine blue	3.5
Hard pencil line	45
Soft pencil line	25
Printer's ink (good quality)	15
Black ink	4
Black velour	0.4

Accent colors	%
White (diffuse)	80
Deep red	14–22
Red	21–31
Orange	38–48
Yellow	60–65
Yellow green	42–46
Saturated green	24–32
Blue	17–23
Violet purple	12–14
Red purple	16–23

Woods	%
Birch and beech	35–50
Whitewood (plain)	45
Maple	42
Satinwood	34
Light oak	25–35
English oak	17
Walnut	16
Black walnut	5–15
Dark oak and cherry	10–15
Mahogany	12

Glass and plastic	%
Mirror glass	80–90
Metabolized plastic	75–85
White structural glass	75–80
Reflective glass	20–30
Clear glass	7
Tinted glass	7
Black structural glass	5

Interior surface colors	%
Dull or flat white	75–90
Cream or eggshell	79
Pale pink, pale yellow	75–80
Ivory	75
Light green, blue, or orchid	70–75
Light beige and pale gray	70
Soft pink and light peach	69
Pink	64
Apricot	56–62
Tan or yellow gold	55
Light gray	35–50
Medium turquoise	44
Yellow green	45
Medium light blue	42
Old gold and pumpkin	34
Rose	29
Cocoa brown and mauve	24
Medium green and blue	21
Medium gray	20
Dark brown and dark gray	10–15
Olive green	12
Dark blue and blue green	5–10
Forest green	7
Aluminum paint	60–70

Recommended Levels of Artificial Illumination

The following is a guide for minimum levels of illumination for certain tasks. The values accommodate young adults with normal and better than 20/30 corrected vision. Values in one category can be used under other categories. The first value is for foot candles (fc) for the task, the second value is for lux (lx) for the task.

Office	*fc*	*lx*
Bookkeeping	150	1610
Typing	70	750
Filing	70	750
Conference rooms	30	320
Reception areas	20	220
Corridors	20	220
Drafting (low value is for rough work, high value is for fine work)	150–200	1610–2150

School	*fc*	*lx*
Chalkboards	150	1610
Desks (for study)	70	750
Drawing (art work)	70	750
Gymnasium	30	320
Auditorium	15	160

Theater	*fc*	*lx*
Lobby	20	220
During intermission	5	54
During movie	0.1	1

Industrial	*fc*	*lx*
Precision manual arc welding	1,000	10,750
Extra-fine machine work and inspection	1,000	10,750
Fine machine work	500	5,380
Medium machine work	100	1,080
Rough machine work	50	540
Sheet metal (scribing)	100	1,080
Steel and sheet metal fabrication	50	540
Paint mixing and matching	200	2,150
Receiving and shipping	10	110

Home	*fc*	*lx*
Reading, studying	30–70	320–750
Writing (with pencil)	70	570
Sewing, hand or machine (low value is for white cloth and high value is for black cloth)	50–200	540–2150
Kitchen sink and range	70	750
Kitchen counters	50–150	540–1600
Laundry work	50	540
Workbench hobbies	70–200*	750–2150
Washer, dryer, games	30	320

*Use if making jewelry.

For instruments	*fc*	*lx*
Business machines, calculators, digital input, etc.	50–100	540–1080
Control panels, consoles	30–50	320–540
Dials	30	320
Meters	30–50	320–540
Gauges	50	540
Scales	30–50	320–540
Scales with 1/64-in divisions	180	1930

Medical	*fc*	*lx*
Operating table	2,500	26,850
Emergency operating	2,000	21,500
Dental work	1,000	10,750
Examination room	50–100	540–1,080

Train	*fc*	*lx*
Dining	50	540
Reading	30	320
Aisle, steps	10	110

Levels of Illumination in Daylight

Light condition	*fc*	*lx*
In direct sunshine (at noon)	6,000–8,000	64,500–87,000
In shade (outdoors at noon)	100–1,000	1,080–10,750
Comfortable reading (in shade at noon)	200	2,150 minimum

COLUMNS, CAPITALS, AND ENTABLATURES
Proportions

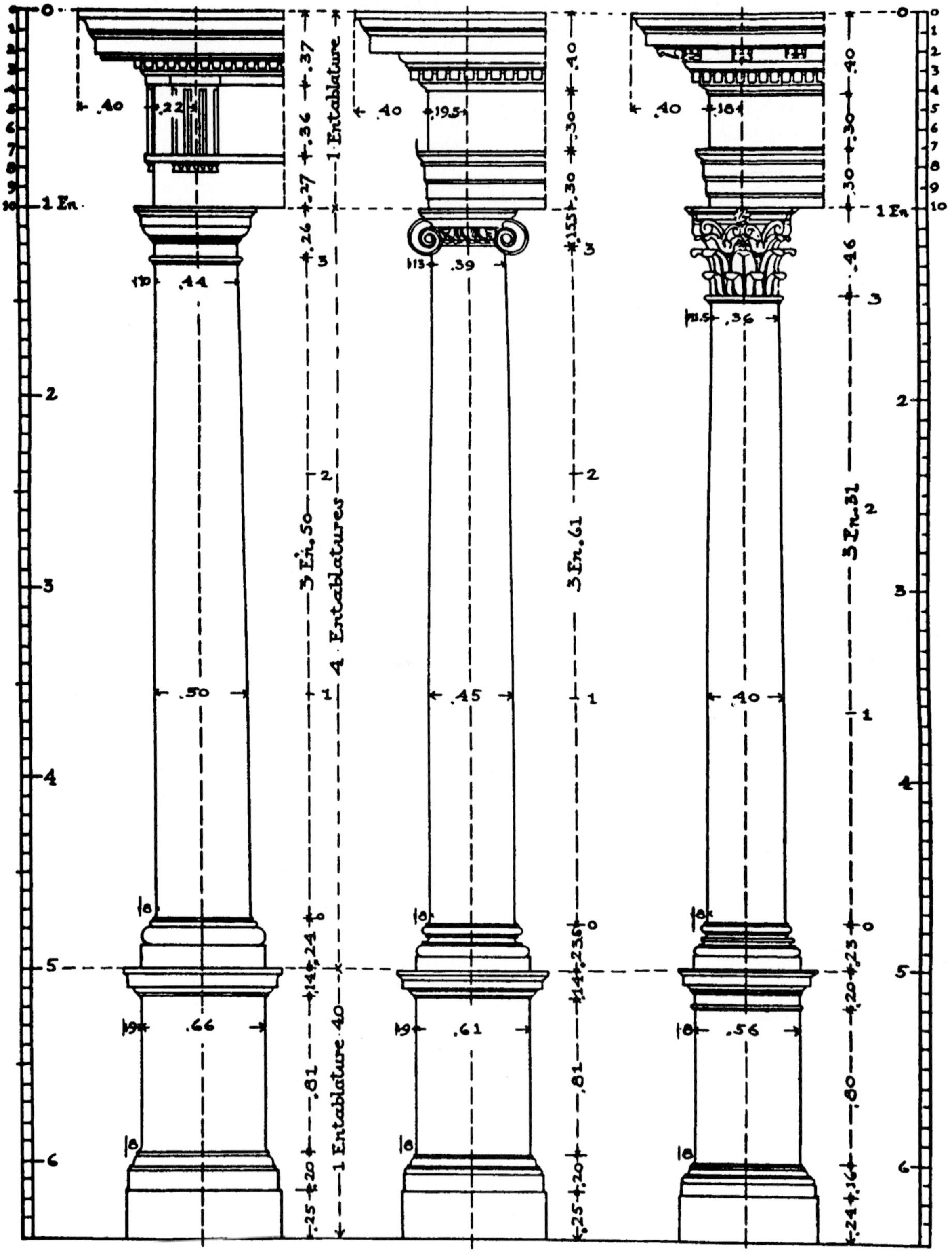

doric ionic corinthian

Wood screws are primarily used for joining wood to wood, the clamping force they provide creating an extremely strong joint that is easily dismantled. They are also used for attaching fittings such as hinges, locks and handles. Most screws are made of steel, which is sometimes case-hardened for extra strength. Brass screws are more decorative, and stainless-steel screws resist corrosion even outdoors. Both can be used in acidic woods such as oak that are stained by ordinary steel hardware. Steel screws may be zinc coated to prevent corrosion, and chrome plating and black japanning are used as decorative coatings. The common types shown here illustrate the principles. In addition, there are a number of other specialized head profiles and drive shapes, the square-recess Robertson pattern being just one example. The most widely known cross-head screw is Phillips, although there are several others.

Screw Sizes

The specified length of a screw corresponds to the part of it that actually enters the wood, as shown in the drawing at left. This measurement can be anywhere from ¼ to 6 in (6 to 150 mm). Select a screw that is about three times as long as the thickness of the piece of wood or board it is to secure. Even if a screw is not long enough to burst through the back of a work piece, it will deform the wood fibers, creating a noticeable bulge in the wood, unless you make sure the point stops at least ⅛ in (3 mm) short of the surface.

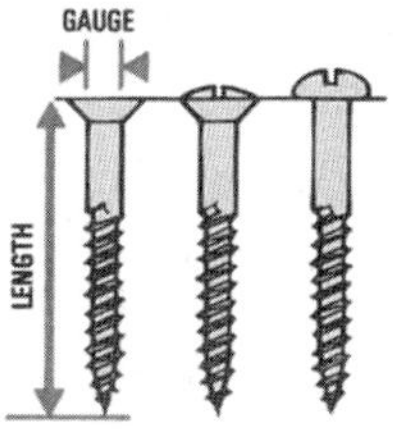

How screws are measured

Screws are also specified by their nominal diameter, or *gauge.* This is never described using a precise measurement. Instead, screw gauges are specified by numbers from 0 to 20—the higher the number, the larger the screw. A no. 5 screw, for example, is about ⅛ in (3 mm) in diameter and a No. 14 screw is about ¼ in (6 mm). For strength, select the largest possible gauge, though the nominal diameter of the screw should never exceed ⅒ of the width of wood into which it is to be inserted. The table of wood-screw sizes shows the lengths commonly available in the various gauges.

Conventional Wood Screws

About 60 percent of the overall length of a conventional wood screw is threaded. The plain cylindrical shank of a wood screw acts like a dowel and is surmounted by a wider head that holds the work piece or attachment in place.

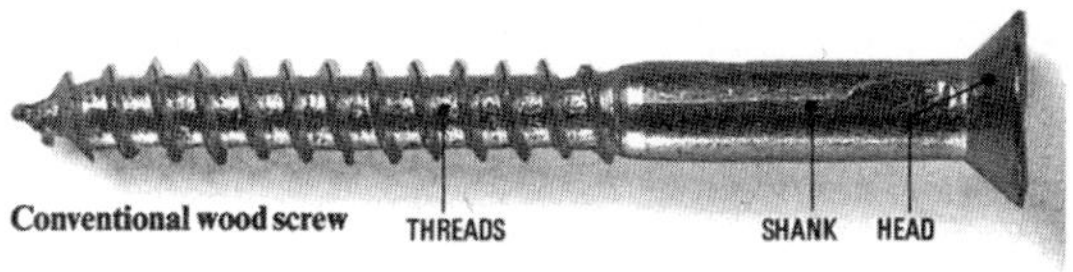

Twin-Threaded Screws

A newer generation of wood screws is made with coarse twin threads that provide a strong hold even in chipboard or MDF. Compared with a conventional screw, more of the overall length is threaded and the shank is much narrower, so there is less risk of splitting the wood. The steep pitch of the threads enables the screw to be driven quickly.

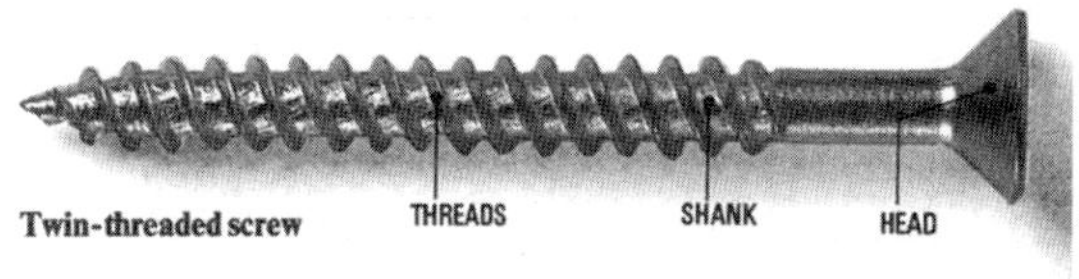

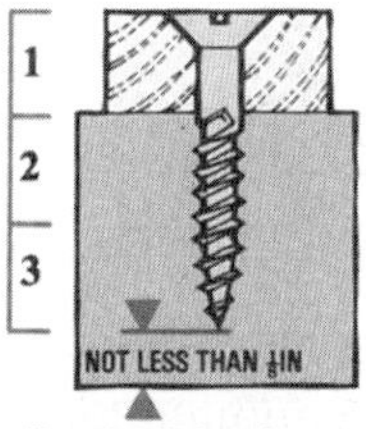

Choosing the length of a screw
A screw should be three times as long as the thickness of the wood it is to secure.

Pilot holes
To prevent the wood from splitting, drill a pilot hole in the work to guide a screw. Use a drill bit that is slightly narrower than the width of the screw thread.

WOOD-SCREW SIZES

LENGTH																	
IMPERIAL	METRIC	GAUGE NUMBER															
¼in	6mm	0	1	2	3	4											
⅜in	9mm	0	1	2	3	4	5	6		8							
½in	12mm		1	2	3	4	5	6	7	8							
⅝in	16mm				3	4	5	6	7	8		10					
¾in	18mm				3	4	5	6	7	8	9	10	12				
⅞in	22mm					4		6	7	8							
1in	25mm				3	4	5	6	7	8	9	10	12	14			
1¼in	32mm					4	5	6	7	8	9	10	12	14			
1½in	38mm					4		6	7	8	9	10	12	14	16		
1¾in	44mm							6	7	8	9	10	12	14	16		
2in	50mm							6	7	8	9	10	12	14	16	18	20
2¼in	57mm							6		8		10	12	14			
2½in	63mm							6		8	9	10	12	14	16		
2¾in	70mm									8		10	12	14			
3in	75mm							6		8		10	12	14	16	18	20
3½in	89mm									8		10	12	14	16		
4in	100mm									8		10	12	14	16	18	20
4½in	112mm											10	12	14			20
5in	125mm											10	12	14	16		
6in	150mm												12	14	16		

NAILS, SCREWS, AND BOLTS

Nails

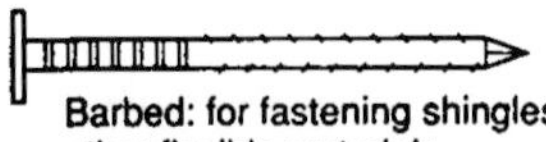
Barbed: for fastening shingles or other flexible materials

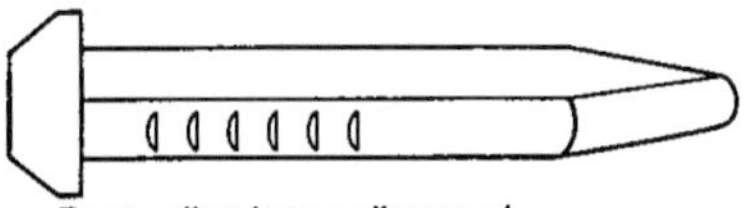
Boat spike: long spike used in timber construction

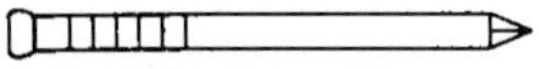
Brad: finishing nail less than 1 inch long

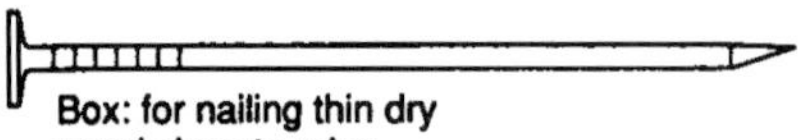
Box: for nailing thin dry wood close to edge

Cement-coated box: coated with resin that increases holding power

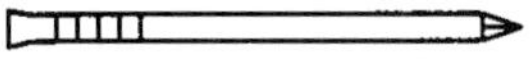
Casing: similar to finishing, but with dulled point to penetrate thin trim without splitting

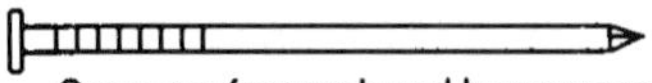
Common: for rough and heavy construction

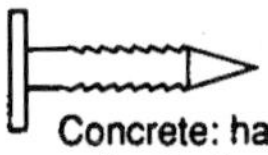
Concrete: hardened steel nail with diamond point

Fluted concrete: hardened steel nail with fluting to increase holding power

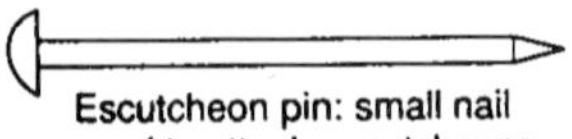
Escutcheon pin: small nail used to attach escutcheons

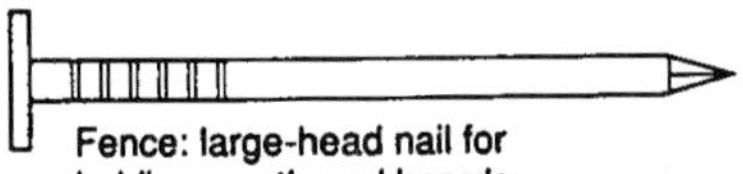
Fence: large-head nail for holding weathered boards

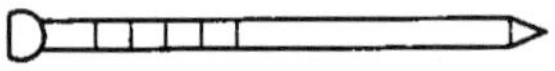
Finishing: slender nail that can be set below surface

Cut finishing: finishing nail used in historic restoration

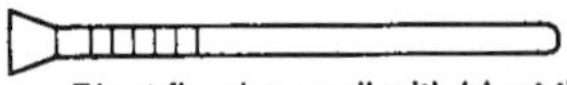
Blunt flooring: nail with blunt tip to prevent splitting hardwood flooring

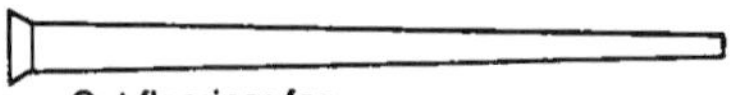
Cut flooring: for historic restoration

Drive-screw flooring: nail with screw-drive to increase holding power

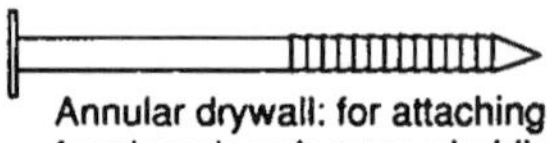
Annular drywall: for attaching drywall to framing; rings increase holding power

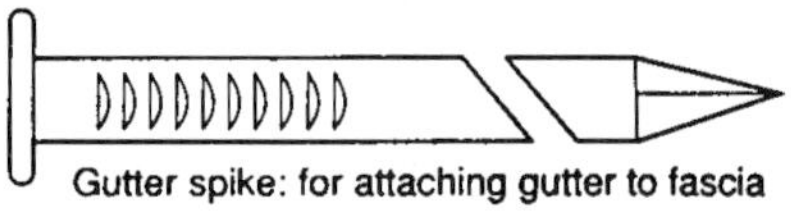
Gutter spike: for attaching gutter to fascia

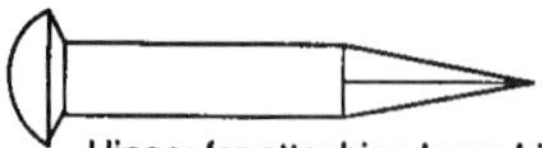
Hinge: for attaching large hinges such as for barn doors

Annular hinge: hinge with rings to increase holding power

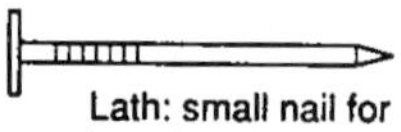
Lath: small nail for installing wood lath

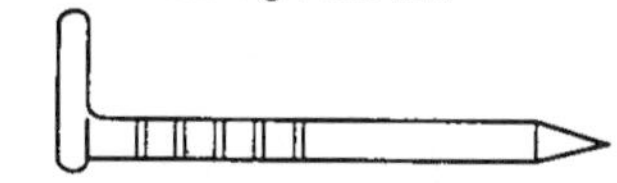
Offset head: for use with power nailer

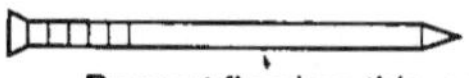
Parquet flooring: thin nail to prevent splitting parquet

Pole barn: large spike for attaching framing to poles

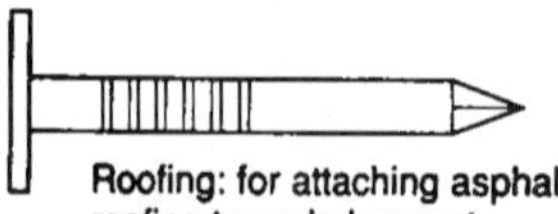
Roofing: for attaching asphalt roofing to underlayment

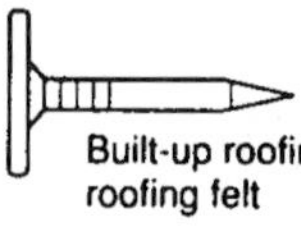
Built-up roofing: for attaching roofing felt

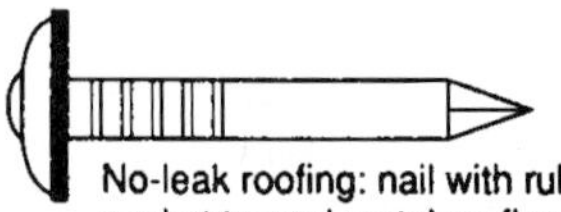
No-leak roofing: nail with rubber gasket to seal metal roofing

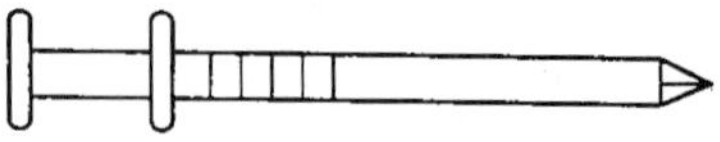
Scaffold: nail with double head to make nail easy to pull for temporary fastening

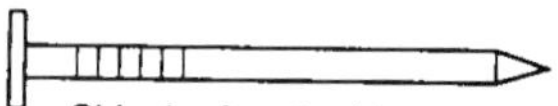
Shingle: for attaching cedar shingles

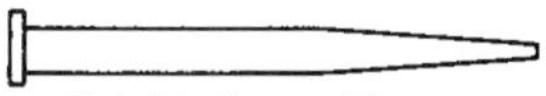
Cut shingle: used in historic restoration

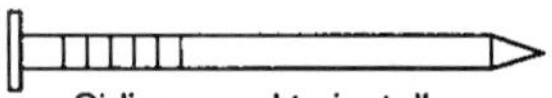
Siding: used to install beveled wood siding

Screw-thread siding: nail with a screw thread to increase holding power

Cement-coated sinker: used to install underlayment

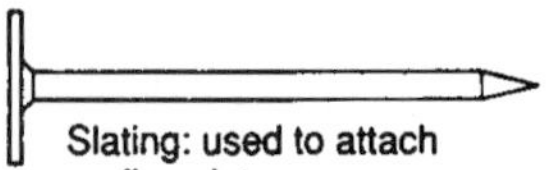
Slating: used to attach roofing slates

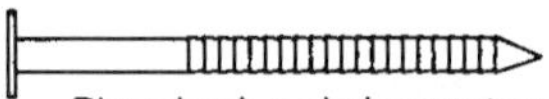
Ring shank underlayment: nail with rings to increase holding power

Spike: common nail 4-1/2 inches or longer

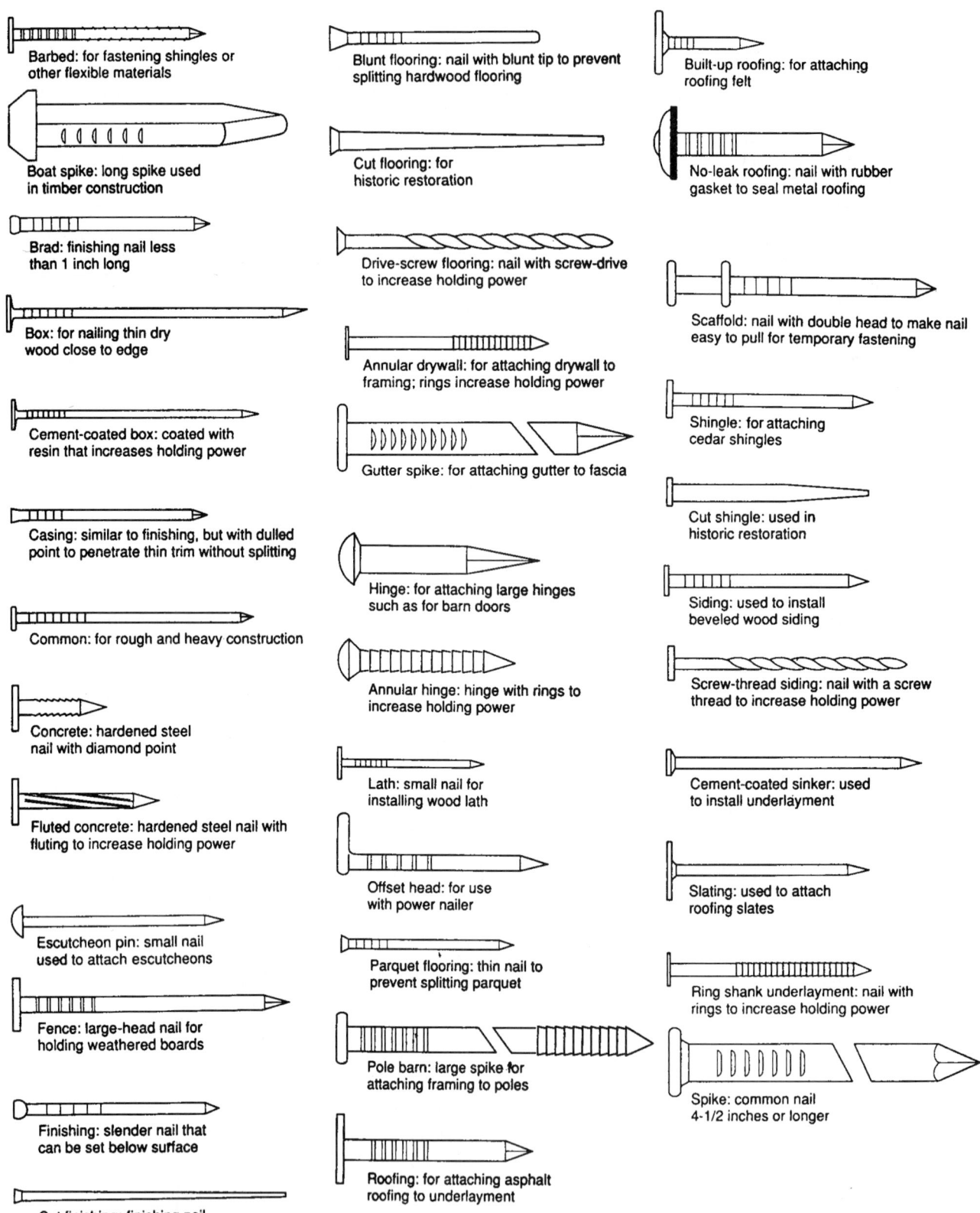

SCREWS

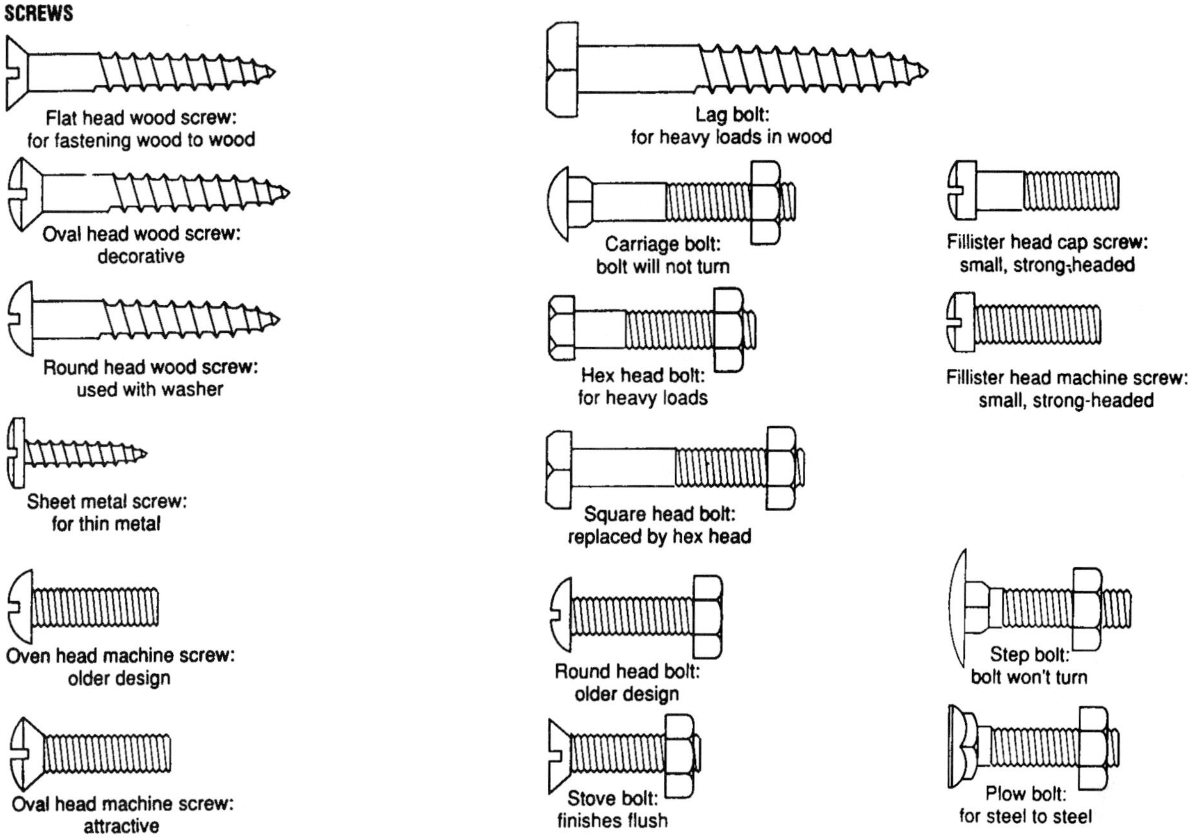
Flat head wood screw:
for fastening wood to wood
Oval head wood screw:
decorative
Round head wood screw:
used with washer
Sheet metal screw:
for thin metal
Oven head machine screw:
older design
Oval head machine screw:
attractive
Lag bolt:
for heavy loads in wood
Carriage bolt:
bolt will not turn
Hex head bolt:
for heavy loads
Square head bolt:
replaced by hex head
Round head bolt:
older design
Stove bolt:
finishes flush
Fillister head cap screw:
small, strong-headed
Fillister head machine screw:
small, strong-headed
Step bolt:
bolt won't turn
Plow bolt:
for steel to steel

SCREW AND BOLT HEADS

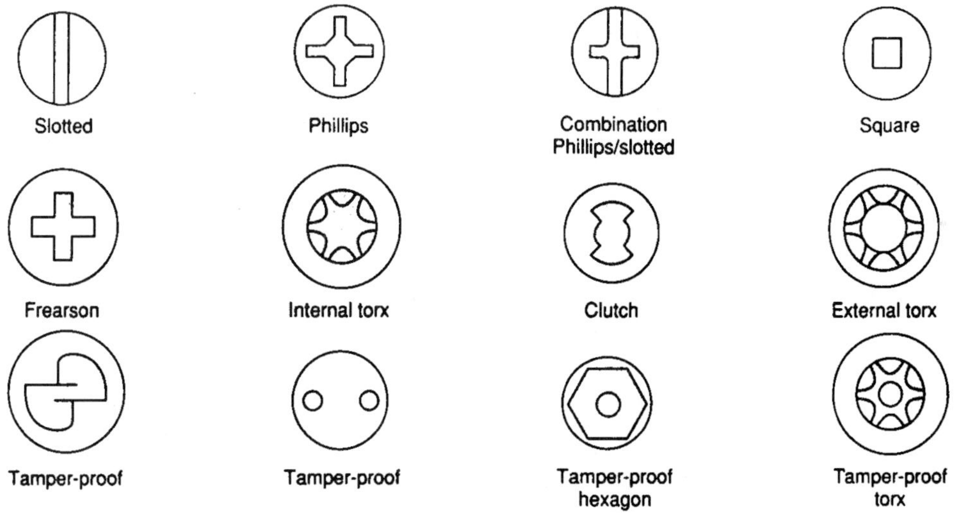
Slotted
Phillips
Combination
Phillips/slotted
Square
Frearson
Internal torx
Clutch
External torx
Tamper-proof
Tamper-proof
Tamper-proof
hexagon
Tamper-proof
torx

WASHERS

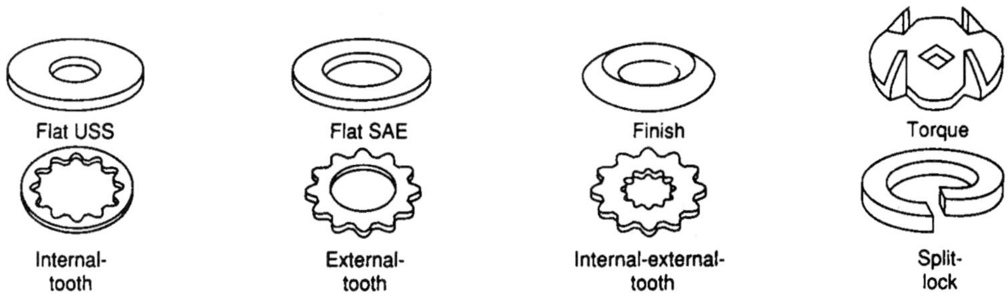
Flat USS
Flat SAE
Finish
Torque
Internal-
tooth
External-
tooth
Internal-external-
tooth
Split-
lock

AUDIOVISUAL

Graphic Projection Image Size and Distance

Image size chart (systems with large optics)

	Image size in feet			
	Wide angle	Standard	Tele	Tele
Distance in feet	135 mm	180 mm	241 mm	318 mm
3				
6				
9	4.60			
12	6.50	4.89		
15	8.25	6.20	4.46	
18	10.00	7.51	5.35	4.04
21	11.75	8.83	6.20	4.75
24	13.50	10.14	7.09	5.46
27	15.30	11.45	7.95	6.18
30	17.00	12.76	8.83	6.90
36	20.50	15.39	10.57	8.33
45	25.75	19.32	13.19	10.47
60	34.50	25.89	17.55	14.06
90	52.00	39.00	26.28	21.20
120	69.50	52.13	35.00	28.30
150	87.00	65.25	43.75	35.50

Image size chart (systems with small optics)

	Image size in feet						
	Wide angle	Wide angle	Standard	Zoom 70–120 mm		Tele	S-Tele
Distance in feet	35 mm	51 mm	85 mm	min.	max.	152 mm	241 mm
3	3.30	2.25	1.32	0.90	1.56		
6	6.60	4.67	2.64	1.80	3.12	1.50	
9	9.90	7.00	3.96	2.70	4.68	2.25	1.32
12	13.20	9.50	5.28	3.60	6.24	3.00	1.76
15	16.50	11.90	6.60	4.50	7.80	3.75	2.21
18	19.80	14.27	7.92	5.40	9.36	4.50	2.65
21	23.10	16.67	9.24	6.30	10.92	5.25	3.09
24	26.40	19.07	10.56	7.20	12.48	6.00	3.53
27	29.70	21.50	11.88	8.10	14.04	6.75	3.97
30			13.20	9.00	15.60	7.50	4.41
36			15.84	10.80	18.72	9.00	5.29
45			19.80	13.50	23.40	11.25	6.62
60			26.40	18.00	31.20	15.00	8.82
90			39.60	27.00	46.80	22.50	13.23

Image Size and Typical Throw Distance of an LCD Projector

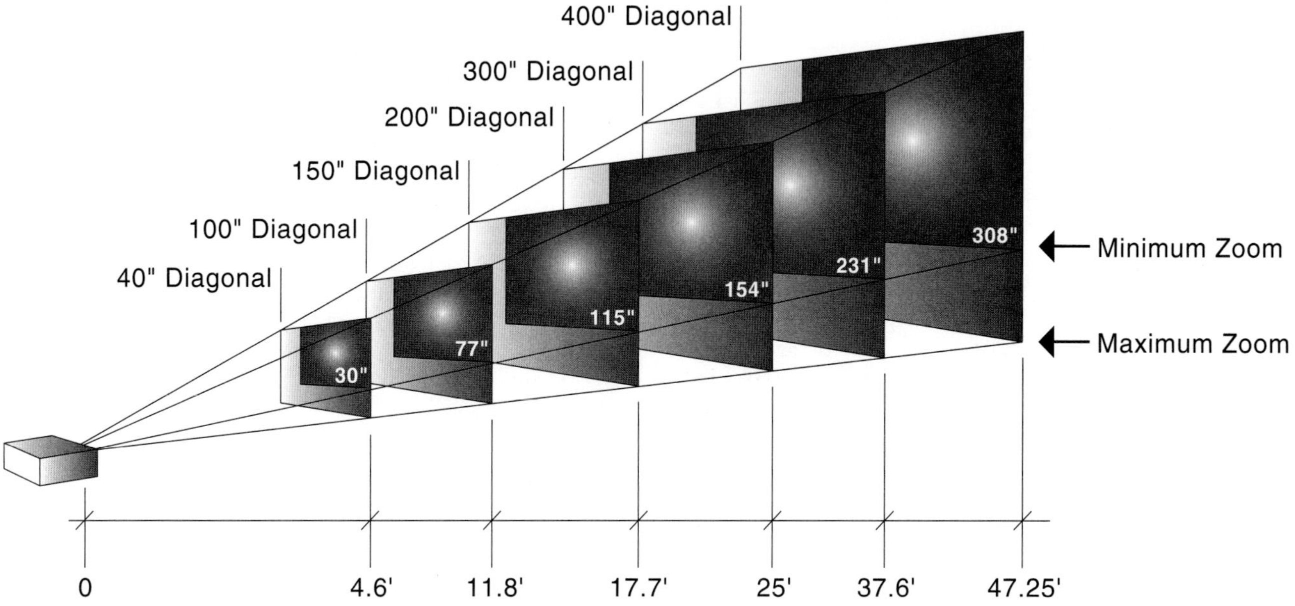

Typical Lens Throw Distance and Image Size

Maximum Zoom (Inches)	40	100	150	200	300	400
Minimum Zoom (Inches)	30	77	115	154	231	308
Throw Distance (Feet)	4'-6"	11'-9"	17'-8"	25'-0"	37'-6"	47'-3"

LINEAR MEASURE

Measures of Length

12 inches	= 1 foot
3 feet	= 1 yard
5½ yards = 16½ feet	= 1 rod, pole or perch
40 poles = 220 yards	= 1 furlong
8 furlongs = 1760 yards = 5280 feet	= 1 mile
3 miles	= 1 league
4 inches	= 1 hand
9 inches	= 1 span

Nautical Units

6080.20 feet	= 1 nautical mile
6 feet	= 1 fathom
120 fathoms	= 1 cable length
1 nautical mile per hr.	= 1 knot

Surveyor's or Gunter's Measure

7.92 inches	= 1 link
100 links = 66 ft. = 4 rods	= 1 chain
80 chains	= 1 mile
33⅓ inches	= 1 vara (Texas)

Length Equivalents

Centimeters	Inches	Feet	Yards	Meters	Chains	Kilometers	Miles
1	0.3937	0.03281	0.01094	0.01	$0.0_3 4971$	10^{-5}	$0.0_5 6214$
2.540	1	0.08333	0.02778	0.0254	0.001263	$0.0_4 254$	$0.0_4 1578$
30.48	12	1	0.3333	0.3048	0.01515	$0.0_3 3048$	$0.0_3 1894$
91.44	36	3	1	0.9144	0.04545	$0.0_3 9144$	$0.0_3 5682$
100	39.37	3.281	1.0936	1	0.04971	0.001	$0.0_3 6214$
2012	792	66	22	20.12	1	0.02012	0.0125
100000	39370	3281	1093.6	1000	49.71	1	0.6214
160935	63360	5280	1760	1609	80	1.609	1

Subscripts after any figure, 0_3, 9_4, etc., mean that that figure is to be repeated the indicated number of times.

MEASURES OF AREA

144 square inches	= 1 square foot
9 square feet	= 1 square yard
30¼ square yards	= 1 square rod, pole or perch
160 square rods = 10 square chains = 43,560 sq. ft. = 5645 sq. varas (Texas)	= 1 acre

640 acres = 1 square mile = 1 "section" of U. S. Govt. surveyed land

Area Equivalents

Square Meters	Square Inches	Square Feet	Square Yards	Square Rods	Square Chains	Roods	Acres	Square Miles or Sections
1	1550	10.76	1.196	0.0395	0.002471	$0.0_3 9884$	$0.0_3 2471$	$0.0_6 3861$
$0.0_3 6452$	1	0.006944	$0.0_3 7716$	$0.0_4 2551$	$0.0_5 1594$	$0.0_6 6377$	$0.0_6 1594$	$0.0_9 2491$
0.09290	144	1	0.1111	0.003673	$0.0_3 2296$	$0.0_4 9184$	$0.0_4 2296$	$0.0_7 3587$
0.8361	1296	9	1	0.03306	0.002066	$0.0_3 8264$	0.0002066	$0.0_6 3228$
25.29	39204	272.25	30.25	1	0.0625	0.02500	0.00625	$0.0_5 9766$
404.7	627264	4356	484	16	1	0.4	0.1	0.0001562
1012	1568160	10890	1210	40	2.5	1	0.25	$0.0_3 3906$
4047	6272640	43560	4840	160	10	4	1	0.001562
2589998	....	27878400	3097600	102400	6400	2560	640	1

(1 hectare = 100 ares = 10,000 centiares or square meters)

Subscripts after any figure 0_3, 9_4, etc., mean that that figure is to be repeated the indicated number of times.

VOLUMETRIC MEASURE

Measures of Volume

1728 cubic inches	= 1 cubic foot
27 cubic feet	= 1 cubic yard
1 cord of wood	= 128 cu. ft.
1 perch of masonry	= 16½ to 25 cu. ft.

Liquid or Fluid Measure

4 gills	= 1 pint
2 pints	= 1 quart
4 quarts	= 1 gallon
7.4805 gallons	= 1 cubic foot

(There is no standard liquid barrel; by trade custom, 1 bbl. of petroleum oil, unrefined = 42 gal.)

Dry Measure

2 pints	= 1 quart
8 quarts	= 1 peck
4 pecks	= 1 bushel

1 std. bbl. for fruits and vegetables = 7056 cu. in. or 105 dry quarts, struck measure

Board Measure

1 board foot = 144 cu. in. = volume of board 1 ft. sq. and 1 in. thick.

No. of board feet in a log = $[\frac{1}{4}(d-4)]^2 L$, where d = diam. of log (usually taken inside the bark at small end), in., and L = length of log, ft. The 4 in. deducted are an allowance for slab. This rule is variously known as the Doyle, Conn. River, St. Croix, Thurber, Moore and Beeman, and the Scribner rule.

Volume and Capacity Equivalents

Cubic inches	Cubic feet	Cubic yards	U. S. Apothecary liquid ounces	U. S. quarts		U. S. gallons		Bushels U. S.	Liters (l)
				Liquid	Dry	Liquid	Dry		
1	$0.0_3 5787$	$0.0_4 2143$	0.5541	0.01732	0.01488	$0.0_2 4329$	$0.0_2 3720$	$0.0_3 4650$	0.01639
1728	1	0.03704	957.5	29.92	25.71	7.481	6.429	0.8036	28.32
46656	27	1	25853	807.9	694.3	202.0	173.6	21.70	764.6
1.805	0.001044	$0.0_4 3868$	1	0.03125	0.02686	0.007813	0.006714	$0.0_3 8392$	0.02957
57.75	0.03342	0.001238	32	1	0.8594	0.25	0.2148	0.02686	0.9464
67.20	0.03889	0.001440	37.24	1.164	1	0.2909	0.25	0.03125	1.101
231	0.1337	0.004951	128	4	3.437	1	0.8594	0.1074	3.785
268.8	0.1556	0.005761	148.9	4.655	4	1.164	1	0.125	4.405
2150	1.244	0.04609	1192	37.24	32	9.309	8	1	35.24
61.02	0.03531	0.001308	33.81	1.057	0.9081	0.2642	0.2270	0.02838	1

Subscripts after any figure, 0_3, 9_4, etc., mean that that figure is to be repeated the indicated number of times.

MEASURES OF WEIGHT

Weights

(The grain is the same in all systems)

Avoirdupois Weight

16 drams = 437.5 grains	= 1 ounce
16 ounces = 7000 grains	= 1 pound
100 pounds	= 1 cental
2000 pounds	= 1 short ton
2240 pounds	= 1 long ton
1 std. lime bbl., small	= 180 lb. net
1 std. lime bbl., large	= 280 lb. net

Also (in Great Britain):

14 pounds	= 1 stone
2 stone = 28 lb.	= 1 quarter
4 quarters = 112 lb.	= 1 hundredweight (cwt.)
20 hundredweight	= 1 long ton

Troy Weight

24 grains	= 1 pennyweight (dwt.)
20 pennyweights = 480 grains	= 1 ounce
12 ounces = 5760 grains	= 1 pound

1 **Assay Ton** = 29,167 milligrams, or as many milligrams as there are troy ounces in a ton of 2000 lb. avoirdupois. Consequently, the number of milligrams of precious metal yielded by an assay ton of ore gives directly the number of troy ounces that would be obtained from a ton of 2000 lb. avoirdupois

Apothecaries' Weight

20 grains	= 1 scruple ℈
3 scruples = 60 grains	= 1 dram ʒ
8 drams	= 1 ounce ℥
12 ounces = 5760 grains	= 1 pound

Mass Equivalents

Kilograms	Grains	Ounces		Pounds		Tons		
		Troy and apoth.	Avoirdupois	Troy and apoth.	Avoirdupois	Short	Long	Metric
1	15432	32.15	35.27	2.6792	2.205	$0.0_2 1102$	$0.0_3 9842$	0.001
$0.0_4 6480$	1	$0.0_2 2083$	$0.0_2 2286$	$0.0_3 1736$	$0.0_3 1429$	$0.0_7 7143$	$0.0_7 6378$	$0.0_7 6480$
0.03110	480	1	1.09714	0.08333	0.06857	$0.0_4 3429$	$0.0_4 3061$	$0.0_4 3110$
0.02835	437.5	0.9115	1	0.07595	0.0625	$0.0_4 3125$	$0.0_4 2790$	$0.0_4 2835$
0.3732	5760	12	13.17	1	0.8229	$0.0_3 4114$	$0.0_3 3673$	$0.0_3 3732$
0.4536	7000	14.58	16	1.215	1	0.0005	$0.0_3 4464$	$0.0_3 4536$
907.2	140_6	29167	320_3	2431	2000	1	0.8929	0.9072
1016	15680_4	32667	35840	2722	2240	1.12	1	1.016
1000	15432356	32151	35274	2679	2205	1.102	0.9842	1

Subscripts after any figure, 0_3, 9_4, etc., mean that that figure is to be repeated the indicated number of times.

METRIC WEIGHT

		Avoirdupois
1 milligram (mg)		= 0.0154 gr.
1 centigram (cg)	= 10 mg	= 0.1543 gr.
1 decigram (dg)	= 10 cg	= 1.5432 gr.
1 gram (g)	= 10 dg	= 15.4323 gr.
1 dekagram (dag)	= 10 g	= 0.3527 oz.
1 hectogram (hg)	= 10 dag	= 3.5274 oz.
1 kilogram (kg)	= 10 hg	= 2.2046 lb.
1 quintal (q)	= 100 kg	= 220.46 lb.
1 metric ton (M.T.)	= 10 q or 1,000 kg	= 2,204.62 lb.

AVOIRDUPOIS WEIGHT

		Metric
1 grain (gr.)		= 0.0648 g
1 dram (dr.)	= 27.34375 gr.	= 1.7718 g
1 ounce (oz.)	= 16. dr.	= 28.3495 g
1 pound (lb.)	= 16 oz.	= 453.5924 g or 0.4536 kg
1 hundredweight (cwt.)	= 100 lb.	= 45.3592 kg
1 short ton (s.t.)	= 2,000 lb.	= 907.18 kg or 0.9072 M.T.

WOOD MEASUREMENTS

	Customary	Metric
1 board foot (bd. ft.)	= 144 cu. in. (1 ft. x 1 ft. x 1 in.)	= .00236 m^3
1 cord foot (cd. ft.)	= 16 cu. ft. (4 ft. x 4 ft. x 1 ft.)	= .4528 m^3
1 cord (cd.)	= 8 cd. ft. (4 ft. x 4 ft. x 8 ft.)	= 3.625 m^3
	Metric	**Customary**
1 stere	1 m^3	1.3079 cu. yd. or 0.2759 cord

LENGTH AND DISTANCE

Customary		Metric
1 inch (in.)		= 2.54 cm
1 foot (ft.)	= 12 in.	= 30.48 cm
1 yard (yd.)	= 3 ft.	= 0.9144 m
1 rod (rd.)	= 5½ yd.	= 5.0292 m
1 furlong (fur.)	= 40 rd. or ⅛ mi.	= 201.168 m
1 statute mile (mi.)	= 5,280 ft.	= 1.6093 km
1 league	= 3 mi.	= 4.8280 km
Metric		**Customary**
1 millimeter (mm)		= 0.03937 in.
1 centimeter (cm)	= 10 mm	= 0.3937 in.
1 decimeter (dm)	= 10 cm	= 3.937 in.
1 meter (m)	= 10 dm	= 39.37 in.
1 dekameter (dam)	= 10 m	= 393.7 in.
1 hectometer (hm)	= 10 dam	= 328.0833 ft.
1 kilometer (km)	= 10 hm	= 0.62137 mi.

SURFACE OR AREA

Customary		Metric
1 square inch (sq. in.)		= 6.4516 cm^2
1 square foot (sq. ft.)	= 144 sq. in.	= 0.0929 m^2
1 square yard (sq. yd.)	= 9 sq. ft.	= 0.8361 m^2
1 square rod (sq. rd.)	= 30¼ sq. yd.	= 25.293 m^2
1 acre (A.)	= 160 sq. rd.	= 0.4047 ha
1 square mile (sq. mi.)	= 640 A.	= 258.998 ha or 2.5899 km^2
Metric		**Customary**
1 square millimeter (mm^2)		= 0.002 sq. in.
1 square centimeter (cm^2)	= 100 mm^2	= 0.1549 sq. in
1 square decimeter (dm^2)	= 100 cm^2	= 15.499 sq. in.
1 square meter (m^2)	= 100 dm^2	= 1.549 sq. in.
1 square dekameter (dam^2)	= 100 m^2	= 119.6 sq. yd.
1 square hectometer (hm^2)	= 100 dam^2	= 2.4710 A.
1 square kilometer (km^2)	= 100 hm^2	= 247.104 A. or 0.3861 sq. mi.

METRIC LAND MEASUREMENTS

	Metric	Customary
1 centiare (ca)		= 1.549 sq. in.
1 are (a)	= 100 ca	= 119.6 sq. yd.
1 hectare (ha)	= 100 a	= 2.4710 A.
1 square kilometer (km^2)	= 100 ha	or 0.3861 sq. mi.

VOLUME MEASUREMENTS

Customary		Metric
1 cubic inch (cu. in.)		= 16.387 cm^3
1 cubic foot (cu. ft.)	= 1,728 cu. in.	= 0.0283 m^3
1 cubic yard (cu. yd.)	= 27 cu. ft.	= 0.7646 m^3
Metric		**Customary**
1 cubic millimeter (mm^3)		= 0.00006 cu. in.
1 cubic centimeter (cm^3)	= 1,000 mm^3	= 0.0610 cu. in.
1 cubic decimeter (dm^3)	= 1,000 cm^3	= 0.0353 cu. ft.
1 cubic meter (m^3)	= 1,000 dm^3	= 1.3079 cu. yd.
1 cubic dekameter (dam^3)	= 1,000 m^3	= 1,307.9 cu. yd.
1 cubic hectometer (hm^3)	= 1,000 dam^3	= 1,307,9000 cu. yd.

METRIC CAPACITY MEASUREMENTS

Metric		Customary
1 milliliter (ml)		= 0.0610 cu. in.
1 centiliter (cl)	= 10 ml	= 0.6102 cu. in.
1 deciliter (dl)	= 10 cl	= 6.1025 cu. in.
1 liter (l)	= 10 dl	= 61.025 cu. in.
		or 1.057 liquid qt.
		or 0.908 dry
1 dekaliter (dal)	= 10 l	= 610.25 cu. in.
1 hectoliter (hl)	= 10 dal	= 6,102.50 cu. in.
1 kiloliter (kl)	= 10 hl	= 35.315 cu. ft.
		or 264.178 gal.
		or 28.38 bu.

HOUSEHOLD CAPACITY MEASUREMENTS

Customary			Metric
1 teaspoon		= ⅙ fl. oz.	= 4.9 ml
1 tablespoon	= 3 teaspoons	= ½ fl. oz.	= 14.8 ml
1 cup	= 16 tablespoons	= 8 fl. oz.	= 236.6 ml
1 pint	= 2 cups	= 16 fl. oz.	= 473.2 ml
1 quart	= 2 pints	= 32 fl. oz.	= 946.4 ml
1 gallon	= 4 quarts	= 128 fl. oz.	= 3.785 l

LIQUID CAPACITY MEASUREMENTS

Customary		Metric	
1 gill (gi.)		= 7.219 cu. in.	= 0.1183 l
1 pint (pt.)	= 4 gi.	= 28.875 cu. in.	= 0.4732 l
1 quart (qt.)	= 2 pt.	= 57.75 cu. in.	= 0.9463 l
1 gallon (gal.)	= 4 qt.	= 231 cu. in.	= 3.7853 l
1 barrel (liquids) (bbl.)	= 31.5 gal.	= 4.21 cu. ft.	= 119.24 l
1 barrel (petroleum) (bbl.)	= 42 gal.	= 5.61 cu. ft.	= 158.98 l
Imperial	**Customary**		**Metric**
1 imperial quart	= 1.2009 U.S. qt.	= 69.355 cu. in.	= 1.13649 l
1 imperial gallon	= 1.2009 U.S. gal.	= 277.420 cu. in.	= 4.54596 l

DRY CAPACITY MEASUREMENTS

Customary			Metric
1 pint (pt.)		= 33.600 cu. in.	= 550.60 cm^3
1 quart (qt.)	= 2 pt.	= 67.20 cu. in.	= 1,101.21 cm^3
1 peck (pk.)	= 8 qt.	= 537.61 cu. in.	= 8,809.85 cm^3
1 bushel (bu.)	= 4 pk.	= 2,150.42 cu. in.	= 0.035239 m^3
1 barrel (bbl.)		= 4.08 cu. ft.	= 0.115627 m^3
Imperial	**Customary**		**Metric**
1 imperial dry quart	= 1.032 U.S. qt.	= 69.354 cu. in.	= 1,136.5 cm^3
1 imperial bushel	= 1.032 U.S. bu.	= 1.284 cu. ft.	= 0.03636 m^3

MATHEMATICAL DATA AND FORMULAS

Fraction, Decimal, and Metric Conversion Tables

DECIMAL OF AN INCH AND OF A FOOT

Fractions of Inch or Foot		Inch Equivalents to Foot Fractions	Fractions of Inch or Foot		Inch Equivalents to Foot Fractions	Fractions of Inch or Foot		Inch Equivalents to Foot Fractions	Fractions of Inch or Foot		Inch Equivalents to Foot Fractions
	.0052	1/16		.2552	3 1/16		.5052	6 1/16		.7552	9 1/16
	.0104	1/8		.2604	3 1/8		.5104	6 1/8		.7604	9 1/8
1/64	.015625	3/16	17/64	.265625	3 3/16	33/64	.515625	6 3/16	49/64	.765625	9 3/16
	.0208	1/4		.2708	3 1/4		.5208	6 1/4		.7708	9 1/4
	.0260	5/16		.2760	3 5/16		.5260	6 5/16		.7760	9 5/16
1/32	.03125	3/8	9/32	.28125	3 3/8	17/32	.53125	6 3/8	25/32	.78125	9 3/8
	.0365	7/16		.2865	3 7/16		.5365	6 7/16		.7865	9 7/16
	.0417	1/2		.2917	3 1/2		.5417	6 1/2		.7917	9 1/2
3/64	.046875	9/16	19/64	.296875	3 9/16	35/64	.546875	6 9/16	51/64	.796875	9 9/16
	.0521	5/8		.3021	3 5/8		.5521	6 5/8		.8021	9 5/8
	.0573	11/16		.3073	3 11/16		.5573	6 11/16		.8073	9 11/16
1/16	.0625	3/4	5/16	.3125	3 3/4	9/16	.5625	6 3/4	13/16	.8125	9 3/4
	.0677	13/16		.3177	3 13/16		.5677	6 13/16		.8177	9 13/16
	.0729	7/8		.3229	3 7/8		.5729	6 7/8		.8229	9 7/8
5/64	.078125	15/16	21/64	.328125	3 15/16	37/64	.578125	6 15/16	53/64	.828125	9 15/16
	.0833	1		.3333	4		.5833	7		.8333	10
	.0885	1 1/16		.3385	4 1/16		.5885	7 1/16		.8385	10 1/16
3/32	.09375	1 1/8	11/32	.34375	4 1/8	19/32	.59375	7 1/8	27/32	.84375	10 1/8
	.0990	1 3/16		.3490	4 3/16		.5990	7 3/16		.8490	10 3/16
	.1042	1 1/4		.3542	4 1/4		.6042	7 1/4		.8542	10 1/4
7/64	.109375	1 5/16	23/64	.359375	4 5/16	39/64	.609375	7 5/16	55/64	.859375	10 5/16
	.1146	1 3/8		.3646	4 3/8		.6146	7 3/8		.8646	10 3/8
	.1198	1 7/16		.3698	4 7/16		.6198	7 7/16		.8698	10 7/16
1/8	.1250	1 1/2	3/8	.3750	4 1/2	5/8	.6250	7 1/2	7/8	.8750	10 1/2
	.1302	1 9/16		.3802	4 9/16		.6302	7 9/16		.8802	10 9/16
	.1354	1 5/8		.3854	4 5/8		.6354	7 5/8		.8854	10 5/8
9/64	.140625	1 11/16	25/64	.390625	4 11/16	41/64	.640625	7 11/16	57/64	.890625	10 11/16
	.1458	1 3/4		.3958	4 3/4		.6458	7 3/4		.8958	10 3/4
	.1510	1 13/16		.4010	4 13/16		.6510	7 13/16		.9010	10 13/16
5/32	.15625	1 7/8	13/32	.40625	4 7/8	21/32	.65625	7 7/8	29/32	.90625	10 7/8
	.1615	1 15/16		.4115	4 15/16		.6615	7 15/16		.9115	10 15/16
	.1667	2		.4167	5		.6667	8		.9167	11
11/64	.171875	2 1/16	27/64	.421875	5 1/16	43/64	.671875	8 1/16	59/64	.921875	11 1/16
	.1771	2 1/8		.4271	5 1/8		.6771	8 1/8		.9271	11 1/8
	.1823	2 3/16		.4323	5 3/16		.6823	8 3/16		.9323	11 3/16
3/16	.1875	2 1/4	7/16	.4375	5 1/4	11/16	.6875	8 1/4	15/16	.9375	11 1/4
	.1927	2 5/16		.4427	5 5/16		.6927	8 5/16		.9427	11 5/16
	.1979	2 3/8		.4479	5 3/8		.6979	8 3/8		.9479	11 3/8
13/64	.203125	2 7/16	29/64	.453125	5 7/16	45/64	.703125	8 7/16	61/64	.953125	11 7/16
	.2083	2 1/2		.4583	5 1/2		.7083	8 1/2		.9583	11 1/2
	.2135	2 9/16		.4635	5 9/16		.7135	8 9/16		.9635	11 9/16
7/32	.21875	2 5/8	15/32	.46875	5 5/8	23/32	.71875	8 5/8	31/32	.96875	11 5/8
	.2240	2 11/16		.4740	5 11/16		.7240	8 11/16		.9740	11 11/16
	.2292	2 3/4		.4792	5 3/4		.7292	8 3/4		.9792	11 3/4
15/64	.234375	2 13/16	31/64	.484375	5 13/16	47/64	.734375	8 13/16	63/64	.984375	11 13/16
	.2396	2 7/8		.4896	5 7/8		.7396	8 7/8		.9896	11 7/8
	.2448	2 15/16		.4948	5 15/16		.7448	8 15/16		.9948	11 15/16
1/4	.2500	3	1/2	.5000	6	3/4	.7500	9	1	1.0000	12

METRIC MEASURES

Linear	Liquid and Dry	Weights
10 millimeters = 1 centimeter	10 milliliters = 1 centiliter	10 milligrams = 1 centigram
10 centimeters = 1 decimeter	10 centiliters = 1 deciliter	10 centigrams = 1 decigram
10 decimeters = 1 METER (m)	10 deciliters = 1 LITER (l)	10 decigrams = 1 GRAM (g)
10 meters = 1 decameter	10 liters = 1 decaliter	10 grams = 1 decagram
10 decameters = 1 hectometer	10 decaliters = 1 hectoliter	10 decagrams = 1 hectogram
10 hectometers = 1 kilometer	10 hectoliters = 1 kiloliter	10 hectograms = 1 kilogram

METRIC CONVERSION FACTORS

METRIC TO AMERICAN

Millimeters ÷ 25.4 = inches
Centimeters × 0.3937 = inches
Meters × 39.27 = inches
Millimeters × 0.003281 = feet
Centimeters × 0.03281 = feet
Meters × 3.281 = feet
Meters × 1.094 = yards
Kilometers × 0.621 = miles
Kilometers × 3280.7 = feet
Square millimeters ÷ 645.1 = square inches
Square centimeters ÷ 6.451 = square inches
Square meters × 10.764 = square feet
Square kilometers × 247.1 = acres
Hectares × 2.471 = acres
Cubic centimeters ÷ 16.383 = cubic inches
Cubic meters × 35.315 = cubic feet
Cubic meters × 1.308 = cubic yards
Cubic meters × 264.2 = gallons
Liters × 61.022 = cubic inches
Liters × 0.2642 = gallons
Liters ÷ 28.316 = cubic feet
Hectoliters × 3.531 = cubic feet
Hectoliters × 2.84 = bushels
Hectoliters × 0.131 = cubic yards
Hectoliters × 26.42 = gallons
Kilograms × 2.2046 = pounds
Kilograms ÷ 1102.3 = tons

AMERICAN TO METRIC

Inches × 25.4 = millimeters
Inches × 2.54 = centimeters
Inches × 0.0254 = meters
Feet × 304.8 = millimeters
Feet × 30.48 = centimeters
Feet × 0.3048 = meters
Yards × 0.9143 = meters
Miles × 1.6093 = kilometers
Feet ÷ 3280.7 = kilometers
Square inches × 645.1 = square millimeters
Square inches × 6.451 = square centimeters
Square feet ÷ 10.764 = square meters
Acres ÷ 247.1 = square kilometers
Acres ÷ 2.471 = hectares
Cubic inches × 16.383 = cubic centimeters
Cubic feet ÷ 35.315 = cubic meters
Cubic yards ÷ 1.308 = cubic meters
Gallons (231 cu. in.) ÷ 264.2 = cubic meters
Cubic inches ÷ 61.022 = liters
Gallons × 3.78 = liters
Cubic feet × 28.316 = liters
Cubic feet ÷ 3.531 = hectoliters
Bushels ÷ 2.84 = hectoliters
Cubic yards ÷ 0.131 = hectoliters
Gallons ÷ 26.42 = hectoliters
Pounds ÷ 2.2046 = kilograms
Tons × 1102.3 = kilograms

MATHEMATICAL DATA AND FORMULAS
Decimals, Fractions, and Millimeters

Fraction	*1/64 ths*	*Decimal*	*Millimeter (approx.)*	*Fraction*	*1/64 ths*	*Decimal*	*Millimeter (approx.)*
—	1	.015625	0.397	—	33	.515625	13.097
1/32	2	.03125	0.794	17/32	34	.53125	13.494
—	3	.046875	1.191	—	35	.546875	13.891
1/16	4	.0625	1.588	9/16	36	.5625	14.288
—	5	.078125	1.984	—	37	.578125	14.684
3/32	6	.09375	2.381	19/32	38	.59375	15.081
—	7	.109375	2.778	—	39	.609375	15.478
1/8	8	.125	3.175	5/8	40	.625	15.875
—	9	.140625	3.572	—	41	.640625	16.272
5/32	10	.15625	3.969	21/32	42	.65625	16.669
—	11	.171875	4.366	—	43	.671875	17.066
3/16	12	.1875	4.763	11/16	44	.6875	17.463
—	13	.203125	5.159	—	45	.703125	17.859
7/32	14	.21875	5.556	23/32	46	.71875	18.256
—	15	.234375	5.953	—	47	.734375	18.653
1/4	16	.250	6.350	3/4	48	.750	19.050
—	17	.265625	6.747	—	49	.765625	19.447
9/32	18	.28126	7.144	25/32	50	.78125	19.844
—	19	.296875	7.641	—	51	.796875	20.241
5/16	20	.3125	7.938	13/16	52	.8125	20.638
—	21	.328125	8.334	—	53	.828125	21.034
11/16	22	.34375	8.731	27/32	54	.84375	21.431
—	23	.359375	9.128	—	55	.859375	21.828
3/8	24	.375	9.525	7/8	56	.875	22.225
—	25	.390625	9.922	—	57	.890826	22.622
13/32	26	.40625	10.319	29/32	58	.90625	23.019
—	27	.421875	10.716	—	59	.921875	23.416
7/16	28	.4375	11.113	15/16	60	.9375	23.813
—	29	.458125	11.509	—	61	.963125	24.205
15/32	30	.46875	11.905	31/32	62	.96875	24.606
—	31	.484375	12.303	—	63	.984375	25.003
1/2	32	.500	12.700	1	64	1.000	25.400

MATHEMATICAL DATA AND FORMULAS
Inches and Millimeters

Length—inches and millimeters—equivalents of decimal and binary fractions of an inch in millimeters (from 1/64 to 1 inch)

½ s	*¼ s*	*8ths*	*16ths*	*32ds*	*64ths*	*Millimeters*	*Decimals of an inch*	*Inch*	*½ s*	*¼ s*	*8ths*	*16ths*	*32ds*	*64ths*	*Millimeters*	*Decimals of an inch*
					1	= 0.397	0.015625							33	= 13.097	0.515625
				1	2	= .794	.03125						17	34	= 13.494	.53125
					3	= 1.191	.046875							35	= 13.891	.546875
			1	2	4	= 1.588	.0625					9	18	36	= 14.288	.5625
					5	= 1.984	.078125							37	= 14.684	.578125
				3	6	= 2.381	.09375						19	38	= 15.081	.59375
					7	= 2.778	.109375							39	= 15.478	.609375
		1	2	4	8	= 3.175	.1250				5	10	20	40	= 15.875	.625
					9	= 3.572	.140625							41	= 16.272	.640625
				5	10	= 3.969	.15625						21	42	= 16.669	.65625
					11	= 4.366	.171875							43	= 17.066	.671875
			3	6	12	= 4.762	.1875					11	22	44	= 17.462	.6875
					13	= 5.159	.203125							45	= 17.859	.703125
				7	14	= 5.556	.21875						23	46	= 18.256	.71875
					15	= 5.953	.234375							47	= 18.653	.734375
	1	2	4	8	16	= 6.350	.2500			3	6	12	24	48	= 19.050	.75
					17	= 6.747	.265625							49	= 19.447	.765625
				9	18	= 7.144	.28125						25	50	= 19.844	.78125
					19	= 7.541	.296875							51	= 20.241	.796875
			5	10	20	= 7.938	.3125					13	26	52	= 20.638	.8125
					21	= 8.334	.328125							53	= 21.034	.828125
				11	22	= 8.731	.34375						27	54	= 21.431	.84375
					23	= 9.128	.359375							55	= 21.828	.859375
		3	6	12	24	= 9.525	.3750				7	14	28	56	= 22.225	.875
					25	= 9.922	.390625							57	= 22.622	.890625
				13	26	= 10.319	.40625						29	58	= 23.019	.90625
					27	= 10.716	.421875							59	= 23.416	.921875
			7	14	28	= 11.112	.4375					15	30	60	= 23.812	.9375
					29	= 11.509	.453125							61	= 24.209	.953125
				15	30	= 11.906	.46875						31	62	= 24.606	.96875
					31	= 12.303	.484375							63	= 25.003	.984375
1	2	4	8	16	32	= 12.700	.5	1	2	4	8	16	32	64	= 25.400	1.000

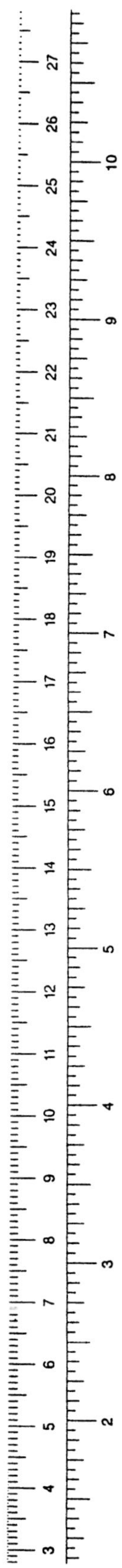

US customary

Linear

12 inches	= 1 foot
3 feet	= 1 yard
5.5 yards	= 1 rod
40 rods	= 1 furlong
8 furlongs	= 1 mile
3 land miles	= 1 league

Area

144 sq inches	= 1 sq foot
9 sq feet	= 1 sq yard
160 sq yards	= 1 acre
640 acres	= 1 sq mile
1 sq mile	= 1 section
36 sections	= 1 township

Weight

27 11/32 grains	= 1 dram
16 drams	= 1 ounce
16 ounces	= 1 pound
100 pounds	= 1 cwt.
20 cwt.	= 1 ton

Conversions

To Convert

Millimeters to:

inches	x .0394
feet	x .00328

Meters to:

feet	x 3.281
inches	x 39.37
yards	x 1.094

Inches to:

millimeters	x 25.40
meters	x .0254

Feet to:

millimeters	x 304.8
meters	x 0.305

Pounds to:

kilograms	x 0.454

Ounces to:

grams	x 28.35

Metric

Linear

10 mm	= 1 cm
10 cm	= 1 decimeter
1000 mm	= 1 meter
10 meters	= 1 dekameter
1000 meters	= 1 kilometer

Area

100 sq dm	= 1 sq meter
10,000 sq cm	= 1 sq meter
1,000,000 sq mm	= 1 sq meter
100 sq meters	= 1 are (a)
1000 sq meters	= 1 hectare (ha)
100 hectares	= 1 sq kilometer
1,000,000 sq m	= 1 sq kilometer

Weight

10 milligrams	= 1 centigram
10 centigrams	= 1 decigram
10 decigrams	= 1 gram
10 dekagrams	= 1 hectogram
1,000 kilograms	= 1 metric ton

Temperature

Celcius	-20		-10		0		10		20		30		40
Fahrenheit		0	10	20	32	40	50	60	70	80	90	100	

Specific ceilings information – quick conversion guide

Inches to millimeters x 25.4

Square feet to square meters x 0.09289

Square meters to square feet x 10.765

Imperial inches	Soft metric mm	Ecophon hard metric equivalent mm
9/16"		15
15/16"		24
24"x24"	610x 610	600x 600
24"x48"	610x1220	600x1200
48"x48"	1220x1220	1200x1200
60"x24"	1525x 610	1600x 600
72"x24"	1830x 610	1800x 600
84"x24"	2135x 610	2000x 600
96"x24"	2440x 610	2400x 600

MATHEMATICAL DATA AND FORMULAS
Metric Units and Symbols

Quantity	*Unit*	*Symbol*	*Accepted alternate*
Length	kilometer	km	
	meter	m	
	centimeter	cm	
	millimeter	mm	
Area	square kilometer	km^2	
	square hectometer	hm^2	hectare
	square meter	m^2	
	square millimeter	mm^2	
Metric ton	ton	t	
Weight (mass)	kilogram	kg	
	gram	g	
	milligram	mg	
Volume	cubic meter	m^3	
	cubic decimeter	dm^3	liter
Force	megapascal	MPa	
	kilonewton	kN	
	newton	N	
Pressure	kilopascal	kPa	
	pascal	Pa	
Temperature	kelvin	K	
	degree Celsius	°C	
Time	second	s	
Electric current	ampere	A	
Amount of substance	mole	mol	
Luminous intensity	candela	cd	
Energy, work quantity of heat	joule	J	
Frequency	hertz	Hz	
Power	watt	W	
Electromotive force	volt	V	
Electric resistance	ohm	Ω	
Luminous flux	lumen	lm	
Illuminance	lux	lx	

10 meters (m)	=	11 yards
10 square meters (m^2)	=	12 square yards
10 cubic meters (m^3)	=	13 cubic yards

Length

1 millimeter (mm)	=	thickness of a thin U.S. dime
25 millimeters (mm)	=	1 inch
300 millimeters (mm)	=	1 foot
1.7 meters (m)	=	height of person (5 ft 8 in)
2 meters (m)	=	residential door height

Area

100 square meters (m^2)	=	floor area of small 3-bedroom home

Volume

1 liter (L)	=	1 cubic decimeter (dm^3) = 1 quart
1 liter (L)	=	contents of a cube 100 millimeters (mm) on a side
208 liters (L)	=	0.2 cubic meters (m^3) = 55 gallons (US) drum for oil, chemicals, etc.

Mass (weight)

1 kilogram (kg)	=	mass of one liter (1) of water = 1 cubic decimeter (dm^3) of water
75 kilograms (kg)	=	mass (weight) of 165-pound man

Temperature, degrees Celsius

0° C	=	freezing point of water
20° C	=	mild, comfortable
30° C	=	hot
37° C	=	body temperature
100° C	=	boiling point of water

Other points

15 kilowatts (kW)	=	20 horsepower
20 megapascals (MPa)	=	3000 psi compressive strength of concrete
1 kilopascal (kPa)	=	20 pounds per square foot (psf)
Residential floor load:		
2 kilopascals (kPa)	–	40 lbs. per square foot (psf)

MATHEMATICAL DATA AND FORMULAS
Units of Measurement Conversion Charts

Units of Length

To convert from **centimeters**

To	*Multiply by*
Inches	0.393 700 8
Feet	0.032 808 40
Yards	0.010 936 13
Meters	**0.01**

To convert from **inches**

To	*Multiply by*
Feet	0.083 333 33
Yards	0.027 777 78
Centimeters	**2.54**
Meters	**0.025 4**

To convert from **yards**

To	*Multiply by*
Inches	**36**
Feet	**3**
Miles	0.000 568 18
Centimeters	91.44
Meters	**0.914 4**

To convert from **meters**

To	*Multiply by*
Inches	39.370 08
Feet	3.280 840
Yards	1.093 613
Miles	0.000 621 37
Millimeters	**1 000**
Centimeters	**100**
Kilometers	**0.001**

To convert from **feet**

To	*Multiply by*
Inches	**12**
Yards	0.333 333 3
Miles	0.000 189 39
Centimeters	**30.48**
Meters	**0.304 8**
Kilometers	**0.000 304 8**

To convert from **miles**

To	*Multiply by*
Inches	**63 360**
Feet	**5 280**
Yards	**1 760**
Centimeters	**160 934.4**
Meters	**1 609.344**
Kilometers	**1.609 344**

All **boldface** figures are exact; the others generally are given to seven significant figures.

In using conversion factors, it is possible to perform division as well as the multiplication process shown here. Division may be particularly advantageous where more than the significant figures published here are required. Division may be performed in lieu of multiplication by using the reciprocal of any indicated multiplier as divisor. For example, to convert from centimeters to inches by division, refer to the table headed "To convert from **inches**" and use the factor listed at "Centimeters" (2.54) as divisor.

Units of Area

To convert from **square centimeters**

To	Multiply by
Square inches	0.155 000 3
Square feet	0.001 076 39
Square yards	0.000 119 599
Square meters	**0.000 1**

To convert from **hectares**

To	Multiply by
Square feet	107 639.1
Square yards	11 959.90
Acres	2.471 054
Square miles	0.003 861 02
Square meters	**10 000**

To convert from **square feet**

To	Multiply by
Square inches	**144**
Square yards	0.111 111 1
Acres	0.000 022 957
Square centimeters	**929.030 4**
Square meters	**0.092 903 04**

To convert from **acres**

To	Multiply by
Square feet	**43 560**
Square yards	**4 840**
Square miles	**0.001 562 5**
Square meters	**4 046.856 422 4**
Hectares	**0.404 685 642 24**

To convert from **square meters**

To	Multiply by
Square inches	1 550.003
Square feet	10.763 91
Square yards	1.195 990
Acres	0.000 247 105
Square centimeters	**10 000**
Hectares	**0.000 1**

To convert from **square inches**

To	Multiply by
Square feet	0.006 944 44
Square yards	0.000 771 605
Square centimeters	**6.451 6**
Square meters	**0.000 645 16**

To convert from **square yards**

To	Multiply by
Square inches	**1 296**
Square feet	**9**
Acres	0.000 206 611 6
Square miles	0.000 000 322 830 6
Square centimeters	**8 361.273 6**
Square meters	**0.836 127 36**
Hectares	**0.000 083 612 736**

To convert from **square miles**

To	Multiply by
Square feet	**27 878 400**
Square yards	**3 097 600**
Acres	**640**
Square meters	**2 589 988.110 336**
Hectares	**258.998 811 033 6**

MATHEMATICAL DATA AND FORMULAS
Architectural Scales and Prefixes

U.S. traditional scales	*Closest ISO scales*	*Corresponds to*
Site plans		
1/16″ = 1′0″	1:200	5 mm = 1 m
1/8″ = 1′0″	1:100	10 mm = 1 m
1″ = 20′	1:200	5 mm = 1 m
1″ = 50′	1:500	2 mm = 1 m
—	1:100	1 mm = 1 m
Building designs		
1/8″ = 1′	1:100	10 mm = 1 m
1/4″ = 1′	1:50	20 mm = 1 m
Details		
1/2″ = 1′0″	1:20	50 mm = 1 m
3/4″ = 1′0″	1:10	100 mm = 1 m
1″ = 1′0″		
1-1/2″ = 1′0″	1:10	100 mm = 1 m
3″ = 1′0″	1:5	200 mm = 1 m
1′ = 1′ (full size)	1:1 (full size)	

SI prefixes

Factor	*Prefix*	*Symbol*	*Multiplication factor*	*U.S. pronunciation*
10^{12}	tera	T	1 000 000 000 000	as in *terra*pin
10^{9}	giga	G	1 000 000 000	jig′ a (*a* as in *a*round)
10^{6}	mega	M	1 000 000	as in *mega*phone
10^{3}	kilo	k	1 000	as in *kilo*watt*
10^{2}	hecto	h	100	heck′toe
10^{1}	deka	da	10	deck-a
10^{-1}	deci	d	0.1	as in *deci*mal
10^{-2}	centi	c	0.01	as in *senti*nel
10^{-3}	milli	m	0.001	as in *mili*tant
10^{-6}	micro	μ	0.000 001	as in *micro*dot
10^{-9}	nano	n	0.000 000 001	nan-o (as in *Nan*cy)
10^{-12}	pico	p	0.000 000 000 001	peek oh
10^{-15}	femto	f	0.000 000 000 000 001	as in *fem*inine
10^{-18}	atto	a	0.000 000 000 000 000 001	as in an*atom*y

*So that the prefix will retain its identity, the first syllable of each prefix should be accented. U.S. citizens already are drifting into an undesirable pronunciation for "kilometer," accenting the second syllable instead of the first.

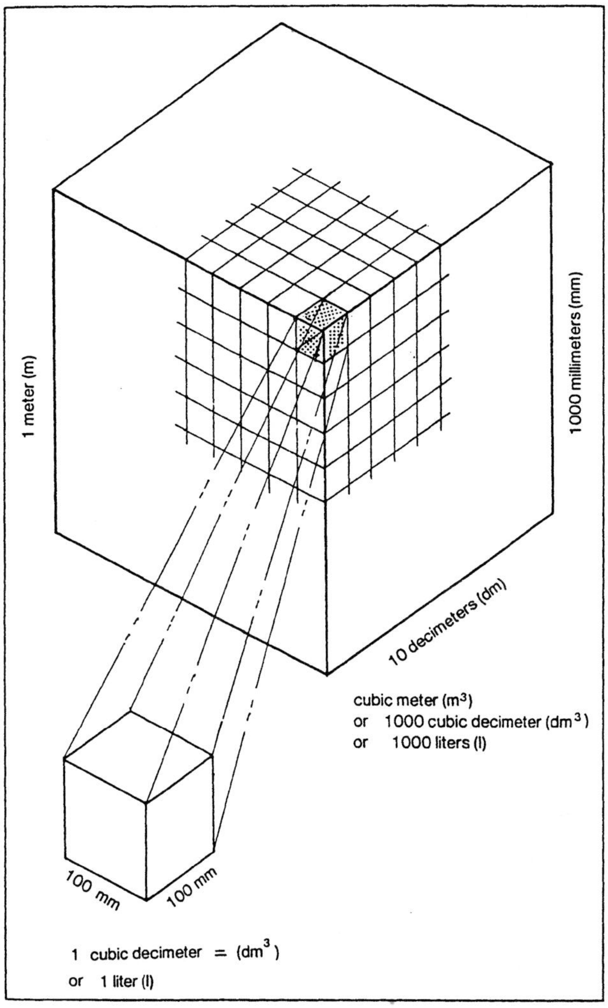

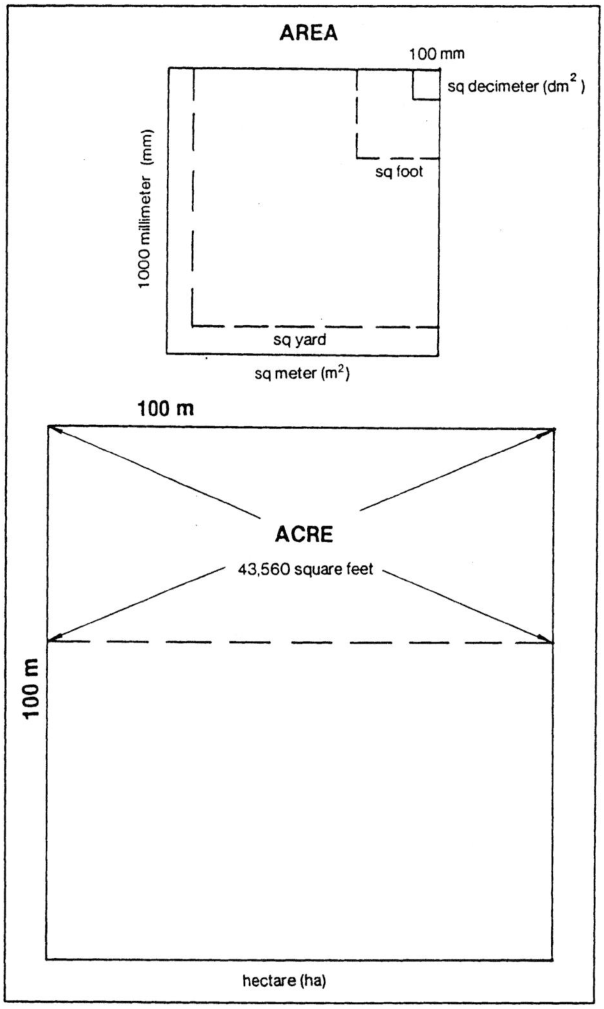

Derivation of Liter from Cubic Meter

The Hectare and the Acre

MATHEMATICAL DATA AND FORMULAS
Lengths, Areas, and Volumes

Lengths

Meters* (m)	Inches (in)	Feet (ft)	Yards (yd)	Rods (r)	Chains (ch)	Miles, U.S. Statute	Miles, U.S. Nautical	Kilo-meters (km)
1	39.37	3.28	1.09	0.199	0.05	$0._0^36214$	$0._0^35396$	0.001
0.025	1	0.083	0.028	$0._0^251$	$0._0^213$	$0._0^4158$	$0._0^4137$	$0._0^4254$
0.305	12	1	0.333	0.06	0.015	$0._0^3189$	$0._0^3165$	$0._0^3305$
0.914	36	3	1	0.18	0.045	$0._0^3568$	$0._0^3493$	$0._0^3914$
5.029	198	16.5	5.5	1	0.25	$0._0^2313$	$0._0^2271$	$0._0^2503$
20.117	792	66	22	4	1	0.013	0.0109	0.020
1609.35	63360	5280	1760	320	80	1	0.868	1.609
1853.25	72962.5	6080.2	2026.7	368.5	92.12	1.15	1	1.853
1000	39370	3280.8	1093.6	198.8	49.71	0.621	0.540	1

*1 meter (m) = 10 decimeters (dm) = 100 centimeters (cm) = 1000 millimeters (mm)

NOTE: Notations $^2_0$, $^3_0$, $^4_0$, etc., indicate the number of zeros. Example: 1 meter = $0._0^36214$ = 0.0006214 statute miles.

Areas

Square meters (sm)	Square inches (si)	Square feet (sf)	Square yards (sy)	Square rods (sr)	Acres (ac)	Hectares (ha)	Square miles statute	Square kilometer (sq km)
1	1550.0	10.76	1.196	0.039	$0._0^3247$	0.0001	$0._0^6386$	$0._0^51$
$0._0^365$	1	$0._0^269$	$0._0^377$	$0._0^626$	$0._0^616$	$0._0^765$	$0._0^925$	$0._0^965$
0.093	144	1	0.111	$0._0^237$	$0._0^423$	$0._0^593$	$0._0^736$	$0._0^793$
0.836	1296	9	1	0.333	$0._0^321$	$0._0^484$	$0._0^632$	$0._0^684$
25.293	39204	272.25	30.25	1	0.006	$0._0^325$	$0._0^598$	$0._0^426$
4046.87	6272640	43560	4840	160	1	0.405	$0._0^216$	$0._0^241$
10000	15499969	107639	11959.9	395.37	2.47104	1	$0._0^239$	0.01
2589999		27878400	3097600	102400	640	259	1	2.59
1000000		10763867	1195985	39536.6	247.104	100	0.386	1

Volumes

Cubic deci-meter or liters	Cubic inches	Cubic feet	Cubic yards	U.S. quarts Liquid	U.S. quarts Dry	U.S. gallons Liquid	U.S. gallons Dry	U.S. bushels
1	61.02	0.035	$0._0^213$	1.057	0.908	0.264	0.227	0.028
0.016	1	$0._0^358$	$0._0^421$	0.017	0.015	$0._0^243$	$0._0^272$	$0._0^247$
28.32	1728	1	0.037	29.92	25.714	7.481	6.429	0.804
764.56	46656	27	1	807.90	694.28	201.97	173.57	21.70
0.946	57.75	0.033	$0._0^2124$	1	0.859	0.25	0.215	0.027
1.1012	67.20	0.039	$0._0^2144$	1.1637	1	0.291	0.25	0.031
3.786	231	0.134	$0._0^2495$	4	3.437	1	0.859	0.107
4.405	268.8	0.156	$0._0^2576$	4.655	4	1.164	1	0.125
35.24	2150.4	1.244	0.0461	37.24	32	9.309	8	1

U.S. dry measure: 1 bushel = 4 pecks = 8 gallons = 32 quarts = 64 pints.

U.S. liquid measure: 1 gallon = 4 quarts = 8 pints = 32 gills = 128 fluid ounces.

1 U.S. gallon = 0.83268 imperial gallon.

MATHEMATICAL DATA AND FORMULAS

Areas of Plane Figures

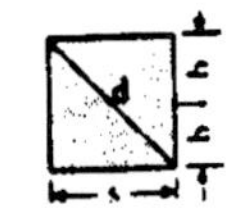

Square

Diagonal $= d = s\sqrt{2}$.
Area $= s^2 = 4b^2 = 0.5d^2$.
Example. $s = 6$; $b = 3$. Area $= (6)^2 = 36$ Ans.
$d = 6 \times 1.414 = 8.484$ Ans.

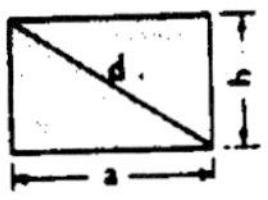

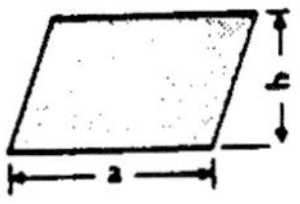

Rectangle and Parallelogram

Area $= ab$ or $b\sqrt{d^2 - b^2}$
Example. $a = 6$; $b = 3$.
Area $= 3 \times 6 = 18$ Ans

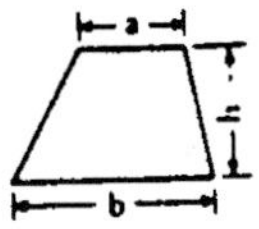

Trapezoid

Area $= \frac{1}{2}h(a + b)$
Example. $a = 2$; $b = 4$; $h = 3$.
Area $= \frac{1}{2} \times 3(2 + 4) = 9$. Ans.

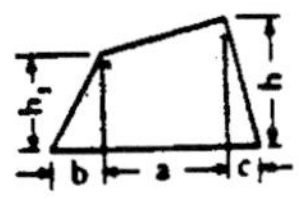

Trapezium

Area $= \frac{1}{2}[a(h + h^1) + bh^1 + ch]$
Example. $a = 4$; $b = 2$; $c = 2$; $h = 3$; $h^1 = 2$.
Area $= \frac{1}{2}[4(3 + 2) + (2 \times 2) + (2 \times 3)] = 15$. Ans.

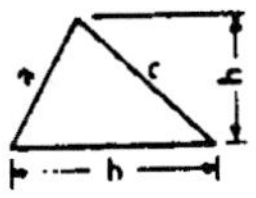

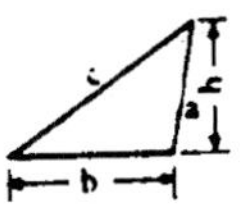

Triangles

Both formulas apply to both figures
Area $= \frac{1}{2}bh$.
Example. $h = 3$; $b = 5$.
Area $= \frac{1}{2}(3 \times 5) = 7\frac{1}{2}$. Ans.

Area $= \sqrt{S(S - a)(S - b)(S - c)}$ when $S = \dfrac{a + b + c}{2}$

Example. $a = 2$; $b = 3$; $c = 4$.
$S = \dfrac{2 + 3 + 4}{2} = 4.5$

Area $= \sqrt{4.5(4.5 - 2)(4.5 - 3)(4.5 - 4)} = 2.9$. Ans.

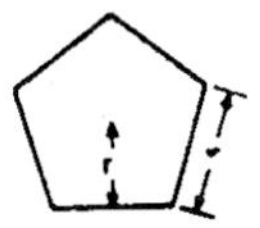

Regular Polygons

Area	5 sides	$= 1.720477\ S^2$	$= 3.63271\ r^2$
	6 "	$= 2.598150\ S^2$	$= 3.46410\ r^2$
	7 "	$= 3.633875\ S^2$	$= 3.37101\ r^2$
	8 "	$= 4.828427\ S^2$	$= 3.31368\ r^2$
	9 "	$= 6.181875\ S^2$	$= 3.27573\ r^2$
	10 "	$= 7.694250\ S^2$	$= 3.24920\ r^2$
	11 "	$= 9.365675\ S^2$	$= 3.22993\ r^2$
	12 "	$= 11.196300\ S^2$	$= 3.21539\ r^2$

n = number of sides; r = short radius;
S = length of side; R = long radius.

Area $= \dfrac{n}{4} S^2 \cot. \dfrac{180°}{n} = \dfrac{n}{2} R^2 \sin. \dfrac{360°}{n}$
$= nr^2 \tan \dfrac{180°}{n}$

Circle

$\pi = 3.1416$; A = area; d = diameter; p = circumference or periphery; r = radius.

$p = \pi d = 3.1416d$. $\quad p = 2\sqrt{\pi A} = 3.54\sqrt{A}$

$p = 2\pi r = 6.2832r$. $\quad p = \dfrac{2A}{r} = \dfrac{4A}{d}$

$d = \dfrac{p}{\pi} = \dfrac{p}{3.1416} \quad d = 2\sqrt{\dfrac{A}{\pi}} = 1.128\sqrt{A}$

$r = \dfrac{p}{2\pi} = \dfrac{p}{6.2832} \quad r = \sqrt{\dfrac{A}{\pi}} = 0.564\sqrt{A}$

$A = \dfrac{\pi d^2}{4} = 0.7854d^2 \quad A = \dfrac{p^2}{4\pi} = \dfrac{p^2}{12.57}$

$A = \pi r^2 = 3.1416r^2 \quad A = \dfrac{pr}{2} = \dfrac{pd}{4}$

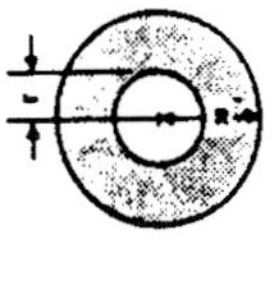

Circular Ring

Area $= \pi(R^2 - r^2) = 3.1416(R^2 - r^2)$
Area $= 0.7854(D^2 - d^2) = 0.7854(D - d)(D + d)$
Area = difference in areas between the inner and outer circles.
Example. $R = 4$; $r = 2$.
Area $= 3.1416(4^2 - 2^2) = 37.6992$. Ans.

Quadrant

Area $= \dfrac{\pi r^2}{4} = 0.7854r^2 = 0.3927c^2$.

Example. $r = 3$. c = chord.
Area $= .7854 \times 3^2 = 7.0686$. Ans.

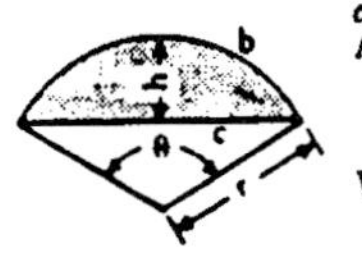

Segment

b = length of arc. θ = angle in degrees
c = chord $= \sqrt{4(2hr - h^2)}$
Area $= \frac{1}{2}[br - c(r - h)]$
$= \pi r^2 \dfrac{\theta}{360} - \dfrac{c(r - h)}{2}$

When θ is greater than 180° then $\dfrac{c}{2} \times$ difference between r and h is added to the fraction $\dfrac{\pi r^2\theta}{360}$

Example. $r = 3$; $\theta = 120°$; $h = 1.5$
Area $= 3.1416 \times 3^2 \times \dfrac{120}{360} - \dfrac{5.196(3 - 1.5)}{2}$
$= 5.5278$. Ans.

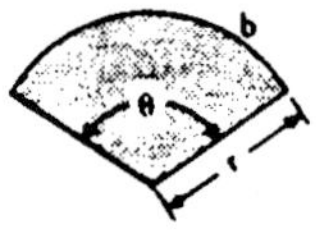

Sector

Area $= \dfrac{br}{2} = \pi r^2 \dfrac{\theta}{360°}$
θ = angle in degrees; b = length of arc.
Example. $r = 3$; $\theta = 120°$
Area $= 3.1416 \times 3^2 \times \dfrac{120}{360} = 9.4248$. Ans.

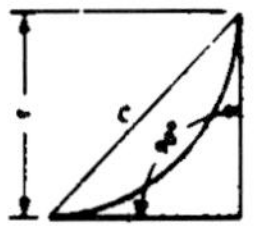

Spandrel

Area $= 0.2146r^2 = 0.1073c^2$
Example. $r = 3$
Area $= 0.2146 \times 3^2 = 1.9314$. Ans

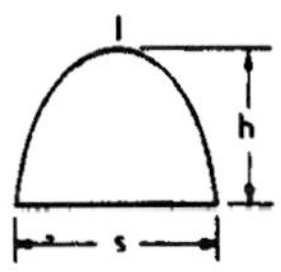

Parabola

l = length of curved line = periphery $- s$

$l = \dfrac{s^2}{8h}[\sqrt{c(1+c)} + 2.0326 \times \log(\sqrt{c}+\sqrt{1+c})]$

in which $c = \left(\dfrac{4h}{s}\right)^2$

Area $= \dfrac{2}{3}sh$
Example. $s = 3$; $h = 4$
Area $= \dfrac{2}{3} \times 3 \times 4 = 8$. Ans.

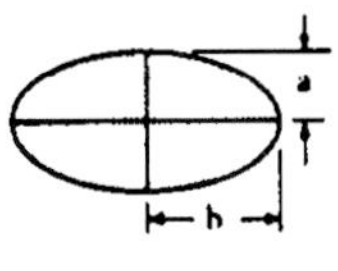

Ellipse

Area $= \pi\ ab = 3.1416ab$

Circum. $= 2\pi\sqrt{\dfrac{a^2 + b^2}{2}}$ (close approximation)

Example. $a = 3$; $b = 4$.
Area $= 3.1416 \times 3 \times 4 = 37.6992$. Ans.

Circum. $= 2 \times 3.1416\sqrt{\dfrac{(3)^2 + (4)^2}{2}}$
$= 6.2832 \times 3.5355 = 22.21$ Ans.

Form		*Method of finding areas*
Triangle		Base × ½ perpendicular height. $\sqrt{s(s-a)(s-b)(s-c)}$, s = ½ sum of the three sides a, b, c.
Trapezium		Sum of area of the two triangles
Trapezoid		½ sum of parallel sides × perpendicular height.
Parallelogram		Base × perpendicular height.
Reg. Polygon		½ sum of sides × inside radius.
Circle		$\pi r^2 = 0.78540 \times \text{diam}^2 = 0.07958 \times$ circumference
Sector of a circle		$\dfrac{\pi r^2 A°}{360} = 0.0087266\ r^2A° = \text{arc} \times \frac{1}{2}$ radius
Segment of a circle		$\dfrac{r^2}{2}\left(\dfrac{\pi A}{180} - \sin A°\right)$
Circle of same area as a square		Diameter = side × 1.12838
Square of same area as a circle		Side = diameter × 0.88623
Ellipse		Long diameter × short diameter × 0.78540
Parabola		Base × ⅔ perpendicular height.

MATHEMATICAL DATA AND FORMULAS
Geometric Shapes and Slopes, Grades, and Angles

Geometric Figures

Plane Shapes (two-dimensional)

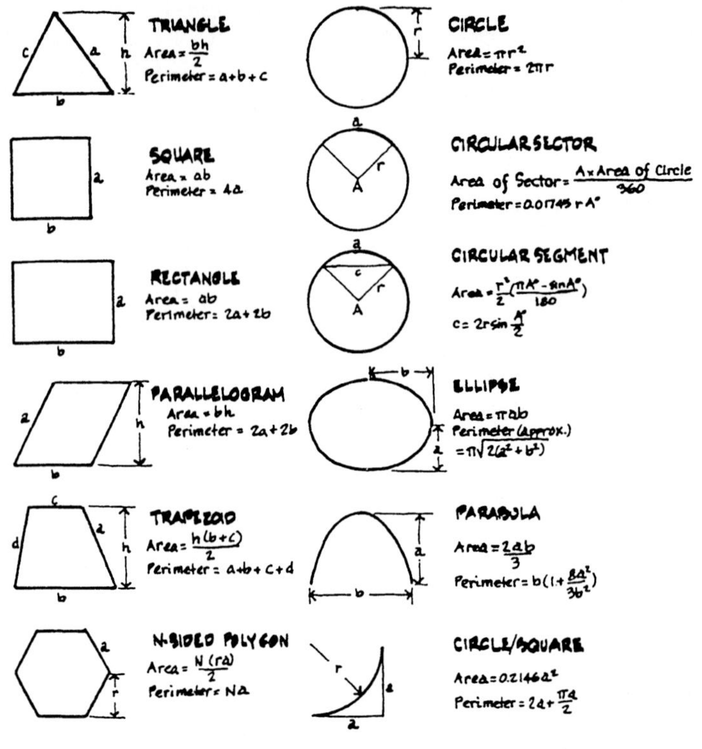

Table of slopes, grades, and angles

% Slope	In/ft	Ratio	Deg. from horiz.	% Slope	In/ft	Ratio	Deg. from horiz.
1	⅛	1 in 100		17	2	approx. 2 in 12	
2	¼	1 in 50		18	2⅛		
3	⅜			19	2¼		
4	½	1 in 25		20	2⅜	1 in 5	11.5
5	⅝	1 in 20	3	25	3	3 in 12	14
6	¾			30	3.6	1 in 3.3	17
7	⅞			35	4.2	approx. 4 in 12	19.25
8	approx. 1	approx. 1 in 12		40	4.8	approx. 5 in 12	21.5
9	1⅛			45	5.4	1 in 2.2	24
10	1¼	1 in 10	6	50	6	6 in 12	26.5
11	1⅜	approx. 1 in 9		55	6⅝	1 in 1.8	28.5
12	1½			60	7¼	approx. 7 in 12	31
13	1⅝			65	7¾	1 in 1½	33
14	1¾			70	8⅜	1 in 1.4	35
15			8.5	75	9	1 in 1.3	36.75
16	1⅞			100	12	1 in 1	45

NO.	SQUARE	CUBE	SQUARE ROOT	CUBE ROOT	LOGARITHM	1000 x RECIPROCAL	NO. = DIAMETER	
							CIRCUM.	AREA
1	1	1	1.0000	1.0000	0.00000	1000.000	3.142	0.7854
2	4	8	1.4142	1.2599	0.30103	500.000	6.283	3.1416
3	9	27	1.7321	1.4422	0.47712	333.333	9.425	7.0686
4	16	64	2.0000	1.5874	0.60206	250.000	12.566	12.5664
5	25	125	2.2361	1.7100	0.69897	200.000	15.708	19.6350
6	36	216	2.4495	1.8171	0.77815	166.667	18.850	28.2743
7	49	343	2.6458	1.9129	0.84510	142.857	21.991	38.4845
8	64	512	2.8284	2.0000	0.90309	125.000	25.133	50.2655
9	81	729	3.0000	2.0801	0.95424	111.111	28.274	63.6173
10	100	1000	3.1623	2.1544	1.00000	100.000	31.416	78.5398
11	121	1331	3.3166	2.2240	1.04139	90.9091	34.558	95.0332
12	144	1728	3.4641	2.2894	1.07918	83.3333	37.699	113.097
13	169	2197	3.6056	2.3513	1.11394	76.9231	40.841	132.732
14	196	2744	3.7417	2.4101	1.14613	71.4286	43.982	153.938
15	225	3375	3.8730	2.4662	1.17609	66.6667	47.124	176.715
16	256	4096	4.0000	2.5198	1.20412	62.5000	50.265	201.062
17	289	4913	4.1231	2.5713	1.23045	58.8235	53.407	226.980
18	324	5832	4.2426	2.6207	1.25527	55.5556	56.549	254.469
19	361	6859	4.3589	2.6684	1.27875	52.6316	59.690	283.529
20	400	8000	4.4721	2.7144	1.30103	50.0000	62.832	314.159
21	441	9261	4.5826	2.7589	1.32222	47.6190	65.973	346.361
22	484	10648	4.6904	2.8020	1.34242	45.4545	69.115	380.133
23	529	12167	4.7958	2.8439	1.36173	43.4783	72.257	415.476
24	576	13824	4.8990	2.8845	1.38021	41.6667	75.398	452.389
25	625	15625	5.0000	2.9240	1.39794	40.0000	78.540	490.874
26	676	17576	5.0990	2.9625	1.41497	38.4615	81.681	530.929
27	729	19683	5.1962	3.0000	1.43136	37.0370	84.823	572.555
28	784	21952	5.2915	3.0366	1.44716	35.7143	87.965	615.752
29	841	24389	5.3852	3.0723	1.46240	34.4828	91.106	660.520
30	900	27000	5.4772	3.1072	1.47712	33.3333	94.248	706.858
31	961	29791	5.5678	3.1414	1.49136	32.2581	97.389	754.768
32	1024	32768	5.6569	3.1748	1.50515	31.2500	100.531	804.248
33	1089	35937	5.7446	3.2075	1.51851	30.3030	103.673	855.299
34	1156	39304	5.8310	3.2396	1.53148	29.4118	106.814	907.920
35	1225	42875	5.9161	3.2711	1.54407	28.5714	109.956	962.113
36	1296	46656	6.0000	3.3019	1.55630	27.7778	113.097	1017.88
37	1369	50653	6.0828	3.3322	1.56820	27.0270	116.239	1075.21
38	1444	54872	6.1644	3.3620	1.57978	26.3158	119.381	1134.11
39	1521	59319	6.2450	3.3912	1.59106	25.6410	122.522	1194.59
40	1600	64000	6.3246	3.4200	1.60206	25.0000	125.66	1256.64
41	1681	68921	6.4031	3.4482	1.61278	24.3902	128.81	1320.25
42	1764	74088	6.4807	3.4760	1.62325	23.8095	131.95	1385.44
43	1849	79507	6.5574	3.5034	1.63347	23.2558	135.09	1452.20
44	1936	85184	6.6332	3.5303	1.64345	22.7273	138.23	1520.53
45	2025	91125	6.7082	3.5569	1.65321	22.2222	141.37	1590.43

MATHEMATICAL DATA AND FORMULAS
Functions of Numbers

(Continued)

NO.	SQUARE	CUBE	SQUARE ROOT	CUBE ROOT	LOGARITHM	1000 x RECIPROCAL	NO. = DIAMETER CIRCUM.	NO. = DIAMETER AREA
46	2116	97336	6.7823	3.5830	1.66276	21.7391	144.51	1661.90
47	2209	103823	6.8557	3.6088	1.67210	21.2766	147.65	1734.94
48	2304	110592	6.9282	3.6342	1.68124	20.8333	150.80	1809.56
49	2401	117649	7.0000	3.6593	1.69020	20.4082	153.94	1885.74
50	2500	125000	7.0711	3.6840	1.69897	20.0000	157.08	1963.50
51	2601	132651	7.1414	3.7084	1.70757	19.6078	160.22	2042.82
52	2704	140608	7.2111	3.7325	1.71600	19.2308	163.36	2123.72
53	2809	148877	7.2801	3.7563	1.72428	18.8679	166.50	2206.18
54	2916	157464	7.3485	3.7798	1.73239	18.5185	169.65	2290.22
55	3025	166375	7.4162	3.8030	1.74036	18.1818	172.79	2375.83
56	3136	175616	7.4833	3.8259	1.74819	17.8571	175.93	2463.01
57	3249	185193	7.5498	3.8485	1.75587	17.5439	179.07	2551.76
58	3364	195112	7.6158	3.8709	1.76343	17.2414	182.21	2642.08
59	3481	205379	7.6811	3.8930	1.77085	16.9492	185.35	2733.97
60	3600	216000	7.7460	3.9149	1.77815	16.6667	188.50	2827.43
61	3721	226981	7.8102	3.9365	1.78533	16.3934	191.64	2922.47
62	3844	238328	7.8740	3.9579	1.79239	16.1290	194.78	3019.07
63	3969	250047	7.9373	3.9791	1.79934	15.8730	197.92	3117.25
64	4096	262144	8.0000	4.0000	1.80618	15.6250	201.06	3216.99
65	4225	274625	8.0623	4.0207	1.81291	15.3846	204.20	3318.31
66	4356	287496	8.1240	4.0412	1.81954	15.1515	207.35	3421.19
67	4489	300763	8.1854	4.0615	1.82607	14.9254	210.49	3525.65
68	4624	314432	8.2462	4.0817	1.83251	14.7059	213.63	3631.68
69	4761	328509	8.3066	4.1016	1.83885	14.4928	216.77	3739.28
70	4900	343000	8.3666	4.1213	1.84510	14.2857	219.91	3848.45
71	5041	357911	8.4261	4.1408	1.85126	14.0845	223.05	3959.19
72	5184	373248	8.4853	4.1602	1.85733	13.8889	226.19	4071.50
73	5329	389017	8.5440	4.1793	1.86332	13.6986	229.34	4185.39
74	5476	405224	8.6023	4.1983	1.86923	13.5135	232.48	4300.84
75	5625	421875	8.6603	4.2172	1.87506	13.3333	235.62	4417.86
76	5776	438976	8.7178	4.2358	1.88081	13.1579	238.76	4536.46
77	5929	456533	8.7750	4.2543	1.88649	12.9870	241.90	4656.63
78	6084	474552	8.8318	4.2727	1.89209	12.8205	245.04	4778.36
79	6241	493039	8.8882	4.2908	1.89763	12.6582	248.19	4901.67
80	6400	512000	8.9443	4.3089	1.90309	12.5000	251.33	5026.55
81	6561	531441	9.0000	4.3267	1.90849	12.3457	254.47	5153.00
82	6724	551368	9.0554	4.3445	1.91381	12.1951	257.61	5281.02
83	6889	571787	9.1104	4.3621	1.91908	12.0482	260.75	5410.61
84	7056	592704	9.1652	4.3795	1.92428	11.9048	263.89	5541.77
85	7225	614125	9.2195	4.3968	1.92942	11.7647	267.04	5674.50
86	7396	636056	9.2736	4.4140	1.93450	11.6279	270.18	5808.80
87	7569	658503	9.3274	4.4310	1.93952	11.4943	273.32	5944.68
88	7744	681472	9.3808	4.4480	1.94448	11.3636	276.46	6082.12
89	7921	704969	9.4340	4.4647	1.94939	11.2360	279.60	6221.14
90	8100	729000	9.4868	4.4814	1.95424	11.1111	282.74	6361.73

WOOD VENEERS

The method by which wood veneers are manufactured provides the designer with a great variety of results. The primary factors influencing these results are the natural characteristics of the wood, including its grain, color, and texture. In addition, the location of the tree from which the veneer is cut and how it is cut will also influence the end result or the "figure" of the veneer.

Generally speaking, the widest figured and longest wood veneers are cut from the main trunk of the tree. Other parts of a tree commonly used for veneers include the "stump" (or "butt"), the "burl" or ("burr"), and the "crotch". Accordingly, commonly used terms describing these veneers include butt veneers, burl or burr veneers, crown-cut veneers, crotch veneers, freak-figured veneers, ray-figured veneers, and striped veneers. These descriptive terms refer to either the method of cutting or the portion of the tree from which the log and, ultimately,the veneer are cut. Section 3 of this book provides the designer with additional information on wood veneer matching patterns as related to the design of architectural woodwork paneling.

The following color plates of wood veneers have been provided by B & B Rare Woods (10946 W. Texas Avenue, Lakewood, CO 80232, 303-986-2585).(www.wood-veneers.com/veneer)

MARBLE

The use of stone as both a structural and decorative building material dates back thousands of years. It continues to be a material that is used today for the interiors and exteriors of all types of buildings. Natural stone materials used for architectural interiors are generally classified as igneous (granite), sedimentary (sandstone, limestone, travertine, and slate), and metamorphic (marble). Typically, these stones are removed from quarries in the form of large blocks or sheets. These blocks and sheets are then refined into smaller slabs, panels, and tiles.

Marble is a metamorphic stone material that is formed as a result of the crystallization of limestone that has been subjected to intense heat and pressure. While considered to be a durable material, it is not as hard and is less strain resistant than granite. Accordingly, careful attention must be given to how one uses marble, especially when utilized on horizontal surfaces such as countertops and flooring. It can also be used for wall surfaces, tabletops, and fireplaces.

Depending on the specific type and application of the marble, there are a variety of finishes available. These are some of the more common types of finishes:

Fine Rubbed: The marble surface receives a smooth finish free from scratches and without any sheen.
Honed: The marble receives a relatively smooth finish with a slight or somewhat dull sheen, generally producing no reflections. It is produced by the use of polishing heads on sanded slabs.
Polished: The stone (marble/granite) receives a mirror gloss finish that produces relative sharp reflections.

The following color plates show marble that is quarried in Greece; however, marbles with similar characteristics, color, and veining are available from many regions in the United States, and from many countries. The designer should realize that there is a far greater range of marbles than can be depicted in a book of this type.

Afromosia

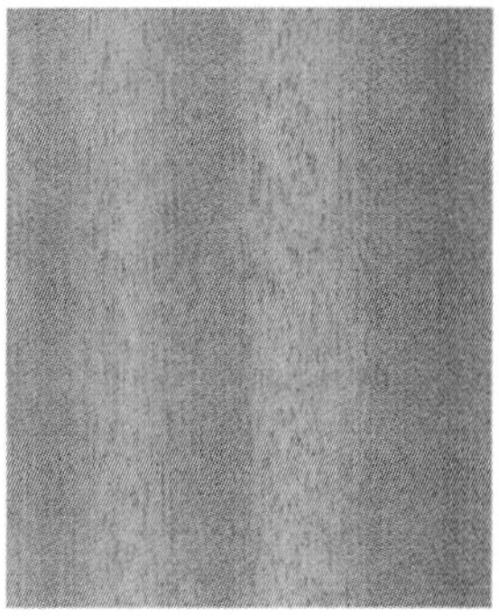

Amapa Ribbon Stripe

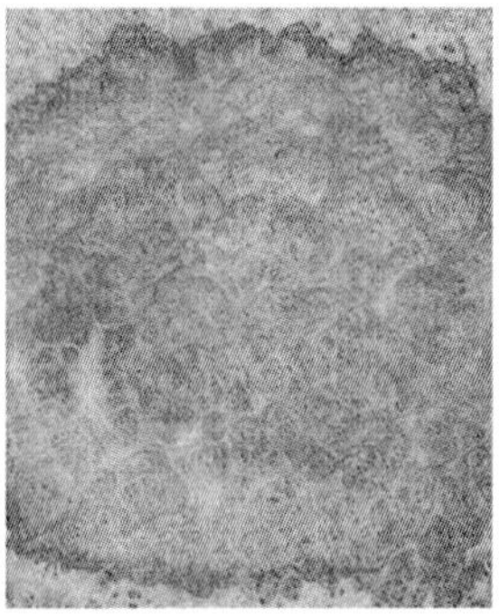

Amboyna Burl Light

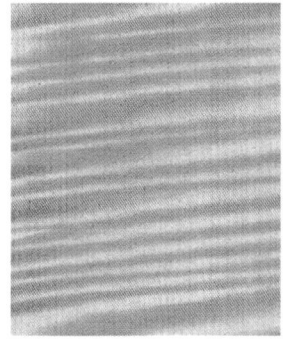

Amboyna Quilt

Amburana Cerejeria

Anagre Fiddleback

Andiroba Mottled

Anagre Curly

WOOD AND MARBLE SAMPLES
Wood Veneers

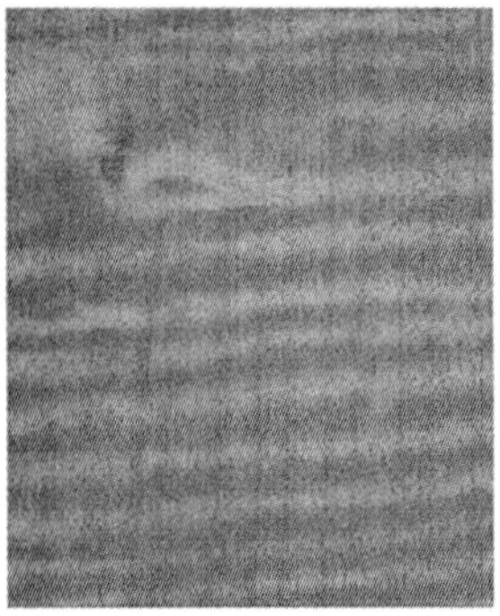
Anagre Figured

Ash Angelstep

Ash Birdseye

Ash Burl French

Ash French Cluster Burl

Ash Olive Burl

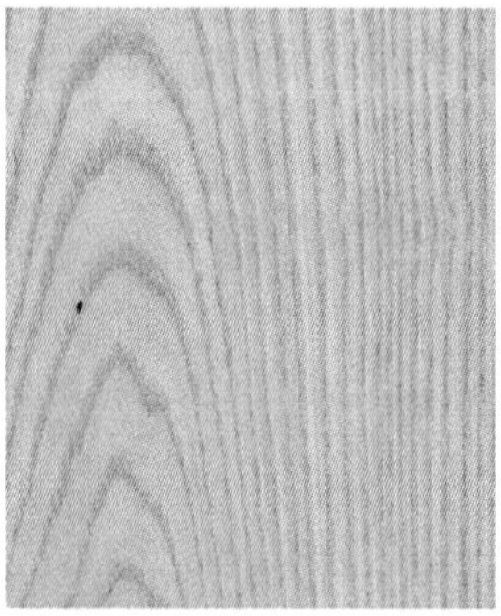
Ash White fc

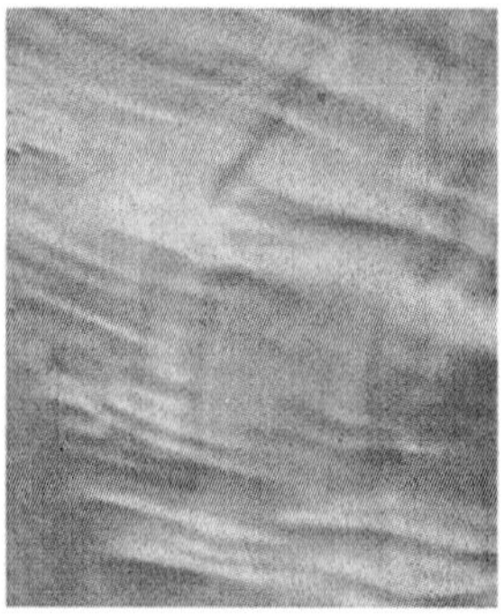
Aspen Figured

Aspen Silver

Avodire Curly

Avodire Flash Figure

Beech European qc

Beech European Steamed qc

Beech European White qc

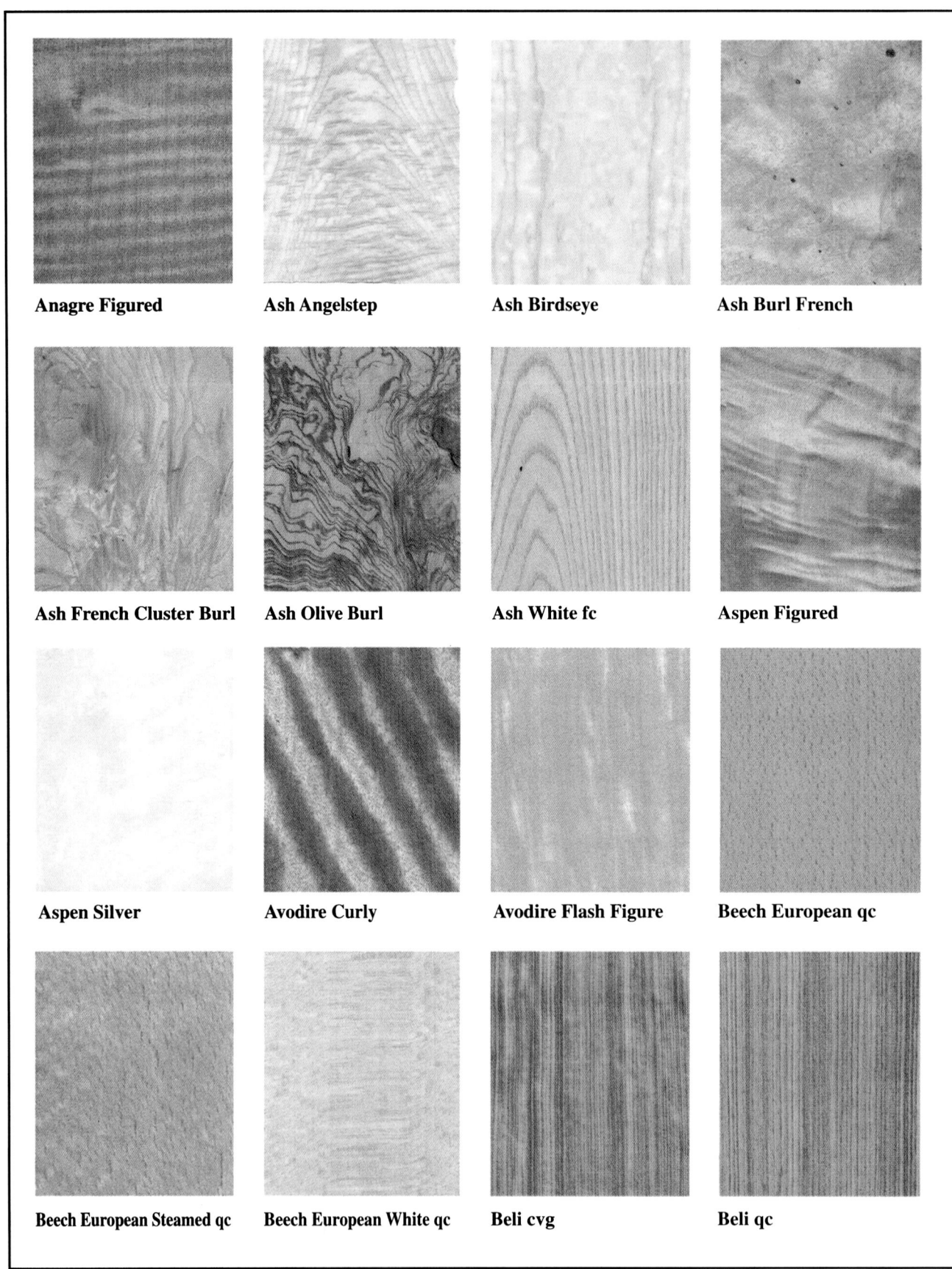

Beli cvg

Beli qc

Birch European Masur Burl

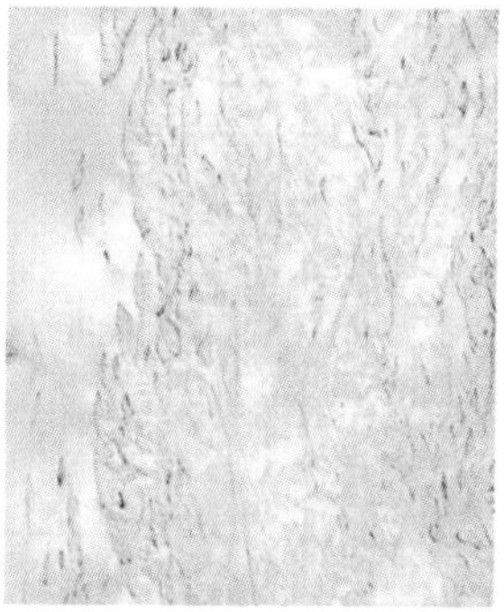
Birch European Masur Burl

Birch fc

Black Palm Sawn

Bloodwood qc

Bocote qc

Boxwood

Bubinga

Bubinga Mottled qc

Bubinga Pommele

Bubinga qc

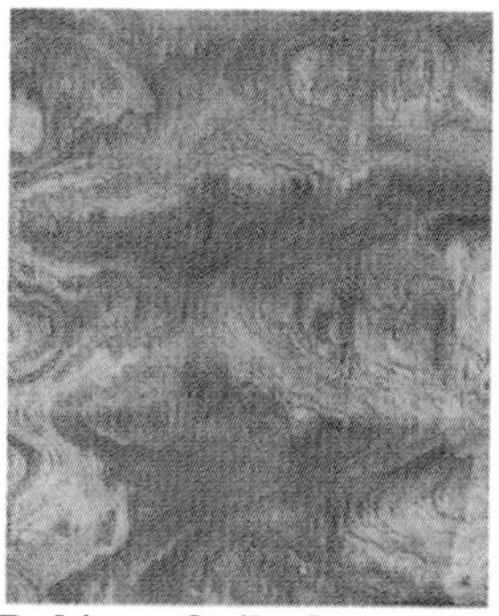
Bubinga Quilted

Butternut

Butternut fc

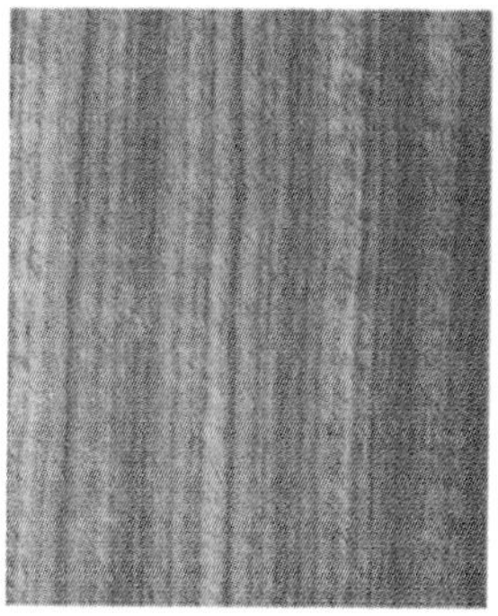
Canarywood

Castello Figured

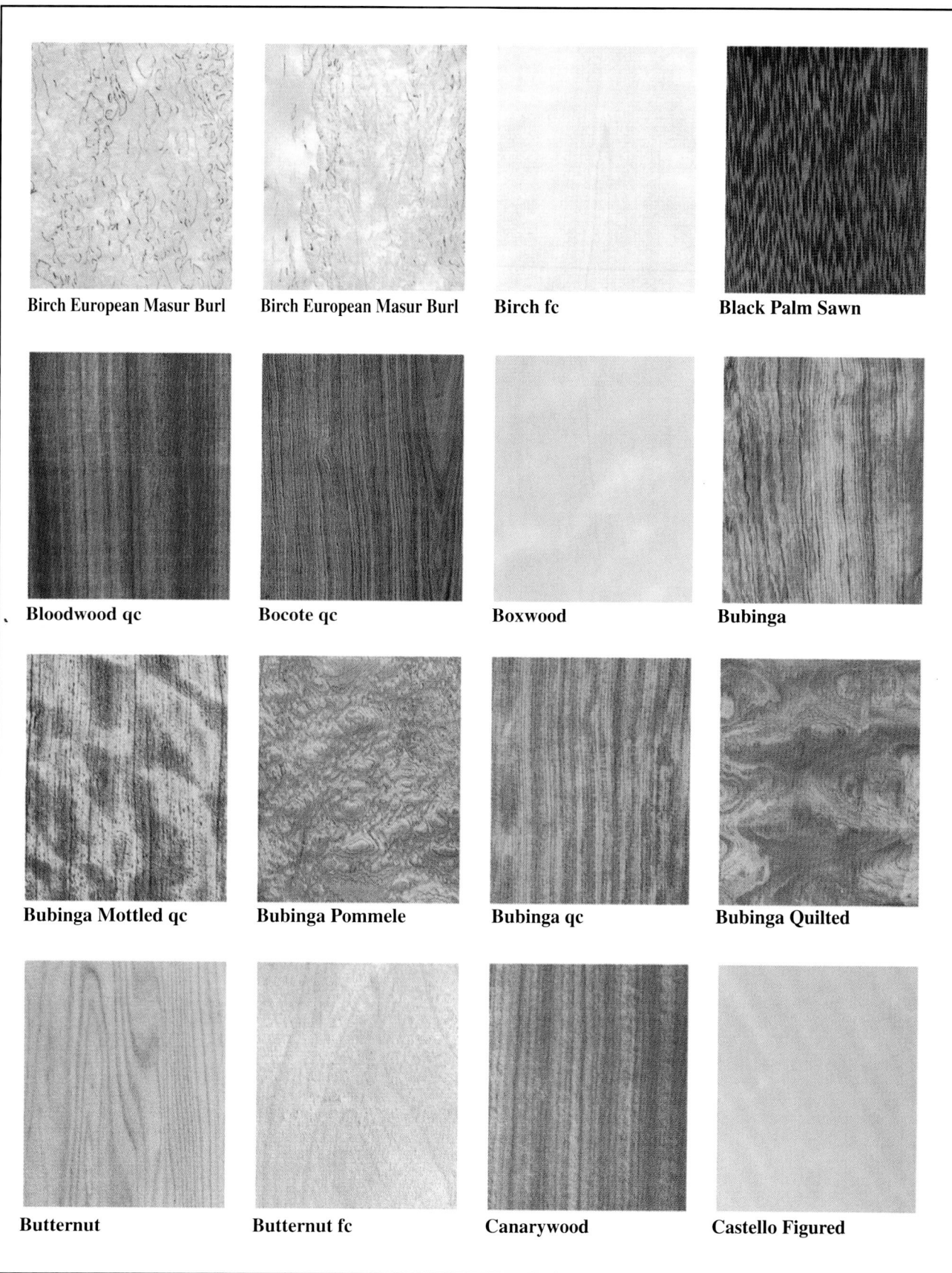

WOOD AND MARBLE SAMPLES

Wood Veneers

Cedar of Lebanon

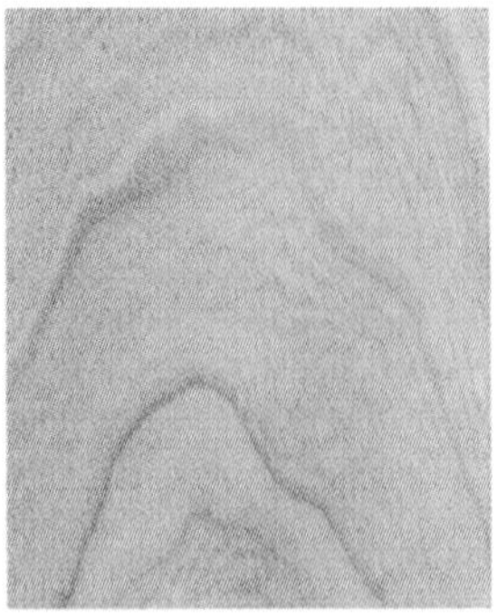
Cherry

Cherry Birdseye

Cherry Dimpled

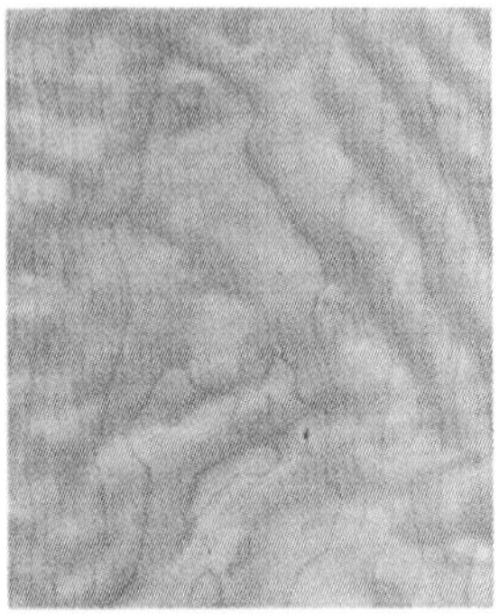
Cherry Rolling Curl

Cherry Ropey

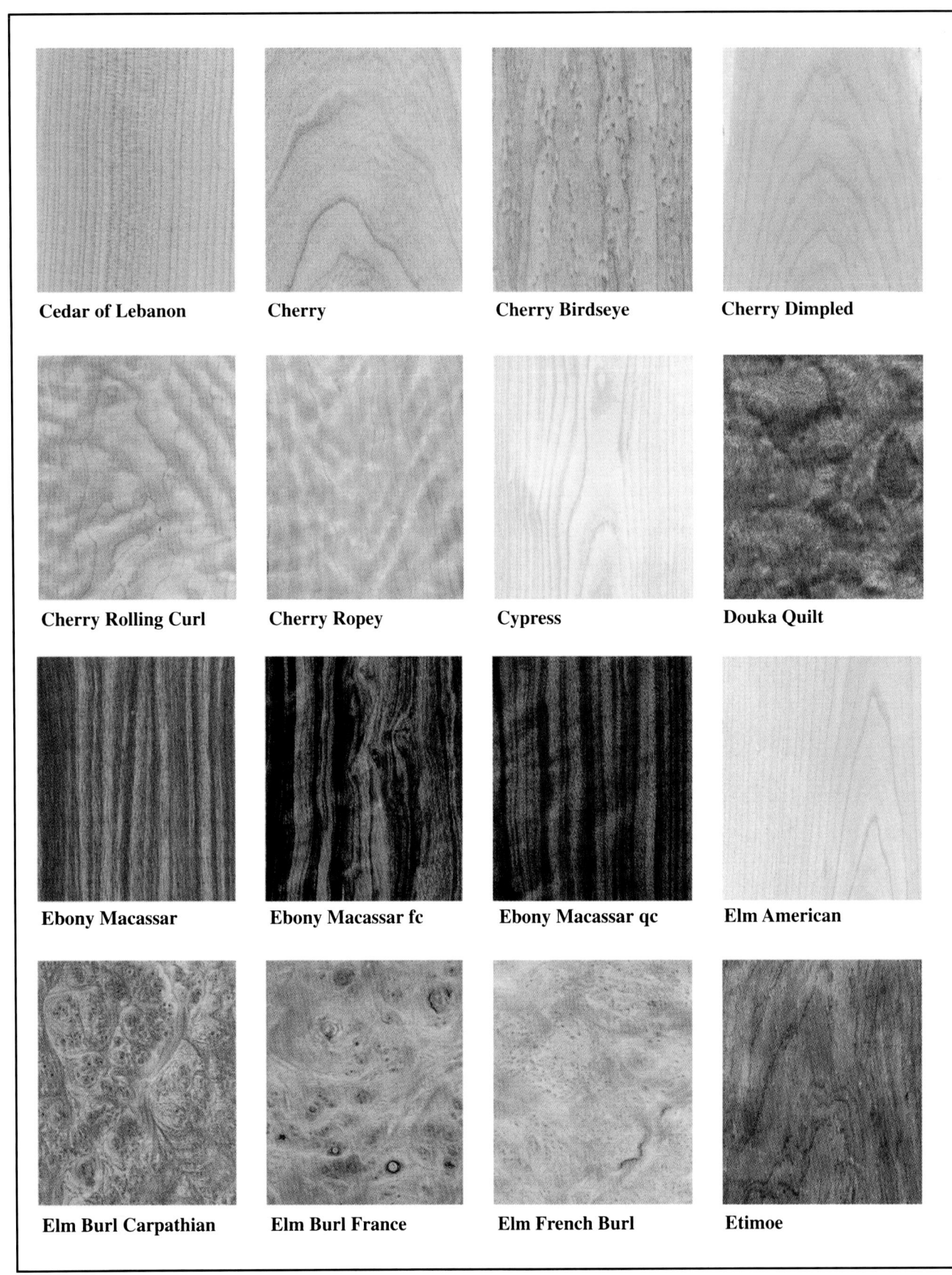

Cypress

Douka Quilt

Ebony Macassar

Ebony Macassar fc

Ebony Macassar qc

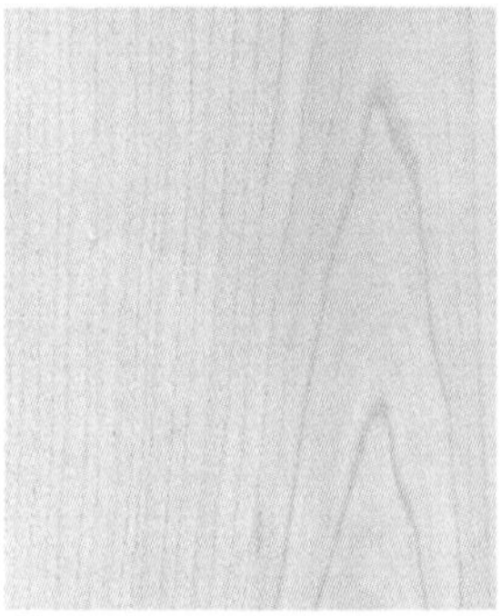
Elm American

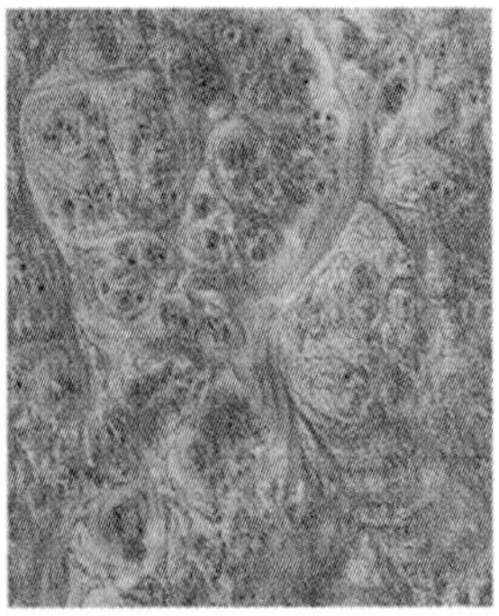
Elm Burl Carpathian

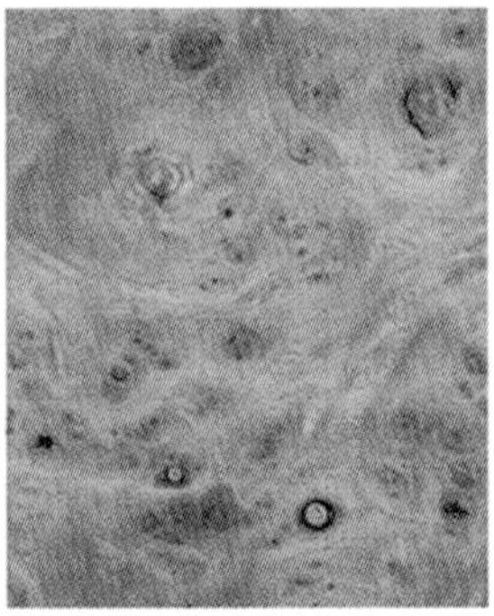
Elm Burl France

Elm French Burl

Etimoe

Etimoe fc

Eucalyptus Mottled

Goncalo Nalves

Guatambu qc

Hickory Pecky

Honeywood

Imbuia

Indian Laurel Fiddleback

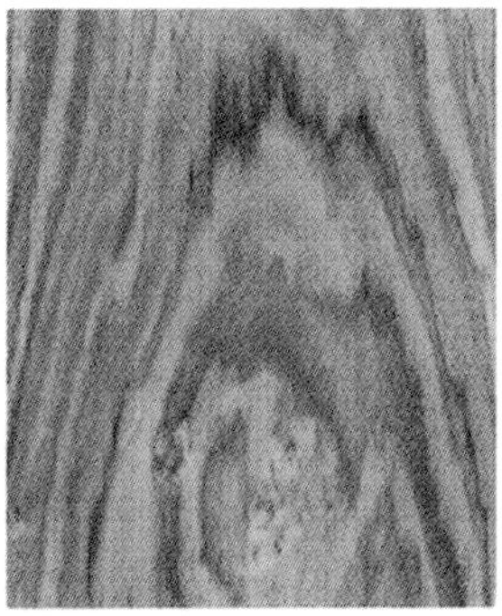
Jacaranda Amarillo

Jatoba

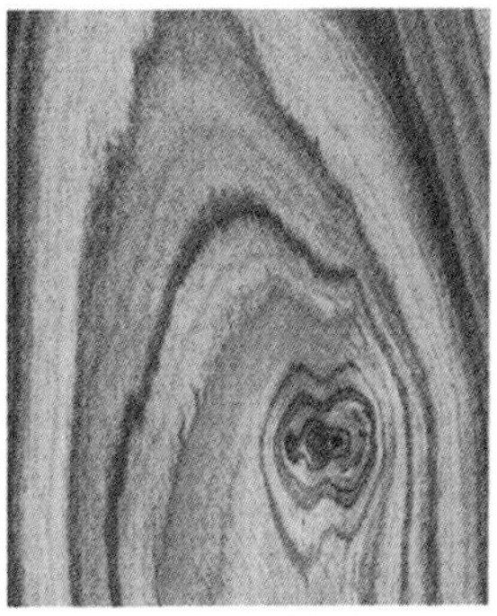
Kingwood Contrasy

Kingwood Dark

Kingwood Light

Koa Fiddleback

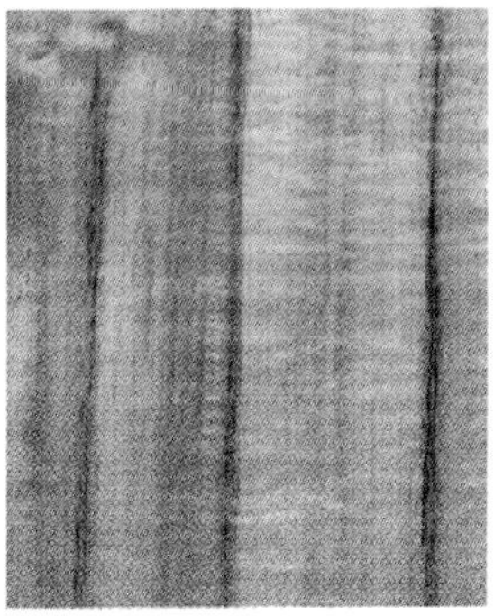
Koa Figured

Koto qc

WOOD AND MARBLE SAMPLES
Wood Veneers

Lacewood

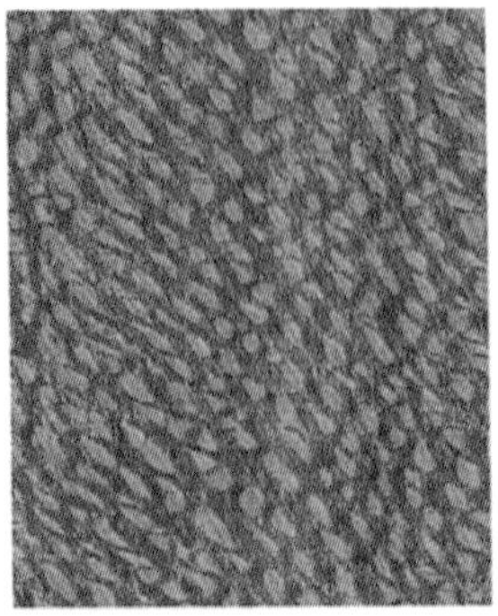
Lacewood Dark

Lacewood qc

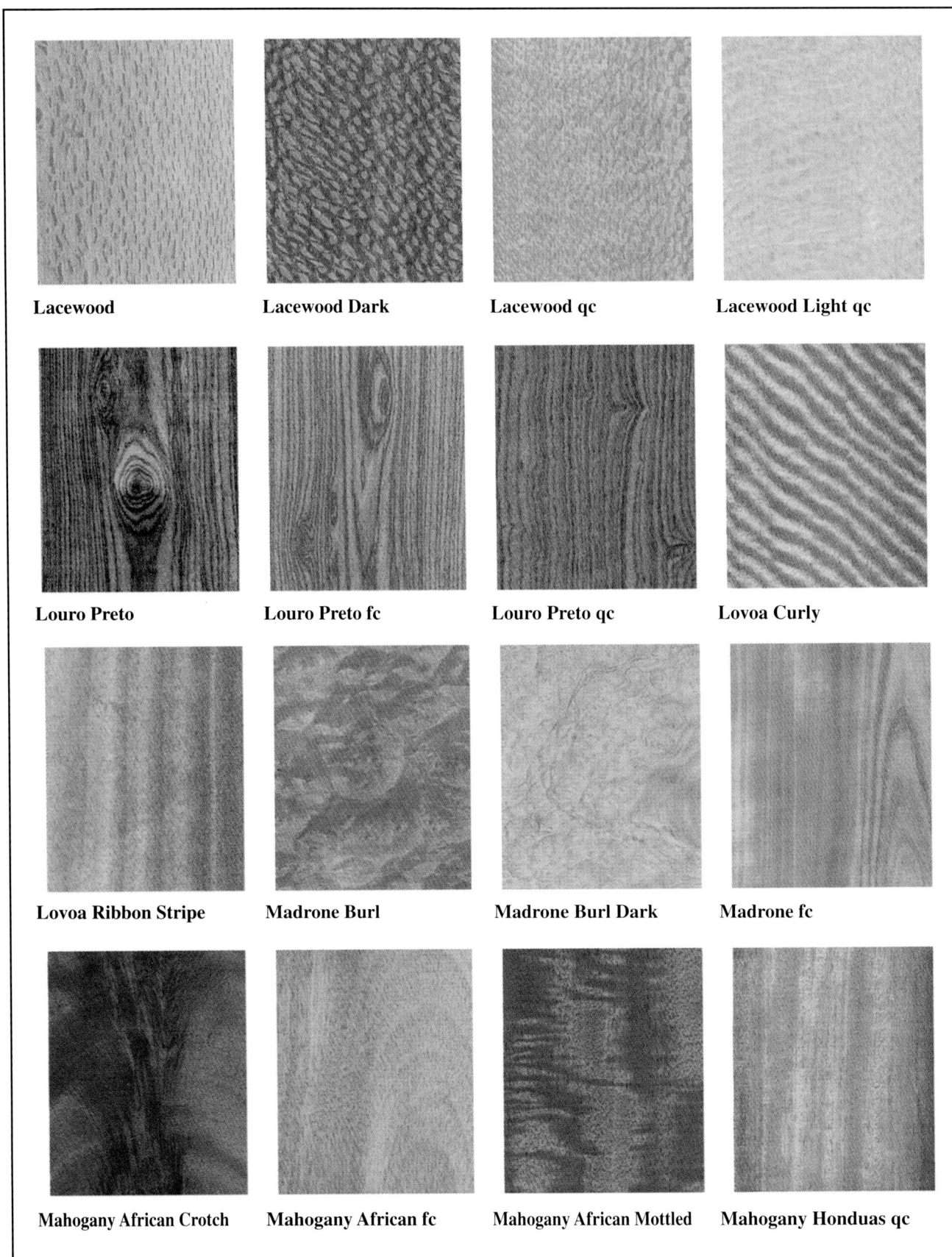

Lacewood Light qc

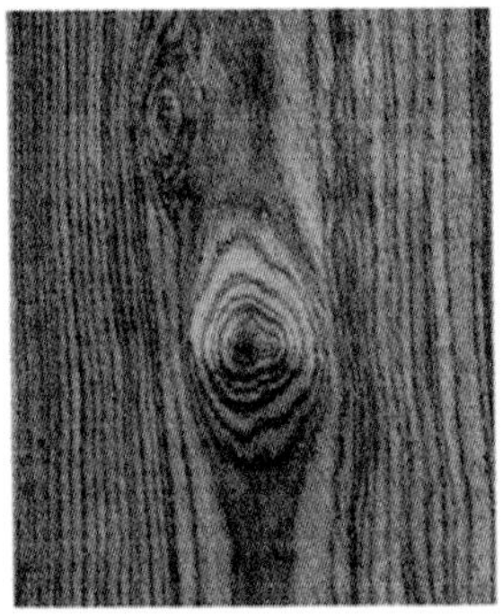
Louro Preto

Louro Preto fc

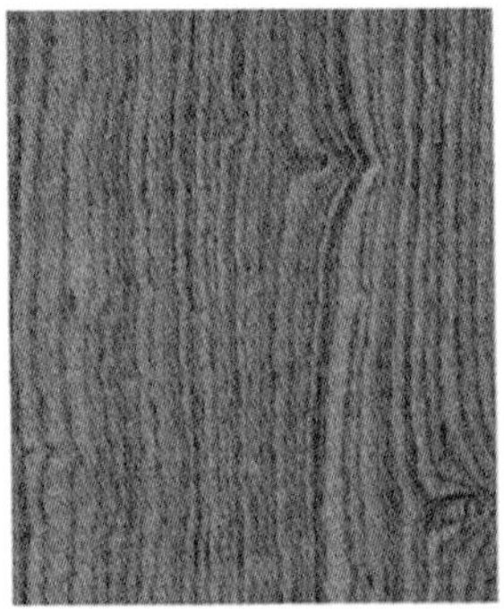
Louro Preto qc

Lovoa Curly

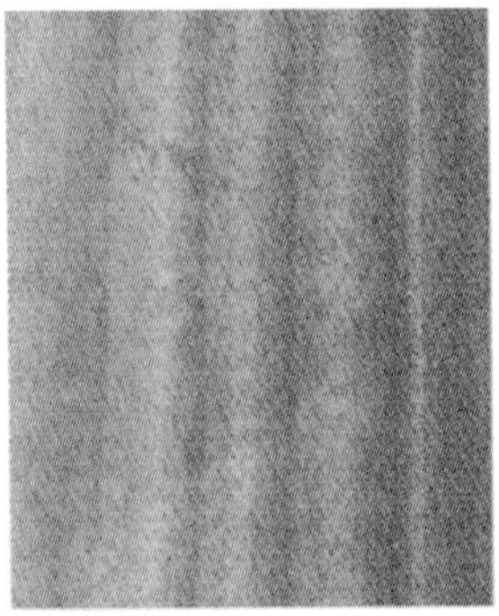
Lovoa Ribbon Stripe

Madrone Burl

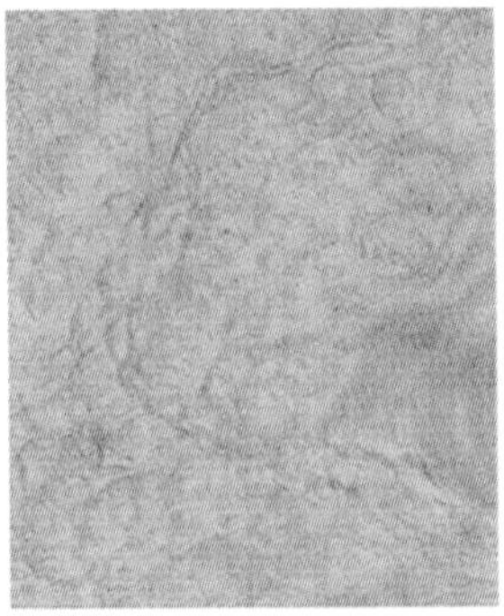
Madrone Burl Dark

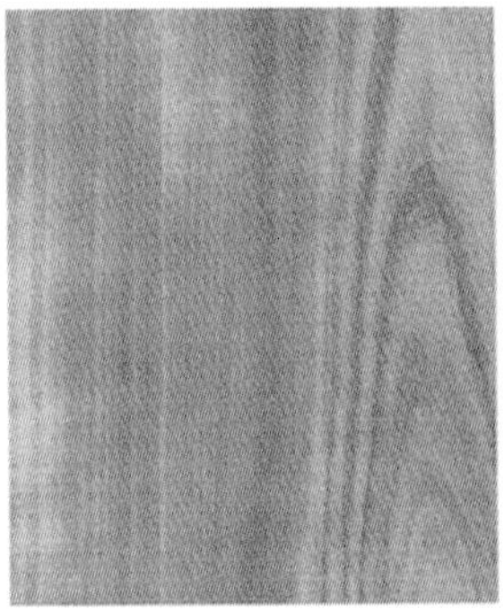
Madrone fc

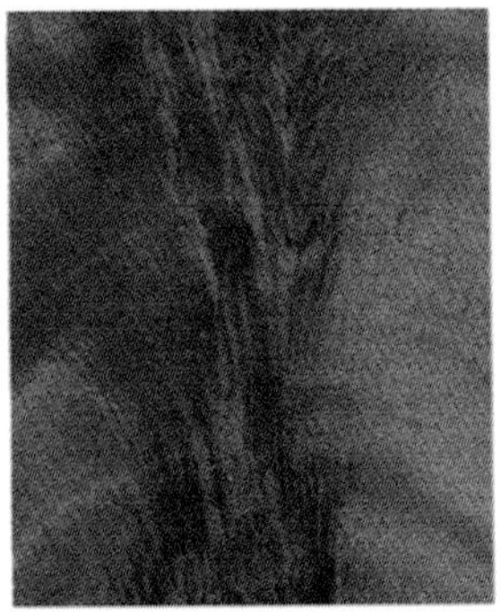
Mahogany African Crotch

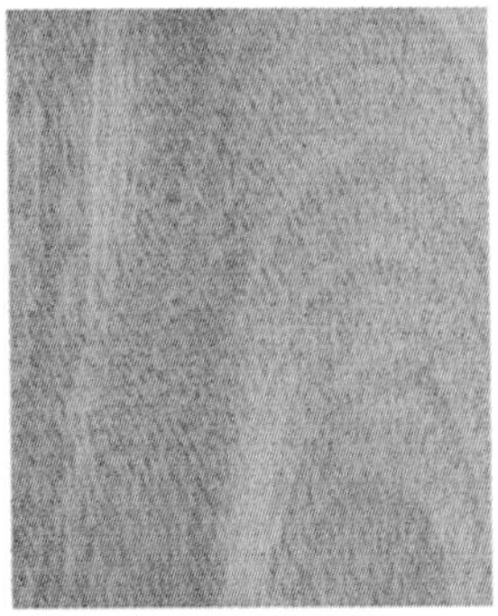
Mahogany African fc

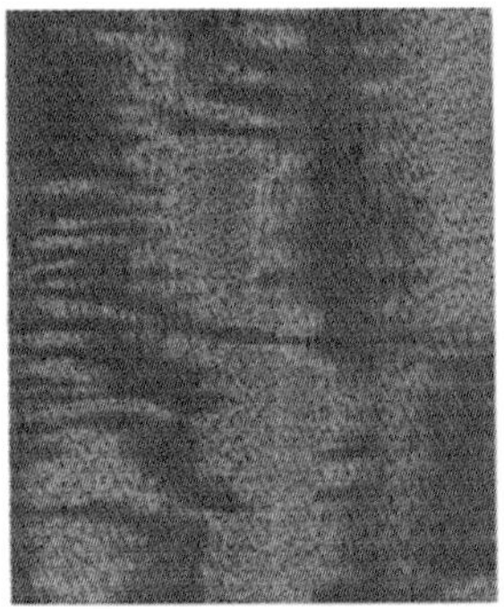
Mahogany African Mottled

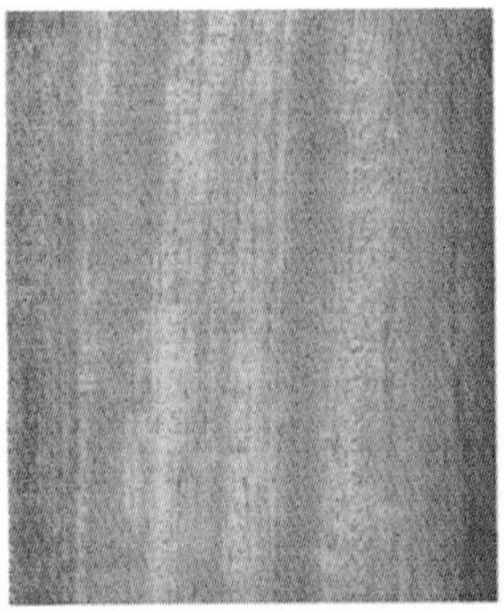
Mahogany Honduas qc

Mahogany Honduras qc

Maidou Burl

Makai qc

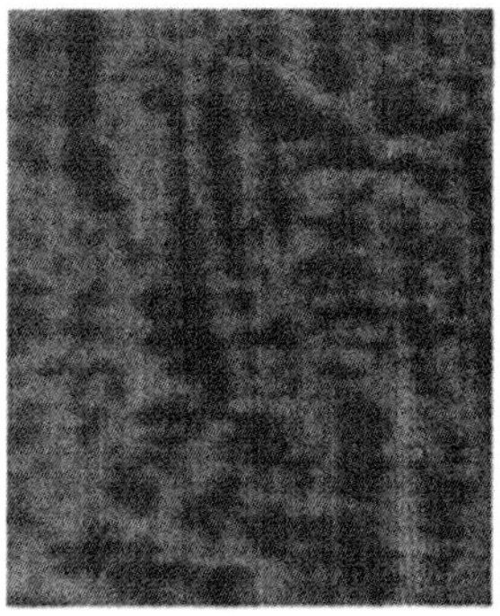

Makore Mottled

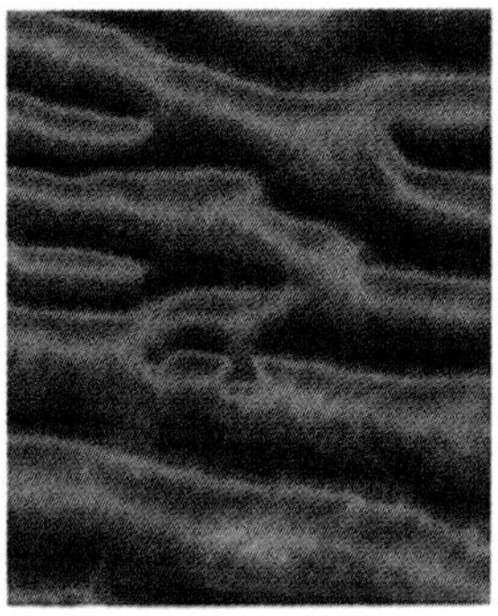

Makore Quilted

Maple Bigleaf Burl

Maple Bigleaf Burl Quilt

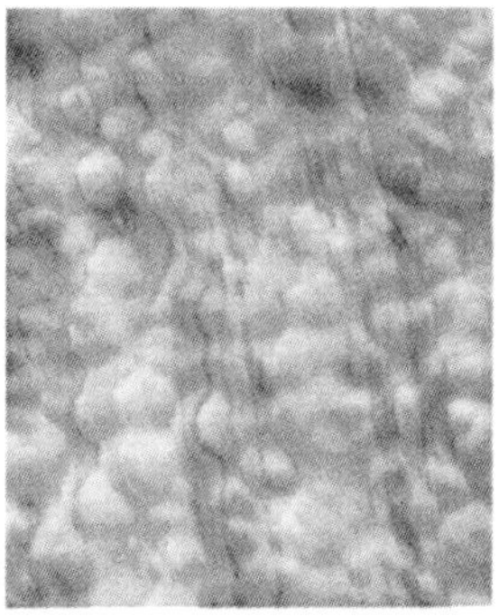

Maple Bigleaf Pommele

Maple Bigleaf Quilt

Maple Birdseye

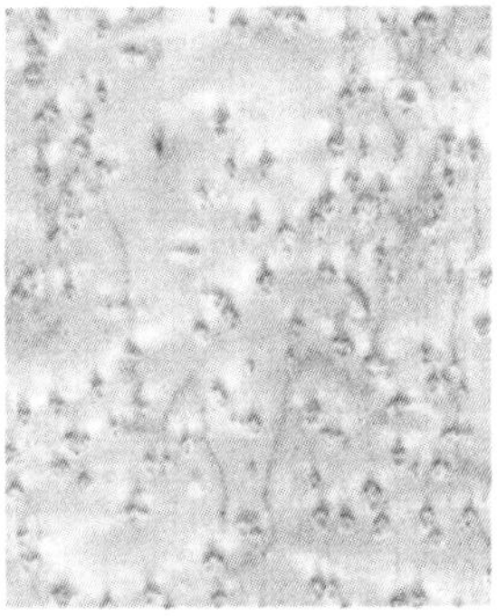

Maple Birdseye

Maple Birdseye Heavy

Maple Birdseye Quilt

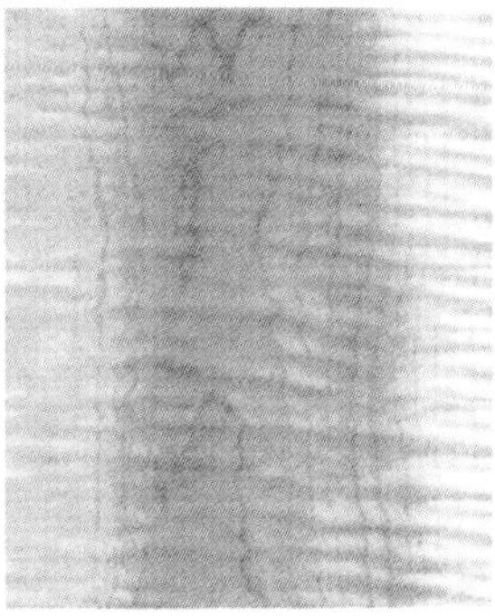

Maple Curly Greenheart

Maple Curly Spalted

Maple Diamond Quilt

WOOD AND MARBLE SAMPLES

Wood Veneers

Maple Drape Curl

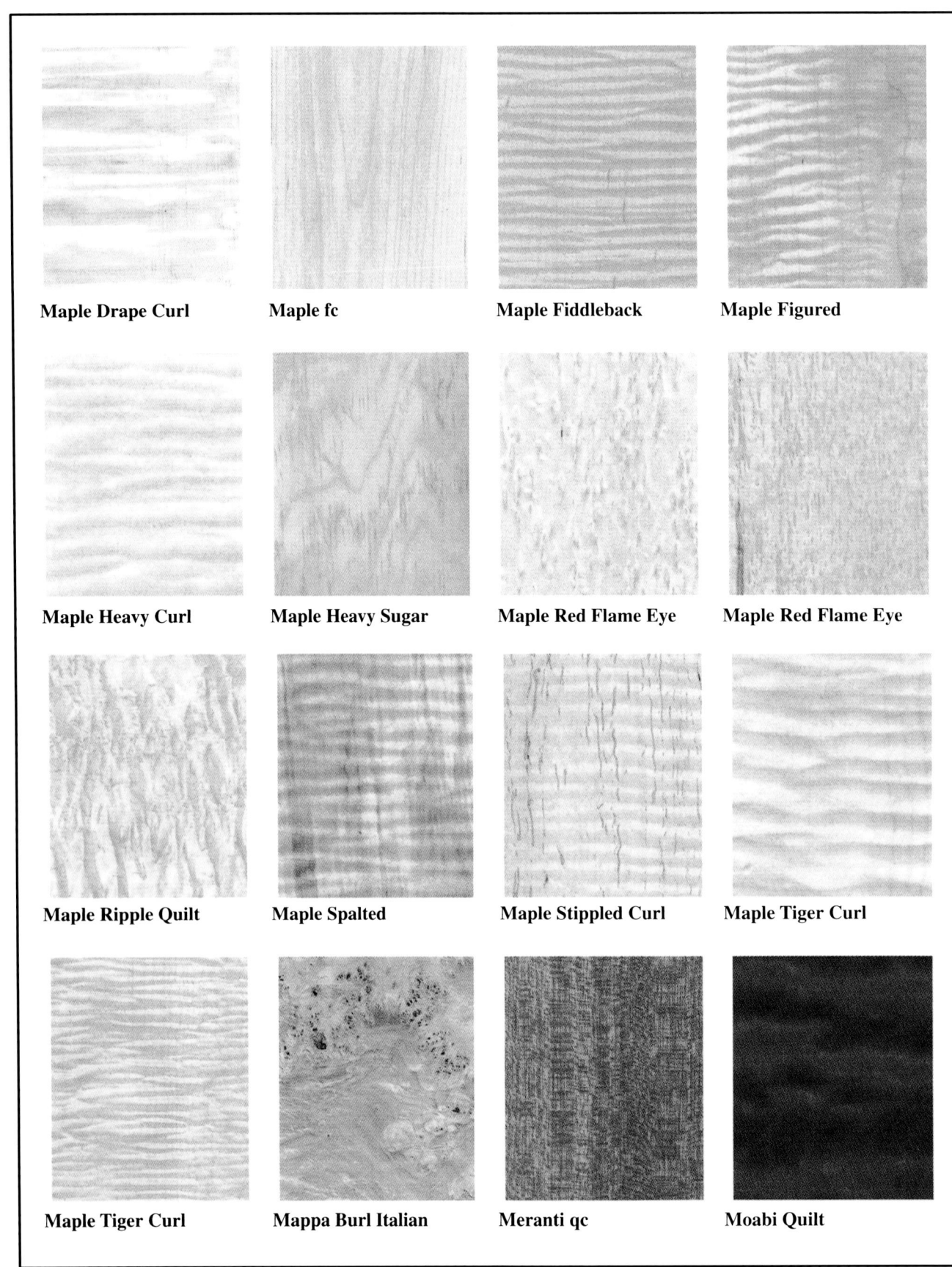

Maple fc

Maple Fiddleback

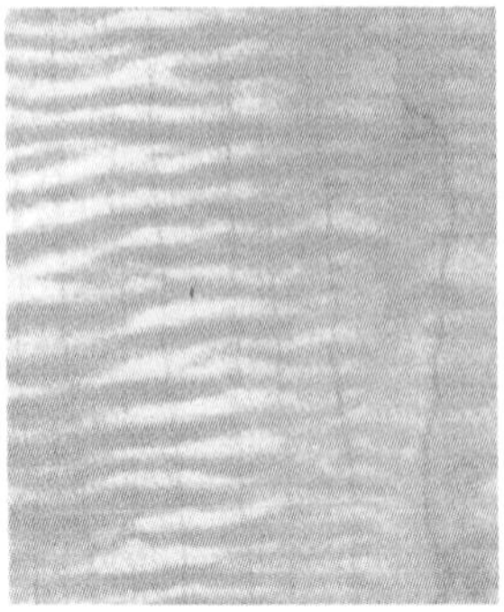

Maple Figured

Maple Heavy Curl

Maple Heavy Sugar

Maple Red Flame Eye

Maple Red Flame Eye

Maple Ripple Quilt

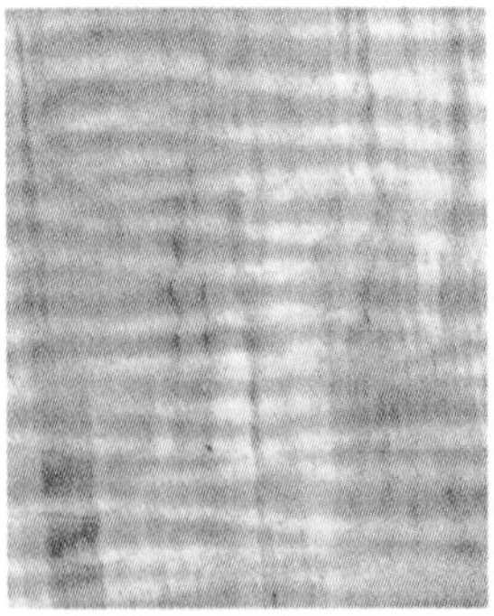

Maple Spalted

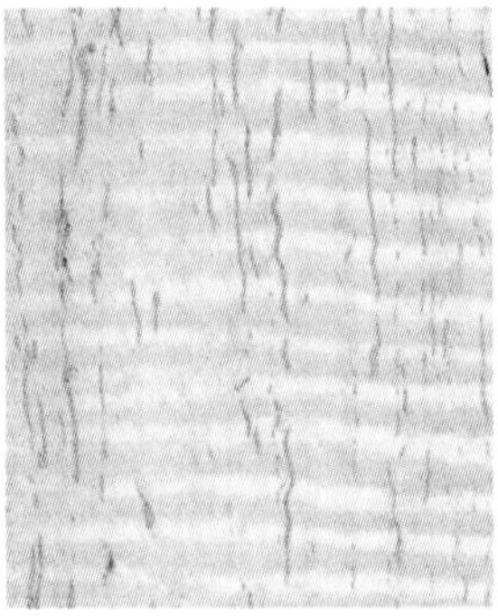

Maple Stippled Curl

Maple Tiger Curl

Maple Tiger Curl

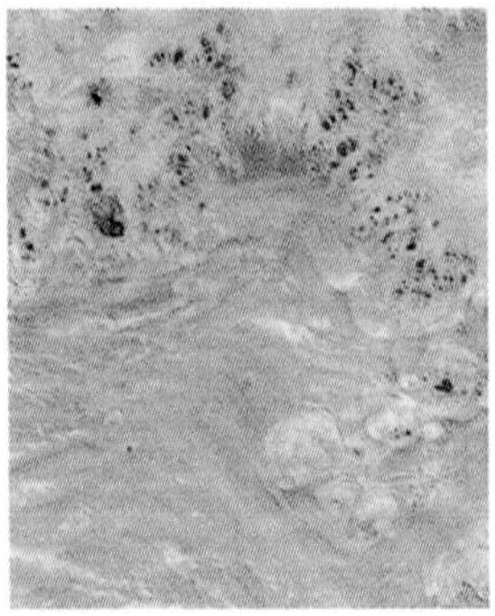

Mappa Burl Italian

Meranti qc

Moabi Quilt

Movingui Mottled

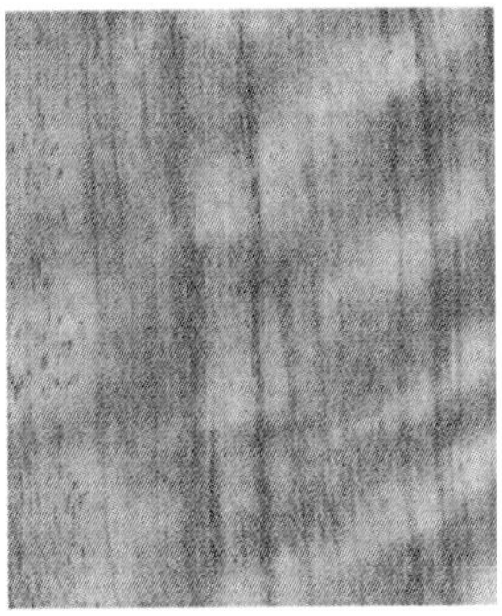
Mozambique

Myrtle Burl Light

Narra Beeswing

Oak California Black

Oak English Curly

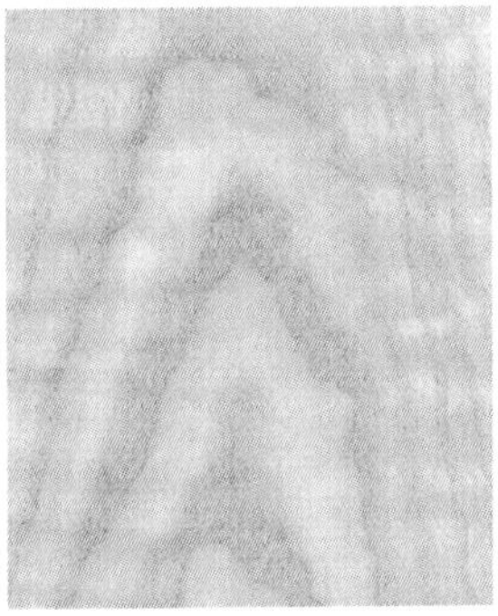
Oak Red Curly

Oak Red fc

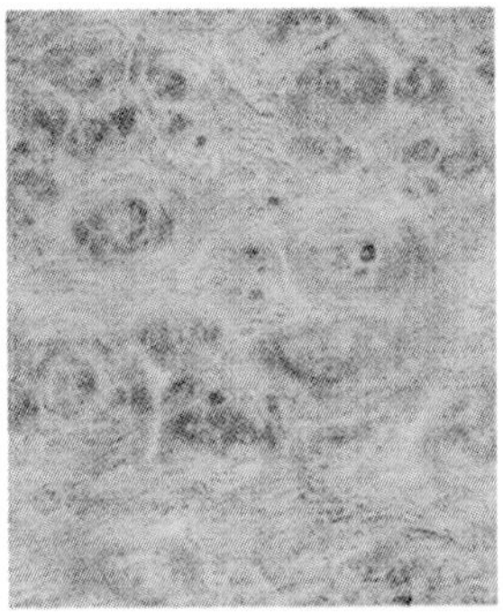
Oak White Cluster Burl

Oak White Rift

Oak White Swirly

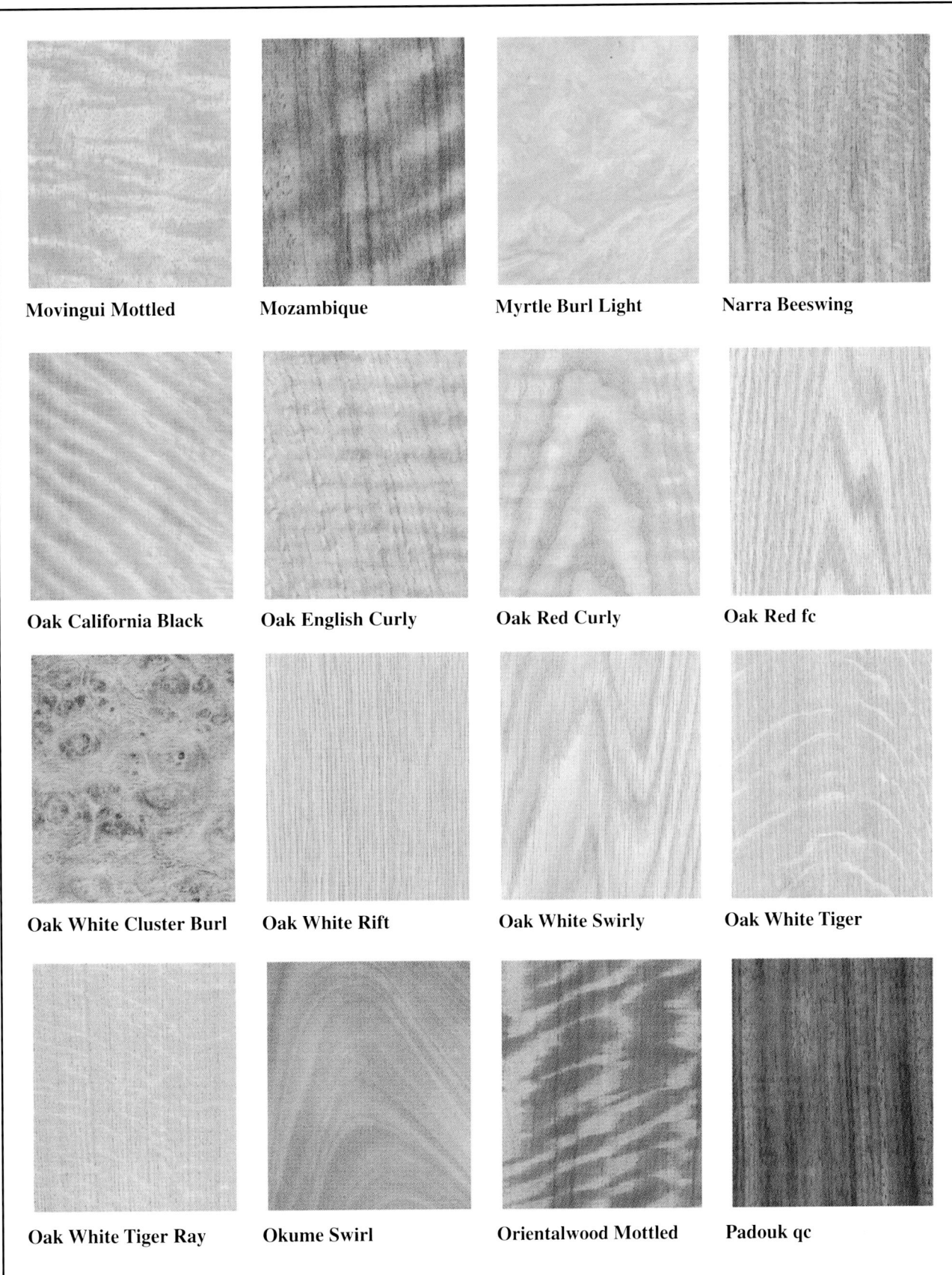

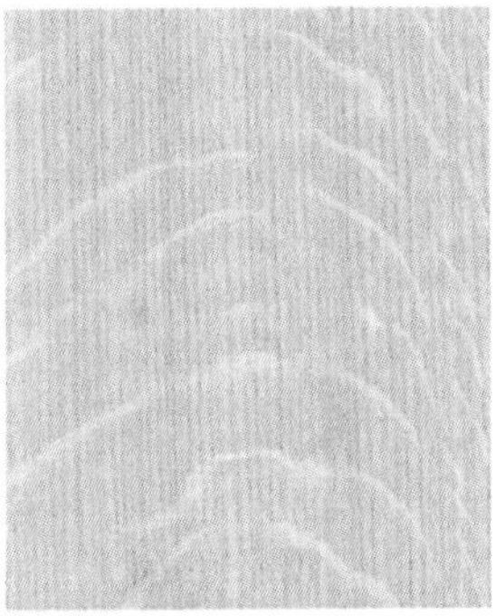
Oak White Tiger

Oak White Tiger Ray

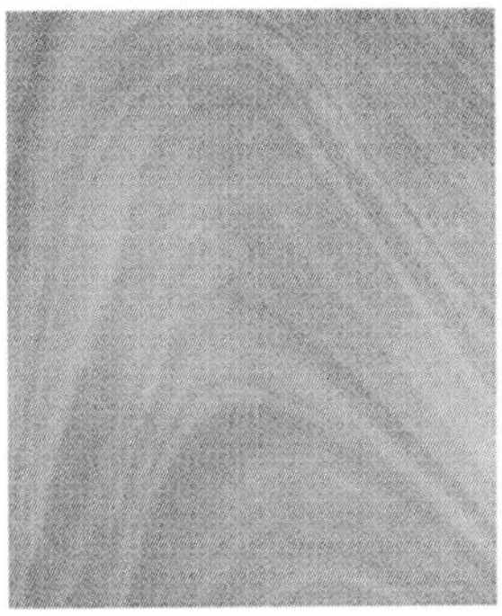
Okume Swirl

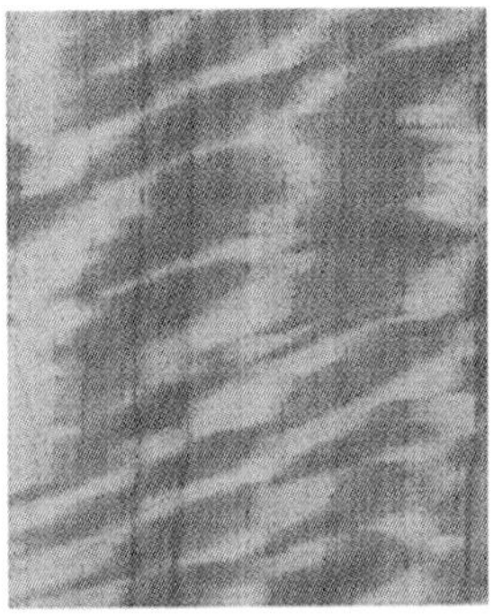
Orientalwood Mottled

Padouk qc

WOOD AND MARBLE SAMPLES

Wood Veneers

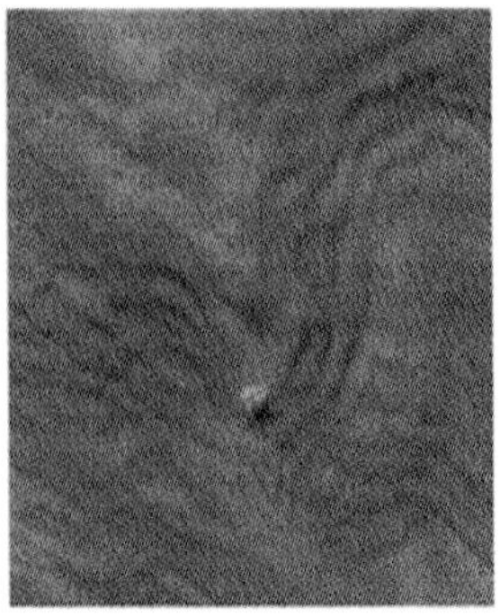

Paldao Swirly

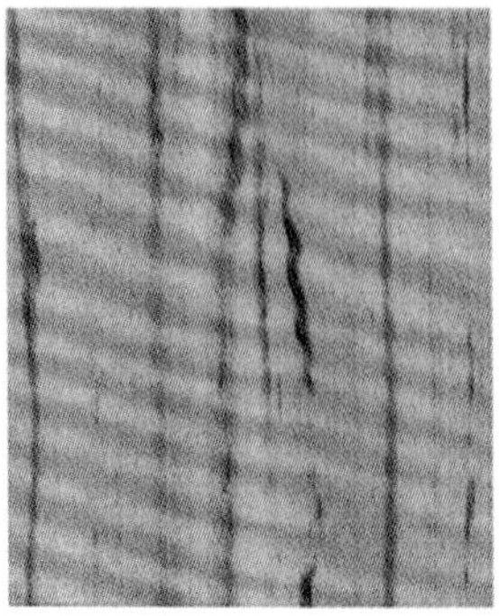

Pau Amarillo

Pau Ferro

Pau Sangue

Pear Swiss qc

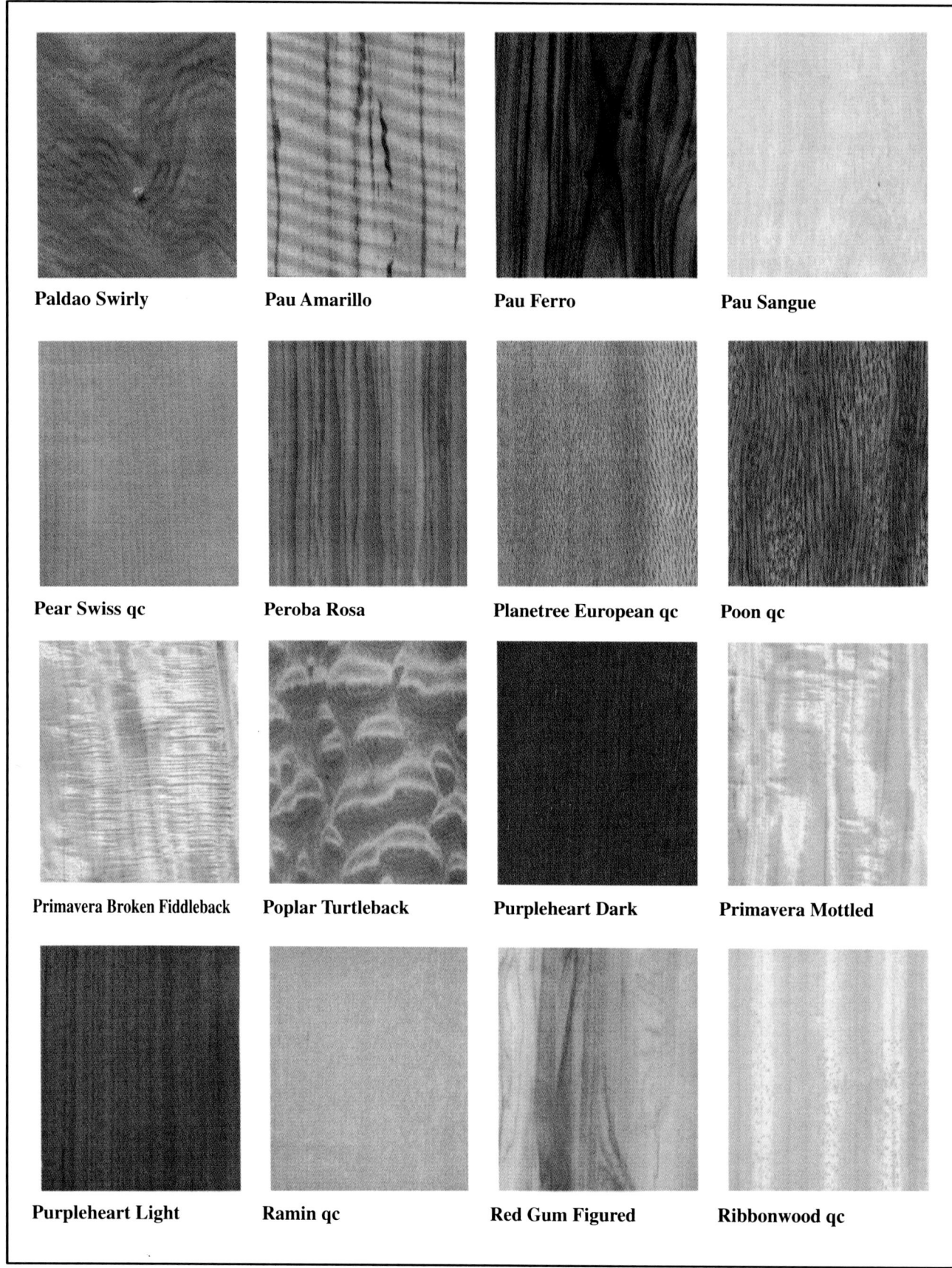

Peroba Rosa

Planetree European qc

Poon qc

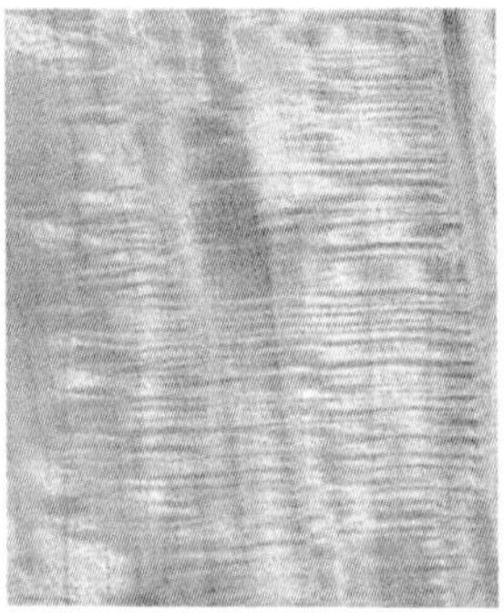

Primavera Broken Fiddleback

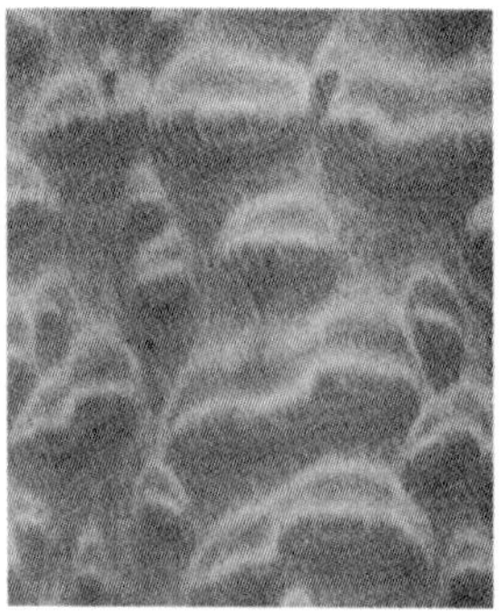

Poplar Turtleback

Purpleheart Dark

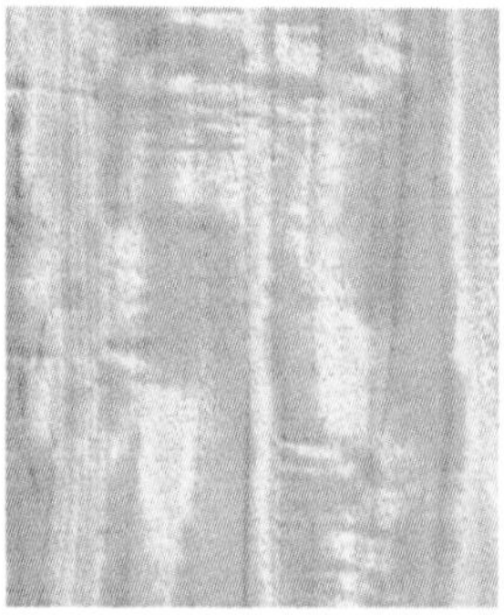

Primavera Mottled

Purpleheart Light

Ramin qc

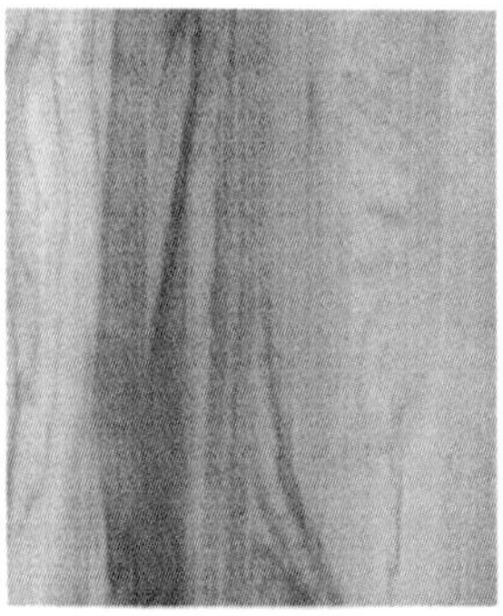

Red Gum Figured

Ribbonwood qc

WOOD AND MARBLE SAMPLES
Wood Veneers

Rosewood Brazilian

Rosewood Brazilian

Rosewood Indian fc

Rosewood Indian Pommele

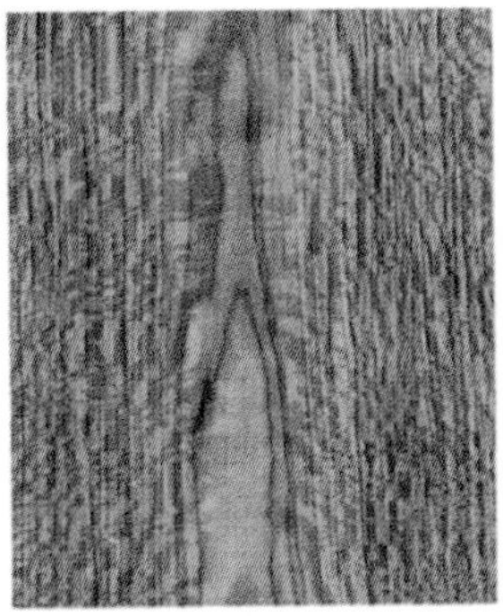
Rosewood Santos Beeswing

Rosewood Siam fc

Santa Rosa

Sapele Crown

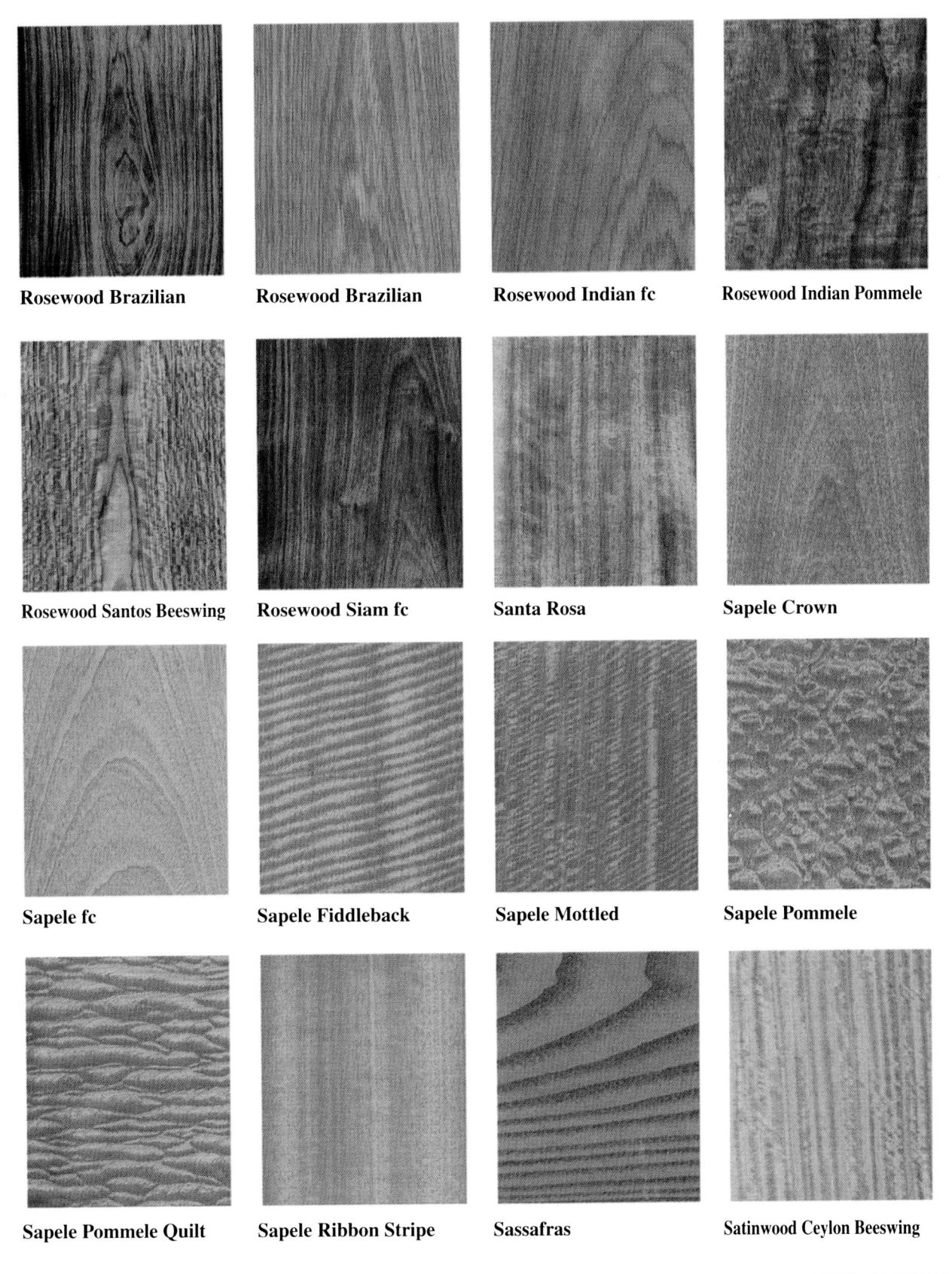

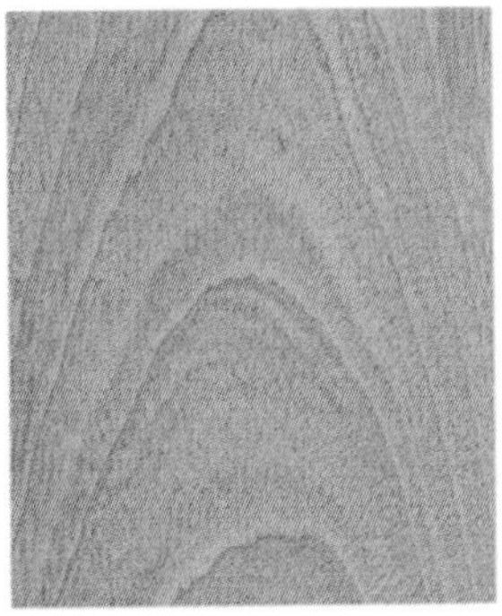
Sapele fc

Sapele Fiddleback

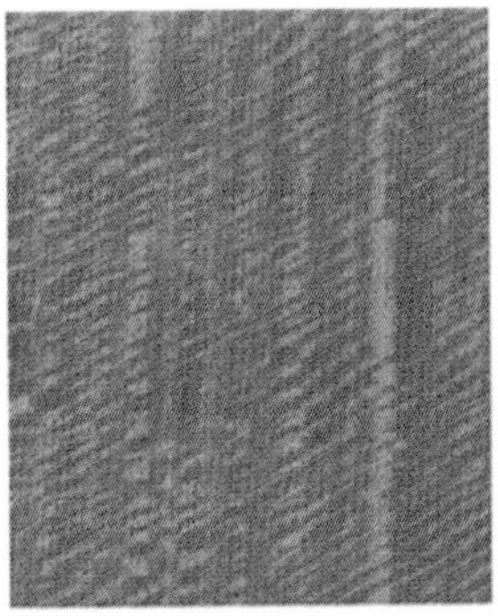
Sapele Mottled

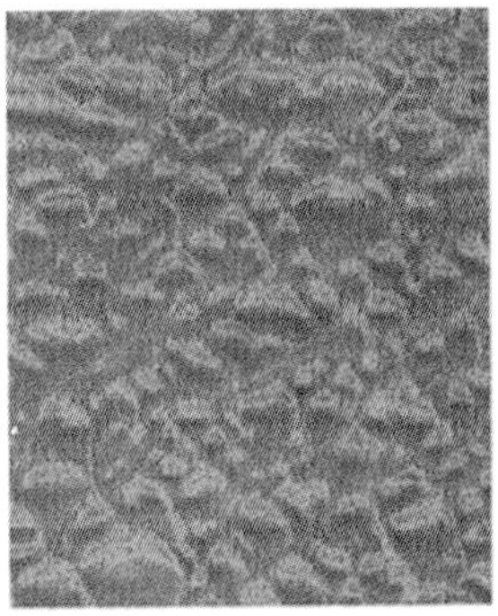
Sapele Pommele

Sapele Pommele Quilt

Sapele Ribbon Stripe

Sassafras

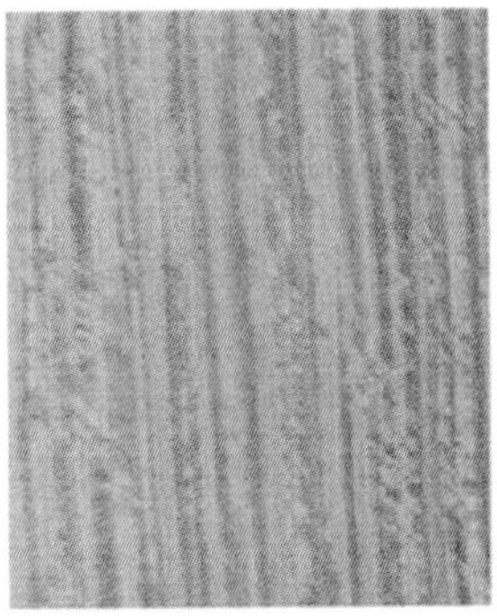
Satinwood Ceylon Beeswing

WOOD AND MARBLE SAMPLES

Wood Veneers

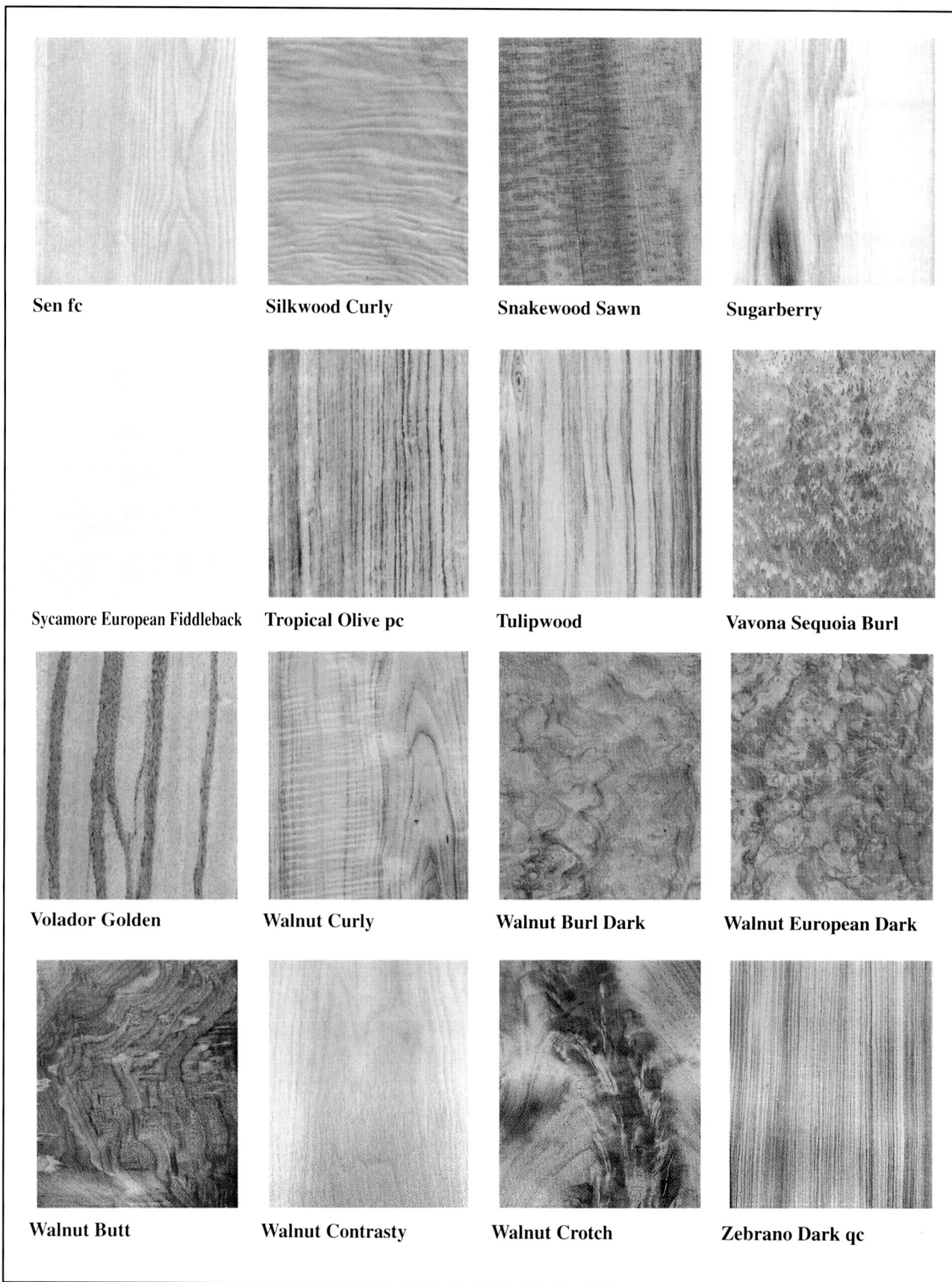

Sen fc

Silkwood Curly

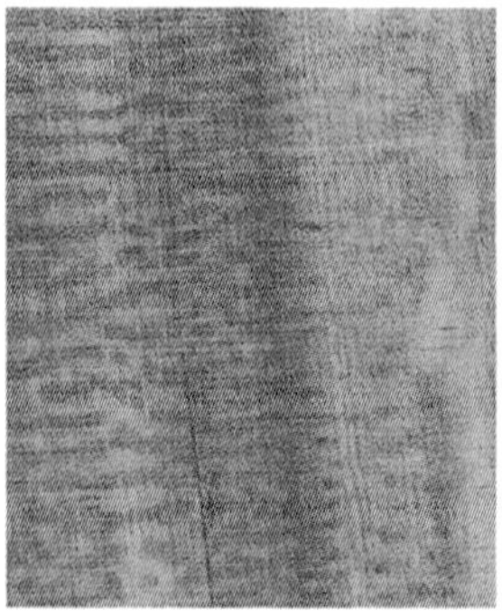

Snakewood Sawn

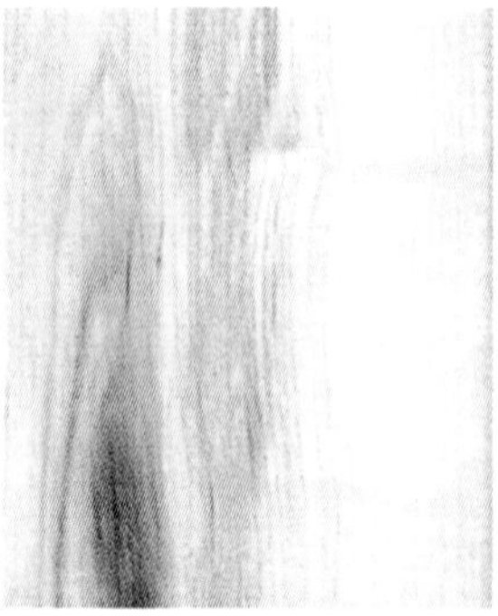

Sugarberry

Sycamore European Fiddleback

Tropical Olive pc

Tulipwood

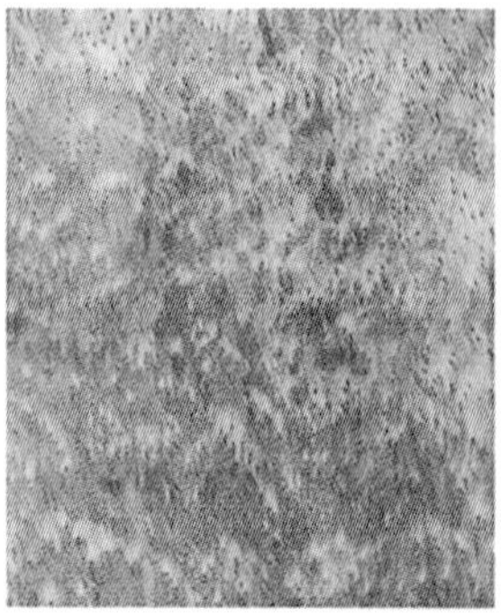

Vavona Sequoia Burl

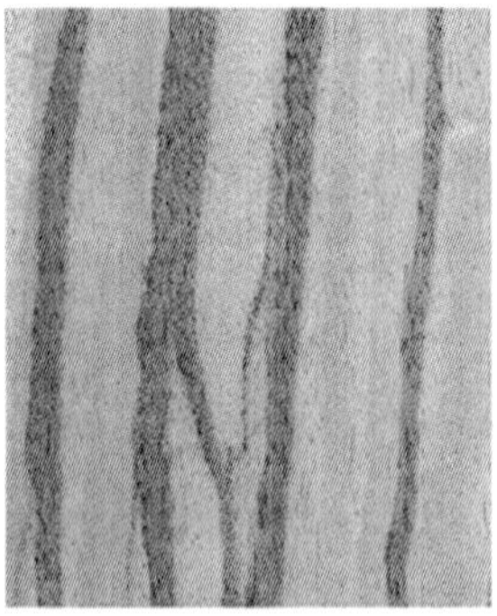

Volador Golden

Walnut Curly

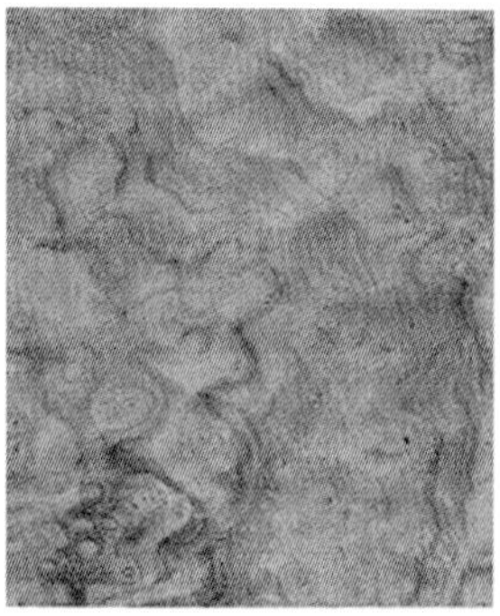

Walnut Burl Dark

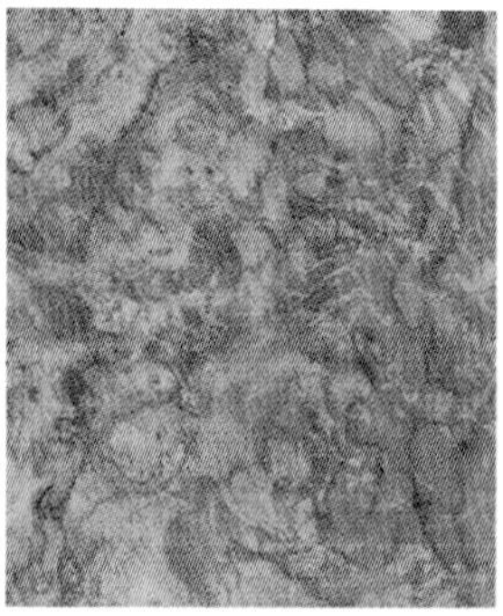

Walnut European Dark

Walnut Butt

Walnut Contrasty

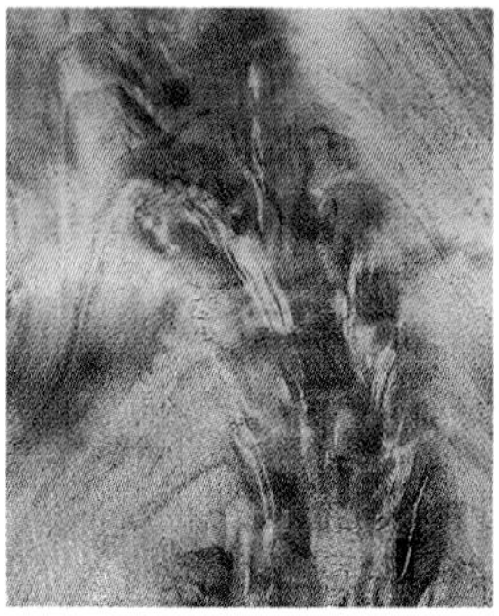

Walnut Crotch

Zebrano Dark qc

Allegerino Limestone

Ash Crystallina Thassos

Ash Crystallina Chalkero

Ash White of Paros

Astoria Black

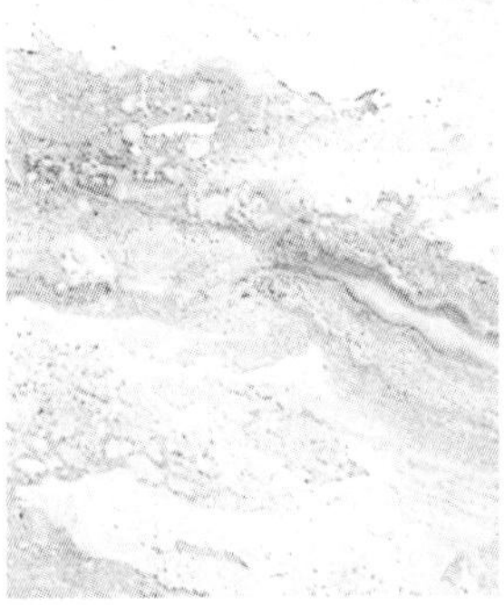

Beige Banded Karnezeika

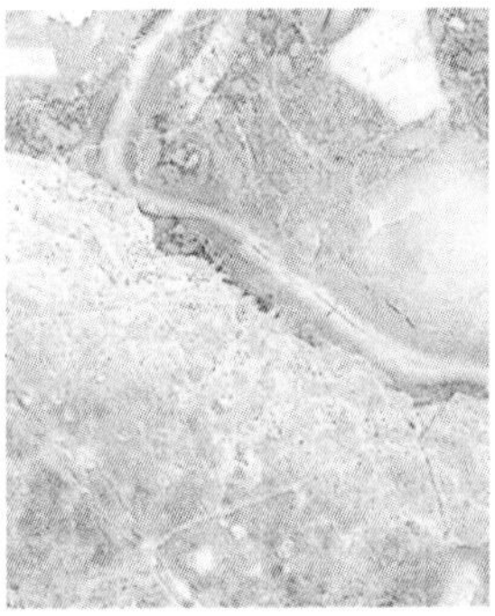

Beige Breccia Karnezeika

Beige Breccia Mycenae

Beige of Ioannina

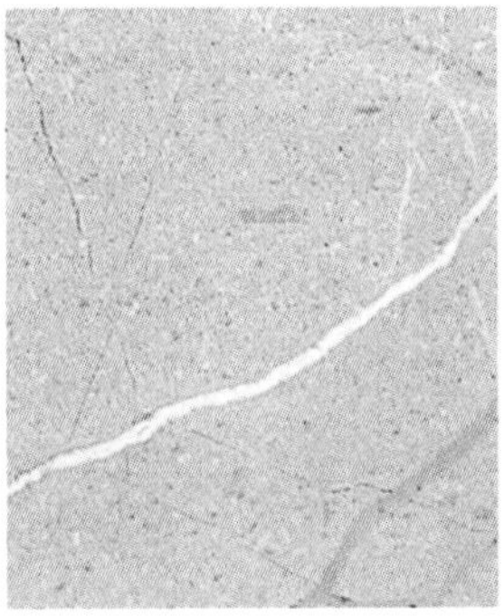

Beige of Ligurio

Bianco Egeo

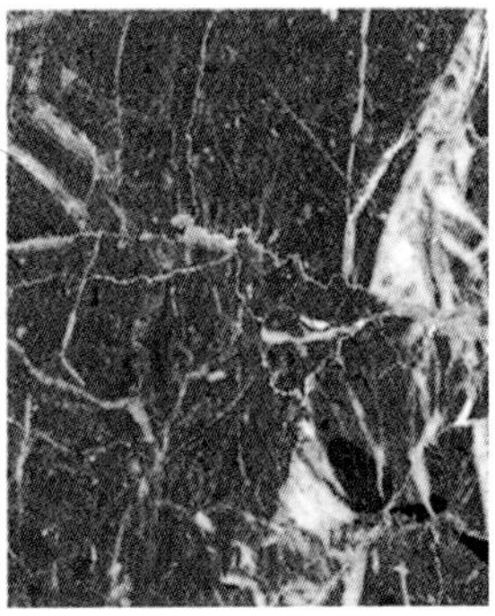

Black of Cresta

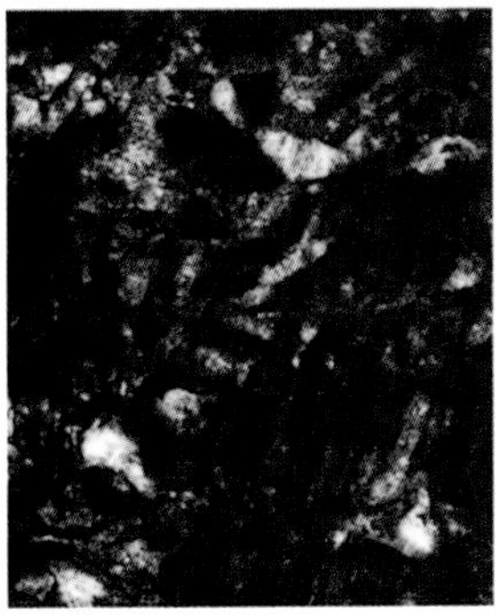

Black of Levadia

Black of Vytina

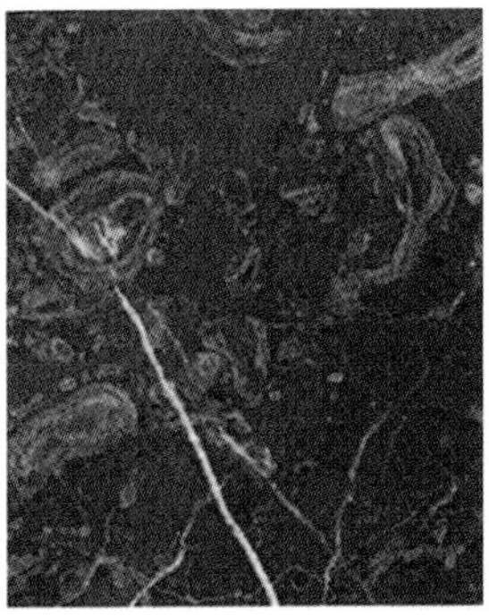

Brown of Chios

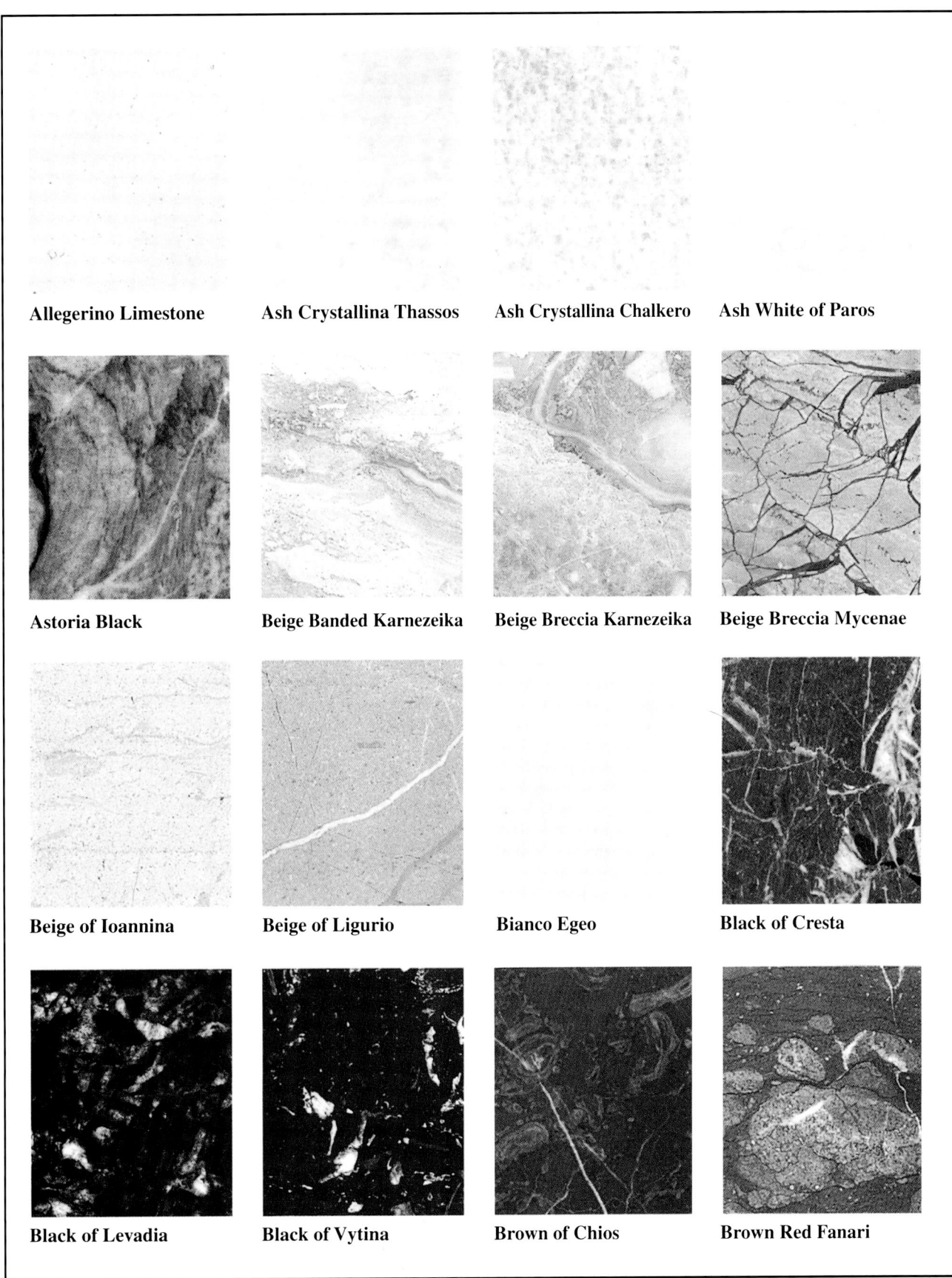

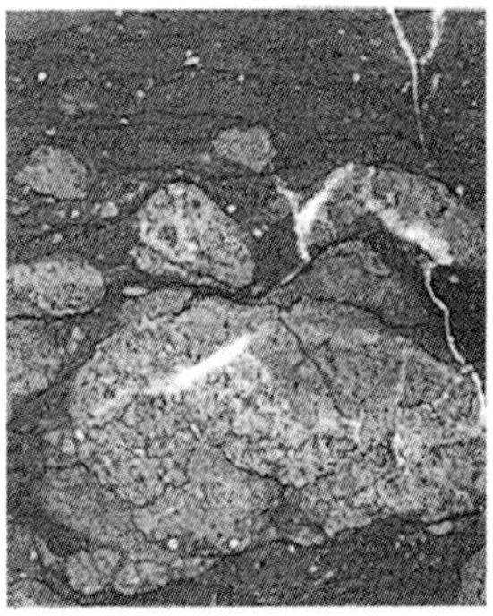

Brown Red Fanari

WOOD AND MARBLE SAMPLES

Marble

Cippolino Verde

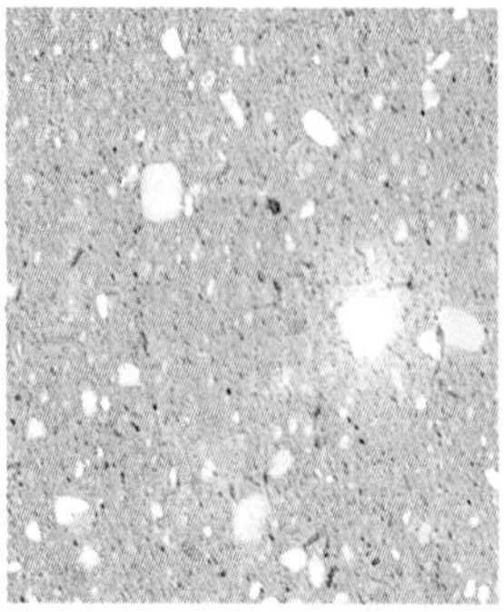
Coral Stellar Pink

Crema

Cremato Egeo

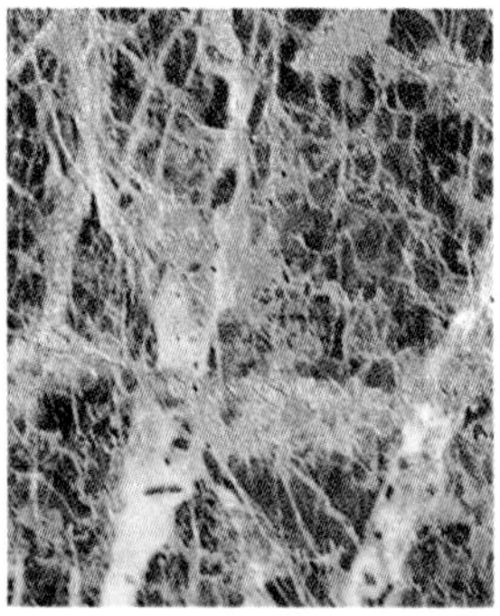
Fiore DeGreco Carnico

French Vanilla

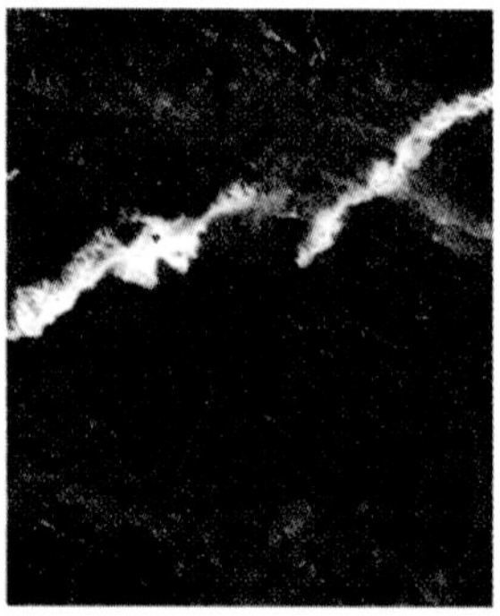
Green of Imathia

Green of Styra

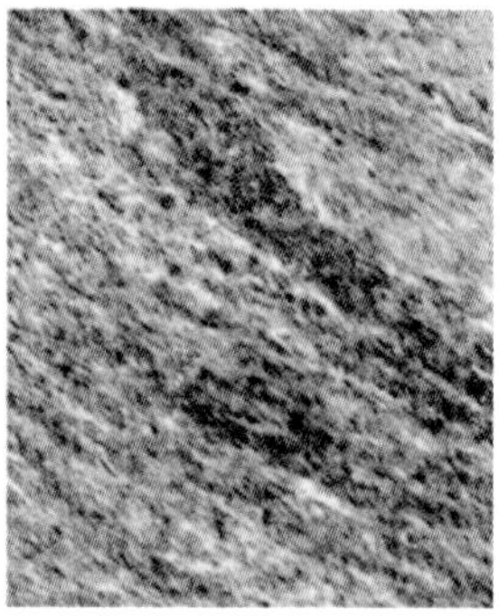
Grey of Aliveri

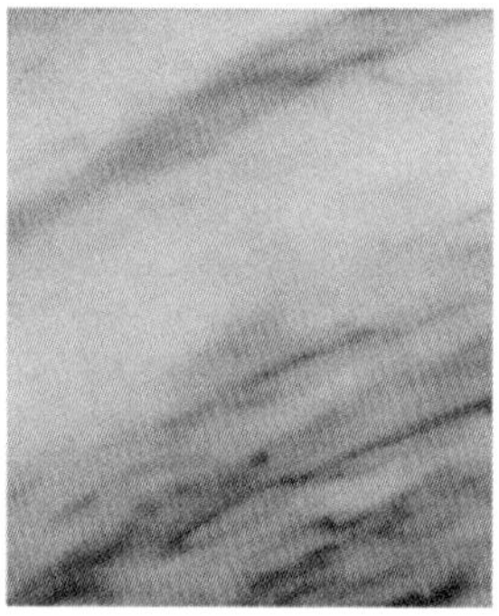
Grey of Tranovaltos

Grey White Achlades

Kandia Red

Lais Blue

Lais Pink

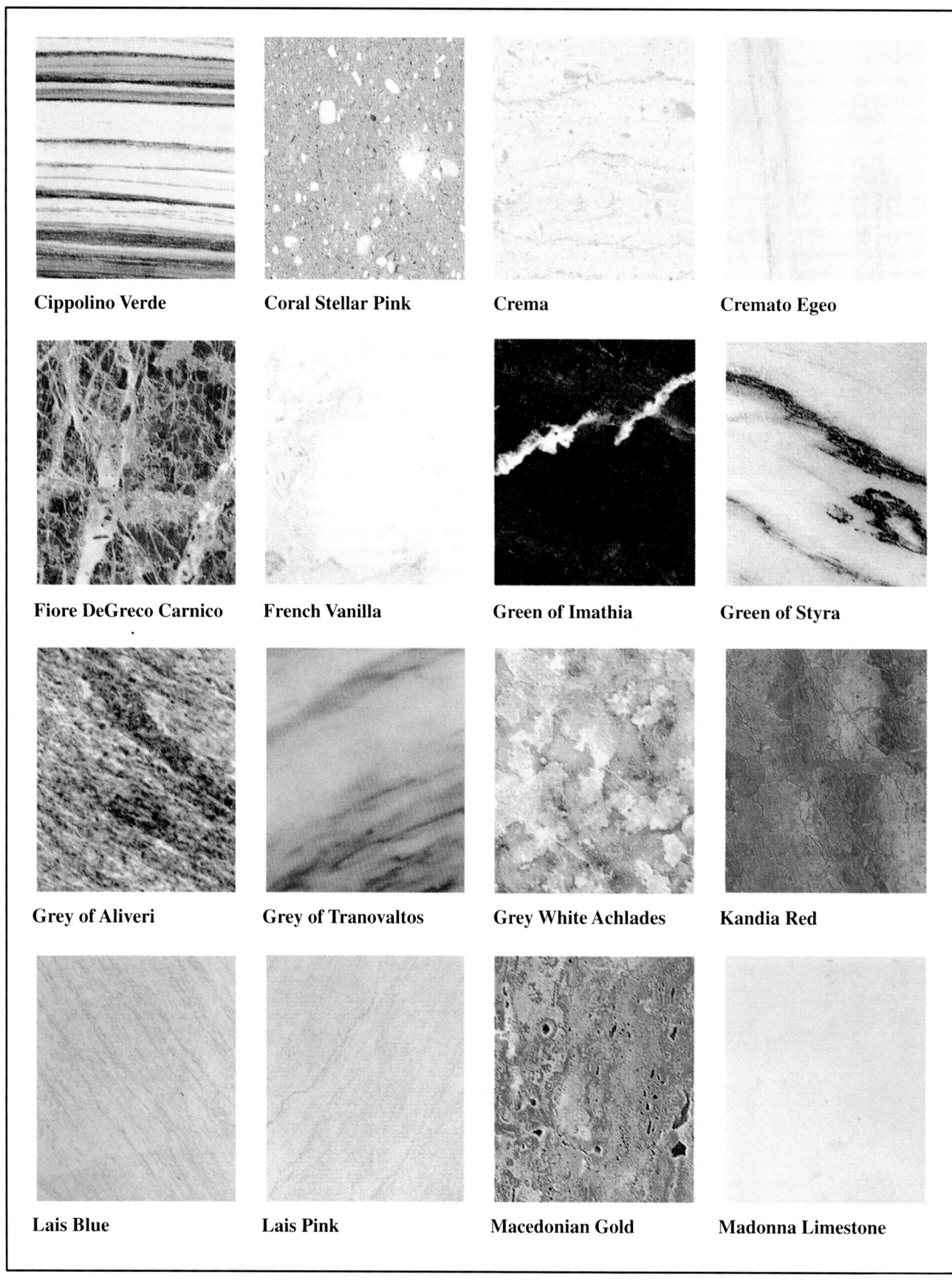

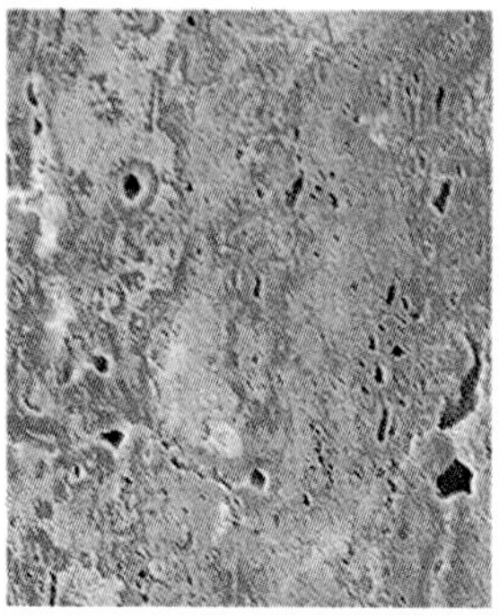
Macedonian Gold

Madonna Limestone

LEGENDS, ABBREVIATIONS, AND NOTES
Communications and Signals

◀W	WALL MOUNTED TELEPHONE OUTLET
◀PC.	WALL MOUNTED, TELEPHONE OUTLET TYPE FOR CRT
◀FAX	WALL MOUNTED, FAX TYPE OUTLET
◀FR	TELEPHONE OUTLET IN FURNITURE
◀FL	TELEPHONE OUTLET FLOOR MOUNTED
T-PNL	TELEPHONE PANEL
PC	COMMUNICATION OUTLET IN FURNITURE
	EXIT LIGHT
	EMERGENCY LIGHT WALL MOUNTED
	EMERGENCY LIGHT CEILING MOUNTED
S	SMOKE DETECTOR
F	FIRE DETECTOR
	PUSH BUTTON
	BUZZER
	BELL
D	ELECTRIC DOOR OPENER
BT	BELL RINGING TRANSFORMER

PV	PULL STATION
R154	ALARM LINE
M	MAGNETIC DOOR
C	CAMERA
	MOTION DETECTOR ALARM
LE	LOCAL ENUNCIATOR
K	A/C KEY PAD
AAC	ALARM A/C CONTROL
AP	ALARM PANEL
	CCTV EQUIPMENT MONITORS UCRS SWITCHES
SP	CEILING SPEAKERS
	LINEAR DIFFUSERS
	RETURN AIR LINEAR DIFFUSERS
T	THERMOSTAT

LEGENDS, ABBREVIATIONS, AND NOTES
Abbreviations

A	Astragal
ADJ	Adjustable
AFF	Above finish floor
AHU	Air handling unit
ALUM	Aluminum
ARCH	Architect
B	Base
BLDG	Building
BLKG	Blocking
BO	By others
BRD	Board
BRK	Brick
BSMT	Basement
C	Carpet, cornice
CH	Ceiling height
CL	Center line, closet
CLG	Ceiling
CLO	Closet
COL	Column
CONC	Concrete
CONT	Continuous
CP	Ceiling paint
CT	Ceramic tile
D	Door, dryer
DBL	Double
DH	Double hung
DIAG	Diagonal
DIAM	Diameter
DIM	Dimension
DISP	Disposal
DTL	Detail
DW	Dishwasher
DWG	Drawing
ELEC	Electrical
ELEV	Elevation
EQ	Equal
EQUIP	Equipment
EXIST	Existing
EXT	Exterior
FD	Floor drain
FF	Finished floor
FIN	Finish
FL	Floor
FOW	Face of wall
FT	Foot
GA	Gauge
GC	General contractor
GL	Glass/glazing
GYP BD	Gypsum board
HM	Hollow metal
HOR	Horizontal
HT	Height
HVAC	Heating, ventilation, air conditioning
ID	Inside diameter
INS	Insulate (D)
INT	Interior
KIT	Kitchen
LAM	Laminate
LAV	Lavatory
LIN	Linen
LR	Living room
M	Mirror
MAX	Maximum
MB	Marble
MDO	Medium density overlay
MECH	Mechanical
MIN	Minimum
MLDG	Molding
NIC	Not in contract
NS	No sill
NTS	Not to scale
OC	On center
OD	Outside diameter
OH	Opposite hand
OPG	Opening
OPP	Opposite
P	Paint, panel molding
PL	Plastic laminate
PLYWD	Plywood
PT	Point
PTD	Painted
PVC	Polyvinyl chloride
QT	Quarry tile
R	Riser, chair rail, wainscot cap, counter edge
R&S	Rod and shelf
RE	Refer to
REF	Reference, refrigerator
RO	Rough opening
REQ	Required
REV	Revision
RM	Room
SC	Solid core, skim coat
SECT	Section
SH	Shelves
SIM	Similar
SPEC	Specification
SQ	Square
SS	Stainless steel
ST	Stone
STL	Steel
T	Tread, door opening, or window trim
TEMP	Tempered
TYP	Typical
UON	Unless otherwise noted
VIF	Verify in field
VT	Vinyl tile
W	Washer
W/	With
WC	Water closet, wall covering
WD	Wood
WF	Wood flooring
W/O	Without
WP	Waterproof

1. The general conditions of the contract for construction (AIA document A201 latest edition) will apply to this contract.
2. Drawings shall not be scaled for dimensional information.
3. The contractor and all subcontractors shall verify all conditions and dimensions in the field and notify the designer of any discrepancies before proceeding with any work. No changes shall be made to any plan without prior comment of the designer.
4. All work shall be done in a first-class workmanlike manner by mechanics skilled in their respective trades.
5. The contractor shall review plans and the area of construction carefully to ensure full understanding of exact scope of work. The designer will be available to review all work on site and resolve any unclear items.
6. The architect shall comply with all rules and regulations of the building owner, and all city, state, and federal regulatory agencies having jurisdiction over the work.
7. The architect shall be responsible for filing all plans with the building department, paying initial fee, and obtaining building notice for this work. Contractor shall obtain building permit, process and complete all controlled inspection reports, and secure final sign-offs.
8. The contractor shall contact the building management to be advised of the rules of the building with respect to construction, when and how deliveries and/or removals can be done on regular or overtime, and, in general, any building requirements which will affect their work.
9. The contractor shall submit to the designer all fabrication shop drawings and fixture cuts for review.
10. The contractor shall furnish a system of temporary lights and water throughout the space under construction, if required.
11. The contractor shall remove from the building all rubbish and waste materials for his/her or subcontractors' work.
12. No work depending on partition locations shall be done until the contractor has marked partition locations on the floor plan in field and the designer has reviewed them.
13. All materials and installations shall be in accordance with manufacturers' latest printed specifications and with code requirements.
14. The contractor's price is to be complete in all ways including taxes, overtime, shipping, etc.
15. Ceiling light fixture layout is the determinant reference for all other ceiling-located items (except where required; access panels are coordinated with the designer by architects and engineers).
    - concealed sprinkler heads and covers
    - emergency light fixtures
    - exit light fixtures
    - smoke detectors
    - linear diffusers
    - speaker system (if necessary to be ceiling located)
16. General contractor and millworker are to submit samples and cuts of all exposed materials and finishes, hardware, devices, linear diffusers and return grills, concealed sprinkler covers, and light fixtures for review by designer.
17. Submit detailed shop drawings of all:
    - millwork, cabinetry, wood panels, trim, doors, etc.
    - custom hardware (architectural metal)
    - location of HVAC grills, etc. in relation to all ceiling lights
18. As noted on the drawings, no substitutions will be allowed for any item(s) specified unless reviewed by designer.
19. Electrical engineer is to specifically coordinate all cable, telephone, and cash register requirements per client's standards.
20. All ceiling height dimensions called out on the drawings (A.F.F.) indicate the dimension from the ceiling to the surface of the finished floor.
21. Contractor shall check and verify all conditions and dimensions and report any discrepancies to designer prior to start of work.
    All dimensions are to finished surface except where otherwise noted. "EQ" indicates equal dimension per each overall dimension.
    All partitions to be wedged tightly to ceiling unless otherwise noted.
    N.I.C. indicates "not in contract." B.O. indicates item furnished "by others."
22. All drawings and construction notes are complementary and what is called for by one will be as binding as if called for by all.
23. Prior to the start of work, the architect consultant and engineer consultant shall be responsible for building department permit and all other fees and permits necessary for the execution of work.
24. All new gypsum board is to be taped with three coats of spackle, flat tape at ceiling, "cover bead" and "L" beads as specified.
25. All dimensions for door or trimmed openings are given between minimum wood surfaces; consult interior elevations and details for frames and trim.
26. The contractor shall obtain full knowledge by personal and careful examination of all existing conditions at the site and of all requirements of the specifications and drawings. The contractor hereby accepts all such conditions and requirements and hereby assumes all responsibility and costs resulting from his/her failure to obtain knowledge of any of them.
27. The contractor shall guarantee all work for a period of one year after date of acceptance of the contract that he/she will make good any and all work which in any way becomes defective as to the quality of the materials and workmanship for any cause other than ordinary wear and tear.
28. The contractor shall indemnify the owner and his/her agents for and against all suits, claims, or liability on account of personal injuries or acts of the contractor in the performance of the work covered by the contract.
29. The contractor shall coordinate all the work of the various trades whether included in this contract or not. The contractor shall make openings as required by other trades and close same. The contractor shall schedule the work of the various trades so as not to impede the progress of the work.
30. Removals of debris shall be made as often as necessary to maintain said premises in a safe, clean, and accessible condition.
31. Where the term "or equal" is used in specifications, it shall be understood that the reference is made to the ruling and judgment of the designer and shall be submitted to the designer for review. Actual samples of the substitutions shall be submitted to the designer for review.
32. The contractor shall submit cuts for all fixtures and equipment called for and actual samples.
33. The contractor shall submit shop drawings and fixture cuts for all fabrication work to designer for review. All shop drawings and cuts signed "reviewed" are for design appearances only. The contractor shall assume responsibility for all errors on their drawings.
34. The contractor shall furnish a field progress schedule to the designer for all phases of erection.
35. The contractor shall provide and maintain all temporary protection of adjacent work, equipment, and occupied areas and same shall be subject to the owner's approval.
36. All existing walls and ceilings to remain shall be plaster patched and prepared for painting.

LEGENDS, ABBREVIATIONS, AND NOTES
Construction and Finish Notes (Sample)

1. All dimensions are to finished surfaces unless otherwise noted.
2. Contractor to check that there is sufficient clearance between doors, openings, walls, etc. for all trims, moldings, and equipment before building interior partitions or locating doors and openings. If there is a problem, notify designer.
3. All millwork items to be supplied and supervised daily by millwork contractor, or supplied daily, but supervised and installed as per agreement with general contractor. Antiques and furniture are supplied and installed by others.
4. The general contractor shall, upon completion, remove all paint from where it was spilled, splashed, or splattered on surfaces, including light fixtures, diffusers and registers, glass, etc. The general contractor shall remove all electrical switch plates and outlet plates, surface hardware, etc. before painting, protecting, and replacing same when painting has been completed.
5. The general contractor shall install wall coverings where designated. All wall coverings shall be smooth with no wrinkles, bubbles, or loose edges. All paste and brush marks shall be thoroughly removed. Wall coverings adjoining wood trim shall be cut straight and square. All workmanship which is not judged to be first quality will not be accepted.
6. All flooring workmanship shall be of the best quality and when the work is complete, seams shall be kept in accurate alignment.
7. All wood to be treated prior to construction for flame retardant. And all new ceilings are required to be incombustible. Comply with UBC table 6-A.

   Department of building and safety: Section "additional corrections"—#2. Supplemental fire/life safety plan correction sheet: Section "construction and general" #2.
8. Whenever the building is occupied, exit signs shall be lighted so that they are clearly visible.

   Department of building and safety: Section "exits"—#18. Supplemental fire/life safety plan correction sheet: Section "exits" #25.

MASONRY

CONCRETE BLOCK COURSING, TYPES, AND SIZES

Concrete Block Types and Sizes

NOMINAL DIMENSIONS W × L × H (ACTUAL DIMENSIONS ARE 3/8" LESS)

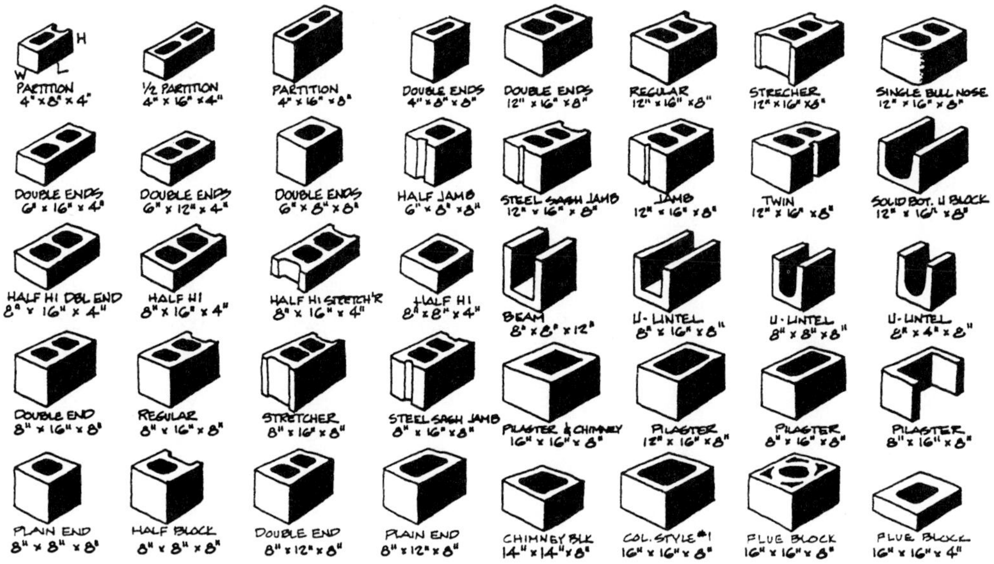

Concrete block coursing

CSC	4″ high blk	8″ high blk.	CSC	4″ high blk.	8″ high blk.	CSC	4″ high blk	8″ high blk.	CSC	4″ high blk.	8″ high blk.
1	4″	8″	38	12′8″	25′4″	20	6′8″	13′4″	57	19′0″	38′0″
2	8″	1′4″	39	13′0″	26′0″	21	7′0″	14′0″	58	19′4″	38′8″
3	1′0″	2′0″	40	13′4″	26′8″	22	7′4″	14′8″	59	19′8″	39′4″
4	1′4″	2′8″	41	13′8″	27′4″	23	7′8″	15′4″	60	20′0″	40′0″
5	1′8″	3′4″	42	14′0″	28′0″	24	8′0″	16′0″	61	20′4″	40′8″
6	2′0″	4′0″	43	14′4″	28′8″	25	8′4″	16′8″	62	20′8″	41′4″
7	2′4″	4′8″	44	14′8″	29′4″	26	8′8″	17′4″	63	21′0″	42′0″
8	2′8″	5′4″	45	15′0″	30′0″	27	9′0″	18′0″	64	21′4″	42′8″
9	3′0″	6′0″	46	15′4″	30′8″	28	9′4″	18′8″	65	21′8″	43′4″
10	3′4″	6′8″	47	15′8″	31′4″	29	9′8″	19′4″	66	22′0″	44′0″
11	3′8″	7′4″	48	16′0″	32′0″	30	10′0″	20′0″	67	22′4″	44′8″
12	4′0″	8′0″	49	16′4″	32′8″	31	10′4″	20′8″	68	22′8″	45′4″
13	4′4″	8′8″	50	16′8″	33′4″	32	10′8″	21′4″	69	23′0″	46′0″
14	4′8″	9′4″	51	17′0″	34′0″	33	11′0″	22′0″	70	23′4″	46′8″
15	5′0″	10′0″	52	17′4″	34′8″	34	11′4″	22′8″	71	23′8″	47′4″
16	5′4″	10′8″	53	17′8″	35′4″	35	11′8″	23′4″	72	24′0″	48′0″
17	5′8″	11′4″	54	18′0″	36′0″	36	12′0″	24′0″	73	24′4″	48′8″
18	6′0″	12′0″	55	18′4″	36′8″	37	12′4″	24′8″	74	24′8″	49′4″
19	6′4″	12′8″	56	18′8″	37′4″						

MASONRY
Brick Coursing

	Nonmodular						*Modular*				
	2 1/4″-thick bricks		*2 5/8″-thick bricks*		*2 3/4″-thick bricks*		*Nominal thickness (height) of brick*				
Course	*3/8″ joint*	*1/2″ joints*	*3/8″ joint*	*1/2″ joint*	*3/8″ joint*	*1/2″ joint*	*2″*	*2 2/3″*	*3 1/5″*	*4″*	*5 1/3″*
1	2 5/8″	2 3/4″	3″	3 1/8″	3 1/8″	3 1/4″	2″	2 11/16″	3 3/16″	4″	5 5/16″
2	5 1/4″	5 1/2″	6″	6 1/4″	6 1/4″	6 1/2″	4″	5 5/16″	6 3/8″	8″	10 11/16″
3	7 7/8″	8 1/4″	9″	9 3/8″	9 3/8″	9 3/4″	6″	8″	9 5/8″	1′0″	1′4″
4	10 1/2″	11″	1′0″	1′0 1/2″	1′0 1/2″	1′1″	8″	10 11/16″	1′0 13/16″	1′4″	1′9 5/16″
5	1′1 1/8″	1′1 3/4″	1′3″	1′3 5/8″	1′3 5/8″	1′4 1/4″	10″	1′1 5/16″	1′4″	1′8″	2′2 11/16″
6	1′3 3/4″	1′4 1/2″	1′6″	1′6 3/4″	1′6 3/4″	1′7 1/2″	1′0″	1′4″	1′7 3/16″	2′0″	2′8″
7	1′6 3/8″	1′7 1/4″	1′9″	1′9 7/8″	1′9 7/8″	1′10 3/4″	1′2″	1′6 11/16″	1′10 3/8″	2′4″	3′1 5/16″
8	1′9″	1′10″	2′0″	2′1″	2′1″	2′2″	1′4″	1′9 5/16″	2′1 5/8″	2′8″	3′6 11/16″
9	1′11 5/8″	2′0 3/4″	2′3″	2′4 1/8″	2′4 1/8″	2′5 1/4″	1′6″	2′0″	2′4 13/16″	3′0″	4′0″
10	2′2 1/4″	2′3 1/2″	2′6″	2′7 1/4″	2′7 1/4″	2′8 1/2″	1′8″	2′2 11/16″	2′8″	3′4″	4′5 5/16″
11	2′4 7/8″	2′6 1/4″	2′9″	2′10 3/8″	2′10 3/8″	2′11 3/4″	1′10″	2′5 5/16″	2′11 3/16″	3′8″	4′10 11/16″
12	2′7 1/2″	2′9″	3′0″	3′1 1/2″	3′1 1/2″	3′3″	2′0″	2′8″	3′2 3/8″	4′0″	5′4″
13	2′10 1/8″	2′11 3/4″	3′3″	3′4 5/8″	3′4 5/8″	3′6 1/4″	2′2″	2′10 11/16″	3′5 5/8″	4′4″	5′9 5/16″
14	3′0 3/4″	3′2 1/2″	3′6″	3′7 3/4″	3′7 3/4″	3′9 1/2″	2′4″	3′1 5/16″	3′8 13/16″	4′8″	6′2 11/16″
15	3′3 3/8″	3′5 1/4″	3′9″	3′10 7/8″	3′10 7/8″	4′0 3/4″	2′6″	3′4″	4′0″	5′0″	6′8″
16	3′6″	3′8″	4′0″	4′2″	4′2″	4′4″	2′8″	3′6 11/16″	4′4 3/16″	5′4″	7′1 5/16″
17	3′8 5/8″	3′10 3/4″	4′3″	4′5 1/8″	4′5 1/8″	4′7 1/4″	2′10″	3′9 5/16″	4′6 3/8″	5′8″	7′6 11/16″
18	3′11 1/4″	4′1 1/2″	4′6″	4′8 1/4″	4′8 1/4″	4′10 1/2″	3′0″	4′0″	4′9 5/8″	6′0″	8′0″
19	4′1 7/8″	4′4 1/4″	4′9″	4′11 3/8″	4′11 3/8″	5′1 3/4″	3′2″	4′2 11/16″	5′0 13/16″	6′4″	8′5 5/16″
20	4′4 1/2″	4′7″	5′0″	5′2 1/2″	5′2 1/2″	5′5″	3′4″	4′5 5/16″	5′4″	6′8″	8′10 11/16″
21	4′7 1/8″	4′9 3/4″	5′3″	5′5 5/8″	5′5 5/8″	5′8 1/4″	3′6″	4′8″	5′7 3/16″	7′0″	9′4″
22	4′9 3/4″	5′0 1/2″	5′6″	5′8 3/4″	5′8 3/4″	5′11 1/2″	3′8″	4′10 11/16″	5′10 3/8″	7′4″	9′9 5/16″
23	5′0 3/8″	5′3 1/4″	5′9″	5′11 7/8″	5′11 7/8″	6′2 3/4″	3′10″	5′1 5/16″	6′1 5/8″	7′8″	10′2 11/16″
24	5′3″	5′6″	6′0″	6′3″	6′3″	6′6″	4′0″	5′4″	6′4 13/16″	8′0″	10′8″

Index

Credits

1. PLANNING AND DESIGN OF INTERIOR SPACES

Residential Spaces

Pages 5–28: Richardson Wright (ed.), *House and Garden's Complete Guide to Interior Decoration,* Simon and Schuster, New York, 1942 (copyright renewed 1970 by The Condé Nasts Publications Inc.).

Pages 29–42: Franklin H. Gottshall, *How to Design and Construct Period Furniture,* Bonanza Books, New York, 1989.

Page 43: *The House and Home Book of Interior Design,* McGraw-Hill, New York, 1976.

Page 47: *New Spaces for Learning, Educational Facilities Lab,* New York, 1966.

Pages 54-58: Charles George Ramsey and Harold Reeve Sleeper, *Architectural Graphic Standards,* 2d Edition, Wiley, New York, 1936.

Pages 60, 61, 80, 81, 204, 205, 208: *Architectural Forum,* October 1937.

Pages 62–65, 68, 69, 96, 113–119, 168: Thompson, Robinson, Toraby.

Page 66: Verna Cook Salomonsky, Architect.

Page 67: Ulrich Franzen, Architect; *Selected Architectural Details,* Reinhold, New York.

Pages 70–73: Parrish Hadley Associates.

Pages 74–76: Panero Zelnik Associates, Architects and Interior Designers.

Pages 79, 98, 99, 159: *House Planning Handbook,* 2d Edition, MWPS-16, Midwest Plan Service, Ames Iowa, 1988 (reproduced with permission).

Page 80: U.S. Department of Housing and Urban Development, Washington, D.C.

Pages 82, 83: Lehigh Furniture Company.

Pages 84, 85, 120–122, 126, 172, 173, 207, 227–229: Naomi Leff & Associates.

Pages 87–89, 160, 161: *Manual of Acceptable Practices,* U.S. Department of Housing and Urban Development, Washington, D.C.

Pages 88, 210, 211: *Internal Spaces of the Dwelling,* Canada Mortgage and Housing Corporation, 1984.

Pages 89, 90, 123–125, 134, 169, 170: Bromley/Jacobsen.

Page 91: Philip G. Knobloch, *Good Practice in Construction,* Pencil Points Press, New York, 1931.

Page 92: *Comparative Architectural Details*, Pencil Points Series (Francis Y. Joannes, Architect), 1935.

Page 94: Gensler Associates; ISD; Bromley/Jacobson.

Pages 95, 96, 155–157, 216, 217: Julius Panero and Martin Zelnik, *Human Dimension & Interior Space,* Whitney Library of Design/Watson-Guptill Publications, New York, 1979.

Pages 97, 98, 212, 213: *Time-Saver Standards: A Manual of Essential Architectural Data,* F. W. Dodge Corporation, New York, 1946.

Pages 101–103: Kohler.

Pages 104, 105, 109, 174 (bottom): Eljer.

Pages 106–108, 110, 111 (top): American Standard.

Pages 112, 200: Caleb Hornbostel, *Architectural Detailing Simplified,* Prentice-Hall, Englewood Cliffs, N.J., 1986.

Pages 127, 162: *A Design Guide for Home Safety,* U.S. Department of Housing and Urban Development, Washington, D.C., 1972.
Page 128: Space Design Group.
Pages 129, 130: Marble Institute of America.
Pages 132, 133, 136: *Handbook for Ceramic Tile Installation,* Tile Council of America, Princeton, N.J. 1987.
Pages 137–140, 187–192: *Adaptable Housing,* Office of Policy Development and Research, U.S. Department of Housing and Urban Development, 1987.
Pages 141, 142, 185, 186: New York City Building Code.
Pages 143, 146, 153, 184: *Uniform Federal Accessibility Standards,* 1985-494-187, U.S. Government Printing Office, Washington, D.C., 1985.
Pages 144, 193: *Handbook for Design*, Veterans Administration, Washington, D.C.
Pages 145, 154, 171, 180, 181, 194, 195, 197, 198: Jerry Caldari, Architect.
Pages 147–152: *Barrier-Free Residential Design*, McGraw-Hill, New York.
Pages 157, 158: Joseph De Chiara and John Hancock Callender (eds.*), Time-Saver Standards for Building Types,* 2d Edition, McGraw-Hill, New York, 1980.
Pages 157, 163–167, 176, 177: Merillat.
Page 161: Formica Corporation.
Page 165: Triangle Pacific Corporation.
Page 175, 179: Euroflair by Frigidaire.
Page 178: *Manual of Millwork,* Woodworking Institute of California.
Pages 182, 183: *Universal Kitchen and Bathroom Planning,* McGraw-Hill, New York.
Page 190: *Adaptable Housing,* Office of Policy Development & Research, U.S. Department of Housing and Urban Development.
Page 199: *Pencil Points,* April 1934.
Pages 201, 202: Panero Zelnik Associates.
Page 203: Putnam Rolling Ladder Company.
Pages 204, 209, 210, 214, 215: Joseph De Chiara, Julius Panero, and Martin Zelnik, *Time-Saver Standards for Residential Development,* McGraw-Hill, New York, 1984.
Page 206: *Design Solutions,* Architectural Woodworking Institute, Winter 1998.
Page 207: Naomi Leff & Associates.
Page 208 (top): *Architectural Forum,* October 1937.
Page 208 (bottom): *Design Solutions,* Architectural Woodworking Institute, Summer 1989.
Page 217, 218: *Council Notes,* University of Illinois.
Page 218: *Architectural Forum,* October 1938.
Page 219 (left): General Services Administration.
Page 219 (right): Illinois Agricultural Experiment Station.
Pages 220, 225, 226: *Pencil Points,* 1935.
Page 221: Bertram Bassuk, FAIA.
Page 221–223: ISD.
Page 224: Charles D. Flayhan Associates.
Page 230: Schulte.
Pages 231–234: Closet Maid Systems.

Office Spaces

Pages 238, 251, 252, 260, 268, 288: Julius Panero and Martin Zelnik, *Human Dimension & Interior Space,* Whitney Library of Design/Watson-Guptill Publications, New York, 1979.
Pages 239, 240, 262–264: William L. Pulgram and Richard E. Stonis, *Designing the Automated Office,* Whitney Library of Design/Watson-Guptill Publications, New York, 1984.
Pages 241, 245–247: Dancker Sellen & Douglas.
Page 248: *Design Solutions,* Architectural Woodworking Institute, Spring 1992.
Pages 256, 257, 259, 276, 294, 295, 305: Gensler Associates.
Pages 256 (left), 317–329: Steelcase.
Page 256 (right): Panero Zelnik Associates.
Pages 258, 292, 311: ISD.
Page 261: Intergraph Corp., Interiors.
Pages 265–268: *Interiors*, November 1985.
Pages 269, 270: Lehigh Furniture Company.
Page 271: Howe Furniture Corp.
Pages 275, 298, 305: *Design Solutions,* Architectural Woodworking Institute, Spring 1986.
Pages 278–286: Bretford.
Pages 291, 296, 297, 308, 309, 331–334, 336, 338: Charles D. Flayhan Associates.
Page 293: Marble Institute of America.
Page 301: *Design Solutions,* Architectural Woodworking Institute, Winter 1992.
Page 302: *Design Solutions,* Architectural Woodworking Institute, Summer 1996.
Page 300, 303, 304: *Design Solutions,* Architectural Woodworking Institute, Fall 1992.
Pages 307, 310: Bertram Bassuk, FAIA.
Page 312: Joseph De Chiara and John Hancock Callender (eds.), *Time-Saver Standards for Building Types*, 2d Edition, McGraw-Hill, New York, 1980.
Page 313–315: Herman Miller.
Page 316: Vecta.
Page 337: *Design Solutions*, Architectural Woodworking Institute, Winter 1991.

Hospitality Spaces

Pages 341, 342: *Architectural Record,* 1943.
Pages 343, 344, 347–349: Panero Zelnik Associates.
Page 346: *Architectural Forum*; *Manual of Acceptable Practices,* U.S. Department of Housing and Urban Development, Washington, D.C.
Pages 350, 351, 368, 425, 427–430, 440: Thomas D. Davies, Jr., and Kim A. Beasley, *Design for Hospitality: Planning for Accessible Hotels and Motels,* Nichols Publishing, New York, 1988.
Pages 352, 353, 430, 435, 436, 450–452, 459: DiLeonardo International Inc.
Pages 354, 355, 357, 360, 363, 364, 366, 376–378, 399, 405, 408, 415, 416, 419–423: Tony Chi and Associates.
Pages 356, 361, 386–397: Julius Panero and Martin Zelnik, *Human Dimension & Interior Space*, Whitney Library of Design/Watson-Guptill Publications, New York, 1979.
Pages 358, 388: Panero Zelnik Associates.
Pages 359, 367, 370, 403, 404, 406, 407, 409: Jerry Caldari, Architect.
Pages 362, 369: Space Design Group.
Pages 365, 371, 372: *Interiors*, October 1985.
Pages 373–375: Gensler Associates.
Page 379: Charles D. Flayhan Associates.
Pages 397, 398, 402: *Interiors,* July 1985.
Page 400: *Selected Architectural Details,* Reinhold, New York.
Pages 401, 409, 410, 413, 446, 447, 449: *Design Solutions,* Architectural Woodworking Institute, Spring 1990.

Pages 411, 412, 443: Hochheiser-Elias Design Group.
Page 414: Bromley Caldari.
Page 417, 418: Naomi Leff & Associates.
Pages 424, 426: Joseph De Chiara and John Hancock Callender (eds.), *Time-Saver Standards for Building Types,* 3d Edition, McGraw-Hill, New York, 1990.
Pages 431–434, 437–439, 443–445, 453–458, 460: Brennan Beer Gorman Monk/Interiors.
Pages 462–464: Richard H. Penner, *Conference Center Planning and Design,* Whitney Library of Design.
Page 466: Centrebrook Architects & Planners, LLC.

Retail Spaces

Pages 469–471: Julius Panero and Martin Zelnik, *Human Dimension & Interior Space,* Whitney Library of Design/Watson-Guptill Publications, New York, 1979.
Pages 472, 496: *Selected Architectural Details,* Reinhold, New York.
Pages 473–477, 491–495, 505, 512–521, 523, 524, 536, 541–548, 558–561, 567, 571–583: Rosenblum Architects.
Pages 479, 480, 489, 498, 490, 501, 503, 504, 506, 507: Tony Chi & Associates.
Pages 481, 482: *Design Solutions,* Architectural Woodworking Institute, Winter 1987, Summer 1988.
Pages 484, 485, 487, 499, 500, 503, 504, 562–566: Passalacqua & Toto.
Pages 488, 525–528, 554, 555, 568–570: Naomi Leff & Associates.
Page 497: Marble Institute of America.
Pages 508–511, 529–534, 537: Walker Group/CNI.
Pages 538–540, 549–551: Panero Zelnik Associates.
Pages 552, 553, 556: PAM International Co., Inc.
Page 557: Reeve Store Equipment Co.

Health Care Spaces

Pages 587–615, 625–634: Norman Rosenfeld Architects LLC.
Pages 616–624: HKS, Inc.

Banking Spaces

Pages 637–666: Andrew Seifer and Associates.
Pages 667, 668: Passalacqua & Toto.

Public Rest Rooms, Toilets, and Coatrooms

Page 675: New York City Building Code.
Page 676: General Services Administration.
Page 677: Norman Rosenfeld Architects LLC.
Pages 678–681: General Services Administration.
Pages 682–688, 735: Bertram Bassuk, FAIA.
Page 689: DiLeonardo International Inc.
Pages 690–695: Joseph De Chiara, *Handbook of Architectural Details for Commercial Buildings*, McGraw-Hill, New York, 1980.
Pages 696, 697: Tony Chi and Associates.
Page 698: Brennan Beer Gorman Monk/Interiors.
Pages 700–703, 708–721: Bobrick.
Pages 703, 704: American Sanitary Partition Corporation.
Pages 705–707: *Access America,* Architectural and Transportation Barriers Compliance Board, Washington, D.C., 1980.
Pages 705–707: *Uniform Federal Accessibility Standards,* 1985-494-187, U.S. Government Printing Office, Washington, D.C., 1985.
Page 722: Rosenblum Architects.
Page 723: A & J Washroom Accessories.
Pages 724–728: Parker/Nutone.
Pages 728, 729: American Specialties, Inc.
Pages 730–733: Rallex.
Page 734: Jerry Caldari, Architect.

2. CONSTRUCTION DETAILS AND FINISHES

Pages 740, 801: Walter McQuade (ed.), *Schoolhouse*, Simon and Schuster, New York, 1958.
Pages 741, 802, 834, 980–985, 1076: *Time-Saver Standards: A Manual of Essential Architectural Data,* F. W. Dodge Corp., New York, 1946.
Pages 742, 744–746: New York State Building Code.
Pages 743, 747, 748, 851: William J. Hornung, *Reinhold Data Sheets,* Reinhold, New York, 1965.
Pages 749, 755, 764, 771, 774–776, 786, 797–799, 806–810, 816, 866, 867, 869–876, 895, 899, 909, 910, 920, 923, 936, 938–940, 962, 976, 979, 1028 (bottom), 1034, 1055, 1062, 1068, 1069: Bertram Bassuk, FAIA.
Pages 750–752 (bottom), 762, 763 (bottom), 971: ISD.
Pages 752 (top), 756, 769, 770, 813, 814, 821, 860, 972–974 (top): Gensler Associates.
Pages 754, 868, 990 (top): William Morgan, FAIA.
Pages 757, 761, 877, 879, 937, 966: Rosenblum Architects.
Pages 758–760, 765, 817–819, 880, 881, 905–907, 1047–1051, 1071, 1072: Naomi Leff & Associates.
Pages 763 (top), 965 (bottom): Charles D. Flayhan Associates.
Pages 766, 872, 901–904, 908, 926, 964, 975: Norman Rosenfeld Architects LLC.
Pages 768, 828, 835, 836, 934, 935, 942, 943: L. O. Anderson, *Wood-Frame House Construction,* Department of Agriculture Handbook No. 73, U.S. Government Printing Office, Washington, D.C., 1970.
Pages 772, 837: *Wood Frame Design,* Western Wood Products Association.
Pages 776, 778, 1128, 1129: Panero Zelnik Associates.
Pages 777, 782, 784, 922, 941, 986, 1040, 1041, 1089: Philip G. Knobloch, *Good Practice in Construction,* Pencil Points Press, New York, 1931.
Pages 779, 780, 848–851: *Handbook for Ceramic Tile Installation*, Tile Council of America, Princeton, N.J., 1988.
Pages 781, 841–847: American Olean Tile.
Pages 783, 804, 1063, 1085, 1086: Marble Institute of America.
Page 785: Buckingham Virginia Slate Co.
Pages 787, 789–795: Pittsburg Corning Glass Block.
Page 796: Norman Rosenfeld Architects LLC.
Page 803: William Radford, *Architectural Details,* R. D. Radford, Chicago, 1938.
Page 805: John Hancock Callender (ed.), *Time-Saver Standards for Architectural Design Data*, 6th Edition, McGraw-Hill, New York, 1982.
Pages 806–813 (top): Walker Group/CNI.
Pages 815, 838: Roppe Rubber Corp.
Page 821: *American Architect and Architecture,* May 1932.
Pages 822, 824, 827: National Terrazzo and Mosaic Association, Inc.
Page 830: *Guide Specifications for Maple Flooring Systems,* Maple Flooring Manufacturers Association.

Page 831: American Parquet Association.
Page 832: Hoboken Wood Flooring Co.
Page 833: Tarkett.
Page 840: Franciscan Tile Company.
Pages 853–855, 857–859, 861–864, 882–893, 900: Hollow Metal Manufacturers Association.
Page 856: Pat Guthrie, *The Architect's Portable Handbook,* 2d Edition, McGraw-Hill, 1998.
Page 861: *Methods and Materials of Commercial Construction.*
Page 894: *New York State Construction Handbook.*
Pages 896, 897, 1013–1020, 1023, 1025, 1031, 1032, 1058, 1059, 1093: Earl P. Baker and Harold S. Langland, *Architectural Metal Handbook,* National Association of Ornamental Metal Manufacturers, Washington, D.C., 1947.
Page 898: General Services Administration.
Page 911: Eggers Industries.
Pages 912, 1007: Antonin Raymond, *Architectural Details*, Architectural Book Publishing Co., Inc., 1947.
Pages 913–916: "Sliding and Folding Door Hardware," Stanley Hardware.
Page 917: Brennan Beer Gorman Monk/Interiors.
Pages 918, 987: Nelson L. Burbank, *House Construction Details,* 3d Edition, Simmons-Boardman Publishing Corp., New York, 1952.
Page 921: Thompson, Robinson, Toraby.
Page 924: *Progressive Architecture*, April 1971.
Pages 925, 963, 990 (bottom), 1001, 1002, 1043–1046, 1053, 1054: Tony Chi & Associates.
Pages 927–933: *Comparative Architectural Details,* Pencil Points Series (Frank J. Forster, Architect), 1935.
Page 944, 945: Philip G. Knobloch, *Good Practice in Construction,* Pencil Points Press, New York, 1931.
Pages 946–950: Schlage.
Pages 951–953: New York City Building Code.
Pages 954–956: U.S. Gypsum Drywall Suspension Systems, "Flat Drywall Ceilings."
Pages 957–959: Sweet's Catalog.
Page 961: Celotex Corporation.
Pages 967, 968: Passalacqua & Toto.
Pages 969, 970, 977, 978: U.S. Gypsum Drywall Suspension Systems.
Page 988: *Design Solutions*, Architectural Woodworking Institute.
Page 989: Simon B. Zelnik, FAIA.
Pages 991, 992, 1042: Jerry Caldari, Architect.
Page 993: *Interiors,* April 1985.
Page 994: John L. Feirer, *Cabinet Making and Millwork,* Charles A. Bennet Co., Peoria, Ill.
Page 995: Ascente.
Pages 997, 1000–1006: Marcel Morin Stairworld, Inc., Ottawa., Canada (www.stairworld.com)
Pages 996, 998, 999: Stairways, Inc.
Pages 1010, 1060: *Selected Architectural Details*, Reinhold, New York.
Pages 1011, 1021, 1022, 1024, 1026–1028 (top), 1029, 1030, 1033, 1035–1039, 1056: National Association of Architectural Manufacturers.
Page 1061: New York City Housing Authority.
Page 1064: Slate Institute.
Page 1065: *Manual of School Planning*, New York City Board of Education.
Pages 1066, 1067, 1070: Uniform Federal Accessibility Standards, 1985-494-187, U.S. Government Printing Office, Washington, D.C., 1985.
Page 1075: Farmers Bulletin #1889, U.S. Department of Agriculture, Washington, D.C., 1971.
Pages 1077, 1078: *Handbook of Successful Fireplaces,* Dunley Bros. Co., Cleveland, Ohio, 1961.
Page 1080: *Pencil Points* (Ely Jacques Kahn, Architect), October 1938.
Page 1081: *Pencil Points* (Richard Neutra, Architect), 1938.
Pages 1082–1084: *The Fireplace Design Handbook,* The Majestic Products Company.
Page 1087: *Pencil Points* (Frank Forster, Architect).
Page 1088: *Pencil Points* (Walker & Gillette, Architects).
Pages 1090–1092: Architectural Paneling, Inc.
Pages 1094, 1095: General Electric Company.
Pages 1096–1099: Nessen Lamp Company.
Pages 1100–1112: *Design with Light,* Lightolier.
Page 1115: Panero Zelnik Associates.
Pages 1116, 1117: Space Design Group.
Pages 1118, 1119: Michael Lynn Associates.
Pages 1120, 1121: Horton Lees Lighting Designs, Inc.
Pages 1122, 1126, 1127, 1135, 1138–1140, 1143, 1156, 1172, 1173: Jean Gorman, *Detailing Light,* Whitney Library of Design.
Pages 1123–1125 (bottom): Naomi Leff & Associates.
Page 1125 (top): Rosenblum Architects.
Pages 1130–1132: Space Design Group.
Pages 1133, 1134: Bromley/Jacobsen.
Pages 1136, 1137: Norman Rosenfeld Architects LLC.
Pages 1141, 1148, 1150–1152: Tony Chi & Associates.
Page 1142: Centrebrook Architects and Planners, LLC.
Page 1144: *Architectural Lighting,* September 1987.
Pages 1145, 1147: Roberts Step Lite Systems, Inc.
Pages 1146, 1149, 1153: National Cathode Corp.
Page 1154: Philips Lighting Co.
Pages 1155, 1159: Just Bulbs Ltd.
Page 1157: Lightolier Inc.
Pages 1160, 1162–1168, 1170: General Electric.
Pages 1161, 1169, 1174: *Product Technology & Specification Guide: Lamp & Ballast Catalog,* Osram Sylvania.
Page 1171: General Electric.

3. ARCHITECTURAL WOODWORK

Pages 1178, 1179, 1187–1189: *Time-Saver Standards: A Manual of Essential Architectural Data*, F. W. Dodge Corp., New York, 1946.
Pages 1180–1182, 1190–1196, 1208–1210, 1214–1216: Woodworking Institute of California.
Pages 1183–1185: Albert Jackson, David Day, and Simon Jennings, *The Complete Manual of Woodworking,* Alfred A. Knopf, New York, 1989.
Page 1186: Ernest Joyce, *Encyclopedia of Furniture Making,* Sterling Publishing Co., Inc., New York, 1987.
Pages 1204–1207: Marble Institute of America.
Pages 1211–1213, 1263, 1292, 1296, 1298, 1300–1302: Architectural Woodwork Institute.
Pages 1212, 1220: *Comparative Architectural Details*, Pencil Points Series (Frank J. Forster, Architect), 1935.
Page 1217: Leroy P. Ward, Architect.
Pages 1218, 1219: *Comparative Architectural Details,* Pencil Points Series (Evans, Moore, Peterson & Woodbridge, Architects), 1935.

Pages 1221–1223, 1226, 1266: Philip G. Knobloch, *Good Practice in Construction,* Pencil Points Press, New York, 1931.
Pages 1224, 1225: Passalacqua & Toto.
Pages 1227, 1253 (right), 1256, 1259, 1261, 1262, 1264 (bottom), 1268–1271, 1274, 1275, 1277–1279, 1288, 1289, 1306–1308: *Design Solutions.*
Pages 1228, 1229: Space Design Group; ISD.
Pages 1230, 1231: *Selected Architectural Details*, Progressive Architecture (Perkins & Wills, Architects).
Page 1232: Thompson, Robinson, Cecil, Inc.
Pages 1233–1237, 1243, 1245–1249: Bertram Bassuk, FAIA.
Pages 1238, 1242, 1250–1252: Charles D. Flayhan Associates.
Page 1239: ISD.
Pages 1240, 1241, 1244, 1245, 1253 (left), 1260: Gensler Associates.
Pages 1254, 1255: Winebarger Church Furniture.
Page 1257: Panero Zelnik Associates.
Page 1258: Hochheiser-Elias.
Page 1267: General Services Administration.
Page 1265: Roger H. Ballard, Architect.
Page 1272: Hyde and Shepherd, Architects.
Page 1273: Howard and Frenaye, Architects.
Page 1275, 1276: *Comparative Architectural Details*, Pencil Points.
Page 1280: Tony Chi & Associates.
Page 1281: Manual of Millwork, Woodworking Institute of California.
Pages 1282–1286, 1305: Architectural Paneling, Inc.
Pages 1287, 1292–1297, 1299–1304: Camden Window and Millwork.
Pages 1309–1311: Ernest Joyce, *Encyclopedia of Furniture Making*, Sterling Publishing Co., Inc., New York, 1987.
Pages 1312–1324: Hafele.

4. SPECIALTIES

Pages 1328–1339: Everett Conklin and Susan Korner, in Andrew Alpern (ed.), *Handbook of Specialty Elements in Architecture*, McGraw-Hill, New York, 1982.
Pages 1340–1349 (top): *The Green Scene,* National Park Service, U.S. Department of the Interior, Washington, D.C., 1973.
Pages 1349 (bottom), 1350–1352, 1357, 1358: Engel/GGP.
Pages 1353, 1354: Caleb Hornbostel, Architectural Detailing Simplified, Prentice-Hall, Englewood Cliffs, N.J., 1986.
Pages 1359–1365, 1371, 1372, 1376–1379: Fred T. Knowles, in Andrew Alpern (ed.), Handbook of Specialty Elements in Architecture, McGraw-Hill, New York, 1982.
Pages 1366–1377: Designers Sign Company/Frank Rispoli.
Page 1368: Innerface Architectural Signage.
Pages 1373–1375: U.S. Department of Transportation, Washington, D.C.
Pages 1380–1390: Jerome Menell, in Andrew Alpern (ed.), Handbook of Specialty Elements in Architecture, McGraw-Hill, New York, 1982.
Pages 1394–1397: Hussey Seating Company.
Pages 1398, 1399, 1401–1408, 1410: J. G. Furniture Systems.
Page 1400: *Design Guide for Music and Drama Centers*, Department of the Army, Washington, D.C., 1981.
Page 1409: Architectural Record.
Pages 1411–1432: *A Design Guide for Improving Residential Security*, U.S. Department of Housing and Urban Development, Washington, D.C., 1973.
Page 1421: Marvin Windows.
Pages 1433, 1448, 1449: Halse, *The Use of Color in Interiors*, McGraw-Hill, New York, 1968.
Pages 1434, 1437, 1460: *The House and Home Book of Interior Design,* McGraw-Hill, New York, 1979.
Pages 1435, 1436, 1438, 1439: Mary Derieux and Isabelle Stevenson, *The Complete Book of Interior Decorating,* Greystone Press, New York, 1950.
Pages 1450–1454: Sweet's Catalog.
Pages 1456–1459: L. O. Anderson, *Wood-Frame House Construction*, Department of Agriculture Handbook No. 73, U.S. Government Printing Office, Washington, D.C., 1970.
Page 1451: Walter McQuade (ed.), *Schoolhouse,* Simon and Schuster, New York, 1958.
Pages 1465–1484, 1488, 1489: Panero Zelnik Associates.
Pages 1485–1487, 1490, 1492: Kirsch.
Page 1494: Armor Elevator.
Pages 1494 (bottom)–1496, 1499: Dover Elevator Co.
Pages 1497–1499, 1501, 1509, 1519–1524: Concord Elevator.
Pages 1502–1504: "The ADA from A to Z," Montgomery KONE Inc., 1995.
Pages 1502–1505: *Uniform Federal Accessibility Standards,* 1985-494-187, U.S. Government Printing Office, Washington, D.C., 1985.
Page 1506: Panero Zelnik Associates.
Page 1507 (top): Ronald L. Mace, *An Illustrated Handbook of the Handicapped Section of the North Carolina State Building Code,* Raleigh, N.C., 1974.
Pages 1508, 1510–1518: Graventa.
Pages 1525, 1528–1530, 1534, 1536: *Outdoor Sports Facilities*, Departments of the Army, Navy, and Air Force, Washington, D.C.
Pages 1526, 1527, 1531–1533, 1535: "Guide Specifications for Maple Flooring Systems," Maple Flooring Manufacturing.
Pages 1537–1540: Cutler Manufacturing.
Page 1541: Phillips and Brooks, Inc.
Pages 1542–1548: Earl P. Baker and Harold S. Langland, *Architectural Metal Handbook,* National Association of Ornamental Metal Manufacturers, Washington, D.C., 1947.
Pages 1549–1551: Brown Manufacturing Co.
Page 1552: Bertram Bassuk, FAIA.
Pages 1553, 1554, 1558–1560: Pittcon Softforms.
Pages 1555: Rosenblum Architects.
Pages 1556, 1557: Passalacqua & Toto.
Pages 1561–1563: Alvarado Manufacturing Co.
Pages 1564, 1565: Haws.
Page 1566: Uniform Federal Accessibility Standards.
Pages 1567–1570: International Steel Revolving Door Company.
Pages 1571–1573: Electric Time Company, Inc.
Pages 1574–1576: Doug Mockett & Company, Inc.

5. ACCESSIBLE DESIGN/ADA

Pages 1580–1582: Eastern Paralyzed Veterans Association (EPVA).
Pages 1583–1598: Architectural and Transportation Barriers Compliance Board (Access Board).

6. GENERAL REFERENCE DATA

Pages 1602–1605: David Kent Ballast, *Architect's Handbook of Formulas, Tables, and Mathematical Calculations,* Prentice-Hall, Englewood Cliffs, N.J., 1988.

Pages 1606–1608: Julius Panero and Martin Zelnik, *Human Dimension & Interior Space,* Whitney Library of Design/Watson-Guptill Publications, New York, 1979.
Pages 1609, 1610: *Access America,* Washington, D.C.
Pages 1611, 1612, 1636, 1637: *The Measure of Man and Woman,* Henry Dreyfuss Associates.
Page 1613 (top): Sister Kenny Institute.
Page 1614: *Uniform Federal Accesssibility Standards,* 1985-494-187, U.S. Government Printing Office, Washington, D.C., 1985.
Pages 1615, 1616: W. E. Woodson, *Human Factors Design Handbook,* McGraw-Hill, New York, 1981.
Pages 1617: *Building for People,* U.S. Department of Commerce, Washington, D.C.
Pages 1619–1621, 1626: Norman Foster, *Practical Tables for Building Construction*, McGraw-Hill, New York, 1963.
Page 1624: U.S. Gypsum.
Pages 1627, 1658, 1667, 1668: Pat Guthrie, *The Architect's Portable Handbook,* 2d Edition, McGraw-Hill, New York, 1998.
Pages 1628, 1629: Mary Derieux and Isabelle Stevenson, *The Complete Book of Interior Decorating,* Greystone Press, New York, 1950.
Page 1630: W. Robert Harris, *Drywall: Installation and Applications,* American Technical Publishers, Inc., Alsip, Ill., 1979.
Pages 1630–1632: Fred W. Zimmerman, *Upholstery Methods,* The Goodheart-Willcox Company, Inc., 1992.
Pages 1634, 1635: Steelcase.
Page 1638: Indiana Limestone Institute.
Pages 1639, 1640: Charles Wing, *The Visual Handbook of Building and Remodeling,* Rodale Press, 1990.
Page 1642: Derksen (USA) Inc.
Page 1643: Audio Unlimited of East Meadow, Long Island.
Pages 1644–1646: *Time-Saver Standards: A Manual of Essential Architectural Data,* F. W. Dodge Corp., New York, 1946.
Pages 1661, 1663, 1664: Naomi Leff & Associates.
Page 1665: Brennan Beer Gorman Monk/Interiors.

About the Authors

Joseph De Chiara is a practicing architect and city planner in New York City. He has taught at Columbia University, Pratt Institute, Cooper Union, New York Institute of Technology, and SUNY/Farmingdale. He is the coauthor of *Time-Saver Standards for Site Planning*, *Time-Saver Standards for Housing and Residential Development*, and *Time-Saver Standards for Interior Design and Space Planning,* and the author of *Handbook of Architectural Details for Commercial Buildings,* all published by McGraw-Hill.

Julius Panero is a practicing architect and interior designer in New York City, and a partner in the architectural firm of Panero Zelnik Associates. He is professor emeritus at the Fashion Institute of Technology/State University of New York, where he taught for 36 years. He is coauthor of *Human Dimension and Interior Space, Time-Saver Standards for Interior Design and Space Planning,* and *Time-Saver Standards for Housing and Residential Development.*

Martin Zelnik is a practicing architect and interior designer in New York City, and a partner in the architectural firm of Panero Zelnik Associates. He is a professor of interior design at the Fashion Institute of Technology/State University of New York, where he taught for over 32 years. He is coauthor of *Human Dimension and Interior Space, Time-Saver Standards for Interior Design and Space Planning,* and *Time-Saver Standards for Housing and Residential Development.* He is a member of the American Insititute of Architects, the American Society of Interior Designers, and the Interior Designers Educators Council.

NOTES

NOTES

NOTES

NOTES

NOTES

NOTES

NOTES

NOTES

NOTES

NOTES

NOTES

NOTES

NOTES